2012 County and City Extra
Annual Metro, City, and County Data Book
20th Edition

2012 County and City Extra

Annual Metro, City, and County Data Book

20th Edition

Edited by Deirdre A. Gaquin
and Mary Meghan Ryan

Lanham, MD

Published in the United States of America
by Bernan Press, a wholly owned subsidiary of
The Rowman & Littlefield Publishing Group, Inc.
4501 Forbes Boulevard, Suite 200
Lanham, Maryland 20706

Bernan Press
800-865-3457
www.bernan.com

ISBN: 978-1-59888-526-2

E-ISBN: 978-1-59888-527-9

ISSN: 1059-9096

∞ ™ The paper used in this publication meets the minimum requirements of American National Standard for
Information Sciences—Permanence of Paper for Printed Library Materials, ANSI/NISO Z39.48-1992.
Manufactured in the United States of America.

Contents

Contents

INTRODUCTION

County and City Extra is an annual publication that provides the most up-to-date statistical information available for every state, county, metropolitan area, and congressional district, as well as all cities in the United States with a 2010 census population of 25,000 or more. Data for places, including towns and cities with populations of fewer than 25,000 people are published by Bernan Press in a separate companion volume, *Places, Towns and Townships*. These two volumes are designed to meet the needs of libraries, businesses, and other organizations or individuals who desire convenient and timely sources of the most frequently sought information about geographic entities within the United States. The annual updating of *County and City Extra* ensures its stature as a reliable and authoritative source for statistical information.

County and City Extra and *Places, Towns and Townships* are large volumes, but are not big enough to accommodate the wealth of information from the decennial census and the American Community Survey. Two additional volumes in the *County and City Extra* series include this information. *County and City Extra—Special Decennial Census Edition* provides detailed population and housing data from the 2010 census and was published by Bernan Press in December 2011. *The Who, What, and Where of America—Understanding the American Community Survey* includes social and economic details from the American Community Survey and was published by Bernan Press in June 2012.

The American Community Survey (ACS) is a new national survey that has replaced the census long form as the key source of detailed social and economic data. *County and City Extra* includes data from both the 2010 census and the ACS.

New and Updated Information for the 2012 Edition

This edition is the first to fully incorporate the new pattern of census data. The basic demographic and housing data come from the census, while detailed social and economic characteristics—formerly from the long form sample of the census—come from the ACS. In addition, this edition uses a new list of cities based on the 2010 census populations and current city definitions, with a new appendix showing 2010 cities with their component counties.

County and City Extra includes updated data including 2011 population estimates for states, and 2010 census counts for counties, metropolitan areas, and cities. Also included are the latest available data for education, vital statistics, income and poverty, employment and unemployment, residential construction, production by industry, health resources, crime, land use, the distribution of federal funds, city government finances, weather statistics, and many other topics.

Table E (Congressional Districts) includes data that were gathered for the 112th Congress, along with the 112th Congressional representative.

Finally, a new map on the percent of persons with no health insurance has been added.

This edition includes data from both the 2010 census and the ACS. In December 2010, the Census Bureau released the first 5-year estimates from the American Community Survey (ACS). While annual ACS data are now available for all states and almost all metropolitan areas (all geographic areas with populations of 65,000 or more), three years are needed to build a sample large enough for reliable estimates for areas of 20,000 to 64,999, and smaller areas need five years of data collection.

With the now annual release of 1-year, 3-year, and 5-year estimates, *County and City Extra* uses ACS data to replace all of the detailed data from the 2000 census. ACS data for 2010 are included in Table A (States), Table C (Metropolitan Areas), and Table E (Congressional Districts)—all areas with populations of 65,000 or more. Table B (Counties) includes 5-year data (2006–2010). The release of 5-year data for even the smallest geographic areas means that annual social and economic characteristics are now available for all counties. Table D (Cities) includes 3-year data from the ACS (2008–2010) because all of the cities in this book are over the 20,000 cutoff for ACS 3-year data.

Although some of the state data are also included in Table B (States and Counties), the separate state data table offers several important features:

* Additional data not available at the county level are provided. Examples include population projections, health insurance coverage, number of immigrants, personal tax payments, information about health service firms not subject to federal tax, and exports by state of origin.

* Additional data that exceeds the space limitations for counties can be found for states. Examples are age of householder, more detailed information about employment in retail trade and services, and the expanded presentation of federal grants and payments to individuals by type.

* State totals can be found more quickly and compared more readily.

Appendix F, **Source Notes and Explanations**, includes Internet references for all data sources. Some of the data can be directly found in data tables on the web sites; some can be assembled through on-line access tools; others can be obtained by downloading files and processing them with statistical software; and some need to be ordered from the agencies.

Rankings

The rankings present the geography types by various subjects, including population, land area, population density, population change, age, immigration, birth rate, housing characteristics, race, Hispanic origin, educational attainment, income, unemployment rate, per capita local taxes, poverty rate, defense contracts, value of agricultural products, and violent crime rate.

Subjects Covered and Volume Organization

A summary of the **subjects covered** in each of the five tables appears on **page ix**. The **colored map** portfolio begins on **page xiii**.

The main body of this volume contains five basic parts. Each part includes a table that is preceded by highlights and rankings, as well as the complete column headings for the table. **Part A**, which begins on **page 1**, contains data for states. **Part B**, beginning on **page 51**, contains information for states and counties. The county geography codes include county typology codes from the Economic Research Service of the Department of Agriculture. These codes characterize counties by size of the largest place as well as by other criteria for nonmetropolitan counties. (See Appendix A for the definition of each code.) **Part C**, beginning on **page 773**, contains information for metropolitan areas. Statistics for cities with a 2010 census population of 25,000 or more can be found in **Part D**, which begins on **page 895**. **Part E**, beginning on **page 1175**, contains data for the congressional districts of the 112th Congress.

Contents pages preceding tables B through E list the page number on which the data for a given geographic area begin. Counties and cities are listed alphabetically by state. Metropolitan areas are listed alphabetically, except that metropolitan divisions are listed alphabetically within the metropolitan statistical area of which they are components. Congressional districts are listed in numeric order within states.

The appendixes include definitions of geographic concepts (**Appendix A**), sources and definitions of each data item included in this volume (**Appendix F**), an alphabetical listing of metropolitan areas with their component counties delineated as of December 2009, with 2010 census populations (**Appendix B**), a listing of metropolitan and micropolitan areas and their component counties as of December 2009, with 2010 census populations (**Appendix C**), a list of cities by county (**Appendix E**), and maps showing congressional districts, counties, and selected places within each state (**Appendix D**).

Symbols

D   Indicates that the number has been withheld to avoid disclosure of information pertaining to a specific organization or individual, or because the number does not meet statistical standards for publication.

NA   Indicates that data are not available.

X   Indicates that data are not applicable or are not meaningful for this geographic unit.

In this volume, a figure that is less than half the unit of measure shown will appear as zero.

Sources

The great majority of the data in this volume have been obtained from federal government sources. A few items are obtained from private sources that are widely recognized as reliable basic sources of those particular data items. For a complete list of these sources, see **Appendix F**.

Data included in this volume meet the publication standards established by the U.S. Census Bureau and the other federal statistical agencies from which they were obtained. Every effort has been made to select data that are accurate, meaningful, and useful. All data from censuses, surveys, and administrative records are subject to errors arising from factors such as sampling variability, reporting errors, incomplete coverage, nonresponse, imputations, and processing error. Responsibility of the editors and publishers of this volume is limited to reasonable care in the reproduction and presentation of data obtained from sources believed to be reliable.

County and City Extra: Annual Metro, City, and County Data Book is part of Bernan Press's *County and City Extra* series. The editors of *County and City Extra* acknowledge the contributions of Courtenay Slater and the late George Hall, the originators of this publication. Their initial contributions continue to enrich the *County and City Extra* series. As always, we are especially grateful to the many federal agency personnel who assisted us in obtaining the data, provided excellent resources on their websites, and patiently answered questions.

Deirdre A. Gaquin has been a data use consultant to private organizations, government agencies, and universities for over 30 years. Prior to that, she was Director of Data Access Services at Data Use & Access Laboratories, a pioneer in private sector distribution of federal statistical data. A former President of the Association of Public Data Users, Ms. Gaquin has served on numerous boards, panels, and task forces concerned with federal statistical data and has worked on five decennial censuses. She holds a Master of Urban Planning (MUP) degree from Hunter College. Ms. Gaquin is also an editor of Bernan Press's *The Who, What, and Where of America: Understanding the American Community Survey*; *Places, Towns and Townships*; *The Congressional District Atlas*, and *The Almanac of American Education*.

Mary Meghan Ryan is the senior research editor for Bernan Press. She is also the editor for the *Handbook of U.S. Labor Statistics*, *State Profiles*, and the associate editor for *Business Statistics of the United States*.

SUBJECTS COVERED, BY GEOGRAPHY TYPE

State data begin on page 24
County data begin on page 72
Metropolitan area data begin on page 796
City data begin on page 910
Congressional district data begin on page 1186

Subject	Column Number				
	Table A. States	Table B. States and Counties	Table C. Metropolitan Areas	Table D. Cities	Table E. Congressional Districts
Land area	1	1	1	1	1
Population					
Total persons, 1990	31	20	20	23	
Total persons, 2000	32	21	21	24	
Total persons, 2010	33	2	2	2	2
Total persons, 2011	2				
Rank, 2010		3	3	3	
Rank, 2011	3				
Persons per square kilometer	4	4	4	4	3
Race and Hispanic or Latino origin, 2000	45–50				
Race and Hispanic or Latino origin, 2010	4–9	5–9	5–9	5–10	4–11
Immigrants	24				
Foreign-born population	22			11	13
Percent born in state of residence	23				14
Age distribution, 2000	52–61				
Age distribution, 2010	10–19	10–18	10–18	12–20	15–23
Median age	20, 62			21	24
Percent female	21	19	19	22	12
Percent population change, 1990–2000	34	22	22	25	
Percent population change, 2000–2010	35	23	23	26	
Percent population change, 2010–2011	36				
Components of population change	37–41	24–26	24–26		
Daytime population		33–34	33–34		
Population projections	42–44				
Households					
Total households, 2000	64				
Total households, 2010	25	27	27	27	29
Percent change in number of households	26, 65	28	28		
Household type	28–30, 67–68	30–31	30–31	29–30	31–34
Persons per household	27, 66	29	29	28	30
Persons in group quarters		32	32	31–33	35–40
Housing					
Housing units in 2000	69–78			47–49	
Housing units in 2010	79–92	87–88	87–96		41–50
Housing units in 2008–2010				50–57	
Housing units in 2006–2010		89–96			
Percent change in number of housing units	70, 80	88	88	48	
Housing costs	73–77, 83–90	91–95	91–95	53–57	44–49
Substandard housing units	78, 91	96	96		50
Percent with no vehicle available				58	
Percent who lived in same house one year ago	92			59	
Percent who lived outside city one year ago				60	
New residential construction	93–95	178–179	178–179	69–71	
Manufactured housing	96				
Persons in group quarters		32	32	31–34	35–40

SUBJECTS COVERED, BY GEOGRAPHY TYPE — Continued

State data begin on page 24
County data begin on page 72
Metropolitan area data begin on page 796
City data begin on page 910
Congressional district data begin on page 1186

Subject	Column Number				
	Table A. States	Table B. States and Counties	Table C. Metropolitan Areas	Table D. Cities	Table E. Congressional Districts
Vital statistics					
Births	97–98	35–36	35–36		
Deaths	99–103	37–38	37–38		
Health					
Persons in nursing homes				33	38
Medicare enrollees	106	41–43	41–43		
Persons lacking health insurance	104–105	39–40	39–40		64
Crime	107–110	44–47	44–47	35–38	
Education					
School enrollment	111–112	48–49	48–49		25–26
Educational attainment	27–28	50–51	50–51	39–41	27–28
Expenditures for education	117–118	52–53	52–53		
Income					
Personal income	134–149	62–74	62–74		
Per capita income	122, 136, 149	54, 64	54, 64	42	51
Household income	123–126	55–58	55–58	43–45	52–53
Poverty	127–133	59–61	59–61	46	54–55
Food stamps					56
Personal income by type	138–140	66–68	66–68		
Earnings by industry	150–158	75–83	75–83		
Transfer payments	141–146	69–74	69–74		
Gross state product	159				
Personal tax payments	147				
Disposable personal income	148–149				
Labor Force and Employment					
Labor force and unemployment	167–171	97–100	97–100	61–68	57–59
Employment in selected occupations	163–166	101–103	101–103		60–63
Employment by industry	172–183, 207–216	104–112	104–112		
Exports of goods produced	119–121				
Establishments, employment, sales, and payroll					
Manufacturing	207–216	151–154	151–154	88–91	
Construction	217–221				
Wholesale trade	222–226	135–138	135–138	72–75	
Retail trade	227–235	139–142	139–142	76–79	
Information	236–246				
Utilities	247–251				
Transportation and warehousing	252–256				
Finance and insurance	257–261				
Real estate and rental and leasing	262–266	143–146	143–146	80–83	
Professional, scientific, and technical services	267–275	147–150	147–150	84–87	
Health care and social assistance	276–289	159–162	159–162	100–103	
Arts, entertainment and recreation	290–294				
Accommodation and food services	295–300	155–158	155–158	92–95	
Other services, except public administration	301–308	163–166	163–166	104–108	

SUBJECTS COVERED, BY GEOGRAPHY TYPE — Continued

State data begin on page 24
County data begin on page 72
Metropolitan area data begin on page 796
City data begin on page 910
Congressional district data begin on page 1186

Subject	Column Number				
	Table A. States	Table B. States and Counties	Table C. Metropolitan Areas	Table D. Cities	Table E. Congressional Districts
Government employment	309–311	194–196	194–196	140	
Agriculture	184–202	113–132	113–132		68–80
Land and water	203–206	133–134	133–134		
Government finances	331–350	180–193	180–193	117–139	
Federal funds and grants	312–330	167–177	167–177	108–116	
Voting and elections	351–355	197–199	197–199		
Climate					141–147

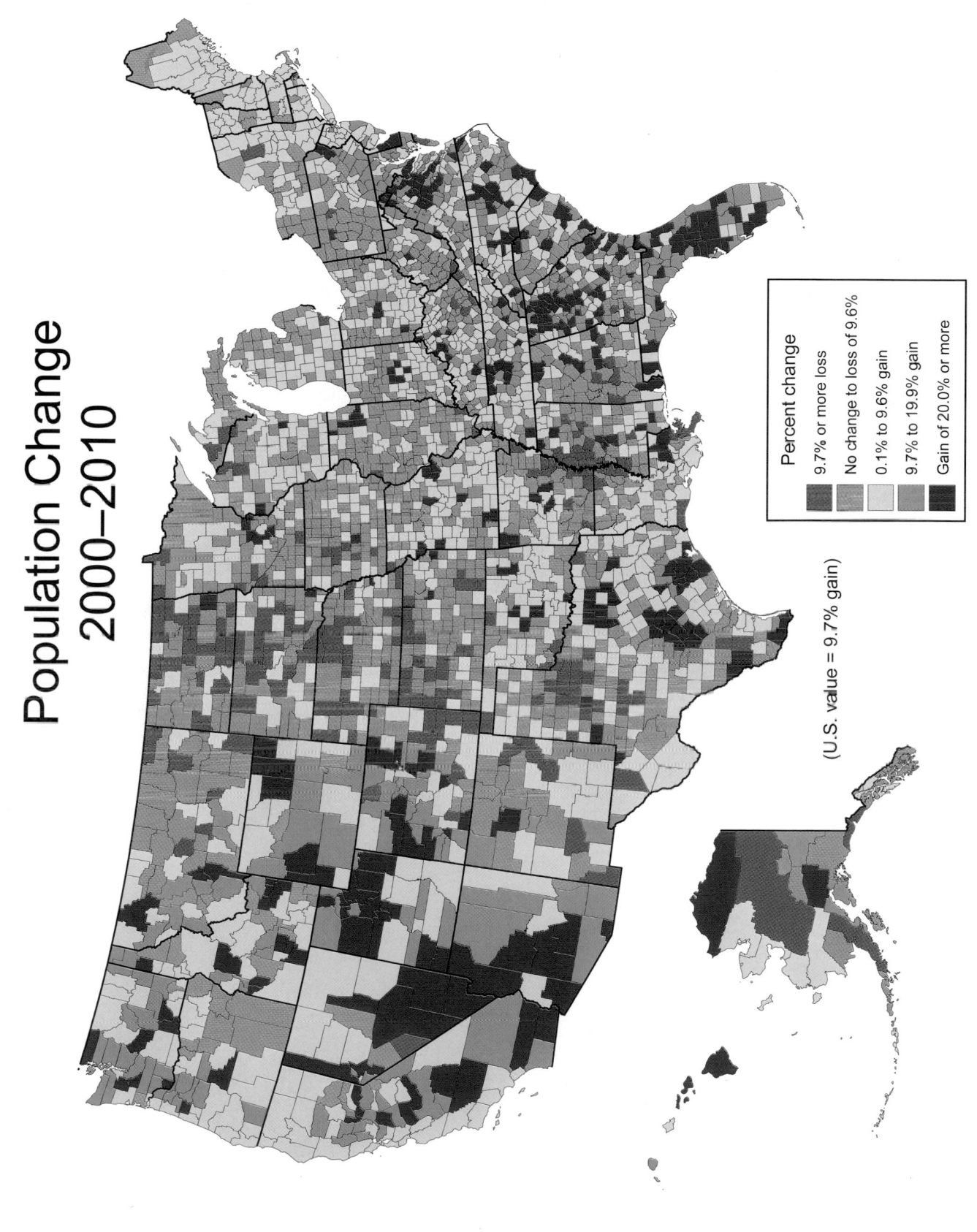

Population Change
2000–2010

Percent change

9.7% or more loss

No change to loss of 9.6%

0.1% to 9.6% gain

9.7% to 19.9% gain

Gain of 20.0% or more

(U.S. value = 9.7% gain)

Black, Not Hispanic or Latino, Population 2010

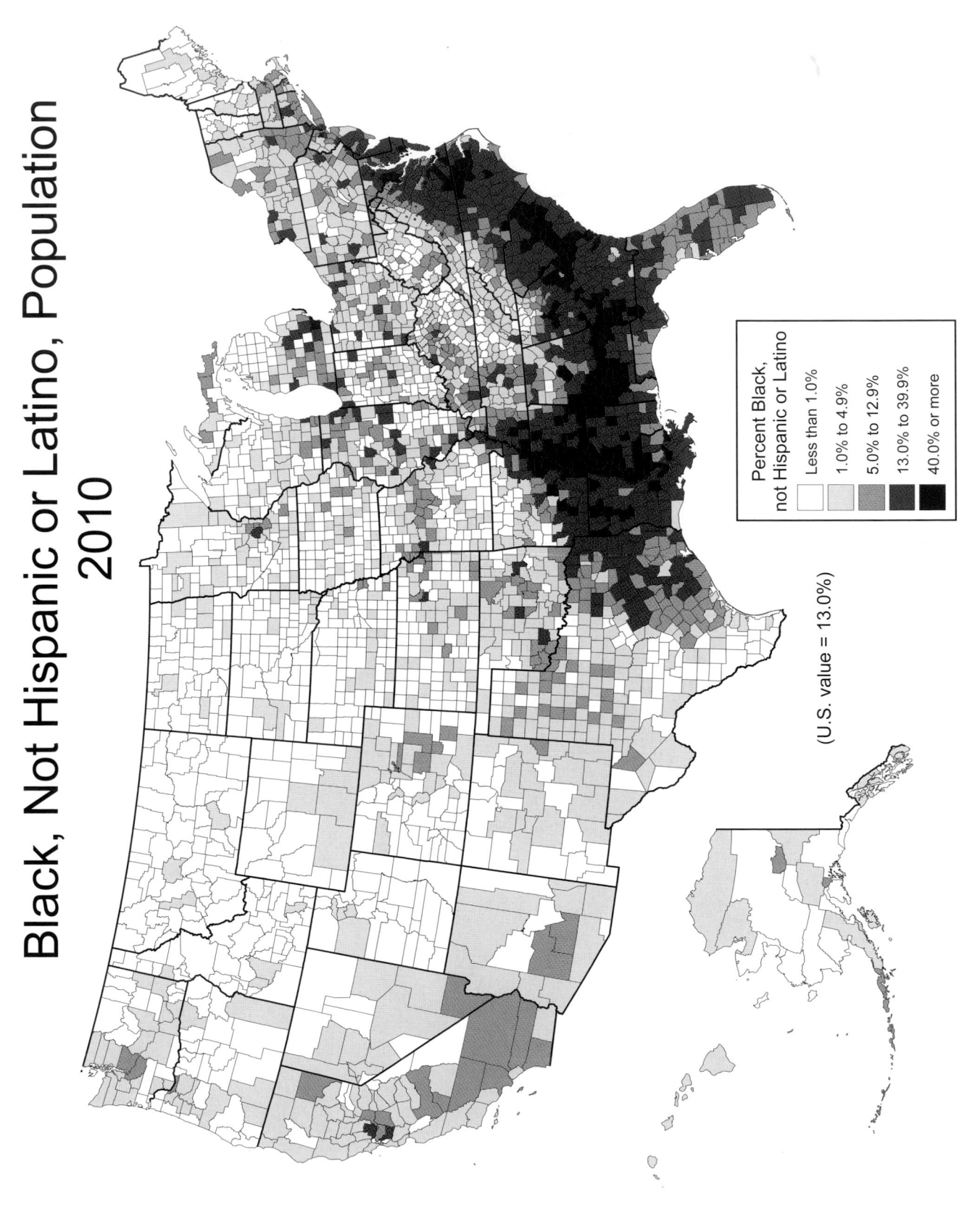

Percent Black,
not Hispanic or Latino

Less than 1.0%
1.0% to 4.9%
5.0% to 12.9%
13.0% to 39.9%
40.0% or more

(U.S. value = 13.0%)

Hispanic or Latino Population
2010

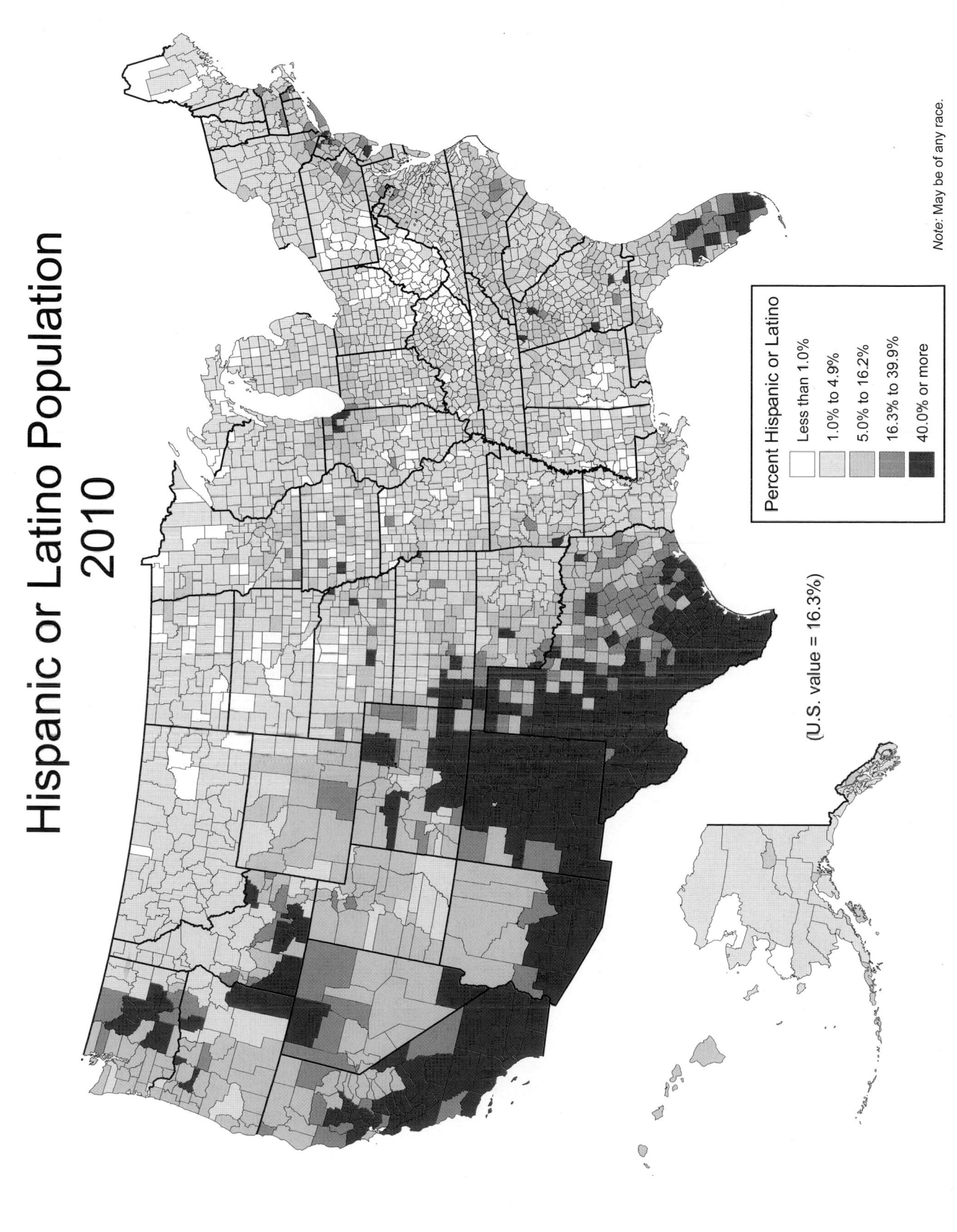

Percent Hispanic or Latino

- Less than 1.0%
- 1.0% to 4.9%
- 5.0% to 16.2%
- 16.3% to 39.9%
- 40.0% or more

(U.S. value = 16.3%)

Note: May be of any race.

Population Under 18 Years Old
2010

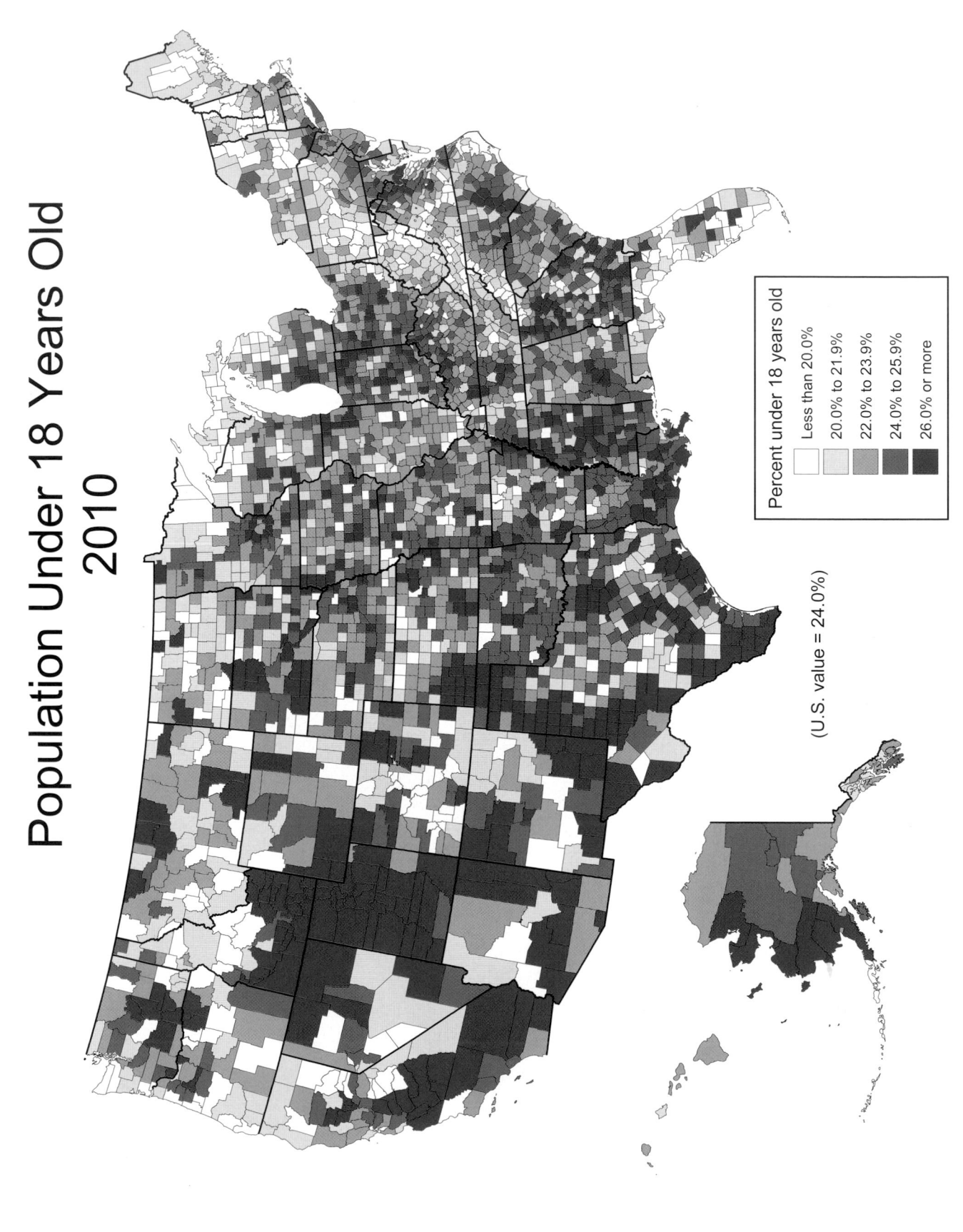

Percent under 18 years old

Less than 20.0%
20.0% to 21.9%
22.0% to 23.9%
24.0% to 25.9%
26.0% or more

(U.S. value = 24.0%)

Population 65 Years Old and Over
2010

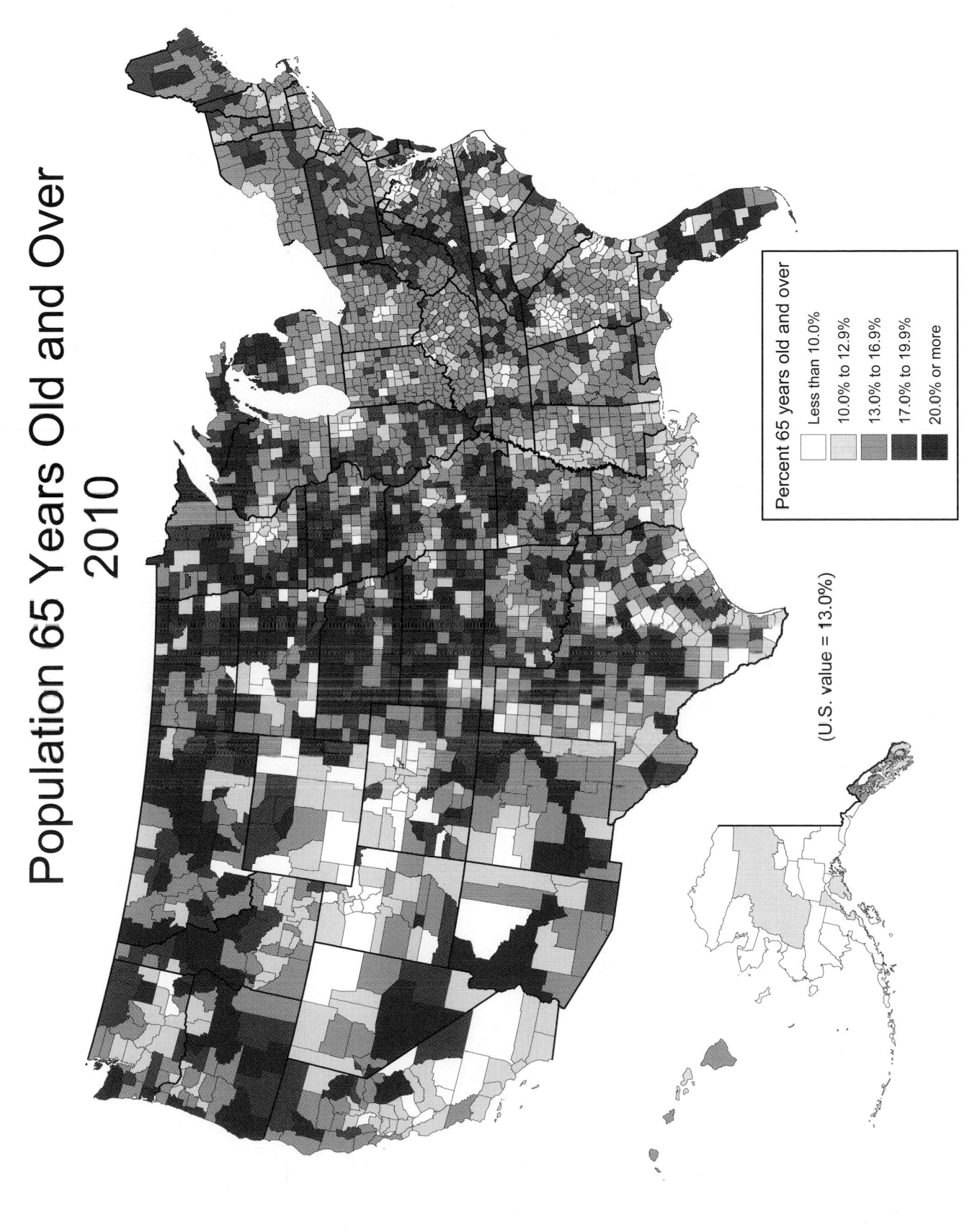

Percent 65 years old and over

	Less than 10.0%
	10.0% to 12.9%
	13.0% to 16.9%
	17.0% to 19.9%
	20.0% or more

(U.S. value = 13.0%)

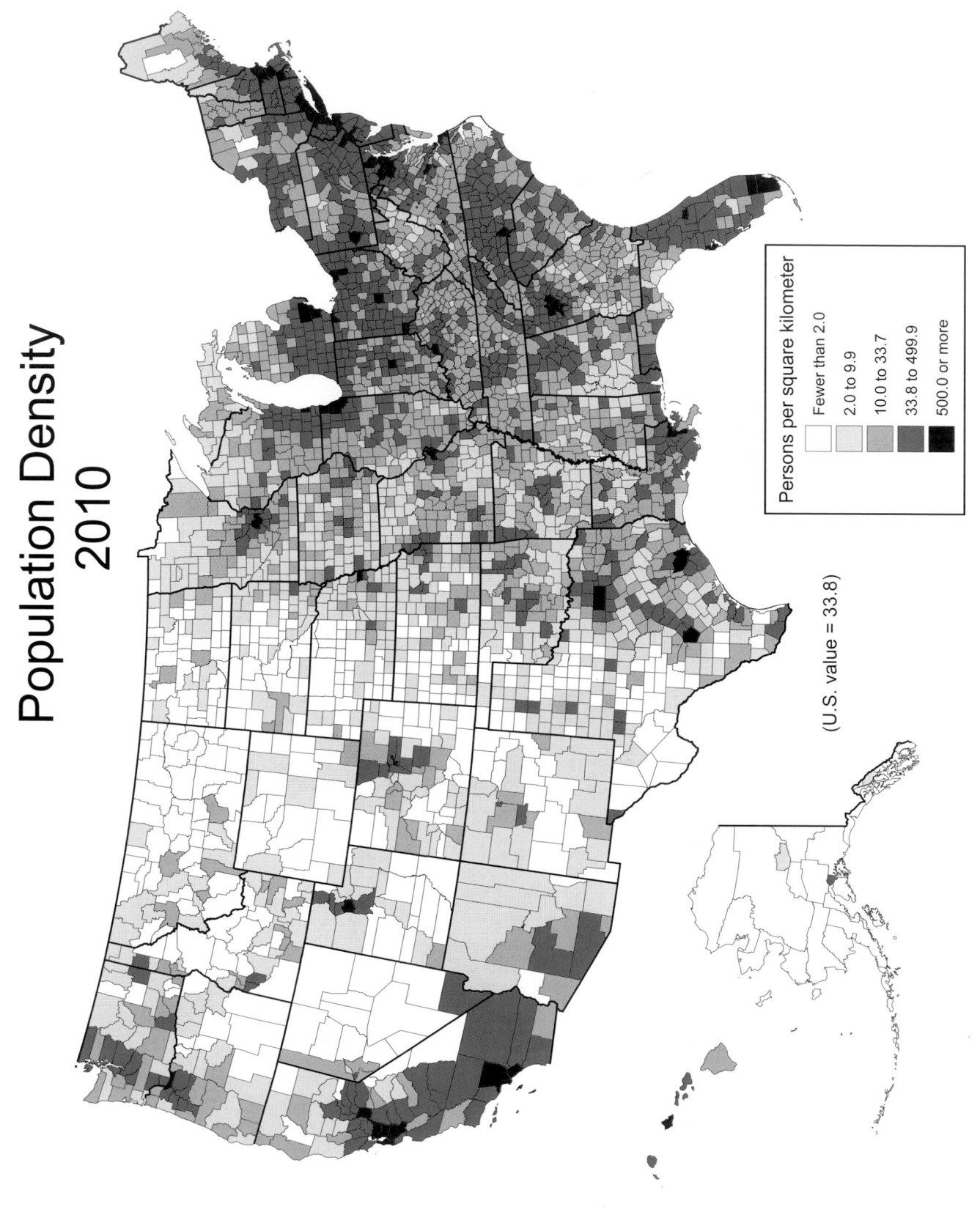

Population Density
2010

Persons per square kilometer

☐	Fewer than 2.0
☐	2.0 to 9.9
☐	10.0 to 33.7
☐	33.8 to 499.9
■	500.0 or more

(U.S. value = 33.8)

Unemployment Rate
2010

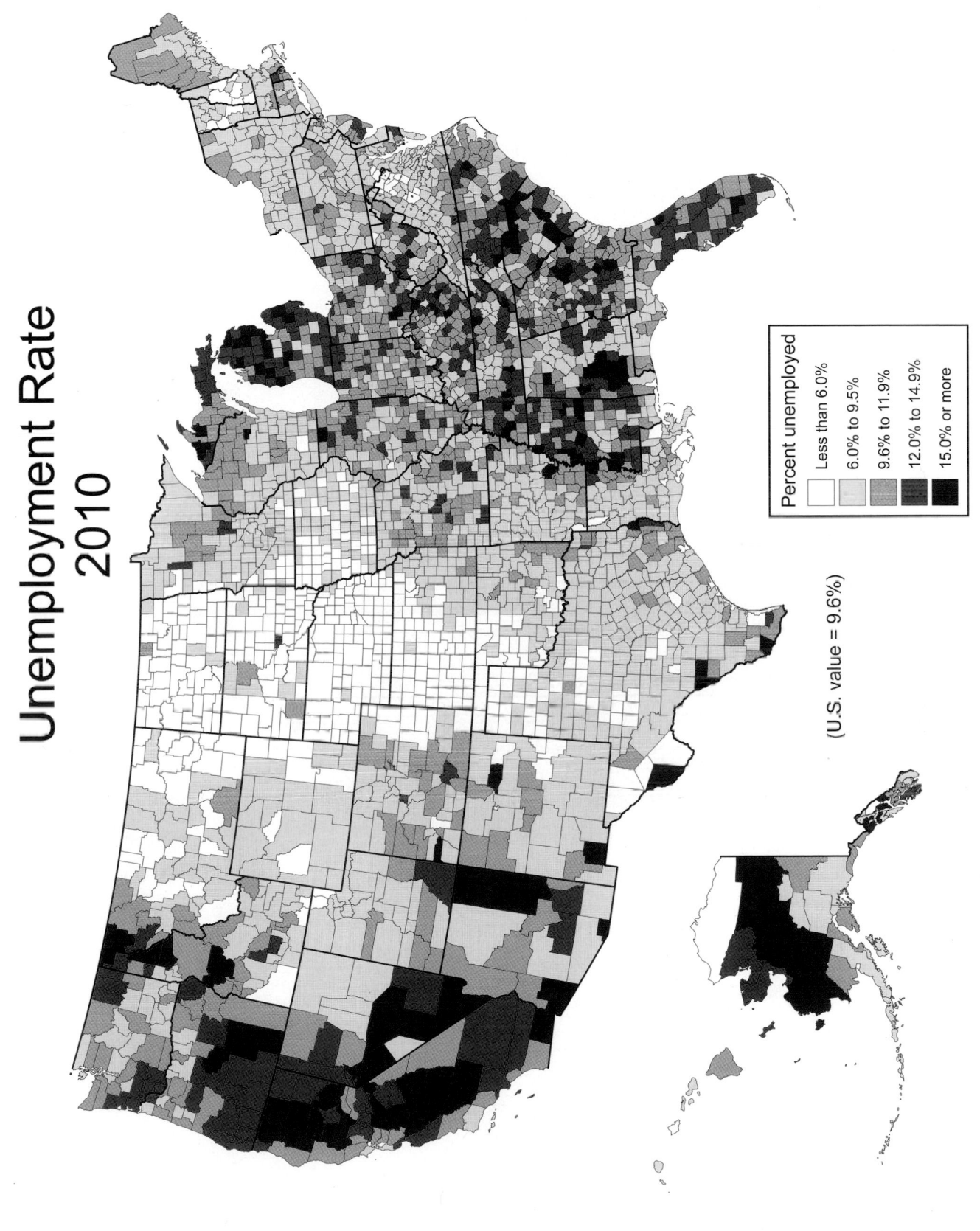

Percent unemployed

	Less than 6.0%
	6.0% to 9.5%
	9.6% to 11.9%
	12.0% to 14.9%
	15.0% or more

(U.S. value = 9.6%)

Educational Expenditures Per Student
2008–2009

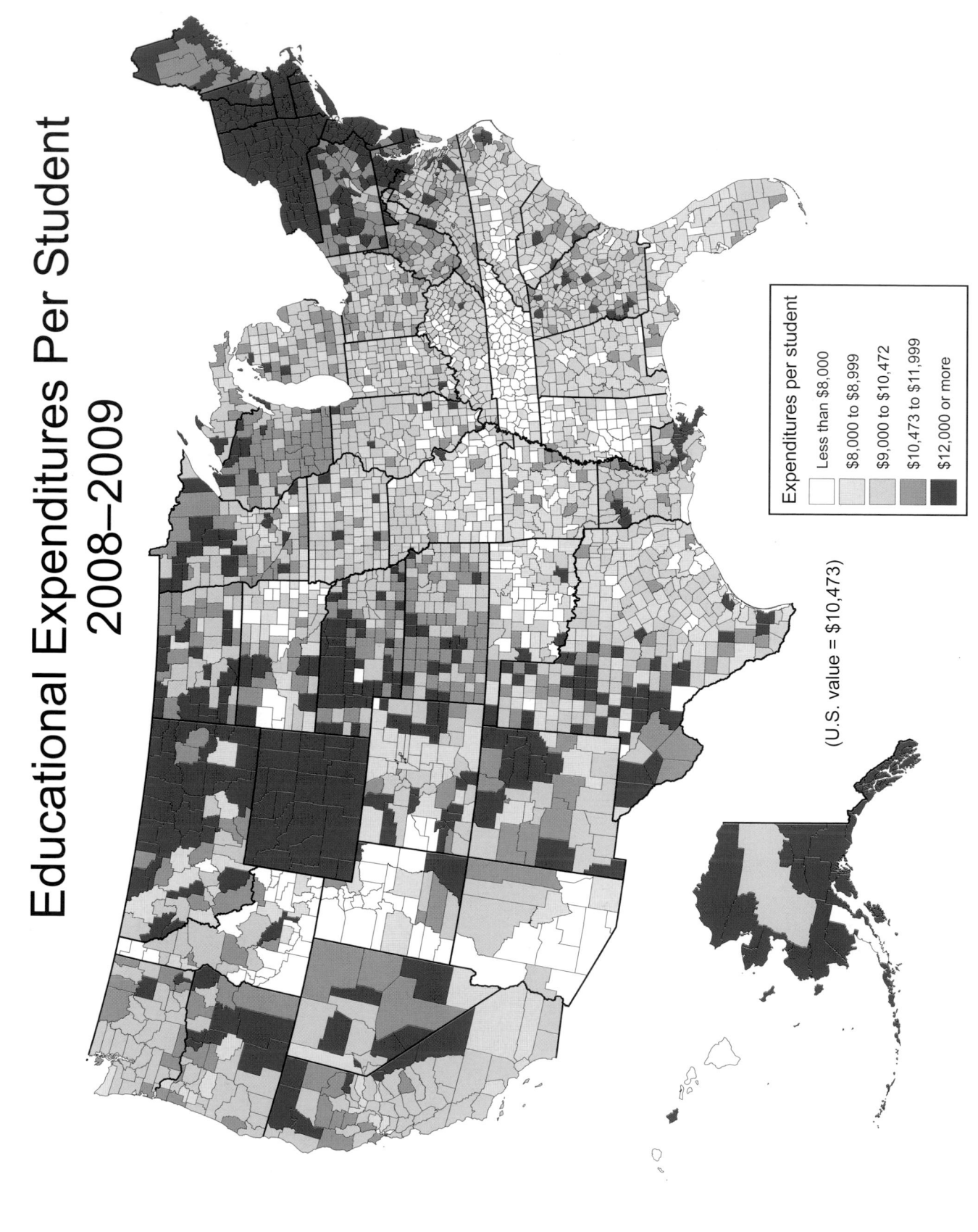

(U.S. value = $10,473)

Expenditures per student

- Less than $8,000
- $8,000 to $8,999
- $9,000 to $10,472
- $10,473 to $11,999
- $12,000 or more

Population with High School Diploma or Less
2006–2010

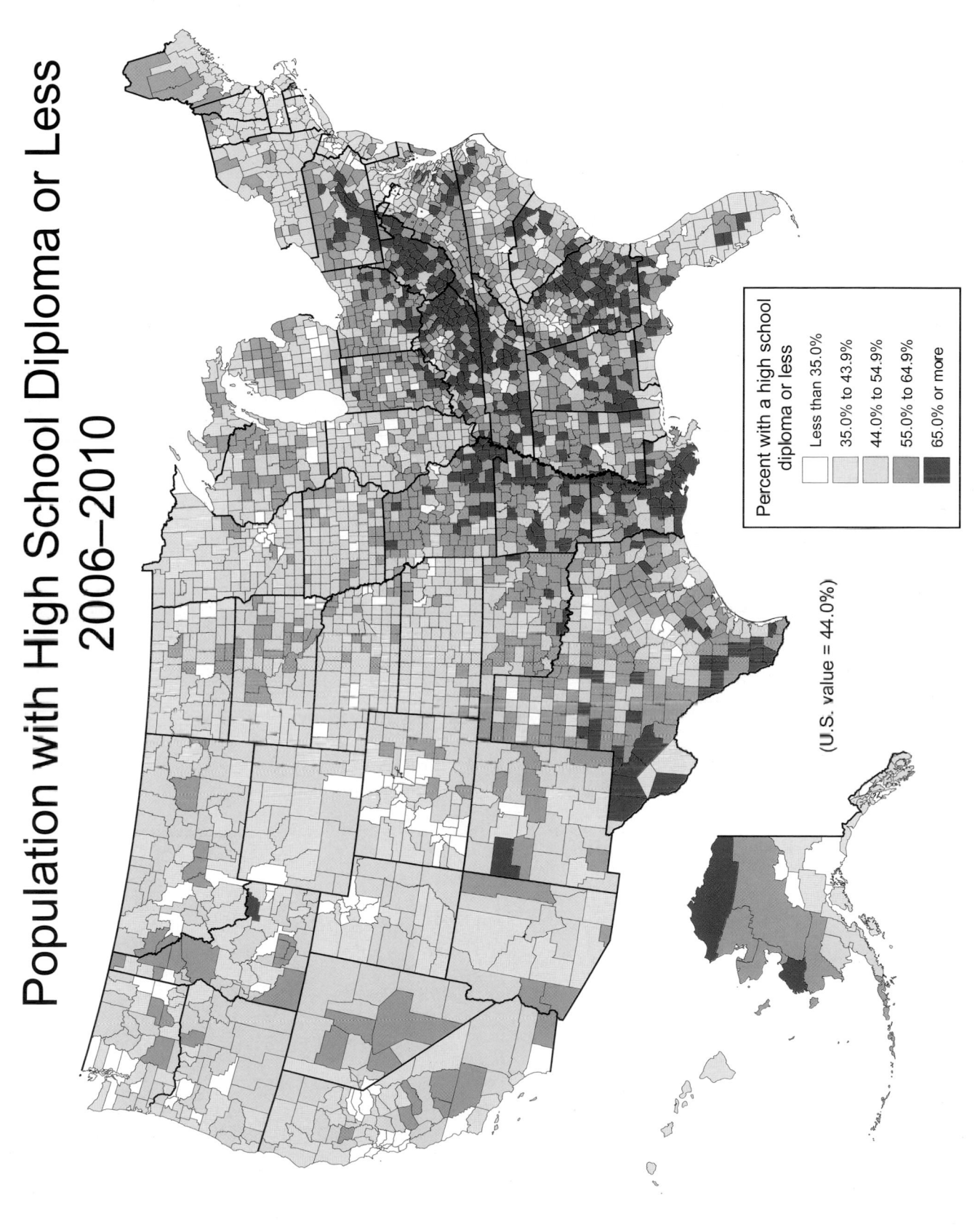

Percent with a high school diploma or less

- Less than 35.0%
- 35.0% to 43.9%
- 44.0% to 54.9%
- 55.0% to 64.9%
- 65.0% or more

(U.S. value = 44.0%)

Earnings from Manufacturing 2009

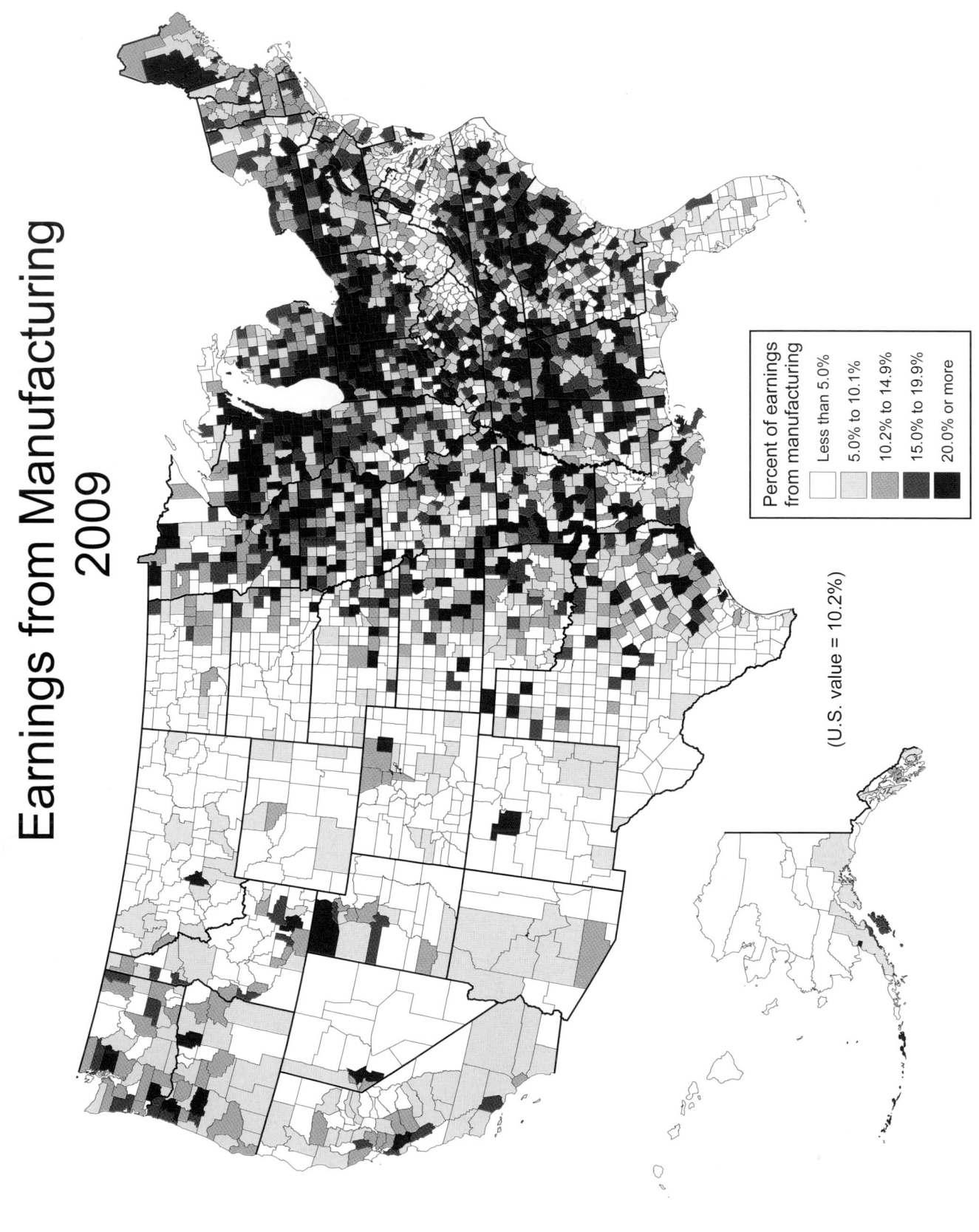

Percent of earnings from manufacturing

- Less than 5.0%
- 5.0% to 10.1%
- 10.2% to 14.9%
- 15.0% to 19.9%
- 20.0% or more

(U.S. value = 10.2%)

Employment in Management, Business, Science, and Arts Occupations: 2006–2010

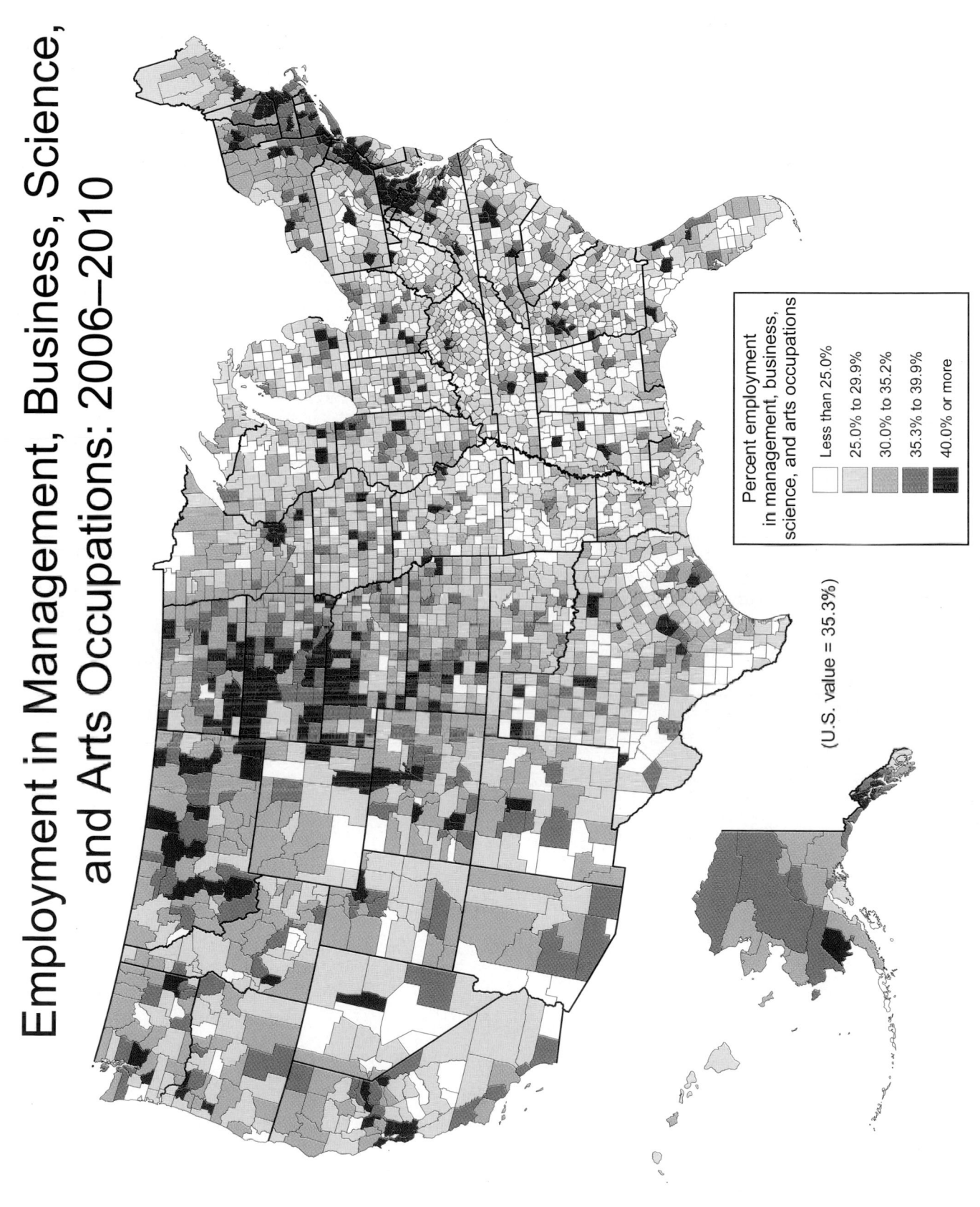

Percent employment in management, business, science, and arts occupations

Less than 25.0%
25.0% to 29.9%
30.0% to 35.2%
35.3% to 39.9%
40.0% or more

(U.S. value = 35.3%)

Land in Farms
2007

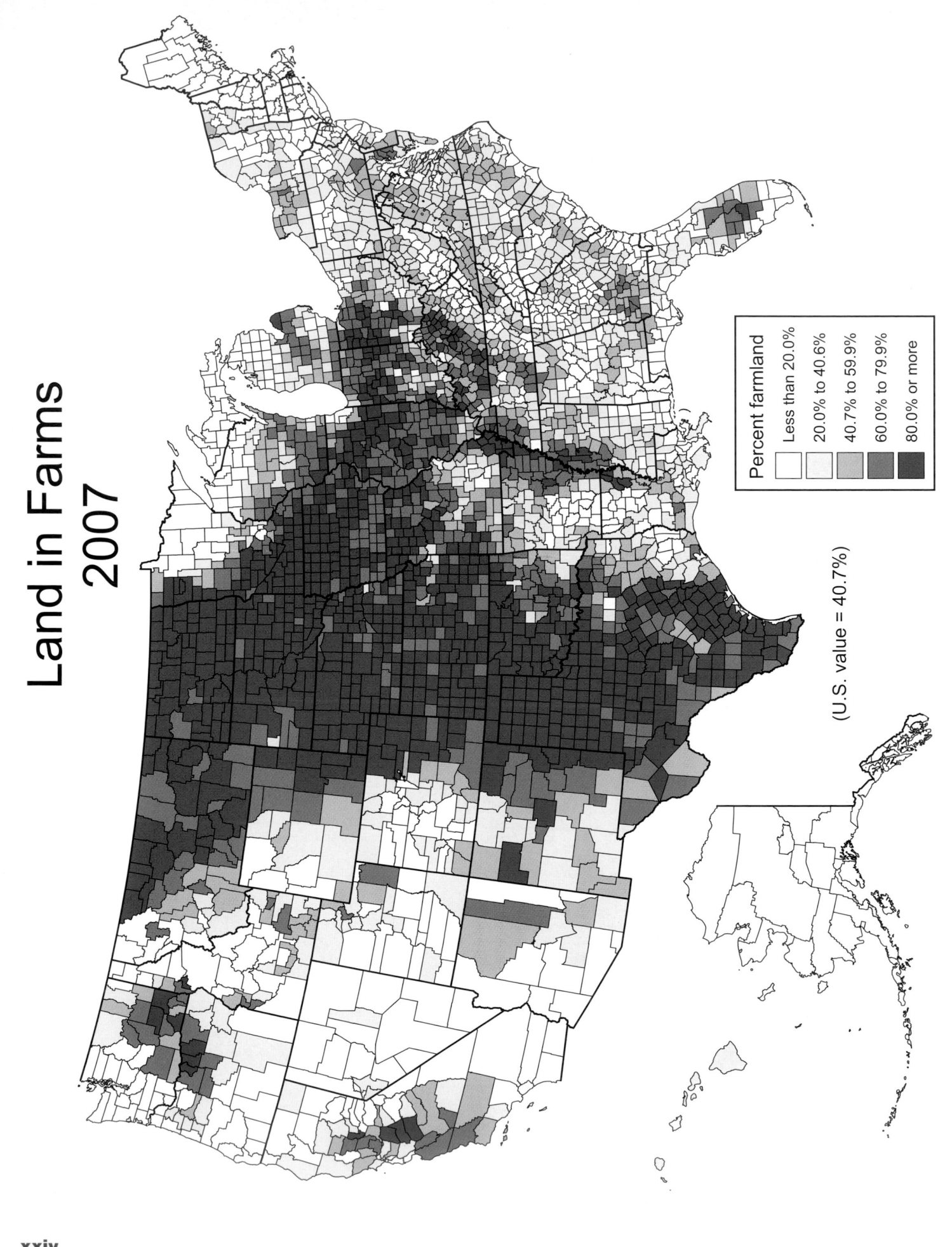

Percent farmland

- Less than 20.0%
- 20.0% to 40.6%
- 40.7% to 59.9%
- 60.0% to 79.9%
- 80.0% or more

(U.S. value = 40.7%)

Percent of Persons Under Age 65 with No Health Insurance
2009

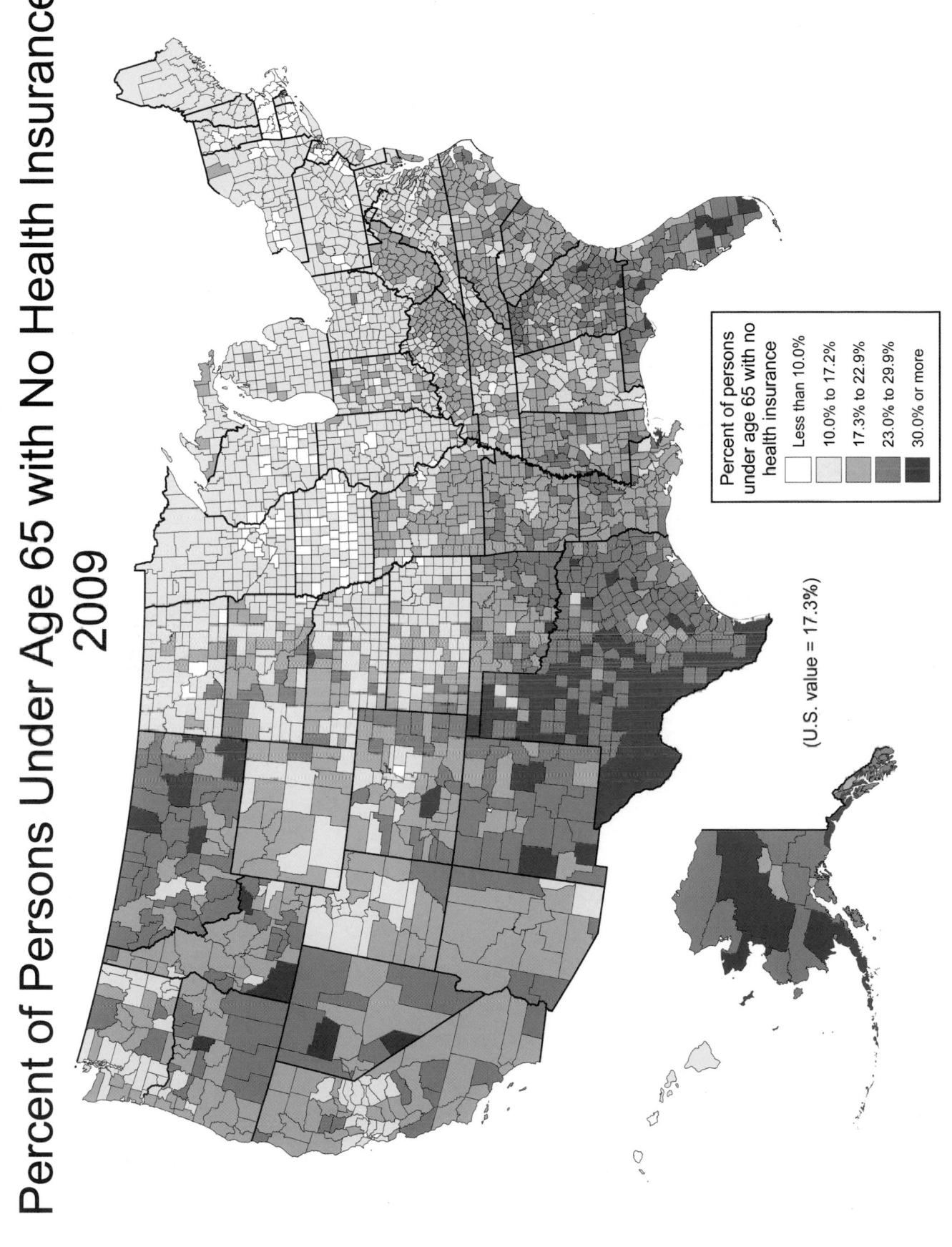

Percent of persons under age 65 with no health insurance

- Less than 10.0%
- 10.0% to 17.2%
- 17.3% to 22.9%
- 23.0% to 29.9%
- 30.0% or more

(U.S. value = 17.3%)

Median Household Income
2010

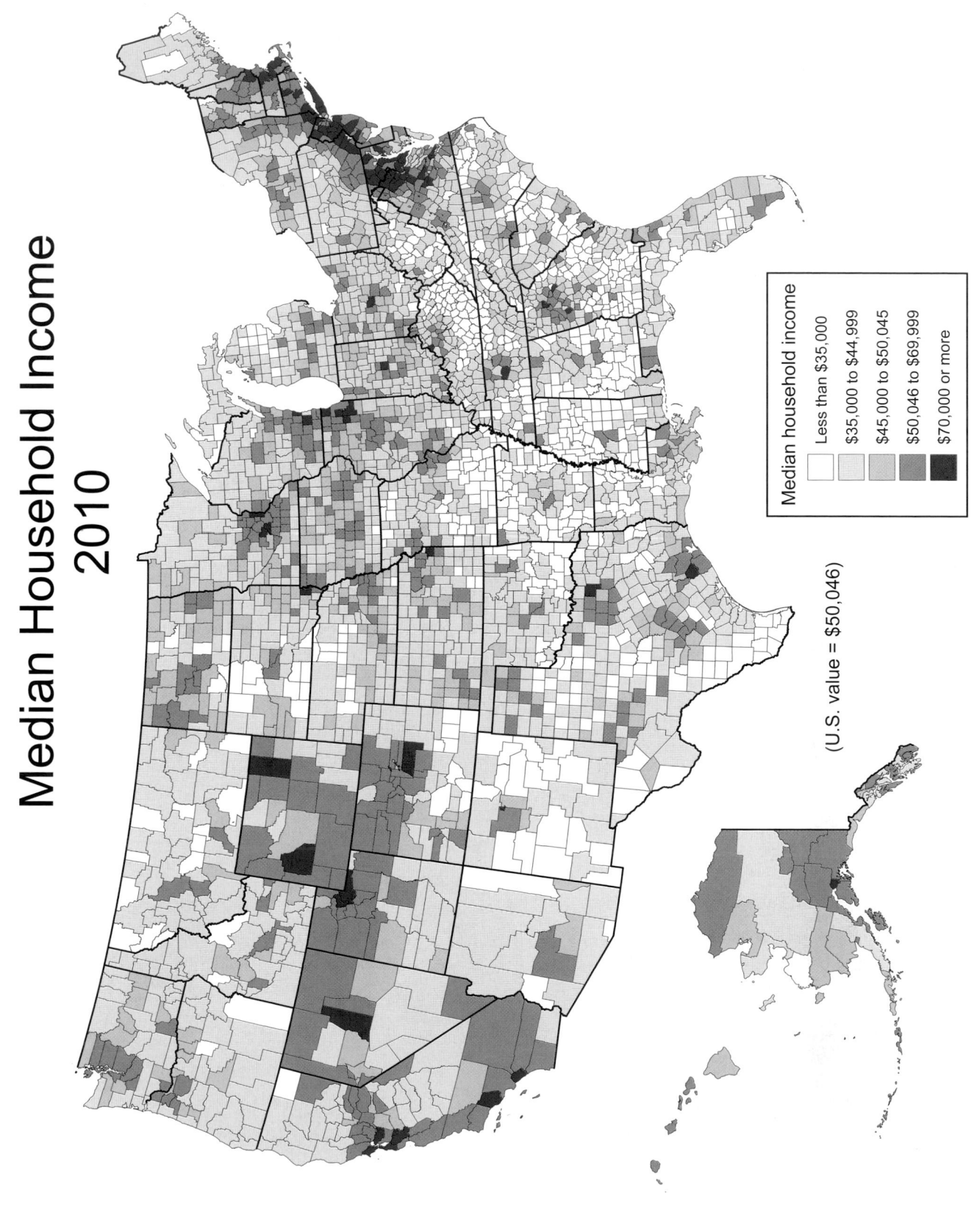

(U.S. value = $50,046)

Median household income

Median household income
- Less than $35,000
- $35,000 to $44,999
- $45,000 to $50,045
- $50,046 to $69,999
- $70,000 or more

Percent in Poverty
2010

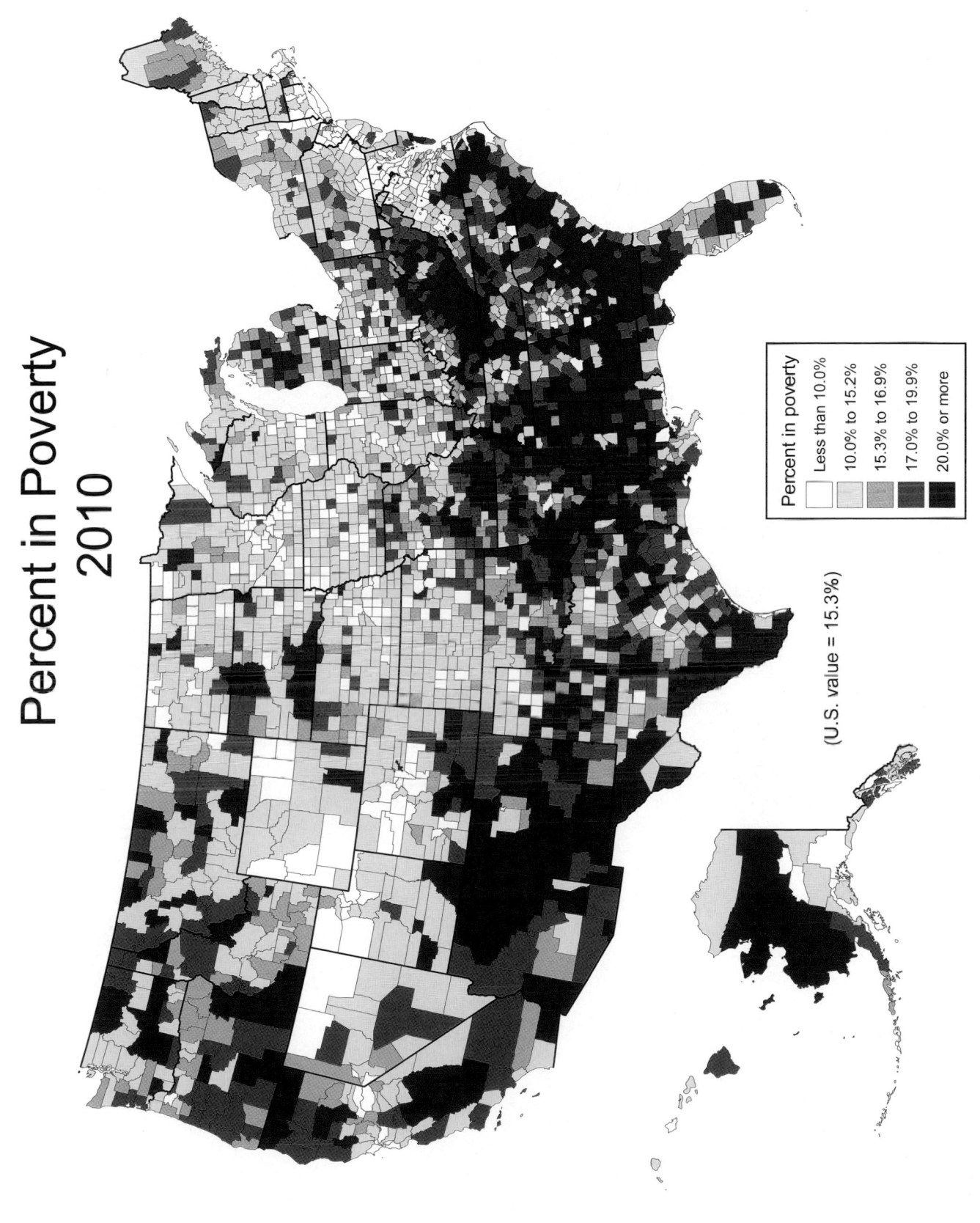

Percent in poverty

Less than 10.0%
10.0% to 15.2%
15.3% to 16.9%
17.0% to 19.9%
20.0% or more

(U.S. value = 15.3%)

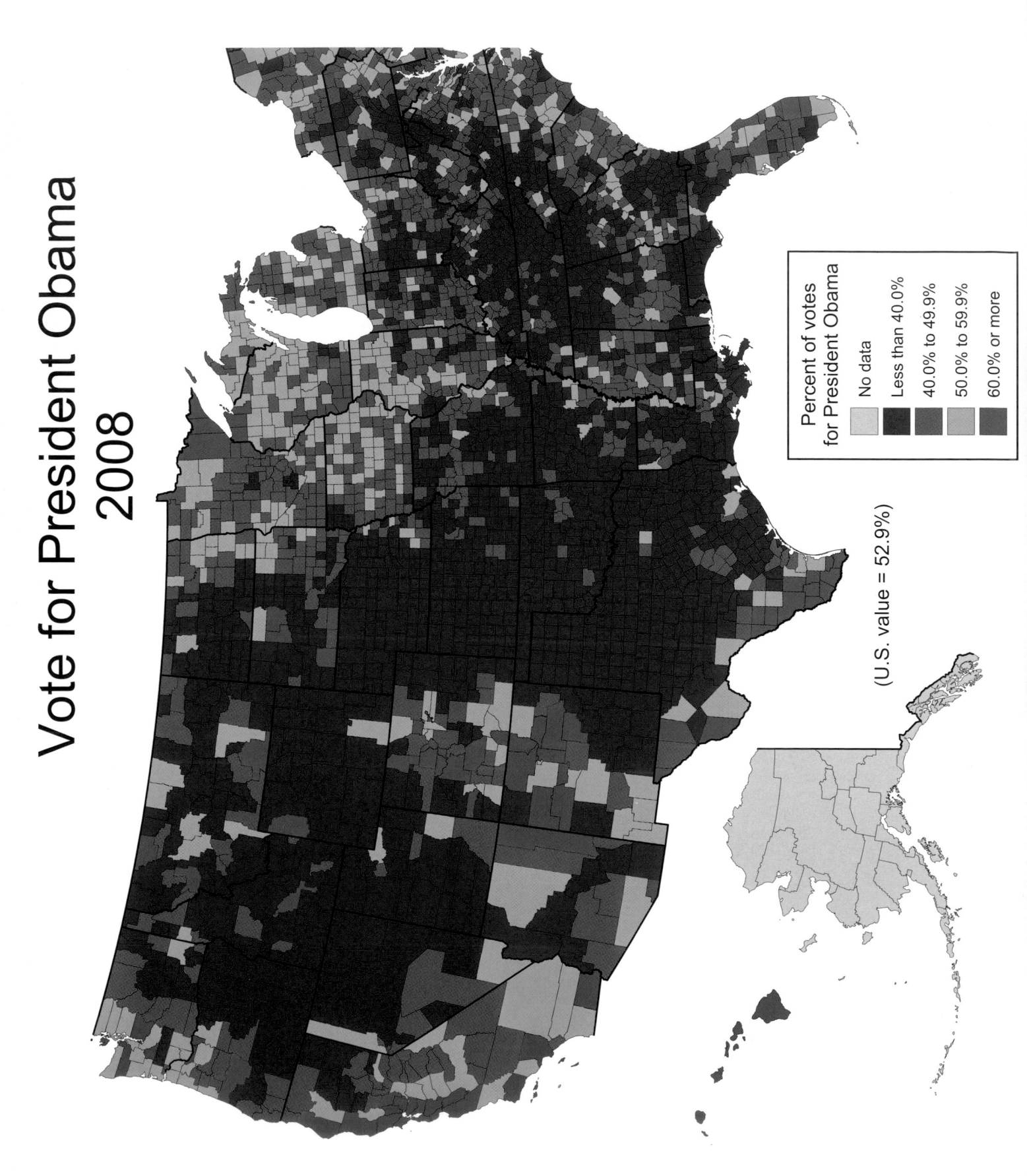

Vote for President Obama
2008

Percent of votes
for President Obama

No data
Less than 40.0%
40.0% to 49.9%
50.0% to 59.9%
60.0% or more

(U.S. value = 52.9%)

PART A.

States

(For explanation of symbols, see page viii)

Part A—States

1

State Highlights and Rankings

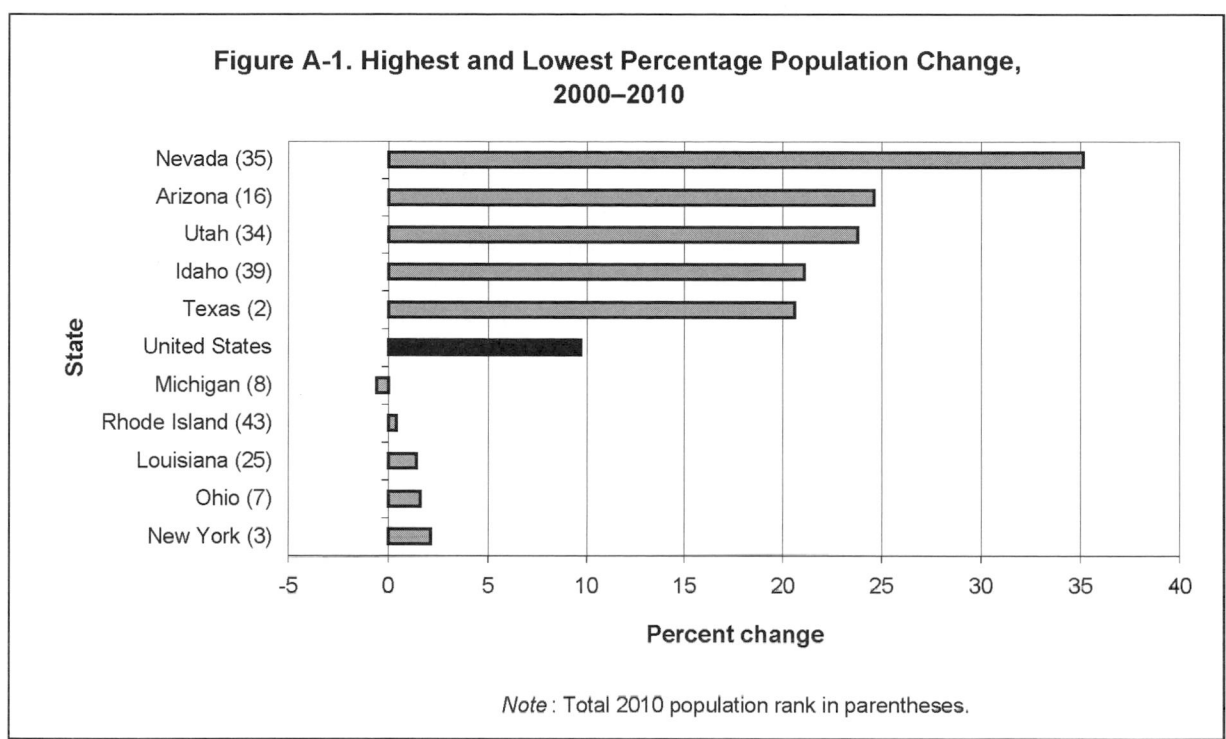

Figure A-1. Highest and Lowest Percentage Population Change, 2000–2010

Note: Total 2010 population rank in parentheses.

There is no simple relationship between population size and land area for most of the geographic entities included in this publication. According to the Census Bureau's 2011 estimates, state populations ranged from a high of nearly 37.7 million in California to a low of 568,158 in Wyoming. (The median population for states—with half having a larger population and half having a smaller population—was about 4.3 million people.) California was also one of the largest states in land area (ranking third). Alaska was by far the largest state in area; it was more than twice the size of Texas, the second-largest state, even though its population rank was close to the bottom (ranked 47th). Texas was also the second-largest state in terms of total population with over 25.6 million residents. At the other end of the geographic size spectrum were many of the New England states (with Rhode Island ranking as the smallest), plus Delaware and Hawaii. As a consequence of differing area size and population rank, New Jersey was the most densely settled state, with 463 persons per square kilometer, while Alaska was the least densely settled, with about 0.5 persons per square kilometer. California, which had the largest population and third-largest land area, ranked 12th in terms of population density (93 persons per square kilometer). Arizona was the 16th most populous state in 2010, jumping from 20th in 2000. From 2000 to 2010, the state's population grew 24.6 percent, second only to Nevada's 35.1 percent. Other states that grew by 20 percent or more during the decade were Utah, Idaho, and Texas. The 15 most populous states remained unchanged between 2000 and 2010, but there were changes within their ranks. Georgia and North Carolina became the 9th and 10th most populous states, pushing New Jersey down to number 11. Washington moved up to number 13, surpassing Massachusetts and Indiana.

Not surprisingly, states with higher population density also had higher proportions of developed land. According to the Department of Agriculture's most recent National Resources Inventory, 35.5 percent of New Jersey's land was developed. Connecticut had the second highest proportion with 32.5 percent, followed by Massachusetts at 32.1 percent. Among the reporting states, Nevada had the lowest proportion of developed land, at just 0.8 percent, followed by Wyoming and Montana, each with 1.1 percent of its land developed. Nearly 85 percent of Nevada's land was owned by the federal government. This was by far the highest percentage in the nation. Federal land accounted for about 20 percent of the United States' total land area. (Estimates are not available for Alaska, Hawaii, and the District of Columbia. See Appendix F for definitions and additional information.)

The total population of the United States increased by 9.7 percent between 2000 and 2010, with 21 states matching or exceeding this rate of growth and the remainder growing more slowly. States with the fastest population growth in the decade were concentrated in the West and in the South. Ranking first was Nevada, whose population increased by 35.1 percent since 2000. Despite its growth, Nevada ranked 35th for total population and was among 9 states with population densities of fewer than 10 persons per square kilometer. Texas, Florida, North Carolina, and Georgia ranked among the top 10 states for total population and for population growth since 2000. Rhode Island and Vermont both ranked among the 10 least populous states, as well as among the 10 states with the lowest population growth from 2000 to 2010. While most states have increased their populations since 2000, Michigan's population dropped by .6 percent. Ohio, Louisiana, and Rhode Island, all experienced increases below 2 percent. However, Louisiana's population has rebounded from a loss of about 250,000 residents after Hurricane Katrina hit the state in August 2005.

States and the District of Columbia
Selected Rankings

Population, 2011			Land Area, 2010				Population density, 2011			
Population rank	State	Population [col 2]	Population rank	Land area rank	State	Land area (square kilometers) [col 1]	Population rank	Density rank	State	Density (per square kilometer) [col 4]
	United States	311 591 917			United States	9 147 593			United States	34.1
1	California	37 691 912	47	1	Alaska	1 477 953	50	1	District of Columbia	3 911.4
2	Texas	25 674 681	2	2	Texas	676 587	11	2	New Jersey	463.1
3	New York	19 465 197	1	3	California	403 466	43	3	Rhode Island	392.6
4	Florida	19 057 542	44	4	Montana	376 962	14	4	Massachusetts	326.1
5	Illinois	12 869 257	36	5	New Mexico	314 161	29	5	Connecticut	285.5
6	Pennsylvania	12 742 886	16	6	Arizona	294 207	19	6	Maryland	231.8
7	Ohio	11 544 951	35	7	Nevada	284 332	45	7	Delaware	179.7
8	Michigan	9 876 187	22	8	Colorado	268 431	3	8	New York	159.5
9	Georgia	9 815 210	51	9	Wyoming	251 470	4	9	Florida	137.2
10	North Carolina	9 656 401	27	10	Oregon	248 608	6	10	Pennsylvania	110.0
11	New Jersey	8 821 155	39	11	Idaho	214 045	7	11	Ohio	109.1
12	Virginia	8 096 604	34	12	Utah	212 818	1	12	California	93.4
13	Washington	6 830 038	33	13	Kansas	211 754	5	13	Illinois	89.5
14	Massachusetts	6 587 536	21	14	Minnesota	206 232	40	14	Hawaii	82.6
15	Indiana	6 516 922	38	15	Nebraska	198 974	12	15	Virginia	79.2
16	Arizona	6 482 505	46	16	South Dakota	196 350	10	16	North Carolina	76.7
17	Tennessee	6 403 353	48	17	North Dakota	178 711	15	17	Indiana	70.2
18	Missouri	6 010 688	18	18	Missouri	178 040	8	18	Michigan	67.4
19	Maryland	5 828 289	28	19	Oklahoma	177 660	9	19	Georgia	65.9
20	Wisconsin	5 711 767	13	20	Washington	172 119	24	20	South Carolina	60.1
21	Minnesota	5 344 861	9	21	Georgia	148 959	17	21	Tennessee	60.0
22	Colorado	5 116 796	8	22	Michigan	146 435	42	22	New Hampshire	56.9
23	Alabama	4 802 740	30	23	Iowa	144 669	26	23	Kentucky	42.7
24	South Carolina	4 679 230	5	24	Illinois	143 793	25	24	Louisiana	40.9
25	Louisiana	4 574 836	20	25	Wisconsin	140 268	20	25	Wisconsin	40.7
26	Kentucky	4 369 356	4	26	Florida	138 887	13	26	Washington	39.7
27	Oregon	3 871 859	32	27	Arkansas	134 771	2	27	Texas	37.9
28	Oklahoma	3 791 508	23	28	Alabama	131 171	23	28	Alabama	36.6
29	Connecticut	3 580 709	10	29	North Carolina	125 920	18	29	Missouri	33.8
30	Iowa	3 062 309	3	30	New York	122 057	37	30	West Virginia	29.8
31	Mississippi	2 978 512	31	31	Mississippi	121 531	49	31	Vermont	26.2
32	Arkansas	2 937 979	6	32	Pennsylvania	115 883	21	32	Minnesota	25.9
33	Kansas	2 871 238	25	33	Louisiana	111 898	31	33	Mississippi	24.5
34	Utah	2 817 222	17	34	Tennessee	106 798	16	34	Arizona	22.0
35	Nevada	2 723 322	7	35	Ohio	105 829	32	35	Arkansas	21.8
36	New Mexico	2 082 224	12	36	Virginia	102 279	28	36	Oklahoma	21.3
37	West Virginia	1 855 364	26	37	Kentucky	102 269	30	37	Iowa	21.2
38	Nebraska	1 842 641	15	38	Indiana	92 789	22	38	Colorado	19.1
39	Idaho	1 584 985	41	39	Maine	79 883	41	39	Maine	16.6
40	Hawaii	1 374 810	24	40	South Carolina	77 857	27	40	Oregon	15.6
41	Maine	1 328 188	37	41	West Virginia	62 259	33	41	Kansas	13.6
42	New Hampshire	1 318 194	19	42	Maryland	25 142	34	42	Utah	13.2
43	Rhode Island	1 051 302	49	43	Vermont	23 871	35	43	Nevada	9.6
44	Montana	998 199	42	44	New Hampshire	23 187	38	44	Nebraska	9.3
45	Delaware	907 135	14	45	Massachusetts	20 202	39	45	Idaho	7.4
46	South Dakota	824 082	11	46	New Jersey	19 047	36	46	New Mexico	6.6
47	Alaska	722 718	40	47	Hawaii	16 635	46	47	South Dakota	4.2
48	North Dakota	683 932	29	48	Connecticut	12 542	48	48	North Dakota	3.8
49	Vermont	626 431	45	49	Delaware	5 047	44	49	Montana	2.6
50	District of Columbia	617 996	43	50	Rhode Island	2 678	51	50	Wyoming	2.3
51	Wyoming	568 158	50	51	District of Columbia	158	47	51	Alaska	0.5

States and the District of Columbia
Selected Rankings

Percent population change, 2000–2010				Percent under 18 years old, 2010				Percent 65 years old and over, 2010			
Popu-lation rank	Percent change rank	State	Percent change [col 35]	Popu-lation rank	Under 18 years old rank	State	Percent under 18 years old [cols 10 + 11]	Popu-lation rank	65 years old and over rank	State	Percent 65 years old and over [cols 17 + 18 + 19]
		United States	9.7			United States	24.0			United States	13.0
35	1	Nevada	35.1	34	1	Utah	31.5	4	1	Florida	17.3
16	2	Arizona	24.6	39	2	Idaho	27.4	37	2	West Virginia	16.0
34	3	Utah	23.8	2	3	Texas	27.3	41	3	Maine	15.9
39	4	Idaho	21.1	47	4	Alaska	26.4	6	4	Pennsylvania	15.5
2	5	Texas	20.6	9	5	Georgia	25.7	30	5	Iowa	14.9
10	6	North Carolina	18.5	16	6	Arizona	25.5	44	5	Montana	14.9
9	7	Georgia	18.3	33	6	Kansas	25.5	48	7	North Dakota	14.6
4	8	Florida	17.6	31	6	Mississippi	25.5	49	8	Vermont	14.5
22	9	Colorado	16.9	36	9	New Mexico	25.1	40	9	Hawaii	14.4
24	10	South Carolina	15.3	38	9	Nebraska	25.1	32	9	Arkansas	14.4
45	11	Delaware	14.6	1	11	California	25.0	45	9	Delaware	14.4
51	12	Wyoming	14.1	46	12	South Dakota	24.9	43	9	Rhode Island	14.4
13	12	Washington	14.1	15	13	Indiana	24.8	46	13	South Dakota	14.3
47	14	Alaska	13.3	28	14	Oklahoma	24.7	7	14	Ohio	14.1
36	15	New Mexico	13.2	25	15	Louisiana	24.6	29	14	Connecticut	14.1
12	16	Virginia	13.0	35	15	Nevada	24.6	18	16	Missouri	14.0
40	17	Hawaii	12.3	32	17	Arkansas	24.4	27	17	Oregon	13.9
27	18	Oregon	12.0	5	17	Illinois	24.4	14	18	Massachusetts	13.8
17	19	Tennessee	11.5	22	19	Colorado	24.3	23	18	Alabama	13.8
1	20	California	10.0	21	20	Minnesota	24.2	16	18	Arizona	13.8
44	21	Montana	9.7	51	21	Wyoming	24.0	8	21	Michigan	13.7
32	22	Arkansas	9.1	30	22	Iowa	23.9	24	21	South Carolina	13.7
19	23	Maryland	9.0	10	22	North Carolina	23.9	20	21	Wisconsin	13.7
28	24	Oklahoma	8.7	18	24	Missouri	23.8	38	24	Nebraska	13.6
46	25	South Dakota	7.9	23	25	Alabama	23.7	42	24	New Hampshire	13.6
21	26	Minnesota	7.8	8	25	Michigan	23.7	11	26	New Jersey	13.5
23	27	Alabama	7.5	26	27	Kentucky	23.6	3	26	New York	13.5
26	28	Kentucky	7.4	20	27	Wisconsin	23.6	28	26	Oklahoma	13.5
18	29	Missouri	7.0	7	27	Ohio	23.6	17	26	Tennessee	13.5
38	30	Nebraska	6.7	11	30	New Jersey	23.5	36	30	New Mexico	13.3
15	31	Indiana	6.6	17	30	Tennessee	23.5	26	30	Kentucky	13.3
42	32	New Hampshire	6.5	13	30	Washington	23.5	33	32	Kansas	13.1
33	33	Kansas	6.1	19	33	Maryland	23.4	15	33	Indiana	13.0
20	34	Wisconsin	6.0	24	34	South Carolina	23.3	10	33	North Carolina	13.0
50	35	District of Columbia	5.2	12	35	Virginia	23.2	21	35	Minnesota	12.9
29	36	Connecticut	4.9	29	36	Connecticut	22.9	31	36	Mississippi	12.8
48	37	North Dakota	4.7	45	36	Delaware	22.9	39	37	Idaho	12.5
11	38	New Jersey	4.5	44	38	Montana	22.6	5	37	Illinois	12.5
31	39	Mississippi	4.3	27	38	Oregon	22.6	51	39	Wyoming	12.4
41	40	Maine	4.2	3	40	New York	22.4	25	40	Louisiana	12.3
30	41	Iowa	4.1	40	41	Hawaii	22.3	13	40	Washington	12.3
6	42	Pennsylvania	3.4	48	41	North Dakota	22.3	19	40	Maryland	12.3
5	43	Illinois	3.3	6	43	Pennsylvania	21.9	12	43	Virginia	12.2
14	44	Massachusetts	3.1	42	44	New Hampshire	21.8	35	44	Nevada	12.0
49	45	Vermont	2.8	14	45	Massachusetts	21.7	1	45	California	11.4
37	46	West Virginia	2.5	4	46	Florida	21.3	50	45	District of Columbia	11.4
3	47	New York	2.1	43	46	Rhode Island	21.3	22	47	Colorado	11.0
7	48	Ohio	1.6	37	48	West Virginia	20.9	9	48	Georgia	10.6
25	49	Louisiana	1.4	41	49	Maine	20.6	2	49	Texas	10.4
43	50	Rhode Island	0.4	49	49	Vermont	20.6	34	50	Utah	9.0
8	51	Michigan	-0.6	50	51	District of Columbia	16.7	47	51	Alaska	7.7

States and the District of Columbia
Selected Rankings

Percent born in state of residence, 2010				Number of immigrants, 2010				Birth rate, 2009			
Population rank	Born in state of residence rank	State	Percent born in state of residence [col 23]	Population rank	Immigrant rank	State	Number of immigrants [col 24]	Population rank	Birth rate rank	State	Birth rate (per 1,000 population) [col 98]
		United States	58.8			United States	1 042 625			United States	13.5
25	1	Louisiana	78.8	1	1	California	208 446	34	1	Utah	19.4
8	2	Michigan	76.6	3	2	New York	147 999	2	2	Texas	16.2
7	3	Ohio	75.1	4	3	Florida	107 276	47	2	Alaska	16.2
6	4	Pennsylvania	74.0	2	4	Texas	87 750	39	4	Idaho	15.4
20	5	Wisconsin	72.1	11	5	New Jersey	56 920	50	5	District of Columbia	15.1
31	6	Mississippi	71.9	5	6	Illinois	37 909	38	6	Nebraska	15.0
30	7	Iowa	71.7	14	7	Massachusetts	31 069	28	7	Oklahoma	14.8
37	8	West Virginia	71.1	12	8	Virginia	28 607	33	8	Kansas	14.7
26	9	Kentucky	70.3	19	9	Maryland	26 450	46	8	South Dakota	14.7
23	10	Alabama	70.0	9	10	Georgia	24 833	40	10	Hawaii	14.6
21	11	Minnesota	68.8	6	11	Pennsylvania	24 130	25	11	Louisiana	14.5
48	12	North Dakota	68.6	13	12	Washington	22 283	31	11	Mississippi	14.5
15	13	Indiana	68.3	8	13	Michigan	18 579	51	11	Wyoming	14.5
5	14	Illinois	67.1	16	14	Arizona	18 243	9	14	Georgia	14.4
18	15	Missouri	65.9	10	15	North Carolina	16 112	36	14	New Mexico	14.4
38	16	Nebraska	65.6	7	16	Ohio	13 585	1	16	California	14.3
46	17	South Dakota	65.1	22	17	Colorado	12 489	35	17	Nevada	14.2
41	18	Maine	64.0	21	18	Minnesota	12 408	16	18	Arizona	14.1
3	19	New York	63.6	29	19	Connecticut	12 222	48	19	North Dakota	13.9
14	20	Massachusetts	63.1	35	20	Nevada	10 803	32	20	Arkansas	13.8
34	21	Utah	62.3	15	21	Indiana	8 539	22	21	Colorado	13.7
32	22	Arkansas	61.3	17	22	Tennessee	8 156	10	22	North Carolina	13.5
17	23	Tennessee	61.0	27	23	Oregon	7 997	15	22	Indiana	13.5
28	24	Oklahoma	60.8	18	24	Missouri	7 151	13	24	Washington	13.4
2	25	Texas	60.5	40	25	Hawaii	7 037	21	24	Minnesota	13.4
43	26	Rhode Island	59.3	20	26	Wisconsin	6 189	5	26	Illinois	13.3
24	27	South Carolina	58.6	34	27	Utah	6 085	12	26	Virginia	13.3
10	28	North Carolina	58.5	33	28	Kansas	5 501	23	26	Alabama	13.3
33	29	Kansas	58.2	26	29	Kentucky	4 930	24	26	South Carolina	13.3
9	30	Georgia	55.2	28	30	Oklahoma	4 627	26	26	Kentucky	13.3
29	31	Connecticut	55.1	24	31	South Carolina	4 401	18	31	Missouri	13.2
40	32	Hawaii	55.0	38	32	Nebraska	4 400	19	31	Maryland	13.2
44	33	Montana	54.1	25	33	Louisiana	4 397	30	31	Iowa	13.2
1	34	California	53.8	30	34	Iowa	4 245	17	34	Tennessee	13.1
11	35	New Jersey	52.4	43	35	Rhode Island	4 027	45	34	Delaware	13.1
36	36	New Mexico	51.7	23	36	Alabama	3 740	3	36	New York	12.7
49	37	Vermont	51.1	36	37	New Mexico	3 528	11	36	New Jersey	12.7
12	38	Virginia	49.9	50	38	District of Columbia	2 897	44	38	Montana	12.6
19	39	Maryland	47.6	32	39	Arkansas	2 684	7	39	Ohio	12.5
39	40	Idaho	46.9	39	40	Idaho	2 556	20	39	Wisconsin	12.5
13	40	Washington	46.9	42	40	New Hampshire	2 556	27	41	Oregon	12.3
27	42	Oregon	45.5	45	42	Delaware	2 198	4	42	Florida	11.9
45	43	Delaware	45.3	31	43	Mississippi	1 709	8	43	Michigan	11.8
42	44	New Hampshire	42.7	47	44	Alaska	1 703	37	44	West Virginia	11.7
22	45	Colorado	42.5	41	45	Maine	1 349	6	45	Pennsylvania	11.6
51	46	Wyoming	41.5	48	46	North Dakota	1 058	14	46	Massachusetts	11.4
47	47	Alaska	39.0	46	47	South Dakota	987	29	47	Connecticut	11.1
16	48	Arizona	37.7	49	48	Vermont	867	43	48	Rhode Island	10.9
50	49	District of Columbia	37.3	37	49	West Virginia	729	41	49	Maine	10.2
4	50	Florida	35.2	44	50	Montana	457	42	50	New Hampshire	10.1
35	51	Nevada	24.3	51	51	Wyoming	452	49	51	Vermont	9.8

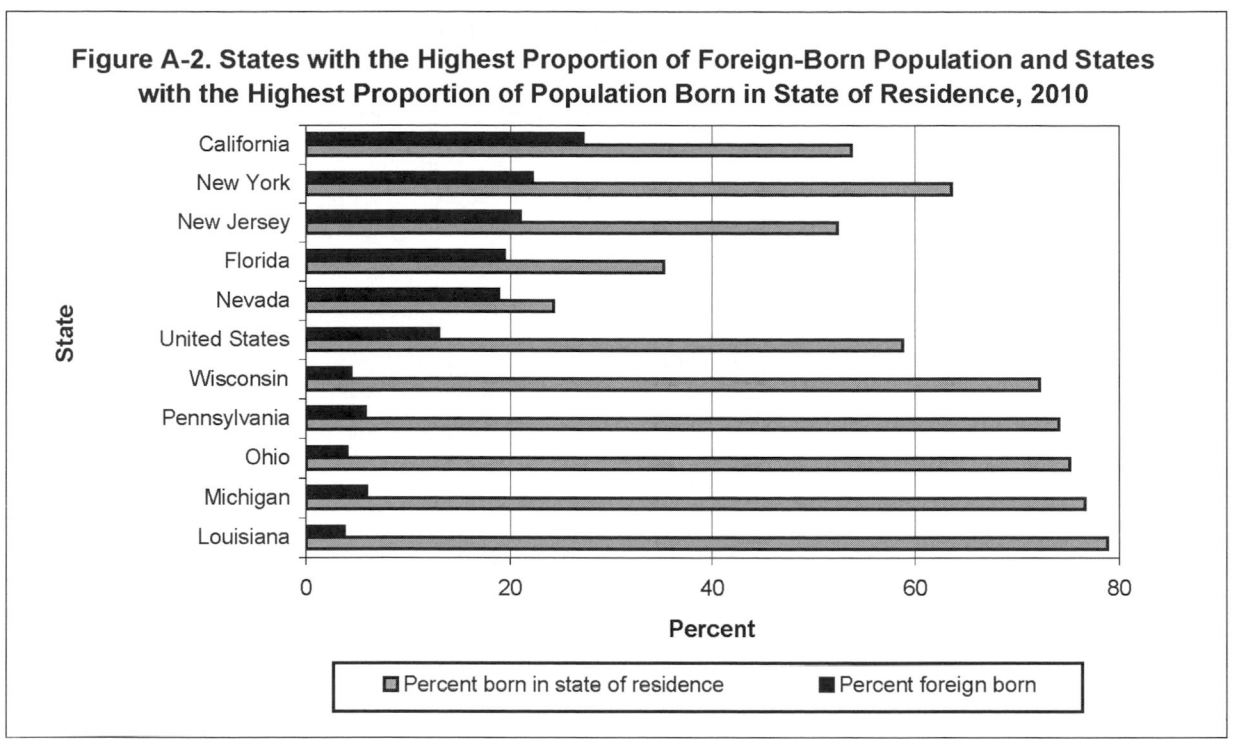

Figure A-2. States with the Highest Proportion of Foreign-Born Population and States with the Highest Proportion of Population Born in State of Residence, 2010

☐ Percent born in state of residence　　■ Percent foreign born

The U.S. median age increased from 35.3 years in 2000 to 37.2 years in 2010, primarily caused by the aging Baby Boomer population. This increase was much less than the jump from 32.1 years to 35.3 years between 1990 and 2000. The population between 55 and 64 years showed the largest proportional increase, while the proportion between 35 and 44 years old showed the largest decrease. The median age by state ranged from 29.2 years in Utah to 42.7 years in Maine. Utah had the highest proportion of young residents; in 2010, 31.5 percent of the state's population was younger than 18 years old. The population age 65 years and over ranged from 7.7 percent in Alaska to 17.3 percent in Florida. Alaska, Wyoming, and North Dakota had the lowest proportions of female residents, and were among just nine states in which males outnumbered females. South Dakota was evenly split at 50 percent each. The District of Columbia had the highest proportion of female residents with 52.8 percent.

Natural growth is the difference between the number of births and the number of deaths. Vermont had the fewest births between 2010 and 2011. West Virginia was the only state to have more deaths than births, but a net migration of more than 3,728 people prevented the state from having a population loss from 2010 to 2011. California, the largest state in the nation, had 339,330 more births than deaths and 98,740 new residents through net migration. From 2010 to 2011, California gained 164,445 residents from foreign countries and lost 65,705 residents to other states. Texas and Florida each had a net gain of over 200,000 new residents during this period. In both states, about 60 percent of these new residents were from other states. Fifteen states had a net loss of residents due to internal migration. New York lost over 100,000 residents to other states, partially offset by about 80,000 new residents from foreign countries. No state had a net loss of residents because of international migration. Michigan and Rhode Island both experienced small population losses during the year.

In ten states, more than 70 percent of the residents were born in that same state. Louisiana ranked highest with 78.8 percent. The ten highest rates were mainly in the Midwest and the South. Thirteen states and the District of Columbia had proportions less than 50 percent. Nevada had the lowest proportion by far, with just 24.3 percent of its residents having been born in the state. Nationally, 58.8 percent of Americans lived in the state of their birth.

The U.S. birth rate in 2009 was 13.5, the lowest rate ever recorded. Utah had the highest birth rate in the nation, with 19.4 births per 1,000 population. Texas and Alaska were tied for second with a birth rate of 16.2. Vermont and New Hampshire had the lowest birth rates in the nation, with rates of 9.8 and 10.1, respectively. Utah and Alaska had the lowest crude death rate with 5.1 deaths per 1,000 population. However, both states had a relatively young population (In Utah, 43.0 percent of the population was under 25 years old while 36.9 percent of the population was under 25 in Alaska). Once adjusted for age, Alaska's death rate increased to 7.5, just below the U.S. rate of 7.7, surpassing 18 states and equaling three others, once it was adjusted for age. However, the age-adjusted death rate for Utah remained much lower at 6.7. West Virginia, Alabama, and Arkansas had the highest crude death rates in the nation. With a very high proportion of persons age 65 and over, West Virginia had the highest age-adjusted death rate along with Mississippi, which had a greater mix of younger and older residents. Florida had, by far, the highest proportion of senior citizens. However, Florida also had a high proportion of younger people, which helped give the state a crude death rate outside the top ten, at 9.3 per 1,000 population. When Florida's death rate was age-adjusted, it dropped to 6.9, which was well below the national age-adjusted rate of 7.7. The District of Columbia, Mississippi, and Alabama had the highest infant mortality rates, while Utah Vermont, and New Hampshire had the lowest infant death rates.

States and the District of Columbia
Selected Rankings

Percent of owners with a mortgage paying 30 percent or more of income for housing expenses, 2010				Median value of owner-occupied housing units, 2010				Median gross rent of renter-occupied housing units, 2010			
Population rank	Percent of income for housing rank	State	Percent owner-occupied [col 83]	Population rank	Median value rank	State	Median value (dollars) [col 88]	Population rank	Median rent rank	State	Median rent (dollars) [col 90]
		United States	37.8			United States	179 900			United States	855
1	1	California	50.9	40	1	Hawaii	525 400	40	1	Hawaii	1 291
40	2	Hawaii	50.0	50	2	District of Columbia	426 900	50	2	District of Columbia	1 198
4	3	Florida	48.3	1	3	California	370 900	1	3	California	1 163
11	4	New Jersey	46.5	11	4	New Jersey	339 200	19	4	Maryland	1 131
35	5	Nevada	44.7	14	5	Massachusetts	334 100	11	5	New Jersey	1 114
43	6	Rhode Island	43.5	19	6	Maryland	301 400	3	6	New York	1 020
27	7	Oregon	42.6	3	7	New York	296 500	12	7	Virginia	1 019
29	8	Connecticut	41.3	29	8	Connecticut	288 800	14	8	Massachusetts	1 009
3	9	New York	41.2	13	9	Washington	271 800	29	9	Connecticut	992
16	10	Arizona	40.9	43	10	Rhode Island	254 500	47	10	Alaska	981
13	11	Washington	40.7	12	11	Virginia	249 100	45	11	Delaware	952
42	12	New Hampshire	40.0	27	12	Oregon	244 500	35	11	Nevada	952
5	13	Illinois	39.7	45	13	Delaware	243 600	42	13	New Hampshire	951
14	14	Massachusetts	39.0	42	14	New Hampshire	243 000	4	14	Florida	947
49	15	Vermont	38.6	47	15	Alaska	241 400	13	15	Washington	908
19	16	Maryland	38.0	22	16	Colorado	236 600	43	16	Rhode Island	868
9	17	Georgia	37.9	34	17	Utah	217 200	22	17	Colorado	863
22	18	Colorado	37.3	49	18	Vermont	216 800	5	18	Illinois	848
45	19	Delaware	37.1	21	19	Minnesota	194 300	16	19	Arizona	844
39	20	Idaho	36.6	5	20	Illinois	191 800	49	20	Vermont	823
8	21	Michigan	36.2	44	21	Montana	181 200	9	21	Georgia	819
44	22	Montana	35.9	51	22	Wyoming	180 100	27	22	Oregon	816
36	22	New Mexico	35.9	41	23	Maine	179 100	2	23	Texas	801
50	24	District of Columbia	35.5	35	24	Nevada	174 800	34	24	Utah	796
34	25	Utah	35.4	20	25	Wisconsin	169 400	21	25	Minnesota	764
31	26	Mississippi	35.2	16	26	Arizona	168 800	6	26	Pennsylvania	763
12	27	Virginia	35.0	6	27	Pennsylvania	165 500	25	27	Louisiana	736
10	28	North Carolina	34.3	39	28	Idaho	165 100	10	28	North Carolina	731
20	29	Wisconsin	34.2	4	29	Florida	164 200	8	29	Michigan	730
41	30	Maine	33.9	36	30	New Mexico	161 200	24	30	South Carolina	728
24	31	South Carolina	33.8	9	31	Georgia	156 200	20	31	Wisconsin	715
21	32	Minnesota	33.3	10	32	North Carolina	154 200	41	32	Maine	707
6	33	Pennsylvania	33.1	18	33	Missouri	139 000	36	33	New Mexico	699
17	33	Tennessee	33.1	17	33	Tennessee	139 000	17	34	Tennessee	697
23	35	Alabama	32.5	24	35	South Carolina	138 100	51	35	Wyoming	693
2	35	Texas	32.5	25	36	Louisiana	137 500	7	36	Ohio	685
47	37	Alaska	32.1	7	37	Ohio	134 400	39	37	Idaho	683
7	38	Ohio	31.8	46	38	South Dakota	129 700	15	37	Indiana	683
26	39	Kentucky	30.1	2	39	Texas	128 100	33	39	Kansas	682
25	39	Louisiana	30.1	38	40	Nebraska	127 600	18	39	Missouri	682
18	39	Missouri	30.1	33	41	Kansas	127 300	31	41	Mississippi	672
28	42	Oklahoma	28.7	23	42	Alabama	123 900	38	42	Nebraska	669
51	43	Wyoming	28.0	30	43	Iowa	123 400	23	43	Alabama	667
32	44	Arkansas	27.4	15	44	Indiana	123 300	28	44	Oklahoma	659
15	44	Indiana	27.4	8	44	Michigan	123 300	44	45	Montana	642
33	46	Kansas	26.4	48	46	North Dakota	123 000	32	46	Arkansas	638
38	47	Nebraska	25.9	26	47	Kentucky	121 600	30	47	Iowa	629
37	48	West Virginia	25.5	28	48	Oklahoma	111 400	26	48	Kentucky	613
46	49	South Dakota	25.4	32	49	Arkansas	106 300	46	49	South Dakota	591
30	50	Iowa	24.7	31	50	Mississippi	100 100	48	50	North Dakota	583
48	51	North Dakota	19.0	37	51	West Virginia	95 100	37	51	West Virginia	571

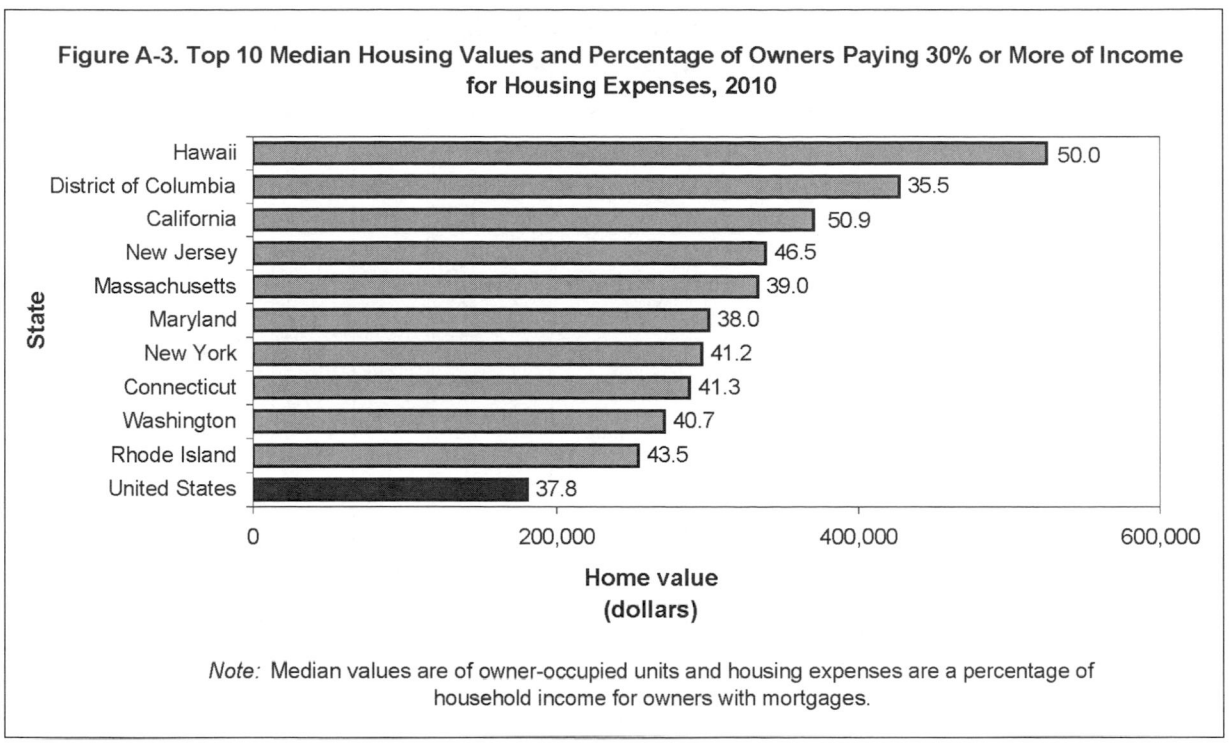

Figure A-3. Top 10 Median Housing Values and Percentage of Owners Paying 30% or More of Income for Housing Expenses, 2010

State	Value
Hawaii	50.0
District of Columbia	35.5
California	50.9
New Jersey	46.5
Massachusetts	39.0
Maryland	38.0
New York	41.2
Connecticut	41.3
Washington	40.7
Rhode Island	43.5
United States	37.8

Home value (dollars)

Note: Median values are of owner-occupied units and housing expenses are a percentage of household income for owners with mortgages.

In 2010, homeowners paid a median of 25.1 percent of their incomes for monthly owner costs (mortgage, insurance, taxes, utilities, fuel, etc.). This ranged from a high of 30.6 percent in California to 19.6 percent in North Dakota. Nationally, 37.8 percent of owners with a mortgage paid 30 percent or more of income for housing expenses in 2010. California had the highest proportion, with 50.9 percent followed by Hawaii, Florida and New Jersey which all had more than 46 percent of homeowners with a mortgage paying 30 percent or more of their income. In 10 states, less than 30 percent of all mortgaged owners paid this high level of owner costs. North Dakota had the lowest proportion in the nation with 19.0 percent. Five states and the District of Columbia had median home values exceeding $300,000 in 2010, led by Hawaii with a median home value of $525,400. Nationally, the median value of owner-occupied housing units was $179,900. Hawaii also had the highest median gross rent, at $1,291. The District of Columbia, California, Maryland, New Jersey, New York, Virginia, and Massachusetts all had median gross monthly rents exceeding $1,000.

Many minority groups had above average growth rates over the past decade. Currently, in four states and the District of Columbia, the minority population outnumbers non-Hispanic Whites. Nationally, 65.4 percent of the U.S. population was non-Hispanic White alone or in combination, but the racial and ethnic compositions of the states varied widely. In Hawaii, the state with the highest proportion of minorities, Asians and Pacific Islanders alone or in combination was the largest race group, representing over 76 percent of the state's population. Hispanics made up over 46 percent of New Mexico's residents and about 37 percent of residents in both California and Texas. The District of Columbia had the highest proportion of Black residents at just over half the population, down from 60.5 percent in 2000. Among the states, Mississippi and Louisiana ranked first and second, with Black populations of 37.4 and 32.5 percent, respectively. Alaska had the highest proportion of American Indians, who made up 18.8 percent of the population. Oklahoma, New Mexico, and South Dakota all had high proportions of American

Indian populations. As might be expected, the states with the largest number of minorities were among the states with the highest total populations. New York was home to nearly 3 million Blacks, and California had the largest number of Hispanics, Asian and Pacific Islanders, and American Indians and Alaska Natives. California had over 380,000 non-Hispanic American Indian and Alaska Native residents, though they made up just 1.0 percent of the state's population. Oklahoma ranked second for both the total number of Native Americans as well as for their representative proportion of the state's population. Despite having only about 79,000 Native American residents, South Dakota had the third highest proportion in the nation.

States and the District of Columbia
Selected Rankings

Population rank	Percent White rank	State	Percent White [col 5]	Population rank	Percent Black rank	State	Percent Black [col 6]	Population rank	Hispanic or Latino rank	State	Percent Hispanic or Latino [col 9]
		United States	65.4			United States	13.0			United States	16.3
49	1	Vermont	95.8	50	1	District of Columbia	51.3	36	1	New Mexico	46.3
41	1	Maine	95.8	31	2	Mississippi	37.4	1	2	California	37.6
37	3	West Virginia	94.4	25	3	Louisiana	32.5	2	2	Texas	37.6
42	4	New Hampshire	93.6	9	4	Georgia	30.9	16	4	Arizona	29.6
48	5	North Dakota	90.3	19	5	Maryland	30.2	35	5	Nevada	26.5
30	6	Iowa	89.9	24	6	South Carolina	28.5	4	6	Florida	22.5
44	6	Montana	89.9	23	7	Alabama	26.6	22	7	Colorado	20.7
26	8	Kentucky	87.7	45	8	Delaware	22.1	11	8	New Jersey	17.7
51	9	Wyoming	87.3	10	8	North Carolina	22.1	3	9	New York	17.6
46	10	South Dakota	86.4	12	10	Virginia	20.1	5	10	Illinois	15.8
39	11	Idaho	85.6	17	11	Tennessee	17.2	29	11	Connecticut	13.4
21	12	Minnesota	84.8	32	12	Arkansas	15.9	34	12	Utah	13.0
20	13	Wisconsin	84.6	4	12	Florida	15.9	43	13	Rhode Island	12.4
38	14	Nebraska	83.5	3	14	New York	15.2	27	14	Oregon	11.7
15	15	Indiana	82.9	5	15	Illinois	15.0	39	15	Idaho	11.2
7	16	Ohio	82.7	8	16	Michigan	14.9	13	15	Washington	11.2
18	17	Missouri	82.6	11	17	New Jersey	13.5	33	17	Kansas	10.5
34	18	Utah	82.0	7	18	Ohio	13.1	14	18	Massachusetts	9.6
27	19	Oregon	81.1	18	19	Missouri	12.3	38	19	Nebraska	9.2
6	20	Pennsylvania	80.7	2	20	Texas	12.0	50	20	District of Columbia	9.1
33	21	Kansas	80.3	6	21	Pennsylvania	11.3	40	21	Hawaii	8.9
8	22	Michigan	78.3	29	22	Connecticut	10.2	28	21	Oklahoma	8.9
43	23	Rhode Island	78.0	15	23	Indiana	9.8	51	21	Wyoming	8.9
14	24	Massachusetts	77.6	35	24	Nevada	8.7	9	24	Georgia	8.8
17	25	Tennessee	76.9	26	25	Kentucky	8.5	10	25	North Carolina	8.4
32	26	Arkansas	76.0	28	26	Oklahoma	8.4	45	26	Delaware	8.2
13	27	Washington	75.8	14	27	Massachusetts	6.8	19	26	Maryland	8.2
28	28	Oklahoma	73.3	20	27	Wisconsin	6.8	12	28	Virginia	7.9
29	29	Connecticut	72.6	33	29	Kansas	6.7	32	29	Arkansas	6.4
22	30	Colorado	71.8	1	30	California	6.5	15	30	Indiana	6.0
47	31	Alaska	69.8	43	31	Rhode Island	6.2	20	31	Wisconsin	5.9
23	32	Alabama	68.2	21	32	Minnesota	6.0	6	32	Pennsylvania	5.7
45	33	Delaware	67.0	38	33	Nebraska	5.2	47	33	Alaska	5.5
12	34	Virginia	66.8	22	34	Colorado	4.5	24	34	South Carolina	5.1
10	35	North Carolina	66.6	13	34	Washington	4.5	30	35	Iowa	5.0
24	36	South Carolina	65.2	16	36	Arizona	4.4	21	36	Minnesota	4.7
5	37	Illinois	64.9	47	37	Alaska	4.3	17	37	Tennessee	4.6
25	38	Louisiana	61.4	37	38	West Virginia	4.1	8	38	Michigan	4.4
11	39	New Jersey	60.5	30	39	Iowa	3.6	25	39	Louisiana	4.2
3	40	New York	59.5	40	40	Hawaii	2.5	23	40	Alabama	3.9
16	41	Arizona	59.4	27	41	Oregon	2.3	18	41	Missouri	3.5
4	42	Florida	59.1	36	42	New Mexico	2.2	26	42	Kentucky	3.1
31	43	Mississippi	58.8	46	43	South Dakota	1.7	7	42	Ohio	3.1
9	44	Georgia	57.1	41	44	Maine	1.6	44	44	Montana	2.9
35	45	Nevada	56.6	48	44	North Dakota	1.6	42	45	New Hampshire	2.8
19	46	Maryland	56.4	42	46	New Hampshire	1.5	31	46	Mississippi	2.7
2	47	Texas	46.4	49	47	Vermont	1.4	46	46	South Dakota	2.7
1	48	California	42.3	34	48	Utah	1.3	48	48	North Dakota	2.0
36	49	New Mexico	41.7	51	49	Wyoming	1.1	49	49	Vermont	1.5
40	50	Hawaii	36.5	39	50	Idaho	0.9	41	50	Maine	1.3
50	51	District of Columbia	36.3	44	51	Montana	0.7	37	51	West Virginia	1.2

1. May be of any race

10

States and the District of Columbia
Selected Rankings

Percent high school graduates,[1] 2010				Percent college graduates (bachelor's degree or more),[1] 2010				Median household income, 2010			
Population rank	Percent high school graduates rank	State	Percent high school graduates [col 115]	Population rank	Percent college graduates rank	State	Percent college graduates [col 116]	Population rank	Median income rank	State	Median income (dollars) [col 123]
		United States	85.6			United States	28.2			United States	50 046
51	1	Wyoming	92.3	50	1	District of Columbia	50.1	19	1	Maryland	68 854
21	2	Minnesota	91.8	14	2	Massachusetts	39.0	11	2	New Jersey	67 681
44	3	Montana	91.7	22	3	Colorado	36.4	47	3	Alaska	64 576
42	4	New Hampshire	91.5	19	4	Maryland	36.1	29	4	Connecticut	64 032
47	5	Alaska	91.0	29	5	Connecticut	35.5	40	5	Hawaii	63 030
49	5	Vermont	91.0	11	6	New Jersey	35.4	14	6	Massachusetts	62 072
30	7	Iowa	90.6	12	7	Virginia	34.2	42	7	New Hampshire	61 042
34	7	Utah	90.6	49	8	Vermont	33.6	50	8	District of Columbia	60 903
38	9	Nebraska	90.4	42	9	New Hampshire	32.8	12	9	Virginia	60 674
41	10	Maine	90.3	3	10	New York	32.5	1	10	California	57 708
48	10	North Dakota	90.3	21	11	Minnesota	31.8	45	11	Delaware	55 847
20	12	Wisconsin	90.1	13	12	Washington	31.1	13	12	Washington	55 631
40	13	Hawaii	89.9	5	13	Illinois	30.8	21	13	Minnesota	55 459
13	14	Washington	89.8	43	14	Rhode Island	30.2	34	14	Utah	54 744
22	15	Colorado	89.7	1	15	California	30.1	3	15	New York	54 148
46	16	South Dakota	89.6	33	16	Kansas	29.8	22	16	Colorado	54 046
33	17	Kansas	89.2	40	17	Hawaii	29.5	51	17	Wyoming	53 512
14	18	Massachusetts	89.1	34	18	Utah	29.3	5	18	Illinois	52 972
27	19	Oregon	88.8	44	19	Montana	28.8	43	19	Rhode Island	52 254
8	20	Michigan	88.7	27	19	Oregon	28.8	35	20	Nevada	51 001
29	21	Connecticut	88.6	38	21	Nebraska	28.6	49	21	Vermont	49 406
6	22	Pennsylvania	88.4	47	22	Alaska	27.9	6	22	Pennsylvania	49 288
39	23	Idaho	88.3	45	23	Delaware	27.8	20	23	Wisconsin	49 001
19	24	Maryland	88.1	48	24	North Dakota	27.6	48	24	North Dakota	48 670
7	24	Ohio	88.1	9	25	Georgia	27.3	2	25	Texas	48 615
11	26	New Jersey	88.0	6	26	Pennsylvania	27.1	38	26	Nebraska	48 408
45	27	Delaware	87.7	41	27	Maine	26.8	33	27	Kansas	48 257
50	28	District of Columbia	87.4	10	28	North Carolina	26.5	30	28	Iowa	47 961
15	29	Indiana	87.0	46	29	South Dakota	26.3	16	29	Arizona	46 789
5	30	Illinois	86.9	20	29	Wisconsin	26.3	27	30	Oregon	46 560
18	30	Missouri	86.9	16	31	Arizona	25.9	9	31	Georgia	46 430
12	32	Virginia	86.5	2	31	Texas	25.9	46	32	South Dakota	45 904
28	33	Oklahoma	86.2	4	33	Florida	25.8	41	33	Maine	45 815
16	34	Arizona	85.6	18	34	Missouri	25.6	8	34	Michigan	45 413
4	35	Florida	85.5	8	35	Michigan	25.2	7	35	Ohio	45 090
3	36	New York	84.9	30	36	New Mexico	25.0	15	36	Indiana	44 613
35	37	Nevada	84.7	30	37	Iowa	24.9	4	37	Florida	44 409
10	37	North Carolina	84.7	7	38	Ohio	24.6	18	38	Missouri	44 301
9	39	Georgia	84.3	24	39	South Carolina	24.5	39	39	Idaho	43 490
24	40	South Carolina	84.1	39	40	Idaho	24.4	10	40	North Carolina	43 326
17	41	Tennessee	83.6	51	41	Wyoming	24.1	44	41	Montana	42 666
43	42	Rhode Island	83.5	17	42	Tennessee	23.1	25	42	Louisiana	42 505
36	43	New Mexico	83.3	28	43	Oklahoma	22.9	36	43	New Mexico	42 090
37	44	West Virginia	83.2	15	44	Indiana	22.7	28	44	Oklahoma	42 072
32	45	Arkansas	82.9	23	45	Alabama	21.9	24	45	South Carolina	42 018
23	46	Alabama	82.1	35	46	Nevada	21.7	17	46	Tennessee	41 461
26	47	Kentucky	81.9	25	47	Louisiana	21.4	23	47	Alabama	40 474
25	47	Louisiana	81.9	26	48	Kentucky	20.5	26	48	Kentucky	40 062
31	49	Mississippi	81.0	32	49	Arkansas	19.5	32	49	Arkansas	38 307
1	50	California	80.7	31	49	Mississippi	19.5	37	50	West Virginia	38 218
2	50	Texas	80.7	37	51	West Virginia	17.5	31	51	Mississippi	36 851

1. Persons 25 years old and over

States and the District of Columbia
Selected Rankings

Unemployment rate, 2011				Per capita state taxes, 2009–2010				Exports of goods by state of origin, 2010			
Population rank	Unemployment rate rank	State	Unemployment rate [col 171]	Population rank	State taxes rank	State	State taxes per capita (dollars) [col 337]	Population rank	Exports rank	State	Exports (milions of dollars) [col 119]
		United States	8.9			United States	X			United States	1 480 665
35	1	Nevada	13.5	47	1	Alaska	6 361	2	1	Texas	249 860
1	2	California	11.7	49	2	Vermont	4 013	1	2	California	159 354
43	3	Rhode Island	11.3	48	3	North Dakota	3 934	3	3	New York	82 894
31	4	Mississippi	10.7	51	4	Wyoming	3 756	4	4	Florida	64 756
4	5	Florida	10.5	40	5	Hawaii	3 556	13	5	Washington	64 632
10	5	North Carolina	10.5	29	6	Connecticut	3 438	5	6	Illinois	64 565
8	7	Michigan	10.3	3	7	New York	3 278	25	7	Louisiana	55 124
24	7	South Carolina	10.3	21	8	Minnesota	3 245	8	8	Michigan	50 802
50	9	District of Columbia	10.2	45	9	Delaware	3 085	7	9	Ohio	46 408
9	10	Georgia	9.8	14	10	Massachusetts	3 062	6	10	Pennsylvania	41 030
5	10	Illinois	9.8	11	11	New Jersey	2 949	11	11	New Jersey	38 241
16	12	Arizona	9.5	1	12	California	2 814	9	12	Georgia	34 713
26	12	Kentucky	9.5	19	13	Maryland	2 637	15	13	Indiana	32 200
27	12	Oregon	9.5	41	14	Maine	2 627	17	14	Tennessee	29 973
11	15	New Jersey	9.3	20	15	Wisconsin	2 527	14	15	Massachusetts	27 711
17	16	Tennessee	9.2	37	16	West Virginia	2 512	10	16	North Carolina	26 964
13	16	Washington	9.2	32	17	Arkansas	2 496	24	17	South Carolina	24 680
23	18	Alabama	9.0	43	18	Rhode Island	2 441	20	18	Wisconsin	22 048
15	18	Indiana	9.0	13	19	Washington	2 395	21	19	Minnesota	20 276
29	20	Connecticut	8.8	6	20	Pennsylvania	2 375	26	20	Kentucky	20 066
39	21	Idaho	8.7	33	21	Kansas	2 276	34	21	Utah	18 929
18	22	Missouri	8.6	10	22	North Carolina	2 257	27	22	Oregon	18 292
7	22	Ohio	8.6	8	23	Michigan	2 247	12	23	Virginia	18 105
22	24	Colorado	8.3	30	24	Iowa	2 235	23	24	Alabama	17 893
3	25	New York	8.2	26	25	Kentucky	2 196	16	25	Arizona	17 501
32	26	Arkansas	8.0	44	26	Montana	2 166	29	26	Connecticut	16 198
37	26	West Virginia	8.0	35	27	Nevada	2 161	18	27	Missouri	14 145
6	28	Pennsylvania	7.9	5	28	Illinois	2 144	30	28	Iowa	13 283
2	28	Texas	7.9	36	29	New Mexico	2 144	33	29	Kansas	11 572
47	30	Alaska	7.6	15	30	Indiana	2 128	31	30	Mississippi	10 926
41	31	Maine	7.5	31	31	Mississippi	2 113	19	31	Maryland	10 879
20	31	Wisconsin	7.5	38	32	Nebraska	2 086	37	32	West Virginia	9 002
14	33	Massachusetts	7.4	12	33	Virginia	2 051	35	33	Nevada	7 978
36	33	New Mexico	7.4	7	34	Ohio	2 044	38	34	Nebraska	7 578
45	35	Delaware	7.3	25	35	Louisiana	1 932	22	35	Colorado	7 334
25	35	Louisiana	7.3	27	36	Oregon	1 903	28	36	Oklahoma	6 218
19	37	Maryland	7.0	28	37	Oklahoma	1 887	39	37	Idaho	5 898
44	38	Montana	6.8	39	38	Idaho	1 883	32	38	Arkansas	5 559
40	39	Hawaii	6.7	34	39	Utah	1 842	45	39	Delaware	5 509
33	39	Kansas	6.7	23	40	Alabama	1 713	47	40	Alaska	5 238
34	39	Utah	6.7	22	41	Colorado	1 707	49	41	Vermont	4 328
21	42	Minnesota	6.4	4	42	Florida	1 675	42	42	New Hampshire	4 294
28	43	Oklahoma	6.2	17	43	Tennessee	1 657	41	43	Maine	3 461
12	43	Virginia	6.2	18	44	Missouri	1 621	48	44	North Dakota	3 379
51	45	Wyoming	6.0	42	45	New Hampshire	1 614	43	45	Rhode Island	2 300
30	46	Iowa	5.9	46	46	South Dakota	1 602	36	46	New Mexico	2 090
49	47	Vermont	5.6	16	47	Arizona	1 596	44	47	Montana	1 581
42	48	New Hampshire	5.4	24	48	South Carolina	1 581	46	48	South Dakota	1 455
46	49	South Dakota	4.7	2	49	Texas	1 567	51	49	Wyoming	1 222
38	50	Nebraska	4.4	9	50	Georgia	1 526	50	50	District of Columbia	1 055
48	51	North Dakota	3.5	50	X	District of Columbia	X	40	51	Hawaii	909

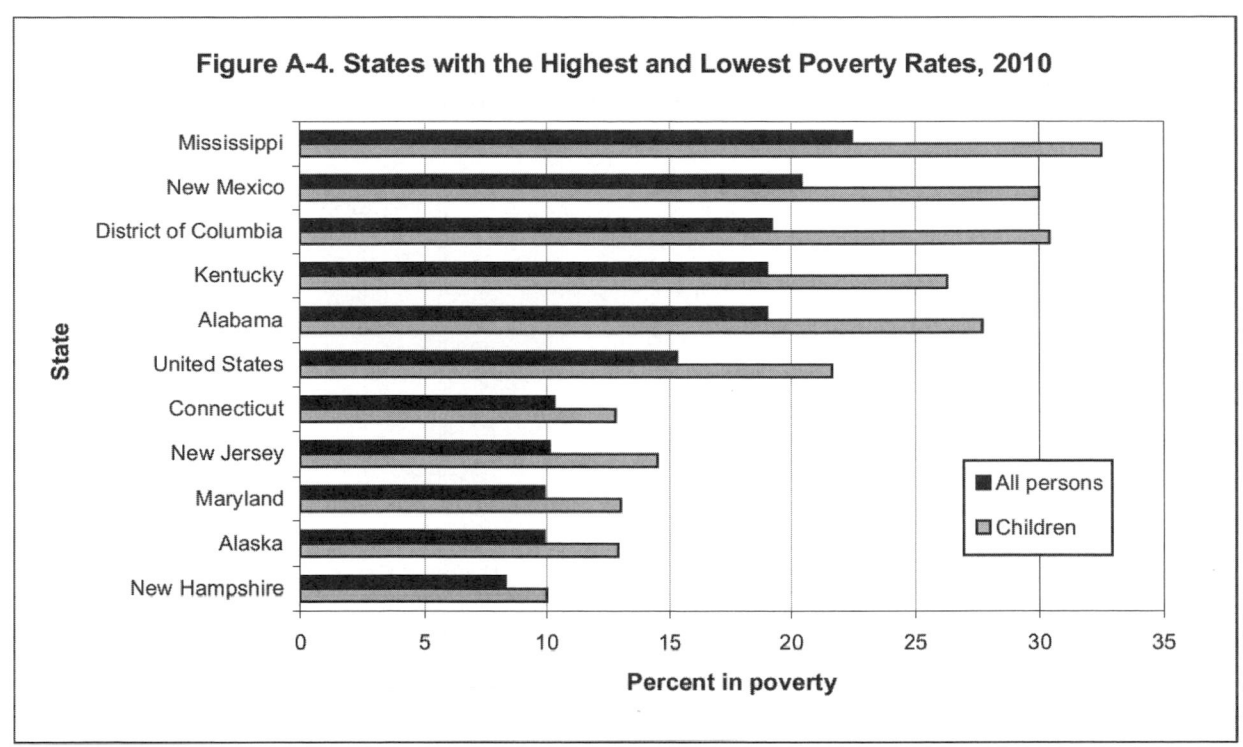

Figure A-4. States with the Highest and Lowest Poverty Rates, 2010

Nationally, 85.6 percent of the population 25 years old and over has graduated from high school. Twelve states had high school attainment levels of 90 percent or more, led by Wyoming with 92.3 percent. States in the Midwest and the West tended to have above average high school attainment rates although California along with Texas had the lowest rate in the nation at 80.7 percent. States with above average high school attainment levels do not necessarily have high proportions of college graduates. Nationally, 28.2 percent of the population held bachelor's degrees. In the District of Columbia, 50.1 percent of the population had graduated from college. Even when compared with other large cities, the District of Columbia had among the 10 highest proportions of college graduates in the nation. Of the 50 states, Massachusetts, Colorado, Connecticut, New Jersey and Maryland each had more than 35 percent of their populations holding bachelor's degrees or more. States in the Northeast tended to have above average college attainment levels, while states in the South had below average rates.

Median household income ranged from $36,851 in Mississippi to $68,854 in Maryland. Nationally, the median household income was $50,046. In nine states—Mississippi, West Virginia, Kentucky, Arkansas, Alabama, Louisiana, South Carolina, Tennessee, and New Mexico—more than 30 percent of households had incomes below $25,000. Maryland and New Jersey had the highest proportions of households earning $100,000 or more, at 32.8 percent and 32.5 percent respectively, followed by the District of Columbia at 30.5 percent and Connecticut at 29.9 percent.

The poverty threshold for an individual was $11,139 in 2010. Mississippi had the highest poverty rate in the nation, with 22.4 percent of its population living in poverty. New Mexico, the District of Columbia, Kentucky, and Alabama all ranked among the top five, with poverty rates of 19 percent or higher. The threshold for a four-person family was $22,314. Among all children under 18 years old, 21.6 percent were living in poverty.

Over 30 percent of children in Mississippi, the District of Columbia, and New Mexico lived in poverty. New Hampshire had the lowest proportion of children in poverty, at 10.0 percent. The District of Columbia had the highest proportion of residents 65 years and over living in poverty at 13.1 percent.

The United States labor force declined by 0.2 percent between 2010 and 2011. From 2000 to 2008, it grew about an average of 1 percent a year but has been declining since then. Nineteen states experienced a decline in their labor force between 2010 and 2011. Arizona experienced the largest decline, dropping 2.1 percent. Meanwhile, the labor force in Mississippi grew by 2.1 percent in the same period. In 2011, eight states and the District of Columbia had unemployment rates at 10 percent or higher. At 13.5 percent, Nevada had the highest unemployment rate in the nation, followed by California at 11.7 percent. Michigan ranked 7th with an unemployment rate of 10.3, after ranking first or second for five straight years. North Dakota, Nebraska, and South Dakota had the lowest unemployment rates in 2011— all below 5 percent.

States and the District of Columbia
Selected Rankings

Percent of persons below the poverty level, 2010				Percent of children under 18 years old below the poverty level, 2010				Percent of persons lacking health insurance, 2010			
Popu-lation rank	Poverty rate rank	State	Poverty rate [col 127]	Popu-lation rank	Poverty rate rank	State	Poverty rate [col 128]	Popu-lation rank	Percent lacking health insurance rank	State	Percent lacking health insurance [col 104]
		United States	15.3			United States	21.6			United States	16.3
31	1	Mississippi	22.4	31	1	Mississippi	32.5	2	1	Texas	24.6
36	2	New Mexico	20.4	50	2	District of Columbia	30.4	36	2	New Mexico	21.6
50	3	District of Columbia	19.2	36	3	New Mexico	30.0	35	3	Nevada	21.3
23	4	Alabama	19.0	23	4	Alabama	27.7	31	4	Mississippi	21.1
26	4	Kentucky	19.0	32	5	Arkansas	27.6	4	5	Florida	20.8
32	6	Arkansas	18.8	25	6	Louisiana	27.3	24	6	South Carolina	20.6
25	7	Louisiana	18.7	26	7	Kentucky	26.3	25	7	Louisiana	20.0
24	8	South Carolina	18.2	24	8	South Carolina	26.1	9	8	Georgia	19.4
37	9	West Virginia	18.1	17	9	Tennessee	25.7	1	8	California	19.4
9	10	Georgia	17.9	2	9	Texas	25.7	39	10	Idaho	19.2
2	10	Texas	17.9	37	11	West Virginia	25.5	16	11	Arizona	19.1
17	12	Tennessee	17.7	10	12	North Carolina	24.9	32	12	Arkansas	18.7
10	13	North Carolina	17.5	9	13	Georgia	24.8	44	13	Montana	18.1
16	14	Arizona	17.4	28	14	Oklahoma	24.7	47	14	Alaska	18.0
28	15	Oklahoma	16.9	16	15	Arizona	24.4	51	15	Wyoming	17.3
8	16	Michigan	16.8	4	16	Florida	23.5	10	16	North Carolina	17.0
4	17	Florida	16.5	8	16	Michigan	23.5	28	16	Oklahoma	17.0
1	18	California	15.8	7	18	Ohio	23.3	27	18	Oregon	16.2
7	18	Ohio	15.8	1	19	California	22.0	11	19	New Jersey	15.4
27	18	Oregon	15.8	35	19	Nevada	22.0	23	19	Alabama	15.4
39	21	Idaho	15.7	15	21	Indiana	21.7	3	21	New York	15.0
15	22	Indiana	15.3	27	22	Oregon	21.6	26	22	Kentucky	14.9
18	22	Missouri	15.3	3	23	New York	21.2	5	23	Illinois	14.8
35	24	Nevada	14.9	18	24	Missouri	20.9	17	24	Tennessee	14.7
3	24	New York	14.9	44	25	Montana	20.1	12	25	Virginia	14.1
44	26	Montana	14.6	5	26	Illinois	19.4	18	26	Missouri	14.0
46	27	South Dakota	14.4	6	27	Pennsylvania	19.1	13	27	Washington	13.8
43	28	Rhode Island	14.0	20	27	Wisconsin	19.1	7	28	Ohio	13.7
5	29	Illinois	13.8	39	29	Idaho	19.0	34	29	Utah	13.6
33	30	Kansas	13.6	43	29	Rhode Island	19.0	37	30	West Virginia	13.5
22	31	Colorado	13.4	33	31	Kansas	18.4	15	31	Indiana	13.4
6	31	Pennsylvania	13.4	38	32	Nebraska	18.2	38	32	Nebraska	13.3
13	31	Washington	13.4	46	32	South Dakota	18.2	48	33	North Dakota	13.1
34	34	Utah	13.2	13	32	Washington	18.2	19	33	Maryland	13.1
20	34	Wisconsin	13.2	45	35	Delaware	18.1	46	35	South Dakota	13.0
48	36	North Dakota	13.0	41	36	Maine	17.8	8	35	Michigan	13.0
41	37	Maine	12.9	22	37	Colorado	17.4	22	35	Colorado	13.0
38	37	Nebraska	12.9	49	38	Vermont	16.7	33	38	Kansas	12.7
49	39	Vermont	12.7	30	39	Iowa	16.3	50	39	District of Columbia	12.5
30	40	Iowa	12.6	48	40	North Dakota	16.2	30	40	Iowa	12.3
45	41	Delaware	11.8	34	41	Utah	15.7	43	41	Rhode Island	11.4
21	42	Minnesota	11.6	21	42	Minnesota	15.2	45	42	Delaware	11.3
14	43	Massachusetts	11.4	11	43	New Jersey	14.5	6	43	Pennsylvania	11.0
51	44	Wyoming	11.2	12	43	Virginia	14.5	29	43	Connecticut	11.0
12	45	Virginia	11.1	14	45	Massachusetts	14.3	42	45	New Hampshire	10.3
40	46	Hawaii	10.7	51	45	Wyoming	14.3	21	46	Minnesota	9.8
11	47	New Jersey	10.3	40	47	Hawaii	13.9	49	47	Vermont	9.5
29	48	Connecticut	10.1	19	48	Maryland	13.0	41	48	Maine	9.4
47	49	Alaska	9.9	47	49	Alaska	12.9	20	48	Wisconsin	9.4
19	49	Maryland	9.9	29	50	Connecticut	12.8	40	50	Hawaii	7.7
42	51	New Hampshire	8.3	42	51	New Hampshire	10.0	14	51	Massachusetts	5.6

States and the District of Columbia
Selected Rankings

Defense contracts, 2009–2010				Value of agricultural products sold, 2007				Violent crime rate, 2010 (violent crimes known to police)			
Popu-rank	Defense contract rank	State	Defense contracts (millions of dollars) [col 314]	Popu-lation rank	Agri-cultural sales rank	State	Value of sales (millions of dollars) [col 197]	Popu-lation rank	Violent crime rate rank	State	Violent crime rate (per 100,000 population) [col 108]
		United States	329 873			United States	297 220			United States	403.6
1	1	California	41 323	1	1	California	33 885	50	1	District of Columbia	1 330.2
12	2	Virginia	40 378	2	2	Texas	21 001	35	2	Nevada	660.6
2	3	Texas	30 331	30	3	Iowa	20 418	47	3	Alaska	638.8
4	4	Florida	12 814	38	4	Nebraska	15 506	45	4	Delaware	620.9
14	5	Massachusetts	12 674	33	5	Kansas	14 413	17	5	Tennessee	613.3
19	6	Maryland	12 018	5	6	Illinois	13 329	24	6	South Carolina	597.7
6	7	Pennsylvania	11 901	21	7	Minnesota	13 180	36	7	New Mexico	588.9
29	8	Connecticut	11 114	10	8	North Carolina	10 314	25	8	Louisiana	549.0
16	9	Arizona	10 831	20	9	Wisconsin	8 967	19	9	Maryland	547.7
18	10	Missouri	10 335	15	10	Indiana	8 271	4	10	Florida	542.4
3	11	New York	8 810	4	11	Florida	7 785	32	11	Arkansas	505.3
20	12	Wisconsin	8 469	18	12	Missouri	7 513	8	12	Michigan	490.3
9	13	Georgia	8 378	32	13	Arkansas	7 509	28	13	Oklahoma	479.5
23	14	Alabama	8 140	9	14	Georgia	7 113	14	14	Massachusetts	466.6
11	15	New Jersey	7 858	7	15	Ohio	7 070	18	15	Missouri	455.0
5	16	Illinois	7 119	13	16	Washington	6 793	2	16	Texas	450.3
7	17	Ohio	6 064	46	17	South Dakota	6 570	1	17	California	440.6
25	18	Louisiana	5 842	48	18	North Dakota	6 084	5	18	Illinois	435.2
22	19	Colorado	5 632	22	19	Colorado	6 061	16	19	Arizona	408.1
26	20	Kentucky	5 181	6	20	Pennsylvania	5 809	9	20	Georgia	403.3
13	21	Washington	5 151	28	21	Oklahoma	5 806	3	21	New York	392.1
50	22	District of Columbia	4 651	8	22	Michigan	5 753	23	22	Alabama	377.8
24	23	South Carolina	4 497	39	23	Idaho	5 689	33	23	Kansas	369.1
15	24	Indiana	4 370	31	24	Mississippi	4 877	6	24	Pennsylvania	366.2
8	25	Michigan	4 080	26	25	Kentucky	4 825	10	25	North Carolina	363.4
10	26	North Carolina	3 627	3	26	New York	4 419	22	26	Colorado	320.8
17	27	Tennessee	3 101	23	27	Alabama	4 416	7	27	Ohio	315.2
34	28	Utah	2 522	27	28	Oregon	4 386	37	28	West Virginia	314.6
28	29	Oklahoma	2 410	16	29	Arizona	3 235	15	29	Indiana	314.5
40	30	Hawaii	2 351	12	30	Virginia	2 906	13	30	Washington	313.8
33	31	Kansas	1 941	44	31	Montana	2 803	11	31	New Jersey	307.7
47	32	Alaska	1 776	25	32	Louisiana	2 618	29	32	Connecticut	281.4
31	33	Mississippi	1 634	17	33	Tennessee	2 617	38	33	Nebraska	279.5
30	34	Iowa	1 557	24	34	South Carolina	2 353	30	34	Iowa	273.5
21	35	Minnesota	1 520	36	35	New Mexico	2 175	44	35	Montana	272.2
36	35	New Mexico	1 520	19	36	Maryland	1 835	31	36	Mississippi	269.7
41	37	Maine	1 336	34	37	Utah	1 416	46	37	South Dakota	268.5
35	38	Nevada	1 315	51	38	Wyoming	1 158	40	38	Hawaii	262.7
32	39	Arkansas	1 138	45	39	Delaware	1 083	43	39	Rhode Island	256.6
42	40	New Hampshire	1 092	11	40	New Jersey	987	27	40	Oregon	252.0
27	41	Oregon	891	49	41	Vermont	674	20	41	Wisconsin	248.7
38	42	Nebraska	793	41	42	Maine	617	26	42	Kentucky	242.6
43	43	Rhode Island	777	37	43	West Virginia	592	21	43	Minnesota	236.0
49	44	Vermont	711	29	44	Connecticut	552	48	44	North Dakota	225.0
46	45	South Carolina	561	40	45	Hawaii	514	39	45	Idaho	221.0
37	46	West Virginia	345	35	46	Nevada	513	12	46	Virginia	213.6
44	47	Montana	313	14	47	Massachusetts	490	34	47	Utah	212.7
48	48	North Dakota	288	42	48	New Hampshire	199	51	48	Wyoming	195.9
39	49	Idaho	265	43	49	Rhode Island	66	42	49	New Hampshire	167.0
45	50	Delaware	218	47	50	Alaska	57	49	50	Vermont	130.2
51	51	Wyoming	155	50	X	District of Columbia	X	41	51	Maine	122.0

15

Table A. States — **Land Area and Population Characteristics**

State code	STATE	Population, 2011				Population characteristics, 2010										
						Race alone or in combination, not Hispanic or Latino (percent)					Age (percent)					
		Land area,[1] 2010 (sq km)	Total persons, 2011	Rank	Per square kilometer	White	Black	American Indian, Alaska Native	Asian and Pacific Islander	Hispanic or Latino[2] (percent)	Under 5 years	5 to 17 years	18 to 24 years	25 to 34 years	35 to 44 years	45 to 54 years
		1	2	3	4	5	6	7	8	9	10	11	12	13	14	15

1. Dry land or land partially or temporarily covered by water. 2. May be of any race.

Table A. States — **Population Characteristics, Immigration, and Households**

STATE	Population characteristics, 2010 (cont.)									Households, 2010					
	Age (percent) (cont.)												Household type		
	55 to 64 years	65 to 74 years	75 to 84 years	85 years and over	Median age	Percent female	Percent foreign born	Percent born in state of residence	Immigrants admitted to legal status, 2010	Number	Percent change, 2000–2010	Persons per house-hold	Married couple	Female house-holder[1]	House-holder living alone
	16	17	18	19	20	21	22	23	24	25	26	27	28	29	30

1. No spouse present.

Table A. States — **Population Change**

STATE	Population, 1990–2010			Population change, 1990–2011								Population, 2020–2030		
	Census counts			Percent change			Components of change, 2010–2011					Projections		
									Migration					
	1990	2000	2010	1990–2000	2000–2010	2010–2011	Births	Deaths	Net migration	Inter-national	Net internal	2020	2025	2030
	31	32	33	34	35	36	37	38	39	40	41	42	43	44

Table A. States — **Population Characteristics**

STATE	Population characteristics, 2000																		
	Race (percent)							Age (percent)											
	White alone	Black alone	American Indian, Alaska Native alone	Asian and Pacific Islander alone	Some other race or two or more races	Percent Hispanic or Latino[1]	Percent foreign born	Under 5 years	5 to 17 years	18 to 24 years	25 to 34 years	35 to 44 years	45 to 54 years	55 to 64 years	65 to 74 years	75 to 84 years	85 years and over	Median age	Percent female
	45	46	47	48	49	50	51	52	53	54	55	56	57	58	59	60	61	62	63

1. May be of any race.

Table A. States — **Households and Housing Units**

STATE	Households, 2000														Housing units, 2000															
					Percent													Occupied units												
																		Owner-occupied							Renter-occupied					
																				Median owner cost										
	Number	Percent change, 1990–2000	Persons per house-hold	Female family house-holder[1]	One person			Total	Percent change, 1990–2000			Total	Percent	Median value[2] (dollars)	With a mort-gage	Without a mort-gage[3]		Median rent[4] (dollars)	Median rent as a percent of income	Sub-standard units[5] (percent)
	64	65	66	67	68			69	70			71	72	73	74	75		76	77	78

1. No spouse present.   2. Specified owner-occupied units.   3. Median monthly costs is often in the minimum category—9.9 percent or less, which is indicated as 9.9 percent.
4. Specified renter-occupied units.   5. Overcrowded or lacking complete plumbing facilities.

Table A. States — **Housing Units**

STATE	Housing units, 2010													
			Occupied units											
						Percent who pay 30 percent or more of income for housing expenses		Median owner cost as a percent of income						
	Total	Percent change, 2000–2010	Total	Percent owner-occupied	Owners with a mort-gage	Renter	With a mort-gage	Without a mort-gage[1]	Median monthly housing costs (dollars)	Median value of units[2] (dollars)	Percent valued over $500,000	Median gross rent[3] (dollars)	Sub-standard units[4] (percent)	Percent living in a different house than 1 year ago
	79	80	81	82	83	84	85	86	87	88	89	90	91	92

1. Median monthly costs is often in the minimum category—10.0 percent or less, which is indicated as 10.0 percent.   2. Specified owner-occupied units.   3. Specified renter-occupied units.
4. Overcrowded or lacking complete plumbing facilities.

Table A. States — **Residential Construction, Vital Statistics, and Health**

STATE	Value of residential construction authorized by building permits, 2010				Births, 2009		Deaths, 2008					Percent lacking health insurance, 2010		
								Number		Rate				
											Total			
	New con-struction ($1,000)	Number of housing units	Percent single family	Manu-factured housing units put in place, 2010 (1,000)	Total	Rate[1]	Total	Infant[2]	Crude[1]	Age-adjusted	Infant[3]	All persons	Children under 18 years	Medicare enrollees, 2010
	93	94	95	96	97	98	99	100	101	102	103	104	105	106

1. Per 1,000 resident population.   2. Deaths of infants under 1 year old.   3. Deaths of infants under 1 year old per 1,000 live births.

Table A. States — **Crime and Education**

STATE	Serious crime known to police,[1] 2010				Public elementary and secondary school enrollment, 2009–2010		Educational attainment[3] (percent)				Local government expenditures for education, 2008–2009	
	Violent Crime		Property Crime				2000		2010			
							High school graduate or more	Bachelor's degree or more	High school graduate or more	Bachelor's degree or more		
	Number	Rate[2]	Number	Rate[2]	Total	Student/ teacher ratio					Total current expenditures (mil dol)	Current expenditures per student (dollars)
	107	108	109	110	111	112	113	114	115	116	117	118

1. Data for serious crimes have not been adjusted for underreporting; this may affect comparability between geographic areas and over time.   2. Per 100,000 population estimated by the FBI.   3. Persons 25 years old and over.

Table A. States — Exports, Income, and Poverty

STATE	Exports of goods by state of origin, 2011 (mil dol)			Income, 2010					Percent below poverty level, 2010						
				Households									Families with children under 18		
	Total	Manu-factured	Non-manu-factured	Per capita income (dollars)	Median income (dollars)	Percent with income of $25,000 or less	Percent with income of $100,000 or more	Median income of family of four	All persons	Children under 18 years	Persons 65 years and over	All families	Married-couple families	Male house-holder[1] families	Female house-holder[1] families
	119	120	121	122	123	124	125	126	127	128	129	130	131	132	133

1. No spouse present.

Table A. States — Personal Income

STATE	Personal income, 2010												
	Total (mil dol)	Percent change, 2009–2010	Per capita[1]		Sources of personal income (mil dol)								
									Transfer payments				
										Government payments to individuals			
			Dollars	Rank	Wages and salaries[2]	Proprietors' income	Dividends, interest, and rent	Total	Total	Social Security	Medical payments	Income main-tenance	Unemploy-ment insurance
	134	135	136	137	138	139	140	141	142	143	144	145	146

1. Based on the resident population estimated as of July 1 of the year shown.   2. Does not include supplements to wages and salaries.

Table A. States — Personal Income and Earnings

STATE	Personal tax payments, 2010 (mil dol)	Disposable personal income, 2010		Earnings, 2010									Gross state product, 2010 (mil dol)
								Percent by selected industries					
						Goods-related[2]		Service-related and other[3]					
		Total (mil dol)	Per capita[1] (dollars)	Total (mil dol)	Farm	Total	Manu-facturing	Total	Retail trade	Finance, insurance, and real estate	Health care and social assist-ance	Government	
	147	148	149	150	151	152	153	154	155	156	157	158	159

1. Based on the resident population estimated as of July 1 of the year shown.   2. Total includes mining, construction, and manufacturing.   3. Includes private sector earnings in forestry, fishing, related activities, and other; utilities; wholesale trade; transportation and warehousing; and information.

Table A. States — Social Security, Employment, and Labor Force

STATE	Social Security beneficiaries, December 2010		Supple-mental Security Income recipients, December 2010	Civilian employment and selected occupations,[2] 2010				Civilian labor force (annual average), 2011				
					Percent						Unemployed	
	Number	Rate[1]		Total	Management, business, science and art occupations	Services, sales, and office occupations	Construction and production occupations	Total (1,000)	Percent change, 2010–2011	Employed (1,000)	Total (1,000)	Rate[3]
	160	161	162	163	164	165	166	167	168	169	170	171

1. Per 1,000 resident population counted in the 2010 census.   2. Persons 16 years old and over.   3. Percent of civilian labor force.

Table A. States — Nonfarm Employment and Earnings

STATE	Private nonfarm employment and earnings, 2011											
	Employed		Manufacturing			Employment (1,000)						
				Average earnings of production workers								
	Total (1,000)	Percent change, 2010–2011	Employment (1,000)	Hourly	Weekly	Construction	Transportation and public utilities	Wholesale trade	Retail trade	Information	Financial activities	Services[1]
	172	173	174	175	176	177	178	179	180	181	182	183

1. Includes professional and business services, educational and health services, leisure and hospitality, and other services.

Table A. States — Agriculture

STATE	Agriculture, 2007											
	Farms					Land in farms					Value of land and buildings (dollars)	
		Percent with:						Acres				
	Number	Fewer than 50 acres	500 acres or more	Farm operators whose principal occupation is farming (percent)	Government payments, average per farm (dollars)	Acreage (1,000)	Percent change, 2002–2007	Average size of farm	Total irrigated (1,000)	Total cropland (1,000)	Average per farm	Average per acre
	184	185	186	187	188	189	190	191	192	193	194	195

Table A. States — Agriculture, Land, and Water

STATE	Agriculture, 2007 (cont.)								Land, 2007			
		Value of products sold				Percent of farms with sales of:						
				Percent from:								
	Value of machinery and equipment, average per farm (dollars)	Total (mil dol)	Average per farm (dollars)	Crops	Livestock and poultry products	$10,000 or more	$100,000 or more	Cropland (percent)	Owned by the federal government (percent)	Developed (percent)	Water consumption, 2005 (mil gal per day)
	196	197	198	199	200	201	202	203	204	205	206

Table A. States — Manufactures and Construction

STATE	Manufactures, 2010										Construction, 2007			
	All employees			Production workers							Employees			
						Wages								
	Number (1,000)	Percent change, 2009–2010	Annual payroll (mil dol)	Number (1,000)	Work hours (millions)	Total (mil dol)	Average per worker (dollars)	Value added by manufacture (mil dol)	Value of shipments (mil dol)	Total capital expenditures (mil dol)	Number of establishments	Number	Percent change, 2002–2007	Value (mil dol)	Annual payroll (mil dol)
	207	208	209	210	211	212	213	214	215	216	217	218	219	220	221

Table A. States — **Wholesale Trade and Retail Trade**

STATE	Wholesale trade, 2007					Retail trade,[1] 2007								
		Employees						Employees						
	Number of estab-lishments	Number	Percent change, 2002–2007	Sales (mil dol)	Annual payroll (mil dol)	Number of estab-lishments	Total	Percent change, 2002–2007	Motor vehicle and parts dealers	Food and beverage stores	Clothing and clothing accessory stores	General merchan-dise stores	Sales (mil dol)	Annual payroll (mil dol)
	222	223	224	225	226	227	228	229	230	231	232	233	234	235

1. Establishments with payroll.

Table A. States — **Information**

STATE	Information, 2007										
		Employees									
	Number of establishments	Number	Percent change, 2002–2007	Publishing, except Internet	Motion picture and sound recording	Broadcasting, except Internet	Internet publishing and broad-casting and web search portals	Telecom-munications	Data processing, hosting, and related services	Receipts (mil dol)	Annual payroll (mil dol)
	236	237	238	239	240	241	242	243	244	245	246

Table A. States — **Utilities, Transportation and Warehousing, and Finance and Insurance**

STATE	Utilities, 2007					Transportation and warehousing, 2007					Finance and insurance, 2007				
		Employees					Employees					Employees			
	Number of estab-lishments	Number	Percent change, 2002–2007	Receipts (mil dol)	Annual payroll (mil dol)	Number of estab-lishments	Number	Percent change, 2002–2007	Receipts (mil dol)	Annual payroll (mil dol)	Number of estab-lishments	Number	Percent change, 2002–2007	Receipts (mil dol)	Annual payroll (mil dol)
	247	248	249	250	251	252	253	254	255	256	257	258	259	260	261

Table A. States — **Real Estate and Rental and Leasing and Professional, Scientific, and Technical Services**

STATE	Real estate and rental and leasing, 2007					Professional, scientific, and technical services, 2007								
		Employees						Employees						
	Number of estab-lishments	Number	Percent change, 2002–2007	Receipts (mil dol)	Annual payroll (mil dol)	Number of estab-lishments	Total	Percent change, 2002–2007	Legal services	Accounting and related services	Architectural, engineering, and related services	Computer systems design and related services	Receipts (mil dol)	Annual payroll (mil dol)
	262	263	264	265	266	267	268	269	270	271	272	273	274	275

Table A. States — **Health Care and Social Assistance**

STATE	Health care and social assistance, 2007													
	Subject to federal tax							Tax-exempt					
		Employees							Employees				
	Number of estab-lishments	Total	Percent change, 2002–2007	Ambulatory health care services	Hospitals	Receipts (mil dol)	Annual payroll (mil dol)	Number of estab-lishments	Total	Percent change, 2002–2007	Ambulatory health care services	Hospitals	Receipts (mil dol)	Annual payroll (mil dol)
	276	277	278	279	280	281	282	283	284	285	286	287	288	289

Table A. States — **Arts, Entertainment, and Recreation and Accommodation and Food Services**

STATE	Arts, entertainment, and recreation, 2007					Accommodation and food services, 2007				
		Employees					Employees			
	Number of establishments	Number	Percent change, 2002–2007	Receipts (mil dol)	Annual payroll (mil dol)	Number of establishments	Total	Percent change, 2002–2007	Food services and drinking places	Receipts (mil dol)	Annual payroll (mil dol)
	290	291	292	293	294	295	296	297	298	299	300

Table A. States — **Other Services, Except Public Administration, and Government Employment**

STATE	Other services, except public administration, 2007								Government employment, 2010		
		Employees									
	Number of establishments	Total	Percent change, 2002–2007	Repair and maintenance	Personal and laundry services	Religious, civic, and similar services	Receipts (mil dol)	Annual payroll (mil dol)	Federal civilian	Federal military	State and local
	301	302	303	304	305	306	307	308	309	310	311

Table A. States — **Federal Funds**

STATE	Federal funds and grants, 2009–2010 (mil dol)											
			Procurement contract awards		Direct payments to individuals							
	Total	Salaries and wages	Defense	Other	Total	Social Security and government retirement	Medicare	Unemploy-ment compen-sation	Food Stamps	Supple-mental Security Income	Agricultural assistance	Housing assistance
	312	313	314	315	316	317	318	319	320	321	322	323

Table A. States — **Federal Funds and State Government Finances**

	Federal funds and grants, 2009–2010 (mil dol) (cont.)							State government finances, 2010							
	Grants								General revenue (mil dol)						
									From federal government		From own sources				
												Taxes		Taxes per capita[2] (dollars)	
STATE	Total[1]	Medicaid and other health-related	Nutrition and family welfare	Disasters and emergency prepared-ness	Housing and community develop-ment	Employ-ment and training	Energy and environ-ment	Total	Total	Per capita[2] (dollars)	Total	Total	Sales and gross receipts	Total	Sales and gross receipts
	324	325	326	327	328	329	330	331	332	333	334	335	336	337	338

1. Includes program categories not shown separately.   2. Based on resident population counted in the 2010 census.

Table A. States — **State Government Finances and Voting**

	State government finances, 2010 (cont.)												Voting and registration, November 2008		Presidential election,[2] 2008 (percent of vote cast)		
	General expenditures (mil dol)										Debt outstanding						
			Direct general expenditures		By selected function												
STATE	Total	To local govern-ments	Total	Per capita[1] (dollars)	Educa-tion	Health and hospitals	High-ways	Public safety	Public welfare	Natural resources, parks, and recreation	Total (mil dol)	Per capita[1]	Percent registered	Percent voted	Demo-cratic	Repub-lican	All other
	339	340	341	342	343	344	345	346	347	348	349	350	351	352	353	354	355

1. Based on resident population counted in the 2010 census.   2. © 2009 Election Data Services, Inc. All rights reserved.

Table A. States — Land Area and Population Characteristics

State code	STATE	Land area,[1] 2010 (sq km)	Total persons, 2011	Rank	Per square kilometer	White	Black	American Indian, Alaska Native	Asian and Pacific Islander	Hispanic or Latino[2] (percent)	Under 5 years	5 to 17 years	18 to 24 years	25 to 34 years	35 to 44 years	45 to 54 years
		1	2	3	4	5	6	7	8	9	10	11	12	13	14	15
00	UNITED STATES	9 147 593	311 591 917	X	34.1	65.4	13.0	1.3	5.7	16.3	6.5	17.5	9.9	13.3	13.3	14.6
01	ALABAMA	131 171	4 802 740	23	36.6	68.2	26.6	1.1	1.5	3.9	6.4	17.3	10.0	12.6	13.0	14.5
02	ALASKA	1 477 953	722 718	47	0.5	69.8	4.3	18.8	8.3	5.5	7.6	18.8	10.5	14.5	13.1	15.6
04	ARIZONA	294 207	6 482 505	16	22.0	59.4	4.4	4.6	3.6	29.6	7.1	18.4	9.9	13.4	12.9	13.2
05	ARKANSAS	134 771	2 937 979	32	21.8	76.0	15.9	1.5	1.7	6.4	6.8	17.6	9.7	12.6	12.6	14.0
06	CALIFORNIA	403 466	37 691 912	1	93.4	42.3	6.5	1.0	14.9	37.6	6.8	18.2	10.5	14.2	13.9	14.1
08	COLORADO	268 431	5 116 796	22	19.1	71.8	4.5	1.3	3.7	20.7	6.8	17.5	9.7	14.4	13.9	14.8
09	CONNECTICUT	12 542	3 580 709	29	285.5	72.6	10.2	0.6	4.4	13.4	5.7	17.2	9.1	11.8	13.6	16.1
10	DELAWARE	5 047	907 135	45	179.7	67.0	22.1	0.9	3.8	8.2	6.2	16.7	10.1	12.3	12.9	14.9
11	DISTRICT OF COLUMBIA	158	617 996	50	3 911.4	36.3	51.3	0.8	4.5	9.1	5.4	11.3	14.5	20.9	13.4	12.6
12	FLORIDA	138 887	19 057 542	4	137.2	59.1	15.9	0.6	3.1	22.5	5.7	15.6	9.3	12.1	12.9	14.6
13	GEORGIA	148 959	9 815 210	9	65.9	57.1	30.9	0.7	3.8	8.8	7.1	18.6	10.0	13.6	14.4	14.4
15	HAWAII	16 635	1 374 810	40	82.6	36.5	2.5	1.7	76.2	8.9	6.4	15.9	9.6	13.3	13.0	14.2
16	IDAHO	214 045	1 584 985	39	7.4	85.6	0.9	1.9	2.1	11.2	7.8	19.6	9.9	13.3	12.2	13.3
17	ILLINOIS	143 793	12 869 257	5	89.5	64.9	15.0	0.5	5.2	15.8	6.5	17.9	9.7	13.9	13.5	14.6
18	INDIANA	92 789	6 516 922	15	70.2	82.9	9.8	0.6	2.0	6.0	6.7	18.1	10.0	12.7	13.0	14.6
19	IOWA	144 669	3 062 309	30	21.2	89.9	3.6	0.7	2.2	5.0	6.6	17.3	10.0	12.6	12.0	14.4
20	KANSAS	211 754	2 871 238	33	13.6	80.3	6.7	1.7	3.0	10.5	7.2	18.3	10.1	13.0	12.2	14.2
21	KENTUCKY	102 269	4 369 356	26	42.7	87.7	8.5	0.6	1.5	3.1	6.5	17.1	9.5	13.0	13.3	14.8
22	LOUISIANA	111 898	4 574 836	25	40.9	61.4	32.5	1.1	1.9	4.2	6.9	17.7	10.5	13.7	12.5	14.4
23	MAINE	79 883	1 328 188	41	16.6	95.8	1.6	1.3	1.4	1.3	5.2	15.4	8.7	10.9	12.9	16.5
24	MARYLAND	25 142	5 828 289	19	231.8	56.4	30.2	0.8	6.4	8.2	6.3	17.1	9.7	13.2	13.8	15.6
25	MASSACHUSETTS	20 202	6 587 536	14	326.1	77.6	6.8	0.5	6.0	9.6	5.6	16.1	10.4	12.9	13.5	15.5
26	MICHIGAN	146 435	9 876 187	8	67.4	78.3	14.9	1.2	3.0	4.4	6.0	17.7	9.9	11.7	12.9	15.3
27	MINNESOTA	206 232	5 344 861	21	25.9	84.8	6.0	1.7	4.7	4.7	6.7	17.5	9.5	13.5	12.8	15.2
28	MISSISSIPPI	121 531	2 978 512	31	24.5	58.8	37.4	0.8	1.1	2.7	7.1	18.4	10.3	12.6	12.6	14.1
29	MISSOURI	178 040	6 010 688	18	33.8	82.6	12.3	1.1	2.2	3.5	6.5	17.3	9.8	12.9	12.5	14.8
30	MONTANA	376 962	998 199	44	2.6	89.9	0.7	7.5	1.2	2.9	6.3	16.3	9.6	12.3	11.4	15.1
31	NEBRASKA	198 974	1 842 641	38	9.3	83.5	5.2	1.3	2.3	9.2	7.2	17.9	10.0	13.2	12.1	14.2
32	NEVADA	284 332	2 723 322	35	9.6	56.6	8.7	1.5	9.6	26.5	6.9	17.7	9.2	14.3	14.2	13.9
33	NEW HAMPSHIRE	23 187	1 318 194	42	56.9	93.6	1.5	0.7	2.7	2.8	5.3	16.5	9.4	11.0	13.6	17.2
34	NEW JERSEY	19 047	8 821 155	11	463.1	60.5	13.5	0.5	9.0	17.7	6.2	17.3	8.7	12.6	14.1	15.7
35	NEW MEXICO	314 161	2 082 224	36	6.6	41.7	2.2	9.2	1.8	46.3	7.0	18.1	9.9	12.8	12.1	14.2
36	NEW YORK	122 057	19 465 197	3	159.5	59.5	15.2	0.7	8.1	17.6	6.0	16.4	10.2	13.7	13.5	14.9
37	NORTH CAROLINA	125 920	9 656 401	10	76.7	66.6	22.1	1.7	2.7	8.4	6.6	17.3	9.8	13.0	13.9	14.4
38	NORTH DAKOTA	178 711	683 932	48	3.8	90.3	1.6	6.2	1.4	2.0	6.6	15.7	12.0	13.1	11.2	14.4
39	OHIO	105 829	11 544 951	7	109.1	82.7	13.1	0.7	2.1	3.1	6.2	17.4	9.5	12.4	12.8	15.1
40	OKLAHOMA	177 660	3 791 508	28	21.3	73.3	8.4	12.2	2.4	8.9	7.0	17.7	10.2	13.5	12.3	14.0
41	OREGON	248 608	3 871 859	27	15.6	81.1	2.3	2.3	5.3	11.7	6.2	16.4	9.4	13.7	13.0	14.1
42	PENNSYLVANIA	115 883	12 742 886	6	110.0	80.7	11.3	0.5	3.2	5.7	5.7	16.2	9.9	11.9	12.7	15.3
44	RHODE ISLAND	2 678	1 051 302	43	392.6	78.0	6.2	1.0	3.5	12.4	5.5	15.8	11.4	12.0	13.0	15.4
45	SOUTH CAROLINA	77 857	4 679 230	24	60.1	65.2	28.5	0.8	1.7	5.1	6.5	16.8	10.3	12.7	13.0	14.3
46	SOUTH DAKOTA	196 350	824 082	46	4.2	86.4	1.7	9.7	1.3	2.7	7.3	17.6	10.0	12.8	11.4	14.4
47	TENNESSEE	106 798	6 403 353	17	60.0	76.9	17.2	0.8	1.8	4.6	6.4	17.1	9.6	12.8	13.5	14.6
48	TEXAS	676 587	25 674 681	2	37.9	46.4	12.0	0.7	4.4	37.6	7.7	19.6	10.2	14.3	13.8	13.7
49	UTAH	212 818	2 817 222	34	13.2	82.0	1.3	1.4	3.9	13.0	9.5	22.0	11.5	16.2	12.0	11.1
50	VERMONT	23 871	626 431	49	26.2	95.8	1.4	1.1	1.7	1.5	5.1	15.5	10.4	11.2	12.5	16.4
51	VIRGINIA	102 279	8 096 604	12	79.2	66.8	20.1	0.8	6.6	7.9	6.4	16.8	10.0	13.6	13.9	15.2
53	WASHINGTON	172 119	6 830 038	13	39.7	75.8	4.5	2.5	9.7	11.2	6.5	17.0	9.7	13.9	13.5	14.7
54	WEST VIRGINIA	62 259	1 855 364	37	29.8	94.4	4.1	0.7	0.9	1.2	5.6	15.3	9.1	11.7	12.8	14.9
55	WISCONSIN	140 268	5 711 767	20	40.7	84.6	6.8	1.3	2.7	5.9	6.3	17.3	9.7	12.6	12.8	15.4
56	WYOMING	251 470	568 158	51	2.3	87.3	1.1	2.8	1.3	8.9	7.1	16.9	10.0	13.6	11.9	14.8

1. Dry land or land partially or temporarily covered by water.   2. May be of any race.

Table A. States — Population Characteristics, Immigration, and Households

| | Population characteristics, 2010 (cont.) | | | | | | | | | Households, 2010 | | | | | |
| | Age (percent) (cont.) | | | | | | | | | | | | Household type | | |
STATE	55 to 64 years	65 to 74 years	75 to 84 years	85 years and over	Median age	Percent female	Percent foreign born	Percent born in state of residence	Immigrants admitted to legal status, 2010	Number	Percent change, 2000–2010	Persons per house-hold	Married couple	Female house-holder[1]	House-holder living alone
	16	17	18	19	20	21	22	23	24	25	26	27	28	29	30
UNITED STATES	11.8	7.0	4.2	1.8	37.2	50.8	12.9	58.8	1 042 625	116 716 292	10.7	2.58	48.4	13.1	26.7
ALABAMA	12.3	7.8	4.4	1.6	37.9	51.5	3.5	70.0	3 740	1 883 791	8.4	2.48	47.9	15.3	27.4
ALASKA	12.1	5.0	2.1	0.6	33.8	48.0	6.9	39.0	1 703	258 058	16.5	2.65	49.4	10.7	25.6
ARIZONA	11.4	7.8	4.4	1.6	35.9	50.3	13.4	37.7	18 243	2 380 990	25.2	2.63	48.1	12.4	26.1
ARKANSAS	12.0	8.0	4.6	1.8	37.4	50.9	4.5	61.3	2 684	1 147 084	10.0	2.47	49.5	13.4	27.1
CALIFORNIA	10.8	6.1	3.7	1.6	35.2	50.3	27.2	53.8	208 446	12 577 498	9.3	2.90	49.4	13.3	23.3
COLORADO	11.9	6.2	3.4	1.4	36.1	49.9	9.8	42.5	12 489	1 972 868	19.0	2.49	49.2	10.1	27.9
CONNECTICUT	12.4	7.1	4.6	2.4	40.0	51.3	13.6	55.1	12 222	1 371 087	5.3	2.52	49.0	12.9	27.3
DELAWARE	12.4	8.1	4.5	1.8	38.8	51.6	8.0	45.3	2 198	342 297	14.6	2.55	48.3	14.2	25.6
DISTRICT OF COLUMBIA	10.6	6.1	3.5	1.8	33.8	52.8	13.5	37.3	2 897	266 707	7.4	2.11	22.0	16.4	44.0
FLORIDA	12.4	9.2	5.7	2.4	40.7	51.1	19.4	35.2	107 276	7 420 802	17.1	2.48	46.6	13.5	27.2
GEORGIA	11.0	6.3	3.1	1.2	35.3	51.2	9.7	55.2	24 833	3 585 584	19.3	2.63	47.8	15.8	25.4
HAWAII	12.9	7.4	4.7	2.3	38.6	49.9	18.2	55.0	7 037	455 338	12.9	2.89	50.5	12.6	23.3
IDAHO	11.5	7.0	3.8	1.7	34.6	49.9	5.5	46.9	2 556	579 408	23.4	2.66	55.3	9.6	23.8
ILLINOIS	11.5	6.6	4.0	1.9	36.6	51.0	13.7	67.1	37 909	4 836 972	5.3	2.59	48.2	12.9	27.8
INDIANA	11.9	7.0	4.3	1.7	37.0	50.8	4.6	68.3	8 539	2 502 154	7.1	2.52	49.6	12.4	26.9
IOWA	12.2	7.4	5.0	2.5	38.1	50.5	4.6	71.7	4 245	1 221 576	6.3	2.41	51.2	9.3	28.4
KANSAS	11.6	6.7	4.3	2.1	36.0	50.4	6.5	58.2	5 501	1 112 096	7.1	2.49	51.1	10.4	27.8
KENTUCKY	12.4	7.5	4.2	1.6	38.1	50.8	3.2	70.3	4 930	1 719 965	8.1	2.45	49.3	12.7	27.5
LOUISIANA	11.8	6.9	3.9	1.5	35.8	51.0	3.8	78.8	4 397	1 728 360	4.4	2.55	44.4	17.2	26.9
MAINE	14.5	8.5	5.3	2.1	42.7	51.1	3.4	64.0	1 349	557 219	7.5	2.32	48.5	10.0	28.6
MARYLAND	12.1	6.7	3.9	1.7	38.0	51.6	13.9	47.6	26 450	2 156 411	8.9	2.61	47.6	14.6	26.1
MASSACHUSETTS	12.3	7.0	4.6	2.2	39.1	51.6	15.0	63.1	31 069	2 547 075	4.2	2.48	46.3	12.5	28.7
MICHIGAN	12.7	7.3	4.5	1.9	38.9	50.9	6.0	76.6	18 579	3 872 508	2.3	2.49	48.0	13.2	27.9
MINNESOTA	11.9	6.7	4.2	2.0	37.4	50.4	7.1	68.8	12 408	2 087 227	10.1	2.48	50.8	9.5	28.0
MISSISSIPPI	11.7	7.2	4.1	1.5	36.0	51.4	2.1	71.9	1 709	1 115 768	6.6	2.58	45.4	18.5	26.3
MISSOURI	12.1	7.5	4.5	2.0	37.9	51.0	3.9	65.9	7 151	2 375 611	8.2	2.45	48.4	12.3	28.3
MONTANA	14.0	8.2	4.7	2.0	39.8	49.8	2.0	54.1	457	409 607	14.2	2.35	49.2	9.0	29.7
NEBRASKA	11.7	6.7	4.7	2.2	36.2	50.4	6.1	65.6	4 400	721 130	8.2	2.46	50.8	9.8	28.7
NEVADA	11.7	7.3	3.6	1.1	36.3	49.5	18.8	24.3	10 803	1 006 250	34.0	2.65	46.0	12.7	25.7
NEW HAMPSHIRE	13.5	7.4	4.4	1.8	41.1	50.7	5.3	42.7	2 556	518 973	9.3	2.46	52.1	9.7	25.6
NEW JERSEY	11.9	7.0	4.6	2.0	39.0	51.3	21.0	52.4	56 920	3 214 360	4.9	2.68	51.1	13.3	25.2
NEW MEXICO	12.5	7.5	4.3	1.5	36.7	50.6	9.9	51.7	3 528	791 395	16.7	2.55	45.3	14.0	28.0
NEW YORK	11.9	7.0	4.5	2.0	38.0	51.6	22.2	63.6	147 999	7 317 755	3.7	2.57	43.6	14.9	29.1
NORTH CAROLINA	11.9	7.3	4.1	1.6	37.4	51.3	7.5	58.5	16 112	3 745 155	19.6	2.48	48.4	13.7	27.0
NORTH DAKOTA	12.2	7.0	5.1	2.5	37.0	49.5	2.5	68.6	1 058	281 192	9.3	2.30	48.6	8.2	31.5
OHIO	12.6	7.4	4.7	2.0	38.8	51.2	4.1	75.1	13 585	4 603 435	3.5	2.44	47.2	13.1	28.0
OKLAHOMA	11.7	7.5	4.4	1.6	36.2	50.5	5.5	60.8	4 627	1 460 450	8.8	2.49	49.5	12.3	27.5
OREGON	13.3	7.8	4.3	2.0	38.4	50.5	9.8	45.5	7 997	1 518 938	13.9	2.47	48.3	10.5	27.4
PENNSYLVANIA	12.8	7.7	5.3	2.6	40.1	51.3	5.8	74.0	24 130	5 018 904	5.1	2.45	48.2	12.2	28.6
RHODE ISLAND	12.4	7.0	4.9	2.5	39.4	51.7	12.8	59.3	4 027	413 600	1.3	2.44	44.5	13.5	29.6
SOUTH CAROLINA	12.6	8.0	4.1	1.6	37.9	51.4	4.7	58.6	4 401	1 801 181	17.4	2.49	47.2	15.6	26.5
SOUTH DAKOTA	12.0	7.1	4.8	2.4	36.9	50.0	2.7	65.1	987	322 282	11.0	2.42	50.1	9.7	29.4
TENNESSEE	12.4	7.7	4.2	1.6	38.0	51.3	4.5	61.0	8 156	2 493 552	11.7	2.48	48.7	13.9	26.9
TEXAS	10.3	5.9	3.3	1.2	33.6	50.4	16.4	60.5	87 750	8 922 933	20.7	2.75	50.6	14.1	24.2
UTAH	8.7	5.0	2.9	1.1	29.2	49.8	8.0	62.3	6 085	877 692	25.2	3.10	61.0	9.7	18.7
VERMONT	14.4	7.9	4.5	2.1	41.5	50.7	4.4	51.1	867	256 442	6.6	2.34	48.5	9.6	28.2
VIRGINIA	11.9	6.9	3.8	1.5	37.5	50.9	11.4	49.9	28 607	3 056 058	13.2	2.54	50.2	12.4	26.0
WASHINGTON	12.4	6.8	3.7	1.8	37.3	50.2	13.1	46.9	22 283	2 620 076	15.4	2.51	49.2	10.5	27.2
WEST VIRGINIA	14.3	8.8	5.2	2.0	41.3	50.7	1.2	71.1	729	763 831	3.7	2.36	49.8	11.2	28.4
WISCONSIN	12.3	7.0	4.6	2.1	38.5	50.4	4.5	72.1	6 189	2 279 768	9.4	2.43	49.6	10.3	28.2
WYOMING	13.0	7.0	3.8	1.6	36.8	49.0	2.8	41.5	452	226 879	17.2	2.42	50.9	8.9	28.0

1. No spouse present.

Table A. States — **Population Change**

STATE	Population, 1990–2010 — Census counts			Percent change			Components of change, 2010–2011		Migration			Population, 2020–2030 — Projections		
	1990	2000	2010	1990–2000	2000–2010	2010–2011	Births	Deaths	Net migration	International	Net internal	2020	2025	2030
	31	32	33	34	35	36	37	38	39	40	41	42	43	44
UNITED STATES	248 709 873	281 421 906	308 745 538	13.2	9.7	0.9	4 998 000	3 045 912	894 291	894 291	(X)	335 804 546	349 439 199	363 584 435
ALABAMA	4 040 587	4 447 100	4 779 736	10.1	7.5	0.5	74 348	59 330	7 922	5 948	1 974	4 728 915	4 800 092	4 874 243
ALASKA	550 043	626 932	710 231	14.0	13.3	1.8	14 027	3 985	2 383	1 643	740	774 421	820 881	867 674
ARIZONA	3 665 228	5 130 632	6 392 017	40.0	24.6	1.4	108 787	57 063	38 891	25 741	13 150	8 456 448	9 531 537	10 712 397
ARKANSAS	2 350 725	2 673 400	2 915 918	13.7	9.1	0.8	47 374	35 237	9 853	4 129	5 724	3 060 219	3 151 005	3 240 208
CALIFORNIA	29 760 021	33 871 648	37 253 956	13.8	10.0	1.2	631 242	291 912	98 740	164 445	-65 705	42 206 743	44 305 177	46 444 861
COLORADO	3 294 394	4 301 261	5 029 196	30.6	16.9	1.7	82 666	38 473	42 899	11 704	31 195	5 278 867	5 522 803	5 792 357
CONNECTICUT	3 287 116	3 405 565	3 574 097	3.6	4.9	0.2	46 560	35 099	-4 634	12 214	-16 848	3 675 650	3 691 016	3 688 630
DELAWARE	666 168	783 600	897 934	17.6	14.6	1.0	13 946	9 531	4 802	2 455	2 347	963 209	990 694	1 012 658
DISTRICT OF COLUMBIA	606 900	572 059	601 723	-5.7	5.2	2.7	11 235	5 871	10 794	2 460	8 334	480 540	455 108	433 414
FLORIDA	12 937 926	15 982 378	18 801 310	23.5	17.6	1.4	264 829	213 354	205 193	86 437	118 756	23 406 525	25 912 458	28 685 769
GEORGIA	6 478 216	8 186 453	9 687 653	26.4	18.3	1.3	166 852	87 328	47 182	29 456	17 726	10 843 753	11 438 622	12 017 838
HAWAII	1 108 229	1 211 537	1 360 301	9.3	12.3	1.1	23 101	11 971	3 496	5 816	-2 320	1 412 373	1 438 720	1 466 046
IDAHO	1 006 749	1 293 953	1 567 582	28.5	21.1	1.1	28 743	13 820	2 429	2 685	-256	1 741 333	1 852 627	1 969 624
ILLINOIS	11 430 602	12 419 293	12 830 632	8.6	3.3	0.3	209 060	125 135	-45 403	34 055	-79 458	13 236 720	13 340 507	13 432 892
INDIANA	5 544 159	6 080 485	6 483 802	9.7	6.6	0.5	106 018	70 621	-2 226	9 186	-11 412	6 627 008	6 721 322	6 810 108
IOWA	2 776 755	2 926 324	3 046 355	5.4	4.1	0.5	47 724	34 328	2 638	3 999	-1 361	3 020 496	2 993 222	2 955 172
KANSAS	2 477 574	2 688 418	2 853 118	8.5	6.1	0.6	49 977	29 497	-2 365	5 563	-7 928	2 890 566	2 919 002	2 940 084
KENTUCKY	3 685 296	4 041 769	4 339 367	9.7	7.4	0.7	70 438	52 431	12 064	6 303	5 761	4 424 431	4 489 662	4 554 998
LOUISIANA	4 219 973	4 468 976	4 533 372	5.9	1.4	0.9	79 540	50 551	12 179	5 094	7 085	4 719 160	4 762 398	4 802 633
MAINE	1 227 928	1 274 923	1 328 361	3.8	4.2	0.0	16 054	15 978	-181	819	-1 000	1 408 665	1 414 402	1 411 097
MARYLAND	4 781 468	5 296 486	5 773 552	10.8	9.0	0.9	91 097	54 169	17 934	20 928	-2 994	6 497 626	6 762 732	7 022 251
MASSACHUSETTS	6 016 425	6 349 097	6 547 629	5.5	3.1	0.6	91 957	65 313	13 684	24 570	-10 886	6 855 546	6 938 636	7 012 009
MICHIGAN	9 295 297	9 938 444	9 883 640	6.9	-0.6	-0.1	142 826	108 447	-42 018	15 216	-57 234	10 695 993	10 713 730	10 694 172
MINNESOTA	4 375 099	4 919 479	5 303 925	12.4	7.8	0.8	85 067	47 762	3 807	11 880	-8 073	5 900 769	6 108 787	6 306 130
MISSISSIPPI	2 573 216	2 844 658	2 967 297	10.5	4.3	0.4	49 979	35 353	-3 513	3 159	-6 672	3 044 812	3 069 420	3 092 410
MISSOURI	5 117 073	5 595 211	5 988 927	9.3	7.0	0.4	94 510	67 711	-4 874	6 957	-11 831	6 199 882	6 315 366	6 430 173
MONTANA	799 065	902 195	989 415	12.9	9.7	0.9	14 884	10 469	4 403	515	3 888	1 022 735	1 037 387	1 044 898
NEBRASKA	1 578 385	1 711 263	1 826 341	8.4	6.7	0.9	32 307	18 240	2 299	3 276	-977	1 802 678	1 812 787	1 820 247
NEVADA	1 201 833	1 998 257	2 700 551	66.3	35.1	0.8	45 934	24 116	948	12 061	-11 113	3 452 283	3 863 298	4 282 102
NEW HAMPSHIRE	1 109 252	1 235 786	1 316 470	11.4	6.5	0.1	15 986	12 128	-2 081	1 564	-3 645	1 524 751	1 586 348	1 646 471
NEW JERSEY	7 730 188	8 414 350	8 791 894	8.9	4.5	0.3	129 618	85 256	-14 936	39 162	-54 098	9 461 635	9 636 644	9 802 440
NEW MEXICO	1 515 069	1 819 046	2 059 179	20.1	13.2	1.1	35 620	19 396	6 761	4 559	2 202	2 084 341	2 106 584	2 099 708
NEW YORK	17 990 455	18 976 457	19 378 102	5.5	2.1	0.4	304 098	182 998	-33 232	80 525	-113 757	19 576 920	19 540 179	19 477 429
NORTH CAROLINA	6 628 637	8 049 313	9 535 483	21.4	18.5	1.3	151 908	97 404	66 062	25 029	41 033	10 709 289	11 449 153	12 227 739
NORTH DAKOTA	638 800	642 200	672 591	0.5	4.7	1.7	11 240	7 141	7 156	788	6 368	630 112	620 777	606 566
OHIO	10 847 115	11 353 140	11 536 504	4.7	1.6	0.1	176 295	134 426	-33 149	11 719	-44 868	11 644 058	11 605 738	11 550 528
OKLAHOMA	3 145 585	3 450 654	3 751 351	9.7	8.7	1.1	67 093	42 458	15 405	6 472	8 933	3 735 690	3 820 994	3 913 251
OREGON	2 842 321	3 421 399	3 831 074	20.4	12.0	1.1	57 969	39 153	22 134	8 498	13 636	4 260 393	4 536 418	4 833 918
PENNSYLVANIA	11 881 643	12 281 054	12 702 379	3.4	3.4	0.3	179 565	155 957	17 746	18 867	-1 121	12 787 354	12 801 945	12 768 184
RHODE ISLAND	1 003 464	1 048 319	1 052 567	4.5	0.4	-0.1	13 773	11 436	-3 586	2 687	-6 273	1 154 230	1 157 855	1 152 941
SOUTH CAROLINA	3 486 703	4 012 012	4 625 364	15.1	15.3	1.2	74 303	51 245	30 686	8 673	22 013	4 822 577	4 989 550	5 148 569
SOUTH DAKOTA	696 004	754 844	814 180	8.5	7.9	1.2	14 731	8 101	3 300	690	2 610	801 939	801 845	800 462
TENNESSEE	4 877 185	5 689 283	6 346 105	16.7	11.5	0.9	100 612	73 507	30 203	9 875	20 328	6 780 670	7 073 125	7 380 634
TEXAS	16 986 510	20 851 820	25 145 561	22.8	20.6	2.1	493 650	205 171	238 956	93 641	145 315	28 634 896	30 865 134	33 317 744
UTAH	1 722 850	2 233 169	2 763 885	29.6	23.8	1.9	65 156	17 734	5 912	6 738	-826	2 990 094	3 225 680	3 485 367
VERMONT	562 758	608 827	625 741	8.2	2.8	0.1	7 485	6 407	-339	502	-841	690 686	703 288	711 867
VIRGINIA	6 187 358	7 078 515	8 001 024	14.4	13.0	1.2	127 114	72 880	41 156	25 618	15 538	8 917 395	9 364 304	9 825 019
WASHINGTON	4 866 692	5 894 121	6 724 540	21.1	14.1	1.6	108 600	60 198	57 054	21 888	35 166	7 432 136	7 996 400	8 624 801
WEST VIRGINIA	1 793 477	1 808 344	1 852 994	0.8	2.5	0.1	25 769	27 020	3 728	914	2 814	1 801 112	1 766 435	1 719 959
WISCONSIN	4 891 769	5 363 675	5 686 986	9.6	6.0	0.4	86 923	57 446	-4 432	6 558	-10 990	6 004 954	6 088 374	6 150 764
WYOMING	453 588	493 782	563 626	8.9	14.1	0.8	9 410	5 355	461	610	-149	530 948	529 031	522 979

Table A. States — **Population Characteristics**

	Population characteristics, 2000																		
STATE	Race (percent)							Age (percent)											
	White alone	Black alone	American Indian, Alaska Native alone	Asian and Pacific Islander alone	Some other race or two or more races	Percent Hispanic or Latino[1]	Percent foreign born	Under 5 years	5 to 17 years	18 to 24 years	25 to 34 years	35 to 44 years	45 to 54 years	55 to 64 years	65 to 74 years	75 to 84 years	85 years and over	Median age	Percent female
	45	46	47	48	49	50	51	52	53	54	55	56	57	58	59	60	61	62	63
UNITED STATES	69.1	12.1	0.7	3.7	1.8	12.5	11.1	6.8	18.9	9.7	14.2	16.0	13.4	8.6	6.5	4.4	1.5	35.3	50.9
ALABAMA	70.3	25.9	0.5	0.7	0.9	1.7	2.0	6.7	18.6	9.9	13.6	15.4	13.5	9.3	7.1	4.4	1.5	35.8	51.7
ALASKA	67.6	3.4	15.4	4.5	5.1	4.1	5.9	7.5	22.8	9.1	14.3	18.2	15.1	7.1	3.6	1.7	0.4	32.4	48.3
ARIZONA	63.8	2.9	4.5	1.9	1.6	25.3	12.8	7.5	19.2	10.0	14.5	15.0	12.2	8.6	7.1	4.6	1.3	34.2	50.1
ARKANSAS	78.6	15.6	0.6	0.8	1.2	3.2	2.8	6.8	18.7	9.8	13.2	14.9	13.1	9.6	7.4	4.8	1.7	36.0	51.2
CALIFORNIA	46.7	6.4	0.5	11.1	2.9	32.4	26.2	7.3	20.0	9.9	15.4	16.2	12.8	7.7	5.6	3.8	1.3	33.3	50.2
COLORADO	74.5	3.7	0.7	2.3	1.8	17.1	8.6	6.9	18.7	10.0	15.4	17.1	14.3	7.9	5.3	3.3	1.1	34.3	49.6
CONNECTICUT	77.5	8.7	0.2	2.4	1.8	9.4	10.9	6.6	18.2	8.0	13.3	17.1	14.1	9.1	6.8	5.1	1.9	37.4	51.6
DELAWARE	72.5	18.9	0.3	2.1	1.4	4.8	5.7	6.6	18.3	9.6	13.9	16.3	13.3	9.1	7.2	4.4	1.3	36.0	51.4
DISTRICT OF COLUMBIA	27.8	59.4	0.2	2.7	2.0	7.9	12.9	5.7	14.4	12.7	17.8	15.3	13.2	8.7	6.3	4.4	1.6	34.6	52.9
FLORIDA	65.4	14.2	0.3	1.7	1.7	16.8	16.7	16.7	16.9	8.3	13.0	15.5	12.9	9.8	9.1	6.4	2.1	38.7	51.2
GEORGIA	62.6	28.5	0.2	2.1	1.2	5.3	7.1	7.3	19.2	10.2	15.9	16.5	13.2	8.1	5.3	3.2	1.1	33.4	50.8
HAWAII	22.9	1.7	0.2	49.7	18.2	7.2	17.5	6.5	18.0	9.5	14.1	15.8	14.1	8.8	7.0	4.8	1.4	36.2	49.8
IDAHO	88.0	0.4	1.2	1.0	1.5	7.9	5.0	7.5	21.0	10.7	13.1	14.9	13.2	8.3	5.9	4.0	1.4	33.2	49.9
ILLINOIS	67.8	14.9	0.1	3.4	1.3	12.3	12.3	7.1	19.1	9.8	14.6	16.0	13.1	8.4	6.2	4.3	1.5	34.7	51.0
INDIANA	85.8	8.3	0.2	1.0	1.1	3.5	3.1	7.0	18.9	10.1	13.7	15.8	13.4	8.7	6.5	4.4	1.5	35.2	51.0
IOWA	92.6	2.1	0.3	1.3	0.9	2.8	3.1	6.4	18.6	10.2	12.4	15.2	13.4	8.8	7.2	5.4	2.2	36.6	50.9
KANSAS	83.1	5.6	0.8	1.8	1.7	7.0	5.0	7.0	19.5	10.3	13.0	15.6	13.2	8.2	6.5	4.8	1.9	35.2	50.6
KENTUCKY	89.3	7.3	0.2	0.8	1.0	1.5	2.0	6.6	18.0	9.9	14.1	15.9	13.8	9.2	6.8	4.3	1.4	35.9	51.1
LOUISIANA	62.5	32.3	0.5	1.2	1.0	2.4	2.6	7.1	20.2	10.6	13.5	15.5	13.1	8.5	6.3	3.9	1.3	34.0	51.6
MAINE	96.5	0.5	0.5	0.7	1.0	0.7	2.9	5.5	18.1	8.1	12.4	16.7	15.1	9.7	7.5	5.0	1.8	38.6	51.3
MARYLAND	62.1	27.7	0.3	4.0	1.7	4.3	9.8	6.7	18.9	8.5	14.1	17.3	14.3	8.9	6.1	4.0	1.3	36.0	51.7
MASSACHUSETTS	81.9	5.0	0.2	3.8	2.4	6.8	12.2	6.3	17.4	9.1	14.6	16.7	13.8	8.6	6.7	5.0	1.8	36.5	51.8
MICHIGAN	78.6	14.1	0.5	1.8	1.8	3.3	5.3	6.8	19.4	9.4	13.7	16.1	13.8	8.7	6.5	4.4	1.4	35.5	51.0
MINNESOTA	88.2	3.4	1.1	2.9	1.5	2.9	5.3	6.7	19.5	9.6	13.7	16.8	13.5	8.2	6.0	4.3	1.7	35.4	50.5
MISSISSIPPI	60.7	36.2	0.4	0.7	0.7	1.4	1.4	7.2	20.1	10.9	13.4	15.0	12.7	8.6	6.5	4.0	1.5	33.8	51.7
MISSOURI	83.8	11.2	0.4	1.1	1.4	2.1	2.7	6.6	18.9	9.6	13.2	15.9	13.3	9.1	7.0	4.7	1.8	36.1	51.4
MONTANA	89.5	0.3	6.0	0.6	1.6	2.0	1.8	6.1	19.4	9.5	11.4	15.7	15.0	9.4	6.9	4.8	1.7	37.5	50.2
NEBRASKA	87.3	3.9	0.8	1.3	1.1	5.5	4.4	6.8	19.5	10.2	13.0	15.4	13.2	8.3	6.8	4.8	2.0	35.3	50.7
NEVADA	65.2	6.8	1.1	4.8	2.6	19.7	15.8	7.3	18.3	9.0	15.3	16.1	13.5	9.5	6.6	3.5	0.9	35.0	49.1
NEW HAMPSHIRE	96.1	0.7	0.2	1.3	1.0	1.7	4.4	6.1	18.9	8.4	13.0	17.9	14.9	8.9	6.3	4.2	1.5	37.1	50.8
NEW JERSEY	66.0	13.0	0.1	5.7	1.8	13.3	17.5	6.7	18.1	8.0	14.1	17.1	13.8	9.0	6.8	4.8	1.6	36.7	51.5
NEW MEXICO	44.7	1.7	8.9	1.1	1.6	42.1	8.2	7.2	20.8	9.8	12.9	15.5	13.5	8.7	6.5	3.9	1.3	34.6	50.8
NEW YORK	62.0	14.8	0.3	5.5	2.3	15.1	20.4	6.5	18.2	9.3	14.5	16.2	13.5	8.9	6.7	4.5	1.6	35.9	51.8
NORTH CAROLINA	70.2	21.4	1.2	1.4	1.1	4.7	5.3	6.7	17.7	10.0	15.1	16.0	13.6	9.0	6.6	4.1	1.3	35.3	51.0
NORTH DAKOTA	91.7	0.6	4.8	0.6	1.1	1.2	1.9	6.1	18.9	11.4	12.0	15.3	13.3	8.3	7.1	5.3	2.3	36.2	50.1
OHIO	84.0	11.4	0.2	1.2	1.3	1.9	3.0	6.6	18.8	9.3	13.4	15.9	13.8	8.9	7.0	4.8	1.6	36.2	51.4
OKLAHOMA	74.1	7.5	7.7	1.4	4.1	5.2	3.8	6.8	19.0	10.3	13.1	15.2	13.1	9.2	7.0	4.5	1.7	35.5	50.9
OREGON	83.5	1.6	1.2	3.1	2.6	8.0	8.5	6.5	18.2	9.6	13.8	15.4	14.8	8.9	6.4	4.7	1.7	36.3	50.4
PENNSYLVANIA	84.1	9.8	0.1	1.8	1.0	3.2	4.1	5.9	17.9	8.9	12.7	15.9	13.9	9.2	7.9	5.8	1.9	38.0	51.7
RHODE ISLAND	81.9	4.0	0.4	2.3	2.8	8.7	11.4	6.1	17.5	10.2	13.4	16.2	13.5	8.5	7.0	5.5	2.0	36.7	52.0
SOUTH CAROLINA	66.1	29.4	0.3	0.9	0.9	2.4	2.9	6.6	18.6	10.2	14.0	15.6	13.7	9.3	6.7	4.1	1.3	35.4	51.4
SOUTH DAKOTA	88.0	0.6	8.1	0.6	1.2	1.4	1.8	6.8	20.1	10.3	12.1	15.3	12.9	8.3	7.0	5.2	2.1	35.6	50.4
TENNESSEE	79.2	16.3	0.2	1.0	1.0	2.2	2.8	6.6	18.0	9.6	14.3	15.9	13.8	9.4	6.7	4.2	1.4	35.9	51.3
TEXAS	52.4	11.3	0.3	2.7	1.2	32.0	13.9	7.8	20.4	10.5	15.2	15.9	12.5	7.7	5.5	3.3	1.1	32.3	50.4
UTAH	85.3	0.7	1.2	2.3	1.5	9.0	7.1	9.4	22.8	14.2	14.6	13.4	10.6	6.4	4.5	3.0	1.0	27.1	49.9
VERMONT	96.2	0.5	0.4	0.9	1.2	0.9	3.8	5.6	18.6	9.3	12.2	16.7	15.4	9.3	6.7	4.4	1.6	37.7	51.0
VIRGINIA	70.2	19.4	0.3	3.7	1.8	4.7	8.1	6.5	18.0	9.6	14.6	17.0	14.1	8.9	6.1	3.9	1.2	35.7	51.0
WASHINGTON	78.9	3.1	1.4	5.8	3.2	7.5	10.4	6.7	19.0	9.5	14.3	16.5	14.4	8.4	5.7	4.1	1.4	35.3	50.2
WEST VIRGINIA	94.6	3.1	0.2	0.5	0.9	0.7	1.1	5.6	16.6	9.5	12.7	15.1	15.0	10.2	8.2	5.3	1.8	38.9	51.4
WISCONSIN	87.3	5.6	0.8	1.7	1.0	3.6	3.6	6.4	19.1	9.7	13.2	16.3	13.7	8.5	6.6	4.7	1.8	36.0	50.6
WYOMING	88.9	0.7	2.1	0.6	1.3	6.4	2.3	6.3	19.8	10.1	12.1	16.0	15.0	9.0	6.3	4.0	1.4	36.2	49.7

1. May be of any race.

Table A. States — Households and Housing Units

STATE	Households, 2000					Housing units, 2000									
				Percent				Occupied units							
										Owner-occupied			Renter-occupied		
											Median owner cost				
	Number	Percent change, 1990–2000	Persons per household	Female family householder[1]	One person	Total	Percent change, 1990–2000	Total	Percent	Median value[2] (dollars)	With a mortgage	Without a mortgage[3]	Median rent[4] (dollars)	Median rent as a percent of income	Sub-standard units[5] (percent)
	64	65	66	67	68	69	70	71	72	73	74	75	76	77	78
UNITED STATES	105 480 101	14.7	2.59	12.2	25.8	115 904 641	13.3	105 480 101	66.2	119 600	21.7	10.5	602	25.5	6.3
ALABAMA	1 737 080	15.3	2.49	14.2	26.1	1 963 711	17.6	1 737 080	72.5	85 100	19.8	9.9	447	24.8	3.5
ALASKA	221 600	17.3	2.74	10.8	23.5	260 978	12.2	221 600	62.5	144 200	22.3	9.9	720	24.8	13.0
ARIZONA	1 901 327	38.9	2.64	11.1	24.8	2 189 189	31.9	1 901 327	68.0	121 300	22.1	9.9	619	26.6	9.3
ARKANSAS	1 042 696	17.0	2.49	12.1	25.6	1 173 043	17.2	1 042 696	69.4	72 800	19.4	9.9	453	24.4	4.4
CALIFORNIA	11 502 870	10.8	2.87	12.6	23.5	12 214 549	9.2	11 502 870	56.9	211 500	25.3	9.9	747	27.7	15.6
COLORADO	1 658 238	29.3	2.53	9.6	26.3	1 808 037	22.4	1 658 238	67.3	166 600	22.6	9.9	671	26.4	4.9
CONNECTICUT	1 301 670	5.8	2.53	12.1	26.4	1 385 975	4.9	1 301 670	66.8	166 900	22.4	13.1	681	25.4	3.2
DELAWARE	298 736	20.7	2.54	13.1	25.0	343 072	18.3	298 736	72.3	130 400	20.8	9.9	639	24.3	3.1
DISTRICT OF COLUMBIA	248 338	-0.5	2.16	18.9	43.8	274 845	-1.3	248 338	40.8	157 200	22.2	9.9	618	24.8	9.5
FLORIDA	6 337 929	23.4	2.46	12.0	26.6	7 302 947	19.7	6 337 929	70.1	105 500	22.8	10.5	641	27.5	6.8
GEORGIA	3 006 369	27.0	2.65	14.5	23.6	3 281 737	24.4	3 006 369	67.5	111 200	20.8	9.9	613	24.9	5.3
HAWAII	403 240	13.2	2.92	12.4	21.9	460 542	18.1	403 240	56.5	272 700	26.3	9.9	779	27.2	16.1
IDAHO	469 645	30.2	2.69	8.7	22.4	527 824	27.7	469 645	72.4	106 300	21.5	9.9	515	25.3	5.4
ILLINOIS	4 591 779	9.3	2.63	12.3	26.8	4 885 615	8.4	4 591 779	67.3	130 800	21.7	11.1	605	24.4	5.3
INDIANA	2 336 306	13.1	2.53	11.1	25.9	2 532 319	12.7	2 336 306	71.4	94 300	19.3	9.9	521	23.9	2.7
IOWA	1 149 276	8.0	2.46	8.6	27.2	1 232 511	7.8	1 149 276	72.3	82 500	19.1	9.9	470	23.2	2.3
KANSAS	1 037 891	9.9	2.51	9.3	27.0	1 131 200	8.3	1 037 891	69.2	83 500	19.3	9.9	498	23.4	3.4
KENTUCKY	1 590 647	15.3	2.47	11.8	26.0	1 750 927	16.2	1 590 647	70.8	86 700	19.6	9.9	445	24.0	2.9
LOUISIANA	1 656 053	10.5	2.62	16.6	25.3	1 847 181	7.6	1 656 053	67.9	85 000	19.6	9.9	466	25.8	5.8
MAINE	518 200	11.4	2.39	9.5	27.0	651 901	11.0	518 200	71.6	98 700	21.4	12.1	497	25.3	2.1
MARYLAND	1 980 859	13.3	2.61	14.1	25.0	2 145 283	13.4	1 980 859	67.7	146 000	22.2	9.9	689	24.7	4.0
MASSACHUSETTS	2 443 580	8.7	2.51	11.9	28.0	2 621 989	6.0	2 443 580	61.7	185 700	21.9	12.4	684	25.5	3.4
MICHIGAN	3 785 661	10.7	2.56	12.5	26.2	4 234 279	10.0	3 785 661	73.8	115 600	19.6	9.9	546	24.4	3.4
MINNESOTA	1 895 127	15.0	2.52	8.9	26.9	2 065 946	11.8	1 895 127	74.6	122 400	20.0	9.9	566	24.7	3.3
MISSISSIPPI	1 046 434	14.8	2.63	17.3	24.6	1 161 953	15.0	1 046 434	72.3	71 400	20.4	9.9	439	25.0	5.7
MISSOURI	2 194 594	11.9	2.48	11.6	27.3	2 442 017	11.0	2 194 594	70.3	89 900	19.5	9.9	484	24.0	2.9
MONTANA	358 667	17.1	2.45	8.9	27.4	412 633	14.3	358 667	69.1	99 500	22.2	10.4	447	25.3	3.8
NEBRASKA	666 184	10.6	2.49	9.1	27.6	722 668	9.4	666 184	67.4	88 000	19.7	10.5	491	23.0	3.0
NEVADA	751 165	61.1	2.62	11.1	24.9	827 457	59.5	751 165	60.9	142 000	23.8	9.9	699	26.5	8.9
NEW HAMPSHIRE	474 606	15.4	2.53	9.1	24.4	547 024	8.6	474 606	69.7	133 300	22.3	13.6	646	24.2	2.1
NEW JERSEY	3 064 645	9.7	2.68	12.6	24.5	3 310 275	7.6	3 064 645	65.6	170 800	23.7	15.3	751	25.5	5.4
NEW MEXICO	677 971	24.9	2.63	13.2	25.4	780 579	23.5	677 971	70.0	108 100	22.2	9.9	503	26.6	8.7
NEW YORK	7 056 860	6.3	2.61	14.7	28.1	7 679 307	6.3	7 056 860	53.0	148 700	23.2	13.6	672	26.8	8.4
NORTH CAROLINA	3 132 013	24.4	2.49	12.5	25.4	3 523 944	25.0	3 132 013	69.4	108 300	21.3	9.9	548	24.3	4.0
NORTH DAKOTA	257 152	6.8	2.41	7.8	29.3	289 677	4.8	257 152	66.6	74 400	19.4	10.2	412	22.3	2.5
OHIO	4 445 773	8.8	2.49	12.1	27.3	4 783 051	9.4	4 445 773	69.1	103 700	20.6	10.6	515	24.2	2.1
OKLAHOMA	1 342 293	11.3	2.49	11.4	26.7	1 514 400	7.7	1 342 293	68.4	70 700	19.2	9.9	456	24.3	4.2
OREGON	1 333 723	20.9	2.51	9.8	26.1	1 452 709	21.7	1 333 723	64.3	152 100	23.2	10.5	620	26.9	5.3
PENNSYLVANIA	4 777 003	6.3	2.48	11.6	27.7	5 249 750	6.3	4 777 003	71.3	97 000	21.6	12.2	531	25.0	2.4
RHODE ISLAND	408 424	8.1	2.47	12.9	28.6	439 837	6.1	408 424	60.0	133 000	22.7	13.4	553	25.7	3.3
SOUTH CAROLINA	1 533 854	21.9	2.53	14.8	25.0	1 753 670	23.1	1 533 854	72.2	94 900	20.5	9.9	510	24.4	3.8
SOUTH DAKOTA	290 245	12.0	2.50	9.0	27.6	323 208	10.5	290 245	68.2	79 600	19.7	10.5	426	22.9	3.6
TENNESSEE	2 232 905	20.5	2.48	12.9	25.8	2 439 443	20.4	2 232 905	69.9	93 000	21.1	9.9	505	24.8	3.3
TEXAS	7 393 354	21.8	2.74	12.7	23.7	8 157 575	16.4	7 393 354	63.8	82 500	20.1	10.9	574	24.4	10.0
UTAH	701 281	30.5	3.13	9.4	17.8	768 594	28.4	701 281	71.5	146 100	22.9	9.9	597	24.9	6.3
VERMONT	240 634	14.2	2.44	9.3	26.2	294 382	8.5	240 634	70.6	111 500	22.4	13.9	553	26.2	2.0
VIRGINIA	2 699 173	17.8	2.54	11.9	25.1	2 904 192	16.3	2 699 173	68.1	125 400	21.4	9.9	650	24.5	3.9
WASHINGTON	2 271 398	21.3	2.53	9.9	26.2	2 451 075	20.6	2 271 398	64.6	168 300	23.8	10.4	663	26.5	5.5
WEST VIRGINIA	736 481	7.0	2.40	10.7	27.1	844 623	8.1	736 481	75.2	72 800	19.5	9.9	401	25.8	2.3
WISCONSIN	2 084 544	14.4	2.50	9.6	26.8	2 321 144	12.9	2 084 544	68.4	112 200	20.9	11.2	540	23.4	2.8
WYOMING	193 608	14.7	2.48	8.7	26.3	223 854	10.1	193 608	70.0	96 600	19.7	9.9	437	22.5	3.2

1. No spouse present.　2. Specified owner-occupied units.　3. Median monthly costs is often in the minimum category—9.9 percent or less, which is indicated as 9.9 percent.
4. Specified renter-occupied units.　5. Overcrowded or lacking complete plumbing facilities.

Table A. States — **Housing Units**

	Housing units, 2010													
STATE			Occupied units											Percent living in a different house than 1 year ago
					Percent who pay 30 percent or more of income for housing expenses		Median owner cost as a percent of income							
	Total	Percent change, 2000–2010	Total	Percent owner-occupied	Owners with a mort-gage	Renter	With a mort-gage	Without a mort-gage[1]	Median monthly housing costs (dollars)	Median value of units[2] (dollars)	Percent valued over $500,000	Median gross rent[3] (dollars)	Sub-standard units[4] (percent)	
	79	80	81	82	83	84	85	86	87	88	89	90	91	92
UNITED STATES..............	131 791 065	13.7	114 567 419	65.4	37.8	48.9	25.1	12.8	976	179 900	10.5	855	3.9	15.4
ALABAMA	2 174 428	10.7	1 815 152	70.1	32.5	46.7	23.0	12.3	723	123 900	3.4	667	2.4	15.7
ALASKA	307 065	17.7	254 610	63.9	32.1	41.5	23.3	10.8	1 167	241 400	7.1	981	10.2	19.6
ARIZONA	2 846 738	30.0	2 334 050	65.2	40.9	49.1	26.5	11.3	974	168 800	6.8	844	5.1	20.0
ARKANSAS	1 317 818	12.3	1 114 902	67.4	27.4	43.3	21.5	10.9	648	106 300	2.1	638	3.2	17.3
CALIFORNIA	13 682 976	12.0	12 406 475	55.6	50.9	54.4	30.6	11.4	1 381	370 900	33.7	1 163	9.1	16.6
COLORADO	2 214 262	22.5	1 960 585	65.9	37.3	49.0	25.2	10.7	1 098	236 600	11.4	863	3.2	19.0
CONNECTICUT	1 488 215	7.4	1 358 809	68.0	41.3	50.5	26.8	17.6	1 362	288 800	17.6	992	2.4	12.4
DELAWARE	406 489	18.5	328 765	73.0	37.1	50.9	24.8	11.8	1 115	243 600	7.4	952	2.9	14.1
DISTRICT OF COLUMBIA ...	296 836	8.0	252 388	42.5	35.5	47.5	24.8	11.0	1 390	426 900	40.3	1 198	3.5	20.5
FLORIDA	8 994 091	23.2	7 035 068	68.1	48.3	55.6	29.5	14.4	1 013	164 200	6.7	947	3.1	16.6
GEORGIA	4 091 482	24.7	3 482 420	66.2	37.9	49.0	25.2	12.3	957	156 200	5.3	819	3.2	16.4
HAWAII	519 992	12.9	445 812	58.0	50.0	51.3	30.1	10.1	1 432	525 400	53.0	1 291	9.1	15.3
IDAHO	668 634	26.7	576 709	69.6	36.6	46.9	24.7	10.6	806	165 100	5.0	683	3.6	17.5
ILLINOIS	5 297 077	8.4	4 752 857	67.7	39.7	48.8	25.9	13.8	1 035	191 800	8.0	848	3.1	13.2
INDIANA	2 797 172	10.5	2 470 905	70.3	27.4	46.7	21.6	11.0	781	123 300	2.2	683	2.2	15.3
IOWA	1 337 563	8.5	1 223 439	72.4	24.7	42.3	21.3	11.5	728	123 400	2.1	629	1.7	15.3
KANSAS	1 234 037	9.1	1 101 658	68.1	26.4	41.8	21.8	11.8	776	127 300	2.5	682	2.2	17.0
KENTUCKY	1 928 617	10.1	1 684 348	68.6	30.1	43.7	22.2	11.3	675	121 600	2.5	613	2.5	15.3
LOUISIANA	1 967 947	6.5	1 689 822	67.6	30.1	46.4	21.6	10.5	721	137 500	3.0	736	3.7	14.7
MAINE	722 217	10.8	545 417	72.7	33.9	45.1	24.1	13.9	835	179 100	5.5	707	2.5	13.5
MARYLAND	2 380 605	11.0	2 127 439	67.0	38.0	48.7	25.4	12.9	1 403	301 400	18.6	1 131	2.4	14.0
MASSACHUSETTS	2 808 727	7.1	2 520 419	62.2	39.0	47.8	26.1	15.3	1 310	334 100	20.5	1 009	2.0	14.0
MICHIGAN	4 531 231	7.0	3 806 621	72.8	36.2	51.2	24.6	13.9	862	123 300	2.6	730	2.1	14.9
MINNESOTA	2 348 242	13.7	2 091 548	73.0	33.3	47.5	24.1	11.9	995	194 300	5.8	764	2.3	14.6
MISSISSIPPI	1 276 441	9.9	1 079 999	69.8	35.2	47.0	23.5	12.0	659	100 100	2.0	672	4.0	14.3
MISSOURI	2 714 017	11.1	2 350 628	69.0	30.1	45.8	22.6	11.7	776	139 000	3.4	682	2.2	16.1
MONTANA	483 006	17.1	402 747	69.7	35.9	39.9	24.1	11.3	714	181 200	6.3	642	2.8	16.0
NEBRASKA	797 677	10.4	719 304	67.4	25.9	41.0	21.4	12.6	776	127 600	2.0	669	2.2	17.0
NEVADA	1 175 070	42.0	989 811	57.2	44.7	50.3	28.1	12.2	1 125	174 800	5.9	952	5.0	23.9
NEW HAMPSHIRE	614 996	12.4	515 431	71.7	40.0	47.7	26.5	16.5	1 227	243 000	7.4	951	1.9	14.2
NEW JERSEY	3 554 909	7.4	3 172 421	66.4	46.5	51.5	28.7	18.9	1 478	339 200	21.7	1 114	4.1	10.0
NEW MEXICO	902 242	15.6	765 183	67.9	35.9	42.4	24.3	10.0	741	161 200	5.9	699	4.7	14.9
NEW YORK	8 108 211	5.6	7 196 427	54.3	41.2	50.2	26.3	15.5	1 156	296 500	24.4	1 020	5.5	11.5
NORTH CAROLINA	4 333 479	23.0	3 670 859	67.2	34.3	47.2	24.0	12.5	835	154 200	5.6	731	2.8	16.5
NORTH DAKOTA	318 099	9.8	280 412	66.9	19.0	36.2	19.6	10.0	625	123 000	1.4	583	1.3	16.4
OHIO	5 128 113	7.2	4 525 066	68.4	31.8	47.7	23.4	13.1	818	134 400	2.3	685	1.8	14.6
OKLAHOMA	1 666 205	10.0	1 432 959	67.8	28.7	41.8	21.9	11.2	701	111 400	2.1	659	3.0	17.5
OREGON	1 676 476	18.4	1 507 137	62.5	42.6	51.2	27.3	12.9	971	244 500	10.2	816	3.4	18.0
PENNSYLVANIA	5 568 820	6.1	4 936 030	70.1	33.1	46.3	23.8	13.7	869	165 500	5.4	763	1.6	12.1
RHODE ISLAND	463 416	5.4	402 295	60.8	43.5	48.1	27.7	15.4	1 144	254 500	10.3	868	2.6	13.6
SOUTH CAROLINA	2 140 337	22.0	1 761 393	68.7	33.8	47.2	23.5	12.0	782	138 100	5.5	728	2.7	15.4
SOUTH DAKOTA..............	364 031	12.6	318 955	68.0	25.4	37.2	21.9	10.9	672	129 700	2.6	591	2.7	15.5
TENNESSEE	2 815 087	15.4	2 440 663	68.1	33.1	46.7	23.7	11.4	765	139 000	4.1	697	2.5	15.6
TEXAS	9 996 209	22.5	8 738 664	63.6	32.5	46.3	23.4	12.5	893	128 100	3.8	801	5.8	17.7
UTAH	981 821	27.7	880 025	69.9	35.4	45.8	24.8	10.0	1 028	217 200	6.7	796	4.6	17.7
VERMONT	322 698	9.6	256 922	70.4	38.6	49.9	26.0	16.3	995	216 800	7.2	823	2.2	13.6
VIRGINIA	3 368 674	16.0	2 992 732	67.7	35.0	46.6	24.7	11.4	1 183	249 100	16.0	1 019	2.6	14.9
WASHINGTON	2 888 594	17.9	2 606 863	63.1	40.7	48.4	26.7	12.1	1 124	271 800	14.8	908	3.4	18.0
WEST VIRGINIA	882 213	4.5	741 940	74.6	25.5	40.2	20.1	10.0	528	95 100	1.5	571	1.8	11.4
WISCONSIN	2 625 477	13.1	2 279 532	68.7	34.2	46.5	24.5	14.0	885	169 400	3.8	715	2.2	14.2
WYOMING	262 286	17.2	222 803	69.7	28.0	34.3	22.0	10.0	773	180 500	6.3	693	2.8	20.2

1. Median monthly costs is often in the minimum category—10.0 percent or less, which is indicated as 10.0 percent. 2. Specified owner-occupied units. 3. Specified renter-occupied units.
4. Overcrowded or lacking complete plumbing facilities.

Table A. States — **Residential Construction, Vital Statistics, and Health**

STATE	Value of residential construction authorized by building permits, 2010			Manu-factured housing units put in place, 2010 (1,000)	Births, 2009		Deaths, 2008					Percent lacking health insurance, 2010		Medicare enrollees, 2010
	New construction ($1,000)	Number of housing units	Percent single family		Total	Rate¹	Number Total	Number Infant²	Rate Crude¹	Rate Age-adjusted	Rate Infant³	All persons	Children under 18 years	
	93	94	95	96	97	98	99	100	101	102	103	104	105	106
UNITED STATES	101 943 061	604 610	74.0	49.9	4 130 665	13.5	2 471 984	28 059	8.1	7.7	6.6	16.3	9.8	46 584 745
ALABAMA	1 546 975	11 261	77.3	2.1	62 475	13.3	47 707	612	10.2	9.4	9.5	15.4	8.9	845 266
ALASKA	204 680	904	83.3	(D)	11 324	16.2	3 494	67	5.1	7.5	5.9	18.0	13.7	65 691
ARIZONA	2 424 190	12 370	86.9	1.0	92 798	14.1	45 823	635	7.1	6.7	6.4	19.1	15.0	930 211
ARKANSAS	880 263	7 177	64.8	1.5	39 808	13.8	29 322	300	10.2	9.1	7.4	18.7	7.4	531 404
CALIFORNIA	9 120 591	43 716	58.8	1.5	527 020	14.3	234 766	2 814	6.4	6.7	5.1	19.4	10.7	4 757 352
COLORADO	2 608 302	11 591	75.8	0.4	68 628	13.7	31 274	437	6.3	7.1	6.2	13.0	7.8	624 824
CONNECTICUT	861 356	3 932	66.9	0.3	38 896	11.1	28 794	242	8.2	7	6.0	11.0	6.0	567 517
DELAWARE	364 135	3 072	87.0	0.3	11 559	13.1	7 622	101	8.7	7.8	8.4	11.3	6.0	149 288
DISTRICT OF COLUMBIA	105 470	739	24.0	X	9 040	15.1	5 140	99	8.7	8.7	10.8	12.5	5.1	78 134
FLORIDA	7 823 544	38 679	77.7	2.7	221 394	11.9	170 703	1 669	9.3	6.9	7.2	20.8	14.2	3 374 563
GEORGIA	2 659 234	17 265	85.6	1.2	141 377	14.4	69 640	1 182	7.2	8.4	8.1	19.4	9.9	1 235 730
HAWAII	773 013	3 442	55.8	(D)	18 887	14.6	9 501	108	7.4	6.1	5.5	7.7	2.3	206 487
IDAHO	732 442	4 153	85.9	0.3	23 737	15.4	10 962	149	7.2	7.3	5.9	19.2	9.0	229 797
ILLINOIS	2 412 386	12 318	61.9	1.1	171 163	13.3	103 471	1 256	8.1	7.8	7.1	14.8	7.6	1 839 383
INDIANA	1 960 774	13 083	74.7	0.4	86 673	13.5	56 752	614	8.9	8.4	6.9	13.4	6.0	1 005 734
IOWA	1 222 077	7 607	78.2	0.2	39 701	13.2	28 541	228	9.5	7.5	5.7	12.3	7.4	517 427
KANSAS	811 584	5 140	77.3	0.3	41 396	14.7	24 975	304	8.9	7.9	7.3	12.7	7.5	432 755
KENTUCKY	1 086 665	7 986	74.9	2.3	57 551	13.3	41 329	402	9.6	9.1	6.9	14.9	6.8	759 956
LOUISIANA	1 765 181	11 343	90.0	4.3	64 973	14.5	41 220	591	9.3	9.2	9.1	20.0	9.0	686 727
MAINE	525 280	3 034	92.7	0.3	13 470	10.2	12 541	75	9.5	7.7	5.5	9.4	4.4	264 883
MARYLAND	1 951 869	11 931	71.2	0.1	75 059	13.2	43 892	619	7.8	7.8	8.0	13.1	9.2	784 770
MASSACHUSETTS	1 816 993	9 075	64.3	0.2	75 016	11.4	53 518	391	8.2	7	5.1	5.6	3.8	1 061 049
MICHIGAN	1 553 300	9 075	85.5	0.4	117 294	11.8	88 445	894	8.8	8.2	7.4	13.0	5.1	1 651 222
MINNESOTA	1 810 528	9 840	71.7	0.3	70 646	13.4	38 499	434	7.4	6.7	6.0	9.8	6.0	785 852
MISSISSIPPI	715 298	5 259	84.2	2.2	42 901	14.5	28 984	448	9.9	9.6	10.0	21.1	13.4	497 155
MISSOURI	1 430 224	9 699	71.2	1.0	78 905	13.2	56 578	585	9.5	8.5	7.2	14.0	8.9	1 004 371
MONTANA	303 528	2 022	65.4	0.2	12 257	12.6	8 913	86	9.2	7.9	6.8	18.1	8.8	169 503
NEBRASKA	744 968	5 401	70.0	0.1	26 936	15.0	15 461	146	8.7	7.5	5.4	13.3	10.3	279 073
NEVADA	759 741	6 443	83.2	0.2	37 612	14.2	19 335	211	7.4	8.2	5.3	21.3	17.5	356 618
NEW HAMPSHIRE	461 754	2 670	70.8	0.1	13 377	10.1	10 268	54	7.8	7	4.0	10.3	5.5	223 259
NEW JERSEY	2 036 521	13 535	54.5	0.2	110 331	12.7	70 026	626	8.1	7.2	5.6	15.4	9.2	1 327 012
NEW MEXICO	779 509	4 533	88.4	1.0	29 000	14.4	16 005	169	8.1	7.7	5.6	21.6	13.7	313 427
NEW YORK	3 165 281	19 568	50.9	1.2	248 110	12.7	148 698	1 374	7.6	6.8	5.5	15.0	7.9	2 988 430
NORTH CAROLINA	5 107 162	33 889	76.9	2.3	126 845	13.5	77 283	1 073	8.4	8.2	8.2	17.0	9.2	1 489 840
NORTH DAKOTA	481 143	3 833	54.4	0.4	9 001	13.9	5 871	52	9.2	7.2	5.8	13.1	10.2	109 307
OHIO	2 297 494	13 710	77.3	0.6	144 841	12.5	109 767	1 144	9.5	8.4	7.7	13.7	8.3	1 900 576
OKLAHOMA	1 225 760	8 140	84.3	1.7	54 553	14.8	37 014	397	10.2	9.4	7.3	17.0	11.9	603 461
OREGON	1 377 070	6 868	76.6	0.7	47 132	12.3	31 967	253	8.5	7.6	5.2	16.2	10.4	621 067
PENNSYLVANIA	3 293 098	19 740	85.5	1.4	146 434	11.6	127 462	1 100	10.1	7.9	7.4	11.0	8.2	2 283 210
RHODE ISLAND	155 072	934	77.8	(D)	11 442	10.9	9 738	71	9.2	7.5	5.9	11.4	5.3	182 972
SOUTH CAROLINA	2 489 139	14 021	90.5	1.4	60 620	13.3	40 289	507	8.9	8.4	8.0	20.6	14.2	773 702
SOUTH DAKOTA	403 140	2 946	74.2	0.6	11 934	14.7	7 083	101	8.8	7.1	8.4	13.0	6.6	136 564
TENNESSEE	2 344 869	16 475	70.6	2.4	82 211	13.1	58 820	693	9.4	8.9	8.1	14.7	7.9	1 057 914
TEXAS	13 739 563	88 461	75.7	7.6	401 977	16.2	164 914	2 504	6.8	7.8	6.2	24.6	16.3	3 001 032
UTAH	1 672 395	9 171	75.1	0.2	53 887	19.4	14 040	266	5.1	6.7	4.8	13.6	11.4	283 032
VERMONT	227 618	1 319	74.3	0.1	6 110	9.8	5 211	29	8.4	7.2	4.6	9.5	4.1	111 526
VIRGINIA	3 246 376	20 992	76.9	1.1	105 059	13.3	59 100	732	7.6	7.7	6.9	14.1	8.3	1 140 524
WASHINGTON	3 891 040	20 691	71.1	0.8	89 313	13.4	48 627	491	7.4	7.3	5.4	13.8	5.9	972 359
WEST VIRGINIA	345 589	2 395	75.0	1.1	21 268	11.7	21 557	165	11.9	9.6	7.7	13.5	2.7	381 765
WISCONSIN	1 793 681	10 864	70.8	0.2	70 843	12.5	46 815	503	8.3	7.4	7.0	9.4	4.6	910 945
WYOMING	435 191	2 298	67.3	0.2	7 881	14.5	4 227	56	7.9	7.8	7.0	17.3	10.2	80 079

Table A. States — **Crime and Education**

STATE	Serious crime known to police,[1] 2010				Public elementary and secondary school enrollment, 2009–2010		Educational attainment[3] (percent)				Local government expenditures for education, 2008–2009	
	Violent Crime		Property Crime				2000		2010			
	Number	Rate[2]	Number	Rate[2]	Total	Student/ teacher ratio	High school graduate or more	Bachelor's degree or more	High school graduate or more	Bachelor's degree or more	Total current expenditures (mil dol)	Current expenditures per student (dollars)
	107	108	109	110	111	112	113	114	115	116	117	118
UNITED STATES...............	1 246 248	403.6	9 082 887	2 941.9	49 373 307	15.4	84.1	25.6	85.6	28.2	518 997	10 591
ALABAMA	18 056	377.8	168 092	3 516.8	748 889	15.8	77.5	20.4	82.1	21.9	6 684	9 042
ALASKA	4 537	638.8	20 259	2 852.5	131 661	16.3	90.4	28.1	91.0	27.9	2 006	15 353
ARIZONA	26 085	408.1	225 893	3 534.0	1 077 831	20.7	85.1	24.6	85.6	25.9	8 625	7 929
ARKANSAS.........................	14 735	505.3	103 775	3 558.9	480 559	12.9	81.7	18.4	82.9	19.5	4 241	8 854
CALIFORNIA........................	164 133	440.6	981 939	2 635.8	6 263 449	20.0	81.2	27.5	80.7	30.1	60 081	9 503
COLORADO.........................	16 133	320.8	134 992	2 684.2	832 368	17.0	89.7	34.6	89.7	36.4	7 187	8 782
CONNECTICUT	10 057	281.4	78 386	2 193.2	563 985	12.9	88.2	31.6	88.6	35.5	8 708	15 353
DELAWARE	5 575	620.9	30 963	3 448.2	126 801	14.7	86.1	24.0	87.7	27.8	1 519	12 109
DISTRICT OF COLUMBIA ...	8 004	1 330.2	28 756	4 778.9	69 433	10.9	83.2	38.3	87.4	50.1	1 353	19 698
FLORIDA.............................	101 969	542.4	669 035	3 558.4	2 634 522	14.3	84.0	22.8	85.5	25.8	23 328	8 867
GEORGIA	39 072	403.3	352 679	3 640.5	1 667 685	14.4	82.6	23.1	84.3	27.3	15 977	9 649
HAWAII...............................	3 574	262.7	45 083	3 314.2	180 196	15.8	87.4	26.3	89.9	29.5	2 225	12 399
IDAHO.................................	3 465	221.0	31 286	1 995.8	276 299	18.2	86.2	20.0	88.3	24.4	1 958	7 118
ILLINOIS.............................	55 835	435.2	343 989	2 681.0	2 104 175	15.2	85.5	27.1	86.9	30.8	23 495	11 592
INDIANA..............................	20 389	314.5	197 260	3 042.4	1 046 661	16.8	84.6	17.1	87.0	22.7	9 681	9 254
IOWA..................................	8 333	273.5	68 315	2 242.5	491 842	13.7	89.7	25.5	90.6	24.9	4 731	10 055
KANSAS.............................	10 531	369.1	89 015	3 119.9	474 489	13.7	88.1	27.3	89.2	29.8	4 805	10 201
KENTUCKY.........................	10 528	242.6	110 709	2 551.3	680 089	15.3	78.7	20.5	81.9	20.5	5 887	9 038
LOUISIANA.........................	24 886	549.0	165 357	3 647.5	690 915	13.9	80.8	22.5	81.9	21.4	7 277	10 625
MAINE................................	1 621	122.0	32 934	2 479.3	189 225	11.6	89.3	24.1	90.3	26.8	2 350	12 183
MARYLAND	31 620	547.7	173 051	2 997.3	848 412	14.6	85.7	32.3	88.1	36.1	11 592	13 737
MASSACHUSETTS	30 553	466.6	153 905	2 350.5	957 053	13.7	85.1	32.7	89.1	39.0	13 943	14 540
MICHIGAN	48 460	490.3	268 201	2 713.6	1 649 082	17.8	86.2	23.0	88.7	25.2	17 218	10 373
MINNESOTA	12 515	236.0	136 431	2 572.3	837 053	15.8	90.8	31.2	91.8	31.8	9 270	11 088
MISSISSIPPI.......................	8 003	269.7	88 574	2 985.0	492 481	14.9	80.3	18.7	81.0	19.5	3 967	8 064
MISSOURI	27 252	455.0	200 414	3 346.4	917 982	13.5	86.6	26.2	86.9	25.6	8 827	9 891
MONTANA...........................	2 693	272.2	25 169	2 543.8	141 807	13.5	89.6	23.8	91.7	28.8	1 436	10 189
NEBRASKA.........................	5 104	279.5	48 821	2 673.2	295 368	13.3	90.4	24.6	90.4	28.6	3 054	10 846
NEVADA	17 841	660.6	74 932	2 774.7	428 947	19.4	82.8	19.3	84.7	21.7	3 606	8 321
NEW HAMPSHIRE	2 198	167.0	28 782	2 186.3	197 140	12.7	88.1	30.1	91.5	32.8	2 491	12 583
NEW JERSEY.....................	27 066	307.7	183 042	2 081.9	1 396 029	12.1	87.3	30.1	88.0	35.4	23 589	17 076
NEW MEXICO	12 126	588.9	70 742	3 435.4	334 419	14.7	82.2	23.6	83.3	25.0	3 186	9 648
NEW YORK	75 977	392.1	376 161	1 941.2	2 766 052	12.9	82.5	28.7	84.9	32.5	48 635	17 746
NORTH CAROLINA.............	34 653	363.4	328 719	3 447.3	1 483 397	14.1	79.2	23.2	84.7	26.5	12 470	8 518
NORTH DAKOTA	1 513	225.0	11 895	1 768.5	95 073	11.4	85.5	22.6	90.3	27.6	929	9 802
OHIO...................................	36 366	315.2	374 381	3 245.2	1 764 297	15.8	87.0	24.6	88.1	24.6	19 398	10 902
OKLAHOMA........................	17 987	479.6	128 126	3 415.5	654 802	15.3	86.1	22.5	86.2	22.9	5 082	7 878
OREGON	9 655	252.0	115 428	3 012.9	582 839	20.3	88.1	27.2	88.8	28.8	5 530	9 611
PENNSYLVANIA..................	46 514	366.2	276 023	2 173.0	1 786 103	13.6	85.7	24.3	88.4	27.1	21 832	12 299
RHODE ISLAND..................	2 701	256.6	26 910	2 556.6	145 118	12.8	81.3	26.4	83.5	30.2	2 139	14 719
SOUTH CAROLINA.............	27 648	597.7	180 407	3 900.4	723 143	15.4	83.0	19.0	84.1	24.5	6 627	9 228
SOUTH DAKOTA................	2 186	268.5	15 082	1 852.4	123 713	13.3	91.8	25.7	89.6	26.3	1 080	8 543
TENNESSEE	38 921	613.3	232 132	3 657.9	972 549	14.9	79.9	22.0	83.6	23.1	7 768	7 992
TEXAS	113 231	450.3	951 246	3 783.0	4 850 210	14.6	79.2	23.9	80.7	25.9	40 688	8 562
UTAH..................................	5 879	212.7	87 880	3 179.6	582 793	22.9	90.7	26.4	90.6	29.3	3 639	6 612
VERMONT	815	130.2	14 281	2 282.3	92 431	10.6	90.0	28.8	91.0	33.6	1 413	15 096
VIRGINIA	17 087	213.6	186 196	2 327.2	1 245 340	17.6	86.6	31.9	86.5	34.2	13 505	10 928
WASHINGTON	21 101	313.8	249 253	3 706.6	1 035 347	19.4	91.8	28.6	89.8	31.1	9 940	9 688
WEST VIRGINIA.................	5 830	314.6	41 500	2 239.6	282 662	13.9	77.1	15.3	83.2	17.5	3 059	10 821
WISCONSIN	14 142	248.7	142 612	2 507.7	872 436	14.9	86.7	23.8	90.1	26.3	9 696	11 183
WYOMING	1 104	195.9	13 874	2 461.6	88 155	12.3	90.0	20.6	92.3	24.1	1 268	14 628

1. Data for serious crimes have not been adjusted for underreporting; this may affect comparability between geographic areas and over time.   2. Per 100,000 population estimated by the FBI.   3. Persons 25 years old and over.

Table A. States — Exports, Income, and Poverty

STATE	Exports of goods by state of origin, 2011 (mil dol)			Income, 2010					Percent below poverty level, 2010						
				Households									Families with children under 18		
	Total	Manu-factured	Non-manu-factured	Per capita income (dollars)	Median income (dollars)	Percent with income of $25,000 or less	Percent with income of $100,000 or more	Median income of family of four	All persons	Children under 18 years	Persons 65 years and over	All families	Married-couple families	Male house-holder[1] families	Female house-holder[1] families
	119	120	121	122	123	124	125	126	127	128	129	130	131	132	133
UNITED STATES	1 480 665	1 094 669	177 468	26 059	50 046	25.0	20.0	72 767	15.3	21.6	9.0	11.3	8.4	22.6	39.6
ALABAMA	17 893	14 438	2 923	21 993	40 474	31.9	14.1	61 593	19.0	27.7	10.7	14.7	9.6	27.3	49.3
ALASKA	5 238	521	4 599	30 598	64 576	17.0	29.5	88 003	9.9	12.9	5.7	7.2	4.0	15.4	29.0
ARIZONA	17 501	11 125	2 707	23 618	46 789	25.2	17.3	61 267	17.4	24.4	7.7	12.5	11.9	23.7	38.0
ARKANSAS	5 559	4 683	681	20 725	38 307	32.4	11.8	56 275	18.8	27.6	10.2	14.1	10.4	30.9	47.1
CALIFORNIA	159 354	102 107	20 207	27 353	57 708	21.5	26.4	74 806	15.8	22.0	9.7	11.8	10.6	23.2	35.4
COLORADO	7 334	5 989	586	28 723	54 046	22.2	22.7	79 905	13.4	17.4	8.1	9.4	6.9	20.0	37.1
CONNECTICUT	16 198	13 744	1 756	35 078	64 032	19.2	29.9	99 440	10.1	12.8	6.6	7.2	3.7	15.4	29.8
DELAWARE	5 509	948	67	27 729	55 847	20.8	22.8	79 829	11.8	18.1	7.7	8.1	5.3	21.0	30.4
DISTRICT OF COLUMBIA	1 055	4 680	76	41 240	60 903	24.0	30.5	115 995	19.2	30.4	13.1	14.1	3.8	19.0	42.3
FLORIDA	64 756	44 767	10 652	24 272	44 409	27.3	15.8	62 742	16.5	23.5	9.9	12.0	10.0	23.9	37.6
GEORGIA	34 713	29 082	2 987	23 383	46 430	27.4	17.7	64 223	17.9	24.8	10.7	13.7	9.7	26.3	41.4
HAWAII	909	613	187	27 537	63 030	18.5	27.8	82 726	10.7	13.9	6.8	7.4	5.0	14.7	29.5
IDAHO	5 899	3 468	608	20 991	43 490	26.8	12.2	61 301	15.7	19.0	7.9	11.6	10.5	24.1	39.4
ILLINOIS	64 565	50 933	4 987	27 325	52 972	23.1	21.9	79 074	13.8	19.4	8.4	10.1	7.1	23.0	38.2
INDIANA	32 200	29 446	628	22 806	44 613	26.6	14.3	67 296	15.3	21.7	6.8	11.0	8.2	22.8	41.1
IOWA	13 283	11 319	1 594	24 883	47 961	24.3	15.2	72 234	12.6	16.3	6.7	8.2	6.3	13.0	39.4
KANSAS	11 572	8 728	1 856	24 911	48 257	24.5	16.6	72 665	13.6	18.4	7.7	9.5	6.7	20.3	41.3
KENTUCKY	20 066	16 799	524	21 706	40 062	32.4	12.7	62 583	19.0	26.3	11.2	14.5	10.4	31.5	48.5
LOUISIANA	55 124	34 873	19 852	22 862	42 505	31.0	15.8	65 778	18.7	27.3	11.5	14.5	7.1	25.7	46.5
MAINE	3 461	2 749	594	24 950	45 815	26.6	14.6	74 738	12.9	17.8	9.5	8.8	5.5	16.2	39.2
MARYLAND	10 879	7 910	1 133	33 772	68 854	16.3	32.8	100 928	9.9	13.0	7.7	6.6	3.2	14.0	25.5
MASSACHUSETTS	27 711	21 919	1 868	33 203	62 072	21.5	29.2	99 067	11.4	14.3	8.7	8.2	3.6	18.3	34.9
MICHIGAN	50 802	43 333	3 350	23 622	45 413	27.5	15.6	70 237	16.8	23.5	8.0	12.1	8.7	25.7	44.5
MINNESOTA	20 276	17 022	1 943	28 563	55 459	21.1	21.4	84 251	11.6	15.2	7.5	7.5	4.6	20.6	35.6
MISSISSIPPI	10 926	9 086	728	19 096	36 851	35.5	11.0	54 765	22.4	32.5	11.9	17.8	10.8	37.5	51.2
MISSOURI	14 145	11 690	1 941	23 920	44 301	27.8	15.2	67 255	15.3	20.9	9.1	10.6	7.5	23.7	40.4
MONTANA	1 581	1 103	414	23 552	42 666	27.8	13.0	68 313	14.6	20.1	7.0	10.0	8.5	21.7	39.8
NEBRASKA	7 578	5 482	1 814	24 744	48 408	24.4	15.7	71 247	12.9	18.2	7.5	8.8	6.7	25.9	36.6
NEVADA	7 978	6 044	967	25 284	51 001	22.9	18.5	65 179	14.9	22.0	7.6	11.1	9.5	18.8	35.2
NEW HAMPSHIRE	4 294	3 202	287	30 949	61 042	17.5	25.6	91 750	8.3	10.0	6.1	5.3	2.5	13.4	31.9
NEW JERSEY	38 241	28 500	3 903	33 555	67 681	18.2	32.5	101 957	10.3	14.5	7.2	7.8	4.5	15.4	34.2
NEW MEXICO	2 090	1 614	99	22 150	42 090	30.0	15.2	54 640	20.4	30.0	12.0	15.7	14.9	28.5	44.2
NEW YORK	82 894	49 368	12 276	30 011	54 148	24.1	24.8	81 212	14.9	21.2	10.9	11.5	8.6	20.5	37.7
NORTH CAROLINA	26 964	22 763	1 948	23 432	43 326	28.5	14.6	65 036	17.5	24.9	9.9	13.3	9.7	29.5	44.4
NORTH DAKOTA	3 379	1 940	1 351	26 021	48 670	25.2	15.7	79 336	13.0	16.2	12.1	7.8	5.1	11.9	43.8
OHIO	46 408	40 664	2 231	23 975	45 090	27.4	15.3	70 599	15.8	23.3	7.7	11.8	7.4	25.3	45.1
OKLAHOMA	6 218	5 057	497	22 254	42 072	29.0	13.3	60 395	16.9	24.7	9.3	12.7	9.9	26.5	45.5
OREGON	18 292	12 693	3 725	24 753	46 560	25.9	16.4	66 616	15.8	21.6	7.9	11.0	9.0	22.0	42.0
PENNSYLVANIA	41 030	31 356	4 813	26 374	49 288	25.4	18.6	76 682	13.4	19.1	7.9	9.3	5.7	21.3	39.4
RHODE ISLAND	2 300	1 402	727	27 667	52 254	25.2	21.4	86 267	14.0	19.0	8.2	9.2	5.7	19.2	34.6
SOUTH CAROLINA	24 680	22 655	731	22 128	42 018	30.6	13.5	62 912	18.2	26.1	9.8	13.8	8.7	27.5	45.1
SOUTH DAKOTA	1 455	1 347	82	23 647	45 904	25.7	14.2	69 006	14.4	18.2	11.1	9.2	5.7	17.4	40.7
TENNESSEE	29 973	22 418	2 005	22 463	41 461	30.2	13.6	60 909	17.7	25.7	9.7	13.4	10.4	26.7	43.8
TEXAS	249 860	195 214	18 136	23 863	48 615	25.5	19.3	63 859	17.9	25.7	10.7	13.8	11.7	22.0	42.0
UTAH	18 929	17 523	835	22 059	54 744	19.9	19.1	64 780	13.2	15.7	6.0	9.7	8.6	21.7	37.6
VERMONT	4 328	2 345	92	26 876	49 406	25.0	16.9	77 296	12.7	16.7	6.8	8.4	5.4	9.1	40.5
VIRGINIA	18 105	13 486	3 251	31 313	60 674	19.5	27.8	87 498	11.1	14.5	7.4	7.7	4.6	16.7	31.5
WASHINGTON	64 632	46 371	15 326	28 364	55 631	21.0	22.1	80 404	13.4	18.2	6.9	9.2	7.5	19.5	36.6
WEST VIRGINIA	9 002	3 419	5 360	20 953	38 218	33.8	10.5	61 691	18.1	25.5	9.9	13.2	11.2	33.6	48.7
WISCONSIN	22 049	19 319	1 237	25 458	49 001	24.1	16.3	76 117	13.2	19.1	7.1	9.1	5.9	22.8	40.0
WYOMING	1 222	1 081	108	27 616	53 512	21.8	19.4	73 362	11.2	14.3	6.8	7.2	6.0	4.8	35.8

1. No spouse present.

Table A. States — **Personal Income**

STATE	Total (mil dol)	Percent change, 2009–2010	Per capita Dollars	Per capita Rank	Wages and salaries[2]	Proprietors' income	Dividends, interest, and rent	Transfer payments Total	Government payments to individuals Total	Social Security	Medical payments	Income maintenance	Unemployment insurance
	134	135	136	137	138	139	140	141	142	143	144	145	146
UNITED STATES................	12 353 577	3.7	39 937	X	6 400 786	1 033 652	2 070 501	2 281 184	2 220 915	690 177	948 254	264 544	139 495
ALABAMA......................	160 332	3.2	33 504	43	77 656	11 213	23 927	37 901	36 885	12 722	14 826	5 049	1 162
ALASKA........................	31 589	4.5	44 233	8	17 530	2 863	4 365	5 020	4 885	959	1 948	591	270
ARIZONA......................	221 503	2.9	34 539	38	109 926	16 925	37 878	47 154	45 884	14 134	19 587	4 878	1 899
ARKANSAS....................	95 844	3.2	32 805	45	44 975	7 170	16 633	23 342	22 778	7 753	9 456	2 680	938
CALIFORNIA..................	1 587 404	4.0	42 514	18	818 605	148 006	291 114	260 021	252 818	64 409	110 045	33 393	22 150
COLORADO....................	213 494	3.7	42 295	15	114 319	21 260	38 366	28 600	27 622	8 935	10 747	2 789	2 216
CONNECTICUT...............	193 932	2.7	54 239	2	98 350	17 984	37 087	28 826	28 140	8 907	12 997	2 408	2 426
DELAWARE....................	36 079	3.8	40 097	23	20 531	2 820	5 941	7 045	6 872	2 396	3 092	598	329
DISTRICT OF COLUMBIA ...	42 773	5.7	70 710	1	58 546	5 613	5 755	5 442	5 325	876	3 009	740	333
FLORIDA.......................	719 828	3.2	38 210	25	325 533	41 737	176 504	149 088	145 252	49 185	61 280	16 612	6 574
GEORGIA	337 468	3.0	34 747	41	182 252	26 043	52 086	60 183	58 290	18 723	21 546	9 195	3 375
HAWAII.........................	56 647	3.7	41 550	16	28 806	3 575	10 606	9 064	8 814	2 941	3 458	1 230	597
IDAHO..........................	50 114	4.0	31 897	48	23 120	5 439	8 911	9 993	9 691	3 400	3 661	1 060	598
ILLINOIS.......................	539 880	2.8	42 040	17	292 745	39 198	91 764	91 767	89 271	27 547	38 097	10 519	7 189
INDIANA.......................	220 555	2.5	33 981	42	114 999	13 562	31 622	45 739	44 487	16 200	17 169	4 747	2 894
IOWA...........................	116 027	3.1	38 039	27	57 553	12 446	18 765	21 376	20 788	7 666	8 068	2 005	1 082
KANSAS........................	111 441	2.7	38 977	24	56 423	10 127	19 304	18 842	18 294	6 526	7 251	1 976	1 144
KENTUCKY....................	140 483	2.0	32 316	49	72 311	7 606	19 976	34 887	34 050	11 053	13 826	4 375	1 715
LOUISIANA....................	168 356	3.6	37 039	29	84 041	14 438	25 514	34 709	33 637	9 648	15 908	4 925	862
MAINE..........................	48 799	1.7	36 763	32	23 589	3 872	7 425	10 974	10 719	3 636	4 692	1 160	420
MARYLAND	283 634	4.0	49 023	5	139 829	18 157	46 022	38 661	37 551	11 450	17 369	3 991	1 902
MASSACHUSETTS.............	336 320	3.6	51 304	4	188 290	26 421	57 704	55 634	54 356	15 053	25 780	6 050	4 835
MICHIGAN.....................	342 874	3.3	34 714	40	173 571	22 726	50 317	81 131	79 210	27 367	31 120	9 708	5 853
MINNESOTA...................	227 288	4.4	42 798	13	124 924	18 442	38 327	37 888	36 862	11 699	16 152	3 526	2 572
MISSISSIPPI...................	92 284	3.8	31 071	51	41 286	7 602	12 113	24 056	23 435	7 205	10 443	3 550	637
MISSOURI	220 635	2.5	36 799	31	114 807	19 991	34 831	45 124	43 963	14 998	19 219	4 551	1 928
MONTANA.....................	34 736	4.7	35 053	37	15 634	1 543	7 382	6 973	6 783	2 404	2 606	635	329
NEBRASKA....................	72 353	3.2	39 534	22	37 786	3 015	12 653	11 572	11 221	4 002	4 610	1 104	357
NEVADA.......................	99 892	1.8	36 938	30	50 806	3 521	20 893	16 359	15 842	5 354	5 605	1 701	1 977
NEW HAMPSHIRE	57 542	2.8	43 698	9	28 610	2 131	8 657	8 632	8 376	3 411	3 408	629	364
NEW JERSEY..................	450 004	3.7	51 139	3	218 118	16 355	73 548	69 299	67 602	21 286	28 398	5 882	7 614
NEW MEXICO	68 882	4.4	33 342	44	33 749	2 522	10 589	15 557	15 163	4 356	6 524	2 089	764
NEW YORK....................	942 523	4.3	48 596	6	519 947	37 535	153 468	180 977	177 201	44 771	91 382	21 642	9 260
NORTH CAROLINA............	334 677	3.7	35 007	39	174 550	13 207	52 250	68 571	66 749	22 614	26 295	8 284	4 605
NORTH DAKOTA..............	28 935	9.4	42 890	11	14 828	1 331	4 799	4 465	4 338	1 488	1 782	419	119
OHIO...........................	417 235	3.0	36 162	33	219 781	17 542	59 380	89 792	87 558	27 911	36 306	10 381	4 700
OKLAHOMA...................	133 070	5.3	35 389	36	62 739	18 224	21 319	27 813	26 793	8 900	10 977	3 241	950
OREGON.......................	139 395	3.2	36 317	34	71 613	10 368	26 031	28 754	28 009	9 371	10 182	3 095	2 570
PENNSYLVANIA...............	516 390	3.3	40 604	21	260 965	40 097	79 957	109 649	107 197	34 837	47 324	9 785	8 267
RHODE ISLAND...............	44 200	3.3	41 995	14	21 566	2 733	7 350	9 341	9 138	2 675	4 080	966	705
SOUTH CAROLINA	150 528	3.6	32 462	46	73 858	9 086	22 073	35 642	34 756	11 920	13 339	4 356	1 689
SOUTH DAKOTA..............	32 271	4.4	39 519	19	14 431	4 755	6 769	5 199	5 041	1 881	2 086	540	86
TENNESSEE	222 007	4.2	34 921	35	111 779	25 010	27 310	49 476	48 249	15 921	20 476	6 604	1 709
TEXAS	953 254	5.3	37 747	26	503 959	116 542	135 207	154 282	149 399	43 235	65 849	21 387	7 023
UTAH	90 250	3.8	32 517	47	49 917	7 585	14 912	12 988	12 444	4 199	4 450	1 591	768
VERMONT	25 120	3.4	40 134	20	12 108	1 958	4 511	5 237	5 116	1 648	2 322	577	224
VIRGINIA.......................	355 193	3.8	44 267	10	197 598	18 925	56 925	48 119	46 595	16 763	18 283	5 356	1 598
WASHINGTON..................	287 175	3.0	42 589	12	148 780	20 597	53 013	48 999	47 704	14 686	16 721	5 835	4 311
WEST VIRGINIA...............	59 417	3.3	32 042	50	27 426	3 664	7 496	16 632	16 277	5 751	6 758	1 813	523
WISCONSIN	217 562	3.8	38 225	28	113 248	15 263	34 990	41 147	40 048	14 210	16 441	4 069	2 873
WYOMING	25 383	4.1	44 961	7	12 474	2 131	6 164	3 544	3 437	1 194	1 304	258	212

1. Based on the resident population estimated as of July 1 of the year shown.   2. Does not include supplements to wages and salaries.

Table A. States — Personal Income and Earnings

STATE	Personal tax payments, 2010 (mil dol)	Disposable personal income, 2010 Total (mil dol)	Per capita[1] (dollars)	Earnings, 2010 Total (mil dol)	Farm	Goods-related[2] Total	Manu-facturing	Service-related and other[3] Total	Retail trade	Finance, insurance, and real estate	Health care and social assistance	Government	Gross state product, 2010 (mil dol)
	147	148	149	150	151	152	153	154	155	156	157	158	159
UNITED STATES	1 192 677	11 160 900	36 081	8 986 229	0.9	16.2	9.9	64.7	6.2	8.3	11.1	18.3	14 551 782
ALABAMA	12 440	147 892	30 905	109 702	0.8	20.2	13.1	55.7	6.9	5.5	10.6	23.3	172 567
ALASKA	2 597	28 992	40 597	26 436	0.0	17.7	2.6	48.2	5.6	4.3	9.7	34.1	49 120
ARIZONA	16 630	204 873	31 946	152 823	0.5	14.8	8.4	66.2	7.9	7.6	12.4	18.5	253 609
ARKANSAS	7 606	88 238	30 202	63 876	2.1	19.6	13.0	58.3	7.0	4.5	11.7	20.1	102 566
CALIFORNIA	172 932	1 414 472	37 883	1 158 629	1.2	15.5	10.3	65.6	6.0	7.2	9.6	17.8	1 901 088
COLORADO	20 623	192 871	38 210	162 492	0.6	14.3	6.0	66.8	5.7	7.8	9.0	18.4	257 641
CONNECTICUT	26 553	167 379	46 813	138 879	0.1	16.2	11.4	70.0	5.6	16.7	11.8	13.6	237 261
DELAWARE	3 792	32 287	35 883	28 189	0.5	13.2	7.9	69.7	6.0	14.2	12.5	16.4	62 280
DISTRICT OF COLUMBIA	4 796	37 978	62 782	81 445	0.0	1.3	0.2	55.1	0.9	4.1	5.2	43.7	103 288
FLORIDA	55 126	664 703	35 284	442 407	0.5	10.5	5.2	70.8	7.9	8.1	12.8	18.1	747 735
GEORGIA	29 766	307 702	31 682	253 212	0.7	14.1	9.0	65.6	6.2	7.3	9.5	19.6	403 070
HAWAII	4 965	51 682	37 908	41 471	0.7	8.8	1.8	55.2	6.1	4.4	9.4	35.3	66 760
IDAHO	3 852	46 262	29 446	34 771	4.5	17.5	10.2	58.9	7.7	5.0	11.5	19.1	55 435
ILLINOIS	52 134	487 745	37 981	400 456	0.9	15.8	10.8	68.1	5.3	9.7	10.4	15.2	651 518
INDIANA	19 998	200 558	30 900	157 733	1.3	26.2	20.0	56.8	6.3	5.2	12.6	15.6	275 676
IOWA	9 964	106 062	34 772	84 489	5.8	21.6	15.8	55.8	6.6	9.4	10.4	16.9	142 698
KANSAS	10 276	101 166	35 383	81 543	2.7	19.0	13.8	56.8	6.0	6.2	10.9	20.7	127 170
KENTUCKY	12 490	127 992	29 442	99 877	0.6	17.4	12.2	57.1	6.7	5.8	12.3	23.0	163 269
LOUISIANA	12 701	155 655	34 245	119 799	0.7	17.8	9.7	57.0	6.5	4.4	10.9	20.4	218 853
MAINE	4 244	44 555	33 566	33 482	0.6	17.0	11.0	63.0	8.4	6.6	16.2	19.4	51 643
MARYLAND	32 239	251 395	43 451	193 608	0.1	12.2	5.3	61.8	5.6	6.9	11.0	25.9	295 304
MASSACHUSETTS	41 235	295 084	45 013	255 329	0.1	14.5	9.8	73.2	4.9	11.4	13.6	12.2	378 729
MICHIGAN	28 984	313 890	31 779	239 069	0.7	20.6	16.1	61.5	6.4	5.7	17.1	13.6	384 171
MINNESOTA	23 708	203 580	38 334	172 507	2.5	17.6	13.1	65.3	5.3	9.0	12.6	14.4	270 039
MISSISSIPPI	6 047	86 237	29 035	60 366	2.2	18.9	12.5	52.5	7.5	4.4	11.0	25.5	97 461
MISSOURI	19 130	201 505	33 608	162 984	1.0	16.5	10.7	65.2	6.5	7.1	11.8	17.2	244 016
MONTANA	3 002	31 734	32 024	23 390	2.5	11.8	4.4	59.7	8.3	5.5	13.5	23.3	36 067
NEBRASKA	6 122	66 231	36 189	55 528	6.2	15.5	9.7	60.2	6.1	7.8	10.9	18.0	89 786
NEVADA	8 089	91 802	33 947	70 425	0.2	11.1	3.7	69.4	7.1	6.3	8.8	17.6	125 650
NEW HAMPSHIRE	4 795	52 747	40 057	40 355	0.1	19.0	13.0	67.2	9.0	7.9	13.2	13.6	60 283
NEW JERSEY	50 582	399 422	45 391	305 418	0.1	13.8	8.9	70.0	6.5	9.6	11.1	16.1	487 335
NEW MEXICO	5 517	63 365	30 672	47 686	2.2	10.8	4.6	55.1	6.8	4.0	11.1	28.4	79 678
NEW YORK	128 487	814 036	41 971	728 218	0.2	9.4	5.2	74.7	5.0	18.3	15.8	15.8	1 159 540
NORTH CAROLINA	30 179	304 498	31 850	242 954	1.0	18.1	12.7	58.7	6.4	7.2	10.3	22.1	424 935
NORTH DAKOTA	2 336	26 599	39 427	23 177	11.2	13.1	6.2	51.9	6.2	5.1	11.4	19.7	34 685
OHIO	38 618	378 616	32 815	304 200	0.6	20.3	15.6	62.5	6.3	6.9	13.2	16.3	477 699
OKLAHOMA	10 848	122 221	32 504	93 128	1.0	14.8	9.6	54.3	6.9	5.1	10.6	23.6	147 543
OREGON	13 929	125 466	32 688	99 691	1.2	17.9	12.3	62.7	6.8	5.7	12.7	18.1	174 151
PENNSYLVANIA	51 708	464 682	36 538	364 140	0.3	16.4	10.9	68.4	6.0	7.6	14.5	14.1	569 679
RHODE ISLAND	4 084	38 115	38 115	29 872	0.1	13.6	8.6	66.9	5.9	9.2	14.9	19.2	49 234
SOUTH CAROLINA	11 648	138 880	29 950	102 475	0.4	19.0	13.5	57.1	7.6	6.2	9.5	23.4	164 445
SOUTH DAKOTA	2 159	30 112	36 875	22 968	10.5	14.5	8.7	55.9	7.1	7.7	13.8	18.9	39 893
TENNESSEE	14 222	207 784	32 684	163 802	0.1	17.8	12.2	66.6	7.4	6.8	14.6	15.3	254 806
TEXAS	72 735	880 519	34 867	736 614	0.6	16.5	9.6	61.7	6.1	7.4	9.6	16.5	1 207 494
UTAH	7 778	82 472	29 715	70 278	0.3	17.6	10.7	61.5	7.6	7.1	8.8	19.3	114 538
VERMONT	2 130	22 990	36 731	17 079	1.0	19.2	12.6	60.3	8.1	5.4	14.5	19.3	25 620
VIRGINIA	38 273	316 920	39 497	268 218	0.1	10.6	5.5	62.6	5.1	5.8	8.5	26.3	423 860
WASHINGTON	22 358	264 817	39 273	207 948	1.3	15.6	9.6	61.6	6.5	5.8	10.3	21.4	340 460
WEST VIRGINIA	4 979	54 438	29 357	38 846	-0.1	15.0	8.7	54.6	7.2	3.6	14.4	23.4	64 642
WISCONSIN	21 183	196 380	34 503	156 332	1.2	24.7	19.4	59.0	6.2	7.2	12.9	15.0	248 265
WYOMING	2 086	23 297	41 265	17 914	0.7	13.7	3.9	46.4	6.3	3.8	7.6	25.0	38 527

1. Based on the resident population estimated as of July 1 of the year shown. 2. Total includes mining, construction, and manufacturing. 3. Includes private sector earnings in forestry, fishing, related activities, and other; utilities; wholesale trade; transportation and warehousing; and information.

Table A. States — Social Security, Employment, and Labor Force

STATE	Social Security beneficiaries, December 2010		Supplemental Security Income recipients, December 2010	Civilian employment and selected occupations,[2] 2010				Civilian labor force (annual average), 2011			Unemployed	
					Percent							
	Number	Rate[1]		Total	Management, business, science and art occupations	Services, sales, and office occupations	Construction and production occupations	Total (1,000)	Percent change, 2010–2011	Employed (1,000)	Total (1,000)	Rate[3]
	160	161	162	163	164	165	166	167	168	169	170	171
UNITED STATES	52 641 311	170.5	7 911 333	139 033 928	35.9	43.0	21.0	153 617	-0.2	139 869	13 747	8.9
ALABAMA	1 012 056	211.7	172 223	1 978 825	31.9	42.0	26.2	2 191	0.6	1 994	197	9.0
ALASKA	78 208	110.1	12 269	337 683	35.1	41.0	23.9	367	0.8	339	28	7.6
ARIZONA	1 067 717	167.0	110 011	2 655 557	35.6	46.2	18.3	3 034	-2.1	2 747	288	9.5
ARKANSAS	635 041	217.8	106 526	1 245 328	30.9	41.8	27.4	1 370	1.0	1 260	110	8.0
CALIFORNIA	4 979 141	133.7	1 267 711	16 243 172	36.5	43.3	20.2	18 385	0.4	16 227	2 158	11.7
COLORADO	693 341	137.9	65 720	2 446 674	39.7	41.9	18.5	2 723	-0.1	2 497	226	8.3
CONNECTICUT	622 167	174.1	58 257	1 736 446	40.6	42.4	17.0	1 918	0.1	1 749	169	8.8
DELAWARE	172 441	192.0	15 865	411 120	37.7	42.7	19.7	439	0.5	407	32	7.3
DISTRICT OF COLUMBIA	74 417	123.7	24 371	299 127	59.2	32.9	8.0	344	0.3	309	35	10.2
FLORIDA	3 784 225	201.3	485 172	7 974 945	33.5	48.3	18.2	9 249	1.3	8 278	970	10.5
GEORGIA	1 468 209	151.6	228 510	4 165 453	35.4	42.1	22.5	4 725	0.6	4 262	463	9.8
HAWAII	227 914	167.5	24 945	638 191	33.0	48.7	18.3	661	1.8	616	44	6.7
IDAHO	269 293	171.8	27 294	681 907	36.1	42.3	24.1	771	1.0	704	67	8.7
ILLINOIS	2 033 345	158.5	273 310	5 911 495	32.3	42.8	21.1	6 566	-0.6	5 925	640	9.8
INDIANA	1 191 768	183.8	118 065	2 898 761	32.3	41.5	26.1	3 188	0.3	2 901	287	9.0
IOWA	584 113	191.7	47 687	1 540 038	33.5	40.7	25.8	1 664	-0.4	1 566	98	5.9
KANSAS	488 765	171.3	45 793	1 373 030	35.6	41.9	22.4	1 505	0.0	1 404	101	6.7
KENTUCKY	894 473	206.1	192 076	1 815 971	32.3	41.2	26.5	2 068	0.4	1 871	197	9.5
LOUISIANA	790 617	174.4	174 731	1 967 523	31.4	43.8	24.9	2 061	-0.4	1 909	151	7.3
MAINE	299 875	225.7	35 426	641 665	35.9	41.5	22.6	704	0.4	651	53	7.5
MARYLAND	850 361	147.3	107 636	2 886 015	44.1	40.1	15.8	3 072	0.5	2 856	217	7.0
MASSACHUSETTS	1 140 830	174.2	192 814	3 225 103	43.5	40.9	15.7	3 456	-0.4	3 202	254	7.4
MICHIGAN	1 964 862	198.8	253 532	4 137 510	34.2	43.8	22.0	4 658	-1.9	4 178	480	10.3
MINNESOTA	882 408	166.4	86 506	2 693 645	38.4	41.1	20.5	2 978	0.6	2 787	191	6.4
MISSISSIPPI	596 637	201.1	125 507	1 175 203	31.0	41.7	27.3	1 344	2.1	1 201	143	10.7
MISSOURI	1 166 223	194.7	133 895	2 733 876	34.4	43.6	22.0	3 046	-0.2	2 786	261	8.6
MONTANA	192 701	194.8	17 632	467 674	35.9	42.5	21.6	505	1.2	470	35	6.8
NEBRASKA	308 790	169.1	25 613	935 104	35.2	41.8	23.0	1 005	1.6	961	45	4.4
NEVADA	408 113	151.1	41 269	1 196 894	28.3	53.6	18.2	1 386	0.2	1 198	188	13.5
NEW HAMPSHIRE	254 752	193.5	17 910	684 575	38.9	41.2	20.0	738	-0.1	698	40	5.4
NEW JERSEY	1 472 335	167.5	168 423	4 143 877	40.3	41.9	17.9	4 556	0.0	4 132	424	9.3
NEW MEXICO	360 242	174.9	60 487	868 276	35.5	44.0	20.4	928	-0.6	859	69	7.4
NEW YORK	3 280 575	169.3	680 057	8 913 640	38.5	44.3	17.2	9 504	-0.9	8 730	775	8.2
NORTH CAROLINA	1 757 135	184.3	219 570	4 128 576	35.0	41.9	23.0	4 654	0.8	4 165	489	10.5
NORTH DAKOTA	120 098	178.6	8 277	362 895	34.6	41.3	24.0	383	1.9	370	13	3.5
OHIO	2 124 650	184.2	285 569	5 176 890	34.0	43.1	22.8	5 806	-1.0	5 305	501	8.6
OKLAHOMA	705 364	188.0	93 855	1 666 604	32.2	43.1	24.7	1 771	0.0	1 662	109	6.2
OREGON	712 216	185.9	74 860	1 701 473	36.2	43.4	20.4	1 992	0.4	1 804	188	9.5
PENNSYLVANIA	2 577 714	202.9	358 197	5 842 790	36.1	42.0	21.9	6 386	-0.1	5 879	507	7.9
RHODE ISLAND	203 660	193.5	32 809	490 964	36.3	44.3	19.4	563	-1.2	500	63	11.3
SOUTH CAROLINA	924 726	199.9	112 094	1 955 035	32.2	44.1	23.8	2 157	0.3	1 936	221	10.3
SOUTH DAKOTA	153 508	188.5	13 812	409 194	35.3	41.7	23.0	446	0.7	425	21	4.7
TENNESSEE	1 251 947	197.3	174 486	2 734 829	33.4	42.6	24.0	3 133	1.6	2 845	288	9.2
TEXAS	3 440 442	136.8	616 968	11 271 851	34.3	42.9	22.9	12 452	1.5	11 465	987	7.9
UTAH	324 136	117.3	28 106	1 229 064	35.3	42.5	22.1	1 338	-1.8	1 248	90	6.7
VERMONT	128 619	205.5	15 265	322 432	38.5	41.1	20.4	359	-0.3	339	20	5.6
VIRGINIA	1 284 823	160.6	148 501	3 814 199	42.1	39.6	18.3	4 306	1.2	4 037	269	6.2
WASHINGTON	1 089 887	162.1	137 546	3 070 269	38.5	40.8	20.6	3 485	-0.9	3 165	319	9.2
WEST VIRGINIA	443 911	239.6	80 367	746 844	30.2	44.3	25.6	800	-0.2	736	64	8.0
WISCONSIN	1 061 501	186.7	107 571	2 805 102	33.6	41.4	25.0	3 062	-0.7	2 833	229	7.5
WYOMING	91 019	161.5	6 337	280 614	33.0	39.4	27.6	304	0.3	286	18	6.0

1. Per 1,000 resident population counted in the 2010 census.   2. Persons 16 years old and over.   3. Percent of civilian labor force.

STATE	Employed: Total (1,000)	Employed: Percent change, 2010–2011	Manufacturing: Employment (1,000)	Manufacturing: Average earnings of production workers — Hourly	Manufacturing: Average earnings of production workers — Weekly	Construction	Transportation and public utilities	Wholesale trade	Retail trade	Information	Financial activities	Services[1]
	172	173	174	175	176	177	178	179	180	181	182	183
UNITED STATES	131 359	1.1	11 733	18.94	784.68	5 504.0	4 847.4	5 528.8	14 642.9	2 659.0	7 681.0	55 877.0
ALABAMA	1 866.5	-0.2	1 867	16.93	685.16	78.9	66.8	71.8	225.7	23.3	92.5	677.5
ALASKA	328.8	1.1	13	19.58	749.41	15.2	21.6	6.2	35.5	6.4	14.8	115.2
ARIZONA	2 405.5	1.0	150	17.60	712.83	111.7	82.7	95.9	294.0	36.6	166.0	1 047.0
ARKANSAS	1 160	-0.1	158	14.52	590.42	46.9	59.5	45.8	129.9	14.6	48.1	427.1
CALIFORNIA	14 060.5	0.9	1 246	19.49	801.10	553.7	471.9	659.0	1 532.0	432.4	761.5	5 977.1
COLORADO	2 255.3	1.5	129	23.64	915.01	112.6	69.8	91.8	239.2	71.5	143.6	977.7
CONNECTICUT	1 623.5	1.0	166	24.76	1 004.01	51.2	50.4	63.9	179.5	31.5	134.9	706.6
DELAWARE	417.3	0.8	26	15.94	645.72	19.6	12.7	12.4	50.1	5.7	42.7	184.5
DISTRICT OF COLUMBIA	727.8	2.2	1	NA	NA	12.0	4.1	4.6	18.5	18.6	26.8	394.5
FLORIDA	7 271.5	1.1	311	18.82	755.74	330.1	231.4	308.7	954.9	134.3	482.9	3 417.0
GEORGIA	3 880	1.0	350	17.69	681.54	145.5	183.2	196.4	441.4	97.3	208.8	1 579.1
HAWAII	592.1	0.9	13	18.20	650.34	28.3	27.0	17.3	66.6	8.2	26.9	279.8
IDAHO	606.8	0.5	55	20.97	856.26	30.1	21.1	26.4	74.3	9.4	29.4	241.2
ILLINOIS	5 663.1	0.9	574	18.01	728.87	195.3	259.2	289.2	591.0	100.4	361.9	2 445.9
INDIANA	2 830.3	1.2	464	18.04	754.67	120.5	127.8	114.8	305.5	34.2	131.4	1 100.5
IOWA	1 477.8	0.6	207	16.50	665.99	62.3	61.8	66.3	173.2	27.9	100.4	526.6
KANSAS	1 337	0.7	161	19.52	801.03	53.0	52.3	59.7	141.1	27.8	72.8	502.6
KENTUCKY	1 790.4	1.1	213	18.90	775.07	67.6	91.8	70.7	201.5	26.7	84.3	682.8
LOUISIANA	1 916.7	1.3	139	21.15	879.09	121.9	80.6	72.9	219.6	23.7	94.9	750.5
MAINE	593.4	0.1	50	20.21	823.32	24.7	17.0	18.9	81.7	8.2	31.7	256.9
MARYLAND	2 548	1.2	113	18.60	766.53	146.2	75.7	86.3	279.9	42.3	142.7	1 154.5
MASSACHUSETTS	3 210.6	0.6	254	20.47	806.98	107.9	84.1	123.1	341.8	83.0	205.8	1 575.1
MICHIGAN	3 935.7	1.9	506	21.08	927.89	124.7	117.6	156.2	446.1	53.4	193.2	1 712.7
MINNESOTA	2 675.7	1.3	301	19.04	775.44	90.9	90.9	125.6	279.4	62.8	174.3	1 146.4
MISSISSIPPI	1 090	-0.1	134	15.12	618.64	48.8	47.8	33.9	132.5	11.9	44.8	380.7
MISSOURI	2 650.3	0.0	247	18.66	738.70	102.3	97.7	116.2	298.7	58.4	159.3	1 128.7
MONTANA	426.1	-0.3	17	21.19	661.95	23.0	16.0	15.6	54.6	7.3	20.9	177.2
NEBRASKA	944	0.4	93	16.58	675.79	41.1	51.2	40.5	104.1	16.9	69.5	359.5
NEVADA	1 125.1	0.7	38	16.28	612.76	52.7	51.3	32.9	128.1	12.6	52.0	594.1
NEW HAMPSHIRE	626.4	0.4	67	18.24	761.55	21.9	14.7	26.3	92.3	11.1	34.7	265.6
NEW JERSEY	3 856.2	0.1	254	19.03	771.74	129.7	164.4	209.3	442.3	74.2	250.9	1 710.1
NEW MEXICO	804.1	0.1	30	16.22	675.27	42.7	22.1	21.0	89.9	14.2	33.0	334.9
NEW YORK	8 683.4	1.4	458	18.46	750.90	306.8	263.9	329.6	891.5	254.9	683.7	4 001.8
NORTH CAROLINA	3 922.4	1.1	434	16.04	661.14	175.6	118.1	166.0	440.8	68.5	203.0	1 612.4
NORTH DAKOTA	394.2	4.8	24	17.02	669.29	24.0	18.7	22.3	44.7	7.1	21.1	137.2
OHIO	5 083.1	1.0	638	19.25	785.97	173.9	182.8	217.3	553.5	76.4	278.1	2 184.8
OKLAHOMA	1 550.3	1.3	129	15.65	650.23	68.3	53.4	58.2	169.5	24.2	79.6	581.2
OREGON	1 618.1	1.0	167	17.96	711.94	68.8	53.3	74.4	184.7	32.3	92.0	643.9
PENNSYLVANIA	5 687.1	1.1	564	17.49	700.63	221.8	238.8	226.7	628.0	90.2	309.5	2 630.5
RHODE ISLAND	460.2	0.2	41	16.30	639.03	15.7	10.7	16.3	46.2	10.2	30.7	229.0
SOUTH CAROLINA	1 832.1	1.1	216	16.73	709.01	76.3	61.1	65.0	224.3	25.9	96.1	723.2
SOUTH DAKOTA	406.2	0.7	39	16.34	661.53	20.9	12.6	19.1	50.5	6.4	28.0	151.8
TENNESSEE	2 656.3	1.6	304	16.63	673.66	109.6	134.8	116.7	307.5	44.1	135.5	1 072.2
TEXAS	10 557.3	2.1	836	16.41	705.18	559.5	432.1	513.3	1 157.9	195.5	639.0	4 174.4
UTAH	1 208.1	2.2	114	18.03	699.95	65.3	48.9	46.2	137.8	29.4	69.0	466.1
VERMONT	299.6	0.7	31	17.24	674.23	13.7	8.9	9.7	37.9	5.0	12.1	127.6
VIRGINIA	3 680.4	1.2	229	18.53	746.63	178.6	115.5	111.8	401.8	74.0	182.5	1 665.8
WASHINGTON	2 820.5	1.2	269	23.98	1 015.33	137.5	90.5	123.3	312.2	103.7	137.4	1 098.9
WEST VIRGINIA	753.9	1.0	50	18.03	706.36	33.0	25.2	23.2	86.7	10.5	27.3	313.2
WISCONSIN	2 740.7	0.4	443	17.71	728.04	90.5	100.0	114.9	293.6	46.4	158.1	1 078.7
WYOMING	285.7	1.0	9	22.19	867.24	20.8	14.4	8.8	29.2	3.9	10.7	88.4

1. Includes professional and business services, educational and health services, leisure and hospitality, and other services.

Table A. States — Agriculture

STATE	Farms			Farm operators whose principal occupation is farming (percent)	Government payments, average per farm (dollars)	Land in farms					Value of land and buildings (dollars)	
		Percent with:						Acres				
	Number	Fewer than 50 acres	500 acres or more			Acreage (1,000)	Percent change, 2002–2007	Average size of farm	Total irrigated (1,000)	Total cropland (1,000)	Average per farm	Average per acre
	184	185	186	187	188	189	190	191	192	193	194	195
UNITED STATES	2 204 792	38.7	14.6	45.1	9 523	922 096	-1.7	418	56 599	406 425	791 138	1 892
ALABAMA	48 753	40.2	7.7	39.8	8 642	9 034	1.5	185	113	3 143	424 674	2 292
ALASKA	686	48.0	13.1	53.2	21 086	882	-2.1	1 285	3 730	86 238	502 342	391
ARIZONA	15 637	80.1	8.1	61.1	49 077	26 118	-1.8	1 670	876	1 205	1 249 929	748
ARKANSAS	49 346	35.9	12.4	44.5	23 510	13 873	-4.3	281	4 461	8 432	658 732	2 343
CALIFORNIA	81 033	65.8	9.5	50.5	32 273	25 365	-8.1	313	8 016	9 465	2 005 768	6 408
COLORADO	37 054	36.8	25.5	40.4	13 479	31 605	1.6	853	2 868	11 484	892 170	1 046
CONNECTICUT	4 916	63.6	2.1	46.2	11 710	406	13.6	83	10	164	1 045 133	12 667
DELAWARE	2 546	57.1	9.6	59.1	9 364	510	-5.5	200	105	433	2 073 605	10 347
DISTRICT OF COLUMBIA	X	X	X	X	X	X	X	X	X	X	X	X
FLORIDA	47 463	69.2	5.5	44.0	9 722	9 232	-11.4	195	1 552	2 953	1 096 718	5 639
GEORGIA	47 846	41.3	9.2	42.0	15 435	10 151	-5.5	212	1 018	4 478	661 201	3 117
HAWAII	7 521	90.2	2.1	51.3	10 908	1 121	-13.8	149	58 635	177 626	1 146 213	7 688
IDAHO	25 349	48.9	16.9	45.7	10 798	11 497	-2.3	454	3 300	5 919	894 497	1 972
ILLINOIS	76 860	38.0	21.0	48.4	8 577	26 775	-2.0	348	474	23 708	1 321 080	3 792
INDIANA	60 938	48.0	12.6	41.9	7 272	14 773	-1.9	242	397	12 716	868 699	3 583
IOWA	92 856	28.6	20.8	52.4	9 425	30 748	-3.1	331	190	26 316	1 122 023	3 388
KANSAS	65 531	18.6	30.9	47.1	9 613	46 346	-1.9	707	2 763	28 216	644 039	911
KENTUCKY	85 260	35.0	5.8	39.8	3 494	13 993	1.1	164	59	7 278	440 213	2 682
LOUISIANA	30 106	45.4	11.4	41.8	15 943	8 110	3.6	269	954	4 691	554 270	2 058
MAINE	8 136	42.1	6.3	43.5	6 042	1 348	-1.6	166	21	529	364 807	2 203
MARYLAND	12 834	47.9	7.1	48.8	7 277	2 052	-1.2	160	93	1 405	1 124 529	7 034
MASSACHUSETTS	7 691	66.1	1.5	48.0	7 763	518	-0.1	67	23	187	829 090	12 313
MICHIGAN	56 014	44.5	8.2	44.3	5 115	10 032	-1.1	179	500	7 804	610 556	3 409
MINNESOTA	80 992	25.5	17.9	48.9	7 869	26 918	-2.2	332	506	21 949	853 968	2 569
MISSISSIPPI	41 959	29.3	10.8	38.0	13 463	11 456	3.2	273	1 369	5 531	510 454	1 870
MISSOURI	107 825	26.9	13.0	41.8	7 084	29 027	-3.1	269	1 200	16 406	586 478	2 179
MONTANA	29 524	25.0	43.0	50.7	16 971	61 388	3.0	2 079	2 013	18 242	1 611 155	775
NEBRASKA	47 712	18.6	39.7	60.5	11 091	45 480	-0.9	953	8 559	21 486	1 104 392	1 159
NEVADA	3 131	48.8	21.2	52.7	12 105	5 865	-7.3	1 873	691	754	1 148 693	613
NEW HAMPSHIRE	4 166	51.8	3.8	46.3	5 848	472	6.1	113	2	129	558 385	4 929
NEW JERSEY	10 327	75.2	2.9	44.8	8 154	733	-9.0	71	95	489	1 089 883	15 346
NEW MEXICO	20 930	52.0	23.1	48.0	13 030	43 238	-3.5	2 066	830	2 334	696 081	337
NEW YORK	36 352	32.2	8.4	54.0	5 913	7 175	-6.3	197	68	4 315	449 010	2 275
NORTH CAROLINA	52 913	48.7	6.7	45.8	10 633	8 475	-6.7	160	232	4 895	656 080	4 096
NORTH DAKOTA	31 970	8.3	51.7	57.9	13 462	39 675	1.0	1 241	236	27 527	957 053	771
OHIO	75 861	42.4	8.9	43.1	6 099	13 957	-4.3	184	38	10 833	649 130	3 528
OKLAHOMA	86 565	26.0	17.6	41.6	7 754	35 087	4.2	405	535	13 008	468 809	1 157
OREGON	38 553	61.4	10.6	46.2	14 954	16 400	-4.0	425	1 845	5 010	804 145	1 890
PENNSYLVANIA	63 163	41.0	3.9	45.5	4 366	7 809	0.8	124	38	4 870	590 376	4 775
RHODE ISLAND	1 219	68.7	0.6	50.9	7 353	68	10.8	56	4	24	936 229	16 828
SOUTH CAROLINA	25 867	42.3	7.4	37.7	8 717	4 889	0.9	189	132	2 151	540 200	2 858
SOUTH DAKOTA	31 169	15.5	46.7	60.2	11 817	43 666	-0.3	1 401	374	19 094	1 255 332	896
TENNESSEE	79 280	44.4	4.6	38.9	5 528	10 970	-6.1	138	81	6 047	467 420	3 378
TEXAS	247 437	37.9	16.2	39.9	15 010	130 399	0.4	527	5 010	33 667	669 154	1 270
UTAH	16 700	55.8	13.2	38.0	7 689	11 095	-5.4	664	1 134	1 838	829 816	1 249
VERMONT	6 984	35.8	7.6	49.6	5 014	1 233	-0.9	177	2	517	512 684	2 903
VIRGINIA	47 383	39.5	7.0	42.8	5 577	8 104	-6.0	171	82	3 274	720 538	4 213
WASHINGTON	39 284	61.1	11.4	45.9	20 042	14 973	-2.3	381	1 736	7 609	759 146	1 992
WEST VIRGINIA	23 618	29.5	5.3	41.5	1 348	3 698	3.2	157	2	942	373 435	2 385
WISCONSIN	78 463	31.6	7.8	47.2	4 124	15 191	-3.5	194	377	10 116	624 428	3 225
WYOMING	11 069	24.0	38.3	49.2	10 092	30 170	-12.3	2 726	1 551	2 576	1 397 691	513

Table A. States — Agriculture, Land, and Water

STATE	Agriculture, 2007 (cont.)							Land, 2007			
	Value of products sold					Percent of farms with sales of:					Water consumption, 2005 (mil gal per day)
	Value of machinery and equipment, average per farm (dollars)	Total (mil dol)	Average per farm (dollars)	Percent from:		$10,000 or more	$100,000 or more	Cropland (percent)	Owned by the federal government (percent)	Developed (percent)	
				Crops	Livestock and poultry products						
	196	197	198	199	200	201	202	203	204	205	206
UNITED STATES	88 357	297 220	134 807	48.3	51.7	40.2	16.2	18.4	20.7	5.7	460 000
ALABAMA	60 810	4 416	90 570	15.3	84.7	30.8	9.7	6.6	3.0	8.8	11 200
ALASKA	78 837	57	83 119	43.4	56.6	41.3	11.2	NA	NA	NA	1 180
ARIZONA	66 291	3 235	206 852	59.1	40.9	18.6	6.7	1.0	41.7	2.7	7 000
ARKANSAS	90 823	7 509	152 166	38.6	61.4	40.4	16.4	21.7	9.1	5.3	12 800
CALIFORNIA	108 145	33 885	418 164	67.6	32.4	53.4	23.5	9.3	45.9	6.1	51 300
COLORADO	99 344	6 061	163 576	32.7	67.3	36.1	13.8	11.4	35.7	2.9	15 300
CONNECTICUT	64 090	552	112 195	72.8	27.2	34.6	10.0	5.4	0.5	32.9	4 210
DELAWARE	119 718	1 083	425 387	19.4	80.6	59.0	38.8	27.4	2.0	18.3	1 140
DISTRICT OF COLUMBIA	X	X	X	X	X	X	X	NA	NA	NA	11
FLORIDA	54 604	7 785	164 027	80	20	35	11	8	10.0	8.3	20 500
GEORGIA	76 948	7 113	148 662	30.1	69.9	32.3	14.2	10.6	5.6	12.3	6 100
HAWAII	40 666	514	68 292	83.7	16.3	34.3	7.0	NA	NA	NA	2 120
IDAHO	114 383	5 689	224 418	40.9	59.1	39.9	17.0	9.8	62.7	1.7	21 900
ILLINOIS	136 609	13 329	173 421	81.6	18.4	53.1	30.3	66.3	1.4	9.4	17 000
INDIANA	103 427	8 271	135 733	64.3	35.7	45.6	20.8	57.1	2.0	10.6	10 500
IOWA	136 771	20 418	219 890	50.7	49.3	61.4	35.6	70.7	0.5	5.3	3 770
KANSAS	114 261	14 413	219 944	33.9	66.1	51.5	21.7	48.7	4.0	4.0	4 240
KENTUCKY	57 591	4 825	56 586	29.1	70.9	33.5	6.9	20.0	5.0	8.1	4 850
LOUISIANA	78 998	2 618	86 959	61.3	38.7	30.7	10.7	NA	4.2	5.9	13 000
MAINE	65 961	617	75 859	52.9	47.1	31.1	9.5	1.8	1.0	4.1	678
MARYLAND	98 823	1 835	142 987	34.3	65.7	41.5	17.6	18.0	2.2	19.0	8 400
MASSACHUSETTS	56 373	490	63 687	74.4	25.6	35.8	10.4	4.5	1.8	32.1	4 030
MICHIGAN	90 742	5 753	102 710	57.9	42.1	38.1	14.2	21.0	8.8	11.3	13 100
MINNESOTA	131 698	13 180	162 738	53.5	46.5	50.7	27.4	38.3	6.2	4.4	4 530
MISSISSIPPI	73 558	4 877	116 227	34.2	65.8	28.8	10.8	15.4	5.9	5.9	3 280
MISSOURI	68 171	7 513	69 677	46.5	53.5	42.0	11.0	29.8	4.3	6.6	9 860
MONTANA	103 494	2 803	94 942	45.4	54.6	46.8	21.6	14.8	28.8	1.1	11 300
NEBRASKA	157 427	15 506	324 992	44.1	55.9	68.5	41.0	39.4	1.3	2.3	14 100
NEVADA	111 799	513	163 931	42.7	57.3	43.0	19.6	0.7	84.6	0.8	2 670
NEW HAMPSHIRE	58 413	199	47 780	53.5	46.5	27.9	6.9	1.8	12.8	11.7	1 480
NEW JERSEY	68 374	987	95 564	86.3	13.7	32.7	11.1	9.4	2.8	35.5	8 280
NEW MEXICO	55 457	2 175	103 922	25.4	74.6	27.1	8.1	1.9	33.9	1.6	3 740
NEW YORK	97 550	4 419	121 551	35.3	64.7	45.4	18.8	15.9	0.7	12.1	17 000
NORTH CAROLINA	76 793	10 314	194 917	25.3	74.7	35.2	15.7	15.5	7.4	14.2	14 400
NORTH DAKOTA	174 683	6 084	190 310	82.8	17.2	57.9	35.9	52.9	3.9	2.2	1 500
OHIO	88 352	7 070	93 200	58.1	41.9	43.7	15.9	41.8	1.4	15.7	12 900
OKLAHOMA	63 642	5 806	67 072	20.5	79.5	37.1	8.3	19.6	2.6	4.6	1 940
OREGON	79 175	4 386	113 769	67.9	32.1	32.5	12.1	5.8	50.3	2.2	8 090
PENNSYLVANIA	72 988	5 809	91 965	32.2	67.8	38.5	16.9	17.0	2.5	15.0	10 600
RHODE ISLAND	65 343	66	54 067	84.4	15.6	36.5	9.6	2.2	0.4	28.6	454
SOUTH CAROLINA	64 977	2 353	90 953	33.9	66.1	23.4	7.0	11.2	5.2	13.4	8 790
SOUTH DAKOTA	155 652	6 570	210 801	51.5	48.5	65.4	38.3	34.0	6.3	2.0	561
TENNESSEE	58 882	2 617	33 015	43.9	56.1	25.2	4.8	15.4	4.8	11.3	12 100
TEXAS	64 350	21 001	84 874	31.3	68.7	29.0	7.1	14.0	1.7	5.0	30 000
UTAH	75 365	1 416	84 771	26.3	73.7	34.9	9.7	2.6	63.1	1.4	5 730
VERMONT	74 500	674	96 465	14.7	85.3	41.1	15.4	8.8	6.9	6.4	586
VIRGINIA	65 870	2 906	61 334	29.5	70.5	32.9	7.9	10.2	9.8	11.4	11 900
WASHINGTON	83 468	6 793	172 917	70.0	30.0	33.9	15.2	14.7	27.1	5.6	6 320
WEST VIRGINIA	38 871	592	25 051	13.2	86.8	20.1	3.2	4.9	7.8	7.4	5 390
WISCONSIN	96 278	8 967	114 288	29.8	70.2	45.2	21.2	27.9	5.1	7.6	9 640
WYOMING	97 356	1 158	104 575	18.5	81.5	47.7	19.2	3.4	45.9	1.1	5 150

Table A. States — **Manufactures and Construction**

STATE	Manufactures, 2010										Construction, 2007				
	All employees			Production workers								Employees			
						Wages									
	Number (1,000)	Percent change, 2009–2010	Annual payroll (mil dol)	Number (1,000)	Work hours (millions)	Total (mil dol)	Average per worker (dollars)	Value added by manufacture (mil dol)	Value of shipments (mil dol)	Total capital expenditures (mil dol)	Number of establishments	Number	Percent change, 2002–2007	Value (mil dol)	Annual payroll (mil dol)
	207	208	209	210	211	212	213	214	215	216	217	218	219	220	221
UNITED STATES	10 567	-3.2	540 001	7 319	14 591	299 823	40 967	2 185 326	4 916 647	127 952	729 345	7 316 240	1.7	1 731 842	331 003
ALABAMA............................	218	-2.6	9 982	163	330	6 480	39 802	39 246	104 183	3 091	9 239	107 166	8.7	24 714	4 188
ALASKA..............................	11	-3.5	437	8	17	293	34 732	2 447	7 274	145	2 404	22 082	3.4	6 263	1 352
ARIZONA............................	129	-3.9	7 755	73	145	3 112	42 880	26 231	48 257	1 074	15 470	221 585	26.7	56 159	9 182
ARKANSAS.........................	145	-4.8	5 782	117	233	4 070	34 831	21 758	54 532	1 566	5 764	50 407	8.1	10 341	1 814
CALIFORNIA	1 128	-4.2	65 387	695	1 379	28 674	41 270	230 198	457 716	12 622	72 173	873 789	0.4	217 933	43 134
COLORADO	108	-4.1	5 777	72	143	3 009	41 512	21 868	44 573	1 051	17 787	173 559	-1.0	42 990	7 711
CONNECTICUT...................	156	-4.8	9 309	95	187	4 506	47 603	29 814	51 410	1 115	9 004	71 649	-6.5	18 056	3 830
DELAWARE........................	29	-0.1	1 480	19	39	781	40 911	7 045	21 055	358	2 724	25 646	2.0	5 609	1 150
DISTRICT OF COLUMBIA	1	-2.9	56	1	2	35	42 455	136	216	13	375	7 833	30.7	2 473	422
FLORIDA	254	-4.8	12 838	164	330	6 294	38 283	44 877	88 149	2 608	51 143	473 703	11.5	117 804	19 587
GEORGIA	315	-3.4	13 896	240	482	8 697	36 221	60 441	131 815	4 190	20 568	223 557	1.0	59 375	9 651
HAWAII.............................	11	-7.2	430	7	13	239	35 278	1 403	6 424	76	2 771	35 523	30.2	10 420	1 907
IDAHO...............................	50	-0.5	2 220	38	73	1 416	37 231	12 069	21 740	584	7 919	50 382	39.6	10 052	1 730
ILLINOIS............................	539	-1.5	28 107	367	742	15 148	41 252	103 657	240 920	6 930	30 236	272 682	-11.9	72 778	14 623
INDIANA............................	415	-0.1	20 534	310	624	13 283	42 884	95 336	207 530	5 155	15 640	147 467	-0.5	30 164	6 456
IOWA................................	183	-4.3	8 737	133	266	5 175	39 025	39 932	89 232	1 804	8 019	70 357	4.7	14 961	2 900
KANSAS............................	148	-5.1	7 382	104	209	4 407	42 260	27 997	77 479	1 829	7 159	67 769	-1.3	13 829	2 793
KENTUCKY........................	197	-2.8	8 900	151	298	6 035	39 966	37 792	105 553	1 994	8 615	83 154	-0.9	16 493	3 131
LOUISIANA........................	122	-3.7	7 129	88	180	4 468	50 706	57 121	202 307	3 711	8 564	135 781	9.7	25 569	5 806
MAINE..............................	48	-6.7	2 249	34	67	1 407	41 395	8 232	15 158	388	4 942	29 908	-1.6	5 441	1 128
MARYLAND........................	107	-2.4	6 060	65	127	2 739	42 037	22 860	39 932	2 130	15 618	191 293	5.5	44 327	8 953
MASSACHUSETTS..............	226	-3.1	13 329	139	276	6 113	44 105	44 047	78 157	2 268	17 194	135 485	-18.2	36 835	7 470
MICHIGAN.........................	438	1.2	23 316	314	632	14 319	45 632	85 629	195 079	5 915	21 790	160 110	-26.9	35 373	7 244
MINNESOTA	288	-3.3	14 708	190	376	7 520	39 656	49 208	107 280	2 892	15 863	134 584	-9.3	37 052	6 821
MISSISSIPPI	129	-7.3	5 340	100	196	3 493	34 970	20 256	54 168	2 439	4 737	55 936	13.7	11 765	2 093
MISSOURI	226	-3.4	10 821	167	327	6 972	41 837	45 616	101 134	1 855	15 230	164 362	6.8	35 463	7 141
MONTANA	13	-9.2	597	9	17	368	42 252	2 522	9 587	269	5 316	30 353	34.9	6 158	1 105
NEBRASKA........................	88	-2.4	3 662	67	138	2 470	36 803	16 851	44 806	953	5 447	44 605	-3.0	8 490	1 667
NEVADA............................	39	-4.9	2 049	25	51	968	37 965	7 575	13 742	503	5 280	122 900	29.0	29 314	5 749
NEW HAMPSHIRE...............	70	-0.4	3 947	43	84	1 709	39 824	10 342	18 606	571	4 357	30 054	-10.4	5 960	1 366
NEW JERSEY	241	-4.5	14 497	152	305	6 365	41 918	46 609	98 261	2 301	23 142	180 251	-14.4	46 383	9 643
NEW MEXICO	26	-0.3	1 251	17	35	699	40 339	11 479	21 197	1 989	5 306	55 006	21.5	10 324	2 003
NEW YORK	422	-3.6	21 770	278	542	11 009	39 618	81 642	150 027	4 233	43 409	349 415	-5.6	90 318	18 393
NORTH CAROLINA	388	-4.3	16 760	291	573	10 395	35 688	92 942	177 658	3 734	25 457	242 488	7.6	55 786	9 364
NORTH DAKOTA	20	-7.2	889	15	31	577	37 561	3 794	10 308	241	2 082	19 373	14.9	3 674	768
OHIO................................	587	-1.3	29 718	423	851	18 069	42 726	110 783	263 667	5 920	22 937	224 342	-12.8	48 315	10 016
OKLAHOMA.......................	118	-7.2	5 478	88	179	3 486	39 647	22 881	60 004	1 379	7 611	69 842	11.4	14 132	2 808
OREGON...........................	125	-3.4	6 042	89	174	3 429	38 550	34 425	55 061	1 300	13 434	102 974	17.0	23 265	4 443
PENNSYLVANIA	525	-2.4	26 504	366	724	15 277	41 773	98 179	219 949	5 353	28 505	265 925	-4.1	59 187	12 480
RHODE ISLAND..................	37	-4.2	1 985	24	50	978	40 063	5 422	10 813	327	3 587	21 658	-20.6	5 777	1 082
SOUTH CAROLINA..............	191	-2.2	8 866	143	287	5 736	40 020	34 567	81 894	2 393	12 118	108 199	-2.4	22 820	3 910
SOUTH DAKOTA	37	-1.0	1 560	28	55	967	35 157	5 261	13 180	256	3 128	20 601	8.2	3 944	723
TENNESSEE	277	-4.7	12 622	202	404	7 666	37 908	56 774	124 090	3 427	10 907	124 488	0.4	27 964	5 210
TEXAS..............................	694	-5.0	36 877	476	959	20 747	43 622	188 200	560 696	13 452	37 200	596 499	7.5	146 638	26 534
UTAH................................	99	-1.2	5 123	63	126	2 601	41 384	25 022	45 720	1 713	10 055	88 880	31.5	20 012	3 375
VERMONT..........................	28	-3.0	1 494	17	35	692	39 890	4 663	10 203	229	2 838	17 475	10.0	3 171	678
VIRGINIA...........................	226	-3.5	11 167	160	316	6 497	40 562	54 674	92 512	2 330	22 431	235 312	11.1	51 968	10 004
WASHINGTON	223	-3.5	12 506	146	295	6 905	47 366	56 331	103 983	2 653	22 382	199 064	18.6	48 104	9 568
WEST VIRGINIA	49	-3.0	2 429	37	72	1 556	42 078	9 461	21 873	543	3 992	31 965	9.3	5 033	1 200
WISCONSIN	414	-1.8	19 767	301	584	11 664	38 736	67 251	149 622	3 812	14 673	126 261	-11.2	28 611	5 941
WYOMING.........................	8	-5.0	502	6	10	314	56 510	2 465	7 913	268	2 803	22 534	30.1	4 250	956

Table A. States — Wholesale Trade and Retail Trade

STATE	Wholesale trade, 2007					Retail trade,[1] 2007								
	Number of establishments	Employees Number	Employees Percent change, 2002–2007	Sales (mil dol)	Annual payroll (mil dol)	Number of establishments	Total	Percent change, 2002–2007	Motor vehicle and parts dealers	Food and beverage stores	Clothing and clothing accessory stores	General merchandise stores	Sales (mil dol)	Annual payroll (mil dol)
	222	223	224	225	226	227	228	229	230	231	232	233	234	235
UNITED STATES..................	434 983	6 227 389	5.9	6 515 709	336 207	1 128 112	15 515 396	5.9	1 914 466	2 827 162	1 644 025	2 763 474	3 917 663	362 819
ALABAMA	5 663	81 076	8.2	68 625	3 600	19 722	238 922	7.4	31 887	35 110	23 832	54 410	57 345	5 112
ALASKA	753	9 063	22.1	7 355	443	2 641	34 977	6.0	4 517	7 519	2 333	8 105	9 303	937
ARIZONA	7 045	102 200	15.4	85 607	5 224	19 384	337 529	25.7	47 174	67 301	28 497	64 405	86 759	8 011
ARKANSAS........................	3 501	47 949	11.8	63 511	2 019	11 906	140 018	4.3	D	18 949	10 948	D	32 974	2 889
CALIFORNIA......................	61 451	888 079	9.5	925 328	53 724	114 438	1 683 023	10.4	212 872	323 171	212 039	262 169	455 032	44 329
COLORADO.......................	7 290	105 366	4.2	101 410	6 147	19 428	261 962	5.9	31 207	46 934	24 488	46 357	65 897	6 538
CONNECTICUT	4 620	75 993	-3.9	143 640	4 923	13 807	196 133	2.3	23 359	41 163	24 850	23 395	52 165	5 160
DELAWARE	983	19 452	-8.1	28 365	1 467	3 907	55 432	6.8	7 360	8 859	5 468	8 764	14 202	1 323
DISTRICT OF COLUMBIA ...	416	5 184	-10.3	3 247	333	1 827	19 117	3.3	D	5 287	4 003	D	3 844	486
FLORIDA...........................	32 361	326 878	9.2	323 340	15 150	73 794	1 016 290	12.6	132 389	199 431	118 091	174 854	262 341	24 050
GEORGIA	14 165	213 227	6.1	254 298	11 604	36 218	475 344	6.2	62 488	83 542	51 939	89 896	117 517	10 760
HAWAII	1 844	20 252	4.3	12 672	836	5 012	70 661	10.8	7 390	12 966	12 215	12 724	17 612	1 766
IDAHO..............................	2 103	26 519	15.6	20 210	1 136	6 300	80 447	15.5	12 293	10 928	4 892	16 553	20 527	1 834
ILLINOIS...........................	20 062	320 942	-3.2	405 962	18 813	43 055	639 147	6.3	72 057	111 756	68 703	117 382	165 451	14 895
INDIANA............................	8 147	115 868	5.7	101 259	5 324	23 692	333 172	-3.0	42 332	50 449	28 083	70 472	78 746	7 123
IOWA................................	5 017	64 891	4.6	55 108	2 724	13 203	177 156	0.5	21 717	34 508	13 035	33 571	39 235	3 561
KANSAS............................	4 544	57 551	-0.6	69 668	2 789	11 463	149 672	3.3	18 661	26 074	12 203	30 111	34 538	3 134
KENTUCKY........................	4 485	70 882	2.4	94 546	3 409	16 404	214 782	0.3	26 128	33 299	17 512	47 875	50 406	4 502
LOUISIANA........................	5 614	75 568	2.7	67 152	3 460	17 135	231 365	1.3	30 846	35 276	22 636	47 780	56 543	5 096
MAINE...............................	1 629	18 734	-3.6	12 458	790	6 911	83 279	3.8	10 679	17 274	6 140	11 617	20 444	1 894
MARYLAND	5 997	99 648	6.6	83 494	5 590	19 601	294 806	3.2	39 773	57 680	35 385	45 187	75 664	7 291
MASSACHUSETTS	8 765	152 513	-1.6	145 729	10 030	25 469	360 218	0.3	36 748	90 032	45 200	38 996	88 083	8 916
MICHIGAN.........................	12 047	172 356	-3.2	226 532	9 367	37 619	470 794	-9.6	48 960	76 602	45 331	105 937	109 103	10 001
MINNESOTA......................	8 623	138 822	9.5	140 335	8 537	20 777	307 034	0.2	32 763	53 089	26 289	57 166	71 384	6 686
MISSISSIPPI......................	2 922	37 214	5.4	27 995	1 466	12 452	141 426	4.1	17 947	18 625	12 686	34 157	33 751	2 911
MISSOURI	8 338	129 138	1.4	117 329	5 802	23 360	317 318	1.8	40 043	45 890	26 639	65 680	76 575	7 155
MONTANA	1 461	14 184	3.3	10 741	559	5 258	58 883	11.3	8 311	8 692	3 659	9 791	14 687	1 318
NEBRASKA........................	3 093	38 752	5.3	34 283	1 721	7 888	108 209	2.4	12 325	18 326	7 804	20 056	26 487	2 231
NEVADA	3 046	41 664	31.1	27 115	2 031	8 492	139 829	24.5	18 723	22 123	19 203	24 415	37 434	3 692
NEW HAMPSHIRE	1 886	24 960	6.0	19 023	1 490	6 603	98 333	4.8	12 937	20 704	8 378	14 523	25 354	2 380
NEW JERSEY.....................	16 174	283 501	3.5	366 292	18 714	34 482	460 843	6.0	48 275	107 638	63 287	57 782	124 814	12 050
NEW MEXICO	2 036	22 943	15.5	14 702	966	7 208	97 385	8.9	13 659	13 897	7 455	20 724	24 470	2 251
NEW YORK	34 672	412 962	-0.1	438 854	23 018	76 637	892 863	6.6	78 920	194 012	138 550	114 888	230 718	22 337
NORTH CAROLINA.............	12 256	180 664	11.4	148 758	9 342	36 592	466 577	7.2	62 076	75 817	47 335	87 515	114 578	10 343
NORTH DAKOTA	1 525	17 596	10.3	15 408	741	3 361	44 054	6.6	5 853	7 242	2 947	8 011	10 527	891
OHIO................................	15 332	243 652	3.8	241 334	12 100	40 075	591 237	-3.4	72 230	99 666	50 924	114 955	138 816	12 729
OKLAHOMA	4 584	61 265	12.0	66 516	2 802	13 554	170 984	1.8	D	21 975	14 278	D	43 095	3 610
OREGON	5 789	77 547	4.0	72 660	3 943	14 991	204 793	11.5	27 048	38 697	17 632	40 184	50 371	4 916
PENNSYLVANIA.................	15 769	246 422	5.3	229 254	13 164	46 532	672 042	1.5	80 992	143 626	65 190	108 007	166 843	14 862
RHODE ISLAND	1 479	21 502	21.6	12 557	1 062	4 080	50 865	0.4	5 484	11 571	5 639	5 973	12 286	1 215
SOUTH CAROLINA.............	5 034	68 229	13.0	55 125	3 111	18 886	231 685	8.8	28 786	41 184	26 215	42 730	54 298	4 878
SOUTH DAKOTA................	1 425	15 655	4.6	14 765	623	4 172	50 842	3.4	6 713	9 025	2 880	9 028	12 266	1 045
TENNESSEE	7 413	123 575	1.3	126 919	6 065	24 234	320 739	5.3	42 090	48 065	31 283	65 120	77 547	7 245
TEXAS..............................	31 898	495 225	12.6	663 680	27 146	78 795	1 138 440	10.9	156 304	192 056	125 866	224 986	311 335	26 395
UTAH................................	3 659	52 935	20.1	38 764	2 503	8 984	142 266	16.9	18 008	22 968	12 114	26 087	36 574	3 241
VERMONT	852	10 628	-1.5	5 893	472	3 852	40 416	0.8	5 116	9 473	3 301	2 499	9 310	939
VIRGINIA	7 740	120 111	13.7	94 659	6 059	29 633	431 634	7.4	57 291	70 445	47 329	75 598	105 663	9 992
WASHINGTON	9 743	132 047	9.0	116 016	6 919	23 075	328 053	10.6	44 839	59 754	29 651	59 721	92 969	8 585
WEST VIRGINIA.................	1 580	20 653	2.4	15 506	868	7 047	92 227	3.2	11 609	16 316	6 260	20 406	20 539	1 776
WISCONSIN	7 326	117 706	4.4	94 009	5 707	21 205	320 140	2.7	37 848	56 874	21 749	60 781	72 283	6 778
WYOMING	826	7 646	22.2	7 699	372	2 951	32 033	11.2	4 644	5 302	1 659	5 766	8 958	758

1. Establishments with payroll.

40

Table A. States — **Information**

STATE	Number of establishments	Employees Number	Percent change, 2002–2007	Publishing, except Internet	Motion picture and sound recording	Broadcasting, except Internet	Internet publishing and broadcasting and web search portals	Telecommunications	Data processing, hosting, and related services	Receipts (mil dol)	Annual payroll (mil dol)
	236	237	238	239	240	241	242	243	244	245	246
UNITED STATES................	141 566	3 496 773	-6.4	1 093 047	335 807	294 876	75 506	1 250 993	393 741	1 072 342.856	228 837
ALABAMA	1 700	40 054	0.1	13 226	2 109	3 991	110	16 907	3 562	NA	1 875
ALASKA	407	6 754	-5.4	983	590	926	D	4 121	103	NA	374
ARIZONA	2 275	52 573	-7.4	15 967	3 690	4 143	524	17 966	9 635	NA	3 006
ARKANSAS.......................	1 034	26 074	-17.1	D	D	D	D	9 273	D	NA	1 343
CALIFORNIA......................	21 068	556 535	-1.3	166 140	142 848	35 660	30 580	129 756	47 851	NA	48 147
COLORADO.......................	3 183	84 564	-17.2	24 635	4 730	5 621	D	35 283	13 369	NA	5 663
CONNECTICUT	1 834	40 345	-16.3	12 288	D	4 073	D	13 380	4 805	NA	2 556
DELAWARE	383	8 565	4.9	D	D	D	D	3 537	D	NA	457
DISTRICT OF COLUMBIA ...	749	24 499	-14.1	10 544	D	D	934	4 689	D	NA	2 129
FLORIDA...........................	8 296	175 382	-5.0	50 552	13 190	17 527	1 783	73 873	17 265	NA	9 663
GEORGIA	4 328	122 496	-15.7	29 487	6 548	12 544	2 971	54 327	14 641	NA	8 156
HAWAII.............................	622	10 083	-13.6	2 409	1 080	1 012	52	4 672	797	NA	510
IDAHO..............................	717	15 163	37.9	3 267	866	1 352	D	7 681	1 828	NA	528
ILLINOIS	5 696	136 589	-8.9	45 443	9 545	9 391	3 221	46 662	20 343	NA	8 630
INDIANA...........................	2 282	45 786	-7.7	14 847	3 746	4 461	112	17 838	4 375	NA	2 089
IOWA................................	1 590	34 397	-22.2	11 130	1 758	2 716	45	10 635	8 066	NA	1 426
KANSAS...........................	1 502	52 737	6.0	9 902	1 653	2 622	182	33 823	3 597	NA	3 064
KENTUCKY.......................	1 594	33 996	15.4	7 694	1 837	3 219	572	12 130	7 836	NA	1 252
LOUISIANA.......................	1 455	30 537	-2.8	5 866	2 191	3 468	68	17 171	1 609	NA	1 361
MAINE..............................	777	13 520	14.7	4 235	646	1 225	102	5 353	852	NA	523
MARYLAND	2 571	63 081	-13.2	15 239	D	6 334	D	26 069	9 536	NA	3 764
MASSACHUSETTS	3 772	110 038	-11.7	51 791	4 212	5 552	D	30 501	13 623	NA	8 623
MICHIGAN	3 791	77 639	-20.0	26 606	6 017	6 296	347	28 682	9 182	NA	4 314
MINNESOTA	2 772	70 314	0.2	32 666	4 123	4 831	637	18 110	9 547	NA	4 232
MISSISSIPPI.....................	1 017	15 902	-19.9	3 290	970	1 930	D	8 728	761	NA	646
MISSOURI	2 627	73 040	-11.1	20 630	3 802	5 463	510	28 911	13 041	NA	3 880
MONTANA.........................	638	9 500	1.5	2 648	D	1 135	D	3 949	1 023	NA	343
NEBRASKA.......................	957	20 217	-10.3	7 748	1 316	1 809	D	5 361	3 338	NA	984
NEVADA	1 109	17 914	0.4	4 621	1 775	2 787	389	6 907	1 368	NA	973
NEW HAMPSHIRE	790	15 482	5.9	8 604	824	666	D	4 387	710	NA	1 149
NEW JERSEY.....................	4 092	134 356	5.0	46 384	D	D	D	61 510	13 802	NA	8 950
NEW MEXICO	828	13 987	-7.6	3 017	1 186	1 503	D	7 737	412	NA	495
NEW YORK	11 326	301 340	-2.1	94 777	34 555	48 850	D	77 655	21 289	NA	22 538
NORTH CAROLINA.............	3 481	76 413	-1.5	23 062	4 656	6 291	609	33 854	6 856	NA	4 263
NORTH DAKOTA................	367	7 124	-7.5	2 910	345	1 261	D	1 790	611	NA	332
OHIO................................	4 199	97 360	-13.8	32 911	5 711	7 982	5 160	34 879	10 095	NA	5 178
OKLAHOMA.......................	1 585	32 481	-10.8	D	D	D	D	17 759	D	NA	1 463
OREGON	1 992	39 258	-1.7	13 074	3 121	3 330	325	12 853	6 211	NA	2 055
PENNSYLVANIA.................	5 302	137 115	-4.7	45 951	7 704	9 256	756	54 148	13 664	NA	7 774
RHODE ISLAND	394	8 059	-8.4	2 778	374	927	D	3 097	386	NA	416
SOUTH CAROLINA	1 410	33 052	11.3	8 239	1 825	3 324	152	16 878	2 213	NA	1 581
SOUTH DAKOTA................	437	7 296	-8.8	1 968	475	1 177	D	3 170	462	NA	313
TENNESSEE	2 491	50 778	-6.3	13 093	5 330	6 313	D	21 126	4 465	NA	2 370
TEXAS	9 541	250 410	-11.4	62 632	14 855	18 854	1 548	111 021	39 565	NA	15 460
UTAH	1 412	33 310	-4.8	11 345	3 278	1 726	918	9 619	6 121	NA	1 762
VERMONT	514	6 048	-17.6	1 993	404	720	D	1 778	637	NA	255
VIRGINIA	4 064	104 147	-20.5	27 600	5 140	7 133	D	48 597	13 230	NA	7 533
WASHINGTON	3 301	111 840	10.0	59 057	5 065	4 532	2 532	29 709	9 182	NA	11 277
WEST VIRGINIA.................	679	10 285	-18.8	2 633	553	1 541	6	4 726	764	NA	387
WISCONSIN	2 286	54 179	-2.0	19 751	3 497	5 327	307	16 856	8 376	NA	2 625
WYOMING	329	4 159	-1.4	1 293	499	515	D	1 549	234	NA	151

Table A. States — Utilities, Transportation and Warehousing, and Finance and Insurance

	Utilities, 2007					Transportation and warehousing, 2007					Finance and insurance, 2007				
STATE	Number of establishments	Employees Number	Employees Percent change, 2002–2007	Receipts (mil dol)	Annual payroll (mil dol)	Number of establishments	Employees Number	Employees Percent change, 2002–2007	Receipts (mil dol)	Annual payroll (mil dol)	Number of establishments	Employees Number	Employees Percent change, 2002–2007	Receipts (mil dol)	Annual payroll (mil dol)
	247	248	249	250	251	252	253	254	255	256	257	258	259	260	261
UNITED STATES	16 578	637 247	-3.9	584 193	51 654	219 706	4 454 383	22.0	639 916	173 183	501 713	6 607 511	0.4	3 669 303	502 417
ALABAMA	373	14 396	-10.1	NA	1 171	3 266	61 799	19.0	8 167	2 210	7 059	72 010	-3.0	NA	3 912
ALASKA	90	1 731	0.6	NA	125	1 125	20 143	30.3	5 495	1 114	810	7 778	9.5	NA	437
ARIZONA	227	11 957	NA	NA	952	3 405	83 777	10.1	9 626	3 271	10 496	147 894	NA	NA	7 997
ARKANSAS	346	7 127	-3.1	NA	514	2 613	60 118	1.9	7 420	2 199	4 579	37 798	11.3	NA	1 685
CALIFORNIA	1 145	63 954	11.3	NA	5 437	21 616	452 017	13.8	70 603	18 055	54 395	720 191	5.7	NA	57 431
COLORADO	371	8 468	-0.4	NA	614	3 463	64 731	36.9	10 471	2 450	10 905	107 119	5.2	NA	6 920
CONNECTICUT	151	10 210	-3.5	NA	997	1 714	44 117	9.7	5 273	1 739	6 431	137 353	-5.9	NA	16 598
DELAWARE	49	2 615	-2.1	NA	224	725	11 638	33.7	1 050	402	2 117	42 443	-11.8	NA	3 031
DISTRICT OF COLUMBIA	37	2 029	NA	NA	201	197	8 810	52.5	3 765	607	1 036	19 474	NA	NA	2 486
FLORIDA	588	30 920	8.6	NA	2 218	13 417	218 128	23.7	40 830	8 204	34 389	371 543	8.8	NA	21 520
GEORGIA	561	24 495	-3.8	NA	1 821	6 430	169 568	44.7	22 064	7 499	15 707	179 053	0.1	NA	11 189
HAWAII	54	2 953	20.8	NA	214	883	32 361	100.0	4 275	1 108	1 672	20 747	13.6	NA	1 095
IDAHO	186	3 330	-10.1	NA	233	1 772	16 991	31.7	2 198	544	2 997	22 586	27.0	NA	980
ILLINOIS	455	27 635	-21.0	NA	2 551	11 753	237 877	30.8	36 208	9 947	24 106	348 163	-0.2	NA	28 584
INDIANA	605	14 982	-2.2	NA	1 016	5 282	118 144	21.7	16 577	4 108	10 453	110 143	1.6	NA	5 739
IOWA	260	7 718	-5.0	NA	507	3 778	54 447	24.4	6 825	1 909	6 261	91 157	-4.1	NA	4 756
KANSAS	230	9 158	38.7	NA	474	2 656	46 861	15.5	5 881	1 647	6 065	61 657	11.6	NA	3 224
KENTUCKY	329	8 282	-9.1	NA	578	3 176	78 936	17.5	11 791	3 517	6 594	66 825	-2.8	NA	3 076
LOUISIANA	532	10 857	-8.8	NA	928	3 805	72 064	11.9	12 491	3 284	7 825	64 290	-1.2	NA	3 096
MAINE	84	2 513	-12.0	NA	165	1 251	15 211	14.9	1 658	523	2 031	26 977	-0.1	NA	1 380
MARYLAND	115	10 058	-17.8	NA	1 162	3 704	67 301	20.1	7 266	2 548	8 553	125 201	2.4	NA	8 944
MASSACHUSETTS	243	13 230	-6.9	NA	1 139	3 741	79 518	11.4	10 036	2 998	9 941	222 383	3.0	NA	22 299
MICHIGAN	397	22 221	NA	NA	1 734	5 876	106 859	16.8	17 723	4 454	15 165	175 299	-1.2	NA	9 308
MINNESOTA	269	11 780	-5.6	NA	876	4 739	80 323	39.9	15 056	3 185	10 114	156 603	2.5	NA	10 928
MISSISSIPPI	586	8 677	0.7	NA	587	2 340	36 419	23.3	4 041	1 251	4 906	35 919	6.6	NA	1 514
MISSOURI	375	16 032	-18.0	NA	1 199	5 091	89 027	13.0	14 974	3 277	11 219	137 221	0.3	NA	7 277
MONTANA	194	2 761	-9.7	NA	184	1 350	11 658	28.2	1 640	375	2 110	17 011	25.1	NA	715
NEBRASKA	130	1 296	8.1	NA	147	2 334	47 793	63.4	6 323	1 629	4 169	64 519	12.5	NA	3 280
NEVADA	108	5 327	-7.0	NA	442	1 543	48 376	68.6	5 319	1 548	4 841	42 034	16.7	NA	2 098
NEW HAMPSHIRE	97	3 178	-3.8	NA	240	847	12 703	-17.5	1 384	439	2 095	28 111	10.2	NA	1 763
NEW JERSEY	337	18 334	-13.7	NA	1 728	7 440	181 595	12.4	25 333	7 536	12 886	213 509	-4.0	NA	18 545
NEW MEXICO	220	5 012	-0.6	NA	331	1 374	17 192	27.7	2 181	577	2 973	25 485	-37.4	NA	1 216
NEW YORK	547	38 328	-17.0	NA	3 490	12 067	242 097	21.2	35 690	9 358	28 241	590 838	-24.4	NA	104 090
NORTH CAROLINA	392	20 490	-0.1	NA	1 648	5 971	116 932	21.8	13 265	4 252	13 722	192 422	8.7	NA	12 575
NORTH DAKOTA	114	3 331	0.5	NA	265	1 051	10 258	26.6	1 579	347	1 666	16 220	24.0	NA	662
OHIO	610	26 511	5.8	NA	2 159	7 612	177 614	10.4	22 380	6 906	19 047	266 335	2.4	NA	15 422
OKLAHOMA	334	9 822	1.5	NA	632	2 704	48 079	35.5	6 441	1 912	6 727	60 399	8.3	NA	2 702
OREGON	268	7 984	-4.7	NA	657	3 254	57 290	17.1	7 203	2 209	6 729	66 714	3.6	NA	3 570
PENNSYLVANIA	611	29 183	-13.8	NA	2 790	8 158	206 663	20.0	21 206	7 109	18 954	279 472	-10.0	NA	18 603
RHODE ISLAND	28	1 283	-17.3	NA	99	703	10 686	14.2	1 275	345	1 594	31 415	19.7	NA	1 882
SOUTH CAROLINA	323	12 139	21.3	NA	769	2 759	56 053	19.8	6 300	2 042	7 549	66 489	1.7	NA	3 036
SOUTH DAKOTA	151	2 122	2.8	NA	127	1 102	9 168	21.8	1 253	286	1 916	29 806	27.3	NA	1 187
TENNESSEE	150	3 249	-7.0	NA	169	4 218	132 044	11.6	15 208	4 701	10 242	116 358	1.4	NA	6 629
TEXAS	1 860	46 175	-11.2	NA	3 958	16 274	373 340	37.3	62 952	15 768	37 761	465 405	11.6	NA	28 764
UTAH	203	4 639	9.9	NA	346	2 194	49 364	30.1	7 522	1 942	5 351	58 648	38.9	NA	2 769
VERMONT	47	1 902	7.6	NA	167	539	6 243	14.0	717	202	1 039	9 422	-17.7	NA	532
VIRGINIA	312	16 629	10.1	NA	1 395	5 358	95 040	14.1	10 993	3 316	12 396	168 511	5.8	NA	10 456
WASHINGTON	297	5 819	3.6	NA	396	5 111	87 038	33.3	14 983	3 626	11 061	119 201	7.4	NA	7 280
WEST VIRGINIA	211	6 448	4.2	NA	463	1 403	16 588	8.3	2 764	613	2 174	19 975	-10.6	NA	752
WISCONSIN	265	15 721	11.1	NA	1 244	5 606	104 717	19.5	12 814	3 723	9 663	144 531	7.6	NA	8 191
WYOMING	111	2 236	0.8	NA	170	916	8 667	47.8	1 425	372	981	6 854	6.0	NA	291

Real Estate and Rental and Leasing and Professional, Scientific, and Technical Services

STATE	Real estate and rental and leasing, 2007					Professional, scientific, and technical services, 2007								
	Number of establishments	Employees Number	Employees Percent change, 2002–2007	Receipts (mil dol)	Annual payroll (mil dol)	Number of establishments	Total	Percent change, 2002–2007	Legal services	Accounting and related services	Architectural, engineering, and related services	Computer systems design and related services	Receipts (mil dol)	Annual payroll (mil dol)
	262	263	264	265	266	267	268	269	270	271	272	273	274	275
UNITED STATES	384 297	2 188 479	12.3	485 059	84 765	847 492	7 870 414	8.7	1 203 763	1 375 685	1 432 209	1 252 197	1 251 004	502 074
ALABAMA	4 554	27 100	27.2	4 073	823	9 489	94 051	15.7	j	15 126	25 354	14 691	13 863	5 072
ALASKA	852	4 370	2.8	841	160	1 828	12 843	11.3	2 010	1 521	5 419	831	2 042	759
ARIZONA	9 441	52 627	NA	10 078	1 994	16 640	129 368	20.7	17 688	21 946	27 186	23 092	17 802	7 311
ARKANSAS	3 162	14 115	15.1	1 968	375	5 609	32 361	6.2	i	7 407	6 711	2 134	3 443	1 325
CALIFORNIA	51 597	312 488	14.1	76 805	13 447	112 709	1 260 896	8.3	145 772	364 118	185 972	169 890	200 037	82 881
COLORADO	10 011	47 568	1.1	8 461	1 793	22 629	160 601	3.0	17 955	17 283	39 320	37 318	29 572	10 800
CONNECTICUT	3 609	22 455	-3.0	5 687	994	9 881	102 071	-4.7	j	11 868	16 515	13 484	15 895	8 029
DELAWARE	1 248	5 807	1.7	11 057	222	2 390	23 389	1.9	h	2 610	3 568	3 902	4 269	1 722
DISTRICT OF COLUMBIA	1 140	9 663	NA	2 748	625	4 595	89 006	6.6	35 547	4 379	6 494	12 379	25 809	9 137
FLORIDA	33 653	170 859	25.3	32 235	6 094	69 263	430 211	13.6	91 579	62 515	89 807	55 962	61 990	24 395
GEORGIA	12 620	65 875	10.1	14 022	2 903	27 752	215 705	12.0	32 613	35 950	44 517	36 072	35 259	12 809
HAWAII	2 084	16 759	13.6	3 974	654	3 291	22 460	5.9	h	3 424	5 908	2 452	3 172	1 229
IDAHO	2 530	8 371	49.7	1 242	234	4 209	31 650	-0.6	4 631	3 580	9 229	1 901	3 822	1 491
ILLINOIS	13 899	87 468	0.7	21 725	3 985	38 934	369 279	5.8	60 900	70 693	47 136	52 381	62 953	24 624
INDIANA	6 389	34 272	1.2	5 448	1 062	13 017	96 189	-1.7	j	19 014	21 049	8 902	12 184	4 809
IOWA	2 969	14 667	7.4	2 556	473	6 214	42 376	12.0	7 996	9 570	5 363	4 530	5 043	1 896
KANSAS	3 314	15 160	3.5	2 429	440	7 078	56 302	5.7	i	12 215	12 266	8 234	7 889	2 753
KENTUCKY	3 898	20 146	11.8	3 894	593	8 114	61 944	11.5	j	11 253	11 185	9 205	7 917	2 852
LOUISIANA	4 625	30 922	5.3	6 015	1 195	11 190	85 415	6.8	20 106	16 657	27 672	4 887	11 967	4 265
MAINE	1 771	6 942	15.0	1 054	209	3 484	22 242	1.5	4 348	3 085	5 191	2 374	2 916	1 087
MARYLAND	6 768	49 766	9.7	12 392	2 263	19 516	251 806	26.9	j	21 041	38 889	72 913	40 162	16 882
MASSACHUSETTS	7 053	48 576	11.6	14 030	2 288	21 974	252 905	5.5	32 489	25 994	46 532	46 723	51 285	21 358
MICHIGAN	8 862	54 874	NA	12 859	1 686	22 691	251 684	-7.5	27 771	51 164	57 694	28 751	29 800	15 402
MINNESOTA	6 889	39 430	6.5	9 208	1 317	16 678	141 819	10.8	21 404	20 086	20 294	22 862	20 575	8 478
MISSISSIPPI	2 517	10 169	5.2	1 735	284	4 770	30 999	6.8	i	6 352	6 128	3 251	3 986	1 357
MISSOURI	7 003	39 625	3.0	7 186	1 249	13 582	132 339	10.3	j	22 088	21 693	25 803	19 916	7 540
MONTANA	1 892	6 410	34.6	848	153	3 455	16 889	8.1	3 210	2 924	4 424	1 415	1 802	685
NEBRASKA	2 032	9 974	6.0	1 646	292	4 220	40 829	31.6	5 560	10 983	5 718	6 226	4 851	2 018
NEVADA	4 613	31 603	62.2	6 187	1 106	7 925	58 085	25.4	9 593	8 275	17 170	5 486	8 991	3 272
NEW HAMPSHIRE	1 534	7 266	-3.1	1 372	248	3 993	29 453	1.7	h	6 964	4 848	6 677	3 758	1 584
NEW JERSEY	9 618	64 021	11.0	16 348	2 939	31 141	331 838	15.5	k	45 727	43 790	76 963	52 696	23 765
NEW MEXICO	2 525	11 678	26.1	1 955	356	4 832	44 310	43.2	5 732	5 561	8 713	3 977	6 186	2 589
NEW YORK	32 588	171 601	7.2	49 867	7 942	58 526	565 273	0.4	129 554	91 780	66 137	63 579	115 484	42 815
NORTH CAROLINA	11 258	53 583	15.9	11 175	1 881	22 488	184 998	17.3	24 385	28 145	31 819	28 769	26 574	10 883
NORTH DAKOTA	770	3 748	10.4	669	96	1 445	9 794	-10.7	1 678	1 666	2 069	1 260	1 122	420
OHIO	10 973	67 048	5.6	15 011	2 339	25 083	228 670	-4.7	39 115	37 230	44 190	33 677	33 028	12 619
OKLAHOMA	4 003	24 887	30.3	3 852	806	9 174	65 879	12.4	12 586	15 304	12 412	9 186	8 084	3 062
OREGON	6 391	30 978	16.1	5 077	950	11 465	85 253	10.0	12 504	14 448	16 090	10 583	9 964	4 967
PENNSYLVANIA	9 904	68 954	7.2	13 603	2 612	29 726	298 754	-2.4	54 156	48 633	58 726	38 256	46 680	18 523
RHODE ISLAND	1 233	6 493	13.4	1 463	227	3 110	22 892	16.9	h	3 561	3 543	6 163	2 796	1 182
SOUTH CAROLINA	5 473	30 417	23.8	5 194	990	9 518	74 923	17.2	15 302	15 902	18 083	5 925	9 484	3 658
SOUTH DAKOTA	888	3 844	8.2	524	90	1 750	10 197	-2.2	1 869	2 052	1 666	919	1 108	391
TENNESSEE	6 087	37 737	14.8	6 950	1 243	11 339	100 859	4.7	15 457	21 889	19 552	10 974	12 836	5 100
TEXAS	26 593	173 745	13.0	36 399	7 067	57 586	540 528	9.1	81 046	76 120	144 800	79 341	91 869	35 742
UTAH	4 886	20 413	41.4	3 391	617	8 255	68 452	31.5	8 319	18 562	11 171	8 730	8 373	3 212
VERMONT	797	3 395	20.2	497	96	2 122	16 534	30.1	2 203	5 776	2 152	1 989	1 637	658
VIRGINIA	9 475	60 502	21.3	12 637	2 409	27 254	387 272	25.0	28 391	29 108	65 996	148 375	68 693	27 939
WASHINGTON	10 480	51 196	7.3	10 467	1 819	19 394	159 711	12.2	22 408	21 957	37 630	24 995	24 809	10 391
WEST VIRGINIA	1 586	7 055	6.6	1 171	175	2 960	22 233	4.3	5 998	3 247	4 715	2 145	2 650	921
WISCONSIN	5 119	27 226	5.4	4 043	789	11 305	98 050	9.0	j	17 712	17 133	12 681	12 871	5 028
WYOMING	1 121	4 651	49.7	992	160	1 899	8 827	21.2	1 559	1 271	2 570	592	1 093	393

Table A. States — **Health Care and Social Assistance**

	Health care and social assistance, 2007												
	Subject to federal tax						Tax-exempt						
		Employees							Employees				
STATE	Number of estab-lishments	Total	Percent change, 2002–2007	Ambulatory health care services	Hospitals	Receipts (mil dol)	Annual payroll (mil dol)	Number of estab-lishments	Total	Percent change, 2002–2007	Ambulatory health care services	Hospitals	Receipts (mil dol)	Annual payroll (mil dol)
	276	277	278	279	280	281	282	283	284	285	286	287	288	289
UNITED STATES	647 120	8 322 326	18.5	4 984 940	601 899	818 395	330 888	137 506	8 469 748	5.5	718 501	4 926 944	849 882	331 832
ALABAMA	8 502	134 925	19.3	71 265	18 878	12 637	5 167	1 890	103 145	3.2	9 310	69 965	9 968	3 723
ALASKA	1 603	15 416	59.8	10 193	1 740	1 821	714	528	25 202	-3.0	4 401	12 925	2 842	1 077
ARIZONA	13 643	154 061	35.1	91 394	j	16 656	6 572	1 803	124 772	26.1	11 535	l	13 751	5 081
ARKANSAS	5 718	77 215	19.8	39 750	9 239	7 151	2 895	1 498	75 649	8.1	6 435	k	6 289	2 387
CALIFORNIA	84 335	883 552	15.2	563 016	63 134	102 703	38 944	12 953	708 878	6.2	55 838	433 199	88 903	33 587
COLORADO	11 557	127 029	21.3	75 024	9 821	12 599	5 234	2 087	111 913	14.6	16 882	64 076	11 729	4 491
CONNECTICUT	7 687	122 425	11.8	68 206	e	11 535	5 062	2 362	130 935	9.0	14 051	l	13 278	5 378
DELAWARE	1 877	25 319	26.8	15 335	f	2 621	1 156	502	29 421	7.1	2 200	17 353	2 810	1 215
DISTRICT OF COLUMBIA	1 419	19 710	9.3	10 263	3 431	2 099	944	711	41 365	-6.7	1 484	23 722	5 151	1 998
FLORIDA	46 687	538 050	13.8	318 090	70 644	61 637	22 586	4 992	365 954	9.4	33 165	219 986	40 393	14 648
GEORGIA	18 379	229 101	14.5	135 432	19 522	23 274	9 145	2 461	190 195	8.8	11 570	132 958	20 669	7 336
HAWAII	2 778	29 023	45.3	20 431	g	2 979	1 244	706	34 617	-4.4	4 955	j	3 586	1 477
IDAHO	3 974	44 499	31.1	24 110	2 799	3 510	1 423	571	29 433	8.2	1 609	20 808	2 701	1 088
ILLINOIS	25 651	325 085	15.9	205 032	11 797	32 056	13 445	5 411	381 584	0.2	20 692	228 320	37 987	14 564
INDIANA	11 919	181 493	21.8	102 701	13 359	17 015	6 813	3 053	188 600	1.4	13 317	115 514	17 754	6 640
IOWA	5 399	70 263	14.1	40 123	b	5 854	2 732	2 458	128 022	6.9	6 804	l	9 518	3 872
KANSAS	5 778	83 531	16.6	48 409	7 241	7 948	3 176	1 917	94 997	3.3	6 005	49 462	7 181	2 968
KENTUCKY	8 686	115 673	13.0	62 383	7 842	10 090	4 218	1 914	119 609	2.8	10 428	78 156	10 507	4 177
LOUISIANA	9 725	145 174	11.6	77 250	21 393	13 179	4 935	1 820	110 905	-3.4	3 396	71 075	10 507	3 926
MAINE	3 203	39 757	10.4	21 408	e	3 016	1 397	1 672	64 394	11.2	7 955	k	5 577	2 294
MARYLAND	12 542	143 677	15.8	91 164	g	15 364	6 218	2 762	172 104	10.2	8 902	l	18 463	6 871
MASSACHUSETTS	12 828	202 678	8.1	113 995	11 095	21 342	9 280	5 027	308 334	6.7	30 689	162 079	30 605	12 896
MICHIGAN	21 150	228 681	10.0	156 808	2 591	21 055	9 169	4 883	320 801	5.4	24 972	207 748	31 703	12 420
MINNESOTA	10 263	157 035	25.2	93 957	e	13 230	6 021	3 733	229 109	1.9	22 776	m	20 768	8 851
MISSISSIPPI	4 858	72 601	18.0	37 002	11 694	7 229	2 753	1 018	74 257	5.4	3 996	54 573	6 885	2 619
MISSOURI	12 881	159 529	14.2	84 426	13 808	14 102	5 912	3 103	202 811	3.3	15 615	124 941	18 785	7 007
MONTANA	2 438	21 763	18.1	13 791	e	1 945	802	863	36 097	8.3	2 481	j	3 026	1 182
NEBRASKA	3 830	49 338	19.7	27 155	2 050	4 447	1 889	1 090	65 590	2.6	2 796	39 933	5 634	2 219
NEVADA	5 269	72 716	37.5	39 241	17 329	9 226	3 345	503	23 917	1.0	1 516	15 577	2 965	1 053
NEW HAMPSHIRE	2 655	32 711	11.4	18 356	h	3 096	1 386	837	51 006	14.5	8 546	k	4 990	1 992
NEW JERSEY	22 056	253 078	18.0	169 075	3 984	26 416	10 530	3 721	250 292	6.5	20 063	149 193	25 498	10 784
NEW MEXICO	3 713	57 423	42.1	28 655	7 403	4 855	1 958	1 019	48 073	14.0	5 072	25 291	3 980	1 823
NEW YORK	41 201	459 964	15.3	341 364	4 431	46 578	18 428	12 747	866 075	3.7	98 596	411 842	82 017	35 995
NORTH CAROLINA	17 964	286 998	36.1	160 857	6 844	22 795	10 133	3 748	236 399	12.4	15 003	155 137	23 894	8 915
NORTH DAKOTA	1 176	14 135	16.4	9 015	1 404	1 427	571	572	38 062	6.3	1 465	18 719	2 480	1 145
OHIO	22 693	346 386	13.0	204 606	6 227	28 637	12 631	5 272	394 808	4.7	30 467	247 224	37 246	14 990
OKLAHOMA	8 577	121 175	26.5	58 561	21 197	10 860	4 172	1 755	79 602	-2.2	6 397	k	7 503	2 653
OREGON	9 011	91 816	18.6	58 522	g	9 445	3 751	2 250	100 417	13.6	10 889	l	10 715	4 144
PENNSYLVANIA	27 138	368 531	20.3	228 474	21 985	35 089	15 093	8 018	506 212	5.7	43 780	252 464	46 889	18 339
RHODE ISLAND	2 502	34 762	20.5	19 520	c	3 015	1 310	772	47 185	6.2	4 505	k	4 146	1 782
SOUTH CAROLINA	7 883	115 669	23.3	64 005	13 933	11 213	4 523	1 408	84 547	-1.5	4 245	57 911	9 195	3 238
SOUTH DAKOTA	1 535	17 404	-0.1	10 080	1 187	1 697	667	706	39 076	7.2	3 632	22 299	3 070	1 372
TENNESSEE	11 720	185 582	23.8	104 883	23 380	19 249	7 600	2 547	152 159	4.6	11 097	97 202	14 550	5 494
TEXAS	48 875	780 459	26.2	450 190	105 928	71 221	27 772	6 116	386 154	2.0	28 558	257 127	42 609	15 346
UTAH	5 731	67 064	19.3	38 665	i	6 411	2 365	661	45 582	10.8	3 873	k	4 449	1 791
VERMONT	1 469	15 381	14.9	8 992		1 147	532	707	26 536	11.1	6 426	j	2 390	963
VIRGINIA	14 942	203 981	19.5	121 014	18 113	19 705	8 418	2 598	167 086	5.9	11 227	101 016	17 817	6 544
WASHINGTON	15 513	172 010	19.4	103 216	h	16 739	6 871	2 961	173 151	10.1	21 900	l	19 148	7 479
WEST VIRGINIA	3 741	51 790	5.0	25 186	6 094	4 339	1 708	1 119	62 873	-2.1	6 739	38 307	5 536	2 121
WISCONSIN	11 149	165 008	14.9	96 982	h	15 006	6 808	3 268	204 281	5.9	19 528	m	18 835	7 274
WYOMING	1 297	11 680	20.6	7 368	644	1 139	470	413	17 562	13.3	718	9 886	1 437	603

Table A. States — Arts, Entertainment, and Recreation and Accommodation and Food Services

STATE	Arts, entertainment, and recreation, 2007					Accommodation and food services, 2007					
		Employees					Employees				
	Number of establishments	Number	Percent change, 2002–2007	Receipts (mil dol)	Annual payroll (mil dol)	Number of establishments	Total	Percent change, 2002–2007	Food services and drinking places	Receipts (mil dol)	Annual payroll (mil dol)
	290	291	292	293	294	295	296	297	298	299	300
UNITED STATES	124 620	2 061 348	11.5	189 417	58 359	634 361	11 600 751	14.6	9 630 090	613 796	170 827
ALABAMA	1 129	17 981	24.2	1 256	300	8 093	150 791	17.5	136 439	6 426	1 751
ALASKA	495	4 456	20.1	350	72	1 996	25 638	8.3	19 114	1 851	530
ARIZONA	1 819	46 524	18.2	4 275	1 322	11 610	250 716	21.5	199 909	13 269	3 766
ARKANSAS	812	9 212	15.4	484	141	5 112	89 933	15.5	79 512	3 560	994
CALIFORNIA	20 090	302 015	5.2	36 444	11 869	75 989	1 366 926	19.3	1 128 817	80 853	22 375
COLORADO	2 414	49 688	9.8	3 911	1 256	12 075	231 721	12.2	186 986	11 440	3 408
CONNECTICUT	1 652	25 179	8.4	2 546	730	7 941	132 001	11.5	100 129	9 138	2 483
DELAWARE	389	6 855	-8.9	545	139	1 850	32 194	19.4	28 359	1 911	469
DISTRICT OF COLUMBIA ...	290	7 318	3.2	876	319	2 148	52 998	22.4	37 156	4 278	1 238
FLORIDA	7 537	166 847	13.7	15 381	4 218	35 012	746 214	20.1	598 276	41 922	11 470
GEORGIA	2 797	45 047	27.7	3 422	1 137	18 640	355 423	21.3	312 688	16 976	4 704
HAWAII	502	11 988	12.1	824	246	3 528	98 353	14.8	60 304	8 042	2 210
IDAHO	718	9 020	30.0	397	126	3 482	56 662	24.7	45 340	2 416	663
ILLINOIS	4 608	79 603	9.2	7 329	2 242	26 774	468 827	11.4	409 186	25 469	6 894
INDIANA	2 175	35 876	14.0	3 025	953	12 932	254 293	10.0	221 408	11 670	3 175
IOWA	1 453	21 677	6.1	1 534	363	7 014	116 838	11.7	96 927	4 738	1 276
KANSAS	1 114	15 643	16.6	807	232	5 866	104 795	13.8	92 897	4 192	1 174
KENTUCKY	1 341	18 556	15.6	1 205	368	7 309	151 551	11.1	136 285	6 301	1 787
LOUISIANA	1 356	24 761	-16.6	2 801	674	8 169	180 289	6.0	142 855	9 730	2 579
MAINE	894	7 792	22.1	505	134	3 938	49 363	9.8	39 919	2 516	748
MARYLAND	2 149	37 507	17.5	2 776	976	10 802	192 619	9.1	170 707	10 758	2 916
MASSACHUSETTS	3 078	52 731	12.7	4 691	1 612	16 039	257 302	6.6	225 602	14 917	4 340
MICHIGAN	3 654	55 118	-7.2	4 792	1 482	19 678	339 181	2.9	302 866	14 537	4 207
MINNESOTA	2 747	42 057	13.4	2 924	1 057	11 340	221 081	8.9	181 622	10 424	2 978
MISSISSIPPI	673	8 179	-12.0	525	146	4 817	119 626	9.3	79 146	7 045	1 812
MISSOURI	2 161	37 529	12.3	3 411	1 254	12 261	241 438	11.9	207 557	11 071	3 109
MONTANA	1 083	10 294	11.3	674	140	3 360	46 137	12.8	36 177	2 079	554
NEBRASKA	841	11 364	10.6	622	168	4 241	69 142	10.3	61 544	2 686	749
NEVADA	1 261	30 274	13.3	3 367	783	5 570	325 544	21.0	97 104	28 816	8 595
NEW HAMPSHIRE	739	11 595	10.6	776	245	3 508	55 268	15.5	45 825	2 631	800
NEW JERSEY	3 543	51 054	16.4	3 867	1 273	19 526	291 327	8.3	221 700	19 994	6 232
NEW MEXICO	664	14 341	5.4	1 488	304	4 090	80 415	14.9	64 319	3 734	1 055
NEW YORK	11 230	158 275	15.6	21 135	6 424	43 791	591 653	12.1	504 817	39 813	10 956
NORTH CAROLINA	3 422	55 306	19.0	4 462	1 458	18 268	343 235	21.8	302 669	16 127	4 395
NORTH DAKOTA	407	4 581	29.4	198	56	1 840	30 307	15.8	23 926	1 214	338
OHIO	4 077	65 326	3.5	5 526	1 849	23 959	436 598	4.2	401 245	17 780	5 079
OKLAHOMA	1 099	26 237	77.3	2 569	487	6 900	129 159	16.2	117 572	5 107	1 401
OREGON	1 597	24 334	8.4	1 476	546	10 241	150 538	15.8	127 821	7 556	2 153
PENNSYLVANIA	4 648	83 594	13.7	6 702	2 299	26 910	420 209	10.0	369 097	19 625	5 454
RHODE ISLAND	524	8 829	32.9	679	192	2 926	44 426	15.2	40 319	2 149	622
SOUTH CAROLINA	1 547	25 300	18.8	1 426	426	9 291	182 899	19.7	156 272	8 383	2 311
SOUTH DAKOTA	661	6 436	17.2	469	101	2 426	36 710	13.9	27 654	1 623	436
TENNESSEE	2 377	32 436	18.2	3 421	1 079	11 592	239 379	18.1	210 513	10 627	3 009
TEXAS	6 260	109 689	12.6	8 824	2 855	43 509	866 189	21.0	768 821	42 055	11 502
UTAH	842	18 487	-1.1	961	336	4 541	91 808	13.7	74 282	3 981	1 149
VERMONT	474	8 009	0.8	379	112	1 942	31 176	4.4	19 700	1 368	428
VIRGINIA	2 730	51 160	11.2	3 803	1 097	15 765	302 446	18.0	256 469	15 340	4 273
WASHINGTON	2 675	57 631	14.4	4 907	1 538	15 893	233 235	16.8	199 322	12 389	3 618
WEST VIRGINIA	699	10 801	12.6	1 354	180	3 650	61 711	18.7	51 734	2 553	713
WISCONSIN	2 738	42 791	22.1	3 028	969	14 439	227 475	13.3	192 650	9 247	2 535
WYOMING	435	4 045	-0.6	269	75	1 768	26 992	11.7	18 532	1 469	412

Table A. States — Other Services, Except Public Administration, and Government Employment

STATE	Other services, except public administration, 2007								Government employment, 2010		
	Number of establishments	Employees					Receipts (mil dol)	Annual payroll (mil dol)	Federal civilian	Federal military	State and local
		Total	Percent change, 2002–2007	Repair and maintenance	Personal and laundry services	Religious, civic, and similar services					
	301	302	303	304	305	306	307	308	309	310	311
UNITED STATES	540 148	3 479 011	0.1	1 261 083	1 337 539	880 389	405 284	99 123	3 037 000	2 101 000	19 542 000
ALABAMA	6 718	40 488	-2.8	18 034	15 757	6 697	4 154	1 050	58 475	32 776	322 775
ALASKA	1 328	7 566	-0.9	2 487	2 387	2 692	811	223	17 569	27 054	63 531
ARIZONA	8 906	68 368	19.6	27 251	24 794	16 323	6 220	1 726	60 128	34 887	353 788
ARKANSAS	4 153	23 188	-3.8	9 961	8 460	4 767	2 188	558	22 913	18 102	196 422
CALIFORNIA	57 626	399 336	-1.4	158 848	149 940	90 548	52 326	11 914	269 008	223 945	2 196 675
COLORADO	10 151	62 767	-2.1	23 065	22 293	17 409	7 789	1 823	56 376	54 045	343 824
CONNECTICUT	7 392	47 992	3.7	14 885	21 839	11 268	5 061	1 395	19 717	14 739	230 697
DELAWARE	1 587	10 012	-14.9	3 300	4 593	2 119	898	265	6 155	8 675	57 571
DISTRICT OF COLUMBIA	3 284	49 853	5.4	703	6 308	42 842	15 500	3 154	208 842	19 756	40 017
FLORIDA	35 597	201 687	5.1	66 378	82 991	52 318	20 757	5 174	142 508	99 118	964 606
GEORGIA	14 588	98 047	15.3	42 248	38 992	16 807	10 386	2 837	107 849	103 507	581 586
HAWAII	2 916	20 119	4.3	3 805	7 864	8 450	1 918	513	34 869	56 267	89 857
IDAHO	2 640	13 681	4.6	6 567	4 464	2 650	1 094	316	13 707	9 899	104 000
ILLINOIS	23 510	167 675	-5.3	62 578	60 360	44 737	20 639	5 203	91 991	47 780	767 944
INDIANA	11 458	75 292	-5.0	29 915	26 816	18 561	8 451	1 893	42 260	22 190	393 228
IOWA	6 088	31 869	-5.5	12 559	11 772	7 538	3 063	779	19 186	13 041	234 815
KANSAS	5 498	31 665	-1.7	12 126	12 139	7 400	3 326	804	28 491	37 108	237 154
KENTUCKY	6 150	40 956	-1.2	17 582	16 359	7 015	3 751	1 009	42 445	58 131	284 025
LOUISIANA	6 637	42 223	-8.7	20 353	14 686	7 184	4 664	1 170	33 655	40 983	334 679
MAINE	2 840	13 297	-4.3	4 697	4 439	4 161	1 280	328	15 439	7 820	87 595
MARYLAND	10 365	77 368	3.9	25 182	32 326	19 860	9 689	2 487	171 994	46 422	347 113
MASSACHUSETTS	13 516	90 268	-0.9	27 823	38 899	23 546	9 841	2 690	51 064	20 569	382 055
MICHIGAN	17 040	101 568	-10.3	38 528	40 665	22 375	10 844	2 648	57 486	20 755	570 937
MINNESOTA	11 137	81 829	4.7	23 556	28 659	29 614	8 301	2 355	34 709	20 891	363 218
MISSISSIPPI	3 853	20 421	-7.9	8 894	7 307	4 220	1 950	490	27 320	31 236	224 765
MISSOURI	11 111	67 476	-6.8	27 126	26 623	13 727	6 771	1 800	63 297	38 072	389 810
MONTANA	2 287	10 323	0.3	4 533	2 727	3 063	995	246	14 853	8 097	74 235
NEBRASKA	4 073	22 543	-1.7	9 368	7 918	5 257	2 391	543	17 364	13 422	146 272
NEVADA	3 571	27 234	15.0	10 557	12 199	4 478	2 584	702	18 740	17 002	135 207
NEW HAMPSHIRE	2 886	16 153	-3.5	5 849	6 420	3 884	1 574	458	8 045	4 705	83 485
NEW JERSEY	19 047	105 659	-0.4	35 166	50 036	20 457	11 204	3 003	60 515	25 495	561 152
NEW MEXICO	2 953	18 061	0.4	8 051	5 410	4 600	1 690	450	33 723	17 136	166 448
NEW YORK	42 575	249 391	-0.5	56 440	98 809	94 142	39 147	8 073	132 803	60 269	1 325 126
NORTH CAROLINA	14 105	85 304	3.4	34 948	32 550	17 806	9 362	2 217	72 114	144 911	645 100
NORTH DAKOTA	1 708	9 261	-5.4	2 869	3 190	3 202	746	199	10 192	11 661	62 879
OHIO	20 349	135 272	-8.6	48 306	57 766	29 200	13 048	3 464	84 802	35 838	714 091
OKLAHOMA	5 541	31 654	-2.5	12 605	12 458	6 591	3 318	759	50 496	39 571	289 575
OREGON	6 888	39 129	4.0	16 415	13 094	9 620	4 462	1 091	30 576	12 350	256 464
PENNSYLVANIA	25 316	154 379	0.2	51 384	62 406	40 589	17 622	3 933	109 752	36 594	679 011
RHODE ISLAND	2 382	14 379	-0.9	4 226	4 306	5 847	1 449	373	10 673	7 317	55 100
SOUTH CAROLINA	7 088	45 520	7.7	18 456	16 777	10 287	3 902	1 127	34 354	54 501	309 529
SOUTH DAKOTA	1 815	8 518	-2.7	3 471	2 725	2 322	750	182	11 963	8 774	64 878
TENNESSEE	8 811	62 425	6.7	23 758	26 667	12 000	6 339	1 681	52 747	23 586	381 235
TEXAS	34 462	253 503	2.5	116 002	93 700	43 801	25 779	6 994	210 413	183 641	1 619 231
UTAH	4 141	26 236	9.5	12 620	9 314	4 302	2 356	653	37 699	16 886	178 789
VERMONT	1 629	7 269	-1.7	2 306	2 133	2 830	799	183	6 810	4 318	46 243
VIRGINIA	15 072	111 129	1.3	34 685	41 436	35 008	16 498	3 915	191 129	152 451	534 989
WASHINGTON	12 324	71 213	3.7	27 026	27 518	16 669	8 921	2 030	75 691	81 698	474 632
WEST VIRGINIA	2 927	16 527	-4.0	6 735	5 647	4 145	1 550	388	24 416	9 997	127 448
WISCONSIN	10 724	66 392	-2.8	23 560	27 506	15 326	6 360	1 679	31 574	16 706	387 749
WYOMING	1 385	6 526	4.0	3 296	1 554	1 676	766	179	8 103	6 306	60 445

Table A. States — **Federal Funds**

STATE	Federal funds and grants, 2009–2010 (mil dol)											
			Procurement contract awards		Direct payments to individuals							
	Total	Salaries and wages	Defense	Other	Total	Social Security and government retirement	Medicare	Unemployment compensation	Food Stamps	Supplemental Security Income	Agricultural assistance	Housing assistance
	312	313	314	315	316	317	318	319	320	321	322	323
UNITED STATES	3 251 309	341 628	329 873	184 951	1 719 574	858 956	508 446	67 420	64 593	47 304	17 287	13 795
ALABAMA	56 496	5 613	8 140	2 342	31 128	16 937	8 286	533	1 226	1 040	241	331
ALASKA	12 615	4 055	1 776	688	2 631	1 531	349	228	159	59	19	21
ARIZONA	64 427	4 980	10 831	1 982	32 273	17 842	7 041	860	1 588	693	133	82
ARKANSAS	28 904	2 418	1 138	613	17 893	9 722	4 417	451	686	641	526	91
CALIFORNIA	333 809	24 585	41 323	16 214	172 819	78 068	56 261	10 191	5 694	6 775	795	1 114
COLORADO	49 687	8 519	5 632	4 735	22 008	12 450	4 655	1 084	688	389	291	155
CONNECTICUT	55 978	1 903	11 114	843	33 820	9 783	20 602	1 335	570	365	33	230
DELAWARE	8 076	708	218	145	4 951	2 957	1 150	168	171	98	67	50
DISTRICT OF COLUMBIA	61 920	23 030	4 651	16 599	6 769	2 624	1 280	197	196	163	54	115
FLORIDA	186 704	12 964	12 814	5 167	127 692	61 448	46 594	2 687	4 417	2 927	335	483
GEORGIA	92 387	17 372	8 378	4 083	45 804	24 719	10 240	1 365	2 565	1 341	395	417
HAWAII	20 855	7 898	2 351	394	7 187	4 218	1 489	328	358	150	15	45
IDAHO	14 252	1 245	265	2 368	7 393	4 391	1 320	306	300	167	267	28
ILLINOIS	109 967	7 949	7 119	4 482	66 357	32 013	19 805	3 605	2 784	1 831	855	740
INDIANA	58 603	4 360	4 370	1 128	36 780	18 937	8 988	1 217	1 291	745	458	288
IOWA	28 379	1 902	1 557	816	17 710	9 175	4 609	587	526	289	879	56
KANSAS	29 046	5 818	1 941	1 119	15 431	8 306	4 125	568	403	280	742	86
KENTUCKY	57 271	9 205	5 181	2 306	31 077	13 649	11 693	784	1 186	1 187	460	196
LOUISIANA	53 214	4 703	5 842	1 449	26 134	11 960	8 703	464	1 286	1 073	350	152
MAINE	14 644	1 134	1 336	400	7 987	4 679	1 837	233	356	213	102	74
MARYLAND	96 261	15 041	12 018	14 505	40 256	18 444	14 531	901	878	674	93	342
MASSACHUSETTS	82 454	4 506	12 674	3 314	39 808	17 313	13 691	2 309	1 172	1 099	40	852
MICHIGAN	90 921	4 798	4 080	2 386	59 079	30 769	17 108	2 571	2 809	1 635	302	333
MINNESOTA	44 376	3 368	1 520	1 430	27 529	13 727	7 575	1 435	632	546	693	193
MISSISSIPPI	31 419	3 017	1 634	1 032	17 865	9 042	4 606	259	847	742	517	106
MISSOURI	70 348	7 321	10 335	2 668	36 022	18 408	9 846	912	1 361	813	547	200
MONTANA	10 758	1 195	313	507	5 805	3 301	1 153	178	177	103	378	27
NEBRASKA	16 532	1 783	793	514	9 935	5 308	2 142	198	238	150	685	43
NEVADA	19 771	1 942	1 315	1 092	11 720	6 993	2 281	901	415	252	25	43
NEW HAMPSHIRE	11 335	880	1 092	343	6 709	4 199	1 478	196	152	105	45	73
NEW JERSEY	80 990	5 578	7 858	2 379	49 719	23 841	16 834	3 639	1 030	983	60	654
NEW MEXICO	27 959	2 768	1 520	5 979	10 972	6 261	2 011	457	642	368	74	36
NEW YORK	202 266	13 936	8 810	5 073	111 343	49 785	37 803	4 730	4 985	4 025	157	2 335
NORTH CAROLINA	90 737	15 349	3 627	2 464	49 198	28 314	10 371	2 289	2 072	1 297	754	304
NORTH DAKOTA	8 696	1 083	288	397	4 690	2 159	921	74	95	46	1 052	20
OHIO	106 449	6 975	6 064	2 765	66 245	33 289	20 460	2 517	2 737	1 850	357	736
OKLAHOMA	38 475	5 575	2 410	965	21 669	11 994	5 584	400	900	578	282	88
OREGON	33 974	2 569	891	1 156	20 664	11 620	4 615	1 240	1 073	458	211	85
PENNSYLVANIA	145 934	8 803	11 901	7 451	88 367	41 144	31 745	4 169	2 333	2 315	139	649
RHODE ISLAND	11 769	997	777	224	6 609	3 140	1 989	381	238	193	10	191
SOUTH CAROLINA	46 578	4 618	4 497	3 675	25 579	15 285	5 204	666	1 256	640	236	206
SOUTH DAKOTA	9 507	1 031	561	352	5 313	2 545	995	47	153	80	706	20
TENNESSEE	68 866	3 837	3 101	7 040	40 793	20 062	13 284	853	1 966	1 054	261	321
TEXAS	225 725	29 926	30 331	10 263	110 580	56 814	27 712	3 555	5 447	3 609	1 368	503
UTAH	23 545	3 195	2 522	1 237	11 606	5 855	3 539	378	368	171	41	19
VERMONT	7 405	724	711	220	3 369	1 929	757	151	128	78	40	30
VIRGINIA	136 083	21 112	40 378	17 960	44 405	27 413	8 408	815	1 213	891	216	264
WASHINGTON	70 437	11 539	5 151	4 890	34 133	19 564	6 976	2 086	1 387	919	539	166
WEST VIRGINIA	21 511	1 936	345	1 438	12 822	7 228	3 417	266	487	513	22	69
WISCONSIN	54 866	2 926	8 469	1 336	30 143	16 180	7 536	1 530	1 000	653	348	118
WYOMING	6 211	709	155	414	2 678	1 608	567	128	52	36	72	14

Table A. States — Federal Funds and State Government Finances

	Federal funds and grants, 2009–2010 (mil dol) (cont.)							State government finances, 2010							
	Grants							General revenue (mil dol)							
									From federal government		From own sources			Taxes per capita² (dollars)	
												Taxes			
STATE	Total¹	Medicaid and other health-related	Nutrition and family welfare	Disasters and emergency preparedness	Housing and community development	Employ-ment and training	Energy and environ-ment	Total	Total	Per capita² (dollars)	Total	Total	Sales and gross receipts	Total	Sales and gross receipts
	324	325	326	327	328	329	330	331	332	333	334	335	336	337	338
UNITED STATES	675 282	357 482	74 796	6 668	35 874	9 978	26 085	X	X	X	X	X	X	X	X
ALABAMA	9 273	4 947	949	47	382	138	370	22 990	9 370	1 960	13 620	8 186	4 234	1 713	886
ALASKA	3 465	1 066	283	16	174	56	260	11 036	2 962	4 170	8 074	4 518	258	6 361	363
ARIZONA	14 361	8 501	1 461	13	711	146	449	26 324	12 577	1 968	13 747	10 199	6 192	1 596	969
ARKANSAS	6 843	3 731	681	77	265	101	109	16 221	5 978	2 050	10 243	7 279	3 705	2 496	1 270
CALIFORNIA	78 869	41 931	11 744	149	4 891	1 300	2 723	196 643	67 805	1 820	128 838	104 841	38 578	2 814	1 036
COLORADO	8 793	3 665	968	8	400	130	569	19 931	6 371	1 267	13 560	8 586	3 516	1 707	699
CONNECTICUT	8 299	4 769	848	20	522	141	189	21 924	6 230	1 743	15 695	12 286	5 369	3 438	1 502
DELAWARE	2 055	983	207	8	78	28	105	7 234	2 035	2 266	5 199	2 770	463	3 085	516
DISTRICT OF COLUMBIA	10 872	2 283	378	17	343	226	866	X	X	X	X	X	X	X	X
FLORIDA	28 066	14 386	3 377	110	1 636	394	808	71 341	25 448	1 354	45 894	31 499	26 241	1 675	1 396
GEORGIA	16 751	8 037	2 202	100	937	217	368	36 480	16 193	1 672	20 286	14 783	6 516	1 526	673
HAWAII	3 026	1 233	331	6	170	50	141	9 627	2 592	1 905	7 035	4 838	3 044	3 556	2 238
IDAHO	2 980	1 473	283	9	71	68	199	6 727	2 673	1 705	4 054	2 952	1 507	1 883	961
ILLINOIS	24 060	12 148	2 914	260	1 735	405	770	55 674	19 346	1 508	36 329	27 512	14 901	2 144	1 161
INDIANA	11 965	6 229	1 305	25	634	226	611	29 802	10 401	1 604	19 401	13 796	8 490	2 128	1 309
IOWA	6 394	2 962	662	245	698	92	100	17 113	6 743	2 213	10 370	6 809	3 186	2 235	1 046
KANSAS	4 736	2 242	600	123	134	63	157	14 215	4 624	1 621	9 591	6 493	2 963	2 276	1 038
KENTUCKY	9 502	5 483	1 065	78	358	137	161	22 862	9 149	2 108	13 713	9 531	4 677	2 196	1 078
LOUISIANA	15 088	6 251	1 239	2 910	1 732	117	213	27 441	13 255	2 924	14 186	8 758	4 843	1 932	1 068
MAINE	3 787	2 187	340	6	152	58	251	8 248	3 213	2 419	5 035	3 490	1 667	2 627	1 255
MARYLAND	14 441	7 702	1 138	53	710	256	631	31 185	10 534	1 825	20 651	15 224	6 258	2 637	1 084
MASSACHUSETTS	22 352	14 088	1 527	87	1 329	215	867	42 209	13 326	2 035	28 883	20 050	6 774	3 062	1 035
MICHIGAN	20 577	11 166	2 753	7	938	542	1 032	52 667	19 528	1 976	33 140	22 206	12 435	2 247	1 258
MINNESOTA	10 528	6 007	1 249	26	437	187	224	31 462	10 025	1 890	21 438	17 209	7 883	3 245	1 486
MISSISSIPPI	7 871	4 460	857	186	233	96	259	17 427	8 808	2 968	8 619	6 269	4 075	2 113	1 373
MISSOURI	14 003	7 869	1 213	87	520	199	969	26 112	11 798	1 970	14 313	9 708	4 529	1 621	756
MONTANA	2 939	1 080	272	7	96	54	254	6 009	2 505	2 531	3 504	2 143	532	2 166	538
NEBRASKA	3 507	1 703	412	38	120	51	132	8 676	3 203	1 754	5 473	3 809	1 898	2 086	1 039
NEVADA	3 702	1 312	424	4	225	92	446	9 937	2 917	1 080	7 020	5 836	4 275	2 161	1 583
NEW HAMPSHIRE	2 311	1 133	210	14	121	43	102	6 222	2 361	1 793	3 861	2 125	802	1 614	609
NEW JERSEY	15 457	8 132	1 858	131	1 042	273	572	51 183	15 477	1 760	35 706	25 928	11 307	2 949	1 286
NEW MEXICO	6 720	3 713	586	4	160	60	251	14 011	6 247	3 034	7 763	4 414	2 338	2 144	1 135
NEW YORK	63 104	39 959	6 704	144	3 570	553	1 202	139 966	55 726	2 876	84 240	63 529	20 912	3 278	1 079
NORTH CAROLINA	20 099	11 595	2 009	25	645	303	976	44 058	15 699	1 646	28 359	21 517	9 434	2 257	989
NORTH DAKOTA	2 237	630	203	141	75	24	280	5 415	1 742	2 590	3 673	2 646	949	3 934	1 411
OHIO	24 399	13 660	3 021	16	1 216	405	848	57 508	22 462	1 947	35 046	23 584	12 245	2 044	1 061
OKLAHOMA	7 855	3 961	1 024	118	353	91	302	19 486	8 007	2 134	11 479	7 080	2 953	1 887	787
OREGON	8 694	4 360	926	49	346	207	457	19 001	6 858	1 790	12 143	7 289	957	1 903	250
PENNSYLVANIA	29 411	16 147	2 977	32	1 242	427	1 337	63 884	21 339	1 680	42 545	30 169	15 465	2 375	1 217
RHODE ISLAND	3 152	1 753	292	53	144	55	58	7 088	2 967	2 819	4 121	2 569	1 405	2 441	1 335
SOUTH CAROLINA	8 210	4 833	854	8	250	144	157	21 512	7 934	1 715	13 578	7 313	4 017	1 581	869
SOUTH DAKOTA	2 250	762	216	56	89	34	233	3 974	1 794	2 204	2 180	1 304	1 072	1 602	1 317
TENNESSEE	14 094	8 036	1 361	200	545	150	286	25 517	11 371	1 792	14 146	10 514	8 028	1 657	1 265
TEXAS	44 624	23 604	5 505	534	3 383	492	1 098	99 924	41 450	1 648	58 474	39 399	31 119	1 567	1 238
UTAH	4 987	2 084	491	11	123	76	654	13 228	4 374	1 583	8 854	5 092	2 263	1 842	819
VERMONT	2 380	1 088	192	0	72	35	161	5 331	1 905	3 044	3 426	2 511	845	4 013	1 351
VIRGINIA	12 228	5 484	1 143	277	593	274	427	37 103	9 780	1 222	27 323	16 411	5 872	2 051	734
WASHINGTON	14 725	7 161	1 608	46	656	259	1 130	33 711	11 176	1 662	22 534	16 106	12 849	2 395	1 911
WEST VIRGINIA	4 970	2 463	511	32	132	53	422	11 561	4 426	2 389	7 135	4 655	2 219	2 512	1 198
WISCONSIN	11 992	6 592	1 312	56	461	210	655	30 845	10 403	1 829	20 442	14 369	6 687	2 527	1 176
WYOMING	2 254	442	115	1	28	25	242	5 586	2 457	4 359	3 129	2 117	874	3 756	1 551

1. Includes program categories not shown separately.   2. Based on resident population counted in the 2010 census.

Table A. States — State Government Finances and Voting

STATE	\multicolumn{10}{c}{State government finances, 2010 (cont.)}									Voting and registration, November 2008		Presidential election,[2] 2008 (percent of vote cast)		
	\multicolumn{10}{c}{General expenditures (mil dol)}									Debt outstanding						
			Direct general expenditures		\multicolumn{6}{c}{By selected function}										
	Total	To local govern-ments	Total	Per capita[1] (dollars)	Educa-tion	Health and hospitals	High-ways	Public safety	Public welfare	Natural resources, parks, and recreation	Total (mil dol)	Per capita[1]	Percent registered	Percent voted	Demo-cratic	Repub-lican	All other
	339	340	341	342	343	344	345	346	347	348	349	350	351	352	353	354	355
UNITED STATES	X	X	X	X	X	X	X	X	X	X	X	X	64.9	58.2	52.9	45.7	1.4
ALABAMA	24 016	6 604	17 412	3 643	10 555	2 652	1 515	740	6 033	372	8 785	1 838	69.7	60.8	38.7	60.3	0.9
ALASKA	9 733	1 655	8 077	11 373	2 304	355	1 447	369	1 800	442	6 381	8 984	70.8	62.4	38.0	59.8	2.2
ARIZONA	27 982	9 180	18 803	2 942	8 807	1 996	2 117	1 301	9 212	357	13 956	2 183	61.3	53.3	45.1	53.6	1.2
ARKANSAS	15 150	4 792	10 358	3 552	6 702	1 015	945	332	4 212	302	4 261	1 461	62.5	51.8	38.9	58.7	2.4
CALIFORNIA	210 359	90 518	119 842	3 217	70 304	18 288	13 327	9 580	63 849	4 580	148 929	3 998	55.1	51.2	61.0	37.0	2.0
COLORADO	21 818	7 178	14 640	2 911	9 091	1 776	1 381	1 117	5 079	431	16 710	3 323	66.0	62.5	53.7	44.7	1.6
CONNECTICUT	21 600	4 877	16 723	4 679	6 624	2 340	1 085	891	6 030	181	30 216	8 454	66.4	60.8	60.7	38.1	1.1
DELAWARE	6 917	1 236	5 682	6 327	2 432	452	522	367	1 657	124	5 515	6 142	69.1	63.0	61.9	36.9	1.1
DISTRICT OF COLUMBIA	X	X	X	X	X	X	X	X	X	X	X	0	69.0	65.3	92.5	6.5	1.0
FLORIDA	68 482	18 478	50 004	2 660	23 044	4 568	5 382	2 945	20 880	1 408	40 404	2 149	62.4	56.5	51.0	48.2	0.8
GEORGIA	36 710	10 748	25 963	2 680	16 985	1 927	2 175	1 736	9 886	648	13 789	1 423	65.9	59.6	47.0	52.2	0.8
HAWAII	9 710	157	9 553	7 023	3 254	1 156	469	241	1 961	196	7 701	5 661	53.5	46.8	71.8	26.6	1.6
IDAHO	7 119	2 023	5 096	3 251	2 761	234	814	276	1 785	232	3 872	2 470	66.0	58.8	36.1	61.5	2.4
ILLINOIS	59 248	15 383	43 865	3 419	17 283	3 579	5 957	1 741	18 858	540	61 412	4 786	64.6	57.1	61.9	36.8	1.3
INDIANA	30 503	9 705	20 798	3 208	14 215	748	2 657	914	7 997	385	23 635	3 645	66.3	58.8	49.9	48.9	1.1
IOWA	16 306	4 528	11 778	3 866	5 947	1 349	1 797	378	4 662	334	5 140	1 687	72.6	66.9	53.9	44.4	1.7
KANSAS	14 176	4 177	9 999	3 504	5 918	1 309	1 177	451	3 342	242	6 478	2 271	65.9	59.8	41.7	56.6	1.7
KENTUCKY	24 193	5 079	19 114	4 405	9 326	1 910	1 972	702	7 191	448	14 393	3 317	71.1	61.4	41.2	57.4	1.4
LOUISIANA	29 561	6 658	22 903	5 052	9 061	2 926	2 065	1 131	6 436	1 059	17 443	3 848	75.7	68.0	39.9	58.6	1.5
MAINE	7 930	1 338	6 591	4 962	2 097	529	588	224	2 908	183	6 034	4 543	78.5	70.2	57.7	40.4	1.9
MARYLAND	32 110	8 593	23 517	4 073	11 686	2 398	2 193	1 858	8 772	650	24 475	4 239	67.0	61.9	61.9	36.5	1.6
MASSACHUSETTS	41 784	9 108	32 677	4 991	11 879	1 542	1 949	1 828	13 772	597	73 940	11 293	66.4	61.3	62.0	36.2	1.7
MICHIGAN	51 510	19 410	32 100	3 248	22 777	3 596	2 644	1 990	14 470	399	32 146	3 252	73.9	65.0	57.4	41.0	1.6
MINNESOTA	31 642	10 428	21 214	4 000	11 744	880	2 366	878	10 727	780	11 683	2 203	75.2	70.8	54.1	43.8	2.1
MISSISSIPPI	17 500	5 272	12 228	4 121	5 582	1 489	1 408	469	5 182	319	6 468	2 180	75.3	68.2	43.0	56.2	0.8
MISSOURI	25 795	6 228	19 567	3 267	8 950	2 847	2 326	934	7 313	406	20 421	3 410	72.8	64.2	49.3	49.4	1.3
MONTANA	6 005	1 334	4 670	4 720	1 824	214	734	232	1 306	253	4 374	4 421	70.6	64.7	47.3	49.5	3.2
NEBRASKA	8 816	2 192	6 623	3 627	3 268	701	663	327	2 281	294	2 330	1 276	71.8	64.5	41.6	56.5	1.9
NEVADA	9 478	3 704	5 775	2 138	4 032	459	707	392	1 943	137	4 436	1 643	59.0	62.8	55.1	42.7	2.2
NEW HAMPSHIRE	6 351	1 261	5 089	3 866	2 003	143	561	174	1 909	87	8 347	6 341	74.5	69.8	54.1	44.5	1.4
NEW JERSEY	49 249	11 941	37 308	4 243	16 526	3 600	2 905	2 029	13 806	1 067	60 958	6 933	62.0	56.0	57.3	41.7	1.0
NEW MEXICO	15 890	4 309	11 582	5 624	5 519	1 454	882	563	4 391	288	8 740	4 244	63.6	57.4	56.9	41.8	1.3
NEW YORK	137 997	54 318	83 678	4 318	39 108	14 657	4 645	4 301	49 596	1 094	129 530	6 684	57.7	51.5	60.8	31.7	7.5
NORTH CAROLINA	43 014	13 430	29 584	3 103	18 645	3 236	3 045	1 957	11 417	813	18 853	1 977	71.6	63.8	49.7	49.4	0.9
NORTH DAKOTA	4 688	1 246	3 443	5 119	1 765	191	595	100	829	264	2 198	3 268	82.3	66.3	44.6	53.3	2.1
OHIO	57 371	18 374	38 997	3 380	22 052	4 882	3 259	1 891	16 882	525	31 177	2 702	71.9	64.5	51.5	46.9	1.6
OKLAHOMA	19 233	4 546	14 687	3 915	7 762	1 020	1 921	763	5 412	341	9 963	2 656	67.4	56.5	34.4	65.6	0.0
OREGON	20 560	5 865	14 695	3 836	7 342	1 936	1 759	925	5 424	496	13 510	3 526	67.5	62.6	56.7	40.4	2.9
PENNSYLVANIA	69 402	18 615	50 786	3 998	21 358	6 016	7 434	2 753	21 610	944	44 738	3 522	68.3	60.8	54.7	44.3	1.0
RHODE ISLAND	6 352	1 124	5 228	4 967	1 768	248	294	252	2 330	47	9 498	9 024	70.6	63.0	63.1}	35.2}	1.6
SOUTH CAROLINA	22 810	5 370	17 440	3 771	7 776	2 458	1 250	634	6 083	327	15 771	3 410	72.0	63.4	44.9	53.9	1.2
SOUTH DAKOTA	3 988	737	3 251	3 993	1 303	198	531	144	978	197	3 483	4 278	74.9	66.1	44.7	53.2	2.1
TENNESSEE	26 324	6 665	19 660	3 098	8 974	1 602	1 595	968	10 039	359	5 835	919	62.3	53.6	41.8	56.9	1.3
TEXAS	102 373	27 461	74 911	2 979	46 705	6 800	5 831	4 511	29 017	1 082	42 034	1 672	58.5	48.8	43.7	55.5	0.9
UTAH	14 183	3 028	11 155	4 036	6 124	1 326	1 596	434	2 681	210	6 478	2 344	56.8	50.5	34.4	62.6	3.0
VERMONT	5 172	1 518	3 654	5 839	2 300	177	387	200	1 405	83	3 493	5 582	70.9	63.2	67.5	30.4	2.1
VIRGINIA	38 154	10 959	27 195	3 399	14 023	4 175	2 780	2 142	8 727	347	24 967	3 120	69.1	63.8	52.6	46.3	1.0
WASHINGTON	36 469	9 798	26 671	3 966	14 818	3 626	3 147	1 379	8 547	920	27 478	4 086	67.2	62.6	57.7	40.5	1.9
WEST VIRGINIA	10 767	2 383	8 385	4 525	3 932	413	1 157	344	3 043	300	7 144	3 856	65.7	53.1	42.6	55.7	1.7
WISCONSIN	31 678	10 253	21 425	3 767	11 092	1 925	2 317	1 267	8 326	718	22 319	3 924	73.5	68.5	56.2	42.3	1.5
WYOMING	4 957	1 761	3 196	5 670	1 614	296	571	190	734	446	1 514	2 687	67.9	62.9	32.5	64.8	2.7

1. Based on resident population counted in the 2010 census.   2. © 2009 Election Data Services, Inc. All rights reserved.

States and Counties

(For explanation of symbols, see page viii)

Part B—States and Counties

County Highlights and Rankings

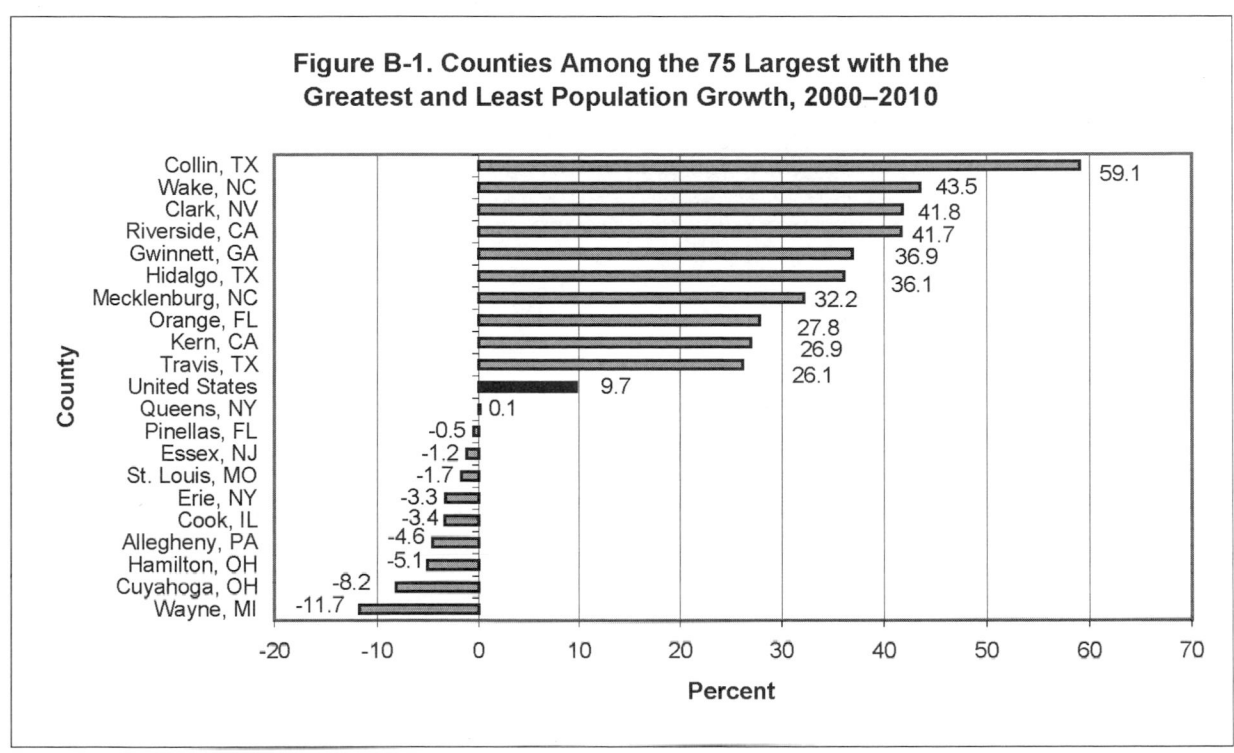

Figure B-1. Counties Among the 75 Largest with the Greatest and Least Population Growth, 2000–2010

County	Percent
Collin, TX	59.1
Wake, NC	43.5
Clark, NV	41.8
Riverside, CA	41.7
Gwinnett, GA	36.9
Hidalgo, TX	36.1
Mecklenburg, NC	32.2
Orange, FL	27.8
Kern, CA	26.9
Travis, TX	26.1
United States	9.7
Queens, NY	0.1
Pinellas, FL	-0.5
Essex, NJ	-1.2
St. Louis, MO	-1.7
Erie, NY	-3.3
Cook, IL	-3.4
Allegheny, PA	-4.6
Hamilton, OH	-5.1
Cuyahoga, OH	-8.2
Wayne, MI	-11.7

While all the results from the 2010 Census have not been released yet, most of the basic information for counties is available. Los Angeles County, CA, remains, by far, the most populous county, with 9.8 million residents. Next is Cook County, IL, which includes Chicago, with nearly 5.2 million people, though its population has declined 3.4 percent from 2000 to 2010. Among the 75 most populous counties, the highest growth rates from 2000 to 2010 were found in the West and the South. Since 2000, the fastest-growing of these large counties was Collin County, TX, in the Dallas-Fort Worth metropolitan area. During the decade, Collin County's population increased by 59.1 percent, bringing it into the 75 most populous counties for the first time in 2008. Wake County, NC (Raleigh); Clark County, NV (Las Vegas); and Riverside County, CA, each had population growth rates exceeding 40 percent while Gwinnett County, GA (Atlanta) and Hidalgo County, TX (at the Mexican border) both had population growth rates over 35 percent. Nearly 1,100 counties lost population during this period. The largest proportional losses were in counties with very small populations, but several Louisiana parishes experienced large out-migrations after Hurricane Katrina. Among the largest counties, those that lost populations were generally located in the Northeast and the Midwest. In addition to Orleans Parish, Cook County, IL (Chicago), Cuyahoga County, OH (Cleveland), and Wayne County, MI (Detroit) each lost more than 100,000 residents between 2000 and 2010. Maricopa County, AZ (Phoenix), gained approximately 745,000 residents, ranking as the fourth most populous in 2010. Thirty-five counties had population growth

rates at or above 50 percent from 2000 to 2010. All except five of these fast-growing counties had more than 50,000 residents, and most of them had more than 100,000.

Within states, the number and physical size of counties varied considerably: Delaware had 3 counties while Texas had 254 counties. For the 3,143 counties (and county equivalents—see Appendix A) in the United States, population in 2010 ranged from 9.8 million in Los Angeles, CA, to 82 in Loving County, TX. Other particularly large counties in terms of population are Cook County, IL (nearly 5.2 million people), encompassing Chicago and its suburbs, Harris County, TX (containing Houston) with 4.1 million people, and Maricopa County, AZ (containing Phoenix), with over 3.8 million people. There were 39 counties with a population of 1,000,000 or more; these counties combined contain more than one-fourth of the U.S. population. Over half of the U.S. population lived in the 167 largest counties, those with a population of 400,000 or more. At the other extreme, there were 35 counties with fewer than 1,000 people in 2010. The median county population size was 25,857.

In terms of land area, counties range from the nearly 377,000 square kilometers of Yukon-Koyukuk Census Area, AK; to Kalawao County, HI, with 31 square kilometers; New York County, NY (Manhattan), with 59 square kilometers; Bristol County, RI, with 63 square kilometers; and Arlington County, VA, with 67 square kilometers.[1] Counties tend to be larger in the western United States (most of the largest 50 in size are in that region). The median land area for all U.S. counties was about 1,600 square kilometers in 2010.

---

[1]Several independent cities in Virginia, which are treated as counties for tabulation purposes, were excluded here.

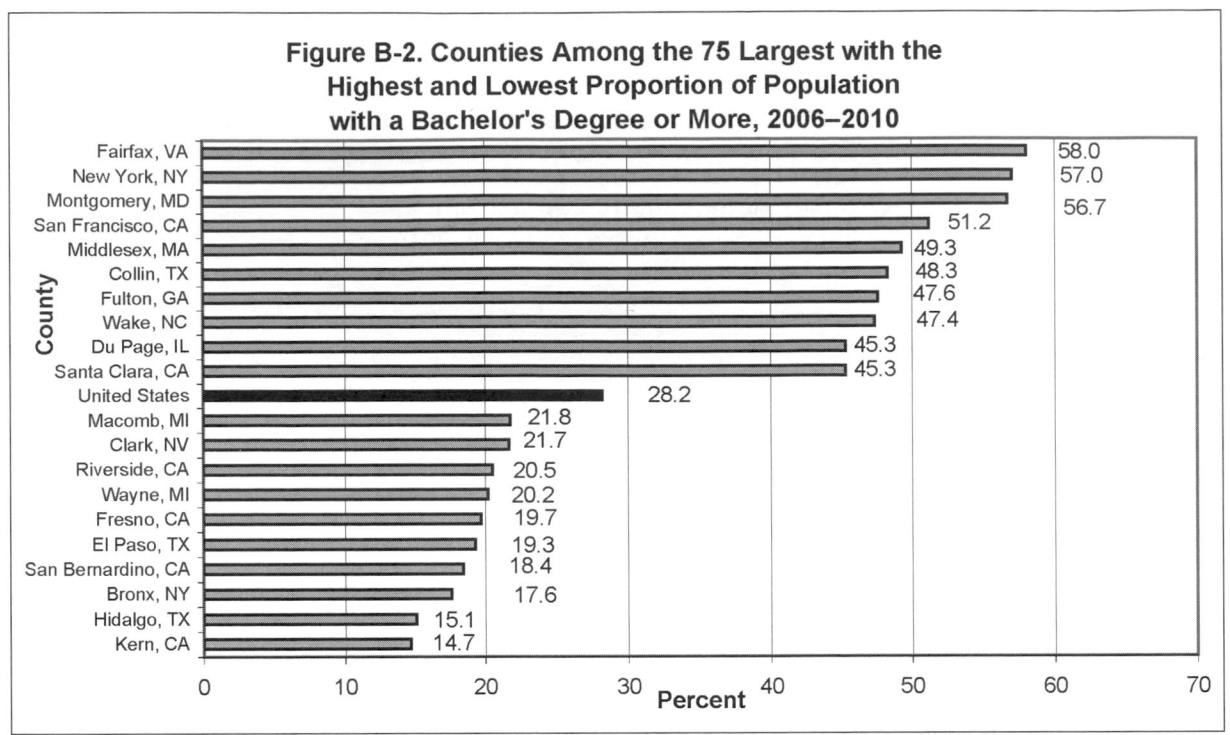

Figure B-2. Counties Among the 75 Largest with the Highest and Lowest Proportion of Population with a Bachelor's Degree or More, 2006–2010

County	Percent
Fairfax, VA	58.0
New York, NY	57.0
Montgomery, MD	56.7
San Francisco, CA	51.2
Middlesex, MA	49.3
Collin, TX	48.3
Fulton, GA	47.6
Wake, NC	47.4
Du Page, IL	45.3
Santa Clara, CA	45.3
United States	28.2
Macomb, MI	21.8
Clark, NV	21.7
Riverside, CA	20.5
Wayne, MI	20.2
Fresno, CA	19.7
El Paso, TX	19.3
San Bernardino, CA	18.4
Bronx, NY	17.6
Hidalgo, TX	15.1
Kern, CA	14.7

While New York County, NY, had one of the smallest land areas, it had by far the highest population density among U.S. counties in 2010, with nearly 27,000 persons per square kilometer. No other county approached that density (although three other New York City boroughs were among the top five counties in population density). San Francisco had the highest population density outside of New York City, with Suffolk County, MA (Boston); Philadelphia County, PA; and Washington, DC, also among the top 10 counties. The median county only had about 17 persons per square kilometer, with only 113 counties having more than 500 persons per square kilometer. The nation's largest county in terms of population (Los Angeles) had a population density of 934.2 persons per square kilometer. This density ranked 20th among the 75 most populous U.S. counties.

Proportionally large year-to-year labor force changes are not unusual for counties with small populations. The 2010 annual averages reflect a national labor force that declined by 0.2 percent. Among the 75 most populous counties, 33 counties' labor forces grew by 0.1 percent or more between 2009 and 2010. El Paso County, TX, Hidalgo County, TX, and Miami-Dade, FL were the only counties among the top 75 most populous that experienced increases in their labor forces of over 3 percent. Four counties experienced increases of between 2.0 and 2.9 percent. Over 1,700 counties experienced declines in their labor forces from 2009 to 2010, with 87 counties losing 5 percent or more. Among the most populous 75 counties, 39 counties had decreases in their labor forces, led by Macomb, MI at 2.3 percent.

The national annual average unemployment rate was 9.6 percent in 2010 up from 9.3 in 2009 and much higher than the unemployment rate of 5.8 percent in 2008. Over 1,300 counties had unemployment rates above the national average

of 9.6 percent in 2010 and over 1,100 counties had unemployment rates greater than 10 percent, up from 1,000 counties in 2009 and only 125 counties in 2008. Of the 10 counties with the highest unemployment rates, only Imperial County, CA, and Yuma County, AZ, had populations over 100,000. Among the 75 most populous counties, 35 exceeded the national unemployment rate of 9.6 percent. Unemployment exceeded 15 percent in three of these large counties, all of them in California and Nevada. Fairfax County, VA, had the lowest unemployment rate at 4.9 percent folllowed by Montgomery County, MD and Honolulu County, HI, at 5.6 percent. In 2009 and 2010, these three counties were the only large counties with unemployment rates below 6 percent, a level held by 43 large counties in 2008.

Among the 75 largest counties, the two with the highest unemployment rates, Fresno and Kern counties in CA, ranked among the top counties for agricultural sales. Meanwhile, two of the seven highest unemployment rates were in counties that topped the rankings for manufacturing employment (Macomb and Wayne counties in MI). Two of the lowest unemployment rates were in the two counties that topped the rankings for employment in professional, scientific, and technical occupations (Fairfax County, VA and Montgomery County, MD.) These two counties were also at the top of the rankings for median household income and educational attainment, with more than 56 percent of residents holding bachelor's, master's, doctoral or professional degrees. Six large counties had college-educated proportions of less than 20 percent, and 4 out of the 6 were among the ten counties with the highest unemployment rates. Nationally, 28.2 percent of the population held bachelor's degrees or higher in 2010.

75 Largest Counties by 2010 Population
Selected Rankings

Population, 2010			Land area, 2010				Population density, 2010			
Popu-lation rank	County	Population [col 2]	Popu-lation rank	Land area rank	County	Land area (Square kilometers) [col 1]	Popu-lation rank	Density rank	County	Density (per square kilometer) [col 4]
1	Los Angeles, CA	9 818 605	12	1	San Bernardino, CA	51 947	20	1	New York, NY	26 879.2
2	Cook, IL	5 194 675	4	2	Maricopa, AZ	23 828	7	2	Kings, NY	13 686.9
3	Harris, TX	4 092 459	41	3	Pima, AZ	23 794	26	3	Bronx, NY	12 707.4
4	Maricopa, AZ	3 817 117	62	4	Kern, CA	21 062	10	4	Queens, NY	7 938.5
5	San Diego, CA	3 095 313	13	5	Clark, NV	20 439	66	5	San Francisco, CA	6 654.8
6	Orange, CA	3 010 232	11	6	Riverside, CA	18 665	21	6	Philadelphia, PA	4 397.7
7	Kings, NY	2 504 700	46	7	Fresno, CA	15 431	73	7	Essex, NJ	2 397.5
8	Miami-Dade, FL	2 496 435	5	8	San Diego, CA	10 895	2	8	Cook, IL	2 122.0
9	Dallas, TX	2 368 139	1	9	Los Angeles, CA	10 510	27	9	Nassau, NY	1 817.5
10	Queens, NY	2 230 722	14	10	King, WA	5 479	45	10	Milwaukee, WI	1 516.4
11	Riverside, CA	2 189 641	28	11	Palm Beach, FL	5 102	54	11	Bergen, NJ	1 501.0
12	San Bernardino, CA	2 035 210	8	12	Miami-Dade, FL	4 915	6	12	Orange, CA	1 469.8
13	Clark, NV	1 951 269	63	13	Ventura, CA	4 774	53	13	Pinellas, FL	1 292.7
14	King, WA	1 931 249	3	14	Harris, TX	4 412	15	14	Wayne, MI	1 148.6
15	Wayne, MI	1 820 584	72	15	Pierce, WA	4 324	51	15	Du Page, IL	1 081.3
16	Tarrant, TX	1 809 034	75	16	Hidalgo, TX	4 069	29	16	Cuyahoga, OH	1 081.2
17	Santa Clara, CA	1 781 642	71	17	Worcester, MA	3 913	36	17	Fairfax, VA	1 067.8
18	Broward, FL	1 748 066	17	18	Santa Clara, CA	3 341	9	18	Dallas, TX	1 049.2
19	Bexar, TX	1 714 773	19	19	Bexar, TX	3 211	64	19	Middlesex, NJ	1 012.3
20	New York, NY	1 585 873	18	20	Broward, FL	3 133	1	20	Los Angeles, CA	934.2
21	Philadelphia, PA	1 526 006	50	21	Erie, NY	2 701	3	21	Harris, TX	927.6
22	Alameda, CA	1 510 271	30	22	Hillsborough, FL	2 642	55	22	Marion, IN	880.5
23	Middlesex, MA	1 503 085	69	23	El Paso, TX	2 623	44	23	Westchester, NY	851.2
24	Suffolk, NY	1 493 350	39	24	Travis, TX	2 565	33	24	Franklin, OH	844.3
25	Sacramento, CA	1 418 788	25	25	Sacramento, CA	2 498	16	25	Tarrant, TX	808.7
26	Bronx, NY	1 385 108	2	26	Cook, IL	2 448	34	26	Hennepin, MN	803.6
27	Nassau, NY	1 339 532	24	27	Suffolk, NY	2 362	22	27	Alameda, CA	789.1
28	Palm Beach, FL	1 320 134	35	28	Orange, FL	2 340	42	28	Montgomery, MD	764.0
29	Cuyahoga, OH	1 280 122	9	29	Dallas, TX	2 257	68	29	Hamilton, OH	763.4
30	Hillsborough, FL	1 229 226	32	30	Oakland, MI	2 247	40	30	St. Louis, MO	759.7
31	Allegheny, PA	1 223 348	16	31	Tarrant, TX	2 237	65	31	Gwinnett, GA	722.3
32	Oakland, MI	1 202 362	74	32	Collin, TX	2 179	23	32	Middlesex, MA	709.7
33	Franklin, OH	1 163 414	56	33	Wake, NC	2 163	59	33	Prince George's, MD	690.7
34	Hennepin, MN	1 152 425	23	34	Middlesex, MA	2 118	49	34	Mecklenburg, NC	677.7
35	Orange, FL	1 145 956	6	35	Orange, CA	2 048	61	34	Macomb, MI	677.7
36	Fairfax, VA	1 081 726	47	36	Shelby, TN	1 977	48	36	Fulton, GA	674.9
37	Contra Costa, CA	1 049 025	58	37	Duval, FL	1 974	31	37	Allegheny, PA	646.9
38	Salt Lake, UT	1 029 655	38	38	Salt Lake, UT	1 923	70	38	Montgomery, PA	639.4
39	Travis, TX	1 024 266	22	39	Alameda, CA	1 914	24	39	Suffolk, NY	632.2
40	St. Louis, MO	998 954	57	40	Hartford, CT	1 904	43	40	Honolulu, HI	612.6
41	Pima, AZ	980 263	31	41	Allegheny, PA	1 891	25	41	Sacramento, CA	568.0
42	Montgomery, MD	971 777	37	42	Contra Costa, CA	1 854	52	42	Fairfield, CT	566.8
43	Honolulu, HI	953 207	52	43	Fairfield, CT	1 618	37	43	Contra Costa, CA	565.8
44	Westchester, NY	949 113	15	44	Wayne, MI	1 585	18	44	Broward, FL	558.0
45	Milwaukee, WI	947 735	60	45	New Haven, CT	1 566	60	45	New Haven, CT	550.8
46	Fresno, CA	930 450	43	46	Honolulu, HI	1 556	38	46	Salt Lake, UT	535.4
47	Shelby, TN	927 644	67	47	Baltimore, MD	1 550	32	47	Oakland, MI	535.1
48	Fulton, GA	920 581	34	48	Hennepin, MN	1 434	19	48	Bexar, TX	534.0
49	Mecklenburg, NC	919 628	33	49	Franklin, OH	1 378	17	49	Santa Clara, CA	533.3
50	Erie, NY	919 040	48	50	Fulton, GA	1 364	67	50	Baltimore, MD	519.4
51	Du Page, IL	916 924	49	51	Mecklenburg, NC	1 357	8	51	Miami-Dade, FL	507.9
52	Fairfield, CT	916 829	40	52	St. Louis, MO	1 315	35	52	Orange, FL	489.7
53	Pinellas, FL	916 542	42	53	Montgomery, MD	1 272	57	53	Hartford, CT	469.5
54	Bergen, NJ	905 116	70	54	Montgomery, PA	1 251	47	54	Shelby, TN	469.2
55	Marion, IN	903 393	59	55	Prince George's, MD	1 250	30	55	Hillsborough, FL	465.3
56	Wake, NC	900 993	61	56	Macomb, MI	1 241	58	56	Duval, FL	437.8
57	Hartford, CT	894 014	29	57	Cuyahoga, OH	1 184	56	57	Wake, NC	416.5
58	Duval, FL	864 263	44	58	Westchester, NY	1 115	39	58	Travis, TX	399.3
59	Prince George's, MD	863 420	65	58	Gwinnett, GA	1 115	74	59	Collin, TX	359.0
60	New Haven, CT	862 477	68	60	Hamilton, OH	1 051	14	60	King, WA	352.5
61	Macomb, MI	840 978	55	61	Marion, IN	1 026	50	61	Erie, NY	340.3
62	Kern, CA	839 631	36	62	Fairfax, VA	1 013	69	62	El Paso, TX	305.2
63	Ventura, CA	823 318	51	63	Du Page, IL	848	5	63	San Diego, CA	284.1
64	Middlesex, NJ	809 858	64	64	Middlesex, NJ	800	28	64	Palm Beach, FL	258.7
65	Gwinnett, GA	805 321	27	65	Nassau, NY	737	71	65	Worcester, MA	204.1
66	San Francisco, CA	805 235	53	66	Pinellas, FL	709	75	66	Hidalgo, TX	190.4
67	Baltimore, MD	805 029	45	67	Milwaukee, WI	625	72	67	Pierce, WA	183.9
68	Hamilton, OH	802 374	54	68	Bergen, NJ	603	63	68	Ventura, CA	172.5
69	El Paso, TX	800 647	21	69	Philadelphia, PA	347	4	69	Maricopa, AZ	160.2
70	Montgomery, PA	799 874	73	70	Essex, NJ	327	11	70	Riverside, CA	117.3
71	Worcester, MA	798 552	10	71	Queens, NY	281	13	71	Clark, NV	95.5
72	Pierce, WA	795 225	7	72	Kings, NY	183	46	72	Fresno, CA	60.3
73	Essex, NJ	783 969	66	73	San Francisco, CA	121	41	73	Pima, AZ	41.2
74	Collin, TX	782 341	26	74	Bronx, NY	109	62	74	Kern, CA	39.9
75	Hidalgo, TX	774 769	20	75	New York, NY	59	12	75	San Bernardino, CA	39.2

75 Largest Counties by 2010 Population
Selected Rankings

Percent population change, 2000–2010				Employment/residence ratio, 2006–2010				Percent White, not Hispanic or Latino, alone or in combination, 2010			
Population rank	Percent change rank	County	Percent change [col 23]	Population rank	Number of employees per resident rank	County	Number of employees per resident [col 34]	Population rank	White rank	County	Percent white [col 5]
74	1	Collin, TX	59.1	20	1	New York, NY	2.8	61	1	Macomb, MI	85.6
56	2	Wake, NC	43.5	48	2	Fulton, GA	1.9	71	2	Worcester, MA	82.2
13	3	Clark, NV	41.8	34	3	Hennepin, MN	1.4	31	3	Allegheny, PA	82.1
11	4	Riverside, CA	41.7	66	3	San Francisco, CA	1.4	70	4	Montgomery, PA	80.3
65	5	Gwinnett, GA	36.9	9	5	Dallas, TX	1.3	50	5	Erie, NY	79.0
75	6	Hidalgo, TX	36.1	35	5	Orange, FL	1.3	23	6	Middlesex, MA	78.3
49	7	Mecklenburg, NC	32.2	49	5	Mecklenburg, NC	1.3	53	6	Pinellas, FL	78.3
35	8	Orange, FL	27.8	55	5	Marion, IN	1.3	32	8	Oakland, MI	76.8
62	9	Kern, CA	26.9	68	5	Hamilton, OH	1.3	38	9	Salt Lake, UT	75.7
39	10	Travis, TX	26.1	3	10	Harris, TX	1.2	72	10	Pierce, WA	75.2
16	11	Tarrant, TX	25.1	14	10	King, WA	1.2	34	11	Hennepin, MN	74.0
4	12	Maricopa, AZ	24.2	21	10	Philadelphia, PA	1.2	24	12	Suffolk, NY	72.6
19	13	Bexar, TX	23.1	29	10	Cuyahoga, OH	1.2	51	13	Du Page, IL	71.7
30	13	Hillsborough, FL	23.1	31	10	Allegheny, PA	1.2	40	14	St. Louis, MO	70.3
3	15	Harris, TX	20.3	32	10	Oakland, MI	1.2	33	15	Franklin, OH	69.5
12	16	San Bernardino, CA	19.1	33	10	Franklin, OH	1.2	68	16	Hamilton, OH	69.2
69	17	El Paso, TX	17.8	39	10	Travis, TX	1.2	60	17	New Haven, CT	68.9
28	18	Palm Beach, FL	16.7	40	10	St. Louis, MO	1.2	14	18	King, WA	68.3
46	19	Fresno, CA	16.4	47	10	Shelby, TN	1.2	52	19	Fairfield, CT	67.4
41	20	Pima, AZ	16.2	51	10	Du Page, IL	1.2	57	19	Hartford, CT	67.4
25	21	Sacramento, CA	16.0	57	10	Hartford, CT	1.2	27	21	Nassau, NY	66.4
38	22	Salt Lake, UT	14.6	58	10	Duval, FL	1.2	74	22	Collin, TX	64.9
72	23	Pierce, WA	13.5	70	10	Montgomery, PA	1.2	67	23	Baltimore, MD	64.3
48	24	Fulton, GA	12.8	2	24	Cook, IL	1.1	56	24	Wake, NC	63.7
36	25	Fairfax, VA	11.5	6	24	Orange, CA	1.1	54	25	Bergen, NJ	63.6
42	26	Montgomery, MD	11.3	8	24	Miami-Dade, FL	1.1	29	26	Cuyahoga, OH	62.8
14	27	King, WA	11.2	15	24	Wayne, MI	1.1	55	27	Marion, IN	61.5
58	28	Duval, FL	11.0	17	24	Santa Clara, CA	1.1	28	28	Palm Beach, FL	61.1
8	29	Miami-Dade, FL	10.8	19	24	Bexar, TX	1.1	4	29	Maricopa, AZ	60.3
37	30	Contra Costa, CA	10.6	23	24	Middlesex, MA	1.1	44	30	Westchester, NY	58.5
5	31	San Diego, CA	10.0	30	24	Hillsborough, FL	1.1	58	31	Duval, FL	58.4
63	32	Ventura, CA	9.3	38	24	Salt Lake, UT	1.1	36	32	Fairfax, VA	57.1
33	33	Franklin, OH	8.8	45	24	Milwaukee, WI	1.1	41	33	Pima, AZ	56.8
43	33	Honolulu, HI	8.8	50	24	Erie, NY	1.1	45	34	Milwaukee, WI	56.1
64	35	Middlesex, NJ	8.0	52	24	Fairfield, CT	1.1	30	35	Hillsborough, FL	55.2
18	36	Broward, FL	7.7	73	24	Essex, NJ	1.1	16	36	Tarrant, TX	53.2
59	36	Prince George's, MD	7.7	1	37	Los Angeles, CA	1.0	39	37	Travis, TX	52.1
9	38	Dallas, TX	6.7	4	37	Maricopa, AZ	1.0	49	38	Mecklenburg, NC	52.0
61	38	Macomb, MI	6.7	5	37	San Diego, CA	1.0	25	39	Sacramento, CA	51.8
67	38	Baltimore, MD	6.7	13	37	Clark, NV	1.0	42	40	Montgomery, MD	51.4
70	41	Montgomery, PA	6.6	16	37	Tarrant, TX	1.0	15	41	Wayne, MI	51.2
71	42	Worcester, MA	6.3	22	37	Alameda, CA	1.0	5	42	San Diego, CA	51.1
17	43	Santa Clara, CA	5.9	25	37	Sacramento, CA	1.0	37	43	Contra Costa, CA	50.9
6	44	Orange, CA	5.8	28	37	Palm Beach, FL	1.0	63	44	Ventura, CA	50.7
24	45	Suffolk, NY	5.2	36	37	Fairfax, VA	1.0	13	45	Clark, NV	50.5
55	46	Marion, IN	5.0	41	37	Pima, AZ	1.0	64	46	Middlesex, NJ	50.3
60	47	New Haven, CT	4.7	43	37	Honolulu, HI	1.0	20	47	New York, NY	49.5
22	48	Alameda, CA	4.6	44	37	Westchester, NY	1.0	35	48	Orange, FL	47.3
57	49	Hartford, CT	4.3	46	37	Fresno, CA	1.0	6	49	Orange, CA	46.2
26	50	Bronx, NY	3.9	53	37	Pinellas, FL	1.0	65	50	Gwinnett, GA	45.4
52	50	Fairfield, CT	3.9	54	37	Bergen, NJ	1.0	2	51	Cook, IL	44.9
66	52	San Francisco, CA	3.7	56	37	Wake, NC	1.0	18	52	Broward, FL	44.6
47	53	Shelby, TN	3.4	62	37	Kern, CA	1.0	66	52	San Francisco, CA	44.6
20	54	New York, NY	3.2	64	37	Middlesex, NJ	1.0	48	54	Fulton, GA	42.1
34	54	Hennepin, MN	3.2	69	37	El Paso, TX	1.0	11	55	Riverside, CA	41.5
1	56	Los Angeles, CA	3.1	75	37	Hidalgo, TX	1.0	62	56	Kern, CA	40.2
44	57	Westchester, NY	2.8	12	57	San Bernardino, CA	0.9	47	57	Shelby, TN	39.6
23	58	Middlesex, MA	2.6	18	57	Broward, FL	0.9	21	58	Philadelphia, PA	38.1
54	59	Bergen, NJ	2.4	24	57	Suffolk, NY	0.9	17	59	Santa Clara, CA	37.7
7	60	Kings, NY	1.6	27	57	Nassau, NY	0.9	22	60	Alameda, CA	37.2
51	61	Du Page, IL	1.4	42	57	Montgomery, MD	0.9	7	61	Kings, NY	36.6
45	62	Milwaukee, WI	0.8	60	57	New Haven, CT	0.9	12	62	San Bernardino, CA	35.0
32	63	Oakland, MI	0.7	61	57	Macomb, MI	0.9	73	63	Essex, NJ	34.3
21	64	Philadelphia, PA	0.6	63	57	Ventura, CA	0.9	46	64	Fresno, CA	34.2
27	65	Nassau, NY	0.4	65	57	Gwinnett, GA	0.9	9	65	Dallas, TX	34.1
10	66	Queens, NY	0.1	67	57	Baltimore, MD	0.9	3	66	Harris, TX	33.9
53	67	Pinellas, FL	-0.5	71	57	Worcester, MA	0.9	43	67	Honolulu, HI	32.3
73	68	Essex, NJ	-1.2	72	57	Pierce, WA	0.9	19	68	Bexar, TX	31.3
40	69	St. Louis, MO	-1.7	74	57	Collin, TX	0.9	1	69	Los Angeles, CA	29.4
50	70	Erie, NY	-3.3	11	70	Riverside, CA	0.8	10	70	Queens, NY	28.6
2	71	Cook, IL	-3.4	37	70	Contra Costa, CA	0.8	59	71	Prince George's, MD	16.2
31	72	Allegheny, PA	-4.6	7	72	Kings, NY	0.7	8	72	Miami-Dade, FL	15.8
68	73	Hamilton, OH	-5.1	10	72	Queens, NY	0.7	69	73	El Paso, TX	13.7
29	74	Cuyahoga, OH	-8.2	26	72	Bronx, NY	0.7	26	74	Bronx, NY	11.4
15	75	Wayne, MI	-11.7	59	72	Prince George's, MD	0.7	75	75	Hidalgo, TX	7.9

75 Largest Counties by 2010 Population
Selected Rankings

Percent Black, not Hispanic or Latino, alone or in combination, 2010				Percent American Indian, Alaska Native, alone or in combination, 2010				Percent Asian or Pacific Islander, alone or in combination, 2010			
Population rank	Black rank	County	Percent black [col 6]	Population rank	American Indian Alaska native rank	County	Percent American Indian, Alaska native [col 7]	Population rank	Asian or Pacific Islander rank	County	Percent Asian or Pacific Islander [col 8]
59	1	Prince George's, MD	65.1	41	1	Pima, AZ	3.0	43	1	Honolulu, HI	79.7
47	2	Shelby, TN	52.6	72	2	Pierce, WA	2.7	66	2	San Francisco, CA	35.9
48	3	Fulton, GA	44.5	4	3	Maricopa, AZ	2.0	17	3	Santa Clara, CA	34.6
21	4	Philadelphia, PA	43.4	14	4	King, WA	1.7	22	4	Alameda, CA	29.8
15	5	Wayne, MI	41.4	25	4	Sacramento, CA	1.7	10	5	Queens, NY	24.7
73	6	Essex, NJ	40.3	34	6	Hennepin, MN	1.5	64	6	Middlesex, NJ	22.5
7	7	Kings, NY	32.8	43	6	Honolulu, HI	1.5	6	7	Orange, CA	19.9
49	8	Mecklenburg, NC	31.4	62	6	Kern, CA	1.5	36	8	Fairfax, VA	19.6
26	9	Bronx, NY	30.8	46	9	Fresno, CA	1.2	14	9	King, WA	17.9
29	10	Cuyahoga, OH	30.3	45	10	Milwaukee, WI	1.1	25	10	Sacramento, CA	17.7
58	11	Duval, FL	30.0	5	11	San Diego, CA	1.0	37	11	Contra Costa, CA	17.3
55	12	Marion, IN	27.9	11	11	Riverside, CA	1.0	42	12	Montgomery, MD	15.5
45	13	Milwaukee, WI	27.6	12	11	San Bernardino, CA	1.0	54	13	Bergen, NJ	15.4
67	14	Baltimore, MD	26.9	13	11	Clark, NV	1.0	1	14	Los Angeles, CA	15.1
18	15	Broward, FL	26.8	22	11	Alameda, CA	1.0	5	15	San Diego, CA	13.3
68	15	Hamilton, OH	26.8	37	11	Contra Costa, CA	1.0	20	16	New York, NY	12.4
2	17	Cook, IL	25.0	38	11	Salt Lake, UT	1.0	74	16	Collin, TX	12.4
40	18	St. Louis, MO	24.1	50	11	Erie, NY	1.0	65	18	Gwinnett, GA	11.5
65	19	Gwinnett, GA	23.9	15	19	Wayne, MI	0.9	7	19	Kings, NY	11.3
33	20	Franklin, OH	22.7	16	19	Tarrant, TX	0.9	13	19	Clark, NV	11.3
9	21	Dallas, TX	22.5	33	19	Franklin, OH	0.9	51	21	Du Page, IL	11.0
56	22	Wake, NC	21.2	58	19	Duval, FL	0.9	46	22	Fresno, CA	10.4
35	23	Orange, FL	20.5	59	19	Prince George's, MD	0.9	23	23	Middlesex, MA	10.3
3	24	Harris, TX	18.9	61	19	Macomb, MI	0.9	72	24	Pierce, WA	10.2
10	25	Queens, NY	18.8	74	19	Collin, TX	0.9	27	25	Nassau, NY	8.4
42	26	Montgomery, MD	17.8	32	26	Oakland, MI	0.8	63	26	Ventura, CA	8.3
8	27	Miami-Dade, FL	17.5	49	26	Mecklenburg, NC	0.8	12	27	San Bernardino, CA	7.5
28	27	Palm Beach, FL	17.5	56	26	Wake, NC	0.8	11	28	Riverside, CA	7.3
30	29	Hillsborough, FL	16.5	63	26	Ventura, CA	0.8	34	29	Hennepin, MN	7.2
16	30	Tarrant, TX	15.2	66	26	San Francisco, CA	0.8	70	30	Montgomery, PA	7.1
32	31	Oakland, MI	14.3	67	26	Baltimore, MD	0.8	21	31	Philadelphia, PA	7.0
31	32	Allegheny, PA	14.2	9	32	Dallas, TX	0.7	2	32	Cook, IL	6.9
44	33	Westchester, NY	14.1	10	32	Queens, NY	0.7	3	33	Harris, TX	6.8
50	34	Erie, NY	13.9	21	32	Philadelphia, PA	0.7	39	34	Travis, TX	6.6
20	35	New York, NY	13.7	39	32	Travis, TX	0.7	32	35	Oakland, MI	6.4
22	36	Alameda, CA	13.4	53	32	Pinellas, FL	0.7	48	36	Fulton, GA	6.3
34	37	Hennepin, MN	13.2	55	32	Marion, IN	0.7	44	37	Westchester, NY	6.2
57	37	Hartford, CT	13.2	6	38	Orange, CA	0.6	56	37	Wake, NC	6.2
60	39	New Haven, CT	12.8	17	38	Santa Clara, CA	0.6	38	39	Salt Lake, UT	6.0
25	40	Sacramento, CA	11.6	26	38	Bronx, NY	0.6	35	40	Orange, FL	5.9
13	41	Clark, NV	11.2	29	38	Cuyahoga, OH	0.6	67	41	Baltimore, MD	5.8
27	42	Nassau, NY	11.1	30	38	Hillsborough, FL	0.6	9	42	Dallas, TX	5.5
52	43	Fairfield, CT	10.8	35	38	Orange, FL	0.6	16	42	Tarrant, TX	5.5
53	43	Pinellas, FL	10.8	40	38	St. Louis, MO	0.6	52	44	Fairfield, CT	5.3
37	45	Contra Costa, CA	10.0	42	38	Montgomery, MD	0.6	49	45	Mecklenburg, NC	5.2
36	46	Fairfax, VA	9.7	48	38	Fulton, GA	0.6	58	45	Duval, FL	5.2
61	47	Macomb, MI	9.4	60	38	New Haven, CT	0.6	73	45	Essex, NJ	5.2
64	47	Middlesex, NJ	9.4	65	38	Gwinnett, GA	0.6	57	48	Hartford, CT	4.8
12	49	San Bernardino, CA	9.3	68	38	Hamilton, OH	0.6	59	48	Prince George's, MD	4.8
70	49	Montgomery, PA	9.3	71	38	Worcester, MA	0.6	62	48	Kern, CA	4.8
1	51	Los Angeles, CA	8.9	1	51	Los Angeles, CA	0.5	33	51	Franklin, OH	4.6
74	51	Collin, TX	8.9	3	51	Harris, TX	0.5	71	51	Worcester, MA	4.6
72	53	Pierce, WA	8.8	7	51	Kings, NY	0.5	4	53	Maricopa, AZ	4.4
39	54	Travis, TX	8.7	19	51	Bexar, TX	0.5	30	54	Hillsborough, FL	4.2
19	55	Bexar, TX	7.5	20	51	New York, NY	0.5	18	55	Broward, FL	4.1
24	55	Suffolk, NY	7.5	24	51	Suffolk, NY	0.5	40	55	St. Louis, MO	4.1
14	57	King, WA	7.3	31	51	Allegheny, PA	0.5	26	57	Bronx, NY	4.0
11	58	Riverside, CA	6.8	36	51	Fairfax, VA	0.5	60	57	New Haven, CT	4.0
66	59	San Francisco, CA	6.7	47	51	Shelby, TN	0.5	24	59	Suffolk, NY	3.9
62	60	Kern, CA	6.0	57	51	Hartford, CT	0.5	45	59	Milwaukee, WI	3.9
5	61	San Diego, CA	5.6	64	51	Middlesex, NJ	0.5	61	61	Macomb, MI	3.7
54	61	Bergen, NJ	5.6	73	51	Essex, NJ	0.5	53	62	Pinellas, FL	3.6
4	63	Maricopa, AZ	5.4	2	63	Cook, IL	0.4	41	63	Pima, AZ	3.5
46	63	Fresno, CA	5.4	18	63	Broward, FL	0.4	31	64	Allegheny, PA	3.3
23	65	Middlesex, MA	5.0	23	63	Middlesex, MA	0.4	15	65	Wayne, MI	3.2
51	66	Du Page, IL	4.9	28	63	Palm Beach, FL	0.4	19	66	Bexar, TX	3.1
71	67	Worcester, MA	4.3	44	63	Westchester, NY	0.4	29	66	Cuyahoga, OH	3.1
41	68	Pima, AZ	3.8	51	63	Du Page, IL	0.4	28	68	Palm Beach, FL	3.0
43	69	Honolulu, HI	3.0	52	63	Fairfield, CT	0.4	50	68	Erie, NY	3.0
17	70	Santa Clara, CA	2.9	69	63	El Paso, TX	0.4	47	70	Shelby, TN	2.7
69	70	El Paso, TX	2.9	70	63	Montgomery, PA	0.4	55	71	Marion, IN	2.6
63	72	Ventura, CA	2.1	27	72	Nassau, NY	0.3	68	71	Hamilton, OH	2.6
6	73	Orange, CA	1.9	54	72	Bergen, NJ	0.3	8	73	Miami-Dade, FL	1.9
38	73	Salt Lake, UT	1.9	8	74	Miami-Dade, FL	0.2	69	74	El Paso, TX	1.4
75	75	Hidalgo, TX	0.4	75	75	Hidalgo, TX	0.1	75	75	Hidalgo, TX	1.0

75 Largest Counties by 2010 Population
Selected Rankings

	Percent Hispanic or Latino,[1] 2010				Percent under 18 years old, 2010				Percent 65 years old and over, 2010		
Population rank	Hispanic or Latino rank	County	Percent Hispanic or Latino [col 9]	Population rank	Under 18 years old rank	County	Percent under 18 years old [cols 10 and 11]	Population rank	65 years old and over rank	County	Percent 65 years old and over [cols 17 and 18]
75	1	Hidalgo, TX	90.6	75	1	Hidalgo, TX	34.6	28	1	Palm Beach, FL	21.6
69	2	El Paso, TX	82.2	62	2	Kern, CA	30.3	53	2	Pinellas, FL	21.2
8	3	Miami-Dade, FL	65.0	69	3	El Paso, TX	30.1	31	3	Allegheny, PA	16.7
19	4	Bexar, TX	58.7	46	4	Fresno, CA	29.8	50	4	Erie, NY	15.7
26	5	Bronx, NY	53.5	12	5	San Bernardino, CA	29.2	29	5	Cuyahoga, OH	15.5
46	6	Fresno, CA	50.3	38	5	Salt Lake, UT	29.2	41	6	Pima, AZ	15.4
12	7	San Bernardino, CA	49.2	65	7	Gwinnett, GA	29.1	27	7	Nassau, NY	15.2
62	7	Kern, CA	49.2	74	8	Collin, TX	28.7	54	7	Bergen, NJ	15.2
1	9	Los Angeles, CA	47.7	11	9	Riverside, CA	28.3	70	9	Montgomery, PA	15.1
11	10	Riverside, CA	45.5	3	10	Harris, TX	28.0	40	10	St. Louis, MO	14.9
3	11	Harris, TX	40.8	16	10	Tarrant, TX	28.0	44	11	Westchester, NY	14.6
63	12	Ventura, CA	40.3	9	12	Dallas, TX	27.6	67	11	Baltimore, MD	14.6
9	13	Dallas, TX	38.3	19	13	Bexar, TX	27.1	43	13	Honolulu, HI	14.5
41	14	Pima, AZ	34.6	26	14	Bronx, NY	26.5	57	13	Hartford, CT	14.5
6	15	Orange, CA	33.7	4	15	Maricopa, AZ	26.4	18	15	Broward, FL	14.3
39	16	Travis, TX	33.5	47	15	Shelby, TN	26.4	60	15	New Haven, CT	14.3
5	17	San Diego, CA	32.0	56	17	Wake, NC	26.1	61	15	Macomb, MI	14.3
4	18	Maricopa, AZ	29.6	63	18	Ventura, CA	25.7	8	18	Miami-Dade, FL	14.1
13	19	Clark, NV	29.1	25	19	Sacramento, CA	25.6	66	19	San Francisco, CA	13.6
10	20	Queens, NY	27.5	15	20	Wayne, MI	25.4	20	20	New York, NY	13.5
17	21	Santa Clara, CA	26.9	49	21	Mecklenburg, NC	25.3	24	20	Suffolk, NY	13.5
35	21	Orange, FL	26.9	13	22	Clark, NV	25.0	52	20	Fairfield, CT	13.5
16	23	Tarrant, TX	26.7	55	22	Marion, IN	25.0	68	23	Hamilton, OH	13.3
20	24	New York, NY	25.4	45	24	Milwaukee, WI	24.9	32	24	Oakland, MI	13.2
18	25	Broward, FL	25.1	72	25	Pierce, WA	24.9	23	25	Middlesex, MA	13.1
30	26	Hillsborough, FL	24.9	73	25	Essex, NJ	24.9	10	26	Queens, NY	12.9
37	27	Contra Costa, CA	24.4	51	27	Du Page, IL	24.8	15	27	Wayne, MI	12.7
2	28	Cook, IL	24.0	52	27	Fairfield, CT	24.8	71	27	Worcester, MA	12.7
22	29	Alameda, CA	22.5	37	29	Contra Costa, CA	24.8	37	29	Contra Costa, CA	12.4
44	30	Westchester, NY	21.8	1	30	Los Angeles, CA	24.6	42	30	Montgomery, MD	12.3
25	31	Sacramento, CA	21.6	6	30	Orange, CA	24.5	64	30	Middlesex, NJ	12.3
73	32	Essex, NJ	20.3	36	32	Fairfax, VA	24.2	4	32	Maricopa, AZ	12.1
65	33	Gwinnett, GA	20.1	17	33	Santa Clara, CA	24.1	21	32	Philadelphia, PA	12.1
7	34	Kings, NY	19.8	42	33	Montgomery, MD	24.1	2	34	Cook, IL	11.9
28	35	Palm Beach, FL	19.0	24	35	Suffolk, NY	24.0	11	35	Riverside, CA	11.8
64	36	Middlesex, NJ	18.4	44	35	Westchester, NY	24.0	30	35	Hillsborough, FL	11.8
38	37	Salt Lake, UT	17.1	48	37	Fulton, GA	23.9	63	37	Ventura, CA	11.7
42	38	Montgomery, MD	17.0	59	37	Prince George's, MD	23.9	6	38	Orange, CA	11.6
52	39	Fairfield, CT	16.9	30	39	Hillsborough, FL	23.9	51	38	Du Page, IL	11.6
24	40	Suffolk, NY	16.5	33	39	Franklin, OH	23.9	7	40	Kings, NY	11.5
54	41	Bergen, NJ	16.1	39	39	Travis, TX	23.9	45	40	Milwaukee, WI	11.5
36	42	Fairfax, VA	15.6	7	42	Kings, NY	23.8	73	40	Essex, NJ	11.5
57	43	Hartford, CT	15.3	2	43	Cook, IL	23.7	34	43	Hennepin, MN	11.4
66	44	San Francisco, CA	15.1	35	44	Orange, FL	23.6	5	44	San Diego, CA	11.3
60	45	New Haven, CT	15.0	58	44	Duval, FL	23.6	13	44	Clark, NV	11.3
59	46	Prince George's, MD	14.9	68	44	Hamilton, OH	23.6	25	46	Sacramento, CA	11.2
74	47	Collin, TX	14.7	32	47	Oakland, MI	23.5	58	46	Duval, FL	11.2
27	48	Nassau, NY	14.6	40	47	St. Louis, MO	23.5	72	48	Pierce, WA	11.1
45	49	Milwaukee, WI	13.3	71	47	Worcester, MA	23.5	17	48	Santa Clara, CA	11.1
51	49	Du Page, IL	13.3	5	50	San Diego, CA	23.4	22	48	Alameda, CA	11.1
21	51	Philadelphia, PA	12.3	27	51	Nassau, NY	23.2	1	51	Los Angeles, CA	10.9
49	52	Mecklenburg, NC	12.2	41	52	Pima, AZ	23.0	14	51	King, WA	10.9
56	53	Wake, NC	9.8	61	52	Macomb, MI	23.0	55	53	Marion, IN	10.6
71	54	Worcester, MA	9.4	57	54	Hartford, CT	22.9	26	54	Bronx, NY	10.5
55	55	Marion, IN	9.3	64	54	Middlesex, NJ	22.9	47	55	Shelby, TN	10.3
72	56	Pierce, WA	9.2	70	54	Montgomery, PA	22.9	19	56	Bexar, TX	10.2
14	57	King, WA	8.9	34	57	Hennepin, MN	22.7	69	56	El Paso, TX	10.2
43	58	Honolulu, HI	8.1	22	58	Alameda, CA	22.6	33	58	Franklin, OH	10.0
53	59	Pinellas, FL	8.0	29	58	Cuyahoga, OH	22.6	46	58	Fresno, CA	10.0
48	60	Fulton, GA	7.9	54	58	Bergen, NJ	22.6	36	60	Fairfax, VA	9.8
58	61	Duval, FL	7.6	21	61	Philadelphia, PA	22.5	35	61	Orange, FL	9.7
34	62	Hennepin, MN	6.7	18	62	Broward, FL	22.4	59	62	Prince George's, MD	9.4
23	63	Middlesex, MA	6.5	60	63	New Haven, CT	22.3	75	63	Hidalgo, TX	9.3
47	64	Shelby, TN	5.6	43	64	Honolulu, HI	22.1	48	64	Fulton, GA	9.0
15	65	Wayne, MI	5.2	67	65	Baltimore, MD	22.0	62	64	Kern, CA	9.0
29	66	Cuyahoga, OH	4.8	8	66	Miami-Dade, FL	21.9	49	66	Mecklenburg, NC	8.9
33	66	Franklin, OH	4.8	50	67	Erie, NY	21.6	12	66	San Bernardino, CA	8.9
50	68	Erie, NY	4.5	14	68	King, WA	21.4	16	66	Tarrant, TX	8.9
70	69	Montgomery, PA	4.3	23	69	Middlesex, MA	21.3	9	69	Dallas, TX	8.8
67	70	Baltimore, MD	4.2	10	70	Queens, NY	20.7	38	70	Salt Lake, UT	8.7
32	71	Oakland, MI	3.5	28	71	Palm Beach, FL	20.4	56	71	Wake, NC	8.5
68	72	Hamilton, OH	2.6	31	72	Allegheny, PA	19.8	3	72	Harris, TX	8.2
40	73	St. Louis, MO	2.5	53	73	Pinellas, FL	17.8	74	73	Collin, TX	7.7
61	74	Macomb, MI	2.3	20	74	New York, NY	14.8	39	74	Travis, TX	7.3
31	75	Allegheny, PA	1.6	66	75	San Francisco, CA	13.4	65	75	Gwinnett, GA	6.8

75 Largest Counties by 2010 Population
Selected Rankings

Percent female-headed family households, 2010				Birth rate, average 2006–2008				Percent under 65 who have no health insurance, 2009			
Population rank	Female households rank	County	Percent female households [col 30]	Population rank	Live birth rate rank	County	Birth rate [col 36]	Population rank	No health insurance rank	County	Percent with no health insurance [col 40]
26	1	Bronx, NY	31.1	75	1	Hidalgo, TX	24.1	75	1	Hidalgo, TX	37.9
21	2	Philadelphia, PA	22.5	38	2	Salt Lake, UT	19.4	8	2	Miami-Dade, FL	33.9
47	3	Shelby, TN	21.7	62	3	Kern, CA	19.3	9	3	Dallas, TX	31.9
15	4	Wayne, MI	20.7	69	3	El Paso, TX	19.3	69	4	El Paso, TX	31.5
73	5	Essex, NJ	20.6	46	5	Fresno, CA	18.9	3	5	Harris, TX	28.6
7	6	Kings, NY	20.5	9	6	Dallas, TX	18.5	18	6	Broward, FL	26.5
59	7	Prince George's, MD	20.4	3	7	Harris, TX	18.1	28	7	Palm Beach, FL	25.6
69	8	El Paso, TX	20.3	55	8	Marion, IN	17.7	35	8	Orange, FL	25.0
8	9	Miami-Dade, FL	18.8	65	9	Gwinnett, GA	17.4	13	9	Clark, NV	24.9
75	9	Hidalgo, TX	18.8	12	10	San Bernardino, CA	17.2	1	10	Los Angeles, CA	24.8
45	11	Milwaukee, WI	17.4	16	10	Tarrant, TX	17.2	16	11	Tarrant, TX	24.6
55	12	Marion, IN	17.1	19	12	Bexar, TX	17.1	19	12	Bexar, TX	23.6
46	13	Fresno, CA	16.9	39	12	Travis, TX	17.1	39	12	Travis, TX	23.6
29	14	Cuyahoga, OH	16.7	49	14	Mecklenburg, NC	17.0	48	14	Fulton, GA	23.4
58	14	Duval, FL	16.7	4	15	Maricopa, AZ	16.8	65	15	Gwinnett, GA	22.9
19	16	Bexar, TX	16.6	26	16	Bronx, NY	16.7	11	16	Riverside, CA	22.5
10	17	Queens, NY	16.4	47	16	Shelby, TN	16.7	53	17	Pinellas, FL	22.3
12	18	San Bernardino, CA	16.2	13	18	Clark, NV	16.5	62	18	Kern, CA	21.9
9	19	Dallas, TX	16.0	7	19	Kings, NY	16.4	46	19	Fresno, CA	21.7
35	20	Orange, FL	15.7	33	19	Franklin, OH	16.4	12	20	San Bernardino, CA	21.6
48	20	Fulton, GA	15.7	11	21	Riverside, CA	16.3	30	21	Hillsborough, FL	21.5
62	20	Kern, CA	15.7	45	21	Milwaukee, WI	16.3	4	22	Maricopa, AZ	20.2
2	23	Cook, IL	15.6	21	23	Philadelphia, PA	16.2	6	23	Orange, CA	19.7
68	24	Hamilton, OH	15.4	58	24	Duval, FL	16.1	58	23	Duval, FL	19.7
1	25	Los Angeles, CA	15.3	56	25	Wake, NC	16.0	2	25	Cook, IL	18.9
3	25	Harris, TX	15.3	5	26	San Diego, CA	15.8	5	26	San Diego, CA	18.8
18	25	Broward, FL	15.3	25	26	Sacramento, CA	15.8	10	26	Queens, NY	18.8
25	28	Sacramento, CA	14.8	35	26	Orange, FL	15.8	73	26	Essex, NJ	18.8
30	28	Hillsborough, FL	14.8	17	29	Santa Clara, CA	15.5	41	29	Pima, AZ	18.2
49	30	Mecklenburg, NC	14.6	59	30	Prince George's, MD	15.3	55	29	Marion, IN	18.2
57	31	Hartford, CT	14.5	63	30	Ventura, CA	15.3	63	31	Ventura, CA	18.1
60	31	New Haven, CT	14.5	73	30	Essex, NJ	15.3	49	32	Mecklenburg, NC	17.1
67	31	Baltimore, MD	14.5	1	33	Los Angeles, CA	15.2	38	33	Salt Lake, UT	17.0
33	34	Franklin, OH	14.4	30	34	Hillsborough, FL	15.1	15	34	Wayne, MI	16.8
40	35	St. Louis, MO	14.2	43	34	Honolulu, HI	15.1	26	35	Bronx, NY	16.7
65	35	Gwinnett, GA	14.2	74	34	Collin, TX	15.1	47	35	Shelby, TN	16.7
16	37	Tarrant, TX	13.8	2	37	Cook, IL	14.9	74	37	Collin, TX	16.5
50	38	Erie, NY	13.7	36	37	Fairfax, VA	14.9	21	38	Philadelphia, PA	16.3
13	39	Clark, NV	13.5	34	39	Hennepin, MN	14.8	59	38	Prince George's, MD	16.3
11	40	Riverside, CA	13.3	48	39	Fulton, GA	14.8	25	40	Sacramento, CA	15.7
72	41	Pierce, WA	13.0	42	41	Montgomery, MD	14.7	33	40	Franklin, OH	15.7
22	42	Alameda, CA	12.9	72	41	Pierce, WA	14.7	7	42	Kings, NY	15.5
41	43	Pima, AZ	12.8	6	43	Orange, CA	14.5	66	43	San Francisco, CA	14.8
44	43	Westchester, NY	12.8	22	43	Alameda, CA	14.5	29	44	Cuyahoga, OH	14.7
43	45	Honolulu, HI	12.7	8	45	Miami-Dade, FL	14.2	72	44	Pierce, WA	14.7
61	45	Macomb, MI	12.7	41	46	Pima, AZ	14.1	22	46	Alameda, CA	14.6
4	47	Maricopa, AZ	12.4	68	47	Hamilton, OH	14.0	64	47	Middlesex, NJ	14.1
37	47	Contra Costa, CA	12.4	10	48	Queens, NY	13.7	45	48	Milwaukee, WI	13.9
52	49	Fairfield, CT	12.3	64	49	Middlesex, NJ	13.6	56	48	Wake, NC	13.9
31	50	Allegheny, PA	12.2	15	50	Wayne, MI	13.5	61	48	Macomb, MI	13.9
71	50	Worcester, MA	12.2	14	51	King, WA	13.4	68	48	Hamilton, OH	13.9
5	52	San Diego, CA	12.1	37	52	Contra Costa, CA	13.1	17	52	Santa Clara, CA	13.8
20	53	New York, NY	11.9	67	52	Baltimore, MD	13.1	37	53	Contra Costa, CA	13.5
53	53	Pinellas, FL	11.9	18	54	Broward, FL	12.9	20	54	New York, NY	13.3
63	55	Ventura, CA	11.8	52	55	Fairfield, CT	12.8	54	55	Bergen, NJ	13.0
64	55	Middlesex, NJ	11.8	20	56	New York, NY	12.7	14	56	King, WA	12.9
24	57	Suffolk, NY	11.7	29	56	Cuyahoga, OH	12.7	42	57	Montgomery, MD	12.4
27	57	Nassau, NY	11.7	24	58	Suffolk, NY	12.5	44	58	Westchester, NY	12.0
28	57	Palm Beach, FL	11.7	51	58	Du Page, IL	12.5	67	59	Baltimore, MD	11.9
6	60	Orange, CA	11.6	44	60	Westchester, NY	12.4	32	60	Oakland, MI	11.6
56	61	Wake, NC	11.5	71	60	Worcester, MA	12.4	24	61	Suffolk, NY	11.5
42	62	Montgomery, MD	11.3	23	62	Middlesex, MA	12.3	52	62	Fairfield, CT	11.4
32	63	Oakland, MI	11.1	28	62	Palm Beach, FL	12.3	36	63	Fairfax, VA	10.9
39	64	Travis, TX	11.0	40	62	St. Louis, MO	12.3	40	64	St. Louis, MO	10.8
38	65	Salt Lake, UT	10.9	70	65	Montgomery, PA	12.2	27	65	Nassau, NY	10.5
54	65	Bergen, NJ	10.9	60	66	New Haven, CT	12.1	31	66	Allegheny, PA	10.4
17	67	Santa Clara, CA	10.7	57	67	Hartford, CT	11.9	51	66	Du Page, IL	10.4
34	68	Hennepin, MN	10.3	61	67	Macomb, MI	11.9	34	68	Hennepin, MN	10.3
23	69	Middlesex, MA	10.1	32	69	Oakland, MI	11.7	60	68	New Haven, CT	10.3
74	70	Collin, TX	9.6	66	70	San Francisco, CA	11.6	57	70	Hartford, CT	9.9
51	71	Du Page, IL	9.5	27	71	Nassau, NY	11.4	50	71	Erie, NY	9.8
70	71	Montgomery, PA	9.5	54	72	Bergen, NJ	11.0	70	72	Montgomery, PA	8.0
36	73	Fairfax, VA	9.2	31	73	Allegheny, PA	10.8	43	73	Honolulu, HI	7.4
14	74	King, WA	9.1	50	73	Erie, NY	10.8	23	74	Middlesex, MA	4.6
66	75	San Francisco, CA	8.3	53	75	Pinellas, FL	10.2	71	74	Worcester, MA	4.6

75 Largest Counties by 2010 Population
Selected Rankings

Percent college graduates (bachelor's degree or more), 2006–2010				Expenditures per student, 2008–2009				Per capita personal income, 2009			
Population rank	College graduates rank	County	Percent college graduates [col 51]	Population rank	Expenditures rank	County	Expenditures per student (dollars) [col 53]	Population rank	Per capita income rank	County	Per capita income (dollars) [col 64]
36	1	Fairfax, VA	58.0	44	1	Westchester, NY	22 092	20	1	New York, NY	105 554
20	2	New York, NY	57.0	27	2	Nassau, NY	21 547	52	2	Fairfield, CT	74 767
42	3	Montgomery, MD	56.7	24	3	Suffolk, NY	19 341	44	3	Westchester, NY	71 728
66	4	San Francisco, CA	51.2	7	4	Kings, NY	19 146	36	4	Fairfax, VA	69 241
23	5	Middlesex, MA	49.3	10	4	Queens, NY	19 146	66	5	San Francisco, CA	68 727
74	6	Collin, TX	48.3	20	4	New York, NY	19 146	42	6	Montgomery, MD	66 323
48	7	Fulton, GA	47.6	26	4	Bronx, NY	19 146	54	7	Bergen, NJ	64 388
56	8	Wake, NC	47.4	73	8	Essex, NJ	18 567	70	8	Montgomery, PA	63 469
17	9	Santa Clara, CA	45.3	54	9	Bergen, NJ	16 501	27	9	Nassau, NY	61 871
51	9	Du Page, IL	45.3	52	10	Fairfield, CT	15 467	23	10	Middlesex, MA	58 744
14	11	King, WA	45.2	42	11	Montgomery, MD	15 447	28	11	Palm Beach, FL	57 461
44	12	Westchester, NY	44.5	64	12	Middlesex, NJ	15 358	14	12	King, WA	56 904
54	12	Bergen, NJ	44.5	70	13	Montgomery, PA	15 066	37	13	Contra Costa, CA	56 703
70	14	Montgomery, PA	44.2	23	14	Middlesex, MA	14 796	17	14	Santa Clara, CA	55 781
34	15	Hennepin, MN	44.0	57	15	Hartford, CT	14 557	34	15	Hennepin, MN	54 008
52	16	Fairfield, CT	43.6	50	16	Erie, NY	14 510	51	16	Du Page, IL	52 449
39	17	Travis, TX	43.5	60	17	New Haven, CT	14 464	40	17	St. Louis, MO	52 214
32	18	Oakland, MI	42.2	59	18	Prince George's, MD	13 756	57	18	Hartford, CT	51 234
27	19	Nassau, NY	40.9	31	19	Allegheny, PA	13 742	48	19	Fulton, GA	50 474
22	20	Alameda, CA	40.3	36	20	Fairfax, VA	13 215	73	20	Essex, NJ	50 349
49	21	Mecklenburg, NC	40.0	21	21	Philadelphia, PA	12 772	32	21	Oakland, MI	50 334
40	22	St. Louis, MO	39.1	29	22	Cuyahoga, OH	12 722	67	22	Baltimore, MD	49 990
64	23	Middlesex, NJ	38.4	71	23	Worcester, MA	12 614	6	23	Orange, CA	49 020
37	24	Contra Costa, CA	38.2	67	24	Baltimore, MD	12 553	24	24	Suffolk, NY	48 691
6	25	Orange, CA	36.0	40	25	St. Louis, MO	12 504	3	25	Harris, TX	48 337
67	26	Baltimore, MD	35.2	45	26	Milwaukee, WI	12 463	22	26	Alameda, CA	48 004
33	27	Franklin, OH	35.0	43	27	Honolulu, HI	12 399	64	27	Middlesex, NJ	47 392
65	28	Gwinnett, GA	34.9	66	28	San Francisco, CA	12 269	60	28	New Haven, CT	47 387
5	29	San Diego, CA	34.1	34	29	Hennepin, MN	12 069	31	29	Allegheny, PA	46 427
31	29	Allegheny, PA	34.1	51	30	Du Page, IL	11 898	2	30	Cook, IL	46 161
57	31	Hartford, CT	33.3	2	31	Cook, IL	11 815	63	31	Ventura, CA	45 908
2	32	Cook, IL	33.2	68	32	Hamilton, OH	11 565	74	32	Collin, TX	45 884
71	33	Worcester, MA	32.9	48	33	Fulton, GA	11 387	5	33	San Diego, CA	45 706
68	34	Hamilton, OH	32.5	32	34	Oakland, MI	11 322	43	34	Honolulu, HI	45 496
24	35	Suffolk, NY	31.9	33	35	Franklin, OH	11 262	9	35	Dallas, TX	45 406
28	36	Palm Beach, FL	31.8	55	36	Marion, IN	10 802	53	36	Pinellas, FL	42 855
60	37	New Haven, CT	31.7	15	37	Wayne, MI	10 727	49	37	Mecklenburg, NC	42 644
73	38	Essex, NJ	31.6	61	38	Macomb, MI	10 330	68	38	Hamilton, OH	42 393
43	39	Honolulu, HI	31.1	1	39	Los Angeles, CA	10 139	71	39	Worcester, MA	42 021
63	40	Ventura, CA	30.8	17	40	Santa Clara, CA	9 792	29	40	Cuyahoga, OH	41 391
35	41	Orange, FL	30.3	14	41	King, WA	9 759	18	41	Broward, FL	41 185
38	42	Salt Lake, UT	30.1	62	42	Kern, CA	9 565	1	42	Los Angeles, CA	40 867
18	43	Broward, FL	29.6	5	43	San Diego, CA	9 541	72	43	Pierce, WA	40 577
41	43	Pima, AZ	29.6	65	44	Gwinnett, GA	9 532	47	44	Shelby, TN	40 547
59	43	Prince George's, MD	29.6	72	45	Pierce, WA	9 417	39	45	Travis, TX	40 544
10	46	Queens, NY	29.5	46	46	Fresno, CA	9 398	56	46	Wake, NC	39 821
50	47	Erie, NY	29.1	22	47	Alameda, CA	9 333	59	47	Prince George's, MD	39 637
1	48	Los Angeles, CA	29.0	39	48	Travis, TX	9 327	16	48	Tarrant, TX	39 380
4	48	Maricopa, AZ	29.0	28	49	Palm Beach, FL	9 296	58	49	Duval, FL	38 937
7	50	Kings, NY	28.8	25	50	Sacramento, CA	9 270	50	50	Erie, NY	38 546
30	50	Hillsborough, FL	28.8	18	51	Broward, FL	9 226	25	51	Sacramento, CA	38 231
16	52	Tarrant, TX	28.7	8	52	Miami-Dade, FL	9 100	30	52	Hillsborough, FL	38 075
29	53	Cuyahoga, OH	28.2	75	53	Hidalgo, TX	9 082	33	53	Franklin, OH	38 020
9	54	Dallas, TX	28.0	37	54	Contra Costa, CA	8 916	55	54	Marion, IN	37 911
25	55	Sacramento, CA	27.8	53	55	Pinellas, FL	8 905	38	55	Salt Lake, UT	37 276
47	55	Shelby, TN	27.8	6	56	Orange, CA	8 897	10	56	Queens, NY	37 148
3	57	Harris, TX	27.7	63	57	Ventura, CA	8 794	45	57	Milwaukee, WI	37 088
55	58	Marion, IN	27.3	12	58	San Bernardino, CA	8 750	13	58	Clark, NV	36 711
53	59	Pinellas, FL	27.1	47	59	Shelby, TN	8 708	19	59	Bexar, TX	36 465
45	60	Milwaukee, WI	26.7	11	60	Riverside, CA	8 643	35	60	Orange, FL	36 400
8	61	Miami-Dade, FL	26.2	69	61	El Paso, TX	8 636	8	61	Miami-Dade, FL	36 357
19	62	Bexar, TX	25.3	49	62	Mecklenburg, NC	8 629	61	62	Macomb, MI	36 004
58	63	Duval, FL	24.9	58	63	Duval, FL	8 593	4	63	Maricopa, AZ	35 319
72	64	Pierce, WA	23.4	30	64	Hillsborough, FL	8 569	21	64	Philadelphia, PA	34 981
21	65	Philadelphia, PA	22.2	3	65	Harris, TX	8 507	7	65	Kings, NY	34 680
61	66	Macomb, MI	21.8	9	66	Dallas, TX	8 480	41	66	Pima, AZ	33 833
13	67	Clark, NV	21.7	19	67	Bexar, TX	8 444	65	67	Gwinnett, GA	32 381
11	68	Riverside, CA	20.5	35	68	Orange, FL	8 198	15	68	Wayne, MI	31 888
15	69	Wayne, MI	20.2	56	69	Wake, NC	8 166	46	69	Fresno, CA	30 646
46	70	Fresno, CA	19.7	74	70	Collin, TX	8 134	11	70	Riverside, CA	29 748
69	71	El Paso, TX	19.3	13	71	Clark, NV	8 120	62	71	Kern, CA	29 630
12	72	San Bernardino, CA	18.4	16	72	Tarrant, TX	8 015	12	72	San Bernardino, CA	29 609
26	73	Bronx, NY	17.6	41	73	Pima, AZ	7 777	69	73	El Paso, TX	29 381
75	74	Hidalgo, TX	15.1	4	74	Maricopa, AZ	7 558	26	74	Bronx, NY	28 523
62	75	Kern, CA	14.7	38	75	Salt Lake, UT	6 285	75	75	Hidalgo, TX	20 509

75 Largest Counties by 2010 Population
Selected Rankings

Median household income, 2010				Median value of owner-occupied housing units, 2006–2010				Median gross rent of renter-occupied housing units, 2006–2010			
Population rank	Median income rank	County	Median income (dollars) [col 58]	Population rank	Median value rank	County	Median value (dollars) [col 91]	Population rank	Median rent rank	County	Median rent (dollars) [col 94]
36	1	Fairfax, VA	102 726	20	1	New York, NY	825 200	36	1	Fairfax, VA	1 492
27	2	Nassau, NY	90 294	66	2	San Francisco, CA	785 200	24	2	Suffolk, NY	1 427
42	3	Montgomery, MD	88 559	17	3	Santa Clara, CA	701 000	6	3	Orange, CA	1 423
17	4	Santa Clara, CA	84 627	6	4	Orange, CA	607 900	42	4	Montgomery, MD	1 417
24	5	Suffolk, NY	81 235	22	5	Alameda, CA	590 900	27	5	Nassau, NY	1 407
74	6	Collin, TX	77 862	63	6	Ventura, CA	568 700	17	6	Santa Clara, CA	1 402
54	7	Bergen, NJ	77 059	7	7	Kings, NY	562 400	63	7	Ventura, CA	1 391
44	8	Westchester, NY	76 993	43	8	Honolulu, HI	559 000	66	8	San Francisco, CA	1 328
64	9	Middlesex, NJ	75 890	44	9	Westchester, NY	556 900	43	9	Honolulu, HI	1 312
70	10	Montgomery, PA	75 369	37	10	Contra Costa, CA	548 200	37	10	Contra Costa, CA	1 270
23	11	Middlesex, MA	75 364	1	11	Los Angeles, CA	508 800	54	11	Bergen, NJ	1 236
52	12	Fairfield, CT	74 634	36	12	Fairfax, VA	507 800	20	12	New York, NY	1 234
37	13	Contra Costa, CA	73 678	27	13	Nassau, NY	487 900	5	13	San Diego, CA	1 228
51	14	Du Page, IL	72 470	5	14	San Diego, CA	486 000	23	14	Middlesex, MA	1 213
63	15	Ventura, CA	71 418	42	15	Montgomery, MD	482 900	52	15	Fairfield, CT	1 206
66	16	San Francisco, CA	70 883	54	16	Bergen, NJ	482 300	44	16	Westchester, NY	1 203
6	17	Orange, CA	70 727	10	17	Queens, NY	479 300	22	17	Alameda, CA	1 188
59	18	Prince George's, MD	69 524	52	18	Fairfield, CT	477 700	64	18	Middlesex, NJ	1 187
43	19	Honolulu, HI	67 519	24	19	Suffolk, NY	424 200	10	19	Queens, NY	1 181
22	20	Alameda, CA	66 937	23	20	Middlesex, MA	420 800	59	20	Prince George's, MD	1 140
14	21	King, WA	66 147	14	21	King, WA	407 700	18	21	Broward, FL	1 133
20	22	New York, NY	63 188	73	22	Essex, NJ	395 700	28	22	Palm Beach, FL	1 129
67	23	Baltimore, MD	62 300	26	23	Bronx, NY	386 200	1	23	Los Angeles, CA	1 117
56	24	Wake, NC	61 594	64	24	Middlesex, NJ	356 000	11	24	Riverside, CA	1 115
71	25	Worcester, MA	61 079	59	25	Prince George's, MD	327 600	12	25	San Bernardino, CA	1 061
32	26	Oakland, MI	60 392	11	26	Riverside, CA	325 300	13	26	Clark, NV	1 036
57	27	Hartford, CT	60 028	25	27	Sacramento, CA	324 200	67	27	Baltimore, MD	1 033
5	28	San Diego, CA	59 759	12	28	San Bernardino, CA	319 000	70	28	Montgomery, PA	1 028
34	29	Hennepin, MN	59 252	51	29	Du Page, IL	316 900	7	29	Kings, NY	1 021
65	30	Gwinnett, GA	57 848	70	30	Montgomery, PA	297 200	51	30	Du Page, IL	1 008
60	31	New Haven, CT	57 070	71	31	Worcester, MA	282 800	8	31	Miami-Dade, FL	1 004
38	32	Salt Lake, UT	56 664	60	32	New Haven, CT	273 300	14	32	King, WA	999
72	33	Pierce, WA	56 446	67	33	Baltimore, MD	269 900	60	33	New Haven, CT	996
40	34	St. Louis, MO	55 290	8	34	Miami-Dade, FL	269 600	35	34	Orange, FL	995
11	35	Riverside, CA	53 981	72	35	Pierce, WA	269 300	25	35	Sacramento, CA	980
48	36	Fulton, GA	53 580	2	36	Cook, IL	265 800	73	36	Essex, NJ	977
25	37	Sacramento, CA	52 655	28	37	Palm Beach, FL	261 900	74	37	Collin, TX	968
1	38	Los Angeles, CA	52 595	13	38	Clark, NV	257 300	65	38	Gwinnett, GA	954
10	39	Queens, NY	52 486	46	39	Fresno, CA	257 000	48	39	Fulton, GA	929
16	40	Tarrant, TX	52 482	48	40	Fulton, GA	253 100	26	40	Bronx, NY	923
49	41	Mecklenburg, NO	52 363	34	41	Hennepin, MN	247 900	4	41	Maricopa, AZ	912
73	42	Essex, NJ	52 288	18	42	Broward, FL	247 500	57	42	Hartford, CT	909
12	43	San Bernardino, CA	52 270	57	43	Hartford, CT	247 400	30	43	Hillsborough, FL	906
39	44	Travis, TX	51 905	4	44	Maricopa, AZ	238 600	53	44	Pinellas, FL	904
2	45	Cook, IL	51 457	38	45	Salt Lake, UT	237 500	72	45	Pierce, WA	902
13	46	Clark, NV	51 427	35	46	Orange, FL	228 600	2	46	Cook, IL	900
3	47	Harris, TX	50 437	56	47	Wake, NC	222 300	39	47	Travis, TX	891
4	48	Maricopa, AZ	50 424	62	48	Kern, CA	217 100	58	48	Duval, FL	880
28	49	Palm Beach, FL	49 891	32	49	Oakland, MI	204 300	32	49	Oakland, MI	871
61	50	Macomb, MI	49 348	39	50	Travis, TX	200 300	71	50	Worcester, MA	862
18	51	Broward, FL	47 917	74	51	Collin, TX	199 000	34	51	Hennepin, MN	853
19	52	Bexar, TX	47 724	30	52	Hillsborough, FL	198 900	56	52	Wake, NC	845
33	53	Franklin, OH	47 621	41	53	Pima, AZ	198 300	16	53	Tarrant, TX	833
31	54	Allegheny, PA	47 490	65	54	Gwinnett, GA	194 200	9	54	Dallas, TX	831
9	55	Dallas, TX	46 909	53	55	Pinellas, FL	185 700	49	55	Mecklenburg, NC	829
50	56	Erie, NY	46 773	49	56	Mecklenburg, NC	185 100	3	56	Harris, TX	820
68	57	Hamilton, OH	46 359	40	57	St. Louis, MO	179 300	21	57	Philadelphia, PA	819
58	58	Duval, FL	46 112	58	58	Duval, FL	175 900	46	58	Fresno, CA	819
30	59	Hillsborough, FL	46 043	45	59	Milwaukee, WI	165 700	38	59	Salt Lake, UT	818
35	60	Orange, FL	45 105	61	60	Macomb, MI	157 000	62	60	Kern, CA	810
62	61	Kern, CA	45 045	33	61	Franklin, OH	155 300	40	61	St. Louis, MO	789
46	62	Fresno, CA	44 869	68	62	Hamilton, OH	148 200	47	62	Shelby, TN	782
41	63	Pima, AZ	44 293	29	63	Cuyahoga, OH	137 200	33	63	Franklin, OH	764
47	64	Shelby, TN	43 859	47	64	Shelby, TN	135 300	19	64	Bexar, TX	761
53	65	Pinellas, FL	42 628	21	65	Philadelphia, PA	135 200	15	65	Wayne, MI	759
7	66	Kings, NY	42 047	16	66	Tarrant, TX	134 900	45	66	Milwaukee, WI	752
29	67	Cuyahoga, OH	41 407	3	67	Harris, TX	131 700	61	67	Macomb, MI	752
45	68	Milwaukee, WI	40 582	9	68	Dallas, TX	129 700	41	68	Pima, AZ	737
8	69	Miami-Dade, FL	40 145	55	69	Marion, IN	122 200	55	69	Marion, IN	715
15	70	Wayne, MI	39 421	15	70	Wayne, MI	121 100	29	70	Cuyahoga, OH	698
55	71	Marion, IN	39 393	50	71	Erie, NY	117 700	31	71	Allegheny, PA	688
69	72	El Paso, TX	36 064	19	72	Bexar, TX	117 100	50	72	Erie, NY	686
21	73	Philadelphia, PA	34 667	31	73	Allegheny, PA	115 200	68	73	Hamilton, OH	652
75	74	Hidalgo, TX	33 070	69	74	El Paso, TX	101 800	69	74	El Paso, TX	618
26	75	Bronx, NY	32 674	75	75	Hidalgo, TX	73 000	75	75	Hidalgo, TX	601

75 Largest Counties by 2010 Population
Selected Rankings

Percent of population below the poverty level, 2010				Percent under 18 years old below the poverty level, 2010				Unemployment rate, 2010			
Population rank	Poverty rate rank	County	Poverty rate [col 59]	Population rank	Poverty rate for children rank	County	Poverty rate for children under 18 years [col 60]	Population rank	Unemployment rate rank	County	Unemployment rate [col 100]
75	1	Hidalgo, TX	33.4	75	1	Hidalgo, TX	44.8	46	1	Fresno, CA	16.8
26	2	Bronx, NY	30.0	26	2	Bronx, NY	42.2	62	2	Kern, CA	15.9
46	3	Fresno, CA	26.8	46	3	Fresno, CA	38.2	13	3	Clark, NV	15.2
21	4	Philadelphia, PA	26.4	21	4	Philadelphia, PA	36.4	11	4	Riverside, CA	14.7
69	5	El Paso, TX	24.6	15	5	Wayne, MI	34.6	15	5	Wayne, MI	14.5
15	6	Wayne, MI	23.9	45	5	Milwaukee, WI	34.6	12	6	San Bernardino, CA	14.2
7	7	Kings, NY	22.9	69	7	El Paso, TX	33.8	61	7	Macomb, MI	13.7
45	8	Milwaukee, WI	21.9	7	8	Kings, NY	33.4	25	8	Sacramento, CA	12.8
62	9	Kern, CA	21.4	55	9	Marion, IN	30.7	26	8	Bronx, NY	12.8
55	10	Marion, IN	20.8	62	10	Kern, CA	30.3	1	10	Los Angeles, CA	12.6
47	11	Shelby, TN	20.4	9	11	Dallas, TX	29.3	8	11	Miami-Dade, FL	12.5
8	12	Miami-Dade, FL	20.3	47	12	Shelby, TN	29.2	32	12	Oakland, MI	12.1
9	13	Dallas, TX	19.0	29	13	Cuyahoga, OH	28.6	30	13	Hillsborough, FL	11.8
33	14	Franklin, OH	18.8	68	14	Hamilton, OH	28.5	75	13	Hidalgo, TX	11.8
39	14	Travis, TX	18.8	3	15	Harris, TX	27.1	28	15	Palm Beach, FL	11.7
3	16	Harris, TX	18.7	8	16	Miami-Dade, FL	25.5	53	15	Pinellas, FL	11.7
68	17	Hamilton, OH	18.5	33	16	Franklin, OH	25.5	58	15	Duval, FL	11.7
29	18	Cuyahoga, OH	18.2	41	18	Pima, AZ	25.1	35	18	Orange, FL	11.4
12	19	San Bernardino, CA	18.1	12	19	San Bernardino, CA	24.7	22	19	Alameda, CA	11.3
41	20	Pima, AZ	17.8	19	20	Bexar, TX	24.6	37	20	Contra Costa, CA	11.2
48	21	Fulton, GA	17.7	1	21	Los Angeles, CA	24.5	17	21	Santa Clara, CA	11.1
1	22	Los Angeles, CA	17.6	2	21	Cook, IL	24.5	73	22	Essex, NJ	11.0
19	23	Bexar, TX	17.0	39	21	Travis, TX	24.5	21	23	Philadelphia, PA	10.9
2	24	Cook, IL	16.8	48	24	Fulton, GA	23.9	49	23	Mecklenburg, NC	10.9
25	25	Sacramento, CA	16.7	25	25	Sacramento, CA	23.6	63	25	Ventura, CA	10.8
30	25	Hillsborough, FL	16.7	4	26	Maricopa, AZ	23.5	48	26	Fulton, GA	10.6
4	27	Maricopa, AZ	16.6	58	26	Duval, FL	23.5	2	27	Cook, IL	10.5
20	27	New York, NY	16.6	11	28	Riverside, CA	23.4	5	27	San Diego, CA	10.5
58	27	Duval, FL	16.6	20	29	New York, NY	23.2	7	29	Kings, NY	10.2
11	30	Riverside, CA	16.4	30	29	Hillsborough, FL	23.2	18	30	Broward, FL	10.1
35	30	Orange, FL	16.4	35	31	Orange, FL	22.8	60	30	New Haven, CT	10.1
73	30	Essex, NJ	16.4	73	31	Essex, NJ	22.8	47	32	Shelby, TN	10.0
49	33	Mecklenburg, NC	15.6	28	33	Palm Beach, FL	22.4	55	32	Marion, IN	10.0
10	34	Queens, NY	15.1	13	34	Clark, NV	22.2	72	34	Pierce, WA	9.9
13	35	Clark, NV	15.0	10	35	Queens, NY	22.0	57	35	Hartford, CT	9.7
5	36	San Diego, CA	14.8	49	36	Mecklenburg, NC	21.3	6	36	Orange, CA	9.6
18	37	Broward, FL	14.7	50	37	Erie, NY	20.9	45	36	Milwaukee, WI	9.6
16	38	Tarrant, TX	14.4	16	38	Tarrant, TX	20.7	29	38	Cuyahoga, OH	9.5
28	39	Palm Beach, FL	14.3	53	39	Pinellas, FL	20.4	66	38	San Francisco, CA	9.5
50	39	Erie, NY	14.3	18	40	Broward, FL	19.8	69	38	El Paso, TX	9.5
53	41	Pinellas, FL	14.2	65	41	Gwinnett, GA	19.2	40	41	St. Louis, MO	9.4
34	42	Hennepin, MN	13.7	5	42	San Diego, CA	19.1	68	41	Hamilton, OH	9.4
38	42	Salt Lake, UT	13.7	34	43	Hennepin, MN	18.7	71	43	Worcester, MA	9.3
65	44	Gwinnett, GA	13.6	38	44	Salt Lake, UT	17.8	65	44	Gwinnett, GA	9.2
22	45	Alameda, CA	13.5	22	45	Alameda, CA	17.2	4	45	Maricopa, AZ	9.1
66	46	San Francisco, CA	12.8	61	46	Macomb, MI	17.1	41	46	Pima, AZ	9.0
61	47	Macomb, MI	12.7	72	46	Pierce, WA	17.1	9	47	Dallas, TX	8.8
72	48	Pierce, WA	12.3	6	48	Orange, CA	16.4	14	47	King, WA	8.8
6	49	Orange, CA	12.2	60	49	New Haven, CT	16.1	64	49	Middlesex, NJ	8.7
14	49	King, WA	12.2	31	50	Allegheny, PA	15.6	3	50	Harris, TX	8.5
56	51	Wake, NC	12.0	14	51	King, WA	15.3	10	50	Queens, NY	8.5
31	52	Allegheny, PA	11.9	63	51	Ventura, CA	15.3	33	50	Franklin, OH	8.5
60	53	New Haven, CT	11.6	56	53	Wake, NC	15.2	56	53	Wake, NC	8.4
57	54	Hartford, CT	11.3	57	54	Hartford, CT	14.8	16	54	Tarrant, TX	8.3
63	55	Ventura, CA	11.0	66	55	San Francisco, CA	14.7	51	54	Du Page, IL	8.3
71	56	Worcester, MA	10.9	40	56	St. Louis, MO	14.0	52	54	Fairfield, CT	8.3
17	57	Santa Clara, CA	10.6	71	56	Worcester, MA	14.0	50	57	Erie, NY	8.2
40	58	St. Louis, MO	10.5	17	58	Santa Clara, CA	13.3	54	58	Bergen, NJ	8.1
32	59	Oakland, MI	10.3	32	58	Oakland, MI	13.3	20	59	New York, NY	8.0
43	60	Honolulu, HI	9.5	37	60	Contra Costa, CA	12.7	67	59	Baltimore, MD	8.0
59	61	Prince George's, MD	9.4	43	61	Honolulu, HI	12.3	31	61	Allegheny, PA	7.7
37	62	Contra Costa, CA	9.3	59	61	Prince George's, MD	12.3	24	62	Suffolk, NY	7.6
52	62	Fairfield, CT	9.3	44	63	Westchester, NY	11.5	74	63	Collin, TX	7.5
44	64	Westchester, NY	9.0	67	64	Baltimore, MD	11.0	19	64	Bexar, TX	7.4
23	65	Middlesex, MA	8.2	52	65	Fairfield, CT	10.8	38	64	Salt Lake, UT	7.4
67	65	Baltimore, MD	8.2	64	66	Middlesex, NJ	10.0	59	64	Prince George's, MD	7.4
64	67	Middlesex, NJ	7.7	74	67	Collin, TX	9.6	70	64	Montgomery, PA	7.4
74	67	Collin, TX	7.7	42	68	Montgomery, MD	9.4	44	68	Westchester, NY	7.2
42	69	Montgomery, MD	7.5	51	69	Du Page, IL	8.8	27	69	Nassau, NY	7.1
51	70	Du Page, IL	6.9	23	70	Middlesex, MA	8.5	23	70	Middlesex, MA	7.0
54	70	Bergen, NJ	6.9	24	71	Suffolk, NY	8.4	34	71	Hennepin, MN	6.9
24	72	Suffolk, NY	6.6	27	72	Nassau, NY	8.1	39	71	Travis, TX	6.9
27	73	Nassau, NY	6.2	54	73	Bergen, NJ	7.8	42	73	Montgomery, MD	5.6
36	74	Fairfax, VA	5.9	36	74	Fairfax, VA	7.3	43	73	Honolulu, HI	5.6
70	75	Montgomery, PA	5.8	70	75	Montgomery, PA	7.2	36	75	Fairfax, VA	4.9

75 Largest Counties by 2010 Population
Selected Rankings

Manufacturing employment as a percent of total nonfarm employment, 2009

Population rank	Manufacturing rank	County	Percent employed in manufacturing [col 107/col 105]
61	1	Macomb, MI	18.6
71	2	Worcester, MA	12.1
45	3	Milwaukee, WI	11.8
57	4	Hartford, CT	11.7
6	5	Orange, CA	11.6
22	5	Alameda, CA	11.6
15	7	Wayne, MI	11.5
1	8	Los Angeles, CA	11.3
16	9	Tarrant, TX	11.2
50	10	Erie, NY	11.1
60	10	New Haven, CT	11.1
29	12	Cuyahoga, OH	11.0
17	13	Santa Clara, CA	10.5
12	14	San Bernardino, CA	10.4
46	14	Fresno, CA	10.4
55	14	Marion, IN	10.4
68	17	Hamilton, OH	10.3
24	18	Suffolk, NY	10.2
63	19	Ventura, CA	10.1
51	20	Du Page, IL	9.6
38	21	Salt Lake, UT	9.5
11	22	Riverside, CA	9.3
70	22	Montgomery, PA	9.3
52	22	Fairfield, CT	9.3
34	25	Hennepin, MN	8.9
3	26	Harris, TX	8.8
41	27	Pima, AZ	8.7
2	28	Cook, IL	8.6
5	29	San Diego, CA	8.4
64	29	Bergen, NJ	8.4
9	31	Dallas, TX	8.3
64	32	Middlesex, NJ	8.2
53	33	Pinellas, FL	8.1
32	34	Oakland, MI	7.8
14	35	King, WA	7.5
23	36	Middlesex, MA	7.3
40	37	St. Louis, MO	7.2
69	38	El Paso, TX	6.9
72	38	Pierce, WA	6.9
65	38	Gwinnett, GA	6.9
4	41	Maricopa, AZ	6.8
73	42	Essex, NJ	6.7
74	42	Collin, TX	6.7
62	42	Kern, CA	6.7
39	45	Travis, TX	6.4
47	45	Shelby, TN	6.4
31	47	Allegheny, PA	5.9
67	47	Baltimore, MD	5.9
37	49	Contra Costa, CA	5.8
33	50	Franklin, OH	5.4
58	51	Duval, FL	5.3
19	51	Bexar, TX	5.3
10	53	Queens, NY	5.0
49	53	Mecklenburg, NC	5.0
25	55	Sacramento, CA	4.9
7	56	Kings, NY	4.5
35	56	Orange, FL	4.5
21	58	Philadelphia, PA	4.4
8	59	Miami-Dade, FL	4.3
30	59	Hillsborough, FL	4.3
56	61	Wake, NC	4.2
18	62	Broward, FL	3.8
27	63	Nassau, NY	3.7
59	64	Prince George's, MD	3.6
44	65	Westchester, NY	3.4
26	66	Bronx, NY	3.2
75	66	Hidalgo, TX	3.2
43	68	Honolulu, HI	3.0
13	69	Clark, NV	2.7
48	69	Fulton, GA	2.7
28	71	Palm Beach, FL	2.6
42	72	Montgomery, MD	2.2
66	73	San Francisco, CA	1.8
36	74	Fairfax, VA	1.5
20	75	New York, NY	1.1

Professional, scientific and technical employment as a percent of total nonfarm employment, 2009

Population rank	Professional services rank	County	Percent employed in professional services [col 110/col 105]
36	1	Fairfax, VA	32.9
42	2	Montgomery, MD	16.6
66	3	San Francisco, CA	16.0
23	4	Middlesex, MA	14.5
20	5	New York, NY	14.0
17	6	Santa Clara, CA	13.6
64	7	Middlesex, NJ	13.0
48	8	Fulton, GA	12.7
32	9	Oakland, MI	12.3
39	10	Travis, TX	12.0
70	11	Montgomery, PA	10.6
5	11	San Diego, CA	10.6
59	13	Prince George's, MD	10.0
34	14	Hennepin, MN	9.8
56	15	Wake, NC	9.6
1	16	Los Angeles, CA	9.4
52	17	Fairfield, CT	9.3
22	17	Alameda, CA	9.3
14	19	King, WA	9.2
2	19	Cook, IL	9.2
3	21	Harris, TX	9.1
9	22	Dallas, TX	9.0
30	23	Hillsborough, FL	8.8
68	24	Hamilton, OH	8.7
63	25	Ventura, CA	8.6
6	25	Orange, CA	8.6
31	25	Allegheny, PA	8.6
40	28	St. Louis, MO	8.4
15	29	Wayne, MI	8.3
37	29	Contra Costa, CA	8.3
35	31	Orange, FL	8.2
73	32	Essex, NJ	8.0
53	32	Pinellas, FL	8.0
65	32	Gwinnett, GA	8.0
51	32	Du Page, IL	8.0
21	36	Philadelphia, PA	7.9
18	37	Broward, FL	7.8
27	38	Nassau, NY	7.7
58	38	Duval, FL	7.7
74	38	Collin, TX	7.7
67	38	Baltimore, MD	7.7
54	42	Bergen, NJ	7.6
24	43	Suffolk, NY	7.5
44	44	Westchester, NY	7.4
25	44	Sacramento, CA	7.4
28	46	Palm Beach, FL	7.3
8	47	Miami-Dade, FL	7.2
49	48	Mecklenburg, NC	6.9
55	49	Marion, IN	6.7
38	50	Salt Lake, UT	6.6
33	50	Franklin, OH	6.6
57	50	Hartford, CT	6.6
29	53	Cuyahoga, OH	6.4
62	54	Kern, CA	6.3
4	55	Maricopa, AZ	6.2
50	56	Erie, NY	6.0
19	57	Bexar, TX	5.7
45	58	Milwaukee, WI	5.6
43	59	Honolulu, HI	5.5
16	59	Tarrant, TX	5.5
71	59	Worcester, MA	5.5
46	62	Fresno, CA	5.3
41	63	Pima, AZ	5.1
13	64	Clark, NV	5.0
60	65	New Haven, CT	4.9
69	66	El Paso, TX	4.7
47	67	Shelby, TN	3.9
72	68	Pierce, WA	3.7
11	69	Riverside, CA	3.5
12	70	San Bernardino, CA	3.2
7	71	Kings, NY	3.1
75	72	Hidalgo, TX	3.0
10	73	Queens, NY	2.4
26	74	Bronx, NY	1.7
61	75	Macomb, MI	0.0

Per capita local government taxes, 2007

Population rank	Local taxes rank	County	Per capita local taxes (dollars) [col 183]
27	1	Nassau, NY	4 802
20	2	New York, NY	4 612
7	2	Kings, NY	4 612
10	2	Queens, NY	4 612
26	2	Bronx, NY	4 612
44	6	Westchester, NY	4 398
24	7	Suffolk, NY	3 925
66	8	San Francisco, CA	3 651
42	9	Montgomery, MD	3 306
54	10	Bergen, NJ	3 227
52	11	Fairfield, CT	3 019
28	12	Palm Beach, FL	2 908
36	13	Fairfax, VA	2 820
29	14	Cuyahoga, OH	2 658
48	15	Fulton, GA	2 622
51	16	Du Page, IL	2 513
33	17	Franklin, OH	2 490
17	18	Santa Clara, CA	2 486
21	19	Philadelphia, PA	2 484
64	20	Middlesex, NJ	2 407
74	21	Collin, TX	2 376
70	22	Montgomery, PA	2 350
22	23	Alameda, CA	2 329
73	24	Essex, NJ	2 328
2	25	Cook, IL	2 315
9	26	Dallas, TX	2 300
57	27	Hartford, CT	2 289
39	28	Travis, TX	2 252
14	29	King, WA	2 220
8	30	Miami-Dade, FL	2 211
68	31	Hamilton, OH	2 210
18	32	Broward, FL	2 115
23	33	Middlesex, MA	2 093
31	34	Allegheny, PA	2 086
60	34	New Haven, CT	2 086
3	36	Harris, TX	2 028
37	37	Contra Costa, CA	2 003
16	38	Tarrant, TX	1 990
50	39	Erie, NY	1 985
35	40	Orange, FL	1 984
59	41	Prince George's, MD	1 958
63	42	Pinellas, FL	1 906
47	43	Shelby, TN	1 888
40	44	St. Louis, MO	1 882
32	45	Oakland, MI	1 833
5	46	San Diego, CA	1 831
67	47	Baltimore, MD	1 825
6	48	Orange, CA	1 804
49	49	Mecklenburg, NC	1 742
1	50	Los Angeles, CA	1 740
13	51	Clark, NV	1 720
65	52	Gwinnett, GA	1 698
30	53	Hillsborough, FL	1 665
63	54	Ventura, CA	1 642
55	55	Marion, IN	1 641
11	56	Riverside, CA	1 601
45	57	Milwaukee, WI	1 600
25	58	Sacramento, CA	1 564
15	59	Wayne, MI	1 561
34	60	Hennepin, MN	1 558
4	61	Maricopa, AZ	1 505
19	62	Bexar, TX	1 461
72	63	Pierce, WA	1 415
58	64	Duval, FL	1 385
71	65	Worcester, MA	1 374
12	66	San Bernardino, CA	1 368
41	67	Pima, AZ	1 333
61	68	Macomb, MI	1 296
62	69	Kern, CA	1 292
38	70	Salt Lake, UT	1 279
56	71	Wake, NC	1 270
69	72	El Paso, TX	1 219
46	73	Fresno, CA	1 189
43	74	Honolulu, HI	1 000
75	75	Hidalgo, TX	968

75 Largest Counties by 2010 Population
Selected Rankings

Violent crime rate, 2010

Population rank	Violent crime rate rank	County	Violent crime rate per 100,000 population [col 46]
21	1	Philadelphia, PA	1 215
47	2	Shelby, TN	1 206
15	3	Wayne, MI	1 157
55	4	Marion, IN	1 136
48	5	Fulton, GA	846
3	6	Harris, TX	777
13	6	Clark, NV	777
35	8	Orange, FL	760
8	9	Miami-Dade, FL	741
45	10	Milwaukee, WI	727
66	11	San Francisco, CA	721
59	12	Prince George's, MD	718
22	13	Alameda, CA	693
58	14	Duval, FL	676
73	15	Essex, NJ	670
2	16	Cook, IL	665
53	17	Pinellas, FL	658
25	18	Sacramento, CA	603
7	19	Kings, NY	595
10	19	Queens, NY	595
20	19	New York, NY	595
26	19	Bronx, NY	595
62	23	Kern, CA	581
49	24	Mecklenburg, NC	557
68	25	Hamilton, OH	556
29	26	Cuyahoga, OH	544
19	27	Bexar, TX	543
67	28	Baltimore, MD	540
46	29	Fresno, CA	535
28	30	Palm Beach, FL	530
33	31	Franklin, OH	513
1	32	Los Angeles, CA	512
9	33	Dallas, TX	498
50	34	Erie, NY	492
18	35	Broward, FL	485
72	36	Pierce, WA	480
71	37	Worcester, MA	465
30	38	Hillsborough, FL	458
34	39	Hennepin, MN	455
16	40	Tarrant, TX	446
12	41	San Bernardino, CA	443
31	42	Allegheny, PA	439
41	43	Pima, AZ	429
69	44	El Paso, TX	421
39	45	Travis, TX	420
60	46	New Haven, CT	416
37	47	Contra Costa, CA	412
4	48	Maricopa, AZ	386
5	49	San Diego, CA	376
38	50	Salt Lake, UT	374
14	51	King, WA	340
57	52	Hartford, CT	332
61	53	Macomb, MI	323
40	54	St. Louis, MO	320
75	55	Hidalgo, TX	314
11	56	Riverside, CA	302
23	57	Middlesex, MA	296
52	58	Fairfield, CT	282
43	59	Honolulu, HI	267
32	60	Oakland, MI	266
17	61	Santa Clara, CA	263
56	61	Wake, NC	263
44	63	Westchester, NY	257
65	64	Gwinnett, GA	252
6	65	Orange, CA	229
63	66	Ventura, CA	212
70	67	Montgomery, PA	195
42	68	Montgomery, MD	185
74	68	Collin, TX	185
64	70	Middlesex, NJ	179
27	71	Nassau, NY	173
24	72	Suffolk, NY	157
51	73	Du Page, IL	102
54	73	Bergen, NJ	102
36	75	Fairfax, VA	99

Military as a percent of all federal employment, 2009

Population rank	Military employment rank	County	military federal employment [col 195/col 194 + 195]
72	1	Pierce, WA	75.7
5	2	San Diego, CA	71.9
69	3	El Paso, TX	64.1
43	4	Honolulu, HI	63.2
12	5	San Bernardino, CA	61.6
74	6	Collin, TX	56.5
13	7	Clark, NV	53.1
19	8	Bexar, TX	53.0
58	8	Duval, FL	53.0
63	10	Ventura, CA	46.7
65	11	Gwinnett, GA	45.6
70	12	Montgomery, PA	45.4
40	13	St. Louis, MO	42.3
41	14	Pima, AZ	41.6
71	15	Worcester, MA	40.8
4	16	Maricopa, AZ	39.7
54	17	Bergen, NJ	38.4
56	18	Wake, NC	37.1
7	19	Kings, NY	36.6
30	20	Hillsborough, FL	36.3
64	21	Middlesex, NJ	35.8
75	22	Hidalgo, TX	34.7
52	23	Fairfield, CT	34.1
32	24	Oakland, MI	33.9
11	25	Riverside, CA	33.8
18	26	Broward, FL	33.2
6	27	Orange, CA	32.7
38	28	Salt Lake, UT	31.9
27	29	Nassau, NY	29.9
3	29	Harris, TX	29.9
53	31	Pinellas, FL	29.7
25	32	Sacramento, CA	29.3
49	33	Mecklenburg, NC	29.1
28	34	Palm Beach, FL	28.9
23	35	Middlesex, MA	27.2
22	36	Alameda, CA	27.1
8	37	Miami-Dade, FL	27.0
34	38	Hennepin, MN	26.7
16	38	Tarrant, TX	26.7
1	38	Los Angeles, CA	26.7
51	38	Du Page, IL	26.7
62	42	Kern, CA	26.1
14	43	King, WA	25.2
47	44	Shelby, TN	24.9
44	45	Westchester, NY	24.7
45	46	Milwaukee, WI	24.4
60	47	New Haven, CT	23.8
37	48	Contra Costa, CA	23.4
17	48	Santa Clara, CA	23.4
26	50	Bronx, NY	23.3
59	51	Prince George's, MD	22.7
33	52	Franklin, OH	22.3
57	53	Hartford, CT	22.1
39	54	Travis, TX	21.9
9	55	Dallas, TX	21.2
2	56	Cook, IL	20.8
31	56	Allegheny, PA	20.8
35	58	Orange, FL	20.4
10	59	Queens, NY	20.3
15	60	Wayne, MI	20.2
55	61	Marion, IN	19.6
68	61	Hamilton, OH	19.6
61	61	Macomb, MI	19.6
48	61	Fulton, GA	19.6
29	65	Cuyahoga, OH	18.5
24	66	Suffolk, NY	18.4
50	67	Erie, NY	16.0
46	68	Fresno, CA	15.3
36	69	Fairfax, VA	15.2
73	70	Essex, NJ	13.9
21	71	Philadelphia, PA	13.0
67	72	Baltimore, MD	12.8
42	73	Montgomery, MD	12.1
20	74	New York, NY	10.6
66	75	San Francisco, CA	10.4

Percent of votes for Barack Obama, 2008

Population rank	Vote for Obama rank	County	Percent of votes for Obama [col 197]
59	1	Prince George's, MD	88.9
26	2	Bronx, NY	88.7
20	3	New York, NY	85.7
66	4	San Francisco, CA	84.2
21	5	Philadelphia, PA	83.1
7	6	Kings, NY	79.4
22	7	Alameda, CA	78.8
2	8	Cook, IL	76.2
73	9	Essex, NJ	76.0
10	10	Queens, NY	75.1
15	11	Wayne, MI	74.1
42	12	Montgomery, MD	71.6
14	13	King, WA	70.3
43	14	Honolulu, HI	69.8
17	15	Santa Clara, CA	69.4
1	16	Los Angeles, CA	69.2
75	17	Hidalgo, TX	69.0
29	18	Cuyahoga, OH	68.9
37	19	Contra Costa, CA	68.0
45	20	Milwaukee, WI	67.3
48	21	Fulton, GA	67.2
18	22	Broward, FL	67.1
69	23	El Paso, TX	65.9
57	24	Hartford, CT	65.2
23	25	Middlesex, MA	64.2
39	26	Travis, TX	63.9
55	27	Marion, IN	63.8
34	28	Hennepin, MN	63.4
44	28	Westchester, NY	63.4
47	28	Shelby, TN	63.4
49	31	Mecklenburg, NC	61.8
28	32	Palm Beach, FL	61.2
60	33	New Haven, CT	61.0
64	34	Middlesex, NJ	60.4
36	35	Fairfax, VA	60.1
70	36	Montgomery, PA	60.0
33	37	Franklin, OH	59.7
40	38	St. Louis, MO	59.5
35	39	Orange, FL	59.0
52	40	Fairfield, CT	58.6
13	41	Clark, NV	58.5
25	41	Sacramento, CA	58.5
50	43	Erie, NY	58.0
8	44	Miami-Dade, FL	57.9
9	45	Dallas, TX	57.3
31	45	Allegheny, PA	57.3
56	47	Wake, NC	56.7
32	48	Oakland, MI	56.5
67	49	Baltimore, MD	56.2
71	50	Worcester, MA	55.8
63	51	Ventura, CA	55.2
72	51	Pierce, WA	55.2
51	53	Du Page, IL	54.7
54	54	Bergen, NJ	54.3
5	55	San Diego, CA	54.1
27	56	Nassau, NY	53.8
53	57	Pinellas, FL	53.6
61	58	Macomb, MI	53.4
30	59	Hillsborough, FL	53.2
68	60	Hamilton, OH	53.0
24	61	Suffolk, NY	52.6
19	62	Bexar, TX	52.4
41	62	Pima, AZ	52.4
12	64	San Bernardino, CA	52.1
3	65	Harris, TX	50.4
11	66	Riverside, CA	50.2
46	66	Fresno, CA	50.2
38	68	Salt Lake, UT	48.7
58	68	Duval, FL	48.7
6	70	Orange, CA	47.6
65	71	Gwinnett, GA	44.5
4	72	Maricopa, AZ	44.1
16	73	Tarrant, TX	43.7
62	74	Kern, CA	40.1
74	75	Collin, TX	36.8

All Counties
Selected Rankings

Defense contracts, 2009–2010				Non-defense contracts, 2009–2010				Federal grants, 2009–2010			
Population rank	Defense contracts rank	County	contracts (millions of dollars) [col 172]	Population rank	Non-defense contracts rank	County	contracts (millions of dollars) [col 173]	Population rank	Grants rank	County	(millions of dollars) [col 174 + 175 + 176 + 177]
36	1	Fairfax, VA	16 145.7	105	1	District of Columbia	16 598.9	1	20	New York, NY	34 534.3
5	2	San Diego, CA	11 593.0	36	2	Fairfax, VA	8 126.3	2	1	Los Angeles, CA	21 340.9
1	3	Los Angeles, CA	10 637.0	42	3	Montgomery, MD	6 596.2	3	25	Sacramento, CA	15 259.3
16	4	Tarrant, TX	9 369.9	1	4	Los Angeles, CA	5 805.2	4	2	Cook, IL	12 589.1
368	5	Winnebago, WI	7 100.1	298	5	Arlington, VA	4 849.9	5	39	Travis, TX	11 329.2
23	6	Middlesex, MA	5 847.4	3	6	Harris, TX	4 427.2	6	105	District of Columbia	10 872.0
41	7	Pima, AZ	5 268.8	59	7	Prince George's, MD	4 171.1	7	80	Suffolk, MA	9 637.6
192	8	Madison, AL	5 246.7	723	8	Anderson, TN	3 681.9	8	4	Maricopa, AZ	7 815.8
298	9	Arlington, VA	4 901.8	352	9	Benton, WA	3 127.6	9	21	Philadelphia, PA	7 464.9
17	10	Santa Clara, CA	4 708.7	22	10	Alameda, CA	2 903.6	10	8	Miami-Dade, FL	7 415.2
105	11	District of Columbia	4 651.0	92	11	Bernalillo, NM	2 894.6	11	100	Baltimore city, MD	7 211.8
40	12	St. Louis, MO	4 569.4	119	12	Jefferson, CO	2 422.3	12	210	Albany, NY	6 947.8
4	13	Maricopa, AZ	4 436.4	386	13	Aiken, SC	2 325.8	13	149	East Baton Rouge, LA	6 872.9
52	14	Fairfield, CT	4 045.9	20	14	New York, NY	2 225.2	14	48	Fulton, GA	6 868.0
77	15	Essex, MA	3 843.8	1 925	15	Los Alamos, NM	2 215.8	15	33	Franklin, OH	6 841.1
19	16	Bexar, TX	3 693.9	48	16	Fulton, GA	2 021.2	16	233	Leon, FL	6 780.4
86	17	Cobb, GA	3 623.6	2	17	Cook, IL	1 997.1	17	243	Dauphin, PA	6 580.6
237	18	New London, CT	3 520.5	89	18	Jackson, MO	1 452.8	18	5	San Diego, CA	5 774.5
25	19	Sacramento, CA	3 511.6	31	19	Allegheny, PA	1 430.4	19	14	King, WA	5 218.8
35	20	Orange, FL	3 417.4	23	20	Middlesex, MA	1 415.4	20	3	Harris, TX	4 941.0
200	21	St. Louis city, MO	3 414.6	561	21	Bonneville, ID	1 359.4	21	15	Wayne, MI	4 934.9
57	22	Hartford, CT	3 292.2	70	22	Montgomery, PA	1 326.0	22	66	San Francisco, CA	4 870.0
9	23	Dallas, TX	3 142.1	5	23	San Diego, CA	1 288.7	23	96	Davidson, TN	4 661.1
78	24	Jefferson, KY	3 079.7	113	24	Brevard, FL	1 237.4	24	55	Marion, IN	4 574.9
342	25	Newport News City, VA	3 013.8	129	25	Chester, PA	1 222.7	25	23	Middlesex, MA	4 530.6
204	26	Loudoun, VA	2 972.3	9	26	Dallas, TX	1 165.9	26	56	Wake, NC	4 489.3
99	27	El Paso, CO	2 888.3	21	27	Philadelphia, PA	1 141.7	27	229	Ingham, MI	4 228.1
95	28	Monmouth, NJ	2 858.3	438	28	Alexandria City, VA	1 128.3	28	315	Sangamon, IL	4 169.2
14	29	King, WA	2 723.5	192	29	Madison, AL	1 127.0	29	22	Alameda, CA	4 003.6
3	30	Harris, TX	2 658.4	799	30	McCracken, KY	1 078.8	30	136	Dane, WI	3 888.9
42	31	Montgomery, MD	2 555.8	17	31	Santa Clara, CA	1 070.8	31	179	Mercer, NJ	3 794.3
189	32	Orleans, LA	2 495.4	24	32	Suffolk, NY	1 038.5	32	29	Cuyahoga, OH	3 602.4
499	33	Potter, TX	2 428.4	51	33	Du Page, IL	947.6	33	106	Denver, CO	3 576.2
61	34	Macomb, MI	2 324.4	100	34	Baltimore city, MD	944.2	34	31	Allegheny, PA	3 499.7
12	35	San Bernardino, CA	2 317.9	67	35	Baltimore, MD	915.4	35	57	Hartford, CT	3 474.4
43	36	Honolulu, HI	2 218.2	13	36	Clark, NV	893.0	36	300	Richmond City, VA	3 338.0
166	37	Prince William, VA	2 205.3	361	37	Monroe, PA	864.9	37	17	Santa Clara, CA	3 243.1
2	38	Cook, IL	2 148.9	4	38	Maricopa, AZ	848.2	38	200	St. Louis city, MO	3 201.5
267	39	Norfolk City, VA	2 126.5	34	39	Hennepin, MN	831.2	39	6	Orange, CA	3 060.1
559	40	St. Mary's, MD	2 123.6	14	40	King, WA	828.5	40	127	Ramsey, MN	2 997.3
113	41	Brevard, FL	2 092.1	244	41	Durham, NC	819.0	41	9	Dallas, TX	2 983.2
150	42	Virginia Beach City, VA	2 086.2	29	42	Cuyahoga, OH	811.3	42	38	Salt Lake, UT	2 896.9
6	43	Orange, CA	2 026.2	66	43	San Francisco, CA	798.8	43	34	Hennepin, MN	2 860.4
51	44	Du Page, IL	1 992.7	80	44	Suffolk, MA	795.3	44	713	Cole, MO	2 797.9
31	45	Allegheny, PA	1 885.2	15	45	Wayne, MI	779.9	45	19	Bexar, TX	2 793.9
116	46	Anne Arundel, MD	1 879.0	275	46	Frederick, MD	718.7	46	79	Multnomah, OR	2 791.1
76	47	Monroe, NY	1 843.6	185	47	Charleston, SC	713.8	47	45	Milwaukee, WI	2 780.4
68	48	Hamilton, OH	1 792.2	82	48	San Mateo, CA	697.8	48	73	Essex, NJ	2 775.4
145	49	Burlington, NJ	1 769.9	39	49	Travis, TX	697.7	49	258	Thurston, WA	2 738.6
109	50	Arapahoe, CO	1 714.8	30	50	Hillsborough, FL	688.4	50	81	Oklahoma, OK	2 673.0
27	51	Nassau, NY	1 713.7	106	51	Denver, CO	654.0	51	97	Providence, RI	2 502.8
47	52	Shelby, TN	1 627.9	499	52	Potter, TX	637.6	52	172	Pulaski, AR	2 460.9
111	53	Bristol, MA	1 585.1	442	53	Kootenai, ID	618.3	53	43	Honolulu, HI	2 409.4
185	54	Charleston, SC	1 578.6	224	54	Howard, MD	594.0	54	41	Pima, AZ	2 291.8
224	55	Howard, MD	1 576.9	47	55	Shelby, TN	593.9	55	60	New Haven, CT	2 265.9
129	56	Chester, PA	1 541.4	85	56	De Kalb, GA	589.1	56	278	Montgomery, AL	2 228.5
341	57	Okaloosa, FL	1 397.5	19	57	Bexar, TX	582.7	57	50	Erie, NY	2 162.0
653	58	Hunt, TX	1 391.0	977	58	Box Elder, UT	572.9	58	264	Hinds, MS	2 131.5
151	59	York, PA	1 323.7	35	59	Orange, FL	568.4	59	68	Hamilton, OH	2 120.9
55	60	Marion, IN	1 290.3	96	60	Davidson, TN	560.2	60	202	Marion, OR	2 105.4
110	61	Delaware, PA	1 289.0	220	61	Boulder, CO	532.6	61	24	Suffolk, NY	2 087.6
206	62	Bell, TX	1 281.2	16	62	Tarrant, TX	531.6	62	12	San Bernardino, CA	2 071.2
199	63	Cumberland, NC	1 227.0	189	63	Orleans, LA	527.4	63	244	Durham, NC	2 066.5
432	64	Cambria, PA	1 180.9	191	64	Hamilton, TN	507.5	64	47	Shelby, TN	2 021.8
308	65	Yolo, CA	1 145.3	448	65	Hampton City, VA	498.1	65	991	Franklin, KY	2 016.9
30	66	Hillsborough, FL	1 144.0	204	66	Loudoun, VA	491.3	66	171	Richland, SC	1 949.8
33	67	Franklin, OH	1 129.9	712	67	Leavenworth, KS	489.9	67	154	Polk, IA	1 943.3
292	68	Linn, IA	1 128.5	79	68	Multnomah, OR	481.1	68	390	Rensselaer, NY	1 879.5
152	69	Jefferson, LA	1 122.5	8	69	Miami-Dade, FL	472.7	69	76	Monroe, NY	1 829.4
245	70	St. Joseph, IN	1 122.3	124	70	Kane, IL	470.0	70	324	Kanawha, WV	1 797.8
130	71	Sedgwick, KS	1 074.6	32	71	Oakland, MI	458.6	71	189	Orleans, LA	1 786.0
380	72	Greene, OH	1 074.1	1 087	72	Hancock, MS	443.7	72	42	Montgomery, MD	1 749.1
140	73	Onondaga, NY	1 051.3	248	73	Rutherford, TN	443.1	73	71	Worcester, MA	1 731.9
74	74	Collin, TX	1 046.7	6	74	Orange, CA	430.5	74	11	Riverside, CA	1 686.2
53	75	Pinellas, FL	978.1	55	75	Marion, IN	429.1	75	188	Washtenaw, MI	1 661.7

75 Counties with Highest Agricultural Sales
Selected Rankings

	Value of agricultural sales, 2007			Average agricultural sales per farm, 2007				Number of farms, 2007		
Value of sales rank	County	Value of sales (millions of dollars) [col 125]	Value of sales rank	Average sales rank	County	Average sales per farm (dollars) [col 126]	Value of sales rank	Number of farms rank	County	Number of farms [col 113]
1	Fresno County, CA	3 731	35	1	Haskell County, KS	2 896 342	19	1	San Diego County, CA	6 687
2	Tulare County, CA	3 335	11	2	Imperial County, CA	2 854 543	1	2	Fresno County, CA	6 081
3	Kern County, CA	3 204	32	3	Scott County, KS	2 753 403	18	3	Lancaster County, PA	5 462
4	Merced County, CA	2 330	34	4	Hartley County, TX	2 569 176	2	4	Tulare County, CA	5 240
5	Monterey County, CA	2 179	43	5	Hansford County, TX	2 437 187	6	5	Stanislaus County, CA	4 114
6	Stanislaus County, CA	1 821	23	6	Yuma County, AZ	2 123 822	8	6	Weld County, CO	3 921
7	San Joaquin County, CA	1 564	22	7	Castro County, TX	2 006 911	7	7	San Joaquin County, CA	3 624
8	Weld County, CO	1 539	5	8	Monterey County, CA	1 816 906	12	8	Yakima County, WA	3 540
9	Kings County, CA	1 358	16	9	Deaf Smith County, TX	1 802 762	20	9	Riverside County, CA	3 463
10	Ventura County, CA	1 316	46	10	Grant County, KS	1 769 655	40	10	Sonoma County, CA	3 429
11	Imperial County, CA	1 290	25	11	Parmer County, TX	1 689 485	54	11	Stearns County, MN	3 368
12	Yakima County, WA	1 204	68	12	Moore County, TX	1 636 750	63	12	Dane County, WI	3 331
13	Sampson County, NC	1 196	3	13	Kern County, CA	1 513 532	59	13	Hillsborough County, FL	2 843
14	Grant County, WA	1 190	38	14	Gray County, KS	1 461 694	48	14	San Luis Obispo County, CA	2 784
15	Duplin County, NC	1 176	73	15	Wichita County, KS	1 389 261	45	15	Marion County, OR	2 670
16	Deaf Smith County, TX	1 148	37	16	Finney County, KS	1 344 046	4	16	Merced County, CA	2 607
17	Sioux County, IA	1 121	47	17	Hendry County, FL	1 319 602	39	17	Miami-Dade County, FL	2 498
18	Lancaster County, PA	1 072	72	18	Sherman County, TX	1 239 944	10	18	Ventura County, CA	2 437
19	San Diego County, CA	1 054	50	19	Dallam County, TX	1 223 139	3	19	Kern County, CA	2 117
20	Riverside County, CA	1 012	9	20	Kings County, CA	1 203 198	52	20	Rockingham County, VA	1 970
21	Madera County, CA	990	64	21	Phelps County, NE	1 119 572	14	21	Grant County, WA	1 858
22	Castro County, TX	973	30	22	Pinal County, AZ	1 018 867	29	22	Maricopa County, AZ	1 793
23	Yuma County, AZ	960	15	23	Duplin County, NC	1 014 902	60	23	Darke County, OH	1 772
24	Santa Barbara County, CA	951	13	24	Sampson County, NC	994 457	49	24	Chester County, PA	1 733
25	Parmer County, TX	938	27	25	Cuming County, NE	992 599	21	25	Madera County, CA	1 708
26	Palm Beach County, FL	932	41	26	Cassia County, ID	973 170	17	26	Sioux County, IA	1 664
27	Cuming County, NE	857	42	27	Gooding County, ID	938 978	53	27	Benton County, WA	1 630
28	Sussex County, DE	849	4	28	Merced County, CA	893 904	24	28	Santa Barbara County, CA	1 597
29	Maricopa County, AZ	814	70	29	Swisher County, TX	860 821	67	29	Plymouth County, IA	1 442
30	Pinal County, AZ	800	44	30	Dawson County, NE	808 444	33	30	San Bernardino County, CA	1 405
31	Texas County, OK	780	69	31	Jerome County, ID	764 237	65	31	Kossuth County, IA	1 395
32	Scott County, KS	763	31	32	Texas County, OK	751 318	28	32	Sussex County, DE	1 374
33	San Bernardino County, CA	744	26	33	Palm Beach County, FL	737 712	51	33	Mercer County, OH	1 302
34	Hartley County, TX	725	36	34	Yuma County, CO	733 393	62	34	Twin Falls County, ID	1 296
35	Haskell County, KS	718	61	35	Ford County, KS	713 970	26	35	Palm Beach County, FL	1 263
36	Yuma County, CO	711	57	36	Wayne County, NC	693 190	13	36	Sampson County, NC	1 203
37	Finney County, KS	694	17	37	Sioux County, IA	673 764	5	37	Monterey County, CA	1 199
38	Gray County, KS	691	74	38	Santa Cruz County, CA	656 037	55	38	Custer County, NE	1 187
39	Miami-Dade County, FL	661	14	39	Grant County, WA	640 576	15	39	Duplin County, NC	1 159
40	Sonoma County, CA	648	2	40	Tulare County, CA	636 453	9	40	Kings County, CA	1 129
41	Cassia County, ID	627	56	41	Fayette County, KY	622 377	71	41	Lyon County, IA	1 087
42	Gooding County, ID	624	28	42	Sussex County, DE	617 862	31	42	Texas County, OK	1 038
43	Hansford County, TX	590	1	43	Fresno County, CA	613 476	75	43	Carroll County, IA	978
44	Dawson County, NE	589	24	44	Santa Barbara County, CA	595 696	36	44	Yuma County, CO	970
45	Marion County, OR	587	21	45	Madera County, CA	579 696	58	45	Morgan County, CO	894
46	Grant County, KS	577	58	46	Morgan County, CO	552 420	66	46	Franklin County, WA	891
47	Hendry County, FL	567	10	47	Ventura County, CA	540 137	27	47	Cuming County, NE	863
48	San Luis Obispo County, CA	561	33	48	San Bernardino County, CA	529 296	56	48	Fayette County, KY	810
49	Chester County, PA	553	66	49	Franklin County, WA	524 145	30	49	Pinal County, AZ	785
50	Dallam County, TX	553	29	50	Maricopa County, AZ	453 704	44	50	Dawson County, NE	728
51	Mercer County, OH	535	75	51	Carroll County, IA	452 612	57	51	Wayne County, NC	723
52	Rockingham County, VA	534	6	52	Stanislaus County, CA	442 529	74	52	Santa Cruz County, CA	682
53	Benton County, WA	526	55	53	Custer County, NE	432 831	42	53	Gooding County, ID	665
54	Stearns County, MN	519	7	54	San Joaquin County, CA	431 665	61	54	Ford County, KS	664
55	Custer County, NE	514	71	55	Lyon County, IA	416 847	41	55	Cassia County, ID	644
56	Fayette County, KY	504	51	56	Mercer County, OH	411 051	16	56	Deaf Smith County, TX	637
57	Wayne County, NC	501	8	57	Weld County, CO	392 520	69	57	Jerome County, ID	604
58	Morgan County, CO	494	62	58	Twin Falls County, ID	364 090	25	58	Parmer County, TX	555
59	Hillsborough County, FL	488	12	59	Yakima County, WA	340 058	70	59	Swisher County, TX	527
60	Darke County, OH	480	65	60	Kossuth County, IA	335 347	37	60	Finney County, KS	516
61	Ford County, KS	474	67	61	Plymouth County, IA	324 065	22	61	Castro County, TX	485
62	Twin Falls County, ID	472	53	62	Benton County, WA	322 649	38	62	Gray County, KS	473
63	Dane County, WI	471	49	63	Chester County, PA	319 267	50	63	Dallam County, TX	452
64	Phelps County, NE	470	20	64	Riverside County, CA	292 244	11	63	Imperial County, CA	452
65	Kossuth County, IA	468	52	65	Rockingham County, VA	271 138	23	63	Yuma County, AZ	452
66	Franklin County, WA	467	60	66	Darke County, OH	270 741	47	66	Hendry County, FL	430
67	Plymouth County, IA	467	39	67	Miami-Dade County, FL	264 652	64	67	Phelps County, NE	420
68	Moore County, TX	463	45	68	Marion County, OR	219 754	72	68	Sherman County, TX	362
69	Jerome County, ID	462	48	69	San Luis Obispo County, CA	201 368	46	69	Grant County, KS	326
70	Swisher County, TX	454	18	70	Lancaster County, PA	196 293	73	70	Wichita County, KS	323
71	Lyon County, IA	453	40	71	Sonoma County, CA	188 854	68	71	Moore County, TX	283
72	Sherman County, TX	449	59	72	Hillsborough County, FL	171 727	34	72	Hartley County, TX	282
73	Wichita County, KS	449	19	73	San Diego County, CA	157 646	32	73	Scott County, KS	277
74	Santa Cruz County, CA	447	54	74	Stearns County, MN	154 226	35	74	Haskell County, KS	248
75	Carroll County, IA	443	63	75	Dane County, WI	141 277	43	75	Hansford County, TX	242

75 Counties with Highest Agricultural Sales
Selected Rankings

Average size of farm, 2007				Average value of land and buildings per farm, 2007				Average value of land and buildings per acre, 2007			
Value of sales rank	Size of farm rank	County	Average size of farm (acres) [col 119]	Value of sales rank	land and buildings per farm rank	County	Average value per farm (dollars) [col 122]	Value of sales rank	Value of land and buildings per acre rank	County	Average value per acre (dollars) [col 123]
34	1	Hartley County, TX	3 230	3	1	Kern County, CA	5 160 784	39	1	Miami-Dade County, FL	27 648
43	2	Hansford County, TX	2 419	5	2	Monterey County, CA	5 144 255	10	2	Ventura County, CA	22 782
50	3	Dallam County, TX	2 073	11	3	Imperial County, CA	5 001 024	74	3	Santa Cruz County, CA	22 423
68	4	Moore County, TX	1 955	30	4	Pinal County, AZ	4 853 351	19	4	San Diego County, CA	19 247
32	5	Scott County, KS	1 636	23	5	Yuma County, AZ	3 893 483	40	5	Sonoma County, CA	15 887
72	6	Sherman County, TX	1 614	47	6	Hendry County, FL	3 673 204	20	6	Riverside County, CA	15 765
73	7	Wichita County, KS	1 609	9	7	Kings County, CA	3 295 061	49	7	Chester County, PA	10 740
35	8	Haskell County, KS	1 608	24	8	Santa Barbara County, CA	3 223 533	28	8	Sussex County, DE	10 234
16	9	Deaf Smith County, TX	1 485	4	9	Merced County, CA	2 879 524	59	9	Hillsborough County, FL	10 190
37	10	Finney County, KS	1 473	21	10	Madera County, CA	2 699 315	7	10	San Joaquin County, CA	10 168
36	11	Yuma County, CO	1 376	40	11	Sonoma County, CA	2 459 725	6	11	Stanislaus County, CA	9 476
55	12	Custer County, NE	1 360	10	12	Ventura County, CA	2 421 700	18	12	Lancaster County, PA	9 324
30	13	Pinal County, AZ	1 334	29	13	Maricopa County, AZ	2 300 844	29	13	Maricopa County, AZ	8 498
22	14	Castro County, TX	1 170	48	14	San Luis Obispo County, CA	2 236 326	23	14	Yuma County, AZ	8 361
31	15	Texas County, OK	1 162	34	15	Hartley County, TX	2 184 140	2	15	Tulare County, CA	8 266
38	16	Gray County, KS	1 155	1	16	Fresno County, CA	2 132 914	1	16	Fresno County, CA	7 927
3	17	Kern County, CA	1 116	7	17	San Joaquin County, CA	2 069 142	4	17	Merced County, CA	7 210
5	18	Monterey County, CA	1 108	28	18	Sussex County, DE	2 006 959	24	18	Santa Barbara County, CA	7 081
47	19	Hendry County, FL	1 082	43	19	Hansford County, TX	1 949 295	45	19	Marion County, OR	6 908
70	20	Swisher County, TX	1 068	2	20	Tulare County, CA	1 843 502	21	20	Madera County, CA	6 783
46	21	Grant County, KS	1 035	6	21	Stanislaus County, CA	1 817 304	56	21	Fayette County, KY	6 594
25	22	Parmer County, TX	1 010	50	22	Dallam County, TX	1 751 802	52	22	Rockingham County, VA	6 150
41	23	Cassia County, ID	1 001	26	23	Palm Beach County, FL	1 712 306	9	23	Kings County, CA	5 465
61	24	Ford County, KS	955	35	24	Haskell County, KS	1 708 092	11	24	Imperial County, CA	5 290
11	25	Imperial County, CA	945	68	25	Moore County, TX	1 677 878	51	25	Mercer County, OH	4 882
44	26	Dawson County, NE	880	41	26	Cassia County, ID	1 665 431	5	26	Monterey County, CA	4 645
58	27	Morgan County, CO	814	64	27	Phelps County, NE	1 663 392	3	27	Kern County, CA	4 626
64	28	Phelps County, NE	810	20	28	Riverside County, CA	1 614 969	48	28	San Luis Obispo County, CA	4 546
66	29	Franklin County, WA	684	74	29	Santa Cruz County, CA	1 561 362	17	29	Sioux County, IA	4 534
9	30	Kings County, CA	603	65	30	Kossuth County, IA	1 553 530	63	30	Dane County, WI	4 330
14	31	Grant County, WA	586	66	31	Franklin County, WA	1 477 309	71	31	Lyon County, IA	4 202
8	32	Weld County, CO	533	14	32	Grant County, WA	1 460 726	60	32	Darke County, OH	4 195
48	33	San Luis Obispo County, CA	492	36	33	Yuma County, CO	1 438 070	57	33	Wayne County, NC	4 160
12	34	Yakima County, WA	466	55	34	Custer County, NE	1 386 763	26	34	Palm Beach County, FL	4 114
23	34	Yuma County, AZ	466	16	35	Deaf Smith County, TX	1 356 340	15	35	Duplin County, NC	4 082
24	36	Santa Barbara County, CA	455	75	36	Carroll County, IA	1 347 857	42	36	Gooding County, ID	3 980
65	37	Kossuth County, IA	431	42	37	Gooding County, ID	1 335 076	13	37	Sampson County, NC	3 738
27	38	Cuming County, NE	417	72	38	Sherman County, TX	1 313 201	75	38	Carroll County, IA	3 681
26	39	Palm Beach County, FL	416	17	39	Sioux County, IA	1 304 456	30	39	Pinal County, AZ	3 638
4	40	Merced County, CA	399	67	40	Plymouth County, IA	1 301 406	67	40	Plymouth County, IA	3 628
21	41	Madera County, CA	398	71	41	Lyon County, IA	1 248 886	65	41	Kossuth County, IA	3 603
53	42	Benton County, WA	388	32	42	Scott County, KS	1 218 245	69	42	Jerome County, ID	3 439
75	43	Carroll County, IA	366	22	43	Castro County, TX	1 209 915	47	43	Hendry County, FL	3 396
33	43	San Bernardino County, CA	366	44	44	Dawson County, NE	1 176 513	33	44	San Bernardino County, CA	3 167
67	45	Plymouth County, IA	359	33	45	San Bernardino County, CA	1 159 028	54	45	Stearns County, MN	2 830
62	46	Twin Falls County, ID	339	37	46	Finney County, KS	1 153 579	14	46	Grant County, WA	2 495
42	47	Gooding County, ID	335	56	47	Fayette County, KY	1 106 925	27	47	Cuming County, NE	2 493
69	48	Jerome County, ID	313	51	48	Mercer County, OH	1 098 779	62	48	Twin Falls County, ID	2 479
71	49	Lyon County, IA	297	73	49	Wichita County, KS	1 077 030	53	49	Benton County, WA	2 323
17	50	Sioux County, IA	288	69	50	Jerome County, ID	1 074 850	66	50	Franklin County, WA	2 161
29	51	Maricopa County, AZ	271	27	51	Cuming County, NE	1 040 286	64	51	Phelps County, NE	2 053
1	52	Fresno County, CA	269	49	52	Chester County, PA	1 034 252	41	52	Cassia County, ID	1 664
13	53	Sampson County, NC	267	25	53	Parmer County, TX	1 029 842	8	53	Weld County, CO	1 550
57	54	Wayne County, NC	242	57	54	Wayne County, NC	1 008 378	12	54	Yakima County, WA	1 530
51	55	Mercer County, OH	225	13	55	Sampson County, NC	998 921	44	55	Dawson County, NE	1 337
2	56	Tulare County, CA	223	38	56	Gray County, KS	983 325	58	56	Morgan County, CO	1 093
15	57	Duplin County, NC	214	53	57	Benton County, WA	901 747	35	57	Haskell County, KS	1 062
54	58	Stearns County, MN	210	58	58	Morgan County, CO	890 238	36	58	Yuma County, CO	1 045
7	59	San Joaquin County, CA	204	19	59	San Diego County, CA	874 683	22	59	Castro County, TX	1 034
60	60	Darke County, OH	198	15	60	Duplin County, NC	873 575	55	60	Custer County, NE	1 020
28	61	Sussex County, DE	196	62	61	Twin Falls County, ID	840 836	25	61	Parmer County, TX	1 019
6	62	Stanislaus County, CA	192	60	62	Darke County, OH	829 604	16	62	Deaf Smith County, TX	913
56	63	Fayette County, KY	168	46	63	Grant County, KS	827 976	68	63	Moore County, TX	858
63	64	Dane County, WI	161	8	64	Weld County, CO	825 561	38	64	Gray County, KS	852
40	65	Sonoma County, CA	155	45	65	Marion County, OR	795 988	50	65	Dallam County, TX	845
52	66	Rockingham County, VA	118	31	66	Texas County, OK	791 501	72	66	Sherman County, TX	814
45	67	Marion County, OR	115	59	67	Hillsborough County, FL	787 847	43	67	Hansford County, TX	806
10	68	Ventura County, CA	106	70	68	Swisher County, TX	775 406	46	68	Grant County, KS	800
20	69	Riverside County, CA	102	39	69	Miami-Dade County, FL	742 119	37	69	Finney County, KS	783
49	70	Chester County, PA	96	52	70	Rockingham County, VA	727 644	32	70	Scott County, KS	744
18	71	Lancaster County, PA	78	18	71	Lancaster County, PA	726 059	70	71	Swisher County, TX	726
59	72	Hillsborough County, FL	77	12	72	Yakima County, WA	712 970	61	72	Ford County, KS	712
74	73	Santa Cruz County, CA	70	63	73	Dane County, WI	696 424	31	73	Texas County, OK	681
19	74	San Diego County, CA	45	61	74	Ford County, KS	680 092	34	74	Hartley County, TX	676
39	75	Miami-Dade County, FL	27	54	75	Stearns County, MN	595 214	73	75	Wichita County, KS	669

Table B. States and Counties — **Land Area and Population**

STATE/ County code	CBSA code[1]	County type[2]	STATE County	Land area,[3] (sq km) 2010	Population and population characteristics, 2010													
								Race alone or in combination, not Hispanic or Latino (percent)					Age (percent)					
					Total persons	Rank	Per square kilometer	White	Black	American Indian, Alaska Native	Asian and Pacific Islander	Percent Hispanic or Latino[4]	Under 5 years	5 to 17 years	18 to 24 years	25 to 34 years	35 to 44 years	45 to 54 years
				1	2	3	4	5	6	7	8	9	10	11	12	13	14	15

1. CBSA = Core Based Statistical Area. See Appendix A for explanation. See Appendix B for list of metropolitan areas with component counties. 2. County type code from the Economic Research Service of USDA Rural-Urban Continuum Codes. See Appendix A for definition. 3. Dry land or land partially or temporarily covered by water. 4. May be of any race.

Table B. States and Counties — **Population and Households**

STATE County	Population, 2010 (cont.)				Population change and components of change, 1990–2010							Households, 2010				
	Age (percent) (cont.)				Total persons		Percent change		Components of change, 2000–2009						Percent	
	55 to 64 years	65 to 74 years	75 years and over	Percent female	1990	2000	1990– 2000	2000– 2010	Births	Deaths	Net migration	Number	Percent change, 2000– 2010	Persons per house-hold	Female family house-holder[1]	One per-son
	16	17	18	19	20	21	22	23	24	25	26	27	28	29	30	31

1. No spouse present.

Table B. States and Counties — **Population, Vital Statistics, Medicare, and Crime**

STATE County	Daytime population, 2006–2010		Births, average 2006–2008		Deaths, average 2006–2008		Persons under 65 with no health insurance, 2009		Medicare, 2011			Serious crimes known to police,[2] 2010	
												Total	
	Persons in group quarters, 2010	Number	Employ-ment/ resi-dence ratio	Total	Rate[1]	Number	Rate[1]	Number	Percent	Eligible for Medicare	Enrolled in Medicare Advantage	Enrolled in a Medicare prescription drug plan	Number	Rate[3]
	32	33	34	35	36	37	38	39	40	41	42	43	44	45

1. Per 1,000 estimated resident population. 2. Data for serious crimes have not been adjusted for underreporting; this may affect comparability between geographic areas and over time. 3. Per 100,000 population estimated by the FBI.

Table B. States and Counties — **Crime, Education, Money Income, and Poverty**

STATE County	Serious crimes known to police,[1] 2010 (cont.)		Education						Money income, 2006–2010				Income and poverty, 2010			
	Rate[2]		School enrollment and attainment, 2006–2010				Local government expenditures,[5] 2008–2009			Households				Percent below poverty level		
			Enrollment[3]		Attainment[4] (percent)						Median income					
	Violent	Property	Total	Per-cent private	High school grad-uate or less	Bach-elor's degree or more	Total current expendi-tures (mil dol)	Current expendi-tures per student (dollars)	Per capita income[6] (dollars)	Dollars	Percent change, 2000 to 2006–2010 (constant 2010 dollars)	Percent with income of $200,000 or more	Median house-hold income (dollars)	All per-sons	Children under 18 years	Children 5 to 17 years in families
	46	47	48	49	50	51	52	53	54	55	56	57	58	59	60	61

1. Data for serious crimes have not been adjusted for underreporting; this may affect comparability between geographic areas and over time. 2. Per 100,000 population estimated by the FBI. 3. All persons 3 years old and over enrolled in nursery school through college. 4. Persons 25 years old and over. 5. Elementary and secondary education expenditures. 6. Based on population estimated by the American Community Survey, 2006–2010.

Table B. States and Counties — **Personal Income**

STATE County	Personal income, 2009												
	Total (mil dol)	Per capita[1]		Wages and salaries[2] (mil dol)	Proprietors' income (mil dol)	Dividends, interest, and rent (mil dol)	Transfer payments (mil dol)		Government payments to individuals				
		Percent change, 2008–2009	Dollars	Rank				Total	Total	Social Security	Medical payments	Income maintenance	Unemployment insurance
	62	63	64	65	66	67	68	69	70	71	72	73	74

1. Based on the resident population estimated as of July 1 of the year shown.   2. Includes supplements to wages and salaries.

Table B. States and Counties — **Earnings, Social Security, and Housing**

STATE County	Earnings, 2009									Social Security beneficiaries, December 2010		Supplemental Security Income recipients, December 2010	Housing units, 2010	
	Total (mil dol)	Percent by selected industries								Number	Rate[2]		Total	Percent change, 2000–2010
		Farm	Goods-related[1]		Service-related and health									
			Total	Manufacturing	Information and professional and technical services	Retail trade	Finance, insurance, and real estate	Health care and social services	Government					
	75	76	77	78	79	80	81	82	83	84	85	86	87	88

1. Includes mining, construction, and manufacturing.   2. Per 1,000 resident population enumerated in the 2010 census.

Table B. States and Counties — **Housing, Labor Force, and Employment**

STATE County	Housing units, 2006–2010								Civilian labor force, 2010				Civilian employment,[5] 2006–2010		
	Occupied units										Unemployment		Percent		
	Total	Percent	Owner-occupied				Renter-occupied		Total	Percent change, 2009–2010			Total	Management, business, science and arts	Construction, production, and maintenance occupations
			Median value[1]	Median owner cost as a percent of income		Median rent[2]	Median rent as a percent of income	Substandard units[3] (percent)			Total	Rate[4]			
				With a mortgage	Without a mortgage										
	89	90	91	92	93	94	95	96	97	98	99	100	101	102	103

1. Specified owner-occupied units.   2. Specified renter-occupied units. A value of 10.0 represents 10 percent or less.   3. Overcrowded or lacking complete plumbing facilities.   4. Percent of civilian labor force.   5. Persons 16 years old and over.

Table B. States and Counties — **Nonfarm Employment and Agriculture**

STATE County	Private nonfarm establishments, employment and payroll, 2009									Agriculture, 2007			
	Number of establishments	Employment						Annual payroll		Farms			Farm operators whose principal occupation is farming (percent)
		Total	Health care and social assistance	Manufacturing	Retail trade	Finance and insurance	Professional, scientific, and technical services	Total (mil dol)	Average per employee (dollars)	Number	Percent with:		
											Fewer than 50 acres	500 acres or more	
	104	105	106	107	108	109	110	111	112	113	114	115	116

Table B. States and Counties — **Agriculture**

	Agriculture, 2007 (cont.)															
STATE County	Land in farms					Value of land and buildings (dollars)			Value of products sold				Percent of farms with sales of:		Government payments	
			Acres					Value of machinery and equipment, average per farm (dollars)				Percent from:				
	Acreage (1,000)	Percent change, 2002–2007	Average size of farm	Total irrigated (1,000)	Total cropland (1,000)	Average per farm	Average per acre		Total (mil dol)	Average per farm (dollars)	Crops	Live-stock and poultry products	$10,000 or more	$100,000 or more	Total ($1,000)	Percent of farms
	117	118	119	120	121	122	123	124	125	126	127	128	129	130	131	132

Table B. States and Counties — **Water Use, Wholesale Trade, Retail Trade, and Real Estate**

	Water use, 2005		Wholesale trade,[1] 2007				Retail trade,[2] 2007				Real estate and rental and leasing,[2] 2007			
STATE County	Total water withdrawn (mil gal/day)	Gallons withdrawn per person	Number of establish-ments	Number of employees	Sales (mil dol)	Annual payroll (mil dol)	Number of establish-ments	Number of employees	Sales (mil dol)	Annual payroll (mil dol)	Number of establish-ments	Number of employees	Receipts (mil dol)	Annual payroll (mil dol)
	133	134	135	136	137	138	139	140	141	142	143	144	145	146

1. Merchant wholesalers, except manufacturers' sales branches and offices.   2. Employer establishments.

Table B. States and Counties — **Professional Services, Manufacturing, and Accommodation and Food Services**

	Professional, scientific, and technical services,[1] 2007				Manufacturing, 2007				Accommodation and food services, 2007			
STATE County	Number of establish-ments	Number of employees	Receipts (mil dol)	Annual payroll (mil dol)	Number of establish-ments	Number of employees	Receipts (mil dol)	Annual payroll (mil dol)	Number of establish-ments	Number of employees	Sales (mil dol)	Annual payroll (mil dol)
	147	148	149	150	151	152	153	154	155	156	157	158

1. Establishment subject to federal tax.

Table B. States and Counties — **Health Care and Social Assistance, Other Services, and Federal Funds**

	Health care and social assistance, 2007				Other services, 2007				Federal funds and grants, 2009–2010			
									Expenditures (mil dol)			
										Direct payments for individuals[1]		
STATE County	Number of establish-ments	Number of employees	Receipts (mil dol)	Annual payroll (mil dol)	Number of establish-ments	Number of employees	Receipts (mil dol)	Annual payroll (mil dol)	Total	Social Security and government retirement	Medicare	Food Stamps and Supplemental Security Income
	159	160	161	162	163	164	165	166	167	168	169	170

1. State totals may include programs not allocated by county.

Table B. States and Counties — Federal Funds, Residential Construction, and Local Government Finances

	Federal funds and grants, 2009–2010 (cont.)							Value of residential construction authorized by building permits, 2010		Local government finances, 2007					
	Expenditures (mil dol) (cont.)									General revenue					
		Procurement contract awards		Grants[1]									Taxes		
STATE County														Per capita[2] (dollars)	
	Salaries and wages	Defense	Other	Medicaid and other health-related	Nutrition and family welfare	Education	Other	New con-struction ($1,000)	Number of housing units	Total (mil dol)	Inter-govern-mental (mil dol)	Total (mil dol)	Total	Property
	171	172	173	174	175	176	177	178	179	180	181	182	183	184

1. State totals may include programs not allocated by county.   2. Based on the resident population estimated as of July 1 of the year shown.

Table B. States and Counties — Local Government Finances, Government Employment, and Voting

	Local government finances, 2007 (cont.)									Government employment, 2009			Presidential election,[2] 2008		
	Direct general expenditure							Debt outstanding					Percent of vote cast:		
			Percent of total for:												
STATE County	Total (mil dol)	Per capita[1] (dollars)	Educa-tion	Health and hospitals	Police protec-tion	Public welfare	High-ways	Total (mil dol)	Per capita[1] (dollars)	Federal civilian	Federal military	State and local	Demo-cratic	Republi-can	All other
	185	186	187	188	189	190	191	192	193	194	195	196	197	198	199

1. Based on the resident population estimated as of July 1 of the year shown.   2. © 2009 Election Data Services, Inc. All rights reserved.

Table B. States and Counties — **Land Area and Population**

STATE/ County code	CBSA code[1]	County type[2]	STATE County	Land area[3] (sq km) 2010	Total persons	Rank	Per square kilometer	White	Black	American Indian, Alaska Native	Asian and Pacific Islander	Percent Hispanic or Latino[4]	Under 5 years	5 to 17 years	18 to 24 years	25 to 34 years	35 to 44 years	45 to 54 years
				1	2	3	4	5	6	7	8	9	10	11	12	13	14	15
00 000	...	X	UNITED STATES	9 147 593	308 745 538	X	33.8	65.4	13.0	1.3	5.7	16.3	6.5	17.5	9.9	13.3	13.3	14.6
01 000	...	X	ALABAMA........................	131 171	4 779 736	X	36.4	68.2	26.6	1.1	1.5	3.9	6.4	17.3	10.0	12.7	13.0	14.5
01 001	33860	2	Autauga	1 540	54 571	917	35.4	78.5	18.1	1.0	1.4	2.4	6.6	20.2	8.5	11.9	15.1	15.0
01 003	19300	4	Baldwin	4 118	182 265	338	44.3	84.7	9.8	1.3	1.0	4.4	6.1	16.9	7.6	11.5	12.9	14.8
01 005	21640	6	Barbour	2 292	27 457	1 516	12.0	47.3	47.2	0.6	0.6	5.1	6.2	15.7	8.9	13.9	13.2	14.6
01 007	13820	1	Bibb..................................	1 612	22 915	1 693	14.2	75.7	22.3	0.7	0.3	1.8	6.0	16.7	9.0	14.2	14.8	14.8
01 009	13820	1	Blount...............................	1 670	57 322	884	34.3	89.8	1.5	1.1	0.4	8.1	6.3	18.3	8.0	12.0	13.8	14.1
01 011	...	6	Bullock	1 613	10 914	2 376	6.8	22.3	70.2	0.5	0.3	7.1	6.8	15.5	9.1	14.2	12.5	15.5
01 013	...	6	Butler	2 012	20 947	1 792	10.4	54.6	43.6	0.5	1.0	0.9	6.5	17.6	8.1	12.1	11.3	14.2
01 015	11500	3	Calhoun	1 569	118 572	505	75.6	74.9	21.1	0.9	1.1	3.3	6.1	16.8	10.9	12.5	12.3	14.3
01 017	46740	6	Chambers	1 545	34 215	1 321	22.1	59.0	39.2	0.5	0.6	1.6	5.7	16.8	8.1	11.1	13.0	14.8
01 019	...	8	Cherokee...........................	1 434	25 989	1 566	18.1	93.4	5.1	1.3	0.3	1.2	5.3	16.1	7.3	9.8	13.0	15.5
01 021	13820	1	Chilton	1 794	43 643	1 093	24.3	81.9	10.0	0.6	0.4	7.8	6.9	18.2	8.4	13.1	13.5	14.2
01 023	...	9	Choctaw............................	2 366	13 859	2 192	5.9	55.9	43.5	0.3	0.2	0.5	5.4	17.3	7.2	10.1	12.4	15.4
01 025	...	7	Clarke	3 208	25 833	1 574	8.1	54.5	44.0	0.7	0.4	1.0	5.7	19.0	7.7	11.1	12.8	15.0
01 027	...	9	Clay..................................	1 564	13 932	2 181	8.9	81.7	15.5	1.2	0.2	2.9	5.7	16.8	7.8	10.6	13.1	15.2
01 029	...	8	Cleburne	1 451	14 972	2 112	10.3	94.1	3.7	0.7	0.3	2.1	6.3	17.5	7.8	10.8	13.8	14.4
01 031	21460	6	Coffee	1 759	49 948	978	28.4	74.3	17.3	2.1	2.0	6.4	6.6	17.6	8.6	13.8	13.2	13.6
01 033	22520	3	Colbert	1 535	54 428	918	35.5	81.0	16.6	1.1	0.6	2.0	5.8	16.4	8.1	11.2	12.7	15.2
01 035	...	9	Conecuh	2 202	13 228	2 236	6.0	51.8	46.7	0.7	0.3	1.2	5.9	17.1	7.7	10.1	11.3	15.2
01 037	10760	8	Coosa	1 686	11 539	2 331	6.8	66.5	31.2	0.8	0.2	2.0	4.9	15.7	7.4	10.0	13.3	16.2
01 039	...	7	Covington	2 669	37 765	1 223	14.1	85.3	13.0	1.2	0.5	1.3	6.0	16.6	7.8	10.9	12.0	15.0
01 041	...	8	Crenshaw	1 577	13 906	2 185	8.8	73.3	24.0	1.1	1.5	1.5	6.0	17.8	8.0	10.8	12.9	15.3
01 043	18980	6	Cullman	1 903	80 406	682	42.3	93.7	1.2	1.1	0.6	4.3	6.1	17.1	8.6	11.9	12.9	14.7
01 045	21460	4	Dale	1 453	50 251	973	34.6	73.2	20.2	1.6	1.8	5.6	7.3	17.5	9.4	14.4	12.2	13.9
01 047	42820	4	Dallas	2 535	43 820	1 089	17.3	29.4	69.7	0.4	0.5	0.7	7.3	19.2	9.2	11.4	11.5	14.9
01 049	22840	6	DeKalb	2 013	71 109	751	35.3	83.3	1.7	2.6	0.5	13.6	7.1	18.7	8.2	12.7	13.6	13.7
01 051	33860	2	Elmore	1 602	79 303	688	49.5	76.1	20.5	0.8	1.1	2.7	6.1	17.5	9.3	13.2	14.7	15.5
01 053	...	6	Escambia...........................	2 448	38 319	1 212	15.7	62.6	32.3	4.1	0.4	1.9	6.2	16.4	8.5	13.1	13.7	14.6
01 055	23460	3	Etowah..............................	1 386	104 430	560	75.3	80.5	15.6	0.9	0.8	3.3	5.9	17.1	8.5	11.5	13.4	14.3
01 057	...	6	Fayette	1 626	17 241	1 967	10.6	86.9	11.8	0.6	0.3	1.2	5.8	16.5	8.4	10.3	12.3	14.8
01 059	...	6	Franklin	1 642	31 704	1 401	19.3	80.6	4.2	0.9	0.3	14.9	7.1	17.7	8.9	12.6	13.2	13.5
01 061	20020	3	Geneva	1 488	26 790	1 538	18.0	86.0	10.0	1.5	0.5	3.4	5.9	16.5	8.2	10.7	12.7	14.8
01 063	46220	3	Greene	1 676	9 045	2 522	5.4	17.5	81.6	0.3	0.2	0.8	6.1	18.1	9.1	10.0	10.2	15.3
01 065	46220	3	Hale	1 668	15 760	2 065	9.4	39.8	59.0	0.4	0.4	0.9	6.1	18.8	8.6	10.9	11.3	15.8
01 067	20020	3	Henry	1 455	17 302	1 962	11.9	68.6	28.9	0.7	0.4	2.2	5.4	17.2	6.9	10.8	12.3	14.4
01 069	20020	3	Houston	1 502	101 547	572	67.6	69.9	26.4	1.0	1.2	2.9	6.6	17.9	8.3	12.7	13.0	14.5
01 071	42460	6	Jackson.............................	2 792	53 227	931	19.1	92.4	3.8	3.1	0.5	2.5	5.6	16.9	7.8	11.1	13.3	15.0
01 073	13820	1	Jefferson...........................	2 878	658 466	93	228.8	52.4	42.3	0.5	1.7	3.9	6.7	16.8	9.8	14.2	12.7	14.5
01 075	...	9	Lamar................................	1 567	14 564	2 143	9.3	87.1	11.8	0.8	0.2	1.2	5.9	16.2	7.2	10.1	12.5	15.2
01 077	22520	3	Lauderdale	1 729	92 709	619	53.6	86.6	10.5	0.8	1.0	2.2	5.6	16.0	10.9	11.0	12.3	14.3
01 079	19460	3	Lawrence	1 789	34 339	1 318	19.2	81.0	11.9	9.3	0.4	1.7	6.3	16.9	8.4	11.1	13.8	16.0
01 081	12220	1	Lee....................................	1 574	140 247	437	89.1	70.9	23.2	0.7	3.1	3.3	6.2	16.3	20.5	13.8	12.3	12.2
01 083	26620	2	Limestone	1 450	82 782	669	57.1	80.0	13.1	1.2	1.5	5.5	6.5	17.5	8.0	13.3	14.8	15.3
01 085	33860	2	Lowndes............................	1 854	11 299	2 344	6.1	25.4	73.6	0.4	0.2	0.8	6.6	17.6	9.3	10.4	11.6	16.5
01 087	46260	6	Macon	1 577	21 452	1 763	13.6	15.9	83.0	0.6	0.5	1.1	5.4	15.2	17.7	10.4	10.5	13.2
01 089	26620	2	Madison.............................	2 076	334 811	192	161.3	68.0	24.7	1.6	3.3	4.6	6.2	17.5	10.3	13.1	13.2	16.1
01 091	...	7	Marengo............................	2 530	21 027	1 785	8.3	46.2	52.0	0.4	0.4	1.7	6.2	18.5	8.4	10.3	12.5	14.5
01 093	...	8	Marion...............................	1 923	30 776	1 416	16.0	93.5	4.2	0.8	0.3	2.1	5.6	16.1	7.7	10.5	13.4	14.7
01 095	10700	4	Marshall	1 466	93 019	618	63.5	85.1	1.9	1.3	0.8	12.1	7.0	18.0	8.8	12.2	13.1	14.0
01 097	33660	2	Mobile...............................	3 184	412 992	163	129.7	60.1	35.1	1.4	2.2	2.4	6.8	18.3	10.0	13.0	12.4	14.5
01 099	...	7	Monroe	2 656	23 068	1 686	8.7	55.9	42.2	1.8	0.5	1.0	6.0	19.3	8.0	10.5	12.5	14.7
01 101	33860	2	Montgomery.......................	2 031	229 363	278	112.9	39.2	55.1	0.6	2.5	3.6	6.9	17.6	11.4	14.3	12.9	13.8
01 103	19460	3	Morgan..............................	1 500	119 490	502	79.7	79.0	12.4	1.6	0.8	7.7	6.3	17.7	8.4	12.6	13.5	15.1
01 105	...	8	Perry.................................	1 864	10 591	2 396	5.7	29.9	68.7	0.3	0.4	1.1	6.4	17.7	13.2	10.5	10.4	13.1
01 107	...	8	Pickens	2 283	19 746	1 853	8.6	56.5	42.0	0.4	0.3	1.6	6.0	17.3	8.6	10.6	11.7	15.3
01 109	45980	6	Pike..................................	1 741	32 899	1 362	18.9	58.5	37.1	1.2	2.3	2.2	5.6	14.7	21.2	12.1	10.7	11.9
01 111	...	6	Randolph	1 504	22 913	1 694	15.2	76.3	20.6	0.8	0.3	2.8	6.0	17.8	8.2	10.6	12.3	14.5
01 113	17980	2	Russell..............................	1 661	52 947	934	31.9	53.5	42.3	1.0	1.2	3.7	7.6	17.9	9.7	13.8	12.5	14.1
01 115	13820	1	St. Clair	1 637	83 593	662	51.1	88.4	8.9	0.8	0.9	2.1	6.6	17.1	7.8	13.6	14.2	15.1
01 117	13820	1	Shelby	2 033	195 085	321	96.0	81.1	11.0	0.6	2.3	5.9	6.7	18.9	7.8	13.9	15.3	15.1
01 119	...	8	Sumter	2 341	13 763	2 203	5.9	24.2	75.0	0.2	0.4	0.6	5.5	16.8	15.0	10.1	10.5	14.6
01 121	45180	4	Talladega	1 908	82 291	672	43.1	65.5	32.2	0.8	0.6	2.0	6.0	17.4	8.6	12.1	13.7	14.9
01 123	10760	6	Tallapoosa	1 856	41 616	1 140	22.4	70.0	27.0	0.7	0.6	2.5	5.8	16.4	8.0	10.6	12.7	14.9
01 125	46220	3	Tuscaloosa	3 423	194 656	323	56.9	65.8	29.9	0.5	1.5	3.1	6.0	15.5	19.7	13.4	11.7	12.2
01 127	13820	1	Walker..............................	2 049	67 023	784	32.7	91.5	6.3	0.9	0.5	2.0	5.8	16.8	8.1	11.4	13.0	14.8

1. CBSA = Core Based Statistical Area. See Appendix A for explanation. See Appendix B for list of metropolitan areas with component counties. 2. County type code from the Economic Research Service of USDA Rural-Urban Continuum Codes. See Appendix A for definition. 3. Dry land or land partially or temporarily covered by water. 4. May be of any race.

Table B. States and Counties — **Population and Households**

STATE County	55 to 64 years	65 to 74 years	75 years and over	Percent female	1990	2000	1990–2000	2000–2010	Births	Deaths	Net migration	Number	Percent change, 2000–2010	Persons per household	Female family householder[1]	One person
	16	17	18	19	20	21	22	23	24	25	26	27	28	29	30	31
UNITED STATES	11.8	7.0	6.0	50.8	248 790 925	281 421 906	13.1	9.7	38 358 804	22 483 225	8 944 170	116 716 292	10.7	2.58	13.1	26.7
ALABAMA	12.3	7.8	6.0	51.5	4 040 389	4 447 100	10.1	7.5	566 363	427 844	136 452	1 883 791	8.4	2.48	15.3	27.4
Autauga	10.7	7.4	4.6	51.3	34 222	43 671	27.6	25.0	6 027	3 753	5 076	20 221	26.4	2.68	13.7	22.0
Baldwin	13.5	9.8	7.0	51.1	98 280	140 415	42.9	29.8	18 726	14 413	34 856	73 180	32.2	2.46	11.1	25.1
Barbour	13.2	8.2	6.1	46.9	25 417	29 038	14.2	-5.4	3 450	2 795	-1 281	9 820	-5.7	2.47	19.8	28.5
Bibb	11.9	7.5	5.2	46.3	16 598	20 826	25.5	10.0	2 459	2 037	1 390	7 953	7.2	2.60	14.4	24.5
Blount	12.7	8.9	5.9	50.5	39 248	51 024	30.0	12.3	6 419	4 898	6 083	21 578	12.0	2.63	9.7	22.2
Bullock	12.9	7.7	5.8	45.8	11 042	11 714	6.1	-6.8	1 518	1 180	-936	3 745	-6.0	2.46	26.8	32.8
Butler	13.5	8.7	7.9	53.0	21 892	21 399	-2.3	-2.1	2 560	2 618	-1 262	8 491	1.1	2.43	19.8	29.7
Calhoun	12.7	8.0	6.4	51.8	116 032	112 249	-3.3	5.6	13 946	12 201	795	47 331	4.5	2.44	15.2	27.7
Chambers	13.9	9.1	7.6	52.2	36 876	36 583	-0.8	-6.5	3 923	4 302	-1 715	13 933	-4.1	2.42	19.1	29.1
Cherokee	15.1	11.2	6.7	50.4	19 543	23 988	22.7	8.3	2 416	2 590	786	10 626	9.3	2.42	10.4	26.0
Chilton	12.1	7.9	5.7	50.5	32 458	39 593	22.0	10.2	5 108	3 965	2 499	16 558	8.3	2.61	12.0	23.5
Choctaw	14.2	10.5	7.6	51.7	16 018	15 922	-0.6	-13.0	1 637	1 610	-1 895	5 866	-7.8	2.34	15.8	31.7
Clarke	12.5	9.1	7.0	52.7	27 240	27 867	2.3	-7.3	3 201	2 611	-2 284	10 337	-2.3	2.47	17.5	28.1
Clay	13.1	9.9	7.6	51.0	13 252	14 254	7.6	-2.3	1 417	1 586	-358	5 670	-1.6	2.41	12.8	27.2
Cleburne	13.7	9.3	6.5	50.2	12 730	14 123	10.9	6.0	1 625	1 522	620	5 891	5.4	2.51	10.3	25.1
Coffee	12.1	8.1	6.4	50.6	40 240	43 615	8.4	14.5	5 505	4 305	4 023	19 849	13.9	2.49	12.9	25.4
Colbert	13.3	9.7	7.7	51.9	51 666	54 984	6.4	-1.0	5 699	5 824	123	22 773	1.4	2.37	13.7	28.8
Conecuh	14.9	10.2	7.7	51.5	14 054	14 089	0.2	-6.1	1 544	1 540	-1 117	5 625	-2.9	2.34	19.1	30.9
Coosa	15.6	10.1	7.0	50.4	11 063	12 202	10.3	-5.4	1 009	1 199	-1 047	4 794	2.4	2.38	14.1	27.9
Covington	13.5	9.9	8.5	51.6	36 478	37 631	3.2	0.4	4 177	4 656	-239	15 531	-0.7	2.39	13.1	28.1
Crenshaw	13.5	8.6	7.3	51.7	13 635	13 665	0.2	1.8	1 583	1 624	232	5 652	1.3	2.44	15.6	28.1
Cullman	12.8	9.2	6.7	50.6	67 613	77 483	14.6	3.8	9 197	8 297	3 917	31 864	3.8	2.49	10.4	25.7
Dale	11.8	7.8	5.7	50.6	49 633	49 129	-1.0	2.3	6 972	4 175	-3 504	20 065	6.3	2.46	14.6	27.3
Dallas	12.6	8.1	6.0	53.8	48 130	46 365	-3.7	-5.5	6 478	5 117	-5 610	17 064	-4.4	2.52	27.1	30.0
DeKalb	12.1	8.0	5.9	50.6	54 651	64 452	17.9	10.3	9 023	6 373	2 676	26 842	6.9	2.62	11.0	24.6
Elmore	11.9	7.2	4.7	51.2	49 210	65 874	33.9	20.4	9 190	5 585	10 066	28 301	24.5	2.61	13.1	22.0
Escambia	12.3	8.8	6.3	48.4	35 518	38 440	8.2	-0.3	4 566	3 889	-1 456	14 157	-1.0	2.48	17.3	27.7
Etowah	13.5	8.7	7.1	51.5	99 840	103 459	3.6	0.9	11 815	12 376	1 411	42 036	1.0	2.43	14.3	28.1
Fayette	14.1	10.3	7.6	50.7	17 962	18 495	3.0	-6.8	1 757	2 030	-759	7 100	-5.2	2.39	12.3	27.5
Franklin	11.7	8.7	6.6	50.1	27 814	31 223	12.3	1.5	4 177	3 440	-746	12 286	0.2	2.56	12.3	26.1
Geneva	13.8	10.0	7.4	51.1	23 647	25 764	9.0	4.0	2 817	2 920	464	10 920	4.2	2.43	13.3	26.7
Greene	15.0	8.4	7.7	52.8	10 153	9 974	-1.8	-9.3	1 204	1 006	-1 296	3 764	-4.2	2.39	24.9	34.4
Hale	13.4	8.2	6.8	52.6	15 498	17 185	10.9	-8.3	2 055	1 758	-485	6 273	-2.2	2.46	21.5	29.5
Henry	15.3	10.1	7.5	52.0	15 374	16 310	6.1	6.1	1 846	1 969	567	6 994	7.2	2.45	14.6	25.9
Houston	12.4	8.0	6.4	52.0	81 331	88 787	9.2	14.4	12 184	8 380	7 891	40 969	14.3	2.44	16.2	27.2
Jackson	13.8	10.0	6.5	50.9	47 796	53 926	12.8	-1.3	5 777	5 649	-1 001	21 513	-0.5	2.45	11.3	26.2
Jefferson	12.2	6.7	6.4	52.6	651 520	662 047	1.6	-0.5	85 382	65 944	-16 377	263 568	0.1	2.44	18.4	30.1
Lamar	14.1	10.6	8.1	51.3	15 715	15 904	1.2	-8.4	1 579	1 759	-1 467	6 103	-5.6	2.35	11.6	28.8
Lauderdale	13.1	9.2	7.6	52.1	79 661	87 966	10.4	5.4	9 058	8 704	1 854	38 680	7.2	2.35	12.2	28.9
Lawrence	13.1	8.8	5.7	51.1	31 513	34 803	10.4	-1.3	3 741	3 213	-1 040	13 654	0.9	2.50	12.6	24.2
Lee	9.5	5.4	3.7	50.7	87 146	115 092	32.1	21.9	13 824	7 455	15 088	55 682	21.8	2.44	13.0	27.9
Limestone	11.9	7.4	4.9	49.4	54 135	65 676	21.3	26.0	8 286	5 689	10 528	31 446	27.4	2.54	11.4	23.7
Lowndes	13.4	8.7	5.9	53.2	12 658	13 473	6.4	-16.1	1 741	1 297	-1 557	4 352	-11.3	2.57	25.4	26.9
Macon	13.4	7.7	6.4	54.2	24 928	24 105	-3.3	-11.0	2 358	2 547	-2 001	8 499	-5.0	2.32	25.6	35.0
Madison	11.3	6.9	5.3	50.9	238 912	276 700	15.8	21.0	35 550	21 504	36 191	134 700	22.5	2.43	12.8	28.7
Marengo	13.3	8.7	7.6	52.9	23 084	22 539	-2.4	-6.7	2 705	2 342	-1 844	8 535	-2.6	2.43	19.5	29.6
Marion	13.7	10.7	7.7	50.3	29 830	31 214	4.6	-1.4	3 240	3 517	-1 662	12 651	-0.4	2.36	12.1	28.4
Marshall	12.0	8.6	6.3	50.7	70 832	82 231	16.1	13.1	12 873	8 830	4 654	35 810	10.0	2.57	12.1	25.4
Mobile	12.1	7.3	5.7	52.0	378 643	399 843	5.6	3.3	55 073	36 423	-4 324	158 435	5.5	2.56	18.8	26.5
Monroe	13.3	8.6	7.1	51.8	23 968	24 324	1.5	-5.2	2 782	2 326	-2 269	9 214	-1.8	2.48	18.1	27.4
Montgomery	11.2	6.4	5.5	52.4	209 085	223 510	6.9	2.6	31 055	18 927	-10 205	89 981	4.5	2.45	20.9	30.4
Morgan	12.4	8.1	6.0	50.7	100 043	111 064	11.0	7.6	14 096	10 069	2 904	47 030	7.9	2.50	12.9	25.9
Perry	12.0	9.1	7.6	53.0	12 759	11 861	-7.0	-10.7	1 602	1 367	-1 442	3 947	-8.9	2.50	27.1	29.3
Pickens	13.6	9.3	7.6	52.3	20 699	20 949	1.2	-5.7	2 330	2 408	-1 562	8 012	-0.9	2.42	18.4	30.1
Pike	11.0	7.4	5.4	52.3	27 595	29 605	7.3	11.1	3 798	2 929	75	13 210	10.7	2.34	16.2	30.3
Randolph	13.6	9.7	7.3	51.5	19 881	22 380	12.6	2.4	2 513	2 520	345	9 164	6.0	2.46	13.9	27.9
Russell	11.7	7.2	5.5	52.2	46 860	49 756	6.2	6.4	6 068	5 130	429	21 229	7.5	2.47	21.3	29.1
St. Clair	12.5	8.0	5.1	49.9	49 811	64 742	30.0	29.1	8 665	6 565	15 285	31 624	31.0	2.58	11.2	22.5
Shelby	11.8	6.4	4.2	51.0	99 363	143 293	44.2	36.1	23 750	9 538	33 914	74 072	35.6	2.60	9.4	23.2
Sumter	12.5	7.7	7.3	54.5	16 174	14 798	-8.5	-7.0	1 602	1 426	-2 085	5 629	-1.4	2.32	24.2	34.8
Talladega	13.2	8.2	5.9	51.3	74 109	80 321	8.4	2.5	9 518	8 248	-846	31 890	4.0	2.48	17.5	26.7
Tallapoosa	14.4	9.9	7.4	51.5	38 826	41 475	6.8	0.3	4 519	4 931	-218	16 985	2.0	2.42	15.9	27.2
Tuscaloosa	10.7	5.8	5.0	51.5	150 500	164 875	9.6	18.1	21 241	13 968	11 496	76 141	18.0	2.42	14.9	29.2
Walker	13.9	9.5	6.8	51.3	67 670	70 713	4.5	-5.2	8 104	8 690	-962	26 571	-6.3	2.49	13.3	25.8

1. No spouse present.

Population, Vital Statistics, Medicare, and Crime

STATE County	Persons in group quarters, 2010	Daytime population, 2006–2010 Number	Daytime population, 2006–2010 Employment/residence ratio	Births, average 2006–2008 Total	Births, average 2006–2008 Rate[1]	Deaths, average 2006–2008 Number	Deaths, average 2006–2008 Rate[1]	Persons under 65 with no health insurance, 2009 Number	Persons under 65 with no health insurance, 2009 Percent	Medicare, 2011 Eligible for Medicare	Medicare, 2011 Enrolled in Medicare Advantage	Medicare, 2011 Enrolled in a Medicare prescription drug plan	Serious crimes known to police,[2] 2010 Total Number	Serious crimes known to police,[2] 2010 Total Rate[3]
	32	33	34	35	36	37	38	39	40	41	42	43	44	45
UNITED STATES	7 987 323	303 849 536	1.0	4 276 494	14.2	2 440 653	8.1	45 041 840	17.3	48 274 594	12 160 221	18 836 211	10 329 135	3 346
ALABAMA	115 816	4 677 103	1.0	64 194	13.8	47 127	10.2	623 621	15.8	874 157	180 831	324 561	186 148	3 895
Autauga	455	41 679	0.5	710	14.2	440	8.8	6 059	13.8	8 767	2 483	2 144	1 664	3 049
Baldwin	2 307	164 644	0.9	2 272	13.2	1 672	9.7	23 971	16.4	37 485	10 047	10 672	4 397	2 412
Barbour	3 193	28 243	1.1	398	14.0	257	9.0	4 781	19.4	5 651	698	2 815	480	1 766
Bibb	2 224	18 352	0.6	269	12.5	225	10.5	3 349	18.4	4 324	1 380	1 382	467	2 038
Blount	489	43 927	0.5	704	12.4	546	9.6	8 591	17.6	10 447	4 080	2 884	329	574
Bullock	1 690	10 219	0.8	D	D	128	11.9	1 982	21.1	1 742	341	891	130	1 191
Butler	333	19 955	0.9	297	14.7	266	13.1	2 896	17.8	4 450	416	2 457	610	2 912
Calhoun	2 919	122 144	1.1	1 535	13.6	1 320	11.7	14 673	15.5	24 180	2 381	9 781	5 163	4 354
Chambers	458	30 626	0.7	D	D	452	13.0	5 196	18.7	8 053	995	4 286	NA	NA
Cherokee	290	21 740	0.6	D	D	297	12.0	3 469	17.8	6 010	1 122	2 706	771	2 967
Chilton	393	35 185	0.6	591	14.0	440	10.4	6 960	19.1	7 857	3 224	2 021	1 203	2 756
Choctaw	129	13 957	1.0	D	D	168	11.7	2 038	18.2	3 576	156	2 117	82	601
Clarke	280	27 258	1.1	319	12.0	268	10.0	3 565	16.8	5 661	621	3 051	379	1 467
Clay	255	12 719	0.8	D	D	175	12.7	1 963	18.0	3 263	353	1 573	104	746
Cleburne	178	12 543	0.6	D	D	151	10.3	2 191	17.8	3 140	360	1 564	308	2 057
Coffee	600	45 606	0.9	671	14.3	473	10.1	6 337	15.6	9 029	720	3 670	1 419	2 841
Colbert	474	55 489	1.0	639	11.7	645	11.8	7 155	16.1	12 600	1 017	5 917	1 416	2 602
Conecuh	45	12 422	0.8	D	D	150	11.3	1 726	16.7	3 290	321	1 824	376	2 974
Coosa	124	9 311	0.5	D	D	133	12.2	1 353	15.9	2 241	231	1 112	3	30
Covington	575	36 980	1.0	449	12.1	509	13.7	5 442	18.7	8 897	549	4 801	859	2 275
Crenshaw	132	12 775	0.8	D	D	190	13.8	2 063	18.3	3 135	572	1 454	172	1 624
Cullman	1 056	73 811	0.8	1 047	13.0	915	11.3	12 629	18.6	16 786	2 986	7 744	2 116	2 632
Dale	917	50 768	1.0	775	16.1	448	9.3	6 748	16.5	8 935	715	3 482	1 144	2 306
Dallas	786	44 312	1.0	712	16.4	564	13.0	5 666	16.5	9 096	1 396	4 863	1 699	3 877
DeKalb	782	66 093	0.9	1 029	15.1	712	10.4	11 897	20.3	13 535	1 811	6 859	374	534
Elmore	5 483	62 584	0.5	1 034	13.4	638	8.3	9 915	14.6	13 499	3 378	3 293	721	909
Escambia	3 199	38 574	1.0	515	13.7	398	10.6	6 008	19.5	7 868	649	4 125	1 009	2 633
Etowah	2 085	99 446	0.9	1 272	12.3	1 373	13.3	14 486	17.1	22 745	3 571	8 503	4 581	4 387
Fayette	291	15 849	0.8	D	D	231	13.0	2 363	16.8	4 508	492	2 199	225	1 398
Franklin	272	29 354	0.8	475	15.5	393	12.8	5 156	19.9	6 308	411	3 490	588	1 872
Geneva	229	22 048	0.6	D	D	310	12.0	4 152	19.8	6 190	552	3 036	521	1 945
Greene	45	8 889	0.9	D	D	112	12.1	1 213	16.9	2 015	108	1 200	304	3 621
Hale	334	13 967	0.6	D	D	180	9.9	2 750	18.4	3 533	172	1 956	243	1 542
Henry	199	14 895	0.7	D	D	220	13.2	2 361	17.5	3 988	719	1 658	234	1 352
Houston	1 416	106 267	1.2	1 375	14.2	917	9.4	13 628	16.6	19 783	2 212	9 134	4 351	4 380
Jackson	597	49 404	0.8	611	11.5	641	12.0	7 221	16.6	11 487	1 091	6 237	975	1 858
Jefferson	15 774	723 422	1.2	9 646	14.7	7 056	10.7	79 450	14.3	114 192	44 644	27 240	28 865	4 545
Lamar	217	13 549	0.8	D	D	186	12.9	2 005	17.6	3 636	228	2 125	74	548
Lauderdale	1 891	87 256	0.9	1 020	11.5	987	11.1	11 773	16.2	19 179	1 608	8 985	2 392	2 580
Lawrence	229	27 572	0.5	414	12.1	366	10.7	5 239	18.1	6 931	505	3 433	141	411
Lee	4 410	126 825	0.9	1 702	13.1	822	6.3	18 579	15.5	17 048	1 656	6 799	3 781	2 696
Limestone	2 907	69 273	0.7	997	13.4	630	8.5	10 607	15.7	13 522	1 664	5 505	1 581	1 910
Lowndes	96	10 557	0.7	D	D	131	10.3	1 722	16.9	2 446	840	856	259	2 292
Macon	1 772	20 683	0.9	254	11.3	270	12.0	3 054	17.4	4 119	781	1 363	1 010	4 708
Madison	8 042	356 921	1.2	4 174	13.4	2 458	7.9	35 550	12.8	50 319	5 257	15 982	14 652	4 420
Marengo	254	20 865	0.9	D	D	253	11.8	3 009	17.6	4 938	356	2 823	687	3 288
Marion	868	30 699	1.0	361	12.1	407	13.7	4 219	18.1	6 633	659	3 457	644	2 093
Marshall	1 047	90 727	1.0	1 505	17.1	1 003	11.4	14 085	18.6	17 931	1 666	8 601	2 881	3 097
Mobile	6 808	415 311	1.0	6 202	15.3	4 051	10.0	60 350	17.2	70 467	26 188	18 767	21 665	5 246
Monroe	230	23 143	1.0	D	D	248	10.9	3 138	17.0	4 779	612	2 567	636	2 964
Montgomery	9 082	264 149	1.4	3 491	15.5	2 065	9.2	26 672	14.1	35 967	8 801	9 527	12 540	5 467
Morgan	2 133	117 751	1.0	1 573	13.6	1 162	10.1	15 242	15.5	21 947	1 711	10 008	4 166	3 486
Perry	721	9 847	0.7	D	D	135	12.5	1 525	17.6	2 418	127	1 433	NA	NA
Pickens	334	16 784	0.6	242	12.2	247	12.5	2 525	16.3	4 663	271	2 481	226	1 181
Pike	1 963	33 573	1.1	D	D	309	10.3	4 457	17.4	5 603	1 004	2 359	1 431	4 350
Randolph	407	20 143	0.7	D	D	277	12.3	3 504	19.2	4 981	488	2 570	450	2 031
Russell	574	44 358	0.6	735	14.6	589	11.7	7 639	18.0	9 643	1 641	3 882	2 096	4 000
St. Clair	1 967	64 773	0.5	1 106	14.2	744	9.6	11 806	17.0	14 161	5 580	3 487	1 642	1 964
Shelby	2 574	170 935	0.8	2 650	14.5	1 093	6.0	17 423	10.2	26 604	9 207	6 282	4 060	2 088
Sumter	718	13 155	0.9	D	D	153	11.4	2 090	19.9	2 764	131	1 736	NA	NA
Talladega	3 143	81 261	1.0	1 051	13.1	938	11.7	10 739	16.1	17 205	3 582	6 974	3 424	4 161
Tallapoosa	576	39 111	0.9	531	13.0	507	12.4	5 572	17.0	9 796	818	5 137	1 286	3 106
Tuscaloosa	10 423	194 742	1.1	2 490	14.1	1 546	8.8	22 163	14.0	29 956	2 225	12 012	8 950	4 598
Walker	866	63 306	0.8	866	12.5	922	13.3	9 864	17.6	16 254	5 072	4 620	1 874	2 796

1. Per 1,000 estimated resident population. 2. Data for serious crimes have not been adjusted for underreporting; this may affect comparability between geographic areas and over time. 3. Per 100,000 population estimated by the FBI.

Table B. States and Counties — **Crime, Education, Money Income, and Poverty**

STATE County	Serious crimes known to police,[1] 2010 (cont.) Rate[2] Violent	Property	Education — School enrollment and attainment, 2006–2010 Enrollment[3] Total	Percent private	Attainment[4] (percent) High school graduate or less	Bachelor's degree or more	Local government expenditures,[5] 2008–2009 Total current expenditures (mil dol)	Current expenditures per student (dollars)	Money income, 2006–2010 Per capita income[6] (dollars)	Households Median income Dollars	Percent change, 2000 to 2006–2010 (constant 2010 dollars)	Percent with income of $200,000 or more	Income and poverty, 2010 Median household income (dollars)	Percent below poverty level All persons	Children under 18 years	Children 5 to 17 years in families
	46	47	48	49	50	51	52	53	54	55	56	57	58	59	60	61
UNITED STATES	404	2 942	80 939 002	16.8	44.0	27.9	512 981.3	10 473	27 334	51 914	-2.4	4.2	50 046	15.3	21.6	19.8
ALABAMA	378	3 517	1 206 731	14.6	50.4	21.7	6 614.1	8 870	22 984	42 081	-2.6	2.3	40 538	18.9	27.4	25.6
Autauga	262	2 787	15 215	17.2	49.9	21.7	73.6	7 420	24 568	53 255	0.1	1.5	53 049	11.9	17.5	16.4
Baldwin	202	2 211	39 293	16.2	42.3	26.8	254.9	9 399	26 469	50 147	-1.6	3.5	47 618	13.3	20.2	18.9
Barbour	92	1 674	5 971	12.9	63.5	13.5	35.3	8 896	15 875	33 219	4.5	0.7	33 074	25.3	36.2	34.3
Bibb	257	1 780	4 862	7.3	67.8	10.0	30.9	8 677	19 918	41 770	5.0	0.5	35 472	20.9	28.6	25.3
Blount	42	532	13 256	11.2	61.8	12.5	75.2	7 665	21 070	45 549	2.1	1.2	42 906	16.5	24.1	21.3
Bullock	229	962	2 451	8.1	61.9	12.0	15.4	9 524	20 289	31 602	21.1	3.3	25 969	31.1	40.3	39.5
Butler	315	2 597	5 208	10.2	63.9	11.0	30.6	9 147	16 916	30 659	-2.3	0.9	29 500	28.1	39.6	38.9
Calhoun	431	3 923	29 209	11.0	56.0	16.1	155.2	8 369	20 574	38 407	-4.5	1.5	37 916	23.5	31.5	30.8
Chambers	NA	NA	8 018	10.4	62.5	10.8	40.8	8 112	16 626	31 467	-16.2	0.5	30 061	28.5	43.5	38.2
Cherokee	323	2 643	5 022	8.3	61.9	10.5	37.2	9 113	21 322	40 690	4.1	1.3	34 410	21.2	33.1	30.2
Chilton	401	2 355	9 458	11.1	64.6	12.2	59.0	7 745	20 517	39 486	-4.3	1.6	38 553	20.4	32.0	30.8
Choctaw	132	469	3 274	21.8	68.2	10.9	17.1	9 064	17 214	31 076	-0.8	1.2	32 003	20.7	29.9	26.2
Clarke	453	1 014	7 226	10.4	65.9	13.5	43.3	8 628	17 372	27 439	-20.9	2.1	33 739	24.9	33.5	29.8
Clay	201	546	3 056	13.1	67.4	9.5	17.8	8 352	18 332	35 595	0.8	0.5	33 035	20.6	29.8	28.1
Cleburne	260	1 797	3 241	5.0	69.2	8.4	22.4	8 413	17 490	36 077	-7.6	0.9	37 566	17.8	26.8	25.5
Coffee	362	2 479	11 278	7.0	49.0	22.1	77.0	8 431	22 797	42 253	-0.9	1.6	40 779	20.1	30.0	30.5
Colbert	233	2 368	12 087	6.3	54.2	16.4	80.2	9 469	21 079	39 610	-2.1	1.4	37 455	19.2	32.2	30.0
Conecuh	538	2 436	3 010	10.6	65.7	9.7	19.5	11 753	15 755	26 944	-3.8	1.1	27 855	25.7	41.0	38.6
Coosa	0	30	2 348	8.9	69.4	10.6	12.3	9 142	19 209	35 560	-6.0	0.6	33 721	18.6	29.5	26.9
Covington	225	2 050	8 235	9.7	60.9	13.1	52.8	8 571	19 822	33 852	1.5	1.4	33 484	20.9	30.2	28.5
Crenshaw	321	1 903	3 281	8.8	64.5	10.1	20.1	8 094	19 793	35 140	6.5	1.5	35 577	20.3	30.3	27.7
Cullman	162	2 470	18 835	11.1	56.7	13.8	110.5	8 626	20 284	38 567	-5.6	1.3	37 948	19.2	26.8	24.7
Dale	306	2 000	12 205	13.1	47.4	17.5	58.8	8 934	21 722	43 353	7.0	1.2	41 287	17.8	25.6	24.4
Dallas	623	3 254	12 280	12.3	59.7	14.3	72.9	8 892	16 646	26 029	-12.0	0.8	26 195	35.6	56.5	53.8
DeKalb	29	505	15 970	5.2	65.7	10.9	101.8	8 538	18 152	35 065	-8.1	1.4	34 822	20.8	31.6	30.8
Elmore	67	842	19 011	19.9	51.4	20.2	103.2	8 037	22 640	53 128	1.7	1.9	51 013	12.5	18.4	17.2
Escambia	483	2 150	8 469	10.4	62.3	10.9	52.5	8 933	16 259	31 927	-11.0	0.8	31 365	26.1	35.6	32.5
Etowah	461	3 926	23 539	12.6	52.0	15.8	135.2	8 299	20 439	36 422	-7.7	1.3	36 088	19.0	28.8	26.3
Fayette	137	1 261	3 798	7.6	62.9	9.5	22.6	8 982	17 711	34 560	-4.4	0.5	32 643	27.3	36.0	34.3
Franklin	315	1 557	6 846	4.9	62.6	11.8	49.3	8 586	18 094	33 942	-1.4	1.1	33 993	21.6	34.2	33.0
Geneva	295	1 650	5 556	5.5	65.1	8.0	31.4	7 933	18 351	34 140	1.9	0.6	34 418	20.3	31.6	31.3
Greene	1 131	2 489	2 386	9.6	64.3	9.9	14.3	10 027	14 738	22 222	-11.5	0.6	27 117	31.0	40.9	38.3
Hale	203	1 339	4 424	11.1	64.2	10.0	26.8	8 914	18 523	29 299	-10.3	0.4	31 790	24.8	35.7	31.4
Henry	295	1 058	3 858	17.3	61.8	15.0	22.4	8 103	19 716	38 379	-0.1	0.5	37 851	18.1	28.8	26.0
Houston	482	3 697	23 155	17.1	51.3	19.0	131.6	8 519	22 725	41 022	-5.9	2.1	39 290	17.9	28.0	26.8
Jackson	175	1 683	11 825	9.5	62.3	12.0	81.2	9 382	18 905	36 312	-10.4	0.6	36 158	19.9	28.6	28.0
Jefferson	403	4 142	169 198	18.0	41.5	28.8	1 001.3	9 540	26 529	45 244	-3.1	3.6	41 740	18.6	27.7	26.7
Lamar	52	496	3 161	6.1	66.3	9.2	19.5	8 308	19 789	33 887	-4.6	1.4	32 993	21.5	31.4	30.2
Lauderdale	151	2 429	22 793	12.3	51.1	21.5	118.8	9 012	22 341	39 345	-6.8	2.1	39 213	17.6	25.7	23.8
Lawrence	64	347	7 830	10.4	64.0	10.7	48.5	8 949	19 370	40 516	1.4	0.4	37 365	18.1	24.1	23.3
Lee	185	2 511	50 743	8.9	41.5	30.9	176.1	8 847	22 794	40 894	4.3	2.0	40 102	21.3	20.6	18.9
Limestone	108	1 802	18 601	13.0	52.2	20.8	104.4	8 870	24 007	46 682	-1.4	2.1	49 667	14.1	19.5	17.8
Lowndes	575	1 717	2 725	19.8	65.8	12.7	22.5	11 497	16 524	29 714	1.8	2.2	28 754	30.7	45.8	44.1
Macon	606	4 102	7 807	39.4	50.4	20.9	26.9	9 205	16 380	27 544	2.7	0.9	27 041	31.2	46.8	42.4
Madison	470	3 950	91 782	17.7	34.4	37.4	469.3	9 121	29 918	55 851	-1.3	4.3	54 633	12.7	18.0	16.5
Marengo	397	2 890	5 250	8.6	57.9	17.9	38.9	8 582	18 323	32 940	-3.7	1.1	33 085	23.6	32.5	30.9
Marion	162	1 930	6 435	6.6	64.2	8.8	41.1	8 097	19 030	32 769	-5.8	1.4	32 080	20.9	31.1	29.9
Marshall	199	2 898	20 365	8.4	58.5	14.5	140.6	8 653	19 875	37 661	-7.5	1.7	38 859	19.4	30.9	28.1
Mobile	582	4 664	109 109	20.0	52.0	19.8	565.2	8 822	21 548	40 996	-4.0	2.2	39 753	20.5	28.9	26.7
Monroe	527	2 437	5 682	15.6	64.5	11.2	36.3	8 625	17 652	30 235	-17.9	0.5	31 744	28.4	49.9	41.3
Montgomery	375	5 093	64 008	20.8	42.8	30.5	276.6	8 834	24 622	43 725	-4.0	2.7	41 556	21.3	32.3	29.3
Morgan	225	3 261	28 093	11.4	50.8	19.1	185.9	9 396	23 090	44 349	-7.4	1.6	44 859	14.1	21.4	20.0
Perry	NA	NA	2 962	21.4	66.4	13.3	18.3	9 336	13 433	25 950	1.4	0.9	24 742	39.5	54.3	52.5
Pickens	240	941	4 759	10.0	63.2	11.5	27.1	8 929	16 278	28 280	-14.9	0.0	31 032	24.4	35.5	33.0
Pike	447	3 903	11 467	7.9	56.0	23.7	41.4	9 357	19 013	29 181	-9.8	1.6	32 771	30.0	37.7	35.1
Randolph	316	1 715	5 298	9.8	64.7	12.2	31.4	8 136	19 844	34 593	-4.7	1.2	32 584	24.8	36.5	33.1
Russell	470	3 531	13 049	12.5	58.4	11.9	82.7	8 733	17 415	32 481	-6.7	0.4	32 733	24.1	35.8	34.1
St. Clair	132	1 833	18 125	14.1	57.2	14.5	99.0	7 910	22 192	48 837	3.4	1.2	48 296	13.0	19.8	19.5
Shelby	191	1 898	50 257	21.0	30.8	39.6	233.3	8 580	33 978	68 380	-2.6	6.0	67 135	9.8	13.2	11.7
Sumter	NA	NA	4 250	9.6	64.8	12.8	21.9	9 386	14 460	25 338	5.8	1.1	25 586	31.3	42.8	38.6
Talladega	269	3 892	20 115	12.8	61.4	11.9	114.4	8 952	18 713	36 948	-7.7	0.8	35 646	22.7	33.6	30.7
Tallapoosa	302	2 804	9 350	9.4	57.9	15.7	58.2	8 988	22 542	36 904	-5.2	1.5	34 440	18.3	29.5	27.6
Tuscaloosa	431	4 167	59 291	9.5	46.6	26.2	234.7	8 439	22 546	42 311	-3.0	2.5	43 098	18.0	23.4	21.7
Walker	157	2 639	14 374	8.0	60.2	9.7	103.9	9 387	20 516	37 191	1.0	1.2	36 044	23.2	34.6	34.2

1. Data for serious crimes have not been adjusted for underreporting; this may affect comparability between geographic areas and over time.   2. Per 100,000 population estimated by the FBI.   3. All persons 3 years old and over enrolled in nursery school through college.   4. Persons 25 years old and over.   5. Elementary and secondary education expenditures.   6. Based on population estimated by the American Community Survey, 2006–2010.

Table B. States and Counties — **Personal Income**

STATE County	Personal income, 2009 Total (mil dol)	Per capita Percent change, 2008–2009	Per capita Dollars	Per capita Rank	Wages and salaries[2] (mil dol)	Proprietors' income (mil dol)	Dividends, interest, and rent (mil dol)	Transfer payments Total	Government payments to individuals Total	Social Security	Medical payments	Income maintenance	Unemployment insurance
	62	63	64	65	66	67	68	69	70	71	72	73	74
UNITED STATES............	12 168 161	-1.7	39 635	X	7 788 815	1 022 360	2 192 960	2 131 880	2 076 109	664 287	892 410	217 858	130 141
ALABAMA	157 324	-0.9	33 411	X	96 697	11 307	25 324	34 907	34 052	12 211	13 621	4 119	1 073
Autauga..............................	1 661	1.3	32 721	1 382	485	111	200	323	314	119	114	37	10
Baldwin..............................	6 199	-1.8	34 461	1 101	2 480	309	1 396	1 242	1 209	537	451	88	34
Barbour..............................	706	-1.0	23 752	2 978	390	47	124	222	217	73	90	34	5
Bibb	527	-1.3	24 396	2 925	186	28	59	172	168	58	74	19	6
Blount................................	1 486	-1.7	25 475	2 807	373	93	202	358	347	148	128	34	10
Bullock..............................	241	1.3	21 971	3 066	114	11	32	88	86	21	39	17	2
Butler................................	560	-0.9	28 040	2 392	242	42	76	189	185	58	78	29	8
Calhoun.............................	3 656	-0.8	32 045	1 519	2 439	173	610	939	919	316	376	104	29
Chambers...........................	906	-0.5	26 388	2 657	311	48	121	317	310	114	124	42	12
Cherokee...........................	665	-0.6	27 210	2 529	202	42	105	201	197	83	75	21	5
Chilton	1 172	-0.9	27 275	2 522	352	48	142	302	294	109	117	36	10
Choctaw.............................	388	0.7	27 769	2 440	216	25	54	130	128	50	51	17	2
Clarke................................	767	-0.1	29 468	2 100	380	54	124	238	234	80	98	34	10
Clay	362	-1.2	26 552	2 631	150	28	50	122	119	43	51	12	5
Cleburne............................	420	0.9	28 472	2 304	116	36	48	105	102	42	41	11	2
Coffee...............................	1 700	1.7	34 959	1 028	583	100	282	363	354	121	147	32	6
Colbert..............................	1 628	0.4	29 798	2 021	1 095	102	249	468	458	184	171	43	16
Conecuh............................	350	-2.0	27 089	2 550	148	24	45	134	132	42	54	20	5
Coosa................................	275	-1.5	26 041	2 718	68	7	36	93	91	38	32	12	4
Covington..........................	1 059	0.8	28 874	2 222	523	76	148	336	329	116	144	35	8
Crenshaw...........................	410	-1.5	29 781	2 025	144	51	51	120	117	40	51	15	3
Cullman.............................	2 378	-1.0	29 081	2 176	1 127	152	377	625	610	234	251	52	19
Dale	1 478	1.4	30 690	1 824	1 722	62	172	402	394	115	184	44	7
Dallas................................	1 204	0.1	28 713	2 257	601	81	173	458	450	115	189	93	18
DeKalb..............................	1 803	-1.2	25 989	2 731	888	170	256	507	495	179	198	56	24
Elmore...............................	2 500	1.7	31 557	1 632	747	99	297	530	516	187	203	57	15
Escambia...........................	1 009	0.1	26 963	2 570	555	76	158	308	301	109	120	39	8
Etowah..............................	3 108	-0.4	29 984	1 983	1 492	184	463	898	880	328	369	88	22
Fayette..............................	441	-1.4	25 367	2 821	162	25	64	149	145	61	54	16	4
Franklin.............................	819	-0.5	26 348	2 661	395	48	119	262	256	87	119	27	9
Geneva..............................	773	-0.4	29 778	2 026	212	57	93	227	222	79	95	24	5
Greene...............................	287	-0.6	32 474	1 434	102	32	54	85	83	25	33	18	2
Hale	478	0.5	26 610	2 622	131	58	61	160	157	45	71	26	5
Henry................................	482	-1.3	28 955	2 209	165	29	75	142	139	53	56	16	3
Houston.............................	3 458	-0.3	34 549	1 085	2 204	217	648	715	697	267	253	92	16
Jackson..............................	1 526	-1.3	28 886	2 220	696	101	219	420	411	160	172	39	17
Jefferson............................	27 761	-3.4	41 745	347	21 035	3 818	5 070	5 109	4 987	1 682	2 078	592	169
Lamar................................	372	-0.7	26 212	2 685	137	26	54	137	134	49	59	13	6
Lauderdale	2 813	0.0	31 398	1 665	1 220	180	540	696	680	282	263	59	22
Lawrence...........................	963	-0.5	28 225	2 360	329	84	103	236	230	100	79	27	10
Lee	3 756	0.0	27 643	2 462	2 190	180	621	671	646	244	214	92	17
Limestone..........................	2 512	2.1	31 968	1 534	1 092	212	343	476	461	186	159	47	16
Lowndes............................	342	-1.2	27 820	2 434	143	38	34	105	103	30	38	25	4
Macon...............................	568	2.3	26 060	2 714	303	17	61	179	175	48	65	37	3
Madison	13 076	1.1	39 897	454	12 323	613	2 189	1 817	1 758	664	668	169	57
Marengo	648	0.5	30 921	1 777	316	59	96	194	190	67	73	32	5
Marion...............................	784	-1.4	26 939	2 578	400	67	119	253	248	92	105	25	10
Marshall............................	2 757	1.5	30 500	1 862	1 373	112	411	688	672	241	293	68	22
Mobile...............................	12 713	0.2	30 878	1 783	8 965	742	1 863	3 109	3 034	1 004	1 246	447	91
Monroe..............................	609	-4.1	27 208	2 530	356	39	85	199	194	67	75	29	9
Montgomery	8 644	-1.9	38 570	571	7 628	694	1 534	1 659	1 618	492	614	292	42
Morgan..............................	3 878	0.2	33 065	1 329	2 270	236	609	846	825	324	339	74	35
Perry.................................	279	-1.7	26 301	2 668	93	16	33	114	112	29	46	26	3
Pickens..............................	559	0.0	29 082	2 175	149	57	77	187	183	60	80	24	5
Pike	1 018	1.8	33 413	1 276	613	63	146	279	273	72	108	35	6
Randolph............................	575	-1.5	25 469	2 809	192	39	88	194	190	68	71	23	7
Russell..............................	1 495	2.1	29 401	2 118	553	49	154	413	403	128	154	68	5
St. Clair	2 473	0.3	30 192	1 938	693	87	274	510	495	203	184	51	20
Shelby...............................	8 108	-2.4	42 118	321	4 204	222	1 428	850	815	405	252	59	26
Sumter..............................	330	0.7	25 655	2 781	155	21	39	125	123	33	47	26	3
Talladega...........................	2 403	-2.2	29 942	1 996	1 364	89	279	686	671	235	279	86	29
Tallapoosa..........................	1 233	-0.6	30 058	1 965	544	52	209	370	362	136	141	44	11
Tuscaloosa.........................	6 301	-0.6	34 239	1 134	4 373	445	1 005	1 273	1 240	432	506	145	36
Walker	2 123	-0.6	30 888	1 780	809	135	290	680	668	236	299	56	17

1. Based on the resident population estimated as of July 1 of the year shown.   2. Includes supplements to wages and salaries.

Table B. States and Counties — Earnings, Social Security, and Housing

STATE County	Earnings, 2009 Total (mil dol)	Farm	Goods-related[1] Total	Manu-facturing	Information and professional and technical services	Retail trade	Finance, insurance, and real estate	Health care and social services	Government	Social Security beneficiaries, December 2010 Number	Rate[2]	Supplemental Security Income recipients, December 2010	Housing units, 2010 Total	Percent change, 2000–2010
	75	76	77	78	79	80	81	82	83	84	85	86	87	88
UNITED STATES	8 811 175	0.8	17.1	10.2	13.5	6.0	8.6	11.0	18.2	52 641 311	171	7 911 333	131 704 730	13.6
ALABAMA	108 004	0.9	20.7	14.2	10.1	6.7	6.2	10.5	23.0	1 012 056	212	172 223	2 171 853	10.6
Autauga	597	3.9	22.1	15.5	4.1	10.5	6.9	8.5	20.8	10 050	184	1 439	22 135	25.3
Baldwin	2 789	0.6	16.4	7.6	6.0	12.9	8.1	12.4	17.6	42 065	231	3 160	104 061	40.1
Barbour	437	4.0	D	30.0	D	6.2	D	6.6	21.8	6 670	243	1 675	11 829	-5.1
Bibb	214	2.1	D	8.6	4.4	6.7	2.1	D	32.6	5 180	226	1 053	8 981	7.6
Blount	466	2.3	21.5	13.1	5.1	8.8	3.2	D	23.3	12 285	214	1 439	23 887	12.9
Bullock	126	5.3	D	D	D	D	2.8	10.6	31.0	2 035	186	721	4 493	-4.1
Butler	284	4.8	18.4	13.9	D	9.3	2.8	D	17.9	5 230	250	1 274	9 964	0.1
Calhoun	2 612	0.4	D	14.4	6.3	6.6	2.5	9.0	37.3	27 935	236	4 671	53 289	3.8
Chambers	359	0.6	19.0	14.7	3.6	10.5	2.5	D	20.4	9 360	274	1 625	17 004	4.5
Cherokee	244	4.4	D	16.8	3.3	11.6	6.0	6.4	26.0	7 110	274	988	16 267	16.0
Chilton	399	2.3	D	14.6	2.4	11.0	3.3	8.1	24.2	9 310	213	1 520	19 278	9.2
Choctaw	241	0.9	D	47.6	2.9	4.9	D	D	11.4	4 255	307	920	7 269	-7.3
Clarke	434	1.3	D	25.1	D	9.9	5.2	D	22.9	6 790	263	1 513	12 638	0.0
Clay	178	4.5	36.1	33.2	D	4.6	3.5	D	26.5	3 780	271	601	6 776	2.5
Cleburne	152	10.8	D	12.7	2.1	7.8	1.9	2.7	27.6	3 730	249	525	6 718	8.5
Coffee	683	3.9	18.8	15.1	9.1	10.7	4.5	12.0	20.3	10 355	207	1 409	22 330	12.6
Colbert	1 197	1.6	27.7	18.4	2.0	8.2	3.5	8.8	29.0	14 680	270	2 172	25 758	3.1
Conecuh	172	3.0	D	9.8	D	4.2	1.4	D	24.9	3 895	294	864	7 093	-2.4
Coosa	75	3.6	41.2	38.7	D	D	1.0	4.6	27.3	3 140	272	554	6 478	5.6
Covington	599	2.8	21.7	16.7	5.6	9.9	3.6	D	18.3	10 205	270	1 543	18 829	1.3
Crenshaw	195	12.1	20.8	16.5	D	4.5	2.9	D	16.6	3 665	264	747	6 735	1.4
Cullman	1 279	1.6	24.4	17.5	3.9	8.2	4.0	13.8	16.7	19 615	244	2 627	37 054	5.2
Dale	1 785	0.7	D	22.7	3.5	2.1	1.0	1.7	54.2	10 365	206	1 847	22 677	4.1
Dallas	683	4.8	D	24.3	D	8.0	2.7	13.7	20.7	10 895	249	4 407	20 208	-1.2
DeKalb	1 058	4.7	D	29.3	3.7	7.2	3.3	9.1	14.9	15 890	223	2 414	31 109	10.9
Elmore	846	0.1	24.8	16.5	5.1	10.3	3.4	9.7	25.3	15 505	196	2 204	32 657	26.9
Escambia	630	1.5	28.4	21.3	2.4	7.9	4.6	D	29.8	9 325	243	1 487	16 488	-0.4
Etowah	1 676	0.1	21.3	16.6	4.8	8.0	5.3	20.7	17.6	26 905	258	4 634	47 454	3.3
Fayette	197	0.5	26.2	18.8	3.2	8.6	3.0	D	31.9	5 195	301	868	8 437	-0.4
Franklin	443	2.6	36.9	33.7	2.0	5.9	4.0	D	22.5	7 430	234	1 182	14 022	2.0
Geneva	268	8.9	D	13.4	D	7.6	3.9	D	26.3	7 105	265	1 215	12 687	4.7
Greene	134	18.9	D	15.0	D	3.2	1.2	D	21.9	2 435	269	926	5 007	-2.1
Hale	189	23.8	19.4	14.5	D	4.9	2.2	D	25.3	4 320	274	1 224	7 655	-1.3
Henry	194	5.2	D	14.7	D	5.3	3.0	D	19.4	4 575	264	668	8 891	10.6
Houston	2 421	0.7	D	9.7	6.0	10.0	4.7	17.0	18.6	22 550	222	3 852	45 319	14.5
Jackson	797	5.2	32.4	27.9	2.9	8.2	2.8	5.5	27.3	13 555	255	1 688	24 786	2.6
Jefferson	24 853	0.0	15.6	7.4	12.1	5.7	9.7	14.8	16.3	131 660	200	24 733	300 552	4.3
Lamar	162	3.1	D	26.9	3.0	6.0	4.2	6.2	19.8	4 275	294	640	7 354	-2.2
Lauderdale	1 401	2.7	16.7	10.5	6.6	10.4	5.2	11.5	25.0	22 270	240	2 747	43 791	8.3
Lawrence	412	10.9	D	30.8	D	6.5	2.0	6.7	19.1	8 290	241	1 411	15 229	1.5
Lee	2 370	0.3	19.8	14.0	4.6	7.2	4.1	6.9	37.8	19 975	142	3 205	62 391	24.0
Limestone	1 304	3.6	D	14.8	10.7	9.2	2.7	5.6	32.6	15 575	188	2 018	34 977	30.0
Lowndes	181	13.3	D	35.1	D	2.8	2.3	2.9	17.1	2 945	261	1 041	5 140	-11.3
Macon	320	2.2	D	D	2.1	3.2	1.1	D	60.7	4 560	213	1 302	10 259	-3.5
Madison	12 936	0.2	17.1	14.7	26.1	4.6	3.1	6.5	29.0	53 945	161	6 529	146 447	21.6
Marengo	375	3.1	27.8	23.7	D	6.7	4.2	D	23.8	5 880	280	1 645	10 237	1.1
Marion	467	3.4	33.7	31.2	5.8	6.5	3.4	12.4	17.2	7 930	258	1 160	14 737	2.2
Marshall	1 484	0.7	D	29.9	4.6	9.2	3.8	6.1	20.7	20 645	222	2 880	40 342	11.0
Mobile	9 707	0.3	19.9	10.8	9.2	6.9	7.8	11.4	18.6	82 220	199	14 411	178 196	7.9
Monroe	395	0.3	36.8	35.0	D	6.7	2.9	D	19.8	5 690	247	1 085	11 333	-0.1
Montgomery	8 321	0.2	14.2	8.9	11.4	5.5	6.9	10.6	33.0	41 170	179	9 826	101 641	6.5
Morgan	2 506	0.5	42.3	34.3	4.0	6.6	3.9	8.1	15.6	25 445	213	3 254	51 193	8.0
Perry	109	10.4	15.9	13.9	D	5.2	3.1	9.0	29.5	2 865	271	1 268	4 737	-12.4
Pickens	206	9.9	D	22.5	2.2	5.7	2.5	D	22.7	5 405	274	1 345	9 483	-0.4
Pike	676	2.6	D	20.2	2.4	7.1	3.7	D	24.5	6 420	195	1 678	15 267	8.9
Randolph	230	5.7	21.8	18.2	3.5	9.3	4.1	D	29.5	5 880	257	926	11 982	16.5
Russell	603	1.6	D	25.7	D	9.6	4.9	D	23.3	11 155	211	2 090	24 595	7.7
St. Clair	779	0.4	D	15.1	4.2	9.9	4.3	7.4	21.4	16 700	200	2 084	35 541	30.2
Shelby	4 426	0.1	16.2	7.9	10.7	7.3	16.0	6.7	10.6	30 000	154	2 365	80 970	36.6
Sumter	176	6.9	14.7	12.6	D	4.6	2.2	D	37.8	3 225	234	1 265	6 786	-2.4
Talladega	1 453	0.9	D	40.4	2.3	5.6	2.3	7.8	19.6	19 985	243	4 238	37 088	7.6
Tallapoosa	596	0.3	D	20.0	5.1	8.0	4.3	D	19.3	11 310	272	1 822	22 111	7.8
Tuscaloosa	4 818	0.1	30.7	19.8	5.4	6.1	4.2	8.7	28.6	35 125	180	6 806	84 872	18.8
Walker	944	0.5	16.8	8.7	6.5	10.6	4.3	15.9	18.7	19 635	293	3 300	30 816	-4.9

1. Includes mining, construction, and manufacturing.   2. Per 1,000 resident population enumerated in the 2010 census.

Table B. States and Counties — Housing, Labor Force, and Employment

STATE County	Housing units, 2006–2010								Civilian labor force, 2010				Civilian employment,[5] 2006–2010		
	Occupied units										Unemployment			Percent	
			Owner-occupied			Renter-occupied										
				Median owner cost as a percent of income											Con-struction, produc-tion, and mainte-nance occu-pations
				With a mort-gage	Without a mort-gage	Median rent[2]	Median rent as a per-cent of income	Sub-stand-ard units[3] (percent)		Percent change, 2009–2010				Manage-ment, business, science and arts	
	Total	Percent	Median value[1]						Total		Total	Rate[4]	Total		
	89	90	91	92	93	94	95	96	97	98	99	100	101	102	103
UNITED STATES	114 235 996	66.6	188 400	25.0	12.7	841	30.5	3.6	154 253 483	0.3	14 860 461	9.6	141 833 331	35.3	22.2
ALABAMA	1 821 210	71.1	117 600	22.1	11.6	644	30.1	2.3	2 179 163	0.4	206 776	9.5	2 036 867	31.2	27.6
Autauga	19 718	77.5	133 900	21.4	10.7	769	26.8	1.8	24 132	0.6	1 933	8.0	24 341	29.3	24.7
Baldwin	69 476	76.7	177 200	24.4	10.9	821	30.1	2.3	81 390	0.7	7 256	8.9	78 520	31.5	24.0
Barbour	9 795	68.0	88 200	21.3	14.1	512	33.8	2.7	9 773	0.3	1 187	12.1	9 909	26.6	36.4
Bibb	7 441	82.9	81 200	19.7	10.9	541	26.1	1.4	8 444	-1.9	905	10.7	9 819	20.1	43.8
Blount	20 605	82.0	113 700	21.9	10.9	574	24.4	3.1	26 016	1.0	2 319	8.9	24 706	24.7	33.7
Bullock	3 732	76.9	66 300	21.4	13.2	400	44.6	1.9	3 651	-0.1	537	14.7	4 310	21.2	39.0
Butler	8 019	69.0	70 200	24.7	13.6	480	28.6	3.3	8 993	1.7	1 091	12.1	8 138	22.2	34.0
Calhoun	46 421	70.7	98 200	21.6	12.0	569	29.2	1.7	52 565	-0.7	5 017	9.5	47 720	27.7	32.5
Chambers	13 681	71.4	82 200	23.8	12.7	572	32.2	2.7	14 060	-0.4	1 931	13.7	13 679	23.5	36.8
Cherokee	11 352	77.5	97 100	21.4	12.5	479	27.5	2.1	11 355	-1.1	1 036	9.1	10 548	25.2	39.5
Chilton	16 563	75.1	103 700	23.2	11.7	570	30.5	3.2	19 067	0.6	1 791	9.4	18 375	23.3	39.4
Choctaw	5 296	85.6	63 400	21.4	12.9	546	28.2	3.4	4 986	-0.3	567	11.4	4 478	29.5	39.2
Clarke	9 144	80.0	73 300	21.7	13.9	444	33.3	4.0	10 057	-0.2	1 585	15.8	8 161	28.0	37.0
Clay	5 851	72.8	82 900	22.3	10.0	398	21.7	3.8	5 356	-2.3	744	13.9	5 744	23.6	46.1
Cleburne	5 397	74.9	87 900	21.3	11.8	557	25.4	3.3	6 292	-1.0	530	8.4	5 681	24.7	41.7
Coffee	18 928	69.7	116 700	20.6	10.0	586	26.8	1.7	21 319	2.5	1 566	7.3	19 338	32.3	30.0
Colbert	22 165	73.5	94 700	21.1	12.3	572	29.1	1.6	25 085	0.6	2 434	9.7	22 858	27.4	30.7
Conecuh	4 861	81.6	72 500	19.4	12.7	514	37.2	2.1	4 577	-4.0	746	16.3	4 449	21.4	36.0
Coosa	4 561	83.7	73 100	21.5	14.0	457	25.3	3.9	4 328	-5.2	565	13.1	4 327	21.7	40.1
Covington	14 663	74.0	85 700	20.7	12.7	499	30.9	2.7	16 235	-0.8	1 475	9.1	15 718	24.6	37.1
Crenshaw	5 641	67.8	71 900	21.7	13.4	473	21.9	3.2	6 489	3.0	563	8.7	5 867	27.8	34.5
Cullman	31 263	74.7	102 200	21.9	11.3	563	28.6	1.9	37 808	0.2	3 323	8.8	34 224	25.5	35.3
Dale	19 545	61.2	93 900	18.8	10.0	612	25.4	1.9	19 916	0.5	1 686	8.5	20 097	25.9	33.3
Dallas	16 795	62.6	70 300	22.8	15.2	538	35.7	5.6	15 020	-2.4	2 593	17.3	16 373	25.2	36.7
DeKalb	25 937	77.5	84 400	22.3	12.5	514	25.9	5.4	29 270	1.1	3 390	11.6	28 636	21.8	44.4
Elmore	27 762	77.6	136 500	21.7	11.0	685	26.6	2.9	35 819	2.0	3 026	8.4	32 740	33.5	26.3
Escambia	13 804	73.5	83 800	21.0	12.8	545	37.7	2.1	14 386	-0.2	1 593	11.1	13 243	25.4	31.8
Etowah	41 584	73.0	98 200	22.0	12.8	587	28.3	2.0	44 377	1.0	4 191	9.4	41 331	29.3	29.9
Fayette	7 164	76.0	71 500	22.4	11.8	448	34.0	0.7	6 638	-2.7	785	11.8	6 796	24.1	41.6
Franklin	12 367	69.2	78 200	21.3	11.8	481	25.7	2.9	13 080	1.6	1 323	10.1	13 397	21.2	42.8
Geneva	10 720	71.6	77 200	22.4	10.0	522	27.2	1.4	10 846	-1.7	974	9.0	11 185	22.6	38.5
Greene	3 522	71.1	71 500	24.2	17.1	466	31.9	5.1	3 223	0.2	544	16.9	2 883	22.4	42.2
Hale	5 843	74.3	70 600	21.8	17.7	466	28.7	3.7	6 767	-1.6	818	12.1	6 015	23.6	40.3
Henry	6 656	81.9	89 700	20.3	12.5	497	30.7	1.5	6 924	-1.5	652	9.4	7 134	25.0	32.0
Houston	38 035	67.4	116 300	20.0	10.0	600	28.3	1.7	45 010	0.5	3 780	8.4	43 872	29.8	26.1
Jackson	21 173	76.6	86 300	21.6	11.2	485	28.7	2.1	26 055	1.1	2 522	9.7	22 247	23.0	41.0
Jefferson	260 441	66.8	138 300	23.7	12.4	748	31.5	1.7	300 697	0.0	28 236	9.4	301 018	35.8	20.0
Lamar	5 944	75.1	68 200	20.7	11.5	389	27.8	1.4	5 234	-3.3	670	12.8	5 669	24.2	41.6
Lauderdale	37 713	73.0	107 400	21.5	11.0	548	33.3	1.6	42 928	1.1	3 796	8.8	38 981	28.3	27.7
Lawrence	13 412	78.7	97 600	22.4	12.3	487	26.7	1.5	15 380	-1.1	1 697	11.0	14 473	22.9	39.4
Lee	54 016	64.2	139 500	22.8	12.6	650	33.8	1.8	64 873	2.3	5 301	8.2	61 882	35.9	23.6
Limestone	30 028	77.1	122 300	21.1	10.0	564	26.7	3.2	37 944	1.8	3 164	8.3	34 257	32.9	30.8
Lowndes	4 205	75.4	64 000	27.2	16.6	505	28.6	5.6	4 673	-4.5	721	15.4	4 202	17.7	39.4
Macon	7 969	68.0	79 200	26.2	13.6	558	37.6	2.3	8 926	-1.8	1 179	13.2	7 986	26.7	23.9
Madison	126 564	70.4	155 600	19.3	10.0	670	27.6	1.6	168 778	1.9	12 405	7.3	154 996	43.7	18.5
Marengo	8 494	73.5	79 000	23.6	12.1	449	32.6	3.2	7 865	-0.4	978	12.4	7 524	28.7	36.8
Marion	12 744	75.8	74 700	22.7	11.3	397	24.9	1.9	11 479	-4.3	1 550	13.5	12 584	23.9	40.1
Marshall	34 433	72.5	101 300	21.3	11.2	550	28.6	3.8	40 462	1.7	3 438	8.5	39 115	24.9	36.8
Mobile	153 302	68.4	120 700	23.0	12.5	695	33.1	2.8	186 352	2.2	19 066	10.2	174 321	29.4	26.4
Monroe	9 191	73.8	80 400	21.3	12.4	510	30.0	1.7	7 981	-5.3	1 366	17.1	8 708	25.0	40.0
Montgomery	88 772	63.2	121 000	22.6	10.3	760	32.8	2.5	103 278	0.2	9 631	9.3	102 224	35.4	20.7
Morgan	46 375	73.1	115 300	20.4	10.0	564	26.1	2.3	55 851	1.6	5 379	9.6	52 500	28.7	31.7
Perry	3 828	67.8	61 000	25.1	16.6	454	39.0	5.6	3 551	-3.0	580	16.3	3 325	23.7	28.9
Pickens	8 008	74.1	81 100	20.6	14.0	440	31.0	2.5	7 787	-1.0	880	11.3	7 246	20.9	37.2
Pike	13 013	56.3	93 900	20.7	11.9	528	35.7	2.6	15 635	1.3	1 213	7.8	14 143	26.5	28.1
Randolph	8 529	75.9	88 100	22.9	11.9	519	27.8	4.0	9 050	-2.1	1 134	12.5	8 944	22.5	42.3
Russell	20 174	62.3	93 300	24.7	12.1	627	31.8	2.9	21 311	0.4	2 232	10.5	20 656	21.0	29.0
St. Clair	29 574	82.2	126 500	22.2	10.6	702	25.6	2.2	35 916	1.4	3 337	9.3	35 338	28.5	30.9
Shelby	71 759	80.6	193 900	22.0	10.1	845	26.9	1.6	98 375	2.0	6 880	7.0	95 469	42.5	16.4
Sumter	4 952	68.3	66 300	21.9	15.7	482	43.8	4.2	4 594	-1.2	654	14.2	5 341	21.5	34.7
Talladega	31 151	73.0	87 000	22.1	13.5	548	29.2	2.1	36 232	-1.6	4 165	11.5	32 482	24.1	36.3
Tallapoosa	16 282	73.3	91 300	22.7	11.3	501	29.1	3.6	17 535	-0.3	2 227	12.7	17 707	27.2	34.7
Tuscaloosa	69 175	63.3	148 400	22.0	10.4	701	35.7	1.7	88 176	1.7	7 337	8.3	85 887	32.2	26.7
Walker	25 800	77.7	83 600	20.6	12.6	557	27.3	1.7	27 712	-0.7	2 943	10.6	25 437	24.2	35.4

1. Specified owner-occupied units.   2. Specified renter-occupied units. A value of 10.0 represents 10 percent or less.   3. Overcrowded or lacking complete plumbing facilities.   4. Percent of civilian labor force.   5. Persons 16 years old and over.

Table B. States and Counties — Nonfarm Employment and Agriculture

STATE County	Private nonfarm establishments, employment and payroll, 2009									Agriculture, 2007			
	Number of establish-ments	Employment						Annual payroll		Farms			
		Total	Health care and social assistance	Manufac-turing	Retail trade	Finance and insurance	Professional, scientific, and technical services	Total (mil dol)	Average per employee (dollars)	Number	Percent with:		Farm operators whose principal occu-pation is farming (percent)
											Fewer than 50 acres	500 acres or more	
	104	105	106	107	108	109	110	111	112	113	114	115	116
UNITED STATES............	7 433 465	114 509 626	17 531 142	11 632 956	14 802 767	6 171 240	7 839 965	4 855 545	42 403	2 204 792	38.7	14.6	45.1
ALABAMA	100 805	1 612 258	239 953	246 259	228 682	71 519	94 230	56 972	35 337	48 753	40.2	7.7	39.8
Autauga............................	877	10 628	1 336	D	2 462	333	327	271	25 458	415	29.4	11.6	36.1
Baldwin.............................	4 812	52 233	6 723	3 930	12 520	1 714	1 919	1 492	28 569	1 139	52.4	8.8	42.0
Barbour.............................	522	7 990	747	3 756	938	219	125	209	26 098	623	19.7	16.1	36.4
Bibb..................................	318	2 927	578	381	544	79	45	84	28 848	211	37.4	9.0	37.9
Blount...............................	749	6 968	849	1 399	1 211	236	201	202	29 012	1 414	45.2	2.6	42.9
Bullock.............................	120	1 919	345	D	232	D	D	49	25 327	277	20.6	31.4	48.7
Butler...............................	446	5 400	D	981	998	159	D	132	24 517	490	28.8	6.7	44.7
Calhoun............................	2 444	38 324	6 617	6 581	6 406	932	1 671	1 155	30 150	735	51.6	2.0	40.7
Chambers..........................	568	6 241	1 288	1 088	1 164	D	123	173	27 653	336	27.1	18.5	37.5
Cherokee..........................	350	3 600	339	1 160	847	113	47	93	25 912	654	36.4	9.3	33.0
Chilton.............................	744	7 048	979	1 407	1 431	227	86	184	26 172	645	38.8	6.4	46.0
Choctaw............................	276	2 969	280	D	358	103	50	131	44 254	264	39.4	10.6	42.4
Clarke..............................	623	6 944	991	1 763	1 475	359	88	201	28 878	321	37.4	10.0	31.5
Clay.................................	204	3 253	650	1 354	307	96	48	82	25 223	432	28.2	6.9	39.1
Cleburne...........................	180	2 071	94	681	356	59	40	59	28 720	380	38.4	2.1	49.5
Coffee..............................	1 016	12 499	1 974	3 155	2 260	556	448	322	25 783	971	29.4	8.5	36.6
Colbert.............................	1 290	19 703	2 841	4 200	2 925	635	1 053	602	30 543	736	47.8	7.2	33.6
Conecuh............................	216	2 612	392	507	250	54	D	74	28 426	401	29.7	9.7	45.4
Coosa...............................	106	1 050	D	695	90	D	14	29	27 991	207	19.3	13.0	36.7
Covington..........................	865	10 810	1 797	2 152	1 874	302	333	303	28 054	1 096	31.2	6.4	40.1
Crenshaw..........................	243	3 212	482	1 033	329	87	40	90	28 078	638	22.4	9.2	35.1
Cullman............................	1 737	22 761	3 669	4 846	3 361	722	496	675	29 670	2 465	49.9	1.9	45.2
Dale.................................	844	13 221	1 397	629	1 251	338	717	543	41 085	528	24.8	12.9	35.4
Dallas..............................	788	11 745	2 125	3 777	1 940	351	213	335	28 495	555	28.1	23.8	36.4
DeKalb.............................	1 127	17 512	2 202	7 059	2 415	484	373	508	28 992	2 426	49.5	2.4	43.0
Elmore.............................	1 143	14 374	2 098	3 185	3 032	406	474	393	27 351	626	47.4	6.5	39.5
Escambia..........................	802	9 769	1 315	1 445	1 748	444	180	285	29 222	502	41.6	13.3	44.4
Etowah.............................	2 079	29 773	6 907	4 611	4 725	1 019	775	865	29 057	1 004	52.7	2.1	33.5
Fayette.............................	328	3 880	920	778	609	99	50	112	28 833	401	21.9	9.0	31.9
Franklin............................	564	8 984	1 330	D	962	395	D	245	27 251	958	29.9	5.2	41.6
Geneva.............................	437	4 199	D	D	787	188	69	113	26 875	1 108	30.3	8.1	40.5
Greene.............................	104	1 430	D	365	193	D	D	41	28 692	316	20.3	20.6	49.7
Hale.................................	201	2 314	D	D	358	76	D	61	26 145	479	24.8	19.8	45.1
Henry...............................	312	2 722	385	238	D	124	D	87	31 903	478	19.2	17.2	44.6
Houston............................	2 823	43 725	9 548	4 924	7 913	1 105	1 278	1 454	33 249	841	37.2	10.2	40.5
Jackson............................	851	11 137	1 516	4 457	1 884	D	262	336	30 182	1 523	44.4	6.4	32.1
Jefferson..........................	16 799	325 281	53 386	26 343	39 984	22 528	19 393	13 697	42 110	470	58.9	2.8	38.5
Lamar..............................	250	2 875	325	D	336	D	60	82	28 483	422	32.5	6.2	30.3
Lauderdale........................	2 018	25 727	4 465	4 090	4 927	849	852	648	25 182	1 697	46.8	4.5	34.1
Lawrence...........................	426	4 748	721	1 262	846	118	132	166	35 062	1 601	43.8	3.9	40.0
Lee...................................	2 431	37 367	6 025	5 771	6 646	851	1 042	1 011	27 061	356	40.4	7.3	46.3
Limestone..........................	1 274	15 993	1 794	4 430	2 660	365	496	470	29 368	1 352	47.6	6.1	35.1
Lowndes...........................	127	2 320	112	1 265	364	45	60	108	46 353	405	24.7	24.2	45.9
Macon..............................	216	6 433	D	D	410	69	51	198	30 796	385	26.8	15.3	32.7
Madison............................	8 143	154 144	19 527	20 946	18 753	3 525	33 214	6 909	44 822	1 187	52.9	6.8	43.9
Marengo...........................	495	5 963	964	1 657	930	D	D	185	31 005	555	25.0	17.1	40.2
Marion..............................	531	7 378	1 230	2 349	1 016	357	76	202	27 432	787	30.1	2.9	35.6
Marshall............................	1 886	29 951	3 494	9 685	4 720	760	668	839	28 013	1 731	55.6	1.8	39.5
Mobile..............................	9 016	150 599	23 433	16 065	20 427	6 297	8 198	5 458	36 245	876	60.8	4.8	39.7
Monroe.............................	401	6 412	782	1 903	907	190	D	219	34 231	505	43.8	11.1	41.6
Montgomery.......................	5 762	104 319	16 600	12 209	13 011	5 415	6 631	3 695	35 425	620	32.6	22.4	42.1
Morgan.............................	2 718	43 314	6 221	12 187	5 760	1 468	1 909	1 456	33 606	1 457	50.2	3.8	37.8
Perry................................	126	1 519	D	419	184	70	D	40	26 645	390	25.6	20.3	43.8
Pickens.............................	286	2 931	714	612	477	209	33	71	24 287	503	29.8	8.7	47.7
Pike.................................	643	10 775	1 295	1 497	1 554	384	D	323	29 949	709	26.8	12.8	37.7
Randolph...........................	367	3 610	753	876	721	153	58	87	24 222	610	26.7	7.0	41.1
Russell.............................	851	11 030	1 425	D	1 956	400	242	316	28 685	303	35.3	14.5	39.3
St. Clair............................	1 230	13 181	1 765	2 171	2 259	465	421	368	27 888	621	46.2	2.7	39.6
Shelby..............................	4 900	76 171	5 778	5 775	9 743	9 839	3 963	3 078	40 409	474	51.3	4.2	39.5
Sumter.............................	220	2 986	471	D	295	64	D	91	30 425	431	24.6	21.8	40.6
Talladega..........................	1 317	21 858	2 887	8 459	2 786	553	249	752	34 419	625	40.2	7.2	40.5
Tallapoosa.........................	782	11 868	2 449	1 325	1 605	333	207	315	26 514	377	31.0	4.5	32.4
Tuscaloosa.........................	4 055	70 373	11 485	12 555	10 033	1 692	2 362	2 477	35 195	613	40.3	8.2	41.3
Walker..............................	1 357	15 960	3 637	1 733	3 400	649	544	467	29 262	629	51.4	3.7	42.0

Table B. States and Counties — **Agriculture**

STATE County	Land in farms					Value of land and buildings (dollars)		Value of machinery and equipment, average per farm (dollars)	Value of products sold				Percent of farms with sales of:		Government payments	
	Acreage (1,000)	Percent change, 2002–2007	Acres			Average per farm	Average per acre		Total (mil dol)	Average per farm (dollars)	Percent from:		$10,000 or more	$100,000 or more	Total ($1,000)	Percent of farms
			Average size of farm	Total irrigated (1,000)	Total cropland (1,000)						Crops	Live-stock and poultry products				
	117	118	119	120	121	122	123	124	125	126	127	128	129	130	131	132
UNITED STATES	922 096	-1.7	418	56 599.3	406 424.9	791 138	1 892	88 357	297 220.5	134 807	48.3	51.7	40.2	16.2	7 983 922	38.0
ALABAMA	9 034	1.5	185	112.8	3 143.0	424 674	2 292	60 810	4 415.6	90 570	15.3	84.7	30.8	9.7	124 692	29.6
Autauga	110	-6.8	266	1.2	42.3	518 368	1 947	61 478	16.8	40 405	D	D	30.8	5.3	1 357	28.4
Baldwin	190	5.0	167	10.2	103.0	544 907	3 270	76 160	100.3	88 087	80.4	19.6	31.9	9.6	5 144	27.0
Barbour	199	4.2	320	2.8	56.9	562 887	1 761	57 809	71.4	114 628	8.4	91.6	27.6	9.1	2 647	60.7
Bibb	38	-15.6	181	0.2	8.6	405 116	2 244	42 852	D	D	D	D	24.6	2.8	61	10.4
Blount	151	5.6	107	0.6	46.7	342 438	3 201	56 286	160.2	113 327	4.2	95.8	35.9	12.7	583	15.3
Bullock	134	-8.2	484	D	32.9	977 472	2 021	80 117	40.8	147 278	67.4	32.6	36.5	9.7	1 074	30.7
Butler	93	12.0	189	0.1	25.2	402 861	2 132	60 671	95.2	194 360	2.3	97.7	27.6	9.6	633	30.2
Calhoun	76	1.3	104	1.7	26.0	329 225	3 176	56 359	69.1	93 960	14.8	85.2	25.3	7.8	391	13.3
Chambers	105	12.9	312	0.3	14.3	565 077	1 809	49 848	6.5	19 386	D	D	26.8	6.0	320	22.0
Cherokee	133	9.9	203	1.2	58.3	442 197	2 176	75 888	60.0	91 744	28.3	71.7	29.5	6.9	2 838	44.6
Chilton	100	2.0	155	0.7	28.8	431 332	2 776	52 825	15.2	23 635	56.4	43.6	31.8	3.9	322	11.0
Choctaw	55	0.0	208	D	9.3	358 189	1 719	50 383	11.2	42 423	4.1	95.9	20.1	3.8	95	12.9
Clarke	74	29.8	230	0.1	10.6	376 945	1 641	39 578	D	D	D	D	19.0	0.6	223	19.9
Clay	74	-11.9	172	0.0	14.2	403 829	2 344	61 856	34.3	79 351	1.8	98.2	35.4	7.2	99	13.2
Cleburne	49	11.4	130	0.5	12.2	400 588	3 076	60 095	66.6	175 330	2.4	97.6	37.6	17.1	58	11.8
Coffee	211	7.1	217	4.2	80.7	472 149	2 171	65 967	196.6	202 436	6.6	93.4	31.3	14.5	5 695	64.1
Colbert	129	-2.3	175	2.4	60.0	377 879	2 158	59 190	42.4	57 648	22.7	77.3	26.0	6.1	2 843	36.3
Conecuh	86	4.9	215	0.1	22.7	394 747	1 834	50 249	7.9	19 756	24.2	75.8	27.4	2.7	903	42.9
Coosa	45	15.4	219	0.0	8.5	457 731	2 087	42 972	D	D	D	0.0	30.9	1.0	19	9.2
Covington	200	-1.0	183	1.2	64.1	409 242	2 241	59 559	85.6	78 110	12.6	87.4	29.8	10.4	3 980	48.2
Crenshaw	132	1.5	208	0.7	33.5	442 221	2 131	56 913	112.0	175 513	1.1	98.9	32.3	14.4	1 516	51.1
Cullman	230	-0.4	93	0.8	87.8	346 699	3 719	68 459	405.9	164 654	2.1	97.9	43.1	21.4	916	13.6
Dale	138	-0.7	262	2.6	54.2	552 202	2 110	66 705	76.3	144 444	10.4	89.6	31.8	13.6	2 307	52.7
Dallas	257	8.9	463	2.9	83.1	763 677	1 649	80 264	43.9	79 187	27.1	72.9	30.3	8.3	5 069	46.1
DeKalb	235	-0.8	97	1.0	91.7	335 689	3 462	58 895	414.3	170 775	2.9	97.1	37.0	17.0	1 383	23.4
Elmore	103	-1.0	164	2.0	43.4	427 939	2 606	59 112	15.0	23 901	62.9	37.1	24.1	5.1	1 526	19.5
Escambia	113	20.2	225	1.9	58.3	473 576	2 107	82 735	23.5	46 754	83.8	16.2	31.3	12.5	5 344	44.0
Etowah	94	4.4	94	0.6	29.6	282 306	3 009	44 457	66.2	65 894	5.3	94.7	23.2	7.0	518	11.2
Fayette	79	5.3	197	0.4	24.1	334 144	1 700	62 850	13.0	32 314	15.7	84.3	25.2	2.7	724	40.9
Franklin	141	-3.4	147	0.2	36.1	310 585	2 112	45 661	133.5	139 302	1.2	98.8	36.5	14.4	491	21.6
Geneva	221	-2.6	199	3.0	90.0	411 435	2 066	57 252	130.6	117 859	14.3	85.7	32.9	13.3	6 583	61.6
Greene	136	6.3	429	0.3	36.3	663 679	1 546	66 754	23.0	72 831	4.3	95.7	30.7	8.9	842	37.7
Hale	169	5.0	353	0.1	35.6	646 418	1 829	86 369	57.8	120 732	D	D	32.2	12.3	1 200	38.6
Henry	166	9.9	347	5.0	79.7	629 450	1 816	79 994	39.6	82 863	35.7	64.3	37.2	10.0	4 820	59.6
Houston	205	9.0	243	13.4	114.9	517 102	2 125	72 552	55.7	66 196	54.3	45.7	33.8	9.5	8 206	57.6
Jackson	243	6.1	159	0.7	112.5	336 077	2 108	55 577	99.7	65 443	14.2	85.8	27.9	7.6	2 037	32.0
Jefferson	40	-4.8	86	0.2	12.2	295 663	3 435	45 990	D	D	0.0	D	17.2	0.9	74	7.2
Lamar	85	-2.3	201	0.1	18.6	285 879	1 425	43 373	D	D	D	0.0	14.7	0.9	416	34.1
Lauderdale	228	9.6	134	1.1	108.2	312 507	2 329	49 841	45.0	26 497	35.1	64.9	26.9	4.7	4 399	33.9
Lawrence	222	-5.1	139	4.1	116.1	361 656	2 603	62 009	145.0	90 589	12.2	87.8	27.4	9.1	6 311	43.4
Lee	63	-14.9	177	0.8	13.9	534 602	3 012	57 383	D	D	D	D	28.7	2.8	497	16.3
Limestone	237	4.9	175	7.4	150.0	466 517	2 659	64 855	70.8	52 359	47.1	52.9	29.3	7.8	7 749	38.3
Lowndes	187	-5.1	461	3.1	42.2	752 337	1 631	82 834	57.8	142 652	D	D	39.8	11.9	1 575	32.8
Macon	117	-9.3	303	2.6	34.8	570 812	1 882	68 543	13.4	34 909	69.4	30.6	26.0	4.7	1 466	32.2
Madison	199	0.5	168	6.5	122.8	449 482	2 677	64 015	37.5	31 582	73.1	26.9	27.4	5.2	5 477	29.8
Marengo	178	-5.8	321	0.0	36.6	537 958	1 676	55 070	16.5	29 747	13.2	86.8	32.6	3.8	1 392	30.1
Marion	117	-1.7	149	0.3	30.3	299 773	2 013	54 228	70.2	89 246	4.8	95.2	26.3	9.1	694	31.9
Marshall	155	-3.7	89	1.2	61.5	330 979	3 707	61 866	238.2	137 603	2.8	97.2	32.5	11.8	1 181	20.6
Mobile	114	12.9	130	3.5	44.2	414 764	3 197	69 495	83.2	94 946	90.1	9.9	29.3	10.0	2 538	12.9
Monroe	119	-0.8	235	0.8	45.9	421 544	1 792	75 376	19.2	38 114	48.4	51.6	30.1	6.5	2 822	44.0
Montgomery	223	4.7	360	0.6	59.8	700 766	1 948	66 319	41.7	67 185	24.8	75.2	36.5	8.9	1 251	24.5
Morgan	162	8.7	111	0.4	72.8	317 198	2 861	52 686	96.9	66 473	6.3	93.7	30.1	7.2	1 432	18.9
Perry	166	0.6	425	0.1	39.7	679 727	1 599	68 219	17.5	44 995	11.1	88.9	32.8	9.2	1 390	38.5
Pickens	131	-8.4	260	0.6	28.6	487 719	1 876	58 308	109.8	218 332	2.4	97.6	38.4	19.7	650	22.9
Pike	179	-4.3	253	2.4	53.0	547 958	2 168	70 915	110.9	156 401	5.7	94.3	34.4	13.3	2 852	47.5
Randolph	115	4.5	188	0.2	19.9	455 760	2 423	57 114	74.9	122 861	1.2	98.8	37.0	14.1	153	19.2
Russell	94	-10.5	311	2.6	24.3	679 298	2 186	68 426	11.9	39 204	59.0	41.0	21.5	2.6	1 551	29.4
St. Clair	72	-13.3	115	1.8	21.0	406 441	3 526	64 661	58.9	94 770	12.8	87.2	28.8	7.9	150	6.0
Shelby	55	-14.1	116	2.2	21.1	428 945	3 710	57 847	9.8	20 599	67.3	32.7	23.4	2.7	543	13.5
Sumter	181	2.3	420	0.5	35.7	605 468	1 442	49 646	17.9	41 434	6.3	93.7	32.3	6.7	887	37.1
Talladega	119	9.2	190	3.2	48.6	442 771	2 325	64 540	28.4	45 414	23.7	76.3	30.2	5.3	1 058	24.5
Tallapoosa	64	-17.9	170	D	13.1	420 894	2 476	52 311	6.6	17 548	21.1	78.9	23.9	2.1	324	16.4
Tuscaloosa	111	7.8	180	1.2	38.2	445 608	2 470	65 369	25.4	41 417	28.4	71.6	23.3	6.5	1 387	18.8
Walker	70	-6.7	112	0.5	20.9	281 205	2 513	55 815	52.6	83 564	5.3	94.7	24.3	7.9	95	9.4

STATE County	Water use, 2005		Wholesale trade,[1] 2007				Retail trade,[2] 2007				Real estate and rental and leasing,[2] 2007			
	Total water withdrawn (mil gal/day)	Gallons withdrawn per person	Number of establish-ments	Number of employees	Sales (mil dol)	Annual payroll (mil dol)	Number of establish-ments	Number of employees	Sales (mil dol)	Annual payroll (mil dol)	Number of establish-ments	Number of employees	Receipts (mil dol)	Annual payroll (mil dol)
	133	134	135	136	137	138	139	140	141	142	143	144	145	146
UNITED STATES............	407 313.9	1 373	369 387	5 098 545	4 174 286.5	260 532.1	1 128 112	15 515 396	3 917 663.5	362 818.7	384 297	2 188 479	485 058.6	84 764.9
ALABAMA	9 957.6	2 185	4 824	70 469	52 252.8	3 032.2	19 722	238 922	57 344.9	5 112.0	4 554	27 100	4 073.2	823.4
Autauga................................	43.7	898	26	D	D	D	182	2 373	598.2	56.4	31	D	D	D
Baldwin................................	69.0	424	183	D	D	D	1 019	12 920	2 966.5	282.6	358	1 987	266.7	59.5
Barbour................................	16.5	580	19	D	D	D	104	994	188.3	17.4	20	D	D	D
Bibb....................................	5.0	231	13	D	D	D	64	515	124.7	10.6	11	27	3.5	0.9
Blount................................	19.0	340	32	D	D	D	155	1 263	319.7	25.4	16	49	3.6	0.7
Bullock................................	5.4	492	6	D	D	D	22	251	43.8	4.8	4	10	0.7	0.1
Butler................................	4.4	211	10	74	56.7	2.9	106	1 084	229.3	19.6	21	88	3.8	0.7
Calhoun................................	29.0	258	104	D	D	D	552	6 854	1 543.0	139.1	93	459	66.3	10.2
Chambers............................	8.4	237	16	D	D	D	130	1 205	264.7	23.9	17	79	7.5	1.3
Cherokee............................	7.2	294	17	74	62.3	2.5	86	884	186.3	17.5	18	58	8.3	1.1
Chilton................................	6.3	150	23	292	155.1	10.5	170	1 503	359.9	31.1	27	87	6.4	1.2
Choctaw............................	49.6	3 348	13	57	52.9	2.1	66	360	84.6	6.1	4	9	0.5	0.1
Clarke................................	4.9	180	14	206	85.8	6.1	153	1 477	344.3	28.7	22	74	6.2	1.5
Clay....................................	2.7	193	5	D	D	D	50	358	70.6	5.3	7	17	1.3	0.5
Cleburne............................	2.4	164	4	10	5.9	0.3	49	362	133.4	10.3	3	D	D	D
Coffee................................	13.0	284	25	275	131.6	9.7	224	2 514	639.6	54.9	62	261	29.7	6.7
Colbert................................	1 363.2	24 939	84	848	351.4	30.2	238	2 912	821.3	66.4	38	211	23.1	4.0
Conecuh............................	2.4	179	7	174	76.7	4.9	46	303	71.2	4.5	8	12	1.0	0.2
Coosa................................	1.0	90	7	37	31.6	1.8	18	89	20.5	1.4	7	10	1.1	0.1
Covington............................	13.5	366	39	610	338.7	17.7	191	1 902	424.9	39.2	33	128	12.1	2.4
Crenshaw............................	3.2	235	13	346	131.9	14.4	50	343	75.5	6.5	7	17	0.9	0.3
Cullman................................	32.7	409	91	D	D	D	341	3 346	867.1	69.6	56	231	26.1	5.9
Dale....................................	12.2	251	22	257	69.3	7.5	149	1 431	332.5	27.0	31	169	21.1	3.6
Dallas................................	17.8	401	31	D	D	D	200	2 085	437.4	41.8	39	119	14.0	2.5
DeKalb................................	16.4	244	43	D	D	D	269	2 532	635.2	55.3	36	153	11.8	3.4
Elmore................................	14.8	200	32	291	104.9	8.8	225	2 479	618.3	50.6	48	125	17.4	3.1
Escambia............................	42.8	1 125	27	221	93.1	6.5	190	1 639	379.6	33.5	25	119	10.3	2.1
Etowah................................	173.9	1 685	96	1 064	518.4	36.1	453	4 786	1 114.8	92.7	79	428	68.7	12.1
Fayette................................	3.9	216	7	34	22.5	1.1	62	633	130.4	11.5	6	15	0.9	0.2
Franklin................................	7.1	231	20	111	67.4	3.5	119	1 060	269.1	19.3	15	45	4.6	0.6
Geneva................................	7.6	296	21	423	231.7	23.0	102	872	170.0	16.0	8	27	1.7	0.4
Greene................................	398.6	41 257	3	D	D	D	28	185	33.6	3.0	1	D	D	D
Hale....................................	28.4	1 550	6	D	D	D	49	361	86.7	7.0	5	D	D	D
Henry................................	5.8	350	14	D	D	D	60	425	92.6	8.2	13	21	1.9	0.3
Houston................................	191.8	1 898	159	D	D	D	618	7 934	1 909.6	179.1	122	553	81.5	17.2
Jackson................................	1 498.2	27 926	38	D	D	D	187	1 923	411.0	37.0	28	106	11.4	2.6
Jefferson............................	81.0	123	1 052	18 937	13 756.8	930.6	3 026	42 765	11 066.3	971.5	810	7 976	1 193.0	289.1
Lamar................................	2.3	150	6	D	D	D	51	349	70.8	6.0	5	22	1.1	0.3
Lauderdale............................	17.2	196	78	1 286	514.6	34.0	445	5 190	1 131.6	100.7	86	345	45.1	8.5
Lawrence............................	67.4	1 949	11	34	23.8	1.0	86	825	167.0	15.6	7	30	2.8	1.0
Lee....................................	21.5	175	68	D	D	D	472	6 391	1 451.6	125.3	122	636	79.4	15.0
Limestone............................	2 013.9	28 578	51	407	248.3	17.8	246	2 611	723.2	58.8	55	156	24.0	3.9
Lowndes............................	6.0	457	2	D	D	D	32	395	103.6	7.1	7	D	D	D
Macon................................	9.9	436	9	D	D	D	50	455	87.5	7.1	11	D	D	D
Madison............................	70.5	236	342	4 519	2 970.4	212.4	1 348	18 840	4 438.7	421.1	432	2 091	345.3	65.4
Marengo............................	26.8	1 224	25	133	64.6	4.2	109	1 039	197.2	18.8	17	85	24.8	3.5
Marion................................	7.8	260	23	195	162.5	6.2	110	976	209.9	18.1	14	33	3.9	0.6
Marshall............................	27.1	316	86	1 486	1 138.7	55.3	465	4 990	1 357.7	102.8	80	603	39.4	8.6
Mobile................................	1 130.9	2 817	546	6 904	3 268.7	296.1	1 644	22 271	5 225.5	483.4	448	2 460	417.2	77.8
Monroe................................	60.0	2 529	15	148	92.8	7.2	93	872	212.6	16.1	13	50	5.5	1.1
Montgomery	69.7	315	290	5 684	3 275.6	235.8	1 009	14 325	3 238.2	314.6	303	2 358	292.8	72.5
Morgan................................	124.8	1 097	163	2 046	1 213.9	86.5	545	5 851	1 637.6	128.4	102	418	60.2	10.4
Perry................................	12.4	1 090	4	69	10.4	1.8	37	178	34.1	3.4	3	D	D	D
Pickens................................	5.7	281	12	72	36.6	1.8	66	524	113.2	9.2	6	31	1.0	0.6
Pike....................................	7.0	236	22	D	D	D	147	1 578	367.9	31.5	28	89	21.5	1.7
Randolph............................	2.8	122	8	61	26.8	0.9	95	714	161.4	15.1	20	49	5.8	1.0
Russell................................	43.7	886	16	D	D	D	165	2 010	428.2	38.5	46	157	23.2	3.5
St. Clair................................	21.0	290	68	726	317.5	30.1	232	2 502	581.3	51.6	45	157	28.4	3.8
Shelby................................	833.3	4 860	328	4 622	4 385.6	255.4	707	10 135	2 520.5	237.8	217	1 474	454.8	57.9
Sumter................................	10.3	743	13	173	76.5	4.8	47	334	59.6	4.4	9	25	3.1	0.9
Talladega............................	78.3	973	59	D	D	D	310	3 233	730.7	63.6	52	400	28.6	4.9
Tallapoosa............................	14.6	360	22	D	D	D	155	1 534	362.3	33.3	38	139	26.6	4.2
Tuscaloosa............................	36.0	213	142	1 655	760.6	72.6	781	10 551	2 445.9	223.5	198	1 170	173.8	32.0
Walker................................	969.5	13 826	52	300	256.4	13.2	322	3 789	903.6	74.7	41	159	24.7	4.2

1. Merchant wholesalers, except manufacturers' sales branches and offices.   2. Employer establishments.

Table B. States and Counties — Professional Services, Manufacturing, and Accommodation and Food Services

STATE County	Professional, scientific, and technical services,[1] 2007				Manufacturing, 2007				Accommodation and food services, 2007			
	Number of establish-ments	Number of employees	Receipts (mil dol)	Annual payroll (mil dol)	Number of establish-ments	Number of employees	Receipts (mil dol)	Annual payroll (mil dol)	Number of establish-ments	Number of employees	Sales (mil dol)	Annual payroll (mil dol)
	147	148	149	150	151	152	153	154	155	156	157	158
UNITED STATES	842 607	7 678 304	1 220 434.1	489 965.4	332 536	13 395 670	5 319 456.3	613 768.6	634 361	11 600 751	613 795.7	170 826.8
ALABAMA	9 437	92 759	13 623.2	4 996.4	4 928	271 986	112 858.8	11 351.6	8 093	150 791	6 426.3	1 751.4
Autauga	61	386	42.3	15.5	33	1 506	D	D	92	2 182	88.2	25.5
Baldwin	458	D	D	D	162	4 795	1 410.3	169.3	414	8 368	437.0	122.4
Barbour	48	D	D	D	38	D	D	D	45	D	D	D
Bibb	14	D	D	D	NA	NA	NA	NA	19	255	10.8	2.6
Blount	47	229	16.7	8.2	53	1 517	341.5	44.3	46	490	20.9	5.1
Bullock	7	20	2.6	0.9	3	D	D	D	8	110	3.7	1.1
Butler	25	85	6.9	2.2	23	1 170	399.1	38.5	40	673	28.4	7.5
Calhoun	171	D	D	D	141	6 961	2 680.0	279.3	224	5 129	186.5	51.5
Chambers	29	D	D	D	27	D	667.3	73.6	47	611	23.2	5.9
Cherokee	17	60	6.3	1.5	24	1 171	307.4	34.7	39	354	13.9	3.7
Chilton	39	D	D	D	52	1 444	D	41.8	60	868	34.1	8.5
Choctaw	18	51	3.3	1.1	7	D	D	D	21	170	11.3	1.5
Clarke	30	94	13.2	2.1	31	1 592	571.5	70.2	53	611	23.6	5.4
Clay	10	56	5.2	0.8	12	2 526	330.9	72.9	12	139	4.4	1.1
Cleburne	8	36	1.7	0.6	NA	NA	NA	NA	13	164	4.1	1.0
Coffee	71	373	45.2	11.2	36	3 128	613.8	80.6	89	1 474	50.1	13.2
Colbert	94	D	D	D	112	4 162	2 083.2	185.2	99	1 560	61.9	16.2
Conecuh	11	19	2.2	0.4	12	672	183.5	21.5	16	202	8.7	1.9
Coosa	6	15	1.7	0.7	9	782	89.6	D	3	5	0.6	0.1
Covington	63	301	28.4	9.7	34	2 476	561.2	76.7	67	745	30.3	7.2
Crenshaw	11	31	2.8	0.8	10	986	270.8	29.1	11	173	5.6	1.4
Cullman	118	566	38.5	14.0	124	5 306	1 393.4	188.9	126	2 457	102.3	25.6
Dale	81	974	129.4	45.3	35	652	115.0	19.8	85	1 219	37.2	10.1
Dallas	45	D	D	D	46	3 594	1 174.8	137.7	63	855	33.7	7.9
DeKalb	79	399	30.1	13.1	134	9 028	1 831.6	304.3	108	1 426	67.9	18.3
Elmore	86	449	79.2	17.0	73	3 312	766.3	130.3	82	1 209	47.9	11.8
Escambia	41	176	16.2	5.4	39	1 660	665.3	80.5	54	728	31.9	7.6
Etowah	156	876	76.6	26.8	118	5 430	1 253.0	203.7	177	3 381	138.0	38.1
Fayette	15	47	3.4	1.1	25	974	186.2	28.5	22	258	10.9	2.6
Franklin	28	123	9.7	2.8	49	4 071	672.0	135.0	51	691	25.4	6.1
Geneva	34	D	D	D	27	960	153.3	27.2	31	313	10.4	2.7
Greene	6	D	D	D	NA	NA	NA	NA	6	58	1.2	0.4
Hale	8	D	D	D	11	820	D	D	12	148	3.1	0.8
Henry	22	D	D	D	17	826	425.8	25.3	25	252	7.4	1.8
Houston	236	D	D	D	126	5 562	1 310.7	201.1	226	4 442	177.2	48.6
Jackson	55	D	D	D	70	5 707	1 525.4	206.5	77	1 068	39.3	10.6
Jefferson	1 946	D	D	D	674	28 833	10 261.0	1 331.4	1 271	26 530	1 268.2	354.2
Lamar	18	51	4.3	1.5	17	1 113	234.9	49.9	19	153	6.0	1.4
Lauderdale	176	D	D	D	91	3 150	1 083.7	116.1	150	3 568	136.6	40.1
Lawrence	35	112	7.7	2.4	24	1 411	D	D	42	543	22.7	6.0
Lee	189	D	D	D	123	D	D	D	271	5 515	201.2	55.8
Limestone	98	666	92.9	34.5	72	4 272	947.3	173.9	96	1 548	68.1	17.2
Lowndes	8	58	9.4	3.3	13	1 103	1 156.9	63.8	6	14	0.6	0.1
Macon	15	D	D	D	NA	NA	NA	NA	22	436	19.4	5.5
Madison	1 276	31 697	5 668.6	2 209.6	319	23 499	8 650.7	1 129.7	643	13 989	596.3	167.6
Marengo	25	88	11.0	2.2	25	1 886	542.1	74.7	41	422	16.7	3.9
Marion	23	75	5.0	1.5	48	3 474	794.5	114.3	46	491	19.1	5.3
Marshall	133	623	54.6	17.9	125	10 842	3 029.5	334.0	169	2 473	103.5	27.5
Mobile	901	D	D	D	385	16 776	12 407.2	840.9	652	13 252	562.4	155.0
Monroe	25	62	4.4	1.3	28	2 329	1 251.9	119.7	32	349	14.8	3.3
Montgomery	662	6 385	890.0	341.8	199	12 828	7 956.6	567.2	473	9 754	402.9	112.8
Morgan	227	1 451	116.6	48.1	199	12 152	D	D	207	3 756	154.7	41.4
Perry	6	D	D	D	NA	NA	NA	NA	11	58	2.6	0.5
Pickens	18	42	2.5	0.7	22	630	107.6	18.7	16	138	6.3	1.7
Pike	34	173	14.6	4.0	32	D	D	D	63	1 197	45.7	11.8
Randolph	20	78	4.2	1.6	21	1 537	401.7	49.3	30	219	9.2	2.4
Russell	48	D	D	D	37	D	D	D	84	1 428	56.4	14.7
St. Clair	93	475	40.8	16.1	76	2 830	985.4	102.2	109	1 641	70.3	18.8
Shelby	570	D	D	D	191	6 672	1 723.0	272.3	334	6 596	301.9	83.6
Sumter	12	32	2.0	0.5	NA	NA	NA	NA	20	262	8.2	2.1
Talladega	72	310	21.8	8.1	88	9 749	9 054.2	514.4	111	1 775	67.1	17.7
Tallapoosa	57	209	24.5	9.2	39	1 473	D	39.7	65	843	28.2	7.9
Tuscaloosa	356	2 555	223.1	83.7	154	13 216	10 852.5	715.5	377	8 183	327.4	87.4
Walker	98	558	46.1	21.7	59	1 679	314.8	52.3	102	1 565	73.9	17.9

1. Establishment subject to federal tax.

Table B. States and Counties — Health Care and Social Assistance, Other Services, and Federal Funds

STATE County	Health care and social assistance, 2007				Other services, 2007				Federal funds and grants, 2009–2010 Expenditures (mil dol)			
										Direct payments for individuals[1]		
	Number of establishments	Number of employees	Receipts (mil dol)	Annual payroll (mil dol)	Number of establishments	Number of employees	Receipts (mil dol)	Annual payroll (mil dol)	Total	Social Security and government retirement	Medicare	Food Stamps and Supplemental Security Income
	159	160	161	162	163	164	165	166	167	168	169	170
UNITED STATES...........	784 626	16 792 074	1 668 276.8	662 719.9	540 148	3 479 011	405 284.0	99 123.3	3 251 308.5	858 961.1	508 581.6	111 896.6
ALABAMA	10 392	238 070	22 604.9	8 890.1	6 718	40 488	4 154.1	1 050.0	56 495.7	16 936.5	8 286.0	2 266.2
Autauga............................	82	1 059	82.1	29.5	65	D	D	D	349.3	196.7	54.1	16.7
Baldwin............................	388	6 647	624.0	230.6	274	1 202	169.0	32.1	1 178.4	733.3	226.1	34.4
Barbour............................	59	D	D	D	32	D	D	D	251.5	85.8	64.9	19.1
Bibb	30	602	33.2	14.3	22	D	D	D	172.2	74.9	42.6	9.7
Blount	47	805	57.0	24.2	59	241	17.5	4.6	304.4	154.1	75.0	17.4
Bullock............................	17	365	25.3	8.9	9	19	1.4	0.3	114.6	26.4	27.0	10.7
Butler	42	798	63.4	25.1	25	152	6.0	3.6	202.5	71.6	56.1	16.2
Calhoun...........................	283	6 307	545.7	206.7	186	944	81.3	22.1	1 726.3	565.6	229.3	61.1
Chambers.........................	66	1 070	95.8	34.1	41	D	D	D	306.3	141.6	82.4	21.0
Cherokee.........................	30	389	28.4	12.3	19	70	5.4	1.3	184.8	90.1	42.5	9.1
Chilton	65	808	53.3	23.4	35	D	D	D	288.6	131.3	78.3	18.4
Choctaw...........................	27	283	18.8	8.4	20	51	5.8	1.2	147.4	56.0	36.3	10.1
Clarke	58	1 007	72.7	29.6	40	190	17.0	3.5	263.3	102.8	58.3	23.2
Clay	23	665	34.4	15.6	13	D	D	D	134.8	55.4	31.5	4.2
Cleburne..........................	13	D	D	D	10	60	6.3	1.6	105.8	51.4	22.6	5.6
Coffee	104	D	D	D	62	D	D	D	2 081.3	234.3	82.6	15.4
Colbert.............................	140	2 680	261.2	103.9	83	572	69.8	16.2	526.1	244.4	114.4	22.5
Conecuh..........................	23	371	30.4	11.2	15	30	4.0	0.8	148.7	51.0	38.7	13.9
Coosa	8	D	D	D	6	14	1.6	0.3	93.1	43.8	19.7	6.1
Covington	98	1 692	136.6	49.2	49	224	20.1	5.4	377.9	154.8	97.1	19.4
Crenshaw	15	D	D	D	15	D	D	D	139.8	50.0	34.5	6.8
Cullman	184	3 542	317.2	123.9	110	515	45.3	12.2	626.1	298.1	154.5	27.4
Dale	72	D	D	D	57	D	D	D	644.3	218.7	92.3	27.5
Dallas	119	2 172	185.6	73.4	64	419	35.7	8.0	614.7	165.9	114.8	62.1
DeKalb............................	109	2 260	160.7	62.4	59	206	16.1	4.0	471.6	209.5	110.1	23.4
Elmore	122	1 880	122.5	48.8	77	D	D	D	525.1	308.5	90.7	22.1
Escambia.........................	79	1 323	98.7	38.8	59	225	17.1	4.0	316.2	132.2	77.5	19.6
Etowah............................	302	6 515	626.7	229.8	121	691	54.0	15.8	966.6	420.9	248.2	51.1
Fayette............................	58	896	48.2	21.4	23	D	D	D	153.9	62.2	36.2	9.4
Franklin...........................	78	1 317	97.3	37.1	37	135	11.6	3.0	275.4	110.2	74.8	13.6
Geneva............................	42	D	D	D	22	D	D	D	255.5	111.5	60.7	11.3
Greene.............................	9	D	D	D	8	30	1.7	0.5	111.5	28.9	23.6	12.9
Hale	17	D	D	D	7	17	1.2	0.3	182.5	66.4	40.0	15.5
Henry...............................	28	D	D	D	18	D	D	D	173.4	70.1	35.4	8.7
Houston	320	9 099	920.9	365.4	198	1 104	104.3	24.4	744.4	372.7	136.6	47.1
Jackson	112	D	D	D	43	161	14.7	3.7	669.1	216.0	99.8	20.9
Jefferson..........................	1 730	54 356	6 502.2	2 422.6	1 192	9 162	1 145.4	295.9	7 448.9	2 361.7	1 540.5	352.9
Lamar..............................	21	346	17.8	8.1	15	46	3.6	0.9	144.2	60.4	36.2	7.5
Lauderdale	265	4 604	399.7	147.1	136	821	51.1	15.7	750.5	403.1	154.8	30.9
Lawrence	40	732	46.9	19.7	32	101	8.3	2.1	239.9	100.5	51.4	13.4
Lee	221	6 157	469.5	191.8	152	748	49.7	14.2	762.5	321.6	107.1	38.7
Limestone........................	130	1 927	136.8	58.8	75	358	26.2	6.9	519.2	259.7	84.1	24.0
Lowndes..........................	9	288	25.9	4.6	4	D	D	D	139.5	34.8	22.7	13.7
Macon..............................	27	1 920	130.1	93.4	17	D	D	D	320.6	90.0	43.6	25.3
Madison...........................	871	18 475	1 883.4	769.3	494	3 661	593.3	96.2	9 801.8	1 302.8	303.7	96.4
Marengo	61	973	71.1	28.3	37	137	9.1	2.0	221.5	71.0	51.4	22.7
Marion.............................	72	1 139	95.0	36.9	32	96	7.9	2.2	264.1	105.3	67.1	10.7
Marshall...........................	201	3 356	290.8	108.0	107	378	27.1	6.8	781.0	352.5	164.4	29.6
Mobile.............................	741	23 845	2 160.0	894.7	666	4 681	412.6	116.5	3 934.1	1 327.4	768.5	269.2
Monroe	31	725	49.6	21.0	22	76	6.9	1.4	211.7	76.7	49.9	14.5
Montgomery	704	16 381	1 747.0	658.7	508	3 504	329.9	96.2	4 910.7	796.3	363.5	149.4
Morgan	344	6 131	501.0	200.4	180	1 058	91.4	26.4	869.8	455.1	179.6	35.3
Perry	18	306	15.5	7.6	4	D	D	D	134.1	33.4	31.6	16.5
Pickens............................	26	646	40.6	17.4	17	D	D	D	238.0	74.9	54.5	16.7
Pike	65	1 086	92.5	34.2	38	D	D	D	360.9	95.7	66.4	21.3
Randolph..........................	41	720	44.4	19.9	24	70	5.1	1.5	193.1	82.3	45.8	11.1
Russell............................	75	1 653	105.4	40.5	68	342	22.5	7.6	459.3	222.9	87.1	33.3
St. Clair	94	1 669	120.3	45.2	91	398	35.5	8.3	425.1	241.2	95.7	23.3
Shelby	392	5 709	522.6	203.0	324	2 137	191.2	61.4	918.4	372.0	135.4	23.1
Sumter.............................	24	447	27.5	10.7	7	24	1.5	0.4	169.2	42.9	30.2	18.4
Talladega.........................	170	3 016	230.4	90.0	79	365	29.2	8.5	743.4	305.0	173.8	52.0
Tallapoosa........................	97	D	D	D	46	204	16.7	4.3	375.7	170.6	85.9	24.8
Tuscaloosa	396	D	D	D	242	1 742	134.7	38.3	1 626.5	543.5	268.3	83.6
Walker.............................	174	3 208	273.4	108.2	85	441	37.0	10.5	694.7	326.2	185.7	31.1

1. State totals may include programs not allocated by county.

Federal Funds, Residential Construction, and Local Government Finances

STATE County	Federal funds and grants, 2009–2010 (cont.)							Value of residential construction authorized by building permits, 2010		Local government finances, 2007				
	Expenditures (mil dol) (cont.)									General revenue				
	Procurement contract awards			Grants[1]								Taxes		
													Per capita[2] (dollars)	
	Salaries and wages	Defense	Other	Medicaid and other health-related	Nutrition and family welfare	Education	Other	New construction ($1,000)	Number of housing units	Total (mil dol)	Inter-governmental (mil dol)	Total (mil dol)	Total	Property
	171	172	173	174	175	176	177	178	179	180	181	182	183	184
UNITED STATES............	341 627.5	329 872.9	184 951.4	357 482.0	74 796.2	57 254.8	185 749.4	101 943 061	604 610	X	X	X	X	X
ALABAMA	5 613.2	8 140.1	2 341.6	4 946.9	949.1	816.7	2 560.7	1 546 975	11 261	X	X	X	X	X
Autauga.............................	26.7	0.0	1.6	35.8	5.4	2.9	2.7	26 030	191	112.8	64.4	31.9	639	206
Baldwin.............................	35.5	3.9	14.1	54.3	16.2	6.7	16.3	131 351	696	616.5	180.5	213.4	1 243	523
Barbour.............................	12.9	0.8	0.9	48.2	5.9	2.7	2.4	2 323	10	73.5	43.3	17.4	623	269
Bibb..................................	15.1	0.0	1.6	21.4	3.4	2.2	0.4	1 343	8	56.0	31.1	7.7	357	143
Blount...............................	9.7	0.0	1.5	35.9	5.2	3.0	0.7	1 895	18	101.6	68.9	18.9	334	165
Bullock..............................	3.9	2.8	0.5	34.6	3.4	0.9	2.8	400	1	31.9	23.0	5.4	504	349
Butler...............................	5.3	0.0	0.9	39.3	5.2	2.7	1.2	334	3	58.6	37.7	15.1	750	266
Calhoun.............................	233.1	415.3	58.5	104.4	16.3	9.1	7.4	15 959	107	507.7	186.6	103.4	915	334
Chambers..........................	7.5	0.0	1.1	40.6	5.8	2.5	1.1	870	10	80.8	40.0	24.1	694	288
Cherokee...........................	13.1	0.0	1.4	19.6	3.0	2.2	0.9	1 099	6	50.7	32.0	13.6	553	278
Chilton..............................	8.0	0.0	1.5	35.8	4.9	3.1	3.9	2 968	22	120.0	55.4	23.3	551	280
Choctaw............................	3.2	0.2	0.6	33.8	3.9	1.1	0.1	200	1	31.8	18.5	6.4	450	390
Clarke..............................	10.0	6.8	1.0	45.7	6.0	2.6	5.1	753	5	68.5	39.5	21.4	808	226
Clay.................................	14.8	0.6	3.6	18.4	2.1	0.9	1.8	295	2	50.6	25.5	4.9	357	199
Cleburne............................	4.8	0.1	1.4	15.9	1.8	1.0	1.0	1 322	8	39.0	27.6	6.7	455	244
Coffee...............................	878.6	776.0	16.5	42.7	6.2	5.7	3.8	21 530	239	166.3	98.8	30.4	650	241
Colbert..............................	16.7	3.3	26.5	51.2	7.6	6.8	13.3	10 082	88	236.0	85.6	44.0	806	364
Conecuh............................	2.5	0.0	0.6	31.9	3.4	1.2	0.8	85	1	31.2	21.9	5.2	398	222
Coosa...............................	4.2	3.2	0.5	12.0	2.1	0.8	0.2	0	0	24.0	15.1	5.1	473	267
Covington..........................	19.5	5.5	1.9	52.5	5.7	4.7	3.5	2 129	12	96.6	55.8	19.0	512	211
Crenshaw...........................	6.7	0.5	0.8	33.3	2.4	1.1	1.0	90	1	31.4	21.1	5.6	408	238
Cullman.............................	30.2	0.1	3.4	73.8	9.3	5.8	3.0	2 822	24	249.2	107.1	34.5	428	206
Dale..................................	130.4	102.3	4.4	41.4	6.7	4.7	3.3	8 188	136	118.1	58.0	21.2	439	192
Dallas...............................	18.9	85.3	4.3	108.6	17.2	8.4	7.5	2 900	36	124.6	77.3	33.4	775	344
DeKalb..............................	14.8	0.1	5.4	77.0	6.8	4.8	3.4	4 229	32	158.5	90.6	37.5	552	219
Elmore..............................	34.2	1.2	2.5	41.8	11.4	5.0	1.0	15 564	128	164.4	85.7	29.5	381	158
Escambia...........................	9.0	4.6	1.2	40.2	6.6	3.5	5.4	459	7	109.0	45.9	25.2	671	278
Etowah..............................	42.2	4.3	15.2	119.3	15.8	11.8	10.7	12 408	105	268.4	133.0	101.5	983	266
Fayette.............................	15.1	0.0	0.8	24.0	2.3	1.3	0.4	220	3	53.5	36.0	10.0	567	211
Franklin............................	7.6	8.7	1.4	47.0	4.2	3.4	1.8	1 478	12	76.4	44.0	14.5	477	236
Geneva..............................	12.5	1.6	2.2	38.4	4.0	1.7	1.2	2 639	18	94.1	36.3	10.4	406	178
Greene..............................	2.2	0.2	0.5	35.0	3.8	1.1	1.5	313	3	27.4	16.7	5.3	579	395
Hale.................................	8.9	0.2	0.9	36.9	5.3	1.7	1.6	2 419	22	41.5	27.9	5.2	288	134
Henry...............................	3.7	0.9	0.8	26.0	3.3	2.7	0.8	5 714	42	44.9	20.6	9.2	554	236
Houston............................	29.1	10.4	7.0	87.1	19.4	8.3	10.5	45 048	261	462.3	111.2	87.2	897	262
Jackson.............................	11.1	2.5	212.1	69.7	7.5	3.4	21.3	4 194	18	167.5	71.5	29.4	554	170
Jefferson...........................	860.4	76.4	344.0	995.0	107.4	58.8	404.8	211 943	1 277	2 986.9	888.6	1 357.7	2 061	781
Lamar...............................	3.9	5.4	0.7	25.1	2.2	1.4	0.5	215	1	35.4	24.2	5.8	398	171
Lauderdale.........................	33.0	4.7	4.4	73.7	11.4	5.7	6.2	12 090	144	578.4	108.7	71.9	812	332
Lawrence...........................	6.3	0.6	1.0	44.5	5.0	2.7	0.4	0	0	89.6	47.4	9.2	270	135
Lee..................................	70.4	22.7	10.2	66.3	18.2	7.9	59.1	150 615	971	728.3	134.9	132.6	1 016	470
Limestone..........................	18.8	7.4	2.8	51.5	6.3	5.2	17.6	25 328	138	197.6	82.2	30.9	418	209
Lowndes............................	4.2	13.3	0.3	29.7	6.9	6.0	2.2	357	3	34.6	20.2	11.3	889	499
Macon...............................	41.4	1.0	19.8	52.9	8.6	8.3	16.1	958	5	52.3	30.2	12.8	571	280
Madison.............................	1 342.0	5 246.7	1 127.0	156.3	28.7	30.3	88.6	271 101	2 137	1 644.2	673.0	333.0	1 065	459
Marengo............................	8.1	4.8	1.0	49.5	6.1	1.7	0.4	3 225	32	64.2	43.1	14.4	675	254
Marion..............................	29.8	0.0	1.2	37.2	3.8	2.0	2.7	660	7	71.8	42.0	17.7	597	206
Marshall............................	26.6	8.2	64.6	85.9	9.3	6.6	10.5	7 539	53	344.2	134.0	64.1	731	314
Mobile..............................	317.4	507.9	65.7	333.9	74.8	37.7	104.8	125 841	1 026	1 348.0	605.0	535.3	1 324	417
Monroe.............................	6.4	0.1	1.0	42.4	5.1	3.7	1.2	255	1	85.2	44.2	10.6	465	262
Montgomery........................	767.6	408.1	93.1	331.9	189.6	378.8	1 328.2	58 229	671	607.0	283.3	258.4	1 144	284
Morgan.............................	44.1	15.9	6.6	83.3	23.8	7.9	9.0	26 375	165	419.4	144.4	95.3	828	400
Perry................................	7.8	0.0	0.4	32.7	5.8	1.7	0.7	0	0	38.2	27.7	6.6	626	219
Pickens.............................	8.9	16.6	5.3	47.9	6.0	1.8	2.7	333	4	45.8	32.6	6.4	325	227
Pike.................................	17.1	0.4	1.2	54.8	11.3	4.3	36.3	7 470	88	70.3	42.1	16.9	565	214
Randolph...........................	4.1	0.6	1.0	32.3	3.3	1.5	0.5	0	0	55.7	34.4	14.0	622	398
Russell..............................	13.3	0.6	2.1	62.3	11.2	4.1	6.1	120 745	934	141.5	77.6	38.8	772	385
St. Clair............................	15.8	6.4	-7.1	32.8	8.9	4.6	1.2	12 937	111	154.5	85.6	46.5	596	249
Shelby..............................	38.4	203.2	28.3	33.0	11.6	6.1	54.1	78 379	473	467.0	175.9	176.0	966	522
Sumter..............................	16.4	0.2	0.7	38.6	7.8	2.7	2.2	1 200	5	36.9	23.7	8.5	639	278
Talladega...........................	42.3	17.1	5.7	97.0	19.6	8.8	11.3	10 206	116	189.6	104.6	55.7	694	324
Tallapoosa.........................	15.0	1.7	1.7	43.9	9.1	4.4	7.2	1 857	9	114.2	66.5	25.8	634	302
Tuscaloosa.........................	102.3	122.5	150.6	156.8	27.8	18.7	79.9	86 412	598	871.6	242.3	163.0	916	347
Walker..............................	23.0	5.3	3.6	75.2	12.7	6.9	5.6	2 944	15	139.8	84.2	34.6	502	153

1. State totals may include programs not allocated by county. 2. Based on the resident population estimated as of July 1 of the year shown.

Table B. States and Counties — Local Government Finances, Government Employment, and Voting

STATE County	Local government finances, 2007 (cont.)									Government employment, 2009			Presidential election,[2] 2008		
	Direct general expenditure							Debt outstanding					Percent of vote cast:		
			Percent of total for:												
	Total (mil dol)	Per capita[1] (dollars)	Educa-tion	Health and hospitals	Police protec-tion	Public welfare	High-ways	Total (mil dol)	Per capita[1] (dollars)	Federal civilian	Federal military	State and local	Demo-cratic	Republi-can	All other
	185	186	187	188	189	190	191	192	193	194	195	196	197	198	199
UNITED STATES............	X	X	X	X	X	X	X	X	X	2 879 000	2 092 000	19 678 000	52.9	45.7	1.4
ALABAMA	X	X	X	X	X	X	X	X	X	54 081	33 131	324 676	38.7	60.3	0.9
Autauga................................	116.2	2 325	62.2	0.2	6.5	0.4	5.6	172.4	3 451	100	246	2 274	25.8	73.6	0.6
Baldwin................................	726.3	4 228	45.6	16.8	4.1	0.1	6.8	1 059.3	6 167	315	872	8 309	23.8	75.3	0.9
Barbour................................	72.1	2 581	49.7	15.4	8.1	0.0	3.7	38.4	1 374	62	155	1 794	49.0	50.4	0.6
Bibb......................................	55.9	2 594	54.3	23.1	3.5	0.0	4.6	60.1	2 790	90	105	1 322	26.6	72.4	1.0
Blount...................................	111.7	1 972	71.8	1.6	5.0	0.1	7.0	49.8	880	97	283	1 986	14.5	84.0	1.5
Bullock.................................	32.3	2 992	51.2	18.4	5.7	0.7	10.3	9.8	909	36	53	730	74.1	25.7	0.2
Butler...................................	63.0	3 126	48.6	8.0	5.4	0.5	8.9	99.7	4 944	41	97	925	43.1	56.5	0.4
Calhoun...............................	494.3	4 370	38.2	35.3	3.6	0.2	4.0	141.5	1 251	5 539	606	8 058	33.2	65.7	1.1
Chambers............................	80.9	2 328	54.1	0.2	8.2	0.0	6.3	67.3	1 936	55	166	1 382	45.5	53.9	0.6
Cherokee.............................	51.3	2 088	72.5	0.1	4.1	0.2	8.8	48.9	1 991	53	118	1 250	23.7	74.9	1.4
Chilton.................................	115.8	2 739	49.8	21.7	5.0	0.0	5.1	28.2	666	73	208	1 798	20.7	78.5	0.8
Choctaw...............................	31.8	2 246	61.3	0.0	5.0	0.0	10.7	42.8	3 017	32	68	546	46.1	53.5	0.4
Clarke..................................	72.7	2 744	64.3	0.2	5.8	0.2	9.3	104.0	3 925	91	126	1 943	44.0	55.6	0.4
Clay.....................................	50.7	3 681	33.5	42.2	4.3	0.1	7.2	3.5	256	51	66	1 006	25.8	73.1	1.1
Cleburne..............................	38.6	2 623	56.6	0.0	4.6	14.2	9.4	33.5	2 281	51	71	825	18.0	80.3	1.7
Coffee.................................	131.6	2 812	67.9	0.5	4.8	0.5	5.3	48.2	1 030	195	235	2 468	25.2	74.1	0.6
Colbert.................................	246.5	4 516	39.4	32.8	3.2	0.2	4.4	140.4	2 572	1 130	265	4 585	39.1	59.3	1.6
Conecuh...............................	36.2	2 747	51.0	0.1	5.3	4.8	13.7	13.7	1 039	34	63	790	49.4	50.0	0.6
Coosa..................................	23.4	2 154	55.7	0.5	6.9	0.9	18.1	11.6	1 066	24	51	406	40.9	58.4	0.8
Covington............................	105.6	2 855	52.2	0.1	7.1	0.5	16.1	209.3	5 655	129	178	2 083	20.5	78.8	0.7
Crenshaw............................	33.7	2 441	59.3	1.1	3.9	0.4	12.4	21.1	1 525	40	67	603	30.8	68.7	0.5
Cullman...............................	246.5	3 060	44.6	35.1	2.9	0.6	3.4	142.7	1 772	242	396	4 124	16.6	81.8	1.5
Dale.....................................	123.2	2 558	47.5	22.5	4.5	0.2	4.7	60.2	1 250	3 018	4 487	2 329	27.3	71.9	0.8
Dallas..................................	121.3	2 815	58.8	0.1	10.5	0.2	5.9	48.4	1 124	155	203	2 748	67.1	32.6	0.3
DeKalb.................................	156.3	2 297	62.1	2.9	3.9	0.5	7.1	99.8	1 467	178	336	2 903	23.6	74.8	1.7
Elmore.................................	149.6	1 930	72.0	0.6	4.6	0.0	6.2	121.0	1 561	145	384	3 859	24.2	75.1	0.7
Escambia............................	107.5	2 859	49.5	25.7	6.0	0.0	5.7	41.8	1 111	64	181	3 930	35.4	63.9	0.8
Etowah................................	274.7	2 661	50.8	1.8	7.6	0.2	3.9	247.2	2 395	360	503	5 178	30.2	68.4	1.4
Fayette................................	40.1	2 273	58.3	0.8	3.6	0.0	8.4	24.7	1 402	45	84	1 266	25.1	73.9	1.0
Franklin...............................	94.4	3 100	59.6	0.1	3.3	0.5	4.6	71.2	2 339	97	151	1 891	29.7	68.8	1.5
Geneva................................	75.2	2 925	45.5	26.8	3.0	0.7	10.1	28.4	1 104	66	126	1 505	18.3	80.8	0.9
Greene.................................	30.1	3 274	57.1	18.1	3.6	0.0	5.1	8.0	874	36	43	628	83.1	16.5	0.4
Hale.....................................	45.0	2 482	60.4	13.6	4.5	0.1	7.5	18.2	1 006	54	87	907	60.7	39.0	0.4
Henry...................................	43.6	2 623	57.4	0.1	4.9	20.1	0.5	33.0	1 984	48	81	764	34.9	64.6	0.6
Houston...............................	493.7	4 976	27.3	46.3	4.4	0.0	8.7	680.4	6 915	844	486	8 144	29.3	70.1	0.6
Jackson...............................	175.8	3 315	47.4	23.6	3.7	0.5	5.0	142.9	2 694	478	256	8 627	30.5	67.5	2.0
Jefferson.............................	2 974.3	4 515	40.7	4.1	6.1	0.1	5.4	8 267.4	12 550	8 034	6 399	52 935	52.2	47.1	0.8
Lamar...................................	35.5	2 455	55.8	3.3	4.0	0.1	11.2	20.2	1 396	40	69	615	22.8	76.6	0.6
Lauderdale	304.3	3 436	44.2	29.0	3.7	0.1	4.3	319.4	3 608	309	438	6 118	35.0	63.2	1.9
Lawrence.............................	87.9	2 568	55.7	10.0	9.9	0.6	9.2	188.0	5 491	90	165	1 450	35.2	63.2	1.6
Lee......................................	542.0	4 153	36.5	35.4	3.4	0.1	4.0	632.6	4 847	315	724	15 418	39.6	59.3	1.1
Limestone............................	208.6	2 822	50.2	24.6	3.7	0.3	4.4	180.3	2 440	1 400	380	5 112	28.4	70.3	1.2
Lowndes..............................	33.8	2 662	67.5	0.4	5.0	0.2	12.8	33.8	2 668	34	60	611	74.9	24.9	0.3
Macon..................................	51.6	2 311	57.2	7.4	3.1	0.0	1.2	103.9	4 653	959	116	2 280	86.9	12.8	0.3
Madison...............................	1 447.7	4 629	31.2	39.9	4.2	0.0	2.9	1 962.4	6 275	16 040	3 125	23 577	41.9	56.9	1.2
Marengo...............................	64.1	3 013	66.4	3.1	3.9	0.4	4.3	27.9	1 309	71	116	1 753	51.7	48.1	0.3
Marion..................................	69.1	2 336	64.6	2.6	2.4	0.1	4.4	85.1	2 878	76	141	1 536	21.0	77.2	1.8
Marshall...............................	348.5	3 977	41.9	34.8	3.9	0.5	2.6	297.6	3 396	262	438	5 773	21.2	77.6	1.2
Mobile..................................	1 241.0	3 069	48.4	3.3	6.9	0.5	4.8	1 144.8	2 831	2 639	2 998	25 823	45.3	54.0	0.7
Monroe.................................	88.1	3 872	42.9	31.8	4.4	0.2	7.4	19.2	844	59	108	1 545	44.7	54.9	0.5
Montgomery	701.0	3 105	40.8	1.6	7.6	0.4	5.5	369.4	1 636	6 524	4 249	27 884	59.4	40.1	0.5
Morgan.................................	445.2	3 870	41.6	21.0	4.3	0.3	2.0	449.0	3 903	297	569	6 905	27.5	71.3	1.3
Perry....................................	39.9	3 763	45.9	21.7	3.2	0.2	7.2	21.4	2 023	27	60	652	72.4	27.3	0.4
Pickens................................	45.4	2 313	63.5	1.2	5.5	0.1	8.5	30.5	1 554	56	93	880	45.6	54.0	0.4
Pike.....................................	77.2	2 578	52.9	0.3	7.9	0.2	10.7	56.4	1 885	94	152	3 359	42.1	57.4	0.5
Randolph..............................	48.0	2 139	68.6	2.7	5.2	0.4	7.6	31.0	1 384	54	109	1 324	29.5	69.1	1.4
Russell.................................	150.1	2 990	61.1	0.1	6.8	0.0	5.2	285.6	5 692	94	246	2 797	53.3	46.0	0.7
St. Clair...............................	163.4	2 094	62.7	0.4	6.5	0.1	5.0	254.7	3 263	114	397	2 901	17.9	81.1	1.0
Shelby..................................	462.1	2 538	58.6	1.4	6.3	0.2	4.4	500.4	2 748	317	932	8 118	22.8	76.2	1.1
Sumter.................................	39.2	2 948	58.2	1.1	4.2	0.1	13.7	16.2	1 217	43	62	1 340	75.0	24.7	0.4
Talladega.............................	313.0	3 900	38.1	3.0	2.8	0.1	3.3	147.4	1 837	485	389	4 945	40.3	58.8	0.9
Tallapoosa...........................	122.3	3 001	51.0	15.5	6.2	0.1	4.1	98.7	2 422	99	199	2 104	31.4	67.9	0.7
Tuscaloosa..........................	904.2	5 082	30.3	43.1	4.0	0.0	5.0	590.5	3 319	1 613	901	21 850	41.6	57.5	0.9
Walker..................................	157.6	2 290	69.4	0.1	5.5	0.1	5.3	105.2	1 529	178	334	3 283	25.9	72.3	1.8

1. Based on the resident population estimated as of July 1 of the year shown. 2. © 2009 Election Data Services, Inc. All rights reserved.

Table B. States and Counties — Land Area and Population

STATE/ County code	CBSA code[1]	County type[2]	STATE County	Land area,[3] (sq km) 2010	Total persons	Rank	Per square kilometer	White	Black	American Indian, Alaska Native	Asian and Pacific Islander	Percent Hispanic or Latino[4]	Under 5 years	5 to 17 years	18 to 24 years	25 to 34 years	35 to 44 years	45 to 54 years
				1	2	3	4	5	6	7	8	9	10	11	12	13	14	15
			ALABAMA—Cont'd															
01 129	...	8	Washington	2 798	17 581	1 944	6.3	65.9	25.2	8.7	0.3	0.9	6.0	19.5	8.1	10.9	12.7	14.9
01 131	...	8	Wilcox	2 301	11 670	2 319	5.1	27.0	72.4	0.4	0.1	0.6	6.1	20.9	8.1	10.6	11.6	14.3
01 133	...	6	Winston	1 588	24 484	1 628	15.4	96.1	0.7	1.3	0.5	2.6	5.4	16.2	7.4	10.4	13.2	15.4
02 000	...	X	ALASKA	1 477 953	710 231	X	0.5	69.8	4.3	18.8	8.3	5.5	7.6	18.8	10.5	14.5	13.1	15.6
02 013	...	9	Aleutians East	18 083	3 141	2 968	0.2	16.4	7.2	30.3	37.7	12.3	3.9	7.9	9.5	16.4	19.0	24.5
02 016	...	7	Aleutians West	11 371	5 561	2 802	0.5	34.6	6.1	17.4	33.1	13.1	3.7	11.0	7.7	17.5	20.4	22.2
02 020	11260	2	Anchorage	4 415	291 826	221	66.1	68.5	7.1	11.5	12.6	7.6	7.5	18.4	11.2	15.6	13.4	15.3
02 050	...	7	Bethel	105 076	17 013	1 985	0.2	14.2	0.8	86.3	1.7	1.1	10.6	26.0	11.6	13.3	10.9	13.0
02 060	...	9	Bristol Bay	1 305	997	3 109	0.8	62.3	0.8	47.4	3.8	2.4	4.8	17.8	6.8	11.2	12.5	22.6
02 068	...	8	Denali	33 026	1 826	3 069	0.1	92.2	0.6	6.2	2.2	2.3	6.2	16.3	4.4	12.7	14.7	20.8
02 070	...	9	Dillingham	48 093	4 847	2 852	0.1	25.0	0.6	79.1	2.3	2.1	9.3	23.6	11.9	11.9	9.9	15.3
02 090	21820	3	Fairbanks North Star	19 006	97 581	594	5.1	79.5	5.5	10.5	4.7	5.8	8.1	17.5	13.4	16.6	12.8	13.9
02 100	...	9	Haines	6 005	2 508	3 008	0.4	87.5	0.6	13.6	1.6	1.9	5.1	14.8	4.7	9.8	12.2	19.1
02 105	...		Hoonah-Angoon	19 489	2 150	3 041	0.1	54.6	1.3	49.1	1.9	3.6	5.8	13.9	7.0	11.2	10.5	18.2
02 110	27940	5	Juneau	6 998	31 275	1 409	4.5	74.7	1.7	18.1	10.1	5.1	6.3	17.1	8.9	13.8	13.8	17.4
02 122	...	7	Kenai Peninsula	41 635	55 400	904	1.3	87.7	0.9	11.2	2.5	3.0	6.3	17.4	8.3	11.4	12.4	17.2
02 130	28540	7	Ketchikan Gateway	12 583	13 477	2 221	1.1	73.9	1.3	20.5	9.1	4.0	6.7	17.2	8.7	13.5	12.6	17.1
02 150	28980	7	Kodiak Island	16 963	13 592	2 212	0.8	58.5	1.2	17.5	22.3	7.3	8.5	20.2	9.7	14.9	13.2	15.7
02 164	...	9	Lake and Peninsula	61 258	1 631	3 079	0.0	30.6	1.6	73.5	2.0	2.6	8.5	21.7	11.3	13.9	9.9	16.8
02 170	11260	2	Matanuska-Susitna	63 734	88 995	637	1.4	88.1	1.7	9.6	2.8	3.7	7.8	21.1	8.4	13.0	13.7	16.1
02 180	...	7	Nome	59 471	9 492	2 480	0.2	21.4	0.6	81.1	1.7	1.2	10.7	23.6	11.6	14.1	11.1	13.0
02 185	...	7	North Slope	229 720	9 430	2 485	0.0	36.2	1.7	57.7	6.9	2.6	7.9	15.9	11.1	14.8	13.0	19.2
02 188	...	7	Northwest Arctic	92 133	7 523	2 642	0.1	16.1	1.0	86.8	1.4	0.8	11.7	23.6	13.7	13.0	11.2	12.5
02 195	...		Petersburg	8 500	3 815	2 920	0.4	76.5	0.7	22.5	5.3	3.4	6.0	17.4	7.6	11.2	12.6	17.5
02 198	...		Prince of Wales-Hyder	10 160	5 559	2 803	0.5	56.8	0.8	46.2	2.7	2.3	7.5	18.1	7.6	10.9	12.7	17.3
02 220	...	7	Sitka	7 434	8 881	2 535	1.2	71.4	0.9	23.3	8.4	4.9	7.0	16.5	8.1	14.1	13.1	16.2
02 230	...		Skagway	1 172	968	3 112	0.8	93.6	0.2	5.2	2.5	2.2	5.1	10.6	5.2	19.5	16.4	16.1
02 240	...	8	Southeast Fairbanks	64 151	7 029	2 684	0.1	83.0	1.4	14.7	1.9	3.3	6.9	19.4	8.0	12.7	13.0	16.7
02 261	...	9	Valdez-Cordova	88 681	9 636	2 466	0.1	78.2	0.8	18.6	5.3	3.6	6.4	17.9	8.3	11.8	12.6	19.3
02 270	...	9	Wade Hampton	44 241	7 459	2 645	0.2	4.2	0.3	96.9	0.5	0.1	12.1	29.5	13.9	11.4	10.4	10.6
02 275	...		Wrangell	6 582	2 369	3 022	0.4	80.4	0.5	24.2	2.9	1.6	5.4	16.5	7.1	8.6	10.2	18.1
02 282	...	9	Yakutat	19 812	662	3 131	0.0	53.8	0.8	49.4	9.7	2.6	6.0	18.4	7.3	11.8	14.2	16.6
02 290	...	8	Yukon-Koyukuk	376 856	5 588	2 801	0.0	27.1	0.5	75.9	0.9	1.2	7.9	19.8	9.9	12.0	10.1	16.2
04 000	...	X	ARIZONA	294 207	6 392 017	X	21.7	59.4	4.4	4.6	3.6	29.6	7.1	18.4	9.9	13.4	12.9	13.2
04 001	...	6	Apache	29 001	71 518	746	2.5	21.5	0.6	73.1	0.5	5.8	8.3	23.4	10.1	11.0	11.3	13.4
04 003	43420	4	Cochise	15 969	131 346	472	8.2	60.5	4.6	1.5	3.3	32.4	6.5	16.6	9.2	12.5	11.2	13.4
04 005	22380	3	Coconino	48 223	134 421	459	2.8	57.1	1.6	27.7	2.1	13.5	6.7	17.0	17.7	13.5	11.5	13.4
04 007	37740	4	Gila	12 323	53 597	927	4.3	66.8	0.5	15.0	0.8	17.9	5.7	15.7	7.0	8.4	9.6	14.0
04 009	40940	6	Graham	11 972	37 220	1 232	3.1	53.3	2.1	14.3	1.0	30.4	8.6	19.8	11.9	14.2	12.1	12.0
04 011	40940	7	Greenlee	4 774	8 437	2 575	1.8	48.8	1.1	2.3	0.7	47.9	7.8	21.4	8.3	12.7	12.1	14.0
04 012	...	6	La Paz	11 654	20 489	1 819	1.8	64.5	1.0	12.3	0.7	23.5	5.0	12.9	5.6	7.8	8.1	11.8
04 013	38060	1	Maricopa	23 828	3 817 117	4	160.2	60.3	5.4	2.0	4.4	29.6	7.4	19.0	9.9	14.2	13.7	13.2
04 015	29420	4	Mohave	34 476	200 186	312	5.8	81.1	1.2	2.7	1.8	14.8	5.5	15.1	6.8	9.1	10.0	14.3
04 017	43320	4	Navajo	25 771	107 449	550	4.2	45.2	1.1	43.6	0.9	10.8	8.1	21.6	9.5	11.1	11.0	13.4
04 019	46060	2	Pima	23 794	980 263	41	41.2	56.8	3.8	3.0	3.5	34.6	6.4	16.6	11.0	12.9	11.8	13.4
04 021	38060	1	Pinal	13 897	375 770	175	27.0	60.2	5.0	5.3	2.7	28.5	8.0	18.5	7.9	15.1	13.4	11.8
04 023	35700	4	Santa Cruz	3 204	47 420	1 017	14.8	16.2	0.3	0.4	0.6	82.8	7.8	23.0	8.5	10.1	12.1	13.6
04 025	39140	3	Yavapai	21 040	211 033	293	10.0	83.5	0.9	2.2	1.4	13.6	5.0	14.1	7.1	8.8	9.7	14.1
04 027	49740	3	Yuma	14 281	195 751	319	13.7	36.3	2.0	1.4	1.7	59.7	7.7	20.5	10.8	12.4	11.7	11.5
05 000	...	X	ARKANSAS	134 771	2 915 918	X	21.6	76.0	15.9	1.5	1.7	6.4	6.8	17.6	9.7	12.9	12.6	14.0
05 001	...	6	Arkansas	2 561	19 019	1 879	7.4	72.1	25.1	0.7	0.6	2.7	6.0	17.2	7.6	12.2	11.9	14.5
05 003	...	7	Ashley	2 397	21 853	1 743	9.1	68.9	26.1	0.6	0.3	4.9	6.5	17.9	8.0	10.8	12.9	14.4
05 005	34260	7	Baxter	1 436	41 513	1 142	28.9	97.2	0.3	1.4	0.7	1.7	4.9	13.2	5.9	8.7	9.8	13.6
05 007	22220	2	Benton	2 195	221 339	283	100.8	78.4	1.5	2.8	3.6	15.5	8.1	19.9	8.3	14.7	14.1	13.0
05 009	25460	7	Boone	1 529	36 903	1 247	24.1	96.8	0.3	1.9	0.7	1.8	6.1	17.2	7.8	11.1	12.3	14.2
05 011	...	6	Bradley	1 682	11 508	2 335	6.8	58.8	28.0	0.5	0.3	13.2	6.7	16.6	8.9	11.3	12.2	13.8
05 013	15780	9	Calhoun	1 628	5 368	2 815	3.3	74.4	22.8	0.8	0.4	2.8	4.9	15.6	8.9	10.6	12.4	16.4
05 015	...	6	Carroll	1 632	27 446	1 517	16.8	85.5	0.4	1.9	0.8	12.7	5.9	16.7	7.1	10.3	11.4	14.4
05 017	...	7	Chicot	1 669	11 800	2 311	7.1	40.7	54.1	0.5	0.6	4.6	6.9	16.2	8.2	11.2	11.1	14.9
05 019	11660	7	Clark	2 243	22 995	1 688	10.3	71.6	24.0	0.8	0.8	4.0	5.4	14.1	21.5	10.3	10.3	12.6
05 021	...	7	Clay	1 656	16 083	2 047	9.7	97.9	0.6	0.9	0.3	1.3	5.6	16.7	7.5	10.0	12.7	14.2
05 023	...	6	Cleburne	1 434	25 970	1 567	18.1	97.0	0.5	1.3	0.4	2.0	5.3	14.6	6.8	9.8	10.8	14.8

1. CBSA = Core Based Statistical Area. See Appendix A for explanation. See Appendix B for list of metropolitan areas with component counties.   2. County type code from the Economic Research Service of USDA Rural-Urban Continuum Codes. See Appendix A for definition.   3. Dry land or land partially or temporarily covered by water.   4. May be of any race.

Table B. States and Counties — **Population and Households**

STATE County	Age (percent) (cont.) 55 to 64 years	65 to 74 years	75 years and over	Percent female	Total persons 1990	2000	Percent change 1990–2000	2000–2010	Components of change, 2000–2009 Births	Deaths	Net migration	Households, 2010 Number	Percent change, 2000–2010	Persons per house-hold	Percent Female family house-holder[1]	One per-son
	16	17	18	19	20	21	22	23	24	25	26	27	28	29	30	31
ALABAMA—Cont'd																
Washington	13.2	8.7	6.0	50.8	16 694	18 097	8.4	-2.9	1 922	1 514	-1 350	6 758	0.8	2.58	13.3	24.5
Wilcox	13.5	8.3	6.7	52.7	13 568	13 183	-2.8	-11.5	1 829	1 362	-1 041	4 484	-6.1	2.58	27.3	28.4
Winston	14.3	10.7	7.0	50.9	22 053	24 843	12.7	-1.4	2 552	2 709	-543	10 163	0.6	2.38	10.9	27.1
ALASKA	12.1	5.0	2.8	48.0	550 043	626 932	14.0	13.3	97 287	28 894	-724	258 058	16.5	2.65	10.7	25.6
Aleutians East	13.8	3.4	1.5	33.4	2 464	2 697	9.5	16.5	173	49	-83	553	5.1	2.56	13.4	26.6
Aleutians West	14.1	2.8	0.6	33.1	9 478	5 465	-42.3	1.8	327	101	-1 058	1 212	-4.6	2.49	9.6	32.4
Anchorage	11.3	4.6	2.7	49.2	226 338	260 283	15.0	12.1	40 260	11 465	-1 541	107 332	13.2	2.64	11.7	24.9
Bethel	8.5	3.9	2.2	47.7	13 660	16 006	17.2	6.3	3 942	827	-1 723	4 651	10.1	3.59	17.2	20.2
Bristol Bay	15.9	5.8	2.5	45.8	1 410	1 258	-10.8	-20.7	106	45	-445	423	-13.7	2.32	6.9	32.4
Denali	17.3	6.0	1.5	45.1	1 682	1 893	12.5	-3.5	195	22	-204	806	2.7	2.22	3.0	35.1
Dillingham	10.6	4.9	2.7	47.6	4 010	4 922	22.7	-1.5	834	226	-562	1 563	2.2	3.07	17.2	25.6
Fairbanks North Star	11.1	4.3	2.3	47.2	77 720	82 840	6.6	17.8	14 991	3 184	-2 173	36 441	22.4	2.56	8.8	26.7
Haines	20.6	8.6	5.1	49.2	2 117	2 392	13.0	4.8	176	137	-19	1 149	15.9	2.18	7.8	31.7
Hoonah-Angoon	20.0	9.6	3.8	45.8	NA	NA	NA	NA	202	126	-526	913	NA	2.35	8.5	31.0
Juneau	14.2	5.5	2.9	49.0	26 752	30 711	14.8	1.8	3 641	1 302	-2 088	12 187	5.6	2.49	10.4	26.9
Kenai Peninsula	15.8	7.3	4.0	47.6	40 802	49 691	21.8	11.5	5 937	2 888	2 210	22 161	20.2	2.42	8.1	28.6
Ketchikan Gateway	14.1	6.2	3.9	48.7	13 828	14 070	1.8	-4.2	1 703	797	-1 931	5 305	-1.7	2.49	11.6	27.9
Kodiak Island	11.1	4.7	2.0	47.0	13 309	13 913	4.5	-2.3	1 994	425	-2 110	4 630	4.7	2.86	10.9	22.1
Lake and Peninsula	10.2	5.6	2.2	47.3	1 666	1 823	9.4	-10.5	240	122	-456	553	-6.0	2.88	14.6	23.0
Matanuska-Susitna	12.0	5.2	2.7	48.3	39 683	59 322	49.5	50.0	9 882	3 300	22 641	31 824	54.8	2.75	8.7	22.3
Nome	9.4	4.1	2.3	46.7	8 288	9 196	11.0	3.2	2 011	536	-1 252	2 815	4.5	3.29	17.5	23.5
North Slope	13.7	3.0	1.3	37.4	5 986	7 385	23.4	27.7	1 585	308	-1 896	2 029	-3.8	3.34	19.9	23.6
Northwest Arctic	8.2	3.5	2.5	46.4	6 106	7 208	18.0	4.4	1 644	360	-1 020	1 919	7.8	3.72	21.0	21.0
Petersburg	16.3	7.4	4.1	48.0	NA	NA	NA	NA	382	261	-595	1 599	NA	2.36	9.4	29.2
Prince of Wales-Hyder	15.9	7.2	2.9	44.8	NA	NA	NA	NA	626	239	-942	2 194	NA	2.51	10.5	29.9
Sitka	13.6	6.5	4.9	49.5	8 588	8 835	2.9	0.5	1 116	455	-717	3 545	8.1	2.43	10.7	29.0
Skagway	18.0	6.5	2.6	48.3	NA	NA	NA	NA	67	23	19	436	NA	2.15	4.6	33.5
Southeast Fairbanks	13.9	6.6	2.9	44.3	5 925	6 174	4.2	13.8	948	308	77	2 567	22.4	2.59	6.7	27.4
Valdez-Cordova	15.3	5.7	2.6	46.6	9 920	10 195	2.8	-5.5	1 133	439	-1 539	3 966	2.1	2.38	8.2	32.0
Wade Hampton	6.7	3.3	2.1	47.1	5 789	7 028	21.4	6.1	2 071	366	-982	1 745	8.9	4.27	23.3	15.1
Wrangell	18.3	9.8	6.0	47.6	NA	NA	NA	NA	212	142	-371	1 053	NA	2.23	9.0	32.6
Yakutat	16.0	6.5	3.2	45.6	725	808	11.4	-18.1	67	37	-153	270	1.9	2.39	10.7	34.1
Yukon-Koyukuk	14.0	6.2	4.0	45.8	6 798	6 551	-3.6	-14.7	822	404	-1 285	2 217	-4.0	2.51	17.1	35.1
ARIZONA	11.4	7.8	6.0	50.3	3 665 339	5 130 632	40.0	24.6	875 726	411 488	986 764	2 380 990	25.2	2.63	12.4	25.1
Apache	11.0	7.2	4.3	50.1	61 591	69 423	12.7	3.0	11 465	4 636	-5 366	22 771	14.0	3.10	21.2	24.8
Cochise	13.4	10.1	7.2	49.0	97 624	117 755	20.6	11.5	16 474	10 405	6 453	50 865	15.9	2.46	11.5	28.2
Coconino	11.4	5.5	3.3	50.4	96 591	116 320	20.4	15.6	18 473	5 751	1 515	46 711	15.5	2.69	12.7	24.5
Gila	16.3	13.5	9.7	50.3	40 216	51 335	27.6	4.4	6 319	6 114	987	22 000	9.2	2.39	11.1	29.3
Graham	9.9	6.4	5.0	46.3	26 554	33 489	26.1	11.1	4 690	2 567	1 562	11 120	9.9	3.01	15.5	21.7
Greenlee	11.6	6.2	5.8	47.9	8 008	8 547	6.7	-1.3	997	518	-1 001	3 188	2.3	2.64	9.6	27.8
La Paz	16.0	20.5	12.1	48.5	13 844	19 715	42.4	3.9	2 082	1 978	299	9 198	10.0	2.19	9.4	32.1
Maricopa	10.4	6.7	5.4	50.5	2 122 101	3 072 149	44.8	24.2	564 289	226 288	632 032	1 411 583	24.6	2.67	12.4	25.9
Mohave	15.7	14.1	9.2	50.0	93 497	155 032	65.8	29.1	20 655	21 291	41 241	82 539	31.4	2.39	10.4	26.7
Navajo	12.0	8.3	5.0	50.9	77 674	97 470	25.5	10.2	16 808	7 344	6 583	35 658	18.7	2.95	17.1	23.0
Pima	12.5	8.3	7.1	50.9	666 957	843 746	26.5	16.2	121 594	73 661	100 945	388 660	16.9	2.46	12.8	29.2
Pinal	11.4	8.8	5.0	47.5	116 397	179 727	54.4	109.1	35 399	17 175	131 833	125 590	104.7	2.78	11.7	20.5
Santa Cruz	11.9	7.8	5.3	52.4	29 676	38 381	29.3	23.6	7 233	2 237	631	15 437	30.7	3.05	17.1	19.0
Yavapai	17.2	13.7	10.4	51.0	107 714	167 517	55.5	26.0	19 235	20 658	50 085	90 903	29.5	2.28	9.0	29.1
Yuma	9.7	8.9	6.8	49.9	106 895	160 026	49.7	22.3	30 013	10 865	18 965	64 767	20.3	2.93	13.8	19.6
ARKANSAS	12.0	8.0	6.4	50.9	2 350 624	2 673 400	13.7	9.1	361 135	258 324	112 923	1 147 084	10.0	2.47	13.4	27.1
Arkansas	14.1	8.6	7.7	51.5	21 653	20 749	-4.2	-8.3	2 345	2 426	-1 605	8 005	-5.3	2.35	15.3	29.4
Ashley	13.2	9.5	6.7	51.5	24 319	24 209	-0.5	-9.7	2 726	2 366	-2 528	8 765	-6.6	2.47	14.9	26.1
Baxter	15.8	15.4	12.7	51.8	31 186	38 386	23.1	8.1	3 491	6 067	6 518	18 748	9.9	2.18	8.6	29.5
Benton	9.8	6.7	5.5	50.7	97 530	153 406	57.3	44.3	27 149	12 108	48 247	82 087	41.0	2.67	9.9	22.5
Boone	13.2	10.0	8.1	51.0	28 297	33 948	20.0	8.7	4 031	3 634	2 695	15 120	9.2	2.41	9.6	26.6
Bradley	12.7	9.2	8.5	51.5	11 793	12 600	6.8	-8.7	1 549	1 501	-786	4 673	-3.3	2.42	15.1	30.3
Calhoun	14.0	9.6	7.5	49.3	5 826	5 744	-1.4	-6.5	513	539	-497	2 262	-2.4	2.30	12.8	30.3
Carroll	15.6	11.0	7.7	50.7	18 623	25 357	36.2	8.2	3 194	2 400	1 959	11 393	11.8	2.39	9.6	28.2
Chicot	13.3	9.6	8.7	50.9	15 713	14 117	-10.2	-16.4	1 685	1 571	-2 363	4 579	-12.0	2.42	21.1	31.6
Clark	11.0	7.7	7.2	52.3	21 437	23 546	9.8	-2.3	2 621	2 287	64	8 783	-1.4	2.32	13.7	29.3
Clay	13.3	11.0	9.0	51.1	18 107	17 609	-2.8	-8.7	1 707	2 188	-1 460	6 845	-7.7	2.33	10.3	29.6
Cleburne	14.3	13.4	10.2	50.8	19 411	24 046	23.9	8.0	2 424	2 893	2 150	11 078	8.7	2.31	8.6	26.9

1. No spouse present.

Table B. States and Counties — **Population, Vital Statistics, Medicare, and Crime**

STATE County	Persons in group quarters, 2010	Daytime population, 2006–2010 Number	Employ-ment/resi-dence ratio	Births, average 2006–2008 Total	Rate[1]	Deaths, average 2006–2008 Number	Rate[1]	Persons under 65 with no health insurance, 2009 Number	Percent	Medicare, 2011 Eligible for Medicare	Enrolled in Medicare Advantage	Enrolled in a Medicare prescription drug plan	Serious crimes known to police,[2] 2010 Total Number	Rate[3]
	32	33	34	35	36	37	38	39	40	41	42	43	44	45
ALABAMA—Cont'd														
Washington	147	17 140	0.9	D	D	162	9.4	2 214	15.6	3 599	323	1 895	209	1 189
Wilcox	108	12 242	1.1	D	D	150	11.7	1 927	18.8	2 860	198	1 821	100	857
Winston	301	24 995	1.0	D	D	303	12.5	3 529	17.9	5 522	658	2 933	491	2 005
ALASKA	26 352	697 587	1.0	11 163	16.4	3 437	5.0	144 785	22.7	68 417	D	25 547	24 796	3 491
Aleutians East	1 726	3 972	1.1	D	D	D	D	974	36.8	134	D	38	NA	NA
Aleutians West	2 543	6 869	1.1	D	D	12	2.5	1 435	32.0	173	D	44	NA	NA
Anchorage	8 450	293 809	1.1	4 588	16.4	1 335	4.8	52 168	20.0	27 931	195	10 488	NA	NA
Bethel	338	17 164	1.1	426	24.8	93	5.4	4 876	29.1	1 171	D	656	NA	NA
Bristol Bay	16	1 197	1.4	D	D	D	D	224	27.6	113	D	24	NA	NA
Denali	36	1 587	1.7	D	D	D	D	374	22.0	184	D	43	NA	NA
Dillingham	52	4 947	1.1	D	D	26	5.2	1 415	30.4	413	D	209	NA	NA
Fairbanks North Star	4 313	93 495	1.0	1 726	18.3	370	3.9	18 922	20.9	8 046	38	2 483	NA	NA
Haines	0	1 638	1.0	D	D	17	7.6	583	28.2	437	D	184	NA	NA
Hoonah-Angoon	0	1 940	0.9	NA	NA	NA	NA	634	34.4	NA	NA	NA	NA	NA
Juneau	887	31 289	1.0	D	D	164	5.3	5 353	19.1	3 515	17	1 118	NA	NA
Kenai Peninsula	1 722	52 583	0.9	662	12.5	330	6.2	12 253	25.7	8 050	72	3 202	NA	NA
Ketchikan Gateway	246	13 702	1.0	D	D	91	6.9	2 934	25.4	1 760	D	715	NA	NA
Kodiak Island	336	13 596	1.0	D	D	56	4.3	3 562	28.9	1 164	11	424	NA	NA
Lake and Peninsula	37	1 717	1.2	D	D	14	9.4	541	38.8	153	D	64	NA	NA
Matanuska-Susitna	1 370	71 983	0.7	1 258	15.2	408	4.9	18 927	23.7	9 189	68	3 469	NA	NA
Nome	219	9 373	1.0	D	D	59	6.4	2 730	30.5	696	D	285	NA	NA
North Slope	2 652	15 763	3.3	D	D	45	6.8	1 754	26.8	431	D	111	NA	NA
Northwest Arctic	382	7 745	1.1	D	D	47	6.2	2 086	29.1	490	D	227	NA	NA
Petersburg	43	4 214	1.2	NA	NA	NA	NA	884	26.7	NA	NA	NA	NA	NA
Prince of Wales-Hyder	50	5 485	1.0	NA	NA	NA	NA	1 408	28.0	NA	NA	NA	NA	NA
Sitka	255	8 994	1.0	D	D	62	7.0	1 994	25.9	1 125	D	344	NA	NA
Skagway	32	1 079	0.9	NA	NA	NA	NA	171	21.8	NA	NA	NA	NA	NA
Southeast Fairbanks	369	7 360	1.1	D	D	32	4.8	1 813	29.4	902	D	351	NA	NA
Valdez-Cordova	201	10 025	1.1	D	D	53	5.5	2 094	24.8	1 093	D	419	NA	NA
Wade Hampton	9	7 407	1.0	229	30.0	50	6.5	2 206	29.1	481	D	326	NA	NA
Wrangell	19	2 344	1.0	NA	NA	NA	NA	482	26.8	NA	NA	NA	NA	NA
Yakutat	18	697	1.2	D	D	D	D	203	32.5	86	D	38	NA	NA
Yukon-Koyukuk	31	5 613	1.0	D	D	55	9.5	1 787	34.7	680	D	285	NA	NA
ARIZONA	139 384	6 222 614	1.0	101 617	16.0	45 914	7.2	1 118 761	19.9	963 677	352 960	266 334	251 978	3 942
Apache	941	69 891	1.0	1 285	18.2	532	7.5	14 918	23.4	9 810	799	5 411	423	591
Cochise	6 271	129 344	1.0	1 821	14.2	1 149	9.0	17 239	16.5	25 576	6 668	6 786	4 008	3 175
Coconino	8 834	132 032	1.0	2 061	16.2	663	5.2	23 124	19.5	14 479	1 759	6 701	4 924	3 663
Gila	917	53 553	1.0	687	13.2	676	13.0	7 682	19.2	13 629	1 486	6 030	1 306	2 484
Graham	3 751	34 930	0.9	590	16.9	292	8.4	6 594	20.5	4 858	1 328	2 073	737	1 980
Greenlee	35	9 842	1.5	D	D	61	7.8	1 083	15.2	1 150	239	440	NA	NA
La Paz	388	21 101	1.1	D	D	232	11.5	3 325	25.1	4 769	681	1 757	651	3 177
Maricopa	53 177	3 793 445	1.0	64 993	16.8	25 013	6.5	707 078	20.2	508 374	213 318	126 755	153 262	4 015
Mohave	2 629	186 273	0.8	2 488	12.8	2 533	13.0	29 500	19.9	50 598	10 444	18 366	6 916	3 455
Navajo	2 227	107 707	1.0	1 956	17.5	858	7.7	19 277	19.5	17 469	2 993	8 554	2 884	2 684
Pima	24 139	964 195	1.0	13 764	14.1	8 041	8.2	154 841	18.2	166 634	73 268	36 708	28 776	2 936
Pinal	26 245	278 635	0.6	5 167	17.3	2 014	6.7	56 434	19.5	53 309	19 342	14 074	11 043	2 961
Santa Cruz	384	46 681	1.0	772	18.0	253	5.9	8 941	24.2	7 238	3 186	1 893	1 106	2 378
Yavapai	3 525	205 757	1.0	2 339	11.0	2 395	11.3	31 768	19.7	58 689	12 143	20 783	5 112	2 422
Yuma	5 921	189 228	1.0	3 332	17.5	1 203	6.3	36 955	23.6	27 095	5 306	10 003	4 866	2 858
ARKANSAS	78 931	2 877 006	1.0	41 003	14.4	28 471	10.0	471 567	19.6	548 761	82 497	263 695	118 510	4 064
Arkansas	247	20 753	1.2	D	D	253	13.0	2 886	18.7	3 963	292	2 479	800	4 206
Ashley	191	22 053	1.0	D	D	258	11.5	3 557	19.7	4 756	427	3 089	618	2 828
Baxter	595	42 321	1.1	D	D	668	16.0	5 933	19.8	13 948	2 791	5 305	1 040	2 505
Benton	2 061	215 808	1.1	3 303	16.3	1 396	6.9	37 704	19.3	32 996	8 845	12 187	4 924	2 230
Boone	465	38 223	1.1	D	D	400	10.9	5 898	20.2	8 883	1 482	3 940	922	2 498
Bradley	220	11 954	1.1	D	D	155	12.9	2 308	24.6	2 483	201	1 554	172	1 611
Calhoun	175	4 998	0.8	D	D	58	10.6	922	22.2	1 150	77	652	38	708
Carroll	230	27 070	1.0	338	12.3	280	10.2	5 727	25.4	6 265	1 361	2 579	733	2 671
Chicot	722	12 179	1.0	D	D	158	12.7	2 065	22.2	2 668	112	1 846	262	2 220
Clark	2 612	23 305	1.0	D	D	242	10.3	4 331	21.9	4 187	602	1 892	806	3 505
Clay	125	14 382	0.7	D	D	225	13.9	2 632	21.7	4 130	442	2 293	148	920
Cleburne	339	24 567	0.9	D	D	327	12.8	4 150	21.4	7 165	609	3 591	847	3 261

1. Per 1,000 estimated resident population. 2. Data for serious crimes have not been adjusted for underreporting; this may affect comparability between geographic areas and over time. 3. Per 100,000 population estimated by the FBI.

Table B. States and Counties — Crime, Education, Money Income, and Poverty

STATE County	Rate² Violent	Rate² Property	Enrollment³ Total	Percent private	Attainment⁴ (percent) High school graduate or less	Attainment⁴ (percent) Bachelor's degree or more	Local government expenditures⁵ 2008-2009 Total current expenditures (mil dol)	Current expenditures per student (dollars)	Per capita income⁶ (dollars)	Median income Dollars	Percent change, 2000 to 2006-2010 (constant 2010 dollars)	Percent with income of $200,000 or more	Median household income (dollars)	All persons	Children under 18 years	Children 5 to 17 years in families
	46	47	48	49	50	51	52	53	54	55	56	57	58	59	60	61
ALABAMA—Cont'd																
Washington	284	904	4 340	7.1	67.4	9.3	30.7	8 815	18 824	36 431	-6.6	0.4	37 639	19.6	28.5	26.0
Wilcox	103	754	3 084	14.2	67.2	13.2	20.2	9 330	12 573	23 491	11.4	0.2	21 611	39.6	52.5	47.5
Winston	151	1 854	5 272	2.9	64.2	11.1	40.2	9 148	18 055	33 685	-6.4	2.3	32 574	20.3	31.9	29.8
ALASKA	639	2 852	190 871	11.8	36.6	27.0	2 025.4	15 552	30 726	66 521	1.9	4.6	63 456	11.0	14.8	12.1
Aleutians East	NA	NA	323	8.0	63.0	9.6	9.0	32 771	22 279	54 375	-10.3	3.0	47 077	16.8	16.4	14.1
Aleutians West	NA	NA	614	15.0	64.0	9.0	10.9	21 017	29 920	72 917	-6.2	2.5	58 517	9.0	11.0	8.6
Anchorage	NA	NA	79 865	12.7	31.0	33.0	648.0	13 191	34 678	73 004	3.8	6.4	70 524	9.6	12.2	9.5
Bethel	NA	NA	5 655	1.6	61.2	13.9	126.7	26 453	18 584	52 214	15.5	5.2	45 481	22.6	30.2	25.9
Bristol Bay	NA	NA	364	5.8	36.9	15.9	20.3	35 910	31 260	84 000	27.2	2.7	62 912	8.8	9.1	7.6
Denali	NA	NA	271	22.5	33.9	27.5	7.3	17 212	42 245	72 500	6.7	2.6	61 004	5.6	6.7	5.4
Dillingham	NA	NA	1 620	3.7	49.2	20.2	29.8	26 224	22 597	60 800	11.5	5.3	46 845	20.6	29.5	25.6
Fairbanks North Star	NA	NA	27 091	12.0	33.6	27.1	227.3	14 440	30 395	66 598	7.2	3.3	60 472	9.4	12.5	11.1
Haines	NA	NA	386	6.0	40.4	33.1	6.1	19 571	27 979	47 981	-7.1	4.4	46 111	12.1	19.5	16.8
Hoonah-Angoon	NA	NA	339	2.4	42.4	27.9	7.7	25 742	24 932	43 750	NA	0.2	38 122	19.4	26.4	23.4
Juneau	NA	NA	8 044	10.9	28.5	34.7	74.8	14 862	34 923	75 517	-3.9	4.1	69 844	8.2	10.0	7.7
Kenai Peninsula	NA	NA	13 360	11.0	40.4	22.4	130.3	13 734	29 127	57 454	-2.2	2.9	57 347	10.7	14.4	12.0
Ketchikan Gateway	NA	NA	3 054	15.1	37.7	24.2	33.9	15 663	29 520	61 695	-5.1	2.5	58 073	10.0	14.8	12.2
Kodiak Island	NA	NA	3 824	21.0	39.5	21.8	44.1	16 837	26 413	60 776	-12.2	4.3	59 847	8.3	10.3	8.3
Lake and Peninsula	NA	NA	651	5.7	53.1	13.5	0.0	0	15 161	40 909	-11.3	1.2	39 794	17.7	25.3	21.8
Matanuska-Susitna	NA	NA	23 777	16.6	39.3	20.8	215.5	13 085	27 910	67 703	4.4	3.2	68 670	10.9	14.1	11.4
Nome	NA	NA	2 859	1.8	58.6	14.9	64.3	27 297	20 549	53 899	3.2	3.9	43 147	24.6	30.7	25.8
North Slope	NA	NA	2 334	1.2	65.4	13.5	69.0	37 914	22 109	68 517	-14.3	2.6	68 744	11.4	13.2	11.0
Northwest Arctic	NA	NA	2 398	2.6	62.7	12.5	52.7	26 216	21 278	55 217	-5.2	0.8	49 466	20.0	21.9	18.7
Petersburg	NA	NA	921	5.8	40.5	27.4	12.1	19 529	30 971	62 317	NA	1.5	52 294	10.6	15.6	12.3
Prince of Wales-Hyder	NA	NA	1 234	4.9	51.1	17.8	28.1	20 392	24 193	45 728	NA	0.9	40 756	17.2	23.9	20.1
Sitka	NA	NA	2 248	6.0	33.9	29.2	21.0	15 710	29 982	62 024	-5.6	4.6	58 000	9.1	11.8	9.7
Skagway	NA	NA	270	16.3	23.3	32.3	3.2	31 670	35 536	73 500	NA	13.0	58 550	4.2	6.8	6.1
Southeast Fairbanks	NA	NA	1 936	11.9	41.1	20.0	23.9	14 629	27 657	59 596	21.4	2.1	54 508	13.4	21.7	17.4
Valdez-Cordova	NA	NA	2 264	8.6	30.1	23.7	30.0	18 997	30 703	60 383	-2.2	2.0	60 297	9.0	11.2	9.3
Wade Hampton	NA	NA	2 785	1.4	69.8	7.7	64.5	25 089	11 269	37 955	-0.7	0.4	30 883	34.1	46.0	39.5
Wrangell	NA	NA	649	13.4	47.6	16.2	5.9	18 089	28 731	50 389	NA	5.1	42 752	13.1	19.8	15.9
Yakutat	NA	NA	218	2.8	40.8	17.9	3.4	27 734	28 576	65 750	11.0	2.3	49 331	14.7	22.6	20.3
Yukon-Koyukuk	NA	NA	1 517	8.0	57.0	11.5	55.6	10 240	18 614	33 712	-7.1	0.6	35 177	27.1	34.9	29.1
ARIZONA	408	3 534	1 655 112	11.1	40.1	26.3	8 357.4	7 700	25 680	50 448	-1.8	3.4	46 787	17.6	25.0	23.0
Apache	67	524	21 786	5.7	59.5	10.3	148.8	11 182	12 294	30 184	2.1	0.9	30 651	34.5	41.8	36.4
Cochise	593	2 582	31 186	10.4	21.4	16.6	8 086	166.9	23 010	44 876	10.4	2.0	43 677	17.7	26.9	24.7
Coconino	377	3 286	44 314	5.3	36.5	31.1	191.6	9 298	22 632	49 510	2.2	2.3	43 051	23.8	28.1	26.2
Gila	436	2 048	10 969	12.0	49.6	15.0	70.5	8 486	19 600	37 580	-4.0	1.2	37 430	19.8	33.6	30.3
Graham	860	1 120	10 496	6.6	51.8	13.4	50.3	7 825	15 644	41 683	11.0	0.7	39 299	21.6	26.3	26.0
Greenlee	NA	NA	2 254	8.8	44.8	13.4	14.1	7 390	21 281	48 696	-2.4	0.6	49 592	12.7	16.7	15.0
La Paz	386	2 792	3 138	4.8	57.2	9.0	26.2	9 928	21 165	32 147	-1.8	1.3	33 818	23.7	38.1	35.8
Maricopa	386	3 629	1 014 437	11.8	38.2	29.0	5 206.3	7 558	27 816	55 054	-4.1	4.3	50 424	16.6	23.5	21.5
Mohave	192	3 262	40 486	10.6	51.6	12.0	187.9	7 027	21 523	39 785	-0.3	1.7	36 446	18.7	33.8	30.7
Navajo	396	2 289	31 603	6.8	49.5	14.4	197.9	9 774	16 745	39 774	9.9	0.9	37 723	27.8	36.4	33.3
Pima	429	2 506	258 366	11.2	36.7	29.6	1 162.8	7 777	25 093	45 521	-2.2	2.8	44 293	17.8	25.1	22.8
Pinal	221	2 740	77 337	11.5	45.3	17.9	391.6	7 708	21 716	51 310	13.0	1.5	49 833	14.4	18.4	17.9
Santa Cruz	125	2 253	14 313	5.9	60.2	17.3	80.2	7 541	16 209	36 519	-2.9	2.2	33 952	28.0	43.5	38.8
Yavapai	325	2 098	43 275	14.1	37.6	23.7	188.7	7 191	25 527	43 290	-2.0	2.4	40 562	18.3	28.0	24.7
Yuma	377	2 482	51 152	7.0	55.4	13.3	269.0	7 115	18 418	40 340	-1.0	1.2	40 609	21.1	32.0	31.6
ARKANSAS	505	3 559	729 777	11.1	53.4	19.1	4 162.9	8 695	21 274	39 267	-3.6	1.8	38 413	18.7	27.3	24.9
Arkansas	373	3 833	4 277	6.9	58.4	14.3	29.2	8 696	22 142	37 230	-3.0	1.3	38 129	18.6	28.3	24.8
Ashley	394	2 434	5 373	2.8	64.0	13.7	35.2	8 579	18 779	34 934	-13.1	1.3	37 042	19.4	31.8	29.9
Baxter	87	2 419	7 651	4.7	53.9	14.5	41.3	8 074	21 513	35 606	-3.4	1.3	34 421	15.7	27.2	26.0
Benton	263	1 967	52 956	13.1	46.9	25.9	293.7	8 066	25 186	50 434	-1.1	3.1	52 417	10.2	13.9	13.3
Boone	287	2 211	8 302	7.9	57.1	14.5	57.4	9 003	20 507	36 977	-2.6	1.5	35 532	16.0	26.3	23.7
Bradley	272	1 339	2 539	6.8	70.3	12.7	19.3	9 425	18 845	29 908	-4.8	2.1	31 047	28.5	43.4	38.6
Calhoun	75	633	1 127	0.7	67.7	6.6	5.6	8 619	16 457	32 450	-9.9	0.1	36 955	15.6	22.6	20.3
Carroll	240	2 430	5 084	9.6	57.6	17.4	30.8	8 073	19 743	34 235	-3.2	1.3	33 789	16.4	26.5	25.4
Chicot	593	1 627	2 653	8.7	71.3	12.6	18.8	10 262	14 668	21 676	-22.3	1.2	27 321	30.7	44.1	41.0
Clark	404	3 101	7 895	24.1	53.7	21.7	46.0	11 496	17 186	31 968	-12.5	1.4	33 433	22.2	28.4	26.3
Clay	87	833	3 646	8.1	68.7	8.8	23.6	8 352	18 892	29 066	-9.4	1.8	31 976	18.3	28.6	24.9
Cleburne	212	3 050	4 791	10.5	56.4	13.8	27.9	8 263	20 371	35 753	-10.5	1.4	35 472	18.6	29.1	28.1

1. Data for serious crimes have not been adjusted for underreporting; this may affect comparability between geographic areas and over time. 2. Per 100,000 population estimated by the FBI. 3. All persons 3 years old and over enrolled in nursery school through college. 4. Persons 25 years old and over. 5. Elementary and secondary education expenditures. 6. Based on population estimated by the American Community Survey, 2006-2010.

Table B. States and Counties — **Personal Income**

STATE County	Personal income, 2009 Total (mil dol)	Percent change, 2008–2009	Per capita¹ Dollars	Per capita¹ Rank	Wages and salaries² (mil dol)	Proprietors' income (mil dol)	Dividends, interest, and rent (mil dol)	Transfer payments (mil dol) Total	Government payments to individuals Total	Social Security	Medical payments	Income maintenance	Unemployment insurance
	62	63	64	65	66	67	68	69	70	71	72	73	74
ALABAMA—Cont'd													
Washington	444	-1.2	26 013	2 728	254	25	51	143	140	52	57	18	5
Wilcox	279	2.3	22 509	3 049	146	14	41	129	126	35	49	30	5
Winston	624	-0.9	26 019	2 725	276	32	96	232	228	77	106	20	10
ALASKA	30 182	-1.2	43 212	X	22 267	2 719	4 622	4 645	4 520	907	1 801	497	212
Aleutians East	82	-5.3	29 944	1 994	82	7	6	10	9	2	2	1	1
Aleutians West	157	-4.8	33 668	1 226	192	17	18	17	16	2	5	2	2
Anchorage	13 907	-1.7	48 598	126	11 151	1 586	2 210	1 882	1 831	356	733	197	76
Bethel	506	2.0	29 173	2 150	337	14	37	147	144	12	76	26	7
Bristol Bay	52	1.7	58 717	36	74	9	7	9	9	2	5	1	0
Denali	100	2.1	54 097	63	114	2	12	23	22	2	15	1	1
Dillingham	178	-0.1	35 828	909	125	16	20	36	35	5	15	6	2
Fairbanks North Star	3 837	-1.3	38 895	548	3 181	202	577	578	562	105	225	52	25
Haines	120	-1.1	50 001	104	44	28	22	21	20	5	8	2	1
Hoonah-Angoon	77	-7.2	35 990	886	31	8	12	21	21	4	10	2	2
Juneau	1 480	-2.9	48 062	131	1 075	63	280	188	183	42	68	19	8
Kenai Peninsula	2 148	-1.6	39 294	508	1 028	203	407	417	407	110	156	35	20
Ketchikan Gateway	674	-1.4	51 850	80	420	85	119	104	102	24	43	11	4
Kodiak Island	539	-1.0	40 393	427	404	65	89	71	68	14	25	8	3
Lake and Peninsula	54	-1.1	36 694	787	37	3	8	12	12	2	5	2	1
Matanuska-Susitna	3 403	0.9	38 508	576	979	227	410	489	472	121	128	50	28
Nome	305	-1.3	32 531	1 416	199	13	27	88	87	9	47	14	4
North Slope	443	1.7	65 564	18	1 403	5	39	41	40	8	16	5	2
Northwest Arctic	233	-0.3	31 285	1 696	195	3	15	71	70	6	42	9	3
Petersburg	165	D	43 606	253	79	31	33	32	31	7	14	3	1
Prince of Wales-Hyder	158	D	28 479	2 302	90	9	24	42	41	10	15	5	3
Sitka	364	-1.9	41 567	361	235	43	81	56	55	13	22	5	2
Skagway	49	-4.8	53 005	69	36	3	8	6	6	1	2	1	1
Southeast Fairbanks	293	-1.2	42 508	293	213	13	32	55	53	10	22	6	3
Valdez-Cordova	421	-2.5	45 177	195	305	44	72	62	60	15	20	7	3
Wade Hampton	152	0.9	19 651	3 098	81	3	9	73	71	5	34	18	4
Wrangell	76	D	35 197	995	36	7	18	20	20	6	8	2	1
Yakutat	28	-3.6	41 145	378	15	3	4	6	5	1	2	0	0
Yukon-Koyukuk	181	1.7	32 135	1 499	106	9	26	68	67	7	36	12	3
ARIZONA	219 027	-2.2	33 207	X	136 364	15 358	40 039	43 592	42 393	13 459	18 765	3 910	1 597
Apache	1 761	7.0	24 947	2 868	1 025	49	166	775	762	105	454	127	19
Cochise	4 435	3.7	34 243	1 132	2 668	171	670	1 225	1 203	352	593	104	27
Coconino	4 481	0.3	34 510	1 091	2 802	309	817	906	883	191	463	99	33
Gila	1 657	1.5	31 748	1 591	680	80	325	647	638	199	341	54	14
Graham	888	-2.8	23 972	2 966	385	31	106	337	330	68	197	32	12
Greenlee	258	-18.0	32 123	1 502	254	5	23	77	76	18	45	5	4
La Paz	527	0.0	26 317	2 666	226	39	87	192	188	63	93	16	4
Maricopa	142 092	-3.3	35 319	980	96 546	11 500	24 867	23 617	22 884	7 320	9 602	2 012	918
Mohave	5 101	-1.7	26 185	2 689	1 968	298	940	1 626	1 590	710	556	140	54
Navajo	2 634	3.7	23 316	3 017	1 318	108	345	1 055	1 035	216	545	156	33
Pima	34 516	-1.1	33 833	1 195	19 481	1 801	7 785	7 659	7 474	2 284	3 674	646	228
Pinal	8 260	1.1	24 225	2 944	2 746	227	1 125	2 215	2 152	705	1 022	195	79
Santa Cruz	1 137	0.3	25 987	2 732	679	77	236	321	313	83	150	48	15
Yavapai	6 284	-2.8	29 134	2 161	2 479	315	1 900	1 659	1 619	815	518	96	53
Yuma	4 994	2.6	25 356	2 823	3 106	349	646	1 281	1 245	330	513	180	104
ARKANSAS	93 374	-0.1	32 315	X	55 698	6 890	16 644	22 035	21 509	7 481	8 820	2 229	1 013
Arkansas	741	-0.9	39 072	532	437	121	109	177	173	55	71	18	19
Ashley	679	1.8	30 962	1 766	401	67	82	207	203	70	86	24	9
Baxter	1 305	-0.1	30 967	1 764	598	59	365	428	421	198	153	22	15
Benton	7 456	-0.3	33 065	1 329	5 531	322	1 512	1 100	1 059	464	348	85	63
Boone	1 056	-0.9	28 673	2 265	619	66	210	305	298	119	117	23	12
Bradley	321	-0.9	27 254	2 523	136	27	51	115	113	35	55	12	5
Calhoun	151	3.2	29 123	2 165	170	6	18	40	39	16	14	4	2
Carroll	715	-2.9	25 590	2 798	344	61	168	197	192	83	71	16	8
Chicot	353	0.0	29 865	2 007	136	61	46	125	122	33	58	19	5
Clark	673	0.1	28 251	2 358	397	46	121	192	188	57	86	16	8
Clay	466	-0.5	29 910	2 000	158	78	65	152	149	53	65	12	8
Cleburne	805	-0.1	31 430	1 656	268	68	170	233	228	99	86	14	8

1. Based on the resident population estimated as of July 1 of the year shown.　　2. Includes supplements to wages and salaries.

Table B. States and Counties — Earnings, Social Security, and Housing

STATE County	Earnings, 2009 Total (mil dol)	Farm	Goods-related[1] Total	Manu-facturing	Information and professional and technical services	Retail trade	Finance, insurance, and real estate	Health care and social services	Govern-ment	Social Security beneficiaries, December 2010 Number	Rate[2]	Supplemental Security Income recipients, December 2010	Housing units, 2010 Total	Percent change, 2000–2010
	75	76	77	78	79	80	81	82	83	84	85	86	87	88
ALABAMA—Cont'd														
Washington	279	3.5	D	41.7	D	2.6	D	D	17.2	4 385	249	824	8 407	3.5
Wilcox	160	3.6	40.2	37.1	D	5.5	2.5	D	25.1	3 570	306	1 645	5 649	-8.6
Winston	307	0.4	D	31.9	2.1	7.0	3.4	8.3	19.5	6 530	267	1 023	13 469	7.7
ALASKA	24 985	0.0	18.5	2.8	8.3	5.6	4.5	9.8	32.6	78 208	110	12 269	306 967	17.6
Aleutians East	89	0.0	D	D	D	1.3	D	D	17.6	150	48	0	747	3.2
Aleutians West	209	0.1	47.7	45.8	D	4.8	3.5	3.6	16.1	190	34	21	1 929	-13.7
Anchorage	12 737	0.0	14.6	1.1	12.5	5.5	5.5	10.5	28.9	29 740	102	5 535	113 032	12.6
Bethel	351	0.0	D	D	2.4	5.0	D	D	43.7	1 510	89	498	5 919	14.1
Bristol Bay	83	0.0	45.4	41.0	D	2.9	D	D	20.3	125	125	0	969	-1.0
Denali	115	0.0	D	0.0	D	D	D	0.4	25.6	210	115	0	1 771	31.1
Dillingham	141	0.0	D	D	D	4.2	D	27.5	26.9	515	106	127	2 427	4.1
Fairbanks North Star	3 383	0.2	12.9	1.5	4.1	5.5	2.9	7.8	51.7	8 790	90	1 086	41 783	25.5
Haines	72	0.0	D	8.2	5.0	7.5	D	D	16.5	475	189	56	1 631	14.9
Hoonah-Angoon	38	0.0	D	D	D	10.5	D	3.5	52.1	360	167	46	1 771	10.3
Juneau	1 139	-0.3	D	1.3	4.2	6.4	3.5	7.6	50.5	3 725	119	635	13 055	6.3
Kenai Peninsula	1 230	0.0	23.3	5.5	4.0	7.4	3.8	12.2	26.4	9 180	166	977	30 578	22.9
Ketchikan Gateway	505	0.0	D	6.0	D	8.2	4.5	10.1	34.8	1 975	147	261	6 166	-1.8
Kodiak Island	469	0.0	20.7	16.9	1.9	3.7	3.1	9.0	41.2	1 320	97	133	5 303	2.8
Lake and Peninsula	39	0.0	D	7.8	D	2.0	D	0.4	45.3	180	110	20	1 502	-3.5
Matanuska-Susitna	1 205	0.3	16.5	1.6	8.4	11.6	4.1	16.2	24.2	10 590	119	1 454	41 329	51.2
Nome	212	0.0	D	D	D	5.2	5.9	21.6	44.8	965	102	222	4 008	9.8
North Slope	1 408	0.0	D	D	D	0.7	D	D	9.4	590	63	26	2 500	-1.5
Northwest Arctic	199	0.0	D	D	D	D	D	D	28.9	655	87	110	2 707	6.6
Petersburg	110	0.0	D	13.7	2.8	6.6	2.8	D	37.0	630	165	45	1 994	0.2
Prince of Wales-Hyder	99	0.0	D	3.6	D	6.8	D	4.9	51.4	815	147	111	2 992	1.7
Sitka	278	0.0	D	5.8	2.8	5.9	3.6	16.1	36.0	1 145	129	95	4 102	12.4
Skagway	39	0.0	15.2	2.4	D	19.3	D	0.7	29.2	80	83	0	636	26.7
Southeast Fairbanks	227	0.0	D	D	8.6	3.8	1.2	D	29.3	1 015	144	166	3 915	21.4
Valdez-Cordova	349	0.0	14.2	9.1	3.8	4.9	5.2	5.2	29.9	1 230	128	124	6 102	18.5
Wade Hampton	83	0.0	D	D	D	6.8	D	D	65.5	700	94	235	2 183	5.8
Wrangell	43	0.0	D	D	D	7.5	D	D	45.1	485	205	48	1 428	5.9
Yakutat	18	0.0	D	D	D	5.7	7.4	1.6	45.6	100	151	0	450	-9.8
Yukon-Koyukuk	115	0.0	D	D	D	5.4	D	9.8	58.9	765	137	204	4 038	3.5
ARIZONA	151 722	0.3	15.3	8.4	10.4	7.6	9.0	12.0	18.8	1 067 717	167	110 011	2 844 526	29.9
Apache	1 074	-1.5	D	0.2	1.5	4.0	D	6.6	68.1	10 915	153	4 616	32 514	2.8
Cochise	2 839	1.3	4.7	1.1	13.6	5.6	2.3	7.2	50.6	28 660	218	2 894	59 041	15.5
Coconino	3 110	0.0	14.3	9.5	4.6	7.6	3.5	15.7	32.9	16 315	121	2 920	63 321	18.5
Gila	759	-0.2	24.0	9.2	D	8.4	3.4	11.7	33.6	15 495	289	1 491	32 698	16.0
Graham	418	2.2	D	2.2	2.8	10.0	1.8	13.2	39.2	5 740	154	807	12 980	13.6
Greenlee	259	0.3	D	0.0	D	1.9	D	2.2	9.4	1 405	167	123	4 372	16.8
La Paz	265	7.2	D	2.5	D	11.4	3.0	5.3	44.6	6 305	259	469	16 049	6.1
Maricopa	108 046	0.2	15.6	8.5	11.3	7.7	10.9	11.6	13.8	563 995	148	54 867	1 639 279	31.1
Mohave	2 267	0.1	14.1	6.8	5.2	13.4	5.1	19.8	20.5	56 875	284	4 014	110 911	38.5
Navajo	1 426	0.6	10.9	3.0	7.4	8.3	2.1	10.6	39.1	19 430	181	5 023	56 938	20.1
Pima	21 282	0.1	17.1	11.5	10.9	6.7	4.9	14.8	25.5	182 545	186	18 785	440 909	20.2
Pinal	2 973	2.1	13.4	6.6	2.9	7.7	3.3	6.9	41.7	58 350	155	5 419	159 222	96.2
Santa Cruz	756	-0.5	D	3.4	D	11.0	3.7	2.5	41.0	7 930	167	1 260	18 010	38.2
Yavapai	2 794	0.2	16.5	5.0	6.0	10.0	5.0	15.6	23.1	64 235	304	3 297	110 432	35.1
Yuma	3 455	5.6	7.3	2.4	4.0	7.2	3.2	10.8	36.8	30 520	156	4 026	87 850	18.5
ARKANSAS	62 587	2.4	19.7	13.3	8.0	6.5	5.1	11.7	20.1	635 041	218	106 526	1 316 299	12.2
Arkansas	558	12.6	31.5	28.7	2.3	6.2	3.5	7.1	11.7	4 565	240	727	9 436	-2.4
Ashley	468	7.5	D	39.8	1.6	4.7	2.7	D	12.7	5 550	254	1 020	10 137	-4.5
Baxter	657	0.7	D	16.5	5.6	10.2	5.7	26.5	14.2	15 815	381	1 083	22 580	13.5
Benton	5 852	0.4	D	9.7	8.8	5.0	4.9	5.9	8.8	37 380	169	3 098	93 084	44.9
Boone	685	0.5	D	12.3	4.8	8.0	5.2	8.5	24.4	10 325	280	1 060	16 827	9.1
Bradley	163	5.6	D	17.0	D	5.5	4.4	13.3	23.2	2 925	254	551	5 860	-1.2
Calhoun	176	0.4	D	72.6	D	D	D	1.2	6.9	1 380	257	179	2 897	-3.8
Carroll	405	8.2	32.1	27.7	2.5	8.3	4.9	D	14.8	7 235	264	612	13 559	14.6
Chicot	197	26.5	8.7	5.3	2.3	5.7	4.9	D	24.5	3 090	262	957	5 421	-9.3
Clark	443	1.6	27.2	25.8	3.8	8.2	3.6	D	25.2	4 860	211	685	10 385	2.2
Clay	237	27.2	15.7	12.5	D	5.1	3.1	7.4	18.8	4 755	296	729	8 031	-5.5
Cleburne	336	1.7	26.4	15.0	3.2	9.3	5.1	D	14.8	8 165	314	727	15 826	15.2

1. Includes mining, construction, and manufacturing.   2. Per 1,000 resident population enumerated in the 2010 census.

Table B. States and Counties — Housing, Labor Force, and Employment

STATE County	Housing units, 2006–2010								Civilian labor force, 2010				Civilian employment,[5] 2006–2010		
	Occupied units										Unemployment			Percent	
			Owner-occupied			Renter-occupied									
				Median owner cost as a percent of income											Con-struction, produc-tion, and mainte-nance occu-pations
	Total	Percent	Median value¹	With a mort-gage	Without a mort-gage	Median rent²	Median rent as a per-cent of income	Sub-stand-ard units³ (percent)	Total	Percent change, 2009–2010	Total	Rate⁴	Total	Manage-ment, business, science and arts	
	89	90	91	92	93	94	95	96	97	98	99	100	101	102	103
ALABAMA—Cont'd															
Washington	6 672	83.0	85 200	23.8	12.0	519	27.8	4.3	6 833	0.9	912	13.3	6 467	20.7	50.0
Wilcox	3 732	76.8	54 200	28.6	14.9	381	34.8	3.7	3 341	-5.1	726	21.7	2 532	22.6	33.7
Winston	9 478	73.8	83 700	23.8	11.4	410	29.3	2.1	9 161	-0.7	1 378	15.0	9 594	24.9	43.2
ALASKA	248 248	64.7	229 100	24.0	11.0	972	27.5	9.7	363 949	1.5	29 010	8.0	332 126	35.1	24.2
Aleutians East	267	59.2	121 600	18.8	12.1	731	19.1	4.9	1 068	-5.3	91	8.5	3 116	6.2	80.6
Aleutians West	521	36.3	163 400	20.9	13.6	1 172	21.4	14.0	2 910	-4.6	190	6.5	5 296	8.7	73.1
Anchorage	104 315	61.7	269 500	24.4	11.4	1 009	28.0	4.8	154 432	-0.1	10 617	6.9	143 069	39.0	18.0
Bethel	4 291	61.3	153 400	18.3	11.5	942	20.4	56.7	7 061	0.8	1 059	15.0	5 984	39.9	20.4
Bristol Bay	410	56.6	171 100	17.5	10.0	933	19.8	3.9	1 052	2.3	41	3.9	437	37.3	23.6
Denali	428	60.7	174 000	16.2	10.0	567	14.6	17.1	1 382	-2.1	128	9.3	633	36.7	29.4
Dillingham	1 408	60.7	199 100	15.8	13.3	959	21.2	27.6	2 107	-2.3	212	10.1	1 908	44.6	17.1
Fairbanks North Star	34 596	59.8	206 800	24.4	10.0	1 009	28.8	8.5	46 563	0.8	3 295	7.1	44 198	34.2	25.7
Haines	744	74.5	205 400	24.3	10.4	778	28.8	6.9	1 392	-0.4	121	8.7	735	41.2	26.4
Hoonah-Angoon	1 004	64.0	184 200	25.7	10.9	683	29.4	17.2	1 100	N/A	169	15.4	937	41.7	26.8
Juneau	12 005	64.0	291 600	25.0	12.6	1 084	27.4	4.3	18 545	0.5	1 068	5.8	17 226	39.2	18.1
Kenai Peninsula	22 303	72.7	193 000	23.2	10.0	788	27.2	10.0	27 238	0.7	2 728	10.0	24 875	29.9	29.0
Ketchikan Gateway	5 629	59.1	242 500	24.4	10.3	956	29.7	5.5	8 216	-1.9	627	7.6	6 802	29.4	30.0
Kodiak Island	4 409	59.2	182 100	23.5	15.8	968	26.9	12.2	6 669	0.9	476	7.1	6 583	20.3	40.9
Lake and Peninsula	492	75.0	156 400	23.7	12.6	722	18.7	24.6	1 076	-2.3	87	8.1	534	31.6	34.6
Matanuska-Susitna	29 361	79.2	212 000	24.7	10.7	917	29.8	9.6	42 616	0.5	3 899	9.1	37 537	31.9	28.6
Nome	2 693	56.2	144 600	21.1	13.8	1 025	20.7	36.8	4 100	2.9	535	13.0	3 499	34.9	23.8
North Slope	1 976	48.3	135 800	14.9	10.0	927	17.0	35.6	5 374	-0.4	273	5.1	3 284	35.7	19.4
Northwest Arctic	1 802	53.7	129 000	21.9	16.3	1 020	19.5	46.7	3 047	3.2	407	13.4	2 529	33.7	30.2
Petersburg	1 559	76.7	195 300	19.2	13.1	625	23.2	4.8	NA	NA	NA	NA	2 034	35.6	31.7
Prince of Wales-Hyder	2 386	69.0	152 100	22.7	11.4	673	20.9	11.8	NA	NA	NA	NA	2 462	33.8	32.8
Sitka	3 729	55.9	309 800	24.6	10.0	977	34.3	6.1	4 684	1.3	294	6.3	4 692	36.9	22.8
Skagway	386	59.1	253 700	25.8	10.8	998	18.6	4.9	663	N/A	89	13.4	697	26.8	11.5
Southeast Fairbanks	2 485	65.2	168 700	21.6	10.0	958	19.9	17.2	3 584	-0.6	381	10.6	2 858	30.7	27.6
Valdez-Cordova	3 941	71.8	165 800	18.2	10.0	796	26.1	13.4	5 232	-2.3	455	8.7	4 698	32.0	29.7
Wade Hampton	1 728	64.8	80 300	14.1	12.9	579	14.5	64.6	2 690	0.0	549	20.4	2 048	33.0	25.7
Wrangell	996	78.7	163 700	24.2	10.0	748	26.9	3.5	NA	NA	NA	NA	1 073	29.0	26.8
Yakutat	257	61.1	151 900	14.5	10.0	986	20.2	21.0	308	-4.0	33	10.7	306	36.3	24.8
Yukon-Koyukuk	2 127	69.1	99 500	20.7	13.2	616	21.2	48.2	2 968	1.3	457	15.4	2 076	35.7	28.4
ARIZONA	2 326 468	67.4	215 000	26.2	10.9	856	30.5	4.9	3 100 253	-1.8	325 485	10.5	2 747 475	34.5	20.3
Apache	18 859	76.3	80 900	21.9	10.0	523	19.2	27.1	23 276	1.2	3 813	16.4	18 833	32.0	26.5
Cochise	48 935	69.0	154 900	23.1	10.2	713	27.0	3.5	64 434	1.9	5 383	8.4	48 973	35.9	18.9
Coconino	45 478	61.2	257 700	25.8	10.0	888	31.0	9.3	76 599	1.5	6 819	8.9	64 410	32.9	21.1
Gila	19 704	78.3	156 100	27.8	11.8	696	31.6	4.5	23 770	1.9	2 642	11.1	18 489	26.3	25.5
Graham	10 822	72.0	119 500	22.2	11.8	604	23.3	6.8	15 271	0.4	2 064	13.5	12 306	25.7	30.7
Greenlee	3 327	46.9	65 800	20.0	11.2	385	0.0	3.2	4 089	-7.2	454	11.1	3 490	29.7	39.4
La Paz	10 158	75.4	100 000	27.5	10.0	533	26.1	10.5	7 774	0.1	773	9.9	7 064	24.3	26.1
Maricopa	1 382 002	66.3	238 600	26.2	11.0	912	30.6	4.3	1 997 744	1.0	180 862	9.1	1 740 825	35.9	19.5
Mohave	80 361	71.5	170 600	28.0	11.5	801	31.1	4.0	92 454	0.3	10 388	11.2	75 389	24.2	23.6
Navajo	35 366	72.5	134 300	24.6	10.0	619	23.5	16.6	42 041	2.1	6 586	15.7	36 993	29.0	26.7
Pima	381 880	64.6	198 300	25.3	11.3	737	31.4	4.2	491 362	0.4	44 400	9.0	423 298	35.9	18.3
Pinal	118 826	77.7	164 000	27.7	11.2	848	30.6	4.5	128 509	3.3	15 482	12.0	125 577	31.2	24.9
Santa Cruz	12 078	71.0	148 200	26.6	10.9	655	32.9	4.7	18 918	2.7	3 076	16.3	16 540	24.6	22.0
Yavapai	89 109	72.5	231 000	28.7	11.8	834	31.2	3.2	98 213	-1.0	10 283	10.5	87 166	30.5	21.5
Yuma	69 563	69.6	142 400	26.3	10.2	730	31.4	8.4	91 707	5.8	23 166	25.3	68 122	24.9	29.6
ARKANSAS	1 117 154	67.7	102 300	21.0	11.1	617	29.4	3.0	1 356 625	0.0	107 712	7.9	1 254 140	30.0	28.7
Arkansas	8 202	64.4	78 900	19.9	10.9	572	30.8	1.9	12 237	-0.6	2 037	16.6	9 224	28.3	33.0
Ashley	8 901	72.4	62 100	19.8	12.5	470	29.6	2.6	9 384	-0.7	950	10.1	8 838	25.0	37.4
Baxter	18 744	76.6	118 400	23.9	10.6	585	29.7	2.7	17 111	-2.2	1 515	8.9	15 771	28.7	27.2
Benton	78 947	70.1	155 000	21.9	10.6	715	26.3	2.7	108 148	2.2	6 892	6.4	98 002	33.9	25.9
Boone	14 317	72.7	105 700	21.5	12.3	532	25.9	2.8	17 038	-0.1	1 249	7.3	15 866	25.3	28.0
Bradley	4 877	70.2	64 800	22.9	10.2	547	32.7	6.4	5 504	0.3	527	9.6	4 787	27.7	41.5
Calhoun	2 123	82.1	51 700	21.8	14.3	524	23.8	0.1	2 578	-3.7	230	8.9	2 469	16.7	53.9
Carroll	11 437	69.5	119 500	25.5	10.1	556	29.9	3.9	13 731	-2.9	906	6.6	12 022	24.3	32.6
Chicot	4 705	69.6	50 700	27.4	17.7	463	31.6	2.9	4 672	-5.2	523	11.2	3 903	28.0	32.2
Clark	8 348	67.6	78 900	21.7	11.1	566	35.1	2.1	10 715	-1.4	868	8.1	10 211	29.7	28.2
Clay	6 787	74.0	59 800	20.8	12.9	453	28.4	1.5	6 553	-2.9	787	12.0	6 470	28.3	33.5
Cleburne	10 755	77.9	110 000	22.9	11.8	608	30.7	2.5	11 795	-1.1	860	7.3	9 577	27.6	35.5

1. Specified owner-occupied units. 2. Specified renter-occupied units. A value of 10.0 represents 10 percent or less. 3. Overcrowded or lacking complete plumbing facilities. 4. Percent of civilian labor force. 5. Persons 16 years old and over.

Table B. States and Counties — **Nonfarm Employment and Agriculture**

STATE County	Private nonfarm establishments, employment and payroll, 2009									Agriculture, 2007			
	Number of establish-ments	Employment						Annual payroll		Farms			
		Total	Health care and social assistance	Manufac-turing	Retail trade	Finance and insurance	Professional, scientific, and technical services	Total (mil dol)	Average per employee (dollars)	Number	Fewer than 50 acres	500 acres or more	Farm operators whose principal occupation is farming (percent)
	104	105	106	107	108	109	110	111	112	113	114	115	116

ALABAMA—Cont'd

STATE County	104	105	106	107	108	109	110	111	112	113	114	115	116
Washington	233	3 056	296	1 504	290	80	47	164	53 678	473	36.6	7.0	39.5
Wilcox	212	2 012	D	607	266	101	D	68	33 808	368	32.9	25.3	53.3
Winston	461	6 622	663	3 149	904	436	64	178	26 909	626	38.5	2.2	41.1
ALASKA	19 901	252 882	42 007	11 927	33 537	7 791	14 628	12 406	49 057	686	48.0	13.1	53.2
Aleutians East	59	D	D	D	69	D	D	D	D	NA	NA	NA	NA
Aleutians West	121	4 953	D	3 316	D	D	D	121	24 468	NA	NA	NA	NA
Anchorage	8 432	144 656	20 663	2 613	15 306	5 113	10 912	7 829	54 122	278	50.4	6.1	52.5
Bethel	202	3 471	D	D	754	D	D	132	37 929	NA	NA	NA	NA
Bristol Bay	67	302	D	D	59	D	D	33	108 391	NA	NA	NA	NA
Denali	100	522	D	0	D	D	D	47	89 906	NA	NA	NA	NA
Dillingham	101	1 256	D	D	181	D	D	59	47 149	NA	NA	NA	NA
Fairbanks North Star	2 445	26 479	4 978	557	4 935	824	1 315	1 171	44 230	212	34.0	22.2	56.1
Haines	128	590	160	D	125	D	D	22	36 886	NA	NA	NA	NA
Hoonah-Angoon	NA	NA	NA	NA	NA	NA	NA	NA	NA				
Juneau	1 107	10 800	2 514	208	1 875	350	510	436	40 346	37	91.9	0.0	51.4
Kenai Peninsula	1 944	13 155	3 114	575	2 339	326	520	558	42 442	124	56.5	5.6	50.0
Ketchikan Gateway	568	4 686	D	354	1 001	241	120	208	44 394	NA	NA	NA	NA
Kodiak Island	471	4 177	D	1 376	475	D	70	160	38 239	NA	NA	NA	NA
Lake and Peninsula	48	138	0	D	D	D	D	13	95 094	NA	NA	NA	NA
Matanuska-Susitna	1 939	14 869	3 086	157	3 074	476	758	588	39 559	NA	NA	NA	NA
Nome	155	2 160	1 008	D	311	D	10	74	34 047	NA	NA	NA	NA
North Slope	140	2 790	D	D	D	D	D	182	65 329	NA	NA	NA	NA
Northwest Arctic	70	1 707	D	0	182	D	D	101	59 199	NA	NA	NA	NA
Petersburg	NA	NA	NA	NA	NA	NA	NA	NA	NA				
Prince of Wales-Hyder	NA	NA	NA	NA	NA	NA	NA	NA	NA				
Sitka	391	3 424	874	251	623	73	41	124	36 287	NA		NA	NA
Skagway	NA	NA	NA	NA	NA	NA	NA	NA	NA				
Southeast Fairbanks	188	783	85	D	202	22	D	27	34 462	NA		NA	NA
Valdez-Cordova	398	2 729	342	145	311	39	64	154	56 564	NA	NA	NA	NA
Wade Hampton	55	556	D	0	309	D	D	11	20 117	NA	NA	NA	NA
Wrangell	NA	NA	NA	NA	NA	NA	NA	NA	NA				
Yakutat	31	118	D	D	D	0	0	6	49 068	NA	NA	NA	NA
Yukon-Koyukuk	113	377	21	0	161	0	D	18	46 960	NA	NA	NA	NA
ARIZONA	134 072	2 122 265	302 595	145 520	316 160	131 858	120 191	82 941	39 081	15 637	80.1	8.1	61.1
Apache	482	7 526	3 174	D	1 143	78	196	237	31 618	4 243	95.3	1.5	70.4
Cochise	2 373	28 407	5 032	512	5 675	561	4 457	919	32 351	1 065	35.1	24.1	48.5
Coconino	3 634	44 916	7 328	D	7 784	834	1 749	1 452	32 330	1 597	94.3	2.8	67.3
Gila	1 086	11 724	2 257	D	2 231	230	339	372	31 771	279	78.5	4.7	60.2
Graham	531	10 078	1 426	D	1 589	107	D	320	31 766	343	60.1	16.0	43.4
Greenlee	79	545	99	0	155	D	21	15	28 134	127	40.2	16.5	57.5
La Paz	357	3 438	521	177	933	85	D	90	26 176	99	28.3	43.4	70.7
Maricopa	85 789	1 451 978	186 527	99 260	203 788	109 786	89 954	60 819	41 887	1 793	79.6	7.8	50.7
Mohave	3 869	42 107	8 511	3 081	9 590	1 234	1 162	1 170	27 785	334	57.8	21.6	48.8
Navajo	1 844	18 493	3 363	830	4 261	482	396	607	32 823	2 949	94.1	2.3	70.8
Pima	20 547	309 243	56 070	26 958	47 950	13 169	15 749	11 041	35 702	622	74.0	12.1	41.2
Pinal	3 225	45 025	9 885	3 052	9 123	887	970	1 303	28 937	785	52.1	23.2	52.5
Santa Cruz	1 153	10 773	1 007	480	2 694	230	149	278	25 809	193	45.1	17.6	39.9
Yavapai	5 875	53 702	10 815	2 649	10 926	1 382	1 674	1 544	28 759	756	63.0	13.8	46.2
Yuma	3 029	42 617	6 580	2 818	8 313	1 378	1 164	1 150	26 983	452	60.6	19.5	57.5
ARKANSAS	65 451	970 748	162 651	163 825	137 421	37 080	34 415	33 065	34 062	49 346	35.9	12.4	44.5
Arkansas	544	8 293	996	3 355	1 130	278	100	261	31 532	539	17.3	42.3	61.0
Ashley	455	6 810	718	D	871	193	D	261	38 320	436	47.9	15.1	43.8
Baxter	1 121	11 156	1 887	2 099	2 283	496	444	313	28 049	668	45.5	5.4	37.3
Benton	5 325	92 837	6 966	9 944	9 928	2 599	5 149	4 393	47 318	2 151	49.2	3.7	46.3
Boone	870	12 094	2 154	1 774	1 973	485	251	358	29 581	1 266	34.7	9.3	41.8
Bradley	267	2 670	485	524	359	116	33	65	24 166	219	37.9	1.8	45.7
Calhoun	77	553	D	D	88	D	D	16	28 920	101	31.7	6.9	30.7
Carroll	733	8 061	D	D	1 200	294	131	200	24 839	1 139	32.0	9.9	47.4
Chicot	232	2 360	776	122	403	108	41	58	24 686	382	20.2	37.7	59.2
Clark	525	7 592	975	2 031	1 202	244	190	200	26 379	430	38.6	8.6	32.1
Clay	298	3 146	640	721	474	112	D	81	25 674	731	27.1	25.0	49.9
Cleburne	633	5 955	810	1 205	1 140	D	D	145	24 360	905	37.7	5.1	34.7

Table B. States and Counties — **Agriculture**

STATE County	Agriculture, 2007 (cont.)															
	Land in farms					Value of land and buildings (dollars)		Value of machinery and equipment, average per farm (dollars)	Value of products sold				Percent of farms with sales of:		Government payments	
			Acres								Percent from:					
	Acreage (1,000)	Percent change, 2002–2007	Average size of farm	Total irrigated (1,000)	Total cropland (1,000)	Average per farm	Average per acre		Total (mil dol)	Average per farm (dollars)	Crops	Live-stock and poultry products	$10,000 or more	$100,000 or more	Total ($1,000)	Percent of farms
	117	118	119	120	121	122	123	124	125	126	127	128	129	130	131	132
ALABAMA—Cont'd																
Washington	84	13.5	177	0.1	19.0	373 658	2 114	57 902	30.8	65 074	8.4	91.6	32.3	10.1	342	20.5
Wilcox	169	5.6	459	0.2	33.4	634 093	1 382	46 064	7.6	20 682	21.7	78.3	22.3	4.3	1 126	46.5
Winston	65	-1.5	103	0.0	20.5	266 819	2 588	50 374	65.5	104 601	1.8	98.2	37.9	17.4	144	12.5
ALASKA	882	-2.1	1 285	3.7	86.2	502 342	391	78 837	57.0	83 119	43.4	56.6	41.3	11.2	1 645	11.4
Aleutians East	NA	NA	NA	NA	NA	NA	NA	NA	NA	NA	NA	NA	NA	NA	NA	NA
Aleutians West	NA	NA	NA	NA	NA	NA	NA	NA	NA	NA	NA	NA	NA	NA	NA	NA
Anchorage	38	-19.1	138	1.7	17.0	488 278	3 536	72 515	31.8	114 216	49.6	50.4	41.0	14.4	110	6.1
Bethel	NA	NA	NA	NA	NA	NA	NA	NA	NA	NA	NA	NA	NA	NA	NA	NA
Bristol Bay	NA	NA	NA	NA	NA	NA	NA	NA	NA	NA	NA	NA	NA	NA	NA	NA
Denali	NA	NA	NA	NA	NA	NA	NA	NA	NA	NA	NA	NA	NA	NA	NA	NA
Dillingham	NA	NA	NA	NA	NA	NA	NA	NA	NA	NA	NA	NA	NA	NA	NA	NA
Fairbanks North Star	111	0.9	523	2.0	63.6	406 163	777	74 337	7.1	33 375	83.2	16.8	42.5	7.5	1 356	23.6
Haines	NA	NA	NA	NA	NA	NA	NA	NA	NA	NA	NA	NA	NA	NA	NA	NA
Hoonah-Angoon																
Juneau	1	NA	14	0.0	0.0	757 354	54 518	216 319	11.8	318 120	7.7	92.3	70.3	35.1	0	0.0
Kenai Peninsula	38	5.6	309	0.0	5.3	409 882	1 327	50 729	D	D	D	D	33.9	4.0	38	6.5
Ketchikan Gateway	NA	NA	NA	NA	NA	NA	NA	NA	NA	NA	NA	NA	NA	NA	NA	NA
Kodiak Island	NA	NA	NA	NA	NA	NA	NA	NA	NA	NA	NA	NA	NA	NA	NA	NA
Lake and Peninsula	NA	NA	NA	NA	NA	NA	NA	NA	NA	NA	NA	NA	NA	NA	NA	NA
Matanuska-Susitna	NA	NA	NA	NA	NA	NA	NA	NA	NA	NA	NA	NA	NA	NA	NA	NA
Nome	NA	NA	NA	NA	NA	NA	NA	NA	NA	NA	NA	NA	NA	NA	NA	NA
North Slope	NA	NA	NA	NA	NA	NA	NA	NA	NA	NA	NA	NA	NA	NA	NA	NA
Northwest Arctic	NA	NA	NA	NA	NA	NA	NA	NA	NA	NA	NA	NA	NA	NA	NA	NA
Petersburg																
Prince of Wales-Hyder																
Sitka	NA	NA	NA	NA	NA	NA	NA	NA	NA	NA	NA	NA	NA	NA	NA	NA
Skagway																
Southeast Fairbanks	NA	NA	NA	NA	NA	NA	NA	NA	NA	NA	NA	NA	NA	NA	NA	NA
Valdez-Cordova	NA	NA	NA	NA	NA	NA	NA	NA	NA	NA	NA	NA	NA	NA	NA	NA
Wade Hampton	NA	NA	NA	NA	NA	NA	NA	NA	NA	NA	NA	NA	NA	NA	NA	NA
Wrangell																
Yakutat	NA	NA	NA	NA	NA	NA	NA	NA	NA	NA	NA	NA	NA	NA	NA	NA
Yukon-Koyukuk	NA	NA	NA	NA	NA	NA	NA	NA	NA	NA	NA	NA	NA	NA	NA	NA
ARIZONA	26 118	-1.8	1 670	876.2	1 205.4	1 249 929	748	66 291	3 234.6	206 852	59.1	40.9	18.6	6.7	55 947	7.3
Apache	D	D	D	9.3	27.5	263 783	194	15 511	12.6	2 975	38.2	61.8	5.3	0.2	28	1.6
Cochise	824	-15.0	774	67.6	141.2	1 475 858	1 907	77 792	117.1	109 981	63.5	36.5	34.3	10.1	3 698	13.8
Coconino	6 102	NA	3 821	2.2	20.5	752 116	197	22 738	D	D	0.0	D	7.4	1.9	372	3.0
Gila	1 166	NA	4 181	3.2	3.7	1 589 706	380	44 594	4.4	15 748	39.2	60.7	20.1	2.2	153	4.3
Graham	1 346	NA	3 923	28.3	35.3	2 161 265	551	157 473	D	D	D	0.0	33.8	12.2	2 974	30.3
Greenlee	35	29.6	278	5.3	6.7	650 667	2 343	71 100	6.2	48 895	23.8	76.2	38.6	7.9	315	28.3
La Paz	D	D	D	100.5	123.3	3 175 260	1 085	363 805	136.6	1 379 731	98.1	1.9	69.7	40.4	4 192	34.3
Maricopa	485	-22.6	271	199.4	267.3	2 300 844	8 498	116 343	813.5	453 704	48.7	51.3	32.8	15.5	17 150	10.3
Mohave	858	8.2	2 570	17.1	31.2	1 450 681	564	57 373	18.6	55 783	65.2	34.8	28.1	5.1	761	4.5
Navajo	4 503	-2.0	1 527	8.6	16.9	421 707	276	19 304	46.5	15 779	9.7	90.3	6.1	0.7	77	2.6
Pima	D	D	D	35.7	49.6	1 951 879	446	80 179	67.5	108 521	73.2	26.8	27.2	9.8	3 771	6.6
Pinal	1 047	-9.9	1 334	215.1	256.0	4 853 351	3 638	240 548	799.8	1 018 867	29.3	70.7	44.5	27.4	17 624	30.8
Santa Cruz	130	-2.3	671	1.7	8.0	1 537 974	2 291	46 385	4.3	22 133	10.7	89.3	31.1	4.1	156	4.1
Yavapai	639	-11.3	845	7.9	25.3	1 503 944	1 779	52 064	D	D	D	D	26.2	5.0	282	3.6
Yuma	210	-9.1	466	174.2	193.1	3 893 483	8 361	373 336	960.0	2 123 822	D	D	60.0	37.4	4 395	20.8
ARKANSAS	13 873	-4.3	281	4 460.7	8 432.2	658 732	2 343	90 823	7 508.8	152 166	38.6	61.4	40.4	16.4	269 448	23.2
Arkansas	405	3.8	752	310.7	359.0	1 568 961	2 088	244 440	180.1	334 046	99.7	0.3	60.1	46.0	14 310	85.2
Ashley	154	-7.8	354	90.8	120.1	811 284	2 294	103 494	64.7	148 425	85.3	14.7	33.9	17.7	5 578	31.7
Baxter	97	-5.8	145	D	18.8	398 818	2 742	42 098	17.5	26 231	4.2	95.8	24.7	2.8	135	10.0
Benton	255	-18.5	118	0.4	101.1	579 942	4 900	68 428	434.0	201 747	1.6	98.4	43.4	17.0	495	6.6
Boone	242	-14.8	191	0.2	57.6	518 871	2 714	56 403	119.8	94 634	1.7	98.3	45.8	11.4	1 476	39.3
Bradley	25	-13.8	115	0.9	9.6	332 369	2 884	54 957	29.9	136 326	11.8	88.2	42.5	18.3	53	8.7
Calhoun	16	-15.8	162	D	6.2	353 653	2 177	55 110	2.9	28 958	D	D	25.7	4.0	65	23.8
Carroll	243	-9.7	213	0.5	64.8	541 070	2 541	62 119	261.1	229 244	0.9	99.1	52.6	20.8	413	14.9
Chicot	286	6.3	747	141.8	221.3	1 320 053	1 766	199 901	129.1	337 977	65.8	34.2	59.7	42.4	9 232	75.7
Clark	82	-16.3	190	0.4	29.9	397 138	2 087	51 666	16.9	39 250	13.4	86.6	29.5	6.5	315	19.5
Clay	330	-3.8	452	227.0	293.4	1 008 541	2 231	166 226	142.1	194 350	98.1	1.9	44.3	28.6	12 282	71.3
Cleburne	130	4.0	143	0.2	38.5	405 826	2 829	57 358	56.1	62 014	2.9	97.1	29.3	8.0	646	18.3

Table B. States and Counties — Water Use, Wholesale Trade, Retail Trade, and Real Estate

STATE County	Water use, 2005 Total water withdrawn (mil gal/day)	Gallons withdrawn per person	Wholesale trade,[1] 2007 Number of establish-ments	Number of employees	Sales (mil dol)	Annual payroll (mil dol)	Retail trade,[2] 2007 Number of establish-ments	Number of employees	Sales (mil dol)	Annual payroll (mil dol)	Real estate and rental and leasing,[2] 2007 Number of establish-ments	Number of employees	Receipts (mil dol)	Annual payroll (mil dol)
	133	134	135	136	137	138	139	140	141	142	143	144	145	146
ALABAMA—Cont'd														
Washington	99.2	5 580	5	78	32.9	2.8	47	325	76.3	5.9	2	D	D	D
Wilcox	23.7	1 828	7	43	21.3	1.4	46	298	75.7	5.5	7	14	0.5	0.1
Winston	1.9	78	29	310	165.6	10.5	108	915	166.7	16.6	11	32	2.4	0.4
ALASKA	1 055.1	1 590	658	8 262	4 563.6	391.6	2 641	34 977	9 303.4	936.8	852	4 370	840.6	160.2
Aleutians East	3.4	1 275	1	D	D	D	9	52	9.3	1.2	2	D	D	D
Aleutians West	4.8	905	10	82	62.1	4.0	14	155	46.8	5.1	6	39	10.0	2.0
Anchorage	107.7	387	339	5 498	2 914.0	261.0	923	15 842	4 482.7	441.8	378	2 416	453.5	94.0
Bethel	0.5	26	4	26	3.5	0.3	54	831	96.8	13.5	6	45	7.9	1.0
Bristol Bay	0.2	158	3	D	D	D	9	50	12.8	1.5	2	D	D	D
Denali	16.2	8 897	NA	NA	NA	NA	10	33	11.0	0.9	NA	NA	NA	NA
Dillingham	0.8	173	2	D	D	D	19	209	42.7	4.8	6	25	3.6	0.6
Fairbanks North Star	38.3	437	72	D	D	D	339	5 236	1 574.3	146.7	136	745	152.5	29.9
Haines	3.5	1 604	2	D	D	D	18	115	16.2	2.9	4	8	0.7	0.1
Hoonah-Angoon			NA	NA	NA	NA	NA	NA	NA	NA	NA	NA	NA	NA
Juneau	603.7	19 352	33	D	D	D	172	1 933	465.3	52.0	58	241	41.1	5.9
Kenai Peninsula	27.4	534	46	353	193.7	16.1	265	2 537	666.9	62.5	66	169	38.2	5.3
Ketchikan Gateway	14.3	1 086	10	D	D	D	109	961	268.9	31.2	22	82	16.1	2.5
Kodiak Island	9.4	692	37	D	D	D	45	481	108.2	11.6	15	75	7.8	2.2
Lake and Peninsula	0.4	265	1	D	D	D	4	D	D	D	3	9	0.5	0.1
Matanuska-Susitna	6.7	90	36	368	137.0	14.9	233	3 200	853.9	86.9	72	272	37.4	6.8
Nome	0.6	67	4	D	D	D	33	399	63.2	7.8	7	24	5.2	0.5
North Slope	175.7	25 489	8	202	135.2	14.6	18	233	70.1	6.7	5	D	D	D
Northwest Arctic	8.0	1 098	1	D	D	D	15	201	41.6	4.9	3	2	0.4	0.0
Petersburg			NA	NA	NA	NA	NA	NA	NA	NA	NA	NA	NA	NA
Prince of Wales-Hyder			NA	NA	NA	NA	NA	NA	NA	NA	NA	NA	NA	NA
Sitka	9.1	1 013	15	D	D	D	62	465	94.9	12.6	15	49	7.8	1.9
Skagway			NA	NA	NA	NA	NA	NA	NA	NA	NA	NA	NA	NA
Southeast Fairbanks	0.7	104	2	D	D	D	38	208	47.3	4.0	8	10	1.0	0.1
Valdez-Cordova	13.1	1 303	14	86	81.2	4.7	56	370	79.7	7.7	17	45	17.1	2.4
Wade Hampton	0.5	61	1	D	D	D	25	283	39.5	4.0	2	D	D	D
Wrangell			NA	NA	NA	NA	NA	NA	NA	NA	NA	NA	NA	NA
Yakutat	0.6	953	3	20	10.0	1.8	6	D	D	D	1	D	D	D
Yukon-Koyukuk	0.7	109	2	D	D	D	34	299	41.6	6.5	3	5	0.3	0.1
ARIZONA	6 244.7	1 051	5 874	84 029	57 573.5	4 116.4	19 384	337 529	86 758.8	8 010.8	9 441	52 627	10 077.6	1 994.3
Apache	35.2	508	12	32	18.1	0.8	104	1 189	276.9	24.1	20	56	5.9	0.9
Cochise	254.4	2 018	54	359	102.3	10.4	455	6 305	1 313.7	129.1	139	504	65.1	12.4
Coconino	48.0	387	98	1 149	475.6	40.2	674	7 861	1 691.7	169.3	237	754	187.5	24.2
Gila	28.0	543	29	D	D	D	186	2 450	550.8	55.6	82	269	35.9	7.5
Graham	172.9	5 228	19	193	68.0	7.5	97	1 602	389.4	36.2	29	D	D	D
Greenlee	31.8	4 195	2	D	D	D	19	159	35.6	2.8	1	D	D	D
La Paz	628.5	31 066	10	107	65.9	3.7	88	1 006	394.4	19.1	17	57	6.0	1.3
Maricopa	1 967.0	541	4 176	66 783	49 760.3	3 457.2	11 468	217 746	58 688.3	5 332.6	6 123	37 987	7 796.5	1 564.0
Mohave	138.6	741	117	976	423.8	33.0	730	10 672	2 837.7	248.0	280	876	133.3	22.7
Navajo	67.5	622	38	289	209.5	12.0	340	4 399	1 237.5	102.4	142	350	56.9	10.1
Pima	306.8	332	744	8 132	3 056.8	324.6	2 982	51 830	11 928.5	1 208.9	1 449	8 133	1 211.7	251.8
Pinal	1 289.2	5 616	110	930	450.4	35.9	524	8 552	2 033.1	175.2	202	689	107.5	18.1
Santa Cruz	19.4	461	157	D	D	D	257	3 058	681.3	60.7	61	265	42.6	5.5
Yavapai	91.5	460	175	1 652	831.4	61.1	920	11 795	2 695.4	266.6	469	1 776	293.9	55.4
Yuma	1 166.1	6 433	133	D	D	D	540	8 905	2 004.6	180.2	190	734	119.2	17.5
ARKANSAS	11 428.3	4 112	2 977	38 988	29 659.8	1 536.3	11 906	140 018	32 974.3	2 889.2	3 162	14 115	1 968.1	374.9
Arkansas	966.4	48 144	30	303	134.6	12.2	111	1 231	286.3	25.4	19	58	6.1	1.3
Ashley	232.3	10 021	18	114	107.3	4.7	95	881	170.8	16.6	13	46	4.8	0.8
Baxter	5.8	145	19	D	D	D	242	2 460	486.8	48.7	50	202	22.7	4.5
Benton	440.9	2 359	216	D	D	D	751	9 896	2 390.6	223.0	308	1 204	165.9	34.3
Boone	3.1	87	32	D	D	D	166	2 038	466.9	42.2	38	104	13.6	2.4
Bradley	1.9	153	10	137	42.8	4.2	50	346	71.5	6.0	9	20	1.6	0.4
Calhoun	0.6	102	2	D	D	D	20	65	17.9	1.0	2	D	D	D
Carroll	11.5	426	14	78	24.1	2.9	167	1 339	265.4	25.8	36	70	6.4	1.3
Chicot	319.9	24 558	13	113	120.6	4.0	50	426	67.0	7.0	11	30	3.5	0.6
Clark	6.6	287	13	D	D	D	102	1 184	247.8	25.8	36	112	11.1	2.2
Clay	478.7	28 876	12	265	116.9	7.9	67	531	132.6	9.8	10	22	1.5	0.4
Cleburne	8.6	338	18	123	54.4	3.0	123	1 131	282.4	23.2	34	83	8.3	2.0

1. Merchant wholesalers, except manufacturers' sales branches and offices.   2. Employer establishments.

Table B. States and Counties — Professional Services, Manufacturing, and Accommodation and Food Services

STATE County	Professional, scientific, and technical services,[1] 2007				Manufacturing, 2007				Accommodation and food services, 2007			
	Number of establish-ments	Number of employees	Receipts (mil dol)	Annual payroll (mil dol)	Number of establish-ments	Number of employees	Receipts (mil dol)	Annual payroll (mil dol)	Number of establish-ments	Number of employees	Sales (mil dol)	Annual payroll (mil dol)
	147	148	149	150	151	152	153	154	155	156	157	158
ALABAMA—Cont'd												
Washington	14	178	25.9	9.1	15	1 397	1 153.4	85.3	9	D	D	D
Wilcox	11	D	D	D	13	876	D	D	19	112	12.9	1.2
Winston	23	70	5.7	1.9	68	4 439	797.8	112.0	40	511	16.6	4.4
ALASKA	1 799	12 509	2 006.8	745.4	544	13 298	8 204.0	489.5	1 996	25 638	1 851.3	529.8
Aleutians East	NA	NA	NA	NA	5	D	D	D	12	D	D	D
Aleutians West	2	D	D	D	14	2 314	634.8	77.1	12	103	14.7	2.9
Anchorage	1 092	D	D	D	194	2 305	D	D	720	14 031	933.3	283.9
Bethel	5	D	D	D	NA	NA	NA	NA	18	39	4.1	0.8
Bristol Bay	1	D	D	D	NA	NA	NA	NA	19	74	13.3	3.9
Denali	2	D	D	D	NA	NA	NA	NA	30	110	37.1	10.5
Dillingham	4	D	D	D	NA	NA	NA	NA	18	51	7.2	1.9
Fairbanks North Star	228	1 329	174.9	64.7	78	745	D	37.3	220	3 430	221.6	60.9
Haines	4	6	0.3	0.1	NA	NA	NA	NA	19	64	6.4	1.5
Hoonah-Angoon	NA	NA	NA	NA	NA	NA	NA	NA	NA	NA	NA	NA
Juneau	95	D	D	D	NA	NA	NA	NA	97	1 228	86.9	21.6
Kenai Peninsula	111	D	D	D	64	982	D	57.4	260	1 677	131.2	33.5
Ketchikan Gateway	26	D	D	D	14	500	D	16.7	57	546	45.6	12.1
Kodiak Island	25	65	12.4	2.5	22	1 644	D	51.5	42	404	26.3	6.9
Lake and Peninsula	3	9	1.0	0.5	NA	NA	NA	NA	14	D	D	D
Matanuska-Susitna	132	D	D	D	NA	NA	NA	NA	185	1 774	113.7	30.2
Nome	5	D	D	D	NA	NA	NA	NA	15	166	10.2	2.9
North Slope	4	14	2.8	1.3	NA	NA	NA	NA	20	414	56.3	20.0
Northwest Arctic	1	D	D	D	NA	NA	NA	NA	4	D	D	D
Petersburg	NA	NA	NA	NA	NA	NA	NA	NA	NA	NA	NA	NA
Prince of Wales-Hyder	NA	NA	NA	NA	NA	NA	NA	NA	NA	NA	NA	NA
Sitka	15	48	4.0	1.1	NA	NA	NA	NA	41	500	27.1	8.2
Skagway	NA	NA	NA	NA	NA	NA	NA	NA	NA	NA	NA	NA
Southeast Fairbanks	11	23	5.5	1.2	NA	NA	NA	NA	30	165	22.2	4.1
Valdez-Cordova	21	D	D	D	14	569	543.4	19.2	56	264	23.1	6.2
Wade Hampton	1	D	D	D	NA	NA	NA	NA	NA	NA	NA	NA
Wrangell	NA	NA	NA	NA	NA	NA	NA	NA	NA	NA	NA	NA
Yakutat	NA	NA	NA	NA	NA	NA	NA	NA	7	21	3.8	1.1
Yukon-Koyukuk	1	D	D	D	NA	NA	NA	NA	12	77	5.4	1.6
ARIZONA	16 563	128 188	17 617.1	7 239.5	5 074	172 438	57 977.8	8 774.3	11 610	250 716	13 268.5	3 766.3
Apache	27	D	D	D	NA	NA	NA	NA	68	1 033	47.8	13.3
Cochise	208	D	D	D	56	576	181.3	20.6	277	4 100	171.4	47.8
Coconino	322	D	D	D	109	4 219	1 526.8	240.5	531	11 181	717.7	181.9
Gila	91	370	34.4	12.2	NA	NA	NA	NA	137	2 021	106.7	29.5
Graham	27	373	10.5	11.2	NA	NA	NA	NA	53	955	34.7	8.3
Greenlee	4	28	0.9	0.4	NA	NA	NA	NA	16	116	4.9	1.2
La Paz	15	D	D	D	NA	NA	NA	NA	73	719	38.0	9.3
Maricopa	11 727	D	D	D	3 398	121 062	40 182.1	6 043.4	6 750	156 678	8 408.9	2 446.3
Mohave	251	D	D	D	164	3 814	1 350.0	139.6	381	6 380	274.3	77.3
Navajo	117	D	D	D	57	D	D	D	244	3 308	191.5	45.7
Pima	2 692	16 250	1 886.4	777.8	760	30 567	10 365.2	1 877.0	1 758	42 002	2 135.2	601.8
Pinal	227	D	D	D	122	3 896	2 149.9	151.8	328	6 063	341.9	88.3
Santa Cruz	63	D	D	D	NA	NA	NA	NA	100	1 481	67.2	19.8
Yavapai	584	D	D	D	233	3 618	764.0	143.6	578	8 737	456.5	126.2
Yuma	208	D	D	D	82	2 856	891.6	88.0	316	5 942	271.9	69.6
ARKANSAS	5 588	D	D	D	3 088	184 568	60 735.6	6 518.4	5 112	89 933	3 559.8	994.1
Arkansas	28	85	7.6	2.7	33	3 964	1 702.2	127.5	43	448	15.5	4.2
Ashley	27	95	9.1	3.0	26	2 733	D	125.4	25	442	15.3	4.1
Baxter	75	413	29.1	11.0	57	2 496	550.1	90.6	108	1 555	60.3	16.1
Benton	535	4 702	472.6	240.4	199	12 403	D	432.3	362	7 511	295.7	85.8
Boone	66	D	D	D	69	D	D	D	63	1 023	41.9	11.7
Bradley	14	36	2.4	0.8	5	916	177.0	27.3	15	176	6.2	1.5
Calhoun	NA	NA	NA	NA	NA	NA	NA	NA	4	30	0.8	0.2
Carroll	51	139	10.0	3.4	41	2 866	D	74.2	143	1 424	54.0	15.8
Chicot	16	53	2.6	1.2	8	503	D	8.5	18	169	6.1	1.6
Clark	28	198	14.7	6.8	28	2 196	433.9	53.9	50	908	32.7	9.5
Clay	16	36	2.7	0.7	17	651	111.8	18.7	16	205	6.3	1.7
Cleburne	31	104	7.0	2.1	40	1 360	205.6	43.3	58	784	29.2	9.0

1. Establishment subject to federal tax.

Table B. States and Counties — Health Care and Social Assistance, Other Services, and Federal Funds

STATE County	Health care and social assistance, 2007				Other services, 2007				Federal funds and grants, 2009–2010 Expenditures (mil dol)			
									Total	Direct payments for individuals[1]		
	Number of establishments	Number of employees	Receipts (mil dol)	Annual payroll (mil dol)	Number of establishments	Number of employees	Receipts (mil dol)	Annual payroll (mil dol)	Total	Social Security and government retirement	Medicare	Food Stamps and Supplemental Security Income
	159	160	161	162	163	164	165	166	167	168	169	170
ALABAMA—Cont'd												
Washington	21	295	16.4	8.4	8	16	1.3	0.2	145.1	60.9	33.2	10.4
Wilcox	20	247	12.7	6.2	10	D	D	D	174.6	43.7	30.4	22.1
Winston	42	915	59.1	23.9	23	D	D	D	218.8	94.0	65.2	10.5
ALASKA	2 131	40 618	4 662.6	1 791.5	1 328	7 566	811.3	222.9	12 615.3	1 531.3	348.7	218.8
Aleutians East	9	D	D	D	2	D	D	D	45.4	3.8	0.3	0.5
Aleutians West	17	146	9.7	4.9	6	29	13.9	1.4	35.4	2.3	1.0	0.3
Anchorage	1 033	20 722	2 678.4	964.1	580	4 060	441.0	125.5	4 812.4	674.3	136.4	72.3
Bethel	11	D	D	D	13	78	8.7	1.9	391.9	13.1	6.7	20.2
Bristol Bay	3	5	1.0	0.4	1	D	D	D	81.0	7.4	1.6	0.1
Denali	2	D	D	D	1	D	D	D	134.2	2.0	2.1	0.0
Dillingham	5	D	D	D	6	15	0.8	0.3	52.3	6.8	0.0	3.7
Fairbanks North Star	267	4 867	570.5	223.9	195	1 081	106.8	31.3	1 546.6	196.7	45.0	19.0
Haines	8	113	6.8	3.0	7	18	1.2	0.3	19.5	7.3	2.6	0.8
Hoonah-Angoon	NA	NA	NA	NA	NA	NA	NA	NA	NA	NA	NA	NA
Juneau	138	2 215	200.8	85.5	85	433	40.0	12.0	779.7	72.9	21.7	7.4
Kenai Peninsula	191	2 671	226.4	97.5	135	602	67.2	18.4	356.7	150.4	40.4	12.7
Ketchikan Gateway	31	D	D	D	35	133	12.7	3.3	147.6	35.6	13.7	5.3
Kodiak Island	42	534	56.7	22.0	26	130	13.7	3.0	182.6	18.0	3.5	3.5
Lake and Peninsula	NA	NA	NA	NA	1	D	D	D	13.5	0.5	2.6	1.7
Matanuska-Susitna	232	2 692	253.8	102.7	113	498	57.1	13.6	361.8	197.4	31.7	21.0
Nome	23	D	D	D	14	74	6.4	1.2	156.1	11.8	3.6	9.1
North Slope	3	D	D	D	8	67	8.3	3.3	64.2	7.9	2.3	1.0
Northwest Arctic	4	D	D	D	6	D	D	D	68.5	8.0	2.5	6.8
Petersburg	NA	NA	NA	NA	NA	NA	NA	NA	NA	NA	NA	NA
Prince of Wales-Hyder	NA	NA	NA	NA	NA	NA	NA	NA	NA	NA	NA	NA
Sitka	28	855	86.1	38.9	21	93	8.2	1.8	98.3	22.8	7.8	2.0
Skagway	NA	NA	NA	NA	NA	NA	NA	NA	NA	NA	NA	NA
Southeast Fairbanks	9	115	7.1	2.8	9	17	1.3	0.4	119.2	15.2	3.4	2.8
Valdez-Cordova	24	470	35.3	13.2	25	96	9.5	2.5	1 253.8	22.8	5.0	2.2
Wade Hampton	3	D	D	D	1	D	D	D	127.3	6.5	2.7	14.4
Wrangell	NA	NA	NA	NA	NA	NA	NA	NA	NA	NA	NA	NA
Yakutat	2	D	D	D	NA	NA	NA	NA	8.9	1.9	0.0	0.1
Yukon-Koyukuk	4	D	D	D	5	D	D	D	121.0	14.3	1.2	7.7
ARIZONA	15 446	278 833	30 406.8	11 653.5	8 906	68 368	6 219.6	1 725.6	64 426.8	17 842.1	7 040.6	2 280.8
Apache	57	2 616	184.3	96.8	35	D	D	D	1 676.0	170.2	60.8	104.4
Cochise	273	4 773	360.3	152.0	162	718	44.2	12.3	3 090.8	624.0	155.9	69.3
Coconino	389	6 628	878.6	305.9	247	1 493	100.8	32.2	1 357.4	341.8	109.5	63.7
Gila	141	2 366	197.5	78.0	64	262	22.1	5.3	635.9	260.0	114.5	34.7
Graham	70	1 242	104.3	41.1	43	287	30.5	10.0	319.6	90.5	39.1	20.2
Greenlee	8	121	6.8	4.2	NA	NA	NA	NA	56.0	21.1	10.1	3.6
La Paz	20	516	59.3	23.4	25	D	D	D	157.7	79.1	0.0	12.9
Maricopa	9 683	175 051	19 740.9	7 610.8	5 509	45 671	4 392.2	1 195.4	31 522.5	9 346.5	4 078.3	1 138.8
Mohave	456	7 612	911.1	284.4	315	1 895	129.4	38.0	1 474.8	868.4	294.3	80.2
Navajo	216	3 152	333.4	133.9	125	1 120	135.7	39.9	1 281.0	318.3	95.0	95.8
Pima	2 672	51 151	5 459.8	2 073.5	1 494	12 045	1 020.6	289.4	14 248.6	3 301.3	1 318.0	381.9
Pinal	325	5 819	476.3	211.5	241	1 445	89.3	28.5	2 009.8	775.8	269.8	103.5
Santa Cruz	70	1 055	89.8	31.8	52	155	11.8	3.5	603.0	112.8	38.1	24.0
Yavapai	737	10 268	930.0	370.7	386	1 822	141.9	41.0	1 624.2	996.3	244.7	51.4
Yuma	329	6 463	654.6	235.7	208	1 217	85.2	26.0	1 761.7	495.9	212.6	96.0
ARKANSAS	7 216	152 864	13 439.6	5 282.0	4 153	23 188	2 187.8	558.0	28 904.0	9 722.2	4 416.7	1 327.7
Arkansas	49	1 087	64.4	26.9	35	137	8.9	2.7	242.2	67.7	46.1	11.9
Ashley	46	567	44.8	19.0	25	131	10.8	2.8	231.7	82.4	50.8	14.7
Baxter	158	3 168	311.6	116.2	99	409	25.9	7.6	413.0	242.7	92.8	12.7
Benton	409	6 176	563.0	220.0	274	D	D	D	957.0	534.3	170.1	26.3
Boone	109	2 109	151.5	59.9	63	D	D	D	344.4	160.0	56.1	12.9
Bradley	31	574	40.8	16.0	22	71	6.8	1.5	134.7	42.1	31.0	8.7
Calhoun	5	D	D	D	2	D	D	D	178.7	16.1	8.5	2.6
Carroll	54	743	59.7	26.3	40	132	8.8	2.4	191.3	98.9	37.0	6.3
Chicot	42	773	49.1	21.0	17	57	4.3	1.0	197.9	42.1	33.7	15.0
Clark	57	D	D	D	38	115	12.9	2.9	202.2	75.2	44.0	9.5
Clay	27	643	31.4	16.3	24	60	5.1	1.3	196.5	64.0	43.7	7.6
Cleburne	43	718	54.9	20.7	42	153	12.2	2.8	224.6	126.9	46.8	8.3

1. State totals may include programs not allocated by county.

Table B. States and Counties — Federal Funds, Residential Construction, and Local Government Finances

STATE County	Salaries and wages	Defense	Other	Medicaid and other health-related	Nutrition and family welfare	Education	Other	New con-struction ($1,000)	Number of housing units	Total (mil dol)	Inter-govern-mental (mil dol)	Total (mil dol)	Total	Property
	171	172	173	174	175	176	177	178	179	180	181	182	183	184
ALABAMA—Cont'd														
Washington	3.7	0.0	0.9	28.9	3.5	1.3	0.9	110	1	42.5	26.9	11.3	656	499
Wilcox	13.4	1.0	1.1	50.7	5.0	1.5	1.0	0	0	39.8	21.8	5.7	450	308
Winston	9.7	0.0	3.6	27.3	3.3	1.7	2.4	0	0	73.9	48.4	13.6	563	202
ALASKA	4 055.1	1 776.3	687.9	1 065.9	283.0	354.9	1 761.4	15 510	64	X	X	X	X	X
Aleutians East	2.2	31.9	0.6	0.0	0.6	1.5	1.3	0	0	24.3	12.2	6.6	2 484	0
Aleutians West	3.0	20.0	3.1	0.7	1.3	1.0	2.2	1 196	8	53.7	16.6	19.2	3 985	869
Anchorage	1 131.2	964.4	298.3	325.6	76.6	45.8	1 024.4	116 574	480	1 185.7	493.7	469.1	1 677	1 461
Bethel	14.6	46.2	3.6	176.2	12.2	36.2	45.8	2 145	10	41.1	18.3	7.5	438	2
Bristol Bay	3.4	8.1	6.1	29.2	0.3	3.8	20.6	250	1	10.7	5.5	2.9	2 929	1 992
Denali	17.1	86.3	26.0	0.0	0.4	0.0	0.0	NA	NA	8.6	5.8	2.2	1 210	130
Dillingham	4.1	0.7	1.5	2.3	3.9	9.3	10.6	NA	NA	30.3	20.6	4.8	962	329
Fairbanks North Star	343.6	493.1	116.7	114.0	33.8	18.3	135.5	8 443	42	327.0	164.7	114.5	1 174	1 041
Haines	1.1	0.2	0.4	4.5	0.5	0.4	1.6	1 254	6	11.4	5.2	4.5	1 989	907
Hoonah-Angoon	NA	NA	NA	NA	NA	NA	NA	NA	NA	NA	NA	NA	NA	NA
Juneau	97.8	2.0	52.7	56.5	51.2	126.1	274.9	12 879	53	256.9	62.8	80.7	2 631	1 223
Kenai Peninsula	33.5	8.1	12.7	53.1	15.4	7.2	18.2	16 417	89	338.5	112.0	101.2	1 906	1 105
Ketchikan Gateway	34.8	0.0	20.0	27.3	3.4	2.3	4.8	3 445	17	103.6	29.2	30.6	2 311	960
Kodiak Island	81.8	1.5	36.7	12.3	5.9	3.2	13.0	4 130	17	87.1	43.1	20.7	1 593	801
Lake and Peninsula	2.3	0.0	0.5	0.0	1.0	0.1	4.0	NA	NA	17.0	12.4	2.1	1 388	0
Matanuska-Susitna	21.2	0.4	19.4	22.2	19.4	6.3	12.1	9 264	53	318.7	179.9	108.4	1 311	992
Nome	10.4	9.3	6.9	49.8	9.9	20.8	13.1	550	1	47.0	24.3	7.2	773	291
North Slope	2.7	0.4	10.3	12.1	2.5	10.8	10.4	2 704	12	357.0	67.9	203.3	30 983	30 944
Northwest Arctic	4.3	3.4	2.3	2.6	5.2	12.7	15.3	600	4	91.0	66.2	3.3	445	0
Petersburg	NA	NA	NA	NA	NA	NA	NA	NA	NA	NA	NA	NA	NA	NA
Prince of Wales-Hyder	NA	NA	NA	NA	NA	NA	NA	NA	NA	NA	NA	NA	NA	NA
Sitka	24.2	0.0	7.4	14.8	2.9	1.6	2.8	2 857	13	73.7	25.6	15.5	1 746	560
Skagway	NA	NA	NA	NA	NA	NA	NA	NA	NA	NA	NA	NA	NA	NA
Southeast Fairbanks	15.5	46.9	4.2	22.6	2.0	1.3	2.9	NA	NA	2.1	1.2	0.0	0	0
Valdez-Cordova	1 125.6	44.5	12.2	14.4	3.7	2.1	18.6	3 749	19	73.8	17.8	35.0	3 688	3 307
Wade Hampton	2.8	0.0	1.2	48.1	1.4	19.3	26.4	NA	NA	13.0	6.0	1.1	140	13
Wrangell	NA	NA	NA	NA	NA	NA	NA	NA	NA	NA	NA	NA	NA	NA
Yakutat	1.5	0.0	1.0	0.5	0.3	0.2	2.6	290	2	6.6	3.5	2.0	2 946	1 496
Yukon-Koyukuk	9.5	8.8	4.2	49.0	4.0	3.8	15.6	0	0	40.5	34.2	0.7	124	47
ARIZONA	4 980.4	10 831.4	1 981.7	8 500.6	1 460.7	1 186.1	3 213.5	2 424 190	12 370	X	X	X	X	X
Apache	138.6	5.3	138.3	611.5	57.9	83.4	184.0	9 303	48	248.0	187.9	26.6	381	301
Cochise	1 063.7	765.6	46.6	254.7	26.6	17.3	40.4	51 295	347	442.4	211.0	125.8	984	710
Coconino	171.0	6.3	128.3	330.2	40.9	50.2	48.2	40 707	315	557.6	231.7	219.0	1 718	965
Gila	29.0	0.2	12.5	129.7	12.5	14.3	17.3	15 025	73	194.1	97.0	68.4	1 316	752
Graham	23.0	0.2	6.6	95.2	7.4	17.0	3.3	11 652	80	133.9	82.0	24.7	711	339
Greenlee	2.4	0.0	0.5	15.2	1.8	0.8	0.2	580	4	34.9	18.3	11.1	1 426	1 208
La Paz	19.0	0.4	11.1	0.7	5.4	8.2	9.7	2 233	16	81.0	49.3	19.6	972	667
Maricopa	1 801.8	4 436.4	848.2	3 913.4	820.8	751.3	2 330.3	1 457 766	6 703	15 566.3	5 955.4	5 840.3	1 505	864
Mohave	36.4	6.0	15.3	84.6	25.0	12.8	29.3	48 555	262	613.2	254.1	253.3	1 299	749
Navajo	91.5	0.9	50.5	433.4	31.4	60.4	29.9	19 872	140	579.2	236.6	122.4	1 100	653
Pima	1 074.4	5 268.8	388.9	1 668.4	174.1	107.4	341.9	424 149	1 938	3 481.7	1 650.1	1 289.2	1 333	911
Pinal	118.4	7.8	85.4	436.0	48.7	25.8	78.7	206 850	1 597	1 134.1	500.3	385.4	1 288	694
Santa Cruz	105.5	7.6	158.1	133.5	12.0	5.4	2.6	13 050	53	189.6	106.2	56.6	1 321	702
Yavapai	70.5	1.1	46.3	147.1	24.0	12.9	5.6	64 053	339	692.9	249.7	293.3	1 380	903
Yuma	235.1	324.8	45.2	209.7	51.8	19.1	30.8	59 100	455	669.9	368.7	193.9	1 017	548
ARKANSAS	2 417.8	1 137.5	613.5	3 731.0	680.6	539.7	1 891.7	880 263	7 177	X	X	X	X	X
Arkansas	20.6	1.2	20.6	41.1	4.5	1.3	2.8	2 649	17	69.8	34.1	14.4	742	300
Ashley	6.4	0.0	1.8	52.4	5.2	1.6	1.2	0	0	67.5	37.1	15.6	700	268
Baxter	15.8	11.4	4.1	22.4	4.5	2.5	-0.1	2 634	17	70.6	36.0	21.0	501	192
Benton	61.1	5.7	52.4	53.4	17.2	8.4	6.5	142 243	769	524.9	265.0	143.6	707	286
Boone	13.3	0.5	4.1	33.5	7.4	4.0	43.0	7 061	71	84.0	57.3	16.7	455	188
Bradley	17.4	0.0	0.6	24.5	5.0	0.8	1.6	11	1	33.0	22.4	6.0	502	198
Calhoun	1.2	129.6	0.2	14.4	1.1	0.3	4.4	45	1	15.7	5.9	2.5	451	259
Carroll	24.2	0.5	2.0	16.8	2.7	1.5	0.3	1 536	10	57.7	29.5	14.1	515	234
Chicot	3.9	1.1	0.6	70.0	5.3	1.8	2.5	442	5	50.3	23.5	8.9	726	289
Clark	13.3	0.2	1.4	33.8	4.0	4.9	1.4	1 974	13	53.7	34.4	10.3	435	170
Clay	6.3	0.8	1.0	49.4	3.0	1.4	6.3	1 194	12	46.9	24.5	7.0	434	240
Cleburne	6.4	2.1	1.4	24.6	3.3	2.2	0.5	1 751	16	45.0	25.9	12.1	477	213

Federal funds and grants, 2009–2010 (cont.) · Expenditures (mil dol) (cont.) · Procurement contract awards · Grants[1] · Value of residential construction authorized by building permits, 2010 · Local government finances, 2007 · General revenue · Taxes · Per capita[2] (dollars)

1. State totals may include programs not allocated by county. 2. Based on the resident population estimated as of July 1 of the year shown.

	Local government finances, 2007 (cont.)									Government employment, 2009			Presidential election,[2] 2008		
	Direct general expenditure							Debt outstanding					Percent of vote cast:		
			Percent of total for:												
STATE County	Total (mil dol)	Per capita[1] (dollars)	Educa-tion	Health and hospitals	Police protec-tion	Public welfare	High-ways	Total (mil dol)	Per capita[1] (dollars)	Federal civilian	Federal military	State and local	Demo-cratic	Republi-can	All other
	185	186	187	188	189	190	191	192	193	194	195	196	197	198	199
ALABAMA—Cont'd															
Washington	44.3	2 570	70.0	2.9	2.8	0.1	10.2	27.0	1 568	39	83	1 005	35.0	64.4	0.6
Wilcox	40.6	3 173	55.2	10.2	2.5	0.5	9.6	42.9	3 357	70	60	771	71.0	28.8	0.2
Winston	76.7	3 162	55.8	22.6	2.7	0.5	5.3	50.6	2 088	81	116	1 126	17.5	80.8	1.7
ALASKA	X	X	X	X	X	X	X	X	X	17 083	27 748	63 825	37.9	59.4	2.7
Aleutians East	29.0	10 877	25.2	30.6	3.1	0.0	2.1	54.2	20 332	24	20	261	NA	0.0	0.0
Aleutians West	44.1	9 139	16.5	0.2	8.3	0.0	10.8	12.6	2 608	18	54	481	NA	0.0	0.0
Anchorage	1 137.1	4 066	49.8	2.1	7.4	0.0	8.5	1 799.6	6 435	9 557	14 111	20 774	NA	0.0	0.0
Bethel	37.9	2 203	0.0	0.4	7.2	0.0	3.2	9.0	525	96	126	2 999	NA	0.0	0.0
Bristol Bay	9.8	9 831	38.2	11.0	7.1	0.0	7.2	1.8	1 846	53	0	169	NA	0.0	0.0
Denali	8.4	4 596	80.0	1.6	0.0	0.0	1.0	1.6	894	225	17	144	NA	0.0	0.0
Dillingham	29.9	5 989	33.5	2.1	3.9	0.0	3.6	25.1	5 022	56	36	685	NA	0.0	0.0
Fairbanks North Star	291.2	2 987	60.0	1.2	2.8	0.0	3.6	185.0	1 898	3 477	9 411	8 000	NA	0.0	0.0
Haines	9.0	3 959	47.0	2.4	5.1	0.2	5.3	20.0	8 769	13	17	193	NA	0.0	0.0
Hoonah-Angoon	NA	NA	NA	NA	NA	NA	NA	NA	NA	101	15	277			
Juneau	245.8	8 008	33.2	26.7	5.4	0.0	3.7	234.1	7 629	834	461	6 304	NA	0.0	0.0
Kenai Peninsula	319.3	6 014	34.2	28.8	2.2	0.0	3.6	121.6	2 290	441	484	4 228	NA	0.0	0.0
Ketchikan Gateway	118.6	8 966	24.2	3.1	3.5	0.0	3.8	202.2	15 284	284	335	1 793	NA	0.0	0.0
Kodiak Island	85.2	6 553	44.4	0.6	4.5	0.1	2.8	32.1	2 471	348	1 058	1 132	NA	0.0	0.0
Lake and Peninsula	20.0	12 979	80.4	0.1	0.0	0.0	0.4	9.6	6 212	45	11	368	NA	0.0	0.0
Matanuska-Susitna	318.4	3 852	65.3	2.8	2.7	0.0	6.2	294.2	3 558	233	641	3 862	NA	0.0	0.0
Nome	50.9	5 461	23.0	0.5	3.5	0.0	3.5	9.5	1 024	62	92	1 656	NA	0.0	0.0
North Slope	271.9	41 440	21.5	3.7	3.3	1.2	7.1	541.4	82 524	22	49	1 916	NA	0.0	0.0
Northwest Arctic	92.0	12 346	70.8	0.1	1.1	0.0	0.4	73.0	9 793	46	54	1 115	NA	0.0	0.0
Petersburg	NA	NA	NA	NA	NA	NA	NA	NA	NA	113	52	488			
Prince of Wales-Hyder	NA	NA	NA	NA	NA	NA	NA	NA	NA	97	40	800			
Sitka	70.5	7 941	31.0	21.2	6.7	0.0	2.7	87.2	9 826	168	249	1 053	NA	0.0	0.0
Skagway	NA	NA	NA	NA	NA	NA	NA	NA	NA	53	0	110			
Southeast Fairbanks	1.8	260	0.1	3.4	0.0	0.0	11.0	1.1	161	337	64	479	NA	0.0	0.0
Valdez-Cordova	63.8	6 715	29.6	19.0	3.4	0.0	5.4	27.5	2 900	170	220	1 212	NA	0.0	0.0
Wade Hampton	11.8	1 547	31.4	1.6	10.1	0.0	1.7	2.0	256	25	56	1 568	NA	0.0	0.0
Wrangell	NA	NA	NA	NA	NA	NA	NA	NA	NA	56	16	261			
Yakutat	5.0	7 194	58.3	3.4	9.1	0.0	7.5	1.3	1 836	28	0	120	NA	0.0	0.0
Yukon-Koyukuk	42.0	7 201	75.5	4.0	1.3	0.0	0.8	6.9	1 186	101	41	1 377	NA	0.0	0.0
ARIZONA	X	X	X	X	X	X	X	X	X	56 811	34 453	362 463	45.1	53.6	1.2
Apache	239.0	3 416	69.7	2.1	1.1	0.5	6.0	387.5	5 537	3 453	151	9 263	63.4	35.2	1.3
Cochise	425.8	3 330	43.8	3.2	8.8	7.0	6.6	151.9	1 188	5 206	5 042	7 161	38.8	59.5	1.7
Coconino	485.8	3 812	39.5	2.6	9.4	1.2	10.3	462.9	3 632	3 049	289	13 690	57.8	40.8	1.3
Gila	186.8	3 592	39.4	3.5	8.8	2.8	8.1	88.0	1 692	500	111	4 564	35.3	63.1	1.6
Graham	132.1	3 799	60.0	1.8	3.7	1.3	9.1	244.4	7 028	416	79	2 225	29.0	69.8	1.2
Greenlee	30.8	3 978	42.5	6.3	2.5	0.0	8.1	43.1	5 555	35	17	500	40.0	58.8	1.2
La Paz	75.5	3 744	34.6	3.6	10.4	0.0	10.5	32.3	1 603	321	43	1 973	34.7	63.2	2.1
Maricopa	15 068.8	3 884	40.5	4.5	7.6	1.7	5.4	26 279.2	6 773	21 437	14 110	198 970	44.1	54.7	1.2
Mohave	607.7	3 117	33.3	2.7	8.5	0.8	7.5	509.9	2 616	527	417	7 746	32.7	65.6	1.7
Navajo	482.1	4 332	51.1	16.2	3.9	0.3	4.0	291.8	2 622	1 724	241	8 631	43.5	55.2	1.3
Pima	3 541.9	3 662	35.0	8.9	8.4	2.7	6.5	4 775.0	4 937	11 799	8 420	66 304	52.4	46.4	1.2
Pinal	1 035.0	3 459	44.2	2.9	6.1	4.3	9.2	861.5	2 879	1 640	728	18 651	42.2	56.7	1.2
Santa Cruz	170.1	3 971	46.8	1.1	9.5	2.5	7.3	99.7	2 328	1 560	93	2 289	65.3	34.0	0.8
Yavapai	676.3	3 181	35.2	1.6	7.3	4.9	10.7	475.8	2 237	1 439	472	9 822	37.0	61.4	1.6
Yuma	749.5	3 933	47.7	1.1	6.0	0.3	6.6	534.1	2 803	3 705	4 240	10 674	42.6	56.3	1.1
ARKANSAS	X	X	X	X	X	X	X	X	X	21 813	19 011	195 065	38.9	58.7	2.4
Arkansas	70.1	3 615	41.4	11.9	4.3	0.0	7.0	67.8	3 499	212	91	1 097	37.5	60.0	2.5
Ashley	60.0	2 689	62.2	0.0	3.5	0.0	5.0	142.8	6 397	82	105	1 214	34.4	62.6	3.0
Baxter	69.5	1 657	56.8	0.2	7.2	0.1	9.7	122.7	2 925	161	202	1 668	32.7	64.3	3.0
Benton	559.1	2 753	59.9	3.9	4.1	0.0	6.6	725.9	3 574	491	1 079	8 442	30.7	67.2	2.1
Boone	81.0	2 209	69.7	0.1	4.6	0.0	4.2	47.2	1 287	193	176	3 128	28.7	68.3	3.0
Bradley	32.9	2 744	67.0	0.1	4.1	0.0	4.8	15.4	1 288	38	56	808	41.6	56.0	2.4
Calhoun	15.0	2 709	42.7	0.2	5.5	1.9	6.2	91.4	16 509	12	25	265	31.2	65.9	2.9
Carroll	54.1	1 973	55.4	0.0	6.7	0.0	6.5	50.7	1 850	85	134	1 080	39.4	57.5	3.1
Chicot	44.8	3 638	43.4	31.9	4.8	0.0	4.8	21.6	1 754	45	57	1 039	58.4	40.7	0.9
Clark	51.9	2 199	65.3	0.1	5.7	0.0	6.0	45.7	1 937	104	114	2 579	46.9	50.7	2.4
Clay	48.5	3 006	54.0	23.4	3.2	0.0	6.4	17.7	1 096	59	75	958	40.7	55.0	4.3
Cleburne	43.4	1 707	68.5	0.1	4.7	0.4	8.7	60.4	2 377	100	123	864	26.0	70.2	3.7

1. Based on the resident population estimated as of July 1 of the year shown.   2. © 2009 Election Data Services, Inc. All rights reserved.

STATE/ County code	CBSA code[1]	County type[2]	STATE County	Land area,[3] (sq km) 2010	Total persons	Rank	Per square kilometer	White	Black	American Indian, Alaska Native	Asian and Pacific Islander	Percent Hispanic or Latino[4]	Under 5 years	5 to 17 years	18 to 24 years	25 to 34 years	35 to 44 years	45 to 54 years
				1	2	3	4	5	6	7	8	9	10	11	12	13	14	15
			ARKANSAS—Cont'd															
05 025	38220	3	Cleveland	1 548	8 689	2 556	5.6	85.7	12.5	0.6	0.2	1.7	6.8	18.0	7.4	11.2	12.6	14.4
05 027	31620	7	Columbia	1 984	24 552	1 623	12.4	60.0	37.2	0.5	0.9	2.2	6.0	16.7	14.2	11.0	11.3	13.2
05 029	...	6	Conway	1 430	21 273	1 776	14.9	84.1	12.0	1.6	0.6	3.6	6.6	17.6	7.9	11.4	12.0	14.9
05 031	27860	3	Craighead	1 832	96 443	598	52.6	80.9	13.8	0.8	1.4	4.4	7.3	17.7	13.0	14.4	12.4	12.6
05 033	22900	2	Crawford	1 536	61 948	838	40.3	89.1	1.6	3.8	1.8	6.1	6.9	19.5	8.4	12.0	13.2	14.8
05 035	32820	1	Crittenden	1 579	50 902	967	32.2	46.0	51.6	0.6	0.8	2.0	8.0	21.1	8.9	13.0	12.8	14.5
05 037	...	6	Cross	1 596	17 870	1 926	11.2	75.5	22.7	0.6	0.6	1.5	6.3	18.9	7.5	11.4	12.7	14.9
05 039	...	6	Dallas	1 729	8 116	2 600	4.7	55.0	42.6	0.8	0.3	2.3	5.8	17.8	7.7	10.0	11.4	14.7
05 041	...	6	Desha	1 990	13 008	2 242	6.5	47.3	47.9	0.5	0.4	4.4	7.6	18.4	8.4	11.5	11.0	14.9
05 043	...	7	Drew	2 145	18 509	1 899	8.6	68.9	28.4	0.6	0.6	2.5	6.3	17.3	12.8	11.7	11.3	14.1
05 045	30780	2	Faulkner	1 678	113 237	527	67.5	83.9	10.9	1.3	1.6	3.9	7.0	17.5	15.7	14.3	12.7	13.0
05 047	22900	2	Franklin	1 577	18 125	1 919	11.5	95.2	1.0	1.9	1.2	2.0	6.6	17.9	8.3	11.3	12.4	14.1
05 049	...	9	Fulton	1 601	12 245	2 288	7.6	98.0	0.7	1.7	0.4	0.8	5.6	15.6	6.2	8.8	11.1	14.4
05 051	26300	3	Garland	1 755	96 024	603	54.7	85.8	8.7	1.4	1.1	4.8	5.6	15.3	7.6	10.8	11.4	14.0
05 053	30780	2	Grant	1 636	17 853	1 931	10.9	94.9	2.4	0.8	0.5	2.2	6.1	18.0	8.1	11.8	13.5	15.5
05 055	37500	6	Greene	1 496	42 090	1 126	28.1	96.5	0.9	1.1	0.4	2.1	6.8	18.4	8.7	12.4	13.5	14.1
05 057	26260	6	Hempstead	1 884	22 609	1 704	12.0	57.7	30.1	1.0	0.6	12.0	7.8	18.2	8.5	12.3	11.6	14.5
05 059	...	6	Hot Spring	1 593	32 923	1 361	20.7	85.5	11.4	1.2	0.5	2.8	6.3	17.1	8.3	12.1	12.2	14.6
05 061	...	7	Howard	1 524	13 789	2 200	9.0	68.3	20.9	1.1	0.8	9.8	7.4	18.8	8.3	11.7	12.2	14.3
05 063	12900	7	Independence	1 979	36 647	1 259	18.5	91.0	2.4	1.0	1.0	5.8	6.7	17.3	9.0	11.9	12.6	14.3
05 065	...	9	Izard	1 504	13 696	2 206	9.1	96.1	1.5	1.5	0.5	1.5	4.7	14.5	6.4	9.9	11.2	14.6
05 067	...	6	Jackson	1 642	17 997	1 922	11.0	80.0	17.2	1.1	0.5	2.4	5.6	15.1	8.3	13.6	13.3	15.3
05 069	38220	3	Jefferson	2 255	77 435	699	34.3	42.2	55.5	0.7	0.9	1.6	6.4	17.4	11.1	12.4	12.0	14.7
05 071	...	6	Johnson	1 709	25 540	1 583	14.9	84.9	1.6	1.7	1.0	12.1	7.0	17.7	10.3	12.3	12.2	14.1
05 073	...	8	Lafayette	1 368	7 645	2 633	5.6	60.6	37.5	0.5	0.4	1.7	5.9	17.3	7.9	10.2	10.7	15.3
05 075	...	6	Lawrence	1 522	17 415	1 955	11.4	97.8	1.0	1.1	0.3	0.9	5.8	17.1	9.4	10.6	12.0	14.3
05 077	...	6	Lee	1 561	10 424	2 412	6.7	42.3	55.8	0.9	0.5	1.6	5.7	15.0	8.8	14.1	13.6	14.0
05 079	38220	3	Lincoln	1 454	14 134	2 164	9.7	66.5	30.1	0.7	0.3	3.2	5.0	14.5	10.5	15.7	15.1	15.5
05 081	...	6	Little River	1 379	13 171	2 238	9.6	76.3	19.8	2.5	0.5	2.7	6.0	17.8	7.6	11.0	12.3	14.3
05 083	...	6	Logan	1 834	22 353	1 717	12.2	93.7	1.7	2.0	1.9	2.3	6.0	18.6	7.6	10.2	12.2	15.1
05 085	30780	2	Lonoke	1 996	68 356	774	34.2	89.3	6.4	1.1	1.3	3.3	7.0	20.5	8.1	13.9	14.3	14.3
05 087	22220	2	Madison	2 161	15 717	2 068	7.3	93.3	0.3	2.1	0.7	4.8	6.2	18.0	7.5	11.1	12.6	15.3
05 089	...	9	Marion	1 546	16 653	2 005	10.8	97.2	0.3	1.7	0.5	1.7	4.6	13.3	6.3	7.7	10.6	15.9
05 091	45500	3	Miller	1 620	43 462	1 097	26.8	71.9	25.1	1.2	0.7	2.4	7.2	17.1	9.2	13.7	12.9	13.9
05 093	14180	4	Mississippi	2 332	46 480	1 035	19.9	61.5	34.6	0.6	0.6	3.6	7.6	20.6	9.0	12.8	12.0	14.1
05 095	...	7	Monroe	1 572	8 149	2 597	5.2	56.7	41.3	0.9	0.5	1.6	6.0	16.6	7.8	9.6	11.0	15.3
05 097	...	8	Montgomery	2 020	9 487	2 481	4.7	94.7	0.3	2.5	0.6	3.8	5.3	15.7	6.7	8.4	11.1	15.3
05 099	26260	7	Nevada	1 600	8 997	2 526	5.6	66.2	31.3	0.7	0.5	2.4	6.6	17.0	7.9	11.1	11.7	14.2
05 101	25460	9	Newton	2 126	8 330	2 586	3.9	96.9	0.2	2.9	0.5	1.7	5.2	15.7	6.7	10.2	10.7	14.9
05 103	15780	7	Ouachita	1 898	26 120	1 558	13.8	57.5	41.0	0.8	0.6	1.6	6.9	16.6	7.9	10.7	11.1	15.5
05 105	30780	2	Perry	1 428	10 445	2 408	7.3	95.0	2.1	1.4	0.4	2.4	5.8	17.2	7.9	10.3	13.2	15.4
05 107	25760	7	Phillips	1 802	21 757	1 746	12.1	35.3	63.3	0.5	0.5	1.3	7.6	20.5	9.0	11.1	10.3	14.2
05 109	...	9	Pike	1 556	11 291	2 345	7.3	89.6	3.2	1.4	0.7	6.4	6.5	18.2	7.9	10.8	12.7	14.4
05 111	27860	3	Poinsett	1 964	24 583	1 621	12.5	90.1	7.7	0.7	0.3	2.2	6.5	17.7	8.6	11.3	12.8	14.3
05 113	...	7	Polk	2 221	20 662	1 811	9.3	91.8	0.4	3.4	0.6	5.8	6.1	17.7	6.9	10.2	11.4	14.0
05 115	40780	5	Pope	2 104	61 754	841	29.4	88.7	3.3	1.7	1.3	6.7	6.7	16.4	14.6	12.2	12.1	13.5
05 117	...	8	Prairie	1 678	8 715	2 552	5.2	86.5	12.5	0.7	0.1	0.9	5.2	16.3	7.0	9.7	12.4	15.2
05 119	30780	2	Pulaski	1 968	382 748	172	194.5	56.7	35.7	0.9	2.4	5.8	7.0	17.1	9.3	15.2	13.1	14.2
05 121	...	7	Randolph	1 689	17 969	1 923	10.6	97.0	1.0	1.2	0.4	1.6	6.1	17.2	8.1	10.7	12.1	14.1
05 123	22620	6	St. Francis	1 644	28 258	1 486	17.2	43.2	52.2	0.8	0.7	4.1	6.7	16.9	8.5	14.8	13.6	15.0
05 125	30780	2	Saline	1 874	107 118	553	57.2	90.1	5.0	1.0	1.2	3.8	6.6	17.8	7.2	13.1	13.8	14.3
05 127	...	6	Scott	2 311	11 233	2 348	4.9	87.4	0.7	3.3	3.7	7.0	6.5	19.1	8.4	10.2	12.0	14.3
05 129	...	9	Searcy	1 725	8 195	2 596	4.8	97.2	0.2	2.9	0.3	1.5	5.0	15.4	6.5	9.7	10.9	15.6
05 131	22900	2	Sebastian	1 378	125 744	484	91.3	75.4	7.2	3.2	4.6	12.3	7.2	18.1	9.7	12.9	12.9	14.4
05 133	...	7	Sevier	1 464	17 058	1 980	11.7	62.7	4.6	3.2	0.5	30.6	8.9	20.7	9.2	12.8	13.0	12.4
05 135	...	7	Sharp	1 565	17 264	1 966	11.0	96.4	0.8	2.1	0.4	1.7	5.4	16.2	6.5	8.8	10.6	13.6
05 137	...	9	Stone	1 571	12 394	2 282	7.9	97.5	0.2	1.9	0.6	1.3	5.6	15.0	6.2	9.5	9.9	15.3
05 139	20980	5	Union	2 692	41 639	1 139	15.5	62.7	33.4	0.8	0.6	3.5	6.6	17.5	7.8	11.9	12.2	15.0
05 141	...	8	Van Buren	1 834	17 295	1 963	9.4	95.8	0.7	2.0	0.4	2.7	5.1	15.4	6.7	9.5	10.9	15.3
05 143	22220	2	Washington	2 440	203 065	303	83.2	76.1	3.5	2.2	4.7	15.5	7.5	17.9	15.0	15.9	12.6	12.0
05 145	42620	4	White	2 681	77 076	706	28.7	91.1	4.6	1.2	0.8	3.7	6.6	17.3	12.8	12.1	12.4	13.7
05 147	...	9	Woodruff	1 520	7 260	2 662	4.8	70.6	28.4	0.8	0.4	1.2	6.0	17.1	7.1	10.3	11.5	14.4
05 149	40780	6	Yell	2 409	22 185	1 728	9.2	77.7	1.6	1.1	1.6	19.1	7.2	19.1	8.5	11.7	12.5	13.9

1. CBSA = Core Based Statistical Area. See Appendix A for explanation. See Appendix B for list of metropolitan areas with component counties.   2. County type code from the Economic Research Service of USDA Rural-Urban Continuum Codes. See Appendix A for definition.   3. Dry land or land partially or temporarily covered by water.   4. May be of any race.

Table B. States and Counties — **Population and Households**

STATE County	55 to 64 years (16)	65 to 74 years (17)	75 years and over (18)	Percent female (19)	Total persons 1990 (20)	Total persons 2000 (21)	Percent change 1990–2000 (22)	Percent change 2000–2010 (23)	Births (24)	Deaths (25)	Net migration (26)	Number (27)	Percent change, 2000–2010 (28)	Persons per household (29)	Female family householder[1] (30)	One person (31)
ARKANSAS—Cont'd																
Cleveland	13.3	9.5	6.8	50.7	7 781	8 571	10.2	1.4	1 004	826	-284	3 416	4.4	2.53	11.7	23.7
Columbia	11.6	8.3	7.7	52.3	25 691	25 603	-0.3	-4.1	2 891	2 693	-1 853	9 759	-2.2	2.38	16.3	30.2
Conway	12.7	9.1	7.7	50.5	19 151	20 336	6.2	4.6	2 411	2 173	347	8 463	6.2	2.48	11.8	26.4
Craighead	10.5	6.7	5.5	51.2	68 956	82 148	19.1	17.4	11 867	7 434	9 316	37 291	15.4	2.49	13.9	26.5
Crawford	12.0	7.9	5.3	50.7	42 493	53 247	25.3	16.3	7 239	4 760	4 703	23 447	19.0	2.62	11.8	23.0
Crittenden	10.9	6.3	4.4	52.5	49 939	50 866	1.9	0.1	8 269	4 607	-1 701	19 026	3.0	2.64	23.6	25.9
Cross	12.9	8.7	6.8	51.8	19 225	19 526	1.6	-8.5	2 301	1 965	-1 219	7 002	-5.3	2.52	15.1	26.2
Dallas	14.5	9.4	8.7	51.0	9 614	9 210	-4.2	-11.9	940	1 129	-996	3 280	-6.8	2.35	15.7	30.0
Desha	13.1	8.6	6.5	53.1	16 798	15 341	-8.7	-15.2	1 977	1 567	-2 355	5 321	-10.1	2.43	21.5	29.6
Drew	11.8	8.1	6.7	51.5	17 369	18 723	7.8	-1.1	2 253	1 656	-610	7 360	0.3	2.41	15.6	27.8
Faulkner	9.8	5.7	4.3	50.9	60 006	86 014	43.3	31.6	12 873	6 402	16 857	42 614	33.7	2.56	11.6	23.4
Franklin	12.8	9.1	7.5	50.5	14 897	17 771	19.3	2.0	2 071	1 849	134	7 037	2.3	2.51	10.8	24.9
Fulton	15.9	13.0	9.4	51.0	10 037	11 642	16.0	5.2	1 031	1 464	436	5 196	8.0	2.32	9.3	28.1
Garland	14.3	11.3	9.6	51.5	73 397	88 068	20.0	9.0	10 300	11 827	12 329	40 994	8.4	2.29	11.9	29.6
Grant	12.4	8.8	5.7	50.3	13 948	16 464	18.0	8.4	1 799	1 516	1 123	6 933	11.1	2.55	10.2	22.4
Greene	11.9	8.2	6.2	51.0	31 804	37 331	17.4	12.7	5 101	3 750	2 566	16 425	11.4	2.53	12.4	24.2
Hempstead	12.1	8.5	6.5	51.8	21 621	23 587	9.1	-4.1	3 086	2 229	-1 308	8 839	-1.3	2.52	16.9	27.2
Hot Spring	13.7	8.8	6.9	48.9	26 115	30 353	16.2	8.5	3 423	3 147	1 359	12 664	5.5	2.48	12.3	25.2
Howard	12.0	8.3	7.0	51.7	13 569	14 300	5.4	-3.6	1 946	1 546	-324	5 365	-1.9	2.54	15.0	26.3
Independence	12.5	8.6	7.1	51.0	31 192	34 233	9.7	7.1	4 344	3 542	-166	14 391	6.9	2.48	10.8	25.9
Izard	15.2	13.4	10.2	48.5	11 364	13 249	16.6	3.4	1 235	1 729	347	5 731	5.3	2.26	8.4	29.7
Jackson	12.8	9.0	6.9	50.4	18 944	18 418	-2.8	-2.3	2 028	2 173	-1 540	6 724	-3.5	2.38	14.4	30.1
Jefferson	12.7	7.3	6.0	50.8	85 487	84 278	-1.4	-8.1	10 682	8 058	-7 793	28 873	-5.5	2.49	21.5	28.4
Johnson	11.6	8.2	6.5	50.4	18 221	22 781	25.0	12.1	3 339	2 277	1 290	9 812	12.3	2.55	11.3	25.3
Lafayette	13.3	11.5	7.9	51.7	9 643	8 559	-11.2	-10.7	871	913	-973	3 150	-8.3	2.39	17.0	29.2
Lawrence	12.5	10.0	8.2	51.4	17 455	17 774	1.8	-2.0	1 973	2 005	-759	6 938	-2.4	2.42	11.0	27.7
Lee	13.4	8.3	7.2	44.3	13 053	12 580	-3.6	-17.1	1 260	1 201	-2 298	3 624	-13.3	2.39	22.0	31.2
Lincoln	11.3	6.7	5.8	39.9	13 690	14 492	5.9	-2.5	1 305	1 143	-1 028	4 207	-1.4	2.54	15.3	25.2
Little River	14.0	10.2	7.0	51.4	13 966	13 628	-2.4	-3.4	1 376	1 321	-672	5 411	-1.0	2.41	14.3	27.9
Logan	13.1	9.7	7.5	49.9	20 557	22 486	9.4	-0.6	2 571	2 505	-83	8 704	0.1	2.50	11.5	25.9
Lonoke	10.6	6.7	4.5	50.8	39 268	52 828	34.5	29.4	7 773	4 534	10 974	25 295	31.3	2.68	12.3	20.5
Madison	13.7	9.1	6.5	49.9	11 618	14 243	22.6	10.3	1 719	1 407	1 370	6 174	13.0	2.53	8.2	24.2
Marion	17.8	14.9	8.9	50.2	12 001	16 140	34.5	3.2	1 280	1 747	1 018	7 411	9.4	2.23	8.2	28.3
Miller	12.3	7.8	5.9	50.8	38 467	40 443	5.1	7.5	5 485	3 260	1 096	17 219	10.1	2.44	17.0	27.4
Mississippi	11.5	6.8	5.4	51.6	57 525	51 979	-9.6	-10.6	7 358	5 152	-7 472	17 741	-8.3	2.58	19.6	27.1
Monroe	14.8	10.1	8.8	52.2	11 333	10 254	-9.5	-20.5	1 076	1 184	-1 951	3 481	-15.2	2.32	16.8	32.8
Montgomery	16.0	12.9	9.5	50.1	7 841	9 245	17.9	2.6	879	1 051	-5	4 000	5.7	2.34	7.7	27.4
Nevada	13.7	9.7	7.9	51.0	10 101	9 955	-1.4	-9.6	1 199	1 059	-889	3 697	-5.0	2.39	16.0	28.5
Newton	16.2	12.2	8.2	49.5	7 666	8 608	12.3	-3.2	794	823	-339	3 571	2.0	2.32	7.9	29.1
Ouachita	14.2	8.9	8.2	52.6	30 574	28 790	-5.8	-9.3	3 305	3 494	-3 030	11 003	-5.3	2.34	18.0	30.5
Perry	13.4	9.6	7.2	50.4	7 969	10 209	28.1	2.3	1 126	1 078	117	4 170	4.5	2.47	10.7	25.8
Phillips	12.4	8.4	6.5	53.4	28 830	26 445	-8.3	-17.7	3 776	2 894	-6 400	8 491	-12.6	2.53	25.8	30.1
Pike	12.3	10.1	7.3	50.4	10 086	11 303	12.1	-0.1	1 082	1 262	-434	4 457	-1.0	2.49	10.5	26.1
Poinsett	13.0	9.3	6.6	51.4	24 664	25 614	3.9	-4.0	3 294	2 931	-1 161	9 754	-2.7	2.49	15.1	26.6
Polk	14.3	11.3	8.2	50.8	17 347	20 229	16.6	2.1	2 434	2 331	58	8 450	5.0	2.43	9.6	26.7
Pope	11.3	7.4	5.7	50.4	45 883	54 469	18.7	13.4	7 217	4 790	3 222	23 353	12.8	2.50	11.5	24.9
Prairie	14.3	11.3	8.4	50.5	9 518	9 539	0.2	-8.6	909	1 058	-761	3 685	-5.4	2.33	11.0	27.7
Pulaski	12.2	6.5	5.5	51.9	349 569	361 474	3.4	5.9	53 952	30 608	-2 881	158 772	7.3	2.36	16.6	31.8
Randolph	13.0	9.9	8.8	51.0	16 558	18 195	9.9	-1.2	1 963	1 967	-127	7 299	0.5	2.41	10.7	27.7
St. Francis	12.3	7.0	5.2	45.5	28 497	29 329	2.9	-3.7	3 933	2 848	-4 030	9 616	-4.3	2.51	23.4	28.7
Saline	12.4	9.0	5.9	50.6	64 183	83 529	30.1	28.2	9 848	7 150	13 636	41 441	30.4	2.55	10.8	21.9
Scott	12.4	10.3	6.8	49.6	10 205	10 996	7.8	2.2	1 318	1 155	24	4 368	1.0	2.55	10.0	26.7
Searcy	16.1	11.5	9.8	50.2	7 841	8 261	5.4	-0.8	792	941	-124	3 574	1.4	2.27	7.4	30.3
Sebastian	11.6	7.2	5.9	51.0	99 590	115 071	15.5	9.3	17 276	10 385	2 407	49 599	9.5	2.49	13.0	28.4
Sevier	10.5	7.0	5.6	50.4	13 637	15 757	15.5	8.3	2 759	1 424	-116	5 975	4.7	2.83	12.2	23.2
Sharp	15.0	13.2	10.7	50.6	14 109	17 119	21.3	0.8	1 690	2 323	1 267	7 360	2.1	2.32	9.8	28.2
Stone	15.8	13.5	9.3	50.6	9 775	11 499	17.6	7.8	1 138	1 321	727	5 325	11.7	2.30	7.2	28.9
Union	13.3	8.2	7.4	51.3	46 719	45 629	-2.3	-8.7	5 466	5 255	-2 796	16 951	-5.8	2.43	15.9	28.5
Van Buren	14.5	12.1	10.6	50.1	14 008	16 192	15.6	6.8	1 625	2 074	761	7 433	8.9	2.30	8.5	29.6
Washington	9.5	5.4	4.3	50.0	113 409	157 715	39.1	28.8	28 464	11 379	24 775	76 389	27.0	2.56	10.6	27.5
White	11.0	7.9	6.2	51.0	54 676	67 165	22.8	14.8	8 932	6 654	7 289	29 342	16.7	2.52	11.2	24.7
Woodruff	15.4	9.7	8.1	52.5	9 520	8 741	-8.2	-16.9	900	1 154	-1 101	3 134	-11.2	2.28	15.7	32.7
Yell	11.7	8.5	6.9	50.1	17 759	21 139	19.0	4.9	3 172	2 244	560	8 219	3.7	2.66	11.4	24.3

1. No spouse present.

Table B. States and Counties — Population, Vital Statistics, Medicare, and Crime

STATE County	Daytime population, 2006–2010 — Persons in group quarters, 2010	Daytime population — Number	Daytime population — Employment/residence ratio	Births, average 2006–2008 — Total	Births — Rate[1]	Deaths, average 2006–2008 — Number	Deaths — Rate[1]	Persons under 65 with no health insurance, 2009 — Number	Persons under 65 — Percent	Medicare, 2011 — Eligible for Medicare	Enrolled in Medicare Advantage	Enrolled in a Medicare prescription drug plan	Serious crimes known to police,[2] 2010 Total — Number	Total — Rate[3]
	32	33	34	35	36	37	38	39	40	41	42	43	44	45
ARKANSAS—Cont'd														
Cleveland	52	6 762	0.4	D	D	94	10.7	1 409	20.2	1 776	134	1 057	120	1 381
Columbia	1 315	25 154	1.0	D	D	295	12.1	3 638	18.8	5 040	408	3 192	728	2 965
Conway	286	19 985	0.9	D	D	257	12.4	3 257	19.0	4 755	763	2 352	860	4 043
Craighead	3 579	98 294	1.1	1 394	15.4	808	8.9	16 167	19.9	15 618	1 641	8 895	3 821	4 015
Crawford	540	54 135	0.8	817	13.8	529	8.9	10 042	19.6	11 528	3 750	4 229	1 755	2 833
Crittenden	701	46 711	0.8	920	17.6	489	9.4	8 780	19.3	7 816	941	4 421	4 267	8 383
Cross	225	16 408	0.8	D	D	204	10.8	3 124	20.3	3 673	494	2 056	428	2 395
Dallas	405	8 890	1.2	D	D	119	14.5	1 334	20.7	1 800	242	1 013	171	2 107
Desha	56	13 420	1.0	D	D	167	12.1	2 359	21.6	2 702	189	1 688	NA	NA
Drew	785	17 581	0.9	259	13.9	178	9.6	3 294	21.2	3 338	190	2 059	586	3 166
Faulkner	4 055	99 209	0.8	1 507	14.5	742	7.1	15 687	16.4	15 376	976	7 856	3 991	3 524
Franklin	447	16 815	0.8	D	D	214	11.7	2 979	20.4	3 838	849	1 645	361	1 992
Fulton	165	11 174	0.7	D	D	174	14.9	1 876	21.4	3 232	510	1 584	160	1 307
Garland	2 166	95 625	1.0	1 183	12.3	1 264	13.1	15 944	21.2	25 009	3 500	11 083	6 163	6 418
Grant	143	13 768	0.5	D	D	170	9.7	2 635	17.6	3 265	324	1 562	388	2 173
Greene	602	41 221	1.0	564	14.0	423	10.5	6 443	18.8	8 393	1 271	4 396	2 071	4 920
Hempstead	301	22 749	1.0	D	D	256	11.0	4 377	22.8	4 109	553	2 301	823	3 640
Hot Spring	1 571	28 387	0.7	D	D	364	11.4	5 044	19.3	6 758	742	3 201	NA	NA
Howard	181	15 348	1.3	D	D	169	11.9	2 698	22.8	2 859	344	1 618	355	2 805
Independence	900	37 190	1.1	491	14.1	390	11.2	5 493	19.3	7 724	569	4 558	1 633	4 456
Izard	769	12 630	0.8	D	D	192	14.6	2 341	23.5	3 700	525	1 771	152	1 110
Jackson	2 000	18 134	1.0	D	D	222	12.9	3 051	22.0	3 833	266	2 438	763	4 436
Jefferson	5 530	81 319	1.1	1 126	14.2	838	10.6	12 708	19.5	14 074	2 443	6 826	5 113	6 688
Johnson	558	25 148	1.0	D	D	260	10.5	4 401	21.1	5 008	1 011	2 267	645	2 525
Lafayette	111	6 792	0.6	D	D	111	14.3	1 407	23.8	1 749	138	1 071	97	1 269
Lawrence	595	16 217	0.8	D	D	203	12.1	2 791	20.9	4 203	466	2 421	280	1 608
Lee	1 756	10 425	0.9	D	D	127	11.5	2 226	26.6	1 998	484	1 109	270	2 590
Lincoln	3 445	13 128	0.8	D	D	127	9.2	2 768	24.7	2 224	275	1 220	98	737
Little River	123	12 473	0.9	D	D	160	12.4	1 900	18.2	2 851	243	1 595	246	1 868
Logan	580	20 562	0.8	D	D	272	12.0	3 528	19.5	5 156	1 035	2 390	562	2 514
Lonoke	572	50 559	0.5	922	14.4	530	8.3	9 797	16.9	10 271	1 191	4 705	2 357	3 597
Madison	79	13 018	0.6	D	D	158	10.2	2 952	23.2	3 255	678	1 404	136	1 017
Marion	141	15 530	0.8	D	D	206	12.3	2 438	19.8	4 847	927	1 977	246	1 477
Miller	1 480	38 824	0.8	666	15.5	425	9.9	7 320	20.3	7 575	1 068	3 802	2 452	5 642
Mississippi	767	49 586	1.2	769	16.4	537	11.4	7 699	19.5	8 272	1 157	4 615	2 449	5 505
Monroe	84	7 967	0.8	D	D	127	14.4	1 426	22.4	2 002	224	1 257	157	1 927
Montgomery	121	8 537	0.7	D	D	120	13.2	1 719	24.9	2 392	199	1 156	23	242
Nevada	157	8 094	0.7	D	D	113	12.1	1 529	20.7	2 067	323	1 067	208	2 312
Newton	51	6 704	0.5	D	D	93	11.1	1 523	23.5	2 210	364	1 030	111	1 333
Ouachita	352	25 201	0.9	370	14.1	378	14.4	3 583	17.6	5 861	1 019	2 963	779	2 982
Perry	152	8 248	0.5	D	D	121	11.6	1 665	19.8	2 539	356	1 200	106	1 015
Phillips	246	21 686	0.9	388	17.4	310	13.9	3 243	19.1	4 269	743	2 489	NA	NA
Pike	196	10 608	0.8	D	D	124	11.5	2 030	24.3	2 484	222	1 381	112	992
Poinsett	341	22 067	0.7	374	15.0	323	13.0	4 329	21.3	5 473	654	3 464	844	3 433
Polk	155	20 269	1.0	D	D	274	13.5	3 612	22.5	5 026	354	2 505	552	2 672
Pope	3 330	62 163	1.1	845	14.4	522	8.9	10 512	20.8	11 093	1 764	5 159	1 929	3 124
Prairie	131	7 674	0.7	D	D	117	13.3	1 474	21.9	1 971	163	1 223	119	1 470
Pulaski	7 938	444 943	1.4	6 016	16.1	3 338	9.0	51 687	16.0	62 947	8 148	27 511	28 972	7 569
Randolph	349	16 645	0.8	D	D	213	11.7	3 064	21.4	4 380	848	2 176	129	718
St. Francis	4 085	29 042	1.1	D	D	285	10.6	4 706	21.5	4 638	897	2 479	1 744	6 172
Saline	1 425	79 683	0.5	1 167	12.1	845	8.8	12 945	15.3	19 836	2 259	8 295	NA	NA
Scott	79	10 631	0.9	D	D	126	11.1	2 153	23.8	2 556	535	1 218	272	2 515
Searcy	71	7 381	0.7	D	D	101	12.6	1 424	23.5	2 325	376	1 203	38	464
Sebastian	2 235	141 882	1.3	1 906	15.7	1 143	9.4	22 933	21.8	22 026	5 487	9 111	6 115	4 891
Sevier	173	16 592	1.0	328	20.0	170	10.4	3 933	27.2	2 686	200	1 535	402	2 357
Sharp	189	16 599	0.8	D	D	252	14.1	2 941	22.3	5 665	897	2 749	NA	NA
Stone	151	12 154	1.0	D	D	147	12.3	2 202	24.3	3 648	458	1 756	199	1 606
Union	524	44 574	1.1	621	14.3	577	13.3	6 293	18.1	9 279	748	5 386	1 699	4 272
Van Buren	189	16 682	0.9	D	D	221	13.3	2 529	20.8	4 881	770	2 277	369	2 134
Washington	7 563	201 692	1.0	3 383	17.6	1 258	6.5	37 001	21.0	25 886	4 487	10 818	6 650	3 275
White	3 252	71 970	0.9	1 043	14.2	724	9.8	13 102	20.6	14 450	1 790	7 251	2 782	3 638
Woodruff	106	6 966	0.8	D	D	121	15.8	1 316	22.3	1 734	142	1 101	NA	NA
Yell	323	19 568	0.7	360	16.5	235	10.8	4 675	25.0	4 218	532	2 151	317	1 429

1. Per 1,000 estimated resident population.   2. Data for serious crimes have not been adjusted for underreporting; this may affect comparability between geographic areas and over time.   3. Per 100,000 population estimated by the FBI.

STATE County	Serious crimes known to police,[1] 2010 (cont.) Rate[2]		Education School enrollment and attainment, 2006–2010 Enrollment[3]		Attainment[4] (percent)		Local government expenditures,[5] 2008–2009		Money income, 2006–2010	Households Median income			Income and poverty, 2010	Percent below poverty level		
	Violent	Property	Total	Per- cent private	High school grad- uate or less	Bach- elor's degree or more	Total current expendi- tures (mil dol)	Current expendi- tures per student (dollars)	Per capita income[6] (dollars)	Dollars	Percent change, 2000 to 2006–2010 (constant 2010 dollars)	Percent with income of $200,000 or more	Median house- hold income (dollars)	All per- sons	Children under 18 years	Children 5 to 17 years in families
	46	47	48	49	50	51	52	53	54	55	56	57	58	59	60	61
ARKANSAS—Cont'd																
Cleveland	69	1 312	2 071	1.5	60.0	14.0	12.2	8 498	19 481	36 957	-9.9	1.1	40 402	15.5	22.7	20.6
Columbia	395	2 570	7 579	7.9	53.8	20.8	30.4	8 228	20 110	35 148	0.4	1.7	34 538	25.6	35.5	31.9
Conway	306	3 737	5 033	7.8	61.3	13.8	36.9	10 996	19 909	32 700	-17.3	1.8	37 475	18.2	26.4	24.0
Craighead	377	3 638	25 962	8.2	51.7	23.1	125.9	7 707	21 728	39 233	-4.4	2.4	37 780	21.1	27.3	24.6
Crawford	375	2 459	15 188	8.3	57.5	13.0	90.5	7 940	18 715	40 197	-3.4	0.6	39 672	15.8	24.2	22.3
Crittenden	1 845	6 538	15 449	6.7	57.5	14.2	95.3	8 565	18 241	33 716	-11.6	1.2	33 938	30.3	45.9	41.6
Cross	386	2 009	4 716	4.2	66.6	12.6	29.3	7 949	18 248	37 021	-0.4	0.5	35 080	19.6	29.5	26.5
Dallas	333	1 774	2 075	13.9	65.7	12.4	8.5	8 104	16 457	29 602	-12.1	0.9	31 350	19.4	33.5	31.0
Desha	NA	NA	3 494	7.0	65.7	13.6	26.3	9 221	17 582	29 051	-4.9	0.2	29 586	28.0	41.7	40.3
Drew	465	2 701	5 274	7.6	56.5	19.4	37.2	11 651	18 903	32 558	-10.2	0.3	34 952	20.9	30.0	28.3
Faulkner	299	3 225	33 545	15.7	44.6	26.4	136.8	7 851	22 811	45 287	-6.4	2.1	46 199	14.8	17.4	15.5
Franklin	221	1 771	4 187	4.1	59.9	11.6	27.1	9 682	18 010	32 064	-17.9	1.5	38 514	17.2	26.6	23.9
Fulton	237	1 070	2 626	8.6	63.1	9.7	13.2	8 389	17 067	30 598	-5.3	0.5	30 191	18.9	31.2	29.5
Garland	595	5 824	20 104	11.4	47.1	20.2	118.9	8 375	22 786	36 844	-8.3	2.2	36 690	21.7	38.0	33.4
Grant	190	1 983	4 042	8.7	61.0	14.7	33.7	6 984	22 229	51 589	9.6	1.4	45 347	11.9	18.5	16.9
Greene	223	4 697	10 524	8.6	63.0	12.0	56.3	7 853	18 225	38 209	-2.1	0.3	36 391	17.0	25.7	23.3
Hempstead	500	3 140	5 740	8.6	57.1	14.7	37.5	9 790	17 177	35 708	-1.5	0.6	31 786	21.8	33.2	31.9
Hot Spring	NA	NA	7 814	6.0	57.5	12.5	44.1	8 119	18 248	37 150	-7.0	0.7	37 243	15.3	26.4	25.3
Howard	284	2 521	3 371	3.1	65.1	12.4	24.9	7 930	18 216	34 554	-4.9	0.9	32 543	21.0	30.5	28.1
Independence	578	3 878	8 572	11.1	56.3	14.7	53.2	8 830	19 912	34 625	-14.3	1.3	35 888	18.2	27.2	24.3
Izard	73	1 037	2 528	7.2	58.2	12.3	19.4	10 477	17 737	31 673	-2.6	0.6	29 883	18.6	32.2	29.2
Jackson	628	3 808	4 003	6.1	71.8	7.0	26.9	8 675	14 874	27 615	-13.1	0.5	30 405	25.8	35.9	33.3
Jefferson	1 008	5 679	21 679	6.3	56.2	16.5	120.4	9 110	18 681	35 998	-9.3	0.8	35 092	22.7	34.1	30.6
Johnson	261	2 275	5 411	14.7	64.1	14.8	34.8	8 081	16 937	30 592	-13.4	1.2	32 326	21.9	31.3	26.8
Lafayette	170	1 099	1 921	6.1	65.3	13.3	11.0	9 485	17 699	27 515	-12.5	2.3	29 084	23.2	35.8	32.8
Lawrence	138	1 470	4 634	22.7	67.5	9.2	31.4	9 510	15 168	30 288	-11.9	0.2	32 869	22.4	35.2	32.5
Lee	365	2 226	2 322	15.2	70.3	8.5	14.5	11 491	13 103	30 494	17.4	0.0	25 944	37.5	46.1	43.2
Lincoln	53	684	3 289	4.6	71.4	8.6	13.7	7 843	15 024	35 737	-4.7	1.9	35 070	28.5	32.7	30.0
Little River	137	1 731	3 021	6.1	58.5	11.9	18.5	8 941	18 808	33 416	-10.3	0.3	37 260	17.8	26.0	23.0
Logan	273	2 241	5 420	9.7	65.3	11.7	34.0	8 327	19 121	37 551	4.6	1.5	36 015	17.1	28.2	25.9
Lonoke	414	3 183	17 814	9.7	50.2	16.6	98.5	7 438	22 473	50 757	-0.6	1.1	50 021	12.4	17.5	15.6
Madison	352	666	3 566	7.1	64.9	13.4	19.5	8 054	18 611	36 502	3.3	1.6	34 547	19.3	29.7	26.9
Marion	174	1 303	3 229	9.3	53.0	14.8	16.1	8 798	19 532	34 109	0.7	2.4	31 438	19.5	36.4	33.6
Miller	716	4 926	10 299	8.9	58.4	12.7	60.0	9 113	19 654	40 307	2.8	1.0	37 806	20.1	30.9	28.8
Mississippi	845	4 660	12 435	2.8	62.1	11.0	79.7	8 746	17 736	33 407	-4.0	1.3	32 169	25.0	36.2	33.9
Monroe	123	1 804	2 070	7.3	65.4	12.3	14.1	10 073	17 084	29 964	4.6	1.4	28 637	26.6	36.9	34.1
Montgomery	32	211	2 050	2.0	58.7	10.1	9.8	8 489	20 010	35 705	-0.8	2.2	32 032	22.2	35.2	32.1
Nevada	256	2 066	2 277	5.6	59.6	10.7	12.7	8 681	21 020	38 375	12.4	1.2	32 896	25.2	38.4	35.6
Newton	84	1 248	1 632	10.7	62.4	12.2	13.4	10 014	15 904	45 121	-12.5	0.2	30 965	23.3	37.1	34.2
Ouachita	375	2 607	6 279	7.3	59.0	13.2	47.2	10 126	18 244	31 259	-15.9	0.5	35 971	20.3	31.2	29.7
Perry	230	785	2 265	4.0	65.1	10.5	13.6	7 901	19 844	43 635	10.9	0.5	39 054	16.8	26.6	24.5
Phillips	NA	NA	6 424	10.8	57.8	12.1	53.2	11 826	15 244	27 361	-2.8	0.8	26 933	36.0	51.8	50.0
Pike	142	850	2 681	7.2	61.8	12.4	10.9	8 185	18 122	32 806	-6.5	1.2	31 569	21.2	32.3	29.1
Poinsett	476	2 957	5 485	5.3	71.0	8.8	44.2	9 566	16 625	32 267	-4.1	0.5	32 130	27.1	39.0	35.7
Polk	305	2 367	4 774	7.6	57.4	10.0	33.5	8 698	16 913	32 525	2.0	0.3	29 938	22.8	36.0	32.8
Pope	243	2 881	16 800	6.8	53.2	20.1	83.3	8 364	19 693	39 841	-1.9	1.4	39 040	17.7	24.8	21.9
Prairie	74	1 396	1 762	3.6	71.6	11.5	10.7	8 172	18 134	35 346	-6.9	0.5	36 898	18.3	29.2	26.5
Pulaski	1 102	6 467	99 618	18.6	39.6	30.7	572.1	10 097	27 158	45 121	-6.5	3.5	44 733	17.1	25.3	23.0
Randolph	22	696	4 472	12.6	61.8	11.1	23.0	8 264	18 751	30 222	-13.5	2.2	33 401	19.2	31.4	29.5
St. Francis	481	5 690	6 394	9.7	63.9	10.5	47.4	9 861	13 693	27 019	-18.4	1.1	29 825	32.7	47.0	43.6
Saline	NA	NA	24 687	11.9	48.1	22.6	104.2	7 198	24 584	51 502	-4.5	1.6	53 430	9.6	14.5	12.5
Scott	139	2 376	2 693	2.8	69.6	9.0	22.9	8 316	17 668	36 417	8.9	0.5	29 863	22.5	36.2	31.7
Searcy	98	366	1 640	15.1	66.8	9.2	17.5	10 530	15 298	28 811	6.3	0.0	27 896	23.7	42.0	39.4
Sebastian	617	4 274	30 321	9.7	51.1	17.9	163.9	8 400	22 284	39 482	-8.0	2.3	38 724	20.5	30.9	27.4
Sevier	252	2 105	3 887	4.7	65.3	9.3	35.1	10 237	15 590	34 383	-9.9	0.8	35 279	23.5	31.8	28.6
Sharp	NA	NA	3 628	6.6	61.6	12.5	22.8	7 669	16 570	31 135	-2.2	0.5	28 933	25.1	39.3	35.3
Stone	258	1 347	2 351	10.4	63.6	10.4	13.7	7 981	16 090	30 380	8.0	0.3	29 182	22.4	37.5	35.1
Union	510	3 761	9 937	8.0	55.3	16.1	66.0	8 312	20 447	36 464	-3.4	1.7	36 934	21.6	33.0	29.7
Van Buren	330	1 804	3 055	7.1	55.9	13.2	19.4	8 104	17 999	31 960	-6.5	1.1	32 142	20.9	33.2	29.4
Washington	413	2 862	58 925	9.4	47.0	27.4	294.2	8 442	22 421	42 303	-3.7	2.5	39 692	19.6	24.7	22.3
White	286	3 351	21 414	26.4	56.4	17.3	103.4	8 200	20 900	39 178	-3.9	1.8	39 974	16.7	22.3	20.9
Woodruff	NA	NA	1 677	1.2	71.8	9.0	6.6	11 602	18 344	27 186	-2.9	1.2	27 003	25.9	43.4	38.3
Yell	194	1 235	5 339	3.4	71.0	10.3	37.6	8 487	16 345	36 606	0.0	0.2	33 522	20.3	30.2	28.1

1. Data for serious crimes have not been adjusted for underreporting; this may affect comparability between geographic areas and over time. 2. Per 100,000 population estimated by the FBI. 3. All persons 3 years old and over enrolled in nursery school through college. 4. Persons 25 years old and over. 5. Elementary and secondary education expenditures. 6. Based on population estimated by the American Community Survey, 2006–2010.

Table B. States and Counties — **Personal Income**

STATE County	Total (mil dol)	Percent change, 2008–2009	Per capita[1] Dollars	Per capita[1] Rank	Wages and salaries[2] (mil dol)	Proprietors' income (mil dol)	Dividends, interest, and rent (mil dol)	Transfer payments (mil dol) Total	Government payments to individuals Total	Social Security	Medical payments	Income mainte-nance	Unemploy-ment insurance
	62	63	64	65	66	67	68	69	70	71	72	73	74
ARKANSAS—Cont'd													
Cleveland	268	-3.3	31 826	1 573	39	12	32	69	68	23	26	7	3
Columbia	777	-2.0	32 554	1 410	403	65	157	216	212	71	85	27	10
Conway	659	0.0	31 679	1 604	302	52	94	194	190	64	85	17	7
Craighead	2 919	0.7	30 580	1 845	1 874	271	463	688	670	215	284	72	31
Crawford	1 541	-1.4	25 638	2 786	792	71	199	436	425	155	171	42	21
Crittenden	1 545	-0.9	29 140	2 159	718	137	161	410	400	107	168	76	23
Cross	517	-1.3	27 858	2 425	210	61	73	152	148	49	63	19	7
Dallas	251	2.8	31 369	1 675	131	18	33	88	87	25	45	9	4
Desha	394	-2.1	29 517	2 089	203	53	55	127	125	34	58	19	6
Drew	536	-0.4	28 761	2 244	253	47	87	158	154	46	63	18	9
Faulkner	3 426	2.1	31 320	1 691	1 858	132	463	685	665	210	284	55	36
Franklin	532	-1.5	29 515	2 091	207	31	86	139	136	52	55	13	6
Fulton	306	1.2	26 440	2 654	73	35	46	113	111	41	47	9	4
Garland	3 320	0.4	33 715	1 216	1 469	143	954	962	944	354	422	66	30
Grant	551	0.5	31 005	1 755	151	25	69	116	113	45	40	9	6
Greene	1 149	0.6	28 018	2 395	598	113	184	321	314	114	126	33	18
Hempstead	594	1.4	25 787	2 762	348	28	84	186	182	56	79	24	8
Hot Spring	855	1.4	26 898	2 585	332	32	131	265	260	95	110	22	12
Howard	375	-4.8	26 250	2 679	278	43	50	116	113	38	52	11	5
Independence	1 076	-0.3	31 078	1 735	637	81	207	297	290	103	123	25	15
Izard	343	1.1	26 331	2 664	112	29	59	132	130	53	50	9	5
Jackson	526	-1.4	31 591	1 626	230	65	74	176	173	51	88	17	8
Jefferson	2 364	1.7	30 034	1 970	1 675	122	338	670	655	181	244	101	34
Johnson	606	-2.4	24 247	2 940	328	36	86	180	175	66	68	19	8
Lafayette	191	-6.2	25 410	2 817	55	19	29	70	68	23	29	9	3
Lawrence	451	-1.5	26 715	2 609	156	56	67	166	163	53	78	14	6
Lee	273	-8.2	26 490	2 645	92	55	37	90	88	24	39	17	4
Lincoln	342	1.0	25 258	2 834	130	28	31	92	89	29	37	12	5
Little River	377	0.3	29 081	2 176	301	16	46	106	104	40	42	10	4
Logan	573	-2.1	25 645	2 783	221	35	90	199	195	67	88	17	9
Lonoke	2 098	2.9	31 458	1 650	529	119	253	442	430	141	178	37	19
Madison	358	-4.0	22 545	3 048	119	32	63	104	102	41	40	9	5
Marion	418	-0.7	25 199	2 845	131	21	87	153	150	66	52	11	7
Miller	1 369	-0.7	31 460	1 648	574	147	199	334	326	101	152	40	11
Mississippi	1 354	-5.0	29 051	2 184	895	113	166	402	394	112	160	64	29
Monroe	232	-1.1	28 380	2 330	83	13	37	86	85	25	40	11	4
Montgomery	218	-0.8	24 234	2 941	62	20	37	79	78	31	30	6	3
Nevada	255	-1.3	27 835	2 429	91	13	39	92	91	26	46	10	4
Newton	199	0.6	24 353	2 930	41	16	29	69	67	28	25	7	3
Ouachita	782	4.2	30 753	1 810	324	24	121	243	239	83	100	29	9
Perry	313	1.3	30 316	1 903	59	24	35	85	83	33	32	8	3
Phillips	632	-3.0	30 212	1 932	260	66	75	243	239	55	112	47	10
Pike	308	-2.7	28 997	2 199	105	32	60	88	86	33	37	7	4
Poinsett	708	-1.5	28 692	2 262	219	100	83	226	222	72	100	30	9
Polk	476	-1.3	23 519	3 002	222	37	81	175	171	66	65	15	6
Pope	1 692	-1.4	28 098	2 385	1 158	54	283	422	412	151	158	37	21
Prairie	273	-1.8	31 765	1 586	62	49	35	78	76	26	35	7	4
Pulaski	16 885	0.2	44 213	231	14 865	1 596	3 455	2 916	2 847	873	1 202	317	122
Randolph	467	0.2	26 015	2 727	175	48	69	167	163	58	66	14	7
St. Francis	711	2.3	27 077	2 553	364	81	80	236	231	61	101	41	11
Saline	3 758	4.4	37 784	666	885	101	516	657	639	285	224	46	31
Scott	249	-1.9	22 424	3 053	104	17	36	91	89	33	37	10	3
Searcy	196	1.7	24 614	2 906	57	17	32	79	78	28	34	7	3
Sebastian	4 517	-2.8	36 547	808	3 252	565	935	899	877	306	357	90	44
Sevier	398	-2.7	23 545	3 001	212	24	49	114	110	35	46	13	4
Sharp	416	1.5	23 577	2 996	133	15	77	187	184	75	74	15	5
Stone	302	-1.7	25 205	2 844	97	18	76	117	115	44	47	9	4
Union	1 708	-2.1	39 929	453	1 021	134	428	387	379	136	153	45	19
Van Buren	448	0.5	27 281	2 521	141	20	88	160	157	66	58	12	7
Washington	6 380	-0.1	31 872	1 559	4 595	312	1 277	1 005	968	351	367	98	58
White	2 138	2.2	28 001	2 398	1 169	133	333	562	548	194	222	48	27
Woodruff	203	-5.9	27 649	2 458	79	14	32	81	80	22	40	9	3
Yell	552	-4.8	24 556	2 910	244	23	78	165	161	56	71	15	8

1. Based on the resident population estimated as of July 1 of the year shown. 2. Includes supplements to wages and salaries.

Table B. States and Counties — Earnings, Social Security, and Housing

STATE County	Earnings, 2009									Social Security beneficiaries, December 2010		Supplemental Security Income recipients, December 2010	Housing units, 2010	
	Total (mil dol)	Farm	Goods-related[1]		Service-related and health					Number	Rate[2]		Total	Percent change, 2000–2010
			Total	Manufacturing	Information and professional and technical services	Retail trade	Finance, insurance, and real estate	Health care and social services	Government					
	75	76	77	78	79	80	81	82	83	84	85	86	87	88
ARKANSAS—Cont'd														
Cleveland	51	9.6	9.1	6.7	D	D	D	6.0	33.5	1 990	229	269	4 064	6.0
Columbia	468	1.5	45.6	31.0	2.6	5.9	4.3	6.5	19.7	5 930	242	1 328	11 596	0.3
Conway	353	5.6	30.4	17.8	1.8	7.9	2.7	D	18.5	5 450	256	972	9 720	7.7
Craighead	2 145	3.1	18.8	13.9	4.7	7.8	4.9	21.2	18.3	18 415	191	3 708	40 515	15.3
Crawford	863	0.2	28.3	17.6	D	6.8	3.4	7.4	14.4	13 870	224	1 997	26 115	22.5
Crittenden	855	6.3	D	12.5	2.6	7.0	4.0	10.8	18.3	9 540	187	3 638	21 489	4.8
Cross	271	16.0	12.7	9.6	2.3	8.6	6.0	D	21.8	4 290	240	945	7 853	-2.2
Dallas	150	0.6	34.0	28.6	D	6.9	2.6	D	12.6	2 180	269	448	4 305	-2.2
Desha	257	19.0	24.0	21.5	2.3	5.9	3.6	D	18.8	3 125	240	810	6 261	-6.0
Drew	300	5.3	11.8	9.9	2.5	9.3	4.5	D	32.4	3 940	213	756	8 408	1.5
Faulkner	1 990	0.1	24.1	12.3	14.5	7.8	3.8	11.4	19.5	17 685	156	2 479	46 612	34.9
Franklin	238	6.1	28.2	17.3	1.9	6.1	3.8	D	27.6	4 545	251	604	8 021	4.5
Fulton	108	6.5	D	2.7	D	5.0	6.5	11.9	28.0	3 715	303	482	6 778	13.5
Garland	1 611	0.4	12.8	6.1	6.2	10.7	4.8	23.4	17.4	28 235	294	3 451	50 548	12.4
Grant	176	0.6	27.6	20.0	3.8	7.5	3.4	D	25.4	3 715	208	397	7 758	11.5
Greene	712	9.9	35.4	32.4	D	6.9	3.0	10.0	15.1	10 090	240	1 756	17 892	10.7
Hempstead	376	1.8	D	20.6	D	6.6	3.1	D	24.1	4 850	215	996	10 419	2.5
Hot Spring	364	1.2	25.6	19.5	D	7.2	3.8	11.7	24.7	8 025	244	1 116	14 332	7.1
Howard	321	7.1	46.9	44.3	1.5	5.5	2.2	D	12.9	3 335	242	495	6 238	-0.9
Independence	718	3.2	27.0	23.3	D	6.8	3.5	18.8	15.5	9 055	247	1 315	16 187	9.1
Izard	142	5.3	D	8.5	D	8.3	5.8	13.1	33.7	4 415	322	534	7 232	9.7
Jackson	295	14.6	D	17.2	2.4	7.2	3.2	D	23.0	4 465	248	928	7 601	-4.5
Jefferson	1 796	2.8	D	15.9	D	5.8	3.6	D	31.7	15 750	203	4 319	33 006	-3.9
Johnson	364	2.5	31.2	27.4	2.0	6.9	3.0	D	17.4	5 920	232	952	11 311	14.0
Lafayette	74	17.7	14.4	2.9	D	5.4	D	D	24.3	1 990	260	516	4 353	-4.5
Lawrence	212	14.8	11.4	8.1	D	7.4	3.7	D	28.1	4 900	281	881	8 000	-1.1
Lee	147	25.4	D	D	D	4.6	2.7	D	28.9	2 350	225	903	4 356	-8.6
Lincoln	158	17.2	D	9.1	D	2.7	2.4	7.4	40.6	2 545	180	531	4 860	-1.9
Little River	316	0.6	D	39.4	D	3.8	1.6	2.1	14.5	3 335	253	436	6 460	0.4
Logan	257	6.0	25.4	18.3	3.5	8.1	5.6	11.4	27.0	6 120	274	889	10 108	1.7
Lonoke	648	8.3	D	11.3	4.0	9.3	6.2	8.8	21.8	11 985	175	1 700	27 239	31.3
Madison	151	7.8	D	24.2	3.7	8.1	3.5	D	22.9	3 835	244	434	7 481	14.4
Marion	152	2.0	D	29.5	D	8.2	6.4	7.7	20.9	5 585	335	575	9 354	13.6
Miller	721	0.7	28.0	21.3	D	7.7	3.1	5.4	16.3	8 590	198	1 864	19 281	8.8
Mississippi	1 008	5.1	41.9	38.7	6.4	5.1	3.3	D	14.8	10 090	217	3 520	20 459	-8.3
Monroe	97	6.5	6.4	4.5	3.1	10.1	5.3	D	25.2	2 280	280	623	4 455	-12.1
Montgomery	82	7.7	D	4.5	D	7.2	5.0	D	31.9	2 745	289	326	6 763	14.2
Nevada	104	5.5	D	D	D	6.3	2.7	12.2	22.8	2 365	263	532	4 563	-4.0
Newton	56	8.2	D	4.9	D	5.1	D	D	40.2	2 610	313	444	4 664	8.1
Ouachita	348	0.3	18.6	13.3	D	9.2	4.1	D	28.7	6 835	262	1 465	13 121	-2.4
Perry	83	15.0	D	2.5	D	4.6	3.0	D	26.8	2 930	281	409	4 907	4.4
Phillips	325	16.5	6.3	4.1	2.9	7.7	4.5	13.5	25.8	5 145	236	2 181	10 126	-6.7
Pike	136	16.1	D	9.1	1.6	7.5	6.2	D	25.3	2 910	258	359	5 580	0.8
Poinsett	319	22.8	D	9.4	2.2	5.8	4.6	6.3	20.1	6 490	264	1 641	10 923	-1.2
Polk	260	1.0	D	18.0	D	9.7	4.3	14.8	22.7	5 885	285	723	10 002	8.3
Pope	1 212	0.4	24.3	16.9	3.0	7.4	3.4	D	18.1	13 000	211	1 944	25 551	11.8
Prairie	111	40.5	D	D	2.6	4.4	3.8	5.5	17.3	2 260	259	389	4 503	-6.0
Pulaski	16 462	0.0	10.2	5.6	15.6	5.1	7.7	12.0	25.4	70 555	184	15 095	175 555	8.9
Randolph	223	13.2	D	11.7	D	7.2	2.9	15.8	24.9	5 110	284	737	8 513	3.0
St. Francis	445	9.6	8.2	6.0	D	7.3	4.1	14.4	33.4	5 500	195	2 082	10 903	-3.0
Saline	987	0.0	D	7.6	3.7	13.7	3.9	12.3	25.7	22 575	211	2 274	44 811	32.5
Scott	120	3.4	D	30.7	D	6.9	2.7	D	22.1	3 070	273	422	5 193	5.5
Searcy	74	2.0	D	8.5	D	7.4	5.1	13.6	30.9	2 775	339	485	4 900	14.2
Sebastian	3 816	0.0	30.2	19.1	9.1	6.4	4.1	15.9	12.2	25 725	205	4 035	54 651	10.8
Sevier	236	3.4	D	D	2.4	6.7	3.2	D	23.2	3 115	183	438	6 887	7.0
Sharp	148	5.9	D	D	5.8	10.2	6.8	D	26.4	6 635	384	854	9 822	5.1
Stone	114	0.9	D	10.8	D	15.9	4.4	D	25.6	4 200	339	641	6 712	17.4
Union	1 155	0.2	38.1	18.5	2.5	5.6	3.4	10.4	11.7	11 000	264	2 066	19 653	-4.9
Van Buren	161	2.6	12.3	1.6	D	10.5	5.2	D	21.5	5 685	329	625	10 345	12.9
Washington	4 907	0.5	18.0	12.6	5.6	6.5	4.7	13.1	21.7	29 760	147	3 806	87 808	36.4
White	1 302	2.1	27.8	10.1	3.7	8.1	3.9	D	14.0	16 890	219	2 292	32 488	17.7
Woodruff	93	14.5	14.3	12.0	D	4.8	4.1	9.1	27.0	2 045	282	466	3 893	-4.7
Yell	267	1.4	D	28.2	D	5.1	3.4	D	26.9	5 045	227	799	9 752	6.5

1. Includes mining, construction, and manufacturing.   2. Per 1,000 resident population enumerated in the 2010 census.

Table B. States and Counties — Housing, Labor Force, and Employment

	Housing units, 2006–2010								Civilian labor force, 2010				Civilian employment,[5] 2006–2010		
	Occupied units										Unemployment			Percent	
			Owner-occupied			Renter-occupied									
STATE County				Median owner cost as a percent of income				Sub-stand-ard units[3] (percent)							Con-struction, produc-tion, and mainte-nance occu-pations
	Total	Percent	Median value[1]	With a mort-gage	Without a mort-gage	Median rent[2]	Median rent as a per-cent of income		Total	Percent change, 2009–2010	Total	Rate[4]	Total	Manage-ment, business, science and arts	
	89	90	91	92	93	94	95	96	97	98	99	100	101	102	103
ARKANSAS—Cont'd															
Cleveland	3 309	78.0	66 900	21.2	10.7	576	32.1	2.7	3 990	-4.5	330	8.3	3 502	30.1	34.3
Columbia	9 895	69.8	76 700	19.6	11.3	517	29.7	2.6	10 476	-2.5	980	9.4	10 040	32.1	26.8
Conway	8 235	75.8	82 100	21.0	12.6	498	29.5	2.4	10 301	-1.0	834	8.1	8 453	26.3	37.6
Craighead	35 864	61.2	107 300	19.4	10.1	600	29.9	2.7	47 226	0.5	3 391	7.2	43 209	32.6	25.3
Crawford	22 882	73.0	98 800	19.9	11.0	593	28.2	2.4	27 744	-1.4	2 177	7.8	27 246	27.1	34.3
Crittenden	18 717	58.2	101 100	23.4	12.9	644	33.1	4.1	21 656	-2.8	2 406	11.1	20 406	27.2	29.8
Cross	6 638	70.7	75 800	21.5	13.4	550	28.0	1.8	8 265	-4.7	706	8.5	7 950	24.4	31.8
Dallas	3 160	70.5	59 200	20.0	11.6	428	33.1	3.0	3 842	-3.4	420	10.9	3 080	24.6	44.9
Desha	5 302	59.1	55 500	19.4	12.7	522	30.9	1.8	5 501	-2.4	637	11.6	5 312	30.8	34.7
Drew	7 383	67.5	73 100	19.4	12.8	598	30.4	2.8	8 177	-1.2	886	10.8	7 879	29.7	33.0
Faulkner	40 928	66.4	127 500	19.6	10.2	662	29.6	2.5	56 642	0.5	4 219	7.4	52 443	34.0	25.8
Franklin	6 741	78.8	81 400	21.8	10.0	535	27.1	1.9	8 104	-3.1	570	7.0	7 293	24.1	35.4
Fulton	4 823	79.6	78 200	21.3	10.8	458	33.1	0.9	5 187	-1.8	385	7.4	4 634	30.1	31.7
Garland	40 146	70.1	126 900	24.0	11.0	662	30.5	2.5	42 151	-1.4	3 405	8.1	39 086	30.1	23.8
Grant	6 761	80.3	96 600	18.7	10.0	654	23.2	2.6	8 491	-2.2	588	6.9	8 418	25.8	34.9
Greene	16 154	65.7	88 900	20.3	10.7	568	28.0	2.9	18 468	-3.6	1 815	9.8	17 874	23.8	38.3
Hempstead	8 715	68.4	68 100	19.1	11.4	546	31.7	3.8	10 687	-0.9	978	9.2	9 869	23.6	38.5
Hot Spring	11 942	76.0	77 400	20.8	11.6	539	23.6	2.4	15 388	0.1	1 179	7.7	13 200	26.0	32.8
Howard	5 158	69.6	71 800	21.1	11.7	519	30.4	5.9	6 009	-4.2	501	8.3	6 369	23.7	44.5
Independence	14 799	72.8	82 400	19.9	10.1	558	30.6	2.6	17 084	0.8	1 401	8.2	15 752	25.9	34.6
Izard	5 762	79.7	76 900	22.1	12.2	472	32.6	2.6	5 270	-2.5	495	9.4	4 806	24.8	29.9
Jackson	6 391	69.8	60 100	20.4	13.1	482	30.7	1.5	7 525	-2.1	795	10.6	6 059	22.7	35.0
Jefferson	28 048	64.4	76 200	19.6	12.6	622	32.7	2.9	35 120	-1.6	3 465	9.9	30 712	27.6	27.5
Johnson	9 350	68.8	83 400	19.8	10.0	538	32.1	3.1	11 364	-2.8	848	7.5	10 385	18.7	45.7
Lafayette	2 775	79.2	49 600	23.6	11.9	455	29.8	0.6	2 941	-2.8	287	9.8	2 742	26.5	30.1
Lawrence	6 768	67.2	57 600	20.8	10.7	460	28.5	1.4	7 280	-1.4	676	9.3	6 608	24.6	35.0
Lee	3 516	66.3	54 200	24.1	13.0	510	28.6	1.6	3 457	-3.5	328	9.5	3 315	20.1	25.0
Lincoln	4 057	69.3	71 900	18.4	12.9	475	32.5	3.4	4 896	-2.8	468	9.6	4 617	24.7	35.5
Little River	5 405	71.2	73 100	18.6	11.2	475	25.4	1.9	6 208	-10.6	466	7.5	5 751	22.0	40.2
Logan	8 323	79.1	78 200	17.5	10.3	509	30.2	2.1	9 888	-3.7	806	8.2	9 044	27.9	36.7
Lonoke	24 136	74.4	117 900	20.3	10.0	666	28.3	3.1	32 469	0.1	2 184	6.7	30 225	30.1	27.5
Madison	5 762	75.3	97 700	19.9	10.0	500	26.1	3.7	7 427	-3.3	498	6.7	6 705	24.9	38.4
Marion	7 239	81.6	91 600	22.9	10.7	525	29.1	3.4	6 463	-3.9	656	10.2	6 419	26.2	32.2
Miller	16 577	66.3	86 400	19.4	10.4	621	28.9	2.3	19 871	-2.2	1 145	5.8	18 229	24.0	32.6
Mississippi	17 202	59.9	68 700	18.5	12.1	554	29.4	4.0	21 380	-0.3	2 448	11.4	18 036	24.3	39.4
Monroe	3 453	61.4	55 600	20.8	13.6	478	32.3	2.6	3 615	-3.2	302	8.4	3 132	25.7	33.3
Montgomery	3 753	82.8	75 300	21.5	11.1	525	34.8	2.6	4 147	-1.1	325	7.8	3 258	29.3	37.1
Nevada	3 782	71.3	62 300	21.1	10.3	561	21.4	3.7	4 197	-2.3	385	9.2	3 827	25.8	41.4
Newton	3 555	79.7	77 700	22.8	10.0	380	27.9	4.0	3 454	-1.6	254	7.4	3 638	22.3	40.5
Ouachita	10 714	69.8	61 900	20.2	12.1	468	27.6	2.1	12 119	-0.8	1 033	8.5	10 123	27.8	33.3
Perry	3 952	81.7	80 200	18.8	11.2	664	26.8	3.0	4 736	-1.9	389	8.2	4 217	22.4	44.0
Phillips	8 325	54.7	60 200	23.2	11.5	537	36.7	5.4	8 862	-1.1	846	9.5	7 766	30.0	24.1
Pike	4 137	74.8	79 400	16.7	12.8	507	28.6	2.7	4 907	-4.1	417	8.5	4 511	23.7	43.8
Poinsett	9 545	66.4	64 900	20.9	12.0	466	29.2	2.8	10 646	-2.3	961	9.0	9 786	21.3	37.8
Polk	8 156	77.4	79 300	23.0	10.2	512	27.9	1.4	8 518	-4.1	643	7.5	8 334	23.8	38.5
Pope	22 535	69.7	99 500	20.1	10.0	590	27.9	2.5	29 712	-1.5	2 278	7.7	27 880	26.1	29.8
Prairie	3 563	72.6	74 200	19.9	12.0	456	27.3	2.0	4 131	-5.0	352	8.5	3 642	29.0	31.8
Pulaski	155 160	60.4	134 300	21.3	11.3	729	30.6	2.4	190 334	-0.8	13 262	7.0	181 831	38.4	18.0
Randolph	7 255	76.6	68 500	20.5	12.6	487	28.2	2.1	7 642	-1.0	723	9.5	6 594	29.4	34.1
St. Francis	9 086	58.7	66 100	23.3	14.7	544	34.3	2.6	10 157	-2.7	1 033	10.2	8 934	26.9	31.2
Saline	39 103	77.7	130 100	19.8	10.3	715	28.8	2.3	49 637	-1.0	3 371	6.8	48 314	32.2	24.0
Scott	4 341	75.1	69 500	21.8	11.1	517	26.4	6.5	4 748	-4.3	324	6.8	4 354	21.1	50.3
Searcy	3 457	75.0	69 500	23.5	10.3	460	41.5	4.6	3 548	-1.9	299	8.4	3 333	21.6	34.0
Sebastian	48 572	63.4	108 000	19.9	10.5	577	28.7	3.6	59 889	-1.4	4 355	7.3	55 548	27.3	31.2
Sevier	5 849	74.2	73 100	24.0	10.4	503	27.9	8.3	7 645	0.2	470	6.1	6 677	20.5	49.8
Sharp	7 189	80.8	78 000	22.4	11.7	546	35.7	3.8	6 274	-0.2	600	9.6	5 800	28.4	34.4
Stone	4 966	80.4	89 000	26.0	11.4	483	27.6	2.9	4 562	-1.1	402	8.8	4 767	27.0	33.1
Union	16 787	71.2	71 200	18.9	12.4	562	30.2	3.1	18 059	-7.6	1 906	10.6	16 638	28.3	32.1
Van Buren	7 065	78.5	79 200	23.2	10.8	512	29.6	3.9	7 006	-0.1	684	9.8	6 045	21.2	40.0
Washington	75 564	56.3	154 900	22.4	10.3	665	29.0	5.4	99 939	-2.6	6 261	6.3	97 300	33.1	24.9
White	29 049	69.0	92 700	19.9	11.3	572	27.0	3.3	34 400	0.1	2 882	8.4	32 648	27.0	29.2
Woodruff	3 323	61.5	55 100	19.8	11.0	352	26.7	2.8	3 393	1.1	368	10.8	3 100	24.0	34.4
Yell	7 912	70.1	75 300	20.3	10.6	538	26.4	8.4	10 509	-1.3	708	6.7	9 335	17.0	43.6

1. Specified owner-occupied units.   2. Specified renter-occupied units. A value of 10.0 represents 10 percent or less.   3. Overcrowded or lacking complete plumbing facilities.   4. Percent of civilian labor force.   5. Persons 16 years old and over.

Table B. States and Counties — Nonfarm Employment and Agriculture

	Private nonfarm establishments, employment and payroll, 2009								Agriculture, 2007			
		Employment					Annual payroll		Farms			
											Percent with:	
STATE County	Number of establishments	Total	Health care and social assistance	Manufacturing	Retail trade	Finance and insurance	Professional, scientific, and technical services	Total (mil dol)	Average per employee (dollars)	Number	Fewer than 50 acres	500 acres or more	Farm operators whose principal occupation is farming (percent)
	104	105	106	107	108	109	110	111	112	113	114	115	116
ARKANSAS—Cont'd													
Cleveland	88	430	D	63	79	D	D	10	23 798	241	44.4	6.2	61.4
Columbia	582	7 448	1 133	2 429	1 092	290	182	225	30 262	306	32.7	7.2	42.8
Conway	416	5 345	572	D	997	144	91	157	29 346	994	33.3	7.5	49.5
Craighead	2 417	36 484	7 919	5 773	6 241	1 201	974	1 079	29 581	736	42.9	25.0	47.7
Crawford	1 071	20 842	1 801	3 824	2 003	409	294	571	27 378	1 026	51.4	3.7	37.3
Crittenden	880	13 652	1 935	1 737	2 188	261	297	399	29 230	266	13.9	51.9	69.2
Cross	387	4 209	727	627	839	192	D	109	26 007	364	23.9	38.7	61.0
Dallas	213	2 980	874	D	337	61	27	79	26 638	106	28.3	8.5	32.1
Desha	338	3 565	611	D	526	D	58	111	31 096	273	22.0	49.1	69.2
Drew	409	4 482	792	797	859	170	95	112	24 885	368	29.3	15.5	40.5
Faulkner	2 309	32 292	4 594	4 036	4 921	973	783	1 063	32 928	1 341	43.0	4.8	35.3
Franklin	279	3 202	513	951	502	170	64	92	28 590	759	29.6	10.1	48.1
Fulton	179	1 405	453	115	197	81	D	32	23 010	702	24.6	13.0	40.7
Garland	2 738	31 558	6 823	2 338	6 035	976	1 162	848	26 859	439	56.9	2.1	38.3
Grant	273	2 959	D	1 189	448	90	50	82	27 747	282	50.4	3.9	43.6
Greene	789	12 565	945	4 326	1 828	646	423	317	25 246	770	37.8	17.1	45.1
Hempstead	407	6 848	1 222	2 123	952	171	83	204	29 834	894	30.4	11.3	43.6
Hot Spring	623	5 810	1 156	1 350	958	234	97	162	27 851	644	49.5	3.4	38.5
Howard	284	6 121	719	3 547	683	116	59	141	23 009	592	28.5	6.6	53.4
Independence	779	14 594	3 232	4 135	1 727	404	196	435	29 815	1 121	32.0	9.7	42.9
Izard	215	1 941	672	218	409	D	D	44	22 599	639	21.0	13.1	43.5
Jackson	335	3 602	809	D	685	97	103	111	30 708	445	24.7	33.7	58.0
Jefferson	1 479	24 421	4 935	5 655	3 657	847	1 301	796	32 582	489	36.6	26.0	50.3
Johnson	380	7 454	934	2 552	963	156	77	179	23 963	607	33.1	6.4	48.1
Lafayette	112	815	202	D	171	61	36	21	26 092	313	31.6	15.7	52.1
Lawrence	307	2 729	586	379	572	D	39	67	24 696	592	20.4	25.0	54.2
Lee	136	904	241	D	179	D	34	26	28 509	251	19.5	45.4	68.9
Lincoln	157	1 542	318	D	195	D	16	43	27 789	384	28.9	20.1	53.9
Little River	172	2 977	339	D	406	92	D	137	46 114	482	31.7	10.2	36.7
Logan	405	3 925	745	D	711	288	D	101	25 758	942	31.4	5.9	46.9
Lonoke	1 013	10 364	1 573	1 382	2 222	419	300	263	25 347	832	34.3	21.6	48.4
Madison	193	1 829	228	D	444	72	D	45	24 686	1 339	30.2	8.7	38.0
Marion	229	2 760	319	1 107	572	D	53	65	23 647	463	28.1	13.6	44.7
Miller	710	10 668	1 064	D	1 483	248	224	343	32 131	601	41.8	10.8	37.4
Mississippi	875	14 751	1 917	5 069	1 895	353	155	482	32 705	369	16.3	52.8	70.5
Monroe	195	1 677	330	104	318	76	D	37	21 893	229	18.8	48.5	65.1
Montgomery	150	973	78	D	156	D	D	24	24 638	456	29.8	6.6	42.1
Nevada	134	1 842	D	D	284	42	D	46	24 822	395	33.9	6.1	34.9
Newton	87	592	216	67	80	D	D	11	18 731	636	28.9	6.3	34.3
Ouachita	553	8 082	1 220	2 618	1 073	218	D	269	33 258	222	36.0	5.0	36.0
Perry	110	866	189	D	202	D	D	25	28 514	453	38.4	5.5	39.1
Phillips	453	4 494	1 048	356	1 137	D	102	114	25 377	307	20.8	54.1	70.0
Pike	188	1 848	D	381	274	108	D	41	22 170	425	32.5	11.5	48.5
Poinsett	363	3 473	456	725	898	157	D	89	25 741	418	20.8	50.7	68.9
Polk	505	5 271	1 026	1 268	908	171	D	122	23 197	1 007	43.2	4.4	42.7
Pope	1 509	22 228	3 027	4 567	3 377	895	513	712	32 054	1 080	41.9	5.9	40.4
Prairie	167	1 044	198	D	210	D	D	23	22 261	539	19.9	32.5	54.4
Pulaski	12 162	209 751	45 902	14 942	24 482	12 608	11 494	8 506	40 552	484	59.3	8.7	39.7
Randolph	324	3 445	802	819	649	128	D	80	23 210	766	28.5	14.8	38.0
St. Francis	486	5 665	1 283	480	1 313	222	129	151	26 742	310	26.1	32.6	58.1
Saline	1 801	18 212	3 854	1 210	3 969	634	D	495	27 173	371	53.9	4.9	38.0
Scott	159	2 103	254	D	303	D	D	52	24 922	593	30.4	5.7	58.3
Searcy	120	957	237	133	287	48	26	20	20 567	617	19.9	16.0	39.2
Sebastian	3 524	64 151	11 643	15 733	8 140	1 629	1 660	2 181	34 000	931	51.2	3.2	35.3
Sevier	267	5 173	612	D	674	148	56	123	23 851	598	39.3	6.5	43.5
Sharp	328	2 620	499	D	725	239	D	56	21 245	723	24.8	13.3	38.5
Stone	242	2 215	486	D	579	121	D	49	22 230	556	24.1	12.1	45.1
Union	1 175	18 819	2 186	4 489	2 430	541	268	705	37 462	356	45.8	2.2	44.1
Van Buren	353	3 493	722	D	617	D	69	93	26 519	566	27.0	7.8	41.3
Washington	4 845	79 069	12 622	13 034	10 931	2 631	3 183	2 668	33 739	2 915	50.4	3.7	39.0
White	1 521	22 485	3 618	2 462	3 604	633	439	656	29 190	2 199	41.7	7.4	35.8
Woodruff	137	1 240	188	D	215	43	D	34	27 498	262	18.7	43.5	66.8
Yell	322	4 401	839	D	554	166	64	112	25 358	993	37.3	7.3	49.1

Table B. States and Counties — **Agriculture**

STATE County	Land in farms — Acreage (1,000)	Percent change, 2002–2007	Acres — Average size of farm	Total irrigated (1,000)	Total cropland (1,000)	Value of land and buildings (dollars) Average per farm	Average per acre	Value of machinery and equipment, average per farm (dollars)	Value of products sold — Total (mil dol)	Average per farm (dollars)	Percent from: Crops	Live-stock and poultry products	Percent of farms with sales of: $10,000 or more	$100,000 or more	Government payments Total ($1,000)	Percent of farms
	117	118	119	120	121	122	123	124	125	126	127	128	129	130	131	132
ARKANSAS—Cont'd																
Cleveland	31	-13.9	129	D	9.3	456 860	3 542	103 715	148.1	614 358	0.2	99.8	46.9	36.1	114	10.8
Columbia	47	-14.5	154	0.1	15.1	378 703	2 463	59 218	45.1	147 521	21.6	78.4	40.2	13.1	14	2.6
Conway	187	8.1	188	11.4	88.5	477 573	2 537	68 347	133.6	134 387	8.2	91.8	42.0	16.7	950	15.3
Craighead	337	-3.7	458	244.4	301.7	1 119 008	2 444	183 029	158.9	215 945	96.5	3.5	45.4	28.9	16 297	49.3
Crawford	119	-21.2	116	2.1	51.7	377 401	3 248	64 864	58.5	57 040	18.5	81.5	28.2	5.9	171	4.1
Crittenden	314	2.6	1 179	138.1	278.8	2 534 662	2 149	311 200	99.6	374 542	99.7	0.3	71.1	47.0	9 794	79.7
Cross	283	-13.2	777	191.6	254.4	1 554 190	1 999	258 712	111.6	306 713	99.2	0.8	55.5	39.8	11 044	76.4
Dallas	20	-23.1	188	D	4.9	319 298	1 699	41 597	1.4	13 069	D	D	13.2	0.9	28	6.6
Desha	306	7.4	1 123	229.7	280.5	2 142 086	1 908	319 493	140.7	515 542	97.5	2.5	67.8	52.0	11 044	80.2
Drew	124	6.9	338	59.3	80.7	663 259	1 963	102 233	57.3	155 809	62.7	37.3	39.1	17.1	3 292	36.1
Faulkner	190	-15.6	142	4.3	71.5	431 415	3 043	52 710	19.9	14 807	29.4	70.6	25.9	2.2	1 080	11.6
Franklin	153	-13.1	201	0.8	52.8	488 050	2 424	57 037	112.2	147 812	2.9	97.1	49.0	17.1	186	7.6
Fulton	177	-29.2	252	0.0	28.9	449 098	1 779	42 612	25.8	36 709	2.5	97.5	37.6	6.3	245	15.4
Garland	39	-15.2	90	0.1	11.4	329 321	3 662	37 905	12.2	27 887	19.4	80.6	19.1	3.4	41	3.2
Grant	35	-5.4	123	0.1	11.8	352 330	2 871	59 597	19.2	68 097	5.0	95.0	29.1	6.7	17	2.5
Greene	267	1.9	347	164.6	229.3	866 235	2 496	132 788	115.8	150 355	91.4	8.6	39.0	18.3	9 479	53.9
Hempstead	211	3.4	236	1.7	66.6	494 672	2 100	79 349	167.1	186 933	3.0	97.0	47.3	18.8	943	18.7
Hot Spring	72	-2.7	112	0.4	25.4	300 367	2 682	47 624	16.2	25 111	9.3	90.7	22.8	3.0	147	6.4
Howard	111	0.9	187	0.9	34.7	489 781	2 619	75 078	184.1	310 915	1.0	99.0	63.5	36.5	98	13.3
Independence	250	-13.2	223	30.3	99.6	480 607	2 158	75 429	123.6	110 286	17.6	82.4	34.9	9.4	1 801	11.9
Izard	170	-20.9	267	0.2	38.0	485 383	1 820	51 103	40.3	63 071	2.9	97.1	39.4	5.5	396	20.3
Jackson	302	-9.0	679	178.1	266.4	1 372 634	2 022	191 313	106.9	240 120	95.7	4.3	55.3	36.6	9 169	63.4
Jefferson	303	9.8	620	200.2	259.2	1 309 975	2 114	177 731	135.9	277 980	86.5	13.5	44.8	24.9	9 774	60.1
Johnson	106	-10.2	174	0.9	40.7	444 923	2 552	62 939	134.7	221 858	2.7	97.3	41.4	15.3	176	4.9
Lafayette	98	-5.8	312	16.8	55.2	599 365	1 922	105 487	91.3	291 576	17.7	82.3	54.6	33.5	1 545	27.2
Lawrence	264	-10.8	445	131.0	200.8	962 044	2 160	148 669	108.0	182 476	77.5	22.5	57.8	25.7	6 375	43.6
Lee	302	8.6	1 205	174.5	288.4	2 420 253	2 008	409 243	128.0	509 932	98.6	1.4	69.7	43.4	9 276	72.1
Lincoln	186	-6.5	484	99.9	131.6	1 053 345	2 174	177 183	171.3	446 044	33.3	66.7	51.3	32.6	5 969	44.8
Little River	139	-5.4	289	2.7	50.9	514 254	1 780	61 524	66.5	137 996	13.1	86.9	41.1	13.5	529	16.2
Logan	160	-20.0	170	1.9	64.1	436 497	2 564	59 457	139.9	148 513	3.9	96.1	45.2	14.3	271	7.9
Lonoke	371	2.8	446	211.4	293.2	961 455	2 154	144 964	152.3	183 071	78.1	21.9	40.9	20.9	11 364	45.8
Madison	260	-11.9	194	0.6	73.1	578 016	2 982	57 534	160.1	119 587	1.7	98.3	42.2	14.4	338	12.2
Marion	130	-9.1	282	0.0	28.7	555 231	1 971	61 396	34.8	75 167	2.2	97.8	41.7	6.9	393	25.7
Miller	175	10.8	291	1.6	101.2	544 285	1 870	62 406	48.7	81 094	41.9	58.1	33.3	11.0	1 309	12.3
Mississippi	461	-1.7	1 250	269.6	451.9	2 804 745	2 243	443 313	195.6	530 072	99.7	0.3	77.5	55.0	22 535	79.7
Monroe	242	4.3	1 058	163.2	211.0	2 121 750	2 006	280 942	93.9	410 189	96.4	3.6	63.3	43.2	7 348	83.0
Montgomery	74	-5.1	162	0.9	27.1	464 258	2 872	60 654	48.2	105 809	2.3	97.7	41.0	17.5	62	4.8
Nevada	65	-20.7	165	0.0	23.8	341 772	2 070	56 264	48.5	122 759	2.6	97.4	43.3	12.7	178	15.7
Newton	113	-13.7	178	0.1	24.5	417 453	2 350	40 388	19.0	29 907	4.9	95.1	32.2	2.5	332	29.7
Ouachita	33	0.0	146	0.0	10.6	336 515	2 298	39 698	16.7	75 083	9.1	90.9	28.4	8.6	49	7.7
Perry	73	7.4	160	5.4	33.0	394 537	2 459	60 564	33.0	72 767	19.0	81.0	42.2	10.6	366	14.3
Phillips	437	32.8	1 424	245.4	424.2	2 575 578	1 808	404 817	185.1	602 891	99.7	0.3	74.3	54.1	15 803	78.5
Pike	84	23.5	197	0.6	23.7	452 519	2 301	77 947	92.9	218 585	0.8	99.2	51.1	25.2	115	13.2
Poinsett	341	-10.7	815	262.2	323.0	1 826 209	2 241	290 355	154.2	368 805	99.5	0.5	68.2	51.4	14 351	78.5
Polk	133	-8.9	132	0.6	45.0	387 972	2 930	52 564	135.5	134 587	1.2	98.8	37.4	15.3	77	3.8
Pope	154	-8.9	142	4.0	65.8	412 029	2 895	64 043	148.9	137 836	4.1	95.9	38.2	13.4	334	6.9
Prairie	332	7.8	616	176.3	234.7	1 142 050	1 855	189 385	102.1	189 402	93.8	6.2	45.6	28.6	10 866	71.2
Pulaski	95	-19.5	196	26.9	61.9	482 049	2 458	59 774	27.4	56 643	67.9	32.1	25.6	8.5	1 371	15.3
Randolph	252	2.4	329	67.3	135.0	641 603	1 948	74 749	64.2	83 876	67.3	32.7	36.2	10.6	3 220	20.8
St. Francis	255	-8.6	823	144.8	225.9	1 668 825	2 028	232 547	91.7	295 816	97.5	2.5	51.6	33.9	8 326	70.0
Saline	45	-19.6	121	0.8	15.6	375 996	3 115	58 900	5.6	15 078	50.4	49.6	21.0	2.4	31	5.4
Scott	96	-22.6	163	D	31.8	405 451	2 492	63 344	112.5	189 790	1.3	98.7	46.2	19.1	111	5.7
Searcy	195	6.6	316	0.0	38.4	565 789	1 791	45 799	12.3	19 881	5.9	94.1	35.0	4.1	392	18.6
Sebastian	104	-14.8	112	0.7	36.8	341 550	3 044	47 115	67.4	72 362	2.7	97.3	29.3	7.5	80	2.5
Sevier	117	-5.6	195	0.3	30.6	472 133	2 422	63 753	149.0	249 103	0.6	99.4	48.7	23.1	154	14.2
Sharp	184	3.4	255	0.3	36.7	473 599	1 860	48 669	56.7	78 375	1.4	98.6	33.3	10.1	146	6.5
Stone	142	-13.4	256	0.2	38.5	519 845	2 030	56 209	43.7	78 570	2.3	97.7	39.0	10.3	566	27.3
Union	38	-5.0	107	0.1	11.6	364 004	3 418	61 407	74.1	208 262	1.2	98.8	33.4	16.3	57	2.5
Van Buren	114	-13.6	202	0.5	33.9	495 478	2 454	54 719	15.5	27 388	8.2	91.8	35.3	5.1	299	15.0
Washington	327	-11.1	112	0.8	112.0	463 747	4 131	52 447	418.0	143 384	1.9	98.1	33.8	11.0	264	3.5
White	411	4.3	187	43.2	202.2	464 706	2 484	50 213	119.2	54 225	28.7	71.3	23.0	5.1	5 848	24.6
Woodruff	274	-0.4	1 047	169.5	246.6	2 110 227	2 015	271 357	91.7	349 856	97.5	2.5	61.8	42.7	6 997	83.6
Yell	175	-3.3	176	4.2	67.0	439 230	2 491	61 287	162.5	163 612	3.4	96.6	40.4	16.7	501	10.3

Table B. States and Counties — Water Use, Wholesale Trade, Retail Trade, and Real Estate

STATE County	Water use, 2005		Wholesale trade,[1] 2007				Retail trade,[2] 2007				Real estate and rental and leasing,[2] 2007			
	Total water withdrawn (mil gal/day)	Gallons withdrawn per person	Number of establishments	Number of employees	Sales (mil dol)	Annual payroll (mil dol)	Number of establishments	Number of employees	Sales (mil dol)	Annual payroll (mil dol)	Number of establishments	Number of employees	Receipts (mil dol)	Annual payroll (mil dol)
	133	134	135	136	137	138	139	140	141	142	143	144	145	146
ARKANSAS—Cont'd														
Cleveland	0.9	104	3	12	1.2	0.2	11	81	12.3	0.8	1	D	D	D
Columbia	5.9	238	22	D	D	D	116	1 100	197.9	19.3	27	139	16.9	4.2
Conway	19.4	936	20	236	124.9	5.9	90	960	270.4	20.1	9	38	11.3	1.1
Craighead	409.7	4 724	129	1 418	605.9	56.8	499	6 536	1 440.9	125.1	103	473	73.6	11.8
Crawford	8.6	148	49	D	D	D	158	1 937	452.5	39.4	60	169	24.3	5.6
Crittenden	160.5	3 093	53	663	795.8	28.3	175	2 313	750.5	44.9	37	153	20.4	4.7
Cross	644.3	33 493	17	265	174.7	9.2	73	693	185.7	15.2	22	149	13.0	3.0
Dallas	1.5	176	6	22	10.9	0.5	52	399	79.7	7.7	7	17	2.1	0.4
Desha	413.6	28 807	22	195	230.9	8.2	85	598	119.2	10.9	18	56	3.9	0.8
Drew	89.6	4 791	12	106	87.6	3.7	96	932	199.0	17.6	21	66	6.5	1.4
Faulkner	17.2	177	71	601	266.1	23.0	381	5 250	1 227.7	102.7	120	384	52.8	9.7
Franklin	3.9	215	7	25	3.1	0.4	55	483	140.2	9.1	7	19	1.1	0.3
Fulton	2.4	204	7	25	8.2	1.1	46	236	42.4	3.4	3	5	0.3	0.1
Garland	19.9	212	91	D	D	D	523	5 898	1 443.4	126.9	158	614	88.0	14.6
Grant	2.7	156	13	130	48.5	4.1	49	460	107.6	9.0	7	41	2.7	0.8
Greene	227.4	5 771	47	D	D	D	180	1 655	373.1	33.6	29	85	12.1	1.7
Hempstead	7.5	322	15	157	32.8	3.8	87	973	204.4	19.2	20	77	9.7	1.7
Hot Spring	323.2	10 337	17	154	77.0	5.7	101	941	207.4	19.2	19	122	8.2	2.9
Howard	5.6	388	12	73	45.1	3.0	63	591	160.8	12.2	12	32	3.3	0.5
Independence	104.6	3 011	29	464	175.0	14.1	167	1 664	384.2	34.4	28	98	10.9	2.3
Izard	5.0	373	4	D	D	D	51	417	104.7	7.7	8	53	3.3	0.8
Jackson	405.7	23 050	27	217	95.4	6.2	72	669	190.9	13.4	18	48	4.6	0.8
Jefferson	349.3	4 276	66	D	D	D	321	4 024	867.4	79.8	76	D	D	D
Johnson	5.3	221	9	83	44.2	2.8	81	938	196.8	16.5	19	57	8.8	1.6
Lafayette	41.2	5 134	3	D	D	D	24	194	32.9	3.1	7	11	0.8	0.1
Lawrence	248.2	14 467	15	114	58.0	3.3	75	644	163.7	14.7	10	30	2.2	0.4
Lee	272.2	23 577	11	136	84.7	4.0	20	205	35.8	3.0	8	18	2.2	0.5
Lincoln	206.4	14 472	8	D	D	D	31	248	57.5	4.1	6	D	D	D
Little River	14.4	1 089	8	32	13.5	1.0	45	335	88.2	7.1	5	12	0.8	0.1
Logan	5.9	257	6	D	D	D	78	700	178.1	13.4	13	31	2.6	0.5
Lonoke	534.3	8 808	42	320	161.6	10.8	185	2 041	407.2	40.9	49	144	13.4	2.5
Madison	2.1	142	3	D	D	D	40	446	114.7	8.2	5	6	0.3	0.1
Marion	2.0	122	4	D	D	D	41	501	87.9	9.5	14	19	2.3	0.3
Miller	125.8	2 914	42	D	D	D	142	1 474	407.7	30.7	21	66	10.5	1.5
Mississippi	279.9	5 842	51	D	D	D	191	1 911	421.9	37.1	45	180	24.3	4.1
Monroe	316.5	34 020	13	100	64.7	3.7	44	364	82.2	6.2	4	9	1.1	0.1
Montgomery	1.5	160	3	D	D	D	25	152	32.4	2.8	10	41	1.4	0.4
Nevada	2.1	219	5	D	D	D	28	295	136.8	5.1	6	14	0.9	0.2
Newton	1.4	166	2	D	D	D	16	67	13.3	1.2	3	9	0.7	0.1
Ouachita	59.5	2 197	22	D	D	D	113	1 086	185.7	18.9	22	D	D	D
Perry	14.6	1 393	3	12	1.5	0.2	22	194	32.8	3.5	6	9	0.9	0.4
Phillips	210.3	8 723	33	D	D	D	99	1 120	229.4	22.1	22	53	5.1	1.2
Pike	1.7	150	17	163	92.1	3.6	35	276	52.8	5.0	8	26	1.5	0.3
Poinsett	772.6	30 479	21	D	D	D	88	883	193.1	14.7	12	72	6.1	1.4
Polk	3.6	176	22	126	47.8	2.5	98	861	176.9	16.8	18	128	10.4	2.6
Pope	1 164.8	20 586	71	426	234.5	16.1	303	3 633	919.3	73.8	78	241	45.3	6.0
Prairie	355.8	39 039	8	59	28.4	2.0	38	201	39.5	3.0	5	9	0.9	0.4
Pulaski	84.0	229	704	13 507	13 419.0	594.4	1 771	25 621	6 163.1	566.9	644	3 614	671.4	113.1
Randolph	141.4	7 657	10	89	39.3	2.1	67	708	137.4	12.4	15	41	3.6	0.6
St. Francis	313.4	11 232	20	D	D	D	136	1 248	353.8	26.3	17	54	4.8	0.8
Saline	9.3	102	68	751	265.2	31.5	301	3 996	1 157.7	90.7	78	225	27.2	4.7
Scott	2.8	251	8	39	9.2	1.2	28	299	48.7	5.3	11		0.8	0.2
Searcy	1.0	124	3	D	D	D	33	299	59.1	5.1	6	31	0.9	0.2
Sebastian	39.4	332	198	2 474	1 313.8	95.9	604	8 058	1 825.5	167.8	170	919	158.6	26.8
Sevier	2.6	156	4	D	D	D	73	657	160.6	12.6	8	32	3.0	0.6
Sharp	5.3	304	7	D	D	D	73	648	156.0	12.1	17	35	4.4	0.7
Stone	2.4	207	8	75	32.6	1.6	62	583	108.4	13.4	10	13	1.8	0.2
Union	20.7	469	55	D	D	D	237	2 457	526.4	47.3	37	184	35.1	5.2
Van Buren	3.0	182	14	81	50.7	2.2	66	603	152.1	12.4	6	34	4.9	0.7
Washington	3.8	21	236	2 578	1 328.1	110.5	798	11 512	2 723.3	247.4	289	2 262	196.0	59.1
White	91.5	1 283	63	D	D	D	311	3 384	803.5	69.1	70	267	34.4	6.8
Woodruff	351.5	43 402	12	183	90.9	7.2	32	263	64.7	3.8	7	11	1.0	0.1
Yell	9.8	458	9	24	5.8	0.6	57	575	109.3	9.4	11	20	1.8	0.3

1. Merchant wholesalers, except manufacturers' sales branches and offices.   2. Employer establishments.

Table B. States and Counties — **Professional Services, Manufacturing, and Accommodation and Food Services**

STATE County	Professional, scientific, and technical services,[1] 2007				Manufacturing, 2007				Accommodation and food services, 2007			
	Number of establishments	Number of employees	Receipts (mil dol)	Annual payroll (mil dol)	Number of establishments	Number of employees	Receipts (mil dol)	Annual payroll (mil dol)	Number of establishments	Number of employees	Sales (mil dol)	Annual payroll (mil dol)
	147	148	149	150	151	152	153	154	155	156	157	158
ARKANSAS—Cont'd												
Cleveland	1	D	D	D	NA	NA	NA	NA	2	D	D	D
Columbia	33	149	10.4	3.9	35	2 688	1 164.3	93.4	38	590	21.8	5.5
Conway	31	94	7.4	2.5	27	1 137	432.6	43.4	36	424	16.2	3.9
Craighead	173	D	D	D	120	6 455	1 830.3	229.9	178	3 963	146.7	41.4
Crawford	90	D	D	D	62	3 576	848.0	97.1	84	1 364	53.2	15.2
Crittenden	53	D	D	D	44	1 396	701.3	55.1	82	1 626	65.1	17.6
Cross	28	74	5.2	1.8	11	664	D	17.9	24	369	12.5	3.3
Dallas	10	23	1.6	0.4	13	749	184.5	27.2	13	115	4.6	1.3
Desha	23	59	4.5	1.4	14	982	400.8	43.4	28	279	9.8	2.5
Drew	28	105	7.6	2.7	24	891	156.1	30.2	31	657	19.7	5.1
Faulkner	214	759	76.5	22.7	100	5 342	1 587.6	216.5	165	3 781	137.9	37.1
Franklin	15	D	D	D	19	954	327.7	28.9	21	262	10.4	2.7
Fulton	15	57	3.6	1.5	NA	NA	NA	NA	16	163	5.3	1.6
Garland	218	D	D	D	119	2 786	661.7	99.9	265	5 080	203.3	62.2
Grant	14	D	D	D	18	1 294	489.9	D	18	249	10.2	2.4
Greene	55	360	20.1	8.0	53	4 942	1 434.1	160.7	61	984	37.6	10.4
Hempstead	15	45	4.1	1.5	30	D	D	D	38	586	21.2	6.0
Hot Spring	22	105	7.0	2.4	33	1 749	858.5	62.4	32	456	16.8	4.4
Howard	18	62	4.1	1.2	23	3 645	1 081.1	100.3	16	307	9.2	2.5
Independence	57	343	17.6	5.6	44	4 491	920.0	147.5	59	990	34.7	9.7
Izard	5	D	D	D	NA	NA	NA	NA	13	111	3.3	1.0
Jackson	24	D	D	D	17	982	D	33.4	26	237	9.7	2.7
Jefferson	89	D	D	D	60	4 684	D	D	140	2 147	87.1	22.4
Johnson	26	99	7.6	2.5	37	2 798	546.8	71.9	35	480	20.5	5.0
Lafayette	7	32	1.4	0.3	NA	NA	NA	NA	5	50	1.5	0.4
Lawrence	13	42	2.4	0.8	NA	NA	NA	NA	19	292	9.3	2.4
Lee	11	47	4.4	1.2	NA	NA	NA	NA	7	84	2.8	0.7
Lincoln	9	D	D	D	5	D	D	D	14	D	D	D
Little River	13	70	5.4	1.6	16	1 339	D	83.8	14	166	6.1	1.5
Logan	28	66	7.5	1.9	23	1 824	692.1	51.9	27	312	10.0	2.9
Lonoke	92	D	D	D	38	1 502	D	56.4	75	1 222	46.4	12.7
Madison	13	D	D	D	21	1 082	D	31.4	13	126	3.2	1.0
Marion	13	40	2.3	0.9	20	1 756	350.1	49.7	32	237	8.6	2.1
Miller	39	187	25.6	6.7	29	2 246	712.9	129.1	66	1 188	43.7	12.7
Mississippi	49	195	17.2	5.6	51	5 962	5 010.2	319.6	81	1 091	45.8	11.8
Monroe	11	33	1.8	0.6	NA	NA	NA	NA	16	212	8.2	2.2
Montgomery	9	22	1.2	0.5	NA	NA	NA	NA	17	232	18.2	5.1
Nevada	4	19	1.6	0.5	8	D	D	D	9	95	3.2	0.9
Newton	6	D	D	D	NA	NA	NA	NA	12	46	3.3	0.7
Ouachita	27	154	17.1	5.0	32	D	D	D	26	421	14.6	3.7
Perry	8	D	D	D	NA	NA	NA	NA	5	58	1.7	0.5
Phillips	39	D	D	D	NA	NA	NA	NA	29	382	13.5	3.7
Pike	3	D	D	D	NA	NA	NA	NA	14	162	6.8	1.7
Poinsett	21	D	D	D	19	834	172.0	29.1	37	361	11.6	2.8
Polk	34	107	8.8	2.6	38	1 218	303.5	34.5	35	418	14.4	3.8
Pope	138	D	D	D	75	4 620	1 436.7	159.3	113	2 349	79.4	21.3
Prairie	7	21	2.2	0.5	NA	NA	NA	NA	14	90	4.3	0.8
Pulaski	1 549	D	D	D	382	15 031	5 969.5	665.4	858	17 807	810.0	231.0
Randolph	21	81	6.0	2.0	35	822	148.1	28.1	22	413	13.9	3.6
St. Francis	35	D	D	D	12	1 011	D	30.7	45	739	28.5	7.5
Saline	136	438	40.4	14.1	74	1 579	366.9	63.9	117	1 919	81.2	23.3
Scott	9	14	1.4	0.3	19	1 070	203.0	27.2	16	100	3.1	0.8
Searcy	8	31	1.5	0.4	NA	NA	NA	NA	11	73	2.9	0.9
Sebastian	297	D	D	D	198	19 654	5 676.5	648.5	262	5 124	207.8	56.8
Sevier	12	47	2.4	0.7	9	D	D	D	14	191	6.9	1.6
Sharp	19	41	2.5	0.7	NA	NA	NA	NA	41	387	13.0	3.3
Stone	8	D	D	D	NA	NA	NA	NA	29	316	12.1	2.9
Union	66	D	D	D	60	4 711	3 901.9	198.3	70	975	40.0	9.8
Van Buren	18	60	4.4	1.5	NA	NA	NA	NA	22	319	12.5	3.1
Washington	570	D	D	D	213	14 703	3 497.6	482.9	454	9 536	355.7	102.3
White	77	343	30.6	11.0	79	3 831	1 168.2	128.4	116	2 005	79.8	20.4
Woodruff	6	D	D	D	NA	NA	NA	NA	7	45	1.3	0.3
Yell	19	D	D	D	17	2 683	449.6	65.3	22	318	9.2	2.5

1. Establishment subject to federal tax.

Table B. States and Counties — **Health Care and Social Assistance, Other Services, and Federal Funds**

STATE County	Health care and social assistance, 2007				Other services, 2007				Federal funds and grants, 2009–2010 Expenditures (mil dol)			
										Direct payments for individuals[1]		
	Number of establishments	Number of employees	Receipts (mil dol)	Annual payroll (mil dol)	Number of establishments	Number of employees	Receipts (mil dol)	Annual payroll (mil dol)	Total	Social Security and government retirement	Medicare	Food Stamps and Supplemental Security Income
	159	160	161	162	163	164	165	166	167	168	169	170
ARKANSAS—Cont'd												
Cleveland	8	D	D	D	7	D	D	D	66.7	30.8	13.6	4.0
Columbia	63	1 190	69.7	27.3	39	169	11.7	3.3	249.8	84.8	50.5	21.0
Conway	45	556	32.1	12.5	16	98	22.6	5.1	203.4	82.3	40.2	10.5
Craighead	307	7 706	769.0	283.2	141	835	67.6	16.9	670.1	274.5	104.2	36.6
Crawford	92	1 542	100.4	46.9	67	420	33.1	9.9	383.4	197.8	71.8	23.1
Crittenden	117	1 897	166.2	65.5	71	476	34.7	9.7	487.2	132.5	80.9	46.5
Cross	47	657	43.2	16.2	22	49	4.1	1.0	189.6	58.4	32.7	11.1
Dallas	22	877	45.3	17.9	14	42	2.9	0.8	88.7	30.0	24.8	6.2
Desha	34	600	42.0	15.6	17	40	2.2	0.6	182.2	41.9	34.9	12.8
Drew	41	1 011	46.4	21.7	21	143	9.9	3.7	169.2	53.9	30.5	7.6
Faulkner	273	4 581	366.0	136.1	121	571	44.6	12.3	607.0	294.5	84.1	30.3
Franklin	28	574	26.5	12.1	15	59	5.7	1.1	147.4	65.9	30.5	6.6
Fulton	27	418	17.8	9.1	10	27	1.4	0.4	108.1	53.4	22.4	8.8
Garland	276	6 590	613.4	244.4	179	1 309	80.6	26.6	1 017.6	513.5	231.6	44.9
Grant	20	237	13.0	5.7	18	D	D	D	108.6	60.7	20.6	4.5
Greene	86	1 572	117.8	42.4	45	145	12.1	3.4	304.9	136.1	56.1	16.6
Hempstead	54	1 160	72.6	26.7	36	D	D	D	192.2	62.5	47.9	13.9
Hot Spring	44	1 070	62.1	27.3	28	135	9.1	2.4	240.9	109.2	58.7	13.4
Howard	30	589	32.7	12.6	21	88	6.8	2.0	126.0	48.9	32.2	5.5
Independence	106	2 730	243.6	90.6	54	249	16.7	5.0	322.1	129.5	59.8	17.0
Izard	22	689	41.6	12.9	16	78	3.0	1.0	139.7	61.8	29.0	6.1
Jackson	56	1 002	67.9	26.0	22	161	7.9	2.3	234.9	53.2	70.6	11.7
Jefferson	267	4 422	387.1	142.7	94	665	44.7	17.2	1 151.3	286.0	138.0	71.5
Johnson	44	977	63.5	26.3	27	161	6.2	2.9	173.2	79.2	34.6	9.5
Lafayette	9	217	7.5	4.0	5	D	D	D	91.4	25.0	22.9	7.0
Lawrence	29	608	34.6	16.2	19	58	4.6	1.0	204.4	70.0	41.6	10.9
Lee	20	243	17.6	6.9	11	18	1.5	0.4	161.7	27.4	23.6	17.0
Lincoln	14	D	D	D	15	D	D	D	111.7	33.9	19.7	8.3
Little River	17	362	19.4	9.9	13	D	D	D	114.0	51.0	24.4	6.0
Logan	44	695	40.6	15.7	27	88	7.0	1.9	198.0	85.8	37.6	11.3
Lonoke	96	1 085	74.7	29.8	59	215	16.1	4.9	424.9	232.8	68.4	16.5
Madison	16	D	D	D	11	D	D	D	113.1	63.6	17.2	4.6
Marion	18	379	12.1	5.8	14	36	2.8	0.6	146.6	77.5	25.5	6.5
Miller	69	1 367	81.7	29.5	40	274	20.9	5.8	359.2	133.8	86.5	31.0
Mississippi	124	1 699	115.5	45.6	44	208	13.8	3.9	492.0	140.3	86.4	45.3
Monroe	21	337	12.4	6.4	13	58	5.0	0.9	141.2	29.5	24.9	11.0
Montgomery	11	D	D	D	7	D	D	D	80.5	37.2	18.2	3.6
Nevada	14	441	17.8	8.4	13	D	D	D	106.9	32.4	25.8	6.1
Newton	9	218	7.0	3.1	4	D	D	D	77.6	31.1	11.3	4.5
Ouachita	61	D	D	D	34	D	D	D	306.0	105.4	64.0	20.4
Perry	16	162	9.4	3.8	6	D	D	D	84.7	42.0	17.5	3.6
Phillips	80	1 168	78.4	28.1	30	D	D	D	368.8	65.2	58.6	38.3
Pike	13	300	10.9	5.0	8	D	D	D	85.7	38.6	21.4	3.9
Poinsett	39	506	23.6	11.3	20	52	4.0	1.1	283.7	83.7	51.8	21.5
Polk	52	947	53.0	22.8	26	84	5.4	1.4	186.7	84.9	40.0	9.6
Pope	146	2 593	180.7	78.6	99	515	33.5	10.3	443.6	191.8	65.6	20.8
Prairie	18	180	10.2	4.5	11	34	1.9	0.5	107.3	31.4	21.5	3.7
Pulaski	1 462	39 444	4 389.9	1 688.5	856	5 641	690.3	155.4	6 517.7	1 391.0	574.8	186.6
Randolph	37	769	53.7	21.7	18	43	3.7	0.9	160.9	65.9	30.8	9.0
St. Francis	59	1 290	76.2	31.5	26	D	D	D	367.4	84.2	50.4	33.1
Saline	174	3 387	248.2	100.2	128	668	53.1	16.7	383.8	207.2	78.2	15.4
Scott	16	269	15.5	6.5	8	38	1.7	1.5	90.3	41.9	17.9	5.1
Searcy	13	292	11.4	5.0	2	D	D	D	97.1	37.0	16.5	5.0
Sebastian	403	11 362	1 021.0	423.8	201	981	81.7	22.2	920.3	398.3	173.5	45.8
Sevier	33	593	28.4	12.8	23	90	4.9	1.4	108.0	45.8	26.8	5.9
Sharp	40	501	19.8	8.7	26	112	7.8	1.9	179.6	92.6	42.8	7.9
Stone	20	458	25.7	11.5	13	41	3.8	1.3	119.6	55.7	23.3	5.8
Union	135	2 440	192.8	79.3	81	446	42.6	10.8	426.9	164.7	94.6	25.3
Van Buren	34	682	39.2	17.1	24	159	13.5	2.6	154.1	79.7	34.4	9.2
Washington	494	11 569	1 179.7	472.0	314	D	D	D	1 252.7	477.0	151.7	43.6
White	154	3 259	282.5	110.2	100	573	46.7	16.1	554.5	268.0	102.4	26.1
Woodruff	22	161	10.0	3.8	9	18	1.4	0.3	126.5	27.1	27.3	7.7
Yell	45	791	46.1	18.4	13	55	4.1	1.0	179.6	75.8	36.3	8.4

1. State totals may include programs not allocated by county.

Table B. States and Counties — Federal Funds, Residential Construction, and Local Government Finances

STATE County	Federal funds and grants, 2009–2010 (cont.)							Value of residential construction authorized by building permits, 2010		Local government finances, 2007				
	Expenditures (mil dol) (cont.)									General revenue				
	Procurement contract awards		Grants[1]									Taxes		
													Per capita[2] (dollars)	
	Salaries and wages	Defense	Other	Medicaid and other health-related	Nutrition and family welfare	Education	Other	New construction ($1,000)	Number of housing units	Total (mil dol)	Inter-governmental (mil dol)	Total (mil dol)	Total	Property
	171	172	173	174	175	176	177	178	179	180	181	182	183	184
ARKANSAS—Cont'd														
Cleveland	1.4	0.0	0.3	13.2	2.1	0.8	0.2	0	0	18.3	14.5	2.0	223	142
Columbia	13.3	5.9	1.1	53.7	4.9	3.2	2.4	1 815	8	71.5	34.9	12.6	519	199
Conway	12.8	0.8	1.2	38.7	4.3	1.6	1.6	749	8	56.9	35.8	10.3	499	193
Craighead	53.7	11.3	9.6	82.0	11.1	8.5	14.8	58 760	590	237.3	130.7	63.4	693	328
Crawford	13.3	8.6	7.0	40.8	10.7	4.0	3.5	10 299	104	143.7	99.5	27.0	458	171
Crittenden	31.2	2.1	3.0	133.2	12.7	6.1	8.0	7 551	42	165.4	98.5	35.3	678	186
Cross	6.7	2.4	1.1	37.4	4.8	1.5	8.2	1 263	8	47.5	33.1	9.3	497	248
Dallas	3.9	0.0	0.5	19.6	2.0	0.8	0.3	470	5	17.9	11.5	4.1	496	160
Desha	6.9	0.4	0.7	46.6	5.2	1.6	3.2	141	2	52.7	28.3	12.0	873	410
Drew	15.4	2.8	1.9	29.9	3.6	3.7	1.8	4 313	86	72.3	38.0	10.6	568	198
Faulkner	45.1	1.3	4.6	42.5	16.3	5.3	56.8	85 800	1 070	241.3	128.2	56.4	538	199
Franklin	17.8	0.9	2.4	17.2	2.7	2.0	0.6	549	8	43.2	31.0	7.9	438	221
Fulton	2.6	0.0	-1.0	17.2	1.9	0.6	0.5	0	0	21.1	13.8	2.9	249	118
Garland	42.3	22.1	39.0	77.7	12.8	8.8	7.4	4 175	38	219.2	115.5	56.9	591	174
Grant	5.7	0.0	0.8	12.0	2.2	1.4	0.2	1 409	39	46.6	34.9	7.2	410	204
Greene	15.7	0.9	1.5	50.7	5.4	2.8	2.7	12 658	168	104.5	57.6	21.4	530	218
Hempstead	9.2	6.3	1.3	34.7	5.5	3.0	1.6	609	5	61.9	41.9	10.6	458	174
Hot Spring	18.1	0.0	1.3	29.2	5.1	2.0	0.5	119	2	66.8	44.6	13.8	435	200
Howard	12.6	0.3	0.8	19.9	2.9	1.1	0.9	862	13	38.7	24.9	7.9	562	195
Independence	21.7	0.1	2.7	54.5	6.8	3.9	13.0	1 440	17	90.4	59.2	16.4	475	256
Izard	2.9	0.1	0.7	20.6	2.1	1.2	7.7	381	2	29.8	21.7	4.9	381	192
Jackson	11.1	0.0	0.8	56.1	3.8	1.6	3.7	869	6	43.1	24.8	10.7	623	284
Jefferson	93.8	256.5	42.6	169.1	19.3	14.9	18.1	8 203	124	213.4	134.7	49.3	624	263
Johnson	7.6	0.1	4.6	28.2	3.6	1.8	1.7	958	10	50.8	33.4	10.9	440	193
Lafayette	2.1	0.1	0.5	27.3	2.3	0.8	-0.1	0	0	19.5	11.7	3.7	477	206
Lawrence	15.1	0.0	1.2	42.0	3.6	1.8	3.1	657	9	59.5	33.4	8.2	486	244
Lee	3.7	4.6	1.0	60.4	5.4	1.3	1.4	2 295	27	23.4	17.0	3.4	317	143
Lincoln	2.0	0.0	0.5	35.0	2.9	0.7	1.3	155	2	20.8	15.3	3.2	237	122
Little River	3.1	2.8	0.6	19.9	2.5	0.8	0.7	195	3	40.9	17.5	7.6	595	269
Logan	19.8	0.0	2.5	33.5	3.8	1.4	1.0	1 865	14	46.0	31.0	8.4	371	190
Lonoke	23.6	0.0	2.4	38.4	7.1	7.9	3.6	27 006	312	160.4	101.3	27.0	424	178
Madison	3.6	0.1	0.7	18.2	2.1	0.9	0.9	1 540	20	27.4	18.9	4.8	310	168
Marion	2.8	5.8	2.5	14.4	2.3	1.0	6.6	1 320	11	24.7	16.2	5.7	341	180
Miller	10.5	1.9	3.1	58.9	10.8	3.2	4.6	6 027	45	104.7	63.6	23.2	545	226
Mississippi	11.0	7.0	5.2	124.2	20.1	6.1	6.2	2 653	35	158.2	79.6	29.3	628	182
Monroe	4.8	0.0	0.7	46.4	3.2	0.9	1.9	165	1	24.6	16.7	4.8	547	315
Montgomery	3.8	0.8	1.2	11.7	1.3	0.3	0.4	NA	NA	17.2	12.9	2.7	299	138
Nevada	17.0	0.0	0.7	19.0	2.3	0.7	2.3	70	1	23.6	12.9	3.7	395	166
Newton	3.5	0.0	1.1	22.1	2.5	0.5	0.8	150	1	25.9	22.2	1.8	219	170
Ouachita	17.8	7.4	2.0	63.5	6.1	1.7	11.4	1 509	6	70.5	51.7	10.7	412	180
Perry	3.7	0.0	0.8	14.1	1.5	0.6	0.1	218	4	18.6	14.1	2.8	267	141
Phillips	12.8	3.7	1.7	131.1	13.8	4.2	3.2	264	2	74.9	54.6	10.3	468	207
Pike	4.2	0.0	0.7	13.2	1.6	1.0	0.4	NA	NA	29.5	20.2	4.8	441	182
Poinsett	11.1	0.2	1.7	70.9	5.5	2.1	2.6	1 570	21	61.2	44.1	9.9	399	189
Polk	17.7	0.2	2.2	20.9	3.6	3.1	0.9	2 050	37	62.8	32.0	6.9	340	127
Pope	45.6	1.6	9.2	54.9	16.0	4.7	8.7	8 383	133	138.6	82.6	34.9	592	209
Prairie	10.3	9.7	0.5	17.5	1.8	0.8	0.5	527	3	20.5	12.8	4.2	480	276
Pulaski	1 083.4	440.8	237.5	523.9	194.3	287.6	1 455.1	172 453	1 283	1 290.8	584.0	373.8	1 000	446
Randolph	2.9	0.0	0.7	29.5	5.6	1.2	1.1	729	6	38.5	25.2	9.5	525	328
St. Francis	42.4	0.4	2.2	109.2	11.0	3.2	8.9	0	0	79.2	50.4	14.2	529	194
Saline	21.9	8.1	2.2	28.3	11.0	3.3	3.5	85 102	851	171.2	102.4	40.5	421	202
Scott	4.9	0.0	1.5	14.1	1.8	0.7	1.7	220	2	22.6	17.2	2.8	252	124
Searcy	5.4	0.0	0.5	27.9	1.7	0.6	1.1	0	0	15.8	10.7	3.3	413	304
Sebastian	123.5	12.0	20.7	73.7	14.6	8.3	13.6	71 472	462	358.6	181.3	115.4	947	305
Sevier	6.3	0.3	1.6	12.6	2.3	1.4	1.3	283	4	48.4	34.0	7.1	435	135
Sharp	4.1	0.0	1.0	24.6	3.1	1.1	1.0	275	3	41.9	27.1	6.0	338	131
Stone	3.4	0.0	1.4	26.4	1.9	0.6	0.1	1 038	9	19.6	13.8	3.9	322	139
Union	20.4	1.0	4.6	83.9	13.1	4.3	7.7	201	3	111.0	63.2	32.5	753	245
Van Buren	3.0	0.0	0.4	22.5	2.6	0.8	0.8	1 229	7	34.1	20.7	8.4	509	217
Washington	133.6	151.4	71.4	77.0	20.4	15.4	75.5	106 857	417	558.8	286.5	168.7	868	263
White	35.8	0.1	3.7	76.7	9.6	6.2	1.4	16 516	151	165.5	108.0	33.1	450	135
Woodruff	5.2	0.1	0.7	38.2	2.7	3.2	0.8	288	4	24.9	16.8	2.8	368	196
Yell	17.2	1.2	2.0	30.7	3.1	1.4	0.7	50	1	54.6	41.7	7.2	329	165

1. State totals may include programs not allocated by county.   2. Based on the resident population estimated as of July 1 of the year shown.

Table B. States and Counties — Local Government Finances, Government Employment, and Voting

STATE County	Local government finances, 2007 (cont.) Direct general expenditure Total (mil dol)	Per capita[1] (dollars)	Percent of total for: Education	Health and hospitals	Police protection	Public welfare	Highways	Debt outstanding Total (mil dol)	Per capita[1] (dollars)	Government employment, 2009 Federal civilian	Federal military	State and local	Presidential election,[2] 2008 Percent of vote cast: Democratic	Republican	All other
	185	186	187	188	189	190	191	192	193	194	195	196	197	198	199
ARKANSAS—Cont'd															
Cleveland	20.1	2 293	64.7	0.1	2.4	0.0	6.8	6.6	751	17	40	374	26.0	69.9	4.1
Columbia	67.8	2 784	45.2	24.3	3.6	0.0	4.6	54.7	2 246	50	114	1 925	37.2	61.3	1.5
Conway	58.0	2 797	69.4	0.1	5.1	0.0	5.1	41.1	1 984	74	100	1 444	38.7	57.6	3.7
Craighead	235.4	2 572	56.3	0.8	5.4	0.1	6.5	446.0	4 871	377	461	7 489	36.5	61.0	2.6
Crawford	161.6	2 738	77.2	0.1	4.1	0.0	3.8	143.9	2 437	103	288	2 165	25.5	71.5	3.0
Crittenden	167.9	3 222	60.1	0.2	6.8	0.0	3.9	290.4	5 573	109	254	2 879	56.6	41.9	1.5
Cross	43.5	2 328	67.2	0.4	4.9	0.3	5.8	20.2	1 080	63	89	1 077	36.2	61.6	2.2
Dallas	17.8	2 162	57.2	2.5	6.4	0.0	5.9	12.2	1 480	23	38	444	44.3	53.0	2.7
Desha	50.7	3 674	55.9	15.7	5.4	0.0	4.7	45.3	3 280	66	64	969	54.9	42.7	2.4
Drew	70.5	3 763	54.5	21.5	4.5	0.0	6.8	24.4	1 302	72	89	2 096	39.3	58.4	2.3
Faulkner	257.6	2 456	63.3	0.0	5.5	0.0	3.8	380.3	3 626	219	531	7 354	36.3	61.6	2.1
Franklin	40.7	2 241	74.5	2.8	3.5	0.1	5.9	37.2	2 048	151	146	888	28.9	68.1	3.0
Fulton	20.9	1 778	62.3	13.2	3.0	0.2	8.0	6.3	539	37	55	658	38.9	57.8	3.3
Garland	214.2	2 223	58.7	0.3	6.5	0.0	3.5	179.2	1 860	586	472	4 352	36.4	61.4	2.3
Grant	44.6	2 552	75.0	0.0	3.7	0.1	4.3	27.1	1 552	35	85	889	23.0	73.9	3.1
Greene	94.0	2 327	61.9	0.2	4.1	0.1	4.3	103.3	2 557	86	196	1 919	33.4	63.0	3.6
Hempstead	60.9	2 621	67.5	0.2	4.4	0.1	5.5	26.0	1 119	89	110	1 736	39.0	58.1	2.8
Hot Spring	68.8	2 159	68.6	0.1	3.8	0.0	5.6	78.3	2 459	77	152	1 875	35.9	60.3	3.8
Howard	36.7	2 622	66.3	0.1	4.1	0.0	5.6	18.5	1 320	68	68	786	36.0	61.0	3.0
Independence	92.4	2 672	60.6	0.1	3.7	0.9	4.6	129.9	3 759	160	166	2 267	30.0	67.1	2.9
Izard	32.7	2 522	78.3	0.1	2.7	0.0	4.5	27.0	2 078	39	62	1 083	34.3	61.2	4.5
Jackson	41.5	2 409	53.4	1.0	6.3	0.5	6.0	36.8	2 138	48	80	1 475	39.5	55.9	4.6
Jefferson	232.7	2 946	64.8	0.2	6.3	0.0	3.3	126.0	1 596	2 109	404	7 547	62.2	35.9	1.9
Johnson	47.6	1 922	70.8	0.0	3.3	0.0	7.4	43.7	1 765	100	120	1 088	37.1	60.2	2.7
Lafayette	15.6	2 008	73.9	0.1	5.5	0.3	4.2	4.2	546	30	36	364	39.0	58.1	2.9
Lawrence	61.3	3 637	53.6	18.8	2.8	3.7	3.9	20.2	1 198	69	81	1 276	36.7	57.6	5.7
Lee	22.6	2 083	62.6	0.5	6.1	0.0	4.7	2.7	245	43	49	832	60.1	38.6	1.2
Lincoln	19.6	1 429	68.1	0.0	3.7	0.0	8.1	16.7	1 214	28	65	1 323	38.8	57.0	4.2
Little River	43.4	3 388	48.2	15.2	3.2	4.8	5.1	90.7	7 077	51	62	913	34.0	63.0	3.0
Logan	45.2	2 000	70.6	1.6	4.3	0.1	4.4	43.8	1 940	131	107	1 415	28.9	67.7	3.4
Lonoke	162.4	2 554	72.3	0.1	3.7	0.0	4.0	114.8	1 803	118	319	2 755	25.1	72.6	2.2
Madison	27.2	1 764	76.6	0.0	6.4	0.0	8.3	18.4	1 194	51	76	629	33.9	62.8	3.4
Marion	24.9	1 498	61.0	0.1	7.3	0.1	14.2	21.1	1 270	44	79	638	33.3	63.2	3.5
Miller	109.4	2 565	61.2	0.1	8.9	0.0	3.8	120.5	2 825	64	208	2 118	32.3	65.8	1.9
Mississippi	155.1	3 325	50.1	0.2	5.1	0.4	3.2	777.7	16 667	123	224	3 127	47.6	49.8	2.6
Monroe	23.8	2 736	63.5	0.5	5.2	0.5	7.0	8.0	917	34	39	508	46.8	50.9	2.3
Montgomery	16.1	1 781	69.4	0.1	2.3	0.0	8.7	22.6	2 501	58	43	513	30.1	65.3	4.6
Nevada	25.0	2 662	48.8	19.0	4.2	0.0	8.0	22.6	2 406	32	44	522	40.6	56.7	2.7
Newton	25.1	3 006	83.3	0.0	2.3	0.0	7.6	12.2	1 467	61	39	459	29.8	65.4	4.8
Ouachita	70.8	2 715	71.5	0.0	3.8	0.0	5.0	37.0	1 421	120	122	2 068	43.6	54.5	1.9
Perry	17.9	1 721	71.3	0.5	4.3	0.1	7.5	10.8	1 039	31	49	444	31.6	64.1	4.3
Phillips	77.1	3 500	65.0	0.1	2.9	0.0	2.5	39.5	1 793	72	100	1 751	63.5	34.5	2.0
Pike	30.0	2 776	71.3	6.2	2.9	0.0	4.6	18.1	1 680	73	51	674	27.5	68.8	3.8
Poinsett	62.6	2 520	73.2	0.1	5.0	0.0	4.8	33.7	1 355	71	118	1 264	34.6	61.8	3.6
Polk	63.5	3 144	52.5	31.0	2.3	0.0	2.6	34.1	1 690	117	97	1 175	25.5	71.3	3.3
Pope	130.6	2 215	65.8	1.2	7.2	0.3	6.0	149.7	2 539	309	289	4 043	27.2	70.5	2.3
Prairie	18.5	2 121	58.9	2.2	6.0	0.0	10.8	10.6	1 207	43	41	343	31.0	65.7	3.3
Pulaski	1 320.8	3 532	43.2	4.6	6.6	0.0	4.5	1 288.0	3 445	9 017	6 886	45 788	55.1	43.5	1.4
Randolph	36.5	2 020	64.8	0.1	6.0	0.0	8.5	7.2	399	39	86	1 302	39.1	57.2	3.7
St. Francis	66.2	2 462	68.1	0.3	6.5	0.2	4.1	14.7	545	658	126	1 668	57.7	41.2	1.1
Saline	191.5	1 991	61.4	0.2	6.2	0.0	5.1	238.4	2 478	96	476	4 582	28.4	69.4	2.2
Scott	20.1	1 782	65.1	0.0	5.9	0.0	8.0	14.1	1 246	79	53	453	26.4	69.9	3.8
Searcy	15.5	1 917	68.5	0.0	5.1	0.0	6.5	4.4	540	52	38	478	25.0	70.9	4.2
Sebastian	336.5	2 764	50.6	0.1	4.6	0.1	9.6	515.8	4 236	1 049	597	6 801	31.6	66.3	2.1
Sevier	44.8	2 744	74.3	0.1	4.1	0.0	4.3	13.0	798	74	81	1 158	28.2	68.2	3.6
Sharp	41.4	2 321	64.3	0.0	4.2	0.0	7.3	31.5	1 763	54	85	858	33.6	62.5	3.9
Stone	19.2	1 601	70.6	0.0	5.6	0.1	10.8	2.6	219	70	57	571	30.0	66.4	3.6
Union	102.1	2 362	63.3	0.1	4.8	0.0	6.8	56.8	1 315	176	206	2 640	36.0	62.2	1.8
Van Buren	31.6	1 917	66.4	0.2	7.9	0.4	7.0	27.7	1 677	42	79	709	32.1	63.8	4.1
Washington	608.4	3 131	52.0	0.2	5.5	0.0	7.9	880.2	4 530	1 911	973	15 501	42.4	55.5	2.0
White	165.7	2 257	67.3	0.1	8.9	0.2	5.1	131.7	1 794	185	366	3 708	25.0	72.2	2.8
Woodruff	25.6	3 345	51.9	0.3	4.8	21.1	6.2	12.1	1 586	47	35	509	51.1	43.7	5.2
Yell	49.6	2 278	72.8	0.1	5.6	0.0	5.7	24.3	1 114	151	108	1 264	33.2	63.1	3.7

1. Based on the resident population estimated as of July 1 of the year shown.   2. © 2009 Election Data Services, Inc. All rights reserved.

Table B. States and Counties — **Land Area and Population**

STATE/ County code	CBSA code[1]	County type[2]	STATE County	Land area[3] (sq km) 2010	Total persons	Rank	Per square kilometer	White	Black	American Indian, Alaska Native	Asian and Pacific Islander	Percent Hispanic or Latino[4]	Under 5 years	5 to 17 years	18 to 24 years	25 to 34 years	35 to 44 years	45 to 54 years
				1	2	3	4	5	6	7	8	9	10	11	12	13	14	15
06 000	...	X	CALIFORNIA	403 466	37 253 956	X	92.3	42.3	6.5	1.0	14.9	37.6	6.8	18.2	10.5	14.3	13.9	14.1
06 001	41860	1	Alameda	1 914	1 510 271	22	789.1	37.2	13.4	1.0	29.8	22.5	6.5	16.1	9.9	15.1	15.1	14.7
06 003	...	8	Alpine	1 912	1 175	3 102	0.6	74.2	0.1	19.4	1.0	7.1	6.0	15.7	6.0	8.3	11.6	18.3
06 005	...	6	Amador	1 540	38 091	1 215	24.7	81.9	2.8	3.0	2.0	12.5	3.8	13.0	6.6	9.6	11.9	16.7
06 007	17020	3	Butte	4 238	220 000	284	51.9	78.3	2.2	3.3	5.4	14.1	5.6	15.3	14.7	12.1	10.6	13.1
06 009	...	6	Calaveras	2 642	45 578	1 056	17.3	86.1	1.2	2.9	2.1	10.3	4.4	15.3	6.2	7.9	10.1	16.6
06 011	...	6	Colusa	2 980	21 419	1 766	7.2	40.9	1.1	2.0	2.1	55.1	8.6	21.3	8.9	13.0	12.5	12.9
06 013	41860	1	Contra Costa	1 854	1 049 025	37	565.8	50.9	10.0	1.0	17.3	24.4	6.4	18.4	8.3	12.4	14.2	15.6
06 015	18860	7	Del Norte	2 606	28 610	1 470	11.0	67.9	3.7	9.2	4.2	17.8	6.0	15.5	8.8	14.3	13.4	15.6
06 017	40900	1	El Dorado	4 423	181 058	339	40.9	82.5	1.1	2.0	4.9	12.1	5.3	17.5	7.4	9.5	12.3	17.9
06 019	23420	2	Fresno	15 431	930 450	46	60.3	34.2	5.4	1.2	10.4	50.3	8.5	21.3	11.7	14.3	12.3	12.4
06 021	...	6	Glenn	3 403	28 122	1 492	8.3	57.4	1.0	2.7	3.0	37.5	7.7	20.2	9.2	12.5	11.9	13.6
06 023	21700	5	Humboldt	9 241	134 623	458	14.6	81.1	1.7	7.8	3.6	9.8	5.7	14.4	12.4	14.9	11.2	13.9
06 025	20940	3	Imperial	10 817	174 528	353	16.1	14.2	3.1	1.2	1.6	80.4	7.8	21.5	10.9	13.9	13.1	12.9
06 027	13860	7	Inyo	26 368	18 546	1 896	0.7	68.3	0.7	11.7	1.9	19.4	5.8	15.3	6.7	10.9	10.6	16.0
06 029	12540	2	Kern	21 062	839 651	62	39.9	40.2	6.0	1.5	4.8	49.2	8.7	21.6	11.2	14.5	12.9	12.9
06 031	25260	3	Kings	3 599	152 982	408	42.5	37.1	7.5	1.3	4.9	50.9	8.4	19.4	11.6	16.7	14.3	13.3
06 033	17340	4	Lake	3 254	64 665	809	19.9	77.1	2.6	4.3	2.1	17.1	5.6	15.5	7.7	10.2	11.0	15.9
06 035	45000	6	Lassen	11 762	34 895	1 302	3.0	69.0	8.5	4.5	2.0	17.5	4.7	13.4	10.7	18.2	15.8	15.6
06 037	31100	1	Los Angeles	10 510	9 818 605	1	934.2	29.4	8.9	0.5	15.1	47.7	6.6	17.9	10.8	15.0	14.6	13.9
06 039	31460	3	Madera	5 535	150 865	414	27.3	39.5	3.6	2.1	2.3	53.7	7.9	20.5	10.5	13.6	12.7	12.8
06 041	41860	1	Marin	1 348	252 409	256	187.2	75.5	3.3	0.8	7.5	15.5	5.5	15.2	5.8	9.8	14.5	16.7
06 043	...	8	Mariposa	3 752	18 251	1 912	4.9	86.1	1.2	4.6	1.8	9.2	4.2	13.5	6.5	9.0	10.0	17.7
06 045	46380	4	Mendocino	9 081	87 841	646	9.7	71.2	1.1	5.7	2.5	22.2	6.1	16.1	8.0	12.2	11.7	14.2
06 047	32900	3	Merced	5 012	255 793	252	51.0	33.4	4.0	1.0	8.3	54.9	8.7	22.9	11.9	13.7	12.5	12.1
06 049	...	6	Modoc	10 147	9 686	2 462	1.0	81.1	1.1	4.8	1.3	13.9	5.6	16.3	6.3	9.3	11.0	14.9
06 051	...	7	Mono	7 897	14 202	2 159	1.8	69.7	0.6	2.4	2.2	26.5	6.3	14.7	10.2	15.9	13.4	16.5
06 053	41500	2	Monterey	8 497	415 057	161	48.8	34.8	3.3	0.8	7.9	55.4	7.8	18.9	11.1	15.0	13.2	12.8
06 055	34900	3	Napa	1 938	136 484	454	70.4	58.3	2.2	1.1	8.2	32.2	6.0	17.1	8.8	12.3	13.1	14.6
06 057	46020	4	Nevada	2 481	98 764	589	39.8	88.8	0.7	2.2	2.2	8.5	4.4	14.9	6.6	9.8	10.6	16.0
06 059	31100	1	Orange	2 048	3 010 232	6	1 469.8	46.2	1.9	0.6	19.9	33.7	6.4	18.1	10.1	13.7	14.6	14.8
06 061	40900	1	Placer	3 644	348 432	187	95.6	79.0	1.9	1.5	7.8	12.8	6.0	18.4	7.6	11.2	13.4	15.3
06 063	...	7	Plumas	6 612	20 007	1 838	3.0	87.9	1.3	4.2	1.4	8.0	4.4	13.6	7.5	8.5	9.5	16.1
06 065	40140	1	Riverside	18 665	2 189 641	11	117.3	41.5	6.8	1.0	7.3	45.5	7.4	20.9	10.4	12.9	13.4	13.4
06 067	40900	1	Sacramento	2 498	1 418 788	25	568.0	51.6	11.6	1.7	17.7	21.6	7.1	18.5	10.1	14.6	13.5	14.1
06 069	41940	1	San Benito	3 597	55 269	908	15.4	39.7	0.9	1.0	3.5	56.4	7.4	21.7	9.2	12.5	13.8	14.9
06 071	40140	1	San Bernardino	51 947	2 035 210	12	39.2	35.0	9.3	1.0	7.5	49.2	7.8	21.4	11.3	13.9	13.4	13.6
06 073	41740	1	San Diego	10 895	3 095 313	5	284.1	51.1	5.6	1.0	13.3	32.0	6.6	16.8	11.9	15.2	13.6	13.9
06 075	41860	1	San Francisco	121	805 235	66	6 654.8	44.6	6.7	0.8	35.9	15.1	4.4	9.0	9.6	20.9	16.6	13.9
06 077	44700	2	San Joaquin	3 604	685 306	87	190.2	38.4	8.1	1.3	16.5	38.9	7.9	21.4	10.4	13.3	13.2	13.4
06 079	42020	3	San Luis Obispo	8 543	269 637	239	31.6	73.3	2.3	1.3	4.4	20.8	4.9	13.9	14.7	11.9	11.0	14.6
06 081	41860	1	San Mateo	1 161	718 451	82	618.8	45.0	3.2	0.6	28.8	25.4	6.5	15.8	7.7	13.8	15.0	15.4
06 083	42060	2	Santa Barbara	7 084	423 895	157	59.8	49.8	2.2	1.0	6.1	42.9	6.5	16.7	14.9	13.6	11.9	13.0
06 085	41940	1	Santa Clara	3 341	1 781 642	17	533.3	37.7	2.9	0.6	34.6	26.9	7.0	17.1	8.9	15.1	15.6	14.8
06 087	42100	2	Santa Cruz	1 153	262 382	250	227.6	62.1	1.4	1.2	5.8	32.0	5.7	15.4	13.8	12.9	12.6	14.8
06 089	39820	3	Shasta	9 778	177 223	349	18.1	85.6	1.4	4.5	3.5	8.4	5.8	16.6	9.0	11.3	11.0	15.0
06 091	...	8	Sierra	2 469	3 240	2 917	1.3	89.7	0.4	2.4	0.9	8.3	4.5	12.5	5.2	7.5	10.3	17.6
06 093	...	7	Siskiyou	16 260	44 900	1 070	2.8	83.3	1.8	6.5	2.2	10.3	5.5	15.3	7.2	9.5	10.1	15.4
06 095	46700	2	Solano	2 128	413 344	162	194.2	44.8	16.2	1.5	18.6	24.0	6.5	18.1	9.8	13.3	13.2	15.5
06 097	42220	2	Sonoma	4 081	483 878	137	118.6	68.6	2.1	1.7	5.4	24.9	5.8	16.2	9.5	12.7	12.5	15.2
06 099	33700	2	Stanislaus	3 872	514 453	125	132.9	48.9	3.2	1.4	7.0	41.9	7.7	20.9	10.5	13.6	13.0	13.5
06 101	40900	3	Sutter	1 560	94 737	608	60.7	53.1	2.5	2.2	16.4	28.8	7.6	20.0	9.6	13.4	12.6	13.4
06 103	39780	4	Tehama	7 640	63 463	821	8.3	74.3	1.0	3.7	1.7	21.9	6.9	18.5	8.4	11.2	11.5	14.6
06 105	...	8	Trinity	8 234	13 786	2 201	1.7	87.6	0.7	7.3	1.7	7.0	4.5	13.8	5.9	9.2	10.1	16.9
06 107	47300	2	Tulare	12 495	442 179	146	35.4	33.8	1.5	1.3	3.9	60.6	9.3	23.3	10.7	14.0	12.4	11.8
06 109	38020	4	Tuolumne	5 752	55 365	905	9.6	84.2	2.3	3.1	1.8	10.7	4.2	13.3	7.6	11.0	10.9	15.5
06 111	37100	2	Ventura	4 774	823 318	63	172.5	50.7	2.1	0.8	8.3	40.3	6.7	19.0	9.9	12.8	13.5	15.0
06 113	40900	1	Yolo	2 628	200 849	308	76.4	52.9	3.0	1.3	15.6	30.3	6.3	16.5	19.1	14.0	11.9	12.4
06 115	49700	3	Yuba	1 636	72 155	744	44.1	62.8	4.2	4.1	8.6	25.0	8.6	20.5	10.4	14.4	12.3	13.2
08 000	...	X	COLORADO	268 431	5 029 196	X	18.7	71.8	4.5	1.3	3.7	20.7	6.8	17.5	9.7	14.4	13.9	14.8
08 001	19740	1	Adams	3 024	441 603	148	146.0	54.7	3.4	1.1	4.3	38.0	8.5	20.0	9.3	16.2	14.8	13.2
08 003	...	7	Alamosa	1 872	15 445	2 085	8.3	51.0	1.2	1.6	1.3	46.0	7.8	17.0	14.8	12.6	10.5	13.9
08 005	19740	1	Arapahoe	2 067	572 003	109	276.7	65.6	11.2	1.1	6.4	18.4	7.1	18.6	8.5	14.7	14.3	14.9
08 007	...	7	Archuleta	3 497	12 084	2 301	3.5	79.7	0.6	2.3	1.0	17.8	4.9	15.0	5.6	9.2	10.1	17.2
08 009	...	9	Baca	6 617	3 788	2 923	0.6	88.9	0.7	2.0	0.2	9.2	5.6	15.9	5.8	9.5	9.9	14.5
08 011	...	7	Bent	3 918	6 499	2 724	1.7	59.5	7.7	1.7	1.1	30.5	4.4	12.4	8.6	16.7	15.9	15.8

1. CBSA = Core Based Statistical Area. See Appendix A for explanation. See Appendix B for list of metropolitan areas with component counties. 2. County type code from the Economic Research Service of USDA Rural-Urban Continuum Codes. See Appendix A for definition. 3. Dry land or land partially or temporarily covered by water. 4. May be of any race.

Table B. States and Counties — **Population and Households**

STATE County	Population, 2010 (cont.) Age (percent) (cont.)				Population change and components of change, 1990–2010							Households, 2010				
					Total persons		Percent change		Components of change, 2000–2009						Percent	
	55 to 64 years	65 to 74 years	75 years and over	Percent female	1990	2000	1990–2000	2000–2010	Births	Deaths	Net migration	Number	Percent change, 2000–2010	Persons per house-hold	Female family house-holder[1]	One per-son
	16	17	18	19	20	21	22	23	24	25	26	27	28	29	30	31
CALIFORNIA	10.8	6.1	5.3	50.3	29 811 427	33 871 648	13.6	10.0	5 058 440	2 179 958	306 925	12 577 498	9.3	2.90	13.3	23.3
Alameda	11.5	6.0	5.1	51.0	1 304 347	1 443 741	10.7	4.6	198 238	87 858	-55 662	545 138	4.2	2.70	12.9	26.0
Alpine	20.0	9.3	4.9	48.4	1 113	1 208	8.5	-2.7	109	53	-224	497	2.9	2.32	8.0	29.4
Amador	17.8	11.7	9.0	45.5	30 039	35 100	16.8	8.5	2 560	3 642	4 030	14 569	14.2	2.30	8.6	26.8
Butte	13.1	7.8	7.6	50.5	182 120	203 171	11.6	8.3	22 583	20 493	16 458	87 618	10.1	2.45	11.6	27.9
Calaveras	18.6	12.7	8.2	49.9	31 998	40 554	26.7	12.4	3 291	3 792	6 799	18 886	14.7	2.39	8.6	24.7
Colusa	11.1	6.4	5.3	48.6	16 275	18 804	15.5	13.9	3 317	1 274	581	7 056	15.7	3.00	11.2	20.9
Contra Costa	12.3	6.7	5.7	51.2	803 731	948 816	18.1	10.6	123 345	63 757	39 187	375 364	9.1	2.77	12.4	22.7
Del Norte	13.0	7.5	6.0	44.4	23 460	27 507	17.3	4.0	2 931	2 461	1 303	9 907	8.0	2.50	13.3	28.1
El Dorado	15.5	8.5	6.1	50.0	125 995	156 299	24.1	15.8	17 155	11 163	16 959	70 223	19.1	2.55	8.8	22.1
Fresno	9.5	5.3	4.7	50.0	667 479	799 407	19.8	16.4	146 819	54 132	29 307	289 391	14.4	3.15	16.9	19.8
Glenn	11.6	7.3	6.0	49.5	24 798	26 453	6.7	6.3	3 977	2 163	207	9 800	6.8	2.84	11.7	22.2
Humboldt	14.4	7.2	6.0	49.8	119 118	126 518	6.2	6.4	14 224	11 346	1 020	56 031	9.4	2.31	10.9	31.8
Imperial	9.5	5.6	4.8	48.6	109 303	142 361	30.2	22.6	27 286	8 568	6 736	49 126	24.7	3.34	19.6	17.0
Inyo	15.7	9.8	9.3	49.6	18 281	17 945	-1.8	3.3	1 911	1 915	-604	8 049	4.5	2.25	10.0	33.9
Kern	9.2	5.2	3.8	48.4	544 981	661 645	21.4	26.9	126 951	48 438	71 540	254 610	22.0	3.15	15.7	19.3
Kings	8.4	4.5	3.4	43.6	101 469	129 461	27.6	18.2	23 111	7 167	4 022	41 233	19.8	3.19	15.9	17.5
Lake	16.4	10.1	7.6	49.8	50 631	58 309	15.2	10.9	6 363	7 209	8 066	26 548	10.7	2.39	12.2	29.7
Lassen	11.8	5.7	4.3	35.8	27 598	33 828	22.6	3.2	2 655	1 953	92	10 058	4.5	2.50	10.3	25.6
Los Angeles	10.3	5.8	5.1	50.7	8 863 052	9 519 338	7.4	3.1	1 402 112	553 030	-474 695	3 241 204	3.4	2.98	15.3	24.2
Madera	10.5	6.5	4.9	51.8	88 090	123 109	39.8	22.5	22 075	8 657	12 821	43 317	19.8	3.28	13.3	16.7
Marin	15.9	9.2	7.5	50.8	230 096	247 289	7.5	2.1	25 767	16 860	-4 088	103 210	2.5	2.36	8.8	30.8
Mariposa	18.0	12.3	8.6	49.2	14 302	17 130	19.8	6.5	1 303	1 571	1 007	7 693	16.3	2.28	7.6	28.4
Mendocino	16.4	8.6	6.8	49.9	80 345	86 265	7.4	1.8	10 304	7 518	-2 472	34 945	5.0	2.46	11.5	29.7
Merced	8.9	5.2	4.2	49.7	178 403	210 554	18.0	21.5	40 173	13 493	8 734	75 642	18.5	3.32	15.8	17.4
Modoc	16.9	11.4	8.2	49.6	9 678	9 449	-2.4	2.5	748	997	-41	4 064	7.4	2.30	10.0	29.4
Mono	13.3	6.5	3.2	46.9	9 956	12 853	29.1	10.5	1 477	463	-901	5 768	12.3	2.42	5.6	27.6
Monterey	10.4	5.5	5.2	48.6	355 660	401 762	13.0	3.3	68 134	21 904	-35 690	125 946	3.9	3.15	12.7	21.7
Napa	13.1	7.7	7.4	50.1	110 765	124 279	12.2	9.8	15 219	11 522	7 498	48 876	7.7	2.69	10.3	25.3
Nevada	18.2	10.7	8.7	50.6	78 510	92 033	17.2	7.3	7 701	8 604	7 153	41 527	12.6	2.35	8.7	26.3
Orange	10.7	6.2	5.4	50.5	2 410 668	2 846 289	18.1	5.8	412 730	157 683	-57 746	992 781	6.1	2.99	11.6	20.9
Placer	12.7	8.3	7.1	51.2	172 796	248 399	43.8	40.3	34 617	21 639	87 515	132 627	42.0	2.60	9.2	23.0
Plumas	19.6	12.7	8.1	50.0	19 739	20 824	5.5	-3.9	1 605	1 906	-200	8 977	-0.8	2.20	8.0	29.8
Riverside	9.8	6.4	5.4	50.2	1 170 413	1 545 387	32.0	41.7	279 418	125 757	432 682	686 260	35.6	3.14	13.3	19.3
Sacramento	11.0	5.9	5.3	51.0	1 066 789	1 223 499	14.7	16.0	191 005	90 135	83 880	513 945	13.3	2.71	14.8	26.0
San Benito	10.7	5.4	4.3	50.0	36 697	53 234	45.1	3.8	8 236	2 423	-3 706	16 805	5.8	3.27	12.6	15.4
San Bernardino	9.7	5.1	3.8	50.3	1 418 380	1 709 434	20.5	19.1	297 930	110 780	130 767	611 618	15.7	3.26	16.2	17.7
San Diego	10.6	5.8	5.5	49.8	2 498 016	2 813 833	12.6	10.0	423 374	181 546	-23 412	1 086 865	9.3	2.75	12.1	24.0
San Francisco	12.0	6.7	6.9	49.3	723 959	776 733	7.3	3.7	80 129	57 268	-25 499	345 811	4.9	2.26	8.3	38.6
San Joaquin	10.0	5.8	4.8	50.2	480 628	563 598	17.3	21.6	100 619	42 408	55 975	215 007	18.4	3.12	15.4	19.7
San Luis Obispo	13.8	7.9	7.4	48.8	217 162	246 681	13.6	9.3	24 628	19 136	16 300	102 016	10.0	2.48	9.3	26.2
San Mateo	12.4	7.0	6.4	50.8	649 623	707 161	8.9	1.6	92 843	43 237	-34 794	257 837	1.5	2.75	10.8	24.5
Santa Barbara	10.6	6.3	6.5	49.8	369 608	399 347	8.0	6.1	55 821	26 635	-19 175	142 104	4.0	2.86	10.9	24.8
Santa Clara	10.4	6.0	5.1	49.8	1 497 577	1 682 585	12.4	5.9	250 140	81 519	-59 871	604 204	6.8	2.90	10.7	21.8
Santa Cruz	13.7	6.0	5.1	50.1	229 734	255 602	11.3	2.7	32 171	15 045	-15 384	94 355	3.5	2.66	10.5	26.4
Shasta	14.4	9.3	7.6	50.8	147 036	163 256	11.0	8.6	19 345	17 279	16 619	70 346	10.9	2.48	12.2	25.9
Sierra	21.4	12.2	8.6	49.2	3 318	3 555	7.1	-8.9	215	320	-262	1 482	-2.5	2.16	7.2	31.2
Siskiyou	17.5	11.0	8.6	50.1	43 531	44 301	1.8	1.4	4 384	4 763	971	19 505	5.1	2.28	9.9	31.1
Solano	12.4	6.3	5.0	50.1	339 469	394 542	16.2	4.8	53 542	24 963	-13 463	141 758	8.7	2.83	14.7	21.9
Sonoma	14.2	7.3	6.6	50.8	388 222	458 614	18.1	5.5	53 617	34 996	-2 730	185 825	7.8	2.55	10.6	27.3
Stanislaus	10.1	5.8	4.9	50.5	370 522	446 997	20.6	15.1	75 988	33 683	23 505	165 180	13.8	3.08	14.6	19.3
Sutter	10.7	6.9	5.8	50.4	64 409	78 930	22.5	20.0	12 871	6 513	7 771	31 437	16.3	2.98	12.8	21.0
Tehama	13.0	9.0	6.9	50.2	49 625	56 039	12.9	13.2	7 059	5 573	3 894	23 767	13.1	2.63	12.8	24.0
Trinity	19.6	12.1	7.9	48.4	13 063	13 022	-0.3	5.9	1 041	1 397	1 477	6 083	8.9	2.20	8.8	32.0
Tulare	9.1	5.2	4.3	49.9	311 932	368 021	18.0	20.2	73 748	25 133	15 609	130 352	18.1	3.36	16.1	16.6
Tuolumne	17.1	11.2	9.2	47.2	48 456	54 501	12.5	1.6	4 305	5 535	2 164	22 156	5.5	2.30	9.2	28.3
Ventura	11.4	6.2	5.5	50.3	669 016	753 197	12.6	9.3	110 905	45 038	-11 182	266 920	9.7	3.04	11.8	19.9
Yolo	10.0	5.3	4.6	51.2	141 212	168 660	19.4	19.1	22 975	10 715	19 537	70 872	19.4	2.74	11.3	22.9
Yuba	10.5	5.8	4.3	49.6	58 234	60 219	3.4	19.8	11 340	4 841	6 540	24 307	18.4	2.92	14.3	21.2
COLORADO	11.9	6.2	4.8	49.9	3 294 473	4 301 261	30.6	16.9	641 107	272 191	357 683	1 972 868	19.0	2.49	10.1	27.9
Adams	9.5	4.8	3.5	49.7	NA	348 618	NA	21.4	66 922	21 019	49 426	153 764	20.0	2.85	13.0	22.3
Alamosa	12.1	6.5	4.8	49.9	13 617	14 966	9.9	3.2	2 314	1 015	-762	5 995	9.7	2.45	13.1	30.2
Arapahoe	11.7	5.6	4.4	51.0	391 572	487 967	24.6	17.2	73 704	28 019	33 573	224 011	17.3	2.53	11.8	28.0
Archuleta	20.5	10.9	6.6	49.5	5 345	9 898	85.2	22.1	1 126	595	2 037	5 267	32.3	2.27	7.8	26.7
Baca	14.7	10.9	13.2	50.4	4 556	4 517	-0.9	-16.1	351	562	-580	1 685	-11.5	2.20	7.4	35.0
Bent	12.4	7.2	6.5	34.3	5 048	5 998	18.8	8.4	592	584	552	1 832	-8.5	2.34	12.8	32.0

1. No spouse present.

Table B. States and Counties — **Population, Vital Statistics, Medicare, and Crime**

STATE County	Persons in group quarters, 2010	Daytime population, 2006–2010		Births, average 2006–2008		Deaths, average 2006–2008		Persons under 65 with no health insurance, 2009		Medicare, 2011			Serious crimes known to police,[2] 2010 Total	
		Number	Employ-ment/resi-dence ratio	Total	Rate[1]	Number	Rate[1]	Number	Percent	Eligible for Medicare	Enrolled in Medicare Advantage	Enrolled in a Medicare prescription drug plan	Number	Rate[3]
	32	33	34	35	36	37	38	39	40	41	42	43	44	45
CALIFORNIA	819 816	36 637 722	1.0	560 211	15.4	235 204	6.5	6 491 176	20.1	4 952 324	1 796 661	1 714 638	1 146 072	3 076
Alameda	37 442	1 485 534	1.0	21 188	14.5	9 292	6.3	192 959	14.6	194 214	81 392	61 679	60 791	4 025
Alpine	24	1 824	2.3	D	D	D	D	150	16.8	184	11	98	87	7 404
Amador	4 551	38 838	1.0	D	D	405	10.5	4 739	15.9	9 045	2 025	3 246	950	2 494
Butte	4 942	217 163	1.0	2 560	11.7	2 299	10.5	32 858	17.9	42 738	2 438	22 282	6 702	3 046
Calaveras	493	38 920	0.6	D	D	440	9.3	5 826	15.7	10 861	1 527	4 459	918	2 014
Colusa	225	21 459	1.0	D	D	135	6.4	4 440	24.2	3 033	226	1 728	547	2 554
Contra Costa	10 314	926 518	0.8	13 397	13.1	6 909	6.7	121 700	13.5	153 172	68 006	41 413	35 006	3 337
Del Norte	3 818	29 054	1.1	345	11.9	268	9.2	5 741	23.3	5 170	433	2 676	858	2 999
El Dorado	1 643	153 753	0.7	1 913	10.8	1 268	7.2	19 807	12.8	32 107	9 646	10 065	3 265	1 803
Fresno	17 523	912 986	1.0	16 978	18.9	6 014	6.7	175 794	21.7	112 620	29 175	48 856	44 374	4 769
Glenn	316	26 996	0.9	D	D	237	8.4	5 856	24.2	4 858	174	2 697	683	2 429
Humboldt	5 014	133 352	1.0	1 615	12.5	1 292	10.0	22 409	20.2	23 591	800	12 678	4 838	3 594
Imperial	10 684	167 010	1.0	3 172	19.6	912	5.6	35 351	24.3	24 259	1 414	15 267	6 390	3 661
Inyo	433	19 317	1.1	D	D	204	11.7	2 798	19.5	3 976	124	2 026	314	1 693
Kern	36 757	814 633	1.0	15 254	19.3	5 327	6.7	156 590	21.9	95 872	32 969	36 161	35 429	4 220
Kings	21 580	149 500	1.0	2 726	18.4	795	5.4	31 296	23.5	14 144	1 613	7 358	3 489	2 281
Lake	1 085	59 979	0.8	D	D	785	12.0	10 591	19.9	14 868	1 432	7 356	2 152	3 328
Lassen	9 779	35 704	1.1	303	8.7	230	6.6	5 774	19.0	4 263	151	1 871	625	1 791
Los Angeles	171 681	9 893 925	1.0	150 540	15.2	58 738	5.9	2 150 986	24.8	1 209 358	467 871	454 198	283 354	2 886
Madera	8 624	144 833	0.9	2 590	17.6	955	6.5	31 570	24.3	20 269	6 245	7 735	3 971	2 632
Marin	9 044	251 514	1.0	2 758	11.1	1 809	7.3	24 435	11.8	47 172	16 551	15 725	5 711	2 263
Mariposa	725	17 509	0.9	D	D	187	10.3	2 391	17.0	4 227	404	1 725	350	1 918
Mendocino	2 044	88 633	1.0	1 141	13.1	799	9.2	15 633	21.9	18 066	1 172	9 512	2 006	2 284
Merced	4 896	238 015	0.9	4 606	18.7	1 459	5.9	46 305	21.4	29 647	2 324	16 186	9 692	3 789
Modoc	357	9 373	0.9	D	D	99	10.6	1 596	22.2	2 331	165	1 164	144	1 487
Mono	222	14 150	1.0	D	D	43	3.4	2 275	21.0	1 227	60	539	362	2 549
Monterey	18 702	406 641	1.0	7 487	18.3	2 273	5.6	86 616	24.0	51 448	1 503	26 045	12 442	2 998
Napa	4 918	140 575	1.1	1 697	12.7	1 186	8.9	19 954	17.7	24 143	9 046	6 569	3 475	2 546
Nevada	1 175	93 393	0.9	846	8.7	921	9.4	12 170	15.6	22 647	3 381	9 081	1 764	1 786
Orange	39 236	3 048 684	1.1	43 584	14.5	17 105	5.7	522 055	19.7	392 778	169 845	115 603	67 754	2 251
Placer	3 807	330 619	1.0	3 994	12.0	2 513	7.5	33 604	11.6	62 113	27 743	14 070	8 547	2 453
Plumas	277	20 216	1.0	D	D	209	10.1	2 510	16.1	5 246	349	2 546	473	2 364
Riverside	35 829	1 961 950	0.8	33 704	16.3	13 953	6.8	414 921	22.5	282 353	138 727	71 123	65 647	2 998
Sacramento	23 787	1 414 598	1.0	21 824	15.8	9 794	7.1	192 214	15.7	198 379	82 920	56 216	59 215	4 174
San Benito	289	47 288	0.7	861	15.6	261	4.7	9 218	18.8	6 419	473	3 252	1 475	2 669
San Bernardino	40 054	1 936 041	0.9	34 559	17.2	12 148	6.1	390 141	21.6	224 851	110 352	59 868	64 211	3 155
San Diego	101 966	3 047 594	1.0	47 074	15.8	19 306	6.5	500 631	18.8	409 903	165 409	113 597	79 489	2 568
San Francisco	24 264	951 627	1.4	8 949	15.8	5 790	7.5	103 131	14.8	126 546	46 142	51 395	39 008	4 844
San Joaquin	14 354	644 561	0.9	11 471	17.1	4 685	7.0	114 489	19.2	87 661	24 766	36 511	33 820	4 935
San Luis Obispo	17 006	262 831	1.0	2 784	10.6	2 104	8.0	38 869	17.5	47 847	6 467	20 131	6 897	2 558
San Mateo	8 853	707 901	1.0	9 831	13.9	4 512	6.4	80 232	12.9	105 834	45 591	25 404	16 979	2 363
Santa Barbara	17 782	428 185	1.1	6 260	15.5	2 837	7.0	67 463	19.5	63 161	11 545	28 774	10 544	2 487
Santa Clara	30 350	1 839 074	1.1	27 056	15.5	8 906	5.1	219 104	13.8	221 196	80 509	79 133	45 125	2 533
Santa Cruz	10 969	245 122	0.9	3 569	14.2	1 584	6.3	40 480	18.1	35 795	4 786	17 558	9 580	3 651
Shasta	2 654	178 182	1.0	2 202	12.2	2 024	11.3	26 528	17.7	40 679	3 855	20 217	6 239	3 520
Sierra	33	3 205	0.9	D	D	36	10.9	467	18.4	758	38	363	65	2 006
Siskiyou	474	45 192	1.0	D	D	537	12.0	6 714	19.0	11 144	977	5 355	987	2 198
Solano	12 452	367 186	0.8	5 755	14.1	2 750	6.7	51 536	14.5	57 475	25 427	10 560	14 281	3 455
Sonoma	10 043	454 717	0.9	5 800	12.4	3 750	8.0	64 511	16.1	79 827	29 492	24 814	10 704	2 212
Stanislaus	6 305	491 315	0.9	8 702	17.0	3 672	7.2	90 325	20.2	69 582	26 846	25 644	23 450	4 558
Sutter	1 060	85 229	0.8	1 514	16.5	689	7.5	17 066	21.5	14 260	819	7 568	2 835	2 992
Tehama	842	59 602	0.9	792	12.9	615	10.0	10 491	20.7	13 064	922	6 761	1 959	3 087
Trinity	385	13 420	0.9	D	D	152	10.7	1 936	19.0	3 373	245	1 584	168	1 219
Tulare	4 772	422 674	1.0	8 443	20.0	2 772	6.6	89 238	23.5	51 446	6 702	27 910	17 832	4 033
Tuolumne	4 482	56 304	1.0	D	D	605	10.8	7 426	17.2	13 240	1 103	6 045	1 337	2 415
Ventura	10 600	768 798	0.9	12 244	15.3	4 954	6.2	126 443	18.1	114 077	30 411	41 166	17 773	2 159
Yolo	6 709	207 156	1.1	2 613	13.5	1 126	5.8	28 444	16.1	23 644	11 018	5 880	6 443	3 208
Yuba	1 171	67 350	0.9	1 319	18.4	529	7.4	12 380	19.1	10 163	904	5 195	1 948	2 700
COLORADO	115 878	4 876 587	1.0	70 530	14.6	30 263	6.2	756 645	17.2	658 484	220 003	189 906	151 125	3 005
Adams	4 027	377 814	0.8	7 119	16.8	2 291	5.4	85 939	21.7	45 682	22 713	9 754	15 683	3 551
Alamosa	740	17 252	1.3	D	D	107	7.0	2 855	21.3	2 292	505	1 088	672	4 351
Arapahoe	4 920	541 379	1.0	7 878	14.4	3 110	5.7	81 923	16.7	67 911	27 822	15 663	18 226	3 186
Archuleta	129	11 993	1.0	D	D	75	6.0	2 333	22.4	2 446	274	1 072	129	1 068
Baca	82	3 814	1.0	D	D	65	16.6	710	25.4	993	D	615	18	475
Bent	2 208	5 795	0.8	D	D	69	11.9	1 679	29.9	942	51	445	38	585

1. Per 1,000 estimated resident population. 2. Data for serious crimes have not been adjusted for underreporting; this may affect comparability between geographic areas and over time. 3. Per 100,000 population estimated by the FBI.

STATE County	Serious crimes known to police,[1] 2010 (cont.) Rate[2] Violent	Property	Education — School enrollment and attainment, 2006–2010 — Enrollment[3] Total	Percent private	Attainment[4] (percent) High school graduate or less	Bachelor's degree or more	Local government expenditures,[5] 2008–2009 Total current expenditures (mil dol)	Current expenditures per student (dollars)	Money income, 2006–2010 Per capita income[6] (dollars)	Households — Median income Dollars	Percent change, 2000 to 2006–2010 (constant 2010 dollars)	Percent with income of $200,000 or more	Income and poverty, 2010 Median household income (dollars)	Percent below poverty level All persons	Children under 18 years	Children 5 to 17 years in families
	46	47	48	49	50	51	52	53	54	55	56	57	58	59	60	61
CALIFORNIA	441	2 636	10 455 359	14.1	40.8	30.1	59 466.3	9 538	29 188	60 883	1.2	6.5	57 664	15.8	22.0	20.8
Alameda	693	3 332	407 491	15.6	34.4	40.3	1 990.3	9 333	33 961	69 384	-2.1	8.4	66 937	13.5	17.2	17.0
Alpine	851	6 553	422	11.6	34.3	29.7	4.4	33 907	32 159	63 478	19.7	3.9	44 241	16.9	29.2	26.7
Amador	289	2 205	7 403	13.0	43.0	19.0	38.8	8 434	26 329	54 758	2.3	2.0	49 516	12.8	17.0	14.9
Butte	346	2 700	68 241	7.6	38.0	24.1	319.5	9 963	23 404	43 170	6.8	1.9	41 168	20.1	25.1	22.9
Calaveras	204	1 810	9 339	11.1	39.4	19.6	66.9	10 293	28 408	54 971	5.8	2.6	50 745	11.1	18.3	16.3
Colusa	224	2 330	5 762	4.2	56.9	11.7	51.5	10 848	21 317	48 016	8.1	2.7	44 981	14.9	22.9	21.2
Contra Costa	412	2 925	279 483	16.3	31.3	38.2	1 488.6	8 916	37 818	78 385	-2.8	10.7	73 678	9.3	12.7	11.2
Del Norte	388	2 611	6 887	12.6	50.5	14.3	46.4	10 148	18 974	36 118	-3.8	1.6	35 438	23.5	30.6	27.8
El Dorado	268	1 535	47 876	13.3	30.6	31.1	264.8	9 161	34 393	70 000	7.4	7.1	65 201	9.4	11.6	10.3
Fresno	535	4 234	283 502	7.6	50.2	19.7	1 821.6	9 398	20 329	46 430	5.6	2.7	44 869	26.8	38.2	36.2
Glenn	260	2 169	7 666	11.8	50.3	16.2	63.9	11 502	19 987	43 074	5.9	2.4	40 859	17.6	25.6	24.0
Humboldt	393	3 201	36 115	8.4	35.6	26.3	176.2	10 084	24 025	40 089	1.4	2.1	38 254	18.0	22.0	21.0
Imperial	354	3 307	52 928	4.5	60.7	12.2	370.8	10 223	16 395	38 685	-4.1	1.7	39 261	22.3	31.8	30.4
Inyo	372	1 321	3 918	9.4	41.9	20.9	38.8	12 676	26 762	44 808	1.1	1.6	44 507	13.9	20.5	18.3
Kern	581	3 639	242 581	8.9	55.7	14.7	1 663.9	9 565	20 100	47 089	4.9	2.6	45 045	21.4	30.3	28.6
Kings	348	1 932	39 912	9.8	58.2	11.8	259.1	9 137	17 875	48 684	7.5	1.5	44 020	22.5	29.7	28.0
Lake	452	2 876	14 486	4.7	46.6	16.4	96.7	10 091	21 531	39 491	5.3	1.3	35 914	21.0	29.8	27.2
Lassen	338	1 453	7 656	15.5	46.9	12.4	50.0	10 924	19 756	50 317	9.4	8.0	50 098	16.8	18.7	17.0
Los Angeles	512	2 374	2 816 868	15.5	45.4	29.0	16 525.5	10 139	27 344	55 476	3.8	6.0	52 595	17.6	24.5	23.7
Madera	434	2 199	39 668	6.2	57.6	13.5	270.5	9 198	18 724	46 039	0.2	3.0	43 596	21.7	31.7	28.1
Marin	206	2 057	56 823	27.3	21.0	54.1	345.8	11 677	53 940	89 268	-1.1	16.8	82 383	9.2	10.9	9.9
Mariposa	203	1 715	3 668	12.7	42.7	20.4	24.1	10 687	27 064	49 098	12.0	2.3	42 222	14.8	22.3	20.3
Mendocino	556	1 728	19 930	11.6	42.0	22.7	152.9	11 689	23 357	43 759	-4.0	2.1	40 339	19.6	28.6	26.2
Merced	566	3 223	80 792	6.0	58.7	12.5	547.2	9 744	18 041	43 844	-2.6	2.4	41 730	23.1	31.4	29.2
Modoc	176	1 311	2 168	8.1	44.7	15.6	19.3	15 935	20 536	34 588	-0.8	0.9	34 579	21.9	32.5	29.1
Mono	415	2 134	2 976	10.8	37.0	29.9	26.9	16 140	27 321	55 087	-3.3	2.0	52 768	10.8	15.0	14.6
Monterey	491	2 507	114 149	10.9	49.9	23.4	726.3	10 295	25 776	59 271	-3.1	5.3	53 735	17.1	25.9	25.0
Napa	477	2 069	33 348	18.6	38.3	30.0	213.6	10 595	34 310	67 389	2.9	8.1	62 893	10.7	14.7	13.3
Nevada	315	1 471	21 810	11.9	28.7	31.9	167.0	9 511	30 727	57 121	-1.6	3.6	54 154	11.7	17.3	15.4
Orange	229	2 021	857 878	15.1	35.2	36.0	4 485.1	8 897	34 017	74 344	-0.2	9.3	70 727	12.2	16.4	15.7
Placer	225	2 228	90 165	15.0	27.9	34.1	511.4	8 009	35 680	74 447	2.2	7.0	68 330	9.1	10.7	10.1
Plumas	545	1 819	4 268	11.7	37.9	19.8	27.9	11 173	28 732	44 000	-4.4	2.0	41 421	15.3	22.3	20.2
Riverside	302	2 696	621 680	11.8	47.0	20.5	3 627.9	8 643	24 431	57 768	6.4	4.2	53 981	16.4	23.4	22.0
Sacramento	603	3 571	405 633	13.0	37.4	27.8	2 183.1	9 270	26 953	56 439	1.7	3.6	52 655	16.7	23.6	22.4
San Benito	385	2 283	16 109	13.0	49.8	18.3	104.4	9 191	25 508	65 771	-9.6	4.5	58 194	12.7	17.4	16.4
San Bernardino	443	2 712	625 508	11.1	49.3	18.4	3 661.4	8 750	21 867	55 845	4.8	3.1	52 270	18.1	24.7	22.9
San Diego	376	2 192	852 740	14.1	34.5	34.1	4 693.7	9 541	30 715	63 069	5.8	6.2	59 759	14.8	19.1	18.4
San Francisco	721	4 123	166 428	28.3	28.7	51.2	677.0	12 269	45 478	71 304	2.0	11.7	70 883	12.8	14.7	14.9
San Joaquin	806	4 129	201 436	12.6	50.5	17.5	1 213.6	9 005	22 851	54 341	4.0	3.5	49 742	19.0	26.0	24.5
San Luis Obispo	266	2 292	75 629	9.5	33.9	30.6	325.9	9 391	29 790	57 365	6.8	4.7	53 620	14.3	15.1	14.3
San Mateo	250	2 113	178 954	23.8	29.3	44.0	934.1	10 449	43 958	85 648	-4.5	13.8	82 417	7.0	8.5	7.7
Santa Barbara	434	2 053	128 572	11.5	38.3	31.0	626.6	9 505	29 731	60 078	1.6	6.2	56 243	17.7	21.7	19.5
Santa Clara	263	2 270	483 177	20.4	30.2	45.3	2 561.0	9 792	39 804	86 850	-7.7	13.5	84 627	10.6	13.3	12.6
Santa Cruz	500	3 151	77 558	11.2	32.7	37.3	386.6	9 993	32 862	65 253	-4.6	7.8	60 247	14.2	19.0	18.1
Shasta	822	2 698	44 997	15.3	38.7	20.0	286.5	10 107	23 772	43 944	1.1	2.5	41 058	18.2	25.4	23.1
Sierra	586	1 420	515	9.7	42.9	23.0	7.3	15 572	27 389	52 950	16.7	1.0	42 800	13.4	18.9	18.0
Siskiyou	307	1 891	10 495	11.9	38.8	22.6	85.2	12 684	22 179	36 981	-1.1	1.2	36 001	21.5	30.7	27.8
Solano	455	3 000	114 536	12.5	38.7	24.0	607.6	8 818	28 649	68 409	-0.1	4.6	62 948	12.2	17.9	14.7
Sonoma	388	1 824	122 618	12.4	34.8	31.5	687.3	9 781	32 597	63 274	-5.9	5.7	58 703	12.8	14.8	13.1
Stanislaus	519	4 039	150 154	8.9	52.4	16.3	994.9	9 415	22 064	51 094	0.6	2.8	47 442	19.7	28.2	26.8
Sutter	379	2 614	26 406	8.7	46.4	18.7	169.0	8 631	22 344	50 944	4.8	2.7	46 188	16.8	23.5	21.8
Tehama	581	2 505	15 973	11.1	50.2	12.6	115.2	10 617	20 198	38 137	-3.5	1.4	38 188	20.4	31.1	29.7
Trinity	247	972	2 757	6.5	37.8	19.5	27.4	15 835	22 073	38 725	10.4	0.6	35 207	18.4	31.3	29.2
Tulare	469	3 563	131 876	6.8	57.3	13.0	905.5	9 395	17 966	43 851	1.9	2.2	42 377	24.6	33.6	32.2
Tuolumne	219	2 196	11 598	12.0	41.9	17.3	70.6	10 250	25 483	47 462	-3.2	3.2	44 751	15.2	21.5	18.8
Ventura	212	1 946	230 815	14.8	37.5	30.8	1 244.1	8 794	32 348	75 348	-0.3	8.4	71 418	11.0	15.3	14.2
Yolo	255	2 953	72 704	7.8	35.8	37.8	271.7	9 183	27 420	57 077	10.6	4.7	54 433	16.4	18.9	17.4
Yuba	346	2 353	20 312	8.1	50.1	12.5	142.9	9 966	19 937	46 807	21.4	1.6	41 045	20.7	28.2	26.4
COLORADO	321	2 684	1 293 504	14.1	34.0	35.9	7 186.3	8 784	30 151	56 456	-5.5	4.5	54 411	13.2	17.1	15.1
Adams	500	3 051	109 310	12.7	49.5	20.3	666.0	8 401	23 999	54 666	NA	2.0	52 785	13.0	17.5	16.0
Alamosa	440	3 911	5 247	6.1	41.2	26.6	31.7	13 022	18 820	35 935	-3.6	1.1	36 339	21.0	29.0	29.1
Arapahoe	339	2 848	146 850	14.9	31.3	37.9	955.4	8 828	31 898	58 719	-13.4	5.3	58 152	11.4	15.0	13.5
Archuleta	108	960	3 670	14.5	29.2	39.0	12.7	8 300	25 421	56 068	16.8	5.4	46 165	13.1	23.1	21.8
Baca	185	290	792	5.2	46.9	19.0	10.8	10 118	21 472	36 017	1.2	2.1	33 086	17.3	26.2	23.8
Bent	31	554	1 121	2.9	54.7	13.2	7.9	9 033	16 505	36 412	2.2	0.7	33 702	30.9	32.1	30.0

1. Data for serious crimes have not been adjusted for underreporting; this may affect comparability between geographic areas and over time. 2. Per 100,000 population estimated by the FBI. 3. All persons 3 years old and over enrolled in nursery school through college. 4. Persons 25 years old and over. 5. Elementary and secondary education expenditures. 6. Based on population estimated by the American Community Survey, 2006–2010.

STATE County	Total (mil dol)	Percent change, 2008–2009	Per capita[1] Dollars	Per capita[1] Rank	Wages and salaries[2] (mil dol)	Proprietors' income (mil dol)	Dividends, interest, and rent (mil dol)	Transfer payments (mil dol) Total	Government payments to individuals Total	Social Security	Medical payments	Income mainte-nance	Unemploy-ment insurance
	62	63	64	65	66	67	68	69	70	71	72	73	74
CALIFORNIA	1 566 999	-2.3	42 395	X	993 700	151 468	306 473	237 560	230 848	61 969	99 718	28 597	18 890
Alameda	71 596	-3.0	48 004	133	50 049	5 141	13 068	9 816	9 544	2 374	4 352	1 071	883
Alpine	44	-1.3	42 717	284	30	4	11	11	10	2	6	1	0
Amador	1 375	-2.0	36 315	844	641	105	341	299	292	129	105	16	19
Butte	7 189	0.6	32 593	1 404	3 448	746	1 484	1 813	1 773	564	701	219	102
Calaveras	1 595	-1.9	34 142	1 147	368	165	397	387	379	156	141	27	27
Colusa	868	8.7	40 721	404	374	289	124	144	140	39	61	14	16
Contra Costa	59 044	-1.1	56 703	47	24 739	4 738	11 617	6 558	6 368	2 112	2 599	522	565
Del Norte	759	0.5	26 081	2 712	388	55	130	251	246	66	108	40	9
El Dorado	8 849	-0.3	49 590	110	2 673	860	1 558	1 162	1 129	449	405	70	98
Fresno	28 050	-0.2	30 646	1 833	16 621	3 094	4 212	6 397	6 230	1 351	2 610	1 167	501
Glenn	913	3.7	32 258	1 470	362	225	153	203	197	62	82	25	14
Humboldt	4 261	-1.0	32 869	1 359	2 119	394	986	1 072	1 049	310	442	125	54
Imperial	4 786	2.5	28 681	2 263	2 718	618	509	1 248	1 217	248	461	231	169
Inyo	655	0.3	37 905	652	371	46	154	138	135	51	57	11	7
Kern	23 924	-0.2	29 630	2 069	15 206	2 561	3 379	4 934	4 787	1 229	1 820	862	398
Kings	3 931	-3.2	26 426	2 655	2 583	406	468	791	765	172	320	129	61
Lake	2 081	-0.5	31 874	1 558	656	145	383	623	611	199	261	71	34
Lassen	942	0.5	27 320	2 513	573	95	139	210	203	54	90	25	12
Los Angeles	402 459	-2.5	40 867	391	268 394	44 759	77 335	67 792	65 996	14 039	32 680	9 559	4 426
Madera	3 982	0.4	26 790	2 598	2 122	505	634	933	905	267	362	135	69
Marin	22 352	-3.5	89 139	4	7 574	2 282	6 903	1 576	1 530	667	547	71	106
Mariposa	596	0.1	33 506	1 252	234	50	135	153	150	59	59	11	8
Mendocino	3 022	-1.9	35 119	1 001	1 354	295	780	765	749	226	338	85	38
Merced	6 750	-1.4	27 517	2 479	3 241	841	950	1 716	1 671	355	735	288	144
Modoc	313	3.4	34 391	1 112	126	49	58	91	89	29	39	10	3
Mono	567	-1.8	43 890	238	337	67	142	52	50	16	17	4	7
Monterey	17 127	-0.7	41 735	348	9 565	2 373	3 832	2 337	2 263	650	896	250	209
Napa	6 706	-3.0	49 805	107	4 018	569	1 565	906	882	310	381	48	60
Nevada	4 310	-2.9	44 092	232	1 481	521	1 237	741	723	316	252	42	51
Orange	148 373	-4.3	49 020	121	94 348	16 911	29 585	16 354	15 802	5 076	6 210	1 450	1 496
Placer	15 899	-2.2	45 614	183	7 568	1 353	3 162	2 188	2 124	849	719	119	195
Plumas	764	-2.4	37 989	643	319	78	200	197	193	69	75	14	14
Riverside	63 228	-2.0	29 748	2 032	29 462	4 720	11 408	12 533	12 145	3 803	4 478	1 446	1 219
Sacramento	53 560	-1.4	38 231	612	40 179	4 145	8 667	10 205	9 949	2 412	4 452	1 369	750
San Benito	1 945	-0.5	35 331	975	751	145	331	286	276	86	96	30	37
San Bernardino	59 741	-1.3	29 609	2 072	34 563	4 091	7 568	12 019	11 654	2 829	4 712	1 884	1 040
San Diego	139 577	-1.7	45 706	181	92 789	11 825	27 493	18 538	18 000	5 140	7 511	1 756	1 501
San Francisco	56 037	-3.7	68 727	14	51 933	7 941	12 443	5 800	5 652	1 383	2 651	655	447
San Joaquin	20 969	-0.7	31 071	1 739	11 198	1 965	3 268	4 851	4 727	1 105	2 157	657	415
San Luis Obispo	10 706	-1.7	40 103	442	5 300	1 100	3 036	1 600	1 551	642	533	116	102
San Mateo	50 014	-2.1	69 562	10	32 442	4 759	13 032	3 814	3 683	1 450	1 316	222	330
Santa Barbara	18 955	-2.1	46 565	155	10 740	1 803	5 856	2 351	2 278	837	836	216	141
Santa Clara	99 550	-4.0	55 781	53	87 522	6 827	20 998	9 854	9 529	2 794	3 805	864	1 109
Santa Cruz	12 592	-2.9	49 145	117	5 122	1 249	3 086	1 537	1 490	466	570	132	156
Shasta	6 170	-0.6	34 068	1 164	3 016	619	1 174	1 734	1 701	539	710	180	117
Sierra	102	-1.9	32 050	1 517	32	5	22	26	26	10	9	2	2
Siskiyou	1 474	-0.3	33 018	1 339	607	168	334	450	442	143	186	48	22
Solano	15 866	-0.3	38 961	542	8 457	787	2 338	2 511	2 438	726	903	268	229
Sonoma	21 142	-4.2	44 784	207	10 392	1 968	5 250	3 032	2 946	1 080	1 142	200	258
Stanislaus	15 949	-0.8	31 248	1 701	8 498	1 450	2 517	3 508	3 415	898	1 400	475	333
Sutter	3 142	1.0	33 921	1 182	1 272	558	527	640	623	172	256	77	58
Tehama	1 617	-0.2	26 446	2 651	734	116	312	500	489	170	181	66	30
Trinity	382	-1.3	26 943	2 577	114	30	84	137	135	45	59	13	7
Tulare	11 911	-0.9	27 721	2 450	6 410	1 374	1 737	2 967	2 889	623	1 229	563	221
Tuolumne	1 951	-2.3	35 354	971	827	140	500	475	465	189	173	34	29
Ventura	36 863	-1.6	45 908	172	19 601	2 564	7 170	4 598	4 452	1 511	1 701	396	408
Yolo	7 437	0.3	37 298	714	5 901	633	1 436	1 112	1 076	294	433	124	87
Yuba	2 036	2.6	27 925	2 415	1 237	148	258	626	613	126	287	92	43
COLORADO	210 513	-2.1	41 895	X	139 028	23 493	38 230	25 930	25 018	8 473	9 850	2 211	1 733
Adams	13 991	-0.6	31 727	1 595	8 472	1 128	1 436	2 027	1 947	607	768	215	167
Alamosa	498	3.0	32 265	1 466	341	51	75	118	115	25	53	17	5
Arapahoe	27 408	-3.8	48 480	128	19 280	5 727	4 841	2 533	2 430	904	823	234	196
Archuleta	365	-2.9	29 344	2 130	137	43	125	68	66	33	18	5	4
Baca	130	9.8	34 990	1 021	48	32	25	30	29	12	13	2	1
Bent	149	3.5	22 777	3 042	65	21	24	43	42	9	20	6	2

1. Based on the resident population estimated as of July 1 of the year shown.   2. Includes supplements to wages and salaries.

STATE County	Earnings, 2009									Social Security beneficiaries, December 2010		Supplemental Security Income recipients, December 2010	Housing units, 2010	
			Goods-related[1]		Service-related and health									
	Total (mil dol)	Farm	Total	Manufacturing	Information and professional and technical services	Retail trade	Finance, insurance, and real estate	Health care and social services	Government	Number	Rate[2]		Total	Percent change, 2000–2010
	75	76	77	78	79	80	81	82	83	84	85	86	87	88
CALIFORNIA	1 145 168	1.1	16.2	10.4	17.1	5.9	8.1	9.4	17.9	4 979 141	134	1 267 711	13 680 081	12.0
Alameda	55 190	0.0	17.5	11.0	17.9	5.3	6.1	10.7	16.8	186 030	123	53 169	582 549	7.8
Alpine	34	0.0	7.2	0.0	D	D	D	2.1	34.0	195	166	40	1 760	16.2
Amador	746	0.1	11.3	4.1	6.8	8.3	3.1	10.4	46.6	9 780	257	669	18 032	19.9
Butte	4 194	4.9	11.0	4.5	6.9	8.6	8.0	18.6	21.3	46 520	211	11 421	95 835	12.1
Calaveras	534	-0.5	D	3.9	7.4	8.5	5.3	7.3	28.5	11 845	260	1 070	27 925	21.7
Colusa	662	44.5	D	7.6	D	3.4	1.6	D	17.7	3 435	160	570	7 883	16.4
Contra Costa	29 477	0.1	D	10.6	14.9	6.1	10.9	12.7	12.8	154 910	148	25 422	400 263	12.9
Del Norte	442	2.1	D	1.4	3.2	8.1	2.9	15.1	49.6	5 805	203	2 062	11 186	7.2
El Dorado	3 533	-0.2	16.7	3.2	13.3	7.1	10.4	11.9	19.8	34 890	193	3 081	88 159	23.7
Fresno	19 715	6.5	13.7	7.7	6.8	6.7	5.3	13.0	22.7	118 240	127	41 602	315 531	16.6
Glenn	587	34.6	D	5.4	D	4.1	2.3	D	22.3	5 330	190	1 160	10 778	8.0
Humboldt	2 512	1.2	D	4.6	6.9	10.4	4.6	13.6	29.7	26 000	193	7 044	61 559	10.1
Imperial	3 336	15.1	D	3.8	2.5	7.1	2.5	4.6	38.6	26 290	151	10 373	56 067	27.7
Inyo	417	1.2	8.6	3.9	D	8.7	2.4	D	47.2	4 105	221	463	9 478	4.8
Kern	17 766	6.6	18.9	5.3	6.2	5.8	3.3	8.7	25.6	107 095	128	33 005	284 367	22.8
Kings	2 989	9.9	D	9.3	2.0	5.7	2.0	8.4	46.3	15 815	103	4 624	43 867	20.0
Lake	800	0.4	9.4	2.0	5.4	9.7	3.5	16.3	27.6	16 685	258	3 806	35 492	9.1
Lassen	668	6.2	D	0.2	D	5.2	2.8	7.6	62.9	4 840	139	1 011	12 710	5.9
Los Angeles	313 153	0.1	14.0	9.8	20.6	5.6	8.3	9.5	15.0	1 148 135	117	413 058	3 445 076	5.3
Madera	2 627	13.3	D	7.2	3.9	6.5	2.1	15.6	25.5	22 500	149	4 740	49 140	21.7
Marin	9 857	0.1	D	1.4	23.2	7.0	14.0	12.5	11.6	46 005	182	3 839	111 214	5.9
Mariposa	284	-0.7	D	1.9	3.5	4.6	3.1	D	42.8	4 740	260	531	10 188	15.4
Mendocino	1 650	-0.2	15.4	8.0	6.5	11.9	4.8	12.7	25.0	18 950	216	3 827	40 323	9.2
Merced	4 082	13.5	D	11.0	3.8	6.8	2.9	9.8	25.8	32 595	127	10 940	83 698	22.1
Modoc	175	20.6	D	D	D	6.1	2.8	D	41.9	2 585	267	455	5 192	8.0
Mono	404	1.2	D	D	4.4	6.4	6.4	D	34.6	1 280	90	104	13 912	18.3
Monterey	11 938	11.1	8.0	3.5	6.4	6.0	3.8	7.7	25.7	54 005	130	9 229	139 048	5.6
Napa	4 587	2.5	26.8	19.3	7.1	5.5	5.4	10.7	16.1	24 595	180	2 416	54 759	12.8
Nevada	2 002	-0.3	20.7	7.4	11.5	8.7	6.4	13.8	18.4	24 440	247	2 003	52 590	18.8
Orange	111 259	0.1	19.5	11.9	15.2	6.0	12.2	8.5	10.6	377 360	125	71 282	1 048 907	8.2
Placer	8 921	0.1	19.3	8.0	10.0	9.6	12.0	13.5	14.0	64 025	184	5 419	152 648	42.3
Plumas	397	1.0	16.9	7.9	D	8.4	6.0	6.5	35.3	5 570	278	695	15 566	16.3
Riverside	34 182	1.2	18.0	7.7	6.8	9.0	5.0	9.9	25.0	306 080	140	57 191	800 707	37.0
Sacramento	44 324	0.2	9.7	3.8	12.8	5.3	8.2	10.8	35.0	201 200	142	63 247	555 932	17.1
San Benito	895	7.7	D	17.1	D	10.2	3.9	4.7	22.4	7 060	128	905	17 870	8.3
San Bernardino	38 653	0.3	14.6	7.9	6.0	7.7	4.7	11.4	26.0	243 380	120	68 723	699 637	16.3
San Diego	104 615	0.4	14.5	8.7	17.6	5.4	7.1	8.0	26.5	415 805	134	82 461	1 164 786	12.0
San Francisco	59 874	0.0	4.5	1.4	28.4	4.0	18.5	5.5	16.1	111 525	138	45 775	376 942	8.8
San Joaquin	13 163	4.8	15.9	9.0	4.4	7.2	5.5	12.6	20.8	93 195	136	28 573	233 755	23.6
San Luis Obispo	6 401	1.3	15.3	5.4	9.7	8.3	5.1	11.5	22.1	50 215	166	5 212	117 315	14.7
San Mateo	37 201	0.2	20.6	16.3	27.9	5.2	10.5	7.0	7.2	103 230	144	12 956	271 031	4.0
Santa Barbara	12 543	4.3	15.6	8.4	13.3	6.4	5.5	10.3	21.6	65 395	154	9 634	152 834	6.9
Santa Clara	94 349	0.1	28.7	25.0	27.0	4.2	4.3	7.5	8.5	205 335	115	47 922	631 920	9.1
Santa Cruz	6 371	5.6	D	5.8	9.3	8.1	4.9	12.6	19.7	37 520	143	5 845	104 476	5.7
Shasta	3 635	0.2	D	3.8	6.8	9.9	4.6	18.5	22.4	44 875	253	9 850	77 313	12.4
Sierra	37	1.7	D	0.0	D	D	D	5.9	57.6	835	258	105	2 328	5.7
Siskiyou	775	6.7	D	5.3	5.9	8.1	3.2	12.4	30.5	12 215	272	2 584	23 910	8.9
Solano	9 243	1.4	21.3	13.4	5.1	6.9	4.5	13.7	27.6	60 430	146	12 167	152 698	13.5
Sonoma	12 360	0.9	22.1	13.0	12.0	7.5	6.1	13.3	15.5	82 525	171	9 779	204 572	11.7
Stanislaus	9 948	5.1	19.9	14.1	4.6	7.6	4.5	15.8	18.4	75 480	147	21 044	179 503	19.0
Sutter	1 830	14.2	12.4	4.8	4.6	9.7	5.1	13.6	15.6	15 165	160	3 812	33 858	19.6
Tehama	850	3.2	D	10.8	3.1	8.9	3.0	11.8	26.4	14 425	227	3 466	26 987	14.6
Trinity	144	-0.3	D	6.0	5.0	8.5	2.6	D	49.2	3 815	277	747	8 681	8.8
Tulare	7 784	10.5	13.5	8.2	4.1	7.5	3.7	7.8	25.2	57 290	130	18 824	141 696	18.4
Tuolumne	967	-0.6	12.7	4.6	6.7	8.0	3.8	16.1	34.6	14 660	265	1 687	31 244	10.3
Ventura	22 165	3.6	22.0	15.9	10.8	6.6	8.2	8.6	18.0	117 290	142	16 484	281 695	11.9
Yolo	6 534	4.6	11.6	5.8	7.0	5.1	3.3	6.7	39.6	24 155	120	5 506	75 054	21.9
Yuba	1 385	5.4	7.6	2.7	3.4	3.9	1.5	D	56.0	11 450	159	4 080	27 635	22.1
COLORADO	162 521	0.5	16.0	6.3	19.5	5.4	8.3	8.8	17.4	693 341	138	65 720	2 212 898	22.4
Adams	9 600	0.4	20.3	8.5	8.0	6.8	4.4	9.5	14.1	50 060	113	6 117	163 136	28.4
Alamosa	392	7.3	D	1.2	8.2	9.4	5.6	D	25.9	2 520	163	532	6 554	7.7
Arapahoe	25 007	0.0	11.2	2.4	30.7	4.8	13.0	9.0	9.2	70 515	123	6 372	238 301	20.8
Archuleta	180	-1.4	13.1	0.9	10.7	13.7	12.3	D	19.8	2 740	227	133	8 762	41.1
Baca	80	35.2	D	D	D	5.7	D	1.4	33.9	1 080	285	83	2 248	-4.9
Bent	86	21.7	D	D	D	2.6	3.8	1.7	41.8	985	152	195	2 242	-5.2

1. Includes mining, construction, and manufacturing.   2. Per 1,000 resident population enumerated in the 2010 census.

STATE County	Housing units, 2006–2010								Civilian labor force, 2010				Civilian employment,[5] 2006–2010		
		Occupied units						Sub-stand-ard units[3] (percent)			Unemployment			Percent	
		Owner-occupied				Renter-occupied									Con-struction, produc-tion, and mainte-nance occu-pations
				Median owner cost as a percent of income										Manage-ment, business, science and arts	
	Total	Percent	Median value[1]	With a mort-gage	Without a mort-gage	Median rent[2]	Median rent as a per-cent of income		Total	Percent change, 2009–2010	Total	Rate[4]	Total		
	89	90	91	92	93	94	95	96	97	98	99	100	101	102	103
CALIFORNIA	12 392 852	57.4	458 500	31.1	11.2	1 147	32.7	8.4	18 316 411	0.6	2 264 898	12.4	16 632 466	36.2	21.0
Alameda	532 026	55.1	590 900	30.7	10.3	1 188	30.9	5.7	755 529	-0.9	85 521	11.3	716 257	44.1	17.3
Alpine	410	73.4	453 600	35.6	10.3	913	28.2	0.0	440	-7.0	69	15.7	513	50.9	17.9
Amador	14 715	77.3	341 400	30.2	13.0	1 059	31.9	1.6	17 472	-2.6	2 336	13.4	14 318	31.5	22.0
Butte	85 465	61.2	265 400	28.7	12.6	861	34.8	3.8	104 580	-0.2	14 587	13.9	90 560	33.6	20.3
Calaveras	18 794	78.8	350 800	29.8	13.6	948	30.5	2.2	20 087	-1.5	3 130	15.6	19 293	31.2	24.3
Colusa	6 972	64.4	275 400	29.6	12.1	830	29.1	8.1	11 928	4.0	2 431	20.4	8 547	24.5	37.5
Contra Costa	368 087	69.5	548 200	31.3	11.3	1 270	32.7	4.1	522 374	-0.7	58 685	11.2	482 898	41.3	16.4
Del Norte	9 906	60.9	240 900	27.9	13.2	845	34.0	4.0	11 695	-0.4	1 559	13.3	9 503	28.1	17.5
El Dorado	68 394	76.5	445 700	30.6	12.7	1 074	32.1	3.3	90 822	-1.1	11 459	12.6	84 829	38.1	17.2
Fresno	283 836	55.0	257 000	28.0	11.1	819	33.2	10.5	438 606	0.0	73 601	16.8	368 278	28.4	27.9
Glenn	9 660	67.5	244 200	29.5	11.2	728	32.3	5.3	12 727	0.5	2 069	16.3	11 602	25.2	33.0
Humboldt	54 276	57.6	324 700	28.9	11.5	827	36.9	3.4	60 854	-0.4	6 972	11.5	60 816	31.8	20.8
Imperial	47 304	56.6	192 600	29.8	12.9	682	32.0	10.5	77 099	1.1	22 860	29.7	57 432	24.2	26.4
Inyo	7 982	64.0	290 000	27.9	12.4	793	32.7	4.6	9 558	0.5	954	10.0	8 646	25.7	22.0
Kern	248 057	61.4	217 100	28.1	11.4	810	32.4	9.2	368 546	0.4	58 554	15.9	310 995	26.0	32.6
Kings	40 606	56.0	220 400	26.8	10.2	815	28.8	10.2	61 350	0.3	10 126	16.5	52 826	23.1	36.2
Lake	25 180	67.1	265 400	32.2	15.2	845	37.8	4.7	25 303	-0.4	4 585	18.1	24 131	29.2	25.1
Lassen	10 276	63.7	217 300	26.3	11.7	895	32.9	5.9	13 755	1.6	1 953	14.2	10 481	31.8	18.8
Los Angeles	3 217 889	48.2	508 800	32.6	11.0	1 117	33.6	12.5	4 910 534	0.3	619 137	12.6	4 522 917	34.6	21.6
Madera	42 089	63.0	276 000	31.2	12.4	864	32.6	11.1	66 960	-0.2	10 420	15.6	52 484	23.7	34.9
Marin	102 727	64.0	868 000	30.5	11.3	1 523	32.5	2.8	131 410	-0.5	10 844	8.3	125 177	51.0	11.3
Mariposa	7 724	70.0	278 500	28.8	10.0	682	26.6	3.4	9 523	0.2	1 150	12.1	7 530	29.0	25.2
Mendocino	34 374	62.8	410 600	33.9	13.7	888	33.9	6.3	43 066	-0.9	4 900	11.4	38 802	29.0	26.7
Merced	73 586	55.9	241 000	30.9	11.1	798	33.2	9.4	107 381	1.6	20 291	18.9	94 778	22.7	36.7
Modoc	3 977	70.2	158 600	24.6	12.6	560	29.2	4.3	4 151	4.6	587	14.1	3 630	36.7	23.4
Mono	5 283	56.4	481 300	32.1	15.8	1 029	34.7	5.4	8 692	-1.5	895	10.3	8 226	35.9	15.5
Monterey	124 963	53.4	566 300	33.6	10.6	1 123	30.9	11.2	219 661	1.4	28 032	12.8	176 225	27.7	30.2
Napa	49 179	65.1	571 500	30.6	11.8	1 211	31.5	6.7	74 424	-1.6	7 308	9.8	63 873	34.6	24.5
Nevada	41 255	74.0	444 100	33.2	14.0	1 119	34.5	3.4	50 612	0.3	5 825	11.5	45 064	37.3	19.2
Orange	984 503	60.8	607 900	30.6	10.1	1 423	32.6	9.4	1 580 859	-0.8	151 169	9.6	1 442 008	39.4	17.8
Placer	129 153	72.9	427 600	29.7	12.4	1 151	31.6	1.9	177 097	-1.0	20 328	11.5	156 296	40.9	15.7
Plumas	10 090	65.6	289 700	27.8	14.4	708	27.7	4.2	10 036	2.4	1 690	16.8	8 895	28.2	30.9
Riverside	666 906	70.0	325 300	32.9	13.3	1 115	35.1	7.3	913 801	0.0	134 317	14.7	865 088	29.1	25.1
Sacramento	508 499	59.5	324 200	29.7	10.6	980	32.9	4.8	674 880	-1.9	86 257	12.8	625 894	37.0	17.6
San Benito	16 812	64.3	542 300	34.3	12.6	1 150	32.7	8.2	25 766	2.8	4 523	17.6	24 698	27.5	32.7
San Bernardino	596 125	65.1	319 000	30.8	11.9	1 061	34.2	9.0	855 660	-1.0	121 889	14.2	823 910	27.9	27.4
San Diego	1 061 789	55.9	486 000	31.6	10.7	1 228	33.4	6.2	1 558 186	0.1	164 320	10.5	1 380 907	39.5	17.0
San Francisco	335 956	37.5	785 200	29.9	10.0	1 328	27.8	7.2	457 989	-0.4	43 579	9.5	444 628	50.5	10.5
San Joaquin	212 905	61.7	318 600	31.7	11.3	972	34.3	8.2	298 937	-0.2	51 786	17.3	271 639	28.2	29.1
San Luis Obispo	102 434	61.4	513 900	31.8	11.5	1 118	36.0	3.2	136 162	-1.1	13 827	10.2	121 560	35.9	17.5
San Mateo	255 758	61.1	784 800	30.8	10.0	1 443	28.7	7.2	372 382	-0.5	33 093	8.9	360 951	43.2	14.8
Santa Barbara	141 793	54.1	576 500	31.2	10.8	1 265	34.7	8.4	220 463	-0.3	20 625	9.4	194 019	34.8	21.9
Santa Clara	596 747	59.2	701 000	30.0	10.0	1 402	28.2	7.3	874 345	-0.4	97 428	11.1	843 854	49.1	15.4
Santa Cruz	93 802	59.6	648 700	33.3	11.9	1 266	33.9	6.8	147 848	-1.3	18 849	12.7	126 380	40.9	20.6
Shasta	69 100	66.0	267 600	30.2	12.7	857	34.9	3.2	83 887	-0.5	13 422	16.0	70 143	32.3	20.3
Sierra	1 437	80.1	323 300	23.7	11.5	734	27.2	0.7	1 593	-2.0	251	15.8	1 616	35.6	28.5
Siskiyou	20 097	65.2	237 400	31.7	13.0	729	35.2	4.5	18 971	-3.5	3 344	17.6	17 370	32.1	23.0
Solano	139 011	65.8	389 800	31.1	10.6	1 195	32.8	4.4	214 954	0.4	25 864	12.0	185 585	32.8	21.9
Sonoma	184 033	62.4	524 400	32.1	12.3	1 201	33.1	5.0	254 195	-1.5	26 630	10.5	233 182	34.3	21.0
Stanislaus	163 841	62.1	285 200	31.1	12.3	941	34.3	7.2	237 400	0.5	41 346	17.4	207 424	27.0	31.0
Sutter	31 373	61.8	262 200	29.0	12.2	856	30.3	6.1	42 103	0.0	8 325	19.8	38 164	28.7	29.8
Tehama	23 510	65.1	221 400	29.8	12.6	770	31.6	6.7	25 116	-1.6	3 973	15.8	23 076	25.3	29.1
Trinity	5 889	73.5	268 200	25.4	10.6	705	30.1	4.8	5 073	0.6	951	18.7	5 213	33.3	22.7
Tulare	126 664	59.3	211 200	28.3	10.9	755	30.3	11.7	207 727	1.1	34 960	16.8	166 451	23.8	36.9
Tuolumne	22 192	70.2	332 500	32.7	13.4	901	34.0	3.1	25 615	-1.5	3 583	14.0	21 022	29.5	22.0
Ventura	264 305	66.4	568 700	30.6	10.8	1 391	32.7	6.4	430 924	-0.1	46 607	10.8	385 262	37.3	20.9
Yolo	69 386	54.1	391 300	28.2	10.0	1 041	33.7	5.3	98 039	-1.2	12 707	13.0	90 422	43.7	18.7
Yuba	23 750	59.8	224 200	29.9	11.7	801	32.3	9.0	28 143	-1.7	5 387	19.1	26 178	27.5	27.9
COLORADO	1 918 959	67.6	236 600	25.3	10.3	852	30.6	2.7	2 725 202	-0.1	243 755	8.9	2 456 139	38.7	19.9
Adams	147 951	68.4	196 100	27.0	12.4	878	31.3	4.4	227 077	0.7	23 201	10.2	208 524	27.5	28.9
Alamosa	5 798	63.2	131 100	22.1	10.0	557	31.9	4.5	9 035	3.9	687	7.6	6 664	35.1	20.5
Arapahoe	218 909	65.9	232 300	25.3	10.0	880	31.7	2.8	310 017	0.2	27 293	8.8	285 347	38.7	17.7
Archuleta	3 377	82.9	304 400	24.3	10.0	753	28.6	3.2	6 138	-2.4	628	10.2	4 964	30.6	25.9
Baca	1 682	74.9	72 700	20.8	13.3	439	19.5	1.8	2 416	-5.6	103	4.3	1 843	34.3	26.7
Bent	1 935	67.4	69 400	22.6	10.4	574	26.1	5.1	2 590	-2.2	209	8.1	1 814	36.0	27.0

1. Specified owner-occupied units.   2. Specified renter-occupied units. A value of 10.0 represents 10 percent or less.   3. Overcrowded or lacking complete plumbing facilities.   4. Percent of civilian labor force.   5. Persons 16 years old and over.

Table B. States and Counties — Nonfarm Employment and Agriculture

STATE County	Private nonfarm establishments, employment and payroll, 2009									Agriculture, 2007			
	Number of establishments	Employment						Annual payroll		Farms			
								Total (mil dol)	Average per employee (dollars)		Percent with:		Farm operators whose principal occupation is farming (percent)
		Total	Health care and social assistance	Manufacturing	Retail trade	Finance and insurance	Professional, scientific, and technical services			Number	Fewer than 50 acres	500 acres or more	
	104	105	106	107	108	109	110	111	112	113	114	115	116
CALIFORNIA	857 831	12 833 709	1 678 778	1 246 464	1 544 327	609 858	1 134 051	621 735	48 445	81 033	65.8	9.5	50.5
Alameda	36 360	581 130	80 069	67 122	62 665	18 965	53 854	31 215	53 715	525	60.4	12.0	37.5
Alpine	43	756	21	0	D	D	11	12	16 393	7	14.3	14.3	28.6
Amador	811	8 378	1 287	D	1 642	D	254	264	31 566	479	54.9	9.4	49.3
Butte	4 794	55 308	13 069	3 744	9 776	2 407	2 528	1 727	31 228	2 048	64.5	7.9	51.6
Calaveras	936	5 819	1 011	395	1 108	172	268	172	29 481	631	59.4	12.4	45.6
Colusa	370	4 133	450	685	585	113	48	131	31 683	814	31.2	26.9	57.0
Contra Costa	22 138	304 803	48 846	17 788	42 645	23 238	25 260	16 872	55 355	634	73.8	9.0	41.8
Del Norte	464	4 401	1 247	D	1 041	118	132	118	26 801	85	52.9	8.2	43.5
El Dorado	4 382	42 602	6 327	2 788	5 825	2 953	2 540	1 587	37 251	1 268	79.1	1.6	42.8
Fresno	15 971	233 208	38 365	24 357	34 040	10 222	12 362	8 277	35 491	6 081	61.3	10.8	57.1
Glenn	482	4 540	480	663	699	137	118	173	38 169	1 242	49.4	15.3	58.8
Humboldt	3 406	33 603	6 993	2 252	7 063	1 133	1 705	982	29 210	852	52.3	16.5	54.7
Imperial	2 441	30 887	4 335	3 324	7 647	993	923	855	27 676	452	28.1	39.4	71.0
Inyo	548	5 193	1 044	D	982	99	136	157	30 193	94	43.6	28.7	50.0
Kern	12 111	179 606	26 613	11 970	26 922	6 165	11 317	6 848	38 130	2 117	43.0	24.7	57.4
Kings	1 638	23 220	4 546	3 666	4 146	582	501	760	32 739	1 129	53.3	17.7	57.8
Lake	1 092	9 280	2 281	341	2 202	249	257	278	29 906	845	66.4	4.9	41.7
Lassen	451	3 610	792	D	926	107	122	102	28 160	459	35.9	22.9	52.7
Los Angeles	245 523	3 703 233	472 035	420 013	389 604	171 200	347 225	178 048	48 079	1 734	86.9	2.8	35.8
Madera	1 955	24 031	5 661	3 367	3 733	635	530	862	35 853	1 708	46.4	13.1	54.4
Marin	9 725	94 673	14 587	1 820	13 388	6 847	8 583	4 961	52 405	255	43.5	31.8	59.2
Mariposa	365	3 064	450	88	391	47	41	85	27 806	302	46.0	21.5	44.7
Mendocino	2 593	22 130	4 165	2 628	4 490	584	685	681	30 756	1 136	50.1	13.4	51.3
Merced	2 921	40 447	6 063	8 678	7 201	1 299	869	1 321	32 671	2 607	55.7	12.6	59.5
Modoc	162	1 310	489	0	214	35	D	41	31 233	448	21.4	36.2	60.0
Mono	573	5 862	D	22	758	48	124	158	26 897	84	33.3	23.8	45.2
Monterey	8 500	100 735	14 540	6 106	16 416	3 683	7 370	3 973	39 440	1 199	45.0	24.9	64.1
Napa	3 996	55 167	10 152	9 896	6 411	1 297	1 980	2 444	44 299	1 638	73.0	5.3	41.4
Nevada	3 097	26 747	4 452	2 300	4 168	860	1 443	918	34 332	690	78.4	3.8	42.8
Orange	87 483	1 336 341	144 177	155 658	143 815	83 532	115 093	62 902	47 070	325	82.8	2.8	40.9
Placer	9 482	123 022	15 186	7 137	20 225	7 307	8 685	5 228	42 499	1 488	81.7	2.6	45.0
Plumas	682	3 812	908	D	619	186	108	134	35 180	142	52.1	15.5	49.3
Riverside	34 055	480 413	61 452	44 887	83 497	12 118	16 984	15 956	33 213	3 463	87.1	2.9	48.0
Sacramento	27 635	417 036	70 781	20 543	57 123	31 560	30 893	17 672	42 376	1 393	70.9	9.0	47.9
San Benito	903	10 894	1 203	2 041	1 465	240	234	369	33 840	625	57.0	21.3	55.5
San Bernardino	31 866	519 247	74 252	54 249	78 747	17 048	16 631	18 063	34 786	1 405	82.6	2.3	48.3
San Diego	76 345	1 119 643	139 226	93 819	138 162	52 930	118 403	50 265	44 894	6 687	91.1	1.3	37.8
San Francisco	30 490	492 689	60 779	9 011	40 480	50 720	78 792	35 300	71 649	6	100.0	0.0	33.3
San Joaquin	11 044	165 952	27 015	20 422	24 982	6 231	4 314	5 972	35 989	3 624	64.1	8.6	55.9
San Luis Obispo	7 950	82 573	14 948	5 508	13 472	2 819	4 991	2 848	34 489	2 784	56.7	12.5	49.6
San Mateo	19 772	336 120	32 003	D	33 708	14 724	50 111	23 739	70 626	329	64.4	7.6	48.6
Santa Barbara	11 203	136 826	19 451	12 022	18 665	4 892	11 178	5 735	41 918	1 597	64.9	11.1	50.9
Santa Clara	44 164	850 828	91 824	89 488	79 026	26 782	115 818	64 936	76 321	1 068	75.2	6.1	46.9
Santa Cruz	6 885	71 708	12 150	4 676	11 992	2 075	4 535	2 851	39 756	682	77.7	2.2	61.9
Shasta	4 428	47 789	10 415	2 335	9 236	2 198	2 125	1 582	33 101	1 473	69.5	8.5	46.8
Sierra	74	322	101	D	D	D	D	10	30 022	50	8.0	16.0	72.0
Siskiyou	1 187	8 517	1 662	699	1 647	312	275	246	28 874	846	36.5	21.2	53.2
Solano	6 839	100 025	19 888	9 514	17 039	3 299	3 750	4 076	40 753	890	62.0	12.1	52.8
Sonoma	13 383	149 366	22 767	19 124	23 094	6 756	8 164	6 315	42 279	3 429	72.4	5.3	47.3
Stanislaus	8 578	127 658	23 533	19 791	21 345	3 711	5 048	4 814	37 707	4 114	64.9	6.1	54.1
Sutter	1 789	20 087	3 971	1 400	4 310	647	589	671	33 400	1 263	50.9	13.5	59.2
Tehama	1 058	11 841	1 831	D	2 136	283	271	377	31 857	1 752	62.9	9.1	50.1
Trinity	281	1 551	332	D	364	49	68	42	27 236	181	50.3	13.8	33.7
Tulare	6 276	87 794	14 409	12 574	14 521	3 310	2 558	2 823	32 160	5 240	64.3	8.0	53.2
Tuolumne	1 436	13 206	3 022	960	2 149	311	525	417	31 566	366	50.5	15.6	47.3
Ventura	19 677	245 788	31 025	24 862	37 200	16 689	21 219	10 889	44 303	2 437	77.8	4.1	47.7
Yolo	3 828	61 609	6 342	6 159	7 238	1 839	3 160	2 445	39 691	983	46.5	17.8	53.9
Yuba	818	9 419	2 365	548	1 309	457	284	294	31 191	828	62.9	8.5	50.4
COLORADO	152 997	2 005 578	252 797	121 919	246 697	99 049	168 070	87 462	43 609	37 054	36.8	25.5	40.4
Adams	8 214	134 044	19 177	9 137	17 179	2 338	4 941	5 334	39 796	895	52.1	20.0	35.6
Alamosa	509	5 315	1 548	92	1 180	343	198	157	29 516	316	20.9	30.4	51.9
Arapahoe	16 994	239 689	28 750	8 140	29 909	22 311	22 114	12 075	50 377	627	59.0	12.6	27.1
Archuleta	508	2 913	208	D	574	117	D	67	22 851	306	35.3	20.3	35.9
Baca	91	563	D	D	151	D	11	14	24 039	777	3.2	58.8	39.6
Bent	63	581	63	D	84	D	D	15	26 566	311	17.4	49.2	56.3

Table B. States and Counties — **Agriculture**

STATE County	Land in farms					Value of land and buildings (dollars)		Value of machinery and equipment, average per farm (dollars)	Value of products sold				Percent of farms with sales of:		Government payments	
	Acreage (1,000)	Percent change, 2002–2007	Acres			Average per farm	Average per acre		Total (mil dol)	Average per farm (dollars)	Percent from:		$10,000 or more	$100,000 or more	Total ($1,000)	Percent of farms
			Average size of farm	Total irrigated (1,000)	Total cropland (1,000)						Crops	Live-stock and poultry products				
	117	118	119	120	121	122	123	124	125	126	127	128	129	130	131	132
CALIFORNIA	25 365	-8.1	313	8 016.2	9 464.6	2 005 768	6 408	108 145	33 885.1	418 164	67.6	32.4	53.4	23.5	240 242	9.2
Alameda	205	-6.0	390	9.7	30.5	1 511 370	3 878	53 082	50.4	95 919	67.9	32.1	40.4	9.3	365	5.7
Alpine	2	NA	259	D	0.5	1 771 429	6 851	71 453	D	D	D	D	42.9	14.3	0	0.0
Amador	163	-16.0	341	10.1	15.6	1 626 088	4 764	46 973	20.7	43 217	63.3	36.7	37.8	9.6	91	2.3
Butte	374	-2.1	183	202.2	222.7	1 371 244	7 513	108 816	342.8	167 366	96.5	3.5	53.6	25.5	14 780	14.3
Calaveras	201	-23.0	319	4.9	12.1	1 167 695	3 665	50 209	16.5	26 146	26.6	73.4	30.0	4.8	49	2.4
Colusa	474	-2.3	582	277.3	299.0	2 317 659	3 979	227 223	386.3	474 570	97.9	2.1	74.8	51.1	21 222	54.8
Contra Costa	147	16.7	232	27.4	35.9	1 531 291	6 605	72 166	70.8	111 687	84.2	15.8	33.6	12.8	192	3.0
Del Norte	18	38.5	214	7.7	8.0	1 453 524	6 800	106 770	32.5	382 445	40.5	59.5	37.6	16.5	D	7.1
El Dorado	107	-8.5	84	9.9	15.3	858 053	10 161	35 905	19.9	15 732	83.9	16.1	26.3	3.0	149	1.8
Fresno	1 636	-15.2	269	984.5	1 102.2	2 132 914	7 927	147 707	3 730.5	613 476	67.0	33.0	71.6	33.6	24 737	9.2
Glenn	489	-3.4	394	236.1	250.3	1 899 672	4 823	147 291	405.4	326 441	76.0	24.0	69.0	39.5	15 457	33.5
Humboldt	597	-5.8	701	17.5	33.9	1 723 851	2 458	84 426	149.8	175 873	D	D	43.5	15.0	515	9.5
Imperial	427	-16.9	945	376.5	396.7	5 001 024	5 290	413 760	1 290.3	2 854 543	54.5	45.5	83.2	61.9	4 885	29.2
Inyo	293	29.1	3 112	32.5	8.3	2 959 058	951	71 730	14.5	153 740	38.7	61.3	52.1	23.4	D	3.2
Kern	2 362	-13.5	1 116	786.3	942.8	5 160 784	4 626	253 255	3 204.1	1 513 532	79.6	20.4	59.6	40.3	27 346	17.1
Kings	681	5.4	603	421.6	512.9	3 295 061	5 465	245 730	1 358.4	1 203 198	48.0	52.0	63.7	41.9	23 258	35.5
Lake	124	-13.9	147	13.6	29.0	1 349 648	9 182	45 940	61.1	72 310	97.7	2.3	33.6	8.3	154	2.4
Lassen	459	-4.8	1 000	69.9	82.6	1 383 204	1 383	108 010	55.5	120 923	65.8	34.2	38.6	12.9	160	4.4
Los Angeles	108	-2.7	63	29.7	49.2	877 388	14 027	67 008	325.9	187 935	92.7	7.3	27.8	11.2	138	1.6
Madera	680	-0.3	398	281.7	290.7	2 699 315	6 783	139 667	990.1	579 696	63.2	36.8	64.8	38.8	4 608	11.3
Marin	133	-11.9	523	1.6	12.0	2 641 781	5 055	83 556	57.9	226 944	10.5	89.5	55.3	25.1	603	13.3
Mariposa	213	-2.7	704	D	4.4	1 160 104	1 649	52 874	11.5	37 960	4.2	95.8	31.8	6.0	131	1.7
Mendocino	609	-13.9	536	27.1	53.8	2 846 283	5 312	57 225	122.4	107 754	87.1	12.9	47.6	15.2	719	7.5
Merced	1 041	3.5	399	514.2	537.7	2 879 524	7 210	198 153	2 330.4	893 904	37.7	62.3	72.7	39.6	11 968	19.8
Modoc	598	-1.8	1 334	132.7	145.8	1 946 852	1 459	122 736	70.8	158 059	61.6	38.4	55.8	26.8	825	20.8
Mono	46	-16.7	531	22.2	10.5	1 639 748	3 088	86 028	9.8	116 313	40.7	59.3	45.2	28.6	0	0.0
Monterey	1 328	5.3	1 108	233.0	311.1	5 144 255	4 645	305 191	2 178.5	1 816 906	98.2	1.8	59.8	37.9	1 316	7.8
Napa	223	-6.3	136	51.6	66.2	3 696 510	27 122	76 502	376.9	230 078	98.7	1.3	72.6	31.2	233	1.6
Nevada	70	-14.6	102	7.2	7.3	745 506	7 331	40 004	9.5	13 722	55.1	44.9	23.3	3.3	227	3.8
Orange	87	27.9	269	9.0	14.6	3 253 936	12 095	166 005	336.4	1 035 046	99.2	0.8	49.5	26.8	38	3.4
Placer	132	0.8	89	30.2	50.3	905 331	10 188	39 564	45.0	30 220	68.1	31.9	24.1	4.3	2 838	4.0
Plumas	120	-29.8	847	20.2	18.5	1 550 857	1 831	68 115	D	D	D	D	32.4	9.9	D	1.4
Riverside	355	-37.9	102	168.1	219.9	1 614 969	15 765	66 421	1 012.0	292 244	71.3	28.7	47.7	13.7	5 740	2.4
Sacramento	329	4.8	236	113.4	133.6	1 585 376	6 721	94 739	346.1	248 485	59.8	40.2	38.5	18.3	3 631	11.1
San Benito	580	0.3	928	30.4	55.2	2 585 410	2 787	107 836	222.9	356 577	83.3	16.7	49.1	17.6	396	7.4
San Bernardino	514	0.0	366	29.0	35.9	1 159 028	3 167	86 262	743.7	529 296	19.9	80.1	41.9	19.3	1 240	4.2
San Diego	304	-25.5	45	62.2	102.5	874 683	19 247	40 032	1 054.2	157 646	91.2	8.8	42.0	10.8	342	0.5
San Francisco	0	NA	1	0.0	0.0	533 333	457 143	53 354	0.6	107 333	100.0	0.0	66.7	16.7	0	0.0
San Joaquin	738	-9.2	204	454.0	492.0	2 069 142	10 168	127 313	1 564.4	431 665	63.4	36.6	65.5	33.9	4 444	8.5
San Luis Obispo	1 370	3.9	492	98.9	299.6	2 236 326	4 546	69 792	560.6	201 368	93.2	6.8	46.3	15.9	4 492	8.2
San Mateo	57	35.7	174	3.6	10.4	1 620 751	9 340	85 246	135.6	412 008	97.6	2.4	45.0	18.8	25	2.7
Santa Barbara	727	-4.0	455	95.1	125.0	3 223 533	7 081	104 111	951.3	595 696	96.0	4.0	57.2	25.9	132	1.0
Santa Clara	300	-6.5	281	22.2	33.3	1 605 690	5 719	77 811	235.9	220 906	94.6	5.4	36.5	11.5	132	2.9
Santa Cruz	47	-29.9	70	19.6	23.6	1 561 362	22 423	101 383	447.4	656 037	96.9	3.1	59.4	30.4	40	0.7
Shasta	391	17.1	265	48.7	40.2	837 861	3 158	43 514	44.7	30 329	D	D	22.6	4.1	252	3.8
Sierra	29	-50.8	576	7.0	6.2	1 502 130	2 609	67 892	2.0	40 062	29.3	70.8	56.0	14.0	47	6.0
Siskiyou	598	-2.0	706	144.1	164.4	1 766 360	2 501	111 641	136.4	161 220	78.9	21.1	39.7	16.2	2 395	22.2
Solano	358	2.0	403	146.0	154.9	1 985 813	4 934	99 718	244.3	274 489	83.1	16.9	41.0	19.3	2 289	17.4
Sonoma	531	-15.3	155	78.3	134.4	2 459 725	15 887	68 139	647.6	188 854	65.2	34.8	56.9	20.6	711	2.6
Stanislaus	789	-0.1	192	375.0	351.2	1 817 304	9 476	119 526	1 820.6	442 529	40.4	59.6	61.4	28.7	4 379	10.0
Sutter	360	-3.2	285	231.7	274.4	1 868 657	6 559	141 018	317.6	251 471	98.0	2.0	67.5	32.2	16 822	26.4
Tehama	532	-38.3	304	76.1	94.2	967 204	3 184	63 403	143.0	81 597	73.0	27.0	43.9	11.7	1 065	7.0
Trinity	125	19.0	690	1.4	3.0	858 580	1 244	43 511	3.2	17 496	32.8	67.2	26.5	3.3	75	8.3
Tulare	1 169	-16.1	223	550.3	638.8	1 843 502	8 266	125 007	3 335.0	636 453	36.2	63.8	69.9	32.8	20 335	11.3
Tuolumne	117	-22.0	320	2.1	5.6	1 086 881	3 398	45 256	18.7	50 965	8.3	91.7	26.5	4.6	37	2.5
Ventura	259	-22.0	106	91.3	113.9	2 421 700	22 782	95 150	1 316.3	540 137	99.0	1.0	62.2	25.2	554	1.9
Yolo	480	-12.7	488	246.3	311.3	2 665 291	5 460	172 234	384.2	390 864	92.9	7.1	57.3	27.9	8 306	30.0
Yuba	161	-31.2	194	71.0	71.0	1 152 483	5 931	96 461	112.9	136 363	84.4	15.6	42.4	20.4	5 161	17.5
COLORADO	31 605	1.6	853	2 868.0	11 483.9	892 170	1 046	99 344	6 061.1	163 576	32.7	67.3	36.1	13.8	155 980	31.2
Adams	702	0.1	784	17.0	546.9	931 948	1 189	102 027	153.4	171 439	88.2	11.8	29.5	13.7	6 242	38.1
Alamosa	177	-13.7	559	94.0	91.1	885 117	1 584	176 244	91.4	289 281	94.1	5.9	51.3	25.9	684	26.6
Arapahoe	252	-24.3	402	1.7	151.3	615 585	1 533	63 458	28.8	45 989	83.4	16.6	17.9	6.1	1 847	27.6
Archuleta	150	45.6	489	14.5	18.9	811 945	1 661	59 412	7.4	24 146	9.8	90.2	24.8	5.9	173	8.8
Baca	1 301	20.5	1 674	55.7	718.7	1 090 687	651	133 172	111.2	143 117	54.6	45.4	42.3	24.3	11 448	80.1
Bent	877	19.2	2 820	50.5	185.7	1 461 869	518	144 804	82.2	264 373	23.1	76.9	55.3	27.3	1 816	56.3

STATE County	Water use, 2005 Total water withdrawn (mil gal/day) [133]	Gallons withdrawn per person [134]	Wholesale trade,[1] 2007 Number of establishments [135]	Number of employees [136]	Sales (mil dol) [137]	Annual payroll (mil dol) [138]	Retail trade,[2] 2007 Number of establishments [139]	Number of employees [140]	Sales (mil dol) [141]	Annual payroll (mil dol) [142]	Real estate and rental and leasing,[2] 2007 Number of establishments [143]	Number of employees [144]	Receipts (mil dol) [145]	Annual payroll (mil dol) [146]
CALIFORNIA	45 719.7	1 265	53 963	745 785	598 456.5	42 334.5	114 438	1 683 023	455 032.3	44 328.9	51 597	312 488	76 805.0	13 446.7
Alameda	171.8	119	2 553	45 364	35 674.0	2 786.6	4 503	67 335	17 909.1	1 882.1	2 032	12 754	3 081.7	508.7
Alpine	15.1	13 037	NA	NA	NA	NA	4	D	D	D	1	D	D	D
Amador	24.1	625	24	D	D	D	163	1 960	1 800.8	49.7	44	98	16.4	2.6
Butte	789.9	3 688	165	1 824	796.4	71.6	798	11 316	2 400.7	256.8	264	1 462	158.8	32.6
Calaveras	17.3	369	20	77	24.2	3.3	151	1 388	292.8	32.6	61	173	29.5	3.9
Colusa	916.3	43 436	18	224	183.2	11.6	60	506	208.5	12.1	17	42	5.8	1.2
Contra Costa	1 679.1	1 650	779	7 116	6 644.0	409.6	2 822	46 065	11 763.8	1 242.9	1 452	7 236	1 607.0	311.8
Del Norte	9.0	314	9	D	D	D	74	1 029	206.3	22.6	35	122	16.6	3.0
El Dorado	46.0	260	118	718	363.6	32.8	591	6 384	1 619.7	175.6	265	1 545	190.8	40.7
Fresno	3 260.2	3 715	814	12 843	7 846.8	582.0	2 579	38 046	9 808.3	905.0	755	4 478	695.2	132.1
Glenn	741.2	26 701	29	415	148.4	14.4	85	766	204.0	18.0	25	97	9.0	2.3
Humboldt	137.2	1 069	99	D	D	D	659	7 782	1 726.4	172.4	186	622	102.8	15.7
Imperial	2 144.9	13 765	212	D	D	D	534	8 052	1 727.3	170.2	134	555	73.4	12.5
Inyo	80.4	4 430	15	D	D	D	116	975	242.0	21.8	28	94	10.6	2.5
Kern	2 663.6	3 519	559	7 850	5 730.5	377.0	1 993	30 123	7 876.0	725.6	627	3 414	565.5	112.8
Kings	1 380.4	9 625	60	D	D	D	326	4 267	1 035.9	93.9	95	343	55.4	7.2
Lake	45.2	694	21	D	D	D	196	2 267	557.9	50.6	67	223	28.2	5.0
Lassen	246.9	7 104	7	D	D	D	95	993	260.4	24.5	25	65	6.1	1.3
Los Angeles	3 811.1	384	21 677	259 831	198 435.8	12 262.9	30 179	418 153	119 111.8	10 849.2	14 085	90 847	26 790.4	4 129.2
Madera	834.8	5 846	79	678	353.1	28.8	368	3 883	1 010.2	89.3	100	409	38.7	9.4
Marin	36.8	149	381	3 631	2 373.1	218.5	1 161	15 432	4 589.3	472.8	633	3 122	1 148.2	137.8
Mariposa	9.2	511	7	D	D	D	72	427	84.5	8.6	21	85	9.3	2.4
Mendocino	58.1	659	84	D	D	D	492	5 097	1 259.1	120.7	141	597	91.3	12.6
Merced	1 624.9	6 723	97	D	D	D	578	8 005	2 001.3	179.9	153	641	85.6	15.1
Modoc	313.8	32 950	8	D	D	D	33	271	53.0	5.4	11	D	D	D
Mono	211.1	16 879	9	D	D	D	90	812	154.3	16.9	65	346	39.5	9.9
Monterey	1 129.2	2 740	392	D	D	D	1 497	18 392	4 541.1	487.8	487	2 423	500.6	86.6
Napa	51.8	390	143	D	D	D	537	6 463	1 665.0	180.7	206	893	153.0	31.1
Nevada	88.9	903	88	D	D	D	443	4 713	1 077.2	124.6	185	820	142.5	26.1
Orange	717.6	240	6 559	94 938	97 963.6	5 642.5	9 991	159 810	45 022.5	4 304.3	5 566	43 366	10 688.2	2 161.6
Placer	209.2	660	334	5 272	3 898.6	275.6	1 254	22 112	6 180.1	604.9	602	4 113	674.9	146.7
Plumas	79.3	3 691	5	D	D	D	118	789	175.3	17.6	42	77	13.7	2.8
Riverside	1 257.5	646	1 601	22 180	16 912.3	979.6	5 320	89 543	24 146.4	2 257.3	2 189	11 787	2 056.8	376.9
Sacramento	774.3	568	1 144	16 959	15 728.1	773.4	3 821	63 609	15 600.0	1 613.6	1 673	9 979	1 677.6	360.4
San Benito	69.4	1 241	36	1 645	319.6	60.7	124	1 522	352.9	40.7	56	115	16.5	3.4
San Bernardino	586.1	298	2 284	33 335	27 579.9	1 434.7	5 018	84 312	21 717.4	2 018.8	1 771	9 935	2 310.1	354.5
San Diego	4 085.1	1 393	4 002	55 934	33 704.9	4 120.7	9 948	151 425	38 710.6	3 889.2	5 810	33 067	7 190.2	1 345.2
San Francisco	1 668.0	2 256	1 195	11 786	10 562.2	668.1	3 710	45 079	12 400.0	1 395.9	1 843	14 332	4 309.7	984.3
San Joaquin	1 483.5	2 234	558	9 517	9 001.3	437.3	1 756	27 329	7 109.7	653.0	634	3 363	577.5	104.4
San Luis Obispo	2 774.1	10 858	277	2 329	955.0	104.1	1 262	14 652	3 548.4	353.6	475	2 050	293.4	56.7
San Mateo	151.1	216	1 076	15 170	12 607.8	1 094.9	2 216	36 139	10 198.8	1 084.2	1 246	8 041	2 077.1	365.1
Santa Barbara	239.6	598	438	5 713	4 023.6	350.4	1 605	20 281	4 983.4	524.4	681	3 452	620.7	119.5
Santa Clara	296.1	174	2 487	61 835	60 644.1	6 157.9	5 297	86 410	26 491.5	2 906.4	2 608	14 831	5 172.6	748.6
Santa Cruz	73.7	295	273	D	D	D	981	12 454	3 725.4	316.0	380	1 793	311.1	58.6
Shasta	236.2	1 313	179	1 748	829.0	69.4	722	10 287	2 526.4	260.1	225	1 201	128.2	26.1
Sierra	63.4	18 465	2	D	D	D	14	D	D	D	NA	NA	NA	NA
Siskiyou	384.8	8 502	37	358	169.1	11.2	209	1 859	403.3	37.2	67	203	22.1	4.1
Solano	467.9	1 137	249	D	D	D	1 167	19 117	4 828.0	482.7	404	1 913	347.9	58.5
Sonoma	114.3	245	585	7 631	3 953.6	454.3	1 925	26 177	6 427.2	718.5	718	3 237	604.1	114.2
Stanislaus	1 457.9	2 884	397	5 460	3 759.1	248.8	1 500	23 394	5 661.9	561.1	500	2 988	472.6	90.3
Sutter	833.7	9 381	66	1 421	879.0	71.7	304	4 614	1 065.4	112.0	99	602	60.4	12.9
Tehama	538.8	8 804	32	D	D	D	180	2 244	735.4	54.7	60	216	23.8	4.7
Trinity	21.6	1 588	4	D	D	D	52	383	69.2	6.7	8	D	D	D
Tulare	2 275.0	5 537	337	D	D	D	1 140	16 005	3 900.9	367.4	294	1 260	189.1	32.3
Tuolumne	33.8	570	37	D	D	D	213	2 419	582.4	56.1	90	271	39.9	6.6
Ventura	1 198.6	1 506	1 024	D	D	D	2 766	40 773	11 083.6	1 074.8	1 051	5 064	1 006.1	196.0
Yolo	738.8	3 995	251	6 048	6 483.6	271.2	500	7 812	1 765.7	189.2	268	1 560	247.0	53.4
Yuba	351.7	5 238	27	D	D	D	126	1 522	423.6	35.0	37	121	20.5	2.6
COLORADO	13 627.7	2 921	5 850	81 144	53 599.0	4 191.0	19 428	261 962	65 896.8	6 537.5	10 011	47 568	8 460.9	1 793.0
Adams	185.3	464	654	15 465	11 193.4	747.5	997	17 192	4 848.9	466.9	455	3 029	458.8	98.1
Alamosa	272.1	17 807	17	136	85.3	4.7	90	1 115	263.0	27.6	26	122	14.2	2.8
Arapahoe	84.9	161	684	9 551	5 774.1	550.7	1 890	32 052	9 932.0	848.7	1 109	6 048	1 207.1	241.7
Archuleta	71.5	6 014	8	29	8.8	0.8	104	647	142.7	14.9	51	178	37.2	4.7
Baca	127.8	31 403	16	43	52.7	1.2	17	124	32.9	2.5	3	3	0.1	0.0
Bent	211.3	38 024	1	D	D	D	16	85	16.4	1.4	2	D	D	D

1. Merchant wholesalers, except manufacturers' sales branches and offices. 2. Employer establishments.

Professional Services, Manufacturing, and Accommodation and Food Services

STATE County	Professional, scientific, and technical services,[1] 2007				Manufacturing, 2007				Accommodation and food services, 2007			
	Number of establish-ments	Number of employees	Receipts (mil dol)	Annual payroll (mil dol)	Number of establish-ments	Number of employees	Receipts (mil dol)	Annual payroll (mil dol)	Number of establish-ments	Number of employees	Sales (mil dol)	Annual payroll (mil dol)
	147	148	149	150	151	152	153	154	155	156	157	158
CALIFORNIA	111 954	1 231 372	194 406.3	80 738.1	44 296	1 448 485	491 372.1	71 247.3	75 989	1 366 926	80 852.8	22 374.8
Alameda	5 143	D	D	D	2 081	81 002	25 236.9	4 645.4	3 385	47 408	2 807.8	770.0
Alpine	5	D	D	D	NA	NA	NA	NA	12	D	D	D
Amador	77	279	26.1	8.9	51	760	143.0	29.4	109	1 249	61.2	17.1
Butte	426	D	D	D	224	4 404	987.4	150.6	429	7 708	355.8	96.7
Calaveras	80	347	36.7	12.9	NA	NA	NA	NA	114	976	42.4	11.1
Colusa	22	50	3.9	1.1	24	745	288.4	27.5	39	1 124	91.6	21.0
Contra Costa	3 273	D	D	D	622	18 551	32 021.4	1 146.1	1 777	28 524	1 562.3	433.1
Del Norte	38	135	13.1	4.2	NA	NA	NA	NA	74	748	32.2	7.9
El Dorado	538	2 808	515.1	151.4	204	3 534	662.2	142.5	447	5 885	301.7	83.5
Fresno	1 564	D	D	D	646	26 898	7 827.3	1 018.0	1 460	25 553	1 147.2	320.9
Glenn	36	149	11.0	3.4	31	721	278.3	27.7	58	608	31.0	8.3
Humboldt	259	D	D	D	158	3 105	877.0	117.7	352	4 649	209.0	58.4
Imperial	153	D	D	D	58	2 846	1 207.9	96.9	261	3 719	167.8	46.2
Inyo	34	D	D	D	NA	NA	NA	NA	98	1 570	91.7	25.3
Kern	1 123	D	D	D	390	12 789	9 456.2	583.7	1 203	19 344	940.3	252.2
Kings	101	535	52.9	16.9	73	4 291	2 107.7	148.7	171	4 209	360.1	77.5
Lake	79	D	D	D	NA	NA	NA	NA	133	1 325	68.1	17.3
Lassen	33	120	11.9	4.0	NA	NA	NA	NA	61	651	29.7	7.6
Los Angeles	30 754	D	D	D	15 158	451 656	153 343.7	20 520.1	19 476	339 815	20 238.1	5 570.1
Madera	124	D	D	D	116	4 143	1 452.9	170.3	192	2 265	125.1	33.1
Marin	1 797	D	D	D	229	2 205	397.2	88.0	694	10 913	626.6	185.9
Mariposa	21	76	5.8	1.9	NA	NA	NA	NA	51	1 430	133.0	27.5
Mendocino	206	D	D	D	146	3 057	773.4	113.6	347	3 796	194.2	53.6
Merced	170	D	D	D	122	9 208	3 954.2	348.6	302	5 130	219.4	55.2
Modoc	11	35	3.7	0.8	NA	NA	NA	NA	26	156	8.8	2.0
Mono	36	217	24.3	9.6	NA	NA	NA	NA	138	3 848	217.4	68.9
Monterey	818	D	D	D	301	7 333	2 227.6	268.4	983	18 026	1 197.1	345.4
Napa	419	D	D	D	436	13 165	4 529.3	632.4	363	8 904	620.4	195.4
Nevada	389	D	D	D	164	2 488	664.6	156.1	235	5 604	199.4	64.4
Orange	14 013	D	D	D	5 351	177 115	49 131.9	8 641.4	6 854	141 702	8 247.8	2 366.7
Placer	1 188	D	D	D	292	9 197	3 023.4	354.3	824	16 575	773.6	228.8
Plumas	57	D	D	D	21	593	130.6	26.5	112	560	30.1	8.5
Riverside	3 174	D	D	D	1 611	56 388	13 623.5	2 314.9	3 292	73 824	4 835.3	1 275.0
Sacramento	3 735	D	D	D	925	26 030	7 282.8	1 126.9	2 634	45 903	2 252.9	628.3
San Benito	70	206	25.8	7.8	63	2 867	630.3	102.0	93	1 109	50.2	14.6
San Bernardino	2 488	D	D	D	2 057	65 702	18 907.3	2 540.2	3 112	54 839	2 754.7	746.0
San Diego	11 972	117 497	18 834.7	7 694.0	3 182	102 168	27 541.1	5 244.6	6 599	144 287	9 551.5	2 567.2
San Francisco	5 600	D	D	D	788	11 339	2 077.5	422.5	3 525	66 365	5 039.2	1 496.8
San Joaquin	801	D	D	D	585	23 442	8 272.5	938.6	1 079	15 195	745.8	199.3
San Luis Obispo	930	5 709	593.8	222.6	377	6 517	2 548.2	260.4	850	14 903	767.9	219.7
San Mateo	2 916	D	D	D	742	30 221	17 918.2	1 975.0	1 785	30 836	2 107.2	613.5
Santa Barbara	1 359	D	D	D	505	13 149	3 174.1	676.8	1 029	21 380	1 361.5	360.1
Santa Clara	7 815	123 627	21 567.5	13 553.6	2 620	142 713	45 088.8	10 295.9	4 097	68 514	4 147.6	1 159.3
Santa Cruz	914	D	D	D	329	6 689	1 502.4	301.6	657	9 774	513.8	148.8
Shasta	400	D	D	D	167	2 794	662.9	117.1	403	5 862	281.0	74.9
Sierra	4	D	D	D	NA	NA	NA	NA	16	D	D	D
Siskiyou	98	D	D	D	38	911	257.8	36.0	149	1 684	78.5	22.0
Solano	598	D	D	D	296	10 357	8 377.3	578.9	731	12 523	573.3	153.4
Sonoma	1 538	D	D	D	885	24 077	5 841.9	1 201.2	1 173	17 739	1 005.4	283.8
Stanislaus	701	D	D	D	443	24 127	9 476.0	1 032.9	842	13 881	615.1	171.7
Sutter	129	D	D	D	71	1 549	494.9	61.3	153	2 498	100.7	28.1
Tehama	75	280	29.1	10.2	47	2 356	556.7	97.0	124	1 215	56.1	14.8
Trinity	22	82	8.1	2.6	NA	NA	NA	NA	53	291	14.6	3.7
Tulare	446	D	D	D	278	12 443	5 016.0	458.3	558	8 282	379.4	102.8
Tuolumne	120	D	D	D	66	1 030	222.5	40.4	169	1 817	86.5	23.6
Ventura	2 597	16 457	6 370.8	1 032.7	954	33 602	8 769.0	1 643.4	1 602	29 832	1 478.2	422.9
Yolo	395	D	D	D	177	5 743	1 853.3	235.7	399	8 693	840.3	159.7
Yuba	70	D	D	D	45	921	170.0	33.3	85	1 055	52.4	14.0
COLORADO	22 522	156 859	28 932.6	10 515.7	5 288	137 880	46 332.0	6 789.7	12 075	231 721	11 440.4	3 408.2
Adams	658	D	D	D	417	11 757	6 161.5	515.1	635	11 997	578.0	164.1
Alamosa	51	D	D	D	NA	NA	NA	NA	48	766	30.3	9.2
Arapahoe	2 727	D	D	D	436	8 358	2 043.0	395.2	1 136	20 947	1 008.5	301.4
Archuleta	43	119	10.1	3.5	NA	NA	NA	NA	64	649	33.2	9.0
Baca	3	5	0.5	0.1	NA	NA	NA	NA	8	D	D	D
Bent	2	D	D	D	NA	NA	NA	NA	10	98	3.0	0.8

1. Establishment subject to federal tax.

Table B. States and Counties — Health Care and Social Assistance, Other Services, and Federal Funds

STATE County	Health care and social assistance, 2007				Other services, 2007				Federal funds and grants, 2009–2010 Expenditures (mil dol)	Direct payments for individuals[1]		
	Number of establishments	Number of employees	Receipts (mil dol)	Annual payroll (mil dol)	Number of establishments	Number of employees	Receipts (mil dol)	Annual payroll (mil dol)	Total	Social Security and government retirement	Medicare	Food Stamps and Supplemental Security Income
	159	160	161	162	163	164	165	166	167	168	169	170
CALIFORNIA	97 288	1 592 430	191 605.7	72 531.1	57 626	399 336	52 326.5	11 913.7	333 809.3	78 067.9	56 261.1	12 469.4
Alameda	4 238	74 258	9 681.4	3 987.0	2 742	19 921	2 359.3	670.7	14 633.9	3 043.5	2 487.2	529.6
Alpine	4	D	D	D	1	D	D	D	7.9	2.6	1.6	0.3
Amador	89	1 281	127.6	48.1	50	158	17.4	4.4	280.5	152.4	78.0	6.1
Butte	737	12 120	1 179.3	427.5	321	2 168	173.6	49.9	1 788.2	699.6	453.6	104.9
Calaveras	99	1 134	106.8	40.4	63	226	18.2	4.9	353.5	181.6	88.9	11.3
Colusa	25	D	D	D	22	94	10.4	2.6	156.4	50.7	36.7	6.5
Contra Costa	2 737	44 257	5 652.4	2 302.8	1 528	8 902	1 054.4	276.2	6 802.1	2 508.5	1 559.0	238.8
Del Norte	75	1 352	117.0	51.3	26	98	10.5	2.1	241.7	89.7	49.9	19.1
El Dorado	452	5 802	624.8	240.9	285	1 513	137.8	38.8	1 057.1	532.1	266.8	29.0
Fresno	2 099	38 707	4 150.8	1 713.0	1 069	7 309	704.7	191.7	5 953.8	1 736.7	991.7	468.5
Glenn	37	479	33.7	14.5	21	51	6.9	1.1	221.0	72.1	51.5	11.3
Humboldt	462	6 762	589.0	217.0	259	1 304	157.0	32.8	1 130.5	385.3	233.2	65.6
Imperial	265	4 257	394.1	142.6	163	1 046	83.2	25.1	1 240.1	314.4	226.8	84.2
Inyo	63	1 047	92.8	38.2	44	164	16.2	4.2	211.4	53.0	44.5	5.1
Kern	1 456	25 119	2 746.4	1 042.9	857	5 637	569.1	145.0	5 744.5	1 632.6	1 074.6	328.6
Kings	204	4 106	433.8	153.1	105	582	47.0	13.4	994.5	260.9	141.1	49.3
Lake	154	2 242	237.7	86.7	79	258	24.4	7.0	621.3	245.0	200.2	37.3
Lassen	61	722	75.5	23.7	29	92	7.4	1.9	315.4	87.7	42.7	10.5
Los Angeles	27 728	444 806	53 200.9	19 568.8	16 089	117 748	15 230.4	3 369.6	82 544.3	16 317.2	17 792.2	4 259.6
Madera	221	5 836	564.7	255.8	119	609	48.9	12.9	847.3	327.4	188.3	45.6
Marin	1 066	13 958	1 595.2	649.1	617	4 249	630.4	167.2	1 694.9	772.6	429.9	32.9
Mariposa	31	456	29.9	13.3	18	62	5.6	1.4	211.5	68.4	34.9	4.4
Mendocino	294	4 185	369.1	147.2	165	674	74.3	16.3	773.3	277.9	177.1	36.3
Merced	443	6 048	592.2	235.3	209	899	73.9	19.3	1 519.8	461.0	273.2	126.0
Modoc	18	D	D	D	7	54	4.5	1.2	263.9	38.4	18.8	4.6
Mono	28	D	D	D	53	199	20.1	5.0	87.7	29.4	7.6	1.1
Monterey	970	13 789	1 876.6	723.7	556	3 651	425.9	104.6	3 298.5	932.2	553.5	91.2
Napa	425	10 004	1 150.0	502.2	219	1 172	142.5	38.4	1 011.6	412.9	312.3	21.3
Nevada	365	4 469	451.4	171.9	176	878	94.0	25.8	808.5	362.2	171.8	18.1
Orange	9 967	133 174	16 300.4	5 915.0	5 111	34 627	3 636.0	967.4	18 041.8	5 889.5	4 181.8	633.2
Placer	979	13 655	1 934.7	676.1	547	7 590	1 955.4	444.6	1 942.3	1 169.9	310.5	43.2
Plumas	53	912	75.2	30.3	41	128	10.6	3.0	249.2	92.2	48.1	5.9
Riverside	3 779	57 969	6 621.0	2 365.0	2 474	15 480	1 335.4	383.7	11 146.5	4 760.9	2 742.7	488.0
Sacramento	3 232	70 675	9 072.3	3 587.6	2 200	17 591	1 974.9	573.8	26 522.5	3 517.6	1 883.2	659.1
San Benito	100	D	D	D	69	251	22.4	5.7	241.6	99.6	51.0	8.2
San Bernardino	3 446	71 731	8 350.6	8 149.6	2 336	16 862	1 592.3	467.0	13 406.5	3 684.2	2 370.5	751.9
San Diego	7 924	133 893	15 954.7	5 872.9	5 176	37 084	3 732.5	1 015.3	37 302.9	7 771.6	4 652.8	790.1
San Francisco	2 967	57 946	7 752.0	3 039.4	2 239	17 261	5 992.0	626.7	11 738.0	1 638.2	1 876.8	363.5
San Joaquin	1 351	26 658	3 045.8	1 141.3	879	5 576	462.8	144.6	4 164.3	1 413.7	851.2	287.4
San Luis Obispo	864	14 341	1 341.2	546.4	464	2 808	222.0	60.3	1 783.4	769.8	416.5	44.5
San Mateo	2 095	30 901	4 046.3	1 591.8	1 411	9 356	2 520.3	331.9	5 434.4	1 785.3	1 106.7	94.8
Santa Barbara	1 322	19 124	2 076.4	784.0	767	5 005	816.9	141.4	3 677.4	1 037.4	621.1	91.6
Santa Clara	5 061	D	D	D	2 901	19 386	2 816.0	658.4	16 008.4	3 253.3	2 064.5	466.3
Santa Cruz	863	11 416	1 441.4	505.0	452	2 702	258.2	72.1	1 598.2	550.8	387.8	56.7
Shasta	661	10 015	1 124.5	420.3	320	1 697	168.2	43.3	1 678.2	724.9	355.0	93.5
Sierra	11	D	D	D	NA	NA	NA	NA	36.2	12.7	9.3	0.8
Siskiyou	117	1 721	151.9	59.3	71	212	20.9	5.1	488.5	193.6	101.0	22.3
Solano	861	18 135	2 136.5	895.9	541	3 240	324.0	92.5	3 454.6	1 261.9	407.1	118.6
Sonoma	1 516	23 219	2 623.9	1 065.9	873	4 877	508.1	138.8	3 142.9	1 300.7	800.3	86.8
Stanislaus	1 108	21 628	2 662.6	967.7	650	4 205	380.9	119.5	3 048.2	1 091.0	705.9	198.7
Sutter	251	3 085	409.2	116.9	132	741	61.9	16.6	575.9	243.5	128.1	28.8
Tehama	129	1 917	171.5	62.1	71	614	31.8	23.9	520.3	183.0	107.2	23.1
Trinity	29	198	12.9	4.7	17	D	D	D	139.3	59.4	29.5	6.6
Tulare	806	13 734	1 295.3	493.8	384	2 298	208.1	62.9	2 559.9	749.5	525.0	196.5
Tuolumne	173	2 662	307.7	112.2	76	435	41.0	11.2	460.8	229.4	111.9	16.5
Ventura	2 317	29 522	3 140.0	1 200.9	1 196	7 303	839.6	195.9	5 559.1	1 945.1	1 102.6	147.1
Yolo	364	5 936	660.5	234.6	282	2 000	208.0	63.8	2 866.1	377.2	208.0	55.2
Yuba	96	2 708	313.1	111.6	54	250	33.9	9.9	789.0	195.8	117.2	45.2
COLORADO	13 644	238 942	24 328.4	9 724.8	10 151	62 767	7 789.2	1 823.2	49 686.9	12 450.4	4 655.3	1 076.3
Adams	582	18 364	2 227.9	770.6	620	4 315	458.5	122.1	2 110.8	726.5	399.6	92.7
Alamosa	69	1 507	114.3	50.8	44	222	11.6	3.6	136.0	37.5	15.6	8.8
Arapahoe	1 714	28 246	3 010.4	1 196.9	1 110	7 321	943.9	242.5	5 218.0	1 576.6	394.3	86.1
Archuleta	37	186	13.3	4.7	29	139	10.0	3.2	66.7	43.7	5.7	1.6
Baca	7	D	D	D	6	D	D	D	62.5	21.6	9.6	1.3
Bent	7	D	D	D	3	D	D	D	57.5	22.9	8.2	3.6

1. State totals may include programs not allocated by county.

Table B. States and Counties — Federal Funds, Residential Construction, and Local Government Finances

STATE County	Federal funds and grants, 2009–2010 (cont.)							Value of residential construction authorized by building permits, 2010		Local government finances, 2007				
	Expenditures (mil dol) (cont.)									General revenue				
	Procurement contract awards			Grants[1]								Taxes		
													Per capita[2] (dollars)	
	Salaries and wages	Defense	Other	Medicaid and other health-related	Nutrition and family welfare	Education	Other	New construction ($1,000)	Number of housing units	Total (mil dol)	Inter-govern-mental (mil dol)	Total (mil dol)	Total	Property
	171	172	173	174	175	176	177	178	179	180	181	182	183	184
CALIFORNIA	24 584.6	41 323.3	16 213.6	41 931.1	11 743.7	6 113.7	19 080.4	9 120 592	43 716	X	X	X	X	X
Alameda	998.9	358.9	2 903.6	2 556.4	318.6	159.9	968.7	397 633	1 727	11 177.5	4 672.4	3 410.6	2 329	1 552
Alpine	0.4	0.4	0.4	1.0	0.3	0.4	0.4	1 237	4	22.6	9.4	8.4	7 298	6 225
Amador	6.9	0.5	2.1	16.6	9.1	0.4	6.2	4 114	29	143.0	64.1	52.4	1 355	1 126
Butte	47.0	0.5	36.4	263.4	44.7	22.7	34.9	61 182	512	1 116.2	653.8	247.0	1 129	888
Calaveras	8.3	4.4	4.3	26.1	11.2	8.1	7.8	13 648	45	196.0	76.1	77.9	1 662	1 464
Colusa	4.3	0.0	0.8	18.6	8.2	1.4	7.6	5 004	19	134.9	76.4	29.4	1 379	1 125
Contra Costa	582.9	245.6	403.6	749.7	189.3	56.4	171.9	304 359	1 676	5 949.8	2 045.3	2 042.3	2 003	1 567
Del Norte	10.1	0.1	8.3	28.8	10.1	2.1	21.3	6 419	29	126.5	81.5	22.5	776	618
El Dorado	54.6	18.6	25.1	62.5	32.4	9.3	18.3	47 090	120	905.5	353.8	309.9	1 764	1 477
Fresno	601.7	72.9	167.6	992.0	274.8	96.6	252.1	398 560	2 248	4 901.8	2 877.0	1 069.3	1 189	832
Glenn	15.7	1.6	7.7	25.3	10.6	2.7	7.4	7 348	45	175.5	105.8	28.4	1 012	815
Humboldt	74.5	3.7	25.3	167.8	36.0	20.9	58.1	23 379	191	682.1	405.0	137.6	1 068	833
Imperial	178.5	47.7	59.2	199.4	50.0	23.2	20.8	17 870	102	1 139.1	670.3	166.9	1 031	684
Inyo	19.8	12.6	35.0	19.8	6.6	4.4	8.9	2 177	8	178.6	65.8	46.9	2 689	1 941
Kern	772.0	484.6	233.1	712.0	203.4	69.5	80.2	256 977	1 656	5 502.3	2 722.3	1 021.3	1 292	1 083
Kings	195.1	28.9	66.6	129.2	37.8	20.1	11.0	39 838	265	632.3	386.7	115.8	778	616
Lake	11.6	1.7	2.7	90.4	15.3	4.5	8.1	8 943	46	274.3	152.0	75.3	1 164	974
Lassen	66.0	37.8	18.4	32.5	7.8	3.9	2.8	2 352	13	147.1	102.0	25.7	733	617
Los Angeles	4 489.4	10 637.0	5 805.2	13 950.6	2 840.6	852.6	3 697.1	1 689 660	7 260	61 779.9	29 562.5	17 192.0	1 740	1 120
Madera	44.6	0.9	7.9	144.3	33.6	9.9	14.9	24 379	192	598.1	351.0	131.1	895	715
Marin	87.4	31.3	32.2	168.7	43.9	10.8	50.5	64 281	186	1 337.5	345.9	672.0	2 709	2 236
Mariposa	33.4	0.0	46.6	10.3	5.2	0.9	6.7	9 917	45	94.9	40.1	29.8	1 655	1 024
Mendocino	22.8	23.3	7.5	126.7	44.5	16.6	25.8	21 586	157	854.4	264.3	130.6	1 513	1 024
Merced	54.0	54.7	64.5	260.0	73.7	26.1	48.7	22 930	106	1 419.6	825.1	251.4	1 024	823
Modoc	163.4	0.0	9.1	11.1	4.9	1.9	4.1	1 968	16	72.2	42.5	11.7	1 272	1 143
Mono	14.1	16.6	8.6	2.7	3.6	1.2	1.8	9 771	22	181.4	41.4	73.4	5 735	4 264
Monterey	588.4	385.9	170.6	285.9	114.4	35.1	93.0	67 126	279	2 775.3	1 150.3	709.4	1 740	1 280
Napa	22.6	24.8	9.1	102.5	32.0	10.9	35.0	61 077	110	773.9	256.2	327.3	2 469	1 962
Nevada	28.0	137.7	8.3	53.8	15.4	5.7	5.9	24 324	142	498.3	164.9	163.7	1 687	1 415
Orange	1 410.9	2 026.2	430.5	1 678.3	610.6	166.1	605.1	691 582	3 134	14 874.7	5 845.1	5 406.3	1 804	1 344
Placer	99.9	18.5	20.5	139.2	44.8	11.6	17.0	299 008	1 166	2 164.9	613.3	790.5	2 374	1 911
Plumas	22.0	0.5	25.9	19.3	7.9	2.7	20.5	5 891	35	183.1	66.1	45.2	2 192	1 924
Riverside	688.7	396.1	149.5	966.4	347.2	121.1	251.5	947 867	4 547	12 026.7	5 366.7	3 319.0	1 601	1 198
Sacramento	895.1	3 511.6	382.0	2 115.5	2 695.9	3 035.5	7 412.4	225 023	1 162	8 376.8	3 982.9	2 168.3	1 564	1 088
San Benito	11.9	18.6	5.6	27.1	12.5	4.0	0.4	10 071	47	325.2	148.3	76.0	1 390	1 254
San Bernardino	1 673.8	2 317.9	299.3	1 236.2	390.1	144.8	300.1	282 842	1 789	11 930.8	6 580.8	2 747.7	1 368	985
San Diego	4 765.8	11 593.0	1 288.7	3 866.8	677.8	239.4	990.5	772 067	3 494	16 065.9	6 632.0	5 448.0	1 831	1 394
San Francisco	1 362.1	509.8	798.8	3 305.9	182.3	149.8	1 232.0	194 472	779	7 150.7	2 481.0	2 793.0	3 651	1 970
San Joaquin	285.9	93.9	65.0	739.1	153.5	47.5	89.5	166 494	813	3 836.6	1 957.0	986.4	1 470	1 065
San Luis Obispo	126.0	56.0	25.0	176.0	70.7	13.3	44.4	114 809	468	1 183.8	434.3	521.1	1 986	1 598
San Mateo	299.5	441.4	697.8	589.1	124.2	35.3	210.6	193 565	253	3 894.9	1 068.6	1 716.6	2 428	1 815
Santa Barbara	416.1	701.1	65.0	332.1	93.3	38.4	201.3	138 930	400	2 499.6	956.2	791.8	1 959	1 459
Santa Clara	953.4	4 708.7	1 070.8	2 000.2	334.3	115.6	793.0	745 489	4 132	11 364.0	3 646.1	4 347.8	2 486	1 854
Santa Cruz	53.2	9.7	19.4	275.4	54.0	21.4	116.7	37 720	158	1 409.1	614.7	454.6	1 806	1 403
Shasta	96.8	3.9	75.2	199.0	50.8	18.4	30.1	42 773	253	953.9	513.4	222.1	1 238	962
Sierra	3.1	0.0	1.5	6.0	0.7	0.3	1.6	2 381	7	28.7	17.8	7.6	2 292	2 079
Siskiyou	42.6	-0.1	21.0	59.6	13.3	5.3	14.2	10 617	58	258.1	160.7	51.1	1 153	950
Solano	689.1	363.8	49.4	264.2	71.7	24.2	163.2	103 818	467	2 176.4	1 047.1	670.5	1 641	1 187
Sonoma	203.3	47.1	78.1	359.9	84.6	26.4	103.0	87 520	477	2 520.7	903.4	933.6	2 010	1 589
Stanislaus	93.7	18.4	33.7	535.9	145.3	36.1	78.6	40 531	292	2 994.5	1 529.2	678.5	1 327	984
Sutter	19.7	0.5	17.0	76.4	20.1	6.1	7.6	16 631	88	479.7	254.2	117.8	1 280	912
Tehama	16.4	0.1	94.8	61.6	17.5	10.1	1.5	13 360	77	262.5	169.4	60.9	997	809
Trinity	15.8	0.0	4.6	12.5	4.9	1.7	3.3	6 442	40	114.5	61.3	11.6	819	718
Tulare	77.9	12.8	73.0	569.1	116.0	40.5	68.2	199 679	1 367	2 844.1	1 469.6	387.4	919	613
Tuolumne	30.2	2.3	12.7	36.9	11.4	2.1	1.9	11 430	57	258.0	95.4	69.2	1 241	1 059
Ventura	602.1	681.1	175.4	445.3	153.9	52.6	159.5	110 971	590	4 288.6	1 876.2	1 310.9	1 642	1 348
Yolo	208.4	1 145.3	61.1	504.8	39.7	17.7	180.3	44 432	254	917.9	389.3	324.8	1 658	1 064
Yuba	224.5	12.4	2.4	125.0	21.8	13.2	6.3	9 028	62	407.1	227.4	84.9	1 178	1 038
COLORADO	8 518.5	5 631.6	4 735.5	3 665.3	967.6	778.9	3 381.1	2 608 302	11 591	X	X	X	X	X
Adams	430.4	33.4	58.6	209.2	47.8	26.2	33.4	130 089	662	1 681.3	572.8	694.2	1 643	1 031
Alamosa	11.4	0.0	5.5	35.3	4.5	2.9	1.2	4 500	38	51.7	30.0	14.1	918	649
Arapahoe	414.5	1 714.8	276.0	463.3	52.7	34.8	141.5	247 081	1 279	2 344.3	696.2	1 054.5	1 935	1 290
Archuleta	3.2	0.2	2.6	5.5	1.5	0.5	1.2	10 335	37	47.5	13.6	23.9	1 898	1 256
Baca	2.1	0.0	0.4	7.3	1.3	0.5	0.1	150	2	60.8	32.3	9.0	2 335	1 473
Bent	2.3	1.3	0.8	11.0	1.8	0.5	0.8	0	0	41.8	12.5	5.5	941	726

1. State totals may include programs not allocated by county.   2. Based on the resident population estimated as of July 1 of the year shown.

Table B. States and Counties — Local Government Finances, Government Employment, and Voting

	Local government finances, 2007 (cont.)									Government employment, 2009			Presidential election,[2] 2008		
	Direct general expenditure							Debt outstanding					Percent of vote cast:		
STATE County	Total (mil dol)	Per capita[1] (dollars)	Education	Health and hospitals	Police protection	Public welfare	Highways	Total (mil dol)	Per capita[1] (dollars)	Federal civilian	Federal military	State and local	Democratic	Republican	All other
	185	186	187	188	189	190	191	192	193	194	195	196	197	198	199
CALIFORNIA	X	X	X	X	X	X	X	X	X	251 441	224 561	2 248 402	61.0	37.0	2.0
Alameda	11 620.2	7 936	23.2	10.8	5.2	5.0	2.3	21 002.9	14 344	10 032	3 738	98 048	78.8	19.3	2.0
Alpine	24.4	21 295	21.9	6.8	8.6	5.6	8.7	2.2	1 927	11	0	190	61.0	36.4	2.6
Amador	154.7	3 998	30.8	5.3	7.9	4.8	7.2	119.7	3 094	100	62	5 502	41.5	56.1	2.3
Butte	1 112.9	5 087	41.0	5.4	4.3	12.0	2.7	441.7	2 019	571	363	14 417	49.8	47.5	2.7
Calaveras	181.4	3 872	42.8	5.4	5.3	7.3	5.9	119.0	2 540	139	76	2 287	42.1	55.1	2.8
Colusa	134.7	6 322	39.8	5.1	5.2	5.4	6.2	28.6	1 344	80	35	2 071	40.0	58.1	2.0
Contra Costa	6 279.4	6 158	37.0	12.8	5.4	6.2	6.1	6 116.2	5 998	5 609	1 715	43 041	68.0	30.2	1.8
Del Norte	128.1	4 413	36.0	9.7	3.7	14.6	2.9	28.8	994	167	59	3 722	45.4	52.1	2.5
El Dorado	935.8	5 327	34.2	4.1	4.5	4.3	6.3	644.1	3 666	859	292	10 062	43.6	54.1	2.2
Fresno	4 984.7	5 543	47.6	6.2	5.4	9.9	3.3	3 891.0	4 326	9 903	1 794	56 953	50.2	48.1	1.7
Glenn	173.1	6 157	41.2	7.6	5.2	12.0	3.6	29.9	1 062	267	46	1 914	37.8	59.8	2.4
Humboldt	669.9	5 199	39.8	9.2	4.2	9.7	3.0	255.4	1 982	807	398	12 299	62.3	34.1	3.6
Imperial	1 068.8	6 603	47.6	16.7	3.8	7.4	2.8	843.5	5 211	2 474	517	15 525	62.2	36.1	1.7
Inyo	179.4	10 284	27.1	37.5	4.3	3.4	3.5	35.2	2 014	421	28	2 685	43.9	53.0	3.1
Kern	5 086.6	6 433	43.2	8.2	3.5	7.3	1.6	2 907.0	3 676	10 347	3 663	48 495	40.1	57.9	2.0
Kings	609.8	4 096	45.4	5.7	5.8	8.7	3.3	264.9	1 780	1 219	5 675	12 100	42.0	56.1	1.9
Lake	286.6	4 432	42.0	7.1	5.3	11.2	3.4	93.7	1 448	160	112	3 955	58.2	38.9	2.9
Lassen	148.1	4 228	51.3	5.5	3.8	9.7	5.7	63.0	1 799	1 568	57	5 073	31.5	65.7	2.8
Los Angeles	56 883.7	5 758	38.2	9.7	7.3	8.0	2.9	73 718.0	7 462	51 046	18 559	552 318	69.2	28.8	2.0
Madera	691.1	4 717	49.3	3.3	3.4	8.0	4.8	386.0	2 635	322	243	11 050	42.4	55.7	1.9
Marin	1 467.3	5 914	32.4	6.4	6.2	3.8	4.0	3 555.3	14 330	904	617	13 455	78.0	20.2	1.8
Mariposa	90.2	5 001	29.2	21.9	6.4	9.6	5.4	29.9	1 655	794	29	1 214	42.5	54.9	2.6
Mendocino	813.6	9 431	27.1	7.8	2.6	6.6	2.5	443.6	5 142	275	173	6 768	69.6	26.8	3.6
Merced	1 437.0	5 853	49.3	3.6	3.8	9.6	3.0	688.0	2 802	772	401	16 315	53.3	45.0	1.7
Modoc	75.0	8 156	37.7	25.9	3.7	6.9	8.2	3.9	421	279	15	1 002	29.7	67.4	2.9
Mono	178.7	13 957	21.9	28.8	5.1	3.3	8.6	98.5	7 692	177	267	1 361	55.5	42.3	2.2
Monterey	2 680.5	6 576	35.2	21.3	4.5	4.9	4.8	1 456.7	3 574	5 345	5 524	26 051	68.2	29.9	2.0
Napa	789.2	5 954	41.2	5.1	6.7	3.7	4.4	766.1	5 779	399	220	9 933	65.1	32.7	2.2
Nevada	491.3	5 063	29.8	21.7	4.8	5.5	5.6	270.6	2 789	390	160	8 087	51.4	46.1	2.5
Orange	14 291.5	4 769	43.2	3.0	7.4	5.6	4.0	21 438.8	7 153	11 730	5 712	141 393	47.6	50.2	2.2
Placer	2 195.6	6 595	38.8	2.4	4.8	4.3	8.1	2 949.2	8 859	736	589	17 968	43.4	54.7	1.9
Plumas	162.4	8 846	29.2	34.4	3.6	4.9	4.8	74.2	3 597	456	33	1 870	42.8	54.7	2.5
Riverside	12 014.0	5 794	40.8	7.9	5.5	6.1	4.5	13 422.4	6 473	6 969	3 559	118 429	50.2	47.9	1.9
Sacramento	8 735.5	6 300	33.6	6.0	5.1	8.8	6.5	15 009.4	11 278	7 614	3 157	183 951	58.5	39.5	2.0
San Benito	313.4	5 732	35.7	24.5	3.4	4.7	8.9	109.4	2 001	153	90	2 590	60.5	37.7	1.8
San Bernardino	11 125.3	5 541	42.3	10.4	5.8	7.2	3.7	10 184.1	5 072	13 341	21 358	105 221	52.1	45.8	2.2
San Diego	16 037.1	5 391	40.2	9.0	6.0	6.5	2.9	17 862.6	5 883	43 765	112 014	187 442	54.1	43.9	1.9
San Francisco	6 597.0	8 624	16.0	22.5	5.2	8.9	3.0	10 649.8	13 922	14 752	1 720	85 486	84.2	13.7	2.2
San Joaquin	3 766.6	5 613	43.4	8.4	5.5	8.1	2.8	3 448.9	5 140	4 188	1 134	34 303	54.4	43.8	1.8
San Luis Obispo	1 122.2	4 276	38.3	5.7	6.4	8.8	5.0	704.1	2 689	638	470	20 482	51.4	46.0	2.6
San Mateo	3 829.0	5 416	31.8	10.9	7.4	5.0	3.5	4 385.4	6 203	3 432	1 331	27 980	73.5	24.7	1.8
Santa Barbara	2 477.1	6 129	37.4	14.0	5.5	5.4	4.7	1 475.7	3 651	3 746	3 437	31 418	60.4	37.5	2.1
Santa Clara	11 104.3	6 349	32.9	16.1	5.0	5.5	2.9	14 916.6	8 529	10 750	3 282	80 663	69.4	28.6	2.0
Santa Cruz	1 495.0	5 939	37.8	6.0	4.3	8.0	3.1	1 194.1	4 743	554	419	17 618	77.5	19.8	2.7
Shasta	983.2	5 480	41.0	6.6	5.0	9.3	2.5	684.3	3 814	1 271	298	12 348	35.9	61.7	2.4
Sierra	30.1	9 032	32.9	8.7	11.1	8.5	11.8	3.3	985	66	0	338	37.3	58.2	4.5
Siskiyou	255.7	5 772	45.4	7.4	5.4	6.9	6.9	32.9	742	778	73	3 483	43.3	53.7	3.1
Solano	2 178.6	5 332	37.7	4.8	8.0	6.8	5.1	2 079.0	5 088	3 918	7 330	21 761	63.4	34.8	1.8
Sonoma	2 662.5	5 733	35.4	8.3	6.4	4.9	4.3	2 522.0	5 430	1 665	1 550	26 050	73.6	24.0	2.3
Stanislaus	2 929.4	5 730	52.0	7.3	4.7	8.4	2.9	3 299.0	6 453	884	838	26 189	49.9	48.1	2.0
Sutter	485.2	5 271	44.3	7.4	5.6	5.7	2.0	241.0	2 618	177	152	4 364	40.7	57.4	1.9
Tehama	268.9	4 401	52.5	5.3	5.2	12.7	4.1	27.0	441	268	100	3 735	36.6	60.7	2.7
Trinity	110.6	7 800	29.9	5.4	2.2	5.7	7.6	30.1	2 124	218	23	1 057	50.7	46.1	3.2
Tulare	2 828.2	6 709	40.6	21.2	3.1	8.7	2.8	1 178.2	2 795	1 309	702	30 376	41.5	56.8	1.7
Tuolumne	277.1	4 966	35.1	18.1	4.7	6.4	3.6	112.5	2 017	379	90	5 219	42.4	55.1	2.4
Ventura	4 176.2	5 231	39.4	8.7	7.5	4.3	4.1	2 696.6	3 378	7 398	6 470	36 318	55.2	42.9	1.9
Yolo	1 018.3	5 200	34.4	4.1	5.4	7.9	6.9	1 052.2	5 372	3 603	337	31 702	67.1	30.8	2.1
Yuba	411.9	5 714	60.2	1.8	3.7	11.6	3.6	202.3	2 806	1 301	3 448	5 755	41.4	56.1	2.5
COLORADO	X	X	X	X	X	X	X	X	X	53 547	49 592	339 098	53.7	44.7	1.6
Adams	1 807.7	4 279	40.3	0.3	5.0	6.2	5.4	3 374.9	7 988	1 699	1 498	20 839	58.2	39.9	1.9
Alamosa	56.4	3 681	50.0	5.3	6.8	4.1	3.5	61.5	4 017	171	40	2 073	56.0	41.9	2.1
Arapahoe	2 432.7	4 463	39.8	1.7	7.1	2.7	5.7	5 251.0	9 633	3 133	2 478	32 184	55.7	42.8	1.5
Archuleta	46.5	3 699	30.0	6.4	5.8	3.5	13.5	70.1	5 572	62	32	615	42.8	54.9	2.3
Baca	57.5	14 857	58.2	16.2	0.9	5.1	7.1	9.0	2 327	42	10	711	24.6	72.3	3.1
Bent	41.6	7 116	21.8	0.4	3.6	12.8	4.8	13.7	2 336	58	24	692	41.6	56.1	2.3

1. Based on the resident population estimated as of July 1 of the year shown.   2. © 2009 Election Data Services, Inc. All rights reserved.

Table B. States and Counties — **Land Area and Population**

STATE/ County code	CBSA code[1]	County type[2]	STATE County	Land area,[3] (sq km) 2010	Total persons	Rank	Per square kilometer	White	Black	American Indian, Alaska Native	Asian and Pacific Islander	Percent Hispanic or Latino[4]	Under 5 years	5 to 17 years	18 to 24 years	25 to 34 years	35 to 44 years	45 to 54 years
				1	2	3	4	5	6	7	8	9	10	11	12	13	14	15
			COLORADO—Cont'd															
08 013	14500	2	Boulder	1 881	294 567	220	156.6	81.1	1.2	0.9	5.3	13.3	5.6	15.7	14.2	13.4	13.9	15.1
08 014	19740	1	Broomfield	86	55 889	896	649.9	81.1	1.3	0.9	7.3	11.1	7.1	19.2	7.7	13.9	16.0	15.5
08 015	...	7	Chaffee	2 625	17 809	1 934	6.8	87.6	1.6	1.4	0.9	9.4	4.3	12.5	6.2	11.6	12.0	16.0
08 017	...	9	Cheyenne	4 606	1 836	3 068	0.4	88.7	0.7	0.8	0.8	9.7	7.1	17.4	6.2	11.2	10.3	15.6
08 019	19740	1	Clear Creek	1 024	9 088	2 520	8.9	93.4	0.8	1.3	0.9	4.7	4.9	12.4	4.8	10.3	14.8	20.6
08 021	...	9	Conejos	3 334	8 256	2 590	2.5	42.7	0.4	1.1	0.5	56.0	7.9	20.4	8.3	10.2	10.8	14.1
08 023	...	9	Costilla	3 178	3 524	2 941	1.1	31.6	0.3	1.3	1.2	66.0	5.0	15.9	6.3	8.1	9.4	15.4
08 025	...	8	Crowley	2 039	5 823	2 782	2.9	58.9	9.7	2.2	1.2	29.0	3.1	10.4	9.7	20.2	17.2	17.4
08 027	...	8	Custer	1 913	4 255	2 887	2.2	93.3	1.1	1.7	0.5	4.7	3.2	14.0	3.3	6.9	9.5	16.6
08 029	...	6	Delta	2 958	30 952	1 413	10.5	84.2	0.7	1.4	0.8	14.0	5.7	16.5	6.6	10.0	10.6	14.8
08 031	19740	1	Denver	396	600 158	106	1 515.6	53.9	10.8	1.2	4.3	31.8	7.3	14.2	10.4	20.5	15.0	12.1
08 033	...	9	Dolores	2 764	2 064	3 046	0.7	93.0	0.2	4.5	0.5	4.0	6.6	15.8	5.0	10.4	12.7	15.1
08 035	19740	1	Douglas	2 176	285 465	225	131.2	87.1	1.6	0.7	5.0	7.5	7.7	22.8	5.4	11.6	18.1	16.6
08 037	20780	5	Eagle	4 363	52 197	952	12.0	68.0	0.6	0.5	1.4	30.1	7.5	17.0	8.5	18.7	17.4	14.6
08 039	19740	1	Elbert	4 794	23 086	1 684	4.8	92.5	1.1	1.2	1.4	5.3	5.0	20.3	5.7	7.2	14.1	22.0
08 041	17820	2	El Paso	5 508	622 263	99	113.0	75.1	7.2	1.6	4.6	15.1	7.3	18.9	10.9	14.1	13.1	14.9
08 043	15860	4	Fremont	3 971	46 824	1 027	11.8	81.7	4.1	2.3	0.9	12.3	4.5	13.0	7.1	13.6	13.8	16.0
08 045	...	5	Garfield	7 634	56 389	893	7.4	69.9	0.6	1.1	1.0	28.3	8.0	19.0	8.4	15.4	14.5	14.8
08 047	19740	1	Gilpin	388	5 441	2 809	14.0	92.2	0.8	1.5	2.0	4.9	5.2	12.5	4.4	10.5	16.3	21.9
08 049	...	8	Grand	4 782	14 843	2 124	3.1	90.8	0.6	0.9	1.2	7.5	5.6	14.7	7.0	13.7	14.2	18.5
08 051	...	7	Gunnison	8 389	15 324	2 092	1.8	90.4	0.5	1.0	1.1	8.2	5.1	13.1	17.3	15.6	13.9	13.4
08 053	...	9	Hinsdale	2 894	843	3 116	0.3	94.9	0.6	1.9	0.7	2.8	7.1	12.8	7.1	9.4	10.3	16.5
08 055	...	6	Huerfano	4 121	6 711	2 711	1.6	62.9	0.4	1.6	0.8	35.3	4.1	13.6	5.5	7.3	8.8	16.0
08 057	...	9	Jackson	4 180	1 394	3 091	0.3	88.2	0.1	1.5	0.1	10.8	4.4	14.2	6.7	9.8	11.6	18.9
08 059	19740	1	Jefferson	1 979	534 543	119	270.1	81.4	1.3	1.0	3.4	14.3	5.7	16.6	8.4	12.3	13.5	17.1
08 061	...	9	Kiowa	4 578	1 398	3 090	0.3	94.0	0.2	0.6	0.2	5.6	5.0	17.5	5.4	9.5	9.4	16.6
08 063	...	7	Kit Carson	5 597	8 270	2 589	1.5	77.2	2.8	1.1	0.7	19.0	6.7	15.6	7.5	14.0	12.9	15.7
08 065	20780	7	Lake	976	7 310	2 659	7.5	59.2	0.5	1.1	0.9	39.1	7.7	17.2	9.8	15.2	14.5	13.9
08 067	20420	6	La Plata	4 382	51 334	960	11.7	82.1	0.7	6.2	1.0	11.8	5.6	14.8	11.8	13.4	12.5	15.5
08 069	22660	2	Larimer	6 724	299 630	212	44.6	86.1	1.2	1.0	2.8	10.6	5.9	15.5	13.9	14.1	12.2	14.2
08 071	...	7	Las Animas	12 361	15 507	2 081	1.3	55.2	1.5	1.8	0.9	41.6	5.6	15.3	9.0	10.4	11.0	15.3
08 073	...	8	Lincoln	6 676	5 467	2 807	0.8	80.7	5.4	1.6	1.0	12.5	5.6	14.9	7.8	14.7	12.6	16.4
08 075	44540	7	Logan	4 762	22 709	1 697	4.8	79.0	4.2	1.2	0.7	15.6	5.2	14.8	11.2	14.4	12.8	15.1
08 077	24300	3	Mesa	8 622	146 723	424	17.0	84.6	0.9	1.3	1.3	13.3	6.8	16.7	9.9	13.1	11.4	14.3
08 079	...	9	Mineral	2 268	712	3 126	0.3	96.1	0.3	1.1	0.4	2.9	2.8	11.4	4.6	8.6	7.4	17.8
08 081	...	7	Moffat	12 285	13 795	2 199	1.1	83.9	0.6	1.4	1.0	14.4	7.8	19.2	8.3	13.5	12.1	15.7
08 083	...	6	Montezuma	5 256	25 535	1 584	4.9	76.7	0.4	12.7	0.8	11.0	6.3	17.2	6.9	10.5	11.6	15.0
08 085	33940	7	Montrose	5 803	41 276	1 148	7.1	78.7	0.5	1.2	1.0	19.7	6.4	18.3	6.5	10.8	11.6	14.6
08 087	22820	6	Morgan	3 316	28 159	1 491	8.5	62.5	2.9	0.8	0.8	33.8	7.7	20.3	8.7	12.2	12.2	14.1
08 089	...	6	Otero	3 268	18 831	1 884	5.8	57.6	0.7	1.3	1.1	40.3	6.3	18.5	8.6	10.5	10.5	13.9
08 091	...	9	Ouray	1 403	4 436	2 874	3.2	94.2	0.3	0.9	1.1	4.4	4.1	13.9	3.5	7.6	12.7	18.4
08 093	19740	1	Park	5 682	16 206	2 042	2.9	93.2	0.8	1.7	1.2	4.8	4.9	14.3	4.7	8.6	13.9	22.1
08 095	...	9	Phillips	1 782	4 442	2 872	2.5	79.9	0.4	0.5	0.9	18.7	6.3	19.0	6.4	10.0	11.1	14.5
08 097	...	7	Pitkin	2 514	17 148	1 974	6.8	88.9	0.8	0.4	1.8	9.1	4.4	13.1	5.9	15.3	16.1	17.3
08 099	...	7	Prowers	4 243	12 551	2 272	3.0	63.4	0.6	0.9	0.4	35.2	7.7	19.4	9.2	11.8	10.9	13.7
08 101	39380	3	Pueblo	6 180	159 063	391	25.7	55.3	2.1	1.2	1.1	41.4	6.6	17.8	9.4	11.9	11.9	14.1
08 103	...	9	Rio Blanco	8 342	6 666	2 717	0.8	87.9	1.1	1.8	0.8	10.0	7.4	17.0	9.5	12.9	11.6	16.8
08 105	...	7	Rio Grande	2 362	11 982	2 305	5.1	56.0	0.4	1.4	0.5	42.4	6.6	18.6	7.6	10.4	11.3	14.9
08 107	...	7	Routt	6 118	23 509	1 665	3.8	91.7	0.6	0.7	1.3	6.8	5.5	15.3	8.1	15.3	15.1	17.3
08 109	...	9	Saguache	8 206	6 108	2 757	0.7	57.6	0.4	2.0	1.1	40.1	6.9	16.3	7.9	10.4	10.6	15.2
08 111	...	9	San Juan	1 004	699	3 128	0.7	86.6	0.1	0.9	1.6	12.0	5.2	13.2	4.3	14.7	13.9	17.3
08 113	...	9	San Miguel	3 332	7 359	2 654	2.2	89.8	0.6	0.9	1.4	8.6	6.2	13.5	6.0	17.2	17.7	17.5
08 115	...	9	Sedgwick	1 419	2 379	3 021	1.7	86.5	0.5	0.7	1.1	12.1	5.1	14.2	6.3	9.5	9.8	15.2
08 117	43540	7	Summit	1 576	27 994	1 498	17.8	83.6	1.0	0.5	1.6	14.2	5.5	11.9	10.0	20.1	16.7	15.3
08 119	17820	2	Teller	1 443	23 350	1 677	16.2	92.4	0.8	1.7	1.4	5.5	4.7	15.8	5.8	7.9	12.2	20.6
08 121	...	9	Washington	6 522	4 814	2 855	0.7	90.5	0.8	0.7	0.7	8.5	5.7	17.7	6.3	10.1	11.1	16.3
08 123	24540	3	Weld	10 327	252 825	255	24.5	68.9	1.1	1.1	1.7	28.4	7.9	19.9	11.0	13.8	13.7	13.5
08 125	...	7	Yuma	6 124	10 043	2 444	1.6	78.4	0.3	0.6	0.3	20.8	7.7	18.7	7.4	12.1	12.2	13.8
09 000	...	X	CONNECTICUT	12 542	3 574 097	X	285.0	72.6	10.2	0.6	4.4	13.4	5.7	17.2	9.1	11.8	13.6	16.1
09 001	14860	2	Fairfield	1 618	916 829	52	566.6	67.4	10.8	0.4	5.3	16.9	6.2	18.6	7.9	11.6	14.3	16.3
09 003	25540	1	Hartford	1 904	894 014	57	469.5	67.4	13.2	0.5	4.8	15.3	5.7	17.2	8.9	12.3	13.3	15.8
09 005	45860	4	Litchfield	2 384	189 927	328	79.7	92.5	1.7	0.6	1.9	4.5	4.8	16.8	6.7	9.2	13.4	18.2
09 007	25540	7	Middlesex	956	165 676	372	173.3	87.8	5.2	0.5	3.2	4.7	5.0	16.2	7.7	10.4	13.8	17.2
09 009	35300	2	New Haven	1 566	862 477	60	550.8	68.9	12.8	0.6	4.0	15.0	5.6	16.7	9.9	12.5	13.2	15.4
09 011	35980	2	New London	1 722	274 055	237	159.1	80.6	6.8	1.8	5.1	8.5	5.5	16.3	9.8	11.9	13.2	16.3

1. CBSA = Core Based Statistical Area. See Appendix A for explanation. See Appendix B for list of metropolitan areas with component counties.   2. County type code from the Economic Research Service of USDA Rural-Urban Continuum Codes. See Appendix A for definition.   3. Dry land or land partially or temporarily covered by water.   4. May be of any race.

Table B. States and Counties — **Population and Households**

	Population, 2010 (cont.) Age (percent) (cont.)				Population change and components of change, 1990–2010							Households, 2010				
					Total persons		Percent change		Components of change, 2000–2009						Percent	
STATE County	55 to 64 years	65 to 74 years	75 years and over	Percent female	1990	2000	1990– 2000	2000– 2010	Births	Deaths	Net migration	Number	Percent change, 2000– 2010	Persons per house- hold	Female family house- holder[1]	One per- son
	16	17	18	19	20	21	22	23	24	25	26	27	28	29	30	31
COLORADO—Cont'd																
Boulder	12.0	5.7	4.3	49.8	NA	269 814	NA	1.1	32 395	13 271	9 349	119 300	4.0	2.39	7.7	29.0
Broomfield	10.8	5.6	4.3	50.4	24 638	38 272	55.3	N/A	6 237	2 041	7 289	21 414	N/A	2.60	8.0	23.9
Chaffee	17.6	11.3	8.5	46.9	12 684	16 242	28.1	9.6	1 317	1 403	1 082	7 601	15.4	2.15	6.7	30.1
Cheyenne	14.3	8.0	9.9	50.4	2 397	2 231	-6.9	-17.7	206	193	-501	786	-10.7	2.28	5.9	33.8
Clear Creek	19.8	8.7	3.7	47.9	7 619	9 322	22.4	-2.5	908	423	-1 070	4 208	4.7	2.14	6.1	31.9
Conejos	13.2	8.1	7.1	50.4	7 453	8 400	12.7	-1.7	1 114	657	-996	3 118	4.6	2.64	11.1	27.5
Costilla	17.1	14.4	8.5	48.3	3 190	3 663	14.8	-3.8	344	323	-531	1 550	3.1	2.27	11.6	33.5
Crowley	11.4	6.0	4.5	27.9	3 946	5 518	39.8	5.5	357	400	951	1 306	-3.8	2.41	10.6	30.2
Custer	24.1	14.9	7.5	48.4	1 926	3 503	81.9	21.5	235	231	481	1 925	30.1	2.13	3.9	30.1
Delta	15.7	11.2	8.9	49.6	20 980	27 834	32.7	11.2	3 178	3 051	3 520	12 703	14.9	2.38	7.9	27.4
Denver	10.3	5.4	5.0	50.0	467 549	554 636	18.6	8.2	97 736	39 799	1 313	263 107	10.0	2.22	10.6	40.6
Dolores	15.6	11.2	7.6	48.5	1 504	1 844	22.6	11.9	217	158	40	899	14.5	2.30	5.9	29.7
Douglas	10.7	4.7	2.5	50.5	60 391	175 766	191.0	62.4	37 125	5 827	81 401	102 018	67.5	2.79	7.1	18.0
Eagle	10.6	4.3	1.4	46.7	21 928	41 659	90.0	25.3	7 646	796	5 379	19 236	27.0	2.71	6.4	22.2
Elbert	16.2	6.5	3.0	50.0	9 646	19 872	106.0	16.2	1 929	903	2 482	8 380	23.8	2.75	5.8	15.5
El Paso	10.9	5.7	4.3	50.2	397 014	516 929	30.2	20.4	80 025	30 690	35 230	235 959	22.6	2.56	11.3	26.0
Fremont	14.4	9.8	7.8	42.3	32 273	46 145	43.0	1.5	3 928	4 542	2 532	16 582	8.9	2.30	9.6	29.0
Garfield	11.5	4.9	3.5	48.4	29 974	43 791	46.1	28.8	8 200	2 596	7 140	20 359	25.4	2.73	8.5	22.3
Gilpin	19.9	7.1	2.3	47.0	3 070	4 757	55.0	14.4	536	212	515	2 460	20.4	2.19	5.1	29.0
Grand	16.0	6.9	3.3	46.6	7 966	12 442	56.2	19.3	1 410	536	649	6 469	27.5	2.26	5.4	29.4
Gunnison	12.8	5.9	3.0	45.8	10 273	13 956	35.9	9.8	1 614	593	446	6 516	15.3	2.22	5.2	30.5
Hinsdale	19.3	11.6	5.8	47.4	467	790	69.2	6.7	72	27	-15	362	0.8	2.17	3.0	27.9
Huerfano	19.5	14.2	10.9	50.4	6 009	7 862	30.8	-14.6	622	897	20	3 137	1.8	2.09	9.3	36.9
Jackson	15.9	11.0	7.5	47.2	1 605	1 577	-1.7	-11.6	114	90	-231	649	-1.8	2.14	4.6	33.3
Jefferson	13.9	7.0	5.6	50.4	NA	525 507	NA	1.4	58 754	31 851	-12 292	218 160	5.9	2.42	9.9	27.4
Kiowa	15.2	11.0	10.4	50.9	1 688	1 622	-3.9	-13.8	137	173	-352	619	-6.9	2.24	5.8	32.3
Kit Carson	11.5	8.5	7.5	43.9	7 140	8 011	12.2	3.2	874	697	246	3 038	1.6	2.37	7.7	31.6
Lake	12.9	5.7	3.2	46.5	6 007	7 812	30.0	-6.4	1 122	322	-563	2 953	-0.8	2.43	8.0	29.6
La Plata	14.6	7.1	4.6	49.1	32 284	43 941	36.1	16.8	4 928	2 425	5 261	21 100	21.7	2.35	8.1	27.0
Larimer	12.3	6.6	5.2	50.4	186 136	251 494	35.1	19.1	31 991	14 535	30 632	120 295	23.8	2.42	8.2	26.9
Las Animas	15.8	9.8	7.9	48.7	13 765	15 207	10.5	2.0	1 657	1 621	845	6 384	3.4	2.29	11.6	32.4
Lincoln	11.1	8.2	8.6	42.1	4 529	6 087	34.4	-10.2	539	485	-949	1 948	-5.3	2.28	8.5	33.6
Logan	11.9	7.1	7.5	43.1	17 567	20 504	16.7	10.8	2 308	1 854	-141	8 047	6.6	2.34	9.5	31.4
Mesa	12.9	7.8	7.1	50.3	93 145	116 255	24.8	26.2	16 500	11 505	24 757	58 095	26.8	2.46	10.0	26.5
Mineral	24.3	15.0	8.0	49.2	558	831	48.9	-14.3	44	50	88	355	-5.8	2.01	4.8	32.4
Moffat	12.7	6.2	4.3	48.9	11 357	13 184	16.1	4.6	1 863	898	-98	5 465	9.7	2.51	9.0	26.6
Montezuma	15.8	9.3	7.5	50.6	18 672	23 830	27.6	7.2	2 952	2 305	1 018	10 541	14.6	2.40	11.5	27.4
Montrose	14.0	9.8	8.0	50.8	24 423	33 432	36.9	23.5	4 719	3 252	6 645	16 484	26.4	2.47	9.1	25.8
Morgan	10.7	7.0	6.9	50.8	21 939	27 171	23.8	3.6	4 143	2 252	-1 078	10 294	7.9	2.68	10.6	25.5
Otero	13.4	9.4	8.9	51.0	20 185	20 311	0.6	-7.3	2 631	2 172	-2 008	7 729	-2.4	2.38	13.8	30.6
Ouray	22.3	12.6	5.0	49.9	2 295	3 742	63.1	18.5	331	204	751	2 022	28.3	2.19	4.9	26.5
Park	19.9	8.7	2.9	47.5	7 174	14 523	102.4	11.6	1 454	622	1 446	7 174	21.7	2.25	5.1	27.0
Phillips	12.1	9.0	11.7	51.1	4 189	4 480	6.9	-0.8	559	466	-78	1 819	2.1	2.41	6.3	31.1
Pitkin	16.4	8.1	3.4	47.0	12 661	14 872	17.5	15.3	1 507	374	111	8 152	19.8	2.09	5.3	38.0
Prowers	12.7	7.5	7.1	50.6	13 347	14 483	8.5	-13.3	2 026	1 139	-2 355	4 935	-7.0	2.48	12.6	28.3
Pueblo	13.0	7.9	7.4	50.8	123 051	141 472	15.0	12.4	18 954	13 894	11 526	62 972	15.4	2.46	14.1	28.9
Rio Blanco	12.5	7.1	5.4	48.5	6 051	5 986	-1.1	11.4	778	437	229	2 647	14.8	2.43	6.5	26.7
Rio Grande	14.3	8.9	7.3	50.3	10 770	12 413	15.3	-3.5	1 585	1 195	-1 162	4 779	1.7	2.47	11.8	26.6
Routt	15.2	5.6	2.5	46.8	14 088	19 690	39.8	19.4	2 229	711	2 355	9 892	24.4	2.34	5.7	26.1
Saguache	18.0	9.8	4.9	48.9	4 619	5 917	28.1	3.2	767	354	785	2 640	14.8	2.31	10.6	33.0
San Juan	19.2	9.3	3.0	43.9	745	558	-25.1	25.3	53	21	-35	344	27.9	2.03	6.7	40.7
San Miguel	15.0	5.4	1.6	45.7	3 653	6 594	80.5	11.6	786	141	337	3 454	14.6	2.13	5.6	37.5
Sedgwick	16.0	11.1	12.8	50.7	2 690	2 747	2.1	-13.4	238	340	-310	1 093	-6.2	2.14	7.1	35.1
Summit	12.8	6.1	1.7	45.1	12 881	23 548	82.8	18.9	3 285	401	923	11 754	28.9	2.36	4.7	25.7
Teller	20.1	9.2	3.7	49.1	12 468	20 555	64.9	13.6	2 003	969	214	9 805	22.7	2.37	6.4	23.6
Washington	13.5	9.7	9.5	48.9	4 812	4 926	2.4	-2.3	416	466	-437	1 980	-0.5	2.34	6.1	31.4
Weld	10.6	5.6	4.0	50.0	NA	180 926	NA	39.7	35 157	11 616	51 045	89 349	41.3	2.76	9.9	21.5
Yuma	12.0	8.1	8.0	50.4	8 954	9 841	9.9	2.1	1 343	991	-396	3 952	4.0	2.49	6.9	28.3
CONNECTICUT	12.4	7.1	7.0	51.3	3 287 116	3 405 565	3.6	4.9	388 331	271 426	16 608	1 371 087	5.3	2.52	12.9	27.3
Fairfield	11.7	6.8	6.7	51.4	827 645	882 567	6.6	3.9	108 655	62 364	-22 755	335 545	3.5	2.68	12.3	24.9
Hartford	12.4	7.1	7.4	51.7	851 783	857 183	0.6	4.3	97 132	72 728	4 154	350 854	4.7	2.47	14.5	28.7
Litchfield	14.9	8.4	7.6	50.9	174 092	182 193	4.7	4.2	17 428	15 402	5 534	76 640	7.1	2.44	9.4	26.6
Middlesex	14.2	8.1	7.4	51.2	143 196	155 071	8.3	6.8	16 169	12 492	7 855	67 202	9.6	2.39	9.4	28.2
New Haven	12.2	7.0	7.3	51.9	804 219	824 008	2.5	4.7	94 809	70 856	5 498	334 502	4.8	2.49	14.5	28.9
New London	12.8	7.4	6.8	50.1	254 957	259 088	1.6	5.8	28 828	20 422	618	107 057	7.2	2.44	11.8	27.6

1. No spouse present.

Table B. States and Counties — Population, Vital Statistics, Medicare, and Crime

STATE County	Persons in group quarters, 2010	Daytime population, 2006–2010 Number	Employment/residence ratio	Births, average 2006–2008 Total	Rate[1]	Deaths, average 2006–2008 Number	Rate[1]	Persons under 65 with no health insurance, 2009 Number	Percent	Medicare, 2011 Eligible for Medicare	Enrolled in Medicare Advantage	Enrolled in a Medicare prescription drug plan	Serious crimes known to police,[2] 2010 Total Number	Rate[3]
	32	33	34	35	36	37	38	39	40	41	42	43	44	45
COLORADO—Cont'd														
Boulder	8 949	316 723	1.2	3 374	11.7	1 510	5.2	37 861	14.0	35 488	11 949	9 859	7 507	2 548
Broomfield	282	55 153	1.1	767	15.0	238	4.7	5 391	10.6	6 572	3 165	1 318	1 208	2 161
Chaffee	1 436	17 940	1.1	D	D	161	9.5	2 844	21.0	4 108	655	1 600	266	1 494
Cheyenne	42	2 387	1.2	D	D	19	10.3	335	23.6	314	15	162	3	163
Clear Creek	84	7 263	0.7	D	D	47	5.2	1 017	13.1	1 242	348	353	220	2 732
Conejos	36	6 847	0.6	D	D	66	8.0	1 438	21.9	1 588	418	799	NA	NA
Costilla	0	3 306	0.8	D	D	33	9.9	582	24.0	947	232	451	NA	NA
Crowley	2 682	5 693	0.9	D	D	44	7.2	1 557	27.5	731	71	383	4	69
Custer	150	3 514	0.8	D	D	30	7.4	693	22.1	1 094	164	375	33	776
Delta	713	29 053	0.9	D	D	344	11.3	5 559	22.5	7 155	1 746	2 535	679	2 194
Denver	15 981	734 217	1.5	11 208	19.2	4 255	7.3	115 432	21.6	74 859	34 455	19 466	24 384	4 063
Dolores	0	1 814	0.8	D	D	20	10.2	416	25.9	451	43	188	28	1 357
Douglas	651	232 386	0.7	4 022	14.8	744	2.7	19 001	7.2	25 304	9 377	6 104	3 720	1 303
Eagle	55	50 826	1.0	D	D	93	1.8	10 996	22.1	3 327	234	1 602	1 175	2 251
Elbert	73	15 163	0.4	D	D	104	4.5	2 646	12.8	2 741	729	793	NA	NA
El Paso	19 141	599 244	1.0	8 868	15.1	3 432	5.8	81 630	15.3	76 650	18 233	18 385	22 110	3 727
Fremont	8 704	46 861	1.0	D	D	484	10.2	8 429	21.8	9 845	2 265	3 320	694	1 482
Garfield	884	53 502	1.0	1 003	18.7	278	5.2	11 801	23.4	5 547	603	2 528	NA	NA
Gilpin	49	7 446	1.8	D	D	28	5.5	532	10.8	603	192	148	253	4 650
Grand	222	14 373	1.0	D	D	57	4.2	2 391	19.3	1 652	181	681	273	1 839
Gunnison	850	15 965	1.1	D	D	58	3.9	2 815	20.5	1 623	63	708	449	2 930
Hinsdale	56	NA	NA	NA	NA	NA	NA	136	20.2	177	D	73	20	2 372
Huerfano	165	6 932	1.0	D	D	107	13.7	1 416	23.9	1 940	252	925	112	1 895
Jackson	2	1 464	1.0	D	D	12	8.5	270	24.3	289	11	150	10	717
Jefferson	7 427	478 095	0.8	6 228	11.8	3 607	6.8	61 556	13.3	79 357	40 294	13 705	15 986	2 991
Kiowa	14	1 633	1.0	D	D	23	16.7	212	22.1	305	D	206	1	72
Kit Carson	1 075	8 270	1.0	D	D	80	10.3	2 009	28.9	1 434	52	871	121	1 590
Lake	133	5 522	0.6	D	D	42	5.3	1 985	27.0	725	42	320	93	1 272
La Plata	1 715	51 378	1.0	D	D	278	5.6	8 979	19.9	7 084	634	2 945	972	1 893
Larimer	8 530	284 022	1.0	3 485	12.2	1 611	5.6	40 094	15.5	42 554	10 156	14 283	8 435	2 815
Las Animas	858	15 754	1.0	D	D	166	10.5	2 787	21.4	3 284	516	1 372	185	1 193
Lincoln	1 030	5 748	1.1	D	D	53	10.0	1 072	25.8	897	32	503	15	317
Logan	3 904	22 018	1.0	D	D	192	9.2	3 648	20.9	3 677	349	2 042	571	2 514
Mesa	3 631	139 644	1.0	1 997	14.4	1 289	9.3	22 255	18.1	25 715	9 745	7 691	4 091	2 802
Mineral	0	1 076	1.1	D	D	D	D	154	22.4	211	25	112	0	0
Moffat	102	12 430	0.8	D	D	93	6.8	2 498	20.1	1 754	67	858	341	2 472
Montezuma	237	24 451	0.9	D	D	252	10.0	4 948	23.3	4 950	457	2 371	559	2 189
Montrose	542	38 919	0.9	538	13.6	373	9.4	8 070	23.9	8 352	1 833	3 181	939	2 275
Morgan	564	27 655	1.0	D	D	242	8.7	5 974	25.3	4 371	251	2 373	471	1 727
Otero	433	18 939	1.0	D	D	239	12.6	3 191	21.2	4 238	577	2 173	402	2 335
Ouray	0	4 071	0.9	D	D	23	5.3	821	21.3	903	137	373	NA	NA
Park	92	11 709	0.5	D	D	70	4.1	2 257	15.3	2 231	556	636	163	1 006
Phillips	60	4 392	1.0	D	D	49	10.8	839	23.6	873	21	593	36	810
Pitkin	72	24 068	1.8	D	D	42	2.8	2 077	14.8	1 989	69	1 101	506	2 951
Prowers	315	12 632	1.0	D	D	126	9.4	2 781	25.4	2 123	49	1 305	164	1 307
Pueblo	4 321	154 182	1.0	2 146	13.9	1 552	10.0	23 471	17.8	30 609	8 389	10 097	7 601	4 779
Rio Blanco	235	7 198	1.2	D	D	50	8.1	973	17.2	937	175	396	78	1 170
Rio Grande	198	11 765	1.0	D	D	131	11.1	2 035	21.5	2 542	495	1 395	179	1 544
Routt	335	24 487	1.1	D	D	89	4.0	3 273	15.3	2 286	146	1 115	454	2 007
Saguache	18	5 716	0.8	D	D	41	5.8	2 169	35.0	861	124	359	92	1 506
San Juan	0	NA	NA	NA	NA	NA	NA	117	23.8	90	D	34	16	2 289
San Miguel	9	8 675	1.3	D	D	17	2.3	1 593	22.6	583	66	246	198	2 691
Sedgwick	35	2 360	0.9	D	D	32	13.5	410	23.4	615	30	366	9	378
Summit	273	28 847	1.1	D	D	47	1.8	5 003	20.0	2 132	177	875	847	3 120
Teller	132	19 953	0.7	D	D	114	5.2	2 562	13.7	3 935	978	1 090	274	1 173
Washington	184	4 270	0.8	D	D	47	10.2	749	22.4	881	17	544	85	1 766
Weld	5 895	218 927	0.8	4 018	16.5	1 296	5.3	43 497	19.0	29 727	6 742	11 612	6 223	2 508
Yuma	196	10 259	1.1	D	D	105	10.8	1 961	24.6	1 746	36	1 220	75	747
CONNECTICUT	118 152	3 533 044	1.0	41 293	11.8	28 902	8.3	299 521	10.2	582 946	115 847	223 469	88 443	2 475
Fairfield	19 168	932 662	1.1	11 507	12.8	6 512	7.3	86 933	11.4	136 463	26 598	55 233	18 552	2 063
Hartford	28 227	962 003	1.2	10 401	11.9	7 752	8.8	72 222	9.9	151 662	32 942	57 130	25 720	2 953
Litchfield	2 804	161 830	0.7	1 792	9.5	1 662	8.8	14 777	9.5	35 143	4 673	14 483	NA	NA
Middlesex	5 085	152 698	0.9	1 664	10.1	1 378	8.4	10 702	7.8	29 338	5 190	10 725	NA	NA
New Haven	29 198	823 960	0.9	10 253	12.1	7 550	8.9	73 071	10.3	143 487	33 068	52 622	28 060	3 469
New London	12 782	276 876	1.0	3 041	11.5	2 216	8.4	20 705	9.3	46 284	5 915	18 140	NA	NA

1. Per 1,000 estimated resident population. 2. Data for serious crimes have not been adjusted for underreporting; this may affect comparability between geographic areas and over time. 3. Per 100,000 population estimated by the FBI.

Table B. States and Counties — Crime, Education, Money Income, and Poverty

STATE County	Serious crimes known to police,[1] 2010 (cont.) Rate[2]		Education						Money income, 2006–2010				Income and poverty, 2010			
			School enrollment and attainment, 2006–2010				Local government expenditures,[5] 2008–2009		Per capita income[6] (dollars)	Households			Median household income (dollars)	Percent below poverty level		
			Enrollment[3]		Attainment[4] (percent)					Median income		Percent with income of $200,000 or more				
	Violent	Property	Total	Per cent private	High school graduate or less	Bachelor's degree or more	Total current expenditures (mil dol)	Current expenditures per student (dollars)		Dollars	Percent change, 2000 to 2006–2010 (constant 2010 dollars)			All persons	Children under 18 years	Children 5 to 17 years in families
	46	47	48	49	50	51	52	53	54	55	56	57	58	59	60	61
COLORADO—Cont'd																
Boulder	203	2 346	90 986	12.8	19.9	57.0	(7)481.0	(7)8 783	36 947	64 839	NA	7.9	62 215	13.6	13.8	12.2
Broomfield	75	2 086	14 571	18.8	25.1	44.4	(7)	(7)	35 836	75 590	-6.6	6.8	76 006	6.0	6.8	6.3
Chaffee	118	1 376	3 210	11.5	38.5	33.3	19.3	9 539	26 110	42 941	-1.3	2.6	42 420	12.9	19.2	17.7
Cheyenne	0	163	476	10.5	46.2	18.5	4.7	15 424	22 999	47 125	0.4	0.4	44 464	12.1	20.0	19.9
Clear Creek	447	2 285	1 659	13.3	28.1	41.6	10.1	10 148	34 506	60 426	-6.4	2.6	64 822	8.6	12.6	11.6
Conejos	NA	NA	2 208	5.2	53.7	18.7	15.3	9 032	17 541	33 627	7.3	0.6	32 254	21.3	28.3	25.8
Costilla	NA	NA	872	0.0	59.5	14.3	6.1	13 267	16 525	24 388	-1.4	0.8	27 305	25.7	37.1	34.4
Crowley	69	0	1 163	14.8	62.9	12.2	4.4	9 045	18 966	38 189	12.5	1.5	34 569	34.7	35.7	32.0
Custer	259	517	684	3.7	39.1	29.2	4.6	8 965	26 860	39 909	-9.3	2.5	42 951	15.0	27.8	24.5
Delta	194	2 000	6 268	7.4	49.9	18.3	42.3	7 683	22 080	40 451	-2.6	1.6	40 288	15.7	22.8	21.7
Denver	565	3 498	137 251	22.3	36.5	40.1	756.3	9 463	30 806	45 501	-9.0	4.7	45 415	21.3	30.8	27.3
Dolores	0	1 357	421	5.5	54.7	14.9	3.1	10 485	19 244	43 058	5.6	0.0	40 511	12.9	14.7	14.4
Douglas	123	1 180	81 484	17.3	16.4	54.4	487.8	8 307	42 418	99 198	-5.5	11.1	97 806	3.5	3.8	3.3
Eagle	146	2 105	10 659	18.3	32.9	45.9	59.3	9 870	36 753	71 337	-10.1	7.1	69 182	8.5	12.0	11.3
Elbert	NA	NA	6 045	10.0	35.1	29.2	32.1	8 377	34 782	78 958	-0.2	5.8	78 550	6.5	9.8	8.0
El Paso	476	3 251	171 453	14.1	30.2	34.9	903.7	8 533	27 945	56 268	-5.1	3.7	51 553	13.4	18.2	15.9
Fremont	250	1 232	7 524	16.1	56.0	16.2	45.5	8 025	19 083	37 847	-12.5	1.5	40 541	16.7	23.2	20.4
Garfield	NA	NA	13 600	11.8	43.1	24.4	105.0	9 069	28 457	64 902	9.0	3.2	60 456	9.6	13.6	12.7
Gilpin	349	4 301	1 006	8.6	27.6	33.7	4.2	11 627	33 591	58 036	-11.8	3.8	63 024	7.5	10.5	7.8
Grand	263	1 577	2 771	15.6	36.9	28.8	18.6	9 670	30 055	60 433	-0.1	0.9	55 818	8.3	12.6	12.3
Gunnison	241	2 689	4 555	9.6	25.7	45.8	15.5	8 419	28 490	49 356	5.6	4.3	47 698	14.5	15.3	13.7
Hinsdale	0	2 372	27	22.2	22.4	42.0	1.3	12 932	43 293	74 659	58.2	5.1	48 195	9.4	16.8	17.2
Huerfano	288	1 607	1 369	10.4	44.2	27.2	8.6	9 083	23 139	30 058	-7.9	2.2	31 696	22.7	36.6	31.3
Jackson	72	646	362	4.4	42.2	21.7	2.6	11 000	23 814	37 222	-7.6	0.6	43 691	15.1	27.4	24.6
Jefferson	235	2 756	132 585	15.3	29.4	39.3	738.7	8 595	34 714	66 075	NA	5.3	64 181	8.8	11.4	10.4
Kiowa	0	72	389	1.8	43.0	20.1	3.4	12 007	22 877	40 089	3.8	2.3	37 600	13.0	18.5	15.8
Kit Carson	145	1 445	2 001	12.1	52.6	14.9	13.9	9 683	21 086	41 678	-0.7	0.2	39 498	14.0	19.6	19.3
Lake	383	889	1 784	1.0	43.2	20.7	19.6	13 919	20 437	41 103	-13.9	0.8	43 565	14.4	21.4	20.8
La Plata	158	1 736	13 064	10.2	27.5	40.6	69.3	9 882	29 836	56 422	11.0	3.6	53 029	11.5	14.1	13.0
Larimer	239	2 576	88 856	10.7	26.6	42.6	362.6	8 535	30 046	56 447	-8.4	3.9	54 739	13.6	13.0	11.2
Las Animas	142	1 051	3 784	4.4	44.6	19.3	24.1	8 599	21 887	38 134	6.5	0.8	37 700	18.8	25.1	23.7
Lincoln	106	211	1 064	8.0	55.6	15.3	18.6	19 889	23 440	41 616	3.0	1.7	39 230	17.9	23.0	22.2
Logan	326	2 189	5 675	10.5	45.0	18.0	28.1	8 960	22 564	40 961	-1.2	1.5	40 637	16.3	19.8	18.2
Mesa	266	2 535	35 062	11.7	41.8	25.4	182.5	7 988	27 067	52 067	14.6	3.2	47 324	14.7	18.0	16.4
Mineral	0	0	115	40.9	33.0	39.1	1.8	15 774	46 358	53 438	21.1	6.4	45 645	11.9	22.7	20.7
Moffat	145	2 327	3 971	7.0	49.4	14.9	20.6	8 643	24 563	53 587	1.9	0.5	55 913	10.1	14.1	13.0
Montezuma	278	1 911	5 135	8.1	41.3	26.5	37.9	9 041	24 616	44 103	8.6	2.4	41 074	17.4	26.5	24.0
Montrose	153	2 122	8 965	14.6	48.5	22.3	52.8	7 701	23 613	46 590	4.4	2.3	44 002	15.0	22.6	20.3
Morgan	110	1 617	7 040	4.9	56.1	14.6	45.0	8 127	20 181	43 111	-1.5	1.2	43 209	14.2	20.5	18.5
Otero	360	1 975	4 936	4.1	51.5	15.4	35.0	10 390	18 056	34 142	-9.3	0.6	34 380	19.9	30.0	27.9
Ouray	NA	NA	946	8.8	28.2	41.3	9.4	14 845	29 051	58 393	9.7	4.9	54 920	9.4	15.9	14.1
Park	136	870	2 986	10.7	35.0	32.6	17.2	9 064	31 663	64 098	-2.5	0.9	66 400	9.3	14.4	12.7
Phillips	90	720	1 062	6.0	48.2	16.0	14.5	16 093	23 453	44 084	8.2	1.5	44 064	11.4	15.6	14.3
Pitkin	128	2 822	3 214	22.2	15.0	59.7	21.0	12 653	64 381	64 502	-14.2	15.1	65 568	7.0	7.9	7.2
Prowers	56	1 251	3 587	2.2	48.6	18.3	26.9	10 806	18 429	33 969	-10.4	0.8	34 488	23.0	31.8	29.1
Pueblo	577	4 202	41 690	9.6	43.9	20.9	225.8	8 235	21 609	40 699	-1.9	1.7	39 107	19.6	25.8	24.1
Rio Blanco	255	915	1 493	7.8	41.6	22.7	15.8	12 729	28 382	57 992	21.4	1.6	59 308	8.6	10.9	10.3
Rio Grande	293	1 250	3 437	7.5	47.6	19.2	18.0	8 210	17 199	39 871	-1.1	0.9	37 300	17.3	29.1	27.5
Routt	239	1 768	4 769	14.1	23.3	45.6	44.8	14 626	33 079	60 876	-10.3	4.5	60 506	7.7	9.9	9.3
Saguache	278	1 228	1 315	2.3	53.3	19.4	10.4	11 410	18 686	30 430	-5.7	1.5	30 985	25.1	37.0	35.9
San Juan	143	2 146	98	39.8	26.6	30.8	1.3	19 719	31 232	43 783	12.4	0.0	37 001	15.9	22.9	23.6
San Miguel	122	2 568	1 314	15.6	19.7	48.8	12.2	12 065	38 247	66 399	8.1	5.0	62 368	10.0	14.1	14.1
Sedgwick	0	378	487	5.1	52.4	12.7	6.9	7 504	21 652	37 625	5.1	1.2	36 749	13.6	22.0	20.5
Summit	118	3 002	4 671	13.0	24.7	49.9	31.5	10 257	35 770	68 750	-4.1	5.3	60 087	10.1	12.9	11.9
Teller	137	1 036	5 135	11.2	32.6	31.0	29.2	8 740	28 726	58 080	-8.6	1.7	59 966	8.7	14.3	12.5
Washington	104	1 662	1 106	9.9	47.8	18.3	10.9	12 062	23 125	39 735	-3.2	1.4	40 914	13.9	20.5	17.7
Weld	277	2 231	71 782	9.9	42.8	25.4	303.9	8 353	24 732	55 596	3.7	2.6	52 334	14.3	18.5	15.9
Yuma	50	697	2 372	3.6	52.1	17.8	17.0	9 541	21 872	42 114	0.3	2.5	43 361	12.5	17.3	16.5
CONNECTICUT	281	2 193	947 117	21.4	40.2	35.2	8 017.1	14 629	36 775	67 740	-0.8	8.1	64 321	10.1	12.8	11.3
Fairfield	282	1 781	245 883	25.3	35.5	43.6	2 256.4	15 467	48 295	81 268	-1.6	16.0	74 634	9.3	10.8	9.9
Hartford	332	2 621	237 284	18.9	41.6	33.3	2 049.3	14 557	33 151	62 590	-2.6	6.0	60 028	11.3	14.8	12.9
Litchfield	NA	NA	46 062	19.3	39.9	32.3	383.2	14 098	35 848	69 639	-2.3	5.8	66 076	6.7	8.4	7.1
Middlesex	NA	NA	41 605	24.7	36.5	37.0	339.0	14 350	37 519	74 906	0.0	6.7	70 805	6.8	6.7	5.6
New Haven	416	3 053	229 534	24.3	43.3	31.7	1 867.1	14 464	31 720	61 114	-1.2	5.4	57 070	11.6	16.1	14.7
New London	NA	NA	67 119	18.9	41.6	30.6	569.7	13 896	32 888	65 419	2.0	5.1	61 792	8.9	11.5	9.9

1. Data for serious crimes have not been adjusted for underreporting; this may affect comparability between geographic areas and over time.   2. Per 100,000 population estimated by the FBI.   3. All persons 3 years old and over enrolled in nursery school through college.   4. Persons 25 years old and over.   5. Elementary and secondary education expenditures.   6. Based on population estimated by the American Community Survey, 2006–2010.   7. Broomfield county is included with Boulder county.

Table B. States and Counties — **Personal Income**

STATE County	Personal income, 2009 Total (mil dol) [62]	Percent change, 2008–2009 [63]	Per capita[1] Dollars [64]	Rank [65]	Wages and salaries[2] (mil dol) [66]	Proprietors' income (mil dol) [67]	Dividends, interest, and rent (mil dol) [68]	Transfer payments (mil dol) Total [69]	Government payments to individuals Total [70]	Social Security [71]	Medical payments [72]	Income maintenance [73]	Unemployment insurance [74]
COLORADO—Cont'd													
Boulder	14 584	-4.3	48 056	132	10 511	1 201	3 644	1 169	1 113	466	375	73	92
Broomfield	2 079	-2.4	37 135	734	2 440	147	356	216	206	85	71	11	18
Chaffee	562	-0.8	32 766	1 374	256	41	175	123	120	51	49	7	5
Cheyenne	83	7.1	47 309	146	37	22	16	13	13	4	7	1	0
Clear Creek	476	-4.6	54 682	57	161	71	99	40	39	17	12	3	3
Conejos	201	3.9	25 620	2 790	52	26	22	72	70	16	37	10	3
Costilla	98	3.0	31 167	1 717	27	8	13	37	37	11	17	5	1
Crowley	96	-2.1	15 036	3 113	52	7	13	35	34	8	16	5	2
Custer	137	0.1	34 232	1 138	35	18	42	30	29	15	9	2	1
Delta	929	-0.7	29 665	2 059	367	57	196	240	235	89	101	17	10
Denver	31 512	-1.8	51 630	82	31 570	6 737	5 577	4 074	3 963	935	2 004	403	231
Dolores	61	-2.4	31 385	1 668	16	12	12	15	14	6	5	1	1
Douglas	17 108	1.8	59 358	32	6 048	394	2 245	747	694	356	109	31	85
Eagle	2 458	-9.3	45 807	178	1 526	364	613	119	109	46	23	7	18
Elbert	986	-2.3	42 352	301	149	37	179	95	91	37	30	5	8
El Paso	23 133	1.2	38 266	608	16 530	1 510	3 765	3 274	3 170	976	1 137	299	206
Fremont	1 245	0.1	26 032	2 722	640	77	226	328	319	119	129	27	15
Garfield	2 089	-9.1	37 099	738	1 441	186	385	203	193	72	67	13	21
Gilpin	229	2.4	40 808	397	255	6	38	19	18	8	4	1	2
Grand	543	-5.3	39 023	537	277	71	133	56	53	23	17	3	5
Gunnison	526	-2.4	34 266	1 131	370	56	151	50	48	20	13	3	4
Hinsdale	31	-0.4	37 525	686	10	4	11	4	4	2	1	0	0
Huerfano	205	2.3	27 166	2 540	80	13	42	80	79	22	38	8	3
Jackson	59	6.3	42 895	276	23	14	14	9	9	4	3	1	0
Jefferson	24 609	-3.9	45 834	176	12 768	1 506	4 945	2 602	2 504	1 059	842	164	190
Kiowa	56	7.0	45 062	199	23	16	9	11	10	4	5	1	0
Kit Carson	263	-5.7	31 338	1 688	122	66	47	45	44	18	18	3	2
Lake	213	-5.2	26 504	2 643	78	14	37	34	33	10	15	3	3
La Plata	2 047	-2.9	39 769	466	1 246	215	496	247	237	91	91	17	15
Larimer	11 292	-1.9	37 844	661	6 833	832	2 367	1 429	1 375	546	494	95	95
Las Animas	478	-1.8	29 819	2 018	247	28	80	152	149	38	74	13	6
Lincoln	148	7.6	28 622	2 274	93	13	28	32	31	11	13	3	1
Logan	699	-5.0	33 647	1 227	378	100	141	127	124	45	49	13	5
Mesa	5 083	-4.1	34 791	1 045	3 108	307	1 025	935	908	326	354	76	59
Mineral	30	-4.3	33 109	1 321	16	2	11	5	5	3	2	0	0
Moffat	538	1.2	38 469	584	310	67	61	72	69	24	29	6	5
Montezuma	825	-1.8	32 502	1 426	370	59	175	170	166	64	66	16	8
Montrose	1 253	-3.0	30 264	1 920	650	173	270	263	255	105	93	23	16
Morgan	834	-1.6	29 958	1 989	500	89	130	168	163	53	75	16	7
Otero	593	1.3	31 787	1 583	256	43	81	228	225	45	122	23	8
Ouray	194	-5.7	42 142	319	66	20	69	25	24	12	6	1	3
Park	561	-4.0	33 452	1 266	95	43	91	69	66	32	15	5	6
Phillips	145	-0.7	32 518	1 421	64	29	28	31	31	11	15	2	1
Pitkin	1 352	-9.9	84 264	5	866	193	575	54	51	27	13	1	6
Prowers	403	0.2	31 026	1 747	188	65	70	106	104	25	54	13	4
Pueblo	4 970	2.7	31 613	1 623	2 696	274	723	1 537	1 509	354	806	156	54
Rio Blanco	280	-7.9	42 882	277	220	45	39	35	34	12	14	2	2
Rio Grande	403	2.5	34 793	1 044	173	70	77	100	98	32	40	15	4
Routt	1 153	-6.2	49 139	118	753	142	328	76	72	31	21	3	9
Saguache	150	6.8	21 118	3 078	70	11	25	39	38	10	18	5	2
San Juan	21	-2.4	38 705	564	9	2	5	4	4	1	2	0	0
San Miguel	361	-6.8	47 827	137	225	59	115	21	19	7	6	1	3
Sedgwick	101	-3.2	43 379	262	32	28	15	21	21	8	10	1	1
Summit	1 138	-6.3	41 789	345	758	95	364	70	65	31	15	3	9
Teller	914	1.6	42 161	317	293	52	145	122	118	55	32	9	8
Washington	161	6.9	36 461	823	50	38	28	29	29	11	13	2	1
Weld	6 926	-3.2	27 186	2 534	4 071	661	1 059	1 148	1 101	374	440	102	86
Yuma	345	-9.1	35 446	960	185	58	79	54	52	21	22	4	2
CONNECTICUT	194 547	-2.9	55 296	X	120 997	17 055	38 137	27 297	26 657	8 664	12 526	1 994	2 086
Fairfield	67 380	-5.4	74 767	6	40 229	6 919	15 952	6 588	6 423	2 090	3 110	455	489
Hartford	45 077	-1.9	51 234	87	36 724	4 271	7 855	7 369	7 209	2 220	3 483	610	537
Litchfield	9 460	-3.4	50 125	100	3 283	835	2 005	1 301	1 267	534	499	55	116
Middlesex	8 695	-1.3	52 475	70	4 451	700	1 664	1 078	1 047	442	405	51	88
New Haven	40 184	-1.3	47 387	144	22 978	3 003	6 699	7 218	7 063	2 104	3 447	588	541
New London	12 499	-0.8	46 841	152	8 978	704	2 276	1 997	1 950	669	869	130	157

1. Based on the resident population estimated as of July 1 of the year shown.   2. Includes supplements to wages and salaries.

Table B. States and Counties — Earnings, Social Security, and Housing

STATE County	Earnings, 2009									Social Security beneficiaries, December 2010		Supplemental Security Income recipients, December 2010	Housing units, 2010	
			Goods-related[1]		Service-related and health									
	Total (mil dol)	Farm	Total	Manu-facturing	Information and professional and technical services	Retail trade	Finance, insurance, and real estate	Health care and social services	Govern-ment	Number	Rate[2]		Total	Percent change, 2000–2010
	75	76	77	78	79	80	81	82	83	84	85	86	87	88
COLORADO—Cont'd														
Boulder	11 712	0.1	17.0	12.5	30.7	4.9	5.5	9.9	15.7	35 790	122	2 313	127 071	14.0
Broomfield	2 587	0.0	25.7	20.9	35.5	6.0	5.2	2.7	3.0	6 550	117	320	22 646	54.5
Chaffee	297	0.3	D	2.1	6.4	11.5	8.8	6.5	29.5	4 330	243	230	10 020	19.4
Cheyenne	59	30.6	D	D	D	3.3	D	0.0	24.8	345	188	16	975	-11.8
Clear Creek	232	0.0	D	D	9.1	3.7	7.5	D	15.5	1 365	150	68	5 685	10.9
Conejos	78	16.5	8.8	0.6	D	7.7	D	6.8	32.7	1 730	210	377	4 286	10.3
Costilla	35	25.8	D	D	D	2.7	D	D	34.0	1 055	299	230	2 613	18.7
Crowley	59	8.8	D	0.1	D	4.7	D	4.8	47.0	780	134	146	1 559	1.1
Custer	53	2.6	D	D	10.7	7.5	13.3	D	19.9	1 175	276	37	3 956	32.4
Delta	424	2.1	22.2	5.3	4.5	9.4	5.3	D	29.4	7 750	250	463	14 572	17.8
Denver	38 308	0.0	13.1	3.5	23.6	2.9	10.7	7.3	15.2	76 070	127	13 913	285 797	13.8
Dolores	27	7.3	D	3.9	D	4.9	D	1.7	25.8	510	247	32	1 468	23.1
Douglas	6 441	0.0	10.8	2.6	24.0	7.6	10.5	6.5	10.4	26 605	93	873	106 859	68.7
Eagle	1 890	0.3	D	1.4	7.5	7.6	13.5	9.0	10.0	3 380	65	84	31 312	41.6
Elbert	187	-4.6	D	3.1	10.8	6.2	7.1	D	24.7	3 065	133	81	8 939	25.7
El Paso	18 040	0.0	11.7	5.5	16.2	5.6	6.0	8.0	35.2	83 460	134	7 420	252 852	24.9
Fremont	717	-0.3	13.1	5.3	3.5	6.8	3.9	11.7	47.1	10 700	229	978	19 242	12.2
Garfield	1 627	0.1	32.2	1.3	6.6	8.1	6.5	8.3	16.6	5 910	105	279	23 309	34.5
Gilpin	260	0.0	D	D	D	0.3	0.4	D	9.8	655	120	25	3 560	21.1
Grand	347	2.5	20.3	1.6	4.8	7.6	8.6	2.7	19.9	1 785	120	53	16 061	47.4
Gunnison	426	0.4	D	0.9	6.3	8.0	5.8	3.5	22.7	1 730	113	75	11 412	24.9
Hinsdale	14	4.2	D	0.0	D	D	D	D	24.0	185	219	0	1 388	6.4
Huerfano	93	-1.0	D	4.4	D	7.6	4.2	D	23.8	1 985	296	276	5 075	10.4
Jackson	37	33.2	D	D	D	5.5	D	1.7	21.6	300	215	11	1 286	12.3
Jefferson	14 274	0.1	20.1	13.2	16.4	6.8	5.8	9.4	17.9	81 655	153	4 950	229 967	8.6
Kiowa	39	43.6	D	D	D	2.4	D	0.0	26.2	320	229	11	805	-1.5
Kit Carson	187	24.2	D	2.9	D	4.8	4.8	3.2	17.8	1 510	183	87	3 527	2.8
Lake	92	0.0	D	D	2.4	6.0	3.7	D	40.7	820	112	64	4 271	9.1
La Plata	1 461	0.2	19.4	1.5	9.7	7.2	6.7	11.6	22.5	7 590	148	398	25 860	24.5
Larimer	7 665	0.2	22.1	12.6	14.2	6.9	4.9	12.6	20.5	44 200	148	2 380	132 722	25.9
Las Animas	274	-0.6	20.0	2.3	D	7.2	6.6	D	31.5	3 495	225	544	8 217	7.7
Lincoln	106	5.6	D	D	D	7.7	4.2	5.1	47.8	950	174	64	2 420	0.6
Logan	478	8.8	12.3	2.9	4.6	8.5	3.9	D	25.4	3 895	172	383	8 981	6.2
Mesa	3 416	0.2	22.8	4.2	6.7	8.0	5.8	14.7	17.5	27 295	186	2 205	62 644	28.6
Mineral	18	-1.9	D	D	D	D	D	D	20.0	215	302	0	1 201	7.3
Moffat	377	5.1	31.0	1.2	D	7.5	2.8	D	17.7	1 985	144	152	6 196	10.0
Montezuma	429	1.5	16.7	3.4	5.3	10.2	4.4	11.6	31.9	5 410	212	440	12 094	15.2
Montrose	824	0.0	26.1	6.0	5.8	9.6	5.1	D	21.4	9 070	220	619	18 250	28.5
Morgan	588	6.0	33.7	20.7	D	5.1	3.0	9.0	18.2	4 615	164	409	11 490	10.4
Otero	299	6.2	D	7.5	3.7	7.6	5.1	D	25.8	4 305	229	795	8 969	1.8
Ouray	86	0.7	24.0	1.6	10.8	7.8	9.7	D	21.0	965	218	25	3 083	43.7
Park	138	0.0	D	1.9	10.6	5.2	7.1	3.2	28.8	2 530	156	93	13 947	30.4
Phillips	92	26.0	D	0.5	3.5	4.1	4.8	D	25.9	955	215	66	2 087	3.6
Pitkin	1 059	0.1	D	0.8	12.4	6.5	12.4	2.9	12.6	1 960	114	25	12 953	28.3
Prowers	254	17.8	11.9	5.1	D	9.0	5.8	6.2	27.3	2 250	179	356	5 942	-0.6
Pueblo	2 969	0.1	D	9.6	4.5	8.0	4.1	19.0	23.8	32 175	202	5 782	69 526	18.0
Rio Blanco	265	1.6	48.8	2.1	2.2	5.7	1.1	1.0	20.6	1 005	151	40	3 309	15.9
Rio Grande	243	6.9	7.2	2.1	2.8	4.9	4.5	D	19.5	2 930	245	437	6 630	10.4
Routt	895	1.6	28.2	0.7	D	8.7	8.1	9.0	10.5	2 405	102	76	16 303	45.4
Saguache	81	17.9	D	1.2	D	5.3	D	D	27.3	895	147	81	3 843	24.5
San Juan	11	0.0	D	D	D	10.5	D	D	27.4	100	143	0	756	19.6
San Miguel	284	0.4	D	2.4	8.7	5.4	15.5	3.1	15.7	640	87	23	6 638	27.7
Sedgwick	61	48.2	D	D	D	4.4	D	D	21.5	660	277	41	1 415	2.0
Summit	853	0.0	D	0.4	8.9	10.6	10.0	5.9	14.6	2 235	80	36	29 842	23.3
Teller	345	-0.5	D	D	D	7.2	5.6	5.7	18.2	4 445	190	182	12 643	22.0
Washington	88	32.5	D	D	D	4.9	D	1.1	22.8	940	195	43	2 434	5.5
Weld	4 732	3.4	29.3	12.7	4.7	6.0	7.4	9.5	15.7	32 020	127	3 065	96 281	45.5
Yuma	242	28.6	15.8	1.4	2.5	5.5	5.5	4.4	19.2	1 790	178	104	4 466	4.0
CONNECTICUT	138 051	0.1	16.8	11.8	12.5	5.5	15.6	11.6	15.4	622 167	174	58 257	1 487 891	7.4
Fairfield	47 148	0.0	D	10.2	15.6	5.6	23.4	8.9	8.8	142 295	155	11 329	361 221	6.4
Hartford	40 995	0.1	16.6	12.3	11.8	4.7	19.4	11.7	15.4	162 425	182	19 481	374 249	6.0
Litchfield	4 118	0.5	26.4	14.5	7.9	8.4	4.0	13.5	15.7	38 030	200	1 632	87 550	10.4
Middlesex	5 151	0.3	D	15.5	7.8	5.8	11.3	15.2	18.2	31 180	188	1 459	74 837	11.2
New Haven	25 981	0.1	D	11.3	11.9	6.0	5.8	15.8	16.5	153 535	178	18 060	362 004	6.2
New London	9 681	0.4	20.3	16.2	9.3	5.1	2.2	10.2	34.2	50 020	183	3 497	120 994	9.3

1. Includes mining, construction, and manufacturing.   2. Per 1,000 resident population enumerated in the 2010 census.

Table B. States and Counties — Housing, Labor Force, and Employment

STATE County	Housing units, 2006–2010								Civilian labor force, 2010				Civilian employment,[5] 2006–2010		
	Occupied units										Unemployment			Percent	
	Owner-occupied					Renter-occupied									
				Median owner cost as a percent of income											Construction, production, and maintenance occupations
				With a mortgage	Without a mortgage	Median rent[2]	Median rent as a percent of income	Substandard units[3] (percent)		Percent change, 2009–2010				Management, business, science and arts	
	Total	Percent	Median value[1]						Total		Total	Rate[4]	Total		
	89	90	91	92	93	94	95	96	97	98	99	100	101	102	103
COLORADO—Cont'd															
Boulder	117 629	63.9	353 300	24.7	10.0	986	34.5	2.7	173 234	-0.5	12 269	7.1	153 341	51.7	12.4
Broomfield	20 116	74.4	270 500	23.7	11.8	982	28.3	2.1	30 411	-0.3	2 393	7.9	28 307	47.2	14.8
Chaffee	7 396	76.9	248 100	27.5	10.4	702	29.6	2.0	8 310	-2.3	660	7.9	7 776	33.1	22.5
Cheyenne	829	80.5	80 700	20.2	10.0	453	14.2	2.3	1 294	-5.1	44	3.4	1 094	39.2	25.1
Clear Creek	4 164	81.3	280 000	28.3	12.2	793	29.6	1.8	5 368	-4.1	456	8.5	5 364	37.3	20.4
Conejos	3 121	75.7	112 200	24.8	11.4	544	30.8	7.4	3 806	1.6	355	9.3	3 295	35.6	26.6
Costilla	1 454	74.6	105 200	29.8	12.6	461	32.8	6.3	1 434	7.0	157	10.9	1 254	27.4	38.0
Crowley	1 163	74.0	81 400	22.7	12.1	539	25.3	3.8	1 938	0.1	204	10.5	1 478	26.6	30.2
Custer	1 850	80.5	218 400	32.5	11.5	688	37.4	2.2	2 029	0.8	140	6.9	1 596	37.3	28.2
Delta	12 700	74.3	193 900	24.8	12.8	715	29.1	2.3	16 286	-3.3	1 577	9.7	13 166	29.4	34.2
Denver	254 181	52.5	240 900	26.0	10.9	798	30.6	3.5	322 060	0.2	31 329	9.7	301 268	40.4	17.8
Dolores	799	78.3	136 200	23.2	10.4	551	23.6	3.0	1 012	-1.4	177	17.5	876	24.9	34.0
Douglas	98 725	82.5	338 700	24.2	10.0	1 174	26.0	0.6	158 979	0.3	11 295	7.1	143 457	52.0	10.0
Eagle	18 183	65.3	530 900	28.4	12.8	1 225	28.5	4.6	29 377	-2.7	2 795	9.5	31 223	32.7	21.4
Elbert	8 135	91.3	346 400	28.0	12.2	909	31.8	1.2	12 801	-0.5	1 067	8.3	11 972	39.8	22.3
El Paso	227 151	66.6	216 800	24.7	10.0	817	29.6	2.3	298 152	0.1	28 745	9.6	275 260	39.8	17.8
Fremont	16 817	76.6	152 800	25.9	13.2	650	34.5	2.1	19 651	-1.0	2 062	10.5	14 239	28.2	21.5
Garfield	19 970	67.5	341 600	26.6	10.0	1 052	28.3	5.4	32 605	-5.7	3 251	10.0	29 896	26.7	30.6
Gilpin	2 530	71.8	316 400	26.1	10.0	1 017	36.0	0.5	3 648	6.8	280	7.7	3 149	38.8	17.1
Grand	5 330	76.9	269 100	26.4	10.0	889	24.7	2.3	8 624	-4.9	774	9.0	8 578	27.5	28.0
Gunnison	6 216	59.1	335 100	29.0	10.0	799	27.6	2.8	9 105	-2.2	650	7.1	9 155	31.6	24.5
Hinsdale	255	83.5	275 000	22.8	10.0	640	21.9	0.0	584	-11.9	27	4.6	243	48.1	9.5
Huerfano	3 154	72.1	154 900	28.8	11.2	624	30.7	6.9	3 279	-6.3	402	12.3	2 568	37.5	20.1
Jackson	690	72.3	144 300	29.9	10.0	656	22.2	2.3	1 209	-6.8	81	6.7	793	33.5	31.4
Jefferson	217 018	71.9	259 300	24.7	10.0	900	29.6	1.8	301 242	-1.1	25 897	8.6	280 327	42.7	17.5
Kiowa	706	66.6	62 200	21.3	11.4	596	27.1	0.7	930	-6.0	47	5.1	837	35.2	20.9
Kit Carson	3 010	69.3	102 300	22.8	13.1	552	19.4	1.5	4 701	-1.9	225	4.8	4 100	28.5	29.6
Lake	2 725	66.9	168 200	24.9	12.2	873	38.4	6.6	3 827	-2.8	483	12.6	3 800	23.6	37.3
La Plata	20 512	69.1	343 400	25.7	10.0	944	28.5	2.9	30 128	-2.6	2 179	7.2	27 585	38.2	20.5
Larimer	117 415	67.5	246 000	25.2	10.0	849	33.4	1.6	175 823	0.2	13 058	7.4	152 467	42.1	18.1
Las Animas	6 420	69.5	142 300	25.2	12.7	697	31.9	3.6	8 186	-4.1	790	9.7	6 671	26.2	34.1
Lincoln	1 919	70.8	103 700	22.5	10.0	600	26.6	2.1	2 995	-2.8	146	4.9	2 190	32.6	23.2
Logan	8 146	68.3	119 900	21.7	12.7	603	23.8	1.9	11 346	-4.3	740	6.5	10 744	26.1	27.6
Mesa	57 123	72.3	221 000	24.5	10.0	810	28.8	2.9	78 853	-3.4	8 330	10.6	69 121	32.2	25.7
Mineral	440	86.4	258 300	21.6	10.0	634	19.5	0.0	461	-8.0	33	7.2	536	45.1	28.0
Moffat	5 360	75.1	166 300	22.5	11.3	735	26.6	1.6	8 587	-5.4	817	9.5	7 069	24.7	35.6
Montezuma	11 027	72.8	191 500	25.2	11.3	593	29.2	5.0	13 087	-0.8	1 199	9.2	11 873	34.5	24.4
Montrose	16 335	74.6	201 700	26.8	11.6	788	29.7	2.9	20 618	-2.0	2 280	11.1	18 588	26.5	30.8
Morgan	10 407	67.3	136 200	25.7	13.3	676	26.2	6.0	14 827	-1.4	1 029	6.9	13 045	24.4	41.5
Otero	7 620	66.1	93 800	23.1	12.0	560	28.0	3.3	9 061	-1.6	786	8.7	7 565	34.2	21.7
Ouray	1 702	74.3	405 800	34.4	11.4	1 153	29.6	1.3	2 773	-3.8	217	7.8	2 087	39.6	21.1
Park	7 070	87.9	245 800	27.1	10.0	1 206	29.3	1.8	9 299	-2.5	825	8.9	8 860	34.1	25.2
Phillips	1 867	73.3	111 600	22.8	12.4	598	26.4	5.4	2 459	-4.8	118	4.8	2 116	31.2	30.5
Pitkin	7 417	62.5	670 200	25.1	10.0	1 259	28.2	2.7	10 672	-3.3	862	8.1	10 475	45.3	12.1
Prowers	4 905	66.7	83 000	19.9	12.0	525	27.0	2.8	6 653	-4.0	439	6.6	6 027	31.8	30.1
Pueblo	61 418	69.9	140 700	25.8	11.7	652	34.4	2.1	74 737	0.8	7 756	10.4	65 445	29.7	22.5
Rio Blanco	2 621	74.1	193 300	21.8	10.0	674	23.2	2.1	4 277	-8.3	282	6.6	3 254	31.8	37.6
Rio Grande	3 630	78.9	129 300	26.4	10.4	555	27.9	2.1	6 901	3.9	554	8.0	4 350	30.1	31.4
Routt	10 146	74.1	422 300	29.6	10.3	1 127	28.5	1.7	14 450	-4.3	1 360	9.4	14 129	37.9	23.4
Saguache	2 684	68.3	120 500	27.9	11.8	549	29.5	5.5	3 439	4.9	332	9.7	2 824	26.1	39.1
San Juan	411	54.3	252 000	22.1	10.0	750	32.6	4.4	556	0.0	60	10.8	530	34.9	18.5
San Miguel	3 228	64.3	493 000	31.1	10.0	973	31.0	2.5	5 119	-1.4	395	7.7	4 886	34.2	14.7
Sedgwick	1 007	72.8	83 100	19.3	11.7	508	20.2	0.7	1 603	-5.9	82	5.1	1 054	27.6	29.0
Summit	10 553	70.5	465 700	28.2	11.1	1 165	29.5	3.2	16 201	-2.1	1 268	7.8	18 086	34.1	21.2
Teller	9 004	86.9	226 000	26.6	10.0	873	33.3	2.3	12 064	-0.7	1 168	9.7	11 354	39.6	18.2
Washington	2 186	68.3	114 300	22.1	12.0	518	24.2	2.1	2 817	-5.0	153	5.4	2 477	35.8	30.7
Weld	86 776	71.7	195 700	25.8	11.7	770	31.4	4.0	119 689	-0.2	12 188	10.2	118 364	31.9	26.8
Yuma	3 941	68.9	116 200	23.2	11.0	547	22.5	4.1	6 551	-7.0	278	4.2	4 799	31.0	38.3
CONNECTICUT	1 359 218	69.2	296 500	26.5	16.9	982	31.0	2.2	1 916 596	1.6	178 138	9.3	1 765 549	40.0	18.2
Fairfield	331 782	70.7	477 500	28.1	17.8	1 206	31.8	2.8	473 538	0.3	39 379	8.3	439 341	42.9	16.0
Hartford	347 625	66.5	247 400	25.2	16.5	909	30.2	2.1	465 733	0.1	44 995	9.7	438 414	39.6	17.7
Litchfield	76 688	78.7	285 800	26.8	16.3	883	29.3	1.3	105 655	0.1	9 341	8.8	100 459	37.9	20.1
Middlesex	66 975	75.8	307 400	26.2	14.8	955	28.5	1.7	95 207	0.4	7 364	7.7	86 275	44.0	17.3
New Haven	330 785	65.3	273 300	27.1	18.6	996	33.0	2.4	454 652	0.9	45 710	10.1	426 766	38.8	19.4
New London	106 590	69.7	268 900	25.8	15.1	974	28.9	1.7	150 822	0.0	13 139	8.7	134 193	37.1	18.7

1. Specified owner-occupied units.   2. Specified renter-occupied units. A value of 10.0 represents 10 percent or less.   3. Overcrowded or lacking complete plumbing facilities.   4. Percent of civilian labor force.   5. Persons 16 years old and over.

Table B. States and Counties — Nonfarm Employment and Agriculture

	Private nonfarm establishments, employment and payroll, 2009								Agriculture, 2007			
	Employment						Annual payroll		Farms			
										Percent with:		
STATE County	Number of establishments	Total	Health care and social assistance	Manufacturing	Retail trade	Finance and insurance	Professional, scientific, and technical services	Total (mil dol)	Average per employee (dollars)	Number	Fewer than 50 acres	500 acres or more	Farm operators whose principal occupation is farming (percent)
	104	105	106	107	108	109	110	111	112	113	114	115	116
COLORADO—Cont'd													
Boulder	11 352	134 041	18 318	14 284	16 474	4 457	25 169	6 484	48 372	746	67.2	6.4	38.6
Broomfield	1 677	29 760	1 119	3 037	4 567	812	4 790	1 750	58 790	24	66.7	12.5	29.2
Chaffee	881	5 039	656	159	989	242	264	136	26 931	223	43.0	17.5	48.4
Cheyenne	61	631	D	0	D	D	5	29	46 414	380	3.4	65.8	46.1
Clear Creek	346	2 681	D	D	231	D	D	78	29 224	27	51.9	18.5	25.9
Conejos	96	544	D	32	152	D	D	14	26 634	535	24.3	22.1	44.1
Costilla	44	187	D	D	31	D	0	4	22 647	241	34.9	19.1	34.9
Crowley	39	587	D	0	84	32	D	14	24 329	268	17.2	43.7	49.6
Custer	146	562	D	D	105	D	D	15	26 511	226	14.2	27.9	41.6
Delta	891	6 554	1 475	509	1 327	316	235	188	28 744	1 294	57.1	7.1	43.0
Denver	21 959	382 765	50 853	16 948	26 459	24 288	34 423	19 752	51 603	24	95.8	0.0	25.0
Dolores	44	204	D	D	D	D	D	5	24 819	279	18.3	28.0	33.7
Douglas	7 396	81 343	7 996	1 385	14 976	5 534	5 236	3 836	47 162	1 080	61.8	7.0	32.6
Eagle	3 341	31 682	1 793	D	3 944	946	1 620	999	31 539	152	40.1	23.0	33.6
Elbert	522	1 909	153	139	236	76	192	62	32 244	1 402	32.4	23.2	35.3
El Paso	15 756	216 331	29 472	11 245	28 669	10 529	20 833	8 458	39 096	1 529	46.8	17.1	34.5
Fremont	868	7 863	2 085	548	1 622	297	148	200	25 489	924	66.6	12.0	36.1
Garfield	2 668	21 417	2 527	274	3 492	711	1 174	878	40 983	623	48.6	16.9	40.1
Gilpin	113	3 910	D	D	D	D	23	154	39 419	27	37.0	18.5	33.3
Grand	905	5 702	273	99	698	149	632	165	28 958	229	27.1	29.3	38.0
Gunnison	1 090	6 773	496	82	965	162	320	192	28 308	217	30.0	29.5	40.6
Hinsdale	74	184	D	0	22	D	D	5	28 902	21	14.3	14.3	61.9
Huerfano	179	1 448	519	70	198	30	D	39	27 208	309	10.0	46.6	41.7
Jackson	63	289	D	D	68	D	D	9	32 152	120	15.8	61.7	55.0
Jefferson	16 231	185 387	21 322	19 434	28 330	8 603	23 065	8 112	43 759	540	68.9	6.9	29.1
Kiowa	43	209	D	0	D	D	D	6	28 938	425	4.7	58.1	40.2
Kit Carson	249	1 931	289	109	327	107	D	55	28 258	786	5.6	59.0	50.5
Lake	206	1 272	D	D	175	D	D	30	23 349	29	37.9	24.1	24.1
La Plata	2 374	19 582	2 692	598	3 236	900	1 355	670	34 239	1 076	45.4	10.8	36.5
Larimer	9 361	104 597	16 756	11 148	16 643	3 569	8 144	3 847	36 780	1 757	60.8	9.2	34.1
Las Animas	408	3 379	646	D	688	154	97	91	28 917	585	16.4	52.1	45.5
Lincoln	125	1 177	257	D	319	60	D	35	29 825	542	6.6	65.3	49.3
Logan	601	5 655	1 146	243	1 241	221	131	149	26 355	1 035	10.7	44.5	45.7
Mesa	4 816	53 464	9 381	2 593	8 734	2 225	2 947	1 828	34 192	1 787	71.0	6.6	36.6
Mineral	60	184	D	D	48	D	D	5	27 799	15	6.7	26.7	0.0
Moffat	446	4 029	479	80	797	D	128	164	40 581	503	26.6	32.4	29.8
Montezuma	784	6 665	1 142	325	1 236	188	281	192	28 842	1 123	47.5	11.8	37.8
Montrose	1 345	11 429	2 170	1 053	2 278	380	511	359	31 427	1 045	51.4	12.0	40.6
Morgan	658	8 562	1 150	2 615	1 012	246	115	277	32 383	894	20.8	30.1	45.2
Otero	469	4 607	D	458	935	187	112	117	25 335	569	33.4	25.1	47.1
Ouray	304	1 060	D	D	D	D	D	33	30 731	105	38.1	25.7	47.6
Park	464	1 292	D	70	221	D	D	32	24 935	282	25.2	28.0	39.0
Phillips	134	956	D	25	145	57	D	30	30 858	334	13.2	54.5	54.8
Pitkin	1 620	16 278	744	147	1 649	287	960	518	31 791	82	32.9	17.1	48.8
Prowers	356	2 972	628	172	D	230	D	75	25 291	636	11.9	47.5	47.0
Pueblo	3 193	46 927	11 707	3 736	7 722	1 368	1 427	1 484	31 618	881	41.2	23.7	38.7
Rio Blanco	248	1 951	D	36	260	D	44	91	46 564	285	31.6	33.0	41.4
Rio Grande	377	2 730	399	57	429	129	75	78	28 557	390	23.6	26.2	60.8
Routt	1 639	18 179	1 188	122	1 653	283	591	641	35 252	610	36.7	25.2	28.4
Saguache	123	778	48	D	88	23	D	21	26 652	242	8.3	45.9	62.4
San Juan	69	196	D	0	33	0	D	6	30 459	0	0.0	0.0	0.0
San Miguel	631	4 704	126	136	460	88	375	130	27 600	123	31.7	29.3	39.8
Sedgwick	76	432	D	37	127	D	14	9	21 106	193	8.8	53.9	62.7
Summit	2 114	21 403	894	129	3 018	292	676	512	23 912	41	12.2	39.0	43.9
Teller	697	5 115	432	D	721	165	258	145	28 294	126	46.8	23.8	32.5
Washington	102	475	31	D	81	37	22	14	29 539	1 010	9.5	47.3	43.9
Weld	5 193	66 870	7 992	11 496	8 049	4 019	1 886	2 533	37 873	3 921	34.4	18.1	40.9
Yuma	352	2 861	593	86	525	D	74	94	32 762	970	11.2	55.2	51.4
CONNECTICUT	90 048	1 468 291	259 507	166 398	180 143	124 950	95 334	78 027	53 141	4 916	63.6	2.1	46.2
Fairfield	27 291	407 342	60 274	37 795	48 617	39 793	37 828	28 989	71 166	310	71.0	2.6	47.4
Hartford	22 935	449 294	76 086	52 544	49 258	62 101	29 488	23 103	51 421	790	65.3	1.8	47.8
Litchfield	5 039	52 370	9 619	9 259	8 443	1 465	1 651	1 928	36 822	979	61.1	3.2	45.5
Middlesex	4 227	61 152	13 752	8 961	8 060	D	2 477	2 584	42 255	393	79.6	0.8	41.5
New Haven	19 893	327 054	70 574	36 209	42 257	12 260	16 064	14 635	44 749	573	70.5	1.4	50.6
New London	5 878	104 745	16 307	D	14 072	2 194	5 785	4 323	41 272	793	58.9	1.5	44.6

STATE County	Acreage (1,000)	Percent change, 2002–2007	Average size of farm	Total irrigated (1,000)	Total cropland (1,000)	Average per farm	Average per acre	Value of machinery and equipment, average per farm (dollars)	Total (mil dol)	Average per farm (dollars)	Crops	Livestock and poultry products	$10,000 or more	$100,000 or more	Total ($1,000)	Percent of farms
	117	118	119	120	121	122	123	124	125	126	127	128	129	130	131	132
COLORADO—Cont'd																
Boulder	138	27.8	185	33.9	54.4	588 686	3 190	66 628	34.0	45 625	76.4	23.6	31.2	6.8	376	11.1
Broomfield	6	NA	260	1.0	4.9	431 533	1 657	50 167	1.0	39 928	51.9	48.1	12.5	8.3	20	25.0
Chaffee	79	11.3	356	15.1	21.9	752 697	2 114	64 166	8.1	36 284	37.9	62.1	35.9	9.9	33	5.8
Cheyenne	900	21.6	2 367	33.0	512.0	1 528 587	646	155 582	71.1	187 099	76.3	23.7	51.6	33.2	6 890	80.3
Clear Creek	12	NA	461	0.1	1.4	579 421	1 256	50 000	0.1	4 690	D	D	7.4	0.0	D	7.4
Conejos	229	-14.6	427	119.1	123.0	534 397	1 250	97 926	31.6	59 007	59.6	40.4	46.5	14.2	671	27.1
Costilla	401	13.3	1 665	63.5	59.0	1 356 077	815	143 398	26.7	110 623	85.7	14.3	34.4	13.3	393	29.5
Crowley	451	20.3	1 684	9.8	62.4	850 123	505	75 316	110.9	413 888	1.4	98.6	34.7	13.4	1 345	49.3
Custer	138	13.1	610	18.2	26.0	1 000 638	1 641	80 386	8.4	37 274	26.7	73.3	33.2	8.4	94	9.7
Delta	253	-3.4	195	66.2	67.3	565 016	2 895	61 140	46.8	36 167	43.1	56.9	34.3	6.6	725	9.1
Denver	1	NA	25	D	0.2	369 472	14 560	46 939	0.6	23 356	D	D	29.2	12.5	1	12.5
Dolores	174	9.4	623	9.4	82.1	657 975	1 056	65 143	8.8	31 719	70.0	30.0	28.7	9.3	1 114	62.7
Douglas	189	-5.0	175	3.5	35.1	563 587	3 217	50 075	15.9	14 760	47.7	52.3	17.4	2.0	163	4.0
Eagle	124	6.9	816	11.1	12.3	932 684	1 143	83 714	4.8	31 816	29.8	70.2	30.9	5.9	210	6.6
Elbert	1 134	6.2	809	12.4	224.0	820 923	1 015	64 340	40.7	29 047	32.5	67.5	26.1	5.8	2 488	18.5
El Paso	616	-24.1	403	15.9	88.7	538 722	1 336	54 664	39.4	25 783	50.5	49.5	21.1	3.2	806	8.8
Fremont	296	11.7	320	11.8	25.6	498 287	1 556	46 486	19.3	20 894	24.8	75.2	18.4	2.2	140	7.6
Garfield	335	-17.1	538	43.7	50.4	974 591	1 811	79 960	22.2	35 639	30.8	69.2	34.3	10.0	358	7.1
Gilpin	13	116.7	492	D	0.3	629 973	1 280	32 368	0.3	12 157	0.6	99.4	18.5	7.4	D	7.4
Grand	208	-5.5	910	43.1	38.8	1 376 888	1 513	110 654	9.4	40 897	15.7	84.3	31.9	10.9	108	5.2
Gunnison	174	5.5	800	40.7	33.8	1 432 979	1 790	80 419	10.7	49 450	16.8	83.2	40.1	12.4	16	2.3
Hinsdale	6	-33.3	281	1.9	0.8	772 668	2 752	40 109	0.8	39 310	0.0	100.0	42.9	28.6	D	9.5
Huerfano	519	-14.6	1 678	13.9	35.8	1 121 356	668	65 511	12.3	39 691	28.2	71.8	35.6	7.1	211	11.3
Jackson	387	-11.6	3 226	89.6	80.3	3 148 162	976	153 620	21.2	176 660	18.3	81.7	51.7	29.2	95	6.7
Jefferson	93	3.3	173	4.2	15.2	588 271	3 405	44 815	11.1	20 568	81.4	18.6	15.4	3.7	42	3.7
Kiowa	958	6.8	2 254	3.3	616.8	1 223 630	543	137 062	68.4	160 918	75.9	24.1	44.5	24.2	7 870	79.1
Kit Carson	1 352	8.4	1 721	118.0	885.8	1 338 431	778	243 340	337.0	428 735	34.1	65.9	53.8	33.8	13 422	79.4
Lake	15	-11.8	512	2.7	6.1	873 671	1 707	44 603	0.6	21 114	D	D	20.7	6.9	D	6.9
La Plata	570	1.2	530	66.0	76.8	734 070	1 385	73 039	19.8	18 393	39.7	60.3	27.7	4.2	1 045	14.6
Larimer	490	-6.1	279	63.4	120.0	695 145	2 494	63 923	128.1	72 921	38.9	61.1	26.0	6.8	803	9.0
Las Animas	2 179	-5.5	3 725	35.1	109.5	1 708 606	459	71 216	25.4	43 414	13.4	86.6	40.3	12.0	1 431	26.3
Lincoln	1 400	-2.0	2 583	9.7	576.0	1 488 765	576	132 201	71.0	130 939	60.1	39.9	50.0	29.9	8 037	69.6
Logan	1 132	1.9	1 094	100.3	603.0	951 244	870	136 747	442.1	427 157	18.0	82.0	55.9	25.6	9 604	74.1
Mesa	373	-3.1	211	64.3	131.2	703 108	3 335	57 102	61.2	34 652	49.4	50.6	28.1	5.7	476	7.9
Mineral	9	125.0	591	0.8	1.8	1 042 017	1 763	27 487	0.1	8 427	D	D	20.0	0.0	0	0.0
Moffat	837	-17.8	1 663	28.5	135.1	1 200 473	722	74 555	28.3	56 269	13.2	86.8	29.4	11.7	1 749	31.4
Montezuma	704	-14.0	627	57.1	103.9	577 679	921	66 298	26.7	23 752	64.8	35.2	30.9	5.5	1 273	14.5
Montrose	321	-4.2	307	85.7	93.3	732 730	2 385	82 249	67.2	64 268	34.6	65.4	39.5	10.1	1 059	18.1
Morgan	728	-4.0	814	94.6	323.0	890 238	1 093	148 005	493.9	552 420	12.9	87.1	51.0	22.9	6 459	58.1
Otero	624	14.3	1 097	55.2	92.9	657 569	599	121 810	111.2	195 408	24.0	76.0	50.8	21.6	1 654	46.0
Ouray	94	-13.0	894	10.7	10.2	1 289 511	1 443	83 245	3.6	34 328	17.0	83.0	41.9	8.6	8	3.8
Park	324	8.7	1 148	9.9	55.9	979 334	853	48 960	5.3	18 659	3.6	96.4	20.2	2.8	42	3.5
Phillips	431	-8.5	1 291	63.7	355.6	1 441 720	1 117	237 350	143.0	428 092	51.9	48.1	63.2	45.2	5 613	78.7
Pitkin	29	20.8	348	10.0	4.8	883 951	2 540	80 543	2.0	24 714	22.1	77.9	29.3	7.3	D	4.9
Prowers	1 037	20.3	1 631	103.2	552.5	1 125 165	690	164 018	263.3	414 027	31.2	68.8	48.7	25.2	7 499	68.2
Pueblo	911	17.7	1 034	24.6	73.5	692 240	670	68 533	49.3	55 904	32.2	67.8	29.3	8.3	1 667	18.8
Rio Blanco	387	2.7	1 356	23.0	55.2	1 302 220	960	86 839	15.6	54 607	10.7	89.3	36.8	14.0	573	24.9
Rio Grande	179	4.7	459	102.8	114.4	1 017 332	2 218	170 004	85.4	218 871	91.4	8.6	56.9	26.9	835	29.0
Routt	533	18.4	874	43.5	129.9	1 192 414	1 365	85 124	34.1	55 926	13.6	86.4	30.5	9.5	1 072	21.1
Saguache	287	-39.8	1 187	103.3	118.2	1 550 459	1 306	252 425	91.5	377 918	85.9	14.1	57.0	36.4	541	33.5
San Juan	0	NA	0	0	0.0	0	0	0	0.0	0	0.0	0.0	0.0	0.0	0	0.0
San Miguel	151	0.0	1 227	12.7	17.8	1 764 631	1 438	69 276	3.4	27 235	19.5	80.5	29.3	5.7	157	13.8
Sedgwick	297	8.4	1 537	40.0	196.4	1 475 381	960	205 608	70.3	364 131	53.1	46.9	68.4	45.6	2 665	78.2
Summit	48	71.4	1 166	10.5	7.1	1 801 830	1 545	87 226	1.1	26 753	42.0	58.0	29.3	9.8	D	2.4
Teller	73	-1.4	581	1.4	8.8	740 055	1 274	42 770	1.1	8 485	4.7	95.3	16.7	1.6	D	0.8
Washington	1 376	-2.3	1 362	37.6	854.4	991 634	728	119 086	130.2	128 884	55.3	44.7	49.1	22.8	12 742	75.3
Weld	2 089	15.3	533	327.8	987.9	825 561	1 550	123 541	1 539.1	392 520	17.7	82.3	39.8	16.4	15 403	39.4
Yuma	1 334	-1.5	1 376	263.8	697.8	1 438 070	1 045	207 395	711.4	733 393	26.9	73.1	56.1	35.3	13 685	69.2
CONNECTICUT	406	13.7	83	9.9	163.7	1 045 133	12 667	64 090	551.6	112 195	72.8	27.2	34.6	10.0	4 122	7.2
Fairfield	40	207.7	128	0.2	6.6	1 850 189	14 505	64 999	37.3	120 273	77.7	22.3	39.4	11.3	19	2.6
Hartford	54	8.0	68	5.7	29.6	992 236	14 651	89 534	133.6	169 091	94.7	5.3	44.6	15.7	422	4.6
Litchfield	87	-7.4	89	0.3	39.2	1 127 534	12 628	54 661	47.4	48 435	57.8	42.2	34.2	7.2	1 533	9.9
Middlesex	17	-5.6	42	0.7	7.4	729 070	17 237	54 704	55.8	141 866	96.9	3.1	22.9	6.6	96	3.3
New Haven	46	76.9	80	1.5	13.8	1 061 198	13 310	64 600	90.2	157 370	90.3	9.7	36.8	12.7	344	6.1
New London	63	6.8	80	0.6	25.1	953 549	11 931	52 855	110.1	138 800	46.5	53.5	29.8	8.1	479	9.6

Table B. States and Counties — Water Use, Wholesale Trade, Retail Trade, and Real Estate

STATE County	Water use, 2005		Wholesale trade,[1] 2007				Retail trade,[2] 2007				Real estate and rental and leasing,[2] 2007			
	Total water withdrawn (mil gal/day)	Gallons withdrawn per person	Number of establish-ments	Number of employees	Sales (mil dol)	Annual payroll (mil dol)	Number of establish-ments	Number of employees	Sales (mil dol)	Annual payroll (mil dol)	Number of establish-ments	Number of employees	Receipts (mil dol)	Annual payroll (mil dol)
	133	134	135	136	137	138	139	140	141	142	143	144	145	146
COLORADO—Cont'd														
Boulder	203.7	726	397	5 129	2 782.1	427.1	1 244	17 620	4 039.3	444.5	669	2 365	441.7	83.2
Broomfield	5.2	120	68	D	D	D	279	5 355	1 139.8	111.3	91	525	105.3	15.3
Chaffee	122.9	7 244	16	71	23.6	1.7	135	989	252.6	24.4	74	210	25.9	4.7
Cheyenne	39.3	20 097	5	46	51.2	1.9	11	67	13.0	1.1	1	D	D	D
Clear Creek	1.7	186	13	33	7.0	0.8	48	238	73.1	6.2	23	180	6.5	1.5
Conejos	359.3	42 205	5	8	3.6	0.2	20	179	33.1	3.6	2	D	D	D
Costilla	173.0	50 529	2	D	D	D	8	24	5.7	0.4	NA	NA	NA	NA
Crowley	34.3	6 343	NA	NA	NA	NA	9	84	15.7	1.8	1	D	D	D
Custer	45.3	11 741	3	D	D	D	21	145	58.7	3.0	15	38	3.0	0.6
Delta	466.0	15 562	25	231	60.9	8.4	141	1 319	312.9	29.1	42	90	14.1	2.6
Denver	236.4	424	1 174	21 245	14 920.9	1 064.5	2 271	27 979	6 835.4	752.6	1 451	11 600	2 536.4	623.7
Dolores	34.7	19 015	5	33	19.2	0.9	8	58	15.0	0.9	NA	NA	NA	NA
Douglas	43.4	174	236	D	D	D	845	15 346	3 765.5	361.9	498	1 368	239.1	45.7
Eagle	156.8	3 300	70	D	D	D	449	4 343	928.8	120.2	414	1 728	268.8	66.5
Elbert	36.6	1 607	17	51	13.8	1.5	38	251	80.7	6.4	18	22	5.5	0.5
El Paso	157.1	278	457	5 400	2 810.6	264.3	2 079	31 302	7 950.2	773.3	1 132	3 870	588.1	114.0
Fremont	160.9	3 158	21	D	D	D	143	1 531	352.4	34.1	46	217	26.5	3.8
Garfield	352.1	7 069	63	625	442.2	32.2	325	3 798	1 184.7	116.0	182	676	114.7	22.6
Gilpin	0.6	126	NA	NA	NA	NA	7	13	3.2	0.1	7	10	0.8	0.2
Grand	230.7	17 460	6	17	5.1	0.5	124	918	193.1	21.3	99	720	75.7	17.4
Gunnison	559.7	39 346	10	D	D	D	142	1 024	211.6	21.9	92	233	27.6	6.0
Hinsdale	70.4	91 961	NA	NA	NA	NA	15	33	7.8	0.8	11	D	D	D
Huerfano	36.5	4 697	1	D	D	D	32	222	55.3	4.4	12	19	3.5	0.4
Jackson	428.5	295 939	1	D	D	D	13	88	19.4	1.9	2	D	D	D
Jefferson	86.9	165	529	4 492	2 514.1	238.5	2 054	31 020	7 282.2	750.6	925	3 134	538.0	104.9
Kiowa	8.6	6 055	8	18	27.0	0.5	6	50	8.0	0.7	NA	NA	NA	NA
Kit Carson	284.8	37 261	17	184	166.3	6.1	46	348	84.4	6.5	7	19	2.4	0.7
Lake	14.7	1 896	1	D	D	D	30	235	51.4	4.6	17	71	6.8	1.4
La Plata	383.5	8 082	59	D	D	D	345	3 345	790.4	83.2	169	552	109.5	17.3
Larimer	504.4	1 855	290	3 156	1 265.2	146.8	1 306	17 510	3 922.9	402.7	562	2 181	327.1	63.6
Las Animas	67.7	4 391	14	119	51.6	3.4	62	733	164.4	16.0	23	84	10.2	1.8
Lincoln	6.4	1 141	2	D	D	D	36	336	134.7	7.3	3	6	0.3	0.0
Logan	290.4	14 017	25	D	D	D	106	1 135	281.3	24.9	22	67	7.2	1.4
Mesa	926.3	7 132	219	2 463	1 179.3	103.2	693	8 856	2 389.5	223.8	323	1 101	246.9	40.1
Mineral	21.8	23 380	1	D	D	D	11	45	6.0	0.7	3	4	0.8	0.0
Moffat	165.4	12 325	27	159	73.2	6.9	77	707	213.0	19.7	20	41	6.5	0.8
Montezuma	249.7	10 075	24	160	52.1	5.6	117	1 335	301.4	31.2	34	111	18.7	2.8
Montrose	705.8	18 831	48	D	D	D	208	2 195	610.9	58.3	67	200	33.8	6.8
Morgan	293.5	10 484	30	D	D	D	105	1 071	232.8	22.1	35	84	7.9	1.6
Otero	393.5	20 183	24	188	59.8	4.9	87	837	171.5	17.4	21	119	14.7	2.4
Ouray	103.9	24 383	3	11	1.0	0.3	46	207	27.0	4.1	9	12	3.1	0.3
Park	22.0	1 296	8	17	3.4	0.5	47	209	55.4	5.1	31	39	4.9	1.0
Phillips	104.5	22 785	11	121	150.9	4.4	23	165	45.6	3.4	4	6	0.4	0.4
Pitkin	130.9	8 776	18	85	64.7	7.1	250	1 864	399.5	57.1	204	1 213	210.3	49.3
Prowers	488.0	35 129	21	174	82.0	4.3	69	709	147.0	14.6	17	49	4.6	0.9
Pueblo	301.3	1 991	85	850	431.0	37.8	548	8 064	1 864.6	192.4	165	667	94.9	18.3
Rio Blanco	241.3	40 405	2	D	D	D	43	247	54.7	5.0	8	11	1.8	0.4
Rio Grande	729.9	59 692	29	435	218.2	13.2	62	465	110.2	10.6	15	55	5.2	0.8
Routt	203.9	9 565	40	246	187.8	12.1	223	1 982	421.5	45.9	148	1 082	165.7	30.9
Saguache	509.2	72 415	12	156	57.1	5.4	18	86	20.9	1.6	1	D	D	D
San Juan	0.3	468	1	D	D	D	14	44	6.6	0.7	1	D	D	D
San Miguel	28.4	3 933	1	D	D	D	75	572	97.8	12.8	89	362	61.5	9.4
Sedgwick	99.7	39 427	5	D	D	D	12	106	33.3	1.9	1	D	D	D
Summit	66.0	2 651	26	D	D	D	371	3 391	641.0	73.9	271	1 980	236.7	51.6
Teller	6.4	293	14	78	26.3	2.0	79	668	169.0	14.4	51	158	15.2	3.2
Washington	120.7	26 041	7	44	42.6	1.9	20	87	23.1	1.3	2	D	D	D
Weld	773.0	3 377	248	D	D	D	650	8 735	2 246.1	212.9	227	838	115.6	23.7
Yuma	397.3	40 590	26	178	193.6	6.2	68	462	106.1	7.8	8	31	5.8	0.9
CONNECTICUT	3 758.4	1 071	3 848	58 291	107 917.0	3 587.9	13 807	196 133	52 165.5	5 160.4	3 609	22 455	5 686.6	994.0
Fairfield	652.0	722	1 220	17 035	78 881.6	1 391.9	3 770	53 738	15 702.2	1 648.8	1 174	7 465	2 283.4	450.7
Hartford	145.4	166	1 014	19 472	15 631.4	1 021.7	3 423	53 241	13 820.7	1 310.7	932	6 289	1 204.5	248.3
Litchfield	99.4	523	176	D	D	D	788	9 059	2 458.2	239.8	162	680	89.9	18.1
Middlesex	224.4	1 375	171	2 189	953.9	111.5	749	8 300	2 129.2	209.8	146	915	233.2	38.1
New Haven	342.7	405	980	14 619	9 890.7	814.1	3 172	46 058	11 785.3	1 112.5	780	5 470	1 611.1	192.9
New London	2 259.1	8 473	147	D	D	D	1 123	15 660	3 883.0	390.4	232	D	D	D

1. Merchant wholesalers, except manufacturers' sales branches and offices. 2. Employer establishments.

Professional Services, Manufacturing, and Accommodation and Food Services

STATE County	Professional, scientific, and technical services,[1] 2007				Manufacturing, 2007				Accommodation and food services, 2007			
	Number of establish-ments	Number of employees	Receipts (mil dol)	Annual payroll (mil dol)	Number of establish-ments	Number of employees	Receipts (mil dol)	Annual payroll (mil dol)	Number of establish-ments	Number of employees	Sales (mil dol)	Annual payroll (mil dol)
	147	148	149	150	151	152	153	154	155	156	157	158
COLORADO—Cont'd												
Boulder	2 447	23 459	5 054.5	1 781.8	534	16 791	3 855.9	896.9	815	14 563	668.9	208.4
Broomfield	271	D	D	D	85	3 939	2 255.5	192.9	137	3 370	163.4	53.3
Chaffee	87	D	D	D	NA	NA	NA	NA	107	1 197	49.2	14.6
Cheyenne	5	5	0.4	0.1	NA	NA	NA	NA	3	10	0.4	0.1
Clear Creek	59	77	9.4	3.9	NA	NA	NA	NA	49	481	25.0	7.6
Conejos	4	5	0.3	0.1	NA	NA	NA	NA	12	49	4.5	0.9
Costilla	1	D	D	D	NA	NA	NA	NA	5	D	D	D
Crowley	1	D	D	D	NA	NA	NA	NA	3	D	D	D
Custer	16	28	1.9	0.8	NA	NA	NA	NA	19	125	5.5	1.5
Delta	80	D	D	D	48	570	141.4	19.1	80	708	26.9	7.6
Denver	3 856	D	D	D	840	19 480	5 189.9	826.0	1 778	38 701	2 279.0	656.3
Dolores	4	4	0.4	0.1	NA	NA	NA	NA	5	22	1.7	0.7
Douglas	1 360	D	D	D	130	6 965	1 950.8	442.7	467	9 878	435.1	136.6
Eagle	422	D	D	D	NA	NA	NA	NA	254	7 882	469.7	152.7
Elbert	80	198	20.3	7.8	NA	NA	NA	NA	16	177	6.9	1.8
El Paso	2 328	D	D	D	499	D	D	D	1 240	24 124	1 153.8	350.5
Fremont	63	184	13.7	4.2	51	663	168.8	29.6	97	1 120	40.8	12.0
Garfield	317	1 270	163.3	63.5	NA	NA	NA	NA	187	2 900	161.2	46.3
Gilpin	16	D	D	D	NA	NA	NA	NA	9	1 610	291.5	49.5
Grand	97	D	D	D	NA	NA	NA	NA	133	1 581	73.9	24.8
Gunnison	121	D	D	D	NA	NA	NA	NA	123	2 501	89.7	29.8
Hinsdale	5	D	D	D	NA	NA	NA	NA	18	58	3.6	0.9
Huerfano	11	26	1.8	0.6	NA	NA	NA	NA	31	221	9.7	2.8
Jackson	3	6	0.8	0.1	NA	NA	NA	NA	11	49	2.4	0.7
Jefferson	2 934	D	D	D	489	16 816	6 566.6	1 063.6	1 109	21 096	960.5	293.0
Kiowa	2	D	D	D	NA	NA	NA	NA	2	D	D	D
Kit Carson	15	41	2.4	1.0	NA	NA	NA	NA	22	194	10.3	2.2
Lake	13	D	D	D	NA	NA	NA	NA	36	412	12.6	4.3
La Plata	342	D	D	D	65	748	D	22.5	204	4 188	206.2	63.3
Larimer	1 327	7 876	867.5	387.3	420	11 764	3 226.8	664.5	807	14 244	604.4	181.9
Las Animas	28	112	15.3	5.6	NA	NA	NA	NA	43	547	22.4	6.0
Lincoln	13	66	6.3	1.8	NA	NA	NA	NA	17	194	8.4	2.4
Logan	39	175	11.5	5.9	NA	NA	NA	NA	43	553	23.3	6.3
Mesa	547	D	D	D	177	2 691	539.6	104.9	301	6 307	268.8	77.6
Mineral	4	4	0.4	0.1	NA	NA	NA	NA	18	62	9.5	2.8
Moffat	41	152	12.2	5.3	NA	NA	NA	NA	37	556	35.3	6.8
Montezuma	79	D	D	D	NA	NA	NA	NA	86	1 424	84.9	22.0
Montrose	138	D	D	D	66	1 436	218.2	38.8	85	1 363	51.1	16.9
Morgan	37	D	D	D	31	2 463	D	85.3	55	741	27.7	8.1
Otero	33	D	D	D	NA	NA	NA	NA	57	558	20.3	5.3
Ouray	36	65	8.5	3.3	NA	NA	NA	NA	56	397	21.2	6.4
Park	58	102	10.3	4.1	NA	NA	NA	NA	44	224	11.1	3.6
Phillips	6	15	1.6	0.4	NA	NA	NA	NA	9	63	1.9	0.5
Pitkin	274	D	D	D	NA	NA	NA	NA	146	4 550	270.8	91.9
Prowers	31	87	12.0	2.7	NA	NA	NA	NA	37	393	16.3	3.9
Pueblo	251	D	D	D	106	3 838	1 705.8	180.3	344	5 602	220.9	61.8
Rio Blanco	20	46	4.0	1.2	NA	NA	NA	NA	31	278	11.3	3.2
Rio Grande	20	58	5.1	2.2	NA	NA	NA	NA	40	328	14.2	3.9
Routt	186	D	D	D	NA	NA	NA	NA	130	4 813	184.4	61.6
Saguache	11	16	1.3	0.6	NA	NA	NA	NA	10	D	D	D
San Juan	4	D	D	D	NA	NA	NA	NA	22	67	5.1	1.6
San Miguel	83	214	27.7	9.1	NA	NA	NA	NA	74	1 422	77.1	22.8
Sedgwick	5	10	0.8	0.2	NA	NA	NA	NA	8	59	1.7	0.5
Summit	220	D	D	D	NA	NA	NA	NA	208	6 952	281.6	97.8
Teller	95	D	D	D	NA	NA	NA	NA	76	1 790	128.0	38.1
Washington	7	17	1.2	0.4	NA	NA	NA	NA	8	46	1.5	0.4
Weld	462	D	D	D	284	10 186	4 193.7	451.8	379	6 099	217.2	63.8
Yuma	23	D	D	D	NA	NA	NA	NA	31	284	8.8	2.3
CONNECTICUT	9 828	101 384	15 771.7	7 988.8	4 924	190 790	58 404.9	10 345.1	7 941	132 001	9 138.4	2 483.1
Fairfield	3 778	38 942	7 103.5	3 058.3	1 029	42 123	20 028.4	2 455.4	2 094	27 883	1 861.9	523.1
Hartford	2 304	29 103	5 011.1	2 180.3	1 392	63 880	15 016.2	3 584.0	1 956	32 809	1 638.0	483.8
Litchfield	457	D	D	D	405	D	509.9	D	424	4 558	245.2	70.5
Middlesex	396	D	D	D	280	10 104	3 336.0	530.4	410	5 266	293.4	89.8
New Haven	2 015	D	D	D	1 289	40 188	10 493.0	1 976.9	1 920	24 768	1 345.9	371.7
New London	555	D	D	D	201	D	D	848.8	690	30 404	3 444.7	856.8

1. Establishment subject to federal tax.

Table B. States and Counties — Health Care and Social Assistance, Other Services, and Federal Funds

STATE County	Health care and social assistance, 2007				Other services, 2007				Federal funds and grants, 2009–2010 Expenditures (mil dol)			
										Direct payments for individuals[1]		
	Number of establishments	Number of employees	Receipts (mil dol)	Annual payroll (mil dol)	Number of establishments	Number of employees	Receipts (mil dol)	Annual payroll (mil dol)	Total	Social Security and government retirement	Medicare	Food Stamps and Supplemental Security Income
	159	160	161	162	163	164	165	166	167	168	169	170
COLORADO—Cont'd												
Boulder	1 158	17 109	1 712.5	716.4	711	4 509	794.5	161.0	3 118.2	722.8	256.8	37.7
Broomfield	110	1 007	89.0	35.0	92	760	127.7	45.5	63.5	7.9	0.0	3.5
Chaffee	60	661	58.9	22.2	43	153	10.4	3.2	123.5	66.4	21.3	3.5
Cheyenne	1	D	D	D	6	11	0.8	0.2	46.2	7.0	6.3	0.2
Clear Creek	15	D	D	D	15	33	3.5	1.0	38.3	23.1	6.6	1.1
Conejos	10	D	D	D	4	D	D	D	86.7	21.4	12.9	5.6
Costilla	7	27	0.9	0.4	2	D	D	D	53.0	14.9	6.7	3.6
Crowley	4	80	3.2	1.5	1	D	D	D	33.7	12.5	6.3	3.0
Custer	3	D	D	D	6	D	D	D	31.1	21.7	3.3	0.7
Delta	82	1 316	91.7	38.5	56	204	20.6	5.1	250.6	118.0	52.3	8.5
Denver	1 981	45 826	5 232.8	2 172.8	1 627	12 532	1 821.5	381.8	8 557.6	1 446.4	1 016.3	279.4
Dolores	5	D	D	D	NA	NA	NA	NA	16.1	7.1	2.4	0.3
Douglas	598	7 186	765.6	283.9	468	2 646	224.2	66.6	575.5	353.9	30.9	4.3
Eagle	144	D	D	D	174	1 998	140.3	36.4	117.6	51.4	8.8	1.1
Elbert	19	138	8.9	3.3	34	83	7.9	2.3	84.7	57.6	10.6	2.3
El Paso	1 733	27 411	2 913.8	1 102.7	1 078	8 039	1 315.5	256.3	11 076.8	2 061.6	467.8	136.8
Fremont	104	2 028	126.5	52.7	48	169	12.8	3.6	392.3	175.2	62.0	13.6
Garfield	143	2 266	286.8	106.0	147	719	64.6	20.0	208.0	99.0	36.0	6.1
Gilpin	5	D	D	D	7	D	D	D	17.2	12.7	1.6	0.3
Grand	32	230	19.0	8.1	42	99	15.3	3.1	55.7	28.9	11.2	0.6
Gunnison	54	513	37.8	14.4	63	183	25.9	4.2	102.4	23.3	6.8	1.5
Hinsdale	1	D	D	D	5	D	D	D	5.0	2.8	0.6	0.1
Huerfano	17	417	18.1	8.9	9	28	3.2	0.5	89.5	31.9	22.4	3.7
Jackson	3	D	D	D	2	D	D	D	11.6	4.7	1.6	0.2
Jefferson	1 441	21 470	1 946.8	821.0	1 124	5 971	579.9	150.6	5 795.9	1 269.9	475.3	59.3
Kiowa	2	D	D	D	3	D	D	D	25.8	9.0	4.3	0.2
Kit Carson	22	328	18.8	8.3	15	46	4.9	0.9	85.4	32.3	13.9	1.3
Lake	13	D	D	D	12	31	2.1	0.5	30.8	12.4	7.0	0.9
La Plata	223	2 766	275.7	106.7	126	582	47.7	15.2	282.2	123.0	45.0	6.3
Larimer	908	15 177	1 400.5	610.6	612	3 126	286.6	77.2	1 879.7	719.3	236.7	38.7
Las Animas	41	543	43.0	15.1	43	580	34.6	11.5	169.0	58.4	30.4	8.7
Lincoln	6	212	15.7	7.9	14	D	D	D	48.2	15.9	11.1	1.0
Logan	72	1 203	81.0	32.7	55	261	26.9	7.3	154.8	56.9	32.9	5.4
Mesa	425	8 480	847.4	336.2	317	1 599	160.1	42.3	1 064.5	462.6	163.9	33.6
Mineral	2	D	D	D	4	D	D	D	4.6	3.0	0.5	0.0
Moffat	43	485	44.5	15.3	29	217	17.2	4.7	83.3	31.5	16.5	2.9
Montezuma	94	1 118	83.6	31.4	55	183	15.4	3.5	235.2	83.8	31.3	7.6
Montrose	157	2 065	164.6	68.3	85	397	33.0	9.2	287.2	143.6	48.0	7.5
Morgan	69	1 093	94.8	36.5	45	146	12.1	3.3	218.2	64.7	39.7	7.9
Otero	62	1 398	79.2	35.4	37	108	8.9	1.9	240.0	75.8	44.1	14.0
Ouray	18	60	4.6	1.7	9	16	2.0	0.3	18.6	12.7	3.1	0.3
Park	16	64	3.5	1.2	29	D	D	D	60.7	44.9	5.4	1.6
Phillips	9	261	15.8	7.3	13	43	5.2	1.1	48.5	14.5	11.9	0.6
Pitkin	80	709	110.5	37.2	105	777	101.4	24.2	42.5	23.5	5.8	0.3
Prowers	32	637	46.1	18.0	24	100	8.1	1.9	107.6	33.3	20.6	6.2
Pueblo	410	11 085	872.7	388.5	237	1 160	92.3	25.4	1 440.6	554.1	256.1	92.2
Rio Blanco	11	258	22.3	9.2	12	50	3.8	0.9	37.2	15.0	8.6	0.7
Rio Grande	34	417	24.3	9.5	31	93	11.1	2.4	108.7	38.3	14.8	9.9
Routt	100	1 147	124.5	50.9	76	362	30.4	8.3	77.9	37.6	10.8	1.4
Saguache	7	49	2.7	1.2	9	D	D	D	50.7	15.2	6.3	4.6
San Juan	2	D	D	D	2	D	D	D	3.5	1.7	0.4	0.1
San Miguel	26	128	8.7	3.4	38	245	37.5	5.7	43.9	9.2	1.9	0.4
Sedgwick	4	D	D	D	4	D	D	D	32.8	9.8	8.5	0.9
Summit	84	942	87.7	34.3	112	478	47.6	12.2	62.0	40.9	4.0	0.4
Teller	63	313	20.6	8.0	49	183	12.7	3.0	117.8	89.1	10.5	3.6
Washington	7	31	1.5	0.5	9	D	D	D	50.4	16.8	9.2	0.7
Weld	429	8 538	763.1	292.3	340	1 513	161.2	40.0	1 076.8	454.9	177.6	43.9
Yuma	27	574	43.7	17.8	24	53	5.5	1.0	134.2	70.9	15.4	1.6
CONNECTICUT	10 049	253 360	24 813.2	10 440.0	7 392	47 992	5 061.3	1 395.4	55 978.3	9 783.0	20 601.7	935.0
Fairfield	2 739	60 497	6 923.5	2 604.2	2 056	13 357	1 722.7	431.1	13 539.9	2 248.1	4 982.5	184.7
Hartford	2 686	72 837	7 022.9	3 107.3	1 989	15 781	1 599.2	458.6	16 782.1	2 484.7	6 135.1	317.9
Litchfield	503	9 629	820.4	349.7	391	1 900	158.3	57.7	1 636.2	585.1	776.3	20.7
Middlesex	476	12 803	1 175.5	543.0	325	1 527	158.7	43.3	1 618.6	490.4	733.6	20.3
New Haven	2 371	68 663	6 467.8	2 792.6	1 772	10 629	948.2	288.9	11 538.3	2 403.0	5 657.1	291.9
New London	703	16 048	1 467.8	617.5	479	2 549	234.3	59.3	6 569.1	887.6	1 336.7	55.3

1. State totals may include programs not allocated by county.

Table B. States and Counties — Federal Funds, Residential Construction, and Local Government Finances

STATE County	Salaries and wages	Defense	Other	Medicaid and other health-related	Nutrition and family welfare	Education	Other	New construction ($1,000)	Number of housing units	Total (mil dol)	Inter-govern-mental (mil dol)	Total (mil dol)	Total	Property
	171	172	173	174	175	176	177	178	179	180	181	182	183	184
COLORADO—Cont'd														
Boulder	317.0	183.9	532.6	216.3	30.3	21.4	757.2	126 879	657	1 187.5	282.9	670.7	2 311	1 403
Broomfield	1.1	25.6	7.1	0.3	0.0	0.6	15.0	55 983	232	185.2	11.5	96.0	1 787	626
Chaffee	6.3	0.1	3.1	15.3	2.9	0.6	3.2	25 219	101	74.1	17.4	21.9	1 304	843
Cheyenne	19.6	0.0	0.2	2.6	0.4	0.1	1.0	80	1	15.0	4.9	5.2	2 969	2 454
Clear Creek	2.7	0.0	0.8	2.1	0.9	0.7	0.0	4 033	13	47.0	12.3	20.9	2 331	1 956
Conejos	3.1	0.0	1.1	37.2	2.8	0.7	0.2	2 088	17	33.3	20.8	5.5	687	498
Costilla	1.0	0.0	0.2	22.1	1.9	0.3	0.8	5 431	24	19.4	12.2	4.9	1 488	1 392
Crowley	1.3	0.0	0.3	7.3	1.3	0.2	0.1	422	4	10.4	6.6	2.8	415	309
Custer	1.3	0.0	0.3	2.6	0.6	0.2	0.1	12 964	67	12.9	4.2	6.1	1 514	1 248
Delta	13.8	0.0	3.0	34.0	5.9	2.1	7.3	1 767	10	142.5	44.4	33.0	1 087	669
Denver	1 009.2	169.1	654.0	1 122.9	402.5	449.0	1 601.8	183 136	1 232	4 170.1	842.5	1 713.4	2 912	1 079
Dolores	0.9	0.0	0.2	2.5	0.5	0.2	0.3	0	0	6.5	3.5	2.3	1 181	979
Douglas	19.1	67.2	53.1	4.9	9.9	3.3	7.4	221 472	915	1 076.3	237.9	561.6	2 064	1 496
Eagle	15.6	7.9	8.1	3.9	3.7	2.1	14.0	48 570	61	378.4	42.2	205.6	4 002	2 534
Elbert	3.9	0.1	0.7	3.7	1.5	0.7	0.1	8 136	33	78.2	28.4	24.9	1 094	976
El Paso	4 744.1	2 888.3	107.2	233.5	67.7	61.3	67.5	513 434	1 718	2 391.6	721.9	756.8	1 289	707
Fremont	74.4	0.0	9.6	42.6	8.5	2.3	2.2	11 713	53	107.9	48.2	39.7	837	554
Garfield	22.2	0.7	8.9	12.8	4.1	2.7	10.2	6 911	37	310.3	76.5	163.2	3 044	2 152
Gilpin	0.9	0.0	0.2	0.6	0.5	0.2	0.1	1 120	4	71.5	15.5	45.5	8 946	4 271
Grand	7.0	0.0	4.0	1.6	1.3	0.9	-0.1	36 680	159	117.2	12.7	54.9	4 035	2 635
Gunnison	8.8	0.4	49.8	3.3	1.5	0.7	3.3	18 792	73	95.4	15.8	40.1	2 680	1 662
Hinsdale	0.1	0.0	0.7	0.5	0.1	0.1	0.1	4 521	11	5.2	1.9	2.4	2 822	1 911
Huerfano	1.3	0.0	1.0	23.0	2.5	0.6	2.2	4 088	30	66.5	24.1	18.4	2 351	1 806
Jackson	2.2	0.0	1.8	0.5	0.2	0.2	0.2	1 081	7	8.1	4.0	2.3	1 690	1 242
Jefferson	757.3	400.4	2 422.3	138.2	48.2	39.2	128.8	143 373	577	1 765.0	511.7	886.8	1 675	1 268
Kiowa	1.4	0.0	0.2	1.6	0.3	0.2	0.0	535	6	14.3	5.1	4.0	2 996	2 595
Kit Carson	3.0	0.4	0.6	7.8	1.5	0.6	0.6	200	2	41.1	15.2	11.2	1 412	1 202
Lake	3.6	0.0	1.1	2.8	1.7	0.5	0.5	3 093	19	102.2	20.9	47.2	5 960	5 555
La Plata	26.6	0.4	16.6	27.2	9.0	4.7	12.9	27 417	222	188.4	41.6	117.0	2 361	1 673
Larimer	212.8	26.2	223.3	157.5	30.1	13.6	166.3	182 921	1 153	1 133.2	287.5	531.6	1 848	1 167
Las Animas	4.7	0.8	0.9	49.4	4.8	3.2	1.5	2 372	20	87.0	35.8	39.7	2 483	1 605
Lincoln	2.0	0.0	0.4	6.6	1.6	0.3	0.1	129	1	39.3	19.5	8.1	1 513	986
Logan	6.7	0.2	4.3	19.4	4.3	1.6	8.1	2 569	15	75.9	31.1	29.9	1 421	847
Mesa	89.3	38.4	99.1	98.5	13.1	8.5	20.1	83 016	408	480.7	186.9	192.8	1 387	752
Mineral	0.3	0.0	0.2	0.0	0.1	0.1	0.4	54	5	6.3	2.9	2.1	2 205	1 599
Moffat	8.9	0.0	12.3	6.0	2.1	0.9	0.4	1 756	7	71.8	19.0	28.6	2 092	1 617
Montezuma	18.9	0.0	31.7	24.6	5.0	4.1	9.8	2 121	14	108.1	41.5	31.9	1 265	787
Montrose	23.5	0.3	15.5	29.5	5.4	2.4	6.2	10 562	62	186.6	53.0	54.4	1 377	722
Morgan	9.9	0.0	42.2	24.8	7.0	2.4	5.2	3 047	22	99.3	34.9	39.5	1 412	1 186
Otero	8.3	0.2	1.5	53.9	12.7	3.6	17.4	832	3	78.6	43.2	23.2	1 229	525
Ouray	1.1	0.0	0.3	0.6	0.4	0.2	0.0	8 373	20	25.3	5.4	13.6	3 102	2 435
Park	3.8	0.1	1.0	1.1	1.6	0.5	0.2	16 329	95	49.3	20.1	22.8	1 339	1 233
Phillips	1.3	0.0	0.4	4.7	0.9	0.4	3.0	402	3	32.2	10.7	7.0	1 558	1 175
Pitkin	6.6	0.1	1.7	1.1	0.8	0.2	2.0	70 907	44	274.9	24.5	125.5	8 306	3 549
Prowers	3.1	0.0	0.6	20.9	3.7	2.0	1.6	150	2	87.7	30.5	17.1	1 296	854
Pueblo	85.8	42.0	20.4	258.3	33.6	16.6	39.7	39 615	234	490.8	226.0	183.4	1 187	747
Rio Blanco	4.7	0.0	1.6	2.7	0.7	0.7	0.6	10 984	22	55.3	16.8	24.2	3 883	2 552
Rio Grande	6.7	0.0	2.0	23.7	4.1	1.2	2.3	4 259	21	46.3	22.5	15.0	1 291	951
Routt	6.9	0.0	8.1	4.2	1.8	1.0	5.2	21 771	27	151.5	30.3	78.8	3 519	1 880
Saguache	3.0	0.0	0.9	12.1	3.5	0.7	0.3	3 671	35	21.6	11.6	7.3	1 055	1 017
San Juan	0.4	0.0	0.4	0.0	0.1	0.1	0.3	200	1	4.4	1.5	2.2	3 900	2 628
San Miguel	3.4	0.0	1.1	2.1	0.7	0.8	24.0	45 422	47	98.0	12.4	53.6	7 114	4 544
Sedgwick	1.5	0.0	0.3	4.7	0.5	0.3	0.1	0	0	18.9	4.8	3.7	1 568	1 286
Summit	3.7	0.6	5.0	2.7	1.8	0.6	1.0	56 395	117	188.1	14.0	106.3	4 004	2 863
Teller	3.8	0.6	2.1	2.3	2.8	0.8	0.7	11 661	42	84.0	33.1	33.3	1 528	1 076
Washington	3.6	0.0	1.2	5.2	1.4	0.4	0.0	914	5	29.2	13.1	7.9	1 713	1 601
Weld	57.0	27.5	23.5	135.0	20.5	17.0	66.4	166 578	863	851.6	256.5	359.0	1 473	1 074
Yuma	4.1	0.0	0.8	8.4	2.2	0.9	2.3	0	0	80.5	19.4	19.4	2 007	1 652
CONNECTICUT	1 902.7	11 113.6	843.0	4 768.8	847.6	497.3	2 185.2	861 356	3 932	X	X	X	X	X
Fairfield	303.9	4 045.9	346.9	869.6	127.7	52.2	278.3	325 061	926	4 018.8	884.0	2 701.7	3 019	2 940
Hartford	632.7	3 292.2	226.2	1 367.9	311.9	291.7	1 502.9	128 378	810	3 596.0	1 271.1	2 007.4	2 289	2 247
Litchfield	39.7	37.2	9.4	113.3	22.9	13.3	8.2	47 723	164	671.9	175.9	440.0	2 337	2 298
Middlesex	38.5	117.2	12.4	140.5	19.0	8.5	21.2	50 594	279	579.7	163.5	372.1	2 267	2 246
New Haven	480.1	79.2	179.4	1 810.1	129.2	70.3	256.3	186 210	1 019	3 404.4	1 294.9	1 764.1	2 086	2 046
New London	342.9	3 520.5	55.9	234.1	35.3	19.9	33.0	64 859	344	1 033.0	375.8	540.4	2 021	1 959

1. State totals may include programs not allocated by county.　　2. Based on the resident population estimated as of July 1 of the year shown.

Table B. States and Counties — Local Government Finances, Government Employment, and Voting

STATE County	Local government finances, 2007 (cont.) Direct general expenditure Total (mil dol)	Per capita[1] (dollars)	Education	Health and hospitals	Police protection	Public welfare	Highways	Debt outstanding Total (mil dol)	Per capita[1] (dollars)	Government employment, 2009 Federal civilian	Federal military	State and local	Presidential election,[2] 2008 Percent of vote cast: Democratic	Republican	All other
	185	186	187	188	189	190	191	192	193	194	195	196	197	198	199
COLORADO—Cont'd															
Boulder	1 157.4	3 987	40.7	0.9	7.7	2.8	6.3	2 072.2	7 139	2 298	890	27 370	72.3	26.1	1.6
Broomfield	237.8	4 429	0.0	1.7	5.2	3.9	4.5	1 531.1	28 518	151	144	1 090	54.9	43.3	1.8
Chaffee	72.5	4 318	28.6	34.2	3.9	2.1	5.5	97.0	5 779	96	44	1 616	49.0	49.1	1.9
Cheyenne	13.3	7 520	37.7	0.8	2.4	17.9	11.2	9.7	5 503	16	11	315	17.8	80.1	2.1
Clear Creek	41.3	4 617	27.2	5.5	6.6	7.1	7.9	31.8	3 550	48	22	639	57.8	39.9	2.3
Conejos	28.5	3 524	56.2	5.2	2.8	2.7	9.1	4.4	542	60	20	556	55.6	42.7	1.7
Costilla	18.1	5 467	37.6	5.9	2.8	4.6	17.7	4.9	1 495	14	0	320	73.4	24.5	2.2
Crowley	11.1	1 667	47.7	0.5	4.3	9.9	8.3	3.2	485	15	16	506	35.4	62.6	1.9
Custer	12.1	3 000	37.3	13.1	6.5	2.4	10.2	5.6	1 391	16	10	236	34.7	63.6	1.7
Delta	138.7	4 574	31.8	31.2	3.4	4.0	6.0	88.1	2 905	187	80	2 271	32.9	65.2	1.8
Denver	3 934.0	6 687	19.1	18.2	4.2	2.8	1.5	9 470.6	16 097	14 153	2 955	59 427	75.5	23.0	1.5
Dolores	9.0	4 689	37.3	2.1	9.3	1.5	27.7	4.6	2 421	12	0	181	30.3	67.2	2.5
Douglas	1 103.2	4 054	44.0	0.5	5.1	1.0	10.3	2 170.4	7 976	438	740	10 977	40.8	58.0	1.2
Eagle	353.5	6 882	18.2	2.8	5.3	0.8	8.0	889.1	17 311	141	138	2 941	60.9	37.8	1.3
Elbert	63.8	2 806	57.0	0.8	3.9	5.0	8.5	200.8	8 839	36	60	1 011	28.9	69.0	2.1
El Paso	2 427.4	4 133	43.5	16.9	5.3	1.7	4.3	3 848.7	6 554	11 944	35 297	35 089	39.9	58.7	1.4
Fremont	103.4	2 183	50.2	0.4	8.4	6.2	5.0	100.2	2 114	1 113	123	4 107	34.4	63.6	2.0
Garfield	336.0	6 265	46.7	7.8	3.9	3.9	5.1	586.6	10 937	330	144	4 612	49.2	49.2	1.6
Gilpin	57.9	11 364	7.4	0.6	8.6	2.0	7.9	99.5	19 553	10	14	396	59.2	38.0	2.8
Grand	109.5	8 044	21.4	11.1	4.4	0.8	8.9	182.9	13 435	156	36	1 131	48.6	49.7	1.7
Gunnison	85.9	5 735	16.8	23.7	5.5	3.3	13.8	76.9	5 136	177	39	1 748	62.6	35.3	2.1
Hinsdale	5.2	6 208	23.6	14.6	7.8	1.1	12.2	1.0	1 223	0	0	84	40.1	57.4	2.5
Huerfano	59.9	7 643	18.9	34.3	8.5	2.4	11.0	16.8	2 146	19	19	486	54.6	43.4	2.0
Jackson	7.9	5 748	38.5	3.2	5.2	1.8	20.7	5.7	4 129	45	0	134	30.3	68.3	1.3
Jefferson	1 778.7	3 360	47.7	1.1	8.2	1.9	4.7	1 876.5	3 545	8 566	1 383	27 140	53.6	44.6	1.8
Kiowa	14.2	10 633	24.6	36.5	3.2	3.7	11.7	0.4	274	28	0	250	20.9	76.3	2.8
Kit Carson	44.1	5 560	32.8	23.5	2.7	3.1	17.2	7.6	956	46	22	797	26.5	71.3	2.2
Lake	100.3	12 671	69.7	15.2	1.2	1.2	1.8	37.4	4 731	67	21	755	61.9	35.9	2.2
La Plata	158.1	3 190	42.3	0.2	9.7	3.1	10.1	235.7	4 756	407	132	5 476	57.4	41.1	1.5
Larimer	1 068.3	3 715	36.2	4.8	7.0	2.5	11.5	1 529.2	5 317	2 514	789	24 724	54.0	44.3	1.7
Las Animas	105.5	6 592	25.2	2.1	6.1	1.3	20.1	25.8	1 580	65	41	1 999	52.7	45.6	1.7
Lincoln	38.3	7 188	44.6	18.6	2.1	6.1	10.7	10.7	2 015	30	13	967	23.7	74.5	1.8
Logan	89.8	4 266	50.8	0.5	4.2	3.4	6.8	57.6	2 737	75	53	2 497	31.7	66.9	1.4
Mesa	515.5	3 707	37.6	1.5	9.2	4.5	14.9	409.8	2 946	1 383	376	8 192	34.5	64.0	1.5
Mineral	6.6	6 842	30.9	27.6	5.0	0.6	10.2	0.0	0	0	0	86	43.3	53.6	3.0
Moffat	70.4	5 161	28.7	26.3	5.4	5.6	9.2	37.3	2 736	178	36	1 086	26.9	70.4	2.6
Montezuma	102.8	4 076	40.5	3.5	6.6	6.9	5.4	44.2	1 751	358	65	2 649	39.4	58.9	1.7
Montrose	184.1	4 658	32.4	29.6	4.5	2.4	4.2	137.0	3 467	319	106	2 808	33.9	63.7	2.4
Morgan	97.7	3 494	48.5	1.5	4.8	4.4	10.4	91.8	3 284	147	71	2 270	37.3	61.3	1.5
Otero	72.4	3 841	50.7	1.7	5.3	13.8	3.5	22.7	1 206	110	48	1 770	44.0	54.5	1.6
Ouray	22.1	5 045	34.8	2.8	4.1	3.4	8.6	31.1	7 100	12	12	365	53.5	44.7	1.9
Park	45.6	2 684	37.7	4.3	6.1	5.7	8.3	27.7	1 627	64	43	823	45.3	52.2	2.5
Phillips	35.0	7 788	36.0	40.8	2.6	1.8	4.4	10.6	2 355	23	11	591	27.5	71.3	1.2
Pitkin	274.4	18 164	17.6	27.8	2.9	1.0	2.4	338.2	22 389	93	41	1 913	73.7	24.9	1.3
Prowers	79.0	5 996	33.2	34.3	4.8	5.0	4.1	362.0	27 467	44	33	1 453	32.2	65.9	1.8
Pueblo	498.3	3 224	43.3	0.9	6.1	4.6	4.6	446.2	2 887	1 042	420	11 624	56.7	41.8	1.5
Rio Blanco	48.7	7 828	25.4	16.2	5.4	1.6	19.1	13.1	2 101	84	17	1 042	20.8	77.4	1.7
Rio Grande	39.7	3 412	51.1	5.2	6.4	0.7	11.5	12.5	1 078	119	30	855	45.0	53.8	1.2
Routt	135.7	6 064	29.1	1.3	4.2	2.3	15.5	174.5	7 796	136	60	1 692	62.7	35.8	1.5
Saguache	21.4	3 088	56.6	3.0	3.4	0.0	16.6	11.3	1 630	48	18	527	63.0	34.7	2.3
San Juan	4.4	7 830	26.5	4.0	10.9	2.4	12.4	1.4	2 460	0	0	65	53.2	44.0	2.8
San Miguel	82.9	11 010	16.2	5.0	5.6	0.8	14.8	142.0	18 854	54	19	764	77.0	21.4	1.6
Sedgwick	21.4	9 162	22.5	52.1	2.5	0.6	4.1	9.8	4 208	24	0	315	34.6	63.4	1.9
Summit	198.3	7 469	27.9	3.0	4.5	1.5	5.5	156.9	5 909	66	70	2 236	65.8	32.8	1.4
Teller	80.8	3 705	38.0	4.8	8.0	4.2	6.3	46.2	2 116	65	56	1 210	35.0	63.1	1.9
Washington	28.8	6 223	41.1	0.3	4.6	4.2	18.9	11.6	2 498	58	11	455	21.1	77.6	1.4
Weld	813.1	3 336	41.4	2.0	5.9	2.3	7.6	908.7	3 728	614	655	14 373	44.7	53.4	1.9
Yuma	84.4	8 737	26.9	42.3	2.8	3.6	7.7	69.0	7 141	55	25	972	24.9	73.3	1.8
CONNECTICUT	X	X	X	X	X	X	X	X	X	19 335	14 456	234 895	60.7	38.1	1.1
Fairfield	3 883.2	4 339	56.0	0.9	5.8	0.7	2.3	3 327.6	3 718	3 329	1 721	44 684	58.6	40.6	0.7
Hartford	3 604.9	4 111	56.9	0.7	5.5	0.9	3.2	1 922.2	2 192	5 980	1 698	67 419	65.2	33.7	1.1
Litchfield	726.3	3 858	67.3	0.8	3.7	0.3	5.0	344.2	1 828	546	356	8 159	51.6	46.7	1.7
Middlesex	625.8	3 813	65.0	0.7	3.6	0.2	5.3	287.5	1 751	378	314	10 719	60.8	37.8	1.5
New Haven	3 336.5	3 946	57.5	0.9	4.8	0.5	3.5	2 951.8	3 491	5 764	1 796	45 551	61.0	37.8	1.2
New London	1 092.9	4 087	63.7	0.4	4.8	0.6	5.1	682.5	2 553	2 734	8 052	35 861	59.9	38.8	1.3

1. Based on the resident population estimated as of July 1 of the year shown.   2. © 2009 Election Data Services, Inc. All rights reserved.

Table B. States and Counties — **Land Area and Population**

STATE/ County code	CBSA code[1]	County type[2]	STATE County	Land area,[3] (sq km) 2010	Total persons	Rank	Per square kilometer	White	Black	American Indian, Alaska Native	Asian and Pacific Islander	Percent Hispanic or Latino[4]	Under 5 years	5 to 17 years	18 to 24 years	25 to 34 years	35 to 44 years	45 to 54 years
				1	2	3	4	5	6	7	8	9	10	11	12	13	14	15
			CONNECTICUT—Cont'd															
09 013	25540	1	Tolland	1 062	152 691	409	143.8	88.9	3.7	0.6	4.0	4.3	4.6	15.6	16.1	10.2	12.9	16.5
09 015	48740	4	Windham	1 328	118 428	506	89.2	87.0	2.4	1.1	1.6	9.6	5.5	16.8	10.6	11.7	13.7	16.4
10 000	...	X	DELAWARE	5 047	897 934	X	177.9	67.0	22.1	0.9	3.8	8.2	6.2	16.7	10.1	12.4	12.9	14.9
10 001	20100	3	Kent	1 518	162 310	378	106.9	67.6	25.2	1.4	2.8	5.8	6.9	18.0	11.0	12.3	12.7	14.3
10 003	37980	1	New Castle	1 104	538 479	115	487.8	63.1	24.3	0.6	4.9	8.7	6.2	17.1	10.9	13.1	13.6	15.2
10 005	42580	4	Sussex	2 424	197 145	317	81.3	77.1	13.6	1.0	1.3	8.6	5.8	14.6	7.3	10.5	11.3	14.4
11 000	...	X	DISTRICT OF COLUMBIA	158	601 723	X	3 808.4	36.3	51.3	0.8	4.5	9.1	5.4	11.3	14.5	20.7	13.4	12.6
11 001	47900	1	District of Columbia	158	601 723	105	3 808.4	36.3	51.3	0.8	4.5	9.1	5.4	11.3	14.5	20.7	13.4	12.6
12 000	...	X	FLORIDA	138 887	18 801 310	X	135.4	59.1	15.9	0.6	3.1	22.5	5.7	15.6	9.3	12.2	12.9	14.6
12 001	23540	3	Alachua	2 266	247 336	263	109.2	65.5	21.0	0.7	6.3	8.4	5.3	12.6	23.2	15.0	10.3	11.9
12 003	27260	1	Baker	1 516	27 115	1 529	17.9	83.7	14.0	1.0	0.7	1.9	7.1	18.9	9.2	13.6	14.0	14.8
12 005	37460	3	Bay	1 964	168 852	365	86.0	81.6	11.6	1.5	3.1	4.8	6.3	15.7	9.5	13.1	12.8	15.7
12 007	...	6	Bradford	761	28 520	1 477	37.5	75.1	20.9	0.8	0.9	3.6	5.9	13.9	8.9	15.2	13.4	15.9
12 009	37340	2	Brevard	2 631	543 376	113	206.5	79.3	10.6	0.8	2.9	8.1	4.9	14.9	7.9	10.1	11.4	16.7
12 011	33100	1	Broward	3 133	1 748 066	18	558.0	44.6	26.8	0.4	4.1	25.1	5.9	16.5	8.4	12.8	14.4	15.8
12 013	...	6	Calhoun	1 469	14 625	2 139	10.0	79.6	14.2	2.3	0.7	5.2	6.2	15.2	8.5	13.6	13.9	15.0
12 015	39460	3	Charlotte	1 762	159 978	387	90.8	87.2	6.0	0.6	1.6	5.8	3.5	10.8	5.4	7.0	8.8	13.3
12 017	26140	4	Citrus	1 507	141 236	436	93.7	90.7	3.2	0.8	1.7	4.7	3.9	11.9	5.7	7.0	9.3	13.7
12 019	27260	1	Clay	1 565	190 865	326	122.0	79.1	10.4	1.0	4.0	7.7	6.2	20.1	8.5	11.4	14.3	15.8
12 021	34940	2	Collier	5 176	321 520	197	62.1	66.3	6.6	0.4	1.5	25.9	5.2	14.2	6.9	10.1	11.1	12.7
12 023	29380	6	Columbia	2 066	67 531	778	32.7	76.2	18.0	1.1	1.2	4.9	6.3	16.2	9.8	12.1	12.0	15.1
12 027	11580	6	DeSoto	1 650	34 862	1 306	21.1	56.8	12.8	0.5	0.7	29.9	6.5	15.9	10.6	13.2	12.0	12.5
12 029	...	6	Dixie	1 826	16 422	2 024	9.0	87.8	8.6	1.2	0.4	3.1	5.3	13.9	7.4	11.3	11.7	15.7
12 031	27260	1	Duval	1 974	864 263	58	437.8	58.4	30.0	0.9	5.2	7.6	6.9	16.7	10.5	14.9	13.5	14.9
12 033	37860	2	Escambia	1 700	297 619	214	175.1	68.5	23.8	1.7	3.9	4.7	6.3	15.2	13.0	12.8	11.4	14.5
12 035	37380	4	Flagler	1 257	95 696	605	76.1	77.5	11.8	0.7	2.7	8.6	5.0	14.9	6.3	9.4	11.2	13.2
12 037	...	6	Franklin	1 385	11 549	2 329	8.3	81.0	14.4	1.1	0.4	4.6	5.1	11.9	7.7	15.6	12.9	14.9
12 039	45220	2	Gadsden	1 337	46 389	1 036	34.7	33.7	56.3	0.6	0.6	9.5	6.9	17.2	8.5	12.5	12.6	15.0
12 041	23540	3	Gilchrist	906	16 939	1 986	18.7	90.7	5.5	1.1	0.5	5.0	5.4	16.1	12.9	9.5	11.5	14.4
12 043	...	6	Glades	2 088	12 884	2 251	6.2	62.3	12.3	4.6	0.4	21.1	5.6	13.2	7.9	13.0	12.9	13.0
12 045	...	6	Gulf	1 461	15 863	2 060	10.9	76.4	19.2	1.3	0.5	4.3	4.1	12.1	7.6	14.9	14.9	16.2
12 047	...	6	Hamilton	1 331	14 799	2 126	11.1	55.9	34.7	1.0	0.7	8.8	5.2	14.4	13.2	13.3	12.9	14.7
12 049	48100	6	Hardee	1 652	27 731	1 506	16.8	48.8	7.2	0.7	1.3	42.9	8.0	19.6	11.3	13.6	12.5	12.1
12 051	17500	4	Hendry	2 986	39 140	1 192	13.1	35.4	13.3	1.7	0.9	49.2	8.0	19.8	10.9	14.2	13.5	12.8
12 053	45300	1	Hernando	1 224	172 778	356	141.2	83.3	5.4	0.7	1.5	10.3	4.9	14.8	6.6	8.9	11.1	13.7
12 055	42700	4	Highlands	2 633	98 786	588	37.5	71.7	9.5	0.8	1.8	17.4	5.0	13.1	6.6	8.7	9.0	11.9
12 057	45300	1	Hillsborough	2 642	1 229 226	30	465.3	55.2	16.5	0.6	4.2	24.9	6.5	17.4	10.5	14.1	14.2	14.5
12 059	...	6	Holmes	1 240	19 927	1 843	16.1	90.7	6.1	2.0	0.8	2.2	5.7	15.8	8.8	11.8	13.0	14.5
12 061	42680	3	Indian River	1 302	138 028	446	106.0	78.4	9.3	0.6	1.6	11.2	4.7	14.1	6.6	9.0	10.3	13.7
12 063	...	6	Jackson	2 377	49 746	982	20.9	67.9	27.3	1.3	0.7	4.3	5.2	14.7	9.2	12.8	14.2	15.2
12 065	45220	2	Jefferson	1 549	14 761	2 129	9.5	59.7	36.3	0.7	0.6	3.7	5.3	13.4	7.6	12.0	13.0	16.4
12 067	...	8	Lafayette	1 407	8 870	2 537	6.3	71.6	16.1	0.8	0.3	12.1	5.5	14.6	12.0	16.1	15.4	13.8
12 069	36740	1	Lake	2 430	297 052	216	122.2	75.7	10.1	0.8	2.3	12.1	5.5	15.3	6.7	9.7	11.9	13.4
12 071	15980	2	Lee	2 032	618 754	101	304.5	72.0	8.3	0.5	1.8	18.3	5.3	14.2	7.7	10.6	11.4	13.2
12 073	45220	2	Leon	1 727	275 487	233	159.5	60.9	30.9	0.8	3.6	5.6	5.6	14.0	22.5	14.5	11.0	12.2
12 075	...	8	Levy	2 896	40 801	1 159	14.1	82.2	9.8	1.1	0.8	7.5	5.6	15.5	7.5	10.0	11.3	15.2
12 077	...	8	Liberty	2 164	8 365	2 582	3.9	74.9	18.3	1.4	0.4	6.2	5.5	15.7	8.8	16.6	15.7	16.4
12 079	...	6	Madison	1 802	19 224	1 867	10.7	55.9	39.2	0.9	0.3	4.7	6.3	15.5	9.5	12.4	12.2	14.5
12 081	35840	2	Manatee	1 924	322 833	196	167.8	74.5	9.1	0.5	2.1	14.9	5.7	14.9	7.1	10.1	11.4	13.6
12 083	36100	2	Marion	4 104	331 298	193	80.7	75.2	12.6	0.8	1.7	10.9	5.2	14.2	7.2	9.6	10.8	13.4
12 085	38940	2	Martin	1 408	146 318	427	103.9	81.2	5.5	0.5	1.4	12.2	4.2	13.4	6.4	8.5	10.5	15.2
12 086	33100	1	Miami-Dade	4 915	2 496 435	8	507.9	15.8	17.5	0.2	1.9	65.0	6.0	15.9	9.9	13.6	14.9	14.7
12 087	28580	4	Monroe	2 547	73 090	739	28.7	72.4	5.7	0.8	1.6	20.6	4.4	10.7	6.8	12.2	13.5	17.6
12 089	27260	1	Nassau	1 680	73 314	737	43.6	89.0	6.7	0.8	1.4	3.2	5.4	16.3	7.8	10.4	12.9	15.8
12 091	18880	3	Okaloosa	2 409	180 822	341	75.1	80.1	10.3	1.3	4.7	6.8	6.4	15.9	10.2	13.8	12.0	15.9
12 093	36380	4	Okeechobee	1 991	39 996	1 174	20.1	66.5	8.3	1.0	1.2	23.9	6.6	17.3	9.1	12.6	12.4	13.5
12 095	36740	1	Orange	2 340	1 145 956	35	489.7	47.3	20.5	0.6	5.9	26.9	6.5	17.1	12.8	15.5	14.4	14.1
12 097	36740	1	Osceola	3 438	268 685	242	78.2	41.5	10.0	0.6	3.5	45.5	6.6	19.6	9.8	13.1	14.7	14.5
12 099	33100	1	Palm Beach	5 102	1 320 134	28	258.7	61.1	17.5	0.4	3.0	19.0	5.4	15.0	8.0	11.1	12.5	14.3
12 101	45300	1	Pasco	1 934	464 697	141	240.3	81.5	4.7	0.7	2.7	11.7	5.5	15.7	7.0	10.6	13.1	14.3
12 103	45300	1	Pinellas	709	916 542	53	1 292.7	78.3	10.8	0.7	3.6	8.0	4.6	13.2	7.3	10.8	12.2	16.1
12 105	29460	2	Polk	4 656	602 095	104	129.3	65.8	15.0	0.7	2.1	17.7	6.5	17.1	8.8	11.8	12.2	13.3

1. CBSA = Core Based Statistical Area. See Appendix A for explanation. See Appendix B for list of metropolitan areas with component counties. 2. County type code from the Economic Research Service of USDA Rural-Urban Continuum Codes. See Appendix A for definition. 3. Dry land or land partially or temporarily covered by water. 4. May be of any race.

STATE County	Population, 2010 (cont.) Age (percent) (cont.)				Population change and components of change, 1990–2010 Total persons		Percent change		Components of change, 2000–2009			Households, 2010			Percent	
	55 to 64 years	65 to 74 years	75 years and over	Percent female	1990	2000	1990–2000	2000–2010	Births	Deaths	Net migration	Number	Percent change, 2000–2010	Persons per house-hold	Female family house-holder[1]	One per-son
	16	17	18	19	20	21	22	23	24	25	26	27	28	29	30	31
CONNECTICUT—Cont'd																
Tolland	12.2	6.7	5.2	49.5	128 699	136 364	6.0	12.0	13 115	8 279	9 954	54 477	10.2	2.51	8.6	24.2
Windham	12.5	6.9	6.0	50.4	102 525	109 091	6.4	8.6	12 195	8 883	5 750	44 810	8.9	2.54	12.3	24.6
DELAWARE	12.4	8.1	6.3	51.6	666 168	783 600	17.6	14.6	106 409	66 314	66 047	342 297	14.6	2.55	14.2	25.6
Kent	11.3	7.8	5.7	51.9	110 993	126 697	14.1	28.1	19 478	10 966	23 051	60 278	27.6	2.62	14.9	23.6
New Castle	11.6	6.6	5.7	51.6	441 946	500 265	13.2	7.6	66 119	38 136	9 875	202 651	7.3	2.57	14.9	26.1
Sussex	15.3	12.3	8.5	51.2	113 229	156 638	38.3	25.9	20 812	17 212	33 121	79 368	26.8	2.45	11.7	25.6
DISTRICT OF COLUMBIA..	10.6	6.1	5.3	52.8	606 900	572 059	-5.7	5.2	73 986	50 911	-17 427	266 707	7.4	2.11	16.4	44.0
District of Columbia	10.6	6.1	5.3	52.8	606 900	572 059	-5.7	5.2	73 986	50 911	-17 427	266 707	7.4	2.11	16.4	44.0
FLORIDA	12.4	9.2	8.1	51.1	12 938 071	15 982 378	23.5	17.6	2 046 244	1 566 658	2 034 234	7 420 802	17.1	2.48	13.5	27.2
Alachua	11.0	5.9	4.9	51.6	181 596	217 955	20.0	13.5	24 747	14 715	16 913	100 516	14.9	2.32	12.8	30.2
Baker	11.6	6.7	4.2	47.8	18 486	22 259	20.4	21.8	3 468	1 873	2 621	8 772	24.5	2.82	14.2	19.3
Bay	12.4	8.1	6.4	50.5	126 994	148 217	16.7	13.9	20 302	13 666	10 716	68 438	14.8	2.41	13.0	27.5
Bradford	12.3	8.1	6.3	43.9	22 515	26 088	15.9	9.3	3 057	2 445	2 657	9 479	11.6	2.53	15.0	25.1
Brevard	13.7	10.6	9.8	51.0	398 978	476 230	19.4	14.1	48 677	51 627	66 900	229 692	15.9	2.33	11.8	28.4
Broward	11.9	7.2	7.1	51.6	1 255 531	1 623 018	29.3	7.7	209 107	142 933	75 947	686 047	4.8	2.52	15.3	28.8
Calhoun	12.2	9.0	6.4	45.6	11 011	13 017	18.2	12.4	1 443	1 338	747	5 061	13.3	2.52	13.7	27.1
Charlotte	17.1	18.1	16.0	51.4	110 975	141 627	27.6	13.0	10 231	20 328	25 749	73 370	14.9	2.14	8.5	28.5
Citrus	16.6	17.4	14.5	51.6	93 513	118 085	26.3	19.6	9 233	20 177	33 766	63 304	20.3	2.20	9.1	28.3
Clay	12.1	7.1	4.6	51.0	105 986	140 814	32.9	35.5	20 010	11 516	38 129	68 792	36.9	2.76	12.9	18.8
Collier	13.4	14.4	12.1	50.7	152 099	251 377	65.3	27.9	35 226	23 589	56 618	133 179	29.3	2.38	8.6	26.7
Columbia	13.1	8.9	6.4	48.2	42 613	56 513	32.6	19.5	7 682	6 161	11 498	24 941	19.2	2.52	14.7	25.7
DeSoto	11.4	10.2	7.6	43.4	23 865	32 209	35.0	8.2	4 271	2 651	1 651	11 445	6.5	2.71	12.8	22.8
Dixie	15.5	12.2	7.1	46.2	10 585	13 827	30.6	18.8	1 553	1 634	1 168	6 316	21.3	2.37	11.7	28.1
Duval	11.5	6.2	5.0	51.5	672 971	778 879	15.7	11.0	118 704	65 563	29 463	342 450	12.7	2.47	16.7	28.4
Escambia	12.3	7.9	6.5	50.6	262 445	294 410	12.2	1.1	38 014	26 784	-539	116 238	4.7	2.41	16.3	28.9
Flagler	15.5	14.2	10.3	51.9	28 701	49 832	73.6	92.0	6 403	7 341	42 701	39 186	84.0	2.42	11.0	23.1
Franklin	14.5	11.1	6.4	42.4	8 967	11 057	23.3	4.4	1 045	1 044	1 503	4 254	3.9	2.29	10.9	29.3
Gadsden	13.6	8.0	5.7	51.2	41 116	45 087	9.7	2.9	6 696	4 267	227	16 952	6.8	2.61	22.6	25.5
Gilchrist	13.4	9.9	7.0	47.8	9 667	14 437	49.3	17.3	1 747	1 448	2 430	6 121	21.9	2.58	11.5	23.4
Glades	13.1	13.4	8.1	42.2	7 591	10 576	39.3	21.8	784	947	557	4 533	17.7	2.52	9.0	25.8
Gulf	13.8	9.5	6.8	40.2	11 504	13 332	15.9	19.0	1 165	1 408	1 488	5 335	8.2	2.33	10.8	28.6
Hamilton	13.0	8.0	5.2	41.1	10 930	13 327	21.9	11.0	1 622	1 189	888	4 617	11.0	2.54	16.6	26.5
Hardee	9.9	7.5	5.4	46.4	19 499	26 938	38.2	2.9	4 536	1 860	-73	8 245	1.0	3.12	14.2	19.2
Hendry	9.3	6.7	4.8	45.8	25 773	36 210	40.5	8.1	6 515	2 625	-380	12 025	10.8	3.09	15.2	19.4
Hernando	14.2	13.4	12.3	52.2	101 115	130 802	29.4	32.1	13 275	21 058	48 506	71 745	29.4	2.38	11.4	25.4
Highlands	13.5	16.8	15.6	51.1	68 432	87 366	27.7	13.1	9 062	12 411	15 239	42 604	13.7	2.28	9.9	28.5
Hillsborough	11.0	6.5	5.3	51.3	834 054	998 948	19.8	23.1	150 497	82 610	134 771	474 030	21.1	2.55	14.8	27.1
Holmes	13.2	10.1	7.0	46.8	15 778	18 564	17.7	7.3	2 054	2 069	626	7 354	6.3	2.47	12.0	26.3
Indian River	14.4	13.1	14.1	51.6	90 208	112 947	25.2	22.2	11 821	15 670	26 537	60 176	22.5	2.26	9.8	29.8
Jackson	13.1	8.8	6.9	45.2	41 375	46 755	13.0	6.4	5 242	4 826	4 027	17 417	4.8	2.40	15.6	28.9
Jefferson	15.8	9.6	6.9	47.7	11 296	12 902	14.2	14.4	1 471	1 420	1 107	5 646	20.3	2.38	15.1	28.1
Lafayette	10.4	7.2	5.0	38.2	5 578	7 022	25.9	26.3	891	619	703	2 580	20.4	2.63	10.9	24.2
Lake	13.3	13.2	11.0	51.5	152 104	210 528	38.4	41.1	28 211	29 756	102 911	121 289	37.2	2.42	10.6	25.2
Lee	14.1	13.1	10.4	50.9	335 113	440 888	31.6	40.3	58 943	52 082	141 120	259 818	37.8	2.35	10.3	26.7
Leon	10.8	5.3	4.1	52.4	192 493	239 452	24.4	15.0	29 002	14 198	12 829	110 945	14.9	2.35	14.0	30.1
Levy	15.5	11.8	7.6	50.8	25 912	34 450	32.9	18.4	4 108	4 225	4 994	16 404	18.3	2.45	13.0	26.0
Liberty	10.7	6.4	4.2	39.1	5 569	7 021	26.1	19.1	893	507	608	2 525	13.6	2.57	13.6	25.1
Madison	13.7	9.0	6.8	47.8	16 569	18 733	13.1	2.6	2 223	1 980	51	6 985	5.4	2.48	18.3	27.6
Manatee	14.0	12.1	11.2	51.6	211 707	264 002	24.7	22.3	33 772	31 133	53 044	135 729	20.7	2.34	10.8	28.5
Marion	13.9	14.2	11.5	52.0	194 835	258 916	32.9	28.0	30 627	35 732	75 565	137 726	29.0	2.35	12.0	26.7
Martin	14.5	13.3	14.0	50.5	100 900	126 731	25.6	15.5	11 840	15 397	17 190	63 899	15.6	2.23	8.6	31.0
Miami-Dade	10.9	7.5	6.6	51.6	1 937 194	2 253 362	16.3	10.8	303 660	170 459	23 116	867 352	11.7	2.83	18.8	23.5
Monroe	17.7	10.5	6.5	46.7	78 024	79 589	2.0	-8.2	6 818	6 402	-6 406	32 629	-7.0	2.18	8.0	30.8
Nassau	15.1	10.1	6.2	50.7	43 941	57 663	31.2	27.1	7 070	5 379	11 506	28 794	31.0	2.53	10.5	21.9
Okaloosa	11.8	7.8	6.2	49.8	143 777	170 498	18.6	6.1	24 131	13 120	-2 606	72 379	9.2	2.43	11.8	26.1
Okeechobee	11.4	9.8	7.2	46.4	29 627	35 910	21.2	11.4	5 334	3 713	2 969	14 013	11.3	2.68	12.5	23.9
Orange	10.0	5.4	4.3	50.8	677 491	896 344	32.3	27.8	144 452	60 510	112 095	421 847	25.4	2.64	15.7	24.9
Osceola	10.7	6.6	4.5	51.0	107 728	172 493	60.1	55.8	32 014	13 923	76 507	90 603	48.6	2.93	16.6	17.9
Palm Beach	12.1	9.9	11.7	51.6	863 503	1 131 184	31.0	16.7	136 768	124 714	135 811	544 227	14.8	2.39	11.7	30.1
Pasco	13.1	10.9	9.8	51.4	281 131	344 765	22.6	34.8	43 006	50 193	134 899	189 612	28.5	2.42	11.0	26.2
Pinellas	14.7	10.4	10.8	52.0	851 659	921 482	8.2	-0.5	85 435	110 717	18 749	415 876	0.2	2.16	11.9	35.4
Polk	12.3	10.1	7.9	51.0	405 382	483 924	19.4	24.4	70 065	50 723	83 146	227 485	21.5	2.59	13.7	23.8

1. No spouse present.

Table B. States and Counties — Population, Vital Statistics, Medicare, and Crime

STATE County	Persons in group quarters, 2010	Daytime population, 2006–2010 Number	Daytime population, 2006–2010 Employment/residence ratio	Births, average 2006–2008 Total	Births, average 2006–2008 Rate[1]	Deaths, average 2006–2008 Number	Deaths, average 2006–2008 Rate[1]	Persons under 65 with no health insurance, 2009 Number	Persons under 65 with no health insurance, 2009 Percent	Medicare, 2011 Eligible for Medicare	Medicare, 2011 Enrolled in Medicare Advantage	Medicare, 2011 Enrolled in a Medicare prescription drug plan	Serious crimes known to police,[2] 2010 Total Number	Serious crimes known to police,[2] 2010 Total Rate[3]
	32	33	34	35	36	37	38	39	40	41	42	43	44	45
CONNECTICUT—Cont'd														
Tolland	16 117	121 175	0.6	1 342	9.1	889	6.0	9 987	7.8	21 428	4 164	7 087	NA	NA
Windham	4 771	101 840	0.7	1 293	11.0	943	8.1	11 125	11.1	19 141	3 297	8 049	NA	NA
DELAWARE	24 413	888 893	1.0	12 083	14.0	7 384	8.5	88 758	12.0	155 791	6 360	74 244	36 538	4 069
Kent	4 322	150 964	0.9	2 257	14.9	1 284	8.5	17 180	12.9	27 402	883	11 325	6 419	3 955
New Castle	17 154	554 168	1.1	7 348	13.9	4 158	7.9	48 426	10.6	80 523	4 221	40 000	22 306	4 142
Sussex	2 937	183 761	0.9	2 478	13.5	1 942	10.5	23 151	15.6	47 866	1 256	22 919	7 960	4 038
DISTRICT OF COLUMBIA	40 021	1 046 036	2.6	8 839	15.1	5 224	8.9	40 951	8.2	80 572	7 898	32 926	36 760	6 109
District of Columbia	40 021	1 046 036	2.6	8 839	15.1	5 224	8.9	40 951	8.2	80 572	7 898	32 926	36 817	6 119
FLORIDA	421 709	18 467 358	1.0	235 804	12.9	169 622	9.3	3 735 524	24.9	3 485 159	1 123 276	1 124 014	771 004	4 101
Alachua	13 920	259 227	1.1	2 887	12.2	1 634	6.9	41 994	20.0	32 874	3 101	13 373	10 766	4 371
Baker	2 344	23 155	0.7	409	15.9	226	8.8	5 305	23.2	3 926	642	1 680	394	1 453
Bay	3 817	169 376	1.0	2 345	14.3	1 506	9.2	31 271	22.8	30 373	2 500	12 373	8 416	4 984
Bradford	4 492	27 243	0.9	360	12.5	274	9.5	5 960	24.4	4 786	473	2 255	683	2 395
Brevard	7 735	533 235	1.0	5 605	10.5	5 668	10.6	83 632	20.1	122 311	37 218	30 498	20 350	3 745
Broward	16 892	1 673 772	0.9	22 867	12.9	14 782	8.4	393 201	26.5	255 947	123 333	66 834	75 974	4 346
Calhoun	1 891	13 154	0.7	D	D	154	11.4	3 054	26.9	2 518	428	1 197	130	889
Charlotte	3 012	155 560	0.9	1 206	7.9	2 137	14.0	23 024	22.8	50 912	11 900	17 360	4 580	2 863
Citrus	2 251	134 658	0.9	1 143	8.2	2 270	16.2	22 749	23.9	48 166	9 988	16 605	3 916	2 773
Clay	1 251	149 376	0.6	2 351	12.9	1 323	7.3	28 923	17.8	29 133	4 214	9 496	5 206	2 728
Collier	4 546	325 059	1.1	4 043	12.8	2 645	8.4	64 812	28.4	72 238	9 724	31 958	6 760	2 103
Columbia	4 606	65 890	1.0	883	13.0	698	10.3	13 048	22.9	12 780	1 327	5 454	2 428	3 595
DeSoto	3 798	33 570	0.9	D	D	269	7.8	10 143	36.3	5 824	879	2 541	1 326	3 804
Dixie	1 430	14 557	0.7	D	D	186	12.4	2 905	25.1	3 687	426	1 714	626	3 812
Duval	19 985	928 693	1.2	13 636	16.1	7 142	8.4	145 732	19.7	121 947	25 221	46 810	46 019	5 325
Escambia	17 959	311 918	1.1	4 306	14.3	2 921	9.7	54 442	21.7	56 142	10 502	17 839	15 468	5 197
Flagler	684	82 679	0.7	943	10.8	920	10.5	14 838	22.0	26 245	8 181	7 031	2 478	2 589
Franklin	1 828	11 229	0.9	D	D	107	10.2	2 901	32.0	2 281	344	1 003	283	2 450
Gadsden	2 161	42 153	0.8	752	16.0	462	9.8	8 828	22.3	8 357	3 050	2 709	1 738	3 796
Gilchrist	1 128	14 351	0.6	D	D	166	9.8	3 616	25.9	3 227	373	1 406	174	1 165
Glades	1 483	11 388	0.7	D	D	103	9.2	2 609	31.3	1 907	371	728	284	2 204
Gulf	3 450	15 090	0.9	D	D	164	11.2	3 465	27.0	2 985	265	1 570	197	1 242
Hamilton	3 064	14 321	0.9	182	12.7	126	8.8	3 504	28.8	2 487	278	1 233	401	2 710
Hardee	1 984	26 894	0.9	522	18.1	202	7.0	8 413	34.1	3 729	457	2 022	921	3 555
Hendry	1 942	38 648	1.0	733	18.4	280	7.0	12 411	36.5	4 684	695	2 379	1 630	4 165
Hernando	1 828	156 185	0.8	1 610	9.5	2 364	14.0	28 689	23.2	48 954	21 558	10 177	5 460	3 160
Highlands	1 733	97 246	1.0	1 096	11.1	1 309	13.2	18 926	28.7	28 666	4 826	11 892	2 907	2 943
Hillsborough	22 065	1 262 199	1.1	17 628	15.1	9 066	7.7	221 763	21.5	175 916	69 952	48 178	42 558	3 462
Holmes	1 732	17 586	0.6	D	D	243	12.6	4 075	26.3	4 435	372	2 100	292	1 465
Indian River	1 794	136 413	1.0	1 403	10.7	1 689	12.9	24 768	25.6	37 816	5 582	14 924	4 696	3 402
Jackson	7 994	48 993	1.0	603	12.2	531	10.7	9 877	23.8	10 108	947	4 590	1 526	3 126
Jefferson	1 339	12 806	0.7	D	D	155	10.6	2 533	22.2	2 889	921	996	386	2 615
Lafayette	2 094	8 105	0.9	D	D	63	7.9	2 410	35.9	908	64	480	59	665
Lake	3 987	265 704	0.8	3 454	11.5	3 234	10.8	50 846	23.9	76 655	14 892	28 323	8 382	2 822
Lee	8 488	595 521	1.0	7 412	12.7	5 842	10.0	113 656	25.6	136 497	32 817	50 272	18 535	2 996
Leon	14 994	287 687	1.1	3 273	12.7	1 528	5.9	40 477	17.4	31 368	11 045	7 788	13 096	4 754
Levy	635	35 495	0.7	484	12.3	468	11.9	7 939	25.5	9 657	1 347	4 320	1 583	3 880
Liberty	1 882	7 678	0.8	D	D	53	6.8	1 971	28.7	1 174	233	476	72	861
Madison	1 933	17 835	0.8	D	D	223	11.7	3 923	25.8	3 723	662	1 863	687	3 574
Manatee	4 817	301 224	0.9	4 049	12.9	3 381	10.7	58 131	24.2	72 442	19 254	24 352	14 915	4 620
Marion	8 239	320 937	1.0	3 660	11.3	4 030	12.5	58 034	24.0	92 672	27 247	29 052	10 090	3 046
Martin	3 933	147 534	1.1	1 329	11.6	1 675	12.0	22 590	22.4	37 104	6 355	14 422	3 914	2 675
Miami-Dade	40 057	2 506 634	1.1	33 911	14.2	18 085	7.5	709 529	33.9	383 142	204 761	123 383	136 434	5 465
Monroe	2 020	75 494	1.1	750	10.2	671	9.1	16 114	26.9	13 100	767	5 956	4 115	5 630
Nassau	543	60 615	0.7	807	11.8	591	8.6	11 824	20.3	14 284	2 551	5 972	1 694	2 311
Okaloosa	4 883	191 081	1.1	2 738	15.2	1 445	8.0	28 277	18.8	30 673	2 272	8 848	5 907	3 267
Okeechobee	2 503	39 265	1.0	599	14.8	419	10.4	10 553	32.1	7 033	1 957	2 643	1 582	3 955
Orange	33 704	1 256 991	1.3	16 798	15.6	6 625	6.2	239 638	25.0	134 884	44 384	40 503	57 301	5 000
Osceola	3 262	228 232	0.7	4 071	16.0	1 581	6.2	63 189	27.1	37 929	16 927	9 325	11 604	4 319
Palm Beach	19 972	1 315 741	1.0	15 550	12.3	13 307	10.5	250 966	25.6	263 061	83 784	91 781	53 165	4 027
Pasco	5 674	390 978	0.6	5 349	11.6	5 472	11.9	86 737	23.6	102 140	47 027	22 770	16 654	3 584
Pinellas	19 678	930 161	1.0	9 346	10.2	11 285	12.3	157 280	22.3	201 071	78 280	55 374	43 546	4 751
Polk	12 261	564 602	0.9	8 239	14.4	5 581	9.8	104 683	22.3	119 134	43 641	33 718	23 218	3 880

1. Per 1,000 estimated resident population.   2. Data for serious crimes have not been adjusted for underreporting; this may affect comparability between geographic areas and over time.   3. Per 100,000 population estimated by the FBI.

Table B. States and Counties — Crime, Education, Money Income, and Poverty

STATE County	Serious crimes known to police,[1] 2010 (cont.) Rate[2] Violent	Property	Education School enrollment and attainment, 2006-2010 Enrollment[3] Total	Per-cent private	Attainment[4] (percent) High school graduate or less	Bach-elor's degree or more	Local government expenditures,[5] 2008-2009 Total current expendi-tures (mil dol)	Current expendi-tures per student (dollars)	Money income, 2006-2010 Per capita income[6] (dollars)	Households Median income Dollars	Percent change, 2000 to 2006-2010 (constant 2010 dollars)	Percent with income of $200,000 or more	Income and poverty, 2010 Median house-hold income (dollars)	Percent below poverty level All per-sons	Children under 18 years	Children 5 to 17 years in families
	46	47	48	49	50	51	52	53	54	55	56	57	58	59	60	61
CONNECTICUT—Cont'd																
Tolland	NA	NA	48 545	9.9	34.8	36.8	310.0	13 648	33 108	77 175	3.2	5.6	74 868	6.4	6.1	5.1
Windham	NA	NA	31 085	10.5	52.6	21.3	242.5	13 650	26 457	59 370	3.9	2.2	56 564	11.8	15.3	12.9
DELAWARE	621	3 448	229 092	21.1	45.1	27.7	1 515.1	12 079	29 007	57 599	-4.0	3.9	56 172	11.9	17.8	15.9
Kent	553	3 402	43 329	15.9	49.8	20.0	280.9	11 343	24 194	53 183	2.6	1.8	51 490	12.1	19.6	17.4
New Castle	685	3 458	147 973	24.2	41.0	32.4	900.7	12 287	31 220	62 474	-5.9	4.9	59 877	11.2	15.2	13.6
Sussex	519	3 519	37 790	14.6	52.2	21.2	333.5	12 189	26 779	51 046	2.8	2.8	48 582	13.9	24.0	21.5
DISTRICT OF COLUMBIA	1 330	4 779	152 806	43.1	33.4	49.2	1 079.8	15 826	42 078	58 526	15.2	9.6	60 729	18.8	31.1	30.9
District of Columbia	1 334	4 785	152 806	43.1	33.4	49.2	1 079.8	15 826	42 078	58 526	15.2	9.6	60 729	18.8	31.1	30.9
FLORIDA	542	3 558	4 455 695	17.9	45.0	25.9	22 979.1	8 760	26 551	47 661	-3.0	3.6	44 390	16.5	23.6	21.9
Alachua	645	3 726	93 297	8.4	31.2	40.9	235.8	8 559	24 741	40 644	2.1	3.5	40 656	25.3	26.3	25.3
Baker	214	1 239	6 139	9.3	71.0	6.2	39.0	7 703	19 593	47 276	-6.7	2.4	45 802	17.5	24.2	22.2
Bay	513	4 471	38 834	10.9	45.2	20.4	211.3	8 139	25 033	47 770	4.5	2.0	44 364	15.1	22.4	21.6
Bradford	291	2 104	5 633	16.3	63.3	8.6	31.2	9 155	16 997	41 126	-2.0	1.6	39 454	19.4	26.2	25.5
Brevard	588	3 157	124 956	20.3	40.1	26.2	602.4	8 241	27 606	49 523	-2.5	3.0	46 331	13.5	20.0	17.7
Broward	485	3 861	448 579	22.0	41.6	29.6	2 365.1	9 226	28 631	51 694	-2.1	4.4	47 917	14.7	18.8	18.7
Calhoun	130	759	2 888	4.5	67.0	11.6	19.9	8 838	15 091	31 699	-5.8	1.3	34 054	22.1	29.6	28.6
Charlotte	238	2 625	25 209	13.8	47.0	21.3	157.3	9 059	26 938	45 037	-2.2	2.1	41 991	13.9	25.5	23.3
Citrus	344	2 429	22 922	13.2	53.8	16.5	138.2	8 624	22 551	37 933	-3.4	1.6	36 174	17.2	30.8	28.5
Clay	428	2 300	53 433	14.2	40.3	23.8	299.0	8 318	26 872	61 185	-1.1	3.0	57 913	11.3	16.1	13.7
Collier	318	1 785	61 902	16.1	43.1	30.8	426.2	10 019	37 046	58 106	-5.0	8.1	53 341	15.7	26.3	24.7
Columbia	555	3 040	15 514	11.0	54.7	14.9	85.7	8 575	19 366	38 214	-2.3	1.0	34 870	19.5	29.9	27.9
DeSoto	769	3 035	6 989	9.3	67.4	11.6	44.7	9 026	15 989	35 979	-7.5	1.1	33 966	32.9	40.1	37.8
Dixie	438	3 374	3 098	13.9	69.6	6.2	18.4	8 690	17 066	32 312	-2.2	0.7	30 967	26.6	37.1	36.4
Duval	676	4 649	226 851	21.3	43.1	24.9	1 053.5	8 593	25 854	49 463	-4.0	2.7	46 112	16.6	23.5	22.7
Escambia	792	4 405	73 474	20.6	42.9	23.4	345.0	8 431	23 474	43 573	-2.3	2.6	41 428	19.1	28.2	27.0
Flagler	239	2 350	18 786	14.3	42.9	22.0	101.4	7 866	24 939	48 090	-5.6	2.3	45 685	15.5	22.0	20.4
Franklin	875	1 576	1 634	8.4	56.4	18.8	14.2	11 051	21 005	36 490	7.7	1.3	34 522	24.2	35.0	32.9
Gadsden	1 031	2 765	10 680	14.2	62.7	12.3	56.1	8 735	16 843	35 728	-9.7	0.7	35 704	23.8	32.7	32.4
Gilchrist	268	897	3 696	14.1	63.3	8.6	24.7	8 991	18 309	37 039	-3.6	1.3	38 517	21.0	26.9	24.7
Glades	303	1 902	2 467	8.1	61.4	11.3	13.2	9 519	17 872	39 429	1.2	0.8	39 089	21.0	29.0	27.8
Gulf	309	933	2 888	3.8	61.6	13.6	18.9	9 228	17 968	39 178	2.2	0.8	39 403	21.1	26.6	24.9
Hamilton	547	2 162	2 735	9.1	69.8	7.8	18.6	9 570	15 794	37 613	15.9	1.7	31 820	30.8	39.4	36.8
Hardee	378	3 177	6 195	6.2	72.4	7.5	44.2	8 644	14 668	37 466	-2.0	0.6	33 732	30.3	40.8	39.8
Hendry	667	3 498	9 795	8.7	74.3	8.2	63.5	9 025	14 734	37 298	-12.3	1.3	37 220	26.7	43.8	41.7
Hernando	383	2 778	35 273	12.7	52.2	16.2	179.2	7 884	22 775	42 011	1.9	1.5	37 867	15.1	24.2	22.5
Highlands	277	2 665	17 259	10.9	57.8	14.6	111.8	9 129	19 579	34 946	-8.5	0.7	34 469	20.7	33.4	31.9
Hillsborough	458	3 004	321 931	16.0	42.3	28.8	1 645.3	8 569	27 062	49 536	-3.8	3.8	46 043	16.7	23.2	20.7
Holmes	301	1 164	3 864	5.0	68.1	11.1	29.0	8 598	15 285	32 247	-8.8	0.1	33 696	22.5	32.1	30.8
Indian River	325	3 078	26 138	15.4	42.1	26.7	150.6	8 555	31 918	47 341	-5.7	5.1	47 525	14.4	25.2	23.9
Jackson	592	2 534	11 130	19.2	57.2	12.8	65.7	8 979	17 177	38 257	1.6	1.2	37 351	19.0	27.0	25.0
Jefferson	1 104	1 511	2 677	36.9	58.3	14.7	12.3	11 145	19 647	41 359	-1.0	1.9	39 113	18.5	29.2	28.2
Lafayette	225	440	2 228	10.5	63.4	9.0	10.7	9 542	18 069	46 445	19.7	0.4	36 001	26.0	28.7	26.0
Lake	402	2 420	59 381	17.1	47.5	20.3	326.1	7 962	25 323	46 477	-0.5	2.2	42 343	13.5	22.4	20.1
Lee	376	2 619	123 302	14.1	45.5	24.6	717.9	9 037	29 445	50 014	-2.0	4.1	44 377	17.1	28.0	25.9
Leon	761	3 993	103 846	12.3	30.7	41.3	280.4	8 623	25 803	44 490	-6.4	2.9	42 393	26.3	25.0	21.7
Levy	402	3 478	9 051	14.5	58.5	12.2	53.2	8 823	18 703	35 737	4.7	1.3	32 197	27.0	41.5	37.3
Liberty	191	669	1 586	6.7	70.0	15.1	14.3	9 605	17 003	40 777	11.7	1.3	37 815	22.9	28.0	25.9
Madison	848	2 726	3 682	6.4	66.5	10.6	25.4	9 370	16 346	37 459	11.5	1.2	31 942	23.4	35.7	34.6
Manatee	659	3 961	64 469	15.5	45.3	25.6	378.2	8 883	28 072	47 812	-2.4	3.4	44 990	14.5	23.4	22.5
Marion	542	2 504	63 473	17.2	53.2	17.1	350.2	8 215	22 384	40 339	-0.3	1.9	37 162	19.6	30.8	28.5
Martin	284	2 391	28 139	16.5	39.7	29.4	158.3	8 761	35 772	53 210	-2.5	6.5	49 539	11.3	17.0	15.3
Miami-Dade	741	4 724	630 404	20.9	50.4	26.2	3 144.3	9 100	22 957	43 605	-4.3	4.0	40 145	20.3	25.5	24.5
Monroe	465	5 165	12 091	14.7	38.9	28.7	98.7	11 924	35 516	53 821	0.5	5.5	50 388	12.6	19.1	19.1
Nassau	281	2 030	16 207	14.7	48.7	21.9	87.2	7 936	29 089	58 712	0.7	4.0	57 605	11.3	17.7	16.2
Okaloosa	367	2 900	43 553	10.4	37.3	26.8	236.6	8 123	28 621	54 242	3.3	3.6	51 173	12.4	19.7	18.3
Okeechobee	565	3 390	8 842	5.8	63.8	11.4	58.2	8 311	19 664	38 339	-0.6	2.3	35 417	22.3	33.0	32.2
Orange	760	4 240	313 921	19.8	40.5	30.3	1 412.1	8 198	25 490	50 138	-4.2	3.6	45 105	16.4	22.8	21.4
Osceola	603	3 716	68 596	14.7	50.8	18.3	429.7	8 272	20 536	46 328	-4.3	1.7	42 165	16.3	24.2	21.6
Palm Beach	530	3 498	291 140	20.6	39.9	31.8	1 587.3	9 296	33 610	53 242	-6.7	6.2	49 891	14.3	22.4	21.0
Pasco	345	3 239	98 157	16.6	49.0	20.0	566.1	8 476	24 164	44 228	5.9	1.9	42 184	15.2	20.8	19.0
Pinellas	658	4 094	186 542	17.4	42.5	27.1	944.5	8 905	28 742	45 258	-3.7	3.2	42 628	14.2	20.4	18.2
Polk	400	3 480	136 211	15.6	54.8	18.0	815.2	8 612	21 881	43 946	-3.7	1.9	41 184	17.5	28.3	25.7

1. Data for serious crimes have not been adjusted for underreporting; this may affect comparability between geographic areas and over time. 2. Per 100,000 population estimated by the FBI. 3. All persons 3 years old and over enrolled in nursery school through college. 4. Persons 25 years old and over. 5. Elementary and secondary education expenditures. 6. Based on population estimated by the American Community Survey, 2006-2010.

Table B. States and Counties — **Personal Income**

STATE County	Total (mil dol)	Percent change, 2008–2009	Per capita[1] Dollars	Per capita[1] Rank	Wages and salaries[2] (mil dol)	Proprietors' income (mil dol)	Dividends, interest, and rent (mil dol)	Transfer payments (mil dol) Total	Government payments to individuals Total	Social Security	Medical payments	Income maintenance	Unemployment insurance
	62	63	64	65	66	67	68	69	70	71	72	73	74
CONNECTICUT—Cont'd													
Tolland	6 834	-0.4	45 424	187	2 382	416	1 071	848	820	327	312	39	79
Windham	4 417	1.1	37 583	682	1 972	207	615	899	878	277	400	67	79
DELAWARE	35 048	-1.6	39 597	X	25 078	2 509	6 319	6 589	6 428	2 294	2 891	481	313
Kent	4 910	1.0	31 127	1 725	3 291	284	702	1 113	1 085	383	442	102	52
New Castle	23 501	-2.8	43 957	237	18 724	1 832	4 145	3 685	3 588	1 227	1 648	270	196
Sussex	6 637	1.0	34 434	1 106	3 063	394	1 472	1 791	1 756	685	801	108	65
DISTRICT OF COLUMBIA..	41 282	1.6	68 843	X	72 028	5 642	6 363	4 823	4 714	846	2 707	644	197
District of Columbia	41 282	1.6	68 843	13	72 028	5 642	6 363	4 823	4 714	846	2 707	644	197
FLORIDA	722 328	-2.3	38 965	X	397 672	40 122	194 177	137 918	134 551	47 211	57 616	12 827	5 941
Alachua	8 665	-0.1	35 573	945	6 413	335	1 881	1 477	1 432	446	623	150	38
Baker	692	-0.1	26 282	2 671	294	19	89	173	168	54	70	21	7
Bay	5 984	0.3	36 316	843	3 758	277	1 232	1 266	1 236	398	527	121	47
Bradford	787	2.1	26 921	2 582	322	29	86	197	192	63	84	23	5
Brevard	20 089	-0.4	37 454	693	11 416	905	4 483	4 368	4 270	1 731	1 697	281	169
Broward	72 752	-4.2	41 185	375	40 559	3 949	17 767	11 433	11 111	3 523	5 101	1 041	590
Calhoun	314	1.9	22 741	3 044	121	14	44	101	99	31	47	12	3
Charlotte	5 628	-2.1	35 858	906	1 788	252	2 089	1 550	1 522	729	569	69	50
Citrus	4 382	0.8	31 224	1 707	1 513	146	1 305	1 459	1 434	685	529	83	38
Clay	6 202	-1.0	33 209	1 305	1 929	162	1 025	1 099	1 066	392	378	90	51
Collier	19 128	-4.8	60 049	30	6 137	875	10 708	2 270	2 212	1 050	798	135	95
Columbia	1 804	1.7	26 047	2 717	1 032	46	304	536	523	169	222	63	16
DeSoto	800	1.8	22 655	3 046	411	46	162	231	224	77	97	27	8
Dixie	330	1.2	22 229	3 060	101	22	58	132	130	47	52	16	3
Duval	33 370	-1.9	38 937	547	28 519	2 108	6 122	5 676	5 523	1 621	2 294	681	299
Escambia	10 354	0.6	34 133	1 149	7 373	422	1 893	2 324	2 271	732	940	262	68
Flagler	2 993	0.6	32 671	1 389	774	21	992	768	751	381	236	50	30
Franklin	330	-0.2	29 298	2 136	133	24	105	86	84	29	38	8	1
Gadsden	1 259	-0.4	26 512	2 639	608	43	193	357	348	106	140	66	13
Gilchrist	498	1.2	29 113	2 167	123	22	67	122	118	43	48	13	4
Glades	278	1.9	25 401	2 819	83	29	66	61	59	30	16	7	2
Gulf	408	-0.6	25 923	2 744	173	18	88	126	123	41	59	10	3
Hamilton	290	5.3	19 891	3 095	219	8	42	104	102	32	43	16	3
Hardee	651	-0.1	22 132	3 063	317	58	101	168	163	47	74	26	6
Hendry	1 048	0.5	26 462	2 647	526	118	160	243	236	62	106	40	14
Hernando	5 128	0.7	29 950	1 993	1 560	177	1 214	1 719	1 688	706	687	109	52
Highlands	2 819	1.4	28 563	2 287	1 095	121	782	956	939	397	385	70	22
Hillsborough	45 511	-0.6	38 075	628	35 755	3 162	8 654	7 745	7 528	2 346	3 049	950	399
Holmes	499	0.5	26 151	2 695	138	29	75	179	175	55	82	20	3
Indian River	7 610	-5.0	56 303	50	2 279	280	4 109	1 242	1 218	549	480	69	49
Jackson	1 331	2.6	26 125	2 704	639	64	205	450	441	130	225	42	7
Jefferson	420	0.3	30 014	1 973	117	16	81	108	105	37	43	14	3
Lafayette	153	-2.1	19 309	3 101	72	7	27	38	37	12	15	5	1
Lake	9 609	-1.9	30 785	1 804	3 561	342	2 340	2 624	2 567	1 069	1 054	168	91
Lee	23 916	-4.3	40 750	403	10 069	1 291	9 140	4 658	4 551	1 933	1 739	328	237
Leon	9 605	-0.7	36 148	867	7 526	530	1 832	1 329	1 280	435	443	165	44
Levy	1 016	-0.4	25 945	2 740	326	44	196	333	326	130	122	36	11
Liberty	195	-0.3	24 437	2 920	138	8	21	48	46	15	20	7	1
Madison	451	0.9	23 841	2 971	185	13	78	161	158	47	72	23	4
Manatee	12 623	-1.3	39 650	474	5 280	968	3 855	2 352	2 294	1 034	805	173	100
Marion	10 217	-1.2	31 097	1 728	4 206	334	2 549	3 009	2 950	1 292	1 083	241	105
Martin	8 208	-5.2	58 712	37	2 904	365	4 256	1 208	1 183	553	471	50	39
Miami-Dade	90 916	-0.8	36 357	833	59 202	7 432	17 340	19 198	18 742	3 941	10 173	2 635	880
Monroe	4 403	-3.8	60 173	29	1 892	228	1 998	486	472	184	198	33	18
Nassau	3 121	-1.6	44 229	229	865	100	839	499	487	205	183	36	19
Okaloosa	7 497	-1.2	42 007	328	5 540	376	1 714	1 228	1 198	400	490	94	36
Okeechobee	1 012	0.2	25 157	2 851	450	41	201	333	325	96	167	31	12
Orange	39 548	-2.8	36 400	828	36 391	2 959	6 680	6 489	6 291	1 761	2 638	832	411
Osceola	6 814	0.6	25 180	2 847	3 127	153	900	1 742	1 692	484	739	244	101
Palm Beach	73 547	-4.9	57 461	43	30 449	4 031	32 147	10 098	9 864	3 977	4 265	625	411
Pasco	13 791	-0.6	29 236	2 141	4 333	278	2 781	3 759	3 673	1 459	1 486	274	142
Pinellas	38 956	-3.1	42 855	279	21 677	2 130	10 372	7 962	7 797	2 831	3 525	521	300
Polk	18 865	-2.2	32 336	1 450	9 568	1 160	3 913	4 274	4 168	1 634	1 547	485	180

1. Based on the resident population estimated as of July 1 of the year shown.   2. Includes supplements to wages and salaries.

Table B. States and Counties — Earnings, Social Security, and Housing

STATE County	Earnings, 2009									Social Security beneficiaries, December 2010			Housing units, 2010	
					Percent by selected industries									
			Goods-related[1]		Service-related and health							Supplemental Security Income recipients, December 2010		
	Total (mil dol)	Farm	Total	Manufacturing	Information and profesional and technical services	Retail trade	Finance, insurance, and real estate	Health care and social services	Government	Number	Rate[2]		Total	Percent change, 2000–2010
	75	76	77	78	79	80	81	82	83	84	85	86	87	88
CONNECTICUT—Cont'd														
Tolland	2 798	0.5	D	7.1	6.7	6.6	3.5	11.8	38.8	23 145	152	917	57 963	12.4
Windham	2 179	0.4	D	16.8	5.0	8.0	2.4	15.3	23.7	21 535	182	1 882	49 073	11.6
DELAWARE	27 587	0.6	D	8.4	12.9	6.1	14.4	12.5	16.5	172 441	192	15 865	405 885	18.3
Kent	3 575	1.5	D	D	4.2	7.9	3.5	11.3	41.5	31 040	191	3 541	65 338	29.4
New Castle	20 556	0.0	D	D	15.9	5.0	17.7	12.3	12.6	88 915	165	9 404	217 511	9.0
Sussex	3 457	3.0	25.1	17.5	4.1	10.7	6.3	15.1	14.0	52 485	266	2 920	123 036	32.2
DISTRICT OF COLUMBIA	77 671	0.0	1.3	0.2	26.6	0.9	4.1	5.3	42.5	74 417	124	24 371	296 719	8.0
District of Columbia	77 671	0.0	1.3	0.2	26.6	0.9	4.1	5.3	42.5	74 417	124	24 371	296 719	8.0
FLORIDA	437 793	0.5	11.4	5.2	12.2	7.6	8.6	12.6	18.0	3 784 225	201	485 172	8 989 580	23.1
Alachua	6 748	0.2	D	3.8	7.7	6.0	5.5	18.0	39.6	36 140	146	5 251	112 766	18.6
Baker	313	0.0	D	4.0	D	7.8	1.9	D	44.3	4 650	171	621	9 687	27.6
Bay	4 035	0.0	11.6	5.5	9.6	7.8	6.4	11.0	31.5	33 940	201	4 301	99 650	27.0
Bradford	352	0.2	D	5.4	3.7	8.1	2.4	D	38.9	5 450	191	835	11 011	14.6
Brevard	12 320	0.1	20.9	16.0	11.6	6.5	4.2	12.9	18.4	134 980	248	10 068	269 864	21.5
Broward	44 508	0.0	10.5	4.3	13.5	8.5	9.8	10.5	16.3	277 735	159	37 583	810 388	9.4
Calhoun	135	2.2	D	D	D	D	1.9	14.6	38.3	2 870	196	564	5 999	14.3
Charlotte	2 041	1.1	8.5	1.4	7.3	12.7	6.2	23.5	18.7	55 725	348	2 301	100 632	26.2
Citrus	1 659	0.1	8.6	1.5	6.2	10.0	3.9	23.3	15.3	53 310	377	2 648	78 026	25.4
Clay	2 091	0.0	11.4	3.6	7.4	12.8	5.3	16.0	21.0	32 630	171	2 379	75 478	40.4
Collier	7 012	2.3	12.8	2.6	8.3	9.1	9.5	14.6	12.4	75 290	234	3 085	197 298	36.5
Columbia	1 079	0.2	13.8	9.5	D	9.0	6.1	14.0	32.7	14 765	219	2 483	28 636	21.5
DeSoto	466	9.9	9.5	5.6	2.4	13.6	3.1	10.9	25.9	6 540	188	886	14 590	7.2
Dixie	123	0.8	20.4	15.9	1.9	7.3	1.6	D	39.0	4 300	262	751	9 319	26.6
Duval	30 627	0.1	11.5	5.9	11.4	6.3	12.4	12.3	18.5	135 145	156	21 663	388 486	17.8
Escambia	7 795	0.1	10.0	4.2	8.0	6.5	5.9	15.3	33.9	62 965	212	9 379	136 703	9.7
Flagler	795	1.5	D	4.4	D	11.7	4.8	13.9	25.5	29 105	304	1 488	48 595	98.7
Franklin	157	0.0	D	D	6.4	9.2	10.9	D	34.6	2 525	219	340	8 652	20.6
Gadsden	651	4.2	20.0	9.1	D	5.4	1.9	4.6	39.7	9 605	207	2 664	19 506	10.2
Gilchrist	145	-0.5	11.9	2.3	D	5.6	2.1	D	39.4	3 760	222	436	7 307	23.7
Glades	113	18.4	D	2.6	1.8	2.9	0.7	D	24.6	2 195	170	179	6 979	20.5
Gulf	191	0.0	14.8	5.0	6.2	6.6	6.6	7.2	37.4	3 345	211	378	9 110	20.0
Hamilton	226	-0.1	D	D	D	2.8	0.9	D	29.0	2 860	193	607	5 778	16.4
Hardee	375	15.0	D	2.6	D	6.9	3.7	12.8	24.2	4 330	156	824	9 722	-1.0
Hendry	645	15.8	D	11.0	D	6.6	2.6	D	20.7	5 385	138	1 229	14 564	18.5
Hernando	1 737	0.2	D	3.3	4.7	11.8	4.2	22.6	21.3	55 595	322	3 428	84 504	34.7
Highlands	1 216	6.7	D	2.0	4.0	11.1	3.6	22.6	19.0	31 595	320	2 358	55 386	13.4
Hillsborough	38 917	0.6	10.2	4.7	16.4	6.4	11.6	11.1	16.1	194 185	158	34 967	536 092	25.9
Holmes	166	-2.5	11.4	4.5	2.7	6.4	4.3	D	41.7	5 065	254	859	8 641	8.0
Indian River	2 559	1.5	D	3.9	9.2	9.9	7.1	18.4	14.2	40 895	296	1 922	76 346	31.9
Jackson	703	3.6	10.8	4.1	D	8.2	2.9	8.8	43.5	11 615	233	1 969	21 003	7.8
Jefferson	132	2.9	D	0.8	D	5.9	6.3	D	31.0	3 200	217	653	6 632	26.3
Lafayette	79	9.9	D	2.0	D	6.9	D	D	47.6	1 090	123	143	3 328	25.1
Lake	3 903	1.1	14.9	4.3	5.8	10.7	4.8	19.2	18.7	83 895	282	5 631	144 996	41.0
Lee	11 360	0.1	12.3	2.1	10.7	10.2	7.1	11.7	20.4	147 530	238	9 953	371 099	51.2
Leon	8 057	0.0	D	1.6	15.0	6.0	6.4	12.5	39.3	33 985	123	4 997	124 136	19.4
Levy	370	4.6	D	4.6	4.7	11.3	5.0	7.0	27.8	11 150	273	1 407	20 123	21.4
Liberty	146	0.0	D	11.0	D	1.8	D	14.9	28.8	1 350	161	277	3 357	6.4
Madison	198	0.2	D	10.2	D	6.6	3.2	12.1	35.8	4 260	222	962	8 481	8.2
Manatee	6 248	2.9	D	8.9	12.5	8.6	4.7	12.4	12.8	78 925	244	4 937	172 690	25.0
Marion	4 540	-0.3	16.6	8.6	6.8	10.3	7.0	15.4	20.7	102 810	310	7 772	164 050	33.7
Martin	3 269	1.2	D	5.7	11.2	9.7	6.4	16.9	11.4	39 825	272	1 452	78 131	19.3
Miami-Dade	66 635	0.3	8.7	3.6	14.0	6.8	9.3	11.1	17.3	371 465	149	140 916	989 435	16.1
Monroe	2 121	0.0	D	0.7	7.6	9.6	5.8	6.8	27.1	14 415	197	1 213	52 764	2.2
Nassau	964	0.1	15.8	11.0	6.0	8.4	5.5	6.0	26.2	15 805	216	1 086	35 009	35.1
Okaloosa	5 916	0.0	9.0	5.0	12.3	6.1	5.9	7.0	44.1	33 895	187	2 690	92 407	17.6
Okeechobee	492	6.9	12.0	5.9	3.4	9.7	2.9	D	26.2	8 095	202	888	18 509	19.4
Orange	39 349	0.2	10.9	5.6	14.5	5.8	8.5	10.2	11.8	150 610	131	28 589	487 839	35.0
Osceola	3 281	0.4	D	2.4	4.4	10.2	6.2	14.2	22.0	43 780	163	8 058	128 170	77.3
Palm Beach	34 480	1.1	10.3	4.0	13.7	7.4	9.9	13.8	13.5	282 895	214	19 165	664 594	19.4
Pasco	4 611	0.4	11.3	4.0	5.6	12.0	4.7	20.5	20.4	116 875	252	9 336	228 928	31.8
Pinellas	23 807	0.0	16.0	9.7	11.7	7.7	9.2	16.0	12.8	220 285	240	18 960	503 634	4.6
Polk	10 728	0.8	16.0	9.6	7.8	7.7	6.9	13.8	15.0	133 160	221	17 248	281 214	24.2

1. Includes mining, construction, and manufacturing.   2. Per 1,000 resident population enumerated in the 2010 census.

Table B. States and Counties — Housing, Labor Force, and Employment

STATE County	Housing units, 2006–2010								Civilian labor force, 2010				Civilian employment,[5] 2006–2010		
	Occupied units							Sub-stand-ard units[3] (percent)		Percent change, 2009–2010	Unemployment			Percent	
	Owner-occupied					Renter-occupied								Manage-ment, business, science and arts	Con-struction, produc-tion, and mainte-nance occu-pations
				Median owner cost as a percent of income											
	Total	Percent	Median value[1]	With a mort-gage	Without a mort-gage	Median rent[2]	Median rent as a per-cent of income		Total		Total	Rate[4]	Total		
	89	90	91	92	93	94	95	96	97	98	99	100	101	102	103
CONNECTICUT—Cont'd															
Tolland....................	54 452	76.4	266 100	24.1	13.6	948	29.5	1.1	86 567	1.0	6 763	7.8	80 523	43.1	17.4
Windham	44 321	70.8	230 100	26.8	15.7	824	28.1	1.9	65 259	0.1	6 718	10.3	59 578	29.2	27.2
DELAWARE	331 639	73.6	242 300	24.5	11.4	938	30.9	2.2	436 822	0.4	35 116	8.0	419 062	36.8	20.1
Kent...........................	57 396	72.9	207 500	25.5	11.8	916	30.2	2.2	72 499	-0.9	6 107	8.4	69 270	31.6	24.4
New Castle..................	198 499	71.3	252 800	23.8	10.5	953	30.7	2.1	261 669	-3.4	22 411	8.6	265 108	40.8	17.3
Sussex........................	75 744	80.0	243 700	26.0	12.5	896	32.1	2.7	91 516	0.8	7 584	8.3	84 684	28.9	25.4
DISTRICT OF COLUMBIA..	257 317	43.5	443 300	24.9	10.8	1 063	29.6	3.4	343 379	3.4	34 690	10.1	297 189	57.7	7.9
District of Columbia...............	257 317	43.5	443 300	24.9	10.8	1 063	29.6	3.4	343 379	3.4	34 690	10.1	297 189	57.7	7.9
FLORIDA......................	7 152 844	69.7	205 600	29.3	14.1	957	34.2	2.9	9 132 470	-0.1	1 030 146	11.3	8 317 203	32.8	19.9
Alachua	97 540	54.9	189 600	25.3	11.5	855	37.9	2.3	131 257	0.5	10 773	8.2	116 528	44.7	12.2
Baker..........................	8 309	76.2	137 900	25.1	10.8	703	28.0	2.7	12 178	-0.6	1 328	10.9	10 565	25.0	28.2
Bay.............................	68 807	66.0	175 500	25.7	11.6	889	29.5	2.4	90 215	0.6	9 249	10.3	76 430	31.2	21.7
Bradford......................	8 931	77.3	120 500	24.3	12.4	673	31.1	3.7	12 625	1.1	1 213	9.6	10 470	24.7	26.2
Brevard........................	220 871	76.4	186 900	27.4	13.0	897	33.0	1.7	268 149	-0.2	30 930	11.5	238 178	36.7	20.0
Broward.......................	668 898	69.3	247 500	32.8	18.4	1 133	35.6	3.5	985 251	-0.2	99 336	10.1	850 849	34.8	17.1
Calhoun.......................	4 765	73.9	89 000	26.4	11.6	530	30.4	4.4	6 168	4.8	553	9.0	4 537	29.3	23.3
Charlotte.....................	71 991	81.1	184 900	30.9	14.4	927	33.3	0.9	69 969	1.4	8 684	12.4	57 368	28.6	21.5
Citrus	59 974	84.6	141 800	27.3	12.2	749	33.8	1.5	58 163	2.8	7 506	12.9	46 517	27.4	22.8
Clay............................	67 493	78.3	189 700	24.8	10.0	971	28.1	1.4	95 766	0.3	10 065	10.5	86 261	34.2	20.5
Collier.........................	119 517	76.5	357 400	31.9	14.4	1 054	33.7	3.6	144 557	0.3	17 293	12.0	133 647	28.7	21.9
Columbia	24 177	71.5	134 300	26.4	11.1	669	30.8	3.5	31 394	-1.0	3 352	10.7	25 649	28.9	28.5
DeSoto	10 656	78.5	114 100	29.5	12.3	715	27.4	6.0	15 197	1.5	1 692	11.1	12 854	21.2	40.0
Dixie...........................	4 909	81.6	98 200	26.9	10.9	526	22.6	2.4	5 815	2.3	735	12.6	5 168	21.9	39.5
Duval..........................	330 276	63.1	175 900	25.8	11.5	880	31.5	2.2	446 118	-0.1	52 274	11.7	408 907	32.8	20.1
Escambia......................	113 313	67.4	148 600	25.8	12.0	816	33.4	2.4	139 787	0.1	15 188	10.9	125 299	31.6	19.9
Flagler........................	36 182	81.1	219 100	31.1	13.2	1 032	34.6	1.4	33 498	2.0	5 186	15.5	35 258	35.0	18.4
Franklin.......................	4 699	65.6	177 000	24.9	13.3	665	34.0	2.3	5 287	7.2	442	8.4	4 710	21.4	28.7
Gadsden......................	16 303	70.9	104 500	25.8	12.7	684	33.2	3.7	21 309	-1.5	2 268	10.6	16 059	25.0	24.2
Gilchrist	5 976	80.5	112 700	22.5	12.5	738	37.5	4.4	7 759	-1.4	772	9.9	6 468	22.0	31.2
Glades	4 165	81.2	106 900	25.3	12.5	744	32.7	2.3	5 475	21.9	524	9.6	4 546	18.9	42.2
Gulf............................	5 347	77.1	131 900	29.1	12.8	739	25.6	2.4	6 342	-1.1	684	10.8	5 595	28.0	25.0
Hamilton	4 532	74.0	75 700	24.4	10.0	528	28.2	3.8	4 726	-3.3	578	12.2	4 392	22.4	34.5
Hardee.........................	7 694	74.7	111 000	26.6	11.2	775	28.4	9.6	12 621	8.8	1 448	11.5	10 423	19.5	47.6
Hendry.........................	11 200	69.2	117 300	27.8	12.5	764	32.1	5.9	17 406	1.2	2 711	15.6	15 330	14.5	43.8
Hernando......................	70 254	83.4	156 400	28.3	13.1	864	36.0	2.1	62 837	-0.9	9 136	14.5	61 570	28.4	21.4
Highlands	40 374	79.9	122 000	27.4	13.2	715	33.0	2.6	41 225	2.1	4 829	11.7	34 083	24.9	27.6
Hillsborough	462 447	63.3	198 900	27.7	13.5	906	32.8	2.7	600 967	0.2	70 778	11.8	577 255	35.6	18.3
Holmes........................	6 768	80.3	87 100	24.4	11.0	611	31.2	1.4	8 952	0.2	768	8.6	6 762	24.2	30.6
Indian River..................	57 560	76.8	198 200	28.8	14.5	899	36.9	2.3	62 464	-0.1	8 743	14.0	54 873	30.6	23.2
Jackson........................	16 767	77.2	97 700	22.3	12.1	554	27.1	2.5	22 415	1.3	1 848	8.2	16 695	31.4	21.1
Jefferson......................	5 233	77.2	127 600	23.7	11.5	693	31.2	0.5	6 621	-4.8	613	9.3	5 721	33.4	18.8
Lafayette......................	2 307	80.6	162 200	22.2	10.0	617	34.8	1.1	3 066	-0.8	253	8.3	3 319	24.3	30.2
Lake	117 544	78.7	178 400	27.7	13.2	904	33.8	1.9	137 687	0.5	16 566	12.0	119 819	31.6	21.3
Lee	245 751	74.8	210 600	30.5	14.2	962	33.4	2.8	277 533	-0.8	35 491	12.8	257 289	29.3	21.5
Leon	109 314	55.4	196 700	24.6	10.8	879	38.4	3.4	148 389	-0.2	12 185	8.2	136 390	44.5	12.6
Levy............................	15 814	76.3	112 100	24.8	12.0	618	30.8	3.5	17 224	3.8	2 107	12.2	15 534	22.5	32.4
Liberty.........................	2 008	77.5	90 700	24.2	12.7	685	26.0	4.3	3 941	1.5	273	6.9	3 025	23.0	35.7
Madison	6 776	73.9	96 400	23.3	12.7	648	30.9	4.4	7 165	-0.5	841	11.7	7 490	25.0	34.5
Manatee.......................	131 200	74.1	214 000	29.3	14.3	930	33.6	2.8	142 026	-2.3	17 427	12.3	135 533	32.1	21.4
Marion	133 966	78.9	150 700	27.4	12.8	829	34.1	2.0	135 005	-0.7	18 671	13.8	122 068	27.3	24.2
Martin	59 203	79.5	254 900	28.9	14.3	1 001	32.0	1.5	63 972	1.6	7 528	11.8	60 387	35.2	18.5
Miami-Dade...................	827 556	58.1	269 600	35.2	17.3	1 004	38.3	5.7	1 231 368	-1.1	153 926	12.5	1 127 602	29.9	21.1
Monroe	29 791	64.5	503 900	39.1	15.2	1 257	34.9	4.9	45 949	1.9	3 400	7.4	37 999	26.9	21.9
Nassau........................	27 255	79.4	213 600	24.2	10.7	859	27.0	2.0	36 317	0.3	3 958	10.9	32 027	29.9	27.9
Okaloosa......................	72 442	67.3	204 400	25.8	11.1	962	30.1	2.1	96 350	-1.9	7 789	8.1	82 822	34.9	19.5
Okeechobee..................	13 642	76.7	136 700	30.1	13.6	788	33.2	6.6	18 987	4.0	2 417	12.7	15 920	22.1	28.7
Orange........................	406 002	59.9	228 600	29.1	12.9	995	34.6	2.9	604 314	0.2	68 805	11.4	561 806	33.7	18.0
Osceola	92 526	66.5	199 200	33.2	14.3	1 036	36.3	2.9	141 058	1.7	17 467	12.4	120 153	25.3	21.9
Palm Beach...................	523 150	73.6	261 900	31.9	16.6	1 129	35.4	2.9	618 694	-0.1	72 439	11.7	585 359	34.3	17.4
Pasco..........................	184 813	78.8	157 400	28.0	13.4	865	33.5	1.6	196 634	-0.7	25 745	13.1	188 298	32.8	20.0
Pinellas........................	405 649	70.4	185 700	29.3	15.9	904	32.7	1.8	442 483	-1.3	51 921	11.7	426 402	36.4	17.1
Polk	223 689	72.1	141 900	26.9	13.1	835	31.3	3.7	275 449	0.0	34 546	12.5	247 262	28.4	26.2

1. Specified owner-occupied units.   2. Specified renter-occupied units. A value of 10.0 represents 10 percent or less.   3. Overcrowded or lacking complete plumbing facilities.   4. Percent of civilian labor force.   5. Persons 16 years old and over.

Table B. States and Counties — Nonfarm Employment and Agriculture

STATE County	Number of establishments	Total	Health care and social assistance	Manufacturing	Retail trade	Finance and insurance	Professional, scientific, and technical services	Annual payroll Total (mil dol)	Average per employee (dollars)	Farms Number	Fewer than 50 acres	500 acres or more	Farm operators whose principal occupation is farming (percent)
	104	105	106	107	108	109	110	111	112	113	114	115	116
CONNECTICUT—Cont'd													
Tolland	2 486	30 274	5 854	3 813	4 722	651	1 092	1 012	33 428	484	62.8	2.1	45.7
Windham	2 159	29 798	6 851	5 512	4 709	689	532	1 035	34 733	594	51.2	2.9	46.3
DELAWARE	24 523	370 846	57 485	30 410	51 130	38 986	23 308	16 777	45 241	2 546	57.1	9.6	59.1
Kent	3 169	48 947	8 129	4 918	9 072	1 339	1 918	1 580	32 286	825	57.0	9.3	58.4
New Castle	15 879	262 628	39 331	14 655	30 060	35 528	19 657	13 315	50 697	347	62.8	8.9	49.9
Sussex	5 408	58 670	10 015	10 837	11 995	1 948	1 623	1 834	31 254	1 374	55.7	10.0	61.8
DISTRICT OF COLUMBIA..	21 210	466 550	67 587	1 800	19 122	16 939	89 927	30 236	64 809	NA	NA	NA	NA
District of Columbia	21 210	466 550	67 587	1 800	19 122	16 939	89 927	30 236	64 809	NA	NA	NA	NA
FLORIDA	491 249	6 861 612	943 823	294 519	921 514	338 098	430 886	253 360	36 924	47 463	69.2	5.5	44.0
Alachua	5 794	82 708	20 606	3 631	13 501	4 139	4 935	2 771	33 499	1 532	71.7	4.6	40.0
Baker	384	5 413	1 837	154	804	131	106	158	29 179	344	77.9	1.7	36.3
Bay	4 510	54 350	9 161	3 285	10 226	2 655	3 310	1 707	31 406	133	69.2	2.3	38.3
Bradford	455	4 321	936	D	920	D	135	112	25 988	479	72.2	1.3	34.9
Brevard	13 005	165 707	26 491	19 994	25 074	5 538	13 099	6 637	40 052	531	79.8	4.9	46.7
Broward	55 289	610 674	88 918	23 288	92 363	33 392	47 802	24 383	39 928	547	92.3	0.5	50.3
Calhoun	216	1 565	518	D	282	55	13	37	23 781	242	52.1	5.0	35.5
Charlotte	3 539	40 953	7 990	400	7 998	1 197	1 244	1 076	26 267	242	57.9	13.6	49.2
Citrus	2 718	24 719	7 067	294	5 308	D	798	782	31 617	411	70.3	4.4	47.0
Clay	3 616	36 229	5 950	1 257	8 480	973	2 844	1 025	28 281	374	78.6	1.9	41.7
Collier	9 860	101 535	15 124	2 485	17 988	3 737	5 096	3 657	36 012	322	70.5	9.9	53.1
Columbia	1 356	17 039	3 882	903	3 105	511	508	526	30 873	982	71.4	3.6	42.0
DeSoto	457	4 902	D	D	916	187	119	152	30 961	1 035	71.3	6.9	39.2
Dixie	179	1 337	124	417	252	D	D	34	25 073	217	59.4	6.9	46.1
Duval	23 830	408 297	57 327	21 547	46 935	44 822	31 472	16 922	41 444	371	79.2	3.2	46.4
Escambia	6 671	98 136	18 531	3 724	15 168	5 298	5 949	3 221	32 821	725	64.0	5.4	38.2
Flagler	1 781	16 572	2 065	755	3 156	560	443	442	26 682	82	47.6	24.4	53.7
Franklin	324	1 986	101	D	408	D	42	47	23 911	15	86.7	0.0	53.3
Gadsden	640	9 200	3 032	1 206	1 227	186	210	281	30 561	385	51.9	4.7	41.8
Gilchrist	215	1 499	425	197	245	43	56	39	26 237	569	65.2	6.5	43.2
Glades	92	811	D	118	D	D	D	26	31 843	311	64.0	13.8	43.1
Gulf	295	2 095	391	D	323	D	189	57	27 372	53	64.2	3.8	47.2
Hamilton	191	2 566	177	D	321	62	D	123	47 774	322	39.8	11.2	35.7
Hardee	363	4 208	1 407	D	708	224	92	123	29 341	1 081	56.1	6.7	39.9
Hendry	558	5 673	757	D	1 162	271	189	165	29 037	430	54.9	19.3	49.5
Hernando	2 923	28 074	6 950	966	6 724	D	1 030	787	27 729	768	79.9	2.6	44.8
Highlands	1 999	19 112	4 937	531	4 542	1 126	707	516	26 957	832	59.9	12.9	48.8
Hillsborough	31 710	490 900	67 647	20 869	61 720	46 027	43 037	20 647	42 059	2 843	83.6	2.3	45.1
Holmes	301	2 030	655	152	307	99	139	45	22 227	1 037	28.8	4.3	34.7
Indian River	3 874	37 847	8 127	1 805	7 628	1 202	1 706	1 252	33 093	415	68.7	9.6	50.1
Jackson	835	8 982	1 795	456	1 937	350	229	234	26 001	1 321	36.3	10.9	42.9
Jefferson	262	1 789	412	88	349	D	D	40	22 428	642	50.2	9.2	34.6
Lafayette	95	753	D	D	156	D	D	15	20 286	236	34.7	9.7	55.5
Lake	6 287	66 820	14 167	3 037	13 891	1 911	2 509	1 965	29 409	1 814	79.4	2.6	40.3
Lee	15 593	169 998	26 724	4 164	33 374	5 935	9 199	5 602	32 954	944	86.4	4.1	37.7
Leon	7 461	90 997	15 588	1 893	15 632	5 007	10 158	3 215	35 333	324	66.7	5.9	34.9
Levy	738	5 456	573	D	1 510	332	200	134	24 530	1 018	70.1	5.6	47.2
Liberty	76	775	116	D	80	23	D	23	30 008	53	47.2	7.5	37.7
Madison	309	2 819	678	D	572	75	82	69	24 395	678	33.9	8.6	42.0
Manatee	7 468	81 154	13 487	8 065	15 566	2 733	3 227	2 608	32 134	794	64.1	8.8	43.8
Marion	6 890	76 897	14 071	6 235	15 166	4 685	3 757	2 349	30 547	3 496	81.9	1.9	50.6
Martin	5 004	48 466	8 543	2 444	8 872	1 930	3 031	1 597	32 942	492	76.4	8.5	40.9
Miami-Dade	72 673	808 269	122 417	34 388	112 584	41 778	58 408	32 730	40 494	2 498	93.2	0.9	50.4
Monroe	3 456	25 940	2 171	177	5 118	839	1 098	774	29 850	23	95.7	0.0	30.4
Nassau	1 612	14 525	2 137	1 109	2 783	402	439	452	31 097	449	76.2	1.1	38.3
Okaloosa	5 005	57 415	8 337	3 419	11 194	2 857	6 196	1 949	33 950	567	47.6	3.5	36.3
Okeechobee	768	6 762	1 447	215	1 602	D	220	189	27 955	656	56.1	17.4	47.9
Orange	31 481	592 186	62 583	26 616	67 297	21 427	48 540	22 860	38 603	825	84.6	3.3	46.5
Osceola	4 766	60 610	8 986	1 660	11 862	1 243	1 452	1 710	28 219	381	65.4	15.2	50.4
Palm Beach	41 763	436 599	68 957	11 166	67 312	21 459	31 794	17 876	40 943	1 263	87.8	5.3	54.4
Pasco	8 237	77 194	15 762	2 737	19 055	2 502	3 157	2 196	28 450	1 210	78.5	4.0	45.1
Pinellas	26 506	354 914	71 836	28 686	46 406	23 001	28 510	13 463	37 933	134	97.0	0.0	24.6
Polk	10 995	163 343	25 371	15 410	23 993	11 169	7 164	5 570	34 103	2 768	66.2	6.4	42.5

Table B. States and Counties — **Agriculture**

STATE County	Land in farms Acreage (1,000)	Percent change, 2002–2007	Average size of farm	Acres Total irrigated (1,000)	Total cropland (1,000)	Value of land and buildings (dollars) Average per farm	Average per acre	Value of machinery and equipment, average per farm (dollars)	Value of products sold Total (mil dol)	Average per farm (dollars)	Percent from: Crops	Live-stock and poultry products	Percent of farms with sales of: $10,000 or more	$100,000 or more	Government payments Total ($1,000)	Percent of farms
	117	118	119	120	121	122	123	124	125	126	127	128	129	130	131	132
CONNECTICUT—Cont'd																
Tolland	39	5.4	81	0.6	16.8	979 030	12 047	64 011	37.6	77 630	53.4	46.6	31.2	7.2	318	6.0
Windham	60	-1.6	101	0.2	25.1	929 269	9 179	66 079	39.7	66 837	30.0	70.0	34.7	10.8	911	9.8
DELAWARE	510	-5.6	200	104.6	432.8	2 073 605	10 347	119 718	1 083.0	425 387	19.4	80.6	59.0	38.8	8 896	37.3
Kent	174	-5.9	211	29.1	146.5	2 091 272	9 926	122 692	188.4	228 352	D	D	46.7	26.1	3 285	37.3
New Castle	67	-5.6	193	2.7	51.9	2 295 500	11 892	102 370	45.7	131 708	D	D	43.8	13.0	1 045	34.0
Sussex	269	-5.3	196	72.8	234.3	2 006 959	10 234	122 313	848.9	617 862	15.1	84.9	70.3	53.1	4 565	38.1
DISTRICT OF COLUMBIA..	NA	NA	NA	NA	NA	NA	NA	NA	NA	NA	NA	NA	NA	NA	NA	NA
District of Columbia	NA	NA	NA	NA	NA	NA	NA	NA	NA	NA	NA	NA	NA	NA	NA	NA
FLORIDA	9 232	-11.4	195	1 552.1	2 953.3	1 096 718	5 639	54 604	7 785.2	164 027	80.4	19.6	34.6	11.0	45 343	9.8
Alachua	173	-22.4	113	13.4	65.6	820 508	7 273	49 395	92.1	60 102	70.6	29.4	27.6	5.5	1 212	7.0
Baker	27	50.0	78	0.7	4.7	496 345	6 389	27 699	D	D	D	0.0	18.0	4.1	50	4.4
Bay	12	9.1	94	D	2.7	718 873	7 667	33 325	5.0	37 813	92.3	7.7	19.5	2.3	5	4.5
Bradford	30	-33.3	62	0.2	8.5	426 399	6 895	33 893	13.9	29 054	16.9	83.1	23.8	3.3	D	0.6
Brevard	167	-11.2	315	20.5	22.1	1 238 223	3 936	56 362	46.7	87 913	85.2	14.8	50.1	9.0	21	1.5
Broward	9	-62.5	16	1.7	4.9	424 408	26 571	32 949	50.3	91 945	97.0	3.0	29.4	10.2	680	5.5
Calhoun	39	-20.4	162	1.5	16.6	707 352	4 378	68 275	16.2	67 048	84.4	15.6	19.4	5.0	772	24.0
Charlotte	166	-13.5	686	20.0	28.7	2 224 000	3 241	61 849	65.6	270 921	89.5	10.5	39.7	16.5	306	2.5
Citrus	40	-14.9	97	1.4	9.7	746 230	7 664	43 628	14.4	35 006	66.2	33.8	20.9	4.9	157	4.1
Clay	42	-46.8	111	0.9	5.7	585 985	5 276	36 344	D	D	0.0	D	13.1	3.2	9	3.2
Collier	110	-39.2	341	31.4	69.9	2 039 523	5 974	87 700	278.8	865 906	98.5	1.5	40.7	20.5	132	4.3
Columbia	86	-4.4	88	2.7	30.0	618 208	7 063	36 690	D	D	D	D	16.3	3.3	334	9.7
DeSoto	260	-33.0	251	56.2	91.3	1 397 534	5 557	59 069	219.9	212 491	84.4	15.6	49.4	13.6	123	1.1
Dixie	42	35.5	194	3.0	7.6	716 085	3 698	45 628	8.4	38 512	32.9	67.1	20.7	1.8	D	5.1
Duval	27	-12.9	72	2.0	5.7	639 475	8 861	32 759	D	D	0.0	D	17.3	3.2	18	2.4
Escambia	82	26.2	113	2.6	52.3	536 368	4 744	56 997	31.9	44 064	87.0	13.0	24.1	7.0	4 193	36.7
Flagler	58	-14.7	712	6.8	8.7	2 833 332	3 979	88 146	35.1	428 538	97.6	2.4	43.9	20.7	27	4.9
Franklin	1	NA	34	0.0	D	87 243	2 566	51 131	0.7	48 282	0.0	100.0	60.0	20.0	0	0.0
Gadsden	47	-30.9	122	2.2	15.2	675 924	5 526	62 515	96.0	249 427	98.2	1.8	24.9	3.9	194	21.0
Gilchrist	71	-12.3	125	7.8	32.8	840 009	6 723	50 514	76.7	134 745	21.1	78.9	26.5	5.1	565	11.4
Glades	402	-1.5	1 294	46.7	50.8	6 796 878	5 252	76 580	85.3	274 330	69.4	30.6	32.2	14.8	237	3.9
Gulf	5	0.0	89	D	1.3	425 195	4 752	41 005	1.1	20 137	22.9	77.2	22.6	9.4	D	3.8
Hamilton	65	25.0	201	5.5	20.0	973 465	4 839	49 506	14.4	44 775	75.9	24.1	25.5	4.7	500	39.8
Hardee	280	-19.1	259	44.1	66.3	1 578 924	6 098	58 750	232.0	214 579	73.1	26.9	56.9	21.2	217	2.4
Hendry	465	-15.8	1 082	188.8	262.4	3 673 204	3 396	136 706	567.4	1 319 602	95.5	4.5	60.5	32.6	626	5.1
Hernando	56	-13.8	73	1.5	16.5	716 829	9 789	37 988	35.7	46 456	49.3	50.7	19.4	5.2	94	1.2
Highlands	476	-17.5	572	73.7	120.5	2 353 234	4 111	87 582	326.0	391 829	80.8	19.2	58.4	25.2	493	3.1
Hillsborough	220	-22.8	77	29.9	86.4	787 847	10 190	52 850	488.2	171 727	89.3	10.7	33.0	10.8	58	0.8
Holmes	152	67.0	146	2.0	46.0	621 851	4 248	40 589	24.1	23 209	16.8	83.2	21.1	3.5	2 726	53.3
Indian River	157	-17.8	379	66.9	81.3	1 986 694	5 245	104 511	136.1	327 910	D	D	61.0	24.1	68	3.6
Jackson	311	37.0	236	20.3	144.0	875 624	3 715	55 873	69.7	52 751	D	D	25.8	7.6	6 638	47.7
Jefferson	147	10.5	230	2.1	34.0	1 035 244	4 508	35 153	22.1	34 427	53.7	46.3	26.9	3.4	1 201	31.3
Lafayette	81	-12.0	344	7.4	17.3	1 306 640	3 794	92 611	138.7	587 594	4.2	95.8	43.6	25.8	458	29.2
Lake	121	-32.8	67	15.0	34.7	705 893	10 546	39 374	188.5	103 925	D	D	40.1	9.4	38	0.9
Lee	86	-31.7	91	14.6	22.0	982 569	10 818	39 788	116.1	122 945	97.1	2.9	26.2	6.1	142	1.2
Leon	91	23.0	280	1.5	13.0	1 070 670	3 823	50 769	4.4	13 646	79.2	20.8	20.7	2.5	165	6.2
Levy	174	-3.3	171	14.5	73.2	891 435	5 209	50 965	75.7	74 354	59.9	40.1	30.9	9.6	2 733	5.9
Liberty	24	140.0	446	D	0.7	828 227	1 859	39 369	1.2	22 034	5.1	94.9	32.1	7.5	D	1.9
Madison	149	-5.1	220	3.1	40.3	1 001 957	4 558	53 827	43.4	63 953	17.6	82.4	28.3	6.6	725	27.3
Manatee	225	-25.2	284	50.8	77.3	1 759 488	6 206	77 276	311.8	392 702	93.6	6.4	40.3	15.9	11	0.4
Marion	267	-1.5	76	9.7	59.9	725 733	9 518	46 830	173.7	49 696	15.7	84.3	22.6	4.6	476	1.3
Martin	129	-37.4	263	48.5	51.9	1 594 655	6 064	61 270	158.5	322 171	84.9	15.1	33.7	12.0	291	6.1
Miami-Dade	67	-25.6	27	39.0	53.8	742 119	27 648	45 341	661.1	264 652	D	D	51.5	18.3	5 450	8.9
Monroe	0	NA	8	0.0	0.2	214 565	26 390	61 786	1.9	83 356	44.0	56.0	47.8	21.7	D	8.7
Nassau	31	NA	70	0.3	4.2	441 968	6 345	28 798	8.3	18 584	9.1	90.9	14.7	1.6	1	0.9
Okaloosa	66	20.0	116	0.4	24.3	628 564	5 410	38 958	D	D	D	D	13.1	3.4	1 641	36.2
Okeechobee	338	-13.8	516	20.5	40.9	2 374 399	4 603	82 412	177.6	270 745	24.8	75.2	37.7	14.0	337	6.6
Orange	136	-7.5	165	11.9	20.7	1 084 345	6 574	60 921	269.9	327 176	98.0	2.0	50.2	24.5	D	0.1
Osceola	646	-1.1	1 696	31.4	44.5	4 339 729	2 558	103 685	90.9	238 571	67.6	32.4	44.9	18.4	230	2.4
Palm Beach	526	-1.9	416	387.8	450.7	1 712 306	4 114	127 234	931.7	737 712	99.1	0.9	41.7	18.8	2 455	6.1
Pasco	150	-11.2	124	10.6	37.8	953 274	7 692	37 716	111.3	91 963	43.7	56.3	31.9	8.4	231	2.1
Pinellas	1	-50.0	11	0.2	D	267 805	24 664	25 608	2.4	17 850	78.6	21.4	29.1	4.5	D	1.5
Polk	549	-12.4	198	98.4	136.3	1 417 168	7 144	57 381	399.0	144 132	91.1	8.9	62.7	22.8	211	1.7

Table B. States and Counties — Water Use, Wholesale Trade, Retail Trade, and Real Estate

STATE County	Water use, 2005		Wholesale trade,[1] 2007				Retail trade,[2] 2007				Real estate and rental and leasing,[2] 2007			
	Total water withdrawn (mil gal/day)	Gallons withdrawn per person	Number of establish-ments	Number of employees	Sales (mil dol)	Annual payroll (mil dol)	Number of establish-ments	Number of employees	Sales (mil dol)	Annual payroll (mil dol)	Number of establish-ments	Number of employees	Receipts (mil dol)	Annual payroll (mil dol)
	133	134	135	136	137	138	139	140	141	142	143	144	145	146
CONNECTICUT—Cont'd														
Tolland	17.6	119	69	571	214.3	25.7	406	5 207	1 206.3	126.3	110	457	62.7	12.2
Windham	17.9	154	71	1 132	546.7	60.0	376	4 870	1 180.6	122.0	73	D	D	D
DELAWARE	1 017.2	1 206	819	9 065	5 727.4	416.9	3 907	55 432	14 202.1	1 322.8	1 248	5 807	11 057.2	222.4
Kent	37.6	261	100	D	D	D	632	9 614	2 589.2	224.6	127	604	91.0	22.0
New Castle	498.4	953	559	D	D	D	2 093	33 010	8 633.4	795.0	823	3 786	10 740.6	155.1
Sussex	481.3	2 726	160	D	D	D	1 182	12 808	2 979.4	303.1	298	1 417	225.5	45.3
DISTRICT OF COLUMBIA..	9.7	17	316	3 680	2 118.0	216.4	1 827	19 117	3 843.7	485.9	1 140	9 663	2 747.8	624.8
District of Columbia	9.7	17	316	3 680	2 118.0	216.4	1 827	19 117	3 843.7	485.9	1 140	9 663	2 747.8	624.8
FLORIDA	18 307.9	1 022	27 442	279 300	221 641.5	12 566.1	73 794	1 016 290	262 341.1	24 049.7	33 653	170 859	32 235.4	6 094.2
Alachua	60.1	249	188	D	D	D	969	14 610	3 152.2	300.1	397	2 048	311.6	59.0
Baker	7.2	300	8	D	D	D	74	888	180.6	16.3	11	D	D	D
Bay	291.9	1 805	174	1 481	645.0	62.9	816	10 186	2 472.0	227.1	314	1 172	167.7	33.6
Bradford	6.7	239	14	D	D	D	87	961	215.6	20.7	22	47	6.2	1.0
Brevard	957.3	1 799	493	3 683	1 852.7	155.1	2 073	28 911	6 594.0	630.4	777	2 795	401.1	74.8
Broward	1 837.9	1 056	3 946	37 891	31 411.6	1 819.5	7 382	104 336	30 886.3	2 710.6	3 624	18 044	3 555.6	648.1
Calhoun	3.4	246	12	D	D	D	42	295	64.8	6.2	5	13	1.1	0.2
Charlotte	40.1	260	94	592	211.7	22.0	582	8 761	1 898.1	187.9	289	877	120.7	22.1
Citrus	1 707.1	12 871	84	D	D	D	516	5 836	1 405.6	131.1	202	605	59.4	12.3
Clay	22.6	133	115	803	394.3	34.8	609	9 363	2 005.7	195.5	230	797	143.2	21.4
Collier	193.2	608	331	2 678	1 649.0	137.9	1 500	20 122	5 186.5	535.5	958	2 874	552.3	118.0
Columbia	12.3	199	75	871	478.6	35.6	265	3 113	862.2	74.2	66	206	31.5	5.4
DeSoto	66.7	2 047	20	D	D	D	75	1 023	280.8	23.1	38	106	13.0	2.2
Dixie	3.8	244	4	D	D	D	34	237	49.1	4.2	7	11	1.1	0.1
Duval	771.6	896	1 154	19 865	17 205.8	969.5	3 464	51 916	13 316.7	1 228.5	1 427	8 481	2 040.1	368.9
Escambia	829.0	1 084	278	3 171	1 838.9	126.6	1 233	16 777	4 055.7	374.3	413	1 539	278.0	45.0
Flagler	19.3	245	53	D	D	D	208	2 899	684.1	66.3	195	508	66.9	13.8
Franklin	2.6	239	8	D	D	D	71	438	92.3	9.3	33	194	20.5	6.1
Gadsden	17.0	355	34	707	384.0	23.9	137	1 462	440.3	29.4	29	88	13.3	2.2
Gilchrist	14.8	911	3	10	2.3	0.2	41	239	52.5	4.7	8	38	4.6	1.0
Glades	104.4	9 731	5	D	D	D	15	83	13.1	1.4	5	14	1.1	0.2
Gulf	2.7	161	3	D	D	D	48	371	76.3	7.3	22	68	8.6	1.6
Hamilton	54.8	3 831	4	D	D	D	54	343	103.2	5.6	4	22	1.8	0.3
Hardee	32.5	1 188	21	D	D	D	75	740	400.1	16.0	25	65	8.3	1.3
Hendry	395.9	10 317	32	273	212.1	8.3	131	1 373	345.7	28.2	29	94	10.3	1.9
Hernando	48.6	322	114	592	177.9	20.8	469	7 191	1 654.1	156.1	192	467	63.0	9.8
Highlands	118.3	1 266	83	D	D	D	364	4 513	1 089.6	99.0	112	337	52.6	8.1
Hillsborough	2 014.0	1 780	1 764	28 080	17 752.9	1 233.9	4 369	70 015	19 110.3	1 745.9	1 983	12 821	2 504.2	500.3
Holmes	3.8	197	14	D	D	D	49	332	73.1	5.5	8	18	1.4	0.3
Indian River	285.7	2 197	132	D	D	D	699	9 096	1 851.7	203.3	260	945	146.5	24.1
Jackson	119.5	2 405	26	185	70.6	5.2	188	2 056	541.9	43.0	47	131	13.1	2.5
Jefferson	13.2	930	9	39	43.7	1.5	55	390	88.7	6.6	10	24	1.9	0.4
Lafayette	7.9	985	4	D	D	D	20	139	66.5	3.1	2	D	D	D
Lake	85.7	326	224	1 745	726.3	62.3	1 003	14 137	3 441.9	310.3	477	2 116	266.9	69.5
Lee	709.1	1 291	589	5 590	2 271.6	225.7	2 624	38 417	9 193.1	923.2	1 307	5 643	1 000.1	171.3
Leon	43.0	159	228	2 254	791.2	88.4	1 043	16 881	3 533.8	343.1	451	2 412	361.5	68.3
Levy	28.7	757	32	170	62.8	4.2	145	1 546	346.4	32.8	44	129	10.2	2.0
Liberty	1.0	136	4	D	D	D	16	76	24.4	1.4	1	D	D	D
Madison	14.3	725	9	D	D	D	71	585	124.8	9.4	13	25	2.4	0.4
Manatee	141.4	465	303	3 314	1 725.5	148.1	1 163	16 937	3 874.8	382.0	550	2 227	390.6	66.0
Marion	54.4	179	318	3 812	1 639.5	149.7	1 208	16 639	4 218.8	379.2	466	1 598	217.9	39.9
Martin	138.7	983	195	1 393	741.6	65.3	809	10 666	2 470.4	243.3	326	1 595	203.0	40.7
Miami-Dade	602.3	249	7 819	65 657	60 760.1	2 818.0	10 293	123 559	34 530.5	3 055.6	4 935	25 546	5 367.9	985.2
Monroe	1.7	20	86	D	D	D	657	6 267	1 387.6	146.7	308	808	150.5	26.5
Nassau	54.9	834	37	D	D	D	280	2 998	630.9	63.0	97	D	D	D
Okaloosa	26.4	140	110	563	236.9	23.0	903	12 427	3 031.0	272.4	398	1 772	260.5	57.0
Okeechobee	54.5	1 443	29	179	85.3	6.0	156	1 680	430.6	37.5	49	115	16.5	3.3
Orange	258.0	247	1 643	23 425	17 080.7	1 148.0	4 670	71 848	19 195.6	1 653.3	2 383	26 517	6 177.0	1 053.1
Osceola	146.8	624	128	1 819	3 044.2	69.6	822	12 171	2 868.7	264.6	504	4 643	732.0	155.4
Palm Beach	1 532.5	1 211	2 007	17 634	12 017.5	900.5	5 564	76 129	19 321.7	1 916.5	2 691	12 359	2 083.2	503.8
Pasco	2 168.2	5 329	311	1 847	807.4	70.4	1 336	18 995	4 746.2	426.6	529	1 602	197.5	35.1
Pinellas	483.8	511	1 247	14 111	12 378.4	625.8	3 850	52 539	14 826.9	1 232.7	1 687	7 648	1 222.6	268.2
Polk	219.3	405	580	8 024	13 241.7	337.4	1 876	25 321	6 420.1	586.4	741	3 423	517.8	95.9

1. Merchant wholesalers, except manufacturers' sales branches and offices.   2. Employer establishments.

Table B. States and Counties — Professional Services, Manufacturing, and Accommodation and Food Services

STATE County	Professional, scientific, and technical services,[1] 2007				Manufacturing, 2007				Accommodation and food services, 2007			
	Number of establishments	Number of employees	Receipts (mil dol)	Annual payroll (mil dol)	Number of establishments	Number of employees	Receipts (mil dol)	Annual payroll (mil dol)	Number of establishments	Number of employees	Sales (mil dol)	Annual payroll (mil dol)
	147	148	149	150	151	152	153	154	155	156	157	158
CONNECTICUT—Cont'd												
Tolland	200	D	D	D	141	3 962	1 021.8	185.1	211	3 472	173.1	48.7
Windham	123	D	D	D	187	6 135	1 776.5	254.7	236	2 841	136.3	38.7
DELAWARE	2 383	D	D	D	673	34 866	25 679.9	1 759.7	1 850	32 194	1 910.8	468.8
Kent	248	D	D	D	87	5 253	2 361.8	213.8	236	5 352	447.9	76.2
New Castle	1 804	D	D	D	421	18 556	20 268.8	1 167.8	1 051	19 118	999.2	267.2
Sussex	331	D	D	D	165	11 057	3 049.3	378.0	563	7 724	463.7	125.4
DISTRICT OF COLUMBIA..	4 373	82 107	24 177.7	8 660.6	137	2 015	332.8	80.8	2 148	52 998	4 278.2	1 238.4
District of Columbia	4 373	82 107	24 177.7	8 660.6	137	2 015	332.8	80.8	2 148	52 998	4 278.2	1 238.4
FLORIDA	69 083	427 536	61 599.8	24 264.5	14 324	355 386	104 832.9	15 227.2	35 012	746 214	41 922.1	11 470.0
Alachua	792	5 262	625.4	263.6	147	3 803	D	D	524	11 170	494.0	133.7
Baker	16	90	7.2	2.9	NA	NA	NA	NA	34	446	19.8	4.8
Bay	406	D	D	D	116	3 702	1 254.3	153.4	442	9 154	480.4	135.8
Bradford	44	163	11.9	4.2	NA	NA	NA	NA	42	752	37.1	9.1
Brevard	1 683	19 711	3 364.7	1 589.6	473	22 772	6 767.6	1 172.5	1 019	19 057	855.5	240.1
Broward	9 509	46 243	6 635.1	2 550.4	1 734	29 333	7 160.8	1 185.5	3 693	70 373	4 209.1	1 140.1
Calhoun	9	19	1.1	0.5	NA	NA	NA	NA	20	285	9.3	2.8
Charlotte	366	D	D	D	NA	NA	NA	NA	240	4 322	178.0	53.2
Citrus	274	D	D	D	NA	NA	NA	NA	188	2 931	109.7	32.4
Clay	423	D	D	D	81	1 464	D	D	274	5 413	213.8	61.9
Collier	1 271	D	D	D	228	3 035	606.7	109.5	704	17 421	1 037.2	308.3
Columbia	115	D	D	D	38	988	351.5	37.5	120	2 220	103.3	25.9
DeSoto	32	189	14.9	6.1	NA	NA	NA	NA	38	579	24.3	6.5
Dixie	13	63	3.5	2.0	11	529	D	D	23	192	7.4	1.6
Duval	3 126	D	D	D	647	26 119	11 222.1	1 242.1	1 811	34 979	1 719.4	488.1
Escambia	778	D	D	D	191	5 152	2 117.0	253.4	534	11 014	493.9	137.2
Flagler	197	674	105.6	46.6	52	1 031	235.7	29.9	131	2 401	114.8	31.6
Franklin	21	41	7.2	2.0	NA	NA	NA	NA	43	623	37.6	10.4
Gadsden	48	D	D	D	33	1 462	262.9	50.8	38	466	18.9	4.7
Gilchrist	18	64	4.4	1.6	NA	NA	NA	NA	19	163	8.1	2.0
Glades	6	D	D	D	NA	NA	NA	NA	11	110	4.9	1.3
Gulf	31	143	14.6	5.4	NA	NA	NA	NA	25	298	18.8	3.4
Hamilton	11	19	1.8	0.3	1	D	D	D	18	151	7.9	1.6
Hardee	23	105	7.0	2.5	NA	NA	NA	NA	25	413	17.9	3.4
Hendry	41	193	17.3	7.0	22	1 014	D	D	71	754	37.3	9.3
Hernando	281	D	D	D	80	1 111	312.5	44.1	237	4 101	166.2	44.3
Highlands	152	D	D	D	56	927	306.1	33.1	133	2 408	100.8	28.0
Hillsborough	4 983	40 574	6 205.8	2 518.5	911	28 213	9 444.9	1 112.6	2 117	47 384	2 619.8	706.8
Holmes	24	160	6.1	3.4	NA	NA	NA	NA	18	206	8.3	2.3
Indian River	473	2 076	235.3	97.2	99	2 179	413.0	87.7	232	4 557	190.5	56.2
Jackson	46	253	23.5	9.1	22	636	180.6	21.1	72	1 014	43.2	11.1
Jefferson	20	98	8.7	3.2	NA	NA	NA	NA	18	79	7.0	1.2
Lafayette	8	28	1.4	0.5	NA	NA	NA	NA	9	47	2.7	0.6
Lake	644	D	D	D	163	3 531	825.5	132.4	428	8 283	436.0	110.6
Lee	1 848	10 115	1 305.2	511.3	403	5 988	1 181.8	222.6	1 095	23 070	1 192.0	344.2
Leon	1 373	D	D	D	100	2 155	593.4	90.3	594	13 745	551.6	150.8
Levy	47	205	15.6	6.1	27	681	131.0	22.3	75	862	32.4	8.2
Liberty	2	D	D	D	NA	NA	NA	NA	4	60	3.4	0.8
Madison	21	111	5.6	2.5	NA	NA	NA	NA	21	356	12.3	3.1
Manatee	919	D	D	D	297	10 012	2 985.1	434.2	529	9 788	443.8	129.5
Marion	698	3 459	361.6	132.0	221	8 904	1 841.5	320.9	443	7 784	353.1	100.0
Martin	675	D	D	D	154	3 242	856.1	118.6	329	6 648	279.0	85.3
Miami-Dade	11 294	60 310	9 603.2	3 755.1	2 312	40 446	9 347.1	1 556.0	4 358	91 230	6 005.9	1 659.8
Monroe	325	D	D	D	NA	NA	NA	NA	484	9 814	748.1	202.4
Nassau	164	495	62.3	23.3	33	D	696.2	68.0	152	3 971	287.0	78.0
Okaloosa	637	D	D	D	98	3 858	656.7	166.4	431	10 619	491.9	148.9
Okeechobee	51	202	14.3	5.1	NA	NA	NA	NA	59	914	46.9	11.5
Orange	4 656	D	D	D	822	30 097	10 921.8	1 555.9	2 426	87 369	6 645.1	1 567.8
Osceola	423	D	D	D	88	1 907	644.9	75.7	532	14 153	890.5	239.0
Palm Beach	6 944	35 002	6 092.8	2 284.2	995	13 919	4 240.7	628.6	2 618	56 542	3 088.6	919.0
Pasco	875	D	D	D	211	3 057	745.2	122.8	581	10 306	432.4	126.7
Pinellas	4 036	D	D	D	1 121	33 564	8 062.0	1 483.6	2 060	37 374	1 925.1	545.3
Polk	1 093	6 654	781.8	310.5	438	16 160	7 178.0	697.4	765	16 084	699.6	199.4

1. Establishment subject to federal tax.

Table B. States and Counties — **Health Care and Social Assistance, Other Services, and Federal Funds**

STATE County	Health care and social assistance, 2007				Other services, 2007				Federal funds and grants, 2009–2010 Expenditures (mil dol)			
									Total	Direct payments for individuals[1]		
	Number of establish-ments	Number of employees	Receipts (mil dol)	Annual payroll (mil dol)	Number of establish-ments	Number of employees	Receipts (mil dol)	Annual payroll (mil dol)		Social Security and government retirement	Medicare	Food Stamps and Supplemental Security Income
	159	160	161	162	163	164	165	166	167	168	169	170
CONNECTICUT—Cont'd												
Tolland	297	5 867	434.0	197.6	201	1 517	177.9	39.1	948.1	351.7	324.7	12.0
Windham	274	7 016	501.3	228.1	179	732	62.2	17.4	1 262.9	330.9	655.7	32.2
DELAWARE	2 379	54 740	5 430.9	2 370.5	1 587	10 012	898.4	264.6	8 076.3	2 957.4	1 149.8	269.6
Kent	354	7 773	672.8	269.3	249	1 460	100.8	32.3	2 016.4	584.1	142.1	46.2
New Castle	1 517	37 843	3 886.5	1 750.7	982	6 854	671.1	195.4	4 010.3	1 475.4	716.4	169.7
Sussex	508	9 124	871.6	350.6	356	1 698	126.5	36.8	1 614.8	897.7	291.3	53.7
DISTRICT OF COLUMBIA..	2 130	61 075	7 250.2	2 942.1	3 284	49 853	15 499.7	3 154.3	61 919.8	2 623.8	1 280.2	358.8
District of Columbia	2 130	61 075	7 250.2	2 942.1	3 284	49 853	15 499.7	3 154.3	61 919.8	2 623.8	1 280.2	358.8
FLORIDA	51 679	904 004	102 029.3	37 234.1	35 597	201 687	20 757.0	5 173.7	186 703.8	61 447.7	46 593.9	7 344.1
Alachua	708	D	D	D	379	2 781	655.1	87.6	2 382.5	652.3	441.7	104.7
Baker	39	1 844	109.1	65.5	30	D	D	D	158.1	73.8	38.8	12.4
Bay	493	9 501	985.3	354.0	315	1 767	122.2	38.1	2 261.4	730.5	337.2	74.5
Bradford	38	913	59.5	26.4	28	139	11.0	3.1	346.7	80.4	68.1	15.5
Brevard	1 417	26 415	2 796.8	1 085.6	1 039	4 868	395.3	121.0	8 154.8	2 539.4	1 110.3	165.0
Broward	5 732	88 155	10 883.5	3 647.7	4 174	22 705	2 171.8	586.7	12 480.1	4 158.7	4 960.3	545.3
Calhoun	28	525	29.7	12.6	7	D	D	D	132.1	39.3	44.3	8.7
Charlotte	474	7 731	897.1	308.2	275	1 186	90.0	24.7	1 438.9	829.2	490.9	31.4
Citrus	340	6 762	661.8	239.8	221	857	52.8	16.3	1 313.3	779.9	398.5	44.8
Clay	376	6 167	611.2	227.6	288	1 423	89.0	29.3	1 111.8	747.9	169.7	31.9
Collier	914	14 861	1 796.1	703.8	828	4 364	393.3	113.0	2 069.4	1 202.8	492.5	54.2
Columbia	155	3 542	372.3	149.5	82	340	29.7	6.6	648.1	253.0	145.2	41.2
DeSoto	53	1 134	96.7	39.1	23	82	4.2	1.3	249.7	90.7	96.9	16.7
Dixie	12	D	D	D	8	25	1.8	0.5	127.7	60.4	34.5	11.5
Duval	2 292	52 877	5 928.8	2 230.4	1 745	11 590	1 242.6	358.0	9 298.6	2 704.4	1 759.9	371.3
Escambia	751	19 847	2 101.2	785.1	477	2 727	229.0	69.1	3 839.2	1 364.1	699.8	161.7
Flagler	149	1 807	175.1	70.7	126	484	35.2	9.4	631.4	469.7	101.0	17.6
Franklin	24	D	D	D	22	99	5.9	1.9	112.0	38.3	42.5	4.7
Gadsden	60	D	D	D	42	147	11.2	3.2	509.9	134.4	151.2	44.6
Gilchrist	21	D	D	D	11	25	3.0	0.7	108.2	57.6	25.5	6.5
Glades	9	D	D	D	6	25	1.5	0.4	47.4	21.9	14.0	0.3
Gulf	25	387	18.1	8.5	18	93	4.4	1.1	150.5	58.7	52.9	7.3
Hamilton	19	275	14.3	5.8	12	41	2.6	0.7	128.8	43.9	38.9	8.5
Hardee	59	1 242	82.1	35.1	28	71	4.9	1.3	226.8	55.0	52.1	20.2
Hendry	63	843	55.0	23.6	49	170	12.3	3.2	283.3	76.9	61.9	25.2
Hernando	411	6 711	741.9	248.6	230	1 115	65.9	21.1	1 619.8	915.0	520.6	58.3
Highlands	300	4 876	483.4	180.7	142	540	40.7	10.4	966.6	478.8	327.5	33.9
Hillsborough	3 248	63 269	7 585.5	2 791.8	2 065	16 278	1 576.0	415.9	11 330.2	3 202.8	2 213.7	521.9
Holmes	33	623	31.4	14.7	16	55	4.4	1.3	236.2	74.6	74.0	14.6
Indian River	446	7 230	836.4	300.9	264	1 169	97.0	26.7	1 224.1	654.7	422.4	26.9
Jackson	91	1 819	135.0	54.3	56	297	27.7	6.9	614.0	181.8	182.0	26.8
Jefferson	27	D	D	D	15	62	2.4	0.8	157.1	46.4	48.1	10.4
Lafayette	10	D	D	D	5	D	D	D	42.8	15.1	11.8	2.5
Lake	704	13 216	1 382.3	533.6	450	1 864	145.2	43.3	2 918.9	1 921.0	644.8	84.4
Lee	1 389	25 867	3 068.2	1 115.8	1 206	6 552	589.9	162.5	4 275.2	2 289.1	1 205.1	133.0
Leon	676	15 657	1 691.6	614.8	629	4 537	704.3	161.8	8 324.6	646.7	314.7	90.5
Levy	59	583	34.1	13.8	61	156	13.3	2.8	327.2	152.9	87.5	19.8
Liberty	11	D	D	D	3	D	D	D	60.7	19.6	18.4	4.0
Madison	39	754	42.5	17.9	21	63	4.5	1.4	224.5	61.5	73.8	13.4
Manatee	793	12 166	1 279.6	448.6	524	2 524	167.0	48.4	2 496.2	1 153.1	688.4	82.8
Marion	817	14 493	1 590.4	566.1	467	2 408	201.6	51.4	2 844.7	1 621.9	717.0	121.2
Martin	506	8 500	859.2	340.2	379	2 024	155.2	49.0	1 188.6	645.1	404.3	28.3
Miami-Dade	8 311	120 152	15 042.3	5 194.3	5 065	27 878	3 185.8	659.3	27 110.5	4 568.7	9 894.6	1 956.9
Monroe	210	2 293	264.8	91.3	257	1 118	110.4	28.1	839.0	249.5	194.7	23.8
Nassau	131	1 974	161.7	63.9	106	D	D	D	671.8	295.9	101.0	17.0
Okaloosa	499	8 357	845.8	312.4	393	2 053	166.4	46.1	3 812.1	1 006.3	281.1	43.9
Okeechobee	103	1 591	153.7	50.6	55	235	16.9	4.8	353.5	134.2	128.7	15.3
Orange	2 611	57 144	5 905.1	2 466.0	2 012	15 428	1 610.4	450.9	10 500.4	2 435.0	1 618.2	397.2
Osceola	407	7 041	965.6	297.2	329	1 411	156.7	33.0	1 243.5	712.1	283.0	107.2
Palm Beach	4 815	67 881	8 382.6	2 978.3	3 180	17 714	1 812.2	460.1	10 665.1	4 385.8	3 739.3	307.3
Pasco	1 016	15 549	1 718.4	624.2	638	2 901	211.0	61.0	3 440.6	1 620.0	1 279.7	119.9
Pinellas	3 194	61 564	6 733.7	2 496.3	2 104	10 928	963.9	283.2	10 365.3	3 904.9	3 329.4	326.1
Polk	971	24 347	2 613.7	926.8	727	3 850	323.5	94.6	4 156.6	1 954.4	1 105.1	266.6

1. State totals may include programs not allocated by county.

Table B. States and Counties — Federal Funds, Residential Construction, and Local Government Finances

	Federal funds and grants, 2009–2010 (cont.)							Value of residential construction authorized by building permits, 2010		Local government finances, 2007				
	Expenditures (mil dol) (cont.)									General revenue				
		Procurement contract awards		Grants[1]								Taxes		
													Per capita[2] (dollars)	
STATE County	Salaries and wages	Defense	Other	Medicaid and other health-related	Nutrition and family welfare	Education	Other	New construction ($1,000)	Number of housing units	Total (mil dol)	Inter-govern-mental (mil dol)	Total (mil dol)	Total	Property
	171	172	173	174	175	176	177	178	179	180	181	182	183	184
CONNECTICUT—Cont'd														
Tolland	32.0	11.4	7.1	84.0	14.8	15.5	62.0	35 611	190	472.6	169.4	255.4	1 724	1 702
Windham	33.0	10.1	5.7	132.2	20.2	8.2	8.7	22 920	200	403.6	205.6	164.2	1 403	1 382
DELAWARE	707.6	218.1	144.5	983.3	207.3	285.8	578.8	364 135	3 072	X	X	X	X	X
Kent	309.0	144.0	10.1	177.8	24.9	223.7	297.7	95 156	813	410.9	241.0	85.8	564	439
New Castle	322.4	71.5	120.9	613.1	106.0	32.6	261.5	55 885	705	1 559.8	739.2	503.8	954	744
Sussex	76.2	2.7	13.5	192.4	22.8	21.0	14.6	213 094	1 554	628.9	320.9	162.8	883	592
DISTRICT OF COLUMBIA	23 029.5	4 651.0	16 598.9	2 282.6	377.8	730.2	7 481.4	105 471	739	X	X	X	X	X
District of Columbia	23 029.5	4 651.0	16 598.9	2 282.6	377.8	730.2	7 481.4	105 471	739	9 746.6	2 999.0	5 192.2	8 826	2 577
FLORIDA	12 964.5	12 814.2	5 166.5	14 386.2	3 377.4	3 471.7	6 831.1	7 823 543	38 679	X	X	X	X	X
Alachua	222.8	16.6	158.6	444.6	39.0	24.3	173.3	58 430	454	879.0	308.3	303.4	1 264	977
Baker	5.7	0.0	2.6	15.4	5.1	2.4	0.9	5 968	35	78.3	41.3	19.6	762	458
Bay	420.0	425.6	56.4	109.4	33.1	14.2	12.5	39 714	309	877.5	228.1	282.9	1 725	1 267
Bradford	134.1	6.0	1.1	33.0	5.4	1.7	0.3	2 076	31	76.0	42.8	20.2	703	465
Brevard	617.8	2 092.1	1 237.4	154.1	63.8	28.4	65.6	248 553	1 144	1 940.6	575.9	770.6	1 437	1 095
Broward	672.6	202.1	285.6	601.0	203.9	104.8	326.9	222 589	1 168	10 074.0	2 472.5	3 722.3	2 115	1 746
Calhoun	2.7	0.0	0.9	29.2	2.8	1.2	1.0	2 272	17	47.7	37.4	6.3	467	330
Charlotte	26.1	0.8	5.5	16.6	19.3	4.9	5.5	59 444	425	668.6	125.2	347.4	2 273	1 705
Citrus	18.8	2.0	4.4	34.3	15.4	6.7	3.8	38 783	199	373.7	114.1	198.3	1 414	1 165
Clay	28.7	15.8	34.2	32.2	17.3	8.8	3.1	86 117	551	614.7	277.7	180.9	994	747
Collier	53.2	61.7	19.9	63.1	62.5	11.5	14.8	371 116	1 259	1 632.7	314.3	935.7	2 963	2 487
Columbia	56.7	2.7	40.9	71.6	15.9	5.5	5.4	10 493	84	196.2	108.9	56.3	828	564
DeSoto	3.5	0.1	0.8	24.6	6.6	3.0	0.9	14 481	96	126.6	62.6	34.8	1 004	657
Dixie	1.3	0.0	0.3	13.4	3.9	1.4	0.4	2 323	18	43.6	24.2	13.0	872	719
Duval	1 367.7	899.9	287.6	768.0	148.7	91.8	255.8	260 241	1 501	3 373.9	1 176.6	1 176.3	1 385	982
Escambia	455.2	482.4	154.1	310.1	60.8	28.6	50.1	132 838	973	1 092.9	466.7	327.9	1 070	727
Flagler	13.8	0.4	3.2	7.1	6.8	2.9	4.1	51 882	278	366.4	107.4	156.2	1 767	1 578
Franklin	2.0	0.7	0.4	18.7	2.7	1.0	0.3	1 199	6	74.6	27.2	34.0	3 385	3 140
Gadsden	11.9	13.1	1.6	107.1	16.5	7.2	17.6	14 768	89	129.1	73.7	33.6	713	429
Gilchrist	2.6	0.0	0.7	9.8	3.2	0.8	0.5	5 277	36	43.3	25.2	12.0	703	566
Glades	1.5	0.3	0.2	2.6	1.5	1.1	0.0	1 090	8	33.0	13.9	13.4	1 208	1 011
Gulf	1.4	0.0	0.3	21.1	5.1	1.2	0.2	10 629	45	63.0	17.7	31.1	2 215	2 035
Hamilton	2.4	0.0	0.5	27.0	3.5	2.4	0.0	1 774	22	88.0	54.0	19.2	1 345	1 124
Hardee	15.0	0.0	0.9	29.2	6.9	2.5	3.0	1 209	12	83.1	42.7	30.3	1 052	859
Hendry	4.4	56.3	0.6	22.5	9.1	2.8	9.3	2 431	22	173.9	58.1	62.1	1 567	1 117
Hernando	27.4	7.1	6.6	38.4	26.5	6.8	3.4	32 102	242	769.7	222.7	387.4	2 291	2 043
Highlands	21.7	6.7	4.3	47.0	13.6	6.3	4.1	26 374	154	285.9	117.4	111.1	1 118	880
Hillsborough	1 636.3	1 144.0	688.4	991.9	182.6	110.8	271.3	926 635	3 950	5 300.4	2 140.9	1 956.4	1 665	1 265
Holmes	12.2	0.2	0.9	45.5	6.8	1.6	3.4	2 633	16	63.2	37.6	10.9	565	295
Indian River	33.2	0.1	10.4	38.1	17.6	6.6	5.8	103 644	307	581.3	109.6	324.0	2 458	1 835
Jackson	43.1	0.1	5.7	129.2	12.3	4.4	7.8	6 936	58	220.3	96.3	32.6	662	353
Jefferson	3.0	0.0	0.6	38.4	3.5	1.6	1.1	3 300	21	35.8	19.7	13.0	898	587
Lafayette	1.2	2.9	0.3	5.6	1.4	0.5	0.2	3 448	19	18.0	11.7	4.2	521	422
Lake	58.1	5.4	25.7	84.7	30.5	16.1	25.5	142 336	552	1 014.6	287.3	370.0	1 229	927
Lee	190.7	4.9	41.8	138.2	62.1	27.1	94.8	239 578	1 276	3 868.3	890.3	1 485.2	2 515	2 088
Leon	187.2	28.9	34.9	680.4	620.2	2 155.9	3 323.9	61 231	434	1 107.2	417.3	357.6	1 370	1 014
Levy	8.9	0.1	1.8	31.7	6.9	5.5	7.1	7 146	56	115.2	52.4	42.8	1 096	902
Liberty	2.6	0.0	0.9	13.0	1.3	0.7	0.0	1 114	12	26.9	19.2	4.5	574	466
Madison	3.4	0.0	1.2	55.2	5.5	3.3	1.3	3 367	27	85.3	45.2	15.9	840	620
Manatee	99.7	212.6	18.5	96.2	41.0	18.7	34.7	238 584	1 247	1 320.2	336.3	547.9	1 739	1 557
Marion	57.6	15.9	17.1	163.8	42.2	18.5	24.2	88 836	481	968.0	357.1	320.2	986	783
Martin	24.8	4.0	9.3	31.7	17.9	5.5	11.8	87 767	199	600.8	145.7	335.9	2 413	2 086
Miami-Dade	1 812.5	396.7	472.7	5 786.5	443.0	166.9	1 018.8	395 139	3 203	14 420.4	4 219.0	5 277.1	2 211	1 651
Monroe	194.8	67.5	15.2	59.6	11.0	4.9	10.7	72 118	271	555.6	152.3	250.2	3 416	2 591
Nassau	198.6	3.6	2.5	35.1	8.6	3.2	3.1	62 622	251	256.3	72.9	129.7	1 895	1 558
Okaloosa	868.9	1 397.5	25.3	84.9	28.9	14.3	25.7	122 079	547	652.5	245.8	266.4	1 468	1 264
Okeechobee	6.3	11.6	1.6	29.5	7.8	3.4	2.3	11 118	48	141.7	74.5	37.4	927	791
Orange	827.1	3 417.4	568.4	467.5	142.8	86.8	219.7	636 208	2 880	5 766.6	1 741.8	2 115.7	1 984	1 352
Osceola	32.8	6.3	7.2	32.2	24.9	13.4	11.0	162 696	892	1 213.1	336.5	456.7	1 785	1 166
Palm Beach	463.0	446.9	309.7	401.8	160.8	57.8	230.1	410 539	1 506	7 017.5	1 555.2	3 682.6	2 908	2 513
Pasco	118.3	17.6	15.0	114.3	53.2	20.1	17.6	212 194	1 612	1 400.0	532.5	500.5	1 082	760
Pinellas	618.1	978.1	331.9	393.4	124.9	56.7	136.9	118 339	697	3 780.7	1 010.6	1 748.4	1 906	1 530
Polk	153.2	49.3	24.1	306.9	97.8	47.9	49.1	208 680	1 200	2 004.3	841.8	655.6	1 141	856

1. State totals may include programs not allocated by county.   2. Based on the resident population estimated as of July 1 of the year shown.

Table B. States and Counties — Local Government Finances, Government Employment, and Voting

STATE County	Total (mil dol)	Per capita¹ (dollars)	Education	Health and hospitals	Police protection	Public welfare	Highways	Total (mil dol)	Per capita¹ (dollars)	Federal civilian	Federal military	State and local	Democratic	Republican	All other
	185	186	187	188	189	190	191	192	193	194	195	196	197	198	199
CONNECTICUT—Cont'd															
Tolland	463.8	3 131	65.8	0.4	2.5	0.6	4.1	305.4	2 062	314	296	14 601	59.6	38.8	1.6
Windham	380.0	3 247	72.0	0.5	2.7	0.3	4.2	167.6	1 432	290	223	7 901	60.7	37.7	1.6
DELAWARE	X	X	X	X	X	X	X	X	X	5 723	8 464	57 627	61.9	36.9	1.1
Kent	421.6	2 769	68.9	0.9	5.1	0.0	1.8	243.8	1 601	1 721	4 275	16 860	54.4	44.6	1.1
New Castle	1 767.4	3 346	58.5	0.8	8.9	0.0	0.9	1 463.8	2 771	3 444	3 066	33 155	69.7	29.1	1.2
Sussex	577.3	3 133	62.5	3.1	4.7	0.0	2.7	433.1	2 350	558	1 123	7 612	45.2	53.8	0.9
DISTRICT OF COLUMBIA..	X	X	X	X	X	X	X	X	X	198 567	19 524	40 697	92.5	6.5	1.0
District of Columbia	8 490.4	14 432	18.2	6.3	5.9	25.5	1.2	10 769.8	18 307	198 567	19 524	40 697	92.5	6.5	1.0
FLORIDA	X	X	X	X	X	X	X	X	X	132 904	99 415	971 706	51.0	48.2	0.8
Alachua	860.4	3 584	41.4	2.6	8.6	0.7	3.1	1 728.0	7 197	4 215	562	38 464	60.2	38.6	1.1
Baker	71.8	2 789	58.9	3.7	6.5	0.8	6.2	35.5	1 378	69	52	2 721	21.0	78.4	0.5
Bay	846.1	5 159	36.6	29.6	5.2	0.0	3.0	797.3	4 862	3 533	4 327	10 618	29.2	69.9	1.0
Bradford	80.3	2 790	47.4	3.4	4.6	0.0	8.8	18.7	651	38	121	2 470	29.4	69.7	0.9
Brevard	1 977.4	3 688	44.4	8.3	6.0	0.3	4.8	2 145.2	4 001	6 282	2 955	23 127	44.3	54.7	0.9
Broward	10 081.9	5 730	30.6	21.2	8.5	1.5	1.6	9 068.5	5 154	7 821	3 887	94 091	67.1	32.4	0.5
Calhoun	48.6	3 575	43.0	1.4	3.8	0.6	27.8	2.1	153	25	27	1 021	29.2	69.6	1.2
Charlotte	645.6	4 225	30.2	3.1	8.6	1.3	9.5	627.2	4 104	280	312	5 930	45.8	53.1	1.1
Citrus	364.3	2 599	45.6	4.9	7.3	1.9	7.4	383.9	2 739	213	278	4 734	41.3	57.4	1.3
Clay	541.8	2 977	57.3	0.9	6.8	0.5	3.3	495.4	2 721	373	368	7 172	28.2	71.1	0.7
Collier	1 757.0	5 563	38.1	2.3	8.8	0.2	8.2	3 007.6	9 523	673	630	12 293	38.3	60.8	0.8
Columbia	191.4	2 815	61.7	3.7	4.9	0.2	7.0	63.2	929	1 177	138	4 710	32.6	66.4	1.0
DeSoto	105.3	3 038	45.7	2.0	6.4	0.6	4.7	52.9	1 526	47	70	2 221	43.3	55.6	1.1
Dixie	41.6	2 782	49.6	6.6	6.2	0.0	6.0	11.8	788	17	29	987	26.5	71.5	2.0
Duval	3 152.0	3 712	43.1	0.7	5.9	2.6	2.7	12 819.4	15 097	15 947	17 997	38 784	48.7	50.6	0.6
Escambia	1 136.7	3 710	42.8	4.8	5.6	0.4	4.2	1 783.8	5 822	5 814	13 223	15 929	39.9	59.2	0.9
Flagler	414.3	4 686	35.3	1.3	4.2	0.2	7.2	447.0	5 057	157	181	3 580	50.4	48.8	0.7
Franklin	71.6	7 138	51.9	7.8	7.9	0.1	6.4	78.9	7 869	16	33	1 078	35.4	63.3	1.3
Gadsden	137.5	2 914	57.6	0.9	5.8	0.7	8.9	31.2	661	118	94	5 143	69.2	30.3	0.5
Gilchrist	45.8	2 690	57.6	2.6	5.4	0.6	7.7	4.9	285	36	34	1 127	25.5	72.3	2.1
Glades	36.5	3 287	50.8	3.0	11.3	0.1	4.0	5.8	523	13	22	519	41.1	57.7	1.2
Gulf	57.3	4 074	36.8	7.1	7.8	0.3	7.6	20.8	1 482	18	31	1 438	29.8	69.1	1.1
Hamilton	74.3	5 198	26.4	1.8	4.1	0.2	13.1	5.6	395	34	29	1 323	42.3	56.9	0.8
Hardee	89.3	3 099	54.0	1.8	10.9	0.0	7.7	14.9	518	50	58	1 681	34.6	64.3	1.1
Hendry	171.9	4 340	43.4	13.1	5.1	1.8	5.0	47.4	1 197	87	78	2 359	45.9	53.1	0.9
Hernando	653.7	3 866	36.0	1.3	4.4	0.1	4.7	658.1	3 893	376	338	6 118	47.7	51.2	1.1
Highlands	291.4	2 933	56.7	2.2	7.1	0.3	4.5	217.9	2 193	251	196	4 052	40.5	58.6	1.0
Hillsborough	4 899.7	4 171	40.9	2.3	6.6	2.4	3.6	6 543.0	5 670	14 460	8 236	65 818	53.2	46.0	0.8
Holmes	60.1	3 124	48.0	12.9	4.3	0.7	7.3	13.0	676	62	38	1 368	16.8	81.9	1.3
Indian River	528.1	4 006	36.5	3.8	7.4	0.6	7.4	540.1	4 097	408	267	5 443	42.1	56.9	1.0
Jackson	202.4	4 106	43.1	31.3	3.3	0.0	6.8	59.4	1 205	480	105	5 376	35.6	63.6	0.8
Jefferson	36.7	2 536	43.4	2.3	9.1	0.0	8.2	8.4	578	41	35	784	51.4	47.7	0.9
Lafayette	18.3	2 285	59.7	4.6	3.5	0.6	5.5	4.3	542	19	16	730	19.1	79.8	1.1
Lake	1 081.5	3 592	42.9	8.4	5.7	0.4	5.3	1 563.5	5 193	624	617	12 862	42.8	56.4	0.8
Lee	3 524.7	5 968	29.1	19.2	4.5	0.4	5.9	4 370.1	7 400	2 483	1 223	33 380	44.5	54.8	0.7
Leon	1 113.7	4 268	41.4	0.9	6.3	0.0	10.2	3 166.0	12 133	1 737	626	52 155	61.7	37.5	0.8
Levy	110.7	2 835	53.9	3.9	8.1	0.7	4.8	27.9	715	80	110	1 988	35.8	62.8	1.4
Liberty	26.0	3 306	60.0	1.8	4.1	1.3	12.1	6.4	819	41	16	823	27.3	71.4	1.3
Madison	87.8	4 633	50.2	12.8	6.7	0.4	3.5	26.1	1 375	49	37	1 429	47.9	51.0	1.0
Manatee	1 493.6	4 740	42.3	1.5	6.5	1.7	3.6	1 825.9	5 795	923	659	11 404	46.1	53.1	0.8
Marion	959.0	2 952	50.3	1.7	10.2	0.7	8.4	760.8	2 342	742	652	16 843	43.7	55.3	1.0
Martin	568.8	4 086	35.2	5.6	8.1	1.6	3.9	377.9	2 715	267	282	5 612	42.8	56.4	0.8
Miami-Dade	14 688.6	6 153	33.7	10.0	6.5	3.0	2.0	20 249.0	8 482	19 895	7 341	130 927	57.9	41.8	0.4
Monroe	599.5	8 187	30.1	4.1	17.2	0.6	2.2	556.4	7 598	1 252	1 543	4 898	51.9	47.0	1.1
Nassau	234.8	3 430	40.2	3.6	6.3	1.1	6.5	241.6	3 529	623	139	2 868	27.7	71.5	0.7
Okaloosa	652.0	3 592	50.0	1.8	7.1	0.3	4.7	355.6	1 959	7 149	15 029	8 050	27.1	72.0	0.9
Okeechobee	129.5	3 212	49.4	0.9	13.0	1.1	5.5	47.2	1 170	75	79	2 257	39.9	59.1	0.9
Orange	5 375.1	5 042	38.8	3.3	6.1	0.7	4.7	10 479.2	9 829	9 535	2 446	60 858	59.0	40.4	0.6
Osceola	1 207.3	4 720	41.1	1.6	5.8	2.1	6.6	2 077.6	8 121	408	536	11 453	59.6	39.8	0.6
Palm Beach	6 853.8	5 412	32.9	3.3	7.3	2.4	2.4	7 088.2	5 597	6 430	2 608	59 707	61.2	38.3	0.5
Pasco	1 443.0	3 119	53.3	1.5	5.0	0.3	4.2	1 492.2	3 225	863	932	16 098	47.7	51.2	1.1
Pinellas	3 564.2	3 885	35.9	2.9	9.6	3.4	3.2	3 766.6	4 106	7 067	2 982	38 844	53.6	45.3	1.1
Polk	1 985.5	3 455	50.8	2.7	6.7	0.9	6.0	2 648.1	4 607	1 378	1 157	28 275	46.5	52.6	0.9

1. Based on the resident population estimated as of July 1 of the year shown. 2. © 2009 Election Data Services, Inc. All rights reserved.

Table B. States and Counties — Land Area and Population

STATE/ County code	CBSA code[1]	County type[2]	STATE County	Land area,[3] (sq km) 2010	Total persons	Rank	Per square kilometer	White	Black	American Indian, Alaska Native	Asian and Pacific Islander	Percent Hispanic or Latino[4]	Under 5 years	5 to 17 years	18 to 24 years	25 to 34 years	35 to 44 years	45 to 54 years
										Race alone or in combination, not Hispanic or Latino (percent)				Age (percent)				
				1	2	3	4	5	6	7	8	9	10	11	12	13	14	15
			FLORIDA—Cont'd															
12 107	37260	4	Putnam	1 885	74 364	729	39.5	73.9	16.6	0.9	0.9	9.0	6.3	16.3	8.2	10.4	10.7	14.8
12 109	27260	1	St. Johns	1 556	190 039	327	122.1	86.7	6.0	0.6	2.8	5.2	5.3	17.8	7.7	9.8	13.5	16.2
12 111	38940	2	St. Lucie	1 481	277 789	232	187.6	62.4	19.5	0.6	2.1	16.6	5.9	16.4	7.7	10.8	12.5	14.1
12 113	37860	2	Santa Rosa	2 620	151 372	411	57.8	87.4	6.0	1.7	3.1	4.3	6.1	17.8	8.5	12.3	13.8	16.4
12 115	35840	2	Sarasota	1 440	379 448	173	263.5	85.9	5.0	0.5	1.7	7.9	3.9	11.9	5.9	8.2	10.0	13.6
12 117	36740	1	Seminole	801	422 718	158	527.7	67.9	11.3	0.6	4.5	17.1	5.5	17.5	10.1	13.0	13.9	15.9
12 119	45540	4	Sumter	1 417	93 420	615	65.9	83.5	9.7	0.7	0.9	6.0	2.4	6.7	3.7	6.9	8.0	9.2
12 121	...	6	Suwannee	1 783	41 551	1 141	23.3	79.0	11.8	1.0	0.8	8.7	6.2	16.5	7.8	11.3	11.6	14.1
12 123	...	6	Taylor	2 702	22 570	1 708	8.4	74.5	21.1	1.6	0.9	3.4	5.7	14.0	8.6	13.3	13.5	15.4
12 125	...	6	Union	631	15 535	2 079	24.6	72.8	22.5	0.8	0.3	4.8	5.3	14.1	9.3	15.5	14.0	16.6
12 127	19660	2	Volusia	2 852	494 593	133	173.4	76.7	10.7	0.8	2.0	11.2	4.9	13.9	9.0	10.3	11.4	15.0
12 129	45220	2	Wakulla	1 571	30 776	1 416	19.6	81.0	15.0	1.2	0.9	3.3	5.7	16.8	7.9	13.9	15.5	16.8
12 131	...	6	Walton	2 687	55 043	910	20.5	87.0	6.2	1.8	1.5	5.3	6.1	14.5	7.6	12.6	12.9	15.8
12 133	...	6	Washington	1 509	24 896	1 604	16.5	80.1	15.6	2.1	0.9	2.9	5.8	15.4	8.7	12.9	14.0	15.3
13 000	...	X	GEORGIA	148 959	9 687 653	X	65.0	57.1	30.9	0.7	3.8	8.8	7.1	18.6	10.0	13.8	14.4	14.4
13 001	...	7	Appling	1 313	18 236	1 914	13.9	71.2	18.9	0.4	0.8	9.3	7.2	18.6	8.2	12.0	13.0	14.7
13 003	20060	9	Atkinson	879	8 375	2 580	9.5	57.7	17.5	0.7	0.5	24.3	8.5	20.6	9.6	13.7	13.6	13.1
13 005	...	7	Bacon	670	11 096	2 358	16.6	77.0	16.0	0.3	0.5	7.1	7.4	18.0	8.5	13.4	13.6	13.0
13 007	10500	3	Baker	886	3 451	2 944	3.9	48.3	47.1	0.5	0.8	4.2	6.4	16.8	8.5	10.4	12.2	15.1
13 009	33300	4	Baldwin	668	45 720	1 054	68.4	54.9	41.9	0.5	1.6	2.0	6.1	14.4	18.4	12.1	11.3	13.9
13 011	...	8	Banks	601	18 395	1 905	30.6	90.9	2.6	0.8	1.1	5.7	6.2	19.1	8.5	11.4	14.5	15.3
13 013	12060	1	Barrow	415	69 367	764	167.1	76.1	12.1	0.7	3.9	8.7	8.4	19.8	8.3	15.5	15.0	13.6
13 015	12060	1	Bartow	1 190	100 157	578	84.2	81.1	10.8	0.8	1.1	7.7	7.0	19.8	8.7	12.8	15.1	14.9
13 017	22340	7	Ben Hill	648	17 634	1 942	27.2	58.5	35.1	0.7	0.8	5.8	7.9	18.5	8.6	12.4	12.2	13.8
13 019	...	6	Berrien	1 170	19 286	1 865	16.5	84.0	10.9	0.6	0.7	4.6	6.9	18.7	8.7	12.0	13.5	14.4
13 021	31420	3	Bibb	647	155 547	401	240.4	43.0	52.7	0.5	2.0	2.8	7.4	18.4	10.6	13.0	12.2	13.9
13 023	...	6	Bleckley	559	13 063	2 241	23.4	69.6	27.5	0.4	1.0	2.3	5.8	16.8	16.5	10.1	11.3	13.7
13 025	15260	3	Brantley	1 146	18 411	1 903	16.1	94.6	3.2	1.1	0.3	1.9	7.2	19.4	8.4	11.5	13.9	14.8
13 027	46660	3	Brooks	1 277	16 243	2 038	12.7	58.9	35.4	0.8	0.5	5.3	6.7	17.0	8.6	11.1	12.4	14.9
13 029	42340	2	Bryan	1 129	30 233	1 423	26.8	79.4	14.9	0.8	2.4	4.4	7.3	22.0	7.7	12.1	14.9	15.9
13 031	44340	4	Bulloch	1 743	70 217	756	40.3	67.0	28.2	0.6	1.9	3.5	6.0	14.5	27.9	12.5	10.3	10.9
13 033	12260	2	Burke	2 142	23 316	1 679	10.9	47.4	49.9	0.6	0.6	2.6	7.6	20.6	9.2	11.5	12.1	14.7
13 035	12060	1	Butts	478	23 655	1 659	49.5	69.4	27.7	0.6	0.7	2.5	6.0	16.5	9.5	13.8	14.2	15.3
13 037	...	8	Calhoun	726	6 694	2 714	9.2	34.1	61.7	0.3	0.6	3.9	5.5	14.2	9.1	15.8	15.6	15.8
13 039	41220	4	Camden	1 588	50 513	969	31.8	73.4	20.4	1.2	2.4	5.1	7.9	19.1	13.0	14.4	13.0	13.7
13 043	...	7	Candler	629	10 998	2 365	17.5	63.8	24.7	0.3	0.7	11.2	7.2	18.5	9.5	11.8	12.2	13.3
13 045	12060	1	Carroll	1 293	110 527	535	85.5	74.5	19.1	0.7	1.1	6.2	7.1	18.4	13.1	13.3	13.3	13.3
13 047	16860	2	Catoosa	420	63 942	816	152.2	93.9	2.7	0.9	1.6	2.3	6.4	18.5	8.1	12.3	14.6	14.4
13 049	...	6	Charlton	2 004	12 171	2 294	6.1	68.0	29.1	1.0	0.9	2.5	6.0	15.7	9.5	14.2	15.2	16.0
13 051	42340	2	Chatham	1 104	265 128	246	240.2	51.7	40.7	0.7	3.1	5.4	7.0	15.6	13.1	15.4	12.0	13.1
13 053	17980	2	Chattahoochee	644	11 267	2 346	17.5	65.8	19.6	1.3	4.2	12.4	9.5	17.6	26.3	21.3	11.3	6.3
13 055	44900	6	Chattooga	812	26 015	1 563	32.0	84.1	11.8	0.6	0.6	4.0	6.1	16.5	8.5	13.0	13.9	14.9
13 057	12060	1	Cherokee	1 092	214 346	290	196.3	82.7	6.1	0.7	2.3	9.6	7.4	20.1	7.7	12.9	16.5	15.4
13 059	12020	3	Clarke	309	116 714	512	377.7	58.5	27.1	0.5	4.9	10.4	6.0	11.5	30.4	16.8	10.1	8.9
13 061	...	9	Clay	506	3 183	2 964	6.3	38.0	61.0	0.5	0.5	0.8	6.4	16.1	7.9	9.5	8.9	14.1
13 063	12060	1	Clayton	367	259 424	251	706.9	15.2	66.5	0.7	5.5	13.7	8.5	20.4	10.7	15.4	15.4	13.8
13 065	...	6	Clinch	2 073	6 798	2 705	3.3	67.8	28.3	0.9	0.5	3.5	7.7	19.4	9.1	11.4	12.7	14.0
13 067	12060	1	Cobb	879	688 078	86	782.8	57.9	25.5	0.7	5.2	12.3	7.0	18.6	9.1	14.7	15.8	15.2
13 069	20060	7	Coffee	1 489	42 356	1 119	28.4	62.1	27.2	0.5	0.9	10.3	7.3	18.9	10.4	13.7	14.0	13.6
13 071	34220	6	Colquitt	1 409	45 498	1 057	32.3	59.5	22.8	0.5	0.8	17.1	8.3	19.3	9.6	13.0	13.2	12.8
13 073	12260	2	Columbia	751	124 053	489	165.2	75.8	15.6	0.8	5.0	5.0	6.7	20.6	8.1	12.3	14.5	15.6
13 075	...	6	Cook	588	17 212	1 970	29.3	65.7	27.7	0.6	0.9	5.9	7.6	19.6	8.9	12.3	13.0	13.4
13 077	12060	1	Coweta	1 142	127 317	481	111.5	74.2	17.8	0.8	2.1	6.7	7.3	20.1	7.6	12.7	15.7	15.0
13 079	31420	3	Crawford	841	12 630	2 268	15.0	74.5	22.9	0.9	0.4	2.4	5.8	16.9	8.4	10.5	13.9	17.3
13 081	18380	6	Crisp	706	23 439	1 668	33.2	52.9	43.4	0.3	1.1	3.2	7.2	18.9	8.6	11.7	12.1	14.0
13 083	16860	2	Dade	451	16 633	2 007	36.9	96.1	1.1	1.1	0.9	1.8	5.5	16.1	12.6	11.0	12.2	15.0
13 085	12060	1	Dawson	546	22 330	1 720	40.9	94.4	0.7	1.0	0.9	4.1	5.7	17.1	8.3	11.5	13.6	15.3
13 087	12460	6	Decatur	1 547	27 842	1 500	18.0	53.2	41.3	0.6	0.6	5.0	6.7	18.7	9.3	12.0	12.7	14.6
13 089	12060	1	DeKalb	693	691 893	85	998.4	30.5	54.7	0.6	5.8	9.8	7.3	16.6	10.1	17.1	15.5	13.9
13 091	...	7	Dodge	1 284	21 796	1 744	17.0	66.2	30.2	0.5	0.6	3.4	6.2	17.1	10.2	12.1	14.0	14.5
13 093	...	6	Dooly	1 015	14 918	2 116	14.7	43.8	49.9	0.3	0.9	5.8	5.7	15.4	8.3	14.0	13.8	15.2
13 095	10500	3	Dougherty	851	94 565	609	111.1	29.6	67.6	0.6	1.1	2.2	7.6	18.2	13.1	13.2	11.4	12.8
13 097	12060	1	Douglas	518	132 403	464	255.6	50.4	40.1	0.8	1.9	8.4	7.4	21.0	8.4	13.2	16.6	14.7
13 099	...	6	Early	1 328	11 008	2 363	8.3	48.1	49.9	0.6	0.5	1.6	6.5	19.8	8.2	10.6	12.0	14.1
13 101	46660	3	Echols	1 075	4 034	2 904	3.8	64.7	4.3	2.3	0.4	29.3	8.9	20.5	10.0	15.7	13.6	12.2

1. CBSA = Core Based Statistical Area. See Appendix A for explanation. See Appendix B for list of metropolitan areas with component counties. 2. County type code from the Economic Research Service of USDA Rural-Urban Continuum Codes. See Appendix A for definition. 3. Dry land or land partially or temporarily covered by water. 4. May be of any race.

Table B. States and Counties — **Population and Households**

STATE County	55 to 64 years	65 to 74 years	75 years and over	Percent female	1990	2000	1990–2000	2000–2010	Births	Deaths	Net migration	Number	Percent change, 2000–2010	Persons per house-hold	Female family house-holder[1]	One per-son
	16	17	18	19	20	21	22	23	24	25	26	27	28	29	30	31
FLORIDA—Cont'd																
Putnam	14.4	10.7	8.2	50.4	65 070	70 423	8.2	5.6	9 078	8 412	2 254	29 409	5.6	2.48	14.4	26.8
St. Johns	14.0	8.8	6.9	51.4	83 829	123 135	46.9	54.3	15 029	11 759	61 015	75 338	51.8	2.49	9.6	23.7
St. Lucie	12.6	10.6	9.4	51.1	150 171	192 695	28.3	44.2	26 913	22 810	70 520	108 523	41.1	2.53	12.9	24.2
Santa Rosa	12.3	8.0	4.9	49.5	81 961	117 743	43.7	28.6	15 761	9 292	27 970	56 910	30.0	2.59	11.4	21.3
Sarasota	15.4	15.4	15.8	52.3	277 776	325 957	17.3	16.4	27 710	44 914	62 513	175 746	17.2	2.13	8.7	32.1
Seminole	12.1	6.5	5.5	51.6	287 521	365 196	27.0	15.8	43 393	25 119	31 979	164 706	18.0	2.55	13.5	24.7
Sumter	19.7	28.6	14.8	48.0	31 577	53 345	68.9	75.1	4 715	7 477	27 086	41 361	99.1	2.04	5.7	25.0
Suwannee	13.5	10.7	8.2	49.6	26 780	34 844	30.1	19.2	4 581	4 337	5 262	15 953	18.5	2.52	13.0	25.6
Taylor	13.8	9.5	6.1	44.4	17 111	19 256	12.5	17.2	2 306	1 979	1 877	7 920	10.4	2.44	14.5	26.9
Union	15.2	6.6	3.4	35.3	10 252	13 442	31.1	15.6	1 458	1 628	1 386	4 048	20.2	2.66	15.1	23.8
Volusia	14.3	10.9	10.2	51.1	370 737	443 343	19.6	11.6	45 857	55 622	64 614	208 236	12.7	2.31	12.1	29.5
Wakulla	12.5	6.9	4.0	44.8	14 202	22 863	61.0	34.6	2 814	1 935	9 123	10 490	24.1	2.61	13.3	22.3
Walton	14.2	9.9	6.3	48.8	27 759	40 601	46.3	35.6	5 391	4 345	13 582	22 301	34.8	2.38	11.1	27.6
Washington	12.6	9.4	6.0	45.5	16 919	20 973	24.0	18.7	2 315	2 354	3 094	8 864	11.8	2.50	13.0	25.6
GEORGIA	11.0	6.3	4.4	51.2	6 478 149	8 186 453	26.4	18.3	1 301 426	616 981	849 133	3 585 584	19.3	2.63	15.8	25.4
Appling	12.8	8.2	5.3	49.8	15 744	17 419	10.6	4.7	2 502	1 730	-71	6 969	5.5	2.56	12.6	26.3
Atkinson	10.4	6.8	3.8	49.4	6 213	7 609	22.5	10.1	1 447	657	-128	2 983	9.8	2.80	15.3	22.9
Bacon	12.7	8.0	5.4	50.5	9 566	10 103	5.6	9.8	1 447	1 123	230	4 214	9.9	2.56	14.8	25.7
Baker	15.2	8.6	6.7	51.5	3 615	4 074	12.7	-15.3	319	286	-493	1 372	-9.4	2.52	15.9	30.5
Baldwin	11.8	7.1	4.9	50.4	39 530	44 700	13.1	2.3	5 167	3 732	455	16 788	13.8	2.45	19.2	26.9
Banks	12.5	8.1	4.4	49.5	10 308	14 422	39.9	27.5	1 955	1 176	1 673	6 700	24.9	2.75	10.2	20.2
Barrow	10.0	5.6	3.7	50.7	29 721	46 144	55.3	50.3	9 636	3 873	20 291	23 971	46.6	2.88	13.4	18.8
Bartow	11.2	6.5	4.1	50.6	55 915	76 019	36.0	31.8	13 685	6 358	13 176	35 782	31.7	2.77	13.5	21.0
Ben Hill	12.5	7.9	6.1	52.1	16 245	17 484	7.6	0.9	2 855	1 936	-759	6 794	1.8	2.55	19.1	26.7
Berrien	12.0	8.3	5.5	50.7	14 153	16 235	14.7	18.8	2 393	1 613	102	7 443	18.9	2.57	13.6	25.2
Bibb	11.9	6.7	5.9	52.9	150 137	153 887	2.5	1.1	22 884	15 251	-4 592	60 295	1.1	2.48	22.0	30.3
Bleckley	10.8	8.1	7.0	52.4	10 430	11 666	11.9	12.0	1 398	1 138	987	4 660	6.6	2.49	15.5	26.5
Brantley	12.5	7.7	4.6	50.1	11 077	14 629	32.1	25.9	1 461	1 360	988	6 885	26.7	2.66	13.2	22.1
Brooks	13.5	9.1	6.7	51.4	15 898	16 450	6.8	-1.3	1 966	1 771	-209	6 457	4.9	2.52	16.8	27.6
Bryan	11.2	5.5	3.5	50.9	15 438	23 417	51.7	29.1	3 891	1 727	7 031	10 738	32.7	2.81	13.9	17.7
Bulloch	8.9	5.3	3.8	50.1	43 125	55 983	29.8	25.4	7 409	3 998	10 047	25 575	23.3	2.56	13.2	25.0
Burke	12.5	7.1	4.7	52.0	20 579	22 243	8.1	4.8	3 608	2 290	-629	8 533	7.5	2.70	24.1	24.3
Butts	12.2	7.5	5.1	47.1	15 326	19 522	27.4	21.2	2 848	1 904	3 927	7 881	22.1	2.70	15.6	21.8
Calhoun	12.0	5.8	6.1	40.9	5 013	6 320	26.1	5.9	856	670	-181	2 002	2.0	2.49	22.6	32.5
Camden	9.9	6.0	3.0	49.4	30 167	43 664	44.7	15.7	7 214	2 104	-353	18 047	22.7	2.69	14.3	20.1
Candler	13.2	8.6	5.8	50.6	7 744	9 577	23.7	14.8	1 670	1 139	619	4 041	19.7	2.65	15.7	25.5
Carroll	10.6	6.5	4.4	51.3	71 422	87 268	22.2	26.7	14 828	7 685	20 611	39 187	24.1	2.73	14.1	21.7
Catoosa	12.1	7.9	5.6	51.5	42 464	53 282	25.5	20.0	6 936	4 393	8 468	24 475	19.8	2.59	12.6	23.1
Charlton	10.8	7.9	4.8	43.7	8 496	10 282	21.0	18.4	1 161	753	67	3 927	17.5	2.64	15.2	23.1
Chatham	11.3	6.8	5.6	51.8	216 774	232 048	7.0	14.3	34 821	21 019	12 430	103 038	14.7	2.45	17.5	28.7
Chattahoochee	4.0	2.4	1.4	37.5	16 934	14 882	-12.1	-24.3	2 167	280	-2 499	2 686	-8.4	2.98	16.2	19.1
Chattooga	12.6	8.1	6.5	48.1	22 236	25 470	14.5	2.1	2 972	2 614	930	9 548	-0.3	2.52	14.0	26.6
Cherokee	10.9	5.9	3.3	50.6	90 204	141 903	57.3	51.1	28 400	8 539	53 761	75 936	53.4	2.80	10.1	18.8
Clarke	7.9	4.6	3.9	52.5	87 594	101 489	15.9	15.0	13 682	5 938	7 777	45 414	14.4	2.37	13.4	30.6
Clay	17.4	11.1	8.5	54.1	3 364	3 357	-0.2	-5.2	454	375	-315	1 331	-1.2	2.35	22.8	31.6
Clayton	9.2	4.2	2.5	52.1	181 436	236 517	30.4	9.7	43 477	12 744	10 012	90 633	10.2	2.82	25.3	25.4
Clinch	13.0	7.7	5.0	51.2	6 160	6 878	11.7	-1.2	1 047	687	-217	2 572	2.4	2.58	19.4	25.7
Cobb	10.8	5.2	3.5	51.4	447 745	607 751	35.7	13.2	99 312	31 328	43 014	260 056	14.3	2.61	13.0	25.6
Coffee	11.0	6.7	4.4	49.3	29 592	37 413	26.4	13.2	6 022	3 188	884	14 817	11.0	2.68	17.4	24.1
Colquitt	10.9	7.3	5.6	50.4	36 645	42 053	14.8	8.2	6 711	4 070	1 189	16 317	5.3	2.73	17.3	24.0
Columbia	12.0	6.2	4.1	51.4	66 031	89 288	35.2	38.9	12 953	5 639	16 810	44 898	44.3	2.75	12.3	18.6
Cook	11.6	8.0	5.5	51.4	13 456	15 771	17.2	9.1	2 331	1 591	189	6 339	7.8	2.69	16.5	23.6
Coweta	11.2	6.5	3.9	51.1	53 853	89 215	65.7	42.7	15 386	6 544	29 284	45 673	45.3	2.77	13.1	19.6
Crawford	14.1	8.5	4.6	49.5	8 991	12 495	39.0	1.1	1 350	967	-570	4 822	8.1	2.59	13.3	22.2
Crisp	13.5	7.5	6.5	52.1	20 011	21 996	9.9	6.6	3 202	2 337	-541	9 079	8.9	2.53	21.3	26.8
Dade	13.2	8.5	5.9	50.7	13 183	15 154	15.0	9.8	1 610	1 387	812	6 291	11.7	2.49	10.4	25.1
Dawson	14.5	9.6	4.5	50.0	9 429	15 999	69.7	39.6	2 460	1 327	5 443	8 433	39.0	2.61	9.5	19.7
Decatur	12.0	7.7	6.2	51.1	25 517	28 240	10.7	-1.4	3 822	2 785	-269	10 390	0.1	2.58	20.0	26.4
DeKalb	10.5	5.1	3.9	52.1	546 174	665 865	21.9	3.9	103 186	37 721	-19 349	271 809	9.0	2.50	18.3	31.4
Dodge	12.0	8.1	5.5	47.5	17 607	19 171	8.9	13.7	2 028	2 028	312	8 177	15.8	2.43	16.4	28.7
Dooly	13.8	8.3	5.5	46.0	9 901	11 525	16.4	29.4	1 579	1 059	-185	5 286	35.2	2.45	19.1	28.8
Dougherty	11.6	6.5	5.6	53.5	96 321	96 065	-0.3	-1.6	14 344	8 033	-5 948	36 508	2.7	2.47	25.6	30.2
Douglas	10.2	5.5	3.0	51.8	71 120	92 174	29.6	43.6	15 998	6 601	28 467	46 624	42.1	2.81	17.3	21.5
Early	12.5	9.1	7.2	52.8	11 854	12 354	4.2	-10.9	1 684	1 318	-1 087	4 228	-9.9	2.56	21.3	27.3
Echols	9.2	5.7	4.2	49.4	2 334	3 754	60.8	7.5	551	187	107	1 329	5.1	3.04	14.0	16.7

1. No spouse present.

Items 16—31

Table B. States and Counties — **Population, Vital Statistics, Medicare, and Crime**

STATE County	Persons in group quarters, 2010	Daytime population, 2006–2010		Births, average 2006–2008		Deaths, average 2006–2008		Persons under 65 with no health insurance, 2009		Medicare, 2011			Serious crimes known to police,² 2010 Total	
		Number	Employment/residence ratio	Total	Rate¹	Number	Rate¹	Number	Percent	Eligible for Medicare	Enrolled in Medicare Advantage	Enrolled in a Medicare prescription drug plan	Number	Rate³
	32	33	34	35	36	37	38	39	40	41	42	43	44	45
FLORIDA—Cont'd														
Putnam	1 407	68 768	0.8	1 050	14.2	914	12.4	13 897	24.4	16 819	2 625	7 743	4 410	5 930
St. Johns	2 798	163 675	0.8	1 802	10.3	1 362	7.8	26 719	17.2	34 953	4 922	13 325	5 134	2 702
St. Lucie	3 053	244 967	0.8	3 506	13.5	2 562	9.9	52 667	25.5	58 481	15 864	19 502	8 483	3 054
Santa Rosa	4 244	121 379	0.6	1 866	12.7	1 070	7.3	26 086	20.0	24 704	4 871	7 429	2 291	1 513
Sarasota	5 622	389 709	1.1	3 161	8.5	4 914	13.2	59 506	23.6	109 439	19 033	43 829	14 439	3 805
Seminole	3 515	390 094	0.9	4 747	11.6	2 738	6.7	72 333	20.2	58 997	16 822	18 281	12 360	2 924
Sumter	8 952	88 253	1.1	D	D	932	13.0	12 794	21.4	44 870	10 286	15 324	1 121	1 209
Suwannee	1 393	38 560	0.9	525	13.3	485	12.2	8 568	27.0	9 651	979	4 738	1 089	2 621
Taylor	3 254	21 755	1.0	D	D	219	10.7	4 381	24.8	4 161	451	1 885	577	2 556
Union	4 778	16 412	1.2	D	D	198	13.2	3 367	26.6	1 749	168	765	197	1 268
Volusia	12 809	469 950	0.9	5 308	10.7	5 968	12.0	93 013	24.3	114 994	43 769	31 004	21 115	4 269
Wakulla	3 428	23 992	0.6	D	D	214	7.1	5 931	21.5	4 328	1 732	1 077	765	2 486
Walton	2 065	53 624	1.0	694	13.1	498	9.4	11 359	25.2	10 104	1 018	4 273	1 570	2 852
Washington	2 694	22 082	0.8	D	D	269	11.6	4 725	23.9	5 008	421	2 293	360	1 446
GEORGIA	253 199	9 468 139	1.0	148 791	15.6	68 593	7.2	1 815 729	21.2	1 302 111	293 450	531 252	391 751	4 044
Appling	426	18 266	1.0	D	D	192	10.7	3 639	23.7	3 195	540	1 711	NA	NA
Atkinson	20	7 634	0.8	D	D	73	9.0	2 069	28.7	1 210	187	714	NA	NA
Bacon	325	10 898	1.0	D	D	131	12.5	2 155	24.0	1 925	309	1 062	NA	NA
Baker	0	3 235	0.7	D	D	37	9.4	783	24.4	679	96	345	5	145
Baldwin	4 569	48 063	1.1	D	D	396	8.6	8 401	21.4	7 369	2 811	2 381	2 354	5 149
Banks	0	15 690	0.7	D	D	137	8.3	3 529	24.3	2 904	611	1 439	614	3 338
Barrow	289	54 551	0.6	1 233	18.4	438	6.5	14 480	22.6	8 720	2 104	3 626	2 413	3 479
Bartow	990	92 482	0.9	1 502	16.1	741	8.0	17 564	20.8	14 189	2 892	6 202	3 880	3 900
Ben Hill	308	17 806	1.0	D	D	192	10.9	3 389	22.9	3 304	627	1 682	NA	NA
Berrien	176	16 613	0.7	D	D	186	11.0	3 295	22.9	3 299	654	1 628	546	2 933
Bibb	6 051	175 779	1.3	2 649	17.1	1 634	10.5	24 322	18.6	26 886	6 344	10 978	11 004	7 084
Bleckley	1 439	11 645	0.7	D	D	127	10.2	2 086	19.3	2 298	268	929	471	3 606
Brantley	66	13 316	0.4	D	D	158	10.2	3 310	24.4	2 894	445	1 533	364	1 977
Brooks	0	12 977	0.5	D	D	182	11.1	3 215	23.8	3 088	554	1 600	692	4 414
Bryan	98	22 496	0.5	D	D	183	6.0	5 227	17.9	3 720	764	1 366	643	2 127
Bulloch	4 818	64 305	0.9	860	13.1	444	6.8	13 270	22.0	8 014	1 389	3 574	2 758	3 928
Burke	283	21 917	0.9	352	15.4	236	10.4	3 952	20.3	3 856	1 083	1 665	1 194	5 350
Butts	2 345	21 176	0.8	351	14.7	229	9.6	4 426	21.2	3 831	947	1 582	714	3 018
Calhoun	1 701	6 126	0.8	D	D	85	13.8	1 420	27.0	1 012	256	600	82	1 225
Camden	1 877	46 973	0.9	874	18.5	271	5.7	7 664	17.9	5 988	1 020	2 317	1 627	3 314
Candler	287	9 789	0.8	D	D	119	11.2	2 507	28.3	2 026	401	1 056	266	2 419
Carroll	3 583	102 109	0.8	1 807	16.3	836	7.5	21 108	21.2	16 561	4 050	7 021	4 395	3 976
Catoosa	461	49 902	0.6	771	12.4	513	8.2	10 023	18.4	10 771	2 094	5 324	1 887	2 951
Charlton	1 791	10 749	0.6	D	D	98	9.1	2 155	23.5	1 772	259	939	222	1 824
Chatham	12 891	285 853	1.3	4 076	16.5	2 289	9.3	44 611	20.6	38 832	9 530	13 781	12 348	4 657
Chattahoochee	3 267	17 406	1.9	D	D	32	2.6	2 697	20.1	522	89	178	NA	NA
Chattooga	1 941	23 358	0.7	D	D	297	11.1	5 280	23.7	5 080	1 131	2 701	280	1 337
Cherokee	1 406	164 159	0.6	3 359	16.5	1 004	4.9	33 675	17.4	24 900	6 255	8 570	3 465	1 621
Clarke	9 183	134 016	1.4	1 655	14.5	628	5.5	23 386	23.0	12 895	2 721	4 863	5 708	4 891
Clay	58	2 728	0.7	D	D	46	14.3	523	20.8	693	176	332	8	251
Clayton	4 037	245 178	0.9	4 892	18.0	1 386	5.1	56 652	23.1	24 733	6 669	9 176	14 432	5 563
Clinch	155	7 037	1.1	D	D	68	9.8	1 419	23.8	1 286	205	787	220	3 236
Cobb	9 068	657 266	0.9	11 095	16.1	3 443	5.0	125 463	20.0	72 971	17 307	24 723	18 459	2 683
Coffee	2 657	42 166	1.0	709	17.6	345	8.6	9 596	27.2	6 115	1 061	3 376	1 077	2 616
Colquitt	1 005	42 610	0.9	800	17.8	438	9.7	10 455	27.0	7 665	1 192	4 014	NA	NA
Columbia	640	96 093	0.6	1 497	13.8	682	6.3	13 838	13.8	15 483	2 977	3 995	2 733	2 203
Cook	143	14 864	0.7	285	17.3	177	10.8	3 429	24.5	2 959	493	1 565	480	3 360
Coweta	588	99 426	0.6	1 776	14.9	793	6.7	18 487	16.6	16 273	3 661	6 489	3 007	2 362
Crawford	133	9 238	0.4	D	D	102	8.1	2 343	21.9	2 151	562	873	533	4 220
Crisp	506	23 886	1.1	381	17.2	245	11.1	4 268	23.0	3 879	870	2 066	1 357	5 789
Dade	993	13 456	0.6	D	D	162	10.0	2 961	21.9	3 006	628	1 477	279	1 677
Dawson	299	19 270	0.8	D	D	167	7.8	4 158	21.6	3 309	642	1 454	496	2 221
Decatur	1 069	27 628	1.0	437	15.2	302	10.5	5 758	23.6	4 997	1 032	2 516	1 051	3 775
DeKalb	13 049	667 851	0.9	11 541	15.7	4 001	5.5	149 309	22.7	77 380	21 600	26 934	41 392	6 048
Dodge	1 951	20 080	0.8	275	13.8	231	11.6	3 802	22.9	3 618	648	1 754	959	4 919
Dooly	1 978	13 936	0.9	D	D	114	9.8	2 322	23.3	2 035	422	963	NA	NA
Dougherty	4 331	109 179	1.4	1 684	17.7	885	9.3	16 953	21.1	15 129	2 800	6 638	5 998	6 343
Douglas	1 368	109 814	0.7	1 993	16.1	763	6.2	22 635	19.5	14 569	3 391	5 480	4 894	3 696
Early	172	11 471	1.1	D	D	154	13.0	1 885	19.9	2 184	524	1 079	331	3 078
Echols	0	NA	NA	D	D	22	5.4	1 289	33.6	448	54	226	53	1 314

1. Per 1,000 estimated resident population. 2. Data for serious crimes have not been adjusted for underreporting; this may affect comparability between geographic areas and over time. 3. Per 100,000 population estimated by the FBI.

Table B. States and Counties — Crime, Education, Money Income, and Poverty

STATE County	Serious crimes known to police,[1] 2010 (cont.) Rate[2] Violent	Property	Education School enrollment and attainment, 2006–2010 Enrollment[3] Total	Per-cent private	Attainment[4] (percent) High school grad-uate or less	Bach-elor's degree or more	Local government expenditures,[5] 2008–2009 Total current expendi-tures (mil dol)	Current expendi-tures per student (dollars)	Money income, 2006–2010 Per capita income[6] (dollars)	Households Median income Dollars	Percent change, 2000 to 2006–2010 (constant 2010 dollars)	Percent with income of $200,000 or more	Income and poverty, 2010 Median house-hold income (dollars)	Percent below poverty level All per-sons	Children under 18 years	Children 5 to 17 years in families
	46	47	48	49	50	51	52	53	54	55	56	57	58	59	60	61
FLORIDA—Cont'd																
Putnam	971	4 959	15 005	8.9	63.3	12.2	102.2	8 893	18 402	34 645	-2.9	0.9	33 300	26.7	38.2	37.9
St. Johns	314	2 387	45 871	21.1	30.3	38.7	237.3	8 178	36 027	62 663	-1.2	7.6	60 841	12.0	14.1	12.4
St. Lucie	406	2 648	62 078	12.4	51.6	17.8	337.4	8 687	23 296	45 196	-1.8	1.9	39 378	17.6	27.2	26.4
Santa Rosa	172	1 341	38 854	13.7	40.4	24.7	203.1	7 998	25 384	55 129	4.0	2.6	51 208	12.6	17.6	15.1
Sarasota	380	3 426	65 457	18.2	40.6	29.1	439.5	10 701	33 045	49 388	-7.0	4.5	46 047	13.1	21.8	18.9
Seminole	367	2 557	117 547	17.5	34.3	33.6	510.3	7 859	29 795	58 971	-5.6	4.8	57 381	11.0	14.1	12.9
Sumter	221	988	8 549	12.2	53.0	19.0	67.7	8 847	24 180	43 079	6.1	1.3	45 165	13.0	33.8	32.2
Suwannee	462	2 159	8 743	10.7	62.5	10.2	46.6	7 802	18 782	36 352	-4.2	1.5	39 259	20.9	30.0	27.7
Taylor	713	1 843	5 011	19.1	60.2	12.0	27.3	8 291	18 649	37 408	-1.6	1.4	35 343	20.6	30.8	30.3
Union	354	914	3 274	7.4	66.7	9.3	20.4	8 794	13 657	41 794	-4.5	0.6	40 523	24.3	25.5	23.3
Volusia	551	3 719	112 724	22.7	46.1	21.0	518.5	8 227	24 768	44 400	-0.4	2.4	41 368	16.5	26.6	24.0
Wakulla	279	2 206	7 059	14.5	52.7	17.3	41.5	7 890	21 892	53 301	13.3	0.7	47 566	14.1	20.0	18.1
Walton	418	2 434	10 752	13.0	44.9	25.0	73.6	10 528	27 746	47 273	15.2	4.3	44 622	16.5	26.6	26.2
Washington	141	1 305	5 384	10.4	60.6	12.8	38.1	10 790	18 470	36 216	2.4	1.2	35 378	21.1	30.9	29.6
GEORGIA	403	3 640	2 617 481	15.7	46.1	27.2	15 924.6	9 649	25 134	49 347	-8.2	3.6	46 252	18.0	25.0	23.0
Appling	NA	NA	4 260	4.4	68.6	8.3	34.6	9 762	18 977	36 155	-5.7	0.4	36 601	24.5	35.7	33.3
Atkinson	NA	NA	2 124	0.2	73.4	8.0	15.5	8 929	15 456	33 834	0.9	1.8	28 579	36.3	58.1	47.9
Bacon	NA	NA	2 370	12.1	72.5	7.4	17.2	9 281	17 110	31 429	-7.8	0.3	31 692	25.6	35.5	32.8
Baker	58	87	1 028	3.3	63.0	12.2	6.4	14 697	16 379	27 462	-28.5	1.9	33 960	26.0	40.6	38.0
Baldwin	766	4 383	13 678	12.8	58.1	18.4	53.5	9 218	17 488	37 237	-16.4	0.9	36 091	27.0	34.5	31.9
Banks	288	3 050	4 185	12.4	69.4	10.5	25.7	8 825	19 497	40 455	-17.1	1.5	42 196	16.4	24.7	22.7
Barrow	507	2 971	16 747	9.2	54.9	14.9	107.9	8 690	20 882	48 958	-14.1	1.4	52 391	12.0	17.7	17.6
Bartow	310	3 590	24 492	11.6	61.3	16.5	170.6	9 128	22 241	49 216	-11.0	1.8	43 825	14.5	21.9	20.9
Ben Hill	NA	NA	4 596	10.5	66.7	12.3	30.7	9 130	15 529	30 134	-12.2	0.9	29 910	27.9	41.5	39.8
Berrien	354	2 578	4 954	6.6	63.4	10.8	26.2	8 402	16 049	32 202	-15.4	0.1	32 859	21.7	33.7	33.0
Bibb	605	6 479	44 712	22.9	50.3	23.1	225.3	9 024	21 436	38 798	-11.3	2.7	36 220	25.9	38.7	36.7
Bleckley	253	3 353	3 861	10.7	70.2	10.1	24.0	9 684	18 960	35 661	-15.8	2.1	38 513	19.8	27.1	25.0
Brantley	206	1 771	4 532	5.6	71.7	4.9	29.7	8 204	18 905	37 343	-2.9	0.2	35 732	23.6	32.4	28.9
Brooks	804	3 610	3 686	4.0	58.3	15.8	23.3	9 797	20 346	41 309	21.2	1.6	32 067	24.5	38.4	37.4
Bryan	116	2 011	8 512	10.5	40.3	27.6	55.0	7 792	28 365	63 244	3.3	2.2	65 478	11.8	16.7	15.2
Bulloch	397	3 630	27 991	4.9	46.7	25.2	95.7	10 207	17 812	34 327	-8.1	1.1	31 943	34.3	31.7	29.0
Burke	887	4 463	6 917	13.3	66.7	9.1	49.7	10 517	15 934	33 155	-6.1	0.6	30 688	32.9	47.0	47.7
Butts	194	2 824	4 956	18.0	68.7	9.1	32.5	9 168	20 963	52 257	3.5	1.3	43 777	16.5	23.5	22.2
Calhoun	149	1 076	1 387	13.5	88.8	8.7	7.9	12 070	12 452	30 522	-2.0	0.9	28 618	36.8	41.0	39.1
Camden	358	2 955	14 319	10.5	44.3	20.4	90.5	9 333	22 022	49 230	-5.3	1.1	48 967	16.5	21.3	21.4
Candler	155	2 264	2 537	7.6	68.2	13.2	18.6	9 321	16 068	35 828	13.1	1.3	30 496	25.2	38.2	37.2
Carroll	727	3 249	31 702	10.5	56.3	18.3	172.6	8 923	20 523	45 559	-7.3	1.6	45 242	19.0	24.3	22.8
Catoosa	195	2 756	16 056	14.4	49.5	17.3	97.9	9 187	22 563	46 544	-8.1	1.6	47 337	14.3	20.6	18.5
Charlton	189	1 635	2 684	8.4	70.0	7.2	17.1	9 493	16 652	40 850	15.8	1.5	32 316	27.9	32.1	30.2
Chatham	396	4 261	69 857	25.1	42.4	29.0	342.5	10 076	25 397	44 928	-6.0	3.0	42 728	19.7	27.5	24.6
Chattahoochee	NA	NA	3 920	13.2	27.8	31.5	9.1	9 865	22 202	51 089	8.7	1.1	46 292	18.5	20.6	20.9
Chattooga	158	1 180	5 913	5.5	68.7	8.0	42.1	9 834	15 158	32 419	-16.5	0.3	33 990	20.5	28.8	26.7
Cherokee	98	1 523	56 618	19.5	35.6	33.6	343.2	9 208	30 217	66 320	-14.0	4.8	63 520	8.6	11.7	11.0
Clarke	329	4 562	49 390	7.0	37.6	41.2	156.3	12 747	19 839	34 253	-4.8	2.6	34 000	33.3	35.6	34.3
Clay	157	94	672	3.3	68.0	8.5	4.3	13 155	13 353	26 250	-3.3	0.0	27 080	35.7	58.3	56.0
Clayton	550	5 013	76 794	13.7	50.5	17.9	506.2	10 225	18 958	43 311	-19.9	0.9	36 595	22.6	34.1	31.3
Clinch	515	2 721	1 538	2.9	66.8	17.1	13.7	9 503	16 709	31 963	-5.7	0.0	30 428	24.7	34.9	32.7
Cobb	273	2 409	189 362	19.2	30.2	43.8	1 109.3	9 678	33 110	65 522	-11.2	6.4	59 471	14.0	19.7	18.0
Coffee	194	2 422	10 764	5.1	63.8	11.0	72.4	9 037	16 664	35 202	-9.5	1.0	33 527	25.9	39.3	35.4
Colquitt	NA	NA	11 285	5.1	66.5	11.2	82.1	9 195	17 362	32 902	-9.0	1.3	32 010	26.2	35.3	33.7
Columbia	122	2 081	33 919	13.4	36.8	33.8	191.6	8 414	29 479	66 333	-5.9	5.1	64 435	8.8	10.6	9.3
Cook	217	3 143	4 617	0.9	65.6	10.4	31.6	9 664	16 528	31 390	-10.1	0.9	32 244	24.7	36.6	34.7
Coweta	187	2 175	32 914	15.7	45.5	25.7	193.8	8 747	26 161	61 550	-7.8	2.6	56 407	11.0	16.9	15.2
Crawford	301	3 919	2 870	9.2	61.3	13.6	18.5	9 825	20 692	37 062	-22.7	2.0	41 593	19.0	29.8	26.3
Crisp	439	5 350	5 910	6.9	65.3	11.7	42.8	9 783	17 187	29 960	-10.9	0.9	35 232	29.9	47.4	46.0
Dade	253	1 425	4 488	31.1	55.0	16.8	22.1	8 694	20 168	39 760	-10.9	1.4	40 161	16.3	22.3	20.6
Dawson	81	2 141	4 943	12.9	54.5	18.8	36.4	10 486	25 557	51 128	-15.0	3.3	51 127	13.9	21.7	20.2
Decatur	467	3 308	7 649	8.2	60.5	12.5	51.0	8 996	17 833	33 297	-8.8	1.1	33 288	25.1	38.8	35.1
DeKalb	641	5 407	187 827	24.4	34.9	38.7	1 061.7	10 348	28 412	51 349	-17.4	4.9	47 068	19.4	26.5	24.0
Dodge	390	4 530	4 689	7.2	65.1	13.8	36.9	10 896	16 288	33 580	-3.9	0.4	33 731	22.5	33.3	31.5
Dooly	NA	NA	2 898	13.6	70.9	9.6	15.2	10 394	14 871	31 038	-12.4	1.2	32 216	25.2	34.9	32.4
Dougherty	781	5 561	29 743	8.5	48.6	19.6	156.6	9 652	19 210	32 435	-17.2	2.2	31 200	35.1	49.2	43.8
Douglas	306	3 390	37 098	14.9	46.4	23.7	215.2	8 677	24 515	55 852	-12.0	2.6	52 887	12.7	19.1	16.9
Early	539	2 539	3 218	5.9	64.8	13.5	25.2	10 283	16 330	26 928	-17.0	1.4	30 572	27.6	40.3	36.6
Echols	198	1 116	1 147	4.0	75.8	6.1	7.0	9 436	14 201	32 390	-1.1	0.2	32 674	27.0	40.6	40.9

1. Data for serious crimes have not been adjusted for underreporting; this may affect comparability between geographic areas and over time. 2. Per 100,000 population estimated by the FBI. 3. All persons 3 years old and over enrolled in nursery school through college. 4. Persons 25 years old and over. 5. Elementary and secondary education expenditures. 6. Based on population estimated by the American Community Survey, 2006–2010.

Table B. States and Counties — **Personal Income**

	Personal income, 2009												
			Per capita[1]						Transfer payments (mil dol)				
										Government payments to individuals			
STATE County	Total (mil dol)	Percent change, 2008–2009	Dollars	Rank	Wages and salaries[2] (mil dol)	Proprietors' income (mil dol)	Dividends, interest, and rent (mil dol)	Total	Total	Social Security	Medical payments	Income mainte-nance	Unemploy-ment insurance
	62	63	64	65	66	67	68	69	70	71	72	73	74
FLORIDA—Cont'd													
Putnam	1 962	1.3	26 923	2 581	848	31	332	677	664	229	277	81	23
St. Johns	8 911	-3.6	47 544	140	2 672	240	2 832	1 163	1 128	491	430	63	43
St. Lucie	7 869	-0.8	29 526	2 085	3 077	264	1 958	2 197	2 148	815	876	193	110
Santa Rosa	5 084	1.5	33 498	1 253	1 582	144	885	931	904	336	342	73	31
Sarasota	20 765	-3.3	56 158	51	7 057	935	9 328	3 689	3 622	1 581	1 577	147	116
Seminole	17 495	-4.0	42 340	302	8 426	1 139	3 309	2 256	2 181	830	785	190	150
Sumter	2 351	5.2	30 259	1 924	869	41	691	938	924	612	197	38	15
Suwannee	1 108	0.3	27 604	2 467	392	74	212	363	356	130	153	38	9
Taylor	554	0.2	25 898	2 747	323	14	94	171	167	57	69	22	5
Union	287	1.8	19 694	3 097	190	10	40	77	74	23	31	11	2
Volusia	15 995	-1.9	32 255	1 473	6 933	507	4 427	4 194	4 104	1 620	1 638	311	170
Wakulla	896	3.8	27 308	2 514	259	29	129	182	176	57	78	18	5
Walton	1 654	-1.3	30 018	1 972	790	87	496	326	316	133	103	29	13
Washington	577	0.7	24 138	2 956	266	17	84	200	196	64	85	22	5
GEORGIA	335 466	-2.2	34 129	X	224 193	28 777	54 169	55 915	54 136	17 753	20 501	7 340	3 395
Appling	464	-0.3	25 746	2 767	327	33	61	131	128	41	55	17	7
Atkinson	175	-4.7	21 314	3 075	65	27	21	60	58	14	27	10	3
Bacon	259	-2.9	24 420	2 924	128	27	34	81	79	24	35	10	3
Baker	107	-8.7	29 554	2 079	25	24	15	23	23	8	7	6	1
Baldwin	1 268	-1.5	27 356	2 507	741	73	213	365	356	98	161	43	18
Banks	523	-2.5	31 137	1 722	166	58	77	99	96	40	33	11	6
Barrow	2 010	1.6	27 855	2 426	672	101	222	363	350	121	141	39	26
Bartow	2 787	-2.6	28 969	2 207	1 581	241	361	556	539	201	193	68	39
Ben Hill	454	-2.2	25 859	2 754	242	34	83	157	154	41	66	23	8
Berrien	500	-1.8	29 331	2 131	160	60	67	147	144	42	63	19	8
Bibb	5 468	-1.1	35 040	1 015	4 075	393	1 001	1 336	1 308	349	576	203	52
Bleckley	345	-2.5	26 805	2 597	131	25	62	87	84	27	27	11	4
Brantley	393	0.1	25 151	2 853	78	17	43	116	113	37	45	15	6
Brooks	465	-2.0	28 424	2 316	109	41	69	119	116	39	44	19	5
Bryan	1 151	0.5	35 361	970	251	83	134	169	163	52	64	16	9
Bulloch	1 673	0.3	24 172	2 952	962	92	285	361	348	105	121	51	22
Burke	585	1.1	25 666	2 779	338	55	71	188	184	52	67	37	8
Butts	614	-1.1	25 157	2 851	239	28	82	169	165	55	72	18	9
Calhoun	143	-2.2	22 634	3 047	55	20	21	49	48	12	23	8	2
Camden	1 465	-0.4	30 340	1 897	1 128	36	181	254	246	83	89	29	13
Candler	264	0.0	24 699	2 893	103	32	35	87	85	24	41	13	3
Carroll	3 199	-1.4	27 871	2 423	1 794	194	491	726	705	234	277	88	40
Catoosa	1 773	-1.3	27 692	2 453	595	135	184	345	334	153	97	35	21
Charlton	233	-0.1	21 750	3 071	91	10	31	78	76	23	34	10	4
Chatham	10 325	-0.9	40 178	439	7 612	514	2 031	1 781	1 736	544	649	208	82
Chattahoochee	371	-1.8	25 757	2 764	1 707	3	36	33	31	7	8	8	3
Chattooga	588	-0.6	22 084	3 065	244	36	72	199	194	69	82	23	10
Cherokee	7 202	-3.9	33 485	1 258	2 121	358	992	834	795	366	237	54	68
Clarke	2 934	-2.5	25 222	2 839	3 385	159	682	587	566	177	214	81	34
Clay	90	-1.5	28 954	2 211	28	5	18	28	27	9	10	6	1
Clayton	6 634	-3.7	24 058	2 959	6 161	335	646	1 560	1 510	332	641	283	111
Clinch	162	1.0	23 172	3 025	93	10	17	62	61	16	30	9	2
Cobb	30 900	-3.2	43 235	264	19 752	2 948	4 787	3 181	3 051	1 082	1 158	292	240
Coffee	1 007	-3.1	24 630	2 904	609	85	144	291	283	78	119	45	18
Colquitt	1 192	0.8	26 134	2 699	575	121	170	326	317	97	129	51	13
Columbia	4 738	-0.4	41 943	334	1 297	181	749	581	560	217	179	43	30
Cook	409	0.2	24 663	2 898	166	50	54	124	121	37	50	19	6
Coweta	4 028	0.3	31 685	1 602	1 441	142	572	657	633	241	236	67	42
Crawford	363	0.1	29 638	2 065	54	28	43	76	74	27	23	12	4
Crisp	591	-1.3	26 626	2 618	303	48	93	186	182	49	80	34	8
Dade	430	-1.7	26 653	2 614	125	22	55	108	106	41	43	9	6
Dawson	725	-2.3	32 126	1 501	267	60	126	123	119	47	47	9	8
Decatur	774	-0.1	26 822	2 592	364	98	129	220	215	63	79	40	11
DeKalb	27 669	-3.2	37 027	750	18 622	3 605	4 231	3 643	3 507	1 049	1 292	568	271
Dodge	488	-2.2	24 694	2 895	219	22	78	156	153	43	71	23	7
Dooly	288	-3.7	24 387	2 926	135	37	44	87	84	24	36	16	3
Dougherty	2 737	0.3	28 555	2 288	2 526	218	481	797	780	200	305	154	33
Douglas	3 823	-0.6	29 476	2 098	1 642	128	427	658	634	211	230	87	50
Early	354	-3.1	30 568	1 850	212	40	53	94	92	28	35	20	4
Echols	91	1.4	21 614	3 072	25	13	11	17	17	6	5	3	1

1. Based on the resident population estimated as of July 1 of the year shown.   2. Includes supplements to wages and salaries.

Table B. States and Counties — Earnings, Social Security, and Housing

STATE County	Earnings, 2009 Total (mil dol)	Farm	Goods-related[1] Total	Manu-facturing	Service-related and health — Information and profes-sional and technical services	Retail trade	Finance, insur-ance, and real estate	Health care and social services	Govern-ment	Social Security beneficiaries, December 2010 Number	Rate[2]	Supple-mental Security Income recipients, December 2010	Housing units, 2010 Total	Percent change, 2000–2010
	75	76	77	78	79	80	81	82	83	84	85	86	87	88
FLORIDA—Cont'd														
Putnam	879	1.4	21.5	16.8	D	8.6	4.4	11.3	28.5	19 380	261	2 951	37 337	10.2
St. Johns	2 912	1.0	D	5.6	7.8	8.7	7.6	11.6	16.8	37 875	199	2 132	89 830	54.9
St. Lucie	3 341	0.7	9.5	3.1	6.4	9.6	5.1	15.3	24.7	64 550	232	5 952	137 029	50.1
Santa Rosa	1 726	0.4	10.0	2.3	9.8	8.9	3.3	10.8	31.0	28 075	185	2 253	64 760	31.8
Sarasota	7 992	0.1	12.3	3.9	11.3	9.3	9.8	20.0	12.1	116 315	307	3 992	228 413	25.2
Seminole	9 565	0.1	12.7	3.9	18.2	8.9	10.8	9.5	11.1	65 335	155	6 278	181 307	23.3
Sumter	910	1.0	16.3	6.4	2.7	9.5	3.3	10.9	32.5	46 395	497	1 439	53 026	110.4
Suwannee	467	6.3	15.8	10.4	3.7	10.6	2.3	10.7	22.9	11 220	270	1 406	19 164	22.2
Taylor	338	0.0	37.6	29.2	3.2	8.9	2.0	D	24.5	4 815	213	757	11 004	14.1
Union	200	0.4	6.7	3.5	D	D	D	D	66.8	2 095	135	359	4 508	20.7
Volusia	7 440	0.6	12.5	6.1	7.4	9.9	5.6	18.8	17.8	128 415	260	10 249	254 226	20.0
Wakulla	288	-0.1	26.5	19.7	6.3	7.4	4.0	D	35.0	4 920	160	586	12 804	30.4
Walton	877	-0.3	D	2.3	4.5	11.5	7.6	9.3	20.4	11 245	204	1 030	45 132	55.2
Washington	283	0.1	D	4.4	D	7.3	3.2	D	44.7	5 795	233	1 007	10 796	13.6
GEORGIA	252 970	0.8	14.5	9.3	14.7	6.0	7.9	9.4	19.2	1 468 209	152	228 510	4 088 801	24.6
Appling	359	4.3	13.1	7.8	D	5.7	2.6	3.4	18.7	3 700	203	703	8 512	8.4
Atkinson	91	23.3	D	25.9	D	5.4	2.7	4.0	21.1	1 395	167	364	3 522	11.1
Bacon	155	9.1	17.4	15.9	D	5.3	D	D	16.7	2 165	195	439	4 801	7.5
Baker	49	52.8	D	D	D	1.7	D	D	15.9	770	223	230	1 652	-5.1
Baldwin	814	0.2	18.9	14.9	3.3	7.5	3.8	13.3	40.0	8 350	183	1 421	20 159	17.3
Banks	224	11.3	18.6	14.2	10.3	11.6	D	D	17.4	3 455	188	395	7 595	30.8
Barrow	773	1.7	D	11.8	D	9.4	4.4	7.7	20.7	10 290	148	1 449	26 400	52.6
Bartow	1 822	1.3	D	26.5	6.2	6.5	4.6	7.9	15.4	16 565	165	2 085	39 823	38.5
Ben Hill	275	3.1	23.1	20.4	D	7.5	4.7	D	25.5	3 715	211	839	7 942	4.2
Berrien	220	18.9	D	15.3	5.4	9.7	6.1	5.5	18.3	3 790	197	713	8 709	22.7
Bibb	4 468	0.0	D	8.3	7.5	7.4	11.3	22.2	13.6	29 880	192	6 756	69 662	3.7
Bleckley	156	5.4	D	D	D	7.7	4.0	6.3	34.6	2 580	198	409	5 304	9.0
Brantley	95	1.7	D	4.9	D	6.6	2.3	4.0	39.3	3 335	181	526	8 086	24.6
Brooks	150	23.2	11.5	8.4	D	5.7	4.1	8.1	22.0	3 610	222	746	7 706	8.3
Bryan	333	1.5	17.3	4.8	4.7	9.0	10.4	D	26.2	4 325	143	524	11 842	36.5
Bulloch	1 054	2.9	15.1	7.4	4.6	8.6	4.6	12.4	32.0	9 130	130	1 626	28 794	26.6
Burke	393	7.5	9.4	7.4	3.1	5.3	2.1	D	18.7	4 705	202	1 267	9 865	11.6
Butts	267	1.3	D	14.0	D	7.1	5.8	7.2	28.9	4 495	190	572	9 357	26.6
Calhoun	75	22.3	D	D	0.7	4.7	8.5	4.4	40.4	1 150	172	326	2 409	4.5
Camden	1 164	0.0	7.6	5.3	3.8	4.6	4.4	4.1	63.1	6 885	136	779	21 114	24.5
Candler	135	7.9	13.1	6.1	7.0	9.5	D	8.6	24.1	2 260	205	495	4 761	22.3
Carroll	1 988	1.1	D	20.5	D	7.6	3.7	14.3	20.4	19 455	176	2 787	44 607	30.9
Catoosa	731	1.1	16.8	10.4	3.7	11.2	4.7	16.0	18.1	12 240	191	1 188	26 606	22.2
Charlton	101	2.4	D	11.4	D	5.0	D	8.4	30.8	2 015	166	346	4 478	16.0
Chatham	8 126	0.0	D	13.1	5.8	6.1	4.4	13.7	23.0	42 755	161	6 093	119 323	19.6
Chattahoochee	1 710	0.0	D	D	D	D	D	D	94.5	665	59	131	3 376	1.8
Chattooga	281	1.7	41.6	38.0	3.8	8.1	2.7	D	25.7	5 930	228	900	10 977	2.8
Cherokee	2 479	0.1	19.8	8.0	8.5	10.0	6.6	9.2	19.4	27 670	129	1 559	82 360	58.5
Clarke	3 543	0.1	D	13.4	4.0	6.4	4.3	16.6	36.7	14 250	122	2 770	51 068	21.2
Clay	33	13.1	D	0.0	D	5.4	D	7.2	41.1	815	256	223	2 102	9.2
Clayton	6 496	0.0	D	4.6	2.2	5.6	2.8	7.4	14.4	29 230	113	6 978	104 705	21.1
Clinch	102	2.9	35.5	33.8	D	3.9	D	4.6	21.1	1 505	221	396	3 007	6.0
Cobb	22 700	0.0	16.9	8.0	18.0	6.2	8.1	8.8	9.5	79 890	116	7 761	286 490	20.6
Coffee	694	6.4	21.4	17.2	3.3	9.8	3.6	D	19.4	7 245	171	1 534	17 061	9.3
Colquitt	697	12.3	21.0	17.7	D	8.4	5.0	D	24.9	8 810	194	1 967	18 311	4.3
Columbia	1 478	0.1	D	12.3	D	10.6	7.2	10.4	18.5	17 240	139	1 227	48 626	45.9
Cook	216	19.6	D	16.5	D	5.6	3.4	D	19.5	3 385	197	639	7 287	11.1
Coweta	1 583	0.6	D	14.3	5.6	10.9	4.5	12.0	18.8	18 795	148	1 814	50 171	51.2
Crawford	82	13.3	D	1.7	D	6.1	1.4	5.8	26.5	2 470	196	463	5 292	8.6
Crisp	351	6.0	14.3	10.7	D	9.0	6.0	D	20.6	4 355	186	1 112	10 734	12.3
Dade	147	0.9	26.5	17.0	5.4	7.9	5.3	5.4	19.4	3 465	208	428	7 305	17.4
Dawson	327	3.1	D	8.1	D	20.0	8.6	D	16.8	3 810	171	305	10 425	45.5
Decatur	462	13.7	D	9.0	2.7	9.5	4.8	D	27.4	5 760	207	1 307	12 125	1.3
DeKalb	22 226	0.0	8.7	4.4	16.6	5.4	7.6	10.8	16.5	84 240	122	15 657	304 968	16.7
Dodge	241	3.3	D	4.9	3.2	8.9	4.6	D	40.3	4 090	188	870	9 857	20.4
Dooly	171	16.5	28.4	27.2	1.7	6.1	4.1	D	21.9	2 305	155	580	6 328	40.7
Dougherty	2 744	0.4	16.9	13.1	7.8	6.7	3.5	15.0	27.0	17 150	181	4 857	40 801	2.9
Douglas	1 770	0.0	D	10.3	4.6	12.0	4.5	11.4	18.2	17 135	129	2 226	51 672	48.3
Early	252	12.3	27.2	25.1	1.8	4.7	D	D	23.6	2 470	224	699	4 975	-6.8
Echols	38	26.9	D	D	0.4	0.9	D	D	20.5	520	129	93	1 558	5.2

1. Includes mining, construction, and manufacturing.
2. Per 1,000 resident population enumerated in the 2010 census.

Table B. States and Counties — Housing, Labor Force, and Employment

STATE County	Total	Percent	Median value[1]	With a mortgage	Without a mortgage	Median rent[2]	Median rent as a percent of income	Substandard units[3] (percent)	Total	Percent change, 2009–2010	Total	Rate[4]	Total	Management, business, science and arts	Construction, production, and maintenance occupations
	89	90	91	92	93	94	95	96	97	98	99	100	101	102	103
FLORIDA—Cont'd															
Putnam	29 168	77.8	109 300	25.5	11.3	587	34.2	3.4	33 226	2.8	4 187	12.6	26 890	23.3	35.3
St. Johns	70 324	77.1	294 100	26.7	12.9	1 025	32.3	1.0	97 450	2.2	9 291	9.5	84 612	41.6	14.0
St. Lucie	103 103	76.0	177 200	33.2	15.3	1 014	34.9	2.4	125 660	1.3	17 759	14.1	110 919	27.4	24.1
Santa Rosa	54 860	77.6	182 300	26.1	11.0	900	30.0	1.9	71 449	0.8	7 026	9.8	64 243	32.0	22.3
Sarasota	169 009	77.4	235 100	30.9	14.7	1 004	34.8	1.4	161 633	-3.5	19 652	12.2	154 284	33.1	19.0
Seminole	152 682	71.3	241 000	27.1	12.1	1 024	31.1	1.8	238 687	-0.6	25 536	10.7	211 051	40.7	14.4
Sumter	38 589	89.3	184 000	26.6	11.9	688	27.7	2.3	33 898	6.9	3 128	9.2	21 467	25.2	25.6
Suwannee	14 983	76.0	111 600	25.6	12.5	650	28.2	2.0	18 384	7.8	1 925	10.5	15 924	22.0	33.6
Taylor	7 724	85.7	87 800	20.5	13.6	534	33.9	2.8	9 194	-0.2	1 056	11.5	8 693	23.0	29.6
Union	3 521	69.5	115 100	23.4	10.0	560	25.7	1.2	5 394	0.2	470	8.7	4 947	22.4	21.8
Volusia	200 346	75.9	186 300	28.5	14.9	879	35.5	1.5	253 470	-0.2	30 403	12.0	213 229	30.3	21.1
Wakulla	10 540	83.6	143 500	23.6	10.5	845	32.6	2.8	16 867	4.8	1 384	8.2	13 026	33.6	21.4
Walton	22 916	75.3	199 800	27.1	11.9	889	33.0	2.0	31 064	-1.2	2 535	8.2	23 190	32.4	23.4
Washington	8 753	80.2	103 800	23.9	11.4	616	44.8	2.8	10 006	-0.4	1 130	11.3	9 257	25.9	25.3
GEORGIA	3 468 704	67.2	161 400	24.3	11.5	808	30.7	2.8	4 694 930	-1.5	481 055	10.2	4 296 760	34.7	23.8
Appling	7 145	72.6	83 600	23.2	11.1	474	19.8	4.1	9 324	-0.7	1 001	10.7	7 864	24.6	43.4
Atkinson	2 758	72.0	54 900	18.0	10.0	399	21.8	5.5	3 062	-7.4	497	16.2	3 225	15.6	57.3
Bacon	3 873	66.4	71 300	19.0	10.0	515	34.1	2.1	4 485	-3.9	460	10.3	4 058	26.6	40.4
Baker	1 342	66.1	66 400	44.7	10.0	472	39.3	7.2	1 548	-6.5	155	10.0	1 303	36.3	38.1
Baldwin	15 902	60.6	112 500	24.3	12.6	661	32.3	2.4	18 842	-8.2	2 963	15.7	17 945	31.0	23.9
Banks	6 463	75.9	146 800	24.4	11.5	597	28.6	7.0	10 110	-4.1	743	7.3	7 868	23.4	39.9
Barrow	23 045	76.7	138 900	24.7	12.3	780	32.9	2.8	34 314	-1.0	3 519	10.3	30 125	26.9	28.2
Bartow	34 301	72.4	146 800	23.5	11.1	746	33.6	2.5	45 189	-2.5	5 267	11.7	43 626	29.6	29.8
Ben Hill	6 582	62.4	73 100	24.3	13.7	584	30.6	4.3	6 998	-2.8	1 005	14.4	6 268	25.0	38.3
Berrien	7 293	72.0	76 200	22.0	12.0	502	32.5	2.1	7 933	-2.5	952	12.0	7 296	25.6	41.8
Bibb	57 222	58.5	118 100	23.2	11.8	689	34.1	2.5	73 526	-1.1	7 791	10.6	62 484	32.8	19.9
Bleckley	4 268	69.0	71 000	18.6	10.1	648	28.0	1.4	5 383	0.1	659	12.2	5 014	21.9	32.9
Brantley	6 629	85.3	68 500	20.6	12.0	473	19.7	4.0	7 210	-4.0	836	11.6	7 366	19.9	39.9
Brooks	6 303	74.3	93 000	23.1	10.7	546	31.5	3.3	7 792	-5.0	689	8.8	7 482	22.0	38.1
Bryan	10 466	74.2	187 400	23.2	10.0	964	33.3	1.5	16 755	0.5	1 399	8.3	13 532	35.5	21.1
Bulloch	24 245	55.6	135 500	23.1	11.0	621	38.5	2.1	31 775	-3.6	3 196	10.1	29 875	32.0	25.5
Burke	7 686	71.7	77 000	23.4	10.3	499	29.0	3.8	9 792	-1.5	1 079	11.0	8 386	23.3	34.7
Butts	7 789	76.7	142 900	23.0	10.0	750	28.5	2.2	9 895	-3.6	1 167	11.8	9 744	25.0	38.8
Calhoun	1 746	70.6	61 700	22.2	16.0	456	30.4	3.2	2 273	-3.4	241	10.6	2 283	18.8	35.6
Camden	17 834	67.3	161 900	23.9	11.0	789	28.1	2.3	19 786	-3.5	1 952	9.9	19 920	27.7	25.3
Candler	3 735	65.9	76 700	26.1	11.5	519	26.2	3.2	4 184	-3.4	411	9.8	4 434	20.9	38.1
Carroll	39 421	68.0	139 900	24.1	12.3	749	32.8	2.5	51 592	-2.4	5 702	11.1	48 461	28.6	30.1
Catoosa	24 098	75.7	132 600	22.8	10.0	652	27.4	2.6	34 363	0.5	2 754	8.0	29 654	30.2	26.5
Charlton	3 720	75.9	73 400	23.2	10.0	656	24.6	2.9	4 276	-4.7	491	11.5	4 504	16.1	35.7
Chatham	100 450	58.7	177 100	25.2	12.2	863	33.3	1.7	129 335	-1.5	11 776	9.1	115 743	33.6	21.6
Chattahoochee	2 537	31.3	91 900	19.4	10.0	1 181	29.4	4.0	2 630	3.3	421	16.0	2 043	30.5	23.7
Chattooga	8 870	72.1	80 400	22.0	13.2	529	25.5	5.9	10 438	-2.0	1 256	12.0	9 887	18.8	49.3
Cherokee	74 339	80.6	201 900	25.0	11.6	936	29.9	1.8	107 921	-1.4	9 640	8.9	102 915	39.7	18.3
Clarke	41 980	45.9	161 400	24.3	10.9	730	36.7	2.9	63 278	-1.1	4 995	7.9	52 950	40.4	17.2
Clay	1 115	71.7	58 500	22.4	16.2	511	33.4	4.5	1 408	-1.1	123	8.7	902	18.5	34.4
Clayton	86 546	59.0	127 800	27.5	11.3	865	33.9	3.8	131 098	-2.0	16 194	12.4	118 323	23.0	30.3
Clinch	2 520	72.5	76 700	24.8	12.1	410	22.9	3.8	2 691	-6.5	313	11.6	2 739	19.8	44.2
Cobb	256 741	69.6	211 000	23.5	10.0	933	29.8	2.7	368 845	-0.7	35 622	9.7	351 327	43.6	16.3
Coffee	14 539	70.1	77 700	22.8	11.0	546	25.7	3.8	15 323	-6.8	2 619	17.1	16 402	22.6	35.0
Colquitt	15 695	61.7	84 300	20.5	11.2	539	30.1	5.3	19 952	-2.3	1 964	9.8	19 296	22.0	41.1
Columbia	41 722	80.9	168 700	22.0	10.0	828	27.7	1.7	60 612	1.0	4 234	7.0	53 816	41.6	18.4
Cook	6 417	72.7	80 000	27.6	12.2	642	35.0	3.5	6 689	-3.7	869	13.0	7 189	26.8	37.4
Coweta	44 137	75.8	177 900	23.7	11.7	887	28.3	2.1	59 998	-0.2	5 906	9.8	57 840	33.0	25.9
Crawford	4 671	80.9	92 400	23.7	11.9	612	45.5	3.1	5 969	-3.8	637	10.7	5 589	29.0	33.3
Crisp	8 835	58.5	93 900	22.9	12.1	562	33.6	4.0	9 285	-5.2	1 246	13.4	8 732	26.9	31.5
Dade	6 262	79.8	123 400	25.2	10.8	576	24.3	1.5	7 979	-2.1	703	8.8	7 589	26.4	27.9
Dawson	8 163	78.9	201 400	29.1	11.0	828	28.7	2.8	11 030	-0.9	1 116	10.1	10 403	26.5	28.6
Decatur	10 532	65.9	98 900	20.7	12.2	526	32.9	7.2	11 098	-7.8	1 529	13.8	11 162	25.7	30.8
DeKalb	264 837	58.6	190 000	26.1	12.6	922	31.8	3.0	374 696	-2.1	39 034	10.4	337 587	41.9	17.4
Dodge	7 821	71.1	75 500	18.8	14.2	468	23.8	0.5	8 806	-3.5	1 045	11.9	7 552	25.4	31.7
Dooly	4 856	66.9	66 000	22.1	11.0	493	33.0	1.9	4 638	-4.0	528	11.4	4 373	26.8	31.7
Dougherty	36 072	48.5	100 300	22.8	12.2	625	32.1	2.4	41 553	-1.6	4 980	12.0	36 911	28.6	25.5
Douglas	44 747	71.5	157 300	25.9	10.0	912	29.5	2.3	63 972	-1.8	7 102	11.1	59 913	32.2	24.9
Early	4 077	66.3	75 000	22.6	12.6	542	36.6	2.7	5 377	-3.4	521	9.7	3 809	26.4	33.2
Echols	1 297	70.8	73 800	24.3	10.0	644	35.6	6.6	2 133	-1.7	152	7.1	1 650	22.2	41.1

1. Specified owner-occupied units. 2. Specified renter-occupied units. A value of 10.0 represents 10 percent or less. 3. Overcrowded or lacking complete plumbing facilities. 4. Percent of civilian labor force. 5. Persons 16 years old and over.

Table B. States and Counties — Nonfarm Employment and Agriculture

	Private nonfarm establishments, employment and payroll, 2009									Agriculture, 2007			
	Employment							Annual payroll		Farms			
											Percent with:		
STATE County	Number of establishments	Total	Health care and social assistance	Manufacturing	Retail trade	Finance and insurance	Professional, scientific, and technical services	Total (mil dol)	Average per employee (dollars)	Number	Fewer than 50 acres	500 acres or more	Farm operators whose principal occupation is farming (percent)
	104	105	106	107	108	109	110	111	112	113	114	115	116
FLORIDA—Cont'd													
Putnam	1 295	13 563	2 658	D	2 711	442	316	412	30 380	469	71.0	8.1	44.1
St. Johns	4 958	44 374	6 644	1 224	8 528	1 803	2 239	1 386	31 235	194	60.8	13.9	61.3
St. Lucie	4 858	51 912	9 244	2 408	12 985	1 551	1 985	1 607	30 956	365	55.3	14.8	49.0
Santa Rosa	2 453	20 786	3 211	391	4 597	602	1 442	631	30 356	594	51.3	3.9	33.3
Sarasota	12 432	121 767	24 256	4 922	21 154	5 832	8 729	4 187	34 383	305	77.4	6.6	43.3
Seminole	12 632	148 232	16 184	6 282	24 199	12 655	11 404	5 371	36 234	395	87.6	2.3	40.5
Sumter	1 091	14 695	1 643	751	2 949	322	343	428	29 116	837	66.1	4.8	43.8
Suwannee	679	8 352	1 491	1 949	1 469	D	259	204	24 424	1 075	50.9	6.9	51.1
Taylor	404	4 935	661	D	985	128	144	156	31 680	132	48.5	9.1	39.4
Union	134	1 728	D	D	139	D	D	54	31 380	275	57.5	4.4	38.2
Volusia	11 881	129 006	25 359	7 644	22 893	4 450	6 566	3 809	29 529	1 243	84.5	2.4	46.7
Wakulla	402	3 179	198	D	786	D	185	91	28 533	147	75.5	4.8	42.9
Walton	1 683	15 377	1 676	D	3 211	297	376	419	27 242	754	36.1	8.4	35.1
Washington	372	3 460	694	388	743	107	161	87	25 264	462	33.8	5.2	38.5
GEORGIA	219 348	3 410 505	431 360	351 203	440 334	168 206	239 870	136 632	40 062	47 846	41.3	9.2	42.0
Appling	386	5 360	D	686	645	146	D	204	38 071	494	41.3	9.1	49.6
Atkinson	92	1 278	31	696	163	D	D	32	25 348	195	20.5	20.5	48.2
Bacon	222	2 704	D	734	330	138	D	73	26 953	326	38.7	9.5	41.4
Baker	30	251	D	D	37	D	D	8	31 789	156	28.2	29.5	66.7
Baldwin	816	13 341	4 322	1 858	2 194	378	649	369	27 625	170	39.4	7.1	48.2
Banks	286	3 489	111	D	991	50	D	80	23 071	530	49.2	1.1	51.5
Barrow	1 038	12 167	1 234	D	2 247	379	564	380	31 195	466	65.9	1.5	40.1
Bartow	1 905	27 795	2 568	7 790	3 681	718	936	910	32 747	501	56.3	5.8	36.1
Ben Hill	347	5 431	726	1 748	901	207	137	142	26 210	227	31.3	17.6	41.4
Berrien	289	3 743	277	1 953	471	163	D	100	26 662	417	27.8	15.6	48.0
Bibb	4 271	72 155	15 300	5 091	10 671	8 053	2 444	2 465	34 165	123	39.8	4.1	48.8
Bleckley	174	2 263	328	D	351	81	66	57	25 346	308	31.2	19.2	43.8
Brantley	180	1 297	D	104	251	D	19	31	23 692	225	46.7	2.7	39.6
Brooks	206	1 949	534	D	311	86	28	50	25 592	457	32.2	19.9	39.8
Bryan	595	5 710	1 111	354	1 035	D	445	140	24 599	77	41.6	9.1	40.3
Bulloch	1 404	17 099	2 476	1 879	3 566	582	579	433	25 348	669	31.8	14.9	39.0
Burke	309	4 657	527	728	752	144	D	194	41 588	468	24.1	19.9	42.1
Butts	356	4 041	545	542	723	D	D	106	26 344	146	41.8	4.8	52.1
Calhoun	81	642	231	D	106	49	4	18	28 757	141	14.9	40.4	58.2
Camden	844	8 658	833	292	2 296	358	D	243	28 121	57	40.4	14.0	28.1
Candler	223	2 159	528	175	399	85	62	56	25 816	283	30.4	12.7	38.2
Carroll	2 025	30 322	4 352	6 686	4 740	998	740	1 037	34 210	1 054	47.5	1.4	41.8
Catoosa	928	13 137	2 384	2 309	2 702	495	269	365	27 821	261	56.7	1.1	34.9
Charlton	148	1 716	D	261	300	43	D	45	26 122	113	34.5	9.7	34.5
Chatham	7 058	114 769	18 306	12 529	15 733	3 225	4 518	4 072	35 481	33	60.6	9.1	42.4
Chattahoochee	65	644	D	D	87	D	109	21	32 842	22	50.0	4.5	22.7
Chattooga	309	4 634	382	2 536	675	148	89	124	26 766	309	30.1	6.5	36.6
Cherokee	4 608	39 429	4 305	3 808	8 070	1 447	2 747	1 126	28 551	452	75.9	1.1	49.8
Clarke	2 938	44 455	9 298	6 121	7 443	1 244	1 649	1 386	31 179	116	57.8	2.6	24.1
Clay	43	D	D	42	81	8	D	D	D	90	22.2	26.7	44.4
Clayton	3 991	71 503	7 204	4 392	11 126	1 824	1 173	2 343	32 768	48	79.2	0.0	45.8
Clinch	115	1 686	D	D	189	22	32	47	27 848	109	47.7	11.0	42.2
Cobb	19 247	303 501	29 405	19 128	35 292	16 152	35 237	14 293	47 094	129	76.7	3.9	35.7
Coffee	851	12 779	1 746	3 103	1 992	355	238	344	26 958	605	28.8	14.2	47.9
Colquitt	870	11 676	2 055	3 426	1 981	317	147	298	25 530	644	33.1	14.4	51.2
Columbia	2 132	26 745	2 395	3 184	5 593	722	909	810	30 301	186	55.4	2.2	30.6
Cook	332	3 245	420	886	505	133	91	79	24 434	253	38.3	11.5	51.8
Coweta	2 082	28 281	3 249	4 464	5 022	743	736	856	30 284	445	53.0	4.7	35.3
Crawford	107	507	D	D	88	20	D	14	26 998	188	35.6	8.5	49.5
Crisp	529	6 659	1 290	1 123	1 486	216	76	167	25 085	229	27.9	17.0	43.7
Dade	211	2 154	175	415	461	91	D	66	30 750	266	47.7	1.9	34.2
Dawson	614	5 645	295	376	2 591	230	190	132	23 387	208	62.5	3.8	45.2
Decatur	618	7 837	988	1 848	2 179	247	D	210	26 808	351	21.9	18.8	46.4
DeKalb	16 116	259 528	39 988	12 389	31 109	10 458	18 012	11 078	42 687	38	86.8	0.0	50.0
Dodge	347	3 987	1 022	D	806	185	D	96	24 083	427	25.3	12.4	38.4
Dooly	173	2 320	175	1 101	293	81	D	64	27 606	329	27.7	24.6	52.0
Dougherty	2 487	40 012	8 032	5 154	6 595	1 357	1 609	1 251	31 256	129	43.4	24.8	49.6
Douglas	2 504	33 992	4 623	3 241	7 494	818	1 323	999	29 387	136	69.9	1.5	37.5
Early	236	2 929	261	D	362	110	55	112	38 279	418	24.2	22.7	40.7
Echols	17	D	D	D	D	D	D	0	D	59	30.5	13.6	39.0

Table B. States and Counties — **Agriculture**

STATE County	Land in farms — Acreage (1,000)	Percent change, 2002–2007	Average size of farm	Total irrigated (1,000)	Total cropland (1,000)	Value of land and buildings (dollars) Average per farm	Average per acre	Value of machinery and equipment, average per farm (dollars)	Value of products sold Total (mil dol)	Average per farm (dollars)	Percent from: Crops	Livestock and poultry products	Percent of farms with sales of: $10,000 or more	$100,000 or more	Government payments Total ($1,000)	Percent of farms
	117	118	119	120	121	122	123	124	125	126	127	128	129	130	131	132
FLORIDA—Cont'd																
Putnam	74	-20.4	159	4.6	12.0	845 062	5 321	48 714	37.5	80 046	86.5	13.5	31.3	7.2	52	2.1
St. Johns	34	-10.5	173	14.4	19.6	1 520 754	8 795	122 298	53.5	275 647	98.0	2.0	33.0	17.0	30	3.6
St. Lucie	153	-31.1	421	69.3	62.6	2 585 978	6 150	93 088	144.3	395 297	92.9	7.1	57.3	28.2	182	2.7
Santa Rosa	70	-16.7	118	2.6	33.3	683 136	5 782	48 021	20.8	34 966	80.8	19.2	25.1	6.4	2 806	43.9
Sarasota	61	-49.6	200	2.3	8.7	1 528 612	7 639	56 547	31.0	101 741	D	D	27.5	10.2	79	2.0
Seminole	36	28.6	90	1.8	4.5	764 620	8 498	24 886	20.8	52 729	91.7	8.3	31.6	5.6	0	0.0
Sumter	160	-14.4	191	2.0	29.4	1 103 939	5 783	46 671	29.4	35 153	D	D	24.1	5.4	222	6.9
Suwannee	167	-1.8	156	20.1	68.2	962 912	6 180	62 945	197.8	183 980	25.0	75.0	34.6	12.7	1 295	13.1
Taylor	34	-37.0	254	D	1.8	1 192 797	4 695	44 450	3.7	27 852	D	D	20.5	3.0	30	6.8
Union	47	-21.7	169	1.0	7.2	779 433	4 604	44 787	D	D	D	0.0	26.5	5.1	56	9.5
Volusia	83	-11.7	67	9.1	18.3	662 001	9 881	38 989	125.5	101 001	94.9	5.1	36.7	10.2	47	1.3
Wakulla	28	154.5	193	0.3	2.0	609 659	3 162	34 966	1.6	11 212	58.6	41.4	21.1	0.7	122	5.4
Walton	127	58.8	168	0.7	46.7	760 624	4 521	47 674	25.5	33 884	19.1	80.9	22.0	5.6	1 972	43.0
Washington	74	39.6	160	0.9	22.7	713 217	4 463	45 794	5.8	12 469	46.7	53.3	18.8	2.4	1 064	52.6
GEORGIA	10 151	-5.5	212	1 017.8	4 478.2	661 201	3 117	76 948	7 112.9	148 662	30.1	69.9	32.3	14.2	224 523	30.4
Appling	102	-14.3	206	9.1	61.6	544 006	2 646	107 135	75.1	152 113	37.0	63.0	43.5	19.0	4 160	43.1
Atkinson	77	8.5	396	5.6	28.4	1 101 543	2 782	111 265	60.0	307 934	24.0	76.0	51.3	25.1	2 021	53.3
Bacon	63	-6.0	194	6.0	29.9	515 224	2 656	105 268	58.2	178 558	31.5	68.5	43.6	15.6	1 128	39.3
Baker	135	7.1	867	22.0	51.6	2 173 489	2 508	249 122	42.1	269 639	61.5	38.5	42.9	32.7	2 986	68.6
Baldwin	30	-16.7	176	0.1	8.7	419 267	2 380	53 128	6.0	35 090	12.1	87.9	27.1	1.8	43	10.6
Banks	47	-19.0	88	0.7	11.9	554 298	6 293	76 605	144.2	272 128	0.3	99.7	47.5	35.7	105	10.2
Barrow	34	-5.6	73	0.1	10.0	452 630	6 229	41 904	41.6	89 249	2.0	98.0	23.8	7.7	39	6.0
Bartow	65	-20.7	130	3.0	24.5	590 027	4 540	63 243	94.0	187 537	13.9	86.1	29.5	15.2	565	16.2
Ben Hill	75	31.6	329	8.0	36.6	727 713	2 210	101 292	20.1	88 530	75.6	24.4	37.9	19.8	2 191	62.1
Berrien	119	-5.6	285	14.5	59.9	786 367	2 760	109 173	61.1	146 503	67.6	32.4	45.8	24.7	3 623	45.3
Bibb	14	-53.3	117	0.1	5.1	440 157	3 758	40 467	6.1	49 512	13.8	86.2	30.1	4.9	82	12.2
Bleckley	88	60.0	286	17.5	57.0	736 698	2 577	94 384	19.0	61 842	93.0	7.0	33.4	17.9	2 982	59.4
Brantley	25	-21.9	113	0.4	10.8	302 862	2 690	59 991	8.3	36 897	37.9	62.1	19.6	4.4	584	23.1
Brooks	189	-6.9	414	19.1	91.8	1 185 393	2 866	108 240	81.2	177 775	75.4	24.6	44.4	20.6	5 997	53.6
Bryan	20	17.6	264	D	6.5	503 395	1 910	67 460	1.9	24 258	82.5	17.5	14.3	3.9	312	18.2
Bulloch	197	-4.4	295	7.8	118.8	772 465	2 623	91 312	55.6	83 061	69.9	30.1	37.7	14.8	7 444	54.6
Burke	192	-12.3	410	17.7	111.1	999 897	2 440	105 946	48.7	104 005	64.1	35.9	39.1	10.9	4 257	38.2
Butts	25	-32.4	174	0.1	6.4	617 679	3 546	50 042	3.5	24 112	33.1	66.9	17.8	6.2	74	26.0
Calhoun	123	4.2	869	30.3	67.0	1 728 410	1 988	316 913	63.1	447 746	58.8	41.2	56.0	39.7	5 142	74.5
Camden	13	8.3	235	0.2	3.3	415 652	1 768	29 533	0.4	7 476	63.6	36.4	15.8	1.8	19	5.3
Candler	74	17.5	261	3.7	36.8	706 614	2 705	102 498	24.4	86 367	71.0	29.0	34.3	13.1	1 776	47.0
Carroll	96	2.1	91	0.7	25.5	484 930	5 313	50 961	155.2	147 228	1.9	98.1	26.5	9.6	295	8.7
Catoosa	21	-22.2	79	0.1	8.2	440 698	5 589	49 795	29.3	112 240	D	D	28.0	10.7	31	7.3
Charlton	20	33.3	181	0.1	3.2	383 047	2 119	47 002	9.5	83 881	4.2	95.8	17.7	4.4	43	3.5
Chatham	4	-55.6	130	0.1	1.2	595 223	4 570	72 863	5.9	179 463	94.9	5.1	30.3	15.2	D	3.0
Chattahoochee	4	0.0	194	0.0	0.4	470 693	2 429	72 661	D	D	0.0	D	9.1	4.5	D	9.1
Chattooga	53	-3.6	172	0.3	16.1	563 567	3 281	60 194	11.1	35 925	11.0	89.0	25.6	5.8	410	24.3
Cherokee	23	-36.1	52	0.1	7.2	467 059	9 018	39 871	40.5	89 588	8.7	91.3	28.3	11.9	51	7.1
Clarke	10	-28.6	90	0.1	3.0	440 776	4 890	40 602	40.1	345 705	D	D	25.0	6.0	69	22.4
Clay	45	7.1	495	9.4	23.8	1 237 349	2 499	108 633	11.5	127 914	94.0	6.0	31.1	17.8	1 542	56.7
Clayton	2	-33.3	35	0.0	0.6	207 059	5 843	32 334	0.2	3 441	72.7	27.3	12.5	0.0	0	0.0
Clinch	19	-38.7	173	1.8	6.0	468 678	2 702	88 055	13.5	123 751	75.6	24.4	46.8	26.6	26	11.9
Cobb	9	-18.2	66	0.0	3.2	375 173	5 693	47 261	2.9	22 475	90.2	9.8	12.4	1.6	32	14.0
Coffee	185	-2.1	306	18.0	98.9	763 316	2 497	122 486	147.9	244 540	30.9	69.1	41.2	20.3	5 872	53.6
Colquitt	197	-13.6	305	44.1	114.6	889 153	2 913	146 905	256.5	398 301	55.5	44.5	48.1	27.0	8 831	55.1
Columbia	19	-17.4	101	0.1	4.7	397 851	3 929	43 121	3.7	20 057	27.6	72.4	17.2	2.7	13	9.1
Cook	65	-4.4	257	10.8	38.4	746 721	2 900	111 437	97.9	386 837	51.9	48.1	41.1	18.6	2 908	57.3
Coweta	75	23.0	168	0.5	18.6	619 703	3 694	59 614	11.3	25 365	39.1	60.9	17.5	1.8	233	5.2
Crawford	38	0.0	200	4.5	15.1	590 638	2 950	77 090	32.9	174 985	43.1	56.9	25.0	14.4	212	14.9
Crisp	83	-20.2	364	17.3	49.2	816 730	2 246	118 230	29.9	130 376	83.1	16.9	41.9	20.5	3 765	57.2
Dade	35	25.0	133	0.0	7.4	421 129	3 177	55 144	14.7	55 381	2.7	97.3	19.2	4.1	67	7.5
Dawson	17	-15.0	81	0.1	4.3	561 380	6 907	91 070	68.2	328 043	1.0	99.0	33.7	23.6	22	6.7
Decatur	180	12.5	513	47.9	106.5	1 363 102	2 659	156 925	114.3	325 749	86.7	13.3	41.3	21.7	7 126	69.8
DeKalb	1	0.0	25	0.0	0.6	258 686	10 208	41 456	0.5	12 184	97.8	2.2	13.2	7.9	7	13.2
Dodge	127	-8.6	298	13.5	46.6	598 796	2 007	58 102	20.9	48 914	87.0	13.0	22.7	8.4	3 355	58.8
Dooly	156	-8.8	473	37.2	106.6	988 541	2 090	188 260	73.9	224 715	66.1	33.9	50.5	34.7	8 570	67.5
Dougherty	88	-10.2	681	15.2	33.1	1 744 680	2 563	167 925	32.2	249 245	94.0	6.0	34.1	22.5	1 442	34.1
Douglas	7	-12.5	52	0.2	2.9	379 781	7 260	43 902	3.8	27 973	32.2	67.8	22.1	3.7	20	7.4
Early	178	11.3	425	33.1	99.5	1 018 724	2 398	138 914	50.7	121 263	87.1	12.9	45.2	26.3	7 543	67.2
Echols	14	-51.7	243	4.0	6.8	786 885	3 240	131 916	17.9	303 237	96.1	3.9	30.5	16.9	129	23.7

Table B. States and Counties — Water Use, Wholesale Trade, Retail Trade, and Real Estate

STATE County	Water use, 2005		Wholesale trade,[1] 2007				Retail trade,[2] 2007				Real estate and rental and leasing,[2] 2007			
	Total water withdrawn (mil gal/day)	Gallons withdrawn per person	Number of establish-ments	Number of employees	Sales (mil dol)	Annual payroll (mil dol)	Number of establish-ments	Number of employees	Sales (mil dol)	Annual payroll (mil dol)	Number of establish-ments	Number of employees	Receipts (mil dol)	Annual payroll (mil dol)
	133	134	135	136	137	138	139	140	141	142	143	144	145	146
FLORIDA—Cont'd														
Putnam	73.9	1 001	24	D	D	D	261	2 918	671.6	60.2	72	182	22.0	3.9
St. Johns	34.9	222	165	1 817	871.1	83.5	763	8 967	2 039.7	189.1	376	1 383	207.0	41.8
St. Lucie	1 352.3	5 634	244	1 899	693.6	72.5	705	13 381	3 697.7	335.1	327	1 014	174.2	31.8
Santa Rosa	29.0	212	72	266	148.9	8.9	363	4 472	1 108.0	96.6	178	469	55.3	10.7
Sarasota	41.0	111	477	3 442	1 560.3	147.8	1 764	22 887	5 599.5	561.1	929	3 175	539.4	103.3
Seminole	68.8	167	661	6 783	2 852.7	314.2	1 800	28 169	6 872.1	642.2	877	3 376	682.0	120.3
Sumter	24.7	333	42	D	D	D	178	2 696	672.1	52.1	90	153	19.7	3.7
Suwannee	103.1	2 700	31	271	108.7	6.3	152	1 606	353.8	33.3	29	66	7.7	1.1
Taylor	49.2	2 311	14	D	D	D	93	980	207.1	18.6	21	76	6.8	1.2
Union	3.3	219	2	D	D	D	28	146	42.0	3.6	2	D	D	D
Volusia	171.2	346	443	4 426	2 002.9	168.8	1 970	26 205	6 099.9	575.9	842	3 978	531.8	101.5
Wakulla	10.9	404	13	63	7.0	1.5	63	908	167.7	17.2	15	41	4.6	0.7
Walton	11.7	218	47	722	205.1	21.7	381	3 317	705.0	72.2	176	950	145.3	33.0
Washington	3.6	156	9	D	D	D	70	805	177.3	16.0	18	42	3.0	0.9
GEORGIA	5 442.4	600	11 545	166 619	141 962.4	8 246.5	36 218	475 344	117 516.9	10 760.2	12 620	65 875	14 021.9	2 903.2
Appling	63.0	3 510	20	112	58.1	3.1	83	705	179.4	14.1	8	38	4.3	0.6
Atkinson	7.9	980	6	D	D	D	26	162	35.7	2.6	1	D	D	D
Bacon	6.4	619	15	171	120.7	5.0	45	313	68.6	5.3	3	9	0.4	0.1
Baker	34.4	8 279	2	D	D	D	5	43	5.3	0.4	2	D	D	D
Baldwin	7.6	169	25	D	D	D	199	2 326	524.2	46.9	34	D	D	D
Banks	3.5	220	12	108	23.3	3.0	68	994	233.9	19.9	4	D	D	D
Barrow	8.6	144	64	1 476	466.3	50.4	159	2 308	660.9	59.8	59	165	22.7	3.4
Bartow	107.8	1 208	120	1 378	649.0	51.3	342	4 069	1 177.4	96.3	137	466	51.6	11.9
Ben Hill	10.7	617	9	D	D	D	96	987	225.0	17.5	11	44	4.5	0.9
Berrien	6.9	411	20	132	68.4	3.3	77	478	129.2	10.4	7	16	1.5	0.2
Bibb	18.7	121	209	2 975	1 613.7	132.6	860	11 834	2 538.2	250.1	223	1 223	221.8	34.9
Bleckley	13.6	1 116	6	42	16.9	2.2	50	385	76.3	6.5	6	36	1.1	1.0
Brantley	2.8	183	3	D	D	D	37	249	62.4	3.9	3	10	0.7	0.1
Brooks	4.5	273	12	66	65.9	2.6	43	302	88.2	6.5	8	D	D	D
Bryan	3.1	109	20	249	154.4	19.0	96	706	225.0	16.6	39	105	21.5	3.2
Bulloch	16.9	275	48	D	D	D	292	3 603	733.4	71.6	88	319	45.9	6.6
Burke	80.8	8 598	22	D	D	D	64	686	177.5	15.4	12	31	3.4	0.6
Butts	3.5	166	17	364	465.4	12.1	69	760	295.5	15.2	28	60	7.6	1.2
Calhoun	27.0	4 528	7	42	16.5	1.4	21	133	19.6	2.0	NA	NA	NA	NA
Camden	6.7	146	10	D	D	D	188	2 512	648.3	55.9	59	201	26.4	3.6
Candler	11.1	1 078	6	43	24.3	0.9	66	468	114.5	8.9	6	20	1.6	0.3
Carroll	14.4	137	78	1 560	985.9	58.9	390	4 606	1 252.5	98.0	98	364	49.7	9.0
Catoosa	6.7	110	40	444	151.2	15.6	203	3 053	795.1	70.5	44	144	24.3	4.1
Charlton	1.2	115	5	34	46.0	1.7	46	258	68.4	4.8	5	33	1.3	0.4
Chatham	241.3	1 012	327	4 287	3 780.1	216.0	1 287	17 094	4 004.2	381.0	409	2 007	351.2	63.6
Chattahoochee	1.2	82	1	D	D	D	11	69	13.0	1.2	1	D	D	D
Chattooga	12.3	462	13	47	66.4	1.8	77	798	147.2	13.8	5	D	D	D
Cherokee	29.3	159	233	1 702	849.0	71.4	545	8 242	2 114.9	193.8	255	721	125.4	20.3
Clarke	7.6	72	106	1 994	1 782.5	84.1	553	7 752	1 669.1	161.5	224	839	128.3	24.3
Clay	0.7	204	5	12	1.5	0.3	9	64	11.0	0.9	2	D	D	D
Clayton	15.6	58	276	6 131	3 582.3	253.8	808	12 447	3 207.0	297.7	231	1 247	302.1	44.0
Clinch	1.9	269	2	D	D	D	26	135	39.8	2.7	4	19	0.6	0.1
Cobb	414.7	625	1 189	20 206	15 524.8	1 094.7	2 413	39 613	10 480.7	961.7	1 235	7 548	2 171.2	383.1
Coffee	16.1	407	47	433	323.9	17.3	208	1 981	458.7	39.9	35	D	D	D
Colquitt	36.8	837	44	370	184.9	10.9	195	1 997	432.4	43.1	42	142	18.6	3.1
Columbia	15.6	150	71	791	357.5	32.5	308	5 023	1 406.3	126.7	93	380	71.4	10.9
Cook	11.1	680	16	125	51.5	5.2	78	530	118.1	9.7	11	34	4.1	0.8
Coweta	42.4	386	68	815	524.6	33.6	343	4 895	1 291.0	111.5	141	390	65.7	12.3
Crawford	4.9	378	5	D	D	D	20	98	18.2	1.5	NA	NA	NA	NA
Crisp	18.8	854	34	D	D	D	131	1 538	326.5	28.8	30	220	16.8	4.3
Dade	2.9	181	4	D	D	D	65	516	189.3	8.3	5	D	D	D
Dawson	2.7	137	16	144	103.9	6.0	185	2 524	466.6	44.2	27	84	27.0	2.3
Decatur	42.0	1 466	28	D	D	D	158	1 945	395.4	33.4	20	55	10.8	1.0
DeKalb	88.8	131	905	11 028	9 361.1	559.4	2 456	35 506	7 973.4	810.1	1 086	5 761	1 542.4	311.4
Dodge	19.9	1 018	13	82	9.8	1.3	91	851	167.1	16.2	15	86	7.5	1.9
Dooly	26.3	2 238	13	115	61.9	3.8	42	303	151.4	7.3	2	D	D	D
Dougherty	158.8	1 673	148	2 086	1 175.7	81.2	538	6 934	1 543.7	136.4	146	654	87.9	17.3
Douglas	27.4	243	114	1 552	929.2	69.7	447	8 396	2 055.8	192.2	135	553	78.5	16.0
Early	123.9	10 277	16	68	131.9	2.1	59	401	75.8	6.3	8	22	1.8	0.4
Echols	6.3	1 477	1	D	D	D	2	D	D	D	1	D	D	D

1. Merchant wholesalers, except manufacturers' sales branches and offices. 2. Employer establishments.

Table B. States and Counties — Professional Services, Manufacturing, and Accommodation and Food Services

STATE County	Professional, scientific, and technical services,[1] 2007				Manufacturing, 2007				Accommodation and food services, 2007			
	Number of establishments	Number of employees	Receipts (mil dol)	Annual payroll (mil dol)	Number of establishments	Number of employees	Receipts (mil dol)	Annual payroll (mil dol)	Number of establishments	Number of employees	Sales (mil dol)	Annual payroll (mil dol)
	147	148	149	150	151	152	153	154	155	156	157	158
FLORIDA—Cont'd												
Putnam	100	D	D	D	40	2 163	982.6	91.3	96	1 103	48.9	11.5
St. Johns	724	D	D	D	104	2 074	533.3	81.9	442	9 172	507.6	153.6
St. Lucie	503	D	D	D	141	2 864	916.5	113.2	336	6 503	268.3	76.3
Santa Rosa	264	D	D	D	55	558	74.9	17.6	184	3 385	135.1	36.4
Sarasota	1 768	D	D	D	333	7 786	1 366.7	328.9	806	16 412	844.4	251.9
Seminole	1 944	D	D	D	400	7 482	1 634.7	296.1	804	16 975	764.1	226.1
Sumter	99	D	D	D	29	889	367.9	33.5	95	2 367	79.9	22.5
Suwannee	53	241	18.6	5.8	23	D	D	D	40	633	31.9	7.5
Taylor	32	138	9.7	3.6	23	1 428	595.5	69.1	41	306	20.0	4.0
Union	10	30	2.0	0.8	NA	NA	NA	NA	20	148	10.5	1.9
Volusia	1 353	D	D	D	369	9 491	1 948.6	366.2	1 006	19 359	899.2	245.8
Wakulla	47	D	D	D	8	D	D	D	34	489	20.1	5.1
Walton	191	D	D	D	NA	NA	NA	NA	165	4 382	312.7	93.2
Washington	30	200	16.3	6.5	13	676	D	16.0	36	525	18.1	4.4
GEORGIA	27 668	213 419	34 966.0	12 689.5	8 699	411 158	144 280.8	16 128.1	18 640	355 423	16 976.2	4 704.4
Appling	20	63	4.8	1.4	23	948	347.1	39.1	31	444	15.8	4.2
Atkinson	5	8	0.4	0.1	12	663	D	D	6	40	0.9	0.2
Bacon	12	57	3.4	1.4	15	817	165.4	20.7	15	141	5.9	1.5
Baker	2	D	D	D	NA	NA	NA	NA	2	D	D	D
Baldwin	57	D	D	D	30	D	D	D	85	1 781	57.9	15.8
Banks	12	37	3.7	1.4	NA	NA	NA	NA	46	950	44.3	12.4
Barrow	89	687	60.2	28.3	65	2 159	768.4	77.4	73	1 711	125.1	25.0
Bartow	142	858	84.3	31.1	143	8 447	3 723.6	359.4	184	3 306	140.7	41.9
Ben Hill	15	178	14.6	6.9	34	2 445	D	D	38	632	20.0	4.9
Berrien	13	29	2.0	0.7	12	1 872	415.9	57.5	21	285	9.3	2.6
Bibb	405	D	D	D	147	5 429	1 693.9	236.8	395	7 493	306.3	81.2
Bleckley	10	45	2.9	1.4	6	D	D	D	10	221	6.6	1.4
Brantley	4	D	D	D	NA	NA	NA	NA	10	94	4.3	1.1
Brooks	13	D	D	D	NA	NA	NA	NA	10	D	D	D
Bryan	66	D	D	D	NA	NA	NA	NA	65	841	34.8	8.3
Bulloch	115	641	64.0	20.8	48	1 904	523.8	63.9	133	2 611	95.3	25.9
Burke	15	D	D	D	15	788	D	29.4	22	306	11.1	2.8
Butts	28	124	10.3	3.1	17	726	287.0	19.9	28	393	18.0	4.2
Calhoun	3	5	0.5	0.1	NA	NA	NA	NA	5	18	0.9	0.2
Camden	76	367	32.8	11.7	NA	NA	NA	NA	101	1 825	71.8	19.8
Candler	16	63	4.9	1.5	NA	NA	NA	NA	20	394	14.7	3.2
Carroll	149	846	63.8	23.3	134	8 222	3 175.6	317.4	201	3 552	142.4	38.6
Catoosa	60	274	25.3	10.1	56	2 563	562.1	90.2	93	1 862	76.5	20.7
Charlton	6	20	1.4	0.5	NA	NA	NA	NA	19	222	9.8	2.6
Chatham	694	D	D	D	185	13 508	D	786.4	807	16 946	872.9	237.9
Chattahoochee	19	D	D	D	NA	NA	NA	NA	4	24	0.8	0.2
Chattooga	18	D	D	D	22	3 502	629.6	84.8	34	D	D	D
Cherokee	711	2 756	381.9	120.5	188	4 008	823.7	146.0	308	6 116	246.9	71.8
Clarke	283	D	D	D	91	6 632	1 971.2	255.2	331	7 062	293.4	80.3
Clay	1	D	D	D	NA	NA	NA	NA	1	D	D	D
Clayton	256	4 947	1 113.8	358.3	127	4 254	1 604.6	179.7	414	8 175	398.9	121.1
Clinch	9	28	3.2	1.1	9	851	D	33.4	11	89	3.3	0.7
Cobb	3 360	23 747	4 225.6	1 464.5	540	20 106	5 651.6	1 033.3	1 460	28 640	1 393.5	395.8
Coffee	58	269	22.7	8.3	48	3 503	D	D	67	1 313	47.1	12.7
Colquitt	63	203	19.6	5.4	59	3 472	599.5	90.0	59	904	35.0	9.5
Columbia	208	D	D	D	52	3 637	2 411.2	183.2	164	3 198	119.1	31.8
Cook	25	102	10.3	3.4	33	976	360.7	32.8	38	410	18.1	4.5
Coweta	202	742	83.0	29.5	87	5 466	2 270.1	227.6	159	3 633	146.6	42.7
Crawford	3	D	D	D	NA	NA	NA	NA	6	59	1.4	0.3
Crisp	25	D	D	D	29	1 405	410.8	54.4	51	1 062	39.0	11.2
Dade	12	D	D	D	15	889	187.8	31.7	22	412	15.8	4.2
Dawson	55	221	24.4	7.8	NA	NA	NA	NA	51	1 049	49.9	14.0
Decatur	38	165	11.5	4.5	34	2 301	1 021.4	74.8	50	600	24.1	5.7
DeKalb	2 872	D	D	D	511	19 626	7 489.0	821.2	1 425	22 495	1 207.7	320.2
Dodge	24	98	8.1	2.9	15	762	199.1	24.5	28	366	12.5	3.5
Dooly	5	11	1.0	0.3	12	1 118	303.8	34.4	16	180	6.6	1.8
Dougherty	214	D	D	D	78	5 380	D	260.0	216	4 151	171.0	42.7
Douglas	251	1 122	115.6	38.2	116	3 656	989.9	149.6	214	5 146	212.3	59.0
Early	14	D	D	D	16	912	832.3	72.6	21	164	6.3	1.5
Echols	NA	NA	NA	NA	NA	NA	NA	NA	NA	NA	NA	NA

1. Establishment subject to federal tax.

STATE County	Health care and social assistance, 2007				Other services, 2007				Federal funds and grants, 2009–2010 Expenditures (mil dol)			
										Direct payments for individuals[1]		
	Number of establishments	Number of employees	Receipts (mil dol)	Annual payroll (mil dol)	Number of establishments	Number of employees	Receipts (mil dol)	Annual payroll (mil dol)	Total	Social Security and government retirement	Medicare	Food Stamps and Supplemental Security Income
	159	160	161	162	163	164	165	166	167	168	169	170
FLORIDA—Cont'd												
Putnam	146	2 213	203.5	70.2	99	444	34.2	9.1	726.8	290.7	221.9	55.2
St. Johns	432	6 152	554.8	213.0	316	D	D	D	1 318.0	669.2	256.9	32.1
St. Lucie	581	8 754	998.2	331.1	355	1 685	132.8	36.8	2 010.2	1 076.9	574.1	88.1
Santa Rosa	232	3 352	311.7	109.1	172	741	54.3	17.1	1 088.8	642.8	177.6	36.4
Sarasota	1 451	23 670	2 493.2	935.9	907	4 837	410.7	111.7	3 891.0	2 130.6	1 274.0	72.0
Seminole	1 141	15 588	1 600.4	612.0	820	5 329	433.5	137.6	2 168.5	1 041.1	531.5	98.9
Sumter	83	1 335	136.0	51.0	59	245	17.9	4.5	608.2	277.5	123.1	24.3
Suwannee	64	1 372	106.0	37.5	43	178	15.2	4.1	368.1	163.9	106.5	19.7
Taylor	45	757	60.6	27.8	29	106	8.8	2.4	218.6	69.3	65.4	13.8
Union	18	D	D	D	6	22	1.3	0.4	93.2	32.1	24.1	15.2
Volusia	1 246	24 171	2 513.9	949.0	1 028	5 409	499.6	119.4	4 310.1	2 079.7	1 282.7	171.3
Wakulla	20	D	D	D	35	79	9.4	2.2	149.6	72.8	34.5	8.3
Walton	100	1 534	133.4	51.6	77	401	42.0	10.4	689.9	178.7	85.4	15.6
Washington	42	1 042	53.0	22.9	22	70	5.6	1.2	269.2	87.1	88.3	13.6
GEORGIA	20 840	419 296	43 943.0	16 481.2	14 588	98 047	10 386.0	2 836.9	92 387.1	24 719.0	10 240.4	3 905.7
Appling	29	811	43.7	19.7	29	118	9.8	2.5	143.0	47.7	32.5	9.7
Atkinson	5	D	D	D	1	D	D	D	69.4	19.7	16.3	4.6
Bacon	17	436	35.8	11.1	18	D	D	D	94.2	28.6	22.6	8.3
Baker	5	D	D	D	2	D	D	D	31.6	4.0	5.8	2.2
Baldwin	107	D	D	D	58	353	21.3	6.6	333.8	127.8	65.3	23.1
Banks	15	130	8.9	2.7	11	47	5.1	1.0	72.2	36.6	14.3	4.0
Barrow	67	1 176	98.4	51.1	77	294	23.0	6.6	369.8	174.5	58.1	19.1
Bartow	158	2 538	286.3	94.7	115	547	53.6	15.1	468.6	246.8	76.3	26.7
Ben Hill	31	601	40.9	17.8	29	D	D	D	159.6	59.8	35.7	12.4
Berrien	25	D	D	D	14	45	3.2	0.7	143.3	61.1	33.0	9.4
Bibb	557	15 350	1 686.3	611.8	302	1 835	190.0	51.3	1 711.4	581.9	343.7	137.1
Bleckley	21	330	20.1	7.4	15	40	4.7	0.9	102.7	34.4	24.7	6.0
Brantley	10	D	D	D	14	39	3.9	0.6	104.7	49.5	21.6	9.5
Brooks	20	D	D	D	23	D	D	D	135.4	45.5	29.2	13.0
Bryan	39	D	D	D	35	163	9.3	2.6	3 496.3	98.1	25.5	10.3
Bulloch	163	2 345	259.9	79.3	99	479	37.6	9.8	370.0	134.8	56.6	24.7
Burke	33	484	32.0	13.1	20	57	3.3	0.8	212.0	68.0	34.7	20.9
Butts	27	700	37.8	16.3	27	178	30.7	3.4	157.3	80.0	30.5	7.7
Calhoun	8	262	13.4	6.9	5	D	D	D	68.2	21.0	14.7	5.8
Camden	99	889	90.2	32.3	53	261	17.7	5.5	587.7	161.8	28.8	14.7
Candler	15	409	25.1	12.2	4	22	1.9	0.4	87.6	29.1	20.2	7.1
Carroll	188	4 028	431.0	169.3	124	596	51.5	12.5	663.9	324.4	132.5	36.6
Catoosa	96	2 366	207.9	82.0	61	359	20.9	6.5	262.7	146.1	52.0	16.4
Charlton	10	218	15.5	5.9	8	16	1.5	0.3	287.1	32.7	18.3	6.1
Chatham	682	18 344	1 941.2	793.5	460	3 091	275.9	83.1	3 475.4	782.4	424.3	148.9
Chattahoochee	5	D	D	D	7	105	8.2	2.7	847.8	12.3	3.1	2.8
Chattooga	24	D	D	D	18	D	D	D	193.0	84.0	46.8	11.3
Cherokee	362	3 977	378.5	141.6	327	1 341	106.2	33.0	580.8	351.4	94.2	18.5
Clarke	394	8 593	871.8	372.4	209	1 635	186.6	31.3	908.7	251.3	103.2	45.2
Clay	7	99	3.6	1.6	2	D	D	D	49.5	9.1	5.3	4.0
Clayton	405	7 206	763.0	298.9	293	1 549	133.4	38.7	1 277.7	598.0	213.7	114.4
Clinch	11	158	13.2	4.3	7	20	1.4	0.4	66.2	19.7	17.6	5.9
Cobb	1 567	29 429	3 293.2	1 282.3	1 259	13 391	902.7	459.0	6 730.9	1 587.2	486.3	113.6
Coffee	95	D	D	D	57	D	D	D	282.9	97.9	57.7	23.9
Colquitt	97	2 018	153.0	59.9	60	326	23.7	7.7	378.0	129.5	71.9	33.9
Columbia	187	2 303	172.5	75.1	148	920	62.3	19.0	1 854.8	308.6	56.7	16.8
Cook	31	437	30.1	10.8	13	50	3.1	0.9	120.9	47.0	26.7	9.6
Coweta	160	2 909	277.0	113.6	143	553	51.2	14.5	576.1	330.8	102.5	28.5
Crawford	9	D	D	D	11	28	1.8	0.6	56.5	25.9	12.3	5.5
Crisp	58	1 212	96.1	34.8	29	D	D	D	213.5	65.1	44.7	21.7
Dade	14	D	D	D	13	D	D	D	106.6	54.2	23.5	5.8
Dawson	32	252	21.6	9.4	40	159	15.8	3.9	107.5	65.3	17.1	4.4
Decatur	60	1 010	71.2	31.8	41	227	11.1	3.5	267.6	74.6	40.2	23.3
DeKalb	1 747	38 838	4 338.3	1 602.9	1 072	7 368	837.2	238.7	5 146.4	1 107.9	741.8	273.7
Dodge	55	1 150	69.9	28.1	20	109	6.9	1.9	195.1	76.0	39.2	12.1
Dooly	12	144	7.5	3.1	9	30	3.2	0.6	115.6	31.8	22.4	8.2
Dougherty	307	8 298	838.5	311.6	188	1 106	85.5	25.7	1 183.2	313.9	154.4	101.8
Douglas	235	4 268	392.5	151.3	212	1 027	121.2	32.5	505.5	285.8	97.2	30.7
Early	23	254	26.1	10.4	14	34	3.2	0.8	127.0	33.0	21.9	13.1
Echols	3	D	D	D	1	D	D	D	15.1	3.9	2.6	1.2

1. State totals may include programs not allocated by county.

Table B. States and Counties — Federal Funds, Residential Construction, and Local Government Finances

STATE County	Federal funds and grants, 2009–2010 (cont.)							Value of residential construction authorized by building permits, 2010		Local government finances, 2007				
	Expenditures (mil dol) (cont.)									General revenue				
	Procurement contract awards			Grants[1]								Taxes		
													Per capita[2] (dollars)	
	Salaries and wages	Defense	Other	Medicaid and other health-related	Nutrition and family welfare	Education	Other	New construction ($1,000)	Number of housing units	Total (mil dol)	Inter-governmental (mil dol)	Total (mil dol)	Total	Property
	171	172	173	174	175	176	177	178	179	180	181	182	183	184
FLORIDA—Cont'd														
Putnam	10.2	2.7	3.3	84.6	17.3	12.5	8.2	4 690	36	424.7	166.8	197.8	2 680	2 486
St. Johns	147.0	51.4	49.6	61.7	15.6	6.6	13.9	302 954	1 268	706.5	182.6	334.3	1 906	1 729
St. Lucie	58.8	1.7	12.4	87.1	30.2	15.3	21.0	32 642	293	1 305.2	387.7	525.8	2 015	1 652
Santa Rosa	58.9	49.8	9.5	59.3	21.6	7.4	5.3	137 714	781	416.8	205.5	129.6	881	763
Sarasota	128.7	11.6	20.4	89.7	35.7	16.3	91.3	194 522	708	2 157.0	280.9	912.6	2 453	1 888
Seminole	126.0	56.4	29.3	124.2	42.4	19.5	31.0	199 372	930	1 430.6	535.1	602.5	1 471	1 075
Sumter	93.1	0.9	36.8	35.5	7.9	3.3	2.9	622 880	2 420	230.4	41.0	80.2	1 110	843
Suwannee	13.8	0.0	1.7	45.6	7.0	3.5	0.5	6 475	50	160.3	94.3	45.2	1 144	887
Taylor	3.1	18.3	1.3	33.2	6.4	2.4	2.8	2 967	33	70.3	33.0	25.3	1 281	1 006
Union	1.7	0.0	0.4	14.9	2.3	0.7	0.7	1 332	13	37.5	27.3	5.2	345	231
Volusia	119.4	115.2	49.7	230.3	58.2	31.4	57.5	158 949	715	2 373.1	574.3	864.5	1 728	1 379
Wakulla	6.4	0.3	3.8	14.5	4.1	1.9	0.9	9 234	81	83.5	44.5	25.8	866	693
Walton	343.7	1.8	1.5	44.4	7.7	2.9	4.2	113 404	388	262.8	60.4	161.9	3 061	2 492
Washington	6.3	0.0	6.1	53.8	4.6	3.3	0.7	3 947	23	81.0	52.3	17.2	752	619
GEORGIA	17 372.0	8 377.5	4 083.2	8 036.6	2 202.4	1 977.0	4 534.7	2 659 234	17 265	X	X	X	X	X
Appling	3.9	0.2	1.7	34.8	5.0	1.7	0.7	222	2	85.1	24.2	27.6	1 539	926
Atkinson	1.9	0.0	0.4	19.1	3.0	0.8	0.0	0	0	25.0	13.7	6.4	780	437
Bacon	1.6	2.8	0.3	17.8	3.6	1.1	1.0	0	0	30.2	15.8	10.7	1 018	559
Baker	0.5	0.3	0.1	9.5	1.2	0.5	0.0	0	0	9.8	4.7	4.3	1 139	873
Baldwin	21.9	0.0	1.2	47.5	11.1	4.3	8.1	7 175	61	187.4	55.2	45.1	980	559
Banks	1.5	0.0	0.3	12.4	2.2	0.8	0.0	4 362	42	43.6	15.0	22.2	1 342	658
Barrow	57.2	10.8	2.1	33.8	6.9	3.2	0.8	5 447	62	176.7	65.2	80.9	1 205	690
Bartow	17.9	16.6	16.1	37.9	18.5	6.1	0.9	14 422	144	340.1	116.5	158.8	1 710	868
Ben Hill	2.6	0.2	1.2	34.8	5.0	1.6	0.7	3 047	36	81.0	26.1	20.7	1 174	631
Berrien	2.9	0.0	0.6	22.4	4.0	1.0	0.7	5 475	28	45.6	22.8	17.7	1 058	632
Bibb	167.9	11.9	44.5	234.9	40.8	22.2	38.8	26 106	210	554.3	201.2	244.8	1 582	867
Bleckley	1.9	0.0	0.5	18.1	2.3	2.3	0.2	1 800	9	34.1	19.5	9.8	797	485
Brantley	2.6	0.0	0.8	13.4	3.3	1.9	0.2	1 896	22	41.5	24.3	13.8	893	491
Brooks	2.1	0.0	0.6	30.7	5.6	2.0	0.8	4 185	24	49.2	19.1	15.0	920	637
Bryan	2 922.3	411.6	2.1	15.6	4.7	1.5	0.1	36 629	223	91.2	36.4	41.9	1 391	802
Bulloch	25.0	1.4	2.3	51.3	11.5	5.6	3.4	22 268	207	190.9	74.7	70.8	1 069	477
Burke	13.8	1.9	1.3	51.1	7.5	2.9	0.8	6 812	41	108.9	26.4	43.6	1 915	1 518
Butts	6.5	0.4	0.9	20.9	8.1	1.4	0.2	889	9	75.3	25.4	36.6	1 541	901
Calhoun	1.4	0.0	0.3	19.3	2.0	0.7	-1.0	85	1	26.3	10.2	5.7	935	606
Camden	213.6	125.0	4.7	15.7	8.7	8.0	0.5	15 156	96	163.6	70.0	63.9	1 313	802
Candler	4.2	0.0	0.4	18.6	3.2	1.0	0.2	0	0	44.6	15.3	11.8	1 114	604
Carroll	21.6	14.1	4.2	70.3	14.4	7.9	8.1	10 743	149	297.7	123.7	118.1	1 055	521
Catoosa	6.9	0.6	2.4	23.1	8.8	3.5	0.2	17 615	123	156.2	70.3	62.1	997	479
Charlton	2.9	0.0	209.8	12.1	3.2	1.7	0.0	3 018	17	44.4	16.3	16.3	1 536	1 121
Chatham	1 181.0	324.2	29.8	256.6	65.2	29.6	48.2	101 681	957	1 573.2	251.8	552.1	2 222	1 376
Chattahoochee	0.8	812.5	8.0	4.6	1.1	1.1	0.2	827	6	10.6	6.7	2.6	272	117
Chattooga	3.2	0.0	0.9	32.8	6.1	2.1	3.2	0	0	63.7	33.1	19.9	742	393
Cherokee	29.9	7.4	10.7	34.1	15.1	5.7	1.4	90 422	549	567.9	184.3	270.2	1 322	991
Clarke	116.6	5.4	31.3	154.2	26.8	15.6	109.1	15 081	94	739.6	115.6	143.5	1 258	890
Clay	2.0	13.9	0.2	11.1	1.3	0.3	0.1	800	10	10.7	5.0	4.2	1 303	835
Clayton	111.7	47.9	12.8	63.3	32.5	24.2	24.0	18 265	143	952.9	336.7	458.1	1 683	937
Clinch	1.7	1.5	0.4	13.7	2.6	0.8	0.1	340	5	35.0	11.5	9.1	1 303	888
Cobb	249.9	3 623.6	259.2	108.9	72.1	34.5	62.9	190 859	1 013	2 215.9	678.3	1 146.8	1 657	1 141
Coffee	17.3	0.0	1.5	50.0	10.1	3.9	0.8	12 654	108	129.0	71.3	41.9	1 046	505
Colquitt	9.9	1.7	1.8	67.6	28.6	4.2	6.3	11 046	67	207.1	69.7	43.1	962	504
Columbia	1 402.0	1.4	3.9	26.3	10.4	3.4	13.0	201 494	1 285	307.9	115.7	141.7	1 299	745
Cook	2.4	0.0	0.6	23.3	4.5	2.8	0.1	4 435	22	50.0	24.0	17.3	1 052	567
Coweta	33.1	1.7	6.1	49.3	12.0	4.8	1.6	114 974	416	292.1	120.2	136.4	1 147	604
Crawford	0.8	0.0	0.2	9.3	1.6	1.0	-1.1	2 700	15	27.6	14.2	9.6	770	600
Crisp	15.7	0.0	0.9	47.2	7.0	3.6	0.7	6 804	75	150.1	38.7	34.0	1 537	736
Dade	2.2	0.0	0.7	16.0	2.9	0.9	0.0	85	1	35.8	16.2	15.8	983	445
Dawson	4.8	0.9	1.1	10.6	2.4	0.4	0.0	10 479	35	72.7	17.2	46.9	2 183	1 220
Decatur	19.2	1.9	4.4	46.9	8.4	3.9	0.6	8 034	89	169.4	53.7	31.9	1 118	573
DeKalb	1 394.9	55.3	589.1	291.0	107.3	55.5	303.5	95 259	432	2 685.0	740.3	1 070.6	1 452	1 050
Dodge	8.8	0.5	0.7	42.0	5.9	2.3	2.9	810	12	100.2	31.1	15.8	789	386
Dooly	3.4	0.0	0.5	29.1	5.0	1.2	2.9	0	0	37.2	13.4	14.0	1 210	724
Dougherty	162.7	111.4	62.3	149.9	35.3	17.3	17.1	4 790	54	372.4	164.5	136.4	1 425	856
Douglas	24.2	0.7	4.6	30.4	12.5	5.7	2.4	8 734	72	431.8	149.4	203.8	1 637	887
Early	3.0	0.0	0.6	33.7	4.1	1.4	7.2	1 874	12	54.6	19.2	16.1	1 358	775
Echols	0.1	0.0	0.0	3.9	0.8	0.4	1.8	327	3	10.1	5.3	4.0	978	804

1. State totals may include programs not allocated by county.   2. Based on the resident population estimated as of July 1 of the year shown.

Table B. States and Counties — Local Government Finances, Government Employment, and Voting

STATE County	Total (mil dol)	Per capita[1] (dollars)	Education	Health and hospitals	Police protection	Public welfare	Highways	Total (mil dol)	Per capita[1] (dollars)	Federal civilian	Federal military	State and local	Democratic	Republican	All other
	185	186	187	188	189	190	191	192	193	194	195	196	197	198	199
FLORIDA—Cont'd															
Putnam	388.8	5 266	39.8	1.5	3.8	0.3	5.0	171.3	2 321	147	144	4 249	39.9	59.2	0.9
St. Johns	871.6	4 968	40.3	1.6	4.4	0.8	6.0	1 605.0	9 148	551	385	7 777	33.8	65.4	0.8
St. Lucie	1 335.9	5 119	44.1	0.7	6.3	0.7	10.7	2 238.9	8 580	813	599	12 906	55.7	43.5	0.8
Santa Rosa	403.6	2 745	57.9	1.0	7.8	0.0	4.7	98.5	670	740	1 383	5 660	25.6	73.5	1.0
Sarasota	1 904.4	5 118	29.5	25.6	5.3	0.0	6.6	1 715.3	4 610	1 052	733	13 660	49.5	49.6	0.9
Seminole	1 396.5	3 410	52.0	0.7	7.6	0.1	8.9	762.8	1 863	1 522	817	16 198	48.2	51.0	0.7
Sumter	215.1	2 977	34.2	1.0	8.4	0.8	4.3	598.0	8 278	1 425	153	2 971	36.1	63.2	0.7
Suwannee	141.7	3 584	68.4	1.2	3.3	0.0	7.0	54.4	1 377	112	79	1 858	27.8	71.0	1.2
Taylor	71.4	3 613	51.2	5.6	6.9	0.4	5.0	47.7	2 411	38	42	1 695	29.9	68.9	1.1
Union	36.8	2 454	54.8	2.9	3.8	0.7	11.3	2.8	184	22	29	2 580	24.6	74.4	1.0
Volusia	2 294.2	4 585	36.0	21.7	6.6	0.5	3.7	3 233.2	6 461	1 432	1 021	20 929	52.4	46.7	0.9
Wakulla	78.4	2 637	57.7	3.5	12.4	0.1	7.7	19.8	667	89	65	1 941	36.9	61.7	1.3
Walton	257.0	4 860	30.3	3.7	11.6	0.6	13.2	131.2	2 482	148	137	2 994	26.5	72.3	1.1
Washington	77.9	3 405	66.7	0.7	6.3	0.0	7.8	15.6	680	42	47	2 348	25.7	73.5	0.8
GEORGIA	X	X	X	X	X	X	X	X	X	98 755	102 818	596 689	47.0	52.2	0.8
Appling	91.2	5 081	37.6	33.7	2.8	1.5	4.9	36.4	2 027	52	56	1 507	26.4	72.7	0.9
Atkinson	26.0	3 159	58.4	1.1	3.8	1.3	4.1	6.1	742	23	25	442	32.3	66.8	0.9
Bacon	30.2	2 872	57.7	1.1	4.0	0.9	7.9	4.3	411	24	33	578	20.7	78.4	0.8
Baker	9.5	2 517	66.0	3.5	4.5	0.7	10.4	0.7	196	11	11	175	50.1	49.1	0.8
Baldwin	176.6	3 835	30.6	41.7	3.7	0.1	3.1	113.8	2 470	65	151	7 517	51.9	47.3	0.8
Banks	47.3	2 859	70.4	2.2	3.6	0.1	4.2	51.1	3 084	17	52	854	16.5	82.1	1.5
Barrow	201.1	2 995	64.2	2.2	6.2	0.4	2.9	260.8	3 885	176	223	2 897	27.1	71.7	1.2
Bartow	329.8	3 553	57.3	1.3	7.0	0.3	5.1	385.6	4 153	186	297	5 076	26.8	72.0	1.3
Ben Hill	81.7	4 631	38.9	28.4	4.1	0.4	3.8	17.3	980	35	54	1 690	42.9	56.6	0.5
Berrien	44.7	2 674	62.9	2.4	4.5	0.2	8.2	26.0	1 557	37	53	917	22.8	76.0	1.2
Bibb	563.4	3 641	45.8	6.5	7.9	0.5	3.4	551.4	3 564	1 275	591	9 903	58.7	40.7	0.5
Bleckley	33.2	2 696	62.7	1.2	8.4	0.9	5.6	3.7	300	28	40	1 284	27.2	72.1	0.7
Brantley	38.9	2 522	74.2	1.8	3.0	0.4	6.2	11.9	768	28	78	797	17.8	80.9	1.2
Brooks	49.9	3 051	46.6	18.4	4.7	0.2	7.5	12.3	752	33	50	737	43.0	56.6	0.4
Bryan	89.6	2 975	60.1	2.0	7.8	0.7	6.1	27.1	898	142	100	1 484	28.3	70.9	0.8
Bulloch	207.3	3 132	53.8	9.7	6.2	0.0	5.2	41.0	620	140	222	6 827	40.1	59.3	0.7
Burke	111.7	4 908	43.4	0.7	3.3	0.4	5.2	721.7	31 720	48	70	1 520	54.4	45.1	0.5
Butts	71.7	3 019	52.4	1.1	6.2	0.2	5.3	78.8	3 315	45	75	1 612	33.7	65.4	0.9
Calhoun	25.1	4 114	43.6	32.6	3.6	0.8	4.4	2.5	405	23	19	780	60.7	39.0	0.3
Camden	167.2	3 435	53.8	2.8	6.2	0.2	6.7	30.5	625	2 204	4 281	2 621	37.9	61.5	0.6
Candler	43.5	4 121	40.2	30.3	3.6	0.1	3.8	12.1	1 149	23	33	715	34.4	65.0	0.7
Carroll	305.8	2 731	61.0	0.6	6.1	0.1	2.7	425.9	3 804	226	355	8 191	33.0	65.9	1.2
Catoosa	157.4	2 529	77.9	0.7	4.0	0.6	1.7	136.2	2 188	100	198	2 465	24.6	74.4	1.0
Charlton	40.2	3 794	44.7	22.9	5.2	0.1	9.0	5.9	556	47	33	622	32.5	66.9	0.6
Chatham	1 581.2	6 364	20.5	34.5	5.8	0.2	4.0	1 231.6	4 957	2 781	7 407	16 127	56.9	42.5	0.6
Chattahoochee	11.8	1 253	71.6	1.5	4.1	5.2	3.3	5.7	604	116	16 413	280	50.2	49.1	0.7
Chattooga	66.5	2 480	62.1	1.3	5.1	0.2	4.3	24.2	904	38	82	1 551	31.3	67.1	1.7
Cherokee	573.7	2 807	66.7	1.4	4.1	0.4	5.5	827.3	4 048	311	664	7 968	23.8	74.9	1.2
Clarke	724.0	6 347	21.2	54.4	3.1	0.1	1.7	345.0	3 025	1 353	671	21 892	65.0	33.7	1.3
Clay	10.6	3 320	48.3	4.1	4.7	1.6	10.5	2.5	792	47	10	251	61.0	38.8	0.2
Clayton	881.9	3 240	57.6	3.2	6.7	0.6	4.5	452.4	1 662	1 424	868	15 395	83.0	16.6	0.4
Clinch	37.9	5 414	37.0	43.9	2.8	0.2	2.9	29.3	4 193	18	22	497	36.7	62.2	1.1
Cobb	2 127.6	3 075	55.3	2.1	6.6	0.7	4.5	1 230.8	1 779	2 482	2 829	33 740	44.8	54.2	1.0
Coffee	125.3	3 127	66.4	0.4	4.7	0.1	6.4	28.6	713	108	126	2 890	35.0	64.5	0.5
Colquitt	209.0	4 665	40.8	32.6	3.0	0.1	4.1	60.4	1 348	133	141	3 574	30.8	68.4	0.8
Columbia	290.5	2 662	68.4	0.5	5.4	0.3	3.9	281.4	2 580	184	348	5 000	28.4	71.0	0.6
Cook	49.7	3 024	57.2	1.3	6.6	0.4	7.2	39.4	2 399	31	51	989	35.2	64.1	0.8
Coweta	296.4	2 492	70.3	0.5	4.8	0.1	4.0	221.7	1 864	232	392	5 115	29.0	70.2	0.9
Crawford	25.3	2 025	72.4	2.0	5.8	0.2	4.0	4.2	340	11	38	469	35.0	64.1	1.0
Crisp	142.4	6 435	31.0	44.7	4.0	0.2	2.8	26.3	1 188	60	69	1 461	40.9	58.6	0.5
Dade	34.0	2 114	66.5	0.8	6.0	0.5	2.5	16.4	1 017	24	50	611	25.2	73.4	1.5
Dawson	77.1	3 589	55.4	2.9	4.4	1.1	3.5	68.6	3 192	44	70	1 149	16.4	82.6	1.0
Decatur	139.3	4 881	41.5	28.2	4.3	0.1	4.9	36.2	1 267	65	89	2 838	42.6	56.8	0.6
DeKalb	2 893.2	3 925	39.7	25.9	4.8	0.4	2.0	2 647.4	3 592	13 316	2 778	34 270	79.0	20.3	0.7
Dodge	82.1	4 096	43.8	36.6	2.9	0.2	3.8	30.1	1 504	47	61	2 170	31.6	67.5	0.9
Dooly	39.0	3 362	62.2	1.8	6.1	0.6	6.8	14.6	1 255	55	36	780	51.4	47.9	0.7
Dougherty	361.3	3 775	49.2	6.9	5.7	0.1	3.1	252.8	2 642	3 229	712	7 296	67.3	32.3	0.4
Douglas	422.5	3 394	59.0	1.4	4.6	0.5	5.9	532.3	4 276	195	401	5 756	50.5	48.7	0.8
Early	53.4	4 509	46.3	24.6	7.5	0.2	4.9	5.5	460	46	36	1 280	48.8	50.8	0.4
Echols	9.0	2 192	74.5	0.3	4.8	0.4	4.0	0.1	27	0	13	206	16.9	82.6	0.4

1. Based on the resident population estimated as of July 1 of the year shown.   2. © 2009 Election Data Services, Inc. All rights reserved.

Table B. States and Counties — **Land Area and Population**

STATE/County code	CBSA code[1]	County type[2]	STATE County	Land area,[3] (sq km) 2010	Total persons	Rank	Per square kilometer	White	Black	American Indian, Alaska Native	Asian and Pacific Islander	Percent Hispanic or Latino[4]	Under 5 years	5 to 17 years	18 to 24 years	25 to 34 years	35 to 44 years	45 to 54 years
				1	2	3	4	5	6	7	8	9	10	11	12	13	14	15
			GEORGIA—Cont'd															
13 103	42340	2	Effingham	1 237	52 250	949	42.2	82.4	14.1	0.9	1.3	2.9	7.0	21.5	8.4	12.9	15.1	15.4
13 105	...	6	Elbert	909	20 166	1 830	22.2	64.9	29.8	0.4	0.8	4.8	6.5	16.8	8.7	11.0	12.3	14.5
13 107	...	7	Emanuel	1 763	22 598	1 705	12.8	61.4	33.8	0.5	0.8	4.1	7.3	18.1	9.2	13.1	12.0	14.0
13 109	...	6	Evans	474	11 000	2 364	23.2	57.4	29.2	0.3	0.8	13.1	7.7	18.1	9.6	13.5	12.9	13.6
13 111	...	8	Fannin	1 002	23 682	1 658	23.6	97.1	0.5	1.0	0.5	1.8	4.8	14.4	6.4	8.8	10.9	15.5
13 113	12060	1	Fayette	503	106 567	555	211.9	69.1	20.7	0.7	4.7	6.3	4.6	21.8	6.8	7.5	13.6	18.6
13 115	40660	3	Floyd	1 321	96 317	601	72.9	74.9	14.8	0.6	1.6	9.3	6.8	17.6	10.3	12.1	13.0	13.9
13 117	12060	1	Forsyth	580	175 511	351	302.6	81.3	2.8	0.5	6.9	9.4	7.7	22.7	5.6	11.0	18.7	15.6
13 119	...	8	Franklin	677	22 084	1 736	32.6	87.0	9.0	0.6	0.7	3.9	5.8	16.6	9.5	10.9	12.6	14.5
13 121	12060	1	Fulton	1 364	920 581	48	674.9	42.1	44.5	0.6	6.3	7.9	6.8	17.1	10.7	16.7	15.5	14.0
13 123	...	6	Gilmer	1 105	28 292	1 482	25.6	89.5	0.6	0.9	0.4	9.5	5.9	16.1	7.0	10.7	12.4	14.8
13 125	...	9	Glascock	372	3 082	2 972	8.3	90.4	8.5	0.9	0.1	1.1	6.5	19.9	7.1	11.5	12.9	15.1
13 127	15260	3	Glynn	1 087	79 626	686	73.3	66.0	26.6	0.6	1.6	6.4	6.7	17.4	8.5	11.9	12.5	14.6
13 129	15660	6	Gordon	922	55 186	909	59.9	81.0	4.1	0.6	1.2	14.0	7.4	19.5	8.8	12.9	14.5	14.0
13 131	...	6	Grady	1 177	25 011	1 600	21.2	60.3	29.0	1.0	0.6	10.0	7.6	18.1	8.5	12.6	12.6	14.2
13 133	...	6	Greene	1 003	15 994	2 049	15.9	55.5	38.6	0.6	0.5	5.6	5.6	15.0	6.7	10.9	10.2	13.3
13 135	12060	1	Gwinnett	1 115	805 321	65	722.3	45.4	23.9	0.6	11.5	20.1	7.7	21.4	8.5	14.3	16.6	15.1
13 137	18460	6	Habersham	717	43 041	1 105	60.0	81.7	3.8	0.7	2.7	12.4	6.7	17.2	8.9	12.6	13.2	13.8
13 139	23580	3	Hall	1 017	179 684	344	176.7	64.6	7.6	0.5	2.1	26.1	7.9	20.1	9.3	13.4	14.3	13.5
13 141	33300	7	Hancock	1 222	9 429	2 486	7.7	23.9	74.2	0.4	0.6	1.5	4.6	13.6	9.0	13.2	12.6	16.3
13 143	12060	1	Haralson	731	28 780	1 461	39.4	93.4	5.3	0.8	0.7	1.1	6.4	18.7	8.8	11.5	14.0	14.5
13 145	17980	2	Harris	1 201	32 024	1 392	26.7	78.8	17.5	0.7	1.4	2.7	5.5	18.3	7.3	9.2	14.3	17.0
13 147	...	6	Hart	602	25 213	1 596	41.9	77.2	19.3	0.4	1.0	3.1	6.1	16.1	7.8	10.4	12.7	14.7
13 149	12060	1	Heard	767	11 834	2 309	15.4	87.6	10.4	0.9	0.6	1.9	6.3	19.5	8.2	10.6	14.3	15.3
13 151	12060	1	Henry	834	203 922	301	244.5	54.0	37.6	0.8	3.6	5.8	6.8	22.5	8.2	12.2	16.9	15.2
13 153	47580	3	Houston	973	139 900	439	143.8	62.4	29.4	0.9	3.4	6.1	7.3	19.5	9.5	14.3	13.5	15.2
13 155	22340	7	Irwin	918	9 538	2 476	10.4	71.1	26.2	0.2	0.8	2.4	6.3	18.0	8.6	12.4	13.5	13.7
13 157	...	6	Jackson	880	60 485	854	68.7	85.0	7.4	0.6	2.1	6.2	7.1	19.4	7.8	12.8	15.2	14.5
13 159	12060	1	Jasper	954	13 900	2 186	14.6	73.8	22.4	0.7	0.5	3.7	6.8	18.2	8.1	11.8	13.5	15.1
13 161	...	7	Jeff Davis	857	15 068	2 103	17.6	74.1	15.2	0.4	0.5	10.5	7.9	19.8	8.7	12.5	12.9	13.8
13 163	...	6	Jefferson	1 364	16 930	1 987	12.4	42.0	54.7	0.3	0.5	3.1	6.9	18.3	8.7	11.6	12.5	13.9
13 165	...	6	Jenkins	899	8 340	2 585	9.3	54.9	40.9	0.6	0.6	4.0	7.4	19.5	8.9	10.7	11.5	13.8
13 167	20140	9	Johnson	785	9 980	2 449	12.7	62.8	35.1	0.4	0.4	1.9	5.5	15.4	7.8	13.8	14.2	16.6
13 169	31420	3	Jones	1 020	28 669	1 469	28.1	73.5	24.9	0.6	0.9	1.1	6.6	19.5	7.7	11.3	14.0	15.7
13 171	12060	1	Lamar	475	18 317	1 907	38.6	66.5	31.7	0.8	0.6	1.9	5.9	15.2	14.6	11.2	12.4	14.1
13 173	46660	3	Lanier	480	10 078	2 441	21.0	70.2	24.6	1.2	1.6	4.6	8.9	18.6	9.6	15.4	13.0	13.5
13 175	20140	6	Laurens	2 091	48 434	1 003	23.2	60.6	36.3	0.5	1.2	2.4	7.1	18.6	8.5	12.2	13.0	14.1
13 177	10500	3	Lee	921	28 298	1 481	30.7	76.8	19.0	0.6	2.8	2.0	6.6	21.5	8.0	12.6	15.8	15.6
13 179	25980	3	Liberty	1 269	63 453	822	50.0	45.5	43.3	1.2	3.7	9.7	10.3	19.9	13.9	16.5	12.2	12.5
13 181	...	8	Lincoln	545	7 996	2 603	14.7	65.8	32.4	0.8	0.6	1.2	5.3	15.4	8.0	8.9	12.5	16.4
13 183	25980	3	Long	1 037	14 464	2 146	13.9	61.0	26.0	1.3	2.0	12.3	9.4	21.2	10.4	15.7	13.7	13.3
13 185	46660	3	Lowndes	1 285	109 233	539	85.0	57.4	36.4	0.7	2.2	4.8	7.6	17.1	17.4	14.4	12.0	12.3
13 187	...	6	Lumpkin	733	29 966	1 429	40.9	93.3	1.4	1.4	0.9	4.5	5.9	14.9	16.1	11.9	11.8	14.1
13 189	12260	2	McDuffie	667	21 875	1 742	32.8	57.4	40.3	0.6	0.6	2.2	7.1	18.9	8.7	11.3	12.4	14.9
13 191	15260	3	McIntosh	1 099	14 333	2 155	13.0	61.6	36.4	0.8	0.5	1.6	5.5	16.0	7.6	9.4	12.3	16.0
13 193	...	6	Macon	1 038	14 740	2 132	14.2	34.2	60.9	0.3	1.7	3.6	5.8	16.3	9.8	13.9	12.9	15.3
13 195	12020	3	Madison	731	28 120	1 493	38.5	86.7	8.7	0.6	0.9	4.1	6.1	18.3	8.2	11.6	13.6	15.7
13 197	17980	2	Marion	948	8 742	2 547	9.2	59.3	33.0	0.9	1.3	6.5	6.5	17.5	9.3	10.0	12.2	16.6
13 199	12060	1	Meriwether	1 298	21 992	1 738	16.9	58.3	39.7	0.7	0.8	1.6	6.5	17.2	8.4	11.3	11.7	15.1
13 201	...	8	Miller	731	6 125	2 755	8.4	70.1	28.3	0.7	0.5	1.5	6.9	16.5	8.0	11.0	12.1	14.1
13 205	...	6	Mitchell	1 326	23 498	1 666	17.7	47.0	48.0	0.6	0.7	4.4	7.4	17.5	9.4	13.0	13.4	14.6
13 207	31420	3	Monroe	1 025	26 424	1 546	25.8	73.1	24.1	0.6	1.0	2.0	5.5	17.0	8.5	11.0	13.2	16.6
13 209	47080	9	Montgomery	620	9 123	2 517	14.7	68.2	26.6	0.4	0.4	5.3	6.1	16.8	12.5	11.9	13.0	14.3
13 211	...	6	Morgan	900	17 868	1 928	19.9	72.7	24.1	0.6	0.8	2.8	5.7	19.1	6.9	10.0	13.4	15.6
13 213	19140	3	Murray	892	39 628	1 179	44.4	85.9	0.9	0.7	0.4	13.0	7.1	19.7	9.1	12.5	14.9	14.7
13 215	17980	2	Muscogee	560	189 885	329	339.1	45.4	46.3	0.8	3.2	6.4	7.4	18.1	11.4	14.9	12.3	13.5
13 217	12060	1	Newton	705	99 958	579	141.8	53.3	41.6	0.7	1.3	4.6	7.6	21.3	8.8	12.7	15.7	13.7
13 219	12020	3	Oconee	477	32 808	1 366	68.8	87.3	5.3	0.3	3.7	4.4	5.9	22.5	6.9	9.3	15.0	16.8
13 221	12020	3	Oglethorpe	1 137	14 899	2 117	13.1	78.3	18.3	0.7	0.7	3.7	5.9	18.0	7.8	11.5	14.0	15.6
13 223	12060	1	Paulding	809	142 324	433	175.9	76.6	17.8	0.8	1.4	5.1	7.9	22.4	7.9	13.6	17.8	14.3
13 225	22980	6	Peach	389	27 695	1 509	71.2	46.2	46.4	0.8	1.1	6.8	6.6	16.2	17.5	11.4	11.4	14.0
13 227	12060	1	Pickens	601	29 431	1 442	49.0	95.5	1.3	0.9	0.6	2.8	5.9	16.6	7.3	10.6	13.6	14.5
13 229	48180	6	Pierce	820	18 758	1 887	22.9	85.6	9.3	0.9	0.6	4.7	7.0	19.1	7.6	11.8	13.6	14.1
13 231	12060	1	Pike	560	17 869	1 927	31.9	87.9	10.8	0.8	0.6	1.1	5.7	21.4	7.4	10.5	15.1	15.6
13 233	16340	6	Polk	804	41 475	1 144	51.6	77.4	13.2	0.6	0.9	11.8	8.0	18.7	9.1	12.7	12.8	13.9
13 235	...	6	Pulaski	645	12 010	2 303	18.6	63.0	32.2	0.4	1.0	3.9	5.9	15.6	7.6	12.6	13.8	15.5

1. CBSA = Core Based Statistical Area. See Appendix A for explanation. See Appendix B for list of metropolitan areas with component counties. 2. County type code from the Economic Research Service of USDA Rural-Urban Continuum Codes. See Appendix A for definition. 3. Dry land or land partially or temporarily covered by water. 4. May be of any race.

Table B. States and Counties — **Population and Households**

STATE County	55 to 64 years (16)	65 to 74 years (17)	75 years and over (18)	Percent female (19)	1990 (20)	2000 (21)	1990–2000 (22)	2000–2010 (23)	Births (24)	Deaths (25)	Net migration (26)	Number (27)	Percent change, 2000–2010 (28)	Persons per household (29)	Female family householder[1] (30)	One person (31)
GEORGIA—Cont'd																
Effingham	10.5	5.9	3.3	50.2	25 687	37 535	46.1	39.2	6 108	2 698	12 672	18 092	37.6	2.85	12.7	17.3
Elbert	13.4	9.2	7.6	52.1	18 949	20 511	8.2	-1.7	2 428	2 280	-164	8 063	0.7	2.47	16.5	26.9
Emanuel	12.3	8.1	5.9	51.2	20 546	21 837	6.3	3.5	3 400	2 424	387	8 430	4.8	2.57	19.1	26.5
Evans	11.0	7.7	6.0	51.0	8 724	10 495	20.3	4.8	1 857	1 075	487	4 033	6.7	2.63	17.4	25.9
Fannin	17.3	13.0	9.0	51.2	15 992	19 798	23.8	19.6	2 312	2 566	3 491	10 187	21.7	2.31	9.5	27.1
Fayette	14.4	7.5	5.2	51.7	62 415	91 263	46.2	16.8	8 806	5 616	12 844	38 167	21.1	2.78	10.3	18.1
Floyd	12.0	7.7	6.5	51.6	81 251	90 565	11.5	8.4	12 998	9 128	2 411	35 930	5.6	2.58	14.8	26.0
Forsyth	9.7	5.7	3.2	50.3	44 083	98 407	123.2	78.4	21 769	6 179	60 472	59 433	71.9	2.94	8.0	15.9
Franklin	13.2	9.7	7.2	50.6	16 650	20 285	21.8	8.9	2 607	2 217	1 188	8 540	8.3	2.51	11.2	26.2
Fulton	10.2	5.1	3.9	51.3	648 776	816 006	25.8	12.8	124 820	54 888	44 899	376 377	17.2	2.36	15.7	35.4
Gilmer	15.4	11.4	6.3	50.0	13 368	23 456	75.5	20.6	3 605	2 221	4 316	11 314	24.7	2.48	8.9	24.5
Glascock	12.0	7.8	7.3	51.8	2 357	2 556	8.4	20.6	324	340	278	1 162	15.7	2.58	13.4	26.6
Glynn	13.2	8.7	6.4	52.5	62 496	67 568	8.1	17.8	9 701	6 864	6 775	31 774	16.8	2.46	16.2	27.5
Gordon	11.2	7.1	4.5	50.6	35 067	44 104	25.8	25.1	7 817	3 853	5 502	19 715	21.9	2.77	12.9	21.6
Grady	12.2	8.3	5.9	51.6	20 279	23 659	16.7	5.7	3 724	2 350	307	9 418	7.1	2.63	16.7	24.3
Greene	17.4	14.0	7.0	51.2	11 793	14 406	22.2	11.0	1 781	1 526	1 169	6 519	19.0	2.43	15.8	25.0
Gwinnett	9.5	4.2	2.6	50.7	352 910	588 448	66.7	36.9	117 981	26 498	131 785	268 519	32.7	2.98	14.2	19.1
Habersham	12.3	8.7	6.6	52.8	27 622	35 902	30.0	19.9	5 474	3 042	5 481	15 472	16.7	2.63	10.5	23.2
Hall	10.5	6.4	4.7	50.1	95 434	139 277	45.9	29.0	28 238	10 211	30 157	60 691	28.1	2.91	12.4	20.3
Hancock	15.1	9.3	6.3	45.2	8 908	10 076	13.1	-6.4	1 042	970	-884	3 341	3.2	2.38	23.7	31.3
Haralson	12.0	8.3	5.7	51.1	21 966	25 690	17.0	12.0	3 578	2 718	2 448	10 757	9.5	2.64	13.3	23.2
Harris	15.2	8.3	4.9	50.1	17 788	23 695	33.2	35.2	2 909	2 002	5 609	11 823	34.0	2.67	10.3	18.5
Hart	14.1	10.2	7.8	50.6	19 712	22 997	16.7	9.6	2 610	2 556	1 175	10 121	11.1	2.43	13.6	27.4
Heard	12.5	8.0	5.2	50.3	8 628	11 012	27.6	7.5	1 295	975	246	4 400	8.8	2.66	13.6	23.8
Henry	9.9	5.3	3.1	52.0	58 741	119 341	103.2	70.9	24 076	8 387	60 406	70 255	69.8	2.89	16.4	18.5
Houston	10.3	6.0	4.4	51.3	89 208	110 765	24.2	26.3	17 415	7 941	15 946	53 051	29.7	2.61	16.2	24.0
Irwin	12.0	8.9	6.6	49.6	8 649	9 931	14.8	-4.0	1 163	984	24	3 495	-4.1	2.54	17.0	25.8
Jackson	11.3	7.5	4.4	50.4	30 005	41 589	38.6	45.4	7 723	4 067	18 297	21 343	41.7	2.80	11.3	18.7
Jasper	13.9	7.7	5.0	50.2	8 453	11 426	35.2	21.7	1 654	1 015	1 936	5 044	20.8	2.74	13.8	20.8
Jeff Davis	12.1	7.7	4.7	50.5	12 032	12 684	5.4	18.8	2 138	1 395	310	5 689	17.8	2.63	15.6	24.2
Jefferson	13.3	8.3	6.5	51.7	17 408	17 266	-0.8	-1.9	2 419	1 928	-1 187	6 241	-1.5	2.63	23.4	26.0
Jenkins	13.2	8.0	7.1	52.5	8 247	8 575	4.0	-2.7	1 193	853	-420	3 192	-0.7	2.59	20.3	28.7
Johnson	12.8	7.8	6.2	44.0	8 329	8 560	2.8	16.6	1 037	918	652	3 347	6.9	2.46	18.3	29.1
Jones	12.7	7.7	4.8	51.6	20 739	23 639	14.0	21.3	2 986	1 855	3 082	10 586	22.3	2.68	14.5	21.4
Lamar	13.0	8.1	5.5	51.7	13 038	15 912	22.0	15.1	1 954	1 651	1 398	6 618	15.9	2.55	15.7	25.6
Lanier	10.1	6.7	4.2	49.6	5 531	7 241	30.9	39.2	1 039	643	806	3 608	39.1	2.72	15.6	22.3
Laurens	12.4	7.9	6.3	52.4	39 988	44 874	12.2	7.9	6 480	4 511	1 713	18 641	9.1	2.54	18.4	26.2
Lee	11.7	5.2	3.2	50.2	16 250	24 757	52.4	14.3	3 172	1 380	5 359	9 706	17.9	2.83	13.6	16.4
Liberty	8.4	4.2	2.1	51.2	52 745	61 610	16.8	3.0	12 680	2 703	-9 209	22 155	14.3	2.75	21.5	20.7
Lincoln	16.1	10.9	6.6	51.3	7 442	8 348	12.2	-4.2	790	855	-326	3 281	0.9	2.42	14.2	27.6
Long	8.1	4.4	2.9	50.5	6 202	10 304	66.1	40.4	1 468	578	1 096	5 023	40.5	2.81	18.1	22.4
Lowndes	9.4	5.7	4.1	51.2	75 981	92 115	21.2	18.6	14 893	6 788	7 117	39 747	21.7	2.59	16.9	24.5
Lumpkin	12.6	8.1	4.6	50.3	14 573	21 016	44.2	42.6	2 950	1 740	5 381	10 989	45.8	2.56	9.6	22.2
McDuffie	13.0	8.1	5.5	53.1	20 119	21 231	5.5	3.0	3 033	2 249	-39	8 289	4.0	2.60	21.4	24.2
McIntosh	15.9	11.2	6.1	51.2	8 634	10 847	25.6	32.1	1 343	1 032	263	5 971	42.1	2.39	14.7	28.4
Macon	13.5	7.6	4.8	45.9	13 114	14 074	7.3	4.7	1 738	1 464	-947	4 999	3.4	2.56	24.0	29.2
Madison	13.1	8.3	5.1	50.6	21 050	25 730	22.2	9.3	3 230	2 281	1 699	10 508	7.2	2.66	12.1	21.5
Marion	14.0	9.4	4.5	50.8	5 590	7 144	27.8	22.4	939	705	-359	3 420	28.2	2.53	16.5	26.9
Meriwether	14.1	9.4	6.3	52.3	22 411	22 534	0.5	-2.4	2 944	2 396	-158	8 522	3.3	2.55	18.7	26.8
Miller	13.0	9.7	8.6	52.2	6 280	6 383	1.6	-4.0	812	746	-192	2 426	-2.5	2.46	15.6	27.3
Mitchell	11.6	7.5	5.6	48.1	20 275	23 932	18.0	-1.8	3 200	2 236	-967	8 055	-0.1	2.65	23.2	25.0
Monroe	14.3	8.2	5.7	49.8	17 113	21 757	27.1	21.5	2 567	1 956	3 109	9 662	25.2	2.61	13.1	21.9
Montgomery	12.6	8.1	4.7	48.5	7 379	8 270	12.1	10.3	1 047	697	336	3 287	12.6	2.55	15.5	24.9
Morgan	13.7	9.3	6.2	51.7	12 883	15 457	20.0	15.6	2 066	1 389	2 696	6 660	19.8	2.66	14.7	20.7
Murray	11.2	7.0	3.8	50.4	26 147	36 506	39.6	8.6	5 800	2 596	1 100	14 080	6.0	2.80	12.8	19.8
Muscogee	10.6	6.0	5.6	52.1	179 280	186 291	3.9	1.9	28 302	16 816	-6 574	74 081	6.1	2.47	21.3	29.9
Newton	10.4	6.0	3.9	52.4	41 808	62 001	48.3	61.2	13 287	5 562	30 237	34 390	56.3	2.85	19.0	19.6
Oconee	12.8	6.5	4.4	51.2	17 618	26 225	48.9	25.1	3 300	1 612	5 503	11 622	28.4	2.81	9.5	16.3
Oglethorpe	13.0	8.7	5.5	50.4	9 763	12 635	29.4	17.9	1 502	1 089	1 355	5 647	16.5	2.61	12.5	23.3
Paulding	8.8	4.6	2.6	51.1	41 611	81 678	96.3	74.3	17 505	5 141	42 669	48 105	71.3	2.94	12.8	16.6
Peach	11.5	6.9	4.5	51.6	21 189	23 668	11.7	17.0	3 401	2 066	2 356	9 958	18.0	2.58	19.2	24.8
Pickens	15.1	10.5	5.8	50.9	14 432	22 983	59.3	28.1	3 214	2 295	7 408	11 291	26.0	2.57	9.9	21.2
Pierce	12.7	8.5	5.5	50.9	13 328	15 636	17.3	20.0	2 398	1 636	2 280	7 083	18.9	2.63	13.6	21.8
Pike	12.0	7.6	4.7	51.1	10 224	13 688	33.9	30.5	1 764	1 193	3 513	6 187	30.1	2.84	11.0	17.6
Polk	11.5	7.7	5.6	50.5	33 815	38 127	12.8	8.8	6 495	4 191	2 116	15 092	7.7	2.72	14.8	23.6
Pulaski	13.5	9.6	6.1	56.8	8 108	9 588	18.3	25.3	1 119	1 057	303	4 475	31.3	2.40	17.6	29.3

1. No spouse present.

Table B. States and Counties — **Population, Vital Statistics, Medicare, and Crime**

STATE County	Persons in group quarters, 2010	Daytime population, 2006–2010		Births, average 2006–2008		Deaths, average 2006–2008		Persons under 65 with no health insurance, 2009		Medicare, 2011			Serious crimes known to police,[2] 2010 Total	
		Number	Employ-ment/resi-dence ratio	Total	Rate[1]	Number	Rate[1]	Number	Percent	Eligible for Medicare	Enrolled in Medicare Advantage	Enrolled in a Medicare prescription drug plan	Number	Rate[3]
	32	33	34	35	36	37	38	39	40	41	42	43	44	45
GEORGIA—Cont'd														
Effingham	607	38 546	0.5	687	13.6	318	6.3	8 361	17.5	6 327	1 297	2 317	643	1 231
Elbert	220	19 846	0.9	D	D	252	12.3	4 026	24.2	4 520	1 097	2 059	1 259	6 243
Emanuel	916	22 131	1.0	D	D	259	11.5	5 247	27.0	4 306	926	2 344	NA	NA
Evans	404	11 861	1.2	D	D	127	11.0	2 562	25.9	1 884	455	895	223	2 027
Fannin	161	21 877	0.8	D	D	272	12.1	4 588	25.7	6 085	976	2 719	497	2 220
Fayette	557	100 227	0.9	894	8.4	627	5.9	9 412	10.4	16 087	3 024	6 201	1 621	1 521
Floyd	3 733	99 758	1.1	1 434	15.0	988	10.3	17 762	22.0	17 533	2 890	9 014	3 853	4 000
Forsyth	642	149 971	0.8	2 316	14.5	700	4.4	19 528	12.5	17 559	4 496	6 043	2 388	1 361
Franklin	610	22 494	1.0	D	D	249	11.4	4 235	23.8	4 636	860	2 363	567	2 659
Fulton	31 392	1 256 406	1.9	14 652	14.8	6 088	6.2	213 991	23.4	102 010	26 757	40 084	59 332	6 445
Gilmer	282	26 595	0.9	D	D	259	9.1	6 435	26.6	5 929	1 053	2 747	453	1 601
Glascock	89	2 253	0.4	D	D	37	13.4	495	21.3	532	90	266	20	827
Glynn	1 453	85 366	1.2	1 150	15.4	766	10.2	13 127	20.7	14 318	2 424	6 245	5 068	6 365
Gordon	670	52 472	0.9	875	16.8	439	8.4	10 986	23.8	8 316	1 199	4 403	1 648	3 016
Grady	200	21 187	0.6	417	16.6	252	10.0	5 298	24.8	4 490	885	2 198	504	2 015
Greene	168	16 554	1.1	D	D	161	10.3	2 774	22.7	4 168	1 049	1 846	498	3 114
Gwinnett	5 682	738 133	0.9	13 442	17.4	3 096	4.0	168 416	22.9	68 557	16 829	24 556	23 499	2 918
Habersham	2 384	41 738	1.0	D	D	331	7.9	9 777	27.0	7 899	1 823	3 508	858	2 082
Hall	3 141	174 271	1.0	3 128	17.4	1 153	6.4	42 755	25.9	25 665	6 164	10 352	4 841	2 694
Hancock	1 471	8 676	0.7	D	D	93	9.8	1 764	23.3	1 936	745	804	143	1 517
Haralson	354	26 989	0.9	D	D	323	11.2	5 437	22.2	5 280	1 308	2 470	1 024	3 558
Harris	442	22 149	0.4	313	10.8	233	8.0	3 852	15.0	4 831	1 021	1 706	595	1 919
Hart	663	22 902	0.8	D	D	282	11.6	4 465	22.9	5 385	955	2 571	917	3 643
Heard	132	9 892	0.6	D	D	109	9.6	2 144	21.7	1 974	492	934	237	2 003
Henry	933	159 185	0.6	2 887	15.6	1 057	5.7	27 637	15.7	22 472	5 580	7 831	5 920	2 903
Houston	1 599	136 760	1.0	2 058	15.8	886	6.8	19 690	16.8	18 795	2 175	5 218	5 302	3 790
Irwin	663	8 983	0.8	D	D	100	9.8	1 949	22.9	1 831	345	997	349	3 659
Jackson	757	52 858	0.8	1 003	17.0	459	7.8	11 490	21.3	9 309	2 198	3 662	1 406	2 396
Jasper	94	10 681	0.5	D	D	117	8.5	2 538	21.1	2 395	591	1 004	244	2 170
Jeff Davis	111	13 958	0.9	D	D	149	11.2	2 817	24.0	2 584	338	1 521	603	4 002
Jefferson	527	16 515	0.9	D	D	210	12.7	3 080	22.6	3 364	686	1 706	NA	NA
Jenkins	84	7 235	0.6	D	D	94	10.9	1 607	22.6	1 541	408	780	NA	NA
Johnson	1 737	8 512	0.6	D	D	102	10.7	1 949	25.2	1 732	308	964	177	1 846
Jones	321	20 409	0.4	D	D	219	8.0	4 157	17.7	4 654	1 460	1 683	685	2 389
Lamar	1 455	15 413	0.7	D	D	188	11.2	3 176	21.4	3 218	1 020	1 315	548	3 095
Lanier	260	7 250	0.4	D	D	72	9.0	1 746	24.0	1 283	185	654	NA	NA
Laurens	1 058	49 104	1.1	753	15.8	505	10.6	7 879	19.6	9 121	2 051	3 954	2 480	5 120
Lee	828	20 070	0.4	361	10.9	159	4.8	5 032	16.3	3 248	538	1 179	659	2 377
Liberty	2 579	65 826	1.1	1 431	23.6	303	5.0	11 765	20.8	4 898	813	1 578	2 423	3 819
Lincoln	67	6 796	0.6	D	D	91	11.1	1 576	24.2	1 726	381	741	NA	NA
Long	328	9 237	0.3	155	13.6	73	6.4	2 895	26.3	1 138	162	464	90	622
Lowndes	6 410	113 660	1.2	1 851	18.3	751	7.4	19 681	21.2	13 976	2 113	6 322	4 231	3 940
Lumpkin	1 782	24 953	0.7	D	D	219	8.3	5 615	23.7	4 663	925	2 014	573	1 912
McDuffie	318	21 318	1.0	D	D	226	10.4	3 881	21.0	3 914	1 209	1 449	425	1 943
McIntosh	71	11 767	0.7	D	D	108	9.5	2 182	23.2	2 403	563	1 020	514	3 586
Macon	1 960	14 016	0.9	D	D	164	12.0	2 731	24.5	2 057	628	1 045	290	2 267
Madison	204	21 504	0.5	D	D	254	9.1	5 593	23.2	5 083	1 249	1 910	919	3 404
Marion	79	7 201	0.6	D	D	80	11.3	1 480	24.4	1 301	314	561	NA	NA
Meriwether	253	19 847	0.7	D	D	248	10.9	4 151	22.0	4 381	1 533	1 918	859	4 151
Miller	168	5 639	0.8	D	D	85	13.7	1 115	22.4	1 151	239	629	91	1 486
Mitchell	2 135	23 550	1.0	D	D	239	9.9	4 678	23.3	4 054	832	2 070	746	3 227
Monroe	1 208	21 785	0.6	D	D	225	9.0	3 812	17.5	4 533	933	1 894	607	2 297
Montgomery	732	7 752	0.6	D	D	80	8.8	1 993	25.9	1 423	292	770	NA	NA
Morgan	154	18 450	1.1	D	D	165	9.1	3 138	20.1	3 487	948	1 387	373	2 183
Murray	254	35 246	0.7	639	15.7	306	7.5	8 635	24.0	6 043	628	3 663	973	2 455
Muscogee	7 017	211 086	1.3	3 335	17.8	1 804	9.6	29 400	18.1	28 535	6 028	9 811	14 545	7 660
Newton	1 792	82 091	0.6	1 584	16.6	637	6.7	18 164	20.8	13 118	3 041	5 243	3 010	3 011
Oconee	117	27 539	0.7	D	D	182	5.8	4 291	14.8	4 503	945	1 444	705	2 149
Oglethorpe	177	10 472	0.3	D	D	120	8.5	2 757	22.7	2 513	517	1 058	570	3 826
Paulding	662	96 620	0.4	1 952	15.3	629	4.9	19 863	16.0	13 455	2 946	4 955	3 265	2 298
Peach	2 028	25 735	0.9	424	16.5	227	8.8	5 182	22.4	4 350	886	1 540	1 536	5 546
Pickens	360	26 215	0.8	D	D	251	8.2	5 160	20.3	6 644	1 216	2 913	436	1 742
Pierce	142	15 016	0.6	D	D	179	10.1	3 675	23.3	3 604	561	1 935	359	1 914
Pike	268	12 934	0.4	D	D	153	8.9	2 984	19.6	2 864	680	1 177	156	873
Polk	373	37 285	0.8	766	18.4	454	10.9	8 715	24.3	7 477	1 388	3 454	1 485	3 593
Pulaski	1 248	10 198	0.7	D	D	116	11.8	1 992	24.2	1 895	273	890	NA	NA

1. Per 1,000 estimated resident population.   2. Data for serious crimes have not been adjusted for underreporting; this may affect comparability between geographic areas and over time.   3. Per 100,000 population estimated by the FBI.

Table B. States and Counties — **Crime, Education, Money Income, and Poverty**

STATE County	Serious crimes known to police,[1] 2010 (cont.) Rate[2]		Education School enrollment and attainment, 2006–2010				Local government expenditures,[5] 2008–2009		Money income, 2006–2010	Households			Income and poverty, 2010 Percent below poverty level		
			Enrollment[3]		Attainment[4] (percent)					Median income					
	Violent	Property	Total	Per-cent private	High school grad-uate or less	Bach-elor's degree or more	Total current expendi-tures (mil dol)	Current expendi-tures per student (dollars)	Per capita income[6] (dollars)	Dollars	Percent change, 2000 to 2006–2010 (constant 2010 dollars)	Percent with income of $200,000 or more	Median house-hold income (dollars)	All per-sons	Children under 18 years	Children 5 to 17 years in families
	46	47	48	49	50	51	52	53	54	55	56	57	58	59	60	61

GEORGIA—Cont'd																
Effingham	134	1 097	14 605	11.5	57.3	15.5	97.8	8 609	23 465	56 903	-3.4	1.4	60 017	10.6	15.1	13.7
Elbert	397	5 846	4 949	10.9	70.0	9.6	35.6	10 340	17 100	30 543	-16.0	0.5	32 888	24.5	37.8	34.6
Emanuel	NA	NA	5 344	9.3	66.8	9.7	40.3	9 107	16 076	30 205	-2.2	1.1	30 985	29.5	43.1	40.9
Evans	218	1 809	2 902	13.7	63.2	13.4	16.6	8 906	19 072	40 796	26.6	0.9	32 427	24.9	37.4	37.3
Fannin	487	1 733	4 293	14.0	61.8	16.2	31.3	9 912	21 103	34 145	-11.9	0.7	33 253	18.2	28.2	27.3
Fayette	79	1 442	31 655	17.4	27.8	41.5	199.7	9 028	35 076	82 216	-8.8	7.3	79 276	6.7	10.0	8.6
Floyd	468	3 532	25 761	23.3	56.8	17.9	173.0	10 682	20 640	41 066	-8.9	2.4	38 289	19.1	26.3	25.3
Forsyth	125	1 236	46 543	17.8	29.9	43.6	284.1	8 776	35 385	87 605	0.4	9.0	81 629	7.2	8.9	7.7
Franklin	89	2 570	5 070	14.5	65.4	13.6	77.0	9 702	19 276	36 739	-9.7	1.0	36 109	18.0	29.0	25.0
Fulton	846	5 599	245 051	23.2	30.2	47.6	1 563.7	11 387	37 211	56 709	-5.4	9.4	53 580	17.7	23.9	22.2
Gilmer	138	1 463	6 015	7.0	60.8	13.4	51.4	12 166	20 439	36 741	-17.4	2.3	39 710	15.9	28.8	26.5
Glascock	0	827	703	9.8	70.8	10.5	6.1	9 377	16 844	37 149	-1.4	0.2	36 433	18.5	23.5	21.1
Glynn	617	5 748	18 833	9.6	44.6	26.4	133.3	10 447	28 040	50 337	2.5	4.0	42 993	18.8	30.2	27.3
Gordon	361	2 655	13 365	10.2	64.6	12.7	94.5	9 143	18 285	40 916	-16.8	1.0	40 656	18.5	26.3	23.7
Grady	156	1 859	6 198	6.0	67.3	10.1	37.7	8 475	17 785	32 247	-11.1	1.0	31 297	28.1	38.3	36.7
Greene	350	2 764	3 514	18.6	63.0	18.9	26.1	13 411	24 943	38 513	-9.2	4.3	36 001	27.4	41.7	38.9
Gwinnett	252	2 666	227 286	15.8	36.1	34.9	1 527.1	9 532	26 901	63 219	-17.5	4.1	57 848	13.6	19.2	18.0
Habersham	187	1 895	11 878	26.8	57.7	18.7	66.0	9 474	19 286	40 192	-12.6	1.9	40 316	17.3	25.6	23.4
Hall	181	2 513	43 660	11.8	54.1	21.0	295.5	9 238	23 675	50 876	-10.5	3.3	47 238	17.8	25.2	24.5
Hancock	127	1 389	2 025	4.2	74.9	10.3	15.3	11 819	10 925	22 283	-20.0	0.2	23 887	33.1	42.0	37.5
Haralson	486	3 072	6 702	5.9	67.7	11.0	52.9	9 038	19 033	38 996	-2.7	1.0	39 046	20.7	28.7	26.2
Harris	90	1 829	8 008	11.9	42.1	27.4	46.2	9 428	31 073	67 018	10.8	5.1	62 264	9.4	13.2	11.9
Hart	346	3 298	5 457	12.2	61.7	15.2	33.2	9 394	19 124	36 109	-13.1	1.3	33 753	23.0	30.1	28.4
Heard	211	1 791	3 062	6.1	68.2	7.3	19.9	9 198	18 077	42 685	2.0	1.0	39 614	21.3	31.2	27.8
Henry	212	2 691	59 725	19.5	43.3	24.4	339.4	8 494	25 773	63 923	-11.9	2.4	59 371	10.2	13.9	12.9
Houston	327	3 463	40 737	9.9	41.4	24.4	246.1	9 364	25 206	55 098	-0.3	2.1	54 977	14.1	21.2	18.7
Irwin	220	3 439	2 164	5.9	66.9	9.2	16.7	9 535	16 561	38 376	0.2	0.6	32 859	24.0	35.1	32.1
Jackson	126	2 270	14 961	11.4	57.7	17.7	110.9	9 794	22 473	51 506	0.8	2.1	50 409	15.7	21.3	20.0
Jasper	133	2 037	3 156	22.4	62.6	13.3	19.3	8 808	20 263	42 081	-16.7	3.3	43 443	18.9	30.3	28.2
Jeff Davis	212	3 789	3 442	6.0	68.9	11.5	24.8	8 545	15 730	32 928	-4.8	0.1	32 380	23.6	34.7	32.1
Jefferson	NA	NA	4 444	15.2	71.4	8.7	27.4	8 783	15 165	29 268	-11.5	0.6	29 683	28.9	44.0	38.2
Jenkins	NA	NA	1 880	7.1	68.2	12.8	14.2	9 289	17 029	27 086	-9.0	2.6	27 682	28.9	45.7	42.1
Johnson	459	1 387	2 176	7.5	70.8	8.9	12.6	10 128	15 659	27 607	-8.6	2.7	28 332	30.5	36.0	32.8
Jones	150	2 239	7 382	16.0	53.0	17.2	47.7	8 409	21 598	50 717	-7.5	1.7	52 215	11.9	18.1	16.5
Lamar	457	2 637	4 466	11.7	65.8	9.7	23.0	9 195	17 725	37 530	-20.1	1.1	40 001	17.8	26.8	25.7
Lanier	NA	NA	2 200	8.2	61.0	9.4	15.2	8 765	16 894	37 522	1.6	1.8	33 430	22.6	33.7	32.9
Laurens	429	4 691	11 962	6.7	62.4	15.9	83.6	8 830	19 387	38 280	-5.6	1.9	36 568	19.7	28.9	28.1
Lee	108	2 269	8 786	11.0	48.2	19.2	47.7	7 704	23 867	59 811	-2.8	2.1	61 489	10.3	14.8	12.9
Liberty	375	3 443	20 098	11.1	45.9	16.3	100.9	9 193	18 662	42 674	0.7	0.8	39 697	21.8	30.9	30.0
Lincoln	NA	NA	1 765	5.9	64.9	9.7	14.5	10 928	19 628	36 399	-10.0	0.7	35 201	20.8	32.0	29.8
Long	69	553	3 687	6.3	61.3	9.1	19.4	7 708	15 068	41 186	6.2	0.0	38 243	20.8	29.6	28.9
Lowndes	296	3 644	33 398	7.9	48.7	22.3	160.6	9 300	20 041	39 096	-3.9	1.4	36 486	23.3	30.4	29.5
Lumpkin	270	1 642	9 009	9.5	54.1	19.5	35.9	9 362	20 088	43 394	-12.5	1.5	44 309	16.5	24.5	23.6
McDuffie	183	1 760	5 605	8.0	65.6	11.5	43.9	10 433	17 261	35 414	-12.4	1.0	36 559	21.4	31.5	30.1
McIntosh	335	3 251	3 130	11.7	62.6	15.0	17.9	9 554	20 964	39 075	2.5	0.7	35 681	19.0	32.8	30.2
Macon	438	1 829	3 700	12.0	69.1	10.7	19.1	10 115	12 902	27 950	-8.9	0.3	27 324	31.7	40.1	36.6
Madison	615	2 790	6 994	16.9	66.9	12.9	46.4	9 715	18 975	41 343	-10.2	0.8	41 267	17.2	25.3	23.3
Marion	NA	NA	2 076	6.1	70.3	6.8	14.1	9 899	17 729	31 581	-14.4	0.0	33 534	23.8	36.7	34.5
Meriwether	261	3 890	5 312	16.8	70.7	9.7	35.6	10 329	18 295	37 845	-6.2	0.8	35 287	20.1	31.2	30.7
Miller	114	1 371	1 525	12.0	65.6	9.4	11.3	9 984	19 895	33 196	-4.1	1.2	32 015	24.4	37.1	34.8
Mitchell	606	2 621	6 027	9.8	69.8	9.6	42.9	10 576	16 322	36 198	7.5	0.8	31 094	29.3	40.7	38.5
Monroe	155	2 142	6 428	21.8	56.5	19.0	37.4	9 366	23 656	48 297	-13.7	2.5	49 839	14.5	21.6	19.6
Montgomery	NA	NA	2 604	30.6	60.5	15.5	12.4	11 309	17 168	35 182	-8.1	0.7	35 133	23.5	32.8	30.5
Morgan	170	2 013	4 404	15.9	54.9	23.8	31.9	9 640	27 732	45 817	-10.1	5.4	45 804	16.5	24.3	21.2
Murray	136	2 319	9 852	4.5	73.4	6.7	66.2	8 453	16 925	38 226	-18.4	0.7	39 911	19.1	27.3	24.9
Muscogee	530	7 130	54 478	10.1	45.6	21.6	312.5	9 590	22 514	41 331	-6.2	2.3	36 359	20.2	29.6	27.3
Newton	380	2 631	28 135	16.8	50.2	19.4	174.8	9 052	21 583	52 361	-7.9	1.5	48 989	15.1	20.8	19.3
Oconee	311	1 838	9 679	19.4	30.0	44.9	60.3	9 336	34 271	74 352	6.3	8.3	76 298	8.2	10.9	9.0
Oglethorpe	336	3 490	3 860	11.1	58.9	11.7	21.6	8 730	17 572	39 319	-12.7	0.6	40 936	16.6	24.2	22.1
Paulding	152	2 146	39 532	11.8	50.6	20.8	234.5	8 401	23 450	62 348	-5.6	1.4	61 496	8.8	12.2	10.8
Peach	650	4 896	9 230	8.9	55.7	18.0	40.7	9 991	18 681	41 014	-6.0	1.1	38 024	25.7	35.6	31.7
Pickens	108	1 634	6 259	10.7	53.3	22.0	45.5	10 043	25 892	49 945	-4.7	3.5	48 532	13.6	22.4	20.9
Pierce	149	1 765	4 731	4.4	63.1	8.8	32.0	8 989	18 283	37 062	-2.1	1.1	37 262	18.3	29.3	26.7
Pike	62	811	4 934	10.0	56.5	15.7	26.8	7 715	21 051	53 213	-5.3	0.8	52 411	12.7	18.3	15.5
Polk	416	3 176	10 031	8.9	62.6	11.4	65.4	8 774	18 214	38 646	-5.6	1.0	36 468	22.1	31.3	29.3
Pulaski	NA	NA	2 454	2.5	69.0	5.6	15.2	9 525	16 621	36 262	-10.2	0.3	36 665	20.8	28.4	26.7

1. Data for serious crimes have not been adjusted for underreporting; this may affect comparability between geographic areas and over time.   2. Per 100,000 population estimated by the FBI.   3. All persons 3 years old and over enrolled in nursery school through college.   4. Persons 25 years old and over.   5. Elementary and secondary education expenditures.   6. Based on population estimated by the American Community Survey, 2006–2010.

STATE County	Total (mil dol)	Percent change, 2008–2009	Per capita[1] Dollars	Per capita[1] Rank	Wages and salaries[2] (mil dol)	Proprietors' income (mil dol)	Dividends, interest, and rent (mil dol)	Transfer payments (mil dol) Total	Government payments to individuals Total	Social Security	Medical payments	Income maintenance	Unemployment insurance
	62	63	64	65	66	67	68	69	70	71	72	73	74
GEORGIA—Cont'd													
Effingham	1 680	1.4	31 378	1 670	464	42	162	250	241	91	80	27	16
Elbert	583	-1.4	28 615	2 275	267	58	104	174	170	59	71	22	9
Emanuel	569	0.2	24 647	2 900	274	36	76	199	195	54	84	31	8
Evans	298	-1.3	25 458	2 810	167	26	46	79	77	23	33	13	3
Fannin	645	-0.3	28 107	2 384	206	59	126	200	196	82	79	14	8
Fayette	4 615	-3.6	43 215	265	1 916	234	915	538	519	238	167	30	30
Floyd	3 065	-0.7	31 840	1 567	1 859	205	531	712	695	249	271	81	37
Forsyth	6 315	-4.9	36 184	862	3 172	45	1 038	557	526	249	155	28	50
Franklin	617	-2.8	28 375	2 331	271	86	101	179	175	64	73	18	9
Fulton	52 178	-5.3	50 474	93	57 139	10 062	10 741	4 845	4 657	1 362	1 649	772	348
Gilmer	786	-2.8	27 067	2 557	316	83	131	216	211	82	90	16	10
Glascock	68	2.1	24 230	2 943	13	3	8	25	24	7	13	2	1
Glynn	2 949	-2.9	38 392	589	1 822	131	795	563	549	204	220	58	24
Gordon	1 397	-2.5	26 208	2 686	873	113	176	330	320	115	123	39	23
Grady	650	-1.2	25 793	2 760	230	72	101	159	154	54	55	28	8
Greene	580	-1.4	36 831	769	233	39	170	142	140	58	52	17	6
Gwinnett	26 169	-1.9	32 381	1 446	18 219	1 299	3 460	2 861	2 713	962	906	331	262
Habersham	1 185	-2.4	27 177	2 537	576	82	266	278	270	108	102	22	14
Hall	5 452	-3.2	29 038	2 188	3 560	398	1 020	968	934	362	343	97	59
Hancock	196	1.9	21 208	3 077	52	10	30	87	85	27	36	14	5
Haralson	817	-2.1	28 291	2 348	325	42	119	210	205	73	84	25	11
Harris	1 366	3.2	45 330	189	150	76	193	163	158	68	45	15	8
Hart	632	-2.8	26 258	2 676	257	51	132	178	174	73	60	20	10
Heard	311	0.1	27 003	2 564	186	13	29	75	73	27	26	11	4
Henry	5 858	0.3	29 986	1 981	2 213	220	717	901	866	323	276	109	66
Houston	4 494	1.4	33 114	1 318	3 805	192	656	774	750	219	292	100	37
Irwin	244	-3.0	24 184	2 951	83	29	42	73	71	23	28	10	4
Jackson	1 770	-0.5	27 847	2 427	790	99	245	366	355	130	146	35	21
Jasper	397	0.5	28 423	2 318	93	17	59	90	87	34	29	12	6
Jeff Davis	346	-1.5	25 296	2 828	159	39	55	104	102	33	42	16	5
Jefferson	419	-0.8	25 429	2 815	220	29	60	153	150	42	66	26	7
Jenkins	197	-1.4	23 332	3 016	55	20	28	74	72	18	32	13	4
Johnson	196	-2.0	21 037	3 081	68	7	24	77	75	21	35	11	3
Jones	904	1.6	32 604	1 403	150	29	107	159	154	66	45	22	9
Lamar	487	-0.7	27 752	2 443	148	38	60	133	130	45	45	15	8
Lanier	221	-1.7	26 207	2 687	55	10	24	60	59	16	26	10	3
Laurens	1 425	-0.5	29 510	2 092	879	84	224	376	368	116	143	60	18
Lee	1 055	3.5	30 668	1 830	227	39	120	136	129	47	42	17	9
Liberty	1 680	-1.9	27 020	2 562	2 620	50	178	304	296	63	105	57	18
Lincoln	221	0.3	27 980	2 402	57	14	34	64	63	23	24	7	3
Long	282	2.2	23 081	3 030	40	7	25	64	62	14	23	12	3
Lowndes	3 187	0.5	29 834	2 014	2 423	174	496	675	656	182	266	95	32
Lumpkin	777	-2.1	28 209	2 364	305	42	148	161	156	63	51	15	11
McDuffie	689	1.8	31 499	1 641	295	44	105	174	170	51	71	27	9
McIntosh	307	-0.4	27 001	2 565	85	16	50	96	94	32	39	12	4
Macon	316	-3.3	23 663	2 984	145	36	41	107	104	25	52	17	5
Madison	821	-2.3	29 088	2 172	141	62	101	190	185	69	73	21	10
Marion	221	-0.5	31 542	1 634	59	15	24	50	49	15	18	10	2
Meriwether	575	-0.8	25 255	2 835	208	34	86	175	171	56	62	28	9
Miller	185	-3.2	29 653	2 064	62	25	35	48	46	15	21	7	2
Mitchell	602	-1.5	25 282	2 831	308	62	87	173	169	49	68	33	8
Monroe	963	2.5	37 860	659	271	28	136	158	154	62	53	18	9
Montgomery	224	-0.2	25 042	2 861	67	16	32	61	60	18	24	9	3
Morgan	628	-2.9	33 494	1 254	252	46	136	124	121	48	45	14	7
Murray	1 011	-0.2	24 883	2 876	457	41	97	239	231	79	91	30	18
Muscogee	7 257	0.0	38 111	625	5 208	336	1 390	1 405	1 372	377	498	236	59
Newton	2 493	0.8	24 948	2 867	1 037	50	316	585	567	185	221	84	40
Oconee	1 540	0.9	46 233	161	387	41	266	147	141	63	48	10	8
Oglethorpe	426	-2.4	29 755	2 029	67	33	54	80	78	33	24	11	5
Paulding	4 584	3.4	33 543	1 244	834	163	388	513	488	194	135	58	48
Peach	804	1.8	29 517	2 089	369	54	113	206	201	53	84	30	9
Pickens	1 018	-4.5	32 550	1 412	310	53	229	216	210	96	74	15	11
Pierce	489	0.2	26 313	2 667	158	32	63	143	140	44	56	16	6
Pike	528	0.4	29 793	2 023	97	30	66	106	102	41	37	11	6
Polk	1 066	-1.3	25 209	2 843	491	42	148	319	311	104	136	35	17
Pulaski	298	-2.2	30 061	1 963	119	7	47	72	70	22	31	10	2

1. Based on the resident population estimated as of July 1 of the year shown. 2. Includes supplements to wages and salaries.

Table B. States and Counties — **Earnings, Social Security, and Housing**

STATE County	Earnings, 2009									Social Security beneficiaries, December 2010		Supplemental Security Income recipients, December 2010	Housing units, 2010	
			Goods-related[1]		Service-related and health									
	Total (mil dol)	Farm	Total	Manu-facturing	Information and profes-sional and technical services	Retail trade	Finance, insur-ance, and real estate	Health care and social services	Govern-ment	Number	Rate[2]		Total	Percent change, 2000–2010
	75	76	77	78	79	80	81	82	83	84	85	86	87	88
GEORGIA—Cont'd														
Effingham	506	0.4	D	25.2	3.3	7.2	3.3	3.6	27.6	7 335	140	834	19 884	40.3
Elbert	325	2.3	40.2	30.0	3.0	6.1	4.0	D	22.8	5 200	258	842	9 583	4.9
Emanuel	309	2.5	26.3	23.4	3.9	7.9	4.1	8.4	29.2	5 040	223	1 297	9 968	5.8
Evans	193	6.6	39.4	32.5	2.2	6.8	3.2	D	16.3	2 150	195	455	4 664	6.5
Fannin	265	0.8	D	D	5.7	10.6	9.3	D	17.6	6 890	291	651	16 207	45.6
Fayette	2 149	0.0	D	9.7	8.9	8.4	5.5	12.4	15.8	17 500	164	787	40 793	24.7
Floyd	2 064	0.6	D	17.1	6.2	6.1	4.0	24.0	17.4	20 185	210	2 973	40 551	10.7
Forsyth	3 216	0.3	D	16.1	11.9	6.4	3.8	7.6	11.9	18 885	108	846	64 052	75.5
Franklin	357	13.9	24.2	19.8	2.2	7.1	4.5	D	15.3	5 505	249	744	10 553	13.4
Fulton	67 201	0.0	D	4.4	29.0	3.4	13.6	7.4	11.5	108 020	117	22 851	437 105	25.4
Gilmer	399	7.1	D	19.1	D	8.9	9.1	6.0	18.2	6 770	239	595	16 564	38.9
Glascock	16	-5.2	D	0.0	D	D	D	D	47.9	660	214	75	1 519	27.4
Glynn	1 953	0.0	D	8.9	5.6	7.7	5.2	10.2	32.0	16 100	202	1 788	40 716	24.8
Gordon	986	2.0	42.4	38.7	2.7	6.7	3.0	8.3	15.5	9 760	177	1 307	22 278	29.9
Grady	302	11.9	D	9.3	2.8	7.3	5.2	7.0	20.2	5 010	200	1 050	10 760	7.7
Greene	272	7.1	D	9.9	4.4	8.0	7.2	D	14.6	4 600	288	579	8 688	30.6
Gwinnett	19 518	0.0	D	9.9	15.0	9.0	8.3	6.5	10.9	75 845	94	9 334	291 547	39.0
Habersham	658	4.3	D	25.8	4.2	7.4	3.5	5.4	22.3	8 850	206	808	18 146	24.0
Hall	3 958	0.7	26.5	20.0	4.6	6.9	6.0	14.8	14.0	28 775	160	2 549	68 825	34.8
Hancock	62	2.2	D	D	D	7.8	D	D	52.4	2 170	230	460	5 360	25.2
Haralson	367	1.3	D	27.7	3.9	9.0	3.1	D	22.2	6 245	217	950	12 287	14.6
Harris	228	-0.2	D	3.1	D	3.7	6.1	D	25.1	5 535	173	451	13 397	30.2
Hart	308	8.9	D	20.6	4.9	7.8	3.8	8.9	19.2	6 110	242	687	13 007	17.0
Heard	199	1.8	D	9.8	D	1.2	D	D	15.7	2 355	199	387	5 148	14.1
Henry	2 434	0.1	13.5	7.2	4.4	9.8	5.6	10.7	25.5	26 325	129	2 813	76 533	77.3
Houston	3 997	0.1	D	7.2	9.1	5.0	2.4	5.2	58.2	20 500	147	3 043	58 325	31.0
Irwin	113	19.4	10.1	6.9	D	4.6	D	D	33.3	2 120	222	393	4 033	-2.8
Jackson	889	7.0	D	22.7	D	10.3	3.2	2.6	18.7	10 805	179	1 288	23 752	46.4
Jasper	110	4.5	D	22.4	2.6	4.5	4.3	D	26.6	2 810	202	347	6 153	28.0
Jeff Davis	198	5.9	21.5	20.2	2.6	9.6	3.2	3.8	19.1	2 980	198	529	6 488	16.2
Jefferson	249	5.0	34.3	21.5	D	6.4	3.2	D	21.2	3 845	227	1 012	7 298	1.1
Jenkins	75	14.8	8.1	5.4	1.0	6.4	D	D	32.9	1 765	212	489	4 221	8.0
Johnson	74	-1.6	15.5	10.4	1.1	4.4	D	D	38.1	1 910	191	495	4 120	13.4
Jones	179	1.0	12.1	1.0	D	6.4	5.3	13.1	32.9	5 435	190	698	11 688	26.1
Lamar	186	7.2	D	14.6	D	7.8	5.9	4.1	31.1	3 745	204	444	7 474	21.6
Lanier	64	10.9	10.3	5.8	D	6.6	D	11.2	32.8	1 530	152	346	4 249	41.1
Laurens	963	1.1	23.0	17.4	D	7.6	8.3	13.2	28.6	10 420	215	2 005	21 368	8.5
Lee	266	5.7	D	2.5	D	8.3	3.4	D	25.8	3 860	136	456	10 276	16.6
Liberty	2 670	0.0	4.0	2.9	D	2.2	1.3	1.4	60.9	5 930	93	1 055	26 731	21.6
Lincoln	71	-0.1	20.3	4.6	D	7.6	4.4	2.8	28.5	1 965	246	257	4 786	6.0
Long	47	4.5	D	D	D	2.8	D	2.9	54.4	1 355	94	297	6 039	42.7
Lowndes	2 596	0.2	D	8.0	4.3	8.6	4.2	11.0	37.4	16 120	148	3 198	43 921	20.1
Lumpkin	347	2.1	D	8.7	D	6.5	4.5	11.1	39.0	5 305	177	527	12 925	56.6
McDuffie	339	6.3	D	23.2	4.1	8.5	3.5	7.2	23.9	4 485	205	941	9 319	4.5
McIntosh	101	0.8	D	1.2	D	11.4	3.8	1.3	34.1	2 800	195	461	9 220	60.8
Macon	182	16.3	D	28.7	1.2	4.2	2.0	D	22.7	2 420	164	678	6 136	11.7
Madison	202	11.8	D	5.7	D	5.8	4.2	D	29.1	5 965	212	848	11 784	12.0
Marion	74	6.2	D	29.4	D	5.5	D	4.9	25.1	1 400	160	306	4 156	32.8
Meriwether	242	2.5	23.5	15.6	1.8	7.1	4.4	D	32.6	4 945	225	934	9 957	8.1
Miller	87	22.5	D	D	D	6.4	5.8	D	32.8	1 340	219	252	2 791	0.8
Mitchell	371	15.7	29.8	27.1	D	5.8	3.0	D	21.3	4 570	194	1 143	8 996	1.3
Monroe	299	1.9	D	2.6	D	5.5	2.2	D	25.4	5 085	192	556	10 710	27.0
Montgomery	83	10.9	11.5	7.2	D	9.7	11.1	D	24.5	1 700	186	316	3 921	12.3
Morgan	298	6.2	22.4	16.0	D	8.3	5.1	3.9	18.6	3 950	221	397	7 472	21.9
Murray	497	1.2	D	46.5	D	6.0	3.2	D	16.6	7 095	179	1 018	15 979	11.6
Muscogee	5 544	0.0	D	6.9	13.6	5.7	10.3	12.9	28.0	32 775	173	6 650	82 690	8.5
Newton	1 086	0.3	D	30.0	3.6	6.9	3.1	9.1	22.8	15 540	155	2 331	38 342	66.5
Oconee	428	4.2	D	5.8	8.9	7.6	8.7	8.6	20.6	4 985	152	305	12 383	30.0
Oglethorpe	100	31.6	12.7	2.9	D	5.2	2.8	D	26.3	2 915	196	420	6 484	20.8
Paulding	997	0.3	D	6.0	5.3	11.2	4.3	8.1	28.2	15 860	111	1 558	52 130	78.2
Peach	422	8.0	33.1	26.5	2.5	8.6	2.4	D	29.0	4 775	172	960	11 050	21.5
Pickens	363	0.8	20.8	10.1	5.6	8.8	8.2	13.9	20.0	7 495	255	536	13 692	28.1
Pierce	189	5.4	18.8	7.2	D	7.2	4.4	6.4	22.9	3 915	209	689	7 986	19.0
Pike	127	0.8	D	5.7	D	4.0	4.9	D	28.0	3 345	187	323	6 820	34.6
Polk	533	1.4	D	29.0	D	8.7	2.8	D	18.3	8 780	212	1 340	16 908	12.3
Pulaski	126	2.7	D	D	6.6	6.6	5.4	D	26.1	2 110	176	377	5 151	30.6

1. Includes mining, construction, and manufacturing.   2. Per 1,000 resident population enumerated in the 2010 census.

STATE County	Total [89]	Percent [90]	Median value[1] [91]	With a mortgage [92]	Without a mortgage [93]	Median rent[2] [94]	Median rent as a percent of income [95]	Sub-standard units[3] (percent) [96]	Total [97]	Percent change, 2009–2010 [98]	Total [99]	Rate[4] [100]	Total [101]	Management, business, science and arts [102]	Construction, production, and maintenance occupations [103]
GEORGIA—Cont'd															
Effingham	17 480	74.5	153 500	23.2	11.3	841	30.2	2.5	28 201	-1.0	2 451	8.7	23 094	27.3	34.0
Elbert	7 733	71.1	81 400	24.6	11.0	509	29.1	2.9	9 436	-7.4	1 285	13.6	8 379	23.3	41.7
Emanuel	8 265	67.1	77 800	24.1	13.4	473	28.5	3.3	9 920	-5.7	1 147	11.6	8 494	25.9	34.6
Evans	4 022	69.6	91 500	20.5	10.5	497	22.5	2.8	4 775	-2.8	445	9.3	4 520	27.5	35.8
Fannin	10 524	80.7	172 400	30.6	11.6	556	29.8	2.1	10 644	-1.0	1 137	10.7	9 603	25.8	32.2
Fayette	37 683	84.5	252 700	24.1	10.0	1 057	31.2	0.9	50 092	-3.0	4 334	8.7	50 690	43.2	17.6
Floyd	34 977	67.1	118 300	23.3	12.3	670	31.4	2.8	48 307	-2.4	5 154	10.7	41 226	30.5	27.4
Forsyth	55 380	86.8	276 700	23.3	10.0	1 078	29.1	1.6	86 114	0.1	7 057	8.2	78 376	45.6	15.2
Franklin	8 691	71.9	124 300	24.9	10.8	530	28.2	2.5	9 992	-1.8	1 174	11.7	9 324	28.0	33.3
Fulton	357 463	56.0	253 100	24.9	13.2	929	30.3	2.9	478 766	-1.2	50 542	10.6	436 762	47.1	12.9
Gilmer	11 741	70.8	137 600	24.7	10.8	673	28.6	4.3	13 179	-2.7	1 397	10.6	12 296	21.2	38.9
Glascock	1 188	71.9	69 500	25.8	10.7	549	34.1	1.5	1 111	-2.0	135	12.2	1 206	21.6	43.3
Glynn	30 617	64.5	180 900	23.2	10.6	762	28.7	3.7	38 740	-3.5	3 660	9.4	35 873	31.9	20.5
Gordon	19 229	69.1	123 200	23.9	11.9	629	30.9	2.1	25 276	0.4	3 125	12.4	24 053	23.4	38.4
Grady	9 477	64.6	90 800	24.2	14.4	611	30.0	3.4	11 335	-2.9	1 048	9.2	9 601	26.4	32.4
Greene	6 064	75.2	124 300	29.3	12.8	651	36.3	2.0	7 151	-5.7	819	11.5	5 823	22.4	31.3
Gwinnett	260 375	72.1	194 200	25.5	10.7	954	30.4	3.1	409 675	-1.0	37 849	9.2	385 981	37.6	21.0
Habersham	15 046	74.1	144 600	23.5	11.0	616	28.3	4.7	19 552	-3.2	1 957	10.0	17 199	27.0	29.9
Hall	60 173	69.0	175 200	24.9	11.5	817	30.0	5.3	89 018	-0.4	8 119	9.1	79 378	27.8	35.2
Hancock	2 907	75.5	73 800	38.5	19.1	635	35.0	5.1	3 029	-9.5	678	22.4	2 910	18.8	38.7
Haralson	10 579	73.5	109 000	23.3	14.8	672	29.0	4.7	12 341	-3.9	1 442	11.7	10 999	25.7	34.8
Harris	11 056	88.5	196 000	22.5	11.3	798	26.4	1.2	16 253	0.3	1 196	7.4	14 259	43.5	18.4
Hart	9 492	76.5	129 900	25.4	10.7	580	39.8	3.1	10 118	-3.3	1 205	11.9	10 027	27.7	32.7
Heard	4 287	73.7	95 300	22.8	11.4	708	28.8	3.4	4 756	-3.3	594	12.5	4 710	20.6	39.7
Henry	66 327	80.2	171 500	25.4	10.5	1 003	30.0	2.0	95 947	-0.8	9 975	10.4	91 632	32.7	22.8
Houston	50 199	67.8	132 500	20.8	10.0	757	27.5	2.0	71 182	1.1	5 408	7.6	60 057	38.2	21.8
Irwin	3 339	78.8	77 500	21.2	12.5	542	31.6	2.8	3 909	-3.8	541	13.8	3 469	25.6	39.1
Jackson	20 917	75.2	166 000	24.8	11.0	714	29.0	1.9	27 099	0.4	2 917	10.8	26 421	29.4	30.7
Jasper	4 998	70.5	121 800	24.7	13.7	676	31.0	1.9	6 261	-3.4	733	11.7	6 036	21.3	38.6
Jeff Davis	5 567	71.0	74 000	23.0	10.0	393	24.1	3.1	5 247	-1.7	754	14.4	5 871	22.1	44.7
Jefferson	6 281	70.9	74 500	23.8	16.1	450	31.4	3.1	6 770	-4.1	973	14.4	6 309	22.8	31.7
Jenkins	3 125	75.8	69 700	30.1	13.8	551	24.6	2.0	2 460	-9.7	479	19.5	3 277	19.0	33.6
Johnson	3 334	69.9	64 000	19.4	13.8	434	26.4	3.0	3 417	-6.5	423	12.4	3 484	21.6	39.9
Jones	10 238	80.8	135 200	23.6	11.5	752	25.0	1.8	14 111	-0.9	1 337	9.5	12 712	31.2	26.3
Lamar	6 377	66.6	114 100	25.8	16.4	659	31.1	2.2	7 869	-1.3	991	12.6	7 576	25.1	33.6
Lanier	3 308	62.6	81 300	26.9	10.0	567	28.7	3.7	4 022	-2.9	376	9.3	3 890	20.6	33.5
Laurens	17 669	67.6	88 800	22.2	11.3	558	25.7	2.3	21 592	-2.0	2 666	12.3	19 608	27.2	31.0
Lee	9 555	77.7	145 300	20.3	12.4	759	21.5	1.5	17 805	-0.5	1 471	8.3	13 209	36.7	24.3
Liberty	22 626	50.8	120 300	23.0	11.5	799	28.5	2.3	26 145	0.9	2 413	9.2	23 155	24.9	27.0
Lincoln	3 435	78.9	98 100	23.7	17.4	568	25.2	3.1	3 717	-4.8	408	11.0	3 249	19.5	34.7
Long	4 553	63.1	75 700	23.5	10.0	604	23.5	3.1	6 683	1.3	480	7.2	5 340	19.3	43.7
Lowndes	38 358	59.1	128 800	23.4	10.6	706	31.7	2.5	52 399	-2.5	4 615	8.8	46 044	28.7	22.5
Lumpkin	10 863	70.5	170 400	28.1	13.1	792	30.0	2.1	12 818	-3.5	1 391	10.9	13 330	28.4	25.0
McDuffie	8 283	65.0	93 600	25.5	12.3	565	27.9	1.8	10 607	-1.6	1 096	10.3	8 801	22.3	33.1
McIntosh	5 687	74.7	103 400	23.0	12.0	592	29.5	4.5	5 073	-4.8	578	11.4	6 230	27.6	30.9
Macon	4 735	64.9	69 000	29.2	13.0	411	26.0	4.4	5 036	-3.1	692	13.7	4 792	24.2	42.9
Madison	9 430	76.8	128 100	23.9	10.0	679	32.8	2.9	15 482	-3.0	1 299	8.4	12 312	26.9	30.4
Marion	3 171	74.4	75 900	27.9	12.9	429	28.0	2.0	3 281	-1.6	325	9.9	3 357	18.2	41.8
Meriwether	8 453	72.5	95 600	24.4	11.5	647	31.7	3.1	9 171	-4.2	1 201	13.1	9 022	20.9	40.8
Miller	2 577	69.9	80 200	20.7	16.5	488	18.8	6.8	3 446	-6.1	286	8.3	2 548	25.2	34.6
Mitchell	8 170	65.4	76 800	22.2	11.1	569	30.5	6.3	9 898	-4.8	1 058	10.7	8 864	22.2	37.7
Monroe	9 206	80.0	152 400	21.6	13.4	660	29.6	1.0	13 490	-1.7	1 250	9.3	11 816	29.8	29.1
Montgomery	3 294	71.3	80 300	21.4	11.0	487	28.7	1.6	4 414	-1.5	473	10.7	3 647	28.5	37.1
Morgan	6 529	74.9	169 400	25.1	10.9	718	29.2	1.1	8 889	-4.4	884	9.9	7 972	36.4	28.0
Murray	14 248	72.5	98 300	21.5	10.1	611	28.8	7.9	19 222	-1.2	2 303	12.0	16 406	18.7	50.4
Muscogee	72 124	56.4	131 900	23.4	11.0	732	30.0	1.8	85 543	0.1	8 078	9.4	75 065	34.1	19.0
Newton	33 536	76.0	148 600	26.5	11.5	907	38.9	2.4	46 040	-2.0	5 606	12.2	43 033	29.9	28.6
Oconee	11 155	82.7	228 700	21.4	10.0	789	28.5	1.5	18 366	0.7	1 212	6.6	15 279	48.8	16.6
Oglethorpe	4 701	80.1	134 400	23.8	13.2	595	23.9	2.9	7 696	-1.2	656	8.5	5 990	26.1	31.4
Paulding	46 440	81.6	149 600	23.8	10.5	907	29.9	2.5	66 848	-0.4	7 111	10.6	64 349	30.8	26.1
Peach	9 016	69.0	113 900	21.6	11.7	628	33.7	3.0	11 980	-2.3	1 436	12.0	10 551	28.5	32.7
Pickens	11 268	80.4	170 600	25.6	11.6	725	32.3	2.3	14 631	-4.0	1 427	9.8	12 749	26.8	28.2
Pierce	6 771	76.6	75 400	19.3	12.5	507	25.1	4.0	8 578	1.1	836	9.7	7 709	24.0	34.0
Pike	5 957	83.1	153 300	26.7	12.0	853	29.7	1.8	7 852	-3.2	816	10.4	7 631	29.3	32.9
Polk	14 623	70.5	108 300	23.4	12.5	641	30.0	3.6	20 336	-4.1	2 160	10.6	16 998	21.6	39.4
Pulaski	4 188	72.3	79 000	23.3	10.0	476	26.3	1.9	4 408	0.6	389	8.8	4 514	18.4	35.0

1. Specified owner-occupied units. 2. Specified renter-occupied units. A value of 10.0 represents 10 percent or less. 3. Overcrowded or lacking complete plumbing facilities. 4. Percent of civilian labor force. 5. Persons 16 years old and over.

Table B. States and Counties — Nonfarm Employment and Agriculture

STATE County	Private nonfarm establishments, employment and payroll, 2009									Agriculture, 2007			
		Employment						Annual payroll		Farms		Percent with:	
	Number of establishments	Total	Health care and social assistance	Manufacturing	Retail trade	Finance and insurance	Professional, scientific, and technical services	Total (mil dol)	Average per employee (dollars)	Number	Fewer than 50 acres	500 acres or more	Farm operators whose principal occupation is farming (percent)
	104	105	106	107	108	109	110	111	112	113	114	115	116

GEORGIA—Cont'd

STATE County	104	105	106	107	108	109	110	111	112	113	114	115	116
Effingham	706	7 112	925	D	1 351	199	503	240	33 807	203	46.3	9.4	36.9
Elbert	477	5 225	572	2 114	724	D	73	142	27 091	507	38.1	4.5	43.4
Emanuel	415	5 360	812	2 100	883	171	212	135	25 250	511	24.1	14.3	35.4
Evans	229	3 771	D	D	470	D	54	101	26 870	212	30.7	16.5	38.7
Fannin	557	4 444	1 014	330	1 053	219	171	113	25 432	243	56.0	1.2	42.0
Fayette	3 155	37 355	4 751	2 973	6 490	1 109	2 463	1 293	34 619	154	50.0	0.6	50.6
Floyd	1 964	34 138	7 890	6 498	4 360	959	850	1 089	31 906	553	42.0	6.5	40.0
Forsyth	5 041	57 948	5 444	6 656	7 936	1 898	4 562	2 244	38 719	306	67.0	1.6	45.8
Franklin	453	5 751	768	1 408	894	160	90	153	26 657	851	47.6	1.9	51.1
Fulton	33 026	714 815	69 220	19 284	48 157	54 310	90 774	40 606	58 807	204	71.6	2.0	45.1
Gilmer	574	6 587	530	D	1 217	326	151	170	25 777	397	49.9	2.3	52.9
Glascock	27	205	D	D	D	D	D	4	20 580	93	14.0	8.6	36.6
Glynn	2 551	31 508	4 778	2 461	4 903	889	1 064	947	30 066	50	74.0	4.0	34.0
Gordon	1 023	16 016	1 640	5 339	2 361	352	230	476	29 744	839	54.1	2.5	42.8
Grady	427	4 017	398	D	823	158	70	101	25 118	445	35.5	12.4	47.0
Greene	393	4 696	D	600	592	193	160	133	28 365	247	30.8	13.4	42.9
Gwinnett	21 349	293 265	23 340	20 187	41 491	14 014	23 510	12 314	41 990	181	75.1	0.6	47.5
Habersham	829	11 341	1 261	D	1 717	643	259	318	28 024	372	57.0	1.1	48.4
Hall	4 007	59 965	10 152	15 239	7 832	2 073	1 629	2 152	35 896	799	60.6	1.6	40.3
Hancock	69	703	D	D	112	D	D	15	21 660	172	20.9	8.1	48.8
Haralson	456	5 375	847	1 823	989	163	99	170	31 617	367	46.3	2.2	34.1
Harris	407	3 324	198	783	287	37	110	81	24 508	371	48.2	5.1	30.5
Hart	404	4 646	629	1 173	892	D	95	128	27 545	657	47.8	2.9	49.2
Heard	122	1 147	D	D	D	D	93	41	35 407	187	36.9	2.7	42.8
Henry	3 347	40 160	5 319	2 594	7 817	D	1 468	1 207	30 054	298	58.4	1.3	49.3
Houston	2 304	33 434	5 006	4 047	6 582	1 186	3 873	974	29 121	298	54.0	5.7	51.0
Irwin	130	1 568	D	128	160	D	D	42	26 570	387	20.9	22.7	47.8
Jackson	1 166	14 955	808	4 325	2 614	298	515	461	30 829	892	55.3	3.3	39.8
Jasper	172	1 611	D	653	D	67	36	37	23 053	333	40.5	6.0	35.7
Jeff Davis	261	3 444	D	1 213	775	91	73	87	25 355	224	39.7	17.0	50.9
Jefferson	330	4 031	525	1 090	653	179	50	123	30 442	315	25.1	17.1	38.7
Jenkins	118	992	245	D	197	37	D	25	25 625	247	19.0	16.6	36.4
Johnson	121	1 187	328	242	D	50	13	28	23 925	281	22.8	11.0	32.7
Jones	327	2 567	382	69	362	147	106	72	28 013	206	35.9	4.9	47.6
Lamar	245	2 633	237	452	564	D	D	63	24 000	271	44.3	5.2	37.6
Lanier	111	885	D	72	139	D	18	21	23 419	107	40.2	15.9	46.9
Laurens	1 064	15 326	2 925	2 875	2 587	525	292	460	30 041	664	30.4	9.3	36.8
Lee	385	3 568	382	D	564	135	84	89	24 966	198	34.8	25.3	44.9
Liberty	829	13 049	1 861	1 277	2 263	255	515	416	31 854	62	50.0	11.3	35.5
Lincoln	155	976	D	D	183	D	35	24	24 330	199	44.2	5.0	34.7
Long	69	385	D	D	55	D	D	8	20 696	73	42.5	9.6	46.2
Lowndes	2 734	38 938	6 714	3 243	7 107	1 071	1 208	1 035	26 576	470	46.8	6.6	33.2
Lumpkin	493	4 426	777	547	761	144	107	124	27 911	292	65.4	2.1	43.8
McDuffie	459	6 388	901	1 893	1 089	157	111	177	27 635	213	43.7	9.4	38.5
McIntosh	214	1 435	D	32	517	D	D	31	21 440	58	58.6	8.6	51.7
Macon	194	2 086	444	727	269	58	28	65	31 041	336	25.6	18.2	47.6
Madison	378	2 195	307	255	442	83	83	53	24 308	771	49.5	1.9	38.7
Marion	86	1 260	D	D	259	D	D	32	25 040	185	30.3	16.2	44.3
Meriwether	318	3 278	577	D	565	149	D	108	32 920	437	41.6	5.9	35.5
Miller	129	1 136	D	D	213	52	D	30	26 504	213	23.0	24.4	57.3
Mitchell	386	6 564	467	D	733	180	199	156	23 810	441	29.0	23.6	52.6
Monroe	505	5 490	695	435	740	111	138	179	32 525	204	39.7	8.8	48.0
Montgomery	125	1 201	55	216	D	99	D	29	24 171	228	30.3	10.1	26.3
Morgan	463	5 291	616	1 038	1 000	172	192	148	27 948	657	39.7	4.9	39.3
Murray	423	8 335	487	4 838	792	D	81	238	28 599	308	51.9	2.6	35.4
Muscogee	4 409	78 925	13 033	6 868	11 340	D	3 764	2 759	34 955	43	32.6	9.3	62.8
Newton	1 386	17 082	2 078	4 079	2 581	530	720	584	34 175	306	58.5	5.6	38.2
Oconee	956	7 815	916	578	1 465	441	682	241	30 823	420	47.1	4.3	32.1
Oglethorpe	180	1 075	120	68	266	45	74	27	24 758	477	40.7	9.0	49.1
Paulding	1 600	14 094	1 696	907	3 731	439	502	373	26 444	181	56.4	0.6	50.3
Peach	494	6 257	706	D	795	122	139	186	29 690	213	55.4	8.9	41.8
Pickens	666	5 863	1 021	625	1 213	343	186	164	27 940	333	60.1	1.2	37.5
Pierce	340	3 073	262	221	366	123	109	77	25 019	431	45.5	5.1	40.6
Pike	243	1 648	D	195	204	D	54	41	25 152	392	49.5	3.6	37.5
Polk	634	9 756	788	3 251	1 510	242	136	271	27 802	363	43.5	2.2	41.3
Pulaski	194	1 918	669	D	397	77	59	56	29 195	190	31.6	19.5	41.6

Table B. States and Counties — Agriculture

STATE County	Land in farms					Value of land and buildings (dollars)		Value of machinery and equipment, average per farm (dollars)	Value of products sold				Percent of farms with sales of:		Government payments	
	Acreage (1,000)	Percent change, 2002–2007	Average size of farm	Total irrigated (1,000)	Total cropland (1,000)	Average per farm	Average per acre		Total (mil dol)	Average per farm (dollars)	Crops	Live-stock and poultry products	$10,000 or more	$100,000 or more	Total ($1,000)	Percent of farms
	117	118	119	120	121	122	123	124	125	126	127	128	129	130	131	132

GEORGIA—Cont'd

STATE County	117	118	119	120	121	122	123	124	125	126	127	128	129	130	131	132
Effingham	40	-24.5	199	0.0	14.7	636 927	3 198	70 116	5.0	24 788	77.9	22.1	27.6	5.4	546	28.6
Elbert	63	0.0	124	0.1	19.2	429 051	3 458	53 690	50.4	99 468	3.4	96.6	23.9	10.5	599	26.4
Emanuel	139	-13.1	271	7.6	54.9	589 051	2 173	77 017	20.4	39 889	79.5	20.5	24.3	10.6	3 814	52.1
Evans	53	10.4	249	2.8	23.4	602 807	2 422	68 410	30.8	145 066	35.8	64.2	35.4	16.5	1 031	41.0
Fannin	19	26.7	77	D	4.5	420 832	5 436	45 444	18.1	74 598	9.1	90.9	19.3	8.6	6	7.8
Fayette	12	-33.3	80	0.1	2.7	535 895	6 689	41 882	2.8	18 473	75.9	24.1	20.8	1.3	6	8.4
Floyd	85	-6.6	153	1.1	28.0	565 269	3 695	63 954	49.4	89 350	5.9	94.1	26.6	8.0	769	16.8
Forsyth	20	-41.2	65	0.2	5.7	539 890	8 344	67 074	40.0	130 628	16.3	83.7	30.7	16.3	44	6.2
Franklin	81	-5.8	96	0.5	25.9	616 510	6 448	70 653	326.2	383 284	0.9	99.1	42.4	27.0	222	13.3
Fulton	16	-42.9	76	0.3	3.6	423 093	5 548	31 360	4.0	19 768	85.5	14.5	21.1	2.0	22	4.4
Gilmer	37	48.0	92	0.1	9.6	694 848	7 550	66 506	194.2	489 115	1.2	98.8	44.3	35.3	166	10.3
Glascock	21	0.0	228	0.1	6.6	491 038	2 151	48 329	1.5	15 659	41.1	58.9	23.7	3.2	386	32.3
Glynn	6	-25.0	117	0.1	0.4	415 516	3 559	77 507	0.3	5 993	37.3	62.3	24.0	0.0	0	0.0
Gordon	79	3.9	94	0.9	31.1	507 095	5 377	57 810	182.0	216 983	1.9	98.1	30.5	15.4	380	15.3
Grady	119	-6.3	267	8.0	56.4	799 170	2 989	89 873	79.5	178 547	65.7	34.3	40.9	15.5	3 857	53.0
Greene	55	5.8	224	0.5	13.7	888 978	3 968	77 363	64.0	259 013	D	D	38.1	13.0	77	14.2
Gwinnett	8	-55.6	46	0.3	3.3	443 536	9 614	61 858	15.9	87 639	81.1	18.9	28.2	11.0	23	3.9
Habersham	29	-25.6	79	0.3	8.4	550 333	6 989	69 204	101.3	272 329	0.8	99.2	46.8	27.4	90	7.0
Hall	57	-8.1	72	0.2	15.4	532 486	7 426	53 349	181.5	227 192	0.6	99.4	31.0	19.3	213	11.3
Hancock	38	-9.5	221	0.1	8.6	556 330	2 517	47 801	3.4	19 970	26.3	73.7	20.3	4.7	52	9.9
Haralson	34	-15.0	94	0.1	11.3	385 787	4 116	48 977	43.3	118 114	1.4	98.6	16.1	4.9	76	11.2
Harris	61	-9.0	164	0.1	11.9	546 578	3 333	37 994	2.7	7 248	66.2	33.8	15.1	0.8	41	4.9
Hart	70	7.7	107	1.5	28.8	613 357	5 724	69 738	204.6	311 413	1.7	98.3	37.3	20.2	420	23.3
Heard	24	-42.9	126	D	5.9	523 055	4 145	67 915	28.3	151 501	3.1	96.9	26.7	7.5	50	10.7
Henry	24	-58.6	79	0.2	8.3	473 022	5 990	43 401	5.3	17 873	70.6	29.4	21.5	3.0	145	11.4
Houston	47	-37.3	157	4.5	20.3	577 908	3 692	64 949	15.6	52 338	44.8	55.2	28.9	6.4	1 095	24.2
Irwin	145	5.1	376	30.6	88.3	845 066	2 249	146 151	46.0	118 822	84.2	15.8	53.0	24.3	7 205	75.7
Jackson	85	-15.0	95	0.6	24.5	588 108	6 181	51 686	166.9	187 137	1.7	98.3	34.2	18.5	165	6.7
Jasper	56	9.8	169	0.3	12.4	649 775	3 835	42 111	20.8	62 329	3.1	96.9	18.9	3.0	75	12.6
Jeff Davis	58	3.6	259	9.3	38.1	578 015	2 228	119 805	23.0	102 856	69.8	30.2	32.6	17.9	2 350	45.5
Jefferson	109	-20.4	346	14.6	61.7	742 772	2 148	86 810	29.3	93 092	69.7	30.3	39.0	15.9	2 569	61.0
Jenkins	85	-10.5	343	10.0	42.0	656 814	1 915	66 491	14.8	59 769	75.7	24.3	25.5	10.9	1 669	51.0
Johnson	67	-11.8	237	1.6	21.2	465 570	1 967	41 804	4.8	16 966	74.5	25.4	19.6	3.2	686	42.0
Jones	32	-8.6	157	0.3	8.6	559 361	3 559	54 788	7.5	36 387	13.5	86.5	30.6	4.9	50	5.8
Lamar	36	-14.3	132	1.3	13.1	548 341	4 165	64 304	43.9	162 151	9.3	90.7	28.8	10.0	88	18.5
Lanier	53	1.9	497	8.4	21.8	1 178 519	2 372	135 457	17.5	163 780	92.3	7.7	29.9	15.9	1 247	41.1
Laurens	165	-14.9	248	6.4	55.3	526 545	2 119	57 077	14.5	21 882	65.7	34.3	20.6	6.0	2 914	53.9
Lee	126	-14.3	638	15.8	50.2	1 595 988	2 502	150 389	30.9	156 095	67.5	32.5	38.9	19.7	2 417	45.5
Liberty	9	-43.8	151	0.0	1.2	307 199	2 032	46 021	0.2	3 080	39.8	60.2	8.1	0.0	34	11.3
Lincoln	28	-9.7	139	0.0	6.9	407 572	2 937	31 999	1.5	7 354	12.4	87.6	18.1	0.5	60	17.1
Long	13	-45.8	180	0.5	4.8	395 719	2 198	92 928	5.3	73 158	14.5	85.5	27.4	6.8	120	19.2
Lowndes	68	-8.1	145	4.2	27.8	534 956	3 702	58 969	22.1	46 931	89.2	10.8	27.2	8.1	1 372	33.2
Lumpkin	22	4.8	75	0.1	5.0	493 787	6 549	45 546	48.8	167 180	1.1	98.9	28.4	15.1	99	14.0
McDuffie	36	-23.4	170	0.5	9.6	483 053	2 849	49 554	24.9	117 022	D	D	29.6	4.2	90	17.4
McIntosh	9	-18.2	157	0.0	2.6	368 010	2 343	43 432	0.6	10 483	6.1	93.9	15.5	1.7	D	3.4
Macon	122	7.0	364	16.9	54.0	1 028 759	2 824	124 100	157.4	468 500	12.6	87.4	47.3	31.3	3 198	50.9
Madison	76	0.0	99	0.3	25.3	500 466	5 044	67 020	140.9	182 719	1.1	98.9	33.1	17.1	289	16.5
Marion	47	-9.6	252	3.4	14.6	632 544	2 510	64 239	32.1	173 291	12.3	87.7	36.8	16.8	372	31.4
Meriwether	81	-3.6	186	0.8	22.2	678 251	3 637	41 468	8.6	19 585	51.0	49.0	20.8	3.7	267	14.9
Miller	102	7.4	478	37.7	65.8	1 273 797	2 667	165 163	42.5	199 486	78.3	21.7	54.0	30.5	4 255	61.0
Mitchell	204	10.3	464	47.7	126.6	1 212 128	2 615	155 875	250.2	567 384	34.2	65.8	53.3	39.0	7 338	56.5
Monroe	39	-37.1	193	0.2	9.1	624 973	3 244	69 841	36.2	177 513	1.0	99.0	33.8	9.8	214	15.2
Montgomery	52	-29.7	226	2.6	17.4	560 558	2 477	49 832	10.2	44 817	79.7	20.3	21.1	7.5	898	46.1
Morgan	92	3.4	141	1.8	31.0	725 864	5 159	64 941	71.9	109 383	6.7	93.3	29.4	10.4	626	28.5
Murray	40	-4.8	130	0.4	15.3	521 263	4 021	54 610	51.5	167 144	3.3	96.7	34.7	14.3	74	10.4
Muscogee	8	-46.7	179	D	2.8	581 738	3 251	37 532	0.1	3 069	41.7	58.3	7.0	0.0	D	4.7
Newton	39	-13.3	126	0.2	9.9	540 261	4 290	44 566	4.7	15 238	19.2	80.8	22.2	4.6	54	12.1
Oconee	49	-9.3	116	1.0	13.6	635 315	5 470	51 107	79.8	190 070	22.2	77.8	31.0	10.2	330	24.5
Oglethorpe	87	55.4	182	0.8	23.7	664 911	3 661	74 478	166.1	348 288	2.7	97.3	35.6	20.8	476	15.9
Paulding	11	-35.3	63	0.0	3.5	416 839	6 609	40 108	17.0	94 050	11.8	88.2	25.4	6.6	2	2.2
Peach	40	2.6	188	5.6	23.5	702 024	3 738	73 240	20.8	97 707	80.5	19.5	24.9	9.4	454	12.7
Pickens	24	41.2	71	0.3	8.0	470 848	6 603	64 071	72.5	217 567	1.1	98.9	28.8	13.2	30	5.7
Pierce	72	-27.3	166	8.3	34.9	475 208	2 855	73 206	24.0	55 743	75.1	24.9	36.7	8.1	2 281	47.8
Pike	46	4.5	118	0.8	14.5	490 571	4 172	54 754	13.9	35 456	23.9	76.1	18.9	3.3	184	18.4
Polk	44	-15.4	121	0.1	15.5	512 580	4 241	61 487	36.3	99 892	3.6	96.4	26.4	8.0	305	18.5
Pulaski	57	-14.9	300	12.7	34.0	794 591	2 651	93 682	18.9	99 467	87.0	13.0	31.6	18.4	2 532	58.4

Table B. States and Counties — Water Use, Wholesale Trade, Retail Trade, and Real Estate

STATE County	Water use, 2005 Total water withdrawn (mil gal/day)	Gallons withdrawn per person	Wholesale trade,[1] 2007 Number of establishments	Number of employees	Sales (mil dol)	Annual payroll (mil dol)	Retail trade,[2] 2007 Number of establishments	Number of employees	Sales (mil dol)	Annual payroll (mil dol)	Real estate and rental and leasing,[2] 2007 Number of establishments	Number of employees	Receipts (mil dol)	Annual payroll (mil dol)
	133	134	135	136	137	138	139	140	141	142	143	144	145	146
GEORGIA—Cont'd														
Effingham	150.8	3 214	12	95	63.0	4.8	108	1 190	322.6	26.1	39	111	14.9	1.9
Elbert	3.4	163	44	377	106.3	11.2	88	650	137.0	13.0	10	23	1.7	0.4
Emanuel	6.7	301	27	172	93.4	4.3	104	896	184.0	17.8	19	54	6.2	1.0
Evans	4.2	371	5	D	D	D	54	451	153.9	11.5	5	21	2.4	0.3
Fannin	2.8	127	22	139	41.8	4.1	122	1 173	293.1	24.1	51	97	18.4	1.9
Fayette	14.8	142	190	1 798	877.2	81.8	464	7 315	1 390.0	147.0	216	535	80.7	15.7
Floyd	588.9	6 252	94	1 274	636.2	46.9	431	4 718	1 039.8	94.0	82	353	58.0	10.1
Forsyth	28.5	203	386	4 565	2 503.5	249.0	541	7 952	1 960.9	194.3	314	829	147.9	30.9
Franklin	4.2	193	20	334	107.8	7.5	115	985	315.1	22.2	17	31	2.1	0.5
Fulton	152.0	166	1 596	28 186	40 824.1	1 744.0	3 625	54 054	13 239.7	1 361.0	2 312	20 719	4 881.9	1 234.2
Gilmer	10.9	400	20	160	45.8	5.2	117	1 298	370.5	32.8	32	84	13.0	1.9
Glascock	0.3	122	NA	NA	NA	NA	3	14	4.8	0.2	NA	NA	NA	NA
Glynn	112.1	1 559	93	598	270.9	20.8	507	4 954	1 351.8	117.0	195	721	93.4	20.4
Gordon	15.1	301	70	D	D	D	249	2 641	659.4	53.3	55	170	32.2	4.4
Grady	10.4	423	23	356	201.3	10.3	87	762	168.1	15.8	21	75	6.5	1.4
Greene	3.9	249	18	90	31.9	4.1	77	638	137.1	12.9	30	54	8.0	1.7
Gwinnett	9.2	13	1 774	33 042	28 829.1	1 851.4	2 959	47 523	13 857.0	1 178.7	1 212	5 730	1 396.1	258.1
Habersham	13.2	333	35	D	D	D	175	1 983	492.1	40.0	33	240	23.3	5.0
Hall	108.6	655	252	3 732	4 914.5	170.8	630	8 134	2 220.7	206.5	229	558	125.5	18.4
Hancock	1.5	153	NA	NA	NA	NA	18	98	21.0	2.4	2	D	D	D
Haralson	3.4	119	19	174	53.2	6.6	96	969	313.1	21.1	14	40	3.5	0.6
Harris	12.6	453	10	D	D	D	51	335	66.1	5.6	15	D	D	D
Hart	3.8	157	19	227	59.0	7.3	94	879	170.7	15.6	19	72	8.9	2.3
Heard	65.9	5 807	2	D	D	D	21	113	24.8	2.1	1	D	D	D
Henry	35.0	208	101	1 508	3 076.6	71.4	556	8 291	1 907.4	183.5	210	636	116.4	19.8
Houston	29.4	233	49	D	D	D	452	6 600	1 524.3	143.9	133	510	72.6	12.5
Irwin	17.6	1 741	14	180	94.1	4.4	34	137	27.3	2.6	4	8	1.1	0.4
Jackson	21.2	405	63	1 050	568.8	32.8	232	2 175	559.4	47.1	62	144	19.4	2.7
Jasper	2.7	202	3	D	D	D	30	228	33.4	3.6	6	D	D	D
Jeff Davis	5.6	427	12	138	35.9	4.2	74	751	204.4	15.4	8	32	4.5	0.7
Jefferson	20.5	1 212	14	141	127.2	8.6	74	694	129.4	12.6	13	D	D	D
Jenkins	4.9	560	2	D	D	D	33	212	53.9	3.8	2	D	D	D
Johnson	3.0	319	11	D	D	D	21	145	25.2	2.2	2	D	D	D
Jones	29.6	1 104	12	86	42.4	4.2	42	364	70.6	6.8	18	D	D	D
Lamar	2.9	177	4	D	D	D	48	480	114.0	10.9	5	D	D	D
Lanier	2.2	287	2	D	D	D	18	D	D	D	4	D	D	D
Laurens	30.1	642	47	663	252.1	18.7	262	2 779	613.1	51.4	46	D	D	D
Lee	7.6	243	10	216	118.3	8.8	48	584	124.0	15.5	25	75	11.3	1.9
Liberty	14.0	243	7	D	D	D	191	1 946	539.3	41.0	51	233	28.9	5.8
Lincoln	0.9	111	6	27	9.4	0.8	31	218	39.6	3.7	4	9	0.7	0.2
Long	3.0	269	2	D	D	D	13	58	17.4	1.0	4	5	0.5	0.1
Lowndes	30.3	314	130	1 731	756.5	55.9	569	7 019	1 804.8	142.9	131	764	80.8	18.7
Lumpkin	3.2	133	12	171	37.4	5.1	86	806	206.6	18.7	28	116	15.5	2.8
McDuffie	5.9	269	10	D	D	D	109	1 196	350.4	26.9	21	90	11.3	2.2
McIntosh	1.1	98	3	D	D	D	69	574	114.0	10.2	12	15	4.1	0.3
Macon	31.5	2 290	12	80	39.5	3.1	38	282	47.9	5.1	7	28	2.6	0.6
Madison	3.6	130	16	186	57.8	5.5	60	501	119.2	8.5	13	D	D	D
Marion	3.1	431	4	D	D	D	25	337	71.7	7.2	NA	NA	NA	NA
Meriwether	2.4	105	8	D	D	D	88	682	100.8	12.0	9	28	1.8	0.5
Miller	22.1	3 547	3	37	15.0	1.2	42	257	53.5	4.3	6	8	0.6	0.1
Mitchell	39.4	1 656	27	302	169.2	8.2	102	816	151.0	14.6	15	70	5.4	1.4
Monroe	62.8	2 640	19	D	D	D	71	526	114.4	10.7	17	D	D	D
Montgomery	2.5	276	8	D	D	D	22	100	24.7	2.1	4	6	0.6	0.0
Morgan	2.9	167	16	200	54.9	5.7	91	1 014	276.4	21.1	27	63	7.8	1.5
Murray	6.3	154	29	338	89.4	12.4	101	818	218.9	18.1	11	40	4.8	1.0
Muscogee	33.9	183	173	1 906	1 173.6	81.2	845	12 642	2 889.2	260.7	259	1 549	292.8	54.0
Newton	14.6	169	52	512	226.6	19.6	223	2 699	679.4	57.2	70	256	33.2	5.8
Oconee	2.0	68	28	254	72.9	10.7	101	1 557	326.4	33.3	60	114	14.4	3.5
Oglethorpe	2.0	146	8	27	8.5	0.9	36	256	69.6	4.7	2	D	D	D
Paulding	4.8	42	62	366	176.5	15.2	233	3 920	973.0	83.7	78	243	44.9	9.5
Peach	10.6	429	19	D	D	D	118	945	317.4	22.1	25	61	11.7	2.1
Pickens	4.9	171	21	108	112.0	4.4	110	1 335	320.5	27.0	49	105	15.3	3.0
Pierce	3.5	204	18	D	D	D	67	460	99.7	8.7	6	22	1.6	0.3
Pike	1.6	98	9	97	16.7	2.9	35	183	33.9	3.1	9	33	2.8	0.4
Polk	8.9	219	17	D	D	D	145	1 500	314.7	29.7	23	68	6.9	1.4
Pulaski	16.7	1 719	8	80	21.4	1.8	47	391	84.5	7.5	12	22	2.2	0.3

1. Merchant wholesalers, except manufacturers' sales branches and offices.   2. Employer establishments.

Table B. States and Counties — Professional Services, Manufacturing, and Accommodation and Food Services

STATE County	Professional, scientific, and technical services,[1] 2007				Manufacturing, 2007				Accommodation and food services, 2007			
	Number of establishments	Number of employees	Receipts (mil dol)	Annual payroll (mil dol)	Number of establishments	Number of employees	Receipts (mil dol)	Annual payroll (mil dol)	Number of establishments	Number of employees	Sales (mil dol)	Annual payroll (mil dol)
	147	148	149	150	151	152	153	154	155	156	157	158
GEORGIA—Cont'd												
Effingham	56	D	D	D	25	D	D	D	49	637	26.1	6.6
Elbert	26	84	5.8	1.5	108	2 522	515.2	82.4	29	437	14.6	4.3
Emanuel	27	189	26.3	9.6	30	1 936	448.4	51.9	33	406	14.8	3.5
Evans	12	60	5.1	1.6	14	1 895	354.8	47.9	17	161	6.4	1.7
Fannin	41	183	12.8	5.2	NA	NA	NA	NA	59	651	29.7	8.4
Fayette	431	D	D	D	113	3 690	1 744.7	170.2	204	4 586	171.2	49.2
Floyd	174	703	80.1	24.8	109	7 726	3 346.1	312.7	198	3 423	144.3	38.1
Forsyth	855	4 197	650.9	207.2	223	8 127	2 318.6	329.8	240	3 904	183.1	48.4
Franklin	31	D	D	D	41	2 180	430.4	69.3	45	664	22.8	6.3
Fulton	6 560	77 813	16 269.2	5 882.0	677	24 993	10 428.5	1 051.8	2 782	66 711	4 133.8	1 154.9
Gilmer	52	207	14.8	5.4	34	2 099	354.6	64.1	57	872	36.6	10.8
Glascock	1	D	D	D	NA	NA	NA	NA	2	D	D	D
Glynn	268	D	D	D	73	2 554	D	123.6	251	7 394	398.3	162.5
Gordon	73	232	23.8	8.3	104	6 291	2 528.1	214.2	89	1 358	62.5	16.2
Grady	14	58	5.6	1.5	22	771	183.2	28.0	26	364	13.1	2.7
Greene	39	120	15.6	5.5	14	533	673.2	20.7	27	897	60.6	15.9
Gwinnett	3 256	D	D	D	772	22 797	6 480.3	1 030.7	1 629	27 397	1 264.7	353.6
Habersham	59	250	23.8	7.1	58	4 357	968.5	140.7	81	995	41.8	10.5
Hall	419	D	D	D	265	17 296	6 069.0	602.5	272	4 930	224.1	62.5
Hancock	3	D	D	D	NA	NA	NA	NA	9	28	1.0	0.3
Haralson	36	141	13.6	4.2	37	2 239	952.1	87.8	34	409	14.6	3.7
Harris	32	D	D	D	20	693	D	D	38	731	43.5	14.2
Hart	34	118	10.9	3.5	31	1 246	244.8	48.7	36	480	16.8	4.4
Heard	7	D	D	D	NA	NA	NA	NA	6	50	1.9	0.5
Henry	305	D	D	D	82	3 092	1 695.8	122.6	348	6 217	243.2	63.1
Houston	281	D	D	D	64	2 511	1 422.9	97.2	248	5 246	206.1	54.8
Irwin	5	30	2.9	0.9	NA	NA	NA	NA	6	97	2.6	0.7
Jackson	98	417	50.4	17.0	77	5 675	1 801.5	202.3	58	811	33.3	9.3
Jasper	8	D	D	D	19	839	187.5	27.7	11	104	3.4	0.9
Jeff Davis	17	87	3.9	1.8	24	1 229	242.9	34.3	21	364	9.9	2.6
Jefferson	13	44	3.0	0.9	30	1 343	303.6	47.6	26	327	11.2	2.6
Jenkins	4	13	0.9	0.4	10	665	116.9	20.6	13	140	3.8	1.0
Johnson	3	8	0.4	0.2	NA	NA	NA	NA	6	39	1.4	0.4
Jones	32	95	7.3	2.9	NA	NA	NA	NA	20	369	13.4	3.5
Lamar	20	83	4.2	1.2	NA	NA	NA	NA	28	379	12.0	3.3
Lanier	6	D	D	D	NA	NA	NA	NA	10	D	D	D
Laurens	73	322	29.7	11.1	47	3 870	D	D	97	1 608	66.8	17.8
Lee	23	79	9.0	2.3	NA	NA	NA	NA	16	205	6.9	2.0
Liberty	54	D	D	D	17	D	D	D	95	1 665	62.9	15.9
Lincoln	9	30	2.5	1.0	NA	NA	NA	NA	11	106	5.2	1.0
Long	3	D	D	D	NA	NA	NA	NA	6	102	1.8	0.6
Lowndes	211	D	D	D	106	4 324	2 237.8	162.9	252	5 498	209.5	55.3
Lumpkin	37	121	9.3	4.5	28	1 063	207.8	30.8	53	757	33.4	9.1
McDuffie	28	D	D	D	36	1 983	D	67.7	41	637	23.6	5.6
McIntosh	16	D	D	D	NA	NA	NA	NA	40	531	19.8	5.4
Macon	9	16	1.5	0.6	17	733	397.4	32.9	19	191	5.6	1.5
Madison	30	D	D	D	30	505	D	17.2	23	182	7.2	1.7
Marion	6	D	D	D	NA	NA	NA	NA	7	18	1.0	0.2
Meriwether	13	41	3.7	1.2	15	812	233.4	33.8	31	434	14.8	4.5
Miller	9	37	1.4	0.5	NA	NA	NA	NA	10	96	2.9	0.9
Mitchell	26	183	8.8	4.1	19	D	D	69.8	29	333	15.4	4.4
Monroe	42	99	9.0	2.8	19	855	118.1	25.9	42	668	23.8	7.2
Montgomery	7	12	0.8	0.2	NA	NA	NA	NA	7	61	2.9	0.7
Morgan	46	222	23.2	8.9	27	1 105	239.5	40.0	56	1 004	40.3	10.8
Murray	20	D	D	D	82	5 446	1 605.7	153.3	43	573	24.6	6.6
Muscogee	348	D	D	D	141	7 055	2 111.4	266.7	418	9 898	428.2	120.7
Newton	127	565	48.1	16.7	90	4 175	2 205.1	187.4	103	1 714	93.5	20.3
Oconee	145	709	58.9	25.7	31	747	D	25.4	58	946	38.9	9.6
Oglethorpe	18	D	D	D	NA	NA	NA	NA	9	45	1.8	0.5
Paulding	141	582	59.3	24.0	61	1 114	255.4	38.9	123	2 863	109.0	31.0
Peach	32	117	8.2	2.7	30	4 378	1 057.8	124.1	49	761	28.7	6.8
Pickens	83	177	18.3	6.4	44	694	104.8	23.0	49	719	27.8	7.8
Pierce	23	D	D	D	NA	NA	NA	NA	19	343	8.7	2.4
Pike	24	59	6.1	1.7	NA	NA	NA	NA	12	53	2.4	0.6
Polk	34	D	D	D	35	3 271	698.6	117.8	63	843	35.2	8.7
Pulaski	12	80	5.0	2.2	NA	NA	NA	NA	21	432	13.7	3.5

1. Establishment subject to federal tax.

Table B. States and Counties — **Health Care and Social Assistance, Other Services, and Federal Funds**

STATE County	Health care and social assistance, 2007				Other services, 2007				Federal funds and grants, 2009–2010 Expenditures (mil dol)			
										Direct payments for individuals[1]		
	Number of establish-ments	Number of employees	Receipts (mil dol)	Annual payroll (mil dol)	Number of establish-ments	Number of employees	Receipts (mil dol)	Annual payroll (mil dol)	Total	Social Security and government retirement	Medicare	Food Stamps and Supplemental Security Income
	159	160	161	162	163	164	165	166	167	168	169	170
GEORGIA—Cont'd												
Effingham	46	D	D	D	43	213	21.2	5.4	213.9	121.8	31.2	13.5
Elbert	39	615	41.6	16.2	27	84	7.5	2.1	193.3	72.6	42.5	13.5
Emanuel	52	897	54.7	24.8	30	127	12.0	2.5	260.2	72.2	43.3	17.2
Evans	20	448	32.8	14.4	16	114	8.4	2.2	86.9	32.6	17.9	6.9
Fannin	67	865	78.7	33.2	26	161	11.2	2.9	200.2	102.5	45.5	7.7
Fayette	301	4 309	437.3	158.9	211	1 273	101.7	31.7	635.1	373.8	66.5	8.6
Floyd	259	7 910	785.1	310.9	108	D	D	D	705.5	304.8	152.1	42.4
Forsyth	368	4 193	403.4	152.7	274	1 618	308.6	83.9	436.6	267.5	55.8	10.4
Franklin	38	768	56.6	21.8	28	171	15.6	3.5	177.2	79.5	41.2	8.3
Fulton	3 204	67 143	8 483.0	3 072.6	2 139	20 887	3 560.9	707.4	16 634.2	2 239.6	1 134.7	608.8
Gilmer	45	625	43.7	16.5	49	424	21.9	6.0	176.9	97.0	38.2	7.2
Glascock	5	D	D	D	3	D	D	D	27.4	10.6	6.8	0.9
Glynn	265	4 708	897.7	183.8	151	912	72.1	21.1	905.8	287.7	141.3	33.7
Gordon	74	1 314	133.1	51.2	50	355	32.4	10.3	286.3	135.4	57.4	15.8
Grady	36	452	41.7	13.6	29	153	14.2	3.7	162.6	62.1	31.2	17.4
Greene	35	393	33.9	13.4	24	98	11.7	3.9	143.2	67.2	25.2	10.5
Gwinnett	1 583	21 698	2 302.0	879.7	1 431	8 527	813.1	257.3	2 250.5	1 097.8	266.8	79.8
Habersham	87	1 406	93.6	41.9	46	170	15.2	4.7	292.2	131.7	64.1	8.5
Hall	398	8 599	1 046.7	384.6	272	1 384	136.1	36.5	1 157.9	440.8	154.3	39.2
Hancock	8	D	D	D	7	20	1.5	0.3	99.8	29.1	23.8	8.6
Haralson	41	608	53.4	22.9	39	171	11.0	3.1	199.7	87.4	43.5	14.4
Harris	23	212	11.1	4.6	19	D	D	D	165.2	98.6	21.1	6.2
Hart	36	697	50.1	20.7	23	80	5.8	1.3	168.0	72.3	35.9	9.5
Heard	6	D	D	D	7	D	D	D	64.4	27.5	14.0	5.7
Henry	351	5 004	459.2	183.6	242	1 172	91.9	27.6	777.4	463.2	96.1	28.5
Houston	256	4 784	461.8	176.5	166	932	67.1	17.0	2 499.9	601.1	113.9	48.8
Irwin	18	529	39.7	13.8	9	D	D	D	80.7	24.2	15.3	5.5
Jackson	63	975	58.9	30.1	67	230	23.7	7.1	335.6	192.3	55.5	17.4
Jasper	13	169	12.5	5.4	13	D	D	D	76.2	36.2	13.7	5.2
Jeff Davis	18	264	19.8	7.6	13	39	1.8	0.6	102.4	39.5	22.4	7.2
Jefferson	25	501	41.1	13.6	19	57	3.3	0.9	188.3	54.5	39.0	15.2
Jenkins	8	258	12.8	6.3	10	23	3.1	0.6	84.1	22.7	19.0	6.4
Johnson	11	D	D	D	9	29	2.3	0.7	84.4	26.1	20.0	7.4
Jones	24	D	D	D	22	57	3.6	1.0	117.3	57.4	23.4	7.5
Lamar	21	204	18.2	5.5	13	147	10.7	4.0	125.6	55.0	24.0	6.5
Lanier	15	D	D	D	4	D	D	D	58.4	20.1	16.9	5.1
Laurens	133	D	D	D	66	335	24.6	6.6	495.6	174.4	73.4	29.5
Lee	25	322	19.4	7.1	27	141	11.6	3.5	112.9	64.9	14.1	6.6
Liberty	66	D	D	D	68	D	D	D	470.3	174.8	32.3	27.5
Lincoln	6	33	2.1	1.1	13	71	5.1	1.1	71.5	30.8	17.9	3.7
Long	4	D	D	D	4	D	D	D	55.7	28.5	6.3	5.1
Lowndes	321	7 074	593.7	243.1	162	794	64.4	21.3	1 032.9	294.2	119.7	58.6
Lumpkin	53	609	52.9	19.8	33	108	9.5	2.3	181.7	71.1	19.5	5.7
McDuffie	48	1 011	55.9	26.0	35	120	39.1	3.3	174.6	69.4	38.4	14.8
McIntosh	13	D	D	D	15	33	3.4	0.8	102.7	43.1	20.6	8.2
Macon	21	460	37.2	13.5	9	D	D	D	158.4	34.3	30.3	7.7
Madison	17	D	D	D	21	D	D	D	181.4	87.7	34.8	14.2
Marion	7	D	D	D	5	D	D	D	54.8	17.2	7.8	6.6
Meriwether	36	717	52.9	25.7	18	48	4.0	1.0	177.7	69.0	35.5	13.8
Miller	14	388	24.0	11.9	10	36	2.7	0.7	62.5	18.7	12.1	4.3
Mitchell	25	500	35.8	14.2	33	191	13.8	3.8	200.7	60.1	35.7	19.9
Monroe	39	D	D	D	30	130	16.3	4.0	139.1	65.9	25.0	8.3
Montgomery	5	15	1.0	0.4	4	10	0.8	0.3	69.4	22.5	14.4	4.4
Morgan	28	500	29.7	15.4	35	135	11.8	2.8	117.9	57.5	24.6	6.5
Murray	33	505	39.2	14.5	28	113	9.1	2.8	180.9	88.4	35.0	10.9
Muscogee	555	13 088	1 332.5	521.1	353	2 323	178.4	54.7	4 790.6	737.8	259.8	142.3
Newton	133	2 037	203.9	75.8	90	414	33.3	9.6	477.4	265.1	83.3	33.9
Oconee	81	D	D	D	47	474	42.8	13.1	133.3	81.7	22.5	4.1
Oglethorpe	10	D	D	D	11	D	D	D	67.8	27.4	13.4	4.6
Paulding	109	1 492	105.5	40.6	108	455	30.3	9.8	328.7	205.0	44.1	17.4
Peach	40	D	D	D	31	D	D	D	269.2	114.7	35.9	20.8
Pickens	50	1 003	72.6	28.5	42	188	15.7	5.0	179.1	112.4	29.6	6.1
Pierce	27	298	11.5	6.2	26	68	4.5	1.0	138.9	67.7	24.9	9.7
Pike	15	D	D	D	15	57	3.4	1.0	371.9	52.1	17.4	4.6
Polk	42	891	53.3	23.2	45	495	46.0	11.2	356.4	131.7	74.1	21.1
Pulaski	24	786	61.5	28.0	10	14	1.0	0.3	95.6	38.3	19.5	5.8

1. State totals may include programs not allocated by county.

Table B. States and Counties — Federal Funds, Residential Construction, and Local Government Finances

STATE County	Salaries and wages	Procurement contract awards — Defense	Other	Medicaid and other health-related	Nutrition and family welfare	Education	Other	New construction ($1,000)	Number of housing units	Total (mil dol)	Inter-governmental (mil dol)	Total (mil dol)	Per capita (dollars) Total	Property
	171	172	173	174	175	176	177	178	179	180	181	182	183	184
GEORGIA—Cont'd														
Effingham	16.7	0.0	1.4	18.6	5.3	1.6	0.0	17 545	121	173.0	67.8	71.3	1 406	759
Elbert	13.2	1.9	2.5	38.2	5.2	1.7	0.5	2 286	18	74.3	26.2	20.5	1 000	599
Emanuel	20.8	0.0	10.2	61.5	10.7	2.0	7.9	398	5	148.3	41.1	22.4	996	527
Evans	2.7	0.3	0.5	18.7	2.8	1.1	0.6	1 997	14	57.6	16.9	9.9	861	416
Fannin	4.5	0.5	1.4	29.5	4.3	1.5	1.7	18 505	106	60.4	22.1	32.1	1 422	810
Fayette	134.7	13.9	7.9	9.7	8.7	2.7	0.1	25 507	82	379.6	108.5	207.1	1 951	1 445
Floyd	35.5	0.0	8.9	86.1	19.0	7.5	5.0	6 526	55	530.9	181.6	115.9	1 212	720
Forsyth	15.5	35.9	7.1	24.2	8.7	8.1	0.4	146 340	1 125	499.7	139.8	274.8	1 729	1 050
Franklin	4.3	1.1	1.1	31.2	3.3	1.8	1.8	137	1	63.8	25.0	28.8	1 322	709
Fulton	2 486.2	825.0	2 021.2	1 802.2	584.2	1 240.0	3 241.6	189 560	1 101	5 576.3	1 414.3	2 601.7	2 622	1 793
Gilmer	6.2	0.0	1.3	20.1	3.9	1.6	0.2	13 530	91	84.9	31.0	42.2	1 486	913
Glascock	0.9	0.0	0.2	6.7	0.5	0.3	0.0	NA	NA	10.3	4.7	4.6	1 669	1 247
Glynn	197.3	11.7	122.0	51.3	20.2	6.5	18.4	78 910	307	509.4	71.8	164.3	2 193	1 434
Gordon	29.3	4.2	5.9	24.7	8.0	3.2	0.5	4 609	33	166.9	68.6	64.9	1 247	579
Grady	3.4	0.0	0.8	32.8	5.9	3.0	0.4	2 781	20	68.1	33.5	24.3	971	521
Greene	7.3	0.0	1.0	24.4	4.8	1.3	0.3	32 259	124	56.7	14.9	33.3	2 124	1 277
Gwinnett	224.1	223.7	118.2	63.3	56.4	26.0	37.0	191 470	1 239	2 583.5	793.0	1 318.2	1 698	1 182
Habersham	8.3	0.5	7.5	29.9	5.7	1.0	34.0	7 220	35	162.0	65.0	54.3	1 286	706
Hall	62.2	264.1	41.1	74.7	41.3	9.3	3.2	29 977	184	1 091.0	200.0	285.5	1 585	843
Hancock	1.4	0.0	0.3	29.4	6.0	1.0	0.0	1 596	12	29.3	11.8	12.9	1 349	1 106
Haralson	4.7	-0.4	1.3	25.3	5.5	2.7	0.6	3 201	17	90.4	40.3	33.3	1 159	602
Harris	6.0	0.2	2.8	22.2	4.5	1.3	0.1	20 636	88	73.2	27.0	36.5	1 254	885
Hart	7.5	2.0	0.7	32.8	4.0	1.8	0.3	4 927	29	61.3	21.8	30.1	1 241	741
Heard	1.3	0.0	0.3	11.1	2.9	0.9	0.1	1 478	11	45.6	13.3	28.1	2 470	1 010
Henry	119.8	0.8	8.6	29.7	11.5	4.6	1.7	45 663	260	629.9	190.0	337.9	1 816	1 157
Houston	982.5	572.7	67.4	55.7	25.1	7.4	2.1	109 400	646	597.5	168.8	172.5	1 316	721
Irwin	5.5	3.6	-3.6	19.0	2.8	1.0	0.4	2 516	19	41.2	15.8	9.3	932	649
Jackson	11.9	0.1	2.5	41.3	7.5	3.1	0.7	14 156	82	249.3	66.3	99.6	1 681	1 010
Jasper	1.9	0.0	1.2	12.7	3.7	0.8	0.2	4 828	36	38.4	13.8	17.2	1 258	953
Jeff Davis	2.1	0.0	0.5	20.1	4.0	0.9	0.2	0	0	62.6	22.2	14.5	1 090	523
Jefferson	3.3	0.0	3.8	56.9	6.7	1.8	1.2	2 266	19	66.1	27.1	20.5	1 245	736
Jenkins	1.5	0.0	0.7	25.5	3.6	1.9	0.3	800	8	28.2	13.5	7.4	857	519
Johnson	1.7	0.0	0.3	23.6	2.9	1.0	0.2	0	0	19.6	10.7	6.7	703	420
Jones	3.0	0.0	2.5	15.7	3.9	3.1	0.0	3 095	25	66.3	35.2	25.7	943	605
Lamar	3.1	0.1	0.7	16.5	3.6	1.0	0.7	7 676	80	44.6	15.7	17.7	1 044	641
Lanier	1.1	0.0	0.2	13.0	2.1	0.7	0.0	5 715	68	21.0	13.5	6.5	812	529
Laurens	52.8	15.5	45.0	77.2	11.7	4.9	1.0	3 690	60	156.4	72.7	45.6	959	425
Lee	3.1	0.1	0.8	11.9	3.5	1.3	0.0	12 686	111	82.4	35.4	35.1	1 061	673
Liberty	120.0	34.7	1.8	26.6	15.0	14.0	11.1	22 215	111	203.9	94.3	63.2	1 045	547
Lincoln	1.4	0.0	0.3	12.4	2.0	0.8	0.1	2 660	16	25.9	12.5	9.8	1 207	805
Long	1.4	0.3	0.2	7.5	1.8	1.0	0.0	NA	NA	26.3	16.6	7.4	658	463
Lowndes	283.1	89.1	4.2	87.7	25.6	9.8	10.0	60 204	757	321.0	135.1	141.2	1 387	660
Lumpkin	51.8	2.5	1.0	17.6	3.2	0.7	2.0	12 032	56	66.2	22.6	31.3	1 178	815
McDuffie	6.6	0.0	0.8	35.3	5.2	2.0	0.4	5 162	33	88.5	39.9	25.1	1 165	559
McIntosh	10.0	0.3	0.4	15.0	3.6	1.0	0.2	9 602	75	31.8	11.3	16.0	1 405	815
Macon	2.2	34.2	0.5	35.3	6.2	1.6	1.1	89	1	35.1	16.0	14.5	1 075	746
Madison	4.6	0.0	1.1	30.8	4.8	1.9	0.4	10 114	58	73.2	41.6	24.4	872	577
Marion	2.3	0.2	0.2	16.3	2.2	0.9	0.2	3 062	17	20.6	11.2	7.4	1 055	765
Meriwether	4.6	0.0	1.3	42.0	7.2	2.4	0.3	4 536	29	90.0	33.4	31.6	1 388	1 056
Miller	1.6	0.1	0.3	12.6	2.1	0.7	0.2	766	4	41.3	10.1	7.7	1 249	831
Mitchell	5.3	1.4	0.8	51.9	8.7	2.5	1.8	4 108	34	94.2	34.4	25.6	1 061	667
Monroe	17.2	0.0	0.8	16.0	2.2	1.4	0.5	15 648	110	91.4	20.4	39.0	1 550	1 131
Montgomery	1.7	0.0	0.4	19.3	2.4	0.8	0.1	1 273	9	23.2	13.3	6.8	750	453
Morgan	3.8	0.0	0.9	18.6	3.4	1.1	0.2	6 970	33	65.6	20.1	35.1	1 934	1 161
Murray	6.7	11.0	2.1	16.3	6.3	2.8	0.2	3 257	31	100.0	50.3	38.6	950	531
Muscogee	3 032.0	266.2	11.5	189.5	51.8	21.4	32.2	31 807	339	707.6	323.8	242.6	1 297	913
Newton	19.5	1.0	4.0	40.0	11.7	5.5	5.8	9 924	58	373.2	109.9	127.0	1 322	893
Oconee	7.4	0.2	1.9	9.3	3.3	1.1	0.4	19 942	74	101.8	32.5	55.7	1 777	1 159
Oglethorpe	1.9	0.0	0.5	15.5	2.8	1.1	0.0	0	0	32.7	15.3	13.7	981	739
Paulding	11.8	1.4	3.0	23.5	9.2	4.0	1.9	42 858	265	350.4	161.9	149.0	1 165	719
Peach	13.6	1.9	12.4	29.5	8.5	7.0	8.8	10 804	78	113.0	32.9	33.3	1 297	695
Pickens	5.6	0.2	1.7	16.0	4.5	1.4	0.6	6 829	28	78.1	22.5	43.7	1 435	895
Pierce	3.3	0.1	1.5	19.6	4.1	1.3	0.1	3 285	34	46.1	25.0	16.9	948	561
Pike	280.7	0.0	0.7	12.6	2.0	0.8	0.0	2 653	17	44.7	22.3	17.6	1 025	787
Polk	26.6	27.8	10.4	49.5	9.6	3.1	0.6	9 986	94	116.4	56.4	43.1	1 039	652
Pulaski	1.5	0.1	0.4	20.6	2.7	0.7	1.1	1 096	14	35.3	21.4	10.5	1 068	629

1. State totals may include programs not allocated by county.　　2. Based on the resident population estimated as of July 1 of the year shown.

Table B. States and Counties — Local Government Finances, Government Employment, and Voting

STATE County	Direct general expenditure — Total (mil dol)	Per capita[1] (dollars)	Education	Health and hospitals	Police protection	Public welfare	Highways	Debt outstanding — Total (mil dol)	Per capita[1] (dollars)	Federal civilian	Federal military	State and local	Democratic	Republican	All other
	185	186	187	188	189	190	191	192	193	194	195	196	197	198	199
GEORGIA—Cont'd															
Effingham	170.9	3 368	58.7	13.7	3.8	0.3	4.2	92.3	1 820	72	165	2 780	24.3	75.0	0.7
Elbert	75.5	3 676	45.3	21.2	6.0	1.7	1.7	17.2	838	136	63	1 489	40.5	58.5	1.0
Emanuel	150.0	6 678	27.2	55.4	1.7	0.1	2.6	64.8	2 884	101	71	1 917	37.2	62.0	0.8
Evans	60.4	5 247	30.6	48.2	2.6	0.0	4.0	2.4	205	37	36	648	35.6	63.9	0.5
Fannin	62.5	2 766	62.6	2.8	4.7	0.7	11.8	24.9	1 103	47	71	968	24.7	73.8	1.6
Fayette	375.6	3 538	60.1	2.2	5.8	1.0	4.8	354.6	3 341	538	329	5 003	34.2	64.9	0.9
Floyd	541.5	5 663	32.4	42.5	2.6	0.1	2.8	233.9	2 446	243	307	6 829	31.2	67.6	1.1
Forsyth	558.6	3 515	60.9	0.2	4.4	0.3	9.4	684.3	4 306	201	538	6 361	20.4	78.5	1.1
Franklin	76.7	3 520	58.1	1.9	8.7	0.4	5.3	47.8	2 193	50	67	1 131	23.7	75.2	1.1
Fulton	4 992.6	5 032	34.2	0.7	7.2	1.6	2.8	15 916.7	16 043	20 912	5 090	81 362	67.2	32.1	0.7
Gilmer	95.7	3 371	66.4	2.8	3.0	0.1	4.0	44.2	1 556	85	90	1 440	23.4	75.4	1.1
Glascock	10.0	3 605	58.0	1.1	3.2	1.3	5.7	1.4	494	11	0	201	14.7	84.2	1.1
Glynn	478.7	6 389	27.5	42.6	3.9	0.1	1.4	447.1	5 967	1 900	274	6 954	38.0	61.4	0.6
Gordon	168.9	3 246	55.5	1.5	4.5	0.3	5.9	64.4	1 238	96	164	2 911	24.2	74.5	1.3
Grady	74.7	2 983	60.3	1.6	4.0	0.3	5.4	64.5	2 576	75	78	1 174	37.8	61.7	0.5
Greene	51.6	3 297	47.2	0.3	8.0	0.8	6.1	26.3	1 680	48	49	756	42.2	57.2	0.6
Gwinnett	2 724.9	3 510	58.7	1.3	5.4	0.2	5.5	3 370.3	4 341	2 983	2 496	32 385	44.5	54.7	0.8
Habersham	174.1	4 119	39.0	39.2	3.2	0.1	2.7	166.6	3 942	116	135	2 917	19.6	79.5	1.0
Hall	1 105.6	6 136	27.0	44.1	2.1	0.6	1.6	1 620.4	8 994	534	580	9 989	24.1	75.0	0.8
Hancock	24.8	2 595	62.6	2.0	4.6	1.3	3.8	16.5	1 728	15	28	795	81.4	18.3	0.3
Haralson	93.8	3 265	63.5	1.6	5.2	0.1	5.5	34.3	1 194	66	89	1 711	20.3	78.0	1.7
Harris	66.4	2 282	67.9	2.1	4.8	0.1	3.6	39.5	1 359	62	93	1 154	28.1	71.4	0.5
Hart	64.2	2 649	59.9	2.1	4.7	0.5	6.9	26.6	1 096	95	74	1 177	33.6	65.4	1.0
Heard	41.2	3 615	50.7	2.1	5.1	1.3	6.8	39.3	3 448	16	36	731	24.7	74.2	1.2
Henry	663.7	3 567	59.0	0.2	5.3	0.7	8.5	1 056.7	5 680	1 069	605	8 641	45.9	53.4	0.7
Houston	604.1	4 611	46.0	28.7	3.8	0.2	4.5	126.5	966	14 648	4 249	9 138	39.5	59.7	0.8
Irwin	42.5	4 279	44.8	30.4	3.8	0.2	7.3	14.3	1 443	25	31	872	31.3	68.1	0.7
Jackson	285.2	4 813	54.9	14.8	4.3	0.2	5.5	406.4	6 858	141	196	3 466	21.6	77.4	1.0
Jasper	42.3	3 095	60.4	11.0	4.7	0.1	2.9	18.1	1 323	23	43	671	32.8	66.3	0.9
Jeff Davis	60.7	4 564	41.7	32.8	3.2	0.1	8.4	17.4	1 305	30	42	828	25.7	73.3	1.0
Jefferson	66.2	4 023	45.1	20.0	3.9	1.4	3.2	20.2	1 226	46	51	1 173	57.4	42.3	0.3
Jenkins	32.6	3 796	57.7	16.8	2.7	0.1	3.3	6.8	797	25	26	567	43.1	56.3	0.6
Johnson	22.6	2 373	54.3	2.4	4.7	0.3	4.7	5.3	552	17	29	685	32.8	66.5	0.6
Jones	65.8	2 418	67.3	0.5	5.0	0.5	5.8	17.1	628	35	86	1 195	36.8	62.6	0.7
Lamar	40.4	2 382	53.6	1.3	5.7	0.1	3.1	46.1	2 717	39	54	1 130	35.8	63.4	0.8
Lanier	20.6	2 596	76.0	0.4	6.9	0.2	4.8	3.6	448	13	26	476	37.0	62.2	0.8
Laurens	172.7	3 634	51.4	11.4	5.1	0.3	6.6	91.9	1 303	1 097	150	6 511	39.0	60.5	0.6
Lee	78.8	2 383	70.6	2.4	3.5	0.1	3.4	55.0	1 664	44	105	1 452	23.7	75.8	0.5
Liberty	209.4	3 462	52.0	15.6	4.5	0.1	3.1	41.2	682	3 887	17 176	3 068	64.0	35.6	0.5
Lincoln	24.9	3 074	54.8	3.0	3.7	5.5	4.5	12.5	1 541	18	24	463	37.4	61.8	0.8
Long	24.9	2 204	71.6	0.7	5.7	1.4	8.8	5.1	448	0	38	620	37.3	61.4	1.2
Lowndes	348.4	3 423	52.0	7.4	6.1	0.6	9.4	52.6	517	810	4 854	10 347	45.0	54.3	0.7
Lumpkin	64.8	2 439	54.5	2.4	5.0	0.5	3.3	81.7	3 075	70	333	2 061	23.3	75.2	1.5
McDuffie	88.6	4 112	53.9	20.9	3.7	1.4	2.7	2.0	91	48	133	1 566	42.3	57.2	0.5
McIntosh	31.6	2 763	55.7	5.3	6.8	0.1	5.6	8.0	704	25	35	698	46.6	52.7	0.7
Macon	34.8	2 573	56.1	1.7	6.4	0.4	5.8	8.2	605	27	41	950	65.3	34.4	0.4
Madison	72.7	2 594	73.5	3.2	2.8	0.3	3.6	23.5	839	55	87	1 227	26.2	72.6	1.3
Marion	19.6	2 786	71.4	0.2	2.3	2.2	2.7	8.6	1 218	38	22	380	43.4	55.7	0.9
Meriwether	88.8	3 904	45.7	17.5	4.2	0.5	3.0	49.8	2 188	47	70	1 776	47.0	52.4	0.6
Miller	43.4	7 039	28.1	51.5	3.5	0.0	4.3	25.0	4 059	23	19	608	29.9	69.4	0.8
Mitchell	97.1	4 021	41.9	23.9	4.8	0.0	4.5	42.3	1 751	79	73	1 673	47.7	51.7	0.6
Monroe	86.7	3 449	43.1	12.9	5.7	0.1	3.9	164.3	6 534	48	78	1 641	33.8	65.4	0.8
Montgomery	22.3	2 466	63.2	2.6	2.5	0.8	8.1	4.2	461	26	28	434	29.1	70.2	0.7
Morgan	66.0	3 634	50.5	6.1	4.3	0.9	9.9	17.5	964	47	58	1 199	33.8	65.4	0.8
Murray	94.8	2 331	72.0	3.0	3.6	0.8	5.6	71.5	1 758	106	125	1 571	26.6	71.9	1.5
Muscogee	680.7	3 639	48.6	7.9	4.9	2.1	3.4	540.0	2 887	5 575	5 553	13 238	59.6	39.9	0.5
Newton	396.1	4 125	41.9	16.8	3.5	0.2	5.0	309.6	3 224	156	308	4 597	50.3	49.1	0.7
Oconee	108.3	3 454	55.6	1.4	3.7	0.8	6.0	105.0	3 349	180	103	1 484	28.2	70.7	1.1
Oglethorpe	33.0	2 365	64.5	2.4	2.1	1.0	2.1	2.9	204	20	44	639	34.6	64.3	1.1
Paulding	376.2	2 941	69.0	0.8	4.1	0.1	4.2	423.1	3 308	135	422	5 207	30.2	68.8	1.0
Peach	100.0	3 894	40.7	13.9	5.0	0.1	2.1	49.5	1 929	106	88	2 412	53.1	46.3	0.6
Pickens	75.5	2 475	59.5	2.6	5.0	0.2	5.6	32.0	1 048	59	96	1 449	20.3	78.2	1.5
Pierce	45.6	2 548	71.6	3.6	3.0	0.6	4.1	7.8	438	45	57	849	18.5	81.0	0.6
Pike	43.7	2 539	72.4	1.8	5.8	0.2	3.0	21.8	1 265	33	55	785	19.2	79.8	1.0
Polk	126.5	3 052	59.5	2.8	5.1	0.5	4.4	42.0	1 014	67	130	1 789	28.7	69.8	1.5
Pulaski	38.6	3 921	40.1	1.6	3.7	0.3	4.0	8.1	825	19	31	756	34.8	64.6	0.6

1. Based on the resident population estimated as of July 1 of the year shown.   2. © 2009 Election Data Services, Inc. All rights reserved.

Table B. States and Counties — Land Area and Population

STATE/ County code	CBSA code[1]	County type[2]	STATE County	Land area,[3] (sq km) 2010	Total persons	Rank	Per square kilometer	White	Black	American Indian, Alaska Native	Asian and Pacific Islander	Percent Hispanic or Latino[4]	Under 5 years	5 to 17 years	18 to 24 years	25 to 34 years	35 to 44 years	45 to 54 years
				1	2	3	4	5	6	7	8	9	10	11	12	13	14	15
			GEORGIA—Cont'd															
13 237	...	6	Putnam	893	21 218	1 778	23.8	66.9	26.4	0.4	0.8	6.3	6.3	15.3	7.5	11.2	11.5	14.3
13 239	21640	9	Quitman	392	2 513	3 007	6.4	50.7	48.0	0.3	0.1	1.4	5.3	15.2	7.8	8.6	11.4	12.6
13 241	...	9	Rabun	958	16 276	2 034	17.0	89.9	1.1	1.1	0.9	8.0	5.0	16.0	7.2	9.2	11.6	14.2
13 243	...	6	Randolph	1 109	7 719	2 627	7.0	36.5	62.0	0.2	0.3	1.5	6.5	15.9	9.1	10.7	10.5	15.2
13 245	12260	2	Richmond	840	200 549	310	238.7	39.7	54.9	0.8	2.5	4.1	7.4	17.2	12.5	15.1	11.6	13.7
13 247	12060	1	Rockdale	336	85 215	656	253.6	42.0	46.9	0.6	2.2	9.5	6.8	20.1	9.0	11.6	14.4	15.5
13 249	11140	8	Schley	432	5 010	2 840	11.6	72.7	23.5	0.4	0.9	3.2	6.3	23.7	7.7	9.7	15.0	13.7
13 251	...	6	Screven	1 671	14 593	2 140	8.7	54.8	43.7	0.7	0.6	1.2	6.8	18.5	8.8	11.0	11.8	14.4
13 253	...	6	Seminole	609	8 729	2 548	14.3	63.9	33.5	0.6	0.4	2.3	5.7	17.2	7.2	10.0	11.5	15.2
13 255	12060	1	Spalding	509	64 073	814	125.9	62.0	33.5	0.7	1.2	3.8	7.2	18.1	9.0	13.0	13.2	14.0
13 257	45740	7	Stephens	464	26 175	1 552	56.4	85.6	11.9	0.7	1.0	2.4	6.2	16.6	9.7	10.8	12.1	14.4
13 259	...	8	Stewart	1 188	6 058	2 762	5.1	27.9	47.2	0.6	1.0	24.0	4.5	11.2	11.3	19.1	15.3	13.1
13 261	11140	6	Sumter	1 250	32 819	1 365	26.3	41.5	52.0	0.6	1.5	5.2	7.2	18.1	13.3	12.7	11.8	12.8
13 263	...	8	Talbot	1 014	6 865	2 697	6.8	39.3	59.5	0.6	0.2	1.3	5.3	16.1	7.5	8.9	11.2	17.8
13 265	...	8	Taliaferro	504	1 717	3 075	3.4	37.6	60.7	0.3	0.7	2.0	5.6	13.2	9.3	9.0	11.4	15.7
13 267	...	6	Tattnall	1 242	25 520	1 586	20.5	60.3	29.6	0.5	0.5	9.8	5.9	15.3	10.1	16.4	15.0	15.1
13 269	...	8	Taylor	976	8 906	2 532	9.1	58.1	39.6	0.4	0.8	1.8	6.1	18.4	8.6	10.8	13.0	15.4
13 271	...	7	Telfair	1 133	16 500	2 018	14.6	51.6	35.8	0.3	0.7	12.3	5.7	14.4	8.2	15.4	15.4	15.2
13 273	10500	3	Terrell	869	9 315	2 495	10.7	36.6	61.5	0.4	0.5	1.7	7.2	17.6	9.6	11.0	11.0	15.1
13 275	45620	4	Thomas	1 410	44 720	1 074	31.7	59.1	37.2	0.8	0.9	2.9	6.8	18.1	8.2	11.5	12.6	15.0
13 277	45700	4	Tift	671	40 118	1 170	59.8	59.5	29.4	0.4	1.5	10.1	7.4	18.4	12.0	12.7	12.3	13.3
13 279	47080	7	Toombs	943	27 223	1 524	28.9	62.9	25.3	0.5	1.0	11.2	8.2	19.8	8.6	12.3	12.5	13.4
13 281	...	9	Towns	431	10 471	2 405	24.3	96.9	0.5	0.5	0.6	2.0	3.7	12.0	10.2	7.0	9.9	12.0
13 283	...	7	Treutlen	517	6 885	2 696	13.3	65.5	32.9	0.4	0.3	1.5	7.2	17.7	9.3	13.7	12.1	14.2
13 285	29300	4	Troup	1 072	67 044	783	62.5	61.4	34.1	0.6	1.8	3.2	7.1	19.5	9.5	12.3	13.2	14.2
13 287	...	6	Turner	739	8 930	2 531	12.1	54.4	41.7	0.4	0.6	3.2	6.7	18.0	9.4	11.9	12.2	13.5
13 289	31420	3	Twiggs	928	9 023	2 525	9.7	57.0	41.6	0.7	0.3	1.4	5.8	14.8	8.7	9.4	11.4	18.2
13 291	...	9	Union	834	21 356	1 772	25.6	96.4	0.5	1.2	0.6	2.4	4.3	13.4	6.1	8.0	10.4	14.0
13 293	45580	6	Upson	838	27 153	1 526	32.4	69.2	28.3	0.6	0.6	2.2	6.2	17.4	8.7	11.1	12.8	14.9
13 295	16860	2	Walker	1 156	68 756	771	59.5	93.5	4.7	0.8	0.7	1.6	6.1	17.5	7.7	12.3	13.6	14.9
13 297	12060	1	Walton	844	83 768	659	99.3	79.5	16.2	0.6	1.5	3.2	6.9	20.0	7.9	11.8	14.9	14.7
13 299	48180	4	Ware	2 311	36 312	1 264	15.7	66.0	30.1	0.7	1.0	3.3	6.9	16.7	9.5	12.9	12.5	14.1
13 301	...	8	Warren	736	5 834	2 781	7.9	37.0	61.8	0.3	0.4	0.9	6.9	16.6	7.9	10.0	11.3	15.5
13 303	...	7	Washington	1 757	21 187	1 779	12.1	44.7	53.1	0.3	0.6	1.9	6.6	17.2	8.8	12.7	12.7	16.1
13 305	27700	6	Wayne	1 662	30 099	1 425	18.1	73.6	20.6	0.8	0.8	5.7	7.2	17.5	8.4	13.2	14.5	14.4
13 307	...	8	Webster	542	2 799	2 992	5.2	54.1	42.6	0.2	0.4	3.5	5.9	19.5	7.4	9.6	13.6	15.2
13 309	...	9	Wheeler	765	7 421	2 649	9.7	60.0	35.2	0.4	0.3	4.8	5.5	13.3	10.3	16.8	14.8	15.3
13 311	...	8	White	623	27 144	1 527	43.6	94.9	2.1	1.1	0.6	2.4	5.9	17.0	8.3	10.0	12.6	14.6
13 313	19140	3	Whitfield	752	102 599	565	136.4	63.2	4.1	0.5	1.5	31.6	7.9	20.6	9.5	13.2	14.1	13.3
13 315	...	9	Wilcox	978	9 255	2 502	9.5	60.4	35.5	0.7	0.5	3.7	5.2	14.1	9.1	15.2	14.7	14.9
13 317	...	6	Wilkes	1 216	10 593	2 395	8.7	53.1	43.6	0.5	0.6	3.4	6.0	16.3	7.2	10.8	11.8	15.1
13 319	...	8	Wilkinson	1 159	9 563	2 475	8.3	58.7	38.8	0.6	0.5	2.2	6.9	17.4	7.9	10.8	11.7	16.2
13 321	10500	3	Worth	1 478	21 679	1 755	14.7	70.2	27.9	0.6	0.6	1.5	6.6	18.0	9.1	10.8	12.5	15.2
15 000	...	X	**HAWAII**	16 635	1 360 301	X	81.8	36.5	2.5	1.7	76.2	8.9	6.4	15.9	9.6	13.6	13.0	14.2
15 001	25900	5	Hawaii	10 434	185 079	334	17.7	48.0	1.3	2.6	68.3	11.6	6.4	16.4	8.4	12.0	11.6	14.9
15 003	26180	2	Honolulu	1 556	953 207	43	612.6	32.3	3.0	1.5	79.7	8.1	6.4	15.7	10.3	14.1	13.1	13.8
15 005	...	9	Kalawao	31	90	3 142	2.9	36.7	0.0	0.0	80.0	1.1	0.0	0.0	3.3	11.1	15.6	18.9
15 007	28180	5	Kauai	1 606	67 091	781	41.8	45.3	1.0	1.9	69.2	9.4	6.4	16.3	7.3	12.1	12.5	15.3
15 009	27980	5	Maui	3 008	154 834	402	51.5	44.9	1.3	1.8	67.2	10.1	6.5	16.7	7.5	13.2	13.8	15.7
16 000	...	X	**IDAHO**	214 045	1 567 582	X	7.3	85.6	0.9	1.9	2.1	11.2	7.8	19.6	9.9	13.3	12.2	13.3
16 001	14260	2	Ada	2 726	392 365	169	143.9	88.5	1.5	1.2	3.7	7.1	7.2	19.2	9.1	14.7	14.2	14.0
16 003	...	8	Adams	3 530	3 976	2 911	1.1	96.1	0.2	2.0	0.7	2.4	4.8	14.4	5.2	8.5	9.3	17.5
16 005	38540	3	Bannock	2 880	82 839	668	28.8	88.1	1.1	3.5	2.3	6.7	8.4	19.0	12.2	15.3	11.0	11.9
16 007	...	7	Bear Lake	2 525	5 986	2 770	2.4	95.5	0.2	0.8	0.6	3.6	6.8	20.5	6.3	10.6	10.0	13.7
16 009	...	6	Benewah	2 011	9 285	2 501	4.6	88.4	0.6	11.1	0.8	2.5	6.5	17.2	6.6	8.9	11.1	15.5
16 011	13940	6	Bingham	5 423	45 607	1 055	8.4	76.0	0.3	6.3	1.2	17.2	9.7	23.3	8.4	12.7	11.3	12.7
16 013	...	7	Blaine	6 847	21 376	1 770	3.1	78.7	0.2	0.5	1.2	20.0	6.6	17.7	5.9	12.4	13.9	16.8
16 015	14260	2	Boise	4 919	7 028	2 685	1.4	95.1	0.3	2.0	0.9	3.5	4.4	17.1	5.0	6.9	11.6	18.5
16 017	...	6	Bonner	4 493	40 877	1 156	9.1	96.3	0.3	1.9	1.1	2.2	5.2	16.4	6.2	9.8	11.3	16.3
16 019	26820	3	Bonneville	4 833	104 234	561	21.6	86.5	0.9	1.0	1.4	11.4	9.6	21.9	8.5	14.7	11.5	12.7
16 021	...	7	Boundary	3 286	10 972	2 368	3.3	93.9	0.6	2.6	1.1	3.7	6.3	19.4	5.8	10.3	10.9	14.7
16 023	...	8	Butte	5 780	2 891	2 987	0.5	94.9	0.2	1.3	0.5	4.1	7.4	20.8	5.7	9.8	9.4	14.6
16 025	...	9	Camas	2 783	1 117	3 105	0.4	92.5	0.2	2.2	0.4	6.7	5.6	15.8	4.9	12.9	11.4	17.7
16 027	14260	2	Canyon	1 521	188 923	330	124.2	73.9	0.8	1.4	1.7	23.9	9.1	22.4	9.4	13.9	12.9	11.8

1. CBSA = Core Based Statistical Area. See Appendix A for explanation. See Appendix B for list of metropolitan areas with component counties.   2. County type code from the Economic Research Service of USDA Rural-Urban Continuum Codes. See Appendix A for definition.   3. Dry land or land partially or temporarily covered by water.   4. May be of any race.

Table B. States and Counties — **Population and Households**

STATE County	55 to 64 years	65 to 74 years	75 years and over	Percent female	Total persons 1990	Total persons 2000	Percent change 1990–2000	Percent change 2000–2010	Births	Deaths	Net migration	Number	Percent change, 2000–2010	Persons per household	Female family householder[1]	One person
	16	17	18	19	20	21	22	23	24	25	26	27	28	29	30	31
GEORGIA—Cont'd																
Putnam	15.7	11.7	6.4	51.3	14 137	18 812	33.1	12.8	2 398	1 712	1 087	8 601	16.2	2.45	14.2	24.7
Quitman	17.1	12.9	9.1	52.2	2 210	2 598	17.6	-3.3	325	276	21	1 053	0.6	2.39	15.8	30.6
Rabun	15.5	12.6	8.7	50.7	11 648	15 050	29.2	8.1	1 719	1 609	1 538	6 780	8.0	2.34	9.6	28.5
Randolph	14.4	9.3	8.5	54.0	8 023	7 791	-2.9	-0.9	941	936	-582	3 187	9.6	2.33	22.7	33.5
Richmond	11.2	6.3	5.0	51.6	189 719	199 775	5.3	0.4	29 694	17 527	-11 013	76 924	4.1	2.47	22.6	30.4
Rockdale	12.0	6.3	4.3	52.4	54 091	70 111	29.6	21.5	10 405	4 985	9 454	30 027	24.8	2.81	18.9	21.0
Schley	10.8	9.3	3.9	52.0	3 590	3 766	4.9	33.0	524	357	409	1 872	30.5	2.68	13.8	25.6
Screven	13.8	8.3	6.6	51.2	13 842	15 374	11.1	-5.1	1 799	1 602	-453	5 596	-3.5	2.53	18.6	27.3
Seminole	14.2	11.0	8.0	52.6	9 010	9 369	4.0	-6.8	1 113	998	-341	3 509	-1.8	2.46	17.9	26.4
Spalding	12.2	7.8	5.5	51.5	54 457	58 417	7.3	9.7	8 872	5 668	3 400	23 565	9.5	2.67	19.4	23.5
Stephens	13.7	9.6	7.0	52.1	23 436	25 435	8.5	2.9	3 168	2 925	137	10 289	3.4	2.49	13.2	25.7
Stewart	11.4	7.5	6.7	39.2	5 654	5 252	-7.1	15.3	538	623	-601	1 862	-7.2	2.35	21.8	32.2
Sumter	11.6	6.9	5.7	52.4	30 232	33 200	9.8	-1.1	4 700	3 185	-2 456	12 123	0.8	2.55	23.0	27.6
Talbot	16.9	10.3	6.0	52.7	6 524	6 498	-0.4	5.6	704	738	-82	2 832	11.6	2.42	19.2	28.9
Taliaferro	15.4	11.1	9.4	51.0	1 915	2 077	8.5	-17.3	195	213	-245	759	-12.8	2.25	22.0	33.2
Tattnall	10.7	7.1	4.6	41.8	17 722	22 305	25.9	14.4	3 143	2 125	1 302	8 210	16.3	2.52	14.1	27.7
Taylor	12.9	9.1	5.8	51.7	7 642	8 815	15.3	1.0	1 045	938	-288	3 522	7.3	2.44	19.6	30.1
Telfair	12.1	7.4	6.3	42.7	11 000	11 794	7.2	39.9	1 524	1 450	908	5 543	33.9	2.41	17.2	30.8
Terrell	13.6	8.7	6.2	51.9	10 653	10 970	3.0	-15.1	1 469	1 165	-899	3 519	-12.1	2.57	24.4	26.7
Thomas	12.8	8.4	6.7	52.6	38 943	42 737	9.7	4.6	5 910	4 319	2 101	17 573	7.8	2.50	18.3	27.2
Tift	11.1	7.1	5.7	52.1	34 998	38 407	9.7	4.5	6 140	3 341	2 009	14 836	6.6	2.60	17.6	25.6
Toombs	11.6	7.9	5.8	52.5	24 072	26 067	8.3	4.4	4 145	2 610	502	10 375	5.0	2.59	18.3	27.2
Towns	16.0	16.4	12.8	52.3	6 754	9 319	38.0	12.4	827	1 268	2 166	4 510	12.8	2.17	7.6	30.1
Treutlen	12.3	7.5	6.2	49.9	5 994	6 854	14.3	0.5	832	674	85	2 543	0.5	2.53	18.1	27.1
Troup	11.8	6.7	5.6	51.9	55 532	58 779	5.8	14.1	8 907	5 971	3 364	24 828	13.3	2.62	20.3	25.1
Turner	12.6	8.7	7.0	51.2	8 703	9 504	9.2	-6.0	1 385	952	-637	3 339	-2.8	2.56	19.4	27.1
Twiggs	15.6	10.0	6.2	51.3	9 806	10 590	8.0	-14.8	1 139	971	-589	3 634	-5.2	2.46	16.5	27.6
Union	17.2	15.8	11.0	51.3	11 993	17 289	44.2	23.5	1 746	2 337	4 604	9 116	27.3	2.30	8.0	26.2
Upson	13.1	9.0	6.7	52.0	26 300	27 597	4.9	-1.6	3 258	3 364	227	10 716	-0.1	2.49	17.6	27.4
Walker	12.9	8.6	6.4	50.9	58 310	61 053	4.7	12.6	7 221	6 267	3 336	26 497	12.3	2.54	18.1	24.7
Walton	11.6	7.1	4.9	51.3	38 586	60 687	57.3	38.0	10 428	5 310	21 634	29 583	38.8	2.81	13.9	18.7
Ware	12.2	7.9	7.4	50.2	35 471	35 483	0.0	2.3	4 744	4 053	-82	13 654	1.3	2.48	17.7	28.4
Warren	13.9	9.9	8.0	53.8	6 078	6 336	4.2	-7.9	775	713	-614	2 315	-4.9	2.48	23.4	28.3
Washington	12.3	7.5	6.1	49.0	19 112	21 176	10.8	0.1	2 461	2 154	-488	7 547	1.5	2.56	22.4	27.2
Wayne	12.0	7.5	5.3	47.8	22 356	26 565	18.8	13.3	3 884	2 500	1 590	10 562	13.3	2.63	14.9	23.6
Webster	13.7	8.5	6.5	51.3	2 263	2 390	5.6	17.1	231	212	-209	1 119	22.8	2.50	16.4	26.6
Wheeler	12.1	6.6	5.3	38.3	4 903	6 179	26.0	20.1	702	501	652	2 152	7.0	2.54	16.5	26.0
White	14.2	10.6	5.3	51.0	13 006	19 944	53.3	22.8	2 687	2 077	4 822	10 646	37.7	2.52	10.7	22.8
Whitfield	10.2	6.5	4.7	50.2	72 462	83 525	15.3	22.9	16 793	6 570	963	35 100	19.7	2.89	13.4	21.4
Wilcox	12.6	7.6	6.7	41.3	7 008	8 577	22.4	7.9	939	904	326	2 891	3.8	2.50	15.7	25.9
Wilkes	14.3	10.4	8.3	51.2	10 597	10 687	0.8	-0.9	1 179	1 255	-291	4 263	-1.2	2.40	18.8	29.6
Wilkinson	13.3	9.2	6.5	52.1	10 228	10 220	-0.1	-6.4	1 446	949	-594	3 666	-4.2	2.58	18.3	24.8
Worth	13.3	8.8	5.7	52.0	19 744	21 967	11.3	-1.3	2 498	1 902	-1 277	8 214	1.3	2.62	17.1	23.4
HAWAII	12.9	7.4	7.0	49.9	1 108 229	1 211 537	9.3	12.3	168 965	83 575	5 843	455 338	12.9	2.89	12.6	23.3
Hawaii	15.9	8.1	6.4	49.8	120 317	148 677	23.6	24.5	21 094	12 004	20 930	67 096	26.6	2.70	12.3	25.1
Honolulu	12.0	7.2	7.3	49.9	836 231	876 156	4.8	8.8	122 222	59 029	-26 320	311 047	8.6	2.95	12.7	22.8
Kalawao	22.2	7.8	21.1	53.3	130	147	13.1	-38.8	0	20	-43	69	-40.0	1.26	1.4	73.9
Kauai	15.2	8.0	6.9	49.8	51 177	58 463	14.2	14.8	7 554	4 197	3 116	23 240	15.1	2.84	12.6	22.6
Maui	13.9	7.3	5.5	49.9	100 374	128 094	27.6	20.9	18 095	8 325	8 160	53 886	23.9	2.82	12.3	24.3
IDAHO	11.5	7.0	5.4	49.9	1 006 734	1 293 953	28.5	21.1	211 735	95 443	134 462	579 408	23.4	2.66	9.6	23.8
Ada	11.0	5.8	4.7	49.9	205 775	300 904	46.2	30.4	49 406	19 068	54 942	148 445	30.9	2.58	10.0	25.0
Adams	19.5	13.8	7.0	48.7	3 254	3 476	6.8	14.4	295	280	38	1 748	23.0	2.26	5.8	26.8
Bannock	11.0	6.0	5.1	50.1	66 026	75 565	14.4	9.6	13 445	5 352	-3 147	30 682	12.8	2.64	10.7	24.9
Bear Lake	13.6	10.1	8.4	50.4	6 084	6 411	5.4	-6.6	742	572	-785	2 281	1.0	2.61	6.3	24.0
Benewah	15.9	11.1	7.2	49.0	7 937	9 171	15.5	1.2	1 076	889	-49	3 837	7.2	2.40	9.3	27.3
Bingham	10.5	6.3	5.1	49.8	37 583	41 735	11.0	9.3	7 410	2 661	-1 549	14 999	12.6	3.02	10.5	18.5
Blaine	15.1	7.8	3.8	49.1	13 552	18 991	40.1	12.6	2 639	739	1 542	8 823	13.4	2.39	7.3	28.7
Boise	20.6	11.5	4.5	47.8	3 509	6 670	90.1	5.4	534	341	606	2 974	13.7	2.35	5.6	25.3
Bonner	17.7	10.6	6.5	49.6	26 622	36 835	38.4	11.0	3 748	3 110	4 110	17 100	16.4	2.37	7.9	26.0
Bonneville	10.3	5.9	5.0	50.1	72 207	82 522	14.3	26.3	16 352	5 963	8 910	36 629	27.4	2.81	10.1	22.4
Boundary	16.0	9.9	6.8	49.4	8 332	9 871	18.5	11.2	1 237	908	793	4 421	19.3	2.47	7.6	27.5
Butte	14.8	10.1	7.4	48.6	2 918	2 899	-0.7	-0.3	363	227	-264	1 129	3.7	2.54	7.8	26.4
Camas	15.7	10.9	5.0	47.9	727	991	36.3	12.7	125	52	47	487	23.0	2.29	5.1	28.3
Canyon	9.7	6.1	4.7	50.5	90 076	131 441	45.9	43.7	29 449	10 176	36 301	63 604	41.3	2.92	12.3	20.1

1. No spouse present.

STATE County	Persons in group quarters, 2010	Daytime population, 2006–2010 Number	Employment/residence ratio	Births, average 2006–2008 Total	Rate[1]	Deaths, average 2006–2008 Number	Rate[1]	Persons under 65 with no health insurance, 2009 Number	Percent	Medicare, 2011 Eligible for Medicare	Enrolled in Medicare Advantage	Enrolled in a Medicare prescription drug plan	Serious crimes known to police,[2] 2010 Total Number	Rate[3]
	32	33	34	35	36	37	38	39	40	41	42	43	44	45
GEORGIA—Cont'd														
Putnam	172	19 467	0.8	D	D	200	9.9	3 544	21.7	4 504	951	1 786	616	2 903
Quitman	0	NA	NA	D	D	32	12.1	530	24.6	646	176	259	71	2 825
Rabun	390	17 191	1.1	D	D	177	10.8	3 376	26.2	3 987	563	2 003	165	1 160
Randolph	308	7 070	0.8	D	D	98	13.5	1 357	23.3	1 483	309	815	NA	NA
Richmond	10 508	229 898	1.4	3 355	17.0	1 887	9.6	33 820	20.0	30 756	7 908	9 748	15 804	7 880
Rockdale	864	81 623	1.0	1 207	14.7	576	7.0	15 582	21.2	11 457	2 897	4 099	3 640	4 272
Schley	0	4 172	0.7	D	D	37	8.9	812	21.8	689	165	330	37	739
Screven	420	13 972	0.8	219	14.5	178	11.8	2 739	21.8	2 753	596	1 287	185	1 320
Seminole	100	8 292	0.8	D	D	106	11.6	1 580	21.6	2 091	408	1 019	155	1 776
Spalding	1 226	61 098	0.9	971	15.4	619	9.8	11 975	21.8	11 468	2 529	5 227	3 525	5 502
Stephens	548	26 038	1.0	D	D	326	12.9	4 719	22.8	5 735	1 048	2 797	1 029	3 931
Stewart	1 675	5 187	0.7	D	D	74	15.9	784	22.0	962	207	520	32	528
Sumter	1 907	33 720	1.1	D	D	317	9.8	5 915	22.0	5 381	1 338	2 609	1 826	5 634
Talbot	17	5 499	0.4	D	D	84	12.8	1 103	21.2	1 391	322	594	90	1 394
Taliaferro	7	NA	NA	D	D	27	14.2	372	27.0	415	128	185	NA	NA
Tattnall	4 859	22 303	0.8	359	15.4	238	10.2	6 489	30.9	3 555	887	1 605	565	2 266
Taylor	322	8 524	0.9	D	D	101	11.5	1 581	22.3	1 612	444	737	99	1 112
Telfair	3 127	16 308	1.1	D	D	152	11.4	2 766	26.0	2 256	395	1 229	250	1 547
Terrell	270	9 194	0.9	D	D	118	11.3	1 947	22.6	1 920	531	872	254	2 727
Thomas	848	47 463	1.2	708	15.6	468	10.3	7 984	21.1	9 024	1 967	4 227	1 580	3 640
Tift	1 568	44 076	1.3	719	17.2	362	8.6	9 281	25.4	6 547	1 339	3 104	2 485	6 194
Toombs	387	28 451	1.1	477	17.1	267	9.6	5 979	25.4	5 044	810	2 873	1 210	5 294
Towns	698	10 868	1.1	D	D	136	12.6	2 040	26.5	3 592	727	1 456	173	1 652
Treutlen	452	5 671	0.5	D	D	74	10.6	1 546	26.2	1 243	301	652	257	3 733
Troup	2 073	70 137	1.2	1 022	16.1	613	9.6	11 531	21.0	10 669	2 374	5 208	2 963	4 419
Turner	371	8 347	0.8	D	D	107	11.5	1 879	24.5	1 770	410	942	224	2 508
Twiggs	89	7 910	0.5	D	D	105	10.2	1 850	21.7	2 044	529	894	178	2 228
Union	379	20 063	0.9	D	D	276	13.1	3 749	24.1	6 288	1 180	2 563	138	646
Upson	474	24 838	0.8	355	12.9	331	12.0	4 935	21.3	5 718	1 616	2 642	963	3 547
Walker	1 323	56 486	0.6	841	13.0	707	10.9	11 409	20.9	12 968	2 664	6 672	2 064	3 002
Walton	682	65 584	0.6	1 265	15.3	577	7.0	14 977	20.0	12 112	2 805	4 942	2 151	2 568
Ware	2 409	40 116	1.3	554	15.5	471	13.2	7 037	23.9	7 316	1 134	4 163	1 850	5 095
Warren	89	5 037	0.6	D	D	78	13.2	1 013	21.9	1 263	342	581	NA	NA
Washington	1 896	21 524	1.1	280	13.4	251	12.0	3 884	22.1	3 724	1 220	1 580	681	3 253
Wayne	2 316	28 334	0.9	471	16.2	292	10.0	5 919	23.6	5 149	951	2 655	1 394	4 631
Webster	0	2 284	0.6	D	D	25	11.1	440	23.9	459	103	221	NA	NA
Wheeler	1 959	7 145	1.0	D	D	62	9.0	1 666	27.8	1 004	184	518	117	1 577
White	365	22 943	0.7	D	D	237	9.5	4 789	23.1	5 474	1 189	2 452	695	2 560
Whitfield	1 002	114 036	1.3	1 853	19.8	744	8.0	23 126	28.3	14 466	1 586	8 510	3 265	3 259
Wilcox	2 019	8 421	0.8	D	D	97	11.1	1 877	25.6	1 530	336	711	101	1 250
Wilkes	344	10 040	0.9	D	D	128	12.4	1 860	23.2	2 413	516	1 204	165	1 558
Wilkinson	110	9 393	0.9	D	D	104	10.4	1 643	19.7	2 075	547	784	186	1 945
Worth	149	17 440	0.5	254	11.8	219	10.2	3 850	21.6	3 572	532	1 725	567	2 667
HAWAII	42 880	1 334 316	1.0	19 200	15.0	9 476	7.4	91 365	8.2	215 707	92 776	58 195	48 657	3 577
Hawaii	3 644	180 358	1.0	2 512	14.5	1 399	8.1	16 123	10.4	31 300	12 041	10 463	5 769	3 117
Honolulu	35 300	937 302	1.0	13 689	15.1	6 611	7.3	57 090	7.4	151 641	66 911	38 177	34 216	3 589
Kalawao	3	NA	NA	NA	NA	NA	NA	NA	NA	18	D	0	NA	NA
Kauai	1 161	65 549	1.0	886	14.0	502	7.9	5 135	9.3	11 127	4 052	3 754	2 722	4 057
Maui	2 772	150 953	1.0	2 114	14.9	962	6.8	13 016	10.2	21 621	9 772	5 801	6 563	4 239
IDAHO	28 951	1 511 099	1.0	24 784	16.6	10 799	7.2	257 017	19.3	240 053	69 373	85 940	34 751	2 217
Ada	9 714	400 884	1.1	5 731	15.4	2 246	6.1	51 541	15.1	51 763	20 869	12 281	9 079	2 314
Adams	21	3 669	0.8	D	D	37	10.5	733	26.7	974	144	388	61	1 534
Bannock	1 792	79 800	1.0	1 462	18.3	570	7.2	12 485	17.4	11 768	3 393	5 177	2 511	3 031
Bear Lake	31	5 647	0.8	D	D	62	10.4	914	19.6	1 253	273	571	110	1 838
Benewah	70	9 777	1.1	D	D	92	9.9	1 533	20.6	2 189	435	948	53	571
Bingham	323	41 951	0.9	829	18.9	291	6.7	8 604	22.1	6 523	1 313	2 947	840	1 842
Blaine	258	22 508	1.1	D	D	82	3.8	4 049	20.5	2 955	312	1 424	338	1 581
Boise	34	6 420	0.8	D	D	41	5.4	1 319	20.6	1 367	534	322	31	474
Bonner	353	39 866	1.0	432	10.5	341	8.3	7 060	20.6	8 547	2 173	3 062	837	2 048
Bonneville	1 172	105 386	1.1	2 005	20.7	698	7.2	15 092	17.0	14 009	2 445	6 390	2 659	2 551
Boundary	73	10 678	1.0	D	D	99	9.1	2 133	23.6	2 341	606	829	96	875
Butte	18	4 900	2.7	D	D	27	9.6	514	23.1	560	53	279	9	311
Camas	0	996	0.6	D	D	D	D	208	21.8	160	20	69	10	895
Canyon	3 335	166 336	0.8	3 569	20.0	1 216	6.8	38 758	24.0	26 053	12 031	6 969	4 626	2 449

1. Per 1,000 estimated resident population. 2. Data for serious crimes have not been adjusted for underreporting; this may affect comparability between geographic areas and over time. 3. Per 100,000 population estimated by the FBI.

STATE County	Serious crimes known to police,[1] 2010 (cont.) Rate[2] Violent	Property	Education — School enrollment and attainment, 2006–2010 Enrollment[3] Total	Per cent private	Attainment[4] (percent) High school graduate or less	Bachelor's degree or more	Local government expenditures,[5] 2008–2009 Total current expenditures (mil dol)	Current expenditures per student (dollars)	Money income, 2006–2010 Per capita income[6] (dollars)	Households Median income Dollars	Percent change, 2000 to 2006–2010 (constant 2010 dollars)	Percent with income of $200,000 or more	Income and poverty, 2010 — Percent below poverty level Median household income (dollars)	All persons	Children under 18 years	Children 5 to 17 years in families
	46	47	48	49	50	51	52	53	54	55	56	57	58	59	60	61
GEORGIA—Cont'd																
Putnam	335	2 569	4 840	18.5	55.2	18.8	32.0	11 573	25 576	41 529	-11.3	3.5	40 037	17.8	33.0	32.1
Quitman	875	1 950	492	2.2	71.4	7.4	3.8	13 587	13 642	28 912	-11.8	0.3	28 102	28.9	44.4	40.5
Rabun	77	1 082	3 235	12.8	50.0	24.7	25.1	11 205	22 471	34 406	-19.8	2.0	37 990	18.1	30.9	27.5
Randolph	NA	NA	2 066	30.1	63.7	13.1	15.5	11 075	17 632	26 194	-6.0	2.4	26 863	27.6	39.4	37.8
Richmond	565	7 315	54 607	14.0	48.9	20.3	308.8	9 438	20 604	37 882	-9.6	1.6	37 866	25.9	39.1	36.0
Rockdale	468	3 803	23 693	18.8	45.0	23.6	155.9	9 926	24 367	55 779	-17.8	2.4	53 899	14.9	24.6	22.0
Schley	80	659	1 384	3.3	64.7	8.7	14.3	10 280	16 122	35 096	-13.5	0.0	37 761	17.6	24.8	21.4
Screven	121	1 199	3 868	7.4	68.3	11.4	25.3	9 355	16 189	32 155	-13.4	0.8	30 925	23.7	33.5	32.9
Seminole	206	1 569	2 121	10.0	60.7	10.3	16.0	9 634	19 263	32 666	-4.8	3.7	30 604	27.5	40.7	36.7
Spalding	437	5 065	15 887	12.9	62.0	13.6	104.7	9 674	19 607	41 100	-10.4	1.6	38 451	22.5	35.1	32.4
Stephens	210	3 721	6 515	22.5	63.7	13.3	NA	NA	18 285	34 938	-6.4	2.9	34 445	22.2	34.2	31.2
Stewart	165	363	1 338	11.4	67.7	11.0	7.5	12 261	15 612	30 954	-1.4	0.3	26 659	38.1	46.1	43.4
Sumter	932	4 702	9 609	13.5	58.1	18.9	50.2	9 625	17 436	32 430	-17.1	1.0	31 871	30.6	43.0	42.3
Talbot	186	1 208	1 622	26.3	68.5	10.9	9.4	14 328	18 007	33 873	0.5	0.1	29 933	21.7	35.8	32.6
Taliaferro	NA	NA	452	8.0	79.1	6.8	3.2	13 688	13 955	22 188	-26.2	0.7	26 863	30.3	48.9	48.0
Tattnall	176	2 089	5 400	12.0	71.3	11.9	31.1	8 940	16 742	38 522	6.1	1.3	35 039	28.0	35.6	32.9
Taylor	135	977	2 209	3.8	72.1	7.4	16.8	10 567	14 693	25 237	-20.7	2.0	30 748	23.6	34.0	30.6
Telfair	247	1 299	3 070	4.7	76.1	8.1	16.5	9 443	13 420	23 876	-27.8	0.1	28 414	32.9	41.2	37.2
Terrell	558	2 169	2 437	15.5	66.9	9.9	16.4	10 836	15 553	27 909	-18.3	0.7	31 143	29.3	42.2	40.4
Thomas	263	3 377	11 000	11.5	56.2	19.6	79.6	9 323	21 261	35 797	-9.1	2.8	35 539	26.4	35.5	30.9
Tift	808	5 387	11 188	8.1	55.0	16.3	66.5	8 802	18 394	36 847	-10.8	1.0	34 702	22.6	33.1	31.3
Toombs	556	4 738	6 702	8.0	60.2	14.3	49.5	8 919	17 974	31 635	-6.8	1.4	32 002	28.1	40.0	37.7
Towns	134	1 518	2 441	45.7	50.9	20.8	13.5	11 600	21 527	39 540	-2.3	1.5	38 207	15.0	28.6	25.7
Treutlen	407	3 326	1 498	7.2	70.1	9.9	11.2	9 102	16 710	36 467	16.9	0.6	30 809	29.6	42.4	39.9
Troup	319	4 100	18 070	14.4	55.5	19.4	117.7	9 384	19 699	41 770	-7.0	1.7	39 422	21.1	29.9	28.5
Turner	325	2 184	2 356	11.5	65.7	13.2	18.4	10 722	15 973	30 763	-5.4	0.4	26 845	28.0	41.0	38.1
Twiggs	150	2 078	2 143	18.9	78.1	6.7	11.9	11 472	15 904	26 521	-33.7	0.7	35 232	25.1	32.1	29.7
Union	52	595	3 949	28.1	46.0	21.6	34.1	10 211	24 182	41 298	2.3	2.9	37 540	19.1	32.6	28.7
Upson	276	3 270	6 804	10.9	63.9	11.3	43.4	9 047	17 398	34 509	-12.7	0.3	33 461	21.3	31.8	30.5
Walker	422	2 580	15 550	13.6	59.2	12.8	96.5	8 995	19 440	38 723	-5.6	1.2	36 854	17.8	25.9	24.3
Walton	192	2 376	20 449	16.5	55.5	17.3	127.6	8 714	22 521	51 721	-12.1	1.6	51 913	14.5	20.8	18.5
Ware	259	4 836	8 827	5.0	61.3	12.2	66.0	10 989	18 295	35 517	-1.1	1.4	33 176	23.2	34.1	32.5
Warren	NA	NA	1 400	8.8	77.3	4.7	8.3	10 601	15 987	31 043	-10.4	1.0	29 764	27.7	39.4	38.0
Washington	368	2 885	4 528	7.6	67.7	10.7	34.5	10 366	15 033	31 382	-17.1	0.5	33 199	30.6	35.4	33.8
Wayne	608	4 023	7 563	6.5	62.3	10.9	48.4	8 919	18 393	37 340	-10.0	1.1	36 562	22.8	35.4	34.8
Webster	NA	NA	675	15.4	66.9	7.9	5.1	10 448	16 295	25 708	-27.5	0.6	31 216	21.8	30.5	27.2
Wheeler	27	1 550	1 327	7.2	76.4	8.6	9.8	9 560	10 043	35 422	16.3	0.0	29 834	33.2	35.3	35.7
White	236	2 825	5 676	16.1	58.1	19.6	51.0	13 250	23 680	41 756	-8.6	1.5	40 120	16.8	25.2	22.6
Whitfield	285	2 993	26 820	7.6	62.1	15.1	190.8	9 473	19 780	42 345	-15.1	2.2	40 117	20.2	27.4	23.8
Wilcox	87	1 163	1 890	6.0	68.7	8.8	12.0	9 091	12 692	30 784	-11.5	0.6	31 442	30.0	38.2	35.1
Wilkes	444	1 114	2 409	5.0	66.5	15.5	16.3	9 339	16 993	28 022	-19.9	0.9	30 461	24.9	38.7	35.3
Wilkinson	188	1 757	2 275	8.3	68.6	12.1	20.1	12 016	17 929	37 902	-8.5	1.3	35 530	21.1	33.0	30.5
Worth	104	2 564	5 470	12.8	65.4	9.4	32.3	8 677	18 348	38 670	-5.7	0.9	37 436	21.2	30.4	28.7
HAWAII	263	3 314	329 081	23.9	39.2	29.4	2 225.4	12 399	28 882	66 420	5.3	5.3	62 774	11.1	14.7	13.0
Hawaii	278	2 839	43 729	19.2	40.9	26.6	(7)	(7)	26 194	54 996	9.1	3.4	46 444	18.3	24.5	22.1
Honolulu	267	3 322	236 895	26.1	38.1	31.1	(7) 2 225.4	(7) 12 399	29 516	70 093	6.6	5.8	67 519	9.5	12.3	10.8
Kalawao	NA	NA	4	0.0	41.9	24.3	(7)	(7)	43 308	41 806	253.7	0.0	N/A	N/A	N/A	N/A
Kauai	367	3 691	14 655	15.9	42.0	22.7	(7)	(7)	26 513	62 531	9.7	3.8	52 714	12.1	15.7	14.7
Maui	191	4 048	33 798	18.6	42.6	25.7	(7)	(7)	29 180	63 989	2.1	5.4	56 206	11.9	16.6	14.4
IDAHO	221	1 996	418 678	14.4	40.7	24.3	1 941.1	7 057	22 518	46 423	-2.4	2.1	43 259	15.8	19.8	17.2
Ada	206	2 107	107 072	12.7	30.1	35.0	483.3	7 001	27 915	55 835	-4.4	3.6	50 909	13.9	16.1	12.9
Adams	201	1 333	876	15.4	50.8	21.3	4.4	9 110	22 730	36 004	0.0	2.1	34 730	15.8	24.8	22.5
Bannock	222	2 809	24 122	8.7	35.4	27.3	92.1	6 627	21 275	44 848	-3.5	1.7	40 946	16.3	20.3	17.9
Bear Lake	150	1 687	1 432	8.8	47.7	16.7	8.1	7 185	19 284	43 374	6.5	0.0	39 469	15.5	20.3	17.6
Benewah	97	474	2 076	5.0	56.4	12.1	14.5	9 321	18 312	37 500	-6.0	0.5	36 906	16.8	25.3	22.4
Bingham	156	1 686	13 208	8.3	48.7	15.9	66.7	6 700	18 633	44 128	-4.3	1.3	43 571	15.6	19.6	17.8
Blaine	285	1 296	4 724	21.1	27.0	43.2	46.8	14 213	32 656	61 854	-3.3	4.7	59 191	10.1	14.6	12.7
Boise	31	443	1 602	17.9	42.3	23.9	9.2	9 255	24 288	48 789	-0.3	0.4	46 871	14.4	20.9	17.4
Bonner	130	1 918	8 216	19.8	42.0	22.5	40.9	7 616	24 745	41 943	1.0	2.9	40 119	17.4	25.3	21.3
Bonneville	261	2 290	27 780	13.7	37.3	26.2	128.0	6 174	23 218	50 445	-4.7	2.3	49 979	13.8	17.3	15.2
Boundary	100	775	2 150	12.7	58.4	12.9	12.3	7 760	18 011	37 712	-4.7	0.6	37 037	17.1	24.9	21.7
Butte	242	69	585	7.9	48.2	17.5	4.1	8 772	20 414	39 413	2.1	0.0	41 368	15.4	21.5	18.7
Camas	0	895	348	7.5	48.3	22.6	1.8	11 284	19 659	44 145	2.0	0.0	46 483	11.3	17.0	13.7
Canyon	265	2 184	51 117	16.3	50.1	16.7	231.1	6 523	18 366	43 218	-4.9	1.4	42 419	19.7	25.1	22.7

1. Data for serious crimes have not been adjusted for underreporting; this may affect comparability between geographic areas and over time. 2. Per 100,000 population estimated by the FBI. 3. All persons 3 years old and over enrolled in nursery school through college. 4. Persons 25 years old and over. 5. Elementary and secondary education expenditures. 6. Based on population estimated by the American Community Survey, 2006–2010. 7. Hawaii, Kalawao, Kauai, and Maui counties are included with Honolulu county.

Table B. States and Counties — **Personal Income**

STATE County	Total (mil dol)	Percent change, 2008–2009	Dollars	Rank	Wages and salaries[2] (mil dol)	Proprietors' income (mil dol)	Dividends, interest, and rent (mil dol)	Total	Total	Social Security	Medical payments	Income maintenance	Unemployment insurance
	62	63	64	65	66	67	68	69	70	71	72	73	74
GEORGIA—Cont'd													
Putnam	691	-3.0	33 712	1 217	275	47	160	160	157	64	56	19	8
Quitman	65	0.6	24 365	2 929	16	3	9	22	22	8	7	4	1
Rabun	492	-2.2	29 635	2 066	190	31	142	131	128	54	52	9	5
Randolph	179	-6.7	24 925	2 870	77	20	28	63	61	18	26	12	2
Richmond	5 974	1.0	29 907	2 002	6 444	219	935	1 601	1 566	412	615	256	96
Rockdale	2 696	-1.4	31 875	1 557	1 534	109	384	474	459	163	160	62	31
Schley	107	-2.2	24 744	2 890	63	8	14	28	27	9	10	4	2
Screven	384	-1.4	25 483	2 806	139	28	58	120	117	36	48	19	7
Seminole	263	-2.9	28 945	2 213	96	32	37	80	79	27	32	13	3
Spalding	1 805	-1.1	27 890	2 421	930	120	276	490	478	155	183	75	29
Stephens	772	0.4	30 053	1 968	417	45	123	224	220	77	95	24	10
Stewart	135	-0.8	29 577	2 075	56	5	16	45	44	11	21	8	2
Sumter	885	-1.8	27 580	2 470	468	63	168	258	252	71	93	50	13
Talbot	163	-0.2	25 701	2 774	37	7	25	52	51	16	17	9	2
Taliaferro	47	0.0	26 037	2 720	8	3	7	17	17	5	7	3	1
Tattnall	595	0.4	24 299	2 935	221	88	70	152	148	43	66	21	6
Taylor	218	-1.1	25 442	2 812	86	19	28	74	73	21	32	13	3
Telfair	270	0.8	21 071	3 080	133	13	41	110	108	28	54	15	5
Terrell	278	-2.5	26 925	2 580	98	29	53	83	82	23	33	18	3
Thomas	1 491	-1.7	32 288	1 460	949	91	295	378	370	118	161	49	14
Tift	1 167	-0.9	27 159	2 542	791	100	194	294	286	87	115	44	15
Toombs	818	1.3	29 246	2 139	464	69	110	226	221	63	97	35	10
Towns	371	-1.2	33 677	1 222	127	23	108	106	104	49	40	5	3
Treutlen	160	2.1	22 727	3 045	46	12	20	53	52	16	21	9	2
Troup	1 959	0.4	30 296	1 907	1 489	84	343	465	453	152	169	71	28
Turner	237	-3.3	25 602	2 795	82	22	34	81	79	21	35	14	5
Twiggs	270	1.3	26 678	2 612	48	3	25	80	78	27	29	13	4
Union	643	-0.4	30 256	1 925	252	36	156	190	186	85	70	10	7
Upson	720	1.2	26 130	2 700	313	35	115	213	208	78	75	29	11
Walker	1 801	-0.7	27 711	2 451	548	74	241	538	526	178	239	50	25
Walton	2 702	1.4	30 947	1 770	878	55	349	508	492	169	209	52	30
Ware	954	-0.6	26 551	2 632	666	64	148	338	331	85	141	40	12
Warren	150	1.7	26 107	2 708	48	4	20	55	53	16	22	9	3
Washington	600	-3.2	28 745	2 250	310	35	128	167	163	49	69	25	8
Wayne	808	-0.9	27 475	2 487	414	48	92	226	220	70	92	29	10
Webster	66	-7.2	29 943	1 995	20	2	13	17	16	5	5	3	1
Wheeler	131	0.6	18 727	3 104	57	6	14	41	40	12	17	6	2
White	671	-1.8	26 544	2 633	227	41	143	177	173	74	64	14	9
Whitfield	2 754	-4.0	29 390	2 122	2 591	188	480	592	575	200	228	66	40
Wilcox	211	-2.9	23 677	2 982	53	31	27	68	66	17	33	10	3
Wilkes	289	-1.2	28 142	2 374	120	23	60	97	95	33	41	12	4
Wilkinson	264	1.5	26 233	2 683	163	6	30	84	83	30	32	12	4
Worth	656	-0.4	30 938	1 773	150	59	87	140	136	45	48	25	7
HAWAII	54 594	-0.2	42 152	X	37 218	3 409	10 011	8 204	7 974	2 813	3 083	996	551
Hawaii	5 695	-0.7	32 023	1 525	3 060	427	1 286	1 272	1 239	417	434	205	103
Honolulu	41 291	0.3	45 496	185	29 472	2 404	7 191	5 539	5 381	1 954	2 053	667	328
Kalawao	(3)	(3)	(3)	(3)	(3)	(3)	(3)	(3)	(3)	(3)	(3)	(3)	(3)
Kauai	2 295	-0.9	35 560	948	1 383	153	476	440	428	149	179	42	37
Maui	(3)5 314	(3)-2.7	(3)36 585	(3)803	(3)3 302	(3)425	(3)1 058	(3)953	(3)926	(3)292	(3)417	(3)82	(3)83
IDAHO	49 245	-2.5	31 857	X	28 945	4 896	9 565	9 190	8 909	3 237	3 337	778	626
Ada	15 320	-3.4	39 827	460	10 420	1 847	3 105	2 029	1 958	710	690	144	184
Adams	109	-0.3	30 924	1 774	42	5	34	29	29	13	8	2	3
Bannock	2 371	0.1	28 726	2 253	1 406	178	348	526	511	153	188	51	27
Bear Lake	168	1.2	29 085	2 173	66	13	26	41	40	17	16	3	1
Benewah	284	-2.8	30 645	1 834	153	24	48	83	81	29	33	6	6
Bingham	1 129	-3.2	25 281	2 832	631	81	175	249	241	88	95	28	11
Blaine	1 287	-7.8	57 636	41	594	139	562	99	95	41	30	4	13
Boise	251	1.8	33 681	1 221	55	7	46	43	41	19	11	3	3
Bonner	1 264	-1.9	30 536	1 855	578	104	338	280	272	115	91	20	22
Bonneville	3 484	-0.9	34 386	1 114	1 867	360	672	584	565	196	244	54	27
Boundary	269	-0.7	24 577	2 909	153	18	53	76	74	30	25	6	6
Butte	97	-3.1	34 989	1 022	768	18	13	21	21	8	10	1	0
Camas	41	0.4	37 217	720	18	7	7	6	5	2	2	0	1
Canyon	4 258	-0.7	22 815	3 040	2 158	281	650	1 126	1 092	335	434	126	105

1. Based on the resident population estimated as of July 1 of the year shown.   2. Includes supplements to wages and salaries.   3. Kalawao county is included with Maui county.

Table B. States and Counties — Earnings, Social Security, and Housing

STATE County	Earnings, 2009									Social Security beneficiaries, December 2010		Supplemental Security Income recipients, December 2010	Housing units, 2010	
			Percent by selected industries											
			Goods-related[1]		Service-related and health									
	Total (mil dol)	Farm	Total	Manu-facturing	Information and profes-sional and technical services	Retail trade	Finance, insur-ance, and real estate	Health care and social services	Govern-ment	Number	Rate[2]		Total	Percent change, 2000–2010
	75	76	77	78	79	80	81	82	83	84	85	86	87	88

GEORGIA—Cont'd														
Putnam	321	1.6	20.6	10.4	2.9	12.2	6.0	D	25.2	5 110	241	464	12 804	24.1
Quitman	19	10.1	D	D	D	3.2	D	D	32.1	725	288	151	2 047	15.5
Rabun	222	2.1	D	11.5	3.3	13.7	9.4	D	19.0	4 485	276	402	12 313	20.6
Randolph	98	11.4	D	D	D	6.0	4.0	D	31.6	1 685	218	462	4 153	22.1
Richmond	6 663	0.0	D	8.7	6.2	4.6	3.4	13.1	45.0	35 270	176	7 547	86 331	4.9
Rockdale	1 643	0.1	D	12.9	10.8	9.0	4.3	11.9	14.3	13 070	153	1 526	33 272	32.7
Schley	71	6.1	D	41.9	D	2.8	D	D	22.6	810	162	152	2 208	37.0
Screven	168	11.2	25.1	18.6	D	5.9	3.8	D	27.9	3 260	223	768	6 739	-1.7
Seminole	129	19.2	D	D	D	7.7	3.9	17.5	17.3	2 345	269	489	4 797	1.2
Spalding	1 049	-0.1	D	16.5	D	8.0	4.0	14.2	22.1	13 270	207	2 303	26 777	16.4
Stephens	462	0.5	D	21.8	3.4	8.4	5.1	D	21.2	6 625	253	1 008	12 662	8.7
Stewart	61	3.3	D	D	D	4.0	3.9	15.2	33.9	1 045	172	272	2 383	1.2
Sumter	532	6.0	D	11.6	D	6.9	2.9	13.4	26.6	6 195	189	1 391	13 909	1.5
Talbot	44	2.1	D	0.0	3.3	3.9	D	D	30.7	1 540	224	327	3 399	18.4
Taliaferro	12	22.9	D	D	D	1.6	D	D	46.7	470	274	114	1 015	-6.5
Tattnall	309	25.4	D	0.9	D	5.2	3.3	D	31.2	4 050	159	876	9 966	16.2
Taylor	105	11.2	D	3.8	D	5.7	2.5	5.6	24.5	1 910	214	455	4 563	14.7
Telfair	146	4.3	D	D	D	5.5	4.0	D	25.6	2 630	159	620	7 297	43.6
Terrell	126	17.9	14.2	12.5	4.3	5.8	5.2	D	25.1	2 170	233	586	4 080	-8.5
Thomas	1 040	2.4	D	16.9	3.6	7.3	5.5	D	18.3	10 205	228	2 150	20 177	10.4
Tift	891	4.9	12.4	8.5	5.5	8.9	3.6	10.1	29.5	7 780	194	1 548	16 434	6.7
Toombs	533	7.0	15.6	9.4	D	8.6	3.4	23.3	14.4	5 750	211	1 307	12 144	6.8
Towns	150	2.4	D	1.8	2.9	7.4	9.7	D	16.5	3 960	378	229	7 731	23.1
Treutlen	58	12.4	D	D	D	11.2	D	D	30.6	1 540	224	387	2 992	4.4
Troup	1 573	0.0	D	24.7	8.7	10.5	4.8	11.2	13.3	12 530	187	2 012	28 046	17.8
Turner	104	14.3	11.5	9.6	D	7.5	D	D	27.9	2 045	229	448	3 841	-1.9
Twiggs	52	-0.4	D	D	0.6	D	D	D	28.3	2 355	261	491	4 235	-1.3
Union	288	1.0	D	3.9	3.9	12.2	6.4	D	25.0	7 045	330	474	14 052	40.5
Upson	348	1.0	26.8	20.7	D	8.3	5.5	18.5	22.1	6 485	239	1 125	12 161	4.7
Walker	622	2.1	D	31.8	3.3	8.9	4.1	5.5	25.2	14 995	218	1 809	30 100	17.7
Walton	933	1.6	D	11.4	5.1	11.8	3.3	7.5	21.9	13 650	163	1 702	32 435	44.1
Ware	730	1.4	11.8	6.3	D	10.6	4.3	D	22.4	7 595	209	1 704	16 326	3.1
Warren	51	3.3	D	24.9	D	7.5	D	D	24.1	1 415	243	309	2 985	7.9
Washington	345	2.7	16.7	8.5	4.3	6.8	4.8	D	28.6	4 340	205	947	9 047	8.6
Wayne	461	2.6	28.7	20.6	D	7.6	3.1	5.9	33.0	5 910	196	1 068	12 199	12.7
Webster	22	7.5	D	D	0.2	4.5	D	0.0	31.6	520	186	97	1 523	36.7
Wheeler	64	7.1	D	D	D	2.5	D	D	22.6	1 140	154	240	2 625	7.3
White	268	2.1	25.5	10.2	D	12.0	5.1	D	23.7	6 240	230	505	16 062	69.9
Whitfield	2 779	0.1	38.5	36.6	9.4	7.6	2.2	8.8	10.9	16 315	159	2 160	39 899	29.8
Wilcox	84	34.3	2.4	0.5	D	3.8	D	6.3	31.4	1 715	185	383	3 510	5.7
Wilkes	144	7.0	18.7	14.9	D	7.1	6.7	5.6	28.1	2 800	264	458	5 158	2.7
Wilkinson	169	0.2	57.7	10.6	3.3	2.4	D	2.6	14.3	2 425	254	346	4 487	0.9
Worth	209	21.7	12.6	7.5	1.8	8.3	3.8	D	22.4	4 105	189	793	9 251	1.7
HAWAII	40 627	0.6	8.9	1.9	8.1	6.0	5.1	9.6	35.1	227 914	168	24 945	519 508	12.8
Hawaii	3 487	1.8	D	D	D	8.4	D	11.2	26.2	35 060	189	5 000	82 324	31.4
Honolulu	31 876	0.2	8.4	2.0	8.9	5.3	5.1	9.6	38.5	156 280	164	17 024	336 899	6.6
Kalawao	(3)	(3)	(3)	(3)	(3)	(3)	(3)	(3)	(3)	0	0	0	113	-34.3
Kauai	1 536	1.4	D	D	D	8.7	D	D	22.6	12 455	186	974	29 793	17.6
Maui	(3)3 728	(3)2.6	(3)D	(3)2.4	(3)5.0	(3)8.7	(3)3.8	(3)D	(3)19.1	24 120	156	1 947	70 379	24.8
IDAHO	33 842	4.0	17.8	10.4	10.6	8.0	5.3	11.3	19.5	269 293	172	27 294	667 796	26.5
Ada	12 267	0.3	19.1	11.9	11.5	7.2	7.1	13.2	16.3	57 135	146	5 597	159 471	34.6
Adams	47	-5.0	9.5	3.1	D	18.0	3.2	3.1	35.8	1 085	273	47	2 636	33.0
Bannock	1 584	0.6	D	8.4	7.3	7.9	6.0	14.4	25.6	12 485	151	1 701	33 191	14.1
Bear Lake	79	6.6	D	D	D	9.8	2.5	D	35.6	1 390	232	99	3 914	19.8
Benewah	177	4.6	D	16.6	1.9	7.1	1.2	5.0	35.5	2 475	267	252	4 629	9.2
Bingham	712	5.4	D	18.5	D	5.5	3.1	9.2	24.0	7 340	161	822	16 141	12.9
Blaine	733	1.7	20.1	4.3	17.6	8.7	7.8	6.9	11.6	3 135	147	100	15 050	23.5
Boise	61	1.1	D	2.1	D	4.0	D	3.2	45.1	1 575	224	112	5 292	21.7
Bonner	683	0.7	24.1	14.0	7.8	15.5	4.7	7.4	17.9	9 755	239	818	24 669	25.6
Bonneville	2 227	1.9	13.1	4.6	11.5	10.0	4.8	16.3	14.6	15 925	153	1 840	39 731	30.3
Boundary	170	9.2	D	9.5	4.3	9.3	3.0	8.1	31.0	2 690	245	270	5 175	26.4
Butte	786	1.8	D	0.2	D	0.3	0.2	D	2.7	615	213	45	1 354	5.0
Camas	25	33.7	D	D	D	D	D	D	23.1	185	166	0	831	38.3
Canyon	2 439	4.7	22.8	15.1	5.2	9.6	3.6	11.4	17.7	29 255	155	4 070	69 409	44.7

1. Includes mining, construction, and manufacturing. 2. Per 1,000 resident population enumerated in the 2010 census. 3. Kalawao county is included with Maui county.

Table B. States and Counties — Housing, Labor Force, and Employment

STATE County	Housing units, 2006–2010								Civilian labor force, 2010				Civilian employment,[5] 2006–2010		
	Occupied units							Sub-standard units[3] (percent)		Percent change, 2009–2010	Unemployment			Percent	
			Owner-occupied			Renter-occupied									Con-struction, produc-tion, and mainte-nance occu-pations
				Median owner cost as a percent of income										Manage-ment, business, science and arts	
	Total	Percent	Median value[1]	With a mort-gage	Without a mort-gage	Median rent[2]	Median rent as a per-cent of income		Total		Total	Rate[4]	Total		
	89	90	91	92	93	94	95	96	97	98	99	100	101	102	103
GEORGIA—Cont'd															
Putnam	8 467	79.9	157 600	24.6	12.4	732	34.1	1.5	9 710	-6.0	1 117	11.5	8 814	26.5	28.9
Quitman	1 015	70.4	66 700	24.6	15.0	562	29.0	3.2	967	-2.2	130	13.4	897	12.7	40.8
Rabun	7 148	73.0	175 700	29.0	11.5	681	29.7	3.7	6 666	-5.1	812	12.2	6 629	28.8	25.4
Randolph	2 952	65.0	64 300	21.3	13.8	438	36.2	5.0	2 677	-3.8	348	13.0	2 713	21.6	34.2
Richmond	74 199	57.0	99 300	24.5	12.3	686	29.9	2.5	90 965	-0.6	9 362	10.3	78 955	30.0	23.5
Rockdale	28 561	68.9	169 900	24.8	10.1	933	31.0	2.6	39 472	-1.4	4 568	11.6	38 544	33.4	25.2
Schley	1 690	66.4	91 300	22.2	15.4	529	26.3	7.8	1 794	-3.3	259	14.4	2 007	29.5	40.8
Screven	4 709	77.4	76 800	23.6	13.4	482	25.3	1.2	6 919	-5.3	975	14.1	5 107	24.1	36.4
Seminole	3 147	78.5	72 900	24.4	11.7	528	34.5	3.2	3 914	-4.2	417	10.7	3 363	22.9	30.7
Spalding	23 105	64.6	124 400	24.0	13.9	762	34.5	3.5	27 974	-3.1	3 716	13.3	26 490	24.2	33.0
Stephens	9 307	72.0	108 100	24.5	14.0	613	32.6	4.8	13 359	-0.9	1 404	10.5	10 753	25.5	30.1
Stewart	2 248	68.9	49 500	24.2	12.2	432	28.5	3.3	2 237	-4.3	237	10.6	2 177	25.8	32.2
Sumter	11 508	63.0	86 300	23.0	13.3	570	30.0	3.4	13 368	-7.3	1 797	13.4	13 455	29.2	30.3
Talbot	2 682	79.6	85 900	25.5	14.9	484	30.9	2.0	3 023	-3.5	263	8.7	2 555	26.1	38.9
Taliaferro	741	71.0	67 200	22.2	19.8	474	31.6	4.6	773	-9.9	103	13.3	646	16.4	47.5
Tattnall	7 750	68.1	80 700	20.6	10.7	443	25.0	2.7	9 224	-1.2	903	9.8	9 080	26.1	37.5
Taylor	3 430	74.2	61 500	21.1	14.7	462	27.5	2.1	3 445	-3.0	457	13.3	2 826	24.9	40.2
Telfair	5 681	61.6	58 900	22.0	15.6	462	34.5	0.8	4 240	-8.4	734	17.3	5 121	24.3	37.8
Terrell	3 457	60.6	75 100	26.6	12.5	487	27.8	4.3	4 340	-2.2	483	11.1	3 309	23.9	33.7
Thomas	17 399	61.8	137 200	23.5	12.2	643	33.9	1.9	21 199	-1.5	1 983	9.4	16 668	33.9	25.0
Tift	14 442	64.9	109 500	22.9	12.1	585	28.1	2.5	18 308	-2.0	2 196	12.0	17 251	29.1	30.1
Toombs	10 077	62.6	86 000	20.3	10.7	527	30.6	1.8	13 538	-3.0	1 437	10.6	10 962	28.3	30.6
Towns	4 758	86.5	194 600	31.0	12.1	677	26.3	1.1	5 610	-2.8	539	9.6	3 940	22.6	30.1
Treutlen	2 496	65.2	69 000	18.4	10.0	468	25.6	0.4	2 864	-2.9	364	12.7	2 511	31.5	30.4
Troup	23 690	65.0	130 300	23.4	12.0	662	31.5	2.9	31 401	4.2	3 590	11.4	28 284	27.9	30.3
Turner	3 096	64.4	83 100	20.9	14.1	469	28.5	3.6	4 274	-8.8	571	13.4	3 194	27.9	30.3
Twiggs	3 070	81.0	65 500	24.5	15.2	543	28.7	0.6	4 565	-3.1	527	11.5	2 875	28.8	29.9
Union	9 471	78.0	197 000	26.4	12.3	623	28.6	1.1	10 887	-0.6	1 010	9.3	8 495	34.9	20.1
Upson	10 502	69.8	93 700	23.3	11.7	564	31.7	3.1	11 420	-7.5	1 420	12.4	10 893	22.0	35.5
Walker	25 901	74.0	108 100	22.9	11.6	604	30.8	2.6	31 686	-1.5	3 075	9.7	28 243	26.3	33.6
Walton	29 147	76.0	164 900	25.0	11.3	784	32.2	2.3	40 517	-1.9	4 160	10.3	38 661	27.7	28.6
Ware	13 053	66.6	78 000	20.0	11.6	556	28.0	1.9	14 732	-1.1	1 663	11.3	13 716	27.1	30.7
Warren	2 357	70.8	61 100	22.5	14.2	468	33.4	2.0	2 514	-4.0	438	17.4	2 205	11.1	50.0
Washington	7 167	71.8	77 500	23.8	13.2	537	33.8	2.7	7 634	-4.7	1 175	15.4	7 404	23.9	29.5
Wayne	10 362	70.0	86 800	20.0	10.0	523	30.9	3.1	11 814	-2.5	1 461	12.4	11 410	25.5	37.9
Webster	1 107	76.1	62 800	18.0	14.7	310	25.9	1.0	1 131	-7.1	116	10.3	1 061	25.8	39.9
Wheeler	1 664	75.5	65 000	20.2	12.1	456	25.4	1.4	2 828	-3.5	309	10.9	1 746	26.1	42.8
White	12 063	76.0	171 000	25.3	10.9	724	35.7	1.2	12 179	-0.8	1 225	10.1	12 409	31.7	26.2
Whitfield	34 292	68.3	130 000	23.7	10.0	645	28.9	5.8	43 116	-1.9	5 181	12.0	44 651	22.5	41.1
Wilcox	2 619	84.0	56 900	24.9	13.8	475	35.9	2.2	3 020	-8.0	376	12.5	2 672	29.3	32.9
Wilkes	3 999	71.5	84 700	25.8	18.7	482	31.3	2.2	4 345	-4.4	510	11.7	3 646	29.2	37.5
Wilkinson	3 511	81.7	71 200	20.4	11.8	474	23.2	3.3	4 416	-6.2	529	12.0	3 362	26.5	38.0
Worth	7 940	70.9	85 400	21.7	11.8	510	30.8	1.9	9 977	-2.4	1 133	11.4	8 614	25.7	33.5
HAWAII	442 267	59.3	537 400	29.2	10.0	1 260	32.5	9.5	649 158	2.8	44 636	6.9	636 454	33.2	18.8
Hawaii	64 382	66.2	361 400	29.1	10.0	1 009	30.7	9.3	83 271	-1.2	8 125	9.8	85 780	29.4	21.7
Honolulu	304 827	57.6	559 000	28.7	10.0	1 312	33.0	9.2	438 993	-1.3	24 478	5.6	439 691	34.9	18.0
Kalawao	67	0.0	N/A	N/A	N/A	278	N/A	N/A	NA	NA	NA	NA	60	51.7	5.0
Kauai	21 710	65.0	583 200	30.6	12.0	1 187	29.0	9.8	31 845	-1.0	2 781	8.7	32 933	29.1	21.1
Maui	51 281	58.8	614 600	32.1	10.0	1 313	31.9	11.9	74 921	-2.1	6 239	8.3	77 990	29.1	19.2
IDAHO	570 283	71.0	172 700	24.3	10.5	689	28.4	3.0	763 498	1.7	66 983	8.8	698 898	32.8	25.8
Ada	145 584	69.6	214 500	23.8	10.5	780	28.8	1.7	194 943	0.7	17 381	8.9	186 690	41.1	17.2
Adams	1 700	80.4	205 100	24.8	12.5	504	24.5	4.1	1 999	-4.3	344	17.2	1 810	24.6	34.4
Bannock	29 860	71.2	135 500	22.7	10.4	576	29.3	1.7	39 931	0.2	3 376	8.5	38 000	32.0	22.5
Bear Lake	2 538	80.9	135 900	18.7	10.2	557	23.0	1.8	3 231	-2.8	213	6.6	2 478	26.7	36.6
Benewah	3 840	74.2	123 000	23.7	11.9	558	27.2	7.9	4 220	2.7	589	14.0	3 882	25.4	36.6
Bingham	14 319	79.9	125 300	22.3	10.0	541	24.6	3.9	23 005	6.0	1 688	7.3	19 092	28.0	31.6
Blaine	9 125	68.3	473 600	29.6	12.0	902	24.6	3.7	12 618	-3.9	1 211	9.6	11 535	35.5	23.4
Boise	3 024	76.8	186 700	24.9	10.0	663	25.9	4.8	3 395	0.1	338	10.0	3 072	36.8	30.2
Bonner	18 206	74.5	236 300	27.9	10.6	716	27.4	3.9	20 434	-1.3	2 621	12.8	18 251	30.2	31.1
Bonneville	35 358	74.1	153 400	22.6	10.0	674	29.6	2.5	50 526	0.9	3 515	7.0	46 196	34.9	23.2
Boundary	4 186	82.5	174 600	28.6	10.0	575	28.8	3.8	4 756	9.8	741	15.6	4 247	26.6	32.8
Butte	1 149	82.9	108 500	24.1	12.7	452	22.0	3.2	1 498	2.9	98	6.5	1 231	33.7	25.8
Camas	427	72.6	226 100	28.7	10.0	788	27.9	2.6	571	-6.5	72	12.6	613	25.6	43.1
Canyon	62 008	71.4	151 300	26.6	11.3	710	29.2	4.7	84 678	1.4	9 597	11.3	76 684	27.6	30.4

1. Specified owner-occupied units.   2. Specified renter-occupied units. A value of 10.0 represents 10 percent or less.   3. Overcrowded or lacking complete plumbing facilities.   4. Percent of civilian labor force.   5. Persons 16 years old and over.

Table B. States and Counties — Nonfarm Employment and Agriculture

	Private nonfarm establishments, employment and payroll, 2009									Agriculture, 2007			
		Employment						Annual payroll		Farms			
												Percent with:	
STATE County	Number of establishments	Total	Health care and social assistance	Manufacturing	Retail trade	Finance and insurance	Professional, scientific, and technical services	Total (mil dol)	Average per employee (dollars)	Number	Fewer than 50 acres	500 acres or more	Farm operators whose principal occupation is farming (percent)
	104	105	106	107	108	109	110	111	112	113	114	115	116
GEORGIA—Cont'd													
Putnam	437	5 119	485	969	1 109	136	D	146	28 509	215	35.8	8.4	34.4
Quitman	34	223	D	D	24	D	D	6	27 807	25	24.0	28.0	40.0
Rabun	490	4 237	494	509	1 010	211	108	115	27 087	121	66.9	0.8	41.3
Randolph	143	1 284	D	D	196	D	25	34	26 491	177	13.0	21.5	37.9
Richmond	4 364	81 854	22 289	7 712	10 183	2 202	3 623	2 880	35 180	154	50.0	1.9	33.1
Rockdale	2 079	28 387	3 506	3 844	4 464	655	1 019	1 004	35 356	108	79.6	1.9	50.0
Schley	65	1 033	D	652	98	D	D	31	30 020	122	22.1	12.3	32.8
Screven	243	2 681	494	916	399	119	D	63	23 520	419	24.1	21.0	39.6
Seminole	184	1 554	440	D	372	D	32	41	26 569	182	25.3	24.2	48.4
Spalding	1 186	16 997	3 761	3 456	2 728	522	448	477	28 062	347	64.8	2.0	35.7
Stephens	577	8 323	1 502	1 867	1 165	218	183	248	29 849	199	51.8	1.5	43.7
Stewart	72	795	172	D	85	34	D	20	25 736	94	16.0	31.9	33.0
Sumter	691	9 008	1 632	1 465	1 606	247	208	227	25 184	429	24.9	18.4	44.1
Talbot	62	547	D	D	43	D	D	17	31 899	149	29.5	14.1	32.2
Tallaferro	22	D	D	D	D	D	0	D	D	71	23.9	9.9	40.8
Tattnall	307	2 698	D	34	542	176	59	74	27 603	589	38.0	9.8	46.9
Taylor	126	1 097	241	84	175	D	13	32	29 297	262	21.4	19.8	45.0
Telfair	216	3 868	429	D	369	95	47	79	20 456	301	21.6	11.6	36.5
Terrell	179	1 601	180	D	296	D	31	39	24 221	274	20.1	28.5	44.9
Thomas	1 089	15 857	D	2 746	2 393	646	466	518	32 697	485	33.4	19.8	42.1
Tift	1 088	15 955	3 077	2 004	2 402	428	553	474	29 716	404	31.4	15.6	52.5
Toombs	716	9 358	1 860	1 755	1 699	368	245	250	26 702	341	31.1	8.5	40.2
Towns	335	2 859	463	79	431	175	64	71	24 813	116	62.1	0.0	38.8
Treutlen	92	754	153	D	133	D	D	13	17 728	151	39.1	7.9	29.8
Troup	1 439	25 649	3 129	6 029	3 113	1 092	453	921	35 890	241	46.1	5.8	39.8
Turner	165	1 491	170	D	167	115	D	34	22 480	278	32.7	24.5	42.4
Twiggs	71	750	D	0	84	D	D	33	44 496	121	34.7	14.0	42.1
Union	578	4 855	1 006	238	798	D	186	149	30 639	281	61.6	2.1	30.2
Upson	464	6 216	1 557	1 198	1 075	D	156	177	28 482	348	44.5	3.7	29.3
Walker	745	10 203	931	3 753	1 400	367	198	273	26 728	538	43.7	4.8	42.9
Walton	1 531	15 458	1 813	1 573	2 648	540	485	462	29 893	490	52.2	3.7	39.6
Ware	931	12 012	3 049	1 075	2 629	376	297	329	27 404	280	43.6	7.5	39.6
Warren	72	645	D	D	D	D	D	18	28 448	188	31.9	8.0	34.0
Washington	366	5 547	859	496	883	189	211	188	33 827	425	27.1	13.9	30.8
Wayne	571	5 550	D	918	1 276	D	122	175	31 488	313	43.8	7.3	44.7
Webster	25	D	D	D	D	D	0	D	D	114	11.4	16.7	36.8
Wheeler	76	1 025	D	0	68	D	D	29	28 738	143	21.0	17.5	32.9
White	608	4 781	432	505	956	176	D	120	25 111	291	59.5	1.0	48.5
Whitfield	2 334	48 195	4 103	18 311	4 946	831	1 240	1 664	34 528	480	45.6	0.8	34.2
Wilcox	92	684	229	21	120	52	D	13	22 925	349	24.6	18.9	44.1
Wilkes	239	2 681	510	D	369	D	102	73	27 295	356	25.0	10.1	43.8
Wilkinson	159	2 053	176	D	148	48	D	81	39 506	168	29.7	9.5	43.0
Worth	303	2 415	420	313	461	99	56	62	25 790	496	30.0	23.4	46.2
HAWAII	32 372	488 403	64 995	12 854	66 960	19 220	23 245	17 743	36 328	7 521	90.2	2.1	51.3
Hawaii	4 197	51 238	7 915	1 377	9 458	1 161	1 825	1 613	31 478	4 650	89.9	1.9	48.6
Honolulu	21 748	338 594	48 340	10 135	44 004	16 747	18 718	12 917	38 150	967	90.6	1.6	71.5
Kalawao	NA	NA	NA	NA	NA	NA	NA	NA	NA	NA	NA	NA	NA
Kauai	1 919	23 802	2 702	272	4 200	428	632	759	31 882	748	90.2	3.3	52.7
Maui	4 450	59 606	6 032	1 070	9 298	835	1 422	1 971	33 075	1 156	91.3	2.8	44.6
IDAHO	44 300	500 226	78 519	55 345	74 343	21 364	31 391	16 328	32 642	25 349	48.9	16.9	45.7
Ada	12 394	166 239	26 963	16 569	20 268	9 426	9 771	6 413	38 576	1 323	81.9	3.4	31.7
Adams	143	480	D	D	83	D	21	11	23 681	258	40.7	22.5	51.2
Bannock	2 040	26 890	5 895	2 124	4 585	1 528	1 288	708	26 325	937	52.6	14.7	35.6
Bear Lake	130	1 003	D	D	269	41	D	23	22 839	445	27.9	21.8	38.4
Benewah	246	2 190	331	577	307	46	D	70	32 142	292	34.2	15.1	39.4
Bingham	851	9 940	D	D	1 385	260	189	307	30 871	1 328	56.3	18.1	47.6
Blaine	1 416	10 949	585	341	1 399	303	777	378	34 503	193	42.0	32.6	45.1
Boise	153	499	D	D	87	D	D	10	19 752	105	49.5	12.4	40.0
Bonner	1 510	11 877	1 408	1 923	2 116	344	520	353	29 738	687	52.7	4.7	47.6
Bonneville	3 244	42 413	7 125	2 391	7 037	1 219	D	1 583	37 332	926	51.6	18.4	37.4
Boundary	400	2 359	554	322	418	D	D	62	26 337	373	47.2	10.2	47.2
Butte	70	449	D	D	96	24	D	21	46 590	222	24.8	26.6	51.8
Camas	33	189	D	D	D	D	0	3	17 000	104	26.9	34.6	44.2
Canyon	3 636	42 564	5 844	7 933	7 203	1 273	1 130	1 189	27 929	2 368	73.8	4.7	40.5

STATE County	Acreage (1,000)	Percent change, 2002–2007	Average size of farm	Total irrigated (1,000)	Total cropland (1,000)	Average per farm	Average per acre	Value of machinery and equipment, average per farm (dollars)	Total (mil dol)	Average per farm (dollars)	Crops	Live-stock and poultry products	$10,000 or more	$100,000 or more	Total ($1,000)	Percent of farms
	117	118	119	120	121	122	123	124	125	126	127	128	129	130	131	132
GEORGIA—Cont'd																
Putnam	38	-7.3	176	0.5	12.4	728 384	4 149	82 524	40.7	189 287	2.1	97.9	30.7	13.0	137	17.2
Quitman	11	-21.4	455	D	5.5	1 164 034	2 556	55 540	D	D	D	0.0	20.0	8.0	248	44.0
Rabun	8	-20.0	66	0.6	2.4	355 197	5 420	47 368	9.1	75 302	38.4	61.6	28.9	9.1	75	5.0
Randolph	90	13.9	509	15.8	55.5	1 091 378	2 146	105 986	19.9	112 191	88.9	11.1	33.3	14.7	2 525	74.6
Richmond	13	8.3	81	0.0	6.3	331 942	4 083	37 369	1.3	8 343	34.6	65.4	21.4	0.0	22	8.4
Rockdale	6	-33.3	59	0.0	1.7	321 986	5 494	49 400	D	D	0.0	D	17.6	0.0	D	1.9
Schley	36	2.9	297	1.3	9.6	896 270	3 015	51 961	33.2	272 317	4.5	95.5	27.0	10.7	552	41.0
Screven	179	-2.7	426	13.6	92.0	1 004 920	2 356	88 440	29.2	69 697	85.7	14.3	33.2	13.1	2 700	65.9
Seminole	104	11.8	569	45.8	71.0	1 295 067	2 276	219 806	48.1	264 180	88.9	11.1	54.9	32.4	4 311	68.1
Spalding	26	0.0	76	0.2	7.1	411 223	5 398	48 106	5.1	14 558	6.9	93.1	12.7	1.2	98	12.7
Stephens	15	-25.0	77	0.0	4.2	394 935	5 109	47 188	43.4	218 314	0.5	99.5	33.7	15.6	50	10.6
Stewart	46	35.3	490	0.4	11.7	1 203 874	2 457	78 741	5.3	56 337	48.0	52.0	35.1	11.7	676	55.3
Sumter	153	-8.4	357	31.9	84.7	834 664	2 341	98 626	78.3	182 423	57.7	42.3	37.5	17.2	4 040	55.9
Talbot	42	-6.7	280	0.1	6.7	590 495	2 112	54 855	1.0	6 555	32.7	67.3	18.8	0.7	83	10.1
Taliaferro	14	-26.3	199	D	5.3	519 870	2 619	56 221	6.0	84 406	2.8	97.2	23.9	8.5	17	11.3
Tattnall	136	-4.9	230	12.5	73.5	641 217	2 786	91 471	210.9	357 986	33.5	66.5	46.7	24.3	1 642	27.2
Taylor	87	16.0	331	4.4	32.6	709 832	2 146	60 830	24.0	91 459	49.0	51.0	31.7	9.2	1 242	48.1
Telfair	62	-15.1	205	7.3	24.2	463 548	2 260	59 316	7.6	25 325	79.8	20.2	32.2	6.6	789	57.1
Terrell	137	11.4	498	29.1	80.1	1 184 295	2 377	138 498	31.0	113 248	97.2	2.8	36.1	24.8	5 735	70.8
Thomas	204	3.0	421	12.5	94.0	1 147 428	2 725	95 260	59.6	122 977	51.3	48.7	45.8	20.8	5 539	48.7
Tift	133	35.7	329	28.8	77.3	848 743	2 582	105 870	68.1	168 561	94.4	5.6	51.2	25.7	5 800	57.7
Toombs	90	-3.2	264	10.7	30.6	564 309	2 141	69 962	46.8	137 239	79.8	20.2	29.9	13.2	1 278	43.1
Towns	7	-36.4	65	D	2.3	408 219	6 319	55 925	5.1	44 192	17.5	82.5	32.8	5.2	80	11.2
Treutlen	30	-14.3	199	5.0	10.5	442 565	2 220	73 182	D	D	D	0.0	13.2	3.3	561	58.3
Troup	38	-37.7	157	D	7.6	600 868	3 824	49 654	3.5	14 669	20.6	79.4	23.2	2.5	106	6.2
Turner	116	18.4	417	22.2	65.8	1 033 969	2 479	132 939	46.0	165 347	74.5	25.5	51.1	27.7	5 335	65.1
Twiggs	45	12.5	371	2.1	13.5	950 523	2 559	86 902	3.3	27 297	79.5	20.5	18.2	5.8	561	28.9
Union	21	-16.0	75	0.0	6.1	443 060	5 941	60 385	18.7	66 385	D	D	25.6	4.6	76	11.0
Upson	48	2.1	137	0.6	12.8	434 761	3 173	43 069	28.1	80 877	4.7	95.3	17.8	5.5	137	10.1
Walker	71	-13.4	132	0.3	22.9	568 791	4 301	67 106	90.3	167 856	1.5	98.5	30.5	9.9	209	15.4
Walton	54	-18.2	110	0.8	19.3	639 545	5 836	42 917	37.3	76 040	28.8	71.2	25.3	8.2	241	25.9
Ware	50	-23.1	180	2.5	18.9	548 590	3 055	47 402	21.4	76 561	44.1	55.9	31.4	7.1	496	26.8
Warren	37	-22.9	198	D	10.7	494 741	2 501	47 957	4.9	26 255	12.3	87.7	20.7	4.3	253	25.0
Washington	110	-11.3	259	2.3	39.8	574 658	2 217	48 376	11.7	27 528	63.8	36.2	27.8	5.6	1 639	48.5
Wayne	57	-10.9	181	4.6	24.1	525 441	2 896	80 308	28.7	91 710	55.6	44.4	29.4	9.3	896	36.4
Webster	55	-16.7	480	3.3	26.4	1 086 376	2 266	75 613	8.9	78 166	56.9	43.1	28.1	10.5	1 156	77.2
Wheeler	57	-5.0	400	4.1	17.5	855 491	2 140	52 972	5.9	41 120	90.2	9.8	34.3	9.8	604	62.9
White	21	-30.0	72	0.1	7.0	519 479	7 200	57 419	70.2	241 148	1.1	98.9	41.2	26.8	29	7.9
Whitfield	43	0.0	89	0.1	13.8	416 808	4 680	56 827	108.4	225 793	0.6	99.4	30.6	12.3	133	6.0
Wilcox	101	-1.0	289	21.4	58.1	645 775	2 235	107 317	68.0	194 772	50.3	49.7	42.4	24.1	4 088	69.9
Wilkes	90	-9.1	252	0.4	19.3	662 337	2 626	56 773	32.5	91 363	5.1	94.9	30.3	6.7	336	26.7
Wilkinson	30	-3.2	189	0.0	9.5	422 091	2 230	56 663	3.4	21 533	21.4	78.6	17.1	1.3	142	20.3
Worth	193	7.8	388	30.2	111.1	940 534	2 423	131 943	72.0	145 192	74.1	25.9	42.3	22.2	10 212	65.1
HAWAII	1 121	-13.8	149	58.6	177.6	1 146 213	7 688	40 666	513.6	68 292	83.7	16.3	34.3	7.0	2 378	2.9
Hawaii	684	-16.7	147	8.1	81.8	1 022 976	6 956	31 981	202.6	43 564	74.2	25.8	32.5	5.6	1 232	2.9
Honolulu	60	-15.5	62	8.4	18.9	1 106 333	17 710	61 269	126.6	130 897	84.4	15.6	48.2	15.1	294	1.8
Kalawao	NA	NA	NA	NA	NA	NA	NA	NA	NA	NA	NA	NA	NA	NA	NA	NA
Kauai	152	0.0	203	14.1	22.3	1 259 559	6 217	49 828	45.2	60 362	90.3	9.7	31.1	4.9	164	2.9
Maui	226	-12.1	195	28.0	54.6	1 601 950	8 210	52 480	139.3	120 524	94.8	5.2	32.2	7.4	688	3.8
IDAHO	11 497	-2.3	454	3 299.9	5 918.9	894 497	1 972	114 383	5 688.8	224 418	40.9	59.1	39.9	17.0	99 494	36.3
Ada	191	-14.3	145	57.0	66.1	607 769	4 199	62 480	153.0	115 670	29.4	70.6	23.3	6.6	667	11.3
Adams	149	-24.0	578	24.9	27.8	777 096	1 346	48 639	9.1	35 379	10.8	89.2	31.0	9.3	268	15.9
Bannock	322	-9.8	344	39.3	185.0	516 233	1 503	58 955	34.3	36 555	60.0	40.0	22.5	6.2	3 878	31.6
Bear Lake	233	9.9	524	38.7	101.5	682 885	1 304	70 615	17.3	38 886	16.0	84.0	40.9	9.7	1 604	49.4
Benewah	154	11.6	526	0.3	83.4	854 158	1 624	71 787	20.4	70 023	95.9	4.0	20.5	8.9	1 415	41.4
Bingham	913	11.2	687	316.9	362.1	1 194 297	1 738	160 921	355.1	267 420	73.5	26.5	43.4	20.6	7 108	29.4
Blaine	192	-15.0	995	44.0	54.2	1 602 365	1 611	154 365	26.4	136 979	52.4	47.6	46.6	24.4	478	37.3
Boise	44	-12.0	416	2.0	4.1	623 161	1 498	34 895	3.5	33 183	75.3	24.7	21.0	5.7	63	6.7
Bonner	94	3.3	137	2.1	28.8	583 313	4 246	48 929	10.7	15 559	62.4	37.6	19.7	2.5	70	3.8
Bonneville	453	-5.2	489	156.0	298.6	991 113	2 026	109 781	189.3	204 402	58.6	41.4	36.9	13.2	5 520	47.0
Boundary	74	-3.9	197	2.8	43.2	751 326	3 813	74 008	30.2	81 033	91.5	8.5	38.3	12.6	942	17.7
Butte	121	0.0	546	54.5	61.9	817 106	1 497	102 308	25.0	112 507	64.6	35.4	57.7	22.1	1 460	57.2
Camas	138	3.0	1 331	16.5	81.4	1 630 469	1 225	145 206	10.1	97 488	82.3	17.7	42.3	15.4	413	58.7
Canyon	260	-4.4	110	197.3	191.7	672 852	6 122	82 719	420.9	177 757	41.4	58.6	35.3	12.1	1 668	19.6

Table B. States and Counties — Water Use, Wholesale Trade, Retail Trade, and Real Estate

STATE County	Water use, 2005		Wholesale trade,[1] 2007				Retail trade,[2] 2007				Real estate and rental and leasing,[2] 2007			
	Total water withdrawn (mil gal/day)	Gallons withdrawn per person	Number of establishments	Number of employees	Sales (mil dol)	Annual payroll (mil dol)	Number of establishments	Number of employees	Sales (mil dol)	Annual payroll (mil dol)	Number of establishments	Number of employees	Receipts (mil dol)	Annual payroll (mil dol)
	133	134	135	136	137	138	139	140	141	142	143	144	145	146
GEORGIA—Cont'd														
Putnam	1 097.2	55 331	16	96	75.5	3.6	95	899	204.1	21.4	34	203	16.3	3.0
Quitman	0.2	85	3	D	D	D	5	26	2.8	0.3	1	D	D	D
Rabun	4.7	292	5	D	D	D	92	949	234.4	23.4	27	54	10.4	1.3
Randolph	10.4	1 425	9	53	41.7	1.5	31	211	44.3	3.6	4	12	0.8	0.2
Richmond	115.7	591	196	2 249	916.4	94.3	895	11 084	2 505.1	233.6	233	1 449	220.1	38.5
Rockdale	14.5	184	101	726	515.6	33.7	329	5 488	1 450.1	138.0	98	389	85.3	14.0
Schley	1.0	252	3	D	D	D	13	110	18.6	1.9	NA	NA	NA	NA
Screven	14.3	929	7	31	17.5	0.6	51	427	93.6	7.7	12	36	1.9	0.5
Seminole	39.4	4 275	11	58	48.8	2.1	53	382	76.5	6.6	5	14	0.8	0.2
Spalding	14.4	234	54	565	604.3	20.9	252	2 948	661.6	63.1	62	243	28.1	5.8
Stephens	4.6	182	30	D	D	D	101	1 164	274.7	24.5	12	30	3.2	0.8
Stewart	1.1	225	3	16	2.6	0.4	22	89	23.9	1.6	1	D	D	D
Sumter	14.0	424	31	462	239.0	12.6	150	1 575	326.1	29.3	24	86	11.3	1.7
Talbot	2.5	367	3	D	D	D	7	23	4.7	0.3	NA	NA	NA	NA
Taliaferro	0.2	104	NA	NA	NA	NA	4	14	1.7	0.2	2	D	D	D
Tattnall	8.2	355	21	446	152.0	11.9	70	518	102.4	9.9	11	31	2.3	0.4
Taylor	5.3	592	5	93	21.4	3.0	28	190	46.4	3.6	4	10	0.7	0.1
Telfair	4.8	360	12	66	30.5	1.7	51	396	77.3	6.5	3	D	D	D
Terrell	16.2	1 512	10	D	D	D	52	343	68.3	5.7	5	D	D	D
Thomas	20.1	451	63	752	575.3	35.4	239	2 567	627.5	55.4	44	167	23.7	4.0
Tift	25.9	634	70	1 205	612.2	41.2	242	2 515	721.6	52.1	61	217	32.4	5.0
Toombs	11.1	406	35	611	665.0	20.7	158	1 702	386.3	33.9	25	86	12.0	1.7
Towns	6.6	638	11	28	6.2	0.7	72	446	102.3	8.6	28	71	16.6	1.8
Treutlen	1.5	228	5	D	D	D	25	199	30.4	3.0	1	D	D	D
Troup	12.6	204	57	D	D	D	295	3 357	798.8	71.3	66	445	41.7	9.0
Turner	15.9	1 675	15	148	103.2	4.8	34	193	64.5	3.4	4	D	D	D
Twiggs	22.2	2 156	2	D	D	D	18	99	30.3	2.1	1	D	D	D
Union	8.1	408	12	99	38.1	3.3	117	981	246.7	20.1	60	153	17.5	3.3
Upson	5.0	182	3	D	D	D	97	1 152	208.7	21.5	18	87	5.5	0.9
Walker	9.9	155	33	D	D	D	170	1 472	344.2	28.5	20	D	D	D
Walton	10.8	142	63	598	260.4	25.3	207	2 660	797.2	64.4	91	193	27.1	4.6
Ware	6.0	173	45	450	762.7	13.5	244	2 811	621.1	55.7	34	139	12.4	2.3
Warren	4.6	754	4	D	D	D	22	154	23.2	3.1	2	D	D	D
Washington	35.7	1 776	17	122	70.0	4.2	94	920	213.7	18.7	17	84	9.9	1.8
Wayne	65.2	2 297	14	D	D	D	134	1 367	310.3	29.3	20	102	7.6	1.5
Webster	2.9	1 284	4	22	3.5	0.3	4	29	4.7	0.5	NA	NA	NA	NA
Wheeler	4.9	723	3	47	8.2	0.8	19	92	18.1	1.2	1	D	D	D
White	3.7	152	18	154	40.4	4.5	137	960	280.7	23.8	28	48	8.1	1.5
Whitfield	36.9	406	235	3 548	1 351.9	136.0	504	5 707	1 440.2	128.8	89	372	56.7	11.0
Wilcox	12.6	1 442	3	D	D	D	24	125	27.4	2.1	NA	NA	NA	NA
Wilkes	1.9	186	6	38	19.0	1.1	60	401	73.4	7.0	7	22	2.5	0.5
Wilkinson	18.5	1 827	7	28	13.3	1.2	26	153	24.3	2.6	NA	NA	NA	NA
Worth	13.8	627	27	188	116.4	5.8	70	497	132.2	11.0	13	34	2.1	0.4
HAWAII	1 893.4	1 485	1 629	17 707	8 894.7	699.1	5 012	70 661	17 611.9	1 766.4	2 084	16 759	3 974.0	653.8
Hawaii	124.8	746	185	1 847	732.2	62.1	722	9 730	2 566.0	250.0	303	2 729	474.1	106.3
Honolulu	1 593.3	1 760	1 244	14 049	7 377.1	565.1	3 058	46 613	11 518.3	1 144.1	1 294	9 867	2 660.2	399.9
Kalawao	NA	180	NA	NA	NA	NA	NA	NA	NA	NA	NA	NA	NA	NA
Kauai	49.4	788	61	525	209.4	16.4	379	4 457	1 052.7	110.3	168	1 387	245.6	50.7
Maui	126.0	900	139	1 286	575.9	55.5	853	9 861	2 474.8	262.0	319	2 776	594.1	96.8
IDAHO	19 510.2	13 652	1 846	21 844	14 286.7	900.0	6 300	80 447	20 526.6	1 833.6	2 530	8 371	1 241.7	233.5
Ada	1 117.3	3 241	561	7 490	6 006.9	371.8	1 483	23 080	5 855.1	545.1	916	3 614	551.8	121.0
Adams	115.9	32 264	1	D	D	D	17	120	20.0	1.8	12	17	1.7	0.2
Bannock	398.0	5 092	78	636	386.6	24.1	350	4 972	1 099.2	97.7	96	323	52.2	6.9
Bear Lake	107.4	17 383	4	63	23.4	1.7	32	288	58.7	4.0	7	16	1.2	0.3
Benewah	4.4	477	5	37	6.1	1.0	39	366	93.9	7.5	5	9	0.6	0.2
Bingham	1 195.7	27 337	50	D	D	D	124	1 357	339.9	27.6	24	75	8.4	1.7
Blaine	349.5	16 510	35	678	285.9	29.8	201	1 579	356.0	44.6	111	363	59.4	10.5
Boise	11.7	1 553	NA	NA	NA	NA	21	100	18.7	1.5	8	13	2.0	0.2
Bonner	72.8	1 780	37	275	149.7	10.8	206	2 126	485.3	48.0	95	257	34.8	7.1
Bonneville	882.0	9 601	158	2 081	1 881.6	89.0	512	7 375	1 871.5	159.4	142	501	86.8	11.5
Boundary	7.0	662	10	39	19.7	1.7	45	369	86.3	8.3	9	9	0.9	0.2
Butte	237.4	84 558	4	31	5.2	0.5	15	98	18.1	1.5	7	26	0.8	0.2
Camas	59.2	56 333	NA	NA	NA	NA	2	D	D	D	NA	NA	NA	NA
Canyon	658.3	3 999	182	1 766	992.9	79.2	510	7 916	2 176.0	196.0	212	643	67.7	12.5

1. Merchant wholesalers, except manufacturers' sales branches and offices.   2. Employer establishments.

Table B. States and Counties — Professional Services, Manufacturing, and Accommodation and Food Services

STATE County	Professional, scientific, and technical services,[1] 2007				Manufacturing, 2007				Accommodation and food services, 2007			
	Number of establishments	Number of employees	Receipts (mil dol)	Annual payroll (mil dol)	Number of establishments	Number of employees	Receipts (mil dol)	Annual payroll (mil dol)	Number of establishments	Number of employees	Sales (mil dol)	Annual payroll (mil dol)
	147	148	149	150	151	152	153	154	155	156	157	158
GEORGIA—Cont'd												
Putnam	37	81	9.5	2.2	27	1 352	316.1	42.7	39	545	19.8	5.2
Quitman	1	D	D	D	NA	NA	NA	NA	3	D	D	D
Rabun	31	119	10.3	4.0	25	591	138.7	19.4	66	676	41.1	10.4
Randolph	9	42	2.4	1.5	NA	NA	NA	NA	14	81	3.9	0.9
Richmond	437	3 181	397.2	144.3	129	9 055	5 256.3	452.0	431	9 726	395.4	108.6
Rockdale	229	1 139	131.5	50.5	87	4 437	1 778.8	192.6	193	4 190	196.6	49.7
Schley	2	D	D	D	12	919	215.9	32.0	6	29	0.9	0.2
Screven	13	39	2.4	0.8	17	1 063	183.8	32.9	20	206	8.3	1.9
Seminole	11	40	3.7	0.9	NA	NA	NA	NA	19	140	5.4	1.3
Spalding	81	481	51.1	19.6	57	4 266	2 285.2	170.1	111	2 023	77.4	20.8
Stephens	42	160	17.9	6.2	52	1 981	535.7	69.0	50	771	26.2	6.8
Stewart	2	D	D	D	NA	NA	NA	NA	7	69	2.7	0.6
Sumter	34	D	D	D	35	1 940	412.0	64.7	56	1 069	33.7	9.8
Talbot	3	5	0.3	0.2	NA	NA	NA	NA	NA	NA	NA	NA
Taliaferro	NA	NA	NA	NA	NA	NA	NA	NA	1	D	D	D
Tattnall	17	78	7.3	2.0	NA	NA	NA	NA	21	269	9.5	2.2
Taylor	9	11	0.8	0.1	NA	NA	NA	NA	8	57	1.6	0.5
Telfair	11	48	3.2	1.2	13	D	D	D	19	216	11.1	2.6
Terrell	8	36	3.3	1.1	14	535	D	17.8	10	D	D	D
Thomas	78	426	44.9	16.2	51	3 166	657.6	112.5	82	1 313	49.9	13.5
Tift	79	559	47.4	20.4	54	2 370	547.5	75.6	102	2 195	92.0	26.1
Toombs	46	225	20.1	6.6	36	D	D	D	65	1 042	42.3	11.2
Towns	21	88	6.7	2.7	NA	NA	NA	NA	42	539	31.0	9.2
Treutlen	3	D	D	D	NA	NA	NA	NA	4	50	1.8	0.5
Troup	88	429	42.3	18.6	92	6 857	2 470.8	288.4	131	2 359	88.7	23.8
Turner	13	33	2.9	0.8	NA	NA	NA	NA	17	172	6.5	1.7
Twiggs	4	D	D	D	NA	NA	NA	NA	7	29	1.3	0.4
Union	49	197	13.8	5.6	NA	NA	NA	NA	43	452	21.6	5.7
Upson	36	D	D	D	24	D	526.5	56.5	50	569	22.9	5.3
Walker	53	197	21.3	9.4	65	5 417	2 060.6	181.2	56	745	25.4	6.4
Walton	151	574	53.1	20.3	55	1 698	591.8	69.5	90	1 397	58.4	15.0
Ware	61	D	D	D	33	1 552	D	43.2	75	1 645	55.5	14.7
Warren	3	D	D	D	NA	NA	NA	NA	7	17	0.7	0.2
Washington	22	193	12.6	8.9	NA	NA	NA	NA	32	516	16.5	4.4
Wayne	28	106	6.9	5.5	28	1 505	663.4	74.0	57	875	32.9	8.7
Webster	1	D	D	D	NA	NA	NA	NA	1	D	D	D
Wheeler	3	8	0.3	0.1	NA	NA	NA	NA	3	D	D	D
White	50	122	10.1	3.1	34	584	103.9	20.3	88	831	51.1	11.6
Whitfield	167	D	D	D	317	22 283	7 524.9	710.4	189	3 428	144.8	38.8
Wilcox	2	D	D	D	NA	NA	NA	NA	3	17	0.6	0.1
Wilkes	16	87	7.3	3.6	17	622	174.3	18.3	18	176	7.1	1.7
Wilkinson	7	69	5.6	1.9	15	973	521.5	52.4	7	39	1.4	0.4
Worth	10	D	D	D	NA	NA	NA	NA	17	178	6.5	1.7
HAWAII	3 254	21 772	3 068.3	1 193.5	984	14 127	8 799.3	511.5	3 528	98 353	8 042.2	2 209.8
Hawaii	321	D	D	D	138	1 516	290.1	53.6	421	12 280	874.7	284.5
Honolulu	2 433	18 508	2 686.9	1 056.8	684	10 996	8 201.9	398.9	2 347	57 064	4 123.8	1 126.5
Kalawao	NA	NA	NA	NA	NA	NA	NA	NA	NA	NA	NA	NA
Kauai	132	D	D	D	NA	NA	NA	NA	234	7 082	591.5	168.8
Maui	368	D	D	D	114	1 319	262.7	50.7	526	21 927	2 452.2	630.1
IDAHO	4 189	D	D	D	1 942	64 778	18 011.0	2 829.4	3 482	56 662	2 416.0	662.7
Ada	1 602	D	D	D	419	21 075	4 942.4	1 248.3	900	17 928	796.0	219.9
Adams	8	D	D	D	NA	NA	NA	NA	16	D	D	D
Bannock	164	D	D	D	58	D	D	D	180	3 056	117.8	31.9
Bear Lake	3	D	D	D	NA	NA	NA	NA	15	D	D	D
Benewah	12	D	D	D	10	576	D	25.0	21	D	D	D
Bingham	49	209	23.0	7.9	45	2 334	624.5	79.9	55	1 046	24.3	6.2
Blaine	163	727	114.2	47.3	NA	NA	NA	NA	114	3 186	153.3	52.2
Boise	12	D	D	D	NA	NA	NA	NA	23	165	5.7	1.7
Bonner	145	576	43.8	26.7	87	2 091	498.6	79.6	124	2 018	63.3	20.8
Bonneville	382	D	D	D	144	2 580	D	92.8	200	3 824	153.5	41.3
Boundary	27	108	6.0	2.6	NA	NA	NA	NA	23	D	D	D
Butte	2	D	D	D	NA	NA	NA	NA	8	D	D	D
Camas	NA	NA	NA	NA	NA	NA	NA	NA	6	89	1.5	0.4
Canyon	252	D	D	D	233	9 848	D	335.1	242	3 905	140.9	38.1

1. Establishment subject to federal tax.

Table B. States and Counties — Health Care and Social Assistance, Other Services, and Federal Funds

STATE County	Health care and social assistance, 2007				Other services, 2007				Federal funds and grants, 2009–2010 Expenditures (mil dol)			
										Direct payments for individuals[1]		
	Number of establishments	Number of employees	Receipts (mil dol)	Annual payroll (mil dol)	Number of establishments	Number of employees	Receipts (mil dol)	Annual payroll (mil dol)	Total	Social Security and government retirement	Medicare	Food Stamps and Supplemental Security Income
	159	160	161	162	163	164	165	166	167	168	169	170
GEORGIA—Cont'd												
Putnam	25	380	27.0	11.2	31	73	5.4	1.2	145.4	77.6	28.1	8.0
Quitman	2	D	D	D	1	D	D	D	23.0	4.3	6.0	2.2
Rabun	32	455	36.0	13.7	34	96	10.0	2.3	138.1	65.0	33.2	4.4
Randolph	8	246	16.2	6.3	8	22	2.2	0.4	88.7	22.8	15.4	8.8
Richmond	617	20 772	2 482.3	911.5	290	1 956	193.4	49.9	2 506.5	829.7	291.1	168.1
Rockdale	228	3 606	335.9	127.4	175	838	65.4	19.0	372.8	215.9	67.4	17.9
Schley	5	D	D	D	5	D	D	D	30.0	11.3	6.2	2.1
Screven	20	468	24.6	11.8	20	65	6.7	1.5	131.5	44.1	29.7	8.9
Seminole	22	464	41.2	14.3	14	48	2.9	0.9	91.6	32.6	18.5	8.9
Spalding	128	3 753	277.7	96.8	88	502	38.6	11.8	475.6	201.9	95.6	40.5
Stephens	49	1 335	108.0	45.9	36	190	20.0	4.3	235.4	108.6	53.5	14.4
Stewart	12	196	12.8	4.3	7	18	1.8	0.4	67.6	16.2	14.2	5.8
Sumter	88	D	D	D	49	D	D	D	438.3	87.7	50.9	26.4
Talbot	2	D	D	D	6	5	0.4	0.1	65.2	30.4	9.6	5.8
Taliaferro	2	D	D	D	3	D	D	D	23.6	6.4	6.0	1.5
Tattnall	26	615	30.8	13.7	14	42	2.9	0.6	180.8	68.0	35.4	14.0
Taylor	19	267	13.4	4.6	8	D	D	D	92.3	31.1	16.5	7.8
Telfair	18	647	32.7	15.6	17	69	7.8	1.6	176.4	50.3	32.2	8.9
Terrell	17	D	D	D	16	D	D	D	112.4	28.3	21.3	11.0
Thomas	134	3 303	369.8	130.7	74	470	41.2	10.2	404.0	160.7	77.9	31.8
Tift	110	2 811	267.4	121.2	65	543	65.3	17.1	315.1	116.7	57.0	24.5
Toombs	117	1 787	151.4	58.2	43	241	19.6	5.4	230.5	87.9	46.0	19.1
Towns	25	416	32.1	12.8	15	35	2.2	0.6	106.1	60.6	19.1	2.1
Treutlen	9	150	5.9	2.8	7	29	1.7	0.5	59.6	18.2	10.7	5.4
Troup	132	3 341	281.4	114.9	96	456	40.6	9.8	461.6	197.3	98.5	33.3
Turner	9	D	D	D	9	31	1.4	0.4	87.7	27.6	20.4	7.8
Twiggs	8	D	D	D	6	16	1.9	0.4	81.4	31.0	15.3	7.1
Union	56	941	74.6	28.9	32	202	19.8	4.4	175.5	104.4	32.7	4.9
Upson	61	1 360	121.7	45.9	38	D	D	D	228.0	84.4	48.3	16.4
Walker	52	D	D	D	48	D	D	D	484.5	239.9	127.5	25.4
Walton	107	1 661	223.7	51.1	113	349	29.1	8.1	448.8	251.8	77.3	24.8
Ware	114	2 824	260.2	94.7	70	349	22.5	6.3	397.3	154.4	82.8	30.3
Warren	5	110	6.4	3.0	7	D	D	D	67.8	19.3	16.2	5.4
Washington	36	949	48.6	23.3	34	88	7.1	1.6	181.7	58.9	43.1	14.4
Wayne	56	1 634	94.1	36.4	29	D	D	D	244.6	89.4	50.3	16.9
Webster	1	D	D	D	2	D	D	D	19.8	5.9	4.0	1.5
Wheeler	9	98	11.5	5.1	5	12	1.3	0.3	56.5	14.8	11.9	3.7
White	33	427	20.9	9.8	46	204	15.6	4.2	147.2	87.6	25.2	4.6
Whitfield	195	3 776	441.3	168.8	138	726	68.5	21.2	515.5	237.9	110.8	29.4
Wilcox	14	213	9.2	3.9	6	17	0.9	0.2	82.4	28.4	18.2	5.6
Wilkes	30	514	28.6	13.1	14	46	4.0	0.8	143.2	41.8	27.9	6.7
Wilkinson	14	141	10.9	3.9	11	40	2.3	0.7	90.2	38.9	20.4	7.2
Worth	27	D	D	D	28	75	7.0	1.4	153.5	55.1	27.5	15.7
HAWAII	3 484	63 640	6 565.0	2 721.4	2 916	20 119	1 917.8	512.6	20 855.2	4 218.0	1 488.9	508.6
Hawaii	452	7 285	623.3	271.8	310	1 673	162.5	42.6	1 258.9	549.4	178.0	111.0
Honolulu	2 473	47 727	5 055.4	2 047.9	2 083	15 228	1 462.7	388.7	17 392.9	3 117.6	1 100.2	333.7
Kalawao	NA	NA	NA	NA	NA	NA	NA	NA	1.3	0.0	1.2	0.0
Kauai	172	2 729	266.5	119.7	134	866	65.6	20.6	523.7	188.4	77.5	22.8
Maui	387	5 899	619.8	282.0	389	2 352	227.1	60.6	771.1	362.5	131.9	41.1
IDAHO	4 545	73 932	6 211.0	2 510.8	2 640	13 681	1 094.0	315.6	14 251.7	4 390.8	1 320.1	467.0
Ada	1 298	25 055	2 433.7	1 020.4	790	4 663	395.2	122.6	3 296.9	1 010.1	241.3	78.7
Adams	9	44	2.1	1.0	3	D	D	D	34.1	17.5	4.4	1.3
Bannock	291	D	D	D	132	669	59.4	14.2	597.4	240.9	71.8	36.5
Bear Lake	14	295	18.1	7.6	8	23	2.2	0.4	46.4	22.2	7.9	1.6
Benewah	19	362	23.0	9.7	16	79	6.4	2.0	114.0	40.5	15.4	4.8
Bingham	84	1 417	105.3	51.0	56	310	27.0	8.5	307.3	106.8	35.6	18.4
Blaine	79	595	69.3	27.7	82	331	45.8	10.9	87.2	44.9	11.3	2.4
Boise	5	22	1.3	0.5	8	D	D	D	46.7	22.9	4.8	1.3
Bonner	132	1 448	112.6	44.2	84	376	22.5	7.1	276.4	147.6	41.2	15.6
Bonneville	464	D	D	D	166	954	83.6	22.4	1 989.3	259.3	83.4	33.2
Boundary	34	507	25.7	13.6	23	36	3.3	0.8	106.0	40.2	9.1	4.4
Butte	8	191	8.5	5.4	3	18	1.2	0.2	40.2	10.2	5.0	0.9
Camas	3	D	D	D	NA	NA	NA	NA	7.3	2.7	0.7	0.2
Canyon	340	5 703	422.5	175.9	207	1 172	83.0	24.4	969.1	448.9	132.1	61.4

1. State totals may include programs not allocated by county.

Table B. States and Counties — Federal Funds, Residential Construction, and Local Government Finances

STATE County	Salaries and wages	Defense	Other	Medicaid and other health-related	Nutrition and family welfare	Education	Other	New construction ($1,000)	Number of housing units	Total (mil dol)	Inter-governmental (mil dol)	Total (mil dol)	Per capita[2] (dollars) Total	Property
	171	172	173	174	175	176	177	178	179	180	181	182	183	184
GEORGIA—Cont'd														
Putnam	5.3	0.0	2.5	15.5	5.9	1.1	0.1	7 922	35	85.6	17.4	40.9	2 020	1 152
Quitman	0.7	0.0	0.2	8.0	1.0	0.3	0.0	526	5	9.1	5.3	3.0	1 124	730
Rabun	4.4	1.5	1.1	23.2	2.6	0.5	1.7	11 098	65	58.9	13.9	37.2	2 251	1 534
Randolph	1.8	0.0	0.4	25.3	4.6	2.8	0.4	75	1	38.0	13.5	8.4	1 157	668
Richmond	300.8	298.1	87.5	330.6	59.0	25.8	61.3	63 583	378	667.8	316.3	198.7	1 007	612
Rockdale	13.6	0.2	2.7	19.8	9.5	6.7	9.6	13 121	40	259.3	81.2	129.2	1 574	994
Schley	0.6	0.0	0.2	7.2	0.9	0.5	0.1	0	0	13.9	8.1	3.6	863	633
Screven	2.7	0.0	0.6	34.3	4.2	1.4	0.2	1 229	7	46.3	21.9	13.7	908	552
Seminole	1.7	0.0	0.4	19.3	2.7	1.0	0.1	4 431	53	27.3	13.4	10.9	1 200	743
Spalding	28.6	2.3	2.5	70.9	13.4	6.7	0.6	15 129	118	231.3	98.8	88.1	1 403	849
Stephens	9.3	0.8	1.7	33.5	5.0	2.1	1.5	141	2	110.0	43.4	33.5	1 325	810
Stewart	7.1	0.0	0.3	19.7	2.4	0.6	0.2	70	1	14.5	7.3	5.7	1 237	855
Sumter	13.3	0.9	2.0	57.1	10.3	3.4	161.0	3 189	19	176.4	65.4	29.6	910	524
Talbot	1.6	0.0	0.4	13.2	2.5	0.6	0.2	714	6	18.8	7.5	9.6	1 451	1 065
Taliaferro	0.6	0.0	0.2	7.7	0.7	0.1	0.0	260	2	9.0	4.2	2.7	1 421	1 142
Tattnall	3.7	0.0	0.8	40.5	5.6	1.4	0.5	2 894	21	53.1	26.0	16.5	713	412
Taylor	1.8	0.0	0.4	21.4	2.3	1.6	8.4	1 306	10	25.8	14.2	8.5	969	567
Telfair	2.9	0.0	41.9	32.0	4.3	1.2	0.3	0	0	30.0	14.9	10.4	778	387
Terrell	5.4	0.0	0.6	31.2	4.8	1.2	0.2	893	14	32.3	15.2	10.7	1 045	669
Thomas	16.9	2.5	4.9	77.1	12.4	6.5	0.9	13 869	72	172.5	75.7	42.9	948	468
Tift	31.5	-0.7	1.9	51.3	9.6	6.6	1.1	5 287	47	318.7	52.5	61.8	1 486	678
Toombs	5.8	0.1	1.5	47.7	7.7	2.4	0.5	2 561	21	156.8	46.6	23.3	839	296
Towns	7.8	0.0	1.6	11.4	1.5	0.4	0.1	10 363	59	37.9	15.1	17.0	1 561	728
Treutlen	1.0	0.0	0.2	18.6	2.2	0.5	0.5	1 053	6	18.6	10.5	5.0	714	440
Troup	16.8	7.7	2.3	78.9	13.5	6.0	3.5	17 999	140	237.9	103.1	92.1	1 449	851
Turner	2.4	0.0	0.7	18.6	3.7	1.4	0.3	1 120	7	34.0	17.5	10.3	1 109	708
Twiggs	4.2	0.7	0.3	16.5	3.1	1.0	1.1	1 208	8	23.6	11.7	9.4	910	629
Union	6.0	0.0	2.5	20.4	3.1	0.5	0.2	11 958	68	56.8	20.4	30.0	1 430	774
Upson	12.7	0.0	1.0	37.4	7.4	2.2	15.8	7 744	71	76.0	34.3	30.2	1 097	658
Walker	10.3	-0.1	2.3	53.6	11.1	5.5	0.8	9 347	75	165.1	91.6	51.6	799	438
Walton	31.6	0.3	5.0	39.0	9.7	3.9	0.9	6 571	45	299.8	82.2	126.1	1 516	1 019
Ware	14.4	0.1	3.6	71.2	19.2	4.9	5.9	9 368	76	138.3	62.8	47.3	1 321	621
Warren	1.5	0.0	0.4	20.9	2.6	0.7	0.2	0	0	17.9	7.7	7.3	1 237	883
Washington	3.8	0.0	0.8	45.4	9.1	2.1	0.6	127	4	95.4	27.1	33.1	1 580	962
Wayne	27.5	0.1	4.5	39.5	6.6	2.3	0.4	345	3	118.2	38.8	33.2	1 142	742
Webster	0.6	0.0	0.1	4.9	0.8	0.1	0.0	NA	NA	7.9	4.2	2.8	1 267	971
Wheeler	1.0	0.0	0.2	16.0	2.5	0.5	4.2	0	0	15.9	9.7	4.5	658	435
White	4.3	0.0	1.1	13.9	3.0	5.3	0.8	6 938	40	72.2	28.2	34.1	1 362	836
Whitfield	25.2	2.1	7.9	58.9	16.3	9.0	0.8	9 122	70	358.4	147.4	112.0	1 200	604
Wilcox	1.9	0.1	0.5	20.6	2.5	0.7	0.3	NA	NA	20.4	12.0	6.7	778	531
Wilkes	2.9	0.0	0.5	24.0	3.3	1.0	34.0	3 004	17	43.1	13.9	12.6	1 226	798
Wilkinson	2.0	0.0	0.5	16.0	3.1	1.5	0.2	351	2	32.4	11.3	18.6	1 849	1 106
Worth	5.2	0.6	0.7	28.9	6.7	2.7	0.8	9 427	69	53.3	28.0	18.3	861	567
HAWAII	7 897.6	2 350.8	394.0	1 232.7	331.2	350.8	1 110.8	773 013	3 442	X	X	X	X	X
Hawaii	104.8	26.2	21.4	113.4	27.1	9.2	92.7	231 078	1 102	321.3	68.5	214.5	1 240	1 048
Honolulu	7 676.7	2 218.2	350.0	983.8	208.1	288.2	929.3	409 780	1 891	1 503.1	212.0	905.8	1 000	754
Kalawao	0.0	0.0	0.0	0.0	0.0	0.0	0.0	NA	NA	NA	NA	NA	NA	NA
Kauai	47.1	98.5	7.6	53.2	8.0	2.7	14.1	68 047	172	179.9	61.5	94.0	1 496	1 232
Maui	66.8	7.9	15.1	74.7	21.2	3.2	30.1	64 108	277	378.9	65.9	240.0	1 693	1 373
IDAHO	1 245.3	264.9	2 368.4	1 473.1	282.9	244.4	979.2	732 442	4 153	X	X	X	X	X
Ada	461.4	33.6	146.1	258.3	77.9	128.5	768.2	292 055	1 285	1 088.3	442.2	367.7	985	914
Adams	4.3	0.2	1.8	3.6	0.5	0.1	0.1	2 787	13	12.8	7.3	4.3	1 200	961
Bannock	58.7	0.4	11.7	102.0	13.6	2.9	16.2	18 314	140	329.8	100.9	58.9	737	692
Bear Lake	3.0	0.0	0.6	8.6	1.3	0.1	0.1	6 710	27	26.3	10.2	3.0	507	481
Benewah	3.5	0.9	2.5	13.0	3.1	2.1	12.3	2 452	19	42.5	14.7	4.7	508	480
Bingham	20.9	12.0	3.0	59.0	10.5	2.5	5.6	6 420	61	148.4	70.1	22.4	516	487
Blaine	6.9	1.7	2.6	4.4	1.6	0.2	8.3	25 139	24	116.6	33.9	63.1	2 927	2 547
Boise	5.5	1.5	3.2	3.1	0.8	0.2	2.9	5 054	24	17.6	10.7	4.1	543	507
Bonner	12.1	2.5	5.1	39.6	5.1	0.9	5.2	2 903	17	94.4	48.0	29.9	729	704
Bonneville	64.4	66.5	1 359.4	84.9	15.0	1.5	4.0	34 073	325	254.6	131.1	64.8	671	642
Boundary	11.7	11.2	1.8	14.1	1.4	0.3	8.3	6 063	29	35.9	16.7	6.8	621	610
Butte	8.2	0.0	1.3	10.4	0.6	0.1	0.2	120	1	16.5	5.0	2.9	1 058	1 031
Camas	1.4	0.0	0.8	1.0	0.1	0.0	0.1	594	4	4.6	3.0	1.2	1 093	1 055
Canyon	44.7	0.2	13.1	206.3	27.4	4.7	13.9	48 830	360	457.9	229.1	125.4	699	610

1. State totals may include programs not allocated by county.   2. Based on the resident population estimated as of July 1 of the year shown.

Table B. States and Counties — Local Government Finances, Government Employment, and Voting

STATE County	Local government finances, 2007 (cont.) Direct general expenditure — Total (mil dol)	Per capita[1] (dollars)	Education	Health and hospitals	Police protection	Public welfare	Highways	Debt outstanding Total (mil dol)	Per capita[1] (dollars)	Government employment, 2009 Federal civilian	Federal military	State and local	Presidential election,[2] 2008 Percent of vote cast: Democratic	Republican	All other
	185	186	187	188	189	190	191	192	193	194	195	196	197	198	199
GEORGIA—Cont'd															
Putnam	73.7	3 638	46.9	22.4	4.4	0.8	5.1	66.9	3 305	71	63	1 763	34.0	65.3	0.7
Quitman	8.2	3 073	54.2	2.0	6.3	1.8	6.0	5.5	2 059	0	0	136	53.6	45.7	0.7
Rabun	58.9	3 565	56.1	4.6	4.8	0.8	7.1	22.5	1 364	52	51	816	26.3	72.2	1.5
Randolph	38.6	5 288	40.9	33.1	2.9	0.0	3.8	6.7	912	26	22	747	57.0	42.6	0.4
Richmond	773.3	3 918	42.9	17.8	4.2	0.1	2.3	1 281.5	6 493	6 871	11 417	22 543	65.7	33.8	0.5
Rockdale	253.2	3 086	56.2	1.6	4.7	0.3	6.0	300.3	3 660	121	262	4 374	54.4	44.9	0.7
Schley	14.6	3 533	71.9	1.7	3.4	0.3	5.3	6.3	1 531	0	13	323	27.6	72.0	0.4
Screven	49.0	3 260	53.3	14.0	5.0	0.3	6.1	6.2	409	42	46	985	46.7	52.8	0.5
Seminole	26.9	2 962	64.1	4.0	5.9	0.0	7.5	1.0	110	18	28	470	41.5	57.9	0.5
Spalding	234.2	3 728	48.8	8.8	5.7	0.1	3.4	146.2	2 328	144	200	4 785	40.2	58.9	0.9
Stephens	114.5	4 533	38.6	36.7	3.5	0.4	1.9	78.9	3 123	70	79	1 959	25.7	73.1	1.2
Stewart	15.0	3 230	54.0	1.0	6.0	0.0	4.5	2.1	453	87	14	297	62.0	37.2	0.8
Sumter	178.8	5 497	31.5	45.1	2.9	0.1	1.3	52.2	1 605	144	99	2 843	52.8	46.7	0.5
Talbot	17.6	2 662	56.9	4.2	5.6	1.1	6.1	8.1	1 222	17	20	305	64.0	35.2	0.8
Taliaferro	7.1	3 794	53.9	2.3	9.3	2.7	3.7	1.5	819	0	0	135	64.9	34.2	0.8
Tattnall	49.0	2 116	62.4	2.8	4.3	0.1	5.9	21.2	914	32	76	2 249	28.8	70.4	0.8
Taylor	25.3	2 893	64.1	3.0	7.3	0.3	8.6	6.1	701	22	26	576	42.9	56.4	0.7
Telfair	32.9	2 464	59.5	2.4	5.7	0.3	5.2	17.7	1 325	40	39	854	42.6	56.8	0.6
Terrell	28.2	2 749	54.6	5.0	6.5	0.1	2.5	170.3	16 600	86	32	568	56.6	42.8	0.6
Thomas	179.0	3 957	46.7	9.3	4.7	0.0	3.7	115.8	2 559	203	143	3 704	41.8	57.7	0.5
Tift	293.6	7 056	23.0	52.6	3.0	0.0	3.0	231.6	5 565	224	133	5 006	33.3	66.1	0.5
Toombs	153.2	5 506	38.6	44.1	2.0	0.1	3.6	14.1	506	68	86	1 604	30.6	68.7	0.7
Towns	33.9	3 112	62.2	5.9	3.9	2.2	3.4	12.5	1 149	28	34	533	24.2	74.8	1.0
Treutlen	18.6	2 687	61.3	3.3	7.9	1.3	3.8	7.0	1 003	13	22	410	37.6	61.8	0.5
Troup	242.3	3 814	51.1	10.6	5.8	0.3	3.0	190.4	2 997	140	199	4 248	40.2	59.1	0.7
Turner	33.6	3 627	56.8	3.8	7.1	0.2	7.1	9.2	991	33	29	642	40.2	59.0	0.8
Twiggs	20.7	2 015	55.7	2.2	8.6	1.1	5.7	5.5	538	11	31	329	53.2	46.2	0.7
Union	55.4	2 640	52.7	3.7	4.0	1.6	5.8	51.5	2 457	61	66	1 570	23.4	75.4	1.3
Upson	74.3	2 694	39.9	2.0	4.3	0.1	3.5	47.0	1 706	43	85	1 623	35.6	63.8	0.6
Walker	159.4	2 469	62.7	12.7	4.5	1.1	2.9	75.8	1 175	119	200	3 459	25.9	72.7	1.4
Walton	295.5	3 554	55.5	12.0	5.0	0.4	4.3	360.8	4 340	160	269	3 673	23.5	75.6	0.8
Ware	147.2	4 108	44.6	14.2	4.4	0.3	4.4	80.7	2 252	145	112	3 243	32.5	66.9	0.6
Warren	16.0	2 713	61.6	3.2	3.2	0.1	10.6	2.1	352	17	18	289	58.4	40.9	0.7
Washington	90.8	4 337	42.1	30.4	3.9	0.1	6.9	19.2	918	47	64	2 274	52.0	47.6	0.5
Wayne	142.6	4 911	31.2	48.8	3.0	0.3	5.5	32.8	1 129	398	91	2 458	27.1	72.0	1.0
Webster	7.9	3 501	57.9	5.5	4.8	0.9	4.2	2.9	1 276	16	0	151	46.4	52.9	0.7
Wheeler	15.9	2 331	73.4	2.9	4.7	0.0	4.2	1.2	180	10	22	336	35.9	63.7	0.4
White	80.0	3 196	64.4	1.9	4.7	0.4	3.9	32.2	1 285	50	78	1 242	20.2	78.7	1.1
Whitfield	676.7	4 086	48.8	11.2	6.7	0.1	4.8	244.5	2 619	189	289	5 668	29.5	69.5	1.0
Wilcox	19.2	2 228	64.7	4.7	6.5	0.7	9.0	1.2	134	28	27	612	30.9	68.3	0.8
Wilkes	42.6	4 149	38.9	28.7	4.6	0.9	3.6	18.4	1 795	43	32	861	45.8	53.5	0.6
Wilkinson	30.6	3 044	56.6	3.0	6.4	1.1	7.2	9.1	906	22	31	573	49.2	50.3	0.6
Worth	55.6	2 614	60.7	1.8	9.4	0.1	7.6	5.8	271	41	65	892	30.4	69.1	0.6
HAWAII	X	X	X	X	X	X	X	X	X	33 379	55 663	91 919	71.8	26.6	1.6
Hawaii	292.2	1 689	0.0	6.3	15.5	2.1	6.7	465.1	2 688	1 361	1 400	11 308	75.9	22.2	1.8
Honolulu	1 403.3	1 550	0.0	2.0	13.7	0.0	9.7	4 105.7	4 534	30 601	52 528	67 775	69.8	28.7	1.4
Kalawao	NA	NA	NA	NA	NA	NA	NA	NA	NA	(3)	(3)	(3)	NA	NA	NA
Kauai	154.6	2 461	0.0	0.0	12.5	7.6	8.1	125.3	1 994	536	573	3 967	75.0	22.9	2.1
Maui	313.2	2 209	0.0	0.3	11.2	4.6	9.1	330.0	2 327	(3)881	(3)1 162	(3)8 869	76.7	21.5	1.8
IDAHO	X	X	X	X	X	X	X	X	X	13 559	10 129	104 642	36.1	61.5	2.4
Ada	1 000.9	2 680	44.1	2.2	8.2	0.5	7.6	865.1	2 317	5 619	1 552	26 814	45.8	52.0	2.1
Adams	11.1	3 119	42.0	1.6	9.9	0.0	10.9	5.6	1 571	112	14	213	31.4	65.4	3.2
Bannock	348.5	4 360	25.3	42.7	4.4	0.4	5.8	139.7	1 748	555	324	7 489	42.1	55.1	2.7
Bear Lake	24.7	4 219	34.0	40.0	2.9	0.7	6.3	3.5	595	65	23	590	17.1	80.8	2.2
Benewah	43.4	4 699	34.2	46.0	1.7	0.4	4.8	2.3	244	70	36	1 279	33.8	63.5	2.7
Bingham	144.4	3 321	45.2	28.4	4.0	0.3	5.1	58.3	1 342	250	175	3 577	25.8	71.3	2.9
Blaine	93.3	4 327	48.3	4.9	4.3	0.3	5.1	47.4	2 199	114	87	1 346	65.7	32.5	1.8
Boise	18.3	2 423	48.6	1.9	8.4	1.0	12.7	4.1	547	175	29	368	32.9	64.5	2.7
Bonner	91.4	2 226	45.3	3.1	6.9	0.4	8.0	23.1	562	206	162	2 182	40.1	57.0	2.9
Bonneville	244.0	2 527	53.4	1.2	5.1	0.3	6.7	164.8	1 707	835	397	5 036	27.4	70.3	2.3
Boundary	33.6	3 086	35.6	26.2	4.8	2.6	7.3	14.8	1 361	164	43	928	31.4	65.0	3.6
Butte	15.1	5 460	25.1	52.2	3.3	0.5	1.2	6.6	2 372	109	23	177	22.6	74.9	2.6
Camas	4.3	3 860	42.1	0.3	12.0	0.2	19.0	4.0	3 622	27	0	96	30.3	68.3	1.5
Canyon	450.8	2 513	51.5	0.2	6.1	0.6	4.7	390.9	2 179	408	731	8 238	31.4	66.5	2.1

1. Based on the resident population estimated as of July 1 of the year shown. 2. © 2009 Election Data Services, Inc. All rights reserved. 3. Kalawao county is included with Maui county.

STATE/ County code	CBSA code[1]	County type[2]	STATE County	Land area,[3] (sq km) 2010	Total persons	Rank	Per square kilometer	White	Black	American Indian, Alaska Native	Asian and Pacific Islander	Percent Hispanic or Latino[4]	Under 5 years	5 to 17 years	18 to 24 years	25 to 34 years	35 to 44 years	45 to 54 years
				1	2	3	4	5	6	7	8	9	10	11	12	13	14	15
			IDAHO—Cont'd															
16 029	...	6	Caribou	4 569	6 963	2 691	1.5	94.2	0.2	1.0	1.1	4.8	7.9	21.1	6.3	11.9	10.6	13.9
16 031	15420	7	Cassia	6 644	22 952	1 690	3.5	73.8	0.3	0.9	0.9	24.9	9.3	23.7	8.4	12.1	11.3	12.3
16 033	...	8	Clark	4 569	982	3 111	0.2	57.9	0.8	0.9	0.7	40.5	8.4	23.0	8.5	12.5	11.4	13.3
16 035	...	6	Clearwater	6 364	8 761	2 545	1.4	93.8	0.4	3.5	1.1	3.1	4.3	13.5	5.9	9.5	11.0	16.0
16 037	...	9	Custer	12 745	4 368	2 879	0.3	94.9	0.2	1.3	0.5	4.0	5.0	14.6	5.1	9.8	11.3	17.0
16 039	34300	4	Elmore	7 964	27 038	1 532	3.4	77.8	3.4	1.9	4.7	15.2	9.3	19.1	12.8	15.7	11.7	12.4
16 041	30860	3	Franklin	1 719	12 786	2 256	7.4	92.8	0.3	0.9	0.4	6.6	9.5	25.6	7.4	12.2	11.3	11.8
16 043	39940	6	Fremont	4 827	13 242	2 234	2.7	86.0	0.3	1.1	0.6	12.8	8.8	22.6	7.7	12.7	10.9	12.6
16 045	14260	2	Gem	1 453	16 719	2 002	11.5	90.8	0.3	1.4	1.1	8.0	6.6	17.9	7.0	9.7	11.3	15.1
16 047	...	7	Gooding	1 888	15 464	2 083	8.2	70.7	0.2	1.2	0.9	28.1	8.3	21.2	8.7	12.5	11.4	12.5
16 049	...	6	Idaho	21 956	16 267	2 036	0.7	93.9	0.4	3.9	0.7	2.6	5.3	15.6	6.1	8.7	10.3	15.4
16 051	26820	3	Jefferson	2 832	26 140	1 557	9.2	88.7	0.3	0.8	1.0	10.1	10.8	24.7	7.9	13.9	11.7	12.3
16 053	46300	7	Jerome	1 547	22 374	1 714	14.5	67.7	0.3	1.2	0.6	31.0	9.5	21.5	9.4	13.8	11.3	12.0
16 055	17660	3	Kootenai	3 222	138 494	442	43.0	93.9	0.6	2.2	1.5	3.8	6.5	18.3	8.7	12.1	12.5	14.3
16 057	34140	7	Latah	2 787	37 244	1 231	13.4	92.7	1.2	1.5	3.1	3.6	5.7	13.0	25.4	14.0	9.7	11.3
16 059	...	7	Lemhi	11 819	7 936	2 607	0.7	96.4	0.6	1.7	0.5	2.3	5.4	14.5	5.4	8.5	9.6	16.0
16 061	...	8	Lewis	1 240	3 821	2 918	3.1	91.2	0.5	6.2	1.0	3.3	6.2	16.0	5.9	9.0	9.0	16.4
16 063	...	9	Lincoln	3 112	5 208	2 828	1.7	70.2	0.6	1.1	0.7	28.3	8.6	24.0	8.1	13.6	11.5	12.0
16 065	39940	6	Madison	1 215	37 536	1 228	30.9	92.2	0.6	0.5	1.8	5.9	9.6	16.4	36.4	14.2	6.4	6.6
16 067	15420	7	Minidoka	1 962	20 069	1 836	10.2	66.2	0.4	1.3	0.6	32.4	8.4	21.0	8.4	11.9	10.5	13.5
16 069	30300	3	Nez Perce	2 197	39 265	1 188	17.9	90.6	0.6	6.7	1.4	2.8	5.6	16.0	10.0	11.8	11.5	14.1
16 071	...	8	Oneida	3 108	4 286	2 883	1.4	95.8	0.3	0.9	0.8	2.9	7.6	22.3	5.7	10.5	10.0	14.1
16 073	14260	2	Owyhee	19 854	11 526	2 334	0.6	69.5	0.2	4.7	0.9	25.8	7.7	21.5	8.0	11.6	11.7	13.6
16 075	36620	6	Payette	1 054	22 623	1 701	21.5	83.1	0.4	1.9	1.7	14.9	7.7	21.0	7.7	11.3	12.0	13.5
16 077	38540	3	Power	3 637	7 817	2 624	2.1	67.4	0.4	3.0	0.8	29.8	9.2	21.7	9.3	12.1	10.8	13.1
16 079	...	6	Shoshone	6 811	12 765	2 259	1.9	95.0	0.3	2.6	0.7	3.0	4.9	16.0	6.4	9.5	11.6	15.0
16 081	27220	9	Teton	1 164	10 170	2 431	8.7	82.1	0.2	0.6	0.8	16.9	9.7	20.1	6.6	17.1	17.3	13.1
16 083	46300	5	Twin Falls	4 976	77 230	703	15.5	83.9	0.6	1.2	1.8	13.7	8.2	19.1	9.8	13.5	11.3	13.0
16 085	...	8	Valley	9 491	9 862	2 452	1.0	95.1	0.2	1.0	0.8	3.9	5.2	14.6	5.3	10.3	12.3	16.3
16 087	...	6	Washington	3 763	10 198	2 428	2.7	81.3	0.2	1.5	1.2	16.8	5.6	19.1	6.5	9.2	11.1	13.7
17 000	...	X	ILLINOIS	143 793	12 830 632	X	89.2	64.9	15.0	0.5	5.2	15.8	6.5	17.9	9.7	13.8	13.5	14.6
17 001	39500	5	Adams	2 215	67 103	780	30.3	94.5	4.4	0.5	0.9	1.2	6.3	16.7	8.9	11.5	11.8	14.6
17 003	16020	7	Alexander	610	8 238	2 592	13.5	62.1	36.6	0.7	0.4	1.9	7.1	15.8	9.0	11.5	11.2	14.6
17 005	41180	1	Bond	985	17 768	1 938	18.0	89.9	6.7	0.8	0.6	3.1	5.4	15.2	10.3	12.9	13.4	15.2
17 007	40420	2	Boone	727	54 165	922	74.5	76.4	2.3	0.5	1.7	20.2	6.9	22.1	7.9	10.8	14.9	14.7
17 009	...	7	Brown	792	6 937	2 694	8.8	75.3	18.6	0.4	0.3	5.8	4.3	11.8	11.3	19.0	15.9	15.3
17 011	36860	6	Bureau	2 251	34 978	1 300	15.5	90.9	1.0	0.5	0.8	7.7	5.8	17.5	7.0	10.8	12.1	15.0
17 013	41180	1	Calhoun	657	5 089	2 836	7.7	98.6	0.2	0.4	0.3	0.8	5.4	16.5	6.8	9.8	12.1	15.6
17 015	...	7	Carroll	1 152	15 387	2 090	13.4	95.7	1.2	0.6	0.6	2.8	4.7	15.8	6.8	9.6	11.0	15.1
17 017	...	6	Cass	973	13 642	2 210	14.0	79.9	3.0	0.4	0.4	16.8	6.8	18.1	8.2	12.2	12.8	14.4
17 019	16580	3	Champaign	2 580	201 081	307	77.9	72.9	13.4	0.6	10.0	5.3	5.8	13.6	23.8	15.0	10.6	11.5
17 021	45380	6	Christian	1 837	34 800	1 308	18.9	96.6	1.8	0.4	0.6	1.4	6.0	16.3	8.1	11.5	12.5	15.4
17 023	...	6	Clark	1 299	16 335	2 030	12.6	98.1	0.4	0.5	0.5	1.1	5.7	17.1	7.7	10.7	12.6	15.5
17 025	...	7	Clay	1 213	13 815	2 197	11.4	97.9	0.5	0.6	0.6	1.1	6.2	16.7	7.8	11.2	11.6	15.1
17 027	41180	1	Clinton	1 228	37 762	1 224	30.8	92.9	3.9	0.5	0.8	2.8	5.8	16.9	8.5	13.3	13.4	16.0
17 029	16660	5	Coles	1 316	53 873	925	40.9	92.8	4.4	0.6	1.3	2.1	5.2	13.2	23.5	11.4	9.6	12.3
17 031	16980	1	Cook	2 448	5 194 675	2	2 122.0	44.9	25.0	0.4	6.9	24.0	6.6	17.1	9.9	16.0	13.7	13.8
17 033	...	6	Crawford	1 149	19 817	1 849	17.2	92.7	5.0	0.5	0.8	1.8	5.1	15.4	8.7	12.5	12.8	15.7
17 035	16660	9	Cumberland	896	11 048	2 362	12.3	98.6	0.5	0.6	0.3	0.7	6.6	16.9	8.0	11.5	12.2	14.9
17 037	16980	1	DeKalb	1 635	105 160	558	64.3	81.0	6.9	0.5	2.8	10.1	6.3	16.0	20.7	14.0	11.4	12.4
17 039	...	6	De Witt	1 030	16 561	2 013	16.1	96.7	0.8	0.5	0.6	2.1	5.8	17.3	7.1	11.5	12.8	15.8
17 041	...	6	Douglas	1 079	19 980	1 840	18.5	93.1	0.6	0.6	0.5	6.1	7.0	18.9	7.9	12.0	11.7	14.6
17 043	16980	1	DuPage	848	916 924	51	1 081.3	71.7	4.9	0.4	11.0	13.3	6.2	18.6	8.5	12.8	13.7	16.3
17 045	...	6	Edgar	1 615	18 576	1 893	11.5	98.3	0.5	0.5	0.3	1.0	5.7	16.4	7.1	11.0	11.8	15.3
17 047	...	9	Edwards	576	6 721	2 709	11.7	98.2	0.7	0.4	0.5	0.9	5.4	17.4	7.2	10.3	12.5	15.3
17 049	20820	7	Effingham	1 240	34 242	1 320	27.6	97.4	0.5	0.4	0.6	1.7	6.6	18.1	8.5	12.2	11.7	15.6
17 051	...	6	Fayette	1 856	22 140	1 730	11.9	93.8	4.6	0.5	0.5	1.4	5.8	16.6	9.0	12.4	12.7	15.1
17 053	16580	3	Ford	1 258	14 081	2 167	11.2	96.7	0.8	0.6	0.5	2.1	5.8	18.0	7.0	10.5	12.0	15.9
17 055	...	5	Franklin	1 059	39 561	1 181	37.4	97.9	0.6	0.7	0.5	1.2	6.0	16.7	7.8	11.2	12.4	14.3
17 057	15900	6	Fulton	2 242	37 069	1 240	16.5	93.6	3.7	0.6	0.5	2.4	5.2	15.7	8.0	12.3	12.9	14.3
17 059	...	8	Gallatin	837	5 589	2 800	6.7	98.2	0.5	1.1	0.2	1.2	5.9	15.2	7.5	10.5	11.6	14.5
17 061	...	6	Greene	1 406	13 886	2 187	9.9	98.0	1.1	0.5	0.2	0.8	5.9	17.2	7.7	11.6	12.1	15.8
17 063	16980	1	Grundy	1 083	50 063	975	46.2	89.8	1.5	0.4	1.0	8.2	7.3	20.0	7.6	13.6	14.7	14.8
17 065	34500	7	Hamilton	1 126	8 457	2 572	7.5	98.0	0.5	0.4	0.5	1.2	5.9	16.9	7.0	11.4	11.0	14.5
17 067	...	7	Hancock	2 056	19 104	1 875	9.3	98.2	0.5	0.6	0.5	1.0	5.9	16.1	7.0	10.4	11.1	15.1

1. CBSA = Core Based Statistical Area. See Appendix A for explanation. See Appendix B for list of metropolitan areas with component counties. 2. County type code from the Economic Research Service of USDA Rural-Urban Continuum Codes. See Appendix A for definition. 3. Dry land or land partially or temporarily covered by water. 4. May be of any race.

STATE County	Population, 2010 (cont.) Age (percent) (cont.) 55 to 64 years	65 to 74 years	75 years and over	Percent female	Population change and components of change, 1990–2010 Total persons 1990	2000	Percent change 1990–2000	2000–2010	Components of change, 2000–2009 Births	Deaths	Net migration	Households, 2010 Number	Percent change, 2000–2010	Persons per house-hold	Percent Female family house-holder[1]	One per-son
	16	17	18	19	20	21	22	23	24	25	26	27	28	29	30	31
IDAHO—Cont'd																
Caribou	12.4	8.8	7.1	49.6	6 963	7 304	4.9	-4.7	951	578	-741	2 606	1.8	2.64	6.1	22.9
Cassia	10.0	6.8	6.1	49.4	19 532	21 416	9.6	7.2	3 715	1 691	-1 632	7 666	8.6	2.96	9.1	21.5
Clark	9.8	8.2	4.9	44.7	762	1 022	34.1	-3.9	170	47	-199	345	1.5	2.84	7.0	24.3
Clearwater	17.5	13.4	9.0	45.9	8 505	8 930	5.0	-1.9	657	852	-667	3 660	5.9	2.23	6.4	29.3
Custer	18.4	11.6	7.1	46.9	4 133	4 342	5.1	0.6	336	303	-118	1 936	9.4	2.25	4.8	30.2
Elmore	9.0	5.9	4.2	48.3	21 205	29 130	37.4	-7.2	4 878	1 439	-3 621	10 140	11.5	2.60	9.4	23.8
Franklin	9.3	6.8	6.1	49.3	9 232	11 329	22.7	12.9	2 025	809	196	4 079	17.3	3.11	6.3	17.9
Fremont	10.8	7.9	6.1	47.4	10 937	11 819	8.1	12.0	2 063	848	-285	4 436	14.2	2.88	7.2	19.7
Gem	13.7	10.3	8.3	50.5	11 844	15 181	28.2	10.1	1 978	1 624	975	6 495	17.3	2.55	9.3	24.3
Gooding	10.3	8.0	7.0	48.3	11 633	14 155	21.7	9.2	2 225	1 265	-608	5 531	9.6	2.79	8.8	24.2
Idaho	17.5	12.7	8.5	47.8	13 768	15 511	12.7	4.9	1 455	1 470	62	6 834	12.3	2.30	6.6	28.6
Jefferson	9.3	5.6	3.9	49.8	16 543	19 155	15.8	36.5	4 088	1 151	2 815	8 146	38.0	3.20	7.4	15.0
Jerome	10.2	6.3	4.9	48.9	15 138	18 342	21.2	22.0	3 430	1 341	937	7 540	19.7	2.95	9.6	20.3
Kootenai	13.2	8.3	6.2	50.7	69 795	108 685	55.7	27.4	15 031	8 820	24 974	54 200	31.2	2.53	10.0	24.3
Latah	10.5	5.8	4.6	48.5	30 617	34 935	14.1	6.6	3 945	1 957	-309	14 708	12.6	2.32	6.1	28.2
Lemhi	18.6	13.2	8.9	49.0	6 899	7 806	13.1	1.7	703	828	260	3 576	9.2	2.20	6.9	31.7
Lewis	15.7	12.7	9.1	49.9	3 516	3 747	6.6	2.0	401	396	-4	1 657	6.6	2.26	7.6	32.6
Lincoln	11.1	5.8	5.2	48.3	3 308	4 044	22.2	28.8	742	321	197	1 705	17.8	3.03	7.1	20.5
Madison	4.9	3.0	2.5	51.6	23 674	27 467	16.0	36.7	7 430	1 096	1 811	10 611	48.8	3.44	4.8	10.1
Minidoka	11.5	8.1	6.7	49.4	19 361	20 174	4.2	-0.5	3 072	1 659	-2 300	7 170	2.8	2.79	9.1	22.0
Nez Perce	12.9	8.8	9.2	50.4	33 754	37 410	10.8	5.0	4 218	3 854	1 585	16 241	6.2	2.36	10.3	28.6
Oneida	13.0	8.5	8.1	48.9	3 492	4 125	18.1	3.9	542	360	-67	1 545	8.0	2.74	6.1	22.5
Owyhee	11.9	8.3	5.7	48.9	8 392	10 644	26.8	8.3	1 613	767	-204	4 076	9.9	2.79	9.6	23.0
Payette	11.5	8.9	6.4	50.5	16 434	20 578	25.2	9.9	3 014	1 707	1 340	8 262	12.1	2.73	10.4	22.1
Power	11.8	7.1	6.0	48.5	7 086	7 538	6.4	3.7	1 169	471	-721	2 641	3.2	2.94	10.1	19.8
Shoshone	16.3	11.4	8.5	49.7	13 931	13 771	-1.1	-7.3	1 173	1 547	-693	5 605	-5.1	2.25	8.7	31.3
Teton	9.7	3.9	2.7	47.7	3 439	5 999	74.4	69.5	1 450	248	2 162	3 651	75.7	2.78	5.9	21.9
Twin Falls	11.1	7.3	6.5	50.6	53 580	64 284	20.0	20.1	10 349	6 024	6 988	28 760	20.6	2.65	10.5	24.3
Valley	19.3	11.5	5.4	48.2	6 109	7 651	25.2	28.9	869	552	780	4 393	36.9	2.23	6.0	27.9
Washington	14.4	11.2	9.3	50.8	8 550	9 977	16.7	2.2	1 222	1 080	54	4 034	7.2	2.50	9.7	25.8
ILLINOIS	11.5	6.6	5.9	51.0	11 430 602	12 419 293	8.6	3.3	1 681 839	960 627	-228 888	4 836 972	5.3	2.59	12.9	27.8
Adams	12.5	8.4	9.1	51.3	66 090	68 277	3.3	-1.7	7 713	7 661	-880	27 375	1.9	2.37	10.7	30.1
Alexander	13.9	9.2	7.7	49.2	10 626	9 590	-9.7	-14.1	1 168	1 142	-1 689	3 329	-12.6	2.31	18.5	33.6
Bond	12.6	7.6	7.5	47.7	14 991	17 633	17.6	0.8	1 883	1 631	314	6 427	4.4	2.44	9.1	26.8
Boone	10.9	7.0	4.8	50.0	30 806	41 786	35.6	29.6	6 469	3 019	8 997	18 505	26.8	2.91	10.2	18.9
Brown	10.0	6.6	5.8	35.9	5 836	6 950	19.1	-0.2	559	554	-333	2 099	-0.4	2.30	8.6	32.2
Bureau	13.6	9.0	9.1	51.1	35 688	35 503	-0.5	-1.5	3 920	3 692	-801	14 262	0.6	2.42	9.2	28.0
Calhoun	13.8	11.0	9.1	50.3	5 322	5 084	-4.5	0.1	490	576	43	2 085	1.9	2.40	7.0	27.3
Carroll	15.7	11.1	10.1	49.9	16 805	16 674	-0.8	-7.7	1 491	1 833	-484	6 622	-2.5	2.29	8.2	29.8
Cass	11.9	8.0	7.7	49.9	13 437	13 695	1.9	-0.4	1 783	1 411	-434	5 270	-1.4	2.55	10.9	26.5
Champaign	9.7	5.1	4.9	50.1	173 025	179 669	3.8	11.9	22 111	10 865	5 958	80 665	14.3	2.29	9.9	33.2
Christian	12.6	8.8	8.8	49.3	34 418	35 372	2.8	-1.6	3 765	3 854	-795	14 055	1.0	2.36	10.3	29.9
Clark	12.7	9.4	8.6	51.3	15 921	17 008	6.8	-4.0	1 726	1 958	-28	6 782	-2.7	2.38	9.7	27.7
Clay	13.5	8.9	9.0	50.9	14 460	14 560	0.7	-5.1	1 620	1 617	-810	5 697	-2.4	2.37	9.4	28.9
Clinton	11.6	7.2	7.2	48.3	33 944	35 535	4.7	6.3	3 881	3 049	229	14 005	9.8	2.55	8.7	25.1
Coles	10.8	6.9	6.9	51.8	51 644	53 196	3.0	1.3	5 330	4 561	-1 633	21 463	2.0	2.30	9.9	31.4
Cook	11.0	6.2	5.7	51.6	5 105 044	5 376 741	5.3	-3.4	746 279	396 730	-449 818	1 966 356	-0.4	2.60	15.6	31.0
Crawford	13.0	8.6	8.3	48.1	19 464	20 452	5.1	-3.1	1 809	2 147	-568	7 763	-1.0	2.36	9.4	29.1
Cumberland	13.3	8.6	8.0	50.1	10 670	11 253	5.5	-1.8	1 197	1 182	-491	4 377	0.2	2.50	8.6	24.3
DeKalb	9.3	5.1	4.7	50.0	77 932	88 969	14.2	18.2	11 531	5 735	12 562	38 484	21.5	2.56	10.2	25.8
De Witt	12.9	9.1	7.6	50.5	16 516	16 798	1.7	-1.4	1 854	1 861	-662	6 811	0.6	2.39	10.0	27.5
Douglas	12.1	7.9	7.9	50.7	19 464	19 922	2.4	0.3	2 709	1 852	-1 535	7 720	1.9	2.57	8.5	26.1
DuPage	12.3	6.3	5.3	51.0	781 689	904 161	15.7	1.4	115 387	52 467	-34 018	337 132	3.5	2.68	9.5	24.3
Edgar	14.0	9.7	9.0	51.5	19 595	19 704	0.6	-5.7	1 960	2 239	-845	7 839	-0.4	2.33	10.7	29.5
Edwards	14.1	8.9	8.9	50.6	7 440	6 971	-6.3	-3.6	698	780	-408	2 840	-2.2	2.35	8.3	28.5
Effingham	12.2	7.7	7.5	50.3	31 704	34 264	8.1	-0.1	4 284	3 023	-898	13 515	4.0	2.50	9.5	26.9
Fayette	12.1	8.4	7.8	47.4	20 893	21 802	4.4	1.6	2 292	2 208	-831	8 311	2.0	2.45	9.7	27.2
Ford	12.1	8.5	10.2	51.3	14 275	14 241	-0.2	-1.1	1 566	1 896	73	5 676	0.7	2.41	9.8	29.2
Franklin	13.3	9.9	8.5	51.1	40 319	39 018	-3.2	1.4	4 448	5 098	1 154	16 617	1.3	2.35	11.6	30.0
Fulton	13.2	9.1	9.0	48.3	38 080	38 250	0.4	-3.1	3 733	4 370	-731	14 536	-2.3	2.37	10.2	28.1
Gallatin	14.3	11.9	8.6	51.3	6 909	6 445	-6.7	-13.3	615	787	-542	2 403	-11.8	2.32	10.0	31.1
Greene	12.5	8.9	8.3	49.5	15 317	14 761	-3.6	-5.9	1 563	1 582	-1 115	5 570	-3.2	2.44	9.4	27.8
Grundy	11.0	6.2	4.9	50.1	32 337	37 535	16.1	33.4	5 859	3 075	8 324	18 546	29.8	2.69	9.7	22.5
Hamilton	13.5	10.1	9.6	51.2	8 499	8 621	1.4	-1.9	796	950	-322	3 489	0.8	2.39	9.2	28.1
Hancock	14.5	10.3	9.5	50.8	21 373	20 121	-5.9	-5.1	1 967	1 985	-1 655	8 040	-0.4	2.35	8.3	28.2

1. No spouse present.

Table B. States and Counties — Population, Vital Statistics, Medicare, and Crime

STATE County	Persons in group quarters, 2010	Daytime population, 2006–2010		Births, average 2006–2008		Deaths, average 2006–2008		Persons under 65 with no health insurance, 2009		Medicare, 2011			Serious crimes known to police,[2] 2010 Total	
		Number	Employment/ residence ratio	Total	Rate[1]	Number	Rate[1]	Number	Percent	Eligible for Medicare	Enrolled in Medicare Advantage	Enrolled in a Medicare prescription drug plan	Number	Rate[3]
	32	33	34	35	36	37	38	39	40	41	42	43	44	45
IDAHO—Cont'd														
Caribou	79	7 302	1.1	D	D	68	9.9	1 039	18.0	1 242	193	513	40	574
Cassia	286	23 195	1.1	D	D	186	8.8	4 398	24.1	3 516	485	1 748	486	2 117
Clark	2	943	1.2	D	D	D	D	246	30.2	131	21	56	6	611
Clearwater	607	8 966	1.1	D	D	97	11.8	1 320	21.4	2 433	363	1 119	176	2 009
Custer	21	4 328	1.0	D	D	33	7.9	787	22.8	925	113	375	NA	NA
Elmore	632	26 170	1.0	540	18.8	162	5.6	5 209	20.4	3 261	329	1 129	472	1 746
Franklin	102	11 247	0.8	D	D	84	6.8	2 159	19.9	1 850	578	800	54	422
Fremont	460	11 004	0.7	D	D	84	6.8	2 778	26.0	2 070	410	888	107	808
Gem	151	13 558	0.5	D	D	179	10.8	2 969	22.7	3 648	1 383	1 082	155	927
Gooding	52	14 368	0.9	D	D	136	9.5	3 147	26.4	2 559	331	1 201	150	970
Idaho	524	15 235	0.9	D	D	164	10.5	2 642	21.8	3 477	566	1 839	186	1 143
Jefferson	111	20 590	0.6	D	D	123	5.3	4 516	20.5	3 080	583	1 322	200	765
Jerome	106	20 982	1.0	420	20.8	152	7.5	4 772	26.2	2 987	779	1 381	323	1 444
Kootenai	1 488	129 697	0.9	1 756	13.1	1 001	7.4	22 178	19.0	25 892	7 453	9 101	3 953	2 854
Latah	3 086	33 713	0.8	D	D	201	5.6	5 921	17.8	4 728	619	1 847	758	2 035
Lemhi	80	7 857	1.0	D	D	88	11.3	1 307	21.4	2 094	287	793	59	743
Lewis	74	3 872	1.1	D	D	47	12.9	557	19.9	1 691	295	836	55	1 439
Lincoln	37	4 390	0.7	D	D	38	8.5	1 038	26.0	914	107	425	NA	NA
Madison	1 036	36 930	1.0	1 041	29.6	127	3.6	5 269	15.2	2 402	856	817	331	882
Minidoka	82	18 117	0.8	D	D	172	9.2	3 741	23.4	3 043	595	1 455	302	1 505
Nez Perce	966	41 855	1.2	458	11.8	418	10.8	5 169	16.4	8 529	1 786	3 223	1 523	3 879
Oneida	50	3 767	0.7	D	D	35	8.5	697	20.2	811	121	387	18	420
Owyhee	160	10 068	0.7	D	D	79	7.3	2 803	30.1	1 829	594	606	284	2 464
Payette	94	19 761	0.7	D	D	195	8.6	4 269	22.2	4 335	1 400	1 480	490	2 166
Power	47	7 401	0.9	D	D	53	6.9	1 645	24.7	1 161	249	541	119	1 522
Shoshone	160	12 913	1.0	D	D	174	13.4	1 887	18.9	3 194	725	1 413	311	2 436
Teton	7	8 283	0.8	D	D	29	3.4	2 342	27.2	873	57	470	81	796
Twin Falls	1 072	75 739	1.0	1 232	16.9	679	9.3	13 635	21.7	12 774	2 504	5 833	1 944	2 517
Valley	66	10 460	1.1	D	D	54	6.1	1 636	22.6	1 785	304	700	251	2 545
Washington	119	9 570	0.9	D	D	125	12.3	2 000	25.3	2 357	686	904	65	637
ILLINOIS	301 773	12 738 249	1.0	179 401	14.0	102 048	8.0	1 658 111	15.0	1 894 424	173 646	918 483	399 824	3 116
Adams	2 287	70 483	1.1	839	12.5	835	12.5	6 178	11.4	13 452	474	7 847	1 777	2 694
Alexander	543	7 902	0.8	D	D	118	14.0	975	15.5	1 736	71	1 040	376	4 564
Bond	2 060	15 579	0.7	D	D	181	10.0	2 258	15.0	3 151	66	1 936	290	1 632
Boone	310	45 039	0.6	716	13.4	353	6.6	6 197	13.2	7 819	1 293	3 215	962	1 776
Brown	2 110	7 873	1.4	D	D	56	8.5	1 225	22.0	987	36	557	46	663
Bureau	456	31 895	0.8	D	D	395	11.3	3 443	12.3	7 020	532	3 798	569	1 701
Calhoun	90	4 068	0.5	D	D	63	12.2	535	13.5	1 174	22	742	68	1 336
Carroll	223	13 512	0.7	D	D	195	12.2	1 726	14.1	3 861	434	1 882	240	1 779
Cass	184	13 210	0.9	D	D	171	12.5	1 712	15.2	2 407	101	1 346	NA	NA
Champaign	16 129	207 724	1.1	2 483	13.1	1 132	6.0	20 837	12.2	23 561	4 468	7 028	6 356	3 185
Christian	1 610	31 312	0.8	D	D	396	11.4	3 467	12.5	7 216	277	4 200	377	1 153
Clark	221	14 686	0.8	D	D	199	11.8	1 713	12.8	3 392	318	1 886	156	1 258
Clay	305	14 021	1.0	D	D	167	12.0	1 483	13.6	3 046	39	1 998	209	1 513
Clinton	2 072	32 024	0.7	D	D	343	9.4	3 662	12.2	6 552	122	3 754	584	1 621
Coles	4 489	55 565	1.1	581	11.3	496	9.7	5 519	12.6	8 563	550	4 394	1 176	2 183
Cook	90 282	5 377 259	1.1	78 821	14.9	40 811	7.7	857 736	18.9	718 709	67 879	354 011	211 258	4 174
Crawford	1 495	20 276	1.0	D	D	227	11.5	2 217	14.0	3 941	105	1 939	NA	NA
Cumberland	117	8 690	0.5	D	D	117	10.7	1 121	12.7	2 118	126	1 199	67	703
DeKalb	6 673	93 908	0.8	1 300	12.6	625	6.0	12 769	13.5	12 341	415	6 097	2 488	2 441
De Witt	249	14 207	0.7	D	D	186	11.3	1 525	11.6	3 184	418	1 465	NA	NA
Douglas	168	18 851	0.9	D	D	211	10.7	2 499	15.8	3 677	852	1 497	143	863
DuPage	12 140	1 000 754	1.2	11 608	12.5	5 700	6.1	84 558	10.4	122 918	6 337	61 099	16 659	1 817
Edgar	283	17 736	0.9	D	D	238	12.6	2 200	14.8	3 973	204	2 341	244	1 314
Edwards	52	6 797	1.0	D	D	81	12.3	634	12.3	1 439	23	930	NA	NA
Effingham	440	38 273	1.2	448	13.1	315	9.2	3 345	11.8	6 177	113	3 643	594	1 735
Fayette	1 784	20 391	0.8	D	D	216	10.1	2 799	16.3	4 324	61	2 552	357	1 612
Ford	410	12 663	0.8	D	D	196	13.9	1 310	11.6	2 774	270	1 452	NA	NA
Franklin	517	35 198	0.7	471	11.9	540	13.6	4 848	15.4	9 073	816	4 834	1 028	2 916
Fulton	2 683	32 395	0.7	389	10.5	462	12.5	4 249	14.5	7 663	1 415	3 924	624	1 886
Gallatin	25	5 280	0.8	D	D	87	14.4	722	16.0	1 382	46	899	107	1 914
Greene	284	11 326	0.6	D	D	177	12.7	1 498	13.6	2 905	42	1 857	130	1 014
Grundy	254	42 779	0.7	721	15.3	351	7.5	4 226	10.1	6 785	138	3 123	1 085	2 167
Hamilton	117	7 154	0.6	D	D	111	13.4	957	15.0	1 884	79	1 146	NA	NA
Hancock	223	15 663	0.6	D	D	207	11.0	1 759	12.1	4 145	221	2 444	NA	NA

1. Per 1,000 estimated resident population.   2. Data for serious crimes have not been adjusted for underreporting; this may affect comparability between geographic areas and over time.   3. Per 100,000 population estimated by the FBI.

Table B. States and Counties — **Crime, Education, Money Income, and Poverty**

STATE County	Serious crimes known to police,[1] 2010 (cont.) Rate[2] Violent	Property	Education — School enrollment and attainment, 2006-2010 — Enrollment[3] Total	Per-cent private	Attainment[4] (percent) High school graduate or less	Bach-elor's degree or more	Local government expenditures,[5] 2008-2009 Total current expenditures (mil dol)	Current expenditures per student (dollars)	Money income, 2006-2010 Per capita income[6] (dollars)	Households Median income Dollars	Percent change, 2000 to 2006-2010 (constant 2010 dollars)	Percent with income of $200,000 or more	Income and poverty, 2010 Median house-hold income (dollars)	Percent below poverty level All per-sons	Children under 18 years	Children 5 to 17 years in families
	46	47	48	49	50	51	52	53	54	55	56	57	58	59	60	61
IDAHO—Cont'd																
Caribou	43	531	1 665	8.2	48.4	16.2	12.8	8 486	20 637	44 958	-5.6	0.6	49 208	12.1	16.1	14.0
Cassia	170	1 948	6 488	8.0	47.9	15.7	33.8	6 558	17 782	39 866	-5.5	1.6	40 739	15.7	21.0	19.0
Clark	204	407	159	0.0	67.5	5.3	2.5	11 686	19 737	40 909	2.3	0.0	41 387	17.9	26.6	23.4
Clearwater	320	1 689	1 565	8.1	57.3	14.4	11.2	9 194	20 507	41 835	3.0	1.6	38 124	15.3	26.3	22.6
Custer	NA	NA	803	2.2	46.8	24.5	6.2	9 591	22 625	41 910	2.9	0.9	42 575	14.9	19.8	16.4
Elmore	303	1 442	7 588	10.5	42.9	14.6	35.1	7 116	20 388	43 089	-3.5	0.9	40 475	15.8	22.1	19.5
Franklin	31	391	3 681	8.4	49.5	18.5	17.7	5 722	17 967	45 682	0.0	1.7	43 936	10.5	14.7	13.2
Fremont	53	755	3 256	10.4	42.8	19.8	17.0	6 885	18 616	42 523	0.5	1.5	38 407	16.4	23.6	21.4
Gem	126	801	4 150	11.0	49.6	12.6	17.8	6 735	20 431	42 794	-1.9	0.6	40 110	17.1	24.7	21.7
Gooding	129	841	3 488	6.2	59.0	11.5	22.2	7 416	17 694	37 228	-7.8	2.2	37 751	16.4	23.1	21.4
Idaho	86	1 057	3 005	9.7	58.2	12.3	18.0	10 462	18 980	34 536	-7.6	1.0	35 715	18.3	26.6	23.2
Jefferson	73	692	7 340	11.9	43.5	17.8	37.2	6 248	19 019	51 579	7.9	1.0	50 123	12.0	15.8	14.4
Jerome	156	1 287	5 534	8.5	58.5	12.1	27.0	6 357	16 947	39 188	-10.8	0.7	40 229	19.1	25.1	22.2
Kootenai	295	2 560	32 971	14.4	38.1	23.2	136.1	6 463	24 418	46 336	-3.1	2.2	43 826	14.6	17.7	15.0
Latah	113	1 922	15 280	7.1	29.3	41.8	43.2	8 559	20 218	36 974	-10.2	0.9	40 942	17.6	14.9	13.0
Lemhi	151	592	1 464	14.2	37.5	22.3	8.5	7 964	21 699	36 411	-4.7	1.2	34 757	21.1	32.6	28.6
Lewis	183	1 256	773	10.6	46.2	16.5	9.5	10 519	18 580	35 808	-10.0	0.3	37 742	17.8	28.6	24.5
Lincoln	NA	NA	1 235	4.7	56.6	11.4	8.5	8 307	19 011	45 714	11.1	0.5	39 517	14.1	19.0	16.6
Madison	53	829	19 122	59.1	24.7	30.0	37.7	6 189	13 735	35 461	-14.1	1.4	36 202	28.4	20.1	19.5
Minidoka	115	1 390	5 225	7.1	59.1	9.4	29.1	7 097	17 747	40 350	-0.5	0.9	39 802	15.8	22.1	19.9
Nez Perce	160	3 718	9 189	10.3	45.6	18.2	50.7	8 989	23 899	44 395	-3.4	1.6	43 580	12.5	17.8	15.2
Oneida	93	327	1 213	4.1	45.1	15.6	6.3	7 044	17 950	44 599	2.7	0.3	44 425	12.4	16.6	14.5
Owyhee	165	2 299	2 880	12.7	61.7	10.3	19.7	7 457	17 373	33 441	-6.8	2.5	36 670	22.7	32.2	28.5
Payette	305	1 861	6 045	10.2	53.7	13.8	28.4	6 441	18 814	43 559	4.1	0.6	39 724	17.1	23.3	20.1
Power	115	1 407	1 936	3.9	49.0	18.9	14.8	8 909	18 412	40 843	0.1	0.9	39 555	16.4	24.3	22.9
Shoshone	345	2 092	2 415	6.6	55.2	11.9	20.0	9 775	19 020	36 654	1.4	0.1	36 129	20.8	27.3	22.6
Teton	39	757	2 129	8.9	34.8	31.6	11.1	6 996	23 633	53 364	0.4	1.4	52 272	11.3	17.2	16.7
Twin Falls	265	2 252	18 575	11.7	46.7	16.8	86.4	6 754	19 892	42 455	-2.8	1.1	42 007	15.4	19.0	17.1
Valley	284	2 261	1 838	19.9	36.4	36.1	14.3	10 865	27 577	50 851	8.7	2.4	45 248	12.6	21.6	19.3
Washington	88	549	2 358	9.5	50.3	17.4	14.6	7 718	20 015	36 542	-5.8	2.8	35 774	17.0	26.4	21.3
ILLINOIS	435	2 681	3 504 636	19.3	41.8	30.3	22 936.4	10 833	28 782	55 735	-5.5	4.7	52 967	13.8	19.4	18.1
Adams	315	2 378	17 177	23.6	50.2	21.1	89.5	9 835	24 308	43 824	-0.5	2.1	41 734	13.2	18.3	16.9
Alexander	1 262	3 302	2 211	8.4	60.7	9.5	17.2	14 159	15 858	28 833	-12.6	0.8	29 278	31.1	49.0	47.4
Bond	51	1 581	4 744	26.2	46.9	24.7	18.5	7 505	24 341	51 946	8.9	1.3	46 364	13.7	18.8	16.2
Boone	174	1 603	15 159	16.5	52.2	20.8	99.4	9 280	26 105	61 210	-7.7	5.1	57 323	11.6	16.9	14.2
Brown	317	346	1 426	5.8	59.4	10.9	6.8	8 408	17 133	38 696	-13.8	0.8	43 640	14.4	13.8	12.9
Bureau	69	1 632	8 042	10.6	52.8	16.1	54.3	9 373	24 103	45 892	-10.3	1.4	45 580	11.2	17.6	15.2
Calhoun	334	1 002	1 099	16.4	58.7	12.5	7.0	9 803	23 109	44 891	3.1	1.4	45 772	10.9	15.4	13.4
Carroll	74	1 705	3 329	8.3	54.4	15.9	25.8	9 499	25 914	44 805	-4.8	1.6	47 032	13.0	21.0	18.2
Cass	NA	NA	3 412	7.2	62.5	12.3	19.7	8 094	19 825	41 544	-6.9	0.7	43 183	12.8	19.5	18.4
Champaign	624	2 560	79 617	6.8	31.1	41.2	238.1	10 143	24 553	45 262	-5.4	2.8	45 803	19.6	20.2	20.0
Christian	257	896	8 113	11.6	56.8	12.1	63.2	9 716	21 519	41 712	-9.9	1.3	44 253	14.2	20.0	17.4
Clark	282	976	4 107	6.5	51.2	16.4	23.9	8 090	23 173	43 597	-4.3	2.0	44 312	12.1	18.6	17.2
Clay	58	1 455	3 060	1.9	56.2	13.8	24.0	8 292	20 802	38 016	-1.9	0.9	38 091	15.3	22.3	19.7
Clinton	125	1 496	9 193	15.7	44.8	18.9	42.9	7 768	25 392	55 278	-2.2	2.0	52 650	8.4	11.9	10.5
Coles	297	1 886	20 071	4.8	45.6	23.3	76.4	11 637	20 601	36 457	-10.8	2.3	38 242	18.7	21.9	20.5
Cook	665	3 509	1 398 209	23.8	41.7	33.2	9 535.8	11 815	29 335	53 942	-7.2	5.3	51 457	16.8	24.5	23.9
Crawford	NA	NA	4 614	11.5	49.6	13.5	28.5	9 060	21 545	41 434	0.6	1.1	41 612	14.9	20.1	17.6
Cumberland	63	640	2 611	7.3	55.0	13.0	14.4	7 920	21 262	42 101	-8.0	1.5	43 448	11.6	17.7	16.2
DeKalb	223	2 219	39 786	7.7	39.0	28.0	190.4	10 832	24 179	54 002	-6.9	2.3	52 106	14.3	14.5	12.9
De Witt	NA	NA	3 938	5.1	56.2	15.7	25.0	8 197	24 320	45 347	-13.2	1.6	48 662	10.9	16.8	14.7
Douglas	115	748	4 745	8.2	57.4	14.9	25.9	8 986	21 438	46 941	-6.0	0.9	48 469	11.1	16.9	14.5
DuPage	102	1 715	259 225	23.8	28.2	45.3	1 914.6	11 898	37 849	76 581	-10.9	8.9	72 470	6.9	8.8	7.9
Edgar	382	931	3 943	7.5	53.6	16.8	28.4	8 771	22 175	39 904	-10.5	1.1	39 386	14.3	21.8	19.0
Edwards	NA	NA	1 539	12.7	45.4	13.1	8.4	8 494	21 113	40 430	0.4	1.3	43 044	11.3	17.4	15.8
Effingham	105	1 630	8 334	13.2	47.4	20.0	45.7	8 452	24 843	49 509	-0.7	2.0	49 001	9.9	14.9	13.4
Fayette	212	1 400	5 331	8.8	59.5	14.3	28.7	7 912	21 663	41 269	2.3	1.0	38 966	15.8	22.7	21.0
Ford	NA	NA	3 383	8.2	53.8	17.8	29.5	9 132	23 401	48 667	0.9	0.5	48 622	11.0	16.9	14.8
Franklin	423	2 494	9 142	4.4	49.7	12.4	60.6	9 139	18 504	34 381	-4.4	0.2	32 853	20.3	27.9	26.7
Fulton	178	1 707	8 373	6.1	54.5	13.4	59.3	8 560	20 309	41 268	-4.0	1.4	40 749	14.5	19.4	17.0
Gallatin	107	1 807	1 115	3.8	58.8	10.1	7.6	9 495	21 537	38 003	14.9	1.5	37 287	18.5	27.7	25.9
Greene	133	882	3 446	12.2	58.5	13.5	18.2	8 261	22 107	41 450	3.1	1.2	40 399	14.9	22.3	20.5
Grundy	100	2 067	12 980	10.1	44.4	18.3	128.7	10 313	27 895	64 297	-1.8	2.3	60 130	8.0	9.4	8.5
Hamilton	NA	NA	1 811	6.0	55.7	12.7	17.7	8 746	21 602	35 032	-9.3	1.2	40 670	14.6	22.5	20.7
Hancock	NA	NA	4 343	7.1	50.2	19.1	32.3	10 320	22 885	42 857	-7.7	1.3	41 520	13.4	20.1	18.2

1. Data for serious crimes have not been adjusted for underreporting; this may affect comparability between geographic areas and over time. 2. Per 100,000 population estimated by the FBI. 3. All persons 3 years old and over enrolled in nursery school through college. 4. Persons 25 years old and over. 5. Elementary and secondary education expenditures. 6. Based on population estimated by the American Community Survey, 2006-2010.

Table B. States and Counties — **Personal Income**

STATE County	Personal income, 2009												
			Per capita[1]					Transfer payments (mil dol)					
									Government payments to individuals				
	Total (mil dol)	Percent change, 2008–2009	Dollars	Rank	Wages and salaries[2] (mil dol)	Proprietors' income (mil dol)	Dividends, interest, and rent (mil dol)	Total	Total	Social Security	Medical payments	Income maintenance	Unemployment insurance
	62	63	64	65	66	67	68	69	70	71	72	73	74
IDAHO—Cont'd													
Caribou	217	-1.1	31 447	1 651	192	17	41	42	40	18	15	3	2
Cassia	675	-8.0	31 129	1 724	396	120	120	132	128	47	55	14	4
Clark	39	-10.5	40 907	388	28	8	4	4	4	1	2	0	0
Clearwater	254	0.6	31 560	1 631	126	19	52	79	78	34	28	5	5
Custer	142	5.2	33 596	1 234	77	20	34	27	27	12	10	1	1
Elmore	888	-1.0	30 826	1 796	646	53	100	139	134	41	46	15	8
Franklin	331	-3.8	26 129	2 701	112	37	43	61	59	25	23	5	1
Fremont	310	1.1	24 433	2 922	121	13	61	71	69	27	26	6	5
Gem	451	-2.4	27 464	2 490	118	21	87	124	121	49	43	9	9
Gooding	467	-19.0	32 355	1 449	256	49	79	89	86	33	35	8	4
Idaho	425	-1.6	27 506	2 481	181	41	104	112	109	45	41	7	7
Jefferson	628	-2.1	25 333	2 824	215	74	83	118	113	42	46	10	7
Jerome	626	-7.1	29 437	2 107	364	110	82	113	110	39	44	12	6
Kootenai	4 428	-0.5	31 770	1 585	2 265	333	917	912	886	358	315	64	64
Latah	1 139	-0.3	29 933	1 997	605	89	226	183	176	67	59	13	7
Lemhi	238	-0.5	30 092	1 957	99	18	67	69	67	27	28	4	3
Lewis	146	-1.5	39 029	536	51	23	26	52	51	22	22	4	1
Lincoln	132	-10.2	28 455	2 307	68	25	18	27	27	11	8	2	3
Madison	674	1.4	17 543	3 108	473	66	97	153	146	34	42	12	5
Minidoka	562	-0.5	29 217	2 148	275	79	81	119	115	40	51	12	5
Nez Perce	1 342	-0.8	34 215	1 140	941	118	246	317	310	119	129	24	8
Oneida	109	-0.3	25 729	2 769	38	10	17	27	26	11	12	2	1
Owyhee	307	-6.2	27 367	2 504	100	51	46	61	59	24	23	6	1
Payette	613	-2.7	26 527	2 637	250	34	125	145	141	57	47	17	8
Power	203	-1.1	26 240	2 682	152	10	34	42	41	15	15	5	2
Shoshone	390	-1.2	30 811	1 800	199	23	61	125	122	46	47	11	10
Teton	249	-7.8	26 667	2 613	121	13	53	33	31	11	12	2	3
Twin Falls	2 317	-3.1	30 773	1 808	1 303	303	418	482	469	171	188	43	23
Valley	334	-5.4	38 313	599	155	25	106	63	61	25	19	3	8
Washington	275	-1.4	27 208	2 530	107	14	60	77	76	30	28	8	4
ILLINOIS	540 380	-2.6	41 856	X	354 969	44 948	99 248	85 333	82 984	26 771	34 817	8 788	6 901
Adams	2 369	-0.8	35 329	976	1 547	130	478	492	479	185	182	42	29
Alexander	204	3.8	25 831	2 756	84	6	22	91	90	22	41	18	4
Bond	562	-2.0	31 055	1 743	210	44	86	123	120	43	47	12	9
Boone	1 679	-3.1	31 072	1 738	696	67	276	293	283	119	83	22	41
Brown	170	1.1	25 861	2 753	157	16	28	34	33	13	14	3	2
Bureau	1 218	-3.8	35 096	1 005	600	101	208	250	244	101	91	17	21
Calhoun	160	-0.7	31 857	1 563	31	13	28	41	40	17	15	2	3
Carroll	505	-2.3	32 037	1 520	180	37	106	131	129	50	49	9	9
Cass	435	1.1	32 050	1 517	258	45	60	99	96	33	41	8	6
Champaign	6 545	0.2	33 450	1 267	5 034	361	1 260	918	882	285	298	111	89
Christian	1 188	-0.6	34 694	1 065	490	142	184	283	277	103	117	22	18
Clark	538	-3.5	32 292	1 458	182	61	95	128	125	47	49	10	11
Clay	433	0.6	31 990	1 531	218	55	66	127	124	39	60	10	8
Clinton	1 310	-3.7	36 011	884	484	103	216	239	233	85	98	14	17
Coles	1 603	-0.1	30 791	1 802	1 062	121	288	352	342	112	132	32	26
Cook	244 055	-2.8	46 161	164	174 356	26 596	47 859	38 490	37 527	9 821	17 816	4 735	2 801
Crawford	670	0.4	34 469	1 100	445	64	114	143	140	57	52	11	10
Cumberland	348	-3.0	32 482	1 433	92	43	48	75	73	29	27	6	6
DeKalb	3 066	-6.1	28 570	2 286	1 761	171	565	532	512	175	174	41	60
De Witt	579	-1.0	36 111	871	306	64	82	122	119	45	47	9	8
Douglas	688	-3.6	35 872	903	354	111	116	122	119	51	41	9	9
DuPage	48 911	-5.3	52 449	71	38 691	4 116	9 208	4 739	4 569	1 867	1 682	260	454
Edgar	595	-3.5	32 192	1 486	284	67	99	149	146	54	59	13	11
Edwards	198	-1.4	30 740	1 813	119	25	40	45	44	19	15	3	3
Effingham	1 187	-1.4	34 473	1 099	846	96	255	228	221	84	92	17	15
Fayette	564	0.6	26 944	2 576	244	55	96	164	160	57	66	16	11
Ford	555	-3.6	39 888	455	214	102	82	100	98	39	39	7	7
Franklin	1 100	3.0	27 979	2 403	381	65	160	372	365	127	149	37	24
Fulton	1 189	-0.4	32 439	1 441	348	87	178	310	303	109	132	23	22
Gallatin	184	0.0	32 259	1 469	54	24	33	56	55	19	24	5	3
Greene	396	1.2	29 218	2 147	108	51	62	109	106	38	44	10	6
Grundy	1 658	-1.9	34 233	1 137	1 033	107	269	271	262	105	92	15	33
Hamilton	256	2.0	31 661	1 613	64	35	41	74	73	25	33	6	4
Hancock	621	-3.8	33 823	1 198	180	94	106	144	140	57	53	10	11

1. Based on the resident population estimated as of July 1 of the year shown.   2. Includes supplements to wages and salaries.

STATE County	Earnings, 2009 Total (mil dol)	Farm	Goods-related[1] Total	Manu-facturing	Service-related and health — Infor-mation and profes-sional and technical services	Retail trade	Finance, insur-ance, and real estate	Health care and social services	Govern-ment	Social Security beneficiaries, December 2010 — Number	Rate[2]	Supple-mental Security Income recipients, December 2010	Housing units, 2010 — Total	Percent change, 2000–2010
	75	76	77	78	79	80	81	82	83	84	85	86	87	88
IDAHO—Cont'd														
Caribou	209	5.3	D	D	4.0	4.0	2.4	D	14.6	1 370	197	71	3 226	1.2
Cassia	516	24.8	15.8	10.7	4.3	8.2	2.5	D	14.8	4 040	176	406	8 372	6.5
Clark	36	29.9	D	D	D	D	3.1	D	21.1	130	132	0	531	1.9
Clearwater	145	2.4	13.9	7.0	2.7	6.5	2.3	D	38.1	2 785	318	252	4 453	7.5
Custer	97	13.2	D	D	4.3	5.0	1.5	2.1	24.6	1 060	243	65	3 103	4.0
Elmore	699	7.4	D	2.5	D	4.1	1.7	2.7	68.1	3 720	138	403	12 162	15.5
Franklin	149	19.4	13.9	4.6	4.4	8.7	2.8	D	24.1	2 100	164	161	4 528	16.9
Fremont	134	3.1	D	1.3	D	6.2	3.9	D	39.7	2 305	174	173	8 531	23.8
Gem	140	4.5	D	4.6	4.1	7.2	4.0	D	28.5	4 160	249	407	7 099	20.6
Gooding	306	31.2	D	13.9	D	4.3	D	D	15.4	2 895	187	280	6 093	10.7
Idaho	222	4.7	17.7	9.2	4.4	8.4	4.2	9.3	31.2	3 925	241	352	8 744	16.0
Jefferson	289	20.1	D	11.1	D	5.4	2.8	4.5	19.2	3 600	138	298	8 722	38.7
Jerome	475	24.8	17.0	12.1	3.5	7.3	1.7	4.3	10.0	3 420	153	363	8 101	20.7
Kootenai	2 598	0.4	18.2	8.1	8.8	10.7	6.6	12.6	20.6	29 290	211	2 315	63 177	35.6
Latah	694	3.8	D	3.0	7.5	8.2	2.6	9.2	46.6	5 295	142	414	15 988	15.5
Lemhi	116	1.4	D	3.4	6.9	9.1	2.6	8.0	39.4	2 350	296	182	4 729	13.8
Lewis	74	25.1	D	8.0	D	8.1	2.5	6.0	25.6	1 940	508	226	1 880	4.7
Lincoln	93	37.4	D	D	D	2.7	D	5.2	27.4	1 035	199	68	1 976	19.7
Madison	539	0.7	D	6.5	7.1	8.2	3.6	D	17.2	2 700	72	202	11 280	47.8
Minidoka	364	25.4	D	16.3	3.8	4.2	1.9	D	17.4	3 470	179	372	7 665	2.2
Nez Perce	1 059	2.1	D	16.1	5.2	8.6	7.7	16.7	19.0	9 515	242	1 048	17 438	7.6
Oneida	47	18.9	D	1.2	2.1	8.0	D	3.3	35.2	920	215	64	1 906	8.6
Owyhee	152	43.9	D	4.1	D	4.2	D	D	20.0	2 130	185	283	4 781	7.4
Payette	284	6.5	D	19.8	D	5.0	4.2	D	17.1	4 980	220	550	8 945	12.5
Power	162	11.6	40.0	38.2	D	2.8	D	1.3	17.6	1 325	170	118	2 944	3.5
Shoshone	222	-0.1	29.2	4.6	4.9	19.1	2.4	6.2	21.4	3 685	289	424	7 061	0.1
Teton	134	5.3	D	3.3	13.3	7.1	5.6	2.1	22.8	975	96	68	5 478	108.2
Twin Falls	1 606	10.0	14.4	9.2	7.4	9.5	5.1	15.2	13.9	14 415	187	1 612	31 072	21.4
Valley	180	0.3	12.5	1.4	6.9	11.1	6.1	D	36.1	2 055	208	89	11 789	45.8
Washington	121	5.8	D	13.9	8.1	7.8	3.4	D	27.1	2 660	261	243	4 529	9.4
ILLINOIS	399 917	1.0	17.0	11.2	14.6	5.2	10.1	10.2	14.8	2 033 345	158	273 310	5 296 715	8.4
Adams	1 676	2.2	D	18.5	5.4	8.1	7.3	17.9	14.0	14 755	220	1 271	29 842	1.6
Alexander	90	2.2	D	8.0	1.6	3.5	1.4	D	36.5	2 000	243	529	4 006	-12.7
Bond	254	9.8	18.5	14.5	3.5	3.3	2.2	D	25.7	3 460	195	332	7 089	6.0
Boone	763	1.9	48.8	38.3	3.1	5.7	2.6	3.9	16.2	8 845	163	460	19 970	29.6
Brown	173	6.2	D	D	D	1.5	D	D	17.2	1 060	153	105	2 462	0.2
Bureau	701	8.4	D	15.2	D	5.0	4.2	D	15.8	7 660	219	352	15 720	2.5
Calhoun	44	15.8	D	D	D	9.6	D	D	27.4	1 330	261	84	2 835	5.7
Carroll	217	8.9	D	18.6	D	6.1	5.9	D	19.2	4 065	264	249	8 437	6.2
Cass	303	11.2	35.5	32.5	4.0	4.9	3.4	D	14.2	2 650	194	246	5 836	0.9
Champaign	5 395	2.3	D	7.8	8.9	5.2	4.4	13.6	37.4	24 400	121	2 850	87 569	16.3
Christian	631	15.5	23.1	15.8	D	6.9	3.5	10.8	15.3	8 085	232	696	15 563	3.8
Clark	243	12.7	32.8	22.4	3.9	6.0	3.4	5.9	17.1	3 795	232	290	7 772	-0.6
Clay	273	8.7	38.5	30.9	D	5.4	3.2	D	17.4	3 325	241	358	6 404	0.2
Clinton	587	7.2	D	6.5	4.8	8.3	5.3	12.6	22.5	6 980	185	456	15 311	11.0
Coles	1 183	4.1	17.3	12.3	D	5.8	3.5	15.3	28.3	9 315	173	1 064	23 425	2.9
Cook	200 953	0.0	13.2	7.8	19.8	4.0	13.5	9.6	12.6	748 985	144	157 804	2 180 359	4.0
Crawford	509	4.3	50.4	41.9	2.7	4.6	2.7	D	18.5	4 490	227	326	8 661	-1.4
Cumberland	135	14.6	D	13.6	D	11.7	D	9.8	17.2	2 425	219	190	4 874	0.0
DeKalb	1 932	2.5	18.1	11.5	4.3	7.6	3.7	11.9	33.6	13 295	126	732	41 079	24.5
De Witt	370	10.1	16.4	8.6	D	6.1	2.6	D	14.2	3 440	208	235	7 521	3.3
Douglas	465	13.5	D	36.3	1.5	6.1	3.2	D	9.9	3 990	200	239	8 390	4.8
DuPage	42 807	0.0	14.9	9.5	17.5	5.6	9.0	8.4	8.3	127 585	139	7 709	356 179	6.1
Edgar	351	13.3	D	25.2	3.6	5.5	7.0	D	17.9	4 370	235	449	8 803	2.2
Edwards	144	6.6	D	D	D	4.0	D	2.3	9.9	1 610	240	96	3 187	-0.4
Effingham	942	2.5	24.4	17.7	D	9.0	3.5	19.1	11.5	6 865	200	443	14 570	4.4
Fayette	299	9.1	18.3	11.4	3.1	8.1	3.9	D	25.5	4 895	221	510	9 302	2.8
Ford	316	20.9	D	10.6	3.2	5.2	3.0	D	13.0	3 065	218	197	6 282	3.7
Franklin	446	2.1	17.7	11.0	D	10.8	3.3	10.3	26.1	10 380	262	1 438	18 525	2.3
Fulton	435	10.5	D	2.8	3.9	8.4	4.3	D	28.7	8 560	231	703	16 195	-0.3
Gallatin	78	23.1	D	D	D	5.8	D	D	16.6	1 575	282	240	2 746	-10.6
Greene	158	25.0	D	6.2	2.4	7.4	5.8	D	21.2	3 195	230	353	6 389	0.9
Grundy	1 140	3.9	24.4	11.9	3.8	6.4	2.5	D	11.8	7 700	154	355	19 996	33.0
Hamilton	99	23.0	10.9	3.2	D	4.4	2.9	5.0	29.5	2 115	250	209	4 104	3.1
Hancock	274	25.4	D	10.8	5.9	4.7	3.9	D	18.6	4 555	238	313	9 274	4.1

1. Includes mining, construction, and manufacturing.   2. Per 1,000 resident population enumerated in the 2010 census.

Table B. States and Counties — Housing, Labor Force, and Employment

STATE County	Housing units, 2006–2010 Total	Occupied units Percent	Owner-occupied Median value[1]	Median owner cost as a percent of income — With a mortgage	Without a mortgage	Renter-occupied Median rent[2]	Median rent as a percent of income	Sub-standard units[3] (percent)	Civilian labor force, 2010 Total	Percent change, 2009–2010	Unemployment Total	Rate[4]	Civilian employment,[5] 2006–2010 Total	Percent — Management, business, science and arts	Construction, production, and maintenance occupations
	89	90	91	92	93	94	95	96	97	98	99	100	101	102	103
IDAHO—Cont'd															
Caribou	2 726	79.2	116 000	19.9	10.4	509	18.8	3.0	3 782	9.7	303	8.0	3 034	28.1	36.3
Cassia	7 550	68.6	114 600	23.2	10.3	515	25.6	4.3	10 960	8.0	777	7.1	9 158	27.5	37.6
Clark	334	77.5	82 800	19.0	10.0	468	16.5	10.8	558	3.1	50	9.0	420	32.9	60.7
Clearwater	3 656	78.2	124 800	21.7	10.8	536	20.3	1.9	3 372	-2.6	524	15.5	3 437	27.3	32.1
Custer	1 918	80.1	127 600	21.8	10.0	445	23.6	1.2	2 557	-4.2	189	7.4	2 152	30.5	34.9
Elmore	9 522	67.5	142 600	23.8	10.0	658	26.5	2.5	11 392	1.2	1 062	9.3	10 353	25.0	32.7
Franklin	4 080	80.9	165 300	24.7	10.0	549	26.4	3.3	5 854	1.7	342	5.8	5 176	26.3	38.2
Fremont	4 504	81.6	125 000	22.4	11.5	616	19.3	5.4	5 736	3.2	577	10.1	6 037	27.3	35.9
Gem	6 512	79.4	161 700	24.0	10.2	666	31.2	2.7	6 937	-0.4	815	11.7	7 079	27.8	28.3
Gooding	5 512	72.7	127 500	26.3	12.2	553	24.4	5.3	8 961	8.3	635	7.1	6 335	25.2	41.7
Idaho	6 596	75.8	140 900	27.8	10.0	510	25.6	4.2	7 321	0.1	848	11.6	5 993	26.2	34.4
Jefferson	7 781	81.9	154 000	23.8	10.0	639	23.2	4.5	11 622	2.7	896	7.7	10 648	29.6	32.8
Jerome	7 229	64.6	135 200	24.4	10.0	660	25.5	5.1	10 328	2.0	883	8.5	9 520	24.8	42.4
Kootenai	54 560	70.7	220 000	26.9	11.6	768	29.8	2.5	71 444	0.5	7 862	11.0	63 529	31.6	24.8
Latah	14 635	54.0	183 800	23.2	11.1	634	37.2	1.8	17 174	-3.3	1 351	7.9	18 215	39.8	18.4
Lemhi	3 545	72.8	174 900	22.4	10.0	496	29.1	3.2	3 807	-2.6	400	10.5	3 572	31.1	31.4
Lewis	1 644	72.6	112 100	22.3	10.1	541	28.1	1.2	1 766	3.1	112	6.3	1 524	29.1	29.0
Lincoln	1 814	75.4	124 600	22.3	10.0	572	25.6	3.6	2 605	2.7	350	13.4	2 353	20.6	42.8
Madison	9 868	52.0	169 700	24.2	10.0	595	34.3	7.6	16 450	3.7	1 082	6.6	16 291	31.2	21.0
Minidoka	6 751	76.7	98 400	22.4	10.7	506	22.2	5.4	10 203	9.5	790	7.7	8 369	23.0	42.8
Nez Perce	16 163	67.6	159 600	22.0	11.3	585	26.7	1.6	18 883	2.1	1 380	7.3	18 522	27.4	27.9
Oneida	1 556	81.2	120 400	25.3	12.3	525	30.9	1.8	2 303	4.7	123	5.3	1 690	35.7	32.1
Owyhee	4 016	67.8	133 500	25.1	11.1	540	24.6	7.2	4 328	3.2	224	5.2	4 448	30.2	38.0
Payette	8 303	74.5	134 800	24.1	10.8	605	28.6	1.8	11 066	3.5	1 076	9.7	9 400	25.9	32.1
Power	2 598	73.2	121 900	25.3	10.0	558	20.5	3.7	3 557	0.0	354	10.0	3 394	31.9	36.0
Shoshone	5 776	71.4	145 000	24.1	12.5	524	25.4	3.5	6 076	-1.9	913	15.0	5 100	25.2	33.2
Teton	3 786	59.7	294 800	30.6	10.4	820	23.8	5.5	5 147	2.0	406	7.9	5 422	28.6	31.3
Twin Falls	27 626	67.9	148 400	24.1	10.5	650	25.6	2.8	38 567	-0.4	3 249	8.4	34 731	26.9	30.7
Valley	4 388	77.7	287 100	24.9	10.2	727	20.5	4.8	4 642	-0.7	756	16.3	4 964	33.0	30.3
Washington	4 010	75.3	140 200	26.2	10.5	520	29.1	3.0	4 736	-2.9	508	10.7	4 251	29.7	31.3
ILLINOIS	4 769 951	69.2	202 500	25.7	13.7	834	30.3	2.9	6 602 654	0.2	691 911	10.5	6 062 848	35.6	22.2
Adams	27 149	73.8	98 400	19.9	11.6	552	27.7	0.9	38 371	0.7	2 846	7.4	32 948	29.8	25.7
Alexander	3 316	71.4	58 200	18.8	14.1	374	30.2	2.5	2 982	-3.7	351	11.8	3 113	22.1	24.0
Bond	6 255	81.2	106 500	21.6	12.4	643	25.1	0.4	8 636	-0.5	870	10.1	8 419	30.0	27.6
Boone	17 908	82.6	174 400	25.8	13.8	719	31.3	3.5	26 452	1.5	4 194	15.9	23 878	28.7	33.8
Brown	2 139	74.6	80 100	22.3	12.9	469	26.4	0.6	3 572	2.8	181	5.1	2 351	29.1	30.6
Bureau	14 580	75.2	102 000	21.5	13.2	582	26.3	1.9	19 555	0.9	2 222	11.4	16 862	23.5	34.6
Calhoun	2 045	78.6	101 900	22.0	13.4	540	28.5	1.8	2 524	-0.6	274	10.9	2 188	29.0	30.8
Carroll	7 010	76.3	98 500	21.9	13.3	511	24.6	0.8	8 424	2.0	954	11.3	7 653	28.9	30.8
Cass	5 057	71.4	77 300	19.5	11.8	603	26.2	2.5	7 793	1.0	607	7.8	6 194	21.7	39.2
Champaign	77 851	55.9	145 200	22.0	11.1	730	35.0	1.6	106 393	1.5	9 567	9.0	99 764	42.9	15.9
Christian	14 135	75.0	80 500	21.2	12.9	576	28.9	2.2	18 266	2.8	1 819	10.0	15 193	26.1	29.0
Clark	6 747	77.1	84 100	19.3	13.1	577	28.2	1.5	8 260	2.3	1 041	12.6	7 826	29.9	33.0
Clay	5 615	76.4	72 700	20.0	12.0	498	27.0	2.6	6 631	2.9	805	12.1	6 020	27.8	36.8
Clinton	13 999	80.0	124 200	21.2	12.0	608	23.4	2.2	18 730	-1.1	1 552	8.3	17 802	30.3	28.1
Coles	20 906	62.5	89 500	21.1	11.9	598	37.0	2.1	27 941	1.8	2 676	9.6	23 670	29.3	29.0
Cook	1 936 481	60.4	265 800	28.8	15.1	900	31.3	4.3	2 604 300	0.1	272 436	10.5	2 438 989	36.8	20.5
Crawford	7 819	80.4	70 400	19.1	11.6	525	27.5	2.1	9 789	0.7	934	9.5	8 879	24.9	34.7
Cumberland	4 172	79.7	81 300	20.4	12.2	518	23.9	1.7	5 628	0.7	586	10.4	5 272	23.9	36.1
DeKalb	37 825	62.7	192 600	26.6	14.6	797	33.3	3.0	60 076	1.0	5 831	9.7	53 681	32.7	23.8
De Witt	6 811	76.0	96 200	19.9	13.1	566	23.6	1.0	9 035	4.8	796	8.8	8 074	26.6	30.5
Douglas	7 572	78.3	93 000	21.1	12.0	609	31.8	2.8	10 281	0.9	955	9.3	9 668	26.4	34.0
DuPage	335 453	76.1	316 900	26.4	14.0	1 008	28.4	2.1	524 521	0.2	43 516	8.3	470 105	43.8	16.2
Edgar	7 877	76.0	74 200	20.0	13.7	544	23.7	0.7	10 360	1.6	1 122	10.8	8 587	26.5	35.6
Edwards	2 788	77.3	61 400	18.8	11.0	461	22.5	1.5	3 186	2.6	292	9.2	3 205	26.1	40.0
Effingham	13 462	79.0	106 500	21.0	11.3	541	26.0	1.5	18 471	1.6	1 548	8.4	17 377	28.5	30.1
Fayette	8 176	79.5	73 200	20.6	11.5	540	26.5	2.1	10 562	3.5	1 216	11.5	10 109	28.0	32.6
Ford	5 638	79.1	90 700	21.0	11.8	573	22.7	1.2	7 130	-1.1	718	10.1	6 772	28.5	30.3
Franklin	16 228	78.5	61 100	21.5	13.1	507	28.2	1.8	18 214	2.4	2 339	12.8	15 565	23.8	30.3
Fulton	14 673	78.4	79 000	22.2	13.9	565	30.0	2.0	18 774	1.5	2 188	11.7	15 400	28.3	29.3
Gallatin	2 377	79.0	56 600	19.0	11.2	374	25.8	2.7	2 688	1.4	271	10.1	2 391	28.1	34.1
Greene	5 789	78.3	72 000	20.4	11.2	472	26.4	2.5	6 976	3.2	671	9.6	6 374	27.4	33.4
Grundy	17 961	76.8	193 300	24.9	13.5	894	27.3	2.1	26 784	1.5	3 325	12.4	23 589	29.1	28.9
Hamilton	3 503	83.7	67 500	19.9	12.2	353	35.3	3.2	4 115	-0.2	400	9.7	3 606	27.7	34.1
Hancock	8 012	79.9	80 200	20.4	12.1	483	22.6	2.0	9 584	1.2	1 104	11.5	9 359	27.9	33.4

1. Specified owner-occupied units.   2. Specified renter-occupied units. A value of 10.0 represents 10 percent or less.   3. Overcrowded or lacking complete plumbing facilities.   4. Percent of civilian labor force.   5. Persons 16 years old and over.

Table B. States and Counties — Nonfarm Employment and Agriculture

STATE County	Private nonfarm establishments, employment and payroll, 2009									Agriculture, 2007			
		Employment					Annual payroll		Farms			
											Percent with:		
	Number of establishments	Total	Health care and social assistance	Manufacturing	Retail trade	Finance and insurance	Professional, scientific, and technical services	Total (mil dol)	Average per employee (dollars)	Number	Fewer than 50 acres	500 acres or more	Farm operators whose principal occupation is farming (percent)
	104	105	106	107	108	109	110	111	112	113	114	115	116
IDAHO—Cont'd													
Caribou	192	2 683	D	709	324	D	247	131	48 690	454	17.0	40.5	50.2
Cassia	641	6 787	1 199	1 094	1 396	223	192	179	26 429	644	36.8	33.9	53.9
Clark	16	269	D	D	39	D	D	5	18 602	81	19.8	51.9	54.3
Clearwater	257	1 824	563	D	268	50	45	56	30 493	241	34.0	15.8	44.0
Custer	156	931	D	D	139	25	D	34	36 436	261	36.8	21.8	51.3
Elmore	449	3 983	728	D	971	207	121	99	24 737	381	54.6	20.5	44.1
Franklin	299	1 997	334	216	514	76	55	48	23 937	739	37.6	17.7	41.9
Fremont	304	1 404	187	46	215	49	D	38	26 709	536	30.8	23.9	48.9
Gem	364	2 110	648	63	342	D	49	48	22 919	822	68.7	6.3	47.9
Gooding	344	2 646	520	553	353	77	72	76	28 535	665	53.4	11.7	57.1
Idaho	490	3 020	605	D	497	141	D	84	27 935	760	26.8	31.2	51.4
Jefferson	457	3 675	321	864	463	D	84	90	24 518	826	55.8	16.3	44.9
Jerome	536	5 768	481	1 374	1 020	97	145	172	29 738	604	51.0	15.1	54.0
Kootenai	4 510	44 289	7 881	3 926	7 406	2 068	3 114	1 380	31 155	826	57.9	8.0	40.0
Latah	907	8 644	1 221	311	1 959	242	479	206	23 819	1 104	30.0	14.5	36.7
Lemhi	314	1 635	457	D	390	36	D	37	22 816	342	48.8	22.5	57.3
Lewis	132	748	D	174	D	D	D	18	24 679	225	15.6	48.4	61.3
Lincoln	92	650	104	D	D	D	D	18	28 423	258	21.3	28.3	61.2
Madison	780	14 136	1 401	1 096	1 640	261	1 069	302	21 389	450	42.9	20.9	50.2
Minidoka	411	4 119	614	694	550	71	105	126	30 665	626	51.9	13.7	53.4
Nez Perce	1 166	16 490	2 965	2 678	2 532	1 224	529	529	32 105	473	35.1	27.7	51.0
Oneida	81	614	D	33	143	D	D	14	22 826	463	21.8	30.5	39.3
Owyhee	177	1 531	135	119	235	27	24	37	24 109	620	43.1	23.9	56.9
Payette	491	4 280	480	D	531	182	124	118	27 527	678	65.6	6.0	43.1
Power	162	2 184	150	D	D	62	D	68	31 137	336	17.6	52.7	50.6
Shoshone	389	3 846	476	D	918	76	224	127	33 113	39	59.0	0.0	43.6
Teton	446	2 048	D	88	283	88	135	64	31 116	299	32.4	21.4	43.1
Twin Falls	2 563	27 170	4 782	2 698	4 771	920	1 595	717	26 398	1 296	48.5	12.6	54.0
Valley	585	2 792	394	D	491	73	107	72	25 957	145	44.8	22.1	46.9
Washington	234	1 736	372	240	269	60	D	39	22 729	594	44.9	19.4	46.8
ILLINOIS	314 977	5 120 970	732 836	566 887	600 315	324 750	359 119	233 993	45 693	76 860	38.0	21.0	48.4
Adams	1 855	29 460	5 186	4 980	4 898	1 688	839	977	33 163	1 295	32.0	19.1	45.9
Alexander	118	1 241	286	D	152	D	D	39	31 700	143	37.8	12.6	52.4
Bond	323	3 899	576	806	373	119	104	107	27 361	673	36.1	22.3	41.6
Boone	841	10 900	837	4 274	1 514	236	528	367	33 631	540	57.2	15.7	56.3
Brown	124	D	D	D	124	D	D	D	D	422	26.3	19.2	39.1
Bureau	776	10 100	2 298	1 800	1 222	475	D	358	35 416	1 189	33.4	26.4	55.5
Calhoun	95	598	100	D	103	77	D	13	22 261	464	31.0	9.7	38.6
Carroll	421	3 451	520	991	422	200	D	102	29 567	676	31.4	21.7	53.8
Cass	258	4 664	408	D	551	151	D	131	28 176	433	33.3	23.8	46.0
Champaign	4 176	68 678	12 204	7 221	10 691	2 552	2 974	2 280	33 203	1 389	32.1	27.3	55.2
Christian	765	8 490	1 661	1 059	1 377	358	283	268	31 512	910	34.2	29.3	53.7
Clark	332	3 281	351	944	362	159	D	95	28 996	588	38.8	23.3	54.4
Clay	349	4 482	603	1 712	489	153	82	137	30 639	707	42.4	18.4	42.7
Clinton	866	8 779	1 761	875	1 474	303	266	242	27 545	1 031	38.0	17.7	45.0
Coles	1 238	18 111	3 964	3 264	2 523	662	511	540	29 831	729	41.0	20.2	52.5
Cook	127 868	2 245 334	336 123	192 628	217 507	168 760	206 588	116 535	51 901	184	84.2	2.2	45.7
Crawford	430	6 352	919	2 023	787	238	D	234	36 917	615	45.2	18.7	41.8
Cumberland	192	1 529	254	393	176	D	34	37	24 354	654	46.3	13.9	37.8
DeKalb	2 014	25 810	4 867	4 055	4 395	971	610	794	30 775	930	36.8	26.2	57.4
De Witt	381	4 556	536	503	734	165	82	196	43 038	508	40.4	26.4	56.5
Douglas	634	6 227	336	2 241	1 148	240	91	190	30 512	657	41.4	22.2	54.9
DuPage	33 330	574 472	58 555	55 014	59 996	35 563	45 856	28 360	49 368	73	82.2	5.5	34.2
Edgar	380	5 635	759	1 785	863	287	96	176	31 312	670	28.8	31.2	56.0
Edwards	163	2 153	134	D	188	63	D	73	33 881	365	43.6	19.5	40.5
Effingham	1 175	18 116	2 675	3 332	2 956	447	309	531	29 289	1 150	41.0	11.3	37.8
Fayette	488	4 958	1 014	690	941	223	118	115	23 206	1 132	40.5	16.4	41.4
Ford	389	4 236	1 038	856	525	150	111	136	32 063	524	26.3	34.0	55.2
Franklin	792	6 761	1 334	457	1 533	292	380	170	25 162	785	50.6	14.0	37.5
Fulton	709	7 084	2 143	302	1 406	348	D	192	27 096	1 005	30.0	21.6	46.3
Gallatin	107	686	D	D	70	23	24	21	30 711	210	36.7	32.9	56.2
Greene	274	1 777	361	200	398	97	67	44	24 971	600	27.2	24.0	50.2
Grundy	1 090	15 037	1 954	1 544	1 995	417	427	711	47 299	450	30.0	27.1	48.0
Hamilton	193	1 356	515	79	177	44	33	31	23 149	685	38.2	15.8	35.6
Hancock	426	2 847	598	D	492	D	136	82	28 723	1 063	29.1	22.1	51.8

STATE County	Acreage (1,000)	Percent change, 2002–2007	Average size of farm	Total irrigated (1,000)	Total cropland (1,000)	Value of land and buildings (dollars) Average per farm	Average per acre	Value of machinery and equipment, average per farm (dollars)	Total (mil dol)	Average per farm (dollars)	Crops	Live-stock and poultry products	$10,000 or more	$100,000 or more	Total ($1,000)	Percent of farms
	117	118	119	120	121	122	123	124	125	126	127	128	129	130	131	132
IDAHO—Cont'd																
Caribou	421	-1.4	928	68.3	229.0	1 000 425	1 078	151 325	55.0	121 172	62.6	37.4	43.0	22.9	4 178	65.6
Cassia	645	-13.3	1 001	249.8	372.8	1 665 431	1 664	255 684	626.7	973 170	28.0	72.0	58.9	34.8	5 062	39.1
Clark	158	-11.2	1 949	32.0	45.5	1 709 390	877	196 453	30.3	374 545	75.6	24.4	54.3	34.6	727	46.9
Clearwater	70	-1.4	289	D	32.4	597 891	2 071	53 036	8.0	32 988	71.3	28.7	23.2	7.9	978	46.5
Custer	124	-6.1	476	56.0	46.9	1 122 682	2 359	89 236	17.8	68 385	25.3	74.7	44.8	16.1	685	17.6
Elmore	347	0.3	910	97.9	120.8	1 253 456	1 378	148 119	284.6	747 055	25.3	74.7	34.9	18.6	886	17.6
Franklin	225	-7.8	304	49.4	131.8	631 735	2 076	96 436	78.8	106 576	20.2	79.8	43.4	15.6	2 456	49.0
Fremont	288	0.3	538	101.8	175.7	1 012 170	1 883	164 650	86.2	160 776	87.9	12.1	42.5	18.8	3 524	55.8
Gem	191	-13.6	232	35.1	34.9	523 969	2 258	54 029	30.8	37 487	39.9	60.1	32.4	8.2	571	23.6
Gooding	223	14.4	335	132.6	133.8	1 335 076	3 980	233 583	624.4	938 978	8.2	91.8	57.9	27.4	1 567	23.8
Idaho	591	-7.5	778	1.2	218.8	1 095 770	1 409	78 506	51.4	67 582	71.5	28.5	42.9	16.7	6 634	52.4
Jefferson	325	6.6	394	210.3	225.1	818 005	2 077	143 918	233.1	282 146	53.4	46.6	50.0	24.2	2 632	39.5
Jerome	189	1.6	313	150.8	157.6	1 074 850	3 439	209 468	461.6	764 237	20.4	79.6	57.9	33.9	1 710	40.6
Kootenai	131	-14.9	158	11.0	71.2	642 680	4 057	52 170	16.4	19 834	75.1	24.9	18.8	3.6	869	17.4
Latah	344	1.2	312	0.3	242.9	647 950	2 077	66 496	60.9	55 192	94.3	5.7	21.7	10.4	6 396	72.3
Lemhi	190	9.2	555	77.0	53.6	879 721	1 586	78 591	21.3	62 274	6.6	93.4	42.1	16.7	828	12.9
Lewis	246	13.4	1 093	0.3	184.1	1 649 738	1 509	176 488	43.7	194 418	92.7	7.3	58.2	37.8	3 920	76.9
Lincoln	117	-8.6	455	68.0	68.4	976 143	2 146	178 150	131.0	507 650	16.2	83.8	60.9	30.2	1 034	50.0
Madison	211	11.1	468	128.2	176.1	1 279 118	2 733	211 179	107.8	239 494	94.4	5.6	52.9	25.6	2 824	51.8
Minidoka	226	-0.9	361	191.6	202.7	875 005	2 422	185 923	257.0	410 606	70.0	30.0	55.4	34.0	3 011	51.3
Nez Perce	353	2.9	747	0.6	203.6	1 095 708	1 467	118 452	58.7	124 086	93.0	7.0	37.0	20.5	5 013	53.7
Oneida	314	-13.5	678	38.3	204.3	794 950	1 173	82 291	27.6	59 533	64.3	35.7	39.3	13.6	4 149	70.0
Owyhee	569	-0.4	918	115.2	136.6	1 256 088	1 368	138 716	206.6	333 148	25.3	74.7	55.6	28.9	1 258	32.4
Payette	166	7.1	245	54.6	56.1	688 178	2 808	98 039	146.5	216 009	19.5	80.5	39.2	13.0	462	23.2
Power	451	6.1	1 343	114.0	351.1	1 400 971	1 043	224 989	164.1	488 493	80.9	19.1	45.5	28.6	8 045	71.7
Shoshone	3	-25.0	81	D	1.3	471 129	5 839	37 528	0.1	3 400	13.5	86.5	5.1	0.0	0	0.0
Teton	122	-2.4	410	52.6	85.1	1 497 180	3 655	141 413	33.0	110 230	87.1	12.9	41.1	14.7	1 016	44.5
Twin Falls	440	-0.2	339	244.5	267.1	840 836	2 479	144 828	471.9	364 090	29.8	70.2	59.6	28.5	2 585	43.1
Valley	62	-6.1	428	22.1	11.4	1 409 537	3 294	57 304	5.1	35 505	10.3	89.7	36.6	11.0	43	9.7
Washington	417	-11.7	702	43.9	88.4	686 593	978	74 774	43.0	72 380	42.6	57.4	42.1	14.1	878	36.5
ILLINOIS	26 775	-2.0	348	474.5	23 707.7	1 321 080	3 792	136 609	13 329.1	173 421	81.6	18.4	53.1	30.3	487 293	73.9
Adams	374	-15.8	289	1.6	284.7	1 013 322	3 507	113 632	156.3	120 673	66.7	33.3	52.3	25.6	5 141	70.6
Alexander	48	-38.5	333	D	36.7	1 030 129	3 093	83 157	13.1	91 674	97.1	2.9	42.0	14.0	715	62.9
Bond	225	16.6	334	0.0	203.3	1 137 540	3 406	134 298	74.3	110 419	83.0	17.0	48.1	26.3	3 327	77.7
Boone	137	-6.8	254	1.8	128.8	1 255 409	4 942	112 280	81.4	150 765	86.1	13.9	48.3	28.3	3 711	54.1
Brown	151	4.9	358	D	92.1	1 091 712	3 050	87 114	42.0	99 448	72.9	27.1	42.7	22.0	2 583	83.2
Bureau	478	-2.6	402	10.2	439.9	1 628 471	4 047	156 932	303.4	255 137	86.2	13.8	63.8	42.9	10 029	81.6
Calhoun	88	-2.2	190	D	49.6	588 974	3 108	66 781	18.7	40 223	83.9	16.1	30.0	9.3	1 697	72.8
Carroll	265	6.9	392	10.5	228.1	1 442 019	3 676	170 529	207.0	306 250	54.0	46.0	59.0	37.1	6 184	80.6
Cass	174	-12.6	401	21.2	143.6	1 426 235	3 559	136 955	92.0	212 370	71.3	28.8	51.3	31.6	3 375	82.4
Champaign	550	-4.7	396	7.1	536.1	1 724 299	4 351	176 444	311.5	224 235	96.0	4.0	72.8	43.3	10 743	88.0
Christian	450	9.5	494	0.0	430.4	2 064 186	4 179	171 450	229.2	251 882	94.4	5.6	63.5	40.8	7 078	80.7
Clark	239	-13.1	406	6.4	206.0	1 312 708	3 234	158 135	103.5	175 937	84.1	15.9	48.5	27.7	4 128	78.4
Clay	210	-13.6	297	D	178.3	871 635	2 937	102 294	72.8	102 946	69.6	30.4	38.9	20.1	3 698	83.7
Clinton	268	5.1	260	1.2	246.4	991 561	3 808	143 602	175.9	170 627	45.4	54.6	58.5	30.6	5 123	85.4
Coles	255	-2.3	350	0.0	235.1	1 354 381	3 874	143 393	123.9	169 906	95.8	4.2	55.0	31.4	4 726	74.1
Cook	8	-66.7	45	0.2	6.5	464 325	10 422	71 712	15.3	82 988	95.0	5.0	34.8	16.8	94	13.0
Crawford	205	-4.2	334	6.8	176.6	1 094 677	3 278	116 138	74.7	121 406	89.9	10.1	36.6	22.3	4 548	85.9
Cumberland	145	-16.2	222	0.0	124.5	781 010	3 523	97 966	71.8	109 811	70.3	29.7	43.9	22.6	3 343	82.7
DeKalb	371	3.3	399	0.1	356.2	1 847 105	4 633	185 559	302.0	324 915	62.8	37.2	66.5	46.6	10 012	73.5
De Witt	199	-2.0	391	D	185.6	1 630 935	4 170	149 395	96.1	189 154	92.6	7.4	59.1	37.6	3 671	75.0
Douglas	262	12.4	398	D	252.8	1 674 156	4 206	148 029	133.9	203 880	94.6	5.4	59.4	34.1	4 785	70.2
DuPage	8	0.0	109	D	6.4	817 586	7 509	57 909	14.1	192 813	99.7	0.4	37.0	19.2	113	13.7
Edgar	353	-0.6	526	0.2	328.3	2 011 584	3 823	182 109	189.9	283 501	88.3	11.7	67.3	40.1	6 337	77.8
Edwards	117	-4.9	320	0.1	100.5	890 959	2 787	101 514	32.8	89 967	87.2	12.8	41.1	21.1	2 237	83.6
Effingham	242	-12.9	210	0.3	204.5	759 757	3 610	101 108	127.3	110 709	55.6	44.4	50.5	22.2	4 565	75.1
Fayette	303	-17.2	268	0.1	254.5	789 210	2 946	103 978	104.3	92 158	86.6	13.4	42.6	20.7	4 381	73.0
Ford	271	-5.2	517	0.1	258.7	2 053 439	3 975	178 916	145.9	278 379	88.4	11.6	74.0	49.2	4 552	87.6
Franklin	208	15.6	265	D	183.7	671 184	2 535	80 319	56.6	72 135	80.3	19.7	28.5	15.4	3 772	68.0
Fulton	385	-6.8	383	0.9	280.1	1 350 626	3 523	121 274	145.6	144 860	84.9	15.1	53.4	26.1	5 104	68.2
Gallatin	186	20.8	885	20.6	171.6	2 628 760	2 972	315 220	72.6	345 538	95.7	4.3	51.9	35.7	3 017	82.9
Greene	273	-13.3	455	3.8	214.8	1 651 273	3 628	150 950	135.5	225 906	63.2	36.8	56.7	30.0	4 644	79.2
Grundy	215	0.9	479	D	206.1	1 988 655	4 153	189 410	105.2	233 714	97.1	2.9	73.6	42.0	3 404	79.3
Hamilton	220	-6.0	321	D	191.9	963 280	3 001	99 151	65.4	95 405	81.0	19.0	34.0	16.5	4 309	83.1
Hancock	393	-9.0	370	1.3	322.2	1 228 769	3 324	119 803	188.5	177 364	71.1	28.9	58.0	32.7	6 781	77.9

STATE County	Water use, 2005		Wholesale trade,[1] 2007				Retail trade,[2] 2007				Real estate and rental and leasing,[2] 2007			
	Total water withdrawn (mil gal/day)	Gallons withdrawn per person	Number of establishments	Number of employees	Sales (mil dol)	Annual payroll (mil dol)	Number of establishments	Number of employees	Sales (mil dol)	Annual payroll (mil dol)	Number of establishments	Number of employees	Receipts (mil dol)	Annual payroll (mil dol)
	133	134	135	136	137	138	139	140	141	142	143	144	145	146
IDAHO—Cont'd														
Caribou	379.4	53 207	14	63	94.6	2.3	34	340	68.4	6.0	5	6	0.6	0.1
Cassia	880.9	41 309	30	267	335.9	8.5	128	1 436	318.9	30.2	26	D	D	D
Clark	95.6	101 326	1	D	D	D	3	D	D	D	NA	NA	NA	NA
Clearwater	15.2	1 809	5	32	13.7	1.1	42	265	69.8	5.8	5	D	D	D
Custer	842.7	206 699	NA	NA	NA	NA	30	150	35.1	2.7	7	20	0.6	0.1
Elmore	424.7	14 830	14	101	53.4	4.0	75	970	241.2	20.1	16	50	5.6	1.0
Franklin	203.8	16 477	19	146	49.5	4.5	42	508	113.5	9.3	11	D	D	D
Fremont	295.0	24 095	14	184	76.7	4.9	41	250	68.2	4.9	6	11	2.5	0.3
Gem	725.8	44 604	11	75	13.6	2.7	47	392	113.9	8.8	20	37	3.8	0.5
Gooding	1 155.5	79 905	19	174	118.9	5.0	44	419	88.2	6.5	9	D	D	D
Idaho	19.2	1 221	17	115	64.8	3.7	68	519	97.6	11.2	14	28	2.8	0.5
Jefferson	2 108.0	97 684	23	D	D	D	56	474	92.4	8.0	13	47	5.0	0.8
Jerome	1 472.9	75 002	36	226	103.7	8.4	73	982	300.4	21.5	26	51	8.2	0.9
Kootenai	73.2	573	142	1 550	843.3	64.0	609	7 398	2 175.2	187.5	249	876	155.3	27.4
Latah	9.7	281	24	D	D	D	156	1 960	361.7	37.1	49	120	17.6	2.9
Lemhi	240.8	30 446	5	D	D	D	53	444	123.0	8.9	19	33	2.7	0.6
Lewis	2.7	720	9	D	D	D	20	138	29.7	2.3	5	15	1.3	0.2
Lincoln	321.9	70 814	NA	NA	NA	NA	13	77	16.9	1.1	4	D	D	D
Madison	625.5	20 194	38	475	162.0	11.6	124	1 718	407.7	37.6	59	174	23.4	3.1
Minidoka	649.7	34 167	40	745	347.0	24.9	66	543	162.9	10.4	10	D	D	D
Nez Perce	28.9	761	45	D	D	D	216	2 822	703.0	70.0	40	160	23.0	4.7
Oneida	152.6	36 263	1	D	D	D	15	145	24.1	2.0	4	D	D	D
Owyhee	816.9	73 778	10	71	34.6	2.8	25	219	50.9	4.4	10	23	0.7	0.1
Payette	285.0	12 841	26	187	133.1	6.3	70	596	145.6	14.2	29	46	6.4	0.8
Power	349.2	45 034	11	D	D	D	23	213	50.4	3.9	7	27	1.8	0.3
Shoshone	5.4	411	9	71	25.0	2.8	80	1 019	623.1	32.1	11	44	3.1	0.7
Teton	166.5	22 291	12	D	D	D	46	329	84.1	6.9	46	56	22.5	2.4
Twin Falls	1 691.8	24 370	123	1 301	497.6	44.6	423	5 363	1 259.1	117.5	113	359	49.1	8.4
Valley	68.2	8 184	11	62	20.5	2.4	83	643	135.6	13.5	60	111	16.5	2.6
Washington	187.4	18 558	12	439	63.4	7.2	38	335	76.3	6.1	13	43	3.3	0.5
ILLINOIS	15 183.7	1 190	16 704	259 758	231 082.8	14 319.6	43 055	639 147	165 450.5	14 895.5	13 899	87 468	21 725.0	3 985.2
Adams	26.1	389	114	D	D	D	330	4 813	928.3	89.9	65	294	34.9	7.0
Alexander	4.9	544	7	D	D	D	24	165	22.9	2.5	2	D	D	D
Bond	2.9	158	18	414	217.6	17.0	60	490	104.5	8.7	13	D	D	D
Boone	8.1	160	35	223	146.2	11.0	103	1 555	454.9	36.6	25	68	7.9	1.3
Brown	0.5	66	7	D	D	D	25	166	30.0	2.7	2	D	D	D
Bureau	13.5	381	42	823	977.6	30.0	120	1 269	332.0	27.2	17	D	D	D
Calhoun	0.6	122	2	D	D	D	15	104	22.3	2.1	2	D	D	D
Carroll	17.3	1 075	23	250	301.8	10.5	59	428	88.7	7.6	10	34	2.8	0.4
Cass	20.5	1 478	17	355	331.3	13.2	50	478	115.4	9.1	6	D	D	D
Champaign	38.6	209	170	3 166	2 576.0	118.7	667	10 960	2 347.1	213.1	233	1 655	349.4	51.0
Christian	835.6	23 753	46	D	D	D	122	1 385	369.9	30.7	20	83	10.4	1.8
Clark	8.7	511	17	154	176.1	4.8	60	390	109.6	8.2	5	18	2.4	0.5
Clay	2.3	161	28	315	168.8	9.7	55	531	114.8	10.2	11	30	3.6	0.7
Clinton	8.1	225	48	544	282.0	19.7	151	1 538	383.2	35.5	22	161	16.5	4.0
Coles	5.5	108	59	496	382.9	19.9	193	2 894	635.1	60.6	47	162	21.8	4.1
Cook	1 758.0	331	6 657	98 030	83 964.6	5 379.0	16 288	241 745	60 585.6	5 793.8	6 626	47 857	13 137.3	2 511.3
Crawford	102.0	5 128	15	157	90.9	4.3	63	709	164.2	14.0	17	39	4.2	0.5
Cumberland	1.8	168	18	D	D	D	27	160	22.9	2.1	NA	NA	NA	NA
DeKalb	15.4	157	72	579	249.7	21.7	320	4 713	1 090.2	94.6	66	524	57.2	11.2
De Witt	938.9	56 500	25	262	248.9	12.4	64	740	188.2	14.5	9	45	6.4	0.6
Douglas	4.0	198	30	318	290.1	13.1	136	1 081	218.4	18.9	11	38	5.2	1.0
DuPage	16.0	17	2 423	46 343	49 574.9	2 924.4	3 512	65 944	18 043.4	1 646.3	1 485	11 690	3 917.2	614.7
Edgar	3.2	167	23	197	126.7	8.0	66	743	197.1	16.3	9	39	3.4	1.1
Edwards	0.9	137	17	213	147.1	7.5	27	191	40.6	3.3	3	D	D	D
Effingham	5.0	145	60	D	D	D	205	3 141	857.8	68.7	44	222	36.8	6.7
Fayette	4.4	201	25	396	322.6	13.3	88	970	227.3	19.1	12	34	3.4	0.7
Ford	5.9	419	30	312	323.1	10.8	62	599	112.3	9.1	6	12	1.1	0.2
Franklin	14.7	370	31	191	72.7	6.6	152	1 545	362.2	33.5	21	75	8.2	1.3
Fulton	158.7	4 208	23	D	D	D	128	1 343	288.9	25.5	18	D	D	D
Gallatin	18.9	3 074	6	44	23.2	1.2	18	108	21.9	2.2	NA	NA	NA	NA
Greene	11.0	756	22	148	151.3	5.1	56	389	95.9	7.6	3	11	0.3	0.1
Grundy	1 560.1	35 587	46	393	438.5	16.4	161	1 928	522.6	42.5	41	149	23.5	3.4
Hamilton	1.0	117	10	D	D	D	33	158	41.9	2.9	6	41	0.5	0.2
Hancock	4.0	210	28	160	200.5	5.2	82	569	106.5	9.8	3	8	3.4	0.1

1. Merchant wholesalers, except manufacturers' sales branches and offices.   2. Employer establishments.

Table B. States and Counties — **Professional Services, Manufacturing, and Accommodation and Food Services**

STATE County	Professional, scientific, and technical services,[1] 2007				Manufacturing, 2007				Accommodation and food services, 2007			
	Number of establish-ments	Number of employees	Receipts (mil dol)	Annual payroll (mil dol)	Number of establish-ments	Number of employees	Receipts (mil dol)	Annual payroll (mil dol)	Number of establish-ments	Number of employees	Sales (mil dol)	Annual payroll (mil dol)
	147	148	149	150	151	152	153	154	155	156	157	158
IDAHO—Cont'd												
Caribou	9	D	D	D	11	D	443.2	D	11	D	D	D
Cassia	45	173	14.6	4.3	28	1 032	371.3	41.2	47	656	33.5	6.5
Clark	2	D	D	D	NA	NA	NA	NA	1	D	D	D
Clearwater	12	D	D	D	NA	NA	NA	NA	34	D	D	D
Custer	8	D	D	D	NA	NA	NA	NA	33	205	11.3	2.7
Elmore	27	D	D	D	NA	NA	NA	NA	55	702	27.0	7.9
Franklin	12	D	D	D	NA	NA	NA	NA	20	194	5.8	1.7
Fremont	12	27	6.0	0.6	NA	NA	NA	NA	33	170	10.1	2.7
Gem	20	61	4.5	1.3	NA	NA	NA	NA	28	342	9.2	2.6
Gooding	20	80	8.5	2.8	25	510	D	20.4	30	D	D	D
Idaho	22	88	16.0	3.6	NA	NA	NA	NA	66	353	14.7	3.5
Jefferson	44	D	D	D	33	1 069	D	26.3	24	238	7.4	1.8
Jerome	30	D	D	D	24	1 246	764.2	36.6	33	329	14.0	3.5
Kootenai	438	D	D	D	246	4 401	992.2	163.3	363	6 773	303.7	96.0
Latah	84	D	D	D	NA	NA	NA	NA	104	1 756	55.2	15.9
Lemhi	24	68	4.0	1.4	NA	NA	NA	NA	34	232	7.7	2.4
Lewis	1	D	D	D	NA	NA	NA	NA	13	D	D	D
Lincoln	4	D	D	D	NA	NA	NA	NA	10	68	2.4	0.7
Madison	64	910	38.1	11.4	35	D	D	D	50	1 090	32.0	9.0
Minidoka	23	98	7.0	2.8	27	864	381.1	32.2	28	336	18.9	3.4
Nez Perce	78	D	D	D	37	2 874	D	D	95	1 687	64.5	20.2
Oneida	1	D	D	D	NA	NA	NA	NA	9	85	2.1	0.5
Owyhee	10	35	2.9	1.1	NA	NA	NA	NA	21	144	4.2	1.2
Payette	28	D	D	D	31	1 228	D	39.9	33	329	12.8	2.4
Power	6	D	D	D	8	D	D	D	17	70	2.6	0.6
Shoshone	27	254	24.2	8.1	NA	NA	NA	NA	50	310	11.1	3.4
Teton	32	D	D	D	NA	NA	NA	NA	29	201	10.7	2.9
Twin Falls	221	D	D	D	101	3 175	970.3	104.3	177	2 825	112.0	29.5
Valley	47	165	31.8	6.2	NA	NA	NA	NA	82	803	43.2	13.0
Washington	17	70	4.2	1.3	NA	NA	NA	NA	25	D	D	D
ILLINOIS	38 797	363 231	61 896.1	24 197.9	15 704	663 586	257 760.7	31 715.9	26 774	468 827	25 469.0	6 894.3
Adams	136	D	D	D	96	D	D	D	142	D	D	D
Alexander	9	D	D	D	NA	NA	NA	NA	19	D	D	D
Bond	23	D	D	D	16	821	D	30.0	31	333	13.1	3.4
Boone	73	D	D	D	71	6 534	5 553.7	387.3	71	883	40.2	10.4
Brown	8	D	D	D	NA	NA	NA	NA	15	D	D	D
Bureau	41	D	D	D	43	2 062	D	D	78	765	27.4	7.5
Calhoun	2	D	D	D	NA	NA	NA	NA	20	138	5.4	1.4
Carroll	19	66	5.4	1.6	28	926	320.8	34.1	40	297	13.0	2.8
Cass	16	59	4.6	1.5	13	D	D	D	33	235	8.1	2.0
Champaign	453	2 913	299.3	127.9	143	8 995	3 248.9	337.2	502	9 836	374.5	104.4
Christian	46	5 377	69.6	32.6	25	1 339	392.4	46.6	76	762	29.3	7.5
Clark	20	132	8.2	3.8	18	1 622	664.4	59.5	38	543	17.0	5.0
Clay	16	57	4.1	1.1	17	1 980	737.1	71.3	30	D	D	D
Clinton	50	244	20.6	8.0	35	1 005	D	30.6	76	808	32.4	8.6
Coles	83	494	43.4	15.2	54	3 537	D	D	127	2 465	75.6	21.7
Cook	18 818	D	D	D	6 018	236 509	77 932.9	11 039.2	10 887	201 766	13 094.4	3 525.6
Crawford	30	124	12.3	4.0	19	2 007	D	120.1	37	423	15.3	3.9
Cumberland	7	30	2.0	0.8	NA	NA	NA	NA	11	140	3.1	0.9
DeKalb	158	D	D	D	140	4 608	1 435.9	191.2	214	3 247	128.2	32.7
De Witt	29	91	7.0	2.3	NA	NA	NA	NA	38	483	13.9	4.1
Douglas	30	108	6.4	2.3	92	2 731	699.9	102.2	54	674	24.5	7.2
DuPage	5 172	D	D	D	1 881	62 578	16 862.5	2 977.7	2 071	41 256	2 226.2	638.5
Edgar	28	105	8.4	2.5	23	2 061	521.8	75.8	28	384	12.0	3.4
Edwards	11	37	2.0	0.7	7	D	D	D	8	83	2.5	0.8
Effingham	57	315	31.9	9.0	63	3 440	890.3	119.2	107	2 265	85.2	24.3
Fayette	26	132	7.8	3.6	21	833	174.6	24.8	46	511	18.3	5.2
Ford	26	93	9.0	2.7	20	D	D	D	36	302	11.4	3.2
Franklin	56	345	23.3	7.6	38	782	223.2	25.7	82	956	34.2	10.1
Fulton	43	D	D	D	NA	NA	NA	NA	84	844	29.4	8.4
Gallatin	7	21	1.6	0.7	NA	NA	NA	NA	10	D	D	D
Greene	16	79	6.7	2.7	NA	NA	NA	NA	24	D	D	D
Grundy	93	D	D	D	49	1 755	2 082.4	D	101	1 406	56.3	14.7
Hamilton	11	25	2.2	0.5	NA	NA	NA	NA	8	95	2.8	0.8
Hancock	25	127	21.2	4.9	24	726	193.2	35.2	34	254	10.9	3.0

1. Establishment subject to federal tax.

Table B. States and Counties — Health Care and Social Assistance, Other Services, and Federal Funds

STATE County	Health care and social assistance, 2007				Other services, 2007				Federal funds and grants, 2009–2010 Expenditures (mil dol)			
									Total	Direct payments for individuals[1]		
	Number of establishments	Number of employees	Receipts (mil dol)	Annual payroll (mil dol)	Number of establishments	Number of employees	Receipts (mil dol)	Annual payroll (mil dol)	Total	Social Security and government retirement	Medicare	Food Stamps and Supplemental Security Income
	159	160	161	162	163	164	165	166	167	168	169	170
IDAHO—Cont'd												
Caribou	20	224	14.8	5.7	18	39	4.0	0.8	43.9	20.8	6.9	1.4
Cassia	83	1 165	74.8	27.8	45	135	11.9	2.5	140.0	53.9	25.1	7.5
Clark	2	D	D	D	NA	NA	NA	NA	6.1	2.1	0.9	0.1
Clearwater	25	551	34.5	17.8	10	98	4.1	1.9	130.2	41.7	13.9	3.9
Custer	9	49	2.1	0.8	3	7	0.3	0.1	38.3	16.2	6.2	1.0
Elmore	52	711	46.7	17.4	40	167	8.6	2.4	469.4	102.2	17.4	6.6
Franklin	27	D	D	D	20	D	D	D	60.5	30.4	10.7	3.0
Fremont	18	209	10.2	4.4	19	62	5.8	1.4	81.7	33.7	11.6	2.6
Gem	41	574	33.9	13.1	29	D	D	D	124.8	64.1	19.4	5.6
Gooding	32	482	28.8	12.2	24	D	D	D	106.4	39.5	18.9	4.2
Idaho	35	535	38.2	17.6	19	51	3.1	0.6	183.1	63.3	22.3	7.1
Jefferson	33	D	D	D	17	24	3.4	0.7	114.0	52.8	17.0	5.6
Jerome	36	471	26.3	13.8	45	214	19.0	4.9	163.4	47.2	20.7	6.4
Kootenai	458	7 004	573.4	238.0	240	1 242	82.8	24.6	1 486.4	487.5	118.9	38.9
Latah	71	1 210	92.7	36.9	59	407	25.4	8.0	289.0	88.2	27.4	8.0
Lemhi	32	431	24.3	10.4	27	69	5.3	1.2	96.4	38.3	15.7	2.1
Lewis	15	59	3.7	1.3	1	D	D	D	83.4	31.2	8.0	3.1
Lincoln	7	D	D	D	2	D	D	D	26.4	10.2	4.2	1.0
Madison	84	1 183	99.2	35.9	31	163	9.6	2.5	133.8	40.0	13.8	4.2
Minidoka	39	588	34.0	13.9	26	186	17.1	4.5	124.6	51.4	26.8	7.8
Nez Perce	140	2 949	271.7	95.2	89	484	31.7	9.5	422.7	163.3	64.7	16.4
Oneida	8	174	7.8	3.5	4	D	D	D	29.2	14.5	5.6	1.2
Owyhee	13	128	6.2	3.0	8	D	D	D	78.7	27.1	8.4	4.5
Payette	39	512	29.6	11.9	21	D	D	D	157.5	65.9	23.3	11.1
Power	12	D	D	D	13	43	4.0	0.9	55.5	17.1	6.1	3.8
Shoshone	32	458	31.1	11.8	23	84	5.9	1.6	148.9	57.0	30.2	13.7
Teton	29	D	D	D	20	75	6.2	1.9	38.3	12.3	6.0	0.5
Twin Falls	311	4 734	373.6	134.8	167	976	70.1	20.6	524.9	220.9	80.2	24.7
Valley	40	399	32.5	12.4	31	109	8.9	2.7	89.5	36.7	11.7	2.9
Washington	22	413	24.3	9.8	11	40	5.5	1.0	88.1	38.4	14.5	7.0
ILLINOIS	31 062	706 669	70 042.9	28 009.4	23 510	167 675	20 639.2	5 203.0	109 967.5	32 012.8	19 805.5	4 615.9
Adams	156	5 096	509.4	185.2	158	D	D	D	548.0	221.0	114.8	22.1
Alexander	8	D	D	D	6	D	D	D	122.9	29.7	24.3	9.3
Bond	30	D	D	D	26	88	7.0	2.0	148.7	52.7	28.0	4.5
Boone	65	745	39.7	16.8	66	345	27.5	7.9	204.7	125.5	39.0	6.3
Brown	7	152	8.7	4.0	10	D	D	D	34.6	14.4	8.3	1.4
Bureau	77	2 024	157.6	64.9	76	304	22.3	6.9	257.0	115.0	66.9	5.6
Calhoun	6	D	D	D	6	6	1.0	0.2	72.7	19.8	11.1	1.5
Carroll	28	550	18.9	8.6	32	164	12.0	3.4	130.5	66.4	32.0	3.7
Cass	23	366	14.8	7.3	23	100	7.2	1.9	94.8	42.6	26.1	3.1
Champaign	363	10 977	1 251.3	490.5	290	2 154	428.6	56.4	1 499.6	374.1	153.2	43.9
Christian	71	1 664	107.0	42.0	68	319	19.1	4.8	258.8	117.7	78.2	10.1
Clark	20	393	18.9	9.1	23	71	4.6	1.0	123.6	55.7	33.3	4.2
Clay	37	711	44.4	17.5	31	116	9.0	1.8	121.1	44.7	32.5	4.3
Clinton	76	D	D	D	62	257	17.0	4.6	226.7	114.8	55.8	5.0
Coles	156	3 631	290.3	105.3	100	498	35.4	10.7	344.9	132.6	80.2	14.9
Cook	13 580	325 243	34 227.7	13 682.6	9 784	79 024	11 900.2	2 789.2	45 944.7	11 361.0	10 015.8	2 820.5
Crawford	44	894	54.7	21.0	44	183	14.2	3.4	141.7	65.0	36.3	4.6
Cumberland	18	229	15.1	6.9	14	84	5.1	1.9	72.0	31.2	17.5	2.8
DeKalb	202	4 374	368.3	143.8	148	838	59.9	16.2	522.7	212.2	95.3	11.9
De Witt	26	473	30.1	12.3	24	128	7.8	2.2	111.6	53.8	30.3	4.7
Douglas	33	331	19.6	8.6	30	140	13.4	2.9	103.7	51.2	26.5	3.5
DuPage	2 894	56 847	6 379.9	2 541.4	2 038	17 829	2 120.8	647.6	7 121.9	2 189.7	1 000.9	90.4
Edgar	32	744	53.7	21.5	29	108	7.4	1.8	144.1	63.9	37.9	5.9
Edwards	15	145	5.9	2.9	15	54	3.0	0.9	48.7	20.7	12.6	1.5
Effingham	120	2 550	231.6	88.4	95	783	48.6	19.2	226.1	107.4	51.6	6.1
Fayette	47	814	50.9	20.6	37	121	12.0	2.4	153.7	61.2	37.6	7.5
Ford	33	D	D	D	25	79	4.8	1.1	96.3	47.9	25.2	2.8
Franklin	70	1 329	77.8	32.8	62	227	20.0	6.1	379.2	167.6	91.3	22.2
Fulton	67	1 528	129.4	47.1	70	375	15.7	4.9	285.7	124.2	90.4	12.9
Gallatin	6	D	D	D	10	23	1.9	0.4	79.2	22.8	15.6	4.3
Greene	26	481	29.3	13.5	19	D	D	D	119.8	48.2	31.6	4.7
Grundy	97	1 780	171.5	67.5	78	400	33.7	9.1	219.8	122.4	57.6	6.3
Hamilton	17	422	21.2	9.4	19	40	3.2	0.6	82.7	29.7	18.2	3.0
Hancock	39	554	32.8	13.5	32	81	5.9	1.5	148.7	71.1	35.5	5.3

1. State totals may include programs not allocated by county.

Table B. States and Counties — Federal Funds, Residential Construction, and Local Government Finances

STATE County	Federal funds and grants, 2009–2010 (cont.) Expenditures (mil dol) (cont.)							Value of residential construction authorized by building permits, 2010		Local government finances, 2007 General revenue				
		Procurement contract awards		Grants[1]								Taxes		
													Per capita[2] (dollars)	
	Salaries and wages	Defense	Other	Medicaid and other health-related	Nutrition and family welfare	Education	Other	New construction ($1,000)	Number of housing units	Total (mil dol)	Intergovernmental (mil dol)	Total (mil dol)	Total	Property
	171	172	173	174	175	176	177	178	179	180	181	182	183	184
IDAHO—Cont'd														
Caribou	2.6	0.0	0.6	3.3	1.5	0.1	0.1	968	7	35.1	15.3	7.3	1 062	1 020
Cassia	11.2	0.0	2.0	21.9	4.4	0.6	0.5	7 653	37	79.8	47.8	11.2	536	509
Clark	2.2	0.0	0.1	0.0	0.1	0.1	0.0	105	2	4.7	3.4	0.8	916	905
Clearwater	11.8	8.7	22.0	21.9	1.8	0.2	1.7	2 455	20	29.8	15.7	8.2	1 002	962
Custer	6.9	0.1	2.4	3.5	0.8	0.1	0.5	1 810	12	15.3	8.4	4.3	1 040	981
Elmore	232.1	77.5	2.4	12.9	4.4	2.8	2.2	7 875	37	85.4	33.5	12.4	429	398
Franklin	4.8	0.0	0.6	7.3	1.9	0.2	0.3	7 843	52	42.0	20.9	4.2	348	324
Fremont	6.8	0.0	2.1	11.5	2.5	0.3	0.1	8 160	52	35.5	17.7	15.1	1 208	1 165
Gem	9.5	0.0	1.7	19.8	2.7	0.4	0.2	1 513	13	48.4	24.1	11.0	669	587
Gooding	8.5	0.0	2.1	23.9	2.3	0.5	3.4	2 299	12	54.4	26.0	10.7	754	744
Idaho	20.0	0.4	25.0	26.1	2.7	1.6	0.8	423	4	47.0	25.4	7.2	467	439
Jefferson	4.9	0.0	2.7	12.6	4.7	0.4	1.4	10 434	65	57.7	37.7	13.4	586	571
Jerome	6.1	0.0	51.3	24.0	2.1	0.6	0.4	7 176	54	69.1	36.7	10.9	545	516
Kootenai	61.7	13.4	618.3	103.5	13.6	2.4	5.8	102 367	627	567.8	168.3	115.8	862	708
Latah	18.3	4.2	16.4	33.8	4.8	4.3	44.3	15 263	107	85.8	43.5	25.6	705	641
Lemhi	11.2	0.0	15.3	10.4	1.4	0.2	0.6	1 721	20	36.1	12.7	4.3	563	523
Lewis	2.6	0.0	0.3	19.8	1.2	0.1	1.2	0	0	18.7	10.2	4.9	1 373	1 344
Lincoln	4.5	0.0	0.5	2.1	0.8	0.2	0.0	411	3	16.8	10.7	3.3	737	707
Madison	8.4	0.3	1.0	10.7	4.9	0.7	0.8	34 786	249	114.1	42.5	20.1	549	403
Minidoka	4.4	0.0	1.5	19.8	4.5	0.5	1.8	5 588	40	69.4	34.0	9.0	485	461
Nez Perce	19.6	0.4	16.5	76.8	10.9	8.4	13.0	7 675	48	121.4	55.8	35.7	916	873
Oneida	0.8	0.0	0.2	3.1	0.7	0.1	0.1	1 252	19	13.9	7.9	2.3	569	552
Owyhee	3.2	9.7	1.3	14.6	2.4	0.5	0.3	1 638	11	38.0	22.3	11.4	1 048	892
Payette	4.4	6.0	1.1	32.7	8.7	0.6	2.0	4 230	38	59.5	34.4	13.6	598	551
Power	1.7	0.0	0.5	5.2	1.4	0.3	3.4	2 115	9	35.3	16.3	10.4	1 360	1 344
Shoshone	4.1	10.8	3.6	25.0	2.1	0.3	1.2	428	2	55.4	22.3	11.6	906	852
Teton	3.4	0.6	0.4	10.4	0.8	0.1	1.5	3 769	16	31.8	11.8	6.1	733	490
Twin Falls	43.7	2.2	11.1	84.7	15.6	1.9	4.3	28 448	199	363.5	131.5	47.8	654	611
Valley	16.1	0.0	12.2	5.2	1.3	0.1	3.0	10 005	46	67.9	19.7	20.8	2 331	1 938
Washington	3.0	0.0	0.5	17.7	2.3	0.3	3.2	2 517	23	49.6	21.6	6.5	642	620
ILLINOIS	7 949.5	7 118.7	4 481.8	12 147.7	2 913.9	2 151.5	6 847.0	2 412 386	12 318	X	X	X	X	X
Adams	44.2	6.5	5.6	75.4	12.3	3.1	7.7	20 439	139	190.5	93.7	61.6	918	780
Alexander	3.3	2.4	0.7	42.6	3.6	0.8	1.0	0	0	31.4	18.5	4.5	535	452
Bond	23.8	0.1	5.7	13.7	2.8	0.3	0.6	4 746	28	38.6	18.7	11.0	610	592
Boone	7.2	0.2	2.0	9.1	4.6	0.8	1.3	7 828	42	142.4	58.2	52.2	976	921
Brown	2.2	0.0	0.4	3.3	1.1	0.1	0.1	0	0	13.5	7.2	4.5	682	658
Bureau	12.3	23.3	0.8	11.6	4.7	0.8	1.1	5 846	27	138.1	46.4	39.7	1 133	1 093
Calhoun	2.1	9.7	0.8	6.2	1.1	1.6	0.1	477	3	12.4	7.0	3.3	645	639
Carroll	5.1	3.4	1.5	8.3	2.7	0.4	0.2	3 751	18	45.6	18.2	21.6	1 357	1 297
Cass	5.2	0.0	0.8	10.4	2.3	0.4	0.1	540	3	39.2	22.3	11.0	800	742
Champaign	132.3	25.0	45.7	243.8	25.8	19.3	377.3	66 983	478	608.1	226.6	268.5	1 411	1 161
Christian	7.3	0.0	2.1	24.0	5.4	0.9	2.5	5 162	35	98.0	53.6	30.2	873	830
Clark	4.8	0.0	1.1	11.1	2.5	0.5	0.2	254	5	45.7	24.9	12.5	741	699
Clay	3.8	0.0	0.8	19.8	2.8	0.4	1.8	405	3	54.9	21.8	8.7	626	595
Clinton	9.0	5.7	1.5	11.6	4.9	0.6	0.0	18 577	104	83.0	36.4	30.7	843	830
Coles	32.8	0.3	3.0	34.4	6.9	2.1	5.4	14 520	127	186.4	86.7	60.8	1 192	1 072
Cook	3 429.7	2 148.9	1 997.1	8 022.8	1 321.0	370.1	2 875.2	674 513	2 734	27 280.1	9 218.1	12 233.3	2 315	1 687
Crawford	4.8	0.0	1.1	13.6	3.2	0.5	3.1	1 750	7	80.5	26.1	17.2	877	856
Cumberland	2.4	0.0	0.6	7.0	5.1	0.2	0.6	221	2	25.1	13.3	7.6	699	689
DeKalb	22.4	2.2	4.7	22.4	8.9	4.5	71.5	9 957	51	383.8	126.7	171.8	1 656	1 396
De Witt	5.1	0.0	1.0	8.3	2.5	0.3	0.6	3 870	24	63.8	15.9	25.7	1 563	1 535
Douglas	5.1	0.0	1.2	7.0	2.5	0.4	0.0	3 723	26	49.4	20.6	22.1	1 128	1 093
DuPage	411.9	1 992.7	947.6	151.4	69.8	20.1	136.6	241 686	618	3 886.1	792.9	2 334.9	2 513	2 226
Edgar	7.3	0.0	1.2	14.5	3.4	0.5	0.6	1 078	6	50.2	24.8	17.9	945	851
Edwards	2.0	0.0	0.5	3.8	1.4	0.1	0.1	NA	NA	14.5	7.8	4.3	656	602
Effingham	22.0	0.3	2.9	17.4	7.5	1.0	2.0	10 550	147	98.7	51.2	29.9	875	822
Fayette	5.5	0.0	1.3	18.2	3.6	0.7	2.9	783	4	50.4	26.1	14.9	692	619
Ford	4.4	0.1	1.0	5.0	2.2	0.3	0.2	1 708	10	42.9	19.9	17.1	1 208	1 113
Franklin	14.6	3.1	7.3	50.8	7.6	1.6	3.3	1 197	15	130.1	68.3	21.2	536	483
Fulton	12.6	0.4	2.0	20.4	6.2	1.3	1.6	5 044	32	121.4	62.6	30.6	832	778
Gallatin	2.1	0.0	8.1	12.8	1.6	0.2	2.7	NA	NA	15.4	10.3	3.6	591	551
Greene	4.1	0.5	1.0	19.0	3.0	0.5	0.3	190	1	32.8	17.8	9.8	706	656
Grundy	9.2	6.1	2.1	5.2	3.9	0.6	0.2	9 686	86	186.2	49.2	104.6	2 218	2 150
Hamilton	3.2	0.1	0.7	12.2	1.7	0.2	0.3	0	0	35.4	15.7	4.8	577	575
Hancock	6.9	0.0	1.6	12.4	3.4	0.5	0.2	565	3	48.6	24.1	16.5	874	840

1. State totals may include programs not allocated by county. 2. Based on the resident population estimated as of July 1 of the year shown.

Table B. States and Counties — **Local Government Finances, Government Employment, and Voting**

STATE County	Local government finances, 2007 (cont.) Direct general expenditure Total (mil dol)	Per capita[1] (dollars)	Percent of total for: Educa-tion	Health and hospitals	Police protec-tion	Public welfare	High-ways	Debt outstanding Total (mil dol)	Per capita[1] (dollars)	Government employment, 2009 Federal civilian	Federal military	State and local	Presidential election,[2] 2008 Percent of vote cast: Demo-cratic	Republi-can	All other
	185	186	187	188	189	190	191	192	193	194	195	196	197	198	199
IDAHO—Cont'd															
Caribou	32.2	4 689	42.3	24.3	5.0	0.2	9.5	4.4	640	51	27	649	16.7	80.4	2.8
Cassia	76.7	3 661	44.1	0.1	5.6	0.4	7.0	49.6	2 366	182	85	1 498	17.0	80.5	2.6
Clark	5.0	5 474	45.1	0.2	6.2	0.4	25.1	3.8	4 177	41	0	124	17.1	81.3	1.6
Clearwater	27.3	3 313	40.9	1.9	7.7	1.0	9.3	8.0	976	206	31	853	31.0	65.8	3.2
Custer	13.3	3 199	48.1	3.7	5.4	0.4	9.2	1.7	408	165	17	306	26.0	72.0	2.0
Elmore	82.7	2 867	38.3	30.7	5.1	0.2	7.2	29.8	1 033	908	4 099	1 378	30.7	67.2	2.1
Franklin	37.4	3 067	50.4	25.2	3.8	0.7	5.0	6.8	559	39	50	911	11.8	83.7	4.5
Fremont	34.1	2 724	46.5	0.9	7.1	0.9	8.1	23.0	1 838	98	50	1 021	18.1	79.9	2.0
Gem	44.1	2 675	43.0	18.4	3.1	0.8	4.5	20.9	1 266	85	64	768	27.3	70.3	2.5
Gooding	45.8	3 214	50.5	22.9	3.2	0.6	6.9	17.5	1 228	70	56	1 043	27.6	69.8	2.5
Idaho	44.2	2 879	38.7	16.2	3.4	0.9	18.3	6.1	397	392	60	861	24.6	71.8	3.6
Jefferson	54.3	2 378	62.9	1.3	4.2	0.6	3.8	21.8	956	58	97	1 343	15.7	81.8	2.5
Jerome	79.3	3 950	50.9	0.4	2.9	0.6	7.7	50.8	2 531	59	83	995	26.2	71.5	2.3
Kootenai	541.9	4 031	32.3	34.0	3.6	0.5	4.0	219.9	1 636	594	546	9 198	35.7	62.0	2.3
Latah	82.4	2 270	51.8	0.3	10.8	0.6	8.0	33.1	911	209	180	6 701	51.9	45.1	3.0
Lemhi	31.6	4 092	28.3	43.4	4.5	0.6	5.1	17.6	2 282	225	31	596	25.8	71.6	2.6
Lewis	17.6	4 907	49.1	1.4	5.9	0.7	12.0	6.6	1 836	38	15	414	26.6	70.7	2.8
Lincoln	16.7	3 708	48.4	1.2	3.4	0.7	36.5	4.8	1 076	100	18	427	29.1	65.9	5.0
Madison	112.3	3 064	31.0	38.8	5.0	0.1	5.0	148.1	4 041	62	150	1 880	12.5	85.2	2.3
Minidoka	65.6	3 534	42.9	19.5	3.7	4.3	4.3	48.6	2 617	67	75	1 412	23.7	73.8	2.5
Nez Perce	122.2	3 138	43.9	4.4	7.0	0.5	6.5	12.6	324	172	154	3 848	40.0	58.1	1.9
Oneida	13.7	3 337	45.2	21.2	5.9	0.2	7.5	4.0	983	22	17	430	17.6	79.7	2.6
Owyhee	36.7	3 389	52.5	0.2	3.9	0.7	7.2	16.4	1 518	57	44	675	23.3	74.5	2.2
Payette	64.0	2 815	60.3	0.2	6.3	0.7	6.4	28.5	1 251	40	90	1 050	28.0	69.5	2.4
Power	33.0	4 296	44.1	17.8	4.7	0.3	9.7	17.4	2 261	27	30	671	36.1	61.7	2.1
Shoshone	62.7	4 883	42.4	16.6	4.3	0.8	12.5	48.6	3 789	91	50	964	44.5	52.1	3.4
Teton	29.5	3 531	36.8	28.3	2.3	0.3	5.2	28.9	3 462	45	37	544	49.4	48.6	2.0
Twin Falls	357.1	4 887	42.0	33.1	2.8	0.9	3.5	165.6	2 266	430	295	4 178	30.4	67.1	2.4
Valley	55.3	6 177	30.1	23.9	2.7	0.3	12.5	87.9	9 822	263	34	902	45.4	52.3	2.2
Washington	41.2	4 061	39.6	16.8	3.6	0.7	7.6	10.7	1 057	54	40	669	27.5	70.3	2.2
ILLINOIS	X	X	X	X	X	X	X	X	X	87 467	48 155	774 657	61.9	36.8	1.3
Adams	181.9	2 713	56.3	2.9	5.6	0.2	7.3	65.1	970	320	135	4 503	38.3	60.7	1.0
Alexander	31.7	3 751	46.7	0.0	4.9	0.7	6.6	5.6	658	31	16	583	55.6	43.0	1.4
Bond	38.4	2 122	45.6	6.8	5.2	0.1	9.6	17.7	978	337	36	719	48.5	49.8	1.7
Boone	183.0	3 418	65.5	0.6	3.1	2.3	4.8	148.8	2 780	83	108	2 184	51.1	47.0	1.9
Brown	12.9	1 972	45.4	2.1	6.0	0.0	14.2	4.9	744	43	13	423	38.4	60.1	1.5
Bureau	137.5	3 924	37.6	21.2	4.0	3.2	8.1	52.9	1 511	143	69	2 211	51.9	46.2	1.8
Calhoun	12.9	2 488	53.0	0.7	3.4	0.1	19.5	5.6	1 086	35	10	236	52.7	45.2	2.0
Carroll	44.8	2 794	58.8	1.3	6.0	0.3	8.0	25.4	1 595	77	31	829	51.7	46.9	1.5
Cass	37.3	2 718	49.9	7.8	4.8	0.4	6.2	10.4	756	65	27	987	49.7	48.4	1.9
Champaign	584.6	3 073	48.8	2.5	5.7	3.6	5.4	333.6	1 754	1 261	426	34 938	57.8	40.3	2.0
Christian	104.1	3 013	62.4	1.4	5.3	0.2	7.5	32.3	934	87	68	1 850	45.8	52.1	2.1
Clark	44.2	2 617	49.8	1.8	5.3	0.2	14.0	20.7	1 224	61	33	886	45.1	53.2	1.7
Clay	56.9	4 099	35.3	30.5	3.3	0.0	5.7	39.6	2 854	47	27	924	37.6	60.8	1.6
Clinton	80.1	2 196	50.0	1.8	7.4	0.0	10.9	46.2	1 267	111	73	2 356	44.2	54.0	1.7
Coles	199.7	3 915	59.2	1.6	4.9	0.2	6.5	73.5	1 440	141	108	6 496	50.8	47.6	1.7
Cook	26 539.5	5 022	36.7	4.6	7.7	1.1	3.7	44 769.2	8 471	41 565	10 910	292 678	76.2	22.8	1.0
Crawford	79.5	4 053	36.8	40.1	2.6	0.0	6.4	31.0	1 582	61	39	1 905	42.5	55.5	1.9
Cumberland	23.6	2 178	57.8	1.6	4.8	0.2	9.6	10.7	982	36	21	482	38.6	59.3	2.1
DeKalb	378.7	3 651	46.6	1.9	5.8	3.2	7.4	264.5	2 550	209	218	13 134	57.5	40.8	1.7
De Witt	59.6	3 627	39.3	20.7	6.1	0.1	8.7	16.5	1 006	55	32	1 111	42.4	55.7	1.9
Douglas	45.7	2 331	51.0	1.5	6.7	0.2	10.2	26.9	1 370	65	38	1 014	38.6	59.9	1.5
DuPage	3 750.1	4 036	52.2	1.0	6.5	1.7	5.2	4 021.9	4 328	5 144	1 869	45 999	54.7	43.9	1.4
Edgar	47.3	2 498	57.8	2.9	5.9	0.1	8.3	15.5	817	70	37	1 110	45.3	53.3	1.4
Edwards	16.0	2 427	52.0	0.8	3.5	0.1	10.4	26.3	4 004	24	13	298	34.0	63.8	2.2
Effingham	95.4	2 788	48.4	2.5	6.2	0.0	8.2	32.3	942	171	70	1 797	31.3	67.3	1.5
Fayette	49.0	2 282	49.6	6.3	6.8	0.1	8.3	36.3	1 689	71	42	1 327	41.0	56.8	2.2
Ford	46.2	3 259	59.6	1.0	5.5	0.0	6.2	16.1	1 135	53	28	851	34.9	63.9	1.3
Franklin	129.5	3 279	45.3	12.5	5.7	0.4	6.2	34.2	866	229	78	1 962	47.6	50.4	1.9
Fulton	121.8	3 305	55.7	3.4	4.4	2.1	6.0	82.5	2 239	109	73	2 440	59.6	38.3	2.1
Gallatin	14.8	2 452	49.1	0.7	2.5	0.6	19.3	4.0	658	30	11	289	55.5	42.4	2.1
Greene	32.3	2 325	53.0	5.2	4.7	0.4	10.9	23.2	1 669	55	27	706	45.1	52.6	2.3
Grundy	210.9	4 474	62.4	0.8	3.7	0.5	4.0	233.8	4 958	118	97	2 438	49.9	48.2	1.9
Hamilton	36.6	4 433	28.4	38.5	0.9	0.1	17.2	8.9	1 083	40	16	608	42.1	55.2	2.7
Hancock	50.6	2 684	56.5	3.5	3.7	0.0	9.3	15.3	812	82	37	1 196	43.7	54.5	1.8

1. Based on the resident population estimated as of July 1 of the year shown.   2. © 2009 Election Data Services, Inc. All rights reserved.

Table B. States and Counties — Land Area and Population

STATE/ County code	CBSA code[1]	County type[2]	STATE County	Population and population characteristics, 2010														
				Land area,[3] (sq km) 2010	Total persons	Rank	Per square kilometer	Race alone or in combination, not Hispanic or Latino (percent)				Percent Hispanic or Latino[4]	Age (percent)					
								White	Black	American Indian, Alaska Native	Asian and Pacific Islander		Under 5 years	5 to 17 years	18 to 24 years	25 to 34 years	35 to 44 years	45 to 54 years
				1	2	3	4	5	6	7	8	9	10	11	12	13	14	15
			ILLINOIS—Cont'd															
17 069	...	9	Hardin	460	4 320	2 882	9.4	97.2	0.5	0.9	0.7	1.3	5.6	14.7	6.4	9.9	11.7	14.9
17 071	15460	9	Henderson	981	7 331	2 658	7.5	98.2	0.5	0.7	0.4	1.1	4.7	15.7	6.3	9.3	11.0	17.0
17 073	19340	2	Henry	2 132	50 486	970	23.7	93.2	2.0	0.5	0.6	4.8	6.0	18.0	7.2	10.9	12.0	15.3
17 075	...	6	Iroquois	2 894	29 718	1 434	10.3	93.4	1.2	0.5	0.5	5.3	5.5	18.1	6.9	10.0	11.5	15.7
17 077	16060	5	Jackson	1 513	60 218	856	39.8	78.0	15.3	1.0	3.8	4.0	5.2	12.6	24.9	14.4	9.8	11.1
17 079	...	7	Jasper	1 281	9 698	2 460	7.6	98.7	0.3	0.4	0.4	0.8	5.7	17.0	7.6	11.2	11.4	16.4
17 081	34500	7	Jefferson	1 479	38 827	1 199	26.3	88.7	9.0	0.6	0.9	2.1	6.3	15.9	8.5	12.3	12.8	14.6
17 083	41180	1	Jersey	956	22 985	1 689	24.0	98.0	0.7	0.7	0.7	1.0	5.6	17.2	9.8	11.0	12.2	15.9
17 085	...	6	Jo Daviess	1 557	22 678	1 699	14.6	96.3	0.8	0.5	0.5	2.7	5.3	15.5	6.2	9.1	11.0	15.2
17 087	...	7	Johnson	891	12 582	2 271	14.1	88.7	8.1	0.7	0.3	3.0	4.5	14.9	8.8	12.4	13.3	15.3
17 089	16980	1	Kane	1 347	515 269	124	382.5	60.1	5.9	0.3	4.0	30.7	7.7	21.2	8.4	13.4	14.8	14.4
17 091	28100	3	Kankakee	1 752	113 449	526	64.8	74.7	16.0	0.6	1.2	9.0	6.8	18.6	10.2	12.5	12.5	14.3
17 093	16980	1	Kendall	830	114 736	519	138.2	75.6	6.2	0.4	3.7	15.6	8.8	22.6	6.9	15.3	17.5	13.0
17 095	23660	4	Knox	1 855	52 919	935	28.5	87.2	8.4	0.6	0.9	4.8	5.2	15.3	10.0	11.5	11.5	14.2
17 097	16980	1	Lake	1 149	703 462	84	612.2	66.6	7.3	0.4	7.1	19.9	6.7	20.7	9.0	11.5	14.2	16.2
17 099	36860	4	LaSalle	2 940	113 924	524	38.7	89.2	2.3	0.5	0.9	8.0	5.8	17.2	8.3	11.7	12.2	15.8
17 101	...	7	Lawrence	964	16 833	1 994	17.5	86.8	9.9	0.5	0.3	3.3	5.2	13.9	9.6	14.9	14.0	14.9
17 103	19940	4	Lee	1 877	36 031	1 273	19.2	89.3	5.2	0.5	0.9	5.0	5.7	15.8	8.1	11.7	13.0	16.6
17 105	38700	4	Livingston	2 705	38 950	1 197	14.4	90.5	5.3	0.4	0.7	3.9	5.7	16.8	8.3	12.3	12.5	16.2
17 107	30660	6	Logan	1 601	30 305	1 422	18.9	88.8	8.0	0.5	0.9	2.9	5.3	14.7	10.9	13.6	12.9	14.9
17 109	31380	5	McDonough	1 527	32 612	1 374	21.4	90.4	5.6	0.7	2.2	2.7	4.6	11.5	28.7	10.8	8.6	10.9
17 111	16980	1	McHenry	1 562	308 760	207	197.7	84.8	1.3	0.4	3.1	11.4	6.4	20.8	7.6	11.3	15.3	17.0
17 113	14060	3	McLean	3 065	169 572	362	55.3	83.7	8.4	0.6	4.8	4.4	6.3	16.4	17.3	13.8	12.4	13.3
17 115	19500	3	Macon	1 504	110 768	534	73.6	80.5	17.8	0.6	1.3	1.9	6.3	16.6	9.3	11.7	11.6	14.7
17 117	41180	1	Macoupin	2 235	47 765	1 008	21.4	97.8	1.0	0.6	0.5	0.9	5.9	16.7	8.4	11.2	12.0	15.4
17 119	41180	1	Madison	1 853	269 282	241	145.3	88.2	8.7	0.7	1.2	2.7	6.1	16.7	10.2	12.7	12.6	15.3
17 121	16460	4	Marion	1 482	39 437	1 184	26.6	93.8	4.9	0.6	0.8	1.4	6.5	16.9	8.2	11.0	11.5	15.1
17 123	37900	2	Marshall	1 002	12 640	2 267	12.6	96.6	0.5	0.4	0.6	2.5	5.4	16.3	7.0	10.0	11.7	15.4
17 125	...	6	Mason	1 397	14 666	2 135	10.5	98.3	0.6	0.6	0.4	0.8	5.2	16.8	7.2	10.1	12.1	15.3
17 127	37140	7	Massac	614	15 429	2 087	25.1	91.6	7.0	0.9	0.5	1.9	6.2	16.6	7.4	10.8	12.6	15.4
17 129	44100	3	Menard	814	12 705	2 261	15.6	97.9	1.0	0.7	0.4	1.0	5.8	17.8	7.1	10.0	12.7	16.5
17 131	19340	2	Mercer	1 454	16 434	2 021	11.3	97.4	0.5	0.3	0.4	1.9	5.9	16.8	7.0	9.9	12.2	15.9
17 133	41180	1	Monroe	997	32 957	1 359	33.1	97.8	0.3	0.5	0.7	1.4	5.9	18.6	7.1	10.8	13.5	17.7
17 135	...	6	Montgomery	1 823	30 104	1 424	16.5	94.7	3.4	0.4	0.6	1.5	5.7	15.6	8.1	12.2	12.9	15.7
17 137	27300	4	Morgan	1 473	35 547	1 287	24.1	91.2	7.0	0.5	0.7	2.0	5.5	15.9	10.3	11.9	11.5	15.2
17 139	...	6	Moultrie	870	14 846	2 122	17.1	98.4	0.5	0.4	0.3	0.9	6.7	18.3	7.4	11.8	11.3	14.2
17 141	40300	4	Ogle	1 965	53 497	929	27.2	89.6	1.3	0.5	0.7	8.9	5.9	18.8	7.7	10.5	13.1	16.3
17 143	37900	2	Peoria	1 604	186 494	333	116.3	74.9	19.2	0.6	3.7	3.8	6.8	17.3	10.3	13.4	12.2	13.7
17 145	...	7	Perry	1 144	22 350	1 718	19.5	88.3	9.1	0.5	0.6	2.7	5.3	15.4	10.0	13.2	13.3	14.6
17 147	16580	3	Piatt	1 138	16 729	2 001	14.7	98.1	0.6	0.5	0.6	1.0	5.6	18.3	6.4	10.5	12.2	17.0
17 149	...	7	Pike	2 153	16 430	2 022	7.6	96.9	1.9	0.5	0.3	1.0	6.2	16.4	7.7	10.7	12.1	14.4
17 151	...	9	Pope	955	4 470	2 871	4.7	91.5	6.5	0.9	0.4	1.4	4.6	13.6	11.0	9.1	9.7	15.0
17 153	...	9	Pulaski	516	6 161	2 750	11.9	65.4	33.1	1.1	0.4	1.6	5.8	17.0	8.5	10.1	10.5	15.6
17 155	36860	8	Putnam	415	6 006	2 766	14.5	94.9	0.8	0.3	0.6	4.2	5.2	16.1	6.8	10.1	11.4	16.9
17 157	...	6	Randolph	1 491	33 476	1 337	22.5	87.2	10.1	0.5	0.4	2.6	5.1	14.7	8.0	14.1	13.5	15.8
17 159	...	7	Richland	932	16 233	2 040	17.4	97.3	0.8	0.4	1.0	1.3	6.0	16.2	8.2	11.3	11.6	15.0
17 161	19340	2	Rock Island	1 108	147 546	422	133.2	77.6	10.0	0.7	2.0	11.6	6.4	16.1	9.2	12.5	11.8	14.5
17 163	41180	1	St. Clair	1 704	270 056	238	158.5	64.6	31.5	0.7	2.0	3.3	6.8	18.6	9.2	13.0	13.0	15.3
17 165	25380	7	Saline	984	24 913	1 603	25.3	93.8	4.8	0.9	0.6	1.4	5.8	17.1	8.3	11.0	11.9	14.2
17 167	44100	3	Sangamon	2 249	197 465	315	87.8	84.4	13.1	0.6	2.0	1.8	6.3	17.4	8.4	12.9	12.5	15.5
17 169	...	7	Schuyler	1 133	7 544	2 640	6.7	95.3	3.3	0.4	0.2	1.2	5.6	15.3	6.8	10.7	13.5	15.5
17 171	27300	9	Scott	650	5 355	2 816	8.2	98.6	0.3	0.5	0.4	0.8	6.0	17.7	6.8	10.7	11.8	16.8
17 173	...	6	Shelby	1 965	22 363	1 716	11.4	98.5	0.4	0.5	0.3	0.8	5.7	16.9	7.4	10.2	11.7	15.3
17 175	37900	2	Stark	746	5 994	2 769	8.0	98.0	0.8	0.5	0.6	1.0	5.3	18.2	6.6	9.5	11.9	14.5
17 177	23300	4	Stephenson	1 462	47 711	1 012	32.6	87.2	10.5	0.5	1.0	2.9	5.9	16.7	7.9	10.2	11.7	15.4
17 179	37900	2	Tazewell	1 681	135 394	456	80.5	96.0	1.4	0.6	1.1	1.9	6.4	17.1	7.5	12.8	12.9	14.8
17 181	...	7	Union	1 071	17 808	1 935	16.6	93.5	1.4	0.9	0.6	4.8	5.8	15.7	8.4	10.5	12.1	15.4
17 183	19180	3	Vermilion	2 327	81 625	676	35.1	82.0	13.9	0.7	0.9	4.2	6.7	17.7	8.1	11.9	11.8	14.5
17 185	...	6	Wabash	578	11 947	2 306	20.7	97.1	1.0	0.7	0.8	1.3	6.0	16.1	8.4	11.4	11.2	15.3
17 187	23660	7	Warren	1 405	17 707	1 941	12.6	89.1	2.3	0.5	0.7	8.4	5.8	16.3	12.0	10.8	11.2	13.8
17 189	...	6	Washington	1 457	14 716	2 133	10.1	97.6	0.9	0.3	0.5	1.3	5.7	16.5	7.8	11.3	12.2	16.5
17 191	...	7	Wayne	1 849	16 760	1 998	9.1	98.1	0.4	0.5	0.6	1.1	6.2	16.3	7.5	11.1	11.7	14.5
17 193	...	6	White	1 281	14 665	2 136	11.4	98.1	0.4	0.5	0.4	1.1	6.0	14.9	7.2	11.0	10.7	15.7
17 195	44580	4	Whiteside	1 772	58 498	874	33.0	87.0	1.8	0.5	0.7	11.0	6.0	17.5	7.8	10.5	12.1	15.2
17 197	16980	1	Will	2 168	677 560	88	312.5	68.5	11.6	0.4	5.1	15.6	7.2	21.8	8.1	12.2	16.0	15.2
17 199	32060	5	Williamson	1 088	66 357	791	61.0	93.0	4.6	0.8	1.1	2.0	6.1	16.0	8.5	12.8	12.7	14.7

1. CBSA = Core Based Statistical Area. See Appendix A for explanation. See Appendix B for list of metropolitan areas with component counties. 2. County type code from the Economic Research Service of USDA Rural-Urban Continuum Codes. See Appendix A for definition. 3. Dry land or land partially or temporarily covered by water. 4. May be of any race.

Table B. States and Counties — **Population and Households**

	Population, 2010 (cont.)				Population change and components of change, 1990–2010							Households, 2010				
	Age (percent) (cont.)				Total persons		Percent change		Components of change, 2000–2009						Percent	
STATE County	55 to 64 years	65 to 74 years	75 years and over	Percent female	1990	2000	1990–2000	2000–2010	Births	Deaths	Net migration	Number	Percent change, 2000–2010	Persons per house-hold	Female family house-holder[1]	One per-son
	16	17	18	19	20	21	22	23	24	25	26	27	28	29	30	31

ILLINOIS—Cont'd

Hardin	16.5	12.2	8.1	50.3	5 189	4 800	-7.5	-10.0	404	596	-228	1 915	-3.6	2.25	9.2	31.7
Henderson	15.2	11.6	9.3	50.7	8 096	8 213	1.4	-10.7	605	814	-609	3 149	-6.4	2.31	8.7	27.3
Henry	13.6	8.8	8.3	50.3	51 159	51 020	-0.3	-1.0	5 259	4 899	-1 755	20 373	1.6	2.44	9.5	26.1
Iroquois	13.3	9.6	9.3	51.1	30 787	31 334	1.8	-5.2	3 252	3 540	-1 164	11 956	-2.2	2.45	9.3	27.2
Jackson	10.4	5.9	5.7	49.1	61 067	59 612	-2.4	1.0	6 268	4 297	-3 233	25 538	5.5	2.20	10.2	35.1
Jasper	13.3	8.7	8.7	50.2	10 609	10 117	-4.6	-4.1	1 090	962	-661	3 940	0.3	2.45	7.9	24.5
Jefferson	13.4	8.6	7.6	48.6	37 020	40 045	8.2	-3.0	4 442	3 889	-417	15 365	-0.1	2.38	11.4	29.1
Jersey	12.5	8.4	7.3	51.0	20 539	21 668	5.5	6.1	2 286	2 161	887	8 828	9.0	2.51	9.7	25.0
Jo Daviess	16.5	11.9	9.4	49.8	21 821	22 289	2.1	1.7	2 112	2 099	-178	9 753	5.8	2.31	7.0	28.4
Johnson	13.6	10.3	6.9	44.2	11 347	12 878	13.5	-2.3	1 166	1 103	813	4 584	9.6	2.41	8.3	25.3
Kane	10.5	5.5	4.2	50.2	317 471	404 119	27.3	27.5	78 015	24 170	52 874	170 479	27.3	2.98	11.0	19.8
Kankakee	11.8	7.0	6.4	50.9	96 255	103 833	7.9	9.3	14 630	9 961	3 934	41 511	8.7	2.61	14.7	25.5
Kendall	8.6	4.5	2.8	50.5	39 413	54 544	38.4	110.4	13 370	3 344	41 668	38 022	102.3	3.01	9.2	16.4
Knox	13.8	9.2	9.3	49.8	56 393	55 836	-1.0	-5.2	5 464	6 336	-3 002	21 535	-2.4	2.27	11.9	32.3
Lake	11.3	5.7	4.6	50.1	516 418	644 356	24.8	9.2	94 657	35 956	8 712	241 712	11.8	2.82	10.4	21.5
LaSalle	12.7	8.1	8.3	50.1	106 913	111 509	4.3	2.2	12 963	11 822	-78	45 347	4.4	2.45	10.5	28.6
Lawrence	11.7	7.9	8.1	44.0	15 972	15 452	-3.3	8.9	1 488	2 066	1 566	6 130	-2.8	2.34	10.7	30.1
Lee	13.4	8.1	7.5	47.5	34 392	36 062	4.9	-0.1	3 569	3 360	-1 183	13 758	3.8	2.41	10.0	28.8
Livingston	12.4	7.9	7.9	49.9	39 301	39 678	1.0	-1.8	4 749	3 844	-2 616	14 613	1.7	2.43	9.9	28.6
Logan	12.0	7.8	8.0	49.3	30 798	31 183	1.3	-2.8	3 058	3 052	-1 269	11 070	-0.4	2.34	10.6	29.2
McDonough	10.6	6.8	7.4	49.9	35 244	32 913	-6.6	-0.9	2 726	2 712	35	13 057	5.6	2.19	8.0	33.9
McHenry	11.4	6.0	4.1	50.1	183 241	260 077	41.9	18.7	39 252	15 823	35 513	109 199	22.1	2.81	8.9	19.8
McLean	10.3	5.3	4.9	51.4	129 180	150 433	16.5	12.7	20 116	9 583	7 620	65 104	14.7	2.44	9.6	28.1
Macon	13.5	8.2	8.2	52.2	117 206	114 706	-2.1	-3.4	13 075	10 972	-8 040	45 855	-1.5	2.33	14.1	30.9
Macoupin	13.4	8.5	8.6	50.7	47 679	49 019	2.8	-2.6	5 234	5 428	-730	19 381	0.7	2.42	9.8	27.0
Madison	12.1	7.3	6.9	51.1	249 238	258 941	3.9	4.0	31 486	24 596	2 350	108 094	6.0	2.46	12.2	26.8
Marion	13.3	9.1	8.4	51.4	41 561	41 691	0.3	-5.4	4 727	4 621	-2 585	16 148	-2.8	2.40	12.8	28.8
Marshall	14.8	9.9	9.6	50.7	12 846	13 180	2.6	-4.1	1 285	1 610	-54	5 161	-1.2	2.40	7.7	26.8
Mason	14.2	9.6	9.5	50.9	16 269	16 038	-1.4	-8.6	1 664	1 824	-1 010	6 079	-4.9	2.38	10.3	28.4
Massac	12.7	9.5	8.9	52.2	14 752	15 161	2.8	1.8	1 785	1 875	-3	6 362	1.6	2.38	12.0	29.2
Menard	14.5	8.8	6.7	51.3	11 164	12 486	11.8	1.8	1 269	1 182	-31	5 140	5.5	2.44	9.6	24.3
Mercer	14.2	9.8	8.5	50.6	17 290	16 957	-1.9	-3.1	1 678	1 648	-619	6 734	1.7	2.41	7.9	25.8
Monroe	12.2	7.1	7.0	50.6	22 422	27 619	23.2	19.3	3 463	2 409	4 277	12 589	22.5	2.59	7.9	21.5
Montgomery	12.7	8.3	9.0	47.7	30 728	30 652	-0.2	-1.8	3 072	3 282	-981	11 652	1.3	2.38	10.2	28.4
Morgan	13.1	8.6	8.1	49.8	36 397	36 616	0.6	-2.9	3 781	3 732	-1 566	14 104	0.5	2.30	11.2	31.5
Moultrie	12.6	8.5	9.1	51.4	13 930	14 287	2.6	3.9	1 696	1 778	275	5 758	6.5	2.51	8.9	25.5
Ogle	12.5	8.3	6.8	50.4	45 957	51 032	11.0	4.8	5 616	4 410	2 582	20 856	8.2	2.54	9.7	24.5
Peoria	12.4	7.2	6.7	51.6	182 827	183 433	0.3	1.7	24 609	16 209	-4 914	75 793	4.2	2.39	14.1	31.0
Perry	12.4	8.2	7.5	45.8	21 412	23 094	7.9	-3.2	2 283	2 322	-500	8 335	-2.0	2.38	11.3	28.6
Piatt	13.7	8.8	7.4	50.6	15 548	16 365	5.3	2.2	1 703	1 458	15	6 782	4.7	2.46	8.0	24.5
Pike	13.4	9.4	9.6	50.1	17 577	17 384	-1.1	-5.5	1 760	1 964	-816	6 639	-3.4	2.38	9.0	27.8
Pope	15.4	12.6	9.0	47.3	4 373	4 413	0.9	1.3	308	428	-300	1 829	3.4	2.23	7.8	29.8
Pulaski	14.2	9.5	8.8	52.2	7 523	7 348	-2.3	-16.2	650	819	-1 144	2 642	-8.7	2.32	14.3	33.4
Putnam	15.7	9.9	7.9	49.5	5 730	6 086	6.2	-1.3	557	486	-113	2 509	3.9	2.39	7.2	26.0
Randolph	12.8	8.2	7.8	45.1	34 583	33 893	-2.0	-1.2	3 463	3 477	-1 034	12 314	1.9	2.37	10.1	28.9
Richland	12.5	9.5	9.7	51.0	16 545	16 149	-2.4	0.5	1 724	1 912	-479	6 726	1.0	2.36	9.6	29.3
Rock Island	13.2	8.3	7.9	50.9	148 723	149 374	0.4	-1.2	18 051	13 374	-6 394	61 303	1.0	2.34	12.7	31.6
St. Clair	11.5	6.4	6.1	51.9	262 852	256 082	-2.6	5.5	34 749	23 442	-4 263	105 045	8.5	2.53	17.7	27.5
Saline	13.3	9.8	8.6	51.2	26 551	26 733	0.7	-6.8	2 868	3 651	-48	10 379	-5.6	2.32	11.7	31.9
Sangamon	13.2	7.2	6.6	52.0	178 386	188 951	5.9	4.5	23 706	16 808	-824	82 986	5.4	2.33	13.2	31.8
Schuyler	14.0	9.3	9.2	47.9	7 498	7 189	-4.1	4.9	705	814	-316	3 040	2.2	2.33	7.6	28.6
Scott	12.1	9.8	8.2	51.1	5 644	5 537	-1.9	-3.3	592	543	-357	2 214	-0.4	2.40	9.1	27.3
Shelby	13.8	9.8	9.1	50.2	22 261	22 893	2.8	-2.3	2 285	2 243	-992	9 216	1.8	2.40	8.0	27.1
Stark	14.0	10.2	9.7	51.2	6 534	6 332	-3.1	-5.3	644	795	-132	2 425	-4.0	2.43	8.0	26.8
Stephenson	13.4	9.4	9.4	51.5	48 052	48 979	1.9	-2.6	5 303	4 872	-2 596	19 845	0.3	2.36	11.2	29.7
Tazewell	12.9	7.9	7.7	50.7	123 692	128 485	3.9	5.4	15 229	11 909	1 477	54 146	7.6	2.45	10.2	26.3
Union	13.9	10.2	8.0	50.1	17 619	18 293	3.8	-2.7	2 042	2 196	-17	7 167	-1.7	2.41	10.6	28.4
Vermilion	13.0	8.5	7.8	50.4	88 257	83 919	-4.9	-2.7	10 275	8 782	-4 898	32 655	-2.2	2.41	14.7	29.8
Wabash	13.7	8.6	9.2	51.1	13 111	12 937	-1.3	-7.7	1 329	1 244	-953	5 012	-3.5	2.37	9.3	29.4
Warren	13.1	9.0	8.0	51.4	19 181	18 735	-2.3	-5.5	1 899	1 918	-1 213	6 918	-3.5	2.40	9.7	28.2
Washington	13.0	8.7	8.3	49.9	14 965	15 148	1.2	-2.9	1 646	1 592	-561	5 926	1.3	2.44	7.3	25.9
Wayne	13.3	10.2	9.2	50.7	17 241	17 151	-0.5	-2.3	1 815	1 905	-674	7 102	-0.6	2.35	9.1	28.4
White	13.5	10.2	10.7	51.7	16 522	15 371	-7.0	-4.6	1 582	2 127	-78	6 313	-3.4	2.26	9.5	30.5
Whiteside	13.4	8.8	8.7	50.9	60 186	60 653	0.8	-3.6	6 874	5 944	-2 294	23 740	0.2	2.42	11.0	27.7
Will	10.2	5.4	3.9	50.3	357 313	502 266	40.6	34.9	89 052	31 123	127 855	225 256	34.4	2.97	10.9	18.5
Williamson	12.9	9.0	7.3	50.5	57 733	61 296	6.2	8.3	7 090	6 849	3 906	27 421	8.1	2.35	11.5	29.1

1. No spouse present.

Table B. States and Counties — Population, Vital Statistics, Medicare, and Crime

STATE County	Daytime population, 2006–2010			Births, average 2006–2008		Deaths, average 2006–2008		Persons under 65 with no health insurance, 2009		Medicare, 2011			Serious crimes known to police,[2] 2010 Total	
	Persons in group quarters, 2010	Number	Employment/residence ratio	Total	Rate[1]	Number	Rate[1]	Number	Percent	Eligible for Medicare	Enrolled in Medicare Advantage	Enrolled in a Medicare prescription drug plan	Number	Rate[3]
	32	33	34	35	36	37	38	39	40	41	42	43	44	45
ILLINOIS—Cont'd														
Hardin	17	4 075	0.8	D	D	68	15.1	534	15.4	1 124	42	617	29	671
Henderson	51	5 753	0.5	D	D	86	11.3	893	15.4	1 607	70	921	165	2 309
Henry	724	42 812	0.7	D	D	517	10.4	4 771	11.9	10 009	1 056	4 635	920	2 034
Iroquois	468	26 191	0.7	D	D	391	12.9	2 990	12.6	6 485	336	3 939	355	1 195
Jackson	4 087	63 780	1.1	688	11.8	464	8.0	7 611	15.3	8 300	122	4 140	2 507	4 163
Jasper	54	8 429	0.7	D	D	105	10.8	977	12.6	2 022	67	1 279	134	1 382
Jefferson	2 203	43 452	1.3	D	D	443	11.0	4 556	13.9	7 484	267	4 515	1 689	4 350
Jersey	848	18 569	0.6	D	D	224	9.9	2 213	11.9	4 421	197	2 536	463	2 014
Jo Daviess	167	20 724	0.8	D	D	220	9.8	2 180	12.7	5 303	1 591	2 475	361	1 699
Johnson	1 553	11 672	0.7	D	D	124	9.2	2 171	19.2	2 673	91	1 184	137	1 229
Kane	6 787	471 438	0.9	8 388	16.7	2 650	5.3	68 976	15.1	57 690	4 635	27 116	9 783	1 899
Kankakee	5 107	108 319	0.9	1 596	14.4	1 055	9.5	14 200	14.8	19 209	462	10 636	3 216	3 176
Kendall	208	80 786	0.5	1 796	18.7	406	4.2	9 278	9.8	10 956	1 266	4 576	1 985	1 730
Knox	3 955	52 120	1.0	545	10.4	669	12.8	5 739	13.9	11 347	1 894	5 861	1 731	3 539
Lake	20 709	710 289	1.0	9 733	13.7	3 948	5.5	74 752	11.9	86 135	2 845	42 011	12 379	1 937
LaSalle	2 950	108 195	0.9	1 359	12.1	1 288	11.4	11 592	12.5	21 451	1 140	10 610	2 180	2 004
Lawrence	2 471	16 281	0.9	D	D	195	12.2	1 984	15.0	3 079	80	1 814	142	996
Lee	2 872	34 908	0.9	D	D	355	10.0	4 034	14.0	6 954	297	3 743	NA	NA
Livingston	3 390	38 545	1.0	497	13.0	402	10.5	3 752	12.1	6 957	708	3 538	741	2 106
Logan	4 361	28 751	0.9	D	D	319	10.6	3 326	13.6	5 443	192	2 543	NA	NA
McDonough	4 036	33 697	1.1	D	D	299	9.3	4 011	14.5	5 510	204	2 814	734	2 251
McHenry	1 647	262 196	0.7	4 058	12.9	1 827	5.8	31 439	11.2	38 544	1 221	18 972	4 614	1 559
McLean	10 676	173 874	1.1	2 213	13.5	1 075	6.6	14 560	9.9	20 841	2 895	7 634	4 531	2 733
Macon	4 059	116 448	1.1	1 426	13.1	1 188	10.9	11 144	12.6	21 843	1 564	12 466	4 250	3 837
Macoupin	876	39 405	0.6	D	D	580	12.0	4 772	12.3	9 695	168	5 536	752	1 662
Madison	3 754	248 199	0.8	3 397	12.7	2 632	9.9	25 526	11.4	47 346	8 801	20 359	6 460	2 619
Marion	758	38 465	0.9	D	D	499	12.6	4 088	13.0	8 647	92	5 289	1 440	3 700
Marshall	255	11 175	0.7	D	D	169	13.2	1 114	11.0	2 702	332	1 265	124	1 105
Mason	206	13 176	0.7	D	D	191	12.5	1 526	12.9	3 521	150	1 782	370	2 841
Massac	292	14 658	0.9	D	D	197	13.0	1 584	13.1	3 435	134	1 731	478	3 098
Menard	154	8 708	0.4	D	D	117	9.4	1 053	10.2	2 296	69	1 010	NA	NA
Mercer	185	12 640	0.5	D	D	164	9.9	1 510	11.6	3 627	516	1 656	280	1 739
Monroe	343	24 967	0.5	D	D	273	8.4	2 265	8.1	5 252	1 076	2 132	372	1 129
Montgomery	2 419	29 573	0.9	341	11.4	351	11.7	3 577	15.0	6 027	105	3 630	659	2 189
Morgan	3 064	36 615	1.1	D	D	411	11.6	3 588	12.6	7 310	253	3 954	762	2 144
Moultrie	395	14 078	0.9	D	D	180	12.5	1 566	13.4	2 765	195	1 473	NA	NA
Ogle	525	47 563	0.8	D	D	456	8.3	5 857	12.6	9 503	1 210	4 577	688	1 382
Peoria	4 979	208 080	1.3	2 744	15.0	1 750	9.6	19 443	12.5	31 381	5 512	13 140	7 628	4 090
Perry	2 500	20 747	0.8	D	D	242	10.7	2 941	15.9	4 186	143	2 627	273	1 221
Piatt	72	13 489	0.6	D	D	162	9.8	1 414	10.5	3 119	660	1 069	243	1 453
Pike	627	15 157	0.8	D	D	198	11.9	2 086	16.2	3 454	103	2 101	31	205
Pope	389	3 481	0.4	D	D	57	13.7	494	16.0	966	38	488	58	1 298
Pulaski	21	6 405	1.1	D	D	89	13.7	759	14.9	1 401	132	788	183	3 284
Putnam	2	5 227	0.7	D	D	58	9.6	548	11.3	1 235	95	584	55	916
Randolph	4 298	33 202	1.0	D	D	351	10.7	4 061	15.2	6 098	204	3 521	343	1 086
Richland	364	15 969	1.0	D	D	201	12.9	1 671	13.6	3 552	139	2 261	434	2 674
Rock Island	4 313	158 260	1.2	1 963	13.3	1 480	10.1	16 205	13.4	27 560	3 832	10 432	4 905	3 340
St. Clair	4 451	252 063	0.9	3 847	14.7	2 498	9.6	28 482	12.7	41 452	8 790	16 279	12 214	4 746
Saline	878	25 754	1.1	304	11.7	380	14.6	2 694	13.2	5 745	198	3 381	782	3 139
Sangamon	3 966	209 946	1.2	2 522	13.0	1 788	9.2	16 926	10.3	33 873	1 883	13 517	10 909	5 639
Schuyler	463	6 630	0.7	D	D	80	11.4	743	14.1	1 530	64	852	60	795
Scott	43	4 223	0.6	D	D	55	10.5	506	12.2	983	28	557	NA	NA
Shelby	205	18 318	0.6	D	D	241	11.0	2 054	11.8	4 664	100	2 634	171	765
Stark	92	5 354	0.7	D	D	73	11.8	578	12.3	1 098	186	533	83	1 385
Stephenson	835	46 467	0.9	570	12.2	505	10.8	4 577	12.3	10 294	2 535	4 298	1 143	2 396
Tazewell	2 843	127 217	0.9	1 711	13.1	1 319	10.1	10 914	10.0	24 114	4 141	9 136	2 354	2 250
Union	566	16 329	0.8	D	D	217	11.9	2 109	14.5	4 129	137	2 112	NA	NA
Vermilion	2 903	80 755	1.0	1 130	13.9	940	11.6	8 539	13.1	16 505	3 927	6 274	3 551	4 422
Wabash	88	10 625	0.7	D	D	129	10.5	1 275	13.2	2 518	69	1 484	178	1 490
Warren	1 116	16 596	0.9	D	D	210	12.0	1 819	12.9	3 147	309	1 827	629	3 655
Washington	246	14 149	0.9	D	D	167	11.3	1 283	10.7	2 848	72	1 687	185	1 267
Wayne	76	15 746	0.9	D	D	203	12.3	1 860	14.4	3 693	68	2 531	286	1 706
White	391	13 267	0.8	D	D	215	14.5	1 652	14.4	3 572	174	2 186	244	1 734
Whiteside	1 012	55 329	0.9	719	12.1	640	10.8	6 332	13.2	12 314	977	7 276	1 546	2 679
Will	8 547	581 259	0.7	9 926	14.7	3 700	5.5	70 178	11.5	77 936	4 136	35 475	12 984	1 958
Williamson	1 870	64 770	1.0	780	12.1	761	11.8	7 426	13.9	13 205	659	6 699	1 738	2 619

1. Per 1,000 estimated resident population. 2. Data for serious crimes have not been adjusted for underreporting; this may affect comparability between geographic areas and over time. 3. Per 100,000 population estimated by the FBI.

Table B. States and Counties — Crime, Education, Money Income, and Poverty

STATE County	Serious crimes known to police,[1] 2010 (cont.) Rate[2]		Education School enrollment and attainment, 2006–2010				Local government expenditures,[5] 2008–2009		Money income, 2006–2010					Income and poverty, 2010			
			Enrollment[3]		Attainment[4] (percent)					Households Median income					Percent below poverty level		
	Violent	Property	Total	Percent private	High school graduate or less	Bachelor's degree or more	Total current expenditures (mil dol)	Current expenditures per student (dollars)	Per capita income[6] (dollars)	Dollars	Percent change, 2000 to 2006–2010 (constant 2010 dollars)	Percent with income of $200,000 or more	Median household income (dollars)	All persons	Children under 18 years	Children 5 to 17 years in families
	46	47	48	49	50	51	52	53	54	55	56	57	58	59	60	61

ILLINOIS—Cont'd

STATE County	46	47	48	49	50	51	52	53	54	55	56	57	58	59	60	61
Hardin	278	394	825	2.8	56.8	11.0	5.5	8 496	18 515	27 578	-21.4	0.2	34 228	19.4	31.0	28.0
Henderson	196	2 113	1 652	9.6	54.9	14.9	8.9	8 586	22 492	43 450	-5.7	1.0	43 212	12.3	20.5	18.6
Henry	177	1 857	12 401	8.6	47.5	20.6	71.3	8 052	24 915	49 164	-2.6	1.9	49 262	10.8	15.9	13.9
Iroquois	64	1 131	7 093	11.8	54.5	13.7	50.0	10 028	23 400	47 323	-1.8	2.2	43 873	11.2	18.2	16.3
Jackson	566	3 597	24 401	9.0	36.0	35.4	80.7	11 099	19 294	32 169	1.8	1.5	32 739	23.5	31.3	31.7
Jasper	206	1 176	2 266	12.4	51.3	13.0	20.7	14 549	21 467	46 546	5.9	0.6	46 000	10.8	16.2	14.6
Jefferson	783	3 567	8 975	10.1	51.9	14.1	54.4	9 255	21 370	41 161	-3.1	1.5	40 527	17.0	24.9	23.4
Jersey	287	1 727	5 656	22.3	49.6	16.0	39.7	8 535	24 368	53 470	0.4	1.5	54 278	10.0	14.3	12.6
Jo Daviess	235	1 464	4 522	14.5	50.2	23.0	34.8	10 432	26 819	50 279	-1.7	1.7	45 972	9.3	15.5	13.9
Johnson	206	1 023	2 541	4.4	54.3	12.8	16.4	7 937	16 402	41 619	-1.4	0.6	41 743	14.2	19.5	17.8
Kane	200	1 699	142 617	16.8	41.6	31.8	1 197.5	9 916	29 480	67 767	-9.8	6.0	65 430	11.0	16.4	15.4
Kankakee	382	2 794	30 538	19.6	49.8	17.4	185.2	9 401	22 888	50 484	-4.0	1.8	45 707	14.8	20.2	18.8
Kendall	158	1 572	31 297	16.2	34.5	32.3	214.3	9 132	30 565	79 897	-2.4	4.2	79 542	4.6	6.2	5.7
Knox	399	3 141	13 005	17.9	53.0	15.2	71.5	9 219	20 908	39 545	-11.8	1.0	39 409	15.4	25.1	22.6
Lake	120	1 817	202 813	18.5	32.8	41.3	1 694.3	12 031	38 120	78 948	-6.9	10.9	74 594	9.0	12.1	10.6
LaSalle	131	1 874	27 019	12.7	50.8	15.8	179.4	10 298	24 982	51 705	1.3	1.7	49 414	13.2	17.6	15.9
Lawrence	225	772	3 602	5.5	56.5	11.1	19.6	8 017	19 297	38 771	0.8	0.6	37 428	17.5	23.5	21.9
Lee	NA	NA	8 666	16.2	50.6	15.0	46.4	9 494	24 440	48 502	-6.5	2.4	48 749	11.0	15.3	13.8
Livingston	202	1 904	9 080	7.6	58.2	13.5	69.6	10 406	23 259	50 500	-3.5	1.5	51 427	11.5	15.7	13.3
Logan	NA	NA	8 331	29.9	54.6	17.0	35.1	10 001	22 063	48 999	-1.8	1.6	48 311	11.5	17.9	16.4
McDonough	126	2 125	13 756	5.3	39.7	32.6	41.1	11 934	18 344	33 702	-17.2	0.9	37 890	22.0	23.2	22.5
McHenry	112	1 447	88 876	16.2	36.0	32.1	536.2	9 898	31 838	76 482	-6.8	5.4	69 290	7.3	9.6	8.5
McLean	367	2 367	56 925	16.6	33.5	40.4	232.5	9 534	28 167	57 642	-3.2	3.0	59 719	11.7	10.3	9.8
Macon	502	3 335	27 567	19.4	49.1	20.5	168.6	9 936	24 726	44 337	-7.5	2.6	42 206	17.7	26.8	22.8
Macoupin	166	1 496	11 735	14.1	52.3	15.0	54.9	7 393	23 222	47 178	2.9	1.4	45 995	13.0	19.3	16.6
Madison	229	2 390	72 728	14.7	44.5	23.0	398.0	9 246	26 127	51 941	-1.3	2.2	51 706	14.3	21.8	18.5
Marion	295	3 405	9 769	8.9	52.2	13.6	72.1	9 924	20 493	38 974	-12.6	0.7	38 182	16.5	26.6	24.8
Marshall	89	1 015	2 893	10.3	52.1	17.1	16.0	9 269	24 991	48 647	-6.7	1.1	48 647	11.4	17.7	15.2
Mason	468	2 373	3 430	9.2	55.1	16.5	27.6	8 793	23 427	42 461	-6.8	2.1	42 529	15.0	23.6	19.2
Massac	350	2 748	3 537	6.1	50.4	14.1	20.8	7 868	20 216	41 077	3.0	0.5	39 636	16.7	26.6	24.8
Menard	NA	NA	2 975	12.0	47.8	24.2	20.7	7 727	26 281	56 230	-4.7	1.5	58 075	9.0	14.0	12.6
Mercer	230	1 509	3 831	13.2	52.0	14.5	27.7	8 855	25 332	50 909	-1.7	2.0	46 871	11.3	14.5	12.5
Monroe	55	1 074	8 472	22.6	41.1	24.7	42.9	8 059	31 091	68 253	-2.6	4.0	69 731	4.9	5.8	4.8
Montgomery	525	1 664	6 898	10.9	58.7	13.3	39.7	8 278	21 700	40 864	-2.6	1.5	42 468	14.4	20.7	18.5
Morgan	253	1 890	9 294	23.1	52.3	20.2	54.0	10 345	23 244	44 645	-4.5	1.3	43 753	14.8	21.0	18.7
Moultrie	NA	NA	8 257	9.8	57.8	16.8	16.2	8 101	22 954	46 364	-8.7	2.1	47 459	10.4	16.5	15.3
Ogle	66	1 316	14 311	10.0	49.9	17.8	100.9	9 836	24 959	55 733	-3.2	1.6	53 402	10.8	15.7	13.4
Peoria	615	3 475	49 731	26.2	40.8	28.1	287.1	10 321	28 157	49 747	-1.7	3.9	50 166	14.3	21.4	19.3
Perry	174	1 047	5 351	6.1	54.7	13.5	23.6	7 901	17 926	40 696	-3.4	0.4	38 916	17.4	24.1	21.1
Platt	263	1 190	4 113	10.0	46.3	22.9	28.4	8 411	26 492	55 752	-3.8	1.6	54 350	7.3	9.5	8.1
Pike	33	172	3 730	6.9	59.5	12.7	24.7	8 870	19 996	40 205	2.0	1.2	37 172	17.0	25.3	23.7
Pope	291	1 007	1 128	9.8	50.4	8.3	4.5	8 319	20 134	39 672	4.3	0.0	37 926	17.9	26.5	25.6
Pulaski	1 418	1 866	1 536	6.4	56.7	11.9	12.0	10 406	18 444	31 173	-2.9	2.0	33 262	20.8	36.2	33.6
Putnam	67	849	1 255	8.1	48.1	15.0	8.7	9 433	27 004	56 458	-2.0	1.9	52 564	7.8	13.7	12.3
Randolph	218	867	6 904	17.3	60.5	12.0	42.6	9 877	19 950	45 020	-3.9	0.8	46 410	13.5	19.2	17.5
Richland	197	2 476	3 669	8.6	47.8	18.1	18.0	8 438	22 874	41 917	6.1	1.9	40 893	14.5	20.7	19.1
Rock Island	470	2 870	36 733	19.7	46.5	21.1	214.0	9 958	25 071	46 226	-5.4	2.4	45 114	12.5	20.2	18.7
St. Clair	978	3 768	76 137	14.4	41.6	23.9	467.4	10 525	24 770	48 562	-2.0	2.2	47 027	15.9	22.7	21.3
Saline	377	2 762	6 302	5.2	47.9	14.3	35.4	8 168	20 903	35 644	-2.2	0.5	37 170	19.4	28.2	25.9
Sangamon	897	4 742	51 159	18.2	38.4	31.0	302.3	10 300	28 394	52 232	-4.0	2.8	51 057	13.2	19.7	17.4
Schuyler	93	703	1 923	5.5	52.9	17.7	12.1	9 477	20 649	43 686	-2.1	0.5	45 481	12.0	17.5	16.5
Scott	NA	NA	1 240	9.1	55.7	18.0	8.3	8 687	27 530	49 462	6.8	3.0	48 890	9.7	13.0	11.7
Shelby	121	644	5 082	4.4	53.7	14.7	21.1	8 259	21 891	44 627	-5.5	1.6	45 474	12.3	17.7	15.4
Stark	184	1 201	1 433	10.2	51.3	15.2	14.1	14 755	25 311	49 195	8.4	4.9	49 280	10.6	16.5	14.5
Stephenson	115	2 280	11 385	12.6	47.7	17.2	71.7	9 995	22 608	43 304	-15.3	1.1	42 869	13.4	21.1	18.7
Tazewell	250	1 999	33 445	14.0	42.7	23.1	180.4	9 020	27 036	54 232	-5.4	2.3	50 737	9.9	13.7	12.3
Union	NA	NA	4 192	5.3	52.1	17.8	27.7	8 753	19 512	39 760	1.3	1.3	39 764	18.4	26.0	24.0
Vermilion	592	3 831	18 996	8.1	55.4	13.7	134.5	9 713	20 218	39 456	-8.5	0.9	38 534	20.9	31.3	28.1
Wabash	184	1 306	3 035	11.5	47.4	15.3	15.0	7 775	23 350	46 026	5.4	1.4	42 129	14.4	20.5	18.6
Warren	389	3 266	5 102	32.1	48.6	19.9	22.6	8 123	20 047	41 636	-9.2	0.4	43 881	13.9	19.3	17.7
Washington	315	952	3 389	13.0	48.5	17.1	17.3	8 607	24 846	51 440	-0.8	1.3	51 209	8.2	12.5	11.1
Wayne	263	1 444	3 893	6.2	51.4	12.1	22.5	8 480	21 493	39 207	1.6	1.2	40 630	14.9	22.6	20.1
White	171	1 564	3 063	6.8	50.3	12.2	24.6	14 481	22 081	39 728	6.0	0.9	39 964	16.9	26.1	24.1
Whiteside	180	2 499	13 969	15.1	53.6	16.1	93.5	9 445	23 405	45 266	-11.4	1.3	45 606	11.7	18.3	15.9
Will	173	1 784	198 673	17.2	38.2	30.7	1 194.0	10 074	29 811	75 906	-3.7	5.0	71 344	8.5	12.2	10.7
Williamson	541	2 078	16 093	8.2	43.9	21.7	89.7	8 798	22 164	40 579	0.2	1.3	43 004	16.0	23.5	21.4

1. Data for serious crimes have not been adjusted for underreporting; this may affect comparability between geographic areas and over time.   2. Per 100,000 population estimated by the FBI.   3. All persons 3 years old and over enrolled in nursery school through college.   4. Persons 25 years old and over.   5. Elementary and secondary education expenditures.   6. Based on population estimated by the American Community Survey, 2006–2010.

Table B. States and Counties — **Personal Income**

STATE County	Personal income, 2009 Total (mil dol)	Percent change, 2008–2009	Per capita[1] Dollars	Rank	Wages and salaries[2] (mil dol)	Proprietors' income (mil dol)	Dividends, interest, and rent (mil dol)	Transfer payments (mil dol) Total	Government payments to individuals Total	Social Security	Medical payments	Income mainte-nance	Unemploy-ment insurance
	62	63	64	65	66	67	68	69	70	71	72	73	74
ILLINOIS—Cont'd													
Hardin	112	4.9	25 789	2 761	37	7	16	45	44	15	20	4	2
Henderson	238	-5.3	32 414	1 443	48	38	32	53	52	22	18	4	4
Henry	1 695	-3.6	34 364	1 118	575	138	314	339	330	142	117	24	26
Iroquois	1 061	-2.8	35 743	923	337	175	186	239	234	93	93	18	17
Jackson	1 853	3.6	31 894	1 552	1 351	119	298	380	370	99	140	50	24
Jasper	299	-2.8	31 416	1 661	115	36	59	67	66	27	25	6	5
Jefferson	1 239	0.5	31 006	1 754	897	97	193	328	321	102	139	34	20
Jersey	787	-2.6	34 889	1 035	210	38	113	156	151	63	56	11	11
Jo Daviess	865	-2.6	39 336	502	347	57	232	157	153	75	49	8	12
Johnson	307	3.6	22 384	3 056	92	24	46	91	88	35	33	7	6
Kane	18 321	-2.1	35 790	913	10 882	825	2 940	2 507	2 414	853	891	230	283
Kankakee	3 598	0.6	31 780	1 584	1 984	174	516	871	850	273	358	90	71
Kendall	3 687	1.6	35 170	997	1 180	86	420	374	355	165	69	29	61
Knox	1 681	1.1	32 545	1 413	905	143	269	482	473	150	210	38	26
Lake	37 218	-4.4	52 231	76	25 768	1 869	8 149	3 499	3 372	1 311	1 216	262	368
LaSalle	3 863	-0.9	34 335	1 121	2 082	269	675	805	785	324	273	62	74
Lawrence	481	1.6	29 296	2 137	197	46	86	138	135	44	66	10	9
Lee	1 144	-1.2	32 772	1 373	606	90	193	259	253	100	102	14	20
Livingston	1 466	-4.8	38 815	553	698	193	208	259	252	104	96	18	20
Logan	964	-1.6	32 373	1 447	434	115	150	206	201	76	80	17	13
McDonough	978	0.9	29 836	2 013	604	92	176	202	196	67	68	18	15
McHenry	11 691	-5.3	36 424	826	5 015	302	1 968	1 492	1 433	596	493	71	179
McLean	6 489	0.5	38 695	565	5 222	459	963	784	753	298	237	75	67
Macon	4 239	-1.2	39 174	517	2 928	359	710	889	869	315	327	94	65
Macoupin	1 576	-3.0	32 990	1 343	465	107	264	377	369	138	152	27	26
Madison	9 614	-1.8	35 811	911	4 910	420	1 539	1 995	1 946	679	781	182	150
Marion	1 252	2.2	32 105	1 507	602	52	200	430	423	111	210	38	23
Marshall	486	-2.3	38 252	609	139	56	79	96	94	40	33	6	8
Mason	529	-1.8	35 769	919	147	61	83	136	133	52	54	11	10
Massac	445	0.4	29 740	2 033	223	26	68	137	134	46	58	15	7
Menard	486	1.1	38 968	540	93	57	68	81	79	33	30	6	5
Mercer	591	-4.6	36 339	838	127	61	90	116	113	51	39	7	9
Monroe	1 314	-2.0	39 521	492	345	62	229	183	177	77	62	7	15
Montgomery	911	2.0	30 876	1 784	443	88	161	238	232	85	99	19	16
Morgan	1 132	-0.2	32 448	1 439	659	108	212	268	261	100	106	23	15
Moultrie	479	-3.3	33 263	1 299	168	60	77	110	108	40	47	6	7
Ogle	1 690	-6.5	30 550	1 853	886	115	292	336	326	139	107	26	35
Peoria	7 660	-1.0	41 223	374	5 837	459	1 330	1 330	1 296	466	472	160	111
Perry	545	1.9	24 290	2 936	212	34	91	166	162	59	62	16	12
Piatt	730	-1.2	44 084	233	153	81	97	108	105	44	42	5	7
Pike	490	1.2	30 138	1 943	166	57	83	130	127	46	57	10	7
Pope	115	4.5	28 716	2 256	29	6	16	38	37	14	14	4	2
Pulaski	179	0.4	28 795	2 232	83	15	17	67	65	18	26	9	3
Putnam	228	0.6	37 904	654	93	11	46	42	41	19	13	2	5
Randolph	915	-0.2	27 992	2 401	535	43	174	239	233	88	94	19	15
Richland	479	2.6	30 887	1 781	266	49	91	136	133	47	53	12	8
Rock Island	5 441	-1.5	37 056	747	4 982	277	979	1 040	1 013	391	375	104	74
St. Clair	9 256	-1.6	35 112	1 003	5 632	338	1 459	2 036	1 989	558	828	269	145
Saline	785	3.8	30 493	1 863	449	53	120	252	247	77	113	26	13
Sangamon	7 939	0.8	40 563	416	5 908	645	1 387	1 319	1 284	477	490	144	82
Schuyler	243	-2.5	36 155	865	96	33	34	49	48	21	16	4	3
Scott	169	-1.2	32 503	1 425	53	23	24	36	35	14	14	3	2
Shelby	690	-2.9	31 669	1 609	202	100	106	169	165	66	67	11	12
Stark	227	-6.5	37 700	675	55	40	41	47	46	16	22	2	3
Stephenson	1 629	-3.5	35 003	1 019	938	92	309	370	361	146	127	36	29
Tazewell	5 061	-3.5	38 209	618	3 835	222	876	917	892	368	331	64	79
Union	521	3.7	28 923	2 215	206	25	76	168	165	51	77	17	9
Vermilion	2 459	0.0	30 713	1 817	1 429	171	371	672	657	231	241	86	46
Wabash	386	-0.1	32 158	1 495	141	42	76	92	90	35	35	8	6
Warren	569	-0.9	32 680	1 388	254	76	84	125	122	43	51	11	7
Washington	518	-0.4	35 554	950	243	53	95	103	101	39	41	6	7
Wayne	525	-3.0	32 197	1 483	187	76	88	138	135	49	59	11	8
White	514	-3.2	35 044	1 013	214	61	107	135	132	48	60	11	7
Whiteside	1 997	-0.7	33 867	1 188	957	135	382	478	467	178	196	34	33
Will	26 352	-0.9	38 457	586	10 583	752	3 395	3 151	3 026	1 165	976	269	381
Williamson	2 079	2.3	31 901	1 549	1 205	104	345	508	496	178	184	52	33

1. Based on the resident population estimated as of July 1 of the year shown.   2. Includes supplements to wages and salaries.

Table B. States and Counties — **Earnings, Social Security, and Housing**

STATE County	Earnings, 2009									Social Security beneficiaries, December 2010		Supplemental Security Income recipients, December 2010	Housing units, 2010	
			Goods-related[1]		Service-related and health									
	Total (mil dol)	Farm	Total	Manu-facturing	Infor-mation and profes-sional and technical services	Retail trade	Finance, insur-ance, and real estate	Health care and social services	Govern-ment	Number	Rate[2]		Total	Percent change, 2000–2010
	75	76	77	78	79	80	81	82	83	84	85	86	87	88

ILLINOIS—Cont'd

STATE County	75	76	77	78	79	80	81	82	83	84	85	86	87	88
Hardin	44	2.3	D	D	D	6.3	D	26.2	24.7	1 275	295	194	2 488	-0.2
Henderson	86	31.7	D	D	D	3.5	D	6.4	21.2	1 755	239	93	3 827	-7.2
Henry	713	9.3	D	9.3	9.2	8.0	5.8	7.2	21.6	10 955	217	628	22 161	4.2
Iroquois	512	27.5	12.5	6.2	3.2	6.4	4.5	D	13.8	7 205	242	491	13 452	0.7
Jackson	1 471	1.2	9.5	2.2	5.2	7.2	3.5	12.8	46.9	8 790	146	1 420	28 578	6.4
Jasper	151	15.4	10.4	5.3	2.4	6.5	3.1	2.5	21.5	2 235	230	161	4 345	1.2
Jefferson	995	1.9	D	18.8	D	6.9	5.3	D	14.8	8 265	213	979	16 954	-0.2
Jersey	248	4.6	11.0	0.9	6.3	10.8	3.1	D	25.4	4 930	214	355	9 848	10.4
Jo Daviess	405	4.6	D	16.7	D	7.7	5.2	D	16.5	5 845	258	205	13 574	13.1
Johnson	115	3.7	D	1.0	D	5.5	D	D	44.5	2 940	234	265	5 598	10.9
Kane	11 707	0.4	24.6	17.1	9.5	6.2	5.8	11.9	17.4	62 260	121	4 566	182 047	31.0
Kankakee	2 159	4.2	D	16.6	D	8.2	4.4	17.6	17.2	21 225	187	2 714	45 246	11.4
Kendall	1 266	2.4	30.4	23.7	4.3	10.1	3.3	5.5	20.9	12 295	107	567	40 321	106.5
Knox	1 048	7.3	D	4.7	4.5	8.6	4.1	D	17.0	11 940	226	1 246	24 077	1.5
Lake	27 637	0.1	D	20.7	9.0	6.9	8.3	7.1	16.4	91 430	130	7 180	260 310	15.2
LaSalle	2 351	4.4	23.9	16.5	5.0	9.0	4.2	10.7	15.6	24 145	212	1 401	49 978	7.6
Lawrence	243	7.7	D	9.4	2.3	5.3	8.1	D	16.8	3 535	210	317	6 936	-1.1
Lee	696	6.0	D	19.9	D	5.7	3.0	15.9	19.9	7 705	214	540	15 049	5.2
Livingston	891	16.2	D	16.1	D	5.7	3.7	8.7	19.6	7 775	200	498	15 895	3.9
Logan	549	14.9	D	12.1	2.7	7.1	4.1	9.8	23.5	5 870	194	383	12 107	2.0
McDonough	696	9.2	D	11.2	3.7	6.6	3.7	D	44.0	5 760	177	578	14 419	8.5
McHenry	5 318	0.6	29.3	19.0	6.2	8.0	3.8	11.2	16.0	42 340	137	1 625	116 040	24.9
McLean	5 681	2.8	D	5.0	D	4.9	22.7	9.1	13.8	22 795	134	1 743	69 656	16.1
Macon	3 287	2.1	35.5	27.5	5.4	5.5	3.4	13.1	10.7	23 855	215	3 137	50 475	0.5
Macoupin	571	9.2	16.8	9.7	4.4	7.0	4.5	D	20.5	10 805	226	905	21 584	2.3
Madison	5 330	0.7	27.8	17.1	7.5	7.6	4.8	11.4	17.3	52 145	194	5 544	117 106	7.5
Marion	654	2.3	24.2	16.3	D	7.1	3.4	16.8	18.1	9 220	234	1 092	18 296	1.5
Marshall	195	20.4	30.1	26.6	3.6	3.6	3.5	7.6	13.0	3 030	240	133	5 914	0.3
Mason	208	23.2	D	3.9	D	4.7	3.3	3.9	28.1	4 050	276	285	7 077	0.6
Massac	250	2.7	17.4	15.1	2.4	6.2	2.5	D	19.4	3 865	251	501	7 113	2.3
Menard	150	26.7	D	0.5	5.2	7.4	5.2	D	21.4	2 570	202	147	5 654	7.0
Mercer	188	24.4	14.9	11.0	2.4	5.4	5.1	8.6	28.0	3 070	242	166	7 658	3.5
Monroe	407	4.4	14.5	4.3	13.7	9.8	6.1	7.2	18.1	5 695	173	170	13 392	24.6
Montgomery	631	8.7	17.7	7.5	4.5	8.7	4.7	D	19.0	6 785	225	629	13 080	4.4
Morgan	767	7.6	20.7	16.8	4.9	7.0	6.0	13.2	17.2	8 055	227	904	15 515	1.5
Moultrie	228	16.3	28.9	22.1	4.7	6.6	4.0	D	12.9	3 090	208	167	6 260	9.0
Ogle	1 001	3.9	23.0	18.0	D	5.5	6.5	5.9	15.4	10 495	196	545	22 561	10.5
Peoria	6 297	0.7	18.0	12.6	16.5	5.1	5.6	22.1	11.5	65 010	188	4 758	86 064	6.2
Perry	246	2.8	D	11.1	3.5	7.9	4.7	D	29.1	4 700	210	480	9 426	-0.3
Piatt	234	26.2	11.8	6.7	3.7	5.0	4.9	9.2	18.2	3 340	200	112	7 269	6.9
Pike	222	15.8	D	1.9	3.3	9.3	6.1	D	22.5	3 810	232	353	7 951	-0.7
Pope	35	6.4	D	10.5	D	2.3	D	D	43.6	1 130	253	123	2 491	6.0
Pulaski	98	8.5	8.5	6.0	D	3.0	D	D	40.5	1 580	256	309	3 155	-5.9
Putnam	104	10.6	D	34.2	2.5	3.2	D	D	12.6	1 390	231	43	3 074	6.4
Randolph	578	3.7	27.6	22.9	2.0	8.0	3.1	7.4	30.0	6 715	201	485	13 707	2.8
Richland	315	7.0	14.7	6.9	2.7	7.7	5.0	D	15.4	3 905	241	397	7 513	0.6
Rock Island	5 259	0.3	D	15.6	5.8	4.9	4.7	9.2	22.4	30 035	204	2 823	65 756	2.0
St. Clair	5 970	0.6	D	5.6	10.2	6.4	3.9	12.6	33.4	45 260	168	8 541	116 249	11.3
Saline	502	1.0	33.2	3.6	4.4	7.1	3.6	D	20.1	6 390	256	1 160	11 697	-5.4
Sangamon	6 554	2.0	D	3.1	8.2	5.2	7.9	18.6	32.4	38 090	193	4 845	89 901	5.2
Schuyler	129	19.3	D	2.5	1.4	4.3	2.6	3.9	19.2	1 680	223	109	3 459	4.7
Scott	76	27.4	D	D	D	3.9	2.9	D	20.3	1 085	203	86	2 459	-0.2
Shelby	303	26.3	D	15.1	D	5.6	3.7	7.8	15.4	5 200	233	383	10 396	3.3
Stark	94	37.4	12.6	10.4	D	7.5	D	3.6	15.0	1 255	209	54	2 674	-1.9
Stephenson	1 030	3.2	36.2	25.1	3.8	5.2	8.5	13.9	14.3	11 340	238	1 001	22 081	1.7
Tazewell	4 057	1.8	50.5	44.7	D	5.1	3.6	5.1	9.3	26 990	199	1 726	57 516	8.6
Union	231	3.3	D	7.8	2.9	9.8	3.7	16.9	33.3	4 530	254	683	7 924	0.4
Vermilion	1 600	5.2	D	20.0	D	5.9	4.9	10.1	23.2	18 625	228	2 797	36 318	-0.1
Wabash	183	6.3	31.2	8.7	5.1	6.6	4.1	D	26.8	2 755	231	226	5 585	-3.0
Warren	331	17.9	D	26.4	D	4.4	D	D	11.8	3 400	192	290	7 682	-1.4
Washington	296	12.1	30.5	23.0	2.8	8.5	3.9	D	13.8	3 030	206	152	6 534	2.3
Wayne	263	13.2	28.7	14.6	2.3	6.5	2.3	11.3	16.3	4 130	246	305	7 975	0.3
White	274	9.2	33.6	4.5	2.3	9.3	3.7	D	14.8	3 950	269	405	7 181	-2.9
Whiteside	1 093	6.1	D	23.4	3.9	10.3	3.4	9.6	21.4	13 875	237	1 070	25 770	3.0
Will	11 336	0.4	22.3	12.7	6.8	7.9	4.5	10.0	18.2	85 745	127	6 392	237 501	35.3
Williamson	1 308	0.2	D	8.4	4.7	8.1	7.6	17.7	27.3	14 600	220	1 676	30 359	9.6

1. Includes mining, construction, and manufacturing.   2. Per 1,000 resident population enumerated in the 2010 census.

Table B. States and Counties — Housing, Labor Force, and Employment

STATE County	Housing units, 2006–2010								Civilian labor force, 2010				Civilian employment,[5] 2006–2010		
	Occupied units							Sub-standard units[3] (percent)			Unemployment			Percent	
	Owner-occupied					Renter-occupied									
				Median owner cost as a percent of income											Construction, production, and maintenance occupations
	Total	Percent	Median value[1]	With a mortgage	Without a mortgage	Median rent[2]	Median rent as a percent of income		Total	Percent change, 2009–2010	Total	Rate[4]	Total	Management, business, science and arts	
	89	90	91	92	93	94	95	96	97	98	99	100	101	102	103
ILLINOIS—Cont'd															
Hardin	1 868	77.0	63 300	18.1	13.1	320	27.0	2.8	1 813	3.5	210	11.6	1 531	27.3	33.8
Henderson	3 246	78.4	77 600	20.4	11.9	503	22.0	1.7	3 820	-1.7	389	10.2	3 542	26.6	33.9
Henry	20 433	77.3	108 800	20.0	12.9	615	25.8	1.5	26 991	0.1	2 479	9.2	24 077	29.9	29.6
Iroquois	11 835	76.2	101 100	22.2	12.1	646	26.0	1.5	17 138	2.8	1 720	10.0	14 295	28.6	31.3
Jackson	23 773	54.4	96 100	20.7	12.2	577	39.0	1.7	32 827	2.7	2 579	7.9	27 610	36.9	16.3
Jasper	4 004	82.2	77 900	20.9	11.9	443	23.1	0.1	5 050	2.5	486	9.6	4 865	27.7	33.6
Jefferson	15 364	75.0	85 800	21.2	13.2	546	29.5	1.8	20 760	1.3	1 994	9.6	16 737	25.3	30.6
Jersey	8 626	78.9	118 200	20.1	11.9	580	27.2	1.4	11 619	-0.2	1 093	9.4	11 141	28.3	30.9
Jo Daviess	10 001	78.1	138 000	22.9	13.4	617	23.8	0.8	13 230	0.3	1 159	8.8	11 769	31.1	28.5
Johnson	4 396	79.8	94 700	21.0	12.0	427	27.1	1.6	5 229	2.5	573	11.0	3 766	32.4	19.8
Kane	168 980	77.6	245 000	28.4	15.4	929	31.6	3.5	271 334	1.0	27 947	10.3	243 846	34.2	25.1
Kankakee	40 943	69.4	148 400	24.3	14.0	721	31.4	2.2	57 222	1.8	7 511	13.1	50 674	27.9	28.6
Kendall	35 687	85.8	248 300	27.8	14.4	1 099	29.7	0.9	60 201	1.2	5 914	9.8	53 143	37.2	22.2
Knox	21 863	68.9	80 600	21.2	12.3	553	28.5	0.9	26 206	0.9	2 498	9.5	22 537	27.9	26.2
Lake	239 246	78.4	287 300	27.0	15.3	963	29.6	2.7	365 683	0.7	38 395	10.5	336 890	41.2	18.5
LaSalle	45 326	76.3	125 500	23.1	13.4	646	27.3	1.4	60 381	1.7	7 880	13.1	54 468	25.7	32.2
Lawrence	6 300	72.3	67 900	20.7	12.0	471	27.0	1.0	8 222	-0.8	785	9.5	6 237	23.9	33.8
Lee	13 731	74.1	113 400	22.5	12.7	571	23.8	1.7	18 496	0.5	2 034	11.0	17 249	27.4	32.4
Livingston	14 630	75.8	101 700	22.5	13.2	593	25.7	0.6	19 206	-0.2	1 996	10.4	17 530	25.5	33.2
Logan	10 981	74.5	95 100	19.0	12.6	568	26.9	1.8	13 687	2.4	1 311	9.6	12 786	28.7	27.6
McDonough	12 923	62.4	85 100	20.7	11.6	652	45.7	1.6	17 094	0.1	1 490	8.7	14 669	35.5	21.1
McHenry	108 106	84.1	249 700	27.6	14.4	998	31.3	1.7	180 783	0.7	17 286	9.6	154 998	36.8	21.7
McLean	63 145	68.3	151 700	21.5	12.4	692	28.8	1.3	93 167	3.4	7 201	7.7	87 367	39.5	15.0
Macon	44 947	71.1	90 500	20.1	11.6	595	28.9	1.2	55 274	0.8	6 502	11.8	49 180	31.3	25.5
Macoupin	19 371	78.4	93 400	21.5	12.5	551	26.7	1.6	24 165	-0.6	2 567	10.6	22 357	28.2	30.7
Madison	106 867	74.5	122 600	22.2	12.3	712	31.2	1.6	138 701	-0.3	13 582	9.8	126 522	33.0	23.8
Marion	16 148	74.6	71 400	21.4	13.8	565	29.9	2.0	18 341	-0.2	2 222	12.1	17 435	24.1	32.1
Marshall	5 160	82.0	102 700	21.7	12.6	574	28.2	0.7	7 137	-0.5	688	9.6	5 874	26.4	33.2
Mason	6 475	80.4	81 400	19.4	12.6	559	28.3	1.6	7 719	1.9	967	12.5	6 523	29.7	34.0
Massac	6 293	80.2	81 800	21.5	13.2	525	24.5	2.1	7 190	-0.8	700	9.7	6 484	23.5	27.9
Menard	5 056	82.5	113 500	19.6	12.5	599	26.4	1.7	7 095	2.5	557	7.9	6 603	34.9	21.7
Mercer	6 862	79.9	102 800	20.6	12.6	582	24.6	1.2	8 770	0.0	951	10.8	8 353	28.7	32.6
Monroe	12 391	81.7	197 400	22.1	11.9	730	23.6	1.1	18 528	1.3	1 442	7.8	16 733	35.1	23.5
Montgomery	11 698	77.8	78 100	20.8	12.4	562	29.1	1.0	13 779	3.3	1 800	13.1	12 631	28.9	28.6
Morgan	14 003	70.4	93 300	20.6	11.7	545	27.9	1.4	17 750	0.1	1 660	9.4	16 790	31.0	22.7
Moultrie	5 627	78.8	89 700	21.4	13.2	548	22.1	2.1	8 046	2.6	693	8.6	6 932	26.8	35.3
Ogle	20 669	75.6	152 400	23.6	14.6	642	23.1	1.5	27 915	1.2	3 778	13.5	25 966	27.2	32.3
Peoria	75 011	68.2	119 000	20.8	12.0	669	27.9	1.8	98 594	1.0	10 610	10.8	86 857	36.6	20.4
Perry	8 268	78.4	76 900	21.2	12.5	499	29.0	1.9	9 514	0.8	1 135	11.9	8 751	29.5	31.8
Piatt	6 555	81.7	119 100	19.5	12.7	651	24.9	1.3	8 952	0.3	753	8.4	8 460	35.4	29.4
Pike	6 648	79.0	76 000	19.7	12.9	472	23.4	1.6	8 780	4.2	776	8.8	7 498	22.4	31.8
Pope	1 847	78.0	88 300	19.0	13.0	399	23.2	1.5	1 917	1.2	208	10.9	1 814	16.5	35.4
Pulaski	2 529	74.0	48 800	20.9	12.7	460	29.9	3.3	2 870	0.2	322	11.2	2 221	26.2	31.4
Putnam	2 535	79.9	123 600	20.0	11.9	559	21.4	4.0	3 267	-1.1	393	12.0	3 051	21.0	37.2
Randolph	11 999	78.7	86 900	20.1	10.9	565	26.1	1.3	15 424	0.9	1 409	9.1	13 601	25.7	33.4
Richland	6 675	78.4	76 000	21.0	11.8	571	23.2	1.6	7 388	1.0	742	10.0	7 662	26.1	34.8
Rock Island	60 454	71.5	111 700	22.0	12.2	598	27.1	1.7	78 729	0.9	7 488	9.5	69 399	29.7	26.3
St. Clair	103 084	67.7	122 400	23.4	13.4	734	30.1	1.6	124 858	0.6	13 666	10.9	120 338	33.2	20.2
Saline	10 583	72.6	69 400	21.1	13.0	523	27.9	1.7	12 961	2.1	1 310	10.1	10 070	32.2	24.7
Sangamon	81 968	70.5	118 900	21.3	11.6	674	29.0	1.6	110 862	3.0	8 876	8.0	97 917	39.2	14.3
Schuyler	3 008	78.8	74 900	19.1	12.7	472	21.2	4.9	4 271	1.8	318	7.4	3 444	24.2	36.4
Scott	2 140	76.3	82 100	18.6	10.0	459	21.1	0.8	2 756	1.9	266	9.7	2 736	31.2	30.3
Shelby	9 035	79.5	84 500	20.0	11.5	573	26.5	2.2	11 266	0.7	1 146	10.2	10 508	28.8	32.5
Stark	2 411	81.7	87 500	18.4	11.5	488	22.0	1.0	2 887	-1.1	313	10.8	2 844	31.4	31.0
Stephenson	19 645	72.4	103 300	22.9	14.2	573	31.6	0.7	24 641	-2.6	2 886	11.7	22 293	28.1	29.4
Tazewell	53 727	77.9	125 700	20.9	12.1	631	25.8	1.2	73 637	0.4	7 458	10.1	63 971	34.0	25.3
Union	7 062	75.8	84 200	20.1	12.8	488	27.8	1.4	8 351	2.3	1 011	12.1	7 047	32.6	27.2
Vermilion	32 236	71.3	76 500	20.5	12.4	584	30.1	1.9	37 494	0.5	4 547	12.1	34 529	25.5	31.8
Wabash	4 901	80.1	77 400	20.1	13.3	540	21.1	3.0	6 112	1.0	609	10.0	5 484	26.6	37.0
Warren	6 878	72.5	83 300	21.0	13.7	576	27.4	2.9	9 421	1.7	794	8.4	8 223	26.8	30.4
Washington	6 057	83.2	103 100	22.4	12.3	600	24.9	1.6	8 341	2.8	656	7.9	7 709	30.0	33.2
Wayne	7 212	75.5	65 100	18.8	12.4	494	25.3	1.3	8 192	0.1	791	9.7	7 699	24.4	37.0
White	6 464	79.9	62 900	19.3	10.6	460	24.4	1.5	7 826	1.4	682	8.7	6 870	26.7	32.7
Whiteside	23 599	75.8	98 100	21.2	13.0	600	28.0	1.8	30 246	-1.0	3 280	10.8	27 715	26.7	32.3
Will	220 135	85.0	240 500	27.2	14.3	890	30.3	2.2	367 626	1.0	38 339	10.4	322 166	35.6	23.2
Williamson	26 324	73.6	87 600	20.3	12.8	586	29.0	1.3	35 622	3.1	3 348	9.4	28 415	31.4	21.7

1. Specified owner-occupied units.　2. Specified renter-occupied units. A value of 10.0 represents 10 percent or less.　3. Overcrowded or lacking complete plumbing facilities.　4. Percent of civilian labor force.　5. Persons 16 years old and over.

Table B. States and Counties — Nonfarm Employment and Agriculture

STATE County	Number of establishments	Employment Total	Health care and social assistance	Manufacturing	Retail trade	Finance and insurance	Professional, scientific, and technical services	Annual payroll Total (mil dol)	Average per employee (dollars)	Farms Number	Percent with: Fewer than 50 acres	500 acres or more	Farm operators whose principal occupation is farming (percent)
	104	105	106	107	108	109	110	111	112	113	114	115	116
ILLINOIS—Cont'd													
Hardin	72	760	357	D	63	35	D	22	29 391	145	22.1	8.3	34.5
Henderson	117	620	D	D	104	84	35	15	24 645	400	21.5	30.0	63.8
Henry	1 125	12 861	1 534	3 639	1 949	573	328	388	30 168	1 473	35.9	23.4	50.6
Iroquois	706	6 496	1 768	973	958	343	118	185	28 542	1 471	27.9	29.4	57.4
Jackson	1 335	16 961	3 792	659	3 717	647	786	467	27 528	810	39.8	13.0	40.7
Jasper	217	1 758	132	D	236	96	D	63	35 856	882	38.8	19.3	46.7
Jefferson	1 006	16 552	3 361	2 914	2 283	486	504	541	32 659	1 156	43.7	10.7	30.8
Jersey	460	4 909	883	96	1 077	197	188	117	23 854	519	34.9	23.7	51.4
Jo Daviess	745	7 114	612	1 171	916	260	266	203	28 585	1 016	34.1	12.1	43.6
Johnson	182	1 559	237	D	221	66	D	25	16 072	568	34.2	6.9	35.7
Kane	12 262	174 964	21 417	28 259	23 559	9 579	9 329	6 625	37 863	759	60.1	14.9	49.9
Kankakee	2 424	35 858	6 651	5 021	5 748	1 639	774	1 130	31 507	835	34.9	26.6	51.0
Kendall	1 920	20 118	1 362	2 372	4 879	665	680	603	29 966	424	42.7	22.4	54.2
Knox	1 143	16 009	3 904	974	3 510	457	381	427	26 692	904	36.7	22.8	53.5
Lake	19 505	319 399	30 719	44 070	43 064	19 607	28 350	18 953	59 340	396	77.5	4.3	47.5
LaSalle	2 849	36 076	5 815	4 930	6 399	1 376	1 146	1 239	34 332	1 622	29.3	27.1	53.7
Lawrence	302	3 349	684	513	463	385	62	106	31 599	421	43.2	27.3	52.5
Lee	753	9 653	1 230	3 083	1 397	291	287	306	31 673	898	31.3	27.1	58.1
Livingston	917	12 321	2 096	3 424	1 807	471	313	389	31 589	1 319	27.4	32.9	58.0
Logan	651	7 573	1 388	969	1 140	313	186	219	28 878	710	31.8	31.1	60.0
McDonough	729	9 341	1 951	1 398	1 670	376	214	245	26 265	761	33.0	24.6	55.3
McHenry	7 810	85 520	10 446	18 166	15 127	2 602	3 192	3 166	37 019	1 035	65.0	11.1	50.6
McLean	3 691	78 893	9 375	4 814	9 593	22 997	2 749	3 469	44 089	1 513	35.1	30.5	53.7
Macon	2 548	46 139	7 782	7 924	5 485	1 516	1 257	1 696	36 748	708	44.1	27.0	54.5
Macoupin	939	9 046	1 835	629	1 509	531	D	260	28 737	1 187	38.6	20.5	49.5
Madison	5 988	83 793	13 279	13 167	12 665	3 306	3 424	3 008	35 892	1 229	46.5	15.7	47.3
Marion	973	10 527	2 712	2 262	1 507	382	225	324	30 784	1 077	39.7	12.3	31.5
Marshall	275	2 878	483	1 043	321	110	43	79	27 305	500	29.2	24.0	57.2
Mason	312	2 473	507	200	400	142	36	71	28 845	447	27.7	40.3	60.0
Massac	242	4 092	616	D	329	111	31	164	40 032	400	41.3	10.0	39.3
Menard	229	1 390	D	30	311	D	67	37	26 714	411	45.7	24.1	46.7
Mercer	292	2 303	372	543	377	168	31	63	27 157	795	34.9	22.5	52.6
Monroe	772	7 516	915	310	1 298	387	623	251	33 332	678	44.7	17.6	43.7
Montgomery	751	7 764	1 254	922	1 562	430	212	243	31 300	1 029	38.1	22.2	50.9
Morgan	890	13 026	2 671	2 076	2 009	821	448	396	30 373	740	30.9	28.1	51.8
Moultrie	316	4 386	778	D	377	114	103	128	29 249	520	51.5	19.6	51.5
Ogle	1 103	13 068	1 494	3 564	1 515	509	239	499	38 187	1 274	44.0	18.7	47.1
Peoria	4 788	108 226	21 259	10 272	11 187	4 571	4 800	5 282	46 805	877	33.6	18.0	47.2
Perry	416	4 409	867	D	664	175	91	129	29 185	589	35.5	20.5	44.5
Piatt	348	2 604	401	D	476	169	117	77	29 827	480	31.7	34.0	58.5
Pike	384	3 172	630	178	597	255	69	85	26 689	967	25.1	23.7	45.1
Pope	62	327	182	D	59	10	D	5	15 514	346	33.5	7.2	36.7
Pulaski	99	965	186	D	87	59	D	30	31 304	276	31.2	22.8	44.2
Putnam	135	1 297	D	358	107	D	20	49	37 446	167	26.9	23.4	52.1
Randolph	681	10 439	2 188	2 893	1 423	332	176	313	29 981	833	34.0	17.4	44.4
Richland	472	5 403	994	550	749	227	D	162	29 982	579	39.0	21.4	48.2
Rock Island	3 353	63 600	9 739	8 328	8 244	2 963	3 071	2 732	42 950	700	44.3	15.1	45.6
St. Clair	5 486	79 282	14 765	5 165	13 742	2 488	5 419	2 634	33 229	895	42.9	20.0	45.8
Saline	602	7 920	1 721	437	1 308	344	189	270	34 123	497	42.7	12.5	32.6
Sangamon	5 140	82 240	18 945	2 923	12 051	5 478	4 898	2 929	35 621	1 153	45.1	22.4	48.0
Schuyler	154	1 217	D	98	D	64	D	35	28 610	534	30.1	21.2	39.1
Scott	77	597	D	110	100	D	D	19	31 591	350	37.1	22.6	47.1
Shelby	457	4 358	739	1 045	571	D	165	126	28 852	1 185	39.5	19.4	44.1
Stark	126	983	D	189	150	82	D	29	29 424	372	29.3	32.8	61.3
Stephenson	1 107	14 488	2 750	2 537	2 313	1 413	442	498	34 342	1 178	44.5	16.2	50.3
Tazewell	2 836	44 395	5 315	7 704	6 710	1 845	D	1 468	33 078	998	37.5	21.4	51.8
Union	359	3 527	1 286	363	678	140	82	90	25 644	620	35.5	8.1	38.4
Vermilion	1 537	24 945	4 795	5 059	3 435	1 343	387	852	34 162	1 014	38.7	27.3	52.4
Wabash	275	2 822	799	200	428	102	131	84	29 871	225	35.1	30.2	51.6
Warren	366	5 595	850	1 722	573	215	78	149	26 557	644	27.0	31.2	56.7
Washington	396	5 482	D	1 751	565	201	112	169	30 745	779	28.0	30.9	54.2
Wayne	351	3 336	824	D	650	119	54	98	29 367	1 233	43.5	13.7	33.8
White	372	3 418	571	D	494	D	80	107	31 194	481	36.4	24.5	45.3
Whiteside	1 287	18 062	3 701	3 948	2 810	651	378	574	31 758	1 132	34.1	22.3	56.3
Will	13 800	184 968	20 895	19 731	28 050	4 961	7 562	6 962	37 638	877	55.0	14.8	52.2
Williamson	1 621	22 148	5 763	2 035	3 651	1 441	527	699	31 577	616	47.1	7.3	32.3

Table B. States and Counties — **Agriculture**

STATE County	\[117\] Acreage (1,000)	\[118\] Percent change, 2002–2007	\[119\] Average size of farm	\[120\] Total irrigated (1,000)	\[121\] Total cropland (1,000)	\[122\] Average per farm	\[123\] Average per acre	\[124\] Value of machinery and equipment, average per farm (dollars)	\[125\] Total (mil dol)	\[126\] Average per farm (dollars)	\[127\] Crops	\[128\] Live-stock and poultry products	\[129\] $10,000 or more	\[130\] $100,000 or more	\[131\] Total ($1,000)	\[132\] Percent of farms
ILLINOIS—Cont'd																
Hardin	35	-12.5	240	0.0	16.4	549 014	2 292	60 083	3.0	20 803	71.1	28.9	23.4	4.1	360	49.0
Henderson	170	-15.4	426	16.6	143.7	1 469 607	3 449	147 170	86.0	215 083	81.6	18.4	76.0	43.5	3 468	86.0
Henry	490	1.9	333	7.2	446.1	1 313 624	3 950	128 465	296.8	201 511	71.4	28.6	60.4	37.1	10 999	78.5
Iroquois	678	-0.1	461	4.1	646.9	1 857 803	4 032	180 847	418.5	284 529	79.3	20.7	70.2	45.8	12 595	85.4
Jackson	224	12.0	277	0.4	177.4	775 182	2 798	107 406	60.8	75 101	88.2	11.8	34.8	15.6	3 118	59.8
Jasper	243	-10.3	276	D	214.4	913 218	3 309	116 937	112.9	128 057	64.8	35.2	52.3	27.6	4 187	85.7
Jefferson	233	-10.0	201	0.0	186.0	570 152	2 834	72 646	51.0	44 084	79.8	20.2	28.9	11.0	3 629	69.2
Jersey	189	9.2	365	0.0	158.1	1 336 206	3 660	129 502	68.7	132 420	92.6	7.4	47.8	30.8	2 559	73.4
Jo Daviess	281	6.4	277	0.1	196.0	1 108 860	4 003	109 864	136.7	134 499	53.3	46.7	46.6	20.6	5 672	78.1
Johnson	100	-17.4	177	D	53.4	414 754	2 344	63 753	12.5	22 085	59.0	41.0	22.4	5.1	1 369	48.1
Kane	192	-3.0	253	2.9	182.0	1 231 861	4 860	175 643	198.1	261 011	88.6	11.4	48.9	28.5	4 614	40.1
Kankakee	386	11.2	462	16.0	376.2	2 000 617	4 330	187 468	244.1	292 276	88.8	11.2	70.2	41.8	5 988	75.0
Kendall	167	-0.6	394	2.1	160.5	1 703 203	4 328	171 639	103.5	244 155	92.5	7.5	63.4	40.8	3 108	61.1
Knox	363	-7.9	401	D	301.5	1 614 027	4 020	146 360	198.7	219 791	73.8	26.2	52.0	30.5	7 008	74.6
Lake	35	-10.3	87	0.6	28.5	551 511	6 326	69 788	30.8	77 839	77.6	22.4	34.8	12.4	444	13.9
LaSalle	643	11.1	397	3.8	614.4	1 665 997	4 201	174 983	329.0	202 834	93.8	6.2	72.1	43.0	11 943	80.9
Lawrence	194	1.0	461	15.7	179.1	1 510 800	3 278	144 458	90.1	213 914	75.3	24.7	49.9	33.3	3 527	79.3
Lee	396	1.8	441	21.7	377.6	1 900 065	4 313	174 859	214.4	238 717	91.4	8.6	65.3	46.5	8 009	80.4
Livingston	629	-1.1	476	0.2	599.1	1 973 244	4 141	186 082	350.7	265 897	84.9	15.1	77.3	52.1	11 434	83.9
Logan	320	-10.9	451	1.3	303.1	1 896 399	4 203	156 048	180.2	253 818	89.2	10.8	63.9	44.4	6 627	86.5
McDonough	308	-5.2	404	0.1	267.2	1 570 176	3 883	143 647	148.5	195 088	90.0	10.0	58.1	32.3	5 135	76.2
McHenry	216	-7.3	208	8.5	198.8	1 049 568	5 039	114 010	156.5	151 231	80.0	20.0	43.4	21.7	4 280	31.1
McLean	676	-1.7	447	2.9	647.4	1 868 207	4 181	175 125	366.5	242 265	89.5	10.5	65.1	44.7	12 275	77.9
Macon	291	-9.3	410	0.0	280.7	1 831 072	4 461	177 853	156.8	221 463	96.8	3.2	58.9	37.3	5 131	74.2
Macoupin	394	-7.7	332	0.0	337.0	1 273 380	3 834	131 387	184.3	155 263	78.7	21.3	50.3	26.8	6 846	75.4
Madison	313	5.7	255	1.0	284.6	1 053 742	4 138	133 828	131.9	107 345	89.5	10.5	47.8	22.4	4 419	60.5
Marion	261	-0.4	242	0.1	212.1	755 440	3 121	93 949	78.3	72 666	84.2	15.8	31.7	15.4	5 471	78.8
Marshall	205	7.3	409	2.3	183.5	1 654 832	4 044	146 222	100.6	201 285	94.4	5.6	65.2	39.4	3 614	81.6
Mason	273	-4.2	612	100.5	251.3	2 017 955	3 300	221 325	121.6	272 053	96.9	3.1	63.1	46.5	4 605	85.5
Massac	90	-28.0	224	8.1	65.0	567 832	2 532	77 963	22.2	55 622	84.0	16.0	36.8	12.5	1 578	69.5
Menard	169	9.0	410	2.7	150.9	1 572 483	3 833	147 681	80.7	196 457	92.1	7.9	45.5	30.4	3 017	77.4
Mercer	306	4.4	390	9.2	265.2	1 438 698	3 687	133 503	145.8	185 717	84.2	15.8	56.3	33.0	6 103	78.1
Monroe	178	0.6	263	3.3	148.7	934 349	3 556	127 779	62.9	92 754	75.2	24.8	44.0	23.2	2 774	63.4
Montgomery	348	-3.9	338	0.4	315.0	1 288 726	3 813	127 417	150.0	145 801	83.4	16.6	54.2	31.1	5 883	78.7
Morgan	321	9.6	433	3.2	281.1	1 703 819	3 934	166 922	149.5	202 050	87.6	12.4	60.8	36.4	5 226	77.2
Moultrie	168	-9.7	323	0.0	159.1	1 364 294	4 228	131 838	90.7	174 510	96.2	3.8	53.7	27.5	2 890	64.0
Ogle	366	-1.6	288	1.2	333.6	1 304 554	4 535	138 105	258.7	203 098	67.1	32.9	54.3	31.6	8 579	69.9
Peoria	259	-2.6	296	2.8	220.2	1 148 306	3 885	116 613	126.3	143 980	85.9	14.1	58.3	28.8	4 239	67.6
Perry	200	3.1	340	D	171.8	953 734	2 804	100 470	41.5	70 377	90.9	9.1	46.2	21.4	2 957	80.5
Piatt	267	3.5	557	0.5	259.5	2 432 020	4 368	206 231	146.5	305 208	92.0	8.0	69.4	47.3	4 850	80.4
Pike	390	-8.5	403	1.3	288.1	1 417 177	3 516	116 504	170.9	176 708	69.7	30.3	48.7	26.2	6 532	77.0
Pope	61	-20.8	176	D	30.9	399 521	2 273	54 068	5.4	15 589	79.5	20.5	19.1	3.2	934	61.6
Pulaski	101	17.4	367	D	83.2	1 084 029	2 957	115 253	29.5	106 751	91.3	8.7	39.5	21.0	1 798	74.6
Putnam	63	-11.3	375	0.5	53.9	1 478 127	3 937	214 337	64.9	388 638	94.9	5.1	61.1	36.5	1 456	81.4
Randolph	253	-0.4	304	0.4	202.3	976 442	3 216	126 178	73.5	88 206	83.1	16.9	48.1	19.8	3 450	75.4
Richland	203	-2.9	350	0.0	185.6	1 076 855	3 074	110 702	82.5	142 524	70.4	29.6	51.5	25.2	3 419	80.7
Rock Island	179	5.3	255	3.2	148.7	1 045 315	4 096	102 621	95.3	136 152	81.5	18.5	47.3	23.7	4 037	66.3
St. Clair	307	13.7	342	1.1	284.8	1 301 234	3 799	150 091	125.6	140 368	87.8	12.2	54.1	27.5	5 099	71.8
Saline	117	-10.0	236	D	96.2	681 789	2 890	77 874	42.0	84 430	66.5	33.5	34.4	13.3	1 779	65.6
Sangamon	518	10.7	449	0.8	485.2	1 748 638	3 891	174 091	294.0	255 016	94.6	5.4	51.3	33.9	9 235	67.0
Schuyler	207	0.0	388	D	138.4	1 266 603	3 260	114 478	65.4	122 398	83.8	16.2	43.4	21.9	3 377	83.1
Scott	136	17.2	388	5.5	109.0	1 397 802	3 640	136 752	54.5	155 664	87.9	12.1	51.7	26.9	2 105	68.0
Shelby	387	-7.9	327	0.1	347.0	1 160 282	3 550	129 810	203.3	171 600	80.7	19.3	52.8	29.1	6 153	74.9
Stark	170	-2.3	456	0.0	159.8	1 881 018	4 122	175 762	87.0	233 758	95.2	4.8	69.9	45.2	3 650	82.5
Stephenson	338	4.3	287	0.1	306.9	1 109 412	3 867	142 964	246.8	209 505	53.8	46.2	50.3	30.7	7 527	69.8
Tazewell	329	0.6	330	31.4	306.4	1 331 434	4 036	126 285	184.8	185 206	85.3	14.7	60.2	34.3	6 352	74.4
Union	122	-19.7	197	0.1	75.0	522 955	2 650	64 280	25.7	41 498	78.2	21.8	26.1	8.2	1 883	60.2
Vermilion	457	1.6	451	0.7	428.1	1 781 695	3 950	178 307	224.0	220 875	95.5	4.5	61.3	37.7	8 500	78.7
Wabash	114	2.7	508	1.1	104.9	1 647 150	3 241	178 399	40.5	180 199	95.9	4.1	61.8	36.0	1 774	78.7
Warren	295	-9.8	458	D	260.6	1 873 134	4 090	161 721	168.2	261 176	77.1	22.9	74.1	46.6	5 320	82.9
Washington	354	6.6	454	D	324.9	1 532 726	3 374	187 882	142.4	182 821	65.7	34.3	62.4	37.6	5 543	87.2
Wayne	333	-6.5	270	2.5	284.3	728 843	2 697	87 931	119.1	96 591	68.0	32.0	32.9	15.6	7 093	84.3
White	297	5.7	617	24.2	265.8	1 753 235	2 840	211 083	102.7	213 483	92.1	7.9	45.5	27.0	4 872	80.9
Whiteside	405	6.9	358	57.0	376.4	1 367 865	3 820	157 131	280.8	248 037	69.3	30.7	62.5	39.4	8 643	77.7
Will	221	-16.6	252	1.9	208.9	1 419 945	5 639	132 564	127.6	145 492	94.6	5.4	49.7	26.1	3 392	51.0
Williamson	94	-10.5	153	0.0	64.8	433 076	2 834	53 815	16.2	26 324	80.3	19.7	23.4	6.8	1 383	47.2

STATE County	Water use, 2005		Wholesale trade,[1] 2007				Retail trade,[2] 2007				Real estate and rental and leasing,[2] 2007			
	Total water withdrawn (mil gal/day)	Gallons withdrawn per person	Number of establish-ments	Number of employees	Sales (mil dol)	Annual payroll (mil dol)	Number of establish-ments	Number of employees	Sales (mil dol)	Annual payroll (mil dol)	Number of establish-ments	Number of employees	Receipts (mil dol)	Annual payroll (mil dol)
	133	134	135	136	137	138	139	140	141	142	143	144	145	146
ILLINOIS—Cont'd														
Hardin	1.8	384	NA	NA	NA	NA	11	70	14.4	1.1	2	D	D	D
Henderson	18.2	2 287	10	D	D	D	18	103	26.1	1.7	2	D	D	D
Henry	12.4	246	60	D	D	D	200	2 173	477.6	45.0	32	74	5.8	1.1
Iroquois	5.8	190	50	463	614.9	16.1	99	964	265.4	20.4	18	46	6.8	1.2
Jackson	89.4	1 543	26	D	D	D	244	3 759	684.1	66.9	76	381	38.6	6.6
Jasper	608.9	60 766	16	142	257.2	4.9	34	282	82.6	5.2	4	D	D	D
Jefferson	2.7	68	49	D	D	D	190	2 262	567.6	50.1	28	101	13.5	3.1
Jersey	2.9	128	24	D	D	D	76	978	250.3	21.2	13	24	2.9	0.4
Jo Daviess	7.1	315	21	107	120.5	4.7	145	1 060	310.7	21.6	29	63	11.5	1.6
Johnson	2.6	200	7	40	16.7	1.0	36	272	65.5	5.3	4	D	D	D
Kane	69.6	144	775	10 899	9 589.6	620.8	1 624	25 240	5 688.3	543.7	502	2 803	430.3	89.0
Kankakee	35.3	327	116	D	D	D	389	5 737	1 258.5	118.1	105	342	63.5	9.5
Kendall	13.3	168	63	1 164	1 299.8	44.8	243	4 360	1 064.0	106.6	67	195	25.4	4.3
Knox	2.4	46	50	D	D	D	206	3 653	681.4	67.7	36	148	19.4	2.8
Lake	855.6	1 218	1 121	26 870	26 053.3	2 054.7	2 530	44 334	20 336.3	1 407.1	846	3 956	1 082.2	213.0
LaSalle	121.9	1 082	131	1 577	1 208.2	59.7	478	6 904	1 739.9	149.9	103	692	76.2	22.4
Lawrence	15.6	977	12	220	82.7	8.3	46	432	81.7	8.7	8	16	1.4	0.2
Lee	26.0	728	31	D	D	D	118	1 421	366.5	31.4	32	162	13.2	2.9
Livingston	9.2	235	51	D	D	D	152	1 841	396.5	34.8	21	61	5.4	1.3
Logan	7.4	243	43	D	D	D	109	1 234	275.5	24.4	29	105	12.2	2.3
McDonough	4.5	141	22	D	D	D	142	1 657	338.1	32.0	26	85	14.5	2.3
McHenry	43.5	143	438	4 815	2 391.2	251.9	979	15 034	3 578.6	331.8	295	1 358	178.3	39.0
McLean	16.0	100	174	2 701	5 309.3	149.1	608	9 660	2 231.4	197.0	153	934	139.2	24.9
Macon	40.4	366	113	D	D	D	432	6 231	1 450.6	132.5	91	454	64.6	12.6
Macoupin	9.3	188	49	610	350.4	24.5	160	1 464	326.0	31.8	24	96	6.1	1.8
Madison	387.5	1 466	231	2 470	1 643.6	113.7	906	12 733	3 104.2	285.8	241	1 284	158.5	32.3
Marion	6.6	165	39	D	D	D	168	1 434	345.7	30.7	29	D	D	D
Marshall	7.0	526	17	D	D	D	42	329	78.5	6.1	6	D	D	D
Mason	276.0	17 536	19	206	192.3	8.1	48	453	98.8	7.3	3	5	1.1	0.1
Massac	630.9	41 105	9	D	D	D	44	287	75.9	6.5	5	D	D	D
Menard	3.9	308	14	113	128.7	4.3	33	352	68.9	5.6	8	58	9.5	0.6
Mercer	8.7	517	16	D	D	D	45	405	85.3	7.8	4	6	0.5	0.1
Monroe	2.9	92	22	D	D	D	105	1 395	405.7	35.1	37	123	13.0	2.9
Montgomery	510.2	16 786	41	312	254.8	18.0	138	1 647	401.5	34.2	19	58	5.2	1.1
Morgan	232.1	6 497	45	697	425.5	23.5	162	1 984	403.1	37.0	24	D	D	D
Moultrie	1.6	112	15	86	95.2	3.5	48	480	118.7	9.3	4	D	D	D
Ogle	64.9	1 196	44	D	D	D	151	1 587	454.3	30.1	45	120	13.0	2.4
Peoria	529.6	2 905	226	3 127	1 609.8	147.6	786	11 618	2 425.9	241.0	230	1 167	194.6	31.7
Perry	2.2	96	8	53	42.9	1.7	58	650	168.3	13.9	7	26	1.6	0.3
Piatt	3.3	199	27	237	263.9	10.1	44	496	118.8	10.7	7	40	1.7	0.5
Pike	33.0	1 929	21	171	265.3	6.1	56	551	136.5	10.5	8	24	2.5	0.4
Pope	0.4	102	NA	NA	NA	NA	11	60	9.2	0.9	1	D	D	D
Pulaski	2.3	343	5	D	D	D	18	96	31.8	1.9	1	D	D	D
Putnam	210.2	34 491	8	D	D	D	14	112	21.7	1.8	1	D	D	D
Randolph	41.4	1 249	32	422	166.4	17.3	116	1 472	332.3	31.0	14	34	3.0	0.7
Richland	3.1	194	22	382	250.3	11.6	70	756	161.5	15.2	8	D	D	D
Rock Island	1 082.3	7 322	163	3 145	1 437.5	131.4	545	8 158	1 711.4	174.9	136	615	96.1	14.1
St. Clair	32.8	126	182	1 800	1 661.6	72.9	976	13 864	3 087.2	299.7	245	1 167	153.2	33.2
Saline	3.3	125	16	D	D	D	120	1 214	271.2	26.0	13	70	6.0	1.4
Sangamon	411.4	2 134	192	2 763	1 841.3	109.2	809	12 446	2 862.6	250.1	227	1 011	153.5	24.6
Schuyler	1.7	233	3	D	D	D	37	285	53.1	6.1	4	D	D	D
Scott	9.4	1 739	2	D	D	D	12	119	34.9	2.3	1	D	D	D
Shelby	3.3	149	27	184	157.3	6.0	72	549	140.9	9.6	11	27	1.7	0.4
Stark	2.0	316	10	D	D	D	19	174	57.3	5.5	1	D	D	D
Stephenson	8.9	186	46	D	D	D	167	2 045	480.6	42.4	37	105	11.6	2.5
Tazewell	123.8	952	134	1 946	1 225.1	86.6	455	6 798	1 758.1	156.7	85	321	55.1	8.9
Union	3.4	187	8	64	20.5	2.0	70	678	145.1	14.2	14	42	4.4	0.9
Vermilion	17.1	208	77	D	D	D	281	3 443	757.9	68.5	59	254	34.3	6.6
Wabash	4.0	316	12	143	89.5	4.5	43	496	109.2	8.4	5	20	1.8	0.4
Warren	3.6	206	20	281	219.8	10.1	66	634	133.7	11.5	8	19	1.7	0.3
Washington	4.0	267	31	482	270.5	18.8	65	610	197.3	15.4	14	30	1.4	0.2
Wayne	4.9	289	16	128	126.6	6.2	68	645	146.3	12.4	8	22	1.9	0.5
White	14.9	974	26	280	400.3	8.9	59	491	123.1	10.0	10	49	4.9	1.4
Whiteside	54.9	918	64	431	926.8	16.7	222	2 823	570.6	57.2	47	179	16.4	3.2
Will	2 630.5	4 092	699	12 694	11 061.8	636.9	1 654	28 627	6 841.5	624.0	530	2 767	424.1	80.9
Williamson	112.9	1 775	58	D	D	D	308	3 900	987.5	84.7	61	242	43.7	9.5

1. Merchant wholesalers, except manufacturers' sales branches and offices.   2. Employer establishments.

Table B. States and Counties — Professional Services, Manufacturing, and Accommodation and Food Services

STATE County	Professional, scientific, and technical services,[1] 2007				Manufacturing, 2007				Accommodation and food services, 2007			
	Number of establishments	Number of employees	Receipts (mil dol)	Annual payroll (mil dol)	Number of establishments	Number of employees	Receipts (mil dol)	Annual payroll (mil dol)	Number of establishments	Number of employees	Sales (mil dol)	Annual payroll (mil dol)
	147	148	149	150	151	152	153	154	155	156	157	158
ILLINOIS—Cont'd												
Hardin	4	D	D	D	NA	NA	NA	NA	7	32	1.0	0.3
Henderson	6	24	1.5	0.4	NA	NA	NA	NA	20	57	1.9	0.5
Henry	67	D	D	D	57	4 272	D	D	97	1 119	42.0	10.4
Iroquois	29	111	8.9	3.6	30	880	338.7	24.3	64	539	20.8	5.6
Jackson	119	D	D	D	31	716	177.4	D	155	3 138	108.3	31.2
Jasper	9	22	1.7	0.6	NA	NA	NA	NA	13	110	3.2	0.8
Jefferson	71	471	39.8	17.1	36	D	D	D	82	1 650	67.8	19.3
Jersey	27	163	13.2	6.0	NA	NA	NA	NA	59	749	26.7	7.4
Jo Daviess	54	184	26.7	8.1	36	1 106	419.5	42.8	101	1 730	81.3	22.7
Johnson	16	361	9.9	3.6	NA	NA	NA	NA	16	163	6.8	1.8
Kane	1 522	D	D	D	885	34 075	9 879.5	1 552.1	904	15 459	680.9	201.2
Kankakee	169	D	D	D	115	5 633	3 418.9	280.8	229	D	D	D
Kendall	169	D	D	D	84	2 766	685.7	D	152	2 153	99.9	25.7
Knox	65	D	D	D	40	D	D	D	132	1 800	68.3	19.1
Lake	3 021	D	D	D	922	49 414	16 381.5	3 717.8	1 492	24 968	1 299.3	365.8
LaSalle	181	D	D	D	155	5 964	2 244.0	274.7	322	4 263	158.6	44.1
Lawrence	19	77	7.8	2.6	12	D	D	D	22	D	D	D
Lee	46	271	26.3	10.7	43	4 115	1 098.2	145.9	89	884	35.0	8.8
Livingston	59	302	24.5	10.9	55	4 021	1 261.5	188.0	79	898	38.3	9.5
Logan	42	177	13.7	5.2	20	1 329	631.6	51.7	73	844	30.4	9.4
McDonough	42	D	D	D	22	1 369	248.8	49.9	107	1 598	52.8	13.5
McHenry	973	3 730	488.0	167.7	576	21 462	5 291.2	958.4	539	8 438	365.6	104.5
McLean	338	D	D	D	115	5 497	2 578.8	270.5	375	8 558	336.1	97.4
Macon	181	1 185	125.8	51.1	112	8 762	9 590.8	409.4	219	4 733	170.9	52.0
Macoupin	55	471	40.2	18.2	40	704	180.4	25.2	84	786	26.1	6.5
Madison	528	D	D	D	213	13 490	18 978.2	769.9	596	10 249	382.7	111.6
Marion	63	232	15.0	6.6	56	2 930	689.7	113.5	88	1 016	36.8	9.9
Marshall	13	D	D	D	21	1 045	D	D	30	345	9.2	2.7
Mason	12	34	3.0	0.8	NA	NA	NA	NA	36	279	10.4	2.5
Massac	12	D	D	D	6	514	D	D	27	D	D	D
Menard	14	77	4.9	1.5	NA	NA	NA	NA	22	185	6.9	1.5
Mercer	13	D	D	D	NA	NA	NA	NA	20	222	5.6	1.8
Monroe	75	766	82.7	43.1	NA	NA	NA	NA	66	971	35.9	10.7
Montgomery	37	217	16.7	5.1	28	1 081	305.6	40.1	74	992	36.4	10.8
Morgan	50	D	D	D	34	2 349	D	D	88	1 248	44.4	13.0
Moultrie	19	100	8.6	3.6	31	1 777	541.2	70.0	19	D	D	D
Ogle	81	729	46.1	21.1	68	4 590	1 137.6	192.5	108	1 140	43.4	11.8
Peoria	426	D	D	D	165	11 683	4 951.3	502.0	486	8 169	343.1	99.3
Perry	21	93	6.2	2.6	19	831	369.0	30.9	34	526	15.4	4.5
Piatt	34	119	8.9	3.9	NA	NA	NA	NA	31	299	10.0	2.7
Pike	18	67	8.1	2.0	NA	NA	NA	NA	40	434	13.7	3.7
Pope	3	D	D	D	NA	NA	NA	NA	10	26	1.2	0.2
Pulaski	NA	NA	NA	NA	NA	NA	NA	NA	9	D	D	D
Putnam	6	D	D	D	10	613	D	D	13	59	2.3	0.5
Randolph	39	201	22.8	5.5	34	3 104	532.2	80.7	74	800	26.8	7.0
Richland	27	84	9.2	3.1	32	543	94.6	17.4	31	357	14.2	3.7
Rock Island	297	D	D	D	166	7 961	3 714.3	395.9	364	5 853	224.2	64.9
St. Clair	514	D	D	D	181	5 788	2 324.5	245.6	564	11 181	615.4	149.4
Saline	48	223	27.0	7.3	27	501	92.4	D	45	833	28.3	7.5
Sangamon	580	4 649	562.7	228.8	117	D	D	D	521	9 265	366.8	110.7
Schuyler	9	19	1.2	0.4	NA	NA	NA	NA	14	D	D	D
Scott	3	D	D	D	NA	NA	NA	NA	9	33	1.7	0.4
Shelby	24	164	15.4	6.3	18	1 163	D	44.9	38	364	14.1	4.1
Stark	14	D	D	D	NA	NA	NA	NA	8	40	1.4	0.3
Stephenson	76	460	48.5	17.0	57	3 631	905.1	168.4	95	1 192	44.8	13.6
Tazewell	183	1 197	106.3	47.0	121	9 985	5 145.7	395.7	334	6 334	353.9	83.9
Union	24	91	9.8	4.7	11	584	176.1	21.0	29	314	10.0	4.0
Vermilion	93	396	44.7	12.9	100	5 458	2 576.4	239.7	156	2 370	85.0	24.6
Wabash	21	108	11.0	3.7	NA	NA	NA	NA	21	301	10.2	2.9
Warren	20	D	D	D	21	D	D	D	29	414	14.3	4.0
Washington	21	97	16.2	6.1	17	1 983	409.2	73.5	37	313	12.3	2.9
Wayne	23	54	4.6	1.1	17	D	D	D	26	D	D	D
White	20	80	5.3	1.4	NA	NA	NA	NA	26	338	11.4	3.2
Whiteside	73	583	128.8	24.9	103	3 985	1 022.5	178.9	119	1 647	60.6	16.4
Will	1 516	D	D	D	642	22 470	13 628.2	1 098.3	1 029	20 905	1 404.9	308.1
Williamson	128	D	D	D	50	1 863	681.4	72.1	145	2 588	118.6	31.0

1. Establishment subject to federal tax.

Table B. States and Counties — Health Care and Social Assistance, Other Services, and Federal Funds

STATE County	Health care and social assistance, 2007				Other services, 2007				Federal funds and grants, 2009–2010 Expenditures (mil dol)			
										Direct payments for individuals[1]		
	Number of establishments	Number of employees	Receipts (mil dol)	Annual payroll (mil dol)	Number of establishments	Number of employees	Receipts (mil dol)	Annual payroll (mil dol)	Total	Social Security and government retirement	Medicare	Food Stamps and Supplemental Security Income
	159	160	161	162	163	164	165	166	167	168	169	170
ILLINOIS—Cont'd												
Hardin	11	311	17.9	8.9	3	D	D	D	48.2	17.2	12.6	3.0
Henderson	8	D	D	D	5	D	D	D	57.2	27.1	12.1	1.7
Henry	87	1 421	116.2	43.3	96	640	48.8	11.7	337.3	170.5	82.4	9.2
Iroquois	78	1 648	93.3	42.0	52	148	15.0	3.8	225.7	107.6	57.3	7.2
Jackson	161	3 872	370.4	127.7	96	436	42.6	7.3	445.8	142.0	73.5	30.2
Jasper	15	130	5.9	2.3	23	89	5.7	1.2	67.9	27.3	16.3	2.3
Jefferson	139	3 158	316.6	118.3	88	391	26.6	8.1	318.8	127.2	81.8	18.0
Jersey	37	D	D	D	33	126	5.6	1.5	132.5	65.9	32.3	5.4
Jo Daviess	41	615	32.0	15.4	58	277	19.9	5.5	152.6	84.6	35.5	2.8
Johnson	20	192	9.4	3.9	10	D	D	D	95.8	46.7	19.5	4.0
Kane	1 068	20 650	2 107.5	861.5	849	5 753	583.3	165.6	2 591.9	1 072.5	425.8	88.7
Kankakee	290	6 260	618.8	228.6	193	1 080	105.7	26.6	794.0	326.4	202.6	42.4
Kendall	128	1 021	95.7	35.6	148	767	55.4	16.9	427.7	140.8	34.2	3.5
Knox	143	4 266	356.7	134.4	83	621	204.5	15.2	427.2	200.4	113.0	17.8
Lake	1 818	30 953	3 380.3	1 372.6	1 246	8 449	787.7	218.6	4 231.8	1 575.2	617.8	89.6
LaSalle	277	5 599	404.0	164.3	249	1 337	87.7	25.5	761.0	360.7	190.2	25.3
Lawrence	27	713	33.8	13.4	28	153	16.5	3.7	130.1	50.7	36.9	5.0
Lee	87	2 082	161.8	71.7	64	338	25.1	7.8	237.6	117.4	55.6	6.8
Livingston	67	1 622	123.6	50.2	77	321	29.4	7.2	233.9	107.3	65.8	8.0
Logan	59	1 296	91.4	33.5	55	222	16.6	3.3	200.7	86.2	53.8	7.0
McDonough	83	1 816	120.0	52.5	72	265	17.8	4.6	201.8	74.7	46.2	9.2
McHenry	667	10 348	1 013.9	409.5	561	3 226	240.5	75.1	1 189.0	760.7	232.7	18.3
McLean	333	8 693	875.8	354.5	260	2 362	187.8	59.7	758.0	353.8	140.8	25.7
Macon	282	7 449	750.1	281.3	197	1 526	222.4	33.5	1 043.4	382.0	189.1	51.9
Macoupin	96	1 761	96.0	39.1	80	276	23.7	5.6	369.0	176.6	105.5	15.0
Madison	655	12 765	1 066.8	412.7	479	3 210	273.5	80.8	2 208.0	921.9	477.6	102.3
Marion	113	2 852	210.8	80.0	77	279	20.3	5.3	401.3	165.8	114.6	19.9
Marshall	22	D	D	D	21	D	D	D	82.4	43.2	22.5	2.4
Mason	27	460	28.2	12.8	27	88	7.3	1.4	137.1	59.5	39.1	5.6
Massac	31	628	40.7	16.7	28	150	8.3	3.0	138.4	56.8	36.3	6.4
Menard	15	D	D	D	19	61	4.8	1.2	80.7	39.1	18.2	2.7
Mercer	27	369	21.7	9.4	23	65	7.3	1.5	116.5	57.0	26.2	3.4
Monroe	70	793	45.2	19.2	68	292	23.6	6.6	173.4	99.4	34.1	2.0
Montgomery	75	1 538	111.7	41.8	57	220	17.2	4.6	237.2	104.5	59.5	10.0
Morgan	125	D	D	D	66	273	17.1	5.0	262.8	114.3	62.9	10.8
Moultrie	30	721	33.9	15.5	23	66	6.6	1.7	110.6	52.7	27.5	2.6
Ogle	92	1 424	86.4	34.6	80	346	28.1	7.8	272.0	148.0	60.6	7.4
Peoria	536	20 744	2 106.8	888.9	688	8 786	332.4	141.5	1 686.2	552.5	305.3	85.3
Perry	44	1 018	61.6	24.8	50	162	13.3	2.6	155.7	71.9	42.3	8.7
Piatt	29	D	D	D	19	70	4.2	0.9	111.7	56.9	26.9	2.1
Pike	31	585	41.0	15.6	29	103	7.8	1.7	136.7	56.0	36.1	5.6
Pope	13	143	4.9	2.5	4	D	D	D	41.6	16.2	8.9	1.9
Pulaski	14	184	6.6	2.8	14	37	5.0	0.7	475.0	21.7	17.1	6.1
Putnam	4	20	1.0	0.3	6	17	1.2	0.3	38.4	21.8	9.6	0.7
Randolph	73	2 120	147.9	69.0	66	248	17.0	5.7	239.2	109.3	63.4	9.2
Richland	48	945	60.5	26.1	44	187	13.3	3.7	134.7	54.3	28.6	5.2
Rock Island	397	9 031	742.0	324.9	263	1 765	152.2	44.1	1 673.8	524.0	247.2	54.0
St. Clair	620	14 718	1 246.8	517.7	439	2 502	196.7	60.3	3 539.8	952.1	472.5	164.6
Saline	62	2 059	116.0	53.1	53	D	D	D	312.6	102.4	56.4	18.0
Sangamon	462	D	D	D	482	3 494	382.6	108.4	5 512.3	575.4	314.8	67.4
Schuyler	15	345	20.3	8.4	13	39	6.0	0.7	52.5	23.7	11.9	1.8
Scott	5	D	D	D	5	14	2.2	0.3	40.3	16.7	9.4	1.0
Shelby	37	683	43.3	16.3	27	96	7.8	1.8	176.3	75.4	45.7	5.0
Stark	7	D	D	D	3	D	D	D	51.5	21.4	15.3	1.1
Stephenson	104	2 586	208.5	88.9	98	594	30.6	9.9	345.8	168.6	74.5	14.8
Tazewell	238	5 102	335.4	135.1	252	1 270	109.9	32.3	785.6	409.7	199.1	24.4
Union	53	1 156	47.5	22.0	20	71	5.3	1.5	157.3	61.6	34.4	9.8
Vermilion	149	4 729	437.7	203.4	138	780	54.8	14.5	774.1	302.8	150.8	44.4
Wabash	28	733	42.2	16.6	23	D	D	D	86.0	39.1	22.3	4.5
Warren	44	732	33.5	13.4	34	112	11.3	1.9	131.4	53.9	32.2	5.1
Washington	26	489	26.2	12.1	28	101	5.8	1.4	119.7	47.9	34.7	2.6
Wayne	32	727	41.8	18.5	28	112	8.1	2.0	141.5	53.8	36.3	4.5
White	38	536	25.7	10.2	34	141	16.1	3.9	166.8	60.1	38.1	5.6
Whiteside	112	3 834	248.3	104.9	135	695	71.1	14.2	433.3	231.4	105.0	14.6
Will	1 127	18 527	1 782.4	714.9	1 013	6 548	638.9	169.8	2 344.2	1 309.4	444.4	83.5
Williamson	210	5 288	539.0	197.2	102	472	44.1	10.8	704.3	224.4	107.5	26.9

1. State totals may include programs not allocated by county.

Table B. States and Counties — Federal Funds, Residential Construction, and Local Government Finances

	Federal funds and grants, 2009–2010 (cont.)							Value of residential construction authorized by building permits, 2010		Local government finances, 2007				
	Expenditures (mil dol) (cont.)									General revenue				
	Procurement contract awards			Grants[1]								Taxes		
													Per capita[2] (dollars)	
STATE County	Salaries and wages	Defense	Other	Medicaid and other health-related	Nutrition and family welfare	Education	Other	New construction ($1,000)	Number of housing units	Total (mil dol)	Inter-govern-mental (mil dol)	Total (mil dol)	Total	Property
	171	172	173	174	175	176	177	178	179	180	181	182	183	184
ILLINOIS—Cont'd														
Hardin	1.1	0.0	0.3	10.7	1.3	0.2	0.8	0	0	12.3	9.5	1.4	302	274
Henderson	2.6	0.6	0.5	4.7	1.5	0.2	0.1	1 659	17	19.6	10.2	6.2	812	798
Henry	31.1	0.5	2.2	14.1	6.8	1.0	3.6	5 158	28	168.5	62.0	50.4	1 015	960
Iroquois	9.1	0.1	11.1	9.1	4.4	0.8	1.3	5 722	44	82.7	36.0	33.6	1 108	1 031
Jackson	29.6	5.8	8.1	76.7	13.2	6.1	20.3	4 784	65	157.6	72.2	53.8	914	696
Jasper	3.3	0.0	0.8	7.0	1.8	0.2	0.0	0	0	34.5	18.0	12.5	1 283	1 270
Jefferson	17.0	0.1	3.1	43.5	8.3	2.4	2.1	0	0	133.7	78.1	34.2	851	660
Jersey	3.7	0.0	0.9	14.9	3.1	0.3	0.9	5 747	65	74.2	23.6	16.3	724	627
Jo Daviess	6.2	0.0	2.6	7.8	3.1	0.4	0.4	9 695	37	82.4	21.4	39.3	1 761	1 700
Johnson	5.5	0.0	1.5	13.2	2.2	0.4	0.2	317	3	26.3	15.8	5.3	408	404
Kane	212.5	45.0	470.0	127.0	50.8	11.7	34.2	102 341	565	2 427.2	666.1	1 310.9	2 617	2 353
Kankakee	53.7	0.2	4.7	96.5	20.0	5.2	18.9	12 972	71	374.3	178.8	129.3	1 168	1 106
Kendall	192.5	32.8	3.9	3.7	4.4	1.2	3.9	32 660	177	342.3	91.9	167.4	1 729	1 583
Knox	20.9	0.0	3.4	37.3	8.3	2.9	3.6	1 263	7	172.0	77.1	54.1	1 043	934
Lake	535.9	685.9	316.9	171.6	68.4	25.9	54.7	138 751	698	3 294.3	796.2	1 949.8	2 745	2 561
LaSalle	56.3	5.5	5.7	52.6	13.5	3.1	22.5	12 002	77	376.1	140.6	162.7	1 445	1 313
Lawrence	7.0	0.1	0.9	16.1	2.9	0.5	0.6	0	0	34.3	20.5	7.8	499	490
Lee	15.5	0.0	2.2	16.2	4.5	0.9	1.0	5 815	29	110.3	41.1	46.8	1 321	1 217
Livingston	16.3	0.1	1.9	12.0	5.3	0.8	1.0	5 339	29	141.7	52.1	54.4	1 421	1 399
Logan	10.4	0.3	1.7	15.0	6.3	2.3	1.2	3 789	17	71.2	30.2	27.3	910	872
McDonough	17.8	0.1	1.7	15.7	4.7	0.9	2.7	929	9	134.5	41.1	25.6	801	771
McHenry	56.4	8.1	13.0	33.0	22.5	3.4	13.0	49 234	305	1 095.7	253.3	625.2	1 979	1 795
McLean	67.4	0.3	18.6	56.5	18.9	5.3	21.8	62 284	427	542.8	157.7	275.3	1 676	1 372
Macon	63.7	2.0	18.1	111.7	20.3	4.3	179.3	28 243	101	391.1	180.1	140.6	1 293	1 103
Macoupin	11.3	0.2	2.9	26.9	9.1	1.1	1.0	9 041	48	116.8	66.6	33.0	684	652
Madison	82.5	164.7	91.0	222.3	55.2	10.5	30.2	103 545	483	883.4	401.0	318.5	1 191	1 084
Marion	14.2	0.1	3.2	44.6	10.8	2.3	3.3	0	0	181.5	90.1	38.6	976	826
Marshall	3.1	0.0	0.7	3.7	1.8	0.2	0.1	2 492	13	32.4	11.6	15.8	1 226	1 180
Mason	5.0	3.2	2.5	11.1	2.9	0.4	0.7	1 134	8	66.1	25.3	19.2	1 269	1 208
Massac	3.5	2.2	2.8	22.7	2.9	0.5	0.3	106	1	67.7	30.6	11.2	743	699
Menard	3.0	0.0	0.7	9.7	1.8	0.3	1.0	1 701	9	41.6	18.0	14.8	1 184	1 150
Mercer	4.4	5.1	0.9	5.8	2.7	0.2	0.2	1 889	10	56.8	23.6	16.7	1 014	1 004
Monroe	8.8	0.4	5.1	12.9	2.8	0.3	0.0	24 728	131	88.0	25.5	38.9	1 202	1 120
Montgomery	17.2	0.0	1.8	22.0	4.9	1.0	3.0	3 844	24	81.8	40.1	28.0	940	901
Morgan	8.0	0.0	1.6	44.4	5.1	1.4	1.8	991	8	95.3	51.1	32.3	915	827
Moultrie	14.9	0.0	0.6	5.8	1.8	0.3	0.0	3 230	33	44.7	15.3	23.2	1 620	1 608
Ogle	11.2	4.0	2.6	13.2	5.7	0.9	1.7	11 693	97	211.1	69.4	88.6	1 610	1 562
Peoria	170.8	250.1	40.9	134.6	33.1	8.1	50.9	71 031	455	694.9	273.2	260.0	1 421	1 144
Perry	4.2	0.0	1.0	16.2	3.4	0.6	0.9	4 165	26	68.3	25.6	11.4	504	471
Piatt	3.5	7.8	0.8	5.0	2.2	0.3	0.1	7 944	41	65.8	32.0	21.6	1 311	1 277
Pike	5.5	0.0	1.3	17.0	3.2	0.5	0.3	1 518	15	44.2	24.2	12.4	744	717
Pope	4.7	0.0	1.9	5.4	1.1	0.1	0.2	0	0	9.6	5.9	2.4	581	576
Pulaski	3.9	380.3	1.1	27.2	6.8	1.0	0.9	600	8	25.0	18.0	2.6	398	351
Putnam	1.9	0.0	0.5	0.8	1.0	0.1	0.1	2 113	15	19.6	11.4	6.5	1 084	1 065
Randolph	13.9	0.3	5.8	19.4	6.9	0.8	0.7	6 580	50	128.2	42.3	22.8	697	642
Richland	4.8	-0.1	1.2	15.9	2.9	1.5	0.8	1 791	10	74.8	44.2	11.6	749	702
Rock Island	343.9	301.2	18.8	86.5	26.1	5.3	35.7	29 159	237	548.0	224.6	203.5	1 381	1 203
St. Clair	698.0	585.9	59.8	438.8	52.5	25.9	37.3	160 488	1 023	1 012.9	517.1	308.7	1 181	966
Saline	7.8	2.9	22.9	50.0	4.9	1.8	33.2	0	0	82.1	45.2	18.9	723	649
Sangamon	269.9	25.2	32.2	272.7	394.3	939.9	2 562.3	72 332	390	661.9	257.4	279.3	1 439	1 255
Schuyler	2.2	0.1	0.5	6.7	1.4	0.2	0.1	NA	NA	36.2	10.8	6.4	921	919
Scott	1.8	0.1	0.4	6.6	1.1	0.1	0.1	NA	NA	17.1	8.9	4.1	779	752
Shelby	16.0	2.5	1.4	15.7	3.3	0.5	0.6	11 719	99	45.3	20.6	16.5	761	743
Stark	2.2	0.0	0.5	3.3	1.2	0.1	0.1	0	0	17.8	6.5	8.1	1 312	1 298
Stephenson	25.9	0.7	2.7	29.6	7.8	1.9	2.3	5 483	27	168.4	74.4	59.4	1 276	1 162
Tazewell	48.6	3.5	9.1	55.1	17.2	2.0	4.7	53 641	242	457.4	181.1	176.4	1 345	1 167
Union	4.2	0.0	0.9	35.6	3.5	0.7	1.7	3 753	27	75.2	31.9	14.1	773	767
Vermilion	56.9	14.7	69.5	79.2	19.3	3.6	9.5	1 384	13	277.9	144.2	79.7	981	836
Wabash	2.4	0.0	0.6	9.1	2.1	1.0	0.2	75	1	49.6	15.8	8.1	668	632
Warren	7.5	0.0	1.1	15.0	5.3	0.4	1.5	8 091	57	44.2	20.5	14.8	850	833
Washington	4.2	0.0	1.0	8.7	2.1	0.3	1.1	4 847	31	44.2	14.9	12.0	816	808
Wayne	5.1	0.0	1.1	16.5	3.1	0.6	1.0	50	1	38.7	23.3	9.4	567	527
White	4.5	0.3	11.8	22.0	7.1	0.4	0.3	0	0	44.8	28.5	9.2	626	582
Whiteside	21.0	0.7	2.7	27.1	13.2	1.4	2.7	8 907	50	281.2	74.0	62.7	1 059	1 002
Will	102.1	81.6	60.8	116.1	53.8	13.9	31.8	131 322	618	2 329.8	670.9	1 202.8	1 786	1 620
Williamson	95.1	109.1	39.0	67.0	9.2	2.5	3.2	12 935	128	212.3	110.3	60.6	939	794

1. State totals may include programs not allocated by county.   2. Based on the resident population estimated as of July 1 of the year shown.

Table B. States and Counties — Local Government Finances, Government Employment, and Voting

	Local government finances, 2007 (cont.)									Government employment, 2009			Presidential election,[2] 2008		
	Direct general expenditure							Debt outstanding					Percent of vote cast:		
			Percent of total for:												
STATE County	Total (mil dol)	Per capita[1] (dollars)	Educa-tion	Health and hospitals	Police protec-tion	Public welfare	High-ways	Total (mil dol)	Per capita[1] (dollars)	Federal civilian	Federal military	State and local	Demo-cratic	Republi-can	All other
	185	186	187	188	189	190	191	192	193	194	195	196	197	198	199
ILLINOIS—Cont'd															
Hardin	9.8	2 201	63.4	3.2	2.7	0.2	7.8	5.1	1 130	13	0	258	39.6	59.0	1.5
Henderson	18.0	2 369	51.6	7.6	3.7	0.1	10.4	4.8	627	44	15	406	58.1	40.4	1.5
Henry	163.6	3 294	42.4	16.9	6.8	1.9	6.5	85.4	1 721	158	98	3 324	53.2	45.4	1.4
Iroquois	86.2	2 847	54.0	2.9	3.7	0.1	8.7	57.7	1 904	114	59	1 496	34.1	64.0	1.9
Jackson	158.1	2 687	49.4	2.5	6.8	6.9	7.7	116.9	1 986	271	124	13 372	59.7	37.9	2.3
Jasper	31.6	3 260	58.9	5.8	4.1	0.1	13.8	7.1	735	45	19	681	40.2	57.8	2.0
Jefferson	124.5	3 098	65.5	0.9	4.3	0.1	4.8	50.8	1 265	164	81	2 753	43.5	54.3	2.2
Jersey	71.8	3 198	34.6	38.4	3.9	0.2	4.3	19.3	859	46	45	1 161	47.6	50.4	2.0
Jo Daviess	79.0	3 543	42.5	14.1	6.0	0.0	9.3	48.5	2 173	78	44	1 311	54.5	44.0	1.5
Johnson	27.0	2 064	58.2	1.4	3.5	0.1	9.4	11.7	893	83	27	765	31.7	66.3	2.0
Kane	2 458.6	4 907	53.3	0.5	6.5	0.1	5.5	3 468.0	6 922	1 799	1 024	29 044	55.2	43.4	1.3
Kankakee	395.4	3 571	54.9	1.0	6.0	0.1	5.7	256.7	2 319	254	227	6 227	51.5	46.9	1.5
Kendall	408.2	4 216	60.2	0.9	3.3	0.7	7.5	672.0	6 941	144	209	4 085	53.1	45.8	1.1
Knox	176.2	3 397	53.4	1.4	5.6	4.2	5.9	74.2	1 431	170	103	3 374	59.2	39.3	1.6
Lake	3 247.6	4 573	54.7	1.8	5.9	0.9	4.5	2 963.3	4 172	5 768	18 190	37 109	59.3	39.6	1.1
LaSalle	362.1	3 216	55.5	1.6	6.0	1.5	8.8	192.2	1 706	367	226	6 354	54.7	43.6	1.7
Lawrence	33.6	2 158	55.2	0.3	4.9	0.1	12.9	17.1	1 095	48	33	918	46.1	52.1	1.8
Lee	107.5	3 032	59.5	1.6	5.2	0.1	6.3	65.9	1 859	92	71	2 191	47.6	50.6	1.8
Livingston	129.0	3 371	54.3	3.1	4.6	3.9	6.1	57.5	1 502	113	75	2 769	39.6	58.8	1.6
Logan	73.6	2 458	46.7	3.5	5.5	0.1	9.0	29.5	983	115	59	2 013	40.7	57.6	1.7
McDonough	128.7	4 022	30.4	38.6	3.2	3.6	6.1	17.6	550	107	69	5 650	52.0	46.4	1.6
McHenry	1 135.3	3 593	49.6	1.6	5.5	1.8	5.9	1 206.1	3 817	561	641	14 860	51.9	46.6	1.5
McLean	563.9	3 434	44.5	1.2	5.4	1.4	5.2	651.5	3 968	728	341	14 407	49.8	48.5	1.7
Macon	379.7	3 492	50.8	2.2	6.6	0.3	7.8	200.6	1 845	318	226	5 963	49.8	48.7	1.5
Macoupin	115.6	2 397	61.0	2.4	7.1	0.2	8.5	58.5	1 213	136	95	2 459	54.0	44.2	1.8
Madison	865.5	3 237	50.4	0.7	6.2	1.3	7.0	897.7	3 358	651	539	16 230	53.7	44.6	1.7
Marion	216.5	5 468	62.2	8.6	2.5	0.2	6.5	77.7	1 964	174	78	2 246	48.1	50.1	1.9
Marshall	29.2	2 274	44.2	1.6	5.2	0.1	12.5	12.2	948	44	25	536	48.6	49.7	1.7
Mason	64.3	4 241	44.7	25.1	2.6	0.1	7.2	29.2	1 924	69	30	1 149	52.0	46.1	1.8
Massac	64.6	4 273	31.3	31.0	3.7	0.0	6.7	65.9	4 360	52	30	938	37.5	60.8	1.7
Menard	43.4	3 482	55.7	1.7	3.5	10.2	8.0	22.1	1 769	36	25	732	41.9	56.8	1.3
Mercer	55.7	3 377	44.9	22.5	3.3	0.1	7.2	61.4	3 722	67	32	1 096	55.2	43.3	1.4
Monroe	93.9	2 899	47.0	1.7	4.3	15.8	9.3	153.5	4 741	79	66	1 432	44.0	54.6	1.4
Montgomery	79.0	2 661	48.7	3.2	5.6	0.1	11.6	49.3	1 652	114	59	1 773	50.4	47.8	1.8
Morgan	92.5	2 622	54.1	1.6	8.5	3.1	9.6	13.2	374	102	70	2 315	48.6	49.4	1.9
Moultrie	41.3	2 882	35.6	1.5	6.9	0.0	7.9	5.8	406	34	29	595	42.6	55.4	1.9
Ogle	215.9	3 924	59.0	1.4	6.6	0.1	6.6	174.7	3 176	140	110	2 943	45.3	52.9	1.8
Peoria	691.5	3 779	38.9	1.4	6.2	2.2	6.3	432.2	2 362	1 554	416	9 882	56.2	42.3	1.5
Perry	65.7	2 909	34.6	33.9	4.1	0.6	7.5	28.1	1 023	51	45	1 242	47.0	50.9	2.1
Piatt	58.6	3 560	46.4	2.9	4.7	10.8	11.7	25.7	1 558	47	33	947	42.9	55.5	1.7
Pike	45.4	2 715	53.6	5.1	4.2	0.5	12.1	19.6	1 175	69	32	969	39.7	58.5	1.8
Pope	9.3	2 233	47.4	0.0	2.2	0.7	11.9	6.9	1 649	84	0	202	37.9	60.2	1.9
Pulaski	25.1	3 870	64.2	1.7	4.7	0.9	5.5	16.3	2 519	85	12	793	50.1	48.7	1.2
Putnam	19.7	3 278	45.9	1.7	3.6	0.3	10.7	1.6	266	24	12	310	56.9	41.3	1.8
Randolph	120.8	3 689	33.0	36.4	4.0	3.2	6.3	39.1	1 193	106	65	2 860	48.6	49.6	1.8
Richland	74.5	4 795	76.0	0.4	2.1	0.1	5.4	20.0	1 286	63	31	967	41.6	56.6	1.8
Rock Island	518.5	3 519	47.5	1.3	6.7	2.8	5.2	281.7	1 912	6 198	564	7 863	61.7	37.1	1.2
St. Clair	954.7	3 654	55.1	1.6	4.9	0.3	5.7	686.3	2 626	6 172	5 347	13 613	60.6	38.1	1.3
Saline	81.2	3 112	63.5	0.0	6.2	0.2	5.8	46.6	1 785	109	51	1 950	44.5	53.4	2.2
Sangamon	635.5	3 274	54.3	1.1	8.6	1.2	5.9	1 061.5	5 468	1 935	409	25 951	51.4	47.0	1.6
Schuyler	34.1	4 875	33.4	43.6	2.6	0.2	7.5	8.7	1 249	31	13	553	49.7	47.9	2.4
Scott	15.8	3 026	48.6	1.1	4.9	15.6	7.6	1.9	360	25	10	350	41.9	56.0	2.1
Shelby	40.8	1 877	48.0	2.6	5.3	0.2	9.4	19.3	888	103	44	879	39.1	58.9	2.1
Stark	18.9	3 056	63.1	0.5	1.7	0.2	8.3	10.0	1 617	31	12	307	46.7	52.0	1.3
Stephenson	163.6	3 512	55.0	1.6	3.9	4.7	4.8	117.2	2 517	134	93	2 969	52.5	45.9	1.6
Tazewell	434.9	3 316	57.0	1.6	5.4	0.2	7.2	263.4	2 008	532	264	7 041	46.0	52.1	1.9
Union	70.9	3 885	53.8	23.8	3.0	0.0	5.0	19.6	1 072	56	36	1 417	43.0	54.9	2.1
Vermilion	256.8	3 163	54.1	1.5	6.1	3.3	6.8	94.9	1 168	1 540	160	4 550	49.4	48.8	1.7
Wabash	48.6	3 998	32.0	37.4	4.7	0.6	8.5	14.4	1 183	37	24	1 040	42.6	56.3	1.1
Warren	42.1	2 420	52.8	0.8	5.5	0.1	9.2	47.7	2 742	73	35	772	53.4	45.3	1.3
Washington	44.5	3 012	38.6	29.4	3.4	0.1	7.2	20.3	1 374	60	29	903	42.1	56.4	1.5
Wayne	44.2	2 666	50.2	1.8	3.5	0.1	8.5	17.1	1 033	61	33	999	31.6	66.8	1.7
White	47.3	3 225	61.8	0.8	4.4	0.2	9.0	6.9	473	59	29	851	44.5	53.5	2.0
Whiteside	268.1	4 528	32.6	42.1	3.2	0.7	3.7	60.4	1 020	175	118	4 164	58.0	40.4	1.5
Will	2 491.9	3 699	53.5	1.3	5.8	0.7	6.2	3 575.2	5 308	1 060	1 381	33 928	56.0	42.8	1.2
Williamson	201.3	3 120	61.2	1.6	4.1	0.4	8.2	143.5	2 223	1 553	131	3 949	41.9	56.4	1.7

1. Based on the resident population estimated as of July 1 of the year shown.   2. © 2009 Election Data Services, Inc. All rights reserved.

Items 185—199

Table B. States and Counties — Land Area and Population

STATE/ County code	CBSA code[1]	County type[2]	STATE County	Population and population characteristics, 2010														
				Land area,[3] (sq km) 2010	Total persons	Rank	Per square kilometer	Race alone or in combination, not Hispanic or Latino (percent)				Percent Hispanic or Latino[4]	Age (percent)					
								White	Black	American Indian, Alaska Native	Asian and Pacific Islander		Under 5 years	5 to 17 years	18 to 24 years	25 to 34 years	35 to 44 years	45 to 54 years
				1	2	3	4	5	6	7	8	9	10	11	12	13	14	15
			ILLINOIS—Cont'd															
17 201	40420	2	Winnebago	1 330	295 266	218	222.0	74.4	13.2	0.7	2.8	10.9	6.7	18.3	8.5	12.4	13.1	14.9
17 203	37900	2	Woodford	1 367	38 664	1 202	28.3	97.4	0.9	0.5	0.8	1.4	6.5	19.3	8.2	10.7	12.2	15.4
18 000	...	X	INDIANA	92 789	6 483 802	X	69.9	82.9	9.8	0.6	2.0	6.0	6.7	18.1	10.0	12.8	13.0	14.6
18 001	19540	6	Adams	878	34 387	1 316	39.2	95.1	0.5	0.4	0.4	4.1	9.3	21.9	8.6	11.5	11.5	12.8
18 003	23060	2	Allen	1 702	355 329	182	208.8	78.6	13.0	0.8	3.2	6.5	7.5	19.5	9.4	13.2	12.9	14.1
18 005	18020	3	Bartholomew	1 054	76 794	707	72.9	88.2	2.4	0.5	3.8	6.2	6.8	18.4	7.9	12.7	13.6	14.3
18 007	29140	3	Benton	1 053	8 854	2 541	8.4	94.4	0.7	0.4	0.3	4.9	7.0	18.8	7.1	11.1	12.6	15.2
18 009	...	6	Blackford	428	12 766	2 258	29.8	98.3	0.7	0.8	0.4	0.9	5.9	16.9	7.7	10.1	12.6	15.4
18 011	26900	1	Boone	1 095	56 640	890	51.7	95.0	1.2	0.5	2.2	2.2	6.9	21.2	6.4	10.7	14.5	17.2
18 013	26900	1	Brown	808	15 242	2 095	18.9	97.8	0.6	0.8	0.6	1.2	5.1	15.7	5.9	8.5	12.0	17.0
18 015	29140	3	Carroll	964	20 155	1 831	20.9	95.9	0.5	0.4	0.3	3.5	6.1	18.5	7.3	10.6	12.6	15.6
18 017	30900	4	Cass	1 067	38 966	1 196	36.5	84.6	1.8	0.6	1.2	12.6	6.8	19.1	7.9	11.8	12.6	14.7
18 019	31140	1	Clark	966	110 232	536	114.1	87.0	8.1	0.7	1.2	4.9	6.6	17.1	8.2	14.2	13.8	14.9
18 021	45460	3	Clay	926	26 890	1 535	29.0	98.0	0.7	0.6	0.4	1.1	5.8	18.1	8.3	11.6	13.1	15.3
18 023	23140	6	Clinton	1 049	33 224	1 345	31.7	85.9	0.6	0.4	0.3	13.2	7.5	19.1	8.3	11.9	12.5	14.4
18 025	...	8	Crawford	792	10 713	2 388	13.5	97.9	0.4	0.9	0.4	1.2	6.1	17.2	8.0	10.3	12.5	16.2
18 027	47780	7	Daviess	1 112	31 648	1 402	28.5	94.5	0.9	0.4	0.7	4.2	8.4	20.4	8.9	11.8	11.3	13.6
18 029	17140	1	Dearborn	790	50 047	976	63.4	97.7	1.0	0.4	0.6	1.0	6.2	18.8	7.6	10.8	13.7	16.4
18 031	24700	6	Decatur	965	25 740	1 578	26.7	97.1	0.5	0.5	0.9	1.7	6.5	19.0	7.7	12.1	12.9	15.3
18 033	12140	4	DeKalb	940	42 223	1 122	44.9	96.5	0.7	0.5	0.7	2.4	6.7	19.7	8.1	11.7	13.2	15.4
18 035	34620	3	Delaware	1 016	117 671	507	115.8	89.9	7.9	0.7	1.5	1.8	5.4	14.6	19.2	11.0	11.0	12.7
18 037	27540	7	Dubois	1 107	41 889	1 134	37.8	93.1	0.4	0.3	0.6	6.0	6.6	18.9	7.0	11.7	12.9	16.1
18 039	21140	3	Elkhart	1 200	197 559	314	164.6	78.9	6.7	0.7	1.3	14.1	8.1	20.3	8.9	12.8	13.1	13.5
18 041	18220	7	Fayette	557	24 277	1 633	43.6	97.2	1.7	0.5	0.4	0.9	6.2	17.8	7.4	11.2	12.8	14.1
18 043	31140	1	Floyd	383	74 578	728	194.7	90.8	6.2	0.6	1.3	2.6	6.1	17.9	8.8	12.0	13.3	16.1
18 045	...	6	Fountain	1 025	17 240	1 968	16.8	97.1	0.4	0.7	0.4	2.2	5.9	18.3	7.2	10.4	12.6	15.3
18 047	17140	1	Franklin	996	23 087	1 683	23.2	98.5	0.3	0.5	0.4	0.9	6.3	19.9	7.1	10.2	13.7	16.0
18 049	...	7	Fulton	954	20 836	1 799	21.8	94.1	1.1	0.7	0.6	4.2	6.5	18.2	7.4	11.1	12.1	14.9
18 051	21780	2	Gibson	1 263	33 503	1 334	26.5	96.1	2.7	0.6	0.6	1.3	6.5	17.8	8.1	11.5	12.6	15.5
18 053	31980	4	Grant	1 072	70 061	757	65.4	88.4	8.2	0.8	0.9	3.6	5.8	15.9	13.3	10.1	11.4	14.4
18 055	14020	3	Greene	1 405	33 165	1 347	23.6	98.2	0.3	0.6	0.5	1.0	6.0	17.8	7.5	11.0	13.1	15.2
18 057	26900	1	Hamilton	1 021	274 569	235	268.9	87.8	4.0	0.4	5.6	3.4	7.9	22.3	5.7	13.1	16.8	15.5
18 059	26900	1	Hancock	793	70 002	759	88.3	95.1	2.4	0.6	1.2	1.7	6.3	19.9	7.0	11.3	14.3	16.0
18 061	31140	1	Harrison	1 255	39 364	1 186	31.4	97.4	0.7	0.6	0.6	1.5	6.1	17.6	7.8	11.8	13.1	16.5
18 063	26900	1	Hendricks	1 054	145 448	429	138.0	89.7	5.5	0.5	2.6	3.0	7.0	20.4	7.1	13.0	15.3	15.4
18 065	35220	4	Henry	1 015	49 462	987	48.7	95.9	2.6	0.6	0.5	1.4	5.4	16.9	7.8	11.4	13.6	15.5
18 067	29020	3	Howard	759	82 752	670	109.0	89.1	8.1	0.8	1.3	2.7	6.2	17.4	7.9	11.5	12.3	15.1
18 069	26540	6	Huntington	991	37 124	1 238	37.5	97.0	0.8	0.7	0.7	1.7	6.0	17.7	10.0	11.5	12.3	15.6
18 071	42980	4	Jackson	1 319	42 376	1 117	32.1	92.5	1.0	0.6	1.1	5.7	6.5	18.1	7.7	12.9	13.5	15.0
18 073	16980	1	Jasper	1 449	33 478	1 336	23.1	93.3	0.9	0.5	0.6	5.4	6.5	19.2	9.2	11.4	12.5	15.0
18 075	...	6	Jay	994	21 253	1 777	21.4	96.5	0.5	0.4	0.6	2.7	7.0	19.6	8.0	10.6	12.8	14.2
18 077	31500	6	Jefferson	934	32 428	1 378	34.7	95.1	2.2	0.6	0.9	2.3	5.8	16.9	9.9	11.7	12.8	15.5
18 079	35860	6	Jennings	975	28 525	1 475	29.3	96.9	1.1	0.6	0.4	2.0	6.6	19.8	8.2	10.9	14.3	15.2
18 081	26900	1	Johnson	830	139 654	441	168.3	93.5	1.6	0.5	2.5	3.1	6.9	19.5	8.3	12.8	14.2	14.7
18 083	47180	4	Knox	1 337	38 440	1 206	28.8	95.0	3.1	0.5	0.8	1.5	5.9	15.4	13.9	11.2	10.8	14.5
18 085	47700	4	Kosciusko	1 376	77 358	701	56.2	90.8	1.1	0.6	1.1	7.3	6.9	18.7	8.9	12.3	12.6	14.8
18 087	...	6	LaGrange	983	37 128	1 236	37.8	95.6	0.4	0.4	0.5	3.5	10.1	24.4	9.1	11.6	11.2	11.6
18 089	16980	1	Lake	1 292	496 005	131	383.9	56.3	26.1	0.6	1.6	16.7	6.7	19.0	8.7	12.7	12.6	14.9
18 091	33140	3	LaPorte	1 550	111 467	531	71.9	83.0	11.7	0.7	0.8	5.5	5.9	16.8	8.4	12.9	13.2	15.3
18 093	13260	4	Lawrence	1 163	46 134	1 041	39.7	97.5	0.6	0.9	0.7	1.2	5.9	17.7	7.1	11.0	12.7	15.3
18 095	11300	3	Madison	1 170	131 636	466	112.5	87.7	9.2	0.6	0.7	3.2	6.2	16.9	9.0	12.4	13.2	14.3
18 097	26900	1	Marion	1 026	903 393	55	880.5	61.5	27.9	0.7	2.6	9.3	7.5	17.5	10.5	16.0	13.2	14.1
18 099	38500	6	Marshall	1 149	47 051	1 022	40.9	90.5	0.8	0.6	0.6	8.4	6.9	20.0	8.0	11.1	12.5	14.6
18 101	...	6	Martin	870	10 334	2 416	11.9	98.6	0.3	0.5	0.4	0.7	6.5	17.5	7.3	10.5	12.6	15.8
18 103	37940	6	Miami	968	36 903	1 247	38.1	91.8	5.1	1.5	0.6	2.5	5.7	17.0	8.3	12.7	14.2	15.2
18 105	14020	3	Monroe	1 022	137 974	447	135.0	88.2	4.1	0.7	6.2	2.9	4.7	11.6	28.9	14.5	10.0	10.7
18 107	18820	6	Montgomery	1 307	38 124	1 213	29.2	93.8	1.2	0.6	0.8	4.6	6.5	17.5	9.7	11.0	12.6	15.3
18 109	26900	1	Morgan	1 046	68 894	769	65.9	97.9	0.6	0.7	0.6	1.2	6.2	18.9	7.7	10.8	13.9	16.3
18 111	16980	1	Newton	1 041	14 244	2 158	13.7	94.0	0.6	0.6	0.4	5.0	5.7	17.3	7.3	10.5	12.4	16.4
18 113	28340	6	Noble	1 064	47 536	1 015	44.7	89.4	0.7	0.5	0.6	9.6	7.3	19.8	8.3	12.0	13.1	14.9
18 115	17140	1	Ohio	223	6 128	2 754	27.5	98.0	0.5	0.5	0.4	1.1	4.9	16.3	7.6	10.0	13.0	17.5
18 117	...	6	Orange	1 032	19 840	1 847	19.2	97.5	1.2	0.9	0.5	1.0	6.2	18.5	7.6	11.0	12.6	15.2
18 119	14020	3	Owen	998	21 575	1 761	21.6	98.1	0.5	0.8	0.5	0.9	5.6	17.6	7.6	10.1	12.8	17.1
18 121	...	6	Parke	1 152	17 339	1 960	15.1	95.9	2.5	0.6	0.3	1.2	5.7	15.7	8.5	12.0	13.1	15.8
18 123	...	6	Perry	989	19 338	1 863	19.6	95.9	2.6	0.5	0.5	1.0	6.0	15.5	8.1	13.4	12.8	15.8

1. CBSA = Core Based Statistical Area. See Appendix A for explanation. See Appendix B for list of metropolitan areas with component counties.   2. County type code from the Economic Research Service of USDA Rural-Urban Continuum Codes. See Appendix A for definition.   3. Dry land or land partially or temporarily covered by water.   4. May be of any race.

Table B. States and Counties — **Population and Households**

STATE County	55 to 64 years (16)	65 to 74 years (17)	75 years and over (18)	Percent female (19)	1990 (20)	2000 (21)	1990–2000 (22)	2000–2010 (23)	Births (24)	Deaths (25)	Net migration (26)	Number (27)	Percent change, 2000–2010 (28)	Persons per household (29)	Female family householder[1] (30)	One person (31)
ILLINOIS—Cont'd																
Winnebago	12.3	7.3	6.5	51.1	252 913	278 418	10.1	6.1	37 436	23 095	4 942	115 501	7.0	2.52	14.0	27.7
Woodford	12.8	7.3	7.5	50.6	32 653	35 469	8.6	9.0	4 180	3 180	2 415	14 276	11.6	2.64	7.5	21.8
INDIANA	11.9	7.0	6.0	50.8	5 544 156	6 080 485	9.7	6.6	810 225	512 148	71 633	2 502 154	7.1	2.52	12.4	26.9
Adams	10.8	6.7	7.1	50.6	31 095	33 625	8.1	2.3	5 850	2 806	-2 219	12 011	1.6	2.83	8.9	24.6
Allen	11.5	6.2	5.7	51.3	300 836	331 849	10.3	7.1	49 299	24 264	-867	137 851	7.1	2.53	13.1	28.1
Bartholomew	12.2	7.8	6.2	50.6	63 657	71 435	12.2	7.5	9 688	6 069	1 413	29 860	6.9	2.53	10.7	25.3
Benton	12.4	8.4	7.4	50.5	9 441	9 421	-0.2	-6.0	1 068	823	-1 001	3 479	-2.2	2.52	9.4	27.0
Blackford	13.6	9.6	8.2	50.7	14 067	14 048	-0.1	-9.1	1 408	1 359	-966	5 236	-8.0	2.41	10.9	24.7
Boone	11.3	6.4	5.4	50.8	38 147	46 107	20.9	22.8	6 358	3 979	8 041	21 149	23.8	2.65	8.4	22.4
Brown	18.6	10.8	6.4	50.4	14 080	14 957	6.2	1.9	1 159	1 222	-271	6 199	5.1	2.43	7.2	23.6
Carroll	13.5	8.8	7.0	49.9	18 809	20 165	7.2	0.0	2 083	1 557	-820	7 900	2.4	2.54	7.3	24.0
Cass	12.0	7.9	7.2	50.0	38 413	40 930	6.6	-4.8	5 187	3 754	-3 092	14 858	-5.5	2.55	11.3	27.3
Clark	12.5	7.2	5.6	51.0	87 774	96 472	9.9	14.3	12 766	9 034	8 993	44 248	14.2	2.46	12.9	27.6
Clay	12.8	8.1	7.0	50.8	24 705	26 556	7.5	1.3	3 132	2 804	-204	10 447	2.3	2.54	10.7	24.0
Clinton	11.8	7.2	7.2	50.6	30 974	33 866	9.3	-1.9	4 785	3 265	-852	12 105	-3.5	2.68	11.1	23.1
Crawford	14.7	9.1	5.9	49.3	9 914	10 743	8.4	-0.3	1 184	1 027	-307	4 303	2.9	2.48	9.7	25.6
Daviess	11.5	7.5	6.6	50.2	27 533	29 820	8.3	6.1	4 661	2 802	-882	11 329	4.0	2.74	10.0	24.6
Dearborn	13.3	7.6	5.5	50.3	38 835	46 109	18.7	8.5	5 686	3 501	2 471	18 743	11.4	2.64	10.0	22.0
Decatur	12.1	7.7	6.8	50.5	23 645	24 555	3.8	4.8	3 376	2 180	-537	9 977	6.3	2.54	10.6	25.0
DeKalb	12.1	7.2	5.9	50.4	35 324	40 285	14.0	4.8	5 295	3 143	-146	15 951	5.4	2.61	10.5	24.3
Delaware	11.4	7.8	6.8	51.9	119 659	118 769	-0.7	-0.9	12 229	10 812	-4 300	46 516	-1.3	2.34	12.2	29.8
Dubois	12.3	7.6	6.9	50.8	36 616	39 674	8.4	5.6	5 078	3 311	240	16 133	8.9	2.54	8.6	24.7
Elkhart	11.1	6.4	5.7	50.7	156 198	182 791	17.0	8.1	30 789	13 222	1 188	70 244	6.2	2.76	12.6	22.7
Fayette	14.0	8.9	7.7	51.0	26 015	25 588	-1.6	-5.1	2 896	2 697	-1 548	9 719	-4.7	2.46	12.4	26.6
Floyd	12.9	7.0	5.9	51.5	64 404	70 823	10.0	5.3	8 123	6 290	2 134	29 479	7.2	2.48	13.6	25.6
Fountain	12.6	9.6	8.0	50.5	17 808	17 954	0.8	-4.0	1 956	1 808	-1 157	6 935	-1.5	2.46	10.0	26.7
Franklin	12.8	7.8	6.3	50.0	19 580	22 151	13.1	4.2	2 669	1 715	164	8 579	9.0	2.67	8.4	20.5
Fulton	13.2	9.0	7.4	50.3	18 840	20 511	8.9	1.6	2 366	2 117	-378	8 237	1.9	2.50	10.2	25.8
Gibson	12.6	7.8	7.5	50.5	31 913	32 500	1.8	3.1	3 828	3 046	-339	13 255	3.2	2.47	9.7	26.5
Grant	12.9	8.7	7.6	51.9	74 169	73 403	-1.0	-4.6	7 680	7 280	-4 611	27 245	-3.8	2.39	13.4	28.8
Greene	13.4	8.9	7.2	50.1	30 410	33 157	9.0	0.0	3 711	3 366	-862	13 487	0.9	2.44	9.4	27.0
Hamilton	10.1	5.0	3.6	51.2	108 936	182 740	67.7	50.3	34 177	9 802	66 788	99 835	51.4	2.73	8.3	20.5
Hancock	12.4	7.5	5.3	50.9	45 527	55 391	21.7	26.4	7 901	4 430	9 745	26 304	27.0	2.64	9.8	20.3
Harrison	13.2	7.9	5.9	50.0	29 890	34 325	14.8	14.7	4 171	2 851	2 118	15 192	17.6	2.56	9.5	22.8
Hendricks	11.1	6.1	4.6	50.2	75 717	104 093	37.5	39.7	15 011	7 210	29 101	52 368	40.5	2.71	9.8	19.8
Henry	13.3	8.7	7.4	49.3	48 139	48 508	0.8	2.0	5 045	5 151	-334	19 077	-2.1	2.43	11.6	27.3
Howard	13.8	8.8	7.4	51.9	80 827	84 964	5.1	-2.6	10 523	8 101	-4 056	34 301	-1.4	2.38	13.1	29.4
Huntington	12.3	7.8	6.9	50.9	35 427	38 075	7.5	-2.5	4 386	3 590	-870	14 218	-0.2	2.52	9.9	24.4
Jackson	12.0	7.8	6.5	50.2	37 730	41 335	9.6	2.5	5 535	3 804	-455	16 501	2.8	2.53	10.8	24.4
Jasper	12.1	8.0	6.0	50.2	24 823	30 043	21.0	11.4	3 950	2 446	1 459	12 232	14.5	2.66	9.3	20.9
Jay	12.3	8.4	7.0	50.7	21 512	21 806	1.4	-2.8	2 813	2 106	-1 287	8 133	-3.2	2.58	10.4	25.6
Jefferson	12.9	8.2	6.4	51.8	29 797	31 705	6.4	2.3	3 408	2 859	920	12 635	4.0	2.42	11.4	27.2
Jennings	12.3	7.9	4.8	49.9	23 661	27 554	16.5	3.5	3 583	2 226	-712	10 680	5.4	2.64	11.5	22.3
Johnson	11.4	6.8	5.5	50.8	88 109	115 209	30.8	21.2	16 375	9 658	18 388	52 242	23.1	2.63	10.2	22.6
Knox	12.5	8.3	7.5	49.7	39 884	39 256	-1.6	-2.1	4 277	4 213	-1 192	15 249	-1.9	2.35	11.1	30.1
Kosciusko	12.2	7.6	5.9	50.3	65 294	74 057	13.4	4.5	10 200	5 599	-1 720	29 197	7.0	2.60	9.5	23.9
LaGrange	10.4	6.8	4.8	49.6	29 477	34 909	18.4	6.4	6 720	2 056	-2 163	11 598	3.3	3.17	7.1	18.4
Lake	12.2	6.9	6.3	51.7	475 594	484 564	1.9	2.4	64 177	43 639	-7 842	188 157	3.6	2.60	17.4	27.4
LaPorte	13.3	7.7	6.5	48.3	107 066	110 106	2.8	1.2	12 719	9 750	-1 371	42 331	3.1	2.48	12.8	27.3
Lawrence	13.8	9.1	7.3	50.6	42 836	45 922	7.2	0.5	5 030	4 527	-267	18 811	1.5	2.42	10.1	27.3
Madison	12.6	8.1	7.2	50.0	130 669	133 358	2.1	-1.3	15 110	13 311	-2 927	51 927	-2.1	2.41	13.6	28.3
Marion	10.6	5.6	5.0	51.8	797 159	860 454	7.9	5.0	136 636	68 960	-32 195	366 176	4.0	2.42	17.1	32.0
Marshall	12.2	7.5	7.2	50.5	42 182	45 128	7.0	4.3	6 255	3 796	-396	17 406	5.4	2.66	9.9	24.1
Martin	14.1	9.1	6.7	49.5	10 369	10 369	0.0	-0.3	1 183	986	-569	4 216	0.8	2.43	9.2	28.7
Miami	12.9	7.6	6.3	46.7	36 897	36 082	-2.2	2.3	4 145	3 011	-1 002	13 456	-1.9	2.49	11.3	26.2
Monroe	9.4	5.3	4.9	50.1	108 978	120 563	10.6	14.4	12 083	7 014	5 848	54 864	17.0	2.24	8.1	32.5
Montgomery	12.0	8.5	7.1	49.6	34 436	37 629	9.3	1.3	4 404	3 413	-540	14 979	2.6	2.47	10.4	25.9
Morgan	13.2	7.7	5.2	50.4	55 920	66 689	19.3	3.3	8 159	5 223	1 657	25 765	5.4	2.65	10.1	20.3
Newton	13.6	9.6	7.0	49.5	13 551	14 566	7.5	-2.2	1 351	1 338	-766	5 503	3.1	2.56	8.7	23.8
Noble	12.2	6.7	5.8	50.0	37 877	46 275	22.2	2.7	6 580	3 568	-1 021	17 355	3.9	2.69	10.0	22.9
Ohio	14.1	10.0	6.6	50.5	5 315	5 623	5.8	9.0	593	472	196	2 477	12.5	2.45	9.8	25.2
Orange	13.2	8.8	6.9	50.3	18 409	19 306	4.9	2.8	2 323	1 942	-10	7 872	3.3	2.49	10.4	26.7
Owen	14.3	8.9	5.9	49.9	17 281	21 786	26.1	-1.0	2 282	2 002	453	8 486	2.5	2.52	9.2	24.0
Parke	13.6	9.1	6.6	53.2	15 410	17 241	11.9	0.6	1 721	1 501	-502	6 222	-3.0	2.51	9.4	24.8
Perry	13.2	7.6	7.6	47.0	19 107	18 899	-1.1	2.3	2 098	1 811	-266	7 476	2.8	2.38	9.7	28.7

1. No spouse present.

Table B. States and Counties — **Population, Vital Statistics, Medicare, and Crime**

STATE County	Daytime population, 2006–2010			Births, average 2006–2008		Deaths, average 2006–2008		Persons under 65 with no health insurance, 2009		Medicare, 2011			Serious crimes known to police,[2] 2010 Total	
	Persons in group quarters, 2010	Number	Employment/residence ratio	Total	Rate[1]	Number	Rate[1]	Number	Percent	Eligible for Medicare	Enrolled in Medicare Advantage	Enrolled in a Medicare prescription drug plan	Number	Rate[3]
	32	33	34	35	36	37	38	39	40	41	42	43	44	45
ILLINOIS—Cont'd														
Winnebago	4 685	298 213	1.0	4 171	14.0	2 500	8.4	37 998	15.0	50 604	8 853	22 970	14 208	4 944
Woodford	1 021	30 203	0.6	D	D	341	8.9	2 931	9.0	6 386	776	2 720	293	853
INDIANA	186 923	6 360 553	1.0	89 079	14.0	55 458	8.7	882 602	16.2	1 040 311	183 257	462 205	217 649	3 357
Adams	421	32 704	0.9	654	19.4	283	8.4	5 231	18.1	5 254	1 925	2 501	NA	NA
Allen	6 107	367 817	1.1	5 470	15.7	2 645	7.6	50 385	16.6	53 070	20 357	21 406	11 023	3 102
Bartholomew	1 147	82 168	1.2	1 090	14.6	666	8.9	9 762	15.4	13 183	1 777	5 886	2 890	3 782
Benton	92	7 730	0.7	D	D	89	10.1	1 167	16.5	1 652	181	910	NA	NA
Blackford	163	11 652	0.8	D	D	137	10.3	1 713	16.1	2 867	331	1 410	272	2 155
Boone	574	47 420	0.7	707	13.0	435	8.0	5 293	11.1	7 815	1 366	3 593	NA	NA
Brown	163	11 977	0.5	D	D	122	8.3	2 002	16.8	3 275	676	1 264	101	663
Carroll	106	15 972	0.6	D	D	182	9.1	2 684	16.4	3 754	563	1 740	277	1 374
Cass	1 066	38 486	1.0	549	13.9	401	10.2	5 659	17.3	7 214	754	3 678	1 141	2 928
Clark	1 515	100 277	0.9	1 484	14.1	959	9.1	14 568	15.8	19 189	3 082	9 246	4 629	4 447
Clay	341	22 756	0.7	D	D	296	11.0	3 592	16.3	5 056	461	2 594	NA	NA
Clinton	830	30 296	0.8	506	14.9	354	10.4	5 400	18.7	5 690	657	2 705	1 144	3 443
Crawford	62	8 886	0.6	D	D	101	9.3	1 683	18.8	2 129	264	1 126	97	905
Daviess	581	28 792	0.8	D	D	314	10.4	5 775	22.2	5 007	257	2 642	705	2 228
Dearborn	530	41 494	0.7	614	12.3	370	7.4	5 754	13.5	8 665	1 805	3 698	NA	NA
Decatur	377	26 501	1.1	D	D	236	9.5	3 463	16.4	4 632	889	2 255	NA	NA
DeKalb	615	42 359	1.0	D	D	342	8.2	5 672	15.9	7 106	2 927	2 866	NA	NA
Delaware	8 830	118 191	1.0	1 277	11.1	1 177	10.2	16 493	17.2	21 394	2 235	9 818	3 309	2 812
Dubois	893	48 291	1.3	D	D	370	9.0	4 661	13.5	7 160	525	4 300	NA	NA
Elkhart	3 804	217 861	1.2	3 501	17.6	1 469	7.4	36 316	20.9	28 684	6 222	13 054	5 428	2 748
Fayette	367	22 787	0.8	D	D	289	11.8	3 401	17.2	5 507	566	3 496	NA	NA
Floyd	1 329	67 689	0.8	874	12.0	706	9.7	8 847	14.2	12 650	1 682	6 339	3 070	4 282
Fountain	172	15 179	0.7	D	D	189	11.0	2 271	16.7	3 594	404	1 757	NA	NA
Franklin	187	18 571	0.5	D	D	199	8.5	3 228	16.5	4 773	1 259	2 196	195	845
Fulton	224	18 391	0.7	D	D	227	11.1	3 150	18.8	4 081	1 384	1 514	193	926
Gibson	738	36 580	1.2	D	D	320	9.7	3 932	14.5	6 039	1 371	2 667	528	1 576
Grant	5 022	70 427	1.0	852	12.3	749	10.8	9 710	17.3	14 596	2 003	6 368	2 276	3 249
Greene	281	27 043	0.6	386	11.7	353	10.7	4 518	16.9	6 483	422	3 194	405	1 309
Hamilton	1 628	240 343	0.8	3 847	14.8	1 142	4.4	22 180	9.1	28 732	5 544	11 673	3 043	1 278
Hancock	649	54 333	0.6	882	13.3	511	7.7	6 934	12.1	11 104	2 039	4 167	708	1 011
Harrison	461	32 155	0.6	D	D	304	8.2	4 953	15.6	6 899	938	3 438	591	1 501
Hendricks	3 360	119 289	0.7	1 780	13.3	859	6.4	14 240	11.8	18 419	3 757	6 624	NA	NA
Henry	3 016	43 486	0.7	510	10.8	548	11.6	6 340	16.1	9 976	1 278	4 052	1 764	3 566
Howard	1 282	88 286	1.1	1 122	13.4	844	10.1	9 794	14.4	17 110	1 178	7 196	3 042	3 676
Huntington	1 330	34 522	0.8	D	D	367	9.7	5 052	16.2	7 033	2 784	2 667	551	1 484
Jackson	595	43 077	1.1	579	13.7	431	10.2	6 126	17.2	7 892	2 003	2 940	1 673	4 243
Jasper	926	29 808	0.8	428	13.2	274	8.5	4 027	14.7	5 793	413	2 875	NA	NA
Jay	243	20 153	0.9	D	D	244	11.4	3 260	18.5	4 188	725	2 042	330	1 734
Jefferson	1 905	31 627	0.9	D	D	317	9.7	4 631	16.9	6 317	594	3 301	NA	NA
Jennings	298	24 400	0.7	D	D	247	8.8	4 366	18.0	5 007	787	2 186	611	2 142
Johnson	2 332	115 899	0.7	1 887	13.9	1 057	7.8	16 394	13.7	20 870	3 844	8 524	3 661	2 725
Knox	2 645	39 650	1.1	496	13.0	458	12.0	5 315	17.1	7 346	440	4 059	1 200	3 378
Kosciusko	1 568	77 361	1.0	1 131	14.8	599	7.9	11 185	17.2	12 708	4 398	4 659	1 451	1 876
LaGrange	324	35 735	0.9	739	19.9	232	6.2	8 741	27.0	4 857	1 324	1 918	244	657
Lake	6 349	477 161	0.9	6 798	13.8	4 630	9.4	67 352	16.2	79 411	3 923	35 261	22 193	4 493
LaPorte	6 623	107 179	0.9	1 395	12.6	1 099	10.0	15 924	17.2	19 330	1 264	10 097	4 358	4 036
Lawrence	653	41 593	0.8	513	11.1	497	10.8	6 407	17.1	9 182	1 090	3 940	807	1 931
Madison	6 277	120 078	0.8	1 623	12.4	1 410	10.8	18 942	17.6	25 617	3 451	9 362	4 688	3 561
Marion	16 675	1 029 639	1.3	15 479	17.7	7 300	8.4	140 148	18.2	123 004	24 052	52 282	57 178	6 669
Marshall	670	45 274	0.9	645	13.8	412	8.8	7 627	19.3	8 037	2 257	3 246	742	1 577
Martin	93	13 390	1.6	D	D	99	9.7	1 423	17.2	2 063	166	906	115	1 113
Miami	3 416	33 445	0.7	430	11.9	324	9.0	5 487	18.1	6 050	715	2 743	332	900
Monroe	14 976	142 760	1.1	1 321	10.4	780	6.2	18 857	16.6	16 855	2 401	8 232	5 258	3 811
Montgomery	1 171	38 071	1.0	463	12.2	369	9.7	4 778	15.3	7 002	1 315	3 062	1 156	3 032
Morgan	592	54 001	0.5	862	12.3	586	8.3	8 718	14.5	11 649	1 868	4 876	NA	NA
Newton	170	12 146	0.7	D	D	142	10.1	2 094	18.2	2 556	200	1 348	227	1 594
Noble	831	45 024	0.9	721	15.1	397	8.3	8 272	19.9	7 444	2 712	2 976	524	1 102
Ohio	52	4 881	0.6	D	D	50	8.7	768	15.8	1 066	190	471	NA	NA
Orange	258	18 808	0.9	D	D	203	10.4	2 890	17.7	4 036	674	1 938	NA	NA
Owen	197	17 977	0.6	D	D	228	10.1	3 419	18.2	4 144	612	1 871	NA	NA
Parke	1 741	14 915	0.6	D	D	168	9.8	2 794	19.8	3 093	291	1 451	149	859
Perry	1 532	18 247	0.9	D	D	198	10.5	2 706	17.3	3 527	216	2 063	NA	NA

1. Per 1,000 estimated resident population. 2. Data for serious crimes have not been adjusted for underreporting; this may affect comparability between geographic areas and over time. 3. Per 100,000 population estimated by the FBI.

Table B. States and Counties — **Crime, Education, Money Income, and Poverty**

STATE County	Serious crimes known to police,[1] 2010 (cont.) — Rate[2] Violent	Rate[2] Property	Education — School enrollment and attainment, 2006-2010 — Enrollment[3] Total	Enrollment[3] Percent private	Attainment[4] (percent) High school graduate or less	Attainment[4] Bachelor's degree or more	Local government expenditures,[5] 2008-2009 Total current expenditures (mil dol)	Current expenditures per student (dollars)	Money income, 2006-2010 Per capita income[6] (dollars)	Households Median income Dollars	Percent change, 2000 to 2006-2010 (constant 2010 dollars)	Percent with income of $200,000 or more	Income and poverty, 2010 Median household income (dollars)	Percent below poverty level All persons	Children under 18 years	Children 5 to 17 years in families
	46	47	48	49	50	51	52	53	54	55	56	57	58	59	60	61
ILLINOIS—Cont'd																
Winnebago	920	4 024	76 216	20.5	49.3	21.1	473.9	9 984	24 008	47 198	-15.1	2.2	44 336	17.5	27.2	23.8
Woodford	50	804	10 577	17.4	40.3	26.0	72.8	8 799	29 475	65 890	1.2	3.1	65 931	7.5	9.6	8.5
INDIANA	314	3 042	1 723 172	16.7	50.0	22.4	9 681.7	9 366	24 058	47 697	-9.4	2.2	44 616	15.3	21.6	19.6
Adams	NA	NA	8 784	26.9	59.7	12.2	39.2	8 306	19 089	43 317	-15.8	0.9	43 121	16.8	29.6	29.7
Allen	238	2 864	98 917	20.5	43.1	26.1	515.4	9 379	24 532	48 714	-9.8	2.3	47 014	13.9	19.8	19.8
Bartholomew	141	3 641	19 359	17.6	47.0	26.7	125.3	10 293	26 860	52 742	-5.7	2.6	49 045	12.8	22.0	19.4
Benton	NA	NA	2 272	13.2	60.6	13.7	18.6	10 115	21 949	46 318	-8.1	0.9	47 520	11.3	17.5	16.0
Blackford	87	2 068	2 862	4.8	64.4	12.2	19.3	9 068	21 783	41 989	-4.6	1.2	38 637	16.0	24.3	21.9
Boone	NA	NA	15 310	16.1	36.4	38.0	95.3	8 832	38 696	68 594	9.1	9.7	66 023	8.0	9.6	8.0
Brown	26	636	3 232	8.7	52.6	21.2	21.5	9 800	24 312	50 139	-9.4	2.9	46 770	13.2	21.0	19.3
Carroll	74	1 300	4 779	13.3	59.8	14.9	22.7	8 162	23 163	48 055	-11.1	1.1	49 966	10.1	16.3	14.8
Cass	92	2 836	9 584	11.2	61.7	14.1	68.1	9 889	20 562	42 587	-14.2	1.5	38 859	16.7	25.5	20.9
Clark	547	3 900	25 076	14.8	51.2	17.8	148.7	9 088	23 592	47 368	-6.7	1.2	44 775	12.5	19.1	17.3
Clay	NA	NA	6 756	12.3	56.0	13.8	39.1	8 542	20 569	44 666	-4.3	0.2	42 233	13.6	22.2	18.8
Clinton	169	3 275	7 808	9.8	62.2	13.1	57.2	9 151	21 131	48 416	-6.2	1.2	47 229	12.8	21.5	20.0
Crawford	140	765	2 230	11.7	68.0	11.5	16.4	9 754	18 598	37 988	-8.1	0.8	39 358	17.0	28.0	26.2
Daviess	107	2 120	7 294	19.6	62.9	12.2	41.7	9 716	20 254	44 592	3.4	1.0	42 318	14.7	23.7	23.0
Dearborn	NA	NA	12 978	18.7	55.4	16.9	80.3	8 867	25 023	56 789	-8.3	2.2	55 817	10.1	14.2	12.5
Decatur	NA	NA	6 522	11.5	61.0	14.8	35.8	7 960	22 719	46 894	-8.3	1.3	49 551	13.6	21.7	19.4
DeKalb	NA	NA	11 308	16.5	55.6	15.7	86.0	10 925	21 779	46 722	-17.8	0.9	46 781	10.6	15.6	14.2
Delaware	246	2 566	38 427	5.9	51.9	22.4	147.6	9 481	20 405	38 066	-13.3	1.5	36 362	24.2	27.5	24.0
Dubois	NA	NA	9 890	13.3	56.2	20.2	71.0	9 533	24 801	52 871	-5.5	2.2	51 885	8.4	9.9	8.7
Elkhart	118	2 629	51 126	15.7	56.5	18.1	340.5	9 490	22 187	47 258	-16.1	2.1	42 168	17.2	26.8	24.7
Fayette	NA	NA	6 001	7.7	66.2	8.8	40.3	9 504	18 928	37 038	-24.7	0.8	36 734	17.0	25.5	22.8
Floyd	172	4 110	18 839	17.6	48.4	22.1	113.0	9 212	25 971	52 422	-6.0	2.1	49 117	12.4	19.3	17.9
Fountain	NA	NA	4 073	11.2	62.5	10.8	26.8	8 353	20 949	42 817	-11.8	0.8	43 947	12.4	19.5	17.1
Franklin	52	793	5 850	18.1	59.5	16.5	39.7	7 872	23 090	51 649	-6.3	1.9	48 938	12.3	18.4	15.8
Fulton	168	758	4 696	10.3	60.2	14.0	21.3	7 903	21 119	40 372	-16.7	1.3	40 856	13.8	21.6	20.8
Gibson	90	1 486	8 139	16.8	55.2	14.3	42.4	8 284	22 542	46 872	-1.3	0.9	45 383	12.1	15.9	14.4
Grant	216	3 033	18 939	27.4	59.5	15.4	106.0	8 918	19 792	38 985	-14.9	1.0	35 976	19.8	29.7	26.9
Greene	55	1 254	7 865	8.9	60.5	11.1	52.8	9 566	20 676	41 103	-4.5	0.5	41 504	14.0	20.7	18.7
Hamilton	45	1 233	78 060	19.8	21.2	53.8	419.4	8 282	38 500	81 947	-8.9	9.2	82 054	4.9	6.3	5.8
Hancock	40	971	17 420	12.3	46.1	24.2	106.8	8 372	28 017	61 052	-14.5	3.3	62 195	8.5	10.6	8.0
Harrison	94	1 407	9 588	14.5	56.0	14.4	53.5	8 724	23 539	51 272	-6.8	1.5	48 775	11.0	16.5	14.4
Hendricks	NA	NA	38 084	16.1	38.9	31.2	218.1	8 801	28 880	67 180	-3.9	3.5	66 080	6.4	8.0	7.0
Henry	47	3 520	11 937	7.4	60.9	13.8	77.5	9 413	19 879	41 087	-14.9	0.7	40 732	16.2	23.5	21.1
Howard	232	3 444	20 353	8.9	50.9	19.7	132.8	9 669	23 759	45 003	-18.3	1.7	41 786	16.0	24.5	21.7
Huntington	86	1 398	9 823	21.0	56.5	14.8	52.1	8 609	21 575	45 964	-12.8	1.1	46 530	11.3	15.8	14.8
Jackson	279	3 964	9 494	22.7	58.6	13.8	56.1	8 324	21 498	43 980	-11.9	1.1	46 562	12.7	18.9	17.6
Jasper	NA	NA	8 711	20.0	57.6	14.2	42.6	7 867	23 676	55 093	0.3	1.3	55 267	9.5	13.9	12.9
Jay	47	1 686	5 486	7.3	64.1	10.7	34.5	9 386	18 946	39 886	-11.8	0.6	38 117	15.6	26.0	23.8
Jefferson	NA	NA	8 333	30.1	55.2	18.2	54.5	11 383	21 278	42 707	-11.7	1.2	41 654	15.9	22.8	21.0
Jennings	116	2 026	7 131	11.1	65.6	7.5	46.6	8 965	18 636	43 755	-12.3	0.4	41 869	14.2	22.4	20.0
Johnson	208	2 518	35 615	17.8	44.8	26.2	212.6	8 580	28 224	61 629	-7.6	3.3	58 695	10.5	14.8	13.3
Knox	73	3 305	10 120	9.2	51.9	14.9	52.2	10 024	20 381	39 523	-0.5	1.3	39 123	17.6	22.9	21.4
Kosciusko	62	1 814	18 882	15.9	53.0	20.2	124.7	8 686	24 019	50 217	-9.7	2.2	47 811	13.4	19.7	17.9
LaGrange	27	630	8 502	30.7	70.2	10.4	54.9	8 990	18 388	47 792	-11.9	0.9	44 151	16.1	26.9	26.5
Lake	411	4 082	132 955	15.3	51.2	18.9	831.7	9 751	23 142	48 723	-8.0	1.8	45 252	17.7	26.0	24.7
LaPorte	211	3 825	26 775	13.6	54.1	16.7	166.5	9 111	22 599	46 014	-12.3	1.5	44 039	16.2	25.0	23.5
Lawrence	101	1 831	10 603	10.9	63.3	12.5	65.9	8 949	21 352	40 380	-12.1	1.6	41 305	15.2	22.6	20.0
Madison	206	3 355	30 301	16.7	55.7	16.6	182.5	9 370	21 722	43 256	-12.2	1.2	39 449	18.0	27.7	25.1
Marion	1 136	5 533	232 720	21.2	46.1	27.3	1 449.9	10 802	24 498	43 541	-14.9	2.3	39 393	20.8	30.7	28.2
Marshall	89	1 488	11 561	17.2	57.4	17.1	76.7	9 860	22 493	50 141	-7.0	1.7	43 283	12.7	19.0	17.2
Martin	68	1 045	2 323	10.9	61.8	8.5	16.0	9 273	21 750	43 406	-5.9	0.8	43 854	13.2	18.9	17.3
Miami	62	837	9 671	9.0	60.7	10.2	52.1	9 120	18 854	39 485	-20.4	0.6	40 466	17.0	23.8	21.5
Monroe	309	3 501	58 822	6.7	33.1	42.7	126.0	9 084	21 882	38 137	-9.6	2.5	38 348	24.3	18.1	16.7
Montgomery	155	2 877	9 570	14.1	58.0	17.5	59.8	9 280	22 788	47 694	-8.8	1.4	41 853	15.3	22.9	20.8
Morgan	NA	NA	17 231	12.6	55.9	13.9	99.7	8 322	23 972	55 427	-8.3	1.7	53 738	11.9	18.1	15.3
Newton	112	1 481	3 453	13.1	61.1	9.5	22.9	9 376	24 055	50 721	-2.2	1.9	48 043	11.1	16.8	15.1
Noble	74	1 029	12 099	14.3	60.6	13.0	68.6	8 766	19 783	45 818	-15.3	0.5	45 269	12.6	19.4	17.6
Ohio	NA	NA	1 289	8.4	64.0	12.1	8.1	8 706	25 703	50 966	-2.7	0.5	47 937	10.0	14.3	12.4
Orange	NA	NA	4 209	12.4	66.2	12.5	37.0	10 867	19 119	37 120	-7.1	1.2	35 999	17.5	26.5	22.9
Owen	NA	NA	4 830	7.2	68.0	8.3	28.9	9 708	20 581	44 285	-4.3	1.0	42 658	14.1	22.5	21.1
Parke	23	836	3 424	13.7	58.5	12.7	23.4	9 567	19 494	40 512	-10.4	1.4	42 749	16.6	27.5	26.3
Perry	NA	NA	3 793	11.9	65.7	8.3	26.9	8 903	20 806	45 108	-1.7	0.9	41 446	13.0	17.3	15.7

1. Data for serious crimes have not been adjusted for underreporting; this may affect comparability between geographic areas and over time.   2. Per 100,000 population estimated by the FBI.   3. All persons 3 years old and over enrolled in nursery school through college.   4. Persons 25 years old and over.   5. Elementary and secondary education expenditures.   6. Based on population estimated by the American Community Survey, 2006-2010.

Table B. States and Counties — Personal Income

	Personal income, 2009												
			Per capita[1]					Transfer payments (mil dol)					
									Government payments to individuals				
STATE County	Total (mil dol)	Percent change, 2008–2009	Dollars	Rank	Wages and salaries[2] (mil dol)	Proprietors' income (mil dol)	Dividends, interest, and rent (mil dol)	Total	Total	Social Security	Medical payments	Income mainte-nance	Unemploy-ment insurance
	62	63	64	65	66	67	68	69	70	71	72	73	74

ILLINOIS—Cont'd

Winnebago	9 630	-2.4	32 131	1 500	6 650	472	1 590	2 087	2 033	756	701	239	223
Woodford	1 532	-0.4	39 425	497	537	106	271	214	207	97	69	11	18
INDIANA	218 527	-2.3	34 022	X	140 089	16 654	31 912	43 570	42 400	15 598	16 481	3 864	3 184
Adams	910	-6.9	26 573	2 627	484	93	152	202	195	79	71	13	21
Allen	12 060	-1.9	34 078	1 160	8 871	994	2 035	2 255	2 190	803	825	222	178
Bartholomew	2 859	-4.5	37 589	681	2 321	227	455	513	499	204	197	35	35
Benton	325	-4.1	37 697	676	103	70	46	59	58	24	22	4	4
Blackford	361	-0.3	27 630	2 463	143	26	53	110	108	44	39	10	9
Boone	2 751	-3.3	48 870	122	925	389	501	287	277	120	102	16	21
Brown	510	-3.6	35 065	1 009	103	44	85	96	93	50	23	6	7
Carroll	639	-4.1	32 333	1 452	202	90	91	119	116	56	34	7	10
Cass	1 161	-3.8	29 718	2 041	623	70	162	307	300	103	132	23	22
Clark	3 496	-1.4	32 182	1 490	2 191	189	417	773	753	272	320	60	47
Clay	782	1.4	29 456	2 103	269	65	96	211	206	74	87	18	14
Clinton	997	-2.1	28 998	2 197	502	89	138	228	221	82	87	19	17
Crawford	284	1.6	26 932	2 579	72	16	29	90	88	29	39	8	6
Daviess	952	-3.8	31 075	1 736	457	86	149	203	198	63	93	17	8
Dearborn	1 684	-0.6	33 349	1 289	711	102	226	323	314	130	118	21	24
Decatur	837	-1.4	33 394	1 279	548	72	133	178	174	68	68	13	15
DeKalb	1 273	-1.0	30 268	1 917	945	62	190	278	271	107	95	22	27
Delaware	3 389	-0.5	29 418	2 112	2 079	215	491	902	881	325	348	84	59
Dubois	1 641	-4.5	39 620	476	1 219	162	377	260	253	105	105	12	16
Elkhart	6 028	-7.8	30 064	1 961	4 745	551	982	1 218	1 182	429	404	114	155
Fayette	666	-2.2	27 652	2 457	273	50	96	235	230	82	103	20	15
Floyd	2 808	-2.6	37 733	671	1 349	158	407	534	520	182	217	47	31
Fountain	533	-3.3	31 636	1 618	213	50	68	137	134	52	55	9	10
Franklin	765	0.0	33 067	1 327	175	43	131	147	143	68	41	12	12
Fulton	595	-3.7	29 355	2 129	275	47	94	150	147	60	53	12	12
Gibson	1 037	-3.8	31 664	1 612	886	66	151	231	225	87	90	14	14
Grant	2 116	1.7	30 751	1 811	1 285	148	268	633	620	218	254	56	39
Greene	1 000	2.1	30 799	1 801	353	55	123	240	234	85	99	19	13
Hamilton	12 723	-1.7	45 556	184	6 252	1 041	2 063	1 010	959	445	291	48	90
Hancock	2 638	-4.5	38 606	569	931	254	342	404	391	173	136	22	30
Harrison	1 175	-2.2	31 280	1 697	454	56	163	252	246	97	94	18	17
Hendricks	4 877	-1.4	34 683	1 068	2 182	360	601	666	641	285	213	33	54
Henry	1 391	-2.0	29 085	2 173	541	90	193	396	387	152	154	30	31
Howard	2 582	-4.8	31 149	1 721	2 016	137	376	718	703	275	271	61	57
Huntington	1 149	-2.0	30 427	1 881	579	58	179	265	258	102	93	18	24
Jackson	1 349	-3.6	31 843	1 566	863	140	189	296	289	115	114	21	23
Jasper	1 078	-5.1	32 849	1 360	512	103	144	213	207	89	75	14	15
Jay	586	-5.8	27 774	2 439	307	55	71	157	153	61	60	11	12
Jefferson	962	0.2	29 151	2 155	556	56	151	267	261	90	118	20	17
Jennings	813	-3.2	29 004	2 196	335	37	85	236	231	74	107	19	18
Johnson	4 852	-1.4	34 288	1 128	1 787	310	698	791	765	321	278	50	59
Knox	1 318	0.2	34 781	1 050	725	151	182	348	341	103	167	28	14
Kosciusko	2 603	-3.8	34 032	1 169	1 880	129	403	466	452	194	151	30	49
LaGrange	802	-7.2	21 544	3 073	431	69	128	183	177	72	56	11	26
Lake	16 538	-2.3	33 464	1 264	10 126	822	2 153	3 784	3 694	1 250	1 515	454	238
LaPorte	3 354	-3.1	30 199	1 936	1 970	179	512	803	783	297	299	75	60
Lawrence	1 353	-1.9	29 505	2 093	543	72	183	367	359	129	153	27	28
Madison	4 025	-3.5	30 627	1 836	1 716	319	501	1 097	1 073	406	436	96	74
Marion	33 774	-1.9	37 911	651	34 947	3 327	4 542	6 329	6 166	1 826	2 435	769	414
Marshall	1 329	-5.2	28 335	2 338	728	89	213	293	284	118	98	20	29
Martin	317	-0.4	31 871	1 561	597	13	43	74	72	26	31	6	4
Miami	934	-3.4	25 934	2 741	432	51	128	265	258	84	99	22	23
Monroe	4 108	1.5	31 424	1 659	3 034	201	776	683	659	245	257	50	43
Montgomery	1 190	-2.9	31 430	1 656	728	97	173	271	264	105	108	19	18
Morgan	2 459	-1.3	34 700	1 064	641	78	262	447	434	178	159	36	32
Newton	416	-8.0	30 280	1 912	156	36	49	93	91	38	32	6	7
Noble	1 336	-2.7	27 827	2 432	704	90	161	293	284	111	97	20	36
Ohio	195	1.4	32 917	1 352	67	5	17	39	38	16	14	2	3
Orange	568	-0.2	29 042	2 187	299	30	72	158	154	53	67	14	11
Owen	636	1.4	28 405	2 323	239	29	73	154	150	60	55	14	10
Parke	461	-0.9	27 304	2 516	131	36	63	126	123	47	51	10	8
Perry	543	-0.9	28 891	2 219	278	27	80	131	127	49	53	9	9

1. Based on the resident population estimated as of July 1 of the year shown. 2. Includes supplements to wages and salaries.

Table B. States and Counties — Earnings, Social Security, and Housing

STATE County	Earnings, 2009 Total (mil dol)	Percent by selected industries — Farm	Goods-related[1] Total	Goods-related[1] Manufacturing	Service-related and health — Information and professional and technical services	Retail trade	Finance, insurance, and real estate	Health care and social services	Government	Social Security beneficiaries, December 2010 — Number	Rate[2]	Supplemental Security Income recipients, December 2010	Housing units, 2010 — Total	Percent change, 2000–2010
	75	76	77	78	79	80	81	82	83	84	85	86	87	88
ILLINOIS—Cont'd														
Winnebago	7 121	0.2	28.0	23.1	5.7	6.4	6.4	17.6	12.7	57 035	193	6 894	125 965	10.1
Woodford	643	10.6	22.6	15.8	D	5.6	3.0	21.5	13.9	7 045	182	273	15 145	12.3
INDIANA	156 743	1.4	27.0	20.8	7.3	6.2	5.6	12.5	15.6	1 191 768	184	118 065	2 795 541	10.4
Adams	577	4.5	D	32.8	D	6.8	3.9	D	16.0	5 990	174	324	13 014	4.9
Allen	9 865	0.2	23.2	17.4	8.5	5.9	7.6	17.1	11.2	60 675	171	6 922	152 184	9.6
Bartholomew	2 548	1.0	D	42.5	4.4	4.7	4.8	8.3	12.5	15 250	199	1 153	33 098	10.9
Benton	173	31.4	13.5	9.1	D	3.6	3.5	D	16.8	1 895	214	114	3 937	3.1
Blackford	169	6.2	D	31.1	3.2	8.8	3.3	8.9	17.5	3 495	274	265	6 051	-1.7
Boone	1 314	2.8	D	7.8	7.1	7.3	3.4	7.8	13.5	8 690	153	402	22 754	26.9
Brown	147	0.8	D	6.3	D	7.5	3.9	D	24.1	3 780	248	180	8 285	15.7
Carroll	292	11.8	D	29.0	3.3	5.2	3.3	5.3	13.6	4 315	214	175	9 472	9.2
Cass	692	4.9	D	26.1	2.7	5.8	3.1	D	28.1	8 075	207	756	16 474	-0.9
Clark	2 380	0.4	D	17.2	2.8	8.3	5.2	8.8	19.6	21 885	199	2 205	47 776	16.0
Clay	334	4.5	D	21.5	2.7	8.2	3.0	D	18.3	5 840	217	607	11 703	5.4
Clinton	591	8.2	39.9	35.5	D	4.2	2.5	D	14.5	6 320	190	426	13 321	0.4
Crawford	88	0.9	D	D	1.4	5.3	4.5	4.8	28.1	2 555	238	307	5 520	7.4
Daviess	543	5.9	33.4	15.1	4.6	8.8	2.5	D	17.9	5 510	174	546	12 471	4.8
Dearborn	813	0.4	D	13.3	3.7	8.3	3.5	6.8	20.6	9 910	198	563	20 171	13.3
Decatur	620	6.5	D	41.9	D	4.9	3.7	3.9	13.4	5 345	208	390	11 209	12.2
DeKalb	1 007	1.4	D	44.1	3.4	4.2	2.4	D	10.7	8 295	196	641	17 558	8.8
Delaware	2 294	1.0	D	11.0	6.8	7.5	5.8	21.2	23.2	24 605	209	2 758	52 357	2.6
Dubois	1 380	2.4	D	34.9	3.5	6.8	2.3	11.8	8.1	8 165	195	378	17 384	12.1
Elkhart	5 295	0.5	D	42.2	3.9	5.3	3.2	9.9	9.0	32 225	163	2 965	77 767	11.4
Fayette	323	5.1	D	16.7	4.0	10.1	3.6	21.3	19.4	6 465	266	814	10 898	-0.8
Floyd	1 506	0.1	D	20.5	6.4	6.6	5.7	12.8	20.2	14 195	190	1 627	31 968	9.9
Fountain	262	10.6	41.5	38.4	2.2	5.9	3.3	D	15.9	4 105	238	289	7 865	2.2
Franklin	218	7.6	D	13.6	D	8.2	D	D	22.6	5 415	235	361	9 538	11.0
Fulton	323	4.0	D	27.0	3.0	7.2	4.7	D	20.0	4 690	225	345	9 708	6.4
Gibson	953	2.9	58.5	50.0	1.7	4.5	1.2	5.2	7.0	6 805	203	482	14 645	3.7
Grant	1 434	2.5	D	20.9	2.9	6.1	2.9	15.9	19.1	16 905	241	1 907	30 443	-0.4
Greene	407	5.4	D	3.7	21.6	7.2	2.9	D	23.6	7 315	221	675	15 211	1.0
Hamilton	7 293	0.4	11.8	4.5	15.0	8.0	17.0	9.8	9.7	31 335	114	1 323	106 772	53.7
Hancock	1 186	2.8	22.6	14.3	15.0	6.2	3.9	7.1	18.3	12 635	180	536	28 125	29.3
Harrison	510	3.7	17.4	11.7	D	7.7	3.9	D	20.6	7 885	200	588	16 534	20.7
Hendricks	2 542	0.9	D	8.1	5.4	9.2	3.3	8.9	18.5	20 535	141	796	55 454	41.4
Henry	631	5.8	D	17.5	3.1	8.8	3.9	D	25.5	11 775	238	930	21 288	3.4
Howard	2 153	1.0	D	43.8	3.6	6.1	3.5	9.1	16.3	20 030	242	2 089	38 679	2.9
Huntington	637	5.0	D	29.1	D	5.8	4.3	9.3	13.3	7 940	214	491	15 805	3.5
Jackson	1 004	5.6	D	34.1	2.8	7.5	3.5	D	15.7	9 165	216	751	18 202	6.2
Jasper	615	11.3	D	12.5	3.1	6.5	3.0	6.2	15.4	6 765	202	348	13 168	17.2
Jay	362	9.2	D	38.6	1.7	4.7	2.7	D	17.5	4 765	224	378	9 221	1.6
Jefferson	611	0.3	30.4	27.0	2.9	7.7	2.7	D	19.6	7 265	224	732	14 311	6.9
Jennings	371	5.1	D	20.3	2.0	5.8	1.8	D	19.0	6 140	215	675	12 069	5.2
Johnson	2 097	1.1	D	12.3	5.8	10.8	5.4	12.4	17.7	23 710	170	1 267	56 649	25.6
Knox	876	7.0	19.2	8.6	4.4	6.1	3.9	11.4	28.5	8 430	219	1 007	17 038	-1.5
Kosciusko	2 009	1.4	D	52.2	2.7	5.0	2.4	7.2	8.1	14 405	186	762	37 038	15.1
LaGrange	499	5.6	D	41.1	2.0	5.9	3.1	D	14.6	5 575	150	303	14 094	8.9
Lake	10 948	0.2	29.2	20.4	5.1	7.5	3.5	16.2	13.7	91 705	185	12 609	208 750	7.1
LaPorte	2 149	1.6	28.8	21.3	3.5	7.5	3.1	13.9	17.9	22 360	201	2 077	48 448	6.2
Lawrence	615	1.5	25.8	20.8	6.2	9.3	4.1	13.5	21.7	10 500	228	911	21 074	2.5
Madison	2 035	1.9	D	18.1	4.3	7.0	4.0	15.8	18.1	30 275	230	3 055	59 060	3.7
Marion	38 274	0.0	22.8	17.1	11.5	4.7	7.7	13.1	14.3	140 795	156	23 028	417 862	7.9
Marshall	817	2.6	D	33.9	D	6.9	5.4	8.9	14.8	9 190	195	634	19 845	9.6
Martin	611	1.3	D	4.2	D	1.3	0.9	0.5	79.9	2 310	224	206	4 786	1.2
Miami	482	5.1	24.3	19.2	D	5.6	3.3	7.8	33.8	6 645	180	704	15 479	1.2
Monroe	3 235	0.2	17.4	12.5	7.8	6.0	3.8	14.0	32.6	18 585	135	1 651	59 107	16.2
Montgomery	825	7.7	D	40.2	2.3	5.7	2.5	D	12.9	8 030	211	551	16 535	5.5
Morgan	719	4.5	23.3	14.8	D	9.1	4.4	11.0	22.6	13 525	196	903	27 754	7.1
Newton	193	18.4	D	15.2	D	3.9	4.0	D	19.6	2 915	205	191	6 030	5.3
Noble	794	1.1	D	47.9	D	5.5	2.4	6.6	13.0	8 750	184	635	20 109	10.3
Ohio	71	0.8	D	D	1.4	2.9	D	D	23.0	1 240	202	75	2 784	14.9
Orange	329	2.9	D	14.7	D	5.4	2.1	D	15.0	4 690	236	537	9 176	9.9
Owen	268	1.6	D	44.3	D	4.3	2.7	D	15.1	4 870	226	386	10 091	2.4
Parke	167	9.3	D	12.6	3.7	5.5	3.7	D	33.4	3 740	216	314	8 085	7.3
Perry	306	1.2	D	33.7	2.9	5.7	3.5	D	26.0	4 105	212	346	8 495	3.3

1. Includes mining, construction, and manufacturing. 2. Per 1,000 resident population enumerated in the 2010 census.

Table B. States and Counties — Housing, Labor Force, and Employment

STATE County	Housing units, 2006–2010								Civilian labor force, 2010		Unemployment		Civilian employment,[5] 2006–2010		
	Total	Occupied units												Percent	
		Percent	Owner-occupied			Renter-occupied									
			Median value[1]	Median owner cost as a percent of income		Median rent[2]	Median rent as a percent of income	Sub-standard units[3] (percent)	Total	Percent change, 2009–2010	Total	Rate[4]	Total	Manage-ment, business, science and arts	Con-struction, produc-tion, and mainte-nance occu-pations
				With a mort-gage	Without a mort-gage										
	89	90	91	92	93	94	95	96	97	98	99	100	101	102	103

ILLINOIS—Cont'd

STATE County	89	90	91	92	93	94	95	96	97	98	99	100	101	102	103
Winnebago	112 466	70.1	128 100	23.8	14.1	675	31.1	2.0	146 319	1.2	22 185	15.2	133 606	29.4	27.5
Woodford	14 192	83.3	151 500	21.0	12.1	675	26.2	1.7	21 478	0.9	1 743	8.1	18 957	38.6	25.3
INDIANA	2 465 402	71.5	123 000	21.8	11.7	683	29.4	1.9	3 176 657	-0.2	320 240	10.1	2 999 570	31.3	27.8
Adams	12 243	78.3	111 700	22.7	10.0	564	25.8	8.2	14 559	-6.5	1 618	11.1	15 637	22.9	38.6
Allen	135 807	70.6	113 200	20.4	10.1	629	26.2	1.8	175 251	-1.4	18 417	10.5	166 132	33.3	24.3
Bartholomew	29 856	72.5	133 100	20.0	11.0	731	27.0	1.9	37 652	-1.4	3 491	9.3	36 794	37.8	26.4
Benton	3 558	78.7	85 200	21.4	11.6	573	23.9	0.6	4 206	-4.3	435	10.3	4 145	26.8	36.2
Blackford	5 389	78.1	77 600	21.1	11.5	531	28.6	1.7	6 313	-2.8	823	13.0	5 435	25.0	36.2
Boone	20 801	79.1	174 300	22.1	12.0	758	26.8	0.8	27 809	-0.5	2 189	7.9	26 671	45.0	18.8
Brown	5 913	84.7	158 500	26.0	13.6	793	29.6	3.3	7 322	-2.6	732	10.0	7 031	25.5	32.2
Carroll	8 033	79.6	107 400	21.3	13.2	559	25.3	2.7	9 674	-4.8	921	9.5	9 602	29.5	34.5
Cass	14 981	75.6	82 400	21.1	11.9	571	25.7	3.0	18 558	-0.1	1 990	10.7	17 410	24.1	42.0
Clark	43 255	71.2	125 800	22.1	11.5	692	29.2	1.6	55 175	-0.3	5 183	9.4	53 496	29.0	25.8
Clay	10 262	79.1	87 100	20.7	11.3	615	27.6	1.0	12 690	-2.1	1 339	10.6	12 703	27.5	32.0
Clinton	11 906	73.4	98 700	21.7	11.4	651	28.1	3.3	16 437	-3.4	1 692	10.3	15 320	23.4	39.6
Crawford	4 344	83.8	86 300	22.1	12.8	471	29.3	2.5	5 148	-3.9	622	12.1	4 544	22.3	43.9
Daviess	11 016	79.6	97 200	19.4	10.3	577	24.6	2.9	14 735	-0.7	923	6.3	14 442	22.7	40.4
Dearborn	18 311	77.2	160 300	21.5	12.1	631	26.7	1.3	25 654	-1.1	2 762	10.8	24 754	26.8	29.6
Decatur	9 952	71.9	118 500	22.7	10.5	610	24.7	1.7	12 528	-0.9	1 447	11.6	12 165	25.3	38.2
DeKalb	15 930	80.1	112 300	22.8	11.8	591	26.6	1.4	19 928	-3.2	2 386	12.0	19 767	26.6	38.3
Delaware	46 212	66.4	92 400	21.2	12.1	632	35.2	1.5	54 114	-0.9	6 074	11.2	51 605	30.7	21.9
Dubois	15 900	79.2	129 600	21.6	10.0	613	23.5	2.2	21 779	-1.5	1 638	7.5	21 276	27.6	35.8
Elkhart	70 035	72.7	128 000	22.5	12.0	695	29.2	3.1	90 354	0.2	12 325	13.6	92 488	25.3	38.2
Fayette	9 864	74.0	84 900	23.2	13.8	592	30.3	2.9	9 674	-2.9	1 391	14.4	9 592	24.7	36.0
Floyd	28 966	73.1	147 100	21.5	10.6	683	27.8	1.3	37 249	-1.7	3 296	8.8	36 580	33.7	24.7
Fountain	6 952	79.2	87 600	20.8	12.6	567	29.1	0.8	8 338	-4.7	980	11.8	7 862	22.6	45.0
Franklin	8 347	78.6	144 500	21.9	11.2	615	27.6	2.6	11 349	-3.2	1 251	11.0	10 420	28.2	34.9
Fulton	8 451	75.2	93 900	21.7	11.6	621	29.4	2.5	9 882	-3.3	1 134	11.5	9 171	24.9	40.1
Gibson	13 001	77.7	99 100	19.1	12.4	561	27.0	2.1	16 561	-0.7	1 300	7.8	15 655	22.0	41.3
Grant	26 711	70.6	83 100	20.7	11.2	571	28.5	1.0	32 874	1.8	3 792	11.5	29 505	29.0	27.4
Greene	13 137	78.2	87 500	19.5	11.5	534	27.2	1.8	15 703	-2.7	1 434	9.1	14 227	26.1	35.2
Hamilton	95 835	80.0	211 200	21.3	10.0	903	25.2	0.8	143 137	1.0	10 028	7.0	135 063	51.0	10.8
Hancock	25 416	80.0	159 200	22.0	10.0	763	29.6	0.9	35 690	-0.6	3 262	9.1	32 911	35.4	24.4
Harrison	14 317	84.2	124 200	21.4	10.0	638	25.8	1.1	19 094	-1.6	1 760	9.2	18 621	24.5	37.2
Hendricks	50 936	82.4	161 100	22.3	11.9	860	27.1	1.0	72 740	0.1	5 925	8.1	70 365	37.9	22.7
Henry	18 971	76.5	95 200	21.3	12.7	616	29.2	1.5	22 241	-2.8	2 911	13.1	19 648	25.8	32.5
Howard	34 330	70.5	108 300	20.5	10.2	643	30.1	1.8	35 112	-0.9	4 369	12.4	34 128	28.4	29.7
Huntington	14 224	79.7	96 700	21.8	12.7	596	26.4	1.1	18 977	-5.4	2 212	11.7	17 953	25.1	35.7
Jackson	16 753	73.6	113 700	22.0	11.3	668	30.0	2.3	20 918	-3.2	2 089	10.0	19 649	25.7	36.6
Jasper	12 230	78.8	142 200	21.3	10.1	657	25.0	1.4	15 256	-1.8	1 570	10.3	15 505	25.6	35.2
Jay	8 288	79.0	81 300	19.2	12.2	495	27.0	2.7	11 205	-3.8	1 097	9.8	9 965	22.7	41.0
Jefferson	12 667	71.8	106 800	22.7	11.9	589	27.7	2.6	15 692	-5.4	1 740	11.1	14 598	27.2	34.4
Jennings	11 007	73.4	92 200	21.5	11.8	657	26.8	3.3	13 377	-2.4	1 662	12.4	12 265	23.0	41.3
Johnson	51 080	75.8	143 400	21.4	11.1	781	27.7	1.2	73 323	-0.9	6 201	8.5	67 246	35.0	23.7
Knox	14 856	69.8	84 700	19.5	12.6	549	29.0	1.7	19 873	2.3	1 454	7.3	17 545	26.2	30.1
Kosciusko	30 555	76.8	134 600	22.0	10.0	667	26.2	2.7	40 665	-1.5	4 170	10.3	37 039	27.3	36.6
LaGrange	12 171	82.9	148 200	24.4	12.2	668	28.0	4.6	14 989	-9.5	1 934	12.9	15 955	22.6	49.6
Lake	182 952	70.9	135 400	23.7	13.9	748	31.4	2.4	220 500	-2.2	24 326	11.0	217 015	28.8	28.7
LaPorte	42 090	75.4	119 800	22.4	11.6	664	30.1	2.3	51 018	-3.1	6 106	12.0	48 968	25.9	32.1
Lawrence	18 679	78.6	97 400	21.9	13.5	547	28.5	2.8	21 320	-3.0	2 562	12.0	19 422	25.5	34.0
Madison	51 436	73.5	96 300	21.9	11.7	647	31.3	1.5	61 538	-0.8	7 035	11.4	56 626	28.7	27.7
Marion	357 081	58.8	122 200	22.6	12.0	715	30.7	2.1	452 662	-0.8	45 298	10.0	430 020	33.8	21.7
Marshall	17 631	78.3	123 400	21.6	12.3	620	25.0	2.8	22 156	-3.1	2 585	11.7	22 225	26.5	37.8
Martin	4 113	83.8	84 100	18.9	10.1	526	26.5	3.2	5 196	4.0	380	7.3	4 765	25.6	39.7
Miami	13 506	76.6	86 100	22.2	12.4	573	33.6	2.1	15 915	-3.2	1 990	12.5	15 393	25.5	34.5
Monroe	51 388	55.2	146 700	21.8	10.9	727	39.8	1.5	69 430	-0.9	5 058	7.3	63 504	43.1	16.9
Montgomery	14 503	73.6	107 100	20.8	10.9	608	27.5	1.3	18 763	-0.6	1 880	10.0	18 004	26.7	36.1
Morgan	24 925	80.1	141 200	23.1	10.3	716	28.6	1.4	36 204	-1.7	3 545	9.8	32 000	27.2	32.0
Newton	5 446	81.9	109 600	21.5	11.4	655	24.7	2.0	6 621	-4.2	726	11.0	6 594	23.4	42.6
Noble	17 498	77.4	112 600	23.3	11.5	592	25.5	2.5	21 349	-7.3	2 962	13.9	21 573	23.1	45.7
Ohio	2 495	75.3	134 200	20.8	11.0	657	24.7	3.0	3 011	-0.5	331	11.0	3 172	20.0	33.2
Orange	7 866	77.4	90 500	21.8	13.0	535	29.8	2.9	10 008	-3.1	1 125	11.2	8 236	24.9	37.4
Owen	8 371	82.1	95 700	22.4	10.0	631	27.4	2.4	11 367	-1.9	1 174	10.3	9 826	21.8	41.4
Parke	6 437	82.5	91 600	22.6	10.0	541	25.5	3.2	8 050	1.5	805	10.0	6 831	23.2	41.1
Perry	7 687	78.2	93 600	20.4	11.5	466	24.9	1.5	9 174	-7.0	928	10.1	8 577	17.8	46.1

1. Specified owner-occupied units.   2. Specified renter-occupied units. A value of 10.0 represents 10 percent or less.   3. Overcrowded or lacking complete plumbing facilities.   4. Percent of civilian labor force.   5. Persons 16 years old and over.

Table B. States and Counties — **Nonfarm Employment and Agriculture**

STATE County	Private nonfarm establishments, employment and payroll, 2009									Agriculture, 2007			
	Number of establishments	Employment						Annual payroll		Farms			
		Total	Health care and social assistance	Manufacturing	Retail trade	Finance and insurance	Professional, scientific, and technical services	Total (mil dol)	Average per employee (dollars)	Number	Percent with: Fewer than 50 acres	500 acres or more	Farm operators whose principal occupation is farming (percent)
	104	105	106	107	108	109	110	111	112	113	114	115	116
ILLINOIS—Cont'd													
Winnebago	6 769	120 990	20 143	24 558	15 162	4 641	4 200	4 326	35 753	860	55.3	11.9	44.2
Woodford	786	8 129	1 293	1 906	967	268	147	269	33 140	932	34.5	19.5	51.8
INDIANA	146 017	2 449 980	381 999	442 399	314 411	101 674	102 098	88 394	36 080	60 938	48.0	12.6	41.9
Adams	728	11 848	1 830	4 418	1 561	293	204	335	28 254	1 315	61.4	5.9	35.1
Allen	9 224	162 419	30 256	26 485	19 915	9 245	6 827	5 843	35 973	1 649	57.7	7.3	36.2
Bartholomew	1 893	40 133	5 349	11 132	4 771	1 208	2 946	1 561	38 898	668	46.0	13.6	39.7
Benton	205	1 534	161	342	218	99	31	43	28 232	399	21.3	39.1	54.6
Blackford	260	2 807	360	1 058	362	D	D	81	28 685	250	52.8	15.6	46.0
Boone	1 373	16 775	2 415	1 353	1 862	339	697	527	31 410	582	50.7	22.2	48.5
Brown	390	2 171	D	181	365	44	D	51	23 293	169	52.7	2.4	43.2
Carroll	397	4 424	246	D	439	96	93	122	27 659	581	43.4	18.8	48.7
Cass	762	13 008	2 884	4 031	1 552	318	311	368	28 321	868	49.3	14.4	44.2
Clark	2 409	42 629	5 573	7 291	6 715	1 841	962	1 354	31 770	585	48.9	6.8	41.5
Clay	487	4 794	647	1 432	803	D	92	121	25 153	666	51.1	12.5	46.4
Clinton	624	8 465	1 223	3 223	1 022	239	148	262	30 929	693	46.2	23.1	49.1
Crawford	140	1 255	D	300	191	D	D	32	25 151	354	29.1	2.8	28.0
Daviess	799	9 995	1 489	1 906	1 567	250	699	279	27 888	969	51.1	10.2	35.4
Dearborn	978	13 609	2 308	1 356	1 881	365	330	419	30 813	564	36.3	3.2	37.6
Decatur	656	9 721	989	3 862	1 263	D	145	318	32 733	639	36.0	20.7	54.3
DeKalb	1 013	16 369	1 619	6 763	1 658	377	465	613	37 453	1 144	55.4	5.9	27.0
Delaware	2 450	38 335	10 622	4 074	6 116	1 606	1 543	1 107	28 867	659	58.0	11.1	48.1
Dubois	1 306	25 123	D	9 593	3 138	477	481	855	34 036	761	33.0	12.4	43.5
Elkhart	4 972	92 665	9 642	41 093	9 043	2 087	2 258	3 187	34 388	1 617	64.1	4.5	37.3
Fayette	459	5 363	1 695	812	1 023	156	178	150	28 000	391	40.2	14.1	41.9
Floyd	1 753	24 167	4 969	5 066	3 113	763	1 031	802	33 176	279	58.1	2.9	33.7
Fountain	326	4 558	D	D	618	161	81	125	27 328	503	39.8	19.3	48.5
Franklin	450	4 406	1 049	557	541	169	63	124	28 197	723	30.8	7.3	44.0
Fulton	472	5 456	D	1 822	801	185	131	169	30 941	639	44.6	16.3	46.5
Gibson	722	15 298	1 490	D	1 736	D	342	629	41 140	590	37.5	21.5	50.0
Grant	1 430	25 832	5 331	3 910	3 264	645	370	813	31 460	524	41.8	24.2	46.6
Greene	605	6 267	1 233	262	1 251	D	D	167	26 684	799	40.8	8.3	44.8
Hamilton	7 347	100 070	13 452	4 897	14 160	10 931	6 939	4 097	40 943	636	65.7	8.6	42.8
Hancock	1 407	17 136	2 323	2 804	1 964	401	1 649	591	34 505	686	59.5	13.0	44.6
Harrison	668	9 425	1 477	1 594	1 464	307	213	265	28 131	1 125	47.7	5.1	38.1
Hendricks	2 864	45 323	5 811	3 030	8 942	884	1 539	1 358	29 952	714	59.8	9.4	39.6
Henry	861	11 344	2 487	2 493	1 697	369	216	310	27 337	781	54.7	11.8	38.0
Howard	1 837	30 438	5 543	8 333	4 775	733	610	1 423	46 748	601	48.1	16.5	52.4
Huntington	890	12 753	1 772	3 499	1 415	413	190	365	28 605	766	53.7	14.5	35.4
Jackson	1 044	17 372	2 247	5 773	2 248	446	369	561	32 304	827	40.1	15.8	44.0
Jasper	743	9 431	1 509	1 409	1 377	273	205	288	30 500	734	34.9	29.6	49.7
Jay	421	6 199	882	2 732	683	183	73	177	28 594	881	49.1	12.0	37.0
Jefferson	739	10 572	2 130	2 383	1 810	230	247	315	29 789	694	45.7	5.2	36.5
Jennings	418	6 195	1 073	1 514	752	D	89	203	32 796	613	46.5	11.6	40.3
Johnson	2 947	39 827	5 820	5 163	8 819	1 292	1 397	1 194	29 979	585	59.1	14.0	45.0
Knox	970	13 313	3 553	1 360	2 176	387	205	387	29 056	568	33.8	27.8	59.0
Kosciusko	1 904	31 158	3 609	12 404	3 304	755	507	1 298	41 667	1 235	54.5	9.5	37.8
LaGrange	773	8 745	838	3 884	1 172	247	149	259	29 644	1 507	56.2	4.3	37.6
Lake	10 059	167 000	31 763	24 082	24 249	5 200	6 445	6 119	36 642	441	55.3	16.8	48.1
LaPorte	2 487	34 772	5 315	7 296	5 840	821	947	1 089	31 311	869	51.6	18.1	44.3
Lawrence	889	10 577	2 614	1 846	2 018	377	522	315	29 787	820	40.1	6.5	39.4
Madison	2 366	33 639	6 641	2 971	5 088	1 137	952	983	29 211	870	55.3	14.3	49.8
Marion	23 496	503 410	75 790	52 494	48 651	29 467	33 594	22 569	44 832	263	82.1	2.3	42.2
Marshall	1 095	15 834	1 933	5 270	2 069	399	371	486	30 711	866	44.3	10.7	42.3
Martin	179	1 788	137	437	332	64	D	50	27 743	278	39.9	11.2	37.8
Miami	576	7 525	1 170	2 125	909	278	127	192	25 498	682	44.4	15.5	40.6
Monroe	3 001	47 533	8 413	6 441	7 331	1 536	1 901	1 509	31 740	481	49.1	3.7	36.4
Montgomery	873	13 161	1 470	5 479	1 637	304	262	451	34 255	745	42.0	23.2	48.3
Morgan	1 196	11 439	2 120	1 419	2 180	457	456	331	28 898	642	60.7	7.8	36.3
Newton	296	2 438	153	651	391	117	45	71	29 013	434	39.2	25.6	47.0
Noble	912	13 971	1 406	6 902	1 490	258	219	422	30 201	1 196	56.0	6.6	31.8
Ohio	79	1 248	65	20	105	26	D	38	30 187	179	39.1	2.2	31.8
Orange	383	7 168	900	1 355	738	144	76	196	27 413	474	35.9	7.4	31.9
Owen	304	4 363	408	1 934	369	134	69	126	28 770	570	42.3	5.6	38.9
Parke	263	2 130	433	443	349	D	69	55	26 008	477	29.8	17.6	48.8
Perry	370	5 011	839	1 629	830	125	79	162	32 336	425	23.8	5.4	40.0

STATE County	Land in farms					Value of land and buildings (dollars)		Value of machinery and equipment, average per farm (dollars)	Value of products sold				Percent of farms with sales of:		Government payments	
	Acreage (1,000)	Percent change, 2002–2007	Acres									Percent from:					
			Average size of farm	Total irrigated (1,000)	Total cropland (1,000)	Average per farm	Average per acre		Total (mil dol)	Average per farm (dollars)	Crops	Live-stock and poultry products	$10,000 or more	$100,000 or more	Total ($1,000)	Percent of farms
	117	118	119	120	121	122	123	124	125	126	127	128	129	130	131	132
ILLINOIS—Cont'd																
Winnebago	184	-3.7	214	0.4	162.6	941 759	4 411	89 695	89.9	104 542	81.9	18.1	40.7	20.6	4 068	56.9
Woodford	288	-7.1	309	0.8	267.3	1 311 286	4 238	134 004	177.5	190 492	80.6	19.4	62.1	38.2	5 461	78.6
INDIANA	14 773	-1.9	242	397.1	12 716.0	868 699	3 583	103 427	8 271.3	135 733	64.3	35.7	45.6	20.8	260 809	58.9
Adams	182	-20.5	139	0.2	165.8	602 154	4 339	83 042	158.8	120 760	38.9	61.1	52.5	24.6	3 446	49.4
Allen	254	-10.6	154	0.7	230.4	620 138	4 024	78 985	117.5	71 264	76.3	23.7	43.0	14.9	5 533	61.3
Bartholomew	166	3.1	249	10.2	148.3	945 855	3 798	108 015	69.5	104 009	87.5	12.5	48.4	19.3	3 817	64.7
Benton	271	9.3	679	4.0	262.6	2 297 119	3 384	232 443	138.4	346 900	94.1	5.9	81.7	50.6	5 606	91.5
Blackford	85	-12.4	339	0.0	77.1	928 317	2 742	118 784	38.6	154 275	79.5	20.5	45.2	22.4	1 478	70.0
Boone	223	-1.3	383	1.0	210.5	1 495 547	3 908	143 000	117.1	201 175	84.8	15.2	53.4	29.7	3 717	57.6
Brown	17	-15.0	100	0.1	8.2	431 476	4 300	41 953	2.5	14 757	D	D	17.2	1.2	110	25.4
Carroll	192	-5.0	331	0.4	178.2	1 364 641	4 122	151 749	151.4	260 518	56.1	43.9	60.9	34.8	4 118	68.2
Cass	228	9.6	263	3.1	208.5	939 498	3 574	113 562	131.4	151 403	75.2	24.8	49.0	23.8	4 632	74.3
Clark	87	-13.9	148	0.4	61.0	530 185	3 579	65 566	23.7	40 597	73.8	26.2	39.8	9.7	1 078	52.1
Clay	158	3.9	237	0.1	134.1	746 315	3 155	100 679	63.9	95 878	88.1	11.9	45.6	20.0	2 706	74.8
Clinton	255	4.1	368	0.8	244.8	1 523 643	4 136	168 228	174.4	251 720	67.8	32.2	59.3	34.8	5 321	63.1
Crawford	45	-18.2	128	0.0	17.1	372 429	2 904	35 406	4.7	13 297	34.7	65.3	20.9	2.0	252	37.9
Daviess	199	-3.9	206	3.7	173.8	748 465	3 638	99 028	166.8	172 137	44.0	56.0	50.6	21.4	3 049	39.5
Dearborn	66	-10.8	117	0.1	35.8	448 519	3 843	44 659	11.5	20 391	66.9	33.1	26.1	5.5	558	41.7
Decatur	205	-1.0	320	D	183.7	1 141 402	3 563	147 662	153.3	239 871	45.7	54.3	57.9	34.7	4 444	65.3
DeKalb	161	-10.1	140	0.8	135.2	509 248	3 626	53 011	62.4	54 557	69.3	30.7	29.7	9.8	4 557	76.7
Delaware	154	-18.9	234	0.5	143.4	824 551	3 518	95 643	68.6	104 109	88.2	11.8	44.6	18.7	2 670	58.4
Dubois	182	-3.7	239	0.4	135.2	773 917	3 233	107 302	200.7	263 763	22.1	77.9	54.1	26.9	2 992	64.3
Elkhart	163	-18.9	101	22.0	141.6	560 281	5 548	72 668	205.8	127 245	26.1	73.9	49.7	26.2	1 909	26.3
Fayette	93	-13.1	237	0.0	75.8	773 927	3 271	95 706	34.2	87 377	80.3	19.7	48.8	21.2	1 777	63.4
Floyd	24	0.0	86	0.0	13.8	398 364	4 632	45 785	4.8	17 050	D	D	25.4	3.9	190	30.1
Fountain	189	-7.8	375	D	163.1	1 294 404	3 450	124 401	76.5	152 136	93.3	6.7	52.1	24.5	3 121	64.0
Franklin	126	-9.4	175	0.1	85.4	642 318	3 676	74 735	35.7	49 364	65.7	34.3	42.2	13.3	2 070	60.6
Fulton	185	-4.1	289	19.6	165.9	969 826	3 353	125 001	88.9	139 054	77.6	22.4	50.2	26.3	3 346	67.9
Gibson	231	9.5	392	4.9	209.3	1 233 872	3 150	154 398	105.3	178 404	87.8	12.2	61.0	31.7	3 902	74.4
Grant	202	2.0	386	D	191.1	1 318 126	3 417	161 000	79.3	151 261	88.3	11.7	52.9	30.0	3 292	69.5
Greene	170	-0.6	212	1.3	119.1	617 546	2 907	84 421	78.8	98 579	49.3	50.7	40.6	10.9	2 288	40.4
Hamilton	124	-11.4	194	1.9	114.3	883 288	4 545	95 016	115.0	180 780	96.6	3.4	39.3	16.7	1 865	38.7
Hancock	172	6.2	250	0.2	159.3	1 026 073	4 100	115 124	86.8	126 545	80.5	19.5	47.1	17.2	2 924	54.5
Harrison	155	-3.1	138	0.1	99.1	447 746	3 250	64 697	50.2	44 587	46.3	53.7	29.9	7.9	2 201	38.4
Hendricks	172	-5.5	241	0.0	157.6	989 541	4 114	95 291	74.0	103 680	90.5	9.5	40.3	16.0	2 557	48.7
Henry	174	0.6	223	D	157.5	770 537	3 451	99 450	86.3	110 517	75.7	24.3	43.0	18.2	3 109	58.0
Howard	162	3.8	270	0.1	151.6	1 119 988	4 148	134 320	95.6	159 044	70.0	30.0	56.2	28.1	3 371	68.6
Huntington	199	-0.5	260	0.3	185.0	899 850	3 463	128 411	122.4	159 804	60.5	39.5	46.7	21.5	3 716	71.8
Jackson	209	1.0	253	2.0	165.5	760 401	3 005	138 912	196.9	238 141	25.1	74.9	47.3	20.0	3 979	65.2
Jasper	340	21.4	464	22.6	315.6	1 550 715	3 344	181 318	293.5	399 924	50.2	49.8	67.0	42.9	5 965	74.0
Jay	197	1.0	224	D	176.8	889 772	3 975	105 379	178.7	202 797	35.8	64.2	49.6	24.6	4 112	71.9
Jefferson	103	-5.5	148	0.0	67.1	502 997	3 405	63 024	27.0	38 922	65.7	34.3	27.4	6.8	1 270	47.8
Jennings	138	-3.5	226	0.6	105.1	719 690	3 189	98 904	63.1	102 912	56.8	43.2	36.5	13.1	2 082	57.1
Johnson	142	5.2	243	2.1	128.9	1 082 177	4 453	119 630	69.8	119 297	85.3	14.7	41.0	20.7	2 754	48.7
Knox	327	9.0	576	30.2	308.1	1 991 953	3 457	203 301	192.0	338 049	85.4	14.6	65.5	39.1	5 634	75.4
Kosciusko	251	-4.2	204	28.0	218.7	759 172	3 730	92 697	196.1	158 823	43.9	56.1	42.8	19.9	4 684	55.4
LaGrange	162	-14.3	107	24.7	127.1	546 508	5 093	61 006	171.2	113 617	26.1	73.9	53.6	22.2	1 955	24.5
Lake	128	0.0	291	9.7	121.4	1 153 687	3 961	111 625	62.1	140 869	90.9	9.1	48.1	25.4	2 406	55.3
LaPorte	256	5.3	295	47.8	231.9	1 077 366	3 655	131 009	152.3	175 238	67.4	32.6	49.0	26.6	5 128	59.7
Lawrence	135	-8.2	164	0.3	68.1	460 299	2 803	52 993	25.9	31 596	47.1	52.9	29.6	5.5	1 597	43.8
Madison	217	-11.1	250	1.5	204.1	933 308	3 736	115 455	115.5	132 730	87.5	12.5	50.9	21.6	4 441	61.0
Marion	17	-29.2	66	0.4	14.2	384 823	5 873	52 273	22.5	85 586	D	D	24.7	9.5	210	18.6
Marshall	179	-12.3	207	8.6	156.0	735 013	3 556	89 027	97.0	112 048	63.6	36.4	49.4	21.6	3 058	57.5
Martin	61	-4.7	221	D	40.2	712 748	3 231	83 254	54.5	195 935	25.7	74.3	41.7	20.5	737	39.6
Miami	178	-6.8	261	2.0	156.3	874 902	3 352	101 607	104.0	152 482	58.7	41.3	47.9	23.3	3 164	72.7
Monroe	54	-11.5	111	0.1	27.1	405 291	3 641	56 066	12.0	24 886	79.5	20.5	28.9	4.8	555	30.8
Montgomery	301	10.3	404	1.6	271.1	1 518 713	3 755	140 585	165.4	221 990	79.9	20.1	57.2	31.0	5 582	71.1
Morgan	114	1.8	178	0.0	93.0	694 578	3 907	83 852	56.5	87 961	84.1	15.9	31.5	13.9	1 621	45.3
Newton	190	4.4	439	5.7	176.3	1 583 756	3 609	203 045	193.4	445 553	41.7	58.3	57.8	35.7	3 540	80.0
Noble	160	-7.5	134	8.4	130.1	494 049	3 696	65 093	80.0	66 869	55.6	44.4	36.5	12.0	3 193	63.9
Ohio	22	-8.3	120	0.2	10.2	428 904	3 571	58 017	3.1	17 485	64.6	35.4	21.8	3.9	134	36.3
Orange	97	-8.5	206	D	58.8	597 393	2 907	82 157	40.4	85 333	42.4	57.6	25.9	7.2	1 461	51.3
Owen	88	-11.1	154	0.1	53.5	494 654	3 211	49 358	18.2	31 965	81.8	18.2	30.7	6.5	982	49.3
Parke	177	7.3	372	1.6	131.6	1 151 369	3 097	129 596	65.6	137 549	85.8	14.2	50.5	29.4	2 514	61.8
Perry	70	-7.9	166	0.0	36.0	441 734	2 666	67 079	24.3	57 076	34.0	66.0	36.9	12.7	559	44.0

Table B. States and Counties — Water Use, Wholesale Trade, Retail Trade, and Real Estate

STATE County	Water use, 2005		Wholesale trade,[1] 2007				Retail trade,[2] 2007				Real estate and rental and leasing,[2] 2007			
	Total water withdrawn (mil gal/day)	Gallons withdrawn per person	Number of establishments	Number of employees	Sales (mil dol)	Annual payroll (mil dol)	Number of establishments	Number of employees	Sales (mil dol)	Annual payroll (mil dol)	Number of establishments	Number of employees	Receipts (mil dol)	Annual payroll (mil dol)
	133	134	135	136	137	138	139	140	141	142	143	144	145	146
ILLINOIS—Cont'd														
Winnebago	43.9	152	363	4 931	2 624.7	209.7	1 051	16 095	3 852.0	346.4	245	1 585	211.3	46.2
Woodford	14.2	378	48	D	D	D	102	1 089	278.3	21.6	30	D	D	D
INDIANA	9 340.1	1 489	6 756	97 219	67 634.9	4 295.6	23 692	333 172	78 745.6	7 123.1	6 389	34 272	5 448.1	1 061.6
Adams	7.8	230	36	D	D	D	150	1 672	369.9	32.3	30	99	8.0	2.3
Allen	55.1	160	548	D	D	D	1 345	21 214	4 774.2	440.3	410	1 913	323.3	54.3
Bartholomew	21.2	289	80	1 012	747.3	50.5	375	5 133	1 075.2	106.7	74	319	50.1	8.9
Benton	0.9	94	16	D	D	D	43	241	50.9	4.0	3	6	0.3	0.2
Blackford	2.2	159	11	112	158.9	3.0	51	435	97.9	9.3	12	38	2.9	0.6
Boone	4.8	92	58	532	386.4	22.8	176	1 769	484.5	37.7	47	110	20.7	3.1
Brown	0.3	21	8	64	4.3	1.0	93	467	61.5	7.1	17	47	6.0	1.6
Carroll	7.7	377	21	D	D	D	58	529	102.1	8.4	14	20	4.6	1.0
Cass	33.6	838	42	458	439.0	14.8	134	1 561	340.9	34.6	21	72	7.5	1.3
Clark	24.1	237	101	1 375	1 062.0	67.1	446	7 214	1 729.5	157.4	100	593	91.4	15.1
Clay	1.6	59	15	D	D	D	96	1 040	312.4	20.8	13	41	4.7	0.5
Clinton	6.4	188	29	D	D	D	115	1 009	223.6	22.1	19	90	5.9	1.5
Crawford	4.9	433	2	D	D	D	32	189	40.7	3.5	6	D	D	D
Daviess	7.1	234	28	282	153.7	10.3	121	1 563	381.5	33.9	16	57	6.2	1.0
Dearborn	749.2	15 263	32	D	D	D	151	1 866	509.7	43.3	39	212	29.7	5.6
Decatur	5.1	203	32	D	D	D	119	1 403	315.0	29.7	21	60	8.7	1.6
DeKalb	10.0	241	45	D	D	D	147	1 744	408.9	36.8	33	184	18.3	5.8
Delaware	17.7	152	97	984	424.1	31.6	484	6 563	1 516.8	130.8	113	575	89.0	17.2
Dubois	7.3	177	64	846	630.6	33.3	242	3 215	763.4	74.3	38	D	D	D
Elkhart	36.5	187	371	6 096	3 231.4	255.2	727	9 710	2 416.9	219.0	180	813	109.4	20.4
Fayette	3.3	134	14	126	85.9	5.7	84	1 018	208.9	19.7	21	61	7.2	1.2
Floyd	268.5	3 729	78	873	1 420.5	33.3	221	3 457	787.4	71.9	81	351	43.9	7.4
Fountain	2.2	125	14	105	124.8	3.6	72	672	142.5	10.8	8	29	0.9	0.3
Franklin	4.2	180	8	61	18.6	2.1	79	614	171.3	11.2	8	36	2.5	0.5
Fulton	15.1	729	15	125	62.1	4.1	82	925	200.8	17.6	19	66	3.5	0.9
Gibson	52.1	1 558	20	D	D	D	133	1 597	442.6	30.4	17	58	10.3	1.4
Grant	12.8	181	44	D	D	D	282	3 380	765.8	69.7	60	217	23.2	5.1
Greene	4.8	144	15	D	D	D	118	1 087	226.1	18.9	14	54	2.4	0.5
Hamilton	78.5	326	346	4 043	2 779.5	231.5	821	14 029	3 295.4	323.6	367	2 871	558.5	129.1
Hancock	7.1	112	51	826	519.9	32.6	165	2 012	568.5	47.9	43	137	22.1	3.1
Harrison	3.6	98	27	296	98.6	8.7	134	1 421	400.9	32.3	19	61	7.4	1.0
Hendricks	9.7	76	103	2 465	2 520.7	103.1	437	8 440	2 088.7	176.6	110	350	54.5	8.4
Henry	6.7	142	23	280	180.2	13.3	167	1 861	455.0	41.3	34	83	8.2	1.5
Howard	21.0	247	62	510	319.5	24.1	374	5 240	1 194.7	105.6	83	320	47.7	7.5
Huntington	5.4	141	38	D	D	D	136	1 539	328.0	29.2	32	109	8.4	1.6
Jackson	8.3	197	42	D	D	D	199	2 193	529.5	49.2	43	171	20.0	3.1
Jasper	53.8	1 687	37	234	163.4	9.8	127	1 425	405.5	28.1	26	112	36.5	3.3
Jay	4.1	190	21	270	413.7	8.3	68	690	139.5	14.7	8	20	1.8	0.4
Jefferson	1 287.6	39 705	14	D	D	D	162	1 754	382.7	37.2	38	126	15.8	2.8
Jennings	3.6	125	15	D	D	D	80	776	223.8	18.0	13	26	3.6	0.8
Johnson	15.5	121	108	1 181	682.3	52.8	513	9 056	2 072.9	189.7	153	532	90.4	13.0
Knox	54.5	1 421	59	618	321.5	21.7	192	2 194	471.8	44.8	39	163	17.1	3.1
Kosciusko	26.4	347	87	D	D	D	314	3 780	794.9	80.9	80	196	49.4	6.3
LaGrange	14.7	400	33	318	104.6	7.3	166	1 212	276.9	25.1	24	65	9.0	1.1
Lake	1 720.7	3 488	396	5 198	3 348.8	254.9	1 715	26 506	7 102.4	559.8	441	2 376	328.0	64.1
LaPorte	37.3	338	123	1 446	856.2	54.1	495	6 054	1 363.6	114.9	102	438	60.4	11.1
Lawrence	6.2	133	22	D	D	D	169	2 041	481.6	44.7	29	85	12.5	1.9
Madison	15.6	119	75	1 113	574.2	44.1	431	5 542	1 234.9	108.0	103	434	61.5	10.2
Marion	311.2	360	1 358	25 490	15 780.3	1 254.1	3 291	53 214	12 951.3	1 278.7	1 297	10 411	1 935.6	390.8
Marshall	7.7	163	65	D	D	D	191	2 164	551.0	41.0	34	98	11.0	1.9
Martin	1.6	153	5	39	51.1	1.0	34	361	81.2	6.2	6	14	1.7	0.2
Miami	35.1	986	30	D	D	D	109	936	235.4	19.8	30	103	6.8	1.8
Monroe	17.0	140	83	1 331	683.2	47.0	508	7 479	1 530.8	146.7	187	1 133	144.0	29.5
Montgomery	5.7	149	43	338	368.6	15.1	147	1 759	429.2	34.9	28	113	11.8	2.0
Morgan	224.2	3 213	44	310	185.0	13.6	212	2 578	586.9	54.2	62	179	21.7	3.7
Newton	7.4	514	17	128	121.6	5.7	55	391	96.7	7.5	10	25	2.5	0.4
Noble	10.3	218	36	D	D	D	149	1 572	357.3	31.6	41	121	13.2	2.3
Ohio	0.8	143	2	D	D	D	11	107	23.7	1.7	4	10	0.6	0.1
Orange	1.4	71	12	83	52.8	2.2	75	729	153.2	13.9	15	60	5.4	1.2
Owen	2.4	106	11	D	D	D	44	427	106.3	8.8	11	19	2.6	0.2
Parke	2.4	137	6	44	24.5	1.5	50	404	84.5	6.7	16	50	5.5	2.1
Perry	2.3	118	10	65	12.9	1.8	72	796	153.4	13.9	16	46	6.2	0.8

1. Merchant wholesalers, except manufacturers' sales branches and offices. 2. Employer establishments.

Table B. States and Counties — Professional Services, Manufacturing, and Accommodation and Food Services

STATE County	Professional, scientific, and technical services,[1] 2007				Manufacturing, 2007				Accommodation and food services, 2007			
	Number of establish-ments	Number of employees	Receipts (mil dol)	Annual payroll (mil dol)	Number of establish-ments	Number of employees	Receipts (mil dol)	Annual payroll (mil dol)	Number of establish-ments	Number of employees	Sales (mil dol)	Annual payroll (mil dol)
	147	148	149	150	151	152	153	154	155	156	157	158
ILLINOIS—Cont'd												
Winnebago	654	D	D	D	685	27 367	7 913.4	1 354.8	591	10 526	452.2	125.1
Woodford	43	137	12.0	4.6	47	1 869	963.3	78.4	62	746	26.0	7.2
INDIANA	12 959	95 701	12 128.9	4 785.9	9 015	536 907	221 877.8	24 474.7	12 932	254 293	11 669.8	3 175.2
Adams	48	198	16.1	6.3	65	5 564	2 127.7	215.6	53	948	27.1	7.8
Allen	889	6 829	716.2	333.7	568	30 612	19 741.9	1 526.0	703	15 470	550.5	169.0
Bartholomew	157	D	D	D	143	11 711	4 843.9	502.9	160	3 416	139.7	39.9
Benton	10	D	D	D	NA	NA	NA	NA	10	81	2.6	0.5
Blackford	14	92	8.6	2.7	30	1 437	397.1	62.4	20	213	8.0	2.0
Boone	154	618	133.3	28.8	74	2 131	D	D	102	1 473	54.5	15.5
Brown	40	D	D	D	NA	NA	NA	NA	47	559	19.8	6.8
Carroll	28	D	D	D	29	2 536	D	D	33	556	18.4	5.3
Cass	48	257	18.3	7.0	49	4 628	1 302.0	151.9	80	1 032	33.8	9.3
Clark	177	848	122.2	30.7	165	8 119	2 114.9	332.5	204	4 834	197.5	60.4
Clay	29	D	D	D	36	1 705	D	D	46	571	18.4	4.7
Clinton	43	149	13.7	3.7	50	3 910	2 283.5	139.2	56	759	25.1	6.9
Crawford	6	D	D	D	NA	NA	NA	NA	19	D	D	D
Daviess	36	346	36.4	14.2	71	2 036	643.4	54.6	62	772	25.9	6.9
Dearborn	76	316	28.4	10.8	48	D	786.1	D	79	D	D	D
Decatur	38	138	13.9	5.5	55	4 294	1 869.7	174.5	56	836	29.9	8.4
DeKalb	72	521	36.7	14.1	120	8 220	3 818.9	381.7	85	1 353	47.5	13.6
Delaware	169	D	D	D	150	5 268	1 280.6	232.7	216	4 981	160.8	48.3
Dubois	86	757	42.4	42.8	125	D	D	D	104	1 649	58.8	17.7
Elkhart	338	D	D	D	852	64 309	15 779.8	2 508.4	385	7 395	272.4	76.0
Fayette	29	D	D	D	30	2 265	486.5	107.8	47	594	21.6	5.6
Floyd	185	D	D	D	119	6 166	1 558.4	250.7	119	D	D	D
Fountain	20	90	4.2	1.4	23	2 228	498.4	90.0	36	387	12.0	3.6
Franklin	34	D	D	D	17	D	D	D	41	676	28.5	7.5
Fulton	30	190	14.9	5.2	51	2 248	524.3	83.6	47	D	D	D
Gibson	46	D	D	D	40	6 362	D	D	71	1 134	38.5	11.0
Grant	87	D	D	D	69	4 653	1 670.1	272.3	148	2 496	88.1	24.3
Greene	41	D	D	D	NA	NA	NA	NA	49	665	19.5	5.2
Hamilton	1 054	D	D	D	200	6 001	1 569.9	241.0	499	10 012	437.2	127.2
Hancock	123	683	59.1	50.5	67	3 118	1 256.0	129.8	97	1 823	66.3	19.0
Harrison	44	D	D	D	46	1 522	410.7	56.4	55	D	D	D
Hendricks	248	1 491	144.9	57.3	109	3 566	2 819.4	139.0	250	5 771	227.6	66.7
Henry	55	D	D	D	49	2 300	1 026.6	118.6	76	1 019	36.2	10.3
Howard	131	D	D	D	76	11 980	2 923.2	877.5	186	3 921	150.5	44.5
Huntington	42	186	16.3	5.2	71	4 357	1 478.6	195.1	100	1 333	44.3	13.4
Jackson	64	372	29.7	11.0	74	7 015	2 585.5	279.3	83	1 557	58.4	17.4
Jasper	54	D	D	D	38	1 549	601.1	62.1	65	1 051	33.9	9.3
Jay	23	90	5.6	1.8	33	2 523	835.1	100.5	36	D	D	D
Jefferson	57	280	18.6	6.5	60	3 881	1 477.0	165.4	77	1 152	43.2	11.3
Jennings	20	D	D	D	43	1 995	377.2	70.5	29	433	16.1	4.4
Johnson	253	1 235	107.4	37.6	133	5 904	1 609.9	233.2	265	5 447	208.4	62.7
Knox	57	227	20.2	5.8	38	1 917	774.3	68.2	83	1 502	56.8	14.9
Kosciusko	129	545	48.8	15.2	198	14 469	5 705.3	706.3	151	2 342	92.3	25.8
LaGrange	35	137	8.8	3.2	147	6 694	1 602.3	280.9	65	761	33.9	9.4
Lake	933	D	D	D	411	26 654	21 914.5	1 489.0	993	19 402	1 069.2	265.5
LaPorte	169	D	D	D	184	8 808	2 364.0	363.9	259	5 254	389.7	80.1
Lawrence	63	406	42.5	16.5	71	3 016	716.5	160.7	74	1 227	43.0	12.5
Madison	202	D	D	D	118	4 652	1 046.9	191.8	246	4 343	155.1	43.6
Marion	2 816	D	D	D	1 016	57 069	24 333.9	3 137.1	2 111	45 923	2 248.4	663.8
Marshall	69	386	28.9	9.9	125	6 310	1 239.4	230.3	98	1 408	50.5	13.8
Martin	10	D	D	D	NA	NA	NA	NA	25	D	D	D
Miami	34	140	9.4	3.9	50	2 576	711.3	88.0	59	805	25.8	6.9
Monroe	282	D	D	D	108	6 389	1 799.3	279.5	335	7 271	287.8	79.1
Montgomery	55	242	17.9	6.3	57	6 258	2 768.4	298.5	86	1 152	48.5	12.6
Morgan	103	342	32.3	10.8	66	D	D	92.5	80	1 530	59.1	17.4
Newton	15	D	D	D	27	1 108	197.5	32.0	32	256	8.0	2.0
Noble	56	259	30.3	8.5	138	9 525	2 454.5	345.8	82	1 028	35.9	9.9
Ohio	2	D	D	D	NA	NA	NA	NA	15	D	D	D
Orange	22	71	4.5	1.6	24	1 414	201.7	45.1	28	D	D	D
Owen	22	D	D	D	33	2 040	D	D	23	316	10.4	3.0
Parke	12	D	D	D	13	660	137.6	21.5	36	D	D	D
Perry	25	76	8.1	2.1	29	2 003	600.2	92.4	41	D	D	D

1. Establishment subject to federal tax.

Table B. States and Counties — Health Care and Social Assistance, Other Services, and Federal Funds

STATE County	Health care and social assistance, 2007				Other services, 2007				Federal funds and grants, 2009–2010			
									Expenditures (mil dol)			
										Direct payments for individuals[1]		
	Number of establishments	Number of employees	Receipts (mil dol)	Annual payroll (mil dol)	Number of establishments	Number of employees	Receipts (mil dol)	Annual payroll (mil dol)	Total	Social Security and government retirement	Medicare	Food Stamps and Supplemental Security Income
	159	160	161	162	163	164	165	166	167	168	169	170
ILLINOIS—Cont'd												
Winnebago	669	19 367	1 909.7	798.6	551	3 698	305.0	89.8	1 903.8	842.2	346.0	99.3
Woodford	42	1 252	56.4	27.8	55	D	D	D	173.3	93.0	45.0	3.7
INDIANA	14 972	370 093	34 768.4	13 453.8	11 458	75 292	8 451.2	1 892.9	58 603.4	18 937.0	8 987.6	2 036.4
Adams	53	1 727	103.5	38.9	73	307	24.5	6.4	196.3	86.3	45.7	7.0
Allen	1 011	28 617	2 769.4	1 073.6	692	5 000	403.4	127.8	3 067.7	929.2	394.3	117.7
Bartholomew	228	5 095	439.1	178.5	120	857	82.8	19.5	709.5	247.2	97.4	15.8
Benton	13	114	6.5	2.9	14	32	3.9	0.8	62.3	29.0	16.1	1.8
Blackford	25	D	D	D	23	65	6.5	1.3	111.6	50.2	22.9	5.2
Boone	116	2 134	175.6	71.9	97	563	40.9	11.6	238.5	133.1	58.3	6.0
Brown	26	228	12.6	5.7	20	65	6.6	1.7	58.5	34.5	10.6	3.1
Carroll	29	299	15.3	7.5	33	87	6.4	1.8	112.5	52.9	23.9	2.9
Cass	75	2 973	173.8	80.2	75	492	26.6	9.2	283.8	126.3	68.0	13.2
Clark	233	5 037	453.1	182.3	182	1 226	105.3	30.9	990.3	360.1	168.0	30.2
Clay	56	D	D	D	46	255	12.1	3.2	233.0	101.9	51.6	8.7
Clinton	50	1 235	77.3	29.7	55	314	26.9	7.3	210.1	98.3	52.5	8.2
Crawford	14	166	8.3	3.6	9	D	D	D	92.2	39.0	19.2	5.0
Daviess	79	1 468	96.7	40.4	64	365	65.4	8.7	208.6	94.4	49.8	6.8
Dearborn	107	D	D	D	71	326	24.3	6.6	276.1	149.0	69.4	10.7
Decatur	58	1 026	78.0	33.1	47	251	19.2	4.2	159.7	76.7	35.6	5.8
DeKalb	89	1 615	121.4	47.6	79	303	20.8	6.3	234.4	134.5	44.8	7.3
Delaware	316	10 078	836.1	335.6	203	1 206	119.8	26.7	932.8	377.0	182.0	52.1
Dubois	125	2 965	239.4	103.7	86	478	56.8	10.9	260.1	118.8	53.7	3.5
Elkhart	347	9 746	1 024.6	358.1	374	2 298	195.7	60.1	913.7	486.1	182.1	45.9
Fayette	65	1 217	114.0	48.1	44	190	17.8	3.9	210.7	94.1	49.5	12.0
Floyd	233	5 234	437.2	172.7	140	846	71.3	16.9	554.6	245.2	115.3	24.6
Fountain	25	493	27.6	10.8	29	90	8.9	1.8	137.8	69.2	32.4	4.6
Franklin	58	D	D	D	37	D	D	D	118.1	57.4	23.8	4.4
Fulton	45	838	68.0	29.8	36	112	11.8	2.6	128.3	65.9	32.2	4.2
Gibson	83	D	D	D	58	267	18.1	5.1	236.6	105.8	58.7	7.7
Grant	176	5 003	435.1	182.6	124	549	38.1	10.4	665.4	278.2	127.7	84.5
Greene	71	1 104	65.8	26.4	50	D	D	D	257.1	126.1	53.2	10.4
Hamilton	729	12 555	1 354.4	494.5	461	3 217	218.4	68.8	807.0	499.9	113.7	15.2
Hancock	131	2 265	187.3	70.9	105	472	39.4	9.4	327.4	212.6	61.6	6.7
Harrison	69	1 327	88.4	36.0	46	150	17.0	3.6	220.4	125.8	44.6	9.7
Hendricks	260	4 706	427.5	170.6	208	1 051	84.9	24.2	570.4	366.8	94.3	8.7
Henry	92	2 418	155.5	68.2	71	316	32.0	5.6	370.3	174.3	87.5	16.8
Howard	223	5 618	513.4	195.6	131	711	53.2	14.1	692.4	353.2	144.9	33.8
Huntington	73	1 823	122.2	47.3	77	341	18.8	5.6	233.1	130.4	47.8	7.1
Jackson	108	2 174	158.1	69.7	80	431	35.9	9.2	284.2	139.0	56.4	11.3
Jasper	56	1 432	92.1	38.3	52	157	14.4	3.4	206.5	107.6	42.1	6.7
Jay	35	707	59.8	22.4	40	123	8.6	2.0	158.7	70.2	38.8	6.1
Jefferson	86	2 209	178.0	82.7	57	254	19.4	4.8	271.9	123.4	54.6	11.1
Jennings	60	886	69.7	29.3	27	D	D	D	193.5	82.6	32.3	9.6
Johnson	276	5 814	446.4	176.6	216	1 434	113.7	35.6	731.2	393.2	125.5	21.8
Knox	129	3 581	296.3	116.5	71	491	32.2	8.8	378.3	136.0	85.9	16.6
Kosciusko	144	3 432	225.9	101.9	160	877	81.6	20.2	370.8	203.8	78.1	9.8
LaGrange	45	770	57.0	21.6	49	217	17.7	4.8	136.1	80.3	28.6	4.1
Lake	1 220	31 776	3 101.6	1 205.3	902	6 829	548.1	167.1	4 006.6	1 530.8	967.5	286.9
LaPorte	236	4 900	521.2	188.2	207	1 172	74.6	22.2	756.1	357.8	183.6	38.0
Lawrence	101	2 407	184.2	75.6	85	417	26.1	7.6	368.0	172.2	77.4	12.6
Madison	266	6 713	556.4	223.6	201	1 239	83.4	24.0	1 214.0	561.7	257.3	55.3
Marion	2 402	74 201	8 186.4	3 168.6	1 780	16 477	2 991.1	535.3	13 113.6	2 379.9	1 427.6	427.4
Marshall	80	1 947	152.3	56.3	87	509	45.3	14.4	244.9	130.8	52.5	8.2
Martin	12	D	D	D	14	D	D	D	847.3	44.8	17.8	3.3
Miami	43	1 226	77.8	29.9	56	295	18.8	5.7	306.2	128.6	53.6	14.0
Monroe	304	7 565	690.6	298.4	211	2 080	609.7	56.0	1 080.3	304.2	111.1	24.8
Montgomery	87	1 367	103.3	47.0	83	525	50.5	13.0	259.3	124.7	57.3	8.8
Morgan	111	1 668	145.8	55.5	110	480	37.5	10.0	396.8	208.7	81.2	15.6
Newton	15	165	7.7	4.0	16	58	7.9	1.4	81.2	39.4	20.7	3.4
Noble	76	1 354	97.2	40.6	82	308	54.2	6.6	224.1	120.1	52.6	9.0
Ohio	8	D	D	D	6	D	D	D	35.8	17.9	7.9	0.9
Orange	43	951	49.1	20.3	30	132	9.2	1.9	148.5	63.9	32.5	6.9
Owen	23	390	18.9	8.6	31	D	D	D	124.5	65.6	22.6	6.6
Parke	27	484	24.6	10.0	27	84	9.7	1.8	114.6	52.7	25.1	3.9
Perry	42	832	69.7	22.2	30	81	7.2	1.7	145.2	57.0	31.5	4.1

1. State totals may include programs not allocated by county.

Table B. States and Counties — Federal Funds, Residential Construction, and Local Government Finances

STATE County	Federal funds and grants, 2009–2010 (cont.)							Value of residential construction authorized by building permits, 2010		Local government finances, 2007				
	Expenditures (mil dol) (cont.)									General revenue				
	Procurement contract awards			Grants[1]								Taxes		
													Per capita[2] (dollars)	
	Salaries and wages	Defense	Other	Medicaid and other health-related	Nutrition and family welfare	Education	Other	New construction ($1,000)	Number of housing units	Total (mil dol)	Intergovernmental (mil dol)	Total (mil dol)	Total	Property
	171	172	173	174	175	176	177	178	179	180	181	182	183	184
ILLINOIS—Cont'd														
Winnebago	117.1	153.3	23.4	176.0	33.5	11.0	37.6	27 816	257	1 065.2	437.3	447.8	1 499	1 317
Woodford	6.7	0.1	1.8	7.8	4.1	0.5	1.3	15 498	83	114.1	45.3	52.2	1 374	1 312
INDIANA	4 359.7	4 369.9	1 128.5	6 228.9	1 304.6	977.7	3 453.6	1 960 774	13 083	X	X	X	X	X
Adams	5.0	0.1	1.3	35.8	3.7	2.0	0.9	5 326	44	126.4	44.8	34.8	1 034	916
Allen	208.3	836.9	169.0	244.6	51.5	12.0	46.7	122 589	721	1 062.8	379.5	383.3	1 097	894
Bartholomew	185.4	19.5	4.0	68.4	12.8	1.3	49.9	23 921	131	398.0	87.4	73.8	988	791
Benton	2.5	0.0	0.6	6.0	0.7	0.1	0.2	1 101	7	38.1	17.4	13.4	1 522	1 357
Blackford	12.5	0.0	0.6	11.9	2.4	0.3	2.2	1 038	8	33.9	17.6	10.1	765	644
Boone	12.8	0.9	2.1	14.0	4.0	0.4	0.1	85 761	767	212.4	58.5	55.4	1 024	806
Brown	1.3	0.0	0.3	6.0	1.9	0.2	0.0	25 779	136	46.5	13.6	24.3	1 658	1 421
Carroll	10.6	0.0	0.9	9.7	2.4	0.3	1.2	2 998	37	56.8	26.4	16.5	825	680
Cass	22.7	0.6	1.7	34.4	8.4	0.8	1.4	2 300	15	151.7	52.5	33.0	843	713
Clark	257.8	9.6	35.5	94.3	17.9	2.0	4.5	39 723	276	429.6	137.3	104.8	997	785
Clay	20.1	0.2	1.4	37.2	3.2	0.7	2.1	1 683	15	102.1	52.5	12.9	484	444
Clinton	9.2	0.0	2.9	24.6	4.9	0.8	1.4	880	13	92.8	46.8	24.8	734	614
Crawford	2.6	0.1	0.6	22.3	1.9	0.8	0.0	0	0	31.3	15.0	8.0	740	600
Daviess	7.8	3.8	1.5	29.0	4.4	1.0	0.5	6 244	42	124.2	34.7	29.4	980	848
Dearborn	10.3	0.0	1.8	32.9	7.7	0.6	1.2	11 368	68	219.0	68.9	52.8	1 060	977
Decatur	5.8	0.0	1.3	23.2	3.5	0.6	0.5	5 820	31	105.6	29.3	24.6	986	766
DeKalb	7.2	0.0	1.5	17.9	4.7	0.6	6.8	11 200	70	187.1	59.3	52.5	1 255	1 101
Delaware	56.0	0.4	20.6	156.3	21.6	4.4	25.1	7 887	50	304.8	150.1	87.5	758	697
Dubois	18.4	17.2	17.0	12.7	5.5	0.3	5.3	12 900	81	140.7	52.7	52.1	1 265	1 114
Elkhart	27.9	21.1	-6.4	103.4	21.7	5.2	14.1	35 050	234	585.9	266.7	200.5	1 013	835
Fayette	5.4	0.1	0.9	35.7	5.7	0.6	3.7	283	4	71.1	37.0	22.2	913	723
Floyd	35.0	4.2	4.5	90.0	11.8	1.1	5.4	28 418	133	340.5	76.8	58.1	795	605
Fountain	4.8	0.0	1.0	14.9	5.1	0.3	0.2	524	5	50.9	24.7	16.3	953	842
Franklin	3.6	0.4	0.8	22.5	1.9	0.3	0.3	5 228	26	44.0	23.3	13.9	599	485
Fulton	4.4	0.0	1.1	9.7	2.7	0.4	2.5	1 953	10	97.0	22.0	15.7	772	633
Gibson	7.5	0.0	1.9	26.1	4.4	1.7	4.9	7 302	45	109.4	46.1	31.0	947	798
Grant	46.6	0.1	37.8	91.6	14.4	2.5	4.3	9 273	46	171.3	90.2	52.2	759	691
Greene	14.8	3.8	1.5	33.5	4.3	1.5	1.3	NA	NA	98.9	40.0	20.5	628	483
Hamilton	39.4	3.3	32.8	42.3	12.6	1.6	27.5	310 799	1 975	820.1	212.6	315.5	1 206	1 080
Hancock	13.4	2.0	2.4	16.4	4.7	0.5	1.3	25 286	151	249.0	65.1	59.1	891	676
Harrison	8.6	0.1	2.2	28.3	4.6	0.5	0.2	1 900	88	133.9	66.9	23.4	635	449
Hendricks	27.8	2.1	59.3	23.0	7.9	1.1	0.4	113 178	631	533.5	132.4	187.5	1 393	1 181
Henry	10.7	0.0	2.0	59.5	9.4	0.8	2.4	3 712	22	148.3	66.4	47.4	1 004	844
Howard	33.9	0.5	5.6	81.1	14.2	1.7	10.2	2 041	13	409.8	113.6	113.9	1 360	1 292
Huntington	16.4	0.8	1.7	15.6	4.5	0.5	0.6	11 176	79	105.8	50.0	39.7	1 052	915
Jackson	14.4	3.5	1.9	40.2	5.7	0.7	1.2	14 726	111	179.7	41.9	31.9	757	681
Jasper	18.8	0.1	1.6	14.1	3.4	0.4	0.2	14 615	80	123.3	37.3	29.2	906	752
Jay	3.5	0.0	0.8	23.1	6.1	0.7	2.9	2 340	14	91.5	32.8	22.6	1 050	814
Jefferson	15.3	4.1	1.7	45.4	7.1	1.0	-0.3	4 419	37	81.5	40.5	24.4	746	653
Jennings	13.5	13.9	1.0	31.3	2.5	0.7	1.5	3 375	37	67.4	40.2	15.8	562	464
Johnson	25.6	67.9	21.1	53.5	10.9	1.5	0.9	92 817	651	444.0	136.3	141.8	1 043	742
Knox	18.3	3.3	6.7	59.5	10.3	3.2	5.2	2 597	17	242.9	43.4	29.8	786	674
Kosciusko	17.8	6.6	5.7	22.3	10.8	1.1	3.0	30 057	193	209.0	84.4	65.8	865	783
LaGrange	5.3	0.0	1.2	9.7	2.4	0.9	0.0	14 207	74	84.4	39.4	28.3	764	602
Lake	155.0	31.3	26.6	709.0	103.6	19.2	95.0	139 744	818	2 093.9	902.5	805.8	1 637	1 561
LaPorte	37.9	4.2	5.8	86.8	17.7	2.6	5.0	27 474	228	386.6	163.7	106.7	972	806
Lawrence	22.4	7.9	4.2	53.7	8.8	1.6	2.9	1 704	8	154.3	54.6	41.0	892	768
Madison	33.7	4.5	13.0	160.5	19.5	3.3	93.3	17 237	80	356.2	165.7	101.0	769	650
Marion	1 693.0	1 290.3	429.1	1 193.1	445.1	506.0	2 430.7	154 998	1 404	3 905.3	1 379.3	1 439.0	1 641	1 393
Marshall	11.9	3.8	2.0	19.5	7.2	0.7	1.1	16 469	88	108.7	54.4	36.9	789	734
Martin	185.5	560.8	0.7	17.1	1.8	0.4	13.5	0	0	29.6	15.3	7.9	785	751
Miami	34.2	31.9	1.4	26.1	6.1	0.8	5.6	1 392	10	167.1	67.7	30.1	823	746
Monroe	74.9	4.7	14.0	393.2	14.9	11.7	87.6	37 149	261	284.9	111.5	106.3	826	744
Montgomery	21.6	0.5	1.8	27.5	4.5	0.7	3.6	4 618	42	115.7	45.5	39.4	1 041	937
Morgan	20.0	6.5	2.6	46.3	7.5	1.0	1.7	14 355	89	192.0	74.8	46.7	669	507
Newton	2.8	0.0	0.7	6.0	2.0	0.2	0.8	3 033	18	53.0	19.6	18.6	1 324	1 201
Noble	7.5	0.0	1.5	20.3	4.3	0.8	1.9	10 539	66	114.8	49.3	23.2	488	431
Ohio	1.4	0.0	0.3	6.0	0.7	0.1	0.0	2 322	15	27.9	12.1	4.0	691	555
Orange	3.8	0.6	1.5	31.3	3.6	0.6	1.9	763	5	46.4	25.5	12.0	614	512
Owen	5.2	0.6	0.9	17.1	2.8	0.5	0.0	293	2	44.8	22.0	15.5	691	571
Parke	5.2	0.1	0.9	17.9	2.9	0.5	0.6	3 571	29	50.5	19.6	11.6	677	521
Perry	15.0	0.1	1.6	23.8	4.7	1.4	1.5	4 978	38	56.5	24.4	16.0	847	714

1. State totals may include programs not allocated by county. 2. Based on the resident population estimated as of July 1 of the year shown.

Table B. States and Counties — Local Government Finances, Government Employment, and Voting

	Local government finances, 2007 (cont.)									Government employment, 2009			Presidential election,[2] 2008		
	Direct general expenditure							Debt outstanding					Percent of vote cast:		
			Percent of total for:												
STATE County	Total (mil dol)	Per capita[1] (dollars)	Education	Health and hospitals	Police protection	Public welfare	Highways	Total (mil dol)	Per capita[1] (dollars)	Federal civilian	Federal military	State and local	Democratic	Republican	All other
	185	186	187	188	189	190	191	192	193	194	195	196	197	198	199
ILLINOIS—Cont'd															
Winnebago	1 071.9	3 588	44.7	1.5	6.0	2.8	5.6	805.9	2 697	1 038	601	14 211	55.6	42.8	1.7
Woodford	106.9	2 812	66.3	1.4	4.0	0.1	6.5	53.1	1 396	75	78	1 820	35.9	62.6	1.5
INDIANA	X	X	X	X	X	X	X	X	X	39 125	22 353	399 289	49.9	48.9	1.1
Adams	124.6	3 704	40.4	28.2	2.4	1.5	4.7	129.7	3 854	71	115	1 969	36.5	62.2	1.3
Allen	1 165.0	3 333	48.8	0.8	4.6	2.9	3.1	857.2	2 453	2 018	1 189	17 169	47.4	51.8	0.8
Bartholomew	413.6	5 533	28.0	41.7	2.3	1.9	2.1	184.1	2 463	208	256	6 253	43.7	55.0	1.3
Benton	45.7	5 186	62.6	1.3	1.9	2.3	6.3	13.6	1 542	34	29	635	41.0	57.2	1.8
Blackford	38.9	2 952	54.9	0.7	3.3	2.4	4.6	44.7	3 388	29	44	617	49.2	49.4	1.4
Boone	245.7	4 538	46.4	20.5	2.2	1.1	3.0	203.1	3 752	106	189	3 199	36.6	62.4	1.0
Brown	43.1	2 936	54.0	1.2	1.8	4.4	7.6	35.4	2 415	18	49	834	47.8	50.4	1.8
Carroll	47.8	2 394	49.6	2.7	3.4	2.6	11.2	25.8	1 289	70	66	767	42.8	55.6	1.6
Cass	168.7	4 305	43.3	24.6	2.6	2.8	3.4	41.0	1 046	114	131	3 639	44.8	53.3	1.9
Clark	491.3	4 677	32.3	28.7	1.6	1.7	1.9	179.3	1 707	2 417	367	6 143	46.0	53.1	0.9
Clay	96.2	3 610	67.1	0.4	1.6	1.1	3.5	49.1	1 843	87	89	1 262	43.5	55.0	1.5
Clinton	125.9	3 725	63.3	0.9	2.8	2.0	3.4	128.8	3 811	72	115	1 632	42.8	55.8	1.3
Crawford	37.0	3 428	56.1	1.8	1.1	4.6	4.6	32.1	2 975	29	35	573	48.2	50.4	1.4
Daviess	123.9	4 125	40.1	32.8	3.5	1.5	3.4	80.1	2 666	80	103	1 778	31.8	67.1	1.1
Dearborn	305.2	6 133	30.0	20.6	1.6	0.9	1.6	87.8	1 765	94	170	2 855	32.1	67.0	0.9
Decatur	110.3	4 420	33.8	31.0	1.7	1.5	3.5	57.1	2 286	88	84	1 482	37.1	61.5	1.4
DeKalb	190.4	4 555	43.1	20.5	2.4	2.0	4.3	93.4	2 235	92	141	1 970	41.8	57.0	1.1
Delaware	373.1	3 232	51.4	1.3	3.9	4.7	2.7	233.5	2 023	371	392	10 360	56.9	41.9	1.1
Dubois	125.8	3 052	63.1	0.8	3.3	1.3	5.6	149.3	3 621	113	139	2 085	47.1	51.3	1.6
Elkhart	815.9	4 122	53.1	1.4	3.8	2.4	2.6	702.5	3 549	295	674	8 353	43.9	55.1	0.9
Fayette	76.0	3 131	49.7	2.0	4.5	4.6	4.9	34.4	1 417	52	81	1 233	46.4	52.0	1.6
Floyd	367.1	5 024	34.0	41.5	2.3	1.4	1.3	351.4	4 809	186	250	5 674	44.5	54.6	0.9
Fountain	51.1	2 981	58.8	2.0	1.5	2.6	7.7	30.6	1 784	61	57	807	41.8	56.1	2.1
Franklin	49.1	2 113	54.8	0.5	1.4	2.2	11.6	20.3	875	51	78	992	32.1	66.1	1.8
Fulton	86.9	4 279	28.7	34.6	2.4	2.5	4.2	40.6	2 002	52	68	1 170	41.1	57.2	1.7
Gibson	121.5	3 709	60.8	1.7	2.2	1.7	4.8	187.7	5 731	99	110	1 188	42.8	56.0	1.3
Grant	207.2	3 010	50.0	0.7	5.8	4.0	4.2	445.1	6 465	1 202	232	3 162	42.9	56.0	1.0
Greene	105.7	3 234	50.9	18.8	1.9	2.8	5.5	56.4	1 725	91	109	1 863	41.9	66.4	1.7
Hamilton	1 162.4	4 442	40.9	12.0	3.1	0.3	5.2	1 556.9	5 950	417	940	11 916	38.5	60.7	0.7
Hancock	299.3	4 515	43.3	27.5	2.2	0.9	3.0	259.8	3 918	122	229	3 945	34.7	64.3	1.1
Harrison	155.0	4 210	40.9	20.7	0.6	1.9	2.3	84.5	2 294	111	126	1 947	40.3	58.3	1.4
Hendricks	544.8	4 049	43.7	25.6	2.6	0.4	1.7	542.2	4 029	281	472	8 249	37.8	61.2	1.0
Henry	160.2	3 396	52.5	1.7	2.7	6.0	9.8	95.1	2 015	106	161	3 151	47.2	51.1	1.7
Howard	415.3	4 958	35.2	32.9	4.5	1.5	2.8	244.7	2 921	268	279	6 544	46.3	52.4	1.3
Huntington	93.5	2 477	58.0	0.5	3.5	2.1	5.3	84.3	2 233	92	127	1 544	35.8	63.0	1.2
Jackson	177.3	4 204	32.7	41.0	2.5	1.2	1.4	226.8	5 376	102	142	2 811	42.3	56.0	1.7
Jasper	126.8	3 928	47.2	25.0	2.7	1.4	3.1	173.0	5 362	87	110	1 915	39.2	59.6	1.3
Jay	96.5	4 486	49.2	20.3	2.1	1.2	4.1	57.4	2 666	51	71	1 287	45.1	52.9	2.0
Jefferson	94.0	2 875	61.2	1.4	2.6	4.3	4.2	71.3	2 180	94	111	2 571	46.4	52.3	1.3
Jennings	75.9	2 700	61.5	1.1	2.4	2.9	4.5	60.5	2 152	89	94	1 286	44.9	52.9	2.2
Johnson	551.3	4 055	50.8	13.8	2.4	0.6	2.1	499.6	3 675	373	475	6 474	36.8	62.2	1.0
Knox	232.8	6 135	22.0	53.1	1.5	1.4	2.3	88.1	2 323	186	127	4 794	46.1	52.6	1.3
Kosciusko	227.2	2 985	58.0	0.8	3.1	0.9	4.1	94.7	1 245	199	257	3 002	30.6	68.0	1.4
LaGrange	96.1	2 595	61.8	0.5	1.4	1.9	4.8	91.4	2 469	69	125	1 306	38.6	60.1	1.3
Lake	2 234.5	4 541	42.9	0.6	6.6	5.8	2.2	2 131.7	4 332	1 494	1 660	26 816	66.7	32.5	0.8
LaPorte	352.4	3 210	57.1	1.3	2.1	2.0	7.3	269.9	2 459	204	391	7 216	60.2	38.2	1.6
Lawrence	173.6	3 771	42.9	24.3	3.0	1.6	3.4	121.0	2 628	146	154	2 503	38.9	59.4	1.7
Madison	426.4	3 247	50.8	0.3	4.1	3.0	3.4	373.2	2 842	283	443	6 481	52.6	46.0	1.4
Marion	4 422.1	5 043	37.8	14.2	4.1	2.6	1.1	7 384.5	8 422	14 497	3 536	67 315	63.8	35.4	0.8
Marshall	143.2	3 066	64.5	1.0	3.1	2.4	5.3	116.2	2 489	101	157	2 422	42.5	56.1	1.4
Martin	29.4	2 921	53.0	0.6	2.0	2.3	8.4	20.9	2 077	3 921	74	517	34.8	63.7	1.5
Miami	161.0	4 393	44.6	19.5	1.8	1.7	4.0	68.4	1 867	606	138	2 184	39.4	58.9	1.7
Monroe	286.0	2 223	47.4	0.8	4.0	4.3	4.0	302.5	2 351	394	453	22 234	65.6	33.4	1.0
Montgomery	134.2	3 543	59.5	0.5	2.6	2.9	5.4	162.5	4 289	102	127	2 059	39.3	59.3	1.4
Morgan	217.5	3 113	52.0	18.1	2.9	0.9	4.0	89.5	1 281	122	238	3 037	35.9	62.9	1.2
Newton	51.8	3 694	48.3	2.5	2.2	3.8	6.3	39.8	2 843	37	46	782	43.4	54.6	2.0
Noble	147.0	3 093	50.9	0.4	0.7	1.3	13.0	142.8	3 004	95	161	1 921	41.6	57.0	1.4
Ohio	35.1	6 082	23.6	0.3	1.8	1.7	4.5	21.6	3 743	13	20	344	39.7	58.7	1.6
Orange	50.8	2 592	61.7	0.7	2.2	1.4	7.7	46.5	2 373	48	66	985	41.9	56.1	2.0
Owen	45.7	2 042	62.2	3.7	1.8	2.9	6.6	50.0	2 234	38	75	854	43.7	54.0	2.3
Parke	41.3	2 404	59.4	1.7	3.3	1.3	8.3	631.0	36 750	57	57	1 217	42.0	56.1	1.9
Perry	54.0	2 855	51.4	0.6	3.4	1.8	6.5	62.1	3 282	81	63	1 502	60.6	37.7	1.7

1. Based on the resident population estimated as of July 1 of the year shown.   2. © 2009 Election Data Services, Inc. All rights reserved.

STATE/ County code	CBSA code[1]	County type[2]	STATE County	Land area,[3] (sq km) 2010	Total persons	Rank	Per square kilometer	Race alone or in combination, not Hispanic or Latino (percent) White	Black	American Indian, Alaska Native	Asian and Pacific Islander	Percent Hispanic or Latino[4]	Age (percent) Under 5 years	5 to 17 years	18 to 24 years	25 to 34 years	35 to 44 years	45 to 54 years
				1	2	3	4	5	6	7	8	9	10	11	12	13	14	15
			INDIANA—Cont'd															
18 125	27540	6	Pike	866	12 845	2 255	14.8	98.3	0.5	0.5	0.4	0.9	6.0	16.4	7.2	10.7	12.5	16.3
18 127	16980	1	Porter	1 083	164 343	374	151.7	87.1	3.3	0.6	1.6	8.5	6.0	18.3	9.3	12.2	13.4	15.4
18 129	21780	2	Posey	1 061	25 910	1 569	24.4	97.6	1.5	0.5	0.4	1.0	5.7	18.0	8.1	10.1	12.5	17.1
18 131	...	6	Pulaski	1 123	13 402	2 225	11.9	96.4	0.8	0.7	0.4	2.4	5.9	18.0	7.4	10.6	12.4	16.1
18 133	26900	1	Putnam	1 245	37 963	1 218	30.5	93.4	4.3	0.6	1.0	1.5	5.1	15.9	13.6	11.9	12.8	15.4
18 135	...	6	Randolph	1 172	26 171	1 553	22.3	95.9	0.8	0.6	0.5	3.0	5.9	18.5	7.7	10.7	12.7	14.7
18 137	...	6	Ripley	1 156	28 818	1 458	24.9	97.5	0.4	0.6	0.7	1.5	6.6	19.7	7.5	11.2	13.1	14.9
18 139	...	6	Rush	1 057	17 392	1 958	16.5	97.5	1.2	0.5	0.4	1.1	5.9	18.8	7.8	10.3	13.0	15.7
18 141	43780	2	St. Joseph	1 186	266 931	245	225.1	77.6	13.9	0.9	2.5	7.3	6.6	18.0	11.3	12.6	12.2	14.0
18 143	42500	6	Scott	493	24 181	1 638	49.0	97.6	0.4	0.4	0.6	1.5	6.1	17.9	8.5	11.7	14.1	15.4
18 145	26900	1	Shelby	1 065	44 436	1 080	41.7	94.5	1.4	0.5	0.8	3.7	6.1	18.3	8.0	11.2	13.3	16.6
18 147	...	8	Spencer	1 028	20 952	1 791	20.4	96.5	0.7	0.4	0.4	2.5	5.9	18.3	6.8	10.9	12.4	16.7
18 149	...	6	Starke	801	23 363	1 655	29.2	96.0	0.5	0.8	0.3	3.3	6.4	18.0	8.2	10.8	12.5	15.4
18 151	11420	7	Steuben	800	34 185	1 323	42.7	95.9	0.7	0.6	0.7	2.9	5.5	17.4	10.5	10.2	12.6	14.9
18 153	45460	3	Sullivan	1 158	21 475	1 762	18.5	93.7	4.7	0.7	0.3	1.4	5.4	16.0	8.8	13.4	13.7	15.2
18 155	...	8	Switzerland	571	10 613	2 392	18.6	97.9	0.5	0.5	0.2	1.4	7.4	18.2	7.9	11.4	12.9	15.2
18 157	29140	3	Tippecanoe	1 294	172 780	355	133.5	81.9	4.7	0.6	6.9	7.5	6.4	14.3	24.6	14.4	10.7	10.9
18 159	29020	3	Tipton	675	15 936	2 052	23.6	97.1	0.5	0.4	0.6	2.2	5.2	18.1	7.1	9.5	13.5	15.6
18 161	...	8	Union	418	7 516	2 643	18.0	97.8	0.6	0.7	0.7	1.1	5.9	19.2	7.8	10.6	13.2	15.2
18 163	21780	2	Vanderburgh	605	179 703	343	297.0	87.1	10.4	0.6	1.6	2.2	6.5	15.7	11.8	13.2	11.6	14.7
18 165	45460	3	Vermillion	665	16 212	2 041	24.4	98.6	0.4	0.5	0.5	0.8	5.5	17.6	7.2	10.5	12.9	14.8
18 167	45460	3	Vigo	1 045	107 848	543	103.2	88.6	8.1	0.8	2.1	2.3	5.8	15.5	14.2	13.2	12.3	13.7
18 169	47340	6	Wabash	1 068	32 888	1 363	30.8	96.3	0.8	1.1	0.6	2.1	5.9	16.8	10.0	10.2	11.7	14.4
18 171	...	8	Warren	945	8 508	2 568	9.0	98.4	0.3	0.4	0.6	0.8	5.8	17.7	7.2	10.0	12.9	16.3
18 173	21780	2	Warrick	997	59 689	862	59.9	95.2	1.8	0.6	2.0	1.6	6.4	19.5	6.8	11.1	13.6	16.0
18 175	31140	1	Washington	1 331	28 262	1 485	21.2	98.1	0.4	0.6	0.5	1.1	6.0	19.2	8.0	11.4	13.5	15.7
18 177	39980	5	Wayne	1 041	68 917	768	66.2	91.1	6.5	0.8	1.2	2.6	6.3	16.7	9.3	11.4	12.4	14.7
18 179	23060	2	Wells	953	27 636	1 511	29.0	97.0	0.6	0.6	0.5	2.0	6.5	18.4	7.9	11.3	11.7	15.8
18 181	...	6	White	1 308	24 643	1 618	18.8	92.1	0.4	0.7	0.6	7.1	6.0	18.2	7.0	10.3	12.3	15.3
18 183	23060	2	Whitley	869	33 292	1 343	38.3	97.5	0.6	0.7	0.6	1.5	6.3	18.3	7.7	11.1	12.9	16.0
19 000	...	X	IOWA	144 669	3 046 355	X	21.1	89.9	3.6	0.7	2.2	5.0	6.6	17.3	10.0	12.6	12.0	14.4
19 001	...	8	Adair	1 474	7 682	2 631	5.2	98.2	0.2	0.3	0.4	1.3	5.8	16.6	6.1	10.3	10.6	16.1
19 003	...	9	Adams	1 097	4 029	2 905	3.7	97.8	0.4	0.7	0.6	0.9	5.8	15.3	6.8	9.7	10.0	17.2
19 005	...	6	Allamakee	1 655	14 330	2 156	8.7	93.4	0.9	0.4	0.4	5.3	6.6	16.5	7.2	10.1	10.8	15.2
19 007	...	7	Appanoose	1 288	12 887	2 250	10.0	97.6	0.7	0.7	0.5	1.4	6.3	16.2	7.4	10.1	10.9	15.2
19 009	...	8	Audubon	1 147	6 119	2 756	5.3	98.7	0.4	0.3	0.6	0.6	5.5	16.4	5.6	8.9	10.7	16.4
19 011	16300	3	Benton	1 855	26 076	1 560	14.1	98.1	0.8	0.4	0.4	1.1	6.3	19.2	6.4	10.8	13.3	16.7
19 013	47940	3	Black Hawk	1 465	131 090	474	89.5	85.7	10.0	0.6	1.9	3.7	6.5	15.3	15.6	13.3	10.7	12.7
19 015	14340	6	Boone	1 480	26 306	1 549	17.8	96.6	1.1	0.6	0.6	1.9	5.9	17.9	7.6	11.9	11.6	15.6
19 017	47940	3	Bremer	1 128	24 276	1 634	21.5	97.4	1.2	0.2	1.0	1.0	5.8	16.9	12.4	10.2	11.5	13.6
19 019	...	6	Buchanan	1 479	20 958	1 790	14.2	98.0	0.7	0.5	0.6	1.2	7.5	19.6	7.3	11.3	11.7	15.1
19 021	44740	7	Buena Vista	1 489	20 260	1 825	13.6	68.5	2.7	0.3	6.4	22.7	7.2	17.8	11.7	11.1	10.8	14.6
19 023	...	8	Butler	1 503	14 867	2 120	9.9	98.6	0.4	0.3	0.5	0.9	6.6	17.0	5.9	10.8	11.3	14.3
19 025	...	9	Calhoun	1 476	9 670	2 463	6.6	98.4	0.4	0.4	0.4	0.9	5.7	15.5	6.3	9.1	10.0	15.1
19 027	...	7	Carroll	1 475	20 816	1 801	14.1	97.4	0.8	0.4	0.6	1.6	7.0	17.8	6.5	10.8	11.3	15.7
19 029	...	6	Cass	1 461	13 956	2 179	9.6	97.2	0.4	0.4	0.6	1.8	6.6	16.2	6.4	10.3	10.3	15.6
19 031	...	6	Cedar	1 501	18 499	1 900	12.3	97.6	0.6	0.5	0.7	1.5	6.2	18.3	6.1	10.6	12.3	16.4
19 033	32380	5	Cerro Gordo	1 472	44 151	1 084	30.0	93.8	2.0	0.5	1.2	3.8	5.8	15.7	8.4	11.2	10.9	15.9
19 035	...	6	Cherokee	1 494	12 072	2 302	8.1	96.4	0.9	0.5	0.7	2.3	5.6	15.5	6.4	9.8	9.9	16.3
19 037	...	6	Chickasaw	1 306	12 439	2 279	9.5	97.2	0.4	0.2	0.4	2.2	6.6	17.8	6.4	10.0	10.8	15.8
19 039	...	6	Clarke	1 117	9 286	2 500	8.3	89.0	0.5	0.5	0.7	10.0	7.4	17.8	7.8	11.1	11.5	14.6
19 041	43980	7	Clay	1 469	16 667	2 003	11.3	95.9	0.8	0.5	0.9	2.9	6.5	16.5	7.1	11.8	11.0	15.2
19 043	...	8	Clayton	2 016	18 129	1 918	9.0	97.5	0.5	0.3	0.6	1.7	6.2	17.0	6.4	9.5	10.8	16.4
19 045	17540	4	Clinton	1 800	49 116	993	27.3	94.0	3.5	0.7	0.8	2.5	6.3	17.3	8.1	11.0	11.8	15.8
19 047	...	6	Crawford	1 850	17 096	1 977	9.2	73.8	1.4	0.3	0.7	24.2	7.4	19.0	8.8	10.8	11.2	14.4
19 049	19780	2	Dallas	1 524	66 135	793	43.4	89.7	1.8	0.4	3.0	6.1	8.7	20.3	6.1	15.9	15.7	13.4
19 051	...	9	Davis	1 301	8 753	2 546	6.7	98.5	0.2	0.6	0.6	1.0	8.5	20.6	7.4	9.7	10.7	13.9
19 053	...	9	Decatur	1 378	8 457	2 572	6.1	94.8	2.0	0.8	1.1	2.1	6.3	16.4	15.0	9.3	9.8	12.9
19 055	...	6	Delaware	1 496	17 764	1 940	11.9	98.5	0.6	0.3	0.4	0.8	6.4	18.8	6.4	10.5	11.7	17.1
19 057	15460	5	Des Moines	1 078	40 325	1 165	37.4	91.3	6.3	0.7	1.1	2.6	6.5	16.6	7.5	11.8	11.6	14.7
19 059	44020	7	Dickinson	986	16 667	2 003	16.9	98.2	0.4	0.3	0.7	1.1	4.9	14.5	5.5	10.4	10.7	15.2
19 061	20220	3	Dubuque	1 576	93 653	613	59.4	94.0	3.2	0.4	1.6	1.9	6.4	17.4	10.6	11.9	11.7	14.6
19 063	...	7	Emmet	1 025	10 302	2 417	10.1	91.2	0.9	0.6	0.7	7.4	6.4	16.6	9.9	11.0	10.1	14.2
19 065	...	6	Fayette	1 893	20 880	1 794	11.0	96.5	1.4	0.4	0.7	1.8	6.0	16.4	9.4	9.8	10.6	15.3
19 067	...	7	Floyd	1 297	16 303	2 032	12.6	95.3	1.5	0.2	1.5	2.0	6.4	17.5	7.1	10.0	11.2	14.3

1. CBSA = Core Based Statistical Area. See Appendix A for explanation. See Appendix B for list of metropolitan areas with component counties. 2. County type code from the Economic Research Service of USDA Rural-Urban Continuum Codes. See Appendix A for definition. 3. Dry land or land partially or temporarily covered by water. 4. May be of any race.

Table B. States and Counties — **Population and Households**

STATE County	55 to 64 years	65 to 74 years	75 years and over	Percent female	1990	2000	1990–2000	2000–2010	Births	Deaths	Net migration	Number	Percent change, 2000–2010	Persons per household	Female family householder[1]	One person
	16	17	18	19	20	21	22	23	24	25	26	27	28	29	30	31
INDIANA—Cont'd																
Pike	13.9	9.5	7.5	50.0	12 509	12 837	2.6	0.1	1 397	1 343	-574	5 186	1.3	2.44	8.5	25.5
Porter	13.1	7.0	5.4	50.9	128 932	146 798	13.9	12.0	17 261	10 964	11 396	61 998	13.4	2.60	10.4	23.3
Posey	14.1	8.0	6.4	50.2	25 968	27 061	4.2	-4.3	2 387	2 124	-1 167	10 171	-0.3	2.52	8.5	23.3
Pulaski	12.8	9.1	7.6	49.5	12 780	13 755	7.6	-2.6	1 499	1 444	-116	5 282	2.2	2.50	9.0	25.6
Putnam	11.7	7.6	5.9	47.2	30 315	36 019	18.8	5.4	3 759	2 859	102	12 917	4.4	2.52	9.0	23.9
Randolph	12.8	9.0	8.1	50.7	27 148	27 401	0.9	-4.5	2 908	2 712	-1 765	10 451	-4.4	2.47	11.1	25.7
Ripley	12.1	8.0	6.9	50.7	24 616	26 523	7.7	8.7	3 627	2 373	-184	10 789	9.6	2.63	10.2	22.8
Rush	12.6	8.3	7.5	50.7	18 129	18 261	0.7	-4.8	2 073	1 661	-1 401	6 767	-2.3	2.54	10.9	24.5
St. Joseph	11.9	6.4	6.9	51.5	247 052	265 559	7.5	0.5	35 444	22 209	-9 690	103 069	2.3	2.48	13.6	29.1
Scott	12.8	8.0	5.4	50.6	20 991	22 960	9.4	5.3	2 879	2 275	189	9 397	6.4	2.54	13.0	24.0
Shelby	12.6	7.6	6.3	50.4	40 307	43 445	7.8	2.3	5 219	3 686	-233	17 302	4.5	2.53	10.5	24.5
Spencer	14.1	8.5	6.5	49.7	19 490	20 391	4.6	2.8	2 194	1 702	-724	8 082	6.8	2.55	8.1	23.2
Starke	13.4	9.2	6.1	50.6	22 747	23 556	3.6	-0.8	2 847	2 486	-238	9 038	3.4	2.58	11.7	23.5
Steuben	13.9	8.8	6.1	49.5	27 446	33 214	21.0	2.9	3 907	2 534	-795	13 310	4.5	2.47	9.3	25.3
Sullivan	12.8	8.1	6.7	45.7	18 993	21 751	14.5	-1.3	2 201	2 271	-385	7 823	0.1	2.45	10.8	26.7
Switzerland	12.4	9.1	5.5	49.0	7 738	9 065	17.1	17.1	1 051	842	453	4 034	17.4	2.60	10.0	24.3
Tippecanoe	9.2	5.0	4.5	49.0	130 598	148 955	14.1	16.0	19 448	9 412	9 864	65 532	18.7	2.42	9.8	29.2
Tipton	13.9	9.5	7.7	50.8	16 119	16 577	2.8	-3.9	1 779	1 496	-871	6 376	-1.4	2.47	9.6	25.4
Union	13.7	8.3	6.2	50.6	6 976	7 349	5.3	2.3	803	583	-492	2 938	5.2	2.54	11.7	23.9
Vanderburgh	12.2	7.1	7.3	51.8	165 058	171 922	4.2	4.5	22 074	17 125	-313	74 454	5.4	2.31	13.1	32.3
Vermillion	14.6	9.2	7.7	50.5	16 773	16 788	0.1	-3.4	1 792	1 997	-320	6 619	-2.1	2.42	11.0	27.3
Vigo	11.8	6.9	6.5	49.4	106 107	105 848	-0.2	1.9	12 202	10 527	-894	41 361	0.9	2.38	13.1	30.6
Wabash	12.9	8.9	9.2	51.4	35 069	34 960	-0.3	-5.9	3 584	3 591	-2 210	12 777	-3.3	2.43	9.5	27.3
Warren	13.5	9.6	7.0	49.8	8 176	8 419	3.0	1.1	838	823	109	3 337	3.7	2.52	8.3	23.1
Warrick	13.4	7.7	5.6	50.7	44 920	52 383	16.6	13.9	6 242	4 326	4 476	22 505	15.8	2.62	9.2	20.7
Washington	12.7	7.8	5.8	50.1	23 717	27 223	14.8	3.8	3 196	2 436	-75	10 850	5.7	2.58	11.1	23.7
Wayne	12.7	8.6	7.9	51.4	71 951	71 097	-1.2	-3.1	8 201	7 322	-3 986	27 551	-3.2	2.41	13.3	28.5
Wells	12.6	8.0	7.7	50.8	25 948	27 600	6.4	0.1	3 186	2 348	-696	10 780	3.6	2.52	8.6	24.8
White	13.8	9.1	8.0	50.8	23 265	25 267	8.6	-2.5	3 112	2 436	-2 402	9 741	0.1	2.50	9.3	24.8
Whitley	13.7	7.3	6.7	50.3	27 651	30 707	11.1	8.4	3 881	2 622	1 080	13 001	11.0	2.53	9.2	24.1
IOWA	13.2	7.4	7.5	50.5	2 776 831	2 926 324	5.4	4.1	361 755	255 370	-15 876	1 221 576	6.3	2.41	9.3	28.4
Adair	13.0	9.7	11.7	50.4	8 409	8 243	-2.0	-6.8	715	1 044	-520	3 292	-3.1	2.29	6.7	30.7
Adams	13.9	10.5	10.8	50.5	4 866	4 482	-7.9	-10.1	391	475	-452	1 715	-8.1	2.28	5.8	29.0
Allamakee	14.1	10.0	9.6	49.0	13 855	14 675	5.9	-2.4	1 762	1 471	-479	5 845	2.1	2.39	6.9	28.3
Appanoose	13.8	9.8	10.3	51.3	13 743	13 721	-0.2	-6.1	1 488	1 662	-786	5 627	-2.6	2.27	9.9	32.3
Audubon	13.3	10.7	12.5	51.7	7 334	6 830	-6.9	-10.4	550	847	-472	2 617	-5.6	2.29	6.3	30.3
Benton	11.8	7.6	7.8	50.0	22 429	25 308	12.8	3.0	2 858	2 134	705	10 302	5.7	2.50	7.7	24.0
Black Hawk	12.1	6.9	7.0	51.4	123 798	128 012	3.4	2.4	15 471	10 338	-3 178	52 470	5.6	2.38	11.5	28.8
Boone	13.4	7.8	8.1	49.8	25 186	26 224	4.1	0.3	2 837	2 583	-237	10 728	3.4	2.38	8.1	27.6
Bremer	12.4	8.9	8.4	51.1	22 813	23 325	2.2	4.1	2 429	2 028	-133	9 385	5.9	2.40	6.6	25.8
Buchanan	12.3	8.0	7.3	50.4	20 844	21 093	1.2	-0.6	2 834	1 827	-1 083	8 161	2.9	2.53	7.8	25.6
Buena Vista	11.7	6.2	8.8	49.9	19 965	20 411	2.2	-0.7	2 463	1 720	-1 456	7 522	0.3	2.56	8.5	28.6
Butler	14.3	9.3	10.5	50.6	15 731	15 305	-2.7	-2.9	1 557	1 782	-647	6 120	-0.9	2.39	6.4	25.8
Calhoun	14.6	10.7	13.1	51.4	11 508	11 115	-3.4	-13.0	934	1 321	-1 009	4 242	-6.0	2.22	7.0	31.5
Carroll	12.2	8.1	10.6	51.3	21 423	21 421	0.0	-2.8	2 447	2 127	-951	8 683	2.3	2.34	7.4	31.2
Cass	13.6	10.2	10.7	51.1	15 128	14 684	-2.9	-5.0	1 478	1 714	-602	5 980	-2.3	2.28	8.3	30.5
Cedar	13.3	8.1	8.7	50.5	17 444	18 187	4.3	1.7	1 871	1 593	-348	7 511	5.1	2.42	7.5	26.2
Cerro Gordo	14.1	8.4	9.5	51.2	46 733	46 447	-0.6	-4.9	4 644	4 786	-2 418	19 350	-0.1	2.22	9.4	33.0
Cherokee	14.8	9.4	12.2	50.7	14 098	13 035	-7.5	-7.4	1 094	1 421	-1 238	5 207	-3.2	2.25	7.5	30.9
Chickasaw	13.5	9.4	9.7	49.7	13 295	13 095	-1.5	-5.0	1 418	1 278	-1 172	5 204	0.2	2.36	6.3	28.8
Clarke	13.0	8.4	8.3	50.2	8 287	9 133	10.2	1.7	1 186	934	-248	3 701	3.3	2.47	8.7	27.8
Clay	13.5	8.2	10.2	51.0	17 585	17 372	-1.2	-4.1	1 918	1 694	-880	7 282	0.3	2.26	8.2	31.7
Clayton	14.3	9.2	10.1	49.9	19 054	18 678	-2.0	-2.9	1 882	1 923	-1 064	7 599	3.0	2.35	6.4	28.9
Clinton	12.9	8.6	8.3	50.8	51 040	50 149	-1.7	-2.1	5 588	4 912	-1 595	20 223	0.6	2.39	10.3	29.1
Crawford	11.9	8.0	8.4	49.2	16 775	16 942	1.0	0.9	2 136	1 547	-1 035	6 413	-0.4	2.57	8.4	27.0
Dallas	10.1	5.3	4.5	51.1	29 755	40 750	37.0	62.3	6 963	2 961	16 772	25 240	62.0	2.60	8.3	23.6
Davis	12.0	8.8	8.3	50.4	8 312	8 541	2.8	2.5	1 219	832	-324	3 201	-0.2	2.70	6.2	24.3
Decatur	12.1	8.8	9.3	49.9	8 338	8 689	4.2	-2.7	918	863	-472	3 223	-3.4	2.42	8.6	29.1
Delaware	12.6	8.3	8.3	50.0	18 035	18 404	2.0	-3.5	1 920	1 465	-1 583	7 062	3.3	2.48	6.8	24.9
Des Moines	13.7	8.8	8.8	51.4	42 614	42 351	-0.6	-4.8	4 826	3 971	-1 926	17 003	-1.5	2.33	12.1	30.3
Dickinson	16.5	11.0	11.3	50.4	14 909	16 424	10.2	1.5	1 583	1 649	386	7 554	6.3	2.18	6.3	30.6
Dubuque	12.2	7.6	7.7	50.7	86 403	89 143	3.2	5.1	11 108	7 771	625	36 815	9.3	2.43	9.2	28.4
Emmet	13.0	8.4	10.4	50.1	11 569	11 027	-4.7	-6.6	1 261	1 193	-802	4 236	-4.8	2.30	8.4	31.7
Fayette	13.0	9.4	10.0	50.0	21 843	22 008	0.8	-5.1	2 091	2 332	-1 497	8 634	-1.6	2.33	7.6	29.7
Floyd	13.6	9.7	10.3	51.0	17 058	16 900	-0.9	-3.5	1 851	1 835	-924	6 886	0.8	2.32	8.1	31.2

1. No spouse present.

Table B. States and Counties — Population, Vital Statistics, Medicare, and Crime

STATE County	Persons in group quarters, 2010	Daytime population, 2006–2010 Number	Employment/residence ratio	Births, average 2006–2008 Total	Rate[1]	Deaths, average 2006–2008 Number	Rate[1]	Persons under 65 with no health insurance, 2009 Number	Percent	Medicare, 2011 Eligible for Medicare	Enrolled in Medicare Advantage	Enrolled in a Medicare prescription drug plan	Serious crimes known to police,[2] 2010 Total Number	Rate[3]
	32	33	34	35	36	37	38	39	40	41	42	43	44	45
INDIANA—Cont'd														
Pike	213	10 909	0.6	D	D	145	11.4	1 585	15.8	2 712	442	1 285	NA	NA
Porter	3 405	143 801	0.8	1 874	11.6	1 252	7.8	18 055	13.1	25 301	1 472	11 250	3 478	2 141
Posey	242	22 960	0.8	D	D	219	8.3	2 547	11.7	4 552	956	2 188	NA	NA
Pulaski	193	13 031	0.9	D	D	162	11.7	1 892	16.9	2 777	303	1 460	231	1 724
Putnam	5 424	36 184	0.9	D	D	313	8.5	5 331	17.2	6 145	1 291	2 582	NA	NA
Randolph	329	22 757	0.7	D	D	290	11.1	3 587	17.0	5 338	619	2 546	552	2 569
Ripley	449	27 821	0.9	D	D	264	9.6	3 879	17.0	4 618	791	2 265	438	1 520
Rush	178	15 422	0.7	D	D	177	10.1	2 497	17.6	3 314	365	1 781	625	3 594
St. Joseph	11 272	274 668	1.1	3 863	14.5	2 420	9.1	36 803	16.3	42 049	10 091	16 349	12 239	4 596
Scott	312	20 831	0.7	D	D	253	10.7	3 477	17.2	4 727	738	2 363	769	3 180
Shelby	683	40 831	0.8	551	12.5	417	9.5	5 960	15.9	7 463	1 155	3 596	1 276	2 878
Spencer	368	18 347	0.7	240	11.8	178	8.7	2 512	15.1	3 712	420	1 849	NA	NA
Starke	16	19 374	0.6	D	D	280	12.0	3 545	18.1	4 981	468	2 449	567	2 427
Steuben	1 300	32 701	0.9	D	D	287	8.6	4 847	17.1	6 259	2 245	2 417	955	2 794
Sullivan	2 298	19 439	0.8	D	D	239	11.1	3 089	17.4	3 945	251	2 095	221	1 283
Switzerland	107	8 615	0.6	D	D	84	8.7	1 591	19.3	1 553	123	810	NA	NA
Tippecanoe	14 463	179 497	1.1	2 268	14.1	1 031	6.4	24 100	16.4	19 754	2 930	9 371	5 001	2 894
Tipton	205	13 668	0.7	D	D	165	10.3	1 747	13.5	3 135	303	1 355	237	1 487
Union	67	5 416	0.4	D	D	63	8.7	1 016	17.4	1 232	212	693	NA	NA
Vanderburgh	7 531	201 916	1.3	2 434	14.0	1 829	10.5	21 925	15.1	32 464	7 996	14 136	6 904	3 842
Vermillion	209	14 789	0.8	D	D	198	12.1	2 035	15.3	3 342	236	1 699	145	894
Vigo	9 545	117 196	1.2	1 345	12.9	1 074	10.3	15 336	17.2	18 540	1 459	10 205	NA	NA
Wabash	1 839	31 999	0.9	D	D	384	11.6	4 252	16.3	7 240	2 647	2 828	243	739
Warren	84	6 911	0.6	D	D	73	8.6	1 028	14.5	1 643	129	869	NA	NA
Warrick	726	46 454	0.6	686	12.0	486	8.5	6 510	13.2	9 664	2 173	3 770	897	1 503
Washington	261	23 085	0.6	D	D	257	9.2	4 444	18.8	5 050	1 117	2 388	NA	NA
Wayne	2 614	71 072	1.1	897	13.1	812	11.9	9 977	18.1	14 305	1 554	8 112	2 030	3 028
Wells	472	26 018	0.9	D	D	268	9.6	3 296	14.5	5 037	1 731	2 250	540	1 954
White	307	22 960	0.8	D	D	248	10.3	3 564	18.6	4 949	551	2 548	190	771
Whitley	436	28 871	0.7	D	D	279	8.5	3 705	13.4	5 674	2 701	2 027	NA	NA
IOWA	98 112	3 014 881	1.0	40 572	13.6	27 708	9.3	247 530	10.0	528 332	69 621	299 542	76 648	2 516
Adair	151	7 161	0.8	D	D	111	14.6	533	9.6	1 637	148	1 103	60	781
Adams	114	3 696	0.8	D	D	48	11.8	357	12.0	994	18	715	84	2 085
Allamakee	332	13 184	0.8	D	D	160	10.9	1 545	13.6	3 079	265	1 883	NA	NA
Appanoose	126	12 712	0.9	D	D	191	14.6	1 136	11.6	3 060	346	1 873	309	2 398
Audubon	136	5 302	0.7	D	D	81	13.2	564	12.4	1 504	61	1 122	36	588
Benton	313	19 457	0.5	D	D	218	8.2	1 894	8.6	4 561	757	2 512	215	913
Black Hawk	5 967	139 097	1.2	1 761	13.8	1 102	8.7	11 573	10.8	22 020	3 057	9 947	4 187	3 194
Boone	768	23 366	0.8	D	D	295	11.2	1 822	8.5	5 075	495	2 995	386	1 467
Bremer	1 718	22 812	0.9	D	D	223	9.4	1 464	7.7	4 581	383	2 516	230	947
Buchanan	343	17 781	0.7	D	D	197	9.4	1 928	11.2	3 700	473	2 002	220	1 050
Buena Vista	1 014	20 581	1.1	D	D	187	9.4	2 369	14.6	3 305	182	2 121	395	1 950
Butler	242	12 037	0.6	D	D	188	12.7	1 042	9.3	3 259	320	2 027	11	74
Calhoun	238	8 910	0.8	D	D	136	13.5	772	10.6	2 484	125	1 686	84	869
Carroll	467	22 257	1.1	D	D	242	11.6	1 441	8.9	4 337	334	3 133	151	725
Cass	304	13 777	1.0	D	D	178	12.8	1 129	10.8	3 338	223	2 283	246	1 763
Cedar	324	14 178	0.6	D	D	170	9.4	1 269	8.7	3 305	547	1 775	160	865
Cerro Gordo	1 158	46 969	1.1	524	11.9	501	11.4	3 367	9.7	9 530	240	5 945	1 266	2 867
Cherokee	371	12 037	1.0	D	D	150	12.8	904	10.5	2 658	395	1 659	199	1 648
Chickasaw	183	11 743	0.9	D	D	124	10.1	1 060	11.1	2 623	90	1 805	30	241
Clarke	152	9 228	1.0	D	D	104	11.4	820	11.2	1 771	130	1 099	152	1 637
Clay	234	17 804	1.1	D	D	192	11.5	1 361	10.4	3 523	71	2 457	337	2 022
Clayton	287	16 432	0.8	D	D	192	10.7	1 757	12.9	4 060	642	2 590	61	336
Clinton	852	49 327	1.0	630	12.8	536	10.9	3 715	9.4	9 709	1 134	5 667	1 683	3 427
Crawford	585	16 627	1.0	D	D	168	10.1	1 842	13.9	3 188	207	2 127	104	608
Dallas	516	53 770	0.8	D	D	340	5.9	4 287	7.7	7 825	1 030	3 988	1 238	1 872
Davis	124	7 709	0.7	D	D	84	9.8	1 124	16.3	1 602	124	938	38	434
Decatur	663	7 801	0.8	D	D	100	11.8	946	14.5	1 636	170	1 060	8	95
Delaware	218	15 958	0.8	D	D	159	9.1	1 449	10.4	3 161	542	2 055	135	760
Des Moines	685	43 170	1.2	548	13.5	426	10.5	3 311	10.1	8 426	599	5 129	1 409	3 494
Dickinson	211	16 698	1.0	D	D	190	11.3	1 166	9.2	4 243	145	2 938	180	1 080
Dubuque	4 268	99 499	1.1	1 225	13.2	868	9.4	6 850	9.0	16 781	6 492	9 978	2 214	2 364
Emmet	540	9 984	0.9	D	D	123	11.7	985	12.1	2 081	41	1 501	146	1 417
Fayette	782	19 792	0.9	D	D	250	12.1	1 608	10.3	4 602	473	2 889	259	1 240
Floyd	304	14 970	0.8	D	D	197	12.1	1 388	11.1	3 643	75	2 476	167	1 024

1. Per 1,000 estimated resident population.   2. Data for serious crimes have not been adjusted for underreporting; this may affect comparability between geographic areas and over time.   3. Per 100,000 population estimated by the FBI.

Table B. States and Counties — Crime, Education, Money Income, and Poverty

STATE County	Serious crimes known to police,[1] 2010 (cont.) Rate[2] Violent	Property	Education — School enrollment and attainment, 2006-2010 Enrollment[3] Total	Percent private	Attainment[4] (percent) High school graduate or less	Bachelor's degree or more	Local government expenditures,[5] 2008-2009 Total current expenditures (mil dol)	Current expenditures per student (dollars)	Money income, 2006-2010 Per capita income[6] (dollars)	Households Median income Dollars	Percent change, 2000 to 2006-2010 (constant 2010 dollars)	Percent with income of $200,000 or more	Income and poverty, 2010 Median household income (dollars)	Percent below poverty level All persons	Children under 18 years	Children 5 to 17 years in families
	46	47	48	49	50	51	52	53	54	55	56	57	58	59	60	61
INDIANA—Cont'd																
Pike	NA	NA	2 769	8.2	63.1	8.3	32.0	15 667	20 005	41 222	-6.3	1.1	39 684	14.7	20.1	17.0
Porter	136	2 005	44 743	19.8	44.4	25.2	229.5	8 329	27 922	60 889	-9.4	2.9	56 648	10.9	13.5	12.0
Posey	NA	NA	6 592	16.7	51.7	18.5	42.0	10 575	26 727	57 530	2.8	1.9	56 159	9.8	13.5	11.6
Pulaski	343	1 380	3 511	11.2	60.7	13.6	23.3	10 714	20 491	44 016	-1.9	0.8	41 794	14.2	21.6	19.6
Putnam	NA	NA	10 039	23.5	54.9	17.6	59.6	9 018	20 441	48 992	-0.5	1.1	44 437	13.9	17.6	15.8
Randolph	19	2 550	6 336	7.9	62.0	10.4	43.3	9 004	19 552	40 990	-6.3	0.6	40 806	16.0	26.2	24.3
Ripley	142	1 378	7 319	13.1	61.4	14.8	34.1	9 716	22 025	48 093	-8.3	1.1	45 951	10.7	15.1	13.6
Rush	86	3 507	4 352	8.9	64.5	13.2	22.7	8 431	21 215	46 685	-3.4	1.2	45 464	13.2	20.5	18.4
St. Joseph	383	4 213	79 868	32.1	47.1	25.6	401.9	9 887	23 082	44 644	-12.8	2.3	42 316	15.9	24.1	20.9
Scott	372	2 808	5 492	4.7	69.0	9.9	36.9	8 636	19 414	39 588	-9.8	1.0	39 134	18.8	28.8	26.9
Shelby	83	2 794	10 505	10.8	58.3	15.2	66.2	8 524	26 398	52 292	-5.4	2.6	46 619	12.8	18.9	16.8
Spencer	NA	NA	4 981	16.9	58.7	15.9	29.8	8 410	23 609	52 105	-3.1	1.7	47 726	11.3	15.2	13.0
Starke	133	2 294	5 292	8.0	65.7	11.2	33.3	8 130	17 991	37 480	-20.5	0.5	38 317	18.2	30.2	27.5
Steuben	108	2 685	8 632	21.4	53.3	18.9	38.4	8 907	22 950	47 479	-15.0	1.4	45 431	12.8	19.9	17.3
Sullivan	99	1 184	4 795	11.8	58.4	14.1	31.1	9 640	20 093	44 184	5.8	1.3	42 481	14.7	21.0	18.8
Switzerland	NA	NA	2 231	10.5	69.1	11.4	13.3	8 871	21 214	44 503	-5.3	1.4	42 268	16.3	27.3	26.4
Tippecanoe	212	2 682	68 012	7.8	38.8	35.7	186.2	8 780	22 203	42 632	-12.9	2.1	41 722	20.9	20.1	17.3
Tipton	82	1 406	3 740	11.4	57.4	13.5	22.9	8 032	23 499	51 485	-16.2	1.5	54 171	8.5	14.5	12.1
Union	NA	NA	2 062	8.2	59.1	15.2	15.8	9 760	19 243	43 257	-6.8	0.2	44 337	12.6	20.1	18.5
Vanderburgh	307	3 535	46 133	18.5	47.6	21.8	224.8	9 958	23 945	42 396	-9.1	2.0	41 024	16.9	25.1	22.0
Vermillion	142	753	3 723	6.2	61.3	12.3	24.4	8 681	22 178	41 904	-5.0	1.8	42 613	13.6	20.2	16.8
Vigo	NA	NA	31 004	14.5	49.6	21.3	149.3	9 351	20 398	38 508	-8.4	1.6	39 089	19.1	27.0	25.4
Wabash	36	702	8 103	20.7	59.4	16.3	54.7	10 053	20 475	43 157	-15.7	0.5	42 990	12.2	18.4	16.7
Warren	NA	NA	1 984	11.2	60.9	13.1	11.5	9 009	23 670	49 238	-7.0	3.1	50 349	9.8	16.1	13.8
Warrick	176	1 327	14 816	19.7	42.5	25.6	72.3	7 491	29 737	62 354	0.9	4.2	59 195	7.3	10.4	9.2
Washington	NA	NA	6 809	14.1	66.7	10.5	38.9	8 217	19 278	39 722	-14.4	0.7	39 945	15.9	24.6	22.8
Wayne	263	2 765	16 823	12.4	56.7	15.8	97.4	9 149	21 789	41 123	-6.9	1.4	36 424	20.3	29.8	24.6
Wells	11	1 943	6 720	13.7	53.6	14.0	46.1	9 718	23 169	47 202	-15.2	1.2	45 492	9.6	14.5	12.8
White	69	702	5 701	8.5	57.2	14.5	45.2	8 731	22 323	45 891	-11.0	0.8	43 487	12.2	18.4	16.6
Whitley	NA	NA	8 001	15.3	50.3	16.6	41.2	8 478	24 644	52 129	-9.5	1.4	49 989	9.3	13.4	11.6
IOWA	274	2 243	802 129	16.5	44.5	24.5	4 732.7	9 707	25 335	48 872	-2.2	2.3	48 031	12.5	16.2	14.2
Adair	65	716	1 632	4.8	53.5	13.6	9.4	9 953	23 497	45 202	1.5	1.6	45 540	9.7	14.1	12.7
Adams	645	1 440	834	8.2	54.2	15.6	5.8	10 804	23 549	40 368	4.7	2.1	39 781	14.1	20.7	19.0
Allamakee	NA	NA	3 316	13.3	59.5	13.5	20.9	9 172	21 349	46 623	8.4	0.8	45 881	13.3	22.3	20.9
Appanoose	287	2 111	2 941	6.0	54.3	16.6	19.5	8 886	20 084	34 689	-4.3	1.5	35 352	15.7	24.2	21.7
Audubon	0	588	1 293	4.2	55.3	15.0	8.2	9 184	24 207	42 717	4.7	2.1	45 563	10.0	15.3	13.0
Benton	93	820	6 855	13.3	48.1	17.8	34.1	8 590	25 111	54 726	1.9	1.2	54 283	8.3	11.4	9.9
Black Hawk	423	2 771	39 091	12.0	45.1	24.6	195.5	11 077	23 357	44 178	-6.4	1.8	44 046	18.0	25.2	21.3
Boone	190	1 277	6 494	10.8	46.5	19.8	34.9	9 136	25 998	49 578	-4.0	2.2	51 723	9.4	12.1	10.2
Bremer	297	651	6 878	31.9	42.3	26.5	40.3	8 466	26 522	55 676	7.7	1.8	55 606	7.6	8.3	7.2
Buchanan	43	1 007	5 482	12.8	51.5	18.5	25.3	8 858	23 437	51 961	7.9	1.5	50 026	11.0	16.4	15.8
Buena Vista	262	1 688	5 674	22.2	50.6	22.6	36.6	9 350	21 256	43 182	-3.4	1.9	44 795	13.0	18.6	16.8
Butler	40	34	3 258	4.1	56.4	14.9	16.1	8 609	24 030	47 702	5.0	1.7	49 703	9.5	12.7	11.6
Calhoun	72	796	2 007	2.9	50.6	18.0	20.7	10 613	23 049	41 611	-1.3	2.1	44 859	12.0	17.4	15.9
Carroll	29	697	4 834	28.5	51.1	20.0	27.7	8 817	25 094	47 507	0.6	2.4	49 536	9.1	11.5	10.5
Cass	165	1 598	2 948	6.2	53.7	14.5	25.1	9 725	21 787	40 820	-2.1	1.1	40 867	13.7	20.4	19.0
Cedar	76	789	4 451	5.8	49.6	18.6	28.9	8 507	24 742	54 321	1.7	0.4	55 413	7.3	9.7	8.5
Cerro Gordo	120	2 747	10 447	10.7	39.7	21.2	55.8	8 926	25 463	44 741	-1.5	1.9	43 982	13.0	17.0	14.7
Cherokee	447	1 201	2 533	8.1	49.3	19.2	15.4	8 627	24 507	44 635	0.3	1.2	46 305	9.6	14.3	12.8
Chickasaw	16	225	2 802	7.6	59.0	13.5	19.0	8 756	22 447	41 372	-13.2	1.3	45 083	10.6	15.3	13.8
Clarke	108	1 529	2 224	4.0	59.7	12.9	14.8	8 605	23 271	45 596	4.4	0.8	43 016	12.4	19.1	17.8
Clay	60	1 962	3 763	12.8	47.3	18.5	23.2	9 418	25 398	43 542	-3.9	1.3	44 395	11.3	15.5	13.4
Clayton	39	298	4 017	8.7	56.9	14.9	39.2	18 281	22 303	45 873	6.3	1.2	41 940	12.2	19.3	17.1
Clinton	381	3 046	12 078	13.5	50.1	17.0	75.3	9 078	23 573	46 170	-2.6	1.5	46 577	13.5	18.7	16.8
Crawford	58	550	4 347	10.4	59.7	15.0	30.0	9 245	21 181	44 377	3.3	1.9	45 637	13.1	18.0	16.2
Dallas	191	1 681	16 264	17.6	32.0	40.2	106.7	8 321	33 051	67 037	9.1	5.8	68 568	6.4	7.7	6.8
Davis	217	217	2 092	20.3	53.1	17.0	10.5	8 532	21 970	46 597	12.0	2.0	40 145	17.0	27.8	26.4
Decatur	12	83	2 519	36.4	56.6	17.8	10.0	8 692	18 195	37 138	7.3	1.1	34 250	19.1	26.2	24.9
Delaware	197	563	4 524	18.3	55.8	14.6	25.9	8 656	22 578	47 078	0.0	0.8	45 910	10.1	13.8	12.5
Des Moines	461	3 033	9 370	9.3	47.2	17.6	57.6	8 887	22 555	41 937	-10.0	1.0	42 191	15.3	24.2	21.9
Dickinson	72	1 008	3 078	6.7	40.2	27.2	22.9	8 673	29 459	50 174	1.5	3.1	49 295	9.1	12.7	10.3
Dubuque	202	2 162	25 042	36.2	48.1	25.3	130.3	9 233	25 045	48 573	-3.1	2.7	49 493	10.7	13.6	12.0
Emmet	214	1 204	2 399	7.7	47.2	18.1	16.4	9 572	24 371	42 286	0.3	2.0	41 519	12.6	18.7	17.8
Fayette	192	1 049	5 353	20.4	54.6	16.5	35.4	9 146	21 566	41 055	-0.1	1.0	41 163	13.3	19.1	17.5
Floyd	61	963	3 620	10.4	52.4	14.9	23.5	8 949	21 416	39 467	-11.5	1.2	42 233	15.2	22.4	18.7

1. Data for serious crimes have not been adjusted for underreporting; this may affect comparability between geographic areas and over time.   2. Per 100,000 population estimated by the FBI.   3. All persons 3 years old and over enrolled in nursery school through college.   4. Persons 25 years old and over.   5. Elementary and secondary education expenditures.   6. Based on population estimated by the American Community Survey, 2006-2010.

Table B. States and Counties — Personal Income

STATE County	Personal income, 2009												
			Per capita[1]					Transfer payments (mil dol)					
									Government payments to individuals				
	Total (mil dol)	Percent change, 2008–2009	Dollars	Rank	Wages and salaries[2] (mil dol)	Proprietors' income (mil dol)	Dividends, interest, and rent (mil dol)	Total	Total	Social Security	Medical payments	Income maintenance	Unemployment insurance
	62	63	64	65	66	67	68	69	70	71	72	73	74
INDIANA—Cont'd													
Pike	369	-1.3	30 126	1 946	189	11	48	103	101	39	43	7	5
Porter	6 725	-2.6	41 110	380	2 724	273	973	988	958	408	345	61	76
Posey	978	-2.8	37 602	680	547	76	153	171	166	70	63	11	10
Pulaski	415	-8.1	30 466	1 870	194	45	74	100	97	41	37	7	7
Putnam	1 115	-2.7	30 262	1 921	478	64	138	223	216	91	75	15	18
Randolph	786	-0.3	30 578	1 846	303	82	102	205	200	80	78	16	15
Ripley	812	-2.0	29 595	2 073	633	33	125	197	192	68	86	13	14
Rush	595	-5.1	34 661	1 073	201	83	79	127	124	48	50	10	9
St. Joseph	9 289	-4.2	34 712	1 063	6 055	1 047	1 430	1 835	1 787	640	700	183	142
Scott	657	1.5	27 829	2 431	270	17	64	199	195	66	83	22	13
Shelby	1 488	-1.8	33 431	1 271	754	66	179	302	294	112	118	22	24
Spencer	665	-0.2	33 169	1 309	309	51	84	136	132	54	51	9	9
Starke	580	-2.6	24 640	2 902	161	29	73	187	183	72	67	17	15
Steuben	988	-2.0	29 410	2 116	531	65	173	234	228	94	79	16	23
Sullivan	576	-1.1	27 226	2 527	234	36	72	163	159	57	71	13	8
Switzerland	281	0.6	29 017	2 194	97	12	25	63	61	23	25	5	4
Tippecanoe	5 048	-0.5	30 056	1 966	4 034	395	806	814	783	298	260	74	72
Tipton	547	-5.9	34 432	1 107	176	45	73	117	114	51	40	6	10
Union	240	0.7	34 131	1 150	55	33	28	49	48	17	20	4	3
Vanderburgh	6 659	-1.5	37 955	647	5 383	650	1 156	1 359	1 327	474	563	124	72
Vermillion	527	0.7	32 618	1 398	254	41	64	128	125	49	47	9	9
Vigo	3 221	0.1	30 398	1 887	2 385	191	523	827	808	266	348	82	49
Wabash	1 019	-3.1	31 309	1 692	472	78	169	276	270	108	107	17	20
Warren	273	-4.2	32 209	1 481	79	47	34	54	52	24	16	3	5
Warrick	2 296	0.4	39 237	514	748	106	350	356	345	149	130	20	23
Washington	794	-0.5	28 627	2 273	228	41	90	198	193	71	74	19	16
Wayne	2 019	-1.7	29 881	2 006	1 272	111	319	585	573	209	238	51	38
Wells	860	-2.8	31 191	1 714	459	50	132	176	171	75	60	10	15
White	781	-3.5	33 307	1 293	344	67	123	193	188	73	78	12	13
Whitley	1 030	-2.9	31 341	1 686	509	35	140	212	206	86	73	11	21
IOWA	113 236	-1.0	37 647	X	70 446	11 729	19 066	20 294	19 746	7 464	7 725	1 666	1 117
Adair	281	-2.2	38 223	617	103	59	47	51	50	21	20	3	3
Adams	147	4.5	37 450	694	49	33	25	34	33	13	16	2	1
Allamakee	422	-5.1	29 273	2 138	182	56	83	99	97	40	38	7	6
Appanoose	361	1.7	28 431	2 315	167	31	59	113	110	40	46	11	6
Audubon	262	-3.5	43 402	260	70	91	45	45	44	20	18	2	2
Benton	974	-1.3	36 444	824	241	134	143	159	154	67	56	10	10
Black Hawk	4 582	0.6	35 445	961	3 585	314	763	905	882	321	349	93	46
Boone	1 032	2.1	39 585	480	443	92	158	236	231	70	123	13	10
Bremer	903	0.6	38 502	577	429	67	158	161	156	67	65	7	8
Buchanan	682	-1.0	32 620	1 397	251	81	121	135	132	53	54	9	8
Buena Vista	706	-2.8	36 030	882	410	128	120	127	123	47	49	10	5
Butler	550	-2.0	38 341	594	144	109	86	107	104	45	42	6	6
Calhoun	388	-5.0	40 145	440	119	101	67	80	79	35	33	4	2
Carroll	808	-1.8	39 075	531	475	115	165	149	145	58	68	8	4
Cass	540	0.4	39 269	512	234	105	97	116	114	45	50	9	5
Cedar	694	-0.5	38 535	574	225	91	115	106	103	48	36	6	7
Cerro Gordo	1 657	0.1	37 992	642	1 091	149	292	352	344	132	135	29	18
Cherokee	472	-2.1	41 389	369	216	104	91	86	84	37	35	4	3
Chickasaw	428	-2.7	35 578	944	193	58	83	88	86	36	34	5	7
Clarke	274	-1.1	30 156	1 942	162	34	37	65	63	23	26	6	4
Clay	635	-4.0	38 225	615	376	110	116	120	117	49	44	8	9
Clayton	564	-3.2	32 275	1 462	266	53	123	129	126	52	49	7	10
Clinton	1 747	0.4	35 708	928	1 028	147	263	420	411	138	155	36	21
Crawford	623	-0.5	37 938	648	322	145	92	110	107	42	46	8	3
Dallas	2 747	1.6	44 337	224	1 643	151	392	254	243	109	82	18	15
Davis	212	-3.3	24 780	2 885	74	20	33	57	55	21	21	4	5
Decatur	203	1.4	24 656	2 899	79	17	31	61	59	21	24	6	2
Delaware	569	-3.9	33 080	1 324	254	56	110	106	103	42	39	7	8
Des Moines	1 427	0.2	34 754	1 053	942	143	251	343	335	123	129	33	18
Dickinson	709	-2.8	42 674	287	319	88	196	129	126	60	45	6	9
Dubuque	3 317	-0.8	35 635	937	2 412	201	689	633	616	240	245	49	38
Emmet	352	-3.1	34 340	1 120	160	60	55	86	84	29	34	5	6
Fayette	636	-2.6	31 533	1 637	266	72	117	169	165	59	63	13	11
Floyd	540	-1.9	33 927	1 181	230	69	104	131	128	52	51	9	9

1. Based on the resident population estimated as of July 1 of the year shown.　　2. Includes supplements to wages and salaries.

Table B. States and Counties — **Earnings, Social Security, and Housing**

STATE County	Earnings, 2009									Social Security beneficiaries, December 2010		Housing units, 2010		
			Percent by selected industries											
			Goods-related[1]		Service-related and health							Supplemental Security Income recipients, December 2010		Percent change, 2000–2010
	Total (mil dol)	Farm	Total	Manu-facturing	Information and professional and technical services	Retail trade	Finance, insurance, and real estate	Health care and social services	Govern-ment	Number	Rate[2]		Total	
	75	76	77	78	79	80	81	82	83	84	85	86	87	88
INDIANA—Cont'd														
Pike	200	2.2	D	4.0	D	3.3	D	D	15.5	3 110	242	269	5 735	2.2
Porter	2 997	0.6	32.6	24.3	6.4	6.8	3.3	13.6	12.4	29 145	177	1 793	66 179	14.9
Posey	623	5.8	50.6	44.6	4.9	4.1	2.0	D	10.1	5 290	204	337	11 207	1.2
Pulaski	239	12.0	D	27.5	2.4	4.9	3.6	D	21.8	3 215	240	232	6 060	2.4
Putnam	542	3.1	22.9	18.6	4.0	6.1	3.3	D	24.6	7 150	188	440	14 706	8.9
Randolph	385	9.3	D	29.3	D	3.8	1.9	D	16.4	6 135	234	483	11 743	-0.3
Ripley	666	2.6	24.3	19.7	5.0	3.5	5.6	8.9	10.7	5 355	186	377	11 952	14.0
Rush	283	20.6	D	18.4	D	5.3	3.7	4.6	20.1	3 835	221	292	7 508	2.3
St. Joseph	7 102	0.4	23.9	19.3	D	6.0	6.0	15.2	11.1	47 900	179	5 279	114 849	7.3
Scott	287	1.6	D	33.6	2.5	9.4	3.5	6.2	24.4	5 685	235	883	10 440	7.2
Shelby	820	6.2	36.3	29.1	2.9	7.2	2.3	D	17.3	8 625	194	632	19 080	8.2
Spencer	359	4.5	25.3	19.6	D	3.7	1.8	D	13.7	4 230	202	296	8 872	6.5
Starke	190	7.9	22.2	18.9	2.4	9.0	2.1	D	24.8	5 855	251	606	10 962	7.5
Steuben	596	1.7	36.7	32.4	4.3	8.7	3.2	D	13.3	7 180	210	420	19 377	11.8
Sullivan	270	5.3	16.0	11.5	4.4	6.1	2.4	5.2	34.1	4 615	215	420	8 939	1.5
Switzerland	109	4.5	D	1.7	1.8	2.5	1.5	4.3	21.3	1 845	174	192	4 969	17.6
Tippecanoe	4 428	0.8	D	21.2	5.4	5.7	4.7	15.7	29.2	22 450	130	1 945	71 096	21.9
Tipton	221	15.8	22.7	16.8	4.2	7.8	2.9	D	22.7	3 600	226	169	6 998	2.2
Union	88	20.2	13.9	10.3	D	5.5	D	D	25.0	1 510	201	112	3 239	5.3
Vanderburgh	6 033	0.3	28.1	15.0	7.3	6.3	3.9	17.2	9.7	36 795	205	4 470	83 003	8.8
Vermillion	295	6.7	D	27.1	3.6	6.7	2.1	7.6	12.6	3 820	236	276	7 488	1.1
Vigo	2 577	0.2	24.0	18.7	4.0	7.4	4.5	17.9	19.7	21 295	197	3 039	46 006	1.8
Wabash	550	4.1	30.3	24.8	4.1	6.8	5.1	D	18.2	8 305	253	611	14 171	1.0
Warren	127	35.7	D	11.1	D	4.0	D	9.4	16.0	1 870	220	94	3 680	5.8
Warrick	855	1.2	34.4	26.0	5.6	4.9	5.8	16.5	12.6	11 075	186	655	24 203	17.8
Washington	269	6.4	D	21.8	5.0	7.1	3.7	6.2	29.4	6 165	218	659	12 220	9.2
Wayne	1 384	2.2	25.1	22.0	D	7.9	4.6	D	17.0	16 440	239	1 953	31 242	2.5
Wells	509	4.8	D	25.2	D	5.5	3.4	13.7	14.1	5 695	206	295	11 659	6.3
White	410	13.6	D	20.4	D	10.5	2.9	D	20.0	5 765	234	286	12 970	7.3
Whitley	544	4.3	46.9	42.4	D	5.8	2.2	D	14.3	6 515	196	284	14 281	13.8
IOWA	82 175	6.3	21.1	15.5	6.6	6.4	9.4	10.5	17.2	584 113	192	47 687	1 336 417	8.4
Adair	162	27.2	D	10.8	2.2	4.3	3.2	D	14.3	1 755	228	86	3 698	0.2
Adams	82	30.5	D	8.5	D	4.2	D	16.6	14.9	1 075	267	96	2 010	-4.7
Allamakee	238	7.4	D	15.9	2.5	7.3	4.1	D	20.3	3 455	241	202	7 617	6.7
Appanoose	198	1.7	D	17.3	3.8	8.9	3.6	D	19.8	3 360	261	466	6 633	-1.0
Audubon	161	39.4	9.3	5.8	D	3.5	D	4.7	12.3	1 675	274	65	2 972	-0.8
Benton	376	10.8	D	9.4	3.1	7.0	3.7	D	20.3	5 245	201	295	11 095	6.9
Black Hawk	3 898	1.1	31.7	27.8	5.9	6.5	5.7	13.7	16.2	24 550	187	3 072	55 887	8.0
Boone	535	11.1	D	6.8	D	5.9	2.6	8.1	26.8	5 520	210	367	11 756	7.2
Bremer	496	8.4	D	20.9	3.1	6.0	12.9	D	18.3	5 055	208	174	9 915	6.2
Buchanan	332	15.1	D	16.1	3.0	7.6	4.3	D	22.2	4 150	198	311	8 968	3.1
Buena Vista	538	16.6	27.6	24.7	D	6.2	3.6	D	15.3	3 645	180	233	8 237	1.1
Butler	253	32.1	D	16.4	2.2	3.4	2.5	D	13.3	3 580	241	169	6 682	1.6
Calhoun	219	36.7	4.5	1.9	2.0	5.1	D	D	17.4	2 705	280	127	5 108	-2.1
Carroll	590	12.2	D	11.1	3.9	7.4	8.8	D	10.4	4 690	225	262	9 376	3.9
Cass	339	21.8	D	8.5	D	7.2	3.9	D	22.6	3 670	263	331	6 591	0.0
Cedar	316	16.6	18.4	11.8	6.1	5.3	3.1	D	16.4	3 695	200	143	8 064	6.5
Cerro Gordo	1 239	4.9	D	14.1	5.7	8.2	5.7	22.9	12.9	10 465	237	761	22 163	3.1
Cherokee	320	25.7	D	14.8	3.1	5.6	2.8	D	17.1	2 865	237	144	5 777	-1.2
Chickasaw	250	13.4	D	21.5	D	6.8	3.0	D	13.0	2 940	236	138	5 679	1.5
Clarke	196	5.3	D	26.3	D	7.9	3.0	D	18.7	1 980	213	158	4 086	3.9
Clay	487	16.4	D	11.6	4.9	10.6	3.4	9.4	17.8	3 910	235	233	8 062	3.0
Clayton	319	7.9	D	11.8	3.0	6.0	4.4	D	21.1	4 485	247	256	8 999	4.4
Clinton	1 175	5.4	D	27.0	2.9	6.5	3.8	13.1	11.3	10 805	220	1 116	21 733	0.7
Crawford	467	24.6	29.9	25.9	D	4.8	2.3	5.3	14.3	3 555	208	193	6 943	-0.2
Dallas	1 795	4.9	D	5.4	5.9	6.8	35.2	8.9	9.3	8 355	126	417	27 260	64.7
Davis	94	-3.9	D	13.4	4.3	7.9	3.4	D	30.4	1 805	206	141	3 600	2.0
Decatur	96	7.4	D	5.0	D	5.0	D	D	28.2	1 820	215	214	3 834	0.0
Delaware	310	4.0	D	21.2	D	6.3	5.3	D	20.2	3 530	199	219	8 028	4.5
Des Moines	1 085	2.6	D	25.7	3.9	8.1	3.3	16.0	13.1	9 315	231	940	18 535	-0.6
Dickinson	407	9.0	D	21.4	3.6	9.7	5.5	7.8	14.8	4 615	277	188	12 849	13.0
Dubuque	2 612	0.8	D	18.9	8.2	7.4	7.9	15.9	9.5	18 820	201	1 472	38 951	9.7
Emmet	221	17.5	20.9	15.6	4.2	6.9	2.9	D	18.6	2 305	224	120	4 758	-2.7
Fayette	338	14.5	D	8.0	2.7	6.5	3.8	D	17.7	5 025	241	463	9 558	0.5
Floyd	299	13.2	D	25.2	3.3	6.1	4.6	D	17.9	4 100	251	315	7 526	2.8

1. Includes mining, construction, and manufacturing.   2. Per 1,000 resident population enumerated in the 2010 census.

STATE County	Housing units, 2006–2010								Civilian labor force, 2010				Civilian employment,[5] 2006–2010		
	Occupied units										Unemployment			Percent	
	Owner-occupied				Renter-occupied										
				Median owner cost as a percent of income											
	Total	Percent	Median value[1]	With a mortgage	Without a mortgage	Median rent[2]	Median rent as a percent of income	Substandard units[3] (percent)	Total	Percent change, 2009–2010	Total	Rate[4]	Total	Management, business, science and arts	Construction, production, and maintenance occupations
	89	90	91	92	93	94	95	96	97	98	99	100	101	102	103
INDIANA—Cont'd															
Pike	5 293	84.3	80 700	20.9	12.3	528	28.0	1.4	5 734	-4.4	513	8.9	5 551	21.5	46.1
Porter	61 370	77.9	164 500	21.6	12.8	791	28.8	2.0	81 418	-2.4	7 265	8.9	77 701	32.4	27.4
Posey	10 035	84.8	120 500	18.5	10.8	535	28.1	2.0	13 114	-0.7	1 023	7.8	13 091	28.3	34.4
Pulaski	5 105	78.8	97 900	21.3	11.7	584	31.9	3.4	6 754	1.0	627	9.3	5 850	29.8	37.1
Putnam	12 785	77.9	119 800	22.3	11.7	682	29.9	1.7	16 946	-3.2	1 883	11.1	16 260	29.2	30.8
Randolph	10 369	77.0	80 100	21.5	11.9	564	26.6	2.1	12 647	-0.9	1 483	11.7	11 625	26.3	39.2
Ripley	10 717	78.2	138 200	23.2	12.3	659	25.7	2.3	13 784	-0.8	1 550	11.2	13 824	23.9	38.0
Rush	6 684	74.0	106 800	22.5	11.7	566	27.1	0.8	9 102	0.5	938	10.3	8 021	25.4	37.2
St. Joseph	100 540	71.5	116 300	21.8	12.1	683	29.1	1.6	127 457	-0.7	14 620	11.5	122 769	33.0	23.9
Scott	9 271	76.0	96 600	23.6	11.8	648	31.8	2.4	10 814	-2.9	1 347	12.5	10 292	22.5	41.6
Shelby	17 196	74.3	126 400	21.6	11.7	671	24.8	1.2	23 099	-2.5	2 302	10.0	21 576	27.3	34.3
Spencer	8 102	83.5	111 600	19.8	10.7	521	23.9	2.7	10 321	-0.6	925	9.0	10 220	25.3	38.2
Starke	8 992	79.8	98 200	25.2	13.2	598	31.2	1.7	10 514	-1.9	1 356	12.9	9 217	21.0	41.9
Steuben	13 944	79.0	121 700	22.6	11.9	636	27.6	1.8	15 919	-2.4	1 971	12.4	17 310	25.6	32.4
Sullivan	8 033	77.1	77 000	19.7	11.4	525	25.1	1.9	8 760	-0.9	921	10.5	8 771	27.1	32.4
Switzerland	4 060	81.1	119 800	23.5	11.6	611	21.8	3.9	5 623	1.2	446	7.9	4 732	19.7	34.6
Tippecanoe	64 093	55.8	128 900	21.8	10.0	729	35.7	1.7	82 345	-1.1	7 473	9.1	81 638	39.2	20.6
Tipton	6 651	78.5	113 500	20.9	12.2	616	22.1	1.3	7 169	0.2	812	11.3	7 541	27.6	34.6
Union	2 933	79.0	112 600	23.7	13.6	594	27.8	1.5	3 522	-0.3	364	10.3	3 651	26.8	31.0
Vanderburgh	73 973	65.1	111 700	21.2	12.0	659	31.6	2.1	91 011	0.9	7 931	8.7	87 315	29.2	25.5
Vermillion	6 639	78.3	77 000	20.3	11.5	564	28.6	2.5	7 896	-0.4	1 003	12.7	7 303	23.8	33.8
Vigo	40 490	65.8	89 900	20.1	12.4	605	30.5	1.9	50 719	0.5	5 671	11.2	46 995	30.8	24.7
Wabash	13 055	78.0	96 400	20.9	11.6	556	27.5	2.0	16 037	-2.2	1 784	11.1	15 064	28.3	35.1
Warren	3 304	77.7	102 600	22.3	11.7	585	27.6	0.9	4 568	-5.1	428	9.4	3 887	29.6	36.1
Warrick	22 093	83.8	140 200	20.8	10.7	714	28.2	1.7	31 082	1.5	2 415	7.8	28 952	33.6	24.2
Washington	10 810	79.2	100 200	23.2	12.7	512	25.5	3.3	13 505	-4.9	1 421	10.5	12 414	23.8	38.5
Wayne	27 953	68.6	99 700	21.7	12.1	590	28.6	1.9	31 158	-4.6	3 893	12.5	30 892	28.8	30.3
Wells	10 728	79.0	110 100	21.4	10.0	563	26.1	1.4	13 810	-4.7	1 319	9.6	13 337	26.7	33.0
White	10 065	77.6	111 000	22.5	12.4	664	29.1	3.0	12 205	-1.1	1 303	10.7	11 820	26.2	33.7
Whitley	13 246	83.2	123 500	22.1	11.3	562	30.0	1.2	17 149	-4.0	1 804	10.5	16 315	25.5	38.0
IOWA	1 215 954	73.2	119 200	21.3	12.0	617	27.3	1.8	1 669 841	0.3	104 823	6.3	1 553 594	33.1	26.1
Adair	3 409	75.8	93 800	21.7	13.0	513	23.7	2.3	4 216	0.8	225	5.3	3 844	29.0	35.5
Adams	1 764	79.0	81 200	18.8	13.8	401	25.4	2.6	2 080	-3.0	109	5.2	2 156	32.3	31.1
Allamakee	5 807	79.7	105 200	22.7	12.3	484	19.8	2.7	7 740	3.6	641	8.3	7 284	26.4	37.3
Appanoose	5 573	74.5	72 400	23.3	14.1	516	29.3	2.8	6 101	-1.7	455	7.5	5 780	30.5	30.7
Audubon	2 700	79.9	72 900	19.5	11.2	445	19.4	0.4	3 248	-0.8	194	6.0	3 128	33.5	27.9
Benton	10 200	80.9	128 900	21.9	12.0	527	23.3	1.2	14 704	1.1	943	6.4	13 151	28.8	33.8
Black Hawk	51 822	69.0	118 600	20.5	11.7	617	31.9	1.5	74 564	0.5	4 480	6.0	64 888	30.1	26.1
Boone	10 801	75.3	115 800	21.7	13.3	572	23.6	1.9	15 456	-1.6	870	5.6	13 936	29.8	29.4
Bremer	9 397	82.1	132 800	20.9	10.9	584	24.0	1.4	13 765	-1.6	687	5.0	12 447	35.7	24.8
Buchanan	8 212	77.9	113 400	21.0	11.2	550	23.1	3.4	10 987	-1.3	701	6.4	10 417	29.5	34.5
Buena Vista	7 551	69.3	87 600	19.6	11.0	555	22.8	4.2	10 845	2.2	538	5.0	10 415	27.4	37.7
Butler	6 059	82.2	90 900	19.2	11.4	537	22.0	1.8	8 502	0.8	499	5.9	7 311	27.0	34.7
Calhoun	4 316	79.7	70 700	18.5	11.4	470	20.0	0.3	5 166	-2.0	276	5.3	4 204	32.4	22.1
Carroll	8 661	75.0	106 700	19.8	10.0	465	25.9	0.9	12 259	-0.7	515	4.2	11 070	29.1	27.6
Cass	6 000	71.1	82 600	20.3	12.9	520	25.5	1.1	7 574	-0.5	479	6.3	7 111	28.0	30.1
Cedar	7 547	79.5	125 900	21.5	12.4	605	21.4	1.0	11 368	-0.2	602	5.3	10 187	31.0	31.6
Cerro Gordo	19 839	71.6	107 900	20.7	11.2	565	26.2	1.6	25 115	-0.9	1 727	6.9	23 275	30.1	28.0
Cherokee	5 373	75.6	77 500	20.7	10.8	471	20.8	0.1	6 763	3.1	319	4.7	6 362	26.4	32.9
Chickasaw	5 328	84.5	93 800	21.1	11.9	468	22.7	1.9	6 672	-3.1	489	7.3	6 027	29.6	39.0
Clarke	3 511	78.0	92 400	19.5	15.7	468	22.5	1.7	4 838	-1.3	375	7.8	4 602	26.8	31.4
Clay	7 459	70.6	98 500	20.7	10.8	482	25.8	1.0	9 610	0.6	555	5.8	8 816	25.7	28.4
Clayton	7 684	77.3	96 500	22.8	11.9	465	21.2	2.7	9 940	0.3	759	7.6	9 323	26.6	37.6
Clinton	20 074	75.2	106 100	21.1	12.6	535	26.6	1.0	27 832	-0.7	1 901	6.8	24 366	27.8	32.8
Crawford	6 475	79.5	81 500	21.7	10.6	472	25.4	3.4	9 510	0.2	421	4.4	8 257	22.2	43.8
Dallas	23 973	77.6	176 600	21.4	11.6	688	24.7	1.2	34 706	1.9	1 775	5.1	33 340	44.7	17.4
Davis	3 122	82.7	101 400	20.3	12.4	483	19.2	4.9	3 955	-1.6	313	7.9	3 923	32.9	38.1
Decatur	3 248	68.3	69 300	22.5	13.0	507	30.0	1.8	4 113	-0.4	277	6.7	4 078	32.8	29.6
Delaware	7 336	80.7	113 700	22.4	12.6	481	21.7	0.8	10 735	-0.2	637	5.9	9 269	28.7	36.2
Des Moines	16 862	73.5	90 400	21.7	12.7	578	26.8	1.7	20 776	-1.0	1 577	7.6	18 676	27.9	31.9
Dickinson	8 103	78.3	153 000	22.9	12.2	535	25.8	0.8	9 381	0.3	637	6.8	8 970	31.7	27.3
Dubuque	36 787	74.7	136 800	21.3	12.4	584	27.0	1.3	53 627	2.8	3 231	6.0	49 193	33.5	24.0
Emmet	4 286	76.6	78 600	18.5	11.9	575	28.6	2.1	5 758	-1.5	417	7.2	5 462	25.5	33.0
Fayette	8 474	78.5	81 200	21.8	12.5	481	24.0	1.5	10 875	0.3	800	7.4	10 161	28.9	33.6
Floyd	6 779	74.5	89 200	19.9	12.2	425	26.3	1.5	8 359	-1.8	613	7.3	7 850	28.5	35.2

1. Specified owner-occupied units.   2. Specified renter-occupied units. A value of 10.0 represents 10 percent or less.   3. Overcrowded or lacking complete plumbing facilities.   4. Percent of civilian labor force.   5. Persons 16 years old and over.

Table B. States and Counties — Nonfarm Employment and Agriculture

	Private nonfarm establishments, employment and payroll, 2009									Agriculture, 2007			
		Employment						Annual payroll		Farms			
											Percent with:		
STATE County	Number of establishments	Total	Health care and social assistance	Manufacturing	Retail trade	Finance and insurance	Professional, scientific, and technical services	Total (mil dol)	Average per employee (dollars)	Number	Fewer than 50 acres	500 acres or more	Farm operators whose principal occupation is farming (percent)
	104	105	106	107	108	109	110	111	112	113	114	115	116

INDIANA—Cont'd

	104	105	106	107	108	109	110	111	112	113	114	115	116
Pike	187	2 517	358	166	278	D	26	113	44 833	334	43.4	12.6	34.7
Porter	3 471	48 317	5 307	9 620	7 140	1 192	2 177	1 618	33 487	517	53.4	13.7	39.5
Posey	513	7 858	601	1 867	749	101	366	357	45 416	438	39.3	24.7	57.3
Pulaski	328	3 575	648	1 177	472	D	D	113	31 566	552	37.9	23.7	49.5
Putnam	705	11 003	1 883	1 902	1 335	290	183	281	25 516	843	54.9	10.2	40.1
Randolph	497	5 589	749	2 202	622	162	105	170	30 397	784	43.5	15.4	51.3
Ripley	643	9 620	1 005	3 006	938	490	D	426	44 243	873	43.5	8.4	38.1
Rush	388	4 063	495	D	511	119	111	119	29 179	607	33.1	22.1	58.5
St. Joseph	6 038	115 156	18 367	14 371	14 753	4 259	5 269	4 116	35 744	712	55.2	11.9	43.1
Scott	435	5 822	962	1 794	1 090	155	152	156	26 860	394	57.1	6.9	32.7
Shelby	918	14 951	1 922	3 959	1 594	220	309	495	33 099	636	45.9	18.9	48.6
Spencer	409	5 194	369	963	898	266	117	164	31 610	632	37.3	10.9	39.7
Starke	327	2 998	396	813	750	79	54	75	24 879	640	53.9	14.1	33.3
Steuben	982	12 767	1 282	3 632	2 242	232	164	328	25 660	719	51.9	6.4	29.5
Sullivan	358	3 726	D	617	608	D	127	109	29 180	447	35.1	23.0	51.5
Switzerland	131	1 748	155	D	85	39	D	50	28 404	374	39.8	3.5	38.8
Tippecanoe	3 277	59 352	8 662	13 141	9 317	2 890	2 315	1 975	33 280	757	54.2	13.5	41.0
Tipton	318	3 081	D	667	442	D	D	103	33 392	458	44.5	21.2	50.2
Union	125	881	143	D	212	38	D	23	25 896	233	26.2	21.5	60.1
Vanderburgh	5 024	108 423	18 468	12 404	12 979	5 408	3 840	3 701	34 139	335	54.9	11.9	45.7
Vermillion	281	4 403	D	855	615	D	D	211	47 840	293	39.9	22.5	45.7
Vigo	2 577	46 392	9 194	8 523	6 921	1 280	1 124	1 481	31 913	518	59.7	11.6	44.4
Wabash	747	10 712	2 232	2 530	1 586	327	341	292	27 286	850	46.5	13.6	41.4
Warren	127	1 114	D	D	99	33	D	35	31 009	391	35.0	24.0	50.6
Warrick	1 102	12 594	2 567	D	1 566	677	519	462	36 722	413	51.1	14.8	32.2
Washington	463	4 360	689	1 384	717	D	125	114	26 142	893	40.3	9.9	43.0
Wayne	1 572	25 353	5 144	5 500	3 861	901	482	790	31 148	894	45.7	9.6	38.0
Wells	632	10 351	1 495	2 431	1 227	192	233	295	28 467	701	46.9	16.3	43.2
White	647	6 371	940	1 649	1 100	218	111	192	30 167	646	43.3	27.4	56.8
Whitley	674	10 593	1 187	4 252	1 538	271	190	316	29 839	809	55.6	8.2	32.8
IOWA	80 971	1 283 769	205 387	203 998	177 640	93 462	47 310	43 832	34 144	92 856	28.6	20.8	52.4
Adair	176	1 591	294	D	255	D	40	43	27 329	766	22.5	23.8	54.7
Adams	121	886	D	D	160	D	23	24	26 965	610	17.0	21.3	48.2
Allamakee	405	4 105	1 008	732	610	210	78	107	26 029	1 032	24.6	16.4	47.5
Appanoose	335	3 527	741	902	683	130	75	92	26 076	731	24.5	14.9	36.7
Audubon	180	1 165	296	142	210	57	D	33	28 260	666	29.9	25.4	51.5
Benton	576	4 417	782	682	781	196	78	125	28 291	1 251	28.0	21.1	52.4
Black Hawk	3 175	63 591	12 055	13 172	8 936	2 817	2 839	2 197	34 549	942	31.8	19.4	51.5
Boone	569	6 833	1 624	721	1 032	205	D	197	28 767	925	35.4	22.3	48.7
Bremer	604	8 387	1 662	1 942	1 231	802	201	271	32 327	995	34.1	14.0	51.3
Buchanan	501	5 662	1 280	1 148	977	239	D	154	27 124	1 174	33.6	19.3	52.7
Buena Vista	590	8 772	1 358	2 935	1 164	480	161	256	29 202	924	26.4	30.7	63.2
Butler	342	2 452	500	613	358	128	70	70	28 484	1 214	36.9	18.5	50.2
Calhoun	283	2 384	690	114	404	135	D	58	24 307	845	31.1	29.6	53.1
Carroll	908	11 121	2 280	1 560	1 730	826	231	332	29 894	978	25.8	24.0	62.0
Cass	484	4 706	1 084	D	938	235	141	132	28 045	763	20.3	28.4	51.5
Cedar	478	4 398	679	691	638	D	102	119	27 087	1 036	30.2	20.5	54.0
Cerro Gordo	1 435	22 705	5 084	3 472	3 902	1 183	622	724	31 897	844	32.5	29.3	54.6
Cherokee	372	4 214	956	828	661	176	75	127	30 115	840	23.1	25.7	59.0
Chickasaw	398	3 797	539	1 298	457	137	53	106	27 871	1 037	32.1	16.7	53.5
Clarke	201	3 424	570	D	603	92	54	82	24 033	690	22.3	14.3	45.5
Clay	628	7 936	1 518	1 230	1 669	262	179	219	27 628	798	24.8	28.6	57.9
Clayton	530	5 245	1 112	687	731	187	D	140	26 610	1 655	24.8	13.1	50.2
Clinton	1 215	23 421	3 901	4 641	2 743	555	382	731	31 197	1 314	31.1	18.3	51.8
Crawford	454	6 292	993	2 398	890	196	107	196	31 103	855	24.0	26.9	57.5
Dallas	1 492	26 494	2 128	D	4 921	D	1 230	980	36 982	912	38.0	20.0	46.3
Davis	169	1 436	422	211	316	45	40	37	25 753	910	22.7	10.7	40.2
Decatur	141	1 984	410	D	218	23	33	39	19 478	738	24.4	17.6	45.5
Delaware	505	5 316	944	1 464	792	267	111	149	27 954	1 470	31.3	12.5	59.6
Des Moines	1 126	19 383	3 472	4 087	3 320	581	360	631	32 556	646	31.0	18.0	47.7
Dickinson	767	7 422	817	2 099	1 132	476	138	226	30 492	566	26.1	27.7	52.8
Dubuque	2 745	52 354	7 666	8 499	7 280	2 793	1 851	1 721	32 879	1 483	26.0	11.1	53.1
Emmet	331	3 514	702	1 072	486	131	89	98	27 922	532	26.7	33.8	68.4
Fayette	591	5 802	1 329	644	827	218	138	140	24 138	1 398	27.3	17.6	54.9
Floyd	425	4 317	1 000	D	733	201	D	131	30 285	991	33.4	20.0	51.5

Table B. States and Counties — Agriculture

STATE County	Acreage (1,000)	Percent change, 2002–2007	Average size of farm	Total irrigated (1,000)	Total cropland (1,000)	Value of land and buildings, Average per farm	Value of land and buildings, Average per acre	Value of machinery and equipment, average per farm (dollars)	Value of products sold, Total (mil dol)	Value of products sold, Average per farm (dollars)	Crops	Livestock and poultry products	$10,000 or more	$100,000 or more	Govt payments Total ($1,000)	Govt payments Percent of farms
	117	118	119	120	121	122	123	124	125	126	127	128	129	130	131	132
INDIANA—Cont'd																
Pike	74	-2.6	220	0.0	58.8	614 145	2 787	76 570	30.6	91 567	74.5	25.5	41.0	18.6	1 221	64.7
Porter	115	-21.2	223	8.9	106.1	926 001	4 161	99 668	53.6	103 649	89.6	10.4	44.7	21.3	2 067	58.0
Posey	204	6.3	466	8.8	186.8	1 419 223	3 047	202 096	97.9	223 479	87.4	12.6	60.5	33.8	3 248	67.4
Pulaski	232	4.0	421	20.0	213.3	1 305 431	3 103	179 033	159.2	288 425	58.7	41.3	52.7	35.1	4 329	76.8
Putnam	168	-7.2	200	D	130.6	718 756	3 597	74 156	69.3	82 149	74.2	25.8	34.8	13.4	2 773	50.1
Randolph	232	-10.1	296	0.1	210.5	931 610	3 151	120 497	113.8	145 116	69.3	30.7	56.8	26.7	3 922	68.6
Ripley	159	-8.1	182	0.0	120.9	633 669	3 479	76 990	54.0	61 843	73.4	26.6	41.0	11.7	2 535	65.6
Rush	217	-3.1	357	0.5	201.6	1 314 403	3 679	151 157	125.8	207 281	62.4	37.6	68.4	37.4	4 265	74.0
St. Joseph	179	8.5	251	25.0	163.6	915 848	3 650	114 265	89.9	126 195	83.5	16.5	49.0	21.5	3 106	62.2
Scott	62	-10.1	157	0.0	48.2	486 203	3 088	57 222	18.9	48 031	94.0	6.0	25.9	7.1	1 046	49.7
Shelby	205	2.5	323	3.3	194.0	1 225 616	3 794	131 092	83.6	131 518	86.6	13.4	55.8	25.5	3 642	65.1
Spencer	150	-3.2	238	0.4	110.8	725 113	3 050	99 922	61.6	97 474	62.7	37.3	48.1	19.0	2 302	67.2
Starke	154	14.9	240	17.3	132.8	728 640	3 035	93 974	59.1	92 399	97.6	2.4	30.9	18.9	4 022	84.4
Steuben	106	-6.2	148	1.5	85.4	579 770	3 918	78 711	40.6	56 490	60.5	39.5	27.5	9.5	2 529	74.1
Sullivan	177	-1.1	397	9.7	157.9	1 189 316	2 997	149 235	74.8	167 313	95.1	4.9	56.4	31.8	2 742	70.7
Switzerland	47	-21.7	127	0.1	25.4	446 818	3 521	48 251	8.3	22 321	66.3	33.7	24.6	3.2	387	33.4
Tippecanoe	218	-1.4	288	5.5	199.8	1 137 312	3 944	121 160	112.8	148 957	85.9	14.1	44.8	22.1	4 096	54.3
Tipton	166	9.2	362	0.1	159.4	1 492 178	4 120	140 884	97.3	212 394	79.3	20.7	67.2	31.2	3 038	82.8
Union	73	-14.1	314	0.0	63.7	1 180 880	3 756	122 174	30.0	128 656	79.8	20.2	63.5	28.8	1 354	72.1
Vanderburgh	72	-12.2	215	D	67.2	736 718	3 431	113 475	32.6	97 288	88.8	11.2	50.4	23.3	1 423	63.6
Vermillion	132	20.0	452	D	112.9	1 436 115	3 179	150 311	64.1	218 703	83.4	16.6	48.8	28.0	2 452	66.2
Vigo	121	-1.6	234	2.1	103.0	720 485	3 073	96 017	47.2	91 150	94.6	5.4	37.1	16.4	1 585	62.5
Wabash	201	-6.5	236	1.1	180.4	844 871	3 578	101 014	151.3	178 016	47.9	52.1	46.7	25.6	3 948	71.6
Warren	196	17.4	501	4.4	178.7	1 770 103	3 532	142 916	103.7	265 142	82.9	17.1	48.3	30.7	3 399	67.0
Warrick	110	17.0	266	0.2	88.9	812 666	3 053	117 708	33.9	82 179	87.8	12.2	36.6	19.6	1 806	67.8
Washington	200	10.5	224	0.1	137.9	632 380	2 824	76 019	88.7	97 035	49.7	50.3	36.1	14.1	2 820	50.3
Wayne	164	-4.1	184	0.2	138.0	600 840	3 273	77 139	66.2	74 067	74.6	25.4	46.2	18.9	3 451	68.7
Wells	195	-13.7	278	0.1	184.1	961 703	3 464	119 797	112.0	159 770	64.3	35.7	58.8	31.7	3 431	69.6
White	318	12.0	492	3.4	301.0	1 888 323	3 835	189 568	232.0	359 066	63.2	36.8	62.5	38.2	6 119	72.6
Whitley	137	-20.3	169	1.0	118.3	647 245	3 820	77 703	85.1	105 153	63.0	37.0	38.1	15.3	2 694	70.5
IOWA	30 748	-3.1	331	189.5	26 316.3	1 122 023	3 388	136 771	20 418.1	219 890	50.7	49.3	61.4	35.6	706 286	80.7
Adair	312	-16.4	407	D	243.7	1 102 777	2 710	128 558	136.8	178 591	59.4	40.6	63.3	30.9	5 826	83.0
Adams	225	-5.5	369	D	167.8	941 061	2 553	102 601	77.6	127 227	57.6	42.4	53.3	25.7	5 889	86.7
Allamakee	275	-15.6	266	0.3	164.4	741 749	2 785	97 243	131.6	127 524	26.2	73.8	45.5	20.3	7 231	86.8
Appanoose	198	-16.1	271	D	120.4	584 408	2 159	71 067	37.9	51 821	60.8	39.2	45.7	13.3	3 872	73.9
Audubon	279	6.9	419	0.0	245.2	1 453 725	3 469	149 587	200.5	301 088	46.3	53.7	58.7	36.8	6 484	79.4
Benton	401	0.0	320	0.0	356.3	1 156 555	3 609	140 267	263.1	210 329	59.1	40.9	64.4	37.1	9 472	82.1
Black Hawk	282	2.5	300	0.2	263.2	1 167 942	3 899	161 236	178.0	189 009	68.5	31.5	69.5	38.7	7 381	79.7
Boone	332	6.1	359	0.1	301.7	1 348 605	3 757	148 616	174.2	188 286	78.9	21.1	59.6	35.0	6 682	79.0
Bremer	243	-4.7	244	0.3	223.0	966 883	3 958	136 806	158.2	158 979	61.9	38.1	63.2	33.7	6 486	81.3
Buchanan	360	5.9	307	0.2	330.8	1 156 930	3 770	154 736	254.6	216 828	55.7	44.3	70.7	41.7	11 678	74.3
Buena Vista	363	6.1	392	0.0	335.8	1 502 243	3 829	158 413	355.3	384 563	39.8	60.2	73.9	55.4	8 657	84.4
Butler	376	14.6	310	0.3	343.2	1 086 765	3 511	117 318	253.1	208 470	58.0	42.0	59.6	34.8	7 982	82.7
Calhoun	359	5.3	425	D	339.5	1 621 138	3 811	171 574	271.9	321 732	57.2	42.8	67.2	46.3	8 348	88.2
Carroll	358	-1.6	366	0.2	329.6	1 347 857	3 681	169 461	442.7	452 612	30.5	69.5	75.6	50.4	7 092	83.2
Cass	318	-5.6	417	0.7	264.1	1 279 235	3 070	147 966	172.9	226 574	53.4	46.6	61.6	37.7	7 019	82.2
Cedar	337	-0.3	325	0.2	299.7	1 195 881	3 678	151 347	198.0	191 160	67.2	32.8	62.2	39.6	8 497	80.1
Cerro Gordo	337	4.3	399	0.5	319.7	1 431 476	3 588	168 157	182.4	216 110	77.6	22.4	63.9	44.9	8 714	83.4
Cherokee	315	-6.0	375	D	275.5	1 423 062	3 796	166 209	266.0	316 698	42.8	57.2	77.6	51.0	5 758	82.7
Chickasaw	289	6.6	279	0.1	260.5	1 010 190	3 623	159 289	226.2	218 110	43.6	56.4	66.3	39.2	8 351	84.6
Clarke	191	-11.6	276	D	105.5	639 372	2 313	65 495	58.1	84 273	30.1	69.9	45.2	12.6	3 050	76.2
Clay	328	5.1	411	0.5	304.8	1 484 677	3 610	148 124	257.2	322 313	48.3	51.7	70.6	47.1	6 621	82.6
Clayton	409	-5.5	247	0.0	296.1	768 155	3 108	98 757	230.0	138 966	37.8	62.2	51.6	31.4	12 658	86.2
Clinton	396	2.1	301	0.1	355.6	1 025 461	3 406	144 814	229.6	174 723	66.0	34.0	63.8	37.0	9 164	81.4
Crawford	432	-3.1	506	D	384.7	1 575 267	3 115	164 491	274.9	321 536	57.1	42.9	69.8	43.5	6 936	80.5
Dallas	297	-3.9	326	0.4	263.7	1 089 116	3 343	138 055	185.9	203 821	59.0	41.0	55.6	28.3	6 532	71.1
Davis	219	-24.7	240	0.1	131.0	564 142	2 347	72 447	63.0	69 248	40.7	59.3	50.1	12.6	4 370	68.1
Decatur	229	-17.6	310	D	116.7	638 036	2 060	74 479	59.2	80 194	40.2	59.8	48.2	15.6	3 619	71.8
Delaware	334	-3.2	227	D	291.0	863 463	3 801	133 723	326.3	221 947	30.3	69.7	68.2	45.9	9 696	85.2
Des Moines	185	2.2	286	2.5	157.1	941 178	3 287	127 308	81.1	125 502	78.6	21.4	58.0	28.6	3 946	84.2
Dickinson	226	11.3	400	0.8	211.5	1 414 772	3 538	149 864	134.6	237 831	65.0	35.0	66.6	38.9	5 263	86.6
Dubuque	311	-1.6	210	D	237.4	711 542	3 395	119 819	271.1	182 789	23.6	76.4	65.3	37.2	7 841	81.2
Emmet	250	6.4	470	0.3	233.9	1 687 378	3 594	203 697	208.7	392 224	49.1	50.9	71.6	51.7	5 549	82.5
Fayette	417	0.5	298	0.5	355.5	1 006 861	3 374	127 904	286.2	204 740	46.9	53.1	63.1	40.3	12 072	85.8
Floyd	298	2.4	301	1.1	274.1	1 122 840	3 728	147 116	176.0	177 627	64.6	35.4	56.8	35.9	7 224	83.9

Table B. States and Counties — Water Use, Wholesale Trade, Retail Trade, and Real Estate

STATE County	Water use, 2005		Wholesale trade,[1] 2007				Retail trade,[2] 2007				Real estate and rental and leasing,[2] 2007			
	Total water withdrawn (mil gal/day)	Gallons withdrawn per person	Number of establishments	Number of employees	Sales (mil dol)	Annual payroll (mil dol)	Number of establishments	Number of employees	Sales (mil dol)	Annual payroll (mil dol)	Number of establishments	Number of employees	Receipts (mil dol)	Annual payroll (mil dol)
	133	134	135	136	137	138	139	140	141	142	143	144	145	146
INDIANA—Cont'd														
Pike	529.5	41 477	8	41	64.7	3.2	35	265	55.9	4.6	3	D	D	D
Porter	720.9	4 569	143	2 004	1 463.1	99.8	500	7 393	1 956.3	162.9	168	779	89.8	18.3
Posey	23.3	869	23	381	346.7	12.1	74	711	268.4	17.1	10	30	4.5	0.6
Pulaski	9.6	693	28	396	262.9	14.1	67	456	112.8	8.5	11	15	0.9	0.2
Putnam	6.8	185	19	134	43.0	4.8	111	1 134	310.8	25.9	23	69	6.3	1.3
Randolph	4.4	163	16	184	113.3	6.8	84	735	273.3	14.6	11	27	2.0	0.3
Ripley	3.4	124	18	112	44.5	3.3	106	1 027	255.4	21.6	22	D	D	D
Rush	3.1	172	17	119	162.3	4.8	56	535	113.4	10.9	10	25	3.1	0.4
St. Joseph	54.8	206	345	D	D	D	951	16 607	3 683.4	349.9	242	1 442	215.2	43.4
Scott	3.5	145	14	D	D	D	95	1 025	241.2	19.9	19	73	6.4	1.0
Shelby	8.8	201	40	739	291.0	18.4	136	1 707	487.6	41.5	44	127	16.6	2.7
Spencer	35.5	1 730	13	223	181.1	8.3	72	908	166.0	22.2	13	37	3.0	0.6
Starke	6.9	301	11	63	61.5	2.4	76	893	156.7	14.8	16	36	3.1	0.6
Steuben	4.7	140	33	246	97.2	8.2	198	2 293	575.1	40.8	46	114	16.4	2.9
Sullivan	463.4	21 295	22	159	201.5	4.8	65	630	146.9	11.3	8	24	1.5	0.3
Switzerland	2.8	285	4	10	3.9	0.3	13	96	19.9	1.6	3	D	D	D
Tippecanoe	34.2	222	99	1 033	413.3	44.0	567	9 881	2 079.6	193.0	196	1 073	185.3	34.5
Tipton	2.0	125	10	132	141.6	4.4	52	425	136.0	11.8	15	35	2.0	0.5
Union	0.8	110	4	D	D	D	27	179	31.0	3.0	4	11	0.7	0.2
Vanderburgh	33.1	191	271	5 495	2 907.8	282.2	855	13 949	3 025.8	297.7	214	1 431	217.0	38.9
Vermillion	646.1	39 013	12	D	D	D	57	687	184.6	12.8	6	27	1.3	0.2
Vigo	567.4	5 531	101	1 212	584.1	46.5	487	7 679	1 668.2	154.6	102	628	80.5	18.4
Wabash	8.2	241	30	420	168.9	12.4	148	1 475	325.6	31.9	29	103	11.2	2.6
Warren	2.1	242	13	154	118.3	5.8	16	106	24.0	1.5	3	D	D	D
Warrick	759.2	13 470	41	342	412.3	17.9	134	1 436	331.2	29.7	39	172	27.5	3.4
Washington	4.3	152	12	67	16.3	1.9	87	750	190.7	15.0	16	45	3.9	0.7
Wayne	11.6	167	58	517	325.2	20.8	302	4 153	1 004.3	85.8	60	274	30.5	6.9
Wells	4.5	162	40	D	D	D	103	1 219	221.3	22.8	26	86	7.6	1.7
White	5.2	211	40	424	235.1	11.6	108	1 205	283.4	25.4	22	90	7.4	1.4
Whitley	4.2	129	23	D	D	D	121	1 644	343.5	30.8	30	103	12.4	2.9
IOWA	3 366.4	1 135	4 361	55 874	41 068.3	2 276.7	13 203	177 156	39 234.6	3 561.1	2 969	14 667	2 556.0	473.0
Adair	2.0	254	6	60	29.4	2.3	31	245	49.6	3.5	5	D	D	D
Adams	1.8	410	4	27	14.2	0.8	25	155	32.6	2.4	3	5	0.7	0.1
Allamakee	214.6	14 586	35	383	154.5	12.3	62	586	128.7	11.0	9	16	2.1	0.4
Appanoose	10.7	786	11	60	23.1	1.7	65	681	133.5	12.5	13	24	1.8	0.3
Audubon	1.7	256	14	81	47.8	2.8	19	200	37.3	3.3	5	4	0.5	0.1
Benton	8.1	118	60	253	213.2	8.5	96	844	176.4	15.9	15	54	5.1	1.4
Black Hawk	37.6	299	149	2 492	1 278.5	95.1	532	8 624	1 929.4	175.3	148	707	114.7	19.2
Boone	3.3	125	30	D	D	D	75	960	210.6	21.5	16	D	D	D
Bremer	3.5	146	23	149	108.6	6.2	94	1 112	268.4	24.6	21	D	D	D
Buchanan	3.6	171	30	357	624.5	12.5	90	861	214.8	18.0	13	D	D	D
Buena Vista	6.4	316	29	D	D	D	104	1 100	260.8	22.2	22	77	9.3	2.6
Butler	2.4	160	29	228	288.4	7.7	66	332	79.1	5.9	7	D	D	D
Calhoun	2.3	217	21	253	200.7	11.1	53	316	103.5	5.9	4	18	1.2	0.3
Carroll	6.1	292	58	1 519	1 350.5	59.9	156	1 572	298.1	32.2	23	125	24.7	4.2
Cass	3.1	217	26	207	151.5	6.7	79	927	178.2	18.1	14	68	11.8	2.2
Cedar	3.5	191	29	290	221.8	10.6	66	585	131.3	10.9	16	23	1.9	0.3
Cerro Gordo	15.3	343	88	800	650.5	32.7	246	3 917	887.1	77.2	63	D	D	D
Cherokee	4.2	344	13	101	114.7	3.7	71	660	139.4	11.8	7	18	1.2	0.2
Chickasaw	2.6	203	31	266	210.1	10.1	52	453	103.9	8.0	5	D	D	D
Clarke	2.5	275	3	16	6.3	0.5	38	436	95.4	8.3	7	D	D	D
Clay	4.0	237	46	542	425.1	19.4	124	1 650	298.7	31.9	27	102	16.9	2.4
Clayton	6.4	347	33	349	564.6	13.7	87	682	163.6	11.6	8	10	1.0	0.2
Clinton	241.3	4 854	49	319	190.1	11.2	219	2 789	635.7	57.5	46	136	27.6	3.9
Crawford	5.1	302	14	126	122.0	5.3	85	854	162.4	14.4	10	21	1.3	0.2
Dallas	4.8	92	49	420	218.3	17.3	263	5 073	905.7	90.7	47	298	68.3	15.0
Davis	1.5	171	7	47	17.9	1.3	32	330	71.6	6.8	7	13	1.4	0.2
Decatur	1.4	160	9	121	76.7	2.6	27	223	39.6	3.3	3	D	D	D
Delaware	6.7	373	34	369	302.4	14.9	82	700	171.4	14.4	11	27	2.0	0.4
Des Moines	105.3	2 580	47	D	D	D	221	3 193	616.9	63.0	41	D	D	D
Dickinson	6.9	412	20	D	D	D	116	1 044	255.2	22.8	49	88	16.4	2.6
Dubuque	86.8	947	154	2 388	1 847.7	91.6	467	7 056	1 433.5	135.0	103	446	73.6	16.6
Emmet	2.5	236	18	105	103.9	3.1	60	510	92.7	9.7	5	D	D	D
Fayette	4.7	220	39	476	304.2	18.4	100	830	157.2	15.4	15	48	9.4	1.1
Floyd	3.2	193	24	143	121.9	7.4	74	762	149.1	12.7	10	30	4.3	0.7

1. Merchant wholesalers, except manufacturers' sales branches and offices. 2. Employer establishments.

Professional Services, Manufacturing, and Accommodation and Food Services

STATE County	Professional, scientific, and technical services,[1] 2007				Manufacturing, 2007				Accommodation and food services, 2007			
	Number of establishments	Number of employees	Receipts (mil dol)	Annual payroll (mil dol)	Number of establishments	Number of employees	Receipts (mil dol)	Annual payroll (mil dol)	Number of establishments	Number of employees	Sales (mil dol)	Annual payroll (mil dol)
	147	148	149	150	151	152	153	154	155	156	157	158
INDIANA—Cont'd												
Pike	7	26	2.0	0.6	NA	NA	NA	NA	11	164	5.6	1.6
Porter	333	2 132	224.9	83.1	152	9 716	7 318.8	615.5	301	5 474	211.3	58.6
Posey	45	D	D	D	24	2 564	D	182.9	41	477	17.1	5.5
Pulaski	22	64	3.9	1.0	20	1 268	D	59.4	28	D	D	D
Putnam	47	172	10.6	3.9	30	3 004	676.0	99.9	79	1 224	45.9	11.6
Randolph	34	90	6.6	2.0	46	2 134	577.4	84.8	42	D	D	D
Ripley	44	142	10.9	3.6	44	2 574	757.4	92.2	40	495	18.7	5.3
Rush	31	122	11.1	3.2	36	1 160	523.3	47.0	27	D	D	D
St. Joseph	561	D	D	D	427	17 667	8 011.0	862.2	555	11 175	439.7	126.6
Scott	31	133	11.1	3.5	32	2 096	978.7	78.0	44	804	30.7	8.6
Shelby	69	379	23.6	11.8	87	5 730	2 354.9	247.4	68	1 322	46.4	13.3
Spencer	23	112	9.8	3.0	26	1 346	D	58.4	29	390	16.3	4.1
Starke	16	54	4.5	1.4	24	996	243.7	32.1	32	D	D	D
Steuben	57	185	12.7	3.8	97	4 542	1 148.0	163.1	100	1 391	57.0	15.8
Sullivan	25	D	D	D	NA	NA	NA	NA	35	396	14.3	3.9
Switzerland	8	D	D	D	NA	NA	NA	NA	20	D	D	D
Tippecanoe	296	D	D	D	125	13 836	D	693.0	389	8 352	316.0	92.3
Tipton	23	D	D	D	24	1 094	362.1	37.4	27	299	9.8	2.8
Union	6	D	D	D	NA	NA	NA	NA	7	88	3.0	0.8
Vanderburgh	455	D	D	D	276	14 248	6 447.6	607.9	457	11 318	516.8	146.4
Vermillion	18	D	D	D	12	816	D	56.3	39	376	16.3	3.5
Vigo	207	1 181	110.8	37.7	126	8 821	3 565.9	393.7	252	4 838	195.5	54.9
Wabash	53	352	24.3	7.9	62	3 950	1 045.4	153.9	62	900	30.3	8.3
Warren	7	D	D	D	15	572	93.1	D	9	173	8.4	2.2
Warrick	94	D	D	D	46	2 973	D	D	72	1 073	36.9	11.1
Washington	32	D	D	D	41	1 763	248.3	60.7	31	D	D	D
Wayne	86	377	30.9	11.5	128	6 830	2 483.1	265.6	147	3 153	107.2	31.8
Wells	42	231	23.1	7.7	54	2 855	699.1	107.5	42	667	19.3	5.5
White	31	112	7.1	2.4	44	2 058	715.2	76.3	70	682	24.5	6.5
Whitley	47	193	14.0	5.2	72	4 783	2 107.5	203.9	58	860	28.3	7.7
IOWA	6 181	42 118	5 015.6	1 883.8	3 802	223 049	97 592.1	9 525.7	7 014	116 838	4 737.7	1 276.0
Adair	12	44	2.7	0.8	NA	NA	NA	NA	14	129	4.1	1.2
Adams	5	D	D	D	NA	NA	NA	NA	7	D	D	D
Allamakee	21	151	9.8	2.7	33	1 557	D	50.6	37	313	8.5	2.1
Appanoose	26	68	4.3	1.4	14	755	151.6	28.8	30	297	8.0	2.2
Audubon	11	D	D	D	NA	NA	NA	NA	8	D	D	D
Benton	32	82	6.3	2.2	30	819	176.8	27.8	42	348	9.6	2.6
Black Hawk	234	D	D	D	163	12 539	5 880.3	531.7	288	6 172	194.6	59.7
Boone	40	170	17.7	5.3	33	782	161.3	30.1	45	592	16.2	4.6
Bremer	44	D	D	D	39	1 950	699.7	99.5	46	546	16.7	4.5
Buchanan	28	115	9.8	2.6	41	1 216	640.8	42.8	39	388	11.5	3.2
Buena Vista	40	178	15.6	6.5	32	2 906	1 578.0	92.9	47	796	25.5	6.9
Butler	19	62	5.2	1.1	26	696	D	22.9	22	D	D	D
Calhoun	16	39	3.7	0.9	NA	NA	NA	NA	19	D	D	D
Carroll	51	224	21.2	6.7	44	1 551	794.0	67.1	56	637	20.8	5.7
Cass	29	121	10.0	3.8	23	560	D	21.6	33	374	11.6	3.1
Cedar	32	96	7.5	2.4	34	530	178.8	19.8	36	326	9.5	2.6
Cerro Gordo	96	D	D	D	54	3 761	1 357.5	152.3	148	2 429	83.9	24.2
Cherokee	17	71	10.8	1.8	21	813	279.3	26.3	30	259	8.7	2.7
Chickasaw	20	58	5.0	1.2	35	1 170	278.3	40.8	30	263	7.4	1.7
Clarke	12	39	3.0	0.8	15	1 054	416.6	33.8	22	791	84.9	12.9
Clay	36	181	16.9	6.4	30	D	D	D	49	618	23.4	6.2
Clayton	27	84	6.6	1.8	31	1 010	206.4	31.6	57	768	53.7	10.1
Clinton	64	366	30.8	13.0	61	4 678	3 914.9	218.3	117	1 440	54.1	14.4
Crawford	20	101	7.0	2.6	26	2 477	1 266.8	91.4	35	412	12.9	3.5
Dallas	133	1 072	167.9	47.8	41	2 384	574.2	79.9	132	2 621	110.4	31.3
Davis	11	41	4.2	0.9	NA	NA	NA	NA	13	128	3.1	0.9
Decatur	7	D	D	D	NA	NA	NA	NA	13	180	4.3	1.2
Delaware	30	131	9.3	3.8	37	1 573	326.4	59.9	34	377	9.0	2.7
Des Moines	55	336	30.0	15.1	67	D	D	D	98	2 012	68.8	20.6
Dickinson	48	D	D	D	37	1 878	647.5	66.3	104	1 284	54.6	16.2
Dubuque	168	D	D	D	150	9 378	4 711.2	380.3	253	4 502	145.7	42.5
Emmet	17	66	7.0	2.5	16	1 138	331.4	40.9	23	252	7.9	2.2
Fayette	39	147	10.0	3.3	32	735	157.7	23.9	50	479	14.6	3.6
Floyd	28	92	6.9	1.8	19	708	461.4	40.5	43	378	13.7	3.1

1. Establishment subject to federal tax.

Table B. States and Counties — Health Care and Social Assistance, Other Services, and Federal Funds

STATE County	Health care and social assistance, 2007				Other services, 2007				Federal funds and grants, 2009–2010 Expenditures (mil dol)			
									Total	Direct payments for individuals[1]		
	Number of establishments	Number of employees	Receipts (mil dol)	Annual payroll (mil dol)	Number of establishments	Number of employees	Receipts (mil dol)	Annual payroll (mil dol)		Social Security and government retirement	Medicare	Food Stamps and Supplemental Security Income
	159	160	161	162	163	164	165	166	167	168	169	170
INDIANA—Cont'd												
Pike	14	359	17.2	6.5	22	78	5.8	1.6	99.3	43.7	24.9	4.0
Porter	363	7 157	632.1	248.0	290	1 827	155.6	44.4	874.1	496.1	183.1	25.5
Posey	44	D	D	D	38	130	12.1	2.7	170.4	72.7	39.4	6.4
Pulaski	33	619	40.4	17.7	27	105	9.2	1.8	99.5	46.7	21.2	3.8
Putnam	74	1 612	93.6	38.7	63	273	19.9	5.3	206.1	100.4	43.6	6.0
Randolph	34	591	44.0	17.0	46	177	13.9	3.2	208.8	96.5	45.9	10.5
Ripley	67	903	43.9	20.9	55	191	17.1	3.6	210.3	98.1	44.3	6.3
Rush	31	528	35.5	14.3	40	138	12.7	2.6	122.6	52.6	32.3	4.2
St. Joseph	668	D	D	D	519	3 816	403.4	96.4	3 015.5	757.3	407.0	99.4
Scott	66	955	68.4	25.0	23	106	8.4	2.0	224.3	84.1	42.1	12.0
Shelby	86	1 604	148.4	56.2	75	525	40.4	11.3	320.8	128.2	63.4	9.5
Spencer	33	404	17.4	7.7	35	110	6.8	2.3	131.3	64.3	29.0	4.7
Starke	31	663	45.7	17.4	39	141	10.6	2.1	157.2	78.8	30.5	9.0
Steuben	77	1 278	86.3	32.0	81	580	56.3	11.5	201.3	108.2	44.8	6.6
Sullivan	40	D	D	D	25	100	6.9	1.6	169.8	69.4	46.0	6.2
Switzerland	16	125	8.9	3.4	13	D	D	D	66.2	26.7	13.7	3.3
Tippecanoe	322	9 181	913.3	342.8	252	1 861	239.1	46.9	1 070.3	356.6	132.6	30.5
Tipton	30	575	58.0	21.3	29	127	13.2	3.1	105.4	54.8	28.7	2.6
Union	12	D	D	D	10	D	D	D	47.3	24.2	9.7	1.8
Vanderburgh	563	17 053	1 720.0	649.2	367	3 041	274.3	82.1	1 573.9	574.3	323.6	76.2
Vermillion	24	D	D	D	22	48	3.7	0.6	139.1	57.7	28.9	5.1
Vigo	357	8 792	917.0	305.2	191	1 408	110.4	30.8	1 006.3	334.4	213.6	43.6
Wabash	73	2 139	134.8	51.1	61	242	21.2	4.8	234.2	118.6	47.2	7.0
Warren	11	D	D	D	8	D	D	D	48.2	21.7	11.6	1.3
Warrick	117	2 329	225.4	75.4	91	440	37.1	11.0	293.5	169.5	57.2	8.7
Washington	45	738	55.2	27.9	31	157	12.8	3.9	187.5	80.9	36.0	9.1
Wayne	184	5 306	530.7	195.2	136	612	52.8	13.4	597.1	245.0	123.5	36.2
Wells	51	1 419	105.3	42.5	67	273	22.0	4.9	146.2	77.8	34.7	4.0
White	36	742	58.2	24.3	46	173	13.0	2.8	182.3	91.9	43.9	5.1
Whitley	52	1 115	69.5	26.1	66	413	31.7	8.1	243.1	103.1	39.7	3.6
IOWA	7 857	198 285	15 371.6	6 603.6	6 088	31 869	3 063.2	779.2	28 378.9	9 174.7	4 608.9	815.2
Adair	16	297	15.3	6.2	15	D	D	D	66.2	24.2	15.7	1.7
Adams	17	301	18.4	8.9	8	21	1.9	0.4	39.5	15.9	9.7	1.2
Allamakee	41	937	41.7	19.9	34	101	11.2	2.1	98.3	45.9	20.2	3.0
Appanoose	39	723	42.3	17.6	27	103	6.6	1.8	140.8	50.3	30.4	7.0
Audubon	14	297	17.4	7.1	20	61	5.4	1.4	50.0	23.3	14.8	1.2
Benton	52	755	39.1	18.1	52	138	12.3	3.1	151.7	75.3	36.3	4.9
Black Hawk	340	10 326	850.4	362.6	212	1 670	127.4	35.5	1 013.1	377.8	219.0	54.0
Boone	57	1 538	87.6	39.8	46	155	15.5	4.1	209.8	86.3	40.3	6.1
Bremer	54	1 604	91.5	43.0	59	D	D	D	173.0	80.0	38.8	3.0
Buchanan	39	1 104	61.6	33.7	31	84	8.2	1.3	143.6	66.5	34.1	4.7
Buena Vista	51	1 322	76.4	33.0	35	D	D	D	144.7	55.2	36.3	3.6
Butler	26	460	19.3	9.3	24	61	5.9	1.1	126.7	56.7	33.1	2.9
Calhoun	31	684	39.3	17.0	16	35	4.9	0.6	95.0	38.4	24.7	2.0
Carroll	108	2 280	146.4	55.0	51	211	17.4	3.8	172.6	71.8	37.7	3.8
Cass	41	1 180	63.3	29.2	42	205	15.2	3.0	122.1	53.1	33.4	4.5
Cedar	57	585	23.9	11.9	37	96	7.5	1.9	111.3	52.3	26.4	3.0
Cerro Gordo	134	D	D	D	115	526	36.3	11.0	382.7	165.5	84.0	13.2
Cherokee	36	911	53.8	27.1	29	61	6.2	1.5	101.7	44.0	25.5	2.3
Chickasaw	30	490	28.8	10.9	40	123	14.2	2.3	96.2	43.2	22.7	2.0
Clarke	30	625	37.6	17.3	21	67	6.1	1.0	68.4	28.8	15.2	2.8
Clay	52	1 341	113.3	48.7	51	239	17.0	4.4	134.0	58.4	28.1	3.6
Clayton	54	897	42.0	18.8	36	72	6.1	1.3	147.4	62.2	34.4	3.0
Clinton	142	3 835	240.7	101.4	114	563	28.6	13.5	567.8	169.2	94.6	19.3
Crawford	37	943	51.8	23.3	31	133	8.3	2.5	152.3	49.1	31.5	4.5
Dallas	147	2 453	183.0	92.3	82	888	105.8	45.0	215.0	114.5	47.9	7.0
Davis	23	413	25.9	10.6	13	30	2.1	0.5	67.7	27.1	14.6	2.0
Decatur	23	408	21.9	9.9	7	D	D	D	79.0	27.0	14.6	3.7
Delaware	44	843	48.4	21.9	31	110	7.1	1.5	112.9	49.4	23.3	3.0
Des Moines	140	D	D	D	92	D	D	D	465.5	153.0	78.7	16.2
Dickinson	57	D	D	D	43	191	13.1	3.4	124.6	66.7	28.0	3.0
Dubuque	242	7 056	592.0	264.0	208	1 505	102.2	27.4	640.7	284.2	148.6	20.4
Emmet	31	666	37.9	16.0	27	85	6.5	1.6	106.7	37.1	22.9	2.5
Fayette	62	1 251	69.1	30.2	54	200	21.0	5.7	188.9	70.4	40.3	6.2
Floyd	58	966	55.6	23.6	35	111	8.3	2.0	159.7	62.9	36.7	5.3

1. State totals may include programs not allocated by county.

Table B. States and Counties — Federal Funds, Residential Construction, and Local Government Finances

STATE County	Federal funds and grants, 2009–2010 (cont.) — Expenditures (mil dol) (cont.) — Procurement contract awards — Salaries and wages	Defense	Other	Grants[1] — Medicaid and other health-related	Nutrition and family welfare	Education	Other	Value of residential construction authorized by building permits, 2010 — New construction ($1,000)	Number of housing units	Local government finances, 2007 — General revenue — Total (mil dol)	Inter-govern-mental (mil dol)	Taxes — Total (mil dol)	Per capita[2] (dollars) — Total	Property
	171	172	173	174	175	176	177	178	179	180	181	182	183	184
INDIANA—Cont'd														
Pike	2.6	0.0	0.6	16.4	1.9	0.2	0.5	3 661	34	30.8	11.9	9.3	741	731
Porter	33.6	5.5	13.3	58.2	14.7	2.0	29.2	65 601	251	704.0	164.8	184.9	1 152	1 101
Posey	5.2	8.2	1.1	18.6	3.4	1.8	1.1	9 713	60	77.6	31.1	35.6	1 357	1 348
Pulaski	3.5	0.0	0.8	9.7	1.8	0.3	2.6	1 712	13	69.9	26.3	13.9	1 010	767
Putnam	17.0	0.0	1.3	21.6	7.6	0.6	1.0	7 624	63	149.6	49.0	30.7	829	686
Randolph	15.0	0.0	1.2	26.8	4.8	0.7	0.7	1 255	12	78.0	40.7	22.3	864	706
Ripley	6.5	2.2	5.8	29.0	3.8	0.5	8.2	10 440	68	86.8	38.9	29.9	1 092	678
Rush	7.4	0.0	0.9	17.2	2.6	0.3	0.0	1 670	10	61.3	22.1	13.3	759	625
St. Joseph	143.5	1 122.3	28.9	264.0	33.5	8.8	83.1	48 096	311	852.3	353.9	309.5	1 163	1 098
Scott	30.1	3.4	0.8	41.7	5.2	0.7	0.3	4 811	44	81.0	35.5	17.9	756	625
Shelby	71.6	1.1	1.6	32.1	5.1	0.7	0.6	6 785	54	110.2	49.8	38.8	882	724
Spencer	5.5	0.0	1.2	18.6	2.1	0.3	0.2	4 549	38	63.1	24.0	28.1	1 381	1 147
Starke	4.5	0.0	1.1	23.1	4.3	0.7	0.2	4 579	31	82.2	39.5	19.5	830	784
Steuben	8.1	1.9	1.3	14.9	4.6	0.9	1.4	15 792	71	125.3	67.3	28.5	852	709
Sullivan	4.5	4.0	1.1	25.3	3.1	0.5	0.4	130	1	78.6	24.3	15.6	731	711
Switzerland	1.9	0.0	0.5	15.6	0.8	0.3	0.8	2 564	44	37.9	23.9	7.7	790	643
Tippecanoe	58.9	17.6	18.6	145.4	16.6	9.9	235.7	82 645	487	392.6	141.4	168.9	1 034	910
Tipton	2.7	0.0	0.6	10.4	1.7	0.2	0.1	613	5	81.2	18.9	21.6	1 344	1 102
Union	1.5	0.0	0.4	6.0	1.6	0.2	0.1	0	0	22.3	11.8	7.1	988	765
Vanderburgh	110.5	135.9	13.4	235.7	34.4	6.3	33.1	30 873	277	556.5	199.5	206.5	1 184	1 026
Vermillion	4.1	17.0	1.3	17.6	2.9	0.3	1.4	1 789	9	43.1	17.6	16.1	980	946
Vigo	117.4	4.3	54.5	161.2	22.5	4.7	18.2	20 505	164	276.6	124.8	90.9	866	716
Wabash	6.3	0.2	1.6	33.5	4.2	0.5	1.4	3 799	23	164.5	50.1	38.5	1 168	949
Warren	1.8	0.0	0.4	5.2	1.1	0.1	0.2	693	11	24.6	11.8	8.4	985	857
Warrick	10.0	0.4	2.6	29.8	6.4	0.5	2.5	37 806	197	124.4	47.6	43.0	754	681
Washington	13.4	0.1	1.1	34.2	4.3	0.8	1.6	4 410	31	79.8	32.8	16.0	575	457
Wayne	31.0	3.5	4.2	116.5	15.0	4.2	3.1	11 352	149	193.9	94.5	64.8	950	720
Wells	5.9	0.0	1.2	12.7	3.4	0.3	0.0	11 012	71	79.6	41.9	21.5	771	619
White	9.2	-1.8	1.3	14.1	4.9	0.4	4.2	8 195	72	108.2	35.5	28.3	1 187	1 049
Whitley	6.4	68.2	2.1	11.6	3.0	0.3	0.1	13 669	93	71.5	29.7	24.6	753	613
IOWA	1 902.3	1 556.7	815.9	2 962.1	661.9	469.7	2 300.6	1 222 078	7 607	X	X	X	X	X
Adair	2.1	0.0	0.5	13.2	1.6	0.3	1.5	635	4	21.7	9.5	9.5	1 251	997
Adams	3.2	0.0	0.3	4.0	0.9	0.2	0.3	205	2	14.7	7.0	5.5	1 346	1 188
Allamakee	3.6	0.2	0.8	13.2	2.8	0.9	3.0	3 292	34	55.1	21.0	18.8	1 285	1 025
Appanoose	5.2	6.7	1.3	29.8	3.0	0.8	0.3	673	8	35.6	18.2	14.1	1 081	793
Audubon	3.7	0.0	1.0	4.1	1.0	0.2	1.0	2 492	30	22.5	8.8	10.9	1 802	1 206
Benton	6.4	0.2	1.9	12.1	3.6	0.5	0.4	3 085	16	67.0	30.0	27.6	1 041	872
Black Hawk	81.0	0.1	32.0	138.4	23.3	8.0	40.7	54 657	318	489.8	202.2	182.9	1 435	1 113
Boone	43.7	0.1	1.3	17.4	4.0	0.6	1.5	4 261	32	99.7	28.8	32.6	1 237	971
Bremer	5.4	15.3	1.1	11.5	3.3	0.5	4.8	12 923	59	107.9	30.1	31.8	1 342	1 076
Buchanan	5.0	0.0	1.2	13.8	2.8	1.2	1.3	3 757	25	67.2	24.1	23.2	1 111	868
Buena Vista	12.9	0.0	1.0	14.5	3.1	0.9	0.1	1 318	12	103.2	36.5	27.3	1 378	1 081
Butler	3.2	0.0	0.8	14.9	2.3	0.6	2.2	4 989	29	36.6	15.7	16.1	1 098	920
Calhoun	3.1	0.0	1.0	9.2	1.9	0.3	0.6	1 606	8	48.8	16.2	26.3	2 634	2 211
Carroll	10.4	0.0	7.3	19.5	5.0	0.4	7.8	5 280	29	71.7	27.1	28.9	1 379	1 098
Cass	6.1	0.1	0.9	12.7	2.9	0.5	0.8	2 690	11	73.2	22.8	21.3	1 535	1 211
Cedar	6.6	0.0	2.3	9.2	2.5	0.3	0.6	6 454	32	58.2	24.2	26.3	1 462	1 185
Cerro Gordo	25.5	3.0	2.5	47.6	8.8	2.3	11.9	9 472	51	178.8	64.3	72.8	1 654	1 250
Cherokee	5.4	0.2	1.4	10.9	2.1	0.6	2.3	1 890	12	37.0	16.0	15.5	1 326	1 104
Chickasaw	3.7	0.2	0.8	9.2	2.1	0.3	0.6	1 536	7	36.5	15.6	16.2	1 328	1 042
Clarke	2.5	0.0	0.5	8.6	2.1	0.3	0.9	4 336	60	45.8	13.8	14.2	1 582	1 216
Clay	6.8	0.0	1.2	16.2	2.8	0.3	6.1	3 506	16	127.4	24.1	25.1	1 504	1 122
Clayton	6.3	0.5	2.9	22.4	3.6	0.4	1.9	3 615	21	68.5	32.9	25.4	1 438	1 148
Clinton	11.3	0.3	2.2	33.7	7.5	1.6	9.2	12 836	80	160.5	70.5	68.5	1 397	1 044
Crawford	13.5	0.0	22.0	16.7	3.4	0.6	0.4	3 174	20	65.8	25.6	19.6	1 182	931
Dallas	10.4	0.1	2.4	14.4	4.8	1.0	1.3	55 743	265	186.9	66.1	84.4	1 473	1 245
Davis	2.6	0.0	0.5	10.3	1.2	0.4	3.0	306	3	40.1	11.3	13.8	1 606	1 434
Decatur	3.3	0.0	0.8	14.6	4.2	1.2	0.4	195	4	32.1	14.4	12.5	1 488	1 040
Delaware	4.2	0.6	0.9	13.2	2.9	0.3	0.5	1 300	10	72.8	22.3	23.6	1 351	1 115
Des Moines	18.2	125.9	2.1	36.8	9.4	2.7	4.7	5 442	33	164.7	73.0	57.2	1 405	1 052
Dickinson	4.9	0.0	1.2	10.4	2.4	0.3	2.2	19 671	92	88.7	13.2	42.1	2 523	2 021
Dubuque	35.9	3.8	5.3	77.2	14.0	3.3	28.3	69 096	548	300.1	111.3	128.9	1 395	1 009
Emmet	11.1	0.0	6.3	9.8	2.1	1.8	1.1	3 743	25	64.0	24.7	16.3	1 563	1 356
Fayette	11.0	0.0	1.2	19.5	4.4	0.8	2.9	941	5	66.1	30.7	26.2	1 281	1 013
Floyd	4.8	0.0	0.9	25.2	2.9	0.5	12.3	1 799	12	70.1	22.1	22.8	1 398	1 110

1. State totals may include programs not allocated by county.   2. Based on the resident population estimated as of July 1 of the year shown.

Table B. States and Counties — Local Government Finances, Government Employment, and Voting

STATE County	Local government finances, 2007 (cont.) — Direct general expenditure — Total (mil dol)	Per capita[1] (dollars)	Education	Health and hospitals	Police protection	Public welfare	Highways	Debt outstanding — Total (mil dol)	Per capita[1] (dollars)	Government employment, 2009 — Federal civilian	Federal military	State and local	Presidential election,[2] 2008 — Percent of vote cast: Democratic	Republican	All other
	185	186	187	188	189	190	191	192	193	194	195	196	197	198	199
INDIANA—Cont'd															
Pike	36.2	2 868	55.9	0.4	1.9	4.7	8.4	31.3	2 481	41	41	658	44.8	53.4	1.8
Porter	746.2	4 647	45.8	25.8	1.7	0.7	2.2	512.1	3 189	406	550	6 710	53.0	45.8	1.2
Posey	86.2	3 283	57.5	1.8	2.0	2.5	9.4	43.3	1 650	78	87	1 173	45.6	53.3	1.1
Pulaski	70.8	5 140	48.4	22.6	2.3	2.9	4.0	37.6	2 727	46	46	1 030	41.3	56.8	1.8
Putnam	165.0	4 457	45.1	31.7	1.3	1.6	3.4	198.6	5 365	85	124	2 701	43.2	55.2	1.5
Randolph	90.9	3 514	55.4	0.6	2.7	4.4	4.9	54.1	2 090	76	86	1 321	44.8	53.6	1.7
Ripley	94.2	3 444	56.1	0.5	1.2	3.4	5.3	61.9	2 262	82	92	1 402	34.4	63.9	1.7
Rush	57.2	3 267	38.5	19.0	3.1	2.3	8.0	13.1	746	52	58	1 147	42.3	56.0	1.7
St. Joseph	903.8	3 396	51.3	0.6	4.8	4.0	2.4	916.7	3 445	1 150	935	13 798	58.0	41.0	1.0
Scott	88.8	3 749	44.9	22.0	2.8	1.9	2.7	38.4	1 620	52	79	1 346	48.1	50.1	1.8
Shelby	146.7	3 329	58.1	1.7	3.8	2.5	4.1	250.0	5 674	148	149	2 538	39.8	58.8	1.4
Spencer	64.7	3 184	58.2	0.5	1.9	1.1	5.3	40.9	2 010	78	67	1 008	49.5	49.1	1.4
Starke	74.3	3 155	66.1	2.2	1.7	3.0	4.0	62.3	2 644	53	79	953	50.5	47.3	2.3
Steuben	105.7	3 161	47.3	0.8	3.1	2.9	10.9	112.7	3 370	82	113	1 609	44.4	54.2	1.3
Sullivan	84.2	3 943	41.3	24.7	0.8	2.1	5.9	88.3	4 132	58	71	1 946	48.8	49.5	1.8
Switzerland	37.7	3 897	36.0	1.5	1.2	2.0	4.1	10.3	1 065	25	32	462	45.0	53.3	1.7
Tippecanoe	438.4	2 684	47.7	0.8	3.1	3.7	6.5	454.4	2 781	570	617	22 084	55.2	43.6	1.2
Tipton	93.2	5 802	26.0	32.6	1.4	3.2	2.3	33.5	2 087	41	53	970	41.5	56.9	1.6
Union	27.7	3 847	66.1	0.4	2.1	0.9	5.0	47.3	6 564	16	24	484	36.6	61.6	1.9
Vanderburgh	619.3	3 551	36.0	1.6	6.6	2.8	2.4	524.7	3 008	971	597	9 355	50.8	48.3	0.9
Vermillion	48.4	2 950	54.2	0.9	2.0	1.1	6.5	38.1	2 322	53	62	705	56.1	42.2	1.7
Vigo	317.6	3 027	46.8	1.1	4.0	2.5	3.0	211.8	2 019	1 195	378	8 024	57.3	41.5	1.2
Wabash	169.6	5 153	39.4	33.3	1.4	2.2	3.6	50.2	1 524	86	109	1 916	39.3	59.4	1.3
Warren	25.8	3 046	53.6	1.5	2.4	3.5	12.0	12.4	1 463	25	38	379	43.9	54.2	1.9
Warrick	155.5	2 724	51.9	1.1	2.7	1.6	3.7	170.3	2 983	135	196	1 926	43.0	55.9	1.1
Washington	95.5	3 421	54.1	16.5	1.3	1.3	3.7	40.1	1 436	66	93	1 470	40.4	57.7	2.0
Wayne	222.4	3 258	46.6	1.6	5.7	1.4	4.0	119.9	1 756	158	228	4 737	47.1	51.0	1.9
Wells	102.7	3 676	61.9	0.5	2.8	1.9	3.7	55.6	1 990	61	93	1 466	33.7	65.1	1.3
White	111.2	4 670	48.4	19.2	1.9	1.1	3.5	168.6	7 078	71	79	1 705	44.9	53.2	1.8
Whitley	81.7	2 502	58.7	0.8	3.4	1.3	5.0	84.1	2 575	79	110	1 472	38.6	60.1	1.3
IOWA	X	X	X	X	X	X	X	X	X	18 597	12 900	206 126	53.9	44.4	1.7
Adair	21.6	2 839	44.3	1.2	4.4	0.1	21.0	12.8	1 685	33	31	491	47.5	50.8	1.7
Adams	17.6	4 301	36.3	5.3	4.6	0.1	19.0	23.0	5 621	28	17	254	50.7	47.4	1.9
Allamakee	64.4	4 410	45.9	20.8	2.9	0.6	8.0	48.2	3 297	60	61	1 039	56.2	42.0	1.8
Appanoose	35.5	2 729	60.4	3.7	5.8	0.3	12.0	14.4	1 108	66	54	712	48.1	49.9	2.0
Audubon	22.5	3 703	56.4	5.1	2.9	0.3	14.1	9.4	1 549	32	25	414	50.6	47.6	1.8
Benton	71.8	2 703	62.0	3.3	3.6	0.2	10.8	64.0	3 166	68	113	1 472	51.5	47.0	1.5
Black Hawk	527.8	4 142	54.2	4.8	4.3	0.9	7.3	355.7	2 791	544	548	11 458	60.5	38.1	1.5
Boone	104.1	3 945	38.4	29.1	3.5	0.6	8.6	286.6	10 861	121	110	2 490	52.8	45.2	2.0
Bremer	111.3	4 688	41.4	31.3	3.3	0.4	5.7	66.0	2 782	70	99	1 736	53.9	44.6	1.5
Buchanan	64.3	3 072	42.2	23.1	4.0	0.5	9.7	25.1	1 201	66	88	1 457	58.5	40.0	1.5
Buena Vista	100.7	5 091	36.3	27.0	3.2	0.4	6.5	79.2	4 007	119	83	1 663	48.4	50.2	1.4
Butler	37.1	2 530	47.0	8.5	5.0	0.8	15.7	17.6	1 201	47	60	694	46.9	51.6	1.4
Calhoun	39.5	3 960	53.8	11.3	4.0	2.9	12.2	7.3	729	44	41	790	45.1	52.8	2.2
Carroll	65.0	3 105	42.0	2.4	6.5	5.1	10.7	64.7	3 093	95	87	1 237	51.0	47.3	1.6
Cass	70.5	5 079	35.1	36.5	3.5	0.2	7.9	16.4	1 178	75	58	1 388	43.7	54.5	1.8
Cedar	61.8	3 436	62.7	3.9	3.8	0.1	10.3	34.5	1 920	103	76	1 010	54.0	44.4	1.6
Cerro Gordo	182.7	4 150	50.7	5.6	5.1	0.6	6.4	121.7	2 764	148	185	2 785	59.7	38.8	1.5
Cherokee	36.8	3 149	47.7	3.5	4.3	0.0	14.0	30.8	2 638	50	48	1 041	45.4	53.0	1.7
Chickasaw	34.1	2 790	57.0	2.3	4.6	1.2	13.7	7.9	647	55	51	633	59.6	38.8	1.6
Clarke	45.1	5 015	33.0	36.7	3.5	0.5	6.9	31.1	3 458	31	38	741	49.9	47.6	2.5
Clay	115.2	6 900	23.1	47.4	2.5	0.1	5.6	106.3	6 370	75	70	1 575	46.7	51.8	1.5
Clayton	74.7	4 224	61.4	0.3	4.1	1.7	11.9	49.1	2 776	119	74	1 251	57.8	40.6	1.6
Clinton	160.2	3 267	53.5	5.7	6.0	0.4	7.8	97.9	1 996	123	206	2 576	60.7	37.7	1.5
Crawford	70.8	4 271	44.9	20.4	2.7	0.8	10.7	28.3	1 706	100	69	1 187	51.7	46.5	1.8
Dallas	199.4	3 481	60.0	10.0	2.9	0.4	7.3	255.7	4 463	113	261	3 158	46.4	51.9	1.7
Davis	32.6	3 804	32.7	40.5	2.8	0.2	11.0	7.5	873	39	36	550	44.0	53.1	2.9
Decatur	29.7	3 527	55.8	3.0	4.2	1.4	15.1	13.6	1 620	43	35	576	48.4	49.2	2.4
Delaware	74.2	4 249	44.2	32.0	2.5	0.1	6.8	23.6	1 351	59	72	1 134	52.2	46.2	1.6
Des Moines	163.4	4 015	61.3	1.0	4.8	1.3	6.7	101.0	2 482	178	175	2 661	60.6	37.5	1.9
Dickinson	93.5	5 599	32.4	23.2	3.3	0.3	8.7	94.7	5 672	68	70	1 123	46.7	52.1	1.2
Dubuque	294.8	3 192	47.5	4.1	5.2	2.1	9.1	144.0	1 559	263	410	4 326	59.7	38.9	1.5
Emmet	63.6	6 103	77.8	2.3	3.2	0.4	5.5	31.3	3 008	48	43	827	51.2	47.3	1.4
Fayette	70.1	3 433	52.3	4.0	4.5	0.3	11.8	42.9	2 098	87	85	1 204	57.6	41.0	1.5
Floyd	66.7	4 088	37.1	29.7	3.4	1.0	8.9	18.7	1 145	52	67	1 017	59.6	37.7	2.7

1. Based on the resident population estimated as of July 1 of the year shown.   2. © 2009 Election Data Services, Inc. All rights reserved.

Table B. States and Counties — **Land Area and Population**

					Population and population characteristics, 2010														
									Race alone or in combination, not Hispanic or Latino (percent)					Age (percent)					
STATE/ County code	CBSA code[1]	County type[2]	STATE County	Land area,[3] (sq km) 2010	Total persons	Rank	Per square kilometer	White	Black	American Indian, Alaska Native	Asian and Pacific Islander	Percent Hispanic or Latino[4]	Under 5 years	5 to 17 years	18 to 24 years	25 to 34 years	35 to 44 years	45 to 54 years
				1	2	3	4	5	6	7	8	9	10	11	12	13	14	15
			IOWA—Cont'd															
19 069	...	7	Franklin	1 507	10 680	2 389	7.1	88.1	0.5	0.5	0.4	11.3	6.3	17.6	6.8	11.0	11.1	14.6
19 071	...	8	Fremont	1 324	7 441	2 647	5.6	96.4	0.6	0.7	0.4	2.5	6.3	16.5	6.5	9.6	10.9	15.5
19 073	...	6	Greene	1 475	9 336	2 494	6.3	97.2	0.4	0.6	0.5	1.8	5.6	17.5	6.2	9.7	10.2	15.9
19 075	47940	3	Grundy	1 300	12 453	2 277	9.6	98.5	0.5	0.2	0.4	1.0	6.3	17.5	6.5	10.3	11.8	15.3
19 077	19780	2	Guthrie	1 530	10 954	2 372	7.2	97.4	0.4	0.5	0.5	1.8	5.6	18.3	5.1	9.6	11.6	15.8
19 079	...	6	Hamilton	1 494	15 673	2 070	10.5	92.5	0.7	0.6	2.3	5.0	6.2	17.8	6.5	10.8	11.9	15.8
19 081	...	7	Hancock	1 479	11 341	2 341	7.7	95.4	0.7	0.4	0.7	3.5	6.0	17.4	5.8	10.6	10.4	16.4
19 083	...	6	Hardin	1 474	17 534	1 948	11.9	94.4	1.6	0.5	0.6	3.7	6.0	17.1	8.1	9.9	10.3	14.7
19 085	36540	2	Harrison	1 805	14 928	2 114	8.3	98.1	0.3	0.7	0.4	1.2	6.2	17.9	6.6	9.8	12.1	16.5
19 087	...	7	Henry	1 125	20 145	1 832	17.9	91.4	2.7	0.6	2.8	3.8	5.8	17.4	8.8	11.7	12.6	14.7
19 089	...	7	Howard	1 226	9 566	2 474	7.8	98.1	0.6	0.3	0.5	1.2	7.2	18.0	6.5	11.2	10.5	15.3
19 091	...	7	Humboldt	1 125	9 815	2 453	8.7	95.4	0.7	0.4	0.5	3.6	6.4	16.6	7.1	10.5	10.2	16.0
19 093	...	8	Ida	1 118	7 089	2 676	6.3	97.9	0.3	0.4	0.4	1.4	6.9	17.1	5.9	10.4	10.0	15.2
19 095	...	8	Iowa	1 519	16 355	2 028	10.8	97.3	0.6	0.3	0.5	1.9	6.1	18.4	6.2	10.4	12.5	16.6
19 097	...	6	Jackson	1 647	19 848	1 845	12.1	97.7	0.6	0.5	0.9	1.1	5.7	17.5	6.6	9.9	11.8	16.4
19 099	35500	6	Jasper	1 892	36 842	1 251	19.5	96.5	1.5	0.5	0.7	1.5	5.9	17.0	7.0	11.9	12.8	16.0
19 101	...	7	Jefferson	1 128	16 843	1 992	14.9	87.5	1.6	0.7	9.0	2.4	4.5	13.7	11.1	12.2	9.9	14.0
19 103	26980	3	Johnson	1 590	130 882	475	82.3	84.8	5.6	0.6	6.0	4.7	6.2	13.6	21.5	17.2	11.4	11.6
19 105	16300	3	Jones	1 491	20 638	1 813	13.8	96.0	2.2	0.4	0.6	1.3	5.9	16.6	6.7	11.7	12.3	16.1
19 107	...	8	Keokuk	1 500	10 511	2 402	7.0	98.4	0.7	0.3	0.3	0.9	5.8	17.4	6.6	10.8	10.8	16.3
19 109	...	7	Kossuth	2 519	15 543	2 078	6.2	97.9	0.6	0.2	0.6	1.4	5.8	17.1	5.7	9.5	9.9	16.3
19 111	22800	5	Lee	1 340	35 862	1 277	26.8	93.1	4.0	0.7	0.8	3.0	5.8	16.4	7.8	11.3	11.8	15.6
19 113	16300	3	Linn	1 857	211 226	292	113.7	91.2	5.1	0.7	2.4	2.6	6.7	17.8	9.8	13.7	13.1	14.3
19 115	34700	8	Louisa	1 041	11 387	2 340	10.9	82.4	0.7	0.5	1.2	15.8	5.9	19.9	7.0	11.6	12.4	15.9
19 117	...	6	Lucas	1 115	8 898	2 533	8.0	98.5	0.3	0.3	0.4	1.0	6.2	18.3	6.5	9.3	10.8	15.2
19 119	...	8	Lyon	1 522	11 581	2 326	7.6	97.8	0.3	0.4	0.3	1.8	8.0	19.7	6.6	11.6	11.3	13.8
19 121	19780	2	Madison	1 453	15 679	2 069	10.8	97.9	0.5	0.4	0.7	1.3	7.0	20.2	5.7	10.7	13.8	15.2
19 123	36820	7	Mahaska	1 479	22 381	1 713	15.1	95.8	1.6	0.5	1.5	1.6	6.8	17.5	9.7	11.7	11.5	14.4
19 125	37800	6	Marion	1 436	33 309	1 342	23.2	96.4	0.9	0.5	1.4	1.6	6.7	18.4	10.2	10.8	11.8	14.6
19 127	32260	4	Marshall	1 483	40 648	1 162	27.4	79.3	2.1	0.5	1.8	17.3	7.1	18.3	8.3	11.4	11.3	14.1
19 129	36540	2	Mills	1 133	15 059	2 104	13.3	96.5	0.7	0.7	0.7	2.4	6.4	19.0	6.4	10.5	12.7	16.7
19 131	...	7	Mitchell	1 215	10 776	2 385	8.9	98.4	0.3	0.3	0.4	1.0	6.2	18.6	6.8	9.1	10.5	15.3
19 133	...	6	Monona	1 798	9 243	2 505	5.1	97.2	0.8	1.3	0.5	1.2	5.4	16.7	5.7	8.9	10.0	15.8
19 135	...	7	Monroe	1 123	7 970	2 605	7.1	97.1	0.6	0.4	0.6	2.1	6.5	17.6	7.1	10.7	11.7	14.1
19 137	...	6	Montgomery	1 098	10 740	2 387	9.8	96.3	0.5	0.7	0.4	2.8	5.5	17.8	5.9	9.7	11.5	15.6
19 139	34700	4	Muscatine	1 133	42 745	1 111	37.7	81.7	1.7	0.5	1.1	15.9	7.2	18.9	8.0	12.1	12.7	14.9
19 141	...	7	O'Brien	1 484	14 398	2 150	9.7	95.1	0.6	0.3	0.8	3.8	6.4	17.2	6.6	11.0	10.2	15.1
19 143	...	7	Osceola	1 033	6 462	2 730	6.3	92.4	0.4	0.5	0.5	6.7	6.2	16.9	7.0	10.4	11.2	16.6
19 145	...	7	Page	1 385	15 932	2 054	11.5	93.8	2.6	0.9	1.2	2.7	5.8	16.2	7.0	10.8	11.6	14.9
19 147	...	7	Palo Alto	1 460	9 421	2 489	6.5	97.3	0.7	0.6	0.6	1.6	6.2	15.7	9.0	10.4	9.6	14.8
19 149	...	6	Plymouth	2 235	24 986	1 601	11.2	95.9	0.6	0.4	0.8	3.0	6.6	19.3	6.3	10.7	11.8	15.8
19 151	...	9	Pocahontas	1 495	7 310	2 659	4.9	96.9	0.6	0.3	0.5	2.3	5.9	15.6	6.1	8.9	9.5	17.4
19 153	19780	2	Polk	1 486	430 640	154	289.8	82.4	6.9	0.6	4.2	7.6	7.6	17.9	9.3	15.7	13.8	14.0
19 155	36540	2	Pottawattamie	2 461	93 158	617	37.9	91.0	1.9	0.9	0.9	6.6	6.8	17.3	9.4	12.4	12.1	15.1
19 157	...	7	Poweshiek	1 515	18 914	1 882	12.5	94.7	1.6	0.5	2.0	2.4	5.3	15.6	13.7	9.5	10.5	14.3
19 159	...	9	Ringgold	1 387	5 131	2 834	3.7	97.3	0.4	0.5	0.5	1.8	6.5	17.8	6.3	9.4	9.3	14.0
19 161	...	9	Sac	1 489	10 350	2 415	7.0	97.5	0.5	0.4	0.3	1.9	5.8	16.7	5.5	9.3	10.6	15.8
19 163	19340	2	Scott	1 186	165 224	373	139.3	85.0	8.5	0.8	2.5	5.6	6.8	17.7	8.9	13.4	12.7	14.8
19 165	...	6	Shelby	1 530	12 167	2 295	8.0	97.3	0.4	0.5	0.5	1.8	5.6	17.9	5.8	8.6	11.4	16.2
19 167	...	6	Sioux	1 990	33 704	1 331	16.9	89.8	0.6	0.3	1.0	8.9	7.8	19.0	13.7	12.0	10.2	12.8
19 169	11180	3	Story	1 484	89 542	631	60.3	88.2	2.9	0.5	6.7	3.0	5.4	12.5	29.0	14.3	9.3	10.4
19 171	...	6	Tama	1 867	17 767	1 939	9.5	85.1	0.7	7.7	0.6	7.4	6.3	19.3	6.8	10.0	11.9	14.5
19 173	...	9	Taylor	1 378	6 317	2 741	4.6	93.6	0.4	0.5	0.4	5.8	5.9	17.4	6.0	10.5	10.5	14.6
19 175	...	6	Union	1 097	12 534	2 273	11.4	96.7	1.0	0.6	0.7	1.8	6.6	16.8	8.8	11.2	10.9	14.5
19 177	...	9	Van Buren	1 256	7 570	2 637	6.0	97.9	0.4	0.4	0.7	1.2	6.5	17.6	6.6	10.4	11.1	14.5
19 179	36900	5	Wapello	1 118	35 625	1 283	31.9	88.5	1.8	0.6	1.1	9.1	6.6	16.2	9.6	12.1	11.7	14.5
19 181	19780	2	Warren	1 476	46 225	1 038	31.3	96.7	0.9	0.5	0.9	1.9	6.4	19.6	9.1	10.9	13.5	15.1
19 183	26980	3	Washington	1 473	21 704	1 753	14.7	93.5	1.0	0.5	0.6	5.2	6.4	18.8	6.5	10.8	12.0	15.0
19 185	...	9	Wayne	1 361	6 403	2 736	4.7	98.2	0.5	0.5	0.4	1.1	6.2	17.2	7.1	9.4	9.7	15.7
19 187	22700	5	Webster	1 853	38 013	1 217	20.5	91.4	4.7	0.5	0.9	3.8	5.9	16.2	11.1	11.8	10.5	14.7
19 189	...	7	Winnebago	1 037	10 866	2 379	10.5	95.0	1.0	0.3	1.1	3.3	5.5	16.2	9.5	9.8	10.7	15.0
19 191	...	7	Winneshiek	1 787	21 056	1 784	11.8	96.2	0.8	0.2	1.3	2.0	5.1	15.3	16.7	9.0	10.1	14.9
19 193	43580	3	Woodbury	2 261	102 172	569	45.2	79.5	3.5	2.5	2.9	13.7	7.8	18.9	10.5	12.8	12.1	13.5
19 195	32380	9	Worth	1 036	7 598	2 636	7.3	97.2	0.5	0.5	0.5	1.9	5.4	17.7	6.2	10.3	11.7	16.3
19 197	...	7	Wright	1 503	13 229	2 235	8.8	89.6	0.5	0.5	0.6	9.6	6.5	16.9	6.8	10.1	10.4	14.8

1. CBSA = Core Based Statistical Area. See Appendix A for explanation. See Appendix B for list of metropolitan areas with component counties. 2. County type code from the Economic Research Service of USDA Rural-Urban Continuum Codes. See Appendix A for definition. 3. Dry land or land partially or temporarily covered by water. 4. May be of any race.

Table B. States and Counties — **Population and Households**

STATE County	55 to 64 years	65 to 74 years	75 years and over	Percent female	Total persons 1990	Total persons 2000	Percent change 1990–2000	Percent change 2000–2010	Births	Deaths	Net migration	Number	Percent change 2000–2010	Persons per house-hold	Female family house-holder[1]	One per-son
	16	17	18	19	20	21	22	23	24	25	26	27	28	29	30	31
IOWA—Cont'd																
Franklin	13.6	8.7	10.3	49.6	11 364	10 704	-5.8	-0.2	1 205	1 162	-143	4 332	-0.6	2.42	6.6	27.1
Fremont	15.1	9.3	10.3	50.3	8 226	8 010	-2.6	-7.1	800	843	-587	3 064	-4.2	2.38	8.6	27.3
Greene	14.1	9.5	11.4	50.6	10 045	10 366	3.2	-9.9	962	1 138	-894	3 996	-5.0	2.30	7.8	31.6
Grundy	13.5	9.0	9.8	50.6	12 029	12 369	2.8	0.7	1 186	1 264	-31	5 131	2.9	2.40	6.3	25.8
Guthrie	14.0	10.0	9.9	50.3	10 935	11 353	3.8	-3.5	1 180	1 293	-355	4 544	-2.1	2.37	6.7	27.6
Hamilton	12.9	8.1	10.0	50.3	16 071	16 438	2.3	-4.7	1 686	1 585	-1 224	6 540	-2.3	2.37	8.4	29.2
Hancock	14.2	9.1	10.0	50.1	12 638	12 100	-4.3	-6.3	1 180	1 163	-1 024	4 741	-1.1	2.35	6.8	28.6
Hardin	12.8	9.6	11.4	50.3	19 094	18 812	-1.5	-6.8	1 934	2 299	-1 206	7 296	-4.4	2.28	7.5	31.2
Harrison	13.1	8.9	9.0	50.8	14 730	15 666	6.4	-4.7	1 616	1 736	-135	5 987	-2.1	2.45	8.2	27.0
Henry	13.0	8.1	8.0	48.8	19 226	20 336	5.8	-0.9	2 182	1 915	-561	7 666	0.5	2.43	9.5	27.0
Howard	11.9	8.7	10.6	50.4	9 809	9 932	1.3	-3.7	1 101	1 070	-510	3 944	-0.8	2.37	6.9	30.4
Humboldt	12.6	9.2	11.4	50.6	10 756	10 381	-3.5	-5.5	1 064	1 107	-815	4 209	-2.0	2.30	7.1	30.2
Ida	13.8	8.8	11.9	50.1	8 365	7 837	-6.3	-9.5	769	920	-893	3 052	-5.0	2.28	6.9	31.5
Iowa	12.6	7.9	9.3	50.7	14 630	15 671	7.1	4.4	1 763	1 495	-35	6 677	8.3	2.41	6.8	27.8
Jackson	13.4	9.4	9.2	50.4	19 950	20 296	1.7	-2.2	2 002	1 955	-483	8 289	2.6	2.37	8.5	28.3
Jasper	12.9	8.3	8.2	49.1	34 795	37 213	6.9	-1.0	4 087	3 312	-1 510	14 806	0.8	2.38	8.9	27.7
Jefferson	19.8	7.6	7.2	46.6	16 310	16 181	-0.8	4.1	1 413	1 380	-666	6 846	3.0	2.21	8.2	33.9
Johnson	10.0	4.7	3.9	50.0	96 119	111 006	15.5	17.9	14 265	4 990	10 144	52 715	19.6	2.33	7.6	30.3
Jones	13.6	8.5	8.8	48.1	19 444	20 221	4.0	2.1	2 052	1 754	-10	8 181	8.2	2.36	8.0	27.0
Keokuk	13.1	9.0	10.3	50.3	11 624	11 400	-1.9	-7.8	1 207	1 175	-810	4 408	-3.9	2.35	7.6	28.9
Kossuth	13.9	10.0	11.9	50.4	18 591	17 163	-7.7	-9.4	1 576	1 692	-1 834	6 697	-4.0	2.28	6.2	30.9
Lee	14.4	8.6	8.4	49.4	38 687	38 052	-1.6	-5.8	3 753	3 960	-2 222	14 610	-3.6	2.35	11.1	29.2
Linn	11.5	6.8	6.2	50.8	168 767	191 701	13.6	10.2	26 033	13 964	5 507	86 134	12.2	2.39	9.9	29.2
Louisa	12.4	8.0	7.0	49.1	11 592	12 183	5.1	-6.5	1 424	1 053	-1 260	4 346	-3.8	2.59	9.4	24.6
Lucas	13.5	9.8	10.4	50.2	9 070	9 422	3.9	-5.6	1 023	1 005	-203	3 689	-3.2	2.39	7.5	29.6
Lyon	12.2	7.2	9.6	50.1	11 952	11 763	-1.6	-1.5	1 472	1 116	-885	4 442	0.3	2.57	5.3	24.6
Madison	12.6	7.8	7.0	50.3	12 483	14 019	12.3	11.8	1 827	1 266	921	6 025	13.1	2.57	7.3	23.0
Mahaska	12.3	7.7	8.4	49.7	21 532	22 335	3.7	0.2	2 656	1 969	-911	8 975	1.1	2.42	9.0	27.4
Marion	11.9	7.9	7.7	50.3	30 001	32 052	6.8	3.9	3 789	3 080	102	12 723	5.9	2.48	7.7	26.4
Marshall	13.1	8.0	8.5	49.7	38 276	39 311	2.7	3.4	5 493	4 382	-971	15 538	1.3	2.53	10.3	27.1
Mills	15.0	7.3	6.1	49.7	13 202	14 547	10.2	3.5	1 660	1 244	131	5 605	5.3	2.58	8.8	22.4
Mitchell	11.9	9.5	12.2	50.7	10 928	10 874	-0.5	-0.9	1 183	1 235	31	4 395	2.4	2.40	6.3	29.1
Monona	13.8	10.9	12.8	51.1	10 034	10 020	-0.1	-7.8	918	1 494	-503	4 050	-3.8	2.23	8.3	33.7
Monroe	13.6	9.4	9.2	50.1	8 114	8 016	-1.2	-0.6	822	924	-318	3 213	-0.5	2.44	8.6	26.9
Montgomery	14.0	8.8	11.2	51.5	12 076	11 771	-2.5	-8.8	1 223	1 428	-730	4 558	-6.7	2.31	9.5	30.7
Muscatine	12.5	7.2	6.5	50.2	39 907	41 722	4.5	2.5	5 747	3 502	-809	16 412	3.6	2.57	10.8	24.5
O'Brien	13.0	8.2	12.2	50.2	15 444	15 102	-2.2	-4.7	1 591	1 768	-924	6 069	1.1	2.31	6.1	31.5
Osceola	12.1	9.2	10.6	49.8	7 267	7 003	-3.6	-7.7	691	742	-674	2 682	-3.5	2.37	5.9	29.2
Page	13.7	9.3	10.6	48.1	16 870	16 976	0.6	-6.1	1 557	1 976	-1 207	6 393	-4.7	2.26	9.0	31.8
Palo Alto	12.9	9.0	12.3	50.8	10 669	10 147	-4.9	-7.2	1 065	1 192	-702	3 994	-3.0	2.27	7.1	31.9
Plymouth	12.8	7.8	8.8	50.5	23 388	24 849	6.2	0.6	2 901	2 250	-1 151	9 875	5.4	2.49	6.6	25.8
Pocahontas	14.5	10.4	11.7	50.3	9 525	8 662	-9.1	-15.6	694	1 015	-968	3 233	-10.6	2.22	6.2	32.4
Polk	10.9	5.7	5.1	51.0	327 140	374 601	14.5	15.0	60 116	26 353	20 009	170 197	14.1	2.48	11.0	28.3
Pottawattamie	12.6	7.4	6.9	51.0	82 628	87 704	6.1	6.2	11 324	7 849	-470	36 775	8.7	2.48	12.6	27.1
Poweshiek	12.6	8.8	9.6	51.1	19 033	18 815	-1.1	0.5	1 809	2 029	-71	7 555	2.1	2.29	8.5	30.4
Ringgold	13.1	10.3	13.3	51.4	5 420	5 469	0.9	-6.2	575	748	-328	2 047	-8.8	2.42	6.0	28.9
Sac	14.2	9.3	12.8	51.1	12 324	11 529	-6.5	-10.2	1 040	1 397	-1 068	4 482	-5.6	2.26	6.5	31.6
Scott	12.6	6.9	6.2	51.0	150 973	158 668	5.1	4.1	21 132	11 921	-754	66 765	7.1	2.42	11.9	28.6
Shelby	13.6	9.1	11.8	51.2	13 230	13 173	-0.4	-7.6	1 147	1 369	-829	5 085	-1.7	2.35	7.4	29.1
Sioux	10.3	6.5	7.8	50.1	29 903	31 589	5.6	6.7	4 472	2 318	-1 317	11 584	8.3	2.70	4.5	22.5
Story	9.2	5.0	5.0	48.2	74 252	79 981	7.7	12.0	8 914	4 398	3 142	34 736	18.2	2.34	6.2	28.3
Tama	12.8	8.8	9.6	50.9	17 419	18 103	3.9	-1.9	2 175	1 840	-957	6 947	-1.0	2.50	8.6	26.0
Taylor	14.0	9.6	11.4	50.2	7 114	6 958	-2.2	-9.2	681	821	-438	2 679	-5.1	2.32	6.7	29.7
Union	13.1	8.8	9.3	51.3	12 750	12 309	-3.5	1.8	1 381	1 430	25	5 271	0.6	2.31	9.7	31.6
Van Buren	13.6	10.4	9.3	49.7	7 676	7 809	1.7	-3.1	849	864	-66	3 108	-2.3	2.40	7.0	29.2
Wapello	12.9	8.0	8.5	51.1	35 696	36 051	1.0	-1.2	4 422	3 820	-1 092	14 552	-1.6	2.39	11.2	29.9
Warren	12.1	7.1	6.3	51.3	36 033	40 671	12.9	13.7	4 820	3 190	3 198	17 262	17.4	2.58	8.9	22.1
Washington	13.2	8.0	9.3	51.0	19 612	20 670	5.4	5.0	2 752	2 145	117	8 741	8.5	2.45	8.1	28.0
Wayne	12.5	10.3	11.8	51.3	7 067	6 730	-4.8	-4.9	761	916	-250	2 652	-6.0	2.38	7.9	30.0
Webster	13.0	7.8	8.8	48.8	40 342	40 235	-0.3	-5.5	4 529	4 286	-1 884	15 580	-1.9	2.27	10.8	32.9
Winnebago	14.0	8.6	10.7	50.5	12 122	11 723	-3.3	-7.3	1 109	1 207	-971	4 597	-3.2	2.26	7.4	31.7
Winneshiek	12.1	8.0	8.8	50.4	20 847	21 310	2.2	-1.2	1 830	1 661	-733	7 997	3.4	2.35	5.6	28.8
Woodbury	11.6	6.5	6.3	50.7	98 276	103 877	5.7	-1.6	15 117	8 438	-7 201	39 052	-0.3	2.55	12.6	28.1
Worth	14.0	8.9	9.3	50.2	7 991	7 909	-1.0	-3.9	742	863	-200	3 172	-3.2	2.37	7.4	27.5
Wright	13.6	9.0	12.0	50.3	14 269	14 334	0.5	-7.7	1 575	1 671	-1 467	5 625	-5.3	2.32	8.2	30.6

1. No spouse present.

Table B. States and Counties — **Population, Vital Statistics, Medicare, and Crime**

STATE County	Persons in group quarters, 2010	Daytime population, 2006–2010		Births, average 2006–2008		Deaths, average 2006–2008		Persons under 65 with no health insurance, 2009		Medicare, 2011			Serious crimes known to police,[2] 2010 Total	
		Number	Employ-ment/resi-dence ratio	Total	Rate[1]	Number	Rate[1]	Number	Percent	Eligible for Medicare	Enrolled in Medicare Advantage	Enrolled in a Medicare prescription drug plan	Number	Rate[3]
	32	33	34	35	36	37	38	39	40	41	42	43	44	45
IOWA—Cont'd														
Franklin	198	9 970	0.9	D	D	123	11.7	1 086	13.1	2 233	56	1 598	24	225
Fremont	135	6 867	0.8	D	D	80	10.6	576	10.0	1 655	108	1 082	NA	NA
Greene	142	8 894	0.9	D	D	109	11.4	762	10.9	2 180	232	1 423	58	621
Grundy	154	10 576	0.7	D	D	139	11.4	742	7.7	2 594	291	1 535	98	787
Guthrie	170	9 224	0.7	D	D	131	11.8	896	10.5	2 547	289	1 542	53	484
Hamilton	198	15 605	1.0	D	D	163	10.4	1 133	9.4	3 199	237	2 028	385	2 456
Hancock	185	10 731	0.9	D	D	127	11.1	889	10.1	2 309	54	1 625	84	741
Hardin	870	17 653	1.0	D	D	249	14.2	1 383	10.5	3 908	192	2 680	284	1 620
Harrison	283	12 384	0.6	D	D	180	11.7	1 144	9.3	2 990	156	1 980	106	710
Henry	1 554	21 214	1.1	D	D	209	10.3	1 486	9.1	3 771	309	2 383	413	2 263
Howard	213	9 298	0.9	D	D	115	12.1	875	12.1	2 034	159	1 366	176	1 840
Humboldt	133	9 159	0.8	D	D	114	11.7	763	10.5	2 133	113	1 416	57	581
Ida	122	7 687	1.1	D	D	95	13.6	566	11.0	1 577	165	1 048	64	903
Iowa	290	16 354	1.0	D	D	164	10.2	997	7.9	3 116	406	1 876	163	997
Jackson	201	17 018	0.7	D	D	216	10.7	1 712	11.0	4 199	849	2 675	261	1 315
Jasper	1 648	31 742	0.7	D	D	375	10.1	2 686	9.1	7 088	702	4 747	713	1 935
Jefferson	1 731	17 617	1.1	D	D	151	9.6	1 687	13.2	2 971	305	1 752	348	2 066
Johnson	7 857	135 730	1.1	1 662	13.4	563	4.5	10 112	8.7	13 926	1 730	6 222	2 788	2 130
Jones	1 304	18 001	0.7	D	D	182	8.9	1 610	9.8	3 944	688	2 338	253	1 226
Keokuk	140	8 562	0.6	D	D	116	10.7	905	10.9	2 269	301	1 329	5	48
Kossuth	257	15 353	0.9	D	D	186	11.9	1 093	9.4	3 803	114	2 483	127	817
Lee	1 594	37 787	1.1	D	D	432	12.1	3 051	10.7	7 421	603	4 777	1 178	3 285
Linn	5 166	221 145	1.1	2 854	13.9	1 583	7.7	14 604	8.2	32 758	8 357	15 281	6 641	3 144
Louisa	116	10 218	0.7	D	D	120	10.1	1 179	12.7	1 951	199	1 094	84	738
Lucas	78	8 944	1.0	D	D	106	11.3	888	12.2	1 911	177	1 136	205	2 304
Lyon	161	10 111	0.8	D	D	122	10.8	935	10.4	2 046	158	1 413	76	841
Madison	192	11 712	0.5	D	D	134	8.7	1 232	9.6	2 625	333	1 503	181	1 154
Mahaska	659	20 240	0.8	D	D	215	9.7	1 918	10.7	4 117	424	2 663	365	1 631
Marion	1 693	34 839	1.1	D	D	327	10.0	2 246	8.5	6 114	457	3 614	314	993
Marshall	1 375	40 651	1.0	D	D	465	11.8	3 571	11.2	7 711	741	5 211	1 317	3 240
Mills	608	12 251	0.6	D	D	134	8.8	1 129	8.9	2 767	218	1 732	376	2 497
Mitchell	247	10 409	0.9	D	D	124	11.5	886	10.7	2 367	91	1 572	55	510
Monona	200	8 506	0.8	D	D	150	16.4	787	12.0	2 272	245	1 511	29	314
Monroe	122	7 491	0.9	D	D	93	12.1	709	12.0	1 668	133	1 000	99	1 242
Montgomery	213	10 831	1.0	D	D	152	13.7	936	11.1	2 462	131	1 669	NA	NA
Muscatine	553	44 439	1.1	D	D	367	8.6	3 861	10.6	7 074	989	3 665	1 108	2 592
O'Brien	366	13 744	0.9	D	D	200	14.1	1 160	10.9	3 176	196	2 227	119	827
Osceola	112	5 896	0.8	D	D	78	11.9	616	12.3	1 331	53	908	16	248
Page	1 468	16 531	1.1	D	D	204	12.8	1 230	10.5	3 592	252	2 428	324	2 034
Palo Alto	344	9 151	0.9	D	D	133	14.0	799	11.3	2 059	32	1 454	73	775
Plymouth	349	23 301	0.9	D	D	244	10.0	1 681	8.5	4 525	606	2 759	340	1 361
Pocahontas	141	6 898	0.8	D	D	112	14.6	574	10.3	1 768	74	1 180	50	684
Polk	9 356	462 078	1.2	6 851	16.4	2 940	7.0	35 001	9.4	57 873	9 548	27 436	15 939	3 701
Pottawattamie	2 076	84 531	0.8	1 233	13.7	858	9.6	8 325	11.1	16 372	3 348	8 165	4 792	5 144
Poweshiek	1 627	20 414	1.1	D	D	214	11.4	1 367	9.4	3 729	267	2 248	306	1 618
Ringgold	179	4 762	0.8	D	D	82	15.8	515	14.0	1 234	96	815	NA	NA
Sac	223	9 232	0.8	D	D	147	14.1	826	10.9	2 440	92	1 678	78	754
Scott	3 334	166 181	1.1	2 275	13.9	1 277	7.8	14 182	10.0	26 523	4 747	10 991	6 508	3 939
Shelby	220	12 239	1.0	D	D	146	11.9	824	9.0	2 921	194	1 948	NA	NA
Sioux	2 410	35 381	1.1	518	16.0	241	7.5	2 636	10.0	5 224	496	3 553	NA	NA
Story	8 174	88 449	1.0	1 014	12.1	499	5.9	5 837	7.7	10 418	972	6 130	2 514	2 808
Tama	399	15 389	0.7	D	D	192	10.8	1 486	10.8	3 607	368	2 114	186	1 249
Taylor	96	5 729	0.8	D	D	89	13.8	629	12.9	1 498	73	1 004	36	570
Union	352	13 274	1.1	D	D	155	12.8	1 004	10.5	2 637	223	1 774	249	1 987
Van Buren	97	6 946	0.8	D	D	87	11.3	834	14.0	1 673	165	1 043	94	1 242
Wapello	867	36 664	1.1	D	D	412	11.5	3 149	11.1	7 358	614	3 983	1 137	3 192
Warren	1 742	32 335	0.5	529	11.9	363	8.2	3 055	8.0	7 124	1 099	3 350	745	1 612
Washington	310	19 373	0.8	D	D	235	11.0	1 943	11.3	4 263	401	2 652	249	1 147
Wayne	91	5 878	0.8	D	D	98	15.4	590	12.4	1 585	150	970	35	547
Webster	2 627	39 847	1.1	D	D	479	12.4	3 577	11.6	7 473	460	4 531	1 633	4 296
Winnebago	488	12 782	1.3	D	D	135	12.2	750	9.0	2 272	86	1 514	68	626
Winneshiek	2 288	21 536	1.0	D	D	170	8.1	1 753	10.6	3 918	546	2 356	90	427
Woodbury	2 636	101 689	1.0	1 663	16.2	929	9.1	11 732	13.5	16 238	3 222	8 318	3 650	3 572
Worth	90	6 288	0.7	D	D	79	10.3	567	9.5	1 523	93	985	111	1 461
Wright	198	13 324	1.0	D	D	168	12.8	1 077	11.0	2 967	102	2 065	113	1 041

1. Per 1,000 estimated resident population.   2. Data for serious crimes have not been adjusted for underreporting; this may affect comparability between geographic areas and over time.   3. Per 100,000 population estimated by the FBI.

Table B. States and Counties — Crime, Education, Money Income, and Poverty

STATE County	Serious crimes known to police,[1] 2010 (cont.) Rate[2] Violent	Property	Education — School enrollment and attainment, 2006-2010 — Enrollment[3] Total	Percent private	Attainment[4] (percent) High school graduate or less	Bachelor's degree or more	Local government expenditures,[5] 2008-2009 Total current expenditures (mil dol)	Current expenditures per student (dollars)	Money income, 2006-2010 Per capita income[6] (dollars)	Households Median income Dollars	Percent change, 2000 to 2006-2010 (constant 2010 dollars)	Percent with income of $200,000 or more	Income and poverty, 2010 Median household income (dollars)	Percent below poverty level All persons	Children under 18 years	Children 5 to 17 years in families
	46	47	48	49	50	51	52	53	54	55	56	57	58	59	60	61
IOWA—Cont'd																
Franklin	9	215	2 279	4.1	50.2	14.4	16.6	8 865	22 507	44 863	-1.7	1.0	45 383	11.8	19.3	17.5
Fremont	NA	NA	1 666	4.3	53.3	17.4	8.7	9 285	23 612	47 225	-2.7	1.6	47 513	11.2	16.9	15.6
Greene	43	578	2 147	3.0	50.7	17.5	15.3	9 382	23 947	43 286	0.9	1.6	46 947	11.1	18.5	15.9
Grundy	24	763	3 109	8.0	43.8	21.6	22.7	8 217	26 916	56 184	12.6	2.2	55 302	6.2	7.5	6.7
Guthrie	0	484	2 608	11.3	48.4	18.9	22.6	8 336	26 590	50 090	8.4	1.9	48 064	10.4	14.6	12.6
Hamilton	300	2 157	3 659	8.0	47.1	16.4	26.2	9 177	24 765	46 188	-5.6	2.0	46 574	11.0	15.3	13.7
Hancock	53	688	2 620	13.3	49.9	15.4	15.9	8 834	22 713	47 318	-0.9	0.7	48 195	9.4	13.4	11.7
Hardin	131	1 489	4 261	8.4	44.1	20.2	30.2	10 578	24 154	44 694	-0.4	2.1	46 411	11.4	17.4	15.2
Harrison	40	670	3 733	7.6	51.4	15.5	28.0	9 256	24 221	51 303	6.2	1.3	50 845	10.0	14.9	13.2
Henry	318	1 945	5 242	14.1	48.6	19.9	40.4	8 702	23 056	41 983	-15.2	2.2	43 228	14.9	19.7	16.6
Howard	94	1 746	2 262	11.8	58.6	11.5	13.2	9 366	22 417	46 068	5.0	1.3	40 919	12.7	19.8	17.9
Humboldt	10	571	2 317	15.4	51.6	15.9	14.4	9 571	24 568	45 282	-6.4	1.6	46 300	10.6	15.5	13.6
Ida	28	875	1 629	5.1	51.0	18.3	10.3	8 314	23 841	44 521	1.0	0.8	47 035	12.8	17.2	14.1
Iowa	147	850	3 999	12.9	48.9	19.2	24.5	9 125	26 721	56 053	7.4	1.5	52 592	8.1	10.4	9.0
Jackson	111	1 204	4 657	12.9	58.3	15.0	30.3	9 228	23 008	42 489	-2.8	1.6	42 274	13.2	19.6	16.9
Jasper	160	1 775	8 399	11.0	52.9	16.6	51.3	8 534	23 160	46 396	-12.1	1.2	46 565	12.4	15.7	13.2
Jefferson	113	1 953	3 974	29.3	41.3	30.1	24.7	9 737	23 853	44 167	3.0	2.0	40 158	14.9	22.5	19.2
Johnson	225	1 905	48 873	7.6	23.1	50.8	139.9	9 496	28 008	51 380	1.3	4.1	51 014	17.0	12.5	11.8
Jones	39	1 187	4 432	11.4	55.7	15.9	28.0	8 904	22 873	47 955	1.1	0.9	46 600	10.9	14.3	12.3
Keokuk	0	48	2 451	4.5	55.7	13.8	11.8	8 765	22 088	42 698	-0.9	0.8	42 999	13.0	18.2	16.4
Kossuth	122	695	3 549	17.8	50.3	16.7	19.8	9 930	27 415	48 277	10.3	3.3	47 930	10.3	13.8	12.6
Lee	580	2 705	8 408	22.5	54.6	14.8	40.8	9 391	21 324	42 444	-7.4	1.2	40 363	15.8	24.1	21.3
Linn	225	2 919	57 113	20.5	35.5	29.6	374.0	10 668	28 239	53 674	-8.3	2.9	54 806	9.9	12.2	10.2
Louisa	88	650	3 181	5.2	60.3	13.1	26.2	9 500	20 367	50 457	1.9	0.4	50 301	11.4	16.4	13.8
Lucas	225	2 079	1 921	4.8	57.8	10.5	12.5	8 103	19 967	43 005	10.0	0.2	39 207	17.5	25.4	22.8
Lyon	221	620	2 691	17.8	53.6	15.9	15.8	8 619	21 613	49 508	8.0	0.6	51 491	8.9	12.0	11.1
Madison	38	1 116	3 988	11.1	50.2	18.2	27.7	8 437	25 711	53 183	0.4	2.7	52 351	9.0	10.9	9.4
Mahaska	264	1 367	6 126	29.6	54.8	17.9	36.1	8 883	21 568	45 025	-4.7	1.2	45 211	15.4	18.0	15.9
Marion	187	807	9 198	35.7	46.0	24.0	49.4	8 329	24 613	53 370	-0.6	2.1	52 845	10.2	11.4	10.3
Marshall	305	2 935	9 778	10.5	60.0	18.7	59.1	8 748	22 407	45 232	-6.7	1.6	45 911	13.3	18.4	16.8
Mills	319	2 178	3 776	9.2	44.6	22.6	28.5	8 774	25 400	59 481	10.7	1.8	57 359	9.4	13.0	11.2
Mitchell	56	455	2 078	17.2	50.3	16.6	17.9	9 109	22 820	48 506	9.9	0.3	47 406	11.1	17.0	15.4
Monona	43	270	1 971	7.0	55.5	14.7	13.2	9 422	22 774	41 398	-1.6	1.7	43 052	11.0	20.0	17.6
Monroe	100	1 142	1 755	7.8	54.3	15.1	10.2	8 658	21 228	43 245	-2.1	0.7	42 631	12.7	18.5	17.2
Montgomery	NA	NA	2 543	7.4	49.7	17.6	17.9	9 660	21 301	38 624	-8.2	0.8	41 068	14.4	22.1	19.1
Muscatine	363	2 230	10 809	5.7	48.8	19.8	65.8	8 661	24 138	51 025	3.6	1.9	47 583	13.8	20.4	16.2
O'Brien	69	757	3 485	18.9	49.3	19.3	21.4	8 990	24 771	44 018	-2.8	3.0	44 209	12.0	15.3	13.0
Osceola	15	232	1 472	9.8	56.1	16.3	7.5	8 608	23 063	43 889	1.1	0.9	51 042	9.3	15.1	13.9
Page	151	1 883	3 527	10.7	53.8	16.7	23.4	8 554	21 204	40 778	-9.2	1.5	40 960	14.6	22.4	19.6
Palo Alto	149	626	2 130	9.2	49.5	16.1	15.1	9 597	23 071	42 800	4.3	1.8	43 360	11.4	14.5	13.1
Plymouth	108	1 253	6 333	18.8	47.6	19.8	36.3	8 428	28 060	56 379	6.9	3.5	61 292	8.0	10.4	9.1
Pocahontas	96	588	1 680	10.7	48.5	16.4	9.4	9 721	23 385	42 105	-0.3	0.7	44 225	12.2	19.4	17.3
Polk	341	3 361	110 078	20.7	36.5	32.8	718.2	10 644	29 246	56 094	-3.9	3.5	54 328	11.0	14.5	12.7
Pottawattamie	726	4 418	22 190	12.3	49.7	17.3	166.7	10 360	23 782	48 728	-4.0	1.5	47 870	14.5	19.4	16.8
Poweshiek	127	1 491	5 605	36.1	50.7	21.7	24.5	8 286	25 218	50 998	6.4	2.4	48 929	12.0	14.8	12.9
Ringgold	NA	NA	1 144	11.1	50.8	20.8	8.7	11 098	21 858	42 336	14.9	1.1	36 810	18.6	29.5	26.7
Sac	48	705	2 158	8.5	54.0	18.2	16.4	9 495	23 837	42 986	3.3	2.6	42 888	10.5	15.2	13.4
Scott	557	3 382	43 328	19.3	38.2	29.7	276.7	9 947	27 408	49 964	-7.6	3.3	47 800	15.0	20.2	17.8
Shelby	NA	NA	2 858	8.8	55.3	16.1	17.1	8 702	22 389	44 085	-7.0	0.9	49 056	10.2	12.5	10.6
Sioux	NA	NA	10 292	49.6	49.3	22.4	38.2	8 529	21 333	51 557	0.4	1.7	53 705	8.0	9.4	8.3
Story	297	2 511	37 836	4.3	24.9	47.2	98.6	9 068	25 450	48 248	-5.8	2.5	49 192	18.5	11.7	10.1
Tama	275	974	4 479	10.4	52.5	16.5	22.8	8 642	23 041	46 288	-2.3	2.0	48 833	12.2	18.2	15.8
Taylor	16	554	1 480	7.1	56.8	12.3	9.6	9 677	21 335	40 300	1.7	1.6	42 768	13.4	18.9	16.6
Union	176	1 811	2 996	7.4	52.5	15.6	24.7	12 281	20 435	40 879	1.2	0.3	39 977	15.3	20.9	19.6
Van Buren	119	1 123	1 557	15.0	56.6	13.5	11.4	9 772	20 209	40 073	1.8	1.6	37 833	16.4	26.0	23.8
Wapello	326	2 866	7 999	9.6	55.5	14.9	67.4	12 346	22 376	40 093	-1.6	1.7	38 569	17.4	24.3	21.2
Warren	173	1 439	12 894	21.8	39.3	26.7	73.0	8 327	28 798	62 034	-2.7	3.3	62 036	7.4	9.2	7.5
Washington	332	816	5 156	15.3	48.8	19.4	33.2	8 727	23 979	50 710	2.4	1.0	47 118	10.0	15.4	13.5
Wayne	62	484	1 429	10.4	62.1	10.8	11.7	9 823	18 795	35 425	-4.8	0.7	35 867	16.8	26.5	24.3
Webster	287	4 009	10 208	15.9	48.2	18.0	73.2	13 791	22 653	40 806	-8.8	1.2	39 565	16.5	21.9	19.1
Winnebago	156	469	2 775	21.7	44.3	19.3	22.7	9 128	22 684	41 871	-13.8	0.9	48 933	10.6	15.7	14.1
Winneshiek	24	404	6 511	47.8	46.7	26.3	27.7	9 679	23 608	50 693	2.9	1.8	51 248	10.0	12.0	10.2
Woodbury	313	3 259	27 710	21.4	49.5	20.8	191.6	10 676	22 069	44 343	-9.1	1.5	42 672	15.1	21.5	18.7
Worth	26	1 435	1 722	7.9	45.1	16.0	9.7	10 323	27 240	49 673	7.6	2.3	46 384	11.6	17.2	14.3
Wright	92	949	2 845	5.8	51.0	15.7	24.4	9 152	23 068	44 035	-3.9	1.6	44 456	11.3	16.8	15.3

1. Data for serious crimes have not been adjusted for underreporting; this may affect comparability between geographic areas and over time. 2. Per 100,000 population estimated by the FBI. 3. All persons 3 years old and over enrolled in nursery school through college. 4. Persons 25 years old and over. 5. Elementary and secondary education expenditures. 6. Based on population estimated by the American Community Survey, 2006-2010.

Table B. States and Counties — **Personal Income**

	Personal income, 2009												
			Per capita[1]					Transfer payments (mil dol)					
									Government payments to individuals				
STATE County	Total (mil dol)	Percent change, 2008–2009	Dollars	Rank	Wages and salaries[2] (mil dol)	Proprietors' income (mil dol)	Dividends, interest, and rent (mil dol)	Total	Total	Social Security	Medical payments	Income mainte-nance	Unemploy-ment insurance
	62	63	64	65	66	67	68	69	70	71	72	73	74
IOWA—Cont'd													
Franklin	394	-4.5	37 388	701	161	98	66	70	69	31	25	4	5
Fremont	286	0.9	38 955	543	130	54	42	59	58	23	25	4	2
Greene	371	1.0	40 099	443	143	73	71	72	70	31	28	4	3
Grundy	513	-3.6	42 162	316	184	74	101	78	76	38	26	3	4
Guthrie	412	-6.2	38 068	630	130	70	72	79	77	36	29	5	3
Hamilton	592	-5.0	38 864	550	294	96	116	113	110	45	44	7	8
Hancock	418	-4.2	37 796	665	249	96	66	79	77	33	28	4	8
Hardin	652	-2.9	38 030	636	326	102	123	138	135	55	56	8	6
Harrison	588	3.2	38 342	593	164	96	72	117	114	41	53	7	3
Henry	617	-4.5	30 959	1 768	414	51	107	143	139	54	52	11	11
Howard	320	-2.9	33 979	1 173	162	49	67	65	64	26	25	4	5
Humboldt	381	-0.4	40 244	436	158	81	70	72	70	30	29	4	3
Ida	315	-5.2	46 551	156	153	89	55	51	50	22	21	3	2
Iowa	597	-3.7	37 747	670	383	78	111	102	99	44	37	5	7
Jackson	646	-0.4	32 729	1 378	231	47	127	154	150	55	63	11	10
Jasper	1 198	-0.4	33 053	1 333	490	150	202	247	240	104	90	18	15
Jefferson	539	-2.7	34 818	1 039	292	51	145	106	103	38	38	12	8
Johnson	5 021	0.8	38 330	595	4 166	317	876	544	520	202	177	58	28
Jones	600	-1.3	29 456	2 103	252	58	114	132	128	55	47	9	9
Keokuk	353	0.0	33 405	1 277	92	55	60	80	78	30	32	6	5
Kossuth	656	-3.8	43 276	263	258	180	120	116	114	53	43	6	5
Lee	1 113	-1.3	31 393	1 666	731	68	199	300	294	105	121	28	18
Linn	8 428	-0.6	40 282	434	6 829	419	1 423	1 297	1 259	490	465	119	82
Louisa	369	-3.4	32 805	1 366	152	34	55	73	71	28	27	6	6
Lucas	250	-0.2	27 246	2 525	134	17	48	67	66	25	27	6	3
Lyon	430	-4.5	38 472	582	146	109	69	61	59	27	23	3	2
Madison	552	-2.0	35 826	910	150	72	81	95	92	37	35	6	8
Mahaska	747	-3.1	33 942	1 178	330	77	131	153	149	56	52	15	12
Marion	1 121	-2.8	34 305	1 126	782	75	224	209	203	85	74	13	14
Marshall	1 406	0.0	35 805	912	854	127	230	311	304	113	123	24	16
Mills	642	-0.4	42 809	282	177	62	63	191	188	37	131	7	2
Mitchell	384	-5.2	35 572	946	175	66	73	75	73	32	30	3	3
Monona	351	-0.5	39 568	482	106	95	52	81	79	31	35	5	3
Monroe	270	0.3	35 749	921	172	20	36	62	61	22	26	4	4
Montgomery	371	-2.2	34 403	1 109	174	59	67	93	91	34	40	7	5
Muscatine	1 522	-3.4	35 443	962	1 131	72	311	279	272	106	98	26	27
O'Brien	563	-3.8	40 397	426	233	104	110	111	108	44	48	5	4
Osceola	247	-7.5	38 969	539	92	66	42	41	40	18	16	2	2
Page	509	-1.5	33 351	1 288	248	61	96	131	128	50	55	10	7
Palo Alto	362	-4.9	38 984	538	143	96	57	73	71	29	31	4	4
Plymouth	1 015	-1.6	41 907	337	487	177	183	143	139	63	54	7	7
Pocahontas	311	-5.0	42 317	305	108	90	48	61	59	24	27	3	2
Polk	18 200	-1.0	42 381	300	15 477	1 783	2 764	2 514	2 436	852	958	264	168
Pottawattamie	3 279	-0.8	36 342	837	1 678	235	400	650	634	219	257	61	17
Poweshiek	710	-1.5	38 528	575	425	97	135	127	124	53	46	8	9
Ringgold	139	4.5	28 133	2 377	56	15	29	39	38	16	16	3	1
Sac	403	-7.6	40 062	446	134	88	81	75	73	33	29	4	3
Scott	6 932	0.8	41 594	359	4 008	535	1 159	1 290	1 260	384	379	129	55
Shelby	502	-0.8	41 966	330	216	94	87	95	93	37	42	5	2
Sioux	1 146	-4.4	35 548	951	734	172	224	170	165	71	65	8	9
Story	3 106	0.6	35 616	941	2 236	254	568	410	394	151	145	32	19
Tama	622	0.5	35 788	914	209	123	99	118	114	50	42	8	7
Taylor	223	-0.2	35 178	996	72	54	33	47	46	19	19	3	2
Union	395	2.0	32 295	1 457	257	36	60	101	99	34	42	9	4
Van Buren	207	-3.3	26 892	2 586	82	19	35	60	58	23	24	4	4
Wapello	1 113	0.6	31 491	1 643	696	66	163	316	309	100	125	34	19
Warren	1 738	0.9	38 378	591	390	73	223	251	243	104	89	15	16
Washington	810	-2.2	38 107	626	296	72	150	147	143	59	61	10	7
Wayne	169	1.6	26 904	2 583	71	11	30	52	51	20	22	4	2
Webster	1 325	-3.2	34 566	1 083	859	140	223	302	295	108	121	24	15
Winnebago	366	-5.1	34 546	1 086	184	53	69	82	81	32	32	5	7
Winneshiek	724	-3.1	35 078	1 007	421	88	146	132	129	51	46	6	8
Woodbury	3 463	-1.7	33 674	1 225	2 267	363	530	675	656	227	278	70	29
Worth	256	-3.0	33 961	1 177	90	42	44	49	48	20	16	3	4
Wright	536	-8.1	42 150	318	243	99	109	107	104	42	44	6	6

1. Based on the resident population estimated as of July 1 of the year shown.   2. Includes supplements to wages and salaries.

STATE County	Total (mil dol)	Farm	Goods-related[1] Total	Manu-facturing	Information and professional and technical services	Retail trade	Finance, insurance, and real estate	Health care and social services	Govern-ment	Number	Rate[2]	Supplemental Security Income recipients, December 2010	Housing units Total	Percent change, 2000–2010
	75	76	77	78	79	80	81	82	83	84	85	86	87	88
IOWA—Cont'd														
Franklin	259	28.4	D	14.2	2.8	4.1	2.9	4.9	13.9	2 475	232	116	4 894	2.8
Fremont	184	25.9	34.1	32.9	2.0	5.4	D	D	11.9	1 945	261	151	3 431	-2.4
Greene	216	27.1	D	15.6	4.5	4.4	4.7	D	18.5	2 430	260	158	4 546	-1.7
Grundy	258	24.6	21.7	8.9	2.4	4.0	6.1	D	11.8	2 855	229	85	5 530	4.3
Guthrie	200	29.7	13.9	7.4	3.0	3.9	9.5	6.8	19.8	2 840	259	144	5 756	5.3
Hamilton	389	19.2	D	24.3	3.2	4.0	3.9	D	15.5	3 515	224	193	7 219	1.9
Hancock	344	19.7	D	37.7	2.3	2.9	2.1	D	9.5	2 580	227	126	5 330	3.2
Hardin	427	20.0	17.5	7.9	3.2	5.3	3.5	D	20.2	4 235	242	216	8 224	-1.1
Harrison	260	31.2	D	4.8	2.7	5.1	3.3	D	17.1	3 305	221	239	6 731	2.0
Henry	465	3.8	D	20.7	5.2	5.6	2.7	D	21.4	4 320	214	315	8 280	0.4
Howard	212	15.1	32.0	27.1	D	6.0	4.4	D	17.6	2 235	234	102	4 367	0.9
Humboldt	239	23.1	D	19.7	2.6	5.2	2.8	D	13.8	2 385	243	137	4 684	0.8
Ida	241	28.8	27.8	22.8	1.3	3.3	4.0	6.6	7.8	1 765	249	69	3 426	-2.3
Iowa	461	8.1	48.7	44.4	2.5	5.6	2.4	4.5	11.5	3 425	209	144	7 258	10.9
Jackson	278	7.6	16.2	11.2	4.5	9.6	4.7	D	21.4	4 675	236	394	9 415	5.2
Jasper	640	16.1	D	12.9	11.3	5.8	3.4	6.7	21.5	8 000	217	482	16 181	3.3
Jefferson	343	4.4	D	14.6	12.0	8.7	4.6	5.7	17.3	3 275	194	306	7 594	4.9
Johnson	4 483	1.3	D	6.9	7.1	5.6	3.9	7.6	45.3	14 810	113	1 422	55 967	22.1
Jones	310	12.0	D	12.6	D	9.9	3.7	D	23.2	4 430	215	241	8 911	9.7
Keokuk	147	25.8	D	4.9	3.0	4.9	D	6.4	18.2	2 490	237	190	4 931	-1.6
Kossuth	438	27.9	D	15.0	3.7	5.1	7.2	D	12.2	4 190	270	188	7 486	-1.6
Lee	800	1.9	36.9	30.7	2.6	7.1	3.4	12.8	16.8	8 235	230	935	16 205	-2.5
Linn	7 248	0.6	29.4	22.8	9.4	6.9	10.1	10.6	10.8	36 510	173	3 031	92 251	14.5
Louisa	185	11.8	D	33.8	D	3.0	2.7	4.0	21.3	2 205	194	169	5 002	-2.6
Lucas	150	-0.1	D	5.4	3.0	6.7	4.4	6.6	23.2	2 105	237	211	4 238	0.0
Lyon	255	35.6	D	11.3	7.8	3.5	3.3	5.3	11.3	2 210	191	64	4 848	1.9
Madison	222	18.3	D	11.2	3.7	6.6	5.1	6.5	23.8	2 975	190	139	6 554	15.8
Mahaska	407	11.5	D	19.8	4.6	7.1	2.9	D	18.7	4 630	207	438	9 766	2.3
Marion	858	4.1	D	43.0	2.3	5.0	3.0	10.2	14.3	6 790	204	360	13 914	9.1
Marshall	982	6.7	D	32.4	3.7	5.6	2.9	11.7	18.6	8 610	212	633	16 831	3.1
Mills	239	15.1	D	4.1	2.5	4.7	4.4	D	41.2	3 070	204	281	6 109	7.7
Mitchell	241	19.4	D	20.8	2.6	3.6	2.9	D	13.9	2 580	239	91	4 850	5.6
Monona	201	40.8	5.5	2.2	D	4.8	3.5	12.3	14.9	2 580	279	159	4 697	0.8
Monroe	192	2.4	50.1	42.6	D	4.1	2.6	D	13.8	1 900	238	145	3 884	8.2
Montgomery	233	20.4	D	9.5	D	8.9	3.4	D	21.4	2 735	255	220	5 239	-3.0
Muscatine	1 202	1.6	41.4	37.1	9.9	5.0	2.6	6.2	12.4	8 110	190	704	17 910	6.7
O'Brien	336	22.0	12.8	8.1	3.2	5.6	5.5	14.2	13.9	3 510	244	202	6 649	2.2
Osceola	158	42.0	D	12.0	D	2.8	2.9	D	10.1	1 485	230	64	2 990	-0.7
Page	308	9.3	D	16.4	D	8.2	3.6	D	25.3	4 040	254	346	7 181	-1.7
Palo Alto	239	37.8	11.0	8.9	2.0	5.1	3.3	D	18.1	2 320	246	140	4 628	-0.1
Plymouth	664	18.7	D	19.5	3.3	4.6	4.0	5.3	11.4	5 015	201	212	10 550	6.8
Pocahontas	198	41.8	D	8.8	D	3.3	D	D	14.9	1 925	263	105	3 794	-4.9
Polk	17 261	0.3	D	5.8	10.0	5.7	22.6	10.2	14.1	63 665	148	6 857	182 262	16.5
Pottawattamie	1 912	4.5	D	13.2	4.6	8.4	3.5	13.4	16.2	17 640	189	2 009	39 330	9.8
Poweshiek	522	12.5	D	14.5	D	4.5	10.9	D	8.5	4 055	214	198	8 949	4.5
Ringgold	71	8.9	D	2.6	D	6.6	2.8	D	33.4	1 390	271	105	2 613	-6.3
Sac	222	28.8	D	7.6	D	4.0	3.6	D	13.3	2 655	257	113	5 429	-0.6
Scott	4 542	0.8	22.3	16.1	9.7	8.5	5.4	14.4	11.0	29 505	179	3 558	71 835	9.4
Shelby	310	26.8	12.7	8.3	6.0	5.2	4.4	D	16.3	3 065	252	165	5 542	2.4
Sioux	906	15.4	31.8	25.6	3.6	4.9	4.0	6.6	11.3	5 595	166	187	12 279	9.0
Story	2 489	3.3	D	12.4	5.6	5.3	3.0	8.2	42.7	11 145	124	644	36 789	20.1
Tama	331	31.1	7.5	4.7	D	4.2	2.3	D	30.1	4 015	226	176	7 766	2.4
Taylor	126	41.9	D	12.8	D	2.2	1.9	4.5	15.3	1 640	260	110	3 107	-2.9
Union	293	5.4	D	24.8	D	7.4	3.7	8.9	23.1	2 905	232	290	5 937	4.9
Van Buren	101	14.3	D	21.1	2.2	4.5	D	3.7	27.9	1 860	246	133	3 670	2.5
Wapello	762	0.8	D	27.0	3.7	8.4	3.3	16.7	17.3	8 195	230	1 124	16 098	1.4
Warren	463	3.7	12.4	5.0	7.0	9.5	4.4	D	24.4	7 905	171	372	18 371	20.2
Washington	368	12.8	D	10.2	3.4	8.7	4.4	8.4	19.7	4 690	216	298	9 516	11.4
Wayne	82	4.6	25.5	22.4	4.2	5.9	D	6.4	33.6	1 735	271	141	3 212	-4.3
Webster	1 000	7.9	D	16.7	5.4	7.0	3.6	14.6	16.9	8 505	224	748	17 035	0.4
Winnebago	237	17.0	D	22.6	D	6.5	3.9	D	15.7	2 520	232	103	5 194	2.5
Winneshiek	509	6.2	D	18.4	4.1	6.6	3.2	D	18.6	4 240	201	191	8 721	6.3
Woodbury	2 630	3.9	D	12.9	4.9	8.6	5.5	16.6	15.8	18 035	177	1 978	41 484	0.2
Worth	132	24.7	D	15.0	2.9	3.4	2.4	4.4	14.1	1 670	220	65	3 548	0.4
Wright	342	26.6	D	17.9	4.1	3.9	2.8	4.6	20.5	3 245	245	168	6 529	-0.5

1. Includes mining, construction, and manufacturing.   2. Per 1,000 resident population enumerated in the 2010 census.

STATE County	Housing units, 2006–2010								Civilian labor force, 2010				Civilian employment,[5] 2006–2010		
	Occupied units							Substandard units[3] (percent)			Unemployment			Percent	
			Owner-occupied			Renter-occupied									Construction, production, and maintenance occupations
				Median owner cost as a percent of income										Management, business, science and arts	
	Total	Percent	Median value[1]	With a mortgage	Without a mortgage	Median rent[2]	Median rent as a percent of income		Total	Percent change, 2009–2010	Total	Rate[4]	Total		
	89	90	91	92	93	94	95	96	97	98	99	100	101	102	103
IOWA—Cont'd															
Franklin	4 189	74.1	82 500	20.2	11.5	479	19.3	1.0	5 912	2.5	381	6.4	5 280	24.8	39.2
Fremont	3 119	77.9	92 800	19.3	12.7	497	24.6	2.5	3 801	1.5	240	6.3	3 740	32.2	28.1
Greene	4 168	76.2	80 400	20.3	12.3	526	23.2	1.8	4 987	-1.8	307	6.2	4 832	31.6	28.1
Grundy	5 042	80.7	111 000	19.5	10.9	513	22.6	1.3	6 928	-0.2	407	5.9	6 362	33.0	29.9
Guthrie	4 669	79.1	94 600	19.7	12.6	476	24.9	0.7	5 703	-1.9	385	6.8	5 458	34.4	25.3
Hamilton	6 603	76.7	90 500	19.6	13.5	572	30.1	1.7	7 779	-5.7	603	7.8	8 124	28.3	36.0
Hancock	4 774	82.6	81 200	20.1	12.3	500	23.5	2.5	5 658	0.6	406	7.2	5 805	27.8	36.1
Hardin	7 353	73.8	85 600	19.8	11.9	513	22.1	0.7	9 100	-3.0	607	6.7	8 530	32.3	30.2
Harrison	6 096	79.4	111 400	21.2	12.9	539	28.9	1.6	7 662	-0.5	390	5.1	7 498	33.8	29.2
Henry	7 657	73.8	96 400	22.0	12.3	569	29.2	2.0	9 533	-2.7	853	8.9	9 848	28.8	34.9
Howard	4 021	79.5	90 300	21.8	12.3	517	25.2	0.3	4 946	-2.5	339	6.9	5 010	26.5	37.6
Humboldt	4 289	76.0	81 600	19.4	10.3	535	23.2	1.9	5 082	-0.9	271	5.3	4 902	30.4	31.3
Ida	3 123	75.6	74 300	17.5	10.0	419	18.4	1.5	3 878	-2.3	199	5.1	3 648	31.4	34.8
Iowa	6 657	77.9	128 400	21.4	11.6	561	20.3	2.3	8 422	-1.3	537	6.4	8 912	31.5	30.7
Jackson	8 381	78.4	106 100	21.9	13.2	502	24.3	1.2	11 019	-1.3	805	7.3	10 174	26.8	36.9
Jasper	15 036	73.4	114 600	23.6	12.2	586	27.1	1.4	17 404	-1.9	1 431	8.2	17 613	29.2	28.6
Jefferson	6 826	72.4	92 400	21.7	12.8	592	24.2	2.2	7 907	-3.7	637	8.1	8 869	38.7	25.1
Johnson	50 985	60.3	177 000	22.1	10.6	735	37.1	1.5	80 319	0.5	3 503	4.4	72 565	44.8	14.1
Jones	8 093	79.2	106 900	21.5	12.4	607	25.4	0.9	10 655	-0.2	690	6.5	9 972	27.5	32.7
Keokuk	4 571	80.1	74 700	21.6	12.4	508	22.4	2.0	5 526	-2.0	371	6.7	5 345	23.4	36.1
Kossuth	6 661	82.2	84 700	18.7	10.0	435	25.2	2.0	8 929	0.5	429	4.8	7 760	36.1	25.9
Lee	14 234	74.1	78 900	19.6	11.5	507	27.0	1.8	17 169	-0.4	1 666	9.7	16 190	25.7	35.7
Linn	85 447	72.9	136 400	21.2	12.2	620	26.1	1.4	122 633	0.5	7 360	6.0	109 889	37.4	21.3
Louisa	4 280	80.1	87 400	21.5	12.1	583	21.1	4.3	5 844	-5.4	411	7.0	5 491	22.2	44.9
Lucas	3 668	75.5	85 200	21.5	12.3	456	28.2	1.1	4 750	1.9	267	5.6	3 939	22.2	33.1
Lyon	4 365	81.9	97 900	20.8	10.0	518	22.5	1.1	6 938	1.0	248	3.6	6 081	32.7	30.2
Madison	5 753	81.5	145 400	23.6	14.5	606	25.7	1.6	8 215	-1.7	574	7.0	8 086	33.8	26.8
Mahaska	8 988	75.1	95 200	19.8	12.5	521	26.9	1.2	11 577	-1.4	815	7.0	11 171	29.5	31.3
Marion	12 522	76.2	137 300	21.0	11.3	625	24.8	1.2	17 028	-1.0	1 066	6.3	17 070	31.3	28.1
Marshall	15 517	75.0	99 600	22.4	12.4	552	26.7	3.3	20 324	-0.5	1 394	6.9	18 578	29.9	32.7
Mills	5 581	82.5	144 200	21.8	10.0	677	28.3	2.3	7 892	-2.3	345	4.4	7 480	30.0	26.1
Mitchell	4 328	83.2	99 200	21.2	10.5	461	24.0	1.3	5 549	-4.4	304	5.5	5 273	30.5	36.3
Monona	4 200	71.5	71 300	18.7	10.0	468	25.8	0.8	4 528	0.1	359	7.9	4 497	27.7	29.5
Monroe	3 384	78.3	80 100	21.6	12.7	503	30.5	3.0	4 268	-1.2	290	6.8	3 626	31.5	35.8
Montgomery	4 519	74.4	80 800	21.0	11.8	534	29.4	1.2	5 092	-2.5	431	8.5	4 931	27.4	29.5
Muscatine	16 481	77.7	120 300	21.8	13.1	606	27.0	2.4	23 351	-0.4	1 767	7.6	20 894	27.6	35.2
O'Brien	6 022	76.9	83 000	18.0	10.5	515	29.2	0.8	7 843	-0.2	385	4.9	7 491	29.0	31.4
Osceola	2 724	75.6	70 200	17.5	10.6	535	21.4	0.6	3 236	-2.3	184	5.7	3 456	29.3	34.3
Page	6 396	74.0	81 900	19.3	12.4	486	27.6	2.3	7 528	-3.5	500	6.6	6 844	32.1	29.3
Palo Alto	3 979	74.6	74 500	20.1	12.8	388	24.9	1.5	5 141	-3.1	295	5.7	4 740	31.8	29.7
Plymouth	9 804	80.8	119 400	18.7	10.0	526	21.5	0.6	14 483	0.1	660	4.6	13 754	29.5	30.4
Pocahontas	3 317	80.3	56 100	17.8	10.0	417	19.2	0.5	4 031	-2.4	213	5.3	3 783	32.0	30.6
Polk	168 352	70.8	149 700	22.2	12.6	714	28.2	2.4	241 570	-0.3	14 848	6.1	225 897	37.6	18.3
Pottawattamie	36 325	71.3	126 100	22.0	12.9	689	28.8	2.3	48 100	-0.6	2 506	5.2	46 954	28.1	25.9
Poweshiek	7 650	78.2	108 900	20.0	10.8	561	31.0	0.4	10 336	0.8	610	5.9	9 974	33.8	25.3
Ringgold	2 072	79.2	83 300	20.3	13.8	500	19.5	2.1	2 454	0.6	125	5.1	2 417	36.9	31.1
Sac	4 535	80.8	76 800	19.2	11.0	499	25.7	1.5	5 787	0.7	272	4.7	5 220	28.1	30.0
Scott	66 318	70.4	134 600	21.3	11.4	636	28.2	1.4	89 952	0.9	6 209	6.9	81 233	34.6	24.2
Shelby	5 070	77.8	103 100	21.0	12.5	582	28.7	1.3	7 524	-0.7	310	4.1	6 120	30.6	25.1
Sioux	11 522	81.3	119 900	20.4	10.0	542	23.7	2.2	19 785	0.8	765	3.9	18 324	32.4	29.8
Story	34 227	54.8	156 000	21.1	10.6	703	33.1	1.6	48 905	0.0	2 268	4.6	49 877	43.9	17.0
Tama	7 058	77.9	96 500	21.8	12.6	559	22.7	1.9	8 857	0.0	611	6.9	8 644	29.2	32.3
Taylor	2 687	80.5	67 000	19.4	12.4	437	21.8	1.6	3 317	-0.7	183	5.5	2 996	30.0	34.6
Union	5 326	71.9	88 100	22.0	12.5	555	37.8	1.7	7 043	2.9	398	5.7	6 273	24.0	37.3
Van Buren	3 098	78.3	67 600	20.5	12.1	482	24.7	3.5	3 793	-0.5	299	7.9	3 659	29.4	31.9
Wapello	14 764	76.5	74 800	20.3	13.5	565	26.5	1.3	18 579	-0.4	1 491	8.0	17 113	23.2	37.4
Warren	17 008	79.1	150 900	21.6	12.4	673	24.4	1.2	25 675	-0.9	1 528	6.0	24 634	37.0	19.3
Washington	8 767	77.0	118 600	22.4	11.6	624	28.2	2.4	11 842	-2.2	626	5.3	11 373	32.1	28.1
Wayne	2 742	79.2	60 500	21.0	13.5	432	25.1	3.6	3 263	1.0	180	5.5	2 734	28.3	39.6
Webster	15 936	68.8	85 600	19.3	11.9	523	25.4	0.7	19 171	-3.3	1 448	7.6	18 988	27.4	28.9
Winnebago	4 711	74.7	90 900	20.0	11.8	457	19.5	1.9	5 631	-1.6	398	7.1	5 538	30.7	33.6
Winneshiek	7 869	75.5	147 600	22.0	12.5	517	24.7	1.5	12 270	0.7	684	5.6	11 618	33.5	27.0
Woodbury	38 739	68.6	94 700	20.7	11.7	601	28.9	3.1	55 733	0.1	3 691	6.6	50 651	28.1	29.0
Worth	3 279	80.1	95 200	21.4	12.8	516	23.1	2.1	4 399	-2.1	305	6.9	4 021	25.8	36.0
Wright	5 545	74.4	72 700	20.3	11.1	457	21.6	1.7	6 933	-0.8	494	7.1	6 546	29.9	31.9

1. Specified owner-occupied units. 2. Specified renter-occupied units. A value of 10.0 represents 10 percent or less. 3. Overcrowded or lacking complete plumbing facilities. 4. Percent of civilian labor force. 5. Persons 16 years old and over.

Table B. States and Counties — Nonfarm Employment and Agriculture

STATE County	Private nonfarm establishments, employment and payroll, 2009									Agriculture, 2007			
	Number of establishments	Employment						Annual payroll		Farms			
		Total	Health care and social assistance	Manufacturing	Retail trade	Finance and insurance	Professional, scientific, and technical services	Total (mil dol)	Average per employee (dollars)	Number	Fewer than 50 acres	500 acres or more	Farm operators whose principal occupation is farming (percent)
	104	105	106	107	108	109	110	111	112	113	114	115	116
IOWA—Cont'd													
Franklin	328	3 057	557	772	286	101	D	94	30 710	923	30.3	30.3	57.1
Fremont	192	2 183	370	551	508	72	D	65	29 766	497	19.5	31.0	61.8
Greene	269	2 715	D	D	357	156	100	74	27 076	820	32.2	29.4	54.3
Grundy	294	2 735	379	D	419	201	D	102	37 249	800	32.6	24.3	56.1
Guthrie	323	2 753	563	D	377	279	78	92	33 329	987	26.6	18.8	42.0
Hamilton	399	5 629	607	1 812	673	175	117	164	29 187	882	36.2	23.4	55.7
Hancock	304	2 946	446	905	399	61	93	85	28 714	949	30.1	25.7	58.9
Hardin	570	5 519	1 056	631	818	240	269	169	30 593	943	33.0	25.0	56.7
Harrison	349	2 974	651	D	479	131	D	85	28 523	817	27.2	28.4	56.8
Henry	517	13 492	1 181	2 091	836	175	345	381	28 233	880	30.0	15.8	44.9
Howard	285	2 834	443	957	375	145	51	75	26 400	877	28.4	17.2	53.7
Humboldt	328	3 287	418	832	438	115	78	104	31 619	632	23.4	32.3	61.2
Ida	262	2 945	437	973	319	D	37	98	33 312	633	28.8	25.6	56.4
Iowa	473	7 778	780	3 497	1 349	109	75	247	31 702	1 144	26.3	15.3	51.0
Jackson	567	5 038	856	886	902	250	83	121	24 069	1 214	27.8	12.5	45.2
Jasper	782	8 359	1 639	958	1 359	297	462	248	29 719	1 166	31.9	21.3	53.4
Jefferson	667	6 804	640	989	1 134	215	618	193	28 429	773	21.3	11.5	43.7
Johnson	3 024	59 393	16 325	5 326	8 616	2 140	1 771	1 994	33 573	1 293	29.5	14.5	53.4
Jones	528	4 822	907	797	1 097	247	118	130	26 969	1 117	29.2	19.2	51.9
Keokuk	251	1 817	D	187	240	117	D	51	28 264	1 163	23.6	17.0	50.1
Kossuth	579	5 624	931	980	895	548	192	165	29 310	1 395	23.9	31.4	65.8
Lee	945	12 993	2 263	3 610	2 136	477	267	396	30 512	883	27.2	17.0	45.2
Linn	5 414	114 445	14 401	16 858	14 336	8 918	5 490	4 471	39 064	1 413	34.9	13.7	47.8
Louisa	209	2 766	303	D	221	88	30	82	29 826	701	29.0	17.8	47.6
Lucas	175	2 646	516	162	376	96	D	86	32 636	699	29.6	11.6	34.3
Lyon	383	2 807	454	D	407	148	109	83	29 438	1 087	28.2	20.8	56.7
Madison	366	2 649	655	169	437	D	115	75	28 297	956	36.3	15.9	41.4
Mahaska	576	7 286	1 050	1 567	1 177	237	125	226	31 041	1 031	26.7	16.8	47.2
Marion	829	15 630	2 483	D	1 840	380	330	544	34 811	951	32.8	15.1	37.3
Marshall	840	16 132	2 237	D	2 109	395	412	517	34 149	928	31.3	22.0	53.0
Mills	295	2 057	667	D	343	113	110	51	24 746	511	27.2	29.5	58.7
Mitchell	332	3 246	596	1 116	389	119	74	94	29 006	893	29.1	23.3	57.2
Monona	238	2 269	688	D	386	122	52	56	24 599	649	20.0	35.9	63.8
Monroe	176	1 748	457	406	269	71	46	45	25 502	660	24.1	15.0	43.3
Montgomery	339	3 904	833	778	507	132	D	111	28 544	558	22.4	27.8	54.8
Muscatine	974	20 132	1 852	7 292	2 207	515	1 150	805	39 970	838	29.0	15.5	47.7
O'Brien	528	5 100	1 358	507	811	236	122	133	26 000	987	27.6	26.6	63.4
Osceola	187	1 540	204	355	175	84	D	40	26 178	663	22.5	27.1	65.6
Page	411	5 636	1 635	1 637	743	188	133	156	27 643	788	25.3	23.6	53.0
Palo Alto	298	2 934	756	309	339	132	186	67	22 852	849	32.9	26.5	54.5
Plymouth	707	9 449	1 157	2 367	1 134	321	289	324	34 292	1 442	24.6	26.1	60.1
Pocahontas	238	2 066	363	359	242	184	51	50	24 378	806	24.4	35.6	65.1
Polk	11 913	243 771	31 272	14 966	27 686	41 703	13 738	10 288	42 204	738	47.6	19.2	48.0
Pottawattamie	1 979	30 836	4 355	5 072	6 143	879	941	903	29 277	1 158	30.7	27.5	59.6
Poweshiek	559	9 008	1 185	1 383	1 096	957	172	278	30 902	938	30.3	20.7	48.4
Ringgold	141	1 000	362	D	189	40	33	26	26 287	733	17.1	19.0	40.0
Sac	350	2 391	522	D	371	128	D	69	28 862	802	26.6	31.3	61.8
Scott	4 495	79 056	11 780	11 594	11 300	2 549	3 023	2 694	34 083	861	32.9	18.2	58.3
Shelby	413	5 406	1 063	531	649	468	120	147	27 132	871	21.9	29.7	62.8
Sioux	1 205	17 203	2 246	4 813	1 830	576	727	504	29 314	1 664	34.5	18.9	60.8
Story	1 998	28 999	4 881	4 350	4 903	895	1 241	887	30 575	1 077	36.1	20.1	50.7
Tama	355	3 513	390	D	510	134	D	102	29 073	1 210	23.1	23.4	54.8
Taylor	135	1 291	224	417	140	D	D	40	30 628	779	18.9	18.4	43.1
Union	330	4 913	868	1 489	775	182	68	141	28 645	681	26.3	18.2	48.3
Van Buren	166	1 656	400	608	197	D	D	46	27 511	808	22.5	13.9	40.6
Wapello	812	14 246	2 649	3 800	2 409	408	419	450	31 622	744	34.3	11.8	38.6
Warren	795	8 066	1 289	476	1 496	266	260	204	25 308	1 189	38.7	9.8	35.7
Washington	696	6 410	1 237	787	977	231	200	170	26 590	1 257	27.5	17.1	52.1
Wayne	162	1 379	350	427	255	D	D	35	25 550	814	21.1	17.6	42.8
Webster	1 068	16 837	3 090	2 069	2 759	589	459	539	32 025	1 103	28.5	26.7	63.0
Winnebago	314	5 931	697	D	508	172	74	176	29 736	679	31.7	27.4	56.4
Winneshiek	606	9 822	1 447	1 437	1 274	245	154	273	27 785	1 418	28.9	11.1	49.9
Woodbury	2 795	48 021	8 486	5 458	7 187	1 523	1 045	1 459	30 389	1 149	27.2	22.3	48.8
Worth	171	1 792	190	517	D	D	18	45	24 995	683	33.7	25.9	50.5
Wright	403	4 349	882	1 253	572	155	143	131	30 235	771	25.3	29.3	56.4

Table B. States and Counties — **Agriculture**

STATE County	Land in farms — Acreage (1,000) [117]	Percent change, 2002–2007 [118]	Acres — Average size of farm [119]	Acres — Total irrigated (1,000) [120]	Acres — Total cropland (1,000) [121]	Value of land and buildings — Average per farm [122]	Value of land and buildings — Average per acre [123]	Value of machinery and equipment, average per farm (dollars) [124]	Value of products sold — Total (mil dol) [125]	Value of products sold — Average per farm (dollars) [126]	Percent from: Crops [127]	Percent from: Livestock and poultry products [128]	Percent of farms with sales of: $10,000 or more [129]	Percent of farms with sales of: $100,000 or more [130]	Government payments — Total ($1,000) [131]	Government payments — Percent of farms [132]
IOWA—Cont'd																
Franklin	367	8.9	397	D	346.0	1 446 396	3 642	170 685	328.7	356 085	46.8	53.2	69.9	50.3	9 350	86.1
Fremont	245	-23.0	494	8.7	214.9	1 510 774	3 061	164 699	99.1	199 424	87.0	13.0	64.8	40.0	4 068	84.7
Greene	354	2.0	431	0.5	321.7	1 641 924	3 809	177 530	231.1	281 867	61.8	38.2	66.8	40.0	7 730	85.6
Grundy	316	-2.5	395	0.0	300.8	1 550 364	3 925	172 202	237.1	296 432	67.8	32.2	69.1	45.6	7 770	79.9
Guthrie	355	9.6	360	2.5	282.2	1 076 917	2 995	155 513	196.2	198 822	47.3	52.7	49.0	23.8	7 892	80.9
Hamilton	347	-0.3	393	0.0	326.3	1 550 641	3 946	184 248	324.1	367 497	47.9	52.1	65.9	43.1	8 141	81.3
Hancock	361	12.1	380	1.0	345.6	1 360 015	3 575	173 651	288.6	304 153	52.8	47.2	70.6	44.7	8 570	87.2
Hardin	339	3.4	359	0.0	307.5	1 360 569	3 785	163 841	379.6	402 514	36.8	63.2	64.7	42.0	7 836	79.4
Harrison	365	-14.7	447	31.2	313.5	1 325 527	2 966	131 420	144.4	176 801	82.4	17.6	60.0	38.8	6 566	79.8
Henry	240	-4.4	272	0.0	192.8	831 807	3 055	98 395	121.8	138 390	57.1	42.9	47.8	27.5	6 002	78.9
Howard	279	3.7	318	0.3	248.8	969 433	3 051	140 611	174.4	198 889	52.6	47.4	59.0	35.6	8 426	85.2
Humboldt	270	-0.4	428	D	256.2	1 603 916	3 751	183 973	159.1	251 816	71.7	28.3	76.4	51.3	5 949	89.9
Ida	273	2.6	431	D	251.2	1 384 465	3 215	182 692	170.3	269 095	58.7	41.3	68.9	42.5	6 043	81.4
Iowa	345	1.5	302	D	281.1	929 623	3 081	115 089	182.6	159 648	53.4	46.6	55.4	30.0	8 753	85.8
Jackson	296	-15.2	244	0.0	191.5	693 239	2 839	99 232	146.2	120 430	36.9	63.1	53.0	20.6	7 306	79.2
Jasper	428	4.4	367	0.6	378.8	1 267 110	3 453	166 231	254.7	218 419	71.3	28.7	63.2	36.5	8 741	76.3
Jefferson	197	-15.5	255	0.0	145.0	726 498	2 846	77 123	67.2	86 990	58.3	41.7	41.0	17.7	5 874	84.2
Johnson	321	6.6	248	2.9	282.0	931 742	3 751	114 199	189.7	146 681	55.5	44.5	61.0	32.9	7 964	74.6
Jones	324	3.8	290	0.6	271.2	1 013 974	3 496	139 930	200.1	179 143	52.0	48.0	65.8	36.5	8 041	83.3
Keokuk	318	-7.6	274	0.0	255.2	813 483	2 974	108 846	145.7	125 307	59.0	41.0	52.1	25.6	9 831	86.9
Kossuth	602	1.7	431	0.6	573.3	1 553 530	3 603	193 168	467.8	335 347	53.4	46.6	75.8	52.2	13 371	85.2
Lee	238	-11.9	270	1.7	174.4	731 239	2 710	88 076	87.8	99 386	71.8	28.2	47.0	24.7	4 811	77.9
Linn	335	-4.0	237	0.6	295.2	892 921	3 762	110 495	165.6	117 202	70.8	29.2	59.6	27.2	7 794	77.3
Louisa	186	-7.5	265	9.4	153.5	846 682	3 191	115 591	103.6	147 838	59.1	40.9	50.6	26.7	5 730	79.2
Lucas	171	-23.0	245	D	91.2	532 190	2 174	54 042	34.3	49 000	41.1	58.9	38.9	12.0	3 108	73.2
Lyon	323	-5.6	297	1.0	290.9	1 248 886	4 202	162 022	453.1	416 847	25.5	74.5	81.6	55.0	5 871	76.8
Madison	283	-6.9	296	1.8	185.2	875 822	2 955	91 832	110.8	115 895	58.6	41.4	46.0	17.1	4 450	71.0
Mahaska	295	-10.3	286	0.1	244.7	878 248	3 068	136 776	211.9	205 553	39.8	60.2	55.3	28.3	7 682	81.6
Marion	246	-11.2	259	0.7	183.3	754 717	2 915	80 451	92.7	97 493	71.4	28.6	45.0	20.6	5 586	76.6
Marshall	324	-3.3	349	0.8	295.3	1 301 147	3 724	147 211	189.8	204 537	73.8	26.2	62.7	36.9	7 638	80.3
Mills	197	-20.2	385	D	175.0	1 283 812	3 333	133 637	71.9	140 662	93.9	6.1	59.1	35.2	3 538	77.9
Mitchell	294	1.7	329	1.3	270.8	1 179 551	3 582	152 635	245.9	275 373	47.1	52.9	73.7	47.9	6 495	80.3
Monona	394	0.5	606	65.7	346.5	1 923 705	3 172	197 756	156.9	241 779	79.1	20.9	70.9	43.5	6 340	78.6
Monroe	201	-20.6	305	0.0	122.9	688 899	2 260	75 532	46.0	69 696	52.8	47.2	52.6	13.9	3 566	77.3
Montgomery	220	-9.5	395	D	176.1	1 153 369	2 919	125 679	112.6	201 722	62.4	37.6	64.5	35.3	4 424	84.2
Muscatine	222	-3.5	265	7.3	188.5	939 422	3 548	115 133	116.2	138 646	69.5	30.5	57.3	29.2	6 455	84.1
O'Brien	346	-4.4	350	D	317.5	1 473 176	4 205	155 574	362.0	366 766	37.1	62.9	81.8	58.7	6 953	80.5
Osceola	251	-2.3	379	2.0	237.6	1 469 454	3 879	178 299	286.6	432 235	34.4	65.6	79.6	55.5	5 396	84.5
Page	271	-20.1	344	0.1	215.1	933 727	2 714	102 944	92.8	117 734	77.8	22.2	59.9	30.6	5 204	80.1
Palo Alto	353	8.0	416	4.4	337.4	1 505 757	3 618	172 807	329.6	388 218	45.8	54.2	66.2	44.8	7 565	84.6
Plymouth	517	-2.6	359	2.8	460.6	1 301 406	3 628	152 681	467.3	324 065	33.7	66.3	74.1	46.7	10 164	82.0
Pocahontas	362	2.3	450	D	348.1	1 655 945	3 683	184 427	216.4	268 499	67.2	32.8	75.8	53.8	8 538	88.7
Polk	249	9.7	338	0.7	232.6	1 299 872	3 846	146 803	122.7	166 278	85.9	14.1	51.2	28.7	5 045	66.7
Pottawattamie	486	-10.0	420	2.0	434.8	1 523 228	3 630	175 050	311.5	268 985	62.1	37.9	61.8	39.4	8 676	71.9
Poweshiek	313	-9.3	334	0.0	267.7	1 107 683	3 321	129 040	165.7	176 636	67.8	32.2	57.2	31.6	7 347	85.1
Ringgold	265	-11.4	361	D	180.8	821 568	2 273	78 930	70.3	95 956	43.5	56.5	47.3	18.4	5 878	81.7
Sac	363	7.1	453	0.7	337.9	1 747 284	3 857	182 827	386.6	482 001	36.4	63.6	76.1	52.1	7 373	84.3
Scott	249	8.7	289	2.0	230.7	1 214 686	4 206	154 580	148.3	172 271	70.5	29.5	69.2	39.8	6 581	76.3
Shelby	358	2.9	411	D	333.7	1 322 099	3 213	136 273	212.0	243 343	65.7	34.3	77.7	49.5	7 647	85.4
Sioux	479	-5.1	288	9.1	441.8	1 304 456	4 534	172 473	1 121.1	673 764	16.1	83.9	83.3	57.5	10 189	71.6
Story	352	-2.2	327	0.3	328.1	1 163 987	3 559	162 630	200.6	186 271	80.6	19.4	64.2	34.2	7 792	73.9
Tama	431	3.1	356	0.0	380.8	1 233 812	3 465	140 953	235.1	194 337	70.2	29.8	61.9	35.3	10 270	82.3
Taylor	283	-8.1	363	D	209.6	902 297	2 487	99 662	119.0	152 754	44.2	55.8	48.8	18.1	6 882	82.3
Union	215	-9.7	315	0.0	139.5	793 544	2 518	89 810	94.0	138 075	39.7	60.3	51.2	19.8	4 414	78.7
Van Buren	222	-12.3	274	0.0	144.9	679 268	2 478	72 135	89.7	111 034	44.4	55.6	40.0	15.6	4 113	72.8
Wapello	166	-19.4	223	D	119.3	689 369	3 086	85 364	55.2	74 247	68.9	31.1	41.8	14.2	3 381	65.3
Warren	242	-19.1	203	0.1	160.3	636 132	3 130	71 015	75.2	63 211	73.8	26.2	40.5	12.6	5 353	66.0
Washington	326	-2.7	259	0.2	268.8	956 033	3 688	123 019	269.1	214 082	35.5	64.5	59.3	34.9	10 232	80.8
Wayne	273	-10.5	336	0.1	192.1	751 524	2 239	90 804	55.8	68 580	70.1	29.9	43.4	15.0	6 793	81.1
Webster	454	8.9	412	0.0	426.6	1 487 541	3 615	174 122	270.7	245 465	70.7	29.3	69.7	43.3	10 462	88.4
Winnebago	252	5.0	370	D	235.6	1 241 478	3 351	170 424	174.7	257 326	58.9	41.1	59.9	43.4	6 794	84.8
Winneshiek	314	-17.4	221	D	244.2	719 078	3 250	110 317	199.7	140 844	35.7	64.3	53.6	29.4	9 875	85.6
Woodbury	446	0.9	388	10.6	385.3	1 155 786	2 981	136 018	244.6	212 862	57.4	42.6	58.1	31.9	6 239	78.0
Worth	232	3.6	339	0.6	213.8	1 200 627	3 541	142 303	105.0	153 778	86.3	13.7	55.1	36.7	6 199	85.5
Wright	328	-4.9	425	0.0	309.1	1 662 127	3 910	253 945	405.9	526 463	34.8	65.2	63.8	45.1	8 517	89.5

Table B. States and Counties — Water Use, Wholesale Trade, Retail Trade, and Real Estate

STATE County	Water use, 2005		Wholesale trade,[1] 2007				Retail trade,[2] 2007				Real estate and rental and leasing,[2] 2007			
	Total water withdrawn (mil gal/day)	Gallons withdrawn per person	Number of establishments	Number of employees	Sales (mil dol)	Annual payroll (mil dol)	Number of establishments	Number of employees	Sales (mil dol)	Annual payroll (mil dol)	Number of establishments	Number of employees	Receipts (mil dol)	Annual payroll (mil dol)
	133	134	135	136	137	138	139	140	141	142	143	144	145	146
IOWA—Cont'd														
Franklin	2.7	254	29	176	154.6	6.3	42	353	65.9	5.6	14	36	3.6	0.4
Fremont	1.8	237	13	93	105.5	3.4	35	478	102.9	8.5	2	D	D	D
Greene	1.8	184	18	380	144.9	14.9	44	374	87.9	6.5	6	19	2.3	0.3
Grundy	2.0	164	17	225	269.9	9.8	57	490	109.4	9.0	8	D	D	D
Guthrie	2.6	226	18	D	D	D	41	350	91.3	5.6	7	22	2.1	0.5
Hamilton	4.2	261	31	772	558.3	31.8	65	683	149.3	11.0	10	19	2.0	0.2
Hancock	3.5	298	27	214	171.7	7.2	52	437	119.3	7.5	13	37	2.4	0.6
Hardin	7.4	410	42	892	1 191.0	40.6	90	815	161.8	14.6	17	31	3.4	0.6
Harrison	7.2	456	29	255	130.2	7.8	55	466	100.9	7.5	10	29	1.7	0.4
Henry	3.1	155	32	207	90.6	6.0	64	900	214.7	17.7	20	50	5.9	0.8
Howard	2.0	201	15	135	143.6	5.1	53	375	83.2	6.8	7	11	3.3	0.4
Humboldt	2.8	284	38	275	183.1	10.7	51	467	82.0	9.3	9	27	1.8	0.5
Ida	2.2	295	13	185	147.1	7.1	41	357	61.1	5.0	8	D	D	D
Iowa	2.8	174	19	115	80.2	4.0	145	1 204	213.4	18.3	4	D	D	D
Jackson	3.9	194	28	200	109.1	6.1	87	935	210.0	15.7	16	35	2.7	0.6
Jasper	7.5	200	41	D	D	D	122	1 424	274.0	25.8	31	81	8.4	1.6
Jefferson	2.2	140	48	319	114.6	9.7	84	1 205	333.5	33.9	20	43	6.2	0.8
Johnson	45.1	386	81	1 183	567.6	48.4	537	8 424	1 653.1	168.8	146	D	D	D
Jones	3.6	175	33	236	144.7	7.7	81	1 060	257.7	23.6	11	15	1.4	0.2
Keokuk	1.8	162	26	215	122.3	7.3	38	265	66.9	3.9	2	D	D	D
Kossuth	4.8	297	43	525	318.4	17.2	107	959	195.8	16.4	16	51	3.6	0.7
Lee	18.4	501	36	400	396.3	15.3	164	2 011	420.8	38.0	28	80	7.7	1.5
Linn	270.1	1 358	300	4 412	2 506.1	207.7	794	14 096	3 592.8	307.0	238	1 696	356.8	91.5
Louisa	10.4	880	12	D	D	D	27	237	56.5	3.7	6	7	0.4	0.1
Lucas	1.2	126	6	30	1.5	0.2	33	372	84.3	6.9	4	7	1.9	0.3
Lyon	5.8	489	23	226	215.3	7.7	54	419	91.1	6.5	7	7	1.0	0.1
Madison	1.7	115	13	D	D	D	52	422	80.6	7.7	7	16	2.1	0.2
Mahaska	4.0	181	36	D	D	D	109	1 229	242.9	22.7	12	56	5.9	1.0
Marion	4.8	146	41	D	D	D	153	1 726	333.1	30.8	40	92	9.9	1.5
Marshall	11.5	291	43	379	298.1	16.4	166	2 126	407.7	41.6	40	400	46.1	10.9
Mills	2.1	137	10	56	23.0	1.8	42	339	78.6	5.8	11	40	10.4	0.9
Mitchell	2.8	253	26	208	228.7	7.7	65	394	93.1	8.0	7	16	1.0	0.2
Monona	11.6	1 214	15	102	77.6	3.7	43	386	99.2	7.0	5	9	0.5	0.1
Monroe	1.8	227	13	162	46.2	4.9	33	290	62.5	5.2	2	D	D	D
Montgomery	2.2	197	13	109	150.7	4.5	56	510	88.3	8.6	9	49	4.9	1.1
Muscatine	306.3	7 164	52	481	377.5	17.2	158	2 086	448.6	42.3	49	160	19.9	4.2
O'Brien	4.4	307	33	407	322.7	13.9	104	844	169.7	14.0	7	33	4.8	0.7
Osceola	4.8	722	9	D	D	D	28	162	40.5	2.8	2	D	D	D
Page	2.8	173	16	155	116.4	5.6	92	738	163.0	12.8	11	20	1.7	0.3
Palo Alto	3.8	390	15	118	132.5	4.1	47	378	65.8	6.1	8	D	D	D
Plymouth	7.6	303	42	345	243.0	12.8	111	1 184	299.7	22.2	22	112	6.9	1.4
Pocahontas	1.8	232	14	229	86.9	6.4	38	306	79.9	3.6	1	D	D	D
Polk	58.0	145	668	11 440	6 697.2	536.1	1 658	28 621	6 714.4	655.9	567	3 399	673.2	120.0
Pottawattamie	509.5	5 678	91	1 618	2 256.7	64.7	326	6 025	1 503.4	117.5	95	425	66.3	10.5
Poweshiek	2.5	129	24	220	118.1	7.6	95	1 109	241.3	22.0	15	36	3.2	0.6
Ringgold	1.1	211	7	49	26.0	1.7	29	213	63.6	4.1	2	D	D	D
Sac	3.8	356	33	223	165.0	9.5	63	391	92.5	6.6	6	6	0.2	0.0
Scott	110.6	687	265	D	D	D	702	11 831	2 853.0	252.6	185	1 826	276.5	47.1
Shelby	2.8	218	25	423	158.6	11.7	66	588	135.1	10.5	7	D	D	D
Sioux	17.6	545	78	1 345	753.1	44.9	173	1 674	394.4	32.6	26	76	13.1	3.2
Story	11.9	149	80	599	432.0	24.7	320	4 611	968.3	91.7	96	371	38.1	10.1
Tama	5.8	325	27	163	154.9	5.4	78	548	112.5	9.3	7	17	0.9	0.2
Taylor	0.9	130	8	72	41.0	2.4	23	154	25.1	1.8	4	D	D	D
Union	5.4	449	16	236	384.7	8.1	60	779	153.8	15.1	18	46	4.8	0.9
Van Buren	0.9	116	6	D	D	D	30	243	36.9	3.0	3	4	0.6	0.1
Wapello	23.6	657	28	D	D	D	160	2 461	500.7	46.1	30	81	13.1	2.0
Warren	2.4	56	43	527	628.1	21.6	104	1 438	328.4	30.4	27	75	8.8	1.6
Washington	4.4	204	40	315	185.7	10.6	102	993	195.0	16.9	11	D	D	D
Wayne	0.8	123	5	36	27.0	1.4	36	247	49.2	3.7	1	D	D	D
Webster	11.3	291	68	D	D	D	194	2 723	577.5	52.3	42	120	18.9	2.9
Winnebago	2.3	200	19	130	170.0	4.6	60	538	115.0	8.2	8	D	D	D
Winneshiek	6.9	323	30	259	167.3	9.6	129	1 221	289.6	24.7	13	41	4.8	0.9
Woodbury	969.2	9 446	155	2 452	1 740.0	104.2	471	7 502	1 512.0	142.8	98	592	92.1	15.5
Worth	4.4	568	12	D	D	D	22	154	28.7	2.9	2	D	D	D
Wright	4.4	324	22	274	291.1	12.0	65	554	100.2	8.7	15	33	2.3	0.5

1. Merchant wholesalers, except manufacturers' sales branches and offices. 2. Employer establishments.

Items 133—146

STATE County	Professional, scientific, and technical services,[1] 2007				Manufacturing, 2007				Accommodation and food services, 2007			
	Number of establishments	Number of employees	Receipts (mil dol)	Annual payroll (mil dol)	Number of establishments	Number of employees	Receipts (mil dol)	Annual payroll (mil dol)	Number of establishments	Number of employees	Sales (mil dol)	Annual payroll (mil dol)
	147	148	149	150	151	152	153	154	155	156	157	158
IOWA—Cont'd												
Franklin	19	89	5.0	2.1	24	798	260.0	28.8	13	169	4.4	1.4
Fremont	8	34	2.4	0.8	7	D	D	D	26	241	14.8	2.0
Greene	24	80	6.6	3.1	NA	NA	NA	NA	14	145	3.9	1.1
Grundy	17	D	D	D	13	648	143.8	21.2	21	167	4.3	1.0
Guthrie	23	68	7.3	1.9	NA	NA	NA	NA	25	259	8.3	2.2
Hamilton	31	122	9.7	3.3	27	2 916	1 162.4	95.9	33	308	12.2	3.1
Hancock	19	109	7.3	2.4	27	1 126	266.8	49.0	17	159	4.1	1.0
Hardin	35	158	12.2	3.6	27	661	743.1	23.5	33	336	11.4	3.0
Harrison	21	D	D	D	NA	NA	NA	NA	31	304	10.4	2.8
Henry	39	D	D	D	32	2 520	889.9	79.3	54	693	22.2	6.1
Howard	15	38	2.9	1.2	26	1 562	273.0	D	21	187	4.8	1.1
Humboldt	20	67	5.6	1.9	27	1 214	289.8	41.4	24	244	7.5	2.0
Ida	12	44	3.8	1.1	15	1 241	373.0	53.3	14	D	D	D
Iowa	22	70	9.2	1.3	37	3 819	1 478.9	152.4	41	684	25.0	8.0
Jackson	32	85	4.9	1.7	34	1 047	248.0	27.0	45	485	14.5	3.3
Jasper	56	566	134.1	18.9	34	733	170.8	24.3	68	960	30.1	8.4
Jefferson	122	D	D	D	37	1 252	246.6	46.9	39	468	16.6	4.3
Johnson	241	D	D	D	83	5 598	D	230.1	329	6 906	258.8	75.7
Jones	33	130	10.6	4.3	30	859	180.8	31.6	34	359	9.8	2.8
Keokuk	6	29	3.7	1.0	NA	NA	NA	NA	11	D	D	D
Kossuth	41	193	22.8	5.5	25	946	474.8	38.2	40	393	11.5	2.8
Lee	50	255	18.9	6.7	66	D	D	D	96	1 154	37.0	9.5
Linn	503	4 587	574.9	244.7	237	17 801	8 229.2	1 123.9	488	9 343	353.6	103.2
Louisa	12	D	D	D	11	1 389	D	41.8	20	139	4.5	1.0
Lucas	12	D	D	D	NA	NA	NA	NA	13	D	D	D
Lyon	20	108	12.2	6.8	23	645	100.9	26.6	17	D	D	D
Madison	32	112	10.1	3.9	NA	NA	NA	NA	26	224	7.6	2.0
Mahaska	33	149	19.8	8.3	34	1 763	1 618.5	75.9	36	495	16.8	4.6
Marion	52	245	22.0	9.7	40	7 392	1 856.9	376.7	68	936	29.0	8.2
Marshall	52	340	50.4	12.0	45	5 546	1 848.0	232.3	86	1 180	40.4	11.1
Mills	25	D	D	D	NA	NA	NA	NA	16	109	5.4	0.8
Mitchell	13	66	5.9	1.5	20	941	252.0	34.8	20	186	5.1	1.1
Monona	15	96	5.1	1.6	NA	NA	NA	NA	28	193	7.2	1.6
Monroe	13	39	3.7	1.1	NA	NA	NA	NA	20	D	D	D
Montgomery	18	81	10.4	2.1	12	813	180.8	36.3	26	256	7.6	2.1
Muscatine	63	D	D	D	68	7 982	D	366.4	88	1 266	44.2	12.1
O'Brien	25	103	11.8	2.9	25	511	305.0	18.7	34	406	9.8	2.6
Osceola	7	25	3.0	0.6	NA	NA	NA	NA	14	D	D	D
Page	20	158	5.8	2.5	24	2 019	348.2	80.9	34	439	12.6	3.6
Palo Alto	12	35	3.3	1.1	21	577	401.4	23.6	23	566	34.6	7.3
Plymouth	40	203	13.7	7.0	30	2 228	D	D	60	982	22.0	6.5
Pocahontas	19	51	3.8	1.1	NA	NA	NA	NA	13	D	D	D
Polk	1 366	11 826	1 761.6	645.1	378	17 620	7 519.9	797.2	1 064	19 898	825.2	243.1
Pottawattamie	143	D	D	D	68	5 371	D	D	193	5 771	451.5	97.0
Poweshiek	40	181	18.9	5.1	34	1 997	462.2	71.6	48	632	17.0	4.9
Ringgold	9	25	3.7	0.7	NA	NA	NA	NA	15	D	D	D
Sac	16	54	6.4	1.1	NA	NA	NA	NA	27	D	D	D
Scott	389	D	D	D	189	12 506	5 745.1	590.4	421	9 171	423.9	112.7
Shelby	26	150	11.4	3.7	NA	NA	NA	NA	27	292	8.7	2.3
Sioux	81	769	67.0	18.4	95	5 479	1 152.4	179.0	78	1 187	31.7	9.2
Story	193	D	D	D	75	4 668	1 970.8	213.4	224	4 388	151.0	43.4
Tama	21	90	14.7	7.7	NA	NA	NA	NA	33	D	D	D
Taylor	9	D	D	D	NA	NA	NA	NA	10	D	D	D
Union	17	60	5.0	1.9	12	1 450	214.3	47.7	27	344	11.2	2.8
Van Buren	11	23	2.3	0.7	12	734	D	22.1	12	D	D	D
Wapello	48	D	D	D	28	4 309	1 840.4	178.0	76	1 116	41.5	11.3
Warren	62	218	18.4	6.3	27	545	D	D	60	792	25.1	6.5
Washington	52	D	D	D	39	1 114	D	33.7	41	1 224	114.7	21.3
Wayne	7	28	2.6	0.6	NA	NA	NA	NA	10	D	D	D
Webster	75	419	31.4	15.1	50	2 483	1 909.4	122.4	81	1 399	61.9	15.7
Winnebago	21	76	7.6	2.0	21	4 215	1 094.3	170.7	18	231	6.4	1.4
Winneshiek	31	145	15.2	5.8	31	1 721	288.7	58.0	58	732	21.5	6.2
Woodbury	190	D	D	D	98	5 073	2 827.5	210.2	262	4 699	158.4	47.3
Worth	10	D	D	D	13	593	248.9	20.7	13	110	4.7	1.0
Wright	24	158	11.2	3.3	26	1 096	863.3	49.5	37	242	7.6	2.0

1. Establishment subject to federal tax.

STATE County	Health care and social assistance, 2007				Other services, 2007				Federal funds and grants, 2009–2010			
									Expenditures (mil dol)			
									Total	Direct payments for individuals[1]		
	Number of establish-ments	Number of employees	Receipts (mil dol)	Annual payroll (mil dol)	Number of establish-ments	Number of employees	Receipts (mil dol)	Annual payroll (mil dol)	Total	Social Security and government retirement	Medicare	Food Stamps and Supplemental Security Income
	159	160	161	162	163	164	165	166	167	168	169	170
IOWA—Cont'd												
Franklin	31	524	28.1	13.3	27	64	5.5	1.5	83.3	35.9	18.7	2.5
Fremont	16	324	18.3	8.0	14	D	D	D	80.8	33.8	19.6	2.6
Greene	27	652	29.8	15.1	23	92	5.6	1.3	84.9	37.1	19.6	2.6
Grundy	29	387	21.1	9.2	23	D	D	D	86.2	40.3	20.9	1.3
Guthrie	33	505	27.2	12.6	25	D	D	D	90.4	41.2	22.0	2.3
Hamilton	36	633	47.0	18.1	36	118	13.1	3.5	131.9	55.7	33.6	3.1
Hancock	17	453	27.1	10.7	30	214	25.9	8.1	87.4	38.4	19.5	2.1
Hardin	41	995	48.9	23.7	49	140	12.5	3.2	171.4	69.9	38.8	4.5
Harrison	36	657	43.3	18.1	23	D	D	D	125.9	54.3	31.6	3.9
Henry	60	1 081	80.3	38.6	41	158	8.7	3.3	138.3	65.2	28.4	4.4
Howard	24	431	24.2	12.3	19	47	3.4	0.8	81.9	32.5	18.6	1.9
Humboldt	22	444	25.6	11.2	18	38	4.0	0.7	80.0	34.2	21.2	2.6
Ida	19	420	23.8	10.8	16	59	4.1	1.3	58.2	24.5	14.7	0.9
Iowa	38	727	36.5	17.8	22	52	5.5	1.1	102.1	51.0	23.6	2.3
Jackson	40	896	45.3	22.1	44	114	13.4	2.3	158.1	67.6	38.7	6.5
Jasper	83	1 565	97.5	46.1	60	249	16.5	4.2	236.6	115.9	58.9	7.2
Jefferson	50	697	48.1	18.8	44	152	21.6	2.9	115.4	45.1	23.3	5.8
Johnson	357	15 466	1 501.0	577.8	213	1 376	173.4	35.3	1 055.6	243.9	79.6	16.4
Jones	44	794	40.3	18.4	40	86	10.2	2.1	128.0	63.3	28.1	4.3
Keokuk	21	373	15.5	7.6	18	49	4.0	0.9	105.7	40.9	25.3	3.4
Kossuth	41	864	57.4	23.1	57	129	17.4	2.5	143.8	58.7	30.5	3.0
Lee	114	D	D	D	73	285	22.5	5.0	305.3	123.9	76.1	15.4
Linn	540	13 371	1 173.9	491.2	402	2 594	243.7	63.2	2 581.4	575.2	228.6	50.7
Louisa	24	322	11.2	5.3	14	D	D	D	108.2	33.8	15.8	3.6
Lucas	29	550	31.0	13.3	9	23	2.3	0.5	91.1	32.7	19.2	4.0
Lyon	23	403	18.2	7.6	31	88	7.2	1.4	70.6	30.2	18.1	1.4
Madison	27	598	30.4	13.6	27	D	D	D	101.2	45.9	24.0	2.3
Mahaska	59	934	61.5	28.0	41	156	12.4	2.9	158.8	65.9	36.0	6.9
Marion	93	2 430	170.3	73.0	65	242	22.1	5.2	244.5	120.6	47.7	6.3
Marshall	84	2 143	139.6	66.8	69	465	33.2	10.0	317.6	139.1	60.6	12.1
Mills	29	733	27.6	14.3	25	D	D	D	121.4	57.3	25.9	4.2
Mitchell	30	561	33.9	13.4	31	70	6.1	1.5	85.6	41.3	21.9	1.3
Monona	23	690	40.7	19.5	16	40	3.2	0.9	104.6	36.1	29.5	2.9
Monroe	22	485	24.8	11.1	7	19	2.2	0.4	77.7	29.6	20.5	2.7
Montgomery	38	849	49.6	22.4	34	93	8.6	1.7	110.6	43.2	29.4	3.7
Muscatine	92	1 866	111.1	50.1	77	D	D	D	314.5	124.9	52.1	14.8
O'Brien	49	1 391	66.5	29.4	43	170	16.9	3.9	123.5	50.8	30.8	2.3
Osceola	14	307	16.1	6.6	15	26	2.5	0.4	47.2	19.4	12.7	1.0
Page	51	1 587	91.4	43.4	33	102	6.6	1.5	143.2	61.9	35.4	4.7
Palo Alto	37	688	40.3	16.8	20	22	2.0	0.4	95.7	35.8	22.7	2.1
Plymouth	54	986	65.3	25.4	55	164	14.4	3.0	160.9	66.9	35.8	2.5
Pocahontas	21	318	17.9	8.0	14	38	2.4	0.5	78.8	29.1	20.9	2.1
Polk	1 021	32 180	3 108.7	1 332.6	965	6 980	751.7	206.0	4 643.2	1 071.3	503.4	124.3
Pottawattamie	194	4 453	364.2	159.4	148	678	52.0	15.7	694.2	309.5	146.0	35.1
Poweshiek	59	1 281	89.6	42.0	35	113	9.3	2.5	130.3	60.1	32.2	3.8
Ringgold	15	337	19.9	8.8	12	32	4.0	0.9	55.0	20.5	11.5	1.6
Sac	24	558	28.5	14.0	24	57	6.1	1.1	95.1	37.9	23.4	1.9
Scott	456	10 963	944.3	414.0	342	2 063	168.0	47.5	1 462.7	539.6	200.1	75.5
Shelby	38	1 065	52.4	24.4	24	85	7.4	1.6	111.2	43.0	32.1	2.7
Sioux	74	2 078	119.2	49.1	87	292	26.9	6.5	197.0	75.2	43.5	2.5
Story	172	5 026	415.3	172.4	148	1 096	212.9	28.7	1 268.6	195.3	80.6	12.0
Tama	30	314	15.3	7.6	21	64	5.3	1.1	134.9	60.0	31.5	3.6
Taylor	15	206	7.8	3.8	12	53	4.2	1.0	65.6	25.5	15.0	2.2
Union	38	904	55.5	24.8	30	139	13.1	2.6	142.0	53.3	25.1	4.8
Van Buren	14	353	17.0	8.5	11	D	D	D	68.1	29.5	16.0	2.0
Wapello	103	2 848	199.1	88.0	58	234	15.9	4.5	353.3	132.5	80.4	18.9
Warren	74	1 230	67.1	31.9	58	218	14.2	4.5	223.6	125.0	43.9	6.0
Washington	66	1 248	61.5	29.4	50	153	19.8	3.4	147.9	69.9	34.8	4.4
Wayne	19	309	18.5	8.2	12	31	2.7	0.5	80.8	26.3	19.1	2.4
Webster	117	2 977	239.7	108.3	77	404	43.4	11.0	368.9	134.3	83.6	14.6
Winnebago	41	628	27.5	12.0	15	37	15.7	0.7	100.2	39.0	21.6	1.8
Winneshiek	58	1 455	90.2	40.4	42	177	16.2	3.1	151.9	62.5	27.1	2.4
Woodbury	333	8 054	718.5	273.3	193	1 279	90.6	28.8	783.5	283.5	171.2	31.1
Worth	13	D	D	D	13	34	4.3	0.7	57.3	25.6	14.3	1.3
Wright	40	915	68.4	26.0	30	73	5.7	1.1	124.0	53.3	31.2	3.0

1. State totals may include programs not allocated by county.

Table B. States and Counties — Federal Funds, Residential Construction, and Local Government Finances

	Federal funds and grants, 2009–2010 (cont.)							Value of residential construction authorized by building permits, 2010		Local government finances, 2007				
	Expenditures (mil dol) (cont.)									General revenue				
		Procurement contract awards		Grants[1]								Taxes		
													Per capita[2] (dollars)	
STATE County	Salaries and wages	Defense	Other	Medicaid and other health-related	Nutrition and family welfare	Education	Other	New con-struction ($1,000)	Number of housing units	Total (mil dol)	Inter-govern-mental (mil dol)	Total (mil dol)	Total	Property
	171	172	173	174	175	176	177	178	179	180	181	182	183	184

IOWA—Cont'd

Franklin	2.6	0.0	0.6	9.8	1.7	0.4	0.4	515	2	50.1	18.4	16.5	1 560	1 325
Fremont	2.4	0.1	0.5	9.8	1.5	0.2	0.1	1 892	12	26.6	12.9	11.4	1 500	1 192
Greene	3.0	0.0	0.7	11.5	1.7	0.2	0.5	3 131	13	49.2	13.4	15.2	1 604	1 397
Grundy	3.3	0.0	0.7	5.2	1.4	0.2	0.2	2 952	14	49.4	16.0	18.1	1 492	1 232
Guthrie	4.2	0.0	0.9	10.9	1.9	0.3	0.2	993	4	53.7	20.5	19.9	1 797	1 459
Hamilton	4.2	0.0	1.1	12.1	2.6	0.3	4.2	200	1	71.7	22.9	24.6	1 580	1 352
Hancock	3.2	0.0	6.5	5.5	1.8	0.2	1.5	1 490	9	46.6	15.7	17.1	1 506	1 260
Hardin	11.5	0.1	1.4	15.5	3.2	1.0	0.4	487	4	81.2	24.6	29.0	1 651	1 331
Harrison	5.3	0.0	3.5	14.9	2.8	0.4	0.6	3 141	20	51.2	24.4	22.6	1 464	1 219
Henry	10.2	0.0	1.3	13.9	2.6	0.9	0.6	2 722	18	89.3	27.3	24.1	1 197	940
Howard	2.4	0.5	0.9	12.0	2.1	0.2	0.9	1 350	7	47.8	14.3	16.8	1 756	1 441
Humboldt	4.3	0.0	1.0	8.1	1.7	0.4	0.6	1 897	9	44.2	12.7	14.0	1 455	1 193
Ida	2.5	0.0	0.5	5.8	1.4	0.2	0.2	1 770	12	21.3	9.0	8.5	1 222	1 000
Iowa	5.1	0.2	1.1	7.5	2.0	0.3	0.4	1 547	10	59.5	20.5	24.0	1 509	1 122
Jackson	5.5	4.8	1.3	22.4	3.7	1.0	0.4	2 987	20	70.1	25.4	23.0	1 148	875
Jasper	8.1	0.0	1.6	24.2	4.9	0.8	3.6	5 357	32	149.7	42.4	55.8	1 518	1 268
Jefferson	12.8	0.0	1.1	10.6	2.0	0.4	4.6	1 248	9	59.1	20.4	17.1	1 097	862
Johnson	124.4	11.9	65.3	413.4	11.9	12.2	41.8	105 349	519	353.8	109.4	175.0	1 392	1 265
Jones	4.4	0.0	1.1	12.7	2.9	0.4	0.3	3 206	21	57.7	25.0	24.1	1 181	930
Keokuk	5.2	0.0	2.5	12.6	1.9	0.5	2.4	350	4	37.6	14.7	15.5	1 437	1 210
Kossuth	16.2	0.0	1.2	16.2	2.4	0.4	1.1	3 339	19	70.4	27.6	24.6	1 576	1 278
Lee	9.9	1.8	26.9	32.2	5.5	1.9	2.1	10 719	133	104.2	46.8	42.8	1 201	868
Linn	96.4	1 128.5	251.2	128.4	28.8	5.6	36.7	77 471	818	818.0	309.3	305.9	1 486	1 353
Louisa	4.2	2.6	5.8	10.3	2.0	0.3	22.5	2 267	14	46.8	20.3	18.6	1 580	1 190
Lucas	5.3	5.1	0.6	14.9	2.1	0.5	1.0	465	3	40.2	13.5	10.4	1 100	889
Lyon	3.1	0.0	0.7	7.5	1.8	0.2	0.2	3 770	20	39.0	16.2	15.9	1 413	1 112
Madison	3.2	0.0	0.7	11.7	2.3	0.2	4.5	6 223	35	64.8	23.7	21.5	1 393	1 159
Mahaska	5.0	0.0	1.0	23.5	3.3	1.1	2.4	1 520	10	84.6	22.8	29.0	1 301	1 048
Marion	13.1	13.2	1.7	24.8	4.6	2.0	1.8	8 885	48	96.2	39.4	40.8	1 244	949
Marshall	19.4	0.0	3.7	35.7	9.1	3.5	20.7	2 519	14	152.1	70.7	54.4	1 384	1 056
Mills	6.5	0.0	0.8	17.2	2.2	0.3	0.7	2 199	16	44.8	20.2	19.3	1 272	1 103
Mitchell	2.9	0.0	0.8	7.5	1.5	0.4	0.9	3 216	24	45.9	12.2	14.4	1 345	1 114
Monona	3.5	0.0	0.8	16.6	2.4	0.3	0.2	2 535	15	34.6	12.9	13.2	1 444	1 207
Monroe	2.7	0.2	0.5	13.2	1.7	0.3	0.6	2 301	16	19.5	9.3	8.2	1 077	802
Montgomery	13.8	0.0	0.8	11.5	2.0	0.5	0.6	1 740	9	57.4	16.1	15.8	1 432	1 165
Muscatine	9.9	50.6	15.0	25.3	6.9	1.0	4.5	4 749	46	151.3	56.6	59.2	1 395	1 102
O'Brien	7.7	0.0	1.0	18.3	2.2	0.9	0.3	1 675	7	61.6	25.3	22.2	1 577	1 245
Osceola	1.9	0.1	1.1	4.6	1.0	0.1	0.2	150	1	17.2	7.8	7.2	1 108	974
Page	5.7	0.0	1.3	21.2	2.9	0.8	1.9	2 371	13	65.6	21.0	18.8	1 184	899
Palo Alto	3.1	0.0	0.7	16.4	5.0	0.2	1.1	671	4	52.1	14.0	17.8	1 888	1 398
Plymouth	18.3	4.1	2.5	13.3	5.3	0.6	0.3	9 542	44	100.1	31.0	34.5	1 416	1 118
Pocahontas	6.7	0.0	0.6	7.5	1.6	0.2	0.9	950	4	30.9	10.2	10.6	1 383	1 161
Polk	618.0	83.0	176.3	398.0	181.5	238.2	1 125.6	400 146	2 233	1 784.5	563.4	784.3	1 875	1 581
Pottawattamie	36.7	0.6	4.2	99.0	14.3	3.7	13.5	26 788	168	380.1	153.0	153.1	1 713	1 264
Poweshiek	4.3	4.5	1.1	11.1	2.4	0.4	0.9	3 243	19	56.8	21.7	23.8	1 276	1 057
Ringgold	2.8	0.0	0.8	7.5	1.5	0.2	1.2	345	2	27.5	8.6	7.5	1 462	1 339
Sac	5.1	0.0	0.8	7.5	2.2	0.4	0.5	446	3	49.6	13.7	14.9	1 435	1 207
Scott	73.1	57.0	7.9	128.9	27.8	5.8	28.9	60 546	427	609.5	239.1	265.9	1 634	1 314
Shelby	4.3	0.0	0.9	14.9	5.5	0.3	0.2	2 212	11	63.5	18.3	17.9	1 456	1 197
Sioux	7.6	0.9	6.3	33.1	3.8	0.5	6.9	17 746	88	128.2	31.9	39.5	1 220	978
Story	85.6	15.0	63.0	61.0	8.3	2.6	699.8	34 489	167	394.2	77.8	112.0	1 321	1 045
Tama	4.9	0.0	1.2	12.9	3.0	1.3	3.6	2 415	15	63.8	30.8	25.7	1 440	1 158
Taylor	3.0	0.0	0.6	9.7	1.8	0.3	0.5	370	2	21.5	10.4	8.2	1 285	1 065
Union	6.4	0.1	1.2	18.9	3.6	0.9	16.6	991	5	88.4	37.1	17.6	1 453	1 137
Van Buren	3.3	0.0	0.7	7.1	1.4	0.4	0.6	120	1	32.2	15.5	8.6	1 117	890
Wapello	17.4	0.2	2.6	63.6	9.2	2.8	4.8	3 086	26	162.8	78.5	43.6	1 228	880
Warren	8.1	0.1	2.9	19.0	5.0	1.7	1.9	38 140	278	124.0	56.2	49.7	1 118	955
Washington	8.8	0.0	1.0	13.9	2.6	0.8	1.0	3 956	34	83.0	27.0	27.0	1 264	975
Wayne	2.6	0.0	0.6	15.5	1.9	0.3	0.7	0	0	28.8	10.5	7.0	1 113	967
Webster	33.1	4.5	4.7	44.8	8.2	1.4	7.6	3 387	23	157.6	68.6	49.6	1 285	1 050
Winnebago	3.5	0.0	1.0	12.2	1.8	0.4	10.7	330	2	44.7	18.7	19.1	1 739	1 322
Winneshiek	10.0	0.0	1.2	11.7	5.7	2.4	4.2	6 443	41	127.6	41.6	29.0	1 388	1 110
Woodbury	85.5	9.6	12.5	103.6	19.9	6.3	19.9	16 504	86	418.3	184.4	161.2	1 576	1 141
Worth	2.4	0.0	0.6	5.8	1.1	0.3	0.3	700	4	22.5	8.6	11.3	1 473	1 192
Wright	9.7	0.0	1.1	12.1	2.4	0.3	1.0	900	6	77.7	21.7	21.7	1 658	1 381

1. State totals may include programs not allocated by county. 2. Based on the resident population estimated as of July 1 of the year shown.

Table B. States and Counties — Local Government Finances, Government Employment, and Voting

STATE County	Local government finances, 2007 (cont.)									Government employment, 2009			Presidential election,[2] 2008		
	Direct general expenditure							Debt outstanding					Percent of vote cast:		
				Percent of total for:											
	Total (mil dol)	Per capita[1] (dollars)	Education	Health and hospitals	Police protection	Public welfare	Highways	Total (mil dol)	Per capita[1] (dollars)	Federal civilian	Federal military	State and local	Democratic	Republican	All other
	185	186	187	188	189	190	191	192	193	194	195	196	197	198	199
IOWA—Cont'd															
Franklin	49.9	4 718	40.1	31.5	3.8	0.2	9.6	18.4	1 739	40	44	751	50.0	48.6	1.4
Fremont	25.7	3 388	53.4	5.2	2.1	0.6	13.7	9.0	1 194	36	31	469	47.4	51.1	1.5
Greene	48.9	5 141	35.5	37.7	2.7	0.0	8.6	15.7	1 652	42	39	827	49.4	48.9	1.7
Grundy	50.4	4 151	43.8	17.9	3.1	0.1	10.2	29.8	2 453	45	51	625	40.9	57.8	1.4
Guthrie	49.3	4 458	53.2	18.2	3.0	0.1	8.3	32.5	2 936	60	46	807	44.9	52.6	2.6
Hamilton	69.2	4 437	38.6	27.5	4.3	0.5	9.8	28.0	1 792	58	64	1 239	49.7	48.4	1.9
Hancock	47.4	4 168	35.3	24.1	3.7	0.3	11.4	19.1	1 676	43	47	691	47.3	50.9	1.8
Hardin	79.4	4 525	41.4	24.4	4.5	0.2	8.7	29.1	1 660	87	72	1 777	49.6	48.7	1.7
Harrison	49.8	3 230	60.3	1.7	5.8	0.1	13.3	40.0	2 599	77	65	857	46.9	51.5	1.6
Henry	86.1	4 278	39.7	32.5	3.2	0.7	6.3	85.1	4 231	76	84	1 830	46.4	51.4	2.2
Howard	44.0	4 608	40.6	31.7	2.4	0.2	8.8	10.2	1 071	37	40	850	62.2	36.4	1.4
Humboldt	45.2	4 696	34.0	25.6	3.0	0.3	9.8	19.2	1 998	59	40	667	42.2	56.5	1.3
Ida	20.9	3 005	54.1	3.0	4.4	0.3	14.0	8.5	1 228	36	28	387	41.0	57.4	1.6
Iowa	60.7	3 817	43.1	16.6	3.7	0.4	12.8	27.4	1 723	67	67	1 022	49.2	49.0	1.8
Jackson	73.6	3 675	44.7	19.0	3.3	0.3	10.2	37.0	1 847	84	83	1 151	61.3	36.9	1.8
Jasper	146.1	3 975	37.8	27.2	4.0	1.4	4.9	92.3	2 511	108	153	2 358	52.8	45.3	1.9
Jefferson	66.5	4 259	29.4	29.8	3.5	0.5	10.6	50.6	3 241	78	65	1 044	58.7	38.5	2.8
Johnson	413.7	3 291	32.3	4.2	4.2	0.5	4.3	678.6	5 399	1 807	568	31 115	69.9	28.4	1.7
Jones	55.2	2 708	56.0	4.5	4.3	0.6	12.8	22.8	1 116	58	86	1 379	54.4	44.0	1.6
Keokuk	42.2	3 915	46.3	25.9	2.1	0.9	11.2	21.0	1 948	64	45	524	47.0	50.6	2.5
Kossuth	71.1	4 558	32.6	31.1	2.7	0.2	12.2	16.1	1 030	81	64	1 047	50.8	47.6	1.6
Lee	102.8	2 885	50.2	4.6	6.2	3.2	7.7	56.3	1 582	103	165	2 243	57.0	41.0	2.0
Linn	801.6	3 894	57.0	3.8	4.6	1.5	5.3	849.1	4 125	1 164	883	12 482	60.0	38.5	1.5
Louisa	44.0	3 733	63.3	1.3	4.3	0.2	9.9	89.9	7 623	63	47	727	51.3	47.0	1.7
Lucas	38.3	4 070	35.1	32.9	2.5	0.2	11.6	44.7	4 748	42	39	678	45.3	52.1	2.6
Lyon	38.0	3 377	53.5	4.0	4.0	0.2	13.1	20.4	1 813	43	47	623	26.9	71.9	1.2
Madison	61.4	3 982	43.8	27.5	3.9	0.4	9.8	105.8	6 860	44	65	1 043	44.0	54.0	2.0
Mahaska	77.3	3 467	36.1	34.0	4.3	0.2	10.2	47.8	2 145	68	93	1 377	40.8	57.4	1.8
Marion	98.6	3 009	58.2	3.9	4.2	0.5	8.6	91.3	2 784	527	138	1 663	43.6	54.3	2.1
Marshall	154.5	3 930	67.9	2.7	4.9	0.5	6.3	85.2	2 167	134	165	3 406	53.7	44.4	1.9
Mills	45.1	2 974	59.4	4.7	5.2	1.6	11.2	39.5	2 604	47	63	1 784	40.9	57.4	1.7
Mitchell	44.7	4 164	35.9	31.6	3.1	1.1	10.6	20.1	1 868	44	45	691	55.1	42.8	2.0
Monona	28.5	3 121	49.3	3.3	5.6	0.4	16.4	9.8	1 070	48	37	680	47.8	50.3	1.9
Monroe	18.2	2 401	60.5	2.3	5.9	0.9	15.0	7.9	1 044	43	32	498	46.4	51.6	2.0
Montgomery	51.7	4 699	34.1	39.8	3.9	0.0	7.1	22.4	2 037	54	45	955	44.0	54.6	1.4
Muscatine	132.0	3 112	50.7	1.9	5.3	1.0	7.2	134.7	3 174	110	181	2 647	57.1	41.5	1.4
O'Brien	59.7	4 245	64.3	4.2	3.9	0.3	9.3	41.2	2 930	54	59	1 047	31.9	66.7	1.4
Osceola	17.4	2 686	46.1	3.9	11.6	0.8	15.2	10.5	1 629	32	27	310	33.1	64.8	2.1
Page	61.2	3 852	39.4	30.6	3.7	0.5	7.8	32.7	2 058	68	64	1 463	39.4	59.1	1.5
Palo Alto	51.2	5 427	33.6	32.5	2.9	0.7	11.7	30.6	3 246	43	39	979	50.5	47.7	1.8
Plymouth	96.1	3 943	38.5	24.1	3.4	2.0	9.2	55.9	2 294	91	102	1 410	37.0	62.0	1.0
Pocahontas	30.8	4 009	32.1	23.1	4.1	1.2	13.3	10.8	1 411	42	31	587	44.9	53.3	1.8
Polk	1 867.4	4 464	47.8	6.6	4.7	1.3	5.0	2 111.8	5 048	5 343	1 940	30 211	56.4	41.8	1.8
Pottawattamie	361.8	4 047	58.7	2.3	5.3	0.5	5.2	230.1	2 573	225	381	5 172	48.3	50.2	1.5
Poweshiek	55.0	2 947	53.0	2.2	4.5	0.7	10.2	42.2	2 262	60	78	855	55.0	43.3	1.7
Ringgold	25.1	4 874	38.0	35.3	1.4	0.0	10.2	6.8	1 327	38	21	458	46.0	52.1	1.9
Sac	48.2	4 637	34.4	39.6	3.5	0.2	9.5	6.8	655	50	42	602	44.6	53.5	1.8
Scott	630.3	3 874	54.0	2.8	5.8	0.3	4.7	500.2	3 074	574	702	7 881	56.6	42.1	1.3
Shelby	60.8	4 937	34.6	36.9	3.0	0.2	9.6	21.4	1 737	58	50	1 014	44.4	54.0	1.6
Sioux	129.3	3 997	35.6	30.3	3.8	0.4	8.3	109.4	3 382	106	136	2 004	18.2	80.9	0.9
Story	363.8	4 292	28.6	44.0	3.1	0.7	3.6	190.7	2 251	1 116	397	18 488	57.0	40.8	2.2
Tama	62.6	3 503	59.7	4.5	3.5	0.6	14.1	28.5	1 594	65	73	2 211	55.3	43.2	1.5
Taylor	21.7	3 387	51.6	6.6	3.8	0.2	14.8	11.7	1 832	49	27	398	44.5	53.1	2.4
Union	86.7	7 136	49.4	29.9	2.2	0.1	3.8	46.4	3 824	75	52	1 281	50.7	47.0	2.2
Van Buren	32.5	4 220	39.3	34.3	2.5	0.1	10.7	10.8	1 408	46	32	590	42.8	55.0	2.2
Wapello	170.3	4 790	64.7	1.4	2.5	0.5	5.3	50.8	1 430	136	149	2 264	55.3	41.8	2.9
Warren	132.6	2 979	64.8	3.5	4.3	0.6	8.0	104.3	2 344	106	191	2 046	49.4	48.8	1.8
Washington	94.8	4 443	36.8	20.7	2.8	0.6	8.6	74.8	3 502	71	90	1 424	48.6	49.4	2.0
Wayne	28.8	4 584	37.6	36.5	2.3	0.4	9.9	6.8	1 083	40	26	575	45.5	52.5	2.0
Webster	168.9	4 378	67.0	3.6	3.0	0.6	5.6	91.4	2 368	237	166	2 833	53.4	44.9	1.6
Winnebago	47.2	4 311	57.7	4.4	3.6	0.3	9.1	23.6	2 152	50	45	750	53.5	44.9	1.7
Winneshiek	132.8	6 349	51.3	31.4	2.0	0.2	5.7	77.6	3 709	87	87	2 031	60.5	37.9	1.6
Woodbury	414.2	4 049	55.6	2.7	5.4	0.6	8.0	329.8	3 225	818	434	6 155	49.1	49.6	1.4
Worth	22.2	2 887	44.5	8.4	6.9	0.1	14.9	13.7	1 787	35	32	372	60.3	37.8	1.9
Wright	84.2	6 444	38.3	35.6	3.4	1.0	6.8	55.0	4 207	83	54	1 241	48.5	50.0	1.5

1. Based on the resident population estimated as of July 1 of the year shown.   2. © 2009 Election Data Services, Inc. All rights reserved.

STATE/ County code	CBSA code[1]	County type[2]	STATE County	Land area[3] (sq km) 2010	Total persons	Rank	Per square kilometer	White	Black	American Indian, Alaska Native	Asian and Pacific Islander	Percent Hispanic or Latino[4]	Under 5 years	5 to 17 years	18 to 24 years	25 to 34 years	35 to 44 years	45 to 54 years
				1	2	3	4	5	6	7	8	9	10	11	12	13	14	15
20 000	...	X	KANSAS	211 754	2 853 118	X	13.5	80.3	6.7	1.7	3.0	10.5	7.2	18.3	10.1	13.2	12.2	14.2
20 001	...	7	Allen	1 296	13 371	2 228	10.3	93.9	2.6	2.0	0.8	2.9	6.6	17.0	9.3	11.0	10.7	14.5
20 003	...	6	Anderson	1 501	8 102	2 601	5.4	97.0	0.7	1.3	0.6	1.5	6.9	18.4	6.7	10.1	11.3	14.2
20 005	11860	6	Atchison	1 117	16 924	1 988	15.2	91.6	6.2	1.4	0.7	2.3	6.5	17.6	14.2	10.4	10.9	13.8
20 007	...	9	Barber	2 937	4 861	2 851	1.7	95.9	0.7	1.2	0.6	2.4	6.3	16.1	6.8	10.5	9.5	16.0
20 009	24460	7	Barton	2 319	27 674	1 510	11.9	84.6	1.8	1.0	0.4	13.3	7.2	17.3	9.1	11.7	10.3	15.1
20 011	...	6	Bourbon	1 646	15 173	2 102	9.2	93.9	3.5	1.8	0.8	2.0	7.4	18.2	9.9	11.1	9.9	13.3
20 013	...	6	Brown	1 479	9 984	2 448	6.8	86.6	1.9	10.5	0.6	3.1	7.3	18.1	6.7	10.8	10.5	14.8
20 015	48620	2	Butler	3 703	65 880	795	17.8	92.7	2.1	1.9	1.1	3.9	6.6	20.3	9.1	11.3	12.6	15.5
20 017	21380	8	Chase	2 002	2 790	2 993	1.4	94.4	1.6	1.1	0.6	3.6	5.4	16.6	6.5	9.0	11.6	14.4
20 019	...	9	Chautauqua	1 655	3 669	2 934	2.2	93.1	0.7	7.0	0.2	2.4	4.9	15.8	6.0	9.5	9.5	15.5
20 021	...	6	Cherokee	1 522	21 603	1 760	14.2	92.9	1.1	7.0	0.9	2.0	6.5	18.5	7.9	10.7	12.5	15.2
20 023	...	9	Cheyenne	2 641	2 726	2 998	1.0	93.8	0.2	0.5	0.8	5.2	5.1	16.2	4.4	8.7	9.5	15.3
20 025	...	9	Clark	2 524	2 215	3 037	0.9	91.2	0.6	2.0	1.2	7.4	6.5	18.7	5.4	9.4	10.1	14.5
20 027	...	7	Clay	1 671	8 535	2 565	5.1	96.9	0.6	1.1	0.6	1.9	6.8	16.9	6.2	10.9	11.2	13.8
20 029	...	7	Cloud	1 853	9 533	2 477	5.1	95.9	0.9	0.8	0.5	3.0	6.5	15.9	10.7	10.3	9.8	13.5
20 031	...	6	Coffey	1 624	8 601	2 559	5.3	96.3	0.8	1.5	0.6	2.0	5.7	18.6	6.4	9.9	11.7	16.2
20 033	...	9	Comanche	2 042	1 891	3 064	0.9	95.4	0.5	1.0	0.3	3.9	5.3	17.7	4.7	9.0	9.8	14.7
20 035	49060	4	Cowley	2 916	36 311	1 265	12.5	84.7	3.6	3.3	2.0	9.1	6.8	17.7	10.5	11.3	11.6	14.1
20 037	38260	4	Crawford	1 527	39 134	1 193	25.6	92.3	2.9	1.9	1.8	4.5	6.4	15.9	17.4	12.8	10.5	12.3
20 039	...	9	Decatur	2 314	2 961	2 984	1.3	97.6	0.9	1.0	0.3	1.0	5.1	13.7	4.8	8.0	8.8	16.2
20 041	...	7	Dickinson	2 194	19 754	1 852	9.0	94.5	1.5	1.3	0.7	3.9	6.5	18.3	6.9	10.9	11.7	15.5
20 043	41140	3	Doniphan	1 019	7 945	2 606	7.8	93.5	3.9	2.1	0.4	2.1	5.7	16.6	12.3	10.0	12.0	14.2
20 045	29940	3	Douglas	1 181	110 826	533	93.8	84.6	5.1	3.6	4.8	5.1	5.6	13.5	24.6	15.8	10.8	11.2
20 047	...	9	Edwards	1 611	3 037	2 976	1.9	81.5	0.4	0.9	0.5	17.6	5.9	17.8	5.4	9.8	11.4	16.8
20 049	...	8	Elk	1 669	2 882	2 989	1.7	95.6	0.6	2.5	0.8	2.7	5.9	15.4	5.5	8.1	10.0	14.5
20 051	25700	5	Ellis	2 331	28 452	1 478	12.2	92.9	1.4	0.7	1.6	4.6	6.5	14.5	18.4	13.7	9.8	12.7
20 053	...	7	Ellsworth	1 854	6 497	2 725	3.5	89.4	5.2	1.2	0.6	5.0	5.3	13.5	7.7	13.1	11.5	16.4
20 055	23780	5	Finney	3 372	36 776	1 254	10.9	47.4	2.4	0.8	3.6	46.7	9.6	22.4	10.9	13.3	12.5	13.5
20 057	19980	5	Ford	2 845	33 848	1 329	11.9	44.9	2.2	0.8	1.8	51.2	9.6	21.3	10.8	14.6	12.4	12.3
20 059	28140	1	Franklin	1 481	25 992	1 565	17.6	94.0	2.1	1.9	0.6	3.6	7.1	18.8	8.8	11.7	12.2	15.5
20 061	31740	5	Geary	996	34 362	1 317	34.5	64.6	20.7	2.0	6.1	12.4	11.1	19.8	13.5	18.0	11.9	10.5
20 063	...	9	Gove	2 776	2 695	3 000	1.0	97.6	0.6	0.2	0.7	1.6	6.7	15.7	5.7	9.7	8.3	14.9
20 065	...	9	Graham	2 327	2 597	3 002	1.1	93.0	4.9	1.8	0.8	2.3	5.5	13.6	5.6	9.6	8.7	16.7
20 067	...	7	Grant	1 489	7 829	2 622	5.3	54.9	0.5	0.9	0.4	43.9	9.0	22.4	8.3	13.6	11.7	13.5
20 069	...	9	Gray	2 250	6 006	2 766	2.7	84.7	0.6	0.7	0.5	14.2	8.5	21.9	7.7	12.3	12.5	13.7
20 071	...	9	Greeley	2 016	1 247	3 097	0.6	85.3	0.4	0.6	0.5	13.7	6.5	14.8	6.3	10.9	8.1	19.2
20 073	...	6	Greenwood	2 961	6 689	2 715	2.3	95.1	0.6	2.1	0.5	3.3	6.0	16.1	5.8	9.4	10.7	15.2
20 075	...	9	Hamilton	2 581	2 690	3 001	1.0	67.8	0.4	1.4	0.5	30.7	9.4	19.0	8.7	14.6	10.7	13.3
20 077	...	8	Harper	2 075	6 034	2 763	2.9	93.6	0.6	1.6	0.3	4.9	6.7	16.9	6.3	10.3	10.5	13.3
20 079	48620	2	Harvey	1 398	34 684	1 311	24.8	86.3	2.3	1.3	1.1	10.8	6.8	18.7	8.6	11.8	10.9	14.1
20 081	...	9	Haskell	1 496	4 256	2 886	2.8	72.2	0.3	1.0	0.4	27.0	8.1	23.0	7.8	11.9	11.9	14.3
20 083	...	9	Hodgeman	2 227	1 916	3 061	0.9	92.2	1.4	0.6	0.6	6.2	5.9	18.1	5.3	8.9	10.0	18.4
20 085	45820	3	Jackson	1 700	13 462	2 222	7.9	88.4	1.0	9.5	0.5	3.3	6.7	19.8	6.6	10.1	12.8	15.3
20 087	45820	3	Jefferson	1 379	19 126	1 873	13.9	96.5	0.8	1.9	0.5	1.8	5.7	19.0	6.4	9.8	12.5	17.4
20 089	...	9	Jewell	2 356	3 077	2 974	1.3	97.0	0.5	1.0	0.2	2.0	4.8	13.9	4.8	7.5	8.5	15.0
20 091	28140	1	Johnson	1 226	544 179	112	443.9	83.8	5.1	0.9	5.0	7.2	7.2	19.1	7.1	14.6	14.3	15.0
20 093	...	9	Kearny	2 255	3 977	2 910	1.8	69.8	0.9	1.7	0.5	28.5	7.8	22.1	8.3	11.2	11.8	13.7
20 095	...	6	Kingman	2 236	7 858	2 616	3.5	96.3	0.3	1.3	0.7	2.5	5.8	18.4	6.6	9.3	10.4	16.3
20 097	...	9	Kiowa	1 872	2 553	3 004	1.4	94.0	0.7	1.4	0.9	3.9	5.2	16.4	11.1	10.0	10.7	13.9
20 099	37660	7	Labette	1 671	21 607	1 758	12.9	89.0	6.0	4.1	0.7	4.0	6.9	17.4	8.9	10.8	11.4	15.1
20 101	...	9	Lane	1 858	1 750	3 072	0.9	94.2	0.9	1.5	0.5	4.2	4.9	17.6	5.3	9.7	11.3	14.7
20 103	28140	1	Leavenworth	1 199	76 227	712	63.6	82.7	10.4	1.6	2.3	5.7	6.8	18.3	7.8	13.5	14.9	15.7
20 105	...	9	Lincoln	1 863	3 241	2 960	1.7	96.9	0.4	0.7	0.4	2.2	6.4	17.6	4.5	9.5	10.0	16.2
20 107	28140	1	Linn	1 539	9 656	2 464	6.3	96.5	0.6	1.7	0.6	1.9	5.6	17.6	6.1	9.7	11.2	15.3
20 109	...	9	Logan	2 779	2 756	2 996	1.0	95.7	1.3	0.8	0.8	2.9	5.5	17.3	6.0	11.0	10.3	16.1
20 111	21380	5	Lyon	2 195	33 690	1 332	15.3	74.9	2.9	1.1	2.7	20.1	7.0	16.6	16.3	12.8	10.6	13.2
20 113	32700	6	McPherson	2 327	29 180	1 449	12.5	94.6	1.6	0.9	0.8	3.5	6.2	17.3	8.7	11.0	10.6	15.1
20 115	...	6	Marion	2 446	12 660	2 265	5.2	96.1	1.1	1.3	0.5	2.3	5.3	17.3	9.1	8.7	10.0	15.5
20 117	...	7	Marshall	2 331	10 117	2 437	4.3	97.3	0.7	0.8	0.5	1.9	6.5	16.6	6.0	10.8	9.8	15.9
20 119	...	9	Meade	2 533	4 575	2 865	1.8	83.3	1.0	1.2	0.8	14.8	7.4	21.6	6.6	10.4	12.2	13.7
20 121	28140	1	Miami	1 491	32 787	1 367	22.0	95.2	1.8	1.4	0.7	2.5	6.5	20.4	6.5	10.9	13.6	16.8
20 123	...	7	Mitchell	1 818	6 373	2 737	3.5	97.9	0.3	0.7	0.5	1.1	5.9	15.5	8.0	10.0	9.8	15.1
20 125	17700	5	Montgomery	1 667	35 471	1 289	21.3	85.0	6.9	6.2	1.0	5.2	6.9	16.8	9.7	11.5	11.0	14.2
20 127	...	9	Morris	1 801	5 923	2 774	3.3	95.2	0.6	1.4	0.7	3.6	5.2	16.3	6.1	9.1	9.9	16.6
20 129	...	9	Morton	1 890	3 233	2 962	1.7	77.5	1.0	1.3	2.4	19.3	6.6	20.4	7.4	10.5	12.0	14.6
20 131	...	8	Nemaha	1 858	10 178	2 429	5.5	97.6	0.8	0.9	0.4	1.2	6.5	19.7	5.4	10.3	11.0	15.4

1. CBSA = Core Based Statistical Area. See Appendix A for explanation. See Appendix B for list of metropolitan areas with component counties.   2. County type code from the Economic Research Service of USDA Rural-Urban Continuum Codes. See Appendix A for definition.   3. Dry land or land partially or temporarily covered by water.   4. May be of any race.

STATE County	55 to 64 years	65 to 74 years	75 years and over	Percent female	1990	2000	1990–2000	2000–2010	Births	Deaths	Net migration	Number	Percent change, 2000–2010	Persons per household	Female family householder[1]	One person
	16	17	18	19	20	21	22	23	24	25	26	27	28	29	30	31
KANSAS	11.6	6.7	6.5	50.4	2 477 588	2 688 418	8.5	6.1	370 672	225 837	-17 574	1 112 096	7.1	2.49	10.4	27.8
Allen	12.8	8.9	9.4	51.2	14 638	14 385	-1.7	-7.0	1 592	1 654	-1 050	5 475	-5.2	2.37	10.2	29.3
Anderson	12.2	10.2	9.9	50.5	7 803	8 110	3.9	-0.1	974	915	-261	3 260	1.2	2.45	7.7	28.2
Atchison	11.1	7.8	7.5	51.3	16 932	16 774	-0.9	0.9	2 019	1 696	-595	6 241	-0.5	2.49	11.2	28.1
Barber	14.4	10.0	10.4	49.6	5 874	5 307	-9.7	-8.4	437	601	-539	2 139	-4.3	2.25	6.6	32.2
Barton	12.3	7.8	9.2	50.9	29 382	28 205	-4.0	-1.9	3 355	2 793	-2 064	11 283	-1.0	2.39	8.9	30.3
Bourbon	12.8	8.4	8.9	51.0	14 966	15 379	2.8	-1.3	1 999	1 800	-599	5 986	-2.8	2.47	10.6	28.9
Brown	13.6	9.0	9.3	51.3	11 128	10 724	-3.6	-6.9	1 276	1 298	-730	4 094	-5.2	2.41	10.3	28.9
Butler	11.8	6.3	6.3	49.6	50 580	59 482	17.6	10.8	7 252	5 057	2 787	23 992	11.5	2.65	9.6	22.8
Chase	15.2	11.0	10.2	49.0	3 021	3 030	0.3	-7.9	378	319	-278	1 150	-7.7	2.30	5.8	31.2
Chautauqua	14.4	12.8	11.6	49.3	4 407	4 359	-1.1	-15.8	349	645	-300	1 612	-10.2	2.23	7.4	34.0
Cherokee	12.9	9.1	6.9	50.3	21 374	22 605	5.8	-4.4	2 400	2 490	-1 337	8 625	-2.8	2.48	10.9	26.9
Cheyenne	14.5	10.2	16.1	49.6	3 243	3 165	-2.4	-13.9	219	388	-281	1 260	-7.4	2.12	5.4	36.4
Clark	13.4	9.6	12.4	51.5	2 418	2 390	-1.2	-7.3	228	261	-270	923	-5.7	2.34	8.3	30.4
Clay	13.9	9.3	11.1	50.5	9 158	8 822	-3.7	-3.3	946	989	-30	3 559	-1.6	2.36	7.2	29.2
Cloud	12.9	9.1	11.3	51.1	11 023	10 268	-6.8	-7.2	1 000	1 412	-542	3 910	-6.1	2.31	7.7	30.4
Coffey	14.3	9.2	8.0	50.6	8 404	8 865	5.5	-3.0	944	1 024	-300	3 497	0.2	2.42	8.6	26.2
Comanche	14.8	12.3	11.7	51.8	2 313	1 967	-15.0	-3.9	160	311	60	824	-5.5	2.22	5.5	33.7
Cowley	12.3	8.1	7.7	50.1	36 915	36 291	-1.7	0.1	4 264	3 833	-2 982	13 940	-0.7	2.46	10.8	28.4
Crawford	10.8	6.9	7.0	50.4	35 582	38 242	7.5	2.3	4 892	4 143	82	15 729	1.5	2.38	10.8	29.8
Decatur	16.1	11.1	16.2	49.9	4 021	3 472	-13.7	-14.7	227	486	-350	1 378	-7.8	2.09	5.5	36.1
Dickinson	12.2	8.5	9.5	50.7	18 958	19 344	2.0	2.1	2 047	2 152	-128	8 073	2.2	2.41	9.0	27.8
Doniphan	12.9	8.0	8.2	49.6	8 134	8 249	1.4	-3.7	733	750	-562	3 136	-1.2	2.40	9.4	29.0
Douglas	9.6	4.7	4.2	49.9	81 798	99 962	22.2	10.9	11 606	5 286	5 836	43 576	13.2	2.34	8.6	29.8
Edwards	13.7	9.6	9.5	50.2	3 787	3 449	-8.9	-11.9	383	381	-367	1 302	-10.5	2.31	6.3	30.9
Elk	16.2	12.9	11.4	50.5	3 327	3 261	-2.0	-11.6	314	461	-89	1 284	-9.1	2.21	8.8	32.2
Ellis	11.0	6.0	7.4	50.3	26 004	27 507	5.8	3.4	3 322	2 253	-680	11 908	6.4	2.30	7.6	31.5
Ellsworth	13.6	9.1	9.8	43.8	6 586	6 525	-0.9	-0.4	454	763	-3	2 463	-0.7	2.24	6.9	29.9
Finney	9.4	4.6	3.7	49.8	33 070	40 523	22.5	-9.2	7 374	1 824	-6 899	12 359	-4.5	2.93	12.7	22.6
Ford	9.0	4.8	5.1	48.4	27 463	32 458	18.2	4.3	5 954	2 273	-2 321	11 145	2.7	2.97	11.8	22.7
Franklin	11.6	7.7	6.4	50.5	21 994	24 784	12.7	4.9	3 470	2 156	76	10 104	6.9	2.53	10.2	25.8
Geary	7.5	4.1	3.6	50.3	30 453	27 947	-8.2	23.0	5 642	1 799	-4 135	12 690	21.3	2.64	16.1	24.1
Gove	15.0	10.9	18.7	50.0	3 201	3 068	-5.0	-12.2	262	345	-531	1 154	-7.3	2.29	4.3	29.0
Graham	14.7	13.0	12.7	51.1	3 543	2 946	-16.9	-11.8	209	343	-371	1 196	-5.3	2.14	5.3	33.2
Grant	11.1	5.9	4.6	48.9	7 159	7 909	10.5	-1.0	1 274	486	-1 333	2 716	-0.9	2.85	8.6	21.1
Gray	10.8	6.8	5.8	50.9	5 396	5 904	9.4	1.7	878	511	-245	2 153	5.3	2.75	6.8	22.6
Greeley	13.2	8.5	12.4	52.3	1 774	1 534	-13.5	-18.7	139	147	-295	525	-12.8	2.33	4.2	30.3
Greenwood	14.7	11.0	11.2	50.7	7 847	7 673	-2.2	-12.8	733	1 094	-613	2 988	-7.6	2.21	7.0	34.2
Hamilton	10.7	6.7	6.9	49.3	2 388	2 670	11.8	0.7	381	246	-170	1 060	0.6	2.54	7.7	29.3
Harper	14.2	10.6	11.0	50.5	7 124	6 536	-8.3	-7.7	637	941	-538	2 545	-8.2	2.32	8.6	30.2
Harvey	12.0	7.7	9.4	51.2	31 028	32 869	5.9	5.5	4 002	3 285	883	13 411	6.6	2.49	8.7	26.9
Haskell	12.3	5.2	5.5	50.0	3 886	4 307	10.8	-1.2	633	263	-665	1 510	2.0	2.80	6.8	21.9
Hodgeman	12.7	9.6	11.1	50.0	2 177	2 085	-4.2	-8.1	197	211	-157	803	0.9	2.37	5.4	27.5
Jackson	13.3	8.4	7.0	49.9	11 525	12 657	9.8	6.4	1 641	1 166	350	5 228	10.6	2.55	9.4	24.9
Jefferson	13.9	8.8	6.7	49.3	15 905	18 426	15.9	3.8	1 948	1 539	-525	7 366	7.8	2.56	8.0	21.6
Jewell	17.5	13.2	14.8	48.8	4 251	3 791	-10.8	-18.8	213	459	-470	1 450	-14.5	2.10	5.3	34.3
Johnson	11.7	5.7	5.2	51.2	355 021	451 086	27.1	20.6	69 592	27 665	51 852	212 882	21.9	2.53	8.7	25.8
Kearny	11.6	6.8	6.7	49.2	4 027	4 531	12.5	-12.2	593	325	-626	1 400	-9.2	2.78	10.4	21.1
Kingman	13.2	9.4	10.6	50.4	8 292	8 673	4.6	-9.4	776	1 004	-845	3 227	-4.3	2.38	6.9	29.4
Kiowa	13.9	8.5	10.3	50.8	3 660	3 278	-10.4	-22.1	297	273	-998	1 014	-25.7	2.37	6.1	28.4
Labette	12.9	8.4	8.2	50.5	23 693	22 835	-3.6	-5.4	2 602	2 685	-833	8 822	-4.0	2.39	11.5	30.2
Lane	15.4	10.1	11.0	51.1	2 375	2 155	-9.3	-18.8	161	240	-333	799	-12.2	2.19	4.9	34.7
Leavenworth	11.9	6.3	4.8	46.9	64 371	68 691	6.7	11.0	8 660	4 892	3 189	26 447	14.6	2.63	10.6	22.8
Lincoln	15.4	8.3	12.0	50.1	3 653	3 578	-2.1	-9.4	324	483	-278	1 423	-6.9	2.24	7.2	32.8
Linn	15.1	10.8	8.5	49.9	8 254	9 570	15.9	0.9	1 046	941	-293	4 020	5.6	2.39	7.1	27.7
Logan	13.0	9.2	11.5	50.5	3 081	3 046	-1.1	-9.5	275	317	-451	1 219	-1.9	2.23	6.6	34.1
Lyon	11.0	6.4	6.1	51.1	34 732	35 935	3.5	-6.2	4 994	2 742	-4 493	13 303	-2.8	2.42	10.0	29.5
McPherson	12.7	8.1	10.2	50.9	27 268	29 554	8.4	-1.3	3 222	3 254	-491	11 748	4.8	2.41	6.7	28.0
Marion	13.2	9.8	11.0	49.7	12 888	13 361	3.7	-5.2	1 156	1 634	-822	5 005	-2.1	2.39	6.4	27.7
Marshall	13.2	9.4	11.6	50.5	11 705	10 965	-6.3	-7.7	1 126	1 316	-592	4 300	-3.5	2.31	6.2	30.6
Meade	11.0	7.3	9.9	49.2	4 247	4 631	9.0	-1.2	559	429	-337	1 713	-0.9	2.60	7.4	25.4
Miami	12.1	7.1	5.9	50.6	23 466	28 351	20.8	15.6	3 779	2 270	1 283	12 161	17.3	2.64	8.9	21.3
Mitchell	14.6	8.8	12.3	49.5	7 203	6 932	-3.8	-8.1	581	857	-267	2 790	-2.1	2.20	6.2	33.1
Montgomery	12.6	8.8	8.6	50.9	38 816	36 252	-6.6	-2.2	4 447	4 359	-1 928	14 382	-3.5	2.39	11.5	29.6
Morris	14.5	10.6	11.7	50.1	6 198	6 104	-1.5	-3.0	536	703	88	2 554	0.6	2.29	6.5	28.7
Morton	11.6	8.0	8.9	51.4	3 480	3 496	0.5	-7.5	487	301	-648	1 250	-4.3	2.52	8.3	27.0
Nemaha	11.6	8.0	12.1	49.4	10 446	10 717	2.6	-5.0	1 196	1 349	-533	4 115	3.9	2.41	5.5	31.3

1. No spouse present.

Table B. States and Counties — Population, Vital Statistics, Medicare, and Crime

STATE County	Persons in group quarters, 2010	Daytime population, 2006–2010		Births, average 2006–2008		Deaths, average 2006–2008		Persons under 65 with no health insurance, 2009		Medicare, 2011			Serious crimes known to police,[2] 2010 Total	
		Number	Employment/residence ratio	Total	Rate[1]	Number	Rate[1]	Number	Percent	Eligible for Medicare	Enrolled in Medicare Advantage	Enrolled in a Medicare prescription drug plan	Number	Rate[3]
	32	33	34	35	36	37	38	39	40	41	42	43	44	45
KANSAS	79 074	2 821 867	1.0	41 602	15.0	24 673	8.9	349 636	14.6	445 060	50 606	234 730	99 546	3 489
Allen	382	13 450	1.0	D	D	173	12.8	1 587	15.0	2 824	165	1 786	373	2 790
Anderson	103	7 069	0.7	D	D	90	11.3	1 009	16.1	1 765	62	1 045	160	2 005
Atchison	1 375	16 295	0.9	D	D	188	11.3	1 922	14.2	2 895	160	1 825	377	2 228
Barber	40	4 795	1.0	D	D	71	14.8	613	16.8	1 164	28	739	NA	NA
Barton	672	27 294	1.0	392	14.2	316	11.4	4 063	18.1	5 192	98	3 564	1 260	4 553
Bourbon	409	14 892	1.0	D	D	192	12.9	1 874	15.5	3 134	181	1 810	544	3 585
Brown	116	10 254	1.1	D	D	146	14.5	1 254	15.7	2 122	46	1 392	104	1 267
Butler	2 309	53 335	0.6	814	12.9	556	8.8	6 812	12.5	9 814	1 001	5 302	1 736	2 664
Chase	145	2 497	0.8	D	D	38	12.9	420	18.9	557	20	339	2	72
Chautauqua	79	3 183	0.7	D	D	64	16.7	568	20.4	950	25	616	17	463
Cherokee	202	19 080	0.7	D	D	283	13.3	2 802	16.2	4 273	256	2 476	473	2 208
Cheyenne	49	2 688	0.9	D	D	44	15.5	363	18.7	740	24	462	31	1 137
Clark	57	2 149	0.9	D	D	29	13.7	267	16.5	496	16	345	27	1 219
Clay	140	7 902	0.9	D	D	117	13.5	1 011	14.7	1 831	118	1 150	157	1 839
Cloud	498	9 157	0.9	D	D	153	16.1	1 062	15.0	2 206	126	1 480	236	2 476
Coffey	130	8 926	1.1	D	D	104	12.2	908	13.1	1 872	64	1 143	81	942
Comanche	65	1 820	1.0	D	D	37	19.4	222	15.8	481	D	323	NA	NA
Cowley	2 004	35 166	0.9	473	13.7	410	11.9	4 454	15.8	6 800	701	4 005	1 238	3 409
Crawford	1 773	39 488	1.0	539	14.0	446	11.6	5 557	17.2	6 621	274	4 232	1 814	4 635
Decatur	81	2 926	0.9	D	D	54	17.9	406	19.6	824	52	527	NA	NA
Dickinson	307	17 874	0.8	D	D	223	11.6	2 131	13.9	3 985	288	2 129	513	2 714
Doniphan	427	6 858	0.7	D	D	74	9.5	1 010	16.2	1 439	34	840	178	2 240
Douglas	8 792	103 562	0.9	1 282	11.3	573	5.1	14 668	14.3	12 410	1 111	6 550	5 079	4 583
Edwards	35	2 737	0.8	D	D	38	12.1	449	18.5	661	21	431	NA	NA
Elk	40	2 547	0.7	D	D	47	15.3	495	22.1	816	29	529	29	1 006
Ellis	1 033	28 702	1.0	D	D	247	9.0	3 212	13.9	4 376	78	2 906	862	3 165
Ellsworth	983	6 372	1.0	D	D	78	12.4	821	16.9	1 346	51	871	112	1 865
Finney	548	36 479	1.0	763	19.3	191	4.8	8 999	23.6	3 785	103	2 395	1 454	3 954
Ford	708	33 532	1.1	678	20.3	224	6.7	6 472	21.8	3 624	89	2 321	1 179	3 483
Franklin	478	23 458	0.8	D	D	247	9.3	2 882	12.8	4 683	267	2 655	721	2 774
Geary	847	34 219	1.3	736	27.4	192	7.2	4 340	15.6	3 296	221	1 153	786	2 287
Gove	56	2 932	1.2	D	D	40	15.2	358	19.6	685	17	478	NA	NA
Graham	40	2 539	0.9	D	D	39	14.7	311	17.9	748	33	487	68	2 618
Grant	79	8 035	1.1	D	D	56	7.5	1 413	21.9	939	D	610	125	1 597
Gray	78	5 677	0.9	D	D	52	9.1	1 153	22.4	838	14	595	37	616
Greeley	26	1 361	1.1	D	D	11	8.2	192	19.7	278	D	207	13	1 043
Greenwood	90	5 864	0.7	D	D	109	15.6	909	17.5	1 627	45	1 086	89	1 331
Hamilton	0	2 696	1.0	D	D	30	11.5	534	24.6	406	D	282	1	37
Harper	129	5 848	0.9	D	D	100	17.1	784	17.8	1 361	30	903	78	1 710
Harvey	1 311	32 522	0.9	D	D	371	11.0	3 957	14.2	6 735	924	3 940	741	2 193
Haskell	33	4 162	1.0	D	D	33	8.1	792	22.7	499	13	338	NA	NA
Hodgeman	14	1 772	0.8	D	D	22	11.0	226	14.7	410	11	251	35	1 827
Jackson	133	11 544	0.7	D	D	138	10.3	1 530	13.6	2 593	98	1 315	248	1 967
Jefferson	235	13 482	0.4	D	D	175	9.4	1 796	11.9	3 428	220	1 680	533	2 787
Jewell	27	2 898	0.8	D	D	48	15.0	404	18.5	903	41	608	NA	NA
Johnson	5 166	555 796	1.1	7 834	14.9	3 208	6.1	46 249	9.8	69 394	17 337	25 572	12 440	2 287
Kearny	81	3 508	0.7	D	D	38	8.9	815	22.5	588	D	400	0	0
Kingman	190	7 113	0.8	D	D	101	12.9	877	14.7	1 697	62	1 079	136	1 731
Kiowa	149	2 708	1.0	D	D	33	11.8	313	17.1	560	13	350	59	2 311
Labette	480	22 021	1.0	D	D	284	12.9	2 682	15.0	4 613	230	2 934	1 056	4 887
Lane	3	1 711	1.0	D	D	28	15.9	248	18.2	430	D	304	23	1 314
Leavenworth	6 561	68 199	0.8	959	13.0	517	7.0	7 915	12.1	10 403	972	3 713	2 348	3 080
Lincoln	50	2 915	0.8	D	D	48	14.5	458	18.8	698	11	459	48	1 481
Linn	63	8 370	0.7	D	D	118	12.0	1 216	16.1	2 109	335	954	163	1 738
Logan	41	2 782	1.0	D	D	40	15.2	324	16.6	623	26	419	35	1 270
Lyon	1 444	34 683	1.0	531	14.9	287	8.0	5 589	19.7	5 188	212	3 240	1 400	4 156
McPherson	925	29 612	1.0	D	D	366	12.5	2 933	12.6	5 727	429	3 390	537	1 897
Marion	723	11 236	0.8	D	D	172	13.9	1 471	15.9	2 840	143	1 850	149	1 229
Marshall	164	10 455	1.1	D	D	126	12.3	1 157	14.8	2 362	113	1 522	121	1 288
Meade	119	4 062	0.8	D	D	48	10.9	771	21.5	792	16	472	40	874
Miami	645	25 128	0.6	D	D	247	8.0	3 393	12.6	5 016	825	2 369	632	1 928
Mitchell	246	6 822	1.1	D	D	96	15.3	698	14.2	1 382	65	954	77	1 304
Montgomery	1 112	37 047	1.1	D	D	470	13.6	4 237	15.4	7 249	357	4 450	1 308	3 688
Morris	66	5 260	0.8	D	D	74	12.2	763	16.7	1 367	87	693	97	1 638
Morton	83	3 335	1.1	D	D	37	12.0	471	18.9	571	D	340	53	1 639
Nemaha	259	10 327	1.0	D	D	143	14.0	1 029	13.3	2 129	44	1 388	147	1 444

1. Per 1,000 estimated resident population.   2. Data for serious crimes have not been adjusted for underreporting; this may affect comparability between geographic areas and over time.   3. Per 100,000 population estimated by the FBI.

Table B. States and Counties — Crime, Education, Money Income, and Poverty

STATE County	Serious crimes known to police,[1] 2010 (cont.) Rate[2] Violent	Property	Education — Enrollment[3] Total	Percent private	Attainment[4] (percent) High school graduate or less	Bachelor's degree or more	Local government expenditures,[5] 2008–2009 Total current expenditures (mil dol)	Current expenditures per student (dollars)	Money income, 2006–2010 Per capita income[6] (dollars)	Households Median income Dollars	Percent change, 2000 to 2006–2010 (constant 2010 dollars)	Percent with income of $200,000 or more	Income and poverty, 2010 Median household income (dollars)	Percent below poverty level All persons	Children under 18 years	Children 5 to 17 years in families
	46	47	48	49	50	51	52	53	54	55	56	57	58	59	60	61
KANSAS	369	3 120	778 515	14.0	39.7	29.3	4 678.6	9 945	25 907	49 424	-3.9	2.9	47 888	13.5	18.1	15.9
Allen	307	2 483	3 511	6.9	46.6	17.7	25.2	10 968	20 195	41 546	4.2	0.5	39 662	18.4	26.4	24.0
Anderson	376	1 629	1 881	7.6	54.1	15.9	13.9	10 077	20 558	40 428	-4.0	1.4	41 054	14.6	21.7	19.6
Atchison	130	2 098	4 882	26.6	55.8	22.3	24.4	10 284	20 995	44 175	1.5	1.7	41 659	15.6	20.0	18.2
Barber	NA	NA	1 031	3.5	42.1	18.7	9.0	11 594	23 542	38 875	-8.1	1.5	42 565	12.5	19.4	18.5
Barton	488	4 065	6 959	5.9	45.6	20.5	44.1	10 181	23 688	43 763	7.4	1.9	43 675	13.3	20.1	19.4
Bourbon	244	3 341	4 056	10.9	43.8	20.4	22.4	8 900	18 596	38 045	-3.7	1.1	37 192	15.9	25.7	24.5
Brown	146	1 121	2 254	4.5	54.2	16.3	18.0	11 521	19 555	37 525	-7.3	1.4	40 464	18.4	27.1	23.8
Butler	183	2 481	18 752	11.2	36.7	24.8	128.3	8 776	26 436	56 290	-2.2	2.7	55 182	9.1	12.0	10.4
Chase	0	72	694	3.6	47.8	18.8	5.1	11 741	21 890	40 372	-2.4	1.7	39 683	13.1	18.8	16.7
Chautauqua	55	409	696	7.2	51.0	17.0	6.1	11 539	21 613	35 848	-1.4	1.1	34 772	15.6	25.2	23.5
Cherokee	280	1 928	4 966	4.9	52.5	14.5	40.6	10 468	20 075	38 154	-1.2	1.7	36 204	20.1	28.2	26.6
Cheyenne	73	1 064	626	5.0	46.9	16.4	5.2	11 826	19 460	31 186	-19.5	0.0	35 730	12.6	18.8	16.5
Clark	90	1 129	601	7.5	45.6	19.7	6.0	11 669	24 605	37 931	-11.5	1.6	41 715	11.2	14.3	13.0
Clay	141	1 699	1 832	6.9	47.0	18.9	16.1	9 258	24 858	42 490	-1.2	1.2	46 421	11.6	17.3	16.1
Cloud	252	2 224	2 440	5.1	48.6	15.2	14.6	10 321	18 690	35 838	-10.9	0.5	37 539	16.0	19.1	17.4
Coffey	128	814	2 126	8.3	46.6	20.0	19.2	11 295	23 744	47 171	-1.6	0.9	49 727	9.7	12.7	11.1
Comanche	NA	NA	396	3.5	48.5	16.4	3.8	11 577	22 974	34 808	-6.6	3.6	38 207	10.4	13.8	11.1
Cowley	355	3 054	9 488	12.7	44.2	19.5	61.3	9 579	20 720	40 749	-6.5	1.4	39 155	17.3	21.9	19.6
Crawford	317	4 318	12 862	10.1	41.1	26.3	60.3	10 064	19 753	35 286	-5.2	1.2	35 407	19.2	26.8	23.3
Decatur	NA	NA	469	2.6	50.3	17.6	4.5	11 710	21 966	35 383	-7.7	0.0	37 081	13.1	20.3	18.9
Dickinson	206	2 508	4 597	13.5	47.9	19.9	39.1	9 815	22 009	46 457	2.0	1.1	45 037	11.6	16.6	14.1
Doniphan	189	2 052	2 036	6.8	51.7	16.3	17.6	12 740	21 704	43 410	5.4	0.9	45 202	13.0	17.4	15.2
Douglas	423	4 160	44 861	11.8	24.8	48.3	129.1	9 397	24 851	45 831	-3.6	3.0	47 335	15.6	13.8	12.4
Edwards	NA	NA	672	8.2	46.1	21.1	5.7	13 655	24 899	39 226	1.5	2.7	41 800	12.1	19.2	17.0
Elk	69	937	570	3.0	47.8	17.1	7.2	12 313	20 958	33 455	-3.1	1.4	32 619	18.3	29.2	28.6
Ellis	283	2 882	9 280	8.2	35.2	33.6	38.3	10 755	24 093	44 543	8.8	2.2	42 409	13.6	13.4	13.2
Ellsworth	200	1 665	1 302	9.1	50.6	19.8	11.6	11 432	21 704	42 200	-6.8	1.5	41 622	10.8	15.2	14.1
Finney	402	3 551	10 641	7.5	54.6	17.3	82.0	10 044	20 976	50 454	3.6	2.7	46 697	15.2	21.3	19.8
Ford	479	3 005	8 943	5.2	56.3	17.2	66.2	9 699	19 348	46 621	-2.8	1.6	43 876	14.1	20.6	17.9
Franklin	312	2 462	7 121	15.6	40.8	18.5	46.8	9 875	22 294	49 459	0.0	0.4	40 905	11.0	16.6	15.0
Geary	533	1 755	8 763	5.5	39.1	19.4	71.2	10 151	20 709	45 559	12.7	1.3	43 691	12.1	15.7	15.4
Gove	NA	NA	523	2.3	51.1	16.9	6.9	16 208	22 775	41 295	-2.7	1.9	41 263	11.6	18.8	18.2
Graham	193	2 426	530	4.7	43.8	24.2	4.5	11 391	25 026	43 980	11.0	1.6	40 049	12.5	17.8	15.6
Grant	204	1 392	2 085	10.8	52.2	15.9	16.1	9 294	25 188	55 514	10.0	1.9	51 460	11.2	16.7	15.7
Gray	50	566	1 604	16.5	54.8	19.8	14.5	11 962	22 606	52 824	4.3	1.8	51 828	8.1	12.7	11.4
Greeley	321	722	327	1.8	46.2	20.7	2.9	12 711	28 698	55 972	27.7	4.1	47 625	10.5	17.0	16.8
Greenwood	135	1 196	1 431	2.1	54.4	14.6	11.2	11 104	21 325	37 180	-2.7	0.5	35 146	17.4	25.6	21.7
Hamilton	37	0	631	2.9	50.1	14.9	5.3	10 541	20 190	36 297	-10.5	1.0	42 586	12.8	20.0	20.1
Harper	175	1 535	1 226	7.3	48.6	16.3	11.6	11 563	22 467	38 168	1.2	1.3	37 468	14.4	22.4	20.6
Harvey	317	1 877	9 280	18.7	42.3	25.5	55.4	9 031	22 890	46 604	-10.0	1.4	46 941	10.1	13.1	12.1
Haskell	NA	NA	1 179	8.1	56.0	14.8	10.4	11 901	21 966	45 859	-6.3	2.8	51 257	11.0	17.7	16.0
Hodgeman	104	1 722	492	3.5	37.0	22.9	4.6	15 976	20 859	41 127	-9.8	0.3	43 338	10.6	14.9	13.6
Jackson	254	1 713	3 609	11.1	51.8	17.7	25.3	10 719	23 306	51 759	1.0	1.2	50 709	11.3	16.0	14.2
Jefferson	204	2 583	4 688	8.6	49.4	22.2	41.9	10 520	25 580	56 886	-1.3	2.1	52 592	9.0	12.5	10.6
Jewell	NA	NA	595	11.1	43.7	18.9	3.9	13 757	22 443	37 759	-2.4	1.5	37 640	13.6	18.6	16.8
Johnson	170	2 117	147 176	20.7	21.1	51.1	846.4	9 553	37 882	73 733	-5.3	7.4	71 389	6.6	7.7	6.5
Kearny	0	0	1 153	2.9	49.5	12.3	11.1	11 335	20 888	46 435	-8.7	0.8	49 426	11.4	18.2	16.3
Kingman	102	1 629	1 750	21.4	43.2	20.2	13.9	10 756	22 861	44 510	-7.0	0.9	46 574	12.4	17.5	15.6
Kiowa	78	2 233	813	45.0	44.5	20.9	7.1	10 481	19 430	37 292	-6.7	1.5	41 166	13.2	20.0	17.5
Labette	731	4 156	5 528	14.6	43.8	17.8	41.2	10 099	21 021	39 049	-0.1	1.0	39 683	17.1	25.1	22.5
Lane	114	1 200	373	9.7	49.7	22.2	4.6	12 316	25 261	42 311	-7.3	2.1	44 288	9.7	15.2	13.1
Leavenworth	487	2 594	20 075	18.6	41.5	28.8	115.1	8 869	25 925	61 107	0.3	2.4	60 848	9.4	12.7	11.4
Lincoln	185	1 296	761	8.0	45.2	17.1	5.9	11 382	23 084	41 071	5.0	0.4	39 442	12.9	18.4	16.2
Linn	213	1 525	1 978	6.4	54.1	13.5	21.0	10 789	22 472	44 379	-2.4	0.8	43 509	14.3	21.9	19.5
Logan	145	1 125	670	13.7	47.1	18.0	6.2	11 054	22 856	39 375	-3.2	1.0	42 297	10.4	15.3	13.0
Lyon	312	3 844	11 228	6.0	47.8	23.5	57.5	9 954	18 245	36 921	-11.2	0.7	39 258	19.6	22.4	20.2
McPherson	194	1 703	7 732	25.7	44.3	25.1	34.8	9 471	26 467	53 026	1.8	2.4	54 881	9.3	11.9	10.3
Marion	124	1 106	3 307	28.3	46.8	19.5	23.4	10 888	21 166	45 713	4.6	1.0	45 899	10.9	14.0	12.3
Marshall	75	1 214	2 137	11.9	57.8	12.7	23.5	11 313	21 295	43 125	6.1	0.4	43 584	11.8	16.9	15.7
Meade	328	546	1 253	9.5	47.9	20.9	7.5	11 219	23 909	46 658	0.2	1.9	48 634	10.2	14.6	12.9
Miami	186	1 742	8 230	12.9	42.4	23.0	46.2	9 341	26 218	60 539	2.4	2.0	58 445	8.8	11.9	10.4
Mitchell	305	999	1 481	15.4	42.2	20.8	12.8	11 468	23 350	44 247	4.7	1.5	42 946	10.3	15.2	14.4
Montgomery	479	3 208	8 701	12.0	46.1	18.6	52.1	9 141	21 037	40 603	3.4	1.3	37 495	18.6	26.2	23.9
Morris	152	1 486	1 324	6.2	55.6	16.6	8.5	10 423	23 967	42 083	3.3	2.7	44 417	11.0	16.8	15.1
Morton	402	1 237	783	2.7	45.8	19.1	10.5	10 573	22 862	42 273	-10.3	1.2	49 526	11.2	18.9	16.3
Nemaha	226	1 218	2 525	11.9	58.3	17.1	16.6	10 133	22 484	46 134	6.2	1.9	44 056	10.0	12.6	11.2

1. Data for serious crimes have not been adjusted for underreporting; this may affect comparability between geographic areas and over time. 2. Per 100,000 population estimated by the FBI. 3. All persons 3 years old and over enrolled in nursery school through college. 4. Persons 25 years old and over. 5. Elementary and secondary education expenditures. 6. Based on population estimated by the American Community Survey, 2006–2010.

Table B. States and Counties — **Personal Income**

STATE County	Personal income, 2009												
			Per capita[1]					Transfer payments (mil dol)					
									Government payments to individuals				
	Total (mil dol)	Percent change, 2008–2009	Dollars	Rank	Wages and salaries[2] (mil dol)	Proprietors' income (mil dol)	Dividends, interest, and rent (mil dol)	Total	Total	Social Security	Medical payments	Income mainte-nance	Unemploy-ment insurance
	62	63	64	65	66	67	68	69	70	71	72	73	74
KANSAS	110 418	-1.4	39 173	X	70 399	10 148	20 023	17 947	17 437	6 312	7 095	1 578	1 096
Allen	426	-1.1	32 267	1 465	231	49	66	116	113	39	48	12	7
Anderson	251	0.2	31 948	1 539	82	28	44	63	62	24	26	5	4
Atchison	500	-2.4	30 492	1 864	261	51	99	119	116	40	50	10	8
Barber	168	-5.1	36 583	804	74	32	33	38	37	16	16	2	1
Barton	1 065	-4.6	38 793	554	567	167	214	202	197	74	88	16	8
Bourbon	446	0.5	29 982	1 984	261	24	83	125	122	41	52	13	6
Brown	386	5.7	38 853	551	223	57	64	78	76	28	34	8	3
Butler	2 435	0.0	37 995	641	821	208	367	387	375	150	135	29	31
Chase	119	-2.0	42 598	292	31	30	21	20	20	8	8	1	1
Chautauqua	122	-0.8	32 528	1 417	30	15	30	34	34	13	15	3	1
Cherokee	674	-0.7	31 984	1 533	263	102	86	174	170	59	74	22	7
Cheyenne	98	-1.1	36 263	852	33	24	21	23	22	10	10	1	0
Clark	76	-2.0	36 349	835	32	11	16	17	17	7	7	1	0
Clay	354	-1.7	40 661	409	121	61	64	62	61	25	26	4	2
Cloud	305	-1.7	32 972	1 344	136	42	57	80	79	29	35	5	2
Coffey	357	2.4	42 329	304	267	46	50	67	66	25	29	5	3
Comanche	63	-3.3	33 640	1 228	23	15	12	15	14	7	7	1	0
Cowley	1 126	-1.3	33 482	1 261	616	68	191	272	266	97	106	26	15
Crawford	1 163	1.1	29 915	1 999	686	12	243	311	304	90	135	35	17
Decatur	124	-1.1	43 410	258	38	27	37	25	24	11	10	1	0
Dickinson	671	-0.4	35 280	983	278	49	115	132	129	51	49	9	6
Doniphan	262	2.7	34 348	1 119	105	49	32	57	56	20	22	5	2
Douglas	3 732	1.1	32 070	1 510	2 176	189	724	516	494	181	184	46	30
Edwards	135	-2.7	44 025	236	42	48	21	24	23	9	11	1	1
Elk	87	-2.2	29 064	2 180	23	12	15	28	28	11	11	3	1
Ellis	1 109	-1.4	39 975	450	663	156	218	168	163	61	71	11	4
Ellsworth	202	-2.8	32 692	1 386	98	28	38	48	47	19	21	3	1
Finney	1 116	-0.5	26 529	2 636	777	106	175	186	178	52	82	29	5
Ford	1 013	0.4	30 077	1 959	734	79	161	158	152	51	66	21	3
Franklin	866	0.4	32 757	1 375	421	42	119	193	188	64	82	15	14
Geary	1 316	1.5	41 444	366	2 431	32	140	158	154	43	49	26	10
Gove	112	0.2	45 259	193	42	29	21	21	21	9	11	1	0
Graham	119	-5.1	48 697	124	41	38	16	26	26	11	12	1	0
Grant	270	0.3	36 726	783	181	49	40	37	36	14	16	4	1
Gray	215	-2.8	35 782	917	118	42	32	28	27	12	12	2	0
Greeley	71	-0.5	57 476	42	24	32	10	9	9	4	4	0	0
Greenwood	213	-2.4	31 918	1 545	66	25	38	62	61	24	28	5	2
Hamilton	93	-10.9	35 322	977	45	24	14	16	16	6	8	1	0
Harper	221	-7.3	39 058	534	93	39	41	48	47	19	20	3	2
Harvey	1 254	-0.5	36 629	798	613	206	196	256	249	92	107	15	15
Haskell	166	-7.4	41 382	370	77	44	30	19	18	8	7	2	0
Hodgeman	61	-4.6	31 910	1 548	21	10	15	13	12	6	5	1	0
Jackson	442	0.5	32 964	1 347	165	51	63	85	82	35	27	7	5
Jefferson	610	1.1	33 486	1 256	166	16	92	118	114	48	41	7	8
Jewell	124	-3.4	40 405	424	34	36	24	25	25	12	10	1	1
Johnson	28 957	-3.4	53 353	67	18 850	2 671	6 345	2 605	2 505	1 050	965	116	188
Kearny	132	-2.3	31 699	1 596	55	24	24	23	22	9	10	2	1
Kingman	284	-3.0	37 514	688	111	33	53	59	57	24	24	3	3
Kiowa	105	0.2	45 291	191	41	25	18	21	20	7	10	1	0
Labette	708	-0.3	32 522	1 420	398	50	105	208	204	60	99	19	12
Lane	70	0.6	40 033	447	35	11	15	14	14	6	6	1	0
Leavenworth	2 601	0.6	34 577	1 081	1 812	135	421	402	389	138	147	32	25
Lincoln	108	-3.8	34 496	1 093	36	21	20	23	22	10	9	2	1
Linn	292	0.3	31 296	1 693	105	13	43	76	75	30	29	6	5
Logan	114	0.3	44 668	212	47	31	24	21	20	8	9	1	0
Lyon	979	-1.5	29 131	2 163	641	36	180	219	213	69	87	22	11
McPherson	1 125	-3.0	38 962	541	661	162	191	200	195	82	83	11	8
Marion	389	-2.7	32 444	1 440	137	51	64	93	91	39	38	5	4
Marshall	409	-5.2	40 386	428	202	82	83	78	76	29	30	5	4
Meade	176	1.5	40 020	449	62	47	33	27	27	11	12	2	1
Miami	1 280	2.1	41 323	372	348	15	164	202	196	70	84	12	15
Mitchell	242	-0.8	38 070	629	137	39	46	52	51	19	25	2	2
Montgomery	1 116	1.2	32 592	1 405	693	60	175	312	306	103	129	29	24
Morris	198	0.5	32 953	1 348	62	11	37	44	43	17	17	3	2
Morton	133	-5.3	43 858	241	63	35	20	23	22	9	11	2	1
Nemaha	385	0.5	38 671	567	187	48	108	67	65	27	29	3	2

1. Based on the resident population estimated as of July 1 of the year shown.   2. Includes supplements to wages and salaries.

Table B. States and Counties — **Earnings, Social Security, and Housing**

STATE County	Earnings, 2009									Social Security beneficiaries, December 2010		Supplemental Security Income recipients, December 2010	Housing units, 2010	
			Goods-related[1]		Service-related and health									
	Total (mil dol)	Farm	Total	Manufacturing	Information and professional and technical services	Retail trade	Finance, insurance, and real estate	Health care and social services	Government	Number	Rate[2]		Total	Percent change, 2000–2010
	75	76	77	78	79	80	81	82	83	84	85	86	87	88
KANSAS	80 546	2.6	21.5	14.6	10.4	5.6	6.3	10.5	20.2	488 765	171	45 793	1 233 215	9.0
Allen	279	3.1	D	29.3	3.0	6.4	3.0	7.4	24.2	3 230	242	333	6 226	-3.5
Anderson	110	10.3	19.3	9.4	2.8	10.0	D	D	21.7	1 965	243	113	3 720	3.4
Atchison	312	5.8	32.2	25.2	D	6.3	D	D	13.7	3 230	191	316	6 990	2.5
Barber	106	8.9	29.4	6.9	D	5.0	7.4	D	25.5	1 250	257	79	2 765	0.9
Barton	734	3.9	31.6	6.5	D	7.7	6.9	D	13.7	5 750	208	462	12 696	-1.5
Bourbon	285	-2.1	D	17.3	3.5	7.2	9.2	D	17.7	3 540	233	404	7 167	0.4
Brown	279	13.9	D	12.1	2.6	4.7	4.4	10.8	27.0	2 330	233	231	4 779	-0.7
Butler	1 029	2.5	D	14.6	3.9	7.0	4.7	13.1	24.9	11 165	169	758	26 058	12.4
Chase	61	9.3	D	4.6	D	3.2	D	D	17.7	630	226	39	1 503	-1.7
Chautauqua	46	-3.3	D	4.8	D	5.3	D	11.5	23.9	1 125	307	105	2 150	-0.9
Cherokee	365	7.2	D	29.0	D	4.8	2.9	D	16.0	5 025	233	685	9 890	-1.4
Cheyenne	58	35.4	D	1.2	D	3.5	D	13.1	17.0	820	301	21	1 518	-7.2
Clark	43	14.9	D	D	D	4.2	D	D	43.5	555	251	26	1 135	2.2
Clay	182	11.9	14.7	9.1	3.1	13.2	3.7	D	21.8	2 055	241	119	4 042	-1.0
Cloud	178	15.3	D	9.5	5.2	8.2	3.7	D	20.5	2 430	255	190	4 659	-3.7
Coffey	313	4.5	7.2	1.7	3.2	3.3	2.3	2.3	17.3	2 065	240	204	3 964	2.2
Comanche	38	25.7	12.6	4.3	D	4.4	6.6	D	26.3	515	272	26	1 044	-4.0
Cowley	685	0.8	34.0	27.8	3.4	7.1	3.2	D	23.9	7 580	209	799	16 030	2.3
Crawford	698	1.3	14.4	14.4	5.0	6.7	2.7	D	30.9	7 400	189	1 017	17 801	3.4
Decatur	65	33.6	D	D	D	4.9	D	12.2	14.7	935	316	42	1 818	-0.2
Dickinson	327	10.9	21.2	17.5	2.6	7.5	3.2	D	22.4	4 220	214	255	8 972	3.3
Doniphan	154	26.3	21.6	17.9	D	2.9	3.3	D	23.9	1 600	201	120	3 576	2.5
Douglas	2 365	0.2	15.7	10.5	11.0	6.5	4.4	7.5	34.3	13 500	122	1 155	46 731	16.1
Edwards	90	49.4	D	8.5	1.1	2.6	1.8	6.6	11.3	695	229	45	1 636	-6.7
Elk	34	12.2	D	D	D	5.4	2.9	D	40.8	900	312	56	1 760	-5.3
Ellis	818	2.1	19.4	4.2	8.1	8.2	6.2	19.0	18.6	4 790	168	299	12 872	6.6
Ellsworth	126	11.4	D	12.7	6.9	3.7	3.4	9.2	31.8	1 495	230	89	3 239	0.3
Finney	883	3.8	27.9	18.4	3.5	8.8	4.3	D	18.5	4 235	115	607	13 276	-3.5
Ford	813	3.8	36.1	32.2	4.3	6.6	2.9	D	17.1	4 040	119	426	12 005	3.0
Franklin	463	1.3	16.5	10.4	3.4	6.8	2.6	D	20.1	5 215	201	484	11 147	9.0
Geary	2 463	0.1	D	1.5	D	1.7	0.8	1.1	84.7	4 015	117	576	14 517	21.8
Gove	71	27.6	13.0	7.6	2.4	7.6	3.7	3.2	23.2	725	269	16	1 373	-3.5
Graham	79	23.3	D	D	D	5.6	4.3	5.1	20.0	815	314	39	1 484	-4.4
Grant	230	11.0	28.5	4.1	D	3.6	3.2	6.1	14.5	1 060	135	81	2 945	-2.7
Gray	160	25.2	D	4.5	5.7	2.9	3.2	D	22.0	880	147	31	2 340	7.3
Greeley	67	57.9	D	0.0	D	3.5	D	D	11.2	290	233	0	629	-11.7
Greenwood	91	10.4	23.8	8.2	D	4.8	D	D	22.2	1 895	283	170	4 068	-4.8
Hamilton	69	41.1	D	0.0	D	3.3	D	D	21.5	440	164	18	1 236	2.1
Harper	133	12.1	23.3	11.3	D	5.8	D	2.3	26.3	1 515	251	85	3 116	-4.7
Harvey	820	3.5	33.3	23.0	3.7	6.1	6.4	D	11.4	7 015	202	447	14 527	8.6
Haskell	121	40.0	D	D	D	1.6	D	D	19.9	560	132	32	1 666	1.6
Hodgeman	31	36.3	D	0.3	D	4.1	4.2	0.2	36.0	430	224	0	973	3.1
Jackson	216	2.4	D	4.4	6.0	6.4	5.3	D	43.7	2 960	220	176	5 779	13.5
Jefferson	182	2.3	D	5.2	D	3.5	3.3	D	28.3	3 795	198	212	8 160	8.9
Jewell	71	37.7	D	D	D	3.8	2.6	1.0	21.6	1 000	325	48	2 032	-3.4
Johnson	21 521	0.0	13.5	7.7	24.3	5.6	11.7	9.7	8.3	73 120	134	3 377	226 571	24.6
Kearny	79	33.2	D	D	D	1.7	D	1.3	36.3	630	158	45	1 556	-6.1
Kingman	143	6.9	29.9	14.7	D	4.5	7.5	11.0	17.0	1 855	236	104	3 818	-0.9
Kiowa	66	28.5	D	D	D	D	2.5	D	22.3	595	233	52	1 220	-25.7
Labette	448	0.4	D	22.5	3.2	5.9	3.4	10.4	29.4	5 100	236	704	10 092	-2.0
Lane	46	24.0	D	D	D	4.3	4.4	D	22.4	480	274	16	990	-7.0
Leavenworth	1 947	0.0	8.5	3.6	8.4	3.2	4.1	5.4	61.5	11 430	150	863	28 697	17.6
Lincoln	57	26.1	D	D	D	4.9	4.1	3.8	28.0	780	241	40	1 864	0.6
Linn	118	1.6	15.0	1.6	3.0	4.2	D	25.8	25.8	2 460	255	165	5 446	15.4
Logan	78	30.5	D	0.5	D	4.4	4.0	3.4	33.5	670	243	40	1 441	1.3
Lyon	677	1.4	29.1	22.1	3.0	7.0	3.1	7.6	30.0	5 590	166	648	15 237	3.3
McPherson	823	4.7	44.4	32.2	2.8	4.5	4.8	10.0	11.1	6 200	212	313	12 721	7.5
Marion	188	16.2	12.5	7.6	4.6	4.6	3.6	D	21.5	3 080	243	151	5 946	1.1
Marshall	284	17.4	D	17.5	4.5	5.6	D	7.2	11.6	2 465	244	183	4 866	-2.7
Meade	109	41.0	6.5	0.8	D	3.2	2.8	D	25.3	880	192	32	1 998	1.5
Miami	363	-0.6	21.6	8.2	3.3	9.0	6.1	11.6	28.5	5 515	168	405	13 190	20.1
Mitchell	176	17.1	D	14.9	3.5	7.6	D	7.0	25.5	1 475	231	73	3 296	-1.3
Montgomery	753	0.2	35.6	28.8	D	6.3	3.0	D	16.2	8 445	238	1 073	16 578	-3.7
Morris	73	8.0	16.1	7.8	D	4.2	D	D	29.2	1 480	250	78	3 206	1.5
Morton	99	37.0	D	D	D	4.1	D	D	30.0	650	201	38	1 467	-3.4
Nemaha	235	16.9	D	18.5	3.6	5.6	D	D	14.2	2 335	229	117	4 562	5.1

1. Includes mining, construction, and manufacturing.   2. Per 1,000 resident population enumerated in the 2010 census.

Table B. States and Counties — Housing, Labor Force, and Employment

STATE County	Housing units, 2006–2010								Civilian labor force, 2010		Unemployment		Civilian employment,[5] 2006–2010		
	Total	Percent	Owner-occupied			Renter-occupied		Sub-stand-ard units[3] (percent)	Total	Percent change, 2009–2010	Total	Rate[4]	Total	Percent	
			Median value[1]	Median owner cost as a percent of income		Median rent[2]	Median rent as a per-cent of income							Manage-ment, business, science and arts	Con-struction, produc-tion, and mainte-nance occu-pations
				With a mort-gage	Without a mort-gage										
	89	90	91	92	93	94	95	96	97	98	99	100	101	102	103
KANSAS	1 101 672	69.4	122 600	21.5	11.9	671	27.6	2.2	1 504 883	-0.2	107 675	7.2	1 390 619	35.5	23.7
Allen	5 575	78.0	64 400	18.3	10.9	476	26.5	0.7	7 593	1.6	574	7.6	6 599	27.9	37.1
Anderson	3 188	83.9	87 300	25.6	11.7	488	24.2	1.7	4 487	1.1	350	7.8	4 012	30.0	33.1
Atchison	6 220	66.4	89 200	21.9	12.2	531	25.4	2.2	8 504	-3.5	761	8.9	7 598	31.5	28.8
Barber	2 304	71.2	52 500	18.5	13.3	517	23.0	1.4	2 809	-3.1	120	4.3	2 544	36.6	28.8
Barton	11 472	74.1	71 000	19.7	11.3	521	22.5	1.0	15 973	0.2	895	5.6	14 126	30.9	26.1
Bourbon	5 833	74.7	76 400	21.4	14.4	556	23.3	1.4	8 633	-1.1	646	7.5	7 053	28.1	27.6
Brown	4 080	70.0	74 800	20.6	13.4	468	24.0	0.9	5 690	-5.6	344	6.0	4 797	30.0	25.7
Butler	23 987	77.8	121 200	21.1	12.3	664	26.2	1.3	32 160	-1.7	2 682	8.3	31 031	33.5	26.6
Chase	1 175	81.7	86 100	23.4	10.0	448	26.5	2.6	1 524	3.3	82	5.4	1 443	36.2	31.7
Chautauqua	1 554	78.6	49 800	21.8	12.7	500	26.5	1.8	1 875	1.4	160	8.5	1 656	26.6	37.1
Cherokee	8 362	79.0	69 100	19.6	11.5	520	30.3	2.1	11 420	-1.2	981	8.6	9 729	26.6	33.4
Cheyenne	1 269	75.3	67 100	23.6	16.0	507	28.1	0.3	1 592	4.6	57	3.6	1 245	30.3	26.5
Clark	954	73.6	59 100	18.6	13.1	474	23.9	1.0	1 259	-0.8	52	4.1	1 128	40.9	24.7
Clay	3 561	73.4	86 500	21.4	11.7	610	24.1	0.7	5 421	2.8	255	4.7	4 150	35.2	26.9
Cloud	3 970	78.0	63 400	21.6	14.0	463	24.9	0.8	5 852	0.6	259	4.4	4 425	29.9	27.9
Coffey	3 445	77.0	98 500	19.2	11.3	515	23.7	1.1	5 594	1.0	368	6.6	4 306	35.2	30.9
Comanche	832	82.9	42 500	23.2	10.0	363	22.8	0.0	1 074	-2.8	45	4.2	967	30.2	39.0
Cowley	13 583	72.2	76 900	19.8	12.6	573	27.3	3.3	18 501	0.2	1 333	7.2	16 472	25.8	35.0
Crawford	15 484	64.9	83 900	19.9	13.6	612	31.5	1.2	20 327	-2.0	1 676	8.2	18 202	31.2	25.0
Decatur	1 517	72.7	57 300	22.5	13.6	424	27.2	0.9	1 706	-6.1	74	4.3	1 444	42.3	22.9
Dickinson	7 559	73.9	97 400	20.7	11.2	559	25.2	1.7	10 961	0.8	666	6.1	9 379	29.5	30.3
Doniphan	3 123	75.2	84 600	20.2	13.1	519	22.9	1.0	4 474	-4.7	414	9.3	3 914	29.7	32.0
Douglas	42 943	53.5	176 500	23.2	12.4	779	35.0	1.6	63 316	0.8	3 922	6.2	59 332	42.7	14.9
Edwards	1 389	75.2	54 600	18.5	11.0	496	25.6	0.6	1 771	-1.1	89	5.0	1 601	34.7	31.8
Elk	1 340	81.0	52 700	24.7	13.4	376	24.1	3.0	1 571	3.2	121	7.7	1 293	34.3	33.3
Ellis	11 721	63.0	123 800	21.1	12.0	611	29.2	0.7	18 784	4.3	694	3.7	16 402	31.6	20.7
Ellsworth	2 564	78.4	67 400	20.5	11.4	463	26.0	0.7	3 910	1.2	171	4.4	3 132	31.8	28.5
Finney	11 974	71.8	102 100	22.6	11.0	599	25.0	6.3	20 056	2.1	982	4.9	18 385	22.4	35.8
Ford	11 010	68.3	82 700	22.4	12.3	596	25.4	5.5	19 686	4.3	740	3.8	16 250	25.0	42.1
Franklin	10 197	72.1	117 100	22.5	14.2	684	26.9	1.5	13 418	-4.6	1 201	9.0	13 085	27.3	29.4
Geary	11 379	49.9	118 600	22.3	11.9	790	26.8	2.7	14 545	4.1	1 174	8.1	11 853	32.5	23.7
Gove	1 182	81.2	66 500	21.2	11.2	465	21.0	0.5	1 635	1.7	49	3.0	1 353	38.3	26.8
Graham	1 157	80.5	71 200	21.7	11.1	427	23.1	1.0	1 465	-0.9	64	4.4	1 395	40.7	23.4
Grant	2 723	73.1	85 500	19.3	10.0	422	18.8	4.4	4 191	1.6	173	4.1	3 721	31.3	38.7
Gray	2 051	75.4	100 000	20.7	12.1	558	18.1	4.9	3 511	1.6	110	3.1	2 959	32.4	32.0
Greeley	507	73.8	67 800	20.6	10.7	473	13.8	0.0	737	1.1	28	3.8	723	35.3	25.0
Greenwood	3 020	73.5	52 400	18.4	12.1	444	23.0	2.8	3 433	-4.1	261	7.6	3 203	29.7	35.7
Hamilton	1 125	74.2	73 300	24.7	12.5	542	22.9	2.7	1 302	-2.5	55	4.2	1 342	28.8	29.2
Harper	2 647	70.7	61 400	20.9	11.2	491	26.2	1.3	3 462	0.3	182	5.3	2 919	32.2	30.8
Harvey	13 252	74.0	103 300	19.9	10.0	588	28.0	1.4	17 829	-1.5	1 319	7.4	16 745	34.3	27.6
Haskell	1 381	76.0	88 100	19.4	11.0	555	15.8	4.9	2 349	3.6	84	3.6	2 150	28.1	36.8
Hodgeman	787	80.8	63 700	15.8	12.4	483	26.9	2.4	994	5.4	40	4.0	977	43.3	26.4
Jackson	5 205	78.2	114 800	22.6	11.0	584	22.9	3.6	7 009	1.1	459	6.5	6 691	30.7	25.2
Jefferson	7 512	85.2	136 200	22.1	12.6	671	24.9	1.7	9 791	-0.1	801	8.2	9 792	36.8	28.1
Jewell	1 455	76.4	45 500	18.1	11.1	423	16.6	2.3	1 921	-4.7	86	4.5	1 493	39.3	25.5
Johnson	210 278	71.9	209 900	21.7	11.1	857	25.4	1.1	295 026	-2.6	19 173	6.5	289 377	48.4	12.1
Kearny	1 433	74.1	85 900	19.9	11.8	482	14.3	6.4	2 227	3.3	99	4.4	1 826	25.6	44.5
Kingman	3 464	78.9	77 100	21.4	10.7	483	18.1	1.7	4 547	-1.7	263	5.8	3 756	34.1	30.9
Kiowa	994	73.2	75 000	19.7	12.3	434	22.6	1.0	1 595	1.6	68	4.3	1 297	35.1	30.0
Labette	8 952	71.5	64 600	19.9	11.9	499	24.6	2.5	11 214	-3.8	1 079	9.6	10 468	26.7	31.1
Lane	757	73.4	55 100	19.3	11.3	535	15.0	0.5	1 164	2.5	40	3.4	836	42.1	27.2
Leavenworth	25 778	69.4	166 700	21.6	12.6	786	27.3	1.5	32 353	-2.5	2 713	8.4	31 461	35.1	22.3
Lincoln	1 444	81.1	64 300	19.9	13.8	482	23.3	0.0	1 962	-2.1	111	5.7	1 716	34.4	29.1
Linn	4 306	84.9	98 800	23.8	12.9	524	28.5	1.6	4 433	-7.2	468	10.6	4 302	31.4	35.0
Logan	1 334	76.3	66 600	20.6	10.4	457	26.0	2.7	1 705	0.4	59	3.5	1 539	33.1	28.5
Lyon	13 752	59.5	91 200	21.7	11.1	570	30.3	3.5	18 410	-1.7	1 182	6.4	17 470	26.5	31.9
McPherson	11 715	76.2	115 300	19.8	10.0	576	20.7	1.4	16 619	-1.5	860	5.2	15 289	31.1	29.3
Marion	5 063	83.7	80 500	20.5	12.4	496	21.6	1.4	6 804	-2.5	393	5.8	6 152	35.0	27.6
Marshall	4 291	76.2	74 700	20.0	11.6	466	20.1	3.4	6 135	0.4	305	5.0	5 359	32.2	32.5
Meade	1 767	78.2	80 800	19.3	12.5	527	21.4	3.3	2 593	1.8	105	4.0	2 126	38.2	23.5
Miami	11 931	79.9	165 500	23.7	13.0	679	29.5	2.0	15 838	-4.4	1 244	7.9	16 058	34.3	26.2
Mitchell	2 692	75.9	68 500	17.8	11.6	451	20.3	0.4	3 642	-4.7	189	5.2	3 481	31.4	24.6
Montgomery	14 564	71.8	68 100	19.4	11.7	533	26.9	2.0	18 364	-0.5	1 905	10.4	16 154	28.4	31.7
Morris	2 604	77.6	76 400	19.1	10.4	480	23.3	2.8	3 083	0.3	225	7.3	2 898	29.7	37.2
Morton	1 278	71.3	64 600	17.8	12.0	531	18.8	2.4	1 728	-2.7	73	4.2	1 641	33.7	32.5
Nemaha	3 955	79.1	85 800	19.5	10.0	426	21.5	1.0	6 042	2.3	246	4.1	5 099	35.4	29.8

1. Specified owner-occupied units.   2. Specified renter-occupied units. A value of 10.0 represents 10 percent or less.   3. Overcrowded or lacking complete plumbing facilities.   4. Percent of civilian labor force.   5. Persons 16 years old and over.

STATE County	Private nonfarm establishments, employment and payroll, 2009									Agriculture, 2007			
		Employment						Annual payroll		Farms			
												Percent with:	
	Number of establishments	Total	Health care and social assistance	Manufacturing	Retail trade	Finance and insurance	Professional, scientific, and technical services	Total (mil dol)	Average per employee (dollars)	Number	Fewer than 50 acres	500 acres or more	Farm operators whose principal occupation is farming (percent)
	104	105	106	107	108	109	110	111	112	113	114	115	116
KANSAS	74 698	1 146 263	185 280	167 416	147 288	60 227	60 099	42 147	36 769	65 531	18.6	30.9	47.1
Allen	392	4 567	653	1 835	602	108	114	130	28 545	611	14.9	23.2	42.2
Anderson	219	1 564	367	223	345	D	D	38	24 496	715	18.5	25.3	47.1
Atchison	389	6 053	1 006	1 507	758	D	71	157	25 929	711	20.3	20.8	46.8
Barber	217	1 511	288	D	236	68	D	41	27 047	427	11.2	48.0	50.6
Barton	982	10 662	2 201	1 376	1 544	421	308	323	30 284	678	15.8	37.5	54.1
Bourbon	371	5 119	1 144	1 012	745	529	D	140	27 314	928	17.2	18.6	39.3
Brown	255	3 509	812	467	365	171	53	94	26 864	637	18.7	27.0	54.2
Butler	1 330	13 535	3 592	1 464	2 074	502	510	389	28 743	1 427	32.0	19.6	42.7
Chase	68	391	D	D	51	19	D	10	26 749	250	14.8	42.8	55.2
Chautauqua	82	518	D	D	D	D	D	11	20 469	359	9.7	32.3	51.5
Cherokee	359	5 442	744	1 976	514	128	90	180	33 038	809	26.1	20.0	51.5
Cheyenne	100	549	170	D	D	34	17	14	26 193	422	8.3	49.8	55.0
Clark	66	D	D	D	50	35	25	D	D	278	6.1	48.2	49.3
Clay	280	2 529	629	D	393	105	61	63	25 059	583	17.0	36.0	52.0
Cloud	317	3 088	712	D	550	D	83	86	28 008	466	12.0	44.4	54.3
Coffey	240	D	437	D	374	116	D	D	D	681	18.2	26.7	42.4
Comanche	82	433	138	D	54	38	8	9	21 349	253	4.7	53.4	53.0
Cowley	779	11 508	2 366	3 331	1 621	378	186	337	29 256	1 027	22.2	21.8	41.6
Crawford	951	14 351	3 030	2 338	1 980	344	593	378	26 309	911	24.8	19.6	40.4
Decatur	102	D	D	D	112	36	D	D	D	303	9.6	59.1	59.1
Dickinson	486	5 153	887	1 042	781	167	D	144	27 897	1 046	16.5	30.1	43.5
DonIphan	152	1 139	70	510	106	71	19	37	32 771	573	19.9	25.0	53.2
Douglas	2 669	37 319	5 388	3 500	6 014	1 063	2 224	1 047	28 047	1 040	38.8	9.2	35.4
Edwards	90	651	D	192	D	D	11	19	28 899	371	6.2	44.7	56.1
Elk	72	401	D	D	36	25	D	7	16 264	361	12.7	38.8	52.4
Ellis	1 109	12 713	3 115	984	2 198	751	334	371	29 146	687	12.7	37.0	43.8
Ellsworth	185	1 725	522	347	170	88	76	49	28 275	408	12.3	40.4	47.8
Finney	988	14 128	2 184	D	2 438	518	357	430	30 407	516	9.9	53.5	55.8
Ford	776	14 724	1 385	6 373	1 650	325	467	458	31 074	664	13.0	41.9	43.7
Franklin	579	9 085	D	756	1 082	190	755	290	31 964	1 051	29.0	13.5	40.7
Geary	694	8 343	1 550	D	1 338	329	316	220	26 316	229	18.3	31.9	52.4
Gove	133	827	238	115	105	60	D	20	24 781	413	8.7	57.4	60.0
Graham	116	688	240	D	106	D	D	18	25 576	475	11.2	39.4	49.1
Grant	220	2 331	D	145	306	110	D	80	34 238	326	10.4	44.8	46.3
Gray	201	1 438	D	D	D	66	32	44	30 697	473	10.6	45.2	48.8
Greeley	44	356	D	0	D	D	D	10	28 888	303	2.3	50.5	47.9
Greenwood	190	1 223	D	84	217	80	D	32	25 834	539	14.8	35.8	49.5
Hamilton	72	606	D	0	81	D	D	15	25 081	431	6.3	47.3	46.4
Harper	211	1 723	D	488	191	103	D	51	29 526	495	12.9	39.2	52.3
Harvey	833	12 437	2 851	3 448	1 379	321	243	370	29 753	829	30.5	23.2	42.1
Haskell	122	811	D	59	56	D	54	27	33 311	248	7.7	54.8	60.9
Hodgeman	48	254	D	0	33	48	D	6	24 496	379	4.7	56.7	59.4
Jackson	264	2 988	540	200	402	106	79	76	25 406	1 127	22.8	13.9	37.7
Jefferson	324	2 405	356	221	344	91	D	82	34 148	1 137	26.2	11.3	39.9
Jewell	86	568	D	D	90	D	D	13	22 512	525	11.0	45.9	66.5
Johnson	17 015	305 554	32 678	20 877	35 419	25 660	28 511	13 981	45 755	610	50.7	9.0	38.7
Kearny	87	595	D	D	56	D	D	17	28 886	337	5.6	49.0	54.3
Kingman	213	1 975	433	349	212	153	D	53	26 833	876	14.5	32.3	44.6
Kiowa	92	795	222	0	D	27	D	23	28 582	399	8.8	42.1	50.6
Labette	489	8 355	3 293	1 883	988	275	109	238	28 505	1 052	22.9	16.9	43.1
Lane	70	402	D	D	D	D	D	15	36 381	284	6.3	54.9	51.1
Leavenworth	1 197	13 704	2 828	935	2 029	1 074	845	437	31 867	1 203	38.1	5.8	39.0
Lincoln	98	620	133	D	D	62	D	15	24 813	473	9.7	40.2	56.7
Linn	180	D	52	81	250	73	14	D	D	918	18.4	13.2	37.3
Logan	122	776	D	D	49	D	23	23	29 515	289	6.6	61.6	51.6
Lyon	844	12 093	2 041	3 008	1 923	310	590	327	27 041	930	24.3	23.4	45.2
McPherson	924	13 216	2 271	4 043	1 386	712	170	439	33 252	1 142	15.9	30.1	51.1
Marion	292	2 786	622	220	338	122	140	62	22 118	974	18.0	32.9	53.0
Marshall	375	3 738	581	980	698	195	102	108	28 938	913	11.5	37.3	57.9
Meade	134	945	D	D	181	D	D	27	28 387	448	5.6	54.5	49.8
Miami	731	6 728	1 927	496	1 067	306	199	191	28 335	1 538	42.2	8.1	34.4
Mitchell	254	2 682	D	D	410	128	53	73	27 142	396	10.4	44.7	65.2
Montgomery	918	14 923	2 519	4 519	1 658	424	265	447	29 976	994	25.8	14.2	39.2
Morris	137	1 147	D	136	167	68	59	28	24 462	479	17.7	34.4	51.8
Morton	104	859	244	D	158	D	18	30	34 632	353	2.3	51.0	39.9
Nemaha	386	4 073	860	1 106	624	208	111	116	28 506	1 054	13.2	26.6	54.8

Table B. States and Counties — **Agriculture**

	Agriculture, 2007 (cont.)														
STATE County	Land in farms					Value of land and buildings (dollars)		Value of machinery and equipment, average per farm (dollars)	Value of products sold				Percent of farms with sales of:		Government payments	
	Acreage (1,000)	Percent change, 2002–2007	Acres			Average per farm	Average per acre		Total (mil dol)	Average per farm (dollars)	Percent from:		$10,000 or more	$100,000 or more	Total ($1,000)	Percent of farms
			Average size of farm	Total irrigated (1,000)	Total cropland (1,000)						Crops	Livestock and poultry products				
	117	118	119	120	121	122	123	124	125	126	127	128	129	130	131	132
KANSAS	46 346	-1.9	707	2 762.7	28 216.1	644 039	911	114 261	14 413.2	219 944	33.9	66.1	51.5	21.7	427 144	67.8
Allen	267	-4.6	438	0.0	145.4	441 021	1 008	81 903	31.0	50 725	49.9	50.1	46.6	13.4	2 057	63.0
Anderson	367	-3.2	514	2.6	214.9	524 621	1 022	103 751	61.1	85 461	54.1	45.9	53.4	18.7	2 651	68.1
Atchison	254	11.9	357	D	172.4	488 263	1 366	88 910	64.0	89 989	66.5	33.5	60.3	24.3	2 170	62.2
Barber	611	-12.3	1 432	10.0	197.7	929 757	649	123 138	64.5	150 994	24.8	75.2	57.8	26.0	2 794	65.1
Barton	559	-14.0	824	40.5	406.2	695 645	844	149 153	282.8	417 089	23.1	76.9	58.7	26.1	4 785	79.2
Bourbon	328	-3.2	353	D	139.9	395 666	1 121	56 674	42.6	45 958	23.3	76.7	44.8	8.9	1 904	43.0
Brown	347	7.1	544	1.5	254.5	928 119	1 705	145 148	116.4	182 682	74.4	25.6	68.3	31.7	4 081	73.5
Butler	787	12.3	552	6.2	314.7	601 671	1 091	81 689	235.1	164 778	17.5	82.5	36.2	15.1	2 959	39.2
Chase	320	-11.6	1 280	0.2	67.9	1 240 483	969	88 836	71.4	285 752	8.7	91.3	59.6	26.8	437	45.6
Chautauqua	308	-21.0	859	D	51.6	757 655	882	58 504	27.5	76 683	18.1	81.9	49.0	15.0	425	27.3
Cherokee	324	11.3	401	0.1	235.3	497 881	1 242	108 936	88.5	109 393	60.4	39.6	51.8	19.4	3 165	49.9
Cheyenne	577	0.2	1 367	43.7	346.8	841 579	616	151 858	82.8	196 240	63.3	36.7	62.8	29.6	5 285	83.2
Clark	486	-1.2	1 748	5.2	165.2	1 104 498	632	105 579	123.5	444 414	12.5	87.5	45.3	23.7	2 822	84.9
Clay	351	-10.7	602	18.3	216.6	702 200	1 167	112 949	78.9	135 317	60.6	39.4	59.3	27.6	4 028	84.9
Cloud	384	-10.9	824	17.9	253.8	836 044	1 015	157 877	71.2	152 756	77.4	22.6	66.1	35.2	3 282	79.8
Coffey	325	-3.3	477	1.3	168.6	465 960	977	76 140	48.5	71 210	52.6	47.4	44.8	17.3	2 287	67.4
Comanche	432	-3.4	1 709	4.4	128.5	908 422	532	98 758	53.8	212 795	24.9	75.1	58.5	31.2	2 017	80.6
Cowley	576	-16.5	560	3.5	225.8	536 077	957	78 995	66.2	64 473	34.9	65.1	43.8	11.6	3 220	60.2
Crawford	342	0.3	376	2.6	180.3	405 629	1 079	77 023	57.4	62 976	60.1	39.9	46.2	13.0	2 854	59.2
Decatur	483	3.0	1 595	8.6	283.7	1 046 797	657	148 823	139.1	459 095	35.8	64.2	74.6	41.3	2 854	82.2
Dickinson	537	-2.5	513	5.0	350.4	544 571	1 061	102 985	135.3	129 343	37.0	63.0	51.6	23.2	6 404	82.1
Doniphan	248	20.4	432	1.6	180.6	740 906	1 713	106 150	75.0	130 813	90.5	9.5	57.9	30.2	2 898	72.6
Douglas	221	10.0	212	1.8	134.7	408 136	1 924	66 492	41.3	39 675	67.8	32.2	34.3	7.9	1 994	44.2
Edwards	439	4.5	1 184	106.4	328.0	1 038 291	877	193 502	173.0	466 280	42.6	57.4	56.6	38.8	5 086	91.1
Elk	317	-14.3	877	0.5	65.2	861 330	982	52 378	29.9	82 706	D	D	51.8	13.0	690	47.4
Ellis	526	-9.0	766	2.5	278.7	592 976	774	92 726	107.8	156 895	25.7	74.3	59.5	17.6	3 617	75.1
Ellsworth	365	-11.6	895	0.6	180.3	675 082	755	107 044	33.0	80 771	58.8	41.2	55.9	22.3	3 521	86.0
Finney	760	-5.2	1 473	179.3	567.7	1 153 579	783	285 752	693.5	1 344 046	20.3	79.7	62.6	45.0	9 060	80.0
Ford	634	-2.3	955	81.9	491.1	680 092	712	170 110	474.1	713 970	18.4	81.6	54.7	28.9	7 550	79.1
Franklin	314	-7.4	298	1.6	167.6	493 012	1 653	71 393	67.2	63 947	48.1	51.9	41.5	8.7	2 028	47.7
Geary	148	-17.8	648	3.0	60.5	813 657	1 255	100 460	25.6	111 764	43.1	56.9	52.4	21.8	959	68.1
Gove	594	0.3	1 437	17.7	371.3	865 618	602	174 232	184.4	446 502	32.0	68.0	72.4	39.2	5 732	82.1
Graham	515	-0.4	1 084	10.4	308.2	669 871	618	106 291	57.7	121 374	73.0	27.0	52.8	27.8	4 757	85.3
Grant	337	11.6	1 035	87.4	272.0	827 976	800	186 057	576.9	1 769 655	11.1	88.9	54.0	39.3	4 856	80.7
Gray	546	9.0	1 155	137.1	425.9	983 325	852	248 223	691.4	1 461 694	15.8	84.2	56.7	39.7	7 427	81.4
Greeley	493	8.1	1 627	23.4	445.2	1 150 144	707	162 830	115.4	380 891	55.9	44.1	49.2	31.7	5 850	93.1
Greenwood	609	2.5	1 130	0.4	108.5	1 082 093	958	78 155	87.7	162 642	9.2	90.8	55.1	17.1	874	43.2
Hamilton	611	14.0	1 417	24.8	455.2	951 306	671	186 927	267.0	619 548	19.4	80.6	38.3	26.7	6 554	85.8
Harper	481	2.3	972	1.8	315.8	717 911	738	134 164	93.4	188 734	19.1	80.9	47.5	20.2	4 470	83.0
Harvey	339	-3.7	408	35.8	273.7	557 519	1 365	105 309	103.7	125 061	47.4	52.6	50.8	20.5	3 807	67.2
Haskell	399	-1.7	1 608	156.5	327.6	1 708 092	1 062	367 208	718.3	2 896 342	16.2	83.8	67.7	58.9	5 686	86.3
Hodgeman	526	11.7	1 387	29.4	334.3	824 336	594	163 440	179.3	473 178	22.9	77.1	65.4	38.8	5 918	90.8
Jackson	339	0.6	301	D	146.8	355 481	1 181	52 976	52.0	46 139	40.7	59.3	42.9	9.6	2 697	48.9
Jefferson	286	2.1	251	7.6	155.6	403 989	1 607	68 357	61.3	53 952	54.5	45.5	42.5	10.3	2 406	46.4
Jewell	471	-5.0	898	14.0	290.8	742 214	827	149 668	101.2	192 826	60.4	39.6	70.3	37.5	4 679	87.4
Johnson	114	-23.5	187	1.4	69.9	375 228	2 004	72 856	40.7	66 655	72.5	27.5	30.5	9.0	676	26.2
Kearny	519	-7.0	1 541	66.6	359.0	1 061 954	689	198 167	221.1	655 989	30.0	70.0	51.3	32.9	5 908	85.8
Kingman	546	-1.8	624	21.9	332.0	523 300	839	97 277	52.1	59 419	49.5	50.5	48.4	14.4	7 204	85.8
Kiowa	440	1.1	1 104	38.9	228.2	695 277	630	124 883	50.5	126 471	68.7	31.3	53.1	23.6	3 909	84.7
Labette	371	2.8	353	D	193.4	361 924	1 026	76 909	89.9	85 490	25.3	74.7	47.3	9.9	3 007	49.9
Lane	401	-12.8	1 413	14.0	284.1	845 541	598	153 133	187.0	658 474	16.6	83.4	54.2	32.4	5 022	89.8
Leavenworth	195	-1.0	162	0.7	102.5	315 933	1 951	49 515	33.2	27 613	63.2	36.8	34.7	5.4	1 256	32.1
Lincoln	432	-3.1	914	1.4	228.8	718 894	786	115 686	55.8	117 941	58.6	41.4	65.3	26.8	3 692	87.9
Linn	265	-14.8	289	D	133.8	387 739	1 342	66 913	32.0	34 868	40.8	59.2	35.3	6.3	2 292	52.7
Logan	567	-7.0	1 960	12.7	340.9	1 196 169	610	177 752	61.5	212 771	77.3	22.7	66.4	41.5	4 095	82.4
Lyon	474	-4.0	509	1.1	210.2	497 850	977	78 578	102.7	110 437	23.9	76.1	46.1	13.7	2 775	65.6
McPherson	566	-1.6	496	33.4	421.8	558 384	1 126	117 556	119.8	104 860	47.8	52.2	60.8	21.4	6 639	76.4
Marion	599	1.9	615	3.1	337.6	614 495	999	102 280	111.2	114 174	39.3	60.7	58.4	24.2	4 950	75.5
Marshall	515	-11.4	564	2.5	338.6	710 582	1 260	130 214	111.0	121 589	73.7	26.3	71.0	33.2	6 556	83.9
Meade	602	-1.5	1 344	105.2	380.5	952 328	708	174 018	194.6	434 356	46.9	53.1	54.9	35.0	6 330	86.8
Miami	307	-4.1	200	1.7	155.0	410 186	2 054	58 177	62.7	40 749	44.2	55.8	31.5	5.8	1 839	29.1
Mitchell	444	-1.1	1 122	7.9	302.8	1 034 656	922	193 541	128.1	323 371	48.2	51.8	71.5	39.1	3 911	85.6
Montgomery	314	-9.2	316	1.3	152.4	360 615	1 142	71 188	39.9	40 157	41.6	58.4	37.5	6.4	1 715	34.4
Morris	414	7.3	863	0.3	154.4	758 291	878	108 849	82.8	172 946	26.3	73.7	63.3	20.5	1 920	66.6
Morton	442	25.2	1 252	47.0	366.1	720 822	576	159 913	119.1	337 520	35.8	64.2	41.6	25.2	5 969	89.8
Nemaha	451	8.2	427	0.3	287.9	602 277	1 409	107 998	146.9	139 370	45.7	54.3	64.7	31.2	5 313	78.1

Table B. States and Counties — Water Use, Wholesale Trade, Retail Trade, and Real Estate

STATE County	Water use, 2005		Wholesale trade,[1] 2007				Retail trade,[2] 2007				Real estate and rental and leasing,[2] 2007			
	Total water withdrawn (mil gal/day)	Gallons withdrawn per person	Number of establishments	Number of employees	Sales (mil dol)	Annual payroll (mil dol)	Number of establishments	Number of employees	Sales (mil dol)	Annual payroll (mil dol)	Number of establishments	Number of employees	Receipts (mil dol)	Annual payroll (mil dol)
	133	134	135	136	137	138	139	140	141	142	143	144	145	146
KANSAS	3 785.3	1 379	3 747	47 285	45 863.9	2 150.4	11 463	149 672	34 538.3	3 133.7	3 314	15 160	2 428.8	439.7
Allen	4.3	310	21	164	37.2	4.6	63	541	121.7	11.2	13	44	2.0	0.5
Anderson	2.1	252	8	56	53.5	1.7	42	309	87.2	6.5	6	15	0.3	0.1
Atchison	4.9	290	17	D	D	D	58	730	130.1	12.4	13	D	D	D
Barber	6.2	1 257	8	39	35.6	1.9	35	250	70.3	4.4	3	D	D	D
Barton	37.2	1 324	62	D	D	D	138	1 543	339.4	33.1	29	113	12.5	3.3
Bourbon	3.4	229	17	541	554.9	21.9	47	567	120.6	11.6	14	53	10.1	1.3
Brown	1.9	181	16	120	87.5	4.2	34	369	67.9	6.6	5	14	0.8	0.1
Butler	14.2	227	44	243	130.1	8.7	194	2 050	567.5	43.5	61	125	18.3	2.6
Chase	1.2	393	2	D	D	D	10	60	10.9	0.7	2	D	D	D
Chautauqua	1.5	360	2	D	D	D	14	81	15.8	1.1	NA	NA	NA	NA
Cherokee	98.9	4 588	18	162	205.5	5.5	67	503	121.7	9.8	4	D	D	D
Cheyenne	45.4	15 407	10	102	54.6	2.6	22	85	12.2	1.1	2	D	D	D
Clark	5.4	2 343	2	D	D	D	14	70	9.9	0.9	1	D	D	D
Clay	13.8	1 597	15	136	99.3	5.7	44	419	76.0	6.3	3	10	1.7	0.2
Cloud	15.0	1 536	18	241	91.8	8.3	61	493	109.7	10.7	7	D	D	D
Coffey	27.2	3 131	10	90	52.3	2.6	50	442	103.0	7.1	4	5	0.5	0.1
Comanche	7.2	3 726	2	D	D	D	19	73	10.3	1.0	1	D	D	D
Cowley	7.8	222	28	D	D	D	135	1 596	317.2	31.1	19	78	6.3	1.2
Crawford	7.2	187	37	D	D	D	174	1 974	395.4	36.3	38	118	15.2	2.3
Decatur	11.3	3 554	13	80	60.5	2.6	19	119	17.2	1.4	4	D	D	D
Dickinson	7.0	362	23	255	232.6	8.5	77	787	191.4	17.4	14	21	2.4	0.3
Doniphan	0.8	104	9	D	D	D	21	132	25.2	2.2	2	D	D	D
Douglas	22.0	213	81	D	D	D	407	6 121	1 202.2	110.5	170	711	93.4	17.5
Edwards	95.9	29 116	5	81	74.7	2.9	12	73	12.4	1.1	1	D	D	D
Elk	1.0	315	2	D	D	D	7	40	8.0	0.5	1	D	D	D
Ellis	6.1	228	43	322	144.9	11.1	183	2 174	497.5	42.6	40	109	14.5	2.5
Ellsworth	3.3	517	9	47	23.0	1.4	30	185	31.9	2.3	2	D	D	D
Finney	248.0	6 361	68	D	D	D	182	2 396	504.2	47.1	34	136	23.7	4.0
Ford	90.6	2 683	57	D	D	D	139	1 632	395.7	34.2	27	115	18.8	2.7
Franklin	3.4	128	14	172	168.7	7.7	96	1 153	234.3	22.6	23	D	D	D
Geary	8.7	352	8	154	70.8	2.7	96	1 292	295.1	26.0	34	138	17.5	2.7
Gove	19.1	6 898	13	79	104.8	2.3	23	96	17.1	1.4	NA	NA	NA	NA
Graham	11.6	4 245	9	23	23.1	0.8	24	114	30.2	2.2	3	D	D	D
Grant	91.7	12 171	17	187	263.1	6.9	39	284	67.0	6.2	5	18	3.3	0.6
Gray	179.4	30 606	20	164	112.7	5.1	28	175	34.8	2.6	1	D	D	D
Greeley	19.8	14 655	1	D	D	D	8	46	9.6	0.9	1	D	D	D
Greenwood	2.3	313	10	70	14.1	1.4	37	220	53.3	3.9	2	D	D	D
Hamilton	64.5	18 207	9	60	84.4	2.4	10	85	25.4	1.4	NA	NA	NA	NA
Harper	3.0	493	15	155	91.0	3.9	38	228	50.2	4.6	NA	NA	NA	NA
Harvey	42.8	1 264	30	173	90.8	6.6	131	1 445	274.7	26.1	30	87	10.4	1.4
Haskell	164.4	38 837	14	133	147.1	4.4	15	70	13.7	0.7	2	D	D	D
Hodgeman	25.6	12 114	4	D	D	D	5	36	5.9	0.5	NA	NA	NA	NA
Jackson	2.2	160	13	89	34.5	2.6	44	413	91.1	8.3	7	18	2.5	0.5
Jefferson	4.1	212	11	35	9.6	0.8	58	392	71.3	5.1	9	D	D	D
Jewell	28.3	8 455	6	38	16.8	1.2	19	77	14.3	0.9	1	D	D	D
Johnson	17.9	35	919	13 922	16 252.0	785.5	2 001	38 008	9 255.3	870.3	1 032	5 454	1 067.3	196.3
Kearny	158.2	35 022	8	20	19.8	0.5	10	43	7.6	0.6	2	D	D	D
Kingman	18.2	2 229	19	124	57.0	4.2	32	237	43.2	3.9	4	6	0.2	0.1
Kiowa	50.4	16 883	8	91	71.5	3.3	14	77	14.6	1.1	NA	NA	NA	NA
Labette	4.5	205	21	D	D	D	109	1 004	204.3	18.3	14	65	6.4	1.3
Lane	15.8	8 337	5	31	12.2	0.7	11	57	13.6	1.0	NA	NA	NA	NA
Leavenworth	8.2	113	17	56	13.2	1.7	188	2 130	493.0	45.7	61	240	27.8	5.7
Lincoln	1.6	481	8	55	24.1	1.5	18	78	11.1	0.9	1	D	D	D
Linn	11.8	1 193	5	18	4.3	0.5	38	269	47.8	3.7	2	D	D	D
Logan	8.0	2 878	13	73	53.6	2.3	19	197	78.6	4.5	NA	NA	NA	NA
Lyon	10.7	301	30	D	D	D	169	2 028	470.7	38.0	40	D	D	D
McPherson	32.9	1 114	32	D	D	D	168	1 495	382.2	31.8	32	70	5.8	1.1
Marion	4.0	308	16	182	106.7	7.3	62	349	70.0	5.7	8	D	D	D
Marshall	3.9	377	26	182	128.9	5.5	75	707	186.0	12.5	4	3	0.3	0.1
Meade	125.2	27 072	14	106	108.3	3.4	20	125	20.3	2.1	NA	NA	NA	NA
Miami	6.9	225	21	48	72.7	2.3	103	1 068	251.7	21.4	40	D	D	D
Mitchell	15.6	2 424	25	212	73.3	7.4	53	419	98.8	7.7	4	45	2.3	0.5
Montgomery	11.3	326	36	D	D	D	167	1 772	364.6	35.4	38	140	20.4	3.0
Morris	1.7	274	5	20	9.2	0.7	34	259	45.0	4.2	3	D	D	D
Morton	31.5	9 862	10	101	54.8	2.5	17	103	28.6	2.4	NA	NA	NA	NA
Nemaha	3.4	321	20	147	79.6	5.1	83	575	106.8	9.3	NA	NA	NA	NA

1. Merchant wholesalers, except manufacturers' sales branches and offices. 2. Employer establishments.

Table B. States and Counties — **Professional Services, Manufacturing, and Accommodation and Food Services**

STATE County	Professional, scientific, and technical services,[1] 2007				Manufacturing, 2007				Accommodation and food services, 2007			
	Number of establish-ments	Number of employees	Receipts (mil dol)	Annual payroll (mil dol)	Number of establish-ments	Number of employees	Receipts (mil dol)	Annual payroll (mil dol)	Number of establish-ments	Number of employees	Sales (mil dol)	Annual payroll (mil dol)
	147	148	149	150	151	152	153	154	155	156	157	158
KANSAS	7 042	55 922	7 781.4	2 736.5	3 170	177 659	76 751.8	7 983.4	5 866	104 795	4 192.3	1 173.7
Allen	25	123	8.6	3.6	24	1 971	434.7	65.6	29	384	12.4	3.1
Anderson	14	40	2.6	0.9	NA	NA	NA	NA	17	193	5.6	1.3
Atchison	20	D	D	D	23	1 994	D	D	35	540	14.9	4.2
Barber	15	55	7.8	1.5	NA	NA	NA	NA	14	93	2.7	0.6
Barton	61	324	29.9	11.5	46	1 685	561.4	58.0	61	921	35.4	9.3
Bourbon	28	129	9.2	3.4	31	1 114	179.0	35.6	34	431	16.3	4.1
Brown	15	74	9.3	2.7	17	544	91.4	19.9	24	279	7.6	2.1
Butler	100	D	D	D	44	1 535	D	78.5	100	1 479	57.4	15.0
Chase	4	D	D	D	NA	NA	NA	NA	7	67	2.3	0.8
Chautauqua	4	7	0.5	0.2	NA	NA	NA	NA	10	D	D	D
Cherokee	28	84	4.3	1.2	34	2 041	512.1	68.8	25	315	8.6	2.3
Cheyenne	7	17	1.4	0.5	NA	NA	NA	NA	5	40	0.9	0.2
Clark	6	22	4.2	0.6	NA	NA	NA	NA	7	D	D	D
Clay	15	61	3.9	1.9	NA	NA	NA	NA	19	196	5.5	1.3
Cloud	17	75	5.3	2.3	NA	NA	NA	NA	24	388	13.7	3.2
Coffey	15	57	2.2	0.7	NA	NA	NA	NA	19	152	4.9	1.3
Comanche	5	D	D	D	NA	NA	NA	NA	7	38	1.5	0.4
Cowley	54	D	D	D	44	3 726	2 025.4	132.0	71	980	34.2	9.0
Crawford	68	D	D	D	64	2 736	757.2	91.5	89	1 611	51.9	14.5
Decatur	6	25	1.8	0.5	NA	NA	NA	NA	9	69	1.5	0.4
Dickinson	32	D	D	D	20	1 236	317.3	38.4	37	454	15.3	3.8
Doniphan	8	D	D	D	13	D	D	33.8	8	74	1.5	0.4
Douglas	285	D	D	D	88	3 848	976.5	143.0	299	5 937	213.7	60.1
Edwards	4	11	0.3	0.2	NA	NA	NA	NA	6	D	D	D
Elk	6	14	1.0	0.4	NA	NA	NA	NA	6	D	D	D
Ellis	65	D	D	D	38	1 003	D	D	101	1 950	72.2	19.6
Ellsworth	7	81	5.9	2.5	NA	NA	NA	NA	12	136	4.6	1.1
Finney	61	D	D	D	27	3 510	D	110.0	74	1 190	54.9	13.3
Ford	46	D	D	D	27	5 951	D	197.1	72	960	40.3	10.0
Franklin	41	D	D	D	30	1 045	384.1	48.0	56	807	27.9	7.5
Geary	37	D	D	D	7	619	D	20.0	73	1 291	52.0	16.4
Gove	7	14	0.7	0.2	NA	NA	NA	NA	9	48	2.0	0.5
Graham	7	15	0.8	0.2	NA	NA	NA	NA	9	52	1.3	0.3
Grant	13	30	3.2	0.7	NA	NA	NA	NA	18	223	7.1	1.8
Gray	14	33	3.2	1.0	NA	NA	NA	NA	10	63	1.3	0.3
Greeley	3	6	0.6	0.2	NA	NA	NA	NA	2	D	D	D
Greenwood	13	42	2.5	0.9	NA	NA	NA	NA	14	106	3.0	0.7
Hamilton	3	14	0.5	0.1	NA	NA	NA	NA	6	35	0.6	0.2
Harper	15	26	1.8	0.5	NA	NA	NA	NA	18	184	4.4	1.3
Harvey	44	D	D	D	68	3 774	D	151.0	61	997	29.4	8.7
Haskell	7	31	3.9	1.3	NA	NA	NA	NA	6	D	D	D
Hodgeman	3	D	D	D	NA	NA	NA	NA	3	9	0.2	0.1
Jackson	19	80	4.2	1.2	NA	NA	NA	NA	19	D	D	D
Jefferson	22	57	4.9	1.6	NA	NA	NA	NA	22	158	4.4	1.2
Jewell	4	7	0.6	0.1	NA	NA	NA	NA	9	55	1.2	0.3
Johnson	2 644	D	D	D	527	20 896	7 847.7	1 004.5	1 099	24 556	1 083.0	328.1
Kearny	8	33	1.3	0.4	NA	NA	NA	NA	6	51	1.2	0.3
Kingman	12	37	2.9	0.8	NA	NA	NA	NA	13	169	4.5	1.2
Kiowa	2	D	D	D	NA	NA	NA	NA	9	71	0.9	0.2
Labette	26	2 328	9.6	17.5	39	2 446	410.2	84.4	39	496	14.2	3.8
Lane	4	17	1.3	0.5	NA	NA	NA	NA	1	D	D	D
Leavenworth	123	D	D	D	37	1 036	107.7	28.3	86	1 384	48.3	13.2
Lincoln	8	10	1.1	0.5	NA	NA	NA	NA	5	49	0.8	0.3
Linn	8	D	D	D	NA	NA	NA	NA	7	50	1.3	0.3
Logan	5	D	D	D	NA	NA	NA	NA	18	124	3.5	0.9
Lyon	45	D	D	D	37	D	D	D	104	1 528	51.0	14.3
McPherson	52	180	14.1	4.5	64	4 288	4 222.6	188.8	64	972	29.8	8.6
Marion	16	139	24.5	4.5	NA	NA	NA	NA	23	239	5.6	1.5
Marshall	17	90	9.5	2.0	19	1 091	257.7	46.6	27	270	8.8	2.3
Meade	7	42	1.5	0.6	NA	NA	NA	NA	7	44	1.5	0.3
Miami	66	D	D	D	31	527	D	D	59	695	24.0	6.7
Mitchell	15	56	3.6	1.0	NA	NA	NA	NA	17	164	5.1	1.4
Montgomery	49	206	17.3	5.7	56	5 438	3 979.7	233.2	78	1 276	43.5	10.2
Morris	12	63	4.1	1.7	NA	NA	NA	NA	16	167	4.6	1.5
Morton	7	18	1.4	0.3	NA	NA	NA	NA	6	72	2.3	0.6
Nemaha	27	D	D	D	28	1 163	243.1	44.7	18	168	4.2	1.0

1. Establishment subject to federal tax.

Table B. States and Counties — Health Care and Social Assistance, Other Services, and Federal Funds

STATE County	Health care and social assistance, 2007				Other services, 2007				Federal funds and grants, 2009–2010 Expenditures (mil dol)			
										Direct payments for individuals[1]		
	Number of establishments	Number of employees	Receipts (mil dol)	Annual payroll (mil dol)	Number of establishments	Number of employees	Receipts (mil dol)	Annual payroll (mil dol)	Total	Social Security and government retirement	Medicare	Food Stamps and Supplemental Security Income
	159	160	161	162	163	164	165	166	167	168	169	170
KANSAS	7 695	178 528	15 128.7	6 143.8	5 498	31 665	3 326.1	803.6	29 045.5	8 305.6	4 125.5	683.0
Allen	41	629	43.6	18.0	29	85	7.9	1.8	128.6	45.8	27.1	4.4
Anderson	25	372	21.8	8.6	14	26	1.8	0.5	61.2	27.1	16.9	1.5
Atchison	52	D	D	D	24	D	D	D	142.5	52.6	31.6	5.4
Barber	14	202	14.7	7.2	21	51	3.7	0.9	45.9	17.5	14.6	0.8
Barton	108	2 143	130.5	55.6	82	300	30.7	6.9	198.4	86.9	56.3	8.0
Bourbon	44	1 105	69.5	30.9	31	67	6.5	1.4	132.4	48.4	36.5	6.0
Brown	30	759	45.8	18.9	20	D	D	D	123.8	34.6	22.5	3.5
Butler	152	D	D	D	84	243	21.5	5.0	348.8	179.9	69.7	12.5
Chase	2	D	D	D	12	24	1.8	0.3	27.6	9.9	6.6	0.9
Chautauqua	10	155	7.4	3.4	5	D	D	D	38.1	14.8	11.7	1.4
Cherokee	39	619	27.2	12.3	28	72	5.4	1.1	189.6	68.9	45.9	10.4
Cheyenne	12	161	9.2	4.6	6	D	D	D	37.9	14.6	9.1	0.3
Clark	9	665	26.8	13.5	6	D	D	D	19.9	7.3	6.9	0.4
Clay	31	641	31.9	15.0	29	77	5.7	1.3	75.4	34.6	19.5	2.0
Cloud	38	775	36.1	16.8	24	85	6.6	1.4	98.9	34.1	28.8	2.4
Coffey	29	477	30.6	18.7	14	36	3.5	0.7	67.3	27.7	19.8	2.1
Comanche	7	D	D	D	8	D	D	D	18.3	7.5	5.3	0.3
Cowley	120	2 091	135.5	53.2	56	218	15.2	4.5	352.3	107.0	62.3	11.9
Crawford	141	3 013	182.6	70.4	69	D	D	D	334.7	124.2	77.5	14.5
Decatur	7	233	10.4	5.0	6	14	1.0	0.3	35.9	14.0	9.2	0.6
Dickinson	47	876	44.1	19.1	45	152	13.4	2.5	174.9	75.0	35.4	3.9
Doniphan	9	D	D	D	8	D	D	D	71.3	24.2	15.0	2.2
Douglas	283	5 331	375.5	163.3	190	1 429	277.4	33.7	689.9	246.9	76.3	18.1
Edwards	7	162	8.5	3.7	8	18	1.2	0.3	37.6	10.8	10.8	0.6
Elk	5	D	D	D	6	D	D	D	32.9	12.2	9.2	1.0
Ellis	115	3 027	252.3	98.6	81	372	37.4	7.3	195.5	74.0	46.7	4.4
Ellsworth	22	508	29.8	13.2	15	46	3.1	0.8	54.7	21.4	17.9	0.8
Finney	96	2 155	159.9	60.1	81	377	36.9	8.2	178.0	69.4	32.5	8.5
Ford	89	1 362	145.7	46.7	59	437	29.9	8.9	180.4	67.2	37.7	7.0
Franklin	66	1 159	80.3	34.4	46	298	24.9	8.4	177.3	73.0	44.7	7.0
Geary	53	1 554	130.2	57.3	51	261	13.9	4.1	3 295.5	109.1	19.1	12.1
Gove	11	201	12.9	5.0	14	38	4.2	0.6	34.1	12.4	8.3	0.2
Graham	14	272	12.5	6.5	9	20	3.1	0.5	35.6	12.6	8.6	0.4
Grant	14	191	15.9	6.8	13	55	6.0	1.1	41.1	18.4	8.3	1.3
Gray	13	164	6.2	3.5	13	26	2.4	0.5	45.0	17.1	7.0	0.6
Greeley	2	D	D	D	6	D	D	D	23.2	6.8	2.3	0.1
Greenwood	13	318	18.5	7.8	16	25	2.2	0.4	73.2	27.3	21.7	3.1
Hamilton	9	D	D	D	9	18	1.6	0.3	29.2	11.4	6.6	0.8
Harper	16	348	19.5	9.0	24	40	4.4	0.6	60.9	20.0	18.0	1.4
Harvey	97	2 877	208.7	86.1	67	277	19.3	5.2	232.7	116.6	58.4	6.4
Haskell	13	175	10.0	4.5	9	D	D	D	31.0	11.5	4.7	0.8
Hodgeman	5	D	D	D	5	D	D	D	19.8	6.4	5.3	0.1
Jackson	28	521	21.4	10.5	26	94	7.4	1.5	92.7	45.6	16.5	3.1
Jefferson	27	345	14.9	7.5	27	91	6.4	1.9	111.9	66.0	22.2	2.5
Jewell	4	D	D	D	7	D	D	D	41.8	13.6	8.4	0.6
Johnson	1 561	32 801	3 409.3	1 365.4	999	8 126	820.0	230.6	2 538.6	1 321.1	490.4	36.6
Kearny	7	D	D	D	8	D	D	D	35.1	12.9	5.9	0.7
Kingman	24	410	20.3	8.7	14	21	1.4	0.4	74.1	26.3	19.5	1.7
Kiowa	9	271	12.9	4.9	9	19	1.3	0.4	30.4	8.4	9.7	0.7
Labette	85	2 003	132.0	58.6	38	164	14.8	3.6	214.2	74.5	51.2	9.9
Lane	5	D	D	D	7	D	D	D	27.3	9.4	5.8	0.3
Leavenworth	122	2 682	247.8	105.6	96	510	40.6	11.4	2 169.6	291.4	79.4	14.0
Lincoln	6	138	6.8	3.5	8	28	1.5	0.4	30.6	10.7	7.7	0.4
Linn	11	84	3.5	1.4	13	62	4.3	1.0	83.9	34.2	22.3	2.4
Logan	8	184	11.4	5.4	14	31	2.0	0.5	34.7	12.5	7.3	1.0
Lyon	103	D	D	D	75	305	25.0	5.9	207.8	97.9	43.9	11.1
McPherson	86	2 275	111.7	51.9	83	389	31.6	8.8	185.9	92.9	47.4	2.9
Marion	30	669	34.6	15.6	27	108	9.3	1.8	105.6	44.2	27.2	2.1
Marshall	40	542	30.2	15.6	36	94	6.1	1.4	107.8	39.8	24.0	2.1
Meade	9	D	D	D	10	20	1.8	0.3	34.3	13.1	10.4	0.4
Miami	51	1 813	98.6	48.6	57	155	11.4	2.9	159.2	77.1	43.5	5.5
Mitchell	25	596	38.6	16.0	18	69	4.8	1.1	63.1	22.6	16.3	0.8
Montgomery	108	2 513	157.1	67.6	65	295	15.2	6.6	334.8	133.3	80.9	15.7
Morris	10	232	12.8	5.2	7	D	D	D	53.5	26.7	12.6	1.6
Morton	8	D	D	D	10	D	D	D	33.7	12.0	7.0	0.4
Nemaha	38	881	39.2	18.8	32	92	6.5	1.6	80.9	32.8	20.7	1.1

1. State totals may include programs not allocated by county.

Table B. States and Counties — Federal Funds, Residential Construction, and Local Government Finances

STATE County	Federal funds and grants, 2009–2010 (cont.) — Expenditures (mil dol) (cont.) — Procurement contract awards — Salaries and wages	Defense	Other	Grants[1] — Medicaid and other health-related	Nutrition and family welfare	Education	Other	Value of residential construction authorized by building permits, 2010 — New construction ($1,000)	Number of housing units	Local government finances, 2007 — General revenue — Total (mil dol)	Inter-governmental (mil dol)	Taxes — Total (mil dol)	Per capita[2] (dollars) — Total	Property
	171	172	173	174	175	176	177	178	179	180	181	182	183	184
KANSAS	5 818.5	1 940.8	1 118.9	2 241.5	600.2	508.5	1 386.0	811 584	5 140	X	X	X	X	X
Allen	12.4	0.0	0.7	23.6	2.8	0.5	1.7	2 147	16	55.1	27.4	16.1	1 203	947
Anderson	3.2	0.0	0.7	4.5	1.4	0.2	0.3	955	7	25.2	11.5	10.8	1 368	1 209
Atchison	4.7	3.0	18.0	15.2	3.4	0.4	1.2	455	4	54.6	24.2	19.7	1 188	871
Barber	1.9	0.0	0.4	3.4	0.9	0.1	1.6	100	1	31.7	6.1	12.4	2 598	2 292
Barton	10.0	0.1	2.0	12.6	5.2	2.3	1.1	1 520	7	115.5	48.0	40.9	1 473	1 144
Bourbon	6.1	0.0	3.9	19.1	2.9	1.0	1.7	90	1	53.8	25.8	16.8	1 132	865
Brown	20.7	0.1	6.8	10.2	6.6	0.6	6.5	375	1	34.2	15.7	12.8	1 274	1 081
Butler	22.3	1.7	3.4	24.2	10.1	2.8	2.0	25 494	147	265.3	124.4	84.8	1 346	1 199
Chase	1.6	0.0	4.4	2.3	0.5	0.1	0.2	0	0	10.8	3.7	5.4	1 864	1 700
Chautauqua	1.6	0.0	0.5	6.2	1.0	0.1	0.0	0	0	13.1	6.6	4.7	1 247	1 094
Cherokee	4.5	2.2	1.8	39.9	4.9	0.8	0.5	141	4	63.1	33.0	18.1	850	642
Cheyenne	1.1	0.0	0.2	2.8	0.6	0.1	0.6	0	0	10.4	3.9	5.0	1 793	1 566
Clark	0.5	0.0	0.2	1.1	0.4	0.1	0.0	292	2	23.0	4.0	7.4	3 529	3 462
Clay	2.9	0.0	0.7	5.6	3.2	0.2	0.5	845	7	39.2	11.0	9.8	1 125	904
Cloud	4.2	0.0	0.9	15.2	1.7	0.4	0.9	898	4	46.9	17.5	14.6	1 558	1 297
Coffey	3.4	4.4	0.6	4.5	1.5	0.2	-0.8	3 296	29	65.5	9.7	32.6	3 852	3 775
Comanche	0.4	0.0	0.1	1.7	0.3	0.1	0.0	0	0	11.8	2.1	5.8	3 071	2 903
Cowley	8.0	93.7	7.9	32.6	7.0	2.0	3.6	5 658	37	174.7	65.9	38.6	1 126	916
Crawford	17.5	0.1	4.1	58.5	11.6	2.4	5.0	5 579	47	125.6	53.1	37.6	968	720
Decatur	1.3	0.0	0.3	2.3	0.6	0.1	0.2	180	1	10.2	3.5	4.6	1 568	1 465
Dickinson	8.7	1.3	21.4	15.8	3.5	0.4	1.0	5 055	33	78.1	32.0	21.4	1 128	937
Doniphan	2.9	0.4	1.4	10.8	1.6	0.4	1.5	1 100	7	39.6	21.2	7.4	957	805
Douglas	52.4	12.5	18.6	110.8	13.8	27.9	77.8	41 580	288	429.5	85.5	157.0	1 384	1 048
Edwards	1.7	0.0	0.4	5.1	0.6	0.1	0.0	0	0	11.6	4.2	6.2	1 998	1 844
Elk	1.8	0.0	0.4	5.1	0.8	0.1	1.1	NA	NA	13.7	6.3	4.2	1 380	1 287
Ellis	22.1	0.0	1.8	18.5	4.8	1.0	3.9	9 604	54	77.1	24.3	40.4	1 470	1 077
Ellsworth	1.6	0.1	0.5	2.8	1.1	0.1	4.7	0	0	20.6	8.2	9.6	1 520	1 318
Finney	9.7	0.0	1.4	20.8	7.2	2.5	2.7	2 388	18	159.3	67.0	63.9	1 669	1 351
Ford	20.9	0.5	2.1	14.1	7.3	1.9	4.7	7 045	52	149.7	76.6	46.8	1 404	1 063
Franklin	13.8	0.1	1.0	20.8	6.0	0.5	1.6	5 707	33	107.0	37.5	34.0	1 284	1 003
Geary	2 790.8	310.4	1.2	22.7	8.3	13.5	1.4	26 221	229	159.0	71.1	33.7	1 341	820
Gove	1.4	0.0	0.3	1.1	0.4	0.1	1.1	0	0	20.8	9.9	5.4	2 053	1 800
Graham	1.6	0.0	0.3	3.4	0.6	0.1	0.7	470	5	16.1	3.1	6.5	2 502	2 325
Grant	0.9	0.0	0.2	1.7	1.4	0.1	0.1	795	5	33.6	5.6	24.4	3 250	3 104
Gray	1.6	0.0	0.3	3.4	0.9	0.2	0.1	4 523	34	22.9	11.4	9.2	1 637	1 489
Greeley	0.5	0.0	0.1	2.2	0.3	0.1	0.0	180	1	7.9	1.9	5.3	4 052	3 846
Greenwood	3.1	0.5	0.7	10.1	1.4	0.2	3.5	0	0	22.5	10.6	9.7	1 381	1 217
Hamilton	0.5	0.0	0.1	1.1	0.4	0.1	0.1	0	0	13.7	3.3	9.2	3 483	3 291
Harper	2.8	0.7	0.6	4.5	1.2	0.2	4.1	442	4	43.2	10.6	11.6	1 999	1 788
Harvey	7.2	0.4	2.9	12.0	4.7	1.4	13.0	7 098	55	115.0	46.4	41.8	1 249	948
Haskell	0.8	0.0	0.1	1.7	0.7	0.2	0.0	0	0	34.0	4.3	19.3	4 775	4 607
Hodgeman	1.0	0.0	0.2	1.1	0.3	0.1	0.0	NA	NA	15.8	4.2	6.3	3 209	3 181
Jackson	4.5	0.0	1.0	8.9	3.0	1.4	4.6	2 917	19	40.9	22.1	13.6	1 015	830
Jefferson	4.5	2.8	1.0	6.2	2.8	0.4	0.5	4 253	36	62.8	34.7	20.7	1 122	1 020
Jewell	2.7	0.0	0.9	5.6	0.7	0.1	0.4	0	0	16.3	5.5	5.7	1 795	1 669
Johnson	233.2	72.4	152.7	84.4	40.9	5.5	30.8	257 291	1 053	2 164.6	534.5	1 158.8	2 202	1 581
Kearny	0.8	0.0	0.2	2.8	0.9	0.1	0.0	695	4	36.0	3.8	21.0	5 065	4 953
Kingman	11.6	2.4	0.6	3.9	1.5	0.2	0.0	1 644	11	27.4	10.2	13.6	1 735	1 628
Kiowa	1.2	0.0	-3.0	2.6	0.6	0.1	5.4	160	1	15.2	4.6	6.9	2 343	2 134
Labette	11.0	8.1	1.2	37.1	4.7	1.8	3.8	1 417	15	117.9	42.8	26.6	1 211	932
Lane	0.7	0.0	0.1	3.9	0.4	0.1	0.1	0	0	12.2	3.2	4.9	2 818	2 727
Leavenworth	961.8	266.1	489.9	33.2	8.6	12.5	2.5	15 483	103	214.8	96.6	81.7	1 110	852
Lincoln	2.0	1.3	0.4	2.3	0.5	0.1	0.1	0	0	16.9	4.7	6.6	1 996	1 862
Linn	3.4	0.0	0.7	11.8	1.8	0.2	4.0	3 022	23	35.0	14.5	17.1	1 753	1 670
Logan	1.1	0.0	0.2	1.1	2.0	0.1	0.2	0	0	20.9	4.0	6.0	2 301	2 087
Lyon	14.4	0.8	0.9	15.6	5.8	2.5	1.0	3 460	27	155.3	51.2	39.9	1 109	849
McPherson	6.7	3.0	1.6	10.7	4.7	0.4	2.1	9 594	56	98.6	34.2	42.4	1 452	1 204
Marion	4.4	8.2	1.0	7.9	2.1	0.3	0.1	1 882	20	52.6	21.2	16.3	1 328	1 153
Marshall	11.2	2.5	1.3	11.8	2.1	0.2	1.7	4 120	29	37.7	17.5	14.7	1 442	1 261
Meade	0.9	0.0	0.2	2.8	0.6	0.1	0.0	85	1	31.2	4.9	9.6	2 189	2 017
Miami	6.9	0.0	1.1	16.9	3.8	0.4	0.8	8 134	38	90.4	32.8	42.8	1 378	1 083
Mitchell	2.5	0.0	3.3	5.6	1.5	0.2	0.3	395	2	38.6	18.8	11.2	1 776	1 455
Montgomery	18.8	3.3	2.1	56.8	7.0	2.8	2.1	603	6	120.2	48.3	43.9	1 272	931
Morris	2.9	0.9	0.5	4.5	1.1	0.1	0.0	464	3	15.7	6.5	7.2	1 205	1 024
Morton	1.2	0.0	0.2	1.1	0.6	0.1	1.9	0	0	43.6	6.8	15.1	4 973	4 837
Nemaha	4.6	0.0	2.2	7.9	1.6	0.2	0.3	1 951	9	30.9	13.8	11.5	1 123	958

1. State totals may include programs not allocated by county. 2. Based on the resident population estimated as of July 1 of the year shown.

STATE County	Local government finances, 2007 (cont.) Direct general expenditure Total (mil dol)	Per capita[1] (dollars)	Education	Health and hospitals	Police protection	Public welfare	Highways	Debt outstanding Total (mil dol)	Per capita[1] (dollars)	Government employment, 2009 Federal civilian	Federal military	State and local	Presidential election,[2] 2008 Percent of vote cast: Democratic	Republican	All other
	185	186	187	188	189	190	191	192	193	194	195	196	197	198	199
KANSAS	X	X	X	X	X	X	X	X	X	25 938	34 418	240 391	41.7	56.6	1.7
Allen	58.1	4 334	66.5	1.5	3.0	0.0	4.8	30.9	2 300	63	56	1 646	37.4	60.7	1.9
Anderson	24.0	3 034	57.2	1.7	4.0	0.0	11.0	27.7	3 509	40	33	531	32.4	65.1	2.5
Atchison	53.5	3 226	48.0	0.9	5.7	4.3	7.0	40.7	2 456	52	69	924	45.1	52.7	2.2
Barber	29.8	6 217	32.1	37.7	2.7	0.2	10.5	7.2	1 508	29	19	679	24.3	74.5	1.3
Barton	106.4	3 833	63.7	2.0	3.4	0.0	5.8	64.2	2 310	88	116	2 273	27.4	70.6	2.1
Bourbon	50.4	3 404	65.8	0.8	2.8	0.0	7.9	33.6	2 269	84	63	1 129	35.3	62.5	2.2
Brown	35.2	3 492	48.5	0.6	3.7	0.0	9.4	28.7	2 849	96	42	1 843	30.1	68.2	1.7
Butler	244.6	3 880	66.6	1.1	2.8	0.0	5.7	450.1	7 139	133	270	5 877	32.9	65.1	2.0
Chase	12.1	4 209	41.3	1.1	2.8	0.6	10.6	4.4	1 521	26	12	274	27.7	70.5	1.8
Chautauqua	12.4	3 255	56.3	3.9	3.0	0.4	12.2	7.2	1 883	17	16	263	21.7	76.6	1.8
Cherokee	60.8	2 848	62.4	2.1	4.4	0.0	7.9	10.2	479	58	89	1 369	37.2	60.9	1.9
Cheyenne	9.5	3 397	54.5	1.2	3.7	0.0	13.8	0.0	0	21	11	261	21.6	76.6	1.8
Clark	22.2	10 617	26.9	54.5	1.6	0.3	4.4	5.0	2 405	13	0	478	21.1	77.4	1.5
Clay	42.4	4 888	27.6	40.7	2.5	0.1	5.1	25.0	2 884	39	37	966	24.9	74.0	1.2
Cloud	48.0	5 120	57.9	2.5	2.8	0.0	6.1	10.4	1 113	45	39	910	27.7	70.1	2.2
Coffey	68.4	8 087	33.0	33.0	2.6	0.0	9.9	21.0	2 488	48	35	1 254	26.5	72.2	1.3
Comanche	11.4	6 044	33.4	26.9	2.4	0.0	10.1	2.6	1 399	0	0	296	19.9	78.5	1.5
Cowley	173.4	5 063	47.4	19.0	3.4	0.0	6.0	102.1	2 981	97	141	3 564	36.4	61.6	2.1
Crawford	122.5	3 152	45.8	12.5	4.8	0.0	3.8	100.5	2 586	117	167	4 839	49.5	48.1	2.4
Decatur	10.9	3 692	48.4	3.5	4.8	0.4	13.2	4.0	1 363	23	12	251	22.2	76.8	1.0
Dickinson	75.5	3 981	47.3	20.2	3.6	0.0	8.0	30.0	1 581	106	80	1 675	27.9	70.2	1.9
Doniphan	40.2	5 189	71.3	1.6	0.7	0.0	6.2	14.2	1 831	38	32	954	31.3	66.6	2.2
Douglas	378.9	3 339	32.9	31.9	6.2	0.1	3.9	522.0	4 600	511	534	14 906	64.4	33.6	2.0
Edwards	11.2	3 610	47.0	4.5	5.6	0.0	14.7	1.2	374	26	13	231	24.5	73.3	2.1
Elk	13.8	4 554	47.6	2.1	2.1	12.9	12.4	4.0	1 307	18	13	389	25.3	72.7	2.0
Ellis	86.1	3 133	43.3	2.8	4.2	0.2	6.2	46.1	1 677	162	117	3 214	32.2	65.9	1.8
Ellsworth	21.0	3 323	52.9	5.5	4.6	0.3	11.3	21.3	3 373	27	26	900	29.0	68.8	2.2
Finney	155.7	4 065	64.2	1.7	5.4	0.0	2.8	104.9	2 740	134	177	3 343	31.6	66.9	1.5
Ford	148.8	4 462	59.8	1.5	4.3	0.0	6.0	109.3	3 279	249	142	2 674	33.7	64.6	1.6
Franklin	102.9	3 886	43.8	23.8	3.5	0.0	5.7	90.2	3 406	81	111	1 826	37.8	60.3	1.9
Geary	148.8	5 917	43.5	30.3	4.7	0.0	2.6	93.0	3 699	3 267	16 709	2 714	43.1	55.5	1.4
Gove	20.2	7 671	37.9	42.1	1.6	0.0	4.9	2.5	960	20	10	428	18.4	80.1	1.5
Graham	15.8	6 059	30.6	35.7	2.8	0.0	9.3	1.5	558	32	10	363	22.8	74.5	2.7
Grant	31.5	4 200	49.3	3.0	5.2	0.0	13.4	7.5	996	21	31	809	23.9	75.0	1.2
Gray	22.5	3 990	62.4	2.2	3.4	0.0	10.7	10.4	1 851	27	25	980	20.6	77.5	1.9
Greeley	6.8	5 261	43.0	5.3	4.2	0.0	11.5	3.1	2 426	12	0	173	20.3	79.3	0.4
Greenwood	20.5	2 926	55.2	3.0	4.0	0.3	10.8	15.2	2 176	50	28	482	27.3	71.0	1.7
Hamilton	10.9	4 154	44.5	2.4	6.4	0.0	14.2	5.9	2 238	14	11	392	21.3	77.0	1.7
Harper	37.7	6 484	30.5	43.8	1.9	0.0	5.9	13.7	2 362	37	24	914	26.3	71.5	2.2
Harvey	118.7	3 544	44.8	0.9	4.0	0.2	5.0	159.1	4 749	75	144	2 024	40.5	57.7	1.9
Haskell	31.8	7 878	40.9	32.1	3.6	0.0	9.0	8.2	2 028	17	17	568	17.7	81.3	1.0
Hodgeman	14.3	7 270	31.4	29.9	2.3	0.0	15.0	13.2	6 687	17	0	313	19.3	78.9	1.8
Jackson	43.1	3 210	62.4	0.7	7.1	0.3	10.2	27.9	2 077	49	56	2 082	36.9	60.9	2.1
Jefferson	58.0	3 140	68.0	3.5	4.3	0.0	7.4	42.8	2 319	67	77	1 115	39.6	68.3	2.1
Jewell	15.5	4 843	40.2	23.3	2.0	0.0	11.0	1.7	537	33	13	389	19.8	77.7	2.5
Johnson	2 110.0	4 009	46.5	2.3	7.8	0.8	5.0	3 523.8	6 695	2 009	2 288	28 946	44.8	53.8	1.3
Kearny	35.9	8 652	31.8	41.0	3.0	0.0	5.7	16.2	3 906	17	18	672	20.9	78.2	0.9
Kingman	27.9	3 566	47.4	2.7	4.1	0.0	14.3	30.6	3 912	36	32	605	26.3	71.0	2.7
Kiowa	13.3	4 515	56.9	2.7	4.0	0.0	9.0	2.3	772	25	10	392	17.6	80.4	2.0
Labette	120.5	5 483	41.2	31.4	2.9	0.0	3.1	60.8	2 767	74	92	2 967	42.5	55.4	2.1
Lane	11.7	6 715	39.3	30.7	4.8	0.0	6.5	1.4	790	16	0	281	18.8	79.3	1.9
Leavenworth	195.6	2 657	54.8	1.2	5.2	0.0	6.1	211.5	2 874	3 924	3 383	4 296	43.3	54.9	1.8
Lincoln	15.7	4 777	37.9	29.0	3.2	0.0	8.9	3.9	1 177	34	13	401	21.9	75.9	2.2
Linn	35.7	3 659	60.8	1.6	4.4	0.0	7.8	14.3	1 462	47	39	702	30.9	66.8	2.3
Logan	17.7	6 744	31.8	38.8	2.8	0.1	5.9	1.0	394	21	11	677	15.6	82.4	1.9
Lyon	152.9	4 250	42.1	28.5	3.7	0.0	3.8	134.1	3 727	119	142	4 440	45.9	51.9	2.2
McPherson	95.3	3 264	46.6	2.8	4.0	0.0	9.5	86.8	2 974	93	121	2 065	31.5	66.8	1.7
Marion	54.1	4 422	43.7	18.5	2.6	0.1	13.4	34.1	2 783	66	50	1 075	29.7	68.6	1.6
Marshall	36.8	3 612	59.5	1.7	3.4	0.0	10.9	9.4	920	57	43	885	35.4	62.7	1.9
Meade	32.1	7 295	24.7	43.6	2.2	3.8	7.8	24.0	5 447	17	19	685	18.5	79.8	1.8
Miami	89.7	2 887	47.8	0.9	5.7	0.0	8.3	164.5	5 294	67	130	2 123	37.3	61.0	1.6
Mitchell	32.9	5 209	57.3	4.4	4.1	0.2	7.9	4.6	721	39	27	1 097	21.9	76.2	1.9
Montgomery	127.8	3 702	59.7	1.8	3.5	0.0	3.9	86.3	2 501	137	144	2 827	31.2	66.9	1.9
Morris	15.5	2 590	53.2	2.5	3.6	0.0	14.0	7.2	1 203	36	25	491	31.9	66.0	2.1
Morton	36.3	11 945	33.7	41.9	0.6	0.0	5.1	14.0	4 592	25	13	676	16.3	82.2	1.4
Nemaha	29.8	2 917	52.3	1.3	4.4	0.0	10.7	21.0	2 059	66	42	758	26.7	71.2	2.1

1. Based on the resident population estimated as of July 1 of the year shown.   2. © 2009 Election Data Services, Inc. All rights reserved.

Table B. States and Counties — Land Area and Population

STATE/ County code	CBSA code[1]	County type[2]	STATE County	Land area,[3] (sq km) 2010	Total persons	Rank	Per square kilometer	Race alone or in combination, not Hispanic or Latino (percent) White	Black	American Indian, Alaska Native	Asian and Pacific Islander	Percent Hispanic or Latino[4]	Under 5 years	5 to 17 years	18 to 24 years	25 to 34 years	35 to 44 years	45 to 54 years
				1	2	3	4	5	6	7	8	9	10	11	12	13	14	15
			KANSAS—Cont'd															
20 133	...	7	Neosho	1 480	16 512	2 017	11.2	93.1	1.6	1.8	0.8	4.2	6.9	17.8	8.8	10.8	11.1	14.6
20 135	...	9	Ness	2 784	3 107	2 971	1.1	91.8	0.8	0.5	0.3	7.4	5.4	17.0	4.6	9.1	9.3	16.8
20 137	...	7	Norton	2 274	5 671	2 792	2.5	92.1	3.2	0.6	0.9	4.2	5.0	15.0	6.9	12.7	12.5	17.0
20 139	45820	3	Osage	1 827	16 295	2 033	8.9	96.8	0.7	1.4	0.4	2.0	6.2	18.6	6.5	9.9	11.3	16.9
20 141	...	9	Osborne	2 312	3 858	2 915	1.7	97.8	0.5	0.7	0.8	1.2	5.4	15.7	5.6	9.3	9.0	16.4
20 143	41460	9	Ottawa	1 867	6 091	2 758	3.3	96.7	1.2	0.9	0.3	2.0	5.7	19.7	5.3	10.2	12.0	16.6
20 145	...	7	Pawnee	1 954	6 973	2 688	3.6	87.7	5.4	1.1	0.7	6.6	5.5	16.4	7.7	11.6	10.9	16.1
20 147	...	7	Phillips	2 294	5 642	2 794	2.5	96.4	0.7	0.6	1.0	2.1	6.2	18.0	5.6	9.8	10.0	14.9
20 149	31740	6	Pottawatomie	2 178	21 604	1 759	9.9	93.1	1.7	1.5	1.3	4.4	8.5	21.2	7.5	13.0	12.1	14.2
20 151	...	7	Pratt	1 904	9 656	2 464	5.1	92.8	1.4	1.3	0.5	5.4	6.6	16.2	10.5	11.0	9.5	14.4
20 153	...	9	Rawlins	2 770	2 519	3 006	0.9	96.0	0.8	0.4	0.2	3.2	5.2	13.7	5.2	8.7	8.2	15.4
20 155	26740	4	Reno	3 251	64 511	812	19.8	87.9	3.8	1.3	0.8	8.1	6.6	17.0	9.1	12.0	11.0	14.5
20 157	...	9	Republic	1 858	4 980	2 841	2.7	97.9	0.7	0.4	0.3	1.1	5.1	14.2	4.9	8.1	9.0	16.2
20 159	...	7	Rice	1 881	10 083	2 440	5.4	87.8	1.6	1.5	0.7	10.1	6.2	17.7	11.8	10.1	10.1	14.2
20 161	31740	5	Riley	1 579	71 115	750	45.0	82.2	7.4	1.2	5.6	6.5	6.8	11.7	33.8	17.5	8.1	7.9
20 163	...	9	Rooks	2 306	5 181	2 830	2.2	96.9	0.7	0.5	0.6	2.1	6.3	17.4	6.7	10.2	10.5	15.5
20 165	...	9	Rush	1 859	3 307	2 958	1.8	96.5	0.4	1.1	0.3	2.5	4.9	14.5	5.6	9.3	10.4	15.8
20 167	...	7	Russell	2 295	6 970	2 689	3.0	96.4	1.4	1.1	0.6	1.6	5.7	15.6	6.3	10.2	10.3	15.1
20 169	41460	5	Saline	1 865	55 606	901	29.8	84.4	4.5	1.1	2.8	9.7	7.2	17.9	9.3	12.6	12.0	14.5
20 171	...	9	Scott	1 858	4 936	2 844	2.7	83.4	0.5	0.9	0.5	15.3	7.6	17.4	6.8	10.5	12.0	14.1
20 173	48620	2	Sedgwick	2 584	498 365	130	192.9	72.6	10.5	2.1	4.9	13.0	7.9	19.3	9.7	14.1	12.4	14.1
20 175	30580	7	Seward	1 656	22 952	1 690	13.9	37.2	3.5	0.9	3.0	56.6	10.0	21.9	12.0	14.4	13.1	11.9
20 177	45820	3	Shawnee	1 409	177 934	346	126.3	78.4	10.0	2.2	1.7	10.8	7.0	17.9	8.7	13.0	11.7	14.4
20 179	...	9	Sheridan	2 321	2 556	3 003	1.1	96.2	0.4	0.9	0.2	3.3	6.7	16.9	5.2	8.9	9.4	16.9
20 181	...	7	Sherman	2 735	6 010	2 765	2.2	88.0	1.3	0.8	0.5	10.8	6.7	15.8	9.0	11.4	10.3	14.5
20 183	...	9	Smith	2 319	3 853	2 916	1.7	97.7	0.5	1.0	0.6	1.5	4.9	15.2	5.2	8.3	8.7	16.7
20 185	...	9	Stafford	2 051	4 437	2 873	2.2	86.7	0.5	1.4	0.5	11.9	5.7	17.7	6.5	9.1	10.0	16.8
20 187	...	9	Stanton	1 762	2 235	3 035	1.3	61.4	0.7	1.4	0.3	37.0	8.2	20.9	7.6	12.3	12.4	12.7
20 189	...	7	Stevens	1 884	5 724	2 787	3.0	66.1	0.6	1.1	0.3	32.6	8.5	22.1	7.9	12.4	12.4	13.8
20 191	48620	2	Sumner	3 061	24 132	1 640	7.9	93.2	1.3	2.4	0.4	4.5	6.7	19.5	7.1	10.8	11.2	16.1
20 193	...	7	Thomas	2 783	7 900	2 609	2.8	93.7	0.9	0.7	0.8	4.7	6.6	16.8	13.4	11.4	10.2	14.3
20 195	...	9	Trego	2 304	3 001	2 980	1.3	97.3	0.6	0.6	0.4	1.7	4.5	15.5	5.2	8.3	9.6	17.9
20 197	45820	3	Wabaunsee	2 057	7 053	2 680	3.4	96.0	0.8	1.4	0.4	2.9	6.6	18.8	5.8	10.5	11.0	17.4
20 199	...	9	Wallace	2 366	1 485	3 085	0.6	92.0	0.8	0.6	0.1	7.3	5.5	19.7	6.0	9.7	8.6	16.6
20 201	...	9	Washington	2 317	5 799	2 785	2.5	96.7	0.7	0.5	0.5	2.5	5.8	17.1	5.4	9.4	10.4	15.3
20 203	...	9	Wichita	1 861	2 234	3 036	1.2	74.4	0.8	0.4	0.3	24.6	7.4	19.8	4.7	11.5	11.7	14.2
20 205	...	7	Wilson	1 477	9 409	2 490	6.4	96.0	0.6	2.3	0.7	2.3	6.5	17.9	6.3	10.8	10.5	15.0
20 207	...	9	Woodson	1 289	3 309	2 956	2.6	96.6	0.8	2.1	0.3	2.1	5.4	14.5	5.7	10.3	9.7	15.7
20 209	28140	1	Wyandotte	393	157 505	395	400.8	45.2	26.3	1.4	2.9	26.4	8.7	19.5	9.6	15.1	12.5	13.4
21 000	...	X	KENTUCKY	102 269	4 339 367	X	42.4	87.7	8.5	0.6	1.5	3.1	6.5	17.1	9.5	13.0	13.3	14.8
21 001	...	7	Adair	1 050	18 656	1 890	17.8	95.1	3.1	0.6	0.4	1.7	6.3	16.3	12.0	10.8	12.2	14.4
21 003	...	6	Allen	892	19 956	1 842	22.4	97.2	1.3	0.7	0.3	1.5	6.7	17.7	8.4	11.5	13.6	14.5
21 005	23180	6	Anderson	523	21 421	1 765	41.0	95.9	2.5	0.6	0.8	1.3	6.7	18.7	7.3	12.3	15.0	15.5
21 007	37140	9	Ballard	639	8 249	2 591	12.9	95.6	3.7	0.7	0.4	1.1	5.2	16.9	7.4	10.7	13.4	15.0
21 009	23980	6	Barren	1 263	42 173	1 124	33.4	92.8	4.6	0.6	0.6	2.6	6.5	17.7	7.7	11.9	13.2	15.0
21 011	34460	8	Bath	722	11 591	2 324	16.1	97.0	1.8	0.6	0.3	1.4	7.1	17.7	7.4	11.3	13.6	15.0
21 013	33180	7	Bell	930	28 691	1 468	30.9	96.6	2.8	1.0	0.4	0.7	5.5	16.2	8.9	11.6	13.3	15.0
21 015	17140	1	Boone	638	118 811	504	186.2	91.4	3.1	0.6	2.7	3.5	7.6	20.7	7.5	13.2	15.5	15.0
21 017	30460	2	Bourbon	750	19 985	1 839	26.6	86.6	7.0	0.5	0.4	6.8	6.2	17.9	7.4	10.8	13.7	15.5
21 019	26580	2	Boyd	414	49 542	986	119.7	94.9	3.4	0.7	0.7	1.4	5.9	15.5	7.3	12.3	13.4	15.3
21 021	19220	7	Boyle	467	28 432	1 479	60.9	88.6	8.6	0.6	1.1	2.8	5.3	16.3	10.7	10.7	13.0	14.4
21 023	17140	1	Bracken	533	8 488	2 570	15.9	98.2	0.7	0.7	0.2	1.1	6.7	18.6	8.2	11.1	13.4	15.7
21 025	...	7	Breathitt	1 275	13 878	2 188	10.9	98.3	0.4	0.4	0.7	0.6	6.1	17.1	8.4	11.9	13.5	15.6
21 027	...	8	Breckinridge	1 469	20 059	1 837	13.7	96.5	2.6	0.8	0.3	0.9	6.1	18.1	7.2	10.7	12.2	15.8
21 029	31140	1	Bullitt	769	74 319	730	96.6	97.0	1.0	0.8	0.8	1.4	6.3	19.0	8.0	12.4	14.8	16.1
21 031	...	8	Butler	1 104	12 690	2 262	11.5	96.8	0.6	0.7	0.2	2.5	6.3	16.8	8.2	12.4	12.7	15.1
21 033	...	6	Caldwell	893	12 984	2 244	14.5	93.3	5.9	0.6	0.4	1.0	6.1	16.2	7.4	10.4	12.8	14.7
21 035	34660	7	Calloway	997	37 191	1 234	37.3	91.8	4.4	0.6	2.1	2.4	5.2	12.8	20.9	11.9	10.3	12.1
21 037	17140	1	Campbell	392	90 336	629	230.4	94.7	3.3	0.5	1.1	1.7	6.4	16.4	11.1	13.8	12.6	15.1
21 039	...	9	Carlisle	491	5 104	2 835	10.4	96.9	1.1	0.8	0.4	1.6	6.3	16.3	7.0	11.1	12.2	14.6
21 041	...	6	Carroll	333	10 811	2 383	32.5	90.3	2.6	0.9	0.7	7.3	7.4	17.7	8.2	13.0	13.5	15.0
21 043	...	6	Carter	1 061	27 720	1 507	26.1	97.9	0.7	0.7	0.3	1.2	6.3	17.2	9.2	12.0	13.0	14.5
21 045	...	9	Casey	1 151	15 955	2 051	13.9	96.8	0.8	0.5	0.3	2.4	6.2	17.4	7.5	11.7	12.9	14.2
21 047	17300	3	Christian	1 858	73 955	733	39.8	70.8	22.4	1.1	2.1	6.1	9.8	18.7	13.9	16.3	11.2	10.8
21 049	30460	2	Clark	654	35 613	1 284	54.5	92.1	5.4	0.5	0.6	2.5	6.3	17.2	7.4	12.2	14.1	15.4

1. CBSA = Core Based Statistical Area. See Appendix A for explanation. See Appendix B for list of metropolitan areas with component counties. 2. County type code from the Economic Research Service of USDA Rural-Urban Continuum Codes. See Appendix A for definition. 3. Dry land or land partially or temporarily covered by water. 4. May be of any race.

Table B. States and Counties — **Population and Households**

STATE County	55 to 64 years (16)	65 to 74 years (17)	75 years and over (18)	Percent female (19)	1990 (20)	2000 (21)	1990–2000 (22)	2000–2010 (23)	Births (24)	Deaths (25)	Net migration (26)	Number (27)	Percent change, 2000–2010 (28)	Persons per household (29)	Female family householder[1] (30)	One person (31)
KANSAS—Cont'd																
Neosho	12.6	8.6	8.7	50.6	17 035	16 997	-0.2	-2.9	2 000	1 865	-1 013	6 645	-1.4	2.42	9.4	28.6
Ness	13.2	11.6	13.0	49.8	4 033	3 454	-14.4	-10.0	275	456	-523	1 365	-10.0	2.22	5.2	33.1
Norton	12.2	9.0	9.6	44.1	5 947	5 953	0.1	-4.7	491	629	-456	2 163	-4.5	2.24	7.5	33.1
Osage	13.6	9.1	7.9	50.3	15 248	16 712	9.6	-2.5	1 735	1 679	-580	6 552	1.0	2.46	8.7	25.8
Osborne	13.3	10.9	14.3	50.3	4 867	4 452	-8.5	-13.3	333	619	-304	1 742	-10.2	2.16	7.1	35.5
Ottawa	13.1	9.3	8.2	48.4	5 634	6 163	9.4	-1.2	644	692	-107	2 456	1.1	2.44	7.5	26.5
Pawnee	14.4	8.7	8.7	44.5	7 555	7 233	-4.3	-3.6	594	739	-890	2 665	-2.7	2.23	8.7	35.6
Phillips	15.3	9.7	10.5	50.5	6 590	6 001	-8.9	-6.0	560	790	-475	2 432	-2.6	2.29	6.6	30.8
Pottawatomie	11.1	6.4	5.9	50.4	16 128	18 209	12.9	18.6	2 776	1 567	673	7 878	16.3	2.70	7.9	23.2
Pratt	12.9	8.7	10.2	50.7	9 702	9 647	-0.6	0.1	1 099	1 107	-286	3 956	-0.2	2.34	8.9	30.8
Rawlins	17.0	12.1	14.5	50.2	3 404	2 966	-12.9	-15.1	184	365	-349	1 176	-7.3	2.11	4.9	35.8
Reno	12.7	8.2	8.9	49.9	62 389	64 790	3.8	-0.4	7 770	6 322	-2 492	25 794	1.2	2.38	10.4	30.0
Republic	15.5	11.2	15.9	50.9	6 482	5 835	-10.0	-14.7	437	812	-631	2 274	-11.1	2.14	5.7	32.8
Rice	12.0	9.0	8.8	49.8	10 610	10 761	1.4	-6.3	1 185	1 182	-634	3 906	-3.6	2.42	7.6	29.0
Riley	6.8	3.6	3.8	47.9	67 139	62 843	-6.4	13.2	8 901	2 820	-620	25 796	16.5	2.40	9.2	27.4
Rooks	13.7	9.2	10.6	51.1	6 039	5 685	-5.9	-8.9	539	631	-591	2 238	-5.2	2.28	8.0	31.3
Rush	15.5	9.6	14.4	50.7	3 842	3 551	-7.6	-6.9	335	488	-240	1 511	-2.4	2.14	6.6	34.1
Russell	14.1	10.2	12.5	50.6	7 835	7 370	-5.9	-5.4	693	970	-461	3 173	-1.1	2.17	8.0	34.7
Saline	12.2	7.3	7.1	50.2	49 301	53 597	8.7	3.7	7 218	4 649	-1 488	22 416	4.6	2.42	10.8	29.7
Scott	13.3	9.2	9.1	49.6	5 289	5 120	-3.2	-3.6	603	481	-665	1 983	-3.0	2.44	5.7	27.3
Sedgwick	11.1	5.9	5.6	50.6	403 662	452 869	12.2	10.0	72 274	35 391	3 931	193 502	9.7	2.54	12.4	28.7
Seward	8.3	4.5	4.0	48.5	18 743	22 510	20.1	2.0	4 787	1 257	-2 978	7 460	0.6	3.01	12.4	21.4
Shawnee	13.0	7.4	7.0	51.7	160 976	169 871	5.5	4.7	23 344	15 531	-279	72 600	5.3	2.39	12.5	30.9
Sheridan	13.9	9.6	12.4	49.1	3 043	2 813	-7.6	-9.1	269	297	-342	1 099	-2.2	2.30	5.3	30.6
Sherman	13.2	9.6	9.4	50.0	6 926	6 760	-2.4	-11.1	699	657	-926	2 608	-5.4	2.27	8.4	33.1
Smith	14.7	10.8	15.6	51.0	5 078	4 536	-10.7	-15.1	313	614	-469	1 748	-10.5	2.17	4.8	32.3
Stafford	13.2	9.6	11.4	50.2	5 365	4 789	-10.7	-7.4	443	581	-298	1 907	-5.1	2.29	6.8	32.9
Stanton	10.4	7.5	8.1	48.9	2 333	2 406	3.1	-7.1	356	165	-491	825	-3.8	2.65	6.8	24.6
Stevens	9.8	6.3	6.8	50.4	5 048	5 463	8.2	4.8	831	427	-732	2 044	2.8	2.77	6.8	23.6
Sumner	12.9	7.6	8.1	50.1	25 841	25 946	0.4	-7.0	2 897	2 510	-2 764	9 454	-4.4	2.51	9.0	26.8
Thomas	12.0	7.4	8.0	50.8	8 258	8 180	-0.9	-3.4	903	695	-1 014	3 196	-0.9	2.36	7.7	30.3
Trego	15.7	10.5	13.0	50.6	3 694	3 319	-10.2	-9.6	301	422	-263	1 358	-3.8	2.16	6.2	32.0
Wabaunsee	14.1	8.6	7.1	49.1	6 603	6 885	4.3	2.4	766	600	-173	2 737	3.9	2.54	6.1	23.5
Wallace	13.5	8.2	12.2	50.0	1 821	1 749	-4.0	-15.1	154	166	-328	620	-8.0	2.36	5.0	31.0
Washington	13.4	10.8	12.3	49.3	7 073	6 483	-8.3	-10.6	556	833	-491	2 474	-7.4	2.30	4.7	32.1
Wichita	12.8	8.9	9.1	48.8	2 758	2 531	-8.2	-11.7	317	210	-522	891	-7.9	2.48	6.3	25.8
Wilson	13.8	10.0	9.3	50.9	10 289	10 332	0.4	-8.9	1 103	1 278	-620	3 933	-6.4	2.36	9.1	29.8
Woodson	16.0	9.7	13.0	50.0	4 116	3 788	-8.0	-12.6	316	546	-301	1 524	-7.2	2.15	7.3	35.2
Wyandotte	10.4	5.7	5.0	50.7	162 026	157 882	-2.6	-0.2	25 885	13 506	-14 495	58 399	-2.2	2.67	18.5	28.5
KENTUCKY	12.4	7.5	5.8	50.8	3 686 892	4 041 769	9.6	7.4	519 005	370 888	126 831	1 719 965	8.1	2.45	12.7	27.5
Adair	12.7	8.9	6.4	50.6	15 360	17 244	12.3	8.2	1 979	1 567	476	7 288	8.0	2.42	10.4	27.4
Allen	12.8	8.7	6.0	50.9	14 628	17 800	21.7	12.1	2 184	1 799	910	7 848	13.6	2.52	11.3	25.2
Anderson	12.5	7.0	5.0	51.1	14 571	19 111	31.2	12.1	2 294	1 577	2 061	8 369	14.3	2.55	11.4	22.3
Ballard	13.8	9.8	7.8	50.3	7 902	8 286	4.9	-0.4	798	985	105	3 397	0.1	2.39	9.2	25.9
Barren	12.5	8.4	7.0	51.5	34 001	38 033	11.9	10.9	4 862	4 008	3 078	16 999	10.8	2.44	11.8	26.8
Bath	13.3	8.7	6.1	50.4	9 692	11 085	14.4	4.6	1 472	1 200	300	4 587	3.2	2.50	12.1	26.4
Bell	13.8	9.2	6.5	51.4	31 506	30 060	-4.6	-4.6	3 472	3 458	-923	11 787	-1.8	2.35	15.8	29.8
Boone	11.1	5.7	3.8	50.5	57 589	85 991	49.3	38.2	15 164	5 659	23 415	43 216	38.3	2.73	10.9	21.3
Bourbon	13.3	8.6	6.7	51.3	19 236	19 360	0.6	3.2	2 228	1 846	108	7 976	3.8	2.48	13.9	26.2
Boyd	13.6	9.0	7.6	50.3	51 096	49 752	-2.6	-0.4	5 526	5 509	-1 025	19 787	-1.1	2.39	12.7	28.2
Boyle	13.4	8.5	7.7	51.3	25 590	27 697	8.2	2.7	2 943	2 819	1 604	11 075	4.7	2.36	12.8	28.4
Bracken	12.5	7.9	5.8	50.2	7 766	8 279	6.6	2.5	1 071	783	141	3 317	2.8	2.55	11.0	24.7
Breathitt	13.9	8.1	5.4	50.0	15 703	16 100	2.5	-13.8	1 642	1 722	-360	5 494	-11.0	2.47	13.4	26.9
Breckinridge	14.4	9.3	6.3	50.1	16 312	18 648	14.3	7.6	2 125	1 889	251	7 827	6.9	2.52	9.7	25.1
Bullitt	12.3	7.2	3.9	50.5	47 567	61 236	28.7	21.4	7 025	3 737	8 142	27 673	24.8	2.67	11.9	19.1
Butler	12.8	9.2	6.6	49.9	11 245	13 010	15.7	-2.5	1 527	1 221	88	5 057	0.0	2.47	11.2	25.1
Caldwell	14.7	9.9	7.9	51.8	13 232	13 060	-1.3	-0.6	1 254	1 553	183	5 393	-0.7	2.38	11.9	27.7
Calloway	11.5	8.6	6.5	51.8	30 735	34 177	11.2	8.8	3 320	3 189	2 257	15 530	12.0	2.20	8.8	33.6
Campbell	11.8	6.8	6.0	51.0	83 866	88 616	5.7	1.9	10 748	7 790	-2 643	36 069	3.8	2.42	11.9	30.1
Carlisle	13.6	9.6	9.3	51.2	5 238	5 351	2.2	-4.6	587	608	-89	2 116	-4.2	2.38	10.1	27.4
Carroll	12.1	7.2	5.7	49.1	9 292	10 155	9.3	6.5	1 431	1 060	239	4 061	3.1	2.58	13.6	25.0
Carter	13.0	8.9	5.9	50.2	24 340	26 889	10.5	3.1	3 306	2 691	-690	10 760	4.0	2.52	11.6	24.6
Casey	14.0	9.4	6.7	51.2	14 211	15 447	8.7	3.3	1 738	1 685	1 085	6 351	1.5	2.44	11.3	28.9
Christian	9.0	5.5	4.7	49.3	68 941	72 265	4.8	2.3	14 111	5 542	-7 575	26 144	5.2	2.62	16.3	25.5
Clark	13.3	7.9	6.3	51.2	29 496	33 144	12.4	7.4	4 045	3 003	2 179	14 267	9.6	2.46	13.6	25.4

1. No spouse present.

Table B. States and Counties — Population, Vital Statistics, Medicare, and Crime

STATE County	Persons in group quarters, 2010	Daytime population, 2006–2010 Number	Daytime population, 2006–2010 Employment/residence ratio	Births, average 2006–2008 Total	Births, average 2006–2008 Rate[1]	Deaths, average 2006–2008 Number	Deaths, average 2006–2008 Rate[1]	Persons under 65 with no health insurance, 2009 Number	Persons under 65 with no health insurance, 2009 Percent	Medicare, 2011 Eligible for Medicare	Medicare, 2011 Enrolled in Medicare Advantage	Medicare, 2011 Enrolled in a Medicare prescription drug plan	Serious crimes known to police,[2] 2010 Total Number	Serious crimes known to police,[2] 2010 Total Rate[3]
	32	33	34	35	36	37	38	39	40	41	42	43	44	45
KANSAS—Cont'd														
Neosho	450	17 091	1.1	D	D	207	12.8	1 992	15.3	3 355	161	2 153	472	2 859
Ness	70	3 252	1.1	D	D	49	16.7	328	16.2	766	19	564	21	676
Norton	822	5 998	1.1	D	D	73	13.4	760	17.9	1 132	62	667	55	970
Osage	194	12 148	0.5	D	D	177	10.7	1 722	13.0	3 268	202	1 706	210	1 353
Osborne	100	3 672	0.9	D	D	66	17.1	502	17.7	1 018	14	650	NA	NA
Ottawa	98	5 072	0.6	D	D	73	12.1	676	14.0	1 219	109	705	134	2 200
Pawnee	1 026	7 403	1.2	D	D	80	12.5	892	17.2	1 328	27	896	139	1 993
Phillips	68	5 688	1.0	D	D	78	14.4	649	16.1	1 327	23	872	37	656
Pottawatomie	299	19 051	0.8	D	D	169	8.7	2 066	12.1	3 109	220	1 672	394	1 824
Pratt	380	9 905	1.0	D	D	121	12.8	1 067	14.4	1 966	57	1 348	298	3 086
Rawlins	40	2 708	1.1	D	D	44	17.3	339	19.5	710	D	433	27	1 072
Reno	3 129	63 105	1.0	857	13.5	705	11.1	8 125	15.8	12 720	761	7 870	3 654	5 783
Republic	103	4 941	0.9	D	D	71	14.4	573	16.8	1 394	82	886	57	1 145
Rice	648	9 599	0.9	D	D	129	12.7	1 398	17.3	2 002	71	1 305	115	1 141
Riley	9 127	71 258	1.1	1 064	15.7	297	4.4	8 097	12.7	6 054	330	3 130	1 797	2 527
Rooks	72	5 061	0.9	D	D	69	13.3	671	17.3	1 212	18	769	29	560
Rush	67	3 105	0.9	D	D	50	15.5	360	15.5	863	24	566	42	1 270
Russell	89	6 712	0.9	D	D	99	14.7	865	17.4	1 743	32	1 141	160	2 296
Saline	1 465	57 598	1.1	818	15.0	571	10.5	6 631	14.6	9 603	1 060	5 404	2 692	4 877
Scott	105	4 891	1.0	D	D	58	12.5	632	17.1	932	11	678	83	1 682
Sedgwick	7 252	507 980	1.1	8 155	17.1	3 836	8.0	65 077	15.4	70 542	10 140	36 876	24 171	4 850
Seward	476	23 847	1.1	539	23.3	134	5.8	5 170	25.0	2 242	64	1 330	765	3 333
Shawnee	4 397	186 498	1.1	2 584	14.9	1 687	9.7	20 775	14.1	32 586	1 919	16 731	9 532	5 401
Sheridan	33	2 422	0.9	D	D	29	11.6	317	17.0	556	14	326	17	665
Sherman	102	6 047	1.0	D	D	76	12.6	772	16.6	1 266	32	862	51	849
Smith	56	3 882	1.0	D	D	63	16.0	456	17.0	1 108	31	662	18	467
Stafford	69	4 192	0.9	D	D	64	14.5	673	21.1	936	26	610	69	1 555
Stanton	47	2 195	1.0	D	D	19	8.6	450	25.5	357	D	257	17	761
Stevens	72	5 103	0.8	D	D	47	9.2	912	20.8	804	29	466	NA	NA
Sumner	409	20 359	0.7	D	D	276	11.5	2 628	13.5	4 443	474	2 595	578	2 528
Thomas	353	7 761	1.0	D	D	78	10.6	847	14.0	1 309	31	859	188	2 380
Trego	64	2 938	1.0	D	D	47	16.0	367	16.6	765	D	463	20	666
Wabaunsee	90	5 272	0.5	D	D	68	9.9	731	13.0	1 281	86	615	100	1 607
Wallace	19	1 373	0.9	D	D	17	11.8	247	22.4	314	19	206	1	67
Washington	114	5 410	0.9	D	D	85	14.6	755	17.8	1 532	74	975	18	310
Wichita	26	2 210	1.0	D	D	21	9.6	377	22.1	427	D	300	38	1 701
Wilson	121	9 606	1.0	D	D	143	14.6	1 213	16.2	2 217	72	1 439	154	1 637
Woodson	39	2 946	0.7	D	D	58	17.1	446	18.4	802	52	502	93	2 811
Wyandotte	1 335	170 440	1.2	2 894	18.7	1 387	9.0	28 462	21.2	21 682	5 828	8 268	9 136	5 800
KENTUCKY	125 870	4 300 530	1.0	58 664	13.8	40 507	9.5	601 743	16.5	786 882	134 283	426 045	121 237	2 794
Adair	1 055	17 003	0.8	D	D	169	9.5	3 391	22.8	3 833	374	2 499	68	364
Allen	197	17 125	0.6	D	D	186	9.8	2 748	17.3	3 870	459	2 351	144	722
Anderson	108	15 464	0.5	D	D	169	8.0	2 659	14.3	3 559	658	1 740	173	808
Ballard	127	7 620	0.8	D	D	106	12.8	1 087	16.6	1 781	167	960	209	2 534
Barren	702	42 040	1.0	555	13.5	438	10.6	5 870	17.1	8 727	1 347	5 235	539	1 278
Bath	103	9 764	0.6	D	D	138	11.8	1 875	19.2	2 451	525	1 427	NA	NA
Bell	952	30 287	1.2	392	13.4	370	12.7	4 881	20.3	6 689	670	4 406	764	2 663
Boone	835	126 906	1.2	1 745	15.5	663	5.9	12 184	11.7	15 199	4 292	6 203	3 322	2 796
Bourbon	236	19 039	0.9	263	13.3	190	9.6	3 072	18.8	3 827	835	1 844	330	1 706
Boyd	2 338	57 658	1.4	617	12.6	593	12.2	6 568	16.4	11 245	1 516	5 313	1 814	3 662
Boyle	2 301	32 010	1.3	D	D	293	10.2	4 081	16.9	5 868	771	3 185	714	2 579
Bracken	41	6 677	0.5	D	D	88	10.2	1 261	17.3	1 586	305	904	120	1 529
Breathitt	322	13 487	0.8	D	D	177	11.2	2 581	19.5	3 359	364	2 279	NA	NA
Breckinridge	301	16 712	0.6	D	D	218	11.4	3 098	19.4	4 142	689	2 172	56	279
Bullitt	340	55 664	0.5	775	10.5	433	5.9	9 749	14.7	11 945	2 877	5 857	1 464	1 970
Butler	203	10 824	0.6	D	D	138	10.4	2 207	19.7	2 675	472	1 518	28	221
Caldwell	148	12 461	0.9	D	D	158	12.3	1 780	17.2	3 156	248	1 905	302	2 326
Calloway	2 952	37 311	1.0	D	D	346	9.6	5 724	19.2	6 883	938	3 945	1 273	3 423
Campbell	2 963	74 891	0.7	1 158	13.3	804	9.3	9 898	13.2	14 049	4 073	5 790	2 982	3 301
Carlisle	60	4 277	0.6	D	D	73	14.1	799	19.2	1 175	81	698	15	294
Carroll	325	13 216	1.6	D	D	106	10.0	1 618	17.8	2 041	393	1 029	92	851
Carter	626	24 667	0.7	D	D	287	10.5	4 310	18.6	5 811	765	3 443	174	628
Casey	480	14 119	0.7	D	D	182	11.2	3 194	23.5	3 419	307	2 254	135	846
Christian	5 389	92 510	1.7	1 522	20.1	592	7.8	12 569	18.0	9 830	1 052	5 719	2 105	2 910
Clark	458	33 883	0.9	D	D	337	9.5	4 917	16.1	6 917	1 313	3 062	1 124	3 156

1. Per 1,000 estimated resident population.   2. Data for serious crimes have not been adjusted for underreporting; this may affect comparability between geographic areas and over time.   3. Per 100,000 population estimated by the FBI.

Table B. States and Counties — Crime, Education, Money Income, and Poverty

STATE County	Serious crimes known to police,[1] 2010 (cont.) Rate[2]		School enrollment and attainment, 2006-2010				Local government expenditures,[5] 2008-2009		Per capita income[6] (dollars)	Households Median income			Median house-hold income (dollars)	Percent below poverty level		
	Violent	Property	Enrollment[3] Total	Per-cent private	High school graduate or less	Bachelor's degree or more	Total current expenditures (mil dol)	Current expenditures per student (dollars)		Dollars	Percent change, 2000 to 2006-2010 (constant 2010 dollars)	Percent with income of $200,000 or more		All persons	Children under 18 years	Children 5 to 17 years in families
	46	47	48	49	50	51	52	53	54	55	56	57	58	59	60	61
KANSAS—Cont'd																
Neosho	224	2 634	4 950	6.3	45.9	16.2	24.9	9 994	18 683	36 702	-9.9	0.8	38 363	16.4	23.7	21.1
Ness	129	547	637	16.0	46.4	18.9	4.9	10 617	27 622	47 639	16.3	3.3	51 717	10.3	15.4	13.4
Norton	53	917	1 036	9.7	46.0	17.3	10.4	11 187	19 080	32 016	-18.6	0.2	40 386	13.9	18.0	16.2
Osage	187	1 166	4 012	7.9	49.8	19.4	29.1	9 929	22 697	48 594	1.2	1.6	45 221	12.1	17.3	14.5
Osborne	NA	NA	830	6.9	51.0	18.0	6.3	12 895	22 536	34 797	-5.7	2.4	36 519	14.4	22.0	19.3
Ottawa	148	2 052	1 445	7.5	41.6	19.6	13.3	10 341	22 665	50 814	5.6	1.6	53 086	9.9	13.1	11.2
Pawnee	316	1 678	1 507	2.4	46.2	16.9	12.7	12 220	17 927	40 048	-10.1	0.9	42 658	14.1	17.8	15.2
Phillips	35	620	1 257	3.4	46.8	17.1	9.5	10 916	21 870	44 381	0.1	0.1	42 071	11.4	16.3	15.2
Pottawatomie	185	1 639	5 552	14.5	38.3	28.4	36.8	9 614	25 157	53 430	5.0	2.5	52 861	9.0	11.6	11.2
Pratt	362	2 724	2 595	11.5	40.0	22.7	16.0	11 365	23 585	43 583	-3.1	1.7	43 987	11.3	17.0	15.7
Rawlins	40	1 032	488	1.4	41.6	19.8	4.0	12 162	22 895	39 797	-2.1	0.8	40 211	13.0	18.9	17.8
Reno	464	5 319	15 488	11.1	44.4	18.8	97.6	9 957	22 149	41 431	-7.9	1.4	41 717	14.6	20.8	18.8
Republic	181	964	868	6.0	40.6	18.6	8.6	11 166	24 731	38 286	-0.9	2.6	38 331	12.3	16.5	15.1
Rice	129	1 012	2 538	20.9	47.6	20.9	20.9	11 759	19 316	43 164	-4.4	0.5	41 687	13.8	18.0	15.4
Riley	287	2 240	30 718	4.6	27.0	42.3	68.1	9 636	19 999	39 257	-3.2	1.8	45 523	21.2	17.7	17.6
Rooks	97	463	1 142	8.6	46.6	20.4	10.8	11 251	23 435	37 861	-1.8	1.7	38 487	14.4	19.2	17.5
Rush	242	1 028	568	1.4	47.9	16.2	6.0	12 340	23 608	39 435	-0.4	1.4	38 595	13.4	22.2	20.0
Russell	402	1 894	1 337	4.9	45.8	20.4	9.8	10 225	23 243	36 135	-2.6	3.0	36 575	15.4	21.4	18.5
Saline	409	4 468	13 549	12.1	44.3	23.6	94.3	10 271	23 669	45 162	-4.4	1.8	43 927	17.2	28.3	23.8
Scott	304	1 378	1 020	9.6	41.6	20.3	9.1	10 252	28 872	68 341	13.7	3.9	46 925	9.2	14.0	13.2
Sedgwick	673	4 177	136 325	16.6	41.1	27.5	766.7	9 945	25 297	47 848	-11.1	2.6	45 996	15.3	20.4	17.5
Seward	462	2 871	5 772	4.0	63.7	13.5	48.9	9 026	18 083	41 373	-11.1	1.2	43 449	15.6	22.4	21.2
Shawnee	439	4 962	45 355	15.6	41.0	28.9	265.0	9 752	25 705	47 464	-8.6	2.5	45 359	17.5	26.0	21.3
Sheridan	0	665	559	6.3	40.5	21.8	6.0	10 761	24 933	46 739	10.0	2.5	46 699	13.1	19.8	18.2
Sherman	100	749	1 306	3.6	43.2	19.1	9.6	10 172	22 651	41 570	0.4	1.2	37 927	16.9	25.6	23.4
Smith	78	389	647	2.2	51.9	14.9	8.8	12 374	23 644	39 836	10.4	1.9	38 120	13.9	19.2	16.9
Stafford	270	1 285	951	5.2	44.7	20.7	11.5	11 915	23 171	39 375	0.0	2.8	39 990	13.8	21.4	18.0
Stanton	89	671	507	10.8	59.4	14.2	5.3	11 707	19 196	49 612	-2.5	1.0	49 580	12.3	18.2	16.8
Stevens	NA	NA	1 349	8.2	49.4	13.9	13.9	10 777	21 633	50 517	-4.6	1.2	50 070	11.5	18.7	17.4
Sumner	210	2 318	6 436	12.2	45.4	18.7	58.0	9 720	23 114	49 562	-0.7	2.0	47 113	12.1	16.4	14.4
Thomas	241	2 139	2 318	5.7	39.9	23.4	10.8	10 424	23 883	47 033	0.3	2.0	45 797	10.5	12.3	10.9
Trego	100	566	542	10.9	48.5	22.2	5.1	11 266	22 095	39 655	5.5	0.5	40 178	11.6	15.7	14.1
Wabaunsee	273	1 334	1 758	9.7	47.4	21.8	11.1	11 399	23 072	52 133	-1.3	0.8	50 740	9.3	13.4	11.8
Wallace	0	67	294	4.8	45.6	23.4	4.1	13 248	23 269	43 953	5.2	2.1	43 553	12.6	15.8	13.9
Washington	34	276	1 240	16.5	49.0	18.2	9.8	11 437	20 577	39 698	6.8	0.4	40 956	9.9	15.8	14.2
Wichita	269	1 432	542	0.9	52.0	15.9	4.9	10 545	20 375	44 318	4.6	0.4	45 019	12.8	21.6	20.0
Wilson	234	1 403	2 197	7.2	59.0	10.7	18.4	10 473	18 708	39 301	4.3	0.4	37 078	16.0	24.5	22.8
Woodson	242	2 569	558	7.0	52.8	12.8	5.2	11 952	23 986	30 385	-5.3	1.7	33 134	17.2	28.1	25.6
Wyandotte	548	5 253	41 836	12.3	57.9	15.2	298.2	10 458	18 827	38 503	-10.0	0.6	37 805	23.9	34.7	33.1
KENTUCKY	243	2 551	1 077 319	14.9	53.4	20.3	5 865.0	8 756	22 515	41 576	-2.5	2.1	40 089	18.9	26.1	23.7
Adair	16	348	4 541	26.1	66.5	14.4	23.2	9 124	15 790	29 834	-2.1	1.1	30 177	24.0	35.4	32.7
Allen	70	651	4 549	6.1	65.8	10.6	23.9	7 855	16 897	35 247	-10.9	0.2	35 617	22.3	31.0	27.0
Anderson	103	705	5 407	8.7	53.6	17.3	31.4	7 837	24 516	55 506	-3.5	1.0	52 660	12.8	18.4	15.9
Ballard	73	2 461	1 911	11.5	59.6	10.7	12.9	9 069	23 001	41 228	1.3	2.1	41 776	14.4	22.5	19.9
Barren	81	1 197	9 693	7.2	63.5	15.0	65.4	8 821	20 067	38 374	-3.0	1.6	38 000	19.4	28.9	26.8
Bath	NA	NA	2 730	9.9	66.0	13.2	17.3	8 510	15 487	30 458	-7.6	0.8	32 091	27.8	38.1	35.4
Bell	125	2 537	6 528	12.9	68.6	11.3	49.6	9 450	14 627	24 724	2.5	0.7	26 911	30.2	41.9	39.4
Boone	107	2 689	32 039	19.4	40.4	28.2	157.5	7 874	28 520	66 549	-1.9	3.4	64 005	9.2	11.5	10.0
Bourbon	119	1 587	4 796	14.0	57.4	17.4	31.6	8 825	21 355	40 849	-7.9	1.0	39 219	17.0	24.7	21.6
Boyd	208	3 454	10 839	10.3	52.8	15.8	64.2	8 599	22 064	38 802	-6.4	2.0	38 029	19.1	28.4	26.2
Boyle	202	2 377	7 411	27.5	52.5	23.3	43.4	9 572	22 534	40 720	-8.8	2.5	39 241	16.6	23.2	21.4
Bracken	13	1 517	2 004	5.2	70.6	11.6	12.3	7 803	18 671	38 481	-12.7	0.6	42 056	16.5	24.7	20.7
Breathitt	NA	NA	2 929	4.0	73.0	10.4	26.8	9 905	16 442	19 906	-17.9	1.3	28 045	28.3	38.7	38.4
Breckinridge	30	249	4 601	15.4	70.0	7.8	28.4	9 515	17 757	37 395	-3.3	0.7	35 428	20.7	29.6	26.6
Bullitt	90	1 880	18 902	16.0	58.5	11.1	96.1	7 540	22 791	51 526	-9.8	0.8	51 409	10.5	15.3	13.6
Butler	16	205	2 682	4.1	68.6	7.8	17.7	8 218	17 236	33 703	-9.5	0.8	35 162	19.5	29.3	27.5
Caldwell	177	2 149	3 038	6.2	63.2	14.0	17.2	8 514	19 498	35 289	-2.9	0.4	36 255	18.8	28.7	26.8
Calloway	102	3 321	12 300	6.6	47.2	28.2	40.0	8 304	20 951	39 194	2.7	1.6	39 038	17.2	22.5	21.3
Campbell	187	3 114	25 252	19.4	47.6	26.3	105.6	9 228	27 096	51 482	-3.0	2.7	47 341	13.0	17.2	15.8
Carlisle	0	294	1 043	15.1	65.0	10.6	7.3	8 998	17 260	33 909	-11.0	0.3	38 182	14.4	24.6	22.4
Carroll	55	795	2 278	3.0	66.1	9.3	18.3	9 226	21 845	43 440	-4.5	1.6	42 192	22.3	36.8	35.3
Carter	36	592	6 868	15.8	67.8	10.2	41.9	8 380	18 147	32 424	-3.1	1.6	34 303	23.2	34.4	31.3
Casey	38	809	3 572	10.9	70.0	9.5	21.2	8 721	14 252	26 592	-2.7	0.1	26 612	27.8	40.8	38.4
Christian	241	2 669	18 772	12.5	53.0	13.7	76.8	8 394	18 476	37 061	-6.1	1.1	36 542	19.7	29.0	28.7
Clark	230	2 926	8 035	11.6	55.6	17.7	43.7	7 843	23 966	46 575	-7.9	1.8	45 016	17.4	26.2	22.2

1. Data for serious crimes have not been adjusted for underreporting; this may affect comparability between geographic areas and over time. 2. Per 100,000 population estimated by the FBI. 3. All persons 3 years old and over enrolled in nursery school through college. 4. Persons 25 years old and over. 5. Elementary and secondary education expenditures. 6. Based on population estimated by the American Community Survey, 2006-2010.

Table B. States and Counties — **Personal Income**

STATE County	Total (mil dol)	Percent change, 2008–2009	Per capita[1] Dollars	Per capita[1] Rank	Wages and salaries[2] (mil dol)	Proprietors' income (mil dol)	Dividends, interest, and rent (mil dol)	Transfer payments Total	Govt payments to individuals Total	Social Security	Medical payments	Income maintenance	Unemployment insurance
	62	63	64	65	66	67	68	69	70	71	72	73	74
KANSAS—Cont'd													
Neosho	497	-2.8	30 991	1 756	275	52	78	136	133	45	57	13	9
Ness	154	-5.5	54 318	61	56	42	31	27	26	11	13	1	1
Norton	188	0.0	35 322	977	105	30	36	36	35	15	15	2	1
Osage	495	0.8	30 748	1 812	120	13	74	119	116	44	42	10	10
Osborne	141	-4.1	36 530	811	48	38	30	33	32	14	14	2	1
Ottawa	185	-2.9	30 980	1 760	50	21	31	39	38	16	14	2	2
Pawnee	228	-3.6	36 663	794	140	30	35	42	41	19	16	3	1
Phillips	219	-1.8	41 544	362	96	38	56	45	44	18	19	3	2
Pottawatomie	718	-0.6	35 924	898	389	60	117	109	105	42	42	7	6
Pratt	360	-4.4	38 744	561	184	55	74	75	74	28	33	4	2
Rawlins	112	-2.8	46 059	168	34	38	21	22	21	10	10	1	0
Reno	2 064	0.4	32 577	1 408	1 191	116	397	483	472	181	197	44	22
Republic	177	0.5	36 803	771	72	40	33	40	39	18	16	2	1
Rice	291	-3.5	28 833	2 225	140	22	52	72	71	29	29	5	3
Riley	2 879	3.1	40 358	430	1 338	56	397	258	246	82	87	24	9
Rooks	181	-3.0	36 399	829	79	29	35	42	42	16	19	2	2
Rush	117	-5.8	37 174	726	43	23	22	30	29	12	13	2	1
Russell	233	-2.9	35 382	967	110	22	61	61	60	24	28	4	1
Saline	2 107	-0.6	38 752	560	1 372	245	441	368	359	135	147	33	18
Scott	160	-1.5	35 059	1 010	82	17	39	26	25	14	8	2	0
Sedgwick	19 297	-2.0	39 312	505	14 068	1 912	3 307	3 214	3 125	1 051	1 220	369	296
Seward	679	-3.2	29 492	2 094	506	95	89	106	102	31	45	16	4
Shawnee	6 705	1.2	38 039	633	5 056	317	1 241	1 321	1 289	439	508	125	63
Sheridan	124	0.3	50 750	90	38	49	23	17	16	8	7	1	0
Sherman	237	0.8	40 399	425	97	64	35	51	50	17	25	4	1
Smith	153	-2.4	40 796	399	47	36	38	32	31	15	13	2	1
Stafford	168	-1.0	38 759	559	54	39	34	38	37	14	18	3	1
Stanton	95	-0.4	45 293	190	39	25	24	12	12	5	5	1	0
Stevens	210	-1.1	40 905	389	86	63	41	28	27	12	11	2	1
Sumner	869	-3.1	37 002	751	252	69	112	177	173	63	68	13	14
Thomas	287	2.0	39 102	528	157	53	51	48	46	19	20	3	1
Trego	107	-4.6	36 590	801	47	18	20	24	23	9	11	1	0
Wabaunsee	236	-2.8	34 436	1 105	62	14	38	44	43	18	15	2	3
Wallace	64	1.2	45 695	182	19	24	11	12	11	4	6	1	0
Washington	182	-3.0	32 060	1 514	73	20	35	45	44	19	19	2	1
Wichita	95	-2.8	44 824	206	40	30	15	14	13	6	6	1	0
Wilson	306	-2.6	32 315	1 455	157	32	53	85	83	29	34	8	7
Woodson	95	0.3	29 474	2 099	27	18	17	30	29	11	13	2	2
Wyandotte	4 463	1.2	28 779	2 237	4 738	181	424	1 161	1 133	300	515	159	71
KENTUCKY	139 166	0.5	32 258	X	90 023	9 289	20 479	33 296	32 513	10 645	13 329	3 732	1 752
Adair	457	3.3	25 321	2 826	176	23	58	168	164	45	80	17	8
Allen	484	-1.4	25 509	2 805	163	55	58	147	143	50	58	15	10
Anderson	641	1.3	29 414	2 114	194	19	83	126	122	51	40	11	9
Ballard	297	5.4	36 378	831	169	34	29	82	81	25	41	6	3
Barren	1 142	0.0	27 366	2 505	662	79	185	321	313	109	128	36	19
Bath	281	1.7	24 191	2 949	71	9	30	96	94	29	37	15	6
Bell	710	4.7	24 513	2 914	394	23	77	323	318	84	151	51	10
Boone	3 945	0.2	33 268	1 298	3 694	154	506	588	566	222	194	41	46
Bourbon	608	-1.5	30 812	1 799	333	25	102	140	137	51	55	14	7
Boyd	1 619	1.3	33 363	1 286	1 489	94	233	467	458	158	195	46	17
Boyle	838	0.1	28 648	2 270	638	28	176	221	216	79	84	21	12
Bracken	246	0.2	28 388	2 327	55	9	26	65	63	21	26	7	4
Breathitt	384	3.3	24 635	2 903	145	13	34	173	170	40	79	34	5
Breckinridge	500	1.3	26 258	2 676	127	33	71	156	153	53	61	17	9
Bullitt	2 115	0.4	27 950	2 410	682	83	219	427	413	171	127	39	35
Butler	308	1.6	23 089	3 029	99	19	36	107	105	34	45	12	6
Caldwell	376	0.6	29 221	2 146	169	31	53	115	113	41	46	11	6
Calloway	1 047	1.5	28 809	2 230	634	84	173	262	256	96	96	20	12
Campbell	3 204	-0.8	36 235	859	1 278	95	500	594	578	203	224	50	37
Carlisle	147	2.7	28 284	2 349	29	22	21	44	44	17	18	3	2
Carroll	350	4.5	32 681	1 387	324	13	37	83	81	27	34	9	6
Carter	648	1.6	24 205	2 947	220	26	65	239	234	74	91	35	14
Casey	369	3.0	22 376	3 057	122	24	44	137	134	39	60	18	6
Christian	2 299	-1.0	28 403	2 324	4 863	118	298	468	456	129	184	66	29
Clark	1 164	-0.1	32 188	1 488	611	96	189	260	254	93	95	29	15

1. Based on the resident population estimated as of July 1 of the year shown.   2. Includes supplements to wages and salaries.

Table B. States and Counties — Earnings, Social Security, and Housing

STATE County	Earnings, 2009									Social Security beneficiaries, December 2010		Supplemental Security Income recipients, December 2010	Housing units, 2010	
			Percent by selected industries											
			Goods-related[1]		Service-related and health									
	Total (mil dol)	Farm	Total	Manu-facturing	Information and professional and technical services	Retail trade	Finance, insurance, and real estate	Health care and social services	Govern-ment	Number	Rate[2]		Total	Percent change, 2000–2010
	75	76	77	78	79	80	81	82	83	84	85	86	87	88
KANSAS—Cont'd														
Neosho	327	4.3	D	16.3	D	8.3	4.1	D	25.1	3 620	219	384	7 513	0.7
Ness	98	23.8	D	1.2	D	5.3	D	0.8	18.5	845	272	26	1 740	-5.2
Norton	135	16.8	D	6.4	3.0	8.1	D	8.8	28.7	1 260	222	56	2 542	-4.9
Osage	133	3.1	D	6.6	D	6.3	D	7.0	39.3	3 700	227	334	7 503	6.9
Osborne	85	25.0	D	7.1	D	6.1	4.9	6.3	15.6	1 175	305	50	2 206	-8.8
Ottawa	71	17.1	D	4.2	3.9	4.0	D	D	26.1	1 325	218	78	2 779	0.9
Pawnee	170	15.0	D	1.2	D	3.6	3.9	5.8	51.2	1 460	209	89	3 152	1.2
Phillips	134	14.6	20.3	14.8	D	3.7	D	7.8	21.9	1 505	267	76	3 049	-1.3
Pottawatomie	448	1.3	30.5	21.2	D	7.1	4.5	D	12.8	3 470	161	191	8 626	18.0
Pratt	239	9.5	20.3	2.1	4.0	8.5	5.1	14.1	20.8	2 120	220	136	4 514	-2.6
Rawlins	72	33.0	D	1.3	D	3.8	D	5.1	18.0	780	310	39	1 458	-6.8
Reno	1 307	2.4	20.2	13.0	5.4	7.8	4.3	18.1	19.3	14 060	218	1 266	28 274	2.3
Republic	112	28.4	D	7.6	2.9	5.2	6.4	11.3	18.6	1 500	301	75	2 877	-7.6
Rice	162	9.0	18.6	9.5	3.8	5.3	4.9	D	25.7	2 260	224	152	4 548	-1.3
Riley	1 394	0.6	D	1.7	5.7	6.4	4.8	10.8	44.6	6 530	92	508	28 212	20.4
Rooks	108	15.9	12.8	4.7	D	7.5	4.1	3.7	24.9	1 370	264	70	2 768	0.4
Rush	66	27.3	D	14.3	D	D	D	D	21.3	940	284	64	1 869	-3.1
Russell	132	7.4	32.0	16.3	4.5	5.6	4.3	10.8	19.2	1 915	275	127	3 910	1.0
Saline	1 617	1.2	D	18.9	5.9	7.3	4.2	14.0	13.5	10 680	192	955	24 101	6.2
Scott	99	18.5	D	0.8	3.8	5.3	D	D	17.2	1 040	211	52	2 193	-4.3
Sedgwick	15 979	0.1	36.7	29.5	6.3	5.6	3.6	11.6	13.5	79 060	159	10 017	211 593	10.7
Seward	601	2.7	D	D	D	8.1	3.3	D	19.0	2 470	108	342	8 061	0.4
Shawnee	5 373	0.2	12.6	7.3	7.8	5.2	9.9	15.6	25.7	34 410	193	4 520	79 140	7.3
Sheridan	88	44.4	D	0.3	D	5.4	5.5	1.9	13.3	605	237	14	1 265	0.2
Sherman	161	32.5	D	2.7	3.4	7.2	5.5	4.1	21.2	1 395	232	127	3 148	-1.1
Smith	83	35.8	D	4.1	1.4	7.0	D	9.4	17.7	1 215	315	44	2 232	-4.0
Stafford	94	38.3	8.1	2.4	D	1.8	3.9	D	26.0	1 045	236	53	2 319	-5.7
Stanton	64	42.3	D	D	D	2.5	D	D	20.9	355	159	17	990	-1.7
Stevens	149	37.7	D	D	D	2.9	D	D	21.9	855	149	45	2 306	1.8
Sumner	321	12.7	17.9	13.8	4.8	6.0	4.8	D	26.2	4 880	202	418	10 865	-0.1
Thomas	210	22.7	D	1.4	4.4	8.6	4.8	D	17.0	1 425	180	75	3 536	-0.7
Trego	65	20.9	D	1.8	5.8	6.2	D	1.8	27.6	835	278	33	1 682	-2.4
Wabaunsee	76	6.4	D	10.7	D	2.8	D	D	25.7	1 465	208	98	3 227	6.4
Wallace	43	51.2	D	D	D	0.8	D	D	14.6	335	226	14	781	-1.3
Washington	93	24.5	D	4.6	D	3.7	D	4.7	29.8	1 635	282	67	2 955	-6.0
Wichita	70	47.8	5.6	3.6	D	2.4	D	D	17.7	445	199	17	1 054	-5.8
Wilson	189	9.0	39.9	31.8	D	8.9	D	5.5	21.9	2 460	261	256	4 682	-5.2
Woodson	45	13.3	D	D	D	5.7	3.1	3.6	21.2	905	273	67	2 022	-2.6
Wyandotte	4 920	0.0	D	17.6	3.1	5.1	2.5	14.8	22.5	24 500	156	4 877	66 747	1.3
KENTUCKY	99 312	1.1	21.4	13.9	7.5	6.4	6.0	12.0	22.0	894 473	206	192 076	1 927 164	10.1
Adair	200	1.3	D	6.2	D	9.0	5.9	D	23.1	4 420	237	1 059	8 568	10.0
Allen	218	3.4	D	12.8	D	18.1	3.9	D	17.2	4 485	225	897	9 307	15.5
Anderson	214	-1.3	D	28.9	3.7	9.1	4.6	D	22.4	4 105	192	437	9 127	17.7
Ballard	203	11.2	D	30.1	6.3	3.1	1.7	2.6	10.2	2 065	250	262	3 885	1.3
Barren	741	1.9	30.6	24.0	5.5	10.0	3.1	15.5	15.2	9 925	235	1 917	19 188	12.2
Bath	80	2.8	D	8.6	D	5.5	5.7	5.9	33.1	2 885	249	968	5 405	8.2
Bell	417	-0.1	29.2	7.3	D	10.1	4.5	14.6	22.6	7 605	265	3 212	13 154	-1.4
Boone	3 847	0.0	D	16.2	5.6	6.7	5.8	5.1	10.0	16 995	143	1 523	46 154	38.4
Bourbon	358	8.4	D	31.5	D	6.3	3.7	D	14.3	4 385	219	656	8 927	6.9
Boyd	1 583	-0.1	D	15.0	6.3	7.3	3.0	24.2	12.0	12 580	254	2 466	21 803	-0.8
Boyle	665	-0.1	D	22.2	D	7.7	3.7	20.9	14.2	6 520	229	1 139	12 312	7.8
Bracken	64	0.6	D	D	D	4.3	4.2	4.0	29.0	1 880	221	321	3 840	3.4
Breathitt	158	-0.1	D	D	2.9	9.4	4.1	21.1	35.1	3 805	274	2 293	6 231	-8.5
Breckinridge	160	4.6	17.9	6.2	3.3	8.9	5.8	D	26.0	4 800	239	958	10 630	7.5
Bullitt	765	0.0	D	16.5	9.0	6.7	3.2	4.6	18.7	14 000	188	1 650	29 318	26.6
Butler	118	7.4	D	22.0	1.9	5.3	4.1	D	24.4	3 110	245	636	5 877	1.1
Caldwell	200	5.0	28.1	23.1	D	11.7	4.2	D	20.6	3 485	268	592	6 292	2.7
Calloway	719	3.4	22.8	17.5	4.2	8.7	2.8	5.9	31.9	7 830	211	832	18 065	12.4
Campbell	1 373	-0.1	D	11.3	7.2	8.0	5.0	12.0	23.8	15 475	171	2 014	39 523	7.1
Carlisle	50	31.6	10.2	3.7	D	6.3	8.2	4.6	23.0	1 355	265	169	2 441	-2.0
Carroll	336	-0.4	55.5	51.3	D	5.6	1.2	D	10.0	2 435	225	494	4 696	5.8
Carter	246	0.3	18.4	10.5	3.6	10.7	4.3	D	26.3	6 730	243	1 767	12 311	6.8
Casey	146	1.6	D	18.2	2.4	7.9	D	11.8	22.1	3 895	244	1 151	7 487	3.4
Christian	4 981	0.9	D	4.8	3.5	1.9	1.0	2.8	78.1	11 570	156	2 584	29 459	8.3
Clark	707	0.5	D	24.5	8.1	7.1	3.7	10.2	11.7	7 860	221	1 364	15 706	14.2

1. Includes mining, construction, and manufacturing.   2. Per 1,000 resident population enumerated in the 2010 census.

Table B. States and Counties — Housing, Labor Force, and Employment

STATE County	Total [89]	Percent [90]	Median value[1] [91]	With a mort-gage [92]	Without a mort-gage [93]	Median rent[2] [94]	Median rent as a per-cent of income [95]	Sub-stand-ard units[3] (percent) [96]	Total [97]	Percent change, 2009-2010 [98]	Total [99]	Rate[4] [100]	Total [101]	Manage-ment, business, science and arts [102]	Con-struction, produc-tion, and mainte-nance occu-pations [103]
KANSAS—Cont'd															
Neosho	6 742	77.2	71 100	20.2	14.3	463	24.8	1.1	8 683	-0.1	745	8.6	7 220	30.6	32.0
Ness	1 369	82.6	47 100	18.1	10.0	502	19.7	1.5	1 840	-0.8	61	3.3	1 524	35.8	25.5
Norton	2 221	68.0	51 200	19.1	12.3	465	25.9	1.4	2 823	-1.9	126	4.5	2 720	31.9	25.3
Osage	6 739	79.0	96 400	21.8	13.0	567	24.8	2.7	8 592	-0.4	714	8.3	8 161	30.6	31.1
Osborne	1 726	78.3	39 700	20.2	12.6	465	23.1	1.7	2 340	3.0	109	4.7	2 019	30.2	32.5
Ottawa	2 311	81.8	83 800	19.7	12.9	565	24.0	0.3	3 296	-3.4	188	5.7	3 003	29.1	29.6
Pawnee	2 520	70.9	63 200	23.2	11.2	569	21.6	0.0	3 894	-1.4	168	4.3	2 822	39.4	17.9
Phillips	2 337	79.8	57 400	21.6	11.1	436	15.1	0.8	3 112	-1.7	150	4.8	2 864	36.0	23.5
Pottawatomie	7 764	81.0	138 600	20.6	11.0	625	22.5	2.1	11 301	2.3	594	5.3	10 575	31.5	29.5
Pratt	3 979	70.4	74 500	19.5	13.3	595	24.7	1.0	5 966	-0.2	292	4.9	4 957	32.4	27.1
Rawlins	1 186	74.5	57 600	21.7	11.8	391	22.9	0.4	1 330	0.8	53	4.0	1 365	46.6	16.6
Reno	25 876	71.6	87 500	21.6	12.7	578	25.8	2.2	34 751	-0.6	2 111	6.1	30 316	28.8	27.7
Republic	2 377	81.1	47 800	19.6	12.9	385	18.2	1.5	2 859	-1.3	118	4.1	2 526	34.7	29.2
Rice	4 011	75.5	62 600	19.6	11.0	557	26.1	2.1	5 917	-0.8	289	4.9	4 890	32.1	31.0
Riley	24 838	43.7	154 800	21.6	11.0	759	34.1	5.3	38 620	2.2	1 923	5.0	32 619	39.4	15.9
Rooks	2 401	77.6	62 900	19.3	12.6	454	24.9	0.4	2 711	-3.0	170	6.3	2 583	33.0	30.0
Rush	1 592	79.7	50 500	20.5	11.5	472	19.1	2.4	1 730	1.9	95	5.5	1 677	36.8	22.3
Russell	3 245	75.3	63 300	19.5	13.7	465	23.0	0.3	3 575	-0.6	186	5.2	3 534	28.5	27.1
Saline	21 932	67.8	114 000	20.8	11.1	604	28.2	1.7	30 896	-2.5	1 898	6.1	28 841	28.4	28.0
Scott	2 129	81.8	100 100	22.4	10.3	544	16.4	1.8	2 903	1.1	101	3.5	2 525	37.2	26.3
Sedgwick	190 832	66.9	117 300	21.2	11.2	639	29.1	2.6	253 045	-1.6	21 981	8.7	235 219	33.5	25.4
Seward	7 472	64.4	82 100	22.0	10.5	623	25.4	6.8	11 017	-0.6	519	4.7	10 429	19.9	43.6
Shawnee	73 066	66.8	115 300	21.5	11.7	642	28.3	2.2	95 017	1.6	6 560	6.9	85 725	34.9	20.5
Sheridan	1 104	77.7	81 600	19.6	10.0	533	25.1	1.8	1 652	3.7	49	3.0	1 349	39.6	23.2
Sherman	2 567	71.9	79 300	23.0	11.7	598	24.9	0.6	3 857	1.9	151	3.9	2 903	39.0	25.1
Smith	1 830	81.1	58 400	19.6	13.2	421	21.5	1.5	2 264	0.9	98	4.3	1 957	33.3	26.6
Stafford	1 860	80.9	50 200	19.1	11.9	450	18.6	2.3	2 268	1.6	115	5.1	2 135	36.8	30.1
Stanton	731	74.8	77 500	17.5	10.0	465	22.1	3.3	1 224	3.8	43	3.5	990	31.3	34.3
Stevens	2 061	68.9	78 200	17.7	12.1	638	25.9	4.7	2 368	0.0	110	4.6	2 454	28.0	38.5
Sumner	9 280	77.4	82 400	21.2	11.5	539	26.5	1.4	11 382	-3.6	1 018	8.9	11 641	32.3	29.6
Thomas	3 039	65.1	83 900	20.9	10.0	448	21.2	0.0	4 243	-1.1	173	4.1	4 138	31.2	22.9
Trego	1 276	82.3	69 700	18.8	14.0	481	22.2	1.5	1 897	1.5	70	3.7	1 409	35.3	28.2
Wabaunsee	2 750	83.2	99 400	21.0	13.6	577	23.3	1.6	3 738	-1.6	242	6.5	3 567	34.3	28.9
Wallace	584	83.4	65 300	17.9	12.4	393	12.5	2.7	927	0.5	50	5.4	780	40.9	32.3
Washington	2 496	78.8	53 600	18.2	12.3	383	18.3	2.4	3 401	-1.2	159	4.7	3 092	31.4	32.2
Wichita	856	80.0	76 800	18.4	13.4	601	23.9	3.5	1 227	-3.3	44	3.6	1 155	30.7	30.0
Wilson	3 872	76.2	58 500	20.1	12.7	491	23.7	2.7	5 052	-3.8	530	10.5	4 280	26.7	32.7
Woodson	1 574	73.8	47 800	21.5	14.6	450	26.0	1.6	1 748	-1.7	139	8.0	1 482	26.8	35.4
Wyandotte	57 207	63.2	97 600	26.0	15.4	698	32.1	4.4	69 259	-3.7	7 223	10.4	67 852	22.4	32.3
KENTUCKY	1 676 708	69.9	116 800	21.7	10.8	601	28.6	2.2	2 060 180	-0.9	210 776	10.2	1 871 531	31.4	27.5
Adair	7 272	74.8	80 000	22.6	11.1	464	30.6	3.1	9 442	2.8	990	10.5	6 920	29.0	31.6
Allen	7 811	74.8	89 500	22.5	11.8	513	27.1	2.4	8 654	-2.0	1 086	12.5	7 491	23.3	34.5
Anderson	8 319	76.3	131 900	21.1	10.0	643	26.3	2.5	11 141	0.5	1 168	10.5	10 493	33.3	30.1
Ballard	3 363	83.3	78 100	18.4	10.0	561	26.0	2.5	4 106	-3.2	419	10.2	3 435	27.3	34.2
Barren	16 727	70.3	96 400	19.8	11.8	530	29.0	2.7	19 195	-1.5	2 311	12.0	18 346	29.8	35.1
Bath	4 338	80.6	70 100	28.7	11.5	428	34.1	3.1	5 052	-3.3	719	14.2	4 131	29.9	33.7
Bell	10 902	68.6	64 500	20.7	10.2	399	32.1	3.2	9 361	-6.5	1 279	13.7	9 226	28.4	29.0
Boone	41 612	76.4	175 900	21.6	10.1	797	28.1	1.4	65 035	1.8	6 200	9.5	59 510	34.8	23.0
Bourbon	8 132	61.4	137 700	22.4	11.8	581	28.0	1.1	9 458	-2.9	937	9.9	8 935	28.4	35.6
Boyd	19 542	69.2	93 200	19.3	10.4	533	29.5	1.0	23 062	-1.0	2 064	8.9	19 283	31.3	23.7
Boyle	10 787	69.0	126 700	21.5	11.0	584	29.1	1.4	12 855	-1.3	1 587	12.3	12 001	30.5	29.4
Bracken	3 177	78.6	87 500	22.3	10.9	484	24.2	2.3	4 308	-0.6	485	11.3	3 593	25.8	40.5
Breathitt	5 257	71.7	50 900	22.0	11.7	405	32.4	2.5	5 739	-0.6	672	11.7	4 068	22.6	26.8
Breckinridge	7 474	79.4	80 800	20.5	10.0	479	27.2	4.4	9 619	1.4	1 090	11.3	7 324	24.9	40.4
Bullitt	27 266	81.3	143 000	22.8	11.7	701	26.9	1.8	40 148	-0.3	4 344	10.8	34 577	24.9	33.1
Butler	5 175	79.4	77 700	23.4	10.2	486	29.8	1.8	5 636	2.1	694	12.3	5 123	19.7	49.4
Caldwell	5 261	76.7	72 300	20.4	12.1	512	19.4	0.9	6 940	-0.4	642	9.3	5 201	29.0	33.3
Calloway	14 844	68.4	105 300	21.8	10.0	523	32.9	2.5	17 849	-1.6	1 550	8.7	17 696	32.3	24.5
Campbell	35 300	72.3	146 300	21.6	12.2	672	28.1	1.1	45 633	0.9	4 892	10.7	44 793	35.2	21.6
Carlisle	2 062	84.0	67 400	23.4	12.1	481	22.0	1.4	2 370	0.6	209	8.8	1 978	18.0	43.3
Carroll	4 222	65.3	109 700	20.2	10.0	551	26.5	4.0	5 468	-0.5	751	13.7	4 666	19.1	40.7
Carter	10 577	77.9	74 500	19.1	10.2	531	29.3	2.5	13 713	-0.1	1 704	12.4	10 668	26.9	34.9
Casey	6 012	85.1	71 000	23.4	11.6	438	30.3	5.0	7 248	0.7	804	11.1	6 346	29.2	33.8
Christian	25 923	56.5	95 500	21.9	11.0	683	27.6	3.0	30 097	0.6	3 448	11.5	24 281	26.7	32.4
Clark	14 535	65.2	134 500	21.4	10.4	631	27.1	2.4	17 311	-1.7	1 872	10.8	16 310	31.9	27.5

1. Specified owner-occupied units. 2. Specified renter-occupied units. A value of 10.0 represents 10 percent or less. 3. Overcrowded or lacking complete plumbing facilities. 4. Percent of civilian labor force. 5. Persons 16 years old and over.

Table B. States and Counties — Nonfarm Employment and Agriculture

	Private nonfarm establishments, employment and payroll, 2009									Agriculture, 2007			
	Employment						Annual payroll		Farms			
											Percent with:		
STATE County	Number of establishments	Total	Health care and social assistance	Manufacturing	Retail trade	Finance and insurance	Professional, scientific, and technical services	Total (mil dol)	Average per employee (dollars)	Number	Fewer than 50 acres	500 acres or more	Farm operators whose principal occupation is farming (percent)
	104	105	106	107	108	109	110	111	112	113	114	115	116
KANSAS—Cont'd													
Neosho	491	6 038	1 216	1 288	881	225	133	163	26 992	775	20.0	21.2	36.3
Ness	143	1 003	D	D	114	52	D	30	29 450	521	5.0	52.0	48.8
Norton	185	1 773	404	D	219	91	43	51	28 560	388	10.3	52.1	55.2
Osage	267	3 258	D	D	370	112	60	58	17 926	1 092	26.2	17.5	35.0
Osborne	154	1 211	270	137	193	81	D	26	21 840	378	11.1	50.3	63.8
Ottawa	123	991	258	D	92	61	31	22	21 905	546	11.5	36.8	49.6
Pawnee	175	2 241	D	D	223	88	65	78	34 898	438	9.1	43.2	46.1
Phillips	219	1 699	349	226	236	116	102	49	28 886	507	18.1	41.4	50.9
Pottawatomie	564	7 612	1 193	1 417	D	219	175	237	31 128	843	19.9	25.9	46.5
Pratt	382	3 623	826	94	808	152	125	99	27 407	538	10.6	32.3	39.4
Rawlins	99	568	179	25	106	47	D	16	27 581	339	11.2	62.5	65.5
Reno	1 686	22 906	5 029	3 396	3 722	891	641	716	31 260	1 749	18.9	23.8	41.9
Republic	198	1 468	336	192	247	98	26	34	23 388	682	14.4	37.0	61.4
Rice	278	2 531	D	360	278	144	140	68	27 052	580	16.9	37.4	49.3
Riley	1 533	20 816	3 444	D	4 131	813	1 175	541	26 000	532	23.9	25.2	43.8
Rooks	187	1 389	242	124	224	D	36	39	28 436	419	8.1	51.1	50.6
Rush	91	805	D	D	69	44	D	24	30 129	481	4.4	43.2	48.9
Russell	283	1 835	D	D	D	82	D	48	26 110	522	6.3	35.4	47.1
Saline	1 638	27 514	4 425	5 530	4 274	1 131	1 324	858	31 189	749	23.5	27.4	42.7
Scott	197	1 364	812	D	233	D	46	43	31 658	277	17.3	50.5	58.1
Sedgwick	12 113	231 442	33 257	51 855	27 415	8 914	10 519	9 014	38 947	1 419	35.2	20.2	43.0
Seward	600	9 889	1 275	D	1 405	199	138	300	30 296	342	7.3	44.4	46.2
Shawnee	4 489	77 264	17 634	6 356	10 105	5 362	3 793	2 785	36 045	885	38.0	11.5	41.2
Sheridan	105	598	D	10	D	43	—	18	29 562	380	4.2	61.3	65.0
Sherman	257	2 021	454	D	381	110	94	48	23 702	436	3.7	48.9	55.3
Smith	138	972	D	71	204	74	25	23	23 483	489	10.0	46.0	57.3
Stafford	133	655	D	D	77	49	D	17	25 206	558	9.9	42.3	48.7
Stanton	72	445	D	D	74	D	13	15	34 362	328	3.4	51.5	51.5
Stevens	192	1 007	D	D	D	73	46	32	31 884	425	8.0	40.7	38.4
Sumner	484	4 844	1 034	1 097	696	265	76	130	26 910	1 099	19.5	31.3	51.0
Thomas	355	3 021	433	D	663	149	76	83	27 344	464	8.8	53.9	59.1
Trego	133	801	D	27	D	33	27	21	26 005	380	7.4	48.2	53.7
Wabaunsee	125	957	124	125	136	65	5	23	23 818	660	19.4	28.5	41.4
Wallace	55	308	D	D	46	D	D	8	26 552	303	6.6	58.7	51.8
Washington	223	1 572	395	122	244	D	D	34	21 815	817	12.7	35.6	52.4
Wichita	93	461	D	D	91	D	D	14	29 924	323	4.0	61.9	60.1
Wilson	241	3 858	674	776	265	99	43	123	36 715	553	16.3	31.8	51.0
Woodson	98	546	189	D	97	D	12	13	23 720	339	12.4	36.3	52.8
Wyandotte	2 995	63 278	12 026	9 890	6 916	1 028	1 244	2 597	41 044	191	71.2	2.6	32.5
KENTUCKY	90 661	1 486 545	238 447	214 746	222 354	68 613	64 883	51 717	34 790	85 260	35.0	5.8	39.8
Adair	311	4 093	878	414	722	D	61	97	23 813	1 424	32.0	3.4	39.7
Allen	233	3 045	D	D	455	142	45	75	24 561	1 208	34.9	3.7	43.4
Anderson	329	3 235	326	D	784	D	131	90	27 769	678	31.6	3.2	31.9
Ballard	135	2 090	D	D	205	60	D	115	55 096	481	38.5	10.2	39.1
Barren	875	12 866	2 298	3 575	2 207	451	241	380	29 503	2 170	40.2	3.7	43.7
Bath	136	1 179	193	288	199	D	D	30	25 707	789	25.9	6.6	43.9
Bell	547	7 261	1 510	943	1 493	272	154	208	28 663	69	40.6	5.8	40.6
Boone	2 874	63 815	4 187	11 177	9 943	4 031	2 435	2 236	35 036	682	53.1	2.8	40.5
Bourbon	387	5 925	636	1 818	775	229	107	204	34 389	918	35.1	9.4	50.0
Boyd	1 441	25 070	D	2 686	4 393	670	1 028	995	39 681	260	41.9	1.5	29.2
Boyle	744	13 687	2 800	2 525	1 936	402	340	420	30 675	649	39.4	6.0	40.2
Bracken	98	845	123	D	152	D	D	23	27 386	618	24.3	5.2	38.2
Breathitt	211	2 341	797	45	550	D	D	62	26 343	199	25.6	10.6	29.6
Breckinridge	271	2 150	454	213	497	149	58	53	24 806	1 509	26.8	5.3	39.9
Bullitt	1 051	13 554	1 119	2 381	1 553	319	356	385	28 374	519	51.3	1.7	43.0
Butler	195	1 578	331	D	274	68	44	41	25 930	778	23.7	9.9	34.8
Caldwell	284	3 429	563	787	680	116	D	89	26 026	625	26.2	8.8	33.4
Calloway	812	13 257	1 982	2 671	1 936	359	278	338	25 470	888	47.1	7.5	34.8
Campbell	1 665	24 325	3 124	2 843	4 010	554	910	796	32 726	535	43.6	1.3	37.4
Carlisle	69	486	D	68	120	77	D	10	20 566	408	35.5	8.8	37.5
Carroll	236	5 498	D	2 614	679	76	93	239	43 540	326	22.1	5.8	45.4
Carter	407	5 504	552	802	1 021	189	101	126	22 828	895	29.5	4.2	36.0
Casey	219	2 629	386	D	327	D	D	64	24 402	1 286	25.7	4.4	43.1
Christian	1 335	22 186	3 907	4 548	3 220	707	840	657	29 616	1 324	28.6	9.7	43.3
Clark	788	12 061	1 507	2 797	1 881	291	328	380	31 476	907	41.8	8.2	42.6

Table B. States and Counties — **Agriculture**

STATE County	Land in farms					Value of land and buildings (dollars)		Value of machinery and equipment, average per farm (dollars)	Value of products sold				Percent of farms with sales of:		Government payments	
			Acres								Percent from:					
	Acreage (1,000)	Percent change, 2002–2007	Average size of farm	Total irrigated (1,000)	Total cropland (1,000)	Average per farm	Average per acre		Total (mil dol)	Average per farm (dollars)	Crops	Livestock and poultry products	$10,000 or more	$100,000 or more	Total ($1,000)	Percent of farms
	117	118	119	120	121	122	123	124	125	126	127	128	129	130	131	132
KANSAS—Cont'd																
Neosho	322	-5.6	415	D	166.1	440 042	1 061	76 761	48.2	62 228	36.9	63.1	43.0	10.7	1 895	55.6
Ness	620	-5.3	1 190	2.5	389.0	642 817	540	102 326	55.8	107 082	67.5	32.5	56.8	26.1	7 662	93.5
Norton	531	2.7	1 369	12.1	301.5	938 997	686	159 964	105.5	271 792	40.4	59.6	62.6	33.0	4 287	80.9
Osage	380	3.5	348	0.4	203.9	419 046	1 204	71 149	48.4	44 367	57.0	43.0	38.3	11.0	2 805	62.5
Osborne	420	-15.8	1 111	3.0	218.7	843 491	759	143 551	52.2	138 021	72.5	27.5	71.4	37.0	2 903	86.5
Ottawa	437	5.0	801	4.5	263.8	662 683	827	112 362	77.0	140 936	46.2	53.8	57.0	24.5	3 373	77.5
Pawnee	487	-6.3	1 113	61.6	380.9	952 707	856	188 646	320.1	730 756	21.0	79.0	59.4	30.8	4 993	85.2
Phillips	495	-15.7	976	7.6	240.1	681 303	698	110 605	75.8	149 453	54.2	45.8	59.0	29.6	2 952	75.1
Pottawatomie	429	-7.7	508	20.2	164.9	606 340	1 193	80 528	85.0	100 864	35.8	64.2	51.5	15.1	2 626	65.7
Pratt	480	-4.2	892	71.2	321.1	798 517	895	160 420	173.6	322 687	36.3	63.7	42.6	23.8	5 258	80.3
Rawlins	591	-9.2	1 742	18.7	329.7	1 111 443	638	176 909	76.8	226 430	77.4	22.6	79.4	48.1	3 403	86.7
Reno	781	6.3	446	42.3	547.8	452 375	1 013	88 113	171.2	97 912	40.6	59.4	41.3	14.6	11 181	75.8
Republic	407	-4.0	596	43.1	282.9	661 603	1 109	151 027	148.1	217 094	53.8	46.2	67.2	33.4	4 655	83.0
Rice	428	2.9	739	24.7	338.8	661 906	896	159 654	184.9	318 840	28.8	71.2	57.9	29.8	5 462	80.5
Riley	232	4.5	436	5.2	103.1	542 879	1 245	89 015	46.8	88 003	50.5	49.5	51.1	19.0	1 738	63.5
Rooks	561	0.2	1 340	1.1	314.2	880 231	657	145 996	86.8	207 254	53.8	46.2	60.9	33.2	4 400	87.4
Rush	406	-2.9	844	11.4	287.1	590 408	700	113 270	53.7	111 574	63.1	36.9	59.0	26.0	4 810	90.0
Russell	444	-8.3	850	0.2	226.0	560 332	659	96 309	36.9	70 777	64.0	36.0	44.6	19.3	4 036	88.9
Saline	431	-1.4	576	2.8	246.7	618 604	1 075	106 018	55.0	73 423	48.9	51.1	48.6	15.0	3 349	75.8
Scott	453	-8.5	1 636	41.6	326.5	1 218 245	744	245 594	762.7	2 753 403	9.4	90.6	69.7	47.3	3 844	78.3
Sedgwick	510	-4.5	360	37.5	405.1	519 179	1 444	97 940	85.1	59 978	66.9	33.1	44.1	13.4	6 982	61.5
Seward	396	9.1	1 158	114.5	293.3	842 235	727	202 410	361.7	1 057 467	22.6	77.4	48.2	35.7	4 570	80.4
Shawnee	206	-5.1	233	18.5	125.1	372 351	1 598	68 821	39.7	44 828	83.1	16.9	36.9	9.9	1 703	43.2
Sheridan	522	2.2	1 374	78.7	369.3	1 064 169	775	251 818	294.9	776 121	32.4	67.6	80.8	52.9	6 197	88.2
Sherman	658	8.4	1 509	103.2	530.0	1 140 642	756	190 457	161.3	370 022	67.2	32.8	63.1	37.6	7 686	90.1
Smith	457	-11.8	935	3.7	285.3	732 236	783	140 317	80.8	165 321	66.8	33.2	71.6	35.0	3 950	82.0
Stafford	502	6.1	900	104.2	386.1	780 017	867	221 555	167.8	300 767	44.5	55.5	50.5	30.1	6 887	84.1
Stanton	414	-5.5	1 263	84.4	358.3	966 134	765	166 328	181.8	554 116	42.1	57.9	50.6	36.0	5 372	87.2
Stevens	503	2.4	1 185	167.1	402.1	935 882	790	231 921	232.9	548 037	53.3	46.7	43.5	27.5	6 031	82.6
Sumner	710	-3.0	646	15.0	571.2	605 771	938	116 856	74.7	67 956	67.9	32.1	44.3	14.5	7 744	74.0
Thomas	657	-4.8	1 417	86.1	561.3	1 157 139	817	253 121	211.0	454 799	61.4	38.6	79.1	50.9	8 815	90.0
Trego	430	-5.5	1 130	4.0	246.4	699 202	618	107 865	44.4	116 844	67.7	32.3	58.4	28.9	3 105	87.1
Wabaunsee	470	1.3	713	7.1	127.5	695 256	975	74 138	62.0	93 969	28.0	72.0	49.7	15.6	1 842	59.5
Wallace	430	3.6	1 418	43.6	287.9	883 716	623	158 099	69.0	227 634	68.4	31.6	57.8	34.7	4 860	88.1
Washington	548	10.3	671	9.1	326.0	693 876	1 034	127 236	151.8	185 858	43.3	56.7	68.3	31.8	5 822	79.7
Wichita	520	10.4	1 609	50.9	398.2	1 077 030	669	238 644	448.7	1 389 261	D	D	62.8	47.1	5 088	85.4
Wilson	333	-1.2	603	0.6	184.8	578 951	961	120 120	44.4	80 246	60.6	39.4	53.2	17.4	2 448	61.1
Woodson	262	2.7	772	0.0	107.4	716 599	929	101 224	37.4	110 230	38.8	61.2	56.6	21.5	1 719	67.8
Wyandotte	18	28.6	95	0.2	12.4	230 441	2 431	36 743	5.1	26 763	D	D	20.4	4.7	98	5.2
KENTUCKY	13 993	1.1	164	58.7	7 278.1	440 213	2 682	57 591	4 824.6	56 586	29.1	70.9	33.5	6.9	103 104	34.6
Adair	188	10.6	132	0.1	85.1	326 191	2 471	52 060	47.4	33 305	16.5	83.5	35.4	6.0	991	40.1
Allen	167	-0.6	138	0.3	69.2	385 115	2 791	45 107	52.8	43 744	14.1	85.9	38.3	3.4	1 184	38.1
Anderson	88	4.8	129	0.1	43.7	351 040	2 716	45 303	11.4	16 847	15.3	84.7	25.2	3.1	245	13.4
Ballard	110	-2.7	229	0.1	85.0	590 043	2 575	116 385	60.4	125 580	41.6	58.4	35.3	13.3	1 469	54.7
Barren	265	10.4	122	0.2	151.2	339 496	2 783	52 186	105.8	48 772	19.0	81.0	42.0	8.2	1 831	29.8
Bath	129	19.4	164	0.1	54.1	330 436	2 020	51 738	17.9	22 689	41.9	58.1	38.3	5.1	344	25.2
Bell	10	42.9	148	0.1	4.1	286 240	1 937	32 776	0.3	4 023	41.4	58.6	10.1	0.0	D	2.9
Boone	75	0.0	110	0.4	35.8	539 948	4 926	55 809	17.5	25 728	51.1	48.9	26.7	4.1	193	18.2
Bourbon	184	-0.5	201	0.2	86.5	944 272	4 703	75 990	179.6	195 624	13.2	86.8	50.0	17.3	644	21.9
Boyd	29	-14.7	111	0.0	7.2	287 599	2 602	47 415	1.9	7 157	12.1	87.9	11.2	0.4	12	6.5
Boyle	94	-5.1	145	0.1	46.5	469 769	3 235	55 041	24.3	37 517	11.1	88.9	33.1	5.7	333	23.3
Bracken	101	7.4	163	0.3	43.1	334 400	2 053	54 627	10.5	16 974	52.5	47.5	32.4	3.2	286	23.5
Breathitt	44	-13.7	219	0.0	9.4	331 771	1 516	39 100	1.6	8 097	25.0	75.0	11.6	0.5	43	18.6
Breckinridge	274	-0.7	182	0.0	124.9	384 909	2 116	55 561	56.1	37 164	37.2	62.8	38.2	5.6	2 440	52.0
Bullitt	51	-16.4	99	0.4	24.8	373 149	3 786	48 241	6.3	12 122	59.8	40.2	21.6	2.5	220	18.1
Butler	174	7.4	224	D	73.6	432 624	1 935	49 124	27.7	35 629	38.4	61.6	26.0	5.1	1 536	46.3
Caldwell	143	-2.7	228	2.4	86.5	452 216	1 980	66 631	23.3	37 234	69.0	31.0	31.0	6.9	1 718	65.8
Calloway	158	-6.5	178	1.7	113.4	501 183	2 821	68 480	69.7	78 459	48.9	51.1	32.8	11.4	2 968	66.1
Campbell	47	-6.0	88	0.2	20.2	345 486	3 905	43 994	5.7	10 651	34.8	65.2	19.4	2.1	89	12.1
Carlisle	96	-10.3	235	0.4	73.9	557 075	2 375	95 525	48.4	118 526	50.6	49.4	27.7	14.5	1 498	76.2
Carroll	64	4.9	195	0.1	25.7	463 198	2 370	49 696	5.4	16 424	45.3	54.7	34.4	2.5	180	27.6
Carter	126	5.0	140	0.0	39.0	249 326	1 778	33 228	7.9	8 774	29.9	70.1	16.0	1.2	206	14.5
Casey	192	0.5	149	0.2	77.9	302 017	2 027	41 100	25.8	20 056	28.6	71.4	37.0	4.7	653	41.4
Christian	346	1.2	262	2.7	239.4	675 113	2 580	84 335	103.0	77 795	63.9	36.1	40.6	16.6	5 958	57.5
Clark	149	4.2	164	0.1	69.0	550 833	3 349	51 024	32.4	35 694	23.7	76.3	37.9	9.9	452	22.1

Table B. States and Counties — Water Use, Wholesale Trade, Retail Trade, and Real Estate

STATE County	Water use, 2005		Wholesale trade,[1] 2007				Retail trade,[2] 2007				Real estate and rental and leasing,[2] 2007			
	Total water withdrawn (mil gal/day)	Gallons withdrawn per person	Number of establishments	Number of employees	Sales (mil dol)	Annual payroll (mil dol)	Number of establishments	Number of employees	Sales (mil dol)	Annual payroll (mil dol)	Number of establishments	Number of employees	Receipts (mil dol)	Annual payroll (mil dol)
	133	134	135	136	137	138	139	140	141	142	143	144	145	146
KANSAS—Cont'd														
Neosho	3.9	235	24	262	180.2	10.0	96	921	199.8	18.3	6	20	1.9	0.4
Ness	4.6	1 519	13	74	42.4	2.3	20	84	16.1	1.2	NA	NA	NA	NA
Norton	10.1	1 785	11	61	40.0	1.6	29	180	37.0	3.0	1	D	D	D
Osage	2.2	129	11	79	19.4	2.0	54	369	70.6	5.7	7	28	2.0	0.4
Osborne	3.5	874	13	97	86.2	3.3	31	198	38.5	2.3	1	D	D	D
Ottawa	3.7	598	9	199	48.0	5.8	17	90	19.3	1.5	1	D	D	D
Pawnee	68.9	10 221	6	92	93.8	3.8	27	215	48.5	4.2	3	12	0.8	0.3
Phillips	6.9	1 245	8	61	33.9	1.6	36	243	46.6	3.6	1	D	D	D
Pottawatomie	43.4	2 266	20	530	161.0	18.2	98	1 463	283.9	30.3	21	51	7.8	1.3
Pratt	79.2	8 340	22	131	108.3	3.7	54	690	170.2	15.4	16	40	3.7	0.7
Rawlins	17.7	6 613	6	54	83.5	2.9	23	101	16.3	1.7	2	D	D	D
Reno	62.8	988	65	749	573.3	27.1	316	3 722	828.6	78.4	64	166	43.2	3.9
Republic	21.4	4 134	19	272	97.4	4.8	40	250	43.7	3.9	2	D	D	D
Rice	24.9	2 378	17	111	64.0	4.1	45	279	46.9	4.2	6	D	D	D
Riley	6.7	107	35	314	93.2	10.8	270	4 028	728.6	66.5	105	489	50.3	10.1
Rooks	2.8	527	16	112	120.3	4.7	33	224	56.4	3.4	1	D	D	D
Rush	8.5	2 501	10	53	27.7	1.3	12	80	30.7	1.9	NA	NA	NA	NA
Russell	1.1	164	14	107	70.3	3.2	41	284	68.0	4.4	9	31	2.9	0.7
Saline	11.2	208	84	1 178	816.4	44.4	284	4 226	1 064.6	86.3	74	D	D	D
Scott	47.7	10 365	21	114	131.5	5.1	33	212	46.8	3.5	3	4	0.4	0.1
Sedgwick	94.8	203	599	8 304	12 449.4	383.6	1 771	26 921	6 574.2	590.0	605	3 411	501.8	93.7
Seward	132.2	5 679	42	392	197.5	15.5	116	1 395	314.6	29.1	27	95	12.4	2.0
Shawnee	36.1	210	166	1 966	915.3	81.2	747	10 406	2 310.1	216.4	241	D	D	D
Sheridan	73.0	28 186	11	92	88.4	4.4	20	96	18.4	1.5	NA	NA	NA	NA
Sherman	106.7	17 348	19	116	119.1	3.7	44	378	110.6	7.6	11	29	3.2	0.7
Smith	3.4	815	11	119	71.1	3.3	30	170	23.6	2.1	3	4	0.4	0.1
Stafford	75.9	16 914	6	24	18.1	0.7	19	88	15.9	1.3	NA	NA	NA	NA
Stanton	81.9	36 481	11	D	D	D	10	73	16.4	1.6	NA	NA	NA	NA
Stevens	162.8	30 085	13	84	113.7	3.0	25	187	40.3	3.4	1	D	D	D
Sumner	9.3	375	25	152	202.2	6.1	63	556	131.4	10.7	16	47	3.3	0.9
Thomas	95.6	12 519	34	242	163.1	8.6	64	633	159.4	12.2	9	23	3.7	0.4
Trego	6.3	2 069	9	34	24.1	0.9	28	127	40.4	2.5	1	D	D	D
Wabaunsee	4.9	707	6	43	13.4	1.7	23	136	26.7	2.1	5	D	D	D
Wallace	51.0	32 416	3	D	D	D	7	47	6.3	0.7	2	D	D	D
Washington	7.5	1 251	15	185	111.3	6.4	41	209	34.8	2.6	2	D	D	D
Wichita	50.6	21 919	10	60	68.2	2.3	15	83	18.5	1.3	1	D	D	D
Wilson	2.6	265	5	D	D	D	41	267	54.2	4.1	6	D	D	D
Woodson	1.9	529	5	43	27.4	1.2	19	79	17.2	1.6	2	D	D	D
Wyandotte	385.1	2 473	234	5 833	4 127.5	289.5	461	7 022	1 710.0	174.6	136	791	129.4	22.7
KENTUCKY	4 329.0	1 037	3 794	59 854	74 680.8	2 869.5	16 404	214 782	50 405.9	4 502.2	3 898	20 146	3 894.3	593.4
Adair	2.9	164	18	131	54.7	2.8	61	486	137.1	9.6	11	51	2.4	0.4
Allen	1.9	102	11	243	97.7	9.4	63	533	112.1	8.6	12	55	3.8	0.8
Anderson	3.8	186	7	D	D	D	58	709	170.7	14.2	14	52	5.3	1.1
Ballard	8.0	963	6	D	D	D	28	208	52.8	3.8	2	D	D	D
Barren	9.1	227	38	D	D	D	193	2 319	552.9	48.5	25	78	9.2	1.8
Bath	5.8	501	NA	NA	NA	NA	40	243	51.5	3.7	6	D	D	D
Bell	4.7	157	20	195	196.1	4.7	133	1 556	374.9	31.7	23	67	10.6	1.7
Boone	18.8	177	160	D	D	D	493	9 371	2 439.2	206.6	133	898	154.9	23.1
Bourbon	3.0	153	10	D	D	D	66	804	175.3	14.9	11	40	3.1	0.6
Boyd	52.6	1 060	64	D	D	D	271	4 016	934.6	75.1	53	233	41.1	6.2
Boyle	6.7	235	18	120	71.2	3.8	150	1 943	430.0	43.0	33	99	12.6	2.1
Bracken	1.7	201	3	D	D	D	19	155	25.9	2.3	2	D	D	D
Breathitt	10.0	629	5	D	D	D	51	501	103.7	9.2	7	D	D	D
Breckinridge	2.1	108	8	47	19.4	1.4	55	445	113.8	9.2	8	21	2.3	0.4
Bullitt	3.2	46	29	563	879.7	26.0	164	1 699	500.5	31.9	33	97	12.3	1.7
Butler	1.6	120	6	D	D	D	40	284	58.0	4.3	6	55	3.2	1.2
Caldwell	3.6	274	7	D	D	D	61	673	151.8	13.6	7	58	2.8	1.6
Calloway	5.9	169	39	D	D	D	158	2 030	454.8	41.2	34	129	12.1	2.2
Campbell	29.5	339	55	D	D	D	282	4 043	970.8	83.6	67	468	89.2	15.2
Carlisle	0.8	148	3	9	2.9	0.2	14	116	23.8	2.2	2	D	D	D
Carroll	81.7	7 810	7	73	13.4	1.3	55	642	182.7	14.2	5	22	5.8	0.7
Carter	4.3	156	13	406	306.2	9.7	114	1 098	268.5	18.7	17	53	3.7	0.7
Casey	1.9	118	10	95	34.9	2.6	48	316	71.8	5.1	2	D	D	D
Christian	14.5	206	65	1 028	878.4	38.6	270	3 263	936.1	70.7	66	299	29.8	5.8
Clark	187.6	5 378	34	D	D	D	147	1 861	461.8	39.2	40	135	16.6	2.5

1. Merchant wholesalers, except manufacturers' sales branches and offices. 2. Employer establishments.

STATE County	Professional, scientific, and technical services,[1] 2007				Manufacturing, 2007				Accommodation and food services, 2007			
	Number of establishments	Number of employees	Receipts (mil dol)	Annual payroll (mil dol)	Number of establishments	Number of employees	Receipts (mil dol)	Annual payroll (mil dol)	Number of establishments	Number of employees	Sales (mil dol)	Annual payroll (mil dol)
	147	148	149	150	151	152	153	154	155	156	157	158
KANSAS—Cont'd												
Neosho	32	133	11.5	4.6	36	1 395	291.0	48.8	35	395	13.1	3.0
Ness	6	19	1.6	0.3	NA	NA	NA	NA	11	71	1.5	0.4
Norton	11	46	2.9	0.7	NA	NA	NA	NA	13	152	5.4	1.4
Osage	16	D	D	D	NA	NA	NA	NA	21	D	D	D
Osborne	9	51	10.4	1.6	NA	NA	NA	NA	9	55	1.4	0.4
Ottawa	10	D	D	D	NA	NA	NA	NA	8	103	1.5	0.5
Pawnee	15	53	4.2	1.2	NA	NA	NA	NA	13	179	5.7	1.5
Phillips	16	84	7.6	2.6	NA	NA	NA	NA	14	146	3.7	0.8
Pottawatomie	43	D	D	D	33	1 626	329.6	64.9	32	355	11.8	3.1
Pratt	31	127	9.6	3.5	NA	NA	NA	NA	25	431	15.0	3.5
Rawlins	8	15	1.0	0.2	NA	NA	NA	NA	9	24	0.7	0.2
Reno	109	D	D	D	93	3 672	908.7	142.1	125	2 289	83.4	23.1
Republic	17	25	2.7	0.5	NA	NA	NA	NA	11	127	3.1	0.6
Rice	19	119	5.8	1.8	NA	NA	NA	NA	18	231	6.6	1.9
Riley	155	D	D	D	28	795	D	24.7	158	3 493	125.4	33.4
Rooks	13	41	3.5	1.3	NA	NA	NA	NA	11	D	D	D
Rush	6	16	1.4	0.6	NA	NA	NA	NA	4	20	0.9	0.2
Russell	14	57	4.4	1.1	NA	NA	NA	NA	20	300	10.0	2.3
Saline	124	D	D	D	77	D	D	222.7	128	2 593	96.1	26.7
Scott	19	67	6.3	1.4	NA	NA	NA	NA	13	D	D	D
Sedgwick	1 120	D	D	D	573	53 568	21 117.1	2 940.1	1 066	21 268	846.9	246.6
Seward	32	127	11.3	4.2	9	D	D	D	49	826	32.2	8.9
Shawnee	472	D	D	D	121	6 097	D	274.4	370	D	D	D
Sheridan	4	21	1.2	0.3	NA	NA	NA	NA	5	31	0.8	0.1
Sherman	18	79	6.6	2.4	NA	NA	NA	NA	23	328	11.0	3.0
Smith	9	23	2.2	0.3	NA	NA	NA	NA	8	79	1.4	0.3
Stafford	9	15	1.8	0.6	NA	NA	NA	NA	12	42	1.2	0.2
Stanton	6	16	1.1	0.4	NA	NA	NA	NA	4	22	0.8	0.1
Stevens	11	53	13.7	4.3	NA	NA	NA	NA	11	D	D	D
Sumner	24	D	D	D	39	1 253	D	43.0	39	537	16.8	4.8
Thomas	32	76	7.7	1.6	NA	NA	NA	NA	29	512	18.3	5.1
Trego	8	23	1.4	0.3	NA	NA	NA	NA	12	106	4.0	1.1
Wabaunsee	5	D	D	D	NA	NA	NA	NA	10	D	D	D
Wallace	2	D	D	D	NA	NA	NA	NA	3	D	D	D
Washington	11	34	3.5	0.9	NA	NA	NA	NA	14	123	2.5	0.7
Wichita	3	D	D	D	NA	NA	NA	NA	3	14	0.5	0.1
Wilson	14	39	4.4	0.9	22	1 428	D	D	18	191	5.8	1.4
Woodson	5	18	0.8	0.3	NA	NA	NA	NA	6	71	1.5	0.4
Wyandotte	158	D	D	D	215	11 083	7 634.5	632.0	248	4 964	241.9	66.8
KENTUCKY	8 075	61 428	7 872.2	2 831.6	4 165	247 096	119 105.4	10 773.2	7 309	151 551	6 300.9	1 787.4
Adair	16	D	D	D	NA	NA	NA	NA	20	188	9.1	1.7
Allen	11	60	5.6	1.3	12	592	164.8	22.1	14	207	8.2	2.0
Anderson	27	102	9.6	3.0	21	1 102	600.9	47.9	26	369	11.3	3.6
Ballard	5	D	D	D	11	727	D	43.3	10	70	1.8	0.5
Barren	49	292	23.2	7.3	49	4 540	1 024.9	164.9	87	1 790	64.7	17.5
Bath	11	D	D	D	NA	NA	NA	NA	10	D	D	D
Bell	37	453	31.0	17.3	21	688	D	D	47	1 044	38.1	10.5
Boone	232	3 501	381.4	146.4	183	13 239	4 691.0	647.7	269	D	D	D
Bourbon	35	D	D	D	26	1 769	D	D	25	327	13.5	3.6
Boyd	104	D	D	D	33	3 024	D	229.1	112	2 820	100.5	27.7
Boyle	72	437	43.7	15.3	28	2 839	D	D	63	1 539	57.7	16.8
Bracken	7	D	D	D	NA	NA	NA	NA	10	D	D	D
Breathitt	11	D	D	D	NA	NA	NA	NA	15	223	8.7	2.3
Breckinridge	12	66	4.6	1.9	NA	NA	NA	NA	18	273	7.9	2.5
Bullitt	76	366	26.3	10.0	47	2 823	D	104.8	84	1 818	73.0	20.1
Butler	6	126	2.4	1.4	15	573	120.5	19.5	16	170	5.4	1.4
Caldwell	18	50	4.0	1.0	16	898	213.2	27.1	24	260	9.4	2.3
Calloway	55	273	22.0	7.5	35	2 658	729.2	96.0	70	1 548	52.5	14.2
Campbell	149	D	D	D	85	2 338	798.2	105.8	192	3 734	163.3	49.0
Carlisle	3	D	D	D	NA	NA	NA	NA	4	42	1.1	0.3
Carroll	20	98	7.7	3.8	12	2 547	4 059.7	183.7	26	426	18.2	5.0
Carter	28	89	5.9	2.3	18	712	D	19.0	39	619	24.4	5.9
Casey	9	D	D	D	28	1 019	189.1	21.1	16	184	6.4	1.9
Christian	89	875	102.4	32.8	73	5 192	1 571.6	202.4	113	2 055	80.1	21.9
Clark	57	321	27.3	11.8	44	3 794	1 252.3	146.2	59	1 264	51.3	13.9

1. Establishment subject to federal tax.

Table B. States and Counties — Health Care and Social Assistance, Other Services, and Federal Funds

STATE County	Health care and social assistance, 2007				Other services, 2007				Federal funds and grants, 2009–2010 Expenditures (mil dol)			
										Direct payments for individuals[1]		
	Number of establishments	Number of employees	Receipts (mil dol)	Annual payroll (mil dol)	Number of establishments	Number of employees	Receipts (mil dol)	Annual payroll (mil dol)	Total	Social Security and government retirement	Medicare	Food Stamps and Supplemental Security Income
	159	160	161	162	163	164	165	166	167	168	169	170
KANSAS—Cont'd												
Neosho	58	1 256	85.1	31.8	41	120	11.2	2.1	135.0	54.0	34.0	6.1
Ness	11	249	13.3	6.1	10	D	D	D	34.6	12.5	12.2	0.2
Norton	23	448	21.5	10.7	14	40	5.0	0.7	97.6	18.5	12.5	0.9
Osage	30	1 533	35.5	20.5	20	D	D	D	114.0	60.2	25.5	3.6
Osborne	16	281	11.5	5.1	10	D	D	D	46.8	15.6	13.5	0.8
Ottawa	9	D	D	D	9	23	3.1	0.5	43.3	18.3	10.7	1.0
Pawnee	16	1 268	72.7	49.0	15	33	4.1	0.8	54.4	15.1	14.8	0.9
Phillips	21	294	17.1	8.0	23	64	24.8	1.2	58.8	21.3	16.0	0.6
Pottawatomie	49	1 466	56.3	28.4	46	139	10.5	2.5	113.2	55.1	28.4	2.6
Pratt	38	641	66.7	22.0	35	122	8.7	2.3	81.6	32.0	25.0	2.0
Rawlins	7	D	D	D	5	D	D	D	37.8	12.9	7.4	0.4
Reno	200	4 751	420.0	173.9	132	536	42.5	10.9	478.9	210.6	120.3	20.6
Republic	16	306	15.5	7.2	19	47	3.3	0.8	54.5	20.6	13.4	0.9
Rice	25	372	20.4	9.9	19	62	4.7	1.2	80.7	34.9	19.8	2.6
Riley	167	3 409	257.9	99.5	135	1 550	279.3	49.4	446.7	141.9	41.2	8.3
Rooks	13	213	11.0	4.9	15	63	6.4	1.5	58.9	20.0	17.5	0.9
Rush	5	128	7.2	3.3	6	D	D	D	37.0	13.5	11.9	0.8
Russell	18	420	21.9	11.0	14	36	3.3	0.4	66.2	27.2	22.0	1.6
Saline	180	D	D	D	123	582	55.4	13.1	438.9	170.0	83.1	13.3
Scott	12	292	15.7	7.9	19	65	6.0	1.0	40.1	13.8	7.9	0.3
Sedgwick	1 298	32 662	3 447.9	1 254.0	853	6 143	554.1	168.3	4 637.8	1 332.7	643.9	156.9
Seward	70	1 110	82.7	31.5	49	226	25.6	5.2	103.0	36.6	20.6	7.7
Shawnee	502	16 040	1 388.4	610.9	410	2 872	284.2	80.6	2 879.8	651.6	244.3	59.3
Sheridan	7	D	D	D	6	D	D	D	31.5	10.1	5.6	0.3
Sherman	35	390	23.0	9.3	23	61	5.6	1.4	76.9	25.5	15.6	1.3
Smith	9	260	11.2	5.4	13	30	3.0	0.6	47.1	17.0	11.7	1.0
Stafford	25	244	10.8	5.0	15	35	1.9	0.4	49.4	20.8	12.1	0.8
Stanton	4	D	D	D	5	D	D	D	31.8	12.0	2.9	0.3
Stevens	10	218	13.8	7.1	7	D	D	D	46.3	16.2	9.0	1.0
Sumner	61	D	D	D	42	112	9.3	2.1	189.1	86.3	47.8	6.7
Thomas	37	465	34.2	13.8	31	124	8.4	2.3	87.0	29.2	15.0	1.1
Trego	7	D	D	D	14	26	2.2	0.4	33.2	11.4	10.1	0.4
Wabaunsee	6	121	4.9	2.2	6	D	D	D	79.5	59.6	10.4	0.9
Wallace	5	D	D	D	6	13	0.9	0.2	23.4	7.2	4.7	0.3
Washington	26	378	14.8	6.9	17	55	5.3	0.8	63.4	21.9	15.5	1.3
Wichita	6	D	D	D	10	20	2.2	0.4	31.4	12.8	3.7	0.4
Wilson	35	588	37.1	16.1	12	26	1.6	0.5	90.5	33.9	21.9	3.0
Woodson	14	110	6.8	2.4	6	D	D	D	36.0	13.6	9.5	1.5
Wyandotte	309	10 811	1 094.6	467.5	234	1 390	232.0	34.5	1 616.6	419.1	331.6	84.2
KENTUCKY	10 600	235 282	22 151.8	8 395.1	6 150	40 956	3 751.1	1 009.3	57 270.5	13 649.1	11 693.5	2 373.7
Adair	41	883	49.2	24.4	15	37	3.0	0.7	208.4	52.2	82.3	10.2
Allen	23	D	D	D	13	42	4.0	1.2	183.8	56.9	67.6	8.6
Anderson	33	336	19.9	8.9	27	91	5.2	1.5	120.0	62.9	31.3	4.7
Ballard	8	D	D	D	9	D	D	D	99.1	42.3	32.6	3.6
Barren	106	2 498	196.0	85.7	48	D	D	D	362.4	124.2	116.6	17.4
Bath	13	198	9.8	4.0	12	D	D	D	122.1	33.8	40.3	11.4
Bell	80	1 525	116.8	46.1	37	D	D	D	278.8	107.4	162.4	41.6
Boone	211	3 754	311.0	123.2	184	1 641	126.9	42.9	668.0	303.8	92.7	17.3
Bourbon	39	D	D	D	24	127	6.3	1.7	168.7	62.0	53.8	8.1
Boyd	246	7 162	811.2	303.0	110	D	D	D	605.9	223.8	186.7	33.2
Boyle	110	2 486	238.4	105.7	50	219	14.2	3.9	275.3	103.9	82.6	13.3
Bracken	9	D	D	D	6	D	D	D	85.5	28.4	29.0	5.9
Breathitt	40	785	72.9	24.8	10	D	D	D	318.2	52.8	105.6	26.4
Breckinridge	30	453	30.9	11.0	23	49	4.4	1.0	192.2	70.0	61.0	10.7
Bullitt	90	906	59.6	22.8	81	1 021	27.2	23.1	340.0	175.4	74.4	18.3
Butler	19	250	14.4	6.4	14	51	2.8	0.8	127.7	37.5	48.6	7.6
Caldwell	30	515	35.2	12.9	17	62	5.4	1.3	129.4	49.9	44.8	5.3
Calloway	109	1 917	152.4	56.0	49	214	14.1	4.1	288.7	114.6	82.2	10.7
Campbell	160	3 393	288.9	114.6	124	916	111.4	26.6	648.0	255.2	200.5	30.9
Carlisle	7	D	D	D	3	D	D	D	53.3	20.7	18.9	2.0
Carroll	21	D	D	D	15	92	5.2	1.7	104.0	32.2	32.8	6.3
Carter	44	572	34.8	13.6	34	182	11.8	3.3	316.2	76.8	105.0	24.0
Casey	24	395	25.2	9.7	12	30	2.9	0.6	173.6	44.6	66.5	10.9
Christian	177	4 734	438.9	153.4	105	739	54.2	16.0	6 240.5	196.8	158.0	34.3
Clark	111	1 459	122.5	45.9	56	294	17.2	4.6	279.8	126.3	77.0	16.1

1. State totals may include programs not allocated by county.

Table B. States and Counties — Federal Funds, Residential Construction, and Local Government Finances

	Federal funds and grants, 2009–2010 (cont.)							Value of residential construction authorized by building permits, 2010		Local government finances, 2007				
	Expenditures (mil dol) (cont.)									General revenue				
	Procurement contract awards			Grants[1]								Taxes		
													Per capita[2] (dollars)	
STATE County	Salaries and wages	Defense	Other	Medicaid and other health-related	Nutrition and family welfare	Education	Other	New construction ($1,000)	Number of housing units	Total (mil dol)	Inter-governmental (mil dol)	Total (mil dol)	Total	Property
	171	172	173	174	175	176	177	178	179	180	181	182	183	184
KANSAS—Cont'd														
Neosho	4.9	1.5	1.1	16.3	3.3	1.8	2.4	4 868	62	90.3	28.0	22.7	1 398	1 059
Ness	1.8	0.0	0.6	1.7	0.6	0.1	0.0	0	0	23.2	3.9	7.6	2 548	2 401
Norton	3.2	0.0	0.4	3.4	1.0	0.1	50.1	0	0	25.4	8.9	7.1	1 316	1 136
Osage	5.6	1.5	1.0	9.0	2.6	0.4	0.9	4 715	24	55.2	29.4	15.9	964	851
Osborne	2.0	0.0	0.4	6.2	0.7	0.1	0.1	0	0	12.0	3.9	5.9	1 511	1 289
Ottawa	1.6	0.0	0.4	5.1	1.0	0.1	0.1	692	4	24.0	11.8	8.7	1 449	1 292
Pawnee	9.3	0.0	0.6	3.9	1.1	0.1	0.5	1 258	12	24.6	10.0	10.4	1 624	1 408
Phillips	3.6	0.0	0.7	7.3	1.0	0.1	1.1	0	0	26.6	11.1	8.2	1 539	1 378
Pottawatomie	4.6	4.3	1.0	9.0	2.7	0.4	0.6	18 924	90	73.9	28.5	34.5	1 781	1 472
Pratt	4.0	0.2	0.5	3.4	1.5	0.5	1.7	180	1	46.4	18.1	19.1	2 026	1 690
Rawlins	1.4	0.0	0.5	3.9	0.5	0.1	0.0	0	0	9.3	3.7	4.4	1 702	1 559
Reno	33.1	0.1	3.0	48.0	13.0	2.6	3.8	10 360	63	220.8	92.7	79.1	1 253	908
Republic	2.5	0.0	0.5	3.9	1.0	0.1	0.2	115	1	21.5	8.5	9.9	2 018	1 787
Rice	3.5	0.0	0.8	5.1	1.9	0.2	1.2	2 917	28	45.3	17.1	15.2	1 505	1 355
Riley	66.0	9.2	18.7	36.7	9.4	7.1	77.5	71 199	511	151.1	48.4	74.0	1 072	765
Rooks	2.1	0.0	0.4	3.9	1.0	0.1	5.6	365	3	32.0	7.3	11.8	2 285	2 115
Rush	1.9	0.0	0.4	2.8	0.7	0.1	0.0	160	1	16.8	4.9	6.2	1 945	1 868
Russell	3.5	0.0	0.6	5.1	1.3	0.1	0.3	583	2	31.4	9.1	16.2	2 403	2 026
Saline	55.1	3.6	45.6	35.7	12.1	1.5	2.6	12 880	98	181.1	70.4	74.9	1 373	946
Scott	1.4	0.0	0.3	2.8	0.8	0.1	0.7	375	3	18.5	6.4	10.4	2 282	2 078
Sedgwick	667.7	1 074.6	149.5	359.7	78.5	23.7	76.1	125 376	1 036	1 644.2	709.8	654.3	1 375	930
Seward	7.3	0.0	0.7	12.4	4.5	1.7	2.6	5 197	58	136.9	38.2	39.8	1 720	1 283
Shawnee	299.1	20.6	54.6	244.1	136.6	225.1	892.2	44 179	285	671.1	224.4	285.2	1 644	1 243
Sheridan	0.9	0.0	0.2	2.3	0.4	0.1	0.1	NA	NA	8.5	2.7	4.5	1 808	1 668
Sherman	6.2	0.0	0.4	4.5	1.1	0.2	0.2	0	0	30.9	11.8	10.4	1 741	1 256
Smith	3.5	0.0	0.5	3.4	0.8	0.1	0.4	437	4	15.4	6.1	6.8	1 730	1 630
Stafford	2.7	0.0	1.7	2.3	1.0	0.2	0.0	698	6	24.5	8.2	10.1	2 293	2 172
Stanton	0.5	0.0	0.1	0.6	0.5	0.1	0.1	0	0	17.6	2.2	10.6	4 888	4 730
Stevens	1.6	0.0	0.3	2.8	0.9	0.1	1.1	0	0	43.7	6.0	26.1	5 164	5 055
Sumner	6.9	0.8	1.5	16.3	4.5	1.1	1.1	3 478	21	91.4	37.7	30.5	1 275	1 063
Thomas	6.2	0.0	0.6	4.5	1.3	0.7	2.4	0	0	41.2	18.1	11.3	1 547	1 160
Trego	1.0	0.0	0.2	3.4	0.6	0.1	0.1	385	2	18.9	3.7	5.8	1 991	1 755
Wabaunsee	2.4	0.0	0.6	2.3	1.0	0.2	0.1	3 005	17	22.0	9.6	9.3	1 347	1 263
Wallace	0.8	0.0	1.8	1.1	0.3	0.1	0.0	0	0	7.4	3.1	3.5	2 387	2 342
Washington	4.2	0.0	0.9	6.8	1.2	0.2	0.1	320	2	29.2	12.6	9.8	1 676	1 557
Wichita	1.0	0.0	0.2	1.8	0.5	0.1	1.2	0	0	15.5	4.2	5.8	2 638	2 331
Wilson	4.2	0.0	0.8	16.3	2.3	0.3	1.7	460	2	37.7	16.2	12.0	1 225	1 049
Woodson	1.4	1.8	0.3	5.1	0.7	0.1	0.0	120	1	10.8	4.5	5.0	1 497	1 290
Wyandotte	200.9	18.3	52.6	405.8	39.6	8.4	29.7	20 534	214	743.6	271.8	268.2	1 742	1 216
KENTUCKY	9 204.7	5 180.5	2 305.6	5 482.6	1 065.1	784.2	2 170.4	1 086 665	7 986	X	X	X	X	X
Adair	3.6	0.0	0.8	42.5	3.1	1.7	2.5	405	8	58.6	21.9	6.7	377	235
Allen	4.0	0.0	0.9	36.1	2.5	1.3	0.2	NA	NA	36.6	21.1	10.3	545	344
Anderson	3.3	0.2	0.7	11.5	2.2	1.2	0.0	8 923	57	44.7	22.8	14.6	689	492
Ballard	2.5	1.1	0.9	8.6	1.6	0.7	0.7	NA	NA	25.1	11.7	5.7	683	449
Barren	24.5	0.6	2.0	57.2	5.1	2.4	3.6	26 600	156	100.1	49.3	33.2	807	450
Bath	2.2	0.2	0.5	25.3	2.4	1.2	1.0	0	0	21.4	14.4	4.3	369	250
Bell	14.8	2.9	-158.7	88.1	11.8	2.8	2.8	2 283	22	74.0	48.1	15.8	545	290
Boone	104.6	91.6	10.9	18.4	8.3	3.1	6.9	64 721	450	290.6	80.8	167.8	1 492	954
Bourbon	3.3	0.0	0.8	21.3	4.2	2.2	3.1	5 513	33	46.4	22.9	17.3	875	433
Boyd	56.9	1.1	15.0	63.1	9.7	5.0	4.9	2 030	15	127.4	59.8	46.0	948	447
Boyle	10.7	0.0	1.4	37.0	3.9	3.8	14.4	7 469	47	71.0	31.2	27.3	952	487
Bracken	2.5	0.0	0.6	13.8	1.4	0.8	0.1	NA	NA	19.4	11.5	5.1	600	436
Breathitt	13.4	1.4	0.7	73.3	8.0	1.7	33.8	168	1	38.2	24.9	6.5	417	181
Breckinridge	4.8	0.1	1.7	29.0	4.4	1.7	3.0	389	6	46.3	23.8	8.8	461	305
Bullitt	6.2	25.1	1.8	23.1	7.6	3.7	0.5	45 515	293	129.1	64.0	49.5	670	502
Butler	2.5	0.3	1.1	24.1	2.3	1.0	0.4	0	0	31.2	21.8	5.7	433	178
Caldwell	2.8	0.0	0.7	18.1	1.8	1.1	1.1	365	3	27.0	15.4	7.2	564	283
Calloway	17.9	0.1	2.8	22.0	9.0	4.4	1.1	6 827	46	209.8	31.5	21.1	582	414
Campbell	49.1	2.2	3.1	56.6	11.3	6.9	9.7	22 282	143	204.2	61.6	102.4	1 179	692
Carlisle	1.3	2.4	0.3	5.8	0.9	0.5	-4.6	NA	NA	9.9	6.3	2.4	461	346
Carroll	9.9	0.0	0.5	15.1	2.3	0.9	1.7	0	0	154.6	12.7	11.1	1 057	453
Carter	10.5	22.2	1.1	57.8	9.2	3.2	0.5	308	3	52.2	37.3	8.6	315	188
Casey	2.3	0.1	0.6	39.1	3.0	1.2	0.6	113	1	43.9	24.3	5.3	330	198
Christian	5 180.4	536.5	13.6	70.9	14.6	6.6	4.5	9 220	115	126.0	69.2	37.6	465	235
Clark	8.3	2.0	3.0	33.6	4.7	2.4	0.8	9 101	49	88.9	41.3	29.6	833	459

1. State totals may include programs not allocated by county.   2. Based on the resident population estimated as of July 1 of the year shown.

Table B. States and Counties — Local Government Finances, Government Employment, and Voting

STATE County	Local government finances, 2007 (cont.) Direct general expenditure — Total (mil dol)	Per capita¹ (dollars)	Percent of total for: Education	Health and hospitals	Police protection	Public welfare	Highways	Debt outstanding — Total (mil dol)	Per capita¹ (dollars)	Government employment, 2009 — Federal civilian	Federal military	State and local	Presidential election,² 2008 Percent of vote cast: Democratic	Republican	All other
	185	186	187	188	189	190	191	192	193	194	195	196	197	198	199
KANSAS—Cont'd															
Neosho	92.5	5 697	39.7	27.9	2.2	0.0	4.6	163.7	10 088	60	68	1 695	35.6	62.2	2.2
Ness	21.5	7 182	25.4	44.1	3.0	0.0	7.6	3.5	1 157	30	12	441	19.0	79.1	1.9
Norton	25.8	4 764	39.6	26.7	3.0	0.0	8.1	20.3	3 737	32	22	891	20.6	77.8	1.7
Osage	53.0	3 222	54.3	2.1	4.6	0.2	9.1	35.2	2 140	82	68	1 248	33.6	63.9	2.5
Osborne	11.5	2 978	35.5	5.5	7.2	0.0	15.0	3.7	958	33	16	328	20.9	77.2	1.9
Ottawa	22.9	3 818	52.2	3.7	6.2	0.0	12.1	31.7	5 282	26	25	441	22.8	75.3	1.9
Pawnee	22.8	3 553	54.7	3.3	4.5	0.0	10.0	4.8	744	47	26	2 044	30.6	67.6	1.8
Phillips	26.1	4 877	41.7	3.9	3.0	7.6	10.4	8.1	1 508	46	22	802	19.7	78.9	1.4
Pottawatomie	74.3	3 832	54.6	7.2	3.1	0.0	9.9	93.7	4 831	56	84	1 326	26.4	70.4	3.1
Pratt	42.8	4 538	60.6	3.0	4.6	0.1	7.8	40.6	4 309	40	39	1 174	30.9	67.4	1.8
Rawlins	7.9	3 098	50.0	3.6	4.3	0.0	11.9	2.3	890	22	10	339	17.6	80.5	1.9
Reno	213.8	3 385	60.6	1.7	4.3	0.1	5.9	274.0	4 339	220	267	5 558	37.4	60.8	1.8
Republic	20.8	4 238	42.9	4.4	2.8	0.1	11.7	13.2	2 700	35	20	558	24.0	74.1	2.0
Rice	43.5	4 312	46.2	19.7	3.7	0.0	10.3	22.3	2 216	47	42	1 077	28.9	69.1	1.9
Riley	142.1	2 056	49.4	1.2	7.6	0.0	5.9	179.6	2 600	477	286	11 184	45.6	52.7	1.7
Rooks	29.8	5 778	34.4	21.7	2.8	8.9	8.1	12.9	2 509	32	21	657	18.1	79.9	2.0
Rush	17.1	5 325	38.4	21.6	3.2	0.0	14.6	0.3	101	28	13	333	28.3	68.8	2.9
Russell	27.2	4 043	43.4	4.7	4.0	0.2	12.0	13.2	1 966	41	28	628	22.4	76.2	1.5
Saline	175.1	3 207	49.0	1.5	4.7	0.0	4.5	140.0	2 565	290	230	4 324	35.9	62.2	1.9
Scott	17.1	3 738	51.7	4.5	4.2	0.0	7.4	18.3	4 008	22	19	372	14.7	83.7	1.6
Sedgwick	1 510.6	3 173	50.7	3.9	7.5	0.6	4.4	2 929.0	6 153	5 614	4 687	26 477	42.7	55.4	1.8
Seward	131.0	5 667	44.3	27.5	2.7	0.0	3.5	70.0	3 029	104	97	2 299	28.0	71.0	1.0
Shawnee	662.5	3 819	53.2	1.7	5.9	0.3	2.9	1 077.0	6 209	2 952	991	20 571	49.0	49.3	1.7
Sheridan	9.0	3 594	44.0	8.2	2.5	0.4	12.3	0.6	247	17	10	323	18.5	80.5	1.0
Sherman	27.9	4 675	51.3	3.5	3.1	0.2	6.9	26.1	4 375	59	25	689	25.4	72.4	2.1
Smith	14.1	3 568	50.6	5.1	2.7	0.1	11.4	4.7	1 198	39	16	359	20.2	78.0	1.8
Stafford	23.7	5 396	48.3	14.8	3.3	0.2	10.2	4.8	1 096	47	18	634	26.1	72.1	1.8
Stanton	14.7	6 805	34.3	27.6	2.3	0.0	11.4	1.4	636	13	0	300	22.7	75.9	1.3
Stevens	37.7	7 448	41.2	21.3	3.9	2.4	9.7	11.1	2 201	24	22	734	13.3	85.3	1.4
Sumner	92.1	3 857	44.7	17.5	1.8	0.0	9.9	98.2	4 112	88	99	1 876	32.4	65.2	2.4
Thomas	39.5	5 400	62.4	1.6	3.6	0.2	4.8	8.9	1 212	42	31	928	21.4	77.2	1.3
Trego	18.5	6 327	25.2	41.5	1.1	0.0	7.9	14.6	5 003	19	12	460	25.1	73.3	1.6
Wabaunsee	19.7	2 871	54.2	1.8	4.8	0.8	10.9	25.8	3 759	31	29	508	29.4	68.0	2.6
Wallace	7.0	4 815	58.0	2.5	3.5	0.0	12.8	2.1	1 408	15	0	164	11.9	85.8	2.2
Washington	25.9	4 441	52.5	13.4	1.3	0.3	10.6	5.7	984	54	24	752	22.1	75.4	2.4
Wichita	15.0	6 835	34.3	34.0	3.4	0.3	9.5	3.7	1 668	25	0	300	16.0	82.4	1.6
Wilson	35.8	3 647	51.8	19.5	3.5	0.2	6.6	16.8	1 711	41	40	942	28.4	69.2	2.5
Woodson	10.3	3 103	47.5	2.6	5.5	0.2	12.7	3.7	1 127	15	14	252	32.0	66.0	2.0
Wyandotte	774.6	5 031	43.1	2.3	6.7	0.0	4.0	3 261.3	21 183	1 964	655	15 857	69.7	28.9	1.4
KENTUCKY	X	X	X	X	X	X	X	X	X	40 064	54 773	276 442	41.2	57.4	1.4
Adair	60.0	3 367	39.5	42.2	2.0	0.0	3.4	86.2	4 832	59	57	891	22.9	75.5	1.6
Allen	36.6	1 935	66.2	3.1	5.0	0.1	3.9	33.1	1 751	46	60	745	27.4	71.2	1.5
Anderson	55.1	2 594	73.0	2.6	3.7	0.1	2.5	89.9	4 232	40	69	1 032	32.8	65.2	1.9
Ballard	27.7	3 336	50.5	4.7	3.2	0.0	4.8	154.2	18 567	39	26	416	35.1	62.5	2.4
Barren	99.2	2 409	64.9	0.9	4.2	0.1	4.4	153.2	3 719	127	131	2 279	32.3	66.2	1.4
Bath	21.5	1 854	70.4	4.3	2.2	0.0	2.0	18.5	1 599	31	37	536	48.6	49.2	2.2
Bell	69.6	2 402	62.2	1.7	3.5	0.0	3.6	45.4	1 566	152	91	1 813	29.0	69.6	1.4
Boone	292.9	2 604	52.7	1.4	4.7	1.9	5.5	957.8	8 517	1 301	374	5 219	32.1	66.6	1.3
Bourbon	50.9	2 575	55.6	2.5	3.9	0.1	4.1	55.0	2 785	46	62	1 035	40.6	57.9	1.5
Boyd	120.5	2 485	51.0	3.5	4.2	0.0	5.0	252.7	5 212	504	153	3 147	43.0	55.3	1.7
Boyle	74.5	2 598	53.0	1.9	4.9	0.3	3.3	227.5	7 936	75	92	1 902	37.7	60.9	1.3
Bracken	17.2	2 004	60.1	1.5	2.9	0.0	7.4	14.2	1 657	29	27	410	36.5	60.8	2.7
Breathitt	36.6	2 338	62.9	0.1	2.6	0.0	5.0	30.7	1 964	68	49	1 055	43.8	53.1	3.1
Breckinridge	43.7	2 291	52.5	0.5	2.1	0.9	5.9	237.6	12 448	72	60	791	36.5	62.0	1.5
Bullitt	130.1	1 760	68.0	1.8	4.9	0.0	2.4	128.0	1 731	74	238	2 611	33.1	65.4	1.5
Butler	28.5	2 151	56.3	2.0	2.6	0.0	5.1	60.5	4 562	31	42	615	29.3	69.6	1.1
Caldwell	24.6	1 928	58.8	1.1	4.7	0.0	5.3	46.1	3 607	42	41	885	35.7	62.4	2.0
Calloway	148.0	4 090	21.9	62.6	2.3	0.0	2.0	118.2	3 266	89	114	5 203	40.0	58.4	1.6
Campbell	219.3	2 524	53.0	0.5	6.8	0.2	5.1	585.2	6 737	325	278	6 056	38.8	59.7	1.6
Carlisle	9.4	1 810	64.8	4.3	1.9	0.0	7.6	2.9	567	20	16	229	33.6	64.9	1.5
Carroll	157.5	14 966	10.3	0.4	0.6	0.0	1.0	5 108.1	485 237	34	34	709	44.8	53.0	2.3
Carter	56.3	2 053	73.4	4.1	3.0	0.0	3.4	51.2	1 867	73	84	1 329	44.0	53.5	2.5
Casey	53.5	3 308	49.8	24.1	1.6	0.0	4.1	55.4	3 427	34	52	718	20.5	78.5	1.0
Christian	129.7	1 604	54.4	0.4	5.4	0.1	3.5	455.8	5 637	4 729	32 229	3 660	39.0	60.1	0.9
Clark	82.6	2 324	43.6	0.6	4.7	0.1	3.2	124.7	3 507	105	114	1 582	36.8	61.8	1.4

1. Based on the resident population estimated as of July 1 of the year shown.   2. © 2009 Election Data Services, Inc. All rights reserved.

Items 185—199

Table B. States and Counties — **Land Area and Population**

STATE/ County code	CBSA code[1]	County type[2]	STATE County	Land area,[3] (sq km) 2010	Total persons	Rank	Per square kilometer	White	Black	American Indian, Alaska Native	Asian and Pacific Islander	Percent Hispanic or Latino[4]	Under 5 years	5 to 17 years	18 to 24 years	25 to 34 years	35 to 44 years	45 to 54 years
				1	2	3	4	5	6	7	8	9	10	11	12	13	14	15
			KENTUCKY—Cont'd															
21 051	...	7	Clay	1 215	21 730	1 747	17.9	93.7	4.4	0.6	0.2	1.8	5.9	16.0	9.1	14.8	15.3	14.8
21 053	...	9	Clinton	511	10 272	2 418	20.1	97.0	0.5	0.8	0.3	2.2	6.3	17.5	7.2	11.0	12.8	15.0
21 055	...	6	Crittenden	932	9 315	2 495	10.0	98.0	1.1	0.7	0.3	0.5	6.7	15.9	7.3	10.9	12.2	14.8
21 057	...	9	Cumberland	790	6 856	2 699	8.7	96.1	3.3	0.5	0.2	0.9	6.4	15.8	7.6	9.8	12.3	15.3
21 059	36980	3	Daviess	1 187	96 656	597	81.4	91.6	5.9	0.4	1.0	2.6	6.9	17.5	8.6	12.4	12.5	15.0
21 061	14540	3	Edmonson	784	12 161	2 296	15.5	97.3	1.7	0.7	0.4	0.8	5.5	16.4	9.0	11.1	12.6	14.8
21 063	...	9	Elliott	607	7 852	2 618	12.9	95.6	3.4	0.4	0.2	0.8	5.7	14.7	7.9	14.2	14.7	14.9
21 065	...	6	Estill	655	14 672	2 134	22.4	98.8	0.3	0.6	0.1	0.7	5.8	16.9	7.2	11.8	13.7	15.5
21 067	30460	2	Fayette	735	295 803	217	402.5	74.9	15.6	0.6	3.9	6.9	6.5	14.7	14.1	16.6	13.3	13.5
21 069	...	7	Fleming	903	14 348	2 153	15.9	97.3	1.6	0.4	0.3	1.0	6.4	18.1	7.6	11.2	13.8	14.8
21 071	...	7	Floyd	1 019	39 451	1 183	38.7	98.4	0.9	0.4	0.3	0.6	6.2	16.2	8.4	12.6	13.4	15.4
21 073	23180	4	Franklin	538	49 285	991	91.6	85.1	11.7	0.7	1.6	2.8	6.1	15.6	9.7	12.5	13.2	15.2
21 075	46460	7	Fulton	532	6 813	2 704	12.8	74.5	24.9	0.6	0.8	0.8	5.9	14.2	8.5	12.4	12.1	14.8
21 077	17140	1	Gallatin	262	8 589	2 560	32.8	94.0	2.0	0.6	0.5	4.3	7.0	19.8	8.3	11.7	14.2	15.5
21 079	...	6	Garrard	596	16 912	1 990	28.4	95.2	2.4	0.4	0.3	2.4	6.2	17.0	7.1	11.3	14.0	14.9
21 081	17140	1	Grant	668	24 662	1 617	36.9	96.2	1.0	0.5	0.6	2.3	7.8	20.3	8.4	13.1	14.2	14.7
21 083	32460	7	Graves	1 429	37 121	1 239	26.0	89.4	5.3	0.7	0.5	5.7	6.6	17.7	8.0	11.7	12.3	14.3
21 085	...	6	Grayson	1 286	25 746	1 577	20.0	97.5	1.3	0.7	0.4	1.0	6.3	17.6	7.7	12.2	13.1	14.6
21 087	...	8	Green	741	11 258	2 347	15.2	96.0	2.4	0.7	0.3	1.4	6.0	16.6	6.9	11.1	12.6	15.7
21 089	26580	2	Greenup	892	36 910	1 246	41.4	97.7	1.0	0.7	0.6	0.8	5.8	16.8	7.2	11.0	13.1	15.3
21 091	36980	3	Hancock	486	8 565	2 563	17.6	97.6	1.3	0.5	0.4	1.1	6.5	19.5	7.0	11.1	13.6	14.9
21 093	21060	3	Hardin	1 614	105 543	557	65.4	80.5	12.9	1.1	3.4	5.0	7.6	18.4	9.9	14.2	13.3	14.8
21 095	...	7	Harlan	1 206	29 278	1 446	24.3	96.6	2.7	0.5	0.4	0.7	6.5	16.4	8.5	11.7	13.0	14.9
21 097	...	6	Harrison	793	18 846	1 883	23.8	95.7	2.7	0.5	0.4	1.8	6.1	18.2	7.3	10.8	13.8	15.9
21 099	...	8	Hart	1 067	18 199	1 916	17.1	93.2	5.5	0.5	0.3	1.4	6.5	18.5	8.2	10.8	12.6	15.5
21 101	21780	2	Henderson	1 131	46 250	1 037	40.9	89.6	8.8	0.4	0.6	1.9	6.7	16.8	7.9	12.6	12.8	15.8
21 103	31140	1	Henry	741	15 416	2 088	20.8	93.9	3.4	0.8	0.3	2.9	6.1	18.7	7.1	10.9	13.3	16.0
21 105	...	9	Hickman	627	4 902	2 848	7.8	89.0	10.0	0.7	0.5	1.2	5.8	15.7	6.7	10.1	12.0	14.8
21 107	31580	4	Hopkins	1 404	46 920	1 026	33.4	91.1	7.7	0.6	0.8	1.6	6.5	16.7	7.8	12.2	12.9	15.0
21 109	...	9	Jackson	894	13 494	2 219	15.1	99.1	0.2	0.5	0.2	0.6	6.1	17.5	7.8	12.4	14.2	15.1
21 111	31140	1	Jefferson	985	741 096	78	752.4	72.2	21.8	0.7	2.7	4.4	6.6	16.6	9.2	14.1	12.9	14.9
21 113	30460	2	Jessamine	446	48 586	1 000	108.9	92.8	3.9	0.7	1.4	2.8	7.3	18.5	10.0	13.2	13.6	14.8
21 115	...	7	Johnson	678	23 356	1 676	34.4	98.8	0.4	0.5	0.5	0.5	5.8	16.6	8.2	11.9	13.8	15.1
21 117	17140	1	Kenton	415	159 720	388	384.9	91.4	5.6	0.5	1.3	2.6	7.2	17.8	8.7	14.9	13.5	15.1
21 119	...	9	Knott	910	16 346	2 029	18.0	98.5	0.8	0.5	0.1	0.6	5.8	15.8	9.8	11.5	13.6	16.1
21 121	...	7	Knox	1 001	31 883	1 396	31.9	97.6	1.4	0.8	0.3	0.8	6.8	17.9	9.5	11.4	13.2	14.1
21 123	21060	3	Larue	677	14 193	2 161	21.0	93.6	3.8	0.4	0.4	2.8	6.2	17.5	8.1	11.9	12.4	15.6
21 125	30940	7	Laurel	1 124	58 849	870	52.4	97.3	1.0	0.8	0.6	1.2	6.5	17.8	8.2	13.0	14.0	15.1
21 127	...	6	Lawrence	1 076	15 860	2 061	14.7	99.0	0.5	0.5	0.3	0.5	6.7	16.5	8.2	11.9	13.1	15.4
21 129	...	9	Lee	541	7 887	2 611	14.6	96.5	2.5	0.6	0.2	0.7	4.7	14.8	8.4	14.0	14.8	16.4
21 131	...	9	Leslie	1 038	11 310	2 342	10.9	99.2	0.4	0.5	0.2	0.4	5.7	15.6	8.5	12.2	13.6	16.9
21 133	...	9	Letcher	875	24 519	1 624	28.0	98.8	0.5	0.4	0.2	0.5	6.2	15.9	7.9	12.5	12.8	15.8
21 135	32500	8	Lewis	1 251	13 870	2 190	11.1	98.9	0.4	0.5	0.1	0.6	6.2	17.7	7.7	11.4	13.5	15.5
21 137	19220	7	Lincoln	865	24 742	1 612	28.6	95.8	2.8	0.8	0.3	1.5	6.6	18.1	7.8	11.6	13.9	14.7
21 139	37140	9	Livingston	811	9 519	2 479	11.7	98.0	0.5	0.8	0.3	1.3	5.7	14.9	7.4	10.0	12.2	16.1
21 141	...	6	Logan	1 430	26 835	1 537	18.8	90.5	7.3	0.6	0.4	2.4	6.4	18.2	7.4	11.9	12.4	15.2
21 143	...	8	Lyon	554	8 314	2 587	15.0	93.2	5.7	0.7	0.4	0.9	4.1	11.4	6.1	11.3	12.8	16.4
21 145	37140	5	McCracken	644	65 565	799	101.8	85.7	12.2	0.8	1.1	2.1	6.0	16.4	7.3	11.9	12.5	15.3
21 147	...	9	McCreary	1 105	18 306	1 909	16.6	91.5	5.7	1.5	0.4	2.1	5.9	16.6	9.2	14.0	15.6	14.3
21 149	36980	3	McLean	654	9 531	2 478	14.6	98.0	0.9	0.5	0.2	1.1	5.8	17.5	7.5	11.0	13.1	14.8
21 151	40080	4	Madison	1 133	82 916	665	73.2	92.1	5.2	0.9	1.3	2.2	6.1	15.4	16.7	13.5	13.0	13.1
21 153	...	9	Magoffin	799	13 333	2 229	16.7	98.8	0.2	0.7	0.1	0.7	6.0	17.9	8.4	12.2	14.2	15.4
21 155	...	6	Marion	888	19 820	1 848	22.3	88.6	9.1	0.5	0.7	2.4	6.7	18.0	7.6	14.0	13.6	15.3
21 157	...	7	Marshall	780	31 448	1 406	40.3	98.2	0.3	0.6	0.4	1.1	5.3	15.5	7.0	10.4	12.7	15.2
21 159	...	8	Martin	595	12 929	2 246	21.7	89.7	6.9	0.6	0.3	3.0	5.7	15.7	8.5	16.7	15.2	14.7
21 161	32500	6	Mason	622	17 490	1 951	28.1	91.2	7.5	0.5	0.8	1.4	6.8	17.5	7.9	10.8	13.6	14.8
21 163	31140	1	Meade	791	28 602	1 471	36.2	92.6	4.0	1.3	1.4	3.0	7.7	19.6	9.2	13.6	13.4	15.2
21 165	34460	9	Menifee	527	6 306	2 742	12.0	97.1	2.2	0.7	0.1	0.8	5.5	17.7	9.3	10.3	12.4	14.7
21 167	...	6	Mercer	644	21 331	1 773	33.1	93.5	4.4	0.7	0.6	2.3	6.0	17.6	7.0	10.8	13.0	15.8
21 169	23980	9	Metcalfe	750	10 099	2 439	13.5	97.1	1.8	0.6	0.2	1.1	6.4	17.6	8.3	10.8	12.9	15.2
21 171	...	9	Monroe	853	10 963	2 369	12.9	95.0	2.7	0.5	0.1	2.6	5.9	17.4	7.3	10.9	12.6	15.3
21 173	34460	6	Montgomery	511	26 499	1 543	51.9	94.1	3.1	0.5	0.4	2.5	6.8	17.7	7.9	13.3	14.5	14.5
21 175	...	7	Morgan	987	13 923	2 184	14.1	94.3	4.5	0.6	0.4	0.8	5.2	15.2	8.4	15.8	14.7	15.0
21 177	16420	6	Muhlenberg	1 210	31 499	1 405	26.0	94.0	5.0	0.5	0.3	1.2	5.6	16.0	8.7	12.0	13.2	14.8
21 179	31140	1	Nelson	1 081	43 437	1 099	40.2	92.2	5.8	0.5	0.8	2.0	6.9	19.1	8.0	12.8	13.7	15.3
21 181	...	8	Nicholas	505	7 135	2 672	14.1	97.7	0.8	0.4	0.4	1.4	6.3	17.9	7.0	11.6	13.9	14.9

1. CBSA = Core Based Statistical Area. See Appendix A for explanation. See Appendix B for list of metropolitan areas with component counties.   2. County type code from the Economic Research Service of USDA Rural-Urban Continuum Codes. See Appendix A for definition.   3. Dry land or land partially or temporarily covered by water.   4. May be of any race.

Table B. States and Counties — **Population and Households**

STATE County	55 to 64 years	65 to 74 years	75 years and over	Percent female	1990	2000	1990–2000	2000–2010	Births	Deaths	Net migration	Number	Percent change, 2000–2010	Persons per household	Female family householder[1]	One person
	16	17	18	19	20	21	22	23	24	25	26	27	28	29	30	31
KENTUCKY—Cont'd																
Clay	12.0	7.4	4.7	46.6	21 746	24 556	12.9	-11.5	2 666	2 136	-1 336	7 732	-9.6	2.52	14.8	25.3
Clinton	13.5	10.0	6.6	50.0	9 135	9 634	5.5	6.6	1 189	1 147	-222	4 358	6.7	2.33	11.4	30.7
Crittenden	14.0	10.6	7.5	50.1	9 196	9 384	2.0	-0.7	951	1 136	-35	3 781	-1.3	2.41	9.9	28.3
Cumberland	13.7	10.6	8.5	50.9	6 784	7 147	5.4	-4.1	762	914	-250	2 883	-3.1	2.35	11.1	29.6
Daviess	12.5	7.7	6.9	51.5	87 189	91 545	5.0	5.6	12 398	8 364	419	38 619	7.2	2.44	12.9	28.3
Edmonson	14.0	9.8	6.8	50.1	10 357	11 644	12.4	4.4	1 119	1 034	250	4 857	4.5	2.44	9.7	25.0
Elliott	13.5	8.8	5.7	44.0	6 455	6 748	4.5	16.4	725	728	2 219	2 773	5.1	2.45	11.8	26.1
Estill	13.8	9.3	6.0	50.7	14 614	15 307	4.7	-4.1	1 796	1 584	-576	5 984	-2.0	2.43	13.4	27.1
Fayette	10.8	5.7	4.8	50.8	225 366	260 512	15.6	13.5	35 765	18 424	11 245	123 043	13.6	2.30	12.3	32.7
Fleming	13.4	8.6	6.1	50.9	12 292	13 792	12.2	4.0	1 741	1 426	635	5 729	6.7	2.50	10.2	25.4
Floyd	14.1	8.1	5.5	51.1	43 586	42 441	-2.6	-7.0	5 100	4 543	-848	16 060	-4.9	2.41	13.5	27.5
Franklin	13.8	7.9	6.1	51.6	44 143	47 687	8.0	3.4	5 739	4 337	134	20 662	3.8	2.29	13.7	31.5
Fulton	14.1	9.4	8.6	50.4	8 271	7 752	-6.3	-12.1	822	1 013	-724	2 864	-11.5	2.22	16.5	34.2
Gallatin	12.1	7.5	3.9	49.8	5 393	7 870	45.9	9.1	1 200	777	-63	3 160	8.9	2.69	12.9	22.3
Garrard	13.4	8.5	6.1	50.7	11 579	14 792	27.7	14.3	1 664	1 271	1 967	6 668	16.1	2.52	9.8	22.4
Grant	10.8	6.7	4.0	50.1	15 737	22 384	42.2	10.2	3 679	1 808	1 398	8 614	5.4	2.81	13.4	19.8
Graves	12.8	9.0	7.6	51.0	33 550	37 028	10.4	0.3	4 463	4 093	546	14 978	0.9	2.44	10.6	27.7
Grayson	13.4	8.9	6.1	49.3	21 050	24 053	14.3	7.0	3 059	2 534	1 140	10 082	5.1	2.48	10.7	25.5
Green	13.8	9.6	7.7	50.7	10 371	11 518	11.1	-2.3	1 182	1 256	133	4 601	-2.2	2.42	9.4	26.6
Greenup	13.8	9.5	7.5	51.6	36 796	36 891	0.3	0.1	3 810	3 782	1 292	14 671	0.9	2.48	11.0	24.5
Hancock	13.5	8.4	5.6	49.5	7 864	8 392	6.7	2.1	1 079	666	-122	3 285	2.2	2.58	9.4	22.6
Hardin	10.8	6.3	4.7	50.1	89 240	94 174	5.5	12.1	14 169	6 547	-1 386	39 853	15.5	2.57	12.9	24.5
Harlan	14.8	8.1	6.2	51.3	36 574	33 202	-9.2	-11.8	3 677	3 932	-1 805	11 789	-11.3	2.43	13.9	27.8
Harrison	13.0	8.4	6.5	51.1	16 248	17 983	10.7	4.8	2 159	1 799	552	7 343	4.7	2.53	11.8	24.1
Hart	13.0	8.8	6.1	50.5	14 890	17 445	17.2	4.3	2 160	1 778	672	7 097	4.8	2.53	10.9	26.2
Henderson	13.2	7.8	6.4	51.7	43 044	44 829	4.1	3.2	5 636	4 081	-610	18 705	3.4	2.41	13.1	28.0
Henry	13.7	8.5	5.7	50.7	12 823	15 060	17.4	2.4	1 929	1 429	596	5 963	2.0	2.57	11.8	23.0
Hickman	14.2	11.0	9.8	52.2	5 566	5 262	-5.5	-6.8	449	582	-248	2 028	-7.3	2.31	11.5	29.9
Hopkins	13.4	8.6	6.8	51.4	46 126	46 519	0.9	0.9	5 490	5 193	-365	18 980	0.9	2.41	12.6	27.0
Jackson	13.2	8.6	5.2	50.3	11 955	13 495	12.9	0.0	1 503	1 364	-316	5 486	3.4	2.44	11.2	26.4
Jefferson	12.3	6.9	6.5	51.7	665 123	693 604	4.3	6.8	92 653	64 567	4 715	309 175	7.7	2.35	15.4	32.0
Jessamine	11.3	6.3	5.0	51.3	30 508	39 041	28.0	24.4	5 692	3 012	6 055	17 642	27.2	2.65	12.9	20.7
Johnson	14.3	8.5	5.7	50.8	23 248	23 445	0.8	-0.4	2 761	2 527	300	9 362	2.8	2.44	11.5	26.2
Kenton	11.6	6.1	6.1	50.6	142 005	151 464	6.7	5.5	21 964	12 200	-1 507	62 768	5.6	2.51	13.0	29.1
Knott	14.1	8.0	5.3	50.2	17 906	17 649	-1.4	-7.4	1 648	1 618	-474	6 414	-4.5	2.44	12.9	27.0
Knox	12.4	8.8	5.8	51.3	29 676	31 795	7.1	0.3	4 388	3 314	56	12 722	2.5	2.46	14.2	28.5
Larue	12.6	8.3	7.3	50.4	11 679	13 373	14.5	6.1	1 513	1 427	288	5 615	6.4	2.47	11.6	25.8
Laurel	12.6	7.8	5.1	51.0	43 438	52 715	21.4	11.6	7 016	4 802	3 100	23 014	13.1	2.53	13.0	24.3
Lawrence	14.0	8.6	5.8	50.6	13 998	15 569	11.2	1.9	1 884	1 631	842	6 239	4.8	2.52	10.6	24.9
Lee	13.6	7.4	5.8	45.2	7 422	7 916	6.7	-0.4	710	901	-352	2 910	-2.5	2.36	13.7	28.8
Leslie	13.3	8.4	5.8	50.5	13 642	12 401	-9.1	-8.8	1 295	1 236	-900	4 555	-6.8	2.43	11.6	26.8
Letcher	14.7	8.6	5.6	50.7	27 000	25 277	-6.4	-3.0	2 820	2 809	-1 527	10 014	-0.7	2.42	12.3	26.7
Lewis	13.3	8.9	5.9	50.1	13 029	14 092	8.2	-1.6	1 623	1 391	-498	5 497	1.4	2.50	10.7	23.7
Lincoln	12.4	8.7	6.2	50.6	20 096	23 361	16.2	5.9	3 108	2 241	1 083	9 777	6.2	2.51	12.7	24.9
Livingston	15.7	10.8	7.3	51.0	9 062	9 804	8.2	-2.9	928	1 054	-22	3 985	-0.3	2.37	9.1	26.0
Logan	12.9	9.1	6.5	51.1	24 416	26 573	8.8	1.0	3 352	2 617	27	10 666	1.5	2.49	11.3	25.9
Lyon	17.1	12.6	8.3	44.9	6 624	8 080	22.0	2.9	531	960	692	3 287	13.4	2.19	7.7	30.0
McCracken	13.9	8.7	8.0	52.0	62 879	65 514	4.2	0.1	7 576	6 962	126	28 227	1.8	2.28	12.6	31.9
McCreary	12.2	7.8	4.5	45.7	15 603	17 080	9.5	7.2	2 172	1 637	286	6 477	-0.7	2.50	14.0	27.1
McLean	13.3	9.6	7.3	50.9	9 628	9 938	3.2	-4.1	1 150	1 064	-361	3 833	-3.8	2.47	10.4	24.5
Madison	11.0	6.4	4.8	51.4	57 508	70 872	23.2	17.0	9 379	5 255	8 673	31 973	17.8	2.42	11.7	26.3
Magoffin	12.9	8.0	4.9	49.9	13 077	13 332	1.9	0.0	1 689	1 249	-535	5 309	5.7	2.49	11.7	25.0
Marion	11.8	7.0	6.0	48.3	16 499	18 212	10.4	8.8	2 413	1 663	648	7 358	11.3	2.52	13.2	26.8
Marshall	14.5	11.1	8.2	50.8	27 205	30 125	10.7	4.4	2 923	3 431	1 753	13 073	5.3	2.37	9.6	25.4
Martin	12.3	6.4	4.8	44.7	12 526	12 578	0.4	2.8	1 501	1 146	214	4 516	-5.4	2.50	13.0	26.8
Mason	13.4	8.2	6.9	51.8	16 666	16 800	0.8	4.1	2 002	1 835	496	7 031	2.7	2.45	13.5	27.7
Meade	11.0	6.4	4.0	49.9	24 170	26 349	9.0	8.6	2 482	1 591	-623	10 471	10.6	2.71	10.8	20.8
Menifee	14.2	10.0	5.9	50.1	5 092	6 556	28.8	-3.8	695	602	-18	2 440	-3.8	2.49	9.2	25.6
Mercer	13.8	9.2	6.7	51.2	19 148	20 817	8.7	2.5	2 476	2 187	947	8 682	3.1	2.44	11.6	26.1
Metcalfe	12.7	9.2	7.1	50.4	8 963	10 037	12.0	0.6	1 196	1 165	51	4 055	1.0	2.46	10.4	26.8
Monroe	13.6	10.2	7.0	50.5	11 401	11 756	3.1	-6.7	1 310	1 285	-148	4 509	-4.9	2.40	11.0	29.8
Montgomery	12.5	7.2	5.6	51.2	19 561	22 554	15.3	17.5	3 281	2 112	2 236	10 435	17.2	2.51	12.6	25.1
Morgan	12.7	7.6	5.4	43.3	11 648	13 948	19.7	-0.2	1 425	1 137	-62	4 860	2.3	2.46	10.1	24.6
Muhlenberg	13.4	9.2	7.0	49.5	31 318	31 839	1.7	-1.1	3 400	3 519	-250	12 052	-2.5	2.45	11.9	24.9
Nelson	12.3	6.9	4.9	50.8	29 710	37 477	26.1	15.9	5 276	2 915	3 943	16 826	20.6	2.55	13.2	24.4
Nicholas	12.9	8.8	6.8	50.3	6 725	6 813	1.3	4.7	846	860	113	2 809	3.7	2.51	11.1	25.6

1. No spouse present.

Table B. States and Counties — **Population, Vital Statistics, Medicare, and Crime**

STATE County	Persons in group quarters, 2010	Daytime population, 2006–2010		Births, average 2006–2008		Deaths, average 2006–2008		Persons under 65 with no health insurance, 2009		Medicare, 2011			Serious crimes known to police,[2] 2010 Total	
		Number	Employ-ment/resi-dence ratio	Total	Rate[1]	Number	Rate[1]	Number	Percent	Eligible for Medicare	Enrolled in Medicare Advantage	Enrolled in a Medicare prescription drug plan	Number	Rate[3]
	32	33	34	35	36	37	38	39	40	41	42	43	44	45
KENTUCKY—Cont'd														
Clay	2 240	21 740	0.9	D	D	223	9.3	4 448	22.1	4 568	369	3 251	169	778
Clinton	136	10 694	1.1	D	D	121	12.6	1 597	21.0	2 465	242	1 717	1	10
Crittenden	210	8 180	0.7	D	D	123	13.5	1 533	21.0	2 172	160	1 212	69	741
Cumberland	86	6 564	0.9	D	D	111	16.0	1 109	21.0	1 625	177	1 115	14	204
Daviess	2 581	96 827	1.0	1 395	14.9	907	9.7	11 541	14.6	18 894	2 216	11 220	2 740	2 835
Edmonson	323	9 350	0.4	D	D	114	9.5	2 128	21.5	2 592	421	1 487	67	551
Elliott	1 061	6 797	0.6	D	D	76	10.5	1 392	21.4	1 497	277	757	NA	NA
Estill	118	12 614	0.6	D	D	161	10.7	2 437	19.5	3 214	442	1 904	217	1 479
Fayette	12 804	320 387	1.2	4 040	14.6	2 013	7.3	40 994	16.0	38 818	7 152	18 894	13 710	4 635
Fleming	22	12 911	0.8	D	D	151	10.3	2 517	20.4	3 090	504	1 863	71	495
Floyd	790	40 431	1.0	572	13.6	503	11.9	7 106	20.1	9 922	1 783	6 027	217	568
Franklin	2 061	59 041	1.4	633	13.1	440	9.1	6 334	15.5	10 842	1 138	7 640	1 379	2 798
Fulton	445	6 776	1.0	D	D	99	14.5	1 025	19.0	1 701	96	1 008	NA	NA
Gallatin	85	7 326	0.9	D	D	81	10.1	1 302	18.5	1 019	179	526	42	510
Garrard	109	12 936	0.4	D	D	154	9.1	2 828	19.8	3 345	476	1 759	149	881
Grant	457	20 312	0.6	D	D	199	7.9	3 806	17.1	4 365	833	2 113	273	1 107
Graves	548	33 679	0.8	514	13.7	435	11.5	5 743	18.7	7 922	810	4 856	518	1 420
Grayson	768	24 095	0.9	D	D	270	10.6	4 020	19.1	5 347	993	2 994	316	1 257
Green	113	9 187	0.5	D	D	136	11.7	2 035	21.8	2 563	269	1 625	26	231
Greenup	454	32 490	0.7	D	D	431	11.5	4 667	15.5	8 769	1 580	4 650	307	855
Hancock	90	9 449	1.3	D	D	70	8.1	1 034	14.0	1 608	148	885	34	397
Hardin	3 256	108 659	1.2	1 615	16.5	739	7.6	12 660	14.9	15 189	1 803	5 999	2 074	1 965
Harlan	627	29 982	1.0	448	14.4	408	13.1	5 192	20.0	7 147	838	4 449	247	844
Harrison	275	16 302	0.7	D	D	193	10.4	2 614	16.6	3 619	579	1 918	587	3 115
Hart	227	16 608	0.8	D	D	205	11.1	3 328	21.7	3 732	417	2 371	42	231
Henderson	1 165	44 862	0.9	643	14.1	449	9.9	5 743	15.2	8 714	1 614	4 782	1 243	2 688
Henry	80	12 496	0.5	D	D	159	10.1	2 320	17.1	2 901	743	1 429	35	271
Hickman	212	4 774	0.9	D	D	62	12.5	748	19.6	1 195	77	732	NA	NA
Hopkins	1 086	47 227	1.0	636	13.7	558	12.0	6 750	17.8	9 679	1 223	5 877	363	774
Jackson	110	11 573	0.6	D	D	145	10.6	2 288	20.6	2 731	327	1 750	101	796
Jefferson	14 153	810 260	1.2	10 539	14.9	6 924	9.8	86 489	14.3	124 925	29 118	59 720	36 171	4 893
Jessamine	1 779	43 104	0.8	703	15.4	347	7.6	7 083	17.1	7 070	1 400	3 327	1 639	3 373
Johnson	528	21 836	0.8	314	13.0	273	11.3	3 807	18.9	5 435	752	3 297	173	741
Kenton	2 332	145 808	0.8	2 516	16.1	1 325	8.7	18 652	13.5	22 768	5 413	10 261	5 391	3 375
Knott	677	15 168	0.7	D	D	187	10.7	2 768	19.0	3 555	588	2 176	22	146
Knox	642	31 095	0.9	478	14.7	373	11.4	5 700	20.7	7 030	688	4 668	417	1 308
Larue	313	11 704	0.6	D	D	152	11.1	1 998	17.9	2 859	484	1 580	62	437
Laurel	699	59 801	1.1	787	13.7	538	9.4	9 694	19.7	11 615	1 276	6 790	723	1 229
Lawrence	108	14 929	0.8	233	14.2	172	10.5	2 725	19.5	3 561	377	2 151	150	946
Lee	1 016	7 936	1.0	D	D	88	11.8	1 294	21.5	1 654	195	1 114	12	152
Leslie	227	10 697	0.8	D	D	123	10.5	1 885	19.5	2 744	360	1 748	NA	NA
Letcher	243	22 860	0.8	D	D	307	12.7	3 761	19.0	5 727	832	3 483	72	294
Lewis	139	11 972	0.6	D	D	137	9.9	2 415	20.9	2 685	312	1 783	79	570
Lincoln	219	20 656	0.6	D	D	254	10.1	4 200	20.0	5 160	758	2 917	123	524
Livingston	69	7 987	0.6	D	D	120	12.4	1 279	16.5	2 329	203	1 278	103	1 082
Logan	277	25 762	0.9	D	D	288	10.6	4 060	18.0	5 437	657	3 540	537	2 067
Lyon	1 123	7 894	0.8	D	D	107	13.0	1 435	22.5	2 069	320	1 063	93	1 119
McCracken	1 189	75 626	1.4	809	12.5	765	11.8	7 798	14.6	14 052	1 390	7 679	1 967	3 000
McCreary	2 111	17 166	0.8	D	D	173	10.0	3 370	22.3	3 682	439	2 468	182	994
McLean	82	7 742	0.5	D	D	124	12.7	1 382	17.6	2 114	418	1 120	38	399
Madison	5 695	78 159	0.9	1 047	13.0	613	7.6	13 044	18.1	12 794	2 589	6 670	3 367	4 061
Magoffin	127	12 556	0.8	D	D	153	11.5	2 095	18.7	2 801	318	1 821	55	413
Marion	1 297	19 651	1.0	D	D	179	9.4	3 108	18.8	3 509	693	2 059	269	1 357
Marshall	464	30 099	0.9	D	D	385	12.3	3 760	15.2	7 610	760	3 922	483	1 536
Martin	1 657	13 431	1.1	D	D	130	11.0	2 244	19.9	2 696	427	1 676	78	603
Mason	298	19 288	1.3	255	14.7	203	11.7	2 416	16.9	3 477	639	2 033	715	4 088
Meade	212	21 742	0.4	D	D	178	6.5	3 680	15.9	4 190	656	1 889	164	573
Menifee	230	5 282	0.5	D	D	71	10.5	1 169	22.1	1 514	415	841	30	476
Mercer	128	19 826	0.8	D	D	251	11.5	3 003	16.5	4 467	753	2 220	223	1 095
Metcalfe	121	9 032	0.7	D	D	117	11.4	1 627	19.8	2 216	489	1 268	61	604
Monroe	143	10 412	0.8	D	D	155	13.3	2 069	21.9	2 603	318	1 810	NA	NA
Montgomery	357	26 524	1.1	405	16.0	245	9.7	3 800	17.4	4 948	1 049	2 651	1 024	3 864
Morgan	1 975	13 519	0.9	D	D	125	8.8	2 638	22.2	2 657	469	1 591	NA	NA
Muhlenberg	1 951	30 222	0.9	353	11.3	400	12.8	4 574	17.9	7 014	765	4 579	135	429
Nelson	496	38 415	0.8	D	D	345	8.1	5 718	15.2	7 478	1 400	4 071	630	1 479
Nicholas	95	5 644	0.5	D	D	102	14.8	1 183	21.0	1 518	174	951	NA	NA

1. Per 1,000 estimated resident population.   2. Data for serious crimes have not been adjusted for underreporting; this may affect comparability between geographic areas and over time.   3. Per 100,000 population estimated by the FBI.

Table B. States and Counties — Crime, Education, Money Income, and Poverty

STATE County	Serious crimes known to police,[1] 2010 (cont.) Rate[2] Violent	Property	Education — School enrollment and attainment, 2006–2010 — Enrollment[3] Total	Per cent private	Attainment[4] (percent) High school graduate or less	Bach-elor's degree or more	Local government expenditures,[5] 2008–2009 Total current expenditures (mil dol)	Current expenditures per student (dollars)	Money income, 2006–2010 Per capita income[6] (dollars)	Households Median income Dollars	Percent change, 2000 to 2006–2010 (constant 2010 dollars)	Percent with income of $200,000 or more	Income and poverty, 2010 — Median house-hold income (dollars)	Percent below poverty level All per-sons	Children under 18 years	Children 5 to 17 years in families
	46	47	48	49	50	51	52	53	54	55	56	57	58	59	60	61
KENTUCKY—Cont'd																
Clay	64	713	4 975	9.9	79.8	7.5	36.3	9 860	12 300	20 175	-2.1	0.8	24 081	38.0	48.9	43.6
Clinton	0	10	2 380	1.4	75.1	3.7	17.4	9 848	14 802	23 788	-4.0	1.5	27 133	25.4	37.5	34.0
Crittenden	21	719	1 892	4.9	66.5	9.3	11.2	8 288	19 463	34 623	-5.9	0.5	33 966	20.0	31.9	31.2
Cumberland	0	204	1 395	9.7	73.0	7.9	10.2	10 076	15 025	28 135	3.0	0.0	27 382	26.3	39.5	38.3
Daviess	133	2 701	24 024	16.5	53.0	18.2	139.7	9 062	22 064	42 821	-8.1	1.3	41 878	16.2	24.6	22.5
Edmonson	41	510	2 593	3.5	70.4	7.2	18.2	8 784	18 959	35 808	11.3	0.4	34 849	18.8	30.1	28.1
Elliott	NA	NA	1 522	3.0	73.2	7.1	10.8	9 469	13 072	22 097	-17.0	0.0	29 335	29.9	36.0	33.7
Estill	95	1 384	2 853	9.3	75.0	6.6	20.8	8 288	15 725	28 324	-4.1	0.7	29 486	28.7	42.2	36.9
Fayette	590	4 045	83 499	16.3	32.8	39.1	336.3	9 312	28 345	47 469	-5.8	3.6	45 820	20.0	23.9	22.0
Fleming	0	495	3 420	11.2	60.9	12.7	20.4	8 659	17 629	31 236	-11.9	0.8	33 141	18.9	30.8	29.1
Floyd	31	537	8 241	8.0	65.8	11.7	56.8	8 811	15 883	27 907	4.1	0.9	28 589	29.9	43.5	37.4
Franklin	183	2 615	11 730	12.0	48.0	27.2	57.1	8 285	26 857	47 976	-5.3	2.3	46 323	16.0	23.0	20.3
Fulton	NA	NA	1 265	17.4	66.2	10.9	11.1	10 495	16 908	31 965	3.5	0.4	30 662	27.1	41.5	40.8
Gallatin	12	498	2 057	2.6	69.1	9.0	14.2	8 912	17 810	41 310	-10.4	0.1	42 761	16.7	25.3	22.9
Garrard	18	863	3 710	7.4	64.6	13.8	21.6	8 147	18 735	37 095	-14.6	0.7	40 834	17.0	25.8	24.2
Grant	24	1 083	6 494	9.8	61.5	10.8	39.2	8 321	20 257	42 475	-12.7	1.4	42 690	18.4	26.1	24.4
Graves	132	1 288	9 114	10.5	59.7	14.4	51.9	8 239	19 976	35 277	-9.8	2.4	34 811	19.7	28.6	28.0
Grayson	36	1 221	6 128	10.6	70.6	7.5	34.0	7 961	17 443	33 965	-3.0	0.6	32 970	20.8	31.8	29.1
Green	27	204	2 410	14.7	68.0	11.4	14.7	8 640	21 281	36 575	13.4	1.5	31 423	21.6	32.4	29.5
Greenup	42	813	8 176	8.1	56.3	14.9	54.1	8 372	21 533	42 377	4.1	1.6	40 762	17.3	23.8	21.7
Hancock	35	362	2 227	4.0	60.4	10.8	14.5	8 409	19 952	44 892	-4.0	0.3	46 729	14.2	20.1	17.8
Hardin	215	1 750	26 941	10.0	47.2	18.5	132.1	8 088	22 997	47 540	-0.5	1.4	44 203	14.7	20.6	20.7
Harlan	79	765	6 791	5.8	68.4	11.1	45.6	8 730	15 224	26 582	12.5	0.6	28 503	33.7	39.2	37.0
Harrison	138	2 977	4 292	8.1	59.7	13.8	25.3	7 879	20 037	40 582	-11.5	0.5	42 124	16.6	24.4	22.3
Hart	27	203	4 295	10.6	70.8	9.2	22.7	9 476	16 726	30 969	-3.6	0.4	31 733	25.3	37.0	33.8
Henderson	69	2 618	10 339	14.0	54.8	16.1	59.0	8 508	22 192	40 438	-11.0	0.9	41 309	16.5	22.4	20.7
Henry	46	224	3 582	4.0	65.3	14.1	23.0	7 759	21 090	43 612	-7.6	1.8	40 806	17.1	25.3	22.2
Hickman	NA	NA	1 106	5.3	59.0	16.5	7.4	9 122	19 953	31 836	-20.5	0.7	39 087	18.7	30.7	27.3
Hopkins	62	712	10 742	7.6	59.1	13.2	65.6	8 340	21 347	39 312	0.6	1.3	39 738	19.3	29.5	25.7
Jackson	8	788	3 172	4.1	75.8	6.2	22.2	9 721	13 995	21 928	-14.2	0.5	26 462	30.2	40.1	36.7
Jefferson	532	4 361	183 683	24.1	42.4	28.5	988.9	9 973	26 473	45 352	-9.2	3.1	42 535	17.3	24.4	22.1
Jessamine	132	3 242	13 084	27.0	45.7	27.4	63.8	8 316	24 097	47 494	-6.5	2.8	43 503	16.1	23.6	21.3
Johnson	47	694	4 645	5.6	67.9	10.5	41.7	9 123	18 486	30 820	-2.3	2.0	34 260	23.4	32.8	29.7
Kenton	291	3 085	41 563	22.9	44.3	27.5	187.9	8 440	27 205	53 213	-4.3	3.5	51 049	13.3	18.3	16.3
Knott	0	146	4 096	23.8	65.8	12.4	23.7	9 434	16 110	29 451	14.2	0.2	30 693	26.4	34.3	31.4
Knox	66	1 242	7 425	11.6	77.2	8.5	48.4	8 808	14 101	21 493	-7.2	1.1	25 965	33.9	45.3	42.3
Larue	14	423	3 361	5.8	63.7	12.1	19.6	8 044	18 474	38 891	-4.2	0.8	37 863	19.1	29.7	26.9
Laurel	58	1 171	13 301	11.2	62.7	13.6	79.7	8 116	19 604	36 787	7.5	1.4	34 712	24.0	33.3	29.8
Lawrence	44	902	3 539	6.8	67.9	8.2	21.8	8 879	15 903	28 865	5.5	1.0	33 313	20.0	29.9	29.5
Lee	25	127	1 571	5.9	75.4	7.8	10.9	9 539	12 983	25 129	7.0	0.0	24 908	37.3	52.2	46.1
Leslie	NA	NA	2 569	8.1	74.5	8.1	19.0	10 049	14 753	26 857	14.4	0.1	30 597	29.2	35.8	33.6
Letcher	41	263	6 261	8.3	64.1	11.7	36.9	9 622	17 393	31 283	17.0	0.6	33 410	23.2	32.6	31.1
Lewis	43	526	3 122	14.0	74.0	11.6	22.1	9 053	14 915	28 376	0.9	0.6	29 453	28.4	39.5	36.9
Lincoln	34	490	5 793	6.4	69.0	10.4	40.1	9 834	16 985	32 314	-3.9	0.3	32 864	23.3	33.9	31.3
Livingston	32	1 051	1 932	8.4	61.1	10.7	12.3	9 421	20 800	39 075	-2.9	0.9	38 608	14.7	23.4	22.6
Logan	123	1 944	5 800	9.7	67.5	10.3	39.8	8 372	19 443	34 647	-15.7	1.4	37 316	17.9	27.5	24.7
Lyon	0	1 119	1 259	6.3	57.7	10.8	7.9	8 416	19 036	42 079	4.8	1.2	39 588	14.9	20.8	18.9
McCracken	204	2 796	15 084	13.7	45.3	21.0	86.3	8 455	24 709	41 630	-2.9	2.3	41 585	16.1	25.6	23.2
McCreary	49	945	4 204	8.6	71.3	8.0	30.0	9 194	12 197	22 643	-7.6	0.0	24 691	36.5	49.3	46.2
McLean	21	378	2 403	6.1	64.7	9.7	13.1	7 800	21 071	39 115	4.1	1.8	38 580	16.4	24.1	21.2
Madison	200	3 861	26 445	15.5	45.9	27.4	96.4	8 116	21 536	41 894	0.7	1.4	41 945	21.4	25.1	22.5
Magoffin	38	375	3 374	2.8	70.7	10.5	22.9	9 762	13 849	22 779	-7.4	0.9	28 943	29.4	41.2	37.1
Marion	66	1 292	4 788	12.2	65.6	11.4	27.0	8 382	18 445	37 488	-2.6	1.7	36 816	18.4	25.9	23.7
Marshall	86	1 450	6 692	8.5	58.1	14.8	41.5	8 573	23 056	43 326	-3.8	1.6	43 825	11.5	18.5	17.9
Martin	23	580	2 881	2.2	68.5	8.9	21.1	9 451	14 785	25 173	8.8	0.0	29 575	36.6	42.2	38.2
Mason	143	3 945	3 871	9.9	60.3	14.3	24.1	8 544	21 717	40 523	6.0	2.3	36 795	21.6	33.9	31.4
Meade	28	545	7 883	7.5	54.5	11.5	38.1	7 656	18 823	43 800	-6.4	0.1	46 671	14.3	21.5	19.5
Menifee	0	476	1 292	4.4	70.7	10.3	10.1	8 964	15 418	29 740	6.4	0.0	28 061	28.4	43.2	37.9
Mercer	108	987	4 891	10.7	58.2	17.0	32.0	8 653	23 645	47 955	6.5	1.7	41 985	15.3	22.9	19.9
Metcalfe	10	594	2 261	9.9	75.2	7.2	14.4	8 138	16 835	34 732	16.5	0.6	28 538	21.4	36.1	33.6
Monroe	NA	NA	2 564	2.7	70.9	11.6	18.6	9 208	15 534	28 439	0.5	0.0	28 074	24.5	39.1	35.6
Montgomery	211	3 653	5 890	7.3	62.9	15.1	35.4	7 548	20 004	36 034	-10.4	0.9	37 678	19.2	26.6	25.4
Morgan	NA	NA	3 139	5.2	68.1	11.8	19.7	9 197	17 705	30 229	9.2	2.2	30 502	31.8	38.8	34.2
Muhlenberg	41	387	6 966	7.4	64.5	10.2	47.4	9 158	18 538	36 750	1.6	1.1	37 614	21.0	30.0	26.9
Nelson	92	1 387	10 512	20.0	57.4	15.4	79.1	7 830	21 763	44 783	-9.3	1.6	43 330	16.0	21.5	19.6
Nicholas	NA	NA	1 498	10.1	69.6	9.4	10.2	8 155	18 452	40 259	6.4	0.6	36 306	18.7	29.2	26.7

1. Data for serious crimes have not been adjusted for underreporting; this may affect comparability between geographic areas and over time.   2. Per 100,000 population estimated by the FBI.   3. All persons 3 years old and over enrolled in nursery school through college.   4. Persons 25 years old and over.   5. Elementary and secondary education expenditures.   6. Based on population estimated by the American Community Survey, 2006–2010.

Table B. States and Counties — **Personal Income**

STATE County	Personal income, 2009												
	Total (mil dol)	Percent change, 2008–2009	Per capita[1]		Wages and salaries[2] (mil dol)	Proprietors' income (mil dol)	Dividends, interest, and rent (mil dol)	Transfer payments (mil dol)	Government payments to individuals				
			Dollars	Rank				Total	Total	Social Security	Medical payments	Income mainte-nance	Unemploy-ment insurance
	62	63	64	65	66	67	68	69	70	71	72	73	74
KENTUCKY—Cont'd													
Clay	499	5.5	21 116	3 079	184	19	46	241	236	52	109	52	8
Clinton	256	6.1	27 187	2 533	141	12	23	115	113	26	64	14	4
Crittenden	242	3.7	26 564	2 629	65	18	32	85	84	31	36	7	4
Cumberland	172	4.6	25 668	2 778	56	7	24	80	79	19	44	9	3
Daviess	3 185	0.5	33 390	1 282	1 926	205	547	760	743	266	308	74	37
Edmonson	290	0.4	24 280	2 937	64	11	33	91	89	32	33	11	6
Elliott	141	3.2	15 506	3 112	37	1	13	62	60	17	24	12	3
Estill	341	3.8	22 950	3 032	92	8	31	148	145	36	66	23	7
Fayette	11 048	-1.8	37 254	718	9 297	937	2 020	1 741	1 687	543	595	156	94
Fleming	340	0.9	23 188	3 024	120	17	49	114	111	37	45	14	7
Floyd	1 158	3.9	27 644	2 461	571	81	102	468	461	133	206	72	14
Franklin	1 727	0.4	35 273	985	1 541	74	293	396	387	146	152	39	18
Fulton	199	5.9	29 172	2 151	101	24	29	74	73	22	32	11	3
Gallatin	228	2.6	27 747	2 445	103	8	16	58	56	15	28	6	4
Garrard	430	0.1	25 169	2 848	83	39	61	118	115	43	41	13	7
Grant	685	1.1	26 810	2 596	197	25	65	179	174	60	67	20	12
Graves	1 068	0.8	28 312	2 343	440	109	161	331	325	111	145	30	13
Grayson	618	4.3	24 171	2 953	278	32	78	221	217	68	96	25	14
Green	277	2.4	24 038	2 961	66	25	36	102	100	30	48	10	5
Greenup	1 247	4.2	32 804	1 367	434	37	126	354	347	106	136	31	14
Hancock	241	2.7	27 874	2 422	258	12	28	59	58	24	20	5	4
Hardin	3 519	2.2	35 269	986	2 954	211	456	723	706	197	292	64	41
Harlan	782	7.0	25 276	2 833	423	23	74	341	335	100	142	54	9
Harrison	527	0.8	28 015	2 396	225	27	72	132	128	47	48	14	9
Hart	420	2.3	22 839	3 038	173	22	56	142	139	43	60	19	7
Henderson	1 459	0.7	32 070	1 510	870	83	214	373	365	128	155	38	20
Henry	463	0.8	28 823	2 228	131	24	57	118	115	40	50	11	7
Hickman	181	5.6	37 392	700	41	54	21	44	43	16	18	4	2
Hopkins	1 438	1.8	31 151	1 720	828	82	204	393	385	137	154	42	18
Jackson	255	5.2	19 274	3 102	87	7	21	119	117	30	52	20	6
Jefferson	29 834	-1.0	41 345	371	23 735	3 138	5 163	5 542	5 411	1 792	2 264	579	315
Jessamine	1 450	0.1	30 464	1 871	666	89	222	268	259	98	85	31	17
Johnson	639	5.1	26 817	2 594	256	41	65	243	239	71	102	36	8
Kenton	6 027	-3.3	37 973	646	3 591	286	958	1 004	975	327	364	97	69
Knott	423	4.5	24 714	2 891	205	15	34	173	170	45	74	30	6
Knox	811	3.0	24 798	2 881	351	95	77	312	306	83	124	63	12
Larue	466	3.1	34 078	1 160	95	24	58	111	109	36	47	11	7
Laurel	1 502	2.3	26 007	2 729	954	88	167	461	451	148	175	64	22
Lawrence	402	6.4	24 233	2 942	153	15	36	162	159	46	67	25	6
Lee	175	4.2	23 813	2 972	70	6	17	81	80	19	38	15	3
Leslie	301	5.1	26 142	2 698	102	11	19	140	138	37	66	23	4
Letcher	652	3.7	27 597	2 469	289	19	51	269	264	79	118	40	8
Lewis	281	3.1	20 439	3 089	79	11	27	122	119	30	52	20	7
Lincoln	605	1.7	24 049	2 960	181	30	70	201	197	62	84	24	11
Livingston	294	2.3	30 617	1 838	116	18	34	90	88	34	38	6	4
Logan	772	1.0	28 392	2 326	370	84	106	224	219	71	101	21	11
Lyon	228	0.7	27 455	2 493	73	15	39	72	71	30	27	4	3
McCracken	2 416	-0.5	36 672	791	1 803	150	466	560	548	198	225	55	23
McCreary	362	6.5	20 344	3 091	133	12	33	191	188	42	91	34	7
McLean	303	0.7	31 574	1 628	64	57	32	82	80	29	35	7	4
Madison	2 210	2.4	26 540	2 635	1 279	64	293	540	525	167	198	56	32
Magoffin	313	6.1	23 759	2 977	89	13	27	148	146	34	68	29	7
Marion	513	-1.3	26 318	2 665	287	17	73	148	145	44	63	18	11
Marshall	968	-1.1	31 010	1 751	527	51	163	268	262	111	99	18	13
Martin	316	8.5	24 147	2 954	177	8	24	135	133	41	54	26	3
Mason	528	-1.7	30 371	1 892	382	24	95	135	132	46	53	16	8
Meade	929	5.1	35 043	1 014	185	30	104	169	164	58	51	16	12
Menifee	136	4.4	20 638	3 085	37	4	12	65	64	18	27	10	3
Mercer	623	0.7	28 417	2 319	336	31	97	155	151	62	53	14	10
Metcalfe	222	1.2	22 102	3 064	78	11	27	90	88	25	41	10	6
Monroe	278	3.7	23 992	2 963	103	20	35	118	116	30	60	14	5
Montgomery	685	1.8	26 512	2 639	409	31	92	190	185	63	70	25	12
Morgan	289	3.4	20 489	3 088	119	10	31	113	111	31	48	19	6
Muhlenberg	833	3.1	26 621	2 621	448	47	124	276	271	99	110	29	12
Nelson	1 326	-0.4	30 447	1 874	648	60	190	293	285	101	109	29	22
Nicholas	196	1.9	28 575	2 285	37	6	18	63	62	19	29	7	3

1. Based on the resident population estimated as of July 1 of the year shown.   2. Includes supplements to wages and salaries.

Table B. States and Counties — Earnings, Social Security, and Housing

STATE County	Earnings, 2009									Social Security beneficiaries, December 2010		Housing units, 2010		
				Percent by selected industries										
			Goods-related[1]		Service-related and health									
	Total (mil dol)	Farm	Total	Manu-facturing	Information and professional and technical services	Retail trade	Finance, insurance, and real estate	Health care and social services	Govern-ment	Number	Rate[2]	Supplemental Security Income recipients, December 2010	Total	Percent change, 2000–2010
	75	76	77	78	79	80	81	82	83	84	85	86	87	88
KENTUCKY—Cont'd														
Clay	203	-0.1	D	0.8	3.7	9.5	2.8	D	45.3	5 230	241	3 717	8 875	-6.0
Clinton	153	2.4	45.1	40.1	1.5	4.0	2.7	D	18.5	2 790	272	963	5 311	8.7
Crittenden	83	9.0	D	9.8	4.8	7.3	4.8	D	22.3	2 535	272	328	4 569	3.6
Cumberland	63	1.9	D	9.5	D	7.8	6.9	24.8	28.4	1 840	268	527	3 690	3.4
Daviess	2 131	2.0	21.0	15.0	5.0	7.9	5.9	10.7	21.7	21 655	224	3 620	41 452	7.9
Edmonson	75	2.9	D	D	D	4.8	D	10.8	48.1	2 950	243	627	6 467	5.9
Elliott	38	-5.7	D	0.0	D	5.0	D	9.9	64.3	1 715	218	661	3 371	8.5
Estill	99	-1.7	D	8.6	2.9	10.1	3.8	16.2	32.4	3 530	241	1 354	6 865	0.6
Fayette	10 235	0.8	16.3	10.5	13.5	6.4	5.5	11.7	23.4	41 840	141	6 571	135 160	16.3
Fleming	137	2.1	D	11.4	4.0	9.5	3.8	8.1	34.5	3 630	253	739	6 623	8.2
Floyd	652	0.0	25.7	0.9	8.3	7.0	2.7	15.4	18.8	12 230	310	4 520	18 175	-2.0
Franklin	1 615	0.1	D	8.3	5.7	5.1	4.4	7.9	53.9	12 230	248	2 828	23 164	8.2
Fulton	124	13.3	D	10.5	3.3	10.4	3.6	12.5	20.1	1 910	280	509	3 372	-8.8
Gallatin	111	0.6	D	D	D	5.2	D	D	19.3	1 270	148	218	3 786	5.9
Garrard	122	1.9	27.6	6.9	D	6.0	5.6	D	25.9	3 850	228	746	7 463	12.6
Grant	222	-0.7	D	11.4	3.5	13.2	4.7	D	26.6	5 280	214	861	9 942	16.4
Graves	549	11.2	18.8	14.0	D	8.8	3.7	D	18.9	9 180	247	1 507	16 777	2.7
Grayson	310	1.4	29.9	23.0	D	9.3	4.8	7.9	25.3	6 305	245	1 366	13 561	5.9
Green	92	14.5	D	3.2	2.6	6.4	7.7	D	34.4	2 925	260	638	5 324	-1.7
Greenup	471	-0.1	D	16.3	D	6.0	2.8	23.4	16.8	8 625	234	1 672	16 330	2.2
Hancock	270	1.8	D	72.6	D	1.7	2.2	2.0	8.0	1 975	231	261	3 734	3.7
Hardin	3 165	0.1	D	8.8	7.3	5.7	3.3	6.5	53.7	17 475	166	2 890	43 261	14.8
Harlan	446	-0.1	39.5	1.1	D	6.8	2.8	6.6	20.0	8 475	289	2 964	13 513	-10.0
Harrison	252	1.4	D	31.7	2.8	6.7	3.3	D	16.9	4 090	217	802	8 208	7.2
Hart	195	1.6	D	38.3	2.0	5.7	2.1	D	21.3	4 340	238	1 088	8 559	6.4
Henderson	953	4.4	36.7	25.2	3.3	6.2	2.9	12.1	14.2	10 155	220	1 737	20 320	4.4
Henry	166	3.0	D	19.1	D	6.2	3.3	D	26.7	3 380	219	556	6 640	4.1
Hickman	95	51.6	D	D	D	5.5	2.7	D	13.0	1 370	279	231	2 342	-3.9
Hopkins	911	3.1	30.4	16.4	3.8	8.0	3.3	16.0	18.7	11 045	235	2 097	21 180	2.5
Jackson	94	-2.3	D	17.4	D	5.1	3.0	D	35.0	3 150	233	1 443	6 523	7.6
Jefferson	26 873	0.0	17.5	11.8	10.6	6.2	10.9	14.8	12.1	137 445	185	23 919	337 616	10.4
Jessamine	755	1.4	D	19.9	D	14.3	3.3	3.7	15.7	8 040	165	1 343	19 331	32.0
Johnson	297	-0.5	D	1.7	7.7	13.2	3.5	D	25.0	8 490	278	2 210	10 624	3.8
Kenton	3 877	0.0	14.7	8.3	9.2	4.4	9.0	15.5	19.0	25 155	157	3 827	68 975	8.5
Knott	220	-0.2	D	D	4.7	3.0	D	6.7	18.6	4 100	251	1 819	7 461	-1.6
Knox	447	-0.4	D	11.1	7.6	9.6	3.5	D	19.5	7 975	250	4 307	14 485	3.5
Larue	119	2.4	D	15.2	D	6.1	5.4	10.1	25.0	3 275	231	510	6 172	5.0
Laurel	1 041	0.1	22.0	13.9	D	10.2	3.6	13.9	15.4	13 350	227	3 689	25 446	14.0
Lawrence	168	-0.5	D	D	D	9.4	3.5	18.2	19.9	4 060	256	1 581	7 286	3.5
Lee	76	-1.8	D	D	D	9.9	D	10.4	27.6	1 880	238	923	3 436	3.5
Leslie	113	-0.1	D	D	7.1	5.1	D	D	25.0	3 255	288	1 309	5 278	-4.1
Letcher	307	-0.2	37.2	2.7	3.5	6.9	1.8	D	18.2	6 895	281	2 349	11 601	1.7
Lewis	90	1.3	D	13.4	1.8	6.0	4.0	D	32.6	2 995	216	1 044	8 481	5.0
Lincoln	211	2.8	23.4	17.7	8.8	9.3	3.0	9.9	25.5	5 860	237	1 501	10 819	6.8
Livingston	134	5.4	30.6	2.4	D	5.7	1.1	8.5	21.2	2 695	283	326	4 824	1.1
Logan	454	9.7	D	37.5	3.1	6.0	2.5	7.2	13.3	6 290	234	951	12 339	3.9
Lyon	88	6.3	D	1.3	D	5.9	D	7.9	39.9	2 330	280	189	4 791	14.4
McCracken	1 954	0.5	D	11.4	8.3	9.6	4.4	19.3	13.0	15 530	237	2 387	31 079	2.4
McCreary	145	-0.9	D	6.7	D	7.8	3.3	D	55.7	4 190	229	2 115	7 507	1.4
McLean	122	41.4	D	5.5	D	6.2	D	3.9	18.7	2 465	259	359	4 264	-2.9
Madison	1 342	0.3	D	16.4	6.1	7.6	3.0	10.8	34.7	14 410	174	2 993	35 043	18.4
Magoffin	103	-0.5	D	D	8.2	7.4	D	10.9	30.6	3 390	254	1 843	5 950	9.2
Marion	304	0.9	48.0	44.0	2.3	6.4	2.6	D	14.6	4 110	207	1 035	8 182	12.4
Marshall	578	1.4	48.3	38.0	D	7.5	3.8	D	14.8	8 745	278	837	15 748	6.9
Martin	185	-0.1	D	D	D	5.6	1.5	5.2	35.8	3 345	259	1 554	5 164	-7.0
Mason	406	0.8	D	21.2	2.7	9.9	3.1	D	15.3	3 975	227	766	8 105	4.5
Meade	216	1.9	28.7	12.6	7.7	8.6	4.4	D	24.1	5 050	177	699	11 762	14.3
Menifee	41	-4.1	D	12.3	D	7.7	D	D	46.5	1 735	275	636	3 744	0.9
Mercer	367	1.5	D	40.9	D	7.0	2.1	D	12.9	5 150	241	705	9 941	7.0
Metcalfe	89	4.0	D	35.5	2.3	6.3	2.7	4.4	26.0	2 585	256	655	4 681	1.9
Monroe	123	6.9	D	12.4	D	9.9	3.3	7.3	32.8	3 035	277	826	5 204	-1.6
Montgomery	440	0.0	D	36.0	D	10.6	4.0	D	13.8	5 745	217	1 285	11 699	20.8
Morgan	129	-2.5	D	6.1	D	8.6	D	10.1	38.9	3 125	224	1 183	5 830	6.3
Muhlenberg	495	3.7	28.7	6.9	2.0	7.2	2.6	D	28.7	8 305	264	1 561	13 699	0.2
Nelson	709	0.7	D	30.1	D	7.9	3.0	10.7	13.5	8 790	202	1 325	18 075	21.0
Nicholas	43	5.3	D	D	D	7.4	D	20.9	35.9	1 765	247	324	3 261	6.9

1. Includes mining, construction, and manufacturing.   2. Per 1,000 resident population enumerated in the 2010 census.

Table B. States and Counties — Housing, Labor Force, and Employment

STATE County	Housing units, 2006–2010								Civilian labor force, 2010				Civilian employment,[5] 2006–2010		
	Occupied units							Sub-stand-ard units[3] (percent)			Unemployment			Percent	
	Owner-occupied					Renter-occupied									
				Median owner cost as a percent of income											
	Total	Percent	Median value[1]	With a mortgage	Without a mortgage	Median rent[2]	Median rent as a percent of income		Total	Percent change, 2009–2010	Total	Rate[4]	Total	Management, business, science and arts	Construction, production, and maintenance occupations
	89	90	91	92	93	94	95	96	97	98	99	100	101	102	103
KENTUCKY—Cont'd															
Clay	6 520	78.7	51 200	23.4	13.5	411	34.1	2.4	7 043	0.2	981	13.9	5 122	23.6	32.1
Clinton	4 184	75.0	62 700	24.7	12.6	378	27.4	2.2	4 861	-0.8	465	9.6	3 664	18.8	44.0
Crittenden	3 749	78.9	69 300	21.3	10.0	383	20.2	0.5	4 106	-1.5	422	10.3	3 577	25.5	37.7
Cumberland	2 660	78.6	67 700	24.3	11.2	354	29.3	4.8	3 095	-1.5	381	12.3	2 800	21.6	37.0
Daviess	37 644	69.6	106 400	20.2	10.2	550	26.2	1.6	49 135	1.2	4 528	9.2	42 297	28.3	30.2
Edmonson	4 752	75.2	84 600	21.5	12.6	545	31.4	3.0	5 390	-1.7	709	13.2	4 930	22.4	39.2
Elliott	2 546	79.9	66 100	27.4	14.1	405	40.5	1.1	3 383	4.4	442	13.1	1 945	27.3	33.9
Estill	5 604	74.3	70 300	24.5	13.1	486	34.3	1.8	6 504	1.0	800	12.3	4 836	22.4	38.5
Fayette	120 917	56.9	159 200	21.5	10.0	693	29.2	2.0	155 425	2.4	12 581	8.1	152 033	41.3	16.3
Fleming	5 568	77.9	82 700	23.1	11.0	524	31.3	3.7	6 581	-0.1	796	12.1	6 326	31.7	36.0
Floyd	15 542	72.0	66 700	24.2	11.4	494	29.0	4.0	15 643	-1.2	1 969	12.6	12 395	26.8	30.1
Franklin	20 878	64.7	138 900	20.1	10.0	597	27.3	2.4	24 654	-1.3	2 195	8.9	23 257	34.6	21.7
Fulton	2 931	64.1	55 300	22.5	13.3	418	23.7	2.9	2 715	-0.5	358	13.2	2 360	21.1	44.3
Gallatin	2 971	73.4	105 500	24.6	13.0	576	35.0	2.3	4 022	-0.7	465	11.6	3 394	14.6	45.3
Garrard	6 294	77.0	109 200	22.3	13.6	573	33.6	3.1	7 811	0.5	918	11.8	7 281	25.3	37.7
Grant	8 906	70.4	117 900	24.0	12.2	665	28.6	3.8	12 915	-1.4	1 492	11.6	10 963	23.7	35.4
Graves	14 679	76.3	83 900	21.9	10.1	539	29.8	2.2	16 279	-1.5	1 663	10.2	15 071	24.5	35.0
Grayson	9 902	76.6	83 700	23.6	13.8	513	26.4	2.9	11 769	0.7	1 712	14.5	9 974	22.7	41.5
Green	4 435	74.5	75 400	18.4	10.0	511	32.1	1.8	5 746	-0.5	687	12.0	4 983	31.1	37.1
Greenup	14 374	80.0	88 400	21.2	11.0	550	31.3	1.2	18 134	0.8	1 796	9.9	14 026	32.7	25.8
Hancock	3 234	82.8	85 500	17.3	10.0	514	23.0	2.0	4 311	-2.3	418	9.7	3 695	22.4	46.3
Hardin	37 426	65.9	131 900	20.8	10.0	629	25.3	2.0	49 256	1.7	4 678	9.5	40 933	31.6	25.2
Harlan	10 700	71.1	52 500	19.3	10.6	444	24.9	5.0	11 043	3.0	1 286	11.6	8 798	30.2	32.5
Harrison	7 275	68.2	112 800	21.3	11.6	494	27.4	2.0	9 482	-0.3	1 038	10.9	8 408	26.1	38.0
Hart	7 050	75.2	80 200	20.7	12.1	465	29.8	3.7	8 475	0.3	882	10.4	6 915	21.4	43.6
Henderson	18 499	67.6	101 200	19.8	10.0	541	28.3	2.1	23 906	1.2	2 435	10.2	21 315	28.6	33.0
Henry	5 917	73.3	123 900	24.7	11.4	656	31.2	1.4	8 018	0.3	809	10.1	6 967	24.7	38.8
Hickman	2 057	80.5	63 600	18.3	15.3	438	24.3	0.7	2 167	1.1	198	9.1	1 854	33.2	31.9
Hopkins	18 401	72.2	77 200	20.8	10.0	539	25.6	2.5	22 438	-4.3	2 109	9.4	19 939	26.5	32.5
Jackson	5 728	76.0	64 700	29.5	13.8	475	33.3	4.5	4 327	0.1	742	17.1	4 718	21.7	44.0
Jefferson	300 561	64.7	145 900	22.5	11.3	667	28.9	1.7	365 635	0.4	38 833	10.6	347 688	35.1	21.9
Jessamine	17 482	66.0	150 200	22.4	11.3	670	28.7	2.2	23 245	-0.8	2 151	9.3	23 168	32.8	23.9
Johnson	9 151	71.9	71 400	19.5	12.9	435	24.0	3.7	10 074	-0.2	1 167	11.6	8 157	22.5	30.6
Kenton	61 912	69.2	145 200	22.0	11.7	667	26.4	2.1	85 123	-0.2	8 914	10.5	79 683	34.7	21.4
Knott	6 012	74.9	60 200	21.7	10.0	419	27.1	1.8	6 305	-6.8	842	13.4	5 185	35.4	33.8
Knox	12 573	66.7	65 000	23.6	13.7	456	32.4	3.0	12 688	-1.9	1 494	11.8	9 696	22.2	31.6
Larue	5 005	77.5	97 200	22.6	10.0	488	29.4	1.0	7 087	-1.5	683	9.6	5 880	24.9	41.5
Laurel	21 714	74.2	96 100	21.1	11.6	522	29.1	1.3	26 253	-2.2	2 907	11.1	23 576	28.2	27.9
Lawrence	5 647	70.7	65 800	21.2	10.0	482	32.9	2.3	6 387	2.0	818	12.8	4 908	26.8	32.0
Lee	2 750	74.5	57 300	27.6	12.1	299	32.8	2.9	2 776	-2.5	349	12.6	2 329	25.0	34.8
Leslie	4 450	73.3	54 600	21.0	10.2	515	18.1	4.4	3 745	2.1	488	13.0	3 347	23.1	39.5
Letcher	9 586	75.4	51 500	18.6	10.0	464	25.4	3.6	8 748	-2.3	994	11.4	8 261	30.6	35.1
Lewis	5 030	84.3	55 800	25.2	14.2	442	29.2	2.8	5 477	-3.7	822	15.0	4 807	29.8	44.2
Lincoln	9 983	76.0	83 000	21.7	11.6	544	28.1	3.7	10 563	-2.1	1 417	13.4	9 912	23.4	35.2
Livingston	3 605	81.6	76 800	19.2	10.0	514	22.5	2.2	4 821	-0.5	522	10.8	4 125	25.4	32.6
Logan	10 697	74.2	87 500	23.8	11.9	525	30.7	3.6	12 823	3.0	1 298	10.1	11 549	25.2	37.9
Lyon	3 272	81.0	84 900	22.9	10.0	508	19.1	2.8	3 396	-1.4	385	11.3	2 672	23.9	28.3
McCracken	27 541	69.2	107 500	19.2	10.0	544	28.8	1.9	31 587	-0.2	2 868	9.1	28 081	31.0	23.7
McCreary	6 351	76.3	62 400	23.9	11.3	394	41.8	2.3	6 071	3.1	877	14.4	4 927	27.4	38.9
McLean	3 736	76.1	71 900	20.7	10.2	472	26.7	1.0	4 636	-0.7	479	10.3	4 226	30.1	32.5
Madison	30 756	62.0	141 100	21.4	10.7	550	28.3	3.0	43 179	0.6	3 791	8.8	39 640	32.8	22.7
Magoffin	4 671	78.2	46 200	19.7	11.7	455	47.3	1.5	4 561	-0.2	900	19.7	3 585	27.9	36.4
Marion	7 135	79.8	97 000	23.0	12.1	563	26.7	1.9	10 309	0.8	1 205	11.7	7 916	26.3	38.3
Marshall	12 795	81.9	96 900	19.8	10.0	540	27.7	1.1	15 015	0.8	1 674	11.1	13 997	25.2	28.1
Martin	4 337	71.5	67 800	17.9	13.2	428	31.6	2.2	3 967	4.6	469	11.8	3 449	24.4	39.9
Mason	6 674	70.9	98 500	19.9	10.0	505	30.8	1.7	8 612	-3.8	900	10.5	7 347	27.4	30.3
Meade	10 043	71.8	107 700	21.5	10.8	693	26.4	1.4	11 639	-2.5	1 533	13.2	11 749	23.6	36.7
Menifee	2 345	82.9	67 100	19.7	11.8	446	38.0	3.9	2 640	-1.6	462	17.5	2 336	23.6	39.3
Mercer	8 464	74.8	129 400	20.3	10.0	542	26.6	2.8	10 562	-0.2	1 221	11.6	9 753	31.5	31.6
Metcalfe	3 991	79.1	73 400	21.2	10.5	483	22.8	2.5	4 294	-5.4	606	14.1	4 294	22.3	44.5
Monroe	4 347	76.1	67 600	24.4	12.6	439	31.3	2.7	4 762	-0.3	549	11.5	4 502	30.6	29.7
Montgomery	10 066	68.7	98 100	22.0	11.9	561	27.1	2.1	12 411	-0.6	1 476	11.9	10 843	25.7	39.6
Morgan	4 433	75.1	72 700	22.7	10.0	394	29.2	3.5	5 272	2.2	740	14.0	4 466	27.9	31.1
Muhlenberg	12 364	79.4	75 700	22.9	10.4	482	27.0	3.4	13 518	-3.6	1 492	11.0	11 385	28.3	35.4
Nelson	16 173	76.9	116 800	22.6	10.0	597	27.3	1.6	22 179	-0.9	2 604	11.7	19 438	26.0	39.0
Nicholas	2 741	76.5	79 800	20.5	10.0	449	30.0	6.4	3 215	1.3	374	11.6	3 123	28.8	36.8

1. Specified owner-occupied units.   2. Specified renter-occupied units. A value of 10.0 represents 10 percent or less.   3. Overcrowded or lacking complete plumbing facilities.   4. Percent of civilian labor force.   5. Persons 16 years old and over.

Table B. States and Counties — Nonfarm Employment and Agriculture

STATE County	Number of establishments	Employment Total	Health care and social assistance	Manufacturing	Retail trade	Finance and insurance	Professional, scientific, and technical services	Annual payroll Total (mil dol)	Average per employee (dollars)	Farms Number	Percent with: Fewer than 50 acres	500 acres or more	Farm operators whose principal occupation is farming (percent)
	104	105	106	107	108	109	110	111	112	113	114	115	116
KENTUCKY—Cont'd													
Clay	253	2 479	845	D	575	D	98	64	25 666	336	29.8	4.8	31.0
Clinton	190	3 230	598	D	233	71	D	81	25 210	629	35.8	4.9	38.8
Crittenden	160	1 468	407	144	D	80	38	34	23 142	740	22.3	8.9	35.1
Cumberland	105	1 061	D	212	190	D	20	25	23 933	507	25.6	9.3	38.1
Daviess	2 272	39 882	7 816	5 462	5 925	1 971	1 048	1 289	32 331	1 008	43.8	11.9	45.1
Edmonson	130	791	224	D	171	D	14	17	21 308	712	35.4	4.1	37.9
Elliott	45	309	112	0	55	D	0	6	19 324	448	22.3	4.7	38.2
Estill	189	1 699	D	D	332	D	21	37	21 511	456	29.6	4.6	36.0
Fayette	8 241	146 031	27 226	9 058	20 621	5 366	10 161	5 623	38 504	810	50.2	8.3	52.3
Fleming	258	2 228	D	375	465	114	D	58	25 864	1 129	26.3	5.8	40.9
Floyd	859	9 771	2 134	D	1 753	277	419	332	33 957	76	28.9	2.6	44.7
Franklin	1 134	14 813	2 201	2 098	2 537	986	681	467	31 555	625	38.2	3.2	37.1
Fulton	135	2 171	D	426	216	71	D	53	24 297	156	28.2	21.8	60.3
Gallatin	89	838	185	155	243	31	D	20	24 094	204	30.9	7.4	46.6
Garrard	228	1 358	D	209	154	61	D	37	27 101	821	32.0	4.8	45.8
Grant	384	4 246	613	D	1 013	168	82	104	24 509	959	31.4	2.0	38.5
Graves	692	8 952	D	2 408	1 471	287	269	243	27 103	1 712	40.7	5.9	35.4
Grayson	471	5 880	928	1 643	1 134	223	87	145	24 629	1 513	27.8	3.6	37.8
Green	159	1 155	419	D	220	D	D	25	21 670	1 064	32.4	4.6	41.6
Greenup	497	5 071	993	522	837	251	197	147	28 965	698	30.7	3.3	35.7
Hancock	138	3 580	107	2 675	107	83	23	171	47 665	383	23.0	5.2	37.6
Hardin	2 136	33 747	5 724	5 140	5 923	1 336	2 115	977	28 952	1 588	43.7	5.4	40.3
Harlan	470	5 994	1 300	D	1 020	161	249	215	35 904	37	40.5	2.7	24.3
Harrison	292	4 009	929	1 279	D	82	63	130	32 308	1 083	31.2	4.7	44.3
Hart	253	3 772	439	D	378	91	54	103	27 429	1 455	32.7	3.1	40.1
Henderson	1 060	16 278	2 587	4 519	2 221	389	374	523	32 099	509	41.7	17.1	42.0
Henry	219	1 938	255	D	336	103	D	54	27 882	962	28.0	5.5	47.4
Hickman	79	1 227	D	D	344	D	10	35	28 500	340	30.6	14.4	45.9
Hopkins	989	14 574	2 914	2 171	2 440	423	398	546	37 445	661	29.0	10.1	37.5
Jackson	118	1 213	D	D	169	D	D	34	28 056	662	34.0	3.2	36.9
Jefferson	19 533	390 000	60 353	37 538	41 017	29 938	23 039	15 563	39 906	476	65.7	1.5	67.1
Jessamine	1 024	13 908	870	2 186	2 316	D	285	427	30 735	711	50.8	4.1	36.4
Johnson	437	4 599	759	101	1 552	236	184	122	26 482	198	25.3	3.0	25.8
Kenton	3 200	74 080	9 695	4 026	D	1 387	2 728	2 932	39 580	481	46.2	1.2	34.5
Knott	185	2 122	351	D	244	37	D	73	34 486	46	23.9	2.2	30.4
Knox	480	7 388	953	D	1 219	237	598	184	24 970	376	39.6	4.3	26.6
Larue	216	1 945	315	667	226	135	D	47	24 682	811	34.8	5.2	40.3
Laurel	1 202	22 526	2 695	3 649	3 236	1 125	494	697	30 935	1 012	43.6	2.3	34.6
Lawrence	213	2 574	689	D	683	89	D	78	30 287	337	21.1	5.6	41.2
Lee	96	1 588	D	D	203	D	14	33	20 700	186	33.9	4.8	28.0
Leslie	110	1 057	395	0	195	D	62	34	32 511	23	39.1	13.0	39.1
Letcher	362	4 582	1 060	46	709	D	116	165	35 927	66	62.1	0.0	24.2
Lewis	125	1 231	D	346	256	75	D	33	26 615	673	19.5	9.7	41.2
Lincoln	298	3 678	547	738	705	D	763	83	22 494	1 278	40.1	5.6	38.3
Livingston	144	1 714	348	75	161	42	28	57	33 265	492	22.8	11.4	33.5
Logan	490	6 421	702	2 615	992	176	167	214	33 287	1 172	30.7	8.5	40.8
Lyon	160	1 152	D	D	210	D	D	25	21 747	270	23.7	6.3	39.3
McCracken	2 116	34 547	7 078	3 295	6 253	1 233	1 049	1 168	33 821	483	49.5	6.4	35.8
McCreary	166	1 451	300	270	340	D	D	33	22 522	139	42.4	1.4	36.0
McLean	167	1 114	D	D	175	73	D	30	27 320	419	34.4	16.7	51.8
Madison	1 568	20 598	3 308	4 160	3 977	662	679	579	28 133	1 328	40.2	8.0	41.6
Magoffin	172	1 587	284	D	267	D	109	43	27 322	470	28.9	2.3	27.0
Marion	354	6 366	1 133	2 989	780	159	D	183	28 682	1 055	33.5	5.3	39.6
Marshall	638	8 916	950	2 461	1 162	358	149	321	35 958	867	46.6	3.2	28.0
Martin	181	2 844	D	D	536	D	38	119	41 737	19	5.3	21.1	42.1
Mason	472	7 402	1 211	1 275	1 440	194	108	229	30 873	753	28.4	9.0	45.6
Meade	322	3 270	286	D	615	107	D	93	28 575	887	45.2	4.3	38.7
Menifee	60	567	D	175	109	D	D	14	24 399	331	29.6	4.2	34.4
Mercer	379	5 237	603	1 926	860	132	62	196	37 411	1 111	43.1	4.4	41.3
Metcalfe	115	1 605	103	923	257	D	D	37	23 318	964	29.8	4.8	41.9
Monroe	207	2 274	506	474	599	118	21	55	24 139	955	27.1	8.8	46.0
Montgomery	527	8 647	1 171	3 162	1 529	D	155	250	28 908	685	35.3	5.4	39.1
Morgan	172	1 903	377	D	408	107	D	54	28 357	795	23.6	7.2	32.2
Muhlenberg	565	6 645	1 324	637	1 232	221	137	211	31 817	636	25.5	8.6	41.4
Nelson	919	11 674	1 345	3 521	1 879	D	235	386	33 077	1 406	43.0	5.0	41.8
Nicholas	75	530	D	D	144	24	D	12	22 438	603	23.1	7.1	43.8

Table B. States and Counties — **Agriculture**

STATE County	Agriculture, 2007 (cont.)															
	Land in farms					Value of land and buildings (dollars)			Value of products sold				Percent of farms with sales of:		Government payments	
			Acres					Value of machinery and equipment, average per farm (dollars)				Percent from:					
	Acreage (1,000)	Percent change, 2002–2007	Average size of farm	Total irrigated (1,000)	Total cropland (1,000)	Average per farm	Average per acre		Total (mil dol)	Average per farm (dollars)	Crops	Live-stock and poultry products	$10,000 or more	$100,000 or more	Total ($1,000)	Percent of farms
	117	118	119	120	121	122	123	124	125	126	127	128	129	130	131	132

KENTUCKY—Cont'd

STATE County	117	118	119	120	121	122	123	124	125	126	127	128	129	130	131	132
Clay	51	-7.3	152	0.0	15.0	285 514	1 874	35 959	4.2	12 567	57.0	42.9	15.8	2.1	60	14.3
Clinton	91	26.4	145	0.0	33.7	332 645	2 297	49 029	30.4	48 357	10.0	90.0	39.0	6.2	359	35.9
Crittenden	160	1.9	216	0.3	84.4	409 032	1 890	50 061	19.2	25 894	46.0	54.0	30.4	4.3	1 967	49.7
Cumberland	103	15.7	204	D	32.6	369 100	1 810	42 029	8.0	15 785	25.4	74.6	28.6	1.4	236	40.8
Daviess	257	1.2	255	3.5	209.0	770 859	3 024	100 771	117.6	116 687	75.0	25.0	41.4	16.5	2 907	51.7
Edmonson	97	3.2	136	0.0	45.1	294 407	2 169	47 761	17.5	24 562	16.0	84.0	27.7	3.2	554	37.1
Elliott	67	19.6	149	D	19.3	232 597	1 559	43 887	2.4	5 426	32.1	67.8	14.5	0.0	101	12.5
Estill	65	1.6	142	0.0	22.5	284 049	1 999	40 149	4.5	9 784	26.7	73.3	23.7	1.5	222	30.3
Fayette	136	14.3	168	0.5	61.7	1 106 925	6 594	83 203	504.1	622 377	3.1	96.9	46.7	23.5	437	15.8
Fleming	182	-1.1	161	0.0	79.5	317 208	1 972	54 062	35.9	31 822	25.0	75.0	41.8	6.8	768	53.9
Floyd	8	14.3	102	0.2	2.0	237 971	2 323	27 122	0.7	9 786	84.4	15.5	10.5	2.6	2	3.9
Franklin	76	-7.3	122	0.4	34.9	396 506	3 248	50 598	14.0	22 449	28.6	71.4	29.9	3.2	166	13.1
Fulton	91	-18.8	586	D	81.5	1 325 193	2 261	152 789	37.5	240 099	69.8	30.2	48.1	29.5	1 446	79.5
Gallatin	34	-10.5	166	0.1	15.6	494 116	2 981	60 543	4.9	24 081	64.6	35.4	38.2	5.4	48	21.1
Garrard	122	1.7	148	0.1	59.0	388 580	2 622	54 863	29.0	35 273	22.1	77.9	41.0	7.1	301	22.5
Grant	115	-0.9	120	0.3	52.6	337 912	2 819	43 732	9.3	9 727	46.8	53.2	23.3	1.3	214	16.3
Graves	278	-7.3	162	3.2	201.7	455 280	2 805	68 139	245.2	143 230	22.8	77.2	29.8	14.4	6 935	67.0
Grayson	216	-7.3	143	0.0	103.5	307 574	2 150	44 973	41.2	27 225	23.7	76.3	30.2	3.8	1 742	40.9
Green	145	7.4	137	0.2	66.9	317 265	2 320	52 588	31.1	29 207	26.5	73.5	42.9	7.4	1 084	45.1
Greenup	92	-10.7	132	0.1	29.5	260 623	1 980	41 988	4.2	5 994	40.7	59.3	15.0	0.3	181	24.9
Hancock	63	-8.7	165	0.2	30.5	354 193	2 151	52 149	10.6	27 634	72.5	27.5	31.1	4.7	535	47.8
Hardin	222	-7.5	140	0.6	121.8	402 378	2 875	56 105	46.9	29 538	56.5	43.5	30.5	5.5	1 599	32.2
Harlan	3	50.0	82	0.0	0.7	137 310	1 675	25 634	0.1	2 020	54.7	44.0	2.7	0.0	0	0.0
Harrison	162	1.9	149	1.7	74.7	400 764	2 683	57 953	24.0	22 180	46.0	54.0	37.1	4.5	627	28.6
Hart	191	-2.1	131	0.1	82.7	316 420	2 410	45 629	34.4	23 673	28.8	71.2	36.8	5.4	1 176	44.4
Henderson	196	2.1	384	4.1	166.4	1 071 805	2 788	113 386	70.5	138 514	91.5	8.5	43.0	18.1	2 654	65.4
Henry	146	2.8	152	0.9	72.7	497 292	3 268	67 967	31.2	32 455	56.1	43.9	41.2	6.3	808	28.3
Hickman	130	4.0	382	13.0	107.1	1 000 739	2 622	136 946	134.2	394 693	28.3	71.7	40.0	25.6	2 383	81.8
Hopkins	159	-3.0	241	0.1	101.8	527 193	2 187	73 155	77.2	116 791	34.0	66.0	31.3	9.5	1 738	50.7
Jackson	83	1.2	125	0.0	33.7	228 127	1 828	41 104	6.3	9 551	30.7	69.3	22.2	0.9	186	19.3
Jefferson	32	-22.0	68	0.2	15.4	496 480	7 302	41 150	11.1	23 403	73.8	26.2	25.1	4.8	136	10.5
Jessamine	80	-2.4	113	0.1	37.7	529 226	4 697	49 652	123.8	174 073	3.7	96.3	34.3	7.2	277	16.9
Johnson	28	16.7	140	D	6.8	299 187	2 134	35 338	1.1	5 533	49.5	50.4	13.6	0.5	27	9.6
Kenton	43	-6.5	88	0.0	21.5	393 811	4 452	47 431	4.6	9 512	39.3	60.7	18.9	2.3	103	13.1
Knott	7	75.0	151	0.0	2.7	300 696	1 994	23 662	0.3	6 735	D	D	23.9	0.0	0	0.0
Knox	51	24.4	136	0.0	17.9	298 061	2 193	39 218	3.0	8 053	25.6	74.4	15.7	1.6	50	12.5
Larue	125	-6.7	155	0.2	72.0	423 765	2 740	59 077	26.6	32 774	52.8	47.2	40.4	6.9	929	40.1
Laurel	102	-5.6	101	0.0	43.2	289 023	2 854	40 800	14.2	14 075	31.6	68.4	23.9	2.3	171	13.3
Lawrence	60	5.3	179	0.0	15.2	262 290	1 468	48 471	1.7	5 018	49.4	50.6	11.3	0.3	35	12.8
Lee	29	26.1	158	0.0	9.2	205 223	1 298	33 899	1.2	6 642	49.6	50.4	14.5	0.5	126	27.4
Leslie	6	100.0	245	D	0.2	195 487	797	21 295	0.0	1 251	D	D	0.0	0.0	0	0.0
Letcher	4	33.3	55	D	0.8	91 932	1 678	39 957	0.2	2 547	46.4	53.6	6.1	0.0	D	6.1
Lewis	147	2.1	218	0.1	41.1	333 249	1 528	44 630	9.7	14 455	47.9	52.1	28.5	2.7	330	36.8
Lincoln	178	4.1	140	0.2	83.9	331 780	2 378	50 492	52.5	41 110	17.2	82.8	37.8	9.4	985	33.3
Livingston	117	-19.9	238	0.0	61.3	467 157	1 964	54 817	12.8	26 117	42.3	57.7	26.6	4.5	1 159	53.5
Logan	290	5.1	247	0.5	198.4	658 369	2 661	76 535	81.0	69 102	56.3	43.7	39.0	10.2	3 560	49.2
Lyon	54	-3.6	201	D	29.4	345 058	1 720	50 969	6.7	24 697	78.8	21.2	26.3	4.1	652	57.8
McCracken	75	-11.8	156	0.2	58.2	456 391	2 926	61 289	21.0	43 422	71.1	28.9	24.8	10.4	918	57.3
McCreary	15	0.0	108	0.1	5.1	258 738	2 389	42 651	0.9	6 559	16.9	83.0	14.4	0.7	15	15.1
McLean	144	11.6	344	D	117.6	1 036 508	3 012	132 390	161.1	384 390	26.3	73.7	57.8	32.0	1 712	71.8
Madison	218	0.0	164	0.4	108.6	484 906	2 951	51 885	42.5	31 994	18.0	82.0	39.3	6.4	680	27.3
Magoffin	62	34.8	131	D	13.9	220 451	1 681	28 809	1.8	3 878	39.6	60.4	7.0	0.6	109	24.7
Marion	161	-5.8	152	0.4	78.8	372 658	2 447	55 914	39.7	37 586	25.5	74.5	43.9	7.8	1 119	41.8
Marshall	98	-19.0	113	0.1	56.0	287 521	2 551	48 562	30.4	35 074	27.7	72.3	18.5	3.9	1 407	51.6
Martin	7	40.0	374	D	1.1	311 793	833	26 840	0.1	4 166	22.8	77.2	10.5	0.0	0	0.0
Mason	140	9.4	186	0.0	78.5	469 349	2 528	57 456	28.4	37 745	39.5	60.5	47.1	8.5	798	41.6
Meade	121	-10.4	137	0.0	65.2	403 270	2 945	67 210	28.7	32 370	42.9	57.1	31.6	4.7	1 213	46.1
Menifee	43	16.2	130	0.0	15.1	245 018	1 881	33 349	2.7	8 153	34.5	65.5	22.7	0.3	106	17.8
Mercer	141	5.2	127	0.1	74.9	435 542	3 421	55 937	43.2	38 865	12.4	87.6	33.8	6.6	1 173	23.4
Metcalfe	149	12.9	155	0.1	69.3	361 808	2 333	54 573	33.4	34 608	19.1	80.9	40.2	7.4	708	35.9
Monroe	176	8.6	184	0.1	73.2	427 772	2 324	59 660	54.3	56 809	10.1	89.9	44.6	8.9	838	36.1
Montgomery	107	17.6	156	0.1	53.9	394 100	2 524	50 070	18.1	26 393	35.2	64.8	37.5	5.1	614	32.6
Morgan	136	17.2	171	0.1	41.3	278 108	1 622	40 588	6.8	8 516	47.1	52.9	24.7	0.3	172	20.4
Muhlenberg	141	2.2	221	0.1	74.5	437 738	1 977	66 153	49.2	77 329	30.7	69.3	34.7	7.7	1 173	45.6
Nelson	196	3.7	140	1.6	104.8	454 205	3 254	58 736	54.8	38 978	30.0	70.0	32.9	7.5	1 189	32.8
Nicholas	110	3.8	183	0.1	55.5	361 083	1 976	63 561	15.7	26 066	42.6	57.4	40.1	6.0	226	15.3

Table B. States and Counties — Water Use, Wholesale Trade, Retail Trade, and Real Estate

STATE County	Water use, 2005		Wholesale trade,[1] 2007				Retail trade,[2] 2007				Real estate and rental and leasing,[2] 2007			
	Total water withdrawn (mil gal/day)	Gallons withdrawn per person	Number of establishments	Number of employees	Sales (mil dol)	Annual payroll (mil dol)	Number of establishments	Number of employees	Sales (mil dol)	Annual payroll (mil dol)	Number of establishments	Number of employees	Receipts (mil dol)	Annual payroll (mil dol)
	133	134	135	136	137	138	139	140	141	142	143	144	145	146
KENTUCKY—Cont'd														
Clay	4.5	187	7	35	13.2	0.6	72	549	138.7	10.3	10	19	1.7	0.3
Clinton	3.8	399	11	79	38.7	1.6	42	232	55.3	3.7	7	28	3.3	0.8
Crittenden	2.2	244	5	108	9.4	2.5	29	286	53.4	4.9	7	27	31.7	0.9
Cumberland	0.9	132	NA	NA	NA	NA	34	225	44.2	3.6	4	D	D	D
Daviess	223.2	2 398	95	1 166	818.1	45.8	442	5 936	1 282.9	123.4	78	518	49.7	10.9
Edmonson	1.3	110	1	D	D	D	27	171	32.5	2.7	NA	NA	NA	NA
Elliott	0.5	65	NA	NA	NA	NA	14	52	12.2	0.9	NA	NA	NA	NA
Estill	1.4	92	3	D	D	D	45	321	84.2	6.0	6	27	1.7	0.4
Fayette	49.9	186	375	8 540	4 442.4	568.5	1 249	22 335	4 778.5	510.4	476	2 268	391.2	68.2
Fleming	1.2	84	19	112	29.8	2.9	70	539	128.5	10.8	7	11	1.8	0.1
Floyd	4.4	105	39	497	404.4	16.8	181	1 535	403.3	33.3	27	99	12.1	2.1
Franklin	11.7	242	23	249	223.6	10.5	198	2 719	622.1	59.4	47	146	23.8	3.6
Fulton	1.8	242	6	D	D	D	40	268	52.2	3.5	3	3	0.6	0.1
Gallatin	2.8	343	3	D	D	D	20	185	37.3	2.7	5	D	D	D
Garrard	2.2	132	5	30	7.1	0.9	38	179	39.6	3.0	5	D	D	D
Grant	2.5	102	9	D	D	D	94	1 053	285.2	22.4	19	51	4.5	1.0
Graves	9.9	262	40	D	D	D	130	1 427	342.5	31.5	25	96	6.4	1.2
Grayson	3.7	148	13	D	D	D	101	1 097	234.9	21.8	14	134	5.8	1.5
Green	3.1	266	5	14	1.9	0.2	36	242	64.4	4.0	4	8	1.8	0.2
Greenup	10.8	290	5	22	3.6	0.4	120	1 431	355.7	25.6	20	72	8.3	1.3
Hancock	266.9	30 982	4	15	3.3	0.3	17	147	28.1	2.0	5	D	D	D
Hardin	14.0	144	54	479	281.1	15.8	433	6 012	1 449.5	132.2	102	D	D	D
Harlan	4.3	136	24	227	159.3	7.5	99	1 045	211.1	19.0	16	50	5.8	0.9
Harrison	3.4	181	10	86	39.8	1.6	64	724	147.0	12.8	11	44	5.4	0.8
Hart	4.6	253	10	41	21.4	1.1	69	429	92.8	6.5	7	D	D	D
Henderson	36.2	794	44	687	545.0	26.3	183	2 508	662.0	54.6	40	218	22.0	5.1
Henry	0.9	57	11	136	46.5	4.8	38	355	153.3	6.8	3	4	0.8	0.1
Hickman	1.4	274	5	36	29.1	0.8	20	301	65.4	5.8	3	7	0.3	0.0
Hopkins	13.5	289	45	D	D	D	203	2 478	560.5	50.9	33	144	13.0	2.8
Jackson	1.3	93	3	D	D	D	32	221	45.2	3.0	4	14	1.2	0.3
Jefferson	794.2	1 135	1 026	16 413	13 000.6	763.2	2 775	43 687	10 002.4	978.5	991	6 888	1 995.1	263.3
Jessamine	6.1	141	37	D	D	D	163	2 388	731.7	60.2	46	202	28.1	6.4
Johnson	2.8	115	19	163	106.1	5.9	106	1 519	350.1	28.7	16	46	5.2	0.8
Kenton	6.4	42	140	D	D	D	426	6 589	1 262.0	124.9	132	856	180.0	26.6
Knott	1.9	108	3	D	D	D	34	203	47.6	3.8	4	11	1.0	0.2
Knox	1.1	35	12	85	63.7	2.6	106	1 260	318.6	26.8	8	75	4.4	1.8
Larue	1.2	90	9	39	19.8	0.9	31	217	49.2	4.0	4	D	D	D
Laurel	12.1	215	60	D	D	D	233	3 306	914.7	75.8	37	179	22.5	3.4
Lawrence	14.0	864	6	D	D	D	54	528	123.6	8.9	10	35	4.8	0.8
Lee	0.8	101	3	D	D	D	25	212	58.6	4.4	6	D	D	D
Leslie	1.3	107	NA	NA	NA	NA	33	306	59.4	4.8	2	D	D	D
Letcher	3.4	140	13	95	51.8	3.2	68	621	124.0	11.4	9	20	3.1	0.4
Lewis	1.8	129	2	D	D	D	38	281	56.8	3.6	5	14	0.6	0.1
Lincoln	3.1	124	15	D	D	D	61	659	127.2	10.8	11	11	2.3	0.2
Livingston	7.8	794	7	D	D	D	25	163	29.7	3.2	2	D	D	D
Logan	1.1	42	20	157	132.9	5.2	101	1 008	230.6	19.8	17	46	5.8	1.0
Lyon	3.1	374	3	D	D	D	29	235	61.0	4.4	9	16	2.1	0.4
McCracken	1 300.5	20 101	102	1 759	3 529.6	70.4	474	6 673	1 570.8	137.6	90	408	62.5	10.3
McCreary	2.0	116	3	9	1.3	0.2	52	406	82.5	6.8	6	29	2.2	0.7
McLean	1.6	157	7	98	38.6	2.8	29	215	48.0	4.4	2	D	D	D
Madison	13.1	168	45	405	242.1	14.3	322	4 190	976.0	82.4	75	241	36.9	5.0
Magoffin	0.9	70	4	28	11.6	0.7	33	248	52.9	4.0	3	10	0.8	0.2
Marion	5.5	290	11	66	22.9	1.3	74	625	136.2	10.5	10	36	4.6	0.9
Marshall	23.0	743	31	284	97.2	9.3	115	1 115	345.7	25.5	24	69	8.3	1.1
Martin	4.9	402	5	59	123.7	2.8	47	412	108.0	7.0	8	142	36.5	7.0
Mason	15.7	917	17	D	D	D	113	1 490	358.0	31.1	14	43	5.6	1.1
Meade	4.7	167	13	72	40.8	2.3	66	673	170.7	11.7	18	56	4.1	0.8
Menifee	0.6	93	NA	NA	NA	NA	17	169	24.2	1.8	4	D	D	D
Mercer	25.9	1 197	12	45	15.0	0.8	74	907	157.0	18.4	17	59	8.2	1.2
Metcalfe	1.0	102	1	D	D	D	32	304	58.0	5.2	5	10	0.6	0.2
Monroe	2.4	208	7	64	28.8	1.5	50	499	100.0	9.1	4	5	0.8	0.1
Montgomery	3.3	136	19	D	D	D	130	1 523	355.8	31.0	25	76	8.2	1.4
Morgan	0.5	36	1	D	D	D	56	408	88.1	7.7	5	13	1.3	0.2
Muhlenberg	496.7	15 745	8	D	D	D	105	1 224	265.6	24.6	22	78	6.5	1.7
Nelson	7.8	190	28	290	217.5	9.6	173	1 926	422.3	39.2	36	108	14.1	2.8
Nicholas	2.7	383	NA	NA	NA	NA	19	124	27.4	2.3	2	D	D	D

1. Merchant wholesalers, except manufacturers' sales branches and offices.   2. Employer establishments.

Table B. States and Counties — Professional Services, Manufacturing, and Accommodation and Food Services

STATE County	Professional, scientific, and technical services,[1] 2007				Manufacturing, 2007				Accommodation and food services, 2007			
	Number of establishments	Number of employees	Receipts (mil dol)	Annual payroll (mil dol)	Number of establishments	Number of employees	Receipts (mil dol)	Annual payroll (mil dol)	Number of establishments	Number of employees	Sales (mil dol)	Annual payroll (mil dol)
	147	148	149	150	151	152	153	154	155	156	157	158
KENTUCKY—Cont'd												
Clay	22	108	12.9	2.5	NA	NA	NA	NA	14	361	12.4	3.5
Clinton	14	34	2.5	0.8	14	1 731	D	44.4	16	223	7.8	1.4
Crittenden	14	42	3.6	0.7	NA	NA	NA	NA	12	152	5.1	1.1
Cumberland	9	24	1.4	0.4	NA	NA	NA	NA	11	122	4.5	1.4
Daviess	167	D	D	D	110	6 486	2 920.0	269.3	172	3 999	147.4	44.5
Edmonson	9	D	D	D	NA	NA	NA	NA	13	144	6.3	1.6
Elliott	1	D	D	D	NA	NA	NA	NA	5	37	3.2	0.5
Estill	9	23	1.0	0.3	NA	NA	NA	NA	19	223	7.9	2.0
Fayette	1 053	D	D	D	255	9 602	3 061.2	401.7	704	17 027	785.7	230.3
Fleming	13	40	3.2	1.0	NA	NA	NA	NA	12	146	6.0	1.8
Floyd	68	D	D	D	NA	NA	NA	NA	46	729	34.9	8.4
Franklin	121	705	88.9	31.4	41	3 566	1 400.8	141.7	95	2 121	80.5	25.5
Fulton	13	D	D	D	10	516	D	D	13	D	D	D
Gallatin	8	D	D	D	NA	NA	NA	NA	8	D	D	D
Garrard	17	36	2.0	0.7	NA	NA	NA	NA	12	126	4.5	1.1
Grant	23	D	D	D	17	D	D	29.1	46	864	30.0	8.7
Graves	36	D	D	D	49	2 240	D	61.8	49	D	D	D
Grayson	19	83	5.8	2.1	29	2 240	692.0	62.9	30	446	16.2	4.2
Green	14	30	2.7	0.7	NA	NA	NA	NA	10	102	4.0	1.0
Greenup	34	D	D	D	15	526	D	21.6	28	504	21.0	5.7
Hancock	7	D	D	D	14	2 709	D	D	10	71	2.2	0.5
Hardin	142	D	D	D	79	5 423	1 792.3	224.5	180	4 566	168.6	52.9
Harlan	47	D	D	D	NA	NA	NA	NA	28	528	20.3	5.1
Harrison	18	64	3.7	1.2	21	1 354	549.6	67.4	19	391	11.3	3.0
Hart	18	69	4.0	1.4	18	1 882	434.6	59.9	22	337	11.5	2.5
Henderson	81	404	34.9	11.1	77	6 420	D	D	88	1 348	54.7	15.1
Henry	21	D	D	D	10	D	D	D	13	D	D	D
Hickman	6	17	0.7	0.3	NA	NA	NA	NA	3	D	D	D
Hopkins	66	D	D	D	52	2 897	896.3	128.8	64	1 406	53.7	13.9
Jackson	6	12	1.1	0.5	NA	NA	NA	NA	5	42	2.1	0.5
Jefferson	2 266	D	D	D	797	45 142	25 695.4	2 233.8	1 561	35 897	1 629.2	480.6
Jessamine	66	224	20.6	6.4	67	2 738	1 015.6	102.8	59	1 183	46.4	13.0
Johnson	33	167	18.3	5.0	NA	NA	NA	NA	36	848	27.2	7.6
Kenton	366	D	D	D	123	4 637	1 236.4	210.3	307	7 033	323.3	94.2
Knott	12	52	5.1	1.8	NA	NA	NA	NA	4	109	3.0	0.8
Knox	40	D	D	D	18	879	210.7	34.0	37	580	27.5	5.7
Larue	14	D	D	D	20	783	90.0	20.6	14	146	5.9	1.6
Laurel	100	431	36.6	11.8	58	3 668	D	124.8	91	2 146	91.0	25.0
Lawrence	14	78	5.4	2.6	NA	NA	NA	NA	15	319	11.5	3.1
Lee	5	D	D	D	NA	NA	NA	NA	6	64	2.5	0.6
Leslie	10	D	D	D	NA	NA	NA	NA	6	81	3.9	0.9
Letcher	23	139	11.5	4.4	NA	NA	NA	NA	23	347	14.1	3.8
Lewis	4	16	0.8	0.4	NA	NA	NA	NA	13	102	3.9	0.8
Lincoln	23	128	9.8	3.3	18	737	D	D	17	259	9.4	2.6
Livingston	7	D	D	D	NA	NA	NA	NA	13	D	D	D
Logan	30	157	12.8	4.6	46	3 021	2 150.6	127.7	29	379	15.3	3.7
Lyon	9	132	2.9	1.3	NA	NA	NA	NA	23	313	12.2	3.5
McCracken	193	D	D	D	54	3 170	D	D	203	4 697	179.2	50.9
McCreary	7	33	2.3	0.5	NA	NA	NA	NA	18	247	7.1	1.9
McLean	8	D	D	D	NA	NA	NA	NA	14	101	3.1	0.8
Madison	120	D	D	D	73	5 473	D	D	143	3 368	127.3	34.7
Magoffin	13	94	13.3	6.2	NA	NA	NA	NA	11	163	7.3	2.0
Marion	23	110	7.7	2.9	30	3 349	620.2	120.1	29	417	12.3	3.6
Marshall	43	169	14.3	7.3	42	2 726	3 095.3	163.9	82	1 249	42.7	11.8
Martin	13	47	2.8	0.8	NA	NA	NA	NA	16	153	4.9	1.1
Mason	29	288	30.2	11.9	13	D	D	D	48	914	36.5	9.4
Meade	19	D	D	D	5	D	D	D	27	D	D	D
Menifee	2	D	D	D	NA	NA	NA	NA	1	D	D	D
Mercer	34	61	4.9	1.4	12	2 212	1 252.4	118.6	35	536	20.7	5.7
Metcalfe	9	16	1.2	0.3	9	979	391.3	32.4	9	101	5.1	0.7
Monroe	7	20	1.3	0.3	28	744	146.5	22.6	17	175	6.5	1.5
Montgomery	34	D	D	D	33	3 384	D	144.8	37	764	30.9	8.3
Morgan	9	42	3.0	0.8	NA	NA	NA	NA	13	226	8.1	1.9
Muhlenberg	41	166	7.1	2.1	26	547	D	22.6	55	786	27.2	7.5
Nelson	47	191	15.1	4.3	65	3 572	1 348.7	144.9	59	D	D	D
Nicholas	7	D	D	D	NA	NA	NA	NA	5	28	0.8	0.2

1. Establishment subject to federal tax.

Table B. States and Counties — Health Care and Social Assistance, Other Services, and Federal Funds

STATE County	Health care and social assistance, 2007				Other services, 2007				Federal funds and grants, 2009–2010 Expenditures (mil dol)			
										Direct payments for individuals[1]		
	Number of establish-ments	Number of employees	Receipts (mil dol)	Annual payroll (mil dol)	Number of establish-ments	Number of employees	Receipts (mil dol)	Annual payroll (mil dol)	Total	Social Security and government retirement	Medicare	Food Stamps and Supplemental Security Income
	159	160	161	162	163	164	165	166	167	168	169	170
KENTUCKY—Cont'd												
Clay	33	1 068	62.3	30.9	11	D	D	D	388.5	62.5	140.7	44.3
Clinton	24	609	35.4	14.3	8	17	1.2	0.3	165.7	31.3	71.4	10.4
Crittenden	17	471	28.3	12.7	14	D	D	D	93.2	33.9	34.8	4.1
Cumberland	14	382	22.4	9.7	7	19	1.9	0.4	105.8	21.8	46.4	5.7
Daviess	302	D	D	D	158	D	D	D	797.0	316.8	219.8	46.2
Edmonson	16	D	D	D	6	14	1.5	0.3	118.4	32.5	34.9	6.5
Elliott	9	D	D	D	4	D	D	D	90.7	35.3	25.0	8.6
Estill	22	388	26.7	9.5	11	22	2.5	0.5	203.6	55.6	76.1	16.7
Fayette	969	26 453	3 046.9	1 172.3	590	4 928	509.8	149.5	3 036.1	707.9	434.4	86.7
Fleming	21	614	42.1	16.0	14	33	2.9	0.5	150.6	44.6	48.5	8.4
Floyd	127	2 271	203.1	71.4	50	257	25.5	6.8	580.2	173.3	187.3	64.6
Franklin	145	2 315	256.7	76.2	142	797	90.9	26.5	2 671.2	197.4	220.3	18.6
Fulton	12	D	D	D	8	D	D	D	118.8	30.8	43.2	7.1
Gallatin	9	D	D	D	NA	NA	NA	NA	60.0	21.6	17.0	3.4
Garrard	21	203	13.3	5.5	14	64	3.4	1.0	122.3	53.8	35.2	6.9
Grant	33	519	43.1	17.5	34	D	D	D	164.2	76.4	44.5	10.7
Graves	94	1 642	113.4	39.1	31	177	25.7	6.6	431.2	140.9	125.7	14.9
Grayson	53	994	80.4	27.7	25	78	6.9	1.1	263.2	88.8	91.0	16.1
Green	27	500	31.4	13.0	15	47	3.2	0.7	107.2	33.6	42.0	6.1
Greenup	79	983	75.9	35.0	30	D	D	D	350.6	159.2	106.8	20.3
Hancock	13	136	6.2	2.1	7	D	D	D	64.0	27.1	19.4	3.0
Hardin	308	D	D	D	153	D	D	D	2 788.9	473.3	160.5	36.6
Harlan	54	1 362	128.9	41.6	26	125	8.9	2.6	639.8	130.2	148.0	196.8
Harrison	46	903	71.3	27.1	22	73	6.8	1.5	172.0	58.3	48.1	9.4
Hart	24	408	28.4	10.9	16	46	3.4	1.0	168.5	51.5	60.9	11.0
Henderson	141	D	D	D	70	D	D	D	360.5	150.1	117.0	22.6
Henry	21	D	D	D	15	55	4.6	1.4	131.3	45.0	46.7	7.0
Hickman	9	148	8.4	3.1	2	D	D	D	52.1	14.7	19.2	2.8
Hopkins	113	3 152	259.2	122.7	72	561	51.2	14.2	523.9	172.9	129.5	28.6
Jackson	17	272	15.8	6.4	4	D	D	D	206.2	38.8	68.8	17.1
Jefferson	2 227	58 914	6 171.5	2 309.4	1 402	12 526	1 315.0	317.2	9 420.0	2 277.8	1 886.6	172.8
Jessamine	76	726	43.7	21.6	73	281	19.6	5.9	243.9	120.5	54.4	15.1
Johnson	62	778	86.5	23.8	32	116	9.5	2.2	321.3	93.5	103.5	29.2
Kenton	337	9 485	1 026.0	418.4	249	1 848	150.4	43.6	1 195.5	415.1	309.3	57.3
Knott	17	380	19.3	7.4	8	D	D	D	236.0	50.8	83.4	23.9
Knox	71	1 071	76.4	29.5	21	74	6.7	1.8	453.8	79.1	148.4	48.1
Larue	15	D	D	D	16	D	D	D	126.0	48.2	42.6	7.0
Laurel	128	2 861	265.9	97.5	73	422	37.7	10.1	497.3	172.2	136.8	40.5
Lawrence	30	D	D	D	15	D	D	D	200.1	61.0	68.2	20.2
Lee	17	853	16.6	9.5	1	D	D	D	113.4	23.4	43.5	12.8
Leslie	15	431	33.1	12.9	3	D	D	D	189.4	42.2	73.5	18.3
Letcher	44	1 097	79.9	35.5	16	49	5.6	1.0	321.5	97.2	111.7	32.4
Lewis	13	307	25.9	10.4	3	D	D	D	155.7	39.5	56.5	13.3
Lincoln	34	543	33.4	15.4	17	45	3.9	0.8	266.1	80.8	90.7	15.8
Livingston	16	D	D	D	6	24	1.5	0.4	175.9	42.7	33.4	3.5
Logan	48	703	54.6	18.3	36	173	12.9	3.6	280.2	87.8	105.7	11.0
Lyon	13	238	10.4	4.7	10	12	1.1	0.3	73.9	37.1	21.1	2.4
McCracken	264	6 501	723.3	257.3	136	D	D	D	1 717.4	258.6	197.9	31.9
McCreary	29	360	17.3	7.3	6	21	1.6	0.3	265.9	54.8	77.5	27.3
McLean	9	D	D	D	13	D	D	D	91.5	35.5	29.6	4.4
Madison	186	3 241	238.4	91.1	89	395	31.5	7.8	1 014.7	228.8	157.4	32.4
Magoffin	14	255	21.5	5.8	8	D	D	D	203.8	41.3	78.3	22.7
Marion	43	1 019	74.2	28.1	17	76	7.4	1.9	176.3	52.9	62.0	10.4
Marshall	52	938	54.1	22.0	42	157	14.6	3.2	263.8	131.9	77.0	8.6
Martin	19	227	12.7	5.0	10	D	D	D	191.0	49.4	51.6	21.8
Mason	71	1 187	107.9	37.2	45	D	D	D	172.6	56.0	58.4	8.1
Meade	36	259	15.2	6.2	24	122	9.0	2.5	159.8	90.4	34.8	7.3
Menifee	7	142	8.7	4.0	3	D	D	D	141.6	25.7	23.4	7.3
Mercer	36	624	41.8	17.2	25	D	D	D	176.1	73.4	48.7	9.0
Metcalfe	16	117	6.4	2.9	6	D	D	D	112.8	30.7	43.0	6.9
Monroe	29	475	32.0	12.6	13	42	3.0	0.7	181.2	35.9	77.4	10.2
Montgomery	74	1 277	76.5	28.5	32	D	D	D	203.6	78.0	63.9	13.1
Morgan	18	445	30.4	11.4	17	38	3.2	0.7	198.3	37.0	59.0	13.9
Muhlenberg	58	D	D	D	43	160	12.4	3.0	400.9	124.5	98.9	19.3
Nelson	86	1 380	113.5	40.9	50	255	16.5	4.5	284.5	114.4	79.9	14.8
Nicholas	10	258	13.3	6.3	7	26	1.5	0.4	85.8	23.1	27.0	4.6

1. State totals may include programs not allocated by county.

Table B. States and Counties — Federal Funds, Residential Construction, and Local Government Finances

	Federal funds and grants, 2009–2010 (cont.)							Value of residential construction authorized by building permits, 2010		Local government finances, 2007				
	Expenditures (mil dol) (cont.)									General revenue				
		Procurement contract awards		Grants[1]								Taxes		
													Per capita[2] (dollars)	
STATE County	Salaries and wages	Defense	Other	Medicaid and other health-related	Nutrition and family welfare	Education	Other	New construction ($1,000)	Number of housing units	Total (mil dol)	Inter-govern-mental (mil dol)	Total (mil dol)	Total	Property
	171	172	173	174	175	176	177	178	179	180	181	182	183	184

KENTUCKY—Cont'd

Clay	25.1	0.0	5.3	96.6	7.8	3.6	1.1	0	0	46.1	33.7	6.2	262	150
Clinton	3.9	2.7	0.4	38.5	2.6	2.8	0.2	0	0	23.0	16.1	4.4	460	228
Crittenden	2.7	0.0	0.5	12.1	1.4	0.9	0.3	499	5	17.6	11.9	3.4	377	253
Cumberland	1.3	0.0	0.2	25.7	1.8	0.7	0.7	0	0	13.8	9.3	2.9	428	205
Daviess	36.5	2.2	7.0	66.5	25.8	5.6	25.9	28 464	332	278.0	107.7	81.9	873	525
Edmonson	11.1	0.9	10.3	17.5	2.1	0.9	0.0	NA	NA	22.5	15.6	4.1	340	253
Elliott	0.7	0.0	0.2	17.5	2.1	0.7	0.1	NA	NA	15.0	12.2	1.6	218	156
Estill	7.2	0.0	0.6	39.2	3.5	1.6	2.0	185	5	29.0	19.1	5.3	357	229
Fayette	255.1	460.0	289.7	340.8	43.0	27.6	131.7	92 725	822	671.8	148.8	426.4	1 528	594
Fleming	3.9	0.1	1.8	26.7	5.7	1.4	4.3	124	2	50.8	18.0	6.6	446	275
Floyd	21.0	0.7	16.9	92.4	9.8	4.0	4.6	272	2	85.1	53.6	21.1	503	402
Franklin	117.9	0.8	3.5	224.6	215.3	351.2	1 225.8	8 786	50	134.4	38.0	58.3	1 203	567
Fulton	3.6	1.4	1.0	20.4	1.9	1.8	1.8	35	1	24.6	15.4	4.7	686	369
Gallatin	1.9	5.7	0.5	6.9	1.3	0.6	0.2	2 001	37	26.6	10.4	7.3	903	542
Garrard	2.1	0.0	0.5	15.8	2.3	1.1	0.4	130	1	30.8	17.8	9.3	547	377
Grant	4.4	0.1	1.0	16.7	4.6	2.0	0.7	5 893	32	56.0	33.9	13.5	536	402
Graves	13.1	0.0	2.6	42.8	5.9	2.3	63.3	147	2	76.2	40.9	20.2	538	360
Grayson	7.5	1.3	1.2	44.0	6.3	1.8	0.2	1 675	21	61.7	40.0	12.7	499	255
Green	1.9	0.0	0.5	16.8	1.8	0.9	0.4	95	1	36.3	13.6	4.6	397	255
Greenup	5.6	5.4	1.3	37.1	5.7	2.0	4.0	4 655	14	76.2	40.5	22.7	610	500
Hancock	1.4	0.0	0.3	9.3	1.1	0.6	0.2	878	5	47.8	11.5	7.8	904	426
Hardin	1 611.9	316.7	92.1	56.2	15.8	5.6	1.8	116 917	1 209	405.5	108.8	66.8	682	383
Harlan	12.3	1.3	51.7	79.0	10.2	5.3	1.8	0	0	65.0	47.3	12.4	400	281
Harrison	12.7	0.8	2.0	22.2	2.8	1.5	9.2	3 687	21	36.0	18.8	13.4	720	309
Hart	3.0	0.1	0.7	31.9	2.6	1.7	1.0	5 448	52	35.6	23.2	7.5	405	234
Henderson	10.6	1.1	1.8	33.3	6.2	3.0	4.8	7 828	63	124.0	53.7	35.0	773	417
Henry	3.5	0.0	0.8	19.7	2.6	1.0	0.2	3 665	28	33.2	18.7	9.1	581	404
Hickman	1.4	0.0	0.3	7.8	0.9	0.6	0.2	NA	NA	9.9	7.0	2.0	402	300
Hopkins	20.6	6.0	89.9	50.0	7.5	5.4	6.9	10 680	82	108.5	58.7	31.3	677	372
Jackson	2.6	4.9	1.9	44.9	4.2	1.7	19.5	0	0	25.3	20.6	3.6	267	172
Jefferson	505.4	3 079.7	177.8	701.0	113.9	95.8	186.3	158 924	1 003	2 164.0	655.6	982.3	1 385	736
Jessamine	6.8	0.6	7.3	21.0	4.6	2.3	3.3	41 954	222	101.7	39.6	47.3	1 039	612
Johnson	4.1	0.4	1.3	55.8	13.6	2.3	15.6	246	1	62.3	38.3	14.6	609	334
Kenton	205.5	2.7	27.8	91.9	22.7	7.8	43.2	33 792	260	547.8	128.7	197.8	1 263	753
Knott	4.0	0.4	0.8	53.4	9.3	2.1	5.7	NA	NA	36.8	28.3	6.0	346	283
Knox	22.3	25.7	1.1	96.8	16.6	3.5	8.3	0	0	80.1	48.6	14.0	432	230
Larue	2.8	0.0	1.6	16.7	2.2	1.1	0.3	5 727	33	29.3	20.2	5.6	409	289
Laurel	30.2	0.3	22.9	72.7	9.7	4.1	5.1	560	9	106.9	62.1	30.6	534	286
Lawrence	3.0	0.1	0.7	40.0	3.8	1.8	0.7	NA	NA	45.6	22.8	6.1	371	258
Lee	1.4	0.0	0.3	27.4	2.3	0.7	1.0	NA	NA	20.4	13.4	3.7	499	285
Leslie	2.2	0.0	0.7	45.3	4.3	1.0	1.9	NA	NA	25.4	19.3	4.4	373	291
Letcher	5.9	0.0	2.0	62.1	6.2	2.2	1.4	0	3	50.8	34.7	10.4	434	338
Lewis	1.8	0.0	0.4	34.1	3.1	1.2	2.1	NA	NA	25.2	19.4	4.3	311	225
Lincoln	13.1	0.0	1.2	51.2	6.5	2.2	0.5	7 046	40	47.6	34.3	9.5	375	224
Livingston	3.7	61.6	15.5	10.6	1.6	0.7	0.0	NA	NA	18.4	11.2	5.1	526	319
Logan	6.0	0.1	1.2	46.6	3.9	1.9	1.1	1 750	24	66.1	37.4	18.8	694	336
Lyon	2.1	0.1	0.3	6.3	0.9	0.4	1.7	1 120	8	19.3	7.8	5.9	721	527
McCracken	46.5	0.5	1 078.8	61.6	11.2	4.1	6.9	28 180	145	165.6	73.2	61.3	946	473
McCreary	28.0	20.5	5.4	43.0	6.0	2.6	0.3	0	0	39.0	28.5	7.4	429	317
McLean	1.6	0.1	0.3	9.3	1.5	0.9	3.4	171	1	26.1	13.9	6.4	661	309
Madison	125.9	315.2	3.5	76.3	14.5	9.9	6.3	14 452	186	155.5	69.1	63.2	779	375
Magoffin	1.4	0.0	0.4	51.9	4.6	1.8	0.6	NA	NA	32.7	23.4	5.1	384	212
Marion	3.9	0.0	1.1	32.2	6.8	1.6	1.1	943	10	45.8	22.7	12.7	668	379
Marshall	14.5	0.0	3.6	18.4	4.1	1.7	0.4	7 075	65	125.3	31.8	32.4	1 038	504
Martin	23.8	0.6	5.3	31.6	3.7	1.4	1.7	NA	NA	28.3	19.7	6.1	521	332
Mason	5.9	0.0	0.9	27.3	2.8	1.6	5.9	3 682	27	50.8	19.6	16.4	952	426
Meade	4.8	0.7	0.8	11.5	3.7	1.3	0.0	21 086	216	52.2	30.9	13.2	485	368
Menifee	58.5	7.6	1.2	14.4	1.3	0.5	0.6	NA	NA	15.0	10.5	2.6	391	257
Mercer	9.7	1.1	0.8	20.7	2.8	1.3	3.8	5 032	42	44.5	21.9	16.6	761	446
Metcalfe	2.2	0.2	0.5	23.6	1.9	1.0	0.1	NA	NA	20.6	13.8	5.0	483	231
Monroe	5.2	0.2	0.5	42.6	2.4	1.0	1.4	NA	NA	24.7	18.3	4.5	386	232
Montgomery	5.4	0.0	1.1	30.0	3.8	2.3	1.5	3 280	29	58.9	29.5	17.8	704	373
Morgan	2.6	0.0	0.6	37.7	6.0	1.2	38.7	143	1	33.4	25.2	4.4	311	199
Muhlenberg	19.3	-3.6	94.6	36.3	5.2	1.9	1.1	176	1	60.7	40.0	11.7	373	288
Nelson	17.6	8.8	2.0	30.6	5.4	2.1	3.4	17 803	146	94.6	45.2	27.3	643	508
Nicholas	10.3	0.0	0.3	13.5	1.5	0.6	0.3	351	2	13.3	8.4	2.8	411	239

1. State totals may include programs not allocated by county.   2. Based on the resident population estimated as of July 1 of the year shown.

STATE County	Total (mil dol)	Per capita[1] (dollars)	Education	Health and hospitals	Police protection	Public welfare	Highways	Total (mil dol)	Per capita[1] (dollars)	Federal civilian	Federal military	State and local	Democratic	Republican	All other
	185	186	187	188	189	190	191	192	193	194	195	196	197	198	199
KENTUCKY—Cont'd															
Clay	45.3	1 909	68.1	1.6	3.1	0.0	4.3	33.2	1 400	366	74	1 191	21.1	77.5	1.4
Clinton	20.0	2 097	73.5	3.2	2.6	0.0	4.6	21.5	2 256	55	30	606	18.2	80.7	1.1
Crittenden	15.8	1 729	60.8	0.9	3.8	0.0	10.6	27.4	3 004	26	29	406	31.9	66.3	1.8
Cumberland	13.7	1 992	66.0	0.3	4.6	0.0	7.0	23.9	3 480	14	21	380	24.9	73.5	1.6
Daviess	275.0	2 933	44.7	1.7	4.5	0.1	3.2	1 042.2	11 117	282	319	8 556	44.2	54.3	1.5
Edmonson	21.2	1 773	70.1	3.9	2.5	0.0	7.0	39.0	3 252	209	38	543	31.3	67.6	1.1
Elliott	13.7	1 912	85.0	4.8	1.4	0.0	0.2	25.3	3 544	0	29	546	61.0	35.9	3.1
Estill	28.7	1 917	69.1	3.8	1.7	0.0	5.4	31.1	2 075	24	47	692	29.3	69.3	1.4
Fayette	637.7	2 285	44.5	3.6	7.9	1.7	0.6	1 151.0	4 125	4 254	960	34 669	51.7	46.9	1.3
Fleming	48.9	3 327	37.5	34.4	1.7	0.0	3.0	194.8	13 259	56	46	943	39.1	58.8	2.1
Floyd	88.5	2 106	65.7	0.1	1.9	0.0	2.4	87.0	2 070	148	132	2 495	48.1	49.4	2.5
Franklin	138.8	2 867	36.2	2.5	3.8	0.4	4.4	182.3	3 765	571	179	14 269	48.9	49.5	1.7
Fulton	24.8	3 652	38.1	0.6	3.5	0.1	4.3	34.9	5 141	27	40	526	43.8	54.2	2.0
Gallatin	36.6	4 559	63.1	1.5	2.3	0.0	2.5	179.9	22 394	35	26	425	40.0	57.6	2.3
Garrard	27.9	1 637	68.2	3.1	3.3	0.0	3.1	14.1	828	28	54	646	27.9	71.0	1.1
Grant	61.3	2 435	68.6	0.4	2.8	0.1	4.0	92.7	3 684	51	80	1 155	35.5	62.9	1.5
Graves	78.6	2 093	60.4	0.2	2.6	0.0	3.6	199.7	5 316	211	119	1 835	36.2	62.2	1.6
Grayson	54.5	2 150	51.0	0.3	2.9	0.7	6.4	111.2	4 387	77	81	1 666	31.8	66.7	1.5
Green	34.7	2 998	36.0	45.1	1.1	0.0	3.9	27.3	2 362	29	36	711	23.7	74.5	1.8
Greenup	74.9	2 011	63.5	1.0	3.6	0.0	3.4	55.6	1 491	76	120	1 588	41.9	56.0	2.1
Hancock	46.3	5 374	25.3	1.1	1.1	0.1	2.3	690.9	80 177	22	27	433	51.5	46.5	2.0
Hardin	383.8	3 919	31.5	49.9	2.1	0.1	2.0	308.9	3 154	5 375	9 173	6 420	39.1	59.8	1.1
Harlan	75.7	2 435	74.2	0.7	2.1	0.2	2.5	118.7	3 820	105	97	1 833	26.1	72.3	1.6
Harrison	33.4	1 799	61.5	1.1	5.7	0.2	7.3	26.5	1 431	51	59	841	38.4	59.6	2.0
Hart	42.8	2 324	66.0	3.2	2.2	0.0	3.3	71.0	3 858	41	58	866	33.6	64.5	1.9
Henderson	115.1	2 540	41.9	0.4	4.9	0.1	4.9	569.6	12 576	130	143	2 642	50.6	47.9	1.5
Henry	31.7	2 017	64.4	4.0	3.8	0.1	4.5	29.4	1 870	100	51	722	39.4	59.0	1.6
Hickman	10.0	2 028	63.6	0.4	3.5	0.0	6.4	9.3	1 885	27	15	244	36.1	62.5	1.4
Hopkins	110.6	2 390	54.2	0.2	5.4	1.2	5.1	377.4	8 154	167	145	3 382	36.7	61.6	1.7
Jackson	25.2	1 852	77.3	1.0	1.2	0.0	6.0	19.8	1 461	36	42	725	14.2	84.4	1.4
Jefferson	1 894.1	2 670	45.8	3.0	6.0	0.8	3.9	4 031.8	5 685	7 209	2 498	40 606	55.5	43.6	1.0
Jessamine	97.2	2 133	59.4	1.8	5.3	0.0	4.0	140.7	3 088	79	151	2 455	30.8	67.8	1.3
Johnson	58.2	2 422	63.7	5.7	3.2	0.1	6.3	57.2	2 382	56	75	1 512	28.3	69.8	1.9
Kenton	529.9	3 382	34.7	3.1	4.9	0.3	3.9	1 949.1	12 440	4 432	500	6 971	38.8	59.7	1.5
Knott	40.7	2 357	47.0	0.1	2.8	0.2	9.3	34.4	1 991	63	54	801	44.9	52.7	2.4
Knox	78.1	2 402	55.9	18.2	1.9	0.1	3.6	92.4	2 841	190	103	1 462	27.0	71.6	1.4
Larue	35.2	2 579	72.0	1.4	2.1	0.0	3.5	48.3	3 537	44	43	680	31.0	67.2	1.8
Laurel	119.1	2 077	73.2	0.3	3.8	0.0	1.9	217.6	3 794	342	182	2 740	20.5	78.5	1.0
Lawrence	44.9	2 749	48.6	0.1	1.7	0.0	5.1	291.8	17 876	38	52	669	36.0	62.0	1.9
Lee	17.6	2 370	55.6	9.8	3.4	0.1	8.2	10.6	1 429	22	23	483	27.1	71.3	1.6
Leslie	24.8	2 109	65.5	0.3	0.5	0.1	5.2	17.1	1 449	28	36	600	17.4	81.3	1.3
Letcher	51.7	2 151	67.8	0.2	2.5	0.1	4.4	34.3	1 426	61	74	1 174	31.9	65.2	3.0
Lewis	27.1	1 952	69.4	0.0	2.2	0.0	1.2	105.7	7 610	25	43	663	31.5	67.1	1.4
Lincoln	46.2	1 830	72.5	0.3	2.2	0.2	4.2	43.3	1 716	61	79	1 127	30.1	68.5	1.4
Livingston	18.9	1 964	56.9	5.3	2.5	0.1	6.8	17.9	1 866	104	30	502	35.3	62.9	1.8
Logan	65.0	2 394	57.7	14.5	4.7	0.0	3.9	48.6	1 792	73	86	1 244	35.0	63.6	1.4
Lyon	16.8	2 036	40.7	5.2	3.1	0.5	6.9	16.2	1 962	30	26	750	40.9	57.6	1.5
McCracken	148.2	2 288	49.0	0.2	4.1	0.1	6.7	148.7	2 296	677	231	3 820	36.7	61.9	1.4
McCreary	37.8	2 183	68.8	2.2	0.8	0.0	3.1	31.3	1 807	452	56	829	23.3	75.4	1.3
McLean	27.1	2 784	47.8	3.4	1.7	0.3	5.5	39.1	4 022	36	30	534	44.4	54.0	1.7
Madison	158.3	1 951	58.7	3.0	4.1	1.4	3.8	371.4	4 580	1 226	271	7 535	38.1	60.5	1.4
Magoffin	36.6	2 779	70.3	0.2	3.0	0.0	4.5	69.0	5 235	17	41	689	45.3	52.3	2.4
Marion	47.2	2 492	52.5	1.7	3.6	0.0	3.8	60.0	3 171	59	61	886	47.2	50.5	2.3
Marshall	123.0	3 936	27.5	11.2	3.5	0.3	2.6	464.2	14 852	97	98	1 736	36.7	61.4	1.9
Martin	26.4	2 270	67.3	3.3	1.8	0.6	5.8	14.4	1 235	375	41	690	21.9	76.5	1.6
Mason	49.6	2 887	39.4	1.1	5.4	0.0	7.8	334.8	19 477	59	55	1 520	40.6	57.6	1.8
Meade	62.5	2 290	74.6	1.9	1.9	0.0	2.2	80.9	2 967	39	83	1 100	38.8	59.7	1.5
Menifee	14.2	2 096	62.1	3.3	4.5	0.3	5.5	17.2	2 546	52	21	338	51.3	46.4	2.3
Mercer	47.1	2 159	65.5	0.4	3.9	0.0	4.7	112.4	5 155	50	69	937	31.4	67.4	1.2
Metcalfe	18.3	1 783	65.3	2.5	3.4	0.0	7.8	13.7	1 333	25	32	528	32.2	65.1	2.7
Monroe	28.5	2 444	70.8	0.2	3.0	0.0	6.7	27.9	2 389	33	36	853	22.9	75.8	1.3
Montgomery	59.9	2 376	59.1	4.1	4.9	0.0	4.4	140.7	5 576	71	81	1 120	41.0	57.6	1.5
Morgan	38.2	2 684	59.9	2.9	2.3	0.0	5.5	22.9	1 608	38	44	1 073	42.9	54.7	2.4
Muhlenberg	64.3	2 053	63.0	0.2	2.7	0.2	5.3	109.7	3 499	604	98	1 768	48.3	50.0	1.7
Nelson	102.9	2 420	55.6	2.0	3.8	0.3	2.5	208.2	4 897	92	137	1 762	42.2	55.9	1.9
Nicholas	12.4	1 796	61.2	1.1	4.3	0.6	7.5	10.1	1 470	15	22	338	42.8	55.0	2.2

1. Based on the resident population estimated as of July 1 of the year shown.   2. © 2009 Election Data Services, Inc. All rights reserved.

Table B. States and Counties — **Land Area and Population**

STATE/ County code	CBSA code[1]	County type[2]	STATE County	Land area[3] (sq km) 2010	Total persons	Rank	Per square kilometer	White	Black	American Indian, Alaska Native	Asian and Pacific Islander	Percent Hispanic or Latino[4]	Under 5 years	5 to 17 years	18 to 24 years	25 to 34 years	35 to 44 years	45 to 54 years
				1	2	3	4	5	6	7	8	9	10	11	12	13	14	15
			KENTUCKY—Cont'd															
21 183	...	6	Ohio	1 521	23 842	1 648	15.7	95.2	1.1	0.5	0.3	3.5	7.1	17.7	8.1	11.9	12.6	14.3
21 185	31140	1	Oldham	485	60 316	855	124.4	90.4	4.8	0.7	1.8	3.5	5.7	22.2	6.2	10.2	16.4	17.7
21 187	...	8	Owen	909	10 841	2 381	11.9	96.5	1.1	0.6	0.3	2.3	6.4	18.1	7.4	11.3	13.2	15.7
21 189	...	9	Owsley	511	4 755	2 860	9.3	98.5	0.5	0.6	0.1	0.8	5.5	16.7	7.7	11.6	12.6	14.8
21 191	17140	1	Pendleton	718	14 877	2 119	20.7	98.4	0.6	0.6	0.3	1.0	6.2	18.5	8.5	11.1	14.0	17.0
21 193	...	7	Perry	880	28 712	1 465	32.6	97.1	2.0	0.5	0.6	0.6	5.9	15.9	8.6	12.6	14.0	15.7
21 195	...	7	Pike	2 038	65 024	805	31.9	98.2	0.8	0.4	0.6	0.7	5.9	16.1	8.3	12.5	13.9	15.6
21 197	...	6	Powell	464	12 613	2 269	27.2	98.0	0.9	0.6	0.3	1.0	6.8	17.8	8.0	12.4	13.8	14.9
21 199	43700	5	Pulaski	1 705	63 063	828	37.0	96.0	1.4	0.7	0.7	2.1	6.1	16.7	7.6	11.7	13.2	14.9
21 201	...	8	Robertson	259	2 282	3 030	8.8	98.7	0.3	0.7	0.2	1.0	6.1	15.3	8.3	10.1	11.7	15.4
21 203	40080	7	Rockcastle	820	17 056	1 981	20.8	98.9	0.2	0.8	0.2	0.6	5.7	17.5	8.0	11.3	14.0	15.8
21 205	...	7	Rowan	725	23 333	1 678	32.2	96.3	1.8	0.5	1.0	1.3	5.8	13.8	21.9	12.2	11.6	12.1
21 207	...	9	Russell	657	17 565	1 945	26.7	95.8	0.8	0.7	0.4	3.3	6.0	16.3	7.5	11.0	13.1	15.0
21 209	30460	2	Scott	730	47 173	1 020	64.6	89.3	6.1	0.6	1.2	4.2	7.5	19.3	9.2	13.9	15.6	14.3
21 211	31140	1	Shelby	983	42 074	1 127	42.8	82.6	8.3	0.6	1.0	9.1	6.6	18.2	7.9	12.8	14.4	15.1
21 213	...	6	Simpson	607	17 327	1 961	28.5	87.8	10.4	0.7	0.8	1.9	6.7	18.0	8.0	12.0	13.2	15.3
21 215	31140	1	Spencer	483	17 061	1 979	35.3	96.3	2.0	0.5	0.7	1.4	6.5	19.2	6.8	11.6	16.1	17.3
21 217	15820	7	Taylor	690	24 512	1 625	35.5	92.5	5.9	0.5	0.7	1.8	6.4	15.9	11.6	11.4	11.5	14.6
21 219	...	8	Todd	970	12 460	2 276	12.8	87.7	8.4	0.6	0.3	4.0	7.9	19.3	8.6	11.8	12.7	14.3
21 221	17300	3	Trigg	1 143	14 339	2 154	12.5	89.9	8.9	0.8	0.6	1.2	5.7	16.8	6.9	9.1	12.7	14.5
21 223	31140	1	Trimble	393	8 809	2 544	22.4	96.3	0.5	0.7	0.7	2.5	6.3	18.8	7.4	11.2	14.5	15.7
21 225	...	6	Union	888	15 007	2 110	16.9	85.6	12.8	0.6	0.5	1.6	6.1	16.8	14.4	11.2	11.1	13.8
21 227	14540	3	Warren	1 403	113 792	525	81.1	83.1	10.0	0.6	3.3	4.5	6.4	16.4	16.2	14.0	12.3	13.2
21 229	...	8	Washington	770	11 717	2 315	15.2	89.9	7.0	0.4	0.5	3.4	5.9	17.2	9.1	10.6	12.9	15.8
21 231	...	7	Wayne	1 187	20 813	1 802	17.5	95.1	2.0	0.7	0.4	2.9	6.1	16.5	8.1	11.5	12.9	14.7
21 233	21780	2	Webster	860	13 621	2 211	15.8	90.9	4.7	0.5	0.7	4.3	6.8	16.7	8.3	11.9	13.1	14.6
21 235	18340	7	Whitley	1 134	35 637	1 282	31.4	97.9	0.8	0.8	0.6	0.9	6.1	17.8	11.1	11.4	12.8	14.1
21 237	...	9	Wolfe	575	7 355	2 656	12.8	99.0	0.2	0.7	0.1	0.6	6.5	17.5	6.9	11.8	12.4	15.8
21 239	30460	2	Woodford	489	24 939	1 602	51.0	87.6	5.6	0.4	0.8	6.7	5.8	18.3	7.2	10.8	13.5	17.2
22 000	...	X	LOUISIANA	111 898	4 533 372	X	40.5	61.4	32.5	1.1	1.9	4.2	6.9	17.7	10.5	13.9	12.5	14.4
22 001	18940	4	Acadia	1 697	61 773	840	36.4	79.6	18.7	0.5	0.3	1.7	7.6	19.7	9.4	12.6	12.0	14.7
22 003	...	6	Allen	1 973	25 764	1 575	13.1	72.1	23.9	3.0	0.9	1.3	6.5	16.4	8.5	15.3	14.4	14.7
22 005	12940	2	Ascension	751	107 215	552	142.8	71.7	22.6	0.6	1.3	4.7	7.8	20.9	8.4	13.9	15.2	14.4
22 007	38200	6	Assumption	877	23 421	1 669	26.7	66.5	30.8	0.9	0.3	2.1	6.3	18.3	9.0	12.1	12.6	15.5
22 009	...	6	Avoyelles	2 156	42 073	1 128	19.5	67.2	30.4	2.0	0.5	1.4	6.7	17.7	8.7	13.1	12.8	14.5
22 011	19760	6	Beauregard	2 998	35 654	1 281	11.9	82.4	13.8	1.8	1.1	2.8	6.9	19.1	8.4	13.3	13.3	14.0
22 013	...	6	Bienville	2 101	14 353	2 152	6.8	53.7	42.6	1.0	0.3	1.4	5.9	17.4	8.8	10.6	11.4	14.7
22 015	43340	2	Bossier	2 176	116 979	509	53.8	70.7	21.6	1.0	2.4	6.0	7.4	18.3	9.7	15.0	13.0	13.8
22 017	43340	2	Caddo	2 275	254 969	254	112.1	48.8	47.7	0.9	1.4	2.4	7.0	17.6	10.1	13.8	11.8	14.0
22 019	29340	3	Calcasieu	2 755	192 768	325	70.0	70.7	25.6	1.0	1.4	2.6	7.2	18.3	10.1	13.4	12.0	14.5
22 021	...	8	Caldwell	1 371	10 132	2 436	7.4	80.1	17.4	0.7	0.3	2.2	6.2	17.2	8.5	12.3	12.8	14.6
22 023	29340	3	Cameron	3 328	6 839	2 701	2.1	95.4	1.9	0.8	0.2	2.3	5.8	18.4	8.5	11.9	12.2	18.2
22 025	...	9	Catahoula	1 834	10 407	2 118	5.7	67.3	31.8	0.5	0.1	0.9	6.3	16.3	8.9	14.2	11.6	15.2
22 027	...	7	Claiborne	1 955	17 195	1 971	8.8	47.6	51.1	0.7	0.4	1.0	5.3	14.4	8.8	14.5	13.2	15.0
22 029	35020	7	Concordia	1 805	20 822	1 800	11.5	57.4	41.2	0.6	0.3	1.0	6.9	18.2	8.7	13.3	11.4	14.4
22 031	43340	2	De Soto	2 268	26 656	1 540	11.8	57.5	39.5	1.2	0.2	2.5	6.7	18.2	8.2	11.5	12.1	15.5
22 033	12940	2	East Baton Rouge	1 179	440 171	149	373.3	47.8	45.7	0.5	3.2	3.7	6.7	16.8	14.2	15.3	11.6	13.2
22 035	...	7	East Carroll	1 090	7 759	2 625	7.1	28.7	69.1	0.4	0.8	1.6	7.3	18.4	10.3	15.0	11.8	14.0
22 037	12940	2	East Feliciana	1 174	20 267	1 824	17.3	53.4	45.4	0.8	0.4	1.0	5.4	15.3	8.9	12.7	12.8	17.1
22 039	...	6	Evangeline	1 716	33 984	1 325	19.8	68.7	28.8	0.6	0.5	2.3	7.5	19.4	9.7	12.4	12.2	14.2
22 041	...	7	Franklin	1 618	20 767	1 805	12.8	67.2	31.7	0.5	0.3	0.9	7.5	18.1	8.6	11.6	11.3	14.2
22 043	10780	3	Grant	1 665	22 309	1 722	13.4	79.1	16.0	1.7	0.5	4.2	6.4	16.7	8.0	16.1	14.9	14.6
22 045	35340	4	Iberia	1 487	73 240	738	49.3	61.9	32.6	0.6	2.8	3.1	7.5	19.6	9.5	12.7	12.2	15.0
22 047	12940	2	Iberville	1 602	33 387	1 339	20.8	48.4	49.4	0.4	0.4	2.0	6.2	16.3	9.8	14.2	13.2	16.1
22 049	40820	6	Jackson	1 474	16 274	2 035	11.0	68.4	30.2	0.7	0.4	1.3	6.7	16.0	8.8	13.1	12.0	13.5
22 051	35380	1	Jefferson	766	432 552	152	564.7	57.0	26.4	0.7	4.3	12.4	6.6	16.0	9.2	14.2	12.6	15.1
22 053	27660	6	Jefferson Davis	1 687	31 594	1 404	18.7	80.1	18.4	1.0	0.4	1.7	7.3	19.3	8.5	12.0	11.9	14.9
22 055	29180	3	Lafayette	696	221 578	282	318.4	68.4	26.3	0.7	1.8	3.9	7.1	17.4	12.5	15.4	12.5	14.2
22 057	26380	3	Lafourche	2 767	96 318	600	34.8	79.3	13.8	3.6	1.0	3.8	7.1	17.5	10.5	13.3	13.0	15.1
22 059	...	6	La Salle	1 618	14 890	2 118	9.2	84.8	12.1	1.4	0.2	2.2	6.4	17.2	9.0	13.8	12.8	13.9
22 061	40820	4	Lincoln	1 222	46 735	1 028	38.2	54.9	40.9	0.6	2.0	2.5	6.1	14.5	24.6	13.5	9.5	10.9
22 063	12940	2	Livingston	1 679	128 026	480	76.3	91.0	5.4	0.8	0.7	3.0	7.6	20.0	8.8	14.4	14.4	14.1
22 065	45260	7	Madison	1 617	12 093	2 299	7.5	36.9	61.4	0.6	0.3	1.6	6.7	18.3	9.6	15.9	12.1	14.2
22 067	12820	6	Morehouse	2 059	27 979	1 499	13.6	51.6	47.2	0.5	0.6	0.9	6.9	17.8	8.6	12.1	11.5	14.5
22 069	35060	6	Natchitoches	3 243	39 566	1 180	12.2	54.9	42.1	1.8	0.7	1.9	6.7	17.5	15.4	12.2	10.7	12.2

1. CBSA = Core Based Statistical Area. See Appendix A for explanation. See Appendix B for list of metropolitan areas with component counties. 2. County type code from the Economic Research Service of USDA Rural-Urban Continuum Codes. See Appendix A for definition. 3. Dry land or land partially or temporarily covered by water. 4. May be of any race.

Table B. States and Counties — **Population and Households**

| | Population, 2010 (cont.) Age (percent) (cont.) | | | | Population change and components of change, 1990–2010 | | | | | | | Households, 2010 | | | | |
	55 to 64 years	65 to 74 years	75 years and over	Percent female	Total persons 1990	Total persons 2000	Percent change 1990–2000	Percent change 2000–2010	Births	Deaths	Net migration	Number	Percent change, 2000–2010	Persons per household	Female family householder[1]	One person
	16	17	18	19	20	21	22	23	24	25	26	27	28	29	30	31
KENTUCKY—Cont'd																
Ohio	12.8	8.9	6.5	50.0	21 105	22 916	8.6	4.0	2 951	2 380	200	9 176	3.1	2.56	10.7	24.0
Oldham	12.3	6.1	3.2	47.4	33 263	46 178	38.8	30.6	5 132	2 679	9 168	19 431	30.8	2.87	9.1	15.5
Owen	13.4	8.6	5.8	50.3	9 035	10 547	16.7	2.8	1 205	1 008	700	4 296	5.1	2.52	9.2	25.3
Owsley	14.3	9.8	7.0	50.5	5 036	4 858	-3.5	-2.1	542	661	-98	1 914	1.1	2.44	13.7	28.4
Pendleton	12.5	7.2	5.1	49.9	12 062	14 390	19.3	3.4	1 660	1 166	86	5 494	6.3	2.67	10.7	21.4
Perry	13.8	8.0	5.4	50.5	30 283	29 390	-2.9	-2.3	3 789	3 278	-633	11 319	-1.2	2.48	14.2	26.3
Pike	14.1	8.1	5.6	51.0	72 584	68 736	-5.3	-5.4	7 000	7 243	-2 635	26 728	-3.2	2.39	12.5	27.2
Powell	13.2	8.0	5.0	50.3	11 686	13 237	13.3	-4.7	1 746	1 299	-47	4 834	-4.2	2.57	13.6	24.8
Pulaski	13.5	9.3	6.9	51.2	49 489	56 217	13.6	12.2	7 032	6 067	4 011	25 722	13.2	2.41	11.9	26.7
Robertson	14.3	10.4	8.3	49.7	2 124	2 266	6.7	0.7	211	258	30	902	4.2	2.47	9.6	24.8
Rockcastle	12.9	9.0	5.8	50.9	14 803	16 582	12.0	2.9	1 901	1 672	-215	6 750	3.1	2.48	12.6	25.6
Rowan	10.4	7.2	5.0	51.4	20 353	22 094	8.6	5.6	2 427	1 736	195	8 864	11.8	2.36	11.2	28.6
Russell	13.7	9.6	7.8	51.1	14 716	16 315	10.9	7.7	1 884	1 761	1 045	7 401	6.6	2.35	11.8	28.7
Scott	10.8	5.5	3.7	50.7	23 867	33 061	38.5	42.7	5 786	2 264	9 381	17 408	43.7	2.63	11.8	22.0
Shelby	12.9	7.3	4.8	51.9	24 824	33 337	34.3	26.2	5 023	2 627	6 510	15 321	26.6	2.64	11.8	21.2
Simpson	12.6	8.2	6.0	51.1	15 145	16 405	8.3	5.6	1 993	1 576	308	6 753	5.3	2.52	12.9	25.3
Spencer	12.2	6.5	3.8	49.2	6 801	11 766	73.0	45.0	1 741	922	5 156	6 165	45.0	2.75	7.9	16.0
Taylor	12.6	8.9	7.2	51.7	21 146	22 927	8.4	6.9	2 673	2 359	1 323	9 832	6.5	2.39	12.4	27.9
Todd	11.1	8.1	6.1	50.8	10 940	11 971	9.4	4.1	1 704	1 201	-147	4 647	1.7	2.64	12.3	24.3
Trigg	15.3	11.8	7.2	50.9	10 361	12 597	21.6	13.8	1 310	1 432	895	5 883	12.8	2.42	10.8	25.0
Trimble	13.1	7.8	5.1	49.1	6 090	8 125	33.4	8.4	1 006	753	628	3 420	9.0	2.56	9.7	23.6
Union	12.8	7.3	6.4	48.9	16 557	15 637	-5.8	-4.0	1 710	1 513	-755	5 549	-2.8	2.46	11.5	26.3
Warren	10.6	6.2	4.8	51.1	77 720	92 522	19.0	23.0	12 682	7 336	11 313	43 674	23.5	2.46	12.0	27.7
Washington	12.5	8.5	7.4	51.0	10 441	10 916	4.5	7.3	1 291	1 070	158	4 507	9.4	2.51	10.5	24.8
Wayne	14.1	9.7	6.2	50.5	17 468	19 923	14.1	4.5	2 254	1 979	664	8 646	9.3	2.37	11.5	27.7
Webster	13.6	8.4	6.7	50.3	13 955	14 120	1.2	-3.5	1 779	1 475	-653	5 272	-5.2	2.51	10.8	25.4
Whitley	12.4	8.4	5.8	51.4	33 326	35 865	7.6	-0.6	4 689	3 943	2 416	13 575	-1.5	2.51	14.6	26.0
Wolfe	13.4	9.5	6.1	50.9	6 503	7 065	8.6	4.1	1 068	896	-107	3 065	8.8	2.36	13.6	29.4
Woodford	14.3	7.7	5.3	52.0	19 955	23 208	16.3	7.5	2 805	1 834	958	9 806	10.3	2.51	11.1	23.5
LOUISIANA	11.8	6.9	5.4	51.0	4 221 826	4 468 976	5.9	1.4	595 844	382 645	-285 765	1 728 360	4.4	2.55	17.2	26.9
Acadia	11.2	7.1	5.6	51.2	55 882	58 861	5.3	4.9	8 628	5 836	-1 205	22 841	8.0	2.66	16.4	24.3
Allen	11.3	7.4	5.5	43.8	21 226	25 440	19.9	1.3	3 184	1 808	-1 057	8 516	5.1	2.53	16.4	26.9
Ascension	10.5	5.5	3.3	50.6	58 214	76 627	31.6	39.9	14 038	5 281	19 729	37 790	41.6	2.82	14.2	18.9
Assumption	12.8	7.7	5.7	51.1	22 753	23 388	2.8	0.1	2 640	1 817	-1 224	8 736	6.0	2.66	15.8	22.3
Avoyelles	12.0	8.1	6.4	49.9	39 159	41 481	5.9	1.4	5 825	4 498	-56	15 432	4.7	2.51	17.2	27.4
Beauregard	11.9	7.7	5.2	49.0	30 083	32 986	9.6	8.1	4 237	3 022	1 446	13 159	8.7	2.61	11.6	24.1
Bienville	12.8	9.4	9.0	51.8	16 232	15 752	-3.0	-8.9	1 788	2 015	-714	6 838	-4.4	2.40	18.5	29.9
Bossier	10.8	6.8	5.2	50.8	86 088	98 310	14.2	19.0	15 123	7 716	8 287	45 215	23.4	2.54	14.4	25.9
Caddo	12.2	7.1	6.5	52.5	248 253	252 161	1.6	1.1	34 556	24 328	-7 271	102 139	4.3	2.44	20.8	30.5
Calcasieu	11.8	7.0	5.6	51.2	168 134	183 577	9.2	5.0	25 479	16 358	-4 000	73 996	7.8	2.55	15.9	26.1
Caldwell	13.5	8.7	6.2	48.8	9 806	10 560	7.7	-4.1	1 221	1 110	-174	3 905	-0.9	2.45	14.1	27.7
Cameron	12.0	7.9	5.0	50.4	9 260	9 991	7.9	-31.5	797	565	-3 670	2 575	-28.3	2.66	8.7	20.8
Catahoula	13.1	8.0	6.4	47.1	11 065	10 920	-1.3	-4.7	1 315	1 114	-612	3 834	-6.1	2.49	15.2	27.1
Claiborne	12.8	8.6	7.4	44.1	17 405	16 851	-3.2	2.0	1 612	1 822	-421	6 017	-4.0	2.37	18.7	30.2
Concordia	12.5	7.9	6.7	49.7	20 828	20 247	-2.8	2.8	2 461	2 045	-1 588	7 613	1.2	2.54	21.6	27.5
De Soto	13.4	8.3	6.1	51.7	25 668	25 494	-0.7	4.6	3 459	2 671	280	10 562	9.0	2.50	18.8	26.5
East Baton Rouge	11.3	6.0	4.9	52.0	380 105	412 852	8.6	6.6	55 185	31 481	221	172 057	10.0	2.49	18.4	28.7
East Carroll	10.6	6.8	5.7	46.5	9 709	9 421	-3.0	-17.6	1 303	883	-1 719	2 552	-14.0	2.62	29.3	29.8
East Feliciana	14.7	8.1	4.8	46.2	19 211	21 360	11.2	-5.1	2 477	2 126	-610	7 022	4.8	2.55	16.6	26.4
Evangeline	11.3	7.6	5.6	49.6	33 274	35 434	6.5	-4.1	4 850	3 560	-1 230	12 829	0.7	2.54	16.6	27.4
Franklin	12.3	8.9	7.4	51.5	22 387	21 263	-5.0	-2.3	2 830	2 422	-1 766	7 904	1.9	2.53	17.6	27.1
Grant	11.2	7.2	4.8	44.0	17 526	18 698	6.7	19.3	2 397	1 848	1 045	7 496	6.0	2.58	13.4	24.1
Iberia	11.3	6.8	5.4	51.2	68 297	73 266	7.3	0.0	10 684	6 160	-2 267	26 778	5.5	2.70	18.5	24.0
Iberville	12.2	7.0	5.0	49.0	31 049	33 320	7.3	0.2	4 247	3 016	-1 886	11 072	3.7	2.66	20.6	25.0
Jackson	13.1	9.5	7.2	49.2	15 859	15 397	-2.9	5.7	1 890	1 820	-317	6 261	2.9	2.43	15.1	27.2
Jefferson	12.8	7.3	6.3	51.4	448 306	455 466	1.6	-5.0	55 168	38 075	-49 969	169 647	-3.7	2.53	16.8	27.9
Jefferson Davis	11.6	7.8	6.8	51.0	30 722	31 435	2.3	0.5	4 356	3 067	-1 475	11 771	2.5	2.64	15.2	25.0
Lafayette	10.7	5.6	4.6	51.2	164 762	190 503	15.6	16.3	27 812	13 664	7 672	87 027	20.2	2.49	15.0	27.8
Lafourche	11.1	7.0	5.5	50.9	85 860	89 974	4.8	7.1	11 254	6 978	-3	35 486	10.7	2.67	13.8	22.1
La Salle	12.0	8.3	6.5	48.5	13 662	14 282	4.5	4.3	1 713	1 528	-429	5 468	3.3	2.50	12.1	26.0
Lincoln	9.8	5.9	5.4	51.2	41 745	42 509	1.8	9.9	5 155	3 103	-1 025	17 599	15.5	2.38	15.7	29.6
Livingston	10.8	6.2	3.7	50.5	70 523	91 814	30.2	39.4	15 467	7 157	23 535	46 007	41.0	2.76	13.1	20.1
Madison	11.3	6.3	5.5	50.5	12 463	13 728	10.2	-11.9	1 834	1 424	-2 732	4 025	-9.9	2.61	26.4	27.3
Morehouse	13.2	7.9	7.5	52.1	31 938	31 021	-2.9	-9.8	3 912	3 485	-3 078	10 853	-4.6	2.51	21.8	27.1
Natchitoches	11.8	7.4	6.1	52.3	37 254	39 080	4.9	1.2	5 542	3 471	-1 702	15 614	9.5	2.39	18.2	31.2

1. No spouse present.

Table B. States and Counties — **Population, Vital Statistics, Medicare, and Crime**

STATE County	Daytime population, 2006–2010			Births, average 2006–2008		Deaths, average 2006–2008		Persons under 65 with no health insurance, 2009		Medicare, 2011			Serious crimes known to police,[2] 2010 Total	
	Persons in group quarters, 2010	Number	Employ-ment/resi-dence ratio	Total	Rate[1]	Number	Rate[1]	Number	Percent	Eligible for Medicare	Enrolled in Medicare Advantage	Enrolled in a Medicare prescription drug plan	Number	Rate[3]
	32	33	34	35	36	37	38	39	40	41	42	43	44	45

KENTUCKY—Cont'd

STATE County	32	33	34	35	36	37	38	39	40	41	42	43	44	45
Ohio	307	22 142	0.8	D	D	259	10.9	3 393	17.5	5 021	875	2 928	151	633
Oldham	4 568	47 337	0.6	D	D	297	5.3	5 084	9.9	7 086	1 568	3 256	582	965
Owen	0	8 599	0.5	D	D	99	8.7	1 741	18.1	2 168	236	1 230	82	756
Owsley	90	4 534	0.8	D	D	74	16.0	726	19.4	1 068	88	856	NA	NA
Pendleton	215	11 664	0.5	D	D	145	9.6	2 160	16.9	2 612	488	1 343	228	1 598
Perry	611	32 629	1.4	D	D	367	12.5	4 623	18.6	6 400	725	4 045	372	1 296
Pike	1 100	67 543	1.1	792	12.0	817	12.4	10 104	18.3	15 769	2 443	8 777	436	681
Powell	188	10 888	0.6	D	D	140	10.1	2 145	19.7	2 820	540	1 554	178	1 411
Pulaski	962	62 991	1.0	796	13.2	670	11.1	9 643	19.6	14 849	2 531	8 221	1 458	2 322
Robertson	57	NA	NA	D	D	30	13.4	384	21.1	462	74	254	NA	NA
Rockcastle	341	15 311	0.7	D	D	188	11.2	2 658	19.5	3 583	452	2 079	139	877
Rowan	2 435	24 453	1.1	D	D	197	8.8	3 951	20.4	4 035	893	2 391	334	1 431
Russell	177	18 158	1.1	D	D	194	11.3	2 906	20.7	3 999	498	2 463	118	672
Scott	1 316	47 512	1.1	D	D	280	6.5	5 370	13.2	5 862	1 334	2 689	1 358	2 879
Shelby	1 696	36 776	0.8	598	14.8	286	7.1	6 167	17.0	6 609	1 349	3 580	751	1 788
Simpson	327	18 530	1.2	D	D	173	10.1	2 369	16.6	3 273	417	1 851	462	2 666
Spencer	113	11 094	0.3	D	D	102	6.0	2 223	14.2	2 486	544	1 242	40	234
Taylor	1 035	25 128	1.1	D	D	257	10.8	3 617	18.4	5 488	590	3 488	611	2 493
Todd	195	10 093	0.6	D	D	133	11.0	2 230	21.6	2 245	198	1 483	53	439
Trigg	78	13 046	0.8	D	D	158	11.8	1 848	17.5	3 357	513	1 699	169	1 179
Trimble	41	7 338	0.6	D	D	78	8.6	1 284	16.7	1 632	318	786	23	261
Union	1 371	14 461	0.9	D	D	161	10.6	2 067	16.4	2 757	263	1 828	91	606
Warren	6 210	117 267	1.1	1 446	13.9	794	7.7	15 877	17.0	16 421	2 194	9 514	3 544	3 114
Washington	389	9 832	0.7	D	D	118	10.2	1 751	18.5	2 357	475	1 381	47	401
Wayne	331	19 787	0.9	D	D	208	10.1	3 632	21.1	4 686	824	2 790	254	1 220
Webster	393	12 647	0.8	D	D	166	12.0	2 148	19.9	2 758	520	1 593	62	516
Whitley	1 590	35 745	1.0	523	13.6	406	10.6	6 256	19.4	7 885	882	4 935	NA	NA
Wolfe	132	6 884	0.7	D	D	88	12.5	1 089	18.6	1 801	233	1 282	21	304
Woodford	329	22 595	0.8	D	D	198	8.1	3 009	14.2	4 148	947	1 744	714	2 863
LOUISIANA	127 427	4 446 683	1.0	64 982	14.9	40 410	9.3	766 181	20.0	711 625	171 933	279 724	190 243	4 197
Acadia	1 050	52 051	0.6	940	15.6	635	10.5	10 411	20.4	9 905	633	5 820	NA	NA
Allen	4 200	25 468	1.0	D	D	NA	NA	5 251	24.4	4 085	499	2 170	NA	NA
Ascension	790	88 864	0.7	1 688	17.0	631	6.3	14 627	15.5	12 726	6 168	3 062	3 464	3 274
Assumption	199	18 341	0.4	284	12.3	207	8.9	3 953	20.3	4 030	861	2 118	563	2 404
Avoyelles	3 343	38 481	0.8	653	15.4	464	11.0	7 752	21.9	8 148	877	4 515	754	2 110
Beauregard	1 300	30 075	0.7	495	14.2	350	10.0	5 987	19.9	5 838	502	2 617	649	1 820
Bienville	319	13 940	0.9	D	D	213	14.3	2 339	20.1	3 124	351	1 519	203	1 414
Bossier	1 961	107 446	0.9	1 755	16.1	836	7.7	16 684	17.3	16 525	1 997	5 352	3 968	3 495
Caddo	6 247	271 715	1.2	3 906	15.4	2 688	10.6	40 395	19.1	42 907	5 931	17 828	11 932	4 748
Calcasieu	3 796	195 217	1.1	2 850	15.4	1 858	10.0	28 538	17.8	31 342	3 773	13 777	9 425	5 096
Caldwell	584	8 797	0.6	D	D	129	12.4	2 058	24.0	1 876	186	912	338	3 336
Cameron	0	8 378	1.3	D	D	53	7.1	1 364	23.2	944	94	420	152	2 223
Catahoula	866	9 418	0.7	D	D	123	11.7	2 077	24.3	2 119	154	1 166	460	4 655
Claiborne	2 917	15 905	0.8	200	12.3	194	12.0	3 053	23.7	3 215	309	1 664	324	2 179
Concordia	1 485	19 202	0.8	307	16.0	252	13.1	3 467	22.5	3 873	290	2 110	611	2 934
De Soto	215	22 795	0.7	397	15.1	292	11.1	4 301	19.6	5 106	314	2 427	907	3 403
East Baton Rouge	11 105	484 048	1.2	6 351	14.8	3 577	8.3	63 902	17.0	60 019	19 777	17 048	24 839	5 643
East Carroll	1 067	7 717	0.9	D	D	96	11.4	1 666	25.4	1 375	37	876	140	1 804
East Feliciana	2 391	17 882	0.7	D	D	226	10.8	3 475	19.7	3 640	865	1 195	117	712
Evangeline	1 379	30 134	0.6	538	15.0	368	10.3	6 376	21.4	6 234	460	3 764	1 077	3 169
Franklin	732	18 878	0.7	317	15.7	247	12.2	3 816	24.1	4 178	344	2 232	213	1 076
Grant	2 937	17 209	0.5	278	14.0	214	10.8	3 298	19.3	3 707	405	1 518	302	1 354
Iberia	944	76 164	1.1	1 195	15.9	711	9.5	13 029	20.3	12 199	904	6 789	2 758	3 766
Iberville	3 979	37 625	1.3	462	14.1	285	8.7	5 395	19.7	5 359	1 991	1 676	1 151	3 654
Jackson	1 038	13 881	0.7	D	D	183	12.1	2 318	19.1	3 163	376	1 571	NA	NA
Jefferson	3 311	422 510	1.0	6 015	14.0	3 965	9.2	76 155	20.4	72 655	37 048	16 505	18 295	4 230
Jefferson Davis	567	28 693	0.8	488	15.6	352	11.3	5 220	20.0	5 310	293	2 905	912	3 348
Lafayette	5 150	242 799	1.3	3 174	15.5	1 589	7.8	32 519	17.6	28 597	1 948	14 542	11 319	5 302
Lafourche	1 625	89 870	0.9	1 339	14.4	792	8.5	15 691	19.4	15 173	3 397	7 210	2 674	2 776
La Salle	1 243	13 835	0.8	D	D	159	11.3	2 402	20.7	2 668	248	1 422	157	1 054
Lincoln	4 883	47 492	1.1	562	13.3	337	8.0	7 506	20.5	5 973	588	2 488	1 849	3 956
Livingston	1 192	91 433	0.4	1 899	16.2	871	7.4	20 534	18.8	16 664	7 775	3 634	4 047	3 161
Madison	1 591	12 111	1.0	D	D	149	12.4	2 221	23.5	1 825	57	1 017	454	3 754
Morehouse	768	25 753	0.7	D	D	397	13.7	5 040	22.1	5 760	737	2 965	1 976	7 062
Natchitoches	2 190	38 662	1.0	611	15.6	367	9.4	7 002	21.3	6 568	506	3 268	1 774	4 484

1. Per 1,000 estimated resident population.   2. Data for serious crimes have not been adjusted for underreporting; this may affect comparability between geographic areas and over time.   3. Per 100,000 population estimated by the FBI.

Table B. States and Counties — Crime, Education, Money Income, and Poverty

STATE County	Serious crimes known to police,[1] 2010 (cont.) Rate[2]		Education School enrollment and attainment, 2006–2010 Enrollment[3]		Attainment[4] (percent)		Local government expenditures,[5] 2008–2009		Money income, 2006–2010	Households Median income			Income and poverty, 2010	Percent below poverty level		
	Violent	Property	Total	Percent private	High school graduate or less	Bachelor's degree or more	Total current expenditures (mil dol)	Current expenditures per student (dollars)	Per capita income[6] (dollars)	Dollars	Percent change, 2000 to 2006–2010 (constant 2010 dollars)	Percent with income of $200,000 or more	Median household income (dollars)	All persons	Children under 18 years	Children 5 to 17 years in families
	46	47	48	49	50	51	52	53	54	55	56	57	58	59	60	61
KENTUCKY—Cont'd																
Ohio	55	579	5 235	8.2	67.7	9.4	33.8	8 369	18 258	36 050	-3.7	1.1	35 975	20.4	29.5	26.9
Oldham	78	887	17 128	17.2	34.3	37.0	90.7	7 684	32 702	79 417	-0.8	9.2	75 724	7.7	8.5	6.5
Owen	0	756	2 383	5.9	60.5	18.6	17.3	9 051	21 754	46 238	9.6	0.4	40 413	16.7	25.1	22.5
Owsley	NA	NA	1 180	5.9	77.7	5.9	9.7	12 238	10 767	19 351	-3.3	0.3	22 335	40.1	54.4	49.4
Pendleton	35	1 563	3 779	11.4	65.7	10.5	22.6	8 276	19 523	44 670	-7.5	0.8	43 517	15.0	23.0	20.3
Perry	98	1 198	6 317	3.7	67.9	11.9	48.2	9 078	19 049	29 547	5.6	1.5	31 604	28.7	37.9	33.6
Pike	20	661	14 246	11.4	67.3	12.0	99.1	8 821	18 973	32 563	7.5	1.2	30 302	27.3	36.8	30.2
Powell	71	1 340	2 630	7.9	74.8	10.4	22.0	8 868	15 796	31 815	-1.5	0.3	32 041	25.2	40.1	37.6
Pulaski	83	2 240	14 289	9.2	60.8	14.5	87.3	8 596	19 540	32 771	-5.4	2.2	33 026	21.5	29.4	27.8
Robertson	NA	NA	639	0.0	73.1	7.4	3.8	9 494	15 374	27 254	-29.6	0.0	32 844	22.6	33.3	30.7
Rockcastle	101	776	3 971	8.5	69.2	11.6	26.8	8 777	15 621	26 946	-9.4	0.8	30 900	23.9	35.1	31.7
Rowan	86	1 346	7 814	5.4	55.9	24.7	28.1	8 607	17 435	31 604	-11.0	1.6	35 145	28.3	32.3	28.8
Russell	57	615	3 359	10.8	64.1	12.7	26.9	8 925	17 868	29 980	7.4	1.4	29 478	27.8	37.4	36.4
Scott	290	2 588	12 781	23.4	44.9	26.3	60.1	7 462	26 838	58 028	-2.7	2.2	56 791	11.3	15.9	14.4
Shelby	126	1 662	10 354	21.4	50.6	23.2	54.1	8 336	27 593	55 296	-4.1	4.1	51 845	12.1	17.7	15.6
Simpson	150	2 516	4 031	8.4	61.6	15.6	24.4	8 225	20 426	41 323	-10.4	0.9	40 905	16.2	25.2	22.5
Spencer	0	234	4 125	14.7	51.7	16.6	NA	NA	25 589	59 326	-0.4	2.1	62 579	9.0	12.6	11.2
Taylor	126	2 366	5 958	22.4	64.2	14.9	32.5	8 639	18 014	35 378	-0.5	0.5	35 962	22.8	35.0	30.1
Todd	58	381	2 981	9.9	67.1	10.0	18.7	8 650	17 460	36 989	-1.7	0.9	36 173	23.6	35.1	33.4
Trigg	84	1 095	3 261	10.1	56.7	15.8	17.8	8 353	23 387	41 825	0.1	2.0	42 387	15.0	25.1	22.1
Trimble	0	261	2 352	9.0	62.8	13.1	12.1	7 978	21 161	47 798	4.3	0.1	44 533	15.0	20.2	18.3
Union	80	526	3 657	8.3	55.9	12.4	21.3	8 826	18 811	39 515	-10.9	0.3	41 209	19.4	27.0	24.2
Warren	157	2 957	34 367	7.4	45.8	27.5	132.0	7 775	23 206	43 954	-4.0	2.0	41 001	20.5	25.5	23.4
Washington	0	401	2 827	18.0	64.0	12.8	15.7	8 995	20 873	43 090	2.7	2.2	38 618	16.7	24.9	22.6
Wayne	96	1 124	4 657	1.3	72.3	9.0	29.9	8 591	16 109	25 993	-1.6	0.6	26 683	28.3	40.7	36.6
Webster	33	483	3 064	8.1	67.7	8.5	16.2	7 075	18 879	39 635	-0.7	0.7	41 516	15.1	21.6	20.7
Whitley	NA	NA	9 586	17.9	67.7	11.9	71.7	8 713	15 258	28 122	0.6	0.7	29 813	26.2	37.6	34.1
Wolfe	0	304	1 632	5.3	77.6	7.6	13.6	10 875	11 214	20 910	-14.5	0.4	25 968	31.8	47.8	44.7
Woodford	84	2 779	5 959	18.6	42.4	33.1	29.7	7 300	28 501	56 537	-9.8	2.9	65 962	11.2	16.9	14.7
LOUISIANA	549	3 648	1 165 624	18.9	53.8	20.9	7 191.6	10 542	23 094	43 445	5.4	2.7	42 510	18.8	27.4	25.0
Acadia	NA	NA	15 773	18.3	69.9	10.9	82.1	8 801	18 116	37 261	10.3	0.9	36 814	21.0	29.6	27.1
Allen	NA	NA	5 928	7.2	68.5	9.1	45.1	10 744	17 108	36 926	5.0	0.6	35 711	20.4	26.6	23.2
Ascension	359	2 915	28 700	18.0	52.1	21.9	190.5	9 974	26 888	63 716	13.6	3.3	62 069	12.8	18.6	15.3
Assumption	465	1 938	5 563	14.4	74.1	8.5	49.7	12 410	20 348	45 235	14.8	1.5	43 503	16.7	23.4	20.5
Avoyelles	333	1 777	9 889	14.1	69.4	10.2	57.1	8 284	16 944	31 412	4.0	0.7	31 523	21.6	29.7	27.9
Beauregard	261	1 559	8 697	10.2	58.9	14.8	54.3	9 114	21 543	45 202	9.6	1.4	43 672	15.7	21.9	19.7
Bienville	139	1 275	3 458	6.7	63.5	12.8	29.3	13 277	18 873	31 870	6.4	2.2	31 421	24.4	35.6	32.5
Bossier	459	3 036	29 259	9.2	47.1	21.6	187.3	9 507	25 630	51 020	2.8	2.7	48 957	14.0	22.0	19.8
Caddo	651	4 097	67 351	13.1	50.6	22.0	435.2	10 213	22 594	37 181	-6.7	2.6	37 739	19.5	31.3	30.5
Calcasieu	659	4 437	49 536	13.1	53.6	19.2	352.1	10 356	23 591	43 758	-2.3	2.7	40 928	17.6	24.2	21.9
Caldwell	257	3 079	2 191	5.5	65.9	11.7	17.5	10 203	19 888	37 423	9.6	1.5	34 855	21.6	31.4	29.0
Cameron	175	2 047	1 966	10.0	65.3	11.7	NA	NA	24 634	59 555	37.4	3.6	47 100	13.1	18.6	16.8
Catahoula	2 267	2 388	2 170	9.3	71.7	10.5	16.9	10 080	17 166	36 398	27.6	0.9	31 325	26.1	37.2	32.6
Claiborne	484	1 695	3 639	11.3	65.3	11.3	24.6	10 460	16 925	32 292	0.6	1.0	34 274	30.9	40.5	37.9
Concordia	634	2 300	5 310	5.4	67.6	11.0	36.4	9 321	15 911	30 062	4.4	0.5	29 891	32.9	44.1	38.1
De Soto	1 065	2 337	6 366	8.4	62.3	13.6	66.4	13 719	20 112	38 007	6.2	1.2	37 379	21.2	30.9	26.0
East Baton Rouge	722	4 921	134 149	21.0	39.4	32.9	654.9	11 400	26 260	46 179	-2.0	3.5	44 911	17.3	26.3	24.9
East Carroll	683	1 121	1 765	9.0	74.3	8.3	16.8	11 887	15 947	24 038	-8.4	3.1	25 442	40.3	53.7	51.0
East Feliciana	73	639	4 604	24.9	61.4	12.4	23.4	10 481	18 376	35 335	-11.8	2.0	42 347	18.6	26.0	22.9
Evangeline	285	2 884	8 445	18.6	70.9	10.7	57.9	9 661	17 561	34 057	31.0	0.6	31 736	22.9	31.9	29.8
Franklin	56	1 020	4 806	13.0	68.6	11.3	31.5	9 505	18 676	32 311	11.1	1.4	30 105	27.4	43.3	41.4
Grant	99	1 255	5 074	12.8	62.9	11.8	28.6	8 281	18 536	40 092	6.9	1.1	38 225	19.3	24.3	23.2
Iberia	617	3 149	18 526	14.3	66.8	13.4	130.2	9 439	20 112	41 783	5.7	2.0	40 914	23.0	34.8	29.7
Iberville	1 073	2 581	8 472	19.8	69.3	11.0	63.3	14 838	19 379	42 215	14.8	1.4	40 140	22.7	29.4	25.8
Jackson	NA	NA	3 703	10.7	59.3	13.5	23.6	10 529	19 308	40 674	13.3	0.3	36 312	19.4	27.3	26.4
Jefferson	508	3 722	103 169	34.8	49.6	23.2	546.7	12 322	25 842	48 175	-1.0	3.5	46 500	16.2	25.4	22.6
Jefferson Davis	415	2 933	7 759	11.7	66.5	11.6	59.5	10 196	20 487	42 907	22.2	1.2	39 246	20.2	26.7	23.9
Lafayette	670	4 632	61 910	20.2	45.7	27.6	288.6	9 731	26 791	47 559	2.8	4.3	48 295	17.8	22.4	20.4
Lafourche	170	2 606	23 680	18.6	66.9	14.3	143.6	9 833	22 898	47 492	7.4	2.3	48 436	13.3	19.5	18.6
La Salle	201	853	3 517	10.2	64.1	13.1	25.6	9 833	20 049	37 572	5.3	1.1	41 563	14.7	21.2	19.5
Lincoln	422	3 535	18 369	7.0	42.2	31.8	64.1	10 786	19 665	35 247	3.2	2.1	36 532	24.2	32.0	29.0
Livingston	243	2 918	31 515	12.1	56.6	16.4	204.1	8 457	23 372	54 708	11.1	1.8	53 125	12.5	17.2	15.2
Madison	786	2 969	3 026	13.1	71.5	10.9	21.7	10 544	13 089	26 441	1.8	1.1	25 565	37.4	50.2	46.5
Morehouse	511	6 551	6 338	8.4	68.6	11.1	48.3	10 174	15 713	31 781	-0.1	0.5	29 526	27.4	40.6	37.3
Natchitoches	581	3 902	11 725	9.6	57.0	21.2	64.5	9 551	18 207	30 326	-6.9	1.6	32 055	25.3	33.8	29.6

1. Data for serious crimes have not been adjusted for underreporting; this may affect comparability between geographic areas and over time.   2. Per 100,000 population estimated by the FBI.   3. All persons 3 years old and over enrolled in nursery school through college.   4. Persons 25 years old and over.   5. Elementary and secondary education expenditures.   6. Based on population estimated by the American Community Survey, 2006–2010.

Table B. States and Counties — **Personal Income**

STATE County	Personal income, 2009 Total (mil dol)	Per capita Percent change, 2008–2009	Per capita Dollars	Per capita Rank	Wages and salaries (mil dol)	Proprietors' income (mil dol)	Dividends, interest, and rent (mil dol)	Transfer payments (mil dol) Total	Government payments to individuals Total	Government payments to individuals Social Security	Government payments to individuals Medical payments	Government payments to individuals Income maintenance	Government payments to individuals Unemployment insurance
	62	63	64	65	66	67	68	69	70	71	72	73	74
KENTUCKY—Cont'd													
Ohio	658	4.4	27 949	2 411	301	34	76	203	199	68	83	23	10
Oldham	2 429	0.1	41 816	343	643	58	400	260	250	106	84	13	19
Owen	273	2.5	23 980	2 964	84	10	34	74	72	27	25	9	4
Owsley	116	6.6	25 197	2 846	26	6	8	62	61	11	34	12	1
Pendleton	394	0.6	26 466	2 646	103	6	46	99	96	35	34	11	7
Perry	877	5.0	30 104	1 953	690	51	74	340	335	86	159	52	10
Pike	2 030	2.5	31 024	1 748	1 257	171	231	684	672	227	276	87	21
Powell	320	3.6	23 571	2 997	92	18	26	116	114	36	41	20	7
Pulaski	1 774	3.4	29 149	2 157	993	98	237	629	618	191	297	64	23
Robertson	57	3.7	25 613	2 792	11	2	6	20	19	6	9	2	1
Rockcastle	384	4.3	23 241	3 023	129	10	40	150	147	42	65	21	8
Rowan	572	3.1	25 018	2 865	388	20	68	182	178	51	70	21	9
Russell	445	3.6	25 592	2 797	218	25	61	168	164	49	76	21	8
Scott	1 527	3.1	33 319	1 291	1 316	50	166	229	221	81	77	24	18
Shelby	1 347	0.9	32 019	1 527	604	44	214	229	221	92	74	20	16
Simpson	505	-2.8	29 680	2 055	334	50	70	129	126	46	49	13	10
Spencer	508	4.7	28 656	2 269	68	4	46	94	91	35	33	7	8
Taylor	671	2.1	27 488	2 483	384	26	94	227	223	71	102	21	12
Todd	334	-0.4	27 236	2 526	85	61	45	90	88	28	38	10	5
Trigg	513	1.7	38 613	568	140	26	65	118	116	46	42	8	8
Trimble	209	7.2	23 337	3 015	264	4	23	64	62	21	26	7	4
Union	499	-0.6	33 317	1 292	258	75	68	126	123	42	55	11	7
Warren	3 438	-0.8	31 640	1 617	2 518	198	523	764	744	225	315	77	46
Washington	306	0.1	27 220	2 528	126	15	54	90	88	29	37	8	6
Wayne	465	3.5	22 402	3 054	193	21	59	190	186	53	83	29	9
Webster	407	3.3	29 710	2 046	193	41	49	109	107	41	43	10	5
Whitley	1 006	3.4	25 915	2 746	508	30	116	413	406	95	196	56	15
Wolfe	162	6.3	22 764	3 043	43	5	15	85	84	20	40	16	3
Woodford	1 020	-2.0	40 813	396	495	58	196	142	137	62	42	11	9
LOUISIANA	169 046	-0.4	37 632	X	103 032	15 109	29 703	32 618	31 802	9 310	15 395	4 090	704
Acadia	1 905	-1.5	31 698	1 597	694	214	269	458	447	126	232	58	8
Allen	613	0.6	23 928	2 970	430	56	79	186	181	53	91	21	4
Ascension	3 916	3.4	37 356	707	2 029	366	452	580	561	183	270	59	15
Assumption	799	-0.1	34 951	1 030	260	37	100	179	175	53	85	24	4
Avoyelles	1 192	4.0	28 032	2 394	440	95	160	368	360	93	187	53	6
Beauregard	1 015	0.1	28 659	2 268	423	51	144	241	235	77	110	22	6
Bienville	412	1.0	27 956	2 409	185	27	57	137	134	39	67	18	3
Bossier	3 880	0.6	34 797	1 043	2 427	284	578	729	710	216	317	78	16
Caddo	10 338	-0.7	40 760	402	6 317	1 447	1 978	1 989	1 943	564	884	290	46
Calcasieu	6 796	-2.0	36 237	857	4 548	470	1 168	1 365	1 331	440	623	146	29
Caldwell	295	3.4	28 277	2 351	106	20	32	107	105	23	65	10	2
Cameron	233	-17.7	35 447	959	187	15	53	31	30	14	10	3	1
Catahoula	298	10.0	28 525	2 293	94	47	33	95	93	24	48	13	2
Claiborne	488	-0.6	30 261	1 922	201	52	88	132	129	39	59	19	3
Concordia	552	2.2	29 061	2 181	226	46	91	173	170	50	76	29	4
De Soto	800	-0.2	30 318	1 901	333	103	105	205	200	65	87	31	5
East Baton Rouge	18 149	1.1	41 756	346	15 115	866	3 417	2 942	2 863	795	1 348	416	67
East Carroll	233	3.7	28 706	2 259	86	28	35	86	84	13	48	18	2
East Feliciana	695	1.5	33 129	1 314	286	37	98	180	176	42	100	21	3
Evangeline	929	1.7	26 287	2 669	350	60	141	302	295	76	155	44	5
Franklin	570	2.8	28 768	2 243	199	84	68	200	196	46	107	28	4
Grant	558	2.8	27 679	2 455	169	29	62	159	156	44	74	19	3
Iberia	2 742	-1.6	36 509	815	1 829	273	474	541	528	162	247	80	12
Iberville	1 035	0.7	31 851	1 565	971	87	147	276	270	69	143	39	6
Jackson	455	1.5	30 208	1 933	171	36	60	150	147	42	79	15	3
Jefferson	19 446	-1.6	43 862	240	11 091	2 027	3 858	3 120	3 039	1 010	1 470	301	66
Jefferson Davis	989	-1.1	31 811	1 577	387	75	170	234	228	71	113	25	4
Lafayette	9 408	-1.5	44 598	213	7 324	1 114	1 755	1 273	1 234	379	563	148	28
Lafourche	3 954	-0.8	42 205	314	2 261	421	660	646	629	211	298	69	11
La Salle	427	0.6	30 610	1 840	173	55	52	122	119	36	65	9	2
Lincoln	1 454	1.5	33 595	1 235	826	179	291	319	311	73	147	38	7
Livingston	3 848	2.5	31 201	1 711	972	165	392	714	692	233	325	74	18
Madison	294	-1.2	25 805	2 758	142	20	36	107	105	20	53	23	2
Morehouse	802	1.6	28 410	2 322	304	68	105	298	293	75	147	48	8
Natchitoches	1 182	2.7	30 100	1 955	600	150	163	303	296	77	128	50	7

1. Based on the resident population estimated as of July 1 of the year shown. 2. Includes supplements to wages and salaries.

Table B. States and Counties — **Earnings, Social Security, and Housing**

STATE County	Earnings, 2009 Total (mil dol)	Farm	Goods-related[1] Total	Goods-related[1] Manufacturing	Service-related and health: Information and professional and technical services	Retail trade	Finance, insurance, and real estate	Health care and social services	Government	Social Security beneficiaries, Dec 2010: Number	Rate[2]	Supplemental Security Income recipients, December 2010	Housing units, 2010: Total	Percent change, 2000–2010
	75	76	77	78	79	80	81	82	83	84	85	86	87	88
KENTUCKY—Cont'd														
Ohio	335	4.8	D	27.7	D	6.1	2.3	6.1	20.6	5 865	246	1 164	10 219	3.1
Oldham	702	0.5	D	7.1	8.9	7.1	9.4	12.3	26.4	7 885	131	491	20 688	31.8
Owen	94	2.9	D	D	D	6.4	3.8	14.6	27.4	2 480	229	492	5 634	5.4
Owsley	32	-1.2	D	D	D	D	2.6	19.3	42.4	1 265	266	940	2 328	3.6
Pendleton	109	-2.4	D	12.5	D	6.0	3.4	D	29.7	3 035	204	530	6 339	10.1
Perry	741	0.0	32.2	2.3	4.7	7.8	2.5	D	16.2	7 560	263	2 915	12 791	0.3
Pike	1 428	0.0	36.7	2.3	6.1	7.8	3.7	D	13.0	19 175	295	5 388	30 304	-2.0
Powell	110	-0.8	D	8.7	3.5	9.7	4.2	D	32.2	3 410	270	1 169	5 598	1.3
Pulaski	1 091	0.4	19.8	13.1	5.0	9.1	3.7	22.8	16.5	17 065	271	3 917	31 443	15.7
Robertson	13	8.1	D	0.0	D	D	1.5	14.7	51.2	530	232	121	1 095	6.0
Rockcastle	139	-1.7	D	7.3	4.6	6.4	3.5	25.5	27.3	4 105	241	1 337	7 703	4.8
Rowan	408	-0.1	D	8.8	2.5	9.5	3.2	D	37.1	4 625	198	1 201	10 102	12.4
Russell	242	1.0	D	25.2	D	10.4	4.0	D	21.5	4 590	261	1 303	9 993	10.2
Scott	1 366	1.4	D	56.2	2.1	3.6	1.9	D	7.5	6 705	142	991	19 303	48.7
Shelby	648	1.4	D	28.9	5.5	7.6	4.6	10.2	15.0	7 435	177	860	16 606	29.2
Simpson	384	6.0	47.2	43.2	D	8.6	2.4	4.1	10.5	3 825	221	554	7 435	6.0
Spencer	72	-2.0	D	D	D	9.4	4.7	D	40.9	2 930	172	345	6 704	47.2
Taylor	410	1.5	D	13.7	D	10.2	3.6	D	22.3	6 300	257	1 285	10 864	6.7
Todd	147	36.2	10.3	6.8	2.2	4.1	2.5	D	19.0	2 570	206	448	5 286	3.2
Trigg	167	7.2	D	13.8	14.8	6.9	3.8	D	22.2	3 740	261	423	7 810	16.6
Trimble	268	0.0	D	D	D	0.8	1.5	D	6.3	1 920	218	303	3 930	14.3
Union	333	12.4	39.3	7.9	D	5.1	2.2	D	10.5	3 305	220	443	6 141	-1.5
Warren	2 716	0.5	25.5	17.2	5.4	7.3	5.5	13.5	17.4	18 570	163	3 337	47 223	23.1
Washington	141	1.4	D	31.8	D	7.7	D	D	17.6	2 720	232	501	5 044	11.1
Wayne	214	6.1	D	26.0	6.6	10.6	4.2	D	22.7	5 285	254	1 989	10 942	11.8
Webster	234	12.0	40.8	6.7	D	3.8	1.9	D	13.3	3 230	237	511	5 936	-5.0
Whitley	538	-0.1	13.2	9.5	9.6	8.2	3.2	D	20.2	8 830	248	3 157	15 166	-0.8
Wolfe	48	-3.2	D	2.7	D	12.4	D	D	40.5	2 110	287	1 258	3 880	12.1
Woodford	553	11.3	D	25.2	7.9	4.8	2.8	4.1	13.7	4 700	188	409	10 711	14.3
LOUISIANA	118 141	0.7	23.8	9.7	8.5	6.3	5.3	10.7	19.9	790 617	174	174 731	1 964 981	6.4
Acadia	908	4.9	26.4	6.9	3.7	7.8	4.9	D	17.3	11 465	186	2 752	25 387	9.4
Allen	486	1.1	D	5.8	2.3	4.2	2.3	D	47.2	4 755	185	936	9 733	6.3
Ascension	2 395	0.2	37.0	22.4	5.0	7.5	6.5	6.8	11.2	14 835	138	2 257	40 784	39.8
Assumption	297	4.8	37.3	30.9	D	4.8	3.0	7.1	19.3	4 610	197	1 128	10 351	7.4
Avoyelles	535	4.8	D	4.6	4.7	7.4	4.6	D	35.0	9 155	218	2 835	18 042	8.8
Beauregard	474	0.0	32.1	16.9	D	7.5	7.7	10.9	17.7	6 740	189	1 001	15 040	3.7
Bienville	212	1.6	29.7	21.3	D	4.5	7.5	6.9	20.3	3 400	237	886	7 718	-1.4
Bossier	2 712	0.2	16.9	4.0	3.6	8.1	3.7	7.5	37.3	18 160	155	3 011	49 351	22.4
Caddo	7 764	0.1	23.8	7.0	7.6	6.1	4.4	16.8	20.2	46 920	184	12 387	112 028	3.5
Calcasieu	5 018	0.0	32.4	18.0	9.7	6.3	3.8	10.8	16.1	35 305	183	5 866	82 058	8.0
Caldwell	126	1.6	D	1.7	4.9	10.6	D	17.6	27.8	2 080	205	452	4 994	-0.8
Cameron	202	0.5	34.3	13.6	D	D	D	2.4	19.4	1 120	164	97	3 593	-32.7
Catahoula	141	21.8	D	D	4.4	6.8	3.2	6.6	23.6	2 325	223	655	4 877	-8.8
Claiborne	252	7.8	23.5	4.9	2.6	4.2	2.0	D	30.2	3 475	202	924	7 761	-0.7
Concordia	272	5.9	10.6	1.4	D	9.8	4.3	10.7	29.5	4 425	213	1 301	9 383	2.6
De Soto	437	1.2	48.6	15.7	1.5	6.6	2.3	D	20.1	5 580	209	1 335	12 290	9.7
East Baton Rouge	15 981	0.0	22.2	7.4	11.8	5.8	5.8	12.0	21.7	65 595	149	14 542	187 353	10.8
East Carroll	115	25.3	2.9	2.0	D	4.8	4.0	D	34.6	1 420	183	688	2 904	-12.1
East Feliciana	323	1.1	D	5.2	1.7	4.2	3.4	D	51.5	3 710	183	926	8 014	1.3
Evangeline	410	3.2	17.9	14.1	4.2	7.4	4.8	21.7	23.1	7 100	209	2 401	14 662	2.8
Franklin	283	20.4	D	3.1	D	9.8	4.4	D	24.2	4 375	211	1 307	9 034	4.8
Grant	198	0.8	19.4	7.3	1.6	2.9	D	D	51.8	4 105	184	828	8 886	4.2
Iberia	2 102	1.0	40.7	12.6	3.4	5.7	6.5	7.2	11.1	14 040	192	3 108	29 698	6.7
Iberville	1 059	1.6	51.2	42.3	2.0	2.9	2.4	D	16.4	5 885	176	1 473	12 707	6.3
Jackson	207	1.6	D	D	1.8	7.7	3.1	D	24.5	3 450	212	620	7 680	4.7
Jefferson	13 118	0.0	19.7	7.2	10.1	7.8	7.5	12.9	11.8	79 220	183	13 399	189 135	0.7
Jefferson Davis	462	6.0	17.6	7.6	4.3	8.0	6.2	D	21.6	6 210	197	1 124	13 306	3.8
Lafayette	8 437	0.1	31.0	6.1	10.5	6.4	6.2	12.5	10.8	31 540	142	5 682	93 656	20.0
Lafourche	2 682	0.7	18.9	7.0	3.4	5.3	5.3	6.3	14.7	17 415	181	3 288	38 582	10.1
La Salle	228	2.0	28.5	3.2	4.0	7.4	3.3	5.4	28.2	3 045	204	498	6 560	4.6
Lincoln	1 005	1.3	18.4	8.8	5.0	8.0	5.0	19.6	25.6	6 370	136	1 420	19 479	14.6
Livingston	1 137	0.0	24.8	9.9	6.2	10.1	4.5	6.3	25.3	19 405	152	2 782	50 170	38.5
Madison	162	10.6	14.0	9.5	1.4	7.4	3.5	D	34.7	2 000	165	732	4 804	-3.5
Morehouse	372	11.9	D	12.7	2.8	8.6	3.8	D	19.7	6 445	230	1 815	12 423	-2.3
Natchitoches	749	3.4	D	21.2	5.2	5.7	4.1	D	29.2	7 205	182	2 136	18 587	10.0

1. Includes mining, construction, and manufacturing. 2. Per 1,000 resident population enumerated in the 2010 census.

Table B. States and Counties — Housing, Labor Force, and Employment

| STATE County | Housing units, 2006–2010 — Occupied units — Owner-occupied | | | Median owner cost as a percent of income | | Renter-occupied | | | Civilian labor force, 2010 | | Unemployment | | Civilian employment,[5] 2006–2010 | Percent | |
	Total	Percent	Median value[1]	With a mortgage	Without a mortgage	Median rent[2]	Median rent as a percent of income	Substandard units[3] (percent)	Total	Percent change, 2009–2010	Total	Rate[4]	Total	Management, business, science and arts	Construction, production, and maintenance occupations
	89	90	91	92	93	94	95	96	97	98	99	100	101	102	103
KENTUCKY—Cont'd															
Ohio	8 770	77.7	78 000	21.4	10.7	476	26.7	2.2	12 911	1.5	1 191	9.2	9 087	19.7	42.6
Oldham	19 280	85.1	234 400	21.8	10.0	671	28.4	1.8	28 379	1.0	2 418	8.5	26 430	45.0	16.7
Owen	4 679	75.1	102 000	19.7	10.4	537	27.1	3.7	5 505	-2.0	527	9.6	5 180	23.5	37.9
Owsley	1 487	79.2	68 500	31.3	14.0	371	24.8	3.3	1 612	0.9	183	11.4	1 177	22.4	28.9
Pendleton	5 326	76.4	101 200	22.2	14.1	611	27.0	3.0	7 381	-1.6	947	12.8	6 452	24.8	37.0
Perry	10 816	72.5	55 900	19.5	10.0	471	32.6	4.2	11 799	-0.7	1 332	11.3	9 906	28.1	29.9
Pike	27 022	75.3	64 700	20.5	10.1	515	29.1	2.2	26 445	-1.3	2 660	10.1	22 286	24.9	32.8
Powell	4 701	69.9	80 700	22.3	14.3	612	38.9	5.8	5 795	-1.3	868	15.0	4 620	24.0	40.7
Pulaski	25 872	73.7	95 500	21.8	11.4	513	33.4	3.2	27 945	-0.2	2 996	10.7	24 816	28.0	29.1
Robertson	852	73.1	64 500	23.8	10.8	381	31.2	2.2	1 082	0.1	103	9.5	763	17.2	48.4
Rockcastle	6 475	78.7	72 300	20.8	13.6	464	35.6	2.7	7 124	-4.0	806	11.3	6 219	25.5	34.9
Rowan	8 285	70.4	90 400	19.3	11.2	498	38.1	1.6	12 458	-1.0	1 142	9.2	9 761	35.0	22.6
Russell	7 466	78.1	81 400	24.3	10.8	487	31.1	2.3	8 638	2.1	961	11.1	6 779	29.2	37.8
Scott	17 242	68.9	158 700	19.3	10.0	684	26.4	3.4	23 325	-0.2	2 223	9.5	22 023	34.9	28.5
Shelby	15 051	73.5	169 500	22.5	10.8	674	24.8	3.3	22 079	0.7	2 011	9.1	20 258	30.6	27.6
Simpson	6 667	70.2	113 700	22.9	12.6	665	29.9	2.0	9 263	0.2	1 166	12.6	7 973	22.4	35.3
Spencer	6 086	88.1	167 300	22.6	11.3	605	25.1	2.5	9 390	0.9	975	10.4	8 139	27.1	32.8
Taylor	9 628	68.8	96 600	22.8	10.0	511	29.4	2.0	13 923	2.6	1 498	10.8	9 998	26.7	31.5
Todd	4 640	72.3	79 700	22.1	11.8	523	24.9	3.0	5 444	1.1	585	10.7	5 015	21.9	39.2
Trigg	6 074	78.4	98 300	22.4	10.1	499	30.8	3.6	6 426	-4.4	781	12.2	5 507	25.7	38.6
Trimble	3 390	78.9	119 900	19.1	12.2	602	28.6	0.5	4 457	-0.2	577	12.9	3 866	25.6	38.0
Union	5 639	78.0	78 600	18.2	12.1	462	27.6	1.8	8 337	6.2	775	9.3	6 265	26.1	40.2
Warren	41 979	62.0	135 400	21.9	10.0	627	29.3	2.3	59 582	1.5	5 351	9.0	53 491	32.9	25.6
Washington	4 463	82.9	107 800	21.6	11.0	553	26.3	0.8	5 481	0.2	627	11.4	5 310	26.5	42.1
Wayne	8 604	73.2	70 600	23.2	10.0	403	29.0	4.2	9 096	3.4	1 195	13.1	7 172	23.2	43.1
Webster	4 992	80.3	66 200	18.6	11.0	498	28.3	3.2	6 634	1.6	616	9.3	5 429	22.6	47.2
Whitley	13 102	70.2	64 400	22.5	11.8	532	29.1	3.2	16 161	1.6	1 895	11.7	12 119	26.5	26.6
Wolfe	2 493	75.9	54 400	30.9	12.6	291	37.7	0.4	2 448	1.6	353	14.4	1 742	28.8	28.5
Woodford	10 001	72.8	180 800	21.7	10.0	724	26.3	1.1	13 201	-1.2	1 071	8.1	12 577	41.0	25.2
LOUISIANA	1 641 165	68.2	130 000	21.5	10.2	712	30.9	3.4	2 070 068	0.5	154 724	7.5	1 952 818	30.7	25.9
Acadia	21 984	69.8	86 700	18.6	10.0	514	29.0	4.1	26 256	-0.9	1 753	6.7	25 089	24.5	32.8
Allen	8 388	72.0	76 500	18.5	10.0	555	26.6	4.2	8 891	0.2	943	10.6	8 975	22.8	31.8
Ascension	35 640	80.8	164 200	19.4	10.0	749	28.6	5.6	51 718	1.8	3 648	7.1	48 872	34.4	26.4
Assumption	8 467	84.2	86 500	17.6	10.1	545	19.7	5.5	10 405	-2.0	1 083	10.4	9 292	22.4	41.2
Avoyelles	15 767	69.4	82 100	20.8	11.6	526	30.3	5.2	16 769	2.1	1 379	8.2	15 432	25.1	28.6
Beauregard	12 787	77.5	83 400	17.7	10.0	583	24.7	3.7	14 618	-0.3	1 099	7.5	13 964	26.9	32.2
Bienville	5 689	74.2	62 700	17.1	11.7	432	37.5	2.9	6 495	3.0	577	8.9	5 277	22.9	39.6
Bossier	43 186	67.4	130 400	20.9	10.0	736	26.5	2.7	54 092	1.2	3 156	5.8	52 655	30.1	26.2
Caddo	97 293	63.5	113 300	22.3	11.1	661	31.8	2.6	119 121	0.2	8 853	7.4	108 929	30.5	21.8
Calcasieu	71 601	71.9	109 400	19.6	10.0	677	28.8	2.6	92 162	0.5	6 463	7.0	84 909	28.5	27.0
Caldwell	3 651	73.5	67 800	18.1	11.5	409	24.1	3.1	4 571	-2.2	447	9.8	3 859	23.4	34.1
Cameron	2 663	84.5	122 700	14.5	10.0	769	19.0	3.1	3 104	-9.7	192	6.2	3 561	29.5	37.5
Catahoula	3 794	78.2	67 900	20.2	10.0	417	23.5	6.1	4 330	1.2	436	10.1	3 636	26.3	33.1
Claiborne	5 890	73.2	61 200	19.6	11.6	574	40.9	4.7	6 675	-1.4	599	9.0	6 549	23.8	32.6
Concordia	7 570	70.8	72 700	20.8	14.3	438	30.3	2.9	7 389	-0.1	803	10.9	7 191	23.4	30.1
De Soto	10 121	76.6	80 300	19.3	10.0	473	32.1	3.5	11 460	-0.1	930	8.1	11 248	25.0	32.5
East Baton Rouge	166 543	61.6	156 100	21.5	10.0	759	33.6	2.9	218 570	0.3	15 751	7.2	213 568	36.4	19.0
East Carroll	2 426	55.6	44 400	20.0	11.8	431	39.0	5.2	2 986	-0.4	454	15.2	2 088	23.5	24.2
East Feliciana	6 662	81.6	101 500	22.8	11.5	557	30.4	3.6	8 153	-0.3	693	8.5	7 439	21.7	31.0
Evangeline	12 304	69.1	76 100	17.7	11.5	464	28.1	5.0	12 775	0.4	1 096	8.6	12 203	26.4	33.3
Franklin	7 844	72.6	72 100	19.2	10.2	502	33.5	3.6	7 876	0.1	879	11.2	7 529	24.0	33.8
Grant	7 407	78.1	83 000	19.1	10.0	631	27.7	3.3	8 745	-0.9	684	7.8	8 438	24.7	35.4
Iberia	26 194	70.1	98 100	21.3	10.3	626	28.0	4.2	33 409	-6.0	2 612	7.8	31 109	24.9	31.8
Iberville	11 118	75.9	88 700	20.3	10.0	542	26.5	4.7	12 457	-1.3	1 297	10.4	13 000	21.5	35.8
Jackson	5 967	68.3	73 600	17.6	10.4	547	25.8	2.7	6 543	-2.5	475	7.3	6 640	24.6	30.9
Jefferson	162 881	64.7	175 100	23.8	10.9	866	31.2	3.0	214 572	-0.9	14 909	6.9	209 432	31.5	24.2
Jefferson Davis	11 786	76.0	83 700	19.6	10.4	579	25.3	3.0	14 690	-0.9	920	6.3	12 514	25.0	36.3
Lafayette	83 810	64.9	151 600	19.8	10.0	690	27.9	2.3	112 610	1.3	6 392	5.7	108 215	34.3	21.6
Lafourche	34 108	77.0	115 500	19.3	10.0	585	27.7	5.0	48 811	0.8	2 530	5.2	42 698	26.3	34.2
La Salle	5 245	84.4	72 800	18.3	10.0	451	26.3	2.8	6 839	6.6	408	6.0	5 522	31.2	33.6
Lincoln	16 248	58.5	110 700	21.6	10.0	608	38.1	2.9	19 657	1.3	1 635	8.3	19 002	34.6	20.9
Livingston	42 962	80.4	142 400	20.4	10.0	719	25.4	4.3	59 150	1.3	4 243	7.2	56 549	27.9	30.9
Madison	3 973	59.1	71 400	18.4	11.1	551	33.0	5.8	4 628	-2.8	489	10.6	3 784	28.3	24.9
Morehouse	10 282	71.4	71 200	21.2	11.6	560	35.1	4.4	11 453	-1.8	1 632	14.2	10 071	22.5	29.2
Natchitoches	14 847	61.4	90 500	20.3	10.8	572	39.5	5.2	17 368	-1.2	1 400	8.1	15 722	27.5	28.0

1. Specified owner-occupied units.   2. Specified renter-occupied units. A value of 10.0 represents 10 percent or less.   3. Overcrowded or lacking complete plumbing facilities.   4. Percent of civilian labor force.   5. Persons 16 years old and over.

Table B. States and Counties — Nonfarm Employment and Agriculture

STATE County	Number of establishments	Employment — Total	Health care and social assistance	Manufacturing	Retail trade	Finance and insurance	Professional, scientific, and technical services	Annual payroll Total (mil dol)	Average per employee (dollars)	Farms Number	Percent with: Fewer than 50 acres	500 acres or more	Farm operators whose principal occupation is farming (percent)
	104	105	106	107	108	109	110	111	112	113	114	115	116
KENTUCKY—Cont'd													
Ohio	359	5 535	930	D	783	147	77	135	24 477	969	31.3	5.5	33.4
Oldham	1 222	10 254	2 133	770	1 528	849	539	320	31 185	461	56.2	6.5	38.2
Owen	133	1 342	236	D	216	D	13	47	34 672	864	21.8	6.7	38.9
Owsley	44	374	216	D	D	D	D	9	22 992	195	21.5	9.7	31.8
Pendleton	181	1 685	274	544	198	66	50	46	27 499	910	29.1	2.7	36.2
Perry	687	11 300	2 732	524	2 038	286	310	407	36 032	57	31.6	5.3	38.6
Pike	1 362	21 209	3 591	609	4 110	D	782	784	36 969	70	42.9	7.1	32.9
Powell	167	1 400	212	154	401	D	D	34	24 216	236	36.9	4.7	34.3
Pulaski	1 417	20 630	5 336	3 322	3 470	580	552	586	28 390	1 808	36.5	3.2	44.0
Robertson	25	147	D	0	D	D	D	3	17 748	289	17.6	6.6	40.5
Rockcastle	233	2 501	781	204	345	96	D	79	31 727	727	33.8	2.8	41.5
Rowan	442	7 133	1 951	937	1 542	196	107	185	25 873	386	37.3	4.1	35.2
Russell	365	4 630	875	1 278	786	D	59	110	23 793	805	41.2	4.2	36.3
Scott	849	19 833	1 313	9 068	1 748	277	339	803	40 497	930	39.7	6.0	43.1
Shelby	887	12 078	1 513	3 703	1 811	365	345	360	29 798	1 651	47.2	3.6	41.0
Simpson	391	7 915	429	3 191	1 154	D	D	219	27 730	494	45.1	9.3	43.1
Spencer	204	1 100	232	20	236	D	D	23	21 103	596	39.1	2.3	38.3
Taylor	645	9 578	1 216	1 681	1 596	237	109	253	26 462	941	39.0	3.9	38.5
Todd	184	1 424	209	D	D	76	D	31	22 011	759	29.5	12.3	45.6
Trigg	246	2 352	295	430	366	73	52	57	24 274	458	29.3	12.2	46.9
Trimble	77	652	D	D	D	D	D	25	37 718	489	32.3	3.3	40.5
Union	294	4 330	873	438	707	80	55	161	37 239	325	29.5	28.0	50.5
Warren	2 638	46 492	7 244	8 274	7 045	1 371	2 158	1 481	31 864	1 824	45.5	4.7	34.2
Washington	243	2 599	221	789	273	D	D	72	27 838	1 119	28.3	4.0	38.1
Wayne	326	4 048	552	1 429	730	D	66	95	23 495	781	31.8	7.9	41.9
Webster	235	2 181	266	292	407	93	D	77	35 239	556	26.3	12.2	37.6
Whitley	674	10 789	2 901	1 123	1 548	288	868	296	27 392	565	33.6	3.9	42.8
Wolfe	81	648	276	29	168	D	D	14	21 772	342	22.5	5.3	36.0
Woodford	552	6 883	602	2 082	745	224	485	246	35 698	712	44.8	8.3	49.9
LOUISIANA	103 384	1 639 104	276 553	134 803	229 875	64 200	89 774	61 388	37 452	30 106	45.4	11.4	41.8
Acadia	1 114	12 485	2 173	1 159	2 589	463	353	363	29 039	905	54.4	12.8	41.7
Allen	338	3 721	856	D	638	148	D	100	26 757	405	47.9	10.1	41.7
Ascension	1 962	31 505	2 700	4 087	5 802	1 005	898	1 299	41 218	277	63.5	7.9	32.1
Assumption	257	2 922	788	362	491	93	74	98	33 425	114	50.0	33.3	60.5
Avoyelles	704	8 929	1 991	408	1 545	458	221	214	23 941	947	39.0	12.9	42.8
Beauregard	589	6 877	1 205	922	1 411	D	153	209	30 348	909	41.3	5.0	38.1
Bienville	250	3 097	424	1 024	314	142	28	91	29 529	194	35.1	5.7	42.3
Bossier	2 375	36 102	3 674	1 997	6 389	1 176	1 007	1 014	28 076	493	55.6	12.0	45.2
Caddo	6 331	108 162	28 032	7 983	14 102	3 660	4 226	3 833	35 441	625	55.5	10.7	41.3
Calcasieu	4 283	69 305	12 227	8 021	10 903	1 995	3 496	2 488	35 895	971	53.1	9.0	36.8
Caldwell	191	1 962	658	39	525	118	78	47	24 070	307	34.9	8.8	34.9
Cameron	159	1 440	D	D	D	D	80	73	50 813	339	36.0	22.7	41.6
Catahoula	173	1 667	551	D	272	77	D	41	24 484	510	26.1	21.6	38.8
Claiborne	252	2 705	708	277	426	D	D	81	29 834	239	36.8	10.0	46.9
Concordia	380	4 305	822	D	967	D	111	109	25 361	462	22.3	24.0	39.2
De Soto	382	4 362	796	D	955	174	76	156	35 809	619	38.8	9.2	45.6
East Baton Rouge	12 169	234 947	36 332	10 916	28 820	12 365	18 425	9 395	39 987	511	55.0	5.9	37.2
East Carroll	124	1 220	281	82	180	35	20	39	31 668	280	15.4	36.4	58.2
East Feliciana	265	3 823	2 100	253	329	D	48	121	31 588	439	40.1	16.4	35.3
Evangeline	523	5 859	2 133	D	1 072	279	140	170	28 962	806	49.5	8.7	32.0
Franklin	396	4 032	1 205	D	1 042	211	208	92	22 895	1 273	28.6	14.4	45.2
Grant	187	1 621	255	D	254	83	7	41	25 526	250	48.8	8.8	29.6
Iberia	1 752	31 660	3 874	6 379	3 584	952	810	1 266	39 985	345	61.7	17.7	45.8
Iberville	536	9 100	980	3 120	1 094	276	D	473	51 953	175	48.0	24.0	52.0
Jackson	250	2 974	601	D	508	114	82	118	39 593	197	56.3	2.0	41.1
Jefferson	11 928	186 338	29 623	11 663	29 341	8 422	10 593	7 227	38 782	71	67.6	7.0	42.3
Jefferson Davis	605	6 772	1 419	545	1 463	273	220	188	27 781	706	44.3	20.1	44.5
Lafayette	7 879	120 998	20 544	8 000	15 939	3 354	8 350	4 498	37 174	713	75.6	3.4	37.6
Lafourche	1 938	28 443	3 505	3 050	4 311	897	948	1 105	38 853	440	47.0	9.8	45.5
La Salle	290	3 204	725	D	583	D	99	89	27 644	165	39.4	3.0	38.2
Lincoln	980	14 920	3 521	1 237	2 441	717	505	426	28 543	321	37.7	5.6	45.8
Livingston	1 647	18 146	1 888	1 778	4 239	689	695	480	26 442	476	70.8	1.3	33.4
Madison	210	2 608	1 050	379	421	55	D	62	23 760	355	19.7	36.3	49.3
Morehouse	485	5 352	1 953	129	1 145	257	103	129	24 097	473	27.3	28.3	50.7
Natchitoches	808	10 631	1 699	2 472	1 839	355	296	284	26 690	571	32.7	18.7	45.7

STATE County	Acreage (1,000)	Percent change, 2002–2007	Average size of farm	Total irrigated (1,000)	Total cropland (1,000)	Average per farm	Average per acre	Value of machinery and equipment, average per farm (dollars)	Total (mil dol)	Average per farm (dollars)	Crops	Live-stock and poultry products	$10,000 or more	$100,000 or more	Total ($1,000)	Percent of farms
	117	118	119	120	121	122	123	124	125	126	127	128	129	130	131	132
KENTUCKY—Cont'd																
Ohio	169	1.2	174	D	84.8	348 348	2 002	53 306	72.8	75 167	27.3	72.7	28.2	6.6	1 104	40.2
Oldham	60	-4.8	130	0.2	29.0	795 673	6 111	63 089	19.3	41 799	39.3	60.7	31.5	6.9	223	16.1
Owen	158	1.9	183	0.4	69.3	416 504	2 279	50 450	17.3	20 050	40.9	59.1	34.0	3.9	466	39.8
Owsley	36	9.1	184	0.1	9.9	274 202	1 491	35 100	1.2	6 262	68.6	31.4	15.9	0.5	55	13.8
Pendleton	126	-4.5	139	1.0	55.0	351 015	2 528	54 781	12.4	13 608	58.1	41.9	21.3	2.7	376	20.3
Perry	11	57.1	187	0.0	2.4	227 787	1 218	48 155	0.9	15 222	5.8	94.2	22.8	7.0	D	1.8
Pike	14	100.0	203	0.0	3.0	190 309	936	32 524	0.4	5 737	20.4	79.4	10.0	1.4	1	4.3
Powell	33	-13.2	139	0.0	13.5	267 393	1 926	36 199	2.5	10 623	64.9	35.1	16.5	2.1	83	26.7
Pulaski	232	0.0	128	0.2	105.0	336 474	2 625	47 179	39.7	21 980	26.2	73.8	37.9	4.6	704	25.4
Robertson	51	18.6	178	0.1	21.7	317 504	1 783	46 423	3.8	13 238	54.3	45.7	30.8	2.4	139	16.6
Rockcastle	90	-4.3	124	0.0	32.5	256 809	2 064	38 363	8.4	11 557	29.9	70.1	24.2	2.6	233	21.9
Rowan	50	-2.0	129	0.0	19.5	256 127	1 979	47 450	4.8	12 515	37.5	62.5	21.8	1.6	89	18.4
Russell	93	-4.1	116	0.3	46.2	358 336	3 100	51 300	43.6	54 217	10.1	89.9	41.1	9.7	633	35.9
Scott	139	1.5	150	1.0	62.5	575 648	3 850	60 387	67.5	72 546	15.2	84.8	34.5	8.0	358	17.5
Shelby	205	1.5	124	1.5	124.2	551 127	4 432	58 291	57.0	34 520	52.0	48.0	37.7	6.7	1 689	20.7
Simpson	119	-7.0	241	0.1	89.1	712 528	2 955	78 935	47.4	95 976	40.9	59.1	39.3	10.5	1 243	48.6
Spencer	73	-6.4	123	0.6	36.1	405 163	3 295	52 129	11.5	19 361	58.3	41.7	32.2	4.0	494	41.3
Taylor	119	6.3	126	0.2	59.6	312 492	2 477	52 818	26.3	27 983	40.1	59.9	34.2	6.2	973	41.7
Todd	198	7.6	261	1.0	136.2	745 593	2 858	102 587	130.4	171 817	30.9	69.1	49.4	20.4	2 626	50.3
Trigg	136	10.6	296	0.9	74.0	765 195	2 583	93 146	27.0	58 866	66.2	33.8	43.9	10.5	1 480	50.7
Trimble	65	0.0	133	0.1	25.9	339 215	2 548	48 029	7.6	15 569	57.9	42.1	30.9	2.0	220	22.3
Union	201	-3.8	618	2.3	166.9	1 596 117	2 583	219 696	78.9	242 919	92.5	7.5	59.4	31.4	3 411	64.6
Warren	265	3.9	145	0.3	147.9	455 845	3 136	60 496	74.7	40 941	29.5	70.5	33.9	5.9	2 342	31.9
Washington	163	8.7	146	0.7	80.6	359 002	2 465	53 052	33.0	29 491	29.8	70.2	37.0	6.3	714	29.8
Wayne	143	2.9	183	0.1	48.5	373 723	2 044	55 378	68.5	87 654	8.9	91.1	35.2	7.8	392	24.5
Webster	155	-2.5	279	D	107.5	648 343	2 326	86 349	97.0	174 497	31.7	68.3	32.9	15.8	2 592	68.9
Whitley	73	14.1	130	D	27.8	319 531	2 459	41 622	4.6	8 192	29.4	70.6	18.9	1.1	81	17.9
Wolfe	58	-3.3	169	0.0	15.6	297 877	1 766	38 921	2.2	6 359	32.8	67.2	14.9	0.3	365	37.7
Woodford	119	-3.3	167	0.6	50.7	1 165 408	6 968	85 678	341.1	479 014	2.9	97.1	48.7	19.8	373	14.7
LOUISIANA	8 110	3.6	269	954.4	4 691.3	554 270	2 058	78 998	2 618.0	86 959	61.3	38.7	30.7	10.7	169 333	35.3
Acadia	233	-9.3	257	72.1	185.6	475 108	1 846	78 924	69.1	76 353	87.8	12.2	30.1	12.3	7 612	56.4
Allen	83	-19.4	205	11.6	48.4	390 076	1 899	57 777	10.0	24 701	73.1	26.9	22.0	6.4	1 918	38.3
Ascension	45	-10.0	164	0.3	27.0	569 319	3 469	88 427	19.4	70 095	89.2	10.8	20.9	6.1	84	4.3
Assumption	64	-3.0	559	D	51.5	1 433 380	2 565	289 435	40.9	358 505	94.4	5.6	59.6	36.0	301	16.7
Avoyelles	278	2.2	294	20.2	203.1	522 377	1 776	81 807	75.2	79 378	90.1	9.9	36.0	11.9	6 185	45.5
Beauregard	179	25.2	197	1.6	44.3	439 565	2 233	48 825	11.5	12 637	31.8	68.2	21.2	1.9	1 401	23.9
Bienville	41	-6.8	210	0.0	10.0	450 136	2 145	87 999	28.3	145 927	2.0	98.0	33.5	7.2	107	10.8
Bossier	104	-2.8	210	0.1	37.8	583 220	2 778	57 427	13.1	26 604	37.6	62.4	28.0	6.1	1 025	13.6
Caddo	151	-12.2	242	9.7	77.5	516 961	2 137	78 107	33.0	52 854	78.3	21.7	26.2	7.4	3 956	12.8
Calcasieu	368	21.5	379	11.9	125.2	674 638	1 781	53 687	18.8	19 330	44.8	55.2	26.6	3.4	2 339	26.2
Caldwell	67	9.8	220	4.0	28.7	414 904	1 888	60 246	8.4	27 235	83.2	16.8	30.6	4.9	1 811	50.2
Cameron	216	-13.3	638	12.1	55.4	1 137 196	1 783	75 618	9.1	26 850	43.5	56.5	29.2	7.7	1 912	38.3
Catahoula	231	-0.4	453	22.2	172.8	741 408	1 636	110 922	57.9	113 471	94.7	5.3	34.7	16.5	8 840	68.2
Claiborne	49	-12.5	203	D	13.2	529 754	2 606	70 425	76.6	320 650	3.0	97.0	46.4	20.5	109	8.4
Concordia	211	-0.5	456	10.7	157.7	794 055	1 742	90 152	50.0	108 188	95.0	5.0	33.8	20.8	6 772	81.0
De Soto	167	21.9	270	0.6	35.9	540 986	2 000	66 155	22.1	35 664	17.2	82.8	28.8	5.2	392	13.1
East Baton Rouge	72	18.0	141	0.2	30.5	569 525	4 033	50 922	10.7	21 004	28.0	72.0	28.2	5.1	179	9.4
East Carroll	261	20.3	931	102.3	225.2	1 483 695	1 594	254 233	96.0	342 990	97.9	2.1	53.6	37.9	10 101	86.1
East Feliciana	128	4.1	292	1.0	33.1	757 251	2 594	49 866	8.6	19 482	17.9	82.1	31.4	3.4	349	15.9
Evangeline	172	-6.5	214	37.2	105.8	377 978	1 769	60 250	35.3	43 850	80.1	19.9	26.3	9.1	5 619	49.0
Franklin	347	34.5	273	94.0	232.4	473 756	1 736	79 317	106.3	83 470	77.1	22.9	35.0	13.1	13 335	77.4
Grant	52	44.4	207	0.7	25.4	383 287	1 852	75 144	6.0	24 115	67.0	33.0	19.6	5.2	572	16.0
Iberia	116	4.5	336	0.4	98.1	839 271	2 498	182 162	62.9	182 391	97.9	2.1	38.0	16.2	890	18.0
Iberville	86	-11.3	490	D	67.0	1 401 691	2 861	198 841	49.4	282 014	93.9	6.1	50.3	21.1	366	24.6
Jackson	20	-4.8	102	D	5.1	320 200	3 141	65 834	34.7	176 385	1.1	98.9	34.5	14.7	63	2.0
Jefferson	15	87.5	213	1.1	5.7	440 306	2 070	D	1.6	23 160	D	D	32.4	7.0	242	15.5
Jefferson Davis	288	-10.8	408	79.1	227.4	721 633	1 768	95 734	64.8	91 733	88.7	11.3	35.8	15.2	7 617	59.6
Lafayette	67	-10.7	95	3.1	49.6	322 934	3 415	57 232	30.1	42 265	91.4	8.6	17.7	3.4	647	14.2
Lafourche	106	-29.8	241	3.2	63.1	586 683	2 433	93 194	42.0	95 386	54.3	45.7	38.6	9.1	154	5.5
La Salle	20	17.6	123	D	5.7	285 172	2 318	39 773	D	D	D	0.0	21.8	0.6	141	17.0
Lincoln	52	-21.2	164	1.0	12.9	521 181	3 187	62 247	119.7	372 981	2.4	97.6	38.0	18.7	252	9.3
Livingston	30	-11.8	63	0.4	8.9	272 876	4 332	43 311	5.6	11 712	20.9	79.1	17.2	1.7	49	3.4
Madison	235	-0.8	661	195.6	195.6	1 061 834	1 607	149 597	71.2	200 681	99.0	1.0	50.4	34.9	8 604	87.3
Morehouse	274	11.8	579	140.4	221.6	939 856	1 624	140 292	94.6	200 047	97.4	2.6	46.7	26.6	11 001	62.6
Natchitoches	222	15.0	388	6.1	98.0	641 833	1 653	83 520	82.4	144 395	27.4	72.6	35.0	13.5	3 673	36.1

Table B. States and Counties — **Water Use, Wholesale Trade, Retail Trade, and Real Estate**

STATE County	Water use, 2005		Wholesale trade,[1] 2007				Retail trade,[2] 2007				Real estate and rental and leasing,[2] 2007			
	Total water withdrawn (mil gal/day)	Gallons withdrawn per person	Number of establishments	Number of employees	Sales (mil dol)	Annual payroll (mil dol)	Number of establishments	Number of employees	Sales (mil dol)	Annual payroll (mil dol)	Number of establishments	Number of employees	Receipts (mil dol)	Annual payroll (mil dol)
	133	134	135	136	137	138	139	140	141	142	143	144	145	146
KENTUCKY—Cont'd														
Ohio	19.1	806	12	363	149.5	6.6	60	627	142.5	12.7	7	31	1.6	0.3
Oldham	5.9	110	47	287	95.5	11.8	135	1 483	374.8	35.3	50	134	24.5	3.2
Owen	2.4	208	5	43	10.4	0.6	26	230	43.2	4.0	4	D	D	D
Owsley	0.3	67	1	D	D	D	11	87	16.7	1.5	2	D	D	D
Pendleton	1.6	102	8	D	D	D	29	233	47.2	4.0	8	21	1.6	0.3
Perry	4.8	162	32	438	267.9	21.7	158	1 952	463.1	39.5	21	64	11.1	1.7
Pike	14.4	215	59	451	589.0	21.3	290	3 876	894.9	80.4	42	122	35.2	3.0
Powell	1.2	90	5	22	3.9	0.5	43	382	95.0	6.1	4	D	D	D
Pulaski	132.8	2 242	60	1 124	989.6	29.4	316	3 495	884.4	73.3	51	181	23.8	5.0
Robertson	0.2	75	NA	NA	NA	NA	5	16	1.6	0.1	NA	NA	NA	NA
Rockcastle	2.5	149	11	D	D	D	53	316	71.6	5.1	6	37	2.5	0.7
Rowan	6.8	307	20	177	54.1	4.2	115	1 359	272.1	24.2	22	69	8.4	1.4
Russell	4.1	241	5	D	D	D	89	783	180.3	13.4	9	57	9.9	1.2
Scott	4.2	105	23	D	D	D	132	1 779	528.6	35.8	53	217	39.3	6.7
Shelby	4.7	124	36	618	320.8	26.8	146	1 755	498.7	37.4	45	169	21.5	3.8
Simpson	2.2	129	11	88	260.0	2.7	69	1 039	415.2	22.6	19	108	8.1	3.3
Spencer	0.9	58	4	11	1.5	0.1	23	236	68.1	4.0	9	28	2.7	0.4
Taylor	5.7	239	24	D	D	D	148	1 770	371.9	35.2	30	157	11.9	2.7
Todd	1.0	81	9	47	23.2	1.3	36	246	58.6	3.6	3	9	0.6	0.1
Trigg	6.1	454	7	D	D	D	40	364	70.9	5.9	15	40	5.0	1.0
Trimble	15.7	1 740	NA	NA	NA	NA	15	116	32.0	1.5	3	4	0.3	0.0
Union	3.8	246	12	103	94.0	3.7	65	678	144.2	12.4	7	24	3.0	0.3
Warren	19.6	198	134	D	D	D	535	7 535	1 691.2	151.0	133	1 113	114.4	28.7
Washington	2.5	217	10	94	67.7	2.5	41	262	63.3	4.6	4	5	0.4	0.1
Wayne	2.7	131	10	76	23.6	1.6	66	697	152.5	13.8	10	52	2.4	0.6
Webster	77.8	5 492	10	D	D	D	42	349	67.5	5.8	6	14	1.1	0.2
Whitley	2.7	72	22	D	D	D	153	1 531	373.3	30.5	26	78	10.5	1.9
Wolfe	0.7	93	3	D	D	D	26	187	45.3	3.3	2	D	D	D
Woodford	54.1	2 233	15	D	D	D	74	770	225.2	18.8	21	45	6.3	0.9
LOUISIANA	11 597.7	2 564	4 839	63 911	51 415.6	2 808.3	17 135	231 365	56 543.2	5 096.1	4 625	30 922	6 014.9	1 194.9
Acadia	293.9	4 935	40	D	D	D	193	2 427	526.0	49.2	39	122	11.2	2.3
Allen	30.0	1 188	8	D	D	D	72	741	142.9	11.7	9	32	2.2	0.5
Ascension	202.8	2 241	103	1 297	665.0	65.5	369	5 189	1 318.0	111.9	87	488	139.5	21.7
Assumption	23.1	994	12	D	D	D	53	553	100.0	8.9	7	13	2.5	0.2
Avoyelles	30.8	732	22	210	171.3	6.4	162	1 440	310.9	25.0	18	63	6.3	1.0
Beauregard	82.9	952	13	D	D	D	100	1 412	317.4	28.6	20	71	7.6	1.1
Bienville	13.7	804	6	D	D	D	45	338	58.7	5.3	5	D	D	D
Bossier	19.0	180	90	1 542	1 028.2	70.1	476	6 359	1 741.9	142.0	116	554	100.6	15.0
Caddo	338.1	1 345	312	4 511	5 467.4	198.9	1 008	14 460	3 706.8	326.5	299	1 857	260.4	49.8
Calcasieu	309.8	1 671	185	2 145	1 342.9	91.5	830	11 704	2 776.0	246.5	210	948	195.1	30.7
Caldwell	3.6	344	5	D	D	D	36	459	112.9	8.0	6	17	2.3	0.3
Cameron	31.8	3 322	13	82	62.8	3.7	23	238	36.8	3.0	5	105	36.4	4.9
Catahoula	25.4	2 428	15	156	193.1	4.5	34	244	52.7	4.2	4	18	5.6	0.6
Claiborne	7.8	476	9	69	125.9	2.3	56	444	74.2	7.3	6	18	1.7	0.3
Concordia	38.6	2 003	14	D	D	D	79	871	194.9	16.6	8	155	6.7	3.9
De Soto	547.0	20 732	11	155	22.0	5.1	73	819	184.5	15.3	7	21	1.5	0.3
East Baton Rouge	168.0	408	610	8 786	7 860.1	401.7	1 930	29 228	7 043.0	664.6	583	3 137	559.9	96.5
East Carroll	45.1	5 154	12	D	D	D	26	225	34.0	3.3	7	19	3.1	0.7
East Feliciana	3.6	175	9	D	D	D	53	394	72.8	6.1	5	D	D	D
Evangeline	141.5	3 981	17	D	D	D	130	1 078	228.6	18.6	22	65	6.0	1.3
Franklin	51.3	2 517	19	191	182.7	4.8	89	988	215.5	18.5	21	61	6.4	1.0
Grant	4.8	244	4	D	D	D	29	273	74.7	6.6	2	D	D	D
Iberia	38.3	515	84	D	D	D	290	3 631	910.2	81.0	101	2 302	553.0	164.9
Iberville	933.8	28 833	28	247	149.9	8.8	95	1 103	274.4	22.6	27	154	26.5	3.8
Jackson	2.3	152	7	D	D	D	47	569	114.5	9.8	11	33	3.8	0.5
Jefferson	1 058.6	2 338	802	10 311	6 049.8	489.5	1 855	30 948	8 106.2	771.5	538	5 527	960.2	183.5
Jefferson Davis	170.6	5 455	21	D	D	D	116	1 496	338.8	28.1	19	303	60.8	13.8
Lafayette	48.2	244	445	6 314	2 651.4	281.7	1 041	15 424	3 814.3	340.3	438	3 387	879.4	175.7
Lafourche	56.5	613	71	1 096	888.4	44.2	304	4 103	917.5	79.0	80	544	116.0	23.5
La Salle	13.5	959	8	D	D	D	58	517	116.4	9.0	10	42	4.5	0.9
Lincoln	8.1	191	27	388	171.3	14.6	184	2 482	527.8	48.1	46	242	51.6	6.5
Livingston	15.8	144	38	308	483.0	14.5	288	3 645	923.7	73.1	55	177	30.5	4.3
Madison	20.2	1 622	12	101	153.2	3.4	39	455	142.5	8.2	9	30	3.7	0.5
Morehouse	131.5	4 384	18	170	255.3	5.4	102	1 181	241.4	24.0	24	52	7.0	1.1
Natchitoches	33.9	878	25	D	D	D	156	1 838	414.0	35.5	46	175	15.3	2.4

1. Merchant wholesalers, except manufacturers' sales branches and offices.   2. Employer establishments.

— **Professional Services, Manufacturing, and Accommodation and Food Services**

STATE County	Professional, scientific, and technical services,[1] 2007				Manufacturing, 2007				Accommodation and food services, 2007			
	Number of establish- ments	Number of employees	Receipts (mil dol)	Annual payroll (mil dol)	Number of establish- ments	Number of employees	Receipts (mil dol)	Annual payroll (mil dol)	Number of establish- ments	Number of employees	Sales (mil dol)	Annual payroll (mil dol)
	147	148	149	150	151	152	153	154	155	156	157	158
KENTUCKY—Cont'd												
Ohio	25	69	5.4	1.6	27	2 377	485.5	70.5	27	416	15.3	4.2
Oldham	174	555	60.3	24.9	46	925	275.1	36.6	60	1 127	47.1	12.6
Owen	8	13	1.0	0.2	NA	NA	NA	NA	13	178	6.6	2.0
Owsley	2	D	D	D	NA	NA	NA	NA	2	D	D	D
Pendleton	9	D	D	D	17	596	D	24.3	11	182	4.5	1.2
Perry	57	D	D	D	12	690	122.2	21.4	50	1 186	43.8	11.8
Pike	104	D	D	D	28	652	D	22.2	91	1 710	75.5	19.3
Powell	7	8	0.6	0.1	NA	NA	NA	NA	14	228	9.3	2.5
Pulaski	96	D	D	D	85	4 129	1 088.0	139.4	92	1 862	73.5	19.3
Robertson	1	D	D	D	NA	NA	NA	NA	1	D	D	D
Rockcastle	14	D	D	D	NA	NA	NA	NA	25	351	11.3	3.3
Rowan	23	D	D	D	20	954	259.8	28.6	43	971	36.1	8.4
Russell	22	68	5.5	1.6	25	1 182	D	36.8	31	372	14.5	2.9
Scott	68	414	34.7	14.1	37	9 905	D	D	79	1 815	73.1	20.8
Shelby	76	317	32.0	10.6	52	4 535	1 373.1	178.2	52	D	D	D
Simpson	17	99	4.9	1.9	33	3 531	1 406.3	141.4	41	654	29.7	8.2
Spencer	13	D	D	D	NA	NA	NA	NA	13	D	D	D
Taylor	50	115	9.3	3.3	35	1 871	315.2	56.2	42	831	25.4	6.4
Todd	10	66	3.3	1.6	NA	NA	NA	NA	12	74	2.3	0.7
Trigg	11	46	3.8	0.9	17	1 134	235.1	39.3	21	344	11.3	3.4
Trimble	4	D	D	D	NA	NA	NA	NA	6	40	1.8	0.5
Union	8	28	3.2	1.1	16	901	250.4	40.7	22	261	9.8	2.4
Warren	205	D	D	D	118	D	D	D	217	5 454	231.2	63.7
Washington	15	46	3.3	1.0	12	986	259.0	35.9	12	201	6.3	1.7
Wayne	23	62	4.2	1.5	36	2 053	378.9	52.8	26	431	18.8	4.3
Webster	10	23	1.8	0.3	NA	NA	NA	NA	17	107	4.7	1.2
Whitley	55	450	53.6	15.6	27	1 233	D	40.5	58	974	39.3	9.6
Wolfe	5	11	0.7	0.2	NA	NA	NA	NA	5	42	0.6	0.1
Woodford	68	D	D	D	30	2 584	D	122.8	34	397	15.7	4.5
LOUISIANA	11 128	84 666	11 856.6	4 234.6	3 442	148 080	205 054.7	7 564.5	8 169	180 289	9 729.9	2 579.0
Acadia	89	307	35.1	13.3	51	1 148	D	38.5	67	1 145	40.8	10.5
Allen	19	59	6.0	1.7	13	655	167.5	27.2	28	422	17.4	3.7
Ascension	150	D	D	D	88	4 348	D	329.2	148	2 747	116.3	30.9
Assumption	26	70	6.0	2.4	NA	NA	NA	NA	13	135	4.1	1.0
Avoyelles	60	173	18.9	5.0	NA	NA	NA	NA	52	2 423	174.7	47.0
Beauregard	40	170	11.4	4.6	19	935	D	D	33	550	19.5	5.2
Bienville	12	31	2.7	1.3	13	1 098	D	29.3	16	164	6.6	1.6
Bossier	162	934	96.1	31.6	73	2 200	D	D	232	9 784	711.7	174.9
Caddo	604	4 224	492.8	173.4	215	9 553	D	486.2	439	12 288	675.3	175.3
Calcasieu	440	D	D	D	128	D	D	D	328	10 346	878.6	181.6
Caldwell	22	66	5.3	1.1	NA	NA	NA	NA	10	138	5.8	1.5
Cameron	15	D	D	D	NA	NA	NA	NA	4	20	1.4	0.2
Catahoula	22	56	5.6	2.4	NA	NA	NA	NA	11	127	5.0	1.3
Claiborne	14	41	4.6	1.1	NA	NA	NA	NA	8	52	2.3	0.6
Concordia	23	108	8.1	2.2	NA	NA	NA	NA	27	410	17.8	4.2
De Soto	22	54	5.1	1.3	15	766	D	D	21	300	10.4	2.6
East Baton Rouge	1 684	D	D	D	334	11 054	D	669.1	896	22 590	998.3	277.2
East Carroll	8	D	D	D	NA	NA	NA	NA	9	59	2.1	0.5
East Feliciana	24	51	4.3	1.5	NA	NA	NA	NA	17	199	6.0	1.5
Evangeline	50	198	18.2	4.8	20	698	D	33.4	22	269	9.3	2.1
Franklin	30	586	12.1	6.1	NA	NA	NA	NA	23	354	14.3	3.1
Grant	8	21	0.8	0.2	NA	NA	NA	NA	4	D	D	D
Iberia	161	754	89.1	25.4	130	6 273	1 586.2	261.8	92	1 941	73.5	18.4
Iberville	34	292	30.7	19.9	31	3 461	7 694.7	283.5	35	491	17.9	5.0
Jackson	20	122	11.4	4.1	9	D	D	D	18	223	7.9	1.9
Jefferson	1 401	D	D	D	348	14 278	2 837.2	563.6	1 032	19 590	982.9	287.8
Jefferson Davis	59	245	20.4	7.7	13	530	189.2	21.2	41	734	26.7	6.7
Lafayette	1 135	D	D	D	286	8 790	2 037.2	352.1	513	12 494	584.6	156.1
Lafourche	161	D	D	D	59	3 265	614.3	120.5	159	2 446	106.6	26.3
La Salle	31	68	6.8	2.0	NA	NA	NA	NA	14	175	7.6	1.9
Lincoln	80	419	44.1	18.4	33	D	D	D	80	1 674	72.5	17.6
Livingston	122	D	D	D	68	1 884	459.9	80.3	121	2 388	89.2	24.4
Madison	11	D	D	D	NA	NA	NA	NA	19	276	9.4	2.0
Morehouse	26	D	D	D	15	741	D	D	26	490	19.8	4.7
Natchitoches	66	D	D	D	19	2 818	1 006.3	99.6	72	1 264	52.4	13.4

1. Establishment subject to federal tax.

STATE County	Health care and social assistance, 2007				Other services, 2007				Federal funds and grants, 2009–2010 Expenditures (mil dol)			
										Direct payments for individuals[1]		
	Number of establishments	Number of employees	Receipts (mil dol)	Annual payroll (mil dol)	Number of establishments	Number of employees	Receipts (mil dol)	Annual payroll (mil dol)	Total	Social Security and government retirement	Medicare	Food Stamps and Supplemental Security Income
	159	160	161	162	163	164	165	166	167	168	169	170
KENTUCKY—Cont'd												
Ohio	37	842	53.3	21.7	33	86	8.3	2.1	204.9	79.4	65.8	15.4
Oldham	110	1 881	139.5	61.0	82	431	30.3	8.8	160.8	86.1	41.2	3.8
Owen	8	201	15.8	6.8	12	40	2.8	0.6	78.1	23.3	27.1	5.5
Owsley	10	208	9.3	4.4	3	D	D	D	104.0	14.8	42.4	12.2
Pendleton	18	219	16.2	5.2	8	D	D	D	100.9	41.7	30.4	7.3
Perry	125	2 613	285.4	96.7	29	116	10.5	2.2	421.8	126.5	133.8	44.3
Pike	183	3 638	381.5	139.7	78	314	27.7	8.1	755.9	291.8	228.3	63.7
Powell	20	246	14.4	5.9	6	D	D	D	126.5	41.5	36.5	15.8
Pulaski	234	4 948	462.8	164.2	73	378	37.0	8.0	665.2	244.3	192.8	42.7
Robertson	4	D	D	D	1	D	D	D	22.0	6.6	8.2	1.4
Rockcastle	36	742	56.1	23.8	13	97	14.5	2.4	191.0	49.3	67.9	16.4
Rowan	74	1 718	153.8	60.1	26	166	6.9	2.1	226.4	62.4	62.6	14.3
Russell	47	802	47.2	19.4	19	54	4.3	0.9	316.5	59.9	73.9	13.1
Scott	80	D	D	D	62	277	21.1	5.8	212.1	101.3	56.5	10.2
Shelby	79	1 333	114.9	44.2	59	405	39.4	11.8	263.8	101.3	60.9	8.8
Simpson	37	378	34.9	10.3	26	126	12.3	3.2	137.5	51.0	49.2	4.9
Spencer	20	259	14.9	6.0	13	D	D	D	79.1	41.3	19.2	3.3
Taylor	79	1 249	100.7	39.8	47	159	10.2	2.6	264.8	90.7	76.6	16.2
Todd	13	193	12.3	3.6	13	50	2.8	1.0	123.0	34.1	46.4	4.8
Trigg	19	308	18.0	7.3	14	88	6.0	1.9	142.0	62.8	39.5	4.2
Trimble	8	D	D	D	5	D	D	D	58.9	24.8	17.7	3.1
Union	29	1 279	66.6	26.9	16	D	D	D	345.5	50.6	41.2	5.6
Warren	314	D	D	D	164	1 181	83.6	24.7	841.7	295.2	215.3	41.3
Washington	16	286	12.8	5.6	20	69	5.4	1.4	99.8	31.0	35.3	4.6
Wayne	38	D	D	D	25	66	4.8	1.1	271.7	60.0	106.9	19.7
Webster	23	D	D	D	22	D	D	D	129.7	49.9	40.0	6.7
Whitley	107	2 726	235.8	85.6	34	145	10.3	3.3	561.9	183.1	168.2	47.2
Wolfe	10	229	17.8	5.1	4	D	D	D	128.5	24.6	47.3	14.1
Woodford	48	D	D	D	39	197	12.4	3.6	146.8	73.3	31.6	5.7
LOUISIANA	11 545	256 079	23 685.4	8 860.6	6 637	42 223	4 664.2	1 170.0	53 214.2	11 959.7	8 702.9	2 359.5
Acadia	125	2 041	148.6	55.7	68	363	29.2	7.8	497.9	150.6	106.5	33.2
Allen	45	801	50.0	20.5	21	100	6.2	1.8	233.7	65.3	49.0	10.6
Ascension	152	2 232	140.7	57.8	138	940	109.6	32.1	451.4	216.4	108.3	29.2
Assumption	21	612	23.4	10.5	20	59	8.0	1.6	176.3	57.8	50.4	13.2
Avoyelles	91	2 066	104.9	41.9	44	128	10.6	2.8	408.6	119.9	91.2	29.7
Beauregard	60	1 182	78.5	31.5	39	140	12.7	3.6	254.7	127.1	54.0	13.2
Bienville	15	D	D	D	12	D	D	D	158.3	48.3	44.9	10.6
Bossier	207	3 397	281.4	119.5	146	990	66.9	20.5	1 327.8	366.8	118.1	95.5
Caddo	801	D	D	D	443	3 136	245.6	68.1	2 100.8	738.0	497.9	95.6
Calcasieu	515	10 926	1 025.2	348.4	280	D	D	D	1 441.4	544.6	331.7	72.1
Caldwell	23	534	32.7	14.4	15	D	D	D	103.0	31.4	33.3	5.5
Cameron	5	132	12.3	4.2	4	D	D	D	45.5	9.6	12.9	1.6
Catahoula	14	544	20.8	10.4	11	D	D	D	140.5	34.7	26.3	7.5
Claiborne	26	780	46.7	17.8	11	66	3.7	0.8	146.1	44.1	36.3	11.9
Concordia	46	743	48.1	20.1	25	99	6.2	1.8	219.5	59.0	43.2	14.6
De Soto	25	D	D	D	17	46	3.6	0.9	211.5	76.2	51.8	19.1
East Baton Rouge	1 386	36 001	3 477.8	1 247.2	909	6 732	776.3	206.2	9 253.9	991.4	663.7	189.6
East Carroll	12	300	15.7	7.4	7	D	D	D	120.0	17.1	27.3	11.1
East Feliciana	31	1 972	120.1	64.2	21	81	7.8	1.8	163.8	50.6	46.8	11.3
Evangeline	102	2 453	159.7	61.5	24	45	3.5	0.6	365.4	89.0	79.2	26.0
Franklin	53	1 068	65.6	26.2	20	69	6.0	1.2	244.3	54.1	60.2	15.6
Grant	17	D	D	D	6	25	1.4	0.4	204.6	62.8	39.3	10.4
Iberia	214	4 177	297.5	104.4	137	1 147	175.4	40.3	531.3	196.6	114.8	40.6
Iberville	47	D	D	D	41	285	25.4	8.6	356.9	88.3	82.7	21.6
Jackson	21	632	35.2	13.5	17	D	D	D	173.1	55.6	48.3	7.2
Jefferson	1 291	29 229	3 294.0	1 196.7	789	5 000	525.7	145.2	4 289.2	1 166.5	919.6	172.4
Jefferson Davis	76	1 485	106.9	42.0	39	133	9.0	2.1	234.1	87.1	56.8	13.7
Lafayette	951	19 023	1 871.8	681.0	448	3 481	311.8	87.5	1 285.4	479.2	250.5	65.5
Lafourche	185	3 167	335.1	120.8	115	586	57.7	15.3	987.2	235.4	155.5	40.7
La Salle	24	647	44.7	17.8	8	D	D	D	120.3	43.8	36.5	4.5
Lincoln	123	2 598	270.8	79.8	47	D	D	D	309.0	95.9	66.3	19.4
Livingston	131	1 632	88.1	35.0	108	620	55.0	14.4	520.4	272.1	128.2	29.4
Madison	35	795	37.6	17.6	17	33	2.6	0.4	150.7	25.5	34.7	10.4
Morehouse	85	1 709	102.7	39.4	29	140	9.1	2.4	357.7	94.0	86.1	23.1
Natchitoches	101	1 602	120.0	48.0	47	207	18.0	4.2	374.4	103.1	66.6	26.7

1. State totals may include programs not allocated by county.

	Federal funds and grants, 2009–2010 (cont.)							Value of residential construction authorized by building permits, 2010		Local government finances, 2007				
	Expenditures (mil dol) (cont.)									General revenue				
		Procurement contract awards		Grants[1]								Taxes		
													Per capita[2] (dollars)	
STATE County	Salaries and wages	Defense	Other	Medicaid and other health-related	Nutrition and family welfare	Education	Other	New construction ($1,000)	Number of housing units	Total (mil dol)	Inter-govern-mental (mil dol)	Total (mil dol)	Total	Property
	171	172	173	174	175	176	177	178	179	180	181	182	183	184
KENTUCKY—Cont'd														
Ohio	7.0	0.0	1.1	25.7	4.3	2.2	0.2	379	4	58.4	33.3	11.2	474	263
Oldham	7.6	0.2	1.7	9.8	4.7	2.2	0.6	25 435	113	127.2	48.9	58.2	1 041	868
Owen	1.8	0.0	0.4	13.4	1.8	1.0	0.0	699	10	27.7	20.2	5.7	497	360
Owsley	0.8	0.0	0.2	28.6	2.6	0.7	0.6	NA	NA	12.5	10.2	1.2	250	160
Pendleton	2.6	0.0	0.7	12.4	2.4	0.9	0.2	0	0	31.6	20.4	7.3	488	353
Perry	15.2	0.7	10.0	74.7	7.5	4.4	3.6	788	9	72.7	45.8	17.8	608	400
Pike	28.2	0.5	6.5	100.3	12.1	5.5	10.6	3 221	19	156.8	94.5	40.4	617	411
Powell	2.7	0.0	0.6	23.9	3.4	1.3	0.1	NA	NA	28.3	19.1	5.1	369	195
Pulaski	17.4	1.3	6.6	105.2	10.6	6.2	33.0	550	7	132.0	71.8	41.5	690	392
Robertson	0.4	0.0	0.1	3.7	0.5	0.4	0.0	NA	NA	5.7	4.2	1.1	518	384
Rockcastle	2.6	0.3	6.8	40.8	3.6	1.5	0.2	NA	NA	31.5	23.4	4.9	296	176
Rowan	18.1	0.1	2.2	36.2	3.3	6.2	2.0	84	3	46.9	23.5	16.2	718	312
Russell	4.6	107.9	0.9	40.7	9.3	1.6	2.4	300	4	53.3	22.9	9.7	569	334
Scott	5.4	0.6	1.3	22.3	3.5	1.8	3.1	24 494	185	145.1	37.9	63.6	1 479	447
Shelby	15.5	1.4	33.1	24.6	7.4	3.9	0.2	18 894	109	87.6	30.7	38.8	958	669
Simpson	2.8	0.0	1.0	18.4	2.2	1.3	0.2	2 687	23	46.0	23.4	14.9	871	423
Spencer	2.4	0.5	0.5	7.2	1.7	0.6	0.1	11 974	89	26.5	15.4	8.4	501	404
Taylor	10.5	22.1	1.6	30.0	3.2	2.0	2.8	3 158	47	102.0	52.7	16.4	684	343
Todd	2.5	0.0	0.5	22.4	2.1	0.9	1.1	914	11	26.4	17.9	4.9	403	227
Trigg	7.2	0.0	3.4	14.4	1.8	1.6	1.4	500	2	23.7	13.9	7.5	558	387
Trimble	1.3	0.0	0.3	5.9	1.9	0.7	0.3	NA	NA	34.0	10.6	4.7	525	327
Union	3.7	0.2	218.7	12.1	2.3	1.4	0.7	484	7	34.0	20.6	8.9	588	386
Warren	53.8	1.0	11.9	77.2	18.4	10.1	60.5	124 400	573	235.5	96.5	107.7	1 035	465
Washington	4.1	0.0	0.5	15.6	1.9	1.0	0.5	170	2	27.9	14.5	8.5	732	427
Wayne	6.0	0.0	0.5	65.8	5.1	1.6	4.2	0	0	40.7	29.6	7.9	383	196
Webster	3.2	0.0	6.2	14.7	2.5	0.9	1.1	216	2	35.7	21.3	6.6	472	351
Whitley	16.2	18.1	28.9	78.7	9.3	3.3	1.9	666	8	99.7	65.9	21.9	572	253
Wolfe	2.0	0.0	0.5	34.2	2.4	1.1	1.3	NA	NA	14.8	12.1	1.9	270	153
Woodford	3.6	0.0	1.0	13.4	2.5	2.2	2.4	6 143	50	63.5	22.3	27.9	1 149	572
LOUISIANA	4 702.5	5 841.7	1 448.9	6 250.9	1 238.6	943.3	6 654.8	1 765 181	11 343	X	X	X	X	X
Acadia	16.4	0.1	26.6	126.2	14.7	4.7	3.9	19 012	108	155.6	80.2	53.2	888	282
Allen	43.2	0.0	4.2	42.7	6.8	1.7	6.8	890	4	84.9	37.5	27.9	1 093	414
Ascension	17.4	0.4	3.8	48.8	13.3	5.1	1.6	96 549	711	291.5	102.4	153.6	1 551	579
Assumption	6.9	0.0	0.9	37.6	6.3	1.9	0.6	6 930	36	65.4	35.3	23.0	999	410
Avoyelles	12.4	1.9	1.9	118.4	11.9	3.4	2.8	4 537	39	97.7	56.6	22.8	541	116
Beauregard	8.1	0.6	1.6	37.1	5.6	2.8	0.5	4 916	28	123.0	43.9	37.9	1 090	466
Bienville	4.5	3.7	0.9	38.8	3.6	1.3	0.5	0	0	54.8	17.7	31.8	2 136	1 303
Bossier	461.0	154.8	6.4	60.9	18.2	7.6	11.8	128 146	956	374.6	123.2	192.7	1 773	566
Caddo	157.8	4.9	51.4	354.7	57.2	31.3	47.9	83 209	344	919.5	335.1	450.6	1 784	851
Calcasieu	99.9	40.8	72.3	147.8	31.9	16.3	47.5	119 984	910	841.8	255.5	382.9	2 075	708
Caldwell	3.5	0.1	0.3	21.3	2.8	1.2	0.6	1 382	7	26.8	15.4	7.5	726	288
Cameron	1.3	5.0	0.4	4.3	2.1	0.8	6.1	8 580	65	67.5	21.0	27.4	3 694	3 615
Catahoula	3.5	0.0	0.9	31.9	6.9	1.1	13.9	1 603	9	31.7	21.2	6.7	636	270
Claiborne	3.5	0.0	0.8	42.3	3.5	1.5	1.2	0	0	64.5	29.6	13.5	832	461
Concordia	5.0	16.4	1.1	51.8	5.5	1.9	5.9	2 104	19	91.9	44.5	18.8	989	504
De Soto	4.3	0.1	-6.7	55.6	6.0	2.3	0.5	0	0	105.8	43.2	47.5	1 810	891
East Baton Rouge	296.5	173.7	-77.1	436.1	273.4	451.3	5 712.1	205 864	1 129	1 551.6	445.1	768.5	1 786	648
East Carroll	1.8	0.0	0.5	38.1	4.2	1.3	1.0	0	0	41.1	26.1	5.5	659	333
East Feliciana	3.4	0.0	0.8	41.0	4.6	1.4	2.8	6 247	36	36.7	23.0	10.0	478	155
Evangeline	6.3	0.0	1.3	134.9	12.8	3.3	1.8	9 736	53	88.6	49.2	30.4	846	282
Franklin	15.1	0.0	1.5	69.6	6.8	2.4	0.6	6 549	35	70.2	36.9	14.6	728	215
Grant	46.2	0.0	5.4	31.8	4.0	1.7	0.8	6 402	37	46.4	30.6	11.3	572	206
Iberia	25.7	11.8	8.9	100.9	13.8	9.0	3.5	18 777	114	283.5	119.3	86.7	1 157	375
Iberville	44.3	23.1	10.0	67.0	9.4	4.9	3.3	6 196	34	120.0	36.5	68.6	2 111	875
Jackson	21.9	0.0	0.7	26.8	5.4	1.2	4.9	5 140	23	62.2	29.7	21.5	1 420	417
Jefferson	253.0	1 122.5	208.1	252.7	65.9	31.5	56.2	44 275	274	1 965.7	501.8	689.0	1 627	575
Jefferson Davis	6.7	0.1	0.9	43.3	7.7	3.0	5.0	11 196	91	94.1	47.0	31.0	994	436
Lafayette	133.0	9.4	31.9	150.2	34.3	24.4	43.4	94 430	689	625.8	195.8	313.3	1 530	499
Lafourche	14.9	84.7	327.2	70.4	18.5	8.4	16.6	39 218	204	438.6	144.7	120.6	1 301	563
La Salle	6.6	0.0	0.7	22.3	2.4	1.0	0.7	349	3	79.2	28.8	12.8	915	536
Lincoln	10.3	0.2	1.7	52.6	9.1	8.9	15.3	5 929	29	118.5	44.7	56.1	1 319	536
Livingston	14.5	0.0	2.4	48.3	13.9	6.1	2.9	114 365	812	281.4	146.1	100.6	863	266
Madison	2.5	0.0	3.3	45.1	7.4	1.7	0.7	1 502	14	40.0	22.9	11.3	957	466
Morehouse	7.1	1.9	1.3	90.3	9.4	3.9	9.2	3 100	21	116.8	47.6	29.6	1 028	423
Natchitoches	22.2	2.2	2.8	101.0	10.9	6.3	5.3	9 623	54	164.3	68.0	45.6	1 156	402

1. State totals may include programs not allocated by county.   2. Based on the resident population estimated as of July 1 of the year shown.

Table B. States and Counties — **Local Government Finances, Government Employment, and Voting**

	Local government finances, 2007 (cont.)										Government employment, 2009			Presidential election,[2] 2008		
	Direct general expenditure							Debt outstanding						Percent of vote cast:		
			Percent of total for:													
STATE County	Total (mil dol)	Per capita[1] (dollars)	Education	Health and hospitals	Police protection	Public welfare	Highways	Total (mil dol)	Per capita[1] (dollars)	Federal civilian	Federal military	State and local	Democratic	Republican	All other
	185	186	187	188	189	190	191	192	193	194	195	196	197	198	199
KENTUCKY—Cont'd															
Ohio	53.7	2 278	53.4	2.0	3.0	0.2	3.9	185.7	7 883	110	74	1 396	40.8	57.2	1.9
Oldham	130.5	2 333	66.5	2.5	4.3	0.0	3.0	459.0	8 206	74	184	3 689	34.1	64.8	1.1
Owen	20.9	1 834	68.6	2.1	2.9	0.0	6.7	10.7	940	27	36	490	35.7	62.5	1.9
Owsley	12.4	2 690	70.6	0.7	3.3	0.0	10.2	6.8	1 483	12	15	319	22.6	75.9	1.5
Pendleton	31.1	2 063	71.3	2.6	2.9	0.0	5.2	42.1	2 799	36	47	672	34.9	63.4	1.7
Perry	74.9	2 565	56.5	2.4	2.1	0.3	6.1	245.3	8 397	158	92	2 472	33.2	65.2	1.6
Pike	142.1	2 168	61.2	1.2	1.6	0.4	5.2	148.5	2 266	328	206	3 220	42.1	55.9	2.0
Powell	30.9	2 241	68.8	6.6	2.4	0.0	2.5	21.0	1 524	35	43	840	41.5	57.1	1.4
Pulaski	131.6	2 187	56.4	3.4	4.0	0.1	5.6	180.1	2 995	191	192	3 866	21.7	77.1	1.2
Robertson	5.3	2 397	66.4	0.8	2.1	0.0	8.0	3.2	1 474	0	0	172	44.4	52.5	3.1
Rockcastle	38.9	2 330	75.4	1.9	2.5	0.0	4.7	37.3	2 233	35	52	757	22.5	75.8	1.7
Rowan	49.2	2 180	51.6	2.1	4.3	0.2	6.9	37.0	1 640	83	76	3 303	50.0	47.9	2.1
Russell	56.2	3 278	49.1	29.8	2.6	0.3	2.8	63.4	3 696	80	55	1 001	21.0	77.3	1.7
Scott	136.7	3 182	44.9	1.7	4.6	5.9	2.9	717.3	16 698	62	144	1 967	39.1	59.7	1.2
Shelby	85.1	2 104	52.5	2.0	3.8	0.1	3.1	188.2	4 652	83	132	1 935	37.1	61.8	1.2
Simpson	45.8	2 682	54.8	2.9	3.7	1.8	3.5	73.1	4 285	35	54	787	38.0	60.7	1.3
Spencer	25.3	1 503	67.6	2.1	3.4	0.2	4.2	38.3	2 273	28	56	572	31.3	66.8	1.9
Taylor	97.6	4 079	28.2	53.1	2.2	0.0	2.1	93.9	3 928	96	77	1 745	29.1	69.7	1.2
Todd	24.4	2 023	62.6	1.9	3.3	0.0	5.8	88.0	7 309	37	39	637	31.2	67.5	1.3
Trigg	23.3	1 742	65.3	2.3	4.3	0.0	7.2	10.2	764	92	42	679	34.4	64.2	1.4
Trimble	32.5	3 614	33.6	0.9	0.6	0.0	3.3	533.2	59 351	16	28	365	38.9	58.7	2.3
Union	34.5	2 283	60.9	0.2	5.1	0.2	3.8	30.0	1 986	50	47	734	46.5	51.7	1.8
Warren	236.2	2 270	50.8	0.6	7.0	0.1	4.3	810.4	7 791	473	347	9 232	40.0	58.9	1.1
Washington	25.9	2 245	50.3	3.3	3.3	0.1	8.3	77.3	6 688	34	35	464	35.8	62.7	1.5
Wayne	47.4	2 295	72.2	2.8	2.7	0.0	4.3	55.1	2 671	41	65	1 033	30.6	67.6	1.8
Webster	36.7	2 642	49.5	1.8	2.9	0.0	4.5	70.6	5 086	42	43	679	43.1	54.8	2.0
Whitley	97.9	2 553	70.6	1.0	2.5	0.0	2.3	110.1	2 870	107	122	2 326	25.4	73.1	1.5
Wolfe	14.4	2 040	74.0	0.1	1.6	0.1	5.0	12.6	1 796	27	22	413	50.3	47.4	2.3
Woodford	54.4	2 237	45.9	2.0	10.3	0.1	5.5	134.4	5 526	47	79	1 458	40.9	58.0	1.1
LOUISIANA	X	X	X	X	X	X	X	X	X	32 144	36 356	336 887	39.9	58.6	1.5
Acadia	143.9	2 400	52.3	6.3	6.1	0.2	4.3	65.6	1 094	104	250	2 998	26.3	72.0	1.7
Allen	76.8	3 010	52.5	17.0	6.1	0.0	4.9	24.5	961	602	107	4 067	30.5	66.9	2.6
Ascension	270.4	2 730	60.0	4.3	5.6	0.0	4.4	210.5	2 125	144	436	4 543	31.4	67.1	1.5
Assumption	54.2	2 357	69.7	0.2	4.6	0.9	3.8	10.7	464	34	95	1 106	43.4	54.6	2.0
Avoyelles	91.4	2 167	48.5	11.1	10.9	0.0	4.5	26.4	627	88	177	4 372	37.4	60.4	2.2
Beauregard	111.6	3 209	44.3	27.3	5.7	0.0	4.8	32.9	946	74	147	1 578	21.8	76.2	2.0
Bienville	44.3	2 969	59.1	2.3	5.1	0.2	7.1	10.4	701	54	61	714	48.3	50.8	0.9
Bossier	338.9	3 118	50.1	2.1	9.5	0.0	5.9	241.0	2 217	1 922	5 622	6 869	27.7	71.4	0.9
Caddo	887.0	3 511	48.5	1.1	7.4	0.0	2.8	919.2	3 639	2 655	1 053	21 728	51.1	48.1	0.8
Calcasieu	775.8	4 204	37.3	6.9	6.3	0.2	6.3	997.3	5 405	618	869	14 394	36.8	61.4	1.8
Caldwell	25.4	2 463	60.6	8.3	3.4	0.2	3.3	2.6	252	28	43	782	22.8	75.5	1.6
Cameron	52.0	7 010	53.0	7.8	4.7	0.1	6.8	14.0	1 885	18	27	755	16.2	81.4	2.4
Catahoula	33.2	3 181	44.2	7.1	5.0	0.5	6.4	3.0	289	51	44	724	31.8	66.7	1.5
Claiborne	61.0	3 747	39.8	25.8	3.4	0.6	2.9	27.9	1 712	41	67	1 474	44.2	54.8	1.0
Concordia	90.6	4 754	40.6	14.9	6.4	0.0	2.0	17.3	910	68	79	1 636	39.5	59.5	1.0
De Soto	103.6	3 942	58.3	1.2	4.1	0.5	4.5	142.9	5 438	53	110	1 541	42.8	56.2	1.1
East Baton Rouge	1 364.3	3 171	41.2	5.4	7.2	0.2	4.8	1 905.5	4 428	2 707	2 230	52 754	50.5	48.3	1.2
East Carroll	41.1	4 945	34.4	16.7	4.4	0.0	2.5	12.4	1 493	26	34	915	63.7	35.2	1.1
East Feliciana	37.0	1 778	62.8	0.3	8.7	0.2	9.7	18.1	868	38	88	2 954	44.1	54.6	1.3
Evangeline	85.6	2 385	63.1	0.4	5.1	0.0	5.0	38.6	1 075	65	147	1 947	36.6	61.3	2.1
Franklin	68.4	3 412	41.0	24.5	8.7	0.3	3.5	6.0	300	64	82	1 376	31.6	67.1	1.3
Grant	43.8	2 216	60.6	0.5	5.3	0.0	9.5	29.2	1 477	646	94	937	17.2	80.7	2.1
Iberia	285.0	3 802	47.4	18.9	5.4	0.1	1.9	128.0	1 708	115	313	4 476	37.7	60.7	1.7
Iberville	106.8	3 286	43.8	0.2	8.9	1.0	8.1	58.2	1 792	143	135	3 186	54.9	43.8	1.3
Jackson	59.0	3 895	40.6	11.1	4.3	0.0	4.9	75.8	5 009	34	63	1 010	31.7	67.1	1.2
Jefferson	1 843.7	4 353	25.7	33.1	5.7	0.5	4.1	1 779.5	4 202	1 530	2 415	21 706	35.9	62.5	1.6
Jefferson Davis	89.3	2 865	61.2	1.2	8.0	0.1	3.8	54.0	1 732	69	129	1 924	29.1	68.7	2.2
Lafayette	581.3	2 838	44.0	0.5	7.3	0.0	6.5	995.1	4 858	1 052	890	13 825	33.6	64.9	1.5
Lafourche	423.6	4 569	34.4	33.4	3.9	0.2	4.0	206.0	2 222	151	400	7 081	25.5	71.5	3.0
La Salle	73.3	5 221	38.9	35.8	4.1	0.0	2.1	5.6	397	35	58	1 364	13.1	85.5	1.4
Lincoln	119.4	2 806	59.5	0.3	5.2	1.4	3.7	53.9	1 266	111	191	4 816	43.2	55.7	1.1
Livingston	304.8	2 614	56.4	0.8	4.6	0.0	10.8	406.7	3 488	147	513	5 466	13.1	85.0	1.9
Madison	36.2	3 049	53.7	0.1	4.4	0.4	5.6	54.0	4 554	42	47	1 143	58.5	40.6	0.9
Morehouse	114.3	3 970	38.0	23.8	4.5	0.1	1.6	183.0	6 359	72	117	1 371	43.9	55.0	1.1
Natchitoches	150.7	3 816	38.8	27.3	4.4	0.5	1.3	63.5	1 609	198	167	4 070	45.7	53.0	1.2

1. Based on the resident population estimated as of July 1 of the year shown.   2. © 2009 Election Data Services, Inc. All rights reserved.

Table B. States and Counties — **Land Area and Population**

STATE/ County code	CBSA code[1]	County type[2]	STATE County	Land area,[3] (sq km) 2010	Total persons	Rank	Per square kilometer	Race alone or in combination, not Hispanic or Latino (percent) White	Black	American Indian, Alaska Native	Asian and Pacific Islander	Percent Hispanic or Latino[4]	Age (percent) Under 5 years	5 to 17 years	18 to 24 years	25 to 34 years	35 to 44 years	45 to 54 years
				1	2	3	4	5	6	7	8	9	10	11	12	13	14	15
			LOUISIANA—Cont'd															
22 071	35380	1	Orleans	439	343 829	189	783.2	31.4	60.4	0.6	3.3	5.2	6.4	14.9	12.8	16.4	12.4	14.2
22 073	33740	3	Ouachita	1 581	153 720	407	97.2	60.4	37.0	0.6	1.2	1.8	7.3	19.0	11.3	13.5	12.2	13.4
22 075	35380	1	Plaquemines	2 020	23 042	1 687	11.4	69.7	21.2	2.4	3.9	4.6	6.9	20.6	8.4	12.6	14.0	15.2
22 077	12940	2	Pointe Coupee	1 444	22 802	1 695	15.8	61.0	36.8	0.4	0.4	2.2	6.2	17.8	7.9	11.1	11.3	15.8
22 079	10780	3	Rapides	3 414	131 613	467	38.6	63.3	32.6	1.4	1.6	2.6	7.0	18.9	9.0	13.0	12.2	14.4
22 081	...	6	Red River	1 008	9 091	2 519	9.0	58.8	39.9	0.5	0.2	1.1	7.3	18.1	8.7	12.2	11.3	14.6
22 083	...	6	Richland	1 448	20 725	1 809	14.3	62.0	36.1	0.5	0.5	1.6	7.1	18.4	8.8	12.8	11.8	14.6
22 085	...	6	Sabine	2 245	24 233	1 636	10.8	71.8	17.3	10.0	0.4	3.4	6.8	17.6	8.2	11.2	11.4	13.9
22 087	35380	1	St. Bernard	978	35 897	1 276	36.7	70.3	18.3	1.3	2.4	9.2	7.9	17.6	11.3	15.8	12.6	15.0
22 089	35380	1	St. Charles	723	52 780	938	73.0	67.2	26.9	0.7	1.1	5.0	7.0	19.9	8.4	12.9	13.8	16.8
22 091	12940	2	St. Helena	1 058	11 203	2 350	10.6	45.2	53.5	0.7	0.2	0.9	7.4	17.2	9.5	11.4	11.1	15.3
22 093	...	6	St. James	626	22 102	1 734	35.3	47.8	50.9	0.5	0.2	1.2	6.9	18.9	9.4	12.1	11.9	15.5
22 095	35380	1	St. John the Baptist	552	45 924	1 049	83.2	40.9	53.8	0.6	1.0	4.7	7.3	19.6	9.4	13.0	13.1	15.5
22 097	36660	4	St. Landry	2 393	83 384	663	34.8	56.1	41.9	0.6	0.5	1.6	7.6	19.6	8.9	12.0	11.6	14.6
22 099	29180	3	St. Martin	1 910	52 160	953	27.3	65.9	31.2	0.7	1.0	2.1	7.3	19.1	9.1	12.9	13.0	15.3
22 101	34020	4	St. Mary	1 438	54 650	915	38.0	58.5	33.2	2.3	2.0	5.3	6.9	18.5	9.4	12.4	12.4	15.8
22 103	35380	1	St. Tammany	2 190	233 740	274	106.7	81.8	12.0	1.0	1.7	4.7	6.5	19.2	7.2	11.6	13.5	16.0
22 105	25220	4	Tangipahoa	2 049	121 097	498	59.1	65.2	30.7	0.7	0.9	3.5	7.2	17.9	12.8	13.7	11.7	13.6
22 107	...	9	Tensas	1 561	5 252	2 824	3.4	42.0	56.8	0.4	0.2	1.2	7.0	18.3	7.4	9.8	9.9	14.9
22 109	26380	3	Terrebonne	3 190	111 860	530	35.1	70.1	19.6	6.8	1.4	4.0	7.3	18.8	10.1	13.9	12.8	14.8
22 111	33740	3	Union	2 271	22 721	1 696	10.0	68.2	27.3	0.5	0.3	4.2	6.5	16.5	8.6	11.7	11.5	14.9
22 113	10020	4	Vermilion	3 039	57 999	879	19.1	80.9	14.8	0.7	2.2	2.4	7.4	19.3	8.7	13.0	12.5	15.0
22 115	22860	4	Vernon	3 439	52 334	944	15.2	75.0	15.3	2.3	3.4	7.2	9.2	18.5	13.4	16.9	12.7	11.0
22 117	14220	6	Washington	1 734	47 168	1 021	27.2	66.6	31.4	0.7	0.4	1.9	6.8	18.4	8.2	12.4	11.8	14.8
22 119	33380	6	Webster	1 536	41 207	1 151	26.8	64.1	33.9	0.8	0.5	1.6	6.4	17.2	8.5	11.7	11.9	14.7
22 121	12940	2	West Baton Rouge	498	23 788	1 652	47.8	59.4	38.2	0.5	0.5	2.3	7.0	17.9	10.0	14.1	12.8	15.6
22 123	...	9	West Carroll	931	11 604	2 323	12.5	81.1	16.0	0.7	0.3	2.6	6.6	18.0	7.9	12.0	11.9	14.2
22 125	12940	2	West Feliciana	1 044	15 625	2 074	15.0	51.5	46.6	0.4	0.3	1.6	4.0	13.4	5.7	14.2	18.3	19.9
22 127	...	6	Winn	2 461	15 313	2 093	6.2	66.9	30.9	1.2	0.4	1.6	6.3	16.1	8.4	13.6	13.1	15.0
23 000	...	X	MAINE	79 883	1 328 361	X	16.6	95.8	1.6	1.3	1.4	1.3	5.2	15.4	8.7	10.9	12.9	16.5
23 001	30340	3	Androscoggin	1 212	107 702	547	88.9	93.6	4.3	1.1	1.1	1.5	6.4	16.2	9.3	12.0	13.4	15.8
23 003	...	7	Aroostook	17 279	71 870	745	4.2	96.3	0.9	2.5	0.6	0.9	4.9	15.1	8.0	9.6	12.0	16.1
23 005	38860	2	Cumberland	2 163	281 674	228	130.2	93.3	2.9	0.8	2.7	1.8	5.2	15.7	9.0	12.1	13.8	16.4
23 007	...	6	Franklin	4 394	30 768	1 418	7.0	97.9	0.5	1.2	0.7	1.0	4.9	14.7	11.6	9.6	11.3	16.5
23 009	...	6	Hancock	4 110	54 418	919	13.2	97.2	0.6	1.0	1.1	1.1	4.8	13.6	8.0	9.7	11.9	16.7
23 011	12300	4	Kennebec	2 247	122 151	495	54.4	96.9	1.0	1.3	1.1	1.2	5.2	15.5	8.6	10.9	13.0	16.8
23 013	40500	7	Knox	946	39 736	1 177	42.0	97.8	0.8	1.2	0.7	0.8	4.8	14.6	6.3	10.1	12.5	16.2
23 015	...	8	Lincoln	1 181	34 457	1 314	29.2	98.0	0.5	0.9	0.8	0.8	4.7	14.1	6.0	8.9	11.7	16.0
23 017	...	6	Oxford	5 379	57 833	881	10.8	97.5	0.6	1.2	0.9	1.0	5.1	16.2	7.1	10.0	12.2	17.4
23 019	12620	3	Penobscot	8 799	153 923	406	17.5	96.0	1.1	2.0	1.3	1.1	5.2	14.5	13.2	11.5	12.3	15.7
23 021	...	8	Piscataquis	10 259	17 535	1 947	1.7	97.4	0.5	1.1	1.0	1.0	4.4	14.8	5.8	8.3	12.2	16.8
23 023	38860	2	Sagadahoc	657	35 293	1 291	53.7	96.8	1.2	0.9	1.2	1.3	5.4	15.6	6.5	10.3	13.4	17.4
23 025	...	6	Somerset	10 164	52 228	950	5.1	97.7	0.7	1.2	0.8	0.8	5.2	16.2	7.0	10.3	13.5	16.1
23 027	...	6	Waldo	1 890	38 786	1 200	20.5	97.9	0.6	1.3	0.6	0.9	5.3	15.7	7.5	10.4	12.3	16.1
23 029	...	7	Washington	6 637	32 856	1 364	5.0	92.8	0.6	6.0	0.7	1.4	5.1	14.9	7.2	9.8	11.6	15.8
23 031	38860	2	York	2 566	197 131	318	76.8	96.8	0.9	0.9	1.4	1.3	5.2	16.1	7.7	10.6	13.3	17.2
24 000	...	X	MARYLAND	25 142	5 773 552	X	229.6	56.4	30.2	0.8	6.4	8.2	6.3	17.1	9.7	13.2	13.8	15.6
24 001	19060	3	Allegany	1 099	75 087	724	68.3	89.6	8.9	0.5	1.0	1.4	4.7	13.3	12.8	12.1	12.4	14.2
24 003	12580	1	Anne Arundel	1 075	537 656	116	500.1	74.5	16.4	0.8	4.5	6.1	6.4	16.8	9.1	13.4	14.1	16.0
24 005	12580	1	Baltimore	1 550	805 029	67	519.4	64.3	26.9	0.8	5.8	4.2	6.0	16.0	10.2	12.9	12.8	15.5
24 009	47900	1	Calvert	552	88 737	642	160.8	81.8	14.5	1.1	2.3	2.7	5.6	20.6	8.0	9.8	14.2	18.6
24 011	...	6	Caroline	827	33 066	1 356	40.0	79.8	14.8	0.8	0.8	5.5	7.0	18.2	8.6	11.9	13.0	15.6
24 013	12580	1	Carroll	1 159	167 134	367	144.2	92.4	3.7	0.5	2.0	2.6	5.4	19.3	8.3	9.2	14.2	17.8
24 015	37980	1	Cecil	897	101 108	576	112.7	89.1	7.0	0.8	1.6	3.4	6.4	18.7	8.6	11.5	14.2	16.4
24 017	47900	1	Charles	1 186	146 551	425	123.6	50.8	42.6	1.7	4.0	4.3	6.4	20.1	8.7	11.7	15.8	16.9
24 019	15700	6	Dorchester	1 401	32 618	1 373	23.3	67.6	28.5	0.9	1.2	3.5	6.2	15.4	7.9	10.8	11.9	15.9
24 021	47900	1	Frederick	1 710	233 385	275	136.5	79.8	9.5	0.8	4.7	7.3	6.4	18.9	8.3	11.8	14.9	16.9
24 023	...	6	Garrett	1 676	30 097	1 426	18.0	97.9	1.2	0.4	0.4	0.7	5.2	17.0	8.1	10.1	12.7	15.6
24 025	12580	1	Harford	1 132	244 826	265	216.3	81.1	13.6	0.7	3.2	3.5	6.1	18.6	8.2	11.5	13.9	16.7
24 027	12580	1	Howard	649	287 085	224	442.3	61.7	18.6	0.7	16.0	5.8	6.0	20.0	7.2	12.3	14.9	17.3
24 029	...	6	Kent	718	20 197	1 829	28.1	79.5	15.9	0.6	1.1	4.5	4.9	12.6	12.6	9.1	10.0	14.5
24 031	47900	1	Montgomery	1 272	971 777	42	764.0	51.4	17.8	0.6	15.5	17.0	6.6	17.5	7.5	13.6	14.5	15.8
24 033	47900	1	Prince George's	1 250	863 420	59	690.7	16.2	65.1	0.9	4.8	14.9	6.8	17.1	11.7	14.6	14.4	14.8
24 035	12580	1	Queen Anne's	963	47 798	1 007	49.6	88.7	7.5	0.7	1.5	3.0	5.7	18.1	7.0	9.1	14.0	17.7

1. CBSA = Core Based Statistical Area. See Appendix A for explanation. See Appendix B for list of metropolitan areas with component counties.   2. County type code from the Economic Research Service of USDA Rural-Urban Continuum Codes. See Appendix A for definition.   3. Dry land or land partially or temporarily covered by water.   4. May be of any race.

Table B. States and Counties — **Population and Households**

STATE County	Population, 2010 (cont.) Age (percent) (cont.) 55 to 64 years	65 to 74 years	75 years and over	Percent female	Population change and components of change, 1990–2010 Total persons 1990	2000	Percent change 1990–2000	2000–2010	Components of change, 2000–2009 Births	Deaths	Net migration	Households, 2010 Number	Percent change, 2000–2010	Persons per household	Percent Female family householder[1]	One person
	16	17	18	19	20	21	22	23	24	25	26	27	28	29	30	31
LOUISIANA—Cont'd																
Orleans	12.0	6.1	4.9	51.6	496 938	484 674	-2.5	-29.1	51 756	38 663	-219 414	142 158	-24.5	2.33	20.9	35.9
Ouachita	11.0	6.6	5.7	52.2	142 191	147 250	3.6	4.4	21 477	12 874	-3 444	58 691	6.3	2.52	20.0	27.9
Plaquemines	11.1	6.4	4.8	49.8	25 575	26 757	4.6	-13.9	3 289	1 843	-7 244	8 077	-10.5	2.82	14.8	20.1
Pointe Coupee	14.4	8.4	7.1	51.5	22 540	22 763	1.0	0.2	2 876	2 215	-861	9 082	8.2	2.50	15.9	26.8
Rapides	12.0	7.6	6.0	51.8	131 556	126 337	-4.0	4.2	17 942	12 369	-151	50 401	7.0	2.52	18.4	27.2
Red River	12.5	8.9	6.4	52.2	9 526	9 622	1.0	-5.5	1 343	993	-919	3 472	1.7	2.57	17.7	25.6
Richland	12.2	8.0	6.4	51.8	20 629	20 981	1.7	-1.2	2 811	2 279	-984	7 551	0.8	2.61	19.2	25.1
Sabine	13.6	10.2	7.0	50.4	22 646	23 459	3.6	3.3	3 039	2 368	-247	9 622	4.3	2.47	13.6	26.5
St. Bernard	10.6	5.3	3.9	49.4	66 631	67 229	0.9	-46.6	6 170	5 437	-41 344	13 221	-47.4	2.69	19.5	23.7
St. Charles	11.4	5.6	4.3	50.6	42 437	48 072	13.3	9.8	6 417	3 282	653	18 557	13.0	2.81	16.3	18.8
St. Helena	14.0	8.2	5.9	50.7	9 874	10 525	6.6	6.4	1 042	946	-16	4 333	11.9	2.56	19.3	28.7
St. James	12.4	7.4	5.5	51.1	20 879	21 216	1.6	4.2	2 872	1 748	-1 191	7 717	10.4	2.84	20.5	20.5
St. John the Baptist	11.8	6.3	4.0	51.4	39 996	43 044	7.6	6.7	6 599	3 067	724	15 965	11.8	2.85	20.9	20.1
St. Landry	12.0	7.7	6.1	52.2	80 312	87 700	9.2	-4.9	12 941	8 457	692	31 857	-1.5	2.58	19.2	26.8
St. Martin	11.7	7.0	4.6	50.7	44 097	48 583	10.2	7.4	6 973	3 929	885	19 216	12.0	2.68	17.0	23.1
St. Mary	11.7	7.5	5.4	50.6	58 086	53 500	-7.9	2.1	7 285	4 717	-5 034	20 457	5.9	2.63	18.0	25.8
St. Tammany	13.3	7.3	5.4	51.2	144 500	191 268	32.4	22.2	27 070	15 525	29 593	87 521	26.4	2.66	12.4	22.0
Tangipahoa	11.7	6.7	4.7	51.4	85 709	100 588	17.4	20.4	15 811	9 603	12 437	45 135	23.5	2.60	17.4	24.9
Tensas	15.4	9.6	7.7	52.5	7 103	6 618	-6.8	-20.6	779	656	-1 112	2 172	-10.1	2.41	23.0	32.6
Terrebonne	11.1	6.6	4.7	50.3	96 982	104 503	7.8	7.0	15 805	8 070	-2 338	40 091	11.4	2.75	15.7	21.9
Union	13.8	9.6	6.9	50.6	20 796	22 803	9.7	-0.4	2 986	2 338	-735	9 144	3.2	2.44	15.3	26.7
Vermilion	11.2	7.0	6.0	51.4	50 055	53 807	7.5	7.8	7 483	4 963	-61	21 889	10.4	2.63	14.5	24.1
Vernon	8.9	5.7	3.7	48.8	61 961	52 531	-15.2	-0.4	8 578	3 101	-11 218	19 165	5.0	2.61	11.5	24.6
Washington	13.2	8.3	6.2	50.5	43 185	43 926	1.7	7.4	5 927	5 182	1 227	18 113	10.0	2.52	18.3	28.1
Webster	12.9	9.1	7.6	51.4	41 989	41 831	-0.4	-1.5	4 909	4 959	-971	16 537	0.2	2.42	17.6	28.7
West Baton Rouge	11.6	6.6	4.4	50.8	19 419	21 601	11.2	10.1	2 942	1 696	-100	8 688	13.4	2.67	18.6	23.3
West Carroll	12.4	9.5	7.3	49.9	12 093	12 314	1.8	-6.8	1 367	1 309	-982	4 452	-0.1	2.51	13.2	26.2
West Feliciana	14.4	6.2	3.9	34.4	12 915	15 111	17.0	3.4	1 079	966	-88	3 971	8.9	2.60	16.0	24.4
Winn	13.1	8.3	6.1	47.6	16 498	16 894	2.4	-9.4	1 837	1 816	-1 517	5 469	-7.8	2.48	17.4	28.0
MAINE	14.5	8.5	7.4	51.1	1 227 928	1 274 923	3.8	4.2	128 319	116 170	38 804	557 219	7.5	2.32	10.0	28.6
Androscoggin	12.8	7.3	6.8	51.1	105 259	103 793	-1.4	3.8	12 088	9 615	871	44 315	5.4	2.37	12.0	28.3
Aroostook	15.3	10.0	9.0	50.8	86 936	73 938	-15.0	-2.8	6 444	7 841	-595	30 961	2.0	2.26	9.4	30.8
Cumberland	13.5	7.3	6.9	51.5	243 135	265 612	9.2	6.0	27 657	22 138	9 011	117 339	8.7	2.32	9.7	29.7
Franklin	14.8	9.5	7.3	51.1	29 008	29 467	1.6	4.4	2 587	2 507	376	13 000	10.1	2.28	9.4	28.9
Hancock	17.0	10.0	8.2	51.0	46 948	51 791	10.3	5.1	4 780	5 192	2 343	24 221	10.8	2.20	8.2	30.3
Kennebec	14.5	8.2	7.3	51.3	115 904	117 114	1.0	4.3	11 554	10 659	3 788	51 128	7.2	2.32	10.6	28.8
Knox	16.4	10.0	9.1	50.5	36 310	39 618	9.1	0.3	3 747	4 090	1 732	17 258	3.9	2.22	9.4	31.0
Lincoln	17.2	11.7	9.8	51.0	30 357	33 616	10.7	2.5	2 823	3 515	1 855	15 149	7.0	2.24	8.8	28.9
Oxford	15.0	9.2	7.8	50.4	52 602	54 755	4.1	5.6	5 176	5 613	2 262	24 300	8.9	2.35	10.4	27.1
Penobscot	13.2	7.6	6.9	50.7	146 601	144 919	-1.1	6.2	14 718	12 774	3 491	62 966	8.4	2.33	10.3	28.0
Piscataquis	17.3	11.5	8.8	50.4	18 653	17 235	-7.6	1.7	1 492	2 024	185	7 825	7.5	2.21	8.5	30.5
Sagadahoc	15.0	9.5	6.9	51.6	33 535	35 214	5.0	0.2	3 786	3 018	552	15 088	6.9	2.32	10.1	27.1
Somerset	14.9	9.2	7.2	50.4	49 767	50 888	2.3	2.6	5 019	4 753	122	21 927	7.0	2.35	10.3	26.9
Waldo	16.5	9.3	6.9	51.0	33 018	36 280	9.9	6.9	3 698	3 246	1 737	16 431	11.6	2.33	9.9	27.7
Washington	16.1	10.7	8.8	50.7	35 308	33 941	-3.9	-3.2	3 230	3 951	-900	14 302	1.3	2.24	9.6	31.6
York	14.5	8.3	7.1	51.3	164 587	186 742	13.5	5.6	19 520	15 234	11 974	81 009	8.6	2.40	9.7	26.5
MARYLAND	12.1	6.7	5.6	51.6	4 780 753	5 296 486	10.8	9.0	698 269	405 035	95 290	2 156 411	8.9	2.61	14.6	26.1
Allegany	12.7	9.1	8.8	48.3	74 946	74 930	0.0	0.2	6 474	8 339	-56	29 177	-0.5	2.30	11.0	31.6
Anne Arundel	12.4	6.9	5.0	50.6	427 239	489 656	14.6	9.8	63 788	33 792	4 603	199 378	11.6	2.63	12.1	23.7
Baltimore	12.6	7.0	7.6	52.7	692 134	754 292	9.0	6.7	89 136	70 860	22 145	316 715	5.6	2.48	14.5	28.3
Calvert	12.3	6.3	4.6	50.7	51 372	74 563	45.1	9.9	9 311	5 325	10 955	30 873	21.3	2.85	11.3	18.1
Caroline	12.3	7.4	5.9	51.2	27 035	29 772	10.1	11.1	4 101	2 886	2 543	12 158	9.6	2.68	13.6	22.7
Carroll	12.7	7.1	5.9	50.6	123 372	150 897	22.3	10.8	17 806	11 724	13 711	59 786	13.9	2.74	8.6	20.0
Cecil	12.6	6.8	4.9	50.3	71 347	85 951	20.5	17.6	11 463	6 992	10 833	36 867	18.1	2.70	12.0	21.8
Charles	10.9	5.8	3.6	51.7	101 154	120 546	19.2	21.6	17 152	7 707	12 796	51 214	22.9	2.83	16.3	19.8
Dorchester	14.2	9.8	7.9	52.3	30 236	30 674	1.4	6.3	3 397	3 550	1 691	13 522	6.4	2.37	16.0	28.4
Frederick	11.8	6.0	5.1	50.8	150 208	195 277	30.0	19.5	27 838	13 001	18 933	84 800	21.0	2.70	10.0	22.0
Garrett	14.1	9.9	7.5	50.3	28 138	29 846	6.1	0.8	2 884	2 799	-204	12 057	5.1	2.45	9.3	25.5
Harford	12.5	7.1	5.4	51.1	182 132	218 590	20.0	12.0	27 353	15 555	13 364	90 218	13.2	2.68	11.3	21.5
Howard	12.1	6.1	4.0	51.0	187 328	247 842	32.3	15.8	32 121	12 154	15 708	104 749	16.3	2.72	10.5	21.9
Kent	14.5	11.4	10.4	52.3	17 842	19 197	7.6	5.2	1 750	2 294	1 690	8 165	6.5	2.29	10.9	29.6
Montgomery	12.2	6.4	5.9	52.0	762 875	873 341	14.5	11.3	125 028	50 457	21 718	357 086	10.0	2.70	11.3	25.0
Prince George's	11.2	5.8	3.6	52.0	722 705	801 515	10.9	7.7	115 573	48 128	-30 306	304 042	6.1	2.78	20.4	26.1
Queen Anne's	13.4	8.9	6.0	50.3	33 953	40 563	19.5	17.8	4 760	3 331	6 120	18 016	17.6	2.63	9.2	20.6

1. No spouse present.

Table B. States and Counties — Population, Vital Statistics, Medicare, and Crime

STATE County	Persons in group quarters, 2010	Daytime population, 2006–2010 Number	Employment/ residence ratio	Births, average 2006–2008 Total	Rate[1]	Deaths, average 2006–2008 Number	Rate[1]	Persons under 65 with no health insurance, 2009 Number	Percent	Medicare, 2011 Eligible for Medicare	Enrolled in Medicare Advantage	Enrolled in a Medicare prescription drug plan	Serious crimes known to police,[2] 2010 Total Number	Rate[3]
	32	33	34	35	36	37	38	39	40	41	42	43	44	45
LOUISIANA—Cont'd														
Orleans	13 165	358 772	1.5	3 689	14.3	2 709	10.5	80 602	26.9	48 258	18 790	16 403	15 517	4 513
Ouachita	5 534	157 813	1.1	2 427	16.2	1 454	9.7	26 666	20.8	23 980	3 292	10 676	8 919	5 933
Plaquemines	272	30 384	1.8	D	D	173	8.0	3 904	21.4	3 066	1 589	669	328	1 423
Pointe Coupee	116	19 449	0.7	306	13.6	242	10.8	3 582	19.5	4 152	1 311	1 485	475	2 083
Rapides	4 501	137 168	1.1	2 013	15.4	1 277	9.7	20 973	18.7	24 250	2 258	10 912	7 413	6 011
Red River	164	8 829	0.9	D	D	111	12.0	1 648	22.3	1 539	210	706	210	2 310
Richland	1 039	19 567	0.9	D	D	233	11.3	4 016	23.9	3 804	307	2 039	514	2 887
Sabine	440	22 200	0.8	D	D	261	11.0	4 590	23.6	4 987	627	2 428	706	2 913
St. Bernard	293	26 978	0.9	D	D	263	10.8	12 394	34.9	4 501	2 203	1 210	1 482	4 128
St. Charles	592	52 502	1.0	723	13.9	364	7.0	7 063	15.5	6 882	3 293	1 423	1 534	2 906
St. Helena	121	8 905	0.5	D	D	114	10.7	1 965	22.5	2 535	494	1 183	353	3 151
St. James	204	21 513	0.9	D	D	199	9.3	2 937	16.5	3 658	1 094	1 339	674	3 049
St. John the Baptist	471	43 492	0.8	761	15.9	364	7.6	7 438	18.1	6 676	2 665	1 975	1 322	2 879
St. Landry	1 105	79 568	0.8	1 493	16.3	941	10.3	16 182	21.2	16 604	1 132	9 662	3 455	4 473
St. Martin	701	42 201	0.6	811	15.7	432	8.4	9 543	21.1	8 354	549	4 658	785	1 505
St. Mary	868	59 490	1.2	823	16.0	526	10.2	8 819	20.6	9 477	1 520	5 081	2 434	4 662
St. Tammany	1 275	209 704	0.8	3 102	13.6	1 856	8.1	33 792	16.8	37 386	16 797	8 554	5 086	2 176
Tangipahoa	3 638	111 236	0.9	1 923	16.7	1 124	9.8	20 307	20.0	17 905	4 366	7 300	9 201	7 598
Tensas	16	5 394	1.0	D	D	67	11.4	1 243	27.6	1 098	46	615	NA	NA
Terrebonne	1 479	117 641	1.1	1 772	16.3	965	8.9	19 306	20.3	17 334	2 291	9 181	5 197	4 646
Union	415	19 779	0.7	D	D	264	11.6	3 786	20.9	4 449	608	2 046	291	1 281
Vermilion	536	50 327	0.7	845	15.1	550	9.8	10 412	21.8	9 347	556	5 218	1 410	2 431
Vernon	2 258	52 461	1.1	919	19.7	337	7.2	7 917	19.5	6 362	337	2 308	1 177	2 362
Washington	1 582	43 497	0.8	677	15.0	558	12.4	8 682	23.1	9 338	1 692	4 488	2 142	4 541
Webster	1 231	39 283	0.9	568	13.9	538	13.1	6 725	20.7	8 578	1 033	3 756	755	1 844
West Baton Rouge	556	23 470	1.0	344	15.3	181	8.0	3 534	18.0	3 430	1 428	891	768	3 229
West Carroll	434	10 674	0.7	D	D	139	12.0	2 189	24.1	2 396	121	1 385	623	5 369
West Feliciana	5 297	16 201	1.1	D	D	110	7.2	3 062	23.6	1 660	414	535	204	1 472
Winn	1 760	15 393	1.0	D	D	184	11.8	3 082	24.5	2 789	215	1 496	576	3 762
MAINE	35 545	1 313 567	1.0	13 960	10.6	12 443	9.4	135 054	12.5	274 275	38 375	138 300	34 555	2 601
Androscoggin	2 760	105 963	1.0	1 414	13.2	1 015	9.5	11 168	12.7	21 063	3 365	11 415	2 752	2 555
Aroostook	2 005	72 247	1.0	723	10.0	813	11.3	8 101	14.3	18 044	1 499	11 328	1 402	1 951
Cumberland	9 190	306 183	1.2	2 995	10.9	2 342	8.5	26 050	11.2	50 443	8 573	22 713	8 009	2 843
Franklin	1 110	30 507	1.0	D	D	297	9.9	3 157	12.8	6 483	930	3 329	717	2 330
Hancock	1 176	53 706	1.0	D	D	546	10.2	6 120	14.2	11 963	1 327	5 673	1 113	2 045
Kennebec	3 636	123 724	1.0	1 246	10.3	1 154	9.5	11 937	12.0	26 927	5 197	12 966	3 646	2 985
Knox	1 361	41 606	1.1	D	D	431	10.6	4 522	14.1	9 462	1 102	4 782	890	2 240
Lincoln	498	31 262	0.8	D	D	389	11.2	3 947	14.7	8 789	1 314	3 832	658	1 910
Oxford	849	51 851	0.8	567	10.0	606	10.7	6 231	13.6	12 781	1 468	7 268	1 312	2 269
Penobscot	7 318	156 265	1.0	1 597	10.8	1 379	9.3	15 168	12.2	30 630	4 265	15 957	4 767	3 097
Piscataquis	220	16 969	0.9	D	D	211	12.3	1 912	14.4	4 608	440	2 602	472	2 692
Sagadahoc	265	33 666	0.9	D	D	313	8.6	3 251	10.8	7 216	1 231	2 909	606	1 717
Somerset	715	49 417	0.9	531	10.3	519	10.0	5 593	13.4	10 552	1 228	6 344	1 488	2 849
Waldo	501	33 943	0.7	D	D	350	9.1	4 222	13.4	8 220	1 165	4 215	831	2 143
Washington	836	32 903	1.0	D	D	406	12.4	4 328	17.1	8 340	607	4 896	730	2 222
York	3 105	173 355	0.8	2 049	10.2	1 670	8.3	19 348	11.6	38 754	4 664	18 071	4 994	2 533
MARYLAND	138 375	5 420 828	0.9	77 626	13.8	43 744	7.8	627 606	12.9	818 777	66 880	318 310	204 671	3 545
Allegany	7 924	78 346	1.1	725	10.0	890	12.3	8 675	14.9	15 898	557	8 170	2 878	3 833
Anne Arundel	14 133	510 317	0.9	6 925	13.5	3 820	7.5	47 859	10.7	74 110	4 508	23 550	18 862	3 508
Baltimore	20 781	750 507	0.9	10 281	13.1	7 663	9.7	78 457	11.9	134 391	12 725	61 134	28 477	3 537
Calvert	650	66 433	0.5	992	11.2	615	6.9	7 712	9.9	11 680	393	3 682	2 234	2 518
Caroline	442	26 737	0.6	493	15.0	314	9.5	4 822	16.9	5 598	115	2 911	1 146	3 466
Carroll	3 319	137 240	0.6	1 930	11.4	1 292	7.6	15 094	10.4	25 998	966	11 655	3 059	1 830
Cecil	1 551	83 827	0.7	1 321	13.2	807	8.1	10 620	12.2	15 038	502	6 483	4 092	4 047
Charles	1 405	110 387	0.5	1 894	13.5	834	5.9	13 119	10.5	16 767	828	4 874	4 425	3 019
Dorchester	506	30 093	0.9	418	13.1	371	11.6	3 873	15.1	6 877	220	3 577	1 188	3 642
Frederick	4 182	212 854	0.9	2 964	13.2	1 435	6.4	20 825	10.5	30 875	1 350	11 664	4 698	2 013
Garrett	515	29 788	1.0	D	D	298	10.0	3 596	14.9	6 079	300	3 441	532	1 768
Harford	2 743	209 503	0.7	2 975	12.4	1 763	7.3	19 526	9.4	36 734	2 632	13 754	5 355	2 187
Howard	2 322	278 809	1.0	3 416	12.5	1 302	4.8	20 133	8.1	32 866	1 891	11 529	7 371	2 568
Kent	1 526	20 451	1.0	D	D	269	13.4	2 602	16.5	4 834	84	2 794	422	2 089
Montgomery	8 900	917 098	0.9	13 827	14.7	5 261	5.6	103 270	12.4	125 155	10 554	40 932	22 643	2 330
Prince George's	19 328	738 466	0.7	12 715	15.3	5 371	6.5	118 644	16.3	96 214	11 849	24 410	43 076	4 989
Queen Anne's	426	38 797	0.7	D	D	350	7.5	4 925	12.3	8 232	151	3 289	1 102	2 306

1. Per 1,000 estimated resident population.   2. Data for serious crimes have not been adjusted for underreporting; this may affect comparability between geographic areas and over time.   3. Per 100,000 population estimated by the FBI.

Table B. States and Counties — Crime, Education, Money Income, and Poverty

STATE County	Serious crimes known to police,[1] 2010 (cont.) Rate[2] Violent	Property	Education — School enrollment and attainment, 2006–2010 Enrollment[3] Total	Percent private	Attainment[4] (percent) High school graduate or less	Bachelor's degree or more	Local government expenditures,[5] 2008–2009 Total current expenditures (mil dol)	Current expenditures per student (dollars)	Money income, 2006–2010 Per capita income[6] (dollars)	Households Median income Dollars	Percent change, 2000 to 2006–2010 (constant 2010 dollars)	Percent with income of $200,000 or more	Income and poverty, 2010 Median household income (dollars)	Percent below poverty level All persons	Children under 18 years	Children 5 to 17 years in families
	46	47	48	49	50	51	52	53	54	55	56	57	58	59	60	61
LOUISIANA—Cont'd																
Orleans	756	3 757	78 573	35.5	43.5	31.6	492.1	14 019	24 929	37 468	9.1	4.2	36 525	27.1	41.2	37.5
Ouachita	433	5 500	43 212	10.0	49.6	23.5	282.3	9 999	21 893	39 823	-1.9	2.3	37 728	20.6	28.3	26.7
Plaquemines	165	1 259	6 522	22.0	52.9	17.4	72.1	16 125	23 378	54 730	13.2	2.4	49 781	15.1	19.2	16.7
Pointe Coupee	513	1 570	5 144	33.5	63.8	15.3	29.6	11 227	21 533	41 177	6.2	2.4	41 277	17.6	27.8	25.2
Rapides	751	5 260	33 188	14.9	53.0	19.4	211.8	8 979	21 982	40 658	7.5	1.9	39 693	19.6	29.3	26.0
Red River	803	1 507	2 400	16.3	64.3	12.5	20.6	13 593	20 044	34 723	18.4	2.7	32 711	23.3	33.0	30.9
Richland	241	2 645	4 894	10.4	64.4	12.2	40.2	10 222	18 060	37 682	25.7	2.1	32 646	25.4	40.0	35.2
Sabine	314	2 600	5 830	7.2	65.8	11.6	42.1	9 893	20 626	35 395	4.9	1.9	36 604	21.9	34.3	31.0
St. Bernard	281	3 847	6 756	20.5	63.8	9.9	66.7	14 365	19 448	39 200	-13.9	0.8	38 700	17.8	28.8	28.7
St. Charles	229	2 677	14 926	20.3	52.4	19.7	123.9	12 994	25 728	60 961	6.7	2.9	54 553	12.7	18.2	16.2
St. Helena	786	2 365	2 809	11.4	66.6	11.1	13.0	10 739	16 387	27 393	-13.4	1.0	32 936	23.9	38.9	37.4
St. James	769	2 280	5 938	16.4	66.0	12.4	54.8	13 419	22 509	51 725	15.8	2.0	45 829	16.3	23.6	21.7
St. John the Baptist	189	2 689	12 840	26.4	55.9	15.8	83.8	13 193	20 842	47 666	-4.6	1.4	45 987	18.6	29.0	27.6
St. Landry	640	3 834	20 692	17.6	67.6	12.5	137.6	9 115	17 839	31 813	9.9	1.6	33 466	26.4	36.4	31.7
St. Martin	293	1 212	12 947	17.2	68.5	11.6	74.2	8 827	20 687	41 302	6.2	1.3	39 444	21.8	33.8	34.2
St. Mary	605	4 056	13 257	13.5	67.8	10.4	104.9	10 597	20 057	40 431	13.7	1.0	40 193	20.6	32.2	29.3
St. Tammany	196	1 980	60 951	24.4	39.6	30.1	377.1	10 624	29 282	60 866	0.4	4.6	59 389	9.2	13.8	11.8
Tangipahoa	1 156	6 442	31 816	14.8	56.8	19.7	166.6	8 587	19 788	38 957	4.6	1.6	37 454	21.7	30.1	27.6
Tensas	NA	NA	1 228	15.9	68.9	12.9	9.6	12 885	15 218	27 157	8.3	0.6	26 976	33.3	49.6	46.4
Terrebonne	557	4 089	28 403	16.8	66.1	13.8	181.8	9 567	22 931	48 437	8.6	2.7	47 847	18.3	26.4	23.1
Union	308	973	4 733	15.5	63.7	13.8	28.8	10 180	20 375	38 930	5.8	1.5	36 863	21.0	34.4	31.6
Vermilion	660	1 771	13 562	13.7	70.0	11.7	83.2	9 310	21 389	42 693	14.3	2.0	43 498	17.5	25.6	23.9
Vernon	379	1 983	12 820	7.9	54.7	15.6	88.1	9 177	20 191	42 554	7.7	1.0	43 752	13.5	21.3	20.9
Washington	634	3 907	11 539	16.8	66.1	11.8	79.2	10 427	17 120	30 363	-1.2	1.4	30 950	26.8	37.1	32.6
Webster	237	1 607	9 185	8.0	64.0	13.5	68.2	9 436	19 254	35 999	0.1	1.0	35 861	22.6	32.3	29.7
West Baton Rouge	454	2 775	6 103	18.2	60.3	16.5	44.2	11 660	22 101	47 298	0.6	1.3	46 783	15.0	21.8	20.3
West Carroll	1 060	4 309	2 608	3.1	70.1	9.8	20.1	8 894	16 462	33 901	8.7	1.6	62 146	22.6	32.6	29.9
West Feliciana	274	1 198	3 287	9.9	69.7	12.8	28.4	12 280	18 118	43 411	-13.6	3.4	48 917	20.9	19.2	16.6
Winn	1 038	2 723	3 113	9.3	70.1	11.2	25.4	9 528	15 833	32 039	-0.6	0.4	33 447	23.9	33.0	29.1
MAINE	122	2 479	311 441	16.9	45.4	26.5	2 316.3	12 362	25 385	46 933	-0.5	2.1	45 882	13.1	18.2	15.8
Androscoggin	159	2 396	26 257	19.5	53.4	18.4	185.5	11 240	22 752	44 470	-1.9	1.3	41 831	14.6	20.4	18.7
Aroostook	74	1 877	16 491	8.1	55.1	16.2	129.0	12 283	20 251	36 574	0.2	1.1	36 344	14.0	20.0	17.8
Cumberland	164	2 680	70 712	19.9	33.0	39.5	475.6	12 665	31 041	55 658	-0.2	4.2	57 424	10.3	13.6	11.8
Franklin	124	2 207	7 318	8.6	49.0	24.5	54.7	14 009	20 838	39 831	0.0	0.9	39 084	15.6	22.8	18.9
Hancock	92	1 953	11 213	15.6	42.6	30.1	92.8	14 340	26 876	47 533	4.8	2.0	41 106	14.0	20.2	17.4
Kennebec	121	2 864	28 816	20.5	47.1	24.1	191.4	11 458	24 656	45 973	-0.5	1.7	44 725	11.7	16.9	14.5
Knox	43	2 197	7 836	13.7	47.5	26.9	87.4	13 901	25 291	45 264	-2.8	2.0	42 593	13.7	19.8	17.3
Lincoln	110	1 799	6 279	18.8	40.2	31.6	46.6	13 964	28 003	47 678	-2.7	2.9	45 520	12.7	20.8	18.3
Oxford	109	2 160	12 535	15.9	55.8	18.5	113.6	11 724	21 254	39 748	-6.1	1.2	38 789	15.0	22.5	20.3
Penobscot	67	3 030	41 142	14.8	47.2	23.3	259.4	11 432	22 977	42 658	-1.7	1.7	42 602	16.0	20.6	17.3
Piscataquis	68	2 623	3 360	16.9	56.6	15.0	28.8	11 032	19 870	34 016	-4.9	0.4	34 420	16.6	27.3	24.3
Sagadahoc	43	1 675	7 655	13.7	43.2	29.6	71.6	21 233	26 983	55 486	4.6	1.5	52 071	10.5	15.3	13.6
Somerset	98	2 751	11 169	13.5	57.2	15.3	102.4	11 836	20 709	36 647	-5.8	1.2	36 249	18.6	25.7	22.9
Waldo	93	2 050	8 397	14.0	49.7	23.1	56.0	13 382	22 213	41 312	-4.0	1.3	37 986	15.6	23.4	20.6
Washington	338	1 884	6 845	13.7	54.0	19.0	67.4	16 584	19 401	34 859	6.4	0.6	32 847	19.4	30.9	28.4
York	113	2 421	45 416	18.2	44.1	26.7	354.0	11 479	27 137	55 008	-0.4	2.0	54 076	10.3	13.7	11.3
MARYLAND	548	2 997	1 549 287	21.3	38.7	35.7	11 348.2	13 449	34 849	70 647	5.5	7.3	68 933	9.9	13.1	11.8
Allegany	416	3 417	17 778	12.1	57.8	15.9	130.0	14 086	20 764	37 747	-3.3	1.3	37 083	17.1	23.9	20.8
Anne Arundel	564	2 944	136 210	23.3	36.2	35.7	926.9	12 585	38 660	83 456	6.7	8.9	80 908	6.6	8.8	7.5
Baltimore	540	2 997	212 531	23.6	38.8	35.2	1 295.2	12 553	33 719	63 959	-0.3	5.4	62 300	8.2	11.0	9.9
Calvert	221	2 297	25 443	12.8	41.7	29.0	212.0	12 434	36 323	90 838	8.8	7.5	86 536	6.2	7.9	6.6
Caroline	387	3 079	8 207	15.1	58.9	15.2	62.9	11 408	24 294	58 799	19.6	1.6	55 480	13.0	19.2	18.1
Carroll	208	1 622	45 635	23.9	41.9	31.1	336.9	12 046	33 938	81 621	7.4	5.9	80 291	5.4	6.9	5.7
Cecil	664	3 384	25 614	19.3	50.5	20.9	190.2	11 733	28 640	64 886	1.4	3.2	61 506	10.5	14.6	12.2
Charles	487	2 533	41 420	15.9	40.7	26.1	329.4	12 323	35 780	88 825	12.8	6.8	83 078	6.2	8.5	7.8
Dorchester	576	3 066	6 906	8.9	59.0	16.5	59.2	12 975	25 139	45 151	4.6	2.2	39 630	16.2	25.8	25.1
Frederick	312	1 701	62 873	20.9	36.0	35.8	489.1	12 206	35 172	81 686	7.0	6.5	80 216	5.6	7.7	6.8
Garrett	163	1 605	6 568	10.5	58.0	17.5	57.2	12 924	23 888	45 760	12.1	2.0	43 637	15.1	24.4	21.4
Harford	348	1 839	64 953	20.6	37.7	30.5	467.2	12 102	33 559	77 010	6.3	5.2	71 848	6.9	9.3	7.9
Howard	197	2 370	82 525	19.5	20.1	58.3	731.1	14 649	45 294	103 273	10.0	15.4	100 992	5.2	6.0	5.3
Kent	272	1 817	4 741	35.4	47.4	30.2	32.5	14 626	29 536	50 141	-0.7	3.9	49 017	14.2	20.4	18.7
Montgomery	185	2 145	258 800	25.2	23.5	56.7	2 151.5	15 447	47 310	93 373	3.1	15.3	88 559	7.5	9.4	9.1
Prince George's	718	4 271	250 512	20.1	42.3	29.6	1 760.4	13 756	31 215	71 260	1.8	5.1	69 524	9.4	12.3	11.8
Queen Anne's	251	2 054	11 381	18.5	40.8	29.6	89.5	11 391	35 964	81 096	12.3	6.6	78 503	7.3	10.1	9.0

1. Data for serious crimes have not been adjusted for underreporting; this may affect comparability between geographic areas and over time. 2. Per 100,000 population estimated by the FBI. 3. All persons 3 years old and over enrolled in nursery school through college. 4. Persons 25 years old and over. 5. Elementary and secondary education expenditures. 6. Based on population estimated by the American Community Survey, 2006–2010.

| | Personal income, 2009 | | | | | | | | | | | | |
STATE County	Total (mil dol)	Percent change, 2008–2009	Per capita[1] Dollars	Rank	Wages and salaries[2] (mil dol)	Proprietors' income (mil dol)	Dividends, interest, and rent (mil dol)	Transfer payments (mil dol) Total	Government payments to individuals Total	Social Security	Medical payments	Income maintenance	Unemployment insurance
	62	63	64	65	66	67	68	69	70	71	72	73	74
LOUISIANA—Cont'd													
Orleans	15 261	-3.4	43 006	269	11 700	2 509	3 840	2 306	2 242	551	1 064	361	56
Ouachita	5 270	1.8	34 788	1 047	3 228	577	908	1 182	1 155	314	541	180	25
Plaquemines	895	-5.7	42 715	285	1 095	128	152	141	137	43	69	15	3
Pointe Coupee	784	2.0	34 932	1 031	270	64	131	172	167	50	81	24	3
Rapides	4 972	0.4	37 121	737	2 963	429	823	1 264	1 239	286	707	136	20
Red River	264	1.2	29 309	2 134	104	41	33	73	72	19	35	12	2
Richland	599	2.0	29 327	2 132	238	60	80	196	192	45	107	27	4
Sabine	643	1.6	27 101	2 548	232	53	100	191	187	65	83	21	4
St. Bernard	1 224	-10.8	30 114	1 951	642	88	207	203	196	58	92	23	6
St. Charles	1 969	-0.6	38 154	622	1 867	69	281	311	301	103	137	36	8
St. Helena	336	-0.3	31 836	1 569	72	20	43	91	89	32	29	20	2
St. James	689	0.3	32 719	1 383	583	21	97	168	164	51	78	22	4
St. John the Baptist	1 618	-0.6	34 372	1 116	967	91	170	332	323	95	147	52	9
St. Landry	2 766	0.5	29 957	1 990	1 115	156	390	778	761	198	388	115	14
St. Martin	1 558	0.0	29 844	2 011	503	59	214	351	342	108	155	50	8
St. Mary	1 996	-1.6	39 280	511	1 543	120	412	424	414	134	193	61	9
St. Tammany	10 406	-0.3	44 949	201	3 775	754	1 954	1 458	1 416	532	648	104	29
Tangipahoa	3 659	0.2	30 833	1 792	1 848	162	504	1 017	995	221	554	133	20
Tensas	185	8.6	33 042	1 335	67	22	44	51	50	12	26	10	1
Terrebonne	4 268	-1.7	39 049	535	3 160	124	716	767	747	243	364	91	13
Union	688	2.2	30 482	1 868	179	50	87	190	186	60	89	21	5
Vermilion	1 731	-1.0	30 830	1 793	722	92	317	382	372	122	176	44	8
Vernon	1 962	2.3	42 079	325	1 611	49	166	306	299	75	146	33	8
Washington	1 291	1.6	28 264	2 355	482	63	189	472	464	121	252	59	7
Webster	1 383	0.6	34 113	1 152	595	92	216	366	358	111	171	43	9
West Baton Rouge	805	1.0	35 557	949	637	49	94	160	156	45	77	21	4
West Carroll	282	7.5	24 892	2 875	104	23	34	110	107	28	58	13	4
West Feliciana	421	1.5	27 979	2 403	352	20	74	74	72	21	37	8	2
Winn	420	2.8	27 372	2 503	222	21	55	133	130	36	67	16	3
MAINE	48 180	-0.2	36 547	X	29 112	3 566	7 481	11 034	10 794	3 521	5 057	1 003	397
Androscoggin	3 777	0.7	35 455	957	2 237	243	389	990	970	271	484	113	39
Aroostook	2 213	2.9	30 961	1 767	1 262	106	264	762	749	218	376	70	24
Cumberland	12 405	-1.7	44 533	214	9 687	986	2 223	2 053	2 002	673	959	157	69
Franklin	884	0.5	29 739	2 034	503	71	129	256	251	84	111	27	11
Hancock	1 905	-1.4	35 647	934	991	183	421	424	414	157	182	29	17
Kennebec	4 289	0.1	35 416	964	2 889	284	544	1 059	1 037	329	464	106	33
Knox	1 486	-2.0	36 411	827	742	195	345	335	327	122	148	29	10
Lincoln	1 298	-1.3	37 535	684	445	122	333	285	278	117	114	21	8
Oxford	1 668	-0.3	29 656	2 063	710	108	230	519	508	165	235	54	24
Penobscot	5 045	1.6	33 767	1 208	3 341	369	630	1 302	1 274	385	594	133	46
Piscataquis	521	1.3	31 018	1 749	227	49	70	178	175	56	78	16	7
Sagadahoc	1 377	-0.8	37 833	662	916	67	235	259	253	96	106	20	9
Somerset	1 517	0.8	29 782	2 024	804	109	158	489	479	134	240	54	20
Waldo	1 196	0.1	31 241	1 703	464	104	192	316	309	103	140	32	12
Washington	977	1.8	30 440	1 877	444	79	120	378	372	101	198	34	11
York	7 621	-0.3	37 751	669	3 448	493	1 196	1 432	1 395	511	627	109	55
MARYLAND	274 980	0.3	48 247	X	171 237	15 596	47 288	36 089	35 055	10 993	16 091	3 355	1 835
Allegany	2 311	3.9	31 860	1 562	1 404	101	366	761	748	211	377	59	27
Anne Arundel	28 446	0.0	54 576	58	20 350	1 685	4 621	2 970	2 877	1 041	1 234	185	158
Baltimore	39 483	-0.6	49 990	105	23 511	2 164	8 004	5 614	5 470	1 973	2 492	408	277
Calvert	3 891	0.9	43 612	252	1 205	112	572	454	437	160	184	30	25
Caroline	1 009	-0.1	30 252	1 926	403	79	151	240	234	78	107	23	13
Carroll	7 192	-0.3	42 285	307	2 691	333	1 167	1 011	980	377	438	47	53
Cecil	3 715	-0.4	36 861	763	1 685	133	494	649	631	216	275	52	40
Charles	6 101	1.1	42 899	275	2 312	201	816	717	691	209	291	67	40
Dorchester	1 069	1.4	33 376	1 284	530	59	207	304	299	93	141	35	15
Frederick	10 200	0.2	44 742	209	5 827	390	1 693	1 098	1 056	417	402	73	67
Garrett	1 037	0.9	35 084	1 006	474	150	176	249	243	81	108	21	11
Harford	11 130	0.9	45 893	173	5 160	377	1 601	1 418	1 374	511	561	100	84
Howard	17 427	0.5	61 823	25	10 534	909	2 699	1 159	1 108	439	405	73	72
Kent	905	-2.1	44 703	211	380	64	316	191	187	78	82	11	7
Montgomery	64 439	-0.6	66 323	17	38 242	4 832	13 670	4 672	4 495	1 568	1 999	321	238
Prince George's	33 079	0.7	39 637	475	21 791	1 171	4 069	4 495	4 344	1 115	2 044	451	274
Queen Anne's	2 198	-0.2	45 828	177	628	118	438	262	254	111	95	15	15

1. Based on the resident population estimated as of July 1 of the year shown.   2. Includes supplements to wages and salaries.

Table B. States and Counties — Earnings, Social Security, and Housing

STATE County	Earnings, 2009									Social Security beneficiaries, December 2010		Housing units, 2010		
				Percent by selected industries										
			Goods-related[1]		Service-related and health							Supplemental Security Income recipients, December 2010		
	Total (mil dol)	Farm	Total	Manu-facturing	Information and profes-sional and technical services	Retail trade	Finance, insur-ance, and real estate	Health care and social services	Govern-ment	Number	Rate[2]		Total	Percent change, 2000–2010
	75	76	77	78	79	80	81	82	83	84	85	86	87	88
LOUISIANA—Cont'd														
Orleans	14 209	0.0	14.6	3.7	15.2	3.2	5.4	7.2	23.2	50 600	147	18 158	189 896	-11.7
Ouachita	3 805	0.3	15.8	9.5	12.2	8.1	6.9	15.5	18.5	26 195	170	6 346	64 481	7.2
Plaquemines	1 223	1.3	38.0	18.9	D	D	4.2	D	15.8	3 450	150	564	9 596	-8.4
Pointe Coupee	334	10.1	17.9	6.4	4.8	7.3	4.7	D	17.3	4 400	193	1 051	11 130	8.1
Rapides	3 392	0.9	18.8	8.7	6.2	7.1	4.1	19.0	25.3	26 490	201	6 866	55 684	7.0
Red River	146	7.1	28.4	4.6	3.1	4.3	3.0	D	20.3	1 690	186	502	4 128	3.5
Richland	298	7.8	10.8	4.5	D	9.7	4.0	D	20.8	4 105	198	1 125	8 621	3.4
Sabine	285	4.5	25.6	18.6	4.1	9.6	5.0	7.7	24.2	5 440	224	1 061	14 130	3.4
St. Bernard	730	1.0	D	26.1	2.8	4.7	1.9	D	15.6	5 355	149	1 325	16 794	-37.3
St. Charles	1 936	0.0	44.6	31.7	4.2	3.4	1.9	D	11.3	8 045	152	1 252	19 896	14.2
St. Helena	91	4.4	19.0	13.5	D	4.7	D	D	34.7	2 945	263	1 044	5 150	2.3
St. James	604	1.4	54.3	50.0	D	3.1	2.7	2.9	14.1	4 155	188	755	8 455	11.3
St. John the Baptist	1 058	0.3	41.3	32.1	3.2	5.9	3.7	6.8	13.0	7 875	171	1 816	17 510	10.2
St. Landry	1 271	2.8	17.7	7.6	4.8	9.5	4.0	15.0	23.8	18 480	222	5 679	35 692	-1.4
St. Martin	562	1.9	28.6	11.5	3.9	10.7	7.7	8.1	20.8	9 730	187	1 993	21 941	8.4
St. Mary	1 663	0.7	37.1	19.5	3.4	4.5	5.8	D	15.9	11 005	201	2 470	23 028	6.4
St. Tammany	4 529	0.1	16.1	4.4	9.6	9.2	6.5	14.3	17.2	41 660	178	4 706	95 412	26.5
Tangipahoa	2 010	0.3	11.3	5.9	4.0	9.9	6.9	10.1	32.5	20 050	166	5 080	50 073	22.7
Tensas	89	24.2	D	1.6	D	2.8	D	D	21.6	1 140	217	444	3 357	-0.1
Terrebonne	3 284	0.5	37.5	14.8	4.3	6.8	5.7	9.0	11.5	20 280	181	4 594	43 887	9.9
Union	230	7.1	23.9	16.1	3.5	8.9	3.2	D	23.6	4 995	220	871	11 346	4.4
Vermilion	813	3.8	31.5	8.3	4.0	8.0	5.7	6.5	20.0	10 795	186	1 895	25 235	12.0
Vernon	1 660	0.1	D	1.1	5.8	2.7	1.2	4.1	73.7	7 220	138	1 213	21 433	1.9
Washington	544	0.1	23.8	15.9	D	7.5	3.7	D	36.3	10 805	229	3 062	21 039	10.1
Webster	687	0.3	34.6	14.7	2.9	8.5	5.3	D	18.0	9 410	228	1 946	19 336	1.8
West Baton Rouge	686	0.9	D	21.8	D	4.9	1.0	D	13.0	3 885	163	755	9 324	11.4
West Carroll	127	10.1	D	D	D	7.5	2.9	D	33.7	2 610	225	512	5 046	1.3
West Feliciana	372	0.4	D	2.2	D	2.0	1.4	4.0	42.3	1 770	113	359	5 097	13.6
Winn	242	1.0	25.8	17.5	D	5.1	3.1	16.2	17.2	3 155	206	695	7 234	-3.6
MAINE	32 678	0.5	D	10.5	8.6	8.3	6.8	16.5	19.8	299 875	226	35 426	721 830	10.7
Androscoggin	2 480	0.5	19.5	12.8	7.6	8.2	7.0	21.8	11.9	23 505	218	3 619	49 090	6.8
Aroostook	1 368	-1.1	15.8	11.8	4.3	9.4	3.8	18.5	27.3	19 975	278	2 794	39 529	2.1
Cumberland	10 673	0.2	11.1	6.1	13.3	7.0	11.9	16.9	14.1	53 360	189	5 283	138 657	13.1
Franklin	574	1.2	D	21.7	D	9.1	3.7	D	17.6	7 215	234	911	21 709	13.3
Hancock	1 175	0.8	19.5	9.6	12.3	10.7	4.3	14.6	14.4	12 905	237	1 007	40 184	18.4
Kennebec	3 172	0.5	D	4.4	6.1	9.3	3.3	16.1	33.5	29 220	244	4 290	60 972	8.2
Knox	937	0.5	18.1	10.1	D	9.4	5.3	15.0	16.9	10 185	256	872	23 744	9.9
Lincoln	567	5.7	D	6.6	7.4	9.9	4.7	13.6	15.2	9 490	275	670	23 493	12.7
Oxford	819	2.3	26.6	20.0	3.1	8.9	2.9	14.6	18.9	14 450	250	1 808	36 055	11.6
Penobscot	3 710	0.2	D	7.6	6.3	9.9	4.0	21.7	21.2	33 585	218	5 190	73 860	10.5
Piscataquis	276	0.6	D	23.7	3.0	9.5	1.5	D	26.0	4 950	282	639	15 340	11.3
Sagadahoc	983	0.1	50.7	44.4	8.0	5.8	2.6	5.2	16.2	7 680	218	676	18 288	10.9
Somerset	912	1.6	D	22.9	3.9	7.7	2.7	14.2	15.7	12 010	230	1 849	30 569	8.3
Waldo	568	1.5	D	12.4	D	8.4	13.6	15.7	15.6	9 150	236	1 206	21 566	14.1
Washington	523	3.2	15.6	10.6	3.0	9.7	3.8	17.4	27.4	9 270	282	1 343	23 001	4.9
York	3 942	0.3	19.7	12.7	5.9	8.3	3.8	12.1	29.6	42 325	215	3 269	105 773	12.2
MARYLAND	186 833	0.2	12.0	5.4	16.6	5.5	7.2	11.2	25.8	850 361	147	107 636	2 378 814	10.9
Allegany	1 506	0.1	14.7	9.4	3.9	7.1	3.0	21.1	27.6	16 965	226	2 214	33 311	1.0
Anne Arundel	22 035	0.0	13.2	7.4	D	5.3	3.6	6.9	36.8	77 930	145	5 448	212 562	13.7
Baltimore	25 676	0.1	14.5	7.0	14.5	7.0	10.7	14.0	18.2	143 220	178	14 203	335 622	7.0
Calvert	1 318	-0.1	D	D	7.4	7.8	4.1	14.8	22.8	12 330	139	863	33 780	22.5
Caroline	482	5.4	D	10.6	3.0	8.0	3.4	D	20.4	6 510	197	747	13 482	12.1
Carroll	3 024	0.8	D	9.9	9.5	8.6	4.1	13.9	17.1	27 960	167	1 274	62 406	15.0
Cecil	1 818	0.7	27.4	22.1	D	5.8	2.5	9.7	27.7	17 030	168	1 538	41 103	19.3
Charles	2 513	0.0	D	1.9	8.4	10.9	4.9	10.2	32.4	17 545	120	1 863	54 963	25.2
Dorchester	589	1.8	D	18.9	D	5.4	4.2	D	24.2	7 620	234	1 129	16 554	12.8
Frederick	6 217	0.5	15.2	6.2	19.8	6.4	9.4	9.6	21.6	32 575	140	2 011	90 136	23.4
Garrett	625	1.7	D	D	5.9	9.3	5.2	D	16.1	6 755	224	696	18 854	12.5
Harford	5 537	0.1	12.4	5.9	11.3	7.4	3.9	9.7	36.8	39 325	161	2 949	95 554	14.9
Howard	11 442	0.1	D	4.2	29.3	5.6	7.5	6.6	10.8	31 990	111	2 684	109 282	17.7
Kent	444	5.3	D	8.5	7.4	6.4	4.8	16.7	14.8	5 785	286	324	10 549	12.1
Montgomery	43 074	0.0	9.1	3.8	24.7	4.2	9.1	9.4	24.1	114 130	117	12 831	375 905	12.3
Prince George's	22 961	0.0	13.8	3.7	12.1	6.1	3.7	7.3	36.9	96 185	111	12 716	328 182	8.5
Queen Anne's	746	2.2	D	8.0	9.8	11.3	3.8	7.2	21.0	8 165	171	361	20 140	20.8

1. Includes mining, construction, and manufacturing. 2. Per 1,000 resident population enumerated in the 2010 census.

Table B. States and Counties — Housing, Labor Force, and Employment

	Housing units, 2006–2010								Civilian labor force, 2010				Civilian employment,[5] 2006–2010		
	Occupied units										Unemployment			Percent	
			Owner-occupied			Renter-occupied									
STATE County	Total	Percent	Median value[1]	Median owner cost as a percent of income — With a mortgage	Without a mortgage	Median rent[2]	Median rent as a percent of income	Sub-standard units[3] (percent)	Total	Percent change, 2009–2010	Total	Rate[4]	Total	Management, business, science and arts	Construction, production, and maintenance occupations
	89	90	91	92	93	94	95	96	97	98	99	100	101	102	103
LOUISIANA—Cont'd															
Orleans	116 638	49.3	184 100	28.3	14.0	899	38.3	3.8	148 632	10.6	13 111	8.8	132 056	37.9	19.1
Ouachita	56 192	63.1	112 400	21.1	10.3	621	30.9	2.6	71 778	1.0	5 532	7.7	66 956	31.7	21.5
Plaquemines	7 718	71.4	203 100	26.1	10.5	1 093	30.3	2.7	8 058	-4.6	533	6.6	9 614	30.6	30.0
Pointe Coupee	8 859	79.5	108 600	20.6	11.0	505	28.1	3.8	9 597	-0.4	813	8.5	9 847	27.1	34.0
Rapides	48 127	67.6	110 500	21.0	10.4	684	32.3	3.5	60 592	-0.5	4 238	7.0	55 529	32.5	22.3
Red River	3 203	78.6	72 200	18.6	10.7	394	27.5	4.4	3 700	5.9	324	8.8	3 496	24.9	33.2
Richland	7 417	68.1	70 000	19.3	10.0	561	25.2	3.5	9 217	3.3	933	10.1	7 875	27.2	30.5
Sabine	9 446	78.0	74 600	18.4	10.0	442	30.0	5.9	9 583	-0.9	661	6.9	9 147	24.7	38.8
St. Bernard	10 295	65.7	132 400	23.2	10.5	809	34.6	4.2	18 403	4.8	1 296	7.0	11 853	20.7	40.6
St. Charles	18 460	81.6	170 200	21.8	10.1	799	31.6	3.8	24 126	-2.3	1 728	7.2	24 824	33.2	27.4
St. Helena	4 072	78.8	82 400	19.3	11.8	508	26.0	3.7	4 304	0.4	561	13.0	4 229	19.3	31.4
St. James	7 455	83.8	116 600	19.4	10.4	587	23.0	7.1	9 551	1.5	1 085	11.4	9 637	23.0	35.8
St. John the Baptist	15 772	77.9	146 700	23.0	10.0	761	30.8	5.2	20 994	-1.2	2 129	10.1	20 915	24.5	30.3
St. Landry	30 082	71.2	82 100	19.8	10.8	504	32.0	2.8	38 783	1.3	3 201	8.3	31 998	25.9	29.8
St. Martin	18 931	79.6	84 300	18.9	10.0	556	27.3	2.9	23 982	-0.2	1 746	7.3	22 304	23.7	31.5
St. Mary	20 054	70.1	85 500	20.2	11.0	598	27.4	3.4	23 132	-2.5	2 154	9.3	24 046	22.3	38.2
St. Tammany	84 536	80.4	201 800	23.6	10.6	944	31.3	2.0	109 259	-1.5	6 386	5.8	104 432	39.2	19.0
Tangipahoa	42 558	68.6	133 400	22.2	10.0	683	29.1	4.0	53 794	1.1	4 797	8.9	49 286	28.9	27.8
Tensas	2 165	60.1	72 400	20.5	14.3	444	33.6	3.0	1 999	-4.4	301	15.1	1 954	27.6	26.2
Terrebonne	38 078	74.0	118 100	20.3	10.0	690	26.1	5.8	54 770	0.4	3 038	5.5	49 171	25.2	35.0
Union	8 309	81.0	79 700	17.8	10.0	454	31.4	3.1	10 082	-3.4	864	8.6	9 292	22.8	38.3
Vermilion	21 786	75.7	93 300	18.9	10.0	551	22.4	3.6	24 373	-2.5	1 731	7.1	24 458	24.4	33.6
Vernon	18 032	56.3	85 400	18.2	10.0	743	24.4	3.3	21 090	1.5	1 465	6.9	17 429	27.6	28.1
Washington	17 292	74.4	84 400	23.3	10.0	520	32.0	4.7	15 773	-0.8	1 549	9.8	16 082	25.3	29.3
Webster	16 565	67.5	76 400	19.9	10.2	510	30.7	3.4	20 214	1.7	1 620	8.0	16 615	23.9	35.0
West Baton Rouge	8 386	73.6	126 500	21.4	10.5	637	30.5	4.8	10 734	-0.3	877	8.2	11 047	27.5	29.5
West Carroll	4 061	73.7	76 600	18.8	11.3	416	28.9	3.0	4 402	-1.9	707	16.1	4 049	25.8	32.5
West Feliciana	4 116	71.1	161 400	20.3	11.5	670	25.2	6.6	4 747	-1.0	395	8.3	4 517	33.5	22.8
Winn	5 462	76.7	59 500	19.0	10.9	399	23.8	3.6	6 660	-0.8	547	8.2	5 199	26.0	32.0
MAINE	551 125	73.1	176 200	24.4	14.0	707	29.8	2.0	700 568	0.3	57 324	8.2	657 556	34.2	23.8
Androscoggin	44 040	67.9	155 700	24.4	16.7	644	29.3	1.8	58 283	-0.2	4 703	8.1	52 653	30.8	24.4
Aroostook	30 672	72.1	85 900	20.7	12.8	498	27.9	2.2	34 176	-2.3	3 305	9.7	32 620	29.0	28.9
Cumberland	116 616	68.5	248 400	25.1	14.8	868	30.9	1.8	157 071	-0.2	9 922	6.3	149 143	41.9	16.9
Franklin	12 498	74.7	128 700	22.2	11.3	544	29.9	2.2	14 097	-2.8	1 382	9.8	14 334	30.3	28.0
Hancock	23 300	76.0	201 600	24.8	13.1	725	29.5	2.8	29 486	-0.1	2 583	8.8	27 995	33.6	27.7
Kennebec	50 869	72.4	148 100	23.0	12.8	626	29.7	1.3	63 162	-1.0	4 678	7.4	59 595	34.6	23.0
Knox	16 945	77.7	203 800	26.9	15.5	726	33.0	2.3	20 529	-1.2	1 520	7.4	20 408	30.6	26.4
Lincoln	15 365	85.7	206 200	27.1	13.4	772	26.4	1.9	17 889	-1.6	1 294	7.2	16 634	35.3	28.3
Oxford	23 276	79.1	146 500	24.7	14.7	606	29.0	2.3	28 024	-1.8	2 864	10.2	25 950	26.3	32.1
Penobscot	62 282	70.5	133 600	22.9	13.4	669	31.1	2.2	78 205	-1.6	6 462	8.3	74 933	32.7	22.3
Piscataquis	8 037	77.9	100 800	23.6	13.9	524	28.5	2.1	7 370	-1.3	828	11.2	7 713	26.5	33.0
Sagadahoc	14 721	76.5	193 100	24.8	13.4	782	30.5	1.5	18 755	-1.1	1 281	6.8	18 418	35.6	22.9
Somerset	21 892	77.0	109 500	22.5	14.7	593	33.1	2.7	24 613	-1.3	2 668	10.8	22 710	28.3	33.2
Waldo	16 136	79.3	150 300	26.2	14.6	647	28.3	3.2	19 086	-0.9	1 701	8.9	18 893	29.8	29.7
Washington	14 177	76.2	102 300	23.1	12.9	496	26.7	3.9	14 212	-2.2	1 581	11.1	13 978	28.0	32.0
York	80 299	75.2	233 300	26.3	14.9	814	29.2	1.6	112 290	-1.0	8 500	7.6	101 579	33.8	23.5
MARYLAND	2 121 047	69.0	329 400	25.4	12.4	1 091	30.1	2.1	3 057 271	1.9	239 441	7.8	2 903 595	43.3	16.6
Allegany	28 777	70.8	116 800	22.1	13.0	537	27.6	1.4	35 639	0.3	3 277	9.2	31 050	27.5	25.0
Anne Arundel	195 999	75.7	370 100	24.4	12.1	1 306	29.1	1.4	281 237	0.4	19 198	6.8	269 717	43.6	16.6
Baltimore	315 542	67.0	269 900	24.6	12.2	1 033	29.6	1.7	425 018	-0.6	33 911	8.0	411 816	42.0	16.2
Calvert	30 313	85.0	392 900	24.9	11.8	1 204	32.8	1.8	47 970	-1.5	2 963	6.2	45 254	40.9	20.5
Caroline	11 828	75.8	228 100	28.8	12.9	862	27.0	2.8	16 436	0.6	1 546	9.4	16 159	30.1	29.4
Carroll	59 412	83.9	350 900	24.9	12.5	933	30.8	0.9	93 251	-0.9	6 271	6.7	87 046	42.6	18.7
Cecil	36 182	74.7	261 200	25.4	13.9	942	29.6	1.6	49 866	-1.9	4 922	9.9	49 353	32.8	25.8
Charles	49 898	81.1	355 800	26.3	11.6	1 307	31.3	1.3	76 580	-1.0	4 779	6.2	74 475	41.1	19.0
Dorchester	13 347	71.1	205 000	27.7	15.6	704	32.0	2.8	16 754	0.9	1 791	10.7	15 158	27.2	30.8
Frederick	83 455	76.8	349 500	24.7	11.3	1 133	28.8	1.1	122 181	-1.0	8 074	6.6	121 237	44.0	17.1
Garrett	12 284	77.5	169 400	23.1	11.4	537	28.7	1.4	16 791	1.1	1 360	8.1	14 430	28.0	32.7
Harford	89 421	81.6	298 800	24.6	12.2	971	28.4	1.0	131 916	-0.4	9 910	7.5	125 237	41.3	18.8
Howard	102 271	74.7	456 200	23.6	10.0	1 346	28.4	1.3	160 359	1.0	8 755	5.5	150 099	59.3	8.9
Kent	7 735	71.8	281 100	26.7	14.4	791	31.2	0.5	11 005	1.9	913	8.3	10 045	33.2	23.4
Montgomery	353 177	69.3	482 900	25.0	10.9	1 417	30.4	2.7	513 884	0.0	28 834	5.6	511 482	56.2	10.0
Prince George's	301 906	64.3	327 600	28.8	12.3	1 140	29.7	3.3	449 371	-0.3	33 412	7.4	452 182	38.4	18.3
Queen Anne's	17 188	84.8	375 700	26.2	12.0	1 050	30.6	1.5	26 484	0.4	1 844	7.0	24 211	37.4	21.1

1. Specified owner-occupied units.   2. Specified renter-occupied units. A value of 10.0 represents 10 percent or less.   3. Overcrowded or lacking complete plumbing facilities.   4. Percent of civilian labor force.   5. Persons 16 years old and over.

STATE County	Private nonfarm establishments, employment and payroll, 2009									Agriculture, 2007			
	Number of establish-ments	Employment						Annual payroll		Farms			
											Percent with:		Farm operators whose principal occu-pation is farming (percent)
		Total	Health care and social assistance	Manufac-turing	Retail trade	Finance and insurance	Professional, scientific, and technical services	Total (mil dol)	Average per employee (dollars)	Number	Fewer than 50 acres	500 acres or more	
	104	105	106	107	108	109	110	111	112	113	114	115	116
LOUISIANA—Cont'd													
Orleans	8 324	150 821	23 251	6 425	11 991	6 179	12 876	6 632	43 974	2	0.0	50.0	50.0
Ouachita	4 203	64 516	12 802	5 856	9 440	3 971	4 268	1 973	30 586	502	50.6	6.4	34.3
Plaquemines	679	10 239	403	1 851	475	105	678	553	54 056	177	53.1	23.7	57.1
Pointe Coupee	390	4 294	D	D	1 005	182	149	143	33 269	441	41.0	17.0	48.3
Rapides	3 268	49 277	13 646	4 124	7 621	1 669	1 678	1 548	31 406	977	54.4	7.4	46.4
Red River	135	1 755	446	125	188	74	27	63	35 910	251	30.7	13.9	45.0
Richland	399	4 747	1 841	330	765	182	119	123	25 963	866	29.1	15.9	34.1
Sabine	456	4 176	607	862	806	D	D	110	26 394	366	41.5	4.9	49.5
St. Bernard	627	6 681	574	1 284	1 087	133	145	262	39 270	45	24.4	51.1	57.8
St. Charles	946	20 046	1 320	4 465	1 632	246	1 115	1 144	57 084	58	43.1	6.9	44.8
St. Helena	117	1 209	348	204	167	D	25	34	27 819	364	38.2	3.3	42.3
St. James	309	6 431	471	2 305	632	D	D	385	59 942	64	35.9	35.9	76.6
St. John the Baptist	740	13 301	1 339	2 527	1 709	288	262	551	41 391	39	45.2	25.8	71.0
St. Landry	1 620	22 032	5 319	1 565	4 143	852	568	689	31 250	1 401	57.2	9.6	40.8
St. Martin	876	11 228	1 626	1 278	1 570	334	642	376	33 446	355	65.6	12.1	40.6
St. Mary	1 410	28 134	1 943	4 041	2 523	540	870	1 170	41 584	142	49.3	28.9	55.6
St. Tammany	5 856	67 769	13 335	2 374	13 074	3 381	5 230	2 394	35 322	602	74.1	2.3	42.7
Tangipahoa	2 293	33 587	7 699	2 753	6 656	1 926	887	923	27 475	1 188	48.9	2.7	44.1
Tensas	92	637	118	D	115	D	D	16	25 554	257	21.0	36.6	42.4
Terrebonne	2 950	50 887	6 636	5 194	7 486	1 085	2 237	2 029	39 864	169	45.6	17.8	42.6
Union	338	3 477	686	D	618	125	74	91	26 201	426	34.3	5.9	53.1
Vermilion	1 037	10 490	1 835	551	2 299	461	261	335	31 935	1 182	47.7	10.7	44.1
Vernon	685	8 785	1 696	274	1 687	323	962	241	27 438	479	53.9	4.2	47.0
Washington	672	7 774	2 247	D	1 387	317	185	226	29 122	916	52.1	2.7	41.2
Webster	816	10 937	2 100	1 724	2 090	405	230	335	30 631	430	49.5	3.3	42.6
West Baton Rouge	499	10 108	356	2 311	1 349	167	D	401	39 649	128	65.6	10.9	40.6
West Carroll	175	1 626	498	D	366	73	D	42	25 721	1 078	29.9	7.1	31.1
West Feliciana	184	2 400	364	D	346	D	34	124	51 473	176	38.1	17.0	33.5
Winn	329	4 289	984	604	549	140	D	129	30 065	150	40.0	5.3	34.7
MAINE	40 616	488 932	107 183	53 059	80 297	26 966	23 832	17 168	35 112	8 136	42.1	6.3	43.5
Androscoggin	2 766	44 030	10 013	6 036	6 147	2 869	1 459	1 507	34 216	378	47.9	5.3	52.4
Aroostook	2 059	22 395	6 351	2 674	4 421	764	563	628	28 063	1 246	18.9	13.3	35.1
Cumberland	10 858	155 966	31 486	9 248	21 650	13 428	11 141	6 231	39 949	630	61.6	2.5	40.2
Franklin	796	9 464	1 966	D	1 683	268	131	260	27 502	388	43.8	2.1	47.4
Hancock	2 129	16 650	3 145	1 681	3 183	541	2 002	611	36 675	386	52.1	4.4	37.6
Kennebec	3 360	43 990	12 484	2 408	8 545	1 127	1 735	1 470	33 416	649	43.1	4.3	47.5
Knox	1 723	13 626	2 771	1 421	2 636	713	780	438	32 129	304	53.9	3.3	49.0
Lincoln	1 421	8 483	1 913	779	1 639	314	292	269	31 683	363	54.3	1.4	44.1
Oxford	1 350	13 943	3 060	2 314	2 135	339	377	410	29 392	545	45.1	4.8	44.4
Penobscot	4 219	59 622	14 516	4 629	10 872	2 228	1 941	1 974	33 104	706	44.8	9.1	49.9
Piscataquis	440	4 301	D	822	881	72	69	120	27 830	190	31.6	9.5	44.2
Sagadahoc	942	13 170	1 431	D	1 783	D	751	540	41 032	183	39.9	1.6	49.2
Somerset	1 170	13 669	2 818	3 252	2 245	258	286	462	33 774	564	34.6	9.8	42.2
Waldo	956	8 756	1 628	D	1 408	D	194	270	30 790	424	37.7	7.8	47.4
Washington	871	7 324	2 000	842	1 719	289	135	209	28 516	472	44.5	5.9	36.9
York	5 492	52 213	10 081	8 788	9 349	1 751	1 914	1 695	32 457	708	53.2	1.8	45.9
MARYLAND	135 633	2 122 388	331 581	111 657	277 332	109 188	227 003	96 621	45 525	12 834	47.9	7.1	48.8
Allegany	1 691	23 725	6 071	2 430	3 846	855	580	700	29 502	302	29.1	1.3	36.8
Anne Arundel	13 729	200 856	22 480	13 513	31 482	6 769	19 173	9 124	45 427	377	62.1	2.9	49.6
Baltimore	20 040	322 180	58 738	19 141	47 078	22 153	24 690	13 827	42 918	751	61.5	3.3	48.6
Calvert	1 741	17 919	3 071	678	2 978	403	1 469	663	37 018	274	51.1	2.6	44.9
Caroline	661	6 826	742	D	998	197	206	203	29 811	574	38.2	13.9	58.4
Carroll	4 400	48 777	9 497	4 010	8 510	1 253	2 230	1 633	33 481	1 148	53.0	4.9	49.2
Cecil	1 792	24 235	4 263	D	4 026	464	605	928	38 303	583	52.7	7.2	50.8
Charles	2 701	32 497	4 351	670	8 761	993	1 934	1 063	32 718	418	45.7	4.8	49.8
Dorchester	748	9 005	1 873	2 063	1 156	276	150	276	30 678	424	35.8	17.5	58.7
Frederick	5 830	82 305	10 420	6 289	11 457	7 953	7 062	3 265	39 667	1 442	46.3	5.9	49.8
Garrett	948	10 568	1 656	909	1 782	D	304	297	28 137	677	26.9	3.0	45.8
Harford	5 321	66 567	9 684	4 599	11 931	2 210	8 046	2 343	35 199	704	58.1	4.1	40.9
Howard	8 520	149 381	12 622	5 248	15 197	6 941	30 732	8 161	54 634	335	68.1	3.9	39.4
Kent	668	6 932	1 416	775	833	241	233	217	31 256	377	31.8	15.1	53.1
Montgomery	26 480	411 814	59 303	9 262	44 868	22 566	68 301	22 760	55 267	561	64.9	4.8	43.5
Prince George's	14 387	247 211	28 444	8 784	36 030	6 674	24 673	10 307	41 693	375	61.9	2.9	42.9
Queen Anne's	1 403	11 056	898	1 174	2 299	365	623	347	31 378	521	35.5	18.0	51.8

Table B. States and Counties — **Agriculture**

STATE County	Land in farms Acreage (1,000) [117]	Percent change, 2002–2007 [118]	Acres Average size of farm [119]	Total irrigated (1,000) [120]	Total cropland (1,000) [121]	Value of land and buildings (dollars) Average per farm [122]	Average per acre [123]	Value of machinery and equipment, average per farm (dollars) [124]	Value of products sold Total (mil dol) [125]	Average per farm (dollars) [126]	Percent from: Crops [127]	Live-stock and poultry products [128]	Percent of farms with sales of: $10,000 or more [129]	$100,000 or more [130]	Government payments Total ($1,000) [131]	Percent of farms [132]
LOUISIANA—Cont'd																
Orleans	D	D	D	0.0	D	D	D	D	D	D	0.0	D	50.0	0.0	0	0.0
Ouachita	85	-10.5	170	7.3	50.5	380 479	2 238	65 946	33.6	67 016	38.4	61.6	24.1	8.4	2 081	24.9
Plaquemines	121	245.7	686	1.6	38.4	865 730	1 261	90 690	21.9	123 996	29.3	70.7	45.2	16.9	400	15.8
Pointe Coupee	191	-4.0	432	7.3	143.4	852 053	1 972	138 232	75.5	171 314	91.3	8.7	43.8	17.9	3 545	35.6
Rapides	177	-11.9	181	9.7	103.1	454 947	2 507	78 127	84.5	86 539	87.2	12.8	36.3	11.8	3 917	18.0
Red River	103	-25.4	412	0.6	37.3	690 202	1 676	78 992	20.8	82 992	45.1	54.9	33.5	8.8	1 574	36.3
Richland	291	34.7	336	77.1	203.2	539 159	1 603	83 110	65.4	75 534	88.1	11.9	33.4	13.4	11 139	80.9
Sabine	51	-19.0	138	0.2	13.7	409 674	2 965	61 291	105.3	287 826	0.5	99.5	38.8	18.3	298	7.9
St. Bernard	32	NA	712	D	3.2	837 797	1 176	102 260	8.2	182 815	1.5	98.5	55.6	26.7	53	15.6
St. Charles	D	D	D	0.0	D	D	D	53 973	D	D	D	D	46.6	3.4	13	12.1
St. Helena	52	2.0	144	0.1	17.1	437 896	3 044	57 715	29.1	79 960	1.6	98.4	30.8	6.3	310	19.2
St. James	43	-18.9	676	D	33.6	1 755 985	2 598	279 329	22.9	357 559	99.0	1.0	64.1	40.6	144	14.1
St. John the Baptist	14	-36.4	442	D	9.8	1 273 012	2 881	174 464	6.2	199 541	98.4	1.6	41.9	25.8	55	25.8
St. Landry	298	2.8	213	33.6	220.3	418 758	1 966	73 553	85.2	60 781	85.9	14.1	27.1	8.4	5 212	32.3
St. Martin	79	-2.5	222	8.4	58.6	534 942	2 408	100 741	31.3	88 102	88.2	11.8	34.1	12.1	1 084	17.2
St. Mary	73	0.0	512	0.0	63.7	1 146 836	2 239	220 985	43.6	307 171	97.7	2.3	37.3	26.8	147	10.6
St. Tammany	46	-9.8	76	0.6	10.4	408 119	5 399	48 897	11.9	19 754	59.0	41.0	23.1	3.3	278	5.5
Tangipahoa	124	5.1	104	1.6	55.9	406 142	3 895	56 686	63.3	53 260	24.2	75.8	30.8	11.3	2 461	21.5
Tensas	225	-0.4	877	27.0	188.8	1 414 564	1 613	202 095	85.1	331 196	99.9	0.1	40.9	31.9	11 020	90.7
Terrebonne	178	235.8	1 056	0.4	22.2	1 256 115	1 189	138 902	27.9	165 181	30.7	69.3	42.0	12.4	38	5.3
Union	67	-8.2	158	0.0	18.6	465 724	2 945	69 425	133.8	314 020	0.9	99.1	43.7	22.1	116	4.5
Vermilion	290	-19.2	246	58.9	184.3	491 297	2 000	75 512	68.2	57 703	73.2	26.8	28.8	9.5	7 386	56.7
Vernon	51	2.0	106	0.0	11.8	329 409	3 116	45 438	9.1	19 073	6.3	93.7	17.7	1.7	94	7.5
Washington	98	-3.9	107	0.3	45.0	351 400	3 295	51 482	34.1	37 211	33.4	66.6	26.1	6.4	1 054	19.5
Webster	49	-14.0	115	0.0	16.9	295 124	2 564	50 632	9.1	21 144	11.1	88.9	17.4	2.3	147	5.1
West Baton Rouge	26	18.2	202	D	19.9	604 352	2 996	126 362	14.4	112 580	74.8	25.2	29.7	14.1	256	14.8
West Carroll	197	7.1	183	36.2	113.7	335 608	1 838	51 273	34.9	32 378	90.7	9.3	18.1	6.3	7 633	88.4
West Feliciana	67	-1.5	379	0.0	12.8	912 760	2 410	62 132	4.3	24 439	43.0	57.0	25.0	2.3	204	22.2
Winn	21	0.0	143	0.1	6.6	308 389	2 162	37 441	16.4	109 101	2.7	97.3	21.3	5.3	59	8.7
MAINE	1 348	-1.6	166	21.0	529.3	364 807	2 203	65 961	617.2	75 859	52.9	47.1	31.1	9.5	8 815	17.9
Androscoggin	51	-8.9	135	0.5	23.1	402 339	2 991	112 469	68.4	181 071	11.2	88.8	36.2	16.4	487	15.1
Aroostook	376	-4.1	301	10.8	200.2	348 246	1 155	95 365	146.5	117 589	D	D	29.1	15.2	2 779	56.6
Cumberland	52	-3.7	82	0.3	18.1	408 345	4 973	64 136	20.0	31 683	D	D	28.1	7.3	357	9.0
Franklin	41	-18.0	105	0.1	12.2	276 055	2 629	43 546	8.4	21 708	25.2	74.8	22.9	5.7	401	17.3
Hancock	53	6.0	137	0.1	17.0	387 719	2 837	53 073	D	D	D	D	37.3	7.3	42	5.7
Kennebec	82	-4.7	127	0.1	38.3	345 766	2 721	65 728	63.5	97 875	13.3	86.7	29.7	8.2	1 520	11.1
Knox	30	3.4	99	0.2	12.1	382 856	3 867	42 360	D	D	0.0	D	35.5	5.9	58	4.9
Lincoln	30	-3.2	83	0.1	9.5	317 823	3 846	45 310	D	D	0.0	D	35.5	7.4	172	6.9
Oxford	69	3.0	126	0.5	19.7	348 394	2 763	44 297	D	D	0.0	D	25.1	3.7	495	13.2
Penobscot	115	7.5	162	1.8	47.1	370 924	2 285	67 340	42.5	60 231	30.2	69.8	32.7	9.1	889	11.5
Piscataquis	34	-12.8	179	0.1	9.3	358 841	2 002	43 773	6.5	34 177	35.2	64.8	26.8	7.9	368	23.2
Sagadahoc	19	-5.0	102	0.1	6.8	378 097	3 717	45 889	2.6	14 115	49.4	50.6	18.6	5.5	171	7.7
Somerset	111	0.9	197	0.1	34.1	371 927	1 883	80 643	53.4	94 687	D	D	34.0	12.9	539	20.0
Waldo	68	-1.4	161	0.1	24.3	364 618	2 266	52 706	22.8	53 820	21.9	78.1	34.0	10.8	331	10.4
Washington	158	3.9	336	4.6	35.7	379 601	1 131	66 977	66.1	140 112	D	D	40.9	9.3	94	5.7
York	59	3.5	84	1.3	22.0	394 389	4 706	53 327	20.7	29 254	D	D	29.2	7.8	113	6.2
MARYLAND	2 052	-1.3	160	92.8	1 405.4	1 124 529	7 034	98 823	1 835.1	142 987	34.3	65.7	41.5	17.6	33 386	35.7
Allegany	37	-5.1	121	0.3	12.5	534 085	4 402	40 200	3.2	10 461	58.3	41.7	28.5	1.0	191	24.5
Anne Arundel	29	-17.1	78	0.3	16.3	1 024 267	13 204	81 946	19.1	50 636	84.8	15.2	33.2	6.1	165	10.6
Baltimore	78	9.9	104	0.9	50.9	959 869	9 209	90 216	68.4	91 109	82.3	17.7	37.5	11.5	541	16.6
Calvert	26	-13.3	97	0.1	14.4	825 428	8 553	67 111	4.1	14 788	82.6	17.4	28.5	3.3	201	18.2
Caroline	131	13.9	229	24.6	107.1	1 260 068	5 510	136 800	186.0	324 109	26.3	73.7	57.3	35.9	3 028	63.4
Carroll	142	-3.4	124	1.0	103.2	974 324	7 881	100 900	87.4	76 138	53.4	46.6	39.5	11.5	2 921	33.0
Cecil	85	10.4	146	1.1	60.1	1 121 597	7 690	103 333	95.8	164 304	46.1	53.9	43.1	16.6	1 336	30.7
Charles	52	0.0	125	0.6	29.6	846 793	6 788	75 488	8.9	21 287	74.2	25.8	23.9	4.8	487	21.8
Dorchester	133	6.4	314	21.0	94.9	1 538 075	4 896	155 113	166.7	393 235	26.0	74.0	49.1	33.5	2 900	71.9
Frederick	202	3.1	140	1.0	143.7	1 169 355	8 344	97 310	127.0	88 095	28.3	71.7	40.0	13.8	2 852	35.0
Garrett	96	-5.0	141	0.4	46.0	816 952	5 791	66 682	25.7	38 000	25.1	74.9	43.3	12.1	295	18.9
Harford	75	-7.4	107	0.4	49.2	1 037 882	9 721	80 025	42.9	60 888	61.1	38.9	33.2	10.8	855	28.0
Howard	29	-23.7	88	0.2	18.7	1 158 349	13 212	66 470	22.7	67 717	78.9	21.1	29.6	7.8	246	12.8
Kent	128	9.4	340	7.9	101.4	2 076 300	6 105	165 727	85.7	227 350	54.1	45.9	56.2	27.9	2 864	73.2
Montgomery	68	-9.3	121	1.3	48.6	1 156 957	9 600	92 413	33.2	59 168	76.4	23.6	31.0	11.4	1 047	19.3
Prince George's	37	-17.8	99	0.7	17.4	933 487	9 460	67 749	18.6	49 652	92.0	8.0	27.2	4.8	208	14.1
Queen Anne's	147	-5.8	282	12.9	120.3	1 631 776	5 786	132 654	113.3	217 520	42.5	57.5	51.2	30.3	3 797	68.5

Table B. States and Counties — Water Use, Wholesale Trade, Retail Trade, and Real Estate

STATE County	Water use, 2005 — Total water withdrawn (mil gal/day)	Gallons withdrawn per person	Wholesale trade,[1] 2007 — Number of establishments	Number of employees	Sales (mil dol)	Annual payroll (mil dol)	Retail trade,[2] 2007 — Number of establishments	Number of employees	Sales (mil dol)	Annual payroll (mil dol)	Real estate and rental and leasing,[2] 2007 — Number of establishments	Number of employees	Receipts (mil dol)	Annual payroll (mil dol)
	133	134	135	136	137	138	139	140	141	142	143	144	145	146
LOUISIANA—Cont'd														
Orleans	456.3	1 003	253	3 030	1 938.4	145.6	1 155	11 877	2 718.0	305.5	362	1 764	354.4	61.8
Ouachita	77.2	521	184	D	D	D	738	9 569	2 221.6	195.7	193	862	149.4	27.4
Plaquemines	154.5	5 328	59	711	921.0	34.0	66	444	113.6	10.9	36	410	102.8	20.3
Pointe Coupee	310.7	13 883	8	79	177.0	3.1	89	1 016	216.3	16.6	12	34	11.0	1.4
Rapides	526.6	4 099	142	D	D	D	603	7 960	1 910.2	169.3	140	D	D	D
Red River	2.3	239	6	D	D	D	27	186	36.7	2.8	2	D	D	D
Richland	39.3	1 914	24	213	172.6	7.7	63	737	228.4	14.8	23	69	9.4	1.3
Sabine	3.9	164	12	D	D	D	81	824	172.7	15.4	14	46	6.5	1.5
St. Bernard	292.2	4 470	26	224	164.2	7.5	104	1 056	291.8	22.6	18	47	7.8	1.7
St. Charles	3 131.8	61 854	78	1 896	2 137.7	95.2	120	1 510	389.2	32.0	38	160	52.1	8.0
St. Helena	4.0	392	2	D	D	D	18	187	35.5	2.6	2	D	D	D
St. James	389.4	18 412	14	D	D	D	50	627	162.9	10.8	7	18	1.0	0.4
St. John the Baptist	619.5	13 353	31	672	2 540.8	36.6	114	1 742	454.8	35.5	36	188	53.2	7.5
St. Landry	65.8	731	59	D	D	D	326	4 132	970.7	83.1	57	184	21.2	4.2
St. Martin	56.7	1 124	45	655	326.1	21.9	137	1 581	407.6	34.5	42	659	213.0	38.7
St. Mary	162.4	3 158	81	D	D	D	209	2 396	508.2	46.7	90	667	155.9	29.0
St. Tammany	25.3	115	236	2 118	2 363.2	106.8	897	13 585	3 481.1	318.5	240	973	169.5	35.1
Tangipahoa	19.8	186	89	1 782	953.7	77.1	452	6 607	1 742.4	140.8	90	417	44.6	9.0
Tensas	20.7	3 378	9	D	D	D	18	116	31.8	2.0	2	D	D	D
Terrebonne	11.4	106	194	2 105	899.0	91.0	492	7 621	1 915.4	180.9	176	1 746	372.0	79.4
Union	5.8	251	6	D	D	D	71	690	148.1	12.3	5	12	1.7	0.3
Vermilion	156.9	2 842	40	D	D	D	197	2 054	518.3	43.8	43	482	55.7	14.2
Vernon	8.1	165	19	98	51.6	3.4	156	1 535	315.7	27.3	30	213	17.3	8.3
Washington	37.5	840	23	D	D	D	152	1 513	326.3	29.0	13	32	3.3	0.7
Webster	10.9	263	27	D	D	D	161	2 045	484.8	39.4	24	216	20.9	6.2
West Baton Rouge	14.4	664	34	578	602.2	27.7	78	1 202	319.7	22.4	11	76	2.1	0.6
West Carroll	29.1	2 487	7	D	D	D	29	397	67.7	6.1	7	24	2.4	0.4
West Feliciana	58.4	3 840	7	D	D	D	35	301	66.0	5.4	8	27	3.1	0.7
Winn	13.6	853	9	D	D	D	56	579	122.5	11.6	14	49	5.1	0.9
MAINE	604.6	458	1 439	16 939	8 823.7	686.4	6 911	83 279	20 444.0	1 893.7	1 771	6 942	1 054.0	209.4
Androscoggin	15.8	146	104	1 277	444.6	51.3	489	6 386	1 704.3	145.2	119	509	82.0	13.4
Aroostook	18.4	252	70	438	230.8	17.8	388	4 657	1 105.9	92.5	74	268	29.0	5.4
Cumberland	131.3	477	474	6 730	3 427.9	290.0	1 541	22 703	5 277.2	533.9	618	2 964	505.3	104.9
Franklin	3.2	107	16	D	D	D	166	1 678	381.3	35.4	29	120	10.7	2.7
Hancock	65.6	1 222	70	409	256.6	13.1	397	3 282	820.0	81.8	86	231	28.0	5.8
Kennebec	12.5	103	107	2 450	1 195.6	102.9	605	8 718	2 382.3	203.6	114	476	70.4	13.8
Knox	5.4	131	62	356	178.0	11.5	291	2 753	640.2	62.7	64	156	23.5	5.3
Lincoln	2.7	77	42	154	65.8	4.9	226	1 773	433.2	40.7	57	143	14.0	3.4
Oxford	38.6	681	30	470	188.3	17.9	253	2 286	489.5	47.4	49	172	17.6	3.7
Penobscot	45.1	307	158	D	D	D	777	10 842	2 983.9	241.6	172	782	124.9	21.8
Piscataquis	2.6	149	11	D	D	D	102	941	196.5	18.7	17	39	4.6	0.8
Sagadahoc	3.6	97	29	144	113.9	4.9	142	1 747	415.5	37.4	44	99	15.0	2.6
Somerset	87.3	1 690	27	350	76.7	9.4	239	2 358	577.3	49.4	35	122	13.6	2.8
Waldo	4.1	106	28	271	522.3	10.3	169	1 476	340.3	33.9	29	85	8.7	2.4
Washington	50.2	1 500	51	161	79.1	3.9	172	1 820	405.2	37.5	26	76	4.6	1.3
York	118.3	585	160	1 349	704.2	55.9	954	9 859	2 291.4	232.1	238	700	102.1	19.3
MARYLAND	7 492.3	1 338	5 020	79 868	51 276.8	4 158.4	19 601	294 806	75 664.2	7 290.8	6 768	49 766	12 391.9	2 262.6
Allegany	44.3	602	42	D	D	D	304	4 042	865.2	72.7	58	D	D	D
Anne Arundel	599.8	1 174	522	10 051	6 922.2	537.1	2 126	33 592	9 465.0	812.4	627	5 356	985.8	199.5
Baltimore	838.9	1 067	829	12 110	5 609.3	624.5	2 991	50 468	12 074.9	1 264.2	955	7 075	2 788.3	310.3
Calvert	3 345.4	38 049	32	151	43.7	5.5	230	3 042	730.6	67.7	107	465	115.1	17.1
Caroline	14.4	452	26	228	129.7	8.4	100	1 109	406.9	27.3	24	D	D	D
Carroll	15.6	92	139	1 604	556.1	63.8	580	8 764	2 141.8	188.9	177	D	D	D
Cecil	10.4	107	72	D	D	D	286	3 925	1 099.7	86.4	80	D	D	D
Charles	985.4	7 098	59	D	D	D	540	9 936	2 369.8	239.0	122	534	74.6	19.6
Dorchester	17.5	558	31	D	D	D	119	1 218	318.6	28.4	34	D	D	D
Frederick	43.1	195	208	2 481	1 252.1	123.6	790	12 349	3 066.3	296.9	267	1 439	231.1	50.5
Garrett	8.4	281	28	D	D	D	160	1 754	431.4	36.0	40	D	D	D
Harford	18.9	79	191	2 439	1 871.3	95.6	774	12 630	3 380.3	308.6	246	1 017	173.2	31.7
Howard	4.5	17	478	11 257	7 170.8	654.1	866	16 094	4 555.0	424.8	406	3 189	1 040.7	176.3
Kent	5.6	282	26	D	D	D	106	990	197.1	20.4	39	D	D	D
Montgomery	649.5	700	735	9 168	7 426.6	576.9	2 952	48 390	13 255.8	1 357.8	1 465	15 301	4 335.6	871.7
Prince George's	720.4	851	582	12 603	10 449.8	634.4	2 265	37 623	9 209.7	944.3	740	6 315	1 118.6	246.8
Queen Anne's	14.3	313	68	509	212.9	22.6	249	2 822	618.3	61.9	68	D	D	D

1. Merchant wholesalers, except manufacturers' sales branches and offices.   2. Employer establishments.

Table B. States and Counties — Professional Services, Manufacturing, and Accommodation and Food Services

STATE County	Professional, scientific, and technical services,[1] 2007				Manufacturing, 2007				Accommodation and food services, 2007			
	Number of establish-ments	Number of employees	Receipts (mil dol)	Annual payroll (mil dol)	Number of establish-ments	Number of employees	Receipts (mil dol)	Annual payroll (mil dol)	Number of establish-ments	Number of employees	Sales (mil dol)	Annual payroll (mil dol)
	147	148	149	150	151	152	153	154	155	156	157	158
LOUISIANA—Cont'd												
Orleans	1 290	D	D	D	141	7 607	3 088.9	402.0	1 058	28 356	2 148.2	602.4
Ouachita	441	D	D	D	135	D	D	D	285	6 554	250.3	67.8
Plaquemines	49	691	123.1	41.4	39	2 253	D	151.0	43	616	43.2	14.5
Pointe Coupee	31	120	13.3	4.3	NA	NA	NA	NA	30	363	14.0	3.3
Rapides	281	1 746	207.2	69.2	77	D	D	192.7	224	D	D	D
Red River	7	26	2.3	0.7	NA	NA	NA	NA	9	86	3.5	1.0
Richland	31	111	9.2	2.5	NA	NA	NA	NA	22	359	14.6	3.4
Sabine	39	165	12.8	5.5	21	893	D	34.8	17	282	14.0	3.2
St. Bernard	39	161	13.6	3.4	34	1 371	D	105.1	61	869	36.3	9.2
St. Charles	85	621	68.9	28.7	38	4 864	27 354.7	440.7	81	951	40.1	10.5
St. Helena	8	42	2.4	0.7	NA	NA	NA	NA	9	47	1.7	0.4
St. James	16	46	4.0	1.3	28	2 396	D	184.1	23	330	12.0	3.1
St. John the Baptist	55	341	42.9	11.7	28	2 426	D	178.5	71	1 427	55.5	13.9
St. Landry	130	605	66.6	23.3	55	1 732	D	68.9	97	1 454	56.6	13.9
St. Martin	78	D	D	D	58	1 361	324.3	51.0	77	983	45.1	10.9
St. Mary	106	694	104.2	42.9	90	4 417	2 011.1	200.6	107	1 597	60.3	15.9
St. Tammany	791	D	D	D	136	2 468	436.3	98.1	484	8 601	370.7	105.3
Tangipahoa	189	D	D	D	92	2 773	D	81.3	225	4 169	164.6	41.3
Tensas	4	D	D	D	NA	NA	NA	NA	7	19	0.5	0.2
Terrebonne	280	D	D	D	126	5 107	1 115.6	240.3	238	4 780	233.1	68.9
Union	21	D	D	D	11	D	D	D	17	244	10.2	2.5
Vermilion	109	288	30.7	9.7	42	903	D	30.4	64	1 038	51.1	10.1
Vernon	45	747	64.7	26.2	NA	NA	NA	NA	62	1 150	39.8	11.5
Washington	49	195	23.0	6.5	35	1 383	D	75.3	61	676	28.1	6.8
Webster	52	274	15.8	5.2	33	2 237	712.0	75.3	64	801	28.7	6.3
West Baton Rouge	28	190	25.4	7.1	36	2 442	D	123.4	47	753	35.2	8.2
West Carroll	11	21	1.8	0.5	NA	NA	NA	NA	10	76	4.1	1.0
West Feliciana	17	39	4.2	1.6	6	D	D	D	27	358	11.8	3.3
Winn	15	D	D	D	19	852	D	34.8	19	316	11.2	2.4
MAINE	3 444	20 504	2 686.1	1 004.9	1 825	58 938	16 363.2	2 524.5	3 938	49 363	2 515.8	747.7
Androscoggin	182	D	D	D	158	6 945	2 186.2	300.2	226	3 422	149.7	44.0
Aroostook	104	D	D	D	103	2 441	621.6	82.3	151	1 833	71.8	20.9
Cumberland	1 350	D	D	D	423	11 005	D	479.2	898	14 351	734.9	222.3
Franklin	49	D	D	D	32	1 721	823.5	83.7	90	1 220	43.0	13.0
Hancock	136	D	D	D	107	1 838	599.1	93.3	304	2 245	167.5	45.8
Kennebec	276	D	D	D	113	2 557	584.1	104.6	300	4 073	198.5	59.6
Knox	138	D	D	D	97	1 676	387.0	65.0	178	1 697	90.1	28.4
Lincoln	105	D	D	D	78	762	122.6	27.6	152	987	72.0	20.9
Oxford	79	D	D	D	72	2 682	865.8	132.6	144	2 402	92.6	29.9
Penobscot	333	D	D	D	155	4 795	1 088.5	171.9	320	5 179	224.2	68.1
Piscataquis	10	D	D	D	27	856	119.4	26.6	49	321	13.6	3.6
Sagadahoc	95	D	D	D	41	D	D	D	81	1 048	51.5	16.7
Somerset	63	394	34.5	17.6	71	3 532	1 566.9	163.6	111	1 070	45.0	13.2
Waldo	62	185	18.9	6.6	54	1 487	210.3	42.8	88	794	37.6	10.3
Washington	39	D	D	D	43	980	444.1	42.4	92	616	24.7	6.6
York	423	D	D	D	251	D	2 904.3	D	754	8 105	499.1	144.3
MARYLAND	19 345	D	D	D	3 680	127 780	41 456.1	6 453.7	10 802	192 619	10 758.4	2 915.9
Allegany	108	D	D	D	60	2 679	D	108.9	174	2 848	124.7	34.4
Anne Arundel	2 032	19 275	3 344.9	1 310.5	333	14 020	3 610.1	995.5	1 052	22 159	1 288.1	344.0
Baltimore	2 770	23 340	3 127.1	1 295.0	512	21 919	9 247.2	1 174.1	1 546	27 814	1 414.1	385.4
Calvert	202	D	D	D	49	D	D	D	122	2 518	110.7	30.9
Caroline	39	D	D	D	35	1 351	329.0	43.8	36	466	18.9	4.5
Carroll	470	D	D	D	155	4 369	1 095.1	203.2	251	5 293	203.8	61.2
Cecil	181	D	D	D	55	4 006	1 301.1	229.2	171	2 648	133.4	35.7
Charles	265	D	D	D	62	910	158.0	35.3	231	4 741	231.6	63.3
Dorchester	49	170	16.0	6.3	56	3 077	991.9	99.3	62	1 274	81.8	20.4
Frederick	815	D	D	D	181	7 076	3 003.7	334.7	392	7 542	356.5	106.0
Garrett	58	305	26.8	13.6	54	909	143.2	29.1	79	1 059	47.3	13.8
Harford	614	D	D	D	161	5 578	2 016.1	256.0	367	7 942	361.9	96.7
Howard	1 700	D	D	D	233	6 736	2 368.3	334.6	535	10 804	565.7	160.0
Kent	59	D	D	D	29	1 065	290.2	36.9	63	676	36.0	10.6
Montgomery	5 584	D	D	D	459	10 798	3 264.1	648.1	1 753	30 058	1 872.8	508.1
Prince George's	1 639	D	D	D	347	9 985	2 504.7	494.2	1 186	20 563	1 205.0	312.2
Queen Anne's	174	D	D	D	50	1 224	238.8	48.0	94	1 937	103.0	30.8

1. Establishment subject to federal tax.

Table B. States and Counties — Health Care and Social Assistance, Other Services, and Federal Funds

STATE County	Health care and social assistance, 2007				Other services, 2007				Federal funds and grants, 2009–2010 — Expenditures (mil dol)	Direct payments for individuals[1]		
	Number of establishments	Number of employees	Receipts (mil dol)	Annual payroll (mil dol)	Number of establishments	Number of employees	Receipts (mil dol)	Annual payroll (mil dol)	Total	Social Security and government retirement	Medicare	Food Stamps and Supplemental Security Income
	159	160	161	162	163	164	165	166	167	168	169	170
LOUISIANA—Cont'd												
Orleans	804	16 725	2 039.5	708.6	601	3 875	654.7	107.0	8 277.8	869.5	1 266.8	403.7
Ouachita	587	12 571	1 137.4	400.5	227	1 524	134.4	37.2	1 174.0	388.3	284.8	82.9
Plaquemines	25	D	D	D	45	D	D	D	376.9	55.2	45.2	10.4
Pointe Coupee	36	588	36.6	15.1	26	D	D	D	213.1	60.2	38.0	12.8
Rapides	487	D	D	D	228	1 192	101.7	27.8	1 407.9	438.8	270.1	75.2
Red River	17	465	27.7	12.0	9	D	D	D	94.1	23.4	22.7	5.4
Richland	65	1 633	95.4	39.5	23	71	5.9	1.3	228.5	53.8	56.1	14.0
Sabine	41	810	42.8	15.7	25	97	6.4	1.5	215.2	78.9	49.4	11.5
St. Bernard	45	374	31.6	10.5	32	D	D	D	882.4	75.0	179.4	21.0
St. Charles	74	1 397	85.3	36.9	56	344	63.0	16.2	370.1	119.1	69.5	15.6
St. Helena	15	376	18.4	8.9	4	D	D	D	83.2	18.9	19.4	7.9
St. James	29	441	32.4	13.6	13	42	4.1	0.9	162.9	62.1	47.0	12.5
St. John the Baptist	73	D	D	D	48	D	D	D	263.8	117.4	63.5	23.3
St. Landry	275	4 794	424.4	150.3	77	363	24.1	7.6	881.1	249.7	188.4	69.7
St. Martin	69	1 334	57.6	27.9	46	109	12.2	2.5	364.7	117.9	70.8	22.1
St. Mary	105	1 931	136.8	50.2	91	447	56.2	14.4	498.4	154.8	100.1	37.2
St. Tammany	715	12 287	1 256.7	485.5	364	2 053	168.1	51.9	1 383.9	716.5	275.7	51.4
Tangipahoa	269	7 321	568.5	226.1	150	919	86.4	21.7	928.9	307.4	224.6	70.6
Tensas	11	D	D	D	NA	NA	NA	NA	104.4	14.2	19.3	6.1
Terrebonne	255	6 396	619.2	253.0	173	1 575	222.5	63.2	792.9	298.0	174.8	58.9
Union	29	740	43.5	15.7	18	49	4.1	0.8	205.0	75.9	64.3	10.8
Vermillion	104	1 458	100.3	38.8	58	248	22.5	5.5	381.0	140.4	99.2	27.3
Vernon	70	1 620	170.7	55.0	50	324	32.7	9.3	2 271.3	171.3	67.2	16.5
Washington	89	1 933	132.1	55.3	42	189	13.5	3.4	493.9	152.3	160.2	34.2
Webster	92	2 374	166.5	59.4	36	227	20.3	5.5	411.4	146.4	106.6	24.7
West Baton Rouge	28	D	D	D	32	201	29.7	7.6	233.3	54.6	40.7	11.0
West Carroll	17	653	32.0	12.8	15	68	3.7	1.2	135.0	33.9	34.3	6.5
West Feliciana	20	321	26.0	9.4	7	D	D	D	71.0	23.8	14.8	4.1
Winn	43	820	52.6	21.9	18	111	10.5	4.1	142.7	43.1	41.3	9.8
MAINE	4 875	104 151	8 592.4	3 691.6	2 840	13 297	1 279.7	328.1	14 643.9	4 679.4	1 837.0	569.4
Androscoggin	421	9 495	872.4	355.7	203	945	69.8	21.2	874.9	352.8	171.4	57.0
Aroostook	252	6 327	419.9	188.5	134	410	37.3	8.8	974.3	305.0	130.3	45.8
Cumberland	1 316	29 849	2 669.0	1 155.5	764	4 199	398.0	107.0	2 505.9	864.5	363.0	88.5
Franklin	100	1 888	132.8	55.7	51	204	19.4	4.1	221.2	90.5	48.8	14.1
Hancock	160	2 936	252.3	110.6	137	749	120.8	22.8	542.7	195.6	77.1	18.4
Kennebec	496	11 949	996.5	435.9	292	1 289	146.4	36.0	2 137.6	455.5	154.2	57.8
Knox	177	3 111	215.9	88.8	118	545	58.5	15.1	361.0	157.9	64.3	15.5
Lincoln	102	1 878	131.4	52.9	97	491	38.4	12.2	298.9	146.6	53.3	10.8
Oxford	155	2 961	217.3	87.0	95	354	32.9	8.1	458.3	197.9	93.1	27.6
Penobscot	563	14 538	1 318.9	561.6	276	1 350	139.8	33.6	1 644.1	537.9	207.0	75.8
Piscataquis	44	1 420	81.8	38.9	21	69	6.0	1.4	170.1	78.1	30.0	10.3
Sagadahoc	117	1 372	80.3	34.0	65	326	27.0	8.3	898.4	138.9	33.2	10.7
Somerset	153	3 119	202.8	88.7	94	340	25.5	6.6	445.4	183.9	72.3	34.8
Waldo	111	1 526	116.3	52.0	75	243	23.3	5.4	333.4	131.5	42.7	20.8
Washington	110	2 256	147.2	70.0	59	191	18.0	5.0	455.3	136.7	61.9	24.9
York	598	9 526	737.7	315.7	359	1 592	118.8	32.6	1 686.8	703.2	239.8	59.8
MARYLAND	15 304	315 781	33 826.6	13 089.4	10 365	77 368	9 688.6	2 487.4	96 260.9	18 444.1	14 530.9	1 552.4
Allegany	256	5 848	558.7	209.7	159	858	63.4	17.4	961.7	292.3	379.7	33.3
Anne Arundel	1 184	21 198	2 092.9	851.2	1 095	7 437	691.4	232.8	8 209.5	1 929.3	1 024.5	78.3
Baltimore	2 645	57 385	5 767.6	2 276.7	1 499	10 625	1 072.8	320.0	9 169.4	2 530.4	1 969.5	231.3
Calvert	173	3 200	300.6	114.6	131	770	58.6	19.2	569.2	317.7	126.6	10.8
Caroline	49	667	33.3	17.6	52	226	19.0	5.4	449.0	100.2	111.0	9.4
Carroll	457	8 597	854.7	308.0	352	2 086	147.9	49.5	1 132.3	581.5	298.5	15.7
Cecil	155	5 507	637.1	280.1	152	838	65.9	19.1	707.0	320.9	172.8	22.4
Charles	311	4 069	384.7	150.7	231	1 471	114.6	38.3	1 367.7	543.9	209.9	27.9
Dorchester	85	1 626	130.9	56.6	63	280	18.0	4.6	508.4	117.4	148.4	15.7
Frederick	531	9 326	936.8	368.8	400	2 549	266.1	76.0	2 645.5	647.9	268.1	23.6
Garrett	73	1 602	95.8	42.7	77	702	44.7	18.3	290.7	98.7	102.2	9.9
Harford	545	8 231	782.3	297.9	436	2 714	196.2	65.0	3 147.6	824.0	372.6	36.9
Howard	804	12 295	1 131.0	458.3	524	4 238	452.0	147.4	3 351.7	695.0	204.8	23.1
Kent	72	1 333	121.6	47.2	52	191	21.4	5.3	222.3	98.2	75.4	4.0
Montgomery	3 376	54 741	6 553.4	2 574.9	1 939	17 446	3 379.3	756.2	20 664.2	2 851.8	1 484.4	128.8
Prince George's	1 763	27 511	2 588.3	1 026.7	1 212	9 385	968.3	278.2	13 879.8	2 979.9	1 424.3	189.0
Queen Anne's	67	873	56.0	24.7	109	596	47.2	12.5	315.3	149.3	72.7	4.9

1. State totals may include programs not allocated by county.

Federal Funds, Residential Construction, and Local Government Finances

	Federal funds and grants, 2009–2010 (cont.)							Value of residential construction authorized by building permits, 2010		Local government finances, 2007				
	Expenditures (mil dol) (cont.)									General revenue				
		Procurement contract awards		Grants[1]								Taxes		
													Per capita[2] (dollars)	
STATE County	Salaries and wages	Defense	Other	Medicaid and other health-related	Nutrition and family welfare	Education	Other	New construction ($1,000)	Number of housing units	Total (mil dol)	Inter-govern-mental (mil dol)	Total (mil dol)	Total	Property
	171	172	173	174	175	176	177	178	179	180	181	182	183	184
LOUISIANA—Cont'd														
Orleans	774.6	2 495.4	527.4	1 176.9	120.2	110.8	378.1	153 978	1 080	1 569.3	514.0	609.2	2 548	1 134
Ouachita	68.3	10.1	9.7	186.6	25.5	17.1	41.4	58 009	423	523.7	232.3	226.6	1 516	474
Plaquemines	37.9	143.9	48.8	23.0	4.8	1.7	4.7	5 197	72	215.6	112.3	62.6	2 906	1 629
Pointe Coupee	11.9	12.2	0.9	58.4	6.4	2.0	0.2	7 379	45	79.0	28.2	29.2	1 305	655
Rapides	229.9	11.0	84.6	185.5	31.6	12.3	44.9	55 649	397	430.3	203.4	167.6	1 288	468
Red River	8.0	0.0	0.3	28.3	2.9	0.8	0.3	0	0	30.6	16.7	9.2	1 002	432
Richland	8.0	0.0	1.2	64.9	5.9	2.0	3.3	19 329	120	86.3	39.5	18.7	914	287
Sabine	5.4	2.0	0.9	54.6	5.7	2.9	1.1	0	0	60.4	35.2	20.3	857	326
St. Bernard	3.9	534.6	0.2	36.7	10.7	4.8	11.0	2 874	24	291.6	188.8	63.5	3 202	1 076
St. Charles	11.6	103.0	3.0	29.3	8.5	3.0	3.9	13 360	91	305.5	58.5	167.8	3 225	1 786
St. Helena	1.2	0.0	0.2	26.1	3.2	2.8	0.8	0	0	33.3	16.5	6.5	614	308
St. James	3.1	0.5	0.7	25.8	6.4	1.8	1.7	8 399	40	111.2	32.7	51.6	2 390	1 505
St. John the Baptist	9.6	0.2	1.2	24.8	9.4	3.0	7.1	7 920	52	156.7	52.1	67.9	1 425	594
St. Landry	17.5	9.8	3.5	273.7	27.3	11.9	6.6	22 777	139	318.6	136.2	88.5	968	267
St. Martin	19.4	22.9	1.7	85.4	9.8	5.3	1.8	22 227	160	130.3	70.5	39.5	764	318
St. Mary	17.1	70.1	16.3	68.4	16.6	6.2	3.4	7 353	56	208.8	85.4	76.8	1 497	664
St. Tammany	78.1	93.5	13.0	81.1	33.4	8.6	17.9	112 032	578	1 134.6	348.3	419.9	1 853	720
Tangipahoa	50.5	4.0	-1.2	195.5	22.0	14.3	7.8	71 937	526	514.9	184.0	114.5	992	260
Tensas	1.2	9.4	0.3	27.7	2.5	1.1	1.4	813	7	25.6	16.1	7.2	1 223	689
Terrebonne	35.7	39.1	41.8	90.9	19.8	10.5	14.6	46 609	161	514.7	167.9	153.2	1 413	368
Union	9.1	0.0	3.6	42.0	4.3	1.6	0.8	2 931	18	52.0	27.3	15.5	679	239
Vermilion	17.1	0.5	2.5	65.1	9.8	4.8	4.9	21 840	131	188.2	77.7	60.0	1 078	433
Vernon	1 435.6	498.6	1.5	46.6	10.8	9.4	7.1	1 175	14	124.3	77.2	37.1	783	265
Washington	18.9	0.5	3.0	101.6	9.6	4.0	3.4	7 979	68	198.2	121.6	44.7	996	389
Webster	23.5	5.3	1.8	76.1	10.9	3.7	4.0	11 052	57	123.1	59.8	47.3	1 155	404
West Baton Rouge	4.4	109.7	-18.9	24.5	4.7	1.5	0.0	25 322	157	87.8	31.0	39.0	1 724	786
West Carroll	5.6	0.0	0.5	37.1	3.2	1.0	0.6	140	1	29.8	17.3	9.6	831	259
West Feliciana	1.7	7.0	0.3	14.0	3.0	0.7	0.0	12 162	38	106.8	19.2	29.3	1 941	1 385
Winn	12.7	0.0	0.8	31.8	3.7	1.8	-4.2	0	0	38.6	22.1	12.6	812	372
MAINE	1 134.0	1 336.2	399.5	2 186.8	340.3	229.6	1 030.8	13 413	101	X	X	X	X	X
Androscoggin	46.5	1.1	5.4	178.8	17.7	6.3	18.2	28 397	206	330.4	146.7	142.8	1 337	1 325
Aroostook	75.4	8.7	99.7	225.5	22.8	4.7	21.3	13 196	93	253.4	109.6	74.7	1 037	1 032
Cumberland	246.1	282.5	79.3	335.9	40.2	11.3	114.7	123 850	585	998.6	258.3	529.9	1 924	1 889
Franklin	9.0	0.6	2.3	39.0	6.7	1.7	0.9	17 594	100	89.0	31.1	49.7	1 659	1 647
Hancock	25.6	4.1	24.2	165.2	10.6	1.8	17.0	35 628	175	169.3	38.0	109.3	2 052	2 036
Kennebec	157.9	5.1	69.5	292.9	88.2	118.4	670.4	39 976	303	337.7	158.7	135.1	1 118	1 109
Knox	13.6	2.1	4.8	82.2	6.8	1.9	4.5	14 221	75	113.8	21.1	77.7	1 906	1 888
Lincoln	9.3	0.0	3.5	42.8	6.7	0.9	21.8	16 276	77	116.0	34.6	68.7	1 974	1 955
Oxford	16.8	0.0	7.4	85.7	15.3	1.8	4.7	23 162	143	173.7	76.3	84.1	1 482	1 473
Penobscot	173.7	131.4	69.6	254.0	28.6	10.5	90.0	38 001	272	413.1	167.1	177.0	1 190	1 173
Piscataquis	4.6	0.7	0.9	34.5	3.7	0.7	3.3	1 432	20	86.1	29.3	21.7	1 261	1 255
Sagadahoc	29.4	647.5	1.5	26.8	6.3	0.9	1.1	18 831	102	119.0	42.1	65.7	1 806	1 791
Somerset	18.2	0.1	4.7	106.9	9.5	2.1	4.7	6 877	60	171.0	85.8	72.2	1 398	1 395
Waldo	11.5	46.0	2.4	63.7	7.1	1.2	0.9	14 413	65	100.0	38.8	52.1	1 353	1 349
Washington	28.8	41.9	13.8	104.0	10.7	4.6	8.5	10 112	84	94.9	43.8	42.1	1 285	1 271
York	267.8	164.4	10.3	148.6	27.1	6.5	41.3	109 901	573	588.9	183.6	343.7	1 707	1 680
MARYLAND	15 041.5	12 017.6	14 504.9	7 701.5	1 138.0	1 112.8	4 489.1	1 951 870	11 931	X	X	X	X	X
Allegany	53.5	1.6	12.2	126.2	18.9	4.6	17.6	16 436	122	294.2	150.8	73.7	1 015	592
Anne Arundel	1 791.7	1 879.0	252.0	321.6	66.4	446.7	294.3	206 116	1 711	1 768.5	444.5	1 040.4	2 032	974
Baltimore	1 572.7	857.3	915.4	542.0	86.2	17.0	394.6	172 951	1 230	2 559.9	799.1	1 440.0	1 825	849
Calvert	10.6	13.0	28.3	40.3	8.2	1.3	5.6	38 762	222	330.9	109.9	171.5	1 944	1 110
Caroline	160.4	1.1	1.8	49.8	5.9	0.9	0.4	6 718	67	113.0	65.2	33.6	1 022	584
Carroll	39.3	40.2	19.2	66.2	14.9	2.0	40.8	41 358	195	413.7	37.1	307.7	1 818	1 009
Cecil	67.8	9.8	37.6	45.5	12.1	2.0	6.8	58 217	364	336.2	144.0	146.5	1 469	856
Charles	154.3	278.3	13.2	72.3	19.8	3.2	13.6	131 599	576	361.7	40.8	264.5	1 883	1 048
Dorchester	12.6	2.3	6.0	59.0	6.5	1.6	133.9	15 778	156	123.5	53.0	47.8	1 500	919
Frederick	268.1	569.7	718.7	82.2	24.1	4.1	14.5	178 134	939	917.8	285.5	466.8	2 078	1 162
Garrett	6.3	7.3	4.0	41.5	11.2	1.2	2.0	22 498	95	129.9	56.0	55.1	1 859	1 198
Harford	878.2	823.5	61.3	90.3	25.3	4.5	12.8	116 270	771	844.1	276.9	432.4	1 802	989
Howard	63.5	1 576.9	594.0	50.0	23.3	4.2	81.9	215 318	1 151	1 187.3	278.0	779.7	2 849	1 403
Kent	6.2	0.0	2.2	22.4	3.6	1.4	1.4	12 754	61	73.7	27.6	37.7	1 889	1 146
Montgomery	5 128.6	2 555.8	6 596.2	876.8	98.2	30.2	743.9	343 322	1 899	4 656.7	909.8	3 077.1	3 306	1 388
Prince George's	3 133.9	750.7	4 171.1	545.9	122.1	37.8	389.9	94 514	707	3 353.2	1 185.9	1 623.1	1 958	1 019
Queen Anne's	7.9	31.2	8.8	21.2	5.2	0.9	6.3	29 159	167	200.8	62.7	94.7	2 034	1 024

1. State totals may include programs not allocated by county.   2. Based on the resident population estimated as of July 1 of the year shown.

Table B. States and Counties — Local Government Finances, Government Employment, and Voting

STATE County	Local government finances, 2007 (cont.) Direct general expenditure Total (mil dol)	Per capita[1] (dollars)	Percent of total for: Education	Health and hospitals	Police protection	Public welfare	Highways	Debt outstanding Total (mil dol)	Per capita[1] (dollars)	Government employment, 2009 Federal civilian	Federal military	State and local	Presidential election,[2] 2008 Percent of vote cast: Democratic	Republican	All other
	185	186	187	188	189	190	191	192	193	194	195	196	197	198	199
LOUISIANA—Cont'd															
Orleans	1 250.0	5 227	19.3	1.2	11.0	0.0	1.7	2 804.5	11 728	9 724	3 513	32 233	79.4	19.1	1.5
Ouachita	493.3	3 299	49.4	2.2	5.7	0.1	4.9	386.4	2 585	502	636	12 394	36.9	62.1	1.0
Plaquemines	179.5	8 331	39.8	1.8	5.5	0.3	1.4	62.4	2 899	628	496	1 786	32.3	66.0	1.7
Pointe Coupee	74.7	3 338	39.6	19.6	6.4	0.1	1.5	45.0	2 009	71	93	1 142	44.4	53.9	1.7
Rapides	409.8	3 151	49.5	0.2	9.4	0.0	4.8	342.3	2 632	2 363	564	11 441	35.0	63.6	1.4
Red River	28.1	3 054	55.6	0.0	4.8	0.0	2.7	8.5	924	24	37	467	44.9	53.7	1.4
Richland	86.2	4 210	36.9	32.6	3.8	0.0	3.0	28.5	1 394	91	85	1 156	36.1	62.6	1.3
Sabine	55.0	2 321	64.5	0.3	5.5	0.0	7.7	31.5	1 329	50	99	1 344	23.3	74.9	1.9
St. Bernard	245.5	12 382	37.6	0.2	8.9	0.2	2.5	164.7	8 308	47	169	2 080	25.8	71.2	3.0
St. Charles	271.0	5 207	45.2	11.6	5.6	0.3	3.6	481.1	9 244	169	215	3 581	33.6	64.8	1.6
St. Helena	31.2	2 937	39.7	33.2	4.6	0.0	7.6	8.6	807	11	49	660	57.7	40.8	1.5
St. James	97.9	4 539	48.9	11.3	5.7	1.7	2.6	103.6	4 800	37	88	1 615	55.7	43.2	1.1
St. John the Baptist	135.0	2 831	50.7	0.4	6.2	0.2	3.6	224.0	4 697	119	196	2 187	57.4	41.2	1.5
St. Landry	302.2	3 308	42.2	27.4	5.2	0.0	2.5	112.5	1 231	182	385	5 673	47.7	50.9	1.4
St. Martin	121.9	2 360	52.8	6.5	8.5	0.1	2.6	102.7	1 988	70	217	2 175	38.8	59.6	1.6
St. Mary	195.8	3 816	46.2	11.9	5.9	0.1	4.0	148.2	2 889	151	325	4 981	40.8	57.6	1.6
St. Tammany	1 020.2	4 502	38.0	27.2	3.6	0.1	4.2	758.2	3 346	521	964	13 635	22.5	75.8	1.7
Tangipahoa	487.7	4 226	30.8	44.7	3.7	0.1	4.3	166.8	1 446	342	495	11 429	33.8	64.7	1.5
Tensas	29.5	5 024	31.5	1.2	5.0	0.0	3.5	23.8	4 062	29	23	377	54.1	45.0	0.9
Terrebonne	467.9	4 315	34.9	32.7	3.9	0.3	1.2	173.5	1 600	296	494	6 673	28.5	69.3	2.2
Union	50.0	2 197	51.0	9.1	4.8	0.2	4.4	10.5	462	96	94	1 012	28.6	70.1	1.3
Vermilion	177.5	3 187	44.3	23.0	5.5	0.1	3.6	30.1	540	148	246	2 955	25.2	72.8	2.0
Vernon	123.4	2 605	67.5	0.4	5.5	0.0	6.0	40.2	849	2 192	8 946	2 666	22.4	75.8	1.8
Washington	193.4	4 306	41.0	10.0	4.1	0.0	3.6	82.9	1 846	114	190	3 665	32.9	65.6	1.5
Webster	129.6	3 168	66.5	0.3	4.6	1.6	3.4	106.5	2 601	117	169	2 170	36.2	62.5	1.3
West Baton Rouge	80.7	3 568	39.1	0.5	8.9	0.5	4.5	61.6	2 722	133	94	1 537	42.5	56.1	1.4
West Carroll	28.1	2 429	62.8	5.1	4.2	0.1	6.1	7.0	609	39	47	847	17.6	81.1	1.3
West Feliciana	76.3	5 049	33.8	11.5	5.2	0.2	3.6	487.8	32 278	17	63	2 581	43.0	56.0	1.0
Winn	40.4	2 605	65.1	0.4	5.4	0.1	4.3	22.6	1 459	62	64	823	30.2	68.4	1.4
MAINE	X	X	X	X	X	X	X	X	X	15 006	8 293	88 154	57.7	40.4	1.9
Androscoggin	325.1	3 043	50.6	0.2	3.6	0.2	4.5	321.5	3 010	362	357	5 202	56.5	41.3	2.1
Aroostook	246.6	3 422	50.3	17.2	2.5	0.3	6.6	83.0	1 151	1 248	240	5 626	53.7	44.2	2.1
Cumberland	962.9	3 497	44.0	1.2	4.8	2.7	5.2	890.9	3 235	2 629	3 180	18 719	64.1	34.2	1.7
Franklin	84.5	2 823	60.7	0.5	3.2	0.1	9.6	71.2	2 378	119	98	1 927	58.9	38.6	2.5
Hancock	168.1	3 155	57.4	0.2	2.9	0.2	7.3	99.0	1 858	354	292	2 964	58.7	39.4	1.8
Kennebec	349.0	2 888	63.0	0.8	3.1	0.3	5.8	231.1	1 913	2 002	405	14 018	56.4	41.6	1.9
Knox	116.8	2 864	49.4	0.5	4.5	0.2	9.0	98.4	2 413	121	212	2 754	59.7	38.4	1.9
Lincoln	130.5	3 751	60.2	0.6	2.5	0.3	5.7	106.9	3 072	105	138	1 619	55.1	43.0	1.9
Oxford	182.6	3 219	66.8	0.4	2.7	0.2	7.7	73.9	1 302	170	186	3 152	56.7	40.6	2.7
Penobscot	434.5	2 920	52.8	0.4	4.1	0.5	4.6	271.7	1 826	1 385	509	13 376	51.7	46.6	1.7
Piscataquis	92.4	5 381	42.2	34.7	2.0	0.2	3.6	27.2	1 580	63	56	1 334	47.0	50.7	2.3
Sagadahoc	123.7	3 400	59.1	0.3	3.9	0.2	5.9	86.9	2 389	336	449	1 608	57.0	40.9	2.0
Somerset	168.8	3 267	69.6	0.5	2.8	0.3	5.8	86.9	1 682	216	168	2 604	51.8	46.1	2.2
Waldo	104.8	2 721	62.1	1.0	2.1	0.4	8.5	82.4	2 139	104	135	1 711	54.8	43.1	2.1
Washington	95.2	2 907	62.0	0.5	3.0	0.2	7.4	24.1	735	408	168	2 375	49.5	48.5	2.0
York	575.5	2 858	58.2	0.3	5.6	0.3	7.0	301.6	1 498	5 384	1 710	8 565	59.4	38.8	1.8
MARYLAND	X	X	X	X	X	X	X	X	X	163 392	46 350	347 418	61.9	36.5	1.6
Allegany	301.8	4 157	55.9	1.8	2.8	7.2	3.9	159.8	2 201	555	213	6 220	36.0	61.9	2.2
Anne Arundel	1 783.0	3 481	55.5	2.2	5.8	0.8	3.4	1 777.5	3 471	37 770	15 138	29 089	48.2	50.0	1.9
Baltimore	2 748.4	3 483	54.5	1.6	6.3	0.4	2.8	2 010.2	2 548	15 831	2 317	40 944	56.2	41.7	2.1
Calvert	331.9	3 762	57.2	1.0	3.3	1.0	6.0	217.9	2 470	150	302	4 022	46.1	52.4	1.5
Caroline	120.1	3 649	56.1	2.0	4.3	0.1	4.0	70.5	2 143	84	98	1 537	37.6	60.6	1.8
Carroll	513.0	3 031	60.7	1.5	3.1	0.8	6.1	412.2	2 436	318	585	8 124	33.1	64.3	2.6
Cecil	331.6	3 327	62.8	1.7	3.7	0.5	6.4	189.5	1 900	1 722	295	4 446	41.6	56.1	2.3
Charles	581.7	4 142	56.7	0.7	8.0	0.7	2.9	433.9	3 089	2 232	1 052	7 025	62.2	36.7	1.1
Dorchester	131.4	4 126	41.8	0.6	8.0	1.8	5.9	46.5	1 460	154	94	2 149	45.3	53.5	1.3
Frederick	907.0	4 036	54.1	1.0	4.7	3.7	4.0	789.9	3 515	3 769	1 788	12 022	48.6	49.6	1.8
Garrett	125.9	4 250	50.1	0.9	2.4	0.0	12.5	18.3	617	76	86	1 691	29.0	69.2	1.8
Harford	855.8	3 566	58.7	0.5	5.6	0.8	5.7	235.5	981	8 663	3 495	9 562	39.4	58.2	2.4
Howard	1 212.9	4 432	62.6	1.0	5.7	1.4	3.3	1 105.8	4 041	628	823	17 309	60.0	38.1	1.9
Kent	72.8	3 642	45.9	1.3	4.9	1.5	5.8	35.1	1 757	80	59	1 053	49.4	49.0	1.6
Montgomery	4 525.1	4 861	50.1	3.0	4.7	3.0	3.9	3 766.8	4 047	46 211	6 381	39 130	71.6	27.0	1.4
Prince George's	3 180.7	3 838	54.8	2.1	6.7	0.6	2.6	2 228.7	2 689	26 057	7 639	64 038	88.9	10.4	0.7
Queen Anne's	201.2	4 321	58.0	1.1	2.7	0.9	3.4	143.7	3 086	97	140	2 567	35.7	62.7	1.6

1. Based on the resident population estimated as of July 1 of the year shown.   2. © 2009 Election Data Services, Inc. All rights reserved.

STATE/ County code	CBSA code[1]	County type[2]	STATE County	Population and population characteristics, 2010				Race alone or in combination, not Hispanic or Latino (percent)					Age (percent)					
				Land area,[3] (sq km) 2010	Total persons	Rank	Per square kilometer	White	Black	American Indian, Alaska Native	Asian and Pacific Islander	Percent Hispanic or Latino[4]	Under 5 years	5 to 17 years	18 to 24 years	25 to 34 years	35 to 44 years	45 to 54 years
				1	2	3	4	5	6	7	8	9	10	11	12	13	14	15
			MARYLAND—Cont'd															
24 037	30500	4	St. Mary's	925	105 151	559	113.7	78.9	15.6	1.0	3.5	3.8	7.2	19.0	9.9	12.7	14.0	16.1
24 039	41540	3	Somerset	828	26 470	1 544	32.0	53.4	42.9	0.9	0.9	3.3	4.8	12.0	19.2	12.4	11.5	14.2
24 041	20660	6	Talbot	696	37 782	1 222	54.3	80.2	13.4	0.5	1.6	5.5	4.9	14.6	6.6	9.2	11.1	14.7
24 043	25180	3	Washington	1 186	147 430	423	124.3	85.3	10.8	0.6	1.9	3.5	6.1	16.8	8.4	12.6	14.2	15.6
24 045	41540	3	Wicomico	970	98 733	591	101.8	68.4	25.2	0.7	3.0	4.5	6.2	16.2	14.7	12.2	11.8	14.2
24 047	36180	4	Worcester	1 213	51 454	958	42.4	81.7	14.4	0.7	1.5	3.2	4.5	13.8	6.7	9.1	11.2	15.5
24 510	12580	1	Baltimore city	210	620 961	100	2 957.0	29.2	64.4	0.9	2.9	4.2	6.6	14.9	12.6	16.7	12.3	14.1
25 000	...	X	MASSACHUSETTS	20 202	6 547 629	X	324.1	77.6	6.8	0.5	6.0	9.6	5.6	16.1	10.4	12.9	13.5	15.5
25 001	12700	3	Barnstable	1 020	215 888	288	211.7	93.0	2.6	1.2	1.5	2.2	4.1	13.2	6.5	8.2	10.6	15.9
25 003	38340	3	Berkshire	2 400	131 219	473	54.7	92.3	3.6	0.6	1.7	3.5	4.7	14.9	9.4	9.8	11.7	16.1
25 005	39300	1	Bristol	1 433	548 285	111	382.6	87.2	4.0	0.6	2.3	6.0	5.7	16.6	9.5	11.8	14.1	15.8
25 007	...	7	Dukes	267	16 535	2 015	61.9	89.0	4.4	2.7	1.2	2.3	5.3	13.9	6.0	11.2	13.2	16.8
25 009	14460	1	Essex	1 276	743 159	77	582.4	77.2	3.2	0.4	3.6	16.5	5.9	17.3	8.8	11.3	13.5	16.3
25 011	44140	2	Franklin	1 811	71 372	749	39.4	94.1	1.7	1.0	1.8	3.2	4.8	14.9	8.2	10.7	12.4	17.0
25 013	44140	2	Hampden	1 598	463 490	142	290.0	69.0	8.5	0.6	2.4	20.9	6.0	17.7	10.6	11.7	12.6	15.0
25 015	44140	2	Hampshire	1 366	158 080	393	115.7	87.9	3.0	0.6	5.4	4.7	3.9	13.0	21.3	10.3	11.1	14.5
25 017	14460	1	Middlesex	2 118	1 503 085	23	709.7	78.3	5.0	0.4	10.3	6.5	5.7	15.6	9.5	14.5	14.2	15.5
25 019	...	7	Nantucket	116	10 172	2 430	87.7	81.9	7.3	0.4	1.6	9.4	6.7	14.0	6.3	15.6	16.6	16.1
25 021	14460	1	Norfolk	1 026	670 850	90	653.8	81.7	6.1	0.4	9.5	3.3	5.6	17.1	8.1	11.8	14.0	16.4
25 023	14460	1	Plymouth	1 707	494 919	132	289.9	85.3	8.2	0.6	1.7	3.2	5.8	18.4	8.0	9.9	14.1	16.6
25 025	14460	1	Suffolk	151	722 023	80	4 781.6	49.5	21.2	0.6	9.1	19.9	5.5	12.0	18.0	20.1	12.9	11.7
25 027	49340	2	Worcester	3 913	798 552	71	204.1	82.2	4.3	0.6	4.6	9.4	5.9	17.6	9.6	11.6	14.2	16.4
26 000	...	X	MICHIGAN	146 435	9 883 640	X	67.5	78.3	14.9	1.2	3.0	4.4	6.0	17.7	9.9	11.8	12.9	15.3
26 001	...	9	Alcona	1 747	10 942	2 373	6.3	97.9	0.2	1.2	0.4	1.1	3.0	11.5	4.6	5.9	8.9	15.6
26 003	...	9	Alger	2 370	9 601	2 471	4.1	88.1	6.6	6.2	0.6	1.2	3.9	13.3	6.6	11.0	11.9	16.4
26 005	10880	4	Allegan	2 137	111 408	532	52.1	91.0	1.7	1.1	0.8	6.7	6.7	19.5	7.7	11.0	13.2	16.3
26 007	10980	7	Alpena	1 481	29 598	1 437	20.0	97.6	0.6	1.0	0.7	1.0	5.1	15.8	7.4	9.9	10.9	17.0
26 009	...	9	Antrim	1 232	23 580	1 661	19.1	96.9	0.4	1.8	0.4	1.7	4.9	16.2	5.7	8.6	11.1	15.4
26 011	...	8	Arenac	941	15 899	2 057	16.9	96.9	0.5	1.8	0.4	1.4	4.7	15.4	7.0	9.7	10.9	16.7
26 013	...	9	Baraga	2 326	8 860	2 540	3.8	78.7	7.6	16.6	0.6	1.0	4.7	15.5	7.0	12.3	13.4	15.1
26 015	24340	2	Barry	1 433	59 173	866	41.3	96.5	0.7	1.0	0.6	2.3	6.0	18.5	7.6	10.4	12.5	16.7
26 017	13020	3	Bay	1 146	107 771	545	94.0	92.7	2.3	1.1	0.7	4.7	5.8	16.4	8.5	11.4	12.2	15.6
26 019	45900	9	Benzie	828	17 525	1 950	21.2	96.2	0.7	2.2	0.4	1.7	5.3	15.7	6.0	9.3	11.8	16.2
26 021	35660	3	Berrien	1 470	156 813	399	106.7	78.0	16.2	1.2	2.1	4.5	6.1	17.3	8.5	11.0	12.2	15.3
26 023	17740	6	Branch	1 311	45 248	1 060	34.5	92.1	3.4	0.9	0.9	4.0	6.6	17.4	8.0	12.0	13.0	15.6
26 025	12980	3	Calhoun	1 829	136 146	455	74.4	82.3	12.4	1.4	2.1	4.5	6.4	17.8	9.3	11.5	12.4	14.8
26 027	43780	2	Cass	1 269	52 293	946	41.2	89.9	6.8	2.0	0.9	3.0	5.8	17.7	7.4	9.8	12.6	15.8
26 029	...	7	Charlevoix	1 078	25 949	1 568	24.1	96.5	0.6	2.6	0.7	1.4	5.3	16.8	6.3	9.4	11.5	16.6
26 031	...	7	Cheboygan	1 853	26 152	1 555	14.1	95.4	0.8	5.0	0.5	0.8	4.7	15.7	6.1	8.8	11.8	15.3
26 033	42300	5	Chippewa	4 036	38 520	1 204	9.5	75.8	6.9	19.6	1.1	1.2	5.2	15.0	11.0	12.9	13.6	15.2
26 035	...	7	Clare	1 462	30 926	1 415	21.2	97.1	0.8	1.5	0.5	1.5	5.7	15.2	7.9	9.5	11.3	15.2
26 037	29620	2	Clinton	1 467	75 382	722	51.4	92.0	2.7	1.0	1.9	3.9	5.9	18.8	10.8	10.7	12.8	15.6
26 039	...	7	Crawford	1 441	14 074	2 169	9.8	97.5	0.6	1.0	0.5	1.3	4.7	15.1	6.4	8.4	10.9	17.7
26 041	21540	5	Delta	3 033	37 069	1 240	12.2	96.2	0.5	3.8	0.7	0.9	5.4	15.4	7.3	9.9	11.2	15.9
26 043	27020	5	Dickinson	1 972	26 168	1 554	13.3	97.6	0.6	1.1	0.8	1.0	5.0	16.4	6.7	9.5	11.8	17.2
26 045	29620	2	Eaton	1 490	107 759	546	72.3	86.8	7.2	1.1	2.1	4.7	5.7	17.6	9.1	11.6	12.4	15.9
26 047	...	7	Emmet	1 211	32 694	1 372	27.0	94.1	0.8	5.0	0.8	1.3	5.2	17.4	7.5	10.3	12.0	15.8
26 049	22420	2	Genesee	1 650	425 790	155	258.1	74.7	21.8	1.3	1.3	3.0	6.4	18.6	8.9	11.8	12.9	15.3
26 051	...	6	Gladwin	1 300	25 692	1 579	19.8	97.8	0.4	1.0	0.4	1.2	4.9	15.2	6.9	8.6	11.0	14.5
26 053	...	7	Gogebic	2 854	16 427	2 023	5.8	92.4	4.4	3.3	0.4	0.9	4.7	12.2	8.4	10.2	12.1	15.4
26 055	45900	5	Grand Traverse	1 203	86 986	647	72.3	94.8	1.7	1.8	1.1	2.2	5.6	16.4	8.1	12.1	12.6	16.2
26 057	10940	6	Gratiot	1 472	42 476	1 114	28.9	88.3	5.8	0.8	0.5	5.4	5.4	16.0	11.3	12.7	13.1	14.8
26 059	...	6	Hillsdale	1 549	46 688	1 031	30.1	97.0	0.7	1.0	0.6	1.8	6.0	17.7	9.8	10.1	11.8	15.3
26 061	26340	5	Houghton	2 614	36 628	1 260	14.0	94.8	0.8	1.2	3.4	1.1	5.8	14.8	20.6	10.6	9.7	12.0
26 063	...	7	Huron	2 164	33 118	1 353	15.3	96.8	0.6	0.7	0.7	2.0	4.9	15.7	6.4	9.2	11.2	15.7
26 065	29620	2	Ingham	1 440	280 895	229	195.1	75.2	13.3	1.3	6.0	7.3	5.7	15.1	19.5	14.0	11.2	12.7
26 067	24340	2	Ionia	1 480	63 905	817	43.2	90.2	5.0	0.9	0.6	4.4	6.4	18.1	9.2	13.7	14.1	15.5
26 069	...	7	Iosco	1 422	25 887	1 571	18.2	96.7	0.8	1.4	0.8	1.6	4.0	13.6	6.0	7.7	9.9	15.6
26 071	...	7	Iron	3 020	11 817	2 310	3.9	97.4	0.4	1.6	0.4	1.4	4.2	12.9	5.3	8.5	8.7	16.3
26 073	34380	5	Isabella	1 483	70 311	755	47.4	89.6	3.2	4.3	2.1	3.1	5.2	12.8	31.9	11.4	9.1	10.8
26 075	27100	3	Jackson	1 817	160 248	385	88.2	87.9	9.2	1.0	1.0	3.0	5.9	17.3	9.3	11.6	13.2	15.6
26 077	28020	2	Kalamazoo	1 455	250 331	260	172.0	82.5	12.4	1.2	2.8	4.0	6.3	16.5	15.0	13.3	11.8	13.5
26 079	45900	7	Kalkaska	1 450	17 153	1 973	11.8	97.3	0.6	1.7	0.5	1.2	6.1	16.6	7.0	10.4	12.4	16.3
26 081	24340	2	Kent	2 194	602 622	103	274.7	77.9	10.7	1.0	2.9	9.7	7.3	18.9	10.5	14.0	12.8	14.4

1. CBSA = Core Based Statistical Area. See Appendix A for explanation. See Appendix B for list of metropolitan areas with component counties. 2. County type code from the Economic Research Service of USDA Rural-Urban Continuum Codes. See Appendix A for definition. 3. Dry land or land partially or temporarily covered by water. 4. May be of any race.

Table B. States and Counties — **Population and Households**

STATE County	55 to 64 years	65 to 74 years	75 years and over	Percent female	Total persons 1990	Total persons 2000	Percent change 1990–2000	Percent change 2000–2010	Births	Deaths	Net migration	Households 2010 Number	Percent change 2000–2010	Persons per household	Female family householder[1]	One person
	16	17	18	19	20	21	22	23	24	25	26	27	28	29	30	31
MARYLAND—Cont'd																
St. Mary's	10.7	6.0	4.3	50.2	75 974	86 211	13.5	22.0	13 033	5 895	10 001	37 604	22.7	2.72	11.7	21.8
Somerset	11.9	7.7	6.2	46.6	23 440	24 747	5.6	7.0	2 425	2 368	1 300	8 788	5.1	2.37	15.3	31.5
Talbot	15.1	13.0	10.8	52.3	30 549	33 812	10.7	11.7	3 420	3 955	3 195	16 157	12.9	2.31	10.1	28.3
Washington	12.1	7.4	6.9	49.2	121 393	131 923	8.7	11.8	16 297	12 248	10 733	55 687	12.0	2.50	12.0	26.6
Wicomico	11.8	7.0	6.1	52.3	74 339	84 644	13.9	16.6	11 485	7 925	6 536	37 220	15.5	2.53	15.2	25.3
Worcester	15.9	13.2	10.1	51.3	35 028	46 543	32.9	10.6	4 483	5 195	3 536	22 229	12.9	2.28	10.9	28.0
Baltimore city	11.1	6.2	5.5	52.9	736 014	651 154	-11.5	-4.6	87 191	68 555	-66 255	249 903	-3.1	2.38	23.8	36.1
MASSACHUSETTS	12.3	7.0	6.8	51.6	6 016 425	6 349 097	5.5	3.1	729 448	508 747	-31 623	2 547 075	4.2	2.48	12.5	28.7
Barnstable	16.5	12.4	12.6	52.4	186 605	222 230	19.1	-2.9	18 189	25 467	7 503	95 755	1.0	2.21	9.6	31.8
Berkshire	14.9	9.0	9.5	51.9	139 352	134 953	-3.2	-2.8	11 642	14 190	-2 251	56 091	0.2	2.23	11.5	33.0
Bristol	12.3	7.1	7.1	51.6	506 325	534 678	5.6	2.5	60 902	46 559	1 642	213 010	3.7	2.50	14.0	27.4
Dukes	17.4	8.9	7.4	50.5	11 639	14 987	28.8	10.3	1 513	1 214	762	7 368	14.7	2.22	8.9	33.4
Essex	12.8	7.0	7.1	52.0	670 080	723 419	8.0	2.7	86 145	59 276	-3 304	285 956	3.8	2.54	13.5	28.1
Franklin	16.6	7.9	7.3	51.2	70 086	71 535	2.1	-0.2	6 327	5 931	287	30 462	3.4	2.29	10.7	30.5
Hampden	12.3	6.9	7.3	52.0	456 310	456 228	0.0	1.6	53 487	41 615	-2 806	179 927	2.6	2.49	17.5	29.2
Hampshire	13.3	6.4	6.2	53.2	146 568	152 251	3.9	3.8	11 653	11 087	4 109	58 702	4.8	2.34	10.3	29.7
Middlesex	11.8	6.6	6.5	51.4	1 398 468	1 465 396	4.8	2.6	167 999	103 765	-24 296	580 688	3.5	2.49	10.1	27.8
Nantucket	12.6	6.8	5.3	48.8	6 012	9 520	58.3	6.8	1 415	582	494	4 229	14.3	2.39	8.3	29.7
Norfolk	12.6	7.1	7.4	52.1	616 087	650 308	5.6	3.2	73 676	51 690	-1 928	257 914	3.7	2.53	10.1	27.6
Plymouth	13.3	7.6	6.3	51.4	435 276	472 822	8.6	4.7	56 868	37 333	8 703	181 126	7.6	2.67	12.6	23.8
Suffolk	9.3	5.5	5.0	51.8	663 906	689 807	3.9	4.7	87 710	47 968	-35 725	292 767	5.0	2.30	16.3	36.3
Worcester	12.0	6.4	6.3	50.8	709 711	750 963	5.8	6.3	91 922	62 070	15 187	303 080	6.7	2.55	12.2	26.2
MICHIGAN	12.7	7.3	6.4	50.9	9 295 287	9 938 444	6.9	-0.6	1 196 297	802 544	-372 082	3 872 508	2.3	2.49	13.2	27.9
Alcona	18.9	18.8	12.7	49.2	10 145	11 719	15.5	-6.6	654	1 565	327	5 089	-0.8	2.13	6.4	29.7
Alger	16.5	11.4	9.2	45.6	8 972	9 862	9.9	-2.6	734	1 039	-217	3 898	3.0	2.20	7.1	31.6
Allegan	12.7	7.3	5.7	50.2	90 509	105 665	16.7	5.4	13 906	7 910	2 407	42 018	10.1	2.63	9.8	22.5
Alpena	14.5	10.1	9.4	50.9	30 605	31 314	2.3	-5.5	2 806	3 231	-1 406	12 791	-0.2	2.27	9.8	30.8
Antrim	15.9	13.0	9.2	50.5	18 185	23 110	27.1	2.0	2 232	2 223	813	9 890	7.2	2.36	8.3	25.5
Arenac	15.3	11.9	8.4	49.3	14 906	17 269	15.9	-7.9	1 561	1 802	-865	6 701	-0.1	2.34	9.6	27.5
Baraga	14.6	9.9	7.4	46.1	7 954	8 746	10.0	1.3	857	954	4	3 444	2.7	2.28	10.9	31.6
Barry	13.8	8.4	6.1	49.8	50 057	56 755	13.4	4.3	6 541	4 472	-53	22 551	7.2	2.60	8.6	21.7
Bay	13.9	8.5	7.7	51.1	111 723	110 157	-1.4	-2.2	11 791	10 262	-3 583	44 603	1.5	2.38	11.8	29.3
Benzie	15.0	11.7	8.9	50.4	12 200	15 998	31.1	9.5	1 830	1 625	1 072	7 298	12.3	2.37	8.4	26.2
Berrien	13.3	8.5	7.8	51.3	161 378	162 453	0.7	-3.5	19 493	14 899	-5 624	63 054	-0.8	2.43	13.6	28.7
Branch	12.7	8.4	6.3	47.3	41 502	45 787	10.3	-1.2	5 616	3 872	-2 605	16 419	0.4	2.58	11.1	25.8
Calhoun	12.9	7.6	7.2	51.1	135 982	137 985	1.5	-1.3	17 334	13 195	-5 694	54 016	-0.2	2.44	14.0	28.8
Cass	14.9	9.3	6.6	50.1	49 477	51 104	3.3	2.3	4 861	4 395	-1 412	20 604	4.7	2.51	10.7	24.3
Charlevoix	15.5	10.4	8.2	50.8	21 468	26 090	21.5	-0.5	2 691	2 251	-575	10 882	4.6	2.36	9.1	27.5
Cheboygan	18.0	12.4	9.1	50.2	21 398	26 448	23.6	-1.1	2 496	2 642	-58	11 133	2.8	2.31	8.8	27.7
Chippewa	12.5	8.1	6.5	44.9	34 604	38 543	11.4	-0.1	3 632	2 838	-365	14 329	6.3	2.34	10.9	29.5
Clare	15.2	11.9	8.0	50.1	24 952	31 252	25.2	-1.0	3 194	3 501	-697	12 966	2.2	2.38	10.0	28.0
Clinton	12.5	7.3	5.6	50.8	57 893	64 753	11.8	16.4	7 576	4 423	2 379	28 766	21.6	2.60	8.6	22.1
Crawford	15.8	12.5	8.3	49.8	12 260	14 273	16.4	-1.4	1 242	1 446	197	6 016	7.0	2.31	9.9	27.0
Delta	15.7	9.7	9.4	50.5	37 780	38 520	2.0	-3.8	3 818	3 796	-1 394	15 992	1.0	2.28	8.8	29.8
Dickinson	14.4	9.0	9.9	50.8	26 831	27 472	2.4	-4.7	2 557	2 971	-214	11 359	-0.2	2.26	9.0	30.6
Eaton	13.8	7.8	6.2	51.2	92 879	103 655	11.6	4.0	11 257	7 631	-588	43 494	8.3	2.44	11.1	27.1
Emmet	15.1	8.8	7.8	50.7	25 040	31 437	25.5	4.0	3 428	2 672	1 639	13 601	8.1	2.37	9.6	28.2
Genesee	12.4	7.3	6.4	51.8	430 459	436 141	1.3	-2.4	56 689	36 619	-29 759	169 202	-0.4	2.48	17.2	28.4
Gladwin	16.2	13.6	9.2	50.0	21 896	26 023	18.8	-1.3	2 483	2 858	173	10 753	1.8	2.36	8.8	27.2
Gogebic	15.7	10.5	10.9	46.7	18 052	17 370	-3.8	-5.4	1 242	2 272	-307	7 037	-5.2	2.11	9.3	35.3
Grand Traverse	14.0	7.8	7.2	50.6	64 273	77 654	20.8	12.0	9 144	6 283	6 243	35 328	16.2	2.39	9.5	27.8
Gratiot	11.7	7.6	7.2	46.8	38 982	42 285	8.5	0.5	4 517	4 005	-580	14 852	2.4	2.49	11.4	26.0
Hillsdale	13.5	8.9	6.8	50.4	43 431	46 527	7.1	0.3	5 410	4 018	-1 997	17 792	2.6	2.53	9.5	24.7
Houghton	11.6	7.9	7.1	45.9	35 446	36 016	1.6	1.7	3 738	3 509	-709	14 232	3.2	2.38	7.7	32.2
Huron	15.2	11.2	10.6	50.4	34 951	36 079	3.2	-8.2	3 127	4 134	-2 666	14 348	-1.7	2.27	8.1	30.7
Ingham	11.2	5.6	4.9	51.4	281 912	279 320	-0.9	0.6	33 711	17 622	-16 623	111 162	2.4	2.36	12.7	31.3
Ionia	11.7	6.5	4.9	46.3	57 024	61 518	7.9	3.9	7 770	4 201	-2 161	22 144	7.5	2.64	10.9	22.9
Iosco	17.1	14.5	11.6	50.7	30 209	27 339	-9.5	-5.3	2 182	3 603	72	11 757	0.3	2.17	8.8	31.8
Iron	17.7	12.3	14.0	50.7	13 175	13 138	-0.3	-10.1	859	1 879	-412	5 577	-3.0	2.06	8.3	36.8
Isabella	9.2	5.3	4.4	51.3	54 624	63 351	16.0	11.0	6 781	3 957	1 326	25 586	14.1	2.49	9.6	25.9
Jackson	12.9	7.4	6.7	49.0	149 756	158 422	5.8	1.2	19 051	14 022	-2 727	60 771	4.5	2.48	13.3	27.1
Kalamazoo	11.4	6.4	5.9	51.0	223 411	238 603	6.8	4.9	29 262	17 705	-121	100 610	7.6	2.40	11.8	29.6
Kalkaska	14.6	10.1	6.4	49.2	13 497	16 571	22.8	3.5	2 059	1 427	-240	6 962	8.3	2.44	8.6	26.1
Kent	10.9	5.7	5.5	51.0	500 631	574 335	14.7	4.9	86 851	38 158	-11 368	227 239	6.7	2.60	12.6	26.0

1. No spouse present.

Table B. States and Counties — **Population, Vital Statistics, Medicare, and Crime**

STATE County	Persons in group quarters, 2010	Daytime population, 2006–2010 Number	Daytime population, 2006–2010 Employment/residence ratio	Births, average 2006–2008 Total	Births, average 2006–2008 Rate[1]	Deaths, average 2006–2008 Number	Deaths, average 2006–2008 Rate[1]	Persons under 65 with no health insurance, 2009 Number	Persons under 65 with no health insurance, 2009 Percent	Medicare, 2011 Eligible for Medicare	Medicare, 2011 Enrolled in Medicare Advantage	Medicare, 2011 Enrolled in a Medicare prescription drug plan	Serious crimes known to police,[2] 2010 Total Number	Serious crimes known to police,[2] 2010 Total Rate[3]
	32	33	34	35	36	37	38	39	40	41	42	43	44	45
MARYLAND—Cont'd														
St. Mary's	2 926	96 396	0.9	1 511	15.1	654	6.5	9 965	11.0	12 419	157	4 258	2 567	2 441
Somerset	5 651	25 183	0.9	D	D	237	9.1	4 433	20.5	4 202	100	2 023	655	2 474
Talbot	383	40 536	1.2	D	D	448	12.4	3 986	14.7	9 627	249	4 664	958	2 536
Washington	8 425	144 824	1.0	1 895	13.1	1 331	9.2	16 489	13.4	25 400	2 381	11 910	3 474	2 356
Wicomico	4 403	96 992	1.0	1 361	14.6	912	9.8	12 764	16.0	15 687	372	7 699	4 597	4 656
Worcester	735	53 653	1.1	D	D	576	11.7	5 946	16.0	12 937	305	5 741	2 616	5 084
Baltimore city	25 199	723 591	1.4	9 865	15.5	6 931	10.9	90 271	16.5	91 159	13 691	44 166	38 489	6 198
MASSACHUSETTS	238 882	6 543 487	1.0	77 555	11.9	53 295	8.2	269 241	4.9	1 095 712	194 917	460 508	184 458	2 817
Barnstable	3 961	211 803	0.9	1 909	8.6	2 661	11.9	8 026	4.9	63 183	5 424	26 581	7 540	3 493
Berkshire	6 159	133 813	1.0	1 233	9.5	1 495	11.5	4 759	4.7	29 510	730	17 083	3 637	2 875
Bristol	15 868	501 591	0.8	6 418	11.8	4 896	9.0	25 375	5.6	100 649	13 385	48 988	16 840	3 071
Dukes	143	16 385	1.0	D	D	129	8.3	832	6.4	3 415	39	1 615	542	3 278
Essex	16 472	685 512	0.9	8 978	12.2	6 275	8.5	30 050	4.8	127 930	18 977	58 886	18 786	2 528
Franklin	1 481	63 921	0.8	D	D	649	9.0	2 620	4.4	13 938	2 644	5 703	1 407	2 077
Hampden	14 791	459 450	1.0	5 796	12.6	4 402	9.6	20 276	5.2	86 349	17 607	37 546	19 758	4 331
Hampshire	20 832	150 034	0.9	1 244	8.1	1 221	7.9	5 100	3.9	25 545	3 818	9 538	3 603	2 314
Middlesex	55 412	1 547 079	1.1	18 170	12.3	10 726	7.3	58 888	4.6	227 874	46 952	85 726	33 092	2 206
Nantucket	58	10 780	1.1	D	D	64	6.0	681	7.0	1 475	16	805	421	4 139
Norfolk	17 611	657 835	1.0	7 658	11.7	5 379	8.2	18 183	3.3	110 502	18 366	41 725	12 028	1 814
Plymouth	11 821	431 289	0.7	5 813	11.8	3 952	8.0	18 268	4.4	85 190	10 724	34 061	12 168	2 459
Suffolk	47 228	932 039	1.6	9 608	13.5	4 793	6.7	44 941	7.0	93 007	12 490	49 105	32 554	4 509
Worcester	27 045	741 956	0.9	9 700	12.4	6 654	8.5	31 241	4.6	127 145	43 745	43 146	20 611	2 611
MICHIGAN	229 068	9 911 106	1.0	124 624	12.4	87 069	8.7	1 173 560	13.9	1 714 511	419 502	603 042	316 661	3 204
Alcona	127	10 164	0.7	D	D	165	14.2	1 277	16.4	4 076	664	1 395	141	1 289
Alger	1 022	9 512	1.0	D	D	117	12.2	1 195	16.0	2 293	416	775	103	1 073
Allegan	954	102 319	0.8	1 520	13.4	872	7.7	13 125	13.5	17 883	6 896	5 339	1 905	1 822
Alpena	514	30 897	1.1	D	D	347	11.6	3 329	14.4	7 695	1 001	3 503	731	2 470
Antrim	226	21 673	0.8	D	D	229	9.4	2 860	15.4	6 268	1 474	2 427	577	2 447
Arenac	207	15 615	0.9	D	D	191	11.4	2 052	15.9	4 052	730	1 628	218	1 371
Baraga	1 010	9 281	1.1	D	D	92	10.7	1 252	17.7	1 703	286	615	NA	NA
Barry	603	46 757	0.5	698	11.8	478	8.1	5 939	12.0	10 535	3 320	3 035	1 083	1 845
Bay	1 438	98 303	0.8	1 233	11.4	1 141	10.6	11 309	12.8	22 583	4 251	8 079	2 971	2 757
Benzie	252	15 145	0.7	D	D	184	10.5	2 101	15.4	4 355	974	1 587	342	1 951
Berrien	3 527	156 108	1.0	2 063	12.9	1 613	10.1	21 079	15.9	31 342	5 782	14 163	4 925	3 185
Branch	3 148	44 153	0.9	D	D	449	9.8	6 231	16.4	8 292	1 283	3 819	936	2 069
Calhoun	4 275	141 757	1.1	1 831	13.4	1 415	10.3	16 249	14.3	26 559	4 303	9 517	5 853	4 352
Cass	474	41 379	0.5	558	11.0	493	9.7	6 279	14.9	10 378	2 161	4 451	1 186	2 268
Charlevoix	279	25 149	0.9	D	D	264	10.1	2 883	13.8	5 882	1 349	2 390	479	1 846
Cheboygan	388	24 582	0.8	D	D	284	10.6	3 488	16.9	6 958	1 281	2 732	601	2 298
Chippewa	4 930	38 935	1.0	D	D	321	8.3	6 412	19.5	7 146	1 285	2 395	1 053	2 734
Clare	391	29 269	0.8	D	D	381	12.4	4 031	16.6	8 177	1 217	3 379	278	899
Clinton	680	57 796	0.5	D	D	472	6.8	6 080	10.3	11 305	2 851	2 986	812	1 077
Crawford	197	14 320	1.0	D	D	151	10.3	1 846	16.1	3 292	605	1 236	355	2 522
Delta	623	36 668	1.0	D	D	404	10.7	4 023	13.7	9 118	1 962	3 637	1 048	2 827
Dickinson	453	28 249	1.1	D	D	298	11.0	2 102	10.0	6 055	1 218	2 319	NA	NA
Eaton	1 559	101 191	0.9	1 135	10.6	851	7.9	10 046	11.3	18 621	4 482	5 218	2 648	2 457
Emmet	505	35 918	1.2	D	D	287	8.6	4 300	15.7	6 678	1 501	2 765	532	1 627
Genesee	5 973	417 920	0.9	5 936	13.6	3 973	9.1	43 547	12.1	77 596	20 529	22 788	18 447	4 413
Gladwin	289	23 300	0.7	D	D	322	12.2	3 046	15.2	7 355	1 170	2 747	443	1 724
Gogebic	1 549	16 479	1.0	D	D	241	14.8	2 139	17.3	4 089	1 016	1 712	NA	NA
Grand Traverse	2 642	95 412	1.2	990	11.6	727	8.5	9 721	13.6	16 281	3 918	5 896	1 501	1 726
Gratiot	5 560	41 580	0.9	465	11.0	434	10.3	5 795	16.4	7 480	1 197	3 257	488	1 149
Hillsdale	1 641	43 156	0.8	567	12.1	410	8.8	5 950	15.5	8 776	1 727	4 007	846	1 812
Houghton	2 715	36 213	1.0	D	D	375	10.7	4 526	15.2	6 716	1 487	2 619	642	1 753
Huron	524	33 253	1.0	D	D	446	13.3	3 573	14.2	8 320	1 097	4 100	506	1 608
Ingham	18 478	315 938	1.3	3 580	12.9	1 919	6.9	34 456	14.2	38 496	7 907	12 712	9 677	3 548
Ionia	5 524	57 148	0.7	846	13.2	465	7.2	8 087	14.9	9 257	2 445	2 953	1 162	1 936
Iosco	400	26 784	1.0	D	D	384	14.6	2 943	15.3	8 171	1 263	2 826	603	2 329
Iron	355	11 757	0.9	D	D	196	16.1	1 254	13.9	3 521	614	1 468	238	2 525
Isabella	6 540	71 342	1.1	745	11.2	409	6.2	9 176	15.5	8 808	1 711	3 471	1 461	2 078
Jackson	9 672	156 228	0.9	1 989	12.3	1 497	9.2	18 035	13.4	28 926	5 879	10 631	4 049	2 561
Kalamazoo	8 455	256 776	1.1	3 174	13.0	1 910	7.8	27 121	12.7	39 171	9 924	12 935	9 353	3 736
Kalkaska	138	15 111	0.7	D	D	159	9.2	2 274	16.2	3 814	586	1 575	563	3 282
Kent	11 353	647 994	1.2	9 329	15.5	4 101	6.8	73 099	13.8	86 035	35 893	24 782	19 025	3 157

1. Per 1,000 estimated resident population.   2. Data for serious crimes have not been adjusted for underreporting; this may affect comparability between geographic areas and over time.   3. Per 100,000 population estimated by the FBI.

STATE County	Serious crimes known to police,[1] 2010 (cont.) Rate[2]		Education						Money income, 2006–2010				Income and poverty, 2010			
			School enrollment and attainment, 2006–2010				Local government expenditures,[5] 2008–2009			Households			Percent below poverty level			
			Enrollment[3]		Attainment[4] (percent)					Median income						
	Violent	Property	Total	Percent private	High school graduate or less	Bachelor's degree or more	Total current expenditures (mil dol)	Current expenditures per student (dollars)	Per capita income[6] (dollars)	Dollars	Percent change, 2000 to 2006–2010 (constant 2010 dollars)	Percent with income of $200,000 or more	Median household income (dollars)	All persons	Children under 18 years	Children 5 to 17 years in families
	46	47	48	49	50	51	52	53	54	55	56	57	58	59	60	61
MARYLAND—Cont'd																
St. Mary's	307	2 134	28 266	17.1	43.8	27.4	201.0	11 999	34 000	80 053	15.6	6.1	81 559	7.5	11.0	9.9
Somerset	325	2 150	8 280	7.9	64.3	14.3	41.7	14 323	16 919	42 443	12.1	1.5	38 134	19.3	29.3	28.5
Talbot	214	2 321	7 511	26.3	39.7	32.7	51.1	11 555	37 958	63 017	14.3	7.0	56 806	9.7	14.9	13.2
Washington	303	2 054	35 185	14.8	54.1	18.7	259.3	11 931	26 588	52 994	3.0	2.8	51 610	11.4	16.8	14.6
Wicomico	739	3 917	29 051	12.1	48.9	24.7	185.7	12 727	25 505	50 752	2.7	3.0	47 702	16.6	23.1	19.8
Worcester	507	4 577	10 403	14.6	45.3	26.1	105.3	15 784	31 520	55 487	7.8	3.7	55 492	10.6	20.3	17.8
Baltimore city	1 509	4 689	168 494	23.0	52.1	25.2	1 182.9	14 379	23 333	39 386	3.4	2.6	38 186	24.7	34.3	31.0
MASSACHUSETTS	467	2 351	1 740 293	28.3	38.1	38.3	13 447.6	14 025	33 966	64 509	0.9	6.7	62 133	11.4	14.4	12.8
Barnstable	475	3 017	43 535	18.9	30.4	40.5	406.4	14 728	35 246	60 317	3.7	4.7	54 871	10.9	15.7	14.5
Berkshire	442	2 433	31 036	22.4	43.1	29.6	278.2	15 337	28 300	48 907	-1.1	3.0	44 792	12.4	18.7	16.7
Bristol	591	2 480	138 478	19.4	50.2	24.7	1 117.0	12 917	27 736	54 955	-0.2	3.2	51 361	12.8	16.6	14.5
Dukes	290	2 988	3 414	17.3	34.6	40.0	51.1	22 428	33 390	62 407	8.2	7.4	56 320	8.3	11.9	11.1
Essex	360	2 168	193 615	23.5	38.7	36.1	1 550.4	13 649	33 828	64 153	-1.8	7.1	61 604	10.4	14.5	13.2
Franklin	348	1 728	16 912	17.6	39.6	32.5	152.1	15 575	27 544	52 002	0.7	2.1	49 361	11.7	16.2	14.0
Hampden	733	3 598	125 527	19.0	49.6	23.8	1 062.0	14 055	24 718	47 724	-5.1	2.5	46 356	17.1	25.5	21.5
Hampshire	247	2 067	57 335	23.8	33.2	41.3	272.3	13 508	28 367	59 505	1.9	3.8	57 558	12.5	11.8	10.2
Middlesex	296	1 910	397 885	33.6	31.0	49.3	3 153.3	14 796	40 139	77 377	0.5	9.8	75 364	8.2	8.5	7.5
Nantucket	649	3 490	1 931	25.7	33.7	40.2	28.4	22 203	53 410	83 347	18.5	14.4	67 969	8.1	10.2	9.6
Norfolk	222	1 592	174 864	32.6	29.8	47.4	1 384.7	13 632	42 371	81 027	0.9	11.2	79 899	6.3	6.8	6.0
Plymouth	456	2 002	130 662	19.5	39.2	32.5	1 019.5	12 433	33 333	73 131	3.8	6.2	71 555	8.3	10.9	9.1
Suffolk	993	3 516	209 236	46.7	42.3	38.9	1 305.2	17 374	30 720	50 597	1.5	5.3	49 584	22.6	30.0	29.2
Worcester	465	2 146	215 863	23.2	41.1	32.9	1 667.2	12 614	30 557	64 152	5.8	5.0	61 079	10.9	14.0	12.6
MICHIGAN	490	2 714	2 756 982	13.4	43.4	25.0	17 190.8	10 473	25 135	48 432	-14.4	2.8	45 354	16.7	23.4	21.2
Alcona	183	1 106	1 834	5.3	57.8	12.4	9.3	9 308	19 904	34 858	-12.2	1.1	33 853	16.5	32.7	27.9
Alger	187	885	1 692	10.7	57.2	16.9	12.2	10 135	19 858	38 262	-15.8	1.3	36 749	14.7	22.4	19.3
Allegan	269	1 563	28 602	16.1	50.1	19.4	149.2	9 727	23 108	50 240	-13.4	1.8	45 879	14.8	17.6	15.9
Alpena	169	2 301	6 785	7.8	47.4	15.5	48.7	10 423	21 140	36 695	-15.2	0.9	36 289	16.8	27.0	23.7
Antrim	195	2 252	4 882	10.0	47.8	23.3	37.5	8 892	23 912	43 123	-10.6	1.9	42 083	15.2	26.7	23.9
Arenac	189	1 182	3 274	6.3	60.4	10.6	22.7	8 952	19 073	36 689	-11.7	0.9	34 116	18.4	32.0	29.0
Baraga	NA	NA	1 781	9.2	60.9	11.4	12.9	9 946	19 107	40 541	-4.9	1.1	38 819	14.1	22.5	20.0
Barry	177	1 668	15 257	9.6	49.4	16.6	69.0	8 879	24 493	51 869	-12.5	1.8	50 062	11.0	15.9	14.0
Bay	339	2 418	26 809	14.1	48.5	18.0	158.4	10 179	23 049	44 659	-8.7	1.4	43 845	15.9	23.0	20.4
Benzie	154	1 797	3 962	8.2	43.9	25.2	21.8	9 103	23 649	44 718	-5.5	1.3	43 136	12.6	21.3	19.2
Berrien	350	2 834	39 604	19.3	45.4	23.3	278.6	10 466	24 025	42 625	-12.7	2.3	40 540	17.5	28.5	26.2
Branch	217	1 852	11 103	13.6	54.6	14.1	76.1	10 369	19 049	42 133	-14.2	1.2	37 629	19.6	28.3	25.9
Calhoun	691	3 662	35 861	13.3	47.4	18.8	245.0	10 868	22 166	42 568	-13.6	1.5	42 665	17.0	25.3	23.3
Cass	134	2 134	12 718	10.7	53.0	15.8	68.5	9 079	22 698	45 177	-13.5	1.6	42 420	15.6	23.7	22.0
Charlevoix	162	1 684	5 509	10.6	43.3	24.5	59.9	14 199	26 403	48 704	-3.3	3.3	43 530	14.0	22.8	19.1
Cheboygan	145	2 153	5 380	11.0	51.7	17.8	39.6	11 355	23 038	37 903	-10.4	2.1	36 508	17.0	27.7	23.1
Chippewa	275	2 468	9 700	6.3	50.6	16.0	61.9	11 697	20 309	40 194	-7.9	1.4	36 253	19.6	25.6	21.7
Clare	123	776	6 532	8.2	58.1	10.3	52.9	10 975	18 491	34 399	-5.8	0.6	31 882	27.9	42.5	37.2
Clinton	81	996	21 280	11.0	38.3	27.2	98.0	9 558	27 223	58 016	-13.2	2.8	58 790	10.6	11.0	9.7
Crawford	306	2 217	3 070	8.9	54.9	14.1	16.0	8 794	21 002	39 665	-6.1	1.5	38 661	16.5	27.8	25.8
Delta	127	2 700	8 371	7.8	47.8	18.7	53.7	10 811	22 064	41 951	-6.7	1.3	39 085	15.0	20.7	18.7
Dickinson	NA	NA	5 983	6.7	50.1	17.9	45.6	10 779	23 854	42 586	-3.4	1.3	41 657	13.1	18.0	15.9
Eaton	189	2 268	29 069	15.1	37.8	24.3	188.8	9 726	25 963	54 885	-12.6	1.3	52 300	11.0	15.2	13.6
Emmet	132	1 496	8 153	10.6	36.4	29.5	52.6	9 397	28 308	49 235	-3.3	4.3	45 875	12.1	17.0	14.7
Genesee	813	3 600	121 088	10.5	46.3	19.0	796.4	10 292	22 458	43 483	-18.1	1.5	39 271	21.0	30.5	27.2
Gladwin	152	1 572	5 262	10.5	56.4	11.1	28.7	8 238	20 571	37 936	-6.4	1.2	36 064	19.5	31.3	27.6
Gogebic	NA	NA	3 027	7.7	49.6	18.6	18.9	9 597	19 933	33 673	-3.0	0.8	31 998	21.0	31.4	28.2
Grand Traverse	147	1 578	20 769	13.3	35.2	28.9	157.9	12 033	27 091	50 647	-7.3	2.8	47 442	12.0	15.6	13.8
Gratiot	111	1 038	11 277	20.1	54.8	13.5	76.4	10 557	18 388	40 114	-15.0	1.0	40 227	18.3	25.6	22.3
Hillsdale	214	1 598	12 048	19.9	56.2	14.2	69.8	9 992	20 006	42 989	-16.0	0.9	41 360	17.4	27.5	24.4
Houghton	76	1 676	12 651	5.8	46.5	26.9	53.6	10 049	18 267	34 174	-6.3	1.5	34 828	19.7	21.2	20.5
Huron	124	1 484	7 328	9.9	58.6	13.8	54.0	11 112	22 098	40 038	-10.5	1.6	38 274	15.8	22.8	19.3
Ingham	583	2 965	103 006	8.3	33.0	35.5	483.4	11 266	23 883	45 808	-11.3	2.6	43 414	20.2	24.2	21.9
Ionia	203	1 733	16 975	11.7	52.3	13.1	116.0	10 166	19 386	46 454	-14.8	0.7	42 719	16.2	21.0	18.2
Iosco	240	2 090	4 940	9.0	55.0	13.6	47.4	9 781	20 513	36 861	-7.1	0.8	33 985	19.9	36.8	31.7
Iron	244	2 281	2 144	5.5	57.5	15.1	14.6	9 345	19 986	33 734	-6.7	0.7	34 911	15.2	27.0	24.1
Isabella	202	1 876	30 693	5.6	43.9	25.8	60.4	9 092	18 510	36 880	-15.0	1.5	35 644	32.5	22.5	19.8
Jackson	382	2 179	41 959	13.5	47.1	17.5	269.2	10 524	21 947	46 117	-15.6	1.5	43 465	19.2	29.6	25.9
Kalamazoo	440	3 296	80 162	11.4	34.3	33.4	353.3	10 113	25 138	44 794	-15.8	2.8	43 957	20.0	25.0	22.0
Kalkaska	466	2 816	3 528	6.8	57.5	11.6	20.8	8 486	19 770	39 350	-13.9	0.8	38 810	17.9	29.2	28.5
Kent	436	2 721	172 358	21.3	39.0	29.9	1 126.4	10 221	24 791	49 532	-14.9	2.9	47 897	16.3	23.1	20.7

1. Data for serious crimes have not been adjusted for underreporting; this may affect comparability between geographic areas and over time.   2. Per 100,000 population estimated by the FBI.   3. All persons 3 years old and over enrolled in nursery school through college.   4. Persons 25 years old and over.   5. Elementary and secondary education expenditures.   6. Based on population estimated by the American Community Survey, 2006–2010.

STATE County	Total (mil dol)	Percent change, 2008–2009	Per capita[1] Dollars	Rank	Wages and salaries[2] (mil dol)	Proprietors' income (mil dol)	Dividends, interest, and rent (mil dol)	Transfer payments (mil dol) Total	Government payments to individuals Total	Social Security	Medical payments	Income mainte-nance	Unemploy-ment insurance
	62	63	64	65	66	67	68	69	70	71	72	73	74
MARYLAND—Cont'd													
St. Mary's	4 295	4.6	41 702	351	3 413	220	583	540	522	158	239	50	26
Somerset	706	1.8	27 180	2 535	355	32	101	210	205	58	93	25	9
Talbot	2 049	-2.9	56 507	48	896	145	748	321	314	139	128	17	12
Washington	5 144	1.5	35 257	988	3 138	176	800	1 023	997	354	423	83	57
Wicomico	3 279	0.7	34 799	1 042	2 222	159	541	721	703	222	319	76	38
Worcester	2 046	0.4	41 645	354	909	113	614	438	429	188	163	29	26
Baltimore city	23 828	2.0	37 383	702	23 176	1 872	2 839	6 572	6 456	1 196	3 491	1 104	252
MASSACHUSETTS	327 395	-1.9	49 653	X	222 021	26 824	56 849	53 092	51 890	14 612	24 873	5 183	4 624
Barnstable	11 086	-2.4	50 128	99	4 572	908	3 040	2 205	2 165	892	882	117	167
Berkshire	5 537	-1.3	42 826	281	3 050	409	1 142	1 325	1 302	407	628	120	93
Bristol	21 759	-0.5	39 747	468	11 038	1 038	2 708	4 985	4 885	1 292	2 334	526	510
Dukes	922	-1.9	57 696	40	421	142	303	114	111	46	43	6	12
Essex	36 599	-1.8	49 286	115	18 073	2 418	6 234	6 045	5 910	1 713	2 746	635	543
Franklin	2 906	-0.7	40 486	421	1 204	214	475	686	673	177	349	60	49
Hampden	17 671	0.7	37 511	689	10 583	934	2 249	5 118	5 032	1 103	2 669	688	349
Hampshire	5 903	-1.1	37 832	663	3 063	386	1 113	928	900	328	316	79	93
Middlesex	88 410	-2.8	58 744	35	66 102	6 609	18 029	9 983	9 709	3 144	4 307	815	935
Nantucket	703	-4.7	62 102	23	341	135	235	58	56	21	21	3	9
Norfolk	41 041	-2.9	61 595	27	21 427	3 197	7 970	4 456	4 334	1 554	1 815	279	432
Plymouth	23 368	-1.3	46 892	151	9 744	1 802	3 348	3 845	3 754	1 166	1 713	307	367
Suffolk	37 717	-1.9	50 050	102	54 095	6 461	5 511	7 301	7 163	1 041	4 370	965	475
Worcester	33 773	-1.2	42 021	327	18 308	2 171	4 493	6 042	5 895	1 727	2 681	583	591
MICHIGAN	342 114	-3.1	34 315	X	212 991	24 921	54 826	76 952	75 135	26 295	29 526	7 950	6 594
Alcona	292	1.5	26 343	2 662	61	17	63	130	128	61	44	8	8
Alger	227	0.9	24 465	2 918	117	11	34	83	81	33	31	5	6
Allegan	3 499	-2.2	30 843	1 789	1 631	327	531	681	661	269	227	59	68
Alpena	951	0.5	32 456	1 437	516	60	159	324	319	111	141	27	20
Antrim	738	-1.8	30 981	1 759	198	64	198	221	216	93	81	15	17
Arenac	454	-0.6	28 209	2 364	176	40	64	171	168	60	71	16	13
Baraga	226	1.1	26 272	2 673	136	10	37	77	76	25	29	6	11
Barry	1 887	-2.3	32 286	1 461	537	179	290	362	351	159	107	33	29
Bay	3 348	-0.4	31 165	1 718	1 765	137	558	952	933	343	361	90	64
Benzie	519	-0.6	30 103	1 954	147	35	129	147	144	62	50	11	12
Berrien	5 377	-1.5	33 507	1 251	3 079	367	875	1 371	1 341	466	563	145	96
Branch	1 176	-1.3	26 283	2 670	604	95	181	336	327	121	126	32	30
Calhoun	4 370	0.4	32 227	1 479	3 135	170	606	1 165	1 140	384	444	144	79
Cass	1 569	-5.7	31 436	1 654	380	94	243	376	367	154	119	40	28
Charlevoix	927	-1.1	35 947	896	449	69	243	210	205	87	74	14	20
Cheboygan	744	-0.8	28 505	2 298	273	49	168	237	232	100	80	21	16
Chippewa	996	2.4	25 705	2 770	619	36	137	298	291	99	116	29	22
Clare	823	1.9	27 333	2 510	283	70	113	325	319	119	116	36	21
Clinton	2 501	-1.4	35 783	916	747	194	349	373	360	177	100	27	35
Crawford	346	1.5	24 382	2 927	142	32	55	119	117	49	41	12	9
Delta	1 138	1.1	30 814	1 798	630	52	181	351	345	128	131	27	24
Dickinson	920	-0.6	34 454	1 102	640	27	165	240	235	85	101	16	16
Eaton	3 546	-0.5	33 429	1 272	1 591	125	505	643	624	294	172	55	59
Emmet	1 267	-1.2	37 644	679	735	106	327	286	280	98	116	20	28
Genesee	12 520	-0.8	29 526	2 085	6 674	719	1 724	3 949	3 871	1 248	1 512	516	300
Gladwin	649	0.3	25 237	2 836	171	12	110	273	268	112	103	23	17
Gogebic	458	1.3	28 718	2 254	218	21	78	173	170	57	78	14	10
Grand Traverse	3 119	-1.1	36 128	869	2 080	427	622	648	633	240	251	44	56
Gratiot	1 152	-1.2	27 463	2 491	569	132	152	331	323	109	140	30	27
Hillsdale	1 216	-2.8	26 642	2 617	556	81	177	352	344	130	126	33	35
Houghton	956	2.6	27 054	2 559	553	36	164	290	284	94	126	22	19
Huron	1 104	-8.3	34 242	1 133	470	159	220	312	306	121	126	22	23
Ingham	9 462	-1.2	34 083	1 155	8 818	610	1 410	2 035	1 985	587	843	222	169
Ionia	1 600	-1.9	25 573	2 799	765	87	199	386	374	139	134	40	41
Iosco	696	1.5	26 973	2 568	273	27	133	307	302	120	123	23	19
Iron	362	0.3	31 094	1 729	151	14	61	134	131	49	58	9	7
Isabella	1 884	0.3	28 049	2 390	1 229	121	261	483	471	128	227	39	33
Jackson	4 713	-1.2	29 488	2 095	2 696	249	702	1 239	1 210	442	458	123	101
Kalamazoo	8 571	-1.7	34 502	1 092	5 990	472	1 490	1 694	1 649	598	612	186	130
Kalkaska	418	-1.5	24 776	2 886	181	26	62	135	132	54	43	14	12
Kent	20 461	-3.2	33 635	1 230	16 562	2 004	3 149	3 738	3 627	1 274	1 301	441	333

1. Based on the resident population estimated as of July 1 of the year shown.   2. Includes supplements to wages and salaries.

Table B. States and Counties — **Earnings, Social Security, and Housing**

STATE County	Earnings, 2009									Social Security beneficiaries, December 2010			Housing units, 2010	
					Percent by selected industries									
			Goods-related[1]		Service-related and health									
	Total (mil dol)	Farm	Total	Manu-facturing	Infor-mation and profes-sional and technical services	Retail trade	Finance, insur-ance, and real estate	Health care and social services	Govern-ment	Number	Rate[2]	Supple-mental Security Income recipients, December 2010	Total	Percent change, 2000–2010
	75	76	77	78	79	80	81	82	83	84	85	86	87	88

MARYLAND—Cont'd														
St. Mary's	3 633	0.1	4.2	1.1	25.1	3.8	1.6	6.6	45.7	13 080	124	1 304	41 282	21.1
Somerset	387	2.8	8.5	4.3	2.3	3.3	2.6	10.3	45.2	4 910	185	700	11 130	10.3
Talbot	1 041	1.6	D	5.2	15.7	8.7	7.2	20.1	11.8	10 140	268	518	19 577	18.6
Washington	3 313	0.6	19.7	13.7	6.6	10.3	10.2	16.1	16.4	28 020	190	2 922	60 814	14.8
Wicomico	2 381	0.7	D	8.9	7.6	8.2	4.9	19.8	18.5	17 805	180	2 222	41 192	19.7
Worcester	1 022	1.7	9.2	2.9	4.9	12.7	5.4	9.2	23.2	14 175	275	778	55 749	17.7
Baltimore city	25 048	0.0	7.1	4.0	D	2.4	8.9	19.3	22.6	100 210	161	35 341	296 685	-1.3
MASSACHUSETTS	248 845	0.1	14.4	9.4	18.6	4.9	11.8	13.6	12.3	1 140 830	174	192 814	2 808 254	7.1
Barnstable	5 479	0.1	D	2.4	10.7	10.3	6.1	17.7	18.6	65 730	304	3 645	160 281	9.0
Berkshire	3 459	0.0	18.6	11.2	9.7	8.3	6.5	19.3	13.2	32 095	245	4 149	68 508	3.3
Bristol	12 075	0.2	20.9	14.9	7.5	8.8	3.4	16.5	14.9	109 435	200	19 918	230 535	6.3
Dukes	563	0.1	D	D	D	10.7	8.8	9.9	15.9	3 440	208	149	17 188	15.9
Essex	20 492	0.0	24.2	18.6	14.2	6.7	5.3	15.3	12.4	132 945	179	23 007	306 754	6.8
Franklin	1 418	1.0	D	14.8	7.2	8.2	4.0	12.7	16.9	14 995	210	2 288	33 758	5.7
Hampden	11 518	0.0	16.7	11.7	7.5	6.7	9.4	18.9	18.3	93 730	202	29 550	192 175	3.4
Hampshire	3 449	0.2	10.9	6.4	6.4	6.7	3.2	12.7	31.6	26 535	168	3 178	62 603	6.7
Middlesex	72 711	0.0	17.2	12.4	29.6	3.9	4.7	8.9	9.1	229 325	153	27 085	612 004	6.1
Nantucket	476	0.0	D	D	D	10.2	8.2	6.9	13.4	1 490	146	41	11 618	26.1
Norfolk	24 624	0.0	14.5	7.7	17.9	6.3	13.4	11.7	9.2	112 680	168	10 711	270 359	6.0
Plymouth	11 646	0.3	14.6	6.7	10.2	8.1	6.6	14.2	18.3	90 695	183	9 405	200 161	10.3
Suffolk	60 556	0.0	D	1.3	18.3	2.0	28.1	16.0	11.5	91 120	126	37 627	315 522	7.9
Worcester	20 479	0.1	19.7	14.2	10.3	6.3	6.9	16.4	15.8	136 615	171	22 061	326 788	9.6
MICHIGAN	237 911	0.5	20.9	15.8	11.8	6.3	6.7	12.9	17.0	1 964 862	199	253 532	4 532 233	7.0
Alcona	79	1.4	18.9	10.2	3.3	9.6	D	19.7	21.6	4 675	427	292	11 073	4.6
Alger	128	0.6	D	D	D	5.6	D	6.9	37.7	2 660	277	199	6 664	9.9
Allegan	1 959	4.6	45.5	38.0	3.3	5.1	5.0	6.2	11.9	20 975	188	1 682	49 426	14.2
Alpena	576	0.5	21.9	16.5	3.8	9.8	4.7	13.3	29.4	9 015	305	1 120	16 053	5.0
Antrim	262	2.1	D	15.9	5.3	7.2	7.5	D	23.9	7 050	299	458	17 824	18.1
Arenac	216	2.8	13.2	8.2	5.0	7.2	5.5	D	21.4	4 805	302	550	9 803	2.5
Baraga	145	0.4	D	17.0	2.5	4.1	D	D	54.1	1 975	223	173	5 270	13.8
Barry	715	1.9	D	21.8	D	4.9	10.4	11.1	16.8	12 170	206	788	27 010	13.1
Bay	1 902	1.3	16.9	13.5	14.0	8.7	4.0	16.3	18.3	26 365	245	2 992	48 220	3.9
Benzie	182	1.2	24.2	9.1	3.8	8.4	7.4	D	20.2	4 870	278	322	12 199	18.3
Berrien	3 446	1.2	31.8	27.8	4.5	5.9	5.1	11.9	14.4	35 485	226	4 905	76 922	4.7
Branch	698	2.1	D	15.8	D	8.2	7.6	6.6	26.9	9 575	212	915	20 841	5.1
Calhoun	3 305	0.5	D	22.9	D	5.5	2.7	12.5	21.0	30 320	223	4 592	61 042	4.0
Cass	474	4.1	25.4	18.8	D	5.9	6.0	7.6	24.0	11 840	226	1 081	25 887	8.4
Charlevoix	518	0.3	D	27.2	D	7.4	5.3	11.4	18.1	6 635	256	425	17 249	12.2
Cheboygan	322	0.7	14.8	3.6	4.6	12.4	6.0	17.7	20.9	8 045	308	674	18 298	10.3
Chippewa	656	0.2	7.5	4.0	2.2	7.4	3.2	5.9	58.2	8 340	217	910	21 253	9.4
Clare	353	0.7	D	13.4	3.8	9.4	6.0	D	23.0	9 445	305	1 308	23 233	4.5
Clinton	941	3.4	24.0	14.3	D	7.5	7.2	7.2	18.6	12 940	172	724	30 695	24.6
Crawford	174	0.0	D	16.4	5.9	8.7	6.5	9.8	28.6	3 905	277	367	11 092	10.5
Delta	682	0.2	29.6	23.4	4.5	8.3	4.7	12.5	19.0	10 290	278	991	20 214	5.2
Dickinson	668	0.1	33.4	21.2	D	8.6	3.4	D	24.8	6 965	266	538	13 990	2.1
Eaton	1 716	0.9	16.8	10.4	D	8.0	20.1	6.5	21.1	21 525	200	1 482	47 050	11.7
Emmet	842	0.3	D	6.7	D	10.7	5.8	24.2	17.5	7 520	230	500	21 304	14.8
Genesee	7 393	0.1	15.7	11.2	8.2	8.4	6.6	18.4	20.1	91 680	215	15 387	192 180	4.7
Gladwin	183	1.0	D	15.3	2.1	15.2	2.5	D	25.2	8 540	332	829	17 672	5.0
Gogebic	239	0.0	13.9	9.9	4.6	8.6	4.4	D	35.5	4 765	290	411	10 795	-0.4
Grand Traverse	2 508	0.2	18.1	9.2	10.1	9.2	8.0	23.4	14.2	18 260	210	1 304	41 599	19.4
Gratiot	701	4.7	15.3	13.0	D	5.2	4.5	D	20.3	8 720	205	961	16 339	5.3
Hillsdale	636	3.5	D	24.8	D	7.7	3.5	D	20.4	10 250	220	1 124	21 757	7.8
Houghton	588	0.2	D	3.8	5.4	7.7	4.7	D	41.7	7 655	209	675	18 636	5.0
Huron	629	14.0	D	15.1	4.6	6.1	4.8	D	15.4	9 495	287	746	21 199	3.8
Ingham	9 427	0.1	12.4	8.8	7.9	4.9	7.9	13.7	35.4	43 705	156	6 606	121 281	5.4
Ionia	852	3.9	D	20.1	D	7.5	6.9	D	28.9	10 970	172	1 234	24 778	12.6
Iosco	300	0.3	D	7.4	3.8	11.0	5.8	D	26.9	9 345	361	733	20 443	0.1
Iron	165	0.5	D	9.0	4.3	7.8	5.8	16.3	30.1	4 065	344	311	9 197	4.8
Isabella	1 350	0.8	16.8	7.5	3.4	8.6	6.6	9.0	38.2	10 085	143	1 263	28 381	15.7
Jackson	2 945	0.2	21.0	16.8	4.4	7.3	3.6	15.0	19.7	33 420	209	4 119	69 458	10.4
Kalamazoo	6 462	0.6	26.8	21.7	6.4	6.3	7.6	16.4	14.8	44 590	178	5 796	110 007	10.8
Kalkaska	206	1.5	30.7	7.2	2.7	5.8	4.2	3.9	19.9	4 405	257	447	12 171	12.4
Kent	18 567	0.2	25.7	20.4	9.9	6.5	6.7	14.8	9.5	97 585	162	14 119	246 901	10.2

1. Includes mining, construction, and manufacturing.   2. Per 1,000 resident population enumerated in the 2010 census.

Table B. States and Counties — Housing, Labor Force, and Employment

STATE County	Housing units, 2006–2010								Civilian labor force, 2010		Unemployment		Civilian employment,[5] 2006–2010		
	Occupied units													Percent	
	Owner-occupied				Renter-occupied										
				Median owner cost as a percent of income											
	Total	Percent	Median value[1]	With a mortgage	Without a mortgage	Median rent[2]	Median rent as a percent of income	Substandard units[3] (percent)	Total	Percent change, 2009–2010	Total	Rate[4]	Total	Management, business, science and arts	Construction, production, and maintenance occupations
	89	90	91	92	93	94	95	96	97	98	99	100	101	102	103
MARYLAND—Cont'd															
St. Mary's	36 253	72.9	327 800	24.2	11.2	1 123	26.8	2.2	52 886	3.0	3 309	6.3	49 952	43.0	20.5
Somerset	8 327	67.0	155 900	27.6	14.4	679	30.0	1.3	10 995	-0.4	1 144	10.4	9 462	29.9	22.2
Talbot	15 603	76.2	352 400	26.8	11.3	912	28.8	1.0	18 630	-1.9	1 454	7.8	18 287	36.7	19.7
Washington	55 419	66.3	238 000	24.5	12.1	763	28.5	1.8	67 526	0.0	6 937	10.3	71 046	30.7	24.6
Wicomico	36 302	65.2	195 100	24.6	13.3	936	32.1	3.0	51 641	-0.2	4 539	8.8	47 637	33.4	24.1
Worcester	22 016	78.6	289 100	27.7	13.5	808	28.8	1.3	27 737	0.8	3 348	12.1	24 227	32.6	19.7
Baltimore city	238 392	49.8	160 400	25.9	16.0	859	33.3	2.6	276 612	-0.8	30 062	10.9	274 033	36.1	17.6
MASSACHUSETTS	2 512 552	64.0	352 300	26.7	15.6	1 006	30.3	2.0	3 469 270	-0.2	288 590	8.3	3 271 535	42.8	16.5
Barnstable	98 164	80.4	392 700	29.9	16.2	1 075	33.3	1.3	123 046	0.1	11 283	9.2	104 121	37.5	18.2
Berkshire	55 623	68.9	207 800	25.3	14.8	715	29.8	1.0	73 531	0.5	6 039	8.2	63 416	36.1	18.7
Bristol	210 789	64.1	306 600	27.2	15.9	774	29.5	1.6	294 127	0.2	32 850	11.2	269 617	33.4	22.6
Dukes	5 530	81.1	681 300	36.4	18.3	1 180	31.1	2.5	11 597	2.3	898	7.7	8 425	30.3	27.9
Essex	282 913	65.4	372 400	27.5	16.1	977	31.7	2.0	385 253	0.6	34 429	8.9	366 590	40.7	17.7
Franklin	30 447	70.0	222 000	26.0	15.0	805	29.8	1.3	38 932	-0.6	3 121	8.0	37 422	38.3	23.7
Hampden	177 725	63.0	200 500	25.3	16.1	741	32.6	2.8	228 320	0.9	23 264	10.2	204 690	33.4	21.9
Hampshire	58 612	68.0	262 200	24.3	14.0	853	31.2	1.5	87 644	-0.9	6 039	6.9	82 431	43.8	16.4
Middlesex	572 847	63.9	420 800	26.1	15.4	1 213	28.7	2.0	830 943	0.5	58 318	7.0	784 372	51.5	12.8
Nantucket	3 623	73.3	0	38.2	14.0	1 714	27.8	0.5	7 876	-0.4	616	7.8	6 084	28.9	26.1
Norfolk	255 180	70.4	408 100	26.2	15.3	1 205	29.0	1.5	360 717	-0.1	27 354	7.6	339 910	49.8	12.3
Plymouth	178 983	77.9	360 700	27.9	15.7	1 042	30.7	1.7	266 445	0.9	24 115	9.1	243 860	37.4	19.1
Suffolk	283 954	36.5	384 500	28.9	16.3	1 181	31.8	3.5	377 923	2.0	30 697	8.1	366 804	42.3	12.4
Worcester	298 162	67.6	282 800	25.2	15.2	862	29.3	1.7	407 924	0.5	38 039	9.3	393 793	39.8	19.4
MICHIGAN	3 843 997	74.2	144 200	24.7	13.8	723	32.2	1.9	4 747 128	-2.3	600 566	12.7	4 369 785	33.6	23.4
Alcona	4 608	90.2	119 300	26.7	13.6	545	37.8	2.2	3 984	-4.5	715	17.9	3 500	23.1	31.9
Alger	3 688	81.7	111 500	25.7	13.7	522	27.2	1.1	4 112	-4.1	543	13.2	3 379	27.1	26.0
Allegan	42 078	83.2	149 400	25.1	12.8	645	27.7	2.5	53 247	-2.2	6 313	11.9	51 416	27.0	34.1
Alpena	13 357	80.6	104 800	23.7	13.9	479	33.4	0.9	14 199	-4.7	1 845	13.0	12 891	30.6	26.1
Antrim	10 043	84.5	156 500	27.3	13.7	663	32.2	2.3	10 757	-6.9	1 657	15.4	9 636	28.1	29.5
Arenac	6 686	83.7	99 000	24.8	13.3	492	32.4	2.0	7 407	-6.2	1 190	16.1	6 176	26.8	32.1
Baraga	3 336	75.5	86 500	21.4	12.4	496	25.6	2.6	4 216	-6.1	981	23.3	3 414	30.4	26.2
Barry	22 843	84.5	147 300	24.8	12.6	652	25.9	1.4	28 462	-2.6	2 778	9.8	27 664	25.4	34.6
Bay	44 345	79.8	107 800	23.0	13.4	556	29.8	0.9	53 266	-2.3	6 209	11.7	48 897	28.5	25.0
Benzie	7 366	85.9	160 200	26.7	13.1	737	33.2	3.0	8 613	-2.0	1 275	14.8	7 722	31.6	24.2
Berrien	62 612	72.8	135 600	22.9	12.6	592	32.2	2.0	76 713	-1.1	9 455	12.3	69 977	32.1	25.0
Branch	16 350	80.6	111 800	24.3	13.4	609	30.6	3.3	20 653	-3.9	2 520	12.2	18 172	26.1	34.9
Calhoun	53 925	72.1	110 300	23.8	13.5	642	31.5	1.4	66 989	-2.7	7 334	10.9	58 865	28.0	30.0
Cass	20 201	82.8	133 700	23.9	13.4	634	29.0	2.3	24 780	-3.0	2 706	10.9	23 405	26.1	35.6
Charlevoix	11 355	83.1	162 600	26.3	12.5	587	28.2	1.7	13 368	-3.1	1 923	14.4	12 085	28.7	30.0
Cheboygan	11 790	80.9	123 400	26.6	12.7	585	32.8	2.5	11 351	-3.5	1 435	12.6	10 233	26.7	26.2
Chippewa	14 836	71.5	103 100	21.4	12.5	541	32.0	2.3	17 016	-0.8	2 209	13.0	15 605	26.9	19.3
Clare	13 145	79.9	92 500	25.8	13.3	586	33.9	3.0	12 580	-3.2	1 963	15.6	10 796	24.4	31.8
Clinton	28 321	82.5	167 700	23.8	12.4	746	31.5	0.8	36 544	-1.4	3 153	8.6	35 532	35.7	22.0
Crawford	5 761	84.3	108 000	24.9	11.3	629	37.0	3.2	6 072	-5.3	793	13.1	5 178	29.3	26.6
Delta	16 339	80.1	100 600	23.3	12.8	522	33.6	2.1	19 080	-2.0	2 279	11.9	16 396	27.3	27.2
Dickinson	11 414	80.4	87 800	22.9	12.9	508	31.3	1.0	14 033	-1.8	1 535	10.9	11 921	26.8	26.9
Eaton	43 358	75.3	152 700	23.8	12.4	714	27.6	1.2	56 477	-2.9	5 083	9.0	53 117	33.3	24.2
Emmet	13 833	76.4	182 900	26.8	12.7	713	29.2	1.1	19 274	-1.4	2 815	14.6	16 100	32.8	19.6
Genesee	168 984	71.8	118 000	24.9	14.0	662	34.0	1.8	190 785	-3.9	26 142	13.7	169 980	29.9	24.9
Gladwin	11 321	85.4	117 700	26.5	13.7	542	34.7	2.4	10 123	-1.9	1 604	15.8	9 183	23.0	32.1
Gogebic	7 302	75.6	69 200	21.6	13.8	497	30.6	0.5	7 348	-1.2	951	12.9	6 500	25.2	29.3
Grand Traverse	34 578	77.1	174 300	25.7	13.6	793	29.8	1.8	47 273	-2.2	5 546	11.7	42 988	33.0	19.1
Gratiot	14 718	78.3	93 600	22.7	13.5	596	33.9	2.5	19 545	-0.2	2 430	12.4	17 137	26.2	27.4
Hillsdale	17 506	81.9	116 500	24.6	13.6	607	29.3	2.7	20 261	-2.6	2 869	14.2	19 710	24.8	37.5
Houghton	13 991	70.0	86 100	22.5	13.6	547	38.0	2.5	17 379	-1.4	1 896	10.9	16 043	34.2	19.1
Huron	14 419	83.2	104 900	24.7	13.9	509	30.5	0.8	16 042	0.6	2 084	13.0	14 800	28.4	33.6
Ingham	108 723	61.7	137 900	24.1	13.2	726	34.0	1.6	148 758	-1.7	15 495	10.4	133 958	38.9	16.3
Ionia	22 645	79.1	123 700	24.6	13.5	616	34.5	1.7	28 524	-4.6	3 586	12.6	26 751	25.6	30.6
Iosco	11 202	85.4	102 300	26.2	12.6	565	35.5	1.3	10 165	-2.0	1 667	16.4	9 081	25.2	26.9
Iron	5 386	84.9	75 700	24.9	16.0	463	31.9	0.8	5 559	-3.5	652	11.7	4 802	24.3	29.0
Isabella	24 804	59.4	128 000	24.3	11.4	652	40.2	1.9	37 565	-2.8	3 317	8.8	32 227	27.2	17.5
Jackson	60 612	76.0	130 000	24.1	13.3	678	31.2	1.8	73 313	-4.1	9 250	12.6	67 946	28.8	26.8
Kalamazoo	99 456	65.2	145 900	22.8	13.1	675	34.3	1.2	129 608	-2.6	13 187	10.2	117 835	36.5	19.6
Kalkaska	7 232	83.5	105 900	26.0	14.3	682	29.6	3.2	8 211	-4.0	1 118	13.6	7 145	21.1	32.2
Kent	227 177	71.3	147 600	23.9	13.4	699	30.6	2.2	308 846	-1.6	31 413	10.2	287 878	33.7	24.0

1. Specified owner-occupied units.   2. Specified renter-occupied units. A value of 10.0 represents 10 percent or less.   3. Overcrowded or lacking complete plumbing facilities.   4. Percent of civilian labor force.   5. Persons 16 years old and over.

Table B. States and Counties — Nonfarm Employment and Agriculture

	Private nonfarm establishments, employment and payroll, 2009									Agriculture, 2007			
		Employment						Annual payroll		Farms			
												Percent with:	
STATE County	Number of establishments	Total	Health care and social assistance	Manufacturing	Retail trade	Finance and insurance	Professional, scientific, and technical services	Total (mil dol)	Average per employee (dollars)	Number	Fewer than 50 acres	500 acres or more	Farm operators whose principal occupation is farming (percent)
	104	105	106	107	108	109	110	111	112	113	114	115	116
MARYLAND—Cont'd													
St. Mary's	1 911	28 070	4 256	D	4 684	466	7 353	1 210	43 110	621	49.1	3.7	45.2
Somerset	385	3 990	1 275	229	363	131	D	140	35 167	329	39.8	9.7	47.1
Talbot	1 556	16 975	3 294	1 520	2 602	649	1 236	597	35 177	305	34.4	20.7	47.2
Washington	3 497	56 565	9 514	6 058	9 750	5 173	1 951	1 873	33 116	844	46.8	4.4	51.9
Wicomico	2 543	37 753	8 044	3 737	6 763	1 172	1 566	1 245	32 983	508	50.4	9.1	53.3
Worcester	2 178	17 311	1 855	445	3 431	504	782	520	30 061	384	42.2	12.8	56.8
Baltimore city	12 333	275 608	67 642	13 830	16 504	19 323	19 656	14 026	50 890	NA	NA	NA	NA
MASSACHUSETTS	170 473	2 967 877	549 052	239 914	343 226	209 550	251 629	153 775	51 813	7 691	66.1	1.5	48.0
Barnstable	8 301	70 322	16 250	2 119	14 118	2 385	4 598	2 687	38 205	406	93.3	0.0	53.4
Berkshire	4 088	55 460	11 857	5 195	8 699	2 091	D	2 009	36 216	522	49.8	4.8	48.7
Bristol	12 828	196 389	37 886	30 255	33 804	6 051	6 014	7 303	37 189	777	71.3	0.9	47.4
Dukes	1 034	4 959	710	106	1 029	D	251	245	49 342	81	82.7	1.2	45.7
Essex	18 005	265 720	55 779	39 660	37 883	10 686	14 367	11 795	44 387	531	75.7	1.9	45.2
Franklin	1 623	20 769	3 733	4 149	3 022	684	459	693	33 380	741	51.0	3.4	47.2
Hampden	9 867	170 748	37 965	21 330	23 441	10 676	6 987	6 382	37 379	508	59.3	1.2	44.5
Hampshire	3 543	53 979	14 813	3 626	7 594	1 479	1 717	1 649	30 541	711	57.9	1.4	50.4
Middlesex	42 023	799 100	103 789	58 334	78 086	30 090	115 985	48 985	61 300	700	75.0	0.6	48.7
Nantucket	904	3 963	D	21	853	144	194	219	55 205	14	85.7	0.0	85.7
Norfolk	19 178	309 660	52 941	21 331	40 418	27 745	21 460	15 227	49 174	264	81.1	1.5	47.7
Plymouth	11 927	150 499	27 981	10 832	27 249	7 106	7 339	6 030	40 066	882	74.3	1.5	52.6
Suffolk	19 210	562 929	125 310	9 849	28 886	93 787	54 230	38 057	67 605	7	85.7	0.0	71.4
Worcester	17 786	272 872	58 787	33 107	38 141	15 950	14 901	11 286	41 360	1 547	59.4	0.8	44.6
MICHIGAN	221 682	3 383 615	568 492	470 900	448 068	156 163	240 983	135 808	40 137	56 014	44.5	8.2	44.3
Alcona	195	1 004	206	148	252	37	25	25	25 083	281	32.4	7.8	52.0
Alger	228	1 735	295	D	277	D	20	53	30 326	86	38.4	10.5	39.5
Allegan	2 342	32 415	3 432	12 048	3 581	D	1 189	1 238	38 190	1 595	51.8	7.0	43.6
Alpena	852	9 778	2 862	1 174	1 802	387	228	297	30 402	573	36.8	6.5	37.9
Antrim	560	3 727	453	634	506	131	195	103	27 752	411	37.7	5.8	47.2
Arenac	327	2 902	643	535	399	D	149	82	28 222	488	39.5	10.2	38.5
Baraga	211	1 717	398	381	269	63	D	45	26 235	76	28.9	14.5	36.8
Barry	929	9 634	1 480	2 598	1 438	715	213	298	30 959	1 164	45.4	6.0	39.5
Bay	2 315	30 816	6 434	3 051	5 370	1 057	1 243	1 057	34 300	851	40.2	12.1	48.3
Benzie	436	2 943	353	391	427	D	D	79	26 889	205	46.8	2.9	48.3
Berrien	3 736	51 686	8 985	8 466	7 003	1 280	2 001	1 839	35 584	1 300	57.8	5.5	49.1
Branch	833	11 022	1 627	3 365	1 734	468	154	607	30 559	1 129	39.1	9.9	37.2
Calhoun	2 723	48 904	9 165	11 438	6 211	D	1 119	1 988	40 650	1 178	37.6	9.3	45.3
Cass	771	6 997	855	2 097	881	230	143	202	28 799	811	43.9	9.9	42.3
Charlevoix	829	7 840	1 031	2 317	919	214	237	264	33 674	336	42.0	4.2	35.1
Cheboygan	781	4 901	1 144	222	1 209	214	127	149	30 355	347	41.2	5.8	38.6
Chippewa	822	8 212	1 810	518	1 638	303	198	217	26 409	401	22.2	14.2	42.1
Clare	525	5 446	1 176	757	991	D	122	148	27 140	450	34.9	6.2	42.7
Clinton	1 241	14 361	2 920	1 548	2 160	639	605	445	30 996	1 231	42.7	9.9	43.6
Crawford	319	3 321	915	567	551	82	D	100	30 035	39	66.7	2.6	46.2
Delta	1 128	12 470	1 830	2 362	2 057	430	523	365	29 282	290	19.3	16.6	47.6
Dickinson	920	12 665	D	1 847	2 045	371	287	478	37 709	161	32.3	5.6	32.9
Eaton	2 111	35 051	3 030	5 141	5 856	4 028	1 234	1 239	35 337	1 231	43.9	9.1	42.4
Emmet	1 515	13 313	3 317	929	2 621	379	538	457	34 302	291	37.5	5.5	41.9
Genesee	7 992	114 954	25 626	9 952	19 613	5 301	4 648	4 014	34 922	988	61.3	5.3	47.5
Gladwin	440	3 715	702	713	704	D	59	103	27 636	557	35.5	3.8	37.2
Gogebic	420	4 370	731	548	860	121	100	101	23 203	42	19.0	2.4	31.0
Grand Traverse	3 419	40 317	8 063	4 107	6 629	2 175	2 992	1 407	34 887	522	53.1	5.0	38.5
Gratiot	744	10 307	2 588	1 909	1 324	412	326	316	30 644	1 036	38.6	13.2	46.5
Hillsdale	840	10 435	1 514	3 070	1 341	283	351	298	28 582	1 674	43.2	6.8	33.6
Houghton	941	8 963	2 195	638	1 746	409	433	225	25 079	155	35.5	6.5	40.6
Huron	979	9 791	1 869	2 389	1 611	404	359	294	30 077	1 394	35.9	17.5	54.1
Ingham	6 321	104 521	20 045	9 872	14 100	7 758	6 142	3 909	37 401	947	58.8	7.6	45.7
Ionia	889	9 910	1 146	2 447	2 049	774	193	274	27 690	1 183	41.7	9.6	46.1
Iosco	639	5 991	1 223	778	1 367	238	153	159	26 507	316	43.0	8.2	40.2
Iron	400	2 713	428	449	473	146	174	71	25 999	111	28.8	8.1	30.6
Isabella	1 452	20 088	3 775	2 062	3 558	722	1 233	532	26 489	1 018	36.0	8.9	42.6
Jackson	3 077	45 403	9 248	7 504	7 059	1 536	2 257	1 737	38 263	1 184	50.3	6.1	40.2
Kalamazoo	5 651	100 997	18 053	15 884	13 337	4 754	5 464	3 761	37 238	854	55.4	8.2	46.6
Kalkaska	316	3 289	551	305	479	62	D	111	33 627	221	48.4	2.3	37.6
Kent	15 488	297 755	43 016	50 017	32 588	13 060	13 944	11 557	38 813	1 193	51.5	5.6	43.4

Table B. States and Counties — **Agriculture**

STATE County	Land in farms Acreage (1,000)	Percent change, 2002–2007	Acres Average size of farm	Acres Total irrigated (1,000)	Acres Total cropland (1,000)	Value of land and buildings (dollars) Average per farm	Value of land and buildings (dollars) Average per acre	Value of machinery and equipment, average per farm (dollars)	Value of products sold Total (mil dol)	Value of products sold Average per farm (dollars)	Percent from: Crops	Percent from: Live-stock and poultry products	Percent of farms with sales of: $10,000 or more	Percent of farms with sales of: $100,000 or more	Government payments Total ($1,000)	Government payments Percent of farms
	117	118	119	120	121	122	123	124	125	126	127	128	129	130	131	132
MARYLAND—Cont'd																
St. Mary's	69	1.5	111	1.1	39.8	804 658	7 279	73 148	15.9	25 680	73.3	26.7	36.6	5.6	612	29.3
Somerset	60	5.3	183	0.4	35.4	1 161 268	6 341	113 801	192.6	585 297	7.8	92.2	55.9	41.9	1 173	64.1
Talbot	109	2.8	357	3.5	87.1	2 204 538	6 169	160 468	50.5	165 708	50.2	49.8	48.2	27.2	3 058	73.4
Washington	114	-8.8	135	0.9	81.6	1 025 346	7 587	96 240	83.7	99 160	24.4	75.6	46.4	23.6	986	26.8
Wicomico	93	5.7	183	7.0	51.7	1 058 847	5 793	89 704	197.8	389 426	20.4	79.6	54.5	36.4	1 858	51.8
Worcester	111	-15.3	289	5.2	75.4	1 272 107	4 407	144 978	185.8	483 780	13.7	86.3	60.4	45.1	1 766	54.2
Baltimore city	NA	NA	NA	NA	NA	NA	NA	NA	NA	NA	NA	NA	NA	NA	NA	NA
MASSACHUSETTS	518	-0.2	67	23.1	187.4	829 090	12 313	56 373	489.8	63 687	74.4	25.6	35.8	10.4	4 603	7.7
Barnstable	5	-16.7	13	1.3	2.0	457 980	35 532	44 526	17.7	43 475	57.5	42.5	46.6	10.3	282	9.6
Berkshire	66	-4.3	127	0.2	22.6	1 113 751	8 762	54 632	20.6	39 465	37.5	62.5	28.4	8.2	205	6.1
Bristol	39	8.3	51	1.9	15.2	806 029	15 955	55 614	44.2	56 944	82.6	17.4	36.6	10.0	555	8.0
Dukes	8	0.0	98	0.1	1.1	1 474 733	15 090	57 758	3.3	41 193	67.8	32.2	40.7	6.2	D	1.2
Essex	28	0.0	52	0.9	12.2	971 091	18 526	59 475	25.0	47 122	75.9	24.1	33.9	10.0	276	4.0
Franklin	79	6.8	107	1.7	24.4	832 320	7 761	65 977	56.8	76 712	63.7	36.3	35.9	12.6	719	13.1
Hampden	37	-2.6	73	1.2	13.0	770 017	10 618	51 866	25.7	50 659	83.2	16.8	30.9	8.7	242	7.1
Hampshire	53	3.9	74	1.0	23.8	666 331	8 980	61 033	38.6	54 314	73.8	26.2	37.1	10.7	486	11.4
Middlesex	34	3.0	48	1.5	15.4	907 619	18 745	56 824	81.7	116 726	84.2	15.8	34.3	11.7	D	2.0
Nantucket	1	NA	44	0.4	0.4	445 903	10 151	104 596	2.9	206 131	D	D	50.0	21.4	0	0.0
Norfolk	12	-7.7	44	0.3	3.3	915 554	20 740	40 925	14.0	52 926	92.9	7.1	29.9	9.5	D	1.9
Plymouth	50	-15.3	56	11.9	18.3	823 166	14 634	66 646	78.4	88 935	93.2	6.8	51.1	17.2	629	10.0
Suffolk	0	NA	14	0.0	0.0	376 684	26 634	19 045	0.2	30 214	D	D	57.1	14.3	0	0.0
Worcester	106	1.9	69	0.9	35.6	810 727	11 792	50 355	80.6	52 069	55.5	44.5	29.2	6.9	1 034	7.6
MICHIGAN	10 032	-1.1	179	500.4	7 803.6	610 556	3 409	90 742	5 753.2	102 710	57.9	42.1	38.1	14.2	118 871	41.5
Alcona	45	9.8	162	0.1	28.3	392 702	2 431	51 035	8.7	30 890	28.3	71.7	26.7	6.0	185	24.6
Alger	18	20.0	213	D	10.4	458 926	2 150	56 784	2.8	32 231	12.2	87.8	24.4	9.3	64	32.6
Allegan	275	13.2	172	21.3	226.5	721 334	4 182	110 690	397.5	249 237	37.8	62.2	42.0	18.8	3 444	29.3
Alpena	86	16.2	150	0.0	59.6	387 180	2 581	66 222	21.5	37 449	30.0	70.0	29.0	8.2	332	31.8
Antrim	67	6.3	164	1.6	37.8	632 314	3 859	71 052	23.3	56 766	73.9	26.1	34.8	11.9	233	28.0
Arenac	95	13.1	194	0.0	74.4	464 302	2 395	86 220	29.7	60 923	59.5	40.5	28.1	12.9	1 657	71.3
Baraga	19	26.7	245	0.0	9.2	502 152	2 047	57 405	1.3	17 646	56.7	43.3	28.9	3.9	13	21.1
Barry	168	-7.7	144	3.1	120.0	504 427	3 491	70 091	94.4	81 088	26.9	73.1	25.8	8.2	2 204	43.9
Bay	186	0.0	219	4.1	166.7	616 830	2 818	117 055	77.2	90 744	89.2	10.8	49.9	20.7	2 424	67.0
Benzie	21	-8.7	103	0.3	9.2	470 889	4 582	68 934	8.0	38 933	68.0	32.0	30.2	10.7	74	14.1
Berrien	169	-2.9	130	18.4	138.6	600 093	4 616	102 068	136.3	104 815	90.5	9.5	47.3	17.0	2 241	27.4
Branch	250	-1.6	222	42.9	202.4	664 231	2 998	91 404	115.4	102 241	60.1	39.9	37.0	15.4	3 804	63.6
Calhoun	228	-5.0	194	9.3	175.1	583 048	3 012	81 935	89.8	76 245	60.6	39.4	37.4	13.1	3 170	49.6
Cass	190	0.5	235	39.0	151.9	822 259	3 504	104 890	101.5	125 214	54.8	45.2	39.0	16.8	2 807	52.7
Charlevoix	41	5.1	123	0.2	23.9	466 944	3 788	46 592	7.6	22 762	57.7	42.3	25.0	3.6	141	21.7
Cheboygan	48	-4.0	137	0.2	25.0	370 846	2 706	63 163	10.3	29 564	44.6	55.4	19.9	5.2	89	21.6
Chippewa	99	5.3	247	0.1	66.1	474 994	1 925	63 441	9.4	23 382	36.6	63.4	36.2	6.0	451	28.9
Clare	68	6.3	152	0.6	37.4	435 856	2 869	60 594	18.3	40 734	14.9	85.1	31.8	8.9	383	36.7
Clinton	272	6.3	221	4.3	233.3	797 743	3 616	107 148	165.5	134 466	39.5	60.5	46.9	17.3	3 794	60.2
Crawford	3	-50.0	65	0.0	0.8	262 422	4 055	49 041	0.3	8 209	D	D	15.4	0.0	D	5.1
Delta	78	5.4	268	0.5	40.4	612 835	2 285	72 055	11.6	40 065	37.9	62.1	40.3	12.1	299	28.3
Dickinson	25	-13.8	155	0.6	12.4	381 732	2 469	59 174	4.6	28 353	43.3	56.7	21.7	8.1	159	28.6
Eaton	222	-6.7	181	1.4	176.9	549 794	3 046	82 105	70.6	57 386	81.3	18.7	37.0	13.6	3 033	48.0
Emmet	40	-9.1	136	0.2	21.7	487 008	3 580	61 225	7.5	25 600	38.3	61.7	28.5	5.5	91	16.8
Genesee	129	-9.8	131	1.1	106.6	488 344	3 733	82 249	58.8	59 489	81.3	18.7	31.4	9.2	1 569	31.6
Gladwin	68	-5.6	121	0.2	43.7	359 504	2 961	47 614	12.1	21 732	54.3	45.7	30.2	3.2	625	46.0
Gogebic	4	0.0	93	D	1.7	317 502	3 413	33 270	0.4	9 390	31.7	68.5	14.3	0.0	D	2.4
Grand Traverse	63	1.6	120	1.9	41.1	668 671	5 578	65 073	19.2	36 865	80.2	19.8	37.2	10.3	284	23.6
Gratiot	287	-0.7	277	6.6	254.4	819 592	2 959	131 785	189.9	183 313	45.3	54.7	49.6	21.0	4 485	72.7
Hillsdale	270	-1.8	161	4.2	212.1	485 755	3 013	66 764	120.6	72 064	54.6	45.4	28.7	9.6	6 019	65.5
Houghton	24	-7.7	153	0.1	11.2	302 836	1 985	43 628	2.7	17 476	37.4	62.6	19.4	2.6	46	19.4
Huron	441	2.1	316	2.4	396.9	986 734	3 119	169 283	374.5	268 654	44.5	55.5	55.7	34.4	6 310	76.9
Ingham	186	0.5	197	2.3	155.7	751 299	3 821	104 278	84.6	89 357	61.3	38.7	35.5	12.7	2 153	29.5
Ionia	238	3.5	202	5.1	193.4	692 622	3 436	104 217	201.2	170 098	27.0	73.0	42.9	16.6	3 349	54.6
Iosco	48	6.7	151	0.0	33.1	407 122	2 695	61 327	15.0	47 452	31.0	69.0	23.7	8.5	459	32.9
Iron	28	-9.7	250	0.4	10.4	681 089	2 726	52 147	1.9	17 560	73.7	26.3	25.2	2.7	44	18.9
Isabella	196	0.5	193	3.4	154.1	573 830	2 979	76 421	71.4	70 170	50.5	49.5	39.0	13.7	2 287	56.6
Jackson	182	-5.7	154	3.8	135.1	534 327	3 469	73 640	56.9	48 039	55.8	44.2	31.0	8.6	2 030	32.3
Kalamazoo	145	-2.0	170	31.3	116.0	709 610	4 183	116 842	179.3	209 900	72.0	28.0	38.3	18.4	1 974	30.1
Kalkaska	23	-4.2	106	1.3	13.7	364 828	3 436	41 075	6.1	27 397	86.8	13.2	20.8	3.6	82	19.9
Kent	170	-1.7	143	9.2	131.5	689 965	4 839	86 968	194.7	163 226	70.6	29.4	41.1	15.9	1 405	26.7

Table B. States and Counties — Water Use, Wholesale Trade, Retail Trade, and Real Estate

STATE County	Water use, 2005		Wholesale trade,[1] 2007				Retail trade,[2] 2007				Real estate and rental and leasing,[2] 2007			
	Total water withdrawn (mil gal/day)	Gallons withdrawn per person	Number of establishments	Number of employees	Sales (mil dol)	Annual payroll (mil dol)	Number of establishments	Number of employees	Sales (mil dol)	Annual payroll (mil dol)	Number of establishments	Number of employees	Receipts (mil dol)	Annual payroll (mil dol)
	133	134	135	136	137	138	139	140	141	142	143	144	145	146
MARYLAND—Cont'd														
St. Mary's	11.4	118	30	D	D	D	314	4 531	1 193.0	97.9	92	466	66.1	15.0
Somerset	4.3	165	17	D	D	D	61	459	105.2	8.4	21	44	4.7	1.1
Talbot	6.4	178	61	557	252.7	23.6	262	2 750	711.9	68.0	85	242	45.9	9.0
Washington	71.0	500	144	1 978	1 265.3	81.8	673	10 226	2 463.3	219.5	131	632	136.9	17.9
Wicomico	20.1	223	112	D	D	D	445	7 431	1 780.8	167.2	152	701	107.8	22.3
Worcester	13.1	269	54	D	D	D	458	3 979	875.1	90.8	185	577	75.6	16.1
Baltimore city	29.7	47	534	9 046	4 843.4	468.9	1 950	16 682	4 348.8	401.5	647	4 677	837.5	214.9
MASSACHUSETTS	3 591.4	561	7 284	123 267	95 275.7	7 644.3	25 469	360 218	88 083.0	8 916.5	7 053	48 576	14 029.8	2 287.6
Barnstable	529.6	2 338	189	D	D	D	1 628	16 213	3 973.2	427.7	385	1 632	270.6	50.3
Berkshire	35.6	270	113	D	D	D	766	8 942	1 901.8	208.8	128	770	123.3	22.9
Bristol	1 057.0	1 935	548	10 224	7 719.8	514.7	2 419	37 079	8 647.7	846.5	472	2 451	382.1	70.6
Dukes	4.0	257	14	D	D	D	207	1 202	349.0	42.8	61	169	31.8	5.9
Essex	505.2	684	806	12 176	12 405.7	806.4	2 690	38 874	9 822.1	962.0	647	3 045	584.1	109.8
Franklin	34.4	475	56	579	460.1	31.6	290	3 153	691.0	71.3	50	127	18.2	2.9
Hampden	167.1	362	408	6 818	4 991.8	321.1	1 686	24 052	5 668.7	548.3	409	2 164	356.8	69.0
Hampshire	37.4	244	91	1 638	2 021.8	68.0	584	7 705	1 546.1	169.8	128	526	88.1	14.6
Middlesex	388.9	267	2 022	39 339	32 873.3	2 847.9	6 306	80 413	19 661.1	2 036.6	1 690	12 621	3 802.7	571.3
Nantucket	5.1	503	12	45	39.8	2.9	159	920	342.8	38.9	59	179	51.0	6.4
Norfolk	49.6	78	974	19 035	12 398.9	1 190.2	2 595	42 427	11 241.4	1 107.3	841	6 719	1 538.9	297.7
Plymouth	170.2	346	531	7 002	5 253.6	456.6	2 016	27 593	6 615.1	684.8	427	1 924	493.9	68.4
Suffolk	161.0	246	689	11 905	8 914.8	683.5	2 385	31 139	7 565.8	800.8	1 083	12 455	5 596.1	859.4
Worcester	446.5	570	831	11 876	6 913.7	603.7	2 738	40 506	10 057.2	971.0	673	3 794	692.2	138.6
MICHIGAN	11 659.9	1 152	9 892	137 315	107 109.3	7 016.1	37 619	470 794	109 102.6	10 001.5	8 862	54 874	12 858.6	1 685.7
Alcona	5.7	487	2	D	D	D	45	277	55.3	5.3	7	D	D	D
Alger	7.2	740	4	D	D	D	50	318	54.4	5.1	7	D	D	D
Allegan	29.9	264	115	1 316	506.7	56.6	362	3 715	881.3	77.4	77	258	46.2	8.5
Alpena	122.5	4 024	31	D	D	D	169	1 890	416.8	38.9	25	143	14.3	2.7
Antrim	40.2	1 645	11	D	D	D	103	636	156.7	13.6	21	77	7.0	1.7
Arenac	34.7	2 025	12	D	D	D	72	488	118.8	8.2	7	D	D	D
Baraga	1.8	200	4	5	4.6	0.2	36	324	67.7	5.5	5	D	D	D
Barry	8.8	146	33	210	72.3	8.4	150	1 528	276.2	24.6	31	100	8.3	2.9
Bay	629.6	5 774	95	D	D	D	430	5 580	1 301.0	115.5	77	316	39.9	6.0
Benzie	3.1	173	7	29	3.5	0.7	77	558	131.3	12.2	23	35	6.7	1.1
Berrien	2 327.2	14 311	143	1 836	689.1	65.2	609	7 360	1 622.8	153.9	189	796	105.6	19.3
Branch	32.6	702	30	D	D	D	148	1 887	396.9	38.5	33	79	10.8	2.2
Calhoun	35.6	255	103	D	D	D	531	7 074	1 571.3	136.0	95	475	62.7	11.7
Cass	23.3	448	44	D	D	D	121	899	183.4	17.4	25	56	10.0	1.0
Charlevoix	21.5	803	14	55	8.4	1.6	136	995	221.2	20.8	41	141	29.8	6.7
Cheboygan	3.6	133	14	D	D	D	183	1 282	316.9	28.7	31	117	15.2	2.9
Chippewa	9.3	241	22	D	D	D	169	1 654	369.5	33.0	29	93	12.1	2.1
Clare	4.1	130	12	D	D	D	127	1 144	246.1	22.8	16	29	4.2	0.7
Clinton	11.1	159	46	815	562.1	31.6	186	2 123	631.9	52.4	65	264	41.1	8.0
Crawford	2.5	168	4	D	D	D	74	621	216.8	12.6	15	28	4.0	0.6
Delta	65.4	1 704	45	D	D	D	213	2 268	459.8	46.2	31	78	7.9	1.2
Dickinson	23.7	846	51	D	D	D	181	1 975	417.3	38.8	28	D	D	D
Eaton	11.1	103	71	1 441	914.3	67.9	404	5 996	1 327.0	116.2	105	488	76.7	12.7
Emmet	7.3	218	34	D	D	D	310	2 583	580.6	62.8	53	195	23.9	5.5
Genesee	20.4	46	296	5 871	3 554.9	382.9	1 614	21 531	4 836.7	440.5	339	1 813	270.2	47.7
Gladwin	2.5	93	6	31	9.0	1.4	88	627	140.2	12.6	20	88	8.5	2.8
Gogebic	10.9	649	10	D	D	D	93	719	138.0	13.0	16	61	3.4	1.0
Grand Traverse	14.5	172	122	1 141	425.0	43.1	622	7 192	1 570.1	149.2	163	546	120.9	16.8
Gratiot	9.0	213	29	D	D	D	146	1 367	316.4	27.9	20	63	4.8	1.2
Hillsdale	10.4	220	37	384	260.6	16.5	150	1 430	323.3	31.2	27	81	10.0	1.4
Houghton	4.3	119	20	D	D	D	176	1 935	335.5	34.1	28	D	D	D
Huron	90.9	2 624	38	456	253.6	17.2	188	1 585	323.1	28.5	12	17	4.4	0.5
Ingham	237.6	853	241	3 168	4 423.7	139.6	1 000	15 174	3 156.2	299.6	286	2 596	282.0	68.2
Ionia	11.9	184	25	243	118.8	8.8	163	2 021	446.7	39.8	27	77	7.6	1.2
Iosco	4.2	155	6	D	D	D	137	1 294	270.6	25.0	24	50	5.3	0.9
Iron	2.7	223	12	47	18.6	1.3	73	519	101.4	8.6	19	65	3.9	1.2
Isabella	8.9	135	44	D	D	D	234	3 757	705.4	69.1	56	729	57.4	13.8
Jackson	22.6	138	146	D	D	D	582	7 462	1 690.9	153.6	118	608	64.9	12.5
Kalamazoo	80.3	334	250	3 102	1 207.2	139.2	918	14 148	2 808.8	278.0	226	2 512	219.2	69.1
Kalkaska	4.4	253	21	182	83.4	10.0	57	465	144.1	10.2	10	55	5.0	1.1
Kent	85.6	144	950	21 881	13 020.8	1 141.5	2 216	33 139	8 058.0	715.9	649	4 013	601.0	109.0

1. Merchant wholesalers, except manufacturers' sales branches and offices.   2. Employer establishments.

Table B. States and Counties — **Professional Services, Manufacturing, and Accommodation and Food Services**

STATE County	Professional, scientific, and technical services,[1] 2007				Manufacturing, 2007				Accommodation and food services, 2007			
	Number of establishments	Number of employees	Receipts (mil dol)	Annual payroll (mil dol)	Number of establishments	Number of employees	Receipts (mil dol)	Annual payroll (mil dol)	Number of establishments	Number of employees	Sales (mil dol)	Annual payroll (mil dol)
	147	148	149	150	151	152	153	154	155	156	157	158
MARYLAND—Cont'd												
St. Mary's	274	D	D	D	35	D	D	D	162	3 011	132.3	34.1
Somerset	23	D	D	D	NA	NA	NA	NA	31	298	9.9	2.9
Talbot	162	1 177	176.0	67.8	47	2 422	D	83.8	124	1 997	104.9	31.8
Washington	235	D	D	D	149	6 969	2 448.7	337.4	290	5 036	229.7	65.1
Wicomico	228	D	D	D	79	D	D	136.1	194	4 002	184.8	50.3
Worcester	158	D	D	D	39	D	154.6	D	406	6 477	506.8	141.6
Baltimore city	1 506	D	D	D	479	16 253	5 730.9	726.5	1 481	21 456	1 434.7	372.1
MASSACHUSETTS	21 773	243 374	49 085.7	20 652.0	7 737	289 256	86 429.0	15 712.0	16 039	257 302	14 917.2	4 339.7
Barnstable	753	D	D	D	210	2 461	533.3	110.3	1 100	12 721	891.0	261.6
Berkshire	366	D	D	D	173	6 204	1 425.5	317.1	516	7 600	401.9	125.6
Bristol	1 110	D	D	D	797	35 101	8 878.1	1 659.4	1 206	20 866	885.2	261.7
Dukes	71	282	38.6	14.6	NA	NA	NA	NA	125	734	95.8	28.3
Essex	2 221	D	D	D	997	47 909	17 488.7	2 877.4	1 708	23 927	1 301.5	377.7
Franklin	120	D	D	D	111	4 537	1 164.4	197.3	157	1 944	80.3	24.4
Hampden	886	D	D	D	673	24 346	6 001.1	1 122.1	978	14 673	661.7	191.7
Hampshire	360	D	D	D	157	3 970	1 098.8	182.1	367	5 430	225.5	67.7
Middlesex	6 883	106 332	21 264.5	9 828.5	1 853	72 842	22 482.6	4 609.2	3 372	54 344	3 250.2	932.3
Nantucket	56	D	D	D	NA	NA	NA	NA	104	752	88.9	26.3
Norfolk	2 704	D	D	D	714	26 614	10 340.8	1 434.6	1 435	24 126	1 294.0	378.9
Plymouth	1 288	D	D	D	541	13 012	2 577.2	566.5	1 023	17 051	794.6	242.1
Suffolk	3 067	52 850	13 301.5	5 485.4	379	12 664	3 703.4	674.8	2 257	48 978	3 795.9	1 090.7
Worcester	1 888	14 149	2 693.0	917.8	1 099	39 334	10 706.1	1 953.9	1 691	24 156	1 150.7	330.8
MICHIGAN	22 552	249 864	29 536.8	15 304.5	13 675	581 739	234 455.8	29 910.3	19 678	339 181	14 536.6	4 207.3
Alcona	8	19	1.7	0.7	NA	NA	NA	NA	26	97	4.2	1.1
Alger	12	36	3.0	1.0	9	629	193.9	28.0	41	358	14.2	3.0
Allegan	169	1 012	61.7	42.4	214	13 077	4 240.7	573.6	216	2 742	118.8	34.3
Alpena	48	D	D	D	46	1 603	587.4	72.2	73	882	32.2	9.2
Antrim	43	135	10.5	3.9	52	1 039	193.6	42.2	68	1 176	35.2	14.3
Arenac	16	149	8.2	4.2	27	695	126.6	23.1	47	398	15.6	4.1
Baraga	2	D	D	D	NA	NA	NA	NA	14	183	5.6	1.3
Barry	68	266	19.6	8.6	68	2 781	977.4	118.6	81	929	32.3	9.8
Bay	174	D	D	D	126	3 532	1 107.2	191.2	238	3 973	134.7	41.3
Benzie	28	D	D	D	NA	NA	NA	NA	54	1 053	44.2	12.9
Berrien	287	D	D	D	332	10 831	2 298.3	474.7	413	5 519	219.5	64.1
Branch	46	157	12.8	4.2	80	2 990	1 061.1	127.2	83	990	44.7	10.7
Calhoun	209	D	D	D	179	11 532	4 954.0	537.5	284	4 558	182.0	54.1
Cass	55	D	D	D	85	3 114	711.3	113.6	63	743	27.1	7.5
Charlevoix	71	194	17.6	6.4	52	2 899	698.6	134.0	87	1 570	60.2	17.4
Cheboygan	55	152	14.3	4.9	NA	NA	NA	NA	116	773	46.0	14.6
Chippewa	46	D	D	D	32	578	D	19.5	114	2 428	189.9	45.0
Clare	28	166	12.5	6.8	31	969	192.5	36.1	68	736	28.9	8.0
Clinton	117	574	61.1	25.2	67	2 159	609.3	106.2	99	1 666	50.8	14.6
Crawford	19	79	9.9	2.0	18	563	152.6	23.3	49	600	19.6	6.4
Delta	81	D	D	D	73	2 695	712.6	124.6	110	1 342	46.4	13.3
Dickinson	54	D	D	D	48	2 214	D	100.4	78	873	28.6	8.1
Eaton	193	1 292	143.3	56.3	96	8 377	D	547.9	201	4 122	155.3	48.3
Emmet	118	485	56.9	22.4	51	1 026	254.4	39.9	142	2 220	108.4	33.4
Genesee	694	D	D	D	309	14 878	12 579.5	1 099.6	762	13 583	528.7	151.9
Gladwin	21	61	4.0	1.3	39	811	174.1	33.6	50	488	17.6	5.1
Gogebic	26	110	8.2	3.7	21	682	80.1	20.2	61	1 188	55.7	14.5
Grand Traverse	408	D	D	D	179	4 727	1 160.7	202.0	236	5 267	237.7	72.0
Gratiot	37	279	16.8	10.2	48	2 010	357.4	73.3	66	1 152	40.1	13.0
Hillsdale	50	346	20.3	8.2	92	3 917	1 330.8	145.8	80	752	31.4	8.0
Houghton	68	D	D	D	48	D	D	28.9	111	1 427	46.5	13.6
Huron	56	271	23.3	13.2	68	2 692	647.3	101.9	105	832	33.6	8.2
Ingham	777	5 944	724.3	293.6	222	9 829	D	533.1	601	11 648	446.1	131.8
Ionia	59	D	D	D	73	3 126	1 117.4	112.0	88	980	37.4	9.5
Iosco	40	169	12.5	5.6	37	973	190.4	33.8	77	663	27.3	7.4
Iron	31	199	8.6	4.0	NA	NA	NA	NA	44	334	11.6	3.1
Isabella	124	1 672	78.3	41.3	61	2 221	528.7	85.0	125	3 431	117.8	33.8
Jackson	235	D	D	D	284	9 250	2 783.0	403.6	300	4 999	185.4	53.5
Kalamazoo	557	D	D	D	334	17 261	7 145.9	904.1	507	11 678	414.6	130.6
Kalkaska	21	213	17.1	9.8	NA	NA	NA	NA	29	363	13.7	3.9
Kent	1 643	D	D	D	1 154	61 608	15 738.3	3 034.1	1 134	24 655	925.2	283.6

1. Establishment subject to federal tax.

Table B. States and Counties — **Health Care and Social Assistance, Other Services, and Federal Funds**

STATE County	Health care and social assistance, 2007				Other services, 2007				Federal funds and grants, 2009–2010 Expenditures (mil dol)			
										Direct payments for individuals[1]		
	Number of establishments	Number of employees	Receipts (mil dol)	Annual payroll (mil dol)	Number of establishments	Number of employees	Receipts (mil dol)	Annual payroll (mil dol)	Total	Social Security and government retirement	Medicare	Food Stamps and Supplemental Security Income
	159	160	161	162	163	164	165	166	167	168	169	170
MARYLAND—Cont'd												
St. Mary's	159	3 563	311.3	126.3	146	877	83.7	27.4	3 449.9	387.6	188.4	17.8
Somerset	40	1 267	77.2	37.7	28	85	11.4	1.8	288.6	74.9	99.1	10.1
Talbot	170	2 946	314.7	114.3	129	833	93.2	23.7	447.4	176.5	114.6	6.9
Washington	407	9 407	822.7	355.5	268	1 838	159.3	43.3	1 171.4	467.8	352.3	34.9
Wicomico	346	7 715	745.9	330.3	179	1 218	100.7	30.2	766.3	277.8	240.6	28.6
Worcester	130	1 896	160.3	64.7	150	925	72.2	22.6	518.0	241.3	142.5	10.8
Baltimore city	1 506	64 978	8 368.9	2 954.3	982	9 180	1 541.6	273.4	17 067.5	1 736.1	4 948.1	578.3
MASSACHUSETTS	17 855	511 012	51 946.1	22 176.0	13 516	90 268	9 841.0	2 690.3	82 453.6	17 313.5	13 690.5	2 271.0
Barnstable	807	15 247	1 466.2	620.7	601	3 279	334.9	88.2	2 650.7	1 059.0	647.7	45.7
Berkshire	450	10 869	981.1	429.8	309	1 742	142.3	38.5	1 352.8	459.3	357.1	48.0
Bristol	1 368	36 372	2 911.7	1 364.1	1 052	5 898	465.7	131.5	6 187.8	1 547.6	1 152.2	215.8
Dukes	61	590	78.1	33.0	55	177	26.1	6.1	126.9	50.7	29.7	1.7
Essex	2 030	47 584	4 272.0	1 909.5	1 470	8 644	1 096.7	254.2	9 423.9	2 019.7	1 518.0	274.1
Franklin	197	3 678	267.2	116.1	137	572	48.5	13.3	536.9	214.7	134.6	24.3
Hampden	1 162	37 111	3 243.2	1 423.3	834	5 453	431.5	133.2	4 304.2	1 347.2	942.5	358.7
Hampshire	419	8 219	764.1	309.8	297	1 550	147.2	38.9	1 153.4	397.2	217.2	28.1
Middlesex	4 386	99 055	10 192.8	4 326.2	3 202	23 744	2 577.2	790.2	20 144.1	3 615.4	3 012.9	287.1
Nantucket	34	369	52.3	17.6	41	173	26.3	6.2	54.3	22.7	14.4	0.4
Norfolk	2 084	53 650	4 430.5	1 984.8	1 535	9 656	1 036.5	297.6	4 792.9	1 437.3	1 466.2	80.5
Plymouth	1 157	26 215	2 209.8	978.5	921	6 294	518.6	185.1	3 745.4	1 414.3	855.1	110.2
Suffolk	1 755	116 467	15 525.9	6 462.1	1 716	15 391	2 216.9	483.0	16 685.5	1 699.2	1 778.8	512.8
Worcester	1 945	55 586	5 551.2	2 200.6	1 346	7 695	772.5	224.3	6 321.4	2 028.3	1 564.3	283.5
MICHIGAN	26 033	549 482	52 758.4	21 588.3	17 040	101 568	10 843.7	2 648.1	90 921.1	30 768.9	17 107.6	4 443.4
Alcona	10	D	D	D	14	36	3.1	0.5	148.1	68.2	29.6	3.5
Alger	21	308	18.1	7.7	14	D	D	D	93.3	40.3	21.0	2.2
Allegan	171	3 104	208.5	88.5	182	807	69.2	19.1	566.3	272.5	111.9	22.2
Alpena	92	2 734	222.1	91.5	78	348	29.5	7.7	338.6	139.7	67.6	14.8
Antrim	44	396	23.4	11.4	34	152	15.1	4.4	201.3	95.2	39.1	5.9
Arenac	32	630	46.8	17.6	25	D	D	D	163.8	76.6	38.3	9.2
Baraga	21	355	26.1	11.4	18	49	3.1	0.6	84.2	32.5	16.1	3.1
Barry	76	1 414	104.4	43.8	94	375	36.5	9.4	286.2	161.3	57.7	11.3
Bay	315	5 902	513.3	209.5	196	1 068	75.9	21.8	897.4	401.0	203.4	50.5
Benzie	34	355	26.4	9.7	25	D	D	D	135.2	70.8	23.4	8.9
Berrien	694	8 821	701.7	282.8	281	1 468	112.2	35.1	1 365.2	568.7	292.2	90.8
Branch	51	D	D	D	72	D	D	D	278.3	131.9	67.5	12.3
Calhoun	341	8 967	898.1	372.5	225	1 249	503.8	42.5	1 481.8	503.1	252.8	76.8
Cass	60	D	D	D	62	272	27.8	6.5	296.2	128.3	62.8	18.1
Charlevoix	75	862	81.4	32.6	63	251	23.8	5.9	177.2	98.3	36.1	5.7
Cheboygan	54	1 158	87.8	35.0	72	206	17.9	5.0	206.8	102.7	45.7	8.8
Chippewa	78	1 546	136.9	46.6	61	D	D	D	392.9	134.4	52.7	12.9
Clare	55	947	79.6	27.1	52	157	12.9	2.9	290.6	133.9	69.2	17.2
Clinton	95	1 370	107.1	37.9	105	592	44.7	12.6	301.2	164.6	57.9	8.9
Crawford	40	1 006	90.7	35.3	25	146	15.5	5.3	151.6	52.8	22.9	4.8
Delta	109	1 819	147.1	53.4	95	586	46.5	12.5	363.7	168.7	73.4	15.3
Dickinson	102	D	D	D	76	D	D	D	267.5	117.6	43.6	7.4
Eaton	239	2 995	231.0	88.7	164	1 040	118.8	38.5	736.6	255.7	100.6	19.0
Emmet	198	3 146	361.7	139.1	109	508	56.0	14.9	241.0	123.1	43.3	6.6
Genesee	1 261	25 790	2 505.1	1 005.4	648	3 695	418.1	103.4	3 751.3	1 495.5	857.8	303.7
Gladwin	35	701	55.6	18.3	32	211	15.5	4.3	237.3	125.2	57.2	13.4
Gogebic	40	738	62.9	24.7	43	131	10.2	2.6	185.0	75.5	45.7	7.3
Grand Traverse	382	7 736	798.1	305.0	232	1 314	121.8	32.0	650.9	321.1	108.4	14.5
Gratiot	110	2 439	216.3	81.7	62	255	30.3	7.2	308.3	129.9	70.4	15.0
Hillsdale	112	1 474	111.2	42.2	57	416	24.4	5.0	302.2	146.0	61.9	15.0
Houghton	86	2 026	146.7	61.5	69	D	D	D	353.5	107.4	63.7	12.1
Huron	98	1 804	130.2	50.7	61	212	18.2	4.0	311.3	134.3	75.5	12.0
Ingham	848	20 580	1 991.5	843.5	595	5 128	584.8	158.0	6 596.0	822.1	417.3	132.3
Ionia	108	1 287	94.2	35.9	82	366	24.1	5.7	326.5	154.6	72.1	18.5
Iosco	58	1 200	93.6	41.5	62	223	14.1	3.7	271.5	145.5	66.1	11.1
Iron	18	395	37.7	14.0	22	D	D	D	133.0	55.8	34.4	3.8
Isabella	224	3 265	193.7	86.9	101	544	34.1	9.0	326.8	150.6	57.4	23.8
Jackson	379	8 717	810.5	346.6	241	1 528	147.0	41.2	1 149.7	513.5	248.9	66.6
Kalamazoo	639	18 148	1 811.4	703.6	430	3 414	480.2	91.8	2 155.8	680.0	300.3	90.1
Kalkaska	25	466	32.7	13.6	36	D	D	D	100.6	48.9	22.6	6.2
Kent	1 497	40 522	3 956.9	1 564.3	1 100	7 828	721.7	198.8	3 612.8	1 489.9	637.8	192.0

1. State totals may include programs not allocated by county.

Table B. States and Counties — Federal Funds, Residential Construction, and Local Government Finances

STATE County	Salaries and wages	Defense	Other	Medicaid and other health-related	Nutrition and family welfare	Education	Other	New construction ($1,000)	Number of housing units	Total (mil dol)	Inter-govern-mental (mil dol)	Total (mil dol)	Per capita Total	Per capita Property
	171	172	173	174	175	176	177	178	179	180	181	182	183	184
MARYLAND—Cont'd														
St. Mary's	587.9	2 123.6	23.6	70.9	11.9	4.1	20.0	81 557	413	317.6	119.3	150.9	1 503	701
Somerset	9.8	0.8	2.1	50.4	5.0	7.7	14.1	7 741	48	88.4	53.0	22.2	853	533
Talbot	33.0	35.0	28.8	33.9	4.8	1.0	3.9	30 550	173	166.1	32.4	80.0	2 211	972
Washington	58.6	18.6	46.8	120.3	23.4	6.9	20.0	46 926	256	509.0	194.6	207.2	1 428	843
Wicomico	35.9	13.3	10.4	94.1	22.3	3.7	12.6	22 048	146	378.3	162.6	134.9	1 441	828
Worcester	15.7	38.2	7.0	45.6	7.8	1.4	1.1	17 648	93	318.7	51.7	207.7	4 207	2 887
Baltimore city	941.5	390.4	944.2	4 233.1	448.6	325.6	2 204.5	45 497	369	3 324.9	1 724.8	1 075.5	1 687	947
MASSACHUSETTS	4 506.0	12 673.5	3 313.8	14 088.0	1 526.5	1 343.7	5 393.6	1 816 993	9 075	X	X	X	X	X
Barnstable	250.1	84.7	75.5	189.4	35.0	11.3	233.0	139 122	418	915.3	212.8	541.7	2 438	2 298
Berkshire	54.6	111.3	29.3	202.4	27.1	12.7	31.0	34 941	139	442.7	189.6	203.0	1 564	1 520
Bristol	153.2	1 585.1	159.1	1 043.2	108.7	44.9	112.4	90 967	505	1 915.3	986.2	693.1	1 276	1 225
Dukes	5.0	5.2	1.7	10.8	2.1	0.8	16.4	58 711	113	120.5	25.0	74.4	4 807	4 617
Essex	269.8	3 843.8	150.9	900.1	132.3	59.5	163.4	193 080	872	2 602.3	1 061.9	1 210.2	1 651	1 609
Franklin	20.4	6.7	7.5	82.8	17.8	5.2	14.4	11 455	58	301.3	161.3	115.0	1 606	1 568
Hampden	379.9	64.8	91.0	755.3	108.0	48.8	102.0	58 697	327	1 722.4	980.0	586.2	1 280	1 254
Hampshire	104.5	35.0	49.7	149.2	21.5	11.5	96.0	57 854	248	431.4	177.6	194.1	1 267	1 232
Middlesex	1 248.1	5 847.4	1 415.4	2 508.9	213.3	356.0	1 452.4	426 550	2 109	6 250.8	1 991.3	3 083.9	2 093	2 040
Nantucket	6.5	0.0	2.3	4.6	0.9	0.3	1.4	45 196	53	92.0	7.3	57.9	5 497	5 092
Norfolk	182.6	645.5	65.7	505.4	82.9	37.5	152.9	251 135	1 417	2 401.7	712.8	1 366.9	2 087	2 027
Plymouth	237.4	75.5	357.4	484.6	72.9	37.5	46.6	169 381	945	1 861.1	854.3	812.2	1 657	1 600
Suffolk	1 280.3	203.1	795.3	5 926.4	433.7	609.0	2 668.5	49 597	480	4 635.6	2 563.9	1 412.8	1 981	1 853
Worcester	313.7	165.3	113.1	1 290.4	135.6	62.6	243.3	230 304	1 391	2 659.9	1 294.8	1 073.9	1 374	1 341
MICHIGAN	4 798.2	4 080.3	2 386.4	11 165.6	2 752.7	1 689.6	4 969.4	7 549	52	X	X	X	X	X
Alcona	2.5	0.0	0.6	29.5	2.4	0.9	9.9	2 010	20	35.2	10.8	13.0	1 130	1 094
Alger	5.0	0.0	2.1	16.6	2.2	1.8	1.5	4 467	35	35.5	19.1	8.8	916	876
Allegan	17.5	2.6	4.1	64.8	19.3	6.0	2.7	30 525	152	358.5	168.6	114.4	1 014	997
Alpena	26.1	13.6	4.5	33.6	24.3	2.9	1.9	1 322	11	213.3	57.8	31.9	1 075	1 055
Antrim	6.0	4.5	22.0	21.4	4.4	1.4	0.3	8 007	42	98.4	30.0	44.8	1 843	1 805
Arenac	3.9	0.5	0.9	24.8	4.1	2.9	0.2	1 407	10	45.1	24.2	14.3	863	851
Baraga	3.3	0.1	0.5	13.3	2.9	2.5	8.7	888	6	51.5	18.2	7.9	926	921
Barry	7.8	1.6	2.0	30.0	8.4	1.6	0.3	10 265	84	153.2	78.4	41.5	700	694
Bay	40.3	1.8	13.8	103.8	22.2	5.9	6.3	8 410	54	514.5	250.3	131.3	1 221	1 199
Benzie	3.8	0.0	9.7	18.8	2.8	1.1	0.4	8 406	58	57.6	19.1	22.6	1 288	1 283
Berrien	31.8	2.9	16.0	249.9	36.3	15.7	32.6	36 640	133	590.1	307.2	173.2	1 085	1 060
Branch	7.7	0.0	1.7	36.6	9.9	3.5	0.5	4 001	19	216.4	80.1	40.3	872	850
Calhoun	156.6	156.0	60.6	190.7	37.0	11.3	11.6	5 066	33	634.9	350.7	166.3	1 217	1 073
Cass	9.5	1.9	1.8	41.7	9.0	3.5	5.6	18 787	72	172.2	93.1	40.3	797	781
Charlevoix	5.6	4.0	1.2	17.5	4.9	1.8	1.0	12 159	57	141.3	43.3	67.6	2 581	2 576
Cheboygan	9.6	0.1	3.2	28.1	5.2	1.7	0.9	11 048	39	83.2	36.1	34.8	1 301	1 281
Chippewa	44.1	12.0	11.1	57.7	18.6	6.4	20.9	5 017	60	135.2	68.4	30.8	792	789
Clare	6.2	0.0	1.4	35.4	9.4	4.0	0.3	2 791	34	120.5	59.2	30.1	981	971
Clinton	21.6	4.5	3.5	18.1	9.6	2.9	0.8	18 081	91	203.6	101.6	59.3	850	826
Crawford	44.5	3.2	8.6	8.5	3.5	1.0	1.4	2 999	38	42.0	19.2	16.0	1 102	1 049
Delta	19.3	7.3	6.1	45.3	12.3	2.6	1.7	7 971	60	141.9	77.0	36.3	972	965
Dickinson	40.5	7.3	22.3	19.2	6.4	1.1	0.6	4 591	36	178.6	60.7	30.9	1 147	1 137
Eaton	172.5	4.2	2.6	43.3	14.2	20.2	91.9	20 869	121	322.2	163.8	99.6	928	906
Emmet	9.8	0.0	2.8	28.5	5.8	2.2	10.1	12 012	47	233.0	110.7	74.9	2 242	2 195
Genesee	129.6	8.1	36.2	510.6	112.4	40.8	46.5	13 006	78	2 037.0	976.1	403.5	928	864
Gladwin	4.5	0.0	1.1	25.1	5.5	1.9	0.6	6 751	42	64.9	32.0	21.7	824	811
Gogebic	10.3	0.0	5.3	28.5	4.5	1.9	-0.6	3 234	18	82.8	43.6	14.2	872	866
Grand Traverse	51.2	1.2	36.7	70.1	20.7	5.2	8.1	33 399	181	460.2	201.3	144.3	1 689	1 649
Gratiot	12.0	0.8	2.0	51.8	9.0	3.1	3.2	1 142	9	149.8	99.7	30.5	724	710
Hillsdale	9.6	0.0	2.3	44.1	9.7	2.9	1.3	7 628	46	135.1	74.9	31.9	681	674
Houghton	30.7	16.0	10.6	52.9	12.1	2.7	33.9	8 236	57	136.7	74.5	25.3	718	709
Huron	9.0	1.7	2.1	45.4	8.6	2.4	0.7	5 533	36	142.2	60.6	47.0	1 412	1 390
Ingham	143.3	512.0	127.5	593.0	505.8	820.3	2 309.0	62 716	465	1 439.6	679.0	433.6	1 552	1 424
Ionia	9.9	0.0	2.2	44.7	11.3	3.7	2.1	4 640	28	203.8	130.1	46.8	731	682
Iosco	9.5	7.8	2.5	17.5	7.2	2.5	0.5	4 003	27	112.1	55.5	31.8	1 212	1 200
Iron	6.6	0.0	1.0	20.7	3.1	0.9	6.0	5 540	43	64.9	31.5	15.8	1 300	1 290
Isabella	14.4	0.5	4.0	46.8	10.7	3.7	5.6	6 173	52	216.0	133.1	40.7	610	591
Jackson	65.1	17.2	7.3	140.0	36.5	10.9	9.0	10 457	63	577.7	311.0	149.1	915	851
Kalamazoo	145.3	38.1	28.2	234.1	46.4	20.0	488.9	59 494	289	905.9	446.6	294.2	1 199	1 167
Kalkaska	2.3	-0.2	0.6	15.1	3.3	1.3	-0.2	3 879	22	66.1	18.1	16.5	961	938
Kent	302.4	87.4	98.1	441.7	93.8	38.3	104.9	122 339	694	2 388.9	1 106.3	776.6	1 285	1 138

1. State totals may include programs not allocated by county.   2. Based on the resident population estimated as of July 1 of the year shown.

STATE County	Local government finances, 2007 (cont.)									Government employment, 2009			Presidential election,[2] 2008		
	Direct general expenditure						Debt outstanding						Percent of vote cast:		
			Percent of total for:												
	Total (mil dol)	Per capita[1] (dollars)	Educa-tion	Health and hospitals	Police protec-tion	Public welfare	High-ways	Total (mil dol)	Per capita[1] (dollars)	Federal civilian	Federal military	State and local	Demo-cratic	Republi-can	All other
	185	186	187	188	189	190	191	192	193	194	195	196	197	198	199
MARYLAND—Cont'd															
St. Mary's	286.7	2 856	62.2	0.8	6.2	0.4	2.8	208.3	2 075	7 692	2 612	4 629	42.8	55.6	1.5
Somerset	90.1	3 465	56.5	1.0	4.7	0.1	3.9	71.1	2 732	62	112	2 943	48.2	50.8	1.1
Talbot	117.6	3 249	39.6	1.9	6.2	0.7	5.9	62.1	1 715	264	126	1 665	44.4	54.1	1.5
Washington	453.9	3 128	57.4	0.8	4.2	0.8	5.3	337.5	2 326	720	443	8 450	42.6	55.5	1.9
Wicomico	365.4	3 904	57.8	0.9	4.8	4.9	4.4	200.1	2 137	339	277	7 475	46.4	52.2	1.4
Worcester	275.7	5 583	35.5	3.9	8.7	0.6	5.3	168.8	3 419	205	178	3 583	41.6	57.1	1.3
Baltimore city	3 158.2	4 954	37.6	4.0	11.2	0.1	5.8	3 044.0	4 775	9 713	2 097	67 745	87.2	11.7	1.2
MASSACHUSETTS	X	X	X	X	X	X	X	X	X	49 494	19 899	384 314	62.0	36.2	1.7
Barnstable	979.9	4 411	46.8	1.1	6.2	0.3	3.2	860.0	3 871	1 765	1 234	12 443	56.1	42.4	1.5
Berkshire	500.5	3 856	60.3	0.5	3.4	0.1	5.3	347.1	2 674	452	322	8 109	75.2	22.6	2.2
Bristol	1 971.6	3 631	59.5	0.7	5.3	0.6	2.6	1 424.2	2 623	1 281	1 352	25 966	60.7	37.5	1.8
Dukes	133.2	8 604	45.9	2.3	4.9	0.0	3.9	93.7	6 051	49	39	1 360	75.1	23.2	1.6
Essex	2 691.9	3 672	57.7	0.4	4.9	0.1	2.6	2 237.1	3 052	3 660	1 919	36 337	59.4	39.0	1.6
Franklin	314.9	4 399	63.5	0.4	2.5	0.1	4.8	156.0	2 179	215	177	4 861	72.7	24.9	2.4
Hampden	1 669.6	3 646	60.7	0.6	5.1	0.6	2.9	1 631.0	3 562	4 303	1 335	29 305	61.5	36.4	2.1
Hampshire	468.7	3 060	59.7	0.6	4.0	0.2	4.2	272.7	1 781	1 371	395	16 549	71.8	26.0	2.3
Middlesex	6 127.7	4 159	50.3	11.8	4.4	0.3	2.7	3 686.3	2 502	13 360	4 989	73 520	64.2	34.1	1.7
Nantucket	100.0	9 495	27.5	0.6	3.8	3.7	0.9	156.8	14 892	66	59	650	67.5	31.0	1.5
Norfolk	2 380.8	3 635	55.8	0.5	5.2	0.1	3.5	1 506.1	2 300	1 814	1 662	30 691	58.5	40.0	1.6
Plymouth	1 828.7	3 730	58.3	0.5	4.7	0.2	2.7	1 192.8	2 433	3 460	1 271	28 539	53.0	45.4	1.5
Suffolk	3 362.6	4 716	33.8	5.1	9.5	2.7	1.7	7 558.8	10 601	14 783	3 137	66 918	77.5	21.1	1.4
Worcester	2 872.2	3 676	59.7	0.6	4.3	0.1	3.5	2 447.7	3 133	2 915	2 008	49 066	55.8	42.1	2.1
MICHIGAN	X	X	X	X	X	X	X	X	X	54 092	20 559	581 947	57.4	41.0	1.6
Alcona	34.5	2 989	26.6	19.4	3.1	8.4	10.7	10.3	890	38	20	304	45.1	53.0	1.9
Alger	31.5	3 274	39.9	1.6	3.4	0.0	25.4	11.9	1 239	89	17	807	52.0	46.1	1.9
Allegan	374.0	3 317	60.4	6.4	3.7	3.3	5.9	1 005.4	8 917	197	208	4 064	43.7	54.4	1.9
Alpena	213.9	7 200	30.4	50.1	2.0	0.3	4.6	47.9	1 613	106	58	2 953	51.1	47.2	1.7
Antrim	90.7	3 733	43.8	4.5	4.3	11.2	10.0	54.1	2 227	82	43	1 172	43.9	54.2	1.9
Arenac	45.8	2 755	53.4	1.1	2.8	0.9	13.8	41.2	2 483	51	29	745	51.1	46.8	2.0
Baraga	50.7	5 936	25.8	40.3	2.2	0.2	13.0	34.6	4 048	34	16	1 690	47.3	50.7	2.0
Barry	156.2	2 639	49.3	4.7	3.6	10.7	7.7	204.6	3 458	102	107	2 021	44.0	53.8	2.2
Bay	497.3	4 625	48.5	16.6	3.8	4.2	5.0	312.7	2 909	282	225	5 827	56.7	41.4	1.8
Benzie	57.5	3 281	38.6	6.2	2.9	10.2	11.1	35.4	2 021	40	46	639	52.9	45.5	1.7
Berrien	592.1	3 710	53.6	7.8	5.6	1.1	4.9	334.7	2 098	368	315	8 789	52.0	46.5	1.5
Branch	209.8	4 542	39.7	33.3	2.2	4.2	6.2	97.1	2 102	92	82	3 021	46.0	52.1	1.8
Calhoun	649.8	4 756	50.9	14.2	3.9	2.4	4.3	580.6	4 250	3 068	283	6 912	53.8	44.5	1.7
Cass	182.7	3 614	55.8	6.5	3.0	3.9	4.6	159.1	3 147	89	91	2 131	51.3	47.1	1.6
Charlevoix	143.2	5 468	44.2	14.7	2.2	7.6	6.8	92.8	3 546	53	68	1 633	47.4	50.9	1.7
Cheboygan	81.2	3 035	55.6	2.1	3.5	1.5	12.4	62.7	2 342	61	113	1 025	48.3	49.8	1.9
Chippewa	134.1	3 444	43.3	9.1	2.8	0.5	12.3	132.6	3 408	452	227	6 543	49.0	49.5	1.5
Clare	126.1	4 109	68.2	0.4	2.0	0.6	6.8	83.9	2 734	63	55	1 517	51.5	46.6	1.9
Clinton	195.8	2 807	53.0	2.1	3.8	0.8	9.6	260.0	3 727	153	446	2 101	49.5	48.8	1.6
Crawford	40.4	2 777	43.2	0.3	5.5	1.3	13.4	23.8	1 638	145	26	628	47.9	49.6	2.5
Delta	142.5	3 814	59.9	3.3	1.7	1.4	8.3	86.8	2 323	215	67	2 098	52.3	46.0	1.7
Dickinson	173.6	6 444	27.1	46.3	1.8	0.2	5.1	151.1	5 610	580	49	2 108	45.0	53.0	2.0
Eaton	342.3	3 187	52.7	3.0	4.4	4.1	6.1	470.1	4 377	249	203	5 745	53.4	45.0	1.7
Emmet	229.2	6 865	28.7	36.9	1.5	5.1	4.7	191.8	5 745	116	62	2 639	46.9	51.3	1.8
Genesee	2 071.2	4 764	47.7	24.0	4.0	0.9	3.3	1 026.1	2 360	1 431	776	23 133	65.5	32.9	1.6
Gladwin	59.2	2 251	50.6	1.6	3.5	0.5	12.5	34.3	1 305	60	47	901	49.8	48.3	2.0
Gogebic	80.1	4 919	37.4	11.0	3.2	10.0	10.1	57.9	3 556	166	29	1 556	57.6	40.3	2.1
Grand Traverse	461.5	5 399	47.5	15.1	2.6	5.5	3.1	515.1	6 026	500	285	5 959	47.7	50.7	1.6
Gratiot	156.9	3 724	61.6	6.5	2.8	1.3	6.6	101.2	2 401	102	77	2 485	51.3	46.9	1.8
Hillsdale	135.2	2 889	52.2	0.7	3.3	10.2	8.0	159.7	3 414	120	83	2 274	42.9	54.9	2.3
Houghton	131.0	3 722	42.5	5.2	1.7	10.4	7.9	99.8	2 836	187	100	4 342	46.8	50.7	2.5
Huron	151.3	4 546	41.4	8.9	2.7	5.7	17.2	138.5	4 161	103	74	1 740	48.8	49.2	1.9
Ingham	1 470.4	5 265	50.4	10.0	4.6	1.8	3.4	1 557.2	5 575	2 077	636	48 199	65.9	32.6	1.6
Ionia	216.9	3 386	59.5	5.9	2.3	0.6	9.2	254.2	3 969	126	114	3 721	46.0	51.8	2.2
Iosco	109.6	4 173	45.6	14.0	1.9	6.4	8.3	94.1	3 583	113	72	1 518	51.5	46.4	2.1
Iron	60.7	4 997	26.3	4.3	2.7	25.2	9.8	56.4	4 645	50	21	960	50.0	47.8	2.2
Isabella	209.4	3 139	28.6	35.2	3.0	4.5	6.3	141.0	2 114	141	128	11 023	58.8	39.6	1.6
Jackson	646.7	3 968	55.8	6.7	2.6	3.5	7.1	487.5	2 991	391	293	9 094	50.3	47.9	1.8
Kalamazoo	908.5	3 703	50.4	13.0	7.3	1.0	5.0	1 057.9	4 312	1 007	459	14 028	58.9	39.4	1.7
Kalkaska	54.7	3 183	26.5	36.6	4.9	1.1	10.3	19.1	1 112	28	31	871	44.5	53.3	2.3
Kent	2 513.5	4 159	54.9	5.5	4.1	1.5	4.5	3 556.9	5 886	3 054	1 136	23 349	49.4	48.9	1.6

1. Based on the resident population estimated as of July 1 of the year shown.   2. © 2009 Election Data Services, Inc. All rights reserved.

Table B. States and Counties — Land Area and Population

STATE/ County code	CBSA code[1]	County type[2]	STATE County	Land area[3] (sq km) 2010	Total persons	Rank	Per square kilometer	White	Black	American Indian, Alaska Native	Asian and Pacific Islander	Percent Hispanic or Latino[4]	Under 5 years	5 to 17 years	18 to 24 years	25 to 34 years	35 to 44 years	45 to 54 years
				1	2	3	4	5	6	7	8	9	10	11	12	13	14	15
			MICHIGAN—Cont'd															
26 083	26340	9	Keweenaw	1 399	2 156	3 040	1.5	99.0	0.3	0.6	0.1	0.7	4.5	13.3	5.3	7.7	9.0	16.1
26 085	...	8	Lake	1 469	11 539	2 331	7.9	87.9	10.3	1.8	0.4	2.1	4.5	13.4	5.5	8.3	10.6	15.9
26 087	19820	1	Lapeer	1 665	88 319	644	53.0	94.1	1.3	1.0	0.6	4.1	5.2	19.0	7.9	9.6	13.6	17.7
26 089	45900	9	Leelanau	899	21 708	1 752	24.1	92.4	0.5	4.0	0.6	3.7	4.3	15.2	5.7	7.1	9.8	15.8
26 091	10300	4	Lenawee	1 941	99 892	580	51.5	89.0	3.1	1.0	0.8	7.6	5.7	17.5	9.5	11.0	13.0	15.3
26 093	19820	1	Livingston	1 464	180 967	340	123.6	96.4	0.6	0.9	1.2	1.9	5.5	20.1	7.0	9.6	14.4	18.1
26 095	...	7	Luce	2 329	6 631	2 720	2.8	82.5	11.3	7.6	0.4	1.2	4.6	13.3	7.0	13.3	14.3	16.0
26 097	...	7	Mackinac	2 646	11 113	2 357	4.2	80.7	0.8	21.9	0.4	1.1	4.2	14.4	5.7	8.4	10.9	16.5
26 099	19820	1	Macomb	1 241	840 978	61	677.7	85.6	9.4	0.9	3.7	2.3	5.8	17.2	8.4	12.1	14.1	15.8
26 101	...	7	Manistee	1 404	24 733	1 613	17.6	92.1	3.4	3.1	0.5	2.6	4.3	14.7	7.1	9.6	11.3	15.8
26 103	32100	5	Marquette	4 684	67 077	782	14.3	94.8	2.1	2.9	0.9	1.1	5.2	13.5	14.7	12.1	10.9	14.7
26 105	...	7	Mason	1 282	28 705	1 467	22.4	94.1	1.1	1.6	0.7	4.0	5.7	16.1	7.3	9.6	11.2	15.7
26 107	13660	6	Mecosta	1 438	42 798	1 108	29.8	94.4	3.4	1.5	0.9	1.7	5.2	14.8	20.9	10.0	9.5	12.2
26 109	31940	7	Menominee	2 704	24 029	1 645	8.9	95.6	0.6	3.3	0.5	1.2	4.9	16.1	6.4	9.6	11.2	16.9
26 111	33220	4	Midland	1 337	83 629	661	62.5	94.3	1.7	0.9	2.3	2.0	5.6	18.1	9.2	10.7	12.7	16.2
26 113	15620	9	Missaukee	1 463	14 849	2 121	10.1	96.9	0.5	1.2	0.4	2.1	6.0	18.2	7.0	10.1	11.4	15.9
26 115	33780	3	Monroe	1 423	152 021	410	106.8	93.9	2.8	0.9	0.8	3.1	5.7	18.4	8.4	10.9	13.3	16.6
26 117	...	6	Montcalm	1 827	63 342	825	34.7	93.8	2.7	1.1	0.6	3.1	6.1	18.1	8.3	12.1	13.5	15.5
26 119	...	9	Montmorency	1 416	9 765	2 456	6.9	98.2	0.4	1.4	0.4	1.0	3.9	13.0	5.3	7.7	9.3	15.6
26 121	34740	3	Muskegon	1 293	172 188	359	133.2	79.4	15.6	1.6	0.9	4.8	6.6	18.3	9.0	12.4	12.4	15.2
26 123	24340	2	Newaygo	2 106	48 460	1 002	23.0	92.4	1.5	1.4	0.6	5.5	6.2	18.7	8.0	10.2	12.0	15.9
26 125	19820	1	Oakland	2 247	1 202 362	32	535.1	76.8	14.3	0.8	6.4	3.5	5.7	17.8	7.6	11.9	14.1	16.5
26 127	...	8	Oceana	1 326	26 570	1 542	20.0	84.8	0.7	1.5	0.4	13.7	6.7	18.2	7.5	10.4	11.2	15.2
26 129	...	9	Ogemaw	1 459	21 699	1 754	14.9	97.3	0.4	1.4	0.5	1.4	4.8	15.6	6.5	9.1	10.4	16.0
26 131	...	9	Ontonagon	3 396	6 780	2 706	2.0	97.7	0.3	1.8	0.4	0.9	3.5	12.3	4.1	6.7	10.0	17.4
26 133	...	7	Osceola	1 467	23 528	1 664	16.0	97.2	1.1	1.4	0.4	1.5	6.2	18.6	7.6	10.0	11.6	15.4
26 135	...	9	Oscoda	1 465	8 640	2 558	5.9	98.2	0.3	1.5	0.2	0.9	5.0	15.6	6.3	7.4	9.4	16.2
26 137	...	7	Otsego	1 334	24 164	1 639	18.1	97.3	0.7	1.5	0.6	1.2	5.9	17.0	7.5	9.6	12.6	16.1
26 139	26100	3	Ottawa	1 459	263 801	247	180.8	87.1	1.9	0.7	3.1	8.6	6.7	19.3	12.8	11.7	12.6	14.2
26 141	...	7	Presque Isle	1 706	13 376	2 227	7.8	97.8	0.6	1.1	0.4	0.9	4.0	13.5	5.1	7.6	9.6	16.1
26 143	...	7	Roscommon	1 346	24 449	1 630	18.2	97.6	0.6	1.3	0.5	1.1	3.9	12.1	5.4	7.2	9.4	15.1
26 145	40980	3	Saginaw	2 072	200 169	313	96.6	72.0	19.6	0.8	1.3	7.8	5.9	17.5	10.6	11.0	12.0	14.7
26 147	19820	1	St. Clair	1 868	163 040	375	87.3	93.7	3.2	1.1	0.7	2.9	5.7	18.0	8.0	10.3	13.5	16.6
26 149	44780	4	St. Joseph	1 297	61 295	845	47.3	89.7	3.5	1.0	1.0	6.6	6.9	19.0	8.1	11.8	12.1	14.7
26 151	...	6	Sanilac	2 493	43 114	1 103	17.3	95.6	0.6	0.8	0.5	3.3	5.8	17.8	7.4	10.0	11.9	15.8
26 153	...	7	Schoolcraft	3 034	8 485	2 571	2.8	90.2	0.2	11.5	0.3	0.8	4.8	15.1	5.9	8.3	11.4	16.5
26 155	37020	4	Shiawassee	1 374	70 648	753	51.4	96.3	0.8	1.0	0.6	2.4	5.6	18.5	8.5	10.8	13.1	16.1
26 157	...	6	Tuscola	2 080	55 729	898	26.8	95.3	1.3	1.0	0.5	2.8	5.6	17.9	7.9	10.5	12.4	16.0
26 159	28020	2	Van Buren	1 573	76 258	711	48.5	84.6	5.0	1.6	0.7	10.2	6.4	19.1	7.8	11.2	12.5	15.8
26 161	11460	2	Washtenaw	1 828	344 791	188	188.6	74.7	14.0	1.0	9.1	4.0	5.6	15.3	16.9	14.3	12.7	13.7
26 163	19820	1	Wayne	1 585	1 820 584	15	1 148.6	51.2	41.4	0.9	3.2	5.2	6.5	18.9	9.7	12.0	13.5	14.8
26 165	15620	7	Wexford	1 463	32 735	1 369	22.4	96.7	0.8	1.3	0.9	1.6	6.8	17.6	7.7	11.3	12.1	15.5
27 000	...	X	**MINNESOTA**	206 232	5 303 925	X	25.7	84.8	6.0	1.7	4.7	4.7	6.7	17.5	9.5	13.5	12.8	15.2
27 001	...	8	Aitkin	4 718	16 202	2 043	3.4	96.2	0.6	3.0	0.4	0.9	4.8	13.2	5.1	7.6	9.3	15.3
27 003	33460	1	Anoka	1 096	330 844	194	301.9	87.3	5.3	1.3	4.7	3.6	6.8	19.3	8.1	13.2	14.6	16.9
27 005	...	6	Becker	3 406	32 504	1 377	9.5	90.5	0.7	9.7	0.7	1.2	6.7	17.9	6.8	10.8	10.9	14.9
27 007	13420	7	Beltrami	6 488	44 442	1 079	6.8	77.0	1.2	22.1	1.1	1.5	7.6	17.4	14.6	12.3	10.0	13.3
27 009	41060	3	Benton	1 057	38 451	1 205	36.4	94.8	2.6	0.8	1.5	1.6	7.4	17.3	10.7	15.7	12.9	13.8
27 011	...	9	Big Stone	1 292	5 269	2 822	4.1	98.4	0.4	0.7	0.3	0.8	5.5	15.5	5.6	9.2	9.2	15.6
27 013	31860	5	Blue Earth	1 937	64 013	815	33.0	92.4	3.3	0.5	2.5	2.5	6.0	13.4	22.9	14.0	10.0	11.7
27 015	35580	7	Brown	1 583	25 893	1 570	16.4	95.8	0.4	0.2	0.8	3.3	6.1	15.9	9.1	10.6	10.5	15.9
27 017	20260	2	Carlton	2 231	35 386	1 290	15.9	91.0	1.8	7.3	0.8	1.4	6.3	17.3	7.4	12.0	13.0	16.1
27 019	33460	1	Carver	918	91 042	626	99.2	91.9	1.6	0.5	3.3	3.9	7.4	22.5	6.5	11.9	15.9	17.4
27 021	14660	9	Cass	5 236	28 567	1 472	5.5	87.3	0.6	12.4	0.7	1.2	6.1	15.6	6.3	9.3	10.3	15.3
27 023	...	7	Chippewa	1 505	12 441	2 278	8.3	92.3	0.8	1.5	1.5	4.9	6.7	16.8	7.1	11.1	10.7	14.7
27 025	33460	1	Chisago	1 074	53 887	924	50.2	95.7	1.5	1.1	1.2	1.5	6.1	19.6	7.3	11.7	15.1	17.3
27 027	22020	3	Clay	2 707	58 999	869	21.8	92.2	2.0	2.0	2.0	3.5	6.9	16.4	17.6	13.2	11.1	12.8
27 029	...	8	Clearwater	2 587	8 695	2 554	3.4	89.3	0.5	11.0	0.5	1.4	7.0	18.0	6.9	10.4	11.0	14.9
27 031	...	9	Cook	3 761	5 176	2 831	1.4	89.5	0.4	10.0	1.0	1.1	4.2	12.6	5.4	9.4	11.2	17.1
27 033	...	7	Cottonwood	1 654	11 687	2 317	7.1	90.1	0.9	0.5	3.2	6.2	6.0	17.9	6.7	9.7	10.8	14.3
27 035	14660	5	Crow Wing	2 588	62 500	832	24.1	97.2	0.9	1.4	0.7	1.0	6.4	16.6	7.5	11.4	11.2	14.7
27 037	33460	1	Dakota	1 456	398 552	168	273.7	84.3	5.7	0.8	5.3	6.0	7.0	19.4	7.7	13.6	14.3	16.6
27 039	40340	3	Dodge	1 138	20 087	1 834	17.7	94.4	0.6	0.5	0.9	4.6	7.4	21.6	6.8	12.3	13.8	15.2
27 041	10820	7	Douglas	1 651	36 009	1 274	21.8	97.9	0.7	0.6	0.7	0.9	6.0	15.8	8.1	11.5	10.7	14.8
27 043	...	7	Faribault	1 845	14 553	2 144	7.9	93.5	0.5	0.5	0.5	5.6	5.7	16.3	6.5	10.2	10.0	15.5

1. CBSA = Core Based Statistical Area. See Appendix A for explanation. See Appendix B for list of metropolitan areas with component counties. Service of USDA Rural-Urban Continuum Codes. See Appendix A for definition. 2. County type code from the Economic Research 3. Dry land or land partially or temporarily covered by water. 4. May be of any race.

STATE County	Population, 2010 (cont.) Age (percent) (cont.) 55 to 64 years	65 to 74 years	75 years and over	Percent female	Population change and components of change, 1990–2010 Total persons 1990	2000	Percent change 1990–2000	2000–2010	Components of change, 2000–2009 Births	Deaths	Net migration	Households, 2010 Number	Percent change, 2000–2010	Persons per house-hold	Percent Female family house-holder[1]	One per-son
	16	17	18	19	20	21	22	23	24	25	26	27	28	29	30	31
MICHIGAN—Cont'd																
Keweenaw	19.9	15.2	8.8	48.7	1 701	2 301	35.3	-6.3	222	215	7	1 013	1.5	2.12	4.9	34.2
Lake	18.1	14.7	9.0	48.9	8 583	11 333	32.0	1.8	1 044	1 398	-35	5 158	9.7	2.16	9.2	32.9
Lapeer	13.7	8.0	5.3	49.6	74 768	87 904	17.6	0.5	9 506	5 945	-998	32 776	6.7	2.64	9.4	21.3
Leelanau	18.6	12.6	10.8	50.7	16 527	21 119	27.8	2.8	1 760	1 708	862	9 255	9.7	2.31	7.1	26.0
Lenawee	13.5	7.9	6.7	49.5	91 476	98 890	8.1	1.0	11 368	8 151	-1 741	37 514	4.4	2.52	10.8	25.1
Livingston	13.4	7.2	4.8	50.0	115 645	156 951	35.7	15.3	18 463	9 600	18 080	67 380	21.7	2.67	8.2	20.1
Luce	13.6	10.3	7.6	42.3	5 763	7 024	21.9	-5.6	559	714	-328	2 412	-2.8	2.25	9.3	31.4
Mackinac	17.5	12.8	9.6	49.5	10 674	11 943	11.9	-6.9	962	1 254	-1 005	5 024	-0.8	2.19	8.1	31.0
Macomb	12.4	7.3	7.0	51.4	717 400	788 149	9.9	6.7	93 285	68 058	18 373	331 667	7.3	2.51	12.7	28.0
Manistee	16.5	11.4	9.3	48.2	21 265	24 527	15.3	0.8	2 302	2 693	440	10 308	4.5	2.27	9.3	29.9
Marquette	14.3	7.7	7.0	49.5	70 887	64 634	-8.8	3.8	5 902	5 769	1 379	27 538	6.9	2.26	8.6	30.4
Mason	15.3	10.8	8.4	50.6	25 537	28 274	10.7	1.5	2 971	2 932	503	11 940	4.7	2.37	9.8	28.3
Mecosta	12.1	9.0	6.4	49.8	37 308	40 553	8.7	5.5	4 264	3 157	360	16 101	8.0	2.45	9.6	25.8
Menominee	15.9	9.8	9.3	49.7	24 920	25 326	1.6	-5.1	2 280	2 493	-990	10 474	-0.5	2.26	9.1	30.4
Midland	12.5	7.7	7.1	50.9	75 651	82 874	9.5	0.9	8 936	5 991	-2 785	33 437	5.3	2.46	8.9	25.8
Missaukee	14.1	9.9	7.4	49.1	12 147	14 478	19.2	2.6	1 615	1 295	116	5 843	7.2	2.51	8.3	24.8
Monroe	13.3	7.3	6.1	50.7	133 600	145 945	9.2	4.2	16 183	11 347	2 839	58 230	8.3	2.59	11.1	23.5
Montcalm	12.3	8.0	6.1	48.3	53 059	61 266	15.5	3.4	7 764	5 115	-821	23 432	6.1	2.57	11.4	23.8
Montmorency	18.3	15.4	11.6	49.6	8 936	10 315	15.4	-5.3	789	1 396	444	4 416	-0.9	2.18	8.6	30.8
Muskegon	12.6	7.1	6.4	50.4	158 983	170 200	7.1	1.2	21 984	14 743	-2 413	65 616	3.6	2.53	15.4	26.4
Newaygo	13.3	9.0	6.5	49.7	38 206	47 874	25.3	1.2	5 907	4 000	-807	18 406	4.6	2.60	10.0	23.3
Oakland	13.2	7.0	6.2	51.5	1 083 592	1 194 156	10.2	0.7	138 094	83 918	-36 761	483 698	2.7	2.46	11.1	28.6
Oceana	13.9	9.8	7.3	49.8	22 455	26 873	19.7	-1.1	3 551	2 181	-523	10 174	4.0	2.58	9.5	24.6
Ogemaw	15.7	12.9	9.1	50.2	18 681	21 645	15.9	0.2	1 973	2 782	515	9 283	5.0	2.31	10.0	28.3
Ontonagon	19.5	15.8	10.5	48.4	8 854	7 818	-11.7	-13.3	448	1 014	-671	3 258	-5.7	2.06	6.0	34.8
Osceola	13.7	9.9	7.2	50.2	20 146	23 197	15.1	1.4	2 759	2 051	-1 094	9 222	4.1	2.50	9.7	25.4
Oscoda	17.0	13.8	9.8	49.6	7 842	9 418	20.1	-8.3	811	1 058	-429	3 772	-3.8	2.27	7.7	30.0
Otsego	14.3	9.5	7.6	50.8	17 957	23 301	29.8	3.7	2 624	2 008	-416	9 756	8.5	2.44	9.2	25.3
Ottawa	10.9	6.3	5.5	51.0	187 768	238 314	26.9	10.7	33 235	14 084	6 089	93 775	14.8	2.73	8.4	20.9
Presque Isle	17.9	13.4	12.7	49.9	13 743	14 411	4.9	-7.2	1 136	1 663	-356	5 982	-2.8	2.20	6.5	29.8
Roscommon	18.8	16.1	11.9	50.1	19 776	25 469	28.8	-4.0	1 884	3 438	853	11 433	1.6	2.11	8.0	32.2
Saginaw	13.0	8.0	7.3	51.7	211 946	210 039	-0.9	-4.7	24 980	19 082	-14 154	79 011	-1.8	2.44	16.0	28.2
St. Clair	13.5	7.9	6.6	50.5	145 607	164 235	12.8	-0.7	18 884	13 748	-953	63 841	2.8	2.52	11.4	25.5
St. Joseph	12.7	8.0	6.8	50.5	58 913	62 422	6.0	-1.8	8 758	5 371	-3 748	23 244	-0.6	2.60	11.7	24.8
Sanilac	13.7	9.6	8.0	50.6	39 928	44 547	11.6	-3.2	4 914	4 236	-2 963	17 132	1.5	2.48	9.8	26.4
Schoolcraft	16.8	11.1	10.1	50.5	8 302	8 903	7.2	-4.7	722	1 058	-400	3 759	4.2	2.22	8.1	30.9
Shiawassee	13.1	7.9	8.4	50.6	69 770	71 687	2.7	-1.4	8 073	5 741	-3 606	27 481	2.2	2.54	11.6	24.2
Tuscola	13.8	9.0	6.8	49.9	55 498	58 266	5.0	-4.4	6 166	4 931	-3 798	21 590	0.6	2.52	9.9	24.0
Van Buren	13.4	7.9	5.9	50.4	70 060	76 263	8.9	0.0	9 726	6 384	-896	28 928	3.4	2.61	12.1	24.0
Washtenaw	11.4	5.6	4.5	50.7	282 937	322 895	14.1	6.8	38 579	17 347	5 434	137 193	9.5	2.38	9.8	30.6
Wayne	12.0	6.5	6.2	52.0	2 111 687	2 061 162	-2.4	-11.7	260 776	177 768	-267 576	702 749	-8.5	2.56	20.7	30.7
Wexford	13.2	8.8	7.1	50.2	26 360	30 484	15.6	7.4	3 805	2 820	259	13 021	10.1	2.48	11.3	25.4
MINNESOTA	11.9	6.7	6.2	50.4	4 375 665	4 919 479	12.4	7.8	654 294	348 464	62 426	2 087 227	10.1	2.48	9.5	28.0
Aitkin	17.5	16.3	11.0	49.4	12 425	15 301	23.1	5.9	1 408	1 706	722	7 299	9.9	2.18	6.6	31.0
Anoka	11.5	5.9	3.8	50.0	243 641	298 084	22.3	11.0	40 688	13 533	8 340	121 227	13.9	2.70	10.6	21.3
Becker	14.6	9.3	8.0	49.8	27 881	30 000	7.6	8.3	3 826	2 976	1 406	13 224	11.7	2.42	8.9	27.3
Beltrami	11.9	6.8	6.1	50.1	34 384	39 650	15.3	12.1	6 032	3 148	2 035	16 846	17.5	2.51	13.6	27.9
Benton	10.3	5.7	6.2	49.9	30 185	34 226	13.4	12.3	5 454	2 899	2 912	15 079	15.4	2.48	9.3	26.4
Big Stone	14.2	10.8	14.3	51.1	6 285	5 820	-7.4	-9.5	514	761	-289	2 293	-3.5	2.24	5.7	32.4
Blue Earth	10.2	5.6	6.2	49.7	54 044	55 941	3.5	14.4	6 700	4 023	2 708	24 445	16.1	2.43	8.2	27.5
Brown	13.0	8.2	10.7	50.3	26 984	26 911	-0.3	-3.8	2 715	2 558	-1 321	10 782	1.7	2.30	7.3	31.1
Carlton	12.8	7.7	7.3	48.0	29 259	31 671	8.2	11.7	3 772	3 097	2 156	13 538	12.2	2.47	9.8	26.8
Carver	10.0	4.6	3.9	50.3	47 915	70 205	46.5	29.7	11 551	3 077	13 755	32 891	35.0	2.74	7.6	21.0
Cass	16.1	13.0	8.1	48.9	21 791	27 150	24.6	5.2	3 279	2 696	917	11 948	9.7	2.37	8.6	26.4
Chippewa	13.6	8.6	10.6	51.0	13 228	13 088	-1.1	-4.9	1 392	1 368	-719	5 241	-2.2	2.33	8.2	30.5
Chisago	11.3	6.5	5.1	48.5	30 521	41 101	34.7	31.1	6 507	2 995	6 151	19 470	34.7	2.68	7.9	20.3
Clay	10.1	5.8	6.2	50.6	50 422	51 229	1.6	15.2	6 210	3 640	3 316	22 279	19.3	2.48	9.3	27.0
Clearwater	13.2	10.1	8.6	49.7	8 309	8 423	1.4	3.2	1 078	909	-304	3 527	5.9	2.43	8.8	28.6
Cook	19.7	11.9	8.4	50.1	3 868	5 168	33.6	0.2	413	412	333	2 494	6.1	2.05	6.4	34.6
Cottonwood	13.4	9.3	11.9	50.7	12 694	12 167	-4.2	-3.9	1 312	1 379	-936	4 857	-1.2	2.36	7.2	32.1
Crow Wing	13.7	10.2	8.3	50.2	44 249	55 099	24.5	13.4	7 057	4 991	5 839	26 033	17.0	2.37	8.8	27.6
Dakota	11.4	5.6	4.4	50.9	275 210	355 904	29.3	12.0	50 473	16 786	9 409	152 060	15.9	2.60	10.1	24.1
Dodge	10.6	6.4	5.8	50.0	15 731	17 731	12.7	13.3	2 618	1 134	669	7 460	16.2	2.67	7.7	22.2
Douglas	13.4	10.1	9.6	49.9	28 674	32 821	14.5	9.7	3 744	3 125	3 107	15 289	15.2	2.32	6.9	28.1
Faribault	13.9	10.0	11.8	50.3	16 937	16 181	-4.5	-10.1	1 521	1 920	-1 198	6 236	-6.3	2.28	8.1	31.0

1. No spouse present.

Table B. States and Counties — Population, Vital Statistics, Medicare, and Crime

STATE County	Persons in group quarters, 2010	Daytime population, 2006–2010 Number	Employ-ment/resi-dence ratio	Births, average 2006–2008 Total	Rate[1]	Deaths, average 2006–2008 Number	Rate[1]	Persons under 65 with no health insurance, 2009 Number	Percent	Medicare, 2011 Eligible for Medicare	Enrolled in Medicare Advantage	Enrolled in a Medicare prescription drug plan	Serious crimes known to police,[2] 2010 Total Number	Rate[3]
	32	33	34	35	36	37	38	39	40	41	42	43	44	45
MICHIGAN—Cont'd														
Keweenaw	10	1 730	0.5	D	D	23	10.4	278	16.7	605	113	222	41	1 902
Lake	397	10 513	0.7	D	D	145	12.8	1 675	19.4	3 457	516	1 504	264	2 288
Lapeer	1 716	76 688	0.6	921	10.0	678	7.4	9 691	12.6	15 169	3 503	4 697	1 275	1 444
Leelanau	284	19 254	0.7	D	D	188	8.6	2 323	13.8	5 635	1 572	1 916	125	576
Lenawee	5 396	90 534	0.8	1 193	11.8	918	9.1	11 886	14.2	18 895	3 684	7 733	1 913	2 038
Livingston	1 152	150 024	0.6	1 822	9.9	1 127	6.1	15 076	9.6	26 983	7 737	8 489	2 563	1 416
Luce	1 211	7 047	1.2	D	D	68	10.1	1 138	21.2	1 464	213	518	153	2 307
Mackinac	95	11 395	1.0	D	D	132	12.2	1 403	17.2	2 906	522	937	554	4 985
Macomb	7 432	782 455	0.9	9 875	11.9	7 500	9.0	96 541	13.9	145 268	33 515	51 483	21 062	2 504
Manistee	1 349	24 554	1.0	D	D	273	11.0	2 957	15.3	6 294	1 180	2 540	463	1 872
Marquette	4 757	66 427	1.0	D	D	595	9.1	7 253	13.2	12 406	2 667	3 538	1 515	2 259
Mason	442	28 241	1.0	D	D	318	11.0	3 481	15.2	6 846	1 060	3 248	802	2 794
Mecosta	3 375	42 483	1.0	432	10.3	339	8.1	5 361	15.4	8 083	2 306	2 891	1 460	3 411
Menominee	382	21 666	0.8	D	D	254	10.4	2 586	13.4	5 438	1 504	2 163	681	2 940
Midland	1 272	87 349	1.1	882	10.6	665	8.0	7 412	10.8	15 013	2 187	4 361	1 398	1 672
Missaukee	194	12 657	0.6	D	D	143	9.5	2 033	16.4	3 146	517	1 330	182	1 226
Monroe	1 462	131 758	0.7	1 713	11.1	1 285	8.4	15 339	11.9	25 662	6 092	8 820	4 014	2 711
Montcalm	3 163	56 991	0.7	D	D	553	8.7	8 433	15.7	11 649	2 785	3 943	1 403	2 407
Montmorency	156	9 794	1.0	D	D	152	14.7	1 207	16.2	3 375	523	1 293	66	676
Muskegon	6 345	167 656	0.9	2 377	13.6	1 590	9.1	20 786	14.0	32 747	10 153	11 729	7 822	4 543
Newaygo	557	43 676	0.7	649	13.2	423	8.6	6 447	15.7	9 834	3 568	2 892	1 195	2 483
Oakland	12 496	1 291 777	1.2	14 122	11.7	9 256	7.7	117 460	11.6	194 465	48 940	71 368	27 323	2 272
Oceana	303	24 048	0.7	D	D	248	8.9	4 174	18.1	5 773	1 541	2 097	658	2 754
Ogemaw	244	21 743	1.0	D	D	290	13.6	2 544	15.6	6 117	750	2 603	558	2 651
Ontonagon	83	6 641	0.9	D	D	120	17.1	710	14.6	2 171	395	899	64	944
Osceola	455	22 584	0.9	D	D	221	9.5	2 766	14.7	5 193	1 067	2 095	550	2 338
Oscoda	65	8 320	0.8	D	D	126	14.0	1 203	18.2	2 631	356	1 134	256	2 963
Otsego	348	25 923	1.1	D	D	223	9.2	2 523	13.1	5 116	1 068	2 102	611	2 529
Ottawa	8 261	250 728	0.9	3 490	13.5	1 594	6.2	25 851	11.5	38 257	19 238	8 970	5 112	1 938
Presque Isle	230	12 666	0.8	D	D	182	13.1	1 586	15.9	4 086	562	1 700	159	1 189
Roscommon	277	24 640	1.0	D	D	371	14.5	2 724	15.0	8 687	1 368	3 302	543	2 221
Saginaw	7 116	212 240	1.1	2 492	12.3	2 090	10.3	21 747	13.0	39 411	8 353	13 310	7 347	3 670
St. Clair	1 999	149 190	0.8	1 917	11.3	1 520	8.9	18 910	13.4	30 246	6 359	10 969	4 221	2 589
St. Joseph	765	59 520	0.9	938	15.0	596	9.5	8 454	16.1	11 304	1 851	4 796	1 374	2 320
Sanilac	566	39 904	0.8	486	11.1	474	10.9	5 481	15.8	9 143	1 469	3 986	747	1 767
Schoolcraft	140	8 597	1.0	D	D	111	13.0	1 081	16.8	2 061	286	831	252	2 970
Shiawassee	821	60 701	0.6	814	11.3	619	8.6	8 016	13.6	13 161	3 003	4 493	1 624	2 317
Tuscola	1 235	49 399	0.7	D	D	547	9.6	6 826	14.7	11 388	2 046	4 110	788	1 585
Van Buren	877	68 170	0.7	1 040	13.3	713	9.1	10 974	16.4	13 889	3 221	5 300	2 022	2 652
Washtenaw	17 812	379 763	1.2	4 028	11.6	1 936	5.6	31 502	10.4	44 137	9 355	13 708	10 607	3 076
Wayne	23 849	1 915 142	1.1	26 541	13.5	18 694	9.5	277 663	16.8	295 568	71 554	106 196	99 845	5 484
Wexford	389	34 987	1.2	D	D	300	9.4	3 827	14.6	6 774	1 148	2 957	1 315	4 017
MINNESOTA	135 395	5 260 646	1.0	73 227	14.1	37 555	7.2	460 534	10.2	813 018	367 951	307 092	148 946	2 808
Aitkin	274	14 931	0.8	D	D	188	11.8	1 522	13.6	4 112	2 115	1 502	384	2 370
Anoka	3 009	269 815	0.7	4 456	13.6	1 478	4.5	27 567	9.4	41 349	22 239	11 547	10 696	3 233
Becker	458	31 398	0.9	448	14.0	319	10.0	3 312	12.6	7 027	3 213	3 002	594	1 827
Beltrami	2 079	44 583	1.0	742	17.0	354	8.1	5 529	14.4	7 101	2 383	3 630	1 652	3 717
Benton	1 048	34 622	0.8	D	D	311	7.9	3 947	11.2	5 184	2 506	2 118	622	1 618
Big Stone	137	5 240	1.0	D	D	74	13.6	507	13.1	1 428	543	744	64	1 215
Blue Earth	4 529	65 953	1.1	D	D	435	7.3	5 763	11.0	9 045	3 579	4 793	1 892	2 956
Brown	1 111	27 387	1.1	D	D	295	11.3	1 894	9.3	5 519	1 871	2 629	244	942
Carlton	1 984	32 605	0.9	D	D	344	10.1	3 181	11.1	6 466	2 766	2 607	888	2 509
Carver	836	79 029	0.8	1 268	14.3	392	4.4	5 698	6.9	9 263	4 886	3 045	1 089	1 196
Cass	223	27 342	0.9	D	D	290	10.1	3 081	13.6	7 837	3 349	3 100	1 112	3 893
Chippewa	237	12 456	1.0	D	D	138	11.0	1 054	10.8	2 434	1 145	1 179	205	1 648
Chisago	1 673	43 157	0.6	668	13.3	324	6.5	4 005	9.1	7 550	3 958	2 187	1 246	2 312
Clay	3 743	47 378	0.7	773	14.0	392	7.1	5 093	10.5	8 344	3 004	3 968	1 183	2 005
Clearwater	115	7 878	0.8	D	D	83	10.0	1 045	15.9	1 783	821	796	235	2 703
Cook	51	5 509	1.1	D	D	53	9.9	607	14.0	1 286	458	529	175	3 381
Cottonwood	244	12 255	1.1	D	D	156	13.6	953	10.8	2 815	938	1 577	148	1 266
Crow Wing	750	63 846	1.1	795	12.9	562	9.1	5 877	11.7	14 158	6 624	5 723	1 369	2 190
Dakota	2 853	355 379	0.8	5 611	14.4	1 886	4.8	30 978	8.8	48 844	23 051	15 229	9 276	2 327
Dodge	149	15 911	0.6	D	D	135	6.9	1 613	9.5	2 793	1 058	953	361	1 797
Douglas	522	36 563	1.0	D	D	331	9.2	3 026	10.6	8 415	4 487	3 686	737	2 047
Faribault	336	13 805	0.9	D	D	191	12.8	1 337	12.0	3 504	1 486	1 948	165	1 134

1. Per 1,000 estimated resident population.　　2. Data for serious crimes have not been adjusted for underreporting; this may affect comparability between geographic areas and over time.　　3. Per 100,000 population estimated by the FBI.

— **Crime, Education, Money Income, and Poverty**

STATE County	Serious crimes known to police,[1] 2010 (cont.) Rate[2] Violent	Property	Education — School enrollment and attainment, 2006–2010 — Enrollment[3] Total	Percent private	Attainment[4] (percent) High school graduate or less	Bachelor's degree or more	Local government expenditures,[5] 2008–2009 Total current expenditures (mil dol)	Current expenditures per student (dollars)	Money income, 2006–2010 Per capita income[6] (dollars)	Households — Median income Dollars	Percent change, 2000 to 2006–2010 (constant 2010 dollars)	Percent with income of $200,000 or more	Income and poverty, 2010 Median household income (dollars)	Percent below poverty level All persons	Children under 18 years	Children 5 to 17 years in families
	46	47	48	49	50	51	52	53	54	55	56	57	58	59	60	61
MICHIGAN—Cont'd																
Keweenaw	93	1 809	360	5.8	49.2	22.0	0.1	28 800	21 307	38 872	9.1	1.0	38 768	13.7	22.8	20.7
Lake	295	1 993	2 287	5.9	64.8	8.5	7.4	12 671	16 084	31 205	-7.4	0.6	28 526	25.2	45.1	42.6
Lapeer	142	1 302	23 767	11.7	49.1	17.0	148.8	9 119	25 110	55 005	-16.0	2.2	49 759	12.7	18.1	15.8
Leelanau	37	539	4 651	17.9	29.8	39.4	25.5	11 133	32 194	56 527	-5.1	5.1	55 149	9.3	14.7	12.8
Lenawee	254	1 785	25 874	16.6	49.1	19.2	178.3	10 467	22 529	48 618	-16.1	1.2	45 887	14.2	19.3	16.9
Livingston	111	1 306	50 742	11.1	34.1	31.2	272.3	9 173	31 609	72 129	-15.5	4.3	65 729	7.2	8.4	7.1
Luce	483	1 825	1 365	4.5	62.2	13.5	9.1	9 772	17 195	40 041	-1.3	1.1	35 813	19.5	28.8	26.0
Mackinac	180	4 805	2 207	12.1	52.2	20.1	15.2	10 402	22 170	39 339	-6.9	1.1	37 072	15.3	22.9	20.8
Macomb	323	2 181	219 774	12.8	44.4	21.8	1 400.3	10 330	26 524	53 996	-18.2	1.9	49 348	12.7	17.1	16.3
Manistee	137	1 735	4 707	15.2	51.8	16.8	34.9	10 540	21 612	40 853	-5.7	1.3	37 479	17.0	25.6	22.8
Marquette	106	2 153	18 406	6.6	41.2	29.7	86.9	10 236	23 347	45 130	0.3	1.8	44 239	14.2	15.8	15.6
Mason	261	2 533	6 523	9.2	47.3	19.4	52.0	11 670	21 760	40 039	-8.9	1.0	38 776	15.8	27.6	25.2
Mecosta	472	2 939	15 152	5.3	50.8	20.1	74.2	11 343	18 745	35 887	-16.3	1.2	36 193	21.8	28.8	27.6
Menominee	224	2 715	5 271	7.3	54.6	13.4	39.4	9 669	21 624	41 332	-0.8	0.8	40 253	13.8	22.0	18.8
Midland	148	1 523	23 874	19.5	37.8	32.2	136.5	9 967	28 363	51 103	-11.6	5.0	50 430	11.1	14.6	12.8
Missaukee	34	1 192	3 443	13.5	56.0	12.9	19.3	8 595	19 560	40 376	-9.5	1.2	36 931	15.9	26.1	24.1
Monroe	265	2 446	39 870	14.1	50.1	17.0	242.8	10 108	25 520	55 366	-15.5	1.8	50 777	12.1	17.1	15.1
Montcalm	256	2 151	16 427	10.1	54.6	12.7	102.4	10 015	18 569	39 775	-15.6	0.5	36 701	20.4	29.8	27.6
Montmorency	92	584	1 650	6.5	59.4	10.6	8.0	8 886	19 102	34 447	-9.3	0.9	33 294	19.5	38.7	34.5
Muskegon	462	4 080	45 266	9.8	48.2	16.5	320.3	10 093	19 719	40 670	-15.5	1.0	39 075	21.0	28.8	24.8
Newaygo	237	2 246	12 267	13.7	55.6	13.2	91.6	10 243	20 870	43 218	-8.1	1.7	38 846	19.8	28.7	26.0
Oakland	266	2 007	327 949	18.1	29.1	42.2	2 248.5	11 322	36 138	66 390	-15.3	7.2	60 392	10.3	13.3	11.9
Oceana	184	2 570	6 214	11.4	55.2	14.3	36.0	9 777	18 402	39 543	-11.6	0.7	37 629	22.0	32.7	29.9
Ogemaw	185	2 466	4 890	10.9	60.7	10.7	21.7	8 957	18 321	35 968	-6.8	0.9	34 595	19.4	30.6	27.9
Ontonagon	88	855	1 178	5.1	51.4	16.5	12.0	14 878	21 448	35 269	-5.8	0.7	36 566	16.1	27.0	22.6
Osceola	264	2 074	5 671	12.7	58.2	11.9	43.7	9 297	17 861	38 341	-11.2	0.5	37 840	20.2	29.0	25.2
Oscoda	440	2 523	1 612	14.2	64.6	8.9	9.4	9 417	18 524	32 346	-9.5	1.1	31 303	21.0	36.0	34.2
Otsego	190	2 308	5 607	14.6	50.0	19.4	37.3	8 667	22 568	45 531	-12.0	1.5	43 601	12.8	21.5	19.5
Ottawa	179	1 759	80 830	19.4	41.2	28.8	427.4	9 812	25 045	55 095	-16.9	2.7	53 454	11.4	13.2	11.6
Presque Isle	150	1 039	2 511	11.7	54.6	14.3	15.1	9 022	20 870	37 383	-6.7	0.9	36 376	14.9	26.4	24.0
Roscommon	225	1 996	4 269	8.7	55.1	13.6	37.0	11 078	20 194	33 542	-11.8	1.0	32 401	22.2	39.4	36.3
Saginaw	860	2 810	55 049	12.2	49.7	18.0	341.7	10 198	21 662	42 954	-12.2	1.6	41 714	17.8	26.7	23.6
St. Clair	257	2 332	42 748	11.4	49.5	15.0	321.8	9 964	23 828	49 120	-16.2	1.6	44 706	15.4	22.1	18.6
St. Joseph	314	2 006	14 912	8.0	56.3	14.0	107.8	9 250	20 192	44 392	-13.1	1.1	41 535	16.7	25.8	23.3
Sanilac	196	1 570	10 531	9.0	60.2	11.0	71.0	9 322	19 645	40 818	-12.6	0.9	39 646	17.2	26.1	23.5
Schoolcraft	295	2 675	1 665	13.8	59.3	13.2	11.7	8 937	20 455	36 925	-6.4	1.1	37 180	15.9	25.9	22.0
Shiawassee	264	2 053	18 632	12.7	49.5	14.9	132.2	9 607	21 869	46 453	-13.8	1.3	45 444	15.0	21.6	18.4
Tuscola	185	1 400	14 358	12.1	56.1	12.4	108.7	10 308	19 937	42 198	-17.1	0.7	40 808	16.3	23.6	21.6
Van Buren	324	2 328	19 798	9.0	49.5	18.3	185.2	10 616	22 002	44 435	-10.9	1.6	43 659	15.6	23.4	21.0
Washtenaw	341	2 735	125 379	10.7	23.1	50.8	544.3	11 405	31 316	59 065	-10.3	5.3	56 177	13.0	13.4	11.1
Wayne	1 157	4 327	535 299	12.7	49.0	20.2	3 524.2	10 727	22 125	42 241	-18.2	2.1	39 421	23.9	34.6	32.7
Wexford	394	3 623	7 571	12.5	52.2	16.4	62.7	11 684	19 952	39 997	-10.7	1.4	36 316	17.0	27.2	25.5
MINNESOTA	236	2 572	1 392 204	17.6	36.5	31.4	9 219.5	11 061	29 582	57 243	-4.0	4.0	55 422	11.5	15.0	13.6
Aitkin	111	2 259	2 732	9.3	51.7	14.4	22.2	10 986	22 966	40 226	2.0	0.8	38 646	13.1	24.1	21.1
Anoka	167	3 066	88 897	15.2	37.7	25.7	655.1	10 176	29 347	69 028	-5.6	3.1	65 732	7.4	10.2	9.1
Becker	95	1 732	7 372	8.7	43.5	21.3	41.8	9 389	24 385	46 056	4.5	2.1	43 970	14.6	22.5	19.8
Beltrami	360	3 357	13 002	7.2	38.8	29.1	96.3	12 830	21 016	43 394	2.6	1.5	40 308	20.8	29.6	28.4
Benton	135	1 482	9 940	12.3	44.2	19.6	47.5	8 743	23 648	50 848	-4.3	1.3	49 736	10.5	12.7	11.4
Big Stone	57	1 158	1 083	8.4	52.4	16.0	9.6	11 073	23 746	42 870	10.2	1.6	40 829	11.3	15.5	14.0
Blue Earth	177	2 779	21 281	9.9	35.9	30.1	93.3	9 355	23 691	47 871	-2.9	1.7	46 835	16.9	14.5	14.6
Brown	39	904	6 701	33.9	51.0	18.5	37.1	10 739	24 591	47 696	-5.4	1.8	43 924	9.3	11.9	11.0
Carlton	133	2 377	8 590	13.6	43.5	21.4	66.1	10 286	23 932	52 858	4.3	1.6	48 959	10.8	13.1	11.6
Carver	54	1 142	26 250	22.9	27.3	42.7	162.9	10 833	35 807	80 280	-3.3	8.3	81 935	4.9	5.6	4.7
Cass	249	3 644	5 776	6.9	46.7	20.2	52.7	12 711	24 348	42 445	-2.4	1.8	40 580	16.4	27.0	25.7
Chippewa	145	1 503	2 859	7.8	50.9	15.8	22.9	10 843	23 610	43 956	-2.4	1.2	44 717	10.0	15.2	14.0
Chisago	67	2 245	13 629	11.4	45.0	17.0	74.3	8 889	26 576	64 726	-1.7	1.7	63 237	7.4	9.4	7.9
Clay	124	1 881	18 158	20.6	36.4	31.5	89.6	10 129	23 011	50 057	4.3	1.5	48 395	12.8	14.6	13.5
Clearwater	495	2 208	1 872	5.8	52.6	14.5	14.7	9 915	20 913	39 310	1.7	1.4	41 913	15.7	24.6	23.6
Cook	193	3 188	864	7.8	33.7	32.9	6.6	10 236	28 873	49 162	6.0	2.3	43 694	9.6	15.8	13.7
Cottonwood	137	1 129	2 582	13.7	53.8	15.7	19.4	9 865	23 162	40 292	-0.4	1.8	44 219	11.0	15.5	13.4
Crow Wing	163	2 027	13 865	11.2	39.8	22.0	116.8	12 011	24 282	44 659	-6.2	1.5	45 068	12.3	17.7	16.8
Dakota	86	2 242	107 773	17.0	28.7	38.1	818.6	10 911	34 142	72 850	-7.0	5.5	69 688	7.0	9.0	7.7
Dodge	204	1 593	5 215	6.0	42.6	21.9	31.9	7 834	26 969	64 438	7.3	1.9	60 398	6.9	9.0	8.2
Douglas	108	1 938	7 783	11.1	41.0	21.4	58.9	11 327	25 633	46 789	-2.0	2.0	48 434	9.6	12.8	11.8
Faribault	131	1 003	3 305	14.2	51.5	15.3	21.3	10 543	22 667	41 631	-4.5	1.0	44 645	10.8	18.4	16.6

1. Data for serious crimes have not been adjusted for underreporting; this may affect comparability between geographic areas and over time. 2. Per 100,000 population estimated by the FBI. 3. All persons 3 years old and over enrolled in nursery school through college. 4. Persons 25 years old and over. 5. Elementary and secondary education expenditures. 6. Based on population estimated by the American Community Survey, 2006–2010.

Table B. States and Counties — **Personal Income**

STATE County	Total (mil dol)	Percent change, 2008–2009	Per capita¹ Dollars	Rank	Wages and salaries² (mil dol)	Proprietors' income (mil dol)	Dividends, interest, and rent (mil dol)	Transfer payments (mil dol) Total	Government payments to individuals Total	Social Security	Medical payments	Income mainte-nance	Unemploy-ment insurance
	62	63	64	65	66	67	68	69	70	71	72	73	74
MICHIGAN—Cont'd													
Keweenaw	73	4.2	31 749	1 590	18	2	15	24	23	9	10	1	2
Lake	287	2.6	26 246	2 681	73	16	43	126	124	49	45	16	7
Lapeer	2 739	-2.5	30 438	1 878	817	145	376	601	585	241	194	42	74
Leelanau	872	-2.3	39 815	463	234	48	261	160	156	85	45	7	10
Lenawee	2 952	-3.8	29 572	2 077	1 248	149	400	765	747	289	282	56	74
Livingston	6 956	-2.7	37 987	645	2 172	366	1 016	951	918	448	259	43	106
Luce	153	3.2	23 490	3 003	80	6	25	61	60	21	27	6	4
Mackinac	356	0.0	33 608	1 232	171	17	71	104	103	42	38	7	9
Macomb	29 934	-2.3	36 004	885	16 709	1 585	4 607	6 129	5 978	2 287	2 293	426	640
Manistee	708	0.7	28 964	2 208	337	36	134	249	245	91	106	20	16
Marquette	2 067	0.8	31 461	1 647	1 309	73	311	550	538	180	226	38	37
Mason	846	-0.2	29 543	2 083	402	60	148	270	265	96	103	24	21
Mecosta	1 071	3.0	25 641	2 784	546	73	154	320	312	119	98	34	25
Menominee	677	-3.3	28 235	2 359	291	40	118	192	188	76	65	17	15
Midland	3 455	-2.2	41 853	341	2 248	137	717	582	567	230	207	54	41
Missaukee	350	-4.6	23 605	2 991	112	37	52	115	112	44	39	12	10
Monroe	4 881	-4.6	31 961	1 535	2 037	230	690	1 069	1 041	405	380	83	106
Montcalm	1 468	0.8	23 406	3 011	648	53	203	478	467	168	177	49	43
Montmorency	259	2.2	25 702	2 773	71	15	51	127	125	50	51	9	8
Muskegon	4 834	-1.5	27 792	2 438	2 726	236	658	1 453	1 422	486	534	195	128
Newaygo	1 295	-0.4	26 597	2 625	481	71	175	368	359	141	123	44	30
Oakland	60 678	-8.1	50 334	95	41 351	7 319	11 832	8 184	7 964	3 144	3 062	497	769
Oceana	743	0.0	26 950	2 574	269	24	122	230	225	82	81	28	22
Ogemaw	555	1.4	26 117	2 705	222	33	88	228	224	89	86	25	13
Ontonagon	199	-0.9	30 304	1 906	77	10	29	81	79	31	33	5	5
Osceola	586	0.7	25 813	2 757	291	34	82	202	198	74	77	22	14
Oscoda	200	-5.5	22 934	3 033	54	16	35	90	89	38	29	9	8
Otsego	708	-0.4	30 223	1 930	411	83	123	188	184	76	64	17	17
Ottawa	8 470	-1.1	32 334	1 451	4 907	406	1 485	1 419	1 371	582	436	89	159
Presque Isle	370	0.1	27 571	2 472	121	9	73	140	137	60	50	9	11
Roscommon	719	3.1	29 129	2 164	245	27	139	320	315	130	124	28	15
Saginaw	6 029	-0.4	30 137	1 944	4 002	333	902	1 767	1 730	612	676	238	119
St. Clair	5 291	-2.4	31 574	1 628	2 141	254	757	1 292	1 261	461	458	114	142
St. Joseph	1 660	-4.7	26 899	2 584	907	86	245	466	454	170	171	48	41
Sanilac	1 221	-5.7	29 028	2 191	413	85	191	389	382	132	159	36	36
Schoolcraft	252	2.6	31 060	1 741	133	10	39	91	90	30	42	7	6
Shiawassee	1 913	-0.9	27 322	2 512	669	61	247	572	559	200	224	48	54
Tuscola	1 445	-1.5	26 094	2 709	516	64	207	473	463	173	183	40	44
Van Buren	2 233	-0.9	28 544	2 291	1 039	58	315	612	597	204	245	68	50
Washtenaw	13 159	-4.4	37 859	660	11 194	845	2 549	1 909	1 846	700	684	144	156
Wayne	61 411	-2.5	31 888	1 554	44 215	4 166	8 087	17 366	17 015	4 577	7 530	2 577	1 420
Wexford	856	-0.5	27 117	2 545	534	38	132	281	275	96	110	29	25
MINNESOTA	220 413	-2.5	41 854	X	149 991	15 506	40 098	35 764	34 804	11 239	15 304	2 925	2 548
Aitkin	473	1.0	30 240	1 928	148	42	96	162	159	56	72	11	9
Anoka	12 483	-2.6	37 646	678	6 044	511	1 625	1 831	1 771	604	718	130	177
Becker	1 110	-0.9	34 615	1 078	513	126	208	276	270	89	118	27	17
Beltrami	1 374	4.0	30 976	1 762	779	101	235	405	396	88	196	59	21
Benton	1 255	-1.4	31 215	1 709	709	151	191	219	211	66	84	19	22
Big Stone	200	-2.8	38 023	637	79	31	41	52	51	18	25	4	2
Blue Earth	2 122	-1.4	34 783	1 049	1 618	227	391	391	380	119	157	32	27
Brown	943	-2.6	36 849	767	572	103	202	199	195	73	85	11	12
Carlton	1 071	1.4	31 201	1 711	590	48	162	289	282	91	126	21	17
Carver	4 753	-1.7	51 601	83	1 832	323	692	382	365	136	143	18	41
Cass	988	0.5	34 643	1 075	339	86	242	301	296	107	118	30	17
Chippewa	487	-4.2	39 563	483	237	92	85	92	90	31	41	7	6
Chisago	1 706	-2.1	33 692	1 219	623	76	250	327	317	110	134	19	30
Clay	1 947	-0.6	34 304	1 127	811	117	296	381	371	109	169	36	18
Clearwater	237	3.3	28 738	2 251	94	25	35	80	78	22	35	8	7
Cook	195	-0.5	35 726	926	100	18	50	43	42	18	16	2	3
Cottonwood	423	-1.8	38 048	632	200	81	82	95	93	36	40	7	5
Crow Wing	1 966	0.8	31 349	1 685	1 135	72	418	548	537	193	217	39	36
Dakota	17 594	-3.5	44 374	223	10 050	713	2 936	1 968	1 896	712	706	119	183
Dodge	713	-1.6	36 055	880	239	84	105	113	109	38	48	6	9
Douglas	1 293	-4.0	35 533	952	751	114	284	284	278	109	114	17	16
Faribault	643	-3.0	44 311	225	333	99	108	131	128	47	58	9	8

1. Based on the resident population estimated as of July 1 of the year shown. 2. Includes supplements to wages and salaries.

STATE County	Total (mil dol)	Farm	Goods-related[1] Total	Manu-facturing	Information and profesional and technical services	Retail trade	Finance, insurance, and real estate	Health care and social services	Govern-ment	Number	Rate[2]	Supplemental Security Income recipients, December 2010	Total	Percent change, 2000–2010
	75	76	77	78	79	80	81	82	83	84	85	86	87	88
MICHIGAN—Cont'd														
Keweenaw	20	0.0	D	D	2.1	3.9	D	D	31.3	720	334	40	2 467	6.0
Lake	89	0.5	D	D	D	5.5	D	D	29.8	3 985	345	601	14 966	10.9
Lapeer	962	1.4	26.7	19.6	D	9.2	6.7	6.6	25.5	17 800	202	1 115	36 332	11.0
Leelanau	281	3.1	15.2	2.7	6.6	5.4	6.7	9.2	33.4	6 210	286	183	14 935	12.3
Lenawee	1 397	1.9	D	25.3	3.8	8.4	5.8	10.3	20.7	22 060	221	1 890	43 452	9.2
Livingston	2 538	0.3	25.2	16.6	7.8	9.9	11.4	8.8	14.7	31 050	172	1 165	72 809	23.6
Luce	87	0.8	5.2	1.7	D	6.9	4.6	·2.4	60.9	1 715	259	237	4 343	8.4
Mackinac	188	0.5	D	2.6	3.6	8.8	3.6	D	28.4	3 330	300	207	11 010	17.0
Macomb	18 294	0.1	D	25.7	8.2	7.1	3.4	11.1	16.2	164 350	195	15 553	356 626	11.3
Manistee	373	0.5	20.3	15.4	2.7	6.9	3.5	D	41.6	7 195	291	633	15 694	10.0
Marquette	1 382	0.1	17.6	3.2	5.7	7.7	5.0	22.5	24.5	14 185	211	1 170	34 330	4.4
Mason	463	2.0	22.1	16.8	D	9.1	6.0	15.0	21.3	7 655	267	750	17 293	7.7
Mecosta	619	1.3	D	12.3	3.4	7.6	3.8	8.0	43.0	9 430	220	1 050	21 131	7.8
Menominee	331	2.4	D	24.1	D	6.2	3.3	D	31.6	6 240	260	437	14 227	4.3
Midland	2 386	0.2	34.5	26.8	D	4.9	3.1	11.4	8.5	17 385	208	1 547	35 960	6.4
Missaukee	149	10.9	D	12.5	D	6.7	4.4	D	17.2	3 675	247	342	9 117	5.7
Monroe	2 267	1.1	D	16.1	8.7	6.8	3.9	10.3	15.4	29 940	197	2 545	62 971	11.5
Montcalm	701	3.3	D	17.4	2.7	9.7	2.7	D	26.1	13 670	216	1 708	28 221	9.0
Montmorency	86	0.5	24.8	10.8	D	8.0	7.4	D	22.0	3 930	402	307	9 597	3.9
Muskegon	2 963	0.6	D	23.2	4.6	10.8	4.1	17.6	17.6	38 330	223	6 031	73 561	7.3
Newaygo	552	4.1	D	18.5	4.2	10.3	8.9	11.1	23.1	11 495	237	1 412	25 075	8.1
Oakland	48 670	0.0	16.3	11.3	21.9	5.8	11.5	12.5	7.5	213 680	178	19 864	527 255	7.2
Oceana	293	7.3	D	21.4	D	5.4	3.2	3.7	30.1	6 735	253	691	15 944	6.2
Ogemaw	254	2.1	11.3	5.3	3.2	16.2	4.4	D	24.5	7 085	327	774	16 047	4.2
Ontonagon	87	0.5	D	D	2.5	9.4	4.8	13.2	23.3	2 495	368	154	5 672	5.0
Osceola	325	1.3	D	25.4	D	4.6	D	10.8	17.8	6 060	258	809	13 632	6.1
Oscoda	70	1.2	D	6.6	D	9.0	5.1	6.8	27.8	3 000	347	276	9 118	4.9
Otsego	494	0.2	23.4	6.0	4.5	15.9	5.0	15.0	14.9	5 975	247	482	14 731	10.1
Ottawa	5 313	1.9	38.6	33.2	5.3	5.5	4.6	7.0	15.3	43 250	164	2 535	102 495	18.0
Presque Isle	130	1.5	D	5.6	1.7	9.9	4.7	7.0	24.3	4 710	352	344	10 428	5.2
Roscommon	273	0.0	D	D	2.0	14.6	5.1	D	29.3	10 030	410	823	24 459	5.8
Saginaw	4 335	0.9	D	19.1	6.4	7.7	5.9	18.2	16.0	45 935	229	8 079	86 844	1.6
St. Clair	2 395	0.4	17.1	12.2	D	8.0	5.4	17.2	19.6	34 875	214	3 079	71 822	7.0
St. Joseph	993	3.3	D	41.1	2.6	7.6	3.4	5.7	19.6	13 035	213	1 282	27 778	4.8
Sanilac	498	7.0	22.4	16.6	2.8	10.0	5.5	11.4	20.8	10 510	244	919	22 725	6.6
Schoolcraft	143	0.6	22.5	10.9	2.7	7.7	5.0	4.7	40.4	2 450	289	224	6 313	10.8
Shiawassee	730	1.5	15.7	11.8	4.2	10.6	4.4	D	26.2	16 210	215	1 554	30 319	4.2
Tuscola	580	5.8	17.5	13.3	3.6	7.7	3.5	10.9	31.6	13 295	239	1 186	24 451	4.6
Van Buren	1 097	4.2	17.3	13.7	9.0	6.2	4.6	5.4	26.6	16 300	214	2 077	36 785	8.3
Washtenaw	12 039	0.1	12.6	10.0	14.5	4.7	4.2	11.2	35.2	48 455	141	4 869	147 573	12.7
Wayne	48 382	0.0	17.2	13.3	13.9	4.9	4.9	13.3	16.7	344 625	189	79 513	821 693	-0.5
Wexford	572	0.3	26.8	23.6	D	9.3	4.1	12.9	20.0	7 875	241	1 022	16 736	12.5
MINNESOTA	165 496	1.9	18.1	12.9	10.9	5.5	9.5	12.8	14.8	882 408	166	86 506	2 347 201	13.6
Aitkin	190	2.3	D	6.2	3.4	9.7	4.5	D	22.8	4 550	281	265	16 029	13.1
Anoka	6 555	0.2	34.7	26.6	4.9	6.9	3.5	12.9	14.9	45 910	139	3 915	126 688	17.2
Becker	639	3.4	D	14.0	3.8	8.9	4.5	D	23.0	7 820	241	678	18 784	13.1
Beltrami	879	0.4	D	6.8	D	10.1	2.8	15.3	30.7	7 995	180	1 230	20 527	20.8
Benton	860	5.0	38.2	28.3	5.5	5.9	3.9	8.9	9.9	5 715	149	531	16 140	19.9
Big Stone	109	19.3	D	1.4	D	4.7	4.1	D	25.6	1 555	295	86	3 115	-1.8
Blue Earth	1 844	4.4	D	10.4	7.8	7.9	4.8	20.1	17.5	9 865	154	1 036	26 202	19.3
Brown	675	8.9	D	25.1	6.2	6.3	4.3	11.9	12.7	6 040	233	267	11 493	3.0
Carlton	639	0.1	D	16.4	2.0	6.1	4.1	10.2	38.3	7 195	203	548	15 656	14.1
Carver	2 155	1.2	35.3	28.7	8.6	5.1	4.4	10.5	12.2	10 115	111	448	34 536	38.8
Cass	425	0.8	8.2	2.5	3.4	7.1	6.7	5.6	41.9	8 915	312	723	24 903	17.0
Chippewa	328	18.2	D	15.6	4.1	5.9	4.5	D	16.8	2 660	214	186	5 721	-2.3
Chisago	699	0.9	D	13.9	D	6.8	3.2	26.1	20.1	8 500	158	488	21 172	36.3
Clay	928	5.7	D	4.9	4.0	7.4	3.7	10.5	25.3	9 015	153	966	23 959	21.3
Clearwater	119	2.0	D	17.4	D	6.0	D	11.4	25.7	2 025	233	218	4 773	16.0
Cook	119	0.0	D	D	3.3	7.8	D	2.8	41.9	1 380	267	40	5 839	24.0
Cottonwood	281	19.9	D	21.0	2.0	4.3	3.2	D	15.7	3 080	264	216	5 412	0.7
Crow Wing	1 207	0.3	D	9.0	7.7	10.5	6.9	17.0	20.7	15 585	249	1 096	40 180	20.0
Dakota	10 763	0.4	19.7	12.4	15.8	6.7	9.3	7.8	12.8	52 700	132	3 744	159 598	19.3
Dodge	322	10.1	D	21.5	D	3.5	5.1	D	18.1	3 095	154	157	7 947	19.6
Douglas	866	1.6	D	16.9	8.6	8.9	4.5	9.6	19.5	9 245	257	487	19 905	19.2
Faribault	432	17.1	15.3	11.8	D	3.1	3.7	D	12.8	3 820	262	240	7 090	-2.2

1. Includes mining, construction, and manufacturing. 2. Per 1,000 resident population enumerated in the 2010 census.

Table B. States and Counties — **Housing, Labor Force, and Employment**

STATE County	Housing units, 2006–2010								Civilian labor force, 2010				Civilian employment,[5] 2006–2010		
	Occupied units										Unemployment			Percent	
			Owner-occupied			Renter-occupied									
				Median owner cost as a percent of income											Con-struction, produc-tion, and mainte-nance occu-pations
	Total	Percent	Median value[1]	With a mort-gage	Without a mort-gage	Median rent[2]	Median rent as a per-cent of income	Sub-stand-ard units[3] (percent)	Total	Percent change, 2009–2010	Total	Rate[4]	Total	Manage-ment, business, science and arts	
	89	90	91	92	93	94	95	96	97	98	99	100	101	102	103
MICHIGAN—Cont'd															
Keweenaw	957	86.2	81 800	22.1	13.8	310	28.3	2.8	1 102	1.3	150	13.6	819	29.4	24.5
Lake	4 078	84.5	92 900	28.9	13.3	495	34.4	2.3	4 074	1.0	633	15.5	3 347	22.2	34.8
Lapeer	32 937	84.4	165 200	25.5	12.4	680	31.5	2.2	42 197	-2.9	6 443	15.3	38 722	29.7	32.2
Leelanau	9 349	85.8	241 200	27.5	11.0	762	28.7	1.8	10 769	-1.0	1 085	10.1	9 755	36.6	23.9
Lenawee	37 831	79.8	140 400	25.1	13.9	646	31.0	2.2	46 425	-3.6	6 491	14.0	45 162	28.3	30.6
Livingston	67 265	87.2	216 400	24.7	13.0	860	30.5	1.1	90 684	-0.2	10 105	11.1	88 094	38.7	21.7
Luce	2 473	80.0	86 000	22.6	10.7	541	32.4	3.0	2 665	-1.8	365	13.7	2 258	24.0	23.7
Mackinac	4 927	81.2	126 100	23.4	13.6	558	29.8	2.2	6 088	-0.4	819	13.5	4 736	26.0	24.8
Macomb	330 322	79.1	157 000	25.0	14.8	752	29.9	1.6	406 679	-2.0	55 553	13.7	385 176	32.5	22.7
Manistee	10 747	80.4	124 000	25.2	12.9	627	30.5	2.0	11 283	-2.6	1 433	12.7	9 846	27.4	25.6
Marquette	25 638	73.2	125 100	20.5	11.9	548	31.6	1.1	35 558	-1.8	3 472	9.8	31 463	32.9	19.8
Mason	12 320	77.6	121 600	25.6	12.9	616	29.8	2.2	14 762	0.8	1 809	12.3	12 845	30.4	27.6
Mecosta	16 081	73.4	119 200	25.0	12.3	629	37.7	2.8	20 208	2.6	2 441	12.1	16 464	28.4	26.4
Menominee	10 841	81.2	97 300	23.0	11.7	487	27.0	1.8	12 657	-3.4	1 278	10.1	10 969	26.1	36.7
Midland	33 562	76.6	132 800	21.0	11.6	631	31.3	1.9	41 800	-2.6	3 936	9.4	37 146	39.7	21.2
Missaukee	5 809	82.8	112 300	26.0	12.9	675	30.3	2.9	6 142	-2.4	905	14.7	6 396	25.7	34.7
Monroe	58 298	80.7	161 800	24.4	13.4	733	29.9	1.3	71 165	-4.9	8 859	12.4	69 703	26.7	31.1
Montcalm	23 133	80.2	112 700	26.0	13.4	618	32.7	2.3	26 253	-0.8	4 000	15.2	25 269	22.2	36.3
Montmorency	4 335	86.7	103 200	27.5	12.6	621	34.6	2.1	3 890	-2.4	769	19.8	3 143	24.9	31.8
Muskegon	65 778	75.7	112 800	24.4	13.5	628	35.2	2.2	84 273	-4.3	11 292	13.4	69 840	26.6	30.7
Newaygo	18 952	83.0	115 800	25.4	13.3	608	29.7	2.3	21 701	-2.9	2 752	12.7	19 735	24.2	37.2
Oakland	481 040	74.6	204 300	24.4	14.3	871	29.0	1.5	600 695	-0.4	72 437	12.1	583 107	46.1	14.6
Oceana	9 974	83.2	115 400	25.7	12.9	618	32.2	2.4	14 085	0.4	2 112	15.0	11 456	22.0	40.2
Ogemaw	8 255	84.2	105 900	26.8	13.4	585	35.4	1.9	9 561	-0.7	1 242	13.0	7 656	25.4	28.1
Ontonagon	3 410	85.4	75 300	23.0	13.7	421	29.6	1.0	3 090	-4.1	528	17.1	2 828	21.5	29.2
Osceola	8 955	81.6	101 100	24.6	13.4	533	30.1	3.1	9 357	-1.3	1 335	14.3	9 232	23.9	40.3
Oscoda	4 052	83.2	93 100	26.8	12.2	514	38.7	3.9	3 745	1.5	723	19.3	2 823	24.1	32.1
Otsego	9 753	81.8	122 300	25.2	12.9	639	30.4	1.9	11 436	-5.0	1 688	14.8	10 758	26.6	23.4
Ottawa	92 526	80.8	161 200	23.8	12.7	726	29.8	2.1	129 037	-1.6	14 232	11.0	127 930	32.5	27.8
Presque Isle	6 332	88.7	108 700	24.7	13.8	470	26.5	1.8	5 899	-2.2	1 040	17.6	5 037	27.0	31.9
Roscommon	11 449	84.6	107 400	31.1	12.9	583	41.6	1.4	9 870	-1.8	1 468	14.9	7 651	23.5	23.5
Saginaw	76 764	74.5	110 000	23.5	13.6	663	35.1	1.4	91 827	-2.5	10 838	11.8	81 017	29.5	21.9
St. Clair	64 606	78.9	150 300	25.6	14.6	691	31.6	1.5	79 660	-3.5	11 909	14.9	70 932	25.9	30.7
St. Joseph	22 478	78.0	116 200	23.2	12.6	600	28.9	2.0	28 432	-1.4	3 485	12.3	25 558	23.0	41.2
Sanilac	17 156	83.2	115 600	26.8	14.0	594	32.7	2.3	20 316	-2.4	3 050	15.0	17 760	25.0	36.9
Schoolcraft	3 621	87.6	87 700	24.7	12.1	518	27.2	1.6	3 903	0.0	539	13.8	3 384	28.6	27.6
Shiawassee	27 639	78.9	129 300	24.2	13.1	637	32.6	1.6	34 074	-3.1	4 442	13.0	30 890	27.9	31.0
Tuscola	21 787	83.2	112 200	25.5	13.3	586	29.7	1.6	26 969	-3.0	3 836	14.2	23 061	24.6	30.8
Van Buren	29 096	80.2	125 600	24.8	13.7	572	32.9	2.2	38 712	-3.3	4 868	12.6	33 682	27.0	32.0
Washtenaw	134 161	63.0	216 000	24.5	13.2	866	33.9	1.4	182 223	-0.9	14 782	8.1	168 393	50.7	12.6
Wayne	690 943	67.2	121 100	26.6	15.6	759	35.3	2.9	850 005	-2.1	123 597	14.5	726 108	30.5	23.0
Wexford	12 721	78.9	111 500	26.4	13.4	624	30.5	2.1	13 888	-3.0	2 177	15.7	13 593	25.1	35.8
MINNESOTA	2 085 917	74.2	206 200	24.4	12.0	759	29.5	2.2	2 958 686	0.3	217 099	7.3	2 730 721	37.8	21.6
Aitkin	7 903	81.1	177 900	26.9	12.6	518	29.7	2.9	7 615	-2.0	758	10.0	6 862	26.9	31.2
Anoka	120 026	82.9	223 100	25.4	12.0	870	29.3	1.8	191 213	-0.7	14 889	7.8	175 434	35.7	23.6
Becker	13 345	79.2	166 800	24.3	12.5	550	28.9	1.7	17 796	3.4	1 391	7.8	15 695	28.7	29.4
Beltrami	16 759	72.6	143 800	24.0	12.5	588	29.2	3.7	22 254	2.4	1 843	8.3	20 353	34.6	20.7
Benton	14 986	70.6	170 800	25.6	12.3	633	28.2	1.3	23 579	-0.1	1 879	8.0	20 287	28.7	28.0
Big Stone	2 366	80.1	81 900	21.6	11.4	447	24.8	0.8	3 086	4.8	186	6.0	2 597	32.7	28.0
Blue Earth	23 889	67.1	163 500	23.6	11.9	675	31.9	1.2	38 215	0.5	2 373	6.2	36 019	29.3	23.9
Brown	10 798	79.7	122 400	22.1	10.9	493	27.0	1.2	15 081	-0.2	1 034	6.9	13 865	26.7	32.6
Carlton	13 724	80.5	163 500	24.7	11.0	630	29.0	2.0	17 923	1.7	1 542	8.6	16 345	33.4	26.2
Carver	32 202	83.6	287 100	25.2	10.8	867	29.3	1.1	51 114	0.4	3 506	6.9	47 670	42.9	17.8
Cass	12 944	83.4	184 900	26.4	12.6	579	27.6	3.1	14 317	-1.1	1 557	10.9	12 370	31.2	24.7
Chippewa	5 193	74.3	94 400	19.9	11.8	542	27.6	1.5	7 292	-0.2	519	7.1	6 486	30.4	32.3
Chisago	19 328	86.6	230 600	28.2	13.2	774	31.7	1.7	27 532	-1.2	2 598	9.4	25 950	31.2	29.5
Clay	21 684	71.2	146 100	22.4	11.3	616	32.0	1.5	33 463	0.5	1 590	4.8	30 783	32.3	22.5
Clearwater	3 698	77.6	113 300	25.9	12.7	512	29.1	5.6	4 350	2.0	594	13.7	3 802	28.1	33.7
Cook	2 607	73.3	247 100	27.0	10.0	582	25.4	8.3	3 283	2.6	224	6.8	2 741	32.6	22.0
Cottonwood	4 912	79.6	81 800	21.4	11.9	454	27.3	1.7	6 882	6.2	394	5.7	5 695	29.8	31.5
Crow Wing	26 913	76.4	187 000	25.6	12.2	630	28.9	1.9	33 494	-0.7	3 009	9.0	29 052	31.3	23.9
Dakota	151 122	78.3	243 700	24.1	11.1	891	28.4	1.7	230 818	-0.6	16 244	7.0	215 427	41.1	18.1
Dodge	7 301	87.0	163 700	23.0	11.7	628	26.7	1.1	11 174	-2.0	775	6.9	10 623	33.9	27.3
Douglas	16 070	76.1	182 600	25.8	12.7	590	29.8	1.0	20 653	-1.6	1 354	6.6	18 365	33.1	24.4
Faribault	6 301	80.9	87 000	20.9	12.5	458	31.0	1.3	7 916	2.6	628	7.9	7 387	28.9	34.1

1. Specified owner-occupied units.   2. Specified renter-occupied units. A value of 10.0 represents 10 percent or less.   3. Overcrowded or lacking complete plumbing facilities.   4. Percent of civilian labor force.   5. Persons 16 years old and over.

Table B. States and Counties — Nonfarm Employment and Agriculture

STATE County	Number of establishments	Total	Health care and social assistance	Manufacturing	Retail trade	Finance and insurance	Professional, scientific, and technical services	Total (mil dol)	Average per employee (dollars)	Number	Fewer than 50 acres	500 acres or more	Farm operators whose principal occupation is farming (percent)
	104	105	106	107	108	109	110	111	112	113	114	115	116
MICHIGAN—Cont'd													
Keweenaw	57	165	0	D	D	D	0	3	20 855	8	37.5	12.5	50.0
Lake	165	1 116	246	D	217	D	D	26	23 031	186	37.6	2.2	41.4
Lapeer	1 630	15 357	2 555	3 590	2 984	495	670	424	27 589	1 317	53.5	6.3	45.5
Leelanau	746	3 967	599	226	608	146	189	122	30 737	449	37.9	3.1	47.4
Lenawee	1 924	25 005	3 600	5 620	4 169	753	1 010	774	30 957	1 686	42.9	11.0	42.2
Livingston	4 042	45 657	5 144	7 054	8 405	4 797	2 496	1 408	30 846	795	60.8	5.3	45.3
Luce	165	1 312	D	D	282	73	D	38	29 297	41	29.3	9.8	41.5
Mackinac	427	1 968	D	91	354	D	D	72	36 785	89	20.2	11.2	39.3
Macomb	18 024	257 875	36 017	47 892	40 590	7 311	D	10 339	40 093	475	60.0	5.9	58.5
Manistee	579	5 534	903	801	932	166	96	172	31 011	358	31.6	3.1	47.2
Marquette	1 696	21 125	5 671	897	3 682	862	693	725	34 327	144	35.4	11.1	50.7
Mason	762	8 568	1 551	1 877	1 471	273	180	268	31 249	450	33.8	7.8	43.6
Mecosta	772	9 047	1 514	1 514	2 080	D	194	238	26 337	845	32.8	4.5	43.8
Menominee	473	4 784	355	1 535	706	163	62	126	26 431	419	27.4	13.6	45.1
Midland	1 864	33 740	6 115	5 399	4 215	978	957	1 790	53 045	571	46.8	7.4	40.8
Missaukee	272	1 869	270	286	381	52	D	49	26 032	391	34.8	10.7	43.2
Monroe	2 424	36 045	5 215	6 003	5 130	954	D	1 296	35 952	1 119	52.4	10.0	44.2
Montcalm	1 065	12 172	2 689	2 188	2 407	382	458	349	28 634	1 227	39.9	7.6	47.1
Montmorency	219	1 465	273	280	259	D	D	38	26 123	140	25.7	5.7	47.1
Muskegon	3 406	49 479	10 322	11 045	7 581	1 108	1 308	1 616	32 665	525	52.2	5.7	45.3
Newaygo	837	9 029	1 643	1 666	1 596	676	357	280	30 959	951	42.5	6.0	41.1
Oakland	38 614	614 878	94 064	47 974	71 209	42 536	75 672	30 925	50 294	588	74.7	1.0	42.0
Oceana	512	4 333	748	1 415	625	128	62	117	27 095	648	38.3	8.0	47.8
Ogemaw	577	5 797	1 429	548	1 540	D	114	146	25 126	321	33.6	11.8	48.3
Ontonagon	208	1 515	373	D	303	67	D	41	26 878	104	15.4	19.2	51.9
Osceola	426	5 651	942	1 906	555	99	D	207	36 593	826	34.4	5.7	36.4
Oscoda	191	1 258	196	169	250	36	20	30	23 525	136	39.7	5.1	45.6
Otsego	818	8 616	1 538	574	2 011	219	223	245	28 438	182	38.5	13.2	45.1
Ottawa	5 748	90 843	10 543	27 905	9 893	2 191	4 125	3 232	35 574	1 451	59.4	4.9	43.2
Presque Isle	341	2 112	338	175	423	100	D	57	26 858	289	21.1	12.5	46.4
Roscommon	597	4 464	604	222	1 436	231	D	105	23 578	54	46.3	1.9	48.1
Saginaw	4 510	76 018	17 179	9 818	12 348	3 094	2 753	2 553	33 585	1 533	43.4	10.0	48.3
St. Clair	3 216	38 474	7 975	6 780	7 033	1 333	1 021	1 266	32 913	1 072	51.5	6.7	46.9
St. Joseph	1 218	17 748	D	7 534	2 406	496	1 518	573	32 274	1 033	45.0	10.6	39.2
Sanilac	883	8 212	1 291	2 348	1 382	417	200	218	26 571	1 535	32.8	14.5	56.5
Schoolcraft	236	1 829	D	D	362	D	37	62	33 689	66	25.8	16.7	36.4
Shiawassee	1 193	12 236	2 385	1 558	2 472	379	475	326	26 653	1 082	45.2	10.8	45.2
Tuscola	910	8 963	2 375	1 624	1 675	329	329	260	29 047	1 372	38.7	12.8	47.7
Van Buren	1 366	16 253	2 592	3 295	2 434	350	1 986	477	29 374	1 232	49.0	3.6	46.8
Washtenaw	7 932	135 600	34 129	12 536	15 783	4 163	12 779	6 356	46 876	1 300	54.9	6.1	45.2
Wayne	32 960	593 483	102 420	68 020	64 934	23 812	49 244	26 511	44 669	313	78.0	1.9	46.6
Wexford	820	12 192	2 197	3 304	1 887	363	404	359	29 484	371	41.5	3.0	35.0
MINNESOTA	146 453	2 417 174	421 935	307 822	291 328	148 621	139 270	102 179	42 272	80 992	25.5	17.9	48.9
Aitkin	430	3 128	672	334	713	D	43	80	25 421	538	19.0	9.7	38.1
Anoka	7 368	105 480	14 387	21 548	15 515	2 154	3 579	4 834	45 831	475	58.5	3.4	37.7
Becker	974	11 808	1 932	1 441	1 878	250	239	334	28 296	1 202	13.6	13.0	40.3
Beltrami	1 130	13 762	2 970	980	3 097	441	400	419	30 462	674	14.7	17.7	36.4
Benton	905	14 671	2 602	3 698	1 965	239	225	447	30 436	919	26.8	8.8	44.4
Big Stone	177	1 554	669	D	221	65	D	36	23 098	452	15.7	34.3	62.2
Blue Earth	1 939	34 374	7 720	4 225	6 001	1 041	1 122	967	28 127	1 247	29.7	21.5	52.5
Brown	756	12 258	2 260	3 200	1 654	459	427	352	28 733	1 129	22.1	18.6	57.9
Carlton	744	8 317	1 909	1 409	1 469	474	187	264	31 739	485	17.9	8.5	40.8
Carver	2 323	34 666	4 462	10 231	3 240	870	1 813	1 435	41 401	800	38.1	8.6	50.3
Cass	895	6 923	1 320	373	913	D	D	173	25 004	563	17.6	12.3	37.8
Chippewa	451	5 315	1 095	1 120	813	D	272	150	28 273	720	23.9	29.2	55.4
Chisago	1 253	13 059	D	1 695	1 942	370	704	411	31 496	867	45.8	5.5	37.8
Clay	1 279	16 723	3 131	886	3 086	474	538	418	25 020	921	19.4	30.7	50.8
Clearwater	191	2 190	674	D	265	58	D	62	28 356	601	12.1	16.3	43.3
Cook	272	1 975	D	D	283	36	D	53	26 667	13	38.5	7.7	38.5
Cottonwood	352	4 430	880	1 572	518	D	67	119	26 959	865	24.6	32.3	59.5
Crow Wing	2 052	24 190	5 194	2 326	4 577	732	829	738	30 515	609	25.8	7.6	35.6
Dakota	9 941	164 132	19 707	17 385	21 157	10 533	8 150	6 891	41 986	1 065	48.4	12.2	46.3
Dodge	456	3 986	220	1 058	477	134	118	147	36 962	723	39.3	18.3	46.2
Douglas	1 324	15 775	2 860	2 870	2 975	452	477	500	31 717	1 199	25.1	9.6	39.1
Faribault	461	4 376	996	1 081	573	257	76	129	29 477	952	22.8	31.5	65.3

Table B. States and Counties — **Agriculture**

	Agriculture, 2007 (cont.)														
	Land in farms		Acres			Value of land and buildings (dollars)		Value of machinery and equipment, average per farm (dollars)	Value of products sold				Percent of farms with sales of:		Government payments	
STATE County	Acreage (1,000)	Percent change, 2002–2007	Average size of farm	Total irrigated (1,000)	Total cropland (1,000)	Average per farm	Average per acre		Total (mil dol)	Average per farm (dollars)	Crops	Live-stock and poultry products	$10,000 or more	$100,000 or more	Total ($1,000)	Percent of farms
	117	118	119	120	121	122	123	124	125	126	127	128	129	130	131	132
MICHIGAN—Cont'd																
Keweenaw	2	100.0	200	0.0	0.4	419 412	2 094	39 254	0.0	741	D	D	0.0	0.0	0	0.0
Lake	21	-8.7	115	0.1	10.5	334 655	2 912	53 529	2.4	13 168	28.2	71.8	15.1	2.2	112	13.4
Lapeer	176	-6.9	134	2.4	135.3	551 299	4 117	80 955	69.0	52 427	65.4	34.6	31.0	11.1	1 532	22.1
Leelanau	56	-9.7	124	1.5	33.7	877 921	7 070	81 423	35.3	78 628	89.7	10.3	54.1	17.8	231	19.6
Lenawee	349	-1.1	207	5.9	304.7	661 311	3 198	88 864	161.1	95 557	67.3	32.7	38.6	15.5	8 609	68.6
Livingston	96	0.0	121	1.4	69.3	611 728	5 044	80 225	41.7	52 422	64.1	35.9	29.2	9.8	844	18.9
Luce	9	-10.0	215	D	3.4	633 653	2 946	65 537	2.6	62 208	86.9	13.1	36.6	14.6	D	7.3
Mackinac	22	10.0	244	D	13.0	515 516	2 115	63 252	4.3	48 288	9.5	90.5	39.3	6.7	43	13.5
Macomb	62	-8.8	131	3.0	54.8	672 691	5 154	111 424	52.7	110 915	88.7	11.3	43.6	18.9	622	28.2
Manistee	46	0.0	129	2.3	24.8	396 087	3 080	58 435	9.2	25 732	81.3	18.7	30.2	5.0	113	14.2
Marquette	30	0.0	209	0.1	10.4	504 620	2 415	61 555	3.8	26 565	36.2	63.8	16.0	6.3	40	8.3
Mason	76	-5.0	170	3.3	55.9	542 279	3 192	82 612	34.5	76 596	59.1	40.9	37.6	15.1	574	28.9
Mecosta	115	-4.2	136	8.7	76.7	394 509	2 906	68 454	72.7	85 979	26.5	73.5	34.3	7.3	653	37.4
Menominee	104	5.1	247	0.0	59.7	551 410	2 229	75 382	33.6	80 236	10.0	90.0	37.7	15.5	699	36.5
Midland	91	7.1	159	0.5	69.6	476 039	3 000	72 947	48.8	85 432	45.8	54.2	31.3	10.2	1 181	39.8
Missaukee	88	-10.2	226	4.6	62.9	659 931	2 920	111 648	70.6	180 652	17.0	83.0	35.8	18.9	756	29.4
Monroe	208	-4.1	186	6.5	189.5	710 533	3 826	102 813	130.1	116 237	93.8	6.2	51.4	18.8	3 127	48.9
Montcalm	243	-4.7	198	40.3	189.9	566 867	2 865	89 122	139.4	113 597	63.7	36.3	35.5	12.6	2 473	49.2
Montmorency	22	4.8	156	D	12.6	370 554	2 380	85 309	4.1	29 572	33.0	67.0	22.1	7.9	64	33.6
Muskegon	80	8.1	152	9.8	58.1	601 241	3 962	100 785	91.2	173 668	44.2	55.8	34.1	14.5	790	23.0
Newaygo	133	-1.5	140	10.3	89.5	479 025	3 415	80 344	101.2	106 382	31.4	68.6	33.4	12.6	878	26.5
Oakland	33	-19.5	55	0.6	20.0	465 550	8 422	51 211	18.8	31 987	80.7	19.3	20.9	6.3	131	6.8
Oceana	123	-3.1	190	6.9	83.3	719 566	3 782	92 217	78.1	120 565	58.6	41.4	40.0	13.0	1 083	21.0
Ogemaw	61	-10.3	190	0.2	40.5	535 342	2 820	89 394	30.5	95 071	13.5	86.5	33.6	13.7	349	40.5
Ontonagon	31	-8.8	296	D	15.2	471 379	1 590	61 361	1.9	18 610	38.9	61.2	31.7	3.8	27	22.1
Osceola	122	5.2	148	2.3	73.2	394 667	2 668	60 954	30.2	36 551	16.5	83.5	25.2	5.9	607	22.2
Oscoda	18	5.9	129	0.0	8.4	330 846	2 560	39 659	4.9	36 054	8.3	91.7	44.9	12.5	18	8.1
Otsego	34	-2.9	185	0.4	15.7	490 725	2 658	59 772	4.3	23 802	74.1	25.9	33.5	2.7	45	30.2
Ottawa	171	3.6	118	15.2	130.0	683 668	5 817	97 890	391.1	269 533	59.3	40.7	51.8	24.7	1 463	24.9
Presque Isle	71	4.4	246	1.5	45.7	554 952	2 256	94 074	13.4	46 387	60.6	39.4	33.2	10.4	284	42.9
Roscommon	5	-28.6	88	D	2.3	367 438	4 169	53 978	0.4	7 016	44.9	55.1	22.2	0.0	10	11.1
Saginaw	324	-0.3	212	1.8	287.2	599 832	2 835	100 851	142.5	92 959	88.8	11.2	49.5	17.6	5 355	70.8
St. Clair	160	-12.1	150	1.3	135.4	574 011	3 834	87 841	50.8	47 365	84.7	15.3	34.1	10.4	1 621	30.8
St. Joseph	215	-6.9	209	102.9	181.1	705 213	3 382	119 780	136.0	131 688	77.0	23.0	41.2	21.1	3 322	46.9
Sanilac	417	-4.1	272	2.0	368.2	792 375	2 916	140 989	216.7	141 197	54.5	45.5	51.1	24.6	5 412	62.9
Schoolcraft	27	92.9	405	0.0	10.8	567 778	1 404	54 036	2.4	36 343	63.4	36.6	37.9	12.1	7	18.2
Shiawassee	227	-3.4	209	1.6	195.5	616 615	2 945	92 640	87.8	81 189	65.9	34.1	44.7	15.5	3 176	57.7
Tuscola	343	2.1	250	5.8	301.4	756 725	3 029	123 592	150.0	109 347	77.7	22.3	41.3	18.3	4 568	58.9
Van Buren	185	5.1	150	30.4	135.0	643 980	4 281	96 842	173.5	140 805	82.2	17.8	42.9	16.1	1 436	21.9
Washtenaw	167	-4.6	128	2.7	133.1	642 197	5 003	83 247	73.2	56 305	74.9	25.1	37.3	12.4	2 193	32.6
Wayne	17	-19.0	56	0.8	13.1	431 377	7 741	73 184	28.8	91 875	97.1	2.9	35.8	11.2	93	10.9
Wexford	38	-17.4	104	1.0	24.7	330 704	3 188	43 496	6.9	18 542	42.7	57.3	25.3	4.0	110	17.5
MINNESOTA	26 918	-2.2	332	506.4	21 948.6	853 968	2 569	131 698	13 180.5	162 738	53.5	46.5	50.7	27.4	445 861	70.0
Aitkin	133	-23.6	247	4.4	64.4	413 719	1 678	54 510	13.5	25 157	53.1	47.0	24.0	5.2	222	22.9
Anoka	46	-23.3	97	2.5	30.1	563 161	5 817	63 665	32.6	68 556	66.9	33.1	26.7	7.8	336	24.2
Becker	396	-5.0	329	8.6	263.0	618 949	1 879	93 061	149.5	124 361	50.0	50.0	32.9	14.1	4 330	64.9
Beltrami	211	-9.4	313	2.8	101.7	486 069	1 554	57 869	21.0	31 116	46.0	54.0	33.5	6.4	1 207	33.2
Benton	186	-5.1	202	14.6	136.9	616 751	3 047	111 263	113.9	123 911	19.1	80.9	48.5	19.4	2 390	62.7
Big Stone	252	-8.0	558	2.2	223.8	1 201 905	2 153	185 267	86.8	192 110	75.8	24.2	64.4	40.7	4 045	85.2
Blue Earth	415	2.2	333	0.6	375.7	1 183 017	3 552	163 234	327.5	262 619	47.3	52.7	60.1	40.4	8 511	79.6
Brown	355	2.0	314	3.0	318.8	929 209	2 957	141 845	256.4	227 086	48.5	51.5	70.8	43.8	7 358	87.3
Carlton	98	-14.0	202	2.1	43.9	421 058	2 086	51 806	8.0	16 578	28.0	72.0	27.8	4.3	123	13.0
Carver	169	-1.7	212	0.5	144.5	834 797	3 942	155 820	92.9	116 181	52.0	48.0	50.4	25.6	3 300	64.1
Cass	169	-14.2	300	7.6	72.2	638 582	2 125	56 372	25.6	45 525	14.5	85.5	33.2	6.2	344	21.8
Chippewa	368	8.2	511	2.7	337.7	1 368 517	2 678	212 258	169.0	234 724	88.3	11.7	57.9	41.0	6 392	88.9
Chisago	115	-1.7	133	1.7	78.4	573 014	4 310	69 152	33.4	38 538	60.8	39.2	34.4	7.2	1 341	37.7
Clay	614	2.2	666	5.9	549.6	1 232 342	1 849	178 337	201.8	219 089	84.3	15.7	48.8	30.9	10 124	77.6
Clearwater	194	-14.2	323	D	91.2	480 463	1 487	68 166	23.1	38 475	37.4	62.6	38.4	6.8	943	41.9
Cook	2	-33.3	185	0.0	0.2	794 042	4 297	27 032	D	D	D	0.0	15.4	7.7	D	23.1
Cottonwood	381	1.6	441	1.1	351.5	1 307 650	2 967	192 402	240.6	278 199	57.6	42.4	69.0	49.4	6 962	84.6
Crow Wing	122	-15.9	200	2.9	50.5	518 482	2 594	63 922	13.5	22 112	38.6	61.4	29.9	5.1	377	26.6
Dakota	246	4.2	231	57.1	217.3	899 176	3 892	137 452	184.7	173 435	63.5	36.5	58.4	25.1	4 232	53.1
Dodge	248	6.4	343	D	226.1	1 266 667	3 691	158 083	173.0	239 228	53.2	46.8	56.3	34.2	4 465	70.7
Douglas	263	-3.7	219	2.0	184.2	527 933	2 410	80 248	65.3	54 459	49.1	50.9	38.3	14.9	3 726	77.0
Faribault	454	5.1	477	0.4	429.2	1 514 439	3 177	232 404	290.1	304 682	67.8	32.2	73.8	53.9	9 176	82.6

Table B. States and Counties — Water Use, Wholesale Trade, Retail Trade, and Real Estate

STATE County	Water use, 2005 Total water withdrawn (mil gal/day)	Gallons withdrawn per person	Wholesale trade,[1] 2007 Number of establishments	Number of employees	Sales (mil dol)	Annual payroll (mil dol)	Retail trade,[2] 2007 Number of establishments	Number of employees	Sales (mil dol)	Annual payroll (mil dol)	Real estate and rental and leasing,[2] 2007 Number of establishments	Number of employees	Receipts (mil dol)	Annual payroll (mil dol)
	133	134	135	136	137	138	139	140	141	142	143	144	145	146
MICHIGAN—Cont'd														
Keweenaw	0.2	100	1	D	D	D	12	22	3.3	0.4	3	D	D	D
Lake	2.2	178	2	D	D	D	32	231	53.3	4.1	7	D	D	D
Lapeer	9.3	100	54	411	170.1	15.7	281	3 217	799.9	62.1	68	239	21.0	5.0
Leelanau	4.5	204	12	83	17.1	2.3	134	739	128.2	13.2	28	74	8.4	2.0
Lenawee	15.1	148	70	526	451.9	21.2	340	4 329	944.7	87.2	69	231	31.4	5.1
Livingston	25.9	143	208	1 475	1 293.3	78.1	611	8 734	2 059.8	186.5	139	673	110.5	16.7
Luce	1.2	174	7	D	D	D	34	317	74.0	5.8	4	D	D	D
Mackinac	10.1	894	6	D	D	D	113	462	155.8	11.0	14	D	D	D
Macomb	12.2	15	856	10 424	5 611.1	522.4	2 941	41 513	10 007.6	950.4	674	3 569	601.9	98.4
Manistee	38.9	1 542	14	D	D	D	117	906	225.4	19.5	23	76	6.1	1.1
Marquette	342.2	5 284	54	437	162.4	15.3	312	3 860	729.8	70.4	71	313	31.2	6.4
Mason	29.0	1 001	15	145	148.6	5.5	143	1 562	330.4	31.5	30	146	20.2	3.9
Mecosta	16.0	377	21	D	D	D	160	2 231	475.0	41.4	46	162	20.4	3.4
Menominee	5.9	237	18	D	D	D	80	690	166.9	12.6	16	41	4.6	0.7
Midland	14.7	175	49	D	D	D	323	4 382	869.3	79.5	82	D	D	D
Missaukee	4.6	303	17	D	D	D	36	329	91.9	7.4	6	18	0.8	0.2
Monroe	1 846.7	11 997	91	D	D	D	427	5 637	1 465.3	120.3	95	373	48.8	7.5
Montcalm	40.1	628	39	221	124.8	8.6	240	2 463	563.1	49.0	26	81	8.0	1.5
Montmorency	1.3	128	8	D	D	D	45	303	70.1	5.2	13	D	D	D
Muskegon	323.1	1 840	119	D	D	D	608	7 878	1 666.7	154.5	112	484	67.0	12.0
Newaygo	12.6	252	26	199	71.7	8.2	169	1 577	355.3	31.1	22	D	D	D
Oakland	62.0	51	2 150	28 244	29 825.7	1 655.5	5 189	75 573	18 183.7	1 798.7	1 821	16 685	2 929.4	642.0
Oceana	7.1	250	13	D	D	D	100	714	171.5	13.5	16	58	5.4	1.1
Ogemaw	3.6	162	18	D	D	D	126	1 501	364.7	31.6	27	82	11.2	1.9
Ontonagon	7.3	991	6	83	16.6	3.6	38	311	60.9	5.6	4	D	D	D
Osceola	7.2	304	8	122	57.7	4.9	80	609	151.6	12.1	13	20	4.3	0.6
Oscoda	1.5	158	2	D	D	D	43	264	57.1	4.7	8	D	D	D
Otsego	4.6	186	41	427	290.7	21.0	157	2 137	499.8	48.0	24	91	15.8	3.6
Ottawa	854.5	3 346	304	3 208	2 120.6	148.0	830	10 670	2 367.8	220.4	186	891	107.9	23.9
Presque Isle	13.6	951	8	37	8.3	0.9	69	494	101.4	9.5	7	D	D	D
Roscommon	3.2	124	12	40	6.8	0.9	133	1 610	338.4	33.1	25	63	6.0	1.2
Saginaw	20.2	97	184	2 319	1 070.8	92.0	973	12 584	2 534.3	243.3	149	751	101.8	17.4
St. Clair	1 668.1	9 731	86	818	872.3	47.0	602	7 629	1 601.6	141.9	107	408	63.0	9.7
St. Joseph	77.8	1 235	47	D	D	D	215	2 428	559.9	50.2	40	143	18.7	3.3
Sanilac	6.9	154	31	309	174.9	10.9	172	1 454	300.9	27.2	25	119	11.7	3.5
Schoolcraft	13.0	1 474	4	D	D	D	61	379	110.8	8.0	5	D	D	D
Shiawassee	8.6	118	42	D	D	D	219	2 556	614.7	54.3	39	112	13.1	2.9
Tuscola	10.3	177	29	387	283.1	15.4	163	1 764	432.3	34.2	21	77	7.4	1.3
Van Buren	146.5	1 859	65	D	D	D	262	2 431	556.7	49.6	45	189	20.0	3.0
Washtenaw	37.9	111	291	3 705	3 631.0	194.4	1 148	16 403	3 681.1	355.3	368	2 595	712.4	98.3
Wayne	1 858.7	930	1 649	26 806	26 102.9	1 405.1	6 361	68 272	17 275.8	1 451.0	1 276	7 929	5 528.0	241.0
Wexford	9.0	281	30	433	157.4	18.2	177	2 089	525.4	42.7	32	106	14.3	2.8
MINNESOTA	4 041.3	787	6 913	110 487	82 878.1	6 417.8	20 777	307 034	71 384.1	6 685.6	6 889	39 430	9 208.0	1 317.4
Aitkin	4.6	284	7	96	53.5	3.6	74	750	147.5	12.4	9	18	1.8	0.3
Anoka	97.9	302	335	8 542	7 335.9	1 054.6	986	16 716	3 738.9	363.0	388	1 857	307.3	43.7
Becker	14.5	456	31	245	88.4	8.6	158	1 680	373.5	32.2	45	113	20.7	2.6
Beltrami	7.7	179	41	D	D	D	228	3 236	627.4	60.8	38	132	15.1	2.9
Benton	24.1	626	43	943	513.0	41.0	118	1 989	495.2	40.3	37	270	16.4	7.6
Big Stone	1.7	317	8	85	185.8	2.9	30	244	32.9	3.2	4	12	0.5	0.1
Blue Earth	32.2	555	90	1 391	1 275.9	60.6	355	6 309	1 211.5	110.9	80	634	74.8	13.4
Brown	4.6	173	37	398	547.1	14.8	126	1 754	301.2	29.6	25	78	5.5	1.6
Carlton	9.8	287	21	D	D	D	130	1 490	357.4	30.8	15	76	9.8	1.0
Carver	10.7	126	129	2 044	1 484.3	132.0	235	3 440	807.1	72.1	112	D	D	D
Cass	6.6	228	17	163	44.3	5.4	160	1 122	276.8	23.1	41	262	22.5	5.7
Chippewa	3.0	231	18	212	201.4	9.0	62	697	168.3	14.2	15	98	4.4	1.2
Chisago	14.8	299	42	D	D	D	167	1 864	428.6	32.9	53	D	D	D
Clay	9.5	177	69	D	D	D	180	2 801	630.3	54.6	40	179	17.4	3.2
Clearwater	5.7	675	6	28	14.2	0.7	35	245	42.9	3.6	NA	NA	NA	NA
Cook	171.5	31 956	3	D	D	D	45	290	61.9	6.6	17	48	4.2	0.7
Cottonwood	4.7	395	25	224	177.2	8.5	66	568	90.3	7.9	8	22	2.9	0.6
Crow Wing	12.6	210	67	604	278.7	19.3	389	4 936	1 141.9	107.2	100	236	38.2	6.9
Dakota	394.6	1 029	552	9 217	4 415.5	491.7	1 178	22 061	5 164.0	498.1	544	2 317	356.9	70.6
Dodge	2.9	145	21	388	244.8	16.9	63	418	91.8	8.1	12	18	4.9	0.5
Douglas	22.9	651	45	D	D	D	237	2 982	625.5	58.0	49	167	32.2	3.9
Faribault	3.1	199	29	177	142.9	5.3	78	610	116.7	10.9	9	14	0.8	0.2

1. Merchant wholesalers, except manufacturers' sales branches and offices.   2. Employer establishments.

Professional Services, Manufacturing, and Accommodation and Food Services

STATE County	Professional, scientific, and technical services,[1] 2007				Manufacturing, 2007				Accommodation and food services, 2007			
	Number of establish-ments	Number of employees	Receipts (mil dol)	Annual payroll (mil dol)	Number of establish-ments	Number of employees	Receipts (mil dol)	Annual payroll (mil dol)	Number of establish-ments	Number of employees	Sales (mil dol)	Annual payroll (mil dol)
	147	148	149	150	151	152	153	154	155	156	157	158
MICHIGAN—Cont'd												
Keweenaw	1	D	D	D	NA	NA	NA	NA	15	102	4.4	1.2
Lake	5	D	D	D	NA	NA	NA	NA	31	175	7.8	1.9
Lapeer	128	D	D	D	135	4 916	1 142.6	177.5	123	1 976	72.6	21.7
Leelanau	59	D	D	D	NA	NA	NA	NA	75	716	40.6	13.3
Lenawee	131	601	43.2	20.1	152	6 797	2 230.8	303.3	178	2 680	94.2	28.3
Livingston	483	2 706	327.3	155.2	268	8 278	2 715.8	377.9	263	4 955	181.0	51.3
Luce	9	16	0.9	0.5	NA	NA	NA	NA	22	231	7.4	2.2
Mackinac	16	45	3.1	1.2	NA	NA	NA	NA	106	718	56.5	15.2
Macomb	1 671	D	D	D	1 732	65 038	23 588.5	3 451.5	1 547	27 891	1 120.9	332.0
Manistee	36	104	9.7	3.6	24	973	391.2	54.7	68	654	26.8	7.4
Marquette	128	D	D	D	45	952	310.4	40.1	190	3 089	100.3	32.7
Mason	52	234	18.8	7.8	42	2 137	518.3	87.7	90	884	39.7	11.1
Mecosta	43	D	D	D	37	1 924	668.2	78.4	76	1 289	44.1	13.2
Menominee	23	89	7.4	3.2	49	1 821	418.5	76.2	38	495	17.2	4.8
Midland	164	D	D	D	55	5 103	2 821.3	363.1	129	2 545	108.0	30.6
Missaukee	8	19	1.3	0.6	NA	NA	NA	NA	24	229	9.4	2.8
Monroe	147	944	84.3	39.6	143	8 555	3 503.0	440.6	274	4 682	171.5	47.8
Montcalm	61	D	D	D	66	2 059	389.0	82.7	103	1 012	45.8	10.2
Montmorency	11	31	2.9	1.1	NA	NA	NA	NA	31	210	7.9	2.2
Muskegon	239	D	D	D	290	13 271	3 675.8	609.1	344	5 763	221.0	64.6
Newaygo	51	D	D	D	49	2 005	560.8	72.8	79	873	32.1	9.4
Oakland	6 414	D	D	D	1 862	58 971	25 885.2	3 228.0	2 700	48 801	2 284.8	661.6
Oceana	28	91	7.5	3.0	40	1 473	364.1	40.2	78	794	32.3	10.3
Ogemaw	39	139	10.9	4.2	39	838	151.7	27.0	60	833	31.1	8.3
Ontonagon	8	9	0.8	0.2	NA	NA	NA	NA	40	275	6.8	1.6
Osceola	23	69	5.8	2.1	44	2 038	968.0	81.2	41	435	19.2	5.8
Oscoda	9	24	1.4	0.7	NA	NA	NA	NA	25	253	9.0	2.6
Otsego	56	D	D	D	37	874	158.0	30.7	73	1 307	58.8	16.7
Ottawa	515	D	D	D	584	31 912	9 210.9	1 395.5	381	7 551	277.2	83.8
Presque Isle	16	36	2.1	0.7	NA	NA	NA	NA	42	262	9.2	2.6
Roscommon	35	D	D	D	NA	NA	NA	NA	80	1 063	37.3	11.7
Saginaw	355	3 009	429.9	121.3	219	11 437	4 604.8	659.0	383	8 620	337.3	102.2
St. Clair	244	D	D	D	261	9 326	2 855.5	394.0	287	4 679	178.3	52.0
St. Joseph	80	499	30.8	11.0	143	9 470	3 106.6	410.4	109	1 474	53.8	15.5
Sanilac	69	D	D	D	87	2 921	595.1	104.5	73	738	30.2	7.8
Schoolcraft	10	38	2.0	0.9	NA	NA	NA	NA	32	250	10.2	2.8
Shiawassee	93	475	39.2	12.5	69	1 865	409.5	69.6	109	1 584	57.5	15.7
Tuscola	58	D	D	D	55	1 953	581.5	78.8	68	719	24.7	7.2
Van Buren	90	D	D	D	100	3 838	1 312.9	160.9	168	2 089	80.5	23.1
Washtenaw	1 215	14 248	1 788.8	1 017.4	324	15 543	5 331.8	881.4	679	13 734	613.5	180.4
Wayne	2 880	D	D	D	1 729	87 991	55 896.9	5 545.3	3 215	57 836	3 112.4	857.5
Wexford	55	438	40.1	16.9	57	4 158	D	D	88	1 344	48.8	14.2
MINNESOTA	16 595	140 786	20 473.1	8 425.3	7 951	340 514	107 563.1	15 999.2	11 340	221 081	10 423.7	2 978.4
Aitkin	17	48	3.8	1.2	NA	NA	NA	NA	60	488	19.7	5.6
Anoka	769	D	D	D	675	23 959	6 460.2	1 247.7	461	9 936	374.9	112.1
Becker	56	272	24.5	10.7	47	1 806	284.8	59.3	88	1 130	43.4	11.4
Beltrami	66	D	D	D	38	1 249	279.8	41.5	100	1 643	65.6	18.3
Benton	48	D	D	D	77	4 248	839.1	162.7	63	1 074	42.1	11.6
Big Stone	12	31	2.2	0.9	NA	NA	NA	NA	17	D	D	D
Blue Earth	131	D	D	D	87	4 181	2 728.7	172.0	167	4 053	139.0	40.9
Brown	51	409	40.8	14.6	42	3 570	1 596.9	128.8	74	1 134	40.5	12.6
Carlton	44	D	D	D	33	1 635	D	D	66	856	32.6	9.6
Carver	306	D	D	D	153	12 361	3 149.5	579.3	138	2 511	91.1	26.9
Cass	45	D	D	D	NA	NA	NA	NA	139	2 255	146.4	41.0
Chippewa	24	107	9.7	3.8	29	1 069	175.8	36.4	32	368	11.6	3.0
Chisago	91	328	29.5	12.0	88	1 851	403.1	68.1	93	1 240	43.0	12.1
Clay	71	D	D	D	48	925	317.1	35.7	89	1 586	58.5	16.5
Clearwater	8	35	2.7	0.9	12	D	D	D	21	D	D	D
Cook	12	24	1.8	0.8	NA	NA	NA	NA	65	806	40.4	12.5
Cottonwood	19	72	7.2	1.8	19	1 590	636.1	48.2	23	282	9.0	2.4
Crow Wing	134	D	D	D	118	2 913	D	119.6	200	3 228	149.6	44.0
Dakota	1 387	8 521	971.0	469.7	490	18 815	12 930.1	929.6	645	14 819	614.3	184.9
Dodge	26	D	D	D	30	1 475	D	68.8	28	386	11.8	3.4
Douglas	74	D	D	D	91	2 672	688.2	109.6	114	2 007	71.0	20.7
Faribault	19	63	6.5	2.4	30	1 063	408.6	41.2	34	363	10.5	2.6

1. Establishment subject to federal tax.

STATE County	Health care and social assistance, 2007				Other services, 2007				Federal funds and grants, 2009–2010 Expenditures (mil dol)			
										Direct payments for individuals[1]		
	Number of establishments	Number of employees	Receipts (mil dol)	Annual payroll (mil dol)	Number of establishments	Number of employees	Receipts (mil dol)	Annual payroll (mil dol)	Total	Social Security and government retirement	Medicare	Food Stamps and Supplemental Security Income
	159	160	161	162	163	164	165	166	167	168	169	170
MICHIGAN—Cont'd												
Keweenaw	NA	NA	NA	NA	1	D	D	D	24.3	13.5	5.5	0.5
Lake	12	236	12.2	6.4	9	D	D	D	114.6	50.2	25.2	8.4
Lapeer	195	2 424	196.2	72.9	118	488	35.1	9.7	480.9	257.8	94.6	16.4
Leelanau	56	541	43.9	17.4	43	86	9.6	2.0	134.9	72.8	24.7	3.3
Lenawee	252	3 345	271.9	104.2	159	787	52.0	12.6	688.7	336.9	157.3	29.6
Livingston	365	4 784	404.9	162.8	279	1 647	131.9	41.4	677.8	406.2	128.3	14.0
Luce	16	D	D	D	11	45	2.9	0.6	67.2	24.0	15.7	3.3
Mackinac	15	283	22.6	9.9	14	D	D	D	103.5	47.2	22.3	2.6
Macomb	2 085	35 424	3 299.3	1 390.3	1 450	8 269	669.0	213.7	7 930.1	2 619.7	1 567.3	174.8
Manistee	73	876	67.4	27.5	53	180	15.0	4.2	219.4	104.3	49.4	10.7
Marquette	228	5 390	500.7	232.0	125	711	56.9	13.1	524.3	239.5	105.6	18.0
Mason	98	1 359	121.4	47.8	65	245	16.9	5.1	260.7	116.4	48.2	10.9
Mecosta	79	1 424	105.1	45.7	66	296	23.3	5.9	286.6	137.6	48.4	16.6
Menominee	45	319	19.7	8.1	30	D	D	D	188.9	89.6	37.5	5.5
Midland	242	5 442	539.3	192.0	144	947	147.4	22.3	497.1	251.5	97.3	23.2
Missaukee	24	258	11.8	4.6	21	60	4.9	1.1	93.2	45.5	19.7	5.1
Monroe	284	4 733	381.3	158.7	195	1 172	93.7	30.3	885.2	468.7	218.6	37.2
Montcalm	105	2 392	188.0	81.3	100	345	28.0	6.2	470.5	202.1	95.8	25.6
Montmorency	17	236	12.5	5.8	15	D	D	D	115.8	63.2	30.4	4.3
Muskegon	398	9 463	864.8	374.1	283	1 440	116.0	27.8	1 299.3	564.9	261.1	96.9
Newaygo	74	1 473	118.8	50.3	78	308	50.4	5.4	279.4	140.9	60.2	17.4
Oakland	5 009	91 463	9 299.4	3 883.1	2 507	16 692	2 102.0	461.0	8 890.3	3 895.3	2 003.9	275.6
Oceana	45	660	40.9	19.4	37	D	D	D	198.4	94.9	40.6	12.9
Ogemaw	75	1 289	92.4	37.9	47	164	10.7	2.9	196.4	101.2	45.4	12.0
Ontonagon	24	376	18.3	11.4	9	D	D	D	83.0	37.7	19.4	2.2
Osceola	43	940	67.8	29.2	31	124	10.4	2.3	198.7	92.1	39.2	13.6
Oscoda	12	D	D	D	18	D	D	D	69.7	34.2	17.7	4.0
Otsego	92	1 486	130.0	52.1	65	229	19.6	5.3	173.1	87.9	29.8	5.4
Ottawa	500	9 536	761.6	294.0	425	2 575	240.5	67.4	1 266.2	660.2	197.4	28.4
Presque Isle	28	336	20.3	8.3	26	D	D	D	136.4	69.9	30.0	4.6
Roscommon	48	569	38.4	14.7	60	178	14.7	3.8	275.4	146.5	76.4	13.9
Saginaw	584	16 811	1 512.5	605.3	369	2 191	178.2	46.5	1 822.0	749.9	366.7	145.4
St. Clair	373	7 957	645.6	286.1	221	989	87.7	22.3	1 078.8	452.7	249.2	48.6
St. Joseph	109	1 928	163.5	62.8	114	494	38.8	10.4	384.3	182.2	92.5	18.7
Sanilac	97	1 354	89.9	37.9	64	270	20.6	5.1	340.5	146.9	86.5	14.5
Schoolcraft	15	341	27.5	13.6	21	D	D	D	95.2	37.7	20.9	4.7
Shiawassee	158	2 594	205.3	88.2	110	515	39.5	9.8	493.3	245.4	120.4	23.7
Tuscola	121	2 284	156.8	71.9	69	246	17.0	4.1	417.4	202.7	93.7	19.7
Van Buren	115	2 369	167.4	73.2	93	568	31.4	11.2	590.1	246.9	119.5	35.9
Washtenaw	958	34 745	3 715.8	1 627.0	557	3 917	443.2	122.6	3 527.0	780.4	357.0	71.1
Wayne	4 200	99 591	10 640.0	4 241.8	2 859	18 419	2 068.3	511.0	19 605.8	5 484.5	4 914.9	1 781.8
Wexford	97	2 040	172.2	68.8	64	258	22.1	5.8	407.7	118.0	47.0	14.1
MINNESOTA	13 996	386 144	33 997.4	14 872.0	11 137	81 829	8 301.3	2 355.0	44 375.7	13 726.9	7 574.7	1 177.8
Aitkin	25	653	57.3	20.1	34	D	D	D	174.5	78.3	41.1	5.2
Anoka	547	13 566	1 396.4	566.1	559	4 311	360.4	113.0	1 265.1	563.9	194.7	33.0
Becker	73	1 753	123.1	54.1	79	411	30.7	6.2	319.2	110.1	61.7	8.8
Beltrami	124	2 971	217.7	102.7	91	516	44.3	10.4	429.3	127.0	78.8	20.5
Benton	76	2 060	87.3	39.0	81	D	D	D	242.5	124.9	34.0	9.1
Big Stone	16	577	31.9	12.5	17	D	D	D	64.1	22.4	15.6	1.1
Blue Earth	205	7 412	541.9	232.6	155	953	69.9	18.8	448.3	166.9	80.2	11.3
Brown	70	2 341	148.1	61.9	85	D	D	D	192.0	85.4	45.1	3.4
Carlton	92	1 833	138.0	57.7	66	249	19.8	4.8	282.5	120.1	61.7	7.5
Carver	177	4 149	351.3	154.5	165	1 108	87.5	23.9	304.3	143.9	50.4	5.2
Cass	78	1 275	62.5	26.2	57	289	23.6	5.4	349.1	115.3	72.4	10.1
Chippewa	39	1 035	54.6	25.2	42	D	D	D	117.2	40.7	21.1	3.0
Chisago	121	3 843	332.3	163.9	91	D	D	D	252.6	147.6	51.5	7.5
Clay	148	2 670	115.1	54.5	113	D	D	D	425.2	144.4	74.2	17.5
Clearwater	15	419	19.6	9.6	15	D	D	D	100.6	27.1	26.0	3.1
Cook	14	D	D	D	10	D	D	D	60.0	21.7	7.8	0.6
Cottonwood	34	861	40.0	16.5	29	D	D	D	94.5	34.5	25.8	2.7
Crow Wing	201	5 075	343.3	139.0	148	764	50.8	11.7	536.9	245.3	113.3	14.0
Dakota	886	16 802	1 399.8	602.6	717	5 742	551.5	161.7	2 156.1	788.7	206.1	36.3
Dodge	29	D	D	D	45	274	24.5	7.0	100.8	43.4	25.5	2.3
Douglas	119	2 674	184.0	77.9	111	D	D	D	291.3	132.7	61.0	5.3
Faribault	39	903	51.9	23.1	31	D	D	D	142.4	54.5	36.2	3.1

1. State totals may include programs not allocated by county.

	Federal funds and grants, 2009–2010 (cont.)							Value of residential construction authorized by building permits, 2010		Local government finances, 2007				
	Expenditures (mil dol) (cont.)									General revenue				
	Procurement contract awards			Grants[1]								Taxes		
STATE County													Per capita[2] (dollars)	
	Salaries and wages	Defense	Other	Medicaid and other health-related	Nutrition and family welfare	Education	Other	New construction ($1,000)	Number of housing units	Total (mil dol)	Inter-govern-mental (mil dol)	Total (mil dol)	Total	Property
	171	172	173	174	175	176	177	178	179	180	181	182	183	184
MICHIGAN—Cont'd														
Keweenaw	0.4	0.0	0.1	1.8	0.6	0.5	0.0	974	9	7.3	2.6	1.8	846	810
Lake	4.0	0.0	1.2	18.7	3.7	1.3	1.2	1 207	42	40.4	21.4	13.3	1 189	1 185
Lapeer	23.6	2.7	3.4	57.9	13.4	4.8	0.9	3 877	22	283.2	155.3	70.8	770	729
Leelanau	7.5	0.2	3.6	5.7	4.1	1.8	5.1	17 357	89	63.8	14.4	34.8	1 590	1 582
Lenawee	21.6	2.5	4.3	86.7	18.8	6.8	0.9	12 134	102	352.8	191.4	100.3	991	958
Livingston	33.3	5.5	9.3	41.3	20.0	6.2	3.2	35 533	178	574.5	272.6	189.8	1 036	1 019
Luce	1.4	0.0	1.1	17.7	1.8	1.0	1.0	438	6	53.2	13.6	5.8	856	845
Mackinac	6.5	0.5	4.6	12.2	2.8	1.3	3.0	3 727	26	66.2	16.4	22.5	2 070	2 022
Macomb	523.0	2 324.4	92.1	327.1	103.7	50.5	79.2	183 495	991	3 140.2	1 386.1	1 077.2	1 296	1 276
Manistee	13.8	0.3	1.9	17.0	4.7	6.7	7.1	1 927	10	123.8	35.8	29.9	1 204	1 188
Marquette	39.9	3.9	6.0	56.9	16.2	5.5	12.8	16 742	126	229.2	105.6	60.6	930	909
Mason	7.5	0.0	36.9	23.6	10.1	1.5	0.3	6 867	39	126.4	48.1	51.0	1 775	1 755
Mecosta	9.9	0.1	2.2	32.5	6.6	2.5	1.2	4 027	35	172.1	75.0	42.8	1 018	966
Menominee	6.5	0.0	2.3	22.4	5.7	2.7	6.2	2 763	29	67.3	39.5	17.7	729	723
Midland	25.1	0.5	10.4	47.3	14.0	4.6	11.2	19 326	123	318.8	137.8	120.5	1 455	1 442
Missaukee	2.9	0.0	0.8	11.1	3.2	1.5	0.2	2 785	19	48.0	28.7	10.7	712	711
Monroe	23.8	1.1	5.6	72.5	25.0	10.1	4.8	19 896	117	529.2	247.3	182.9	1 191	1 160
Montcalm	24.0	0.0	3.4	62.7	19.0	5.6	20.6	6 746	59	226.2	136.9	54.1	859	843
Montmorency	1.3	0.0	0.3	12.4	2.4	0.9	0.0	2 032	20	28.6	10.5	9.9	963	945
Muskegon	41.1	37.2	6.6	195.6	44.5	17.7	13.4	16 996	106	697.5	353.7	177.1	1 016	945
Newaygo	7.0	0.0	1.5	34.3	10.7	3.4	0.8	3 695	37	165.6	98.2	44.2	899	895
Oakland	481.6	251.4	458.6	568.3	166.3	68.0	525.3	236 985	1 230	5 275.9	2 006.3	2 211.2	1 833	1 775
Oceana	6.1	0.0	8.6	23.6	6.7	1.9	0.1	2 244	32	94.2	40.2	28.1	1 009	1 004
Ogemaw	5.5	0.0	1.3	22.9	3.8	1.2	0.2	4 669	29	91.6	30.1	18.2	852	837
Ontonagon	3.4	0.3	1.5	14.4	1.8	0.8	0.1	1 379	9	42.5	15.9	10.1	1 448	1 444
Osceola	5.2	1.7	1.3	34.0	5.9	1.8	1.2	2 290	19	73.3	43.8	19.9	860	856
Oscoda	4.3	0.0	0.5	5.3	2.0	0.8	0.3	1 250	15	22.0	10.5	8.9	1 000	986
Otsego	15.6	0.1	7.3	19.9	4.1	1.2	0.3	2 818	17	83.1	32.7	36.9	1 524	1 522
Ottawa	41.7	105.5	62.4	68.2	32.7	11.3	12.0	75 699	434	809.0	388.8	287.7	1 110	1 090
Presque Isle	3.9	0.0	0.9	20.3	3.1	1.0	0.3	3 009	20	43.2	23.9	14.0	1 009	1 007
Roscommon	3.0	0.1	0.9	20.2	6.0	1.8	0.4	4 623	28	98.6	35.8	42.1	1 648	1 638
Saginaw	102.1	16.2	31.3	262.1	58.9	19.0	55.0	25 203	137	749.6	432.9	168.2	831	732
St. Clair	61.2	29.9	32.5	124.4	31.1	11.4	16.6	7 777	54	658.0	342.3	201.9	1 187	1 129
St. Joseph	10.5	0.0	2.2	52.0	11.7	5.4	0.4	4 877	32	295.4	119.3	58.7	939	932
Sanilac	9.6	6.0	2.6	43.9	9.6	3.1	0.2	2 192	23	173.6	103.6	38.4	880	863
Schoolcraft	3.7	1.6	0.8	19.2	2.2	1.3	2.3	1 693	19	55.8	13.0	8.3	980	978
Shiawassee	19.3	0.0	2.8	55.4	13.2	5.1	0.3	4 742	29	239.9	146.3	52.0	725	712
Tuscola	12.0	0.2	2.8	55.7	13.2	5.3	0.6	3 234	29	205.1	120.6	43.4	765	750
Van Buren	18.0	0.9	4.8	110.9	24.3	4.7	15.3	12 871	78	396.4	182.4	90.3	1 158	1 145
Washtenaw	231.6	107.4	209.4	1 194.4	49.9	31.5	388.9	56 890	368	1 351.8	485.7	589.1	1 683	1 660
Wayne	1 265.6	104.6	779.9	3 645.7	580.9	207.1	501.2	128 178	735	10 286.1	4 751.5	3 099.1	1 561	1 241
Wexford	18.9	156.4	5.4	33.6	6.7	2.0	3.2	4 675	39	118.2	58.3	38.8	1 220	1 217
MINNESOTA	3 368.3	1 520.3	1 430.1	6 006.5	1 249.2	755.2	2 516.9	1 810 528	9 840	X	X	X	X	X
Aitkin	3.9	0.0	0.8	38.4	3.5	1.0	0.3	17 396	112	60.2	33.8	14.9	937	923
Anoka	34.9	235.7	27.8	94.1	42.6	15.6	7.2	137 994	642	1 183.6	640.5	333.1	1 021	972
Becker	18.3	0.1	7.4	64.8	14.7	3.0	8.3	19 181	157	115.4	67.0	25.5	798	774
Beltrami	29.7	0.6	7.4	91.2	15.8	13.9	9.9	7 519	65	203.3	126.1	30.4	698	641
Benton	32.4	0.0	1.1	28.8	5.1	1.4	0.0	7 521	41	118.6	66.4	31.7	802	765
Big Stone	3.9	0.0	0.6	10.7	1.7	0.5	0.4	2 023	14	41.9	15.6	5.0	927	904
Blue Earth	55.6	0.5	5.8	63.1	11.8	4.3	13.0	29 269	174	257.9	130.0	57.0	952	840
Brown	14.9	0.1	1.8	21.5	4.2	1.4	2.8	4 344	27	110.6	56.7	21.8	839	776
Carlton	9.8	0.1	1.7	51.0	8.4	4.8	7.0	8 081	68	155.6	77.7	27.8	819	797
Carver	24.1	0.4	35.9	17.5	7.2	2.4	7.2	81 103	294	352.7	144.2	117.4	1 327	1 220
Cass	15.8	0.2	5.7	81.7	11.4	8.4	13.1	25 985	158	122.5	70.5	29.1	1 012	1 000
Chippewa	15.8	3.0	0.7	13.9	5.7	0.9	2.2	438	3	57.2	32.7	11.3	909	881
Chisago	9.5	0.4	2.3	21.4	5.9	1.8	0.5	7 312	43	176.2	81.7	53.3	1 064	1 029
Clay	24.9	50.0	2.7	50.3	11.4	3.4	6.8	33 931	211	239.6	129.1	34.5	628	588
Clearwater	2.6	0.0	0.6	34.1	3.0	1.3	0.5	305	3	35.6	21.7	8.5	1 032	1 028
Cook	7.8	0.0	1.5	6.0	1.1	0.5	12.7	4 478	37	37.4	12.6	8.0	1 483	1 196
Cottonwood	4.7	0.0	1.0	12.8	2.5	1.1	1.5	850	5	62.8	29.1	10.4	920	910
Crow Wing	34.0	3.0	4.5	84.3	11.8	3.7	10.9	34 573	207	303.6	124.4	74.4	1 207	1 141
Dakota	468.3	405.0	57.4	70.7	39.5	15.9	34.0	119 754	507	1 549.7	719.4	460.5	1 179	1 126
Dodge	3.5	0.0	0.8	12.8	3.0	1.0	0.7	8 022	39	78.5	40.4	15.8	810	794
Douglas	16.1	0.4	2.4	48.0	7.1	1.8	5.4	36 111	396	181.2	62.4	34.6	959	908
Faribault	4.5	0.0	1.4	20.3	3.4	1.1	6.0	1 652	9	76.1	30.9	11.5	772	745

1. State totals may include programs not allocated by county.   2. Based on the resident population estimated as of July 1 of the year shown.

Table B. States and Counties — Local Government Finances, Government Employment, and Voting

STATE County	Total (mil dol)	Per capita[1] (dollars)	Education	Health and hospitals	Police protection	Public welfare	Highways	Total (mil dol)	Per capita[1] (dollars)	Federal civilian	Federal military	State and local	Democratic	Republican	All other
	185	186	187	188	189	190	191	192	193	194	195	196	197	198	199
MICHIGAN—Cont'd															
Keweenaw	7.6	3 522	1.7	0.9	5.7	2.6	34.8	2.0	917	35	0	121	43.3	53.6	3.1
Lake	32.5	2 914	35.8	1.8	4.0	1.7	15.5	34.0	3 050	67	20	448	55.2	42.9	2.0
Lapeer	277.5	3 016	50.7	6.6	4.0	5.9	8.2	204.1	2 218	173	166	4 307	47.3	50.3	2.4
Leelanau	60.9	2 782	39.5	2.8	3.4	0.8	8.8	44.4	2 027	143	40	1 879	50.9	48.0	1.2
Lenawee	365.4	3 610	56.4	6.0	3.3	4.2	6.8	373.6	3 690	226	182	4 895	51.6	46.6	1.8
Livingston	583.8	3 187	57.4	5.5	3.1	0.4	5.3	1 146.7	6 260	278	334	5 757	42.5	55.8	1.7
Luce	53.5	7 955	19.9	57.8	0.9	0.2	7.8	15.4	2 283	17	12	881	43.5	54.4	2.2
Mackinac	65.3	6 007	24.4	31.6	2.5	0.1	13.4	58.0	5 330	62	65	1 032	47.3	51.1	1.6
Macomb	3 218.2	3 872	55.3	6.3	6.7	2.1	4.5	3 339.8	4 019	7 611	1 854	30 354	53.4	44.8	1.9
Manistee	118.4	4 773	31.0	30.9	2.1	7.2	5.7	87.8	3 540	102	65	2 741	55.6	42.4	2.0
Marquette	222.1	3 405	43.5	2.7	3.3	5.8	10.9	152.3	2 335	317	141	5 893	59.2	38.9	1.9
Mason	131.3	4 567	61.4	0.9	2.5	6.0	7.1	61.9	2 151	106	67	1 847	51.3	46.9	1.7
Mecosta	166.3	3 951	44.4	26.0	3.2	0.6	5.0	90.2	2 142	96	77	4 520	48.8	49.5	1.7
Menominee	62.1	2 560	54.5	3.8	6.2	0.6	10.2	23.4	963	79	44	2 312	54.0	43.8	2.1
Midland	281.0	3 392	53.7	2.5	3.8	1.8	6.9	271.3	3 276	161	151	3 207	47.4	50.9	1.7
Missaukee	52.7	3 517	36.7	24.7	3.1	0.7	18.3	8.1	541	35	27	503	38.7	59.7	1.7
Monroe	519.5	3 382	55.8	6.3	3.9	0.7	7.7	565.9	3 684	263	280	5 666	51.3	46.9	1.8
Montcalm	232.1	3 688	60.2	3.0	2.2	0.6	5.7	188.6	2 996	143	114	3 057	48.8	49.1	2.0
Montmorency	26.2	2 539	33.7	0.9	4.2	0.7	10.5	14.9	1 442	23	18	375	44.8	53.0	2.2
Muskegon	748.6	4 293	53.1	10.7	3.7	2.9	4.2	815.1	4 674	366	343	8 265	63.9	34.6	1.5
Newaygo	165.2	3 360	60.4	7.4	2.5	4.9	6.0	148.8	3 027	115	89	2 307	46.7	51.3	2.0
Oakland	5 346.4	4 433	64.0	5.3	5.8	0.4	5.5	5 480.4	4 544	4 523	2 317	49 242	56.5	42.0	1.4
Oceana	88.3	3 175	42.3	5.3	3.4	14.9	11.0	248.8	8 951	175	50	1 519	51.2	46.8	2.0
Ogemaw	93.7	4 391	24.7	46.1	2.8	1.4	8.9	43.5	2 040	60	39	1 158	50.1	47.7	2.3
Ontonagon	41.1	5 894	34.7	29.5	1.5	0.1	16.6	27.7	3 964	44	12	355	50.6	46.9	2.5
Osceola	74.5	3 221	58.7	2.8	3.4	0.5	9.7	55.4	2 394	61	41	1 004	44.0	54.2	1.8
Oscoda	21.7	2 425	47.9	3.3	4.1	1.6	16.3	5.5	616	73	16	322	43.6	53.6	2.8
Otsego	79.3	3 275	46.7	2.4	2.4	1.0	11.8	65.4	2 700	170	44	1 052	44.7	53.5	1.8
Ottawa	823.2	3 176	56.8	5.0	3.3	1.0	7.2	1 132.8	4 370	459	546	13 567	37.3	61.2	1.5
Presque Isle	41.6	3 004	37.2	0.8	3.2	1.1	13.8	16.3	1 174	61	25	572	49.6	48.0	2.4
Roscommon	100.7	3 946	60.3	2.3	3.5	1.0	7.9	30.0	1 177	37	45	1 395	50.4	47.9	1.7
Saginaw	770.9	3 811	48.9	13.1	4.2	0.7	5.5	503.7	2 490	1 197	386	10 344	57.9	40.6	1.5
St. Clair	648.9	3 815	47.3	12.8	3.9	0.9	7.7	468.1	2 752	681	378	6 611	50.3	47.6	2.1
St. Joseph	304.3	4 873	44.3	33.5	2.2	0.4	3.7	269.0	4 308	120	113	3 569	47.9	50.1	1.9
Sanilac	175.3	4 017	42.5	12.0	2.6	5.1	10.3	155.3	3 558	124	77	1 872	44.9	52.9	2.2
Schoolcraft	56.4	6 621	26.4	35.6	1.8	12.1	9.0	26.1	3 067	53	15	1 101	50.5	47.6	1.9
Shiawassee	256.4	3 573	62.3	6.3	2.7	5.4	6.5	152.9	2 191	148	128	3 618	53.3	44.7	2.1
Tuscola	209.4	3 686	62.3	2.0	2.9	5.8	8.5	163.4	2 876	152	102	3 083	48.6	49.4	2.0
Van Buren	395.8	5 079	48.3	26.6	2.2	0.7	6.3	452.0	5 799	169	143	5 157	53.5	44.7	1.9
Washtenaw	1 453.7	4 153	53.1	3.4	5.9	0.9	5.5	1 701.4	4 861	2 917	690	67 464	69.8	28.8	1.4
Wayne	10 151.2	5 114	39.6	3.2	6.4	4.6	3.5	17 567.5	8 850	15 921	4 023	94 406	74.1	24.7	1.2
Wexford	110.1	3 463	55.0	0.0	3.6	1.5	8.3	58.2	1 832	148	59	1 904	47.0	51.2	1.8
MINNESOTA	X	X	X	X	X	X	X	X	X	33 825	20 620	362 034	54.1	43.8	2.1
Aitkin	60.6	3 809	34.9	1.3	3.9	8.3	18.9	38.5	2 421	57	59	774	48.8	48.8	2.4
Anoka	1 243.9	3 813	56.4	1.5	4.8	5.3	5.7	1 269.8	3 892	428	1 244	15 386	47.7	50.1	2.1
Becker	115.1	3 601	35.8	0.9	4.1	13.4	17.5	65.1	2 036	251	120	2 543	45.3	52.2	2.5
Beltrami	209.5	4 804	50.9	1.0	3.5	7.5	8.2	197.0	4 517	269	166	4 671	54.1	43.9	2.0
Benton	106.3	2 692	46.4	0.8	4.2	7.9	13.6	247.7	6 271	87	152	1 491	43.7	53.5	2.8
Big Stone	40.2	7 474	24.3	36.8	3.2	5.6	11.9	322.1	59 808	42	20	588	51.9	45.6	2.5
Blue Earth	263.0	4 397	42.1	0.5	4.1	6.7	15.1	240.4	4 020	340	231	5 083	55.1	42.1	2.7
Brown	105.1	4 040	35.2	10.2	5.0	7.4	14.7	121.8	4 683	82	96	1 598	42.7	54.7	2.6
Carlton	163.0	4 809	38.6	22.3	7.3	7.5	7.9	189.5	5 591	86	129	4 903	62.3	35.5	2.2
Carver	432.6	4 890	49.9	0.7	3.4	4.4	8.4	753.1	8 513	235	346	4 236	41.6	56.7	1.8
Cass	122.9	4 280	45.2	2.3	4.5	7.8	10.8	85.6	2 979	224	107	3 969	44.6	53.1	2.3
Chippewa	61.4	4 925	47.6	0.5	4.8	13.1	13.2	39.0	3 129	53	46	1 024	51.6	45.7	2.7
Chisago	192.6	3 841	42.0	1.2	4.1	6.5	13.9	265.2	5 291	111	190	2 406	43.6	53.9	2.5
Clay	257.0	4 688	32.2	2.3	4.1	7.3	10.5	467.4	8 523	121	213	4 098	57.0	40.9	2.1
Clearwater	37.5	4 543	43.6	0.0	3.9	10.2	17.7	36.9	4 477	34	31	611	44.1	53.8	2.2
Cook	35.3	6 542	18.6	28.9	5.1	5.1	12.1	24.9	4 615	162	20	821	60.3	37.0	2.7
Cottonwood	66.7	5 881	31.9	21.9	2.8	6.7	10.4	59.8	5 266	67	42	851	45.7	52.3	2.0
Crow Wing	314.2	5 097	31.5	16.4	4.0	5.9	9.5	389.3	6 314	185	236	4 215	45.1	52.8	2.1
Dakota	1 608.1	4 118	52.4	0.7	4.8	5.7	7.0	2 275.4	5 827	2 404	1 488	18 005	51.8	46.3	1.9
Dodge	76.8	3 930	44.6	1.3	5.0	14.8	11.4	71.7	3 669	48	74	1 155	43.7	53.5	2.8
Douglas	178.7	4 954	29.6	34.2	2.8	4.2	7.3	117.2	3 248	137	136	3 001	44.2	53.7	2.0
Faribault	76.1	5 119	31.0	23.5	3.7	1.7	13.7	42.0	2 823	62	54	1 122	45.8	51.5	2.7

1. Based on the resident population estimated as of July 1 of the year shown.   2. © 2009 Election Data Services, Inc. All rights reserved.

STATE/ County code	CBSA code[1]	County type[2]	STATE County	Land area,[3] (sq km) 2010	Total persons	Rank	Per square kilometer	White	Black	American Indian, Alaska Native	Asian and Pacific Islander	Percent Hispanic or Latino[4]	Under 5 years	5 to 17 years	18 to 24 years	25 to 34 years	35 to 44 years	45 to 54 years
				1	2	3	4	5	6	7	8	9	10	11	12	13	14	15
			MINNESOTA—Cont'd															
27 045	...	8	Fillmore	2 231	20 866	1 797	9.4	98.3	0.5	0.3	0.6	1.0	6.9	17.3	6.5	10.9	11.1	15.1
27 047	10660	7	Freeborn	1 831	31 255	1 410	17.1	89.5	1.0	0.5	1.1	8.8	6.1	15.8	7.2	10.7	11.2	15.3
27 049	39860	4	Goodhue	1 960	46 183	1 039	23.6	94.4	1.5	1.5	1.0	2.9	6.3	17.4	7.0	11.5	11.8	16.2
27 051	...	9	Grant	1 420	6 018	2 764	4.2	97.8	0.6	0.5	0.4	1.6	6.2	15.2	6.0	10.8	9.9	15.6
27 053	33460	1	Hennepin	1 434	1 152 425	34	803.6	74.0	13.2	1.5	7.2	6.7	6.6	16.1	9.9	16.3	13.4	14.8
27 055	29100	3	Houston	1 430	19 027	1 878	13.3	98.1	1.0	0.4	0.8	0.7	5.9	17.2	6.8	10.3	11.4	16.8
27 057	...	7	Hubbard	2 397	20 428	1 822	8.5	95.2	0.7	3.7	0.4	1.6	6.2	15.7	6.0	9.3	10.6	15.8
27 059	33460	1	Isanti	1 129	37 816	1 221	33.5	96.5	1.0	1.1	1.3	1.5	7.2	18.8	8.0	13.0	13.2	16.4
27 061	...	6	Itasca	6 909	45 058	1 064	6.5	94.9	0.7	4.8	0.6	0.9	5.5	16.4	6.9	10.1	10.8	15.5
27 063	...	7	Jackson	1 821	10 266	2 420	5.6	95.3	0.8	0.3	1.7	2.7	5.9	16.7	7.0	10.3	11.3	15.7
27 065	...	6	Kanabec	1 351	16 239	2 039	12.0	97.4	0.7	1.4	0.6	1.3	6.0	18.0	6.6	10.9	12.0	16.4
27 067	48820	4	Kandiyohi	2 064	42 239	1 121	20.5	85.8	2.5	0.5	0.7	11.2	6.9	17.1	9.5	11.6	11.0	14.8
27 069	...	9	Kittson	2 846	4 552	2 866	1.6	97.8	0.3	0.3	0.5	1.5	4.9	16.7	5.3	7.8	10.5	16.0
27 071	...	7	Koochiching	8 040	13 311	2 231	1.7	95.6	0.9	3.5	0.5	1.1	4.8	16.1	6.8	8.9	11.4	16.5
27 073	...	9	Lac qui Parle	1 981	7 259	2 663	3.7	97.7	0.5	0.4	0.7	1.5	5.2	15.9	5.1	8.8	9.6	16.3
27 075	...	6	Lake	5 463	10 866	2 379	2.0	98.3	0.4	1.2	0.5	0.7	5.4	13.6	6.5	9.8	10.0	16.6
27 077	...	9	Lake of the Woods	3 361	4 045	2 903	1.2	97.2	0.6	2.1	1.2	0.9	5.2	15.0	5.2	8.6	10.2	18.5
27 079	...	6	Le Sueur	1 162	27 703	1 508	23.8	93.5	0.5	0.6	0.9	5.2	6.7	18.7	6.7	12.1	13.1	15.7
27 081	...	9	Lincoln	1 390	5 896	2 779	4.2	98.1	0.4	0.4	0.4	1.2	6.5	15.8	5.7	10.2	10.4	14.1
27 083	32140	7	Lyon	1 851	25 857	1 572	14.0	88.6	2.8	0.7	3.1	6.0	7.2	17.0	13.4	13.2	11.0	13.9
27 085	26780	6	McLeod	1 273	36 651	1 258	28.8	93.5	0.8	0.4	1.1	4.9	6.7	18.6	7.4	12.2	13.1	15.0
27 087	...	8	Mahnomen	1 445	5 413	2 811	3.7	57.9	0.6	48.0	0.1	1.8	8.9	20.4	7.3	10.9	10.2	13.8
27 089	...	8	Marshall	4 597	9 439	2 484	2.1	95.5	0.4	0.9	0.3	3.6	5.8	17.8	5.7	10.6	11.4	15.7
27 091	21860	7	Martin	1 845	20 840	1 798	11.3	95.3	0.5	0.4	0.7	3.6	5.8	16.4	6.5	10.2	10.4	15.7
27 093	...	6	Meeker	1 575	23 300	1 680	14.8	95.9	0.5	0.4	0.4	3.3	7.0	18.4	6.7	10.9	11.6	15.6
27 095	...	6	Mille Lacs	1 482	26 097	1 559	17.6	91.9	0.8	6.9	0.6	1.4	7.1	18.2	7.7	11.8	12.4	15.2
27 097	...	6	Morrison	2 914	33 198	1 346	11.4	97.9	0.6	0.8	0.6	1.2	6.8	17.7	7.6	11.8	11.7	15.7
27 099	12380	4	Mower	1 842	39 163	1 191	21.3	85.3	2.7	0.5	2.1	10.6	7.2	18.0	8.1	12.0	11.4	14.1
27 101	...	9	Murray	1 825	8 725	2 550	4.8	96.0	0.4	0.4	1.0	2.8	6.0	16.2	5.9	9.5	10.1	15.1
27 103	31860	5	Nicollet	1 162	32 727	1 370	28.2	92.6	2.5	0.6	1.8	3.7	6.5	16.0	15.0	13.4	11.0	14.1
27 105	49380	7	Nobles	1 852	21 378	1 769	11.5	68.0	3.8	0.6	5.9	22.5	7.9	17.7	9.0	12.5	11.7	13.8
27 107	...	8	Norman	2 261	6 852	2 700	3.0	93.8	0.5	3.1	0.6	4.0	6.0	18.3	5.4	9.6	10.5	15.8
27 109	40340	3	Olmsted	1 692	144 248	430	85.3	85.1	5.5	0.5	6.3	4.2	7.5	17.8	7.8	15.3	12.6	15.4
27 111	22260	6	Otter Tail	5 108	57 303	885	11.2	95.6	1.0	1.0	0.8	2.6	5.8	16.0	6.6	9.9	10.1	15.9
27 113	...	6	Pennington	1 597	13 930	2 182	8.7	93.9	1.7	2.3	0.9	2.7	6.8	17.0	9.0	12.5	11.8	14.7
27 115	...	6	Pine	3 655	29 750	1 433	8.1	92.1	2.4	4.0	0.8	2.4	5.8	16.4	7.1	12.6	12.7	16.4
27 117	...	6	Pipestone	1 204	9 596	2 472	8.0	93.9	1.0	1.9	1.0	3.7	6.9	18.0	6.8	10.4	11.0	15.0
27 119	24220	3	Polk	5 105	31 600	1 403	6.2	91.7	1.1	2.3	1.0	5.4	6.6	17.2	10.3	11.0	11.0	14.8
27 121	...	8	Pope	1 735	10 995	2 366	6.3	98.2	0.6	0.6	0.5	0.9	5.9	15.3	6.2	10.9	10.5	14.9
27 123	33460	1	Ramsey	394	508 640	127	1 291.0	69.2	12.3	1.4	12.6	7.2	6.9	16.4	12.1	15.2	12.0	13.9
27 125	...	8	Red Lake	1 120	4 089	2 898	3.7	96.0	0.6	1.9	0.2	2.5	6.9	17.7	5.8	12.4	10.5	16.0
27 127	...	7	Redwood	2 275	16 059	2 048	7.1	89.4	0.8	5.9	3.6	2.1	6.7	18.3	6.7	10.1	11.1	14.6
27 129	...	9	Renville	2 546	15 730	2 067	6.2	92.2	0.5	1.0	0.6	6.6	5.7	17.5	6.5	10.3	11.0	16.3
27 131	22060	4	Rice	1 284	64 142	813	50.0	86.3	3.7	0.7	2.6	8.0	6.3	17.3	14.4	11.9	12.5	14.4
27 133	...	6	Rock	1 250	9 687	2 461	7.7	96.4	0.9	0.7	1.1	2.0	7.1	18.8	6.2	10.9	11.0	14.3
27 135	...	7	Roseau	4 329	15 629	2 073	3.6	95.2	0.5	2.0	2.9	0.7	6.4	19.8	6.3	10.4	13.3	17.2
27 137	20260	2	St. Louis	16 181	200 226	311	12.4	94.3	2.1	3.3	1.3	1.2	5.5	14.3	12.5	11.6	10.8	15.1
27 139	33460	1	Scott	923	129 928	477	140.8	86.2	3.2	1.3	6.5	4.4	8.2	22.0	6.3	13.9	17.1	15.8
27 141	33460	1	Sherburne	1 121	88 499	643	78.9	94.1	2.5	1.0	1.8	2.2	7.7	21.4	8.5	14.0	15.7	15.1
27 143	...	8	Sibley	1 525	15 226	2 096	10.0	91.7	0.5	0.4	0.9	7.2	6.9	18.8	6.6	11.7	11.8	16.0
27 145	41060	3	Stearns	3 479	150 642	415	43.3	91.8	3.7	0.6	2.4	2.8	6.5	16.7	15.6	13.1	11.5	13.9
27 147	36940	5	Steele	1 113	36 576	1 261	32.9	90.0	3.3	0.5	1.0	6.2	7.3	19.1	7.1	12.3	13.0	14.9
27 149	...	7	Stevens	1 460	9 726	2 458	6.7	93.4	1.1	1.8	1.8	3.5	6.2	14.8	19.5	10.6	9.2	12.3
27 151	...	7	Swift	1 922	9 783	2 455	5.1	95.4	0.9	0.5	0.3	3.6	5.7	16.6	6.9	10.4	11.2	15.5
27 153	...	6	Todd	2 447	24 895	1 605	10.2	93.6	0.7	0.8	0.8	5.2	6.8	18.2	7.4	10.5	10.7	15.4
27 155	...	9	Traverse	1 486	3 558	2 938	2.4	94.4	0.6	4.5	0.2	1.4	4.9	16.9	5.8	8.9	9.6	14.6
27 157	40340	3	Wabasha	1 355	21 676	1 756	16.0	96.3	0.7	0.4	0.7	2.7	6.1	17.2	6.7	10.8	12.3	15.9
27 159	...	7	Wadena	1 389	13 843	2 193	10.0	97.1	1.3	1.4	0.5	1.3	6.6	17.4	7.3	10.0	10.5	14.5
27 161	...	7	Waseca	1 096	19 136	1 872	17.5	91.4	2.5	1.0	0.9	5.1	6.4	17.3	7.2	13.9	12.6	15.4
27 163	33460	1	Washington	995	238 136	270	239.3	87.4	4.3	0.9	5.8	3.4	6.4	20.3	7.2	12.1	14.4	17.0
27 165	...	7	Watonwan	1 127	11 211	2 349	9.9	77.5	0.8	0.3	1.0	20.9	6.9	18.2	7.2	11.0	11.0	14.2
27 167	47420	6	Wilkin	1 945	6 576	2 722	3.4	96.6	0.4	1.4	0.4	2.0	5.6	18.3	6.7	9.8	11.7	17.4
27 169	49100	4	Winona	1 622	51 461	957	31.7	93.9	1.6	0.5	2.5	2.4	5.3	14.1	21.3	11.1	9.9	13.2
27 171	33460	1	Wright	1 713	124 700	486	72.8	94.9	1.6	0.7	1.7	2.4	8.6	21.4	6.6	14.0	15.4	14.8
27 173	...	9	Yellow Medicine	1 966	10 438	2 409	5.3	92.7	0.4	3.6	0.4	3.8	6.3	17.4	7.2	10.9	10.8	15.4

1. CBSA = Core Based Statistical Area. See Appendix A for explanation. See Appendix B for list of metropolitan areas with component counties. Service of USDA Rural-Urban Continuum Codes. See Appendix A for definition. 3. Dry land or land partially or temporarily covered by water. 2. County type code from the Economic Research 4. May be of any race.

Table B. States and Counties — **Population and Households**

STATE County	55 to 64 years	65 to 74 years	75 years and over	Percent female	Total persons 1990	Total persons 2000	Percent change 1990–2000	Percent change 2000–2010	Births	Deaths	Net migration	Households 2010 Number	Percent change 2000–2010	Persons per household	Female family householder[1]	One person
	16	17	18	19	20	21	22	23	24	25	26	27	28	29	30	31
MINNESOTA—Cont'd																
Fillmore	13.1	8.8	10.4	50.3	20 777	21 122	1.7	-1.2	2 559	2 256	-447	8 545	3.9	2.40	7.0	28.3
Freeborn	13.5	9.7	10.5	50.5	33 060	32 584	-1.4	-4.1	3 478	3 369	-1 504	13 177	-1.3	2.32	8.5	30.1
Goodhue	13.4	8.1	8.4	50.4	40 690	44 127	8.4	4.7	5 239	3 986	748	18 730	10.3	2.42	8.3	27.1
Grant	14.2	10.6	11.6	50.6	6 246	6 289	0.7	-4.3	633	782	-267	2 601	2.6	2.27	6.3	30.4
Hennepin	11.6	5.8	5.6	50.9	1 032 431	1 116 200	8.1	3.2	152 041	71 349	-34 429	475 913	4.3	2.37	10.3	32.7
Houston	14.2	8.1	9.3	50.4	18 497	19 718	6.6	-3.5	2 021	1 705	-672	7 849	2.8	2.39	8.2	26.9
Hubbard	15.6	12.0	8.7	49.6	14 939	18 376	23.0	11.2	1 965	1 606	-3	8 661	16.5	2.34	7.4	26.8
Isanti	11.2	7.0	5.4	49.6	25 921	31 287	20.7	20.9	4 347	2 300	6 188	13 972	24.4	2.67	8.9	21.5
Itasca	16.0	10.3	8.7	49.5	40 844	43 992	7.7	2.4	4 558	4 350	805	18 773	5.5	2.35	8.2	28.2
Jackson	13.2	8.6	11.3	49.4	11 677	11 268	-3.5	-8.9	1 038	1 121	-346	4 429	-2.8	2.29	7.1	30.9
Kanabec	13.7	9.4	6.9	49.4	12 802	14 996	17.1	8.3	1 702	1 165	414	6 413	11.4	2.49	8.5	24.9
Kandiyohi	12.8	8.0	8.2	50.1	38 761	41 203	6.3	2.5	5 402	3 369	-1 854	16 732	5.0	2.46	8.6	26.7
Kittson	16.2	10.1	12.5	49.8	5 767	5 285	-8.4	-13.9	401	641	-648	1 986	-8.4	2.24	5.1	33.7
Koochiching	15.9	10.2	9.4	50.4	16 299	14 355	-11.9	-7.3	1 186	1 448	-889	5 874	-2.7	2.23	8.8	32.4
Lac qui Parle	15.3	10.3	13.4	50.0	8 924	8 067	-9.6	-10.0	660	952	-622	3 155	-4.9	2.25	5.9	30.7
Lake	15.7	11.3	11.0	49.6	10 415	11 058	6.2	-1.7	926	1 293	-25	4 825	3.9	2.21	6.7	30.5
Lake of the Woods	17.1	11.1	9.2	48.9	4 076	4 522	10.9	-10.5	376	414	-597	1 784	-6.3	2.24	6.0	29.8
Le Sueur	12.6	7.8	6.5	49.5	23 239	25 426	9.4	9.0	3 269	1 944	1 459	10 758	11.7	2.55	7.3	23.8
Lincoln	12.9	10.9	13.6	49.8	6 890	6 429	-6.7	-8.3	634	866	-437	2 574	-3.0	2.24	5.1	34.0
Lyon	10.7	6.2	7.4	50.3	24 789	25 425	2.6	1.7	3 143	2 104	-1 277	10 227	5.3	2.42	7.9	29.6
McLeod	11.7	7.7	7.6	50.1	32 030	34 898	9.0	5.0	4 846	2 703	123	14 639	8.8	2.47	7.7	27.1
Mahnomen	12.7	8.6	7.2	49.2	5 044	5 190	2.9	4.3	803	474	-473	2 019	2.5	2.64	16.6	26.3
Marshall	13.8	9.5	9.7	49.3	10 993	10 155	-7.6	-7.1	989	824	-1 116	3 981	-2.9	2.35	6.3	28.8
Martin	14.2	9.2	11.5	50.9	22 914	21 802	-4.9	-4.4	2 210	2 261	-1 386	9 035	-0.4	2.27	7.9	31.4
Meeker	13.3	8.4	8.1	49.2	20 846	22 644	8.6	2.9	2 896	2 131	-113	9 176	6.8	2.50	7.0	25.6
Mille Lacs	11.4	8.5	7.6	49.8	18 670	22 330	19.6	16.9	3 148	2 291	3 277	10 166	17.7	2.52	10.6	26.6
Morrison	12.6	8.1	8.0	49.6	29 604	31 712	7.1	4.7	4 003	2 827	208	13 080	10.7	2.60	8.2	26.4
Mower	11.7	7.3	10.1	50.2	37 385	38 603	3.3	1.5	4 967	3 639	-1 487	15 828	1.6	2.43	9.6	30.0
Murray	14.8	10.4	11.9	50.4	9 660	9 165	-5.1	-4.8	866	903	-675	3 717	-0.1	2.30	5.4	29.5
Nicollet	11.8	6.2	5.7	50.0	28 076	29 771	6.0	9.9	3 659	1 817	789	12 201	14.6	2.46	9.0	26.3
Nobles	11.3	7.3	8.7	48.9	20 098	20 832	3.7	2.6	3 022	1 689	-1 501	7 946	0.1	2.64	8.4	26.7
Norman	13.0	9.5	11.9	50.1	7 975	7 442	-6.7	-7.9	672	931	-690	2 863	-4.9	2.34	7.2	32.0
Olmsted	11.1	6.6	5.9	51.1	106 470	124 277	16.7	16.1	19 681	7 540	8 425	57 080	19.4	2.48	8.9	27.2
Otter Tail	14.9	10.7	10.3	49.9	50 714	57 159	12.7	0.3	5 652	5 927	66	24 055	6.1	2.33	6.5	28.3
Pennington	12.3	7.7	8.1	50.7	13 306	13 584	2.1	2.5	1 702	1 297	-71	5 836	5.6	2.33	10.0	31.0
Pine	12.7	9.4	6.9	46.4	21 264	26 530	24.8	12.1	2 984	2 299	1 281	11 373	14.4	2.46	9.1	26.7
Pipestone	12.1	8.1	11.7	51.3	10 491	9 895	-5.7	-3.0	1 184	1 186	-482	4 054	-0.4	2.32	7.6	32.2
Polk	12.6	7.8	8.7	49.9	32 589	31 369	-3.7	0.7	3 445	3 284	-566	12 704	5.3	2.38	9.2	30.1
Pope	15.0	10.4	10.9	49.5	10 745	11 236	4.6	-2.1	1 117	1 336	-70	4 736	4.9	2.28	6.7	29.5
Ramsey	11.6	6.0	6.1	51.5	485 760	511 035	5.2	-0.5	68 401	35 976	-35 361	202 691	0.7	2.42	12.6	33.1
Red Lake	13.5	8.9	8.2	49.1	4 525	4 299	-5.0	-4.9	456	411	-132	1 737	0.8	2.33	6.3	30.5
Redwood	12.8	9.2	10.5	50.4	17 254	16 815	-2.5	-4.5	1 890	1 893	-1 260	6 580	-1.4	2.38	8.0	31.4
Renville	13.3	8.8	10.5	49.5	17 673	17 154	-2.9	-8.3	1 818	1 878	-1 288	6 564	-3.2	2.34	7.4	29.6
Rice	10.8	6.5	5.8	48.9	49 183	56 665	15.2	13.2	7 146	4 033	3 289	22 315	18.1	2.55	9.0	25.9
Rock	12.9	8.2	10.7	50.6	9 806	9 721	-0.9	-0.3	1 221	1 174	-232	3 918	2.0	2.41	6.8	29.1
Roseau	12.2	7.6	6.8	48.9	15 026	16 338	8.7	-4.3	1 958	1 241	-1 055	6 300	1.8	2.45	7.0	27.1
St. Louis	14.3	7.9	8.0	50.0	198 232	200 528	1.2	-0.2	19 487	19 592	-1 377	84 783	2.6	2.25	9.5	32.9
Scott	9.0	4.6	3.1	50.2	57 846	89 498	54.7	45.2	19 083	4 191	27 814	45 108	47.0	2.85	8.3	17.9
Sherburne	9.4	4.7	3.5	48.8	41 945	64 417	53.6	37.4	11 905	3 685	14 631	30 212	40.0	2.86	8.1	17.7
Sibley	12.0	7.8	8.4	49.8	14 366	15 356	6.9	-0.8	1 879	1 311	-922	6 034	4.5	2.49	7.4	27.2
Stearns	10.6	6.1	6.0	49.6	119 324	133 166	11.6	13.1	17 455	7 371	2 385	56 232	18.1	2.53	8.2	25.1
Steele	11.9	7.1	7.3	50.5	30 729	33 680	9.6	8.6	4 810	2 498	1 014	14 330	11.6	2.51	9.1	26.1
Stevens	11.1	6.7	9.7	50.7	10 634	10 053	-5.5	-3.3	1 005	736	-629	3 726	-0.7	2.37	5.7	29.6
Swift	13.6	8.7	11.4	49.7	10 724	11 956	11.5	-18.2	1 072	1 113	-1 069	4 236	-2.7	2.27	7.0	32.8
Todd	13.6	9.6	7.8	48.8	23 363	24 426	4.5	1.9	2 847	2 085	-1 175	9 756	4.4	2.52	6.9	26.4
Traverse	12.9	10.3	16.0	50.3	4 463	4 134	-7.4	-13.9	337	492	-389	1 524	-11.2	2.27	6.4	33.0
Wabasha	13.9	9.1	8.0	49.9	19 744	21 610	9.5	0.3	2 488	1 772	-300	8 822	6.6	2.43	6.8	25.4
Wadena	12.7	9.8	11.3	50.7	13 154	13 713	4.2	0.9	1 636	1 807	-206	5 705	5.1	2.34	8.7	32.2
Waseca	12.5	7.0	7.8	53.1	18 079	19 526	8.0	-2.0	2 389	1 554	-1 481	7 281	3.1	2.44	8.7	26.9
Washington	12.2	6.1	4.4	50.5	145 860	201 130	37.9	18.4	27 135	10 019	15 027	87 859	22.9	2.67	9.4	21.2
Watonwan	12.5	8.6	10.4	49.9	11 682	11 876	1.7	-5.6	1 459	1 089	-1 300	4 520	-2.3	2.45	8.6	29.5
Wilkin	12.7	8.1	9.6	49.3	7 516	7 138	-5.0	-7.9	709	657	-895	2 690	-2.3	2.39	6.4	28.6
Winona	11.7	6.8	6.6	50.8	47 828	49 985	4.5	3.0	5 002	3 696	-1 563	19 554	4.3	2.40	8.0	29.0
Wright	9.6	5.5	4.0	49.8	68 710	89 986	31.0	38.6	17 853	5 453	19 852	44 473	41.3	2.78	8.1	20.2
Yellow Medicine	12.6	8.9	10.6	49.0	11 684	11 080	-5.2	-5.8	1 165	1 225	-1 096	4 292	-3.3	2.36	6.7	29.4

1. No spouse present.

Table B. States and Counties — Population, Vital Statistics, Medicare, and Crime

STATE County	Persons in group quarters, 2010	Daytime population, 2006–2010		Births, average 2006–2008		Deaths, average 2006–2008		Persons under 65 with no health insurance, 2009		Medicare, 2011			Serious crimes known to police,[2] 2010 Total	
		Number	Employment/residence ratio	Total	Rate[1]	Number	Rate[1]	Number	Percent	Eligible for Medicare	Enrolled in Medicare Advantage	Enrolled in a Medicare prescription drug plan	Number	Rate[3]
	32	33	34	35	36	37	38	39	40	41	42	43	44	45
MINNESOTA—Cont'd														
Fillmore	359	17 705	0.7	D	D	226	10.8	2 294	13.8	4 362	1 665	2 001	73	350
Freeborn	637	29 863	0.9	D	D	344	11.0	3 062	12.5	7 137	2 864	3 430	568	1 817
Goodhue	901	44 961	1.0	D	D	424	9.2	3 577	9.5	8 549	4 027	3 266	1 030	2 230
Grant	110	5 595	0.8	D	D	83	13.8	510	11.6	1 559	695	766	96	1 595
Hennepin	25 084	1 356 471	1.4	16 746	14.8	7 700	6.8	103 890	10.3	156 234	76 291	50 915	43 947	3 813
Houston	257	15 584	0.6	D	D	177	9.1	1 491	9.6	3 874	1 254	1 868	214	1 324
Hubbard	154	18 375	0.8	D	D	174	9.2	1 750	12.1	4 907	1 989	2 265	577	2 825
Isanti	465	30 600	0.6	526	13.5	256	6.6	3 648	10.6	5 661	3 020	1 860	588	1 555
Itasca	1 021	43 639	0.9	D	D	460	10.3	4 053	11.2	10 373	3 801	3 986	831	1 844
Jackson	110	10 370	1.0	D	D	94	8.6	861	10.4	2 192	426	1 405	140	1 364
Kanabec	246	13 430	0.6	D	D	131	8.1	1 656	12.6	3 357	1 500	1 109	549	3 381
Kandiyohi	1 058	42 285	1.0	610	14.9	350	8.6	3 823	11.3	8 144	4 084	4 024	979	2 318
Kittson	111	4 258	0.8	D	D	71	15.6	445	13.5	1 105	374	589	35	769
Koochiching	241	13 331	1.0	D	D	165	12.3	1 268	12.3	3 154	1 402	1 623	317	2 381
Lac qui Parle	154	6 980	0.9	D	D	97	13.2	567	10.5	1 752	774	900	74	1 019
Lake	224	10 644	1.0	D	D	143	13.3	864	10.5	2 731	819	1 289	94	865
Lake of the Woods	53	3 845	0.9	D	D	42	10.1	428	14.4	964	362	401	15	371
Le Sueur	270	22 420	0.6	D	D	197	7.0	2 423	10.3	4 433	2 042	1 983	299	1 079
Lincoln	135	5 115	0.7	D	D	87	14.8	485	11.5	1 453	431	873	6	102
Lyon	1 092	27 845	1.2	374	15.1	225	9.1	2 404	11.5	4 235	1 182	2 635	461	1 783
McLeod	476	36 485	1.0	D	D	275	7.4	2 910	9.4	6 418	3 145	2 792	686	1 872
Mahnomen	79	6 132	1.3	D	D	57	11.2	602	14.3	858	319	419	25	462
Marshall	76	7 840	0.6	D	D	85	8.8	915	12.5	1 982	731	1 098	102	1 081
Martin	348	21 021	1.0	D	D	245	11.9	1 655	10.6	4 987	1 832	2 540	325	1 560
Meeker	354	20 019	0.7	D	D	223	9.6	1 976	10.5	4 351	2 500	1 788	491	2 107
Mille Lacs	523	25 559	1.0	375	14.3	263	10.0	3 030	14.0	5 220	2 699	1 831	598	2 291
Morrison	528	30 524	0.8	453	13.8	297	9.1	3 378	12.5	6 452	3 467	2 896	379	1 142
Mower	632	37 075	0.9	D	D	386	10.1	3 612	11.8	7 859	2 126	3 111	1 037	2 648
Murray	163	7 809	0.8	D	D	97	11.4	777	12.1	2 037	508	1 233	57	653
Nicollet	2 720	31 019	0.9	D	D	206	6.5	2 665	9.7	4 684	2 027	2 356	592	1 809
Nobles	385	21 852	1.1	D	D	179	8.8	2 449	14.5	3 825	897	2 246	317	1 483
Norman	149	6 058	0.8	D	D	100	14.8	675	13.5	1 571	569	796	47	686
Olmsted	2 770	156 650	1.2	2 288	16.4	845	6.1	9 402	7.6	21 396	5 719	6 960	3 009	2 086
Otter Tail	1 188	54 953	0.9	D	D	600	10.5	5 214	11.9	13 524	6 869	5 903	747	1 304
Pennington	327	15 955	1.3	D	D	129	9.4	1 241	10.9	2 594	1 088	1 302	186	1 335
Pine	1 797	26 536	0.8	D	D	253	8.9	3 154	13.5	5 567	2 815	1 877	810	2 723
Pipestone	205	9 600	1.0	D	D	128	13.6	882	12.1	1 938	452	1 203	118	1 230
Polk	1 330	29 575	0.9	D	D	360	11.7	2 817	11.2	5 987	2 171	3 025	573	1 813
Pope	184	10 269	0.9	D	D	141	12.7	931	11.0	2 448	1 128	1 184	80	728
Ramsey	18 384	566 705	1.3	7 685	15.4	3 767	7.6	49 687	11.5	73 891	35 926	23 140	21 734	4 367
Red Lake	34	3 281	0.6	D	D	45	10.8	427	12.7	794	487	435	20	489
Redwood	373	15 876	1.0	D	D	194	12.4	1 439	11.8	3 457	1 306	1 862	261	1 625
Renville	342	15 113	0.9	D	D	202	12.5	1 490	11.9	3 279	1 139	1 809	290	1 844
Rice	7 278	58 511	0.9	D	D	416	6.7	5 907	11.0	9 249	4 316	3 994	1 530	2 385
Rock	260	8 510	0.8	D	D	125	13.2	863	11.4	2 054	597	1 189	52	537
Roseau	191	16 552	1.1	D	D	127	7.9	1 522	11.3	2 600	1 381	1 045	96	614
St. Louis	9 433	207 371	1.1	2 148	10.9	2 065	10.5	18 281	11.2	39 807	14 525	15 624	6 898	3 445
Scott	1 287	103 176	0.7	2 119	16.7	495	3.9	10 131	8.4	12 238	6 119	4 171	2 830	2 178
Sherburne	2 174	67 643	0.6	1 355	15.7	406	4.7	7 260	9.1	9 409	4 746	3 065	1 612	1 821
Sibley	230	12 607	0.7	D	D	125	8.3	1 485	12.1	2 826	1 368	1 350	8	53
Stearns	8 213	155 418	1.1	1 983	13.6	801	5.5	12 801	10.1	21 961	9 704	9 519	3 865	2 566
Steele	594	38 357	1.1	D	D	260	7.2	2 815	9.1	5 991	2 872	2 539	638	1 845
Stevens	892	10 617	1.2	D	D	86	8.8	787	10.1	1 653	594	925	209	2 149
Swift	150	9 913	1.0	D	D	119	11.0	1 058	12.2	2 098	764	1 158	152	1 554
Todd	346	21 513	0.7	D	D	210	8.7	2 504	12.8	5 031	2 835	2 073	425	1 707
Traverse	100	3 664	1.0	D	D	56	15.0	347	13.6	952	330	520	77	2 164
Wabasha	246	18 349	0.7	D	D	179	8.1	1 913	10.7	4 089	1 730	1 547	258	1 407
Wadena	482	14 646	1.1	D	D	179	13.4	1 226	12.0	3 405	1 695	1 528	273	1 972
Waseca	1 344	18 024	0.9	D	D	166	8.5	1 598	10.2	3 454	1 656	1 790	303	1 583
Washington	3 570	194 418	0.7	2 933	12.9	1 156	5.1	14 191	6.9	30 361	14 910	7 949	5 990	2 515
Watonwan	150	10 487	0.9	D	D	128	11.6	1 282	14.8	2 192	805	1 147	149	1 329
Wilkin	152	5 726	0.7	D	D	74	11.4	517	10.2	1 384	532	691	96	1 460
Winona	4 499	51 603	1.0	550	11.1	400	8.1	4 342	10.4	7 869	2 490	3 589	769	1 494
Wright	1 104	97 402	0.6	2 145	18.3	604	5.2	10 454	9.7	14 532	7 819	4 939	2 351	1 885
Yellow Medicine	290	9 875	0.9	D	D	122	12.0	835	10.9	2 311	761	1 254	87	833

1. Per 1,000 estimated resident population. 2. Data for serious crimes have not been adjusted for underreporting; this may affect comparability between geographic areas and over time. 3. Per 100,000 population estimated by the FBI.

STATE County	Serious crimes known to police,[1] 2010 (cont.) Rate[2] Violent	Rate[2] Property	Education School enrollment and attainment, 2006-2010 Enrollment[3] Total	Enrollment[3] Percent private	Attainment[4] (percent) High school graduate or less	Attainment[4] Bachelor's degree or more	Local government expenditures,[5] 2008-2009 Total current expenditures (mil dol)	Current expenditures per student (dollars)	Money income, 2006-2010 Per capita income[6] (dollars)	Households Median income Dollars	Percent change, 2000 to 2006-2010 (constant 2010 dollars)	Percent with income of $200,000 or more	Income and poverty, 2010 Median house-hold income (dollars)	Percent below poverty level All persons	Children under 18 years	Children 5 to 17 years in families
	46	47	48	49	50	51	52	53	54	55	56	57	58	59	60	61
MINNESOTA—Cont'd																
Fillmore	34	316	4 595	11.3	50.3	19.3	25.6	9 710	23 758	45 888	-1.1	1.5	45 476	12.4	18.6	18.4
Freeborn	134	1 683	6 591	7.9	52.5	13.8	47.7	11 674	23 645	43 090	-7.9	1.9	42 250	12.3	17.2	15.1
Goodhue	110	2 120	10 496	11.5	42.8	22.7	73.8	9 032	27 472	56 366	-5.2	2.2	55 687	8.3	11.5	10.4
Grant	83	1 512	1 175	7.5	47.3	18.1	11.1	9 654	23 233	41 697	-2.5	1.2	44 039	10.8	16.2	15.0
Hennepin	455	3 359	302 241	19.8	27.7	44.0	1 862.8	12 069	35 902	61 328	-6.3	6.6	59 252	13.7	18.7	17.7
Houston	87	1 238	4 456	17.4	45.8	22.0	37.0	9 109	24 865	50 855	-1.3	1.5	50 732	9.3	12.5	11.3
Hubbard	73	2 751	4 114	7.2	42.5	23.3	23.4	9 741	24 413	45 066	0.8	2.1	42 021	12.8	20.4	18.3
Isanti	87	1 468	9 768	11.1	47.6	16.0	53.7	8 802	25 165	57 260	-9.8	1.9	55 431	8.9	11.9	11.2
Itasca	193	1 651	9 833	10.2	41.7	20.8	104.2	15 747	23 465	45 621	-0.6	1.6	45 813	12.2	19.2	17.6
Jackson	117	1 247	2 315	11.4	45.9	16.2	13.3	8 916	25 144	46 869	0.7	1.9	50 251	9.7	14.6	13.3
Kanabec	388	2 993	3 976	9.7	55.1	13.9	22.3	8 883	21 304	45 672	-6.4	0.5	42 737	13.6	20.4	18.5
Kandiyohi	204	2 114	10 275	10.4	43.9	21.0	56.0	9 852	25 844	49 512	-1.7	2.9	44 926	14.6	22.3	19.4
Kittson	22	747	935	5.0	47.0	19.1	9.2	12 484	25 030	47 568	15.5	2.0	43 980	10.0	14.5	12.5
Koochiching	180	2 201	2 794	13.2	50.6	16.3	21.4	10 642	24 576	39 571	-13.8	1.4	41 695	14.6	22.0	18.9
Lac qui Parle	55	964	1 496	6.2	50.4	16.2	15.8	10 524	24 291	45 550	10.3	1.7	44 852	9.8	14.6	13.2
Lake	138	727	1 879	8.6	44.4	20.1	21.3	14 772	26 087	46 765	-8.6	0.9	47 499	11.2	15.8	14.0
Lake of the Woods	49	321	854	3.7	45.5	18.6	6.0	11 112	27 192	46 080	10.7	3.0	39 391	11.7	19.1	17.7
Le Sueur	112	967	7 023	12.9	47.6	21.2	38.2	8 747	25 958	57 477	-1.2	1.7	55 946	9.2	11.7	10.7
Lincoln	17	85	1 272	4.2	52.4	17.8	10.1	10 196	24 922	44 672	11.6	1.9	43 358	10.0	14.5	14.1
Lyon	147	1 636	7 495	12.5	43.1	25.7	151.0	35 959	23 755	46 872	-5.1	1.5	49 218	11.4	14.0	13.1
McLeod	131	1 741	9 050	17.4	46.6	18.3	50.0	8 872	27 590	58 544	0.6	2.0	53 426	8.5	11.7	10.0
Mahnomen	185	277	1 367	7.1	53.7	13.5	16.0	11 956	17 999	38 523	1.2	0.9	35 978	22.1	33.9	33.0
Marshall	127	953	2 116	6.7	52.9	16.0	17.9	12 653	24 552	48 565	10.2	1.2	47 504	8.2	12.9	11.4
Martin	67	1 492	4 815	18.2	48.4	17.5	37.3	11 711	25 321	43 960	-0.3	3.0	47 910	11.6	18.1	16.7
Meeker	189	1 918	5 552	10.0	50.5	15.7	31.2	8 942	23 839	51 173	-1.2	1.8	49 784	8.9	12.4	11.4
Mille Lacs	88	2 203	6 245	12.7	51.1	14.8	60.9	9 129	21 744	45 273	-3.3	0.6	41 944	13.1	18.3	17.0
Morrison	87	1 054	7 463	11.3	53.1	14.5	50.3	9 783	22 934	47 085	0.4	1.7	42 898	13.4	18.4	16.5
Mower	230	2 418	9 180	9.9	49.6	15.9	58.5	10 082	23 740	44 497	-4.1	1.5	43 122	12.3	16.4	15.4
Murray	23	630	1 767	12.5	50.7	15.0	12.1	10 671	24 045	45 657	3.1	1.5	50 262	8.9	13.3	12.5
Nicollet	107	1 702	9 862	35.1	34.4	33.6	31.2	13 749	25 656	57 540	-1.6	2.2	58 065	9.0	11.0	9.8
Nobles	145	1 338	5 093	9.4	54.7	16.0	36.8	9 728	20 953	43 040	-4.8	1.7	44 777	13.8	18.7	17.6
Norman	73	613	1 502	5.9	53.1	14.9	12.3	10 351	22 817	41 784	1.4	1.2	41 375	11.3	17.7	16.1
Olmsted	191	1 895	36 355	18.7	29.5	39.1	202.9	9 159	32 704	64 090	-1.4	5.3	61 362	8.5	11.1	10.0
Otter Tail	56	1 248	12 025	10.0	46.4	19.7	112.2	14 429	23 445	43 478	-3.0	1.2	44 006	13.4	19.2	16.7
Pennington	72	1 263	3 198	10.6	48.3	15.4	72.7	33 083	22 687	44 926	3.7	1.3	43 266	11.5	15.1	14.4
Pine	124	2 598	6 415	10.7	55.7	12.9	30.2	9 272	21 328	43 838	-7.2	0.9	42 035	15.2	21.7	20.2
Pipestone	10	1 219	2 274	22.1	49.1	15.4	11.4	9 783	22 289	40 589	0.5	1.5	44 880	10.5	15.9	13.9
Polk	209	1 604	7 852	9.1	45.2	20.6	51.0	9 973	23 105	47 283	6.3	1.3	46 500	11.7	15.6	14.0
Pope	64	664	2 102	12.6	48.8	18.4	15.9	11 913	25 935	47 196	4.6	2.3	45 149	10.5	15.1	14.1
Ramsey	486	3 881	142 773	26.8	33.9	36.9	1 127.0	13 606	28 956	51 915	-10.3	4.1	50 224	17.2	24.9	23.6
Red Lake	73	416	853	14.2	54.3	13.0	8.7	11 760	23 171	47 835	17.9	1.2	44 964	11.0	16.1	14.7
Redwood	168	1 457	3 740	14.1	51.9	16.4	25.8	9 445	23 548	44 181	-6.6	2.1	46 900	9.6	13.9	12.7
Renville	140	1 704	3 683	11.0	52.3	16.0	18.5	9 004	23 956	47 623	-0.1	1.3	49 896	11.3	17.0	14.9
Rice	150	2 236	19 083	35.5	43.0	27.1	75.1	8 949	24 678	58 771	-4.6	2.3	55 905	10.3	12.1	10.4
Rock	248	289	2 287	10.9	49.3	16.8	13.8	8 875	23 079	45 411	-5.9	1.4	44 751	10.8	14.0	11.0
Roseau	77	537	3 952	8.2	53.4	16.4	30.4	9 731	22 975	49 400	-2.1	1.5	47 212	9.4	12.5	10.8
St. Louis	231	3 214	51 267	13.6	38.4	25.6	293.6	11 491	25 014	44 941	-2.2	1.8	42 087	17.4	21.6	17.4
Scott	155	2 023	36 259	19.4	30.9	36.0	183.9	8 902	33 612	82 190	-2.6	5.9	78 307	5.1	6.2	5.4
Sherburne	124	1 697	24 728	13.3	36.8	24.2	167.7	8 731	27 376	71 704	-0.7	2.5	69 699	7.2	8.4	7.3
Sibley	0	53	3 564	13.8	55.3	13.4	21.5	9 478	24 073	51 449	-2.0	1.7	47 048	10.0	14.8	12.9
Stearns	187	2 378	46 256	21.9	41.3	23.6	227.0	9 885	24 816	51 779	-3.6	2.6	50 195	12.1	13.0	11.5
Steele	113	1 732	9 223	12.7	46.2	22.0	58.5	9 005	25 062	55 321	-5.2	1.9	51 069	10.4	13.6	11.7
Stevens	134	2 015	2 930	8.2	47.8	23.5	14.5	10 611	24 585	47 055	-0.3	1.9	48 885	11.4	11.0	9.5
Swift	112	1 441	2 094	7.3	54.5	15.2	15.0	9 880	21 571	41 486	-5.9	1.1	43 357	9.9	13.7	12.1
Todd	68	1 639	5 261	13.2	52.2	12.2	48.7	12 770	21 014	42 927	5.0	1.6	40 183	16.9	25.3	23.6
Traverse	309	1 855	761	4.1	52.5	14.7	6.2	11 638	24 188	41 287	6.5	1.8	41 666	13.2	19.5	17.2
Wabasha	115	1 293	5 031	8.7	50.1	17.9	29.5	8 225	26 282	51 112	-4.2	1.9	51 702	7.5	10.8	10.1
Wadena	224	1 748	3 216	4.7	49.4	14.8	24.4	8 545	19 344	34 686	-10.6	0.4	36 412	16.8	24.1	22.8
Waseca	152	1 432	4 501	12.2	48.8	18.3	35.9	9 997	23 121	50 552	-5.9	1.0	50 149	10.7	15.0	13.7
Washington	87	2 428	66 708	18.1	27.9	40.0	370.4	9 494	36 248	79 109	-5.8	7.4	77 591	5.8	7.1	5.9
Watonwan	107	1 222	2 706	9.2	57.6	15.0	18.8	9 524	22 334	44 228	-1.5	1.3	43 699	11.4	17.2	15.0
Wilkin	15	1 445	1 517	10.2	42.9	18.4	11.1	9 501	24 447	48 692	0.9	0.9	48 611	9.5	13.6	11.9
Winona	95	1 399	17 293	22.8	41.9	25.1	72.1	12 819	21 864	44 217	-9.8	1.4	42 113	15.4	15.1	13.9
Wright	86	1 800	32 736	13.4	40.9	23.8	221.8	8 761	28 454	67 963	-0.5	2.9	66 714	5.8	7.2	6.8
Yellow Medicine	153	680	2 437	8.0	47.9	18.4	19.2	11 485	23 171	50 288	15.5	1.4	46 595	12.7	18.1	16.8

1. Data for serious crimes have not been adjusted for underreporting; this may affect comparability between geographic areas and over time. 2. Per 100,000 population estimated by the FBI. 3. All persons 3 years old and over enrolled in nursery school through college. 4. Persons 25 years old and over. 5. Elementary and secondary education expenditures. 6. Based on population estimated by the American Community Survey, 2006-2010.

Table B. States and Counties — **Personal Income**

STATE County	Total (mil dol)	Percent change, 2008–2009	Per capita[1] Dollars	Rank	Wages and salaries[2] (mil dol)	Proprietors' income (mil dol)	Dividends, interest, and rent (mil dol)	Transfer payments (mil dol) Total	Government payments to individuals Total	Social Security	Medical payments	Income mainte-nance	Unemploy-ment insurance
	62	63	64	65	66	67	68	69	70	71	72	73	74
MINNESOTA—Cont'd													
Fillmore........................	702	-1.2	33 709	1 218	230	86	132	163	160	55	77	9	10
Freeborn.......................	1 080	-1.6	34 839	1 038	511	103	204	256	250	97	102	19	16
Goodhue........................	1 763	-0.8	38 455	587	1 029	155	327	316	308	119	130	16	22
Grant.............................	215	-7.2	36 912	758	81	38	43	54	53	20	24	3	3
Hennepin.......................	62 444	-3.6	54 008	64	59 210	5 047	12 566	7 963	7 752	2 252	3 623	774	528
Houston.........................	717	-1.2	37 245	719	189	53	139	140	136	51	57	8	10
Hubbard.........................	604	-1.0	32 423	1 442	227	25	133	176	173	66	71	14	11
Isanti.............................	1 295	-1.2	32 838	1 362	460	116	171	239	232	81	93	16	24
Itasca............................	1 403	1.2	31 369	1 675	709	68	265	414	406	146	167	33	28
Jackson.........................	426	0.9	39 541	486	201	94	73	77	75	28	34	5	4
Kanabec.........................	473	-0.3	29 762	2 028	145	45	80	126	124	41	50	10	12
Kandiyohi.......................	1 595	-1.1	38 789	555	943	170	318	317	310	102	131	27	18
Kittson...........................	171	-26.1	39 072	532	61	29	35	40	39	14	18	2	2
Koochiching...................	452	2.7	34 398	1 110	265	17	69	128	126	45	54	10	7
Lac qui Parle.................	301	6.9	42 274	309	95	84	55	63	62	22	29	4	3
Lake..............................	408	-0.7	38 471	583	188	31	73	103	101	36	40	5	6
Lake of the Woods..........	120	-4.2	30 922	1 776	54	11	27	36	35	13	16	2	2
Le Sueur.......................	947	-2.6	33 763	1 209	325	90	168	190	185	61	84	11	17
Lincoln..........................	213	1.5	37 211	721	66	36	44	50	49	17	25	3	2
Lyon..............................	958	-1.6	38 187	620	656	114	182	180	175	55	84	13	10
McLeod..........................	1 223	-2.4	33 121	1 316	796	88	218	243	236	88	98	14	21
Mahnomen.....................	149	-1.1	29 718	2 041	78	10	23	54	53	10	29	8	2
Marshall........................	345	-13.7	37 573	683	107	50	63	79	77	25	37	5	6
Martin...........................	827	-5.0	40 855	392	403	122	169	181	177	66	77	13	10
Meeker..........................	764	-4.2	33 003	1 341	285	90	137	164	160	58	67	10	13
Mille Lacs......................	723	0.7	27 391	2 501	352	28	118	237	232	72	110	18	17
Morrison........................	1 022	-3.3	31 090	1 731	455	108	173	253	247	78	106	18	23
Mower...........................	1 401	-0.5	36 670	792	770	94	253	320	313	108	143	24	15
Murray..........................	368	-2.0	43 720	247	111	102	67	68	67	25	30	4	4
Nicollet.........................	1 165	-2.7	36 158	864	603	57	217	176	170	64	59	13	14
Nobles...........................	781	-1.6	38 001	639	443	156	134	144	140	49	64	13	7
Norman..........................	254	-14.6	39 282	510	76	53	48	63	62	20	30	5	3
Olmsted.........................	6 315	0.7	43 864	239	5 552	350	1 062	863	837	297	365	65	55
Otter Tail.......................	1 908	-1.5	33 720	1 215	885	147	402	482	471	176	193	31	27
Pennington.....................	542	-3.1	39 138	523	389	35	116	113	111	32	47	9	9
Pine..............................	807	1.5	28 453	2 309	318	35	128	234	229	78	92	20	18
Pipestone......................	366	-2.6	39 137	524	172	77	64	74	73	23	36	6	4
Polk..............................	1 110	-3.7	36 080	874	523	74	177	261	255	77	125	23	12
Pope.............................	402	-3.2	37 029	748	162	52	76	90	88	31	40	6	5
Ramsey..........................	22 469	-2.4	44 381	222	20 885	1 408	4 270	4 233	4 141	1 017	2 151	451	229
Red Lake.......................	125	-4.0	29 750	2 031	55	6	21	31	30	9	14	2	3
Redwood........................	595	-2.3	38 493	580	266	121	121	123	121	44	54	8	6
Renville.........................	602	-7.5	38 318	598	249	116	115	122	119	42	52	10	8
Rice..............................	2 003	0.0	31 938	1 542	1 091	126	365	367	356	131	142	25	32
Rock.............................	352	-6.8	37 139	732	121	68	71	69	67	26	30	4	3
Roseau..........................	557	-10.0	35 009	1 018	399	28	107	102	99	34	44	7	8
St. Louis........................	7 216	-1.4	36 485	819	4 553	500	1 310	1 758	1 722	545	750	156	111
Scott.............................	5 203	-1.5	39 435	496	2 138	217	734	524	500	177	180	30	60
Sherburne......................	2 721	-0.2	30 984	1 758	1 088	109	397	395	379	135	132	26	50
Sibley...........................	542	-2.4	36 331	841	156	74	102	105	102	36	46	7	8
Stearns.........................	5 095	-1.8	34 206	1 143	3 809	323	956	934	907	280	371	67	72
Steele...........................	1 357	-1.1	36 895	761	1 024	73	221	239	232	83	98	18	20
Stevens.........................	361	-10.0	37 460	692	228	41	79	68	66	21	32	4	3
Swift.............................	349	-2.7	32 257	1 471	173	42	63	86	84	26	43	6	5
Todd.............................	676	-2.5	28 325	2 341	242	45	120	196	191	60	85	16	13
Traverse........................	144	-6.6	40 329	431	47	35	35	35	34	12	17	2	1
Wabasha.......................	808	-2.1	36 944	755	282	36	145	157	153	56	69	8	10
Wadena.........................	394	0.7	29 661	2 062	247	16	65	138	135	41	65	13	8
Waseca.........................	648	-3.9	34 528	1 088	330	62	121	127	124	46	49	11	10
Washington.....................	10 718	-3.0	46 208	162	3 587	262	2 076	1 084	1 042	458	325	62	103
Watonwan......................	369	-3.8	33 860	1 189	161	55	67	85	83	28	37	6	5
Wilkin...........................	230	-16.6	36 781	776	94	22	44	54	53	17	26	4	2
Winona..........................	1 697	-1.8	34 327	1 122	1 065	74	375	328	319	106	134	23	25
Wright...........................	4 040	-3.3	33 139	1 312	1 585	207	565	612	590	208	233	35	68
Yellow Medicine..............	401	2.3	40 610	411	194	65	73	93	91	30	42	5	4

1. Based on the resident population estimated as of July 1 of the year shown. 2. Includes supplements to wages and salaries.

Table B. States and Counties — **Earnings, Social Security, and Housing**

STATE County	Total (mil dol)	Farm	Goods-related[1] Total	Manu-facturing	Information and profes-sional and technical services	Retail trade	Finance, insur-ance, and real estate	Health care and social services	Govern-ment	Social Security beneficiaries, December 2010 Number	Rate[2]	Supple-mental Security Income recipients, December 2010	Housing units, 2010 Total	Percent change, 2000–2010
	75	76	77	78	79	80	81	82	83	84	85	86	87	88
MINNESOTA—Cont'd														
Fillmore	316	12.8	D	14.1	3.4	7.1	5.3	D	18.5	4 750	228	214	9 732	9.3
Freeborn	614	7.6	D	19.5	3.3	8.9	6.0	D	13.3	7 915	253	470	14 231	1.7
Goodhue	1 184	5.0	D	15.8	3.4	5.5	3.0	11.8	18.3	9 355	203	429	20 337	13.7
Grant	119	23.1	11.6	1.7	D	4.5	4.0	D	15.4	1 725	287	69	3 324	7.3
Hennepin	64 258	0.0	12.9	9.8	17.0	4.5	14.7	9.7	10.5	163 820	142	24 067	509 469	8.7
Houston	242	6.8	D	9.2	D	5.5	4.3	13.2	22.6	4 240	223	208	8 601	5.3
Hubbard	252	3.1	D	15.6	D	10.0	4.2	17.1	23.3	5 555	272	377	14 622	19.6
Isanti	576	1.0	18.7	11.1	D	9.4	5.2	D	18.5	6 440	170	372	15 321	27.0
Itasca	777	0.3	20.8	9.7	D	8.2	3.8	16.0	23.6	11 860	263	935	27 065	10.3
Jackson	295	27.9	28.1	25.2	1.5	2.8	2.3	D	11.2	2 410	235	115	4 990	-2.0
Kanabec	190	2.0	25.0	9.2	3.9	8.6	4.8	8.8	28.3	3 825	236	265	7 849	14.7
Kandiyohi	1 113	7.2	D	13.6	4.7	7.9	4.0	D	20.1	8 590	203	688	19 476	5.8
Kittson	90	28.4	D	3.8	D	4.1	5.3	D	21.2	1 230	270	57	2 605	-4.2
Koochiching	282	0.3	31.8	27.1	2.5	6.5	12.1	D	21.2	3 535	266	313	7 900	2.3
Lac qui Parle	179	35.4	13.9	10.0	D	4.7	4.6	7.2	18.4	1 930	266	98	3 692	-2.2
Lake	220	0.0	D	13.0	2.2	5.6	5.1	D	20.9	2 830	260	145	7 681	12.3
Lake of the Woods	65	2.8	13.4	11.4	D	8.0	3.3	D	25.4	1 105	273	45	3 672	13.4
Le Sueur	415	6.5	D	27.6	D	4.7	5.8	5.8	15.2	4 855	175	235	12 416	14.3
Lincoln	102	25.8	D	0.5	2.8	4.7	2.9	D	12.3	1 540	261	64	3 108	2.1
Lyon	770	9.0	20.0	14.2	4.3	7.7	8.1	6.0	19.7	4 640	179	405	11 098	7.8
McLeod	884	3.8	D	39.2	3.3	5.7	3.6	13.0	10.8	7 085	193	337	15 760	11.9
Mahnomen	88	5.5	D	D	D	3.5	3.3	D	60.4	980	181	153	2 786	3.2
Marshall	157	27.1	D	7.9	2.3	4.8	D	5.0	21.2	2 195	233	105	4 812	0.4
Martin	525	16.8	17.4	14.7	D	6.7	4.5	D	12.4	5 520	265	357	10 009	2.1
Meeker	375	10.6	24.4	16.6	9.2	6.3	4.7	7.2	16.9	4 870	209	213	10 674	8.7
Mille Lacs	380	1.8	D	7.5	6.1	5.8	3.5	14.3	41.8	5 950	228	390	12 750	21.8
Morrison	563	12.2	D	12.7	6.1	7.6	3.8	D	21.8	7 175	216	519	15 731	13.4
Mower	864	4.9	D	20.4	D	6.2	3.3	D	15.9	8 725	223	674	17 027	4.8
Murray	213	36.9	13.0	5.3	2.5	4.6	4.1	D	13.9	2 210	253	106	4 558	4.6
Nicollet	660	6.8	D	26.6	D	2.9	2.7	D	25.2	5 050	154	300	12 873	14.5
Nobles	599	16.7	27.0	23.8	3.3	8.0	3.0	D	12.1	4 115	192	284	8 535	0.8
Norman	129	35.7	D	D	7.3	5.3	D	10.5	16.3	1 770	258	140	3 421	-1.0
Olmsted	5 901	0.4	16.1	12.3	3.9	4.7	3.0	51.2	8.8	22 970	159	2 100	60 495	22.4
Otter Tail	1 031	4.1	22.3	15.4	5.4	8.1	3.6	14.8	18.0	14 860	259	828	35 594	5.1
Pennington	423	2.0	16.3	13.1	2.4	6.3	2.8	D	18.3	2 740	197	210	6 297	4.4
Pine	353	2.5	D	3.0	D	7.4	3.1	9.4	45.2	6 330	213	489	17 276	12.5
Pipestone	250	17.6	16.4	11.0	D	6.6	2.8	D	18.1	2 075	216	126	4 483	1.1
Polk	597	10.4	19.0	14.3	4.3	5.8	2.9	D	22.7	6 595	209	598	14 610	4.3
Pope	214	15.1	19.3	13.9	1.8	5.7	3.8	D	18.4	2 600	236	122	6 435	10.4
Ramsey	22 293	0.0	D	11.9	9.3	4.1	8.8	13.0	18.4	77 050	151	15 353	217 197	5.2
Red Lake	61	10.1	D	D	D	4.1	D	D	39.0	865	212	40	1 948	3.5
Redwood	387	26.4	D	10.0	3.3	4.9	4.2	6.3	22.6	3 740	233	221	7 272	0.6
Renville	365	32.3	D	15.1	3.0	2.8	3.7	D	15.1	3 580	228	211	7 355	-0.8
Rice	1 217	2.7	26.7	18.5	2.8	6.6	3.5	9.5	19.6	10 145	158	658	24 453	21.9
Rock	190	31.9	10.7	7.6	2.4	5.6	9.5	8.5	17.3	2 200	227	116	4 262	3.0
Roseau	427	1.8	59.5	58.0	1.3	4.2	2.6	D	14.0	2 890	185	169	7 469	5.2
St. Louis	5 053	0.1	15.9	4.9	6.7	6.7	8.4	23.0	19.9	43 790	219	5 268	103 058	7.6
Scott	2 355	1.2	25.8	15.1	8.5	5.8	2.4	8.8	22.5	13 455	104	973	47 124	49.1
Sherburne	1 197	1.2	D	14.6	4.3	7.5	3.2	13.7	20.3	10 840	122	590	32 379	41.9
Sibley	230	32.3	18.6	10.4	2.0	2.7	2.8	D	18.3	3 070	202	140	6 582	9.3
Stearns	4 132	2.6	20.9	13.7	6.2	7.6	5.5	18.0	18.6	24 040	160	1 964	61 974	23.2
Steele	1 097	2.5	D	31.2	D	7.8	16.4	9.8	10.5	6 735	184	461	15 343	15.3
Stevens	270	17.9	D	12.6	4.3	5.4	4.5	D	23.9	1 790	184	105	4 160	2.1
Swift	215	17.0	D	17.0	D	3.8	3.4	D	21.1	2 315	237	166	4 835	0.3
Todd	287	6.8	D	25.6	2.1	6.9	3.9	9.7	23.5	5 460	219	427	12 917	8.6
Traverse	82	40.3	3.8	1.7	D	4.8	D	4.5	23.6	1 040	292	46	2 073	-5.7
Wabasha	318	6.5	D	28.1	2.3	6.9	4.5	9.1	18.1	4 515	208	181	9 997	10.3
Wadena	263	1.2	9.1	6.9	2.5	8.7	3.3	D	23.4	3 715	268	396	6 899	8.9
Waseca	392	12.0	D	31.4	D	4.9	3.9	10.2	19.3	3 815	199	218	7 903	6.4
Washington	3 849	0.8	21.9	15.9	6.7	8.6	8.9	13.2	16.7	33 160	139	1 793	92 374	25.5
Watonwan	216	21.6	D	21.1	D	3.2	3.9	8.3	17.4	2 375	212	133	5 047	0.2
Wilkin	116	17.2	D	0.1	D	4.4	4.8	17.6	17.9	1 460	222	91	3 078	-0.9
Winona	1 139	2.3	D	27.7	D	7.0	3.4	8.9	17.8	8 605	167	651	20 760	6.2
Wright	1 792	2.4	D	12.8	D	9.0	D	9.7	18.8	16 455	132	793	49 000	42.6
Yellow Medicine	258	22.3	D	3.5	4.2	2.9	2.1	D	25.2	2 560	245	155	4 760	-2.3

1. Includes mining, construction, and manufacturing.   2. Per 1,000 resident population enumerated in the 2010 census.

Table B. States and Counties — Housing, Labor Force, and Employment

STATE County	Housing units, 2006–2010								Civilian labor force, 2010				Civilian employment,[5] 2006–2010		
	Occupied units										Unemployment			Percent	
		Owner-occupied				Renter-occupied									
				Median owner cost as a percent of income			Median rent as a percent of income	Sub-standard units[3] (percent)		Percent change, 2009–2010				Management, business, science and arts	Construction, production, and maintenance occupations
	Total	Percent	Median value[1]	With a mortgage	Without a mortgage	Median rent[2]			Total		Total	Rate[4]	Total		
	89	90	91	92	93	94	95	96	97	98	99	100	101	102	103
MINNESOTA—Cont'd															
Fillmore	8 546	79.7	133 900	23.6	13.1	536	26.0	3.1	11 598	2.5	855	7.4	10 534	33.6	30.0
Freeborn	13 186	80.4	111 800	23.7	12.6	539	26.9	1.4	16 705	0.3	1 304	7.8	15 765	24.8	33.3
Goodhue	18 758	78.6	192 900	24.3	13.5	667	29.9	0.7	26 114	1.0	1 879	7.2	24 324	32.0	28.4
Grant	2 663	78.4	102 700	22.8	13.8	503	31.0	0.7	3 264	3.6	268	8.2	3 073	31.8	30.5
Hennepin	473 856	65.2	247 900	24.6	12.7	853	29.8	2.7	658 523	-0.5	45 186	6.9	613 633	44.9	14.5
Houston	7 770	81.7	149 200	21.9	13.2	534	26.1	1.4	11 193	0.6	868	7.8	10 064	32.6	28.8
Hubbard	8 616	82.2	175 500	24.6	12.2	605	31.5	2.7	9 585	0.1	951	9.9	8 940	33.2	27.4
Isanti	13 988	83.2	203 700	27.4	12.4	802	30.0	2.2	21 827	-1.5	2 014	9.2	18 757	28.2	33.1
Itasca	18 998	81.6	146 800	24.7	11.3	587	31.8	2.1	23 444	1.6	2 283	9.7	19 810	30.7	27.2
Jackson	4 531	78.6	100 300	18.8	11.4	543	22.3	1.5	7 074	-1.4	359	5.1	5 463	34.3	29.5
Kanabec	6 439	83.1	162 800	28.0	13.9	704	29.8	2.8	8 120	-0.1	986	12.1	7 795	25.5	34.1
Kandiyohi	17 069	75.7	157 400	23.5	11.7	560	29.6	2.1	24 278	1.2	1 541	6.3	21 767	33.2	27.1
Kittson	1 954	86.0	64 200	17.7	10.0	435	23.8	0.7	2 617	2.6	189	7.2	2 293	31.6	33.9
Koochiching	6 246	76.3	99 800	21.0	12.9	480	30.4	2.5	6 824	0.4	599	8.8	6 120	23.0	33.2
Lac qui Parle	3 137	83.7	77 100	19.6	10.0	449	25.8	0.8	4 525	4.8	266	5.9	3 662	35.1	27.1
Lake	5 181	79.8	142 000	22.4	11.3	567	26.2	2.2	6 386	4.2	486	7.6	5 395	27.1	28.9
Lake of the Woods	1 784	87.6	135 500	25.7	11.3	559	34.0	1.7	2 286	-0.1	146	6.4	2 088	21.9	35.1
Le Sueur	10 758	83.8	191 900	26.1	11.9	585	25.7	2.0	14 540	0.2	1 406	9.7	14 782	29.2	32.2
Lincoln	2 587	83.9	76 300	19.5	13.2	477	23.9	1.0	3 550	4.9	186	5.2	3 105	34.6	27.9
Lyon	10 263	68.2	136 300	19.8	11.4	543	27.8	2.1	14 991	0.9	828	5.5	14 176	35.1	25.9
McLeod	14 510	79.8	169 400	24.0	12.8	631	24.9	1.7	20 174	-0.4	1 819	9.0	19 264	33.5	30.4
Mahnomen	1 994	74.7	86 500	22.7	12.3	449	28.6	5.3	2 572	3.5	208	8.1	2 271	26.7	23.3
Marshall	4 141	83.2	84 600	18.9	10.1	494	24.8	1.2	5 567	2.3	508	9.1	4 927	32.7	30.8
Martin	8 982	78.0	96 200	20.1	11.0	521	29.6	1.0	11 689	0.1	830	7.1	10 161	30.2	33.2
Meeker	9 394	81.6	165 600	25.3	12.6	674	30.0	2.4	12 692	1.0	1 124	8.9	11 568	28.2	35.4
Mille Lacs	10 538	77.4	167 600	27.9	14.3	579	29.3	2.6	12 303	-2.9	1 479	12.0	12 226	27.7	32.5
Morrison	13 496	80.4	159 500	25.8	12.2	549	27.6	1.4	18 328	-1.1	1 749	9.5	16 352	26.9	35.3
Mower	16 018	74.7	108 600	21.9	11.9	608	29.7	3.5	21 270	-0.5	1 254	5.9	19 093	28.8	34.6
Murray	3 831	83.3	90 000	22.2	12.1	521	32.7	1.8	6 074	5.5	336	5.5	4 454	37.2	28.0
Nicollet	12 150	74.3	169 700	23.4	11.3	687	26.2	1.1	20 154	0.0	1 211	6.0	18 218	35.8	23.1
Nobles	8 065	73.2	97 200	21.8	11.4	554	28.0	5.6	11 760	-0.4	617	5.2	10 562	24.2	38.2
Norman	2 889	79.0	79 300	21.2	12.2	452	24.1	1.8	3 764	4.4	237	6.3	3 355	35.0	26.4
Olmsted	56 066	76.6	174 000	22.3	10.3	728	26.9	1.7	82 084	0.0	4 853	5.9	76 151	46.8	16.2
Otter Tail	24 691	78.6	158 600	23.9	12.0	532	29.5	2.0	30 768	1.7	2 216	7.2	27 807	30.6	29.7
Pennington	5 720	77.5	91 600	21.4	11.7	499	26.9	0.9	9 233	0.8	759	8.2	7 372	26.9	30.6
Pine	11 600	81.7	162 400	26.3	13.6	609	26.0	4.2	14 780	0.3	1 522	10.3	13 428	25.0	29.9
Pipestone	3 926	76.8	85 100	21.0	12.4	576	28.0	1.0	5 565	-0.9	336	6.0	4 764	31.7	28.0
Polk	12 509	73.0	115 800	20.7	11.9	556	30.9	1.6	17 475	0.9	993	5.7	15 534	31.3	25.2
Pope	4 824	78.0	148 700	24.0	11.6	557	23.5	1.4	6 413	3.2	421	6.6	5 642	33.2	28.4
Ramsey	203 382	62.2	222 700	24.7	11.9	784	31.0	3.5	271 904	-0.7	19 932	7.3	255 766	42.5	16.9
Red Lake	1 751	83.4	80 800	18.2	11.1	434	24.6	1.8	2 454	-3.7	234	9.5	2 184	29.3	30.8
Redwood	6 661	78.3	88 300	22.0	11.4	557	27.9	2.0	8 690	2.2	568	6.5	7 711	34.0	27.7
Renville	6 539	79.3	97 100	21.5	11.5	520	29.5	1.0	9 254	8.1	707	7.6	8 016	31.0	32.6
Rice	22 213	77.1	210 400	26.1	11.4	729	27.3	2.0	33 665	0.1	2 719	8.1	32 533	32.8	27.4
Rock	3 885	79.3	99 200	21.4	11.3	567	27.3	1.3	5 186	2.1	269	5.2	4 992	31.1	28.5
Roseau	6 331	80.4	96 200	21.0	11.2	555	24.2	2.0	9 309	-5.2	565	6.1	8 412	22.7	46.0
St. Louis	86 561	72.6	140 400	22.7	11.8	619	32.2	1.9	106 190	-0.4	8 420	7.9	94 402	33.9	20.8
Scott	43 814	86.6	274 800	25.1	11.9	891	27.2	1.3	75 292	0.6	5 244	7.0	68 428	40.8	18.7
Sherburne	29 224	85.3	226 300	26.2	11.0	818	31.3	1.3	49 355	-1.9	4 180	8.5	44 263	33.0	28.3
Sibley	6 117	81.9	148 500	24.2	13.2	597	26.3	2.1	9 144	6.1	655	7.2	8 148	28.8	35.2
Stearns	56 365	72.9	174 500	24.0	11.9	670	29.8	1.8	85 413	0.3	6 134	7.2	79 035	31.0	26.6
Steele	14 138	78.9	156 300	24.7	12.3	650	29.0	1.5	21 289	1.4	1 633	7.7	19 304	30.3	29.9
Stevens	3 725	68.2	120 300	19.6	10.2	557	29.8	1.0	5 817	4.3	311	5.3	5 154	38.0	24.8
Swift	4 190	73.6	97 600	21.5	11.1	453	25.8	0.9	5 472	-1.7	438	8.0	4 635	30.9	26.6
Todd	10 065	82.8	139 400	25.9	12.8	560	26.2	3.4	12 915	2.4	1 019	7.9	11 934	24.9	39.5
Traverse	1 636	80.3	69 200	19.8	12.5	448	24.5	1.8	1 896	7.1	117	6.2	1 785	32.3	29.5
Wabasha	8 799	81.9	157 300	24.3	12.7	575	32.4	1.2	12 254	-2.2	827	6.7	11 681	30.5	28.4
Wadena	5 959	76.4	113 800	26.4	12.8	479	33.2	1.6	6 563	-1.7	653	9.9	5 961	29.7	31.3
Waseca	7 284	80.3	141 400	24.3	13.0	566	26.8	0.9	10 560	-1.2	797	7.5	9 747	30.8	29.8
Washington	86 315	84.4	264 800	24.5	10.7	992	29.8	1.3	129 470	-0.5	8 977	6.9	122 007	44.0	17.0
Watonwan	4 399	79.4	89 300	21.7	11.2	546	23.4	2.0	5 613	-0.1	436	7.8	5 564	28.5	38.3
Wilkin	2 779	83.0	102 800	21.2	10.8	496	20.6	0.5	3 648	3.8	178	4.9	3 382	31.0	30.7
Winona	19 414	71.5	159 200	24.2	11.7	585	31.7	1.1	28 866	-1.6	1 979	6.9	27 853	31.2	25.7
Wright	44 413	85.1	222 300	26.2	12.9	765	30.2	2.1	68 094	-0.5	5 604	8.2	63 962	32.6	25.7
Yellow Medicine	4 213	79.5	97 100	18.9	10.0	505	28.9	2.0	5 931	0.1	359	6.1	5 359	32.9	29.4

1. Specified owner-occupied units.   2. Specified renter-occupied units. A value of 10.0 represents 10 percent or less.   3. Overcrowded or lacking complete plumbing facilities.   4. Percent of civilian labor force.   5. Persons 16 years old and over.

Table B. States and Counties — **Nonfarm Employment and Agriculture**

STATE County	Number of establishments	Total	Health care and social assistance	Manufacturing	Retail trade	Finance and insurance	Professional, scientific, and technical services	Total (mil dol)	Average per employee (dollars)	Number	Fewer than 50 acres	500 acres or more	Farm operators whose principal occupation is farming (percent)
	104	105	106	107	108	109	110	111	112	113	114	115	116
MINNESOTA—Cont'd													
Fillmore	626	5 168	1 332	833	711	306	140	129	25 006	1 667	25.1	15.1	50.0
Freeborn	829	11 721	D	2 556	1 947	516	303	355	30 269	1 257	35.3	21.4	53.1
Goodhue	1 356	21 362	3 354	6 142	2 591	487	416	708	33 141	1 644	31.9	11.6	48.2
Grant	208	1 581	574	46	228	90	D	44	27 935	675	22.5	24.7	48.3
Hennepin	39 222	824 275	119 949	73 241	74 090	75 838	80 604	43 128	52 323	582	57.0	5.5	46.7
Houston	467	4 216	1 017	467	641	138	D	103	24 437	1 041	17.8	10.3	44.7
Hubbard	571	4 708	819	890	1 162	187	81	122	25 995	468	15.4	10.9	36.1
Isanti	771	8 335	2 058	1 355	1 662	334	165	268	32 187	910	45.8	5.8	34.3
Itasca	1 164	13 064	2 968	D	2 442	406	552	424	32 474	419	23.6	7.9	39.9
Jackson	316	5 184	1 374	D	344	110	44	138	26 612	969	20.8	30.5	60.7
Kanabec	304	3 143	966	510	516	143	D	88	28 124	701	21.8	8.3	39.8
Kandiyohi	1 388	18 799	5 509	2 418	2 921	573	597	571	30 361	1 386	26.4	16.1	44.4
Kittson	141	1 076	349	71	194	90	22	27	25 543	677	6.8	40.5	45.6
Koochiching	415	4 309	697	D	678	D	73	133	30 800	214	14.0	15.0	36.0
Lac qui Parle	201	2 000	D	D	301	102	24	55	27 420	932	17.7	29.8	51.4
Lake	295	2 955	D	D	332	179	D	87	29 369	34	32.4	2.9	41.2
Lake of the Woods	158	1 195	D	D	220	D	D	27	22 271	225	8.9	20.0	32.9
Le Sueur	692	6 050	822	1 934	852	178	142	191	31 479	1 091	35.9	11.1	42.8
Lincoln	201	1 483	506	15	238	52	25	36	24 195	784	18.1	22.4	52.6
Lyon	816	12 356	1 936	1 958	1 959	1 141	570	403	32 628	1 011	22.7	32.1	62.0
McLeod	1 024	17 311	3 439	6 446	2 149	415	281	590	34 075	1 021	34.6	13.9	54.2
Mahnomen	103	1 647	D	D	179	54	D	43	25 981	374	9.6	28.3	48.1
Marshall	272	1 641	294	213	261	107	D	53	32 425	1 405	8.4	31.5	41.9
Martin	634	8 409	D	1 419	1 398	349	275	285	33 880	960	21.5	32.2	63.4
Meeker	588	5 705	972	1 567	874	170	138	165	28 991	1 146	33.9	14.4	44.2
Mille Lacs	658	7 567	1 648	893	1 023	222	70	201	26 623	762	30.4	6.7	42.9
Morrison	887	9 096	1 418	1 988	1 647	375	289	241	26 539	1 867	18.1	8.9	47.9
Mower	885	13 830	2 619	3 871	2 068	363	277	441	31 901	1 088	35.8	21.2	53.3
Murray	310	2 281	454	D	337	141	73	57	25 195	1 023	25.3	28.6	57.0
Nicollet	628	11 984	D	3 474	828	227	266	396	33 024	827	23.2	20.0	60.1
Nobles	621	9 586	D	D	1 458	291	296	274	28 626	1 094	22.4	25.0	59.2
Norman	204	1 380	419	D	261	D	D	41	29 589	692	14.6	38.3	50.0
Olmsted	3 392	77 113	D	D	10 426	1 814	2 104	3 188	41 348	1 384	37.3	10.0	45.5
Otter Tail	1 706	18 648	4 256	3 602	3 003	568	410	546	29 258	3 296	16.7	13.7	41.3
Pennington	399	7 713	1 143	D	1 044	D	D	256	33 228	630	12.1	27.0	40.6
Pine	590	6 727	1 156	D	1 274	182	105	159	23 573	945	20.1	9.3	45.0
Pipestone	348	4 295	752	914	536	140	D	103	24 059	676	23.4	22.9	69.3
Polk	773	9 446	2 358	1 754	1 387	270	222	278	29 442	1 609	13.5	34.0	47.9
Pope	390	3 584	674	615	308	134	D	113	31 456	1 055	20.3	17.2	41.6
Ramsey	13 313	288 523	54 364	24 948	26 980	19 620	13 745	13 210	45 787	30	90.0	0.0	80.0
Red Lake	101	781	D	D	145	49	19	20	25 307	382	9.7	31.7	45.8
Redwood	524	5 178	1 002	641	D	230	70	144	27 745	1 215	17.0	34.3	68.5
Renville	504	4 789	1 409	925	620	202	160	143	29 805	1 119	21.4	33.6	60.8
Rice	1 504	22 952	3 099	4 191	2 574	520	499	723	31 486	1 494	40.5	6.8	37.7
Rock	262	2 624	623	243	452	364	87	69	26 153	696	26.6	26.1	65.4
Roseau	399	7 181	745	4 150	717	196	94	200	27 877	1 182	10.5	25.8	40.0
St. Louis	5 523	81 634	21 789	4 378	12 583	3 655	3 269	2 702	33 102	761	24.4	7.4	45.3
Scott	3 089	37 129	4 214	5 778	4 856	755	1 037	1 361	36 664	795	48.7	5.0	42.6
Sherburne	1 908	20 205	4 427	3 377	3 039	557	527	652	32 289	549	45.7	9.1	44.3
Sibley	366	3 211	591	793	380	148	76	89	27 739	1 029	25.6	18.4	57.4
Stearns	4 326	73 943	14 126	11 086	10 631	3 625	3 384	2 546	34 432	3 368	25.4	8.0	56.5
Steele	1 008	18 918	2 257	D	2 891	D	191	705	37 280	934	37.0	13.6	43.8
Stevens	352	4 072	1 244	574	573	D	118	127	31 307	639	24.6	34.3	59.0
Swift	309	3 459	593	D	381	128	138	101	29 337	888	22.1	27.0	51.8
Todd	550	4 825	D	1 686	758	206	101	125	25 896	1 910	18.1	6.3	44.9
Traverse	124	775	D	D	243	42	8	21	26 566	479	23.0	36.3	55.5
Wabasha	580	5 846	788	D	887	181	92	163	27 935	976	22.6	14.1	57.6
Wadena	403	5 397	2 283	349	961	149	D	149	27 551	657	16.6	8.5	39.6
Waseca	500	6 713	1 131	D	794	181	156	210	31 287	848	30.8	19.1	53.4
Washington	5 388	67 048	9 273	7 554	11 671	5 069	3 562	2 411	35 967	729	59.8	4.7	44.0
Watonwan	304	3 480	440	1 256	388	160	D	84	24 226	604	24.2	27.3	58.3
Wilkin	171	1 825	D	D	195	D	D	54	29 399	428	18.0	48.8	65.7
Winona	1 233	22 151	3 606	4 871	3 092	619	531	652	29 430	1 203	21.7	12.0	53.8
Wright	3 043	32 006	4 732	4 967	6 493	769	957	1 046	32 685	1 531	39.8	7.4	42.0
Yellow Medicine	327	4 924	1 104	D	422	108	70	169	34 412	986	21.4	30.6	55.0

Table B. States and Counties — **Agriculture**

STATE County	Land in farms — Acreage (1,000) [117]	Percent change, 2002–2007 [118]	Acres — Average size of farm [119]	Total irrigated (1,000) [120]	Total cropland (1,000) [121]	Value of land and buildings (dollars) — Average per farm [122]	Average per acre [123]	Value of machinery and equipment, average per farm (dollars) [124]	Value of products sold — Total (mil dol) [125]	Average per farm (dollars) [126]	Percent from: Crops [127]	Live-stock and poultry products [128]	Percent of farms with sales of: $10,000 or more [129]	$100,000 or more [130]	Government payments — Total ($1,000) [131]	Percent of farms [132]
MINNESOTA—Cont'd																
Fillmore	446	1.1	268	0.0	330.4	771 600	2 882	120 697	223.1	133 838	47.7	52.3	55.8	27.5	9 213	72.2
Freeborn	388	-1.5	309	1.4	359.6	960 388	3 107	163 464	256.1	203 773	62.8	37.2	61.7	37.5	8 345	78.3
Goodhue	397	3.4	241	2.8	322.8	861 849	3 571	135 327	264.0	160 566	47.1	52.9	60.3	29.3	7 038	68.2
Grant	322	1.6	476	4.0	292.1	1 064 207	2 234	151 436	103.3	153 057	86.7	13.3	43.4	28.6	6 105	93.3
Hennepin	67	3.1	114	0.6	49.1	627 606	5 488	91 035	51.4	88 364	83.4	16.6	39.5	12.9	940	36.1
Houston	244	-3.9	235	0.2	127.6	628 865	2 679	92 548	91.0	87 415	30.5	69.5	47.6	19.4	4 096	79.9
Hubbard	126	-10.0	270	22.2	70.8	624 765	2 317	73 567	32.6	69 702	84.6	15.4	30.6	7.3	525	28.2
Isanti	126	-9.4	139	1.3	87.7	554 566	3 999	60 956	27.1	29 795	59.8	40.2	24.3	5.7	1 398	43.3
Itasca	93	-22.5	223	D	43.9	442 079	1 986	56 386	7.4	17 706	49.6	50.4	28.6	3.3	70	14.1
Jackson	401	0.8	413	0.6	371.2	1 258 129	3 044	173 834	267.3	275 827	57.2	42.8	74.9	48.4	7 720	83.4
Kanabec	142	-10.7	202	0.4	70.8	496 715	2 454	62 147	19.7	28 086	37.3	62.7	31.5	6.8	680	30.7
Kandiyohi	417	2.2	301	17.5	349.0	855 562	2 843	133 113	309.1	222 992	37.1	62.9	42.7	25.5	8 249	81.5
Kittson	542	-2.5	801	1.4	439.6	948 150	1 184	165 001	105.4	155 619	95.8	4.2	39.7	27.3	9 536	88.3
Koochiching	55	-25.7	258	0.0	26.0	348 110	1 352	60 052	4.6	21 331	29.0	71.0	27.6	4.7	126	19.2
Lac qui Parle	412	-5.3	442	5.0	362.1	1 014 997	2 296	151 422	157.6	169 089	72.7	27.3	59.5	35.2	8 032	90.6
Lake	3	-40.0	101	D	1.2	335 244	3 324	31 748	0.3	7 546	D	D	11.8	2.9	0	0.0
Lake of the Woods	97	-36.2	431	D	58.3	515 267	1 196	71 663	7.4	32 951	86.1	13.9	28.4	7.1	512	55.1
Le Sueur	251	5.5	230	1.3	211.0	805 168	3 504	112 952	139.6	127 993	52.0	48.0	48.6	26.1	5 605	81.5
Lincoln	286	5.5	365	0.7	246.3	824 131	2 257	121 826	135.1	172 323	53.2	46.8	54.2	30.4	5 794	88.0
Lyon	429	6.2	424	0.0	389.5	1 164 716	2 747	167 766	305.7	302 397	45.7	54.3	64.2	48.3	7 804	84.3
McLeod	244	-7.2	239	0.0	218.7	812 093	3 399	154 659	125.4	122 859	62.7	37.3	60.6	26.4	4 385	74.2
Mahnomen	191	-2.1	510	D	144.7	710 387	1 392	107 799	43.9	117 432	83.1	16.9	45.2	25.1	2 883	79.9
Marshall	911	-2.6	648	0.4	786.3	837 318	1 292	152 148	189.8	135 124	94.8	5.2	38.9	24.4	17 581	87.3
Martin	450	6.4	468	1.0	426.7	1 442 048	3 079	206 965	403.0	419 783	45.8	54.2	77.9	55.1	9 969	81.3
Meeker	322	-5.6	281	9.1	273.9	844 406	3 007	129 037	204.0	178 043	40.4	59.6	47.1	23.5	5 707	77.9
Mille Lacs	125	-5.3	164	0.4	76.5	456 157	2 782	71 842	27.3	35 807	30.7	69.3	34.1	9.4	954	45.1
Morrison	431	-4.6	231	18.5	250.7	536 832	2 324	109 015	261.0	139 810	10.6	89.4	46.8	20.2	4 598	61.8
Mower	420	1.9	386	1.1	391.6	1 227 730	3 181	172 683	287.6	264 341	57.9	42.1	65.3	42.6	7 847	73.7
Murray	429	5.4	419	D	390.7	1 112 129	2 653	162 878	237.1	231 812	56.6	43.4	64.4	43.5	8 860	86.5
Nicollet	274	6.6	331	D	250.0	1 116 870	3 371	173 257	236.8	286 292	40.5	59.5	72.7	47.0	5 489	81.5
Nobles	422	4.5	386	D	389.6	1 212 829	3 142	177 674	343.8	314 272	43.5	56.5	75.2	48.4	7 727	85.6
Norman	513	-2.7	741	0.6	465.2	1 161 374	1 567	176 120	168.3	243 178	89.8	10.2	50.6	35.8	8 071	85.0
Olmsted	296	-5.4	214	0.1	227.6	768 778	3 594	107 327	154.9	111 939	53.6	46.4	48.4	22.1	5 508	70.5
Otter Tail	899	2.0	273	56.0	597.8	548 339	2 011	87 495	300.1	91 041	44.5	55.5	36.1	16.0	11 652	75.2
Pennington	325	-2.1	516	0.1	265.3	709 612	1 374	87 299	41.8	66 388	88.2	11.8	36.7	15.6	6 477	85.2
Pine	208	-18.4	220	0.8	103.0	474 096	2 158	69 700	49.7	52 585	23.0	77.0	36.5	8.0	1 389	36.4
Pipestone	245	-1.6	362	2.5	211.6	982 841	2 715	150 618	176.5	261 049	36.0	64.0	67.9	39.6	3 804	79.0
Polk	1 100	-1.0	684	10.4	976.4	1 026 875	1 502	193 256	341.4	212 193	93.1	6.9	45.1	28.9	20 228	84.5
Pope	360	2.9	341	38.1	285.2	748 080	2 192	119 598	116.9	110 774	62.6	37.4	42.1	21.6	6 256	83.3
Ramsey	1	NA	31	0.1	0.3	262 658	8 374	56 302	D	D	D	D	80.0	26.7	D	3.3
Red Lake	223	-1.8	585	0.2	186.1	789 273	1 349	119 195	42.7	111 670	82.1	17.9	45.3	23.0	4 165	87.7
Redwood	554	1.7	456	0.0	508.7	1 379 768	3 027	194 731	364.1	299 637	55.7	44.3	75.9	55.6	10 378	86.7
Renville	620	-6.6	554	D	587.5	1 613 409	2 913	223 829	420.5	375 784	63.3	36.7	72.8	52.5	9 440	85.3
Rice	253	1.6	169	0.5	205.6	714 669	4 219	100 601	137.2	91 832	48.4	51.6	41.4	15.9	5 490	71.2
Rock	279	-6.7	401	1.2	251.3	1 303 843	3 252	173 081	282.9	406 468	34.8	65.2	78.6	55.0	4 533	76.6
Roseau	591	-15.9	500	0.0	462.2	552 170	1 104	91 271	84.8	71 736	75.4	24.6	32.8	14.0	9 852	80.2
St. Louis	149	-14.9	195	0.2	70.7	383 167	1 961	47 155	13.6	17 813	46.5	53.5	23.7	4.3	120	5.4
Scott	118	-9.9	148	0.4	94.8	741 776	5 017	101 196	63.3	99 663	45.0	55.0	44.9	16.0	2 293	54.2
Sherburne	106	-15.9	193	30.7	78.5	743 910	3 848	106 346	63.9	116 465	78.4	21.6	31.7	14.4	1 294	41.3
Sibley	346	2.1	336	0.3	313.7	1 115 472	3 320	178 970	244.0	237 103	50.9	49.1	69.5	40.5	5 784	77.6
Stearns	708	4.0	210	41.5	527.6	595 214	2 830	130 988	519.4	154 226	14.2	85.8	57.7	32.0	12 639	70.7
Steele	266	-5.7	285	0.5	242.1	960 446	3 370	133 080	184.8	197 809	60.2	39.8	52.0	30.2	5 635	78.7
Stevens	340	8.6	533	16.5	319.0	1 325 623	2 489	275 467	244.0	381 846	44.2	55.8	61.0	43.0	5 623	85.3
Swift	388	-6.7	437	31.4	348.2	1 091 685	2 496	173 531	206.1	232 081	55.2	44.8	54.6	33.8	7 878	87.3
Todd	379	2.4	198	15.6	228.7	433 841	2 188	85 346	148.6	77 805	20.9	79.1	40.9	13.9	4 042	63.3
Traverse	328	-4.7	684	D	311.7	1 493 667	2 184	245 120	111.3	232 276	89.3	10.7	57.0	43.4	5 492	93.3
Wabasha	262	-1.9	269	0.6	181.7	786 131	2 926	143 312	144.2	147 758	36.2	63.8	61.8	32.7	4 647	76.8
Wadena	151	-9.0	230	18.4	81.3	441 947	1 920	83 045	39.9	60 798	35.7	64.3	31.4	10.5	1 420	59.8
Waseca	255	10.4	300	0.1	229.6	1 042 991	3 475	156 845	201.8	237 983	49.6	50.4	62.4	39.5	5 602	82.5
Washington	81	-15.6	111	3.4	57.5	638 102	5 726	79 429	69.9	95 857	88.7	11.3	38.8	12.5	856	25.7
Watonwan	269	-1.1	446	1.6	252.9	1 332 434	2 991	184 735	184.7	305 812	57.6	42.4	68.0	47.0	5 534	86.9
Wilkin	425	0.0	993	1.6	407.6	1 945 976	1 960	278 651	130.5	304 910	98.3	1.7	66.6	49.5	5 541	88.5
Winona	306	-1.6	254	0.0	191.3	757 355	2 982	123 159	187.2	155 608	25.2	74.8	56.5	27.1	5 219	68.5
Wright	265	-0.4	173	2.7	207.3	696 111	4 016	95 428	140.1	91 481	44.7	55.3	44.1	15.8	3 714	56.4
Yellow Medicine	409	-8.7	415	0.6	371.3	1 050 878	2 532	178 186	209.0	212 014	63.6	36.4	62.3	43.4	7 587	87.4

Table B. States and Counties — Water Use, Wholesale Trade, Retail Trade, and Real Estate

STATE County	Water use, 2005		Wholesale trade,[1] 2007				Retail trade,[2] 2007				Real estate and rental and leasing,[2] 2007			
	Total water withdrawn (mil gal/day)	Gallons withdrawn per person	Number of establishments	Number of employees	Sales (mil dol)	Annual payroll (mil dol)	Number of establishments	Number of employees	Sales (mil dol)	Annual payroll (mil dol)	Number of establishments	Number of employees	Receipts (mil dol)	Annual payroll (mil dol)
	133	134	135	136	137	138	139	140	141	142	143	144	145	146
MINNESOTA—Cont'd														
Fillmore	5.3	246	26	197	116.1	8.4	107	728	176.8	13.8	12	23	1.9	0.4
Freeborn	5.5	171	47	541	412.1	21.3	154	2 137	492.1	41.9	23	49	4.2	0.8
Goodhue	619.3	13 586	42	603	313.9	24.3	241	2 664	595.8	53.4	46	D	D	D
Grant	1.7	276	11	177	293.8	7.7	37	259	56.4	4.5	5	3	0.4	0.0
Hennepin	320.8	287	2 280	39 155	34 472.5	2 340.5	4 405	80 179	22 278.8	2 080.8	2 318	18 498	6 322.6	746.8
Houston	2.9	146	20	D	D	D	77	597	152.5	11.5	6	10	1.5	0.2
Hubbard	13.9	738	7	29	35.3	0.9	120	1 071	200.9	18.1	15	61	3.7	0.7
Isanti	4.6	122	18	D	D	D	108	1 560	405.2	34.2	27	D	D	D
Itasca	185.0	4 168	31	274	160.6	13.8	227	2 414	521.6	47.2	36	100	13.6	2.1
Jackson	2.2	194	13	182	151.7	6.6	51	399	80.3	6.0	3	13	0.7	0.1
Kanabec	1.9	115	4	15	4.9	0.4	54	582	150.5	10.4	6	59	2.5	0.9
Kandiyohi	22.0	533	77	D	D	D	231	2 921	597.6	56.7	51	198	27.2	5.8
Kittson	1.4	292	19	131	217.5	3.9	31	206	41.3	3.0	4	7	0.3	0.0
Koochiching	47.5	3 418	10	55	16.8	1.6	83	698	165.0	14.6	15	47	5.5	1.2
Lac qui Parle	4.5	589	12	121	96.2	4.4	47	302	61.6	4.8	7	30	2.3	0.7
Lake	130.9	11 733	4	D	D	D	46	384	119.8	8.9	10	67	3.1	1.3
Lake of the Woods	1.4	310	5	24	11.6	0.6	29	229	39.9	3.3	3	7	0.5	0.1
Le Sueur	19.7	716	23	299	132.0	11.4	108	884	206.2	16.5	24	91	3.8	3.0
Lincoln	1.8	302	9	64	77.6	2.3	40	274	53.1	3.9	7	11	0.8	0.1
Lyon	6.5	266	46	D	D	D	142	1 907	378.9	36.1	35	120	8.6	2.6
McLeod	6.7	183	31	D	D	D	170	2 263	477.1	43.1	38	D	D	D
Mahnomen	3.3	653	4	23	9.9	1.2	20	187	20.2	2.5	3	8	0.6	0.1
Marshall	1.3	127	24	214	246.7	8.4	43	271	118.6	5.8	2	D	D	D
Martin	17.8	846	46	D	D	D	109	1 343	268.2	22.9	16	42	4.4	0.9
Meeker	7.8	335	19	197	98.6	7.5	90	737	174.1	14.3	14	39	2.2	0.6
Mille Lacs	3.1	122	20	207	160.1	5.2	115	1 229	251.8	21.5	18	46	3.8	0.9
Morrison	17.9	547	26	280	249.7	11.0	130	1 501	361.2	31.2	13	34	4.5	0.5
Mower	9.2	238	28	198	229.8	9.7	171	1 946	347.7	33.9	25	138	8.3	1.9
Murray	2.0	227	15	149	283.2	5.3	44	321	46.6	4.3	9	49	1.7	0.7
Nicollet	6.5	212	31	349	194.3	14.0	86	790	164.9	15.5	25	132	10.1	2.7
Nobles	5.1	248	38	680	478.2	25.6	122	1 495	303.6	27.7	15	49	3.9	0.6
Norman	0.8	110	17	95	58.4	3.6	33	260	52.5	4.4	4	7	0.5	0.1
Olmsted	48.0	355	111	1 141	777.9	51.6	606	10 543	2 182.1	227.4	160	821	114.7	21.5
Otter Tail	150.6	2 612	67	432	322.5	13.2	287	3 177	704.5	61.9	67	137	22.2	2.9
Pennington	2.7	196	23	D	D	D	89	1 076	209.5	21.5	11	26	4.1	0.6
Pine	3.6	126	13	24	6.8	0.7	108	1 180	243.5	21.4	26	40	4.9	0.7
Pipestone	5.0	533	21	400	158.3	10.9	54	460	110.9	8.2	2	D	D	D
Polk	24.7	792	47	459	336.9	16.0	122	1 418	297.8	27.0	17	89	3.9	1.4
Pope	22.3	1 985	51	553	305.5	22.4	55	359	103.5	7.5	5	11	0.7	0.1
Ramsey	198.5	401	647	14 603	9 278.4	835.5	1 719	29 640	6 156.5	636.5	762	5 417	832.0	194.8
Red Lake	1.7	387	5	D	D	D	23	193	41.1	3.3	1	D	D	D
Redwood	3.0	188	29	371	210.7	17.7	93	774	156.8	14.8	16	37	2.8	0.6
Renville	4.0	238	29	236	277.7	9.1	82	582	117.0	8.4	6	9	0.6	0.1
Rice	9.8	161	59	D	D	D	219	2 596	599.2	55.9	51	168	51.4	3.7
Rock	3.1	325	15	161	88.5	6.6	47	416	109.1	7.9	9	32	1.9	0.4
Roseau	1.9	114	11	D	D	D	89	837	179.9	15.1	12	32	2.0	0.4
St. Louis	287.7	1 459	200	2 095	1 128.2	89.2	1 020	13 128	2 760.5	264.9	217	974	160.2	22.7
Scott	17.8	149	135	1 671	1 300.8	93.9	361	4 709	1 169.7	103.5	166	428	58.0	10.4
Sherburne	92.9	1 136	66	471	231.7	20.6	218	3 484	844.3	73.9	80	D	D	D
Sibley	3.3	215	14	99	69.3	4.5	61	426	75.5	6.4	9	17	1.5	0.3
Stearns	49.5	347	182	4 375	1 813.6	187.0	724	11 566	2 423.6	225.5	169	856	105.0	19.8
Steele	7.8	217	35	474	323.5	23.6	206	3 004	543.9	54.6	32	264	16.6	4.7
Stevens	6.5	659	19	90	130.8	3.4	52	594	170.1	12.1	11	43	2.5	0.6
Swift	12.5	1 106	18	282	665.6	12.1	50	376	80.6	6.8	6	82	2.4	1.3
Todd	12.7	515	12	89	18.0	2.8	100	758	160.0	13.4	20	31	2.0	0.4
Traverse	0.4	110	10	71	82.6	3.0	29	233	45.5	3.6	3	5	0.4	0.1
Wabasha	4.9	223	20	223	92.2	7.7	106	899	210.8	19.0	7	20	1.1	0.2
Wadena	13.0	952	16	487	243.4	22.4	98	892	177.7	17.3	7	25	0.7	0.3
Waseca	3.1	158	27	220	105.2	7.2	68	839	163.6	15.4	15	35	2.1	0.4
Washington	359.9	1 633	191	1 432	1 743.6	65.7	729	12 945	2 690.7	262.1	338	1 292	174.6	33.4
Watonwan	3.7	332	15	99	145.9	3.6	49	408	70.4	6.1	4	18	0.5	0.3
Wilkin	0.9	129	12	D	D	D	25	210	56.3	5.6	6	6	1.8	0.2
Winona	9.0	183	61	D	D	D	198	3 157	666.1	62.9	50	156	19.7	3.0
Wright	334.0	3 016	96	985	440.7	50.6	470	6 766	1 458.8	131.5	124	342	51.3	8.3
Yellow Medicine	3.2	307	17	205	302.3	8.1	50	449	112.9	7.7	4	10	0.9	0.2

1. Merchant wholesalers, except manufacturers' sales branches and offices.   2. Employer establishments.

Professional Services, Manufacturing, and Accommodation and Food Services

STATE County	Professional, scientific, and technical services,[1] 2007				Manufacturing, 2007				Accommodation and food services, 2007			
	Number of establish-ments	Number of employees	Receipts (mil dol)	Annual payroll (mil dol)	Number of establish-ments	Number of employees	Receipts (mil dol)	Annual payroll (mil dol)	Number of establish-ments	Number of employees	Sales (mil dol)	Annual payroll (mil dol)
	147	148	149	150	151	152	153	154	155	156	157	158
MINNESOTA—Cont'd												
Fillmore	35	145	11.1	3.5	48	880	377.4	32.0	62	487	14.5	3.4
Freeborn	39	D	D	D	59	2 746	767.0	100.5	82	1 076	33.8	9.8
Goodhue	87	358	39.5	14.4	86	4 204	1 332.3	167.6	125	3 132	254.6	62.1
Grant	12	51	4.0	1.4	NA	NA	NA	NA	11	D	D	D
Hennepin	6 938	84 413	13 992.3	5 782.2	1 883	82 304	20 957.7	4 397.5	2 640	62 847	3 279.1	1 017.7
Houston	28	D	D	D	23	647	D	19.3	42	208	8.0	1.8
Hubbard	35	102	6.7	2.3	36	1 284	328.6	43.2	68	468	20.6	5.3
Isanti	59	D	D	D	70	1 515	317.7	62.1	68	936	30.4	9.2
Itasca	70	D	D	D	48	1 367	627.2	63.0	116	1 298	51.0	15.4
Jackson	13	50	3.8	1.1	11	1 025	409.6	36.2	22	454	7.8	2.1
Kanabec	17	83	5.4	1.6	19	647	114.5	22.3	28	315	10.0	2.5
Kandiyohi	89	D	D	D	71	2 957	818.7	104.6	96	1 481	52.0	14.7
Kittson	6	30	2.4	1.0	NA	NA	NA	NA	11	D	D	D
Koochiching	24	81	5.5	2.1	22	1 053	D	D	43	463	21.3	6.0
Lac qui Parle	13	37	1.7	0.5	NA	NA	NA	NA	15	D	D	D
Lake	15	74	3.3	1.2	17	612	156.8	24.6	55	661	33.9	8.9
Lake of the Woods	5	8	0.4	0.2	NA	NA	NA	NA	38	444	20.4	5.1
Le Sueur	46	174	15.4	6.4	53	2 356	623.9	91.2	47	531	17.0	4.7
Lincoln	8	22	2.3	0.5	NA	NA	NA	NA	11	D	D	D
Lyon	50	600	24.7	23.7	38	1 976	697.0	70.3	64	1 182	37.3	11.7
McLeod	68	293	24.1	9.1	75	7 486	1 603.4	362.1	67	1 111	39.8	11.3
Mahnomen	3	D	D	D	NA	NA	NA	NA	10	D	D	D
Marshall	11	32	6.3	1.3	NA	NA	NA	NA	20	D	D	D
Martin	43	217	21.4	6.9	45	1 398	779.4	55.9	49	761	24.4	7.4
Meeker	35	214	12.9	6.1	60	1 500	692.6	60.3	39	469	13.9	4.0
Mille Lacs	31	79	9.5	2.5	43	1 038	215.1	37.7	75	2 035	200.5	37.5
Morrison	33	129	13.2	4.9	58	1 953	504.1	72.1	92	953	32.1	8.7
Mower	43	267	29.1	8.9	37	3 701	D	155.4	86	1 132	41.8	11.5
Murray	15	76	5.7	1.5	NA	NA	NA	NA	19	D	D	D
Nicollet	38	D	D	D	53	4 722	872.3	136.9	47	787	25.6	7.7
Nobles	30	D	D	D	31	2 898	952.0	100.5	51	730	26.1	6.8
Norman	11	37	4.6	1.7	NA	NA	NA	NA	17	D	D	D
Olmsted	275	D	D	D	100	9 150	2 971.4	579.2	311	7 364	326.9	93.7
Otter Tail	93	D	D	D	84	4 005	1 054.4	119.3	157	1 456	62.7	17.5
Pennington	21	325	44.4	15.8	20	1 656	D	55.5	34	1 083	43.3	15.8
Pine	26	D	D	D	NA	NA	NA	NA	63	D	D	D
Pipestone	17	60	5.0	1.1	13	620	D	15.8	20	D	D	D
Polk	39	D	D	D	39	1 733	954.1	67.2	61	1 010	36.7	10.1
Pope	19	244	23.0	11.0	30	524	82.7	19.2	37	325	12.6	3.0
Ramsey	1 859	13 562	1 962.6	807.4	639	27 716	7 578.9	1 580.0	1 114	21 976	963.5	291.7
Red Lake	5	20	1.4	0.4	NA	NA	NA	NA	8	D	D	D
Redwood	26	83	6.5	2.3	30	685	148.1	23.6	38	1 286	81.5	21.4
Renville	27	120	13.5	5.9	28	908	D	40.3	31	D	D	D
Rice	130	572	61.6	27.1	78	4 215	1 397.9	179.4	114	1 936	80.6	21.1
Rock	17	43	6.1	1.5	NA	NA	NA	NA	14	D	D	D
Roseau	24	93	6.2	1.9	20	4 317	D	144.4	38	643	24.5	8.6
St. Louis	420	D	D	D	228	5 670	D	D	579	9 962	498.6	118.8
Scott	393	D	D	D	182	6 024	1 925.0	344.1	185	6 552	527.5	129.9
Sherburne	145	419	43.3	17.6	150	3 592	683.3	150.9	119	2 211	75.3	22.0
Sibley	25	73	6.2	2.6	24	928	548.5	30.9	25	D	D	D
Stearns	303	D	D	D	253	13 255	3 745.5	531.3	389	7 167	251.2	71.9
Steele	63	193	17.0	5.6	70	5 727	1 485.0	263.8	85	1 477	67.7	16.6
Stevens	15	109	10.7	4.4	17	687	192.9	27.9	27	352	11.7	2.9
Swift	15	58	5.1	1.9	NA	NA	NA	NA	28	D	D	D
Todd	25	94	6.7	2.2	48	1 794	648.1	65.3	46	439	15.1	3.8
Traverse	4	D	D	D	NA	NA	NA	NA	7	D	D	D
Wabasha	33	D	D	D	30	1 822	D	63.4	56	464	17.0	4.6
Wadena	18	49	4.5	2.3	NA	NA	NA	NA	35	400	10.9	3.0
Waseca	33	132	8.5	4.2	29	2 365	633.9	106.0	39	383	13.5	3.4
Washington	785	D	D	D	227	9 698	5 751.8	532.2	385	8 209	340.9	101.4
Watonwan	12	60	8.8	2.2	20	1 283	327.5	38.6	22	268	9.1	2.2
Wilkin	6	D	D	D	NA	NA	NA	NA	16	D	5.1	1.5
Winona	80	D	D	D	103	6 754	1 711.1	223.2	109	1 924	65.4	16.6
Wright	270	864	86.7	32.2	217	5 625	1 124.6	229.2	188	3 362	106.7	31.9
Yellow Medicine	12	96	13.4	5.4	NA	NA	NA	NA	27	577	38.3	8.8

1. Establishment subject to federal tax.

Table B. States and Counties — Health Care and Social Assistance, Other Services, and Federal Funds

STATE County	Health care and social assistance, 2007				Other services, 2007				Federal funds and grants, 2009–2010 Expenditures (mil dol)			
										Direct payments for individuals[1]		
	Number of establishments	Number of employees	Receipts (mil dol)	Annual payroll (mil dol)	Number of establishments	Number of employees	Receipts (mil dol)	Annual payroll (mil dol)	Total	Social Security and government retirement	Medicare	Food Stamps and Supplemental Security Income
	159	160	161	162	163	164	165	166	167	168	169	170
MINNESOTA—Cont'd												
Fillmore	50	1 005	44.6	21.0	46	155	16.0	3.1	182.6	69.5	49.3	3.4
Freeborn	76	2 686	192.7	84.1	74	D	D	D	264.7	112.9	65.0	7.6
Goodhue	134	3 093	235.5	110.5	97	D	D	D	308.2	138.6	65.4	4.8
Grant	20	601	32.6	13.6	17	D	D	D	73.6	26.2	16.9	1.0
Hennepin	3 556	110 510	11 773.3	5 161.1	2 653	21 236	2 352.2	583.1	11 103.5	2 800.8	1 990.1	372.4
Houston	44	D	D	D	42	D	D	D	131.1	61.2	31.3	2.2
Hubbard	50	942	71.8	30.9	37	D	D	D	166.3	72.6	41.5	4.4
Isanti	76	2 104	179.4	71.1	62	D	D	D	189.9	87.4	37.9	4.5
Itasca	140	2 936	209.2	90.0	85	D	D	D	415.4	180.6	90.9	12.7
Jackson	25	1 425	42.4	21.3	30	D	D	D	92.7	34.1	20.6	1.6
Kanabec	31	951	69.6	26.9	26	D	D	D	105.8	48.0	21.6	3.8
Kandiyohi	179	5 098	293.6	146.8	92	D	D	D	356.7	124.5	66.5	10.2
Kittson	8	297	13.9	6.7	13	D	D	D	72.8	17.4	15.0	0.7
Koochiching	46	735	41.1	18.8	30	D	D	D	144.4	55.5	31.0	3.8
Lac qui Parle	18	575	26.4	12.0	18	D	D	D	87.3	31.6	17.9	1.2
Lake	31	568	24.9	12.4	21	219	12.1	3.6	104.3	47.8	22.2	1.7
Lake of the Woods	10	D	D	D	9	D	D	D	43.7	16.3	9.8	0.4
Le Sueur	58	812	37.3	16.5	55	249	15.8	3.7	177.4	84.7	40.9	3.5
Lincoln	15	553	31.6	12.5	14	D	D	D	63.1	20.1	17.9	0.8
Lyon	80	1 941	122.4	49.4	59	D	D	D	201.1	73.7	41.2	4.8
McLeod	107	2 595	183.7	78.2	94	D	D	D	203.0	102.0	47.1	4.2
Mahnomen	11	189	10.0	4.5	8	D	D	D	73.1	16.7	12.8	2.4
Marshall	18	306	10.3	5.7	27	D	D	D	118.1	32.0	26.4	1.6
Martin	61	1 954	124.6	60.0	57	D	D	D	173.3	79.2	43.9	4.6
Meeker	52	984	57.8	23.7	46	D	D	D	149.4	65.4	34.9	3.0
Mille Lacs	60	1 500	89.6	38.5	55	224	18.6	3.0	221.0	98.0	64.9	4.9
Morrison	69	1 402	96.8	40.4	82	399	37.6	7.4	325.4	106.2	61.7	7.0
Mower	89	2 587	169.4	79.8	97	D	D	D	335.4	133.5	88.1	8.9
Murray	19	431	35.1	10.8	22	D	D	D	76.8	28.3	19.4	1.1
Nicollet	65	2 111	152.9	89.2	65	373	135.2	9.6	146.5	64.9	26.2	3.2
Nobles	63	1 361	73.3	34.7	50	D	D	D	161.4	53.1	38.7	3.8
Norman	17	384	19.7	10.2	14	D	D	D	89.1	24.8	18.6	2.1
Olmsted	344	18 305	1 975.0	801.4	248	D	D	D	766.0	328.6	149.5	26.4
Otter Tail	171	4 370	232.5	109.3	134	D	D	D	501.9	212.2	118.1	9.0
Pennington	43	1 255	95.8	38.7	41	247	11.8	3.1	148.1	40.1	30.5	2.6
Pine	62	1 240	55.3	23.0	50	306	18.8	4.9	233.8	97.5	47.9	7.5
Pipestone	29	722	42.7	15.1	29	D	D	D	99.3	28.5	23.5	1.9
Polk	90	2 367	124.2	60.5	62	D	D	D	314.6	94.1	72.7	10.9
Pope	25	605	33.8	15.6	28	D	D	D	105.9	38.5	25.8	2.1
Ramsey	1 730	51 661	4 816.8	2 087.2	1 150	10 015	1 313.1	301.5	6 838.8	1 562.5	1 050.0	230.2
Red Lake	5	D	D	D	7	D	D	D	42.9	11.4	10.4	0.7
Redwood	43	959	56.3	22.6	52	D	D	D	140.5	52.2	33.4	2.6
Renville	46	1 317	50.7	24.3	37	D	D	D	144.8	48.3	33.8	3.8
Rice	149	3 197	206.3	90.5	133	D	D	D	341.1	150.4	71.0	7.7
Rock	15	600	30.4	12.2	18	D	D	D	72.4	30.3	18.0	0.9
Roseau	32	798	50.3	20.0	41	D	D	D	138.1	38.5	27.4	1.6
St. Louis	681	22 334	2 078.2	971.3	427	2 581	218.6	55.2	2 056.7	737.7	447.8	67.2
Scott	214	4 023	340.3	139.1	220	1 372	94.2	26.8	317.9	192.0	45.0	8.6
Sherburne	147	3 811	244.8	124.5	152	D	D	D	232.4	133.0	38.5	6.2
Sibley	29	454	22.8	9.8	31	D	D	D	97.2	37.0	27.6	1.9
Stearns	411	13 006	1 270.1	598.4	369	D	D	D	974.7	388.9	166.2	20.9
Steele	120	2 225	170.1	74.0	83	532	45.7	10.6	197.0	95.8	44.6	5.5
Stevens	40	D	D	D	24	D	D	D	102.6	26.6	22.1	1.9
Swift	20	593	34.7	14.8	27	D	D	D	115.8	35.6	26.8	2.0
Todd	51	728	45.3	19.2	45	D	D	D	211.9	72.1	50.9	5.7
Traverse	11	218	12.8	4.5	9	D	D	D	53.2	21.4	11.1	1.1
Wabasha	48	D	D	D	52	170	13.0	2.6	171.2	73.4	38.1	2.0
Wadena	46	1 976	128.2	57.9	28	D	D	D	149.4	51.8	38.0	4.6
Waseca	54	1 241	51.4	21.0	39	D	D	D	132.8	50.5	26.6	2.9
Washington	511	9 218	826.0	327.4	384	2 490	171.5	52.7	646.4	362.0	111.5	13.2
Watonwan	24	546	36.7	15.5	27	D	D	D	78.5	35.0	19.1	2.2
Wilkin	23	D	D	D	13	D	D	D	89.7	23.2	12.5	1.5
Winona	129	3 066	187.2	80.8	90	D	D	D	305.0	125.8	70.6	8.3
Wright	219	4 309	315.0	134.5	225	1 270	89.9	22.0	459.5	242.6	88.9	9.0
Yellow Medicine	28	1 044	59.6	27.2	24	D	D	D	113.6	41.6	26.8	1.8

1. State totals may include programs not allocated by county.

	Federal funds and grants, 2009–2010 (cont.)							Value of residential construction authorized by building permits, 2010		Local government finances, 2007				
	Expenditures (mil dol) (cont.)									General revenue				
		Procurement contract awards		Grants[1]								Taxes		
STATE County	Salaries and wages	Defense	Other	Medicaid and other health-related	Nutrition and family welfare	Education	Other	New construction ($1,000)	Number of housing units	Total (mil dol)	Inter-governmental (mil dol)	Total (mil dol)	Per capita[2] (dollars) Total	Property
	171	172	173	174	175	176	177	178	179	180	181	182	183	184
MINNESOTA—Cont'd														
Fillmore	6.0	0.0	1.5	32.0	6.0	1.5	1.2	8 769	55	71.2	39.8	15.7	747	737
Freeborn	15.0	0.3	2.3	36.4	5.6	1.9	4.2	5 323	34	111.6	63.7	25.1	802	726
Goodhue	11.1	32.2	3.1	31.1	7.6	2.6	2.3	7 895	42	202.0	88.7	58.3	1 273	1 225
Grant	2.3	0.0	0.5	11.7	3.4	0.4	0.5	320	2	35.7	23.6	6.5	1 078	1 075
Hennepin	977.5	613.5	831.2	2 046.6	181.6	93.8	538.4	391 116	1 915	5 614.0	2 424.2	1 770.6	1 558	1 400
Houston	5.0	0.6	1.0	21.4	3.1	1.1	0.5	5 642	40	66.2	42.0	14.3	733	725
Hubbard	3.5	0.0	0.8	34.2	4.4	1.5	1.2	3 418	25	78.2	48.0	19.8	1 052	1 036
Isanti	13.2	-0.4	1.8	23.5	5.0	2.4	0.8	5 241	34	119.3	69.5	30.2	775	739
Itasca	13.7	4.3	4.3	73.6	13.6	4.4	12.4	12 688	79	230.5	94.9	40.8	917	906
Jackson	5.5	0.0	0.6	11.7	2.3	0.7	6.9	2 189	17	46.4	23.3	11.9	1 092	1 086
Kanabec	3.2	1.5	0.7	18.3	5.7	0.8	0.0	1 416	11	77.2	30.9	11.7	727	712
Kandiyohi	20.6	0.1	47.5	50.4	10.2	2.9	3.3	13 264	82	262.7	92.0	38.0	933	846
Kittson	3.9	0.0	1.3	11.7	1.4	0.5	5.3	375	2	27.9	15.8	4.9	1 093	1 076
Koochiching	12.2	0.1	2.3	26.8	3.7	1.2	3.1	1 805	14	64.0	36.3	7.8	578	559
Lac qui Parle	10.7	0.0	0.6	8.5	1.9	0.5	5.4	1 800	11	44.9	23.5	6.2	854	847
Lake	2.1	0.2	0.5	13.9	2.2	0.7	12.8	7 688	48	56.3	29.0	12.0	1 121	1 081
Lake of the Woods	2.7	0.0	0.5	9.6	1.1	0.3	1.3	3 364	21	23.2	14.1	4.2	1 032	970
Le Sueur	6.4	0.1	1.9	26.7	4.0	1.6	2.0	5 051	35	90.8	48.4	22.6	806	779
Lincoln	1.9	0.0	0.5	11.7	1.5	0.5	0.3	1 700	15	20.6	12.3	4.8	819	811
Lyon	27.1	0.0	4.0	25.6	6.1	2.5	0.4	3 507	20	149.2	62.9	23.6	954	922
McLeod	11.5	0.2	1.7	19.4	4.4	1.9	1.8	3 104	16	199.4	69.5	32.4	871	856
Mahnomen	1.7	0.1	0.3	17.1	2.5	4.3	4.9	0	0	36.1	22.5	4.5	874	869
Marshall	4.3	0.1	0.9	19.3	3.2	0.9	1.3	425	3	43.4	29.4	6.9	714	706
Martin	6.7	0.2	1.2	17.1	4.5	1.6	2.1	2 345	13	77.5	41.0	16.5	804	786
Meeker	10.1	0.0	1.3	20.3	4.6	1.4	0.5	3 546	23	121.9	59.3	20.9	899	882
Mille Lacs	5.7	0.0	2.0	38.1	6.6	2.3	1.5	2 727	18	105.5	67.2	22.7	861	841
Morrison	67.7	2.2	1.8	54.8	10.5	2.9	1.6	5 407	61	111.2	64.3	25.2	769	744
Mower	18.2	0.0	2.4	48.0	6.3	2.9	6.7	5 853	29	157.0	89.4	23.2	611	588
Murray	3.7	0.0	0.9	10.7	1.9	0.6	0.6	3 924	26	40.8	21.1	8.1	950	940
Nicollet	6.7	5.6	0.8	15.0	3.6	1.3	2.5	15 535	157	94.0	37.7	22.1	697	672
Nobles	7.5	5.3	4.5	28.8	5.1	1.7	2.5	5 521	41	107.2	48.9	16.2	807	780
Norman	3.2	0.0	0.8	12.8	2.0	0.6	6.4	946	7	34.4	23.7	5.6	842	835
Olmsted	98.0	3.2	21.5	70.3	17.6	7.8	18.1	78 028	398	567.3	246.7	157.6	1 128	990
Otter Tail	19.4	0.8	4.0	89.7	13.1	3.3	3.3	5 971	36	269.7	110.6	44.7	783	759
Pennington	7.7	0.1	3.7	35.2	3.2	1.2	6.2	1 019	5	122.0	37.0	12.1	876	853
Pine	24.7	3.1	-8.1	42.7	5.6	1.8	6.3	5 719	46	91.5	54.8	21.2	752	734
Pipestone	5.9	0.0	1.1	18.1	2.4	0.7	11.2	1 579	10	61.8	28.1	8.3	887	868
Polk	13.7	0.8	2.3	60.2	15.4	2.2	6.0	11 163	56	166.2	96.2	29.1	947	876
Pope	2.9	10.6	0.8	13.9	2.7	0.7	0.1	9 469	52	41.7	23.3	9.5	859	846
Ramsey	533.8	80.8	126.7	853.6	265.3	385.2	1 493.2	27 399	122	2 668.9	1 240.7	622.0	1 244	1 114
Red Lake	1.6	0.7	0.3	7.5	3.7	0.4	0.3	194	2	21.6	15.2	2.9	705	691
Redwood	7.1	0.0	1.7	25.6	3.0	1.3	0.6	4 461	23	85.6	39.0	15.0	965	936
Renville	6.5	0.0	1.2	23.7	3.7	1.4	5.7	2 953	15	81.6	42.8	15.0	931	915
Rice	17.0	0.1	3.2	59.5	7.6	3.0	10.4	12 830	85	305.2	98.6	47.6	768	699
Rock	4.4	0.0	0.5	7.5	1.9	0.7	1.8	3 086	19	41.8	24.7	7.9	829	773
Roseau	7.6	8.4	7.1	22.5	5.0	1.1	0.2	250	3	85.4	61.7	11.2	701	691
St. Louis	160.3	28.0	42.9	369.6	50.9	19.2	84.5	52 264	326	945.8	459.1	193.9	986	868
Scott	14.7	0.8	7.6	16.1	13.3	3.8	3.3	117 835	483	434.5	188.5	141.8	1 120	1 041
Sherburne	12.2	0.3	3.2	22.4	7.9	2.6	0.4	18 413	135	324.7	168.4	95.2	1 103	1 071
Sibley	5.6	0.0	0.9	11.7	2.5	0.9	0.1	1 720	9	72.5	31.0	15.8	1 055	1 024
Stearns	96.1	0.9	55.6	116.5	24.4	8.0	15.5	50 091	273	582.1	284.4	139.3	954	836
Steele	9.5	1.7	1.6	20.4	4.8	1.8	1.1	7 029	41	137.2	72.7	31.8	873	838
Stevens	13.6	0.1	4.8	14.9	2.2	0.6	3.5	2 462	14	38.1	21.9	8.5	882	858
Swift	15.1	0.0	0.9	18.1	2.9	0.8	1.1	801	5	64.2	27.1	9.9	883	874
Todd	8.7	0.0	1.8	53.4	6.9	2.1	2.9	7 657	49	123.2	72.3	18.2	756	720
Traverse	1.5	0.4	0.3	5.3	1.3	0.3	0.3	1 220	9	33.9	11.7	5.6	1 507	1 504
Wabasha	6.1	0.2	18.5	20.3	3.4	1.4	2.0	8 578	40	86.7	45.7	20.7	949	836
Wadena	7.0	0.3	0.9	38.5	3.7	1.2	0.5	4 697	38	59.4	36.4	9.4	705	690
Waseca	19.0	0.5	5.9	14.9	3.4	1.4	0.4	3 619	23	79.4	42.7	17.5	898	819
Washington	56.8	2.8	12.5	45.1	21.5	7.6	3.1	196 347	1 069	800.8	340.1	259.8	1 147	1 077
Watonwan	5.9	0.0	1.4	5.3	2.4	0.8	0.6	1 050	8	45.9	28.6	9.2	831	821
Wilkin	2.2	6.3	0.5	9.7	1.6	0.6	0.2	963	7	31.0	20.4	6.0	935	925
Winona	14.6	3.3	2.3	42.8	7.2	3.1	4.9	15 201	113	152.0	89.0	35.5	712	670
Wright	39.9	0.5	4.5	44.4	13.5	4.0	4.3	35 491	211	468.5	199.8	115.1	981	922
Yellow Medicine	3.8	0.1	1.0	17.1	2.7	1.0	1.8	1 223	7	65.5	28.2	9.8	964	944

1. State totals may include programs not allocated by county.　　2. Based on the resident population estimated as of July 1 of the year shown.

STATE County	Total (mil dol)	Per capita[1] (dollars)	Educa- tion	Health and hospitals	Police protec- tion	Public welfare	High- ways	Total (mil dol)	Per capita[1] (dollars)	Federal civilian	Federal military	State and local	Demo- cratic	Republi- can	All other
	Local government finances, 2007 (cont.)									Government employment, 2009			Presidential election,[2] 2008		
	Direct general expenditure							Debt outstanding					Percent of vote cast:		
			Percent of total for:												
	185	186	187	188	189	190	191	192	193	194	195	196	197	198	199
MINNESOTA—Cont'd															
Fillmore	80.4	3 822	37.4	3.1	4.1	3.9	18.8	70.6	3 354	84	78	1 223	52.7	44.4	2.8
Freeborn	106.6	3 411	41.0	2.2	5.0	9.3	13.5	63.0	2 015	92	117	1 387	57.4	40.2	2.4
Goodhue	201.5	4 396	40.8	7.6	4.8	4.3	11.5	176.8	3 857	122	172	4 259	48.1	49.5	2.3
Grant	33.3	5 529	34.8	1.1	3.4	9.2	15.7	24.0	3 993	32	22	343	51.3	45.7	3.0
Hennepin	5 718.3	5 031	33.6	13.6	5.9	8.1	5.4	7 621.7	6 706	13 854	5 050	79 775	63.4	34.8	1.8
Houston	69.9	3 583	50.3	2.5	5.3	6.0	11.1	55.6	2 848	82	72	1 058	54.3	43.6	2.2
Hubbard	69.0	3 672	38.9	0.0	3.9	15.4	14.7	75.9	4 039	48	70	1 092	41.9	56.3	1.8
Isanti	126.5	3 250	47.2	1.1	5.8	7.6	15.4	184.1	4 730	84	148	1 938	41.1	56.5	2.4
Itasca	238.9	5 364	30.3	22.0	3.6	9.8	11.4	197.6	4 436	198	167	3 306	55.2	42.3	2.6
Jackson	47.1	4 331	30.5	5.3	3.4	11.9	16.2	56.4	5 187	40	40	681	46.6	50.8	2.6
Kanabec	75.6	4 701	30.3	36.6	2.2	4.6	9.5	71.5	4 443	44	60	1 067	44.0	52.7	3.3
Kandiyohi	268.9	6 593	22.7	34.4	3.0	4.6	10.2	237.3	5 818	175	155	3 844	46.2	51.7	2.1
Kittson	26.0	5 773	39.6	0.2	3.4	4.4	27.1	6.2	1 368	49	16	297	58.1	39.6	2.3
Koochiching	72.7	5 401	33.9	1.7	4.3	12.8	18.8	64.6	4 803	187	49	822	53.6	43.5	2.8
Lac qui Parle	47.0	6 470	37.8	20.5	3.0	3.8	15.4	16.9	2 332	39	27	721	51.5	45.6	2.9
Lake	59.8	5 563	28.2	4.2	4.8	11.7	12.3	142.7	13 290	30	40	878	59.9	37.8	2.3
Lake of the Woods	20.9	5 097	32.6	0.3	3.4	6.6	27.2	298.3	72 846	37	19	259	42.0	55.3	2.8
Le Sueur	110.0	3 925	47.0	1.9	3.3	5.6	18.3	136.5	4 870	77	105	1 294	46.6	50.9	2.5
Lincoln	21.2	3 600	28.2	0.2	5.2	7.9	23.7	11.2	1 913	31	21	260	48.5	47.7	3.8
Lyon	162.9	6 594	39.8	21.8	3.6	2.4	11.5	155.2	6 286	133	94	2 795	48.1	49.7	2.2
McLeod	191.2	5 136	27.0	29.5	4.1	4.3	7.0	190.8	5 125	84	138	1 639	39.4	57.8	2.8
Mahnomen	40.0	7 795	43.0	16.7	5.4	5.7	13.9	31.1	6 063	30	19	1 317	61.3	36.0	2.7
Marshall	44.6	4 635	45.9	0.3	3.4	2.6	21.1	11.2	1 167	67	34	569	48.8	48.2	3.0
Martin	89.3	4 366	49.9	0.2	4.5	5.0	13.6	69.3	3 386	72	76	1 327	41.0	56.3	2.7
Meeker	124.7	5 372	47.0	15.8	3.9	7.0	7.0	116.0	4 997	82	87	1 133	42.9	53.7	3.4
Mille Lacs	107.4	4 076	58.8	0.9	3.0	5.2	7.9	107.1	4 063	67	99	3 472	44.8	52.0	3.1
Morrison	118.9	3 633	43.4	1.5	5.1	7.1	17.9	116.8	3 567	439	123	1 695	39.1	58.1	2.8
Mower	150.6	3 960	42.5	1.6	4.0	7.6	11.9	1 209.8	31 803	159	143	2 355	60.5	36.9	2.6
Murray	44.0	5 171	34.9	14.5	3.6	2.2	17.5	16.0	1 877	47	32	571	48.7	48.2	3.1
Nicollet	100.7	3 177	29.9	13.3	5.2	0.9	15.3	119.4	3 768	52	121	2 912	54.2	43.7	2.1
Nobles	105.3	5 231	32.2	21.6	4.4	6.8	6.4	87.6	4 353	100	77	1 356	48.2	49.6	2.3
Norman	35.4	5 297	68.2	1.0	3.6	8.2	19.1	15.1	2 255	44	24	451	62.0	35.1	2.9
Olmsted	603.7	4 320	37.0	1.6	4.3	9.3	5.2	1 588.4	11 367	924	543	7 060	50.6	47.3	2.0
Otter Tail	280.7	4 922	45.3	7.9	3.1	6.0	10.8	205.0	3 594	241	212	3 257	42.4	55.3	2.3
Pennington	119.5	8 687	68.0	0.0	3.2	4.4	7.4	67.4	4 902	76	52	1 606	49.8	47.6	2.6
Pine	93.5	3 320	40.9	1.4	4.2	8.0	17.0	108.7	3 861	314	106	3 115	49.3	47.7	3.0
Pipestone	65.4	7 031	31.1	28.8	2.4	5.9	14.0	40.4	4 346	58	35	935	42.1	55.3	2.6
Polk	176.2	5 737	29.6	1.0	3.8	9.4	14.7	171.2	5 576	139	115	2 557	51.2	46.6	2.2
Pope	39.6	3 575	36.2	4.8	5.2	6.4	18.0	19.0	1 714	46	41	711	50.7	47.0	2.3
Ramsey	2 647.8	5 297	40.0	1.8	5.9	7.5	3.6	5 096.1	10 194	3 656	1 916	53 924	66.0	32.1	2.0
Red Lake	23.0	5 581	52.7	0.1	4.0	5.4	13.1	12.0	2 908	155	16	277	51.1	44.9	4.0
Redwood	83.3	5 370	31.4	19.9	4.0	7.9	14.7	85.2	6 492	69	58	2 077	41.6	55.2	3.2
Renville	79.9	4 950	24.2	11.2	3.8	6.8	19.1	41.4	2 567	72	59	1 042	48.0	48.6	3.4
Rice	309.8	5 001	25.3	37.9	3.2	2.8	9.6	326.9	5 277	149	235	4 017	54.7	43.2	2.2
Rock	39.3	4 134	36.9	0.2	3.9	6.0	22.2	59.5	6 263	35	36	698	41.8	55.8	2.4
Roseau	91.8	5 757	37.1	0.3	3.7	4.5	22.9	64.4	4 042	109	60	1 022	40.2	57.6	2.1
St. Louis	967.2	4 917	29.9	7.9	4.9	8.9	9.3	946.6	4 812	1 528	867	15 496	65.1	32.6	2.3
Scott	553.1	4 368	50.4	0.3	5.5	3.2	14.6	1 011.9	7 990	177	494	9 355	43.5	54.7	1.8
Sherburne	323.8	3 752	52.6	0.5	4.2	4.1	9.1	768.1	8 902	146	329	3 841	39.9	58.1	2.0
Sibley	70.7	4 713	35.5	15.6	4.0	10.1	12.2	49.6	3 304	45	56	831	38.8	58.1	3.1
Stearns	581.9	3 984	41.7	8.3	4.8	3.9	12.4	1 010.5	6 919	2 030	563	10 082	45.3	52.3	2.4
Steele	134.3	3 693	44.6	1.6	4.4	11.6	11.6	118.9	3 267	79	138	2 008	45.9	51.2	2.9
Stevens	38.7	4 019	38.7	3.5	5.0	6.3	17.1	56.8	5 901	85	36	1 179	49.4	48.1	2.5
Swift	70.1	6 262	22.5	28.0	3.6	5.9	19.6	22.1	1 971	57	41	933	55.4	41.6	2.9
Todd	128.1	5 333	45.1	15.2	2.7	5.6	11.4	61.8	2 570	89	89	1 380	43.1	54.1	2.8
Traverse	34.4	9 265	19.3	20.6	3.1	12.5	12.2	20.3	5 466	27	13	426	51.3	45.8	2.9
Wabasha	93.1	4 276	38.3	2.0	5.9	4.5	11.0	76.0	3 491	69	82	1 077	47.5	49.9	2.6
Wadena	60.1	4 490	47.6	1.6	4.3	17.7	10.8	33.0	2 465	52	50	1 333	40.2	57.6	2.2
Waseca	85.3	4 366	45.6	1.6	4.1	11.3	12.2	67.6	3 460	264	70	1 165	44.5	52.7	2.8
Washington	816.5	3 605	49.2	1.8	5.8	3.7	8.3	1 172.3	5 176	457	869	9 948	51.3	46.9	1.8
Watonwan	50.1	4 549	41.1	1.2	5.9	7.5	18.3	38.7	3 514	55	41	761	48.7	48.0	3.2
Wilkin	33.0	5 138	36.5	2.2	4.5	6.3	23.5	12.3	1 923	36	23	362	45.4	52.3	2.3
Winona	156.1	3 134	43.5	2.0	5.0	5.8	17.2	85.1	1 708	156	185	3 465	58.4	39.3	2.3
Wright	539.7	4 598	47.7	8.4	3.6	3.2	14.1	984.7	8 389	215	458	5 930	40.2	57.6	2.2
Yellow Medicine	69.1	6 821	29.2	24.2	2.2	9.5	13.5	38.5	3 797	49	37	1 517	50.6	46.3	3.1

1. Based on the resident population estimated as of July 1 of the year shown.   2. © 2009 Election Data Services, Inc. All rights reserved.

Table B. States and Counties — Land Area and Population

STATE/ County code	CBSA code[1]	County type[2]	STATE County	Land area,[3] (sq km) 2010	Total persons	Rank	Per square kilometer	White	Black	American Indian, Alaska Native	Asian and Pacific Islander	Percent Hispanic or Latino[4]	Under 5 years	5 to 17 years	18 to 24 years	25 to 34 years	35 to 44 years	45 to 54 years
				1	2	3	4	5	6	7	8	9	10	11	12	13	14	15
28 000	...	X	MISSISSIPPI	121 531	2 967 297	X	24.4	58.8	37.4	0.8	1.1	2.7	7.1	18.4	10.3	13.1	12.6	14.1
28 001	35020	5	Adams....................	1 198	32 297	1 384	27.0	39.3	53.7	0.6	0.6	6.7	6.2	16.1	8.2	12.3	11.9	15.8
28 003	18420	7	Alcorn....................	1 036	37 057	1 242	35.8	85.3	11.8	0.5	0.4	2.7	6.7	17.6	7.9	12.3	13.2	13.9
28 005	32620	8	Amite.....................	1 891	13 131	2 240	6.9	57.6	41.4	0.4	0.3	0.8	6.7	15.8	7.7	10.4	11.0	15.7
28 007	...	6	Attala....................	1 904	19 564	1 860	10.3	55.9	42.1	0.4	0.4	1.7	7.5	18.5	7.9	10.9	12.1	13.3
28 009	...	8	Benton....................	1 053	8 729	2 548	8.3	60.5	37.5	0.8	0.1	1.7	6.6	18.1	8.3	11.9	12.8	14.7
28 011	17380	5	Bolivar...................	2 270	34 145	1 324	15.0	33.3	64.3	0.3	0.7	1.9	7.5	17.8	12.7	13.0	11.4	13.1
28 013	...	7	Calhoun...................	1 519	14 962	2 113	9.8	66.7	28.2	0.5	0.2	5.4	7.1	17.9	7.8	11.4	12.9	13.7
28 015	24900	9	Carroll...................	1 627	10 597	2 394	6.5	66.0	32.9	0.5	0.4	1.0	6.0	15.5	7.7	11.0	12.1	15.8
28 017	...	7	Chickasaw.................	1 300	17 392	1 958	13.4	53.8	42.4	0.4	0.4	3.7	7.3	19.0	9.0	11.7	12.1	14.2
28 019	...	9	Choctaw...................	1 083	8 547	2 564	7.9	68.7	30.4	0.5	0.3	0.9	6.4	17.9	7.5	10.4	11.3	15.1
28 021	...	6	Claiborne.................	1 262	9 604	2 470	7.6	14.4	84.4	0.3	0.6	0.8	6.2	17.5	17.0	11.1	10.1	12.9
28 023	32940	9	Clarke....................	1 791	16 732	2 000	9.3	64.2	34.7	0.5	0.3	0.8	6.5	18.2	8.0	10.8	12.1	14.6
28 025	48500	7	Clay......................	1 062	20 634	1 814	19.4	40.4	58.4	0.4	0.3	1.0	7.0	18.7	9.2	11.9	11.5	14.5
28 027	17260	5	Coahoma...................	1 431	26 151	1 556	18.3	22.9	75.6	0.2	0.5	1.1	8.1	21.2	10.9	12.0	11.2	13.3
28 029	27140	2	Copiah....................	2 013	29 449	1 441	14.6	46.0	51.1	0.4	0.4	2.6	7.3	17.8	11.3	11.8	11.3	14.6
28 031	...	8	Covington.................	1 072	19 568	1 859	18.3	62.9	35.1	0.3	0.4	1.9	7.3	18.7	9.1	12.1	11.9	13.8
28 033	32820	1	DeSoto....................	1 233	161 252	382	130.8	71.5	22.4	0.6	1.7	5.0	7.2	21.1	8.1	13.6	15.5	14.0
28 035	25620	3	Forrest...................	1 208	74 934	725	62.0	59.3	36.7	0.6	1.0	3.5	7.2	16.4	15.8	15.2	11.6	12.2
28 037	...	9	Franklin..................	1 460	8 118	2 599	5.6	64.9	34.5	0.5	0.2	0.6	6.8	18.4	7.3	11.6	11.6	14.7
28 039	37700	3	George....................	1 240	22 578	1 707	18.2	89.3	8.3	0.8	0.3	2.0	7.3	19.5	9.1	12.2	13.7	14.1
28 041	...	8	Greene....................	1 846	14 400	2 148	7.8	72.6	26.4	0.6	0.2	0.9	5.7	16.2	8.7	17.2	15.0	14.7
28 043	24980	7	Grenada...................	1 093	21 906	1 740	20.0	56.9	42.0	0.4	0.4	0.9	6.6	18.0	8.7	11.4	13.0	14.5
28 045	25060	3	Hancock...................	1 227	43 929	1 087	35.8	88.1	7.8	1.2	1.5	3.3	6.3	17.6	8.0	11.0	12.6	15.7
28 047	25060	3	Harrison..................	1 487	187 105	332	125.8	69.1	22.9	1.0	3.8	5.3	7.4	17.1	10.8	14.3	12.6	14.7
28 049	27140	2	Hinds.....................	2 253	245 285	264	108.9	28.5	69.4	0.4	0.9	1.5	7.3	19.2	11.7	14.1	12.1	13.8
28 051	...	6	Holmes....................	1 960	19 198	1 869	9.8	15.9	83.4	0.3	0.3	0.7	8.7	20.4	11.9	11.5	10.6	13.6
28 053	...	7	Humphreys.................	1 084	9 375	2 493	8.6	23.3	74.6	0.3	0.4	2.2	9.1	19.7	9.3	12.5	11.2	14.5
28 055	...	9	Issaquena.................	1 070	1 406	3 089	1.3	34.4	64.4	0.4	0.4	0.6	5.0	15.0	12.4	13.9	11.2	16.2
28 057	46180	7	Itawamba..................	1 380	23 401	1 670	17.0	92.3	6.1	0.4	0.3	1.3	6.2	16.9	11.2	11.2	13.3	13.6
28 059	37700	3	Jackson...................	1 872	139 668	440	74.6	71.3	22.1	0.9	2.7	4.6	6.8	18.7	8.7	13.0	13.4	15.1
28 061	29860	3	Jasper....................	1 751	17 062	1 978	9.7	46.4	52.8	0.2	0.3	0.8	6.5	17.7	8.2	11.2	12.1	14.9
28 063	...	7	Jefferson.................	1 347	7 726	2 626	5.7	13.8	85.7	0.3	0.1	0.4	6.2	17.4	10.2	13.4	11.6	16.2
28 065	...	8	Jefferson Davis...........	1 058	12 487	2 275	11.8	38.8	60.1	0.5	0.3	0.8	6.5	17.1	8.6	10.6	12.3	14.6
28 067	29860	4	Jones.....................	1 800	67 761	777	37.6	66.1	28.5	0.7	0.6	4.7	7.5	18.1	9.9	12.5	12.1	13.7
28 069	32940	9	Kemper....................	1 984	10 456	2 406	5.3	35.4	60.5	4.1	0.2	0.5	6.7	16.7	10.8	11.5	12.1	13.8
28 071	37060	6	Lafayette.................	1 636	47 351	1 019	28.9	71.6	24.0	0.5	2.5	2.3	5.4	13.1	26.9	14.0	10.3	10.7
28 073	25620	3	Lamar.....................	1 287	55 658	900	43.2	76.8	19.9	0.5	1.4	2.2	7.6	18.6	11.2	15.3	13.4	13.1
28 075	32940	5	Lauderdale................	1 822	80 261	684	44.1	54.5	43.0	0.4	0.9	1.8	7.1	17.9	9.8	12.9	12.5	13.7
28 077	...	8	Lawrence..................	1 115	12 929	2 246	11.6	66.7	30.9	0.4	0.4	2.1	7.3	17.9	8.1	11.8	12.2	15.0
28 079	...	6	Leake.....................	1 510	23 805	1 649	15.8	49.3	40.8	6.0	0.3	4.3	8.0	23.0	8.8	12.2	11.8	12.3
28 081	46180	5	Lee.......................	1 165	82 910	666	71.2	69.5	27.8	0.4	0.9	2.4	7.3	19.3	8.3	13.2	13.4	14.2
28 083	24900	5	Leflore...................	1 535	32 317	1 383	21.1	24.8	72.3	0.3	0.7	2.3	8.0	19.0	11.8	13.9	11.4	13.2
28 085	15020	6	Lincoln...................	1 518	34 869	1 305	23.0	68.5	30.2	0.4	0.5	0.9	7.3	18.8	8.3	12.2	12.5	14.3
28 087	18060	5	Lowndes...................	1 309	59 779	861	45.7	54.0	43.9	0.5	1.0	1.5	7.0	18.2	10.8	12.8	12.4	14.2
28 089	27140	1	Madison...................	1 851	95 203	607	51.4	56.5	38.4	0.3	2.4	2.9	7.4	19.6	8.6	13.5	13.8	15.2
28 091	...	6	Marion....................	1 405	27 088	1 530	19.3	65.9	32.7	0.4	0.5	1.2	7.5	18.1	8.5	12.7	12.2	14.0
28 093	32820	1	Marshall..................	1 829	37 144	1 235	20.3	49.5	47.2	0.4	0.3	3.2	6.6	16.8	9.9	12.7	12.8	15.7
28 095	...	7	Monroe....................	1 982	36 989	1 244	18.7	67.8	31.2	0.4	0.3	1.0	6.7	17.8	8.6	11.3	12.6	14.3
28 097	...	7	Montgomery................	1 054	10 925	2 375	10.4	53.1	45.6	0.3	0.4	0.9	6.8	17.6	8.3	10.6	11.5	14.5
28 099	...	7	Neshoba...................	1 477	29 676	1 435	20.1	60.8	21.6	16.8	0.5	1.6	8.4	20.3	8.6	12.3	12.0	13.0
28 101	...	7	Newton....................	1 497	21 720	1 748	14.5	63.3	30.5	5.3	0.3	1.3	7.0	19.0	9.8	11.5	12.7	13.2
28 103	...	7	Noxubee...................	1 800	11 545	2 330	6.4	27.3	71.7	0.3	0.3	0.8	7.3	19.8	9.8	11.6	11.7	14.8
28 105	44260	5	Oktibbeha.................	1 187	47 671	1 013	40.2	59.3	37.0	0.5	2.8	1.4	5.7	12.6	30.8	14.1	8.9	10.4
28 107	...	6	Panola....................	1 775	34 707	1 309	19.6	49.6	48.9	0.6	0.3	1.4	7.4	19.6	9.4	12.0	12.5	14.7
28 109	38100	6	Pearl River...............	2 100	55 834	897	26.6	83.7	12.9	1.3	0.8	2.9	6.9	17.7	9.3	11.4	12.6	14.3
28 111	25620	3	Perry.....................	1 676	12 250	2 287	7.3	78.5	20.5	0.6	0.2	1.0	7.1	18.4	8.3	11.9	12.6	14.8
28 113	32620	7	Pike......................	1 059	40 404	1 163	38.2	46.5	51.7	0.5	0.7	1.2	7.6	19.6	8.7	12.1	11.8	13.6
28 115	46180	7	Pontotoc..................	1 289	29 957	1 430	23.2	79.6	14.3	0.7	0.3	6.2	7.3	19.7	8.5	12.7	13.4	14.3
28 117	...	7	Prentiss..................	1 075	25 276	1 593	23.5	84.7	14.4	0.4	0.2	1.2	6.5	16.8	11.2	11.5	12.6	13.7
28 119	...	6	Quitman...................	1 049	8 223	2 593	7.8	29.2	69.9	0.6	0.2	0.7	6.9	19.3	9.8	11.3	11.7	14.3
28 121	27140	2	Rankin....................	2 008	141 617	435	70.5	77.1	19.2	0.5	1.4	2.7	7.0	18.1	8.1	15.1	14.5	14.1
28 123	...	6	Scott.....................	1 578	28 264	1 484	17.9	51.5	37.8	0.4	0.4	10.7	8.1	18.9	9.8	13.3	12.4	13.6
28 125	...	9	Sharkey...................	1 118	4 916	2 846	4.4	28.0	71.1	0.1	0.3	0.8	6.8	18.7	8.7	10.9	10.9	15.6
28 127	27140	2	Simpson...................	1 526	27 503	1 513	18.0	62.9	35.4	0.4	0.5	1.4	7.3	19.1	8.5	11.8	12.0	14.5
28 129	...	8	Smith.....................	1 648	16 491	2 019	10.0	75.8	23.1	0.3	0.2	1.2	6.8	19.0	8.2	10.9	12.8	14.2
28 131	25060	3	Stone.....................	1 154	17 786	1 937	15.4	78.6	19.4	0.9	0.6	1.3	6.6	17.7	12.4	12.2	12.8	14.0

1. CBSA = Core Based Statistical Area. See Appendix A for explanation. See Appendix B for list of metropolitan areas with component counties.   2. County type code from the Economic Research Service of USDA Rural-Urban Continuum Codes. See Appendix A for definition.   3. Dry land or land partially or temporarily covered by water.   4. May be of any race.

Table B. States and Counties — **Population and Households**

	Population, 2010 (cont.)				Population change and components of change, 1990–2010							Households, 2010				
	Age (percent) (cont.)				Total persons		Percent change		Components of change, 2000–2009						Percent	
STATE County	55 to 64 years	65 to 74 years	75 years and over	Percent female	1990	2000	1990–2000	2000–2010	Births	Deaths	Net migration	Number	Percent change, 2000–2010	Persons per house-hold	Female family house-holder[1]	One per-son
	16	17	18	19	20	21	22	23	24	25	26	27	28	29	30	31
MISSISSIPPI	11.7	7.2	5.6	51.4	2 575 475	2 844 658	10.5	4.3	403 008	263 192	-18 973	1 115 768	6.6	2.58	18.5	26.3
Adams	13.7	8.3	7.5	50.1	35 356	34 340	-2.9	-5.9	4 023	3 759	-3 746	12 643	-7.6	2.37	22.2	31.8
Alcorn	12.5	9.2	6.7	51.1	31 722	34 558	8.9	7.2	4 376	3 944	1 064	15 039	5.7	2.44	13.9	28.5
Amite	14.4	10.5	7.7	51.5	13 328	13 599	2.0	-3.4	1 523	1 385	-643	5 351	1.5	2.43	15.7	29.7
Attala	12.6	9.1	8.1	52.4	18 481	19 661	6.4	-0.5	2 695	2 484	-6	7 619	0.7	2.52	18.9	28.1
Benton	12.3	8.5	6.9	50.9	8 046	8 026	-0.2	8.8	1 089	800	-298	3 404	13.5	2.54	17.0	26.8
Bolivar	12.4	6.8	5.2	53.5	41 875	40 633	-3.0	-16.0	5 734	3 911	-5 542	12 727	-7.6	2.56	26.9	28.4
Calhoun	12.7	8.9	7.6	52.2	14 908	15 069	1.1	-0.7	1 881	1 600	-861	5 988	-0.5	2.46	17.0	27.8
Carroll	14.8	10.4	6.7	50.0	9 237	10 769	16.6	-1.6	1 076	912	-614	4 188	2.9	2.45	14.9	26.1
Chickasaw	12.3	8.0	6.4	52.5	18 085	19 440	7.5	-10.5	2 723	1 727	-1 671	6 639	-8.5	2.59	19.7	26.6
Choctaw	13.9	10.0	7.4	52.1	9 071	9 758	7.6	-12.4	1 004	827	-859	3 446	-6.5	2.45	15.5	29.0
Claiborne	13.1	6.9	5.3	52.9	11 370	11 831	4.1	-18.8	1 446	986	-1 522	3 440	-6.6	2.53	26.6	31.4
Clarke	13.5	9.3	7.1	52.4	17 313	17 955	3.7	-6.8	2 169	1 781	-1 037	6 733	-3.5	2.48	17.3	27.0
Clay	13.0	7.5	6.8	53.1	21 120	21 979	4.1	-6.1	2 873	2 063	-1 994	8 029	-1.5	2.53	24.2	26.8
Coahoma	11.0	6.6	5.6	54.1	31 665	30 622	-3.3	-14.6	4 909	3 078	-5 433	9 461	-10.3	2.89	30.2	28.4
Copiah	12.3	7.6	6.1	51.7	27 592	28 757	4.2	2.4	4 202	2 682	-1 027	10 708	5.6	2.65	20.7	25.6
Covington	11.9	8.3	6.8	51.4	16 527	19 407	17.4	0.8	2 827	2 133	548	7 430	4.3	2.60	18.1	26.6
DeSoto	10.3	6.2	4.0	51.3	67 910	107 199	57.9	50.4	18 759	8 338	41 442	57 748	48.9	2.78	15.1	19.8
Forrest	9.9	6.2	5.3	52.2	68 314	72 604	6.3	3.2	10 719	6 591	4 734	28 746	5.7	2.48	18.5	29.3
Franklin	13.4	8.9	7.3	51.4	8 377	8 448	0.8	-3.9	1 041	796	-330	3 211	0.0	2.51	14.8	27.7
George	11.3	8.1	4.6	49.4	16 673	19 144	14.8	17.9	3 285	1 982	2 324	7 982	18.4	2.76	11.1	21.5
Greene	11.2	7.0	4.3	40.9	10 220	13 299	30.1	8.3	1 403	1 086	797	4 306	3.8	2.64	13.3	23.9
Grenada	12.9	8.3	6.6	52.8	21 555	23 263	7.9	-5.8	2 928	2 730	-279	8 779	-0.5	2.47	20.6	29.0
Hancock	13.6	9.2	6.0	50.4	31 760	42 967	35.3	2.2	4 735	3 816	-2 882	17 380	2.9	2.50	13.3	26.2
Harrison	11.4	6.8	4.9	50.3	165 365	189 601	14.7	-1.3	26 531	15 917	-18 302	71 476	-0.1	2.54	17.2	26.4
Hinds	10.9	5.9	4.9	53.0	254 441	250 800	-1.4	-2.2	36 419	18 937	-19 432	91 351	0.4	2.60	25.4	28.3
Holmes	10.8	6.9	5.7	53.2	21 604	21 609	0.0	-11.2	3 576	2 269	-2 542	6 926	-5.3	2.69	32.6	29.2
Humphreys	11.2	6.9	5.6	53.2	12 134	11 206	-7.6	-16.3	1 895	1 098	-2 172	3 373	-10.4	2.75	30.7	27.1
Issaquena	11.9	8.7	5.8	42.0	1 909	2 274	19.1	-38.2	166	106	-720	472	-35.0	2.45	19.3	32.6
Itawamba	11.9	9.1	6.7	51.1	20 017	22 770	13.8	2.8	2 628	2 565	311	8 881	1.2	2.53	11.8	24.5
Jackson	11.9	7.5	4.9	50.7	115 243	131 420	14.0	6.3	17 184	10 826	-4 140	52 205	9.5	2.65	16.4	23.1
Jasper	13.5	9.2	6.8	51.2	17 114	18 149	6.0	-6.0	2 384	1 667	-828	6 798	1.3	2.50	18.2	28.1
Jefferson	12.0	7.3	5.6	50.4	8 653	9 740	12.6	-20.7	1 206	760	-1 223	2 929	-11.5	2.50	28.3	29.9
Jefferson Davis	13.8	9.6	6.9	52.2	14 051	13 962	-0.6	-10.6	1 621	1 336	-1 634	4 977	-3.9	2.49	20.8	29.2
Jones	11.9	7.8	6.5	51.3	62 031	64 958	4.7	4.3	9 875	6 649	4	25 247	4.0	2.61	16.8	25.6
Kemper	12.9	8.3	7.3	51.1	10 356	10 453	0.9	0.0	1 219	924	-868	3 920	0.3	2.49	20.9	30.2
Lafayette	9.2	5.8	4.7	50.6	31 826	38 744	21.7	22.2	4 564	3 048	3 897	18 356	27.7	2.31	11.6	31.1
Lamar	10.0	6.3	4.5	51.6	30 424	39 070	28.4	43.5	6 560	2 968	7 523	21 542	49.6	2.57	13.5	24.1
Lauderdale	11.9	7.4	6.7	51.8	75 555	78 161	3.4	2.7	11 041	8 678	-947	31 090	3.7	2.46	20.0	29.8
Lawrence	12.8	8.8	6.1	50.9	12 458	13 258	6.4	-2.5	1 729	1 296	-309	5 078	0.8	2.55	14.6	26.1
Leake	10.9	7.1	6.0	48.1	18 436	20 940	13.6	13.7	3 543	2 388	1 155	8 272	8.7	2.65	18.4	26.8
Lee	11.2	7.2	5.7	52.1	65 579	75 755	15.5	9.4	11 484	7 466	2 594	32 086	9.9	2.55	16.9	26.4
Leflore	10.7	6.1	5.8	52.0	37 341	37 947	1.6	-14.8	5 621	3 570	-5 290	11 577	-10.6	2.59	29.2	29.9
Lincoln	12.5	7.5	6.7	52.2	30 278	33 166	9.5	5.1	4 510	3 507	878	13 296	6.0	2.57	16.3	25.1
Lowndes	11.8	7.0	5.9	52.6	59 308	61 586	3.8	-2.9	8 325	4 960	-4 988	23 487	2.8	2.49	19.2	27.9
Madison	11.6	5.6	4.8	52.1	53 794	74 674	38.8	27.5	12 181	9 156	15 695	35 829	31.6	2.61	15.8	25.5
Marion	12.3	7.7	6.9	51.7	25 544	25 595	0.2	5.8	3 683	3 098	-303	10 135	8.6	2.60	17.1	25.6
Marshall	12.8	7.5	5.2	50.5	30 361	34 993	15.3	6.1	4 843	3 390	620	13 369	9.9	2.65	19.3	24.4
Monroe	12.8	8.9	6.9	52.5	36 582	38 014	3.9	-2.7	4 781	3 666	-2 030	14 485	-0.8	2.53	18.2	26.4
Montgomery	13.6	9.2	8.0	52.5	12 387	12 189	-1.6	-10.4	1 493	1 282	-1 222	4 438	-5.4	2.44	20.3	29.2
Neshoba	11.9	7.1	6.3	52.0	24 800	28 684	15.7	3.5	4 740	2 932	-12	10 856	1.5	2.70	19.2	25.2
Newton	11.8	7.9	7.0	52.1	20 291	21 838	7.6	-0.5	3 232	2 150	-231	8 214	-0.1	2.57	16.7	26.2
Noxubee	11.5	7.3	6.2	52.1	12 604	12 548	-0.4	-8.0	1 840	1 034	-1 686	4 305	-3.7	2.64	25.4	28.3
Oktibbeha	8.4	5.1	4.1	50.2	38 375	42 902	11.8	11.1	5 406	2 611	-927	18 820	18.0	2.30	14.1	31.6
Panola	11.9	7.4	5.3	51.9	29 996	34 274	14.3	1.3	5 286	3 377	-720	12 839	5.0	2.68	21.2	25.7
Pearl River	13.2	8.8	5.8	50.6	38 714	48 621	25.6	14.8	6 635	4 855	7 722	20 816	15.1	2.63	13.5	23.1
Perry	12.9	8.8	5.4	51.2	10 865	12 138	11.7	0.9	1 611	1 130	-517	4 674	5.7	2.60	15.5	25.3
Pike	12.5	7.6	6.5	52.4	36 882	38 940	5.6	3.8	6 061	4 318	-627	15 370	3.9	2.57	21.4	28.0
Pontotoc	11.3	7.1	5.7	50.7	22 237	26 726	20.2	12.1	3 890	2 219	1 000	11 172	10.6	2.66	13.5	23.6
Prentiss	12.0	8.8	6.9	51.1	23 278	25 556	9.8	-1.1	3 032	2 292	-449	9 812	-0.1	2.49	14.5	26.3
Quitman	12.6	8.1	6.0	52.2	10 490	10 117	-3.6	-18.7	1 299	1 030	-1 986	3 058	-14.2	2.64	26.2	28.4
Rankin	11.6	6.8	4.6	51.6	87 161	115 327	32.3	22.8	17 846	7 889	18 448	52 836	25.5	2.57	13.5	24.0
Scott	11.5	6.8	5.6	51.1	24 137	28 423	17.8	-0.6	4 516	2 479	-980	10 248	0.6	2.74	19.6	24.5
Sharkey	13.9	6.6	7.8	54.2	7 066	6 580	-6.9	-25.3	923	545	-1 532	1 834	-15.2	2.62	27.1	29.7
Simpson	12.8	7.9	6.1	51.8	23 953	27 639	15.4	-0.5	3 739	2 803	-500	10 330	2.5	2.60	16.5	26.0
Smith	12.8	9.1	6.2	51.3	14 798	16 182	9.4	1.9	1 939	1 646	-570	6 221	2.9	2.63	14.3	23.6
Stone	12.3	7.4	4.7	49.9	10 750	13 622	26.7	30.6	1 936	1 410	2 530	6 165	29.9	2.68	14.4	22.5

1. No spouse present.

Table B. States and Counties — Population, Vital Statistics, Medicare, and Crime

STATE County	Persons in group quarters, 2010	Daytime population, 2006–2010 Number	Daytime population Employment/residence ratio	Births, average 2006–2008 Total	Births Rate[1]	Deaths, average 2006–2008 Number	Deaths Rate[1]	Persons under 65 with no health insurance, 2009 Number	Persons under 65 Percent	Medicare, 2011 Eligible for Medicare	Medicare Enrolled in Medicare Advantage	Medicare Enrolled in a Medicare prescription drug plan	Serious crimes known to police,[2] 2010 Total Number	Total Rate[3]
	32	33	34	35	36	37	38	39	40	41	42	43	44	45
MISSISSIPPI	91 964	2 898 175	1.0	45 831	15.7	28 601	9.8	509 923	20.5	512 621	49 878	289 420	96 577	3 255
Adams	2 320	33 202	1.0	436	13.7	421	13.2	5 164	21.1	6 664	454	3 970	1 690	5 233
Alcorn	435	37 211	1.0	504	14.1	425	11.9	6 112	21.0	8 444	155	6 024	NA	NA
Amite	116	11 280	0.5	D	D	168	12.6	2 343	22.3	2 912	208	1 730	NA	NA
Attala	343	18 059	0.8	D	D	280	14.3	3 399	21.5	3 812	256	2 390	NA	NA
Benton	78	6 715	0.4	D	D	90	11.3	1 440	22.3	1 770	146	1 180	NA	NA
Bolivar	1 564	34 322	0.9	646	17.1	439	11.6	6 692	21.5	6 344	215	4 350	1 062	3 495
Calhoun	215	13 264	0.7	D	D	171	11.7	2 643	22.7	3 414	292	2 284	NA	NA
Carroll	334	7 923	0.3	D	D	100	9.7	1 906	23.0	2 357	39	1 536	88	830
Chickasaw	206	17 198	0.9	295	15.6	179	9.4	3 697	23.8	3 777	424	2 457	NA	NA
Choctaw	121	7 592	0.7	D	D	99	10.8	1 678	23.1	1 636	138	1 081	98	1 147
Claiborne	899	9 834	1.0	D	D	108	9.7	1 862	20.5	1 586	347	899	160	1 666
Clarke	52	13 632	0.5	D	D	198	11.3	3 086	22.0	3 733	279	2 189	NA	NA
Clay	303	19 565	0.8	308	14.7	209	9.9	3 839	22.5	3 988	442	2 495	NA	NA
Coahoma	667	27 132	1.1	532	19.2	321	11.6	4 883	21.5	4 669	191	3 395	NA	NA
Copiah	1 027	27 001	0.8	486	16.6	299	10.2	4 992	20.5	5 444	967	2 747	NA	NA
Covington	240	17 214	0.7	320	15.7	240	11.7	3 643	21.4	3 734	399	2 201	NA	NA
DeSoto	610	127 461	0.6	2 254	15.1	949	6.3	24 248	17.5	21 266	2 210	10 020	4 649	2 883
Forrest	3 601	86 274	1.4	1 270	16.3	694	8.9	14 397	21.0	11 742	1 532	6 144	2 806	3 745
Franklin	67	6 957	0.6	D	D	81	9.7	1 513	22.3	1 731	99	974	55	678
George	564	19 494	0.7	D	D	228	10.3	4 295	22.2	3 752	425	1 965	162	718
Greene	3 042	12 164	0.5	D	D	118	8.9	3 190	25.9	2 183	122	1 325	54	387
Grenada	256	24 027	1.2	338	14.7	277	12.1	4 045	21.4	4 791	471	3 090	772	3 524
Hancock	547	43 512	1.1	502	12.5	358	8.9	7 489	22.1	7 580	1 211	3 248	NA	NA
Harrison	5 452	198 345	1.2	2 854	16.3	1 612	9.2	33 085	21.4	29 509	2 421	12 283	9 095	4 861
Hinds	7 843	268 462	1.2	3 999	16.1	2 020	8.1	38 616	18.4	36 088	7 198	17 104	17 084	7 075
Holmes	591	18 021	0.7	407	19.7	217	10.5	3 840	22.6	3 825	184	2 625	NA	NA
Humphreys	83	9 497	1.0	D	D	114	11.3	1 887	22.8	1 761	38	1 287	NA	NA
Issaquena	251	NA	NA	D	D	13	7.6	376	29.5	163	D	114	NA	NA
Itawamba	934	19 596	0.6	D	D	261	11.3	3 883	20.4	5 119	168	3 475	NA	NA
Jackson	1 290	132 436	0.9	1 931	14.8	1 142	8.8	22 107	19.6	22 919	2 742	10 191	5 510	3 945
Jasper	87	15 411	0.7	268	14.7	183	10.1	3 115	21.2	3 598	410	2 157	NA	NA
Jefferson	393	7 442	0.8	D	D	76	8.5	1 760	23.4	1 493	71	1 018	49	802
Jefferson Davis	116	10 807	0.6	D	D	146	11.3	2 140	21.0	2 438	112	1 533	NA	NA
Jones	1 810	70 738	1.1	1 151	17.2	725	10.8	12 641	22.6	12 942	1 026	7 736	2 208	3 528
Kemper	708	8 925	0.5	D	D	101	10.0	2 089	25.9	1 882	112	1 053	40	383
Lafayette	5 038	47 633	1.1	528	12.4	345	8.1	7 643	20.3	6 001	329	3 769	NA	NA
Lamar	338	46 684	0.8	813	17.0	341	7.1	8 275	18.9	7 433	932	3 644	889	1 597
Lauderdale	3 847	85 017	1.2	1 234	16.0	910	11.8	12 364	18.9	13 806	769	7 788	3 217	4 008
Lawrence	0	11 566	0.7	206	15.4	145	10.8	2 313	21.0	2 956	123	1 875	NA	NA
Leake	1 845	22 494	0.9	417	18.3	270	11.8	4 350	22.5	4 028	407	2 413	113	475
Lee	1 065	96 828	1.4	1 278	15.9	942	11.7	13 525	19.6	14 996	743	9 439	2 683	3 417
Leflore	2 279	36 448	1.3	620	17.5	360	10.2	6 674	23.0	5 481	130	3 977	1 601	4 954
Lincoln	714	33 497	0.9	553	16.0	385	11.1	5 864	20.4	6 747	524	4 081	594	1 704
Lowndes	1 318	61 916	1.1	915	15.4	533	8.9	10 694	21.4	10 166	860	5 761	1 647	2 755
Madison	1 765	93 171	1.0	1 459	16.3	1 048	11.7	11 972	15.0	12 911	1 688	6 576	1 459	1 779
Marion	693	25 356	0.9	430	16.7	335	13.0	4 757	22.3	5 252	495	3 247	648	2 392
Marshall	1 737	29 610	0.5	560	15.3	374	10.2	6 977	22.7	6 310	753	3 561	NA	NA
Monroe	408	33 512	0.7	532	14.3	390	10.5	6 234	20.7	7 821	532	5 035	NA	NA
Montgomery	99	9 977	0.7	D	D	148	12.9	1 954	22.0	2 478	37	1 712	NA	NA
Neshoba	386	29 704	1.0	534	17.6	316	10.4	5 922	23.0	5 296	285	3 393	499	1 681
Newton	600	19 302	0.7	358	16.0	224	10.0	3 766	20.0	4 460	316	2 624	NA	NA
Noxubee	173	11 286	0.9	D	D	110	9.2	2 523	26.2	2 234	62	1 724	NA	NA
Oktibbeha	4 367	47 525	1.1	609	14.1	290	6.7	8 626	22.4	5 732	623	3 491	1 142	2 396
Panola	315	33 225	0.9	593	16.7	393	11.1	6 418	21.6	6 405	781	3 724	1 335	3 925
Pearl River	1 124	48 332	0.7	809	14.1	590	10.3	11 112	23.0	11 284	1 700	5 267	1 396	2 500
Perry	102	10 416	0.6	D	D	124	10.2	2 053	20.1	2 326	192	1 508	NA	NA
Pike	865	42 024	1.1	711	17.8	489	12.2	6 779	20.8	7 822	1 083	4 435	1 528	3 782
Pontotoc	236	27 385	0.8	454	15.7	225	7.8	5 079	20.5	5 504	483	3 405	24	80
Prentiss	864	22 817	0.7	D	D	249	9.7	4 548	21.6	5 316	113	3 627	405	1 733
Quitman	164	7 785	0.7	D	D	122	13.6	1 657	23.9	1 689	67	1 220	NA	NA
Rankin	5 629	129 453	0.9	2 096	15.1	890	6.4	20 634	16.8	21 617	3 318	9 882	2 097	1 572
Scott	229	28 595	1.0	538	18.7	268	9.3	6 140	24.7	4 941	671	2 965	345	1 528
Sharkey	108	4 773	1.0	D	D	64	11.3	1 016	22.3	1 020	22	764	NA	NA
Simpson	642	24 570	0.7	419	15.0	289	10.3	5 193	22.3	4 984	608	2 824	NA	NA
Smith	107	14 000	0.6	218	13.7	193	12.1	2 721	20.6	3 280	309	1 818	NA	NA
Stone	1 288	15 795	0.8	231	14.6	155	9.8	3 158	22.3	2 990	451	1 439	250	1 406

1. Per 1,000 estimated resident population.   2. Data for serious crimes have not been adjusted for underreporting; this may affect comparability between geographic areas and over time.   3. Per 100,000 population estimated by the FBI.

Table B. States and Counties — Crime, Education, Money Income, and Poverty

STATE County	Rate² Violent	Property	Enrollment³ Total	Percent private	Attainment (pct) High school graduate or less	Bachelor's degree or more	Total current expenditures (mil dol)	Current expenditures per student (dollars)	Per capita income⁶ (dollars)	Households Median income Dollars	Percent change, 2000 to 2006–2010 (constant 2010 dollars)	Percent with income of $200,000 or more	Median household income (dollars)	All persons	Children under 18 years	Children 5 to 17 years in families
	46	47	48	49	50	51	52	53	54	55	56	57	58	59	60	61
MISSISSIPPI	270	2 985	800 133	13.0	51.3	19.5	3 966.3	8 075	19 977	37 881	-4.5	1.8	36 992	22.4	32.4	30.2
Adams	359	4 874	8 315	19.2	53.0	19.3	37.1	9 308	17 473	27 096	-15.2	1.7	28 587	30.8	41.8	40.3
Alcorn	NA	NA	8 346	8.0	59.2	16.0	44.1	7 746	17 954	32 342	-12.1	1.1	33 299	22.5	32.4	29.4
Amite	NA	NA	2 650	30.9	65.0	9.2	11.4	8 952	16 861	27 615	-16.2	1.1	31 799	22.5	34.7	34.5
Attala	NA	NA	4 995	11.9	56.8	17.1	26.0	7 601	17 659	28 508	-9.2	1.2	29 317	24.3	35.1	33.1
Benton	NA	NA	1 853	11.5	68.8	9.6	9.9	7 386	14 998	29 202	-4.5	1.1	27 586	25.9	38.4	35.7
Bolivar	244	3 252	10 695	8.3	55.8	20.4	61.4	9 285	16 051	26 005	-12.3	2.0	28 984	33.9	52.0	48.3
Calhoun	NA	NA	3 393	9.6	65.7	10.1	21.1	8 237	15 183	28 484	-17.0	0.4	30 281	22.3	31.8	30.2
Carroll	104	727	2 315	24.4	56.9	16.4	8.7	9 280	16 025	29 290	-19.9	0.0	34 436	18.8	28.2	27.4
Chickasaw	NA	NA	4 779	5.2	64.7	11.2	25.4	7 797	15 985	30 092	-9.9	0.7	31 702	24.8	35.2	32.9
Choctaw	199	948	1 932	8.6	59.9	10.9	16.2	10 211	16 545	30 994	-9.4	0.6	31 632	23.4	38.1	35.2
Claiborne	885	781	3 403	10.0	52.7	17.5	15.6	8 880	12 571	24 150	-15.7	0.0	22 750	34.9	51.1	47.1
Clarke	NA	NA	4 477	11.1	63.3	8.3	24.7	8 420	16 467	29 103	-13.6	0.4	31 999	25.4	39.0	37.1
Clay	NA	NA	5 633	11.5	54.0	18.1	29.9	8 470	17 604	31 727	-8.5	1.4	30 777	28.4	41.3	37.6
Coahoma	NA	NA	8 483	9.1	54.8	14.3	45.8	8 583	15 687	24 726	-12.6	1.5	25 719	38.7	55.0	48.6
Copiah	NA	NA	8 232	15.8	55.1	14.1	32.3	7 178	17 473	36 637	9.8	1.1	31 275	23.4	35.7	33.9
Covington	NA	NA	5 354	12.0	57.0	15.8	26.4	8 159	17 713	32 456	-3.9	0.7	32 900	21.7	33.1	31.6
DeSoto	168	2 715	43 240	14.8	43.9	21.1	201.7	6 588	24 531	59 418	-2.7	1.5	58 979	10.4	15.1	13.8
Forrest	183	3 562	23 392	11.9	44.1	25.9	102.2	8 923	19 272	34 448	-0.8	1.4	32 555	29.0	36.9	33.7
Franklin	197	480	2 071	9.9	68.1	13.2	14.1	9 569	21 583	33 324	5.8	2.4	32 376	20.8	31.2	29.5
George	75	642	5 283	6.9	61.1	11.0	28.5	6 775	19 452	45 492	3.4	1.1	43 487	17.2	25.5	23.6
Greene	50	337	2 864	5.2	69.8	8.3	16.4	8 076	14 064	40 828	13.8	0.2	37 348	23.9	26.9	24.2
Grenada	333	3 191	5 737	11.5	55.2	18.6	32.0	7 219	19 701	32 901	-5.1	1.9	32 715	21.5	33.3	31.3
Hancock	NA	NA	10 642	13.5	48.3	21.7	57.8	9 621	21 935	44 494	-0.2	1.3	42 255	18.9	30.0	28.1
Harrison	234	4 627	44 927	15.0	45.7	20.0	251.1	9 043	22 880	45 668	1.2	2.1	41 522	19.7	30.4	27.8
Hinds	757	6 318	77 856	17.9	41.0	27.2	337.7	7 999	20 676	39 215	-8.9	2.4	37 265	22.9	34.1	32.9
Holmes	NA	NA	6 047	8.3	66.1	11.2	32.6	8 445	11 586	21 375	-2.1	0.3	22 536	41.2	53.1	52.8
Humphreys	NA	NA	2 851	11.0	66.3	11.5	13.6	7 360	13 282	25 131	-3.5	1.5	24 205	42.2	61.1	58.9
Issaquena	NA	NA	462	21.4	79.8	4.3	NA	NA	11 810	21 360	-15.4	0.7	27 124	43.3	60.1	57.8
Itawamba	NA	NA	5 867	5.1	61.0	12.4	27.0	7 534	18 517	37 588	-4.7	0.4	37 184	17.2	25.6	23.7
Jackson	291	3 654	35 326	10.1	48.9	18.4	216.9	8 821	22 655	47 906	-3.3	1.9	45 766	16.6	24.9	21.3
Jasper	NA	NA	4 450	11.6	60.0	11.6	22.8	8 263	18 268	30 177	-2.5	1.3	32 501	19.6	30.1	29.0
Jefferson	442	360	1 989	2.5	68.9	20.5	12.2	8 307	12 534	24 304	4.0	0.5	24 671	37.9	52.4	47.0
Jefferson Davis	NA	NA	2 834	10.6	59.0	11.9	14.7	8 102	15 120	25 986	-6.0	0.8	27 988	25.0	39.8	38.5
Jones	326	3 202	15 997	9.9	54.0	15.8	92.3	8 267	18 632	36 017	-1.2	2.0	35 696	23.4	34.9	31.9
Kemper	77	306	2 604	8.8	68.3	8.9	10.8	8 521	12 903	25 649	-15.6	0.1	27 711	26.6	36.6	34.9
Lafayette	NA	NA	19 320	6.5	35.1	39.3	51.3	8 847	21 267	39 080	8.2	3.4	38 725	20.9	22.4	21.2
Lamar	93	1 504	15 205	13.5	37.1	31.8	71.6	7 944	26 052	48 048	0.8	4.0	49 742	16.2	21.5	20.1
Lauderdale	309	3 699	20 688	9.6	48.9	18.8	105.8	7 995	20 116	33 926	-12.9	2.3	34 199	24.4	34.9	32.1
Lawrence	NA	NA	3 037	8.3	60.1	11.8	18.9	8 471	19 142	35 593	-1.4	1.0	36 844	18.2	27.3	26.5
Leake	17	458	6 690	12.5	63.6	9.6	24.8	7 585	14 617	31 986	-6.6	0.5	31 672	27.1	39.1	37.3
Lee	149	3 268	21 161	9.1	47.1	20.9	134.8	8 182	21 831	39 049	-14.7	3.0	41 026	20.5	31.3	30.0
Leflore	628	4 326	11 077	10.2	60.2	16.6	48.8	8 472	12 957	22 020	-19.2	1.0	26 037	37.2	51.0	50.6
Lincoln	146	1 557	8 645	14.7	54.4	17.2	44.8	7 327	20 620	38 405	11.2	2.0	35 523	17.8	26.2	24.8
Lowndes	214	2 541	17 036	13.7	49.9	20.1	83.0	8 460	21 273	37 607	-7.5	1.8	35 774	25.8	37.2	32.5
Madison	116	1 663	26 677	23.8	31.5	42.6	109.0	7 341	31 517	59 585	0.2	6.5	57 089	12.8	17.3	16.6
Marion	210	2 182	6 382	11.3	63.7	12.5	37.0	8 561	17 549	31 332	0.8	1.5	31 026	24.7	37.4	35.9
Marshall	NA	NA	8 411	22.7	66.7	10.2	36.6	7 430	16 825	34 183	-6.1	1.1	35 443	25.3	36.7	33.4
Monroe	NA	NA	8 664	6.2	61.5	13.2	47.4	8 304	18 884	35 685	-7.0	1.0	34 468	24.1	35.1	32.6
Montgomery	NA	NA	2 814	17.5	56.0	16.3	15.6	9 367	16 584	31 488	-1.6	1.1	30 197	23.5	34.9	33.5
Neshoba	131	1 550	8 089	8.0	57.9	12.4	30.4	7 015	17 609	34 905	-2.6	1.4	34 698	22.4	33.0	31.8
Newton	NA	NA	6 154	8.3	53.4	12.7	30.7	7 985	16 727	36 154	-0.6	0.5	34 123	21.6	32.2	29.3
Noxubee	NA	NA	3 583	15.9	64.0	13.1	18.2	9 230	12 759	22 178	-21.6	0.1	24 699	32.6	46.8	44.7
Oktibbeha	183	2 213	20 661	6.9	36.7	39.9	47.0	9 268	19 356	30 320	-3.8	2.4	33 008	26.5	30.8	31.1
Panola	362	3 563	8 360	9.5	60.5	12.5	51.2	8 139	15 987	34 030	0.3	0.5	32 377	27.9	38.8	36.8
Pearl River	149	2 352	13 252	14.8	53.8	14.6	73.2	8 129	20 014	40 038	2.3	1.5	39 424	21.5	31.9	28.2
Perry	NA	NA	2 831	16.3	56.9	10.0	16.7	8 130	18 238	38 887	12.9	0.4	34 470	21.7	33.0	31.5
Pike	332	3 450	11 146	15.3	54.0	15.7	57.1	8 004	17 620	30 779	-1.0	1.0	29 601	27.1	41.2	37.5
Pontotoc	13	67	7 425	5.1	61.3	11.4	41.0	7 326	17 820	38 420	-5.3	0.9	37 493	16.0	24.7	23.2
Prentiss	248	1 485	6 529	2.7	59.2	11.8	29.2	8 177	17 068	31 262	-13.2	0.4	33 940	21.8	30.6	28.6
Quitman	NA	NA	2 242	14.8	63.8	11.0	12.9	9 739	13 080	24 169	-7.5	0.1	25 507	36.9	53.2	50.2
Rankin	121	1 452	35 671	19.9	39.0	28.0	169.1	7 679	26 637	54 028	-5.1	2.9	51 007	13.8	20.0	18.5
Scott	221	1 306	6 775	7.4	66.0	10.3	38.0	7 142	16 608	35 765	5.8	2.1	32 711	21.0	32.1	31.0
Sharkey	NA	NA	1 311	20.8	58.9	17.8	10.3	8 970	14 322	30 129	6.8	0.4	24 987	37.9	58.9	55.0
Simpson	NA	NA	6 628	18.6	59.2	14.3	30.9	7 254	18 397	36 739	2.4	1.2	34 843	21.9	34.0	32.9
Smith	NA	NA	4 045	9.0	61.3	14.8	22.1	7 313	18 686	37 176	-4.8	1.7	36 912	20.8	31.0	28.3
Stone	129	1 276	3 885	10.1	52.3	13.5	22.3	7 940	21 691	43 728	13.2	2.1	37 975	19.3	28.3	26.4

1. Data for serious crimes have not been adjusted for underreporting; this may affect comparability between geographic areas and over time.   2. Per 100,000 population estimated by the FBI.   3. All persons 3 years old and over enrolled in nursery school through college.   4. Persons 25 years old and over.   5. Elementary and secondary education expenditures.   6. Based on population estimated by the American Community Survey, 2006–2010.

Table B. States and Counties — **Personal Income**

STATE County	Personal income, 2009												
			Per capita[1]					Transfer payments (mil dol)					
									Government payments to individuals				
	Total (mil dol)	Percent change, 2008–2009	Dollars	Rank	Wages and salaries[2] (mil dol)	Proprietors' income (mil dol)	Dividends, interest, and rent (mil dol)	Total	Total	Social Security	Medical payments	Income mainte-nance	Unemploy-ment insurance
	62	63	64	65	66	67	68	69	70	71	72	73	74
MISSISSIPPI	89 743	-0.7	30 401	X	52 210	6 873	12 735	22 360	21 825	6 949	9 713	2 957	607
Adams	958	-4.9	31 192	1 713	489	82	175	287	282	93	124	45	6
Alcorn	977	-0.1	27 282	2 520	561	47	145	314	307	116	139	29	9
Amite	345	-2.2	26 458	2 649	79	39	40	112	109	38	47	16	3
Attala	497	-1.0	25 163	2 850	205	42	70	170	166	50	80	22	5
Benton	175	1.4	21 949	3 068	52	8	17	72	71	22	34	10	2
Bolivar	1 006	0.5	27 359	2 506	509	88	128	323	316	79	143	68	8
Calhoun	359	0.0	24 905	2 872	131	19	46	133	130	44	61	16	3
Carroll	316	0.4	30 699	1 821	47	4	31	81	79	30	30	11	3
Chickasaw	469	1.2	25 084	2 856	226	40	69	159	156	49	75	20	5
Choctaw	207	0.5	22 931	3 034	90	16	26	67	66	21	31	9	2
Claiborne	256	2.9	23 781	2 975	228	4	24	103	101	21	41	21	3
Clarke	429	-0.3	24 916	2 871	125	33	53	147	144	51	65	16	4
Clay	578	-2.1	27 897	2 419	241	73	107	165	162	56	64	27	6
Coahoma	780	0.4	28 972	2 206	368	61	105	284	279	58	134	58	6
Copiah	714	1.8	24 538	2 911	309	45	80	264	259	72	119	38	6
Covington	525	0.5	25 560	2 801	205	73	59	160	156	49	73	21	4
DeSoto	4 938	-3.3	31 113	1 727	1 938	448	502	731	703	311	243	63	27
Forrest	2 190	-0.4	27 013	2 563	1 847	254	353	638	623	164	309	71	14
Franklin	195	0.9	23 393	3 013	76	8	24	67	66	23	29	9	2
George	582	1.0	25 681	2 777	225	21	59	171	167	54	86	15	5
Greene	297	1.2	20 722	3 083	89	22	22	90	87	28	41	11	3
Grenada	612	-1.3	26 559	2 630	394	28	91	212	208	64	103	26	6
Hancock	1 526	0.0	37 259	717	943	95	396	294	287	104	130	27	7
Harrison	6 564	0.2	36 225	860	5 061	323	1 115	1 314	1 283	380	623	138	32
Hinds	8 881	-0.9	35 865	905	7 262	1 382	1 299	1 813	1 768	505	727	315	48
Holmes	478	1.0	23 556	3 000	157	20	49	234	230	43	106	50	7
Humphreys	239	0.3	24 321	2 932	112	15	28	101	99	21	49	23	3
Issaquena	46	-2.2	28 543	2 292	12	14	3	9	9	2	4	2	0
Itawamba	630	-2.2	27 405	2 499	229	26	81	188	184	73	58	14	6
Jackson	4 695	0.8	35 321	979	3 258	167	646	917	893	338	371	93	25
Jasper	484	0.6	26 992	2 566	203	45	47	152	148	48	70	20	4
Jefferson	181	-1.0	20 316	3 092	53	11	17	77	75	18	34	17	3
Jefferson Davis	325	-3.1	25 930	2 742	112	22	34	108	106	32	46	19	3
Jones	2 125	-1.2	31 358	1 680	1 374	155	301	614	602	179	315	58	11
Kemper	239	6.6	24 279	2 938	75	13	26	93	91	23	34	11	2
Lafayette	1 395	-1.1	31 730	1 593	887	115	238	268	260	81	120	20	8
Lamar	1 724	2.5	34 487	1 095	668	56	225	251	242	104	87	26	8
Lauderdale	2 497	-2.2	31 569	1 630	1 730	119	393	628	614	187	282	80	16
Lawrence	391	1.2	29 415	2 113	150	30	34	132	129	42	63	14	3
Leake	579	2.6	25 024	2 864	225	66	58	184	180	53	90	23	4
Lee	2 698	-0.6	32 932	1 350	2 281	169	414	585	570	212	247	62	21
Leflore	939	-1.2	27 162	2 541	638	80	168	322	315	69	155	61	8
Lincoln	934	-2.2	26 823	2 591	496	78	134	271	265	94	117	32	7
Lowndes	1 857	-0.3	31 135	1 723	1 377	93	272	433	423	138	178	60	13
Madison	4 138	-1.0	44 454	218	2 132	318	766	511	494	184	194	70	15
Marion	711	0.4	27 622	2 464	339	49	101	234	229	72	108	33	5
Marshall	938	-0.1	25 423	2 816	284	39	78	271	264	84	112	42	9
Monroe	999	-1.6	27 068	2 556	441	79	143	297	291	107	122	32	11
Montgomery	303	0.8	27 253	2 524	98	39	37	112	110	32	57	14	3
Neshoba	913	-4.2	30 133	1 945	575	119	101	218	212	70	94	28	6
Newton	597	1.5	26 456	2 650	241	43	64	217	213	59	110	21	4
Noxubee	272	-2.2	23 376	3 014	100	38	31	105	103	26	46	23	3
Oktibbeha	1 270	-0.4	28 503	2 300	863	75	196	264	256	76	102	35	8
Panola	908	-1.0	25 755	2 765	457	92	106	271	264	85	112	45	9
Pearl River	1 478	1.3	25 545	2 802	445	73	195	445	434	160	180	43	9
Perry	275	0.4	22 865	3 036	122	8	30	96	94	34	39	13	3
Pike	1 064	-1.4	26 722	2 608	595	50	146	361	354	100	162	55	8
Pontotoc	751	0.1	25 666	2 779	424	55	92	191	186	74	76	19	6
Prentiss	608	0.1	23 655	2 986	289	20	82	216	211	70	99	18	7
Quitman	220	-3.8	26 197	2 688	56	26	23	89	88	20	44	18	2
Rankin	4 885	-1.5	34 129	1 151	2 735	287	680	841	815	316	363	65	22
Scott	724	3.3	24 686	2 897	476	62	72	226	221	64	111	31	5
Sharkey	130	-4.4	24 028	2 962	50	-3	19	57	56	13	27	13	1
Simpson	850	2.7	30 426	1 882	267	85	78	251	246	68	134	27	5
Smith	418	2.8	26 443	2 652	135	63	46	115	112	43	45	15	3
Stone	477	4.3	28 698	2 260	181	9	47	149	146	42	64	14	3

1. Based on the resident population estimated as of July 1 of the year shown. 2. Includes supplements to wages and salaries.

Table B. States and Counties — **Earnings, Social Security, and Housing**

STATE County	Earnings, 2009 Total (mil dol)	Farm	Goods-related[1] Total	Manu- facturing	Service-related and health — Infor- mation and profes- sional and technical services	Retail trade	Finance, insur- ance, and real estate	Health care and social services	Govern- ment	Social Security beneficiaries, December 2010 — Number	Rate[2]	Supple- mental Security Income recipients, December 2010	Housing units, 2010 — Total	Percent change, 2000– 2010
	75	76	77	78	79	80	81	82	83	84	85	86	87	88
MISSISSIPPI	59 084	2.0	20.3	13.1	6.4	7.1	4.7	10.7	25.6	596 637	201	125 507	1 274 719	9.7
Adams	572	0.3	23.7	5.3	4.9	9.9	4.5	D	18.2	7 780	241	1 928	14 656	-3.4
Alcorn	608	0.1	29.1	25.2	D	10.1	3.9	10.4	25.0	9 945	268	1 768	17 077	8.0
Amite	118	8.4	D	11.5	D	8.0	3.2	D	18.2	3 285	250	754	6 635	2.9
Attala	246	2.0	D	9.9	3.9	10.1	3.7	D	24.9	4 505	230	995	9 126	5.6
Benton	60	1.9	D	13.8	D	7.1	D	7.2	26.2	2 075	238	524	4 186	21.1
Bolivar	597	11.5	15.6	12.9	D	10.1	3.3	13.9	23.8	7 525	220	3 139	14 070	-5.8
Calhoun	151	-2.3	27.9	24.2	D	12.7	3.3	D	26.5	4 025	269	833	6 913	0.2
Carroll	51	-6.7	D	11.7	2.1	5.9	D	D	34.9	2 690	254	574	5 052	3.4
Chickasaw	266	2.7	45.9	43.9	2.7	6.9	2.5	D	16.8	4 365	251	906	7 514	-5.9
Choctaw	106	2.6	D	9.4	2.8	3.6	D	D	22.1	1 950	228	416	4 150	-2.3
Claiborne	232	0.3	D	2.1	2.1	2.4	D	D	33.2	1 935	201	735	4 223	-0.7
Clarke	159	3.9	25.9	15.7	D	6.5	4.4	11.4	23.8	4 455	266	841	7 876	-2.7
Clay	313	12.1	D	14.7	5.5	8.3	3.6	D	15.5	4 710	228	1 162	9 180	4.2
Coahoma	429	9.6	8.7	7.0	7.0	7.0	5.7	D	23.8	5 525	211	2 343	10 792	-6.1
Copiah	354	3.3	30.1	23.3	2.9	7.1	2.6	D	26.6	6 390	217	1 611	12 184	9.8
Covington	278	11.2	D	16.8	D	6.2	2.3	6.2	20.3	4 455	228	1 038	8 496	5.1
DeSoto	2 386	0.5	20.7	10.2	5.0	10.2	5.5	11.1	14.4	24 215	150	2 422	61 634	51.1
Forrest	2 101	0.3	11.5	6.5	5.1	7.4	3.9	16.7	32.2	13 610	182	2 834	32 289	7.9
Franklin	83	3.3	D	D	11.9	4.8	D	D	35.1	1 985	245	402	4 154	0.8
George	245	1.4	27.5	6.8	4.1	9.5	3.3	D	29.7	4 570	202	667	9 330	24.2
Greene	111	6.4	D	D	D	4.8	1.4	4.6	45.4	2 645	184	483	5 123	3.6
Grenada	422	0.5	30.0	28.0	D	10.0	4.2	D	24.8	5 580	255	1 343	10 155	1.8
Hancock	1 038	-0.1	15.2	9.5	11.8	4.4	2.4	D	38.4	8 540	194	1 135	21 840	3.6
Harrison	5 384	0.0	D	D	6.1	6.6	3.7	7.8	39.9	33 370	178	5 454	85 181	7.0
Hinds	8 644	0.1	10.9	3.0	12.4	4.6	7.2	14.4	28.6	41 780	170	10 720	103 421	3.1
Holmes	177	5.8	D	10.0	D	7.8	7.0	D	36.2	4 395	229	2 039	8 415	-0.3
Humphreys	127	11.2	D	D	5.7	5.6	7.0	D	17.6	2 065	220	1 079	3 855	-6.8
Issaquena	26	47.1	D	0.0	D	D	D	D	15.7	205	146	66	560	-36.1
Itawamba	255	1.3	D	19.5	D	7.2	2.6	D	26.0	6 155	263	726	10 126	3.3
Jackson	3 425	-0.1	49.5	40.3	6.7	4.6	2.3	5.8	19.5	26 735	191	3 135	60 067	16.2
Jasper	248	7.5	39.8	20.5	9.3	5.4	2.9	D	19.2	4 285	251	974	8 212	7.1
Jefferson	64	12.9	D	D	D	D	D	10.7	44.2	1 835	238	784	3 673	-3.8
Jefferson Davis	135	5.6	39.3	0.6	2.1	6.7	1.6	D	23.8	2 985	239	710	5 876	-0.3
Jones	1 529	1.5	39.2	21.1	3.7	6.1	3.1	4.6	21.5	15 250	225	2 880	28 424	5.6
Kemper	87	3.3	19.6	17.6	D	5.4	D	D	35.1	2 145	206	576	4 722	4.2
Lafayette	1 002	0.2	D	5.3	9.7	6.8	4.1	14.0	41.1	6 795	144	988	22 729	37.0
Lamar	724	1.3	13.1	5.6	D	15.1	6.0	21.7	16.0	8 410	151	1 095	24 070	56.0
Lauderdale	1 849	0.0	D	9.4	4.7	8.6	4.4	19.8	25.9	15 785	197	3 449	34 698	3.8
Lawrence	179	8.6	42.1	35.7	D	5.0	D	4.7	19.8	3 480	260	581	6 019	5.8
Leake	291	15.6	D	D	D	7.6	4.2	D	19.7	4 815	202	1 062	9 415	9.6
Lee	2 450	0.3	24.6	21.5	6.5	8.2	5.0	19.9	12.3	17 775	214	2 838	35 872	12.5
Leflore	718	5.1	16.8	11.6	5.7	6.7	3.3	8.1	30.7	6 465	200	2 677	13 199	-6.4
Lincoln	574	1.9	21.1	9.8	3.5	9.6	3.9	13.2	14.8	7 915	227	1 545	15 255	8.6
Lowndes	1 470	0.4	27.0	20.1	3.4	7.6	3.4	10.6	25.9	11 885	199	2 405	26 556	5.8
Madison	2 450	0.2	25.0	16.2	12.7	8.4	11.2	7.4	9.8	14 225	149	2 282	38 558	34.0
Marion	388	4.2	25.4	7.2	3.7	9.3	5.1	D	20.0	6 300	233	1 327	11 838	13.9
Marshall	323	0.2	23.6	13.6	2.6	9.8	4.6	D	21.8	7 355	198	1 706	14 881	12.3
Monroe	520	2.5	35.4	25.8	D	7.0	2.7	D	17.0	9 045	245	1 507	16 455	1.3
Montgomery	136	1.9	5.6	2.2	D	10.5	3.4	D	25.0	2 905	266	674	5 194	-3.9
Neshoba	694	7.5	D	4.8	2.6	6.6	2.0	2.7	41.2	6 425	217	1 253	12 357	3.2
Newton	283	8.4	D	16.0	D	6.5	2.3	D	33.9	5 155	237	921	9 373	1.2
Noxubee	138	15.7	D	19.3	D	7.1	2.5	D	29.1	2 580	223	1 065	5 170	-1.1
Oktibbeha	938	0.3	11.2	7.9	D	5.8	2.4	5.2	54.1	6 465	136	1 606	20 947	20.8
Panola	549	3.3	21.9	17.6	7.8	9.1	4.4	D	20.2	7 630	220	2 098	14 697	7.0
Pearl River	518	-0.5	17.9	10.2	D	12.8	4.9	D	32.2	13 340	239	1 925	23 968	16.3
Perry	130	3.6	D	38.9	2.4	5.4	D	7.6	19.3	2 840	232	600	5 519	8.0
Pike	645	0.7	16.8	13.3	4.5	11.3	4.9	D	30.4	9 005	223	2 329	17 861	6.8
Pontotoc	479	0.7	50.4	47.3	2.8	5.2	2.5	D	12.9	6 570	219	972	12 440	15.0
Prentiss	309	1.3	29.5	25.1	5.3	6.5	3.6	D	25.0	6 265	248	910	11 054	3.5
Quitman	82	26.4	D	2.8	D	6.0	4.7	D	24.4	1 905	232	788	3 589	-8.5
Rankin	3 022	0.9	16.6	7.4	5.5	9.0	8.1	11.1	17.6	24 650	174	2 791	56 487	25.3
Scott	538	8.3	D	44.2	D	6.7	2.4	6.2	14.1	5 835	206	1 363	11 470	3.2
Sharkey	47	-1.5	D	D	2.1	10.4	5.6	D	42.8	1 200	244	506	2 100	-13.1
Simpson	352	13.3	D	2.0	D	9.1	4.3	D	22.4	5 810	211	1 251	11 934	5.5
Smith	198	26.0	D	25.6	3.4	3.3	1.5	3.8	16.0	3 815	231	710	7 237	3.3
Stone	190	0.5	D	14.2	5.9	9.2	3.1	10.5	30.9	3 630	204	549	7 161	34.0

1. Includes mining, construction, and manufacturing.   2. Per 1,000 resident population enumerated in the 2010 census.

Table B. States and Counties — **Housing, Labor Force, and Employment**

STATE County	Housing units, 2006–2010 — Occupied units — Total	Percent	Median value[1]	Median owner cost as a percent of income — With a mortgage	Without a mortgage	Renter-occupied — Median rent[2]	Median rent as a percent of income	Sub-standard units[3] (percent)	Civilian labor force, 2010 — Total	Percent change, 2009–2010	Unemployment — Total	Rate[4]	Civilian employment,[5] 2006–2010 — Total	Percent — Management, business, science and arts	Construction, production, and maintenance occupations
	89	90	91	92	93	94	95	96	97	98	99	100	101	102	103
MISSISSIPPI	1 081 052	70.8	96 500	23.1	12.3	648	31.6	3.4	1 317 216	1.7	138 445	10.5	1 216 050	29.7	28.6
Adams	12 354	67.1	77 500	24.3	13.5	554	35.1	3.0	13 182	0.8	1 392	10.6	12 034	28.6	21.6
Alcorn	13 685	73.3	85 700	20.9	12.5	476	28.4	1.5	15 422	2.1	1 806	11.7	14 255	27.5	33.3
Amite	4 993	81.4	72 300	24.9	14.4	564	38.0	2.3	5 057	-0.3	615	12.2	4 459	21.0	40.0
Attala	7 286	75.4	72 200	25.1	13.8	478	28.3	3.6	7 142	0.8	1 000	14.0	7 414	27.6	34.8
Benton	3 303	79.0	79 100	28.0	17.5	543	26.5	9.5	2 862	2.0	388	13.6	3 205	17.3	52.4
Bolivar	12 666	56.2	77 800	25.9	15.6	578	33.4	6.0	15 436	3.9	1 780	11.5	13 020	30.3	29.1
Calhoun	5 835	68.8	60 700	21.9	12.7	468	27.2	1.8	6 204	6.3	638	10.3	5 859	24.4	45.2
Carroll	3 989	81.4	65 400	26.6	15.6	495	43.1	1.7	4 808	-0.1	525	10.9	3 702	25.4	30.4
Chickasaw	6 775	71.7	59 800	25.9	10.0	474	34.4	3.0	7 530	6.2	988	13.1	6 928	19.5	45.8
Choctaw	3 593	76.9	72 800	26.1	13.2	506	23.0	4.5	3 369	-0.7	441	13.1	3 392	24.6	36.5
Claiborne	3 308	79.0	53 500	34.1	17.7	528	29.8	4.2	3 897	5.7	637	16.3	3 563	20.6	33.7
Clarke	6 787	78.0	59 900	23.1	13.9	574	34.5	3.9	6 889	-0.2	858	12.5	6 339	21.8	38.5
Clay	7 857	71.5	74 500	23.9	14.0	571	30.1	2.8	7 386	-0.5	1 432	19.4	7 759	28.4	32.0
Coahoma	9 351	57.0	53 400	26.8	15.5	545	33.5	4.6	10 408	4.3	1 449	13.9	9 188	25.2	23.8
Copiah	10 275	78.2	73 200	21.3	12.1	536	30.0	4.1	12 168	0.3	1 356	11.1	11 399	23.8	40.1
Covington	7 257	83.7	81 600	22.7	12.1	525	34.4	2.2	8 802	1.3	854	9.7	7 873	27.4	35.5
DeSoto	55 768	77.5	152 300	23.1	10.5	888	27.5	2.0	77 986	1.3	6 097	7.8	75 548	32.2	25.8
Forrest	28 115	58.2	110 400	24.0	13.0	632	33.7	3.4	37 865	2.8	3 507	9.3	32 310	32.8	23.7
Franklin	2 995	85.8	70 000	22.0	10.6	507	39.3	2.1	3 145	4.7	379	12.1	2 811	29.7	41.0
George	7 858	83.0	92 400	20.6	10.6	542	27.8	5.2	9 810	2.3	987	10.1	8 091	26.7	43.3
Greene	4 181	89.3	72 600	20.0	14.4	538	25.8	2.2	5 014	3.5	622	12.4	4 134	23.9	39.6
Grenada	8 945	65.5	85 900	22.8	12.5	521	31.6	2.6	9 348	4.1	1 121	12.0	8 920	28.5	32.0
Hancock	15 818	75.4	150 700	24.1	12.2	819	31.3	7.1	18 749	1.4	1 713	9.1	17 470	30.3	29.3
Harrison	66 990	66.5	142 700	24.5	11.4	844	31.2	3.3	87 933	1.1	7 848	8.9	81 361	28.7	23.5
Hinds	88 201	60.9	105 000	23.4	11.7	756	34.4	3.6	118 137	1.4	11 184	9.5	108 631	31.7	20.7
Holmes	6 739	71.8	46 900	37.5	18.0	465	28.7	5.3	7 102	0.4	1 383	19.5	5 943	24.4	41.4
Humphreys	3 364	62.4	60 100	27.0	17.3	483	41.2	6.4	4 263	1.7	617	14.5	2 997	25.9	34.0
Issaquena	587	65.2	62 000	32.8	18.3	389	32.3	5.1	683	0.7	85	12.4	574	16.4	38.5
Itawamba	8 907	79.9	80 000	21.0	11.2	506	24.2	1.9	10 063	3.3	1 175	11.7	10 118	24.4	42.0
Jackson	49 137	72.7	125 500	22.8	10.9	819	31.0	2.5	64 127	4.0	6 047	9.4	59 399	29.6	28.2
Jasper	6 817	83.6	67 100	25.2	14.3	507	24.0	1.1	7 256	-2.7	855	11.8	6 878	24.3	37.0
Jefferson	2 831	75.0	67 000	29.7	14.5	416	30.0	0.8	2 967	6.2	499	16.8	2 225	29.8	32.0
Jefferson Davis	4 904	81.7	58 800	27.2	13.2	429	48.0	4.4	5 090	1.5	633	12.4	4 439	21.2	38.0
Jones	25 060	73.7	79 500	21.9	12.1	595	30.0	4.2	30 102	-0.4	2 556	8.5	27 171	26.5	36.0
Kemper	3 793	76.4	61 700	22.2	13.9	479	30.6	4.1	3 954	-1.2	527	13.3	3 390	19.0	39.2
Lafayette	16 418	59.9	149 800	22.1	11.4	737	37.6	3.0	22 181	-1.1	1 909	8.6	20 409	40.7	18.0
Lamar	20 345	70.1	157 200	21.6	10.5	785	30.3	2.8	24 440	2.0	1 894	7.7	24 811	37.7	21.7
Lauderdale	30 231	66.0	83 200	22.8	12.3	593	29.8	2.8	33 354	1.9	3 629	10.9	30 939	31.5	24.7
Lawrence	4 983	81.6	71 500	22.4	12.3	567	25.1	4.9	5 213	-2.3	639	12.3	4 832	28.7	37.7
Leake	7 500	78.6	70 100	24.3	13.7	577	28.0	4.5	8 680	2.1	937	10.8	8 184	26.6	36.2
Lee	31 508	69.5	107 100	22.4	11.3	574	30.7	2.5	38 409	4.6	4 006	10.4	36 272	28.5	27.0
Leflore	11 271	51.3	63 400	23.2	15.4	482	33.3	4.6	13 353	0.4	1 849	13.8	10 609	25.4	29.2
Lincoln	13 269	77.5	80 000	20.5	11.5	543	28.0	2.1	13 856	-0.1	1 518	11.0	13 644	29.5	31.7
Lowndes	23 067	66.2	104 200	23.4	10.5	586	32.0	2.5	25 633	0.2	3 117	12.2	24 107	26.3	30.2
Madison	34 708	69.7	181 100	21.6	10.8	803	27.5	4.0	47 081	2.6	3 555	7.6	44 222	45.9	16.0
Marion	9 651	80.3	79 600	21.6	13.7	546	32.3	2.1	10 646	-0.4	1 281	12.0	9 732	25.3	34.9
Marshall	12 738	77.5	84 800	23.7	14.0	616	32.3	3.4	15 109	-1.1	1 955	12.9	14 480	19.6	41.0
Monroe	14 725	78.8	79 500	22.3	11.7	487	29.8	2.6	16 141	2.5	2 156	13.4	15 235	25.5	36.2
Montgomery	4 347	76.1	68 400	25.8	15.2	566	32.7	1.2	4 690	3.1	653	13.9	4 212	27.9	35.6
Neshoba	10 597	76.2	69 200	22.7	11.4	535	26.4	4.3	13 466	1.8	1 262	9.4	11 315	28.3	27.7
Newton	7 989	80.3	67 100	22.4	12.4	537	25.2	4.2	9 279	1.7	954	10.3	8 818	27.3	30.5
Noxubee	4 169	73.9	55 900	27.7	16.4	477	47.2	5.1	3 809	6.4	708	18.6	3 680	20.6	44.4
Oktibbeha	17 933	50.9	106 900	21.8	11.1	632	40.2	1.5	20 014	-2.0	2 121	10.6	20 397	40.9	17.5
Panola	12 325	76.3	75 000	23.9	14.6	620	30.1	6.4	15 355	3.9	1 965	12.8	12 902	25.6	34.6
Pearl River	20 628	78.0	121 700	24.1	12.0	675	33.8	3.4	21 450	0.2	2 276	10.6	22 308	29.5	33.1
Perry	4 753	83.4	71 500	20.7	10.0	608	27.1	3.7	5 044	-1.0	603	12.0	4 972	24.8	41.6
Pike	14 785	72.9	82 000	24.2	12.7	561	34.8	3.0	15 347	0.9	1 783	11.6	14 983	25.7	32.0
Pontotoc	10 200	77.6	84 000	22.9	11.1	589	26.9	2.9	13 388	5.4	1 447	10.8	12 715	23.9	38.8
Prentiss	9 570	79.4	70 800	22.6	11.8	448	34.8	2.0	11 092	1.0	1 398	12.6	10 144	24.3	41.0
Quitman	3 173	68.9	46 200	26.7	13.3	382	31.2	5.6	3 536	1.9	482	13.6	2 792	21.8	34.8
Rankin	51 774	75.8	142 400	21.5	10.0	826	31.6	2.8	75 099	2.3	5 027	6.7	67 948	38.6	20.2
Scott	9 811	80.4	63 800	22.9	13.4	597	29.2	4.9	14 082	3.7	1 108	7.9	11 999	21.2	46.3
Sharkey	1 651	67.0	65 300	25.4	13.5	460	35.9	5.9	2 493	2.4	322	12.9	1 679	33.0	30.0
Simpson	10 343	76.6	75 100	23.1	11.8	606	25.3	4.7	11 687	0.5	1 091	9.3	11 372	24.2	34.8
Smith	6 052	86.8	72 600	20.1	13.2	557	22.5	4.3	6 449	1.2	658	10.2	6 791	29.8	35.3
Stone	5 995	77.4	105 400	22.1	10.0	617	27.5	3.2	8 013	2.9	708	8.8	6 600	26.3	33.0

1. Specified owner-occupied units.   2. Specified renter-occupied units. A value of 10.0 represents 10 percent or less.   3. Overcrowded or lacking complete plumbing facilities.   4. Percent of civilian labor force.   5. Persons 16 years old and over.

STATE County	Private nonfarm establishments, employment and payroll, 2009									Agriculture, 2007			
		Employment						Annual payroll		Farms			
											Percent with:		
	Number of establishments	Total	Health care and social assistance	Manufacturing	Retail trade	Finance and insurance	Professional, scientific, and technical services	Total (mil dol)	Average per employee (dollars)	Number	Fewer than 50 acres	500 acres or more	Farm operators whose principal occupation is farming (percent)
	104	105	106	107	108	109	110	111	112	113	114	115	116
MISSISSIPPI	59 607	904 037	154 190	149 363	137 660	35 142	32 607	28 452	31 472	41 959	29.3	10.8	38.0
Adams	856	10 031	1 924	470	2 164	D	256	271	27 024	245	35.5	13.9	38.4
Alcorn	809	11 746	2 387	2 690	2 141	293	333	337	28 682	540	29.6	5.9	28.7
Amite	173	1 285	D	315	153	D	D	30	23 214	599	25.0	7.3	42.1
Attala	352	5 072	D	594	830	D	61	147	28 944	559	23.6	9.8	34.3
Benton	53	750	D	D	88	D	D	21	28 616	336	19.9	8.6	31.3
Bolivar	703	8 273	1 606	1 747	1 447	276	D	227	27 489	430	23.0	45.6	66.5
Calhoun	257	2 482	493	741	430	D	48	64	25 841	708	19.9	11.4	33.3
Carroll	94	576	D	D	87	D	D	13	22 950	581	19.6	17.2	34.3
Chickasaw	357	4 632	D	2 461	627	112	46	123	26 581	657	21.5	13.1	32.3
Choctaw	118	1 137	D	145	155	D	D	42	36 651	293	15.7	10.2	28.0
Claiborne	114	1 853	346	D	167	D	D	108	58 157	261	20.3	16.1	41.4
Clarke	267	2 500	D	537	355	89	58	57	22 974	373	36.5	6.4	37.0
Clay	367	4 418	639	947	742	138	D	130	29 313	505	19.6	13.1	39.4
Coahoma	570	6 797	1 974	720	1 027	228	178	209	30 713	261	19.5	44.8	56.7
Copiah	422	6 319	679	2 507	883	204	D	152	24 044	642	30.2	7.2	36.8
Covington	324	4 135	478	1 514	543	116	95	109	26 255	623	29.2	5.3	41.1
DeSoto	2 543	41 123	5 021	4 215	7 520	1 040	826	1 187	28 864	490	46.9	10.2	34.5
Forrest	1 872	32 522	7 927	4 320	4 171	1 111	1 169	1 037	31 900	391	44.0	2.3	36.3
Franklin	121	1 089	250	D	135	D	36	32	29 052	196	26.5	11.7	36.7
George	335	3 244	714	336	906	71	121	97	29 894	604	54.6	3.3	40.1
Greene	127	817	D	D	175	D	D	21	25 419	398	36.7	4.3	32.7
Grenada	581	7 969	1 273	2 173	1 389	220	157	214	26 830	356	18.3	15.2	24.2
Hancock	714	10 372	1 025	1 004	1 566	263	1 858	391	37 720	286	44.8	4.5	37.4
Harrison	4 185	69 999	12 816	3 254	10 810	2 924	2 922	2 320	33 148	367	70.3	0.5	37.1
Hinds	5 809	100 697	26 257	4 816	11 526	5 749	6 781	3 834	38 077	1 071	33.7	8.9	31.7
Holmes	262	2 183	306	436	473	92	56	48	22 166	556	21.8	17.3	36.3
Humphreys	151	2 154	281	D	271	126	D	53	24 381	213	21.6	42.7	67.1
Issaquena	9	98	D	0	0	D	0	2	19 969	104	21.2	44.2	53.8
Itawamba	348	4 168	524	1 132	593	134	41	120	28 851	491	22.2	7.3	25.1
Jackson	2 343	48 842	5 240	D	5 345	1 116	1 751	2 058	42 132	454	62.8	1.8	37.2
Jasper	217	2 962	D	D	341	110	94	88	29 805	528	27.5	7.2	37.7
Jefferson	53	513	203	D	83	D	0	17	33 209	356	23.3	12.9	41.6
Jefferson Davis	168	1 386	D	29	266	D	D	59	42 323	437	30.4	4.6	47.6
Jones	1 407	26 659	3 122	D	3 342	D	548	821	30 781	1 027	44.4	1.5	40.3
Kemper	116	1 064	137	420	175	61	D	25	23 482	455	20.4	12.1	40.9
Lafayette	1 047	13 000	2 357	1 460	2 363	432	989	360	27 721	487	16.6	9.4	27.1
Lamar	1 327	16 279	2 991	394	4 880	732	587	407	24 991	500	43.8	4.6	36.2
Lauderdale	1 989	31 026	8 110	2 622	5 298	1 124	904	957	30 835	409	34.5	7.8	36.9
Lawrence	199	2 004	205	733	333	D	21	76	37 702	460	25.0	7.4	41.3
Leake	307	5 080	345	D	744	192	47	114	22 524	735	27.6	5.4	44.8
Lee	2 426	44 281	7 333	9 526	6 777	2 355	1 402	1 451	32 763	590	36.4	7.5	34.2
Leflore	764	12 356	2 610	2 608	1 703	365	323	357	28 869	296	8.8	46.3	55.4
Lincoln	769	10 303	1 511	1 136	1 866	308	475	315	30 530	725	32.0	5.2	36.8
Lowndes	1 535	20 664	3 043	3 775	3 583	511	637	667	32 273	497	33.0	13.5	28.8
Madison	2 765	42 198	3 811	D	6 449	3 358	2 690	1 516	35 937	747	30.7	11.9	31.1
Marion	625	6 979	869	986	1 276	281	198	189	27 042	611	31.1	4.9	40.8
Marshall	441	6 182	D	624	884	287	D	157	25 394	577	25.8	14.6	31.9
Monroe	693	7 791	1 577	2 177	1 319	D	107	235	30 204	730	25.5	12.6	39.3
Montgomery	233	2 477	635	354	505	94	29	57	23 212	363	16.3	11.0	36.4
Neshoba	528	7 704	1 207	669	1 224	311	98	286	37 138	728	28.0	5.1	47.9
Newton	318	3 906	711	1 223	778	145	36	99	25 231	652	25.3	7.1	47.5
Noxubee	199	1 669	262	474	302	D	24	42	25 100	606	21.1	18.2	39.9
Oktibbeha	837	11 438	1 612	1 389	2 091	425	401	280	24 485	451	28.6	8.2	29.7
Panola	626	8 860	1 144	1 989	1 608	335	D	236	26 598	767	16.3	15.9	27.5
Pearl River	838	7 477	1 015	662	2 222	369	301	189	25 294	878	48.4	5.2	41.7
Perry	170	1 775	256	726	287	D	D	68	38 522	347	39.5	1.7	41.8
Pike	1 024	13 369	2 661	2 696	2 665	472	258	348	26 004	593	39.3	2.7	41.3
Pontotoc	465	9 065	717	5 587	881	203	105	233	25 671	919	29.8	5.8	23.7
Prentiss	507	6 433	1 034	2 631	911	164	183	157	24 329	576	25.9	5.2	31.3
Quitman	119	824	299	39	148	D	D	20	23 867	349	14.3	31.8	40.1
Rankin	3 433	50 766	7 790	3 763	8 081	2 780	1 752	1 668	32 861	782	37.9	7.0	43.9
Scott	496	9 674	897	5 186	1 266	220	95	250	25 823	803	36.9	5.5	43.8
Sharkey	116	801	237	0	162	D	D	20	24 456	114	11.4	58.8	59.6
Simpson	416	5 658	2 102	444	998	419	164	126	22 227	727	32.3	4.3	44.2
Smith	185	2 411	D	D	292	81	D	70	29 052	757	27.5	3.6	48.1
Stone	285	2 939	436	D	654	109	78	81	27 416	323	45.5	5.0	37.5

Table B. States and Counties — **Agriculture**

	Agriculture, 2007 (cont.)														
STATE County	Land in farms				Value of land and buildings (dollars)		Value of machinery and equipment, average per farm (dollars)	Value of products sold				Percent of farms with sales of:		Government payments	
			Acres							Percent from:					
	Acreage (1,000)	Percent change, 2002–2007	Average size of farm	Total irrigated (1,000)	Total cropland (1,000)	Average per farm	Average per acre		Total (mil dol)	Average per farm (dollars)	Crops	Live-stock and poultry products	$10,000 or more	$100,000 or more	Total ($1,000)	Percent of farms
	117	118	119	120	121	122	123	124	125	126	127	128	129	130	131	132
MISSISSIPPI	11 456	3.2	273	1 368.7	5 530.8	510 454	1 870	73 558	4 876.8	116 227	34.2	65.8	28.8	10.8	231 382	41.0
Adams	70	-23.1	285	0.0	25.9	478 041	1 675	50 718	4.9	20 087	75.9	24.2	21.2	3.3	586	25.3
Alcorn	94	1.1	174	0.2	43.6	289 875	1 667	54 242	8.2	15 209	69.0	31.0	17.2	2.2	1 165	55.0
Amite	110	-29.9	184	0.2	27.4	435 105	2 370	61 001	63.2	105 555	3.2	96.8	25.2	8.0	547	28.7
Attala	137	8.7	246	0.4	37.7	384 718	1 567	45 167	17.3	30 912	25.7	74.3	17.7	2.9	1 694	46.0
Benton	86	-14.0	256	D	27.1	367 272	1 432	55 927	7.3	21 766	45.2	54.8	19.3	3.0	958	53.3
Bolivar	428	-2.7	996	228.3	389.5	1 986 810	1 995	322 868	182.9	425 263	99.3	0.7	76.5	47.2	14 569	77.4
Calhoun	202	18.8	286	1.8	89.9	397 483	1 392	72 351	50.7	71 653	86.6	13.4	28.1	8.9	4 547	70.3
Carroll	190	13.1	327	8.8	64.0	491 667	1 502	65 965	19.9	34 197	71.2	28.8	26.3	6.0	3 603	48.5
Chickasaw	178	3.5	271	1.7	69.3	396 016	1 459	56 640	36.7	55 798	36.6	63.4	28.2	10.2	2 868	57.7
Choctaw	72	12.5	246	0.4	18.3	435 184	1 768	44 334	13.9	47 295	22.6	77.4	14.7	4.1	536	48.8
Claiborne	94	-6.9	360	D	26.6	576 860	1 603	53 073	9.7	37 026	62.1	37.9	19.5	5.7	1 405	44.8
Clarke	65	16.1	174	0.3	15.4	322 918	1 861	41 713	20.9	56 025	20.0	80.0	27.9	3.8	169	19.3
Clay	142	10.1	282	0.6	41.4	412 641	1 464	56 104	80.6	159 691	5.7	94.3	30.7	9.5	1 811	47.3
Coahoma	303	11.4	1 160	130.9	265.6	2 090 970	1 803	310 055	128.8	493 664	93.2	6.8	65.1	43.3	12 949	80.1
Copiah	131	-17.1	205	0.9	30.1	394 956	1 928	58 722	55.6	86 599	7.4	92.6	23.2	6.1	792	21.2
Covington	116	12.6	187	0.5	37.3	462 975	2 478	61 060	163.1	261 727	3.3	96.7	40.0	19.6	599	27.1
DeSoto	142	-0.7	289	22.0	94.0	678 017	2 346	81 087	30.3	61 866	86.9	13.1	24.3	8.4	2 659	21.8
Forrest	46	2.2	116	1.0	15.1	352 027	3 023	59 200	23.2	59 281	23.0	77.0	23.3	6.1	999	26.9
Franklin	47	6.8	240	D	10.0	446 787	1 863	53 535	5.9	30 145	16.2	83.8	23.5	2.6	303	27.0
George	68	7.9	113	0.7	24.6	330 376	2 927	61 447	17.4	28 847	70.7	29.3	26.0	6.0	1 739	19.0
Greene	51	-13.6	128	0.1	13.0	303 572	2 365	52 010	34.0	85 520	D	D	22.9	6.3	395	9.8
Grenada	112	23.1	314	3.2	36.5	503 090	1 604	50 608	8.2	23 132	76.6	23.4	14.6	2.5	1 304	60.4
Hancock	42	10.5	148	0.4	10.1	441 511	2 988	49 321	3.0	10 391	D	D	20.3	2.8	343	17.1
Harrison	21	-16.0	58	0.1	5.7	280 585	4 799	54 071	3.1	8 403	60.4	39.6	15.8	1.4	59	6.8
Hinds	260	-6.8	243	0.4	74.9	452 184	1 862	53 114	65.8	61 465	22.4	77.6	20.1	2.7	3 872	36.1
Holmes	228	4.1	410	33.3	125.2	687 556	1 676	81 660	47.6	85 646	93.7	6.3	22.5	9.4	7 664	60.4
Humphreys	195	7.1	914	63.3	145.4	1 545 824	1 690	284 136	101.1	474 475	61.5	38.5	72.8	47.4	7 082	72.8
Issaquena	121	3.4	1 165	15.3	79.1	2 012 618	1 727	254 474	30.3	291 593	97.7	2.3	51.9	34.6	3 634	69.2
Itawamba	93	-3.1	190	0.0	35.1	285 841	1 504	53 365	21.9	44 553	21.0	78.9	21.6	6.7	967	52.1
Jackson	41	-4.7	91	0.2	17.2	329 620	3 611	52 171	8.0	17 572	51.8	48.2	21.8	1.8	273	9.7
Jasper	91	13.8	172	0.0	21.1	351 626	2 046	51 204	99.2	187 962	0.9	99.1	30.7	14.6	627	30.1
Jefferson	100	9.9	282	D	35.3	507 666	1 799	47 020	26.1	73 438	31.1	68.9	25.3	8.4	1 609	29.8
Jefferson Davis	68	6.3	155	0.1	21.7	318 553	2 049	59 945	37.1	84 975	11.3	88.7	28.4	8.7	582	34.8
Jones	110	-16.7	107	0.4	32.2	333 008	3 114	53 341	181.0	176 229	2.8	97.2	32.2	15.1	683	20.6
Kemper	136	10.6	299	0.1	26.2	413 304	1 381	45 722	22.0	48 287	4.6	95.4	26.6	4.8	597	33.8
Lafayette	114	-15.6	235	0.2	35.0	469 020	1 997	52 238	8.1	16 653	60.0	40.0	18.9	2.1	1 390	49.5
Lamar	73	-2.7	146	0.3	15.2	397 566	2 721	56 395	21.8	43 624	17.1	82.9	29.6	6.2	1 080	23.0
Lauderdale	84	-9.7	204	0.0	25.8	350 594	1 715	43 943	5.0	12 247	46.5	53.5	20.3	1.5	327	17.6
Lawrence	80	21.2	174	D	27.0	385 626	2 219	64 128	70.3	152 816	4.5	95.5	28.9	10.0	720	30.9
Leake	127	15.5	173	0.3	30.6	389 175	2 244	63 652	225.0	306 180	0.6	99.4	35.1	19.2	1 031	35.2
Lee	146	1.4	248	0.6	82.1	441 930	1 781	58 723	25.8	43 729	62.3	37.7	25.1	5.3	1 720	43.2
Leflore	315	11.3	1 064	144.8	263.0	1 820 563	1 711	321 857	162.1	547 508	70.6	29.4	60.5	41.2	13 073	77.4
Lincoln	125	11.6	172	0.2	34.3	393 366	2 290	50 192	54.7	75 489	4.9	95.1	25.9	8.0	647	18.6
Lowndes	130	-13.3	262	0.5	62.9	467 721	1 785	61 277	23.7	47 738	39.0	61.0	28.2	7.8	2 245	43.7
Madison	223	16.1	298	2.6	81.8	583 497	1 958	59 420	19.6	26 246	75.6	24.4	19.8	5.1	4 512	46.2
Marion	92	-7.1	151	0.2	27.3	370 329	2 457	53 958	74.1	121 218	2.0	98.0	27.8	10.6	1 003	29.8
Marshall	193	0.0	335	0.7	67.6	604 850	1 808	62 359	14.9	25 759	56.9	43.1	22.5	5.0	2 496	48.2
Monroe	199	8.7	272	1.7	84.0	403 486	1 483	58 655	26.9	36 852	51.6	48.4	24.4	7.0	3 229	58.9
Montgomery	97	12.8	268	0.6	25.8	408 119	1 522	56 437	10.1	27 784	56.7	43.3	28.9	5.8	1 460	59.8
Neshoba	121	-17.1	166	0.5	29.8	402 260	2 428	70 614	227.0	311 871	0.7	99.3	39.8	21.4	349	18.0
Newton	120	0.8	185	0.2	29.7	376 253	2 038	63 432	120.9	185 464	1.7	98.3	34.4	15.0	592	23.9
Noxubee	222	5.7	366	4.9	98.5	561 124	1 534	93 174	66.2	109 289	27.6	72.4	44.6	23.3	4 209	59.4
Oktibbeha	101	7.4	225	0.8	26.2	401 869	1 788	47 316	13.1	29 147	9.5	90.5	24.6	3.3	995	39.5
Panola	270	-0.7	352	25.1	138.8	541 174	1 538	61 652	42.7	55 636	73.3	26.7	20.9	6.3	6 450	61.3
Pearl River	136	13.3	155	1.3	30.6	418 301	2 707	50 349	20.8	23 679	43.6	56.3	26.4	4.6	2 159	19.2
Perry	41	17.1	118	0.5	12.0	289 564	2 444	49 014	16.8	48 368	14.5	85.5	25.9	4.3	663	24.8
Pike	73	-8.8	124	0.2	25.7	335 978	2 714	59 513	73.7	124 302	2.2	97.8	30.4	10.3	494	20.1
Pontotoc	146	4.3	159	1.9	61.4	262 986	1 658	41 731	17.6	19 117	46.0	54.0	18.3	3.3	2 506	61.5
Prentiss	101	-1.0	176	0.2	44.6	246 792	1 401	41 611	8.1	13 983	59.0	41.0	17.5	2.4	1 724	69.1
Quitman	220	20.9	631	49.8	176.5	977 714	1 548	139 386	52.2	149 647	95.8	4.2	38.1	23.5	7 979	92.0
Rankin	140	6.9	179	0.4	40.6	449 109	2 504	64 390	123.2	157 561	5.1	94.9	31.6	11.5	1 575	21.5
Scott	127	11.4	158	0.1	34.4	327 233	2 074	66 589	231.6	288 383	1.2	98.8	35.7	18.2	842	23.0
Sharkey	180	9.1	1 576	47.6	156.2	2 461 920	1 562	393 451	73.8	647 533	94.5	5.5	62.3	51.8	7 449	82.5
Simpson	118	13.5	162	0.2	29.7	391 132	2 418	62 826	185.9	255 752	1.2	98.8	36.5	17.9	518	22.1
Smith	110	5.8	145	0.4	25.1	360 426	2 486	62 731	238.7	315 279	1.3	98.7	41.5	25.5	415	19.6
Stone	52	-8.8	161	0.0	10.9	439 555	2 738	43 883	7.9	24 581	D	D	22.3	1.9	567	17.0

Table B. States and Counties — Water Use, Wholesale Trade, Retail Trade, and Real Estate

STATE County	Water use, 2005		Wholesale trade,[1] 2007				Retail trade,[2] 2007				Real estate and rental and leasing,[2] 2007			
	Total water withdrawn (mil gal/day)	Gallons withdrawn per person	Number of establish-ments	Number of employees	Sales (mil dol)	Annual payroll (mil dol)	Number of establish-ments	Number of employees	Sales (mil dol)	Annual payroll (mil dol)	Number of establish-ments	Number of employees	Receipts (mil dol)	Annual payroll (mil dol)
	133	134	135	136	137	138	139	140	141	142	143	144	145	146
MISSISSIPPI	2 927.7	1 002	2 556	32 382	23 003.6	1 276.0	12 452	141 426	33 751.4	2 910.9	2 517	10 169	1 734.6	283.7
Adams	6.9	214	38	D	D	D	191	2 037	427.7	41.5	41	148	18.9	4.0
Alcorn	5.3	150	37	D	D	D	196	2 237	527.6	46.6	23	200	10.7	3.5
Amite	2.4	175	8	29	17.9	0.8	33	177	36.3	3.1	2	D	D	D
Attala	2.9	146	21	87	37.0	3.1	95	845	171.4	16.0	9	22	2.3	0.4
Benton	2.3	295	NA	NA	NA	NA	15	130	25.1	2.2	1	D	D	D
Bolivar	331.8	8 586	31	D	D	D	167	1 558	303.4	27.8	38	126	15.4	2.4
Calhoun	3.2	217	11	75	29.0	1.8	68	443	94.1	7.6	3	D	D	D
Carroll	7.0	669	3	D	D	D	21	159	24.2	1.7	2	D	D	D
Chickasaw	9.1	473	18	188	101.5	4.5	84	681	128.0	10.6	12	30	3.0	0.6
Choctaw	5.6	585	2	D	D	D	31	185	30.8	2.9	2	D	D	D
Claiborne	29.1	2 529	3	D	D	D	31	183	39.3	3.5	1	D	D	D
Clarke	2.6	149	6	D	D	D	51	377	58.1	4.7	5	D	D	D
Clay	6.1	288	14	D	D	D	77	634	126.0	10.7	9	39	4.5	0.8
Coahoma	139.7	4 817	26	D	D	D	127	1 112	260.3	22.7	38	111	14.1	2.4
Copiah	5.8	198	11	D	D	D	92	733	143.1	13.0	9	58	2.9	1.0
Covington	7.6	374	13	68	66.6	2.0	74	567	171.6	11.3	10	18	1.7	0.2
DeSoto	32.0	234	100	2 098	1 676.8	80.1	471	7 895	2 069.5	178.0	110	434	90.0	12.1
Forrest	32.4	431	77	858	424.1	31.1	382	4 496	2 121.6	104.1	99	D	D	D
Franklin	1.2	137	3	D	D	D	20	119	20.9	1.7	2	D	D	D
George	3.3	154	11	D	D	D	81	888	231.5	16.4	9	18	1.7	0.3
Greene	2.9	222	3	79	27.6	2.6	29	194	39.1	2.9	5	12	1.7	0.2
Grenada	10.1	441	29	D	D	D	136	1 378	377.0	31.1	26	92	16.3	2.4
Hancock	10.8	232	21	D	D	D	116	1 411	383.2	32.7	32	69	12.5	1.6
Harrison	195.3	1 007	156	1 618	839.7	70.4	821	11 071	2 903.2	254.4	252	968	175.6	29.3
Hinds	46.3	186	292	4 183	2 118.8	188.3	962	12 358	2 992.6	279.3	286	1 689	412.2	60.1
Holmes	49.9	2 366	10	121	31.1	2.9	81	534	114.4	8.8	14	D	D	D
Humphreys	122.3	11 617	6	35	15.1	1.2	35	298	81.4	5.2	3	D	D	D
Issaquena	11.1	5 825	2	D	D	D	NA	NA	NA	NA	NA	NA	NA	NA
Itawamba	10.9	468	10	222	59.4	7.0	80	635	135.0	12.8	2	D	D	D
Jackson	54.4	400	51	D	D	D	453	5 356	1 305.0	116.0	105	370	48.8	9.3
Jasper	2.5	140	11	89	89.5	3.4	42	370	68.9	7.2	4	38	5.4	0.9
Jefferson	0.7	69	1	D	D	D	13	89	18.6	1.3	2	D	D	D
Jefferson Davis	2.5	192	2	D	D	D	52	345	57.3	5.2	5	D	D	D
Jones	17.2	260	79	664	402.7	28.0	284	3 367	816.4	70.0	60	314	59.4	12.9
Kemper	1.8	171	3	D	D	D	31	176	46.7	2.9	1	D	D	D
Lafayette	3.6	88	22	D	D	D	205	2 419	507.1	48.5	54	177	25.0	3.6
Lamar	21.7	485	35	D	D	D	320	4 871	991.8	90.5	64	D	D	D
Lauderdale	12.0	155	84	1 696	1 127.6	65.7	449	5 400	1 320.6	112.8	73	294	39.3	6.1
Lawrence	38.6	2 861	3	D	D	D	43	301	46.8	5.1	2	D	D	D
Leake	5.8	257	10	93	22.7	2.6	88	799	180.4	15.4	5	12	0.6	0.2
Lee	4.6	58	159	1 859	847.9	65.3	541	6 753	1 439.5	136.4	99	511	88.6	14.7
Leflore	213.6	5 862	39	D	D	D	182	1 803	438.7	34.7	47	D	D	D
Lincoln	5.5	161	28	D	D	D	178	1 998	502.0	41.8	28	102	14.5	2.3
Lowndes	41.7	697	60	D	D	D	349	3 950	809.3	80.4	75	233	33.3	5.1
Madison	13.9	164	131	2 958	3 305.9	119.5	457	6 441	1 268.4	135.6	139	719	159.0	24.1
Marion	5.1	201	24	233	155.7	7.4	132	1 253	259.0	23.4	24	79	18.8	2.2
Marshall	4.1	116	13	68	43.5	2.3	114	886	166.4	17.0	17	47	6.4	1.1
Monroe	27.7	734	23	245	111.1	7.4	146	1 432	282.0	26.1	16	42	3.8	0.8
Montgomery	1.8	153	7	30	7.6	0.9	59	526	136.6	9.1	4	D	D	D
Neshoba	4.8	162	19	197	286.9	9.2	126	1 227	255.8	23.7	19	53	5.7	1.1
Newton	3.1	139	5	32	9.2	0.7	85	811	146.7	14.0	7	18	2.0	0.2
Noxubee	29.9	2 450	10	77	26.8	1.5	52	395	82.9	6.0	1	D	D	D
Oktibbeha	6.4	156	17	416	166.2	13.4	161	2 105	387.9	39.8	49	170	25.6	3.5
Panola	29.0	820	31	572	484.5	21.1	185	1 664	384.4	30.0	17	72	10.2	1.8
Pearl River	6.8	129	30	D	D	D	209	2 452	615.6	52.1	25	76	9.3	1.3
Perry	21.2	1 745	3	D	D	D	37	280	60.4	4.6	3	D	D	D
Pike	8.1	206	50	454	188.7	12.9	235	2 583	544.7	51.1	43	D	D	D
Pontotoc	2.2	79	16	155	57.5	4.3	84	886	203.6	15.3	5	D	D	D
Prentiss	2.3	91	13	43	17.8	1.0	109	763	162.0	14.7	43	96	8.1	1.3
Quitman	80.4	8 449	6	35	19.1	0.9	20	158	24.7	2.2	5	10	1.5	0.2
Rankin	21.6	164	215	3 621	2 629.6	169.1	521	8 124	2 226.2	183.0	147	646	121.9	20.6
Scott	10.9	381	21	71	41.2	1.9	125	1 156	235.1	21.8	8	30	2.5	0.6
Sharkey	32.0	5 368	13	91	64.2	3.1	23	199	31.0	2.8	7	18	2.1	0.3
Simpson	5.3	190	12	D	D	D	93	1 044	212.6	19.8	13	44	4.7	0.9
Smith	4.8	298	8	34	12.6	0.8	36	312	51.1	4.8	3	7	0.4	0.1
Stone	3.2	217	14	D	D	D	65	716	190.7	15.7	11	38	3.1	0.6

1. Merchant wholesalers, except manufacturers' sales branches and offices.   2. Employer establishments.

Table B. States and Counties — Professional Services, Manufacturing, and Accommodation and Food Services

STATE County	Professional, scientific, and technical services,[1] 2007				Manufacturing, 2007				Accommodation and food services, 2007			
	Number of establish-ments	Number of employees	Receipts (mil dol)	Annual payroll (mil dol)	Number of establish-ments	Number of employees	Receipts (mil dol)	Annual payroll (mil dol)	Number of establish-ments	Number of employees	Sales (mil dol)	Annual payroll (mil dol)
	147	148	149	150	151	152	153	154	155	156	157	158
MISSISSIPPI	4 751	30 855	3 971.9	1 350.3	2 598	159 235	59 869.5	5 756.6	4 817	119 626	7 045.1	1 812.3
Adams	62	248	24.6	6.6	NA	NA	NA	NA	88	1 728	98.0	22.2
Alcorn	60	298	26.6	8.6	49	2 994	944.6	122.4	70	1 157	42.5	11.0
Amite	6	D	D	D	10	599	D	21.9	4	28	1.3	0.3
Attala	23	58	5.4	1.4	23	984	319.5	27.8	26	326	13.7	3.4
Benton	2	D	D	D	NA	NA	NA	NA	NA	NA	NA	NA
Bolivar	50	219	19.7	7.1	18	1 345	287.0	48.5	44	777	31.1	7.0
Calhoun	14	50	5.8	1.6	21	876	235.3	26.9	12	90	2.5	0.6
Carroll	4	D	D	D	NA	NA	NA	NA	5	28	0.7	0.2
Chickasaw	15	47	3.5	1.1	51	2 668	427.2	79.1	19	253	11.5	2.2
Choctaw	6	17	1.5	0.6	NA	NA	NA	NA	8	43	1.7	0.3
Claiborne	7	21	1.6	0.4	NA	NA	NA	NA	12	181	4.7	1.4
Clarke	15	D	D	D	22	584	D	16.8	11	108	4.5	1.1
Clay	22	D	D	D	23	1 122	393.0	46.5	34	465	15.8	3.8
Coahoma	47	D	D	D	22	738	D	27.3	42	1 353	120.6	21.8
Copiah	24	66	6.4	1.8	26	2 644	D	D	33	484	15.7	3.8
Covington	17	82	7.5	2.5	12	1 505	D	34.9	21	359	11.2	3.2
DeSoto	175	921	77.9	28.8	133	4 822	1 663.5	208.2	260	6 230	256.8	67.1
Forrest	184	D	D	D	72	D	883.4	137.5	176	4 078	158.8	42.8
Franklin	8	36	2.9	1.3	NA	NA	NA	NA	5	D	D	D
George	18	D	D	D	NA	NA	NA	NA	27	342	13.4	3.0
Greene	4	19	1.2	0.5	NA	NA	NA	NA	4	42	1.7	0.4
Grenada	33	151	14.0	5.6	24	2 910	732.5	101.7	61	875	36.2	8.5
Hancock	93	D	D	D	32	863	D	58.5	78	1 616	133.8	33.0
Harrison	393	D	D	D	110	3 234	D	137.4	353	17 953	1 619.1	435.9
Hinds	710	D	D	D	160	5 610	1 406.2	243.1	451	9 284	403.8	107.2
Holmes	13	59	20.1	4.7	6	622	208.0	17.5	25	178	5.5	1.5
Humphreys	5	12	1.3	0.4	4	D	D	D	9	139	4.4	1.2
Issaquena	NA	NA	NA	NA	NA	NA	NA	NA	NA	NA	NA	NA
Itawamba	17	D	D	D	40	1 531	D	46.8	27	365	12.3	3.2
Jackson	203	D	D	D	82	D	D	D	227	4 167	178.0	47.2
Jasper	18	136	7.2	3.3	13	1 283	256.5	41.6	13	117	4.4	1.0
Jefferson	1	D	D	D	NA	NA	NA	NA	3	D	D	D
Jefferson Davis	13	14	3.8	1.4	NA	NA	NA	NA	9	144	6.2	1.5
Jones	97	598	55.1	16.0	72	8 571	1 760.0	265.3	105	5 520	442.8	106.5
Kemper	5	D	D	D	NA	NA	NA	NA	5	36	1.4	0.4
Lafayette	113	D	D	D	27	1 479	D	47.5	128	2 298	96.2	26.3
Lamar	102	604	72.1	22.9	28	D	D	19.7	100	2 701	103.5	30.2
Lauderdale	120	D	D	D	66	2 880	750.9	99.6	159	3 620	135.8	38.0
Lawrence	8	12	1.6	0.2	12	717	D	42.1	16	104	4.0	0.9
Leake	14	45	3.3	0.8	7	D	D	D	23	299	13.0	3.1
Lee	189	D	D	D	149	11 736	2 986.8	427.4	195	4 096	148.2	41.3
Leflore	50	D	D	D	34	D	D	D	62	1 137	51.4	13.1
Lincoln	56	469	44.0	15.4	33	1 146	275.7	45.4	58	883	41.2	9.6
Lowndes	116	617	78.4	24.7	63	3 879	2 075.5	172.6	111	2 456	88.6	23.4
Madison	323	D	D	D	75	7 495	6 471.9	320.7	228	4 619	180.6	49.6
Marion	43	185	16.0	6.7	23	950	166.3	22.0	44	529	20.1	4.6
Marshall	21	71	6.6	1.8	31	D	D	D	28	422	14.2	3.8
Monroe	40	121	8.7	2.5	53	3 144	1 472.7	130.0	51	541	21.8	4.9
Montgomery	14	27	3.7	0.7	NA	NA	NA	NA	23	229	7.3	1.8
Neshoba	19	90	8.2	3.8	14	628	192.4	23.2	42	665	24.2	5.8
Newton	17	48	2.9	1.0	21	1 693	290.8	51.2	22	356	11.2	3.0
Noxubee	6	12	0.8	0.2	18	792	198.9	26.1	11	81	4.6	1.3
Oktibbeha	73	D	D	D	29	1 506	514.3	63.9	100	2 129	77.3	20.5
Panola	29	157	15.1	3.8	41	2 083	495.3	74.2	54	866	32.6	9.2
Pearl River	63	281	22.1	9.8	36	637	D	25.3	83	1 210	43.2	10.9
Perry	6	D	D	D	10	811	D	40.9	5	34	1.2	0.4
Pike	76	D	D	D	34	2 777	D	68.1	76	1 311	50.9	13.2
Pontotoc	22	D	D	D	78	6 833	D	198.6	30	434	14.8	3.8
Prentiss	26	165	34.4	5.8	40	2 609	975.2	79.1	33	507	17.5	4.8
Quitman	4	D	D	D	NA	NA	NA	NA	5	62	1.9	0.4
Rankin	314	1 450	204.0	67.5	131	3 897	1 865.8	161.8	241	4 832	197.8	52.7
Scott	21	93	5.2	1.9	23	5 072	1 057.5	143.6	38	518	19.7	4.5
Sharkey	8	18	1.2	0.3	NA	NA	NA	NA	4	35	1.6	0.4
Simpson	27	121	8.9	2.6	NA	NA	NA	NA	37	552	20.6	5.2
Smith	14	94	8.1	1.8	13	1 052	402.6	37.5	10	73	1.8	0.5
Stone	18	D	D	D	23	616	D	23.1	27	482	18.6	4.8

1. Establishment subject to federal tax.

Table B. States and Counties — Health Care and Social Assistance, Other Services, and Federal Funds

| STATE County | Health care and social assistance, 2007 | | | | Other services, 2007 | | | | Federal funds and grants, 2009–2010 Expenditures (mil dol) | | | |
| | | | | | | | | | | Direct payments for individuals[1] | | |
	Number of establishments	Number of employees	Receipts (mil dol)	Annual payroll (mil dol)	Number of establishments	Number of employees	Receipts (mil dol)	Annual payroll (mil dol)	Total	Social Security and government retirement	Medicare	Food Stamps and Supplemental Security Income
	159	160	161	162	163	164	165	166	167	168	169	170
MISSISSIPPI	5 876	146 858	14 113.8	5 371.7	3 853	20 421	1 949.6	489.6	31 418.9	9 042.0	4 606.0	1 588.6
Adams	102	1 881	178.3	62.7	47	213	16.9	4.3	306.1	113.5	57.3	27.1
Alcorn	101	2 008	215.4	68.5	58	171	12.7	3.6	325.6	134.9	66.4	15.9
Amite	10	D	D	D	7	D	D	D	111.7	41.5	25.7	8.2
Attala	24	579	42.6	15.4	25	224	11.7	2.5	188.8	68.2	43.1	11.5
Benton	9	D	D	D	3	D	D	D	75.9	28.0	16.0	4.4
Bolivar	72	1 942	135.8	49.2	50	218	16.6	4.2	423.2	98.9	66.8	40.7
Calhoun	23	429	25.9	10.0	14	34	2.4	0.6	158.1	49.2	32.8	6.9
Carroll	5	D	D	D	5	D	D	D	80.8	31.0	15.6	6.3
Chickasaw	29	D	D	D	23	50	3.4	0.8	182.8	61.2	37.4	11.0
Choctaw	9	D	D	D	11	29	2.5	0.6	79.3	24.3	12.8	5.1
Claiborne	18	368	21.4	9.2	5	D	D	D	92.1	25.2	20.0	10.8
Clarke	21	402	26.3	10.1	18	D	D	D	151.2	62.6	32.4	8.1
Clay	27	690	57.3	22.3	23	88	8.4	2.0	169.8	62.5	30.5	15.4
Coahoma	77	1 897	179.5	61.3	36	194	8.1	2.7	382.5	71.0	66.0	34.4
Copiah	31	610	53.4	14.9	33	130	9.5	2.2	305.1	101.1	58.4	21.3
Covington	29	506	37.1	14.6	22	110	8.6	2.0	165.7	62.8	33.6	12.9
DeSoto	208	4 172	424.4	157.5	171	993	101.2	24.0	648.1	406.8	92.0	23.4
Forrest	188	7 667	787.3	357.7	102	747	52.0	15.4	1 105.6	287.6	129.3	43.6
Franklin	10	258	14.0	6.6	4	D	D	D	70.6	25.5	15.6	4.7
George	30	637	52.8	24.7	23	88	7.1	1.8	159.4	79.4	36.7	10.1
Greene	10	99	5.9	2.2	10	D	D	D	74.5	27.7	18.8	6.0
Grenada	69	1 053	95.7	36.1	40	113	10.8	2.5	244.7	83.3	55.7	15.0
Hancock	59	D	D	D	46	174	16.7	4.7	895.0	140.0	71.1	17.0
Harrison	437	12 887	1 498.9	570.4	289	1 778	181.3	47.3	2 420.3	704.2	320.0	82.8
Hinds	735	25 347	2 673.9	985.5	462	3 256	316.5	88.2	4 018.6	686.7	382.2	171.8
Holmes	33	252	17.8	6.9	18	185	9.0	2.6	289.7	52.8	55.7	30.8
Humphreys	19	262	15.8	6.5	14	41	2.5	0.6	148.9	24.7	29.4	14.2
Issaquena	2	D	D	D	NA	NA	NA	NA	28.0	2.4	2.5	1.4
Itawamba	28	D	D	D	24	64	5.1	1.2	250.0	61.7	33.5	4.7
Jackson	288	5 343	569.6	219.1	152	761	64.7	18.1	1 067.0	451.9	179.4	44.1
Jasper	14	289	16.4	7.9	14	47	3.9	1.2	158.4	58.0	32.5	10.2
Jefferson	12	210	14.1	5.9	4	D	D	D	124.8	21.5	16.1	7.4
Jefferson Davis	13	296	18.9	7.0	12	26	2.3	0.4	141.4	37.1	25.2	11.0
Jones	118	3 373	257.7	116.3	98	690	80.7	19.1	554.6	222.7	123.4	29.2
Kemper	7	175	6.2	2.8	4	D	D	D	109.4	28.8	16.7	6.4
Lafayette	107	2 270	243.9	82.0	66	402	121.4	9.9	320.1	95.0	31.7	8.0
Lamar	121	2 445	268.5	88.9	54	240	18.4	4.6	193.0	96.0	88.5	13.2
Lauderdale	207	8 113	919.1	320.4	139	675	59.3	14.6	744.1	268.5	144.8	44.9
Lawrence	20	200	13.0	4.4	10	D	D	D	147.5	59.9	32.1	7.5
Leake	24	521	31.2	14.9	15	43	4.1	1.2	192.1	68.3	48.4	10.3
Lee	254	7 385	910.0	337.6	143	1 055	92.7	31.7	610.3	275.4	104.8	27.8
Leflore	77	D	D	D	47	D	D	D	419.9	87.5	79.0	36.9
Lincoln	72	1 556	139.9	50.4	42	274	20.1	7.4	267.4	110.0	50.7	17.5
Lowndes	166	2 987	282.4	97.3	104	514	36.0	10.9	684.6	202.2	73.0	32.9
Madison	198	2 810	222.5	81.4	133	813	94.1	26.2	812.5	231.1	75.1	34.8
Marion	43	756	58.5	24.4	46	159	14.5	3.1	246.4	84.8	55.1	18.6
Marshall	24	1 149	76.2	24.6	19	D	D	D	319.3	117.6	48.8	24.5
Monroe	64	1 478	119.2	49.2	48	132	11.1	3.0	304.3	123.4	67.9	14.3
Montgomery	21	434	28.4	12.4	16	76	7.0	1.6	148.8	40.8	32.0	8.1
Neshoba	39	1 155	94.9	39.8	33	191	16.0	4.3	276.1	74.1	50.2	14.1
Newton	31	671	46.8	18.6	29	89	4.3	1.2	254.0	94.5	57.4	11.2
Noxubee	18	269	18.3	7.2	15	D	D	D	125.2	30.3	17.9	13.5
Oktibbeha	73	1 625	116.2	50.9	66	330	64.0	5.7	419.8	104.7	36.2	19.7
Panola	60	1 311	84.1	38.4	25	118	7.1	1.9	323.7	103.0	53.4	23.9
Pearl River	94	937	64.3	25.1	58	272	20.8	6.3	441.9	197.8	87.1	26.3
Perry	20	289	18.8	7.1	11	46	2.8	0.9	88.7	36.9	16.8	7.5
Pike	120	D	D	D	56	D	D	D	385.5	139.7	81.7	30.0
Pontotoc	39	D	D	D	32	88	6.9	1.6	176.0	79.0	38.4	7.8
Prentiss	39	982	51.0	18.4	32	D	D	D	221.8	91.3	42.9	10.3
Quitman	17	299	17.0	7.3	8	12	0.8	0.2	123.4	24.2	23.1	11.6
Rankin	265	7 288	705.5	276.3	214	1 210	112.5	32.6	776.3	363.6	111.2	23.3
Scott	46	1 040	65.6	25.7	36	141	10.6	3.0	240.2	85.5	55.6	11.9
Sharkey	12	207	15.2	5.5	9	42	1.5	0.6	80.8	15.1	14.2	7.8
Simpson	53	2 198	104.8	45.4	33	139	9.8	2.6	295.5	81.7	48.5	14.5
Smith	8	D	D	D	8	D	D	D	113.3	41.5	23.4	6.1
Stone	19	D	D	D	14	31	3.4	1.0	145.7	61.1	27.2	7.4

1. State totals may include programs not allocated by county.

Table B. States and Counties — Federal Funds, Residential Construction, and Local Government Finances

	Federal funds and grants, 2009–2010 (cont.)							Value of residential construction authorized by building permits, 2010		Local government finances, 2007				
	Expenditures (mil dol) (cont.)										General revenue			
		Procurement contract awards		Grants[1]								Taxes		
													Per capita[2] (dollars)	
STATE County	Salaries and wages	Defense	Other	Medicaid and other health-related	Nutrition and family welfare	Education	Other	New construction ($1,000)	Number of housing units	Total (mil dol)	Inter-govern-mental (mil dol)	Total (mil dol)	Total	Property
	171	172	173	174	175	176	177	178	179	180	181	182	183	184
MISSISSIPPI	3 016.7	1 634.0	1 031.9	4 459.9	856.9	632.9	1 921.4	715 297	5 259	X	X	X	X	X
Adams	11.4	0.0	6.3	67.9	14.1	2.1	1.5	654	5	133.0	45.0	28.5	897	798
Alcorn	17.8	-0.1	1.8	52.7	4.7	3.0	10.5	1 643	13	200.6	60.6	18.6	523	501
Amite	3.5	0.1	0.9	27.6	2.8	0.9	0.3	0	0	21.9	12.6	5.2	392	380
Attala	5.3	0.2	0.9	47.6	4.6	1.8	4.6	691	2	56.5	26.4	12.8	653	623
Benton	1.8	0.1	0.4	20.5	2.8	0.4	0.1	0	0	16.1	11.4	3.8	470	449
Bolivar	7.9	0.7	1.7	129.7	18.0	5.3	5.8	2 154	16	106.7	61.5	29.0	771	727
Calhoun	19.8	3.1	0.6	35.5	3.0	0.6	2.6	150	1	42.5	19.5	7.9	539	514
Carroll	1.9	-0.3	0.4	19.8	1.8	0.4	0.4	NA	NA	20.0	8.5	6.0	579	566
Chickasaw	14.9	0.0	0.8	45.6	4.2	1.1	1.8	140	2	47.3	28.6	10.5	551	486
Choctaw	12.0	0.0	2.4	19.2	2.2	0.7	0.3	250	1	22.0	13.6	4.4	485	472
Claiborne	1.6	0.0	0.4	27.2	3.0	0.8	1.7	0	0	38.9	23.1	5.0	452	415
Clarke	4.0	1.9	1.8	34.7	3.5	1.0	0.3	480	3	36.9	23.0	9.6	549	530
Clay	8.2	0.0	1.4	39.0	5.2	2.3	1.5	2 148	14	47.6	28.1	15.2	724	708
Coahoma	19.4	15.7	1.2	100.8	13.1	7.9	9.2	451	8	121.4	72.3	22.7	822	685
Copiah	23.2	1.2	16.2	60.2	6.3	2.6	0.6	310	3	92.7	46.7	15.4	524	502
Covington	6.3	0.1	0.7	39.2	4.0	1.4	3.4	700	4	52.6	26.4	10.1	497	477
DeSoto	40.0	6.9	5.8	49.4	10.4	2.8	1.5	61 091	456	349.2	162.3	135.9	910	854
Forrest	305.4	87.8	12.2	87.1	18.6	7.2	74.2	7 686	52	562.4	122.3	73.4	939	825
Franklin	4.2	0.0	0.7	15.4	1.9	0.4	0.6	0	0	22.8	14.7	5.0	597	576
George	11.0	0.0	2.0	13.7	4.3	0.9	0.0	110	3	83.3	35.1	11.9	541	523
Greene	1.4	0.0	0.3	16.8	2.2	0.5	0.0	0	0	36.7	25.3	7.1	541	533
Grenada	23.7	11.8	2.9	39.0	4.2	1.4	1.5	1 580	13	102.4	36.7	17.6	762	726
Hancock	135.9	57.2	443.7	15.9	6.3	1.6	3.8	50 621	428	267.5	137.2	38.7	976	854
Harrison	644.5	287.4	80.2	133.7	38.7	8.2	94.5	137 790	1 304	1 200.9	552.7	198.2	1 126	913
Hinds	332.5	35.6	127.3	472.2	219.7	314.7	1 124.9	47 501	323	848.9	432.4	259.8	1 043	980
Holmes	4.8	0.5	1.2	95.6	7.2	3.5	2.7	382	3	84.0	52.6	13.9	680	660
Humphreys	2.0	0.4	9.1	40.6	3.7	1.0	0.4	70	2	31.4	16.6	7.8	781	757
Issaquena	0.5	8.4	0.1	3.7	0.8	0.1	0.0	0	0	5.4	0.6	1.3	777	762
Itawamba	3.8	0.0	0.6	29.0	3.2	1.6	81.3	1 310	18	92.6	46.3	19.1	831	827
Jackson	102.9	118.1	46.0	45.6	22.1	7.8	37.9	49 410	326	766.3	253.9	150.1	1 153	1 077
Jasper	7.7	0.0	0.7	43.0	4.3	1.1	0.3	0	0	54.4	30.4	12.3	682	651
Jefferson	11.4	0.0	0.4	32.6	2.7	6.6	9.8	184	3	29.7	14.1	5.5	611	589
Jefferson Davis	3.0	16.4	0.4	34.2	10.0	1.1	2.7	0	0	35.0	23.6	6.9	537	528
Jones	34.7	0.9	17.1	88.6	11.8	4.3	3.8	3 494	56	367.1	160.7	44.3	663	624
Kemper	3.5	0.1	0.5	28.9	2.5	0.7	0.6	NA	NA	59.5	31.6	8.2	812	799
Lafayette	41.8	1.4	17.4	41.5	5.3	3.0	46.9	12 093	82	91.5	42.8	34.9	817	765
Lamar	9.1	0.4	1.7	24.0	4.9	1.7	0.2	2 392	22	113.9	54.6	38.7	810	791
Lauderdale	79.1	32.5	6.4	118.3	13.6	4.7	12.6	17 547	109	239.6	135.6	58.9	763	719
Lawrence	14.1	0.0	0.9	25.3	2.7	1.4	1.9	191	3	41.5	22.2	10.0	746	737
Leake	6.2	0.0	0.8	51.1	4.1	1.6	0.2	0	0	42.2	27.2	9.7	426	404
Lee	77.9	0.8	25.2	71.6	8.5	4.6	3.1	15 063	99	230.5	123.4	71.2	886	856
Leflore	28.7	7.8	7.9	98.4	10.5	10.7	5.3	942	9	222.2	54.7	25.4	723	686
Lincoln	32.0	0.3	2.5	43.4	5.9	1.9	0.7	1 702	11	81.2	47.0	22.3	645	608
Lowndes	124.8	109.1	2.9	80.3	10.2	6.0	29.3	10 981	109	186.8	89.3	43.4	727	702
Madison	25.2	291.1	31.8	76.4	11.4	3.9	14.6	123 428	581	249.3	112.3	99.0	1 107	1 030
Marion	10.9	0.0	6.5	52.7	13.9	1.7	0.3	295	2	93.6	47.3	17.6	682	574
Marshall	7.4	0.8	1.8	71.5	32.0	4.2	2.4	7 811	47	64.1	39.6	19.8	540	516
Monroe	10.2	1.0	6.0	57.6	6.6	2.2	8.5	1 215	9	79.1	44.9	22.3	601	557
Montgomery	12.4	-0.1	0.7	40.3	9.9	0.8	1.5	2 276	39	28.1	18.2	6.7	587	552
Neshoba	13.1	20.7	0.9	45.0	8.3	7.1	7.5	469	3	52.8	34.4	13.3	441	423
Newton	19.7	0.0	1.2	42.7	4.0	0.9	10.4	0	0	73.4	47.7	11.4	508	475
Noxubee	3.1	0.0	1.7	48.0	3.7	1.0	0.6	0	0	37.2	17.6	8.0	675	662
Oktibbeha	38.9	21.9	6.8	56.5	7.0	7.2	89.1	10 327	83	135.1	45.7	25.8	589	573
Panola	22.2	18.3	9.2	69.0	7.7	2.1	0.5	914	14	97.3	50.9	23.9	676	622
Pearl River	23.0	31.6	4.8	36.8	8.0	3.3	5.2	26 801	238	246.5	177.3	36.8	645	616
Perry	3.1	0.0	0.4	17.6	2.7	0.8	0.1	0	0	34.7	19.6	7.9	648	626
Pike	27.6	0.9	1.8	70.5	8.4	3.7	10.8	5 465	62	237.4	76.8	27.2	684	655
Pontotoc	4.8	0.0	1.8	35.5	3.7	1.1	1.0	1 008	17	67.4	39.9	14.9	516	489
Prentiss	11.8	0.1	0.7	45.0	3.9	1.3	0.7	1 475	8	84.7	52.1	13.0	510	487
Quitman	1.9	0.0	-0.6	42.1	2.9	0.7	0.4	807	9	22.4	14.6	6.2	696	660
Rankin	155.7	27.5	6.8	49.9	12.6	4.9	5.4	83 818	475	286.7	135.9	103.0	744	700
Scott	18.6	0.0	10.2	48.9	6.5	1.5	0.4	1 148	16	59.6	38.2	14.3	495	455
Sharkey	2.0	0.0	0.7	19.6	1.9	0.7	0.1	290	2	17.9	11.3	4.9	874	832
Simpson	15.9	0.0	0.9	38.0	5.0	2.4	87.3	1 321	9	52.5	33.3	11.3	406	389
Smith	6.5	-0.1	0.5	30.6	3.1	0.8	0.0	175	2	38.5	23.2	8.3	521	505
Stone	7.1	0.0	3.4	10.1	2.4	0.7	2.3	1 200	12	143.2	84.7	27.0	1 719	1 683

1. State totals may include programs not allocated by county.   2. Based on the resident population estimated as of July 1 of the year shown.

Table B. States and Counties — Local Government Finances, Government Employment, and Voting

STATE County	Total (mil dol)	Per capita[1] (dollars)	Education	Health and hospitals	Police protection	Public welfare	Highways	Total (mil dol)	Per capita[1] (dollars)	Federal civilian	Federal military	State and local	Democratic	Republican	All other
	185	186	187	188	189	190	191	192	193	194	195	196	197	198	199
MISSISSIPPI	X	X	X	X	X	X	X	X	X	26 758	31 078	226 703	43.0	56.2	0.8
Adams	122.8	3 872	30.1	33.3	5.5	0.2	3.9	157.0	4 951	133	195	1 967	57.5	41.8	0.7
Alcorn	198.8	5 582	23.4	53.7	2.3	0.0	2.6	69.0	1 939	100	218	2 799	27.2	71.2	1.6
Amite	20.3	1 521	59.7	1.5	4.3	0.2	13.4	0.7	53	34	79	400	43.8	55.5	0.7
Attala	58.2	2 970	46.9	21.5	3.0	0.1	7.6	13.0	662	72	120	1 214	41.9	57.4	0.7
Benton	16.7	2 080	62.8	0.9	5.5	0.0	9.0	3.0	369	27	49	318	48.0	50.2	1.8
Bolivar	102.6	2 727	60.2	1.8	6.6	0.2	6.5	45.1	1 199	93	224	2 977	67.2	31.8	1.0
Calhoun	40.3	2 765	45.9	28.8	3.9	0.0	7.1	12.0	820	39	88	855	35.9	63.5	0.6
Carroll	20.8	2 015	45.0	0.9	4.5	0.2	11.7	13.6	1 325	26	62	323	34.1	65.4	0.4
Chickasaw	46.9	2 473	57.3	1.6	5.4	7.4	5.1	18.4	969	53	114	886	50.7	48.5	0.8
Choctaw	22.6	2 495	66.6	1.0	5.2	1.2	10.6	6.7	739	43	55	480	35.3	63.6	1.1
Claiborne	39.5	3 590	39.4	13.4	3.7	0.2	9.9	143.5	13 045	31	65	1 703	85.9	13.7	0.4
Clarke	38.4	2 204	65.9	1.3	4.2	0.1	10.4	15.9	912	36	105	823	37.2	62.3	0.6
Clay	42.7	2 035	64.8	0.7	6.5	0.7	4.9	26.5	1 265	64	126	925	59.1	40.3	0.6
Coahoma	105.8	3 839	60.1	0.7	4.3	0.1	3.6	156.2	5 670	74	164	2 146	71.9	27.6	0.5
Copiah	92.4	3 152	66.1	11.5	4.2	0.1	6.5	20.0	681	71	177	2 107	53.2	46.2	0.6
Covington	54.9	2 695	50.0	25.6	3.3	0.2	6.7	17.3	848	70	125	1 135	40.7	58.4	0.9
DeSoto	366.8	2 455	54.8	1.2	7.4	0.0	7.2	496.9	3 326	252	965	6 071	30.5	68.8	0.7
Forrest	539.6	6 897	20.2	62.0	2.4	0.0	2.6	361.7	4 622	760	698	11 345	42.8	56.3	1.0
Franklin	22.1	2 658	64.3	2.3	3.3	0.0	15.4	2.4	288	60	51	840	37.0	62.1	0.9
George	76.1	3 468	39.8	36.7	3.0	0.1	7.8	22.0	1 001	44	138	1 388	16.4	82.6	1.1
Greene	36.9	2 813	41.1	0.8	3.9	0.0	43.8	10.7	813	16	87	1 133	23.6	75.3	1.1
Grenada	104.4	4 525	29.5	40.9	5.0	0.1	5.9	56.1	2 432	253	140	1 723	44.4	55.1	0.5
Hancock	238.5	6 009	30.9	14.9	3.2	0.1	3.7	160.8	4 051	1 884	746	2 036	22.1	76.3	1.6
Harrison	1 110.3	6 305	27.0	23.6	4.8	0.1	3.7	889.0	5 048	6 502	10 385	12 785	36.6	62.6	0.9
Hinds	854.5	3 429	54.2	0.6	5.5	0.6	5.2	1 048.4	4 208	5 280	1 555	34 906	69.2	30.3	0.5
Holmes	86.3	4 217	77.2	1.4	3.5	0.3	4.8	38.2	1 866	58	123	1 332	81.4	18.0	0.7
Humphreys	32.1	3 212	49.8	13.1	4.7	0.1	11.7	14.6	1 461	28	60	466	70.9	28.5	0.6
Issaquena	5.1	3 034	1.1	2.0	14.3	0.0	11.8	3.6	2 173	0	10	105	60.9	38.3	0.7
Itawamba	83.5	3 627	83.5	0.5	2.0	0.1	2.8	46.8	2 032	52	140	1 245	20.9	77.0	2.1
Jackson	699.7	5 378	32.3	35.1	2.9	0.1	3.7	479.5	3 686	803	1 224	9 499	32.7	66.3	1.0
Jasper	52.9	2 929	47.4	14.2	3.2	0.2	12.9	8.6	477	57	109	979	54.6	44.9	0.5
Jefferson	27.5	3 066	45.3	20.5	5.4	0.2	6.0	10.2	1 134	18	58	620	86.7	12.3	1.0
Jefferson Davis	27.3	2 131	63.1	4.9	4.8	0.1	7.8	12.7	993	26	76	700	60.4	39.0	0.6
Jones	366.4	5 488	36.7	35.3	2.2	0.1	3.6	304.3	4 558	239	412	6 911	30.2	68.9	0.9
Kemper	59.4	5 878	75.7	0.7	2.0	0.1	6.0	14.7	1 451	36	60	624	62.3	37.0	0.6
Lafayette	98.3	2 302	59.7	1.0	6.0	0.1	8.1	108.4	2 538	346	282	7 064	43.3	55.7	1.0
Lamar	130.1	2 728	70.2	0.4	4.1	0.2	9.1	79.7	1 671	114	304	2 251	21.6	77.4	1.1
Lauderdale	244.9	3 176	56.6	2.6	5.5	0.0	4.3	181.5	2 354	865	1 692	5 797	40.3	59.1	0.6
Lawrence	40.8	3 062	49.9	16.7	3.5	0.1	9.1	3.4	254	47	81	738	36.9	62.3	0.8
Leake	43.3	1 898	55.0	1.4	5.5	0.2	10.1	28.9	1 267	62	141	1 167	44.4	55.0	0.6
Lee	229.2	2 853	55.2	1.0	7.6	0.3	8.9	215.1	2 678	536	499	5 193	34.4	64.9	0.7
Leflore	206.6	5 889	23.8	53.8	3.4	0.1	2.3	266.1	7 584	114	210	4 385	68.1	31.4	0.5
Lincoln	72.5	2 101	60.0	1.5	6.5	0.0	9.9	65.2	1 889	103	212	1 723	33.6	65.7	0.7
Lowndes	157.1	2 635	52.4	0.9	5.5	0.2	6.4	165.4	2 774	858	1 734	3 447	48.1	51.0	1.0
Madison	259.7	2 905	47.5	0.4	10.7	0.2	8.9	324.1	3 626	226	566	4 265	42.0	57.5	0.5
Marion	88.9	3 456	41.6	18.5	3.7	0.0	5.7	30.0	1 165	65	156	1 578	34.0	65.4	0.6
Marshall	66.8	1 820	59.1	1.8	5.9	0.2	11.1	23.8	647	84	224	1 267	58.8	40.6	0.7
Monroe	81.2	2 189	57.7	0.6	7.0	0.2	9.1	43.6	1 177	145	224	1 589	41.0	58.2	0.8
Montgomery	28.2	2 452	57.9	2.4	5.0	0.2	13.8	9.6	832	35	68	710	45.7	53.8	0.6
Neshoba	52.2	1 725	58.2	1.6	5.7	0.2	9.6	32.8	1 086	91	184	6 545	27.3	72.0	0.7
Newton	77.3	3 464	64.1	0.7	4.0	0.0	9.0	13.4	600	83	137	2 015	32.7	66.8	0.6
Noxubee	37.2	3 132	49.3	24.9	3.8	0.2	5.6	13.3	1 118	48	71	760	76.3	23.1	0.5
Oktibbeha	135.1	3 077	35.4	36.7	4.0	0.0	5.6	35.9	817	275	276	9 608	49.6	49.6	0.8
Panola	92.9	2 623	53.3	17.2	5.5	0.2	7.4	41.9	1 183	124	214	2 143	52.9	46.4	0.6
Pearl River	244.8	4 289	49.1	0.4	2.3	0.1	3.2	53.4	935	141	352	3 246	19.2	79.7	1.1
Perry	34.7	2 847	56.5	1.5	4.6	0.0	11.6	82.5	6 759	21	73	574	27.1	71.8	1.1
Pike	230.3	5 787	35.6	46.1	2.3	0.0	3.4	68.1	1 711	127	242	3 572	51.4	47.9	0.7
Pontotoc	70.2	2 431	57.3	1.0	5.4	0.4	5.8	35.7	1 236	56	178	1 168	23.2	75.6	1.2
Prentiss	90.1	3 551	79.0	1.0	3.6	0.0	4.0	47.0	1 850	52	156	1 553	27.6	70.4	2.0
Quitman	23.5	2 641	59.4	1.1	6.5	0.0	9.2	12.5	1 405	28	51	424	67.3	32.0	0.7
Rankin	273.0	1 973	56.9	0.9	6.1	0.2	8.0	318.0	2 298	588	872	9 847	22.8	76.3	0.9
Scott	56.9	1 971	65.9	1.5	6.7	0.3	7.0	19.1	662	227	178	1 215	43.1	56.4	0.5
Sharkey	17.1	3 063	67.2	1.5	5.5	0.8	7.2	3.8	683	31	33	411	68.2	31.2	0.5
Simpson	50.2	1 806	60.0	5.9	2.6	0.0	6.9	35.5	1 275	48	170	1 650	38.2	60.6	1.2
Smith	38.5	2 408	65.0	1.0	5.1	0.0	10.9	10.5	655	32	96	638	23.7	75.4	0.9
Stone	157.2	9 992	74.2	0.4	2.1	0.0	1.4	74.8	4 755	72	101	1 203	27.5	71.1	1.4

1. Based on the resident population estimated as of July 1 of the year shown.   2. © 2009 Election Data Services, Inc. All rights reserved.

Table B. States and Counties — **Land Area and Population**

STATE/ County code	CBSA code[1]	County type[2]	STATE County	Land area,[3] (sq km) 2010	Total persons	Rank	Per square kilometer	White	Black	American Indian, Alaska Native	Asian and Pacific Islander	Percent Hispanic or Latino[4]	Under 5 years	5 to 17 years	18 to 24 years	25 to 34 years	35 to 44 years	45 to 54 years
				1	2	3	4	5	6	7	8	9	10	11	12	13	14	15
			MISSISSIPPI—Cont'd															
28 133	26940	5	Sunflower	1 807	29 450	1 440	16.3	25.4	72.9	0.4	0.4	1.4	7.2	17.0	11.7	16.1	12.9	14.0
28 135	...	7	Tallahatchie	1 671	15 378	2 091	9.2	36.9	56.7	0.6	0.9	5.6	6.7	16.0	11.4	16.0	14.0	13.5
28 137	32820	1	Tate	1 048	28 886	1 456	27.6	67.0	30.8	0.6	0.4	2.2	6.8	19.0	11.5	11.5	12.5	14.1
28 139	...	7	Tippah	1 186	22 232	1 726	18.7	79.4	16.6	0.4	0.2	4.4	7.1	18.3	9.2	11.9	13.0	14.0
28 141	...	8	Tishomingo	1 099	19 593	1 858	17.8	94.2	2.9	0.5	0.2	2.8	6.0	17.2	7.5	10.5	12.9	14.4
28 143	32820	1	Tunica	1 178	10 778	2 384	9.1	23.4	73.8	0.4	0.9	2.3	8.9	20.9	9.5	14.6	12.3	13.6
28 145	...	7	Union	1 076	27 134	1 528	25.2	80.7	15.0	0.4	0.4	4.5	7.1	18.7	8.5	12.4	13.5	13.5
28 147	...	9	Walthall	1 046	15 443	2 086	14.8	53.5	44.7	0.7	0.4	1.5	7.1	19.3	8.0	12.2	11.3	13.5
28 149	46980	4	Warren	1 524	48 773	999	32.0	50.1	47.3	0.5	1.0	1.8	6.9	19.0	8.2	12.6	12.2	15.2
28 151	24740	5	Washington	1 877	51 137	963	27.2	27.0	71.4	0.3	0.7	1.0	7.6	20.4	9.5	12.2	11.5	14.1
28 153	...	7	Wayne	2 100	20 747	1 807	9.9	59.6	39.2	0.4	0.4	1.2	7.3	18.9	8.9	12.4	11.9	14.8
28 155	...	9	Webster	1 090	10 253	2 422	9.4	78.7	20.3	0.4	0.2	1.0	6.6	18.6	7.7	11.5	12.5	15.2
28 157	...	8	Wilkinson	1 756	9 878	2 451	5.6	28.8	70.7	0.3	0.1	0.4	6.6	16.4	9.4	14.8	12.0	15.1
28 159	...	7	Winston	1 573	19 198	1 869	12.2	52.1	46.0	1.3	0.3	1.0	7.2	17.7	8.1	11.8	11.8	13.7
28 161	...	7	Yalobusha	1 210	12 678	2 264	10.5	60.6	38.2	0.4	0.3	1.2	6.8	17.1	8.1	11.1	12.2	13.9
28 163	49540	6	Yazoo	2 390	28 065	1 495	11.7	37.9	57.1	0.5	0.6	4.6	7.4	17.9	8.6	16.0	14.1	13.8
29 000	...	X	MISSOURI	178 040	5 988 927	X	33.6	82.6	12.3	1.1	2.2	3.5	6.5	17.3	9.8	12.9	12.5	14.8
29 001	28860	7	Adair	1 469	25 607	1 581	17.4	94.2	2.1	0.8	2.3	2.0	5.6	13.8	26.5	9.9	9.7	11.7
29 003	41140	3	Andrew	1 121	17 291	1 964	15.4	97.2	0.8	0.8	0.6	1.7	5.8	18.3	7.6	11.0	12.7	15.6
29 005	...	9	Atchison	1 418	5 685	2 791	4.0	98.4	0.4	0.6	0.3	1.0	5.1	15.7	6.5	9.3	11.6	14.9
29 007	33020	6	Audrain	1 793	25 529	1 585	14.2	90.1	7.4	0.7	0.8	2.6	6.8	18.2	8.1	12.7	12.2	14.1
29 009	...	6	Barry	2 016	35 597	1 285	17.7	89.9	0.4	1.9	1.5	7.7	6.4	17.8	7.7	10.3	11.8	15.0
29 011	...	6	Barton	1 533	12 402	2 280	8.1	96.5	0.6	2.6	0.5	1.9	6.7	19.2	7.5	10.9	11.2	14.9
29 013	28140	1	Bates	2 167	17 049	1 982	7.9	96.8	1.1	1.3	0.3	1.6	6.6	18.3	7.2	10.9	11.5	15.3
29 015	...	9	Benton	1 824	19 056	1 876	10.4	97.3	0.5	1.4	0.5	1.5	4.3	13.7	5.7	7.2	9.9	15.2
29 017	16020	9	Bollinger	1 600	12 363	2 284	7.7	98.1	0.3	1.1	0.4	0.8	6.2	17.4	7.7	10.3	12.3	15.8
29 019	17860	3	Boone	1 775	162 642	377	91.6	83.3	10.6	1.0	4.5	3.0	6.2	14.8	20.9	15.2	11.4	12.2
29 021	41140	3	Buchanan	1 057	89 201	634	84.4	88.1	6.3	0.9	1.3	5.2	6.9	16.6	10.9	13.4	12.1	14.6
29 023	38740	7	Butler	1 799	42 794	1 109	23.8	91.8	6.1	1.4	1.0	1.6	6.4	16.9	8.3	11.7	12.1	14.6
29 025	28140	1	Caldwell	1 104	9 424	2 487	8.5	97.4	0.8	1.2	0.6	1.5	6.3	19.2	6.7	10.6	12.0	15.4
29 027	27620	3	Callaway	2 162	44 332	1 082	20.5	92.7	5.3	1.3	0.8	1.6	5.9	16.6	11.6	12.6	12.9	15.6
29 029	...	7	Camden	1 699	44 002	1 085	25.9	96.4	0.7	1.0	0.7	2.3	4.9	14.1	6.5	9.3	10.1	15.5
29 031	16020	5	Cape Girardeau	1 498	75 674	715	50.5	89.5	7.9	0.7	1.5	2.0	6.2	15.7	14.0	12.5	11.7	13.7
29 033	...	6	Carroll	1 799	9 295	2 499	5.2	96.6	2.2	0.5	0.4	1.3	5.7	17.9	6.9	10.7	12.1	14.2
29 035	...	9	Carter	1 314	6 265	2 745	4.8	97.0	0.3	1.9	0.6	1.7	7.0	17.1	8.4	10.4	11.9	15.0
29 037	28140	1	Cass	1 805	99 478	583	55.1	91.2	4.1	1.2	1.1	4.0	6.8	19.7	7.6	12.2	13.3	15.3
29 039	...	6	Cedar	1 229	13 982	2 175	11.4	97.6	0.3	1.6	0.5	1.5	6.0	17.7	6.6	9.0	10.9	13.5
29 041	...	9	Chariton	1 946	7 831	2 621	4.0	97.1	2.5	0.5	0.2	0.5	6.2	16.4	6.4	9.7	10.2	15.8
29 043	44180	2	Christian	1 457	77 422	700	53.1	95.8	1.0	1.4	1.0	2.5	7.4	19.9	7.6	13.3	14.0	14.4
29 045	22800	9	Clark	1 307	7 139	2 671	5.5	98.7	0.5	0.8	0.4	0.6	6.9	17.2	7.1	10.6	11.8	14.8
29 047	28140	1	Clay	1 029	221 939	281	215.7	86.0	6.0	1.2	2.9	5.9	7.3	18.5	8.1	14.4	14.4	14.8
29 049	28140	1	Clinton	1 085	20 743	1 808	19.1	95.9	2.0	1.3	0.7	1.6	6.3	18.3	7.4	10.8	12.7	16.1
29 051	27620	3	Cole	1 020	75 990	713	74.5	84.7	12.1	0.8	1.7	2.4	6.6	17.0	9.1	13.8	13.5	15.1
29 053	...	6	Cooper	1 463	17 601	1 943	12.0	91.0	7.7	0.8	0.7	1.3	6.1	16.5	9.6	13.7	11.7	14.8
29 055	...	6	Crawford	1 923	24 696	1 614	12.8	97.5	0.5	1.2	0.5	1.5	6.7	17.6	8.0	11.3	12.0	15.5
29 057	...	8	Dade	1 269	7 883	2 612	6.2	96.9	0.5	2.6	0.5	1.5	5.2	17.5	6.0	9.0	11.2	15.6
29 059	44180	2	Dallas	1 401	16 777	1 997	12.0	97.1	0.4	2.0	0.5	1.5	6.8	18.0	7.5	10.4	11.5	15.6
29 061	...	8	Daviess	1 459	8 433	2 576	5.8	98.3	0.6	0.9	0.2	1.0	7.4	19.3	7.0	10.6	11.3	13.6
29 063	41140	3	DeKalb	1 091	12 892	2 249	11.8	86.3	11.4	0.7	0.5	1.7	4.6	13.3	8.5	15.8	15.9	16.9
29 065	...	7	Dent	1 950	15 657	2 071	8.0	97.5	0.7	1.8	0.6	0.9	6.2	17.2	7.4	10.5	11.5	15.4
29 067	...	6	Douglas	2 107	13 684	2 207	6.5	98.2	0.4	1.9	0.5	0.8	5.9	16.4	7.3	9.5	10.7	15.2
29 069	28380	7	Dunklin	1 401	31 953	1 394	22.8	84.3	10.5	0.6	0.5	5.4	6.9	18.4	8.2	11.3	12.3	13.8
29 071	41180	1	Franklin	2 390	101 492	574	42.5	97.0	1.2	0.8	0.7	1.4	6.4	18.3	8.3	11.7	13.0	16.4
29 073	...	6	Gasconade	1 341	15 222	2 097	11.4	98.2	0.4	0.7	0.6	1.0	5.5	16.6	6.8	9.7	11.4	16.1
29 075	...	8	Gentry	1 273	6 738	2 708	5.3	98.7	0.5	0.6	0.4	0.5	6.7	17.8	7.9	10.1	10.6	14.9
29 077	44180	2	Greene	1 749	275 174	234	157.3	91.7	3.8	1.5	2.3	3.0	6.2	15.0	13.7	14.2	11.9	13.4
29 079	...	7	Grundy	1 127	10 261	2 421	9.1	96.9	0.7	1.0	0.5	1.7	7.0	17.1	9.3	9.9	10.4	13.8
29 081	...	7	Harrison	1 871	8 957	2 530	4.8	97.5	0.5	0.7	0.4	1.6	7.3	17.5	7.2	10.3	10.5	14.4
29 083	...	6	Henry	1 805	22 272	1 724	12.3	96.6	1.3	1.2	0.5	1.7	6.0	16.2	7.3	10.9	11.4	15.0
29 085	...	8	Hickory	1 034	9 627	2 468	9.3	97.8	0.4	1.9	0.4	0.9	4.6	12.7	5.3	7.0	9.4	13.7
29 087	...	8	Holt	1 198	4 912	2 847	4.1	97.7	0.2	1.3	0.4	0.8	5.7	14.1	6.6	10.3	11.0	16.1
29 089	17860	3	Howard	1 201	10 144	2 435	8.4	89.7	6.2	1.0	0.6	1.2	5.9	15.6	13.4	10.8	10.6	15.1
29 091	48460	7	Howell	2 402	40 400	1 164	16.8	96.7	0.6	1.6	0.8	1.7	7.1	17.8	8.4	11.4	11.7	13.7
29 093	...	6	Iron	1 425	10 630	2 391	7.5	96.9	1.5	1.3	0.3	1.3	5.8	16.8	7.8	10.6	12.0	15.2
29 095	28140	1	Jackson	1 566	674 158	89	430.5	65.3	25.1	1.2	2.4	8.4	7.1	17.5	9.4	14.6	12.9	14.7

1. CBSA = Core Based Statistical Area. See Appendix A for explanation. See Appendix B for list of metropolitan areas with component counties. 2. County type code from the Economic Research Service of USDA Rural-Urban Continuum Codes. See Appendix A for definition. 3. Dry land or land partially or temporarily covered by water. 4. May be of any race.

Table B. States and Counties — **Population and Households**

STATE County	55 to 64 years	65 to 74 years	75 years and over	Percent female	1990	2000	1990–2000	2000–2010	Births	Deaths	Net migration	Number	Percent change, 2000–2010	Persons per house-hold	Female family house-holder[1]	One per-son
	16	17	18	19	20	21	22	23	24	25	26	27	28	29	30	31
MISSISSIPPI—Cont'd																
Sunflower	10.8	5.6	4.6	46.6	35 129	34 369	-2.2	-14.3	4 494	3 074	-6 034	8 822	-8.5	2.81	30.4	24.9
Tallahatchie	10.6	6.7	5.1	45.2	15 210	14 903	-2.0	3.2	1 919	1 327	-2 827	4 856	-7.7	2.67	25.7	27.5
Tate	12.3	7.5	4.9	51.7	21 432	25 370	18.4	13.9	3 662	2 323	789	10 035	13.4	2.75	17.3	22.0
Tippah	11.9	8.5	6.2	51.1	19 523	20 826	6.7	6.8	3 034	2 307	243	8 597	6.0	2.55	13.4	26.6
Tishomingo	13.5	10.1	7.9	51.7	17 683	19 163	8.4	2.2	2 104	2 371	247	8 148	2.9	2.37	11.0	29.5
Tunica	10.7	5.6	3.8	52.8	8 164	9 227	13.0	16.8	1 948	972	267	3 927	20.5	2.72	26.6	29.5
Union	11.9	8.0	6.5	51.1	22 085	25 362	14.8	7.0	3 527	2 430	964	10 317	5.4	2.60	12.8	24.2
Walthall	12.8	8.7	7.1	51.4	14 352	15 156	5.6	1.9	2 038	1 569	-253	5 888	5.7	2.60	16.9	26.5
Warren	13.0	7.4	5.5	52.5	47 880	49 644	3.7	-1.8	7 070	4 698	-3 615	18 941	1.0	2.55	20.1	27.5
Washington	12.5	6.8	5.5	53.5	67 935	62 977	-7.3	-18.8	9 075	5 854	-11 423	18 936	-14.5	2.67	28.7	26.5
Wayne	11.9	8.2	5.7	52.0	19 517	21 216	8.7	-2.2	2 839	1 904	-1 417	8 104	3.1	2.54	17.6	26.7
Webster	12.2	8.8	6.9	51.4	10 222	10 294	0.7	-0.4	1 284	1 327	-357	4 060	4.0	2.51	14.4	25.8
Wilkinson	12.0	7.3	6.5	47.1	9 678	10 312	6.6	-4.2	1 298	1 241	-174	3 455	-3.4	2.52	24.9	31.1
Winston	13.1	8.7	7.8	51.9	19 433	20 160	3.7	-4.8	2 539	2 049	-1 244	7 494	-1.1	2.51	20.1	28.0
Yalobusha	14.3	9.5	7.0	52.3	12 033	13 051	8.5	-2.9	1 813	1 474	463	5 166	-1.8	2.42	19.0	30.0
Yazoo	10.4	6.2	5.6	45.6	25 506	28 149	10.4	-0.3	4 051	2 614	-1 457	8 860	-3.5	2.71	26.7	26.0
MISSOURI	12.1	7.5	6.5	51.0	5 116 901	5 595 211	9.3	7.0	726 153	507 227	105 461	2 375 611	8.2	2.45	12.3	28.3
Adair	10.2	6.7	5.8	52.3	24 577	24 977	1.6	2.5	2 683	2 013	-378	9 877	2.2	2.30	8.6	32.8
Andrew	13.5	8.6	6.9	50.8	14 632	16 492	12.7	4.8	1 720	1 566	506	6 700	6.8	2.55	8.3	21.9
Atchison	15.4	10.8	10.8	50.4	7 457	6 430	-13.8	-11.6	557	763	-168	2 498	-8.2	2.24	6.8	31.5
Audrain	11.9	7.9	8.1	53.8	23 599	25 853	9.6	-1.3	3 621	2 769	-993	9 590	-2.6	2.44	12.3	28.3
Barry	13.4	10.3	7.3	50.4	27 547	34 010	23.5	4.7	4 721	3 598	952	14 057	4.9	2.51	9.8	24.7
Barton	12.5	8.5	8.6	50.7	11 312	12 541	10.9	-1.1	1 540	1 253	-385	4 929	0.7	2.50	9.9	26.6
Bates	12.4	9.3	8.4	50.7	15 025	16 653	10.8	2.4	2 031	1 899	71	6 744	3.6	2.48	8.4	27.2
Benton	18.2	16.0	9.9	49.9	13 859	17 180	24.0	10.9	1 512	2 417	2 267	8 449	13.9	2.23	7.0	28.9
Bollinger	13.7	9.8	6.8	50.0	10 619	12 029	13.3	2.8	1 360	1 177	-328	4 847	5.9	2.52	9.0	23.1
Boone	9.9	5.0	4.3	51.5	112 379	135 454	20.5	20.1	17 990	8 102	11 887	64 077	20.7	2.40	10.7	28.7
Buchanan	11.5	7.1	6.9	50.0	83 083	85 998	3.5	3.7	11 010	8 647	-586	34 509	2.8	2.45	13.4	29.0
Butler	13.1	9.2	7.8	51.4	38 765	40 867	5.4	4.7	5 302	4 898	463	17 614	5.4	2.38	13.4	29.4
Caldwell	13.1	8.8	7.9	49.8	8 380	8 969	7.0	5.1	1 120	963	86	3 676	4.3	2.51	9.5	25.8
Callaway	12.4	7.1	5.2	48.6	32 809	40 766	24.3	8.7	4 735	3 127	1 610	16 333	13.3	2.48	10.8	25.9
Camden	17.8	14.0	7.7	50.3	27 495	37 051	34.8	18.8	3 802	3 766	3 777	19 068	20.8	2.27	7.8	25.8
Cape Girardeau	11.8	7.2	7.1	51.6	61 633	68 693	11.5	10.2	8 484	6 421	3 622	29 848	10.6	2.41	11.0	27.7
Carroll	13.4	9.6	9.5	51.2	10 748	10 285	-4.3	-9.6	1 036	1 195	-530	3 865	-7.3	2.38	9.2	29.9
Carter	13.5	10.1	6.5	51.2	5 515	5 941	7.7	5.5	738	700	-71	2 559	7.6	2.43	11.1	28.7
Cass	11.5	7.5	6.1	51.2	63 808	82 092	28.7	21.2	11 526	7 053	13 614	37 150	23.1	2.65	10.8	21.7
Cedar	14.0	12.1	10.2	50.8	12 093	13 733	13.6	1.8	1 493	1 791	187	5 838	2.7	2.37	9.6	29.1
Chariton	13.9	9.9	11.5	50.7	9 202	8 438	-8.3	-7.2	799	1 058	-541	3 242	-6.5	2.35	7.1	29.0
Christian	11.1	7.2	5.0	51.4	32 644	54 285	66.3	42.6	8 938	4 449	18 818	29 077	42.4	2.64	10.5	20.1
Clark	14.1	9.6	8.1	50.0	7 547	7 416	-1.7	-3.7	796	783	-268	2 933	-1.1	2.40	8.0	27.8
Clay	11.3	6.3	5.0	51.2	153 411	184 006	19.9	20.6	28 060	13 437	23 457	87 217	20.2	2.51	11.3	26.2
Clinton	12.7	8.6	7.1	49.8	16 595	18 979	14.4	9.3	2 385	2 243	1 978	7 951	11.2	2.55	9.3	23.2
Cole	12.6	6.5	5.8	49.5	63 579	71 397	12.3	6.4	8 954	5 434	548	29 722	9.9	2.39	11.3	29.3
Cooper	12.2	7.8	7.5	47.3	14 835	16 670	12.4	5.6	1 829	1 664	566	6 554	10.5	2.45	10.0	27.1
Crawford	12.7	9.2	7.1	50.2	19 173	22 804	18.9	8.3	2 963	2 414	657	9 831	11.0	2.48	10.8	26.4
Dade	15.1	10.9	9.6	49.9	7 449	7 923	6.4	-0.5	774	1 118	-218	3 271	2.2	2.37	7.3	28.5
Dallas	13.2	9.6	7.4	50.3	12 646	15 661	23.8	7.1	2 048	1 645	663	6 524	8.2	2.54	9.3	24.3
Daviess	13.8	9.8	7.3	50.3	7 865	8 016	1.9	5.2	1 148	786	-250	3 214	1.1	2.58	8.1	24.6
DeKalb	11.3	7.0	6.7	37.3	9 967	11 597	16.4	11.2	1 044	1 082	-837	3 839	8.8	2.43	8.2	29.9
Dent	12.9	10.6	8.4	50.4	13 702	14 927	8.9	4.9	1 647	1 767	319	6 338	6.0	2.44	9.6	26.5
Douglas	15.0	11.1	8.7	50.6	11 876	13 084	10.2	4.6	1 372	1 352	582	5 587	7.4	2.43	8.9	25.4
Dunklin	12.6	9.2	7.3	52.0	33 112	33 155	0.1	-3.6	4 392	4 211	-2 113	12 837	-4.3	2.44	15.1	29.3
Franklin	12.1	7.7	6.1	50.4	80 603	93 807	16.4	8.2	12 204	8 295	4 144	39 170	12.1	2.57	10.0	24.2
Gasconade	13.7	10.4	9.7	51.0	14 006	15 342	9.5	-0.8	1 588	1 885	142	6 250	1.3	2.40	8.5	27.9
Gentry	11.5	9.8	10.7	51.6	6 854	6 861	0.1	-1.8	726	859	-597	2 674	-2.7	2.45	8.2	29.0
Greene	11.6	7.2	6.8	51.3	207 949	240 391	15.6	14.5	31 116	22 062	21 541	114 244	16.7	2.31	10.7	30.4
Grundy	12.1	10.6	9.9	52.3	10 536	10 432	-1.0	-1.6	1 188	1 332	-179	4 204	-4.1	2.36	8.7	31.1
Harrison	12.0	10.4	10.3	50.4	8 469	8 850	4.5	1.2	1 022	1 134	85	3 669	0.3	2.40	8.3	28.3
Henry	13.7	10.5	9.0	51.1	20 044	21 997	9.7	1.3	2 588	2 743	458	9 405	3.0	2.34	10.4	28.9
Hickory	17.7	17.3	12.2	50.9	7 335	8 940	21.9	7.7	710	1 239	530	4 371	11.8	2.19	7.6	30.2
Holt	15.1	9.6	11.6	50.6	6 034	5 351	-11.3	-8.2	521	623	-354	2 133	-4.6	2.26	7.2	28.7
Howard	12.7	8.2	7.6	50.3	9 631	10 212	6.0	-0.7	1 057	1 034	-315	3 981	3.8	2.37	8.3	28.8
Howell	12.8	9.2	7.9	51.6	31 447	37 238	18.4	8.5	4 828	4 369	1 451	16 192	9.7	2.46	10.7	27.2
Iron	14.0	10.5	7.4	50.6	10 726	10 697	-0.3	-0.6	1 200	1 503	-406	4 378	4.3	2.37	10.5	30.0
Jackson	11.5	6.5	6.0	51.7	633 234	654 880	3.4	2.9	95 657	55 469	-21 589	274 804	3.2	2.41	15.7	31.8

1. No spouse present.

STATE County	Persons in group quarters, 2010	Daytime population, 2006–2010		Births, average 2006–2008		Deaths, average 2006–2008		Persons under 65 with no health insurance, 2009		Medicare, 2011			Serious crimes known to police,[2] 2010 Total	
		Number	Employ-ment/resi-dence ratio	Total	Rate[1]	Number	Rate[1]	Number	Percent	Eligible for Medicare	Enrolled in Medicare Advantage	Enrolled in a Medicare prescription drug plan	Number	Rate[3]
	32	33	34	35	36	37	38	39	40	41	42	43	44	45
MISSISSIPPI—Cont'd														
Sunflower	4 654	31 036	1.1	507	16.3	334	10.7	6 382	25.3	4 413	197	3 155	NA	NA
Tallahatchie	2 421	13 710	0.7	242	18.1	141	10.6	2 541	24.5	2 622	54	1 959	NA	NA
Tate	1 281	23 731	0.6	D	D	250	9.3	4 677	20.2	4 857	600	2 518	325	1 194
Tippah	287	20 793	0.9	D	D	241	11.4	4 099	22.7	4 919	175	3 499	108	486
Tishomingo	280	18 861	0.9	D	D	256	13.4	3 352	22.1	4 803	83	3 260	NA	NA
Tunica	104	18 776	2.7	242	23.2	112	10.8	1 673	18.8	1 601	205	998	595	5 521
Union	283	25 650	0.9	412	15.2	260	9.6	4 626	20.3	5 603	308	3 590	333	1 227
Walthall	128	13 504	0.6	D	D	174	11.2	2 933	23.4	3 114	227	1 940	229	1 483
Warren	524	52 288	1.2	774	15.9	494	10.1	7 452	18.3	8 266	837	3 908	2 514	5 154
Washington	548	52 878	1.0	976	17.4	614	10.9	9 662	21.1	9 457	754	6 037	3 092	6 047
Wayne	137	19 636	0.8	337	16.1	213	10.2	3 942	22.8	3 773	339	2 405	NA	NA
Webster	56	9 125	0.7	D	D	146	14.7	1 734	21.8	2 730	60	1 915	NA	NA
Wilkinson	1 168	9 435	0.8	D	D	130	12.7	2 108	25.2	1 773	200	1 162	NA	NA
Winston	408	17 971	0.8	D	D	229	11.6	3 359	21.5	4 393	477	2 522	150	781
Yalobusha	155	11 677	0.7	D	D	167	12.3	2 277	20.5	3 308	201	2 118	NA	NA
Yazoo	4 020	26 100	0.7	464	16.7	262	9.4	6 070	25.8	4 637	251	3 176	NA	NA
MISSOURI	174 142	5 968 449	1.0	81 426	13.8	55 142	9.3	764 772	15.2	1 032 534	223 888	444 795	227 666	3 801
Adair	2 900	26 209	1.1	D	D	205	8.3	3 790	17.7	4 121	169	2 494	840	3 280
Andrew	192	11 594	0.4	D	D	168	9.9	2 023	14.1	2 887	140	1 607	174	1 006
Atchison	98	5 197	0.8	D	D	80	13.1	798	16.9	1 365	47	874	58	1 020
Audrain	2 100	25 852	1.0	D	D	299	11.5	3 778	17.9	4 861	421	2 827	470	1 841
Barry	296	37 395	1.1	528	14.5	394	10.9	5 608	19.0	7 354	2 035	2 909	1 026	2 882
Barton	90	11 656	0.8	D	D	131	10.3	1 863	18.4	2 723	376	1 464	212	1 709
Bates	311	14 433	0.6	D	D	201	11.8	2 514	18.4	3 647	388	1 902	439	2 575
Benton	244	17 123	0.7	D	D	283	15.3	2 635	19.6	5 886	864	2 767	450	2 361
Bollinger	163	9 584	0.4	D	D	127	10.4	1 796	18.3	2 688	290	1 471	115	930
Boone	8 998	162 981	1.1	2 083	13.8	914	6.1	17 605	12.8	19 564	1 807	10 435	5 598	3 442
Buchanan	4 495	95 413	1.2	1 321	15.2	946	10.8	11 382	15.1	15 391	874	8 454	4 225	4 736
Butler	884	45 488	1.2	596	14.4	521	12.6	5 907	17.6	9 975	867	5 937	2 058	4 809
Caldwell	214	7 289	0.5	D	D	114	12.2	1 219	16.3	1 725	193	836	178	1 889
Callaway	3 907	37 740	0.7	517	11.9	340	7.9	5 617	14.9	7 215	515	3 469	1 469	3 314
Camden	774	44 520	1.1	D	D	414	10.2	5 467	17.4	10 329	948	5 047	973	2 211
Cape Girardeau	3 823	80 608	1.2	958	13.2	709	9.8	8 971	14.5	13 037	803	6 825	3 484	4 604
Carroll	88	8 350	0.7	D	D	125	12.6	1 346	17.7	2 135	217	1 260	104	1 119
Carter	40	5 318	0.7	D	D	79	13.3	1 054	22.0	1 482	138	914	57	910
Cass	1 044	75 005	0.5	1 301	13.4	810	8.3	11 048	12.8	15 930	4 986	4 529	2 150	2 161
Cedar	156	12 903	0.8	D	D	193	14.0	1 973	19.0	3 594	846	1 538	359	2 568
Chariton	213	6 610	0.6	D	D	106	13.4	968	16.7	1 815	94	1 153	138	1 762
Christian	582	56 802	0.5	1 046	14.3	513	7.0	10 088	15.1	12 495	4 745	3 899	1 447	1 869
Clark	90	5 847	0.6	D	D	85	11.7	1 092	18.9	1 559	97	1 007	80	1 121
Clay	2 646	195 342	0.8	3 234	15.3	1 531	7.2	23 274	11.7	31 608	5 562	12 986	10 833	4 881
Clinton	445	16 491	0.6	D	D	244	11.7	2 437	13.9	3 340	266	1 675	379	1 827
Cole	4 968	89 308	1.4	1 006	13.6	598	8.1	8 229	12.8	11 727	764	5 500	2 318	3 050
Cooper	1 533	16 257	0.8	D	D	188	10.8	2 557	17.8	3 257	405	1 728	454	2 579
Crawford	332	21 512	0.7	D	D	265	11.0	3 833	19.3	5 120	818	2 521	611	2 474
Dade	133	7 255	0.8	D	D	109	14.3	1 043	18.3	1 847	497	743	76	964
Dallas	199	13 514	0.5	D	D	180	10.7	2 745	19.9	3 741	1 407	1 316	337	2 009
Daviess	152	7 060	0.6	D	D	81	10.1	1 365	20.6	1 669	108	905	88	1 044
DeKalb	3 560	12 622	0.9	D	D	123	10.0	2 089	20.5	1 949	99	1 045	222	1 722
Dent	202	14 175	0.8	D	D	188	12.4	2 366	19.7	3 584	176	2 028	349	2 229
Douglas	123	12 552	0.8	D	D	147	10.9	2 102	19.3	3 072	1 060	1 173	201	1 469
Dunklin	672	30 398	0.8	493	15.5	436	13.7	4 735	18.8	7 245	537	4 876	983	3 076
Franklin	857	92 066	0.8	1 343	13.4	951	9.5	12 546	14.6	17 678	5 740	5 979	2 495	2 458
Gasconade	250	14 362	0.9	D	D	197	12.8	1 990	16.6	3 500	511	1 748	272	1 787
Gentry	177	6 303	0.9	D	D	88	14.0	913	19.7	1 757	73	1 124	32	475
Greene	11 242	303 317	1.3	3 615	13.8	2 409	9.2	38 007	16.8	48 441	17 789	16 604	19 436	7 063
Grundy	350	9 800	0.9	D	D	138	13.6	1 391	17.8	2 351	91	1 469	238	2 319
Harrison	145	8 437	0.9	D	D	117	13.2	1 267	18.7	2 064	80	1 364	102	1 139
Henry	233	21 630	0.9	D	D	296	13.2	2 951	16.9	5 697	833	2 837	866	3 888
Hickory	75	8 448	0.7	D	D	134	14.7	1 394	22.3	3 054	800	1 165	134	1 392
Holt	101	4 388	0.8	D	D	65	13.1	697	18.4	1 101	63	631	121	2 463
Howard	714	8 532	0.7	D	D	113	11.4	1 412	17.4	1 922	220	1 049	76	749
Howell	608	41 203	1.1	D	D	483	12.5	6 281	20.2	9 417	1 460	5 053	1 573	3 894
Iron	276	10 461	0.9	D	D	150	14.9	1 495	18.7	2 507	141	1 577	140	1 317
Jackson	11 219	729 009	1.2	10 628	15.9	6 091	9.1	103 833	17.3	105 077	32 061	34 532	37 284	5 530

1. Per 1,000 estimated resident population.   2. Data for serious crimes have not been adjusted for underreporting; this may affect comparability between geographic areas and over time.   3. Per 100,000 population estimated by the FBI.

Table B. States and Counties — Crime, Education, Money Income, and Poverty

STATE County	Serious crimes — Rate² Violent (46)	Property (47)	Education — Enrollment³ Total (48)	Percent private (49)	Attainment⁴ High school graduate or less (50)	Bachelor's degree or more (51)	Local gov't expenditures⁵ 2008–2009 Total current expenditures (mil dol) (52)	Current expenditures per student (dollars) (53)	Money income 2006–2010 Per capita income⁶ (dollars) (54)	Households Median income Dollars (55)	Percent change, 2000 to 2006–2010 (constant 2010 dollars) (56)	Percent with income of $200,000 or more (57)	Income and poverty 2010 Median household income (dollars) (58)	Percent below poverty — All persons (59)	Children under 18 years (60)	Children 5 to 17 years in families (61)
MISSISSIPPI—Cont'd																
Sunflower	NA	NA	8 928	15.6	60.5	13.0	39.2	8 322	11 993	25 012	-20.9	1.1	26 921	39.2	53.9	52.3
Tallahatchie	NA	NA	3 991	16.7	68.6	9.0	21.1	9 211	12 687	24 668	-12.4	0.5	27 352	34.8	44.2	40.8
Tate	48	1 147	7 815	17.1	53.0	14.1	34.2	6 933	18 318	41 102	-9.4	1.4	41 465	18.2	25.8	23.4
Tippah	67	418	5 313	11.5	63.6	10.4	30.5	7 577	16 365	32 109	-13.5	1.0	33 223	20.7	31.6	29.9
Tishomingo	NA	NA	4 164	4.9	63.4	10.7	24.8	7 565	17 017	30 211	-15.7	0.8	33 775	17.7	27.1	25.3
Tunica	640	4 880	3 070	13.5		14.6	24.2	10 707	15 711	29 994	1.8	1.3	29 808	28.1	43.1	42.4
Union	29	1 198	6 681	8.5	59.2	14.5	36.2	7 398	17 945	35 928	-13.2	0.6	37 403	20.0	28.6	25.9
Walthall	65	1 418	4 280	9.6	60.2	14.0	18.8	7 456	16 157	33 054	13.8	1.4	30 278	24.5	39.4	35.9
Warren	449	4 705	12 931	12.8	43.8	24.4	70.8	7 812	22 079	40 404	-9.0	1.8	37 578	23.3	33.5	29.9
Washington	276	5 771	15 039	10.3	56.4	17.6	87.6	8 172	15 946	27 797	-14.8	1.1	25 559	42.2	57.1	51.4
Wayne	NA	NA	5 118	10.6	65.8	11.3	29.3	7 813	17 099	31 081	-5.3	1.3	32 355	24.8	36.1	33.6
Webster	NA	NA	2 402	10.9	58.3	17.2	14.0	7 729	17 888	34 107	-6.6	1.0	32 798	23.4	34.3	30.2
Wilkinson	NA	NA	2 143	23.4	72.5	9.0	12.0	8 975	14 333	28 066	17.1	0.9	27 622	33.3	42.2	40.2
Winston	141	641	4 585	12.3	58.8	14.7	22.5	8 254	17 244	30 738	-14.1	0.7	31 021	29.7	43.6	39.7
Yalobusha	NA	NA	2 877	6.2	61.9	12.3	15.6	8 033	16 623	29 911	-10.2	0.9	31 644	23.9	37.9	36.3
Yazoo	NA	NA	7 108	16.2	62.0	11.9	36.0	7 944	14 339	27 356	-12.9	1.2	28 474	39.0	51.4	50.0
MISSOURI	455	3 346	1 542 979	19.6	46.4	25.0	8 746.2	9 601	24 724	46 262	-3.7	2.5	44 306	15.3	21.0	18.5
Adair	445	2 835	9 998	8.3	49.7	25.5	27.8	9 040	17 098	31 176	-7.7	0.8	32 015	22.2	23.6	20.9
Andrew	52	954	4 201	10.6	51.9	20.5	24.5	8 490	24 009	52 720	2.3	0.8	53 150	10.1	13.6	11.8
Atchison	176	844	1 159	5.7	53.3	21.0	9.0	9 714	23 659	42 375	8.1	2.5	43 587	11.6	14.5	12.6
Audrain	227	1 614	6 177	13.9	63.6	14.0	28.0	8 027	18 800	40 935	0.8	1.0	40 899	18.4	28.1	25.5
Barry	303	2 579	8 226	8.5	61.3	12.4	51.0	7 998	19 363	36 143	-1.3	1.1	34 838	18.9	28.6	26.4
Barton	153	1 556	2 825	7.9	60.6	13.2	17.2	8 093	19 117	39 573	6.7	0.9	36 851	17.6	26.7	22.6
Bates	223	2 352	4 028	13.3	64.6	11.7	19.0	8 112	19 056	38 882	-0.1	0.4	39 265	15.7	22.7	21.0
Benton	226	2 136	3 266	7.6	64.7	12.5	20.9	7 907	19 955	33 305	-1.3	1.2	30 920	20.6	35.1	31.3
Bollinger	121	809	2 867	6.0	69.3	10.1	14.3	7 345	18 172	33 938	-12.0	1.1	36 972	19.5	29.7	26.2
Boone	411	3 031	57 248	12.4	31.4	45.2	203.8	9 091	25 124	45 786	-3.5	2.6	42 202	18.8	16.6	15.4
Buchanan	374	4 362	22 632	13.6	53.8	19.4	112.4	8 769	21 638	42 393	-3.5	1.4	41 210	15.9	22.5	19.9
Butler	491	4 318	9 766	13.8	60.0	14.1	50.2	7 615	19 368	33 525	-2.8	1.0	32 919	19.3	30.6	28.7
Caldwell	371	1 517	2 152	8.0	60.2	11.8	9.7	9 378	19 499	39 439	-0.3	0.5	39 216	13.9	19.9	18.1
Callaway	289	3 025	11 282	23.5	53.1	20.4	43.8	8 568	22 602	49 544	0.0	1.3	47 098	13.8	18.9	16.6
Camden	184	2 027	8 511	16.4	45.7	21.0	47.5	8 808	25 509	44 617	-1.7	3.0	42 955	14.6	26.8	23.3
Cape Girardeau	517	4 087	21 060	14.5	48.1	26.9	78.5	8 128	23 014	44 479	-3.7	2.0	44 569	15.2	20.4	16.5
Carroll	118	1 001	2 109	11.3	60.4	17.9	15.0	9 099	25 021	41 619	7.3	2.3	39 071	15.7	22.7	18.6
Carter	144	766	1 500	2.1	62.5	11.1	11.1	8 330	15 881	28 408	-1.9	0.0	28 524	24.5	38.1	38.5
Cass	157	2 004	25 896	14.1	45.4	21.4	157.3	8 536	26 326	60 097	-4.2	1.9	57 368	8.5	12.0	10.0
Cedar	250	2 317	3 371	24.7	63.0	11.9	18.0	7 808	16 432	32 800	-3.0	0.5	31 542	20.1	32.9	29.8
Chariton	332	1 430	1 732	19.1	61.8	14.2	10.4	9 189	19 978	41 558	1.7	0.3	39 800	14.0	18.9	17.6
Christian	278	1 591	20 214	15.3	39.6	26.9	104.6	7 449	23 720	51 135	6.0	2.0	48 041	11.1	16.9	15.0
Clark	210	910	1 760	9.7	59.4	12.9	8.5	7 692	19 114	38 133	2.2	0.8	36 809	16.3	25.8	24.8
Clay	730	4 151	55 867	18.4	37.9	30.2	349.2	9 355	28 204	58 559	-4.3	2.4	55 835	9.5	13.4	11.6
Clinton	231	1 596	4 917	9.5	50.9	17.6	38.1	8 956	24 629	51 915	-1.5	1.5	51 846	11.1	15.8	13.8
Cole	346	2 704	20 763	23.1	42.2	30.5	87.4	8 225	25 935	53 877	-0.9	1.8	52 835	11.2	15.4	13.5
Cooper	119	2 460	4 230	20.7	56.0	15.7	23.7	9 344	19 234	42 586	-4.8	1.0	41 925	16.7	22.3	20.1
Crawford	186	2 288	5 764	12.5	63.6	10.8	30.6	7 989	17 317	34 506	-11.7	0.5	34 555	19.3	29.2	26.0
Dade	127	837	1 611	14.4	64.3	9.1	26.1	8 774	16 638	32 714	-11.2	0.3	33 452	21.7	33.8	27.4
Dallas	215	1 794	3 289	11.6	67.1	10.7	15.2	8 325	18 400	38 101	10.0	1.8	37 589	19.5	31.2	29.3
Daviess	119	925	1 998	12.1	59.7	14.4	19.2	9 397	19 900	39 925	2.2	1.9	38 279	17.2	28.5	26.5
DeKalb	155	1 567	2 859	8.3	63.9	12.0	11.3	9 836	16 916	43 267	7.9	1.0	41 804	16.5	16.1	14.3
Dent	198	2 031	3 167	8.6	62.3	11.2	18.2	7 803	18 111	36 118	4.9	0.4	34 327	19.1	29.5	27.2
Douglas	205	1 264	3 363	13.1	65.4	10.2	14.0	8 198	15 107	30 968	-5.6	0.6	29 830	23.3	37.8	34.5
Dunklin	369	2 707	7 236	5.0	70.4	10.1	48.7	8 121	16 619	29 375	-6.8	0.9	29 372	27.3	40.0	34.1
Franklin	182	2 276	25 156	17.3	51.5	16.5	140.7	8 405	23 365	49 120	-10.8	1.9	47 530	14.1	19.3	17.3
Gasconade	223	1 564	3 361	12.6	58.7	14.1	24.7	8 226	21 240	40 837	-8.0	1.0	39 688	12.7	20.4	17.8
Gentry	30	445	1 542	12.6	62.7	12.0	11.8	10 393	19 021	35 556	-2.3	1.1	35 755	14.5	21.2	19.5
Greene	568	6 496	72 789	17.3	41.2	27.5	286.3	7 876	23 443	41 059	-5.1	1.9	38 059	19.1	24.1	19.6
Grundy	127	2 193	2 214	12.1	57.3	12.8	13.9	9 041	18 148	35 239	1.8	0.4	35 017	17.5	26.9	24.4
Harrison	112	1 027	1 872	6.1	66.2	7.6	14.1	9 488	18 967	35 000	-3.7	0.7	34 324	17.1	26.6	24.7
Henry	409	3 480	4 655	13.5	58.9	15.1	30.1	9 033	20 304	35 706	-8.9	0.7	37 016	17.2	26.9	22.9
Hickory	42	1 350	1 505	11.7	65.9	8.1	9.1	9 246	18 215	28 097	-12.5	1.3	27 957	22.6	41.4	37.7
Holt	81	2 382	925	6.5	60.9	16.3	7.0	10 388	21 666	40 261	7.9	1.4	39 141	14.2	21.9	20.7
Howard	128	621	2 675	35.4	56.5	21.6	11.7	7 868	21 829	42 067	5.1	1.5	39 383	15.5	21.2	18.7
Howell	292	3 601	9 539	6.2	59.5	14.1	55.4	8 071	17 135	35 282	8.7	0.6	33 211	21.3	32.9	30.1
Iron	216	1 101	2 250	6.1	66.2	9.1	15.2	9 922	17 200	29 803	-9.8	0.3	33 059	21.0	32.0	28.5
Jackson	715	4 815	170 420	18.2	42.8	26.9	1 170.1	11 037	25 213	46 252	-7.0	2.3	44 620	16.8	23.9	21.0

1. Data for serious crimes have not been adjusted for underreporting; this may affect comparability between geographic areas and over time.   2. Per 100,000 population estimated by the FBI.   3. All persons 3 years old and over enrolled in nursery school through college.   4. Persons 25 years old and over.   5. Elementary and secondary education expenditures.   6. Based on population estimated by the American Community Survey, 2006–2010.

Table B. States and Counties — **Personal Income**

STATE County	Personal income, 2009												
			Per capita[1]						Transfer payments (mil dol)				
										Government payments to individuals			
	Total (mil dol)	Percent change, 2008–2009	Dollars	Rank	Wages and salaries[2] (mil dol)	Proprietors' income (mil dol)	Dividends, interest, and rent (mil dol)	Total	Total	Social Security	Medical payments	Income mainte-nance	Unemploy-ment insurance
	62	63	64	65	66	67	68	69	70	71	72	73	74
MISSISSIPPI—Cont'd													
Sunflower	758	1.0	25 611	2 793	389	88	102	250	244	56	104	57	7
Tallahatchie	354	-0.9	27 995	2 400	110	47	38	116	114	30	53	23	3
Tate	774	-0.1	28 301	2 345	240	44	81	204	199	66	73	22	6
Tippah	533	-1.1	24 594	2 907	240	19	64	199	196	64	98	18	6
Tishomingo	461	0.1	24 222	2 946	210	16	68	181	178	65	89	12	5
Tunica	291	-5.3	27 862	2 424	503	24	44	83	81	20	34	20	3
Union	713	-1.0	26 162	2 693	350	46	113	192	187	76	77	18	6
Walthall	369	-1.1	24 129	2 957	113	27	45	125	122	40	53	20	3
Warren	1 700	-3.5	35 288	981	1 171	80	269	374	365	105	173	55	11
Washington	1 511	-1.5	27 664	2 456	821	122	216	493	483	125	207	117	15
Wayne	541	-0.4	26 181	2 691	226	57	83	155	151	50	63	26	4
Webster	236	1.2	23 954	2 968	82	7	32	97	95	35	43	11	2
Wilkinson	228	2.4	22 506	3 050	95	10	30	83	81	22	39	15	2
Winston	473	-9.7	24 508	2 915	193	29	76	166	162	57	65	24	6
Yalobusha	348	-0.7	25 290	2 829	126	16	46	135	132	43	62	16	4
Yazoo	690	0.7	24 644	2 901	301	70	93	229	223	62	102	44	6
MISSOURI	216 637	-1.4	36 181	X	143 352	16 030	36 534	42 828	41 739	14 495	18 562	3 754	1 799
Adair	681	1.9	27 111	2 547	416	43	123	179	174	52	89	13	7
Andrew	698	2.4	40 911	386	99	56	85	95	92	41	34	6	5
Atchison	231	8.9	38 273	607	68	71	35	45	44	19	19	2	2
Audrain	776	-3.2	30 366	1 893	393	108	130	197	192	68	90	16	7
Barry	987	-1.6	27 496	2 482	603	96	153	284	277	95	128	27	9
Barton	349	-1.3	28 193	2 367	136	64	57	97	94	35	41	10	4
Bates	547	-0.9	32 656	1 392	146	80	81	141	138	51	65	10	5
Benton	513	2.3	27 766	2 441	134	39	82	209	205	82	89	14	5
Bollinger	333	10.3	28 157	2 371	112	27	37	98	95	34	41	9	4
Boone	5 731	1.6	36 649	796	4 131	399	972	916	887	271	405	78	35
Buchanan	2 834	1.5	31 542	1 634	2 291	152	405	697	680	212	325	67	27
Butler	1 387	0.7	33 444	1 269	784	174	178	441	433	120	211	48	12
Caldwell	311	0.3	33 976	1 176	63	48	32	67	66	24	30	5	3
Callaway	1 226	0.9	28 048	2 391	735	71	170	284	276	101	118	24	12
Camden	1 341	-1.4	32 946	1 349	638	103	301	335	327	153	118	21	13
Cape Girardeau	2 535	0.7	34 282	1 130	1 838	197	459	501	487	177	201	42	19
Carroll	322	-1.2	33 722	1 214	106	56	58	79	77	28	36	6	3
Carter	157	3.8	26 783	2 600	50	13	21	67	66	19	34	7	2
Cass	3 390	0.6	33 840	1 192	1 023	156	467	598	580	229	237	38	34
Cedar	348	-0.6	25 683	2 776	116	31	61	132	129	46	60	11	4
Chariton	267	-0.2	35 205	994	65	66	45	63	61	23	28	4	3
Christian	2 167	-0.7	27 972	2 405	586	138	289	428	414	169	154	35	21
Clark	215	1.5	30 117	1 949	51	42	31	56	55	21	23	4	3
Clay	8 195	0.5	35 887	901	5 096	583	1 005	1 255	1 214	470	506	80	63
Clinton	716	0.8	34 079	1 158	200	33	88	138	134	49	61	7	6
Cole	2 969	0.8	39 578	481	2 678	235	489	482	469	172	204	38	18
Cooper	511	-1.4	29 525	2 087	234	50	83	123	120	43	54	9	5
Crawford	678	-2.2	28 347	2 337	256	61	94	201	197	70	86	20	9
Dade	205	-2.8	28 079	2 388	64	27	34	63	62	24	26	5	2
Dallas	432	-4.6	25 979	2 735	96	40	62	132	129	47	54	13	5
Daviess	219	-0.3	27 172	2 538	59	37	34	56	55	22	22	4	2
DeKalb	280	1.6	23 129	3 028	123	19	35	65	63	27	24	4	3
Dent	407	1.8	27 075	2 554	149	27	61	146	143	47	71	13	4
Douglas	323	-1.7	23 705	2 981	114	37	45	106	103	38	43	12	4
Dunklin	917	-0.8	29 546	2 082	329	88	107	370	364	90	201	47	10
Franklin	3 492	-2.6	34 487	1 095	1 567	155	582	684	666	263	272	45	41
Gasconade	465	-0.7	30 791	1 802	192	21	99	126	123	49	54	8	6
Gentry	220	2.2	35 986	888	86	34	33	63	62	21	33	3	1
Greene	9 354	0.0	34 691	1 067	7 275	889	1 855	1 882	1 833	640	756	162	73
Grundy	300	3.1	29 863	2 008	139	33	49	89	87	28	40	6	2
Harrison	246	0.9	28 089	2 387	94	29	43	77	75	25	38	6	2
Henry	698	1.8	31 460	1 648	321	45	125	211	207	76	96	16	7
Hickory	208	2.6	23 310	3 018	38	11	36	98	96	42	38	6	3
Holt	181	7.5	37 122	736	51	43	25	41	40	15	19	2	1
Howard	348	2.3	35 286	982	93	29	55	80	78	25	37	6	3
Howell	1 036	1.3	26 624	2 620	582	68	160	351	344	118	148	38	12
Iron	314	5.2	31 599	1 624	210	9	33	108	106	33	54	10	3
Jackson	26 152	-0.4	37 058	746	23 104	2 640	3 609	4 989	4 860	1 515	2 275	495	221

1. Based on the resident population estimated as of July 1 of the year shown.   2. Includes supplements to wages and salaries.

Table B. States and Counties — Earnings, Social Security, and Housing

STATE County	Earnings, 2009									Social Security beneficiaries, December 2010			Housing units, 2010	
			Percent by selected industries											
			Goods-related[1]		Service-related and health							Supplemental Security Income recipients, December 2010		
	Total (mil dol)	Farm	Total	Manufacturing	Information and professional and technical services	Retail trade	Finance, insurance, and real estate	Health care and social services	Government	Number	Rate[2]		Total	Percent change, 2000–2010
	75	76	77	78	79	80	81	82	83	84	85	86	87	88
MISSISSIPPI—Cont'd														
Sunflower	477	16.0	6.5	5.3	1.8	5.3	2.7	D	37.3	5 255	178	2 123	9 685	-6.3
Tallahatchie	157	25.4	3.6	1.5	D	5.8	1.9	D	26.5	3 070	200	1 291	5 530	-3.2
Tate	283	2.8	D	9.0	7.2	9.4	3.6	D	30.5	5 605	194	868	10 947	17.0
Tippah	259	0.9	D	27.9	D	7.6	3.6	D	21.1	5 835	262	1 085	9 696	9.3
Tishomingo	226	0.4	36.7	31.8	1.9	7.3	3.3	D	19.2	5 665	289	749	10 295	7.8
Tunica	527	5.0	1.6	0.9	1.1	2.0	1.1	1.3	8.9	1 950	181	816	4 803	29.6
Union	396	1.7	28.4	24.5	D	7.8	2.6	D	15.8	6 575	242	949	11 520	7.7
Walthall	140	8.9	19.9	14.1	2.7	7.8	4.1	7.5	25.4	3 695	239	864	7 132	11.1
Warren	1 251	0.8	18.6	14.6	7.0	7.2	2.8	12.1	30.4	9 365	192	2 002	21 896	5.3
Washington	943	7.8	D	8.1	6.1	7.8	3.3	8.2	28.2	11 300	221	4 689	21 708	-11.0
Wayne	283	11.7	26.2	12.2	2.7	8.3	3.1	D	20.8	4 425	213	1 163	9 213	1.7
Webster	90	0.2	18.5	14.7	D	9.3	D	D	24.5	3 180	310	634	4 804	10.6
Wilkinson	104	2.4	8.7	6.9	D	6.6	2.3	D	29.0	2 150	218	743	5 037	-1.4
Winston	222	3.4	D	20.0	3.2	9.5	2.6	D	17.9	5 040	263	1 013	8 745	3.2
Yalobusha	142	1.9	D	24.6	D	6.8	3.6	2.4	29.9	3 845	303	868	6 344	1.9
Yazoo	371	5.1	D	11.7	1.9	4.8	4.7	D	34.9	5 445	194	1 881	10 074	0.6
MISSOURI	159 382	1.1	16.7	10.9	11.8	6.4	7.0	11.8	17.5	1 166 223	195	133 895	2 712 729	11.1
Adair	459	0.9	11.7	7.4	5.2	9.4	6.2	D	27.1	4 570	178	672	11 263	4.0
Andrew	156	11.3	D	1.5	D	8.4	5.3	D	23.1	3 215	186	231	7 306	9.7
Atchison	139	39.4	2.7	0.5	3.2	4.8	5.6	D	13.6	1 490	262	82	2 985	-3.8
Audrain	501	11.0	21.9	18.7	2.6	8.2	4.2	D	25.2	5 425	213	529	10 852	-0.3
Barry	699	4.6	33.5	30.7	D	7.3	4.2	5.1	12.2	8 695	244	946	17 523	9.8
Barton	200	20.5	D	10.6	4.5	7.3	5.4	4.0	20.0	3 100	250	323	5 600	3.5
Bates	226	13.9	12.0	6.3	5.0	7.9	6.1	6.2	25.6	4 240	249	392	7 842	8.2
Benton	173	1.8	D	7.1	3.6	13.4	9.0	6.3	29.8	6 695	351	530	14 150	11.5
Bollinger	139	1.1	D	3.7	2.5	5.9	D	5.2	16.1	3 125	253	453	5 878	6.4
Boone	4 530	0.2	9.4	4.3	6.0	7.6	6.7	12.9	38.1	21 870	134	2 538	69 551	22.7
Buchanan	2 443	1.0	D	23.3	5.4	7.1	5.1	15.8	15.2	17 200	193	2 303	38 427	5.1
Butler	958	6.9	D	13.4	4.4	8.2	4.4	19.0	21.7	11 365	266	2 481	19 731	5.5
Caldwell	111	17.0	12.6	1.2	D	6.5	5.9	D	24.2	1 945	206	157	4 605	2.5
Callaway	806	2.8	18.2	11.9	2.5	4.3	2.5	D	26.1	8 365	189	799	18 522	14.6
Camden	741	-0.2	D	6.2	6.3	15.6	6.8	16.1	12.7	11 690	266	607	41 183	23.0
Cape Girardeau	2 036	0.6	16.7	11.0	6.3	8.2	4.9	25.6	15.0	14 540	192	1 603	32 616	10.8
Carroll	161	27.4	D	4.5	D	6.4	4.9	D	17.4	2 380	256	224	4 630	-5.5
Carter	63	-0.4	15.1	9.4	D	9.5	D	6.5	35.1	1 825	291	360	3 247	7.2
Cass	1 179	1.4	15.1	3.7	5.5	11.8	4.9	9.1	23.6	17 825	179	989	40 030	26.4
Cedar	147	-1.3	D	9.0	3.7	10.5	4.5	9.7	28.6	4 075	291	426	7 224	6.0
Chariton	131	27.1	10.5	6.7	2.1	7.1	4.8	4.5	15.6	1 955	250	156	4 167	-2.0
Christian	724	-0.4	D	6.8	8.8	10.8	4.8	6.8	20.7	14 265	184	1 104	31 576	44.7
Clark	93	26.1	D	6.2	2.1	8.9	3.9	3.1	21.9	1 775	249	136	3 473	-0.3
Clay	5 680	0.2	20.6	15.3	15.3	9.0	4.5	8.0	15.5	35 225	159	2 178	93 918	23.2
Clinton	234	6.9	D	2.4	3.0	5.4	9.4	D	30.7	3 840	185	272	8 876	12.7
Cole	2 913	0.0	D	4.5	9.7	6.7	5.5	10.9	39.6	13 910	183	1 395	32 324	11.8
Cooper	284	9.9	D	14.2	2.6	7.1	5.6	D	22.0	3 665	208	286	7 463	11.8
Crawford	317	-1.3	D	23.2	3.4	13.5	4.9	D	14.8	6 085	246	740	11 955	10.2
Dade	91	13.0	D	7.7	1.9	5.4	D	1.6	26.7	2 140	271	184	3 965	5.5
Dallas	136	-3.5	D	4.1	3.9	10.9	6.9	D	24.8	4 255	254	542	7 662	10.8
Daviess	96	25.6	D	8.4	2.4	7.3	D	D	24.4	1 920	228	127	4 199	9.0
DeKalb	142	8.4	D	D	D	9.8	6.5	D	41.9	2 165	168	149	4 329	12.7
Dent	176	-2.4	14.2	9.0	3.5	10.4	5.9	D	25.4	4 180	267	579	7 285	4.2
Douglas	151	-2.4	D	D	D	8.4	3.3	D	17.4	3 595	263	475	6 519	10.1
Dunklin	417	11.3	6.5	3.9	3.4	10.8	3.6	D	21.1	8 440	264	2 449	14 419	-1.8
Franklin	1 722	0.3	31.5	24.4	5.0	8.7	4.0	10.7	14.1	20 765	205	1 530	43 419	13.4
Gasconade	213	0.8	D	26.2	D	9.0	4.9	D	23.5	4 050	266	244	8 205	5.0
Gentry	120	26.3	15.5	6.6	D	6.9	3.5	15.8	17.9	1 930	286	156	3 209	-0.2
Greene	8 164	0.0	D	8.8	8.4	7.9	6.7	19.6	14.7	53 070	193	6 070	125 387	20.0
Grundy	172	10.1	D	18.8	3.4	7.6	3.2	13.7	25.5	2 475	241	246	5 023	-1.5
Harrison	123	13.1	D	1.1	D	15.4	5.9	7.7	28.4	2 285	255	200	4 407	2.1
Henry	366	3.9	D	17.4	2.6	8.5	5.1	8.8	24.7	6 360	286	678	10 886	6.1
Hickory	49	3.9	D	1.2	D	12.2	D	6.3	34.6	3 550	369	292	6 835	10.5
Holt	94	40.2	D	8.0	D	7.1	2.0	3.9	16.6	1 260	257	71	2 806	-4.3
Howard	121	12.5	D	8.8	2.8	6.2	D	D	18.4	2 105	208	253	4 582	5.4
Howell	650	-0.5	21.8	19.3	6.2	9.8	3.8	D	16.8	11 020	273	1 624	18 021	10.3
Iron	219	-0.8	D	12.3	D	3.8	1.8	7.2	13.2	2 910	274	544	5 329	8.6
Jackson	25 744	0.1	12.8	6.7	19.9	4.8	10.2	10.3	18.0	117 350	174	15 745	312 105	8.3

1. Includes mining, construction, and manufacturing. 2. Per 1,000 resident population enumerated in the 2010 census.

Table B. States and Counties — **Housing, Labor Force, and Employment**

STATE County	Total	Percent	Median value[1]	With a mortgage	Without a mortgage	Median rent[2]	Median rent as a percent of income	Substandard units[3] (percent)	Total	Percent change, 2009–2010	Total	Rate[4]	Total	Management, business, science and arts	Construction, production, and maintenance occupations
	89	90	91	92	93	94	95	96	97	98	99	100	101	102	103
MISSISSIPPI—Cont'd															
Sunflower	8 534	57.2	63 300	30.5	14.4	508	31.3	4.0	10 564	1.5	1 647	15.6	8 682	25.5	31.1
Tallahatchie	4 739	72.6	51 600	30.7	13.8	442	34.1	3.5	6 145	5.0	710	11.6	5 271	21.5	32.7
Tate	9 950	75.8	100 500	24.3	13.2	660	31.8	4.3	11 710	-0.5	1 344	11.5	12 667	24.7	33.2
Tippah	8 591	75.1	71 100	24.3	11.3	532	29.9	4.4	8 427	1.3	1 215	14.4	8 764	21.9	41.2
Tishomingo	7 709	79.8	73 200	24.4	10.2	445	35.9	1.7	7 716	1.2	991	12.8	7 170	22.8	42.3
Tunica	4 039	52.1	73 000	24.0	12.4	669	30.8	9.0	4 483	1.4	779	17.4	4 575	17.4	20.7
Union	10 163	75.9	78 600	23.2	12.0	562	30.8	3.2	11 678	0.2	1 339	11.5	11 420	22.5	37.9
Walthall	5 476	84.0	83 800	25.4	15.9	575	27.1	3.6	5 829	0.4	754	12.9	5 533	30.1	37.2
Warren	19 267	67.3	99 700	21.2	11.9	632	33.4	2.8	22 094	-0.2	2 445	11.1	21 651	31.8	26.1
Washington	19 039	56.2	72 800	24.4	14.4	570	34.7	5.6	22 269	1.5	3 384	15.2	18 284	28.3	26.1
Wayne	8 375	82.0	60 500	23.8	14.6	501	27.3	2.6	8 494	1.0	1 046	12.3	7 882	21.1	41.7
Webster	3 892	70.1	72 500	19.9	12.6	476	28.9	4.2	3 501	1.9	501	14.3	3 932	28.5	35.8
Wilkinson	3 464	75.0	55 400	33.4	11.4	430	27.7	5.1	4 115	6.1	511	12.4	2 884	26.4	30.2
Winston	7 360	79.3	71 900	22.7	15.2	608	32.7	3.1	7 668	-2.0	1 386	18.1	7 541	24.2	32.1
Yalobusha	4 981	72.5	61 700	24.4	14.5	460	24.4	2.4	5 692	5.2	740	13.0	4 526	21.4	46.0
Yazoo	8 640	63.7	70 500	27.0	15.9	528	35.6	4.2	10 517	3.1	1 310	12.5	9 366	25.3	28.0
MISSOURI	2 349 955	70.0	137 700	22.4	11.4	667	28.9	2.0	3 052 847	0.1	285 541	9.4	2 796 027	33.5	23.6
Adair	9 584	61.1	97 800	19.4	11.8	507	41.8	2.0	12 914	-4.9	945	7.3	11 340	37.8	20.7
Andrew	6 633	78.6	125 500	19.7	10.4	613	25.9	1.6	9 931	-1.8	782	7.9	8 794	31.4	30.1
Atchison	2 474	72.4	69 500	19.3	11.1	461	20.6	0.3	3 112	-3.8	258	8.3	2 826	28.7	30.1
Audrain	9 532	76.5	84 700	20.1	10.0	556	24.5	2.2	11 797	-3.4	1 065	9.0	10 764	25.0	31.7
Barry	14 256	74.9	101 600	22.2	10.0	517	28.1	5.0	16 752	-3.7	1 450	8.7	15 232	26.0	37.2
Barton	4 984	75.8	84 000	20.7	10.6	489	27.0	4.4	5 116	-2.4	580	11.3	5 638	27.4	35.2
Bates	6 605	74.8	102 000	22.5	12.7	614	32.4	3.0	7 504	-5.1	878	11.7	7 416	24.0	38.8
Benton	8 273	84.0	97 500	23.7	12.1	554	31.9	3.2	8 076	-1.9	854	10.6	7 020	25.5	33.8
Bollinger	4 807	78.7	92 800	20.0	10.0	550	32.5	4.2	5 495	-3.3	542	9.9	5 157	19.9	42.5
Boone	63 420	57.6	153 900	21.2	10.0	729	31.2	2.0	89 078	1.7	5 682	6.4	84 408	42.7	15.0
Buchanan	33 913	67.9	107 800	20.9	11.1	617	28.1	1.7	48 490	-2.0	4 229	8.7	40 779	29.2	28.1
Butler	17 071	67.1	87 700	20.9	10.7	529	30.4	1.5	20 762	-2.2	1 723	8.3	18 189	28.7	29.5
Caldwell	3 759	74.6	97 600	22.2	10.3	555	29.1	3.5	4 101	-5.3	409	10.0	4 088	25.7	34.8
Callaway	16 643	75.4	122 700	21.0	10.0	588	24.5	2.0	22 743	-0.6	1 832	8.1	20 927	30.3	23.9
Camden	18 349	81.3	187 200	23.3	10.0	598	28.3	1.7	20 212	-9.3	2 208	10.9	19 732	32.2	22.9
Cape Girardeau	29 624	67.4	132 500	21.2	10.0	594	26.8	1.2	38 367	-0.3	2 935	7.6	37 333	31.1	24.4
Carroll	3 868	78.2	72 600	19.5	11.3	490	22.9	2.0	4 852	-5.2	537	11.1	4 563	30.9	34.3
Carter	2 435	77.2	88 100	22.5	12.1	359	24.7	1.5	3 100	1.1	289	9.3	2 558	27.1	33.3
Cass	36 399	80.1	152 900	23.3	11.7	863	28.6	1.6	49 507	-2.4	4 995	10.1	48 535	32.0	26.0
Cedar	6 135	76.3	92 300	24.4	12.1	540	28.0	2.9	6 585	4.9	569	8.6	5 377	27.0	29.2
Chariton	3 145	80.1	76 500	18.8	11.5	408	18.9	1.6	4 265	5.5	380	8.9	3 631	30.7	34.5
Christian	28 385	75.7	146 800	22.3	12.0	684	26.9	2.0	40 605	1.6	3 417	8.4	36 692	34.8	22.3
Clark	2 811	76.0	68 700	18.7	10.5	437	27.7	1.4	3 497	-2.7	378	10.8	3 125	26.3	39.2
Clay	86 034	72.6	153 900	22.9	11.7	736	26.0	1.4	119 048	1.1	10 497	8.8	112 471	37.0	20.2
Clinton	8 091	76.4	150 200	23.4	11.2	647	23.4	2.3	10 054	-3.9	1 087	10.8	9 988	26.1	30.6
Cole	29 111	68.0	136 300	19.4	10.0	561	22.4	1.0	40 315	-0.2	2 795	6.9	37 323	39.0	18.0
Cooper	6 397	72.3	112 400	20.6	11.7	548	24.3	1.2	8 663	-4.8	797	9.2	7 854	30.0	29.6
Crawford	9 467	74.8	105 400	23.4	11.8	551	28.9	3.0	11 775	-3.5	1 323	11.2	10 007	17.7	41.1
Dade	3 276	77.5	73 000	22.0	12.5	449	24.1	3.1	3 484	-2.2	311	8.9	3 124	23.0	37.2
Dallas	6 444	81.8	96 800	23.1	10.0	484	26.0	2.7	7 295	-2.1	853	11.7	7 033	22.8	42.2
Daviess	3 288	74.7	99 100	23.9	12.7	529	19.8	3.1	3 777	-2.6	369	9.8	3 719	28.6	33.0
DeKalb	3 961	67.8	115 100	22.3	13.0	463	24.6	1.9	5 051	-3.6	491	9.7	4 778	29.0	27.9
Dent	6 124	77.9	84 100	23.3	10.5	508	31.6	2.1	6 843	1.3	652	9.5	6 307	25.7	34.5
Douglas	4 913	82.0	87 800	24.8	13.2	455	27.3	3.5	6 144	-4.6	634	10.3	5 027	23.3	39.2
Dunklin	12 885	62.4	67 300	21.9	13.0	469	29.4	2.5	14 307	-3.2	1 556	10.9	11 151	23.7	33.5
Franklin	38 556	76.8	147 200	22.2	11.2	620	25.6	2.7	52 682	-1.9	5 814	11.0	48 373	27.2	34.8
Gasconade	6 470	79.1	111 900	23.3	10.7	477	23.0	1.8	7 490	-6.7	789	10.5	7 230	26.2	35.4
Gentry	2 670	76.6	79 500	23.1	12.0	442	24.4	4.4	3 560	0.0	252	7.1	3 121	28.6	32.4
Greene	112 993	61.8	125 500	21.9	10.2	633	29.9	1.5	139 255	-0.1	11 722	8.4	132 829	32.2	20.4
Grundy	4 259	70.4	71 700	21.2	11.5	436	25.6	2.7	4 791	-0.8	373	7.8	4 566	24.3	33.4
Harrison	3 534	75.2	77 700	20.9	14.3	474	25.3	2.6	4 327	-7.2	375	8.7	3 957	24.5	36.1
Henry	9 459	73.3	103 300	22.9	12.6	515	28.0	1.3	10 624	-2.9	1 070	10.1	9 690	26.4	31.6
Hickory	4 478	84.0	89 900	25.7	12.7	438	29.9	1.0	3 508	0.4	439	12.5	3 421	25.6	30.7
Holt	2 219	78.1	74 600	21.0	10.9	456	23.2	2.5	2 700	-3.3	205	7.6	2 354	29.2	31.2
Howard	3 856	78.4	98 300	21.8	10.4	482	25.3	1.8	5 138	-0.8	409	8.0	4 760	29.2	28.3
Howell	15 404	72.0	94 200	22.5	10.0	510	28.7	1.8	19 448	-2.2	1 782	9.2	15 959	27.0	35.7
Iron	4 287	72.8	77 200	20.6	10.0	466	31.0	3.3	4 947	-14.3	573	11.6	3 587	24.6	30.7
Jackson	271 192	63.2	129 900	23.0	13.0	723	30.4	2.0	340 864	1.3	37 400	11.0	323 116	34.6	21.4

1. Specified owner-occupied units.   2. Specified renter-occupied units. A value of 10.0 represents 10 percent or less.   3. Overcrowded or lacking complete plumbing facilities.   4. Percent of civilian labor force.   5. Persons 16 years old and over.

Table B. States and Counties — Nonfarm Employment and Agriculture

STATE County	Number of establishments	Total	Health care and social assistance	Manufacturing	Retail trade	Finance and insurance	Professional, scientific, and technical services	Total (mil dol)	Average per employee (dollars)	Number	Fewer than 50 acres	500 acres or more	Farm operators whose principal occupation is farming (percent)
	104	105	106	107	108	109	110	111	112	113	114	115	116
MISSISSIPPI—Cont'd													
Sunflower	427	5 359	D	735	837	D	111	141	26 361	370	17.8	41.9	57.6
Tallahatchie	184	1 876	311	50	238	D	30	52	27 834	488	14.5	26.2	42.0
Tate	384	4 077	586	796	956	199	73	103	25 142	622	29.7	11.1	38.4
Tippah	345	5 443	664	1 775	693	D	126	138	25 356	691	25.3	5.6	24.6
Tishomingo	358	4 259	597	1 665	554	D	D	111	25 988	349	19.5	3.7	26.6
Tunica	228	11 370	D	D	490	D	D	317	27 856	103	4.9	61.2	65.0
Union	479	8 044	1 206	2 712	1 033	189	88	222	27 551	751	28.5	5.5	24.8
Walthall	231	2 282	410	579	395	72	D	55	24 008	768	30.1	5.1	42.1
Warren	1 074	21 108	3 025	3 935	2 578	396	813	625	29 588	278	33.8	21.6	35.6
Washington	1 217	15 012	2 581	1 057	2 867	352	380	417	27 782	346	21.4	43.6	62.7
Wayne	379	4 698	D	904	1 023	194	88	128	27 334	521	31.5	6.3	42.8
Webster	164	1 683	D	366	399	D	62	43	25 471	392	18.6	9.9	27.8
Wilkinson	156	1 582	398	128	295	D	D	41	25 798	207	16.4	26.6	48.8
Winston	390	4 891	D	1 597	852	119	93	124	25 283	536	27.8	6.3	36.4
Yalobusha	196	2 169	346	671	326	D	D	60	27 541	377	15.4	14.1	34.2
Yazoo	404	3 768	817	D	647	D	69	105	27 776	668	17.2	23.4	36.7
MISSOURI	150 892	2 358 706	373 344	259 237	307 984	131 275	144 024	88 809	37 652	107 825	26.9	13.0	41.8
Adair	700	8 302	2 029	888	1 505	261	D	204	24 619	944	22.6	15.4	40.0
Andrew	304	1 806	348	D	308	D	D	47	26 901	988	28.9	13.6	39.2
Atchison	213	1 241	269	D	327	81	57	30	24 202	501	17.6	35.5	62.5
Audrain	581	6 934	1 294	1 646	1 119	272	118	198	28 609	1 102	22.6	22.7	50.0
Barry	751	14 082	1 396	5 124	1 708	298	D	480	34 095	1 606	33.4	7.4	45.6
Barton	274	2 783	395	575	567	180	D	71	25 441	1 046	21.6	20.8	46.7
Bates	356	2 799	729	247	578	222	94	70	25 010	1 345	23.6	16.2	40.8
Benton	379	2 359	278	D	721	D	D	49	20 825	822	19.6	12.4	49.5
Bollinger	202	1 352	316	D	345	D	28	30	21 883	853	17.6	11.7	44.8
Boone	4 311	64 724	14 954	4 156	11 166	5 455	2 971	2 101	32 457	1 322	39.3	8.9	29.8
Buchanan	2 494	44 384	7 486	11 159	5 849	1 844	1 187	1 470	33 110	881	30.8	10.7	40.2
Butler	1 356	14 641	3 924	D	2 634	490	414	397	27 129	607	27.2	21.9	52.1
Caldwell	162	854	D	D	180	57	D	23	26 737	1 048	27.2	10.4	36.7
Callaway	762	11 404	2 266	1 486	1 532	342	194	388	33 996	1 503	29.9	9.5	34.6
Camden	1 494	12 640	2 117	764	3 121	514	419	348	27 547	544	16.5	13.1	40.4
Cape Girardeau	2 728	38 042	9 591	3 935	5 881	1 336	959	1 152	30 273	1 449	29.4	9.5	42.4
Carroll	229	1 689	411	185	266	116	38	46	27 056	1 199	18.6	16.2	36.3
Carter	192	952	208	191	162	D	D	18	18 471	203	21.2	12.3	33.0
Cass	1 852	17 583	2 480	1 790	3 812	661	495	481	27 356	1 773	45.7	8.4	38.4
Cedar	286	2 236	688	179	418	114	35	48	21 320	840	22.9	10.4	46.3
Chariton	207	1 328	D	180	231	D	D	31	23 184	1 173	18.8	18.2	41.7
Christian	1 635	12 670	1 284	1 271	2 768	593	581	312	24 602	1 265	37.6	5.8	38.5
Clark	142	1 036	110	124	314	68	15	22	20 873	709	12.6	18.1	45.7
Clay	4 903	85 807	12 934	10 672	11 547	3 346	D	3 375	39 332	752	52.5	8.5	35.8
Clinton	371	2 925	801	97	664	D	83	82	27 976	914	34.9	10.4	40.3
Cole	2 240	33 274	6 079	2 179	5 263	1 929	1 731	1 155	34 699	1 103	23.4	4.6	37.3
Cooper	430	4 489	834	648	770	209	87	105	23 433	942	20.7	18.9	42.4
Crawford	605	5 118	938	1 522	736	D	D	137	26 841	679	21.5	13.1	38.9
Dade	149	1 254	95	D	175	D	17	34	27 129	883	24.1	16.5	47.6
Dallas	270	2 513	D	D	536	134	D	44	17 366	1 369	35.4	6.6	41.5
Daviess	182	957	92	D	237	62	D	20	20 676	1 169	20.9	12.9	34.3
DeKalb	226	1 933	360	D	570	279	D	49	25 469	978	25.7	11.8	37.0
Dent	436	3 529	788	614	551	149	D	113	31 968	651	21.8	14.3	41.0
Douglas	207	2 167	214	720	460	D	D	41	19 024	1 124	22.4	8.7	43.9
Dunklin	812	7 962	2 298	315	1 472	273	D	170	21 317	453	24.9	42.2	66.9
Franklin	2 631	31 991	3 776	7 795	4 938	1 157	1 218	970	30 331	2 004	36.6	4.5	35.5
Gasconade	428	4 250	796	1 119	748	196	109	102	23 959	867	14.8	9.8	41.8
Gentry	215	1 972	899	185	253	52	D	40	20 502	839	19.7	15.7	35.2
Greene	8 081	142 628	27 153	12 891	18 846	7 969	7 043	4 578	32 099	1 960	49.0	4.0	36.1
Grundy	247	2 586	750	656	450	85	55	68	26 287	798	23.8	13.5	38.8
Harrison	222	2 079	477	51	685	109	37	44	21 130	1 160	18.0	17.2	34.2
Henry	609	6 761	1 711	1 294	1 234	D	156	214	31 631	1 125	26.1	16.5	44.1
Hickory	143	631	129	D	204	46	D	12	19 209	492	17.9	13.0	47.6
Holt	130	868	D	156	142	51	D	23	26 007	462	16.2	27.7	54.8
Howard	189	1 741	399	245	281	93	43	40	22 820	867	16.7	15.2	37.7
Howell	1 117	12 481	2 878	2 570	2 315	521	422	325	26 028	1 590	30.6	9.9	40.8
Iron	460	2 103	682	87	318	36	D	54	25 749	299	18.1	13.4	43.5
Jackson	17 024	334 290	49 057	31 360	34 361	26 446	27 251	14 239	42 594	838	58.6	6.0	40.2

Table B. States and Counties — **Agriculture**

STATE County	Acreage (1,000) [117]	Percent change, 2002–2007 [118]	Average size of farm [119]	Total irrigated (1,000) [120]	Total cropland (1,000) [121]	Average per farm [122]	Average per acre [123]	Value of machinery and equipment, average per farm (dollars) [124]	Total (mil dol) [125]	Average per farm (dollars) [126]	Crops [127]	Live-stock and poultry products [128]	$10,000 or more [129]	$100,000 or more [130]	Total ($1,000) [131]	Percent of farms [132]
MISSISSIPPI—Cont'd																
Sunflower	378	12.5	1 021	187.7	330.9	1 776 934	1 741	272 845	190.2	513 941	74.0	26.0	66.2	44.9	13 815	75.4
Tallahatchie	316	7.8	647	90.6	236.3	989 326	1 529	155 503	81.5	166 987	98.0	2.0	36.9	18.6	8 424	75.4
Tate	157	1.3	252	2.2	75.0	511 056	2 026	70 526	30.3	48 644	62.7	37.3	28.1	7.4	3 289	42.3
Tippah	137	13.2	199	0.2	52.8	289 384	1 455	43 082	16.8	24 322	52.2	47.8	16.2	2.9	1 720	63.1
Tishomingo	57	7.5	163	D	20.1	251 060	1 544	43 727	4.9	13 899	36.0	64.0	13.5	2.3	602	57.3
Tunica	201	0.0	1 952	73.8	186.3	3 530 822	1 809	461 482	79.4	771 143	D	D	67.0	58.3	6 410	83.5
Union	135	-2.9	180	D	50.3	274 040	1 523	45 051	13.5	18 033	46.9	53.1	19.7	3.6	2 016	60.9
Walthall	128	19.6	167	0.1	38.7	410 004	2 456	47 600	76.4	99 531	2.9	97.1	26.7	10.3	1 301	39.8
Warren	112	-2.6	403	3.9	42.1	712 095	1 769	73 859	14.5	52 274	90.0	10.0	25.5	9.7	2 460	50.7
Washington	333	3.7	964	166.4	310.2	1 723 694	1 788	318 831	158.8	459 035	88.2	11.8	66.8	46.5	14 660	67.1
Wayne	86	2.4	166	0.2	26.9	413 040	2 494	56 764	157.0	301 369	2.8	97.2	41.5	22.8	146	13.1
Webster	84	9.1	214	0.2	26.0	319 966	1 496	46 235	14.9	38 111	48.6	51.4	18.4	4.8	1 787	64.8
Wilkinson	113	7.6	547	0.3	17.6	989 648	1 809	54 488	5.4	25 858	21.6	78.4	26.6	3.9	357	30.9
Winston	95	-5.9	178	0.2	22.4	303 787	1 705	48 693	40.3	75 185	3.0	97.0	27.2	5.2	596	39.4
Yalobusha	99	-1.0	263	D	36.2	405 643	1 540	64 838	8.9	23 580	71.5	28.5	25.5	4.2	1 396	56.2
Yazoo	356	-1.1	532	37.5	194.3	899 793	1 691	114 685	92.6	138 629	84.9	15.1	27.2	15.0	13 798	66.5
MISSOURI	29 027	-3.1	269	1 200.0	16 405.6	586 478	2 179	68 171	7 512.9	69 677	46.5	53.5	42.0	11.0	319 519	41.8
Adair	280	4.1	296	0.1	144.4	552 068	1 862	54 312	33.4	35 395	54.0	46.0	40.1	7.6	3 309	50.0
Andrew	239	7.2	241	D	169.9	584 611	2 421	70 435	54.8	55 422	74.0	26.0	44.9	12.8	3 938	67.5
Atchison	304	-4.4	607	9.0	264.2	1 487 826	2 452	190 814	105.1	209 731	95.6	4.4	68.7	39.5	4 051	80.4
Audrain	425	2.4	386	15.5	337.9	1 005 728	2 609	104 907	136.6	123 967	65.4	34.6	55.8	25.0	6 482	65.0
Barry	290	-9.7	180	0.4	114.2	465 670	2 582	54 234	332.0	206 718	1.9	98.1	45.5	15.7	730	11.0
Barton	349	3.6	334	13.8	237.3	620 450	1 858	86 689	90.7	86 721	53.4	46.6	52.8	16.4	5 352	64.8
Bates	474	1.3	352	1.2	277.7	688 518	1 955	78 014	88.0	65 461	56.4	43.6	48.6	11.4	3 804	52.6
Benton	222	-14.3	270	0.3	89.0	514 178	1 901	59 288	50.0	60 802	21.0	79.0	45.0	7.9	819	25.7
Bollinger	208	-8.8	244	12.0	94.1	456 393	1 873	53 928	24.7	28 899	45.2	54.8	40.2	5.3	1 124	42.7
Boone	259	-4.1	196	3.6	152.5	549 026	2 805	54 231	45.5	34 435	64.1	35.9	33.0	6.6	1 927	31.5
Buchanan	198	-1.0	224	0.0	143.9	605 935	2 702	64 008	50.5	57 272	85.4	14.6	44.6	12.5	2 711	67.3
Butler	251	1.2	413	134.0	214.8	935 745	2 266	116 325	89.6	147 541	96.7	3.3	46.3	22.9	6 838	50.6
Caldwell	250	8.7	239	0.2	155.3	477 143	1 999	49 453	43.4	41 398	44.4	55.6	31.2	7.3	4 923	72.9
Callaway	323	-9.8	215	4.0	166.3	547 519	2 548	57 645	69.3	46 083	42.5	57.5	35.2	7.1	2 651	37.3
Camden	144	-19.1	265	0.1	36.4	493 143	1 858	50 000	20.2	37 060	5.6	94.4	37.7	4.6	176	11.2
Cape Girardeau	303	16.1	209	18.3	202.9	530 425	2 540	70 527	79.6	54 937	57.1	42.9	40.7	10.4	3 835	56.6
Carroll	402	-3.6	335	3.0	294.7	707 980	2 114	78 746	83.5	69 654	84.1	15.9	43.3	12.7	7 550	80.9
Carter	63	-32.3	312	D	14.6	508 658	1 630	57 540	3.8	18 772	9.1	90.9	31.5	4.4	72	10.8
Cass	327	4.1	184	5.3	205.0	522 325	2 839	56 921	81.4	45 834	71.6	28.4	30.9	7.9	2 601	31.9
Cedar	191	-16.2	227	0.2	72.3	413 509	1 823	51 994	24.1	28 670	16.2	83.8	39.9	5.2	568	21.4
Chariton	384	1.3	328	2.5	261.6	645 306	1 969	86 630	105.9	90 273	64.0	36.0	50.1	17.1	5 228	71.7
Christian	189	-11.3	150	0.2	76.0	416 435	2 785	43 351	37.6	29 736	9.2	90.8	35.4	5.0	278	8.8
Clark	263	3.5	371	1.9	181.7	731 041	1 971	85 578	54.4	76 779	78.0	22.0	46.5	17.6	3 600	74.2
Clay	144	12.5	191	0.0	75.1	545 272	2 850	62 280	32.7	43 528	43.5	56.5	27.4	7.7	1 125	25.1
Clinton	237	4.9	260	D	154.1	605 438	2 330	66 328	62.0	67 823	52.4	47.6	38.7	10.1	3 459	51.0
Cole	181	-2.7	164	0.4	79.5	395 059	2 410	53 619	34.7	31 470	24.2	75.8	44.9	3.9	830	31.2
Cooper	302	2.7	321	0.4	189.1	714 630	2 226	80 908	82.9	88 053	51.2	48.8	53.6	16.2	3 410	61.8
Crawford	187	-14.2	275	0.1	49.6	512 067	1 859	53 004	11.5	16 945	15.4	84.6	35.6	2.1	125	12.2
Dade	276	-6.8	313	8.6	127.1	568 901	1 819	65 472	51.1	57 828	38.5	61.5	49.4	9.9	1 534	29.1
Dallas	223	-5.1	163	0.2	84.3	361 993	2 223	43 527	46.4	33 893	6.6	93.4	37.2	6.3	381	10.7
Daviess	331	0.3	283	0.6	203.7	548 197	1 937	59 182	76.8	65 678	49.1	50.9	35.3	10.9	5 850	73.2
DeKalb	260	15.6	266	D	161.4	521 522	1 958	60 644	58.7	59 996	45.0	55.0	39.8	9.9	4 432	69.3
Dent	177	-15.7	271	0.2	41.1	456 640	1 683	38 881	11.7	17 914	10.9	89.1	38.2	3.1	118	9.4
Douglas	254	-18.6	226	0.3	64.9	417 328	1 845	40 944	29.4	26 131	6.4	93.6	35.7	6.1	185	8.3
Dunklin	325	9.4	718	159.5	317.1	1 773 930	2 472	239 059	124.2	274 118	98.9	1.1	66.0	41.9	14 086	75.7
Franklin	300	0.0	150	1.1	150.3	447 562	2 992	48 504	52.5	26 222	45.7	54.3	30.6	3.9	1 596	27.9
Gasconade	213	-4.1	245	0.2	81.4	540 805	2 205	59 395	22.6	26 033	35.8	64.2	42.4	5.3	668	32.2
Gentry	276	-5.5	329	0.0	173.7	614 719	1 869	55 826	94.1	112 146	27.8	72.2	38.0	12.9	4 798	77.0
Greene	232	-15.6	118	0.1	105.6	387 845	3 277	40 074	36.2	18 490	15.0	85.0	28.6	3.6	519	8.5
Grundy	232	9.4	291	0.3	156.2	540 989	1 861	50 575	47.9	60 007	64.9	35.1	35.3	10.0	4 283	69.2
Harrison	388	0.0	335	0.0	236.8	615 154	1 837	56 790	71.0	61 206	57.9	42.1	38.5	10.0	6 966	75.9
Henry	345	2.1	307	0.5	184.8	552 808	1 803	66 408	59.9	53 256	43.4	56.6	48.1	10.9	2 369	39.2
Hickory	147	-5.8	298	0.4	52.7	465 990	1 562	56 905	15.3	31 027	12.8	87.2	45.3	6.3	336	26.8
Holt	237	-6.0	513	23.0	199.4	1 257 203	2 452	159 917	81.2	175 706	92.2	7.8	67.5	29.0	3 763	84.2
Howard	277	2.6	319	12.0	172.3	672 799	2 109	72 927	45.1	51 973	76.4	23.6	45.1	12.6	3 596	62.5
Howell	385	-7.0	242	0.1	83.3	419 964	1 734	43 670	57.5	36 140	3.1	96.9	38.2	6.3	449	10.0
Iron	70	-1.4	233	0.0	19.0	398 775	1 708	46 826	6.9	22 931	6.0	94.0	30.4	2.7	35	5.7
Jackson	139	-4.1	166	0.3	102.8	542 557	3 266	54 414	32.1	38 267	86.5	13.5	25.3	8.1	885	26.3

Table B. States and Counties — Water Use, Wholesale Trade, Retail Trade, and Real Estate

STATE County	Water use, 2005		Wholesale trade,[1] 2007				Retail trade,[2] 2007				Real estate and rental and leasing,[2] 2007			
	Total water withdrawn (mil gal/day)	Gallons withdrawn per person	Number of establish-ments	Number of employees	Sales (mil dol)	Annual payroll (mil dol)	Number of establish-ments	Number of employees	Sales (mil dol)	Annual payroll (mil dol)	Number of establish-ments	Number of employees	Receipts (mil dol)	Annual payroll (mil dol)
	133	134	135	136	137	138	139	140	141	142	143	144	145	146
MISSISSIPPI—Cont'd														
Sunflower	283.0	8 757	22	D	D	D	106	913	211.3	15.8	12	36	4.7	0.7
Tallahatchie	103.1	7 265	9	85	62.4	2.7	47	265	56.8	5.1	6	9	1.4	0.1
Tate	3.5	133	13	70	18.7	2.0	93	974	237.7	20.0	16	30	2.8	0.5
Tippah	5.2	243	18	137	131.8	4.6	88	660	130.9	11.6	4	D	D	D
Tishomingo	2.8	148	20	196	54.7	4.4	82	588	112.6	10.6	12	28	5.0	0.5
Tunica	127.5	12 356	6	47	40.7	2.3	80	581	130.7	8.7	11	26	6.1	0.5
Union	2.9	108	17	173	174.7	6.1	106	998	267.3	19.4	17	45	2.8	0.6
Walthall	3.3	211	8	D	D	D	44	485	124.7	9.4	2	D	D	D
Warren	257.7	5 245	42	D	D	D	249	2 696	606.5	54.4	47	186	30.6	5.3
Washington	228.3	3 855	69	D	D	D	284	3 067	577.7	57.8	62	276	31.5	7.9
Wayne	3.4	159	27	220	221.1	12.0	89	899	178.9	16.1	8	29	3.0	0.4
Webster	1.7	165	6	13	2.0	0.4	45	289	69.6	5.7	3	D	D	D
Wilkinson	4.2	406	9	65	44.2	1.8	38	289	59.8	5.5	3	3	0.7	0.1
Winston	3.9	196	15	266	187.9	16.2	96	879	183.2	16.7	11	82	3.0	1.6
Yalobusha	4.6	340	5	17	14.1	0.6	42	328	59.7	4.6	7	6	1.0	0.1
Yazoo	46.4	1 647	20	D	D	D	92	770	230.5	15.6	21	47	5.9	0.9
MISSOURI	8 793.4	1 516	6 903	96 451	81 032.9	4 533.6	23 360	317 318	76 575.2	7 155.3	7 003	39 625	7 186.3	1 248.8
Adair	3.2	132	25	178	54.7	5.4	118	1 536	310.1	28.9	23	95	12.0	2.1
Andrew	1.5	91	12	77	36.9	3.0	45	362	80.0	6.4	18	D	D	D
Atchison	6.3	1 013	10	74	67.8	1.8	46	364	86.6	6.4	4	D	D	D
Audrain	13.6	528	28	D	D	D	109	1 115	247.8	21.8	18	56	5.6	1.1
Barry	20.8	585	24	331	134.8	13.8	154	1 753	413.8	35.9	33	97	11.3	2.3
Barton	12.1	923	11	106	76.0	3.4	55	726	135.1	12.4	7	25	2.8	0.6
Bates	4.3	250	11	104	77.4	3.2	62	540	135.4	11.8	7	D	D	D
Benton	3.7	197	11	56	18.4	1.1	79	739	174.3	13.9	19	40	6.1	0.7
Bollinger	14.0	1 137	13	D	D	D	33	327	59.6	6.2	6	D	D	D
Boone	20.4	143	125	1 422	610.4	56.7	646	11 317	3 012.3	239.7	243	D	D	D
Buchanan	102.9	1 212	101	1 393	1 015.5	55.4	382	5 943	1 438.7	128.5	108	462	49.9	9.7
Butler	339.7	8 217	56	D	D	D	242	2 705	634.8	52.7	38	231	24.8	6.1
Caldwell	1.2	133	6	38	21.2	1.0	29	228	34.1	3.1	2	D	D	D
Callaway	34.4	807	25	165	70.8	5.8	133	1 336	331.1	24.6	32	D	D	D
Camden	14.7	373	43	267	109.4	9.4	311	3 184	677.9	72.0	90	316	47.1	7.7
Cape Girardeau	30.0	422	125	2 111	1 792.0	77.8	445	6 137	1 353.0	122.1	115	427	63.0	9.8
Carroll	3.9	386	16	76	70.1	2.4	42	279	60.6	5.1	9	D	D	D
Carter	0.8	140	9	57	13.6	1.2	22	157	27.7	3.1	3	4	0.4	0.1
Cass	5.8	62	60	424	351.6	15.8	270	3 715	898.7	79.0	78	264	36.2	7.1
Cedar	2.2	153	8	54	13.7	1.1	63	478	119.9	8.5	12	47	5.4	1.6
Chariton	1.2	145	15	184	198.0	7.0	44	215	51.8	4.0	9	D	D	D
Christian	8.8	131	71	623	166.4	21.0	236	2 971	716.8	67.2	77	156	24.3	3.0
Clark	1.5	210	11	D	D	D	36	269	88.7	4.8	4	11	0.4	0.1
Clay	178.7	884	300	4 532	4 517.3	232.9	683	12 599	3 366.9	280.9	247	1 057	193.9	35.1
Clinton	2.5	121	11	59	96.8	1.9	64	641	147.2	13.3	17	41	5.0	0.8
Cole	11.3	155	71	2 541	706.1	76.6	359	5 504	1 203.7	115.4	73	252	44.8	6.2
Cooper	2.9	169	16	114	75.7	3.4	73	787	225.6	15.4	15	48	5.2	0.8
Crawford	3.1	129	16	201	105.2	6.6	78	726	174.3	15.0	25	105	9.7	2.1
Dade	5.5	699	9	305	62.4	6.9	29	165	46.9	2.9	3	2	0.3	0.1
Dallas	2.6	159	7	94	59.9	2.4	65	540	144.7	10.5	9	32	2.5	0.5
Daviess	2.3	280	10	73	41.8	1.6	39	178	45.3	3.4	1	D	D	D
DeKalb	0.8	68	7	D	D	D	38	569	128.0	10.7	16	D	D	D
Dent	32.5	2 156	7	D	D	D	56	549	124.5	11.0	19	106	3.7	1.0
Douglas	21.1	1 549	10	D	D	D	44	446	93.7	8.0	6	6	0.9	0.1
Dunklin	89.4	2 747	35	298	132.8	8.9	167	1 527	371.3	29.0	32	407	21.8	7.0
Franklin	1 155.5	11 662	97	937	386.4	36.3	422	4 955	1 326.7	112.0	95	461	34.5	8.3
Gasconade	2.6	164	18	183	63.1	5.1	80	683	146.0	12.8	16	D	D	D
Gentry	2.3	352	12	76	35.2	2.9	42	258	59.2	4.8	7	152	3.0	1.8
Greene	221.2	882	432	7 514	5 076.0	316.1	1 253	19 282	4 710.4	421.0	458	2 781	340.0	68.3
Grundy	2.7	263	5	55	76.5	2.0	51	452	88.3	7.4	8	18	2.4	0.4
Harrison	1.3	148	10	203	55.5	5.1	53	720	143.5	13.1	6	D	D	D
Henry	417.5	18 491	24	194	101.1	5.9	125	1 237	284.3	25.2	22	84	10.0	1.9
Hickory	1.4	154	2	D	D	D	32	194	50.0	3.6	3	D	D	D
Holt	7.5	1 468	9	97	84.7	3.5	20	152	35.8	2.6	3	D	D	D
Howard	3.3	335	6	81	19.3	2.3	43	312	88.1	5.7	2	D	D	D
Howell	4.3	113	46	340	180.7	11.2	260	2 356	545.8	45.5	54	151	17.5	3.6
Iron	4.3	421	4	11	1.6	0.2	48	301	65.8	5.0	9	D	D	D
Jackson	546.8	825	850	13 194	11 179.9	661.9	2 326	35 780	8 460.8	825.3	904	6 335	1 474.2	222.6

1. Merchant wholesalers, except manufacturers' sales branches and offices.   2. Employer establishments.

STATE County	Professional, scientific, and technical services,[1] 2007				Manufacturing, 2007				Accommodation and food services, 2007			
	Number of establishments	Number of employees	Receipts (mil dol)	Annual payroll (mil dol)	Number of establishments	Number of employees	Receipts (mil dol)	Annual payroll (mil dol)	Number of establishments	Number of employees	Sales (mil dol)	Annual payroll (mil dol)
	147	148	149	150	151	152	153	154	155	156	157	158
MISSISSIPPI—Cont'd												
Sunflower	28	D	D	D	18	918	D	D	31	349	15.1	4.1
Tallahatchie	14	36	3.2	0.7	NA	NA	NA	NA	8	106	3.6	0.9
Tate	25	74	6.2	2.0	15	922	244.3	28.7	29	384	14.6	4.2
Tippah	18	103	7.3	2.8	37	2 635	566.2	83.9	24	291	11.8	2.9
Tishomingo	19	96	4.7	1.8	34	1 856	305.4	57.9	29	219	9.2	2.4
Tunica	7	17	2.2	0.5	NA	NA	NA	NA	34	13 817	1 308.6	349.9
Union	27	88	11.5	3.3	36	2 512	418.1	75.6	32	629	20.8	5.4
Walthall	11	22	3.0	0.7	19	684	167.3	20.7	16	D	D	D
Warren	98	885	77.8	31.7	48	4 399	1 856.7	165.7	105	4 199	384.6	71.9
Washington	91	D	D	D	47	1 994	840.3	75.2	86	1 529	93.8	20.2
Wayne	21	66	4.6	1.2	16	1 128	287.5	33.7	29	355	15.3	3.8
Webster	8	34	3.7	1.1	NA	NA	NA	NA	12	68	3.2	0.8
Wilkinson	7	22	1.3	0.3	NA	NA	NA	NA	6	71	3.4	0.8
Winston	24	87	14.5	2.1	25	1 856	483.4	76.9	28	485	16.5	4.6
Yalobusha	11	D	D	D	7	598	D	D	12	47	2.9	0.6
Yazoo	26	D	D	D	19	801	371.8	27.9	25	311	12.4	3.2
MISSOURI	13 524	130 786	19 749.8	7 454.7	6 886	295 313	110 907.6	12 996.5	12 261	241 438	11 070.6	3 109.1
Adair	40	D	D	D	14	987	D	31.6	60	1 400	38.7	11.6
Andrew	15	D	D	D	NA	NA	NA	NA	14	125	4.5	1.2
Atchison	9	D	D	D	NA	NA	NA	NA	14	189	4.5	1.1
Audrain	24	120	8.1	3.8	40	1 935	1 337.1	75.2	39	471	18.6	5.0
Barry	53	D	D	D	55	5 548	1 409.8	176.1	63	795	25.8	6.1
Barton	15	125	6.9	2.4	26	1 041	174.3	30.6	20	315	8.4	2.3
Bates	18	D	D	D	NA	NA	NA	NA	26	348	12.3	2.9
Benton	19	D	D	D	NA	NA	NA	NA	60	470	13.2	3.4
Bollinger	8	D	D	D	NA	NA	NA	NA	14	D	D	D
Boone	382	D	D	D	96	4 601	D	D	422	8 458	315.1	93.0
Buchanan	177	D	D	D	95	D	D	D	197	4 175	154.5	45.6
Butler	64	591	53.9	18.7	49	2 657	632.7	72.8	87	1 666	57.9	17.4
Caldwell	8	D	D	D	NA	NA	NA	NA	15	73	2.1	0.5
Callaway	37	161	12.2	4.3	39	918	D	33.6	60	845	33.2	9.5
Camden	85	433	53.5	14.3	54	1 117	251.1	35.5	187	3 061	157.6	47.4
Cape Girardeau	156	D	D	D	97	4 574	D	D	177	4 043	145.9	42.6
Carroll	15	D	D	D	NA	NA	NA	NA	17	170	5.5	1.5
Carter	4	D	D	D	NA	NA	NA	NA	15	107	3.5	1.0
Cass	164	D	D	D	84	1 867	483.7	64.7	143	2 343	82.4	25.4
Cedar	14	D	D	D	NA	NA	NA	NA	32	340	9.8	2.7
Chariton	11	D	D	D	NA	NA	NA	NA	10	61	2.0	0.4
Christian	137	606	52.2	16.4	106	1 327	255.6	44.9	105	1 662	59.7	18.6
Clark	9	16	0.8	0.2	NA	NA	NA	NA	10	73	2.1	0.5
Clay	464	D	D	D	219	12 349	10 903.5	773.8	389	11 292	822.1	192.9
Clinton	24	D	D	D	NA	NA	NA	NA	27	430	16.2	4.3
Cole	238	1 409	174.0	63.0	64	3 384	1 568.1	146.9	157	3 134	127.6	37.1
Cooper	22	D	D	D	16	594	155.3	20.2	39	1 070	112.7	19.2
Crawford	27	D	D	D	44	1 479	271.7	46.1	55	496	25.5	6.3
Dade	4	D	D	D	NA	NA	NA	NA	13	48	2.1	0.5
Dallas	16	D	D	D	19	562	D	11.1	23	234	8.4	2.3
Daviess	8	D	D	D	NA	NA	NA	NA	12	80	2.2	0.6
DeKalb	9	D	D	D	NA	NA	NA	NA	13	118	5.2	1.3
Dent	13	D	D	D	19	654	246.6	25.1	20	286	10.8	3.1
Douglas	9	D	D	D	15	D	D	D	13	211	7.7	2.1
Dunklin	40	107	8.7	2.2	18	626	D	D	59	739	24.9	6.5
Franklin	195	D	D	D	227	9 233	2 432.1	350.1	184	3 096	109.3	32.7
Gasconade	36	137	7.0	2.2	42	1 413	172.4	45.2	44	445	13.5	4.2
Gentry	7	D	D	D	NA	NA	NA	NA	13	112	2.0	0.6
Greene	792	D	D	D	330	14 842	3 845.4	560.0	663	14 922	578.3	170.4
Grundy	13	D	D	D	9	649	D	24.9	16	174	6.2	1.8
Harrison	11	D	D	D	NA	NA	NA	NA	19	269	11.0	2.8
Henry	40	127	9.5	2.5	34	1 426	566.6	49.7	61	718	25.0	6.8
Hickory	9	D	D	D	NA	NA	NA	NA	14	45	1.6	0.4
Holt	2	D	D	D	NA	NA	NA	NA	18	140	4.0	1.0
Howard	12	D	D	D	NA	NA	NA	NA	15	157	3.4	1.0
Howell	59	325	21.7	8.9	82	3 113	682.1	85.3	71	1 251	47.6	13.3
Iron	11	D	D	D	NA	NA	NA	NA	18	168	5.3	1.5
Jackson	2 115	D	D	D	721	29 100	8 939.0	1 337.1	1 431	29 957	1 505.8	416.6

1. Establishment subject to federal tax.

Table B. States and Counties — Health Care and Social Assistance, Other Services, and Federal Funds

STATE County	Health care and social assistance, 2007				Other services, 2007				Federal funds and grants, 2009–2010 Expenditures (mil dol)			
										Direct payments for individuals[1]		
	Number of establishments	Number of employees	Receipts (mil dol)	Annual payroll (mil dol)	Number of establishments	Number of employees	Receipts (mil dol)	Annual payroll (mil dol)	Total	Social Security and government retirement	Medicare	Food Stamps and Supplemental Security Income
	159	160	161	162	163	164	165	166	167	168	169	170
MISSISSIPPI—Cont'd												
Sunflower	44	1 198	83.5	33.4	33	176	19.6	3.9	326.9	59.6	56.9	32.2
Tallahatchie	17	353	21.6	9.3	11	31	2.5	0.7	176.8	34.0	29.4	12.2
Tate	35	525	43.8	16.2	23	148	10.2	3.2	218.2	80.1	35.0	9.4
Tippah	32	603	37.6	16.6	14	45	2.5	0.9	194.1	77.7	46.3	9.7
Tishomingo	29	581	44.2	15.6	29	110	13.2	2.0	189.9	86.4	42.4	6.4
Tunica	16	192	11.7	4.4	9	D	D	D	107.4	25.0	14.7	8.4
Union	47	977	90.9	30.7	23	99	7.6	2.3	176.4	80.8	39.0	8.3
Walthall	24	403	24.2	9.9	14	41	2.5	0.6	133.6	40.0	29.2	9.8
Warren	104	3 313	385.9	149.9	74	342	22.1	6.2	914.3	177.5	101.5	28.1
Washington	161	2 889	236.1	95.3	94	477	51.0	10.8	695.6	154.0	105.3	69.4
Wayne	27	646	41.6	20.9	23	73	4.4	1.5	142.5	51.7	27.0	13.9
Webster	11	412	35.5	12.4	11	26	1.9	0.6	98.5	37.5	20.6	6.1
Wilkinson	15	374	27.0	11.7	8	33	5.2	0.6	89.1	25.6	18.3	9.1
Winston	33	577	41.6	15.2	21	65	5.7	1.1	170.6	60.4	32.8	11.9
Yalobusha	17	317	17.1	7.7	9	15	1.2	0.3	148.0	58.9	34.7	8.5
Yazoo	48	617	55.9	21.9	29	83	5.8	1.6	339.0	69.1	55.4	25.0
MISSOURI	15 984	362 340	32 886.6	12 918.6	11 111	67 476	6 770.7	1 799.9	70 348.1	18 407.8	9 846.3	2 174.6
Adair	105	D	D	D	72	D	D	D	198.3	60.0	45.9	8.3
Andrew	21	D	D	D	19	D	D	D	113.3	40.5	19.9	3.3
Atchison	18	D	D	D	20	34	3.0	0.5	59.3	23.3	14.0	1.9
Audrain	83	1 602	112.6	47.8	46	227	18.1	5.5	204.1	79.2	60.3	8.0
Barry	77	1 193	74.3	28.8	60	192	13.5	3.4	279.3	131.0	60.2	12.5
Barton	30	525	26.3	11.0	19	46	4.1	0.8	96.6	38.1	23.2	4.5
Bates	39	725	49.6	18.9	22	D	D	D	137.8	57.6	34.5	6.7
Benton	32	262	15.0	6.0	37	90	6.3	1.4	192.3	104.2	43.3	7.2
Bollinger	20	D	D	D	16	D	D	D	107.0	38.0	19.2	5.7
Boone	562	15 933	1 695.8	615.7	323	D	D	D	1 173.4	360.3	160.1	43.8
Buchanan	288	7 250	708.8	284.3	195	1 259	108.1	37.6	718.2	283.2	173.5	41.1
Butler	218	3 809	413.0	129.8	78	310	22.4	5.7	513.5	165.9	87.3	29.3
Caldwell	12	88	5.1	2.1	13	D	D	D	72.6	32.8	18.1	2.6
Callaway	76	2 348	134.5	65.4	66	300	22.3	6.3	436.7	125.5	60.0	12.0
Camden	120	1 950	227.0	78.6	114	384	31.8	7.6	281.5	161.9	67.2	9.1
Cape Girardeau	279	9 550	972.9	354.9	162	D	D	D	542.0	221.3	87.6	22.9
Carroll	24	440	23.0	8.9	19	43	4.3	1.2	106.1	35.0	24.7	3.8
Carter	27	173	5.4	2.5	7	34	3.2	0.6	69.3	26.5	12.1	4.6
Cass	127	2 842	187.5	76.7	130	548	36.7	11.6	590.5	281.2	95.3	15.1
Cedar	44	674	32.5	15.0	19	34	2.2	0.6	140.1	59.8	31.8	5.8
Charlton	14	198	7.0	3.0	14	32	4.5	1.0	83.6	27.9	20.7	2.0
Christian	110	1 174	59.8	24.8	109	415	28.9	7.8	353.3	216.5	50.9	12.5
Clark	11	D	D	D	14	48	4.6	0.6	63.8	24.0	13.9	2.3
Clay	515	11 678	1 189.7	480.0	362	2 009	162.9	50.6	932.1	414.1	249.6	21.5
Clinton	56	956	70.2	27.6	28	98	6.6	1.9	146.3	69.4	32.9	5.3
Cole	244	5 943	612.2	230.3	238	1 584	169.1	49.2	3 231.6	230.9	106.5	15.8
Cooper	56	652	39.0	14.9	24	88	6.8	1.6	128.5	52.3	30.8	3.9
Crawford	66	896	64.6	24.2	30	120	9.6	2.3	159.6	71.8	38.0	11.1
Dade	14	67	3.4	1.4	11	D	D	D	73.4	30.4	16.6	3.0
Dallas	26	1 112	24.3	12.8	18	60	2.9	0.7	125.1	53.6	25.4	7.0
Daviess	16	109	5.6	2.1	11	41	3.8	1.2	64.1	25.1	15.1	2.1
DeKalb	34	D	D	D	13	54	4.4	1.3	57.0	26.6	12.6	2.3
Dent	51	716	35.7	14.7	21	53	3.8	0.9	171.8	58.2	33.1	10.8
Douglas	18	211	10.0	4.4	14	43	4.4	1.0	111.5	40.1	21.2	5.7
Dunklin	122	2 179	111.2	43.4	54	152	10.5	2.7	460.2	111.6	81.1	33.0
Franklin	216	3 558	281.7	103.4	183	796	59.8	17.4	624.2	329.5	133.8	25.5
Gasconade	41	587	33.8	14.9	28	85	7.4	1.7	118.9	60.2	31.6	3.1
Gentry	31	675	32.5	13.8	11	D	D	D	86.5	27.7	21.5	1.4
Greene	719	D	D	D	632	4 597	412.5	120.8	1 963.7	845.0	342.6	88.9
Grundy	28	610	46.6	15.1	27	64	5.0	1.3	108.0	37.3	24.5	4.0
Harrison	21	527	26.0	10.9	20	D	D	D	95.5	33.1	24.5	2.8
Henry	51	1 376	117.0	43.9	44	153	9.4	2.9	212.7	97.7	52.7	9.2
Hickory	7	111	5.3	2.4	5	D	D	D	92.8	46.2	24.0	3.8
Holt	12	D	D	D	7	8	1.1	0.2	68.0	21.7	14.0	1.5
Howard	31	377	14.2	6.7	11	D	D	D	99.0	29.2	24.1	3.4
Howell	157	3 094	233.5	89.4	72	283	21.7	4.9	364.3	153.4	67.4	17.5
Iron	105	545	30.9	10.0	36	55	3.5	0.7	113.5	42.6	25.0	7.1
Jackson	1 741	46 973	4 847.2	1 977.2	1 413	9 953	1 641.9	295.1	8 910.3	2 357.9	1 298.3	238.9

1. State totals may include programs not allocated by county.

STATE County	Federal funds and grants, 2009–2010 (cont.)							Value of residential construction authorized by building permits, 2010		Local government finances, 2007				
	Expenditures (mil dol) (cont.)									General revenue				
	Procurement contract awards			Grants[1]								Taxes		
													Per capita[2] (dollars)	
	Salaries and wages	Defense	Other	Medicaid and other health-related	Nutrition and family welfare	Education	Other	New construction ($1,000)	Number of housing units	Total (mil dol)	Inter-govern-mental (mil dol)	Total (mil dol)	Total	Property
	171	172	173	174	175	176	177	178	179	180	181	182	183	184
MISSISSIPPI—Cont'd														
Sunflower	20.4	0.0	1.0	78.2	12.7	2.9	3.4	850	8	115.9	60.2	19.9	643	614
Tallahatchie	4.0	16.0	0.6	54.6	4.6	1.5	2.1	50	1	41.4	25.2	8.3	629	590
Tate	17.6	0.6	1.6	39.5	4.7	1.3	0.2	6 186	66	111.2	57.3	24.9	927	884
Tippah	5.4	0.0	1.2	45.4	3.7	1.1	0.7	1 770	8	55.4	29.5	9.5	448	413
Tishomingo	5.8	9.0	1.1	33.5	3.2	0.6	0.5	92	1	42.8	28.9	8.6	452	403
Tunica	2.0	0.4	0.4	28.9	2.9	1.2	0.9	884	11	79.1	55.5	20.0	1 915	1 291
Union	6.1	0.0	1.1	34.2	3.6	1.4	0.0	895	2	55.7	35.9	13.1	488	468
Walthall	11.3	0.0	0.4	37.1	3.7	0.9	0.0	180	1	43.5	21.9	8.0	521	503
Warren	143.5	358.9	16.1	64.2	9.1	4.0	2.0	0	0	147.5	69.4	57.8	1 183	958
Washington	46.8	1.1	44.2	179.8	24.8	6.4	16.4	1 125	14	253.0	94.6	51.7	930	845
Wayne	4.5	0.0	0.7	37.2	4.7	1.0	0.6	325	2	75.1	33.5	10.9	516	497
Webster	4.3	1.9	0.5	21.8	2.1	0.5	0.5	280	2	21.2	13.6	5.1	522	510
Wilkinson	0.7	0.0	0.2	30.8	2.7	0.7	0.1	100	1	35.5	13.0	5.5	537	523
Winston	12.1	0.0	0.6	44.3	4.3	1.1	1.2	0	0	58.8	23.3	9.2	468	446
Yalobusha	5.2	0.4	0.8	32.2	2.7	0.9	1.1	274	9	40.3	19.0	7.6	555	536
Yazoo	39.8	25.0	8.8	73.5	6.7	1.9	2.1	134	2	60.9	35.9	18.5	680	657
MISSOURI	7 320.6	10 334.5	2 667.9	7 868.9	1 212.9	936.2	3 984.6	1 430 225	9 699	X	X	X	X	X
Adair	10.5	7.6	1.1	46.2	4.7	2.4	1.1	3 921	17	75.6	21.4	42.0	1 706	1 275
Andrew	15.1	0.1	0.7	10.9	1.9	0.4	15.1	835	6	30.5	14.7	9.5	561	435
Atchison	2.6	0.0	0.5	6.7	1.0	0.2	0.9	100	1	16.9	6.5	7.9	1 298	960
Audrain	7.5	0.0	1.3	24.8	3.3	1.7	5.6	797	8	76.3	30.2	31.2	1 203	820
Barry	14.8	0.6	2.4	47.0	5.1	2.7	1.5	2 467	22	81.5	37.6	27.9	772	531
Barton	4.9	0.0	0.7	11.9	1.7	1.2	0.0	1 511	7	37.9	18.2	10.5	822	552
Bates	4.4	0.0	0.9	22.8	2.5	0.9	0.5	2 928	22	38.7	16.8	12.5	734	526
Benton	5.9	5.0	1.2	20.0	2.4	1.0	0.1	65	1	42.2	18.8	14.7	796	587
Bollinger	2.6	0.0	0.6	36.5	1.8	0.8	0.0	75	1	18.2	10.5	5.8	479	351
Boone	111.1	7.6	49.2	180.0	18.9	28.1	138.8	97 917	607	447.0	137.4	201.6	1 323	773
Buchanan	34.6	14.8	8.7	115.7	9.2	6.1	9.4	16 196	118	268.8	89.1	113.3	1 310	843
Butler	33.6	0.1	13.8	140.3	6.9	4.0	10.1	1 425	24	112.3	43.1	38.1	921	469
Caldwell	3.1	0.0	0.8	8.5	1.2	0.6	0.9	3 343	17	23.3	12.5	6.7	726	524
Callaway	180.9	0.3	5.3	35.2	4.0	1.7	2.9	6 779	43	79.0	28.5	32.3	744	527
Camden	6.6	0.4	1.5	25.3	3.9	2.2	2.4	7 964	85	115.6	35.5	53.8	1 330	854
Cape Girardeau	55.5	9.1	8.4	68.5	7.0	5.0	29.0	12 734	98	165.0	58.5	79.8	1 097	578
Carroll	5.2	0.0	7.2	14.2	1.7	1.0	0.8	2 065	14	23.9	12.4	7.9	804	638
Carter	4.2	0.0	2.6	16.6	1.6	0.5	0.4	400	2	13.4	8.3	3.2	538	425
Cass	120.0	4.0	3.6	24.8	7.3	5.2	25.7	36 810	186	344.0	111.2	120.8	1 244	827
Cedar	3.7	8.0	0.8	26.1	1.7	0.7	0.3	455	8	49.3	15.8	14.0	1 019	718
Chariton	3.7	0.0	0.9	16.1	1.1	0.6	0.6	0	0	15.7	6.3	6.3	798	615
Christian	11.7	0.0	3.0	30.4	5.3	4.1	5.7	51 917	286	156.0	65.3	59.7	816	539
Clark	2.9	4.0	0.7	6.7	1.1	0.6	0.2	870	9	21.8	6.4	9.8	1 352	987
Clay	74.3	34.6	40.3	56.7	14.8	8.4	5.9	26 218	141	1 143.2	169.2	318.9	1 505	1 062
Clinton	5.7	0.0	1.3	19.0	2.1	1.0	5.6	4 248	21	46.4	21.0	18.3	875	689
Cole	27.3	9.9	13.0	183.5	243.8	403.7	1 966.9	29 022	178	171.4	50.1	91.5	1 241	748
Cooper	6.2	0.0	0.9	24.2	2.0	1.0	0.1	6 200	42	50.8	15.0	15.9	906	588
Crawford	3.6	0.0	0.9	29.0	3.1	1.5	0.1	503	10	52.2	20.0	14.7	611	407
Dade	2.7	0.0	0.6	14.7	1.4	1.7	0.0	80	2	22.8	8.6	5.4	711	529
Dallas	3.0	0.0	0.7	32.2	2.1	0.9	0.0	0	0	24.1	13.9	7.6	453	291
Daviess	3.3	1.1	0.7	9.5	1.5	0.8	0.4	345	3	19.9	10.2	6.9	870	659
DeKalb	2.4	0.0	0.5	4.3	1.2	0.9	1.9	0	0	17.1	7.5	6.3	515	368
Dent	4.5	17.7	1.0	42.2	2.5	1.2	0.2	145	1	52.1	15.3	8.9	592	405
Douglas	3.8	0.0	0.7	36.1	2.1	1.1	0.2	89	1	19.7	10.5	6.2	466	327
Dunklin	9.7	1.9	2.8	165.0	8.6	3.6	4.6	488	3	71.6	38.4	23.8	752	488
Franklin	39.4	1.1	5.6	59.4	9.8	5.5	1.1	28 522	184	230.2	83.6	110.8	1 107	744
Gasconade	3.9	0.0	0.9	15.2	1.8	1.0	0.1	263	2	53.0	15.1	17.8	1 157	797
Gentry	11.9	0.0	0.7	13.3	1.3	0.7	0.1	624	4	16.7	8.0	6.1	969	758
Greene	235.9	8.7	42.1	226.3	37.2	15.1	37.3	106 905	1 004	757.8	210.2	340.5	1 290	684
Grundy	7.2	0.0	0.8	16.7	3.2	1.3	2.4	160	1	45.9	22.6	8.3	824	604
Harrison	6.3	0.0	1.1	14.2	1.6	1.2	1.0	0	0	35.9	10.3	8.4	948	656
Henry	9.3	2.4	1.5	30.1	2.8	1.4	1.4	4 505	54	110.8	26.0	21.6	966	542
Hickory	2.2	1.3	0.4	11.9	1.7	0.9	0.1	NA	NA	21.7	12.7	6.4	696	536
Holt	2.9	0.0	1.0	8.1	0.8	0.2	0.2	270	3	13.4	5.6	5.9	1 185	896
Howard	2.8	1.3	0.6	22.3	1.3	0.9	5.3	95	0	20.8	9.2	7.4	751	485
Howell	18.7	0.0	2.3	79.0	10.7	2.9	4.3	3 285	73	92.0	44.9	28.7	744	408
Iron	1.9	0.0	0.5	32.2	2.2	1.8	0.0	150	1	27.0	14.4	9.8	983	814
Jackson	1 254.4	953.5	1 452.8	770.7	103.5	60.1	213.6	106 794	670	3 265.6	849.9	1 543.8	2 315	1 115

1. State totals may include programs not allocated by county.   2. Based on the resident population estimated as of July 1 of the year shown.

STATE County	Total (mil dol)	Per capita[1] (dollars)	Educa-tion	Health and hospitals	Police protec-tion	Public welfare	High-ways	Total (mil dol)	Per capita[1] (dollars)	Federal civilian	Federal military	State and local	Demo-cratic	Republi-can	All other
	185	186	187	188	189	190	191	192	193	194	195	196	197	198	199
MISSISSIPPI—Cont'd															
Sunflower	108.5	3 504	59.3	18.3	3.8	0.2	4.5	33.4	1 079	62	180	3 781	70.0	29.0	1.0
Tallahatchie	41.1	3 098	54.3	11.8	5.3	0.4	6.2	4.1	309	40	77	883	59.1	40.1	0.7
Tate	112.1	4 166	78.9	0.6	3.0	0.0	4.6	62.6	2 326	89	166	1 756	39.2	60.1	0.8
Tippah	57.4	2 713	54.7	23.6	3.4	0.3	6.0	7.9	373	55	132	1 131	27.0	71.3	1.7
Tishomingo	46.8	2 456	58.2	1.4	4.4	0.0	10.3	11.5	601	70	116	851	23.3	74.2	2.5
Tunica	75.1	7 180	30.6	2.9	8.4	0.7	10.8	51.4	4 916	22	63	970	75.7	23.5	0.8
Union	55.6	2 065	64.1	1.3	4.6	0.2	7.9	29.0	1 078	60	166	1 220	24.5	74.4	1.1
Walthall	41.8	2 722	48.6	25.8	4.0	0.1	7.1	4.6	296	27	93	754	44.4	54.7	0.9
Warren	139.2	2 848	50.3	2.4	7.8	0.5	7.4	122.5	2 507	2 017	333	2 629	48.2	51.2	0.6
Washington	250.3	4 499	35.6	37.6	4.0	0.2	4.2	100.4	1 805	524	353	4 214	67.1	32.4	0.5
Wayne	65.1	3 084	44.9	33.4	2.9	0.1	4.7	19.5	924	43	126	1 171	38.8	60.6	0.6
Webster	20.9	2 135	62.8	1.3	6.0	0.3	10.0	6.9	703	37	60	434	24.7	74.6	0.7
Wilkinson	34.7	3 382	37.5	40.5	3.8	0.2	5.6	5.5	536	0	62	606	68.8	30.4	0.9
Winston	41.1	2 085	56.2	1.4	6.1	0.1	9.0	12.0	611	41	117	788	45.5	53.8	0.7
Yalobusha	39.9	2 916	39.5	25.3	5.9	0.0	5.3	16.8	1 225	83	84	795	46.2	53.1	0.7
Yazoo	59.5	2 189	61.0	1.2	6.5	0.3	8.3	31.6	1 164	594	170	1 510	53.3	46.1	0.6
MISSOURI	X	X	X	X	X	X	X	X	X	60 996	42 079	396 068	49.3	49.4	1.3
Adair	86.7	3 517	68.5	1.7	2.9	0.4	4.3	32.1	1 302	84	105	2 541	48.3	49.6	2.1
Andrew	37.2	2 207	61.2	3.1	2.3	0.3	3.2	41.6	2 470	41	70	737	38.1	60.1	1.9
Atchison	17.2	2 823	53.7	6.4	3.3	0.0	21.2	2.2	355	35	25	387	33.6	65.1	1.3
Audrain	78.5	3 033	64.1	1.0	5.3	5.1	6.5	37.6	1 454	89	105	2 668	41.1	57.2	1.7
Barry	91.2	2 519	68.8	0.9	4.4	0.0	6.9	66.9	1 848	118	148	1 677	31.6	66.6	1.7
Barton	43.1	3 385	38.3	43.7	3.1	0.0	4.9	29.3	2 305	37	51	864	24.5	74.2	1.3
Bates	42.6	2 501	62.2	1.1	4.0	6.3	7.0	59.9	3 516	66	69	1 179	39.5	58.3	2.2
Benton	42.2	2 283	56.6	3.3	4.5	11.7	3.8	36.5	1 974	105	76	955	37.9	60.2	1.9
Bollinger	19.1	1 573	75.7	1.1	4.9	0.0	8.5	4.9	406	33	48	463	29.2	68.7	2.1
Boone	473.4	3 105	47.7	2.2	4.3	1.6	7.0	527.9	3 463	2 194	679	28 504	55.2	43.2	1.6
Buchanan	260.0	3 007	45.5	1.4	5.0	0.1	6.4	452.4	5 231	507	384	6 548	49.1	48.9	2.0
Butler	102.2	2 472	64.3	0.0	4.5	0.0	5.4	57.1	1 381	683	171	2 914	30.7	68.1	1.3
Caldwell	22.6	2 435	71.8	1.8	2.6	3.5	6.8	13.8	1 486	40	37	627	39.7	58.2	2.1
Callaway	89.8	2 069	54.1	3.5	3.9	0.0	5.7	75.2	1 731	260	209	4 300	39.2	58.9	1.8
Camden	123.6	3 053	50.9	5.7	4.0	0.0	7.9	94.4	2 333	71	167	1 869	35.1	63.6	1.3
Cape Girardeau	178.6	2 456	62.1	1.4	4.2	0.0	7.5	175.1	2 407	427	305	6 182	32.7	66.3	1.0
Carroll	28.1	2 855	58.7	3.7	2.7	0.0	10.1	3.9	394	54	39	592	33.8	65.1	1.1
Carter	13.8	2 329	83.2	2.3	1.4	0.0	3.9	5.8	979	89	24	369	34.0	63.5	2.6
Cass	333.1	3 429	56.5	9.5	5.8	0.0	6.4	418.2	4 805	254	583	4 682	39.5	59.2	1.3
Cedar	46.3	3 372	38.9	12.8	3.1	0.0	30.5	28.6	2 084	65	55	832	32.4	66.0	1.6
Chariton	16.8	2 138	63.2	3.3	4.9	0.0	10.6	5.7	723	53	31	451	42.7	55.5	1.8
Christian	165.1	2 259	64.0	0.9	4.9	1.0	6.4	230.8	3 158	130	317	2 740	31.5	67.3	1.1
Clark	21.5	2 972	59.5	2.3	2.4	14.9	7.4	6.2	857	37	29	475	45.5	51.6	3.0
Clay	1 144.5	5 400	34.7	43.4	1.9	0.0	1.7	875.4	4 130	537	1 244	13 889	49.0	49.7	1.2
Clinton	48.9	2 339	68.7	1.7	5.6	0.0	6.2	43.0	2 058	72	86	1 410	43.5	54.6	1.9
Cole	168.9	2 292	53.4	1.4	8.1	0.0	7.6	190.8	2 589	542	307	21 663	36.0	62.9	1.0
Cooper	58.8	3 350	40.9	20.9	3.3	4.1	5.5	47.4	2 704	52	71	1 306	37.3	61.1	1.6
Crawford	58.6	2 433	66.9	4.7	4.4	0.0	6.2	34.4	1 428	38	98	951	38.8	59.6	1.7
Dade	19.2	2 558	55.7	1.2	2.0	13.2	14.2	7.0	927	35	30	575	28.8	69.6	1.6
Dallas	25.6	1 523	62.4	4.9	10.4	0.0	7.3	1.4	81	41	68	613	34.6	63.7	1.7
Daviess	20.0	2 518	67.9	2.3	3.2	0.1	11.4	7.6	959	43	33	503	37.0	59.8	3.2
DeKalb	18.1	1 477	66.1	2.6	2.6	0.0	6.6	10.0	820	35	50	1 267	36.1	61.7	2.2
Dent	43.8	2 906	46.7	32.1	3.8	0.0	4.3	3.3	219	63	62	865	29.9	67.8	2.3
Douglas	20.5	1 532	70.8	1.8	3.8	0.0	3.9	20.7	1 545	58	56	459	31.9	65.6	2.5
Dunklin	74.0	2 340	68.1	2.1	3.5	0.0	5.8	25.4	803	102	127	1 771	38.6	59.9	1.5
Franklin	250.2	2 501	60.9	3.1	5.6	0.1	8.0	238.9	2 388	242	416	4 512	43.1	55.5	1.4
Gasconade	65.5	4 256	56.2	21.3	2.6	1.0	5.4	72.7	4 723	53	62	1 052	37.3	61.3	1.4
Gentry	18.3	2 933	63.0	3.9	2.1	0.0	11.1	5.3	847	44	25	459	37.5	59.7	2.8
Greene	729.1	2 762	49.1	1.4	9.9	0.5	11.5	1 086.4	4 115	2 323	1 132	18 058	41.4	57.2	1.3
Grundy	41.9	4 155	70.1	3.4	2.7	6.1	3.0	26.8	2 655	57	41	1 018	33.3	63.4	3.2
Harrison	37.0	4 170	38.4	34.2	2.0	0.1	8.1	15.5	1 745	56	36	754	32.9	64.2	3.0
Henry	115.9	5 173	36.6	41.5	3.7	0.1	4.1	53.2	2 376	88	91	1 625	43.6	54.6	1.7
Hickory	23.6	2 588	77.9	1.6	2.1	0.0	5.4	17.3	1 892	45	36	305	42.4	55.7	1.8
Holt	14.1	2 835	51.0	2.8	1.7	0.3	17.6	4.1	831	46	20	324	30.5	68.1	1.4
Howard	21.7	2 192	57.8	2.9	4.1	0.0	8.7	15.4	1 555	42	40	477	41.9	55.8	2.3
Howell	94.1	2 435	67.1	2.6	4.8	0.0	4.0	30.0	777	100	160	2 171	33.7	64.5	1.8
Iron	26.9	2 690	74.3	1.3	4.1	0.0	7.4	13.5	1 346	20	41	647	50.1	47.3	2.5
Jackson	3 351.0	5 025	37.3	2.8	8.2	0.2	4.4	5 888.0	8 829	17 988	3 021	47 617	62.1	36.8	1.1

1. Based on the resident population estimated as of July 1 of the year shown.   2. © 2009 Election Data Services, Inc. All rights reserved.

Table B. States and Counties — Land Area and Population

STATE/ County code	CBSA code[1]	County type[2]	STATE County	Land area,[3] (sq km) 2010	Total persons	Rank	Per square kilometer	White	Black	American Indian, Alaska Native	Asian and Pacific Islander	Percent Hispanic or Latino[4]	Under 5 years	5 to 17 years	18 to 24 years	25 to 34 years	35 to 44 years	45 to 54 years
				1	2	3	4	5	6	7	8	9	10	11	12	13	14	15
			MISSOURI—Cont'd															
29 097	27900	3	Jasper	1 654	117 404	508	71.0	88.6	2.7	2.9	1.6	6.8	7.6	18.2	10.4	13.7	12.3	13.4
29 099	41180	1	Jefferson	1 701	218 733	286	128.6	96.6	1.2	0.8	1.0	1.6	6.8	18.3	8.3	13.0	13.8	16.5
29 101	47660	4	Johnson	2 148	52 595	939	24.5	90.3	5.2	1.3	2.5	3.1	6.8	16.1	19.9	13.1	10.9	12.8
29 103	...	9	Knox	1 305	4 131	2 896	3.2	98.5	0.5	0.7	0.5	0.8	6.4	18.6	6.4	9.3	10.7	15.8
29 105	30060	6	Laclede	1 981	35 571	1 286	18.0	96.1	1.1	1.6	0.9	2.0	7.1	17.9	8.0	11.9	12.3	14.9
29 107	28140	1	Lafayette	1 628	33 381	1 340	20.5	94.6	2.9	1.2	0.8	2.2	6.3	18.3	7.9	11.0	12.3	15.5
29 109	...	6	Lawrence	1 584	38 634	1 203	24.4	92.3	0.5	1.7	0.5	6.3	6.9	19.4	7.4	11.3	12.5	14.3
29 111	39500	9	Lewis	1 308	10 211	2 427	7.8	94.7	3.8	0.7	0.5	1.6	6.4	17.1	12.0	10.6	11.2	14.7
29 113	41180	1	Lincoln	1 623	52 566	941	32.4	95.4	2.6	1.0	0.7	2.0	7.7	20.3	8.1	13.2	13.3	15.8
29 115	...	7	Linn	1 594	12 761	2 260	8.0	97.3	1.3	0.5	0.3	1.5	6.7	18.0	6.7	10.4	11.1	15.0
29 117	...	6	Livingston	1 379	15 195	2 100	11.0	95.8	3.0	0.6	0.5	1.2	6.0	15.9	7.7	12.6	12.7	14.1
29 119	22220	2	McDonald	1 397	23 083	1 685	16.5	83.6	0.9	4.7	2.3	11.2	7.3	20.7	8.4	11.9	13.1	14.7
29 121	...	7	Macon	2 075	15 566	2 077	7.5	96.1	3.0	0.8	0.6	1.0	6.8	17.5	7.0	10.5	11.4	13.9
29 123	...	7	Madison	1 280	12 226	2 291	9.6	97.1	0.4	0.7	0.5	2.0	6.5	17.5	8.5	11.0	11.4	15.0
29 125	...	8	Maries	1 365	9 176	2 512	6.7	98.2	0.4	1.3	0.2	0.8	6.1	17.3	7.5	10.2	11.6	16.0
29 127	25300	5	Marion	1 132	28 781	1 460	25.4	92.8	6.0	0.8	0.8	1.4	6.9	17.1	9.3	12.2	11.8	14.5
29 129	...	9	Mercer	1 175	3 785	2 924	3.2	98.2	0.4	1.0	0.6	0.7	6.9	18.5	6.2	9.2	10.7	15.5
29 131	...	6	Miller	1 535	24 748	1 611	16.1	97.3	0.7	1.3	0.6	1.4	6.5	18.3	7.7	11.3	12.4	15.1
29 133	...	7	Mississippi	1 066	14 358	2 151	13.5	74.0	24.4	0.6	0.2	1.6	6.2	16.0	8.3	13.8	13.5	14.8
29 135	27620	3	Moniteau	1 075	15 607	2 075	14.5	91.7	3.9	1.1	0.6	3.8	6.9	18.2	8.0	13.0	13.6	14.9
29 137	...	9	Monroe	1 677	8 840	2 543	5.3	95.5	3.7	0.7	0.5	1.0	6.1	17.2	7.2	10.0	11.0	15.5
29 139	...	8	Montgomery	1 389	12 236	2 290	8.8	96.4	2.1	1.0	0.4	1.4	6.3	17.0	7.0	10.6	11.2	15.9
29 141	...	8	Morgan	1 548	20 565	1 816	13.3	96.6	0.9	1.6	0.6	1.8	6.1	15.9	7.0	8.8	10.6	14.3
29 143	...	7	New Madrid	1 748	18 956	1 881	10.8	82.4	16.5	0.7	0.6	1.1	6.6	17.2	8.0	11.4	12.4	15.0
29 145	27900	3	Newton	1 618	58 114	877	35.9	90.3	1.2	4.2	2.6	4.4	6.7	18.7	8.8	11.1	12.4	14.6
29 147	32340	6	Nodaway	2 271	23 370	1 672	10.3	94.4	2.7	0.5	1.9	1.3	5.2	13.0	27.4	11.0	9.2	11.4
29 149	...	9	Oregon	2 046	10 881	2 378	5.3	97.2	0.2	2.4	0.5	1.2	5.7	16.6	7.6	8.5	11.1	15.6
29 151	27620	3	Osage	1 565	13 878	2 188	8.9	98.8	0.3	0.4	0.2	0.6	6.4	18.3	9.3	10.9	13.0	15.2
29 153	...	9	Ozark	1 929	9 723	2 459	5.0	97.8	0.3	1.5	0.3	1.3	5.1	15.0	6.2	8.6	10.0	15.3
29 155	...	7	Pemiscot	1 276	18 296	1 910	14.3	70.9	27.5	0.7	0.3	1.9	7.7	19.8	8.8	11.4	11.7	13.9
29 157	...	7	Perry	1 229	18 971	1 880	15.4	97.2	0.6	0.6	0.7	1.7	6.6	18.5	7.8	12.0	12.5	14.6
29 159	42740	4	Pettis	1 767	42 201	1 123	23.9	88.7	3.9	0.9	1.0	7.2	7.5	18.1	9.4	12.7	11.7	14.5
29 161	40620	5	Phelps	1 740	45 156	1 062	26.0	92.2	2.8	1.3	3.6	2.0	6.2	15.5	17.2	12.3	10.6	13.6
29 163	...	6	Pike	1 736	18 516	1 898	10.7	90.3	7.9	0.6	0.5	1.8	6.1	16.1	8.5	13.2	12.6	15.7
29 165	28140	1	Platte	1 088	89 322	633	82.1	86.0	6.6	1.1	3.4	5.0	6.4	18.3	7.8	13.0	14.3	16.4
29 167	44180	2	Polk	1 646	31 137	1 412	18.9	96.3	1.1	1.5	0.6	2.0	6.4	18.2	11.6	10.7	11.5	14.1
29 169	22780	5	Pulaski	1 417	52 274	947	36.9	75.8	12.7	1.8	4.6	9.0	7.5	16.4	22.7	17.1	11.7	10.4
29 171	...	9	Putnam	1 340	4 979	2 842	3.7	98.5	0.3	0.6	0.6	0.7	6.0	17.3	6.1	9.9	10.6	14.4
29 173	25300	9	Ralls	1 217	10 167	2 432	8.4	97.5	1.3	0.6	0.4	1.0	6.3	17.1	5.9	10.7	12.0	16.5
29 175	33620	6	Randolph	1 250	25 414	1 591	20.3	91.8	6.8	0.9	0.7	1.6	6.3	16.9	9.4	13.7	13.2	14.7
29 177	28140	1	Ray	1 473	23 494	1 667	15.9	96.2	1.6	1.0	0.5	1.8	6.2	18.7	7.5	10.6	13.0	16.4
29 179	...	9	Reynolds	2 094	6 696	2 713	3.2	97.6	0.9	1.8	0.3	1.0	5.9	17.0	6.4	9.1	12.1	15.3
29 181	...	9	Ripley	1 630	14 100	2 166	8.7	97.4	0.5	1.8	0.5	1.0	5.9	17.6	7.8	10.6	11.8	14.6
29 183	41180	1	St. Charles	1 452	360 485	181	248.3	90.5	4.8	0.6	2.7	2.8	6.7	19.0	8.6	13.2	14.0	15.9
29 185	...	8	St. Clair	1 735	9 805	2 454	5.7	97.0	0.8	1.6	0.3	1.7	5.0	15.0	6.5	8.4	10.8	15.6
29 186	...	6	Ste. Genevieve	1 293	18 145	1 917	14.0	97.9	1.0	0.8	0.4	0.8	5.6	17.6	7.4	10.5	11.9	17.0
29 187	22100	4	St. Francois	1 170	65 359	802	55.9	93.8	4.6	0.9	0.6	1.2	6.1	15.9	9.4	14.3	13.2	15.2
29 189	41180	1	St. Louis	1 315	998 954	40	759.7	70.3	24.1	0.6	4.1	2.5	5.9	17.6	8.7	12.2	12.3	15.6
29 195	32180	6	Saline	1 957	23 370	1 672	11.9	85.0	6.3	0.8	1.5	8.2	6.4	16.6	11.7	11.7	11.1	14.1
29 197	28860	9	Schuyler	796	4 431	2 875	5.6	98.9	0.3	0.5	0.4	0.7	6.6	19.1	7.8	9.4	11.3	14.3
29 199	...	9	Scotland	1 131	4 843	2 853	4.3	98.4	0.2	0.5	0.3	0.7	7.9	20.2	7.7	10.2	10.6	13.7
29 201	43460	5	Scott	1 088	39 191	1 190	36.0	86.2	12.1	0.8	0.5	1.8	7.0	18.1	8.3	11.9	12.5	14.6
29 203	...	9	Shannon	2 600	8 441	2 574	3.2	97.1	0.3	2.7	0.3	1.6	6.1	17.3	8.0	9.6	11.1	16.1
29 205	...	9	Shelby	1 297	6 373	2 737	4.9	98.0	0.9	0.4	0.4	1.1	6.9	18.1	6.2	11.4	9.9	14.9
29 207	...	7	Stoddard	2 132	29 968	1 428	14.1	97.4	1.1	0.8	0.3	1.2	6.0	16.8	8.2	11.4	12.2	14.6
29 209	14700	8	Stone	1 202	32 202	1 388	26.8	97.2	0.3	1.4	0.5	1.7	4.4	14.3	5.8	8.0	10.4	15.1
29 211	...	9	Sullivan	1 678	6 714	2 710	4.0	80.3	0.6	0.9	0.3	18.6	6.3	17.9	7.3	11.2	12.7	14.4
29 213	14700	6	Taney	1 638	51 675	955	31.5	92.8	1.2	1.7	1.1	4.8	6.1	16.0	9.8	11.5	11.9	13.7
29 215	...	9	Texas	3 049	26 008	1 564	8.5	94.0	3.7	1.8	0.6	1.6	6.2	15.8	8.4	11.7	11.2	15.4
29 217	...	7	Vernon	2 140	21 159	1 780	9.9	96.7	0.7	1.6	0.7	1.6	6.9	18.0	8.7	11.0	11.4	14.4
29 219	41180	1	Warren	1 110	32 513	1 376	29.3	94.4	2.7	0.9	0.7	2.9	7.1	17.9	7.8	12.0	12.0	16.3
29 221	41180	1	Washington	1 968	25 195	1 598	12.8	96.1	2.5	1.0	0.3	1.0	6.6	17.5	8.2	12.3	13.4	16.1
29 223	...	9	Wayne	1 966	13 521	2 217	6.9	98.0	0.5	1.5	0.4	1.0	5.2	15.5	7.4	9.1	11.5	15.2
29 225	44180	2	Webster	1 535	36 202	1 270	23.6	96.5	1.2	1.5	0.4	1.7	7.5	20.3	7.9	11.4	13.3	15.0
29 227	...	9	Worth	691	2 171	3 038	3.1	97.7	0.6	0.4	0.4	1.1	4.5	15.9	6.9	9.2	9.5	16.3
29 229	...	6	Wright	1 766	18 815	1 885	10.7	97.4	0.6	1.3	0.5	1.3	6.8	19.0	7.8	10.2	11.4	14.7

1. CBSA = Core Based Statistical Area. See Appendix A for explanation. See Appendix B for list of metropolitan areas with component counties.   2. County type code from the Economic Research Service of USDA Rural-Urban Continuum Codes. See Appendix A for definition.   3. Dry land or land partially or temporarily covered by water.   4. May be of any race.

Table B. States and Counties — **Population and Households**

STATE County	55 to 64 years	65 to 74 years	75 years and over	Percent female	Total persons 1990	Total persons 2000	Percent change 1990–2000	Percent change 2000–2010	Births	Deaths	Net migration	Number	Percent change, 2000–2010	Persons per household	Female family householder[1]	One person
	16	17	18	19	20	21	22	23	24	25	26	27	28	29	30	31
MISSOURI—Cont'd																
Jasper	11.0	7.1	6.3	51.2	90 465	104 686	15.7	12.1	16 475	10 152	7 815	45 639	10.2	2.52	12.4	27.4
Jefferson	12.2	6.8	4.4	50.2	171 380	198 099	15.6	10.4	26 291	14 884	10 824	81 700	14.3	2.65	11.3	20.9
Johnson	9.7	6.0	4.7	49.5	42 514	48 258	13.5	9.0	6 816	3 222	1 049	19 311	10.9	2.53	9.2	23.9
Knox	12.7	10.9	9.1	50.8	4 482	4 361	-2.7	-5.3	457	541	-271	1 708	-4.6	2.37	7.5	32.0
Laclede	12.2	9.0	6.7	50.7	27 158	32 513	19.7	9.4	4 507	3 300	1 894	14 081	10.4	2.50	10.4	24.8
Lafayette	12.3	8.6	7.8	50.6	31 107	32 960	6.0	1.3	3 861	3 506	-551	13 022	3.6	2.51	10.4	25.2
Lawrence	12.0	8.7	7.7	50.7	30 236	35 204	16.4	9.7	4 705	3 831	1 797	14 869	9.6	2.56	10.1	25.4
Lewis	11.8	8.6	7.7	49.9	10 233	10 494	2.6	-2.7	1 030	1 040	-655	3 874	-2.1	2.43	8.8	28.3
Lincoln	10.7	6.4	4.5	50.1	28 892	38 944	34.8	35.0	6 389	3 373	11 432	18 906	36.5	2.75	11.2	19.8
Linn	13.1	9.6	9.4	51.9	13 885	13 754	-0.9	-7.2	1 551	1 678	-942	5 299	-7.0	2.38	9.2	30.3
Livingston	12.7	8.5	9.7	55.2	14 592	14 558	-0.2	4.4	1 574	1 796	-18	5 871	2.4	2.36	10.0	29.9
McDonald	11.4	7.8	4.7	49.5	16 938	21 681	28.0	6.5	3 366	1 838	-35	8 404	3.6	2.73	11.2	22.5
Macon	13.5	10.0	9.5	51.1	15 345	15 762	2.7	-1.2	1 774	2 030	-62	6 412	-1.4	2.38	9.5	29.4
Madison	12.4	9.7	8.0	50.9	11 127	11 800	6.0	3.6	1 392	1 471	689	4 898	4.0	2.46	10.5	27.1
Maries	13.3	10.4	7.6	49.5	7 976	8 903	11.6	3.1	916	874	-82	3 705	5.3	2.46	8.0	26.2
Marion	12.6	7.5	8.1	51.9	27 682	28 289	2.2	1.7	3 720	3 215	-211	11 377	2.8	2.41	12.3	28.8
Mercer	12.9	10.3	9.9	49.7	3 723	3 757	0.9	0.7	398	373	-288	1 560	-2.5	2.39	6.9	30.6
Miller	13.0	8.5	7.2	50.2	20 700	23 564	13.8	5.0	2 997	2 503	883	9 917	6.8	2.47	10.4	26.9
Mississippi	12.2	8.8	6.4	46.4	14 442	13 427	-7.0	6.9	1 786	1 624	-274	5 180	-3.8	2.41	18.3	29.5
Moniteau	11.6	7.1	6.7	47.3	12 298	14 827	20.6	5.3	1 948	1 336	-216	5 532	5.2	2.58	9.2	25.5
Monroe	14.4	10.4	8.2	50.0	9 104	9 311	2.3	-5.1	982	1 015	-233	3 638	-0.5	2.39	8.1	28.4
Montgomery	13.3	9.8	8.9	50.0	11 355	12 136	6.9	0.8	1 467	1 497	-337	4 868	1.9	2.43	9.3	27.5
Morgan	15.1	12.9	9.2	50.2	15 574	19 309	24.0	6.5	2 376	2 406	1 342	8 450	7.6	2.40	8.3	27.9
New Madrid	13.3	8.9	7.2	52.0	20 928	19 760	-5.6	-4.1	2 276	2 206	-2 255	7 742	-1.0	2.41	15.3	28.7
Newton	12.5	8.6	6.6	50.4	44 445	52 636	18.4	10.4	6 931	4 957	1 830	22 021	9.3	2.60	10.4	23.0
Nodaway	9.6	6.5	6.6	49.3	21 709	21 912	0.9	6.7	2 172	1 791	-23	8 545	5.0	2.31	6.9	30.2
Oregon	15.1	11.7	8.1	50.4	9 470	10 344	9.2	5.2	1 060	1 228	172	4 527	6.2	2.38	9.1	27.7
Osage	11.8	7.7	7.2	48.0	12 018	13 062	8.7	6.2	1 666	1 148	71	5 328	8.2	2.53	7.0	26.0
Ozark	16.4	14.1	9.3	49.5	8 598	9 542	11.0	1.9	964	1 171	21	4 194	6.2	2.29	7.4	27.8
Pemiscot	11.9	7.8	6.9	52.5	21 921	20 047	-8.5	-8.7	2 964	2 173	-2 564	7 350	-6.4	2.46	20.1	30.1
Perry	12.4	7.8	7.8	50.1	16 648	18 132	8.9	4.6	2 322	1 709	213	7 357	6.6	2.54	8.6	25.1
Pettis	11.4	7.4	7.3	50.8	35 437	39 403	11.2	7.1	5 601	3 800	489	16 428	5.5	2.52	11.3	27.4
Phelps	11.0	7.3	6.3	47.7	35 248	39 825	13.0	13.4	4 968	3 870	1 539	17 564	12.0	2.40	10.3	28.9
Pike	12.3	8.7	6.9	45.2	15 969	18 351	14.9	0.9	2 073	1 860	-53	6 560	1.7	2.49	10.7	27.1
Platte	12.7	6.5	4.6	50.8	57 867	73 781	27.5	21.1	9 894	4 693	9 146	36 103	23.3	2.45	9.7	27.0
Polk	11.4	8.5	7.6	50.7	21 826	26 992	23.7	15.4	3 572	2 824	3 043	11 677	17.7	2.54	9.3	24.7
Pulaski	7.0	4.2	3.0	44.1	41 307	41 165	-0.3	27.0	6 269	2 586	1 657	16 004	19.1	2.64	10.9	24.2
Putnam	14.1	11.9	9.7	50.3	5 079	5 223	2.8	-4.7	542	677	-302	2 132	-4.3	2.31	6.9	30.3
Ralls	15.1	10.5	6.0	49.4	8 476	9 626	13.6	5.6	971	807	-104	4 091	9.5	2.47	6.9	23.1
Randolph	11.7	7.4	6.8	47.7	24 370	24 663	1.2	3.0	3 188	2 561	339	9 342	1.6	2.40	12.8	27.7
Ray	12.7	8.7	6.1	50.2	21 968	23 354	6.3	0.6	2 697	2 146	-408	8 957	2.4	2.59	9.4	22.8
Reynolds	14.2	12.0	8.1	49.0	6 661	6 689	0.4	0.1	691	748	-307	2 778	2.1	2.37	8.4	27.8
Ripley	13.0	10.8	7.9	50.5	12 303	13 509	9.8	4.4	1 618	1 687	12	5 637	4.1	2.49	11.3	25.8
St. Charles	11.3	6.4	4.8	50.9	212 751	283 883	33.4	27.0	41 862	17 611	48 658	134 274	32.1	2.64	9.8	22.0
St. Clair	15.3	13.4	10.0	49.5	8 457	9 652	14.1	1.6	869	1 260	72	4 161	3.0	2.31	8.3	29.7
Ste. Genevieve	13.8	8.6	7.4	49.5	16 037	17 842	11.3	1.7	1 773	1 534	-459	7 040	6.9	2.54	8.1	23.4
St. Francois	11.5	7.9	6.5	46.8	48 904	55 641	13.8	17.5	7 171	6 470	7 881	23 981	15.3	2.45	12.4	27.5
St. Louis	12.9	7.4	7.5	52.7	993 508	1 016 315	2.3	-1.7	113 502	87 455	-43 946	404 765	0.1	2.42	14.2	29.5
Saline	12.5	7.9	7.9	50.5	23 523	23 756	1.0	-1.6	2 727	2 578	-963	8 883	-1.5	2.46	11.5	27.9
Schuyler	11.9	10.7	8.9	51.4	4 236	4 170	-1.6	6.3	409	489	78	1 796	4.1	2.44	8.6	30.3
Scotland	11.6	9.2	9.0	51.4	4 822	4 983	3.3	-2.8	604	581	-175	1 880	-1.2	2.54	7.7	28.8
Scott	12.6	8.4	6.6	51.8	39 376	40 422	2.7	-3.0	5 449	3 764	-992	15 538	-0.6	2.49	14.1	26.7
Shannon	14.6	10.7	6.6	50.2	7 613	8 324	9.3	1.4	919	834	0	3 448	3.9	2.42	8.9	27.8
Shelby	13.1	9.6	9.9	51.0	6 942	6 799	-2.1	-6.3	795	844	-392	2 581	-6.0	2.39	8.0	28.6
Stoddard	12.9	9.5	8.3	51.4	28 895	29 705	2.8	0.9	3 331	3 402	-415	12 255	1.6	2.39	10.9	27.4
Stone	17.5	15.6	8.9	50.7	19 078	28 658	50.2	12.4	2 811	2 963	3 004	13 690	15.8	2.33	7.2	22.8
Sullivan	13.2	9.0	8.1	48.9	6 326	7 219	14.1	-7.0	918	789	-482	2 740	-6.3	2.41	9.2	29.5
Taney	13.2	10.6	7.1	51.3	25 561	39 703	55.3	30.2	5 571	4 060	6 990	20 755	28.5	2.41	10.9	26.2
Texas	13.4	10.1	7.9	48.0	21 476	23 003	7.1	13.1	2 699	2 710	1 702	10 057	7.2	2.40	9.5	27.4
Vernon	13.2	8.4	8.0	51.5	19 041	20 454	7.4	3.4	2 600	2 268	-509	8 396	5.4	2.42	10.2	29.4
Warren	12.2	8.7	5.9	50.2	19 534	24 525	25.6	32.6	3 739	2 151	5 471	12 339	34.3	2.61	10.7	22.0
Washington	12.6	8.3	5.2	48.7	20 380	23 344	14.5	7.9	3 100	2 309	407	9 355	11.3	2.58	11.7	23.4
Wayne	14.7	12.8	8.6	49.9	11 543	13 259	14.9	2.0	1 344	1 778	-384	5 717	3.0	2.34	9.3	27.7
Webster	11.6	7.7	5.4	49.5	23 753	31 045	30.7	16.6	4 879	2 602	3 430	13 062	18.0	2.70	9.9	21.2
Worth	14.0	11.9	11.8	50.9	2 440	2 382	-2.4	-8.9	188	274	-280	944	-6.4	2.24	6.5	28.6
Wright	12.5	9.7	7.8	51.2	16 758	17 955	7.1	4.8	2 456	1 999	-396	7 499	5.9	2.48	10.5	27.4

1. No spouse present.

Table B. States and Counties — Population, Vital Statistics, Medicare, and Crime

STATE County	Persons in group quarters, 2010	Daytime population, 2006–2010		Births, average 2006–2008		Deaths, average 2006–2008		Persons under 65 with no health insurance, 2009		Medicare, 2011			Serious crimes known to police,[2] 2010 Total	
		Number	Employment/residence ratio	Total	Rate[1]	Number	Rate[1]	Number	Percent	Eligible for Medicare	Enrolled in Medicare Advantage	Enrolled in a Medicare prescription drug plan	Number	Rate[3]
	32	33	34	35	36	37	38	39	40	41	42	43	44	45
MISSOURI—Cont'd														
Jasper	2 478	121 248	1.1	1 843	16.0	1 117	9.7	17 980	18.0	19 930	2 968	10 260	5 319	4 531
Jefferson	1 983	162 202	0.5	2 948	13.6	1 694	7.8	25 863	13.6	33 114	10 633	10 929	4 752	2 173
Johnson	3 671	49 001	0.9	782	15.2	368	7.1	7 659	16.7	6 711	818	2 809	1 391	2 645
Knox	87	3 647	0.7	D	D	66	16.3	699	22.6	929	48	585	107	2 590
Laclede	345	35 145	1.0	514	14.5	369	10.4	5 426	18.7	7 464	2 598	2 683	1 284	3 610
Lafayette	724	28 036	0.7	420	12.8	369	11.2	4 069	15.3	6 654	1 174	2 904	641	1 920
Lawrence	559	34 035	0.7	D	D	426	11.3	5 877	18.9	7 856	2 357	3 042	1 344	3 479
Lewis	782	8 898	0.7	D	D	124	12.3	1 467	18.4	1 946	106	1 208	136	1 332
Lincoln	632	40 331	0.5	769	14.9	385	7.5	7 189	15.4	7 664	1 711	3 289	840	1 598
Linn	152	12 605	1.0	D	D	168	13.2	1 623	16.3	2 982	222	1 784	256	2 006
Livingston	1 340	15 679	1.1	D	D	203	14.3	1 954	17.3	3 094	255	1 853	309	2 034
McDonald	157	19 946	0.7	D	D	210	9.2	4 272	21.4	3 559	785	1 585	456	1 975
Macon	286	14 703	0.9	D	D	219	14.0	2 245	18.2	3 595	166	2 133	295	1 895
Madison	168	11 166	0.8	D	D	167	13.7	1 914	19.2	2 903	277	1 629	140	1 145
Maries	67	7 144	0.5	D	D	92	10.1	1 393	19.2	1 716	131	893	85	926
Marion	1 368	29 984	1.1	435	15.4	356	12.6	3 507	15.0	5 842	351	3 656	1 559	5 417
Mercer	51	3 996	1.2	D	D	34	9.7	522	19.2	831	38	467	29	766
Miller	271	22 726	0.8	D	D	272	10.9	4 292	21.0	4 479	319	2 411	480	1 940
Mississippi	1 874	13 370	0.9	D	D	178	13.0	2 185	20.1	2 851	78	1 997	384	2 674
Moniteau	1 316	13 369	0.7	D	D	143	9.4	2 403	18.7	2 541	135	1 346	167	1 070
Monroe	128	7 401	0.6	D	D	108	11.7	1 209	16.8	1 947	137	1 141	163	1 844
Montgomery	394	10 636	0.7	D	D	163	13.6	1 695	18.2	2 599	235	1 474	169	1 381
Morgan	302	18 835	0.8	285	13.7	259	12.4	3 482	22.0	5 518	434	2 822	475	2 310
New Madrid	332	19 017	1.0	D	D	250	14.0	2 381	16.7	3 621	252	2 498	271	1 525
Newton	880	56 092	0.9	785	14.0	551	9.8	8 279	17.6	10 759	1 542	5 348	1 887	3 247
Nodaway	3 611	22 874	1.0	D	D	201	9.2	2 870	15.5	3 437	112	2 207	357	1 528
Oregon	121	10 197	0.9	D	D	133	12.9	1 729	21.1	2 656	355	1 483	106	974
Osage	405	10 913	0.6	D	D	121	9.0	1 752	15.5	2 274	112	1 253	144	1 038
Ozark	123	8 702	0.7	D	D	125	13.4	1 584	22.3	2 737	625	1 138	130	1 337
Pemiscot	202	18 492	1.0	D	D	237	12.6	2 498	16.5	3 914	511	2 522	836	4 569
Perry	286	18 949	1.0	D	D	178	9.5	2 451	15.8	3 387	112	2 122	374	1 971
Pettis	851	43 506	1.1	D	D	389	9.5	6 540	19.0	7 732	776	4 166	1 763	4 178
Phelps	3 001	46 124	1.1	566	13.4	439	10.4	6 441	18.2	7 952	583	4 123	1 694	3 751
Pike	2 162	18 397	1.0	228	12.3	194	10.5	3 031	19.9	3 461	255	1 990	279	1 507
Platte	869	84 521	0.9	1 075	12.7	524	6.2	7 175	9.1	11 936	2 103	4 850	4 186	4 686
Polk	1 511	28 631	0.8	D	D	312	10.4	4 998	19.9	6 003	2 042	2 217	856	2 749
Pulaski	9 989	52 103	1.1	749	16.9	280	6.3	7 139	17.2	5 103	357	1 842	1 078	2 062
Putnam	57	4 642	0.8	D	D	73	14.6	691	18.7	1 222	92	771	23	462
Ralls	54	8 452	0.7	D	D	78	7.9	1 191	15.0	2 071	162	1 115	218	2 144
Randolph	2 455	26 748	1.1	D	D	263	10.3	3 992	18.8	4 686	603	2 723	729	2 868
Ray	311	17 758	0.5	D	D	233	9.9	2 695	13.8	4 210	371	1 903	481	2 047
Reynolds	101	7 119	1.2	D	D	78	12.1	942	19.2	1 649	92	976	84	1 254
Ripley	63	12 606	0.7	D	D	195	14.3	2 171	20.2	3 406	245	2 082	328	2 326
St. Charles	5 426	297 507	0.7	4 678	13.6	2 019	5.9	28 015	9.1	49 295	14 834	16 851	7 195	1 996
St. Clair	207	8 502	0.7	D	D	135	14.3	1 457	20.8	2 575	471	1 149	173	1 764
Ste. Genevieve	277	16 299	0.8	D	D	162	9.1	2 107	14.4	3 478	210	1 999	235	1 295
St. Francois	6 652	62 880	0.9	850	13.5	702	11.2	9 241	17.4	12 977	682	7 384	1 432	2 530
St. Louis	19 454	1 096 566	1.2	12 215	12.3	9 302	9.3	88 603	10.8	172 244	48 722	61 687	32 165	3 220
Saline	1 484	22 905	1.0	312	13.7	274	12.1	3 489	18.5	4 524	643	2 516	412	1 763
Schuyler	47	3 682	0.6	D	D	56	13.5	638	19.9	965	59	587	24	542
Scotland	76	4 488	0.9	D	D	61	12.5	852	21.7	934	37	590	60	1 239
Scott	559	38 420	0.9	612	15.0	410	10.0	5 655	16.7	8 526	661	5 465	1 440	3 674
Shannon	80	7 584	0.7	D	D	88	10.5	1 463	21.1	1 867	213	1 017	179	2 121
Shelby	198	5 569	0.7	D	D	93	14.3	925	18.5	1 415	89	862	96	1 506
Stoddard	689	29 373	0.9	D	D	379	12.8	4 445	19.0	7 092	812	4 120	643	2 146
Stone	300	27 852	0.7	D	D	335	10.6	4 527	19.0	8 543	2 497	3 065	719	2 233
Sullivan	108	6 838	1.0	D	D	74	11.1	1 133	20.6	1 447	71	938	89	1 326
Taney	1 744	55 008	1.2	668	14.7	447	9.8	8 383	21.7	11 084	2 719	4 170	2 100	4 064
Texas	1 897	24 249	0.8	304	12.8	299	12.5	4 167	21.2	5 283	468	2 734	354	1 361
Vernon	866	21 321	1.0	D	D	241	12.0	3 116	19.0	4 094	520	2 032	819	3 871
Warren	317	25 191	0.6	D	D	250	8.2	3 867	14.6	5 649	1 704	2 041	758	2 331
Washington	1 091	21 720	0.6	D	D	267	11.0	3 996	19.4	4 609	328	2 667	348	1 381
Wayne	133	12 023	0.7	D	D	190	14.9	1 917	20.2	3 484	353	2 013	205	1 516
Webster	879	28 582	0.5	563	15.7	287	8.0	6 061	19.4	6 566	2 886	2 034	627	1 732
Worth	52	1 804	0.7	D	D	30	14.1	328	21.7	516	12	312	37	1 704
Wright	195	18 003	0.9	D	D	214	11.6	2 941	20.5	4 609	1 282	2 065	288	1 531

1. Per 1,000 estimated resident population.   2. Data for serious crimes have not been adjusted for underreporting; this may affect comparability between geographic areas and over time.   3. Per 100,000 population estimated by the FBI.

Table B. States and Counties — **Crime, Education, Money Income, and Poverty**

STATE County	Serious crimes known to police,[1] 2010 (cont.) Rate[2] Violent	Property	Education — School enrollment and attainment, 2006–2010 — Enrollment[3] Total	Percent private	Attainment[4] (percent) High school graduate or less	Bachelor's degree or more	Local government expenditures,[5] 2008–2009 Total current expenditures (mil dol)	Current expenditures per student (dollars)	Money income, 2006–2010 Per capita income[6] (dollars)	Households — Median income Dollars	Percent change, 2000 to 2006–2010 (constant 2010 dollars)	Percent with income of $200,000 or more	Income and poverty, 2010 Median household income (dollars)	Percent below poverty level All persons	Children under 18 years	Children 5 to 17 years in families
	46	47	48	49	50	51	52	53	54	55	56	57	58	59	60	61
MISSOURI—Cont'd																
Jasper	428	4 102	29 194	13.0	51.9	18.6	154.5	7 479	19 899	37 894	-4.5	1.3	37 565	17.6	23.4	20.3
Jefferson	260	1 913	56 114	15.4	49.2	16.1	309.7	8 720	24 586	56 756	-3.3	1.3	52 841	12.1	15.7	13.2
Johnson	160	2 485	17 733	6.5	41.6	24.1	67.3	8 690	20 405	44 985	0.4	0.9	43 327	17.8	20.0	17.2
Knox	194	2 397	881	14.5	66.3	13.9	5.2	9 413	18 481	33 029	-3.8	2.1	33 076	21.0	32.6	29.6
Laclede	793	2 817	8 236	11.3	60.8	13.0	46.9	7 682	19 858	37 294	-0.4	1.3	35 688	18.2	29.2	25.9
Lafayette	141	1 779	7 491	15.0	55.6	15.9	50.5	9 062	23 043	48 257	-0.3	0.7	45 621	11.9	16.8	15.3
Lawrence	318	3 160	8 895	11.5	60.6	13.3	49.2	8 129	18 777	38 350	-3.1	0.9	38 800	16.7	25.8	21.7
Lewis	78	1 254	2 870	42.6	60.0	13.0	12.9	8 339	18 973	40 399	4.1	1.0	36 501	16.4	24.9	22.8
Lincoln	264	1 334	13 418	17.6	59.4	11.9	65.8	7 487	21 862	52 897	-1.9	1.0	50 307	11.2	15.2	13.7
Linn	172	1 834	2 855	7.8	62.7	14.3	22.8	9 258	20 742	37 706	5.4	1.5	35 323	15.9	24.1	22.0
Livingston	151	1 882	3 277	10.6	59.6	19.0	21.1	9 445	20 295	39 683	-2.9	0.8	39 821	16.7	23.7	20.9
McDonald	329	1 646	5 954	9.3	61.4	8.9	32.3	8 528	17 070	36 619	7.1	1.0	33 352	19.7	29.8	26.8
Macon	173	1 722	3 334	11.8	60.5	15.0	20.9	8 770	18 411	36 429	-4.7	0.7	37 130	15.1	24.4	22.1
Madison	41	1 104	2 581	3.2	61.1	10.7	16.4	7 783	17 239	33 456	3.2	0.7	33 841	19.1	29.2	26.7
Maries	76	850	2 024	13.9	63.6	14.2	11.3	8 490	19 155	40 185	-0.6	0.4	38 877	15.2	23.2	21.0
Marion	281	5 156	6 929	19.3	56.9	16.9	41.0	8 224	20 718	40 859	1.6	1.5	39 975	16.4	22.4	19.5
Mercer	291	476	883	4.4	59.6	14.2	5.9	10 235	19 031	34 008	-9.4	0.7	35 184	14.8	21.4	19.6
Miller	251	1 689	5 703	10.6	61.4	11.9	42.7	8 308	18 202	35 838	-8.6	0.6	34 266	21.3	30.6	27.4
Mississippi	467	2 208	2 951	7.1	74.8	10.5	18.7	8 283	15 927	29 586	1.5	0.8	30 252	27.5	38.8	35.8
Moniteau	122	948	3 706	12.6	58.7	17.1	19.6	8 161	19 267	47 162	0.2	0.4	44 475	14.4	20.0	18.2
Monroe	317	1 527	2 108	14.5	62.7	11.9	14.6	9 025	19 834	38 750	-0.9	0.3	36 950	15.3	23.8	21.5
Montgomery	123	1 259	2 736	12.9	65.2	12.2	15.6	8 532	19 634	39 369	-5.1	0.6	38 145	16.8	26.7	24.2
Morgan	214	2 096	3 718	22.5	62.7	11.8	18.6	8 360	18 789	36 696	-5.5	0.5	34 374	20.6	34.2	31.3
New Madrid	326	1 199	4 313	6.8	68.0	12.2	27.8	9 398	18 811	32 895	-3.2	1.1	32 921	24.5	36.2	31.5
Newton	277	2 970	14 262	15.1	49.6	18.3	63.7	7 247	20 832	41 163	-7.2	1.7	40 955	15.5	23.7	20.9
Nodaway	141	1 386	8 671	7.3	50.6	23.7	28.5	10 315	18 909	38 621	-4.0	1.1	39 823	17.0	15.0	14.0
Oregon	175	800	2 443	6.5	65.6	10.2	13.6	7 760	15 093	26 144	-7.7	0.9	27 646	25.0	35.8	32.8
Osage	144	894	3 445	29.2	60.8	13.2	13.9	8 344	21 484	45 746	-8.7	1.4	49 058	10.8	13.8	12.3
Ozark	226	1 111	1 749	3.1	65.1	11.1	14.8	8 966	17 298	31 960	-2.4	0.6	28 709	24.5	40.2	36.1
Pemiscot	557	4 012	5 008	4.5	69.7	9.8	40.3	10 359	15 841	30 120	8.6	0.7	28 152	31.3	47.5	42.5
Perry	264	1 708	4 457	30.2	66.2	12.2	19.3	7 699	22 200	45 713	-1.5	1.9	43 200	13.6	17.6	14.8
Pettis	415	3 763	10 594	11.8	53.6	16.8	50.1	7 779	19 351	37 658	-6.5	1.3	36 882	17.9	24.5	22.9
Phelps	376	3 375	14 660	11.5	47.4	25.3	53.9	8 429	20 817	40 260	8.2	1.6	39 765	18.0	22.1	21.0
Pike	205	1 302	3 767	22.8	63.6	12.6	24.1	8 775	18 769	42 082	2.7	1.2	37 169	17.8	24.3	22.6
Platte	676	4 010	23 202	23.4	30.7	36.9	144.3	9 769	34 037	65 948	-6.7	5.1	67 791	7.3	9.3	7.7
Polk	337	2 412	8 529	90.0	58.9	16.6	46.3	8 626	18 138	35 831	-4.6	1.3	34 837	21.0	30.3	27.0
Pulaski	260	1 802	14 118	12.7	45.9	18.4	73.7	8 509	19 800	43 155	-0.5	0.4	48 374	15.1	17.3	16.0
Putnam	100	362	1 123	12.2	58.0	15.6	7.5	9 371	20 005	34 545	3.8	1.8	32 643	19.5	27.1	24.3
Ralls	89	2 056	2 334	18.3	62.2	16.1	5.6	7 365	22 605	45 194	-3.8	1.7	43 763	11.0	16.2	14.0
Randolph	134	2 736	6 062	13.3	59.1	11.7	34.2	8 773	17 049	36 458	-8.5	1.2	37 537	17.7	25.4	21.8
Ray	166	1 881	5 683	10.8	58.3	13.5	30.7	8 264	25 244	53 343	0.6	1.7	50 278	11.1	16.3	13.7
Reynolds	209	1 045	1 375	1.1	69.5	6.7	12.3	10 675	16 964	32 059	-2.1	0.2	29 819	24.0	36.1	33.0
Ripley	149	2 177	3 041	7.0	68.1	12.2	17.7	7 421	15 115	29 369	1.9	0.7	29 213	26.6	42.9	38.1
St. Charles	150	1 846	97 659	26.0	35.3	33.4	512.6	8 889	30 664	70 331	-3.0	3.3	65 281	6.1	7.2	6.0
St. Clair	194	1 571	1 751	11.7	64.9	14.1	8.8	8 537	18 309	32 217	0.5	0.2	30 998	21.2	33.6	29.6
Ste. Genevieve	187	1 108	4 157	25.6	61.6	11.6	17.8	8 779	22 665	46 911	-5.5	1.0	48 031	11.2	17.4	14.6
St. Francois	230	2 300	15 277	12.1	56.3	14.8	85.4	7 952	18 852	38 589	-2.3	1.1	35 630	18.9	25.0	23.1
St. Louis	320	2 900	273 158	30.2	32.5	39.1	1 800.6	12 504	33 344	57 561	-10.0	6.1	55 290	10.5	14.0	12.0
Saline	128	1 635	6 252	24.0	58.1	17.7	31.2	8 410	18 581	38 818	-6.4	0.5	37 537	21.0	27.3	23.7
Schuyler	68	474	908	9.9	62.4	9.6	5.9	8 662	18 410	31 358	-9.6	0.5	31 978	20.7	32.0	28.7
Scotland	83	1 156	839	33.5	59.4	17.8	6.3	8 421	19 895	39 722	14.4	2.0	36 272	16.6	26.9	24.7
Scott	732	2 942	9 712	11.3	66.9	13.7	55.0	7 919	19 566	37 716	-5.0	1.0	37 457	18.5	27.6	24.6
Shannon	261	1 860	1 919	5.3	65.5	13.7	7.6	9 019	15 309	30 766	16.4	0.4	26 600	25.6	41.9	39.0
Shelby	63	1 444	1 487	10.8	56.3	13.4	10.4	9 268	18 056	35 012	-6.1	0.0	37 829	14.9	24.1	22.0
Stoddard	207	1 939	6 643	8.7	67.7	11.7	40.7	7 719	20 911	35 932	5.1	1.0	35 994	18.2	27.0	23.4
Stone	286	1 947	5 946	8.6	53.6	16.8	37.7	8 508	21 748	41 351	0.1	1.6	37 788	16.3	30.5	26.6
Sullivan	298	1 028	1 407	2.9	64.2	9.9	10.8	9 315	16 633	30 459	-7.9	0.8	33 932	17.6	24.8	20.8
Taney	495	3 568	11 942	25.4	49.0	20.0	60.7	7 940	21 474	39 026	-0.3	2.1	34 281	20.0	31.3	25.6
Texas	73	1 288	5 612	10.2	64.9	11.8	32.5	8 150	15 790	31 552	1.5	1.4	32 076	23.8	33.2	29.1
Vernon	440	3 431	4 944	16.9	61.6	14.3	28.6	8 873	18 314	34 387	-9.5	0.6	34 985	19.0	27.3	25.3
Warren	237	2 095	7 256	23.6	55.4	16.9	34.9	7 673	24 358	50 231	-3.3	2.3	49 157	12.7	20.2	17.2
Washington	183	1 199	5 516	6.5	71.4	7.7	30.8	7 911	16 867	35 901	4.6	0.7	32 823	24.0	34.9	31.7
Wayne	96	1 420	2 647	7.3	67.3	8.7	15.1	8 230	17 105	30 621	0.7	0.4	28 626	23.4	38.8	35.2
Webster	97	1 635	8 510	13.2	58.0	14.7	53.1	7 318	18 699	40 889	1.1	1.0	42 966	17.2	29.0	26.5
Worth	368	1 336	462	8.9	63.4	12.8	3.4	8 823	18 229	38 220	9.9	0.5	34 246	15.8	23.3	19.9
Wright	165	1 366	4 365	12.9	65.0	11.3	29.7	8 077	16 413	29 636	-5.2	0.6	29 608	23.9	34.9	32.2

1. Data for serious crimes have not been adjusted for underreporting; this may affect comparability between geographic areas and over time.   2. Per 100,000 population estimated by the FBI.   3. All persons 3 years old and over enrolled in nursery school through college.   4. Persons 25 years old and over.   5. Elementary and secondary education expenditures.   6. Based on population estimated by the American Community Survey, 2006–2010.

Table B. States and Counties — **Personal Income**

STATE County	Personal income, 2009 Total (mil dol)	Percent change, 2008–2009	Per capita[1] Dollars	Per capita[1] Rank	Wages and salaries[2] (mil dol)	Proprietors' income (mil dol)	Dividends, interest, and rent (mil dol)	Transfer payments (mil dol) Total	Government payments to individuals Total	Social Security	Medical payments	Income mainte-nance	Unemploy-ment insurance
	62	63	64	65	66	67	68	69	70	71	72	73	74
MISSOURI—Cont'd													
Jasper	3 388	1.0	28 666	2 267	2 672	221	507	904	883	276	428	89	30
Jefferson	7 145	-2.0	32 617	1 399	2 137	336	797	1 329	1 289	504	520	90	79
Johnson	1 447	-0.7	27 488	2 483	951	118	200	294	285	93	117	23	14
Knox	124	0.4	31 245	1 702	40	24	22	35	34	12	18	2	1
Laclede	920	-1.3	25 973	2 737	472	50	162	276	270	94	114	29	13
Lafayette	1 200	-0.3	36 850	765	346	105	164	277	271	93	135	18	10
Lawrence	970	-1.4	25 775	2 763	349	45	148	270	263	101	107	25	10
Lewis	281	0.3	28 693	2 261	101	33	40	72	71	25	32	5	3
Lincoln	1 463	-1.6	27 442	2 496	483	77	179	323	313	115	135	27	20
Linn	383	3.1	30 350	1 896	193	36	61	116	114	36	54	8	4
Livingston	476	2.9	33 439	1 270	251	53	101	117	115	41	54	9	4
McDonald	570	-1.1	24 697	2 894	251	22	58	146	142	46	64	19	5
Macon	464	3.5	30 205	1 935	196	42	79	133	130	47	61	9	4
Madison	311	2.0	25 214	2 840	121	13	42	116	114	39	54	11	4
Maries	244	0.1	27 706	2 452	54	16	35	64	62	22	27	5	2
Marion	893	1.5	31 374	1 673	591	64	135	256	250	75	126	22	9
Mercer	100	2.6	28 833	2 225	40	17	15	28	27	10	12	2	1
Miller	641	-1.3	25 881	2 750	251	42	85	200	195	59	96	18	9
Mississippi	376	-2.4	28 349	2 335	151	45	49	130	128	37	64	18	3
Moniteau	465	-1.4	30 700	1 820	158	38	70	96	93	35	41	7	4
Monroe	269	1.8	29 931	1 998	83	49	44	71	70	26	31	4	3
Montgomery	371	-2.9	31 685	1 602	116	33	65	104	102	36	49	7	5
Morgan	593	-3.1	28 870	2 223	141	44	157	194	190	77	79	14	7
New Madrid	524	-5.5	30 005	1 977	335	60	51	175	172	49	89	22	5
Newton	1 813	-0.4	32 300	1 456	861	94	252	361	351	141	129	35	14
Nodaway	609	4.8	27 534	2 477	390	61	93	126	122	44	51	7	5
Oregon	251	2.3	24 369	2 928	92	21	32	105	103	31	49	11	3
Osage	455	-1.1	33 528	1 246	144	29	65	83	80	31	35	5	3
Ozark	219	1.1	23 479	3 005	53	9	37	88	87	36	34	8	2
Pemiscot	564	-2.9	31 010	1 751	236	65	57	210	207	47	112	33	6
Perry	552	0.5	29 299	2 135	366	30	85	130	126	47	58	9	5
Pettis	1 248	-0.3	30 125	1 947	780	80	194	332	325	100	152	31	12
Phelps	1 326	2.3	31 386	1 667	787	62	206	325	317	100	148	27	10
Pike	505	-0.5	27 447	2 495	240	46	79	137	133	47	64	10	5
Platte	3 833	0.3	42 266	310	2 148	168	538	434	418	182	153	23	24
Polk	796	1.0	25 978	2 736	321	36	123	253	247	76	121	22	9
Pulaski	1 969	6.3	42 392	299	1 933	31	150	254	248	63	105	25	10
Putnam	126	-1.8	26 500	2 644	47	7	25	42	41	14	19	3	1
Ralls	311	0.9	32 244	1 475	107	27	47	65	64	27	24	4	3
Randolph	722	-1.3	28 294	2 347	419	54	100	217	213	58	98	19	9
Ray	805	-0.5	34 475	1 098	175	75	91	161	157	62	66	11	7
Reynolds	176	1.4	28 349	2 335	80	6	21	75	74	23	38	6	2
Ripley	343	3.4	25 627	2 788	94	25	40	154	152	43	78	17	4
St. Charles	13 680	-1.8	38 494	579	6 143	539	1 843	1 815	1 750	757	672	84	105
St. Clair	244	1.4	26 272	2 673	74	15	41	90	88	34	38	7	3
Ste. Genevieve	580	-0.8	33 080	1 324	291	15	99	126	123	51	49	8	6
St. Francois	1 723	2.3	26 974	2 567	906	81	209	547	536	178	245	52	21
St. Louis	51 817	-4.9	52 214	77	38 570	3 194	12 602	6 896	6 715	2 639	2 903	496	294
Saline	797	1.6	34 918	1 033	367	131	114	220	216	59	122	15	6
Schuyler	105	3.4	25 440	2 813	27	9	15	39	38	12	21	3	1
Scotland	133	0.6	27 607	2 466	45	25	25	33	32	12	16	2	1
Scott	1 299	0.8	31 802	1 578	614	135	189	369	361	110	173	42	11
Shannon	184	2.7	21 952	3 067	54	21	23	70	69	23	29	8	3
Shelby	204	2.6	32 289	1 459	69	39	35	52	50	18	24	4	2
Stoddard	895	-4.2	30 782	1 805	411	104	123	276	271	90	130	24	9
Stone	974	-1.8	30 991	1 756	236	106	174	273	268	123	96	18	12
Sullivan	219	-2.7	32 028	1 522	126	37	28	57	56	17	29	5	2
Taney	1 383	0.5	28 790	2 234	953	86	226	395	386	149	155	32	21
Texas	579	2.6	23 567	2 998	224	22	84	197	192	66	83	19	7
Vernon	580	-3.4	28 750	2 247	255	74	82	184	180	55	94	16	5
Warren	1 023	-1.3	32 497	1 429	290	35	152	222	216	86	91	16	12
Washington	602	0.7	24 689	2 896	174	17	53	217	213	62	103	28	9
Wayne	332	4.4	26 782	2 601	89	13	36	151	148	46	76	14	4
Webster	935	1.3	25 568	2 800	258	36	116	246	240	88	104	21	10
Worth	60	7.5	29 553	2 080	14	8	11	17	16	6	7	1	1
Wright	417	0.2	23 304	3 019	155	3	70	169	166	56	75	19	5

1. Based on the resident population estimated as of July 1 of the year shown. 2. Includes supplements to wages and salaries.

Table B. States and Counties — **Earnings, Social Security, and Housing**

	Earnings, 2009								Social Security beneficiaries, December 2010			Housing units, 2010	
		Percent by selected industries											
			Goods-related[1]		Service-related and health								
STATE County	Total (mil dol)	Farm	Total	Manu-facturing	Infor-mation and profes-sional and technical services	Retail trade	Finance, insur-ance, and real estate	Health care and social services	Govern-ment	Number	Rate[2]	Supple-mental Security Income recipients, December 2010	Total	Percent change, 2000–2010
	75	76	77	78	79	80	81	82	83	84	85	86	87	88
MISSOURI—Cont'd														
Jasper	2 894	0.4	24.2	20.4	4.9	8.3	4.3	11.4	12.5	23 795	203	3 356	50 668	11.2
Jefferson	2 472	0.0	21.4	11.2	6.2	8.2	4.5	11.7	19.6	39 275	180	2 939	87 626	15.9
Johnson	1 069	2.4	D	5.1	2.7	5.1	3.6	4.4	59.9	7 645	145	649	21 528	14.0
Knox	64	24.0	D	8.9	6.3	3.0	D	3.0	21.8	1 085	263	112	2 289	-1.2
Laclede	521	-0.8	36.1	32.2	3.0	11.8	4.5	10.5	15.5	8 660	243	1 118	15 778	10.2
Lafayette	451	11.3	15.2	9.3	5.9	8.1	5.2	D	24.1	7 465	224	522	14 718	7.4
Lawrence	394	4.2	D	15.8	3.8	9.5	3.7	6.0	26.8	9 105	236	884	16 649	12.6
Lewis	134	19.3	D	3.8	D	6.1	3.4	D	21.6	2 235	219	196	4 535	-1.4
Lincoln	560	3.8	26.9	15.0	D	9.0	4.5	4.5	23.2	9 195	175	803	21 011	35.5
Linn	229	7.8	19.5	17.4	6.3	7.2	4.4	7.7	17.1	3 185	250	365	6 429	-1.9
Livingston	304	8.4	D	8.8	3.5	10.1	5.8	11.3	22.8	3 510	231	376	6 730	4.1
McDonald	273	-0.4	D	34.2	D	13.2	2.8	D	19.2	4 255	184	622	9 925	6.9
Macon	238	7.9	14.6	10.2	5.6	7.0	4.3	D	35.0	4 050	260	327	7 665	2.2
Madison	134	0.1	D	10.1	D	12.0	3.7	8.7	28.4	3 440	281	495	5 970	5.6
Maries	70	-2.6	D	16.8	D	9.9	D	6.4	22.0	1 945	212	158	4 611	11.1
Marion	654	3.9	D	15.0	D	8.3	3.8	D	15.2	6 450	224	1 037	12 826	3.1
Mercer	57	44.6	D	D	D	D	D	D	19.4	925	244	95	2 135	0.5
Miller	293	4.8	20.9	9.6	D	10.1	5.1	D	23.0	5 340	216	598	12 758	13.3
Mississippi	197	15.2	7.0	5.2	1.4	7.5	4.7	D	27.2	3 370	235	740	5 711	-2.2
Moniteau	195	8.5	D	17.4	2.5	6.5	4.0	D	24.7	3 040	195	211	6 176	7.6
Monroe	132	26.3	D	11.7	3.8	4.2	4.4	4.3	24.9	2 230	252	174	4 798	5.1
Montgomery	149	10.7	D	12.6	D	7.1	6.1	6.3	23.4	3 000	245	287	6 130	7.1
Morgan	184	13.1	D	8.4	3.2	12.8	5.6	D	24.9	6 255	304	520	15 517	11.7
New Madrid	394	11.8	29.1	27.1	1.2	10.0	1.6	D	12.8	4 435	234	1 022	8 531	-0.8
Newton	956	2.6	20.5	15.7	2.8	8.3	2.8	28.9	12.8	12 325	212	1 224	24 313	11.0
Nodaway	451	8.1	D	23.0	D	6.1	6.0	10.7	26.7	3 720	159	265	9 524	6.9
Oregon	112	0.3	D	7.2	2.3	11.3	5.5	D	21.3	2 965	272	651	5 486	9.8
Osage	173	4.7	30.2	23.8	D	8.8	3.4	6.3	20.4	2 630	190	153	6 533	10.7
Ozark	62	-1.1	D	5.5	4.9	8.8	8.1	D	33.4	3 190	328	342	5 652	10.5
Pemiscot	301	15.5	D	12.6	1.3	6.5	3.8	7.3	28.7	4 620	253	1 590	8 161	-7.2
Perry	396	0.6	D	34.4	D	7.6	4.4	D	13.7	3 895	205	376	8 568	9.6
Pettis	860	1.9	30.1	25.5	7.2	7.6	4.3	D	19.1	8 760	208	1 132	18 249	7.6
Phelps	848	-0.2	9.3	5.9	4.0	8.1	3.6	12.4	40.6	8 940	198	1 147	19 533	11.6
Pike	286	8.1	16.5	11.5	4.9	11.8	3.3	D	27.9	3 890	210	415	7 875	5.1
Platte	2 316	0.9	D	7.1	6.3	8.0	6.4	6.0	10.2	13 225	148	569	39 223	26.9
Polk	358	-1.3	D	3.9	D	10.0	5.0	D	32.0	6 720	216	790	13 304	19.0
Pulaski	1 964	-0.1	D	0.3	1.8	2.5	1.2	1.4	83.8	6 110	117	781	17 904	16.2
Putnam	54	5.7	8.1	5.3	D	8.9	8.9	3.1	37.6	1 320	265	134	2 982	2.4
Ralls	134	16.9	D	28.5	1.2	5.5	2.0	D	16.0	2 325	229	159	5 183	13.6
Randolph	474	2.1	D	10.6	D	9.2	6.4	12.0	21.0	5 060	199	766	10 714	-0.2
Ray	250	5.8	D	9.5	5.1	9.8	7.0	D	26.8	4 860	207	294	9 984	6.5
Reynolds	86	-1.6	D	8.0	D	5.0	D	10.7	21.6	1 980	296	278	4 033	7.3
Ripley	119	2.6	16.3	13.9	D	9.0	4.8	11.2	29.8	4 080	289	850	6 597	3.2
St. Charles	6 682	0.4	18.1	10.4	11.3	8.6	9.6	10.6	13.6	54 995	153	2 335	141 016	33.6
St. Clair	89	3.7	D	2.4	D	8.6	3.8	9.8	36.8	2 935	299	302	5 640	8.4
Ste. Genevieve	306	1.2	41.9	25.4	D	5.0	2.9	D	16.6	4 025	222	267	8 637	7.7
St. Francois	987	-0.4	15.0	8.7	3.0	9.2	6.5	16.0	27.9	15 070	231	2 365	28 458	16.4
St. Louis	41 764	0.0	17.6	11.6	14.7	5.8	8.2	12.4	8.8	187 330	188	15 721	438 032	3.4
Saline	498	14.5	20.3	18.2	D	5.4	3.0	D	19.8	5 050	216	611	10 117	1.0
Schuyler	36	6.5	9.6	1.6	D	9.9	2.2	3.5	37.5	1 065	240	109	2 102	3.7
Scotland	70	19.4	D	4.5	D	6.9	D	D	37.8	1 055	218	64	2 369	3.4
Scott	750	4.3	D	12.2	12.2	5.6	4.7	D	16.6	9 700	248	1 779	16 987	0.2
Shannon	75	0.1	D	20.4	D	6.4	4.2	D	28.3	2 290	271	374	4 164	7.8
Shelby	108	25.8	D	11.8	D	5.3	3.2	2.4	22.2	1 580	248	137	3 206	-1.2
Stoddard	514	12.0	D	24.5	2.5	7.9	4.3	D	14.7	8 100	270	1 140	13 609	2.9
Stone	342	-0.9	D	1.4	D	14.5	8.9	8.6	16.4	9 615	299	519	20 373	25.4
Sullivan	164	22.3	D	D	3.3	3.4	3.9	2.9	15.3	1 650	246	202	3 358	-0.2
Taney	1 039	-0.2	D	2.3	4.4	12.0	9.4	9.4	11.3	12 635	245	1 017	29 255	48.6
Texas	247	-1.5	D	14.2	2.1	9.0	5.3	5.6	37.0	6 115	235	827	11 685	8.6
Vernon	329	11.8	9.5	7.0	3.5	7.7	6.2	D	26.6	4 780	226	644	9 495	7.0
Warren	325	3.0	D	24.3	2.4	9.8	4.4	D	19.5	6 620	204	395	14 685	32.9
Washington	191	-0.5	D	15.7	D	7.7	3.8	6.4	42.0	5 540	220	1 202	11 017	11.4
Wayne	102	0.1	D	10.9	D	10.0	4.1	7.9	30.9	4 110	304	716	8 083	7.8
Webster	294	-1.0	19.0	10.3	4.3	11.4	5.0	5.0	26.1	7 710	213	803	14 417	19.6
Worth	22	20.8	D	D	D	D	3.3	3.8	37.8	585	269	46	1 281	2.9
Wright	159	-2.3	D	10.3	3.0	14.9	5.2	D	27.6	5 300	282	828	8 700	9.3

1. Includes mining, construction, and manufacturing.   2. Per 1,000 resident population enumerated in the 2010 census.

Table B. States and Counties — Housing, Labor Force, and Employment

STATE County	Housing units, 2006–2010								Civilian labor force, 2010				Civilian employment[5] 2006–2010		
	Occupied units										Unemployment			Percent	
			Owner-occupied			Renter-occupied									
				Median owner cost as a percent of income				Sub-stand-ard units[3] (percent)		Percent change, 2009–2010				Manage-ment, business, science and arts	Con-struction, produc-tion, and mainte-nance occu-pations
	Total	Percent	Median value[1]	With a mort-gage	Without a mort-gage	Median rent[2]	Median rent as a per-cent of income		Total		Total	Rate[4]	Total		
	89	90	91	92	93	94	95	96	97	98	99	100	101	102	103
MISSOURI—Cont'd															
Jasper	44 505	65.7	93 400	21.9	11.5	612	30.9	2.8	57 887	1.1	4 845	8.4	52 822	27.4	29.0
Jefferson	80 083	83.9	154 700	22.4	10.8	670	27.9	1.6	116 155	-0.7	12 021	10.3	107 488	27.8	29.2
Johnson	19 184	64.5	133 100	22.6	11.3	653	29.9	2.3	25 562	-2.5	2 320	9.1	22 493	27.9	26.5
Knox	1 746	74.9	56 500	22.3	13.6	416	26.9	4.6	2 255	-3.8	152	6.7	1 954	30.2	35.2
Laclede	14 352	70.8	93 000	23.1	10.8	555	25.2	3.8	16 254	-3.0	1 924	11.8	15 553	19.9	39.6
Lafayette	13 394	74.0	121 000	21.8	11.5	566	20.6	2.5	15 799	-4.3	1 727	10.9	16 124	26.6	33.8
Lawrence	15 043	72.5	94 700	23.0	11.1	580	29.6	3.1	18 658	-2.5	1 574	8.4	16 780	27.0	35.5
Lewis	3 764	76.2	79 400	20.0	10.0	464	21.9	3.2	5 424	-2.0	459	8.5	4 790	23.8	34.6
Lincoln	18 061	82.0	155 600	23.5	10.2	674	29.3	2.4	27 151	-0.5	3 133	11.5	23 525	24.1	35.2
Linn	5 062	75.0	66 800	20.0	11.8	491	32.4	1.5	6 024	-9.0	671	11.1	5 406	24.4	36.0
Livingston	5 688	66.6	92 700	18.7	10.0	548	31.0	1.8	7 004	-5.4	566	8.1	6 856	29.3	30.6
McDonald	8 016	70.3	86 800	20.9	12.4	517	23.9	5.2	10 844	-1.1	999	9.2	9 752	18.8	37.7
Macon	6 348	76.5	84 200	22.5	11.9	506	26.9	3.6	8 027	-2.2	673	8.4	6 875	29.0	32.3
Madison	4 757	77.3	83 400	21.0	12.7	509	31.6	2.1	6 223	-0.1	650	10.4	5 042	20.9	38.8
Maries	3 615	82.0	112 500	21.8	10.0	421	28.0	2.2	4 846	0.2	384	7.9	4 132	33.9	30.8
Marion	11 384	67.3	91 200	19.6	11.2	513	26.8	2.0	14 856	-0.1	1 320	8.9	13 295	27.7	30.1
Mercer	1 554	75.7	69 600	19.0	12.8	445	24.0	2.3	1 838	4.4	143	7.8	1 583	41.1	27.7
Miller	10 410	75.3	108 200	22.0	11.0	530	27.7	3.5	12 183	-4.8	1 505	12.4	11 468	23.9	31.2
Mississippi	5 287	62.8	67 400	21.4	11.2	463	36.0	3.3	6 015	-1.4	595	9.9	5 619	23.7	30.9
Moniteau	5 475	78.3	111 900	21.1	10.0	558	23.5	2.2	7 419	-1.1	611	8.2	6 960	30.6	33.5
Monroe	3 835	76.4	79 100	22.4	10.9	488	24.6	2.1	3 888	-9.0	506	13.0	4 274	28.7	34.5
Montgomery	4 869	76.8	107 300	22.4	10.0	510	24.5	2.2	5 943	-3.1	644	10.8	5 479	20.5	36.9
Morgan	8 414	81.7	114 400	23.9	11.1	522	24.6	6.6	8 895	-4.7	1 126	12.7	7 483	27.1	33.7
New Madrid	7 719	64.3	67 100	19.1	11.7	443	24.9	2.1	8 508	0.6	757	8.9	7 882	25.4	35.5
Newton	21 618	74.6	103 400	21.4	10.2	558	26.8	4.1	27 953	0.7	2 504	9.0	26 296	28.3	30.8
Nodaway	8 341	60.6	94 900	19.7	10.0	488	30.9	1.4	11 965	-6.4	794	6.6	11 903	26.5	29.3
Oregon	4 470	74.9	69 200	23.7	12.2	473	28.6	3.9	4 560	-1.5	427	9.4	3 759	19.1	38.5
Osage	5 301	84.6	120 400	19.7	10.0	494	25.4	0.9	7 295	-0.5	500	6.9	6 760	27.5	35.3
Ozark	3 964	82.4	107 000	23.4	10.6	475	34.0	2.6	4 342	-3.3	398	9.2	3 489	24.2	36.4
Pemiscot	7 026	56.1	61 200	19.3	11.7	479	31.0	3.8	8 303	-2.1	873	10.5	6 677	23.5	31.2
Perry	7 691	78.1	122 400	21.6	10.4	576	25.8	3.1	10 524	-0.5	693	6.6	9 350	22.6	37.1
Pettis	16 288	71.5	93 200	23.0	11.4	581	29.0	3.2	20 055	-2.9	1 787	8.9	18 974	23.9	36.8
Phelps	16 726	65.5	114 700	22.3	10.0	584	28.9	1.5	21 743	-1.5	1 667	7.7	19 555	35.9	21.3
Pike	6 721	71.6	97 900	19.5	10.4	524	26.0	4.3	9 022	-3.0	846	9.4	7 721	25.4	28.7
Platte	35 065	67.7	185 100	21.6	10.5	809	25.1	1.7	49 214	0.9	3 997	8.1	46 317	40.3	18.3
Polk	11 718	72.0	112 300	23.3	11.7	566	28.8	3.0	14 115	-0.6	1 391	9.9	12 293	30.4	30.5
Pulaski	15 412	56.2	120 200	22.7	10.5	823	26.0	1.5	20 871	-0.2	1 649	7.9	15 187	30.8	22.0
Putnam	2 224	74.1	98 200	26.6	14.2	530	27.8	2.9	2 390	-4.1	181	7.6	2 365	32.9	30.4
Ralls	4 139	81.8	106 800	19.4	11.7	562	27.4	0.9	5 576	-2.6	465	8.3	5 012	27.8	32.5
Randolph	9 070	73.6	81 100	21.7	11.5	560	28.4	2.4	12 660	-4.2	1 260	10.0	10 207	26.9	28.2
Ray	9 196	78.7	126 100	22.7	12.2	641	26.2	1.8	11 035	-3.5	1 252	11.3	11 153	25.6	37.6
Reynolds	2 878	73.8	76 300	21.8	10.7	370	22.1	3.9	2 524	-8.7	342	13.5	2 465	20.6	45.4
Ripley	5 558	73.4	68 100	23.7	11.0	493	31.0	3.1	6 618	-0.9	658	9.9	5 286	23.2	33.0
St. Charles	130 973	82.0	197 300	22.4	11.5	819	27.6	1.2	195 009	0.7	16 898	8.7	184 890	39.9	17.9
St. Clair	4 320	80.9	82 800	24.1	12.4	431	30.2	3.3	4 041	-4.6	442	10.9	4 366	31.5	29.8
Ste. Genevieve	7 369	83.5	124 700	22.4	10.0	590	25.8	1.8	9 787	-3.5	935	9.6	9 011	25.3	39.6
St. Francois	24 122	73.6	120 800	20.9	11.1	530	28.0	2.1	29 675	-2.7	3 365	11.3	25 502	29.9	27.4
St. Louis	404 777	72.5	179 300	22.8	12.1	789	29.6	1.3	513 534	-0.6	48 145	9.4	489 501	41.9	15.3
Saline	8 939	69.8	84 000	19.9	12.2	511	28.8	2.4	11 318	-4.9	941	8.3	10 604	27.7	34.1
Schuyler	2 097	71.5	55 900	22.1	14.0	405	26.0	5.0	2 063	-4.8	181	8.8	1 895	24.6	33.7
Scotland	1 980	79.2	75 000	20.8	11.6	394	24.8	4.5	2 396	-3.5	185	7.7	2 313	32.2	27.8
Scott	15 520	69.6	95 000	19.5	10.2	526	26.0	2.0	19 581	-3.6	1 812	9.3	17 936	23.5	30.7
Shannon	3 402	78.0	72 100	23.4	11.3	411	30.3	3.6	3 263	-13.1	457	14.0	3 195	26.8	40.3
Shelby	2 705	70.2	69 400	23.4	13.3	400	20.8	1.6	3 174	-4.0	277	8.7	3 016	26.1	35.6
Stoddard	12 130	70.6	80 800	19.6	10.5	513	29.6	1.8	14 972	-0.6	1 364	9.1	12 677	24.3	35.0
Stone	13 529	76.0	139 900	23.2	11.1	645	27.4	2.8	15 527	-4.7	1 923	12.4	13 265	26.3	24.2
Sullivan	2 642	70.6	68 700	22.4	12.0	490	26.9	3.7	3 586	-0.3	253	7.1	2 825	25.6	36.5
Taney	20 281	67.7	132 100	23.5	11.4	655	27.1	1.8	27 357	-2.1	3 458	12.6	23 519	28.2	16.6
Texas	9 523	74.3	92 100	22.1	11.0	470	28.1	2.6	11 134	-0.7	1 055	9.5	8 800	22.8	34.7
Vernon	8 329	70.0	82 600	25.1	12.2	512	29.9	2.0	9 575	3.3	753	7.9	9 467	29.4	27.9
Warren	12 122	78.4	161 000	23.4	11.6	679	32.7	1.9	16 562	-0.6	1 824	11.0	14 682	26.2	32.1
Washington	9 070	80.5	82 400	20.4	10.6	498	24.1	3.3	10 009	-1.7	1 410	14.1	8 763	18.6	40.1
Wayne	5 838	73.3	72 200	19.0	12.3	426	34.3	2.3	6 005	1.1	563	9.4	5 213	29.3	33.1
Webster	12 928	76.6	120 500	22.3	10.0	596	26.9	4.7	16 819	-0.5	1 684	10.0	15 165	22.8	36.3
Worth	977	77.2	57 600	16.1	11.8	276	17.2	1.1	1 124	-1.8	79	7.0	1 114	32.1	30.2
Wright	7 499	71.5	89 300	24.7	10.9	440	24.9	3.4	8 026	-2.9	850	10.6	6 882	28.0	35.4

1. Specified owner-occupied units.   2. Specified renter-occupied units. A value of 10.0 represents 10 percent or less.   3. Overcrowded or lacking complete plumbing facilities.   4. Percent of civilian labor force.   5. Persons 16 years old and over.

Table B. States and Counties — Nonfarm Employment and Agriculture

STATE County	Private nonfarm establishments, employment and payroll, 2009									Agriculture, 2007			
		Employment						Annual payroll		Farms			
												Percent with:	
	Number of establishments	Total	Health care and social assistance	Manufacturing	Retail trade	Finance and insurance	Professional, scientific, and technical services	Total (mil dol)	Average per employee (dollars)	Number	Fewer than 50 acres	500 acres or more	Farm operators whose principal occupation is farming (percent)
	104	105	106	107	108	109	110	111	112	113	114	115	116

MISSOURI—Cont'd

Jasper	3 024	53 169	7 367	9 561	8 080	1 280	1 162	1 658	31 180	1 369	34.8	8.0	41.5
Jefferson	4 069	40 732	5 979	4 734	7 040	1 224	1 001	1 190	29 225	697	41.2	3.9	37.6
Johnson	1 020	9 477	2 007	1 328	1 774	432	290	231	24 355	1 947	33.2	11.3	39.9
Knox	113	673	49	D	98	57	D	16	23 423	696	15.9	19.0	43.1
Laclede	823	12 107	1 294	5 194	1 990	350	162	355	29 342	1 264	25.1	11.9	39.6
Lafayette	736	6 376	1 133	833	1 240	299	188	152	23 767	1 299	31.6	13.6	47.2
Lawrence	699	7 496	1 470	1 543	1 308	187	179	209	27 882	1 873	36.0	7.5	43.2
Lewis	190	1 996	314	D	284	109	37	44	21 944	750	20.8	17.1	41.1
Lincoln	894	8 173	1 144	1 365	1 464	338	177	237	28 976	1 108	33.2	11.3	40.5
Linn	325	3 470	553	1 062	540	156	73	101	29 107	1 077	20.8	16.0	37.5
Livingston	420	4 838	809	479	1 113	D	D	129	26 630	913	20.9	16.5	41.7
McDonald	313	5 092	217	D	1 113	D	D	125	24 623	996	27.6	8.7	48.4
Macon	374	3 118	543	D	585	160	89	81	26 112	1 451	21.6	13.4	36.8
Madison	285	2 858	D	D	523	77	D	65	22 869	376	19.1	11.4	39.1
Maries	138	1 057	D	218	226	D	D	28	26 921	898	18.5	13.0	48.1
Marion	852	10 628	2 021	1 527	1 803	392	291	305	28 742	749	22.4	16.0	41.7
Mercer	76	412	D	D	52	34	4	11	25 784	553	14.5	17.5	35.8
Miller	722	6 279	424	D	1 466	275	251	164	26 076	1 080	17.6	10.7	41.7
Mississippi	270	2 596	611	191	452	129	D	61	23 500	228	17.1	51.3	73.7
Moniteau	336	2 727	363	D	440	123	56	68	25 050	1 138	22.6	10.2	43.0
Monroe	194	1 702	D	570	288	87	D	38	22 310	1 036	20.8	12.5	37.5
Montgomery	276	2 085	389	D	302	124	13	53	25 236	859	22.4	16.5	41.1
Morgan	498	2 818	231	544	788	128	D	66	23 358	1 036	27.8	8.7	43.8
New Madrid	398	5 678	663	D	1 400	141	72	192	33 736	350	10.9	57.1	72.6
Newton	1 288	19 669	5 414	3 028	2 140	576	311	616	31 314	1 590	36.2	5.2	43.5
Nodaway	492	7 529	1 138	2 588	1 210	223	136	214	28 455	1 540	19.7	20.6	49.5
Oregon	212	1 575	407	190	454	67	29	30	18 945	776	24.4	13.7	45.2
Osage	272	2 934	322	1 003	475	125	20	82	28 061	1 181	15.6	10.0	44.9
Ozark	183	908	108	83	197	76	33	18	19 528	742	16.3	16.4	51.9
Pemiscot	379	4 671	1 464	758	650	180	D	125	26 753	258	17.4	56.2	70.2
Perry	602	8 887	1 026	D	1 095	230	D	254	28 580	983	22.6	9.9	39.6
Pettis	1 056	17 284	2 805	4 336	2 406	429	374	494	28 608	1 398	22.6	16.0	45.8
Phelps	1 133	13 099	3 407	904	2 423	420	377	363	27 732	826	30.0	9.0	35.7
Pike	396	4 207	773	D	659	167	396	111	26 413	1 102	23.3	16.7	39.5
Platte	2 247	39 973	2 919	D	6 747	3 650	1 556	1 373	34 351	726	36.9	10.3	36.2
Polk	601	7 047	1 841	D	1 351	226	178	173	24 522	1 707	31.1	8.4	41.1
Pulaski	732	8 253	1 438	147	1 761	D	647	217	26 295	481	18.3	15.0	35.6
Putnam	101	625	D	68	169	49	D	16	25 102	663	17.3	19.8	48.0
Ralls	186	3 495	D	1 379	228	49	27	142	40 508	803	25.9	15.8	41.0
Randolph	597	8 209	1 510	904	1 127	389	153	230	28 020	1 000	29.5	8.6	32.4
Ray	381	2 996	600	D	681	137	76	74	24 762	1 321	31.6	8.7	36.5
Reynolds	212	1 553	237	314	132	D	D	64	41 068	350	23.1	14.0	39.1
Ripley	409	2 294	619	D	425	D	27	43	18 858	471	19.7	14.6	48.2
St. Charles	7 954	115 826	13 808	10 285	18 867	9 332	5 937	3 886	33 552	644	36.8	13.2	46.4
St. Clair	169	1 449	611	D	282	D	15	34	23 297	844	22.3	18.1	47.9
Ste. Genevieve	399	5 528	D	1 950	504	146	156	174	31 556	717	27.3	12.0	36.0
St. Francois	1 491	17 171	4 537	1 459	3 065	826	311	456	26 553	719	33.5	5.3	35.5
St. Louis	30 182	563 427	79 772	40 454	65 479	32 575	47 350	26 062	46 257	276	53.3	4.0	36.6
Saline	535	7 133	1 538	1 967	1 048	260	111	200	27 984	995	21.5	24.8	48.0
Schuyler	92	361	44	D	153	20	D	8	21 709	544	18.8	14.5	40.3
Scotland	124	771	228	56	163	48	D	19	24 411	716	18.7	18.3	41.5
Scott	1 108	13 408	3 427	2 322	1 407	536	495	373	27 831	538	31.2	21.6	47.8
Shannon	170	1 032	D	421	143	50	D	19	18 086	447	25.1	13.0	39.1
Shelby	177	1 231	122	281	205	63	D	29	23 413	707	18.7	21.9	40.7
Stoddard	718	8 089	1 536	2 447	1 455	339	188	214	26 505	1 045	32.5	21.1	47.4
Stone	703	4 981	528	125	960	181	92	119	23 917	753	32.0	7.4	38.1
Sullivan	122	2 142	248	D	177	42	D	66	30 648	882	13.8	21.5	43.1
Taney	1 827	22 932	2 199	499	5 106	412	556	590	25 733	434	23.3	11.8	38.9
Texas	503	4 518	887	857	784	224	97	106	23 571	1 327	21.0	11.7	46.6
Vernon	523	5 649	1 386	1 083	928	296	127	147	25 962	1 383	23.8	16.1	44.4
Warren	567	5 858	532	1 039	1 144	D	158	169	28 922	723	39.0	10.2	39.8
Washington	553	3 145	921	448	504	D	33	72	22 973	558	29.9	11.1	40.1
Wayne	273	1 888	333	397	454	111	33	43	22 523	387	11.1	12.4	41.9
Webster	668	5 061	542	825	1 071	239	D	125	24 782	1 821	35.0	5.4	41.4
Worth	50	184	21	17	57	D	8	4	21 076	455	16.9	18.9	38.9
Wright	409	3 440	468	D	1 062	D	78	78	22 643	1 206	20.5	12.8	48.8

Table B. States and Counties — **Agriculture**

STATE County		Land in farms			Value of land and buildings (dollars)		Value of machinery and equipment, average per farm (dollars)	Value of products sold				Percent of farms with sales of:		Government payments	
	Acreage (1,000)	Percent change, 2002–2007	Average size of farm	Total irrigated (1,000)	Total cropland (1,000)	Average per farm	Average per acre		Total (mil dol)	Average per farm (dollars)	Crops	Live-stock and poultry products	$10,000 or more	$100,000 or more	Total ($1,000)	Percent of farms
	117	118	119	120	121	122	123	124	125	126	127	128	129	130	131	132

MISSOURI—Cont'd

STATE County	117	118	119	120	121	122	123	124	125	126	127	128	129	130	131	132
Jasper	259	-10.4	189	5.2	135.7	417 814	2 210	53 862	92.7	67 688	40.7	59.3	41.4	8.2	2 983	34.8
Jefferson	92	-26.4	132	0.4	39.4	407 554	3 080	47 941	11.1	15 948	50.0	50.0	22.0	2.6	280	12.9
Johnson	424	2.7	218	1.4	244.7	485 494	2 227	72 306	104.1	53 460	36.7	63.3	40.8	8.3	3 575	44.1
Knox	254	2.0	364	D	170.2	691 276	1 897	90 240	57.3	82 325	69.0	31.0	47.4	18.8	4 269	75.4
Laclede	289	-9.4	228	0.1	94.2	440 349	1 928	52 580	40.2	31 835	9.3	90.7	40.5	6.2	870	16.5
Lafayette	353	-2.8	272	2.1	262.4	734 948	2 705	87 125	120.6	92 830	70.5	29.5	52.6	17.8	4 684	63.0
Lawrence	323	2.2	172	2.4	150.7	425 204	2 467	61 081	172.5	92 077	10.1	89.9	41.4	8.8	2 967	23.4
Lewis	261	-8.1	348	2.3	178.3	742 403	2 131	86 827	73.0	97 383	60.5	39.5	44.5	17.9	3 529	72.5
Lincoln	249	-1.2	225	3.1	167.8	704 052	3 135	77 809	69.1	62 352	56.8	43.2	38.2	10.6	3 103	57.8
Linn	330	-2.9	306	1.3	197.0	559 578	1 826	59 902	53.7	49 867	57.0	43.0	44.4	11.9	5 210	66.9
Livingston	309	3.0	338	D	221.1	685 568	2 025	68 844	60.1	65 843	79.1	20.9	44.7	13.7	5 144	74.4
McDonald	200	-7.4	201	0.3	54.9	475 350	2 370	66 772	110.9	111 352	2.2	97.8	39.3	10.0	181	5.5
Macon	394	-3.0	272	0.1	219.6	486 951	1 792	55 367	63.5	43 746	49.7	50.3	39.5	9.0	5 303	60.0
Madison	98	-20.3	261	D	28.1	446 826	1 710	42 331	10.5	27 806	6.8	93.2	32.2	2.7	129	10.1
Maries	240	2.6	268	0.0	70.3	455 995	1 704	60 038	26.1	29 021	9.2	90.8	49.1	4.1	311	16.4
Marion	237	3.0	316	3.0	166.2	705 986	2 231	91 129	76.5	102 172	64.4	35.6	49.1	17.1	3 030	75.3
Mercer	201	-5.2	364	D	105.8	659 442	1 811	84 188	81.5	147 386	17.4	82.6	38.7	8.0	2 921	74.1
Miller	246	-8.2	227	1.2	77.1	453 770	1 996	57 707	95.4	88 326	4.0	96.0	46.5	9.4	354	14.5
Mississippi	258	-5.1	1 134	80.2	249.4	2 681 455	2 365	350 985	108.4	475 525	96.3	3.7	77.2	56.6	4 459	87.7
Moniteau	243	-5.8	213	0.2	122.6	506 981	2 375	63 334	123.0	108 126	13.9	86.1	53.2	12.7	1 727	39.3
Monroe	288	-8.9	278	1.5	183.3	630 118	2 264	66 285	69.9	67 478	59.9	40.1	40.3	12.0	5 014	72.7
Montgomery	248	-4.2	289	3.4	167.2	822 951	2 850	85 520	52.2	60 717	74.9	25.1	46.1	15.8	2 949	63.8
Morgan	217	-2.3	209	0.4	93.5	463 405	2 216	48 802	124.9	120 528	9.0	91.0	47.5	18.2	638	18.5
New Madrid	381	-3.5	1 088	198.8	373.4	2 637 463	2 425	320 207	141.3	403 606	100.0	0.0	85.7	58.0	13 667	91.1
Newton	246	-8.6	155	1.2	107.9	405 698	2 623	63 521	235.6	148 163	4.6	95.4	38.4	9.1	864	13.6
Nodaway	543	7.3	353	0.0	377.5	741 588	2 102	81 566	124.6	80 885	70.9	29.1	57.8	21.0	8 340	75.3
Oregon	239	-10.2	308	0.1	46.2	526 402	1 706	47 366	26.9	34 665	4.1	95.9	37.6	5.4	453	10.7
Osage	297	-5.7	252	0.7	100.2	488 220	1 938	65 056	66.2	56 026	11.8	88.2	52.8	9.2	771	32.9
Ozark	248	-12.1	334	0.2	55.3	569 530	1 705	44 650	31.4	42 372	2.6	97.4	41.5	8.9	250	8.0
Pemiscot	310	4.7	1 203	121.1	304.0	2 599 770	2 161	298 933	100.5	389 355	99.6	0.4	76.0	55.0	11 368	85.7
Perry	239	7.7	243	D	129.4	528 499	2 175	69 282	47.0	47 773	54.5	45.5	43.2	9.9	1 951	61.4
Pettis	409	1.7	293	0.6	262.5	691 718	2 365	82 096	166.3	118 983	31.7	68.3	48.4	17.0	3 907	50.1
Phelps	176	-12.4	213	0.2	51.6	439 592	2 065	43 698	11.3	13 705	13.3	86.7	28.3	1.9	244	9.7
Pike	373	8.4	339	1.4	245.0	801 938	2 368	85 472	79.8	72 387	62.3	37.8	46.5	14.7	4 156	61.2
Platte	179	-3.2	246	2.4	128.0	699 645	2 843	76 224	53.0	73 070	82.9	17.1	37.2	10.9	1 885	51.7
Polk	350	-5.1	205	1.3	144.1	444 350	2 165	49 062	80.4	47 120	7.5	92.5	44.2	8.0	715	17.1
Pulaski	123	-13.4	256	D	33.6	476 513	1 862	53 712	8.9	18 476	10.7	89.3	35.3	2.5	138	13.5
Putnam	273	-6.8	411	D	113.9	709 547	1 725	70 906	75.9	114 537	18.3	81.7	52.3	15.7	2 796	52.8
Ralls	246	-2.8	306	0.9	168.4	725 659	2 373	75 561	56.7	70 653	75.0	25.0	36.5	12.5	3 383	69.6
Randolph	222	-9.8	222	0.7	119.9	450 571	2 033	44 895	36.1	36 064	51.6	48.4	31.9	6.1	2 849	56.8
Ray	292	0.0	221	4.1	180.5	486 006	2 200	58 551	64.5	48 837	55.5	44.5	36.6	6.7	3 475	47.8
Reynolds	107	-9.3	307	0.0	24.9	436 578	1 424	41 467	3.4	9 739	9.5	90.5	26.9	0.9	36	10.9
Ripley	137	-2.1	291	8.6	47.6	503 899	1 729	52 967	13.6	28 875	48.8	51.2	36.5	6.8	521	22.7
St. Charles	156	-15.7	242	0.9	121.8	793 152	3 271	88 341	48.4	75 141	84.7	15.3	47.5	16.5	1 853	55.1
St. Clair	265	-1.1	314	0.2	126.6	561 172	1 787	66 000	34.3	40 625	45.1	54.9	46.9	9.0	1 760	39.3
Ste. Genevieve	189	2.7	263	0.4	86.0	570 917	2 168	57 750	25.7	35 834	47.7	52.3	39.2	7.1	1 029	45.7
St. Francois	113	-12.4	157	0.3	44.5	412 621	2 636	46 680	12.1	16 796	22.1	77.9	27.5	2.5	218	12.4
St. Louis	32	-17.9	117	1.4	20.2	431 316	3 686	62 075	23.8	86 203	98.4	1.6	35.1	9.1	130	21.4
Saline	449	8.7	452	1.5	340.2	997 734	2 209	120 500	178.4	179 320	65.5	34.5	61.0	28.4	6 365	78.7
Schuyler	152	4.1	280	0.0	79.0	476 248	1 700	54 568	20.4	37 541	32.2	67.8	46.1	9.7	1 902	66.2
Scotland	232	-0.9	324	0.3	148.3	635 897	1 965	80 735	53.2	74 306	58.5	41.5	47.8	17.5	4 444	76.1
Scott	228	1.8	424	67.3	203.0	1 097 463	2 585	144 494	108.7	202 062	76.7	23.3	49.4	25.7	4 998	71.4
Shannon	111	-17.8	248	0.1	28.1	435 741	1 756	46 021	7.7	17 332	8.2	91.8	40.5	2.9	145	13.4
Shelby	289	-3.3	409	1.4	201.3	847 723	2 073	108 076	87.2	123 375	59.7	40.3	51.2	22.5	3 844	74.5
Stoddard	461	11.1	441	228.6	418.3	1 045 580	2 369	152 911	228.1	218 293	73.1	26.9	43.3	23.7	14 415	67.7
Stone	122	7.0	162	0.1	36.8	398 716	2 465	44 398	25.3	33 625	7.1	92.9	32.8	3.7	149	5.8
Sullivan	334	-8.5	379	0.0	151.8	592 933	1 566	96 832	131.6	149 171	9.9	90.1	46.3	9.9	4 326	64.6
Taney	107	-30.5	245	D	21.0	466 897	1 902	45 112	7.2	16 552	11.0	89.0	31.6	2.8	55	5.5
Texas	355	-24.8	268	0.1	97.3	465 063	1 737	47 457	42.0	31 667	9.3	90.7	40.8	7.4	273	10.6
Vernon	456	7.0	330	7.6	268.0	606 988	1 842	75 820	129.4	93 530	30.4	69.6	42.5	11.2	4 692	43.0
Warren	147	3.5	203	0.9	85.2	674 902	3 324	65 961	28.8	39 898	62.9	37.1	34.6	10.5	1 586	47.2
Washington	137	3.0	246	0.2	41.3	458 676	1 864	40 773	8.7	15 643	8.1	91.9	29.9	2.0	80	5.7
Wayne	106	-7.0	274	0.0	29.2	467 545	1 706	44 728	6.8	17 535	20.5	79.5	32.3	3.9	223	22.0
Webster	271	-15.3	149	0.2	99.1	389 098	2 613	48 426	67.0	36 767	7.5	92.5	41.5	8.7	349	8.5
Worth	152	8.6	334	0.0	82.1	545 475	1 635	63 513	19.1	41 973	58.0	42.0	40.7	9.9	2 655	79.3
Wright	284	-10.7	236	0.9	91.2	426 822	1 811	52 647	50.4	41 828	3.9	96.1	45.1	11.3	261	11.5

Table B. States and Counties — Water Use, Wholesale Trade, Retail Trade, and Real Estate

STATE County	Water use, 2005 Total water withdrawn (mil gal/day)	Gallons withdrawn per person	Wholesale trade,[1] 2007 Number of establishments	Number of employees	Sales (mil dol)	Annual payroll (mil dol)	Retail trade,[2] 2007 Number of establishments	Number of employees	Sales (mil dol)	Annual payroll (mil dol)	Real estate and rental and leasing,[2] 2007 Number of establishments	Number of employees	Receipts (mil dol)	Annual payroll (mil dol)
	133	134	135	136	137	138	139	140	141	142	143	144	145	146
MISSOURI—Cont'd														
Jasper	28.7	259	140	1 528	793.4	59.1	596	8 171	1 967.4	165.8	141	654	76.4	16.1
Jefferson	793.8	3 715	143	1 438	782.8	66.2	524	6 796	1 709.8	154.1	171	592	69.1	13.5
Johnson	6.2	122	16	D	D	D	157	1 958	412.9	37.0	40	D	D	D
Knox	1.5	357	9	45	29.9	1.3	21	107	27.8	1.8	1	D	D	D
Laclede	17.0	494	28	D	D	D	192	2 059	469.7	43.6	38	99	10.7	2.0
Lafayette	4.6	140	36	277	140.6	9.1	151	1 402	301.4	25.1	23	99	5.2	1.7
Lawrence	6.9	185	25	222	63.7	5.9	138	1 257	419.5	30.9	33	95	9.4	1.3
Lewis	2.6	258	8	D	D	D	38	296	59.3	5.0	4	7	0.6	0.0
Lincoln	6.7	140	36	242	91.8	8.3	138	1 500	433.2	35.9	38	D	D	D
Linn	2.5	187	14	58	38.9	2.8	59	554	117.7	9.7	11	27	1.6	0.3
Livingston	2.8	195	20	218	86.2	7.1	85	1 124	234.5	22.3	13	54	13.3	1.2
McDonald	7.3	318	13	D	D	D	69	1 055	223.3	19.0	7	9	0.5	0.1
Macon	3.5	226	16	189	50.6	5.1	71	725	156.5	12.5	16	44	3.7	0.7
Madison	1.4	114	9	23	6.9	0.5	41	536	106.6	12.2	7	22	1.5	0.3
Maries	1.5	167	5	19	7.4	0.5	26	186	46.3	3.1	2	D	D	D
Marion	7.9	278	30	234	114.4	7.0	149	1 901	423.0	34.5	26	D	D	D
Mercer	2.3	651	2	D	D	D	12	58	20.2	0.8	NA	NA	NA	NA
Miller	4.6	185	20	122	68.9	4.1	134	1 734	451.8	39.8	60	155	27.0	4.7
Mississippi	82.6	6 077	17	176	235.2	6.7	58	458	161.5	8.4	6	24	1.5	0.3
Moniteau	3.0	200	13	219	106.3	5.5	60	490	159.7	8.6	5	D	D	D
Monroe	5.8	614	9	52	36.6	1.9	35	263	48.0	3.9	5	13	1.1	0.1
Montgomery	2.2	178	19	143	117.2	4.4	44	342	81.5	6.3	10	14	1.3	0.2
Morgan	12.1	592	18	149	22.1	2.1	101	948	191.5	18.2	24	55	7.0	1.1
New Madrid	1 027.2	55 326	31	432	288.0	14.3	85	1 479	509.8	28.1	12	26	2.6	0.4
Newton	10.8	194	42	1 233	491.8	33.5	203	1 925	605.7	42.4	41	181	18.7	3.1
Nodaway	2.8	130	18	D	D	D	83	1 099	206.8	17.6	22	50	6.1	0.7
Oregon	2.0	189	5	85	14.2	1.8	45	415	90.9	8.0	9	24	1.5	0.3
Osage	61.8	4 581	9	62	26.7	1.7	64	478	132.8	10.0	6	11	0.5	0.1
Ozark	26.9	2 830	8	D	D	D	33	218	46.0	3.1	7	10	1.7	0.3
Pemiscot	83.8	4 318	23	224	382.6	7.6	72	705	209.5	11.3	17	58	10.8	1.7
Perry	2.8	152	14	388	97.3	14.8	90	1 027	263.5	22.5	16	47	5.9	0.6
Pettis	9.1	228	36	418	169.4	15.6	202	2 398	547.3	50.9	54	353	38.4	9.1
Phelps	10.0	237	31	329	103.5	10.9	208	2 361	632.5	48.7	45	140	17.0	3.1
Pike	12.6	669	25	289	252.2	8.7	76	702	161.3	13.9	9	19	2.2	0.5
Platte	432.9	5 273	102	1 593	3 535.5	90.3	302	5 691	1 737.4	132.0	143	1 279	197.2	33.9
Polk	5.0	178	25	170	43.3	4.1	105	1 249	276.0	26.0	22	78	7.2	1.3
Pulaski	7.3	165	11	76	18.2	2.1	144	1 556	376.5	32.4	39	127	16.4	2.8
Putnam	1.9	375	1	D	D	D	26	152	38.6	2.8	6	21	4.8	0.3
Ralls	1.7	174	15	D	D	D	31	199	60.2	4.5	5	D	D	D
Randolph	581.0	22 931	17	D	D	D	107	1 224	293.5	24.6	26	118	19.3	2.7
Ray	5.7	234	15	152	92.2	5.0	66	695	141.7	13.1	11	27	1.2	0.3
Reynolds	5.9	894	5	30	8.3	0.6	26	150	28.7	2.4	1	D	D	D
Ripley	31.0	2 239	5	29	8.0	0.6	48	475	92.4	8.0	11	42	5.2	0.7
St. Charles	628.8	1 906	349	3 773	9 325.6	184.0	1 115	17 972	4 408.5	414.5	378	1 629	420.4	50.7
St. Clair	1.8	187	7	D	D	D	36	289	64.7	4.8	6	D	D	D
Ste. Genevieve	5.6	307	12	146	73.6	5.1	64	515	148.2	9.3	10	19	1.4	0.3
St. Francois	7.4	120	37	D	D	D	250	3 208	685.8	63.6	61	265	26.8	5.3
St. Louis	789.6	786	1 719	27 191	27 366.6	1 590.7	4 151	72 067	17 237.5	1 929.5	1 537	12 311	2 477.9	474.1
Saline	4.5	197	33	D	D	D	108	1 103	230.3	19.9	21	58	6.5	0.8
Schuyler	0.5	114	3	D	D	D	27	179	32.1	2.4	NA	NA	NA	NA
Scotland	0.9	172	6	D	D	D	31	168	39.4	3.0	3	D	D	D
Scott	107.9	2 622	57	538	252.4	16.0	190	1 515	358.4	29.1	48	D	D	D
Shannon	1.1	129	8	59	14.3	1.0	21	167	26.2	1.9	7	30	1.5	0.3
Shelby	2.1	308	12	71	30.5	2.0	35	229	49.1	3.8	4	7	0.4	0.0
Stoddard	334.8	11 267	31	230	196.3	7.0	143	1 409	436.1	29.7	23	62	5.3	1.0
Stone	4.5	146	15	35	14.2	0.8	116	1 086	222.9	21.9	53	262	26.8	5.0
Sullivan	3.6	520	2	D	D	D	28	183	45.0	3.2	3	3	0.3	0.0
Taney	32.7	760	33	199	76.0	5.7	447	4 576	833.0	84.4	137	1 343	295.8	52.2
Texas	4.4	179	22	121	50.7	3.1	92	789	167.8	13.9	12	30	2.4	0.7
Vernon	6.0	294	18	130	61.2	4.6	79	839	200.6	17.0	18	44	5.6	0.9
Warren	2.5	88	29	D	D	D	109	1 166	318.0	22.2	27	97	13.4	2.0
Washington	3.3	136	14	D	D	D	53	499	124.3	9.7	5	D	D	D
Wayne	1.9	147	8	44	29.8	1.2	46	388	65.8	6.4	2	D	D	D
Webster	4.7	134	31	146	69.5	5.3	122	1 123	294.2	23.4	23	56	5.3	0.9
Worth	0.3	156	5	14	7.7	0.4	13	64	13.2	1.0	1	D	D	D
Wright	3.3	179	16	101	31.7	1.9	99	989	237.9	19.7	18	47	4.1	0.6

1. Merchant wholesalers, except manufacturers' sales branches and offices.   2. Employer establishments.

Table B. States and Counties — **Professional Services, Manufacturing, and Accommodation and Food Services**

STATE County	Professional, scientific, and technical services,[1] 2007				Manufacturing, 2007				Accommodation and food services, 2007			
	Number of establishments	Number of employees	Receipts (mil dol)	Annual payroll (mil dol)	Number of establishments	Number of employees	Receipts (mil dol)	Annual payroll (mil dol)	Number of establishments	Number of employees	Sales (mil dol)	Annual payroll (mil dol)
	147	148	149	150	151	152	153	154	155	156	157	158
MISSOURI—Cont'd												
Jasper	200	D	D	D	189	10 351	3 336.6	383.6	247	4 792	182.3	52.8
Jefferson	227	976	75.8	27.1	202	5 784	1 538.1	229.5	272	5 399	203.3	58.0
Johnson	70	D	D	D	36	2 030	D	D	94	1 797	56.7	16.8
Knox	8	D	D	D	NA	NA	NA	NA	5	26	0.6	0.2
Laclede	41	169	11.1	3.7	63	4 892	1 225.6	151.8	74	1 233	50.3	13.9
Lafayette	50	D	D	D	36	1 123	225.7	32.8	67	793	25.4	7.2
Lawrence	48	181	11.2	3.6	48	1 622	608.7	58.5	55	686	20.5	6.1
Lewis	7	D	D	D	NA	NA	NA	NA	12	D	D	D
Lincoln	47	190	12.6	4.5	47	1 400	528.3	68.0	66	1 037	31.1	8.7
Linn	23	82	6.6	1.9	19	1 107	166.9	37.4	21	269	9.3	2.5
Livingston	30	160	10.0	3.2	17	610	130.3	22.4	32	534	17.4	5.0
McDonald	16	43	2.3	0.8	24	2 413	D	60.7	29	265	10.0	2.5
Macon	18	79	7.2	2.8	NA	NA	NA	NA	36	486	15.2	4.2
Madison	11	D	D	D	NA	NA	NA	NA	23	278	6.7	2.0
Maries	6	D	D	D	NA	NA	NA	NA	15	154	2.6	0.7
Marion	48	D	D	D	43	1 843	D	72.9	74	1 275	41.8	12.7
Mercer	3	D	D	D	NA	NA	NA	NA	9	22	0.6	0.2
Miller	42	199	24.5	9.5	23	699	74.8	21.2	58	650	30.0	9.1
Mississippi	10	D	D	D	NA	NA	NA	NA	23	271	10.0	2.8
Moniteau	18	62	4.5	1.3	26	747	D	25.2	27	280	8.2	2.4
Monroe	8	D	D	D	10	731	D	20.3	21	139	4.4	1.1
Montgomery	12	D	D	D	19	561	121.7	18.2	16	195	6.0	2.4
Morgan	26	D	D	D	28	537	108.1	14.7	43	428	13.3	3.9
New Madrid	17	D	D	D	17	1 768	D	87.0	28	383	15.0	4.2
Newton	69	D	D	D	80	3 434	646.7	107.1	105	1 962	69.6	20.4
Nodaway	27	114	8.4	3.0	19	2 064	866.6	65.7	40	934	28.8	8.2
Oregon	11	D	D	D	NA	NA	NA	NA	11	178	5.9	1.6
Osage	10	21	1.8	0.5	31	943	433.1	33.5	23	167	4.1	1.1
Ozark	9	D	D	D	NA	NA	NA	NA	22	174	6.4	1.9
Pemiscot	17	D	D	D	12	D	D	D	34	398	14.4	3.5
Perry	28	128	9.1	4.0	38	3 339	711.6	105.7	43	599	20.2	5.8
Pettis	69	328	30.2	9.1	60	5 058	1 535.8	162.4	92	1 590	55.4	17.2
Phelps	66	371	33.0	12.0	51	1 224	454.8	51.5	106	1 893	73.6	19.1
Pike	16	77	5.4	1.6	20	722	308.9	32.8	28	318	11.3	3.0
Platte	248	1 331	180.9	60.2	65	2 816	2 077.4	128.3	198	6 301	465.6	109.4
Polk	48	182	13.4	4.5	35	697	D	17.9	54	667	23.3	5.5
Pulaski	47	D	D	D	NA	NA	NA	NA	87	2 033	74.3	32.2
Putnam	4	D	D	D	NA	NA	NA	NA	4	18	0.5	0.1
Ralls	9	D	D	D	15	1 481	D	69.9	16	127	3.6	1.1
Randolph	32	79	9.7	1.7	30	1 165	196.9	38.5	40	600	21.8	5.5
Ray	24	79	6.3	2.1	NA	NA	NA	NA	31	329	10.2	2.8
Reynolds	6	D	D	D	NA	NA	NA	NA	17	45	4.1	0.9
Ripley	10	D	D	D	NA	NA	NA	NA	12	140	5.7	1.6
St. Charles	761	D	D	D	271	15 683	6 532.8	806.9	677	14 650	537.7	161.9
St. Clair	8	D	D	D	NA	NA	NA	NA	15	88	5.4	0.9
Ste. Genevieve	22	84	6.3	2.0	32	1 678	368.5	68.7	37	411	11.4	3.3
St. Francois	88	D	D	D	65	2 228	341.8	69.5	116	D	D	D
St. Louis	3 774	42 378	6 944.0	2 652.2	1 098	54 752	22 654.6	3 285.3	2 142	50 401	2 440.7	703.9
Saline	32	99	6.7	2.0	20	1 768	803.5	62.2	41	511	15.9	5.4
Schuyler	2	D	D	D	NA	NA	NA	NA	5	19	0.4	0.1
Scotland	7	D	D	D	NA	NA	NA	NA	10	61	2.2	0.6
Scott	75	435	41.6	14.0	72	D	976.9	D	83	D	D	D
Shannon	5	D	D	D	NA	NA	NA	NA	21	125	4.4	1.2
Shelby	11	D	D	D	NA	NA	NA	NA	13	76	1.7	0.5
Stoddard	28	184	15.6	4.4	42	2 753	888.0	99.0	39	630	20.5	6.0
Stone	39	139	7.7	3.0	NA	NA	NA	NA	101	641	47.6	10.4
Sullivan	5	D	D	D	6	D	D	D	6	21	0.6	0.1
Taney	110	581	45.4	16.2	50	535	D	D	303	6 283	360.7	106.6
Texas	25	D	D	D	48	987	214.7	28.7	38	381	11.0	3.3
Vernon	29	116	9.9	3.0	28	1 135	D	45.3	40	498	18.7	4.4
Warren	33	175	15.1	5.3	44	1 039	297.4	42.7	47	658	22.4	6.1
Washington	14	D	D	D	20	512	104.2	16.5	17	401	17.3	5.2
Wayne	10	D	D	D	NA	NA	NA	NA	21	128	4.4	1.2
Webster	40	D	D	D	48	977	161.5	30.7	36	638	22.2	5.6
Worth	4	D	D	D	NA	NA	NA	NA	5	15	0.5	0.1
Wright	21	D	D	D	24	526	146.6	18.0	30	301	38.0	5.8

1. Establishment subject to federal tax.

Table B. States and Counties — Health Care and Social Assistance, Other Services, and Federal Funds

STATE County	Health care and social assistance, 2007				Other services, 2007				Federal funds and grants, 2009–2010 Expenditures (mil dol)	Direct payments for individuals[1]		
	Number of establishments	Number of employees	Receipts (mil dol)	Annual payroll (mil dol)	Number of establishments	Number of employees	Receipts (mil dol)	Annual payroll (mil dol)	Total	Social Security and government retirement	Medicare	Food Stamps and Supplemental Security Income
	159	160	161	162	163	164	165	166	167	168	169	170
MISSOURI—Cont'd												
Jasper	396	5 138	349.6	164.1	252	1 297	92.5	27.5	953.0	383.2	195.6	47.1
Jefferson	445	5 598	366.7	155.4	336	1 668	139.3	42.8	1 068.4	593.6	222.8	48.6
Johnson	112	1 779	123.5	51.0	59	D	D	D	678.4	145.9	48.1	12.3
Knox	8	59	2.8	1.1	13	37	3.2	0.5	51.9	15.6	14.0	1.4
Laclede	73	1 228	108.3	42.8	64	223	17.7	4.3	283.1	138.5	47.3	11.3
Lafayette	65	1 130	62.7	26.3	49	166	10.3	2.7	260.5	112.7	66.6	8.7
Lawrence	80	1 522	97.2	45.6	42	116	8.5	2.5	255.7	110.9	54.4	11.3
Lewis	18	311	10.5	5.2	11	D	D	D	99.4	33.0	19.6	3.1
Lincoln	65	1 291	67.9	28.8	76	276	22.2	5.4	250.9	133.4	50.2	11.3
Linn	34	549	30.3	12.4	29	119	8.4	1.8	135.6	52.0	40.1	4.6
Livingston	45	846	58.9	22.5	39	182	9.9	2.4	149.2	52.1	32.9	5.2
McDonald	26	D	D	D	18	D	D	D	151.6	55.7	28.0	11.2
Macon	37	528	31.5	12.7	36	91	7.0	1.7	143.0	56.6	39.6	4.1
Madison	29	713	27.3	13.6	20	42	3.6	0.6	109.5	45.4	25.4	6.7
Maries	12	167	5.7	2.6	6	D	D	D	62.2	27.3	16.1	2.6
Marion	105	2 778	210.2	85.6	75	352	19.4	4.8	266.1	105.7	60.2	14.3
Mercer	10	86	3.7	1.7	5	27	2.0	0.5	89.2	13.1	8.8	1.3
Miller	34	444	24.7	10.1	45	261	16.6	5.8	188.8	88.2	48.7	9.2
Mississippi	30	540	24.2	9.3	16	43	3.3	0.9	187.1	44.2	29.0	14.6
Moniteau	33	355	20.1	6.8	23	68	3.5	0.8	91.9	40.1	25.6	3.0
Monroe	27	251	8.6	3.2	13	28	4.2	0.5	97.4	36.3	22.0	2.4
Montgomery	21	357	17.0	7.2	19	72	7.5	2.1	110.0	45.8	26.8	4.4
Morgan	31	247	10.6	4.3	34	95	12.0	2.0	173.0	89.8	40.5	7.5
New Madrid	42	639	32.5	12.2	27	69	5.6	1.0	278.4	55.9	37.0	16.5
Newton	111	7 121	739.8	271.7	92	378	24.7	7.1	330.0	129.5	62.9	13.8
Nodaway	52	1 096	87.0	32.5	35	127	10.0	2.6	165.5	59.1	30.9	3.8
Oregon	32	358	14.2	6.8	20	37	3.9	0.7	113.4	41.8	20.6	6.1
Osage	21	412	15.0	6.4	14	35	4.9	0.5	84.7	34.7	23.1	1.9
Ozark	17	104	4.6	2.2	18	D	D	D	104.0	43.0	18.5	5.3
Pemiscot	47	1 256	66.8	26.9	17	101	5.3	1.6	313.3	55.9	50.0	23.4
Perry	53	1 036	59.5	24.7	30	D	D	D	129.7	54.5	30.4	6.8
Pettis	146	2 640	182.0	76.0	98	D	D	D	348.9	139.7	71.8	16.1
Phelps	151	3 275	288.8	101.3	86	329	22.0	5.9	419.9	167.2	63.4	17.4
Pike	42	744	37.7	16.5	25	79	6.8	1.1	153.8	55.0	35.2	5.7
Platte	172	2 586	221.3	89.4	165	1 057	107.2	29.4	451.4	107.3	64.7	66.6
Polk	78	1 895	124.5	55.0	50	138	11.8	2.2	229.7	104.9	47.9	8.6
Pulaski	65	1 496	131.3	52.4	65	334	20.8	7.0	2 245.3	170.8	40.2	14.4
Putnam	12	143	8.3	4.2	9	D	D	D	53.8	18.5	14.4	1.8
Ralls	15	189	8.6	3.8	15	89	10.2	2.0	75.4	26.7	14.2	2.2
Randolph	89	1 422	119.9	40.1	47	139	10.3	2.8	221.2	85.4	56.6	12.3
Ray	33	516	33.9	13.3	28	87	6.2	1.4	140.8	66.2	37.8	4.9
Reynolds	18	141	5.4	2.6	3	D	D	D	73.2	25.4	14.7	4.4
Ripley	41	544	20.3	10.7	15	44	3.7	0.7	161.9	54.1	28.7	12.0
St. Charles	738	12 709	1 145.5	439.2	596	3 813	272.6	90.1	1 970.7	944.4	258.7	44.2
St. Clair	25	512	26.2	14.2	9	D	D	D	102.9	40.5	21.2	5.0
Ste. Genevieve	35	769	45.9	18.9	36	151	10.5	2.9	116.3	57.3	26.3	4.1
St. Francois	233	4 516	300.1	121.7	108	885	33.7	10.9	523.0	224.4	113.3	35.0
St. Louis	3 357	78 505	7 776.5	3 129.0	2 050	16 511	1 702.5	517.0	12 747.8	3 202.5	1 860.1	253.0
Saline	69	1 467	93.4	35.5	38	113	10.3	2.8	213.3	70.3	51.8	7.3
Schuyler	4	D	D	D	8	D	D	D	47.4	17.0	11.7	1.4
Scotland	12	223	15.1	7.7	15	D	D	D	49.0	15.0	12.8	1.4
Scott	123	2 713	175.7	73.4	77	D	D	D	385.6	144.4	70.8	27.2
Shannon	20	90	4.6	2.0	5	13	1.4	0.3	77.3	26.4	13.4	5.4
Shelby	8	90	4.6	1.5	12	31	3.9	0.8	66.3	24.0	17.5	2.1
Stoddard	77	1 558	69.0	31.2	39	165	16.4	3.8	325.1	109.7	60.9	13.7
Stone	50	549	43.6	15.7	52	260	18.3	5.2	221.4	135.1	43.9	9.6
Sullivan	17	262	14.1	5.8	12	26	2.7	0.6	85.9	20.8	19.4	2.6
Taney	111	2 196	243.6	93.9	110	512	47.6	11.1	328.3	182.5	67.7	12.1
Texas	58	954	49.9	20.6	37	79	6.4	1.3	212.5	96.6	37.3	12.8
Vernon	103	1 272	87.7	30.4	38	184	14.1	4.1	172.6	71.7	37.0	8.8
Warren	42	517	26.6	10.7	42	153	9.1	2.9	173.5	92.6	37.7	5.2
Washington	55	676	39.2	15.2	23	66	4.5	1.1	200.6	73.2	32.7	18.7
Wayne	29	319	12.6	4.9	10	D	D	D	230.6	65.7	32.9	10.3
Webster	48	D	D	D	42	136	8.9	2.3	265.1	119.4	43.5	10.7
Worth	3	D	D	D	3	13	0.9	0.2	24.6	9.5	4.6	0.9
Wright	43	479	25.8	10.2	29	81	6.0	1.4	198.9	74.4	38.7	11.3

1. State totals may include programs not allocated by county.

Table B. States and Counties — Federal Funds, Residential Construction, and Local Government Finances

STATE County	Federal funds and grants, 2009–2010 (cont.)							Value of residential construction authorized by building permits, 2010		Local government finances, 2007				
	Expenditures (mil dol) (cont.)									General revenue				
	Procurement contract awards			Grants[1]								Taxes		
													Per capita[2] (dollars)	
	Salaries and wages	Defense	Other	Medicaid and other health-related	Nutrition and family welfare	Education	Other	New construction ($1,000)	Number of housing units	Total (mil dol)	Inter-governmental (mil dol)	Total (mil dol)	Total	Property
	171	172	173	174	175	176	177	178	179	180	181	182	183	184
MISSOURI—Cont'd														
Jasper	51.4	37.7	27.8	141.4	20.1	9.6	14.8	16 556	157	307.9	106.1	122.2	1 060	546
Jefferson	49.0	8.7	7.0	81.2	21.4	9.0	9.1	82 883	636	479.8	196.8	217.0	1 004	731
Johnson	227.7	176.3	2.5	23.1	5.8	8.9	6.0	12 106	110	166.9	48.8	43.9	845	536
Knox	2.9	0.0	0.6	7.6	0.7	0.4	0.0	0	0	10.6	5.1	3.7	910	707
Laclede	15.4	0.1	1.4	57.9	4.7	2.3	1.9	6 333	55	108.9	49.2	34.4	972	607
Lafayette	22.2	5.3	1.9	21.6	3.2	2.9	2.2	7 134	42	79.3	34.6	29.3	898	600
Lawrence	17.4	0.0	4.4	41.3	4.7	3.8	4.5	620	5	70.2	34.5	23.6	627	421
Lewis	4.0	10.2	0.8	14.7	1.6	0.9	0.9	387	5	26.6	11.5	7.3	727	509
Lincoln	8.8	2.2	1.9	29.5	3.7	0.8	2.5	10 371	94	122.5	42.3	39.2	761	538
Linn	4.7	0.0	1.1	23.2	2.2	1.1	1.1	160	1	37.8	17.2	13.2	1 041	659
Livingston	15.8	0.0	1.4	28.0	2.0	1.0	1.3	5 956	29	66.5	28.0	15.7	1 109	849
McDonald	10.1	2.4	0.8	36.6	3.2	1.6	0.9	1 005	15	43.0	24.2	13.7	599	343
Macon	9.8	0.3	1.2	22.1	2.2	1.1	0.3	900	12	51.8	19.2	14.5	929	595
Madison	1.7	0.0	1.6	23.7	2.0	0.9	1.1	75	1	33.9	11.6	6.1	497	374
Maries	0.9	0.0	0.2	12.8	1.1	0.6	0.1	440	5	14.0	6.1	5.9	643	479
Marion	7.9	0.4	2.3	52.9	8.3	2.0	1.2	9 236	56	111.8	42.3	45.1	1 601	1 036
Mercer	1.4	0.0	0.3	7.6	0.7	0.1	51.2	300	1	11.4	4.5	4.6	1 315	1 033
Miller	5.3	0.0	1.2	29.4	3.5	1.7	0.2	2 521	12	73.7	25.6	34.7	1 395	978
Mississippi	3.1	0.0	0.7	71.7	4.3	1.9	3.3	593	12	31.6	16.8	9.7	709	482
Moniteau	3.3	0.0	0.7	14.7	1.5	1.1	0.1	180	1	28.2	13.3	10.4	683	549
Monroe	4.4	4.0	0.8	17.1	1.3	0.9	0.7	4 040	23	30.0	12.5	9.1	987	760
Montgomery	4.2	0.0	1.0	19.0	1.5	1.2	0.0	3 771	26	22.7	10.1	8.9	745	526
Morgan	3.8	0.0	1.0	21.8	2.4	1.2	3.6	75	1	34.1	13.5	14.6	700	534
New Madrid	8.6	2.5	0.9	98.6	12.9	2.4	24.7	1 748	20	58.7	21.2	30.9	1 737	1 465
Newton	36.5	0.1	3.5	47.7	6.9	7.2	10.0	4 635	45	104.0	51.2	33.0	588	366
Nodaway	18.2	1.3	2.1	20.9	4.2	4.2	0.9	3 568	27	54.5	21.3	23.1	1 042	706
Oregon	2.6	0.0	0.6	37.9	2.3	1.0	0.2	208	2	25.5	14.9	5.8	559	390
Osage	3.0	0.0	0.7	15.2	1.0	0.7	1.1	0	0	19.0	8.1	8.0	596	445
Ozark	2.2	0.0	0.6	30.8	2.0	1.4	0.1	193	6	21.6	13.0	5.8	633	527
Pemiscot	4.4	0.4	1.0	142.7	7.4	4.0	4.0	1 510	14	60.2	35.5	13.7	730	477
Perry	5.7	7.1	0.8	20.5	2.2	0.8	0.0	3 833	25	35.8	10.4	18.2	969	583
Pettis	20.6	3.9	3.1	61.1	6.6	3.5	1.7	902	28	194.7	45.6	43.7	1 070	591
Phelps	42.9	3.2	5.5	58.0	5.4	3.0	44.5	7 848	98	229.4	41.7	36.0	847	429
Pike	5.1	0.1	1.9	26.1	2.4	2.1	10.7	495	6	37.7	16.2	14.1	765	494
Platte	62.3	30.7	34.0	14.8	5.8	4.0	33.3	33 052	137	241.2	55.2	132.0	1 555	1 083
Polk	8.2	0.0	1.7	44.0	3.6	4.4	0.3	2 191	21	134.5	73.7	21.8	720	432
Pulaski	1 513.7	422.1	1.3	40.7	10.5	22.1	0.2	7 630	54	106.3	64.4	24.7	557	354
Putnam	2.4	0.0	1.1	10.0	0.8	0.5	0.0	40	2	20.2	4.9	5.8	1 178	972
Ralls	5.5	2.8	1.3	7.1	1.0	0.5	9.7	0	0	11.7	4.5	5.4	544	411
Randolph	8.4	0.2	1.5	35.6	2.9	1.8	1.1	590	5	88.6	29.6	38.7	1 513	1 018
Ray	5.9	0.0	0.9	12.8	3.1	1.4	1.2	1 646	14	94.9	26.1	23.4	997	681
Reynolds	2.0	0.0	0.6	23.2	1.4	0.8	0.3	582	6	16.7	8.3	4.9	761	652
Ripley	4.6	0.0	2.7	53.5	3.4	1.2	0.2	75	2	23.8	14.4	6.1	453	347
St. Charles	86.5	436.8	57.3	67.8	20.2	9.7	9.4	261 239	1 799	1 051.3	252.0	579.6	1 685	1 122
St. Clair	2.4	0.0	0.6	16.6	6.0	1.0	7.4	30	1	47.8	16.7	5.7	609	499
Ste. Genevieve	3.1	7.7	0.5	12.5	1.9	0.8	0.0	1 266	8	58.3	20.7	15.5	869	659
St. Francois	21.0	0.1	4.8	81.2	11.7	5.3	13.1	28 602	352	156.0	70.0	54.0	859	482
St. Louis	1 567.0	4 569.4	372.2	511.3	88.2	57.0	162.1	202 465	673	3 322.7	890.3	1 872.3	1 882	1 386
Saline	15.5	0.0	1.1	40.3	6.8	2.0	2.0	2 585	23	77.2	35.5	27.6	1 217	911
Schuyler	4.9	0.0	0.5	8.0	0.8	0.4	0.1	168	1	11.4	4.6	4.0	964	736
Scotland	1.4	0.0	0.3	6.7	0.7	0.4	2.3	584	5	28.4	7.6	3.9	813	635
Scott	6.9	0.8	1.5	101.2	6.9	3.3	5.5	3 304	28	92.0	40.8	35.2	865	492
Shannon	2.5	0.0	0.6	22.7	5.2	0.5	0.1	0	0	63.8	7.6	53.6	6 352	6 220
Shelby	3.3	0.5	0.8	10.0	1.0	0.6	0.1	240	3	22.7	9.6	6.7	1 023	746
Stoddard	12.4	0.5	7.1	85.8	5.2	2.4	3.2	1 174	18	69.6	28.8	28.3	951	610
Stone	3.4	0.2	0.9	21.2	3.5	2.6	0.1	19 764	97	82.0	29.0	44.0	1 395	966
Sullivan	4.1	0.0	2.2	22.3	1.5	0.4	8.9	65	1	23.6	9.0	7.0	1 047	706
Taney	9.9	14.9	1.4	27.1	3.9	1.5	1.0	46 806	464	155.5	41.5	81.1	1 773	727
Texas	6.8	0.0	1.1	46.0	4.3	3.2	0.9	1 025	9	73.4	26.8	12.9	555	351
Vernon	11.3	0.2	1.4	27.5	3.1	1.6	0.7	315	5	44.6	21.3	16.1	805	501
Warren	17.2	0.6	1.0	12.9	2.3	1.0	0.1	16 764	124	60.7	20.5	30.6	1 005	624
Washington	4.9	0.0	1.4	49.5	4.9	1.8	12.9	610	6	62.8	23.2	18.9	778	589
Wayne	4.3	70.9	0.7	40.7	3.0	1.1	0.5	NA	NA	22.2	12.7	6.5	514	342
Webster	7.4	0.2	1.6	47.4	4.0	2.4	27.3	3 425	27	57.5	26.9	19.4	539	294
Worth	1.9	0.0	0.5	4.3	0.4	0.2	0.0	0	0	6.7	2.8	1.7	799	643
Wright	4.8	0.0	1.2	60.2	3.3	1.7	1.3	290	5	43.4	23.1	11.0	602	448

1. State totals may include programs not allocated by county.   2. Based on the resident population estimated as of July 1 of the year shown.

STATE County	Local government finances, 2007 (cont.)							Debt outstanding		Government employment, 2009			Presidential election,[2] 2008		
	Direct general expenditure												Percent of vote cast:		
			Percent of total for:												
	Total (mil dol)	Per capita[1] (dollars)	Educa-tion	Health and hospitals	Police protec-tion	Public welfare	High-ways	Total (mil dol)	Per capita[1] (dollars)	Federal civilian	Federal military	State and local	Demo-cratic	Republi-can	All other
	185	186	187	188	189	190	191	192	193	194	195	196	197	198	199
MISSOURI—Cont'd															
Jasper	307.7	2 670	53.2	9.2	6.7	0.1	7.9	280.2	2 431	333	486	6 872	32.8	65.9	1.3
Jefferson	495.6	2 294	71.2	2.3	4.9	0.0	6.3	385.0	1 782	346	896	8 446	50.6	48.1	1.4
Johnson	158.5	3 052	42.5	31.9	4.8	0.0	5.1	226.6	4 364	1 075	3 362	6 317	42.9	55.2	1.9
Knox	10.3	2 534	50.0	9.2	3.8	20.6	5.7	2.2	553	38	16	317	37.5	59.9	2.6
Laclede	112.0	3 165	67.3	0.5	2.7	0.1	8.4	49.8	1 408	97	145	1 552	32.0	66.6	1.4
Lafayette	88.2	2 699	59.4	1.5	6.9	0.0	7.0	83.4	2 552	124	137	2 255	41.6	56.9	1.5
Lawrence	77.8	2 066	65.0	1.7	4.2	4.6	9.5	68.6	1 821	83	154	2 127	30.6	67.7	1.7
Lewis	25.2	2 511	55.7	1.2	3.9	16.5	6.3	9.6	955	63	40	638	40.8	57.6	1.6
Lincoln	126.0	2 446	50.1	19.4	6.3	0.0	6.5	127.9	2 483	121	218	2 285	43.5	54.9	1.7
Linn	43.3	3 412	57.2	3.3	4.2	0.0	10.7	16.1	1 272	63	52	798	44.5	52.9	2.6
Livingston	69.8	4 914	62.4	2.7	2.9	5.7	5.8	34.1	2 405	86	58	1 420	37.2	60.9	1.9
McDonald	48.6	2 121	74.9	2.4	3.2	0.0	4.9	41.9	1 831	94	94	947	30.2	67.6	2.2
Macon	52.6	3 379	41.6	19.4	3.5	15.8	4.7	24.8	1 592	76	63	1 746	37.2	61.4	1.4
Madison	35.9	2 947	45.4	39.8	1.5	0.0	3.8	11.0	902	26	50	849	40.6	57.6	1.8
Maries	17.1	1 871	74.6	3.7	2.9	0.0	8.3	8.7	952	15	36	352	35.2	62.7	2.1
Marion	120.8	4 286	70.1	3.2	3.4	4.8	3.4	116.6	4 138	72	116	1 988	37.5	61.4	1.2
Mercer	12.6	3 587	62.8	4.0	2.3	0.0	15.3	7.3	2 080	20	14	249	29.7	66.9	3.4
Miller	74.8	3 004	63.3	4.8	3.3	3.8	4.9	55.0	2 208	56	101	1 412	30.8	67.6	1.6
Mississippi	33.2	2 425	60.9	4.8	4.3	0.4	4.2	18.0	1 316	38	54	1 152	42.0	56.6	1.4
Moniteau	29.7	1 961	70.2	4.9	2.8	0.0	6.8	24.4	1 609	48	62	1 027	31.3	67.0	1.7
Monroe	28.4	3 090	53.2	5.7	4.1	7.5	5.9	60.5	6 578	78	37	655	39.5	58.7	1.8
Montgomery	26.1	2 190	59.2	8.0	2.9	0.0	10.4	16.5	1 388	52	48	715	40.1	58.5	1.4
Morgan	36.4	1 746	48.9	2.3	8.3	15.3	8.5	36.0	1 728	52	84	1 006	39.0	59.6	1.5
New Madrid	63.0	3 541	67.8	3.0	3.8	0.0	5.8	28.3	1 592	68	72	1 030	41.6	56.8	1.6
Newton	124.9	2 228	69.7	0.5	3.5	0.0	5.5	78.9	1 408	153	230	2 402	29.3	69.4	1.3
Nodaway	56.1	2 536	54.2	3.5	4.3	0.0	11.4	32.0	1 445	100	91	2 693	44.0	54.5	1.6
Oregon	25.3	2 458	64.0	1.5	1.3	0.0	4.5	4.9	480	36	42	517	39.4	57.8	2.8
Osage	20.4	1 521	69.7	5.1	3.0	0.0	6.0	10.9	815	40	55	814	26.9	71.5	1.6
Ozark	22.8	2 464	63.2	7.6	2.5	0.0	6.1	3.2	342	26	38	472	35.4	62.3	2.3
Pemiscot	62.6	3 332	68.9	1.2	4.1	0.0	4.2	14.0	744	66	74	1 836	43.0	56.1	0.9
Perry	35.7	1 900	55.3	3.0	6.2	0.9	6.8	31.0	1 651	54	77	1 137	34.8	63.9	1.3
Pettis	193.6	4 744	37.4	44.1	2.5	0.0	4.6	58.7	1 438	158	170	3 264	38.1	60.5	1.4
Phelps	232.3	5 460	25.9	55.8	2.0	0.3	3.5	95.2	2 238	392	306	5 784	38.0	60.2	1.7
Pike	41.7	2 259	61.6	6.0	5.2	0.0	7.1	20.9	1 132	80	75	1 690	44.2	54.2	1.6
Platte	264.2	3 113	52.7	0.8	4.9	0.0	8.0	425.7	5 015	326	373	3 481	46.2	52.6	1.2
Polk	131.7	4 359	84.1	51.9	2.7	0.0	5.2	57.2	1 892	91	125	2 116	33.2	65.4	1.4
Pulaski	100.5	2 267	73.7	3.9	3.7	0.1	3.3	30.5	689	4 284	13 094	2 056	35.0	63.7	1.3
Putnam	18.8	3 834	35.9	35.5	0.6	0.2	5.9	21.7	4 419	30	19	442	29.7	68.0	2.3
Ralls	11.1	1 127	54.3	3.7	5.7	0.2	16.1	16.2	1 647	69	39	360	40.1	58.8	1.1
Randolph	88.0	3 437	72.1	1.5	3.8	0.4	3.8	50.2	1 962	86	104	2 136	37.5	60.8	1.7
Ray	85.4	3 638	37.7	29.5	2.6	2.8	8.6	49.7	2 118	58	96	1 426	47.4	50.6	2.0
Reynolds	18.0	2 779	63.8	3.5	2.5	0.6	6.6	2.8	430	25	25	390	43.1	54.2	2.6
Ripley	24.9	1 834	73.0	5.9	4.7	0.0	5.3	1.9	68	56	55	712	33.5	63.5	3.0
St. Charles	1 063.7	3 093	52.8	1.9	5.6	0.0	10.7	1 646.2	4 786	791	1 456	14 686	44.7	54.4	1.0
St. Clair	38.8	4 111	31.2	32.5	7.7	0.0	4.1	24.6	2 614	37	38	677	37.8	59.8	2.4
Ste. Genevieve	54.3	3 041	30.7	53.8	4.0	0.0	3.7	42.1	2 361	35	72	954	56.4	42.3	1.3
St. Francois	161.0	2 563	68.0	3.1	7.3	0.3	3.8	156.1	2 485	130	261	5 829	47.0	51.6	1.4
St. Louis	3 250.1	3 266	56.9	1.6	7.2	0.7	4.8	2 992.6	3 007	5 602	4 102	52 974	59.5	39.6	0.9
Saline	79.1	3 484	72.6	3.3	4.6	0.2	4.6	14.3	628	89	93	2 114	47.8	50.4	1.8
Schuyler	11.1	2 706	56.1	3.7	2.8	15.1	12.5	7.8	1 911	37	17	311	39.1	57.4	3.5
Scotland	27.5	5 703	22.8	44.7	0.8	14.0	0.9	6.3	1 305	26	20	578	37.8	59.5	2.7
Scott	100.1	2 456	62.1	2.8	9.1	0.0	3.6	219.7	5 393	97	167	2 351	34.7	64.1	1.1
Shannon	14.2	1 690	53.2	7.5	2.0	0.0	19.1	4.7	558	51	34	418	42.7	54.1	3.3
Shelby	26.8	4 118	40.3	5.2	2.3	18.4	25.0	6.6	1 006	42	26	588	33.6	65.3	1.1
Stoddard	71.1	2 391	60.8	3.7	5.4	0.0	13.4	57.7	1 941	187	119	1 379	29.4	69.2	1.4
Stone	79.0	2 504	68.4	0.9	3.4	0.0	7.0	57.4	1 818	39	129	1 184	30.7	68.0	1.3
Sullivan	23.5	3 527	46.3	26.3	7.2	0.0	6.1	4.5	667	56	28	488	40.9	56.0	3.1
Taney	202.1	4 421	35.2	4.6	3.2	0.0	6.7	300.1	6 563	107	196	2 199	30.8	68.0	1.1
Texas	86.9	3 724	38.7	31.9	1.9	0.0	16.9	42.8	1 836	90	100	1 880	31.4	66.5	2.1
Vernon	44.8	2 240	62.8	3.2	5.2	0.0	9.4	14.1	707	99	82	1 745	38.1	60.1	1.8
Warren	70.9	2 327	66.5	4.0	4.9	0.0	6.2	94.2	3 091	66	130	1 236	43.0	55.7	1.3
Washington	58.7	2 413	51.4	32.7	3.3	0.0	3.2	34.9	1 436	64	100	1 568	49.0	48.9	2.0
Wayne	23.6	1 867	65.8	7.2	3.9	0.0	9.2	13.4	1 058	93	51	587	36.4	61.5	2.1
Webster	56.0	1 559	64.2	1.5	3.8	6.0	7.4	32.7	911	84	150	1 524	34.8	63.8	1.5
Worth	6.9	3 306	53.1	1.6	1.7	23.2	9.4	4.8	2 304	25	0	190	36.4	60.2	3.4
Wright	46.2	2 528	67.1	1.3	2.4	8.5	5.5	14.5	793	57	73	911	30.0	67.9	2.0

1. Based on the resident population estimated as of July 1 of the year shown.   2. © 2009 Election Data Services, Inc. All rights reserved.

Items 185—199

Table B. States and Counties — Land Area and Population

STATE/ County code	CBSA code[1]	County type[2]	STATE County	Land area,[3] (sq km) 2010	Total persons	Rank	Per square kilometer	White	Black	American Indian, Alaska Native	Asian and Pacific Islander	Percent Hispanic or Latino[4]	Under 5 years	5 to 17 years	18 to 24 years	25 to 34 years	35 to 44 years	45 to 54 years
				1	2	3	4	5	6	7	8	9	10	11	12	13	14	15
			MISSOURI—Cont'd															
29 510	41180	1	St. Louis city	160	319 294	200	1 995.6	43.8	50.3	0.9	3.5	3.5	6.6	14.5	12.3	18.1	12.6	14.0
30 000	...	X	MONTANA	376 962	989 415	X	2.6	89.9	0.7	7.5	1.2	2.9	6.3	16.3	9.6	12.4	11.4	15.1
30 001	...	7	Beaverhead	14 353	9 246	2 504	0.6	93.9	0.3	2.2	1.1	3.7	5.3	14.8	12.5	10.4	9.9	14.8
30 003	...	6	Big Horn	12 938	12 865	2 253	1.0	32.5	0.4	64.7	0.7	4.0	10.5	22.6	10.4	11.4	10.8	13.0
30 005	...	9	Blaine	10 949	6 491	2 726	0.6	49.6	0.2	49.9	0.3	1.8	8.9	21.2	9.0	10.9	10.1	14.5
30 007	...	9	Broadwater	3 089	5 612	2 799	1.8	95.9	0.4	2.2	0.6	2.2	5.8	16.7	6.0	8.9	12.0	17.1
30 009	13740	3	Carbon	5 306	10 078	2 441	1.9	96.8	0.4	1.4	0.4	1.9	4.1	15.6	4.9	9.1	11.0	18.6
30 011	...	9	Carter	8 653	1 160	3 103	0.1	98.2	0.3	1.3	0.1	0.7	3.4	14.1	6.8	8.2	8.5	17.7
30 013	24500	3	Cascade	6 988	81 327	678	11.6	90.3	1.9	6.0	1.7	3.3	6.8	16.1	10.1	12.8	11.1	14.7
30 015	...	8	Chouteau	10 289	5 813	2 783	0.6	76.7	0.4	22.2	0.8	1.6	7.1	19.5	7.4	9.6	10.0	14.6
30 017	...	7	Custer	9 799	11 699	2 316	1.2	95.5	0.5	2.5	0.7	2.2	6.2	16.5	8.4	11.1	10.9	15.4
30 019	...	9	Daniels	3 694	1 751	3 071	0.5	95.9	0.3	3.3	0.5	1.5	5.6	15.4	4.1	8.6	8.6	16.2
30 021	...	7	Dawson	6 143	8 966	2 528	1.5	95.8	0.5	2.5	0.4	2.0	6.1	14.7	9.1	11.4	10.3	15.7
30 023	...	7	Deer Lodge	1 908	9 298	2 498	4.9	95.6	0.9	4.2	0.7	2.9	4.5	14.4	8.4	9.7	11.9	15.5
30 025	...	9	Fallon	4 198	2 890	2 988	0.7	97.8	0.6	0.7	0.9	1.2	7.5	16.0	6.1	12.6	10.0	16.4
30 027	...	7	Fergus	11 240	11 586	2 325	1.0	97.0	0.3	2.0	0.5	1.5	5.4	14.8	5.7	9.9	10.5	15.6
30 029	28060	5	Flathead	13 177	90 928	627	6.9	95.8	0.5	2.2	1.1	2.3	6.3	17.1	7.4	11.9	12.0	15.9
30 031	14580	5	Gallatin	6 741	89 513	632	13.3	94.8	0.6	1.5	1.8	2.8	6.4	14.5	15.9	16.9	12.5	13.3
30 033	...	9	Garfield	12 109	1 206	3 100	0.1	98.9	0.3	0.8	0.1	0.2	6.6	16.5	4.6	10.3	10.1	13.7
30 035	...	7	Glacier	7 759	13 399	2 226	1.7	33.1	0.4	67.0	0.3	1.8	9.2	22.4	10.0	11.9	10.7	15.0
30 037	...	8	Golden Valley	3 044	884	3 115	0.3	94.2	0.0	2.1	0.7	3.5	3.1	18.7	5.8	6.4	10.6	16.4
30 039	...	8	Granite	4 474	3 079	2 973	0.7	97.9	0.2	1.5	0.4	1.4	3.8	13.3	4.0	8.0	9.0	17.2
30 041	25660	7	Hill	7 508	16 096	2 046	2.1	75.6	0.6	23.3	1.1	2.3	7.8	19.0	10.7	12.4	10.6	14.3
30 043	25740	9	Jefferson	4 290	11 406	2 338	2.7	96.1	0.4	2.8	0.7	2.0	5.1	18.0	5.4	7.8	11.8	18.9
30 045	...	8	Judith Basin	4 843	2 072	3 043	0.4	97.9	0.1	1.3	0.3	1.2	4.7	15.9	5.3	8.3	9.8	17.9
30 047	...	6	Lake	3 859	28 746	1 462	7.4	74.6	0.6	27.2	0.8	3.5	7.4	17.9	8.1	10.3	10.2	14.5
30 049	25740	5	Lewis and Clark	8 958	63 395	824	7.1	94.5	0.6	3.4	1.1	2.5	6.2	16.4	8.8	11.9	11.7	16.1
30 051	...	9	Liberty	3 704	2 339	3 027	0.6	99.1	0.4	0.9	0.6	0.3	5.4	16.5	8.0	10.3	10.3	16.5
30 053	...	7	Lincoln	9 357	19 687	1 855	2.1	96.2	0.4	2.4	0.7	2.3	4.8	15.0	5.6	9.0	9.9	16.5
30 055	...	9	McCone	6 846	1 734	3 074	0.3	98.6	0.5	1.2	0.3	0.7	5.6	15.3	5.2	8.7	9.3	16.4
30 057	...	9	Madison	9 292	7 691	2 630	0.8	96.5	0.4	1.3	0.4	2.4	4.5	13.2	5.4	9.4	10.4	16.1
30 059	...	9	Meagher	6 195	1 891	3 064	0.3	97.7	0.2	1.3	0.4	1.5	4.7	14.6	5.3	9.4	9.0	16.2
30 061	...	8	Mineral	3 158	4 223	2 890	1.3	95.8	0.6	2.9	1.0	1.9	4.7	13.2	6.1	8.5	10.0	16.9
30 063	33540	3	Missoula	6 717	109 299	538	16.3	93.2	0.8	3.7	1.9	2.6	5.8	14.2	15.0	15.9	11.6	13.5
30 065	...	8	Musselshell	4 838	4 538	2 868	0.9	95.6	0.4	2.3	0.3	2.6	4.5	16.1	5.0	7.7	10.8	16.9
30 067	...	7	Park	7 260	15 636	2 072	2.2	96.5	0.3	1.6	0.7	2.1	5.2	14.5	5.1	11.2	13.3	17.1
30 069	...	9	Petroleum	4 286	494	3 137	0.1	99.0	0.6	0.2	0.0	1.0	5.1	17.8	5.1	7.7	9.3	19.4
30 071	...	9	Phillips	13 313	4 253	2 888	0.3	89.6	0.1	11.4	0.5	1.9	5.6	17.6	5.5	9.2	9.2	17.6
30 073	...	7	Pondera	4 203	6 153	2 751	1.5	84.0	0.5	15.7	0.4	1.4	7.1	17.9	7.1	10.0	10.3	15.7
30 075	...	9	Powder River	8 540	1 743	3 073	0.2	96.2	0.2	3.2	0.2	1.4	3.8	17.0	4.6	8.1	9.4	16.5
30 077	...	7	Powell	6 025	7 027	2 686	1.2	92.6	1.2	5.0	0.7	1.7	4.3	13.0	7.4	11.9	13.2	18.3
30 079	...	9	Prairie	4 498	1 179	3 101	0.3	98.0	0.2	1.9	1.2	1.4	4.9	12.8	4.5	7.8	8.1	14.2
30 081	...	6	Ravalli	6 192	40 212	1 168	6.5	95.5	0.3	1.8	1.0	3.0	5.3	16.6	6.1	9.3	11.3	15.5
30 083	...	7	Richland	5 398	9 746	2 457	1.8	95.0	0.4	2.8	0.6	3.0	6.5	17.0	7.6	11.5	11.7	17.0
30 085	...	7	Roosevelt	6 099	10 425	2 411	1.7	38.4	0.3	62.4	0.7	1.3	9.6	22.1	10.2	11.7	10.2	14.5
30 087	...	9	Rosebud	12 977	9 233	2 506	0.7	62.4	0.5	35.2	0.9	3.4	8.0	21.5	8.0	10.7	11.0	15.4
30 089	...	8	Sanders	7 150	11 413	2 337	1.6	93.3	0.4	6.5	0.6	2.0	5.1	15.5	5.4	8.2	9.3	15.5
30 091	...	9	Sheridan	4 344	3 384	2 948	0.8	96.3	0.4	2.8	0.7	1.5	4.5	14.9	5.0	8.1	9.5	17.3
30 093	15580	5	Silver Bow	1 861	34 200	1 322	18.4	93.7	0.5	2.8	0.8	3.7	5.8	15.2	10.8	11.3	11.3	15.5
30 095	...	8	Stillwater	4 650	9 117	2 518	2.0	96.5	0.4	1.3	0.8	2.3	6.0	16.9	5.1	9.5	11.5	17.3
30 097	...	9	Sweet Grass	4 805	3 651	2 935	0.8	97.1	0.2	1.5	1.1	1.4	5.5	17.6	4.8	8.5	11.5	15.6
30 099	...	8	Teton	5 885	6 073	2 759	1.0	97.1	0.2	2.8	0.5	1.3	5.3	18.0	5.6	9.3	10.7	16.0
30 101	...	7	Toole	4 962	5 324	2 818	1.1	92.2	0.8	5.7	0.8	2.4	5.3	15.4	7.9	13.3	12.7	17.2
30 103	...	8	Treasure	2 531	718	3 125	0.3	95.0	0.3	2.5	0.7	3.5	5.0	13.6	4.6	7.9	8.8	19.8
30 105	...	7	Valley	12 758	7 369	2 653	0.6	88.2	0.4	11.2	0.8	1.2	5.6	17.5	5.4	9.3	10.1	16.0
30 107	...	9	Wheatland	3 686	2 168	3 039	0.6	97.2	0.8	1.8	0.6	1.5	7.1	16.5	6.8	9.0	10.6	13.4
30 109	...	9	Wibaux	2 303	1 017	3 107	0.4	97.8	0.3	0.6	0.8	1.3	5.2	16.1	4.5	9.4	8.7	16.0
30 111	13740	3	Yellowstone	6 820	147 972	421	21.7	90.2	1.1	4.9	1.2	4.7	6.8	16.8	9.0	13.6	12.0	15.0
31 000	...	X	NEBRASKA	198 974	1 826 341	X	9.2	83.5	5.2	1.3	2.3	9.2	7.2	17.9	10.0	13.4	12.1	14.2
31 001	25580	5	Adams	1 459	31 364	1 407	21.5	89.3	1.1	0.6	1.6	8.1	6.7	17.3	12.0	11.1	11.0	14.2
31 003	...	9	Antelope	2 220	6 685	2 716	3.0	96.5	0.5	0.3	0.4	2.7	6.5	17.0	5.8	9.4	9.1	16.0
31 005	...	9	Arthur	1 853	460	3 139	0.2	95.2	0.0	1.1	0.2	4.1	7.6	19.6	4.3	12.4	9.6	12.6
31 007	42420	9	Banner	1 932	690	3 130	0.4	95.8	0.0	0.7	0.4	3.8	5.2	17.1	6.1	7.4	7.7	19.0

1. CBSA = Core Based Statistical Area. See Appendix A for explanation. See Appendix B for list of metropolitan areas with component counties. 2. County type code from the Economic Research Service of USDA Rural-Urban Continuum Codes. See Appendix A for definition. 3. Dry land or land partially or temporarily covered by water. 4. May be of any race.

Table B. States and Counties — **Population and Households**

STATE County	Population, 2010 (cont.) Age (percent) (cont.) 55 to 64 years	65 to 74 years	75 years and over	Percent female	Population change and components of change, 1990–2010 Total persons 1990	2000	Percent change 1990–2000	2000–2010	Components of change, 2000–2009 Births	Deaths	Net migration	Households, 2010 Number	Percent change, 2000–2010	Persons per house-hold	Percent Female family house-holder[1]	One per-son
	16	17	18	19	20	21	22	23	24	25	26	27	28	29	30	31
MISSOURI—Cont'd																
St. Louis city	10.8	5.5	5.5	51.7	396 685	348 189	-12.2	-8.3	48 788	34 305	-52 780	142 057	-3.4	2.16	19.4	42.6
MONTANA	14.0	8.2	6.7	49.8	799 065	902 195	12.9	9.7	108 579	77 395	42 980	409 607	14.2	2.35	9.0	29.7
Beaverhead	15.4	9.9	7.0	48.8	8 424	9 202	9.2	0.5	844	732	-291	4 014	9.0	2.19	6.4	33.0
Big Horn	11.2	6.1	3.9	50.3	11 337	12 671	11.8	1.5	2 459	984	-1 077	4 004	2.0	3.18	17.3	23.0
Blaine	12.1	6.9	6.6	50.0	6 728	7 009	4.2	-7.4	1 049	575	-968	2 357	-5.8	2.66	16.0	28.7
Broadwater	15.7	10.5	7.2	48.8	3 318	4 385	32.2	28.0	365	448	510	2 347	34.0	2.37	6.2	26.6
Carbon	17.9	10.6	8.2	49.3	8 080	9 552	18.2	5.5	780	866	347	4 571	12.4	2.19	6.1	31.2
Carter	18.1	11.4	11.8	49.5	1 503	1 360	-9.5	-14.7	60	124	-93	532	-2.0	2.16	4.3	30.3
Cascade	12.7	8.2	7.4	50.1	77 691	80 357	3.4	1.2	10 392	7 008	-3 770	33 809	3.9	2.33	10.2	30.5
Chouteau	14.5	8.8	8.5	50.8	5 452	5 970	9.5	-2.6	400	543	-639	2 294	3.1	2.48	10.1	29.1
Custer	14.0	8.3	9.2	50.3	11 697	11 696	0.0	0.0	1 279	1 280	-446	5 031	5.5	2.24	9.0	34.3
Daniels	16.6	10.9	14.0	49.7	2 266	2 017	-11.0	-13.2	122	228	-201	798	-10.5	2.14	4.6	35.1
Dawson	14.7	8.7	9.2	49.5	9 505	9 059	-4.7	-1.0	858	972	-342	3 749	3.4	2.26	6.7	31.2
Deer Lodge	16.4	10.3	8.9	47.1	10 356	9 417	-9.1	-1.3	724	1 139	-161	4 018	0.6	2.11	9.2	36.1
Fallon	13.9	8.1	9.3	49.3	3 103	2 837	-8.6	1.9	307	276	-134	1 233	8.2	2.32	5.7	30.1
Fergus	16.6	11.0	10.5	49.8	12 083	11 893	-1.6	-2.6	952	1 424	-157	5 099	4.9	2.18	6.5	32.6
Flathead	15.0	8.2	6.2	50.2	59 218	74 471	25.8	22.1	9 985	6 615	12 091	37 504	26.8	2.40	8.7	27.2
Gallatin	11.0	5.2	4.2	48.1	50 484	67 831	34.4	32.0	9 867	3 618	16 503	36 550	38.9	2.36	6.6	27.3
Garfield	17.7	11.7	8.9	48.8	1 589	1 279	-19.5	-5.7	149	110	-141	532	0.0	2.27	5.1	30.3
Glacier	10.2	5.9	4.6	51.1	12 121	13 247	9.3	1.1	2 428	1 044	-1 018	4 361	1.3	2.91	19.1	24.9
Golden Valley	17.6	12.1	9.3	47.6	912	1 042	14.3	-15.2	82	68	2	363	-0.5	2.19	5.2	29.5
Granite	20.4	15.7	8.7	49.1	2 548	2 830	11.1	8.8	200	212	73	1 417	18.1	2.14	5.7	29.5
Hill	12.6	6.5	6.2	49.5	17 654	16 673	-5.6	-3.5	2 517	1 312	-1 160	6 275	-2.8	2.47	11.9	29.8
Jefferson	19.0	9.2	4.8	49.0	7 939	10 049	26.6	13.5	890	775	1 360	4 512	20.4	2.48	5.4	22.6
Judith Basin	17.2	11.7	9.1	48.1	2 282	2 329	2.1	-11.0	145	160	-258	924	-2.8	2.24	5.2	30.3
Lake	14.7	9.7	7.1	50.5	21 041	26 507	26.0	8.4	3 597	2 371	1 052	11 432	12.2	2.46	11.5	26.5
Lewis and Clark	15.1	7.8	6.0	50.6	47 495	55 716	17.3	13.8	6 558	4 532	4 509	26 694	16.8	2.30	9.4	30.7
Liberty	13.2	9.1	10.7	51.9	2 295	2 158	-6.0	8.4	144	194	-358	822	-1.3	2.36	4.7	32.2
Lincoln	18.7	13.0	7.6	49.2	17 481	18 837	7.8	4.5	1 649	1 878	197	8 846	13.9	2.20	7.4	30.6
McCone	17.5	11.3	10.7	48.7	2 276	1 977	-13.1	-12.3	133	161	-324	774	-4.4	2.22	3.2	31.7
Madison	20.0	12.5	8.5	48.0	5 989	6 851	14.4	12.3	481	681	843	3 560	20.4	2.11	4.5	32.6
Meagher	18.1	12.4	10.3	49.4	1 819	1 932	6.2	-2.1	196	206	-6	806	0.4	2.13	6.2	33.3
Mineral	18.7	14.2	7.7	48.2	3 315	3 884	17.2	8.7	413	399	-51	1 911	20.6	2.20	7.3	29.7
Missoula	12.7	6.4	5.0	49.7	78 687	95 802	21.8	14.1	11 186	6 412	8 520	45 926	19.5	2.30	9.2	30.3
Musselshell	20.2	11.2	7.7	50.2	4 106	4 497	9.5	0.9	422	526	219	2 046	8.9	2.19	6.5	33.5
Park	16.9	9.3	7.3	50.2	14 515	15 694	8.1	-0.4	1 504	1 357	181	7 310	7.1	2.12	7.0	35.7
Petroleum	14.8	14.0	6.9	46.0	519	493	-5.0	0.2	35	27	-60	225	6.6	2.20	4.0	35.1
Phillips	15.1	10.6	9.7	50.7	5 163	4 601	-10.9	-7.6	364	463	-551	1 819	-1.6	2.27	7.4	32.2
Pondera	13.0	9.0	9.9	51.7	6 433	6 424	-0.1	-4.2	693	661	-619	2 285	-5.2	2.41	9.4	29.9
Powder River	17.9	10.7	12.0	49.2	2 090	1 858	-11.1	-6.2	104	168	-121	755	2.4	2.26	5.0	28.3
Powell	15.5	9.8	6.5	38.9	6 620	7 180	8.5	-2.1	498	663	113	2 466	1.8	2.23	8.8	32.2
Prairie	21.5	13.7	12.3	49.0	1 383	1 199	-13.3	-1.7	69	148	-10	551	2.6	2.10	4.2	34.1
Ravalli	16.7	11.3	8.0	50.4	25 010	36 070	44.2	11.5	3 893	3 383	3 992	16 933	18.5	2.35	7.7	27.1
Richland	13.9	7.8	7.1	48.5	10 716	9 667	-9.8	0.8	936	938	-307	4 167	7.5	2.33	7.6	29.8
Roosevelt	11.0	5.8	5.0	50.7	10 999	10 620	-3.4	-1.8	1 963	1 052	-1 189	3 553	-0.8	2.88	20.5	24.2
Rosebud	13.8	6.8	4.7	49.4	10 505	9 383	-10.7	-1.6	1 578	663	-1 004	3 395	2.7	2.70	10.6	27.6
Sanders	19.5	13.5	8.0	48.7	8 669	10 227	18.0	11.6	955	1 076	1 060	5 121	19.8	2.19	6.2	32.8
Sheridan	17.5	10.4	12.7	49.8	4 732	4 105	-13.3	-17.6	195	538	-511	1 587	-8.8	2.08	5.7	37.1
Silver Bow	13.7	8.7	7.7	49.5	33 941	34 606	2.0	-1.2	3 556	3 884	-1 175	14 932	3.5	2.22	10.6	35.1
Stillwater	17.3	9.6	6.8	48.7	6 536	8 195	25.4	11.3	905	671	405	3 796	17.4	2.37	6.0	25.8
Sweet Grass	16.0	10.5	10.2	49.4	3 154	3 609	14.4	1.2	348	330	59	1 590	7.7	2.27	6.5	30.4
Teton	14.4	11.0	9.7	50.7	6 271	6 445	2.8	-5.8	579	576	-327	2 450	-3.5	2.29	6.0	29.3
Toole	14.2	7.0	6.9	44.3	5 046	5 267	4.4	1.1	436	490	-341	2 015	2.7	2.26	7.4	34.3
Treasure	16.4	13.8	10.0	48.6	874	861	-1.5	-16.6	43	53	-240	335	-6.2	2.14	2.1	32.5
Valley	15.4	10.5	10.2	50.3	8 239	7 675	-6.8	-4.0	742	833	-792	3 198	1.5	2.26	8.0	33.4
Wheatland	15.8	10.9	9.8	50.7	2 246	2 259	0.6	-4.0	195	230	-175	887	4.0	2.28	6.4	35.4
Wibaux	16.1	10.2	13.7	49.6	1 191	1 068	-10.3	-4.8	59	164	-65	457	8.6	2.17	6.1	35.4
Yellowstone	12.7	7.3	6.8	51.1	113 419	129 352	14.0	14.4	17 296	11 154	10 026	60 672	16.5	2.38	10.5	29.7
NEBRASKA	11.7	6.7	6.8	50.4	1 578 417	1 711 263	8.4	6.7	241 832	139 626	-9 156	721 130	8.2	2.46	9.8	28.7
Adams	12.3	7.3	8.2	50.3	29 625	31 151	5.2	0.7	3 919	2 778	-645	12 466	2.7	2.39	9.5	30.3
Antelope	15.2	10.0	11.0	50.2	7 965	7 452	-6.4	-10.3	688	699	-753	2 841	-3.8	2.33	5.9	30.0
Arthur	13.5	10.9	9.6	50.4	462	444	-3.9	3.6	47	33	-122	187	1.1	2.46	8.0	26.7
Banner	17.8	10.7	9.0	48.7	852	819	-3.9	-15.8	42	36	-185	293	-5.8	2.35	4.1	25.6

1. No spouse present.

STATE County	Persons in group quarters, 2010	Daytime population, 2006–2010 Number	Employ-ment/resi-dence ratio	Births, average 2006–2008 Total	Rate[1]	Deaths, average 2006–2008 Number	Rate[1]	Persons under 65 with no health insurance, 2009 Number	Percent	Medicare, 2011 Eligible for Medicare	Enrolled in Medicare Advantage	Enrolled in a Medicare prescription drug plan	Serious crimes known to police,[2] 2010 Total Number	Rate[3]
	32	33	34	35	36	37	38	39	40	41	42	43	44	45
MISSOURI—Cont'd														
St. Louis city	11 978	433 778	1.8	5 492	15.7	3 404	9.7	58 480	19.2	47 314	12 916	21 022	34 279	10 736
MONTANA	28 849	972 754	1.0	12 514	13.1	8 670	9.1	176 837	21.7	176 164	26 297	80 080	27 862	2 816
Beaverhead	444	9 176	1.0	D	D	77	8.8	1 841	25.4	1 836	127	872	127	1 374
Big Horn	137	13 074	1.1	284	22.0	128	9.9	3 217	27.6	1 528	76	794	131	1 018
Blaine	220	6 476	1.0	D	D	68	10.4	1 667	30.0	1 000	92	511	34	643
Broadwater	52	4 749	0.8	D	D	60	12.9	859	23.3	1 113	145	460	65	1 158
Carbon	53	8 629	0.7	D	D	92	9.4	1 799	22.7	2 116	357	955	146	1 449
Carter	11	1 227	0.9	D	D	14	11.2	315	34.2	269	30	148	5	431
Cascade	2 562	80 994	1.0	1 186	14.6	741	9.1	13 370	19.8	15 227	3 371	6 256	3 194	3 927
Chouteau	135	5 307	0.8	D	D	56	10.6	1 198	29.4	1 097	198	627	47	809
Custer	413	11 427	1.0	D	D	138	12.3	1 879	20.8	2 327	285	1 181	267	2 282
Daniels	41	1 667	1.0	D	D	21	12.6	297	23.8	444	24	270	7	400
Dawson	498	8 758	1.0	D	D	104	12.1	1 427	20.9	1 694	127	990	216	2 409
Deer Lodge	811	8 779	0.9	D	D	112	12.6	1 408	20.5	2 147	283	948	250	2 689
Fallon	34	2 981	1.1	D	D	41	15.0	484	22.0	515	18	310	32	1 107
Fergus	465	11 522	1.0	D	D	151	13.3	2 084	24.2	2 774	309	1 316	58	501
Flathead	992	89 477	1.0	1 200	13.8	734	8.4	16 840	22.4	16 741	3 130	6 749	2 711	2 981
Gallatin	3 260	88 208	1.0	1 237	14.4	436	5.1	15 549	19.3	10 183	1 381	3 965	2 312	2 583
Garfield	0	1 280	1.1	D	D	13	10.4	359	38.8	247	18	174	2	166
Glacier	690	13 138	1.0	D	D	124	9.3	3 484	28.9	1 682	82	857	161	1 202
Golden Valley	89	735	0.8	D	D	D	D	293	34.0	256	48	119	3	339
Granite	40	2 703	0.7	D	D	21	7.2	650	29.6	788	67	334	78	2 533
Hill	593	16 318	1.0	D	D	148	9.0	3 540	24.7	2 582	257	1 540	586	3 641
Jefferson	230	9 000	0.6	D	D	84	7.5	1 604	16.2	2 081	228	833	91	798
Judith Basin	0	1 953	1.0	D	D	17	8.4	458	29.1	500	120	239	7	338
Lake	587	27 546	0.9	429	15.0	273	9.6	6 416	27.1	5 719	723	2 616	710	2 470
Lewis and Clark	1 946	64 223	1.1	775	12.9	519	8.6	8 922	16.8	10 849	1 438	3 993	1 555	2 453
Liberty	403	2 269	1.0	D	D	22	12.1	308	23.7	416	24	311	NA	NA
Lincoln	209	19 260	1.0	D	D	227	11.9	3 711	25.5	5 458	1 176	2 351	378	1 920
McCone	19	1 686	1.0	D	D	21	12.4	371	29.4	320	29	202	12	692
Madison	163	7 409	1.0	D	D	78	10.4	1 481	25.2	1 692	150	767	69	897
Meagher	174	2 018	1.0	D	D	24	12.4	387	26.6	501	34	291	16	846
Mineral	22	4 078	0.9	D	D	49	12.5	683	23.3	1 109	123	543	7	166
Missoula	3 634	111 463	1.1	1 293	12.3	717	6.8	19 384	20.6	15 952	1 534	7 658	3 574	3 270
Musselshell	52	3 886	0.8	D	D	59	13.1	1 014	27.8	1 086	169	527	88	1 939
Park	108	14 753	0.9	D	D	151	9.4	3 060	23.1	3 022	259	1 533	245	1 567
Petroleum	0	658	1.2	D	D	D	D	96	28.9	90	D	50	NA	NA
Phillips	127	4 136	1.0	D	D	51	12.8	901	29.9	942	103	554	62	1 458
Pondera	645	5 923	0.9	D	D	62	10.4	1 260	26.9	1 251	205	658	55	894
Powder River	35	1 616	1.0	D	D	20	11.5	412	32.3	356	49	166	NA	NA
Powell	1 523	7 165	1.0	D	D	71	10.0	1 570	26.9	1 333	114	600	57	811
Prairie	21	1 066	1.0	D	D	13	12.3	218	27.0	339	39	200	5	424
Ravalli	478	36 346	0.8	412	10.2	381	9.4	7 429	23.1	9 455	1 500	3 477	738	1 878
Richland	34	9 758	1.1	D	D	102	11.1	1 624	20.8	1 721	50	1 137	95	975
Roosevelt	186	10 397	1.0	D	D	115	11.3	2 329	25.6	1 460	58	839	201	1 976
Rosebud	65	9 755	1.2	D	D	73	7.9	1 880	23.0	1 385	130	715	102	1 105
Sanders	188	10 918	0.9	D	D	122	11.1	2 521	29.7	3 072	347	1 352	168	1 472
Sheridan	85	3 512	1.0	D	D	63	18.7	520	21.9	901	50	615	62	1 832
Silver Bow	998	33 639	1.0	D	D	414	12.6	4 974	18.6	6 747	1 024	3 244	1 574	4 602
Stillwater	112	8 560	0.9	D	D	76	8.7	1 305	18.0	1 766	300	792	94	1 031
Sweet Grass	45	3 830	1.1	D	D	40	10.6	651	22.2	775	75	392	45	1 233
Teton	462	5 896	0.9	D	D	56	9.3	1 216	25.5	1 349	397	733	67	1 103
Toole	766	5 433	1.1	D	D	52	10.2	1 160	26.9	833	110	438	108	2 029
Treasure	0	814	0.9	D	D	D	D	137	29.7	204	20	112	NA	NA
Valley	126	7 402	1.0	D	D	87	12.6	1 322	25.3	1 702	82	977	95	1 289
Wheatland	147	2 160	1.1	D	D	22	11.3	475	30.2	458	55	232	1	46
Wibaux	24	1 009	0.9	D	D	22	24.3	199	30.0	229	13	141	2	197
Yellowstone	3 695	146 592	1.0	1 979	14.1	1 290	9.2	24 278	19.8	24 525	5 144	11 416	6 188	4 182
NEBRASKA	51 165	1 816 432	1.0	26 883	15.2	15 208	8.6	202 324	13.3	285 635	32 857	156 863	53 925	2 953
Adams	1 554	31 803	1.0	D	D	300	9.1	3 799	13.8	5 802	456	3 750	897	2 860
Antelope	70	6 184	0.8	D	D	75	11.1	804	15.8	1 454	57	1 039	20	393
Arthur	0	380	0.8	D	D	D	D	52	20.2	110	D	77	0	0
Banner	0	NA	NA	D	D	D	D	107	19.4	194	D	104	NA	NA

1. Per 1,000 estimated resident population.   2. Data for serious crimes have not been adjusted for underreporting; this may affect comparability between geographic areas and over time.   3. Per 100,000 population estimated by the FBI.

STATE County	Serious crimes known to police,[1] 2010 (cont.) Rate[2]		Education School enrollment and attainment, 2006-2010				Local government expenditures,[5] 2008-2009		Money income, 2006-2010	Households Median income			Income and poverty, 2010 Percent below poverty level		
			Enrollment[3]		Attainment[4] (percent)										
	Violent	Property	Total	Per-cent private	High school graduate or less	Bach-elor's degree or more	Total current expendi-tures (mil dol)	Current expendi-tures per student (dollars)	Per capita income[6] (dollars)	Dollars	Percent change, 2000 to 2006-2010 (constant 2010 dollars)	Percent with income of $200,000 or more	Median house-hold income (dollars)	All per-sons	Children under 18 years	Children 5 to 17 years in families
	46	47	48	49	50	51	52	53	54	55	56	57	58	59	60	61
MISSOURI—Cont'd																
St. Louis city	1 987	8 749	86 236	33.1	46.5	26.9	486.4	13 268	21 406	33 652	-2.1	1.4	32 767	27.7	40.7	38.6
MONTANA	272	2 544	235 983	11.7	40.3	27.9	1 424.5	10 047	23 836	43 872	4.9	1.9	42 303	15.2	21.1	18.7
Beaverhead	249	1 125	2 586	9.0	37.7	30.4	12.4	10 501	21 110	38 264	4.3	1.2	35 952	18.1	25.3	23.2
Big Horn	210	808	3 732	7.2	52.1	12.6	29.6	13 527	15 066	36 550	4.3	0.8	34 507	25.9	34.3	30.8
Blaine	113	530	1 749	7.5	45.1	17.2	18.5	16 536	16 813	37 034	15.8	0.9	31 724	28.3	38.8	34.9
Broadwater	249	909	1 375	7.8	56.7	15.2	5.9	7 966	19 606	44 667	7.9	0.6	40 730	11.8	17.5	15.8
Carbon	218	1 230	2 049	8.4	44.7	28.5	15.9	11 629	24 983	49 010	20.4	0.9	42 256	13.1	17.0	13.9
Carter	86	345	229	6.1	46.4	15.2	2.2	16 632	20 681	35 703	7.2	1.2	34 240	18.6	29.2	25.0
Cascade	205	3 722	19 511	15.9	39.6	23.9	105.2	8 940	22 963	42 389	1.5	1.4	41 827	13.5	20.8	19.1
Chouteau	155	654	1 467	8.2	45.4	22.5	9.5	14 495	20 202	41 064	11.2	2.0	38 434	16.6	21.7	19.4
Custer	188	2 094	2 588	8.0	45.5	19.2	15.2	8 785	21 676	38 913	2.4	1.0	39 469	14.9	20.6	18.3
Daniels	228	171	328	1.5	38.6	19.7	3.6	13 718	24 737	38 125	10.3	1.7	39 453	11.1	13.5	12.1
Dawson	156	2 253	1 901	9.2	41.6	18.4	13.8	10 605	24 602	50 752	27.7	1.3	44 548	12.4	15.7	14.0
Deer Lodge	462	2 226	1 539	3.8	51.6	18.8	11.3	9 956	21 921	35 310	6.0	0.8	36 135	18.7	27.7	22.9
Fallon	104	1 003	554	4.0	54.3	15.7	7.7	16 192	26 819	52 529	38.5	1.9	48 347	9.5	13.0	13.1
Fergus	112	388	2 333	3.4	44.1	23.0	20.8	12 123	22 295	37 607	-2.3	1.6	37 669	13.6	20.2	18.2
Flathead	326	2 656	19 434	15.5	40.6	26.7	119.2	8 781	24 721	44 998	3.1	2.3	42 278	14.8	21.0	18.6
Gallatin	197	2 386	26 485	11.0	25.1	45.0	92.7	8 886	27 423	50 136	3.9	3.1	49 354	12.9	13.5	12.2
Garfield	0	166	279	6.5	57.7	14.1	2.4	14 094	22 424	42 955	30.9	1.0	36 638	19.1	28.3	25.4
Glacier	172	1 030	3 987	8.2	48.8	15.6	35.2	13 347	17 053	38 075	7.7	0.2	32 460	28.8	38.2	35.4
Golden Valley	339	0	154	5.2	50.6	23.7	2.5	15 201	19 319	35 726	3.3	0.6	33 265	21.1	35.4	29.9
Granite	130	2 403	576	12.8	45.8	23.9	4.7	11 990	23 222	36 052	2.4	1.3	36 448	14.8	26.4	22.6
Hill	460	3 181	4 532	11.8	38.5	20.4	38.0	12 651	21 420	43 606	11.9	1.1	39 678	18.5	26.2	22.8
Jefferson	184	614	2 383	15.6	40.2	32.0	15.0	9 093	26 437	56 695	7.9	2.0	58 241	10.0	12.6	10.7
Judith Basin	0	338	308	1.3	38.9	28.5	4.7	15 115	24 029	41 473	12.0	2.3	35 631	16.0	23.8	20.5
Lake	508	1 962	6 588	8.5	41.5	25.2	42.9	10 155	20 164	37 274	2.4	0.9	35 558	21.5	30.8	28.0
Lewis and Clark	292	2 161	14 576	19.9	32.9	34.7	84.7	8 886	25 894	50 238	6.2	1.9	50 889	11.4	15.2	13.3
Liberty	NA	NA	416	5.8	51.7	17.0	3.2	13 077	19 097	40 212	4.9	2.5	31 851	21.9	25.7	22.5
Lincoln	264	1 656	3 338	12.1	51.7	16.4	26.0	9 566	19 626	30 823	-9.0	0.6	33 908	18.7	33.3	29.4
McCone	115	577	351	9.7	51.3	18.6	2.9	11 227	23 265	48 167	28.0	1.9	39 062	16.2	24.9	21.2
Madison	52	845	1 190	15.0	36.7	33.8	12.0	12 756	32 205	42 998	12.3	3.4	42 174	11.6	17.8	15.9
Meagher	53	793	441	14.5	57.7	15.8	2.9	11 687	17 318	31 577	-15.1	1.4	29 026	19.5	31.0	27.9
Mineral	47	118	739	9.7	60.5	13.6	8.9	13 283	19 209	37 266	8.4	0.2	33 333	17.9	28.6	25.2
Missoula	286	2 984	31 843	8.8	32.7	38.4	125.0	9 536	24 343	42 887	-1.7	2.3	44 084	15.0	18.6	16.8
Musselshell	176	1 763	787	4.3	54.4	13.4	6.8	10 376	20 875	37 033	14.6	0.7	36 188	17.7	31.6	28.3
Park	243	1 324	3 528	9.9	40.5	31.4	21.0	9 963	24 717	38 830	-3.4	2.5	37 835	13.9	21.2	18.6
Petroleum	NA	NA	122	9.0	52.0	13.8	1.3	13 000	21 008	36 875	20.8	1.8	29 656	20.6	28.4	23.3
Phillips	282	1 176	913	2.5	53.4	15.8	10.5	14 075	24 227	36 453	0.3	0.6	36 144	16.5	21.7	18.2
Pondera	130	764	1 440	14.8	44.8	19.3	12.3	12 394	18 989	36 419	-5.6	1.4	35 091	19.4	28.2	25.8
Powder River	NA	NA	392	4.8	41.3	16.1	3.9	12 145	21 543	37 685	4.8	2.6	36 550	14.5	18.6	15.1
Powell	100	712	1 267	7.5	53.2	18.7	10.6	12 176	17 849	39 851	2.8	0.6	36 872	20.5	24.0	20.2
Prairie	85	339	173	0.0	49.4	13.4	1.9	14 630	21 296	34 896	8.3	2.2	32 963	15.6	26.9	23.6
Ravalli	288	1 591	8 207	15.7	43.5	25.0	50.0	8 535	23 908	43 000	6.1	2.2	39 409	17.5	26.4	22.8
Richland	41	934	1 909	8.5	54.2	16.6	21.9	13 316	26 888	52 516	29.2	3.5	49 444	11.4	15.4	13.3
Roosevelt	265	1 711	3 162	2.2	51.7	17.3	36.4	16 321	17 821	37 451	19.1	1.2	35 141	27.3	38.0	36.0
Rosebud	303	801	2 605	7.6	47.9	17.6	26.2	14 725	19 844	44 776	-1.5	1.4	44 683	18.8	27.2	25.2
Sanders	315	1 157	2 117	11.7	56.9	15.6	17.9	12 018	18 472	30 622	-9.9	0.2	30 710	19.4	30.7	28.8
Sheridan	207	1 625	557	10.1	44.7	15.7	8.2	17 205	26 537	39 578	5.9	2.3	40 974	11.7	15.7	12.9
Silver Bow	275	4 327	8 275	9.0	47.7	22.9	40.5	8 865	21 357	37 986	-1.3	0.5	37 851	17.7	23.4	19.9
Stillwater	143	888	1 865	9.8	47.1	22.3	15.4	10 870	27 168	57 227	15.3	1.0	51 830	10.2	13.9	11.7
Sweet Grass	301	931	794	13.2	44.2	28.8	5.9	10 065	22 785	43 723	6.5	1.3	41 211	11.4	15.5	13.7
Teton	82	1 021	1 269	14.0	47.2	22.9	13.0	11 364	20 509	39 516	3.3	2.2	39 076	15.5	20.9	17.7
Toole	526	1 503	1 116	23.2	47.2	17.4	8.8	10 655	20 464	42 949	12.4	0.3	44 175	15.9	18.8	15.8
Treasure	NA	NA	166	6.0	49.5	20.9	1.6	14 670	20 882	37 969	0.5	0.0	39 931	11.4	18.8	17.5
Valley	136	1 153	1 624	10.1	50.0	16.9	15.1	12 213	24 305	42 050	7.2	1.7	40 522	13.4	21.4	18.7
Wheatland	0	46	230	20.9	59.4	16.4	4.5	12 311	18 474	30 321	-2.2	0.0	29 187	17.2	23.2	23.2
Wibaux	0	197	224	9.8	56.0	15.9	2.1	14 486	22 579	40 417	13.1	1.8	37 508	12.9	15.8	14.1
Yellowstone	221	3 961	33 700	12.5	39.4	29.0	194.3	8 982	26 152	48 641	4.6	2.4	48 059	12.9	17.3	14.4
NEBRASKA	279	2 673	492 832	17.7	39.6	27.7	2 934.8	10 045	25 229	49 342	-0.7	2.4	48 415	12.6	17.3	15.5
Adams	118	2 742	8 216	23.3	43.1	21.5	55.2	11 509	23 084	44 443	-5.6	2.4	45 149	12.5	17.7	15.7
Antelope	20	374	1 487	13.9	50.7	16.5	20.6	18 855	20 419	37 058	-2.8	1.1	40 652	13.7	22.5	20.9
Arthur	0	0	104	5.8	32.6	17.9	1.4	15 912	19 722	43 250	24.8	0.0	34 804	11.9	16.4	16.1
Banner	NA	NA	177	9.0	36.8	25.1	2.5	14 892	22 042	34 063	-14.2	3.8	37 151	13.2	25.6	23.4

1. Data for serious crimes have not been adjusted for underreporting; this may affect comparability between geographic areas and over time.   2. Per 100,000 population estimated by the FBI.   3. All persons 3 years old and over enrolled in nursery school through college.   4. Persons 25 years old and over.   5. Elementary and secondary education expenditures.   6. Based on population estimated by the American Community Survey, 2006-2010.

Table B. States and Counties — **Personal Income**

STATE County	Total (mil dol)	Percent change, 2008–2009	Per capita[1] Dollars	Per capita[1] Rank	Wages and salaries[2] (mil dol)	Proprietors' income (mil dol)	Dividends, interest, and rent (mil dol)	Transfer payments (mil dol) Total	Government payments to individuals Total	Social Security	Medical payments	Income mainte-nance	Unemploy-ment insurance
	62	63	64	65	66	67	68	69	70	71	72	73	74
MISSOURI—Cont'd													
St. Louis city	11 420	-1.7	32 026	1 524	15 515	1 303	1 571	2 950	2 885	621	1 398	475	118
MONTANA	33 957	-0.5	34 828	X	19 646	3 148	7 644	6 476	6 299	2 311	2 392	504	302
Beaverhead	288	0.3	32 117	1 503	153	16	75	68	66	23	28	4	2
Big Horn	315	2.2	24 191	2 949	228	12	42	89	87	18	38	18	4
Blaine	169	-1.0	26 050	2 716	78	21	38	47	45	12	20	6	1
Broadwater	142	0.8	29 716	2 043	54	13	31	38	37	15	14	2	2
Carbon	354	-0.3	36 247	855	95	20	108	65	64	29	23	3	3
Carter	38	-9.9	31 321	1 690	12	3	15	7	7	3	3	0	0
Cascade	3 077	1.0	37 437	696	1 860	272	636	592	577	202	232	44	19
Chouteau	172	-18.5	33 299	1 296	53	22	48	35	34	14	14	2	1
Custer	367	-0.1	32 844	1 361	208	25	86	79	77	29	30	5	3
Daniels	68	-1.7	39 714	469	26	13	19	14	14	6	7	0	0
Dawson	277	0.8	32 318	1 454	173	12	54	62	61	22	23	3	2
Deer Lodge	268	2.1	30 530	1 857	122	14	50	81	79	30	33	6	3
Fallon	108	5.8	39 534	489	85	9	19	17	17	7	7	1	1
Fergus	386	-2.5	34 453	1 103	184	41	105	88	86	35	36	5	3
Flathead	3 085	-2.6	34 424	1 108	1 654	329	780	601	585	222	205	42	46
Gallatin	3 141	-3.1	34 769	1 052	1 937	319	827	366	349	138	99	23	29
Garfield	33	-18.2	27 748	2 444	11	3	13	7	7	3	3	0	0
Glacier	375	1.3	27 648	2 459	209	41	64	106	104	20	47	20	5
Golden Valley	34	0.4	32 172	1 491	8	1	12	7	7	3	2	0	0
Granite	89	0.1	31 055	1 743	30	10	26	22	22	10	7	1	1
Hill	597	-0.6	35 874	902	327	59	142	124	121	30	48	13	4
Jefferson	416	1.6	36 307	845	109	44	75	69	66	28	23	4	3
Judith Basin	64	-2.9	31 358	1 680	16	8	21	14	14	6	5	1	0
Lake	785	0.6	27 437	2 497	340	49	209	208	203	73	78	21	9
Lewis and Clark	2 402	1.5	38 771	557	1 776	166	482	389	378	150	129	30	15
Liberty	67	-6.8	38 249	610	20	15	22	15	15	6	7	0	0
Lincoln	536	2.0	28 631	2 272	229	45	118	175	172	68	63	13	11
McCone	55	-1.3	33 828	1 196	24	9	12	10	10	4	4	1	0
Madison	256	-3.9	34 310	1 125	144	14	72	50	49	23	18	1	2
Meagher	54	-0.4	28 224	2 361	19	3	19	15	15	6	6	1	1
Mineral	110	2.7	28 596	2 280	38	11	20	40	40	15	16	3	2
Missoula	3 819	0.6	35 156	999	2 519	413	792	632	612	209	229	54	32
Musselshell	125	13.2	27 122	2 544	58	1	27	39	38	14	16	3	1
Park	533	-3.8	33 428	1 274	210	42	147	103	100	34	35	6	6
Petroleum	13	1.5	29 627	2 070	5	2	3	3	3	1	1	0	0
Phillips	133	0.8	33 804	1 202	60	19	30	33	32	12	15	2	1
Pondera	198	-3.7	33 979	1 173	73	28	54	49	48	16	22	4	1
Powder River	42	-3.2	25 026	2 863	17	-1	13	9	9	4	3	0	0
Powell	175	1.7	24 629	2 905	108	5	35	47	46	17	18	3	2
Prairie	32	-5.1	28 727	2 252	14	0	10	9	9	4	3	0	0
Ravalli	1 239	-0.4	30 640	1 835	429	106	351	296	288	121	104	20	15
Richland	375	-3.0	40 310	432	239	30	81	62	60	23	26	3	2
Roosevelt	272	3.7	26 361	2 660	151	20	38	88	86	18	43	15	3
Rosebud	310	1.8	33 509	1 250	254	14	44	63	61	18	23	9	2
Sanders	289	1.5	26 063	2 713	109	25	65	102	100	39	36	7	6
Sheridan	139	1.3	42 934	271	52	30	37	28	27	12	12	1	1
Silver Bow	1 244	0.5	37 761	668	717	148	232	271	265	98	109	22	10
Stillwater	301	-2.3	34 234	1 136	188	14	60	57	55	23	20	2	2
Sweet Grass	105	-6.9	28 748	2 248	72	3	45	22	21	9	7	1	1
Teton	227	-1.5	37 307	712	77	40	66	42	41	17	16	2	1
Toole	186	-6.2	36 079	875	104	35	46	27	26	11	9	2	1
Treasure	22	0.5	36 492	817	7	2	7	5	5	3	2	0	0
Valley	263	0.5	38 788	556	122	34	63	59	58	21	25	4	2
Wheatland	58	0.5	28 152	2 372	21	4	20	15	15	5	6	1	1
Wibaux	25	7.0	27 895	2 420	11	1	6	7	7	3	3	0	0
Yellowstone	5 707	-0.4	39 412	498	3 807	514	1 133	907	881	328	338	69	35
NEBRASKA	70 665	-1.3	39 332	X	46 280	7 651	12 860	10 984	10 657	3 895	4 486	884	289
Adams	1 085	-1.0	32 566	1 409	659	102	232	211	205	81	84	16	6
Antelope	292	0.5	43 845	242	84	114	40	48	47	19	20	3	1
Arthur	13	-7.3	37 900	655	6	-1	4	3	3	1	1	0	0
Banner	20	-22.7	30 566	1 851	8	1	4	3	3	2	1	0	0

1. Based on the resident population estimated as of July 1 of the year shown.   2. Includes supplements to wages and salaries.

STATE County	Earnings, 2009									Social Security beneficiaries, December 2010		Supplemental Security Income recipients, December 2010	Housing units, 2010	
					Percent by selected industries									
			Goods-related[1]		Service-related and health									
	Total (mil dol)	Farm	Total	Manu-facturing	Infor-mation and profes-sional and technical services	Retail trade	Finance, insur-ance, and real estate	Health care and social services	Govern-ment	Number	Rate[2]		Total	Percent change, 2000–2010
	75	76	77	78	79	80	81	82	83	84	85	86	87	88
MISSOURI—Cont'd														
St. Louis city	16 818	0.0	D	10.9	16.0	2.0	5.6	14.1	16.6	53 685	168	16 900	176 002	-0.2
MONTANA	22 793	1.4	15.4	4.7	8.3	8.2	6.3	13.6	23.2	192 701	195	17 532	482 825	17.0
Beaverhead	169	1.2	D	1.7	4.4	6.6	10.1	D	31.3	1 960	212	105	5 273	15.5
Big Horn	240	3.4	24.1	1.0	2.0	3.2	1.9	D	48.0	1 795	140	350	4 695	0.9
Blaine	98	13.3	D	0.5	D	5.5	D	D	40.7	1 150	177	220	2 843	-3.5
Broadwater	67	9.3	D	21.2	D	5.1	4.4	5.7	19.2	1 245	222	69	2 695	34.7
Carbon	115	-1.1	16.9	1.6	6.9	8.4	5.4	8.7	25.5	2 350	233	110	6 441	17.2
Carter	15	24.4	D	0.0	D	4.7	D	D	29.0	310	267	0	810	0.0
Cascade	2 132	0.4	9.9	2.7	6.8	7.8	7.3	17.2	30.0	16 785	206	1 789	37 276	5.8
Chouteau	75	29.2	4.0	1.4	D	6.2	D	8.3	26.2	1 190	205	55	2 879	3.7
Custer	234	0.9	D	1.2	4.8	10.4	7.5	17.8	28.8	2 535	217	240	5 560	3.7
Daniels	39	24.6	D	D	D	3.9	5.3	9.8	17.2	470	268	15	1 111	-3.8
Dawson	185	2.0	D	1.1	4.9	7.7	3.6	15.2	20.2	1 750	195	94	4 233	1.6
Deer Lodge	136	-0.7	D	3.7	6.5	6.8	3.0	18.2	32.8	2 365	254	244	5 122	3.3
Fallon	94	1.8	46.8	0.6	2.6	4.1	D	6.1	13.3	560	194	17	1 470	4.2
Fergus	225	3.1	20.3	7.3	D	8.0	6.5	D	22.7	2 985	258	181	5 836	5.0
Flathead	1 983	0.0	18.4	7.5	7.7	9.5	8.0	15.2	15.0	18 410	202	1 268	46 963	35.1
Gallatin	2 256	0.5	18.2	5.9	13.0	9.9	7.2	9.2	20.8	11 085	124	573	42 289	43.4
Garfield	14	14.4	D	D	D	7.0	D	D	38.3	270	224	10	844	-12.2
Glacier	250	9.6	8.4	0.2	1.8	5.6	D	4.2	50.8	1 930	144	568	5 348	2.0
Golden Valley	9	11.8	D	D	D	D	D	D	35.0	285	322	19	476	5.8
Granite	40	-1.4	D	3.4	D	5.9	D	0.9	30.1	840	273	39	2 822	36.0
Hill	386	7.9	8.9	1.1	7.7	7.8	3.3	10.7	28.1	2 575	160	415	7 250	-2.7
Jefferson	153	-1.0	D	6.4	5.1	7.6	7.0	8.9	25.5	2 365	207	136	5 055	20.4
Judith Basin	24	32.0	D	D	2.7	1.8	D	1.0	31.6	550	265	29	1 336	0.8
Lake	389	0.2	15.2	7.0	6.5	9.0	4.2	13.3	35.4	6 375	222	670	16 588	21.9
Lewis and Clark	1 942	0.1	7.3	2.0	11.0	6.8	8.3	10.2	38.9	12 295	194	1 261	30 180	17.6
Liberty	34	45.1	D	D	D	3.8	D	D	18.5	420	180	46	1 043	-2.5
Lincoln	274	-0.3	16.0	3.2	D	8.6	4.3	13.9	30.3	5 780	294	571	11 413	22.5
McCone	34	24.9	D	D	D	3.8	D	D	17.1	366	210	12	1 008	-7.3
Madison	168	-2.7	19.2	2.4	D	5.2	10.1	5.0	15.8	1 930	251	47	6 940	48.5
Meagher	23	0.6	D	D	D	10.9	D	D	29.3	535	283	66	1 432	5.1
Mineral	49	-1.1	24.0	12.3	D	12.5	2.2	8.8	29.6	1 235	292	124	2 446	24.7
Missoula	2 932	-0.1	11.3	4.4	9.5	8.9	9.9	17.3	19.9	17 190	157	1 691	50 106	21.3
Musselshell	59	-9.5	43.7	2.6	3.0	4.6	2.9	8.7	18.7	1 205	266	101	2 654	14.5
Park	252	1.7	14.1	5.5	6.8	9.1	6.0	12.6	15.7	3 025	193	239	9 375	13.7
Petroleum	7	40.6	D	0.0	D	D	0.8	D	27.3	105	213	0	324	11.0
Phillips	78	13.1	D	1.4	D	6.5	5.6	D	25.6	1 020	240	62	2 335	-6.7
Pondera	101	20.8	13.5	1.9	3.2	7.6	4.9	D	16.7	1 280	208	177	2 659	-6.2
Powder River	17	-11.2	D	D	7.3	10.1	D	D	47.9	390	224	11	1 022	1.5
Powell	113	-3.8	D	D	D	4.6	2.8	D	57.2	1 425	203	106	3 105	6.0
Prairie	14	-2.8	D	D	D	4.1	5.1	0.6	63.8	355	301	0	673	-6.3
Ravalli	535	-0.9	D	7.1	D	9.5	6.0	10.3	22.8	10 395	259	644	19 583	22.8
Richland	269	3.0	29.0	5.1	5.2	6.0	4.7	D	13.6	1 885	193	120	4 550	-0.2
Roosevelt	172	5.4	6.3	1.0	1.7	6.9	2.6	9.9	51.7	1 710	164	446	4 063	0.5
Rosebud	268	1.0	D	D	1.9	2.9	1.1	D	31.2	1 565	170	226	4 057	3.6
Sanders	134	1.0	15.0	5.4	4.3	7.6	3.7	14.5	26.1	3 465	304	272	6 678	26.7
Sheridan	83	30.1	D	0.7	3.3	4.7	3.6	D	22.5	970	287	46	2 089	-3.6
Silver Bow	865	0.0	D	4.5	12.3	10.2	2.8	15.1	17.9	7 615	223	905	16 717	3.3
Stillwater	201	-0.7	D	7.1	4.6	3.8	1.8	3.6	10.6	1 940	213	84	4 803	21.7
Sweet Grass	75	-4.1	D	4.2	3.3	7.1	5.0	D	20.1	830	227	19	2 148	15.5
Teton	117	20.1	D	2.2	D	5.2	4.8	11.4	18.3	1 460	240	111	2 892	-0.6
Toole	138	12.4	D	D	D	4.8	3.0	2.8	29.9	880	165	117	2 336	1.6
Treasure	10	29.9	D	D	D	D	D	D	26.4	220	306	10	422	0.0
Valley	155	15.3	D	0.8	4.4	8.0	D	D	25.0	1 790	243	156	4 879	0.7
Wheatland	25	7.0	D	D	D	6.0	3.3	D	28.4	450	208	42	1 197	3.7
Wibaux	12	4.2	D	0.5	D	1.3	2.4	D	31.4	245	241	14	538	-8.3
Yellowstone	4 321	0.0	18.2	6.7	9.0	8.3	6.7	17.7	13.8	26 590	180	2 364	63 943	17.2
NEBRASKA	53 931	6.1	15.4	9.8	8.8	5.9	8.0	10.8	17.8	308 790	169	25 613	796 793	10.3
Adams	761	8.7	23.3	15.0	3.9	6.5	3.6	D	15.7	6 365	203	507	13 350	2.6
Antelope	198	48.0	D	2.8	D	4.2	D	5.3	12.0	1 645	246	85	3 284	-1.9
Arthur	5	28.1	D	D	D	D	0.0	1.4	31.6	120	261	0	254	-7.0
Banner	9	33.1	D	2.4	0.0	0.0	D	0.0	31.1	220	319	0	369	-1.6

1. Includes mining, construction, and manufacturing. 2. Per 1,000 resident population enumerated in the 2010 census.

STATE County	Housing units, 2006–2010								Civilian labor force, 2010		Unemployment		Civilian employment,[5] 2006–2010		
	Occupied units												Percent		
			Owner-occupied			Renter-occupied									
				Median owner cost as a percent of income											
	Total	Percent	Median value[1]	With a mortgage	Without a mortgage	Median rent[2]	Median rent as a percent of income	Substandard units[3] (percent)	Total	Percent change, 2009–2010	Total	Rate[4]	Total	Management, business, science and arts	Construction, production, and maintenance occupations
	89	90	91	92	93	94	95	96	97	98	99	100	101	102	103
MISSOURI—Cont'd															
St. Louis city	140 439	47.2	122 200	24.6	13.9	658	31.8	2.8	158 404	0.2	19 438	12.3	147 153	35.0	17.5
MONTANA	401 328	69.0	173 300	24.0	11.7	629	27.8	2.4	498 677	0.4	34 463	6.9	476 195	34.1	23.3
Beaverhead	3 918	64.7	169 700	24.6	11.5	519	26.8	0.3	5 158	0.7	292	5.7	4 579	35.6	18.6
Big Horn	3 584	66.6	89 700	20.0	13.6	505	21.4	9.3	5 202	-0.1	599	11.5	4 904	32.2	22.9
Blaine	2 338	63.4	73 100	18.9	11.1	312	17.1	5.0	2 721	-5.9	163	6.0	2 375	41.2	23.1
Broadwater	1 878	78.7	159 700	25.0	11.7	561	18.7	1.3	2 374	-1.0	177	7.5	2 321	30.5	33.1
Carbon	4 149	72.9	200 700	22.6	10.9	627	22.4	2.4	5 196	-1.5	322	6.2	5 196	34.3	26.3
Carter	580	75.0	66 200	28.3	10.8	434	16.9	5.5	679	-6.0	28	4.1	746	57.0	17.4
Cascade	33 164	66.8	146 600	23.2	11.9	557	26.0	2.1	40 712	0.6	2 476	6.1	36 519	32.4	21.9
Chouteau	2 170	66.3	107 000	21.9	11.3	392	19.6	2.7	2 547	-1.5	113	4.4	2 530	41.0	20.9
Custer	5 168	65.6	86 700	20.0	12.7	462	20.7	3.0	5 949	1.3	283	4.8	5 876	32.9	24.1
Daniels	773	81.9	77 300	26.3	11.0	377	18.9	0.6	741	-5.6	33	4.5	844	42.8	16.5
Dawson	3 715	74.0	100 300	16.7	10.5	459	18.4	0.5	4 209	-3.9	187	4.4	4 483	34.9	29.2
Deer Lodge	4 136	72.7	102 600	20.9	13.2	511	28.3	1.6	4 037	3.3	313	7.8	4 631	25.1	30.6
Fallon	1 193	76.2	86 700	15.0	11.5	417	19.4	0.9	1 887	-0.9	54	2.9	1 618	33.1	36.3
Fergus	4 966	71.7	104 100	19.4	13.8	512	28.6	3.8	5 996	-0.2	379	6.3	5 673	38.0	21.5
Flathead	36 348	71.5	231 800	27.3	12.1	707	29.1	2.1	44 046	-1.1	5 180	11.8	42 483	29.8	27.7
Gallatin	35 753	62.3	277 300	25.3	11.7	807	30.3	1.6	47 965	-1.1	3 422	7.1	49 662	36.7	22.2
Garfield	506	79.4	68 800	19.3	10.9	348	16.8	3.4	615	-4.2	26	4.2	669	38.4	25.7
Glacier	4 253	59.0	73 600	15.9	10.0	459	19.2	7.6	5 895	4.9	598	10.1	5 742	34.2	19.0
Golden Valley	334	76.0	90 900	26.0	10.1	714	35.0	1.8	509	-11.9	30	5.9	370	31.9	38.4
Granite	1 461	76.4	169 900	26.6	10.0	486	24.0	6.2	1 264	0.6	132	10.4	1 307	34.4	27.2
Hill	6 086	68.2	109 000	21.2	10.9	493	23.1	3.6	8 359	1.5	466	5.6	7 432	34.4	25.3
Jefferson	4 428	85.5	225 300	22.9	10.0	637	26.9	1.2	6 003	-0.1	348	5.8	5 526	40.5	22.0
Judith Basin	867	77.0	101 500	20.3	11.0	417	16.9	2.2	1 064	1.1	61	5.7	863	62.1	17.3
Lake	12 015	67.9	201 900	26.2	11.0	589	25.4	4.7	11 324	-0.3	1 143	10.1	11 819	34.5	24.1
Lewis and Clark	26 075	72.8	185 500	23.9	11.9	658	29.0	1.5	34 114	0.7	1 872	5.5	32 012	42.6	15.7
Liberty	816	62.7	71 400	19.6	10.9	426	31.1	5.1	725	-2.3	36	5.0	937	37.8	25.9
Lincoln	9 237	76.5	148 500	27.1	12.0	491	25.5	5.9	7 910	2.2	1 237	15.6	7 628	30.0	31.0
McCone	694	77.7	82 800	22.2	10.0	387	18.8	1.6	1 041	3.5	31	3.0	943	50.2	18.0
Madison	3 813	68.9	240 100	27.3	11.8	647	21.5	3.0	3 910	-8.9	295	7.5	3 943	42.5	25.1
Meagher	767	64.0	96 500	30.9	13.8	479	25.0	2.1	836	-2.2	75	9.0	904	28.5	30.3
Mineral	1 760	66.5	159 400	27.0	12.1	601	28.7	1.4	1 919	1.7	220	11.5	1 782	24.2	28.3
Missoula	44 172	60.7	233 700	25.5	11.6	705	33.7	2.3	58 534	0.5	4 246	7.3	55 801	36.1	17.3
Musselshell	2 035	76.7	112 200	25.8	10.6	542	34.8	4.1	2 409	-2.8	162	6.7	1 998	27.3	34.7
Park	6 983	70.4	207 300	28.4	12.9	620	26.9	1.0	8 357	-2.0	677	8.1	7 872	29.1	29.6
Petroleum	283	68.6	106 800	26.3	11.2	708	0.0	5.3	233	-1.7	15	6.4	280	48.6	36.8
Phillips	1 816	75.8	79 100	18.6	10.0	418	20.4	2.3	2 231	0.9	139	6.2	2 018	34.7	26.3
Pondera	2 311	69.9	86 200	20.4	13.5	482	24.7	6.1	2 505	-2.6	165	6.6	2 670	35.8	25.9
Powder River	688	66.4	99 700	17.6	11.1	478	17.9	1.6	902	0.0	38	4.2	887	43.1	24.1
Powell	2 397	74.6	114 600	22.7	12.7	529	23.1	3.2	2 766	3.9	247	8.9	2 703	31.1	25.7
Prairie	497	86.9	69 400	15.5	11.8	444	29.0	2.0	565	-3.4	27	4.8	532	46.8	26.7
Ravalli	16 643	77.9	235 500	29.8	13.3	720	29.4	3.1	17 965	-0.7	1 749	9.7	17 799	32.4	27.4
Richland	4 072	66.4	106 500	16.9	10.0	507	18.2	0.5	5 745	4.6	210	3.7	5 132	27.4	37.0
Roosevelt	3 374	63.7	61 700	14.2	10.7	464	19.6	4.4	4 131	4.9	309	7.5	4 274	36.0	19.5
Rosebud	3 225	70.4	102 900	17.3	10.0	530	16.1	4.3	3 942	-2.6	295	7.5	3 911	30.5	31.6
Sanders	5 119	78.5	172 500	32.4	12.3	574	30.5	3.8	4 384	-1.2	642	14.6	4 712	28.3	30.0
Sheridan	1 674	75.2	68 400	20.3	11.8	466	22.9	0.3	1 701	-4.4	68	4.0	1 683	30.2	30.7
Silver Bow	14 847	65.8	117 200	21.7	12.6	517	29.7	1.0	17 559	2.7	1 080	6.2	16 070	30.0	21.8
Stillwater	3 752	75.1	170 100	21.5	11.2	622	20.5	2.3	4 236	-5.0	268	6.3	4 640	30.5	35.5
Sweet Grass	1 510	81.3	184 100	23.1	11.4	543	24.8	0.7	2 300	-5.5	93	4.0	1 867	31.8	35.8
Teton	2 458	75.7	133 700	26.8	13.0	583	23.0	3.5	2 974	-1.4	174	5.9	2 755	37.9	22.6
Toole	1 992	63.2	97 900	15.8	10.8	479	27.7	2.2	2 448	-3.4	115	4.7	2 260	35.0	22.4
Treasure	319	67.7	66 200	23.2	12.6	681	21.4	0.0	394	-4.1	19	4.8	393	36.9	30.8
Valley	3 152	75.5	81 400	19.6	10.0	474	21.2	2.4	3 541	-1.4	180	5.1	3 590	33.5	23.8
Wheatland	929	78.0	85 000	25.0	17.7	508	14.5	7.2	1 010	-2.9	63	6.2	759	35.2	39.3
Wibaux	389	79.2	60 000	14.6	10.0	325	22.4	0.0	554	-2.3	21	3.8	517	35.2	28.0
Yellowstone	59 746	70.3	168 800	22.6	11.7	652	27.5	1.6	81 110	-0.9	4 469	5.5	74 755	32.3	22.9
NEBRASKA	711 771	68.6	123 900	22.0	12.6	648	26.9	2.1	988 509	0.8	46 434	4.7	937 574	34.8	23.9
Adams	12 403	70.4	95 000	21.5	11.4	583	27.3	1.7	16 921	-3.3	789	4.7	15 995	29.1	28.9
Antelope	2 792	72.0	67 000	21.7	13.0	488	23.9	2.4	3 779	2.2	126	3.3	3 319	36.5	28.2
Arthur	178	63.5	76 100	18.8	13.4	547	16.3	1.7	240	1.7	18	7.5	222	49.1	33.8
Banner	320	66.3	76 900	28.1	14.5	429	20.0	0.0	345	-13.1	16	4.6	392	50.0	22.4

1. Specified owner-occupied units.   2. Specified renter-occupied units. A value of 10.0 represents 10 percent or less.   3. Overcrowded or lacking complete plumbing facilities.   4. Percent of civilian labor force.   5. Persons 16 years old and over.

Table B. States and Counties — Nonfarm Employment and Agriculture

STATE County	Number of establishments	Total	Health care and social assistance	Manufacturing	Retail trade	Finance and insurance	Professional, scientific, and technical services	Total (mil dol)	Average per employee (dollars)	Number	Fewer than 50 acres	500 acres or more	Farm operators whose principal occupation is farming (percent)
	104	105	106	107	108	109	110	111	112	113	114	115	116
MISSOURI—Cont'd													
St. Louis city	9 061	238 347	34 441	18 426	11 093	12 108	17 814	11 039	46 313	NA	NA	NA	NA
MONTANA	36 326	341 357	61 813	17 226	56 989	18 201	17 194	10 654	31 211	29 524	25.0	43.0	50.7
Beaverhead	363	2 238	389	86	437	131	75	55	24 637	431	29.5	43.4	49.7
Big Horn	216	2 148	D	D	322	68	51	86	39 890	695	16.8	51.4	53.1
Blaine	150	1 059	252	D	209	41	D	36	33 789	655	6.1	66.0	56.3
Broadwater	143	899	D	D	150	D	D	24	27 100	302	21.5	39.7	56.6
Carbon	407	2 244	275	51	363	D	108	47	20 806	715	23.5	29.1	46.9
Carter	30	D	D	D	27	D	D	D	D	308	6.2	80.5	72.4
Cascade	2 498	29 975	6 041	1 006	5 389	2 170	1 373	887	29 586	1 112	30.5	33.3	44.6
Chouteau	150	765	D	30	108	45	D	19	24 759	849	4.7	72.7	67.4
Custer	394	4 260	1 142	73	824	D	157	110	25 754	411	20.9	48.7	56.2
Daniels	71	D	D	D	78	37	8	D	D	397	5.0	70.5	57.2
Dawson	313	2 865	D	D	556	102	63	76	26 624	535	8.2	66.0	60.0
Deer Lodge	237	2 748	D	D	272	69	42	76	27 759	123	35.8	29.3	47.2
Fallon	131	860	D	D	143	D	12	30	34 970	296	9.8	63.9	55.1
Fergus	456	3 325	847	339	517	D	82	93	28 018	898	12.9	61.6	60.2
Flathead	4 054	32 182	5 066	2 456	5 584	1 689	1 565	947	29 441	1 094	55.3	7.0	35.3
Gallatin	4 782	37 703	4 034	2 462	6 785	1 225	2 456	1 178	31 241	1 071	46.3	19.8	41.8
Garfield	28	172	D	D	66	D	0	2	14 140	288	3.5	85.4	76.7
Glacier	248	2 013	437	D	450	D	46	71	35 259	625	13.8	53.8	51.4
Golden Valley	13	D	D	D	D	0	D	D	D	153	9.8	60.8	69.7
Granite	101	474	D	D	112	D	7	12	25 437	166	17.5	55.4	54.8
Hill	538	5 311	1 083	48	1 111	218	285	143	27 016	854	6.8	59.4	50.6
Jefferson	265	1 675	231	D	189	D	56	51	30 739	370	27.8	24.9	34.3
Judith Basin	54	179	D	D	24	D	D	4	24 480	306	11.8	67.0	69.3
Lake	825	5 380	1 103	D	1 169	233	D	144	26 854	1 280	52.9	9.9	44.1
Lewis and Clark	2 178	23 930	4 616	681	4 011	2 096	1 721	780	32 580	675	48.9	19.3	39.6
Liberty	61	326	D	D	D	24	D	7	20 549	299	2.0	81.6	65.6
Lincoln	642	3 972	800	239	668	138	149	110	27 758	350	49.1	5.4	33.7
McCone	60	337	D	D	64	20	D	11	31 368	489	2.6	75.9	68.5
Madison	360	1 423	157	D	166	65	51	41	28 969	585	26.0	37.6	47.2
Meagher	71	269	104	D	51	D	D	6	20 810	138	18.1	61.6	58.7
Mineral	127	781	D	D	213	21	36	17	22 344	99	44.4	14.1	37.4
Missoula	4 203	47 442	9 152	1 767	8 376	2 674	2 811	1 481	31 211	699	59.2	8.0	30.8
Musselshell	124	694	190	D	162	30	16	20	28 416	373	12.1	41.8	50.9
Park	754	4 244	760	256	623	D	D	123	28 968	535	28.6	37.6	48.2
Petroleum	11	D	D	D	0	D	0	D	D	103	4.9	74.8	71.8
Phillips	142	924	D	27	186	56	D	22	23 368	556	8.3	63.8	64.6
Pondera	180	1 319	297	D	248	78	D	36	27 065	542	14.0	61.3	60.0
Powder River	68	278	0	D	107	D	D	5	17 892	319	7.5	74.0	64.9
Powell	162	976	199	D	D	D	D	25	25 566	273	20.1	40.7	54.9
Prairie	36	168	D	D	29	20	D	3	20 274	173	6.4	73.4	67.6
Ravalli	1 443	8 655	1 379	891	1 477	419	510	221	25 496	1 532	67.2	4.9	43.0
Richland	467	4 275	D	333	621	127	185	144	33 724	548	10.8	65.9	57.3
Roosevelt	188	1 678	D	D	393	86	D	43	25 333	728	4.7	58.9	48.4
Rosebud	186	2 597	252	D	286	59	D	103	39 773	478	11.3	51.3	58.8
Sanders	369	2 111	471	247	367	D	D	47	22 215	508	34.4	17.5	39.8
Sheridan	147	972	329	D	154	70	31	22	22 611	602	2.7	67.9	53.5
Silver Bow	1 156	13 046	3 107	D	2 160	332	727	414	31 717	175	25.7	24.0	32.6
Stillwater	262	2 298	250	D	237	60	49	101	43 977	635	21.7	40.0	45.7
Sweet Grass	155	915	25	53	137	D	33	37	40 348	355	18.0	48.7	49.9
Teton	189	1 114	210	D	202	D	D	31	27 540	770	14.9	48.3	55.1
Toole	196	1 584	238	D	185	D	43	50	31 392	428	5.4	74.3	55.8
Treasure	22	78	D	D	D	D	D	2	25 897	101	8.9	66.3	56.4
Valley	267	2 108	D	55	311	101	66	54	25 594	770	5.7	60.0	58.3
Wheatland	59	342	D	D	76	D	9	8	22 810	137	13.9	65.0	54.7
Wibaux	34	203	D	0	21	D	D	5	26 931	208	5.3	58.2	62.5
Yellowstone	5 465	67 175	12 344	3 717	10 361	4 426	3 536	2 404	35 790	1 407	42.9	23.7	38.2
NEBRASKA	51 633	779 508	117 081	93 831	106 713	60 412	49 650	27 475	35 246	47 712	18.6	39.7	60.5
Adams	963	14 205	2 803	3 290	1 843	362	314	401	28 212	485	18.4	47.6	69.7
Antelope	218	1 383	275	108	292	86	21	35	25 592	716	13.1	42.7	68.8
Arthur	13	D	0	D	D	D	D	D	D	68	5.9	88.2	73.5
Banner	6	D	0	0	0	D	0	D	D	218	1.8	62.4	55.5

Table B. States and Counties — **Agriculture**

STATE County	Land in farms Acreage (1,000)	Percent change, 2002–2007	Acres Average size of farm	Total irrigated (1,000)	Total cropland (1,000)	Value of land and buildings (dollars) Average per farm	Average per acre	Value of machinery and equipment, average per farm (dollars)	Value of products sold Total (mil dol)	Average per farm (dollars)	Percent from: Crops	Live-stock and poultry products	Percent of farms with sales of: $10,000 or more	$100,000 or more	Government payments Total ($1,000)	Percent of farms
	117	118	119	120	121	122	123	124	125	126	127	128	129	130	131	132
MISSOURI—Cont'd																
St. Louis city	NA	NA	NA	NA	NA	NA	NA	NA	NA	NA	NA	NA	NA	NA	NA	NA
MONTANA	61 388	3.0	2 079	2 013.2	18 241.7	1 611 155	775	103 494	2 803.1	94 942	45.4	54.6	46.8	21.6	221 977	44.3
Beaverhead	1 239	-3.1	2 875	203.5	180.5	3 463 155	1 205	134 772	86.1	199 829	16.5	83.5	50.1	28.1	318	13.9
Big Horn	2 900	3.2	4 172	59.7	383.6	1 702 078	408	112 582	94.9	136 480	43.6	56.4	55.5	26.3	3 182	30.9
Blaine	2 331	3.1	3 558	61.8	673.8	2 180 686	613	138 487	71.6	109 385	48.2	51.8	57.6	29.9	9 664	63.4
Broadwater	475	1.1	1 572	44.1	139.0	1 733 015	1 102	114 051	25.5	84 539	57.6	42.4	45.0	19.9	2 000	48.0
Carbon	794	5.3	1 110	73.8	138.1	1 589 309	1 432	83 201	45.3	63 309	31.3	68.7	47.0	11.5	1 229	32.7
Carter	1 698	1.9	5 514	7.1	267.2	2 174 291	394	140 539	42.8	139 001	19.8	80.2	75.6	43.2	1 766	59.7
Cascade	1 380	-0.6	1 241	35.6	506.6	1 130 619	911	85 783	83.6	75 148	49.0	51.0	37.5	15.3	5 971	52.2
Chouteau	2 278	-1.0	2 683	12.1	1 310.4	1 803 549	672	165 019	147.2	173 432	84.0	16.0	62.9	44.5	19 766	83.4
Custer	2 127	11.7	5 175	31.4	186.7	2 708 137	523	115 823	73.2	178 113	13.0	87.0	56.9	28.5	1 500	43.1
Daniels	860	5.5	2 167	1.5	591.6	1 279 818	591	139 598	51.1	128 779	79.9	20.1	55.4	32.2	7 732	88.7
Dawson	1 379	-2.3	2 577	19.7	446.4	1 316 501	511	112 011	56.6	105 835	56.0	44.0	64.1	31.2	6 290	73.6
Deer Lodge	79	-41.5	645	19.7	19.1	948 727	1 471	64 555	4.0	32 727	12.3	87.7	30.9	13.8	32	8.9
Fallon	979	5.0	3 307	1.5	247.8	1 922 086	581	133 305	35.9	121 412	19.4	80.6	64.2	33.4	2 548	72.0
Fergus	2 446	7.2	2 724	19.8	664.7	2 522 967	926	122 288	101.2	112 658	41.5	58.5	62.5	33.7	6 187	55.0
Flathead	252	7.2	230	23.3	88.5	892 403	3 880	51 610	33.5	30 644	52.3	47.7	26.1	5.6	1 001	19.5
Gallatin	777	9.6	725	81.7	283.7	1 639 919	2 261	85 074	95.1	88 840	50.3	49.7	37.8	15.4	1 761	22.2
Garfield	2 392	9.6	8 305	4.2	409.8	3 583 051	431	170 684	41.8	145 280	38.0	62.0	75.7	44.8	4 514	65.6
Glacier	1 700	3.3	2 720	30.7	552.4	1 547 675	569	123 194	55.4	88 666	41.1	58.9	49.4	19.8	6 205	46.9
Golden Valley	672	1.7	4 391	8.6	157.4	3 307 409	753	93 040	14.6	95 589	35.0	65.0	51.6	28.1	1 902	61.4
Granite	303	7.1	1 825	31.3	35.5	2 515 494	1 378	103 724	13.1	78 804	7.3	92.7	53.6	25.9	121	13.9
Hill	1 697	-6.2	1 987	9.1	1 202.9	1 321 231	665	130 016	86.6	101 444	81.9	18.1	48.9	29.5	18 178	72.0
Jefferson	391	1.0	1 057	26.7	54.5	1 293 519	1 223	65 666	13.7	37 037	13.2	86.8	30.5	9.5	451	12.2
Judith Basin	838	1.0	2 740	16.6	285.0	2 303 311	841	148 766	54.4	177 819	36.7	63.3	70.6	39.5	2 586	64.7
Lake	637	5.8	498	86.5	98.8	774 473	1 555	64 012	51.6	40 337	45.4	54.6	44.4	7.3	698	15.5
Lewis and Clark	971	15.3	1 439	50.3	104.5	1 410 544	980	73 664	32.3	47 837	32.2	67.8	28.0	8.7	998	13.8
Liberty	904	-0.1	3 025	11.3	637.6	1 401 882	464	195 232	49.6	165 976	75.4	24.6	67.2	46.2	10 009	89.0
Lincoln	52	-3.7	148	4.3	16.6	550 718	3 715	44 123	2.7	7 728	19.7	80.3	12.9	1.1	24	2.6
McCone	1 507	12.0	3 081	7.2	576.6	1 466 376	476	151 834	51.6	105 470	62.5	37.5	63.6	33.1	7 628	84.9
Madison	1 061	3.1	1 813	104.9	152.2	2 864 249	1 579	82 009	53.2	90 917	25.4	74.6	44.6	20.9	743	15.4
Meagher	812	-5.3	5 887	40.5	113.1	6 879 211	1 169	154 634	25.3	183 181	11.6	88.4	53.6	33.3	572	29.7
Mineral	23	43.8	229	1.3	4.8	840 038	3 671	44 871	0.9	8 714	28.9	71.1	16.2	2.0	33	16.2
Missoula	282	9.3	403	16.6	27.9	895 806	2 221	39 176	7.6	10 839	35.8	64.2	16.9	2.9	102	6.4
Musselshell	1 133	9.6	3 038	9.0	148.9	1 847 667	608	85 049	23.6	63 165	21.2	78.8	34.0	14.5	2 011	30.3
Park	763	-9.9	1 426	51.9	110.2	2 589 171	1 816	74 336	27.7	51 814	27.2	72.8	42.1	13.6	726	17.8
Petroleum	641	19.1	6 220	15.8	100.9	3 032 164	487	165 748	16.2	157 197	20.4	79.6	74.8	48.5	1 240	65.0
Phillips	2 006	5.7	3 608	48.7	610.0	1 805 753	500	140 094	60.9	109 597	33.5	66.5	58.1	31.5	7 935	68.2
Pondera	944	4.9	1 743	74.5	617.9	1 239 958	712	155 750	75.1	138 576	64.4	35.6	63.5	37.1	9 108	75.8
Powder River	1 620	6.4	5 079	10.0	178.1	3 287 235	647	130 906	41.0	128 401	12.7	87.3	72.7	38.6	925	44.8
Powell	670	8.2	2 456	74.1	71.0	2 218 812	904	106 676	25.7	94 306	10.2	89.8	44.7	20.1	232	16.8
Prairie	768	23.9	4 436	14.5	151.1	2 748 958	620	121 418	24.4	140 778	32.6	67.4	72.8	42.2	2 200	78.6
Ravalli	263	7.3	172	72.2	63.0	664 936	3 875	44 925	34.9	22 756	23.3	76.7	25.1	4.0	164	7.7
Richland	1 279	6.5	2 334	56.0	568.3	1 637 408	701	175 695	107.0	195 177	49.7	50.3	60.2	32.8	6 194	73.0
Roosevelt	1 452	0.8	1 994	14.1	783.9	1 416 662	710	127 540	67.8	93 117	76.9	23.1	52.3	25.3	9 791	78.2
Rosebud	2 714	6.8	5 678	34.6	238.9	2 185 210	385	88 039	56.8	118 877	24.4	75.6	54.0	22.8	2 688	32.4
Sanders	342	-1.2	673	16.9	38.5	1 018 914	1 514	54 424	14.0	27 579	45.7	54.3	27.8	6.1	183	13.0
Sheridan	1 066	1.8	1 770	7.4	716.3	1 174 858	664	154 210	90.7	150 706	86.6	13.4	56.3	34.7	8 646	89.7
Silver Bow	101	36.5	578	8.8	15.8	1 252 542	2 169	61 857	4.8	27 328	8.0	92.0	30.3	9.1	30	4.0
Stillwater	857	-3.7	1 350	28.7	234.6	1 381 295	1 023	69 855	43.4	68 401	20.9	79.1	42.2	12.8	2 833	38.0
Sweet Grass	813	-6.2	2 289	43.2	98.0	2 780 320	1 214	93 463	21.7	61 169	10.0	90.0	43.7	15.5	561	23.4
Teton	1 153	-6.3	1 497	111.3	600.9	1 269 349	848	107 382	97.7	126 889	52.1	47.9	49.0	26.5	10 506	72.5
Toole	1 115	2.5	2 605	4.2	725.1	1 546 725	594	166 176	47.7	111 513	73.2	26.8	54.4	31.5	10 315	82.7
Treasure	462	-23.9	4 572	20.3	36.1	2 270 543	497	183 532	30.4	300 765	37.6	62.4	66.3	41.6	585	36.6
Valley	2 061	0.4	2 677	51.9	921.5	1 575 621	589	122 993	80.4	104 406	55.7	44.3	55.3	26.4	11 345	76.4
Wheatland	822	-2.4	6 002	20.8	151.4	3 347 775	558	158 881	25.7	187 370	26.3	73.7	61.3	32.1	1 689	61.3
Wibaux	493	-8.0	2 368	1.1	160.0	998 788	422	112 747	18.6	89 538	52.5	47.5	61.5	25.5	2 246	83.7
Yellowstone	1 616	3.0	1 148	77.1	344.0	891 477	776	74 338	164.6	117 020	24.8	75.2	34.9	13.9	4 109	32.1
NEBRASKA	45 480	-0.9	953	8 558.6	21 486.0	1 104 392	1 159	157 427	15 506.0	324 992	44.1	55.9	68.5	41.0	387 340	73.2
Adams	306	-11.0	632	203.5	265.4	1 409 216	2 231	222 342	249.3	513 932	52.5	47.5	76.3	57.9	5 462	76.7
Antelope	517	-1.9	721	261.3	369.1	1 192 984	1 654	212 581	339.8	474 627	43.4	56.6	75.1	55.3	6 560	79.7
Arthur	454	4.1	6 671	8.2	31.0	2 226 136	334	133 787	19.3	284 278	D	D	83.8	60.3	232	32.4
Banner	395	-3.9	1 811	16.1	169.4	993 859	549	104 855	67.3	308 599	19.3	80.7	57.3	27.5	2 732	81.7

STATE County	Total water withdrawn (mil gal/day) 133	Gallons withdrawn per person 134	Number of establishments 135	Number of employees 136	Sales (mil dol) 137	Annual payroll (mil dol) 138	Number of establishments 139	Number of employees 140	Sales (mil dol) 141	Annual payroll (mil dol) 142	Number of establishments 143	Number of employees 144	Receipts (mil dol) 145	Annual payroll (mil dol) 146
MISSOURI—Cont'd														
St. Louis city	141.0	409	522	9 422	5 042.1	462.3	1 028	11 368	2 496.7	263.5	418	2 633	606.6	94.7
MONTANA	10 115.9	10 811	1 254	12 849	8 202.8	503.4	5 258	58 883	14 686.9	1 317.8	1 892	6 410	848.3	153.3
Beaverhead	1 185.6	135 142	5	64	24.3	1.9	57	466	122.9	10.0	16	69	8.5	2.1
Big Horn	279.0	21 217	5	D	D	D	48	433	87.4	7.1	10	45	2.1	0.4
Blaine	236.5	35 675	9	32	27.6	0.8	25	174	44.2	3.2	4	10	0.6	0.1
Broadwater	241.3	53 423	6	27	10.3	0.5	16	157	59.2	2.9	7	8	0.6	0.3
Carbon	417.6	42 177	12	55	21.0	2.3	59	330	60.7	5.7	20	31	5.0	0.7
Carter	10.8	8 167	NA	NA	NA	NA	5	30	11.9	0.4	2	D	D	D
Cascade	189.2	2 378	118	1 077	672.0	42.5	388	5 507	1 302.3	121.0	137	378	56.3	8.3
Chouteau	80.3	14 695	12	62	38.4	1.9	19	125	44.7	2.0	6	D	D	D
Custer	121.7	10 798	17	128	75.1	4.4	67	847	199.9	16.5	14	34	3.3	0.6
Daniels	3.1	1 661	4	13	9.9	0.3	12	72	26.6	1.7	NA	NA	NA	NA
Dawson	53.9	6 207	15	157	107.6	3.5	54	506	118.3	9.6	8	20	1.5	0.3
Deer Lodge	67.3	7 520	1	D	D	D	38	264	71.5	5.9	12	32	2.5	0.5
Fallon	2.2	791	4	33	32.9	1.7	16	145	26.3	2.3	2	D	D	D
Fergus	71.4	6 180	15	155	400.2	5.8	76	512	135.4	10.7	19	65	4.8	1.2
Flathead	74.3	894	98	959	863.6	40.1	550	6 076	1 581.3	147.8	269	936	113.6	23.5
Gallatin	470.1	6 011	127	1 405	508.8	50.8	621	7 467	1 791.8	184.6	361	1 265	193.6	33.4
Garfield	16.0	13 336	1	D	D	D	6	63	10.2	0.8	NA	NA	NA	NA
Glacier	87.0	6 418	10	59	125.2	2.3	45	449	106.3	9.5	7	16	1.3	0.2
Golden Valley	44.1	38 007	1	D	D	D	1	D	D	D	NA	NA	NA	NA
Granite	137.8	46 459	1	D	D	D	17	120	23.8	2.0	4	3	0.1	0.1
Hill	20.0	1 228	26	182	190.2	5.8	87	1 020	231.1	19.5	18	49	5.4	1.0
Jefferson	161.5	14 456	8	D	D	D	26	177	39.9	2.9	7	15	0.9	0.3
Judith Basin	71.4	32 475	5	18	4.6	0.4	8	25	5.5	0.3	3	3	0.5	0.1
Lake	291.8	10 310	20	43	8.7	1.0	152	1 201	277.0	26.1	49	77	10.9	1.5
Lewis and Clark	220.3	3 770	48	445	199.6	16.9	302	4 070	972.9	94.0	98	657	83.2	14.2
Liberty	57.5	28 727	4	12	10.5	0.4	13	69	15.6	1.2	4	10	0.4	0.1
Lincoln	34.0	1 769	10	42	12.1	1.0	93	721	170.6	13.3	29	66	7.2	0.8
McCone	26.6	14 715	1	D	D	D	11	68	18.0	1.2	1	D	D	D
Madison	647.7	89 042	7	D	D	D	49	184	48.9	4.0	29	38	4.7	0.9
Meagher	377.2	188 704	NA	NA	NA	NA	13	69	16.4	1.1	1	D	D	D
Mineral	8.1	2 008	1	D	D	D	23	242	46.1	4.5	4	3	0.4	0.1
Missoula	112.7	1 126	169	1 825	860.1	69.5	587	8 668	2 179.4	194.6	227	952	126.3	21.6
Musselshell	97.8	21 741	5	11	6.0	0.3	24	140	33.6	2.6	4	6	0.7	0.1
Park	508.0	31 812	15	58	26.8	2.5	112	723	208.9	15.4	30	52	8.3	1.1
Petroleum	42.1	89 596	NA	NA	NA	NA	2	D	D	D	1	D	D	D
Phillips	166.2	39 773	7	65	80.8	1.6	27	161	34.0	3.1	3	4	0.5	0.0
Pondera	239.5	39 340	13	119	46.1	4.1	34	262	64.7	4.9	5	D	D	D
Powder River	39.9	23 408	1	D	D	D	13	87	13.8	1.3	2	D	D	D
Powell	247.4	35 346	3	D	D	D	17	168	35.0	3.1	8	13	2.0	0.3
Prairie	54.1	48 968	1	D	D	D	8	32	7.4	0.5	1	D	D	D
Ravalli	293.5	7 349	38	220	165.0	7.4	185	1 567	344.8	31.2	72	206	16.7	4.5
Richland	374.5	41 175	19	149	235.8	5.9	60	598	128.6	10.9	18	64	8.0	1.7
Roosevelt	93.3	8 862	11	41	66.3	1.4	40	359	99.9	6.5	7	29	1.1	0.2
Rosebud	245.0	26 592	1	D	D	D	32	306	53.4	4.5	6	33	3.0	0.6
Sanders	57.0	5 152	9	D	D	D	53	366	82.1	6.6	17	41	3.4	0.6
Sheridan	13.8	3 905	5	20	5.0	0.7	21	167	31.5	2.5	2	D	D	D
Silver Bow	66.7	2 024	31	D	D	D	189	2 183	504.7	44.3	45	144	14.9	3.0
Stillwater	107.0	12 593	3	9	14.2	0.5	43	308	103.2	4.5	7	10	1.6	0.2
Sweet Grass	292.0	79 532	2	D	D	D	27	170	42.7	3.1	11	16	3.3	0.4
Teton	561.7	90 010	9	D	D	D	29	220	43.9	4.4	9	21	1.7	0.3
Toole	16.0	3 184	9	114	96.3	3.6	26	202	54.8	3.8	8	17	1.5	0.2
Treasure	72.5	105 269	1	D	D	D	4	D	D	D	1	D	D	D
Valley	236.7	33 132	13	148	80.4	5.1	54	331	81.3	6.8	3	D	D	D
Wheatland	123.9	60 800	1	D	D	D	13	74	18.3	1.0	1	D	D	D
Wibaux	2.3	2 397	NA	NA	NA	NA	4	22	4.3	0.2	NA	NA	NA	NA
Yellowstone	347.7	2 544	297	4 467	2 772.5	196.0	757	10 151	2 840.7	249.2	263	907	142.3	26.5
NEBRASKA	12 604.4	7 167	2 668	32 329	24 019.9	1 323.5	7 888	108 209	26 486.6	2 230.5	2 032	9 974	1 645.5	292.0
Adams	277.7	8 396	56	783	499.7	27.1	163	1 863	360.8	34.7	54	D	D	D
Antelope	217.7	31 088	27	225	136.3	6.5	45	278	57.0	4.4	3	3	0.8	0.0
Arthur	8.4	22 222	NA	NA	NA	NA	3	7	0.9	0.1	NA	NA	NA	NA
Banner	26.4	36 003	NA	NA	NA	NA	NA	NA	NA	NA	NA	NA	NA	NA

1. Merchant wholesalers, except manufacturers' sales branches and offices.   2. Employer establishments.

Table B. States and Counties — Professional Services, Manufacturing, and Accommodation and Food Services

STATE County	Professional, scientific, and technical services,[1] 2007				Manufacturing, 2007				Accommodation and food services, 2007			
	Number of establish-ments	Number of employees	Receipts (mil dol)	Annual payroll (mil dol)	Number of establish-ments	Number of employees	Receipts (mil dol)	Annual payroll (mil dol)	Number of establish-ments	Number of employees	Sales (mil dol)	Annual payroll (mil dol)
	147	148	149	150	151	152	153	154	155	156	157	158
MISSOURI—Cont'd												
St. Louis city	1 005	D	D	D	543	21 432	10 920.6	998.2	934	20 372	1 059.3	311.4
MONTANA	3 403	16 547	1 770.9	670.6	1 324	19 525	10 638.1	808.2	3 360	46 137	2 079.4	554.2
Beaverhead	30	78	7.3	2.0	NA	NA	NA	NA	48	408	16.1	3.9
Big Horn	15	D	D	D	NA	NA	NA	NA	27	248	13.6	3.1
Blaine	10	D	D	D	NA	NA	NA	NA	18	112	2.4	0.6
Broadwater	5	25	1.9	0.7	NA	NA	NA	NA	19	140	5.7	1.4
Carbon	31	110	13.8	4.8	NA	NA	NA	NA	50	557	18.5	5.6
Carter	3	D	D	D	NA	NA	NA	NA	1	D	D	D
Cascade	199	D	D	D	81	1 094	670.9	44.8	247	3 997	174.3	48.6
Chouteau	9	21	2.1	0.4	NA	NA	NA	NA	19	104	3.8	0.8
Custer	23	143	8.9	3.6	NA	NA	NA	NA	40	624	22.1	5.9
Daniels	4	8	0.7	0.1	NA	NA	NA	NA	7	25	1.0	0.2
Dawson	16	64	3.7	1.3	NA	NA	NA	NA	31	396	21.2	4.1
Deer Lodge	23	51	5.1	1.5	NA	NA	NA	NA	36	378	16.4	4.3
Fallon	8	D	D	D	NA	NA	NA	NA	17	99	4.0	0.7
Fergus	29	93	6.5	1.7	NA	NA	NA	NA	49	489	14.1	4.3
Flathead	380	D	D	D	177	3 464	919.4	149.7	347	4 617	232.9	63.0
Gallatin	631	2 552	301.5	113.3	188	2 425	512.6	95.2	376	6 788	325.8	89.9
Garfield	NA	NA	NA	NA	NA	NA	NA	NA	6	19	0.6	0.2
Glacier	15	D	D	D	NA	NA	NA	NA	48	265	37.6	6.4
Golden Valley	1	D	D	D	NA	NA	NA	NA	4	12	0.4	0.1
Granite	6	9	0.8	0.3	NA	NA	NA	NA	15	66	2.5	0.6
Hill	36	D	D	D	NA	NA	NA	NA	49	658	23.8	6.2
Jefferson	26	52	5.1	1.9	NA	NA	NA	NA	31	273	7.3	2.0
Judith Basin	3	D	D	D	NA	NA	NA	NA	9	34	1.3	0.3
Lake	58	D	D	D	44	654	119.8	21.8	78	817	34.7	8.0
Lewis and Clark	243	1 713	207.8	84.6	54	655	D	24.3	190	2 961	118.6	32.9
Liberty	4	7	0.8	0.1	NA	NA	NA	NA	6	24	0.8	0.2
Lincoln	42	D	D	D	NA	NA	NA	NA	66	501	26.5	6.7
McCone	1	D	D	D	NA	NA	NA	NA	5	17	0.7	0.1
Madison	21	D	D	D	NA	NA	NA	NA	65	221	15.0	4.2
Meagher	1	D	D	D	NA	NA	NA	NA	13	74	2.1	0.5
Mineral	8	41	3.0	1.2	NA	NA	NA	NA	22	139	6.7	1.6
Missoula	458	D	D	D	112	2 159	674.9	93.8	332	6 209	269.1	70.0
Musselshell	8	13	1.3	0.4	NA	NA	NA	NA	9	74	3.5	0.7
Park	62	182	20.4	6.6	NA	NA	NA	NA	120	1 083	61.9	16.9
Petroleum	1	D	D	D	NA	NA	NA	NA	3	15	0.4	0.1
Phillips	9	22	1.8	0.5	NA	NA	NA	NA	16	114	4.1	0.9
Pondera	13	43	3.4	1.2	NA	NA	NA	NA	15	168	4.2	1.1
Powder River	6	22	1.4	0.3	NA	NA	NA	NA	9	46	2.2	0.6
Powell	9	57	3.1	1.1	NA	NA	NA	NA	26	177	7.3	2.0
Prairie	2	D	D	D	NA	NA	NA	NA	5	16	0.9	0.1
Ravalli	111	D	D	D	105	1 048	130.2	38.9	105	992	36.5	10.6
Richland	35	156	20.1	6.0	NA	NA	NA	NA	37	502	19.7	4.5
Roosevelt	11	D	D	D	NA	NA	NA	NA	30	269	9.7	2.5
Rosebud	4	15	1.0	0.2	NA	NA	NA	NA	29	274	9.0	2.1
Sanders	17	41	2.5	1.0	NA	NA	NA	NA	36	313	12.2	3.5
Sheridan	8	33	1.8	0.7	NA	NA	NA	NA	17	142	4.8	1.2
Silver Bow	107	D	D	D	NA	NA	NA	NA	133	1 946	78.3	22.7
Stillwater	27	52	5.3	1.6	NA	NA	NA	NA	23	220	9.8	2.6
Sweet Grass	15	34	3.4	1.0	NA	NA	NA	NA	18	158	6.2	1.7
Teton	9	D	D	D	NA	NA	NA	NA	17	118	3.0	0.7
Toole	18	49	4.2	1.4	NA	NA	NA	NA	26	180	10.6	2.8
Treasure	2	D	D	D	NA	NA	NA	NA	2	D	D	D
Valley	18	D	D	D	NA	NA	NA	NA	29	268	11.0	3.0
Wheatland	2	D	D	D	NA	NA	NA	NA	11	55	1.6	0.3
Wibaux	4	12	0.8	0.2	NA	NA	NA	NA	5	31	1.1	0.2
Yellowstone	566	3 170	367.2	135.7	187	3 974	5 740.0	D	368	7 687	361.7	97.3
NEBRASKA	4 205	40 692	4 836.4	2 011.0	1 984	99 547	40 158.0	3 788.6	4 241	69 142	2 685.6	749.1
Adams	61	312	33.2	12.0	67	D	D	D	79	1 185	43.7	10.9
Antelope	13	22	2.4	0.6	NA	NA	NA	NA	13	98	2.4	0.6
Arthur	1	D	D	D	NA	NA	NA	NA	1	D	D	D
Banner	NA	NA	NA	NA	NA	NA	NA	NA	NA	NA	NA	NA

1. Establishment subject to federal tax.

Table B. States and Counties — Health Care and Social Assistance, Other Services, and Federal Funds

STATE County	Health care and social assistance, 2007				Other services, 2007				Federal funds and grants, 2009–2010 Expenditures (mil dol)			
										Direct payments for individuals[1]		
	Number of establishments	Number of employees	Receipts (mil dol)	Annual payroll (mil dol)	Number of establishments	Number of employees	Receipts (mil dol)	Annual payroll (mil dol)	Total	Social Security and government retirement	Medicare	Food Stamps and Supplemental Security Income
	159	160	161	162	163	164	165	166	167	168	169	170
MISSOURI—Cont'd												
St. Louis city..........................	1 036	34 294	3 510.6	1 207.0	694	5 574	635.1	165.4	10 370.1	816.3	1 036.9	372.6
MONTANA	3 301	57 860	4 970.8	1 983.7	2 287	10 323	995.4	245.8	10 758.4	3 301.0	1 153.2	279.4
Beaverhead...........................	38	382	31.4	11.9	21	65	3.8	0.8	91.2	30.5	15.6	2.1
Big Horn	19	D	D	D	12	23	2.3	0.6	147.7	27.0	12.6	7.5
Blaine.................................	11	D	D	D	9	40	2.7	0.6	99.4	17.8	7.3	3.2
Broadwater...........................	7	79	5.2	2.1	6	D	D	D	40.2	22.9	5.9	1.4
Carbon................................	26	243	13.4	6.8	16	43	2.5	0.6	72.0	35.0	15.2	1.8
Carter	2	D	D	D	1	D	D	D	12.9	4.8	1.6	0.2
Cascade	269	6 050	517.8	206.6	166	845	65.4	18.8	1 022.7	329.7	119.7	23.9
Chouteau.............................	17	236	10.9	5.7	5	D	D	D	74.5	18.2	8.4	0.7
Custer.................................	48	926	70.2	30.5	26	112	10.9	2.4	112.9	41.6	17.3	3.3
Daniels	5	153	7.2	3.0	5	D	D	D	81.2	13.0	4.2	0.2
Dawson...............................	26	567	40.5	16.9	33	122	8.4	2.2	94.7	34.9	13.7	2.0
Deer Lodge	46	1 240	68.6	39.8	14	57	4.9	1.1	98.9	39.5	20.4	4.1
Fallon.................................	5	D	D	D	10	D	D	D	21.9	9.3	4.2	0.6
Fergus................................	51	770	47.6	20.8	31	107	9.7	1.4	131.5	48.3	23.8	2.1
Flathead..............................	350	5 001	471.0	166.6	222	967	80.5	21.7	630.3	325.6	80.3	17.9
Gallatin...............................	349	3 634	330.0	120.5	245	1 072	133.4	30.6	526.9	189.1	42.5	7.1
Garfield...............................	3	D	D	D	2	D	D	D	11.4	3.4	2.0	0.1
Glacier................................	18	D	D	D	20	D	D	D	210.4	31.4	14.2	10.3
Golden Valley.......................	2	D	D	D	NA	NA	NA	NA	10.6	4.2	1.6	0.3
Granite................................	3	D	D	D	2	D	D	D	21.9	11.3	3.7	0.6
Hill....................................	45	1 016	86.8	34.9	45	174	14.1	3.1	221.9	53.9	24.0	6.8
Jefferson.............................	19	205	8.9	3.5	15	D	D	D	111.0	41.5	8.8	1.4
Judith Basin.........................	5	23	0.3	0.2	1	D	D	D	24.7	9.0	3.0	0.2
Lake...................................	77	1 136	84.7	36.0	45	141	10.0	2.6	313.3	90.2	32.8	9.3
Lewis and Clark	247	4 736	462.8	182.3	202	D	D	D	1 637.6	223.2	63.9	40.1
Liberty................................	2	D	D	D	2	D	D	D	39.3	10.4	3.8	0.8
Lincoln................................	50	743	48.2	21.0	39	145	12.2	2.6	221.3	93.2	23.7	8.7
McCone..............................	3	D	D	D	3	D	D	D	25.4	7.3	3.7	0.6
Madison..............................	16	142	8.5	4.0	16	35	5.7	1.0	51.3	26.9	9.3	0.3
Meagher..............................	5	D	D	D	4	D	D	D	18.9	7.7	3.0	0.4
Mineral...............................	14	139	6.7	2.9	4	D	D	D	41.1	22.1	5.4	1.9
Missoula..............................	451	8 022	754.8	278.8	288	1 618	150.7	37.8	818.8	299.5	93.6	28.0
Musselshell..........................	9	D	D	D	8	18	1.4	0.3	41.4	18.7	8.0	2.5
Park...................................	45	702	61.1	25.4	53	221	17.3	4.9	107.4	53.1	23.1	2.7
Petroleum............................	1	D	D	D	NA	NA	NA	NA	5.7	1.6	0.7	0.0
Phillips................................	10	216	10.0	4.4	11	D	D	D	61.7	15.1	8.6	1.3
Pondera..............................	20	304	16.6	7.5	11	37	2.3	0.4	80.1	20.4	12.3	2.2
Powder River........................	1	D	D	D	4	D	D	D	11.7	5.4	2.0	0.2
Powell................................	17	178	12.1	4.6	9	20	2.2	0.3	48.3	23.1	8.9	1.4
Prairie................................	1	D	D	D	3	D	D	D	13.2	6.0	2.6	0.1
Ravalli................................	118	1 257	80.6	32.8	86	265	21.9	5.8	318.8	170.9	44.4	7.9
Richland..............................	32	687	41.9	17.9	32	98	9.4	2.2	81.5	31.7	17.0	2.2
Roosevelt	15	D	D	D	13	54	3.9	0.7	271.2	30.8	15.9	9.7
Rosebud..............................	15	259	10.4	5.0	11	37	3.2	1.0	106.7	24.0	8.7	3.6
Sanders..............................	34	423	25.4	11.6	18	46	5.0	0.9	103.7	55.0	15.4	3.5
Sheridan	10	224	12.3	6.7	8	D	D	D	63.4	19.7	8.5	0.5
Silver Bow	157	2 804	184.9	75.9	66	346	32.6	7.7	336.1	124.4	67.3	14.5
Stillwater.............................	19	229	10.8	4.4	11	D	D	D	55.7	31.6	10.1	0.9
Sweet Grass.........................	7	22	0.7	0.3	10	30	2.1	0.5	23.0	12.5	4.4	0.5
Teton.................................	19	228	9.4	4.9	8	31	4.2	1.1	69.0	22.3	10.5	1.2
Toole..................................	10	226	19.0	8.0	9	19	1.8	0.3	57.5	10.7	9.2	0.8
Treasure	3	D	D	D	1	D	D	D	7.4	3.0	1.4	0.1
Valley.................................	19	544	34.1	13.7	21	57	4.6	1.0	107.9	34.7	13.4	2.5
Wheatland	3	D	D	D	4	5	0.3	0.1	22.1	8.2	6.2	0.4
Wibaux	3	D	D	D	NA	NA	NA	NA	11.3	4.3	1.3	0.2
Yellowstone..........................	504	11 503	1 168.5	474.6	380	1 972	198.3	48.7	1 131.6	451.3	164.2	32.6
NEBRASKA......................	4 920	114 928	10 081.0	4 107.3	4 073	22 543	2 391.3	542.8	16 531.8	5 307.5	2 142.1	387.3
Adams................................	120	2 780	229.1	100.8	67	369	23.9	6.5	236.7	98.2	41.8	6.4
Antelope	16	268	18.2	6.7	19	39	3.7	0.7	86.8	23.0	12.9	1.4
Arthur.................................	NA	NA	NA	NA	2	D	D	D	2.5	1.5	0.5	0.1
Banner................................	NA	NA	NA	NA	NA	NA	NA	NA	7.7	1.5	0.6	0.0

1. State totals may include programs not allocated by county.

Table B. States and Counties — Federal Funds, Residential Construction, and Local Government Finances

STATE County	Salaries and wages	Defense	Other	Medicaid and other health-related	Nutrition and family welfare	Education	Other	New construction ($1,000)	Number of housing units	Total (mil dol)	Inter-governmental (mil dol)	Total (mil dol)	Per capita[2] (dollars) Total	Per capita[2] (dollars) Property
	171	172	173	174	175	176	177	178	179	180	181	182	183	184
MISSOURI—Cont'd														
St. Louis city	890.9	3 414.6	389.6	2 094.7	120.1	63.5	923.2	32 630	259	2 068.9	636.4	759.0	2 164	918
MONTANA	1 194.6	312.7	506.7	1 080.2	271.7	263.5	1 324.0	303 528	2 022	X	X	X	X	X
Beaverhead	21.3	0.1	5.1	9.6	1.4	0.6	0.7	1 000	13	40.9	10.3	7.8	888	883
Big Horn	22.1	0.0	11.3	17.3	7.0	11.5	14.2	0	0	49.8	31.5	10.7	838	828
Blaine	10.4	0.0	2.5	15.6	3.6	9.2	8.3	0	0	32.1	20.7	5.5	833	826
Broadwater	2.3	0.1	0.9	3.7	0.7	0.1	0.2	173	3	12.8	5.4	3.8	835	802
Carbon	4.0	0.2	3.6	8.1	1.4	0.3	0.3	1 332	9	28.2	12.6	11.3	1 160	1 071
Carter	1.0	0.0	0.3	1.5	0.2	0.1	0.4	0	0	6.4	3.7	1.9	1 469	1 415
Cascade	238.8	90.2	17.2	136.8	15.5	7.4	11.5	28 242	150	227.1	110.8	63.8	781	755
Chouteau	2.4	0.0	0.5	2.2	0.9	0.4	3.5	0	0	24.0	8.3	8.5	1 609	1 606
Custer	14.8	0.1	6.3	20.5	1.9	1.5	0.9	890	6	37.5	16.9	8.7	775	773
Daniels	3.1	0.4	2.8	1.1	0.3	0.1	38.2	200	1	10.3	3.4	5.4	3 253	3 010
Dawson	3.4	17.9	0.7	8.2	2.4	1.4	2.0	140	1	37.0	15.0	11.1	1 294	1 286
Deer Lodge	6.0	0.0	4.7	15.7	3.0	1.0	3.3	2 381	17	22.8	13.2	6.3	711	707
Fallon	0.8	0.0	0.2	1.5	0.4	0.3	1.0	681	6	32.5	24.7	3.6	1 343	1 250
Fergus	11.3	1.2	8.9	16.2	2.8	1.5	3.1	188	1	37.2	16.9	12.2	1 095	1 075
Flathead	64.4	4.5	40.8	52.4	11.8	5.3	11.3	25 142	154	247.7	88.9	92.9	1 070	969
Gallatin	60.6	18.0	19.4	61.8	8.5	2.9	90.9	77 312	398	223.3	70.1	91.5	1 048	911
Garfield	1.4	0.0	0.2	0.8	0.2	0.2	0.2	55	2	5.2	2.2	1.7	1 421	1 364
Glacier	24.2	1.4	47.8	28.6	7.8	15.6	10.7	130	1	47.7	32.8	9.4	700	694
Golden Valley	0.5	0.0	0.1	0.0	0.2	0.1	0.0	0	0	3.6	1.6	1.6	1 449	1 441
Granite	1.8	0.0	1.3	2.3	0.4	0.1	0.0	0	0	13.7	4.5	4.4	1 534	1 527
Hill	18.7	0.0	5.2	25.4	8.1	12.3	25.5	726	7	58.0	33.8	14.1	854	848
Jefferson	44.6	0.0	1.8	8.9	1.2	0.9	0.9	160	1	27.1	11.4	9.0	806	799
Judith Basin	1.8	0.1	0.5	2.2	0.4	0.1	0.0	0	0	8.4	3.7	3.8	1 835	1 821
Lake	6.7	51.6	8.4	36.9	8.3	14.1	27.9	5 003	25	78.7	38.6	24.8	870	858
Lewis and Clark	166.3	10.9	49.8	105.8	55.6	100.7	785.7	25 593	168	172.8	68.6	57.9	965	946
Liberty	1.6	6.4	0.6	0.7	0.3	0.1	1.1	0	0	7.9	4.0	2.9	1 615	1 610
Lincoln	23.8	27.3	12.8	20.9	4.8	2.2	3.2	455	10	54.0	25.0	14.0	739	696
McCone	0.9	0.0	0.2	2.2	0.2	0.1	0.0	0	0	6.4	2.8	2.7	1 546	1 528
Madison	3.6	0.0	0.9	3.7	0.9	0.5	3.7	418	2	33.6	8.4	13.7	1 851	1 840
Meagher	1.7	0.0	1.0	2.9	0.3	0.1	0.2	0	0	12.4	2.5	3.0	1 573	1 558
Mineral	2.7	0.0	3.0	3.8	0.9	0.4	0.2	0	0	21.0	6.9	4.9	1 261	1 221
Missoula	103.8	5.5	52.8	117.3	17.7	8.6	58.9	35 510	368	266.9	105.7	114.6	1 085	1 048
Musselshell	1.2	0.0	0.5	4.4	0.8	0.2	2.1	100	1	13.1	5.6	4.1	909	907
Park	4.9	0.0	1.9	14.9	2.5	1.6	1.3	2 772	15	42.2	15.3	15.2	944	908
Petroleum	0.3	0.0	0.8	0.0	0.1	0.0	0.0	0	0	2.2	1.2	0.6	1 470	1 468
Phillips	8.6	0.0	2.6	11.8	0.8	0.4	2.1	206	1	26.4	14.8	4.9	1 229	1 218
Pondera	2.9	0.8	11.5	8.8	1.3	2.4	0.3	150	1	29.0	10.8	5.7	958	946
Powder River	0.8	0.0	0.2	0.8	0.3	0.5	0.0	0	0	8.6	3.7	2.9	1 705	1 478
Powell	4.0	0.0	1.4	5.2	1.1	1.6	0.5	0	0	20.0	10.3	5.7	799	793
Prairie	0.6	0.0	0.1	1.5	0.2	0.1	0.0	0	0	6.2	2.2	1.5	1 417	1 368
Ravalli	37.5	0.3	19.4	24.4	7.0	2.3	2.5	1 935	36	79.2	40.2	27.7	687	667
Richland	7.5	0.0	1.1	9.8	1.8	0.7	1.8	5 799	27	53.9	38.9	8.1	884	880
Roosevelt	12.9	65.7	5.0	15.6	5.6	11.6	80.0	590	3	54.7	34.1	11.1	1 094	1 074
Rosebud	11.5	0.0	5.3	14.6	3.9	11.8	12.3	1 064	6	56.4	24.1	14.1	1 531	1 497
Sanders	6.1	0.3	6.9	11.8	2.0	1.4	0.2	0	0	32.0	15.3	12.0	1 087	1 075
Sheridan	6.2	-0.3	1.2	6.0	0.7	0.5	0.0	209	1	17.7	10.4	4.3	1 269	1 251
Silver Bow	26.2	3.1	10.2	58.9	8.7	3.9	10.5	10 376	122	92.0	40.7	31.1	952	926
Stillwater	2.4	0.0	3.9	2.2	1.0	0.8	0.5	1 882	9	28.1	10.3	12.8	1 479	1 474
Sweet Grass	1.9	0.0	0.2	1.5	0.4	0.3	0.2	0	0	18.3	4.8	5.4	1 428	1 424
Teton	3.2	0.4	9.7	6.6	1.1	0.3	0.1	360	4	29.2	10.3	7.5	1 251	1 233
Toole	12.5	0.0	2.4	4.4	0.9	0.1	2.2	320	2	29.3	9.2	5.6	1 094	1 084
Treasure	0.7	0.0	0.2	0.0	0.2	0.0	0.0	0	0	3.2	1.2	1.5	2 246	2 229
Valley	11.4	3.1	1.4	11.0	1.3	1.3	6.3	365	3	30.7	14.2	10.6	1 539	1 517
Wheatland	1.2	0.0	0.4	2.4	0.4	0.1	0.0	0	0	7.1	3.3	2.8	1 410	1 386
Wibaux	0.6	0.0	0.1	2.2	0.2	0.0	0.0	0	0	5.8	4.1	0.9	1 021	958
Yellowstone	158.4	3.3	108.5	126.8	32.1	10.4	13.5	71 670	448	459.4	158.1	128.0	915	841
NEBRASKA	1 782.8	793.2	513.6	1 703.0	411.7	308.7	1 083.6	744 968	5 401	X	X	X	X	X
Adams	20.5	4.8	2.6	33.6	8.1	2.4	3.8	21 482	176	221.2	45.8	63.9	1 937	1 488
Antelope	2.5	0.0	2.0	7.9	1.5	0.4	24.6	2 071	16	26.5	8.9	13.8	2 036	1 801
Arthur	0.2	0.0	0.0	0.0	0.0	0.1	0.0	NA	NA	2.7	0.9	1.6	4 596	4 438
Banner	0.2	0.0	0.0	0.0	0.1	0.1	0.0	NA	NA	3.4	1.2	2.0	2 768	2 514

1. State totals may include programs not allocated by county.   2. Based on the resident population estimated as of July 1 of the year shown.

Table B. States and Counties — Local Government Finances, Government Employment, and Voting

STATE County	Total (mil dol)	Per capita[1] (dollars)	Education	Health and hospitals	Police protection	Public welfare	Highways	Total (mil dol)	Per capita[1] (dollars)	Federal civilian	Federal military	State and local	Democratic	Republican	All other
	185	186	187	188	189	190	191	192	193	194	195	196	197	198	199
MISSOURI—Cont'd															
St. Louis city	1 963.2	5 597	31.2	2.2	8.4	0.0	1.0	3 967.4	11 311	15 644	2 064	22 968	83.7	15.5	0.8
MONTANA	X	X	X	X	X	X	X	X	X	14 177	8 004	73 414	47.3	49.5	3.2
Beaverhead	37.0	4 198	35.9	40.0	3.3	0.0	3.6	17.3	1 965	215	45	767	33.9	63.2	2.9
Big Horn	50.0	3 906	70.4	1.4	3.3	0.6	4.3	3.2	252	427	65	1 976	67.4	31.2	1.4
Blaine	31.6	4 828	66.0	1.5	4.1	0.0	5.8	4.0	616	196	32	523	58.2	39.0	2.8
Broadwater	13.3	2 907	46.5	2.0	6.0	0.6	2.5	6.1	1 329	46	24	214	31.8	65.8	2.4
Carbon	28.1	2 889	60.3	0.6	6.5	0.3	10.2	34.2	3 519	88	49	492	42.5	54.1	3.4
Carter	6.2	4 928	40.2	7.7	7.4	1.7	22.5	0.3	267	20	0	95	15.6	80.1	4.3
Cascade	225.3	2 755	48.3	2.4	8.2	0.6	3.2	95.4	1 166	1 734	3 477	4 221	49.9	47.6	2.4
Chouteau	23.2	4 421	44.9	22.8	3.4	0.3	8.6	3.2	614	38	26	448	39.2	57.1	3.7
Custer	37.4	3 345	61.1	3.7	7.6	0.5	5.3	4.8	431	221	56	924	41.6	55.9	2.5
Daniels	10.1	6 129	41.2	5.0	3.9	0.0	6.1	3.1	1 899	27	0	125	32.0	64.7	3.4
Dawson	36.4	4 257	58.7	2.6	5.0	0.1	5.4	13.0	1 523	32	43	777	35.9	59.5	4.5
Deer Lodge	20.2	2 287	56.8	1.4	9.3	0.1	2.3	6.2	698	81	44	838	67.0	29.6	3.4
Fallon	20.4	7 565	39.8	5.4	4.0	0.0	12.4	1.5	543	13	14	245	22.2	74.3	3.5
Fergus	40.0	3 678	54.1	3.3	4.6	0.0	5.8	10.6	945	171	56	848	31.0	65.9	3.1
Flathead	276.2	3 180	57.1	3.0	5.0	0.4	5.4	149.6	1 723	843	449	4 092	36.9	58.5	4.6
Gallatin	239.6	2 743	44.0	1.3	6.2	3.6	3.8	163.4	1 871	647	463	8 677	50.3	46.9	2.8
Garfield	6.0	4 902	41.3	5.7	3.7	0.0	29.7	0.5	386	29	0	119	15.1	82.3	2.6
Glacier	51.0	3 809	76.5	1.0	3.3	0.1	2.8	4.1	308	463	68	1 960	68.9	29.2	1.9
Golden Valley	3.9	3 476	71.1	1.4	3.8	0.4	6.4	0.6	562	0	0	73	25.3	69.9	4.9
Granite	13.2	4 617	39.4	0.7	5.4	28.3	7.2	7.2	2 540	38	14	221	35.0	59.1	5.9
Hill	56.9	3 432	67.4	3.0	4.6	0.9	4.9	12.4	747	161	88	1 966	54.3	42.1	3.6
Jefferson	27.5	2 472	56.3	2.2	6.5	0.0	5.7	6.5	587	50	67	736	40.7	55.8	3.5
Judith Basin	8.8	4 297	62.1	0.2	1.4	0.7	8.7	3.8	1 835	37	12	145	32.1	64.8	3.1
Lake	78.3	2 752	61.5	1.9	4.1	0.3	3.5	31.6	1 112	109	143	2 603	48.6	46.7	4.7
Lewis and Clark	173.8	2 897	48.4	3.2	6.3	4.1	4.7	154.6	2 576	1 975	319	8 960	52.1	45.5	2.4
Liberty	7.4	4 115	47.1	9.5	5.3	0.0	10.3	1.7	944	27	0	123	36.7	59.3	4.0
Lincoln	60.1	3 183	46.3	2.5	8.7	0.0	6.9	15.7	831	488	94	797	32.8	61.8	5.4
McCone	6.8	3 969	47.8	5.5	4.3	1.4	7.3	1.8	1 029	22	0	148	29.4	66.5	4.0
Madison	33.4	4 496	37.3	11.3	5.4	15.7	9.0	7.9	1 067	70	37	457	35.2	61.8	3.0
Meagher	12.5	6 584	25.2	2.6	4.0	0.0	5.3	0.1	27	32	10	109	30.8	64.6	4.6
Mineral	21.0	5 392	41.3	24.2	3.8	0.0	3.6	6.7	1 722	54	19	265	42.4	52.8	4.9
Missoula	281.7	2 666	46.3	3.9	5.5	0.7	4.4	200.7	1 900	1 422	550	8 521	61.8	35.1	3.0
Musselshell	13.1	2 915	55.2	2.2	5.7	0.0	5.6	1.1	249	15	23	246	27.6	68.6	3.9
Park	44.6	2 769	50.1	2.4	8.8	0.0	4.3	9.1	563	81	80	659	46.9	49.2	3.9
Petroleum	2.5	5 616	55.3	3.0	2.3	0.0	15.8	0.6	1 386	0	0	66	22.7	75.7	1.7
Phillips	21.7	5 491	55.5	1.9	6.0	0.0	12.0	4.9	1 253	81	20	336	30.1	67.0	2.9
Pondera	28.4	4 776	46.7	35.3	4.6	0.0	4.9	7.1	1 188	37	29	325	42.4	55.0	2.6
Powder River	8.8	5 201	44.7	1.4	5.0	21.6	8.2	0.5	285	15	0	184	20.0	77.3	2.7
Powell	21.0	2 953	58.2	3.0	5.7	0.2	2.3	3.1	435	91	36	1 059	36.3	59.8	3.9
Prairie	6.3	6 069	34.2	1.5	3.5	33.9	6.6	1.9	1 824	35	0	149	28.7	68.4	2.9
Ravalli	80.5	1 992	66.7	1.7	6.3	0.0	4.4	35.7	884	546	202	1 441	38.0	58.9	3.1
Richland	41.7	4 542	59.7	3.1	4.1	0.2	9.1	9.2	1 004	100	47	593	26.6	70.5	2.9
Roosevelt	57.1	5 622	67.9	7.7	4.2	0.1	3.4	5.8	568	212	51	1 595	61.8	35.5	2.7
Rosebud	48.4	5 273	56.5	1.5	5.6	0.2	3.8	339.8	37 003	224	46	1 482	50.4	46.4	3.2
Sanders	33.0	2 993	58.9	1.7	5.4	0.1	6.2	5.4	490	150	55	537	33.7	60.9	5.4
Sheridan	15.7	4 652	57.6	3.3	6.3	0.2	9.5	3.1	929	90	16	262	47.5	49.2	3.3
Silver Bow	91.2	2 793	43.6	4.5	6.0	0.2	3.3	49.7	1 522	307	175	2 252	68.8	28.4	2.8
Stillwater	26.8	3 095	63.5	1.5	5.4	0.0	5.9	9.3	1 074	33	44	415	32.4	64.1	3.5
Sweet Grass	19.7	5 174	32.9	2.6	4.1	29.4	3.7	2.6	696	38	18	336	26.0	71.7	2.3
Teton	29.9	4 965	47.9	20.5	3.1	5.5	3.3	8.6	1 432	68	30	443	39.5	57.3	3.2
Toole	31.8	6 183	30.2	34.0	3.9	0.4	6.4	11.1	2 161	181	26	532	34.7	62.1	3.2
Treasure	3.1	4 822	54.5	4.0	4.8	0.0	7.4	0.7	1 058	10	0	65	32.1	64.6	3.3
Valley	32.7	4 734	53.5	1.7	3.7	0.0	8.4	6.9	995	146	34	588	42.1	54.2	3.7
Wheatland	7.2	3 611	63.3	2.8	6.7	0.1	4.8	0.3	144	25	10	140	29.5	67.0	3.6
Wibaux	5.5	6 097	46.3	6.5	5.2	0.0	15.5	1.0	1 072	13	0	95	26.0	67.6	6.4
Yellowstone	450.0	3 216	46.7	6.0	5.7	0.2	6.2	205.1	1 466	1 891	742	7 160	45.5	51.8	2.7
NEBRASKA	X	X	X	X	X	X	X	X	X	16 559	13 752	145 853	41.6	56.5	1.9
Adams	230.2	6 976	46.6	35.6	2.1	0.1	3.4	61.1	1 851	113	143	2 251	35.5	62.5	2.1
Antelope	27.6	4 090	67.9	0.0	1.4	0.2	14.0	5.5	807	39	29	503	23.8	74.8	1.4
Arthur	2.4	6 820	55.8	0.3	1.5	0.0	15.6	0.1	154	0	0	46	14.8	82.5	2.7
Banner	3.3	4 557	73.3	0.1	1.3	0.0	11.6	0.0	0	0	0	74	14.9	83.7	1.4

1. Based on the resident population estimated as of July 1 of the year shown.   2. © 2009 Election Data Services, Inc. All rights reserved.

Items 185—199

Table B. States and Counties — **Land Area and Population**

STATE/ County code	CBSA code[1]	County type[2]	STATE County	Land area,[3] (sq km) 2010	Total persons	Rank	Per square kilometer	Race alone or in combination, not Hispanic or Latino (percent)				Percent Hispanic or Latino[4]	Age (percent)					
								White	Black	American Indian, Alaska Native	Asian and Pacific Islander		Under 5 years	5 to 17 years	18 to 24 years	25 to 34 years	35 to 44 years	45 to 54 years
				1	2	3	4	5	6	7	8	9	10	11	12	13	14	15
			NEBRASKA—Cont'd															
31 009	...	9	Blaine	1 841	478	3 138	0.3	99.8	0.2	0.6	0.0	0.0	4.6	19.9	3.1	8.6	11.5	18.0
31 011	...	9	Boone	1 778	5 505	2 805	3.1	98.0	0.5	0.3	0.3	1.2	6.1	17.6	6.5	8.7	10.6	16.4
31 013	...	7	Box Butte	2 785	11 308	2 343	4.1	86.0	0.8	3.9	0.6	10.2	6.9	18.3	6.3	11.5	11.2	15.7
31 015	...	9	Boyd	1 398	2 099	3 042	1.5	96.9	0.2	0.8	0.8	1.6	4.7	16.8	5.0	7.5	9.3	15.3
31 017	...	9	Brown	3 163	3 145	2 967	1.0	98.5	0.3	0.9	0.3	0.9	4.7	16.9	5.2	9.0	10.1	15.0
31 019	28260	5	Buffalo	2 507	46 102	1 043	18.4	90.1	1.2	0.6	1.5	7.4	7.2	16.8	15.8	13.8	10.9	12.7
31 021	...	8	Burt	1 273	6 858	2 698	5.4	96.0	0.5	2.1	0.6	1.8	5.7	16.8	5.1	8.9	10.5	15.3
31 023	...	6	Butler	1 515	8 395	2 579	5.5	96.9	0.4	0.4	0.4	2.3	5.9	18.9	5.7	9.5	11.0	16.6
31 025	36540	2	Cass	1 444	25 241	1 595	17.5	96.5	0.7	0.9	0.7	2.4	6.3	19.0	6.5	10.6	12.8	16.5
31 027	...	9	Cedar	1 917	8 852	2 542	4.6	98.3	0.2	0.5	0.2	1.3	6.9	18.5	6.2	8.8	10.3	16.2
31 029	...	9	Chase	2 317	3 966	2 913	1.7	88.6	0.3	0.3	0.3	11.1	7.1	16.7	6.5	10.6	10.4	15.0
31 031	...	7	Cherry	15 437	5 713	2 789	0.4	92.3	0.5	7.4	0.6	1.7	5.4	16.7	5.8	10.4	11.2	15.9
31 033	...	7	Cheyenne	3 098	9 998	2 446	3.2	91.5	0.4	0.9	1.8	6.1	6.6	17.4	6.4	13.0	11.9	16.2
31 035	25580	9	Clay	1 482	6 542	2 723	4.4	91.5	0.6	0.6	0.3	7.7	6.2	19.1	6.8	10.0	10.4	16.0
31 037	...	7	Colfax	1 066	10 515	2 401	9.9	57.7	0.6	0.5	0.3	41.0	9.3	19.8	9.0	12.8	11.8	13.7
31 039	...	7	Cuming	1 478	9 139	2 514	6.2	91.2	0.3	0.5	0.4	8.3	6.2	18.7	5.7	9.9	11.0	15.1
31 041	...	7	Custer	6 671	10 939	2 374	1.6	97.3	0.5	0.8	0.2	2.0	6.2	17.4	5.7	9.7	10.5	15.5
31 043	43580	3	Dakota	684	21 006	1 786	30.7	56.1	3.4	2.6	3.5	35.3	9.0	21.0	9.4	13.2	12.0	13.3
31 045	...	7	Dawes	3 617	9 182	2 511	2.5	89.9	1.9	5.0	2.1	3.3	5.4	13.8	21.6	10.8	9.0	11.9
31 047	30420	7	Dawson	2 624	24 326	1 631	9.3	64.1	3.1	0.6	0.8	31.8	7.9	20.6	8.2	11.9	12.4	13.4
31 049	...	9	Deuel	1 139	1 941	3 059	1.7	95.5	0.3	1.0	0.3	3.9	5.8	15.2	5.5	7.1	11.4	16.7
31 051	43580	3	Dixon	1 233	6 000	2 768	4.9	88.7	0.5	0.6	0.3	10.4	6.7	19.0	6.6	9.9	11.4	14.6
31 053	23340	4	Dodge	1 369	36 691	1 257	26.8	88.4	0.9	0.7	0.8	10.1	6.8	17.1	8.5	11.8	11.3	14.1
31 055	36540	2	Douglas	851	517 110	122	607.6	73.7	12.7	1.1	3.3	11.2	7.8	18.3	10.3	15.7	13.0	13.6
31 057	...	9	Dundy	2 382	2 008	3 053	0.8	93.2	1.1	0.6	0.2	5.8	5.2	17.0	4.3	9.0	11.0	15.4
31 059	...	9	Fillmore	1 490	5 890	2 780	4.0	95.8	0.6	0.5	0.4	3.0	5.6	18.2	5.2	9.0	10.3	15.2
31 061	...	9	Franklin	1 491	3 225	2 963	2.2	98.5	0.1	0.8	0.5	1.0	5.6	16.0	5.4	8.3	9.7	16.2
31 063	...	9	Frontier	2 524	2 756	2 996	1.1	98.3	0.3	0.5	0.2	1.3	5.4	16.2	11.5	8.8	9.9	15.2
31 065	...	9	Furnas	1 863	4 959	2 843	2.7	96.6	0.5	0.6	0.6	2.7	5.2	18.1	5.1	8.0	10.4	15.0
31 067	13100	6	Gage	2 205	22 311	1 721	10.1	97.1	0.6	1.0	0.6	1.7	6.2	16.8	7.1	10.2	11.3	15.8
31 069	...	9	Garden	4 414	2 057	3 047	0.5	95.4	0.4	1.3	0.0	3.9	5.1	13.5	5.5	8.0	9.9	16.9
31 071	...	9	Garfield	1 476	2 049	3 049	1.4	98.9	0.2	0.2	0.1	0.7	4.3	16.7	4.7	7.7	9.1	15.3
31 073	30420	9	Gosper	1 187	2 044	3 051	1.7	96.8	0.7	0.9	0.5	2.4	5.7	16.7	4.7	9.3	10.2	16.2
31 075	...	9	Grant	2 010	614	3 135	0.3	98.5	0.3	0.7	0.2	1.1	6.2	12.5	8.1	9.6	8.5	19.5
31 077	...	9	Greeley	1 476	2 538	3 005	1.7	97.0	0.9	0.5	0.1	2.0	6.9	16.6	6.3	9.7	8.9	14.8
31 079	24260	5	Hall	1 415	58 607	872	41.4	73.4	1.9	0.7	1.4	23.3	8.1	19.2	8.3	13.4	12.5	13.8
31 081	...	7	Hamilton	1 406	9 124	2 516	6.5	97.4	0.4	0.3	0.4	2.0	5.8	19.9	6.0	9.6	12.0	16.6
31 083	...	9	Harlan	1 433	3 423	2 947	2.4	98.1	0.1	0.5	0.4	1.3	5.3	16.2	4.5	8.6	10.0	15.7
31 085	...	9	Hayes	1 847	967	3 113	0.5	96.1	0.0	0.1	0.5	3.4	4.8	18.3	5.7	9.1	7.5	18.9
31 087	...	9	Hitchcock	1 839	2 908	2 986	1.6	97.8	0.3	0.9	0.3	1.4	5.5	15.9	5.0	9.8	9.5	15.8
31 089	...	7	Holt	6 248	10 435	2 410	1.7	96.4	0.2	0.5	0.3	2.9	6.4	17.1	5.5	9.4	10.0	16.9
31 091	...	9	Hooker	1 868	736	3 123	0.4	98.4	0.0	1.0	0.0	1.1	4.8	16.6	4.2	9.1	9.1	14.1
31 093	24260	9	Howard	1 475	6 274	2 744	4.3	97.5	0.5	0.6	0.5	1.7	6.3	18.3	5.9	9.9	12.1	15.2
31 095	...	7	Jefferson	1 477	7 547	2 639	5.1	96.5	0.4	0.7	0.5	2.7	5.6	15.7	5.8	10.0	10.7	14.9
31 097	...	8	Johnson	974	5 217	2 827	5.4	83.8	5.4	1.3	1.4	8.3	5.3	13.6	6.4	14.4	12.5	17.9
31 099	28260	7	Kearney	1 337	6 489	2 727	4.9	95.5	0.4	0.5	0.4	3.8	6.8	17.4	6.0	10.5	11.4	16.1
31 101	...	7	Keith	2 750	8 368	2 581	3.0	93.3	0.4	0.9	0.7	5.7	5.6	16.0	5.9	9.3	10.2	16.4
31 103	...	9	Keya Paha	2 002	824	3 117	0.4	99.3	0.0	0.5	0.1	0.5	5.1	16.6	1.7	8.4	8.9	17.4
31 105	...	6	Kimball	2 465	3 821	2 918	1.6	91.9	0.7	1.6	0.9	6.4	6.4	16.0	6.5	9.2	10.6	15.2
31 107	...	9	Knox	2 871	8 701	2 553	3.0	89.5	0.3	9.3	0.4	1.8	6.0	18.1	5.3	8.6	9.7	15.2
31 109	30700	2	Lancaster	2 169	285 407	226	131.6	86.4	4.6	1.2	4.2	5.8	7.1	16.0	14.7	15.4	12.0	13.0
31 111	35820	5	Lincoln	6 641	36 288	1 267	5.5	91.1	1.0	0.8	0.8	7.2	7.1	18.0	7.8	12.2	11.7	14.3
31 113	35820	9	Logan	1 478	763	3 122	0.5	97.1	0.1	1.2	0.1	1.7	7.1	18.1	5.0	10.1	12.1	14.8
31 115	...	9	Loup	1 472	632	3 134	0.4	97.6	0.2	0.2	0.0	2.1	6.0	16.3	5.7	6.8	9.2	18.2
31 117	35820	9	McPherson	2 225	539	3 136	0.2	99.3	1.5	0.0	0.0	0.4	8.5	19.5	3.2	10.8	9.8	17.3
31 119	35740	5	Madison	1 483	34 876	1 303	23.5	84.3	1.7	1.4	0.7	12.9	7.4	17.6	10.4	12.3	10.8	15.2
31 121	24260	7	Merrick	1 256	7 845	2 619	6.2	95.1	0.3	0.8	1.1	3.5	6.0	18.8	6.7	10.0	11.7	15.1
31 123	...	9	Morrill	3 688	5 042	2 839	1.4	85.1	0.4	1.2	0.4	13.6	6.4	17.6	6.5	9.9	11.2	15.2
31 125	...	9	Nance	1 144	3 735	2 926	3.3	97.8	0.3	0.7	0.1	1.7	6.2	17.3	6.3	10.4	9.9	16.0
31 127	...	7	Nemaha	1 055	7 248	2 665	6.9	96.6	1.0	0.8	0.6	1.8	6.0	15.6	13.4	9.7	9.6	14.3
31 129	...	9	Nuckolls	1 490	4 500	2 870	3.0	97.3	0.3	0.8	0.5	2.2	5.2	16.0	4.4	8.8	9.6	15.6
31 131	...	6	Otoe	1 594	15 740	2 066	9.9	92.9	0.7	0.6	0.8	5.7	6.4	17.7	6.5	10.2	11.6	16.0
31 133	...	9	Pawnee	1 116	2 773	2 995	2.5	97.9	0.6	0.6	0.6	1.3	5.3	16.8	5.0	7.0	10.6	14.4
31 135	...	9	Perkins	2 288	2 970	2 982	1.3	96.2	0.4	0.2	0.2	3.2	6.5	18.2	6.0	10.3	10.2	14.3
31 137	...	7	Phelps	1 398	9 188	2 510	6.6	95.3	0.3	0.5	0.5	4.1	6.5	18.1	6.3	10.2	11.4	15.4
31 139	35740	9	Pierce	1 485	7 266	2 661	4.9	98.2	0.3	0.5	0.2	1.3	6.2	19.7	5.7	10.3	11.4	16.6

1. CBSA = Core Based Statistical Area. See Appendix A for explanation. See Appendix B for list of metropolitan areas with component counties. 2. County type code from the Economic Research Service of USDA Rural-Urban Continuum Codes. See Appendix A for definition. 3. Dry land or land partially or temporarily covered by water. 4. May be of any race.

Table B. States and Counties — **Population and Households**

STATE County	55 to 64 years	65 to 74 years	75 years and over	Percent female	Total persons 1990	Total persons 2000	Percent change 1990–2000	Percent change 2000–2010	Births	Deaths	Net migration	Number	Percent change 2000–2010	Persons per household	Female family householder[1]	One person
	16	17	18	19	20	21	22	23	24	25	26	27	28	29	30	31
NEBRASKA—Cont'd																
Blaine	14.4	12.3	7.5	48.3	675	583	-13.6	-18.0	46	32	-142	196	-17.6	2.44	2.0	21.9
Boone	13.1	8.8	12.3	50.1	6 667	6 259	-6.1	-12.0	544	628	-727	2 336	-4.8	2.32	5.3	31.2
Box Butte	14.9	6.9	8.2	51.0	13 130	12 158	-7.4	-7.0	1 418	1 124	-1 525	4 738	-0.9	2.35	8.8	30.6
Boyd	15.0	12.2	14.3	50.5	2 835	2 438	-14.0	-13.9	164	297	-229	942	-7.1	2.20	4.5	35.0
Brown	14.9	11.4	12.7	51.3	3 657	3 525	-3.6	-10.8	289	380	-355	1 449	-5.3	2.14	6.2	34.7
Buffalo	10.7	6.0	6.1	50.5	37 447	42 259	12.9	9.1	5 975	3 120	953	18 037	13.2	2.43	8.5	28.1
Burt	14.6	10.1	13.0	51.0	7 868	7 791	-1.0	-12.0	725	974	-587	2 906	-7.9	2.32	6.2	28.9
Butler	13.4	8.8	10.3	49.8	8 601	8 767	1.9	-4.2	887	932	-370	3 391	-1.0	2.42	7.1	27.3
Cass	13.9	7.9	6.4	49.8	21 318	24 334	14.1	3.7	2 944	1 949	306	9 698	5.9	2.57	7.7	22.2
Cedar	12.7	8.6	11.8	49.2	10 131	9 615	-5.1	-7.9	1 000	983	-1 234	3 539	-2.3	2.46	4.7	27.4
Chase	13.3	9.1	11.3	50.5	4 381	4 068	-7.1	-2.5	438	486	-376	1 681	1.1	2.32	5.9	29.9
Cherry	13.7	10.4	10.4	50.2	6 307	6 148	-2.5	-7.1	643	583	-712	2 530	0.9	2.24	6.6	33.6
Cheyenne	12.6	7.2	8.7	50.3	9 494	9 830	3.5	1.7	1 241	1 034	-273	4 298	5.6	2.30	8.2	31.4
Clay	13.8	8.5	9.3	49.9	7 123	7 039	-1.2	-7.1	690	710	-780	2 649	-3.9	2.43	7.0	28.0
Colfax	10.0	6.0	7.6	48.4	9 139	10 441	14.2	0.7	1 833	869	-1 074	3 618	-1.7	2.88	8.0	24.8
Cuming	12.6	8.9	11.9	50.4	10 117	10 203	0.9	-10.4	1 134	1 082	-1 085	3 756	-4.8	2.40	5.6	28.3
Custer	14.1	10.0	10.9	50.4	12 270	11 793	-3.9	-7.2	1 197	1 440	-709	4 714	-2.3	2.29	6.7	31.2
Dakota	10.5	6.4	5.0	50.1	16 742	20 253	21.0	3.7	3 623	1 463	-1 698	7 218	1.7	2.88	13.4	22.8
Dawes	11.1	8.1	8.2	50.3	9 021	9 060	0.4	1.3	931	800	-398	3 684	4.9	2.19	8.1	34.9
Dawson	11.7	6.9	7.0	49.5	19 940	24 365	22.2	-0.2	3 959	2 018	-1 113	8 899	0.8	2.70	9.7	25.3
Deuel	14.6	11.8	11.9	50.9	2 237	2 098	-6.2	-7.5	181	259	-172	867	-4.5	2.21	7.4	30.0
Dixon	14.1	8.3	9.5	50.6	6 143	6 339	3.2	-5.3	734	635	-149	2 370	-1.8	2.50	7.5	26.9
Dodge	12.1	8.5	9.9	51.0	34 500	36 160	4.8	1.5	4 571	3 748	-1 134	14 990	3.9	2.38	9.8	29.2
Douglas	10.8	5.5	5.1	50.8	416 444	463 585	11.3	11.5	76 137	33 353	6 992	202 411	11.1	2.49	12.6	30.1
Dundy	15.1	9.9	13.1	49.9	2 582	2 292	-11.2	-12.4	182	266	-244	897	-6.7	2.19	4.7	35.1
Fillmore	14.1	10.1	12.3	50.9	7 103	6 634	-6.6	-11.2	621	836	-418	2 483	-7.7	2.28	5.8	30.6
Franklin	14.8	10.8	13.2	50.0	3 938	3 574	-9.2	-9.8	291	469	-295	1 406	-5.3	2.25	6.7	31.4
Frontier	14.0	9.8	9.1	49.2	3 101	3 099	-0.1	-11.1	257	239	-603	1 168	-2.0	2.26	5.1	30.1
Furnas	15.4	10.5	12.2	51.1	5 553	5 324	-4.1	-6.9	465	725	-489	2 185	-4.1	2.23	6.0	34.9
Gage	13.2	9.0	10.4	50.9	22 794	22 993	0.9	-3.0	2 556	2 583	-171	9 422	1.1	2.31	8.4	30.3
Garden	13.9	13.6	13.7	49.3	2 460	2 292	-6.8	-10.3	148	304	-400	961	-5.8	2.10	6.0	33.6
Garfield	15.0	13.6	13.5	51.0	2 141	1 902	-11.2	7.7	164	301	-45	935	15.0	2.16	4.5	35.2
Gosper	16.0	10.9	10.2	49.9	1 928	2 143	11.2	-4.6	200	241	-253	849	-1.6	2.36	5.8	26.6
Grant	16.1	11.9	7.5	45.3	769	747	-2.9	-17.8	57	38	-210	277	-5.1	2.21	2.5	28.9
Greeley	13.8	10.7	12.4	49.6	3 006	2 714	-9.7	-6.5	278	296	-440	1 069	-0.7	2.32	5.4	32.2
Hall	11.3	6.5	6.9	50.0	48 925	53 534	9.4	9.5	8 782	4 648	114	22 196	9.0	2.59	10.9	27.6
Hamilton	13.7	8.2	8.2	50.0	8 862	9 403	6.1	-3.0	976	869	-170	3 563	1.7	2.53	6.9	23.0
Harlan	16.2	12.1	11.5	49.7	3 810	3 786	-0.6	-9.6	289	402	-429	1 519	-4.9	2.22	4.3	32.5
Hayes	15.9	10.7	9.1	47.3	1 222	1 068	-12.6	-9.5	85	68	-132	414	-3.7	2.34	3.4	28.0
Hitchcock	15.6	11.5	11.4	50.3	3 750	3 111	-17.0	-6.5	284	382	-196	1 301	1.1	2.22	7.1	32.9
Holt	14.2	9.3	11.2	50.3	12 599	11 551	-8.3	-9.7	1 127	1 206	-1 425	4 447	-3.5	2.31	6.2	30.7
Hooker	15.9	10.2	16.0	53.0	793	783	-1.3	-6.0	69	106	-20	326	-2.7	2.18	5.2	32.5
Howard	13.6	9.4	9.4	49.1	6 057	6 567	8.4	-4.5	677	623	-142	2 625	3.1	2.38	6.4	28.5
Jefferson	15.4	10.0	12.0	50.7	8 759	8 333	-4.9	-9.4	772	1 004	-843	3 348	-5.1	2.22	7.5	31.7
Johnson	12.3	8.1	9.5	42.2	4 673	4 488	-4.0	16.2	476	517	636	1 847	-2.1	2.31	7.1	29.9
Kearney	13.6	8.7	9.6	50.9	6 629	6 882	3.8	-5.7	705	618	-476	2 681	1.4	2.39	6.3	27.1
Keith	15.5	11.7	9.5	49.9	8 584	8 875	3.4	-5.7	828	895	-1 028	3 753	1.2	2.22	7.1	31.7
Keya Paha	16.4	14.0	11.7	49.6	1 029	983	-4.5	-16.2	96	71	-207	381	-6.8	2.16	3.4	30.4
Kimball	14.0	11.1	11.0	50.2	4 108	4 089	-0.5	-6.6	374	502	-372	1 673	-3.1	2.26	7.3	32.0
Knox	14.3	10.3	12.5	51.0	9 564	9 374	-2.0	-7.2	937	1 199	-697	3 647	-4.3	2.32	7.2	32.1
Lancaster	11.0	5.6	5.3	49.9	213 641	250 291	17.2	14.0	37 359	15 823	11 351	113 373	14.3	2.40	9.7	30.0
Lincoln	13.4	7.8	7.8	50.6	32 508	34 632	6.5	4.8	4 577	3 168	-169	15 025	6.7	2.37	8.9	30.0
Logan	14.7	10.0	8.3	50.1	878	774	-11.8	-1.4	91	71	-63	325	2.8	2.35	6.5	27.4
Loup	16.1	12.8	8.9	48.7	683	712	4.2	-11.2	57	55	-52	275	-4.8	2.30	4.4	28.0
McPherson	13.0	8.5	9.5	48.6	546	533	-2.4	1.1	51	24	-73	211	4.5	2.55	3.8	23.2
Madison	11.6	6.7	8.0	50.4	32 655	35 226	7.9	-1.0	5 153	3 214	-2 528	13 939	3.7	2.43	9.3	30.0
Merrick	13.7	9.3	8.8	50.5	8 062	8 204	1.8	-4.4	799	773	-522	3 151	-1.8	2.43	6.8	26.7
Morrill	13.8	9.7	9.8	50.1	5 423	5 440	0.3	-7.3	562	513	-550	2 085	-2.5	2.38	7.1	28.7
Nance	14.9	8.2	10.8	49.9	4 275	4 038	-5.5	-7.5	383	504	-447	1 525	-3.3	2.36	6.5	31.0
Nemaha	13.5	8.3	9.7	51.1	7 980	7 576	-5.1	-4.3	744	811	-626	2 952	-3.1	2.29	7.6	31.8
Nuckolls	14.3	12.1	14.0	50.5	5 786	5 057	-12.6	-11.0	473	682	-492	2 079	-6.3	2.14	5.5	34.9
Otoe	12.7	8.6	10.3	51.0	14 252	15 396	8.0	2.2	1 772	1 683	-175	6 362	5.0	2.42	8.5	27.4
Pawnee	15.0	11.5	14.5	50.3	3 317	3 087	-6.9	-10.2	226	412	-283	1 230	-8.1	2.22	6.0	34.5
Perkins	14.1	9.8	10.5	49.5	3 367	3 200	-5.0	-7.2	327	355	-392	1 239	-2.8	2.36	4.4	28.9
Phelps	13.2	8.7	10.3	50.5	9 715	9 747	0.3	-5.7	1 079	1 035	-714	3 779	-1.7	2.37	6.6	29.2
Pierce	12.1	8.8	9.1	49.5	7 827	7 857	0.4	-7.5	813	760	-689	2 911	-2.3	2.46	5.5	25.9

1. No spouse present.

Table B. States and Counties — Population, Vital Statistics, Medicare, and Crime

STATE County	Daytime population, 2006–2010 — Persons in group quarters, 2010	Number	Employment/residence ratio	Births, average 2006–2008 — Total	Rate[1]	Deaths, average 2006–2008 — Number	Rate[1]	Persons under 65 with no health insurance, 2009 — Number	Percent	Medicare, 2011 — Eligible for Medicare	Enrolled in Medicare Advantage	Enrolled in a Medicare prescription drug plan	Serious crimes known to police,[2] 2010 — Total — Number	Rate[3]
	32	33	34	35	36	37	38	39	40	41	42	43	44	45
NEBRASKA—Cont'd														
Blaine	0	509	0.9	D	D	D	D	72	22.1	109	D	69	NA	NA
Boone	95	5 471	1.0	D	D	67	12.1	570	13.7	1 225	34	850	NA	NA
Box Butte	186	11 592	1.0	D	D	119	10.8	1 170	12.8	1 966	119	1 294	184	1 627
Boyd	27	1 944	0.9	D	D	30	14.2	336	22.3	609	D	412	18	858
Brown	40	3 286	1.1	D	D	41	12.8	429	19.0	778	20	470	36	1 145
Buffalo	2 225	46 932	1.1	689	15.4	359	8.0	5 135	13.0	6 391	668	3 786	1 185	2 570
Burt	122	6 096	0.7	D	D	100	14.1	734	14.0	1 690	139	1 096	NA	NA
Butler	173	7 230	0.7	D	D	95	11.2	841	12.5	1 740	80	1 146	77	917
Cass	297	18 200	0.5	D	D	212	8.2	2 337	10.8	4 079	443	1 909	381	1 509
Cedar	144	7 968	0.8	D	D	101	11.8	922	14.2	1 783	341	1 052	21	237
Chase	66	4 230	1.2	D	D	52	14.0	436	15.6	840	19	610	42	1 059
Cherry	57	5 747	1.0	D	D	59	10.2	897	20.6	1 213	43	774	67	1 173
Cheyenne	102	11 062	1.2	D	D	103	10.3	962	12.0	1 798	77	1 156	NA	NA
Clay	96	5 980	0.8	D	D	80	12.5	725	14.8	1 338	54	920	NA	NA
Colfax	108	9 447	0.9	D	D	88	8.8	1 713	19.4	1 406	43	954	NA	NA
Cuming	130	8 840	0.9	D	D	115	12.1	1 203	16.9	2 045	128	1 481	28	306
Custer	128	10 732	1.0	D	D	147	13.4	1 280	15.4	2 314	103	1 572	143	1 307
Dakota	249	21 405	1.1	D	D	165	8.1	3 375	18.5	2 820	831	1 240	348	1 657
Dawes	1 132	9 248	1.0	D	D	79	9.1	1 354	19.0	1 691	233	870	196	2 135
Dawson	299	24 799	1.0	D	D	220	8.9	4 107	19.3	3 713	512	2 347	549	2 257
Deuel	22	1 750	0.8	D	D	24	12.6	207	15.3	461	36	288	21	1 082
Dixon	81	5 118	0.7	D	D	64	10.2	705	14.8	1 044	332	500	60	1 000
Dodge	1 003	36 092	1.0	D	D	420	11.7	3 736	13.1	7 472	605	4 168	1 036	2 891
Douglas	12 188	560 781	1.2	8 592	17.3	3 628	7.3	60 107	13.5	68 200	13 873	29 667	21 114	4 090
Dundy	41	1 838	0.9	D	D	34	16.4	319	21.4	493	12	342	NA	NA
Fillmore	222	5 613	0.9	D	D	88	14.5	582	12.8	1 447	40	1 027	NA	NA
Franklin	59	2 947	0.8	D	D	48	15.1	313	13.9	850	68	542	10	310
Frontier	113	2 609	0.9	D	D	27	10.2	345	17.7	543	44	367	NA	NA
Furnas	81	4 720	0.9	D	D	76	15.8	541	15.9	1 293	109	811	NA	NA
Gage	523	21 536	0.9	D	D	288	12.4	2 249	12.7	5 158	359	3 339	686	3 075
Garden	36	2 016	1.0	D	D	31	16.4	200	17.0	581	65	369	NA	NA
Garfield	30	2 179	1.1	D	D	29	16.9	259	21.4	491	28	285	NA	NA
Gosper	40	1 635	0.6	D	D	23	11.9	184	13.4	486	86	277	NA	NA
Grant	3	706	1.1	D	D	D	D	84	19.3	179	26	110	NA	NA
Greeley	53	2 435	0.9	D	D	30	12.7	334	20.6	588	18	372	NA	NA
Hall	1 118	61 728	1.2	993	17.8	516	9.2	7 614	15.7	8 925	934	5 060	2 717	4 636
Hamilton	124	8 402	0.8	D	D	91	9.7	848	11.1	1 789	190	1 053	70	767
Harlan	47	3 229	0.9	D	D	45	13.4	385	16.1	826	97	482	1	29
Hayes	0	874	0.7	D	D	D	D	189	24.0	183	D	100	NA	NA
Hitchcock	26	2 549	0.7	D	D	40	14.1	332	16.0	723	19	525	27	928
Holt	160	10 470	1.0	D	D	133	12.8	1 294	16.8	2 455	33	1 814	NA	NA
Hooker	26	753	1.2	D	D	12	16.2	92	18.3	212	11	147	1	136
Howard	35	5 058	0.6	D	D	78	11.7	736	14.2	1 288	50	825	NA	NA
Jefferson	105	7 605	1.0	D	D	119	15.6	710	13.1	1 851	155	1 240	NA	NA
Johnson	955	4 894	0.9	D	D	58	12.7	729	17.9	877	43	559	16	307
Kearney	84	5 558	0.7	D	D	61	9.3	624	12.0	1 174	81	749	118	1 818
Keith	55	8 008	0.9	D	D	98	12.2	917	15.5	1 985	126	1 257	199	2 378
Keya Paha	0	669	0.8	D	D	D	D	185	30.9	249	D	179	0	0
Kimball	48	3 707	0.9	D	D	52	14.5	404	15.2	912	21	603	NA	NA
Knox	234	8 357	0.9	D	D	133	15.3	1 056	16.7	2 077	192	1 387	25	287
Lancaster	13 816	286 403	1.0	4 164	15.2	1 748	6.4	30 424	12.4	37 216	2 663	19 963	12 082	4 233
Lincoln	642	37 235	1.1	514	14.4	345	9.7	3 622	12.4	6 745	1 221	4 573	1 356	3 737
Logan	0	604	0.8	D	D	D	D	130	23.0	163	16	122	NA	NA
Loup	0	NA	NA	D	D	D	D	104	20.4	140	19	87	NA	NA
McPherson	0	NA	NA	D	D	D	D	82	20.5	84	16	51	NA	NA
Madison	1 071	38 072	1.2	D	D	351	10.2	4 168	14.6	6 193	729	3 786	855	2 452
Merrick	197	6 382	0.6	D	D	84	10.8	886	14.6	1 699	170	1 034	133	1 695
Morrill	82	4 497	0.8	D	D	53	10.4	640	16.6	923	66	622	70	1 388
Nance	143	3 370	0.8	D	D	52	14.4	447	16.7	689	25	488	30	803
Nemaha	486	7 716	1.1	D	D	92	13.0	694	12.7	1 492	76	950	77	1 062
Nuckolls	59	4 294	0.9	D	D	71	15.7	455	14.4	1 199	42	807	15	333
Otoe	338	14 727	0.9	D	D	187	11.9	1 370	11.2	3 149	271	1 833	NA	NA
Pawnee	39	2 476	0.8	D	D	45	16.8	299	15.8	678	29	443	27	974
Perkins	44	2 942	1.0	D	D	40	13.6	354	16.4	611	19	420	25	842
Phelps	249	9 891	1.1	D	D	109	11.8	884	12.4	1 947	316	1 093	159	1 731
Pierce	116	5 952	0.7	D	D	75	10.1	856	14.6	1 310	30	928	34	618

1. Per 1,000 estimated resident population. 2. Data for serious crimes have not been adjusted for underreporting; this may affect comparability between geographic areas and over time. 3. Per 100,000 population estimated by the FBI.

STATE County	Serious crimes known to police,[1] 2010 (cont.) Rate[2]		Education						Money income, 2006–2010				Income and poverty, 2010			
			School enrollment and attainment, 2006–2010				Local government expenditures,[5] 2008–2009			Households				Percent below poverty level		
			Enrollment[3]		Attainment[4] (percent)						Median income					
	Violent	Property	Total	Percent private	High school graduate or less	Bachelor's degree or more	Total current expenditures (mil dol)	Current expenditures per student (dollars)	Per capita income[6] (dollars)	Dollars	Percent change, 2000 to 2006–2010 (constant 2010 dollars)	Percent with income of $200,000 or more	Median household income (dollars)	All persons	Children under 18 years	Children 5 to 17 years in families
	46	47	48	49	50	51	52	53	54	55	56	57	58	59	60	61
NEBRASKA—Cont'd																
Blaine	NA	NA	108	0.0	49.5	19.8	2.0	16 113	20 586	39 000	21.8	0.0	31 119	20.3	37.3	32.0
Boone	NA	NA	1 139	10.7	50.5	15.8	10.7	11 793	22 790	40 703	2.2	1.8	42 265	9.7	13.2	11.6
Box Butte	150	1 477	2 717	9.7	47.5	19.5	19.3	9 828	23 434	44 404	-10.9	0.5	47 640	13.1	19.8	17.1
Boyd	95	762	393	11.5	51.9	13.2	5.0	14 260	21 003	34 906	5.7	0.9	34 564	13.9	23.3	21.1
Brown	32	1 113	642	22.9	53.3	16.8	8.4	16 882	17 330	28 038	-21.9	0.7	34 659	13.9	20.4	17.4
Buffalo	163	2 408	13 770	10.0	37.8	32.0	76.4	10 545	22 616	47 120	1.2	1.6	45 307	12.4	14.7	13.5
Burt	NA	NA	1 547	7.6	48.4	18.3	13.1	9 710	23 302	43 817	1.9	1.9	44 360	12.1	16.6	15.0
Butler	119	798	2 107	29.4	49.3	15.7	12.1	10 453	22 494	44 595	-3.1	0.9	47 490	9.1	12.0	10.1
Cass	48	1 462	6 595	14.4	39.3	23.5	35.6	9 435	27 584	62 039	5.3	2.4	59 392	7.2	11.2	9.5
Cedar	56	181	2 338	26.3	55.1	15.1	15.2	12 678	20 595	40 497	-4.3	0.8	43 923	11.1	14.9	13.8
Chase	177	883	906	2.1	53.2	14.6	8.9	11 786	22 730	38 314	-6.5	0.5	43 271	11.7	16.2	14.7
Cherry	280	893	1 290	11.5	44.4	22.6	10.3	13 030	22 601	43 431	17.2	1.5	38 977	13.7	25.7	22.5
Cheyenne	NA	NA	2 385	15.4	37.5	27.1	17.5	10 272	26 983	49 493	16.9	2.4	49 417	10.7	15.2	13.5
Clay	NA	NA	1 661	10.5	49.8	16.4	16.8	11 306	21 147	42 909	-1.1	1.3	46 199	11.0	15.7	14.0
Colfax	NA	NA	2 317	6.3	59.4	12.7	21.0	9 307	20 872	48 133	6.0	1.3	45 039	10.9	15.2	14.7
Cuming	22	284	2 219	24.4	52.9	15.7	15.3	9 987	22 783	44 278	5.4	1.5	45 234	10.3	13.1	10.9
Custer	110	1 198	2 471	5.9	47.4	18.0	21.0	11 409	21 685	42 364	9.1	1.5	39 801	14.0	21.3	19.6
Dakota	100	1 557	5 158	12.2	64.3	10.8	38.4	9 395	19 048	43 729	-11.1	0.3	43 351	13.2	20.4	18.0
Dawes	218	1 917	3 018	2.9	30.9	36.5	12.6	10 770	18 573	34 937	-6.4	0.9	36 333	17.6	20.7	16.5
Dawson	197	2 060	6 134	6.3	59.7	14.7	49.9	9 539	19 384	41 830	-8.6	0.8	43 899	11.7	17.5	15.8
Deuel	0	1 082	366	2.0	44.7	18.2	3.4	13 518	23 758	37 148	-11.1	2.0	40 325	12.7	22.5	20.6
Dixon	100	900	1 551	3.0	55.4	13.0	11.7	9 990	20 478	42 388	-2.1	0.7	43 505	9.7	15.1	13.4
Dodge	151	2 740	9 058	18.9	53.1	17.3	58.7	9 724	22 049	42 849	-9.0	1.5	41 435	12.7	19.0	16.4
Douglas	471	3 619	145 356	23.0	33.7	35.8	809.4	9 408	28 092	51 878	-5.2	3.9	50 270	14.7	20.5	18.5
Dundy	NA	NA	454	0.7	36.3	25.9	11.8	14 248	24 701	37 031	8.3	2.3	37 071	13.5	19.1	16.8
Fillmore	NA	NA	1 438	9.2	46.8	17.6	14.9	11 259	21 990	43 167	-3.1	0.6	47 551	9.0	14.0	12.1
Franklin	0	310	689	7.8	47.3	16.3	3.5	10 082	19 764	37 220	0.3	1.0	39 516	14.3	19.6	17.6
Frontier	NA	NA	638	10.8	41.8	19.8	7.6	12 985	22 374	42 009	0.4	1.8	40 359	14.1	17.9	15.6
Furnas	NA	NA	1 145	7.1	53.6	16.3	12.6	10 740	21 644	37 938	-1.8	1.8	39 234	13.4	21.2	17.5
Gage	235	2 837	5 259	10.3	48.8	19.1	35.5	11 180	21 619	43 311	-2.0	0.8	45 169	12.5	18.4	16.3
Garden	NA	NA	321	9.3	46.0	20.2	3.6	12 204	19 740	32 962	-1.6	0.0	32 677	15.9	26.6	25.5
Garfield	NA	NA	487	6.8	49.9	13.8	3.9	10 480	19 235	38 709	11.5	0.7	34 998	14.6	19.6	17.0
Gosper	NA	NA	426	12.4	46.4	16.4	2.9	11 434	23 132	41 442	-11.1	2.9	49 286	9.5	15.8	14.4
Grant	NA	NA	122	4.1	64.1	17.3	2.2	18 463	20 518	39 261	-11.0	0.0	40 151	12.1	24.4	23.6
Greeley	NA	NA	585	12.3	56.6	12.5	6.7	13 987	19 235	41 181	14.6	0.0	34 998	13.7	22.1	21.8
Hall	300	4 336	13 851	9.1	50.6	16.3	114.8	10 406	22 552	46 138	-1.5	1.6	46 807	13.1	19.1	15.6
Hamilton	55	712	2 289	8.1	42.2	21.8	16.4	9 793	23 240	60 702	-0.6	1.8	55 535	8.5	11.4	9.5
Harlan	29	0	721	2.9	46.7	16.9	3.3	10 481	25 050	44 656	14.9	2.4	45 732	10.9	17.9	15.8
Hayes	NA	NA	210	9.5	44.7	16.6	2.4	15 396	21 977	45 595	35.0	1.4	40 125	17.1	27.1	24.3
Hitchcock	103	825	550	10.7	54.5	13.7	5.2	22 274	20 853	35 549	-0.8	0.6	36 329	15.2	28.9	26.6
Holt	NA	NA	2 277	17.1	49.2	16.1	21.3	13 079	22 498	43 452	11.6	1.8	44 835	13.7	19.3	18.0
Hooker	0	136	172	2.3	36.4	22.1	2.5	13 754	21 197	38 750	9.8	1.3	34 687	9.7	13.2	11.3
Howard	NA	NA	1 534	5.9	51.2	13.9	11.6	8 766	22 325	45 453	7.8	1.0	45 091	10.5	15.1	13.6
Jefferson	NA	NA	1 698	8.8	51.0	14.7	11.6	10 611	21 976	42 665	3.3	0.7	41 131	12.6	20.3	17.6
Johnson	19	288	865	6.8	61.2	11.8	8.4	10 974	17 606	42 083	2.4	0.3	42 038	12.3	15.6	14.4
Kearney	92	1 726	1 449	5.6	39.9	25.0	14.1	10 617	27 227	54 518	9.7	1.7	53 293	9.0	12.6	11.9
Keith	96	2 283	1 615	10.7	45.6	19.5	21.0	15 343	25 315	42 898	4.8	2.0	41 493	12.0	19.6	16.9
Keya Paha	0	0	91	9.9	52.7	14.0	1.6	17 031	20 691	32 000	1.4	0.9	31 764	22.6	37.4	32.8
Kimball	NA	NA	838	3.5	48.5	19.8	6.3	10 663	22 263	42 010	8.5	0.4	40 455	13.0	20.6	19.1
Knox	0	287	2 058	9.5	51.6	17.5	18.4	11 809	19 894	36 798	5.4	1.4	36 806	14.7	21.9	19.2
Lancaster	452	3 782	85 813	18.8	31.0	35.3	357.3	9 168	25 949	50 849	-4.0	2.5	50 197	14.8	17.6	16.1
Lincoln	190	3 547	8 623	10.8	42.0	19.0	52.8	9 168	25 319	45 181	-2.4	2.7	46 616	12.3	17.8	15.7
Logan	NA	NA	112	3.6	45.3	18.8	3.7	14 883	22 320	45 192	7.7	0.0	42 257	12.5	21.4	20.6
Loup	NA	NA	156	34.6	58.7	10.0	1.5	11 935	20 004	34 219	2.9	0.0	34 805	17.3	24.6	22.4
McPherson	NA	NA	115	0.0	34.8	24.3	NA	NA	21 000	50 625	55.3	0.0	33 950	18.9	33.6	33.0
Madison	152	2 300	9 112	18.5	43.7	20.0	52.6	9 560	22 157	44 089	-2.8	1.6	43 491	13.1	18.3	16.0
Merrick	191	1 504	1 862	9.0	50.5	13.5	9.7	9 406	21 819	46 116	4.2	0.6	43 244	11.8	16.1	13.6
Morrill	60	1 329	1 185	10.0	50.6	21.0	10.9	11 461	21 367	37 717	-1.5	1.1	40 465	15.6	23.5	20.1
Nance	54	750	794	6.0	53.4	11.6	8.2	9 439	21 457	41 610	5.1	0.8	41 950	12.7	18.6	16.7
Nemaha	41	1 021	1 973	5.5	45.0	23.0	16.2	14 075	22 151	42 534	3.1	1.0	45 292	13.2	16.1	14.4
Nuckolls	22	311	993	6.6	56.8	12.4	4.8	10 652	20 299	31 761	-13.4	1.5	36 985	12.4	20.8	18.5
Otoe	NA	NA	3 693	16.1	48.2	21.5	24.5	9 304	23 773	47 493	0.5	1.2	48 980	10.6	15.7	12.6
Pawnee	108	865	496	13.3	61.2	14.8	5.9	12 277	21 865	41 969	14.3	0.2	34 294	14.1	22.1	19.6
Perkins	0	842	751	14.1	37.3	18.4	5.3	14 133	23 542	47 000	8.5	0.4	45 820	10.6	14.0	12.7
Phelps	54	1 676	2 187	13.2	40.7	22.7	19.7	12 055	23 951	45 221	-4.3	1.7	49 532	10.0	13.4	11.9
Pierce	36	582	1 767	11.6	50.6	14.3	13.9	10 676	21 419	48 318	18.4	0.8	45 521	9.6	12.7	11.0

1. Data for serious crimes have not been adjusted for underreporting; this may affect comparability between geographic areas and over time. 2. Per 100,000 population estimated by the FBI. 3. All persons 3 years old and over enrolled in nursery school through college. 4. Persons 25 years old and over. 5. Elementary and secondary education expenditures. 6. Based on population estimated by the American Community Survey, 2006–2010.

Table B. States and Counties — **Personal Income**

STATE County	Total (mil dol)	Percent change, 2008–2009	Per capita[1] Dollars	Rank	Wages and salaries[2] (mil dol)	Proprietors' income (mil dol)	Dividends, interest, and rent (mil dol)	Transfer payments (mil dol) Total	Government payments to individuals Total	Social Security	Medical payments	Income maintenance	Unemployment insurance
	62	63	64	65	66	67	68	69	70	71	72	73	74
NEBRASKA—Cont'd													
Blaine	13	-18.8	29 179	2 149	7	-1	4	3	3	1	1	0	0
Boone	211	3.3	38 943	545	87	47	40	39	38	15	17	2	1
Box Butte	384	-6.1	35 225	992	284	26	67	77	75	22	29	6	3
Boyd	73	0.8	35 342	972	19	22	13	19	19	7	10	1	0
Brown	93	0.7	30 386	1 888	47	6	23	25	24	10	9	1	0
Buffalo	1 576	-2.6	34 396	1 111	1 089	148	309	248	240	89	98	20	6
Burt	276	4.5	39 855	457	74	56	40	60	58	22	28	3	1
Butler	322	-0.1	38 294	603	104	71	50	53	52	23	20	3	1
Cass	992	0.2	38 938	546	209	94	130	152	148	57	59	8	4
Cedar	351	-1.9	41 962	332	106	118	57	51	49	22	20	2	1
Chase	142	-17.8	39 152	521	68	26	32	28	27	12	13	1	0
Cherry	180	-4.3	32 907	1 353	81	15	47	38	37	15	16	3	1
Cheyenne	398	-7.9	40 908	387	280	48	68	61	60	25	25	4	1
Clay	250	-6.9	40 360	429	118	55	35	45	43	18	19	3	1
Colfax	353	1.3	34 146	1 146	207	52	51	66	64	18	38	4	1
Cuming	382	6.1	41 833	342	155	104	69	60	58	27	24	3	1
Custer	384	-2.0	35 646	935	176	67	73	78	76	30	34	5	1
Dakota	579	0.8	28 036	2 393	518	41	66	112	108	39	46	13	4
Dawes	253	-2.7	28 981	2 203	137	20	47	61	59	21	21	5	1
Dawson	747	0.2	29 794	2 022	466	105	107	137	132	51	55	14	4
Deuel	62	-5.3	33 981	1 172	21	7	16	15	15	7	6	1	0
Dixon	205	3.2	32 644	1 393	77	35	27	40	38	13	20	2	1
Dodge	1 308	0.8	36 703	786	689	154	234	265	258	105	111	18	6
Douglas	23 429	-2.1	45 921	171	18 713	2 352	5 060	3 082	2 989	967	1 336	316	87
Dundy	80	-19.7	40 886	390	29	14	22	15	15	6	7	1	0
Fillmore	250	-7.6	41 986	329	97	62	50	45	44	20	17	2	1
Franklin	121	-2.0	39 306	507	32	32	23	27	26	11	11	1	0
Frontier	96	-1.9	38 285	605	35	26	14	17	16	7	7	1	0
Furnas	174	-9.1	38 229	614	78	29	31	42	41	16	19	2	1
Gage	834	-1.9	36 795	773	365	102	140	223	219	69	119	11	5
Garden	80	-9.0	45 888	174	26	14	22	19	19	8	9	1	0
Garfield	64	6.1	37 174	726	26	11	15	14	14	4	8	1	0
Gosper	93	0.9	50 668	91	21	31	15	15	14	7	6	1	0
Grant	15	-12.1	27 579	2 471	8	-2	6	5	5	2	2	0	0
Greeley	73	2.4	32 590	1 406	26	14	15	18	17	7	8	1	0
Hall	2 062	-0.1	35 869	904	1 464	236	366	360	350	121	145	35	8
Hamilton	370	-5.8	39 835	459	145	90	61	55	53	25	19	3	1
Harlan	137	-1.2	42 315	306	36	45	18	26	26	11	10	1	0
Hayes	39	-24.6	40 714	405	10	19	4	5	4	2	1	0	0
Hitchcock	88	-3.6	31 409	1 663	34	11	17	23	23	9	9	1	1
Holt	403	-6.3	40 283	433	174	105	71	79	77	30	36	5	1
Hooker	20	-4.7	27 817	2 435	10	-1	5	6	6	3	2	0	0
Howard	214	0.5	33 187	1 307	56	34	33	42	41	17	16	2	1
Jefferson	255	-7.6	35 269	986	128	27	53	59	58	24	24	4	1
Johnson	165	5.8	32 535	1 415	84	23	23	29	28	11	13	2	1
Kearney	275	-2.5	42 496	295	91	65	41	49	48	17	26	2	1
Keith	265	-6.2	34 139	1 148	122	38	53	59	58	27	22	4	1
Keya Paha	22	-20.9	27 737	2 448	7	2	6	6	6	3	2	0	0
Kimball	133	-6.5	37 197	723	58	24	25	29	28	13	11	2	1
Knox	267	-0.8	31 896	1 551	102	39	50	71	69	25	34	5	1
Lancaster	10 509	-0.5	37 330	710	7 833	664	1 927	1 487	1 436	520	571	125	44
Lincoln	1 305	-1.7	36 598	800	831	166	193	261	254	73	95	20	7
Logan	25	-8.5	34 480	1 097	8	4	4	5	5	2	2	0	0
Loup	11	-18.3	17 216	3 109	5	-3	4	4	4	2	1	0	0
McPherson	8	-13.3	16 998	3 110	3	-3	3	3	3	1	2	0	0
Madison	1 198	-0.5	34 724	1 058	890	106	232	225	219	82	95	19	5
Merrick	270	5.1	35 240	990	88	42	42	57	55	23	23	4	1
Morrill	193	-8.8	39 392	499	67	52	31	37	36	13	16	3	1
Nance	133	-1.6	38 493	580	40	31	20	29	28	10	14	2	0
Nemaha	275	6.4	40 084	444	190	46	39	55	53	20	23	3	1
Nuckolls	166	-7.7	38 305	602	53	42	29	37	36	16	16	2	1
Otoe	557	3.7	36 629	798	267	74	94	103	100	43	40	6	3
Pawnee	94	-2.9	35 978	890	31	18	19	21	21	8	10	1	0
Perkins	113	-26.1	40 973	384	51	28	18	21	21	9	9	1	0
Phelps	375	0.0	41 503	363	210	72	61	67	65	28	28	4	1
Pierce	251	-2.8	34 989	1 022	82	48	40	41	40	18	16	2	1

1. Based on the resident population estimated as of July 1 of the year shown.   2. Includes supplements to wages and salaries.

Table B. States and Counties — Earnings, Social Security, and Housing

STATE County	Earnings, 2009 Total (mil dol)	Farm	Goods-related[1] Total	Manufacturing	Information and professional and technical services	Retail trade	Finance, insurance, and real estate	Health care and social services	Government	Social Security beneficiaries, December 2010 Number	Rate[2]	Supplemental Security Income recipients, December 2010	Housing units, 2010 Total	Percent change, 2000–2010
	75	76	77	78	79	80	81	82	83	84	85	86	87	88
NEBRASKA—Cont'd														
Blaine	6	1.7	D	1.0	0.0	D	D	1.2	61.8	115	241	0	326	-2.1
Boone	134	34.6	7.6	6.0	1.3	4.2	3.7	4.7	20.4	1 295	235	49	2 649	-3.1
Box Butte	310	4.3	6.9	4.9	2.6	3.8	3.1	D	17.2	1 815	161	175	5 478	-0.2
Boyd	41	37.3	3.2	2.1	D	3.4	4.1	4.1	21.1	650	310	33	1 390	-1.1
Brown	53	9.2	6.2	2.6	D	9.5	D	7.5	35.6	890	283	53	1 865	-2.7
Buffalo	1 236	4.8	19.5	14.5	4.5	8.3	4.3	17.2	16.8	7 025	152	463	19 064	13.3
Burt	129	35.7	8.1	4.9	D	2.9	D	5.2	20.7	1 860	271	107	3 467	-6.9
Butler	175	38.0	D	17.4	D	4.1	D	D	16.1	1 885	225	96	4 053	0.9
Cass	303	18.4	16.5	8.9	3.5	6.2	5.2	D	22.2	4 420	175	190	11 117	9.2
Cedar	223	40.0	9.4	4.3	2.7	4.4	4.1	3.2	14.6	1 945	220	69	4 148	-1.2
Chase	94	25.2	D	3.7	4.6	9.2	3.9	2.1	21.7	920	232	41	1 946	1.0
Cherry	97	9.4	9.2	3.1	5.7	10.0	4.7	7.1	27.8	1 325	232	77	3 157	-2.0
Cheyenne	329	6.0	11.5	9.1	D	9.8	2.8	6.3	11.9	1 925	193	124	4 888	7.0
Clay	174	30.2	D	8.9	1.6	2.9	D	3.9	23.2	1 460	223	73	3 001	-2.1
Colfax	259	18.1	D	D	1.7	3.0	3.0	4.5	12.4	1 515	144	82	4 097	0.2
Cuming	258	40.7	D	7.9	2.4	3.5	4.8	D	12.0	2 205	241	85	4 204	-1.8
Custer	243	25.6	17.8	13.9	2.8	6.0	3.6	9.4	16.7	2 540	232	150	5 579	-0.1
Dakota	559	3.4	D	38.6	D	5.0	8.4	D	11.6	3 180	151	285	7 631	1.4
Dawes	157	2.9	D	1.1	3.8	11.4	4.1	11.0	36.8	1 780	194	128	4 252	6.2
Dawson	571	15.0	D	29.4	2.9	6.4	3.1	D	18.5	4 125	170	316	10 123	3.2
Deuel	27	19.8	D	0.9	D	9.5	D	D	28.9	520	268	20	1 044	1.2
Dixon	112	24.2	D	D	D	1.3	D	2.6	16.1	1 145	191	54	2 688	0.6
Dodge	842	12.2	23.2	19.5	2.7	9.0	3.9	D	17.8	8 155	222	460	16 584	7.2
Douglas	21 066	0.1	D	6.0	13.9	5.5	11.3	12.2	12.3	73 655	142	8 867	219 580	14.0
Dundy	44	37.3	3.5	2.2	D	2.7	D	4.8	26.5	520	259	30	1 125	-5.9
Fillmore	159	36.0	D	5.0	D	3.6	D	3.9	18.1	1 570	267	60	2 913	-2.6
Franklin	64	46.6	D	D	D	4.7	3.9	3.1	22.8	905	281	53	1 734	-0.7
Frontier	61	34.9	D	D	D	5.9	D	1.9	21.9	620	225	28	1 574	2.1
Furnas	107	31.0	6.5	3.4	6.9	4.7	D	D	21.5	1 390	280	86	2 721	-0.3
Gage	467	13.2	D	17.5	D	7.0	3.8	D	24.3	5 635	253	364	10 446	4.1
Garden	40	40.0	D	D	D	10.4	4.1	D	27.4	640	311	31	1 314	1.2
Garfield	37	21.8	D	7.0	D	6.9	D	8.0	19.7	445	217	16	1 178	15.4
Gosper	51	59.0	D	D	D	0.8	7.6	D	13.2	535	262	20	1 267	-1.1
Grant	6	-7.3	4.4	0.0	D	D	D	1.3	49.2	185	301	0	391	-12.9
Greeley	41	33.6	5.0	2.5	D	3.7	4.1	3.4	26.5	660	260	32	1 300	8.4
Hall	1 701	2.6	28.3	23.1	3.8	9.3	5.0	12.0	17.0	9 875	168	871	23 549	9.1
Hamilton	235	31.4	15.2	13.0	D	3.7	3.4	D	11.8	1 995	219	83	3 968	3.1
Harlan	81	45.0	D	D	D	5.2	D	4.1	15.2	905	264	49	2 375	2.1
Hayes	29	76.2	D	D	D	D	D	0.2	12.9	170	176	0	511	-2.9
Hitchcock	44	19.4	24.7	17.7	D	2.2	D	D	28.5	795	273	54	1 763	5.2
Holt	279	24.7	10.7	8.3	2.3	6.8	4.2	D	12.8	2 700	259	186	5 215	-1.2
Hooker	9	-19.1	D	D	0.0	D	2.8	D	38.6	225	306	0	431	-2.0
Howard	91	32.4	3.2	0.6	D	5.3	D	3.3	30.3	1 410	225	54	2 951	6.1
Jefferson	155	16.0	D	13.5	3.7	9.0	3.0	D	15.3	2 010	266	148	3 918	-0.6
Johnson	107	12.7	D	4.1	D	4.3	D	6.1	38.9	920	176	49	2 191	3.5
Kearney	156	41.2	13.3	9.8	D	1.9	3.0	7.3	14.2	1 265	195	68	2 886	1.4
Keith	160	13.1	D	6.3	4.5	9.5	5.9	D	16.8	2 125	254	111	5 424	4.8
Keya Paha	9	32.6	D	D	D	D	D	D	27.7	275	334	14	549	0.2
Kimball	82	17.5	21.7	9.6	D	6.0	D	D	22.4	1 000	262	45	1 963	-0.5
Knox	141	24.3	7.0	4.3	D	6.5	D	4.8	34.3	2 295	264	125	4 788	0.3
Lancaster	8 497	0.5	D	9.5	8.4	6.0	8.9	14.0	23.2	39 805	139	4 182	120 875	16.0
Lincoln	997	9.1	D	1.6	3.7	7.0	3.8	15.0	16.8	6 225	172	695	16 583	7.4
Logan	13	39.1	D	D	D	D	D	D	23.6	145	190	10	395	2.3
Loup	2	-100.7	D	0.0	0.0	D	D	5.0	112.3	155	245	0	426	13.0
McPherson	0	-1 746.8	0.0	0.0	D	D	D	0.0	1 136.5	90	167	0	283	0.0
Madison	997	4.3	D	16.9	4.2	8.4	5.0	14.4	18.6	6 750	194	556	15 014	4.0
Merrick	130	29.3	D	7.7	2.3	3.7	5.1	D	19.0	1 805	230	142	3 698	1.3
Morrill	119	41.3	D	1.8	D	5.2	D	3.6	19.6	1 045	207	92	2 442	-0.7
Nance	72	39.3	D	D	D	3.2	D	7.6	23.1	830	222	77	1 801	0.8
Nemaha	236	14.5	D	7.3	3.0	3.5	2.7	4.7	53.0	1 635	226	119	3 498	1.7
Nuckolls	96	33.7	1.6	0.4	2.5	7.2	4.0	13.7	17.4	1 305	290	69	2 465	-2.6
Otoe	340	15.1	25.0	19.4	D	6.4	4.3	D	20.8	3 415	217	202	7 025	7.0
Pawnee	49	31.3	D	11.8	1.0	3.7	4.0	7.6	26.2	705	254	43	1 588	0.1
Perkins	80	26.0	13.1	5.3	D	2.9	D	2.5	19.8	665	224	23	1 450	0.4
Phelps	282	23.0	D	D	D	4.6	5.0	D	12.8	2 105	229	114	4 175	-0.4
Pierce	130	31.1	D	4.0	D	4.2	D	6.5	18.1	1 460	201	58	3 222	-0.8

1. Includes mining, construction, and manufacturing.   2. Per 1,000 resident population enumerated in the 2010 census.

Table B. States and Counties — Housing, Labor Force, and Employment

STATE County	Housing units, 2006–2010 Total	Owner-occupied Percent	Median value[1]	Median owner cost as a percent of income With a mortgage	Median owner cost as a percent of income Without a mortgage	Renter-occupied Median rent[2]	Median rent as a percent of income	Substandard units[3] (percent)	Civilian labor force, 2010 Total	Percent change, 2009–2010	Unemployment Total	Rate[4]	Civilian employment[5] 2006–2010 Total	Percent Management, business, science and arts	Percent Construction, production, and maintenance occupations
	89	90	91	92	93	94	95	96	97	98	99	100	101	102	103
NEBRASKA—Cont'd															
Blaine	242	65.3	57 600	25.8	10.0	631	26.8	2.1	267	2.7	13	4.9	303	44.9	32.7
Boone	2 382	74.6	71 100	21.5	11.8	415	16.8	0.9	3 380	1.9	103	3.0	2 870	34.3	29.2
Box Butte	4 793	67.4	90 600	19.5	11.4	503	24.9	2.6	5 333	-4.7	286	5.4	5 721	28.5	39.7
Boyd	932	75.1	52 100	22.0	12.7	364	13.3	1.4	1 128	0.7	42	3.7	1 135	40.5	26.6
Brown	1 340	70.3	56 400	21.4	16.9	440	26.1	0.3	1 856	1.2	65	3.5	1 360	30.0	34.8
Buffalo	17 268	65.5	128 600	22.3	11.8	619	26.8	1.6	27 436	0.1	948	3.5	24 979	31.3	25.3
Burt	2 951	74.3	83 100	22.7	12.4	561	26.2	1.3	3 929	-1.3	214	5.4	3 346	33.4	25.9
Butler	3 451	75.3	87 800	19.9	12.3	551	21.0	1.4	4 827	2.4	180	3.7	4 353	30.3	37.5
Cass	9 610	82.6	142 800	23.0	13.6	662	23.2	1.0	13 544	-2.5	774	5.7	13 095	33.5	26.6
Cedar	3 419	81.0	85 100	19.9	14.1	455	21.4	1.1	4 849	1.2	160	3.3	4 500	33.5	30.4
Chase	1 710	75.8	82 600	18.7	14.3	434	25.4	0.6	2 089	1.6	62	3.0	2 060	30.6	29.2
Cherry	2 505	65.9	95 300	20.4	14.4	609	26.4	1.6	3 581	3.1	95	2.7	3 177	40.8	22.2
Cheyenne	4 348	70.1	94 200	19.3	13.2	555	23.1	1.6	4 887	-3.3	197	4.0	5 570	35.3	20.0
Clay	2 621	77.2	73 700	20.2	13.1	473	19.5	1.0	2 937	-3.9	136	4.6	3 182	32.1	28.3
Colfax	3 706	80.8	85 400	21.0	13.1	618	24.8	6.0	5 815	1.3	215	3.7	5 184	21.9	52.6
Cuming	3 841	75.0	88 000	21.4	11.7	553	21.6	2.6	5 102	3.1	179	3.5	4 774	35.4	30.8
Custer	4 585	77.1	71 500	18.1	12.2	391	20.1	1.7	6 220	1.7	220	3.5	5 510	34.4	30.3
Dakota	7 281	67.2	97 800	22.4	13.1	630	30.3	5.0	11 075	1.8	882	8.0	10 701	18.2	39.8
Dawes	3 594	63.2	91 800	23.6	16.5	521	27.1	3.2	4 706	-1.5	212	4.5	5 125	30.9	22.5
Dawson	8 908	71.8	83 400	20.9	13.0	565	27.6	4.2	12 502	0.3	637	5.1	12 072	21.8	45.2
Deuel	931	78.3	65 600	22.3	13.8	500	23.0	0.0	1 030	-2.9	39	3.8	1 014	22.3	33.7
Dixon	2 389	77.1	75 200	21.4	12.6	488	23.8	2.0	3 250	-2.3	160	4.9	3 057	27.5	33.0
Dodge	14 994	66.7	110 500	21.7	13.3	613	26.6	2.3	19 278	-2.5	960	5.0	18 089	25.2	32.3
Douglas	198 410	64.4	141 400	22.6	13.0	725	29.0	2.2	269 726	-1.0	14 202	5.3	263 173	38.5	18.1
Dundy	879	79.1	63 400	20.0	14.8	340	14.0	0.0	1 063	0.5	37	3.5	1 013	52.7	21.6
Fillmore	2 572	77.3	75 100	18.4	13.1	480	24.0	0.1	3 161	-0.9	123	3.9	3 051	35.9	28.2
Franklin	1 385	80.4	50 400	21.1	14.4	578	21.5	1.0	1 784	0.1	70	3.9	1 460	33.0	30.3
Frontier	1 156	75.6	73 600	22.2	12.0	504	16.7	0.3	1 649	-0.2	55	3.3	1 472	34.9	28.8
Furnas	2 149	78.5	55 700	23.8	12.2	457	23.9	0.3	2 556	0.4	83	3.2	2 376	31.0	25.8
Gage	9 219	72.7	97 800	21.8	13.7	553	24.0	1.2	11 936	0.1	649	5.4	11 078	30.4	29.3
Garden	969	68.3	58 700	25.9	12.7	483	24.6	0.0	1 106	16.1	50	4.5	1 064	36.6	21.2
Garfield	875	79.4	73 900	19.6	15.3	393	22.5	0.0	1 100	2.0	33	3.0	1 160	31.8	29.8
Gosper	801	76.8	94 900	22.8	13.5	535	22.7	0.0	960	-6.0	36	3.8	1 056	29.5	29.3
Grant	293	62.8	41 100	19.4	10.5	509	18.8	1.4	398	9.3	16	4.0	402	44.0	35.8
Greeley	965	82.7	52 100	20.5	12.6	363	22.5	3.5	1 373	4.0	46	3.4	1 235	38.9	28.6
Hall	21 878	66.9	107 700	21.3	12.9	593	25.5	5.0	31 851	0.4	1 416	4.4	30 094	24.6	31.3
Hamilton	3 464	77.0	108 600	20.4	13.1	581	21.8	1.3	5 562	1.0	179	3.2	4 767	33.2	28.0
Harlan	1 547	82.2	69 900	21.3	10.7	443	23.7	0.1	1 854	-2.0	59	3.2	1 781	39.6	26.9
Hayes	440	70.2	84 500	24.8	10.0	543	24.6	4.1	515	5.7	23	4.5	542	34.3	34.3
Hitchcock	1 280	76.5	48 700	20.9	13.1	452	16.2	1.2	1 463	-1.9	67	4.6	1 381	32.6	34.5
Holt	4 244	75.7	82 300	18.8	12.9	485	22.2	1.2	6 282	1.5	203	3.2	5 469	34.2	28.2
Hooker	320	84.7	67 800	18.8	17.6	421	22.1	3.4	418	3.0	22	5.3	354	37.0	33.3
Howard	2 681	78.3	89 300	23.0	13.2	561	20.5	0.7	3 584	-3.5	145	4.0	3 228	31.0	31.4
Jefferson	3 279	80.1	74 400	20.3	13.4	463	23.5	1.1	4 342	1.5	199	4.6	3 973	29.5	26.6
Johnson	1 980	75.4	76 400	20.7	14.1	506	19.9	3.4	2 982	-0.5	121	4.1	2 192	22.8	38.1
Kearney	2 630	79.4	101 100	19.5	12.4	548	24.2	1.6	3 584	-1.4	128	3.6	3 480	34.1	30.1
Keith	3 735	73.0	88 200	21.5	13.3	553	22.4	2.9	4 484	1.0	181	4.0	4 325	32.5	29.3
Keya Paha	346	83.8	57 500	48.8	12.9	455	15.0	1.2	402	2.3	20	5.0	402	51.7	21.6
Kimball	1 662	70.8	76 800	22.7	14.6	610	24.1	2.5	1 916	0.7	97	5.1	2 014	31.6	32.7
Knox	3 847	75.4	67 000	20.5	13.1	391	19.3	2.0	4 874	0.7	193	4.0	4 360	35.2	26.7
Lancaster	111 933	62.1	145 400	22.7	11.3	668	28.3	1.9	157 637	-0.8	6 685	4.2	154 077	38.6	19.5
Lincoln	15 038	68.3	109 100	20.8	13.6	596	25.3	1.3	21 589	0.0	851	3.9	18 048	28.1	32.1
Logan	320	68.1	72 200	24.2	12.8	588	21.2	3.8	459	1.1	20	4.4	384	36.2	33.1
Loup	242	85.1	58 900	22.5	13.0	525	16.6	0.0	347	4.5	20	5.8	304	39.5	44.1
McPherson	204	58.8	74 400	25.8	10.0	444	17.5	0.0	288	-5.6	10	3.5	281	29.2	35.6
Madison	13 663	67.9	100 500	20.2	11.9	523	26.0	2.2	18 797	0.6	779	4.1	18 138	27.0	32.3
Merrick	3 145	73.3	78 900	19.8	12.8	551	25.2	1.1	4 135	-2.0	180	4.4	3 953	28.5	29.1
Morrill	2 136	67.7	79 800	19.9	13.7	600	22.2	3.4	2 786	-2.3	106	3.8	2 523	29.8	34.8
Nance	1 528	76.0	60 200	16.8	12.1	487	22.2	3.4	2 129	-0.3	73	3.4	1 815	35.8	34.0
Nemaha	3 024	71.2	78 200	18.6	11.7	440	23.1	1.4	3 306	-2.9	196	5.9	3 379	35.9	23.8
Nuckolls	2 060	79.7	54 200	22.9	13.1	475	19.5	0.3	2 295	0.2	96	4.2	2 141	24.2	30.5
Otoe	6 335	73.9	114 000	21.1	12.5	580	24.8	1.2	8 830	-0.7	416	4.7	7 944	31.4	31.2
Pawnee	1 309	78.2	55 100	22.0	12.5	468	25.3	2.1	1 583	3.7	61	3.9	1 395	29.9	28.9
Perkins	1 240	73.3	77 100	18.7	12.6	593	21.2	1.6	1 682	-0.8	56	3.3	1 576	40.2	23.3
Phelps	3 832	74.6	90 200	19.6	13.9	479	22.0	1.0	5 099	-1.5	175	3.4	4 717	32.0	27.2
Pierce	2 917	82.6	87 800	21.8	12.6	460	23.2	0.4	3 855	-1.2	154	4.0	3 961	31.6	34.6

1. Specified owner-occupied units.   2. Specified renter-occupied units. A value of 10.0 represents 10 percent or less.   3. Overcrowded or lacking complete plumbing facilities.   4. Percent of civilian labor force.   5. Persons 16 years old and over.

Table B. States and Counties — Nonfarm Employment and Agriculture

STATE County	Private nonfarm establishments, employment and payroll, 2009									Agriculture, 2007			
	Number of establishments	Employment						Annual payroll		Farms			
		Total	Health care and social assistance	Manufacturing	Retail trade	Finance and insurance	Professional, scientific, and technical services	Total (mil dol)	Average per employee (dollars)	Number	Percent with: Fewer than 50 acres	500 acres or more	Farm operators whose principal occupation is farming (percent)
	104	105	106	107	108	109	110	111	112	113	114	115	116
NEBRASKA—Cont'd													
Blaine	9	D	0	0	D	D	0	D	D	114	6.1	70.2	75.4
Boone	194	1 452	D	D	270	74	25	40	27 533	619	8.1	42.3	66.1
Box Butte	324	3 072	619	338	482	119	102	78	25 461	466	11.8	55.4	61.6
Boyd	78	400	D	D	87	36	D	8	20 198	259	8.5	52.5	66.8
Brown	137	906	185	D	255	D	24	19	20 976	292	14.7	55.5	55.1
Buffalo	1 476	21 201	3 929	3 320	3 539	612	610	631	29 777	949	20.7	38.9	61.7
Burt	199	1 174	200	70	185	D	104	30	25 150	549	20.6	30.6	58.8
Butler	194	1 997	D	567	D	D	D	58	28 870	809	15.6	30.3	60.9
Cass	533	3 314	D	394	656	209	74	96	29 060	682	34.6	26.0	50.9
Cedar	304	1 853	172	D	366	118	D	44	23 940	924	16.9	32.3	63.6
Chase	142	1 054	D	D	239	D	15	30	28 471	347	12.7	57.1	62.8
Cherry	215	1 661	D	35	413	D	59	37	22 122	560	10.4	70.4	70.7
Cheyenne	300	4 085	409	D	1 011	145	56	162	39 640	603	8.5	56.6	58.7
Clay	193	1 174	177	65	219	83	26	32	27 402	454	18.7	48.7	77.3
Colfax	249	3 468	279	D	321	118	50	109	31 298	519	24.1	29.7	61.5
Cuming	360	2 672	394	388	414	158	88	75	28 161	863	19.7	27.7	63.5
Custer	386	2 639	656	D	533	142	87	71	26 839	1 187	16.3	55.5	66.0
Dakota	433	10 103	540	D	932	657	69	330	32 664	278	26.3	23.7	57.2
Dawes	286	2 187	392	D	654	76	D	46	20 906	469	10.4	55.2	57.1
Dawson	725	9 607	1 025	D	1 567	317	192	268	27 875	728	21.2	40.9	63.5
Deuel	56	390	D	0	100	D	D	10	24 467	240	8.3	52.5	62.5
Dixon	123	938	92	D	D	46	D	38	40 100	668	17.6	29.4	49.6
Dodge	1 032	14 316	2 437	3 271	2 447	475	215	451	31 472	715	23.6	31.3	62.7
Douglas	14 812	307 059	43 067	22 686	35 024	32 962	30 071	12 912	42 049	362	54.4	15.5	43.9
Dundy	63	374	146	23	51	D	D	10	27 826	263	4.9	63.9	70.7
Fillmore	223	1 637	273	197	228	142	D	50	30 443	478	9.6	51.5	78.2
Franklin	76	458	D	0	106	D	D	12	25 389	312	13.5	48.7	68.6
Frontier	75	449	50	0	78	29	D	10	23 118	283	11.0	62.9	67.5
Furnas	184	1 348	295	86	290	D	D	37	27 361	365	13.2	55.9	67.7
Gage	643	7 840	2 059	1 832	1 142	194	119	188	23 977	1 280	21.9	29.0	52.0
Garden	50	392	D	D	88	24	D	8	21 158	297	9.8	63.0	60.9
Garfield	97	600	116	97	126	D	D	12	19 393	223	9.9	51.1	69.1
Gosper	67	249	D	D	D	36	D	6	25 687	218	9.2	56.9	69.7
Grant	26	D	0	D	D	D	D	D	D	84	10.7	64.3	79.8
Greeley	69	378	D	D	84	D	D	8	22 447	334	12.3	44.3	64.7
Hall	1 821	29 887	4 355	7 266	4 925	1 541	617	911	30 492	608	23.0	33.6	62.7
Hamilton	296	2 749	298	740	300	112	71	81	29 579	550	16.2	43.1	70.5
Harlan	96	632	D	D	94	35	D	13	21 024	384	19.0	47.1	65.1
Hayes	23	D	D	D	D	D	D	D	D	275	5.1	53.5	62.9
Hitchcock	66	443	D	80	D	D	D	13	28 871	272	8.5	53.7	58.5
Holt	424	3 430	745	358	697	177	65	86	25 161	1 171	10.3	55.1	70.6
Hooker	28	104	D	D	D	D	D	3	25 462	88	9.1	79.5	73.9
Howard	150	906	D	D	242	73	D	19	21 379	564	24.1	31.6	57.4
Jefferson	237	2 551	D	555	489	D	48	68	26 672	601	16.8	35.3	57.7
Johnson	119	993	324	D	165	57	11	31	31 476	541	17.0	20.1	44.5
Kearney	172	1 978	D	155	161	80	D	47	23 539	381	13.1	56.2	78.0
Keith	341	2 530	316	D	496	144	124	66	25 908	398	15.3	42.2	54.8
Keya Paha	22	50	D	D	D	D	D	1	25 220	206	6.3	75.7	72.8
Kimball	131	990	D	D	197	D	D	28	28 646	372	8.3	54.0	48.1
Knox	253	1 505	284	49	390	109	67	30	20 227	863	11.4	42.6	68.9
Lancaster	7 731	127 177	21 266	11 687	16 934	12 129	8 616	4 274	33 610	1 698	45.5	13.5	41.2
Lincoln	1 034	11 477	2 347	265	2 403	503	376	321	28 002	1 053	19.9	48.1	57.1
Logan	20	D	D	D	D	D	0	D	D	152	11.8	56.6	67.8
Loup	13	28	0	D	D	D	0	0	13 714	137	13.9	60.6	70.1
McPherson	8	D	0	0	7	D	0	D	D	143	7.0	75.5	72.0
Madison	1 283	18 015	3 521	3 265	2 976	674	563	557	30 899	699	22.6	28.8	58.1
Merrick	243	1 646	D	197	203	100	43	45	27 109	473	21.8	36.2	66.0
Morrill	116	862	D	D	194	39	D	22	26 089	495	13.7	52.5	58.6
Nance	98	494	126	0	96	49	D	10	20 654	362	15.2	40.9	64.9
Nemaha	202	1 727	350	D	264	111	41	46	26 803	449	18.0	29.0	55.2
Nuckolls	186	1 138	390	6	249	76	64	26	22 941	405	11.1	48.4	61.2
Otoe	482	5 197	D	1 339	839	207	96	139	26 751	804	23.4	25.4	48.9
Pawnee	69	523	130	D	63	49	D	16	31 029	489	12.9	29.0	46.8
Perkins	122	798	D	D	116	38	23	24	30 604	446	7.6	54.0	60.8
Phelps	334	3 802	778	D	391	163	91	114	30 000	420	14.3	51.9	73.1
Pierce	220	1 377	353	110	186	88	35	37	26 883	645	18.8	31.3	59.7

STATE County	Acreage (1,000)	Percent change, 2002–2007	Average size of farm	Total irrigated (1,000)	Total cropland (1,000)	Average per farm	Average per acre	Value of machinery and equipment, average per farm (dollars)	Total (mil dol)	Average per farm (dollars)	Crops	Live-stock and poultry products	$10,000 or more	$100,000 or more	Total ($1,000)	Percent of farms
	117	118	119	120	121	122	123	124	125	126	127	128	129	130	131	132
NEBRASKA—Cont'd																
Blaine	443	0.5	3 888	13.7	43.2	1 759 495	453	127 929	28.7	251 544	11.7	88.3	78.1	47.4	457	29.8
Boone	405	-6.0	655	173.1	282.7	1 213 396	1 853	221 725	300.2	484 998	35.0	65.0	83.7	53.0	5 211	84.2
Box Butte	671	-0.6	1 440	143.0	384.4	1 186 522	824	196 449	188.8	405 125	51.0	49.0	68.7	43.1	4 575	75.5
Boyd	252	-18.2	972	4.5	90.3	759 552	781	123 492	46.9	181 042	24.3	75.7	79.2	35.1	954	74.1
Brown	662	-3.5	2 266	51.9	114.8	1 133 653	500	172 599	165.0	565 057	12.2	87.8	67.1	42.1	1 448	47.6
Buffalo	612	1.8	645	269.1	371.6	1 083 891	1 680	164 249	259.7	273 629	58.1	41.9	70.3	43.3	6 979	67.1
Burt	275	-11.3	501	42.9	246.6	1 249 668	2 494	144 533	145.9	265 707	63.2	36.8	66.8	44.1	5 191	78.9
Butler	356	-5.1	440	118.0	295.6	1 081 926	2 458	137 671	182.6	225 679	66.4	33.6	69.3	40.5	6 797	85.9
Cass	281	-12.2	412	3.0	246.9	1 057 235	2 567	122 385	98.2	143 918	89.8	10.2	59.5	33.6	4 008	70.4
Cedar	475	3.3	514	112.1	366.0	1 020 642	1 986	147 754	268.0	290 071	43.3	56.7	75.0	44.2	6 106	78.0
Chase	556	3.0	1 602	185.3	309.6	1 607 310	1 003	324 228	189.1	544 867	66.2	33.8	70.0	51.3	6 471	77.5
Cherry	3 760	-0.5	6 714	44.7	414.7	2 725 129	406	126 883	142.5	254 457	9.8	90.2	75.4	50.7	1 218	22.3
Cheyenne	755	-6.0	1 251	51.3	556.0	927 431	741	138 262	151.9	251 880	44.4	55.6	67.0	36.3	7 452	88.4
Clay	365	-2.4	804	218.1	291.5	1 841 728	2 290	270 725	261.7	576 322	49.4	50.6	79.7	61.9	6 296	76.0
Colfax	213	-12.7	411	62.5	187.7	1 007 713	2 453	169 620	250.8	483 193	30.3	69.7	74.4	44.9	3 301	77.3
Cuming	360	-1.6	417	51.2	305.1	1 040 286	2 493	189 440	856.6	992 599	14.5	85.5	80.8	54.3	5 279	77.4
Custer	1 614	7.5	1 360	333.4	574.1	1 386 763	1 020	184 323	513.8	432 831	38.1	61.9	72.5	42.5	8 350	58.5
Dakota	167	9.9	599	20.4	147.8	1 057 606	1 765	187 147	63.4	228 168	87.1	12.9	55.0	29.9	2 966	75.5
Dawes	849	8.0	1 810	17.6	202.9	1 019 756	563	91 765	45.8	97 732	25.2	74.8	65.9	27.3	2 527	69.1
Dawson	641	2.9	880	263.9	330.7	1 176 513	1 337	199 439	588.5	808 444	25.7	74.3	72.8	47.3	6 721	60.4
Deuel	279	-5.1	1 162	17.9	231.8	823 459	709	146 724	53.1	221 120	D	D	75.0	40.8	2 716	86.3
Dixon	249	-10.1	438	21.6	188.7	806 327	1 843	98 801	143.3	252 301	39.6	60.4	55.3	30.3	4 759	79.8
Dodge	338	-0.3	473	116.1	305.1	1 256 529	2 654	180 820	250.4	350 205	51.7	48.3	76.9	46.2	5 063	77.2
Douglas	84	-11.6	233	13.8	72.9	848 960	3 642	130 134	46.3	128 012	94.6	5.4	46.1	23.5	1 230	48.6
Dundy	595	4.9	2 262	112.7	254.2	1 856 209	821	240 571	145.6	553 728	50.8	49.2	76.8	57.0	4 277	86.3
Fillmore	362	-0.5	758	223.5	323.0	1 825 852	2 410	271 419	223.8	468 147	67.9	32.1	86.2	65.3	7 130	83.9
Franklin	292	-11.8	934	87.3	165.0	1 207 777	1 293	187 213	78.3	250 944	77.3	22.7	74.7	46.2	4 072	82.7
Frontier	475	-2.5	1 679	53.7	189.8	1 315 651	783	173 872	97.9	346 111	55.3	44.7	75.6	50.5	3 410	72.1
Furnas	446	1.1	1 221	51.9	276.5	1 195 189	978	162 841	141.9	388 895	47.0	53.0	74.8	49.0	5 057	85.5
Gage	540	-2.2	422	59.3	413.2	757 853	1 796	118 186	173.8	135 785	62.4	37.6	61.3	31.3	10 711	81.6
Garden	1 049	-2.1	3 530	44.9	188.0	1 646 862	466	151 788	81.1	273 185	35.9	64.1	75.8	43.1	1 995	70.7
Garfield	366	24.9	1 640	20.6	78.1	913 687	557	104 819	61.1	274 071	13.1	86.9	76.2	40.4	1 076	60.1
Gosper	226	-13.7	1 035	81.4	130.4	1 269 983	1 227	227 140	74.0	339 652	73.4	26.6	78.4	55.5	2 713	78.9
Grant	495	1.0	5 899	1.5	45.3	1 784 493	303	121 056	16.6	197 923	0.6	99.4	73.8	53.6	25	8.3
Greeley	282	-3.8	845	76.4	127.6	1 004 897	1 189	164 361	111.6	333 990	36.0	64.0	67.4	41.6	2 363	73.7
Hall	328	3.8	540	206.9	247.1	1 104 247	2 045	189 582	228.9	376 545	51.4	48.6	73.2	47.2	5 315	65.6
Hamilton	319	-8.3	580	257.7	291.8	1 511 457	2 605	232 598	235.5	428 170	66.1	33.9	84.4	63.1	6 941	82.2
Harlan	351	13.6	914	107.6	224.5	1 047 538	1 146	180 364	134.3	349 860	59.2	40.8	73.7	45.3	4 315	76.3
Hayes	454	11.3	1 650	65.7	210.3	1 118 669	678	173 453	115.5	419 885	45.7	54.3	71.6	41.5	4 301	89.8
Hitchcock	348	-19.8	1 279	19.0	192.6	982 992	768	124 248	58.8	216 017	64.7	35.3	65.4	37.9	3 521	79.0
Holt	1 533	3.5	1 309	339.1	667.6	1 172 798	896	176 114	373.6	319 063	49.5	50.5	74.4	44.9	8 615	58.0
Hooker	457	7.8	5 190	3.0	22.1	1 778 035	343	65 409	11.0	124 700	0.7	99.3	72.7	37.5	157	22.7
Howard	279	-5.1	494	104.3	157.8	770 669	1 559	120 972	145.4	257 879	37.3	62.7	67.0	37.6	3 140	70.9
Jefferson	326	-10.4	542	81.0	232.7	970 708	1 792	124 799	131.7	219 132	59.2	40.8	63.1	35.8	5 722	78.7
Johnson	176	-14.1	324	11.3	114.0	498 010	1 535	71 863	44.0	81 323	56.9	43.1	47.3	20.1	3 804	86.0
Kearney	324	-2.1	851	216.3	272.2	1 708 240	2 007	302 401	264.3	693 652	50.9	49.1	85.6	66.1	5 840	78.7
Keith	582	-7.3	1 461	116.1	260.2	1 251 849	857	173 593	142.1	357 112	57.7	42.3	66.8	39.9	3 319	68.8
Keya Paha	483	4.3	2 347	18.1	101.4	1 302 181	555	148 106	48.5	235 218	20.1	79.9	78.6	42.2	555	46.6
Kimball	528	-4.0	1 418	33.3	346.0	993 252	700	113 483	35.8	96 204	80.3	19.7	41.4	20.2	4 869	82.0
Knox	536	-10.5	622	51.8	273.6	905 312	1 456	139 020	226.5	262 510	28.4	71.6	76.2	39.6	4 976	78.9
Lancaster	421	-6.2	248	15.6	323.6	629 050	2 535	82 805	125.9	74 152	78.5	21.5	39.9	17.0	6 864	66.8
Lincoln	1 601	4.7	1 521	322.9	527.0	1 268 708	834	179 875	431.9	410 131	45.6	54.4	63.5	37.8	7 902	52.5
Logan	363	1.1	2 391	24.8	70.0	1 220 963	511	129 154	31.4	206 756	44.3	55.7	73.7	39.5	872	60.5
Loup	355	5.0	2 589	10.4	35.3	1 163 578	449	97 833	26.1	190 485	12.4	87.6	76.6	36.5	546	62.0
McPherson	542	2.5	3 793	9.7	34.9	1 383 080	365	72 724	24.0	167 650	4.0	96.0	73.4	37.1	267	24.5
Madison	315	-7.9	451	107.9	258.0	977 194	2 167	141 271	220.5	315 519	42.5	57.5	69.7	38.2	4 325	70.2
Merrick	248	-12.4	524	163.8	199.6	959 888	1 831	181 984	198.0	418 604	48.0	52.0	70.4	45.5	3 811	71.7
Morrill	902	3.4	1 822	144.6	266.3	1 177 907	646	146 539	245.4	495 780	25.4	74.6	70.7	41.4	4 865	76.6
Nance	226	-1.3	625	69.4	138.2	910 496	1 456	157 768	99.3	274 375	52.5	47.5	75.7	47.0	2 856	78.7
Nemaha	213	-16.5	474	8.4	169.5	926 483	1 956	133 302	72.1	160 652	82.6	17.4	60.1	34.7	3 097	82.6
Nuckolls	307	-12.5	758	61.1	205.2	1 249 559	1 648	183 177	108.1	266 801	62.4	37.6	81.2	49.1	4 686	85.7
Otoe	322	-6.1	401	4.2	258.4	874 306	2 182	108 819	103.6	128 855	77.4	22.6	58.3	30.2	5 061	80.6
Pawnee	218	-15.2	445	4.6	139.4	583 162	1 310	92 757	47.0	96 122	70.9	29.1	50.7	20.7	4 456	85.7
Perkins	558	1.8	1 252	133.4	444.5	1 223 128	977	193 983	135.5	303 846	82.0	18.0	69.3	46.2	6 594	87.2
Phelps	340	-7.1	810	246.8	281.7	1 663 392	2 053	278 688	470.2	1 119 572	30.8	69.2	86.0	70.2	5 666	79.5
Pierce	317	-4.8	491	128.9	247.2	979 168	1 994	162 655	178.9	277 421	47.1	52.9	73.2	42.8	4 385	74.0

Table B. States and Counties — Water Use, Wholesale Trade, Retail Trade, and Real Estate

STATE County	Water use, 2005		Wholesale trade,[1] 2007				Retail trade,[2] 2007				Real estate and rental and leasing,[2] 2007			
	Total water withdrawn (mil gal/day)	Gallons withdrawn per person	Number of establishments	Number of employees	Sales (mil dol)	Annual payroll (mil dol)	Number of establishments	Number of employees	Sales (mil dol)	Annual payroll (mil dol)	Number of establishments	Number of employees	Receipts (mil dol)	Annual payroll (mil dol)
	133	134	135	136	137	138	139	140	141	142	143	144	145	146
NEBRASKA—Cont'd														
Blaine	9.5	19 628	NA	NA	NA	NA	4	D	D	D	NA	NA	NA	NA
Boone	165.5	28 664	12	179	92.7	5.6	45	290	81.6	4.8	5	25	3.2	0.4
Box Butte	193.0	16 969	19	197	90.0	6.6	55	474	82.2	7.6	17	46	9.1	1.1
Boyd	6.0	2 645	2	D	D	D	14	120	13.2	1.0	1	D	D	D
Brown	80.6	24 207	4	50	26.3	1.4	29	226	48.1	4.0	1	D	D	D
Buffalo	258.3	5 927	66	776	659.3	33.4	250	3 653	739.9	67.8	62	210	34.1	5.1
Burt	45.4	6 089	21	183	70.4	5.2	34	146	40.6	2.8	3	10	0.3	0.1
Butler	123.6	14 179	13	107	118.8	4.5	26	402	72.3	5.9	1	D	D	D
Cass	20.4	791	18	103	99.1	3.6	74	734	183.6	13.3	24	41	3.9	0.6
Cedar	84.1	9 275	22	124	69.7	3.8	55	348	121.8	6.4	8	14	1.2	0.3
Chase	170.4	44 069	15	161	135.1	7.1	31	307	60.4	5.4	3	7	1.1	0.1
Cherry	52.4	8 600	6	D	D	D	48	468	78.3	7.6	6	7	1.2	0.2
Cheyenne	77.9	7 792	15	76	97.9	3.2	57	D	D	D	10	19	7.6	0.4
Clay	161.1	23 928	19	141	155.6	4.1	28	212	60.7	4.3	2	D	D	D
Colfax	78.4	7 514	15	99	63.6	3.9	48	400	107.6	8.6	3	4	0.2	0.1
Cuming	51.5	5 312	29	158	117.4	5.0	61	429	174.6	8.1	3	7	1.0	0.1
Custer	258.3	22 641	14	113	52.8	3.6	81	511	118.0	8.8	9	D	D	D
Dakota	22.0	1 082	19	D	D	D	73	878	170.3	16.5	16	D	D	D
Dawes	27.9	3 234	5	33	10.0	0.7	58	706	164.6	12.9	12	15	1.6	0.3
Dawson	319.2	12 965	32	403	424.7	14.1	123	1 576	345.3	32.8	22	46	4.1	0.6
Deuel	28.7	14 326	3	D	D	D	12	125	102.0	2.3	1	D	D	D
Dixon	21.5	3 493	9	D	D	D	18	219	37.1	2.5	1	D	D	D
Dodge	113.7	3 151	63	D	D	D	176	2 356	665.0	53.5	45	162	21.1	3.2
Douglas	789.5	1 621	760	10 589	6 079.8	494.7	1 863	36 151	8 109.0	805.7	719	5 588	961.6	186.2
Dundy	110.4	51 749	5	D	D	D	9	51	14.0	0.9	2	D	D	D
Fillmore	163.1	25 551	21	162	113.4	5.1	38	219	39.7	3.6	3	4	0.2	0.0
Franklin	124.4	36 352	8	68	51.2	1.8	18	117	17.3	1.7	NA	NA	NA	NA
Frontier	59.2	21 163	4	D	D	D	14	90	14.8	1.1	2	D	D	D
Furnas	57.5	11 462	12	91	88.6	2.6	35	224	50.2	4.0	3	3	0.6	0.0
Gage	102.6	4 403	32	D	D	D	118	1 164	235.1	22.4	22	69	8.1	1.3
Garden	57.6	28 778	5	D	D	D	11	72	12.4	0.9	NA	NA	NA	NA
Garfield	20.2	11 096	4	64	9.2	0.9	24	124	27.1	1.9	1	D	D	D
Gosper	67.6	33 475	5	D	D	D	7	23	2.3	0.2	4	13	4.3	0.5
Grant	2.9	4 358	4	26	8.3	0.5	6	D	D	D	NA	NA	NA	NA
Greeley	97.4	38 786	4	45	23.8	1.1	19	91	25.4	1.7	1	D	D	D
Hall	240.2	4 358	100	1 192	707.9	50.5	336	5 113	1 087.7	99.4	68	261	44.6	7.2
Hamilton	299.4	30 666	13	322	375.5	12.9	41	308	101.1	5.1	8	D	D	D
Harlan	80.0	23 094	11	55	55.1	1.4	17	96	26.0	1.8	1	D	D	D
Hayes	52.7	51 344	NA	NA	NA	NA	2	D	D	D	NA	NA	NA	NA
Hitchcock	45.9	15 465	7	28	18.7	0.5	10	D	D	D	NA	NA	NA	NA
Holt	271.2	25 145	37	395	149.3	8.6	87	716	143.2	10.3	9	25	4.2	1.1
Hooker	4.3	5 780	1	D	D	D	7	D	D	D	NA	NA	NA	NA
Howard	131.2	19 567	7	49	38.4	1.6	30	260	48.4	3.8	2	D	D	D
Jefferson	60.0	7 576	16	132	139.0	4.8	38	496	124.8	9.3	10	21	1.0	0.3
Johnson	13.8	2 946	4	D	D	D	28	144	34.4	2.5	2	3	D	D
Kearney	176.2	26 004	14	154	151.7	4.4	25	172	29.7	2.6	3	4	0.6	0.1
Keith	165.7	19 887	15	100	54.7	3.9	70	628	203.8	12.4	14	22	2.0	0.5
Keya Paha	19.7	21 829	2	D	D	D	4	D	D	D	NA	NA	NA	NA
Kimball	50.8	13 421	4	D	D	D	29	191	49.0	3.9	2	D	D	D
Knox	53.8	6 031	10	92	61.8	2.5	62	395	82.4	6.4	5	21	0.9	0.3
Lancaster	23.9	90	272	3 823	2 729.9	166.3	1 052	17 169	3 662.7	345.8	367	1 558	250.6	43.1
Lincoln	938.7	26 340	39	356	245.4	13.4	204	2 419	634.9	47.6	35	152	20.7	2.9
Logan	24.0	32 365	2	D	D	D	3	D	D	D	NA	NA	NA	NA
Loup	15.7	22 886	1	D	D	D	3	D	D	D	1	D	D	D
McPherson	96.0	189 428	NA	NA	NA	NA	3	D	D	D	NA	NA	NA	NA
Madison	18.8	530	65	1 797	1 880.2	61.8	230	3 067	649.7	57.8	61	D	D	D
Merrick	201.5	24 976	18	162	208.7	5.4	37	195	45.6	3.3	4	D	D	D
Morrill	228.0	44 143	13	134	48.1	4.9	24	152	46.2	2.7	2	D	D	D
Nance	82.3	22 460	5	24	35.0	0.9	18	113	22.4	1.7	2	D	D	D
Nemaha	1 125.0	161 525	11	56	59.9	2.1	44	305	59.3	4.7	4	10	1.0	0.1
Nuckolls	48.4	10 211	14	81	147.0	2.6	32	252	53.3	4.3	3	D	D	D
Otoe	471.9	30 429	19	139	238.0	5.4	84	858	146.8	14.1	16	48	6.0	1.1
Pawnee	5.2	1 803	2	D	D	D	13	73	14.4	1.1	1	D	D	D
Perkins	125.3	40 988	15	82	128.3	2.5	15	114	44.7	2.7	3	14	0.7	0.2
Phelps	205.0	21 693	24	285	152.0	10.1	50	385	94.5	7.8	11	34	1.5	0.3
Pierce	111.9	14 726	18	162	77.6	4.7	36	215	41.4	3.0	4	D	D	D

1. Merchant wholesalers, except manufacturers' sales branches and offices. 2. Employer establishments.

Table B. States and Counties — Professional Services, Manufacturing, and Accommodation and Food Services

STATE County	Professional, scientific, and technical services,[1] 2007				Manufacturing, 2007				Accommodation and food services, 2007			
	Number of establishments	Number of employees	Receipts (mil dol)	Annual payroll (mil dol)	Number of establishments	Number of employees	Receipts (mil dol)	Annual payroll (mil dol)	Number of establishments	Number of employees	Sales (mil dol)	Annual payroll (mil dol)
	147	148	149	150	151	152	153	154	155	156	157	158
NEBRASKA—Cont'd												
Blaine	NA	NA	NA	NA	NA	NA	NA	NA	1	D	D	D
Boone	7	23	4.1	0.6	NA	NA	NA	NA	17	113	3.6	0.8
Box Butte	25	100	7.3	2.3	NA	NA	NA	NA	34	410	12.4	3.3
Boyd	3	D	D	D	NA	NA	NA	NA	5	D	D	D
Brown	6	32	2.3	0.7	NA	NA	NA	NA	11	111	2.9	0.7
Buffalo	93	527	44.2	18.6	59	4 292	D	D	137	2 585	103.1	28.3
Burt	11	62	13.5	2.5	NA	NA	NA	NA	12	68	2.0	0.4
Butler	11	98	3.7	1.8	10	612	D	D	13	60	2.0	0.4
Cass	35	D	D	D	NA	NA	NA	NA	46	537	14.2	4.1
Cedar	11	56	5.0	1.3	NA	NA	NA	NA	17	176	3.5	0.9
Chase	11	20	2.5	0.5	NA	NA	NA	NA	11	69	2.0	0.6
Cherry	14	53	5.7	1.1	NA	NA	NA	NA	21	276	9.7	2.7
Cheyenne	12	32	3.4	1.0	NA	NA	NA	NA	39	507	21.1	5.4
Clay	6	22	2.5	0.6	NA	NA	NA	NA	7	36	1.4	0.3
Colfax	9	39	3.9	0.7	6	D	D	D	16	124	3.5	0.8
Cuming	20	D	D	D	NA	NA	NA	NA	20	229	6.5	2.0
Custer	25	81	7.1	1.8	NA	NA	NA	NA	31	292	8.2	2.3
Dakota	17	D	D	D	39	D	D	D	35	499	19.2	5.6
Dawes	21	148	5.7	1.9	NA	NA	NA	NA	41	538	13.7	4.1
Dawson	60	D	D	D	31	D	D	D	57	694	24.7	6.1
Deuel	4	7	0.6	0.2	NA	NA	NA	NA	7	93	4.1	1.3
Dixon	2	D	D	D	3	D	D	D	14	35	1.9	0.3
Dodge	53	D	D	D	61	3 299	1 233.8	121.2	98	1 454	53.0	13.9
Douglas	1 631	D	D	D	513	23 258	10 012.8	961.2	1 237	25 985	1 118.9	321.6
Dundy	6	14	1.3	0.3	NA	NA	NA	NA	6	24	0.5	0.1
Fillmore	8	20	1.3	0.3	NA	NA	NA	NA	21	196	3.5	0.8
Franklin	4	18	0.8	0.3	NA	NA	NA	NA	5	20	1.0	0.2
Frontier	2	D	D	D	NA	NA	NA	NA	4	25	0.6	0.1
Furnas	9	16	1.4	0.4	NA	NA	NA	NA	14	D	D	D
Gage	30	132	11.7	3.7	44	1 994	602.6	66.8	47	580	23.4	4.8
Garden	2	D	D	D	NA	NA	NA	NA	6	D	D	D
Garfield	5	18	1.3	0.4	NA	NA	NA	NA	9	66	1.3	0.3
Gosper	3	D	D	D	NA	NA	NA	NA	4	23	1.7	0.2
Grant	1	D	D	D	NA	NA	NA	NA	2	D	D	D
Greeley	NA	NA	NA	NA	NA	NA	NA	NA	3	9	0.4	0.1
Hall	99	D	D	D	79	D	D	D	136	2 551	96.9	28.1
Hamilton	19	68	8.0	2.8	24	617	463.4	20.6	13	160	5.1	1.5
Harlan	10	25	2.3	0.6	NA	NA	NA	NA	12	82	2.8	0.6
Hayes	2	D	D	D	NA	NA	NA	NA	3	3	0.3	0.0
Hitchcock	NA	NA	NA	NA	NA	NA	NA	NA	6	19	1.0	0.2
Holt	22	72	9.3	2.6	NA	NA	NA	NA	35	333	10.2	2.4
Hooker	NA	NA	NA	NA	NA	NA	NA	NA	5	D	D	D
Howard	8	D	D	D	NA	NA	NA	NA	12	63	2.8	0.5
Jefferson	12	44	3.4	1.1	13	531	127.9	19.7	22	187	6.4	1.5
Johnson	3	8	0.6	0.1	NA	NA	NA	NA	9	78	3.1	0.7
Kearney	10	16	1.5	0.5	NA	NA	NA	NA	14	94	2.8	0.7
Keith	28	114	9.2	3.1	NA	NA	NA	NA	46	562	22.8	5.0
Keya Paha	2	D	D	D	NA	NA	NA	NA	1	D	D	D
Kimball	9	21	1.4	0.2	NA	NA	NA	NA	15	82	3.1	0.7
Knox	18	64	5.6	1.5	NA	NA	NA	NA	23	74	3.3	0.5
Lancaster	773	8 282	1 102.6	383.8	252	13 413	D	540.6	651	12 028	472.5	132.9
Lincoln	81	D	D	D	NA	NA	NA	NA	96	D	D	D
Logan	1	D	D	D	NA	NA	NA	NA	NA	NA	NA	NA
Loup	NA	NA	NA	NA	NA	NA	NA	NA	NA	NA	NA	NA
McPherson	NA	NA	NA	NA	NA	NA	NA	NA	2	D	D	D
Madison	85	D	D	D	53	D	D	D	87	1 451	48.5	14.0
Merrick	10	D	D	D	NA	NA	NA	NA	16	176	3.9	1.1
Morrill	1	D	D	D	NA	NA	NA	NA	13	82	3.2	0.7
Nance	4	13	0.4	0.2	NA	NA	NA	NA	8	25	0.8	0.2
Nemaha	14	45	3.5	1.3	NA	NA	NA	NA	23	326	7.0	2.3
Nuckolls	10	31	2.7	0.6	NA	NA	NA	NA	8	81	2.1	0.5
Otoe	26	77	8.6	2.8	12	1 395	405.4	48.3	41	612	17.0	5.1
Pawnee	4	D	D	D	NA	NA	NA	NA	6	42	0.9	0.2
Perkins	7	19	1.7	0.3	NA	NA	NA	NA	4	34	0.8	0.2
Phelps	31	110	9.3	3.8	9	D	D	D	20	297	9.1	2.3
Pierce	10	D	D	D	NA	NA	NA	NA	9	81	1.6	0.4

1. Establishment subject to federal tax.

Table B. States and Counties — Health Care and Social Assistance, Other Services, and Federal Funds

STATE County	Health care and social assistance, 2007				Other services, 2007				Federal funds and grants, 2009–2010 Expenditures (mil dol)			
										Direct payments for individuals[1]		
	Number of establishments	Number of employees	Receipts (mil dol)	Annual payroll (mil dol)	Number of establishments	Number of employees	Receipts (mil dol)	Annual payroll (mil dol)	Total	Social Security and government retirement	Medicare	Food Stamps and Supplemental Security Income
	159	160	161	162	163	164	165	166	167	168	169	170
NEBRASKA—Cont'd												
Blaine	NA	NA	NA	NA	NA	NA	NA	NA	4.1	1.5	0.7	0.0
Boone	16	416	24.7	11.0	10	29	2.5	0.7	49.8	20.3	10.8	0.8
Box Butte	27	617	40.7	17.1	35	115	9.6	2.1	90.5	41.6	13.0	3.0
Boyd	9	98	4.2	1.9	7	12	1.1	0.2	23.6	8.2	7.3	0.3
Brown	14	191	9.2	4.1	15	36	3.4	0.7	29.2	13.1	5.8	0.4
Buffalo	151	3 954	365.2	145.3	114	553	45.3	10.9	257.0	112.8	43.0	6.9
Burt	16	196	12.3	5.0	15	60	6.2	2.0	74.3	26.7	17.6	2.0
Butler	16	360	22.6	9.4	15	D	D	D	62.3	27.8	11.6	1.3
Cass	28	350	19.1	7.9	41	132	9.4	2.4	159.9	93.2	29.0	4.2
Cedar	16	108	6.0	2.1	22	52	5.7	1.3	66.9	24.7	13.4	0.7
Chase	9	176	10.0	4.7	10	45	3.0	0.7	53.5	15.3	7.9	0.6
Cherry	15	297	22.0	8.1	18	41	4.9	0.7	42.7	17.6	8.4	1.0
Cheyenne	19	392	39.7	12.0	28	91	9.6	1.9	86.6	30.1	17.0	2.2
Clay	11	151	4.8	2.7	11	28	1.4	0.4	66.1	24.1	10.3	1.0
Colfax	13	254	21.3	7.8	28	83	6.0	1.7	69.5	24.6	23.6	1.3
Cuming	25	404	37.6	13.4	34	156	16.4	3.0	67.4	27.4	15.8	1.1
Custer	35	684	39.2	16.7	32	60	5.5	0.9	101.1	39.4	20.4	2.4
Dakota	32	D	D	D	38	D	D	D	103.2	36.7	23.0	4.0
Dawes	30	390	27.0	11.5	26	73	4.2	1.0	76.3	30.1	10.5	2.7
Dawson	67	D	D	D	59	D	D	D	145.2	59.6	28.6	5.4
Deuel	4	D	D	D	4	22	0.5	0.2	22.2	8.6	4.2	0.1
Dixon	10	D	D	D	7	D	D	D	54.5	26.3	10.0	0.9
Dodge	109	2 771	199.9	78.0	85	381	31.3	6.5	266.7	128.4	59.2	7.0
Douglas	1 552	42 408	4 430.8	1 793.5	1 085	8 366	1 051.5	224.7	4 258.6	1 462.3	631.9	157.5
Dundy	8	152	7.8	4.1	1	D	D	D	33.9	8.3	6.0	0.2
Fillmore	15	290	18.1	7.4	21	71	4.3	1.0	55.4	22.8	10.9	0.7
Franklin	8	138	7.7	3.5	7	19	1.2	0.2	32.9	12.8	7.4	0.6
Frontier	11	87	2.7	1.1	6	D	D	D	27.8	10.2	4.4	0.2
Furnas	15	282	15.9	6.5	15	33	3.4	0.5	57.9	21.0	12.7	0.6
Gage	62	1 697	91.0	39.6	68	252	13.0	3.5	188.7	89.8	31.7	4.7
Garden	1	D	D	D	1	D	D	D	32.8	10.6	5.3	0.2
Garfield	7	100	4.6	2.1	7	29	1.8	0.4	16.5	7.6	4.4	0.3
Gosper	5	D	D	D	2	D	D	D	19.3	9.9	3.2	0.2
Grant	NA	NA	NA	NA	3	D	D	D	4.6	2.5	1.0	0.1
Greeley	4	D	D	D	4	12	1.0	0.2	23.7	9.4	4.5	0.4
Hall	171	3 816	320.6	125.5	158	976	68.8	16.8	416.0	172.2	65.9	14.5
Hamilton	18	388	17.5	7.8	25	74	8.0	2.0	65.7	20.0	11.3	1.0
Harlan	7	168	8.9	4.0	6	D	D	D	37.5	13.4	7.1	0.8
Hayes	1	D	D	D	1	D	D	D	14.6	2.6	1.7	0.1
Hitchcock	4	17	0.7	0.3	3	D	D	D	32.2	13.1	5.5	0.3
Holt	36	696	49.5	20.5	33	93	12.6	2.0	113.7	34.5	21.8	2.2
Hooker	2	D	D	D	3	D	D	D	6.2	3.2	1.6	0.1
Howard	11	D	D	D	17	62	3.6	0.9	49.2	22.3	10.9	0.7
Jefferson	14	376	23.3	9.9	20	73	3.8	0.8	71.4	29.8	13.7	1.8
Johnson	14	306	19.6	7.8	11	D	D	D	33.8	14.6	7.4	0.4
Kearney	15	654	22.6	10.6	13	44	4.9	1.0	52.0	20.2	11.3	0.7
Keith	30	330	26.8	10.1	26	104	7.6	2.0	63.4	30.2	11.1	1.2
Keya Paha	1	D	D	D	3	9	0.7	0.1	6.9	2.6	1.3	0.1
Kimball	9	D	D	D	10	26	1.4	0.4	35.6	15.7	5.7	0.4
Knox	20	318	15.6	6.2	13	27	1.8	0.5	90.6	30.7	19.0	1.9
Lancaster	842	21 431	1 932.6	789.3	660	4 233	546.6	118.0	2 822.6	714.2	223.3	55.0
Lincoln	120	D	D	D	83	D	D	D	299.0	143.8	45.9	9.3
Logan	1	D	D	D	2	D	D	D	7.6	3.0	1.3	0.1
Loup	NA	NA	NA	NA	1	D	D	D	3.8	1.6	1.3	0.0
McPherson	NA	NA	NA	NA	NA	NA	NA	NA	5.0	1.6	0.7	0.3
Madison	158	D	D	D	107	D	D	D	269.3	107.7	41.1	7.1
Merrick	13	D	D	D	20	40	4.6	0.9	60.1	27.4	13.9	1.0
Morrill	5	122	8.2	3.7	5	D	D	D	41.1	17.0	7.9	1.3
Nance	10	D	D	D	16	33	2.7	0.5	34.8	12.3	7.3	0.6
Nemaha	23	359	23.3	10.5	19	61	2.9	0.7	60.2	25.1	12.2	1.6
Nuckolls	16	395	18.8	9.4	20	55	3.4	0.6	50.3	18.8	10.8	0.8
Otoe	41	915	51.3	21.6	38	186	10.3	3.7	106.9	52.6	21.8	2.5
Pawnee	8	143	8.2	3.8	5	D	D	D	32.8	11.1	7.2	0.5
Perkins	6	211	11.2	4.6	12	D	D	D	37.1	10.5	5.9	0.2
Phelps	25	743	51.3	17.5	36	118	16.9	3.0	78.1	32.3	14.9	1.4
Pierce	18	D	D	D	15	D	D	D	47.2	19.4	11.4	1.0

1. State totals may include programs not allocated by county.

Table B. States and Counties — Federal Funds, Residential Construction, and Local Government Finances

	Federal funds and grants, 2009–2010 (cont.)							Value of residential construction authorized by building permits, 2010		Local government finances, 2007				
	Expenditures (mil dol) (cont.)									General revenue				
		Procurement contract awards		Grants[1]								Taxes		
													Per capita[2] (dollars)	
STATE County	Salaries and wages	Defense	Other	Medicaid and other health-related	Nutrition and family welfare	Education	Other	New construction ($1,000)	Number of housing units	Total (mil dol)	Inter-govern-mental (mil dol)	Total (mil dol)	Total	Property
	171	172	173	174	175	176	177	178	179	180	181	182	183	184

NEBRASKA—Cont'd

County	171	172	173	174	175	176	177	178	179	180	181	182	183	184
Blaine	0.4	0.0	0.1	0.7	0.1	0.0	0.0	NA	NA	3.0	1.1	1.8	3 915	3 696
Boone	2.5	0.0	0.6	5.2	1.2	0.4	0.1	540	3	32.7	3.8	11.9	2 146	1 892
Box Butte	3.2	0.0	0.8	7.2	2.1	1.0	0.7	2 200	18	57.1	14.6	18.1	1 648	1 121
Boyd	1.4	0.0	0.3	2.6	0.6	0.3	0.2	0	0	12.3	3.2	6.9	3 233	2 857
Brown	1.4	0.0	0.3	4.6	0.7	0.3	0.2	141	1	23.9	5.1	10.2	3 194	2 749
Buffalo	29.2	0.0	4.4	20.3	10.6	2.7	2.1	17 248	109	137.4	45.7	63.8	1 418	1 074
Burt	2.4	0.0	0.6	8.5	1.5	0.3	4.7	933	8	30.4	7.2	15.0	2 130	1 854
Butler	3.7	0.5	0.7	7.2	1.2	0.4	0.4	1 060	8	35.1	4.6	18.6	2 222	1 828
Cass	6.0	0.0	1.4	11.2	4.3	1.2	1.9	10 587	65	77.1	22.1	38.5	1 504	1 225
Cedar	5.2	2.8	0.8	7.2	1.9	0.6	0.2	814	6	29.2	7.8	15.3	1 789	1 518
Chase	1.8	0.0	0.6	2.6	0.8	0.2	0.4	195	1	27.4	4.3	10.6	2 862	2 611
Cherry	3.0	0.0	0.9	5.9	1.3	0.4	0.8	1 817	8	35.8	7.1	14.9	2 614	2 130
Cheyenne	4.3	0.0	0.8	9.2	1.5	0.5	4.2	1 814	8	36.9	11.1	17.6	1 764	1 390
Clay	12.0	0.0	2.8	3.3	1.1	0.7	0.2	1 100	4	31.8	11.1	16.6	2 630	2 177
Colfax	5.0	0.0	0.6	7.9	1.5	0.3	0.2	1 091	8	33.1	11.5	17.1	1 718	1 543
Cuming	2.8	0.0	0.7	4.6	4.2	0.7	2.6	959	7	32.4	7.1	16.6	1 778	1 524
Custer	5.3	0.0	1.1	14.4	2.1	0.8	0.6	0	0	38.5	12.6	19.2	1 767	1 539
Dakota	5.5	0.0	1.0	22.3	4.2	1.5	1.0	12 356	112	67.9	32.3	26.8	1 318	846
Dawes	10.5	0.0	2.3	6.8	3.3	1.1	2.2	245	2	29.3	11.2	11.7	1 327	980
Dawson	8.4	1.4	1.1	19.7	4.1	0.9	1.5	4 554	38	125.4	39.4	34.6	1 400	1 124
Deuel	0.5	0.0	0.1	3.3	0.3	0.2	0.0	0	0	11.2	3.3	6.9	3 649	3 077
Dixon	2.4	0.0	1.7	4.6	0.9	0.4	0.1	436	3	25.2	7.9	11.9	1 903	1 558
Dodge	19.5	1.0	2.1	23.6	6.1	3.1	5.2	6 143	40	190.5	34.7	51.5	1 429	1 153
Douglas	458.6	226.7	257.9	663.4	94.3	44.4	142.9	215 451	1 916	1 985.9	588.8	943.2	1 896	1 386
Dundy	0.9	0.0	0.2	2.6	0.3	0.1	0.1	0	0	13.7	2.4	4.2	2 069	1 915
Fillmore	2.6	0.0	0.8	5.9	1.1	0.2	0.3	545	3	32.9	5.1	14.9	2 461	2 002
Franklin	1.6	0.0	0.4	2.6	0.6	0.3	0.6	225	1	13.6	3.1	4.8	1 528	1 341
Frontier	1.4	0.0	0.4	2.6	0.5	0.1	0.0	476	4	14.1	4.1	7.4	2 789	2 575
Furnas	2.5	0.0	0.6	10.5	1.0	0.4	0.5	411	3	27.4	8.7	11.1	2 355	1 960
Gage	15.5	0.0	1.9	25.7	3.4	1.4	1.2	1 872	17	69.4	24.4	31.0	1 336	1 068
Garden	1.2	0.0	8.6	2.6	0.4	0.1	0.0	400	1	16.3	1.7	7.6	4 153	3 835
Garfield	0.7	0.0	0.1	2.1	0.3	0.1	0.2	376	3	7.0	2.7	2.5	1 472	1 293
Gosper	0.7	0.0	0.1	0.0	0.2	0.1	0.0	870	10	10.6	1.5	5.8	2 929	2 508
Grant	0.5	0.0	0.1	0.0	0.1	0.0	0.0	NA	NA	3.8	0.5	3.0	4 824	4 563
Greeley	1.6	0.0	0.4	2.0	0.8	0.2	0.0	0	0	11.7	3.1	6.1	2 606	2 199
Hall	51.8	1.8	11.6	48.2	8.5	5.0	8.1	17 791	119	203.5	73.5	81.8	1 471	1 103
Hamilton	2.9	0.0	0.7	7.9	1.2	0.5	0.8	5 910	31	30.6	7.8	16.1	1 730	1 393
Harlan	1.8	4.3	0.3	2.6	0.5	0.3	0.0	475	3	14.5	3.9	3.6	1 055	926
Hayes	0.4	0.0	0.0	0.7	0.2	0.1	0.0	0	0	4.4	1.7	2.4	2 437	2 271
Hitchcock	1.4	1.6	0.3	3.3	0.5	0.1	0.0	0	0	10.6	3.7	4.5	1 578	1 335
Holt	15.3	0.0	0.7	14.4	2.5	0.6	7.2	1 096	9	38.1	11.4	21.5	2 086	1 767
Hooker	0.3	0.0	0.0	0.7	0.2	0.0	0.1	260	3	5.1	0.8	2.8	3 792	3 336
Howard	2.0	0.0	0.4	4.6	1.2	0.4	0.1	2 238	18	33.9	8.0	9.2	1 389	1 243
Jefferson	2.6	0.0	0.5	10.5	4.1	0.4	0.6	983	6	36.9	8.1	17.2	2 295	2 000
Johnson	2.4	0.0	0.4	3.9	0.8	0.6	0.6	125	2	25.5	5.1	10.8	2 403	2 053
Kearney	2.0	0.9	0.4	3.3	0.8	0.3	0.1	3 590	28	29.8	5.2	15.6	2 365	2 146
Keith	3.3	0.0	0.8	5.2	1.3	0.4	1.0	1 214	6	30.6	10.3	15.7	1 959	1 460
Keya Paha	0.2	0.0	0.0	1.3	0.2	0.1	0.0	180	2	4.0	1.3	2.4	2 812	2 636
Kimball	1.1	0.0	0.2	2.5	0.6	0.1	1.7	0	0	29.2	3.6	8.7	2 413	1 721
Knox	3.6	0.3	0.8	12.9	3.1	2.2	4.0	3 692	20	33.4	16.1	13.5	1 554	1 380
Lancaster	325.3	19.0	89.3	278.9	114.3	159.7	773.3	131 008	979	942.0	239.2	482.6	1 751	1 304
Lincoln	27.5	0.0	3.8	32.3	5.1	2.3	6.0	10 153	83	243.3	46.7	73.2	2 062	1 275
Logan	0.2	0.0	0.1	1.3	0.2	0.1	0.0	NA	NA	3.2	1.1	1.8	2 459	2 136
Loup	0.2	0.0	0.0	0.0	0.1	0.0	0.0	548	4	2.3	0.6	1.5	2 306	2 208
McPherson	0.2	0.0	0.0	1.3	0.0	0.1	0.0	NA	NA	2.3	0.4	1.7	3 430	2 827
Madison	25.3	14.2	10.7	31.5	5.3	1.8	8.7	11 787	68	151.2	44.7	68.7	2 011	1 593
Merrick	2.5	0.0	0.7	6.6	1.2	0.7	0.1	2 645	23	33.6	7.4	10.4	1 354	1 166
Morrill	1.4	0.0	0.3	3.9	1.2	0.4	0.1	0	0	27.1	9.6	7.9	1 560	1 268
Nance	0.8	0.0	0.2	7.2	0.8	0.1	0.1	1 294	11	19.0	3.5	8.4	2 339	2 022
Nemaha	2.1	0.0	0.4	7.3	1.1	0.7	0.5	1 050	9	29.8	9.3	9.4	1 333	1 112
Nuckolls	2.5	0.0	0.5	6.6	0.8	0.2	2.0	300	2	7.8	1.7	2.9	643	499
Otoe	6.3	0.2	1.1	11.2	2.1	0.7	0.3	5 581	38	50.0	13.6	23.9	1 527	1 224
Pawnee	1.6	0.0	0.4	4.6	0.6	0.2	3.1	0	0	19.2	6.7	4.8	1 771	1 569
Perkins	0.9	0.0	0.2	0.0	0.4	0.3	0.0	0	0	21.5	3.1	7.0	2 388	1 974
Phelps	2.8	0.1	0.8	7.2	1.3	0.8	0.6	4 744	34	37.7	8.7	18.6	2 025	1 596
Pierce	2.2	0.0	0.5	3.9	1.2	0.5	0.1	1 228	9	32.1	6.2	16.1	2 213	1 764

1. State totals may include programs not allocated by county.　　2. Based on the resident population estimated as of July 1 of the year shown.

Table B. States and Counties — Local Government Finances, Government Employment, and Voting

	Local government finances, 2007 (cont.)									Government employment, 2009			Presidential election,[2] 2008		
	Direct general expenditure							Debt outstanding					Percent of vote cast:		
			Percent of total for:												
STATE County	Total (mil dol)	Per capita[1] (dollars)	Education	Health and hospitals	Police protection	Public welfare	Highways	Total (mil dol)	Per capita[1] (dollars)	Federal civilian	Federal military	State and local	Democratic	Republican	All other
	185	186	187	188	189	190	191	192	193	194	195	196	197	198	199

NEBRASKA—Cont'd															
Blaine	2.6	5 728	72.1	0.0	1.8	0.5	9.9	0.0	0	31	0	56	13.6	84.2	2.2
Boone	32.5	5 879	31.7	45.1	1.7	0.0	7.5	3.1	564	34	23	600	26.2	72.0	1.8
Box Butte	53.4	4 855	36.5	31.9	2.6	0.2	4.0	12.9	1 173	57	47	1 029	37.9	58.9	3.2
Boyd	7.8	3 702	64.7	0.0	1.8	0.0	9.2	7.9	3 725	14	0	228	22.5	75.6	1.9
Brown	18.9	5 884	45.8	27.1	1.8	0.3	6.5	13.8	4 297	25	13	377	19.8	77.1	3.1
Buffalo	138.2	3 074	54.0	0.1	6.6	0.2	9.9	107.6	2 392	161	197	3 852	30.4	67.9	1.7
Burt	28.3	4 005	45.9	14.3	3.4	0.2	11.6	18.3	2 588	36	30	625	41.7	56.3	2.0
Butler	33.6	4 012	36.4	26.9	3.9	0.1	12.6	27.5	3 281	54	36	548	31.0	66.6	2.4
Cass	66.2	2 588	51.6	0.1	4.4	8.2	6.6	149.5	5 844	76	109	1 331	39.2	58.7	2.1
Cedar	28.1	3 289	53.4	0.2	1.6	6.5	10.4	9.4	1 106	98	36	607	28.5	69.8	1.7
Chase	23.8	6 425	35.9	30.4	3.2	0.5	9.0	7.9	2 123	26	16	465	18.5	80.1	1.4
Cherry	30.7	5 375	36.4	30.2	2.5	0.5	11.2	3.7	649	58	23	517	19.6	77.1	3.3
Cheyenne	33.5	3 363	50.4	0.6	4.5	1.0	8.0	31.4	3 148	43	42	802	24.2	73.8	1.9
Clay	31.2	4 934	70.4	0.6	1.8	0.5	8.6	10.6	1 671	157	27	615	25.7	71.8	2.5
Colfax	31.6	3 163	67.5	0.3	3.5	0.1	10.7	12.5	1 257	79	44	604	35.1	63.0	1.9
Cuming	32.2	3 442	50.8	0.2	2.8	6.3	14.2	45.6	4 872	41	39	679	31.2	66.8	2.0
Custer	37.3	3 434	62.3	0.1	2.8	0.2	13.5	14.4	1 329	56	46	837	21.4	77.1	1.5
Dakota	63.2	3 113	55.5	0.3	6.4	0.1	6.1	61.7	3 035	79	89	1 111	46.8	51.5	1.7
Dawes	25.4	2 875	48.3	0.5	5.1	12.5	9.3	5.9	664	140	37	1 083	34.0	62.9	3.0
Dawson	120.7	4 880	38.7	28.6	4.2	0.1	4.5	96.3	3 891	109	108	2 035	30.0	68.4	1.6
Deuel	10.7	5 650	50.2	0.4	3.5	13.6	7.7	3.8	2 023	0	0	204	24.5	73.7	1.8
Dixon	27.3	4 366	63.7	0.0	3.3	8.6	8.5	10.0	1 596	42	27	405	33.9	63.9	2.3
Dodge	179.9	4 996	32.6	44.4	2.6	0.2	5.1	108.7	3 018	119	154	2 781	43.0	55.0	2.0
Douglas	1 879.9	3 779	49.2	2.8	5.8	0.4	3.9	4 585.7	9 219	5 727	2 410	35 095	51.5	46.9	1.6
Dundy	13.2	6 520	32.0	44.6	3.9	0.1	8.0	0.9	429	15	0	236	21.4	76.8	1.8
Fillmore	32.1	5 309	36.2	27.3	3.4	7.1	12.3	11.0	1 816	40	26	664	32.6	64.9	2.4
Franklin	12.6	3 979	28.7	33.7	2.1	0.4	14.2	1.4	447	27	13	340	28.5	69.5	2.0
Frontier	14.3	5 369	63.7	0.7	3.1	0.7	10.1	1.9	701	16	11	329	24.9	73.6	1.5
Furnas	24.9	5 257	59.0	0.1	3.3	0.2	6.3	17.9	3 773	39	20	558	23.9	74.1	2.0
Gage	72.1	3 104	55.9	0.1	4.9	0.3	11.9	32.4	1 396	114	97	2 183	44.0	53.5	2.5
Garden	14.6	7 915	28.0	33.5	2.6	0.0	6.5	0.2	83	22	0	247	24.9	74.2	1.0
Garfield	6.3	3 658	57.1	0.2	3.3	0.0	9.1	2.0	1 174	0	0	165	20.6	77.7	1.7
Gosper	9.2	4 681	33.3	0.6	3.2	23.1	11.3	23.0	11 657	14	0	162	24.8	74.0	1.1
Grant	3.8	6 117	72.2	0.6	1.7	0.1	8.3	0.1	220	0	0	77	11.2	86.6	2.2
Greeley	10.6	4 559	59.0	0.1	3.1	11.3	10.0	3.9	1 690	18	10	288	38.2	59.6	2.2
Hall	221.5	3 981	51.3	0.1	4.5	0.3	6.1	233.7	4 200	732	248	4 342	36.9	61.0	2.1
Hamilton	34.3	3 688	64.5	1.7	2.7	0.5	12.1	20.0	2 156	39	40	600	27.8	70.6	1.6
Harlan	12.8	3 784	23.9	35.1	1.9	0.0	5.5	10.6	3 119	38	14	277	22.8	75.3	2.0
Hayes	6.1	6 216	74.3	0.2	1.4	0.0	12.0	1.0	1 067	13	0	84	15.4	83.4	1.3
Hitchcock	12.0	4 230	63.3	0.0	1.1	0.0	11.1	3.8	1 324	16	12	292	25.1	72.6	2.3
Holt	35.4	3 436	56.8	0.0	3.0	0.3	12.7	11.7	1 133	56	43	773	21.9	75.3	2.8
Hooker	4.7	6 418	49.3	24.4	1.5	0.1	6.2	1.9	2 635	0	0	99	17.1	81.1	1.8
Howard	32.6	4 925	38.3	33.5	2.1	0.2	7.6	14.5	2 189	34	28	587	36.1	61.6	2.2
Jefferson	28.6	3 806	57.6	2.1	4.4	0.1	10.7	4.0	535	43	31	500	41.1	56.9	2.0
Johnson	22.8	5 095	37.2	27.8	1.6	0.1	7.4	18.5	4 143	41	22	866	43.3	54.1	2.6
Kearney	27.9	4 233	49.4	20.5	2.2	0.4	8.8	10.9	1 657	31	28	476	27.8	70.6	1.6
Keith	31.4	3 917	56.3	0.4	4.6	1.1	7.2	10.9	1 354	37	33	534	24.5	74.1	1.3
Keya Paha	4.1	4 839	50.7	0.2	1.9	0.0	21.5	0.1	165	0	0	65	21.6	76.7	1.7
Kimball	23.3	6 471	29.0	27.9	1.9	13.2	7.1	5.7	1 575	18	15	440	24.2	74.3	1.4
Knox	33.0	3 812	65.6	0.2	1.9	0.0	12.5	12.6	1 459	55	36	1 185	30.7	66.8	2.5
Lancaster	1 006.3	3 651	47.6	3.4	4.2	2.2	7.6	1 773.4	6 433	2 963	1 234	31 010	51.6	46.6	1.8
Lincoln	221.7	6 244	34.1	37.1	3.1	0.2	3.7	88.3	2 488	228	153	2 697	31.0	66.5	2.5
Logan	3.2	4 259	71.3	0.4	1.8	0.0	10.2	0.1	107	0	0	80	19.5	78.6	1.9
Loup	2.3	3 607	60.6	0.7	3.3	0.0	10.8	0.1	132	0	0	55	21.9	76.8	1.3
McPherson	2.0	3 944	63.4	0.2	1.8	0.1	16.3	0.4	797	0	0	33	15.4	81.9	2.7
Madison	156.2	4 575	62.9	1.8	4.3	3.8	5.5	99.0	2 900	225	149	3 564	29.5	68.7	1.8
Merrick	26.4	3 432	34.8	32.8	2.7	0.8	10.0	20.2	2 622	30	33	550	28.7	69.2	2.0
Morrill	24.6	4 868	42.3	18.5	2.4	7.5	7.1	8.3	1 641	22	21	469	23.7	73.4	2.9
Nance	17.2	4 806	47.9	26.8	3.5	0.0	11.6	2.8	789	19	15	364	32.2	65.4	2.5
Nemaha	30.9	4 391	49.7	23.7	2.3	0.1	8.2	8.2	1 160	33	29	1 583	35.7	61.4	2.9
Nuckolls	6.0	1 321	0.0	1.2	8.5	0.8	36.9	16.8	3 699	35	19	353	29.6	67.4	3.0
Otoe	47.2	3 015	48.4	12.8	4.4	0.6	8.5	21.4	1 367	60	65	1 171	41.1	56.9	2.0
Pawnee	18.1	6 740	29.7	24.8	1.0	0.1	8.4	2.2	831	25	11	270	34.9	62.1	3.0
Perkins	22.6	7 727	27.2	47.5	1.7	0.3	11.7	5.9	2 014	20	12	370	21.8	76.9	1.3
Phelps	35.6	3 882	57.7	3.7	3.2	0.2	10.5	17.3	1 882	38	39	720	23.5	75.1	1.4
Pierce	28.9	3 972	46.7	18.5	1.6	0.0	12.8	7.6	1 041	35	31	497	24.3	73.9	1.8

1. Based on the resident population estimated as of July 1 of the year shown.   2. © 2009 Election Data Services, Inc. All rights reserved.

Table B. States and Counties — **Land Area and Population**

STATE/ County code	CBSA code[1]	County type[2]	STATE County	Population and population characteristics, 2010														
				Land area,[3] (sq km) 2010	Total persons	Rank	Per square kilometer	Race alone or in combination, not Hispanic or Latino (percent)				Percent Hispanic or Latino[4]	Age (percent)					
								White	Black	American Indian, Alaska Native	Asian and Pacific Islander		Under 5 years	5 to 17 years	18 to 24 years	25 to 34 years	35 to 44 years	45 to 54 years
				1	2	3	4	5	6	7	8	9	10	11	12	13	14	15
			NEBRASKA—Cont'd															
31 141	18100	5	Platte	1 746	32 237	1 385	18.5	84.9	0.7	0.6	0.7	13.8	7.4	19.0	7.9	12.0	11.7	15.1
31 143	...	9	Polk	1 135	5 406	2 813	4.8	96.7	0.2	0.6	0.5	2.9	6.0	18.4	4.7	8.8	11.7	15.3
31 145	...	7	Red Willow	1 857	11 055	2 361	6.0	94.4	1.0	0.8	0.4	4.2	6.1	16.9	8.9	11.3	10.1	15.4
31 147	...	7	Richardson	1 429	8 363	2 583	5.9	95.3	0.5	4.2	0.5	1.3	5.1	16.4	6.0	9.0	10.4	16.0
31 149	...	9	Rock	2 612	1 526	3 082	0.6	98.8	0.3	0.7	0.2	0.1	5.6	14.7	4.3	10.5	7.8	17.0
31 151	...	6	Saline	1 487	14 200	2 160	9.5	77.0	0.9	0.7	1.8	20.2	7.1	17.4	12.6	11.4	11.9	14.1
31 153	36540	2	Sarpy	619	158 840	392	256.6	85.9	5.0	0.9	3.2	7.3	8.4	20.4	8.8	15.4	14.4	14.3
31 155	36540	2	Saunders	1 943	20 780	1 804	10.7	97.0	0.6	0.5	0.6	2.0	6.7	19.1	6.3	10.3	12.2	16.8
31 157	42420	5	Scotts Bluff	1 915	36 970	1 245	19.3	76.4	0.6	1.9	0.8	21.1	7.2	17.6	8.7	12.1	10.9	13.8
31 159	30700	2	Seward	1 480	16 750	1 999	11.3	97.2	0.7	0.6	0.7	1.6	6.1	17.6	13.2	10.1	11.0	14.7
31 161	...	9	Sheridan	6 322	5 469	2 806	0.9	85.9	0.5	12.7	0.6	3.1	6.0	17.6	5.4	9.4	10.3	13.5
31 163	...	9	Sherman	1 465	3 152	2 965	2.2	98.5	0.2	0.2	0.4	1.0	5.8	16.7	5.1	7.6	11.6	14.3
31 165	...	9	Sioux	5 353	1 311	3 095	0.2	95.7	0.4	1.0	0.1	4.0	4.9	17.5	5.3	9.5	9.5	15.9
31 167	35740	9	Stanton	1 108	6 129	2 753	5.5	94.2	0.8	0.8	0.2	4.6	7.6	19.9	6.5	12.3	11.5	15.7
31 169	...	9	Thayer	1 486	5 228	2 826	3.5	97.9	0.5	0.6	0.3	1.5	5.8	15.6	4.9	8.1	9.9	14.8
31 171	...	9	Thomas	1 847	647	3 132	0.4	97.5	0.2	0.2	0.6	1.9	5.1	17.8	4.3	9.4	11.1	13.8
31 173	...	8	Thurston	1 019	6 940	2 693	6.8	40.6	0.6	57.3	0.2	2.7	10.6	24.9	9.7	10.8	10.1	12.4
31 175	...	9	Valley	1 471	4 260	2 885	2.9	97.6	0.2	0.4	0.6	1.9	5.8	16.2	5.4	9.6	10.4	14.5
31 177	36540	2	Washington	1 010	20 234	1 827	20.0	96.7	0.9	0.6	0.5	2.1	5.9	19.3	8.0	9.9	12.4	16.8
31 179	...	6	Wayne	1 147	9 595	2 473	8.4	93.4	1.7	0.5	1.0	4.2	5.4	14.0	26.2	9.8	8.7	12.0
31 181	...	9	Webster	1 489	3 812	2 921	2.6	95.2	0.7	0.9	0.8	3.5	6.1	16.5	6.2	7.9	9.9	16.8
31 183	...	9	Wheeler	1 490	818	3 118	0.5	98.7	0.1	0.2	0.9	0.7	5.9	18.7	5.3	9.4	9.4	16.4
31 185	...	7	York	1 483	13 665	2 208	9.2	93.8	1.4	0.6	0.7	4.1	6.4	16.0	9.0	11.0	10.8	15.2
32 000	...	X	**NEVADA**	284 332	2 700 551	X	9.5	56.6	8.7	1.5	9.6	26.5	6.9	17.7	9.2	14.3	14.2	13.9
32 001	21980	6	Churchill	12 770	24 877	1 606	1.9	79.1	2.2	5.3	4.3	12.1	6.7	18.5	8.3	12.1	11.8	14.3
32 003	29820	1	Clark	20 439	1 951 269	13	95.5	50.5	11.2	1.0	11.3	29.1	7.1	17.9	9.2	15.1	14.8	13.6
32 005	23820	4	Douglas	1 838	46 997	1 023	25.6	85.3	0.7	2.6	2.7	10.9	4.9	15.3	6.3	9.0	10.8	16.4
32 007	21220	5	Elko	44 470	48 818	998	1.1	70.6	0.9	5.6	1.6	22.9	8.4	20.8	9.5	13.4	13.0	15.1
32 009	...	9	Esmeralda	9 277	783	3 120	0.1	79.9	0.3	5.7	1.0	15.3	5.0	11.9	3.8	8.0	9.7	15.6
32 011	21220	9	Eureka	10 815	1 987	3 056	0.2	84.8	0.3	2.9	1.2	12.0	7.2	17.0	6.8	10.1	12.3	18.5
32 013	...	7	Humboldt	24 969	16 528	2 016	0.7	70.5	0.7	4.7	1.1	24.4	7.7	19.7	8.5	12.6	12.8	15.6
32 015	...	7	Lander	14 219	5 775	2 786	0.4	74.7	0.4	4.3	0.5	21.1	7.8	19.8	8.6	11.7	12.6	15.0
32 017	...	8	Lincoln	27 540	5 345	2 817	0.2	89.5	2.5	1.8	1.6	6.2	5.9	20.9	7.7	10.5	10.6	12.6
32 019	22280	6	Lyon	5 183	51 980	954	10.0	80.6	1.3	3.3	2.6	14.8	6.5	18.3	6.8	11.0	12.5	14.8
32 021	...	7	Mineral	9 720	4 772	2 859	0.5	71.5	4.9	15.8	1.8	9.1	4.7	13.7	7.6	8.6	9.4	16.3
32 023	37220	6	Nye	47 091	43 946	1 086	0.9	81.2	2.6	2.5	2.7	13.6	5.0	15.7	6.2	8.1	10.0	15.2
32 027	...	8	Pershing	15 635	6 753	2 707	0.4	69.7	3.9	3.8	1.9	22.3	5.1	14.5	7.7	13.6	16.1	17.9
32 029	39900	2	Storey	681	4 010	2 907	5.9	89.9	1.3	2.6	2.6	5.7	4.3	13.1	5.2	7.5	10.0	19.9
32 031	39900	2	Washoe	16 323	421 407	160	25.8	68.2	2.8	2.0	7.1	22.2	6.6	16.9	10.6	13.4	13.1	14.6
32 033	...	7	White Pine	22 988	10 030	2 445	0.4	77.9	4.2	4.9	1.5	13.2	6.3	15.3	7.7	13.7	12.5	15.6
32 510	16180	3	Carson City	375	55 274	907	147.4	72.4	2.2	2.8	3.1	21.3	5.8	15.5	8.5	12.0	12.6	15.2
33 000	...	X	**NEW HAMPSHIRE**	23 187	1 316 470	X	56.8	93.6	1.5	0.7	2.7	2.8	5.3	16.5	9.4	11.0	13.6	17.2
33 001	29060	4	Belknap	1 037	60 088	858	57.9	96.9	0.7	0.8	1.5	1.2	5.1	15.7	6.7	10.3	12.8	16.9
33 003	...	8	Carroll	2 411	47 818	1 006	19.8	97.8	0.5	0.9	0.8	1.0	4.1	14.5	5.7	8.2	12.0	17.5
33 005	28300	4	Cheshire	1 830	77 117	704	42.1	96.6	0.9	0.8	1.6	1.4	4.8	14.8	13.8	10.2	12.0	15.6
33 007	13620	7	Coos	4 648	33 055	1 358	7.1	97.4	0.7	1.1	0.8	1.2	4.4	14.5	6.7	9.7	12.4	16.9
33 009	30100	5	Grafton	4 426	89 118	636	20.1	93.8	1.2	1.0	3.6	1.8	4.6	13.8	14.3	10.6	11.4	15.6
33 011	31700	2	Hillsborough	2 269	400 721	167	176.6	89.1	2.4	0.6	3.8	5.3	5.9	17.5	8.6	12.3	14.4	17.1
33 013	18180	4	Merrimack	2 419	146 445	426	60.5	95.4	1.4	0.8	2.0	1.6	5.2	16.7	8.9	11.0	13.5	17.2
33 015	14460	1	Rockingham	1 799	295 223	219	164.1	95.3	0.9	0.6	2.2	2.1	5.1	17.8	7.3	9.9	14.6	18.8
33 017	14460	1	Strafford	956	123 143	490	128.8	94.3	1.5	0.7	3.2	1.8	5.5	15.1	15.2	12.0	13.0	15.7
33 019	17200	7	Sullivan	1 392	43 742	1 092	31.4	97.5	0.7	1.0	0.9	1.1	5.3	15.7	6.9	10.3	13.2	16.8
34 000	...	X	**NEW JERSEY**	19 047	8 791 894	X	461.6	60.5	13.5	0.5	9.0	17.7	6.2	17.3	8.7	12.6	14.1	15.7
34 001	12100	2	Atlantic	1 439	274 549	236	190.8	60.0	15.9	0.7	8.2	16.8	6.0	17.3	9.3	11.4	13.2	16.3
34 003	35620	1	Bergen	603	905 116	54	1 501.0	63.6	5.6	0.3	15.4	16.1	5.6	17.0	7.4	11.6	14.3	16.3
34 005	37980	1	Burlington	2 068	448 734	145	217.0	72.4	17.2	0.7	5.2	6.4	5.8	17.4	8.3	11.5	13.9	16.8
34 007	37980	1	Camden	573	513 657	126	896.4	61.6	19.4	0.6	5.7	14.2	6.5	17.9	9.0	13.0	13.6	15.3
34 009	36140	3	Cape May	651	97 265	595	149.4	88.2	5.2	0.6	1.2	6.2	4.7	14.2	8.0	9.4	10.6	15.8
34 011	47220	3	Cumberland	1 253	156 898	397	125.2	51.7	20.0	1.5	1.5	27.1	6.9	17.1	9.5	14.4	14.1	14.2
34 013	35620	1	Essex	327	783 969	73	2 397.5	34.3	40.3	0.5	5.2	20.3	6.9	18.0	9.5	13.7	14.8	14.3
34 015	37980	1	Gloucester	834	288 288	223	345.7	82.5	10.7	0.6	3.1	4.8	6.0	18.3	9.4	11.5	14.1	16.3
34 017	35620	1	Hudson	120	634 266	94	5 285.6	31.8	11.9	0.4	14.2	42.2	6.7	14.0	10.0	20.7	15.2	13.1
34 019	35620	1	Hunterdon	1 108	128 349	479	115.8	88.7	2.8	0.3	3.9	5.2	4.7	18.9	6.9	8.2	14.0	20.1

1. CBSA = Core Based Statistical Area. See Appendix A for explanation. See Appendix B for list of metropolitan areas with component counties.   2. County type code from the Economic Research Service of USDA Rural-Urban Continuum Codes. See Appendix A for definition.   3. Dry land or land partially or temporarily covered by water.   4. May be of any race.

Table B. States and Counties — **Population and Households**

	Population, 2010 (cont.)				Population change and components of change, 1990–2010							Households, 2010				
	Age (percent) (cont.)				Total persons		Percent change		Components of change, 2000–2009						Percent	
STATE County	55 to 64 years	65 to 74 years	75 years and over	Percent female	1990	2000	1990–2000	2000–2010	Births	Deaths	Net migration	Number	Percent change, 2000–2010	Persons per house-hold	Female family house-holder[1]	One per-son
	16	17	18	19	20	21	22	23	24	25	26	27	28	29	30	31
NEBRASKA—Cont'd																
Platte	11.9	7.3	7.6	49.9	29 820	31 662	6.2	1.8	4 265	2 276	-954	12 658	4.8	2.51	8.5	26.8
Polk	15.4	8.9	10.8	50.1	5 655	5 639	-0.3	-4.1	567	580	-518	2 212	-2.1	2.39	5.8	27.5
Red Willow	12.6	8.6	10.1	50.4	11 705	11 448	-2.2	-3.4	1 281	1 219	-798	4 663	-1.0	2.29	8.2	31.6
Richardson	14.2	10.9	12.0	50.6	9 937	9 531	-4.1	-12.3	771	1 307	-834	3 718	-6.9	2.21	8.0	33.6
Rock	17.0	10.1	13.2	50.0	2 019	1 756	-13.0	-13.1	135	186	-196	685	-10.2	2.18	4.5	30.5
Saline	11.0	6.5	8.1	49.7	12 715	13 843	8.9	2.6	1 782	1 423	-247	5 131	-1.1	2.57	7.8	26.8
Sarpy	9.8	5.1	3.4	50.3	102 583	122 595	19.5	29.6	22 402	5 889	15 076	58 102	33.8	2.71	10.2	21.4
Saunders	13.1	8.0	7.5	49.4	18 285	19 830	8.4	4.8	2 306	1 700	-256	8 040	7.2	2.54	6.9	23.8
Scotts Bluff	13.0	8.0	8.8	51.8	36 025	36 951	2.6	0.1	5 026	4 026	-867	14 928	0.3	2.42	11.0	29.4
Seward	12.2	7.6	7.6	49.1	15 450	16 496	6.8	1.5	1 807	1 522	-204	6 266	4.2	2.47	5.4	26.1
Sheridan	15.6	9.7	12.4	51.5	6 750	6 198	-8.2	-11.8	626	731	-811	2 380	-6.6	2.25	7.9	33.7
Sherman	15.6	11.1	12.2	50.9	3 718	3 318	-10.8	-5.0	308	391	-345	1 392	-0.1	2.22	5.4	32.7
Sioux	15.9	11.0	10.4	48.7	1 549	1 475	-4.8	-11.1	94	64	-232	577	-4.6	2.27	5.5	29.1
Stanton	12.4	7.4	6.8	50.5	6 244	6 455	3.4	-5.1	767	473	-404	2 387	3.9	2.57	7.5	24.2
Thayer	15.1	11.1	14.6	51.2	6 635	6 055	-8.7	-13.7	499	780	-740	2 296	-9.6	2.21	4.7	33.0
Thomas	17.6	10.7	10.2	49.3	851	729	-14.3	-11.2	57	54	-165	291	-10.5	2.22	1.7	33.0
Thurston	9.6	5.6	6.3	50.3	6 936	7 171	3.4	-3.2	1 491	672	-651	2 158	-4.3	3.19	20.8	21.3
Valley	14.5	10.9	12.7	50.5	5 169	4 647	-10.1	-8.3	434	549	-403	1 922	-2.2	2.19	4.9	35.0
Washington	13.6	7.5	6.6	50.2	16 607	18 780	13.1	7.7	2 070	1 496	474	7 761	11.8	2.54	7.6	23.0
Wayne	10.1	6.4	7.3	49.8	9 364	9 851	5.2	-2.6	944	597	-899	3 507	2.0	2.38	5.6	27.8
Webster	13.0	11.2	12.5	52.2	4 279	4 061	-5.1	-6.1	329	576	-367	1 604	-6.1	2.28	7.1	32.4
Wheeler	16.0	11.1	7.8	49.6	948	886	-6.5	-7.7	72	65	-129	350	-0.6	2.34	2.3	27.7
York	13.3	8.7	9.5	51.2	14 428	14 598	1.2	-6.4	1 637	1 314	-1 011	5 564	-2.8	2.32	6.6	29.1
NEVADA	11.7	7.3	4.7	49.5	1 201 675	1 998 257	66.3	35.1	333 232	165 152	485 443	1 006 250	34.0	2.65	12.7	25.7
Churchill	13.0	9.0	6.2	49.7	17 938	23 982	33.7	3.7	3 651	2 107	-507	9 671	8.5	2.53	11.3	25.2
Clark	11.0	6.9	4.4	49.7	741 368	1 375 765	85.6	41.8	246 666	111 822	399 902	715 365	39.7	2.70	13.5	25.3
Douglas	17.0	12.0	8.2	50.0	27 637	41 259	49.3	13.9	3 574	3 252	4 086	19 638	19.7	2.38	8.9	24.0
Elko	11.4	5.6	2.9	48.1	33 463	45 291	35.3	7.8	6 100	2 308	-1 081	17 442	11.5	2.77	9.1	22.5
Esmeralda	20.2	16.6	9.2	44.6	1 344	971	-27.8	-19.4	36	83	-310	389	-14.5	2.01	5.9	40.6
Eureka	15.1	7.8	5.2	47.3	1 547	1 651	6.7	20.4	167	98	-20	836	25.5	2.38	4.2	33.0
Humboldt	12.8	6.4	3.9	47.6	12 844	16 106	25.4	2.6	2 244	1 050	-989	6 289	9.7	2.60	8.9	25.6
Lander	12.8	7.8	4.0	49.3	6 266	5 794	-7.5	-0.3	677	363	-953	2 213	5.7	2.60	9.4	25.8
Lincoln	13.5	11.6	6.5	46.2	3 775	4 165	10.3	28.3	388	444	667	1 988	29.1	2.57	7.7	30.4
Lyon	14.2	10.2	5.6	49.6	20 001	34 501	72.5	50.7	5 336	3 845	16 751	19 808	52.3	2.61	10.2	22.1
Mineral	17.3	13.1	9.5	50.8	6 475	5 071	-21.7	-5.9	395	714	-68	2 240	2.0	2.11	11.2	36.7
Nye	16.3	15.1	8.3	49.5	17 781	32 485	82.7	35.3	3 515	4 806	13 183	18 032	35.5	2.42	9.3	26.8
Pershing	12.2	9.0	3.9	36.8	4 336	6 693	54.4	0.9	546	386	-545	2 018	2.9	2.51	9.1	26.6
Storey	21.5	13.0	5.4	49.0	2 526	3 399	34.6	18.0	180	153	1 025	1 742	19.2	2.30	7.6	26.0
Washoe	12.7	7.2	4.8	49.5	254 667	339 486	33.3	24.1	51 994	26 961	52 237	163 445	23.7	2.55	11.3	27.2
White Pine	14.0	8.6	6.3	41.4	9 264	9 181	-0.9	9.2	832	836	41	3 707	12.9	2.37	8.8	30.2
Carson City	13.8	8.7	7.8	48.1	40 443	52 457	29.7	5.4	6 931	5 924	2 024	21 427	6.2	2.41	12.0	30.4
NEW HAMPSHIRE	13.5	7.4	6.2	50.7	1 109 252	1 235 786	11.4	6.5	135 471	92 897	53 460	518 973	9.3	2.46	9.7	25.6
Belknap	15.9	9.1	7.7	50.9	49 216	56 325	14.4	6.7	5 461	5 406	5 270	24 766	10.3	2.39	9.8	25.7
Carroll	17.4	11.5	9.1	50.5	35 410	43 666	23.3	9.5	3 726	4 359	5 048	21 052	14.7	2.25	8.1	28.4
Cheshire	14.1	7.9	6.8	51.2	70 121	73 825	5.3	4.5	7 130	6 117	2 626	30 204	6.7	2.40	9.4	26.2
Coos	16.0	10.0	9.4	49.2	34 828	33 111	-4.9	-0.2	2 780	3 804	-401	14 171	1.5	2.23	9.2	30.3
Grafton	14.3	8.3	7.2	50.5	74 929	81 743	9.1	9.0	7 570	6 459	3 890	35 986	13.9	2.28	8.4	29.4
Hillsborough	12.4	6.4	5.5	50.5	335 838	380 841	13.4	5.2	46 552	26 013	6 914	155 466	7.6	2.53	10.5	25.3
Merrimack	13.8	7.1	6.5	50.8	120 240	136 225	13.3	7.5	14 279	11 007	10 211	57 069	10.1	2.46	9.9	25.4
Rockingham	13.9	7.2	5.5	50.6	245 845	277 359	12.8	6.4	30 644	17 932	10 952	115 033	10.0	2.54	8.9	23.5
Strafford	11.5	6.3	5.6	51.3	104 233	112 233	7.7	9.7	12 920	8 040	7 145	47 100	10.6	2.44	10.5	26.3
Sullivan	15.2	9.1	7.4	50.6	38 592	40 458	4.8	8.1	4 409	3 760	1 805	18 126	9.7	2.37	9.9	26.1
NEW JERSEY	11.9	7.0	6.5	51.3	7 747 750	8 414 350	8.6	4.5	1 038 937	664 523	-60 000	3 214 360	4.9	2.68	13.3	25.2
Atlantic	12.4	7.7	6.5	51.5	224 327	252 552	12.6	8.7	32 749	24 188	12 152	102 847	8.2	2.61	15.5	26.9
Bergen	12.7	7.5	7.7	51.8	825 380	884 118	7.1	2.4	90 828	66 352	-8 340	335 730	1.5	2.66	10.9	24.6
Burlington	12.4	7.2	6.6	50.9	395 066	423 394	7.2	6.0	48 149	33 913	10 819	166 318	7.7	2.62	12.0	24.4
Camden	11.9	6.6	6.2	51.8	502 824	508 932	1.2	0.9	64 312	43 183	-12 492	190 980	2.8	2.65	16.4	26.3
Cape May	15.7	11.3	10.2	51.4	95 089	102 326	7.6	-4.9	8 935	11 919	-2 581	40 812	-3.2	2.32	11.0	31.2
Cumberland	11.1	6.7	5.9	48.5	138 053	146 438	6.1	7.1	21 247	13 643	4 684	51 931	5.7	2.79	18.6	24.0
Essex	10.9	6.1	5.4	52.0	777 964	793 633	2.0	-1.2	108 429	60 910	-67 037	283 712	0.0	2.68	20.6	27.7
Gloucester	12.0	6.7	5.7	51.4	230 082	254 673	10.7	13.2	29 600	21 517	25 240	104 271	14.9	2.72	12.4	22.0
Hudson	9.8	5.7	4.7	50.5	553 099	608 975	10.1	4.2	78 249	39 649	-48 083	246 437	6.9	2.54	16.4	29.9
Hunterdon	14.4	7.3	5.4	50.1	107 852	121 989	13.1	5.2	12 239	7 442	4 097	47 169	8.0	2.62	7.0	22.0

1. No spouse present.

Table B. States and Counties — Population, Vital Statistics, Medicare, and Crime

STATE County	Persons in group quarters, 2010	Daytime population, 2006–2010 Number	Employ-ment/resi-dence ratio	Births, average 2006–2008 Total	Rate[1]	Deaths, average 2006–2008 Number	Rate[1]	Persons under 65 with no health insurance, 2009 Number	Percent	Medicare, 2011 Eligible for Medicare	Enrolled in Medicare Advantage	Enrolled in a Medicare prescription drug plan	Serious crimes known to police,[2] 2010 Total Number	Rate[3]
	32	33	34	35	36	37	38	39	40	41	42	43	44	45
NEBRASKA—Cont'd														
Platte	476	34 706	1.2	483	15.1	237	7.4	3 469	13.1	5 426	247	3 228	634	1 967
Polk	124	4 591	0.7	D	D	56	10.7	503	13.0	1 121	40	739	63	1 165
Red Willow	369	11 305	1.0	D	D	135	12.5	1 176	14.0	2 319	53	1 625	225	2 035
Richardson	155	7 511	0.8	D	D	131	15.6	959	15.5	2 132	68	1 392	75	897
Rock	30	1 578	0.9	D	D	19	12.5	276	24.3	178	D	164	4	262
Saline	1 038	14 488	1.1	D	D	148	10.6	1 557	13.7	2 334	96	1 549	256	1 803
Sarpy	1 277	128 047	0.7	2 554	17.4	689	4.7	12 660	9.2	16 999	2 163	5 838	2 829	1 781
Saunders	335	15 451	0.5	D	D	198	9.8	1 855	11.1	3 548	216	2 090	139	669
Scotts Bluff	847	37 029	1.0	559	15.3	434	11.9	4 592	15.4	7 323	833	4 340	1 236	3 419
Seward	1 296	14 819	0.8	D	D	167	10.0	1 398	10.2	2 864	105	1 881	NA	NA
Sheridan	113	4 988	0.8	D	D	78	14.3	790	19.7	1 257	151	685	65	1 189
Sherman	56	2 641	0.7	D	D	44	14.4	376	17.4	771	87	436	12	381
Sioux	0	1 097	0.6	D	D	D	D	247	24.1	230	41	137	0	0
Stanton	0	4 631	0.5	D	D	49	7.7	730	13.8	904	119	535	48	783
Thayer	156	5 504	1.1	D	D	76	14.6	475	13.2	1 351	44	951	82	1 568
Thomas	2	764	1.0	D	D	D	D	108	24.8	145	D	97	NA	NA
Thurston	58	7 073	1.1	D	D	76	10.6	1 150	18.0	943	71	609	NA	NA
Valley	49	4 402	1.1	D	D	59	13.8	499	16.5	1 035	36	690	NA	NA
Washington	535	18 513	0.8	D	D	161	8.1	1 422	8.5	3 252	409	1 700	141	697
Wayne	1 262	9 400	1.0	D	D	65	7.0	1 101	14.2	1 428	176	969	135	1 407
Webster	156	3 512	0.8	D	D	67	18.5	358	14.6	990	59	660	45	1 180
Wheeler	0	831	1.2	D	D	D	D	142	23.5	147	D	94	5	611
York	737	14 549	1.1	D	D	142	9.9	1 427	12.8	2 780	82	1 832	217	1 588
NEVADA	36 154	2 647 958	1.0	40 238	15.7	18 965	7.4	565 573	24.5	374 609	115 039	106 227	92 773	3 435
Churchill	366	24 484	1.0	D	D	255	10.2	4 780	22.7	4 554	366	1 739	595	2 392
Clark	21 992	1 908 764	1.0	30 085	16.5	12 789	7.0	417 112	24.9	248 286	87 967	63 881	71 098	3 644
Douglas	230	47 368	1.0	D	D	390	8.6	6 772	19.0	11 074	691	4 461	879	1 870
Elko	570	45 808	0.9	777	16.5	279	5.9	10 558	24.3	5 080	285	2 333	1 008	2 065
Esmeralda	1	889	1.0	D	D	13	18.5	144	32.7	227	33	84	3	383
Eureka	1	4 839	4.7	D	D	13	8.4	388	26.1	282	13	113	26	1 309
Humboldt	183	16 509	1.1	D	D	121	6.9	3 868	24.0	2 144	155	958	237	1 434
Lander	16	5 226	0.9	D	D	40	7.7	1 006	22.1	756	62	319	138	2 390
Lincoln	239	4 968	0.9	D	D	53	11.0	907	26.7	957	64	444	46	861
Lyon	358	44 698	0.7	D	D	439	8.4	9 909	22.2	10 450	1 948	3 501	856	1 647
Mineral	52	4 855	1.0	D	D	75	15.7	839	23.3	1 249	160	406	53	1 111
Nye	334	42 570	0.9	453	10.4	580	13.3	7 546	22.5	12 403	5 422	2 292	1 589	3 616
Pershing	1 681	6 786	1.0	D	D	47	7.4	1 737	31.1	905	75	438	144	2 132
Storey	5	NA	NA	D	D	20	4.7	835	22.0	837	112	273	55	1 372
Washoe	5 272	415 439	1.0	6 034	14.9	3 098	7.7	86 085	23.9	62 953	16 910	19 190	13 490	3 201
White Pine	1 229	9 761	1.0	D	D	97	10.6	1 747	22.7	1 709	91	840	169	1 685
Carson City	3 625	62 211	1.3	D	D	655	11.9	11 339	24.9	10 743	685	4 955	1 295	2 343
NEW HAMPSHIRE	40 104	1 273 087	0.9	14 076	10.7	10 210	7.8	133 464	12.0	228 953	13 873	102 075	30 980	2 353
Belknap	858	57 793	0.9	D	D	594	9.7	6 609	13.2	13 541	832	6 049	2 092	3 662
Carroll	437	46 921	1.0	D	D	465	9.8	5 696	15.3	12 006	814	5 385	1 222	3 033
Cheshire	4 627	74 369	0.9	D	D	665	8.6	8 042	12.7	14 506	878	6 763	NA	NA
Coos	1 467	32 662	0.9	D	D	399	12.3	3 677	14.8	8 606	289	4 591	NA	NA
Grafton	7 001	100 447	1.3	833	9.7	719	8.4	9 884	14.0	16 739	785	6 974	1 863	2 703
Hillsborough	7 759	383 940	0.9	4 903	12.2	2 904	7.2	40 995	11.8	61 092	4 042	28 265	9 594	2 541
Merrimack	6 335	147 720	1.0	1 553	10.5	1 177	7.9	14 507	11.6	25 997	1 489	10 977	2 827	2 298
Rockingham	2 498	281 515	0.9	2 907	9.8	1 992	6.7	27 052	10.6	48 073	3 379	20 004	6 043	2 152
Strafford	8 421	110 109	0.8	1 354	11.2	883	7.3	12 273	11.6	19 570	884	9 037	3 178	2 618
Sullivan	701	37 611	0.7	480	11.2	413	9.7	4 728	13.7	8 823	481	4 030	NA	NA
NEW JERSEY	186 876	8 482 907	0.9	114 598	13.3	70 015	8.1	1 071 584	14.4	1 368 007	181 500	586 563	210 097	2 390
Atlantic	6 046	282 749	1.1	3 641	13.4	2 521	9.3	35 494	15.5	46 504	4 150	21 678	11 236	4 093
Bergen	10 422	889 460	1.0	9 902	11.0	7 024	7.8	98 292	13.0	148 731	17 012	65 819	12 479	1 379
Burlington	13 214	428 211	0.9	5 237	11.7	3 606	8.1	41 817	11.1	73 383	12 146	26 471	8 349	1 861
Camden	7 414	479 490	0.9	7 277	14.1	4 551	8.8	64 622	14.6	80 791	14 021	35 150	19 434	3 783
Cape May	2 628	96 145	1.0	930	9.6	1 259	13.0	10 530	14.2	23 924	2 360	11 495	4 793	4 928
Cumberland	12 111	154 746	1.0	2 495	16.0	1 400	9.0	24 955	18.6	25 054	3 112	12 910	6 064	3 865
Essex	23 772	808 157	1.1	11 870	15.3	6 233	8.0	124 263	18.8	104 180	17 473	45 371	25 882	3 301
Gloucester	4 223	250 793	0.8	3 413	12.0	2 316	8.1	27 661	11.1	44 217	7 193	17 990	8 369	2 903
Hudson	9 378	582 058	0.9	9 638	16.1	4 042	6.8	121 003	23.0	73 347	12 499	36 345	15 559	2 453
Hunterdon	4 569	120 339	0.9	1 204	9.3	821	6.3	8 240	7.3	19 540	1 722	8 119	1 106	862

1. Per 1,000 estimated resident population.　　2. Data for serious crimes have not been adjusted for underreporting; this may affect comparability between geographic areas and over time.　　3. Per 100,000 population estimated by the FBI.

STATE County	Serious crimes known to police,[1] 2010 (cont.) Rate[2]		Education School enrollment and attainment, 2006-2010				Local government expenditures,[5] 2008-2009		Money income, 2006-2010	Households			Income and poverty, 2010			
			Enrollment[3]		Attainment[4] (percent)					Median income				Percent below poverty level		
	Violent	Property	Total	Percent private	High school graduate or less	Bachelor's degree or more	Total current expenditures (mil dol)	Current expenditures per student (dollars)	Per capita income[6] (dollars)	Dollars	Percent change, 2000 to 2006-2010 (constant 2010 dollars)	Percent with income of $200,000 or more	Median household income (dollars)	All persons	Children under 18 years	Children 5 to 17 years in families
	46	47	48	49	50	51	52	53	54	55	56	57	58	59	60	61
NEBRASKA—Cont'd																
Platte	136	1 830	8 300	24.7	44.7	18.9	48.4	10 054	23 358	49 523	-0.6	1.4	52 031	8.4	11.6	10.5
Polk	37	1 128	1 278	8.8	47.8	16.1	13.1	10 351	23 831	48 444	1.2	1.6	48 665	8.6	12.3	10.5
Red Willow	100	1 936	2 461	5.9	43.3	21.6	19.4	10 682	21 246	41 927	2.5	0.8	40 830	13.3	18.6	15.9
Richardson	48	849	1 778	15.1	58.3	15.2	15.0	11 132	20 516	35 165	-7.1	0.5	37 980	12.7	19.9	17.3
Rock	0	262	315	5.1	46.2	23.3	3.0	15 900	23 871	39 159	19.9	1.3	34 679	16.1	25.3	23.5
Saline	106	1 697	4 242	27.5	54.8	15.3	27.1	9 491	20 431	45 469	0.0	1.6	43 489	10.6	12.8	12.0
Sarpy	82	1 699	46 638	16.4	28.7	36.1	219.4	9 523	29 212	68 280	0.2	2.8	69 501	5.8	7.9	7.4
Saunders	96	573	5 259	24.5	43.8	23.7	28.2	10 019	26 898	57 699	8.0	2.6	55 070	8.4	10.1	8.7
Scotts Bluff	149	3 269	8 968	11.6	46.3	19.5	66.3	10 461	21 212	39 004	-3.8	1.3	40 088	15.8	24.8	22.0
Seward	NA	NA	5 030	37.8	38.3	27.3	31.8	12 309	26 386	55 877	3.3	2.6	55 507	7.8	9.1	7.9
Sheridan	238	951	1 187	13.1	47.0	22.6	11.7	12 198	20 066	33 608	-10.0	0.4	36 228	17.2	30.9	27.8
Sherman	63	317	619	0.8	56.3	15.7	5.5	11 280	20 900	38 631	6.5	1.2	37 852	12.9	20.5	18.3
Sioux	0	0	294	10.5	37.9	26.0	2.2	21 088	25 824	42 386	12.1	2.5	40 362	16.8	29.4	26.3
Stanton	33	751	1 537	14.1	44.7	12.0	4.4	9 744	23 018	47 713	2.7	1.4	50 352	8.9	14.1	13.6
Thayer	19	1 549	1 019	10.8	56.1	16.1	11.4	14 238	21 648	39 159	0.6	0.7	41 488	11.5	17.6	15.7
Thomas	NA	NA	156	2.6	38.6	16.2	1.8	15 820	31 499	48 250	39.6	2.7	35 901	15.7	22.4	21.6
Thurston	NA	NA	2 412	5.8	50.0	13.2	13.8	12 472	15 686	39 048	9.5	1.7	36 343	26.1	37.2	36.4
Valley	NA	NA	879	9.7	51.8	17.1	8.0	12 471	21 058	38 588	9.1	1.4	38 036	14.2	19.8	20.3
Washington	49	647	5 831	23.2	40.3	29.1	30.9	8 689	27 884	61 940	0.9	3.4	65 554	6.6	8.6	7.1
Wayne	104	1 303	3 857	3.1	39.6	28.0	22.2	14 704	19 681	45 000	9.8	0.3	43 061	14.2	15.3	13.1
Webster	184	997	789	5.4	55.4	12.7	6.2	9 721	18 906	38 015	0.0	0.7	37 647	12.0	17.0	15.6
Wheeler	0	611	113	7.1	37.3	23.5	2.0	18 796	20 614	37 222	9.8	1.2	34 357	19.9	34.8	30.6
York	44	1 544	3 236	23.2	45.5	21.5	19.5	10 870	25 412	47 689	1.5	2.5	46 247	9.8	15.4	14.3
NEVADA	661	2 775	640 986	10.2	45.4	21.8	3 629.8	8 422	27 589	55 726	-1.3	3.5	50 987	14.8	21.3	19.2
Churchill	273	2 118	6 316	8.7	48.1	18.2	40.3	9 253	22 997	51 597	-0.2	1.4	48 235	11.6	18.2	16.8
Clark	777	2 867	456 325	10.6	46.4	21.7	2 539.5	8 120	27 422	56 258	-0.4	3.5	51 427	15.0	22.2	20.1
Douglas	130	1 741	10 149	11.3	34.8	25.9	62.8	9 560	35 239	60 721	-7.5	5.9	57 176	9.3	14.5	12.8
Elko	227	1 837	12 830	6.1	48.6	15.8	102.1	10 644	26 879	67 038	9.4	1.8	66 210	8.3	11.2	10.0
Esmeralda	255	128	136	2.9	53.1	21.1	2.0	30 104	34 571	39 712	-5.5	7.1	40 929	14.4	17.1	16.4
Eureka	403	906	386	6.0	48.5	17.8	8.6	33 815	30 306	61 400	17.1	2.3	58 391	10.1	12.5	12.3
Humboldt	375	1 059	4 023	5.1	54.8	13.4	33.0	9 914	25 965	55 656	-6.8	3.1	59 960	9.9	14.5	13.3
Lander	745	1 645	1 296	6.6	56.8	12.9	11.3	9 478	25 287	66 525	14.0	1.3	70 176	10.0	12.4	11.9
Lincoln	131	730	1 378	11.5	46.3	15.8	16.1	16 196	18 148	44 695	10.4	0.0	42 637	13.4	18.3	17.0
Lyon	227	1 420	12 783	12.5	51.0	12.7	80.3	8 000	21 041	48 433	-6.0	0.7	47 108	11.4	15.9	15.2
Mineral	461	650	760	3.7	61.5	8.2	8.2	14 569	23 226	35 446	-14.9	0.0	39 940	15.4	24.6	22.0
Nye	760	2 856	8 437	6.3	56.7	10.5	67.4	10 618	22 687	41 181	-9.7	1.6	41 054	18.7	27.8	24.2
Pershing	578	1 555	1 474	1.2	66.0	12.4	9.6	13 517	17 519	56 491	9.7	0.6	44 684	18.5	22.0	20.9
Storey	125	1 247	792	4.3	36.4	13.9	6.4	14 825	31 079	61 525	6.8	3.6	57 763	8.7	13.6	12.5
Washoe	420	2 781	107 983	9.8	38.6	26.7	552.4	8 444	29 687	55 658	-4.1	4.1	60 839	15.3	20.4	17.4
White Pine	329	1 356	2 605	13.0	53.2	13.4	16.4	11 569	21 615	48 545	4.5	1.4	49 376	12.6	15.2	14.0
Carson City	293	2 050	13 314	7.4	44.1	21.6	73.4	9 105	27 568	52 067	-1.7	2.2	49 386	15.1	21.5	19.0
NEW HAMPSHIRE	167	2 186	334 796	21.9	38.8	32.9	2 361.8	11 987	31 422	63 277	1.0	4.5	60 917	8.6	10.8	9.0
Belknap	233	3 430	12 820	14.2	42.6	26.9	125.5	12 423	28 517	54 929	-0.5	2.7	53 851	9.5	13.0	11.2
Carroll	136	2 896	9 683	17.6	40.5	30.3	101.9	14 072	28 411	49 897	-1.5	3.8	48 236	10.3	16.6	14.0
Cheshire	NA	NA	21 549	18.8	43.7	29.8	128.5	14 166	27 045	53 828	0.3	3.0	49 126	11.3	13.4	11.3
Coos	NA	NA	6 499	10.5	56.5	16.1	61.9	13 797	22 976	41 534	-2.4	1.4	37 708	14.3	21.4	18.7
Grafton	158	2 545	24 306	30.6	40.1	35.3	179.8	15 435	28 170	53 075	-0.1	4.1	50 834	11.6	13.4	10.9
Hillsborough	230	2 311	103 096	25.1	37.4	34.5	667.1	11 154	33 108	69 321	2.5	5.2	67 650	7.6	10.5	8.8
Merrimack	129	2 169	37 287	25.5	37.9	32.7	281.7	11 564	30 544	63 012	2.6	4.0	60 932	9.5	10.8	8.8
Rockingham	118	2 034	74 310	20.7	34.2	36.6	554.9	11 290	35 889	75 825	3.0	6.1	73 402	5.7	6.7	5.6
Strafford	220	2 398	35 727	14.5	40.3	30.0	174.2	11 902	28 059	57 809	1.9	3.1	52 527	11.1	12.2	10.1
Sullivan	NA	NA	9 519	17.3	48.7	25.9	86.3	13 237	26 322	50 689	-2.2	2.3	50 549	11.2	15.4	12.7
NEW JERSEY	308	2 082	2 281 944	20.6	42.5	34.6	22 396.6	16 297	34 858	69 811	0.0	8.2	67 719	10.2	14.3	13.1
Atlantic	531	3 561	72 440	13.4	50.8	23.6	756.3	16 212	27 247	54 766	-1.6	3.4	51 457	13.6	19.3	16.4
Bergen	102	1 277	227 371	24.4	34.5	44.5	2 209.9	16 501	42 006	81 708	-1.1	12.1	77 059	6.9	7.8	7.3
Burlington	145	1 715	118 333	18.6	39.4	33.5	1 181.2	16 101	34 802	76 258	2.8	6.6	73 788	5.7	7.8	7.1
Camden	598	3 185	137 925	18.6	47.1	27.9	1 366.0	16 271	29 478	60 976	0.1	4.6	56 939	12.3	18.5	17.1
Cape May	251	4 677	19 471	16.7	48.4	26.4	247.0	18 073	33 571	54 292	3.1	3.8	51 585	11.4	18.6	16.6
Cumberland	504	3 361	37 687	11.0	64.0	13.3	438.0	16 383	21 883	50 651	2.2	2.0	49 964	17.0	26.0	24.1
Essex	670	2 631	214 117	19.7	47.0	31.6	2 320.6	18 567	31 535	55 155	-3.1	8.1	52 288	16.4	22.8	20.8
Gloucester	172	2 731	79 794	17.4	45.9	26.9	710.4	14 270	31 210	72 664	5.7	5.0	70 012	6.8	8.7	7.9
Hudson	452	2 001	148 307	20.6	46.7	34.6	1 403.6	17 615	31 024	55 275	8.3	6.1	53 547	16.5	24.4	25.3
Hunterdon	49	813	34 158	18.7	29.3	47.5	400.6	17 482	48 489	100 980	-0.2	17.5	97 532	4.0	4.2	3.5

1. Data for serious crimes have not been adjusted for underreporting; this may affect comparability between geographic areas and over time. 2. Per 100,000 population estimated by the FBI. 3. All persons 3 years old and over enrolled in nursery school through college. 4. Persons 25 years old and over. 5. Elementary and secondary education expenditures. 6. Based on population estimated by the American Community Survey, 2006-2010.

Table B. States and Counties — **Personal Income**

| | Personal income, 2009 | | | | | | | | | | | | |
STATE County	Total (mil dol)	Percent change, 2008–2009	Per capita[1] Dollars	Rank	Wages and salaries[2] (mil dol)	Proprietors' income (mil dol)	Dividends, interest, and rent (mil dol)	Transfer payments (mil dol) Total	Government payments to individuals Total	Social Security	Medical payments	Income mainte-nance	Unemploy-ment insurance
	62	63	64	65	66	67	68	69	70	71	72	73	74
NEBRASKA—Cont'd													
Platte	1 154	-0.1	35 494	955	861	137	203	157	151	76	47	12	5
Polk	237	3.8	46 588	154	60	83	32	35	34	16	14	2	1
Red Willow	385	-3.6	36 108	872	214	54	78	84	82	31	35	5	2
Richardson	299	3.7	36 857	764	94	54	55	70	69	27	30	4	2
Rock	43	-10.9	28 757	2 245	20	7	10	8	8	2	4	0	0
Saline	464	-2.9	33 484	1 260	316	52	67	83	80	32	32	5	2
Sarpy	5 964	1.9	38 851	552	3 590	124	675	654	627	238	205	45	23
Saunders	798	0.5	39 765	467	197	81	108	126	122	49	53	6	3
Scotts Bluff	1 287	-0.1	34 915	1 034	793	179	188	277	270	101	112	27	7
Seward	624	-1.6	37 892	657	253	75	93	93	90	40	34	4	2
Sheridan	169	-4.4	32 027	1 523	61	20	37	41	40	16	16	3	1
Sherman	95	-0.6	32 811	1 364	29	20	17	24	24	10	10	1	0
Sioux	46	2.1	35 737	924	12	9	8	5	5	3	1	0	0
Stanton	215	7.8	34 049	1 167	85	32	28	26	25	12	8	2	1
Thayer	205	-7.9	40 959	385	94	43	41	44	43	18	20	2	1
Thomas	19	-5.4	34 211	1 141	12	0	6	4	4	2	1	0	0
Thurston	233	2.4	31 834	1 571	136	46	22	55	54	12	26	11	2
Valley	161	1.3	39 215	515	70	39	27	33	32	13	15	2	1
Washington	822	-0.7	41 712	349	472	49	122	111	107	47	43	5	3
Wayne	301	-1.0	32 554	1 410	158	47	49	51	50	19	19	3	1
Webster	130	-3.9	38 033	634	38	26	22	32	32	13	14	2	0
Wheeler	25	-1.7	32 807	1 365	15	4	6	4	4	2	2	0	0
York	532	-0.2	38 462	585	301	106	91	97	95	39	41	5	2
NEVADA	99 566	-4.9	37 670	X	64 107	6 734	21 539	15 083	14 603	5 093	5 350	1 272	1 770
Churchill	947	-3.4	38 032	635	512	128	140	178	174	59	70	14	14
Clark	69 855	-5.3	36 711	784	46 708	4 785	14 045	10 488	10 142	3 391	3 734	961	1 288
Douglas	2 504	-3.8	55 080	55	899	123	919	306	298	155	82	13	30
Elko	1 730	-0.2	36 122	870	1 081	35	233	198	190	67	65	18	20
Esmeralda	31	-10.0	49 658	109	11	3	6	6	6	3	2	0	0
Eureka	64	-2.4	37 376	704	451	5	9	8	8	4	3	0	1
Humboldt	605	2.3	33 142	1 311	434	41	89	84	81	29	31	7	7
Lander	228	8.1	44 272	227	215	14	25	30	29	10	12	2	3
Lincoln	114	-3.2	23 787	2 973	69	5	21	33	32	12	14	2	2
Lyon	1 437	-2.1	27 300	2 517	542	49	268	341	331	141	102	21	41
Mineral	158	-1.8	33 827	1 197	84	12	25	47	46	15	21	4	2
Nye	1 400	-3.5	31 647	1 614	615	54	281	406	398	178	136	27	29
Pershing	152	-3.4	24 224	2 945	90	7	23	35	33	12	13	3	3
Storey	143	-4.7	32 245	1 474	148	5	34	23	22	14	2	1	3
Washoe	17 629	-5.1	42 499	294	10 378	1 289	4 840	2 422	2 346	845	860	169	285
White Pine	349	-3.1	37 989	643	219	13	50	62	61	23	25	4	4
Carson City	2 219	-4.2	40 218	437	1 649	166	533	416	406	137	177	26	37
NEW HAMPSHIRE	56 488	-2.3	42 646	X	34 549	4 888	8 962	8 295	8 053	3 262	3 335	509	388
Belknap	2 433	-1.3	39 656	473	1 226	230	486	464	453	196	180	29	21
Carroll	2 013	-2.5	42 067	326	812	221	576	388	380	167	160	20	13
Cheshire	2 973	-1.7	38 591	570	1 653	271	532	513	499	209	208	30	18
Coos	1 095	-0.5	34 790	1 046	554	95	161	335	329	118	155	25	13
Grafton	3 803	-1.4	44 074	234	3 039	368	778	606	590	233	265	33	17
Hillsborough	17 948	-2.7	44 217	230	12 343	1 364	2 405	2 357	2 283	879	943	169	130
Merrimack	6 050	-0.9	40 582	413	4 004	490	978	938	911	371	372	58	44
Rockingham	14 279	-3.1	47 713	138	7 727	1 459	2 180	1 635	1 580	695	626	68	82
Strafford	4 321	-1.5	34 966	1 027	2 553	242	586	740	717	266	293	56	42
Sullivan	1 571	-1.4	36 793	774	639	149	281	318	311	127	133	21	8
NEW JERSEY	435 216	-2.9	49 980	X	264 854	33 848	73 980	64 465	62 879	20 626	26 626	4 741	6 781
Atlantic	10 639	-1.5	39 156	519	7 255	1 182	1 619	2 313	2 264	679	967	205	267
Bergen	57 643	-5.5	64 388	20	31 682	5 836	12 844	6 018	5 854	2 311	2 302	244	618
Burlington	20 751	-0.8	46 516	158	12 992	1 239	3 029	3 134	3 053	1 138	1 179	156	337
Camden	21 379	-0.1	41 282	373	12 101	1 296	2 880	4 327	4 233	1 182	1 918	419	441
Cape May	4 452	0.2	46 329	160	1 876	287	967	1 037	1 020	364	445	50	106
Cumberland	5 028	1.1	31 877	1 556	3 286	266	620	1 370	1 341	368	605	148	146
Essex	38 751	-2.7	50 349	94	26 609	3 394	6 619	6 601	6 461	1 500	3 116	851	629
Gloucester	11 478	1.1	39 591	478	5 499	468	1 332	1 957	1 904	670	719	119	243
Hudson	25 943	-0.3	43 388	261	19 466	1 698	2 829	4 451	4 342	914	2 066	576	520
Hunterdon	8 497	-4.8	65 344	19	3 464	846	1 484	744	720	314	261	18	80

1. Based on the resident population estimated as of July 1 of the year shown.   2. Includes supplements to wages and salaries.

Table B. States and Counties — **Earnings, Social Security, and Housing**

STATE County	Earnings, 2009									Social Security beneficiaries, December 2010			Housing units, 2010	
			Goods-related[1]		Service-related and health							Supplemental Security Income recipients, December 2010		
	Total (mil dol)	Farm	Total	Manu-facturing	Information and professional and technical services	Retail trade	Finance, insurance, and real estate	Health care and social services	Govern-ment	Number	Rate[2]		Total	Percent change, 2000–2010
	75	76	77	78	79	80	81	82	83	84	85	86	87	88
NEBRASKA—Cont'd														
Platte	998	8.4	38.5	32.3	3.7	5.6	3.6	7.0	14.3	5 960	185	308	13 378	4.5
Polk	142	54.3	D	0.4	D	3.7	D	4.1	15.4	1 235	228	52	2 731	0.5
Red Willow	268	12.5	12.9	8.9	4.4	9.0	5.4	D	19.2	2 470	223	169	5 267	-0.2
Richardson	149	29.3	8.4	3.8	3.7	6.9	3.3	10.1	17.6	2 325	278	153	4 393	-3.7
Rock	26	32.0	D	D	D	3.6	D	D	33.0	170	111	0	912	-2.5
Saline	368	11.3	42.2	41.4	D	4.2	3.0	D	16.9	2 545	179	133	5 762	2.7
Sarpy	3 714	0.6	10.9	4.1	10.5	5.3	7.2	4.7	31.9	18 460	116	1 124	61 938	37.7
Saunders	278	22.9	D	6.7	D	6.4	4.8	D	22.4	3 800	183	189	9 221	11.6
Scotts Bluff	972	3.1	D	4.9	4.5	7.7	7.9	17.4	16.6	8 140	220	803	16 408	1.8
Seward	328	18.3	21.3	16.7	3.4	4.6	4.5	D	18.1	2 990	179	136	6 875	7.0
Sheridan	81	19.0	D	1.6	D	7.7	D	2.5	34.9	1 395	255	70	2 936	-2.6
Sherman	49	36.4	2.6	1.1	D	4.7	3.7	5.6	23.4	865	274	32	1 941	5.5
Sioux	21	68.4	D	1.0	D	1.7	D	0.0	17.4	265	202	0	815	4.5
Stanton	116	23.9	D	D	D	0.7	1.9	D	11.6	1 060	173	32	2 633	7.4
Thayer	137	25.0	D	17.9	D	3.9	4.5	D	21.0	1 455	278	78	2 731	-3.4
Thomas	12	5.1	D	D	D	13.5	D	0.0	30.7	160	247	0	402	-9.9
Thurston	182	23.9	8.7	5.4	5.7	2.2	D	6.4	40.9	1 105	159	197	2 408	-2.4
Valley	109	34.2	D	4.1	D	5.0	3.7	3.0	27.5	1 105	259	59	2 273	0.0
Washington	521	6.6	28.2	16.9	6.3	8.7	3.4	D	24.6	3 545	175	141	8 301	12.1
Wayne	205	20.5	16.7	14.7	D	3.7	6.9	8.2	27.3	1 545	161	77	3 776	3.1
Webster	64	37.1	D	D	D	4.3	4.7	5.4	22.4	1 110	291	88	1 912	-3.0
Wheeler	19	63.8	D	D	0.3	D	D	0.0	13.5	160	196	0	576	2.7
York	406	20.7	D	12.5	4.0	6.7	5.1	D	14.9	3 015	221	167	6 231	1.0
NEVADA	70 840	0.2	15.2	3.9	8.6	6.7	7.0	8.5	17.4	408 113	151	41 269	1 173 814	41.9
Churchill	640	0.8	D	2.9	6.2	6.2	5.3	9.5	33.7	5 000	201	432	10 826	11.2
Clark	51 494	0.0	13.6	2.9	8.6	6.7	7.1	8.2	16.1	271 030	139	30 893	840 343	50.1
Douglas	1 022	0.4	D	12.3	7.6	7.4	5.9	7.2	14.7	11 795	251	335	23 671	24.5
Elko	1 116	0.9	24.4	1.1	4.0	7.1	2.4	6.7	21.0	5 615	115	488	19 566	6.0
Esmeralda	14	17.4	D	D	3.7	D	0.7	0.0	30.6	255	326	20	850	2.0
Eureka	456	1.7	D	0.0	D	0.2	D	D	2.6	305	153	12	1 076	5.0
Humboldt	476	4.6	40.6	3.1	D	6.8	1.2	2.7	19.1	2 425	147	218	7 123	2.4
Lander	230	4.0	D	D	D	2.9	D	0.6	14.3	815	141	80	2 575	-7.4
Lincoln	74	1.8	D	D	24.3	6.6	2.7	2.2	48.4	1 035	194	71	2 730	25.3
Lyon	590	4.0	27.5	20.5	3.9	12.9	2.0	D	22.0	11 470	221	736	22 547	57.9
Mineral	96	0.8	D	D	D	4.0	5.0	D	35.4	1 350	283	140	2 830	-1.3
Nye	669	2.0	16.6	0.9	22.6	7.1	2.3	5.0	20.1	13 940	317	940	22 350	40.1
Pershing	98	9.9	28.2	2.4	1.5	5.3	1.0	D	44.4	985	146	83	2 464	3.1
Storey	153	0.0	D	14.2	D	D	D	D	10.5	930	232	43	1 990	24.7
Washoe	11 666	0.0	15.3	7.0	9.6	6.8	9.0	11.5	17.6	67 910	161	5 828	184 841	28.4
White Pine	232	1.4	D	0.5	D	4.6	1.9	D	43.1	1 850	184	144	4 498	1.3
Carson City	1 815	0.0	D	8.6	6.6	6.8	4.6	9.7	41.8	11 400	206	806	23 534	10.6
NEW HAMPSHIRE	39 437	0.1	19.6	13.2	11.7	8.6	8.1	13.2	13.7	254 752	194	17 910	614 754	12.4
Belknap	1 456	0.1	20.3	12.5	8.0	11.6	4.1	13.6	16.2	15 245	254	988	37 386	16.4
Carroll	1 032	-0.1	D	D	7.8	12.6	4.9	12.9	14.8	13 165	275	696	39 813	14.6
Cheshire	1 924	0.1	D	D	5.4	9.4	8.5	14.0	14.1	16 365	212	1 085	34 773	9.1
Coos	649	0.1	D	9.6	2.9	10.2	3.5	17.1	21.8	9 820	297	885	21 321	8.6
Grafton	3 407	0.3	14.1	10.4	9.0	7.8	3.1	24.4	11.4	18 200	204	961	51 120	16.9
Hillsborough	13 707	0.0	22.1	16.7	15.8	7.9	9.8	11.8	11.1	68 120	170	6 090	166 053	10.7
Merrimack	4 493	0.2	14.6	8.5	8.2	8.0	7.8	15.0	22.6	29 135	199	2 285	63 541	13.0
Rockingham	9 186	0.1	19.7	11.7	13.1	9.0	7.4	9.9	10.0	52 540	178	2 177	126 709	12.1
Strafford	2 795	0.1	15.9	10.8	7.4	8.1	13.3	14.2	22.6	22 095	179	1 840	51 697	13.5
Sullivan	788	0.2	D	26.1	6.7	10.0	5.5	9.6	16.4	10 065	230	903	22 341	10.8
NEW JERSEY	298 702	0.1	13.8	8.8	15.7	6.0	10.0	11.3	16.5	1 472 335	167	168 423	3 553 562	7.3
Atlantic	8 437	0.9	D	2.0	6.7	7.6	3.7	13.0	21.2	51 835	189	6 246	126 647	11.0
Bergen	37 517	0.0	12.8	8.6	15.9	6.0	8.1	14.7	9.6	153 595	170	11 112	352 388	3.7
Burlington	14 231	0.2	15.6	10.2	11.8	6.9	11.1	11.2	19.0	80 750	180	5 275	175 615	8.9
Camden	13 397	0.1	13.9	8.4	12.2	6.6	5.1	17.4	19.7	89 255	174	15 049	204 943	2.9
Cape May	2 163	0.3	D	1.4	6.0	10.2	6.7	11.8	30.2	26 685	274	1 774	98 309	8.0
Cumberland	3 552	2.1	21.9	15.5	4.0	7.5	2.9	13.2	29.9	28 655	183	5 212	55 834	5.6
Essex	30 003	0.0	10.7	7.5	14.5	4.1	10.7	11.4	22.9	111 085	142	27 188	312 954	4.0
Gloucester	5 967	0.8	23.6	14.3	8.1	10.0	2.9	10.5	20.2	49 930	173	4 183	109 796	14.9
Hudson	21 164	0.0	D	2.8	12.9	4.6	31.9	6.7	16.3	76 470	121	21 876	270 335	12.4
Hunterdon	4 311	0.0	D	4.5	20.4	12.1	10.7	10.1	15.9	20 885	163	767	49 487	9.9

1. Includes mining, construction, and manufacturing. 2. Per 1,000 resident population enumerated in the 2010 census.

Table B. States and Counties — Housing, Labor Force, and Employment

STATE County	Housing units, 2006–2010 Occupied units — Total	Owner-occupied Percent	Median value[1]	Median owner cost as a percent of income — With a mortgage	Without a mortgage	Renter-occupied Median rent[2]	Median rent as a percent of income	Sub-standard units[3] (percent)	Civilian labor force, 2010 — Total	Percent change, 2009–2010	Unemployment — Total	Rate[4]	Civilian employment,[5] 2006–2010 — Total	Percent — Management, business, science and arts	Construction, production, and maintenance occupations
	89	90	91	92	93	94	95	96	97	98	99	100	101	102	103
NEBRASKA—Cont'd															
Platte	12 378	73.8	108 100	20.3	10.3	541	23.3	2.4	18 213	-0.4	730	4.0	16 843	26.7	35.3
Polk	2 230	75.1	86 400	21.4	13.6	538	21.3	1.5	2 975	-1.9	114	3.8	2 700	32.9	32.5
Red Willow	4 658	69.6	77 300	19.0	13.9	539	23.3	0.6	5 990	-1.2	221	3.7	5 736	26.0	27.9
Richardson	3 862	76.3	63 700	19.4	10.9	501	25.4	1.6	4 159	-1.0	268	6.4	3 942	33.3	29.3
Rock	713	85.1	57 300	18.3	11.9	600	20.7	2.9	898	3.7	26	2.9	940	42.2	23.4
Saline	5 020	66.8	95 100	20.1	12.7	622	25.1	1.7	8 346	0.9	326	3.9	6 822	30.6	33.8
Sarpy	56 512	72.4	158 600	22.7	11.7	813	25.8	1.5	78 286	-0.5	3 795	4.8	79 488	40.4	16.4
Saunders	7 985	82.8	137 500	21.5	13.3	697	24.1	1.1	10 608	-2.6	528	5.0	10 999	32.4	28.5
Scotts Bluff	14 902	65.5	95 900	22.5	14.5	593	28.5	3.5	19 142	-1.7	1 028	5.4	17 833	30.6	24.0
Seward	6 394	73.1	136 400	21.3	11.5	535	22.7	0.2	8 667	-3.5	345	4.0	8 814	35.6	27.1
Sheridan	2 434	69.9	63 300	22.0	14.9	481	22.1	4.3	3 058	-1.2	97	3.2	2 655	39.8	22.7
Sherman	1 362	84.7	53 200	22.0	13.5	469	26.2	1.2	1 964	-1.3	65	3.3	1 603	28.3	33.6
Sioux	598	71.7	109 300	27.7	14.0	395	16.1	1.3	737	0.3	31	4.2	685	43.4	30.1
Stanton	2 419	78.0	87 800	22.4	10.0	615	19.2	2.1	3 475	-0.5	146	4.2	3 354	25.5	34.9
Thayer	2 247	82.6	61 900	20.0	13.0	426	20.0	0.4	2 808	1.2	104	3.7	2 630	36.1	29.4
Thomas	332	77.1	71 100	27.3	12.3	588	16.8	4.5	345	-1.4	18	5.2	424	40.6	26.7
Thurston	2 054	65.6	67 100	17.8	12.1	454	23.4	10.1	3 129	0.0	287	9.2	2 568	35.1	24.5
Valley	1 913	77.4	72 900	18.4	12.5	370	28.3	0.2	2 547	-0.5	93	3.7	2 133	36.2	27.6
Washington	7 431	81.5	167 200	22.7	12.6	673	26.9	0.7	10 855	-2.9	524	4.8	10 348	39.1	23.9
Wayne	3 316	70.0	102 400	20.2	11.9	492	23.9	1.2	5 253	2.4	205	3.9	5 048	31.2	23.9
Webster	1 478	75.7	58 700	18.5	14.0	419	21.5	0.7	1 785	-1.3	77	4.3	1 534	31.0	30.2
Wheeler	336	68.2	66 100	20.9	10.0	455	18.8	0.0	451	-0.7	19	4.2	506	52.6	26.7
York	5 771	76.2	92 300	19.7	11.8	527	22.4	1.5	7 127	0.8	343	4.8	7 326	31.8	25.0
NEVADA	979 621	60.1	254 200	28.9	11.7	998	30.7	4.4	1 385 729	2.3	190 420	13.7	1 254 163	27.4	20.6
Churchill	8 801	64.5	188 300	23.7	12.3	782	25.3	4.0	13 153	-3.9	1 526	11.6	10 288	25.7	27.5
Clark	695 701	58.2	257 300	29.5	11.5	1 036	30.9	4.8	969 098	-1.4	147 501	15.2	907 510	26.4	19.4
Douglas	19 183	76.2	375 800	29.7	12.9	1 030	31.0	2.1	22 062	-2.6	3 506	15.9	22 192	32.7	19.7
Elko	17 324	71.1	178 200	20.8	10.0	753	21.7	4.8	27 738	-0.3	2 311	8.3	24 256	25.1	33.6
Esmeralda	507	64.7	77 300	22.5	10.0	413	19.9	1.4	494	0.0	40	8.1	383	22.2	46.5
Eureka	724	73.1	87 400	17.1	10.0	588	13.3	5.1	911	2.9	83	9.1	859	44.1	41.6
Humboldt	6 087	72.4	138 100	21.3	10.0	617	22.0	4.6	8 849	2.3	850	9.6	7 479	24.4	41.9
Lander	1 945	72.1	103 400	15.0	10.0	723	23.9	3.7	4 099	1.3	309	7.5	2 438	19.5	44.0
Lincoln	1 759	71.5	151 900	21.5	10.5	712	25.9	1.4	1 703	-0.5	228	13.4	1 834	35.8	22.1
Lyon	17 766	72.2	185 000	28.6	12.1	935	30.5	2.8	22 815	-2.2	4 485	19.7	20 271	23.3	30.9
Mineral	2 331	78.1	114 200	22.3	16.3	604	23.1	0.7	2 323	-2.2	375	16.1	1 968	26.4	26.0
Nye	17 943	71.8	161 700	26.6	13.2	852	34.5	2.5	17 786	-1.8	3 194	18.0	14 771	21.0	31.5
Pershing	1 980	70.5	134 500	19.0	12.7	627	23.7	5.9	2 585	-1.5	316	12.2	2 082	29.6	33.7
Storey	1 826	90.2	239 200	27.2	11.6	686	23.6	2.1	2 456	-0.9	355	14.5	1 961	26.6	33.3
Washoe	160 797	60.2	295 700	28.8	12.6	911	30.9	4.1	220 539	-1.6	31 189	14.1	206 736	31.9	20.9
White Pine	3 480	76.6	117 500	19.3	11.0	730	30.0	0.9	5 069	1.6	481	9.5	4 122	26.8	27.5
Carson City	21 467	62.3	270 500	26.4	11.8	885	29.9	2.8	28 632	-2.3	4 024	14.1	25 013	31.2	21.1
NEW HAMPSHIRE	513 804	72.6	253 200	26.8	16.3	933	29.4	1.8	739 349	-0.8	45 364	6.1	695 283	38.4	20.9
Belknap	24 942	76.9	232 300	29.4	14.9	817	27.8	1.5	32 089	-1.6	2 134	6.7	30 884	32.0	23.9
Carroll	19 955	80.6	240 800	26.7	14.1	822	32.9	2.0	25 733	0.4	1 511	5.9	23 749	30.9	22.2
Cheshire	30 087	71.5	201 800	26.4	17.1	906	29.5	2.0	41 674	-1.0	2 425	5.8	40 317	33.5	24.6
Coos	14 915	71.5	131 400	25.7	15.9	594	29.5	2.2	16 185	-0.5	1 272	7.9	15 681	28.0	29.8
Grafton	34 312	70.8	210 600	24.6	15.4	873	28.7	1.9	48 967	0.7	2 415	4.9	45 949	39.0	20.4
Hillsborough	153 120	69.0	269 900	26.7	16.4	1 007	29.3	2.0	229 175	0.1	14 442	6.3	213 942	40.6	19.9
Merrimack	56 948	72.0	243 600	26.8	17.2	902	29.8	2.2	81 514	-0.1	4 490	5.5	77 135	40.1	21.4
Rockingham	114 722	78.6	306 800	27.0	16.8	1 026	29.0	1.2	176 035	1.0	11 047	6.3	159 707	40.7	19.0
Strafford	46 576	67.2	229 100	26.8	17.2	885	30.8	2.0	69 970	0.8	4 073	5.8	64 878	36.1	19.6
Sullivan	18 227	73.7	181 800	25.4	16.2	760	28.0	2.1	22 610	-0.5	1 286	5.7	23 041	32.8	27.1
NEW JERSEY	3 176 069	66.9	357 000	28.5	18.7	1 092	30.9	3.7	4 554 076	0.6	437 436	9.6	4 230 560	39.4	18.3
Atlantic	101 645	70.7	264 400	30.9	19.1	955	33.1	2.8	136 064	-0.3	16 930	12.4	130 065	28.1	16.9
Bergen	333 874	67.5	482 300	29.5	19.4	1 236	29.3	2.5	477 342	-0.7	38 654	8.1	447 824	45.2	14.1
Burlington	165 284	79.0	270 200	26.7	17.3	1 095	31.2	1.3	238 898	-1.2	21 522	9.0	220 207	40.9	16.9
Camden	190 670	69.7	223 700	27.2	18.5	897	32.6	2.2	268 338	-1.1	28 354	10.6	246 454	36.9	18.7
Cape May	45 420	74.3	337 300	29.8	17.8	973	33.0	1.7	58 308	0.7	6 939	11.9	44 311	33.5	20.5
Cumberland	50 825	67.4	175 500	26.8	16.4	869	35.1	3.8	70 675	-0.5	9 430	13.3	64 292	25.7	28.2
Essex	277 426	47.2	395 700	31.1	19.5	977	31.0	5.4	362 780	-1.4	39 950	11.0	358 120	36.3	19.5
Gloucester	102 632	80.9	236 900	26.8	18.7	964	32.5	1.2	158 153	-0.5	15 805	10.0	142 108	38.3	19.5
Hudson	237 726	34.3	383 900	31.6	20.3	1 071	28.7	7.6	297 664	-0.4	32 079	10.8	319 965	36.1	20.4
Hunterdon	47 182	85.6	446 700	27.6	16.7	1 154	31.8	1.5	71 983	-0.8	5 054	7.0	64 890	49.1	12.8

1. Specified owner-occupied units.   2. Specified renter-occupied units. A value of 10.0 represents 10 percent or less.   3. Overcrowded or lacking complete plumbing facilities.   4. Percent of civilian labor force.   5. Persons 16 years old and over.

STATE County	Private nonfarm establishments, employment and payroll, 2009									Agriculture, 2007			
	Number of establishments	Employment						Annual payroll		Farms			Farm operators whose principal occupation is farming (percent)
		Total	Health care and social assistance	Manufacturing	Retail trade	Finance and insurance	Professional, scientific, and technical services	Total (mil dol)	Average per employee (dollars)	Number	Percent with:		
											Fewer than 50 acres	500 acres or more	
	104	105	106	107	108	109	110	111	112	113	114	115	116
NEBRASKA—Cont'd													
Platte	1 019	15 068	1 461	5 348	2 208	505	545	488	32 387	882	18.6	33.7	66.4
Polk	149	841	248	22	132	66	D	22	25 653	505	17.0	39.2	68.3
Red Willow	426	3 907	509	D	989	209	153	101	25 896	386	18.1	47.2	56.2
Richardson	262	1 818	396	212	339	84	60	42	23 231	707	14.6	23.8	48.8
Rock	45	D	D	D	40	D	D	D	D	237	9.3	62.9	66.2
Saline	302	6 183	877	2 782	715	147	45	198	31 969	702	18.8	28.6	57.0
Sarpy	3 075	39 910	3 762	2 527	6 941	2 118	2 951	1 382	34 634	360	50.6	19.4	50.3
Saunders	492	3 515	609	409	578	194	122	95	27 045	1 131	27.4	23.7	56.1
Scotts Bluff	1 141	13 268	2 789	1 078	2 571	633	378	375	28 279	730	21.6	23.4	57.1
Seward	445	5 246	735	899	619	221	91	137	26 082	893	29.5	25.9	49.2
Sheridan	167	1 109	D	D	311	123	46	21	18 849	574	13.4	56.4	61.7
Sherman	83	531	D	D	71	D	D	12	22 578	411	16.3	38.0	56.9
Sioux	20	50	0	0	D	D	D	1	20 980	366	3.3	66.7	72.4
Stanton	119	D	D	D	135	D	D	D	D	636	17.5	23.7	55.5
Thayer	207	1 709	D	393	229	126	D	51	29 776	483	10.8	46.6	61.7
Thomas	25	179	0	D	D	D	D	7	37 307	103	9.7	70.9	67.0
Thurston	107	1 324	320	D	170	49	D	43	32 252	372	20.2	34.1	58.9
Valley	179	1 336	364	69	318	77	67	34	25 460	391	14.6	48.1	71.6
Washington	531	6 219	723	904	954	269	229	234	37 680	762	39.8	19.2	50.5
Wayne	253	2 835	D	D	360	242	105	69	24 365	573	20.1	32.3	64.4
Webster	83	632	194	D	148	26	D	14	21 832	430	13.3	42.3	57.4
Wheeler	18	104	0	D	D	D	0	2	14 644	205	7.3	64.9	66.8
York	511	5 888	1 023	833	1 040	D	155	167	28 420	549	16.4	45.9	73.4
NEVADA	59 785	1 042 166	97 368	42 775	131 285	37 257	52 666	39 137	37 554	3 131	48.8	21.2	52.7
Churchill	536	5 577	843	388	947	191	D	177	31 757	529	56.9	8.1	49.9
Clark	39 755	762 726	66 048	20 784	94 865	28 107	38 325	28 432	37 276	193	74.6	5.2	40.4
Douglas	1 565	15 961	1 251	1 753	1 847	456	872	540	33 803	179	60.3	13.4	49.2
Elko	1 080	18 869	1 290	236	2 395	371	501	867	45 960	456	32.0	36.2	59.6
Esmeralda	18	D	D	0	D	D	0	D	D	19	26.3	42.1	78.9
Eureka	38	1 264	D	D	31	D	5	88	69 613	86	12.8	48.8	75.6
Humboldt	394	6 021	550	282	1 002	D	D	267	44 363	254	37.0	39.8	57.1
Lander	95	1 337	D	D	211	D	D	75	55 724	84	27.4	50.0	54.8
Lincoln	94	591	D	0	209	D	24	13	22 531	98	35.7	17.3	62.2
Lyon	767	9 309	633	1 914	1 402	167	477	279	29 994	325	55.7	17.2	53.5
Mineral	65	D	D	D	D	29	16	D	D	84	69.0	2.4	66.7
Nye	689	7 122	789	256	1 480	163	166	223	31 253	173	50.9	19.1	49.1
Pershing	81	1 071	D	D	D	D	D	38	35 020	135	19.3	44.4	68.9
Storey	91	352	D	D	47	D	D	8	21 435	5	80.0	0.0	0.0
Washoe	12 015	173 120	21 429	13 719	22 588	6 189	10 027	6 681	38 590	393	67.4	6.1	38.2
White Pine	202	2 467	300	D	407	57	38	102	41 503	97	26.8	36.1	50.5
Carson City	2 178	22 258	3 549	3 101	3 627	1 227	1 453	833	37 425	21	66.7	9.5	42.9
NEW HAMPSHIRE	37 873	568 043	84 913	71 259	97 524	25 617	31 241	23 628	41 596	4 166	51.8	3.8	46.3
Belknap	1 870	21 721	3 740	2 680	5 657	697	673	740	34 053	270	51.9	2.2	46.7
Carroll	1 887	17 471	2 788	832	3 975	505	482	493	28 246	274	48.9	4.0	51.8
Cheshire	1 968	29 405	4 136	5 176	5 981	1 692	645	1 075	36 572	419	49.4	5.0	47.5
Coos	915	9 784	2 186	815	2 010	309	148	280	28 665	262	32.1	8.4	34.7
Grafton	2 988	55 230	10 532	5 536	8 139	1 020	1 387	2 041	36 961	552	40.9	6.3	45.1
Hillsborough	10 841	177 056	27 517	27 815	27 153	7 378	12 151	8 600	48 572	615	57.9	1.8	48.1
Merrimack	4 166	59 765	11 844	5 898	9 919	4 098	2 670	2 224	37 219	583	52.8	4.1	47.7
Rockingham	9 563	126 519	14 197	14 548	25 465	5 978	8 774	5 197	41 078	594	67.3	0.8	47.3
Strafford	2 561	36 649	6 614	5 064	6 858	3 238	1 420	1 462	39 894	303	56.1	1.0	47.5
Sullivan	1 025	10 667	1 359	2 895	2 366	465	235	382	35 840	294	45.6	6.5	42.2
NEW JERSEY	231 186	3 443 211	514 099	252 418	444 550	201 941	325 784	177 071	51 426	10 327	75.2	2.9	44.8
Atlantic	6 630	115 605	17 539	2 040	15 934	3 167	5 164	4 080	35 289	499	75.2	1.6	45.3
Bergen	31 669	421 205	62 984	35 259	53 111	17 585	32 066	23 000	54 606	89	98.9	0.0	57.3
Burlington	10 563	180 644	24 108	17 946	27 042	14 303	19 990	8 419	46 608	922	74.6	4.7	48.0
Camden	11 977	173 417	36 632	13 771	22 824	6 455	13 612	7 342	42 340	225	86.7	1.3	40.4
Cape May	3 869	24 315	4 572	459	5 337	1 104	1 074	896	36 864	201	80.6	1.0	50.7
Cumberland	2 978	46 428	8 533	8 259	7 833	1 546	1 223	1 667	35 897	615	62.0	5.7	52.7
Essex	19 225	296 105	55 962	19 967	25 794	22 175	23 820	15 749	53 186	13	100.0	0.0	46.2
Gloucester	5 894	86 094	11 878	8 937	16 546	1 917	4 577	3 194	37 102	669	76.5	2.4	45.7
Hudson	12 732	208 770	24 766	8 464	21 598	36 086	13 236	12 640	60 546	0	0.0	0.0	0.0
Hunterdon	3 928	45 355	7 399	3 582	6 862	D	4 255	2 590	57 106	1 623	75.8	1.8	39.4

STATE County	Acreage (1,000) [117]	Percent change, 2002–2007 [118]	Average size of farm [119]	Total irrigated (1,000) [120]	Total cropland (1,000) [121]	Average per farm [122]	Average per acre [123]	Value of machinery and equipment, average per farm (dollars) [124]	Total (mil dol) [125]	Average per farm (dollars) [126]	Crops [127]	Live-stock and poultry products [128]	$10,000 or more [129]	$100,000 or more [130]	Total ($1,000) [131]	Percent of farms [132]
NEBRASKA—Cont'd																
Platte	426	-2.1	483	208.4	355.3	1 098 136	2 275	212 464	413.1	468 401	34.6	65.4	79.7	54.2	6 185	79.4
Polk	269	1.9	533	164.6	228.6	1 315 269	2 467	190 828	254.7	504 435	39.0	61.0	85.3	56.8	4 564	84.6
Red Willow	446	4.0	1 157	55.1	247.1	1 218 841	1 054	167 928	166.0	430 069	40.9	59.1	69.4	42.0	4 194	71.8
Richardson	279	-13.1	395	2.2	209.0	749 213	1 898	100 623	97.9	138 492	67.8	32.2	59.5	27.9	4 868	85.6
Rock	632	0.5	2 666	43.6	154.6	1 360 295	510	157 509	77.2	325 558	26.2	73.8	73.0	46.4	1 876	54.0
Saline	298	-13.6	425	81.9	241.9	891 706	2 098	143 339	116.8	166 363	78.4	21.6	68.2	38.3	5 595	85.8
Sarpy	101	-3.8	280	11.8	86.7	939 807	3 355	145 436	68.1	189 178	51.6	48.4	48.6	26.9	1 631	64.4
Saunders	428	-6.6	378	93.4	359.9	1 010 408	2 672	129 388	230.8	204 093	59.1	40.9	63.7	32.9	7 451	79.0
Scotts Bluff	360	-15.7	494	155.6	192.8	537 511	1 089	116 047	214.5	293 848	30.9	69.1	60.8	27.8	3 019	65.3
Seward	333	-8.5	372	127.4	272.4	943 216	2 532	141 694	221.9	248 540	53.2	46.8	58.8	32.8	6 784	77.9
Sheridan	1 540	3.6	2 683	57.0	286.0	1 293 556	482	114 056	94.5	164 573	32.5	67.5	65.5	34.7	2 713	58.0
Sherman	270	-14.6	657	72.3	125.6	718 838	1 094	110 428	73.2	178 136	57.3	42.6	65.7	34.3	2 370	74.9
Sioux	1 292	17.1	3 530	51.5	119.6	1 684 596	477	142 906	108.9	297 621	12.5	87.5	77.0	44.3	2 067	58.5
Stanton	236	-2.9	371	31.2	177.9	686 690	1 853	114 363	134.7	211 758	41.4	58.6	59.7	33.8	4 294	78.5
Thayer	351	-7.6	727	131.4	266.1	1 325 009	1 821	152 136	165.3	342 249	61.4	38.6	76.2	49.9	5 959	85.5
Thomas	425	21.8	4 125	3.2	10.2	1 405 772	341	66 827	14.7	142 407	D	D	82.5	39.8	190	21.4
Thurston	200	-6.5	537	7.8	173.2	1 057 191	1 969	169 075	153.7	413 284	39.3	60.7	67.2	40.3	4 015	83.6
Valley	356	13.0	911	99.3	147.8	1 022 526	1 122	182 060	138.2	353 563	35.0	65.0	77.7	44.5	3 210	79.0
Washington	217	-10.3	285	18.5	188.1	875 349	3 069	119 687	131.4	172 487	49.8	50.2	55.5	29.4	3 193	65.0
Wayne	277	-1.4	483	42.7	238.3	1 154 595	2 392	141 598	177.9	310 491	49.6	50.4	68.4	46.1	3 849	78.4
Webster	306	-3.8	710	62.4	178.0	896 346	1 262	144 463	140.9	327 780	37.5	62.5	66.0	37.0	4 237	77.9
Wheeler	360	6.5	1 757	44.1	113.2	1 231 349	701	173 726	196.4	957 846	8.1	91.9	78.5	50.7	2 328	64.9
York	346	-2.3	630	254.7	314.7	1 661 830	2 636	269 338	278.4	507 169	59.6	40.4	84.9	66.3	7 215	78.0
NEVADA	5 865	-7.4	1 873	691.0	753.7	1 148 693	613	111 799	513.3	163 931	42.7	57.3	43.0	19.6	4 007	10.6
Churchill	131	-12.1	248	40.3	36.4	496 430	1 998	73 720	66.9	126 504	20.2	79.8	44.2	12.5	494	13.6
Clark	88	27.5	458	6.5	6.2	1 391 798	3 039	64 840	10.2	53 060	46.1	53.9	21.2	7.3	91	6.7
Douglas	91	-56.9	509	31.2	20.9	1 234 191	2 426	73 444	D	D	D	0.0	34.6	10.1	D	2.2
Elko	2 085	-15.7	4 573	182.2	190.9	1 407 787	308	97 535	53.6	117 541	4.5	95.5	49.1	22.6	460	8.3
Esmeralda	25	NA	1 313	13.7	12.8	1 769 708	1 348	284 228	7.7	405 921	D	D	84.2	68.4	D	10.5
Eureka	783	194.4	9 110	46.2	50.9	1 305 630	143	218 521	25.0	290 877	D	D	76.7	58.1	113	8.1
Humboldt	756	-0.7	2 978	116.3	153.3	1 718 038	577	187 751	74.4	292 736	62.6	37.4	54.3	36.6	682	21.7
Lander	339	-45.3	4 037	31.4	38.0	1 647 807	408	196 558	19.1	227 357	54.7	45.3	63.1	47.6	179	16.7
Lincoln	46	NA	472	18.3	17.9	698 218	1 479	129 086	15.3	156 518	50.1	49.9	54.1	17.3	D	2.0
Lyon	261	15.5	802	81.5	78.9	1 016 512	1 267	154 740	91.1	280 331	68.2	31.8	41.8	20.3	59	3.4
Mineral	D	D	D	D	6.4	2 781 061	982	30 927	2.9	35 035	D	D	20.2	4.8	938	71.4
Nye	91	-7.1	525	21.5	28.1	674 881	1 285	109 264	58.2	336 638	5.6	94.4	39.9	14.5	115	2.9
Pershing	244	86.3	1 809	48.4	69.2	1 288 595	712	165 140	42.4	314 097	54.3	45.7	63.7	41.5	344	26.7
Storey	D	D	D	D	0.0	206 200	14 123	47 212	D	D	D	0.0	20.0	0.0	0	0.0
Washoe	486	-39.4	1 236	18.7	19.0	980 996	793	66 268	18.4	46 771	55.3	44.7	21.6	4.6	284	2.0
White Pine	D	D	D	30.9	23.8	1 685 545	830	185 911	15.2	156 412	28.6	71.4	60.8	29.9	131	4.1
Carson City	3	-25.0	131	D	1.2	408 435	3 112	67 740	1.1	54 131	D	D	23.8	14.3	0	0.0
NEW HAMPSHIRE	472	6.1	113	2.5	128.9	558 385	4 929	58 413	199.1	47 780	53.5	46.5	27.9	6.9	2 474	10.2
Belknap	23	0.0	87	0.1	6.1	496 272	5 732	47 338	7.7	28 400	61.3	38.7	20.7	5.2	120	8.1
Carroll	32	6.7	117	0.1	6.8	549 028	4 695	43 292	5.3	19 268	62.7	37.3	28.5	4.0	209	13.1
Cheshire	48	17.1	115	0.1	11.8	531 220	4 614	61 699	15.4	36 768	28.6	71.4	30.1	5.7	143	10.0
Coos	51	15.9	194	0.0	13.9	465 518	2 396	65 407	13.0	49 630	21.2	78.8	30.5	6.9	413	8.8
Grafton	100	16.3	181	0.1	24.9	710 052	3 921	65 838	34.4	62 306	14.0	86.0	27.4	8.7	579	18.3
Hillsborough	50	25.0	82	0.8	13.1	560 697	6 864	55 096	17.1	27 799	67.6	32.4	24.6	5.4	60	4.6
Merrimack	65	-17.7	111	0.7	16.3	527 966	4 762	56 192	55.3	94 831	81.8	18.2	29.2	8.6	360	9.1
Rockingham	34	6.3	57	0.4	13.6	541 137	9 575	61 082	26.0	43 829	75.1	24.9	27.4	7.4	118	6.2
Strafford	26	-23.5	85	0.2	9.0	526 318	6 195	56 796	9.9	32 712	60.5	39.5	32.0	5.9	224	9.2
Sullivan	43	19.4	147	0.1	13.4	584 232	3 976	65 438	15.0	50 926	28.0	72.0	31.0	8.8	249	18.0
NEW JERSEY	733	-9.1	71	95.3	488.7	1 089 883	15 346	68 374	986.9	95 564	86.3	13.7	32.7	11.1	6 988	8.3
Atlantic	30	0.0	61	11.7	18.6	902 470	14 827	113 651	128.3	257 193	98.0	2.0	44.9	20.6	349	5.0
Bergen	1	0.0	13	0.2	0.6	915 051	69 192	52 244	8.7	97 685	96.4	3.6	51.7	23.6	D	2.2
Burlington	86	-22.5	93	12.6	53.7	1 114 826	11 981	73 154	86.3	93 603	93.3	6.7	38.9	13.6	958	8.7
Camden	9	-10.0	39	2.6	5.0	602 414	15 473	52 844	18.6	82 464	99.0	1.0	36.4	10.2	62	2.2
Cape May	8	-20.0	40	2.3	4.3	637 097	16 055	59 369	14.6	72 567	96.2	3.8	35.8	8.0	20	4.0
Cumberland	69	-2.8	113	18.4	52.3	1 056 005	9 346	118 184	156.9	255 186	97.4	2.6	48.0	22.9	413	9.3
Essex	0	NA	14	0.0	0.0	1 302 885	92 052	28 014	0.7	54 631	98.7	1.4	69.2	23.1	0	0.0
Gloucester	47	-7.8	70	12.9	34.7	1 078 215	15 459	73 867	93.9	140 333	93.8	6.2	34.4	13.5	453	9.4
Hudson	0	NA	0	0.0	0.0	0	0	0	0.0	0	0.0	0.0	0.0	0.0	0	0.0
Hunterdon	100	-8.3	62	1.5	66.6	1 243 324	20 174	49 814	69.7	42 973	87.0	13.0	23.4	4.9	729	8.4

STATE County	Water use, 2005 Total water withdrawn (mil gal/day)	Gallons withdrawn per person	Wholesale trade,[1] 2007 Number of establishments	Number of employees	Sales (mil dol)	Annual payroll (mil dol)	Retail trade,[2] 2007 Number of establishments	Number of employees	Sales (mil dol)	Annual payroll (mil dol)	Real estate and rental and leasing,[2] 2007 Number of establishments	Number of employees	Receipts (mil dol)	Annual payroll (mil dol)
	133	134	135	136	137	138	139	140	141	142	143	144	145	146
NEBRASKA—Cont'd														
Platte	229.0	7 326	49	529	517.8	22.9	174	2 136	494.3	41.2	38	118	19.0	2.4
Polk	171.3	31 603	9	109	103.3	3.5	24	116	35.5	2.1	2	D	D	D
Red Willow	53.2	4 807	20	244	140.9	8.3	88	789	175.9	17.3	20	59	3.8	0.7
Richardson	3.2	364	27	130	186.9	3.8	48	337	70.4	6.2	6	26	1.5	0.4
Rock	39.4	25 163	5	66	23.4	1.6	10	D	D	D	NA	NA	NA	NA
Saline	71.8	5 056	15	139	157.0	6.1	55	552	102.4	10.1	8	23	1.5	0.3
Sarpy	28.3	203	159	2 584	3 005.9	128.5	373	6 783	2 285.8	157.2	131	543	99.7	15.6
Saunders	148.9	7 280	25	145	147.8	5.1	64	570	149.0	10.7	13	17	1.1	0.3
Scotts Bluff	264.1	7 186	65	D	D	D	200	2 451	519.8	49.3	42	133	17.9	2.9
Seward	135.8	8 111	25	182	127.1	8.0	56	577	109.8	10.4	9	17	2.2	0.2
Sheridan	96.5	17 027	11	166	64.8	3.6	46	281	50.3	4.0	3	D	D	D
Sherman	88.4	28 419	3	33	11.3	0.9	15	69	35.5	1.5	1	D	D	D
Sioux	49.8	34 156	4	D	D	D	4	D	D	D	NA	NA	NA	NA
Stanton	30.2	4 620	3	D	D	D	15	136	33.0	2.7	1	D	D	D
Thayer	107.6	19 801	19	146	98.6	5.7	41	254	54.9	4.0	2	D	D	D
Thomas	2.7	4 334	2	D	D	D	4	D	D	D	1	D	D	D
Thurston	13.4	1 822	9	73	115.0	2.5	24	199	54.1	4.1	4	D	D	D
Valley	139.2	31 613	12	89	48.4	2.8	36	316	66.8	5.9	3	D	D	D
Washington	581.7	29 420	19	159	211.4	5.9	60	926	642.6	35.6	15	30	2.2	0.5
Wayne	36.3	3 944	11	139	51.9	3.4	44	394	79.5	6.7	7	20	1.1	0.4
Webster	49.5	13 163	15	75	58.9	2.1	20	155	23.7	1.8	1	D	D	D
Wheeler	50.6	61 671	2	D	D	D	3	D	D	D	NA	NA	NA	NA
York	281.5	19 551	32	332	239.1	12.1	77	1 045	241.3	20.8	18	39	3.9	0.5
NEVADA	2 377.5	985	2 614	36 052	19 255.9	1 698.5	8 492	139 829	37 434.0	3 691.7	4 613	31 603	6 187.3	1 106.5
Churchill	179.3	7 302	19	153	33.3	2.7	84	1 195	265.3	28.6	38	140	11.9	2.6
Clark	607.7	355	1 698	23 067	11 493.1	1 114.8	5 744	99 817	26 676.6	2 656.9	3 356	25 654	5 235.4	925.5
Douglas	52.0	1 106	57	D	D	D	198	2 817	670.4	66.1	140	639	94.0	19.5
Elko	356.9	7 831	58	D	D	D	179	2 307	791.4	57.3	39	297	26.7	5.9
Esmeralda	41.7	53 037	NA	NA	NA	NA	2	D	D	D	NA	NA	NA	NA
Eureka	84.6	59 265	NA	NA	NA	NA	6	35	16.3	1.4	NA	NA	NA	NA
Humboldt	263.9	15 405	16	140	71.5	7.5	76	1 042	333.6	24.9	11	43	5.6	0.9
Lander	107.3	20 987	3	D	D	D	22	237	55.0	4.0	3	4	0.7	0.1
Lincoln	50.9	11 601	2	D	D	D	17	247	31.1	3.0	3	19	0.8	0.2
Lyon	217.8	4 583	40	D	D	D	117	1 080	371.4	25.3	45	138	14.9	3.0
Mineral	19.3	2 705	2	D	D	D	11	D	D	D	3	5	0.3	0.0
Nye	68.6	1 694	16	D	D	D	135	1 554	396.8	37.9	52	141	14.5	2.9
Pershing	131.8	20 730	2	D	D	D	18	154	43.0	3.2	3	9	0.4	0.1
Storey	3.8	923	NA	NA	NA	NA	22	54	6.8	1.1	2	D	D	D
Washoe	116.9	300	602	10 370	6 317.7	461.6	1 555	25 026	6 667.4	671.0	763	D	D	D
White Pine	71.1	7 902	8	D	D	D	44	458	88.8	8.4	8	37	3.0	0.6
Carson City	9.9	177	92	D	D	D	262	3 698	991.5	99.5	147	569	73.4	16.0
NEW HAMPSHIRE	1 323.7	1 010	1 561	21 457	14 564.5	1 196.3	6 603	98 333	25 353.9	2 380.5	1 534	7 266	1 371.8	248.2
Belknap	8.7	141	48	D	D	D	372	5 212	1 348.7	133.2	88	399	56.6	10.2
Carroll	6.1	129	34	D	D	D	424	3 891	889.0	96.0	84	D	D	D
Cheshire	8.5	111	66	D	D	D	382	5 775	1 649.0	139.3	69	296	49.3	10.0
Coos	40.2	1 193	21	D	D	D	197	2 229	602.9	50.3	27	D	D	D
Grafton	13.1	154	80	D	D	D	592	8 158	1 961.3	195.5	140	582	72.8	17.5
Hillsborough	58.6	146	515	6 535	3 873.1	386.1	1 657	27 793	7 647.3	678.7	443	2 664	554.7	96.4
Merrimack	245.3	1 670	159	3 811	2 812.4	173.4	673	10 315	2 605.6	244.8	168	900	222.5	32.8
Rockingham	916.0	3 104	520	6 810	5 844.8	426.4	1 667	25 911	6 414.9	605.5	364	1 542	284.2	58.2
Strafford	20.7	174	81	856	351.1	50.2	439	6 640	1 672.9	173.9	111	428	65.7	10.6
Sullivan	6.4	150	37	D	D	D	200	2 409	562.4	63.3	40	136	16.4	3.1
NEW JERSEY	7 390.5	848	14 033	221 729	233 413.0	13 266.6	34 482	460 843	124 813.6	12 050.0	9 618	64 021	16 347.6	2 939.1
Atlantic	51.4	190	196	2 916	1 342.2	127.1	1 291	17 258	4 429.4	428.6	287	1 867	378.7	56.9
Bergen	123.8	137	3 046	40 189	66 117.9	2 584.6	4 128	55 875	16 475.0	1 768.6	1 441	7 655	2 294.7	412.7
Burlington	104.9	233	572	11 618	15 040.9	649.7	1 594	27 383	7 005.1	706.9	409	3 744	881.0	182.1
Camden	55.4	107	645	D	D	D	1 911	24 858	5 859.3	601.8	457	3 080	575.7	118.0
Cape May	217.6	2 191	65	561	276.1	25.3	746	6 103	1 584.9	164.8	258	836	177.1	27.0
Cumberland	58.1	379	160	D	D	D	564	7 602	1 952.7	185.4	125	540	88.3	16.2
Essex	32.5	41	1 081	17 340	12 622.5	1 116.1	2 892	30 136	7 750.6	764.8	947	5 988	1 411.3	243.8
Gloucester	75.0	271	314	8 732	8 962.5	426.2	989	17 301	4 352.5	386.0	180	D	D	D
Hudson	609.5	1 010	829	16 313	14 524.9	885.7	2 267	22 579	6 099.9	552.6	725	4 635	1 442.8	235.2
Hunterdon	23.1	177	157	1 283	629.5	62.0	572	6 676	2 186.6	193.2	112	407	102.1	17.6

1. Merchant wholesalers, except manufacturers' sales branches and offices.   2. Employer establishments.

Table B. States and Counties — Professional Services, Manufacturing, and Accommodation and Food Services

STATE County	Professional, scientific, and technical services,[1] 2007				Manufacturing, 2007				Accommodation and food services, 2007			
	Number of establish-ments	Number of employees	Receipts (mil dol)	Annual payroll (mil dol)	Number of establish-ments	Number of employees	Receipts (mil dol)	Annual payroll (mil dol)	Number of establish-ments	Number of employees	Sales (mil dol)	Annual payroll (mil dol)
	147	148	149	150	151	152	153	154	155	156	157	158
NEBRASKA—Cont'd												
Platte	59	D	D	D	79	6 253	2 353.6	248.9	80	1 110	39.1	10.6
Polk	13	25	2.0	0.3	NA	NA	NA	NA	8	44	1.1	0.2
Red Willow	33	139	10.8	4.3	NA	NA	NA	NA	27	540	16.4	4.5
Richardson	16	69	3.8	1.3	NA	NA	NA	NA	23	142	4.1	1.1
Rock	1	D	D	D	NA	NA	NA	NA	3	23	0.3	0.1
Saline	17	55	4.1	1.0	19	2 907	951.8	112.2	33	340	11.3	2.8
Sarpy	255	D	D	D	79	2 573	587.7	115.2	224	4 211	160.3	47.6
Saunders	41	D	D	D	25	645	D	D	39	361	9.2	2.3
Scotts Bluff	70	D	D	D	42	D	177.9	33.7	104	1 488	52.9	14.4
Seward	31	79	9.7	2.4	20	977	D	36.8	34	438	13.5	3.4
Sheridan	9	43	3.1	0.8	NA	NA	NA	NA	18	104	2.9	0.8
Sherman	5	7	0.6	0.1	NA	NA	NA	NA	8	50	2.1	0.4
Sioux	1	D	D	D	NA	NA	NA	NA	2	D	D	D
Stanton	6	D	D	D	NA	NA	NA	NA	6	46	1.6	0.4
Thayer	7	16	1.0	0.3	NA	NA	NA	NA	16	80	1.9	0.5
Thomas	1	D	D	D	NA	NA	NA	NA	3	31	1.0	0.3
Thurston	6	D	D	D	NA	NA	NA	NA	8	D	D	D
Valley	12	65	5.1	1.7	NA	NA	NA	NA	13	110	2.7	0.7
Washington	45	418	36.6	19.4	23	1 181	724.2	54.8	40	393	12.5	3.2
Wayne	13	188	8.3	2.6	12	821	180.0	22.8	21	361	9.3	2.2
Webster	3	D	D	D	NA	NA	NA	NA	7	D	D	D
Wheeler	NA	NA	NA	NA	NA	NA	NA	NA	7	D	D	D
York	30	156	17.6	6.2	25	936	353.2	37.8	40	705	28.9	7.7
NEVADA	7 895	57 357	8 881.4	3 241.1	2 035	51 958	15 735.8	2 290.8	5 570	325 544	28 815.5	8 594.6
Churchill	36	500	38.5	23.5	NA	NA	NA	NA	52	725	33.0	8.9
Clark	5 282	43 063	6 982.5	2 498.8	1 096	26 478	7 180.7	1 086.3	3 797	266 845	24 857.8	7 431.8
Douglas	240	1 032	106.0	46.4	78	2 652	751.8	140.6	130	9 342	680.4	200.0
Elko	100	D	D	D	NA	NA	NA	NA	127	5 776	474.1	122.0
Esmeralda	1	D	D	D	NA	NA	NA	NA	2	D	D	D
Eureka	5	D	D	D	NA	NA	NA	NA	4	51	2.2	0.5
Humboldt	20	123	9.5	3.6	NA	NA	NA	NA	57	1 024	52.0	14.6
Lander	3	D	D	D	NA	NA	NA	NA	17	126	5.4	1.5
Lincoln	8	12	1.4	0.3	NA	NA	NA	NA	16	D	D	D
Lyon	52	288	24.8	10.7	101	2 171	573.6	85.1	67	798	35.0	9.5
Mineral	4	D	D	D	NA	NA	NA	NA	13	326	20.2	4.8
Nye	53	214	14.9	6.1	NA	NA	NA	NA	74	1 519	88.1	21.8
Pershing	4	8	0.6	0.2	NA	NA	NA	NA	14	226	9.2	3.3
Storey	8	12	1.5	0.3	NA	NA	NA	NA	13	93	4.8	1.5
Washoe	1 688	10 089	1 442.8	548.7	505	D	D	D	990	35 447	2 399.4	729.2
White Pine	10	D	D	D	NA	NA	NA	NA	30	472	22.0	6.5
Carson City	381	D	D	D	143	3 528	621.6	141.7	167	2 664	127.7	37.8
NEW HAMPSHIRE	3 961	29 160	3 730.8	1 570.2	2 104	81 592	18 592.4	4 196.2	3 508	55 268	2 631.0	799.8
Belknap	161	D	D	D	102	3 274	687.1	142.4	229	2 742	151.6	48.3
Carroll	145	D	D	D	86	992	213.4	35.5	304	3 900	214.9	63.8
Cheshire	150	D	D	D	150	5 483	1 095.2	258.2	161	2 643	110.3	35.0
Coos	44	D	D	D	42	1 166	295.9	43.6	117	1 747	85.7	25.0
Grafton	251	D	D	D	130	6 138	1 314.3	272.5	356	5 844	272.8	83.7
Hillsborough	1 347	D	D	D	633	31 243	7 707.6	1 944.4	875	15 987	732.3	224.9
Merrimack	456	2 625	412.7	152.0	230	7 043	1 539.6	315.1	306	4 900	223.5	68.4
Rockingham	1 101	D	D	D	475	17 081	3 912.6	801.3	832	13 262	660.7	198.6
Strafford	234	D	D	D	152	5 739	1 186.0	243.3	256	3 500	146.8	42.8
Sullivan	72	D	D	D	104	3 433	640.8	140.0	72	743	32.3	9.4
NEW JERSEY	31 040	330 133	52 442.8	23 639.9	9 250	310 606	116 608.1	16 399.3	19 526	291 327	19 993.6	5 232.4
Atlantic	648	D	D	D	140	2 974	D	113.8	862	56 370	6 093.0	1 505.4
Bergen	4 367	D	D	D	1 313	42 288	11 973.8	2 236.6	2 222	27 945	1 848.3	489.0
Burlington	1 374	D	D	D	418	20 568	6 072.3	1 150.1	907	13 306	657.0	180.6
Camden	1 613	D	D	D	486	17 283	4 150.1	819.3	1 019	13 550	678.8	185.1
Cape May	250	D	D	D	81	662	D	18.9	832	5 615	517.0	144.9
Cumberland	231	D	D	D	175	9 037	2 591.4	341.6	262	3 263	155.1	40.0
Essex	2 443	D	D	D	914	27 302	10 422.7	1 472.5	1 514	19 727	1 335.8	357.1
Gloucester	538	D	D	D	276	10 190	15 679.4	573.7	472	8 461	379.4	104.3
Hudson	1 255	D	D	D	477	9 898	2 614.2	404.6	1 297	13 289	880.7	218.3
Hunterdon	644	D	D	D	148	D	D	194.1	284	3 243	175.8	47.2

1. Establishment subject to federal tax.

STATE County	Health care and social assistance, 2007				Other services, 2007				Federal funds and grants, 2009–2010 Expenditures (mil dol)	Direct payments for individuals[1]		
	Number of establishments	Number of employees	Receipts (mil dol)	Annual payroll (mil dol)	Number of establishments	Number of employees	Receipts (mil dol)	Annual payroll (mil dol)	Total	Social Security and government retirement	Medicare	Food Stamps and Supplemental Security Income
	159	160	161	162	163	164	165	166	167	168	169	170
NEBRASKA—Cont'd												
Platte	84	1 587	125.4	47.5	78	497	25.0	8.6	195.3	88.6	25.7	5.2
Polk	7	233	12.9	5.6	16	24	3.1	0.6	40.4	17.1	9.9	0.4
Red Willow	36	D	D	D	31	107	7.8	2.0	88.8	42.4	18.8	3.0
Richardson	22	369	24.4	9.9	22	64	4.1	0.7	91.1	35.2	20.3	2.5
Rock	4	D	D	D	5	11	1.1	0.3	13.2	5.0	2.5	0.2
Saline	29	583	31.8	14.0	26	111	6.1	1.5	133.1	41.4	17.4	1.8
Sarpy	233	3 559	246.5	105.4	206	1 307	107.8	31.8	1 457.1	332.6	45.2	8.2
Saunders	32	536	30.1	13.0	28	87	8.7	2.2	166.5	61.3	27.7	2.5
Scotts Bluff	127	2 980	274.2	115.9	97	459	29.8	9.3	306.1	129.7	51.2	16.6
Seward	32	744	45.5	21.7	40	139	14.5	3.1	89.8	47.0	15.9	1.6
Sheridan	16	192	11.7	5.1	19	47	2.9	0.5	50.1	20.7	10.5	1.9
Sherman	6	D	D	D	7	D	D	D	37.1	12.3	5.9	0.3
Sioux	NA	NA	NA	NA	2	D	D	D	6.6	2.4	0.7	0.0
Stanton	8	D	D	D	5	D	D	D	24.6	9.9	4.4	0.6
Thayer	11	446	23.6	10.7	20	57	7.1	1.1	52.1	22.2	10.7	1.0
Thomas	NA	NA	NA	NA	1	D	D	D	7.9	2.2	1.6	0.1
Thurston	10	361	29.4	13.2	7	30	4.1	0.9	106.1	15.7	12.6	3.4
Valley	21	369	21.3	9.7	14	45	4.1	0.8	48.6	16.3	9.2	0.7
Washington	37	733	47.9	21.5	35	82	7.0	2.1	103.5	57.6	20.5	1.6
Wayne	23	365	23.1	10.5	20	D	D	D	58.8	20.3	9.1	0.9
Webster	6	209	9.5	4.1	4	19	1.9	0.3	40.8	16.1	9.0	0.7
Wheeler	NA	NA	NA	NA	NA	NA	NA	NA	7.7	2.4	1.3	0.0
York	41	952	62.2	27.7	57	300	19.3	4.9	98.5	45.8	20.2	2.3
NEVADA	5 772	96 633	12 191.2	4 398.5	3 571	27 234	2 584.3	701.7	19 771.0	6 993.0	2 281.3	666.6
Churchill	45	862	82.8	33.3	40	160	12.6	3.7	339.5	101.5	33.0	5.6
Clark	3 978	67 163	8 517.4	3 017.6	2 313	18 791	1 602.5	473.7	11 254.2	4 651.5	1 579.7	494.2
Douglas	113	1 064	117.7	39.7	70	470	48.3	14.1	256.9	159.0	42.0	5.1
Elko	121	D	D	D	81	549	62.7	17.8	233.4	90.2	21.3	7.0
Esmeralda	NA	NA	NA	NA	1	D	D	D	13.2	3.5	0.9	0.1
Eureka	3	D	D	D	NA	NA	NA	NA	8.2	4.1	2.0	0.0
Humboldt	31	D	D	D	31	166	19.9	5.8	98.5	41.4	13.0	5.2
Lander	8	D	D	D	6	D	D	D	35.1	12.7	5.2	0.4
Lincoln	4	D	D	D	2	D	D	D	49.9	31.1	6.4	0.6
Lyon	47	D	D	D	38	195	22.3	4.9	308.6	191.3	41.7	12.6
Mineral	6	D	D	D	5	D	D	D	136.0	25.4	10.3	4.8
Nye	60	848	76.2	23.1	50	196	13.8	3.6	355.3	252.2	43.3	12.6
Pershing	10	162	14.0	6.0	6	D	D	D	28.3	12.3	4.9	0.6
Storey	1	D	D	D	4	D	D	D	11.1	7.7	1.2	0.2
Washoe	1 112	D	D	D	761	D	D	D	3 484.5	1 159.7	381.2	98.9
White Pine	13	337	31.8	15.1	14	65	4.6	1.7	83.1	29.6	10.0	5.0
Carson City	220	3 407	453.3	164.1	149	948	83.3	25.4	1 497.0	208.9	85.3	13.9
NEW HAMPSHIRE	3 492	83 717	8 085.7	3 377.8	2 886	16 153	1 574.3	457.9	11 335.3	4 198.8	1 477.6	257.0
Belknap	146	4 011	310.9	143.1	148	629	54.4	15.2	458.3	239.5	91.0	16.3
Carroll	138	D	D	D	113	407	34.1	9.7	338.5	201.3	65.2	10.6
Cheshire	166	3 980	330.1	134.0	145	933	73.0	26.8	515.2	254.5	93.5	16.9
Coos	105	D	D	D	72	355	26.3	8.8	325.6	141.7	74.0	10.1
Grafton	278	9 894	1 483.6	559.2	198	1 083	91.7	24.6	901.2	301.1	109.1	10.6
Hillsborough	1 020	26 771	2 503.8	1 065.3	828	5 317	501.5	155.6	3 353.3	1 143.0	408.1	88.2
Merrimack	415	11 751	1 002.1	454.0	398	1 940	280.1	63.3	1 562.7	417.8	168.1	28.2
Rockingham	803	14 595	1 324.2	540.6	702	3 817	377.6	106.8	2 031.8	902.1	284.8	33.0
Strafford	310	6 170	638.1	267.0	202	1 255	103.4	34.1	869.3	377.5	123.1	28.2
Sullivan	111	1 594	107.2	47.5	80	417	32.3	12.8	431.3	218.7	60.6	14.9
NEW JERSEY	25 777	503 370	51 913.7	21 313.6	19 047	105 659	11 203.7	3 003.1	80 990.1	23 840.6	16 833.7	2 013.4
Atlantic	821	16 172	1 780.0	702.6	547	3 496	270.1	81.7	2 365.5	831.2	563.0	79.3
Bergen	3 435	65 456	7 781.4	2 953.4	2 581	12 322	1 348.6	355.7	5 911.9	2 552.0	1 735.3	84.3
Burlington	1 134	21 970	2 400.1	864.6	850	4 976	384.6	128.9	5 531.3	1 484.5	674.0	56.1
Camden	1 580	35 383	3 701.1	1 521.5	939	6 051	479.3	157.1	4 688.9	1 505.8	1 107.5	207.4
Cape May	268	D	D	D	288	1 124	91.2	29.5	961.9	429.9	310.1	20.2
Cumberland	399	8 351	820.8	333.3	273	1 439	103.0	31.1	1 295.5	434.9	354.9	63.3
Essex	2 540	56 955	5 884.7	2 599.3	1 720	10 832	1 188.8	341.0	8 433.4	1 708.7	1 899.1	450.8
Gloucester	614	11 646	980.0	422.4	530	3 301	272.0	77.5	1 616.9	802.3	433.1	43.3
Hudson	1 337	24 006	2 231.5	898.1	1 118	4 826	463.3	126.1	5 003.1	983.7	1 261.1	272.4
Hunterdon	361	6 893	634.4	274.0	285	1 717	127.5	40.9	613.3	342.9	150.5	5.6

1. State totals may include programs not allocated by county.

Federal Funds, Residential Construction, and Local Government Finances

	Federal funds and grants, 2009–2010 (cont.)							Value of residential construction authorized by building permits, 2010		Local government finances, 2007				
	Expenditures (mil dol) (cont.)									General revenue				
		Procurement contract awards		Grants[1]								Taxes		
STATE County													Per capita[2] (dollars)	
	Salaries and wages	Defense	Other	Medicaid and other health-related	Nutrition and family welfare	Education	Other	New construction ($1,000)	Number of housing units	Total (mil dol)	Inter-governmental (mil dol)	Total (mil dol)	Total	Property
	171	172	173	174	175	176	177	178	179	180	181	182	183	184
NEBRASKA—Cont'd														
Platte	33.1	3.4	6.3	15.3	4.0	1.3	1.8	18 836	88	108.5	30.7	47.7	1 497	1 017
Polk	1.8	0.0	0.4	2.6	0.7	0.3	0.9	475	2	26.3	3.9	13.8	2 657	2 412
Red Willow	5.5	0.0	1.0	6.6	2.0	0.9	0.3	0	0	52.4	28.5	15.3	1 427	1 152
Richardson	3.0	0.0	0.8	11.1	3.3	0.5	8.1	260	1	25.0	9.6	12.9	1 545	1 266
Rock	0.5	0.0	0.1	1.3	0.4	0.1	0.7	0	0	5.9	1.5	3.6	2 372	2 211
Saline	5.3	0.0	43.5	8.9	1.8	1.1	2.9	3 217	20	57.0	17.4	22.7	1 634	1 456
Sarpy	485.7	495.6	9.2	22.4	12.6	14.6	5.0	166 466	939	412.6	136.1	181.5	1 237	1 013
Saunders	41.2	13.1	1.2	7.2	2.5	0.8	0.5	9 876	62	65.6	15.7	29.8	1 476	1 251
Scotts Bluff	19.0	0.0	5.7	47.5	11.5	3.5	5.4	2 912	21	160.1	61.4	60.4	1 660	1 113
Seward	6.4	0.0	2.1	5.3	2.0	1.0	0.1	8 141	53	49.2	14.6	27.8	1 678	1 472
Sheridan	1.5	0.0	0.5	4.6	1.4	0.4	0.3	71	1	28.8	8.2	8.5	1 553	1 324
Sherman	1.2	0.0	0.3	5.2	4.9	0.2	2.1	600	3	10.4	3.7	5.3	1 771	1 576
Sioux	0.6	0.0	0.1	0.7	0.1	0.1	0.0	280	2	3.6	0.9	2.4	1 807	1 651
Stanton	1.7	0.0	0.2	2.6	0.7	0.2	0.4	1 714	10	10.0	3.1	5.1	793	708
Thayer	2.5	0.0	0.6	6.7	1.2	0.2	0.2	1 161	6	32.5	6.0	13.8	2 679	2 369
Thomas	1.8	0.0	1.1	0.0	0.1	0.1	0.0	NA	NA	3.8	1.4	2.0	3 330	3 162
Thurston	10.7	0.8	9.0	20.4	5.0	10.8	9.2	462	5	42.6	19.9	7.0	969	728
Valley	2.1	0.0	0.8	11.1	0.8	0.3	0.6	2 021	18	34.9	6.2	9.9	2 311	1 752
Washington	3.9	-0.2	0.8	9.2	1.8	1.0	0.8	7 220	37	59.7	20.6	31.8	1 595	1 397
Wayne	5.2	0.2	0.5	4.6	1.2	0.7	4.7	1 691	9	28.2	9.4	13.7	1 475	1 283
Webster	1.9	0.0	0.4	5.2	0.6	0.4	0.4	692	4	20.6	5.0	6.4	1 779	1 407
Wheeler	0.4	0.0	0.1	0.0	0.2	0.1	0.0	0	0	3.4	0.7	2.4	2 913	2 712
York	7.3	0.3	0.9	6.6	1.8	1.0	0.8	2 571	14	48.1	11.1	26.1	1 820	1 390
NEVADA	1 941.7	1 315.0	1 092.1	1 312.3	423.8	339.0	1 626.7	759 740	6 443	X	X	X	X	X
Churchill	42.7	99.6	3.5	36.6	3.9	3.0	5.2	308	3	129.7	61.4	20.7	832	600
Clark	1 452.3	443.1	893.0	790.9	162.4	87.6	466.0	577 931	5 474	9 530.4	3 523.8	3 157.6	1 720	1 078
Douglas	7.5	6.4	9.1	5.1	5.8	3.3	10.9	19 609	56	195.4	81.4	70.6	1 556	1 180
Elko	24.8	1.1	17.0	33.7	8.5	4.5	14.7	19 230	136	200.0	114.9	46.9	998	649
Esmeralda	7.1	0.0	0.3	0.9	0.1	0.2	0.0	NA	NA	11.7	9.0	1.2	1 794	1 770
Eureka	0.3	0.0	0.0	0.9	0.2	0.2	0.1	NA	NA	31.6	14.0	13.5	8 643	8 508
Humboldt	9.5	0.0	3.7	15.0	2.6	1.8	1.9	1 831	18	96.6	41.7	19.4	1 105	870
Lander	4.8	0.0	1.7	5.3	0.8	1.1	1.1	786	5	36.7	16.2	10.7	2 093	1 784
Lincoln	2.3	0.2	1.3	1.8	1.4	0.5	2.2	1 751	11	26.8	15.7	6.0	1 259	1 221
Lyon	16.0	7.7	1.4	18.9	4.9	2.7	7.6	9 321	53	171.6	93.5	43.5	829	661
Mineral	4.1	66.0	1.1	13.2	0.9	1.1	8.0	506	7	29.6	11.9	5.1	1 066	854
Nye	15.7	1.3	7.9	10.1	4.0	2.8	2.7	NA	NA	156.7	93.1	44.4	1 006	806
Pershing	0.8	0.1	0.2	4.4	0.8	0.2	0.4	249	2	36.6	16.4	6.0	942	851
Storey	0.4	0.0	0.4	0.0	0.3	0.4	0.3	1 005	6	16.8	6.9	7.5	1 790	1 410
Washoe	274.3	674.8	135.1	292.3	58.3	34.9	315.5	117 001	600	1 793.8	774.2	626.1	1 542	1 086
White Pine	12.1	0.3	6.0	11.5	2.1	2.1	2.2	249	1	60.4	23.6	10.7	1 167	909
Carson City	66.8	14.4	10.5	71.7	107.2	177.7	730.6	9 963	71	198.2	99.8	49.3	897	577
NEW HAMPSHIRE	880.0	1 091.9	343.5	1 132.7	209.8	195.7	772.8	461 754	2 670	X	X	X	X	X
Belknap	15.1	6.6	4.6	60.5	7.6	3.6	8.3	33 755	178	253.8	76.7	144.7	2 370	2 340
Carroll	12.5	0.8	4.1	30.6	5.9	2.4	0.6	40 842	167	186.1	63.1	105.0	2 217	2 192
Cheshire	24.6	6.7	3.5	70.4	11.7	4.6	8.6	17 559	102	282.2	100.3	147.0	1 891	1 878
Coos	11.9	3.5	6.4	51.8	9.4	3.1	8.9	6 494	39	154.0	64.0	63.3	1 933	1 917
Grafton	43.1	47.4	57.4	244.0	10.6	7.7	52.7	55 205	401	359.4	103.5	208.1	2 433	2 411
Hillsborough	369.5	700.2	111.2	271.3	39.2	22.6	101.1	94 983	682	1 330.6	420.3	697.9	1 735	1 686
Merrimack	115.3	14.8	26.8	152.7	63.3	108.6	409.2	33 147	180	497.2	157.3	284.1	1 916	1 899
Rockingham	218.8	282.4	94.1	117.3	26.2	20.2	27.0	128 009	593	1 043.1	285.1	644.8	2 174	2 150
Strafford	60.6	7.5	16.7	86.6	14.9	10.1	119.1	36 207	256	381.0	135.4	199.5	1 641	1 600
Sullivan	8.7	21.9	18.6	47.5	6.0	3.3	26.8	15 551	72	141.6	54.6	73.3	1 716	1 705
NEW JERSEY	5 577.9	7 857.5	2 378.8	8 131.6	1 857.8	1 236.6	4 230.7	2 036 521	13 535	X	X	X	X	X
Atlantic	301.1	40.6	95.9	278.6	51.5	10.0	40.2	79 406	512	1 515.6	456.0	828.2	3 060	2 999
Bergen	284.9	438.1	108.7	387.5	89.5	16.2	120.9	293 868	1 226	4 209.5	720.4	2 890.3	3 227	3 172
Burlington	941.0	1 769.9	204.5	217.4	56.7	19.2	15.8	93 812	682	1 895.9	572.3	1 011.2	2 263	2 230
Camden	271.5	352.0	428.7	533.3	95.2	24.2	86.0	47 342	487	2 913.8	1 153.9	1 079.0	2 100	2 065
Cape May	75.3	7.4	17.1	61.7	15.9	4.0	5.8	110 258	434	633.6	155.7	372.3	3 861	3 709
Cumberland	61.2	42.0	14.4	232.9	41.0	11.5	17.7	28 038	246	758.8	469.5	192.0	1 234	1 205
Essex	692.5	384.7	318.8	1 545.9	216.6	60.0	952.9	106 211	663	3 608.7	1 368.3	1 807.1	2 328	2 225
Gloucester	55.7	27.9	12.5	134.2	35.0	6.6	28.8	84 079	716	1 187.7	391.9	614.0	2 149	2 116
Hudson	576.9	116.5	165.0	1 148.0	135.7	31.3	151.7	119 190	917	2 391.4	1 005.0	939.1	1 570	1 510
Hunterdon	29.6	8.7	8.4	42.0	10.8	1.6	9.0	35 482	275	611.2	99.6	432.6	3 345	3 297

1. State totals may include programs not allocated by county. 2. Based on the resident population estimated as of July 1 of the year shown.

Table B. States and Counties — Local Government Finances, Government Employment, and Voting

STATE County	Total (mil dol) 185	Per capita[1] (dollars) 186	Education 187	Health and hospitals 188	Police protection 189	Public welfare 190	Highways 191	Total (mil dol) 192	Per capita[1] (dollars) 193	Federal civilian 194	Federal military 195	State and local 196	Democratic 197	Republican 198	All other 199
NEBRASKA—Cont'd															
Platte	91.8	2 883	53.8	0.3	5.4	1.3	11.7	1 832.3	57 531	89	139	2 582	28.3	69.8	1.9
Polk	29.9	5 747	53.1	24.4	1.5	0.1	5.8	24.1	4 631	26	22	505	26.3	71.6	2.1
Red Willow	39.8	3 706	46.8	0.4	3.3	14.1	5.6	48.1	4 479	76	46	1 073	24.1	74.0	1.8
Richardson	23.8	2 855	63.3	0.0	4.3	0.2	9.9	14.5	1 735	44	35	568	38.1	59.0	2.8
Rock	6.6	4 327	48.7	5.1	4.1	0.1	11.8	0.4	232	0	0	217	17.4	79.9	2.7
Saline	53.1	3 826	45.6	16.1	3.4	0.5	9.7	22.7	1 638	65	59	1 296	50.9	46.4	2.7
Sarpy	441.0	3 005	49.3	1.6	4.5	0.3	6.5	630.0	4 293	2 713	6 453	6 398	41.2	57.1	1.8
Saunders	80.8	4 004	35.9	30.3	3.8	0.5	7.4	52.9	2 622	98	86	1 299	36.9	60.6	2.5
Scotts Bluff	169.4	4 657	54.1	0.2	4.0	1.3	4.0	67.2	1 847	186	158	3 056	32.2	65.9	1.9
Seward	50.2	3 033	58.8	0.0	4.6	0.6	9.0	54.9	3 316	58	71	1 094	35.9	61.7	2.4
Sheridan	29.0	5 329	45.8	26.2	2.7	0.6	6.1	10.2	1 871	29	23	651	18.4	78.8	2.7
Sherman	10.1	3 349	53.1	0.2	4.0	1.6	15.7	9.1	3 023	13	12	296	37.2	60.4	2.4
Sioux	3.3	2 429	62.0	1.9	2.7	0.0	12.2	0.0	11	13	0	84	16.0	82.4	1.6
Stanton	11.1	1 738	44.4	0.0	4.6	0.0	6.4	20.4	3 195	29	27	275	26.6	71.4	2.0
Thayer	29.2	5 650	37.5	27.6	1.6	0.1	6.7	11.5	2 220	39	21	641	32.3	65.8	1.9
Thomas	4.7	7 763	37.2	0.2	1.3	0.0	12.6	0.2	328	0	0	90	13.1	84.9	2.1
Thurston	37.5	5 202	57.5	25.5	1.9	0.0	5.0	27.3	3 789	208	31	1 327	52.7	45.7	1.6
Valley	33.9	7 951	21.8	40.4	1.4	0.3	6.5	14.2	3 332	36	18	668	29.1	68.4	2.5
Washington	64.2	3 217	49.2	0.1	4.3	0.1	14.6	48.2	2 416	50	85	1 600	36.0	62.3	1.8
Wayne	26.6	2 853	55.8	0.3	4.2	0.8	11.2	13.1	1 411	38	40	1 136	32.8	65.7	1.5
Webster	20.0	5 629	31.8	19.2	1.7	0.1	6.5	8.0	2 208	31	15	309	30.4	67.9	1.8
Wheeler	3.6	4 433	61.4	0.0	2.4	0.1	15.7	0.1	103	0	0	61	21.8	75.9	2.3
York	52.2	3 634	46.0	0.6	3.8	0.3	10.8	53.5	3 722	56	59	1 112	24.5	73.8	1.7
NEVADA	X	X	X	X	X	X	X	X	X	17 873	15 940	135 895	55.1	42.7	2.2
Churchill	122.7	4 930	37.3	0.6	6.2	1.3	4.5	47.6	1 913	589	898	1 446	32.9	64.4	2.6
Clark	8 762.7	4 772	34.3	7.6	8.9	2.7	10.3	18 383.2	10 011	11 710	13 283	85 158	58.5	39.5	2.0
Douglas	192.2	4 233	35.2	1.7	8.2	2.4	2.2	62.6	1 378	104	107	2 206	41.2	56.5	2.3
Elko	199.3	4 240	55.8	0.7	7.2	0.6	5.0	63.7	1 143	416	113	3 337	28.3	68.5	3.2
Esmeralda	6.6	9 446	29.9	2.7	15.1	0.2	9.4	0.4	550	0	0	91	23.7	69.0	7.3
Eureka	22.5	14 424	39.2	4.0	5.6	0.5	16.5	5.0	3 203	0	0	207	19.3	75.7	5.0
Humboldt	87.8	5 013	37.9	25.4	5.9	1.2	5.6	79.7	4 548	170	43	1 268	33.7	63.3	3.0
Lander	30.1	5 889	41.5	24.9	6.4	0.9	4.4	14.4	2 826	87	12	450	27.5	69.7	2.8
Lincoln	28.7	6 038	50.7	1.8	4.5	2.8	8.6	8.4	1 770	44	11	604	24.6	71.1	4.3
Lyon	177.4	3 380	57.6	1.4	6.7	4.2	5.6	211.2	4 025	81	124	2 181	39.8	57.6	2.6
Mineral	26.6	5 580	33.6	36.9	6.2	0.5	5.2	7.5	1 575	91	12	519	46.9	49.0	4.1
Nye	148.4	3 363	43.9	2.7	14.0	0.8	6.9	78.0	1 768	159	149	1 863	41.3	54.5	4.2
Pershing	33.6	5 264	34.6	35.0	7.2	1.5	4.1	13.7	2 155	13	15	715	36.7	58.6	4.8
Storey	20.4	4 873	47.2	0.1	11.6	0.1	5.1	14.6	3 485	0	10	253	45.6	51.6	2.9
Washoe	1 635.1	4 027	33.1	1.4	7.4	3.8	6.5	3 073.0	7 568	3 585	1 003	24 247	55.2	42.6	2.1
White Pine	56.6	6 190	32.5	33.0	6.6	0.6	5.6	46.2	5 056	218	22	1 257	32.0	63.5	4.5
Carson City	199.1	3 625	39.8	3.2	11.6	1.0	5.7	200.1	3 642	592	133	10 093	49.1	48.2	2.7
NEW HAMPSHIRE	X	X	X	X	X	X	X	X	X	7 792	4 544	83 846	54.1	44.5	1.4
Belknap	251.7	4 124	50.0	0.5	5.2	5.9	4.2	107.4	1 759	240	202	4 219	50.0	48.8	1.2
Carroll	197.2	4 162	60.4	1.1	4.4	6.3	5.4	95.8	2 023	145	158	2 917	52.4	46.1	1.5
Cheshire	286.3	3 683	59.1	0.7	4.2	7.2	5.8	120.1	1 545	182	255	5 301	63.0	35.5	1.5
Coos	150.6	4 596	44.5	1.4	3.6	13.6	5.1	47.7	1 454	155	104	2 822	58.3	40.1	1.6
Grafton	367.6	4 299	57.5	1.0	4.6	5.2	5.3	174.8	2 044	517	292	6 770	63.0	35.5	1.5
Hillsborough	1 345.6	3 345	51.1	0.7	5.8	3.9	4.3	1 045.4	2 599	3 940	1 364	18 555	51.2	47.5	1.3
Merrimack	541.2	3 650	53.3	0.4	4.6	9.7	4.5	348.5	2 350	918	492	16 036	56.3	42.5	1.3
Rockingham	1 037.4	3 498	59.0	0.5	6.1	3.7	3.2	484.7	1 635	1 272	1 117	13 810	49.9	48.8	1.3
Strafford	406.3	3 342	50.1	0.2	5.2	6.8	5.1	306.2	2 518	320	419	10 843	59.5	39.2	1.3
Sullivan	144.4	3 382	48.3	0.5	3.7	12.1	6.7	42.7	999	103	141	2 573	58.2	40.3	1.5
NEW JERSEY	X	X	X	X	X	X	X	X	X	59 839	25 538	573 525	57.3	41.7	1.0
Atlantic	1 447.7	5 349	53.0	0.9	7.2	2.0	2.4	1 176.7	4 348	2 700	882	20 516	57.0	41.9	1.1
Bergen	4 392.2	4 903	56.6	4.9	7.1	0.8	2.0	3 023.0	3 375	2 948	1 841	46 077	54.3	44.9	0.8
Burlington	1 976.6	4 424	63.4	1.4	4.2	2.0	2.6	2 020.7	4 522	5 743	5 627	25 726	58.8	40.2	1.0
Camden	2 877.5	5 601	51.6	2.8	5.3	3.2	1.9	3 868.2	7 529	2 742	1 066	32 830	67.6	31.3	1.1
Cape May	730.0	7 570	37.5	1.2	5.3	3.6	5.2	626.5	6 497	467	1 258	9 147	45.0	53.7	1.3
Cumberland	747.9	4 808	62.4	2.2	3.5	3.7	1.8	357.1	2 296	644	324	14 381	60.1	38.5	1.4
Essex	3 931.0	5 065	39.8	2.4	8.9	3.7	1.3	3 435.1	4 426	9 935	1 598	71 075	76.0	23.4	0.6
Gloucester	1 246.3	4 361	60.3	0.5	4.5	2.1	1.8	1 091.3	3 819	1 050	596	18 163	55.4	43.3	1.3
Hudson	2 466.9	4 124	33.5	1.5	9.0	2.4	2.0	2 717.4	4 543	5 856	1 344	38 296	72.9	26.2	0.9
Hunterdon	638.9	4 939	64.2	0.7	2.9	0.8	5.7	535.6	4 141	334	267	9 341	42.6	56.0	1.4

1. Based on the resident population estimated as of July 1 of the year shown.   2. © 2009 Election Data Services, Inc. All rights reserved.

Table B. States and Counties — **Land Area and Population**

STATE/ County code	CBSA code[1]	County type[2]	STATE County	Land area,[3] (sq km) 2010	Total persons	Rank	Per square kilometer	White	Black	American Indian, Alaska Native	Asian and Pacific Islander	Percent Hispanic or Latino[4]	Under 5 years	5 to 17 years	18 to 24 years	25 to 34 years	35 to 44 years	45 to 54 years
				1	2	3	4	5	6	7	8	9	10	11	12	13	14	15
			NEW JERSEY—Cont'd															
34 021	45940	2	Mercer	582	366 513	179	629.7	55.8	20.3	0.5	9.8	15.1	5.9	16.8	10.9	12.8	14.1	15.2
34 023	35620	1	Middlesex	800	809 858	64	1 012.3	50.3	9.4	0.5	22.5	18.4	6.2	16.7	10.2	13.8	14.5	15.1
34 025	35620	1	Monmouth	1 214	630 380	95	519.3	77.8	7.6	0.4	5.6	9.7	5.5	18.3	7.8	10.3	13.7	17.6
34 027	35620	1	Morris	1 192	492 276	134	413.0	76.3	3.3	0.3	9.8	11.5	5.6	18.4	7.1	10.5	14.7	17.3
34 029	35620	1	Ocean	1 629	576 567	108	353.9	86.8	3.3	0.4	2.1	8.3	6.7	16.7	7.5	10.6	11.6	13.6
34 031	35620	1	Passaic	478	501 226	128	1 048.6	46.3	11.5	0.4	5.6	37.0	6.8	18.0	10.3	13.3	13.8	14.6
34 033	37980	1	Salem	860	66 083	794	76.8	78.2	14.6	0.8	1.1	6.8	5.8	17.6	8.2	11.1	12.7	16.0
34 035	35620	1	Somerset	782	323 444	195	413.6	63.7	9.1	0.3	15.1	13.0	5.9	19.0	6.5	11.3	15.1	17.8
34 037	35620	1	Sussex	1 344	149 265	419	111.1	89.9	2.1	0.5	2.3	6.4	5.3	18.6	7.6	9.5	14.4	18.7
34 039	35620	1	Union	266	536 499	117	2 016.9	46.3	21.5	0.4	5.2	27.3	6.7	17.8	8.6	12.9	14.6	15.5
34 041	10900	2	Warren	924	108 692	540	117.6	86.8	3.9	0.4	2.9	7.0	5.6	18.0	7.9	9.8	14.2	17.6
35 000	...	X	NEW MEXICO	314 161	2 059 179	X	6.6	41.7	2.2	9.2	1.8	46.3	7.0	18.1	9.9	13.0	12.1	14.2
35 001	10740	2	Bernalillo	3 007	662 564	92	220.3	43.0	3.0	4.7	3.0	47.9	6.8	17.2	10.4	14.5	12.7	14.2
35 003	...	9	Catron	17 932	3 725	2 928	0.2	77.7	0.6	4.0	0.2	19.0	4.1	11.7	3.5	7.2	6.5	15.4
35 005	40740	5	Chaves	15 709	65 645	797	4.2	44.8	1.9	1.2	0.9	52.0	8.0	20.0	10.1	12.1	11.1	13.1
35 006	24380	6	Cibola	11 757	27 213	1 525	2.3	22.5	1.1	40.3	0.8	36.5	7.0	18.2	9.4	13.6	12.7	14.6
35 007	...	7	Colfax	9 733	13 750	2 204	1.4	51.0	0.4	1.7	0.7	47.2	5.3	15.4	6.9	10.1	10.4	15.6
35 009	17580	5	Curry	3 638	48 376	1 004	13.3	52.5	6.6	1.2	2.0	39.5	8.9	19.5	11.2	15.0	11.8	12.6
35 011	...	9	De Baca	6 016	2 022	3 052	0.3	60.9	0.2	1.6	0.2	38.5	5.6	16.7	4.3	10.2	8.9	15.2
35 013	29740	3	Dona Ana	9 861	209 233	296	21.2	30.9	1.7	1.1	1.4	65.7	7.4	19.3	13.1	13.2	11.2	12.7
35 015	16100	5	Eddy	10 815	53 829	926	5.0	53.2	1.4	1.3	0.9	44.1	7.1	19.0	8.7	12.6	11.7	14.4
35 017	43500	7	Grant	10 261	29 514	1 438	2.9	49.7	0.8	1.4	0.6	48.3	6.0	15.9	7.7	9.8	9.6	13.4
35 019	...	7	Guadalupe	7 849	4 687	2 862	0.6	16.4	1.5	1.4	1.6	79.6	5.7	16.1	8.1	14.3	11.7	16.4
35 021	...	9	Harding	5 505	695	3 129	0.1	56.4	0.3	0.4	0.0	43.0	4.0	9.2	3.9	7.2	8.1	15.7
35 023	...	7	Hidalgo	8 901	4 894	2 849	0.5	42.1	0.4	0.7	0.8	56.6	6.7	19.0	8.4	9.6	11.6	14.5
35 025	26200	5	Lea	11 372	64 727	808	5.7	43.8	4.1	1.2	0.6	51.1	9.1	20.3	10.1	14.6	12.0	13.1
35 027	40760	7	Lincoln	12 512	20 497	1 818	1.6	67.3	0.6	2.7	0.5	29.8	4.8	14.2	6.0	8.6	9.9	16.0
35 028	31060	6	Los Alamos	283	17 950	1 925	63.4	77.9	0.9	1.2	6.9	14.7	5.3	18.9	4.2	9.5	13.0	18.6
35 029	19700	6	Luna	7 680	25 095	1 599	3.3	36.5	0.9	1.1	0.6	61.5	7.3	19.2	8.7	10.4	10.5	12.0
35 031	23700	4	McKinley	14 115	71 492	747	5.1	11.6	0.9	74.9	1.0	13.3	8.6	22.7	11.5	12.4	11.9	13.4
35 033	...	8	Mora	5 002	4 881	2 850	1.0	18.2	0.3	0.6	0.3	81.0	5.1	16.2	6.6	9.3	11.5	15.2
35 035	10460	4	Otero	17 128	63 797	818	3.7	54.7	4.0	6.7	2.2	34.5	7.5	17.5	10.4	13.0	11.2	13.7
35 037	...	7	Quay	7 445	9 041	2 524	1.2	54.8	1.2	1.4	1.2	42.4	5.7	16.0	6.6	9.8	10.9	14.6
35 039	21580	6	Rio Arriba	15 179	40 246	1 167	2.7	13.4	0.4	14.6	0.5	71.3	6.7	17.9	8.9	11.5	12.4	15.0
35 041	38780	7	Roosevelt	6 339	19 846	1 846	3.1	56.7	1.9	1.6	1.1	39.9	7.9	18.6	16.5	13.0	10.7	11.5
35 043	10740	2	Sandoval	9 611	131 561	468	13.7	49.0	2.4	12.9	2.1	35.1	6.9	19.8	7.8	11.8	13.3	15.3
35 045	22140	3	San Juan	14 279	130 044	476	9.1	44.1	0.8	37.1	0.7	19.1	8.4	20.6	9.8	13.8	11.7	14.0
35 047	29780	6	San Miguel	12 214	29 393	1 444	2.4	20.3	1.3	1.2	0.9	76.8	5.5	16.5	10.8	10.9	11.0	15.6
35 049	42140	3	Santa Fe	4 945	144 170	431	29.2	44.9	0.9	2.8	1.6	50.6	5.7	15.3	7.4	11.5	12.6	15.5
35 051	...	6	Sierra	10 823	11 988	2 304	1.1	70.0	0.5	2.4	0.7	28.0	4.7	11.3	5.7	6.7	8.5	13.8
35 053	...	6	Socorro	17 215	17 866	1 929	1.0	38.6	1.0	11.2	1.5	48.5	6.7	17.2	12.5	11.5	10.8	14.1
35 055	45340	7	Taos	5 706	32 937	1 360	5.8	37.5	0.5	6.2	0.9	55.8	5.5	15.1	6.9	10.2	12.0	15.6
35 057	10740	2	Torrance	8 663	16 383	2 026	1.9	57.5	1.5	2.6	0.7	39.1	5.7	18.4	7.8	10.3	12.0	15.9
35 059	...	9	Union	9 903	4 549	2 867	0.5	56.9	1.9	1.7	0.7	39.7	5.6	14.8	7.7	14.4	12.2	15.5
35 061	10740	2	Valencia	2 761	76 569	709	27.7	37.2	1.4	3.3	0.7	58.3	6.9	19.5	8.8	11.7	12.6	15.1
36 000	...	X	NEW YORK	122 057	19 378 102	X	158.8	59.5	15.2	0.7	8.1	17.6	6.0	16.4	10.2	13.7	13.5	14.9
36 001	10580	2	Albany	1 354	304 204	210	224.7	77.7	13.2	0.6	5.4	4.9	5.0	14.9	13.2	13.0	12.2	14.9
36 003	...	7	Allegany	2 666	48 946	995	18.4	96.4	1.4	0.6	1.2	1.4	5.4	16.2	15.8	9.9	10.6	14.0
36 005	35620	1	Bronx	109	1 385 108	26	12 707.4	11.4	30.8	0.6	4.0	53.5	7.4	19.1	11.6	14.7	13.5	13.4
36 007	13780	2	Broome	1 828	200 600	309	109.7	88.2	5.6	0.7	4.1	3.4	5.2	15.0	13.0	11.5	11.1	15.3
36 009	36460	4	Cattaraugus	3 389	80 317	683	23.7	93.4	1.9	3.7	0.9	1.7	6.3	17.1	9.6	10.6	11.8	15.4
36 011	12180	4	Cayuga	1 791	80 026	685	44.7	92.8	4.7	0.8	0.7	2.4	5.3	16.3	8.7	11.8	12.9	16.4
36 013	27460	4	Chautauqua	2 746	134 905	457	49.1	90.8	3.0	0.9	0.7	6.1	5.6	16.2	11.3	10.4	11.5	15.1
36 015	21300	3	Chemung	1 055	88 830	639	84.2	89.6	7.8	0.8	1.5	2.5	5.9	16.4	8.9	11.8	12.3	15.7
36 017	...	6	Chenango	2 314	50 477	971	21.8	96.7	1.0	0.8	0.7	1.8	5.4	17.3	7.5	10.4	12.2	16.5
36 019	38460	5	Clinton	2 688	82 128	673	30.6	92.3	4.1	0.8	1.4	2.5	5.0	14.4	13.5	12.4	13.0	16.3
36 021	26460	6	Columbia	1 644	63 096	827	38.4	89.8	5.3	0.6	2.0	3.9	4.8	15.5	7.4	9.4	12.3	16.8
36 023	18660	4	Cortland	1 292	49 336	990	38.2	95.2	2.1	0.8	1.2	2.2	5.5	15.6	17.4	10.6	11.4	14.3
36 025	...	6	Delaware	3 736	47 980	1 005	12.8	94.2	1.9	0.7	1.1	3.3	5.0	14.6	9.9	9.2	10.9	15.6
36 027	39100	2	Dutchess	2 061	297 488	215	144.3	76.1	10.2	0.6	4.1	10.5	5.1	17.1	10.9	10.6	13.4	16.9
36 029	15380	1	Erie	2 701	919 040	50	340.3	79.0	13.9	1.0	3.0	4.5	5.3	16.3	10.5	11.7	12.2	15.4
36 031	...	6	Essex	4 647	39 370	1 185	8.5	93.9	2.8	0.8	0.9	2.5	4.7	14.6	7.3	11.5	12.6	16.4
36 033	31660	5	Franklin	4 219	51 599	956	12.2	83.7	5.7	8.0	0.6	2.9	5.5	15.3	10.4	13.7	13.3	16.2
36 035	24100	4	Fulton	1 283	55 531	902	43.3	95.0	2.4	0.6	0.9	2.3	5.5	16.7	7.9	11.3	13.1	15.9

1. CBSA = Core Based Statistical Area. See Appendix A for explanation. See Appendix B for list of metropolitan areas with component counties.   2. County type code from the Economic Research Service of USDA Rural-Urban Continuum Codes. See Appendix A for definition.   3. Dry land or land partially or temporarily covered by water.   4. May be of any race.

Table B. States and Counties — **Population and Households**

STATE County	55 to 64 years	65 to 74 years	75 years and over	Percent female	1990	2000	1990–2000	2000–2010	Births	Deaths	Net migration	Number	Percent change, 2000–2010	Persons per house-hold	Female family house-holder[1]	One per-son
	16	17	18	19	20	21	22	23	24	25	26	27	28	29	30	31
NEW JERSEY—Cont'd																
Mercer	11.7	6.4	6.2	51.2	325 759	350 761	7.7	4.5	42 596	26 783	1 914	133 155	5.8	2.61	14.2	26.9
Middlesex	11.2	6.3	6.0	50.9	671 712	750 162	11.7	8.0	97 004	51 374	-548	281 186	5.8	2.80	11.8	22.5
Monmouth	13.0	7.0	6.7	51.4	553 192	615 301	11.2	2.5	69 361	48 921	-2 609	233 983	4.3	2.66	10.5	25.0
Morris	12.6	7.2	6.6	51.0	421 330	470 212	11.6	4.7	54 614	31 579	-1 851	180 534	6.4	2.68	8.5	23.5
Ocean	12.3	10.1	10.9	52.1	433 203	510 916	17.9	12.8	68 622	64 228	58 118	221 111	10.3	2.58	9.8	27.8
Passaic	11.1	6.4	5.7	51.5	470 872	489 049	3.9	2.5	70 611	35 861	-31 000	166 785	1.8	2.94	17.5	22.6
Salem	13.5	7.7	7.3	51.3	65 294	64 285	-1.5	2.8	6 976	6 525	2 028	25 290	4.1	2.56	14.4	25.4
Somerset	12.0	6.4	6.0	51.3	240 222	297 490	23.8	8.7	38 612	19 187	11 943	117 759	8.1	2.71	9.5	23.3
Sussex	14.0	7.1	4.9	50.4	130 936	144 166	10.1	3.5	15 161	9 231	1 805	54 752	7.7	2.69	9.0	21.0
Union	11.3	6.3	6.3	51.8	493 819	522 541	5.8	2.7	68 802	39 932	-22 366	188 118	1.1	2.82	15.6	23.6
Warren	12.7	7.3	6.8	51.4	91 675	102 437	11.7	6.1	11 841	8 186	4 107	41 480	7.3	2.57	10.2	25.0
NEW MEXICO	12.5	7.5	5.8	50.6	1 515 069	1 819 046	20.1	13.2	265 766	136 175	70 558	791 395	16.7	2.55	14.0	28.0
Bernalillo	12.0	6.6	5.6	51.0	480 577	556 678	15.8	19.0	84 361	42 429	48 156	266 000	20.4	2.45	14.1	30.4
Catron	23.5	18.3	9.6	47.7	2 563	3 543	38.2	5.1	209	304	-13	1 787	12.8	2.03	4.8	34.8
Chaves	11.3	7.2	6.9	50.5	57 849	61 382	6.1	6.9	9 043	5 658	-753	23 691	5.0	2.70	14.9	25.2
Cibola	11.8	7.4	5.4	49.4	23 794	25 595	7.6	6.3	3 951	1 957	-439	8 860	6.4	2.79	20.8	24.9
Colfax	16.4	11.4	8.6	49.1	12 925	14 189	9.8	-3.1	1 436	1 346	-1 500	6 011	3.3	2.22	10.9	32.9
Curry	9.6	6.2	5.3	49.8	42 207	45 044	6.7	7.4	7 882	3 378	-4 970	18 015	7.4	2.63	14.2	26.4
De Baca	16.2	12.1	10.8	50.9	2 252	2 240	-0.5	-9.7	171	230	-360	912	-1.1	2.21	8.3	32.7
Dona Ana	10.7	7.0	5.4	51.0	135 510	174 682	28.9	19.8	30 311	11 251	13 752	75 532	26.8	2.71	16.0	24.2
Eddy	12.5	7.3	6.7	50.1	48 605	51 658	6.3	4.2	6 838	4 949	-528	20 411	5.3	2.59	13.0	25.5
Grant	16.3	11.9	9.5	50.9	27 676	31 002	12.0	-4.8	3 471	2 937	-1 517	12 586	3.6	2.30	12.6	30.9
Guadalupe	12.1	8.6	6.9	43.5	4 156	4 680	12.6	0.1	456	410	-471	1 766	6.7	2.33	15.2	32.4
Harding	22.7	12.7	16.5	47.2	987	810	-17.9	-14.2	36	68	-120	349	-5.9	1.99	5.4	34.7
Hidalgo	13.3	9.1	7.6	49.8	5 958	5 932	-0.4	-17.5	591	452	-1 007	1 936	-10.0	2.49	14.2	29.1
Lea	9.9	5.8	5.0	48.9	55 765	55 511	-0.5	16.6	9 386	4 442	54	22 236	12.9	2.82	13.4	22.6
Lincoln	18.5	13.7	8.2	50.9	12 219	19 411	58.9	5.6	2 067	1 540	1 144	9 219	12.4	2.21	9.8	30.5
Los Alamos	15.4	8.0	6.9	49.7	18 115	18 343	1.3	-2.1	1 703	969	-962	7 663	2.2	2.33	6.4	28.5
Luna	12.4	10.7	8.9	50.3	18 110	25 016	38.1	0.3	3 838	2 454	776	9 593	2.1	2.56	14.5	27.8
McKinley	10.0	5.5	4.0	51.6	60 686	74 798	23.3	-4.4	12 707	4 373	-12 507	21 968	2.3	3.22	24.5	22.4
Mora	17.3	10.7	8.0	48.8	4 264	5 180	21.5	-5.8	425	379	-266	2 114	4.8	2.31	10.9	33.2
Otero	11.8	8.6	6.4	49.5	51 928	62 298	20.0	2.4	7 989	4 598	-2 204	24 464	6.4	2.51	12.7	27.1
Quay	15.7	11.9	8.8	50.7	10 823	10 155	-6.2	-11.0	1 021	1 131	-1 078	4 072	-3.1	2.21	12.7	34.2
Rio Arriba	13.5	8.2	5.8	50.6	34 365	41 190	19.9	-2.3	6 491	3 221	-3 625	15 768	4.8	2.53	16.0	28.2
Roosevelt	9.8	6.4	5.5	49.7	16 702	18 018	7.9	10.1	2 967	1 390	-673	7 299	9.9	2.57	11.7	28.3
Sandoval	13.0	7.2	4.9	51.1	63 319	89 908	42.0	46.3	13 077	6 335	28 971	47 602	51.5	2.75	12.5	22.0
San Juan	11.0	6.1	4.7	50.4	91 605	113 801	24.2	14.3	18 809	7 409	-491	44 404	17.7	2.89	15.6	21.9
San Miguel	14.5	9.3	5.9	50.1	25 743	30 126	17.0	-2.4	3 413	2 465	-2 608	11 978	7.6	2.34	14.9	32.5
Santa Fe	16.8	9.3	5.8	51.3	98 928	129 292	30.7	11.5	15 180	8 099	11 881	61 963	18.1	2.28	11.0	33.7
Sierra	18.5	16.8	13.8	49.7	9 912	13 270	33.9	-9.7	1 015	2 020	678	5 917	-3.2	1.98	8.9	40.8
Socorro	12.9	8.5	5.7	48.7	14 764	18 078	22.4	-1.2	2 315	1 312	-920	7 014	5.1	2.46	12.9	30.8
Taos	17.7	10.4	6.7	50.8	23 118	29 979	29.7	9.9	3 408	2 251	527	14 806	16.8	2.19	12.6	36.0
Torrance	15.6	9.0	5.2	48.4	10 285	16 911	64.4	-3.1	1 719	1 151	-956	6 264	4.0	2.52	12.0	27.6
Union	11.9	9.5	8.4	43.0	4 124	4 174	1.2	9.0	417	445	-324	1 695	-2.2	2.29	10.1	33.2
Valencia	12.8	7.6	5.1	49.6	45 235	66 152	46.2	15.7	9 063	4 822	2 911	27 500	21.2	2.73	13.9	22.1
NEW YORK	11.9	7.0	6.5	51.6	17 990 778	18 976 457	5.5	2.1	2 323 103	1 417 221	-846 993	7 317 755	3.7	2.57	14.9	29.1
Albany	12.8	6.8	7.1	51.7	292 812	294 565	0.6	3.3	29 592	25 622	1 507	126 251	4.8	2.27	12.2	33.8
Allegany	12.8	8.0	7.2	49.5	50 470	49 927	-1.1	-2.0	4 992	4 394	-1 083	18 208	1.1	2.44	9.5	27.9
Bronx	9.6	5.8	4.7	53.1	1 203 789	1 332 650	10.7	3.9	209 058	90 419	-121 472	483 449	4.4	2.77	31.1	28.2
Broome	12.6	7.8	8.6	51.0	212 160	200 536	-5.5	0.0	19 533	19 231	-4 987	82 167	1.8	2.32	12.0	32.4
Cattaraugus	13.7	8.1	7.3	50.5	84 234	83 955	-0.3	-4.3	9 196	7 703	-5 272	32 263	0.7	2.41	11.3	29.5
Cayuga	13.3	7.7	7.6	49.0	82 313	81 963	-0.4	-2.4	7 873	6 859	-2 944	31 445	2.9	2.41	11.6	28.5
Chautauqua	13.3	8.2	8.3	50.7	141 895	139 750	-1.5	-3.5	13 964	13 449	-5 945	54 244	-0.5	2.37	11.8	29.9
Chemung	13.2	7.7	8.0	50.3	95 195	91 070	-4.3	-2.5	9 812	8 603	-3 424	35 462	1.2	2.37	13.0	30.3
Chenango	14.0	9.2	7.5	50.2	51 768	51 401	-0.7	-1.8	5 105	4 959	-601	20 436	2.6	2.43	10.8	27.5
Clinton	12.2	7.2	6.2	48.7	85 969	79 894	-7.1	2.8	7 314	5 957	855	31 582	7.3	2.37	10.6	27.5
Columbia	15.6	9.8	8.3	49.7	62 982	63 094	0.2	0.0	5 605	6 242	-420	25 906	4.5	2.35	10.6	28.8
Cortland	12.1	7.0	6.1	51.2	48 963	48 599	-0.7	1.5	5 034	3 990	-1 371	18 671	2.5	2.45	10.9	28.0
Delaware	15.4	10.6	8.8	49.8	47 352	48 055	1.5	-0.2	4 160	5 066	-1 348	19 898	3.3	2.29	9.4	30.5
Dutchess	12.5	7.2	6.3	50.2	259 462	280 150	8.0	6.2	29 452	20 644	6 354	107 965	8.5	2.57	11.0	26.0
Erie	12.7	7.6	8.1	51.8	968 584	950 265	-1.9	-3.3	95 696	90 268	-40 674	383 164	0.6	2.32	13.7	33.0
Essex	14.7	9.6	8.6	48.2	37 152	38 851	4.6	1.3	3 361	3 731	-545	16 262	8.2	2.26	8.5	30.9
Franklin	12.3	7.3	6.1	45.1	46 540	51 134	9.9	0.9	4 585	3 989	-1 133	19 054	6.3	2.37	11.7	29.7
Fulton	13.5	8.3	7.7	50.5	54 191	55 073	1.6	0.8	5 425	5 404	302	22 554	3.1	2.40	12.5	28.2

1. No spouse present.

Table B. States and Counties — Population, Vital Statistics, Medicare, and Crime

STATE County	Persons in group quarters, 2010	Daytime population, 2006–2010 Number	Daytime population Employment/ residence ratio	Births, average 2006–2008 Total	Births Rate[1]	Deaths, average 2006–2008 Number	Deaths Rate[1]	Persons under 65 with no health insurance, 2009 Number	Persons under 65 Percent	Medicare, 2011 Eligible for Medicare	Medicare Enrolled in Medicare Advantage	Medicare Enrolled in a Medicare prescription drug plan	Serious crimes known to police,[2] 2010 Total Number	Serious crimes Rate[3]
	32	33	34	35	36	37	38	39	40	41	42	43	44	45
NEW JERSEY—Cont'd														
Mercer	18 805	414 376	1.3	4 713	12.9	2 895	7.9	40 818	13.0	57 810	7 153	23 633	9 354	2 552
Middlesex	23 835	783 858	1.0	10 730	13.6	5 491	7.0	96 740	14.1	112 820	14 207	47 677	15 476	1 911
Monmouth	7 670	590 235	0.9	7 246	11.3	5 223	8.2	66 962	12.2	101 272	11 845	42 454	15 237	2 417
Morris	8 866	529 390	1.2	5 494	11.2	3 398	6.9	36 171	8.7	75 831	7 032	31 302	5 590	1 136
Ocean	7 163	497 553	0.7	7 994	14.1	6 785	12.0	57 531	12.9	135 636	19 762	54 060	12 127	2 103
Passaic	11 019	452 636	0.8	7 684	15.6	3 688	7.5	83 571	19.7	71 561	10 613	32 888	13 402	2 674
Salem	1 257	59 808	0.8	817	12.3	723	10.9	7 005	12.5	12 308	870	6 860	1 814	2 745
Somerset	3 970	330 640	1.1	3 930	12.1	2 058	6.3	26 310	9.3	44 614	3 419	18 579	4 508	1 394
Sussex	1 742	118 611	0.6	1 591	10.5	1 001	6.6	12 647	9.6	22 359	1 953	9 379	1 877	1 257
Union	6 804	518 768	1.0	7 527	14.3	4 062	7.7	76 224	16.9	76 070	11 749	30 234	14 708	2 741
Warren	1 968	94 884	0.7	1 265	11.5	917	8.3	10 728	11.5	18 055	1 209	8 149	1 576	1 450
NEW MEXICO	42 629	2 007 676	1.0	30 242	15.4	15 594	7.9	394 687	22.9	326 559	85 811	125 356	82 868	4 024
Bernalillo	11 945	676 796	1.1	9 652	15.4	4 909	7.8	109 893	19.8	97 995	44 257	24 321	34 670	5 233
Catron	106	3 518	0.9	D	D	33	9.6	784	31.6	1 123	128	423	13	349
Chaves	1 784	62 945	0.9	1 059	16.9	613	9.8	13 458	25.3	11 114	408	6 849	3 125	4 760
Cibola	2 531	26 037	0.9	441	16.1	221	8.1	5 648	24.2	4 054	350	1 980	600	2 205
Colfax	408	13 886	1.0	D	D	148	11.2	2 132	21.2	3 163	368	1 579	284	2 236
Curry	1 041	47 240	1.0	866	19.3	358	8.0	8 577	22.5	6 640	557	3 695	2 248	4 710
De Baca	9	1 775	1.0	D	D	22	11.5	403	31.1	542	34	334	NA	NA
Dona Ana	4 581	198 825	1.0	3 340	16.9	1 308	6.6	46 430	26.3	30 444	6 939	12 732	7 013	3 414
Eddy	995	54 969	1.1	791	15.4	519	10.1	8 681	19.4	9 140	257	5 794	2 398	4 455
Grant	590	29 455	1.0	D	D	343	11.5	4 797	20.5	7 462	1 327	3 067	966	3 273
Guadalupe	571	4 616	0.9	D	D	45	10.3	1 058	30.6	943	86	604	105	2 240
Harding	0	943	1.0	D	D	D	D	145	29.5	196	20	93	NA	NA
Hidalgo	64	5 150	1.1	D	D	46	9.3	1 173	28.6	984	173	450	24	490
Lea	2 057	63 350	1.0	1 193	20.5	497	8.5	13 680	25.9	8 087	119	5 389	2 881	4 451
Lincoln	116	20 280	1.0	D	D	166	7.9	4 549	27.7	4 954	714	2 085	549	2 888
Los Alamos	94	26 155	1.9	D	D	105	5.6	739	4.8	2 866	151	487	NA	NA
Luna	551	25 290	1.0	D	D	287	10.6	6 352	30.1	6 097	1 443	2 555	894	3 562
McKinley	780	71 246	1.0	1 396	19.7	485	6.8	18 287	28.5	8 642	439	4 969	2 259	3 160
Mora	8	4 306	0.7	D	D	46	9.1	995	24.8	1 211	134	673	7	143
Otero	2 306	60 579	0.9	918	14.6	511	8.1	14 092	26.5	10 821	1 306	3 860	1 600	2 535
Quay	22	9 026	1.0	D	D	118	13.0	1 723	25.1	2 379	269	1 257	430	4 756
Rio Arriba	425	34 930	0.7	715	17.5	375	9.2	8 342	23.8	7 601	1 446	3 292	829	2 060
Roosevelt	1 083	19 050	1.0	D	D	164	8.8	4 478	27.5	2 714	75	1 747	555	2 797
Sandoval	761	103 339	0.6	1 555	13.2	795	6.7	20 660	18.6	19 695	8 501	4 327	2 358	1 792
San Juan	1 754	127 020	1.0	2 253	18.2	862	7.0	30 070	27.1	16 202	404	8 759	3 604	2 771
San Miguel	1 310	27 406	0.8	D	D	269	9.3	4 893	20.7	5 743	448	3 641	NA	NA
Santa Fe	2 613	145 324	1.1	1 694	11.8	945	6.6	29 922	24.0	25 745	6 298	9 842	6 406	4 443
Sierra	265	11 902	1.0	D	D	217	17.4	2 476	27.9	3 996	824	1 560	275	2 294
Socorro	583	17 760	1.0	D	D	150	8.3	4 194	27.3	2 988	386	1 374	511	3 019
Taos	470	32 130	1.0	D	D	265	8.4	7 226	27.8	6 904	1 099	3 257	904	2 901
Torrance	615	14 639	0.7	D	D	142	8.4	3 598	25.5	2 783	1 072	794	230	1 404
Union	662	4 403	1.0	D	D	44	11.6	804	26.1	918	29	545	29	638
Valencia	1 529	63 386	0.6	997	14.0	579	8.1	14 431	22.9	12 413	5 750	3 022	2 863	3 739
NEW YORK	585 678	19 548 402	1.0	251 313	12.9	148 395	7.6	2 172 693	13.2	3 073 761	964 055	1 001 835	452 138	2 333
Albany	17 024	378 209	1.5	3 109	10.4	2 670	8.9	23 381	9.3	50 868	18 462	11 425	11 023	3 624
Allegany	4 584	45 196	0.8	513	10.3	451	9.1	4 665	11.5	9 145	2 815	2 871	835	1 786
Bronx	46 710	1 206 423	0.7	22 931	16.7	9 299	6.8	200 555	16.7	171 991	76 906	56 733	(4)	(4)
Broome	10 141	209 084	1.1	2 112	10.8	2 068	10.6	18 033	11.4	40 752	11 026	15 263	6 007	2 995
Cattaraugus	2 679	77 924	0.9	1 008	12.5	789	9.8	8 250	12.6	15 903	6 325	4 576	2 057	2 561
Cayuga	4 245	71 903	0.8	830	10.3	732	9.1	8 010	12.2	14 158	2 864	5 007	1 753	2 191
Chautauqua	6 514	135 942	1.0	1 478	11.0	1 418	10.6	12 954	11.9	27 664	10 958	9 129	3 859	2 861
Chemung	4 916	89 942	1.0	1 025	11.6	951	10.8	8 268	11.4	18 079	4 391	6 317	2 080	2 342
Chenango	796	48 270	0.9	542	10.6	534	10.4	4 935	12.0	10 718	2 811	4 329	976	1 966
Clinton	7 153	81 972	1.0	794	9.7	644	7.8	9 066	13.2	15 177	1 919	5 706	1 826	2 223
Columbia	2 136	57 335	0.8	595	9.5	644	10.3	6 270	12.6	13 060	2 798	4 443	1 097	1 739
Cortland	3 561	47 603	0.9	542	11.2	431	8.9	4 669	11.5	8 174	1 520	3 434	1 066	2 161
Delaware	2 435	48 139	1.0	D	D	549	11.8	4 627	13.0	9 990	1 969	3 972	749	1 561
Dutchess	19 965	277 752	0.9	3 041	10.4	2 203	7.5	27 566	11.1	49 086	6 504	16 493	5 644	2 126
Erie	28 387	948 734	1.1	9 910	10.8	9 459	10.3	72 931	9.8	176 390	92 495	29 857	32 474	3 533
Essex	2 647	38 888	1.0	D	D	407	10.7	4 392	14.4	8 032	956	3 320	569	1 445
Franklin	6 400	52 031	1.0	D	D	435	8.6	7 665	18.2	9 556	1 590	3 607	895	1 735
Fulton	1 474	51 899	0.8	589	10.7	554	10.0	5 387	12.0	11 271	3 934	4 363	1 692	3 047

1. Per 1,000 estimated resident population.   2. Data for serious crimes have not been adjusted for underreporting; this may affect comparability between geographic areas and over time.   3. Per 100,000 population estimated by the FBI.   4. Bronx, Kings, Queens, and Richmond counties are included with New York county.

STATE County	Violent (46)	Property (47)	Enrollment Total (48)	Percent private (49)	High school graduate or less (50)	Bachelor's degree or more (51)	Total current expenditures (mil dol) (52)	Current expenditures per student (dollars) (53)	Per capita income (dollars) (54)	Median income Dollars (55)	Percent change, 2000 to 2006–2010 (constant 2010 dollars) (56)	Percent with income of $200,000 or more (57)	Median household income (dollars) (58)	All persons (59)	Children under 18 years (60)	Children 5 to 17 years in families (61)
NEW JERSEY—Cont'd																
Mercer	452	2 101	103 202	24.5	39.4	38.2	1 000.0	16 686	36 016	71 217	-0.7	9.7	70 228	11.7	15.7	14.3
Middlesex	179	1 732	215 230	16.5	40.1	38.4	1 676.4	15 358	33 289	77 615	-0.2	7.2	75 890	7.7	10.0	9.4
Monmouth	204	2 213	168 545	23.1	36.1	39.2	1 819.4	15 602	40 976	82 265	1.1	11.7	80 462	6.8	8.7	7.3
Morris	71	1 064	130 023	25.5	30.6	48.4	1 287.6	16 065	47 342	96 747	-1.2	15.6	91 403	5.7	5.6	4.9
Ocean	122	1 982	134 139	30.8	48.9	24.3	1 071.0	14 068	29 826	59 620	1.4	4.0	56 924	11.0	19.2	17.2
Passaic	510	2 164	133 550	18.9	53.6	25.2	1 323.7	16 651	26 095	54 944	-11.8	4.6	53 363	15.6	23.6	23.1
Salem	262	2 483	17 070	14.6	53.5	18.3	184.9	15 407	27 296	59 441	3.0	2.7	55 274	11.2	17.0	14.7
Somerset	77	1 316	84 841	20.4	29.5	49.8	854.0	15 593	47 067	97 440	0.0	16.0	93 777	5.2	6.3	5.6
Sussex	56	1 201	40 539	18.8	40.2	31.4	431.9	16 732	35 982	83 089	0.5	7.1	81 330	5.7	6.9	6.2
Union	467	2 274	137 254	17.6	47.2	31.2	1 434.0	16 671	34 096	66 791	-4.7	8.8	65 937	10.9	15.6	14.0
Warren	101	1 349	27 948	17.3	45.8	28.6	280.1	15 119	32 985	71 364	0.5	5.3	69 658	7.4	9.1	8.2
NEW MEXICO	589	3 435	547 061	10.9	44.3	25.5	3 112.6	9 437	22 966	43 820	1.4	2.4	42 186	19.8	28.5	26.7
Bernalillo	771	4 462	179 778	14.8	38.1	31.5	852.5	8 785	26 143	47 481	-3.3	2.8	47 405	16.4	23.9	22.5
Catron	27	322	491	11.2	46.9	21.3	6.1	17 382	20 895	31 914	5.5	0.1	28 427	23.1	41.7	40.0
Chaves	593	4 168	17 504	11.9	53.0	15.7	102.7	8 987	18 504	37 524	3.9	1.3	34 681	22.8	33.0	31.6
Cibola	625	1 580	7 129	8.8	61.3	11.5	39.1	10 849	14 712	37 361	6.2	0.7	33 782	27.6	38.7	37.6
Colfax	386	1 850	2 868	3.8	48.9	19.9	24.5	11 338	21 047	39 216	0.7	1.2	36 468	17.9	28.3	25.9
Curry	507	4 203	13 321	7.5	46.4	18.2	77.7	8 502	19 925	38 090	4.0	1.2	36 085	19.8	29.9	27.9
De Baca	NA	NA	302	5.6	60.2	19.7	5.0	15 082	20 769	30 643	-4.9	0.9	31 442	18.6	31.2	30.0
Dona Ana	352	3 062	64 427	4.7	46.7	25.4	366.3	9 255	18 315	36 657	-2.9	1.5	35 584	25.4	34.6	31.7
Eddy	550	3 905	13 811	8.0	53.3	15.1	101.1	9 855	24 587	46 583	15.0	2.8	43 240	16.6	23.2	21.9
Grant	396	2 877	7 338	8.8	42.3	24.1	48.7	10 370	21 164	36 591	-0.8	0.8	36 756	18.9	29.5	27.7
Guadalupe	405	1 835	1 141	6.8	61.0	7.4	10.8	14 593	13 710	28 488	-9.2	0.5	28 402	23.7	30.5	28.3
Harding	NA	NA	273	0.0	50.4	18.2	3.3	34 989	14 684	33 750	2.1	1.2	30 941	13.5	18.0	18.5
Hidalgo	102	388	1 223	3.8	54.9	15.6	13.1	13 997	17 451	36 733	16.9	0.0	30 280	25.2	38.9	35.9
Lea	522	3 929	16 539	8.2	57.1	12.9	107.1	8 508	19 637	43 910	16.4	1.7	43 171	18.0	24.1	23.2
Lincoln	600	2 289	4 362	5.8	40.4	23.9	35.8	11 110	24 290	43 750	2.0	1.6	38 623	18.3	33.8	30.5
Los Alamos	NA	NA	4 785	10.8	10.7	64.0	39.3	11 610	49 474	103 643	3.6	12.3	105 987	3.2	3.2	2.7
Luna	562	3 001	6 384	3.3	61.3	13.5	51.3	9 421	15 687	27 997	6.4	1.2	27 257	30.7	48.3	48.4
McKinley	636	2 523	22 376	6.1	65.3	10.9	148.5	10 550	12 932	31 335	-1.0	0.9	29 473	32.6	42.8	42.0
Mora	61	82	1 397	5.5	55.7	15.4	11.4	16 824	22 035	37 784	21.7	0.3	29 321	21.8	32.7	29.4
Otero	358	2 177	16 685	6.4	43.8	17.7	72.0	9 441	19 255	39 615	1.4	1.0	36 628	21.8	30.6	30.7
Quay	542	4 214	2 116	1.9	69.5	14.8	18.7	12 083	18 234	28 773	-8.7	0.8	27 856	24.6	38.3	34.6
Rio Arriba	430	1 630	9 195	15.9	53.7	16.1	78.7	12 475	19 913	41 437	11.2	0.8	36 570	21.0	27.7	25.5
Roosevelt	403	2 393	6 197	4.9	52.2	21.2	35.7	10 502	16 933	37 762	12.2	1.1	33 068	24.5	28.8	28.2
Sandoval	256	1 536	34 123	12.6	37.5	28.4	181.2	8 781	25 979	57 158	0.4	3.4	52 778	13.8	17.5	15.3
San Juan	631	2 141	33 135	6.7	52.1	15.0	219.5	9 285	20 725	46 189	8.0	2.0	44 155	23.9	34.7	31.2
San Miguel	NA	NA	8 205	8.1	48.4	23.3	53.4	12 048	18 508	32 213	-4.1	0.8	31 762	25.7	32.4	31.9
Santa Fe	375	4 069	32 602	21.5	34.9	40.0	143.6	9 118	32 188	52 696	-1.4	4.8	48 507	16.5	23.6	23.2
Sierra	450	1 844	2 135	3.4	53.4	16.8	14.6	9 726	16 667	25 583	-16.4	1.0	26 240	21.2	40.4	39.2
Socorro	632	2 387	5 144	7.0	53.1	22.3	26.6	11 262	17 801	33 284	12.1	1.4	31 254	27.4	39.1	36.7
Taos	523	2 378	6 991	7.8	38.7	30.1	46.5	11 273	22 145	35 441	4.6	2.0	32 940	18.6	29.4	28.1
Torrance	122	1 282	3 929	9.4	55.0	14.0	46.5	9 883	17 278	37 117	-3.7	0.6	36 588	23.8	34.3	30.2
Union	44	594	978	5.3	54.3	17.8	9.2	13 536	19 228	39 975	12.4	2.6	33 195	18.9	26.6	25.8
Valencia	481	3 258	20 174	9.1	49.8	16.8	122.1	9 129	19 955	42 044	-2.6	1.2	40 552	22.5	33.3	31.1
NEW YORK	392	1 941	5 056 560	24.4	43.8	32.1	49 011.6	18 156	30 948	55 603	1.2	6.1	54 047	15.0	21.5	20.0
Albany	390	3 234	85 046	22.6	36.3	37.6	547.6	16 326	30 863	56 090	3.2	4.0	53 783	13.2	17.4	15.1
Allegany	190	1 596	14 657	28.6	51.8	18.6	126.3	16 581	20 058	41 305	1.6	0.9	41 384	17.2	23.0	21.0
Bronx	(7)	(7)	399 010	20.3	59.4	17.6	(7)	(7)	17 575	34 264	-2.0	1.2	32 674	30.0	42.2	41.0
Broome	248	2 747	54 595	8.5	44.9	25.1	448.8	15 281	24 314	44 457	-0.7	2.2	43 920	16.5	23.4	21.2
Cattaraugus	225	2 336	20 577	21.4	53.9	18.1	227.8	15 519	20 824	42 466	0.4	0.9	41 266	15.0	22.1	20.0
Cayuga	197	1 993	18 657	17.6	51.7	18.4	154.3	14 972	22 959	48 415	2.0	1.3	48 453	12.6	19.0	17.3
Chautauqua	231	2 630	33 943	8.6	50.7	20.3	321.0	14 922	21 033	40 639	-4.1	0.9	39 981	17.3	25.4	23.6
Chemung	229	2 113	21 714	21.3	49.0	20.9	186.4	14 942	23 457	44 502	-3.5	2.2	46 130	15.6	22.7	20.4
Chenango	109	1 857	11 964	7.9	54.6	17.0	144.0	16 442	22 036	43 943	3.0	1.3	41 418	16.0	23.6	21.5
Clinton	106	2 117	21 559	8.5	52.8	21.7	204.4	17 067	22 660	47 489	1.3	1.7	44 193	15.7	18.8	16.0
Columbia	136	1 602	14 349	19.3	45.1	28.2	153.5	18 598	31 844	55 546	4.7	4.3	50 620	9.5	15.9	14.2
Cortland	132	2 029	15 610	7.7	47.2	24.3	107.3	15 325	22 078	45 338	4.2	1.4	41 903	14.8	19.5	18.1
Delaware	121	1 440	10 486	9.5	52.1	19.1	128.3	18 684	22 928	42 967	4.5	1.4	40 252	12.3	20.9	19.7
Dutchess	266	1 860	83 783	27.8	40.4	32.0	735.0	15 880	31 642	69 838	3.9	5.4	68 831	8.2	10.7	9.2
Erie	492	3 041	246 718	19.0	41.7	29.1	1 850.9	14 510	26 378	47 372	-3.0	2.7	46 773	14.3	20.9	18.3
Essex	102	1 344	8 438	14.2	45.8	25.5	84.2	20 000	24 390	45 216	2.5	1.8	42 053	13.0	19.3	17.5
Franklin	105	1 630	10 905	16.9	57.0	17.3	138.0	16 699	19 807	42 050	5.4	0.9	41 062	16.1	22.2	20.3
Fulton	221	2 825	12 162	6.4	56.5	14.3	127.1	13 674	23 147	43 240	1.4	1.5	39 939	15.6	24.2	22.5

1. Data for serious crimes have not been adjusted for underreporting; this may affect comparability between geographic areas and over time.   2. Per 100,000 population estimated by the FBI.   3. All persons 3 years old and over enrolled in nursery school through college.   4. Persons 25 years old and over.   5. Elementary and secondary education expenditures.   6. Based on population estimated by the American Community Survey, 2006–2010.   7. Bronx, Kings, Queens, and Richmond counties are included with New York county.

Table B. States and Counties — **Personal Income**

	Personal income, 2009												
			Per capita[1]					Transfer payments (mil dol)					
									Government payments to individuals				
STATE County	Total (mil dol)	Percent change, 2008–2009	Dollars	Rank	Wages and salaries[2] (mil dol)	Proprietors' income (mil dol)	Dividends, interest, and rent (mil dol)	Total	Total	Social Security	Medical payments	Income mainte-nance	Unemploy-ment insurance
	62	63	64	65	66	67	68	69	70	71	72	73	74
NEW JERSEY—Cont'd													
Mercer	19 024	-3.3	51 947	78	16 297	1 687	3 347	2 837	2 771	870	1 245	233	257
Middlesex	37 475	-2.8	47 392	143	28 316	2 516	5 501	5 117	4 973	1 705	1 969	297	598
Monmouth	35 279	-4.2	54 771	56	15 822	2 473	6 771	4 455	4 338	1 583	1 800	209	462
Morris	33 342	-4.3	68 251	16	24 060	3 336	6 078	2 964	2 875	1 197	1 087	90	319
Ocean	22 762	-0.6	39 677	471	7 539	1 276	4 496	5 333	5 229	2 129	2 165	208	414
Passaic	19 886	-2.5	40 436	423	10 506	1 252	2 897	3 874	3 784	1 014	1 670	439	443
Salem	2 542	1.0	38 311	600	1 416	124	340	595	583	191	259	46	56
Somerset	22 680	-4.1	69 385	11	15 962	2 203	4 256	1 765	1 705	712	580	74	216
Sussex	7 178	-2.9	47 497	142	2 018	440	980	921	894	352	323	35	120
Union	25 816	-4.0	49 040	119	16 609	1 842	4 389	3 851	3 755	1 151	1 622	288	420
Warren	4 674	-1.0	42 631	291	2 080	186	701	801	781	281	326	39	86
NEW MEXICO	66 856	0.1	33 267	X	42 020	4 608	10 793	14 346	13 981	4 166	6 225	1 676	539
Bernalillo	23 661	0.0	36 825	770	18 172	1 472	4 046	4 328	4 211	1 293	1 828	457	177
Catron	89	5.8	25 872	2 752	29	7	20	31	31	15	10	2	1
Chaves	1 902	-4.6	29 891	2 004	926	274	298	509	498	145	239	71	15
Cibola	670	2.3	24 795	2 883	360	28	66	206	201	53	95	27	6
Colfax	427	1.7	33 528	1 246	215	45	81	123	120	42	52	11	4
Curry	1 572	2.2	35 390	965	981	164	205	347	340	80	162	48	8
De Baca	63	2.8	34 718	1 060	21	11	11	20	20	6	10	2	0
Dona Ana	5 814	3.6	28 165	2 370	3 284	385	828	1 444	1 406	356	635	215	50
Eddy	2 041	-0.4	38 731	562	1 357	244	249	414	405	129	195	45	12
Grant	889	-2.0	29 713	2 045	420	39	168	307	301	102	132	29	11
Guadalupe	106	5.7	24 981	2 866	49	9	11	45	44	10	24	5	1
Harding	22	-5.2	33 774	1 206	9	4	4	5	5	2	2	0	0
Hidalgo	145	1.6	28 772	2 242	83	12	18	46	45	13	22	6	2
Lea	2 106	-7.8	34 971	1 025	1 489	169	225	432	421	113	220	46	17
Lincoln	618	1.8	29 428	2 111	261	45	154	172	168	67	69	14	5
Los Alamos	1 083	-1.6	59 936	31	1 463	34	218	76	73	36	27	2	2
Luna	657	3.0	24 275	2 939	323	43	92	239	235	74	97	31	16
McKinley	1 666	4.7	23 622	2 990	979	36	167	538	525	84	256	108	18
Mora	121	4.0	24 430	2 923	36	3	15	52	51	14	24	7	2
Otero	1 685	4.8	26 653	2 614	1 094	75	249	411	400	134	162	41	14
Quay	265	2.8	29 707	2 048	122	18	41	97	96	29	44	11	2
Rio Arriba	1 123	2.1	27 619	2 465	474	58	125	349	341	90	169	43	12
Roosevelt	533	-7.4	28 309	2 344	265	33	70	151	148	33	71	18	3
Sandoval	4 053	3.7	32 172	1 491	1 558	106	556	722	699	259	263	63	36
San Juan	3 811	-2.4	30 702	1 819	2 683	255	497	779	756	214	344	90	34
San Miguel	870	3.5	30 731	1 814	367	45	102	310	305	66	161	42	8
Santa Fe	6 292	-2.6	42 645	289	3 334	707	1 624	904	877	342	353	74	37
Sierra	354	2.3	27 457	2 492	124	26	62	150	147	51	65	15	3
Socorro	502	0.3	27 739	2 446	271	28	63	147	143	34	64	28	4
Taos	1 002	0.0	31 792	1 580	442	125	204	271	265	81	119	32	12
Torrance	476	1.7	28 909	2 217	136	22	48	132	129	35	57	20	5
Union	120	2.3	31 378	1 670	57	10	22	34	33	11	15	3	1
Valencia	2 119	0.5	29 057	2 183	635	77	253	555	541	152	241	71	20
NEW YORK	908 997	-3.0	46 516	X	613 551	77 777	161 934	171 768	168 208	43 527	87 139	19 058	8 301
Albany	13 747	0.3	46 086	167	14 107	1 287	2 446	2 478	2 423	750	902	224	110
Allegany	1 264	-1.0	25 705	2 770	611	62	173	383	374	130	152	41	21
Bronx	39 855	1.2	28 523	2 294	13 544	2 009	3 632	14 066	13 811	1 994	8 234	2 401	666
Broome	6 694	0.6	34 391	1 112	4 546	338	1 157	1 704	1 669	593	707	188	82
Cattaraugus	2 571	1.9	32 257	1 471	1 438	185	345	739	724	224	277	66	37
Cayuga	2 544	0.2	31 989	1 532	1 208	145	357	598	584	205	242	57	35
Chautauqua	4 004	0.1	29 995	1 979	2 267	202	619	1 200	1 175	398	501	144	56
Chemung	2 904	-0.7	32 881	1 357	1 843	116	458	778	762	262	325	85	37
Chenango	1 549	0.1	30 608	1 841	767	93	238	422	412	150	169	45	22
Clinton	2 653	1.4	32 507	1 423	1 710	145	348	650	635	206	268	74	38
Columbia	2 345	-0.9	38 050	631	911	148	471	520	509	192	215	41	24
Cortland	1 435	1.0	29 900	2 003	787	92	206	353	344	113	147	41	23
Delaware	1 409	-0.1	30 966	1 765	747	122	247	389	381	145	165	30	19
Dutchess	12 427	-2.7	42 331	303	6 919	497	2 103	2 067	2 013	762	849	139	114
Erie	35 048	0.2	38 546	572	23 743	2 202	5 657	7 821	7 656	2 627	3 187	867	398
Essex	1 230	0.8	32 643	1 394	679	69	226	336	330	114	156	24	17
Franklin	1 429	1.4	28 424	2 316	929	58	198	391	382	127	164	43	20
Fulton	1 842	2.1	33 466	1 263	790	118	258	505	495	162	223	53	27

1. Based on the resident population estimated as of July 1 of the year shown.   2. Includes supplements to wages and salaries.

Table B. States and Counties — **Earnings, Social Security, and Housing**

STATE County	Total (mil dol)	Farm	Goods-related[1] Total	Goods-related[1] Manufacturing	Service-related and health Information and professional and technical services	Service-related and health Retail trade	Service-related and health Finance, insurance, and real estate	Service-related and health Health care and social services	Government	Social Security beneficiaries, December 2010 Number	Social Security beneficiaries, December 2010 Rate[2]	Supplemental Security Income recipients, December 2010	Housing units, 2010 Total	Housing units, 2010 Percent change, 2000–2010
	75	76	77	78	79	80	81	82	83	84	85	86	87	88
NEW JERSEY—Cont'd														
Mercer	17 984	0.0	7.3	4.2	21.6	3.8	10.3	9.4	25.3	62 400	170	8 654	143 169	7.4
Middlesex	30 831	0.0	16.0	11.7	18.2	5.0	7.4	8.4	15.0	119 270	147	11 957	294 800	7.7
Monmouth	18 294	0.2	10.9	3.6	18.7	7.1	9.1	14.4	18.5	109 490	174	7 389	258 410	7.3
Morris	27 396	0.1	D	12.5	20.8	5.3	11.5	8.5	9.4	78 435	159	4 142	189 842	8.9
Ocean	8 815	0.0	12.7	3.2	7.3	10.5	5.1	20.6	22.9	149 365	259	6 271	278 052	11.8
Passaic	11 758	0.0	17.8	11.8	9.5	7.7	6.6	12.6	19.1	76 530	153	14 324	175 966	3.5
Salem	1 540	2.6	D	15.0	5.6	4.3	2.9	10.3	18.9	14 215	215	1 494	27 417	4.8
Somerset	18 165	0.0	D	13.4	26.4	4.8	10.6	6.5	7.8	46 765	145	2 735	123 127	9.9
Sussex	2 458	-0.1	14.0	5.2	11.2	8.6	6.4	14.8	22.2	25 085	168	1 590	62 057	9.8
Union	18 451	0.0	D	13.7	15.3	6.2	5.5	10.6	13.8	81 660	152	9 893	199 489	3.4
Warren	2 265	0.6	31.8	24.9	5.5	9.3	2.9	12.9	17.3	19 975	184	1 292	44 925	9.2
NEW MEXICO	46 628	1.2	14.8	4.5	13.2	6.9	4.4	11.1	28.1	360 242	175	60 487	901 388	15.5
Bernalillo	19 643	0.0	11.0	4.4	17.3	6.5	5.6	12.3	25.9	106 585	161	15 732	284 234	19.0
Catron	37	13.6	D	1.5	D	D	D	D	50.9	1 290	346	76	3 289	29.1
Chaves	1 200	4.5	23.1	5.0	5.9	7.8	3.6	14.7	21.3	12 665	193	2 344	26 697	4.1
Cibola	387	0.3	D	1.4	D	7.4	1.5	12.3	42.7	4 550	167	925	11 101	7.5
Colfax	260	8.7	D	2.6	4.2	9.0	4.9	D	31.9	3 490	254	403	10 023	11.9
Curry	1 145	11.8	D	2.5	D	6.0	2.8	11.1	39.4	7 170	148	1 623	20 062	4.4
De Baca	32	30.3	D	D	D	4.9	3.9	7.8	27.8	565	279	87	1 344	2.8
Dona Ana	3 669	3.2	9.3	4.4	9.6	6.0	3.2	13.9	36.2	33 220	159	7 169	81 492	25.0
Eddy	1 601	0.9	39.7	5.4	5.1	4.9	3.9	8.4	17.0	10 500	195	1 517	22 585	1.5
Grant	459	0.7	22.0	0.8	3.4	7.1	3.0	9.0	39.3	8 350	283	914	14 693	4.5
Guadalupe	58	9.7	D	D	D	10.6	D	11.0	34.0	1 065	227	295	2 393	10.8
Harding	14	15.3	D	D	D	D	D	0.4	31.8	205	295	16	526	-3.5
Hidalgo	95	11.7	D	D	D	6.4	D	D	52.3	1 160	237	168	2 393	-16.0
Lea	1 658	0.9	45.2	5.4	3.7	5.2	3.5	6.3	11.5	9 260	143	1 521	24 919	6.5
Lincoln	306	2.0	11.4	1.0	6.9	11.8	6.1	10.7	24.0	5 485	268	365	17 519	14.5
Los Alamos	1 497	0.0	D	D	75.7	0.9	1.6	3.5	8.0	2 780	155	82	8 354	5.2
Luna	366	3.3	D	9.1	2.6	9.6	2.3	D	40.2	6 860	273	1 332	10 999	-2.6
McKinley	1 015	-0.4	8.7	3.7	2.2	9.7	2.2	11.3	47.4	9 230	129	4 411	25 813	-3.4
Mora	39	0.9	D	D	D	5.3	D	D	43.2	1 365	280	351	3 232	8.7
Otero	1 169	1.7	6.1	0.7	5.1	5.7	2.3	8.9	58.4	12 060	189	1 661	30 992	5.9
Quay	140	7.9	D	D	1.8	10.0	4.6	9.9	33.0	2 640	292	447	5 569	-1.7
Rio Arriba	532	1.6	8.6	1.9	D	8.6	2.6	13.9	45.0	8 740	217	1 561	19 638	9.0
Roosevelt	298	12.1	D	6.0	3.1	7.1	2.9	5.6	36.8	3 050	154	662	8 163	5.4
Sandoval	1 664	0.2	36.8	27.0	7.3	6.7	3.5	4.0	23.5	21 780	166	2 487	52 287	48.8
San Juan	2 938	0.3	30.0	2.8	3.2	7.2	3.0	10.3	21.3	18 805	146	4 025	49 341	14.2
San Miguel	412	1.8	D	0.7	2.7	6.9	3.0	D	52.2	6 465	220	1 826	15 595	9.4
Santa Fe	4 041	0.2	D	1.9	D	9.6	6.5	11.8	29.6	27 605	191	2 676	71 267	23.5
Sierra	150	6.3	D	2.8	6.2	7.7	3.1	D	32.8	4 360	364	556	8 356	-4.2
Socorro	300	4.1	D	2.9	10.4	5.3	2.6	D	50.9	3 315	186	1 083	8 059	3.2
Taos	567	0.2	14.8	1.2	6.2	16.9	4.0	14.7	21.3	7 600	231	1 093	20 265	16.4
Torrance	158	6.8	D	2.6	D	9.3	2.5	D	37.5	3 245	198	591	7 798	7.5
Union	66	14.7	D	D	D	6.1	6.3	D	28.3	1 010	222	109	2 305	3.6
Valencia	713	2.4	10.9	4.5	D	9.1	3.2	12.2	32.1	13 770	180	2 379	30 085	22.1
NEW YORK	691 328	0.1	10.0	5.5	17.5	4.8	17.2	11.4	16.2	3 280 575	169	680 057	8 108 103	5.6
Albany	15 394	0.0	7.9	3.4	14.6	5.1	8.2	11.2	32.8	55 860	184	7 453	137 739	6.0
Allegany	673	0.2	25.9	20.0	2.9	5.5	1.8	8.2	31.8	10 635	217	1 550	26 140	6.7
Bronx	15 553	0.0	D	2.5	5.2	5.8	5.5	32.2	13.6	176 450	127	104 759	511 896	4.3
Broome	4 883	0.1	21.6	15.7	7.0	6.6	5.1	16.0	24.4	46 050	230	6 705	90 563	2.0
Cattaraugus	1 623	0.7	20.8	16.6	2.9	8.6	2.8	13.5	34.2	18 445	230	2 598	41 111	3.2
Cayuga	1 354	3.0	D	14.9	5.0	8.1	2.2	13.4	28.2	16 030	200	1 987	36 489	2.9
Chautauqua	2 470	1.1	28.2	23.0	3.7	8.0	2.8	13.5	23.3	31 820	236	4 803	66 920	3.1
Chemung	1 958	0.0	24.9	18.7	4.4	7.9	4.1	17.2	23.3	20 820	234	3 500	38 369	1.7
Chenango	860	1.0	D	22.2	5.7	7.0	9.5	9.1	27.4	12 370	245	1 735	24 710	3.4
Clinton	1 855	1.6	20.5	15.4	3.6	8.6	2.4	15.8	30.2	17 340	211	2 980	35 888	8.5
Columbia	1 059	1.2	D	D	9.4	9.3	3.8	17.7	24.4	14 685	233	1 643	32 775	8.5
Cortland	879	0.5	23.8	18.9	7.2	7.3	4.0	D	23.9	9 340	189	1 287	20 577	2.3
Delaware	869	0.8	35.1	28.1	4.2	7.4	4.0	D	25.0	11 420	238	1 223	31 222	7.8
Dutchess	7 417	0.1	24.8	19.5	6.5	6.3	4.2	14.3	22.4	54 615	184	5 441	118 638	11.8
Erie	25 944	0.1	18.3	13.5	10.2	5.9	7.5	13.0	19.9	197 455	215	28 845	419 974	1.0
Essex	747	0.0	17.6	8.2	4.2	7.6	2.6	12.6	37.0	9 105	231	1 025	25 603	10.8
Franklin	987	0.8	D	1.9	4.6	6.9	1.9	16.0	52.7	10 920	212	1 919	25 306	5.7
Fulton	907	0.1	D	9.3	5.6	9.2	3.1	18.3	26.0	13 260	239	2 100	28 562	2.8

1. Includes mining, construction, and manufacturing. 2. Per 1,000 resident population enumerated in the 2010 census.

Table B. States and Counties — Housing, Labor Force, and Employment

STATE County	Housing units, 2006–2010								Civilian labor force, 2010				Civilian employment,[5] 2006–2010		
	Occupied units							Substandard units[3] (percent)			Unemployment		Percent		
	Owner-occupied					Renter-occupied									
				Median owner cost as a percent of income											Construction, production, and maintenance occupations
	Total	Percent	Median value[1]	With a mortgage	Without a mortgage	Median rent[2]	Median rent as a percent of income		Total	Percent change, 2009–2010	Total	Rate[4]	Total	Management, business, science and arts	
	89	90	91	92	93	94	95	96	97	98	99	100	101	102	103
NEW JERSEY—Cont'd															
Mercer	129 213	67.9	309 300	26.0	17.0	1 046	30.7	2.6	203 947	0.2	15 934	7.8	176 170	42.9	15.5
Middlesex	277 398	67.0	356 000	27.8	17.9	1 187	27.5	3.8	422 895	-0.9	36 676	8.7	395 702	42.7	17.9
Monmouth	232 513	75.9	424 800	28.4	18.3	1 137	32.8	2.1	333 370	-0.7	28 629	8.6	309 684	42.4	15.6
Morris	178 638	76.6	474 700	27.1	17.0	1 221	27.4	1.9	270 282	-1.5	19 642	7.3	251 987	48.9	13.1
Ocean	222 396	82.4	294 100	29.6	20.2	1 258	37.6	2.2	263 270	0.1	26 580	10.1	243 895	33.9	20.6
Passaic	161 428	55.3	382 600	31.7	22.4	1 080	36.4	9.6	243 037	-0.7	27 344	11.3	230 707	30.3	25.3
Salem	25 117	74.2	196 600	26.1	17.2	859	31.7	1.3	31 494	-2.2	3 571	11.3	30 024	30.9	29.2
Somerset	114 431	79.7	431 200	27.1	16.9	1 295	29.4	1.8	180 580	-0.4	13 351	7.4	163 535	51.4	13.7
Sussex	55 842	84.8	322 400	28.5	18.5	1 111	33.6	1.3	84 561	-1.0	7 890	9.3	78 033	38.1	21.0
Union	184 808	61.5	397 200	29.7	20.1	1 084	31.5	8.7	269 452	-1.0	25 997	9.6	257 956	34.8	22.4
Warren	41 601	75.8	307 300	28.1	18.9	941	30.9	1.1	59 357	-0.9	5 406	9.1	54 631	37.2	21.3
NEW MEXICO	756 112	69.6	158 400	23.5	10.0	683	29.1	4.3	934 380	-0.8	74 176	7.9	888 761	34.4	22.3
Bernalillo	259 165	64.6	188 800	24.3	10.0	717	29.4	2.7	313 345	-0.6	26 583	8.5	313 659	38.8	18.4
Catron	1 824	86.1	129 400	26.5	10.0	524	35.9	4.1	1 604	-3.5	152	9.5	1 292	19.6	40.9
Chaves	23 479	69.3	86 200	20.5	10.0	566	28.6	3.9	27 507	-2.7	2 240	8.1	26 840	26.2	25.9
Cibola	8 089	68.3	74 800	18.3	10.0	518	23.4	8.9	12 532	1.2	975	7.8	8 753	22.4	30.6
Colfax	5 768	68.1	103 100	24.0	10.0	554	27.1	2.5	6 686	-1.4	572	8.6	6 186	27.7	25.1
Curry	17 318	61.4	98 500	21.4	10.8	547	27.3	3.0	21 795	0.0	1 179	5.4	20 417	25.5	29.0
De Baca	784	79.5	71 100	22.4	12.9	397	27.5	1.5	839	-8.7	48	5.7	724	36.5	25.4
Dona Ana	71 748	65.5	137 200	23.4	11.2	631	33.7	4.3	93 644	3.0	7 639	8.2	84 880	32.3	22.8
Eddy	19 320	74.7	90 700	18.1	10.0	605	24.1	3.4	28 869	0.6	1 734	6.0	23 792	29.9	29.4
Grant	12 531	77.0	125 000	22.9	10.2	541	26.6	2.5	11 638	-3.0	1 269	10.9	12 387	35.2	24.2
Guadalupe	1 492	77.5	74 500	25.6	13.4	537	28.8	1.8	1 805	-1.4	187	10.4	1 609	24.3	26.8
Harding	321	91.3	70 300	18.1	15.2	333	15.0	14.0	384	-9.4	20	5.2	335	22.7	28.4
Hidalgo	1 705	69.1	90 800	16.4	10.0	393	30.1	4.6	2 716	-6.8	214	7.9	2 182	30.2	24.4
Lea	21 255	71.0	87 500	19.5	10.0	629	23.8	6.5	28 275	-2.1	2 165	7.7	25 204	24.3	35.1
Lincoln	8 629	77.5	166 600	23.6	11.5	701	24.7	3.6	11 002	-2.2	753	6.8	9 173	30.1	21.4
Los Alamos	7 566	77.2	297 100	19.1	10.0	974	19.8	1.2	10 330	3.1	381	3.7	9 424	66.9	8.9
Luna	9 204	69.5	91 700	25.6	10.2	487	27.7	3.8	12 996	0.7	2 436	18.7	8 601	22.3	29.7
McKinley	17 631	73.4	69 300	20.4	10.0	495	23.6	19.1	27 521	0.3	2 652	9.6	23 970	25.8	27.5
Mora	1 815	83.6	107 500	24.5	10.0	552	29.0	6.6	2 046	-2.1	321	15.7	2 230	30.0	28.8
Otero	24 031	67.6	104 500	21.8	10.0	582	26.9	3.4	26 451	0.3	1 962	7.4	24 218	28.2	24.5
Quay	3 840	74.1	65 200	22.6	11.7	569	27.0	2.6	4 029	-4.1	351	8.7	3 525	30.8	27.5
Rio Arriba	14 934	79.8	136 300	21.9	10.0	614	23.6	5.9	20 438	-1.4	1 777	8.7	17 117	32.1	23.5
Roosevelt	6 794	63.0	94 800	20.5	10.0	534	34.7	3.3	9 338	-1.2	553	5.9	7 958	32.4	26.1
Sandoval	44 860	81.3	184 400	24.7	10.0	925	30.2	4.1	56 829	1.0	5 294	9.3	56 828	37.8	18.8
San Juan	41 767	73.9	149 400	20.5	10.0	683	25.0	9.7	56 513	-1.3	5 406	9.6	52 735	27.0	32.7
San Miguel	11 786	66.8	112 200	24.6	12.5	579	29.6	2.3	13 364	-1.1	1 134	8.5	11 167	32.6	18.0
Santa Fe	60 144	71.2	291 700	27.1	10.1	866	31.6	3.6	77 296	-0.3	5 452	7.1	71 308	41.5	16.5
Sierra	4 747	78.3	92 800	24.6	12.5	513	32.1	0.9	6 111	-0.4	417	6.8	3 630	22.5	24.6
Socorro	5 996	74.0	108 400	22.8	12.1	562	31.3	3.7	9 526	-1.1	583	6.1	6 546	37.8	22.8
Taos	13 146	73.2	212 400	27.4	10.0	718	30.7	5.4	17 636	0.4	1 761	10.0	14 617	31.0	22.1
Torrance	5 849	82.2	92 300	24.4	14.1	589	32.2	8.5	6 975	-0.5	720	10.3	5 649	27.1	29.3
Union	1 739	73.7	91 900	23.8	13.3	578	18.8	2.6	1 906	-12.5	122	6.4	1 923	35.2	27.7
Valencia	26 835	79.6	129 900	24.2	10.5	662	32.8	4.3	31 377	-0.2	3 154	10.1	29 882	29.3	27.7
NEW YORK	7 205 740	55.2	303 900	26.3	15.4	977	30.9	5.1	9 586 931	-0.9	824 668	8.6	9 045 999	37.9	17.7
Albany	124 391	58.9	202 500	22.8	12.8	855	28.5	1.6	155 850	-2.8	11 149	7.2	154 819	43.1	13.3
Allegany	18 987	75.6	66 100	21.6	14.3	568	30.1	2.2	23 998	-0.1	2 246	9.4	21 930	31.9	28.7
Bronx	472 464	20.7	386 200	33.0	12.7	923	32.9	11.6	543 429	1.3	69 436	12.8	537 067	24.4	19.3
Broome	80 806	66.6	99 500	20.5	13.8	613	29.8	1.8	95 682	-2.2	8 449	8.8	92 922	35.1	19.6
Cattaraugus	32 666	73.4	77 000	22.8	13.7	582	29.3	2.3	41 163	-2.1	3 729	9.1	36 751	28.5	28.7
Cayuga	32 038	71.8	98 100	22.0	14.8	629	26.2	1.7	41 211	-1.6	3 431	8.3	37 592	29.4	29.7
Chautauqua	55 044	69.8	79 600	21.3	14.5	581	30.5	1.5	64 640	-2.9	5 659	8.8	60 439	30.3	27.8
Chemung	35 418	68.1	85 900	20.0	13.6	647	31.0	1.5	40 742	-0.8	3 478	8.5	39 180	32.9	22.0
Chenango	19 989	77.2	88 200	22.0	14.1	566	27.1	3.3	24 191	-1.8	2 209	9.1	22 809	30.7	29.7
Clinton	31 056	70.3	117 800	22.6	13.6	659	29.6	2.0	39 017	-2.5	3 971	10.2	37 261	31.8	23.3
Columbia	25 686	73.2	221 900	24.2	15.8	751	28.0	2.0	30 709	-2.9	2 330	7.6	31 015	38.4	22.7
Cortland	17 901	66.3	95 100	22.7	14.0	655	28.6	2.4	24 020	-1.0	2 185	9.1	22 915	33.6	21.7
Delaware	20 110	75.9	126 700	22.6	13.7	598	26.6	3.2	22 003	-1.8	1 923	8.7	21 913	30.0	29.2
Dutchess	106 952	70.6	323 300	27.5	16.5	1 038	31.4	2.5	143 405	-1.9	11 320	7.9	142 968	39.6	18.4
Erie	378 080	66.2	117 700	22.2	14.7	686	31.0	1.2	466 074	-1.4	38 333	8.2	432 738	36.6	18.1
Essex	16 098	73.0	148 100	24.5	14.3	675	24.7	1.4	18 112	-2.2	1 685	9.3	17 587	33.4	25.4
Franklin	19 115	72.6	88 800	21.9	13.6	583	31.0	2.5	22 710	-1.6	2 046	9.0	20 804	30.2	23.2
Fulton	23 006	69.8	95 200	22.3	13.9	635	31.7	1.8	27 240	0.0	2 752	10.1	24 117	27.1	29.4

1. Specified owner-occupied units. 2. Specified renter-occupied units. A value of 10.0 represents 10 percent or less. 3. Overcrowded or lacking complete plumbing facilities. 4. Percent of civilian labor force. 5. Persons 16 years old and over.

Table B. States and Counties — Nonfarm Employment and Agriculture

	Private nonfarm establishments, employment and payroll, 2009									Agriculture, 2007			
	Employment							Annual payroll		Farms			
												Percent with:	
STATE County	Number of establishments	Total	Health care and social assistance	Manufacturing	Retail trade	Finance and insurance	Professional, scientific, and technical services	Total (mil dol)	Average per employee (dollars)	Number	Fewer than 50 acres	500 acres or more	Farm operators whose principal occupation is farming (percent)
	104	105	106	107	108	109	110	111	112	113	114	115	116
NEW JERSEY—Cont'd													
Mercer	9 818	177 461	27 279	7 195	19 399	15 206	22 319	9 792	55 176	311	70.7	2.3	40.8
Middlesex	21 281	369 072	43 378	30 154	37 248	13 237	48 128	20 113	54 496	236	78.4	3.8	44.9
Monmouth	18 976	220 430	38 241	8 792	38 513	10 950	21 060	9 698	43 997	932	86.4	2.4	47.7
Morris	17 161	284 054	32 217	16 724	28 651	20 546	36 234	18 531	65 239	422	82.0	1.7	37.4
Ocean	11 907	123 065	31 060	4 794	25 363	3 553	6 019	4 139	33 630	255	85.9	1.2	44.3
Passaic	11 683	146 599	23 262	20 160	21 934	4 877	9 271	6 549	44 671	103	94.2	0.0	41.7
Salem	1 205	17 576	3 224	3 075	2 200	495	442	850	48 365	759	61.7	7.0	52.2
Somerset	9 802	189 390	20 554	11 537	32 365	14 019	29 132	12 285	64 867	445	77.3	2.9	37.5
Sussex	3 397	31 479	6 283	1 994	5 635	1 208	1 688	1 097	34 850	1 060	73.3	1.9	40.6
Union	13 715	208 348	28 323	25 271	24 454	8 871	22 828	11 210	53 805	15	100.0	0.0	66.7
Warren	2 583	29 691	5 774	4 038	5 905	598	1 013	1 290	43 432	933	68.9	3.0	47.5
NEW MEXICO	44 986	615 879	106 196	28 623	97 027	24 255	47 801	21 379	34 712	20 930	52.0	23.1	48.0
Bernalillo	16 270	251 058	41 945	14 257	35 209	12 167	20 397	9 152	36 452	635	76.7	6.3	38.3
Catron	62	292	95	D	D	D	D	5	18 322	259	13.5	52.9	52.1
Chaves	1 483	17 113	4 001	1 038	3 363	712	701	482	28 138	584	35.8	36.6	50.2
Cibola	344	5 842	1 164	D	987	D	75	173	29 618	317	44.2	30.3	41.0
Colfax	488	3 788	516	D	712	191	134	101	26 773	302	12.3	50.7	60.3
Curry	1 040	12 006	2 437	504	2 545	475	395	322	26 837	681	18.5	41.7	42.9
De Baca	58	352	64	D	56	D	D	10	27 642	173	31.2	45.7	55.5
Dona Ana	3 731	50 549	12 096	2 203	8 015	1 766	4 069	1 378	27 263	1 762	80.5	5.6	41.4
Eddy	1 272	19 476	2 821	1 297	2 599	534	670	794	40 768	543	42.7	27.8	45.9
Grant	676	7 324	1 480	D	1 242	209	156	214	29 255	327	30.6	39.8	56.0
Guadalupe	106	1 005	D	D	236	23	D	26	25 584	258	15.9	57.8	52.3
Harding	11	D	D	0	D	D	D	D	D	168	3.0	70.8	56.0
Hidalgo	97	864	126	D	356	D	D	17	19 796	162	9.9	58.0	51.9
Lea	1 553	20 773	2 547	D	2 820	D	611	805	38 771	572	31.1	38.8	40.2
Lincoln	759	5 220	489	79	1 185	268	155	129	24 751	361	30.2	45.2	49.9
Los Alamos	375	D	902	40	471	D	D	D	D	7	100.0	0.0	57.1
Luna	419	4 284	822	610	855	D	89	107	25 008	206	26.7	33.5	59.7
McKinley	1 029	16 457	4 527	D	3 860	455	236	480	29 140	2 624	74.1	8.5	56.9
Mora	53	388	195	0	D	D	D	8	19 972	589	25.1	26.1	38.5
Otero	1 027	12 617	2 223	198	2 905	436	531	309	24 508	493	62.7	15.6	43.6
Quay	244	2 081	397	55	553	114	D	46	22 256	636	12.4	51.3	47.5
Rio Arriba	642	6 981	1 430	D	1 407	244	106	232	33 278	1 312	57.2	14.8	45.7
Roosevelt	354	4 034	627	414	654	125	104	104	25 750	876	15.6	43.7	43.0
Sandoval	1 626	24 511	1 943	2 475	3 696	D	D	985	40 205	652	71.3	10.1	46.2
San Juan	2 852	40 754	6 117	1 470	6 982	1 091	1 386	1 547	37 963	1 897	85.7	2.2	55.4
San Miguel	472	5 668	D	D	1 186	173	120	234	41 334	765	23.5	37.4	45.5
Santa Fe	4 875	45 986	8 530	764	9 289	2 024	2 537	1 609	34 981	489	66.9	13.5	42.7
Sierra	237	2 526	793	D	501	80	35	54	21 513	265	34.0	32.8	57.7
Socorro	247	2 987	D	87	554	D	446	81	27 041	536	52.1	26.1	49.4
Taos	1 162	9 518	1 576	96	1 567	233	431	225	23 648	637	64.7	8.6	41.8
Torrance	240	1 876	222	D	510	D	45	46	24 480	561	19.3	41.2	47.1
Union	118	1 049	D	D	99	D	D	28	26 399	380	6.3	71.8	56.6
Valencia	941	11 114	2 744	810	2 493	316	332	257	23 146	901	82.9	4.3	41.4
NEW YORK	515 819	7 332 392	1 364 923	462 496	859 320	545 967	580 129	400 790	54 660	36 352	32.2	8.4	54.0
Albany	9 403	168 693	31 673	7 349	21 887	13 556	15 139	6 973	41 336	498	41.2	4.4	42.8
Allegany	803	13 204	1 951	3 187	1 385	205	255	326	24 708	847	23.3	6.0	47.2
Bronx	16 015	223 386	90 956	7 168	23 949	3 943	3 876	9 367	41 934	1	100.0	0.0	100.0
Broome	4 287	74 702	14 587	9 816	11 955	2 938	4 904	2 595	34 743	580	28.8	3.6	43.4
Cattaraugus	1 763	23 922	3 551	4 167	4 159	620	495	777	32 460	1 122	26.7	4.7	49.0
Cayuga	1 624	18 002	2 955	3 083	3 691	351	580	557	30 966	936	28.5	14.2	54.8
Chautauqua	2 992	43 560	8 619	10 136	6 561	955	1 081	1 265	29 046	1 658	35.4	4.2	53.5
Chemung	1 869	32 016	6 936	5 986	5 385	1 085	754	1 071	33 460	373	22.3	7.8	49.1
Chenango	975	11 316	1 731	2 519	2 106	1 126	356	382	33 715	908	24.8	7.7	54.6
Clinton	1 911	25 590	5 133	3 497	5 113	465	D	906	35 407	590	23.4	11.5	55.9
Columbia	1 724	14 811	4 043	1 496	2 378	D	838	475	32 104	554	39.7	9.6	51.8
Cortland	1 024	14 271	3 002	2 668	2 141	365	D	433	30 363	587	25.0	11.6	51.3
Delaware	1 065	12 390	2 047	4 741	1 594	452	218	422	34 067	747	22.8	10.2	58.5
Dutchess	7 497	94 659	18 224	12 969	14 265	3 172	4 093	3 929	41 512	656	46.2	6.3	55.5
Erie	22 372	400 380	72 554	44 328	53 120	28 047	23 998	14 738	36 809	1 215	47.8	4.4	52.3
Essex	1 181	9 766	1 879	D	1 815	D	212	307	31 408	243	34.2	12.8	45.7
Franklin	1 048	10 635	3 064	D	1 982	259	401	314	29 553	604	26.0	9.3	57.0
Fulton	1 232	14 113	3 240	1 961	2 270	305	309	448	31 746	222	29.7	6.8	47.7

STATE County	Acreage (1,000) [117]	Percent change, 2002–2007 [118]	Average size of farm [119]	Total irrigated (1,000) [120]	Total cropland (1,000) [121]	Average per farm [122]	Average per acre [123]	Value of machinery and equipment, average per farm (dollars) [124]	Total (mil dol) [125]	Average per farm (dollars) [126]	Crops [127]	Live-stock and poultry products [128]	$10,000 or more [129]	$100,000 or more [130]	Total ($1,000) [131]	Percent of farms [132]
NEW JERSEY—Cont'd																
Mercer	22	-12.0	70	1.0	15.4	1 314 520	18 813	64 690	18.6	59 956	80.5	19.5	41.2	11.9	286	13.2
Middlesex	19	-13.6	79	2.7	12.9	1 609 071	20 289	79 639	41.9	177 346	96.1	3.9	41.9	19.5	109	7.6
Monmouth	44	-6.4	47	6.0	28.0	1 123 048	23 718	67 217	105.4	113 104	76.1	23.9	36.2	11.1	258	3.5
Morris	17	0.0	40	0.9	9.3	992 865	24 606	54 184	27.3	64 720	84.7	15.3	30.1	8.3	91	3.6
Ocean	10	-16.7	39	1.1	4.4	698 579	18 116	48 171	11.5	45 159	80.9	19.1	31.4	7.1	128	3.1
Passaic	2	0.0	19	0.1	0.4	787 880	40 965	31 834	6.3	61 343	95.8	4.2	20.4	3.9	D	2.9
Salem	97	1.0	127	18.0	78.1	1 332 268	10 475	102 704	80.0	105 351	75.9	24.1	37.2	16.3	1 624	21.7
Somerset	33	-8.3	74	0.4	19.9	1 505 463	20 474	59 654	18.9	42 496	50.9	49.1	24.7	5.6	213	5.8
Sussex	65	-13.3	62	0.5	32.9	838 636	13 625	42 621	21.2	20 040	55.6	44.4	20.3	4.9	328	4.5
Union	0	NA	8	0.0	0.1	1 119 405	133 263	59 995	2.5	165 549	99.4	0.6	46.7	20.0	0	0.0
Warren	75	-3.8	80	2.4	51.5	992 474	12 350	63 855	75.5	80 897	57.8	42.2	29.0	10.5	949	13.3
NEW MEXICO	43 238	-3.5	2 066	830.0	2 334.0	696 081	337	55 457	2 175.1	103 922	25.4	74.6	27.1	8.1	43 377	15.9
Bernalillo	238	NA	374	7.8	22.8	499 833	1 335	38 871	17.9	28 162	32.9	67.1	14.8	2.5	145	3.0
Catron	1 483	-9.8	5 724	3.1	5.1	1 463 469	256	50 545	11.0	42 586	2.4	97.6	39.0	11.6	95	3.1
Chaves	2 455	-2.4	4 203	63.1	85.4	1 289 541	307	126 473	339.1	580 629	12.2	87.8	50.5	27.4	1 970	17.0
Cibola	1 479	-12.5	4 665	2.3	17.0	843 304	181	33 189	D	D	D	D	18.3	2.8	232	7.9
Colfax	2 152	-2.9	7 127	21.1	25.2	2 383 502	334	76 638	33.3	110 378	4.8	95.2	50.0	18.5	266	13.2
Curry	887	-3.2	1 303	72.9	411.5	854 927	656	110 887	347.3	510 020	10.8	89.2	43.0	23.2	8 457	68.4
De Baca	1 071	-24.0	6 188	11.5	16.1	1 425 675	230	68 705	19.9	115 033	26.2	73.8	59.0	22.5	683	38.2
Dona Ana	589	1.4	334	79.0	95.8	636 656	1 903	77 539	388.8	220 651	43.2	56.8	36.8	9.9	2 338	13.1
Eddy	1 108	-6.3	2 040	53.0	67.5	770 228	377	85 775	94.8	174 674	42.5	57.5	47.7	16.4	1 702	29.1
Grant	1 213	-0.4	3 711	3.4	8.8	871 368	235	41 904	7.8	23 908	1.5	98.5	30.3	5.8	134	6.4
Guadalupe	1 405	-3.9	5 446	2.3	13.2	991 767	182	44 337	10.9	42 056	1.6	98.4	44.6	10.1	286	15.1
Harding	944	-4.8	5 621	D	19.9	1 311 240	233	67 689	13.4	79 528	D	D	44.6	16.1	754	48.2
Hidalgo	1 029	-8.8	6 349	11.9	32.2	1 074 236	169	104 085	17.5	108 222	57.7	42.3	51.2	17.3	503	29.0
Lea	2 365	4.7	4 135	39.1	128.4	926 712	224	70 813	93.6	163 713	18.2	81.8	37.1	15.7	3 237	27.1
Lincoln	1 750	9.0	4 849	3.7	9.3	1 352 329	279	56 628	13.3	36 755	4.0	96.0	39.6	10.5	499	10.8
Los Alamos	0	NA	1	D	D	82 734	64 349	7 891	D	D	D	0.0	0.0	0.0	0	0.0
Luna	654	-7.9	3 173	23.2	42.8	1 111 198	350	138 772	48.9	237 334	63.0	37.0	51.5	22.3	1 476	34.5
McKinley	3 173	0.1	1 209	4.5	31.4	157 075	130	14 709	7.9	3 004	14.8	85.2	4.4	0.2	71	5.2
Mora	915	-4.2	1 553	12.7	52.7	807 497	520	42 796	7.6	12 843	23.9	76.1	21.7	3.6	330	5.1
Otero	1 126	-6.8	2 285	7.0	18.6	735 337	322	43 619	15.2	30 887	60.0	40.0	37.3	5.7	406	6.1
Quay	1 490	-9.8	2 342	18.8	245.9	846 037	361	66 660	35.9	56 451	25.5	74.5	43.1	13.5	5 168	61.2
Rio Arriba	1 460	2.0	1 113	30.8	80.3	523 845	471	46 275	12.8	9 728	30.5	69.5	19.8	1.1	323	6.7
Roosevelt	1 494	-0.5	1 706	70.2	403.3	801 954	470	95 021	254.0	289 897	14.1	85.9	39.0	18.4	8 936	65.3
Sandoval	592	-22.4	908	9.0	22.8	327 487	361	28 442	9.1	13 887	62.0	38.0	18.6	2.1	121	3.4
San Juan	1 631	-7.2	860	78.4	107.4	268 195	312	37 574	57.2	30 153	82.6	17.4	8.9	1.3	900	4.6
San Miguel	2 241	7.1	2 930	8.7	61.4	953 077	325	34 935	17.2	22 465	7.5	92.5	19.1	3.1	502	6.0
Santa Fe	569	-16.8	1 164	50.0	21.5	778 559	669	42 309	12.6	25 795	68.1	31.9	20.2	3.5	49	4.5
Sierra	1 344	-1.4	5 073	6.7	D	1 102 667	217	51 354	23.6	88 891	26.4	73.6	46.0	11.7	144	8.7
Socorro	1 430	-6.1	2 668	14.8	23.8	737 418	276	55 712	40.1	74 816	15.6	84.4	38.6	8.6	284	6.5
Taos	457	-1.9	717	19.4	26.2	447 020	623	38 659	6.0	9 406	38.9	61.1	14.3	1.6	81	11.0
Torrance	1 796	5.8	3 202	29.9	81.1	1 059 220	331	67 957	40.4	72 082	41.6	58.4	30.1	9.6	601	12.8
Union	2 193	-2.2	5 770	47.0	122.6	1 778 268	308	114 132	137.0	360 451	23.2	76.8	64.5	30.5	2 569	32.1
Valencia	506	37.1	561	21.0	25.2	364 132	649	48 131	36.3	40 313	17.7	82.3	17.2	3.4	113	2.0
NEW YORK	7 175	-6.3	197	68.0	4 315.0	449 010	2 275	97 550	4 418.6	121 551	35.3	64.7	45.4	18.8	62 652	29.1
Albany	61	-11.6	123	0.4	32.0	392 854	3 206	75 116	22.4	45 010	51.6	48.4	34.9	7.6	270	21.1
Allegany	151	-16.1	178	0.2	74.6	253 899	1 426	53 782	46.1	54 390	12.5	87.5	29.8	10.0	1 285	34.6
Bronx	D	D	D	0.0	D	D	D	D	D	D	D	0.0	100.0	100.0	0	0.0
Broome	87	-11.2	149	0.2	43.6	275 676	1 846	62 296	29.9	51 526	18.6	81.4	28.8	7.1	754	21.6
Cattaraugus	183	-9.4	163	0.5	91.6	284 810	1 742	67 862	75.2	66 980	20.2	79.8	38.7	11.7	1 102	37.0
Cayuga	249	4.6	267	0.2	193.0	566 337	2 125	147 985	214.4	229 063	22.6	77.4	53.8	25.2	2 791	41.3
Chautauqua	236	-7.8	142	1.2	127.2	280 124	1 969	80 228	138.6	83 581	41.7	58.3	52.4	17.2	1 882	19.1
Chemung	65	-5.8	175	0.2	32.9	319 539	1 830	69 729	16.6	44 526	18.9	81.1	29.2	9.4	394	27.9
Chenango	177	-6.8	195	0.1	86.7	351 914	1 803	76 894	65.8	72 460	11.8	88.2	44.2	19.5	2 015	34.3
Clinton	149	-11.8	253	0.2	70.9	442 944	1 751	108 357	124.2	210 508	19.8	80.2	40.5	19.8	1 023	26.1
Columbia	107	-10.8	192	2.0	63.7	823 806	4 282	103 984	65.8	118 718	38.3	61.7	46.8	16.8	945	19.9
Cortland	125	-1.6	213	0.0	61.5	331 184	1 557	72 069	54.9	93 500	10.0	90.0	39.2	17.4	1 514	41.1
Delaware	166	-13.5	222	0.1	69.0	502 668	2 268	83 894	55.1	73 820	14.3	85.7	46.6	19.0	1 247	33.6
Dutchess	102	-8.9	156	1.3	46.9	873 887	5 601	88 862	44.9	68 393	52.2	47.8	47.3	15.2	392	11.7
Erie	149	-8.0	123	3.0	98.6	364 369	2 964	90 447	117.0	96 322	35.6	64.4	37.8	15.5	1 401	22.0
Essex	50	-9.1	207	0.2	22.2	486 131	2 352	81 258	11.5	47 156	42.1	57.9	32.5	13.2	274	16.5
Franklin	131	-5.1	217	0.4	69.7	314 833	1 453	83 318	68.1	112 743	15.2	84.8	47.0	20.5	943	29.1
Fulton	34	-10.5	152	0.1	18.3	331 316	2 173	71 071	9.1	40 919	24.5	75.5	38.7	10.4	136	21.6

Table B. States and Counties — Water Use, Wholesale Trade, Retail Trade, and Real Estate

STATE County	Water use, 2005 Total water withdrawn (mil gal/day)	Gallons withdrawn per person	Wholesale trade,[1] 2007 Number of establishments	Number of employees	Sales (mil dol)	Annual payroll (mil dol)	Retail trade,[2] 2007 Number of establishments	Number of employees	Sales (mil dol)	Annual payroll (mil dol)	Real estate and rental and leasing,[2] 2007 Number of establishments	Number of employees	Receipts (mil dol)	Annual payroll (mil dol)
	133	134	135	136	137	138	139	140	141	142	143	144	145	146
NEW JERSEY—Cont'd														
Mercer	691.6	1 888	359	9 737	8 421.0	816.7	1 412	20 683	5 089.1	505.0	357	D	D	D
Middlesex	645.1	817	1 687	33 964	32 631.8	1 994.9	2 826	40 815	11 131.0	1 048.5	731	6 267	2 206.4	316.6
Monmouth	82.9	130	931	8 184	11 058.9	484.6	2 860	42 007	11 225.1	1 095.8	764	3 716	750.0	139.6
Morris	76.0	155	1 011	15 352	17 440.0	989.0	2 107	31 238	8 756.3	877.7	672	7 848	2 066.6	522.5
Ocean	1 466.2	2 626	453	D	D	D	1 984	27 149	7 307.4	674.0	576	2 485	460.9	83.1
Passaic	164.0	329	802	10 498	7 021.1	539.0	1 912	23 180	6 598.0	579.0	447	5 992	1 103.1	211.4
Salem	2 700.6	40 704	36	D	D	D	197	2 311	669.4	52.0	58	D	D	D
Somerset	146.8	459	528	11 335	14 634.5	863.8	1 216	19 972	5 756.0	530.3	304	1 592	453.3	63.9
Sussex	16.4	107	146	D	D	D	488	5 806	1 722.4	150.3	96	D	D	D
Union	22.0	41	908	14 610	12 948.7	823.8	2 085	25 619	7 312.1	644.5	600	3 270	988.0	135.5
Warren	27.8	252	107	D	D	D	441	6 292	1 550.6	140.4	72	D	D	D
NEW MEXICO	3 331.9	1 728	1 763	19 891	10 589.3	805.8	7 208	97 385	24 470.0	2 250.8	2 525	11 678	1 954.7	355.6
Bernalillo	149.9	248	833	12 139	6 135.0	503.5	2 253	36 900	9 396.1	903.3	1 000	5 337	898.3	155.2
Catron	19.2	5 617	NA	NA	NA	NA	13	77	7.2	0.7	3	7	0.4	0.2
Chaves	256.9	4 152	52	D	D	D	260	3 271	836.1	69.7	85	283	43.2	8.1
Cibola	14.0	506	9	35	15.9	0.8	79	850	217.4	18.8	15	40	3.7	0.7
Colfax	51.9	3 771	12	54	45.1	1.8	91	719	158.8	14.3	34	126	14.6	2.0
Curry	130.4	2 845	49	251	171.5	8.4	198	2 519	591.3	62.1	49	170	25.6	4.4
De Baca	45.1	22 386	NA	NA	NA	NA	11	63	12.4	0.9	NA	NA	NA	NA
Dona Ana	465.2	2 456	120	1 076	448.2	34.1	536	7 881	1 925.6	159.5	229	1 009	143.2	22.2
Eddy	204.9	3 984	58	D	D	D	208	2 384	562.8	51.7	39	226	30.2	7.3
Grant	50.9	1 712	19	D	D	D	132	1 257	261.4	25.4	45	121	16.4	2.6
Guadalupe	24.8	5 672	2	D	D	D	20	290	109.9	4.9	NA	NA	NA	NA
Harding	3.5	4 716	NA	NA	NA	NA	4	8	1.3	0.1	NA	NA	NA	NA
Hidalgo	89.5	17 418	2	D	D	D	36	279	113.4	4.9	1	D	D	D
Lea	163.0	2 874	90	879	376.7	40.0	213	2 759	765.9	67.8	69	617	138.8	32.7
Lincoln	23.2	1 103	8	D	D	D	150	1 162	245.6	25.1	66	175	23.4	3.7
Los Alamos	3.8	203	4	D	D	D	35	490	97.9	9.7	19	78	14.2	2.1
Luna	182.6	6 890	19	D	D	D	76	1 111	236.8	20.2	27	83	13.0	1.6
McKinley	17.2	239	45	D	D	D	262	3 778	926.9	85.1	48	162	21.7	3.0
Mora	20.4	3 991	NA	NA	NA	NA	9	58	14.1	0.9	1	D	D	D
Otero	42.0	660	25	D	D	D	193	2 385	527.8	46.2	62	246	27.8	4.2
Quay	41.6	4 489	4	9	1.7	0.2	53	450	143.9	7.2	7	20	0.7	0.2
Rio Arriba	110.1	2 698	10	D	D	D	101	1 402	319.5	32.0	24	95	10.9	1.9
Roosevelt	180.0	9 871	12	D	D	D	56	660	166.7	13.5	13	46	3.4	0.6
Sandoval	69.5	645	40	262	113.1	12.1	197	3 168	1 117.4	78.1	85	272	35.5	5.8
San Juan	332.7	2 636	146	1 454	866.4	70.4	482	6 671	1 742.0	155.5	120	879	211.5	45.2
San Miguel	35.9	1 214	9	D	D	D	103	1 187	277.2	23.4	16	60	4.4	0.8
Santa Fe	47.4	336	134	D	D	D	887	9 949	2 426.3	261.6	311	1 092	206.0	40.8
Sierra	40.6	3 167	NA	NA	NA	NA	52	375	82.8	6.9	13	36	3.3	0.5
Socorro	145.6	8 022	2	D	D	D	46	574	126.2	10.7	17	54	10.3	1.0
Taos	108.3	3 413	25	D	D	D	245	1 624	309.2	35.7	67	241	23.9	4.6
Torrance	41.0	2 345	8	42	13.7	1.2	42	562	157.5	10.5	7	36	8.7	0.9
Union	48.0	12 457	1	D	D	D	18	100	27.5	1.8	3	D	D	D
Valencia	173.4	2 499	25	110	51.6	3.3	147	2 424	571.3	52.6	50	162	21.5	3.5
NEW YORK	15 175.2	788	30 863	357 459	313 461.9	19 609.0	76 637	892 863	230 718.1	22 336.7	32 588	171 601	49 867.2	7 941.7
Albany	128.5	432	423	6 321	3 642.6	319.4	1 379	22 854	5 404.4	519.3	424	3 112	619.8	107.2
Allegany	7.1	141	20	165	51.4	4.2	157	1 457	276.7	24.7	17	62	6.8	1.5
Bronx	4.1	3	695	10 432	8 039.8	553.9	3 462	24 355	5 539.8	522.1	2 274	8 916	1 703.5	270.6
Broome	117.6	597	194	3 831	1 958.8	150.2	753	11 949	2 573.0	237.6	157	1 114	191.8	31.2
Cattaraugus	19.5	237	55	678	465.7	22.7	372	4 040	1 009.0	84.4	56	197	26.8	4.3
Cayuga	14.8	181	57	D	D	D	273	3 852	884.0	81.6	60	189	27.6	4.2
Chautauqua	461.0	3 380	99	1 610	2 621.3	60.6	555	6 699	1 364.1	133.2	87	480	66.4	12.6
Chemung	15.7	175	86	1 077	357.9	43.2	388	5 580	1 207.2	111.0	79	410	65.6	10.7
Chenango	7.4	143	28	254	126.3	10.2	188	2 203	518.2	47.4	33	84	8.1	2.1
Clinton	13.9	169	97	1 223	679.4	42.8	378	4 890	1 195.0	102.8	85	315	51.1	7.8
Columbia	8.9	140	62	D	D	D	259	2 555	638.4	62.4	69	180	22.6	3.8
Cortland	8.7	180	29	D	D	D	194	2 268	523.1	45.9	40	285	21.5	3.6
Delaware	453.6	9 543	21	361	441.0	14.7	207	1 726	389.6	36.3	35	106	13.7	2.3
Dutchess	38.7	131	228	2 069	982.3	109.1	1 095	14 632	3 599.2	356.2	387	1 844	287.9	63.2
Erie	802.4	862	1 089	20 509	19 416.1	964.4	3 360	53 571	11 217.1	1 096.8	831	6 025	929.8	172.6
Essex	9.0	232	9	95	17.9	1.9	231	1 852	429.2	39.7	35	99	16.5	2.5
Franklin	19.0	373	30	D	D	D	214	2 257	476.4	45.8	40	125	14.9	2.7
Fulton	9.6	172	67	D	D	D	199	2 338	577.1	50.9	41	152	28.4	5.0

1. Merchant wholesalers, except manufacturers' sales branches and offices.   2. Employer establishments.

Table B. States and Counties — Professional Services, Manufacturing, and Accommodation and Food Services

STATE County	Professional, scientific, and technical services,[1] 2007				Manufacturing, 2007				Accommodation and food services, 2007			
	Number of establishments	Number of employees	Receipts (mil dol)	Annual payroll (mil dol)	Number of establishments	Number of employees	Receipts (mil dol)	Annual payroll (mil dol)	Number of establishments	Number of employees	Sales (mil dol)	Annual payroll (mil dol)
	147	148	149	150	151	152	153	154	155	156	157	158
NEW JERSEY—Cont'd												
Mercer	1 646	30 900	5 790.4	2 345.3	293	9 352	D	420.1	834	12 103	695.8	197.7
Middlesex	4 053	D	D	D	847	36 047	12 207.3	1 840.4	1 614	21 554	1 275.1	337.5
Monmouth	2 754	D	D	D	511	11 717	3 468.4	538.0	1 642	21 953	1 153.5	316.0
Morris	2 796	43 496	7 752.3	3 425.8	628	22 068	7 631.7	1 181.6	1 290	18 119	1 129.8	314.1
Ocean	1 167	D	D	D	315	D	D	251.0	1 087	12 584	703.0	182.7
Passaic	1 162	D	D	D	872	22 028	5 178.3	1 042.9	905	9 296	538.7	133.2
Salem	84	D	D	D	43	3 113	1 440.4	204.7	112	1 580	82.3	21.6
Somerset	1 830	D	D	D	337	17 673	6 401.5	1 159.7	712	10 739	656.1	180.0
Sussex	379	D	D	D	128	D	D	89.0	299	3 245	172.4	46.5
Union	1 546	D	D	D	712	31 897	18 574.7	2 106.8	1 110	12 763	748.0	199.9
Warren	260	D	D	D	136	4 603	2 212.2	240.2	250	2 622	118.0	31.3
NEW MEXICO	4 789	43 001	5 975.8	2 516.7	1 574	35 409	17 122.7	1 560.5	4 090	80 415	3 734.3	1 054.8
Bernalillo	2 248	D	D	D	661	16 573	D	719.8	1 319	29 908	1 398.0	410.5
Catron	3	D	D	D	NA	NA	NA	NA	11	57	2.6	0.4
Chaves	111	780	108.2	34.2	45	1 098	661.5	37.7	121	2 306	92.4	25.0
Cibola	21	D	D	D	NA	NA	NA	NA	43	1 403	117.3	25.0
Colfax	37	D	D	D	NA	NA	NA	NA	76	1 426	56.9	17.2
Curry	76	D	D	D	28	530	D	20.6	86	1 934	68.3	17.8
De Baca	1	D	D	D	NA	NA	NA	NA	3	D	D	D
Dona Ana	315	D	D	D	141	2 349	931.9	84.2	298	5 955	238.7	64.9
Eddy	76	D	D	D	37	1 302	D	84.5	110	1 778	80.5	20.8
Grant	45	D	D	D	NA	NA	NA	NA	76	957	35.5	9.1
Guadalupe	1	D	D	D	NA	NA	NA	NA	29	373	16.7	4.5
Harding	NA	NA	NA	NA	NA	NA	NA	NA	3	16	0.3	0.1
Hidalgo	2	D	D	D	NA	NA	NA	NA	16	275	9.9	2.6
Lea	78	522	60.7	24.9	38	815	280.4	36.4	115	1 944	85.1	21.0
Lincoln	61	D	D	D	NA	NA	NA	NA	103	1 114	60.2	15.1
Los Alamos	79	D	D	D	NA	NA	NA	NA	36	467	17.7	4.8
Luna	22	D	D	D	14	759	D	21.5	57	945	36.9	8.4
McKinley	50	D	D	D	33	685	D	37.7	148	2 474	109.1	27.3
Mora	1	D	D	D	NA	NA	NA	NA	3	D	D	D
Otero	83	D	D	D	NA	NA	NA	NA	103	1 798	92.4	24.3
Quay	10	D	D	D	NA	NA	NA	NA	35	555	17.9	4.9
Rio Arriba	42	D	D	D	NA	NA	NA	NA	79	1 184	66.8	18.3
Roosevelt	19	D	D	D	NA	NA	NA	NA	26	607	17.6	5.0
Sandoval	174	D	D	D	65	5 705	D	321.5	144	3 392	150.8	45.5
San Juan	239	D	D	D	91	1 649	668.7	64.3	192	4 108	173.2	45.8
San Miguel	32	D	D	D	NA	NA	NA	NA	66	773	33.1	8.2
Santa Fe	693	D	D	D	153	980	D	34.5	398	9 203	540.4	166.3
Sierra	17	D	D	D	NA	NA	NA	NA	39	423	14.9	4.1
Socorro	25	D	D	D	NA	NA	NA	NA	47	673	24.2	6.5
Taos	125	D	D	D	NA	NA	NA	NA	173	2 330	100.1	31.3
Torrance	9	D	D	D	NA	NA	NA	NA	29	309	12.9	3.1
Union	8	D	D	D	NA	NA	NA	NA	14	178	6.6	1.6
Valencia	86	378	26.4	9.5	35	1 114	D	D	92	1 501	55.7	14.8
NEW YORK	58 087	539 635	112 045.6	41 604.5	18 629	533 835	162 720.2	24 268.0	43 791	591 653	39 813.5	10 956.3
Albany	1 142	11 543	1 773.4	706.6	256	8 253	3 351.5	417.3	957	14 776	738.9	207.1
Allegany	56	D	D	D	44	2 826	965.9	115.8	94	1 151	40.2	10.9
Bronx	631	D	D	D	393	8 668	D	315.7	1 368	10 987	743.2	180.9
Broome	327	D	D	D	210	11 107	2 525.4	D	511	7 795	326.4	92.6
Cattaraugus	104	D	D	D	91	3 972	738.7	169.0	197	4 131	264.8	62.2
Cayuga	100	641	45.6	20.3	92	3 338	1 109.9	150.7	174	1 897	76.4	19.7
Chautauqua	196	D	D	D	212	11 887	4 461.9	489.2	355	4 951	181.2	55.0
Chemung	115	D	D	D	93	6 348	1 280.8	285.8	198	3 151	123.1	35.2
Chenango	74	513	31.5	25.6	86	2 489	595.6	93.2	90	777	32.2	9.6
Clinton	128	D	D	D	88	3 873	1 599.8	155.8	187	2 627	126.6	35.6
Columbia	212	D	D	D	73	1 896	619.2	82.0	165	1 392	65.1	19.5
Cortland	86	D	D	D	65	3 201	603.7	134.6	135	2 079	84.6	21.7
Delaware	73	D	D	D	41	5 120	1 432.9	223.6	125	862	41.2	11.0
Dutchess	778	D	D	D	217	15 948	3 823.0	1 263.0	701	8 172	424.7	117.2
Erie	2 100	D	D	D	1 111	48 058	15 873.8	2 444.8	2 112	36 944	1 462.8	434.5
Essex	65	D	D	D	34	842	D	45.8	217	2 094	125.6	39.4
Franklin	75	D	D	D	NA	NA	NA	NA	113	927	42.7	11.3
Fulton	82	325	25.3	9.0	90	2 346	520.6	84.0	126	1 089	46.6	12.3

1. Establishment subject to federal tax.

STATE County	Health care and social assistance, 2007				Other services, 2007				Federal funds and grants, 2009–2010 Expenditures (mil dol)			
										Direct payments for individuals[1]		
	Number of establishments	Number of employees	Receipts (mil dol)	Annual payroll (mil dol)	Number of establishments	Number of employees	Receipts (mil dol)	Annual payroll (mil dol)	Total	Social Security and government retirement	Medicare	Food Stamps and Supplemental Security Income
	159	160	161	162	163	164	165	166	167	168	169	170
NEW JERSEY—Cont'd												
Mercer	1 147	26 724	2 609.3	1 180.7	860	6 084	828.6	214.7	6 657.9	1 020.4	810.3	91.2
Middlesex	1 970	39 959	4 285.8	1 742.4	1 581	10 420	1 588.0	354.1	5 185.6	1 838.2	1 278.4	113.9
Monmouth	2 300	37 165	4 035.3	1 558.5	1 518	8 075	720.8	214.3	7 482.7	1 946.0	1 183.0	80.8
Morris	1 660	31 028	3 263.2	1 484.4	1 271	7 416	1 016.6	232.4	3 525.7	1 327.4	660.4	31.7
Ocean	1 497	29 082	2 698.1	1 085.8	1 065	5 305	486.8	125.2	4 702.5	2 430.9	1 433.1	71.0
Passaic	1 325	24 170	2 259.9	957.3	1 001	5 020	386.3	118.6	3 670.4	1 115.9	963.3	157.5
Salem	164	2 988	240.8	99.2	116	364	28.8	7.0	519.2	215.4	158.6	15.4
Somerset	1 081	19 020	2 016.6	793.7	713	4 064	574.1	130.4	1 673.1	799.8	342.4	24.0
Sussex	328	D	D	D	330	1 293	112.9	31.6	754.4	418.3	190.1	12.7
Union	1 526	30 202	2 934.9	1 280.0	1 218	6 401	626.3	175.7	3 731.0	1 318.7	1 113.0	118.3
Warren	290	5 884	498.8	205.5	243	1 133	106.2	29.7	737.5	332.8	212.4	14.3
NEW MEXICO	4 732	105 496	8 834.1	3 781.1	2 953	18 061	1 689.7	449.5	27 959.0	6 260.7	2 011.0	909.7
Bernalillo	1 713	42 659	3 957.7	1 724.2	1 089	8 015	670.7	211.2	9 573.0	2 142.0	658.6	238.2
Catron	5	D	D	D	4	D	D	D	39.5	20.6	3.4	1.1
Chaves	181	3 596	342.3	122.8	90	528	39.8	10.3	564.8	194.3	79.4	40.6
Cibola	45	1 043	70.7	34.1	22	94	7.2	1.8	302.3	70.4	0.0	16.8
Colfax	37	577	51.5	22.2	29	110	11.7	2.4	129.9	55.3	22.7	8.1
Curry	101	2 865	190.8	97.7	85	460	40.9	8.1	734.8	153.0	53.7	15.9
De Baca	5	D	D	D	4	D	D	D	23.7	8.5	4.6	0.8
Dona Ana	474	10 748	798.2	323.2	230	1 237	94.1	27.7	2 062.5	567.9	160.8	130.9
Eddy	117	2 773	225.3	88.8	85	461	40.5	9.3	706.6	160.7	84.7	24.4
Grant	94	1 506	116.4	49.4	57	207	14.7	4.1	306.3	129.8	43.4	14.4
Guadalupe	9	45	5.4	0.9	9	38	4.7	1.3	70.8	13.4	8.0	2.3
Harding	1	D	D	D	NA	NA	NA	NA	8.1	3.4	1.5	0.2
Hidalgo	10	102	3.8	1.6	4	D	D	D	96.2	16.5	7.9	4.1
Lea	116	2 483	199.9	74.8	100	709	134.5	23.5	392.8	135.7	86.6	31.6
Lincoln	48	634	54.9	24.5	42	160	16.4	3.3	152.4	87.3	22.4	6.0
Los Alamos	59	965	92.7	34.9	22	151	9.0	2.7	2 347.6	46.5	16.3	0.9
Luna	46	804	77.0	24.9	30	109	6.8	1.5	248.0	91.0	34.5	18.8
McKinley	94	4 020	292.3	155.2	83	528	35.7	9.6	944.8	153.6	55.5	67.3
Mora	6	230	10.0	5.6	3	D	D	D	86.3	19.4	6.4	3.8
Otero	111	2 152	174.8	70.1	66	348	19.2	5.4	941.6	252.4	52.5	20.8
Quay	27	448	31.4	13.0	21	115	13.1	2.8	114.2	40.6	18.5	8.1
Rio Arriba	95	1 808	119.6	66.0	27	134	14.4	2.8	481.7	120.8	45.4	25.3
Roosevelt	35	728	43.6	18.2	16	78	5.4	1.5	178.2	45.4	28.1	10.9
Sandoval	159	1 861	134.8	53.8	94	498	42.3	11.8	675.6	333.7	78.6	28.2
San Juan	265	6 274	534.2	226.2	192	1 363	170.4	37.1	995.9	299.9	102.4	51.5
San Miguel	84	2 532	164.2	69.9	26	92	7.4	2.0	402.8	94.2	40.2	26.9
Santa Fe	518	8 465	809.4	318.0	341	1 849	231.0	54.1	2 153.9	470.9	117.4	28.7
Sierra	21	538	33.1	15.9	20	116	7.2	2.2	160.3	70.0	31.7	6.9
Socorro	30	763	45.9	27.0	15	45	2.9	0.7	189.7	49.8	15.9	17.2
Taos	109	1 548	112.1	48.0	68	270	19.9	5.3	390.6	110.4	31.0	17.7
Torrance	20	361	12.4	6.4	9	23	2.3	0.5	113.4	48.0	11.6	9.7
Union	9	D	D	D	11	D	D	D	49.9	15.0	7.9	1.6
Valencia	88	2 682	113.5	56.1	60	242	20.0	5.2	504.1	239.8	79.5	32.0
NEW YORK	53 948	1 326 039	128 595.2	54 422.4	42 575	249 391	39 147.4	8 073.4	202 266.2	49 784.8	37 802.8	9 010.1
Albany	1 010	30 989	2 855.4	1 165.0	792	6 198	716.3	200.7	9 559.2	842.4	463.1	92.8
Allegany	95	1 994	106.1	50.1	73	265	17.5	3.8	350.7	148.8	75.7	21.3
Bronx	1 997	86 879	8 795.8	3 868.5	1 621	7 061	680.8	184.8	(2)	(2)	(2)	(2)
Broome	435	14 029	1 253.0	505.5	326	2 032	161.7	44.0	1 795.6	682.4	363.4	83.6
Cattaraugus	189	3 656	263.6	110.7	127	794	49.7	12.5	922.4	277.9	137.3	30.3
Cayuga	201	3 683	257.5	112.0	124	487	41.2	8.9	583.8	241.0	129.4	26.0
Chautauqua	297	8 735	581.0	235.6	255	1 558	110.3	23.3	1 234.7	471.2	239.7	63.4
Chemung	221	6 722	587.1	247.0	129	786	59.9	15.7	754.7	306.1	159.0	39.0
Chenango	116	1 795	134.8	55.4	77	270	21.0	6.0	374.1	171.5	70.0	20.1
Clinton	240	5 056	399.7	180.2	123	585	43.2	12.2	652.0	268.0	105.9	31.7
Columbia	170	3 928	274.7	130.3	97	395	38.3	9.8	518.3	219.7	106.4	17.9
Cortland	130	3 262	202.1	93.4	103	557	37.9	10.7	302.6	131.3	62.5	16.1
Delaware	118	2 235	146.6	55.3	83	357	59.3	8.2	391.9	161.0	85.1	15.9
Dutchess	908	17 764	1 631.3	682.5	614	2 577	260.9	68.7	1 990.3	881.2	401.9	52.9
Erie	2 709	73 571	6 357.2	2 520.7	1 773	13 107	1 091.7	322.8	8 851.9	3 203.3	1 767.1	410.1
Essex	137	1 755	114.9	54.8	79	374	35.7	8.7	340.6	140.2	69.4	12.4
Franklin	155	3 205	236.2	102.9	84	250	17.9	4.8	414.5	145.5	73.2	20.6
Fulton	187	3 419	228.8	106.1	87	492	37.8	12.4	405.0	171.8	86.0	20.8

1. State totals may include programs not allocated by county.   2. Bronx, Kings, Queens, and Richmond counties are included with New York county.

STATE County	Federal funds and grants, 2009–2010 (cont.) Expenditures (mil dol) (cont.) — Procurement contract awards			Grants[1]				Value of residential construction authorized by building permits, 2010		Local government finances, 2007 — General revenue		Taxes	Per capita[2] (dollars)	
	Salaries and wages	Defense	Other	Medicaid and other health-related	Nutrition and family welfare	Education	Other	New construction ($1,000)	Number of housing units	Total (mil dol)	Inter-governmental (mil dol)	Total (mil dol)	Total	Property
	171	172	173	174	175	176	177	178	179	180	181	182	183	184
NEW JERSEY—Cont'd														
Mercer	320.8	177.4	175.7	690.6	349.7	578.2	2 175.8	94 561	655	1 979.0	683.1	990.7	2 711	2 675
Middlesex	337.1	165.8	246.0	665.1	88.7	16.8	260.5	164 983	1 568	3 387.0	919.5	1 897.9	2 407	2 350
Monmouth	544.7	2 858.3	192.1	449.0	82.8	17.1	68.2	164 153	915	3 126.6	803.2	1 814.6	2 826	2 770
Morris	392.5	629.8	177.4	153.9	44.8	6.7	56.5	120 912	579	2 299.5	375.6	1 571.1	3 216	3 168
Ocean	218.1	100.2	34.4	223.0	75.3	17.9	39.7	200 986	1 325	2 124.3	556.3	1 255.3	2 220	2 181
Passaic	102.0	375.7	26.4	613.7	106.7	28.2	70.6	49 432	402	1 897.2	681.0	1 034.7	2 103	2 080
Salem	23.0	2.2	12.3	65.8	11.1	2.4	3.8	10 588	105	320.1	134.6	127.5	1 931	1 887
Somerset	118.3	113.1	61.2	97.2	33.5	3.8	13.7	100 790	716	1 524.2	262.5	1 043.1	3 224	3 180
Sussex	32.0	5.2	9.4	56.5	15.4	3.0	4.3	41 851	210	660.1	181.5	395.2	2 609	2 566
Union	156.7	209.5	64.8	479.6	78.9	15.4	67.9	67 489	730	2 753.2	949.6	1 402.5	2 673	2 609
Warren	43.1	32.6	5.3	55.5	17.4	3.7	9.0	23 090	172	501.1	186.9	244.4	2 227	2 198
NEW MEXICO	2 768.0	1 519.7	5 979.2	3 712.9	585.8	619.3	1 802.3	146 588	844	X	X	X	X	X
Bernalillo	1 221.7	755.9	2 894.6	1 015.6	111.6	73.7	242.7	195 461	1 133	2 368.5	1 203.9	740.8	1 177	606
Catron	4.9	0.0	1.3	5.8	0.7	0.5	1.1	NA	NA	12.6	10.0	1.6	465	385
Chaves	45.7	4.0	18.8	143.9	13.4	6.4	11.5	4 744	21	205.0	146.6	31.1	496	384
Cibola	23.7	0.0	124.5	1.5	9.9	5.4	17.5	NA	NA	61.9	41.8	9.6	352	172
Colfax	7.3	2.9	0.8	28.0	3.6	0.6	1.1	6 020	16	58.1	35.1	12.4	935	651
Curry	196.4	143.3	2.9	93.0	10.9	4.2	38.6	33 976	161	157.2	97.0	36.8	812	227
De Baca	0.9	0.0	0.2	6.3	0.8	0.1	0.8	NA	NA	9.7	6.7	1.6	842	568
Dona Ana	218.7	309.3	203.7	273.0	47.7	15.0	64.9	166 683	974	633.2	389.2	159.6	803	331
Eddy	70.2	7.6	202.4	103.3	16.4	3.0	29.5	15 068	89	206.8	116.4	63.3	1 242	588
Grant	17.3	0.0	4.9	66.4	7.8	1.6	12.2	NA	NA	160.0	66.6	27.5	927	312
Guadalupe	3.0	2.3	0.3	37.1	1.5	0.2	2.2	NA	NA	24.8	15.0	6.5	1 461	822
Harding	0.7	0.0	0.2	1.5	0.2	0.0	0.2	NA	NA	6.8	5.1	0.9	1 278	635
Hidalgo	17.6	31.6	0.3	14.2	1.4	0.9	0.6	NA	NA	25.1	19.0	3.3	672	546
Lea	8.7	4.5	1.5	94.5	14.7	3.5	1.4	11 356	77	297.4	135.3	89.9	1 549	513
Lincoln	7.8	0.5	1.8	19.0	4.4	1.1	1.2	9 272	53	82.2	48.0	21.5	1 034	641
Los Alamos	21.3	1.4	2 215.8	19.1	1.7	0.6	22.9	500	2	139.4	72.8	44.6	2 405	705
Luna	38.2	3.0	3.4	45.1	6.5	2.5	2.6	4 580	25	91.3	57.7	18.8	697	335
McKinley	142.5	6.4	116.6	287.0	26.6	65.8	10.8	3 275	17	219.4	158.6	33.8	483	231
Mora	2.5	0.0	0.7	40.0	3.2	0.3	9.3	NA	NA	17.4	12.9	2.6	515	488
Otero	316.8	174.9	9.3	67.7	12.7	4.5	10.3	442	2	139.3	90.9	31.1	492	247
Quay	2.9	0.1	0.7	28.3	5.4	0.6	1.6	NA	NA	45.9	29.8	6.1	676	319
Rio Arriba	22.6	2.4	6.7	198.7	14.0	11.2	17.3	319	3	147.6	91.5	37.8	925	426
Roosevelt	6.3	4.1	4.0	44.1	4.3	3.5	1.4	7 905	51	59.8	42.3	11.2	585	261
Sandoval	26.2	13.8	11.3	111.4	17.3	14.4	24.8	97 426	544	364.7	187.7	104.4	886	422
San Juan	106.8	1.2	79.4	196.6	23.1	38.8	10.4	43 935	273	501.8	314.6	117.3	958	569
San Miguel	20.5	1.2	2.3	184.3	10.2	5.5	7.0	NA	NA	118.7	83.0	24.3	850	349
Santa Fe	136.2	45.2	43.5	254.6	123.5	151.5	743.4	12 802	96	511.3	237.0	184.0	1 287	676
Sierra	6.9	0.7	1.6	32.8	2.8	0.6	4.3	62	1	35.5	22.2	9.3	756	413
Socorro	12.9	2.7	9.8	49.2	5.2	4.2	16.0	506	4	64.9	40.4	15.7	867	600
Taos	29.3	0.0	9.4	115.8	9.1	10.3	52.2	7 260	60	114.6	66.8	28.7	907	432
Torrance	3.7	0.0	1.4	30.6	4.0	0.6	2.8	NA	NA	75.5	54.0	13.0	781	529
Union	4.2	0.0	0.6	13.2	0.9	0.2	3.4	NA	NA	15.1	11.0	2.6	674	306
Valencia	23.7	0.7	4.5	91.0	19.2	5.2	2.8	11 329	87	190.8	140.0	36.8	516	292
NEW YORK	13 936.5	8 809.8	5 073.4	39 959.0	6 704.4	4 360.8	12 079.4	3 165 282	19 568	X	X	X	X	X
Albany	498.7	45.1	198.4	725.5	152.3	2 323.0	3 747.0	62 354	321	1 621.8	493.0	796.5	2 661	1 767
Allegany	10.1	0.6	2.4	62.7	16.1	3.7	2.1	5 020	53	258.6	146.9	84.5	1 702	1 339
Bronx	(3)	(3)	(3)	(3)	(3)	(3)	(3)	123 742	1 064	(3)	(3)	(3)	(3)	(3)
Broome	65.2	177.3	19.2	235.1	54.8	19.7	69.9	11 815	60	1 049.2	455.6	431.0	2 200	1 429
Cattaraugus	37.4	4.5	56.3	111.8	27.5	99.8	45.9	12 648	116	460.1	242.5	147.6	1 843	1 360
Cayuga	16.7	2.1	5.4	108.7	22.0	7.4	10.1	9 535	85	386.2	180.4	133.2	1 663	1 199
Chautauqua	67.8	86.4	16.3	192.8	43.8	11.9	15.2	20 420	130	727.8	336.1	254.1	1 897	1 369
Chemung	36.0	2.0	7.9	143.0	26.0	6.1	19.8	11 868	76	422.5	199.0	150.5	1 710	1 109
Chenango	9.8	3.2	2.3	70.0	16.7	4.5	3.0	4 734	76	272.8	148.7	89.2	1 742	1 374
Clinton	67.2	7.5	10.7	107.9	23.3	8.3	9.3	16 326	115	438.0	201.5	159.5	1 940	1 355
Columbia	14.4	0.3	4.8	113.3	16.4	2.7	8.4	17 927	67	321.9	113.7	166.0	2 662	2 034
Cortland	10.1	0.2	4.4	52.2	13.9	4.5	4.1	8 483	63	234.1	112.3	89.9	1 858	1 336
Delaware	22.9	4.4	2.8	72.5	14.6	2.9	7.0	10 602	65	304.1	139.4	121.0	2 614	2 127
Dutchess	85.3	2.7	51.5	362.1	59.2	17.3	36.9	70 796	336	1 442.7	464.9	773.8	2 643	2 030
Erie	651.8	231.5	213.0	1 541.5	274.2	86.9	259.4	209 613	1 261	4 525.9	2 169.6	1 813.0	1 985	1 342
Essex	25.4	0.5	4.7	66.8	11.9	1.8	4.5	16 908	74	231.3	73.9	116.8	3 063	2 374
Franklin	15.6	0.1	4.0	103.4	15.9	5.2	20.4	7 346	68	277.2	145.6	89.6	1 776	1 400
Fulton	11.7	2.4	3.5	74.7	14.9	4.0	6.9	10 699	92	275.6	128.9	99.4	1 804	1 283

1. State totals may include programs not allocated by county.　2. Based on the resident population estimated as of July 1 of the year shown.　3. Bronx, Kings, Queens, and Richmond counties are included with New York county.

STATE County	Local government finances, 2007 (cont.)									Government employment, 2009			Presidential election,[2] 2008		
	Direct general expenditure							Debt outstanding					Percent of vote cast:		
	Total (mil dol)	Per capita[1] (dollars)	Percent of total for:					Total (mil dol)	Per capita[1] (dollars)	Federal civilian	Federal military	State and local	Demo-cratic	Republi-can	All other
			Educa-tion	Health and hospitals	Police protec-tion	Public welfare	High-ways								
	185	186	187	188	189	190	191	192	193	194	195	196	197	198	199
NEW JERSEY—Cont'd															
Mercer	2 085.4	5 706	53.1	1.0	5.4	4.4	1.3	1 899.1	5 197	2 382	791	49 093	67.4	31.4	1.2
Middlesex	3 668.9	4 652	55.3	1.2	5.7	3.4	2.3	3 699.0	4 690	3 128	1 745	57 344	60.4	38.5	1.1
Monmouth	3 225.6	5 024	56.7	0.8	5.7	2.4	2.4	2 828.7	4 406	7 835	1 962	34 127	47.6	51.3	1.1
Morris	2 404.4	4 922	59.1	0.8	5.4	1.5	2.8	2 029.0	4 154	5 588	1 079	26 313	45.5	53.6	0.9
Ocean	2 223.9	3 933	51.9	0.4	6.3	2.5	4.7	2 186.1	3 866	2 885	1 721	25 040	40.2	58.6	1.3
Passaic	1 873.1	3 806	50.1	1.0	7.1	4.1	1.7	1 286.6	2 614	1 184	1 011	29 181	60.4	38.7	0.8
Salem	333.4	5 050	57.8	1.1	3.5	4.4	3.8	454.1	6 879	179	136	4 510	51.2	47.2	1.6
Somerset	1 584.8	4 898	59.9	1.3	4.8	0.7	3.8	1 217.0	3 761	1 891	672	16 428	52.5	46.4	1.1
Sussex	647.5	4 275	66.1	1.0	3.7	1.6	3.9	697.4	4 604	385	311	7 706	38.9	59.6	1.5
Union	2 808.8	5 354	54.5	1.9	6.3	1.8	2.0	2 182.8	4 160	1 690	1 082	32 347	63.7	35.5	0.9
Warren	529.4	4 824	57.6	2.1	3.3	3.2	3.7	237.2	2 162	273	225	5 884	42.2	56.2	1.7
NEW MEXICO	X	X	X	X	X	X	X	X	X	31 957	15 252	168 746	56.9	41.8	1.3
Bernalillo	2 068.8	3 287	48.6	0.8	9.1	2.1	6.6	1 797.5	2 856	14 659	5 254	54 113	60.0	38.7	1.3
Catron	9.9	2 886	61.8	1.5	7.0	0.0	8.4	2.4	709	114	0	212	31.4	66.2	2.4
Chaves	201.7	3 222	50.8	0.3	5.4	2.8	4.3	120.7	1 928	328	189	4 496	37.1	61.7	1.2
Cibola	62.1	2 277	61.7	0.2	3.9	1.9	3.2	30.0	1 102	341	72	3 078	64.1	34.4	1.5
Colfax	52.7	3 989	51.7	6.6	5.9	0.4	6.4	11.2	846	58	34	1 520	54.7	43.9	1.4
Curry	146.5	3 232	64.1	0.1	5.2	0.9	5.8	42.3	933	828	2 842	2 657	32.3	66.5	1.2
De Baca	9.1	4 768	53.9	1.5	3.3	0.0	14.6	3.6	1 896	15	0	203	34.4	64.8	0.9
Dona Ana	605.1	3 044	58.2	3.1	4.2	0.8	2.8	401.1	2 018	4 050	594	17 629	58.1	40.5	1.3
Eddy	218.6	4 286	49.2	7.1	6.9	1.9	4.4	77.6	1 521	855	140	3 121	36.6	62.2	1.2
Grant	164.1	5 525	31.7	38.6	4.7	0.0	2.0	44.3	1 493	216	80	3 495	59.2	39.3	1.5
Guadalupe	22.3	5 004	49.3	0.1	2.4	1.1	2.4	6.8	1 523	30	11	444	70.9	28.2	0.9
Harding	6.3	8 853	52.1	0.7	1.9	0.0	16.8	2.3	3 258	15	0	95	41.5	57.2	1.3
Hidalgo	21.2	4 297	57.7	0.6	10.7	0.6	4.4	5.9	1 183	274	13	432	50.9	48.0	1.1
Lea	288.1	4 964	49.7	10.2	6.2	1.4	5.8	87.0	1 499	106	160	3 559	27.4	71.6	1.0
Lincoln	80.4	3 871	47.4	3.1	7.1	0.9	3.5	61.7	2 966	119	56	1 216	36.5	61.9	1.7
Los Alamos	134.6	7 253	29.7	0.0	5.4	0.7	3.8	137.5	7 411	299	50	1 660	52.6	45.7	1.6
Luna	92.5	3 425	52.0	1.9	5.9	1.1	5.8	26.3	974	558	72	1 715	51.7	46.4	1.9
McKinley	236.6	3 377	71.2	0.6	4.2	1.4	3.5	121.7	1 737	2 575	188	5 641	71.4	27.5	1.1
Mora	18.6	3 668	67.8	0.0	2.5	0.0	2.6	4.8	947	49	13	286	78.6	20.6	0.8
Otero	131.6	2 084	53.9	0.1	8.0	2.3	5.7	59.4	941	1 912	3 732	4 639	39.6	58.8	1.6
Quay	39.2	4 374	70.1	1.4	1.6	0.7	3.4	6.5	728	52	24	920	38.7	59.2	2.1
Rio Arriba	132.1	3 236	55.9	0.5	4.2	0.9	7.8	75.9	1 859	369	108	4 765	75.0	24.1	0.9
Roosevelt	58.6	3 061	61.2	1.0	5.6	0.0	5.3	14.1	737	59	50	2 210	34.3	64.2	1.6
Sandoval	382.9	3 249	45.6	0.4	6.1	1.7	7.6	585.9	4 971	401	335	7 213	55.7	43.0	1.3
San Juan	519.0	4 239	59.6	0.9	5.4	1.2	4.5	941.0	7 686	1 548	334	9 931	38.8	59.9	1.3
San Miguel	118.1	4 121	61.8	0.1	4.3	0.6	4.5	65.0	2 268	159	75	4 175	79.7	19.1	1.1
Santa Fe	462.7	3 237	43.5	3.0	6.5	3.1	5.8	626.5	4 382	1 040	396	17 886	76.9	21.9	1.2
Sierra	36.1	2 927	47.1	0.9	2.2	1.5	3.8	17.6	1 430	122	34	784	42.9	55.0	2.1
Socorro	58.6	3 235	53.2	1.2	6.9	2.8	5.0	12.6	694	221	48	2 827	59.5	38.4	2.1
Taos	103.6	3 278	50.3	0.9	2.6	1.3	2.0	24.7	781	318	84	1 986	81.8	17.0	1.2
Torrance	68.6	4 133	69.2	0.0	3.3	0.4	3.0	28.4	1 709	90	44	1 142	44.5	53.8	1.7
Union	17.9	4 724	58.8	5.5	5.3	0.0	2.8	2.2	578	61	10	317	28.2	70.4	1.3
Valencia	192.0	2 691	66.4	0.1	4.4	1.8	2.8	103.4	1 449	116	194	4 379	53.2	45.5	1.4
NEW YORK	X	X	X	X	X	X	X	X	X	127 052	60 058	1 338 718	62.9	36.0	1.0
Albany	1 653.7	5 525	40.9	3.1	4.9	12.6	3.3	2 110.9	7 053	5 401	894	61 754	63.8	34.4	1.8
Allegany	259.4	5 227	50.2	3.5	3.2	12.3	8.0	280.0	5 641	130	80	3 962	38.2	60.0	1.8
Bronx	(3)	(3)	(3)	(3)	(3)	(3)	(3)	(3)	(3)	7 603	2 313	15 726	88.7	10.9	0.4
Broome	1 130.8	5 770	46.4	2.7	2.8	11.2	4.3	954.4	4 870	678	331	20 310	53.2	45.2	1.6
Cattaraugus	475.0	5 930	52.4	4.2	2.3	12.4	7.8	363.1	4 534	265	133	10 061	43.9	54.5	1.6
Cayuga	380.6	4 753	50.0	4.6	2.5	10.5	6.3	277.7	3 468	173	129	6 106	53.3	44.8	1.8
Chautauqua	728.1	5 436	50.6	2.5	2.9	12.9	5.9	534.3	3 989	375	217	9 513	49.6	48.6	1.8
Chemung	429.2	4 877	43.9	2.8	3.2	18.3	6.8	316.2	3 593	309	144	6 909	48.8	50.0	1.1
Chenango	262.1	5 118	54.7	5.1	2.2	8.2	8.8	162.0	3 163	120	82	4 403	48.4	49.6	2.0
Clinton	431.6	5 250	50.3	5.2	1.8	11.1	6.3	375.9	4 572	733	134	7 570	60.7	37.8	1.6
Columbia	311.5	4 995	50.3	3.8	2.1	13.5	7.7	140.6	2 255	179	100	4 732	55.9	42.5	1.6
Cortland	241.4	4 991	44.9	5.3	3.0	10.6	9.5	145.6	3 011	120	79	3 595	54.2	44.2	1.6
Delaware	300.8	6 498	39.5	3.5	1.1	12.3	14.9	181.5	3 922	144	74	4 498	46.4	51.6	2.0
Dutchess	1 461.9	4 994	53.7	4.1	3.3	7.7	4.2	1 173.4	4 008	1 255	476	21 408	53.7	45.1	1.2
Erie	4 605.8	5 043	48.0	3.3	4.1	11.3	3.3	4 139.9	4 533	9 077	1 728	67 750	58.0	40.5	1.6
Essex	250.1	6 562	33.9	4.4	7.8	9.7	10.1	258.6	6 785	348	61	4 310	55.9	42.6	1.5
Franklin	279.0	5 530	52.7	3.5	1.3	11.9	5.3	159.2	3 156	180	81	8 443	60.4	38.2	1.4
Fulton	293.9	5 332	53.6	2.4	2.4	14.2	4.9	226.0	4 101	97	90	3 887	44.5	53.7	1.8

1. Based on the resident population estimated as of July 1 of the year shown.   2. © 2009 Election Data Services, Inc. All rights reserved.   3. Bronx, Kings, Queens, and Richmond counties are included with New York county.

Table B. States and Counties — Land Area and Population

STATE/ County code	CBSA code[1]	County type[2]	STATE County	Land area,[3] (sq km) 2010	Total persons	Rank	Per square kilometer	White	Black	American Indian, Alaska Native	Asian and Pacific Islander	Percent Hispanic or Latino[4]	Under 5 years	5 to 17 years	18 to 24 years	25 to 34 years	35 to 44 years	45 to 54 years
								Race alone or in combination, not Hispanic or Latino (percent)					Age (percent)					
				1	2	3	4	5	6	7	8	9	10	11	12	13	14	15
			NEW YORK—Cont'd															
36 037	12860	4	Genesee	1 277	60 079	859	47.0	92.9	3.4	1.6	0.8	2.7	5.6	16.4	9.2	10.9	12.7	16.7
36 039	...	6	Greene	1 676	49 221	992	29.4	88.4	6.1	0.7	1.1	4.9	4.7	14.6	9.5	9.9	12.8	16.7
36 041	...	8	Hamilton	4 448	4 836	2 854	1.1	97.4	0.8	1.1	0.6	1.1	3.5	13.0	5.0	7.4	10.9	17.3
36 043	46540	2	Herkimer	3 656	64 519	811	17.6	96.6	1.5	0.5	0.7	1.6	5.6	16.6	9.2	10.3	12.1	15.7
36 045	48060	4	Jefferson	3 286	116 229	515	35.4	87.8	5.8	1.1	2.2	5.3	8.3	17.2	12.2	15.3	12.6	13.1
36 047	35620	1	Kings	183	2 504 700	7	13 686.9	36.6	32.8	0.5	11.3	19.8	7.1	16.7	10.6	17.0	13.6	12.9
36 049	...	6	Lewis	3 301	27 087	1 531	8.2	97.5	0.8	0.5	0.5	1.3	6.6	18.2	8.0	11.0	12.2	16.3
36 051	40380	1	Livingston	1 636	65 393	801	40.0	93.4	2.7	0.7	1.6	2.8	4.9	15.3	14.5	10.2	12.1	16.4
36 053	45060	2	Madison	1 696	73 442	736	43.3	94.9	2.2	1.1	1.1	1.8	5.3	16.5	13.7	9.8	12.0	16.2
36 055	40380	1	Monroe	1 702	744 344	76	437.3	74.4	15.6	0.7	3.9	7.3	5.8	16.8	11.3	12.2	12.5	15.1
36 057	11220	4	Montgomery	1 044	50 219	974	48.1	86.2	2.1	0.6	0.9	11.3	6.1	17.4	8.2	11.4	12.2	14.7
36 059	35620	1	Nassau	737	1 339 532	27	1 817.5	66.4	11.1	0.3	8.4	14.6	5.5	17.7	8.4	10.6	13.3	16.3
36 061	35620	1	New York	59	1 585 873	20	26 879.2	49.5	13.7	0.5	12.4	25.4	4.8	10.0	11.4	21.5	14.8	12.8
36 063	15380	1	Niagara	1 353	216 469	287	160.0	89.0	7.9	1.7	1.2	2.2	5.3	16.1	9.4	11.0	12.3	16.5
36 065	46540	2	Oneida	3 140	234 878	273	74.8	86.3	6.8	0.6	3.2	4.6	5.7	16.2	10.0	11.4	12.4	15.3
36 067	45060	2	Onondaga	2 016	467 026	140	231.7	81.3	11.8	1.4	3.6	4.0	5.9	17.1	11.2	12.0	12.3	15.3
36 069	40380	1	Ontario	1 668	107 931	542	64.7	93.1	2.8	0.6	1.4	3.4	5.4	17.1	9.0	9.8	12.8	16.3
36 071	39100	2	Orange	2 102	372 813	177	177.4	69.8	10.2	0.8	2.9	18.0	7.1	20.1	9.7	11.2	14.0	15.6
36 073	40380	1	Orleans	1 013	42 883	1 107	42.3	89.3	6.5	1.0	0.6	4.1	5.3	16.9	9.3	11.1	13.1	17.0
36 075	45060	2	Oswego	2 465	122 109	496	49.5	96.1	1.1	0.9	0.8	2.1	5.8	17.3	12.4	10.7	12.8	16.1
36 077	36580	6	Otsego	2 594	62 259	836	24.0	94.0	2.1	0.7	1.4	3.1	4.4	14.3	16.2	9.2	10.8	14.8
36 079	35620	1	Putnam	597	99 710	582	167.0	84.0	2.4	0.5	2.4	11.7	5.1	18.6	7.3	9.5	14.7	18.8
36 081	35620	1	Queens	281	2 230 722	10	7 938.5	28.6	18.8	0.7	24.7	27.5	5.9	14.8	9.8	16.2	14.6	14.5
36 083	10580	2	Rensselaer	1 690	159 429	390	94.3	87.5	7.2	0.7	2.7	3.8	5.5	15.8	11.6	12.2	12.8	15.6
36 085	35620	1	Richmond	151	468 730	139	3 104.2	65.1	10.1	0.4	8.1	17.3	6.0	17.3	9.5	12.8	14.0	15.3
36 087	35620	1	Rockland	449	311 687	205	694.2	66.3	11.8	0.4	6.8	15.7	7.6	20.5	8.8	11.2	12.4	14.4
36 089	36300	5	St. Lawrence	6 942	111 944	529	16.1	94.0	2.4	1.6	1.3	1.9	5.9	15.4	15.0	11.2	11.9	14.4
36 091	10580	2	Saratoga	2 098	219 607	285	104.7	94.1	2.0	0.6	2.3	2.4	5.5	17.2	7.9	11.3	14.5	16.6
36 093	10580	2	Schenectady	530	154 727	403	291.9	79.5	10.5	0.9	4.4	5.7	6.0	17.0	9.2	12.0	12.8	15.7
36 095	10580	2	Schoharie	1 611	32 749	1 368	20.3	95.0	1.7	0.7	0.9	2.8	4.6	15.4	11.5	10.0	12.0	15.7
36 097	...	6	Schuyler	850	18 343	1 906	21.6	97.3	1.2	0.8	0.5	1.3	4.8	16.4	7.7	9.7	12.6	16.8
36 099	42900	6	Seneca	838	35 251	1 293	42.1	91.9	4.8	0.8	0.8	2.7	5.6	15.7	9.4	11.9	12.5	15.6
36 101	18500	4	Steuben	3 602	98 990	585	27.5	95.6	2.1	0.7	1.4	1.4	5.9	17.6	7.8	11.1	12.5	15.6
36 103	35620	1	Suffolk	2 362	1 493 350	24	632.2	72.6	7.5	0.5	3.9	16.5	5.8	18.2	8.7	11.2	14.3	16.5
36 105	...	4	Sullivan	2 507	77 547	698	30.9	76.1	9.3	0.8	1.8	13.6	6.0	16.7	8.4	11.1	12.6	16.4
36 107	13780	2	Tioga	1 343	51 125	964	38.1	97.0	1.0	0.5	1.0	1.4	5.8	17.6	7.3	10.4	12.3	17.7
36 109	27060	3	Tompkins	1 229	101 564	571	82.6	82.7	4.9	0.9	9.8	4.2	4.3	12.1	26.2	13.5	10.2	11.8
36 111	28740	3	Ulster	2 912	182 493	337	62.7	83.5	6.6	0.9	2.2	8.7	4.9	15.2	10.0	10.9	13.2	16.8
36 113	24020	3	Warren	2 245	65 707	796	29.3	96.4	1.3	0.7	0.9	1.8	4.9	15.7	7.5	10.5	12.7	16.6
36 115	24020	3	Washington	2 153	63 216	826	29.4	94.2	3.1	0.6	0.6	2.3	5.3	15.8	8.7	11.6	13.6	16.3
36 117	40380	1	Wayne	1 564	93 772	612	60.0	92.5	3.8	0.7	0.8	3.7	5.9	17.9	7.5	10.4	13.4	17.0
36 119	35620	1	Westchester	1 115	949 113	44	851.2	58.5	14.1	0.4	6.2	21.8	6.0	18.0	8.1	11.4	14.0	15.7
36 121	...	6	Wyoming	1 535	42 155	1 125	27.5	90.9	5.5	0.5	0.5	3.0	5.0	15.7	8.0	13.3	14.3	16.9
36 123	...	6	Yates	876	25 348	1 592	28.9	97.0	1.2	0.5	0.5	1.7	6.2	18.3	10.5	9.3	10.2	15.0
37 000	...	X	**NORTH CAROLINA**	125 920	9 535 483	X	75.7	66.6	22.1	1.7	2.7	8.4	6.6	17.3	9.8	13.1	13.9	14.4
37 001	15500	3	Alamance	1 098	151 131	412	137.6	68.5	19.5	0.8	1.5	11.0	6.3	17.2	10.6	11.4	13.7	14.5
37 003	25860	2	Alexander	673	37 198	1 233	55.3	88.9	6.1	0.6	1.2	4.3	5.9	16.8	7.2	11.8	14.3	15.5
37 005	...	9	Alleghany	609	11 155	2 353	18.3	89.1	1.4	0.6	0.6	9.0	5.2	14.8	6.9	9.7	12.2	14.7
37 007	16740	1	Anson	1 376	26 948	1 534	19.6	46.7	49.1	1.0	1.2	3.0	5.8	16.3	8.8	13.2	13.8	14.8
37 009	...	9	Ashe	1 104	27 281	1 520	24.7	94.0	0.8	0.7	0.5	4.8	5.3	14.1	6.5	10.9	12.5	15.0
37 011	...	8	Avery	640	17 797	1 936	27.8	90.7	4.1	0.8	0.5	4.5	4.3	12.8	9.8	12.4	14.3	15.1
37 013	47820	6	Beaufort	2 142	47 759	1 009	22.3	67.2	26.0	0.6	0.5	6.6	5.8	16.2	7.1	10.6	11.7	14.5
37 015	...	9	Bertie	1 811	21 282	1 775	11.8	35.2	62.9	0.9	0.6	1.3	5.5	15.3	8.6	11.5	11.8	16.2
37 017	...	6	Bladen	2 264	35 190	1 294	15.5	55.6	35.4	2.7	0.3	7.1	6.1	17.0	7.9	11.3	12.4	14.9
37 019	48900	2	Brunswick	2 194	107 431	551	49.0	82.1	12.0	1.3	0.8	5.2	5.4	13.3	6.2	10.7	11.4	13.5
37 021	11700	2	Buncombe	1 701	238 318	269	140.1	86.0	7.1	1.0	1.5	6.0	5.7	14.8	8.6	13.4	13.3	14.5
37 023	25860	2	Burke	1 313	90 912	628	69.2	84.3	7.3	0.7	3.9	5.1	5.6	16.6	9.1	10.7	13.4	15.2
37 025	16740	1	Cabarrus	937	178 011	345	190.0	73.0	15.9	0.7	2.4	9.4	7.3	20.1	7.5	12.7	16.0	14.6
37 027	25860	2	Caldwell	1 221	83 029	664	68.0	89.7	5.6	0.6	0.7	4.6	5.6	17.0	7.7	10.6	14.6	15.4
37 029	21020	8	Camden	623	9 980	2 449	16.0	82.9	13.9	1.0	1.9	2.2	6.0	19.7	6.5	10.0	15.8	17.3
37 031	33980	4	Carteret	1 311	66 469	789	50.7	89.0	6.8	1.0	1.5	3.4	4.9	14.0	7.2	10.8	12.0	16.0
37 033	...	8	Caswell	1 101	23 719	1 656	21.5	62.3	34.6	0.9	0.5	3.1	5.0	15.6	7.3	10.7	13.3	16.9
37 035	25860	2	Catawba	1 033	154 358	404	149.4	79.3	9.2	0.6	3.8	8.4	6.3	17.6	8.1	11.7	14.3	15.1
37 037	20500	2	Chatham	1 767	63 505	820	35.9	72.3	13.7	0.6	1.5	13.0	6.2	15.6	6.3	10.3	13.5	14.9
37 039	...	9	Cherokee	1 180	27 444	1 518	23.3	94.5	1.7	2.8	0.7	2.5	5.0	14.2	5.9	9.2	11.6	13.9

1. CBSA = Core Based Statistical Area. See Appendix A for explanation. See Appendix B for list of metropolitan areas with component counties. 2. County type code from the Economic Research Service of USDA Rural-Urban Continuum Codes. See Appendix A for definition. 3. Dry land or land partially or temporarily covered by water. 4. May be of any race.

Table B. States and Counties — **Population and Households**

STATE County	55 to 64 years	65 to 74 years	75 years and over	Percent female	Total persons 1990	Total persons 2000	Percent change 1990–2000	Percent change 2000–2010	Births	Deaths	Net migration	Households 2010 Number	Percent change, 2000–2010	Persons per house-hold	Female family house-holder[1]	One per-son
	16	17	18	19	20	21	22	23	24	25	26	27	28	29	30	31
NEW YORK—Cont'd																
Genesee	12.7	8.0	7.7	50.5	60 060	60 370	0.5	-0.5	6 146	5 309	-3 005	23 728	4.2	2.45	11.1	27.2
Greene	14.6	9.6	7.7	47.8	44 739	48 195	7.7	2.1	4 200	4 896	1 756	19 823	8.6	2.31	10.6	30.7
Hamilton	19.6	13.5	9.9	49.4	5 279	5 379	1.9	-10.1	367	601	-194	2 262	-4.2	2.10	6.8	32.7
Herkimer	13.8	8.6	8.2	51.1	65 809	64 427	-2.1	0.1	6 394	6 607	-1 582	26 324	2.3	2.40	11.1	29.3
Jefferson	10.0	5.9	5.3	49.1	110 943	111 738	0.7	4.0	15 859	8 008	-7 700	43 451	8.4	2.53	12.4	25.6
Kings	10.6	6.1	5.4	52.8	2 300 664	2 465 326	7.2	1.6	370 723	161 770	-258 520	916 856	4.1	2.69	20.5	29.0
Lewis	12.7	7.7	7.3	49.7	26 796	26 944	0.6	0.5	3 032	2 143	-1 535	10 514	4.7	2.55	8.5	24.5
Livingston	12.9	7.2	6.5	49.8	62 372	64 328	3.1	1.7	5 909	4 670	-2 331	24 409	10.2	2.44	10.4	26.3
Madison	12.6	7.7	6.3	50.9	69 166	69 441	0.4	5.8	6 906	5 307	-664	27 754	9.4	2.46	10.7	26.3
Monroe	12.3	7.0	6.9	51.8	713 968	735 343	3.0	1.2	81 407	57 892	-20 978	300 422	4.9	2.39	14.1	30.5
Montgomery	13.4	7.5	9.1	51.3	51 981	49 708	-4.4	1.0	5 581	5 748	-630	20 272	1.2	2.43	13.2	29.7
Nassau	12.9	7.3	7.9	51.6	1 287 873	1 334 544	3.6	0.4	143 551	101 185	-65 832	448 528	0.3	2.94	11.7	20.1
New York	11.2	7.3	6.2	53.1	1 487 536	1 537 195	3.3	3.2	188 619	100 872	-35 375	763 846	3.4	1.99	11.9	46.3
Niagara	13.4	7.8	8.0	51.5	220 756	219 846	-0.4	-1.5	21 882	21 405	-4 396	90 556	3.1	2.34	12.9	31.4
Oneida	12.8	7.9	8.4	50.2	250 836	235 469	-6.1	-0.3	23 740	23 157	-3 589	93 028	2.8	2.38	13.1	31.1
Onondaga	12.2	6.8	7.2	51.9	468 973	458 336	-2.3	1.9	52 015	37 256	-15 545	187 686	3.6	2.40	13.7	30.7
Ontario	14.2	8.2	7.2	51.1	95 101	100 224	5.4	7.7	10 528	8 520	4 017	43 019	12.1	2.43	10.4	26.9
Orange	11.3	6.0	5.0	50.0	307 571	341 367	11.0	9.2	48 318	23 094	18 764	125 925	9.7	2.86	12.3	22.1
Orleans	12.8	7.8	6.6	50.5	41 846	44 171	5.6	-2.9	4 254	3 477	-2 675	16 119	4.9	2.50	12.4	26.2
Oswego	12.4	7.0	5.6	50.2	121 785	122 377	0.5	-0.2	12 855	9 606	-3 492	46 400	1.9	2.52	11.7	25.1
Otsego	13.8	8.8	7.8	51.6	60 390	61 676	2.1	0.9	5 125	5 473	592	24 620	5.7	2.31	9.2	29.4
Putnam	13.5	7.3	5.2	50.1	83 941	95 745	14.1	4.1	10 180	5 485	-671	35 041	7.1	2.77	8.9	20.3
Queens	11.4	6.8	6.1	51.6	1 951 598	2 229 379	14.2	0.1	283 412	141 976	-200 487	780 117	-0.3	2.82	16.4	25.6
Rensselaer	13.0	7.0	6.6	50.6	154 429	152 538	-1.2	4.5	16 207	13 423	1 177	64 702	8.0	2.38	12.5	29.3
Richmond	12.5	7.0	5.7	51.5	378 977	443 728	17.1	5.6	53 982	32 960	8 225	165 516	5.9	2.78	14.7	24.2
Rockland	11.7	7.1	6.3	51.0	265 475	286 753	8.0	8.7	42 498	18 803	-18 173	99 242	7.1	3.07	11.1	21.1
St. Lawrence	12.4	7.5	6.4	49.2	111 974	111 931	0.0	0.0	11 522	9 746	-3 339	41 605	2.7	2.43	10.8	27.9
Saratoga	13.4	7.6	6.0	50.8	181 276	200 635	10.7	9.5	22 318	13 970	12 224	88 296	13.0	2.44	9.1	26.1
Schenectady	12.4	6.9	8.0	51.6	149 285	146 555	-1.8	5.6	16 858	14 152	3 840	62 886	5.4	2.39	13.8	30.6
Schoharie	14.9	8.9	7.0	50.0	31 840	31 582	-0.8	3.7	2 757	2 757	135	13 166	9.8	2.37	9.4	27.8
Schuyler	15.0	9.4	7.6	50.3	18 662	19 224	3.0	-4.6	1 695	1 696	-390	7 530	2.1	2.39	10.2	27.2
Seneca	13.7	8.0	7.5	47.6	33 683	33 342	-1.0	5.7	3 409	3 035	520	13 393	6.0	2.42	10.5	27.3
Steuben	13.8	8.3	7.6	50.4	99 088	98 726	-0.4	0.3	10 576	9 263	-2 888	40 344	3.3	2.41	10.9	28.9
Suffolk	11.9	7.2	6.3	50.8	1 321 339	1 419 369	7.4	5.2	178 762	105 399	-30 466	499 922	6.5	2.93	11.7	20.6
Sullivan	14.0	8.6	6.1	48.9	69 277	73 966	6.8	4.8	8 239	6 547	599	30 139	9.0	2.45	12.9	29.1
Tioga	13.2	8.6	7.1	50.4	52 337	51 784	-1.1	-1.3	5 405	3 875	-2 989	20 350	3.2	2.49	10.4	24.7
Tompkins	11.1	5.6	5.1	50.7	94 097	96 501	2.6	5.2	8 394	5 484	2 088	38 967	7.0	2.27	8.7	33.3
Ulster	14.0	7.9	6.9	50.2	165 380	177 749	7.5	2.7	16 887	14 309	2 250	71 049	5.3	2.40	11.4	29.0
Warren	14.9	9.1	8.1	51.2	59 209	63 303	6.9	3.8	5 981	5 740	2 806	27 990	8.8	2.32	10.6	29.5
Washington	13.4	8.2	7.1	48.2	59 330	61 042	2.9	3.6	5 903	5 449	1 668	24 142	7.5	2.49	11.2	25.0
Wayne	13.6	7.8	6.4	50.4	89 123	93 765	5.2	0.0	10 345	7 374	-4 891	36 585	4.8	2.53	11.0	24.5
Westchester	12.1	7.2	7.4	51.9	874 866	923 459	5.6	2.8	113 932	66 695	-31 244	347 232	3.0	2.65	12.8	27.2
Wyoming	13.3	7.6	6.0	45.6	42 507	43 424	2.2	-2.9	3 954	3 331	-2 414	15 501	4.0	2.46	9.5	25.7
Yates	13.8	9.0	7.8	51.6	22 810	24 621	7.9	3.0	2 719	2 246	-456	9 517	5.4	2.53	10.2	26.9
NORTH CAROLINA	11.9	7.3	5.6	51.3	6 632 448	8 049 313	21.4	18.5	1 143 251	685 324	889 589	3 745 155	19.6	2.48	13.7	27.0
Alamance	11.9	7.6	7.0	52.4	108 213	130 800	20.9	15.5	17 491	12 555	15 422	59 960	16.2	2.45	14.5	27.8
Alexander	13.3	9.1	6.0	49.4	27 544	33 603	22.0	10.7	3 875	2 824	2 350	14 425	9.8	2.50	10.9	24.1
Alleghany	15.9	11.5	9.2	50.4	9 590	10 677	11.3	4.5	949	1 280	671	4 778	4.0	2.31	9.3	28.2
Anson	12.9	7.9	6.5	48.0	23 474	25 275	7.7	6.6	2 944	2 702	-310	9 755	6.0	2.51	19.8	28.4
Ashe	15.5	11.5	8.7	50.6	22 209	24 384	9.8	11.9	2 474	2 759	1 862	11 755	12.9	2.29	9.3	27.4
Avery	13.9	9.6	7.8	45.6	14 867	17 167	15.5	3.7	1 607	1 763	1 033	6 664	2.0	2.31	8.9	28.1
Beaufort	15.6	10.8	7.6	51.8	42 283	44 958	6.3	6.2	5 558	5 053	1 199	19 941	8.9	2.37	13.6	28.3
Bertie	13.9	9.1	8.1	50.5	20 388	19 773	-3.0	7.6	2 299	2 323	-300	8 359	8.0	2.39	19.9	30.8
Bladen	14.9	9.3	6.3	52.0	28 663	32 278	12.6	9.0	4 162	3 590	-301	14 430	11.9	2.40	16.9	29.8
Brunswick	18.2	14.3	7.2	51.0	50 985	73 143	43.5	46.9	9 141	7 957	32 844	46 297	52.1	2.30	10.4	25.0
Buncombe	13.7	8.4	7.5	51.8	174 357	206 330	18.3	15.5	24 504	20 598	22 403	100 412	17.1	2.30	11.2	30.5
Burke	13.3	9.1	7.0	50.0	75 740	89 148	17.7	2.0	9 589	7 929	-708	35 804	3.7	2.45	12.3	27.3
Cabarrus	10.6	6.4	4.9	51.2	98 935	131 063	32.5	35.8	22 156	11 367	30 882	65 666	32.6	2.69	12.6	22.1
Caldwell	13.7	9.1	6.3	50.8	70 709	77 415	9.5	7.3	8 706	7 331	904	33 388	8.5	2.46	12.5	25.4
Camden	12.0	7.7	5.2	49.8	5 904	6 885	16.6	45.0	899	598	2 557	3 675	38.1	2.71	9.9	19.1
Carteret	16.1	11.1	7.9	50.6	52 407	59 383	13.3	11.9	5 830	6 414	5 515	28 870	14.5	2.27	10.4	28.4
Caswell	15.3	9.4	6.4	49.1	20 662	23 501	13.7	0.9	2 186	2 277	-259	9 190	6.0	2.43	14.7	26.9
Catawba	12.8	8.0	6.1	51.3	118 412	141 685	19.7	8.9	18 989	12 513	11 830	60 887	9.6	2.50	12.4	26.2
Chatham	14.9	9.8	8.5	51.7	38 979	49 329	26.6	28.7	6 659	4 756	13 715	25 845	30.9	2.43	9.8	25.6
Cherokee	17.3	13.9	9.0	51.4	20 170	24 298	20.5	12.9	2 463	2 975	2 653	11 753	13.7	2.30	9.7	27.2

1. No spouse present.

Table B. States and Counties — **Population, Vital Statistics, Medicare, and Crime**

STATE County	Persons in group quarters, 2010	Daytime population, 2006–2010 Number	Daytime population Employment/residence ratio	Births, average 2006–2008 Total	Births Rate[1]	Deaths, average 2006–2008 Number	Deaths Rate[1]	Persons under 65 with no health insurance, 2009 Number	Persons under 65 Percent	Medicare, 2011 Eligible for Medicare	Enrolled in Medicare Advantage	Enrolled in a Medicare prescription drug plan	Serious crimes known to police,[2] 2010 Total Number	Total Rate[3]
	32	33	34	35	36	37	38	39	40	41	42	43	44	45
NEW YORK—Cont'd														
Genesee	1 908	54 990	0.8	661	11.3	593	10.2	4 695	9.9	11 314	5 869	2 102	1 459	2 428
Greene	3 400	45 063	0.8	D	D	524	10.6	5 708	14.3	10 309	2 349	3 001	820	1 666
Hamilton	80	4 704	0.9	D	D	62	12.2	539	14.3	1 340	248	439	52	1 075
Herkimer	1 426	55 102	0.7	668	10.7	674	10.8	5 822	11.5	13 375	3 843	5 432	1 353	2 256
Jefferson	6 170	118 219	1.1	1 873	16.1	848	7.3	12 824	12.7	17 453	3 483	5 932	2 405	2 069
Kings	35 609	2 170 477	0.7	41 402	16.4	16 454	6.5	340 105	15.5	315 876	109 397	129 390	(4)	(4)
Lewis	313	24 005	0.7	D	D	228	8.6	2 623	12.1	4 444	961	1 807	459	1 695
Livingston	5 758	57 238	0.7	620	9.8	503	7.9	5 838	11.0	11 032	6 125	1 991	1 125	1 720
Madison	5 133	64 847	0.8	D	D	566	8.1	6 489	11.0	11 997	3 103	4 123	1 205	1 871
Monroe	26 283	779 533	1.1	8 774	12.0	6 227	8.5	57 986	9.4	130 087	79 035	25 002	25 982	3 491
Montgomery	920	47 370	0.9	641	13.1	608	12.4	4 419	11.3	10 891	3 053	4 498	1 163	2 423
Nassau	21 666	1 259 065	0.9	15 168	11.4	10 591	8.0	118 561	10.5	229 139	47 012	77 933	20 166	1 505
New York	67 373	3 083 102	2.8	20 587	12.7	10 312	6.4	184 607	13.3	246 946	70 357	99 637	(4)189 688	(4)2 320
Niagara	4 319	194 796	0.8	2 236	10.4	2 282	10.6	18 376	10.4	43 874	20 296	7 843	7 114	3 286
Oneida	13 405	243 236	1.1	2 603	11.2	2 451	10.5	21 702	11.5	47 430	12 436	16 433	6 204	2 641
Onondaga	17 069	497 164	1.2	5 519	12.1	3 999	8.8	40 295	10.6	81 378	19 696	24 903	12 980	2 779
Ontario	3 329	106 966	1.0	1 119	10.7	930	8.9	8 561	9.8	20 525	10 764	4 191	1 992	1 846
Orange	12 230	341 221	0.8	5 440	14.4	2 512	6.6	41 451	12.4	51 290	5 762	18 948	9 042	2 505
Orleans	2 586	37 809	0.7	D	D	366	8.6	4 698	13.4	7 712	3 803	1 514	1 028	2 397
Oswego	4 954	105 741	0.7	1 382	11.3	1 032	8.5	11 804	11.4	21 419	5 758	7 641	3 268	2 676
Otsego	5 320	62 595	1.0	D	D	561	9.0	6 232	12.4	12 298	1 852	4 962	1 143	1 836
Putnam	2 592	79 875	0.6	D	D	600	6.0	6 853	8.0	14 946	1 433	5 322	918	940
Queens	28 000	1 846 101	0.7	31 025	13.7	14 515	6.4	370 994	18.8	303 007	112 768	104 492	(4)	(4)
Rensselaer	5 607	136 948	0.7	1 786	11.5	1 427	9.2	12 734	9.7	26 844	9 221	6 027	4 824	3 026
Richmond	7 838	381 322	0.6	5 879	12.2	3 513	7.3	41 732	9.9	72 906	27 637	20 414	(4)	(4)
Rockland	7 183	280 856	0.8	4 860	16.4	2 015	6.8	27 027	10.6	48 802	7 144	17 573	4 736	1 519
St. Lawrence	10 751	109 158	0.9	1 250	11.3	1 053	9.5	11 685	12.7	20 857	3 343	7 209	2 394	2 171
Saratoga	3 950	188 687	0.7	2 340	10.8	1 516	7.0	17 208	9.2	36 815	12 754	9 099	3 197	1 456
Schenectady	4 434	146 029	0.9	1 851	12.3	1 482	9.8	13 391	10.7	27 794	9 893	9 529	6 018	3 889
Schoharie	1 556	29 334	0.8	D	D	272	8.5	3 130	12.1	5 690	1 117	2 098	466	1 423
Schuyler	354	15 981	0.7	D	D	172	9.0	1 950	12.9	3 989	760	1 392	192	1 047
Seneca	2 809	32 698	0.8	D	D	325	9.5	3 856	13.8	6 651	2 507	1 776	644	1 859
Steuben	1 583	98 782	1.0	1 109	11.4	986	10.1	9 065	11.4	19 751	4 461	6 112	1 907	1 970
Suffolk	29 406	1 387 548	0.9	18 546	12.5	11 117	7.5	148 908	11.5	245 178	42 863	78 654	32 313	2 166
Sullivan	3 825	73 410	0.9	964	12.6	725	9.5	9 408	14.9	14 698	1 011	6 564	1 700	2 192
Tioga	523	44 440	0.7	587	11.6	426	8.4	4 134	10.8	9 817	2 537	3 277	560	1 095
Tompkins	13 232	110 797	1.2	D	D	600	5.9	9 274	10.5	13 128	1 993	4 030	2 487	2 449
Ulster	11 773	166 185	0.8	1 839	10.1	1 510	8.3	20 641	13.6	33 637	5 800	11 817	3 836	2 102
Warren	738	72 077	1.2	624	9.4	631	9.6	6 216	11.7	14 514	4 751	3 927	1 286	1 957
Washington	3 164	52 737	0.6	649	10.3	556	8.8	7 008	13.6	11 507	3 831	3 277	874	1 383
Wayne	1 390	80 431	0.7	1 112	12.1	802	8.7	8 491	11.1	18 632	9 487	4 863	1 940	2 069
Westchester	28 704	931 894	1.0	11 797	12.4	7 022	7.4	96 446	12.0	151 973	27 292	53 277	15 167	1 598
Wyoming	3 961	39 634	0.8	D	D	344	8.2	4 813	13.8	7 406	3 720	1 310	473	1 122
Yates	1 287	22 989	0.8	D	D	228	9.3	2 772	14.0	5 076	2 287	1 229	472	1 862
NORTH CAROLINA	257 246	9 273 514	1.0	129 912	14.3	76 015	8.4	1 431 168	18.0	1 552 171	276 237	683 478	363 372	3 811
Alamance	4 229	138 618	0.9	1 984	13.6	1 405	9.7	23 815	19.0	26 857	10 729	9 009	6 368	4 214
Alexander	1 161	30 752	0.6	D	D	330	9.1	6 282	20.4	6 909	1 006	3 533	943	2 535
Alleghany	111	10 961	1.0	D	D	135	12.4	2 038	23.7	2 822	562	1 345	NA	NA
Anson	2 484	25 149	0.8	D	D	300	11.9	4 119	20.0	4 836	185	2 897	1 105	4 266
Ashe	369	25 516	0.9	D	D	292	11.4	4 317	21.2	6 361	861	3 372	69	253
Avery	2 414	19 073	1.2	D	D	177	10.0	3 659	25.5	3 531	440	1 784	268	1 508
Beaufort	503	46 790	1.0	586	12.7	529	11.5	7 270	19.8	11 453	608	6 064	1 520	3 218
Bertie	1 324	20 351	0.9	247	13.0	240	12.6	3 092	19.9	4 862	71	3 357	334	1 569
Bladen	511	33 480	0.9	438	13.5	374	11.5	5 007	18.7	6 923	524	4 087	1 142	3 245
Brunswick	843	93 798	0.8	1 144	11.5	952	9.6	15 645	18.9	28 106	2 897	12 069	3 598	3 433
Buncombe	7 673	248 288	1.1	2 786	12.3	2 264	10.0	34 646	18.3	47 022	7 547	20 451	6 679	2 811
Burke	3 352	85 699	0.9	1 037	11.6	878	9.8	15 606	21.1	17 771	2 863	8 690	2 107	2 357
Cabarrus	1 480	157 842	0.8	2 617	16.1	1 280	7.9	23 784	16.0	25 214	4 092	11 256	4 859	2 733
Caldwell	968	75 689	0.8	915	11.5	811	10.2	13 590	20.6	16 170	3 725	8 320	2 898	3 490
Camden	17	6 775	0.3	D	D	74	7.8	1 298	15.6	1 705	89	606	90	902
Carteret	987	60 971	0.9	636	10.0	683	10.8	9 060	17.8	14 775	693	6 215	2 489	3 745
Caswell	1 368	18 898	0.4	214	9.2	235	10.1	3 450	18.4	4 978	1 449	1 975	560	2 361
Catawba	2 408	168 405	1.2	2 057	13.2	1 408	9.1	25 687	19.3	29 357	4 901	14 949	6 369	4 136
Chatham	778	52 466	0.7	747	12.1	547	8.9	9 517	17.7	12 933	3 195	4 471	1 403	2 209
Cherokee	436	27 033	1.0	282	10.7	334	12.6	4 061	20.2	7 529	1 318	3 469	NA	NA

1. Per 1,000 estimated resident population.   2. Data for serious crimes have not been adjusted for underreporting; this may affect comparability between geographic areas and over time.   3. Per 100,000 population estimated by the FBI.   4. Bronx, Kings, Queens, and Richmond counties are included with New York county.

Table B. States and Counties — Crime, Education, Money Income, and Poverty

STATE County	Serious crimes known to police,[1] 2010 (cont.) Rate[2] Violent	Property	Education — School enrollment and attainment, 2006–2010 Enrollment[3] Total	Percent private	Attainment[4] (percent) High school graduate or less	Bachelor's degree or more	Local government expenditures,[5] 2008–2009 Total current expenditures (mil dol)	Current expenditures per student (dollars)	Money income, 2006–2010 Per capita income[6] (dollars)	Households Median income Dollars	Percent change, 2000 to 2006–2010 (constant 2010 dollars)	Percent with income of $200,000 or more	Income and poverty, 2010 Median household income (dollars)	Percent below poverty level All persons	Children under 18 years	Children 5 to 17 years in families
	46	47	48	49	50	51	52	53	54	55	56	57	58	59	60	61
NEW YORK—Cont'd																
Genesee	178	2 250	14 184	9.6	47.3	20.2	145.3	15 362	24 323	49 750	-3.1	1.1	47 387	12.1	16.9	15.4
Greene	187	1 479	9 384	16.9	54.0	19.2	120.6	17 071	23 461	46 235	0.1	2.0	45 070	17.2	21.0	18.8
Hamilton	83	993	798	6.9	46.6	25.9	17.1	31 067	29 965	49 557	21.2	2.5	45 474	10.6	17.4	14.1
Herkimer	275	1 981	15 175	9.1	50.5	18.2	149.6	14 211	21 908	42 318	1.5	0.9	42 876	15.6	22.7	20.1
Jefferson	186	1 883	28 403	11.4	48.8	20.2	246.7	13 208	21 823	43 410	0.8	1.3	43 448	14.3	20.8	21.4
Kings	(7)	(7)	670 299	29.1	51.1	28.8	(7)	(7)	23 605	43 567	7.1	3.6	42 047	22.9	33.4	32.8
Lewis	89	1 606	6 216	12.4	61.5	14.4	67.6	15 232	20 970	42 846	-1.5	1.0	41 093	15.0	21.8	20.6
Livingston	69	1 652	18 771	12.3	46.9	23.4	129.3	14 615	22 923	51 690	-3.0	1.3	50 094	13.5	16.7	13.9
Madison	76	1 795	20 608	23.0	46.4	23.7	163.5	14 717	24 311	53 345	4.8	2.4	50 270	11.5	16.1	13.7
Monroe	379	3 112	209 475	26.0	37.3	34.8	1 799.9	15 716	26 999	51 303	-9.7	3.1	49 564	15.1	21.0	18.3
Montgomery	150	2 273	11 709	12.1	55.2	15.9	111.8	14 536	22 347	42 603	4.7	1.1	40 035	17.1	27.9	25.5
Nassau	173	1 332	359 868	26.4	35.8	40.9	4 448.9	21 547	41 387	93 613	2.6	13.9	90 294	6.2	8.1	7.0
New York	(7)595	(7)1 726	339 502	44.7	28.7	57.0	(7)18 795.1	(7)19 146	59 149	64 971	9.1	15.8	63 188	16.6	23.2	25.0
Niagara	383	2 903	52 748	18.4	49.0	19.6	465.4	14 540	24 224	45 964	-4.8	1.6	44 006	14.1	19.9	18.8
Oneida	248	2 394	58 987	17.5	48.1	21.5	521.0	14 858	23 458	46 708	2.7	1.7	46 409	15.1	23.7	21.3
Onondaga	344	2 435	130 666	24.7	38.6	32.0	1 131.9	15 315	27 037	50 676	-2.0	3.0	50 298	14.1	19.5	17.6
Ontario	119	1 727	27 017	19.9	37.1	31.0	257.3	14 574	28 950	56 468	0.0	3.3	53 137	10.1	14.5	13.0
Orange	275	2 231	109 657	22.0	44.0	27.7	1 119.0	17 248	28 944	69 523	5.5	5.0	65 512	11.4	16.9	15.2
Orleans	180	2 218	10 816	8.3	57.0	16.1	100.3	14 011	20 812	48 063	0.0	0.8	44 783	14.0	21.9	18.9
Oswego	154	2 522	35 206	7.6	56.3	15.7	344.1	15 189	21 604	45 333	-2.2	1.0	44 371	16.9	23.7	21.0
Otsego	204	1 632	18 122	15.4	47.3	25.5	135.5	16 173	22 902	45 268	6.9	1.7	42 837	15.7	18.9	17.0
Putnam	69	871	26 410	21.5	35.4	38.0	331.4	20 216	37 915	89 218	-2.5	10.4	82 685	6.2	8.0	5.2
Queens	(7)	(7)	541 958	24.4	48.6	29.5	(7)	(7)	25 553	55 291	2.9	3.5	52 486	15.1	22.0	21.4
Rensselaer	342	2 683	41 449	25.6	43.1	26.7	330.3	15 953	27 457	54 152	-0.3	2.2	51 720	13.5	19.6	16.6
Richmond	(7)	(7)	122 406	29.0	46.2	28.5	(7)	(7)	30 843	71 084	2.0	6.1	69 163	12.1	17.2	15.8
Rockland	146	1 374	91 077	40.8	35.9	40.7	871.8	21 050	34 304	82 534	-4.1	11.1	79 798	11.6	18.3	16.5
St. Lawrence	125	2 046	33 370	28.3	52.9	18.7	256.5	15 882	20 143	42 303	3.2	1.0	40 008	17.4	25.4	22.4
Saratoga	67	1 389	53 493	18.7	36.8	34.6	448.2	13 922	32 186	65 100	3.9	4.4	65 508	7.0	8.4	7.5
Schenectady	483	3 407	39 210	20.2	41.6	28.7	355.0	14 439	27 500	55 188	4.4	2.7	52 062	12.0	18.7	16.5
Schoharie	52	1 371	8 598	8.5	52.6	21.0	85.7	16 981	25 105	50 864	9.8	1.8	47 350	13.3	17.1	14.8
Schuyler	55	992	4 473	15.5	52.2	17.4	38.7	16 161	22 123	47 404	4.0	1.1	46 870	13.1	23.4	20.7
Seneca	150	1 709	7 598	20.3	51.9	18.1	73.6	15 800	21 818	46 707	-0.7	1.2	45 961	14.0	22.1	20.3
Steuben	167	1 802	23 594	11.0	49.4	19.9	260.6	15 520	23 279	43 867	-2.4	1.6	45 231	14.4	21.6	19.2
Suffolk	157	2 009	396 722	16.3	41.2	31.9	4 969.2	19 341	35 755	84 506	2.2	9.2	81 235	6.6	8.4	7.3
Sullivan	280	1 912	18 184	14.7	50.5	20.3	223.0	21 484	23 422	48 103	2.7	2.6	43 882	19.1	27.9	25.4
Tioga	70	1 025	12 703	10.0	48.3	22.7	120.7	14 685	24 596	51 948	1.9	1.8	50 043	9.8	15.7	13.9
Tompkins	117	2 332	42 104	54.5	28.4	49.7	201.0	16 716	25 737	48 655	3.1	3.4	50 156	19.6	15.4	13.7
Ulster	224	1 878	45 182	14.0	41.9	29.5	492.2	18 768	28 954	57 584	6.9	3.7	51 194	12.5	15.3	13.9
Warren	146	1 811	14 586	15.7	43.4	27.3	162.0	16 912	27 744	51 619	4.0	2.2	50 269	10.4	17.0	15.3
Washington	142	1 240	14 335	11.0	56.0	16.8	150.3	15 568	22 347	48 327	1.3	1.2	46 629	12.0	19.0	17.1
Wayne	179	1 890	22 449	12.2	47.6	21.6	246.9	15 517	24 092	52 562	-6.0	1.4	50 213	10.6	16.3	13.9
Westchester	257	1 341	249 510	26.5	35.6	44.5	3 294.2	22 092	47 814	79 619	-1.1	15.8	76 993	9.0	11.5	10.6
Wyoming	78	1 044	9 022	11.2	55.4	14.8	72.4	14 667	20 605	50 075	-0.9	0.9	46 846	10.8	15.9	13.9
Yates	71	1 791	6 343	39.3	54.7	22.1	42.1	15 711	23 255	46 822	6.7	2.3	43 820	17.0	29.0	26.5
NORTH CAROLINA	363	3 447	2 425 377	14.6	44.7	26.1	12 732.5	8 556	24 745	45 570	-8.2	2.9	43 417	17.4	24.6	22.6
Alamance	405	3 809	37 655	19.3	48.6	21.4	184.1	7 782	22 819	44 167	-11.0	1.8	41 519	18.5	29.0	23.8
Alexander	153	2 382	8 303	12.0	63.0	11.8	44.1	7 847	20 716	40 014	-18.3	2.0	40 441	16.9	25.7	23.3
Alleghany	NA	NA	2 014	4.2	58.7	16.1	17.1	10 574	18 919	30 845	-16.7	0.9	32 210	23.0	33.9	30.4
Anson	483	3 784	6 047	5.3	68.0	8.4	39.9	9 869	16 856	34 745	-8.1	1.4	32 268	22.6	32.3	30.0
Ashe	15	238	5 313	7.3	56.0	17.2	31.9	9 036	20 350	34 538	-5.4	1.2	31 965	20.0	30.2	27.1
Avery	84	1 424	4 041	23.3	49.4	20.3	24.5	10 060	23 465	34 918	-10.0	2.8	35 568	23.5	33.9	28.7
Beaufort	385	2 832	10 678	8.4	54.3	19.0	67.6	8 470	22 728	40 653	3.3	1.7	38 194	20.7	32.3	29.5
Bertie	103	1 466	4 388	12.7	65.8	10.1	33.6	10 807	17 614	29 110	-8.7	0.6	30 586	27.0	39.1	34.9
Bladen	213	3 032	8 498	6.4	59.1	9.8	51.1	9 493	17 890	30 471	-10.5	1.5	31 637	22.3	31.2	29.4
Brunswick	221	3 212	18 828	11.2	46.2	23.4	113.8	8 954	26 315	45 806	0.8	2.5	44 186	16.5	26.1	24.8
Buncombe	252	2 559	52 382	18.7	39.5	31.2	274.4	9 007	25 665	44 190	-4.8	2.6	42 846	17.1	24.2	22.6
Burke	145	2 212	21 934	7.7	56.7	15.1	120.5	7 702	19 220	37 139	-17.7	1.1	38 541	18.7	26.6	24.6
Cabarrus	143	2 589	45 643	13.2	42.8	23.5	266.5	7 933	26 165	53 928	-7.7	3.5	49 355	12.5	16.6	14.8
Caldwell	160	3 330	20 430	10.2	59.4	12.3	104.1	7 954	19 686	37 261	-17.7	1.2	36 860	18.4	28.5	23.9
Camden	60	842	2 845	14.3	43.6	19.0	17.1	8 959	25 544	61 091	22.2	0.6	59 522	9.7	13.4	11.6
Carteret	332	3 412	13 369	10.3	41.4	23.8	81.0	9 265	26 791	46 155	-4.9	2.2	43 356	14.1	23.6	22.3
Caswell	211	2 150	5 570	16.8	62.6	11.1	29.7	8 613	17 814	36 927	-16.7	1.1	37 115	20.8	30.2	26.7
Catawba	301	3 836	37 329	13.2	50.6	19.4	206.1	8 118	22 969	43 484	-15.3	2.3	41 782	14.5	23.3	21.6
Chatham	205	2 005	13 268	14.6	41.7	35.1	84.3	9 904	29 991	56 038	3.3	4.5	53 958	14.2	21.5	20.6
Cherokee	NA	NA	5 308	11.9	50.5	15.9	36.9	9 497	20 747	38 144	7.6	0.6	32 963	18.1	32.8	30.9

1. Data for serious crimes have not been adjusted for underreporting; this may affect comparability between geographic areas and over time. 2. Per 100,000 population estimated by the FBI. 3. All persons 3 years old and over enrolled in nursery school through college. 4. Persons 25 years old and over. 5. Elementary and secondary education expenditures. 6. Based on population estimated by the American Community Survey, 2006–2010. 7. Bronx, Kings, Queens, and Richmond counties are included with New York county.

Table B. States and Counties — **Personal Income**

STATE County	Personal income, 2009												
			Per capita[1]						Transfer payments (mil dol)				
										Government payments to individuals			
	Total (mil dol)	Percent change, 2008–2009	Dollars	Rank	Wages and salaries[2] (mil dol)	Proprietors' income (mil dol)	Dividends, interest, and rent (mil dol)	Total	Total	Social Security	Medical payments	Income mainte- nance	Unemploy- ment insurance
	62	63	64	65	66	67	68	69	70	71	72	73	74
NEW YORK—Cont'd													
Genesee	1 894	-0.8	32 724	1 380	1 036	121	275	466	455	167	184	36	26
Greene	1 630	0.1	33 299	1 296	682	54	258	404	395	150	159	37	21
Hamilton	178	2.4	36 238	856	70	9	41	46	45	20	18	2	2
Herkimer	1 920	2.8	30 853	1 788	690	75	262	543	532	186	231	51	26
Jefferson	4 641	3.0	39 091	530	3 840	130	470	769	751	246	292	96	44
Kings	89 027	0.0	34 680	1 070	25 033	3 525	10 213	24 708	24 240	3 505	14 957	3 717	1 162
Lewis	776	0.8	29 664	2 061	301	58	109	189	184	63	79	18	11
Livingston	1 953	-0.3	31 059	1 742	888	114	279	459	448	166	186	41	27
Madison	2 316	0.1	33 113	1 320	957	127	375	503	491	171	211	44	30
Monroe	30 078	-1.0	40 994	382	21 157	2 276	5 231	6 264	6 131	1 994	2 719	748	303
Montgomery	1 580	0.6	32 490	1 431	843	43	252	483	474	154	219	53	24
Nassau	83 985	-4.6	61 871	24	39 452	6 611	18 850	10 417	10 169	3 741	4 714	526	492
New York	171 953	-8.0	105 554	3	262 177	37 618	39 809	18 033	17 736	3 258	10 117	2 075	820
Niagara	7 060	0.7	32 906	1 354	3 344	186	1 013	1 864	1 825	667	750	178	109
Oneida	7 837	1.0	33 920	1 183	5 297	366	1 245	2 028	1 986	650	885	230	84
Onondaga	17 877	0.2	39 311	506	13 762	965	2 848	3 638	3 555	1 223	1 496	401	183
Ontario	4 044	0.5	38 275	606	2 321	218	661	818	799	304	331	60	42
Orange	14 027	-0.2	36 574	806	7 274	652	2 060	2 569	2 500	789	1 143	248	144
Orleans	1 189	0.2	28 264	2 355	606	40	161	322	315	117	125	35	18
Oswego	3 604	2.4	29 695	2 050	1 652	108	434	934	912	323	369	102	60
Otsego	1 902	0.3	30 882	1 782	1 117	69	344	479	468	173	199	38	24
Putnam	5 097	-3.9	51 347	86	1 527	174	824	623	605	241	261	20	38
Queens	85 690	-2.1	37 148	731	29 667	3 180	11 851	22 039	21 618	3 828	13 200	2 744	991
Rensselaer	5 940	1.1	38 186	621	2 839	207	873	1 204	1 175	395	509	115	64
Richmond	21 485	-1.4	43 693	248	4 975	691	2 721	5 150	5 060	1 116	2 987	539	210
Rockland	15 572	-5.0	51 877	79	7 129	1 113	2 872	2 422	2 367	762	1 186	174	108
St. Lawrence	3 003	0.7	27 374	2 502	1 735	127	414	898	878	293	375	96	50
Saratoga	9 262	0.3	42 087	324	3 966	450	1 626	1 376	1 336	559	510	85	78
Schenectady	6 183	0.6	40 636	410	4 027	267	1 228	1 253	1 225	411	553	127	57
Schoharie	1 064	1.3	33 735	1 211	398	31	150	235	229	82	99	19	14
Schuyler	584	0.0	31 189	1 715	213	46	76	149	146	57	56	15	9
Seneca	1 081	0.0	31 750	1 589	537	55	156	256	249	94	104	20	13
Steuben	3 347	-3.1	34 662	1 072	2 193	250	444	809	792	278	313	82	46
Suffolk	73 937	-3.5	48 691	125	39 573	3 661	13 981	11 134	10 857	3 884	4 947	698	591
Sullivan	2 679	1.1	35 332	974	1 189	158	417	733	719	214	362	73	32
Tioga	1 714	1.0	34 239	1 134	878	56	244	367	358	143	133	37	22
Tompkins	3 428	0.1	33 684	1 220	2 795	149	688	563	544	198	201	56	33
Ulster	6 626	-0.2	36 519	813	2 948	297	1 192	1 413	1 379	495	609	123	71
Warren	2 353	-0.1	35 644	936	1 701	141	466	543	531	210	210	44	29
Washington	1 910	1.7	30 436	1 879	779	51	253	479	468	166	202	46	25
Wayne	3 162	0.6	34 632	1 077	1 438	97	401	738	722	272	304	62	41
Westchester	68 570	-5.3	71 728	8	32 084	5 259	16 421	7 561	7 387	2 428	3 564	544	354
Wyoming	1 179	-2.3	28 472	2 304	641	41	176	287	280	109	110	22	19
Yates	712	0.3	29 081	2 176	274	23	128	197	193	73	79	16	9
NORTH CAROLINA	327 199	-0.8	34 879	X	213 944	21 128	55 518	65 444	63 751	21 557	26 355	6 775	4 283
Alamance	4 612	-2.2	30 671	1 829	2 530	273	831	1 097	1 070	388	433	97	91
Alexander	1 066	-1.8	28 976	2 204	348	105	160	263	256	93	102	22	26
Alleghany	322	-0.1	29 325	2 133	118	26	77	100	98	36	46	8	4
Anson	673	-2.0	26 879	2 587	312	56	92	238	234	65	107	35	12
Ashe	749	0.1	29 019	2 193	307	55	149	229	225	82	100	18	14
Avery	517	1.6	28 806	2 231	278	57	106	146	142	47	72	9	6
Beaufort	1 510	1.0	32 542	1 414	736	109	310	445	436	156	185	48	20
Bertie	597	4.8	30 835	1 791	298	43	72	210	206	59	103	31	6
Bladen	951	1.8	29 407	2 117	517	81	109	309	303	89	134	42	15
Brunswick	3 343	2.6	31 222	1 708	1 257	182	736	937	917	406	351	59	44
Buncombe	8 048	-1.8	34 774	1 051	5 297	475	1 948	1 770	1 728	634	739	147	87
Burke	2 660	-0.2	29 710	2 046	1 247	246	406	709	693	250	287	65	48
Cabarrus	5 870	-3.1	34 083	1 155	3 005	340	800	1 094	1 062	367	448	94	95
Caldwell	2 235	-0.7	27 969	2 406	1 048	155	325	686	671	230	268	67	67
Camden	344	1.3	35 379	969	110	21	47	59	57	21	22	4	4
Carteret	2 477	1.1	38 455	587	895	173	567	510	498	196	192	34	21
Caswell	686	-1.0	29 830	2 015	132	28	78	195	190	68	77	24	11
Catawba	4 941	-3.1	31 052	1 745	3 651	207	1 001	1 166	1 137	427	425	107	113
Chatham	2 777	0.8	42 870	278	640	227	670	405	393	186	136	26	24
Cherokee	689	0.5	26 185	2 689	296	50	130	278	273	100	110	19	27

1. Based on the resident population estimated as of July 1 of the year shown.   2. Includes supplements to wages and salaries.

Table B. States and Counties — Earnings, Social Security, and Housing

STATE County	Total (mil dol) [75]	Farm [76]	Goods-related[1] Total [77]	Manu- facturing [78]	Information and professional and technical services [79]	Retail trade [80]	Finance, insurance, and real estate [81]	Health care and social services [82]	Govern- ment [83]	Social Security beneficiaries, December 2010 Number [84]	Rate[2] [85]	Supple- mental Security Income recipients, December 2010 [86]	Housing units, 2010 Total [87]	Percent change, 2000– 2010 [88]
NEW YORK—Cont'd														
Genesee	1 157	4.0	20.3	14.7	3.9	8.0	3.4	10.0	28.8	12 760	212	1 170	25 589	5.8
Greene	737	0.5	D	9.2	4.5	9.4	3.0	7.5	38.5	11 640	236	1 307	29 210	10.1
Hamilton	79	0.0	13.6	2.5	1.6	8.2	D	D	49.2	1 520	314	81	8 694	9.2
Herkimer	765	0.7	22.8	16.5	3.4	9.0	2.8	10.9	30.5	15 335	238	1 848	33 381	4.2
Jefferson	3 970	0.6	7.5	3.5	2.3	5.2	1.9	7.9	64.6	20 720	178	3 044	57 966	7.2
Kings	28 558	0.0	11.0	3.7	7.5	7.1	8.5	28.5	11.2	301 475	120	144 281	1 000 293	7.5
Lewis	359	6.0	D	18.9	3.1	6.7	D	D	37.1	5 235	193	622	15 112	-0.1
Livingston	1 002	1.7	D	9.8	3.5	7.7	2.7	9.6	39.0	12 780	195	1 226	27 123	12.9
Madison	1 084	1.3	D	11.3	6.2	7.8	4.0	13.7	23.0	13 440	183	1 386	31 757	10.9
Monroe	23 433	0.1	21.8	17.3	12.2	5.2	5.3	13.4	14.2	145 920	196	24 404	320 593	5.3
Montgomery	886	1.1	22.2	18.3	2.8	9.9	2.4	21.7	20.7	12 550	250	1 967	23 063	2.4
Nassau	46 063	0.0	9.7	3.7	16.0	7.1	9.2	17.9	17.0	244 900	183	17 919	468 346	2.2
New York	299 796	0.0	3.0	1.2	26.9	2.7	30.1	5.2	11.6	235 805	149	80 279	847 090	6.1
Niagara	3 529	0.7	D	17.4	4.4	8.0	2.3	13.6	27.0	50 345	233	5 798	99 120	3.6
Oneida	5 664	0.3	12.5	9.1	7.1	6.7	7.6	16.9	31.2	53 205	227	8 469	104 180	1.3
Onondaga	14 727	0.2	17.2	12.2	10.5	5.8	7.4	13.4	18.4	91 750	196	14 352	202 357	2.9
Ontario	2 539	1.4	23.0	14.2	7.2	10.2	2.9	13.7	20.5	23 095	214	1 985	48 193	13.0
Orange	7 927	0.2	9.9	5.3	7.8	9.1	3.8	14.1	32.9	58 920	158	6 900	137 025	11.6
Orleans	646	5.0	21.3	17.6	2.9	5.2	6.5	D	40.6	9 070	212	940	18 431	6.2
Oswego	1 760	0.6	16.6	12.1	2.5	7.7	2.4	11.3	28.6	25 525	209	3 388	53 598	1.4
Otsego	1 186	0.2	D	4.9	3.7	8.5	6.4	25.6	24.4	13 900	223	1 535	30 777	8.1
Putnam	1 701	0.1	17.6	7.1	9.1	5.8	4.7	17.7	24.3	16 515	166	862	38 224	9.1
Queens	32 847	0.0	D	4.8	5.2	5.9	7.7	18.3	10.6	300 695	135	76 827	835 127	2.2
Rensselaer	3 046	0.1	13.7	5.7	11.1	6.4	5.5	15.6	24.4	30 170	189	3 875	71 475	8.1
Richmond	5 666	0.0	D	D	10.6	8.3	4.0	28.2	11.3	81 015	173	14 732	176 656	7.7
Rockland	8 242	0.0	D	13.1	15.2	5.8	5.2	14.7	20.3	51 725	166	5 615	104 057	9.6
St. Lawrence	1 861	0.8	16.9	11.6	3.0	8.2	2.4	14.8	33.8	24 185	216	4 020	52 133	4.9
Saratoga	4 416	0.2	D	8.6	10.5	8.6	9.7	10.2	19.9	41 385	188	2 959	98 656	13.8
Schenectady	4 294	0.0	D	14.0	22.1	5.4	3.8	14.2	17.2	31 210	202	4 890	68 196	4.9
Schoharie	429	1.0	D	2.6	4.6	8.1	5.6	10.1	37.2	6 520	199	709	17 231	8.3
Schuyler	250	2.9	D	12.9	3.1	8.9	D	D	26.3	4 570	249	486	9 455	3.0
Seneca	592	1.3	D	19.7	D	9.9	3.2	D	32.7	7 575	215	791	16 043	8.4
Steuben	2 444	0.9	26.1	22.8	13.4	5.1	4.3	9.3	20.1	22 555	228	3 286	48 875	5.9
Suffolk	43 233	0.2	16.5	9.3	10.5	6.9	9.6	11.9	21.0	270 480	181	22 279	569 985	9.1
Sullivan	1 346	0.6	9.0	3.5	5.4	8.3	6.3	19.8	31.8	16 845	217	2 860	49 186	10.0
Tioga	934	0.5	57.6	54.5	2.4	4.7	1.5	4.9	16.2	11 370	222	1 210	22 203	3.7
Tompkins	2 943	0.4	11.2	8.1	6.8	4.8	3.1	D	13.7	14 600	144	1 783	41 674	7.9
Ulster	3 245	0.6	11.7	6.4	5.5	10.2	4.4	13.8	31.6	37 585	206	4 428	83 638	7.8
Warren	1 842	0.0	D	13.6	7.7	9.6	6.2	18.3	15.7	16 585	252	1 713	38 726	11.1
Washington	831	0.8	26.2	19.6	D	7.1	1.8	6.5	39.0	13 330	211	1 547	28 844	7.7
Wayne	1 535	3.1	D	22.3	3.9	6.6	2.3	7.3	30.9	21 350	228	2 228	41 057	5.9
Westchester	37 343	0.0	D	5.9	16.5	5.2	10.3	13.4	16.4	159 370	168	17 252	370 821	6.1
Wyoming	681	3.6	D	14.5	2.9	7.2	2.3	D	40.4	8 655	205	688	17 970	6.1
Yates	298	6.2	20.3	15.5	3.0	6.7	2.8	D	23.6	5 775	228	561	13 491	11.8
NORTH CAROLINA	235 072	1.0	18.4	12.8	10.2	6.4	7.0	10.5	22.1	1 757 135	184	219 570	4 327 528	22.9
Alamance	2 803	0.4	D	16.5	5.7	8.4	4.8	15.5	12.5	30 590	202	2 934	66 576	20.0
Alexander	453	8.1	D	30.7	4.4	5.5	3.5	4.8	20.5	7 770	209	587	16 189	14.8
Alleghany	144	6.5	D	14.0	4.0	6.8	3.4	12.6	19.6	3 265	293	322	8 094	26.0
Anson	368	6.9	D	15.6	D	6.7	2.0	D	32.0	5 600	208	1 119	11 576	13.3
Ashe	362	3.4	D	17.9	3.6	9.5	4.3	12.9	16.3	7 280	267	848	17 342	30.7
Avery	335	2.8	D	2.0	D	8.4	4.6	13.7	21.6	4 055	228	374	13 890	16.6
Beaufort	845	5.0	31.3	23.8	D	7.4	3.0	11.3	16.9	13 005	272	1 862	24 688	11.5
Bertie	341	10.6	D	24.0	D	2.7	1.7	D	19.9	5 630	265	1 416	9 822	8.6
Bladen	599	9.6	40.9	38.5	2.3	3.8	1.6	D	19.7	8 040	228	1 868	17 718	15.7
Brunswick	1 439	0.8	D	4.8	6.5	9.0	8.5	8.5	19.2	31 435	293	2 074	77 482	50.7
Buncombe	5 772	0.3	18.2	11.9	7.7	8.0	5.0	19.8	17.8	51 330	215	5 345	113 365	20.7
Burke	1 493	0.8	D	23.0	4.8	5.8	3.1	16.2	25.6	20 580	226	1 996	40 879	9.2
Cabarrus	3 345	0.6	D	13.2	6.7	9.9	3.5	7.9	20.7	28 905	162	2 537	71 937	36.1
Caldwell	1 204	0.9	26.4	22.2	3.1	8.7	3.2	10.2	17.1	19 005	229	1 711	37 659	12.7
Camden	132	9.0	9.1	3.9	D	7.5	2.0	1.9	18.0	1 860	186	152	4 104	38.0
Carteret	1 068	0.5	D	3.6	7.1	10.5	5.6	8.7	26.2	16 280	245	1 233	48 179	17.7
Caswell	161	7.3	D	6.8	3.5	4.9	2.8	10.7	41.5	5 855	247	836	10 619	10.6
Catawba	3 858	0.4	D	27.9	4.0	7.6	3.3	11.7	13.8	33 455	217	2 717	67 886	13.3
Chatham	867	2.7	D	18.4	9.8	7.3	4.0	12.5	15.2	13 905	219	732	28 753	34.6
Cherokee	347	2.0	D	9.3	4.4	12.1	5.2	D	22.9	8 640	315	849	17 515	29.8

1. Includes mining, construction, and manufacturing. 2. Per 1,000 resident population enumerated in the 2010 census.

STATE County	Housing units, 2006–2010								Civilian labor force, 2010				Civilian employment,[5] 2006–2010		
	Occupied units										Unemployment			Percent	
			Owner-occupied			Renter-occupied									
				Median owner cost as a percent of income											Construction, production, and maintenance occupations
				With a mortgage	Without a mortgage	Median rent[2]	Median rent as a percent of income	Substandard units[3] (percent)		Percent change, 2009–2010				Management, business, science and arts	
	Total	Percent	Median value[1]						Total		Total	Rate[4]	Total		
	89	90	91	92	93	94	95	96	97	98	99	100	101	102	103
NEW YORK—Cont'd															
Genesee	23 790	73.7	101 400	23.5	14.6	670	28.0	1.7	32 729	-1.6	2 495	7.6	29 809	30.2	28.6
Greene	18 502	73.6	180 500	25.7	17.0	723	30.1	1.4	24 068	-0.8	2 061	8.6	20 915	31.1	22.5
Hamilton	2 381	81.8	172 300	20.7	13.6	627	21.7	1.0	3 016	-1.3	253	8.4	2 406	30.4	28.3
Herkimer	26 291	71.6	87 600	20.8	14.1	576	29.7	1.2	30 903	-1.6	2 590	8.4	29 539	30.5	25.7
Jefferson	44 109	57.2	116 800	21.8	14.0	769	29.2	2.7	49 859	0.1	4 803	9.6	46 076	29.3	23.9
Kings	903 991	30.3	562 400	32.9	16.9	1 021	31.9	10.4	1 133 377	0.7	115 355	10.2	1 086 160	35.3	17.1
Lewis	10 761	77.8	100 700	21.6	13.6	595	29.0	1.7	12 588	-1.4	1 154	9.2	12 173	29.7	33.2
Livingston	24 135	75.7	112 300	22.8	14.3	664	29.9	1.7	31 916	-1.7	2 762	8.7	30 941	33.4	26.1
Madison	26 851	76.1	111 700	22.1	14.4	691	24.5	1.5	35 584	-2.2	2 975	8.4	34 321	35.0	23.7
Monroe	291 195	66.7	130 400	23.0	14.5	757	33.0	1.4	372 154	-1.4	29 603	8.0	349 817	41.2	17.2
Montgomery	20 320	69.1	95 000	22.7	16.5	666	29.5	2.5	23 999	-2.8	2 353	9.8	22 320	29.4	29.1
Nassau	442 833	82.1	487 900	30.1	19.5	1 407	33.0	2.6	687 538	-1.3	49 094	7.1	650 246	43.2	14.2
New York	732 204	22.8	825 200	20.9	10.0	1 234	27.7	6.5	935 428	-0.7	74 529	8.0	848 016	57.5	6.8
Niagara	88 152	70.9	97 600	22.3	15.5	614	30.1	1.3	112 269	-1.6	10 264	9.1	99 402	29.9	24.1
Oneida	92 058	67.9	101 900	21.5	14.0	638	29.3	1.6	109 617	-1.9	8 509	7.8	105 467	34.7	20.8
Onondaga	183 542	66.0	124 400	21.9	14.0	708	30.2	1.4	230 520	-2.0	18 411	8.0	221 848	38.7	17.0
Ontario	42 952	75.5	129 600	22.9	14.6	711	29.8	1.3	56 569	-0.3	4 259	7.5	53 792	38.9	21.6
Orange	124 379	71.3	312 100	28.7	18.0	1 031	33.0	4.3	179 090	-0.9	14 785	8.3	170 431	35.8	20.3
Orleans	15 736	76.7	86 400	23.3	17.7	630	28.6	1.8	19 310	-1.2	1 910	9.9	18 586	27.2	33.8
Oswego	45 749	73.6	88 000	22.5	14.6	665	33.9	1.8	59 491	-2.0	6 275	10.5	54 150	27.0	30.5
Otsego	24 926	72.5	129 000	23.3	14.1	733	35.3	1.7	31 489	-0.7	2 439	7.7	29 822	34.2	21.6
Putnam	34 907	84.6	418 100	29.6	18.0	1 216	34.0	1.3	54 286	-1.8	3 743	6.9	49 230	42.8	16.3
Queens	774 311	45.5	479 300	32.9	14.8	1 181	31.5	9.6	1 141 560	0.7	97 516	8.5	1 065 977	31.1	19.7
Rensselaer	63 518	65.1	171 200	24.0	14.6	779	28.0	1.9	82 250	-2.8	6 395	7.8	80 598	37.3	18.8
Richmond	164 279	70.3	461 700	29.0	16.2	1 107	32.5	3.7	249 607	1.4	21 623	8.7	207 886	36.3	17.4
Rockland	97 557	71.0	476 900	28.9	18.7	1 240	33.2	6.0	151 930	-1.3	10 862	7.1	140 952	43.6	14.0
St. Lawrence	42 019	71.7	79 600	21.4	14.0	610	31.3	2.1	49 071	-1.6	5 191	10.6	46 253	30.7	23.4
Saratoga	86 658	73.8	221 100	23.4	13.5	871	27.2	1.1	119 723	-1.6	8 095	6.8	111 718	40.9	17.3
Schenectady	58 583	69.2	160 200	23.8	14.7	789	29.9	1.4	75 377	-2.4	5 840	7.7	73 149	37.8	16.7
Schoharie	12 989	77.4	139 000	22.4	14.2	671	36.1	2.1	15 310	-3.8	1 446	9.4	15 343	31.2	27.2
Schuyler	7 482	79.1	86 700	21.9	12.6	602	26.9	1.6	10 005	-0.5	841	8.4	8 606	31.4	25.3
Seneca	13 118	77.4	88 900	23.4	14.3	661	28.5	2.6	17 211	-0.4	1 361	7.9	15 503	32.4	28.1
Steuben	40 558	72.9	83 000	21.4	13.5	597	29.7	1.8	45 194	-2.0	4 470	9.9	43 918	32.9	27.9
Suffolk	495 289	81.4	424 200	31.2	19.3	1 427	34.6	2.4	786 747	-1.2	60 052	7.6	728 324	37.3	19.3
Sullivan	29 722	67.5	186 900	28.0	16.0	795	31.9	3.2	35 020	-1.5	3 216	9.2	34 273	33.6	23.2
Tioga	20 402	80.0	98 200	22.0	13.0	588	25.5	1.3	25 573	-2.9	2 074	8.1	24 696	33.8	26.7
Tompkins	38 446	55.0	162 100	22.7	13.1	851	33.1	1.6	56 653	-0.1	3 431	6.1	50 549	50.0	13.9
Ulster	70 691	69.6	242 100	27.3	17.7	939	31.4	2.0	88 883	-1.7	7 273	8.2	89 787	37.5	19.9
Warren	28 533	68.5	183 000	24.0	14.0	781	29.3	1.4	36 104	-0.7	3 061	8.5	31 829	33.7	22.2
Washington	24 603	74.0	137 000	24.7	14.7	720	31.0	2.0	32 149	-1.0	2 517	7.8	28 991	27.7	31.4
Wayne	36 619	76.3	107 400	22.3	14.5	657	29.9	2.0	47 481	-1.4	4 183	8.8	45 612	32.8	28.8
Westchester	345 795	62.7	556 900	27.4	18.0	1 203	31.2	4.4	481 042	-1.7	34 873	7.2	451 799	45.5	13.8
Wyoming	15 453	76.3	97 300	22.5	13.5	629	30.1	1.2	20 654	-1.8	1 907	9.2	18 456	29.3	31.6
Yates	9 544	78.2	114 200	24.3	14.1	559	30.3	2.8	13 315	0.1	897	6.7	11 486	31.7	28.1
NORTH CAROLINA	3 626 179	68.1	149 100	23.3	11.8	718	29.5	2.5	4 616 767	1.4	504 883	10.9	4 234 087	34.4	25.0
Alamance	59 000	68.1	137 100	23.5	11.5	699	29.7	3.1	69 940	0.5	7 971	11.4	70 874	30.8	26.4
Alexander	13 419	79.9	119 400	23.4	10.0	569	30.0	2.7	17 742	0.2	2 299	13.0	16 401	23.1	43.3
Alleghany	4 971	74.0	133 100	27.7	13.1	532	38.4	1.0	4 642	-4.9	536	11.5	4 701	25.3	45.1
Anson	9 535	71.0	78 400	24.3	14.7	594	29.6	2.7	9 917	-2.0	1 419	14.3	9 924	21.8	41.4
Ashe	11 848	79.2	145 700	24.3	11.6	542	29.6	2.8	12 387	-6.5	1 529	12.3	11 976	24.7	35.7
Avery	7 194	72.8	155 100	30.1	10.0	677	32.7	3.4	7 878	-17.3	853	10.8	7 552	27.8	27.6
Beaufort	20 059	73.4	107 000	24.0	15.1	584	29.0	2.4	20 481	-6.2	2 340	11.4	19 756	29.7	33.3
Bertie	8 160	76.9	77 400	25.4	14.5	588	40.0	2.3	8 691	-9.3	1 011	11.6	8 312	22.0	37.9
Bladen	13 974	69.0	77 300	23.9	15.5	566	28.3	3.1	15 527	-3.2	1 893	12.2	13 581	25.0	38.9
Brunswick	45 409	77.5	190 500	25.7	12.1	790	30.2	2.1	50 413	3.1	5 631	11.2	44 009	29.7	27.9
Buncombe	99 309	67.6	188 300	24.3	11.6	738	29.0	2.2	121 447	2.8	10 186	8.4	113 559	36.2	21.3
Burke	34 888	74.1	108 800	23.1	11.7	565	29.1	2.3	38 809	0.0	5 213	13.4	38 866	27.9	32.5
Cabarrus	63 680	73.3	164 100	22.6	12.2	727	27.8	2.2	84 098	1.2	9 474	11.3	81 311	34.9	24.0
Caldwell	31 296	75.6	106 900	21.9	11.7	569	29.4	1.7	37 171	-0.3	5 354	14.4	35 439	24.0	39.7
Camden	3 442	85.1	221 000	23.4	10.6	830	35.4	1.4	4 375	-6.6	357	8.2	4 247	34.8	24.6
Carteret	28 632	73.5	207 500	24.4	12.6	699	28.2	1.1	32 186	-6.3	2 839	8.8	29 724	30.8	25.7
Caswell	8 788	75.2	97 500	24.3	12.0	590	36.3	1.3	10 613	-2.6	1 261	11.9	9 281	29.0	33.6
Catawba	59 251	71.8	130 300	21.7	10.5	627	27.5	2.6	75 238	0.8	9 850	13.1	71 515	29.4	31.1
Chatham	24 877	79.1	193 900	22.8	12.0	728	29.2	2.9	33 614	0.9	2 474	7.4	28 832	40.6	25.4
Cherokee	11 497	83.2	146 100	24.4	10.0	524	26.8	1.9	10 002	-5.2	1 423	14.2	11 363	26.0	35.6

1. Specified owner-occupied units. 2. Specified renter-occupied units. A value of 10.0 represents 10 percent or less. 3. Overcrowded or lacking complete plumbing facilities. 4. Percent of civilian labor force. 5. Persons 16 years old and over.

Table B. States and Counties — Nonfarm Employment and Agriculture

STATE County	Private nonfarm establishments, employment and payroll, 2009									Agriculture, 2007			
		Employment						Annual payroll		Farms			
											Percent with:		
	Number of establishments	Total	Health care and social assistance	Manufacturing	Retail trade	Finance and insurance	Professional, scientific, and technical services	Total (mil dol)	Average per employee (dollars)	Number	Fewer than 50 acres	500 acres or more	Farm operators whose principal occupation is farming (percent)
	104	105	106	107	108	109	110	111	112	113	114	115	116
NEW YORK—Cont'd													
Genesee	1 326	15 765	1 947	2 786	2 805	377	377	483	30 663	551	36.1	12.5	58.4
Greene	1 136	11 541	1 172	944	2 374	337	241	329	28 516	286	35.7	6.3	50.7
Hamilton	198	826	D	D	151	D	D	25	30 081	20	85.0	0.0	45.0
Herkimer	1 170	12 100	2 387	2 835	2 229	270	248	356	29 381	672	20.4	9.5	61.8
Jefferson	2 424	29 392	5 684	2 451	6 735	816	931	926	31 500	885	21.2	14.7	54.5
Kings	46 445	484 947	165 791	21 878	57 072	17 152	15 262	17 888	36 886	1	100.0	0.0	100.0
Lewis	518	4 590	868	1 299	779	91	104	138	30 032	616	18.2	12.0	63.8
Livingston	1 264	12 684	2 045	2 260	2 644	256	370	348	27 437	792	31.9	12.9	52.7
Madison	1 426	17 519	2 967	2 517	2 700	556	779	520	29 691	744	23.4	14.1	55.6
Monroe	16 990	336 930	57 427	41 425	40 274	12 516	20 526	13 307	39 495	585	54.9	11.3	55.4
Montgomery	1 109	15 256	4 161	3 232	2 416	376	319	489	32 053	604	24.0	8.3	65.1
Nassau	47 087	512 737	97 797	19 203	76 116	37 495	39 602	24 075	46 953	59	88.1	0.0	40.7
New York	103 528	1 996 595	232 961	22 802	128 239	295 668	279 850	180 588	90 448	0	0.0	0.0	0.0
Niagara	4 467	57 730	9 590	8 737	9 814	1 123	1 897	1 742	30 169	865	46.7	5.8	50.8
Oneida	4 905	89 433	20 331	10 690	11 871	7 327	3 922	2 889	32 302	1 013	27.3	8.1	55.7
Onondaga	11 779	212 993	35 567	21 495	27 769	13 824	16 169	8 421	39 536	692	42.6	11.6	53.9
Ontario	2 801	42 307	7 169	6 629	8 920	846	1 703	1 432	33 838	859	39.6	11.1	53.7
Orange	9 237	100 407	18 978	6 802	21 303	3 789	5 155	3 582	35 671	642	46.4	4.0	61.2
Orleans	682	7 997	1 504	2 067	1 242	D	132	232	28 989	554	38.1	8.7	52.5
Oswego	2 107	23 616	4 848	3 018	4 481	658	579	813	34 420	639	28.5	4.7	54.6
Otsego	1 434	17 962	4 900	860	3 385	D	584	589	32 772	980	22.7	6.1	54.9
Putnam	2 926	21 142	4 365	1 643	2 959	665	1 207	862	40 751	72	70.8	1.4	48.6
Queens	42 420	485 341	114 388	24 312	54 040	17 477	11 687	20 437	42 109	4	100.0	0.0	0.0
Rensselaer	2 966	41 085	8 719	2 536	5 869	1 688	3 029	1 523	37 076	506	35.8	6.7	53.6
Richmond	8 321	91 660	28 777	1 140	15 012	2 806	3 447	3 417	37 276	14	100.0	0.0	28.6
Rockland	9 148	99 816	21 350	9 828	13 030	3 547	7 089	4 287	42 945	21	90.5	0.0	42.9
St. Lawrence	2 080	27 527	6 346	2 871	5 518	746	629	830	30 158	1 330	14.9	12.1	52.0
Saratoga	4 919	61 563	7 889	4 646	11 372	4 111	3 805	2 252	36 576	641	51.5	3.4	54.8
Schenectady	3 090	50 635	10 950	4 152	7 264	1 346	D	2 161	42 676	104	46.4	3.1	50.5
Schoharie	567	5 711	1 073	208	1 171	243	218	166	29 045	525	23.4	6.9	57.7
Schuyler	354	3 637	D	537	782	D	31	118	32 358	394	25.9	6.9	55.8
Seneca	702	8 000	1 277	1 265	2 059	158	106	264	33 008	513	32.7	12.5	62.4
Steuben	1 838	27 992	5 761	6 289	4 264	1 025	D	1 177	42 044	1 578	17.2	10.3	48.9
Suffolk	47 573	550 192	90 925	56 006	78 095	24 741	41 243	25 540	46 420	585	74.2	1.2	64.4
Sullivan	1 995	17 709	4 878	953	2 942	847	511	556	31 383	323	31.0	7.1	50.8
Tioga	796	12 973	1 454	1 567	1 340	247	D	625	48 147	565	26.2	7.4	43.5
Tompkins	2 297	45 542	5 178	2 867	5 115	1 081	2 537	1 563	34 320	588	40.5	9.0	45.9
Ulster	4 682	45 021	8 572	3 567	8 731	2 763	1 921	1 417	31 468	501	42.1	5.0	57.1
Warren	2 371	31 537	6 801	4 124	5 624	D	843	1 094	34 684	86	59.3	2.3	37.2
Washington	1 082	9 498	1 413	2 800	1 845	D	241	317	33 358	843	29.9	13.4	49.7
Wayne	1 728	19 395	2 743	5 649	3 606	552	581	667	34 414	938	39.4	7.6	58.6
Westchester	31 590	372 772	73 448	12 557	47 480	20 591	27 629	21 150	56 736	106	69.8	3.8	43.4
Wyoming	785	8 670	1 261	1 901	1 399	D	284	254	29 350	761	30.9	13.9	59.0
Yates	534	5 090	1 175	759	722	110	D	141	27 147	864	25.6	3.8	64.0
NORTH CAROLINA	218 987	3 353 931	539 670	439 637	447 417	169 721	180 238	124 323	37 068	52 913	48.7	6.7	45.8
Alamance	3 212	49 711	7 341	10 201	7 861	1 563	1 295	1 469	29 541	753	42.6	3.9	43.0
Alexander	603	7 259	570	3 591	845	158	127	182	25 100	627	55.5	2.4	42.3
Alleghany	280	2 268	513	D	330	D	D	58	25 419	519	49.3	7.3	47.2
Anson	419	4 781	586	1 366	769	D	132	124	26 011	487	30.2	8.6	42.1
Ashe	566	5 817	1 137	D	1 104	172	82	152	26 120	1 125	51.4	3.0	42.5
Avery	527	4 693	832	234	833	85	80	117	24 861	477	63.3	1.0	40.7
Beaufort	1 179	13 162	2 421	2 923	2 324	362	384	388	29 458	369	36.3	22.0	50.9
Bertie	362	5 169	1 502	D	368	76	D	116	22 537	279	28.3	25.8	64.5
Bladen	526	10 974	1 440	D	855	D	D	311	28 317	500	41.0	14.0	50.8
Brunswick	2 321	23 533	3 283	D	4 314	792	614	676	28 707	264	59.1	6.8	54.5
Buncombe	7 261	98 997	20 990	9 852	14 745	2 658	3 995	3 182	32 144	1 077	67.2	1.3	36.4
Burke	1 505	23 033	4 302	8 645	2 616	403	462	684	29 696	481	65.5	1.2	45.7
Cabarrus	3 958	58 666	10 054	7 137	10 598	921	1 740	1 976	33 685	611	52.9	3.6	36.3
Caldwell	1 438	19 649	3 177	6 298	2 923	483	443	552	28 077	459	62.5	1.1	34.4
Camden	126	824	31	D	113	D	30	32	39 386	76	35.5	30.3	53.9
Carteret	2 049	18 188	2 902	1 103	4 127	538	617	488	26 812	159	78.0	4.4	33.3
Caswell	242	1 808	465	D	253	52	43	39	21 688	562	29.9	8.4	47.2
Catawba	4 267	76 532	10 500	23 226	9 743	1 448	1 754	2 512	32 818	737	51.8	3.0	36.4
Chatham	1 269	14 232	2 734	4 001	2 137	243	550	390	27 378	1 089	47.2	1.5	44.8
Cherokee	641	6 647	1 588	1 136	1 543	209	249	173	26 007	288	59.4	1.4	47.9

Table B. States and Counties — Agriculture

	Agriculture, 2007 (cont.)															
STATE County	Land in farms					Value of land and buildings (dollars)		Value of machinery and equipment, average per farm (dollars)	Value of products sold				Percent of farms with sales of:		Government payments	
			Acres								Percent from:					
	Acreage (1,000)	Percent change, 2002–2007	Average size of farm	Total irrigated (1,000)	Total cropland (1,000)	Average per farm	Average per acre		Total (mil dol)	Average per farm (dollars)	Crops	Livestock and poultry products	$10,000 or more	$100,000 or more	Total ($1,000)	Percent of farms
	117	118	119	120	121	122	123	124	125	126	127	128	129	130	131	132
NEW YORK—Cont'd																
Genesee	184	4.0	333	7.8	146.0	583 415	1 751	165 883	177.8	322 703	35.4	64.6	46.5	22.1	1 989	49.5
Greene	44	-24.1	155	0.7	22.2	452 548	2 920	77 318	16.4	57 249	43.5	56.5	36.0	9.4	225	22.0
Hamilton	0	-100.0	23	D	0.2	97 714	4 343	D	0.4	18 116	97.8	2.5	25.0	10.0	0	0.0
Herkimer	140	-11.9	208	0.2	77.9	363 264	1 743	89 577	62.1	92 472	12.3	87.7	53.1	23.2	992	37.5
Jefferson	262	-20.8	296	0.3	166.2	410 806	1 386	114 803	139.2	157 335	12.2	87.8	51.2	22.7	1 906	35.1
Kings	D	D	D	D	D	D	D	D	D	D	D	0.0	100.0	0.0	0	0.0
Lewis	167	-15.2	272	0.1	92.0	435 764	1 605	119 007	112.6	182 839	5.9	94.1	60.2	39.3	1 012	39.4
Livingston	222	6.2	281	0.5	165.8	565 547	2 014	126 034	153.8	194 243	30.7	69.3	40.9	19.7	2 999	49.4
Madison	188	11.9	253	0.5	115.9	425 987	1 683	113 067	86.3	116 036	18.7	81.3	50.7	24.9	1 629	32.5
Monroe	133	24.3	227	1.6	105.7	587 711	2 584	106 178	72.2	123 436	85.1	14.9	44.3	19.8	1 327	26.0
Montgomery	125	-17.8	206	0.2	84.1	445 455	2 160	106 802	73.6	121 873	16.8	83.2	53.5	20.5	1 231	38.2
Nassau	1	0.0	22	0.2	0.3	2 161 159	98 997	86 665	15.8	267 787	76.1	23.9	59.3	25.4	0	0.0
New York	0	NA	0	0.0	0.0	0	0	0.0	0.0	0	0.0	0.0	0.0	0.0	0	0.0
Niagara	143	-3.4	165	2.6	113.6	351 933	2 134	109 484	103.6	119 820	58.6	41.4	39.9	12.9	1 534	28.3
Oneida	192	-12.7	190	0.3	108.9	367 253	1 935	92 561	90.1	88 956	27.4	72.6	46.0	20.1	2 077	32.4
Onondaga	150	-3.8	217	1.6	106.2	521 122	2 396	127 052	137.4	198 515	26.6	73.4	48.8	22.8	2 104	33.2
Ontario	199	2.1	232	1.0	153.1	510 387	2 204	127 424	153.8	179 101	32.2	67.8	53.0	22.1	2 293	40.0
Orange	81	-25.0	126	4.6	46.3	649 645	5 150	102 810	73.7	114 873	69.4	30.6	50.8	21.3	769	25.7
Orleans	140	5.3	252	3.5	106.3	433 158	1 717	132 141	101.0	182 357	88.1	11.9	44.6	21.1	2 135	44.0
Oswego	100	-2.9	157	1.1	49.0	295 224	1 883	81 275	39.3	61 568	66.2	33.8	41.9	13.5	482	21.9
Otsego	176	-14.6	180	0.2	88.2	341 977	1 899	64 459	51.4	52 457	17.1	82.9	40.3	15.6	977	24.3
Putnam	6	-14.3	78	D	1.3	1 092 842	13 964	64 379	D	29 293	D	D	30.6	11.1	D	1.4
Queens	D	D	D	0.0	D	D	D	D	0.1	29 293	D	D	100.0	0.0	0	0.0
Rensselaer	85	-7.6	168	1.0	45.2	529 827	3 153	89 289	37.5	74 133	37.6	62.4	46.4	13.4	818	30.2
Richmond	D	D	D	0.0	D	379 581	120 776	81 523	5.2	369 589	100.0	0.0	50.0	35.7	0	0.0
Rockland	D	D	D	0.0	0.1	651 265	56 515	82 463	2.6	121 890	D	D	38.1	33.3	0	0.0
St. Lawrence	347	-13.9	261	0.3	176.9	351 391	1 346	81 940	140.2	105 377	10.6	89.4	41.3	14.8	1 853	23.0
Saratoga	76	1.3	118	0.5	42.9	515 230	4 365	81 832	58.2	90 836	26.0	74.0	34.2	9.0	566	16.5
Schenectady	19	-13.6	99	0.4	10.5	354 700	3 597	57 727	3.5	18 014	73.8	26.2	25.3	5.2	D	3.6
Schoharie	95	-15.9	182	0.5	53.0	389 261	2 140	79 647	35.2	66 959	27.9	72.1	49.3	14.1	596	26.1
Schuyler	66	-10.8	168	0.3	37.1	366 960	2 178	67 088	33.1	83 907	38.0	62.0	41.6	14.7	475	20.6
Seneca	128	0.8	249	0.2	102.9	502 185	2 013	129 110	84.1	163 889	39.3	60.7	63.9	35.7	1 214	34.9
Steuben	372	-0.3	236	1.5	211.2	370 465	1 572	88 340	135.3	85 732	28.0	72.0	39.0	14.1	2 616	35.2
Suffolk	34	0.0	59	13.6	26.3	1 065 327	18 115	183 312	242.9	415 270	92.5	7.5	70.9	38.1	253	9.4
Sullivan	50	-21.9	156	0.1	24.6	545 478	3 493	81 001	42.1	130 393	5.0	95.0	44.6	11.8	243	20.1
Tioga	107	-16.4	189	0.4	53.8	331 150	1 751	70 301	36.7	64 894	13.4	86.6	33.1	15.6	1 053	34.3
Tompkins	109	7.9	185	0.3	67.3	418 353	2 262	94 081	60.2	102 356	25.4	74.6	39.6	17.0	955	30.4
Ulster	75	-9.6	150	4.7	31.7	598 130	3 985	92 909	65.6	130 928	89.7	10.3	42.9	15.8	284	11.0
Warren	9	50.0	99	0.0	1.3	345 406	3 472	45 201	D	D	D	D	25.6	2.3	0	0.0
Washington	203	-1.5	241	0.5	112.0	512 622	2 130	104 900	112.3	133 166	11.9	88.1	49.6	21.4	2 189	27.5
Wayne	168	1.8	180	2.2	119.7	410 385	2 285	125 569	169.0	180 131	76.0	24.0	53.0	26.2	1 535	27.2
Westchester	9	-10.0	80	0.2	2.5	2 557 300	31 812	105 460	11.0	103 754	50.2	49.8	45.3	22.6	D	0.9
Wyoming	218	1.4	287	3.7	157.3	509 515	1 778	158 822	229.9	302 159	12.4	87.6	47.7	26.5	2 810	40.5
Yates	126	9.6	146	0.5	86.6	415 303	2 845	92 975	88.4	102 294	36.0	64.0	68.6	37.5	1 107	24.8
NORTH CAROLINA	8 475	-6.7	160	232.1	4 895.2	656 080	4 096	76 793	10 313.6	194 917	25.3	74.7	35.2	15.7	147 334	26.2
Alamance	88	-10.2	117	1.6	35.9	538 124	4 610	60 524	42.6	56 598	19.2	80.8	34.3	10.5	459	18.2
Alexander	55	-5.2	88	0.7	21.5	479 054	5 465	58 998	112.0	178 560	2.9	97.1	42.1	26.5	224	8.3
Alleghany	77	5.5	148	0.4	29.2	838 316	5 676	67 003	34.0	65 500	54.5	45.5	45.5	9.6	389	13.1
Anson	91	-9.0	186	0.5	27.8	664 850	3 567	62 579	157.7	323 815	4.5	95.5	36.6	23.6	951	50.3
Ashe	108	0.0	96	0.3	38.0	555 859	5 766	44 922	41.7	37 070	76.5	23.5	36.4	6.8	128	2.6
Avery	28	-9.7	58	0.4	12.6	440 933	7 561	60 203	20.5	43 024	98.0	2.0	39.8	10.1	92	3.1
Beaufort	160	-5.9	435	0.9	139.0	1 115 057	2 566	146 130	98.8	267 732	65.9	34.1	48.2	29.3	4 038	64.2
Bertie	147	2.8	528	8.5	92.7	1 349 552	2 555	206 421	161.6	579 071	24.4	75.6	63.4	46.2	5 475	77.1
Bladen	127	-12.4	254	11.1	70.6	838 266	3 296	108 439	338.5	676 987	13.3	86.7	46.0	30.0	2 260	43.0
Brunswick	44	7.3	167	2.5	27.4	714 480	4 279	95 917	45.1	170 959	44.8	55.2	31.8	11.4	335	23.1
Buncombe	72	-24.2	67	0.5	20.3	475 105	7 098	52 613	37.2	34 578	75.7	24.3	18.5	2.8	203	9.3
Burke	29	-9.4	60	2.1	14.4	355 410	5 881	62 632	35.6	73 999	55.0	45.0	24.5	7.7	104	8.3
Cabarrus	67	-8.2	109	0.4	34.6	614 341	5 621	56 510	52.4	85 752	14.1	85.9	23.7	6.4	675	17.5
Caldwell	33	-5.7	71	1.5	11.4	360 485	5 077	48 611	20.8	45 208	63.3	36.7	20.9	7.2	51	4.4
Camden	55	NA	726	0.0	47.6	2 138 048	2 945	251 941	28.2	371 476	98.9	1.1	53.9	31.6	681	52.6
Carteret	55	-8.3	348	0.2	38.0	1 070 514	3 073	99 640	20.3	127 430	95.5	4.5	33.3	10.1	376	16.4
Caswell	102	-12.8	182	1.5	37.9	568 243	3 122	50 942	20.7	36 839	44.9	55.1	34.0	6.4	950	26.2
Catawba	72	-8.9	98	1.1	36.7	517 123	5 300	51 627	30.5	41 413	40.7	59.3	25.4	6.0	456	16.8
Chatham	104	-12.6	96	0.9	32.8	535 597	5 599	49 890	171.7	157 713	4.0	96.0	36.1	14.9	530	12.3
Cherokee	20	-9.1	71	0.2	6.5	478 486	6 747	59 654	D	D	0.0	D	20.1	3.5	170	10.4

Table B. States and Counties — Water Use, Wholesale Trade, Retail Trade, and Real Estate

STATE County	Water use, 2005		Wholesale trade,[1] 2007				Retail trade,[2] 2007				Real estate and rental and leasing,[2] 2007			
	Total water withdrawn (mil gal/day)	Gallons withdrawn per person	Number of establishments	Number of employees	Sales (mil dol)	Annual payroll (mil dol)	Number of establishments	Number of employees	Sales (mil dol)	Annual payroll (mil dol)	Number of establishments	Number of employees	Receipts (mil dol)	Annual payroll (mil dol)
	133	134	135	136	137	138	139	140	141	142	143	144	145	146
NEW YORK—Cont'd														
Genesee	11.9	200	68	1 164	811.7	44.7	217	2 616	705.7	55.2	47	197	33.4	7.3
Greene	5.8	117	18	309	232.2	12.0	206	2 553	623.0	58.5	49	217	24.8	5.8
Hamilton	1.1	214	NA	NA	NA	NA	31	191	31.9	3.2	8	15	1.5	0.2
Herkimer	14.8	232	37	577	186.8	22.1	222	2 045	503.1	45.4	44	192	20.2	2.7
Jefferson	15.6	134	71	D	D	D	506	7 188	1 867.7	163.4	122	543	98.9	14.3
Kings	13.9	6	3 342	26 145	13 802.2	914.5	8 365	58 365	15 431.9	1 347.7	4 068	13 786	2 886.4	411.2
Lewis	8.1	304	12	96	33.0	3.5	77	738	175.8	13.9	12	49	4.8	1.0
Livingston	8.2	128	42	418	219.8	16.8	215	2 587	586.5	56.8	48	199	28.9	4.0
Madison	7.1	101	32	318	109.5	13.1	227	2 700	665.9	61.9	60	150	18.7	3.9
Monroe	226.9	309	809	13 783	6 778.3	728.2	2 376	40 062	8 496.1	845.7	803	6 215	1 025.4	193.7
Montgomery	13.2	270	45	D	D	D	197	2 469	621.8	52.2	27	112	13.1	3.3
Nassau	551.5	414	3 078	D	D	D	6 356	84 280	24 312.6	2 273.8	2 501	D	D	D
New York	287.6	181	8 941	99 779	108 757.4	6 717.5	11 665	134 567	38 797.5	4 490.7	9 469	68 786	28 476.7	4 350.0
Niagara	291.0	1 341	181	2 476	1 059.3	105.4	746	9 522	2 075.1	191.8	131	614	71.4	14.5
Oneida	42.9	183	176	2 098	939.4	80.7	869	12 369	2 751.0	264.4	206	822	151.8	19.7
Onondaga	147.5	322	668	12 250	17 121.5	571.3	1 776	28 722	6 363.1	613.2	629	3 439	663.2	124.4
Ontario	14.2	136	119	1 291	536.7	60.1	556	8 689	1 894.2	180.1	98	450	67.4	10.2
Orange	855.1	2 293	447	7 417	6 859.2	335.0	1 586	22 345	5 729.2	517.4	424	1 591	379.5	45.1
Orleans	5.4	125	21	259	88.6	9.2	111	1 282	262.6	25.9	19	44	9.3	1.0
Oswego	1 255.0	10 172	55	429	210.8	13.3	365	4 290	994.1	87.1	74	310	32.8	5.8
Otsego	6.7	107	44	D	D	D	301	3 661	932.4	86.1	47	184	26.5	3.8
Putnam	111.4	1 108	119	928	504.7	43.3	342	3 171	922.3	84.8	110	300	68.0	11.0
Queens	1 738.3	776	2 886	26 189	15 308.5	1 249.2	6 725	54 013	14 587.1	1 322.4	2 839	13 751	2 943.0	522.5
Rensselaer	26.7	172	100	997	1 387.7	42.1	421	5 833	1 384.4	133.0	98	481	74.1	13.1
Richmond	653.9	1 408	366	1 791	1 320.1	77.2	1 242	16 274	3 850.1	358.9	322	1 157	269.4	33.9
Rockland	1 007.5	3 439	508	6 549	3 228.2	282.0	1 186	14 122	3 866.8	346.8	458	1 752	406.8	51.6
St. Lawrence	16.4	147	53	463	116.1	13.2	447	5 183	1 238.8	105.9	66	289	33.0	5.8
Saratoga	23.9	111	182	2 958	2 239.4	160.4	775	11 807	4 506.4	256.4	177	988	181.6	30.5
Schenectady	28.9	194	100	1 124	601.6	44.6	498	7 600	1 664.3	161.8	117	668	114.3	21.0
Schoharie	170.8	5 293	18	126	86.0	4.7	98	1 106	268.9	23.2	21	50	6.8	1.0
Schuyler	3.3	169	6	D	D	D	66	713	179.9	15.8	10	43	2.9	0.7
Seneca	4.7	133	26	D	D	D	201	2 141	426.2	39.1	25	106	20.4	2.4
Steuben	23.8	241	36	D	D	D	363	4 336	1 076.9	89.5	66	249	29.4	7.5
Suffolk	1 508.0	1 022	3 039	42 142	38 208.9	2 400.2	6 750	83 958	23 319.9	2 217.8	1 813	D	D	D
Sullivan	107.8	1 408	67	714	299.1	22.3	318	3 035	815.2	71.1	156	507	66.3	10.1
Tioga	7.9	154	23	D	D	D	151	1 310	302.2	27.3	12	24	3.4	0.4
Tompkins	254.2	2 541	54	426	189.6	15.5	372	5 068	1 018.3	106.1	95	748	116.2	19.8
Ulster	472.5	2 586	150	1 607	946.5	86.5	794	9 242	2 241.1	216.3	209	676	125.2	18.4
Warren	12.0	182	72	758	342.0	32.5	452	5 899	1 382.2	138.7	86	377	67.9	10.4
Washington	10.3	163	30	246	85.1	8.5	206	1 934	485.6	43.7	20	58	4.8	1.1
Wayne	459.9	4 913	68	484	189.4	19.1	289	3 451	816.7	76.7	61	273	27.3	4.5
Westchester	2 529.0	2 688	1 419	17 179	20 059.6	1 155.2	4 058	50 195	14 205.1	1 423.2	2 162	9 027	2 373.8	416.9
Wyoming	10.3	242	30	288	297.2	11.5	144	1 463	338.0	30.6	21	72	7.7	1.7
Yates	71.2	2 874	16	136	42.7	4.4	105	690	178.9	15.2	18	105	9.6	2.4
NORTH CAROLINA	12 852.2	1 480	10 049	142 342	88 795.9	6 969.2	36 592	466 577	114 578.2	10 342.7	11 258	53 563	11 175.1	1 881.4
Alamance	24.3	173	153	1 839	655.8	73.3	631	8 251	1 968.8	168.1	135	523	83.0	14.7
Alexander	5.1	145	22	157	49.8	5.9	91	914	216.8	19.7	14	41	4.0	0.7
Alleghany	4.1	378	5	21	1.5	0.4	44	385	73.7	6.5	11	31	4.8	0.5
Anson	10.9	427	14	333	153.5	13.9	92	825	180.0	16.2	8	18	2.1	0.5
Ashe	3.3	132	15	155	55.9	4.2	117	1 176	292.4	23.5	40	83	15.7	1.8
Avery	12.4	701	22	132	41.6	3.9	94	1 029	197.6	20.0	35	119	13.0	3.2
Beaufort	84.7	1 840	58	487	285.4	18.1	216	2 459	573.4	49.8	39	109	12.8	2.0
Bertie	10.5	540	16	98	51.2	3.1	59	390	93.0	8.1	9	D	D	D
Bladen	56.6	1 719	22	166	174.2	5.6	98	847	196.7	15.9	14	52	6.5	1.5
Brunswick	1 568.4	17 591	74	578	206.7	20.5	392	4 264	1 004.2	90.1	214	689	113.2	22.5
Buncombe	303.8	1 388	257	2 838	1 162.9	114.1	1 205	15 865	3 597.9	342.4	427	1 534	277.8	51.2
Burke	18.9	211	65	757	289.5	27.9	277	2 689	661.2	57.0	53	164	18.2	3.4
Cabarrus	17.7	118	188	2 962	1 412.3	131.7	732	11 058	2 807.8	239.7	214	763	107.6	21.6
Caldwell	11.6	147	74	577	236.8	23.0	276	2 676	648.6	56.4	60	193	26.1	5.2
Camden	0.9	96	5	31	9.5	1.2	17	96	27.0	1.6	2	D	D	D
Carteret	7.9	126	66	577	254.3	21.1	429	4 148	979.6	91.1	134	575	70.7	14.5
Caswell	3.1	130	3	D	D	D	49	260	53.0	4.9	4	3	0.7	0.1
Catawba	1 182.2	7 796	253	6 524	4 087.3	263.5	797	10 577	2 683.1	233.9	193	700	142.2	20.2
Chatham	159.4	2 747	46	360	128.7	13.0	190	2 197	559.4	47.7	42	128	12.6	3.1
Cherokee	31.5	1 222	12	146	60.5	3.1	153	1 675	404.0	34.7	54	151	18.3	2.8

1. Merchant wholesalers, except manufacturers' sales branches and offices.   2. Employer establishments.

Professional Services, Manufacturing, and Accommodation and Food Services

STATE County	Professional, scientific, and technical services,[1] 2007				Manufacturing, 2007				Accommodation and food services, 2007			
	Number of establishments	Number of employees	Receipts (mil dol)	Annual payroll (mil dol)	Number of establishments	Number of employees	Receipts (mil dol)	Annual payroll (mil dol)	Number of establishments	Number of employees	Sales (mil dol)	Annual payroll (mil dol)
	147	148	149	150	151	152	153	154	155	156	157	158
NEW YORK—Cont'd												
Genesee	83	D	D	D	99	3 206	815.5	128.9	130	1 727	79.5	20.5
Greene	75	265	21.4	7.7	35	1 088	591.1	56.0	195	2 556	90.6	25.0
Hamilton	4	D	D	D	NA	NA	NA	NA	56	228	22.6	4.9
Herkimer	72	D	D	D	68	2 839	546.4	109.7	156	1 274	54.2	14.6
Jefferson	123	899	103.8	37.4	73	2 624	839.9	108.5	320	3 748	172.0	49.7
Kings	3 411	20 021	1 888.6	653.2	1 932	24 955	4 555.6	893.8	3 266	23 522	1 544.4	395.6
Lewis	21	D	D	D	23	1 254	511.6	54.3	68	480	18.0	4.8
Livingston	99	D	D	D	68	2 292	463.9	86.0	146	1 790	70.8	19.5
Madison	121	D	D	D	61	2 696	941.4	101.1	157	1 943	77.6	22.6
Monroe	1 947	22 172	2 654.9	1 237.9	939	49 854	16 615.4	2 345.4	1 531	24 626	1 061.3	307.5
Montgomery	67	D	D	D	74	3 483	719.5	132.6	120	1 073	42.0	12.0
Nassau	7 008	D	D	D	1 221	D	D	1 034.1	3 192	39 540	2 439.4	680.0
New York	17 114	263 221	72 850.5	26 601.0	2 731	37 037	8 315.1	1 396.0	8 583	175 329	17 182.6	4 753.4
Niagara	338	D	D	D	270	10 209	3 433.1	526.8	490	8 908	662.4	150.8
Oneida	390	D	D	D	261	10 874	3 251.8	437.3	506	5 862	260.5	74.7
Onondaga	1 214	D	D	D	482	23 308	7 251.5	1 213.7	1 112	17 535	784.3	229.2
Ontario	245	D	D	D	156	6 949	2 097.3	295.7	281	4 645	206.3	62.0
Orange	901	D	D	D	337	7 510	2 353.5	321.0	792	8 755	454.7	123.2
Orleans	37	D	D	D	36	1 853	465.2	67.5	64	652	21.3	5.9
Oswego	127	D	D	D	90	3 535	2 441.3	152.4	258	3 262	128.1	34.9
Otsego	105	D	D	D	58	919	177.8	34.9	193	2 170	121.7	31.0
Putnam	339	D	D	D	92	2 030	D	103.5	209	1 704	94.4	24.5
Queens	2 858	D	D	D	1 433	29 325	5 654.4	1 159.3	3 619	32 175	2 223.4	577.7
Rensselaer	305	D	D	D	111	3 040	D	133.8	309	3 929	171.8	47.8
Richmond	895	D	D	D	137	1 325	D	53.5	658	7 506	401.6	101.9
Rockland	1 225	D	D	D	266	10 344	13 670.4	540.7	689	7 222	435.3	121.2
St. Lawrence	122	D	D	D	82	3 601	2 141.6	180.7	247	3 033	116.6	31.5
Saratoga	589	D	D	D	132	5 287	1 783.6	274.6	487	6 869	333.5	99.7
Schenectady	288	D	D	D	120	4 317	1 702.5	207.6	293	3 421	151.8	44.1
Schoharie	36	D	D	D	NA	NA	NA	NA	64	450	21.6	5.2
Schuyler	15	D	D	D	29	D	D	D	61	387	25.5	6.8
Seneca	32	D	D	D	39	1 197	428.1	58.2	70	685	33.0	8.7
Steuben	151	D	D	D	82	6 168	1 821.2	305.7	221	2 295	103.4	27.7
Suffolk	5 588	D	D	D	2 356	64 453	19 089.7	3 021.9	3 274	39 934	2 376.4	651.5
Sullivan	171	D	D	D	52	1 129	243.8	33.5	243	2 027	120.7	33.2
Tioga	59	D	D	D	38	1 700	535.8	D	79	868	32.7	10.2
Tompkins	273	D	D	D	92	3 152	742.8	137.3	308	3 742	177.7	51.9
Ulster	455	D	D	D	202	D	D	165.3	533	6 542	321.4	103.9
Warren	180	944	94.7	37.4	74	4 240	1 130.5	170.1	418	4 956	300.0	91.2
Washington	70	252	19.0	6.4	102	3 023	832.2	132.7	111	623	25.0	6.6
Wayne	105	D	D	D	134	6 009	1 889.0	242.2	148	1 406	52.3	14.8
Westchester	4 401	27 021	4 865.8	2 046.8	697	14 835	4 122.9	669.0	2 176	25 314	1 799.3	483.6
Wyoming	51	D	D	D	54	2 185	457.0	77.6	78	692	31.1	8.5
Yates	33	D	D	D	32	844	D	30.6	55	446	24.4	6.5
NORTH CAROLINA	22 385	182 224	26 003.8	10 698.3	10 150	506 013	205 867.3	19 589.8	18 268	343 235	16 126.9	4 395.1
Alamance	233	D	D	D	236	11 733	3 163.1	445.0	281	5 080	219.4	62.8
Alexander	37	D	D	D	80	3 931	604.8	120.1	44	697	22.6	6.4
Alleghany	13	56	4.6	1.2	17	628	109.2	18.2	21	186	11.3	3.2
Anson	31	D	D	D	25	1 449	D	49.1	27	D	D	D
Ashe	25	105	4.7	2.6	22	1 122	206.3	35.3	45	634	22.6	6.5
Avery	39	117	11.1	3.1	NA	NA	NA	NA	49	604	33.6	11.9
Beaufort	91	330	25.8	9.6	56	3 317	1 215.6	147.4	80	1 450	49.9	13.1
Bertie	12	57	4.7	1.4	17	2 099	D	52.2	14	152	5.6	1.4
Bladen	31	154	18.6	4.3	31	5 738	1 530.9	164.7	41	448	23.3	5.3
Brunswick	212	D	D	D	75	2 008	D	80.1	238	3 285	150.6	42.5
Buncombe	826	D	D	D	310	11 987	3 211.7	470.5	658	13 930	684.3	203.1
Burke	125	D	D	D	158	9 740	2 271.2	307.2	126	2 637	107.7	28.0
Cabarrus	347	D	D	D	188	8 103	D	394.6	324	6 659	321.5	90.2
Caldwell	93	413	39.9	14.0	142	9 418	1 558.4	255.5	117	1 623	63.7	16.4
Camden	5	D	D	D	NA	NA	NA	NA	4	30	1.4	0.4
Carteret	164	666	65.1	24.7	76	1 488	292.2	43.4	226	3 424	151.0	45.1
Caswell	20	43	4.3	1.4	NA	NA	NA	NA	17	149	5.4	1.4
Catawba	329	1 780	202.9	70.0	465	27 597	6 291.1	935.4	358	6 654	272.1	76.2
Chatham	135	D	D	D	82	4 982	1 129.7	167.6	74	1 036	39.6	12.7
Cherokee	61	230	14.5	5.5	28	1 258	265.4	42.1	63	898	36.8	9.7

1. Establishment subject to federal tax.

Table B. States and Counties — Health Care and Social Assistance, Other Services, and Federal Funds

STATE County	Health care and social assistance, 2007				Other services, 2007				Federal funds and grants, 2009–2010 — Expenditures (mil dol)			
										Direct payments for individuals[1]		
	Number of establishments	Number of employees	Receipts (mil dol)	Annual payroll (mil dol)	Number of establishments	Number of employees	Receipts (mil dol)	Annual payroll (mil dol)	Total	Social Security and government retirement	Medicare	Food Stamps and Supplemental Security Income
	159	160	161	162	163	164	165	166	167	168	169	170
NEW YORK—Cont'd												
Genesee	138	2 647	175.3	76.3	114	697	46.0	12.6	494.5	209.5	98.9	13.1
Greene	88	1 144	83.7	35.5	84	378	29.5	8.3	356.3	171.7	80.2	14.8
Hamilton	7	D	D	D	11	28	2.6	0.5	44.5	22.3	11.3	0.9
Herkimer	114	2 288	136.2	57.2	101	517	31.0	8.9	473.5	199.7	119.1	20.0
Jefferson	234	5 780	429.1	201.9	195	898	78.3	18.3	3 939.9	353.0	132.6	37.4
Kings	5 583	161 022	14 296.4	6 402.9	3 728	15 019	1 389.0	367.8	(2)	(2)	(2)	(2)
Lewis	55	855	63.8	25.6	44	158	15.2	3.2	234.2	80.0	33.1	8.6
Livingston	132	1 722	134.3	54.6	95	341	33.1	7.9	391.1	189.2	85.2	17.8
Madison	166	3 088	238.0	98.8	110	377	33.0	7.8	441.0	214.5	84.5	15.7
Monroe	1 842	57 096	4 771.0	2 015.8	1 188	7 877	802.1	210.9	8 153.1	2 203.1	1 242.2	302.7
Montgomery	177	3 928	341.6	131.3	93	471	34.8	9.3	431.0	182.9	120.0	19.0
Nassau	5 468	93 663	10 928.4	4 452.3	3 837	19 915	1 990.6	549.8	11 807.8	4 184.1	3 074.2	168.7
New York	7 612	221 081	26 406.6	10 594.3	8 951	77 817	22 175.4	3 558.5	(2)84 734.2	(2)15 179.6	(2)18 481.9	(2)5 935.4
Niagara	525	10 180	700.6	294.5	347	1 603	108.7	30.2	1 844.5	814.0	405.1	75.4
Oneida	613	19 752	1 470.7	696.7	412	3 017	192.8	57.4	2 369.5	847.3	440.4	104.5
Onondaga	1 276	34 330	3 449.0	1 451.7	875	6 075	549.0	157.6	4 842.0	1 424.2	706.8	180.3
Ontario	233	6 834	523.6	257.8	213	1 115	83.8	23.1	851.6	372.2	145.8	22.6
Orange	993	19 291	1 706.1	771.0	740	3 887	436.7	98.5	3 184.7	978.8	488.2	93.8
Orleans	92	1 541	92.8	40.8	63	198	14.5	3.3	287.9	131.1	61.4	12.7
Oswego	216	4 739	316.5	138.8	173	706	47.1	12.4	950.8	382.5	157.6	43.3
Otsego	166	5 311	528.4	232.3	109	599	83.4	10.4	477.8	204.0	100.2	15.7
Putnam	269	4 944	483.4	199.1	244	1 081	126.3	35.3	490.4	264.3	126.8	6.9
Queens	4 492	113 126	10 607.0	4 480.8	4 042	18 673	1 754.2	509.4	(2)	(2)	(2)	(2)
Rensselaer	364	8 983	702.4	317.7	241	1 427	143.4	43.5	2 796.0	485.2	249.3	50.7
Richmond	1 155	27 313	2 449.3	1 101.3	763	3 659	309.0	82.8	(2)	(2)	(2)	(2)
Rockland	1 129	21 162	1 829.5	815.0	688	3 019	297.1	81.4	2 132.0	823.8	515.7	56.9
St. Lawrence	294	6 372	455.2	200.8	147	707	55.3	14.2	1 001.0	362.4	164.2	50.1
Saratoga	500	7 674	608.5	245.7	285	1 860	145.7	45.8	1 170.4	652.3	217.7	30.5
Schenectady	451	10 861	867.2	407.5	207	1 481	128.2	33.4	1 684.8	533.0	282.0	55.1
Schoharie	62	1 202	72.4	30.4	37	182	15.4	4.0	229.6	102.6	47.9	8.8
Schuyler	40	828	61.1	23.0	28	134	12.6	2.7	135.7	62.2	24.8	6.0
Seneca	66	1 457	83.2	37.8	44	193	14.3	3.8	231.8	110.1	49.4	7.3
Steuben	250	5 902	447.9	194.8	152	723	55.8	12.6	842.1	357.7	158.8	37.9
Suffolk	4 546	85 581	8 923.6	3 788.5	3 767	17 775	1 746.8	492.8	12 110.2	4 475.1	2 501.9	230.0
Sullivan	257	4 074	361.5	155.5	163	497	165.2	14.6	728.1	243.1	166.7	25.7
Tioga	74	855	49.9	20.4	67	221	19.0	5.2	1 020.2	152.3	57.5	16.5
Tompkins	250	4 919	388.7	152.9	149	945	129.2	21.6	939.3	220.0	84.8	21.6
Ulster	520	D	D	D	316	1 559	117.0	30.2	1 284.7	551.4	269.0	46.9
Warren	259	6 492	526.3	243.7	145	743	71.0	20.9	510.6	251.7	97.0	15.2
Washington	106	1 424	84.5	39.5	75	286	26.8	6.9	416.9	200.8	86.3	18.5
Wayne	155	2 322	153.3	68.8	134	408	33.6	8.0	719.3	308.7	138.1	24.2
Westchester	3 543	70 365	7 454.7	3 252.3	2 733	13 610	2 092.1	482.3	7 147.3	2 609.5	2 007.8	207.9
Wyoming	66	1 294	84.9	37.6	60	242	19.8	5.4	286.9	121.6	56.5	8.8
Yates	55	D	D	D	38	130	11.8	2.3	181.3	88.4	37.3	7.4
NORTH CAROLINA	21 712	523 397	46 688.8	19 047.4	14 105	85 304	9 362.1	2 216.6	90 736.7	28 314.0	10 370.8	3 369.2
Alamance	335	6 483	549.1	227.9	201	1 165	93.5	27.7	925.3	465.3	191.6	35.2
Alexander	45	637	35.9	15.0	46	200	12.3	2.5	195.1	105.1	39.4	7.2
Alleghany	29	504	27.7	11.6	13	26	2.7	0.6	105.0	45.0	20.6	3.4
Anson	43	668	36.8	15.1	24	76	7.1	1.4	237.8	77.5	49.3	19.5
Ashe	53	1 151	64.3	30.9	34	118	10.4	2.6	256.8	96.1	41.1	10.8
Avery	42	1 137	75.6	27.1	34	241	15.7	5.3	153.8	64.1	33.8	7.8
Beaufort	140	2 810	170.8	79.7	90	363	28.7	8.3	498.6	201.9	69.3	29.2
Bertie	68	1 684	69.8	33.2	26	94	8.1	1.9	242.3	71.2	40.0	19.5
Bladen	73	1 375	79.3	33.1	29	136	8.7	3.3	330.6	109.7	52.3	26.2
Brunswick	189	2 834	216.4	88.0	103	542	41.7	10.5	913.2	531.7	112.3	35.0
Buncombe	757	20 467	2 071.2	821.5	437	2 703	222.9	64.3	1 966.7	841.3	327.5	91.5
Burke	205	4 028	380.6	148.4	97	357	32.3	8.0	579.1	278.2	117.3	25.7
Cabarrus	333	9 224	692.5	325.0	246	1 272	120.1	30.7	905.2	477.0	202.2	40.0
Caldwell	128	3 262	228.5	88.4	85	439	35.1	10.2	517.3	260.6	106.5	25.8
Camden	6	D	D	D	9	76	5.4	2.1	72.4	42.7	10.4	2.7
Carteret	176	3 206	234.8	97.8	143	657	52.6	14.3	592.4	321.3	85.5	21.6
Caswell	29	463	18.1	9.9	17	62	4.0	1.0	188.8	72.8	29.6	12.3
Catawba	383	9 682	953.0	378.2	255	1 587	177.8	46.5	932.7	504.8	163.8	41.6
Chatham	117	3 903	236.4	89.8	85	377	29.3	10.2	320.3	166.7	64.4	11.5
Cherokee	84	1 489	109.2	44.9	37	128	8.7	2.4	258.1	125.2	42.5	11.8

1. State totals may include programs not allocated by county. 2. Bronx, Kings, Queens, and Richmond counties are included with New York county.

Table B. States and Counties — Federal Funds, Residential Construction, and Local Government Finances

	Federal funds and grants, 2009–2010 (cont.)							Value of residential construction authorized by building permits, 2010		Local government finances, 2007				
	Expenditures (mil dol) (cont.)									General revenue				
		Procurement contract awards		Grants[1]								Taxes		
													Per capita[2] (dollars)	
STATE County	Salaries and wages	Defense	Other	Medicaid and other health-related	Nutrition and family welfare	Education	Other	New construction ($1,000)	Number of housing units	Total (mil dol)	Inter-govern-mental (mil dol)	Total (mil dol)	Total	Property
	171	172	173	174	175	176	177	178	179	180	181	182	183	184

NEW YORK—Cont'd

Genesee	32.8	1.7	36.4	58.7	14.0	5.9	5.4	7 435	47	363.9	149.6	118.5	2 039	1 336
Greene	11.7	0.1	2.8	50.0	13.1	3.9	4.3	17 616	93	271.3	103.3	133.8	2 717	2 064
Hamilton	1.8	0.0	0.4	2.9	1.3	1.4	1.8	10 472	48	50.3	8.9	36.8	7 247	6 576
Herkimer	9.7	4.7	2.8	81.5	16.9	5.8	2.0	16 862	96	326.4	163.9	114.8	1 836	1 408
Jefferson	2 943.0	230.5	12.3	140.2	33.4	25.9	9.2	26 799	291	544.9	266.1	179.5	1 532	964
Kings	(3)	(3)	(3)	(3)	(3)	(3)	(3)	242 122	2 093	(3)	(3)	(3)	(3)	(3)
Lewis	6.2	50.5	1.4	40.5	8.3	1.5	0.2	8 519	104	183.5	72.8	46.4	1 754	1 346
Livingston	13.9	1.1	3.8	52.4	15.3	4.8	1.2	11 446	95	316.0	138.3	118.8	1 880	1 421
Madison	12.7	0.2	3.3	69.7	18.1	5.5	8.8	14 853	92	327.5	148.0	128.8	1 845	1 521
Monroe	356.6	1 843.6	154.8	1 221.5	188.8	136.7	282.4	151 659	872	3 806.5	1 598.4	1 653.3	2 266	1 679
Montgomery	9.6	5.7	3.4	64.2	14.0	3.2	4.4	15 105	140	266.7	122.6	92.5	1 900	1 334
Nassau	626.4	1 713.7	170.4	1 205.6	243.0	64.2	112.2	169 369	523	9 563.1	2 092.4	6 273.3	4 802	3 885
New York	(3)4 625.6	(3)611.4	(3)2 225.2	(3)25 615.8	(3)2 238.1	(3)908.3	(3)5 772.1	80 137	704	(3)79 683.6	(3)27 746.0	(3)38 163.8	(3)4 612	(3)1 595
Niagara	101.6	54.3	13.9	253.9	57.2	16.1	16.3	42 047	237	1 116.5	490.8	424.7	1 977	1 433
Oneida	226.9	157.4	21.1	408.8	64.3	21.7	38.5	32 882	218	1 130.5	557.2	409.5	1 763	1 096
Onondaga	355.8	1 051.3	204.8	545.7	116.8	45.5	126.7	117 976	845	2 450.7	1 091.0	970.5	2 138	1 475
Ontario	63.8	65.7	40.6	82.7	22.8	7.4	7.4	55 957	320	541.4	207.5	243.1	2 339	1 682
Orange	869.6	196.3	43.5	340.6	80.8	24.6	32.6	107 578	1 007	2 111.5	755.0	1 059.5	2 809	2 125
Orleans	8.0	0.5	10.7	38.4	13.3	3.7	1.2	3 479	27	197.4	103.7	66.9	1 578	1 241
Oswego	28.4	139.5	6.3	135.5	34.9	9.5	7.5	24 325	202	618.7	297.9	216.9	1 786	1 328
Otsego	13.4	2.2	17.3	94.4	18.3	3.2	3.6	6 018	62	289.3	126.9	115.0	1 843	1 240
Putnam	14.8	2.2	3.8	37.7	17.0	7.5	6.9	26 721	81	558.6	147.0	356.6	3 585	3 027
Queens	(3)	(3)	(3)	(3)	(3)	(3)	(3)	272 502	2 358	(3)	(3)	(3)	(3)	(3)
Rensselaer	65.2	7.0	12.0	584.4	1 070.4	11.8	212.9	50 805	332	831.2	336.9	320.2	2 062	1 562
Richmond	(3)	(3)	(3)	(3)	(3)	(3)	(3)	82 093	508	(3)	(3)	(3)	(3)	(3)
Rockland	76.1	70.9	28.1	349.5	70.8	20.8	49.4	49 438	294	1 909.0	467.2	1 165.1	3 930	3 196
St. Lawrence	51.2	32.1	32.8	205.0	33.7	9.8	43.3	14 490	176	562.7	263.3	174.0	1 584	1 193
Saratoga	44.0	29.9	11.9	106.3	44.0	7.5	15.6	137 195	612	906.0	308.3	471.9	2 186	1 615
Schenectady	113.9	301.9	34.0	185.5	37.3	13.0	108.5	23 598	130	805.1	299.0	370.8	2 459	1 776
Schoharie	7.0	0.0	1.7	46.1	9.6	2.4	1.3	5 897	34	173.9	83.2	76.6	2 389	1 842
Schuyler	4.5	0.0	1.2	27.4	5.5	2.0	1.3	3 569	40	85.9	40.5	33.0	1 735	1 266
Seneca	7.6	4.1	2.6	38.6	7.2	1.6	1.5	11 167	68	161.6	69.9	65.9	1 925	1 312
Steuben	48.7	31.7	28.0	122.1	28.6	8.7	3.9	13 208	104	536.4	259.9	185.7	1 917	1 402
Suffolk	931.2	744.7	1 038.5	1 520.4	286.3	88.0	192.9	380 576	971	9 421.8	2 747.3	5 704.5	3 925	2 946
Sullivan	18.9	0.1	17.5	203.7	21.7	7.8	14.4	35 040	244	521.8	173.2	250.9	3 288	2 718
Tioga	13.1	725.4	2.1	33.4	14.1	3.0	1.1	7 036	48	233.9	119.7	85.8	1 700	1 210
Tompkins	39.8	18.9	15.5	210.4	23.7	11.1	260.2	22 337	153	478.3	175.8	213.9	2 117	1 557
Ulster	54.7	6.1	10.4	260.8	43.2	12.7	10.8	43 306	334	984.4	317.9	535.2	2 943	2 321
Warren	22.8	1.2	5.3	78.5	17.4	3.4	7.4	29 140	151	371.8	120.3	194.9	2 947	2 031
Washington	12.1	0.4	3.0	66.2	19.1	5.5	1.2	11 593	128	308.7	145.8	112.3	1 791	1 470
Wayne	18.1	28.5	43.3	114.3	24.1	7.8	4.5	21 524	135	465.3	215.0	173.6	1 902	1 566
Westchester	408.7	102.7	157.3	1 066.0	190.4	62.2	166.8	118 180	357	7 597.5	1 831.6	4 184.1	4 398	3 576
Wyoming	9.3	0.8	40.1	31.7	9.8	3.4	0.2	4 123	28	198.1	77.2	60.1	1 433	1 058
Yates	9.8	0.2	1.4	24.1	5.8	1.4	0.6	8 253	44	104.1	40.7	49.1	2 001	1 578
NORTH CAROLINA	15 349.4	3 626.5	2 464.0	11 594.5	2 009.1	1 865.6	4 629.7	5 107 163	33 889	X	X	X	X	X
Alamance	28.0	5.2	9.0	128.2	19.4	10.3	9.6	79 992	847	402.1	208.0	128.4	883	667
Alexander	5.5	0.0	1.1	23.9	5.7	2.7	2.2	10 838	47	70.3	40.9	20.0	550	337
Alleghany	3.4	0.0	1.2	27.3	1.8	0.9	0.5	7 854	39	30.5	17.2	10.4	952	714
Anson	12.1	0.1	2.2	58.4	6.2	3.4	1.5	4 667	31	86.2	55.3	18.3	726	556
Ashe	10.5	0.0	1.4	68.8	4.4	2.0	20.4	16 601	90	61.7	33.8	21.9	858	591
Avery	4.4	0.5	1.3	33.5	4.2	1.6	0.3	21 789	50	52.1	24.3	22.4	1 263	954
Beaufort	15.6	25.0	2.7	90.7	9.7	6.2	19.8	21 845	211	145.2	81.7	41.0	895	645
Bertie	6.1	0.0	2.2	84.0	7.2	2.3	0.1	2 507	24	60.4	41.0	12.3	660	478
Bladen	13.5	4.8	1.2	90.2	7.2	5.2	2.0	5 908	38	148.2	61.3	26.7	826	605
Brunswick	25.6	85.6	6.9	73.1	11.0	4.0	19.0	184 875	1 079	334.9	99.6	147.9	1 491	1 097
Buncombe	214.1	27.9	116.1	226.2	36.9	19.2	25.9	186 373	1 588	757.9	315.7	298.7	1 317	949
Burke	13.9	6.4	5.4	89.4	14.8	13.6	1.0	24 514	113	243.3	150.0	53.0	595	478
Cabarrus	41.6	1.9	8.7	88.3	18.9	9.5	9.2	84 035	671	531.3	215.0	193.4	1 185	923
Caldwell	16.4	0.0	4.0	66.2	13.4	6.8	3.9	20 099	132	213.9	126.5	55.0	692	498
Camden	3.7	0.0	0.4	7.9	1.3	0.4	0.1	4 922	16	28.4	18.3	8.3	877	628
Carteret	49.1	12.3	10.2	46.0	14.4	4.7	15.2	40 683	216	308.4	95.0	86.1	1 361	958
Caswell	3.4	0.0	0.8	54.3	4.1	1.7	1.2	7 579	40	51.7	31.8	13.7	590	392
Catawba	68.3	2.3	14.6	75.5	18.8	11.4	12.3	40 537	156	625.4	225.5	145.7	936	676
Chatham	13.9	1.1	1.7	42.1	7.1	2.7	5.3	59 434	263	148.0	57.6	65.0	1 057	784
Cherokee	6.1	0.6	4.7	51.1	7.1	2.1	2.4	19 133	108	80.3	43.3	25.2	951	639

1. State totals may include programs not allocated by county.   2. Based on the resident population estimated as of July 1 of the year shown.   3. Bronx, Kings, Queens, and Richmond counties are included with New York county.

490 NY(Genesee)—NC(Cherokee)   Items 171—184

STATE County	Total (mil dol)	Per capita[1] (dollars)	Education	Health and hospitals	Police protection	Public welfare	Highways	Total (mil dol)	Per capita[1] (dollars)	Federal civilian	Federal military	State and local	Democratic	Republican	All other
	Local government finances, 2007 (cont.)									Government employment, 2009			Presidential election,[2] 2008		
	Direct general expenditure							Debt outstanding					Percent of vote cast:		
			Percent of total for:												
	185	186	187	188	189	190	191	192	193	194	195	196	197	198	199
NEW YORK—Cont'd															
Genesee	364.2	6 266	49.9	4.2	2.6	10.9	5.1	188.7	3 246	720	95	5 384	40.1	58.5	1.5
Greene	265.5	5 392	48.1	4.6	1.6	9.3	9.3	180.5	3 665	117	79	4 335	44.1	54.0	1.8
Hamilton	50.9	10 026	37.3	5.3	1.4	3.1	13.8	17.7	3 496	20	0	726	35.9	62.8	1.3
Herkimer	318.3	5 089	54.6	3.1	1.7	9.8	9.5	212.3	3 393	121	103	4 542	44.5	53.8	1.7
Jefferson	553.1	4 719	50.1	3.3	2.3	9.3	8.0	410.6	3 503	3 448	18 148	8 387	46.8	52.0	1.2
Kings	(3)	(3)	(3)	(3)	(3)	(3)	(3)	(3)	(3)	7 907	4 573	28 603	79.4	20.0	0.6
Lewis	170.8	6 452	37.7	24.8	1.0	6.7	8.3	80.9	3 056	65	42	2 422	44.8	53.6	1.6
Livingston	307.4	4 864	44.3	5.3	2.4	18.2	7.6	285.5	4 517	168	102	6 841	45.3	53.2	1.5
Madison	310.4	4 446	52.4	4.0	2.1	7.6	8.4	335.1	4 799	155	113	4 567	49.3	48.5	2.2
Monroe	4 099.3	5 618	47.3	3.7	4.0	11.2	2.6	2 659.9	3 645	2 895	1 268	45 901	58.3	40.5	1.2
Montgomery	270.1	5 547	49.4	2.3	2.0	11.9	6.7	210.9	4 331	119	79	3 033	45.0	53.1	1.9
Nassau	9 819.3	7 516	46.5	7.1	8.4	5.4	3.2	7 779.0	5 954	6 140	2 622	79 114	53.8	45.4	0.7
New York	(3)70 161.5	(3)8 479	(3)26.7	(3)9.9	(3)5.5	(3)15.2	(3)2.1	(3)116 285.7	(3)14 053	24 204	2 866	430 849	85.7	13.5	0.8
Niagara	1 117.2	5 200	50.3	2.6	3.5	9.8	3.1	984.1	4 580	1 112	371	13 943	49.7	48.7	1.6
Oneida	1 147.4	4 939	50.3	2.4	3.3	11.4	6.4	1 212.2	5 218	2 640	442	25 745	46.1	52.2	1.6
Onondaga	2 606.9	5 742	46.5	3.7	3.8	10.8	4.1	2 425.0	5 341	4 166	1 015	36 926	59.3	38.9	1.8
Ontario	554.5	5 334	56.8	3.0	2.8	7.8	6.7	484.6	4 662	1 232	173	7 232	49.2	49.3	1.5
Orange	2 169.5	5 752	54.6	3.2	3.7	9.9	3.3	1 367.0	3 624	5 309	6 645	22 678	51.6	47.4	1.0
Orleans	190.2	4 488	52.1	4.4	2.1	15.2	5.5	135.1	3 187	97	68	4 209	39.9	58.6	1.5
Oswego	600.3	4 943	57.7	2.9	2.0	9.7	5.9	464.2	3 822	283	224	9 084	50.3	47.9	1.8
Otsego	280.4	4 494	49.5	3.1	1.6	13.5	8.8	236.1	3 784	153	101	4 866	52.0	46.1	1.9
Putnam	568.4	5 713	58.6	2.5	3.7	3.8	5.1	391.6	3 936	172	161	4 615	45.8	53.3	1.0
Queens	(3)	(3)	(3)	(3)	(3)	(3)	(3)	(3)	(3)	14 699	3 746	22 297	75.1	24.3	0.6
Rensselaer	863.1	5 557	52.3	3.8	3.0	12.6	3.2	916.6	5 902	440	263	11 179	53.7	44.4	1.9
Richmond	(3)	(3)	(3)	(3)	(0)	(3)	(3)	(3)	(3)	1 272	1 289	5 698	47.6	51.7	0.7
Rockland	1 999.7	6 745	46.1	9.5	4.7	6.4	3.3	1 991.3	6 716	586	487	21 650	52.6	46.7	0.6
St. Lawrence	553.7	5 043	46.8	10.1	2.3	10.5	7.7	449.1	4 090	632	199	9 902	57.5	41.1	1.4
Saratoga	933.7	4 325	56.3	4.0	2.6	7.8	5.9	779.4	3 611	431	1 646	12 329	50.9	47.5	1.6
Schenectady	798.4	5 294	45.3	2.5	3.7	15.1	3.9	547.6	3 631	663	259	10 610	55.3	42.8	2.0
Schoharie	165.3	5 155	52.4	4.3	1.2	8.8	10.6	111.2	3 469	90	51	2 819	41.8	56.1	2.1
Schuyler	82.5	4 336	38.9	5.1	1.8	10.7	11.5	49.1	2 581	55	30	1 230	45.7	52.8	1.6
Seneca	170.3	4 976	49.5	4.0	2.6	9.3	5.3	259.1	7 571	101	59	3 132	50.4	47.8	1.8
Steuben	533.0	5 502	56.0	3.7	1.6	11.4	8.4	357.9	3 694	1 033	157	7 472	40.9	57.8	1.3
Suffolk	9 396.9	6 466	53.7	3.8	5.5	5.4	3.4	6 883.1	4 736	11 967	2 706	96 499	52.6	46.6	0.9
Sullivan	507.4	6 649	47.4	4.6	2.7	12.4	7.8	371.8	4 873	233	123	6 189	54.1	44.6	1.3
Tioga	216.4	4 290	53.9	4.1	2.0	9.1	6.3	125.6	2 488	172	88	2 627	44.1	54.3	1.7
Tompkins	492.8	4 876	48.5	4.3	2.7	7.5	7.6	461.8	4 570	300	182	6 596	70.2	28.1	1.7
Ulster	971.0	5 340	51.6	2.6	3.4	12.6	4.9	738.4	4 060	460	314	14 005	61.0	37.4	1.7
Warren	374.5	5 662	44.0	3.9	2.6	9.9	6.4	328.4	4 965	219	108	4 835	50.6	47.9	1.5
Washington	313.9	5 003	57.4	3.4	1.6	11.0	8.0	175.2	2 793	160	102	5 489	49.5	48.7	1.7
Wayne	454.6	4 980	57.5	4.2	2.0	10.6	5.3	264.8	2 900	204	150	8 044	44.3	54.2	1.4
Westchester	7 721.6	8 117	42.3	12.0	4.6	6.3	2.7	5 783.0	6 079	4 717	1 548	61 631	63.4	35.8	0.8
Wyoming	194.8	4 646	36.8	25.1	2.7	7.3	8.6	106.7	2 544	112	67	4 318	36.1	62.3	1.6
Yates	101.6	4 135	43.0	6.1	3.8	8.4	10.7	88.6	3 608	76	40	1 228	47.6	51.3	1.0
NORTH CAROLINA	X	X	X	X	X	X	X	X	X	67 749	142 715	645 164	49.7	49.4	0.9
Alamance	417.6	2 873	49.4	8.4	5.8	6.2	2.8	191.4	1 317	258	379	6 952	44.9	54.2	0.9
Alexander	69.5	1 909	60.4	6.1	3.1	10.0	0.6	16.8	461	53	92	1 942	29.9	68.3	1.7
Alleghany	29.8	2 729	54.7	4.1	4.0	9.2	0.2	7.3	665	55	28	679	38.4	59.4	2.2
Anson	87.3	3 464	64.5	2.9	3.9	7.8	1.0	9.5	376	55	63	2 628	60.2	39.2	0.7
Ashe	57.3	2 245	52.7	2.4	3.7	12.4	0.8	16.4	643	63	65	1 262	37.3	60.6	2.2
Avery	48.1	2 707	46.5	4.6	4.6	7.8	3.0	23.6	1 325	53	45	1 580	27.4	71.5	1.1
Beaufort	154.8	3 382	55.9	2.6	4.2	8.8	0.9	84.3	1 841	141	117	2 865	41.1	58.5	0.4
Bertie	59.2	3 180	64.4	0.9	3.9	12.0	1.1	25.4	1 363	97	49	1 312	65.2	34.6	0.2
Bladen	149.6	4 631	39.2	19.9	2.9	6.4	0.7	26.2	810	113	81	2 358	50.7	48.7	0.6
Brunswick	345.4	3 482	32.5	11.1	5.7	5.2	1.6	231.5	2 333	428	323	4 759	40.5	58.5	1.0
Buncombe	784.7	3 460	40.5	7.5	4.3	5.9	1.5	412.7	1 820	2 972	629	13 539	56.3	42.4	1.3
Burke	242.3	2 723	54.2	10.3	4.8	8.1	0.8	121.5	1 366	142	225	7 934	39.8	59.0	1.2
Cabarrus	557.8	3 416	48.5	4.9	5.4	5.7	2.6	658.2	4 031	293	433	13 106	40.4	58.9	0.7
Caldwell	219.8	2 767	58.6	4.1	4.7	9.1	1.7	103.6	1 304	136	201	4 376	34.4	64.1	1.6
Camden	24.2	2 554	63.0	0.3	4.5	5.7	0.0	10.8	1 143	20	24	483	33.1	65.1	1.7
Carteret	308.0	4 870	31.2	34.5	3.9	3.7	1.8	158.8	2 510	300	450	4 656	32.2	66.9	1.0
Caswell	49.7	2 138	55.8	6.1	3.7	10.3	0.0	10.2	440	47	58	1 414	51.0	47.9	1.0
Catawba	617.0	3 964	38.1	30.9	3.5	6.9	1.4	248.1	1 594	539	402	9 720	36.9	61.9	1.2
Chatham	144.9	2 358	55.9	3.9	4.9	8.1	0.8	112.3	1 828	148	163	2 423	54.3	44.6	1.1
Cherokee	81.1	3 061	51.9	5.7	4.1	6.2	0.5	26.2	989	114	66	1 563	30.1	68.7	1.3

1. Based on the resident population estimated as of July 1 of the year shown.   2. © 2009 Election Data Services, Inc. All rights reserved.   3. Bronx, Kings, Queens, and Richmond counties are included with New York county.

Table B. States and Counties — **Land Area and Population**

STATE/ County code	CBSA code[1]	County type[2]	STATE County	Population and population characteristics, 2010				Race alone or in combination, not Hispanic or Latino (percent)					Age (percent)					
				Land area,[3] (sq km) 2010	Total persons	Rank	Per square kilometer	White	Black	American Indian, Alaska Native	Asian and Pacific Islander	Percent Hispanic or Latino[4]	Under 5 years	5 to 17 years	18 to 24 years	25 to 34 years	35 to 44 years	45 to 54 years
				1	2	3	4	5	6	7	8	9	10	11	12	13	14	15
			NORTH CAROLINA—Cont'd															
37 041	...	7	Chowan	447	14 793	2 127	33.1	62.0	34.7	0.6	0.5	3.2	5.9	16.5	7.0	10.4	10.4	14.8
37 043	...	9	Clay	556	10 587	2 397	19.0	96.4	0.9	1.0	0.5	2.4	4.7	14.0	6.0	9.0	10.7	14.2
37 045	43140	4	Cleveland	1 202	98 078	593	81.6	75.4	21.5	0.6	1.0	2.8	5.9	17.5	9.1	10.6	13.4	15.0
37 047	...	6	Columbus	2 428	58 098	878	23.9	61.3	31.0	3.9	0.5	4.6	6.0	17.2	8.5	12.1	12.8	14.7
37 049	35100	5	Craven	1 836	103 505	563	56.4	68.9	23.3	1.0	2.9	6.1	7.4	16.0	12.1	13.2	11.0	13.1
37 051	22180	2	Cumberland	1 689	319 431	199	189.1	50.0	37.8	2.6	3.8	9.5	8.3	18.5	12.7	15.8	12.6	13.0
37 053	47260	1	Currituck	678	23 547	1 662	34.7	90.0	6.4	1.0	1.1	3.0	5.6	18.1	7.2	10.4	14.5	18.2
37 055	28620	5	Dare	993	33 920	1 327	34.2	90.0	3.1	0.9	1.0	6.5	5.4	14.6	6.5	12.0	13.4	17.1
37 057	45640	4	Davidson	1 431	162 878	376	113.8	83.0	9.3	0.8	1.5	6.4	6.1	17.7	7.5	11.2	14.6	15.6
37 059	49180	2	Davie	684	41 240	1 150	60.3	86.8	7.0	0.7	0.8	6.1	5.7	17.9	6.4	9.8	13.8	15.8
37 061	...	6	Duplin	2 114	58 505	873	27.7	53.6	25.5	0.7	0.4	20.6	7.3	18.1	8.5	12.5	13.0	14.0
37 063	20500	2	Durham	741	267 587	244	361.1	43.4	38.6	0.8	5.3	13.5	7.4	15.1	12.0	18.3	14.1	12.8
37 065	40580	3	Edgecombe	1 309	56 552	891	43.2	38.4	57.8	0.6	0.4	3.7	6.6	18.0	8.7	11.5	12.0	15.1
37 067	49180	2	Forsyth	1 057	350 670	184	331.8	60.0	26.5	0.7	2.3	11.9	6.8	17.5	10.1	12.8	13.4	14.5
37 069	39580	2	Franklin	1 273	60 619	851	47.6	64.5	27.2	1.0	0.7	7.9	6.6	17.9	8.2	11.6	14.6	15.7
37 071	16740	1	Gaston	922	206 086	299	223.5	77.2	15.9	0.8	1.5	5.9	6.4	17.5	8.5	12.0	14.8	15.0
37 073	...	8	Gates	882	12 197	2 292	13.8	64.2	34.2	1.3	0.6	1.4	5.7	18.1	7.8	9.7	13.2	17.0
37 075	...	9	Graham	756	8 861	2 539	11.7	91.1	0.3	7.4	0.5	2.2	5.7	15.9	7.4	10.3	11.7	14.5
37 077	...	6	Granville	1 377	59 916	860	43.5	58.8	33.3	0.9	0.8	7.5	5.7	16.6	8.5	12.0	15.8	16.3
37 079	24780	3	Greene	689	21 362	1 771	31.0	47.7	37.6	0.8	0.5	14.3	6.5	16.7	8.6	14.2	13.8	15.4
37 081	24660	2	Guilford	1 672	488 406	135	292.1	55.7	33.3	1.0	4.5	7.1	6.3	17.2	11.7	13.2	13.7	14.2
37 083	40260	4	Halifax	1 875	54 691	914	29.2	40.2	53.7	4.1	0.8	2.1	6.0	17.1	8.4	10.7	12.2	15.6
37 085	20380	4	Harnett	1 541	114 678	520	74.4	66.2	22.0	1.7	1.7	10.8	8.1	19.6	10.1	14.2	14.3	13.0
37 087	11700	2	Haywood	1 434	59 036	868	41.2	94.7	1.3	1.0	0.6	3.4	4.9	14.6	6.9	9.8	12.7	14.9
37 089	11700	2	Henderson	966	106 740	554	110.5	85.7	3.6	0.9	1.4	9.8	5.6	14.9	6.2	10.5	12.2	13.9
37 091	...	7	Hertford	914	24 669	1 616	27.0	35.1	60.9	1.7	0.7	2.6	5.7	15.3	10.4	11.5	12.0	15.3
37 093	22180	2	Hoke	1 012	46 952	1 025	46.4	43.4	34.8	10.7	2.2	12.4	9.7	20.5	8.9	17.9	14.0	12.6
37 095	...	9	Hyde	1 587	5 810	2 784	3.7	60.2	32.2	0.7	0.4	7.1	5.0	13.5	7.0	15.0	14.5	15.0
37 097	44380	4	Iredell	1 486	159 437	389	107.3	79.1	12.5	0.7	2.2	6.8	6.3	19.2	7.8	11.4	15.0	15.7
37 099	...	6	Jackson	1 271	40 271	1 166	31.7	83.0	2.2	10.3	1.1	5.1	5.1	12.6	19.5	11.5	10.7	12.3
37 101	39580	2	Johnston	2 049	168 878	364	82.4	70.9	15.6	0.9	0.9	12.9	7.6	20.2	7.4	12.8	16.4	14.4
37 103	35100	8	Jones	1 219	10 153	2 433	8.3	62.6	33.3	1.1	0.6	3.9	6.1	15.7	8.2	10.2	10.9	16.4
37 105	41820	4	Lee	660	57 866	880	87.7	60.4	20.4	0.9	1.2	18.3	7.3	18.4	8.4	13.0	13.3	14.1
37 107	28820	4	Lenoir	1 038	59 495	865	57.3	52.1	41.0	0.6	0.7	6.6	6.4	17.7	8.0	11.0	11.8	15.4
37 109	30740	4	Lincoln	772	78 265	694	101.4	86.9	6.0	0.7	0.8	6.7	5.9	17.7	7.5	10.8	15.3	16.2
37 111	...	6	McDowell	1 141	44 996	1 067	39.4	89.8	4.1	0.8	0.9	5.3	5.8	16.0	7.4	11.6	14.1	14.9
37 113	...	7	Macon	1 335	33 922	1 326	25.4	91.1	1.5	0.8	0.8	6.6	5.2	14.1	7.3	9.4	10.4	13.8
37 115	11700	2	Madison	1 164	20 764	1 806	17.8	96.1	1.3	1.0	0.6	2.0	4.5	15.2	9.8	10.0	12.7	14.8
37 117	...	6	Martin	1 195	24 505	1 626	20.5	52.8	43.9	0.6	0.4	3.1	5.7	16.5	7.6	9.6	11.9	15.8
37 119	16740	1	Mecklenburg	1 357	919 628	49	677.7	52.0	31.4	0.8	5.2	12.2	7.4	17.9	9.6	16.8	15.8	13.8
37 121	...	9	Mitchell	573	15 579	2 076	27.2	95.0	0.5	0.8	0.5	4.1	4.9	14.5	6.9	10.2	12.4	15.1
37 123	...	6	Montgomery	1 274	27 798	1 503	21.8	65.1	19.3	0.7	1.7	14.1	6.2	18.0	7.7	11.6	12.7	14.3
37 125	43860	4	Moore	1 807	88 247	645	48.8	78.8	14.0	1.3	1.2	6.0	5.7	16.0	6.2	10.2	11.9	13.5
37 127	40580	3	Nash	1 400	95 840	604	68.5	55.0	37.8	1.1	1.0	6.3	6.1	17.8	8.2	11.5	13.4	15.5
37 129	48900	2	New Hanover	496	202 667	304	408.6	78.2	15.3	0.9	1.8	5.3	5.8	14.2	12.5	14.6	13.2	13.5
37 131	40260	9	Northampton	1 390	22 099	1 735	15.9	39.5	58.8	0.8	0.3	1.4	5.4	15.4	7.8	9.6	11.2	15.7
37 133	27340	3	Onslow	1 975	177 772	348	90.0	71.8	16.7	1.3	3.4	10.1	9.6	15.7	23.0	16.3	10.5	10.2
37 135	20500	2	Orange	1 031	133 801	462	129.8	72.5	12.5	0.9	7.7	8.2	5.1	15.8	18.2	13.0	12.7	14.1
37 137	35100	9	Pamlico	872	13 144	2 239	15.1	75.9	20.6	0.9	0.7	3.1	4.6	13.4	6.9	9.8	10.8	15.6
37 139	21020	7	Pasquotank	588	40 661	1 161	69.2	56.5	38.7	0.8	1.7	4.0	6.6	16.0	12.7	12.8	12.2	14.5
37 141	48900	2	Pender	2 253	52 217	951	23.2	75.1	18.3	1.1	0.7	6.1	5.9	16.9	7.8	11.3	13.6	15.6
37 143	21020	9	Perquimans	640	13 453	2 223	21.0	72.4	25.3	0.7	0.5	2.1	5.5	15.0	7.0	9.9	10.7	14.7
37 145	20500	2	Person	1 016	39 464	1 182	38.8	67.9	27.8	1.0	0.5	4.0	6.0	17.1	7.5	10.7	13.4	16.3
37 147	24780	3	Pitt	1 689	168 148	366	99.6	58.4	34.8	0.7	2.1	5.5	6.7	15.8	18.4	14.4	12.2	12.4
37 149	...	8	Polk	616	20 510	1 817	33.3	89.5	4.9	0.7	0.5	5.5	4.5	14.7	6.0	7.7	11.5	14.8
37 151	24660	2	Randolph	2 027	141 752	434	69.9	82.3	6.2	0.9	1.2	10.4	6.3	18.1	8.0	11.3	14.5	15.1
37 153	40460	4	Richmond	1 227	46 639	1 033	38.0	60.2	31.2	3.3	1.2	5.9	6.6	17.8	9.1	11.7	13.2	14.1
37 155	31300	4	Robeson	2 458	134 168	460	54.6	28.2	25.0	39.4	1.0	8.1	7.6	19.2	11.1	12.9	12.9	13.4
37 157	24660	2	Rockingham	1 465	93 643	614	63.9	74.7	19.6	0.9	0.7	5.5	5.6	16.6	7.6	10.5	13.7	15.9
37 159	41580	4	Rowan	1 324	138 428	443	104.6	74.8	16.7	0.8	1.2	7.7	6.5	17.3	9.0	12.0	13.3	14.9
37 161	22580	4	Rutherford	1 461	67 810	776	46.4	85.5	11.0	0.7	0.6	3.5	5.7	16.7	7.6	10.3	13.1	14.9
37 163	...	6	Sampson	2 447	63 431	823	25.9	54.2	27.5	2.4	0.6	16.5	6.9	18.7	8.1	12.0	13.6	14.1
37 165	29900	6	Scotland	826	36 157	1 271	43.8	47.5	39.2	12.2	1.0	2.1	6.9	18.2	9.2	11.4	12.7	14.4
37 167	10620	6	Stanly	1 023	60 585	852	59.2	83.3	11.5	0.6	2.0	3.6	5.9	16.7	9.2	11.0	13.5	14.9
37 169	49180	2	Stokes	1 163	47 401	1 018	40.8	92.6	4.5	0.8	0.4	2.6	5.3	16.9	7.2	9.9	14.2	16.6
37 171	34340	4	Surry	1 378	73 673	735	53.5	85.9	4.1	0.6	0.6	9.7	5.9	17.4	7.5	10.7	13.8	14.8

1. CBSA = Core Based Statistical Area. See Appendix A for explanation. See Appendix B for list of metropolitan areas with component counties. 2. County type code from the Economic Research Service of USDA Rural-Urban Continuum Codes. See Appendix A for definition. 3. Dry land or land partially or temporarily covered by water. 4. May be of any race.

Table B. States and Counties — **Population and Households**

STATE County	55 to 64 years	65 to 74 years	75 years and over	Percent female	1990	2000	1990–2000	2000–2010	Births	Deaths	Net migration	Number	Percent change, 2000–2010	Persons per household	Female family householder[1]	One person
	16	17	18	19	20	21	22	23	24	25	26	27	28	29	30	31
NORTH CAROLINA—Cont'd																
Chowan	15.3	10.8	8.9	52.5	13 506	14 526	7.6	1.8	1 687	1 723	757	6 059	8.6	2.40	16.3	27.4
Clay	17.8	13.5	10.1	50.7	7 155	8 775	22.6	20.6	778	1 113	1 917	4 660	21.1	2.25	8.2	28.2
Cleveland	13.4	8.5	6.4	51.8	84 958	96 287	13.3	1.9	11 280	9 530	1 974	38 555	4.1	2.49	15.0	25.8
Columbus	13.5	8.9	6.3	50.5	49 587	54 749	10.4	6.1	7 094	6 019	-1 283	22 489	5.5	2.45	17.1	28.7
Craven	11.9	8.4	6.8	50.3	81 812	91 436	11.8	13.2	14 765	8 309	-2 035	40 299	16.5	2.45	13.4	25.5
Cumberland	9.6	5.5	3.9	51.7	274 713	302 963	10.3	5.4	50 700	19 044	-18 062	122 431	14.0	2.53	19.0	26.5
Currituck	13.1	8.1	4.8	50.4	13 736	18 190	32.4	29.5	2 237	1 621	5 475	8 880	28.7	2.64	9.6	19.7
Dare	15.8	9.3	5.9	50.0	22 746	29 967	31.7	13.2	3 843	2 420	3 032	14 335	13.0	2.36	9.2	25.4
Davidson	12.8	8.3	6.0	51.0	126 688	147 246	16.2	10.6	17 868	13 379	7 792	64 515	10.9	2.50	12.5	24.3
Davie	14.0	9.3	7.3	51.2	27 859	34 835	25.0	18.4	4 147	3 240	5 891	16 245	18.1	2.52	10.4	22.8
Duplin	12.5	8.0	6.2	50.8	39 995	49 063	22.7	19.2	7 472	4 722	1 643	22 495	23.1	2.57	15.1	26.7
Durham	10.5	5.3	4.5	52.3	181 844	223 314	22.8	19.8	37 700	15 783	25 869	109 348	22.8	2.35	14.8	32.3
Edgecombe	13.8	8.1	6.3	53.6	56 692	55 606	-1.9	1.7	7 087	5 542	-4 984	21 680	6.3	2.54	23.4	27.1
Forsyth	11.8	6.9	6.1	52.5	265 855	306 067	15.1	14.6	44 264	26 090	25 533	141 163	14.0	2.41	15.0	30.1
Franklin	12.8	7.5	5.1	50.2	36 414	47 260	29.8	28.3	6 498	4 187	10 662	23 023	29.0	2.56	13.4	24.2
Gaston	12.5	7.4	5.8	51.6	174 769	190 365	8.9	8.3	24 586	18 227	13 271	79 867	8.0	2.54	15.4	24.6
Gates	13.6	8.9	6.1	51.1	9 305	10 516	13.0	16.0	1 100	1 090	1 290	4 665	19.6	2.60	13.6	23.2
Graham	14.8	11.1	8.5	50.7	7 196	7 993	11.1	10.9	932	920	39	3 701	10.3	2.37	10.7	26.6
Granville	12.7	7.3	5.1	46.6	38 341	48 498	26.5	23.5	5 803	4 396	7 932	20 628	23.9	2.57	15.1	24.2
Greene	12.3	6.9	5.5	46.4	15 384	18 974	23.3	12.6	2 291	1 674	1 161	7 313	9.2	2.60	17.4	26.0
Guilford	11.5	6.6	5.7	52.4	347 431	421 048	21.2	16.0	56 158	33 034	38 833	196 628	16.6	2.41	15.1	29.8
Halifax	13.9	8.7	7.4	52.2	55 516	57 370	3.3	-4.7	6 722	6 090	-3 095	21 970	-0.7	2.42	21.6	29.9
Harnett	10.1	6.2	4.3	51.0	67 833	91 025	34.2	26.0	14 008	7 233	18 410	41 594	23.1	2.68	14.9	23.4
Haywood	15.0	11.8	9.3	51.7	46 948	54 033	15.1	9.3	5 305	6 205	4 278	25 563	10.7	2.28	10.4	28.5
Henderson	14.2	11.7	10.7	51.7	69 747	89 173	27.9	19.7	10 762	11 228	15 314	45 448	21.5	2.32	9.1	28.3
Hertford	13.9	8.7	7.1	51.1	22 317	22 601	1.3	9.2	2 796	2 694	316	9 334	4.3	2.40	20.8	29.5
Hoke	9.0	4.5	2.9	51.3	22 856	33 646	47.2	39.5	7 006	2 384	7 046	16 532	45.4	2.80	18.9	20.8
Hyde	14.9	8.3	6.7	44.5	5 411	5 826	7.7	-0.3	544	597	-554	2 119	-3.0	2.35	13.7	31.2
Iredell	11.8	7.5	5.4	50.8	93 205	122 660	31.6	30.0	17 778	11 257	29 536	61 215	29.3	2.58	12.2	23.2
Jackson	13.1	9.1	6.0	50.2	26 835	33 121	23.4	21.6	3 528	2 904	3 310	16 446	24.7	2.23	9.7	32.1
Johnston	11.0	6.3	3.9	50.8	81 306	121 965	50.0	38.5	21 348	9 649	35 354	61 909	32.9	2.70	12.4	22.1
Jones	15.3	9.6	7.7	51.9	9 361	10 381	10.9	-2.2	862	1 055	-96	4 167	2.6	2.41	14.6	27.1
Lee	11.8	7.5	6.2	51.2	41 370	49 040	18.5	18.0	8 160	4 636	1 759	22 058	19.5	2.58	15.0	25.5
Lenoir	13.8	8.7	7.3	52.3	57 274	59 648	4.1	-0.3	7 300	6 462	-3 771	24 327	1.9	2.39	19.1	30.5
Lincoln	13.4	8.1	5.1	50.4	50 319	63 780	26.8	22.7	8 256	5 649	9 994	30 343	26.2	2.56	11.1	22.3
McDowell	13.9	9.3	7.1	50.0	35 681	42 151	18.1	6.7	4 822	4 062	1 851	17 838	7.4	2.43	11.7	25.8
Macon	16.1	13.2	10.6	51.4	23 504	29 811	26.8	13.8	3 245	3 784	4 095	14 591	13.7	2.29	9.4	28.9
Madison	15.3	10.0	7.7	50.5	16 953	19 635	15.8	5.7	1 940	2 087	1 061	8 494	6.2	2.32	9.4	27.1
Martin	15.4	9.9	7.7	53.3	25 078	25 593	2.1	-4.3	2 847	3 057	-1 886	10 318	3.0	2.36	16.8	29.9
Mecklenburg	9.8	5.0	3.9	51.6	511 211	695 454	36.0	32.2	124 154	44 298	142 330	362 213	32.5	2.49	14.6	29.2
Mitchell	14.9	11.8	9.1	51.2	14 433	15 687	8.7	-0.7	1 525	1 892	427	6 685	2.0	2.30	9.9	28.3
Montgomery	13.6	8.9	6.6	51.6	23 359	26 822	14.8	3.6	3 679	2 439	-163	10 544	7.1	2.53	13.1	27.2
Moore	13.8	11.4	11.2	52.2	59 000	74 769	26.7	18.0	8 855	8 710	12 642	37 540	22.2	2.33	10.8	28.1
Nash	13.5	7.8	6.2	51.7	76 677	87 420	14.0	9.6	11 396	8 484	4 918	37 782	12.3	2.48	16.4	27.4
New Hanover	12.4	7.7	6.2	51.5	120 284	160 307	33.3	26.4	20 834	13 741	28 537	86 046	26.2	2.28	12.1	30.7
Northampton	15.3	10.8	8.8	51.5	21 004	22 086	5.2	0.1	2 244	2 654	-1 418	9 193	5.8	2.32	19.6	32.1
Onslow	7.3	4.5	3.0	46.4	149 838	150 355	0.3	18.2	30 997	7 500	-537	60 092	24.9	2.66	13.1	20.3
Orange	11.5	5.6	4.0	52.2	93 662	118 227	26.2	13.2	12 400	6 545	8 245	51 457	12.2	2.41	10.0	27.9
Pamlico	17.2	12.6	9.1	49.0	11 368	12 934	13.8	1.6	1 009	1 358	-86	5 490	6.0	2.27	11.1	27.8
Pasquotank	11.6	7.3	6.3	50.9	31 298	34 897	11.5	16.5	4 895	3 394	5 301	14 956	15.9	2.51	16.3	25.7
Pender	13.9	9.0	6.1	50.0	28 855	41 082	42.4	27.1	4 823	3 771	10 484	20 333	26.7	2.51	12.2	23.3
Perquimans	15.7	13.1	8.4	52.1	10 447	11 368	8.8	18.3	1 188	1 379	1 617	5 598	20.5	2.39	12.2	25.4
Person	13.7	8.6	6.6	51.5	30 180	35 623	18.0	10.8	4 280	3 619	1 588	15 826	12.4	2.47	15.0	25.9
Pitt	10.2	5.5	4.3	52.8	108 480	133 798	23.3	25.7	19 654	10 109	16 551	67 577	28.6	2.39	15.6	30.0
Polk	16.4	12.1	12.2	52.1	14 458	18 324	26.7	11.9	1 517	2 634	2 150	8 989	13.7	2.24	8.8	31.2
Randolph	12.6	8.1	6.0	50.7	106 546	130 454	22.4	8.7	16 835	10 990	6 738	55 373	9.3	2.54	12.2	24.4
Richmond	13.1	8.1	6.2	50.8	44 511	46 564	4.6	0.2	5 986	4 887	-1 407	18 430	3.1	2.47	18.2	28.7
Robeson	11.6	6.7	4.6	51.4	105 170	123 339	17.3	8.8	19 524	11 037	-1 396	47 997	9.9	2.71	22.3	24.4
Rockingham	14.0	9.0	7.2	51.8	86 064	91 928	6.8	1.9	10 184	9 756	513	38 693	4.6	2.39	14.4	28.1
Rowan	12.5	7.8	6.6	50.6	110 605	130 340	17.8	6.2	15 871	12 485	7 793	53 140	6.4	2.52	14.1	25.2
Rutherford	14.3	9.8	7.5	51.7	56 956	62 899	10.4	7.8	7 169	7 245	973	27 466	9.0	2.42	13.3	27.3
Sampson	12.3	8.1	6.2	51.0	47 297	60 161	27.2	5.4	8 449	5 717	1 200	24 005	7.8	2.60	15.8	26.1
Scotland	13.6	7.8	5.8	51.7	33 763	35 998	6.6	0.4	4 654	3 436	-707	13 614	1.6	2.53	22.4	27.2
Stanly	13.1	8.8	6.9	50.3	51 765	58 100	12.2	4.3	6 770	5 603	876	23 589	6.1	2.48	11.8	25.8
Stokes	14.0	9.4	6.6	51.2	37 224	44 711	20.1	6.0	4 462	4 052	1 329	19 416	10.4	2.42	10.9	26.0
Surry	13.3	9.2	7.5	51.2	61 704	71 219	15.4	3.4	8 432	7 386	747	29 914	5.3	2.43	11.4	27.3

1. No spouse present.

Table B. States and Counties — Population, Vital Statistics, Medicare, and Crime

STATE County	Daytime population, 2006–2010			Births, average 2006–2008		Deaths, average 2006–2008		Persons under 65 with no health insurance, 2009		Medicare, 2011			Serious crimes known to police,[2] 2010 Total	
	Persons in group quarters, 2010	Number	Employ-ment/resi-dence ratio	Total	Rate[1]	Number	Rate[1]	Number	Percent	Eligible for Medicare	Enrolled in Medicare Advantage	Enrolled in a Medicare prescription drug plan	Number	Rate[3]
	32	33	34	35	36	37	38	39	40	41	42	43	44	45
NORTH CAROLINA—Cont'd														
Chowan	273	14 847	1.0	D	D	177	12.1	2 090	17.9	3 555	130	2 060	390	2 636
Clay	91	9 667	0.8	D	D	122	12.0	1 572	20.2	2 966	358	1 393	194	1 832
Cleveland	2 050	92 478	0.9	1 199	12.2	1 070	10.8	15 119	18.5	20 474	1 806	11 612	3 212	3 298
Columbus	2 925	53 395	0.8	766	14.1	670	12.3	9 020	20.2	12 157	582	7 510	2 421	4 349
Craven	4 939	104 253	1.1	1 659	17.3	920	9.6	13 650	17.0	19 189	525	8 741	3 651	4 465
Cumberland	10 157	333 939	1.1	5 655	18.5	2 105	6.9	45 009	16.4	40 917	5 802	13 115	19 505	6 106
Currituck	135	18 819	0.6	244	10.2	189	7.9	3 715	17.9	3 616	228	1 354	687	2 918
Dare	152	35 497	1.1	D	D	253	7.5	5 394	19.0	6 191	231	2 728	1 755	5 174
Davidson	1 691	134 306	0.6	1 951	12.4	1 482	9.4	25 770	19.3	29 439	12 655	9 685	4 627	2 870
Davie	365	33 948	0.6	D	D	363	9.0	5 544	16.2	8 155	3 232	2 359	1 031	2 560
Duplin	679	54 463	0.9	832	15.7	504	9.5	11 515	25.6	9 200	453	5 341	1 469	2 583
Durham	10 121	310 654	1.4	4 400	17.2	1 740	6.8	41 477	17.7	32 931	4 774	12 148	14 550	5 437
Edgecombe	1 430	54 256	0.9	773	14.6	600	11.3	7 970	18.0	10 530	651	6 611	2 430	4 297
Forsyth	9 851	367 769	1.2	5 079	15.0	2 867	8.5	51 711	17.1	56 851	25 864	15 623	19 262	5 493
Franklin	1 640	46 859	0.5	743	13.0	464	8.1	10 010	19.4	9 164	1 721	4 255	1 472	2 428
Gaston	3 317	184 950	0.8	2 792	13.8	2 007	9.9	33 057	17.9	36 560	6 765	17 065	6 256	3 152
Gates	61	8 834	0.4	D	D	118	10.1	1 702	17.4	2 167	192	1 042	NA	NA
Graham	93	8 394	0.9	D	D	98	12.5	1 427	22.8	1 951	295	1 004	NA	NA
Granville	6 948	54 157	0.8	634	11.4	521	9.4	9 253	18.9	9 563	1 206	4 465	1 976	3 298
Greene	2 320	17 623	0.6	242	11.9	175	8.6	4 264	24.4	3 011	95	1 793	711	3 328
Guilford	15 492	531 501	1.2	6 267	13.5	3 626	7.8	75 682	18.6	74 824	27 371	23 944	22 942	4 697
Halifax	1 416	53 431	0.9	698	12.6	644	11.7	8 200	18.6	12 835	998	7 711	2 487	4 634
Harnett	3 380	89 973	0.6	1 611	14.8	802	7.4	19 241	18.9	15 561	1 328	7 655	3 587	3 128
Haywood	813	54 796	0.9	583	10.3	678	12.0	8 380	18.9	15 010	2 472	6 279	1 769	2 996
Henderson	1 299	99 449	0.9	1 238	12.3	1 296	12.9	15 572	19.8	26 974	4 560	11 232	2 366	2 217
Hertford	2 297	24 993	1.1	311	13.3	274	11.7	3 656	19.4	4 668	95	3 030	657	2 749
Hoke	670	35 385	0.5	849	19.9	268	6.3	8 713	21.5	4 964	818	2 354	672	1 431
Hyde	830	5 953	1.1	D	D	62	11.9	1 052	24.9	959	23	583	NA	NA
Iredell	1 292	153 306	1.0	1 995	13.2	1 312	8.7	23 238	17.3	25 724	4 660	11 597	3 691	2 315
Jackson	3 574	40 243	1.1	406	11.2	332	9.1	6 825	22.2	6 810	798	2 994	966	2 399
Johnston	1 771	134 820	0.7	2 450	15.5	1 073	6.8	28 231	19.1	23 627	2 289	11 627	4 665	2 864
Jones	91	8 099	0.5	D	D	115	11.3	1 670	20.6	2 098	152	1 149	NA	NA
Lee	999	58 477	1.1	951	16.4	493	8.5	10 165	20.3	9 948	888	4 975	1 385	2 393
Lenoir	1 242	61 170	1.1	773	13.5	673	11.8	8 842	19.4	12 624	370	7 729	2 080	3 529
Lincoln	679	64 517	0.7	903	12.3	652	8.9	12 796	19.7	12 558	1 223	6 748	2 176	2 780
McDowell	1 666	43 462	0.9	D	D	453	10.4	7 276	20.2	9 753	1 910	4 486	1 091	2 425
Macon	439	32 726	0.9	D	D	423	13.0	5 198	21.1	9 444	872	4 568	749	2 208
Madison	1 028	17 161	0.6	D	D	227	11.2	3 242	19.6	4 722	737	2 250	236	1 221
Martin	156	21 983	0.7	D	D	310	13.1	3 399	18.2	5 189	117	3 268	981	4 003
Mecklenburg	16 015	1 011 416	1.3	14 687	17.0	4 960	5.8	137 674	17.1	101 470	17 735	44 728	44 043	4 789
Mitchell	204	15 635	1.0	D	D	205	13.0	2 552	20.7	3 928	659	1 831	NA	NA
Montgomery	1 093	26 480	0.9	D	D	235	8.5	5 298	23.0	4 758	666	2 756	828	2 979
Moore	848	85 966	1.0	997	11.8	962	11.4	11 726	17.7	21 906	2 788	9 486	2 230	2 583
Nash	2 210	94 566	1.0	1 254	13.5	915	9.8	14 147	18.2	17 364	1 060	10 047	3 734	3 896
New Hanover	6 698	213 838	1.2	2 463	13.1	1 554	8.2	28 699	17.7	33 859	2 067	16 441	9 588	4 778
Northampton	752	20 134	0.7	D	D	272	13.0	2 730	17.6	5 190	383	3 057	516	2 894
Onslow	17 805	169 889	1.0	3 640	22.8	847	5.3	24 555	15.9	17 545	868	6 711	5 178	2 913
Orange	9 557	136 285	1.1	1 340	10.8	701	5.7	15 833	14.2	16 189	2 776	5 341	3 829	2 862
Pamlico	705	11 697	0.7	D	D	143	11.3	1 826	19.4	3 322	111	1 578	278	2 115
Pasquotank	3 063	41 430	1.1	569	14.1	356	8.8	6 569	19.0	6 822	455	3 032	1 138	2 799
Pender	1 090	42 167	0.6	D	D	447	9.0	8 607	19.9	9 702	896	4 679	994	1 917
Perquimans	84	10 255	0.4	D	D	148	11.3	1 752	17.9	3 310	214	1 518	190	1 412
Person	442	33 638	0.7	477	12.8	406	10.9	5 071	16.2	7 646	1 774	3 130	1 349	3 418
Pitt	6 526	162 895	1.0	2 291	15.1	1 117	7.4	26 194	19.1	22 259	901	11 981	NA	NA
Polk	330	18 183	0.7	D	D	297	15.5	2 780	19.6	5 286	659	2 454	242	1 222
Randolph	1 298	123 907	0.7	1 829	13.0	1 266	9.0	24 746	20.7	25 243	9 935	8 999	4 865	3 438
Richmond	1 160	45 335	0.9	678	14.7	540	11.7	8 061	21.1	10 182	315	6 068	3 046	6 531
Robeson	4 105	127 597	0.9	2 227	17.3	1 216	9.4	28 920	25.3	21 150	1 507	12 724	9 391	7 022
Rockingham	1 055	85 845	0.8	1 076	11.6	1 077	11.6	13 537	17.9	20 040	7 615	7 034	3 808	4 067
Rowan	4 286	129 135	0.9	1 809	13.1	1 362	9.9	22 359	19.2	26 024	6 110	10 251	4 292	3 101
Rutherford	1 223	63 832	0.9	755	11.9	825	13.0	10 306	20.1	14 650	1 972	7 418	2 111	3 325
Sampson	1 087	57 074	0.8	930	14.6	609	9.6	11 514	21.4	11 625	885	6 570	1 937	3 103
Scotland	1 730	37 860	1.1	539	14.7	396	10.8	5 681	18.5	7 445	654	4 232	1 654	4 683
Stanly	2 051	53 605	0.7	724	12.2	615	10.4	9 232	18.8	11 743	774	6 539	1 500	2 854
Stokes	456	36 359	0.5	460	10.0	453	9.8	6 372	16.8	8 587	4 502	2 373	1 311	2 766
Surry	870	72 429	1.0	919	12.7	837	11.5	12 479	21.2	15 428	5 929	5 733	2 402	3 327

1. Per 1,000 estimated resident population. 2. Data for serious crimes have not been adjusted for underreporting; this may affect comparability between geographic areas and over time. 3. Per 100,000 population estimated by the FBI.

	Serious crimes known to police,[1] 2010 (cont.)		Education						Money income, 2006–2010				Income and poverty, 2010			
	Rate[2]		School enrollment and attainment, 2006–2010				Local government expenditures,[5] 2008–2009			Households				Percent below poverty level		
			Enrollment[3]		Attainment[4] (percent)						Median income					
STATE County	Violent	Property	Total	Percent private	High school graduate or less	Bachelor's degree or more	Total current expenditures (mil dol)	Current expenditures per student (dollars)	Per capita income[6] (dollars)	Dollars	Percent change, 2000 to 2006–2010 (constant 2010 dollars)	Percent with income of $200,000 or more	Median household income (dollars)	All persons	Children under 18 years	Children 5 to 17 years in families
	46	47	48	49	50	51	52	53	54	55	56	57	58	59	60	61

NORTH CAROLINA—Cont'd

STATE County	46	47	48	49	50	51	52	53	54	55	56	57	58	59	60	61
Chowan	291	2 346	3 826	16.1	54.9	15.7	25.8	10 548	20 900	36 761	-6.1	2.0	36 176	21.1	33.6	29.3
Clay	151	1 681	2 254	5.8	50.8	18.6	13.7	9 336	20 474	35 109	-11.7	0.8	35 314	18.8	32.0	28.2
Cleveland	243	3 055	25 504	11.7	54.3	15.7	146.8	8 633	19 284	38 208	-14.5	1.2	38 392	20.9	32.3	28.4
Columbus	415	3 934	13 331	6.8	54.8	12.0	86.3	8 650	18 784	35 421	4.4	1.5	32 518	26.9	40.8	38.5
Craven	367	4 098	24 112	11.6	40.9	21.3	119.8	8 092	24 591	44 599	-2.1	1.9	41 791	17.5	25.1	25.3
Cumberland	525	5 581	94 104	13.1	39.7	21.8	455.9	8 365	22 285	43 834	-7.6	1.7	43 356	18.2	26.4	24.9
Currituck	208	2 709	5 697	13.3	49.1	17.2	38.4	9 462	26 083	55 376	7.1	2.6	53 939	11.1	18.1	16.3
Dare	254	4 920	6 576	12.1	35.4	32.1	55.1	11 167	30 327	53 889	0.3	2.9	50 203	12.3	24.0	20.7
Davidson	239	2 631	38 008	11.0	56.0	16.3	204.4	7 626	22 268	44 249	-9.6	1.4	40 618	17.3	26.3	23.8
Davie	226	2 334	9 881	13.0	48.3	23.6	53.1	7 972	26 139	49 727	-2.3	3.7	46 957	14.0	21.6	19.1
Duplin	331	2 252	13 445	8.8	61.8	10.1	78.0	8 698	16 693	32 816	-13.3	0.8	34 672	23.7	32.8	31.9
Durham	628	4 809	74 953	29.1	32.6	44.1	342.6	9 628	27 503	49 894	-9.1	3.5	48 023	18.4	24.2	22.6
Edgecombe	608	3 689	14 777	6.4	61.7	10.1	65.8	8 162	16 747	32 665	-16.7	0.4	33 146	24.5	38.7	34.0
Forsyth	538	4 955	90 007	20.9	41.3	31.2	485.8	8 852	26 213	46 749	-12.3	3.6	44 443	16.7	24.2	22.8
Franklin	134	2 295	14 363	13.9	54.2	15.2	70.3	8 144	21 331	43 710	-11.4	1.1	45 592	16.0	22.3	20.2
Gaston	365	2 787	50 172	13.4	51.2	18.1	254.9	7 570	22 305	43 253	-13.5	2.2	40 332	19.9	27.7	24.8
Gates	NA	NA	2 938	9.4	56.2	10.5	19.6	9 769	19 893	45 682	1.2	1.2	43 010	17.5	24.1	20.9
Graham	NA	NA	1 624	8.3	55.3	13.0	12.9	10 470	17 825	28 447	-15.7	1.2	31 863	22.5	34.2	32.0
Granville	345	2 952	14 266	11.1	54.7	13.8	73.5	7 911	21 733	48 210	-4.7	1.3	45 828	15.5	19.9	17.5
Greene	276	3 052	5 128	6.5	61.4	9.2	33.1	9 908	17 362	41 488	2.1	0.1	38 428	23.7	35.1	33.7
Guilford	466	4 232	132 824	14.1	39.7	32.4	672.4	9 010	26 267	45 676	-15.4	3.5	42 415	17.9	26.7	24.2
Halifax	581	4 053	13 571	11.4	61.9	11.4	88.4	9 870	17 228	30 439	-9.2	1.0	30 861	26.2	36.7	33.9
Harnett	290	2 838	32 861	20.2	50.0	16.0	143.2	7 553	19 274	42 853	-3.6	0.9	40 956	16.7	24.3	24.4
Haywood	268	2 729	11 512	13.4	47.1	20.6	69.1	8 681	24 233	41 377	-3.7	1.6	39 987	14.6	25.2	23.0
Henderson	170	2 047	20 795	13.9	40.3	27.3	108.1	7 992	26 061	46 446	-3.8	2.3	43 589	15.8	24.6	21.6
Hertford	230	2 519	6 306	18.1	58.6	15.7	35.1	10 460	17 002	30 878	-7.7	0.8	32 410	26.1	35.5	33.2
Hoke	94	1 338	13 000	13.1	48.3	15.1	69.1	8 703	17 630	42 927	2.0	0.3	43 679	19.0	26.3	27.0
Hyde	NA	NA	1 364	30.9	60.4	11.7	10.9	16 563	14 992	38 265	6.2	0.5	35 206	21.9	29.7	28.6
Iredell	166	2 149	38 984	13.6	47.2	21.6	230.1	7 991	25 610	48 962	-7.8	3.3	46 576	13.3	17.9	16.6
Jackson	328	2 071	11 827	5.2	45.9	27.0	34.8	8 924	20 228	37 190	-9.8	1.5	36 741	19.3	25.7	24.7
Johnston	218	2 646	42 518	10.9	48.2	19.3	262.3	8 260	22 437	49 745	-3.9	1.6	46 922	16.1	22.8	20.5
Jones	NA	NA	2 066	5.1	59.5	10.7	15.8	11 029	20 066	38 354	-1.9	1.4	38 578	18.4	31.8	30.8
Lee	161	2 233	13 983	9.3	49.6	18.0	82.9	8 337	21 061	44 120	-10.4	0.9	41 999	18.6	28.1	25.5
Lenoir	562	2 967	15 347	7.7	54.7	14.5	82.9	8 389	19 017	33 625	-14.9	0.8	36 455	23.2	35.6	31.0
Lincoln	134	2 646	18 958	9.5	51.0	17.8	103.6	7 739	23 560	47 450	-9.5	2.3	45 332	15.0	22.9	20.0
McDowell	136	2 289	9 803	6.8	57.7	14.0	54.7	8 305	18 798	64 953	-14.8	1.1	34 383	19.9	29.6	27.2
Macon	109	2 099	5 803	13.2	48.8	19.5	39.3	8 857	26 156	38 615	-5.1	2.5	36 229	19.3	31.2	27.9
Madison	57	1 164	4 985	28.9	56.9	19.2	24.3	9 205	18 792	38 580	-1.7	0.7	36 158	19.7	28.1	25.1
Martin	420	3 583	5 995	8.2	57.6	12.2	40.0	10 012	18 728	34 766	-4.6	0.9	34 814	23.4	37.4	35.4
Mecklenburg	557	4 232	241 669	20.1	32.0	40.0	1 206.9	8 629	31 848	55 294	-13.7	5.7	52 363	15.6	21.3	19.6
Mitchell	NA	NA	3 174	6.6	60.9	14.4	21.9	10 146	18 804	32 743	-15.2	0.6	35 032	18.5	28.2	26.3
Montgomery	198	2 781	6 336	9.8	59.0	14.8	42.9	9 436	18 618	33 861	-18.7	1.8	34 608	24.6	34.3	30.4
Moore	227	2 356	19 544	13.7	38.8	29.8	108.8	8 491	25 786	48 319	-7.5	3.1	47 705	16.6	26.0	23.4
Nash	575	3 321	24 706	13.8	51.8	19.1	159.2	8 374	23 909	44 499	-5.4	2.6	42 315	15.6	24.7	22.8
New Hanover	449	4 329	52 286	12.4	33.0	36.1	229.5	9 337	29 363	48 553	-4.6	4.1	46 129	18.1	23.2	21.9
Northampton	292	2 602	5 108	14.1	66.6	12.0	35.8	8 954	17 128	30 578	-9.4	0.3	32 168	22.5	34.8	33.2
Onslow	237	2 675	40 529	12.5	42.6	17.7	193.5	8 056	21 048	43 561	1.9	1.2	41 969	15.8	22.0	23.0
Orange	168	2 694	47 562	11.4	27.0	54.4	203.9	10 698	32 912	52 981	-1.3	8.5	51 434	17.4	17.4	14.9
Pamlico	152	1 963	2 584	11.3	51.0	17.5	19.5	10 621	23 320	40 561	-6.0	2.3	41 442	15.2	29.9	28.2
Pasquotank	413	2 386	11 248	9.7	47.0	18.7	56.3	8 825	21 736	44 085	14.4	2.2	39 381	22.9	31.3	28.7
Pender	276	1 641	11 651	10.1	51.9	17.8	70.3	8 516	22 872	44 338	-2.5	1.7	43 573	16.7	25.1	22.8
Perquimans	104	1 308	3 067	11.1	53.7	18.1	19.9	11 260	22 085	43 041	15.1	2.0	40 772	16.4	29.4	27.8
Person	322	3 096	9 919	10.5	57.4	13.8	53.8	8 823	21 848	44 668	-5.1	0.7	42 621	16.4	24.8	21.9
Pitt	NA	NA	58 120	9.9	41.1	28.2	195.1	8 306	21 935	38 592	-7.3	2.4	39 519	21.6	26.6	25.7
Polk	71	1 151	3 902	9.0	44.7	27.2	27.3	10 404	24 008	43 692	-4.8	1.0	44 756	14.4	24.7	22.9
Randolph	126	3 312	32 709	9.4	59.4	13.0	187.8	7 846	21 297	40 346	-16.9	1.5	39 648	18.1	26.9	24.5
Richmond	512	6 019	11 804	9.9	62.0	10.0	71.3	9 028	17 692	30 439	-16.6	1.1	31 568	28.1	37.7	35.2
Robeson	879	6 143	37 110	4.3	64.2	12.1	218.7	8 846	15 321	29 667	-16.9	1.1	30 627	31.5	45.5	41.1
Rockingham	325	3 742	21 443	7.7	58.9	12.5	124.0	8 533	20 801	39 231	-8.3	1.1	38 063	18.5	27.2	24.8
Rowan	310	2 791	33 161	14.9	54.3	17.0	174.3	8 252	21 525	43 596	-8.2	1.7	38 658	20.1	29.0	26.7
Rutherford	238	3 087	16 081	9.6	53.8	14.6	92.7	8 838	18 961	35 364	-10.3	1.1	35 057	25.0	33.5	31.1
Sampson	219	2 883	16 201	7.3	60.1	12.4	97.6	8 327	19 086	35 740	-11.2	1.1	37 047	21.4	31.2	28.9
Scotland	462	4 222	9 589	10.9	60.1	14.0	70.6	10 108	16 297	29 368	-25.2	1.2	31 805	27.2	38.1	36.3
Stanly	200	2 655	15 186	16.8	55.9	15.3	83.8	8 452	21 139	44 802	-4.1	1.7	42 854	15.4	22.4	21.2
Stokes	367	2 399	10 517	11.6	63.4	10.9	60.7	8 163	20 852	42 689	-13.1	0.7	43 178	14.3	21.8	19.9
Surry	217	3 110	16 442	9.0	56.1	14.9	91.8	8 321	20 541	37 294	-10.9	1.2	36 622	19.3	30.8	28.3

1. Data for serious crimes have not been adjusted for underreporting; this may affect comparability between geographic areas and over time. 2. Per 100,000 population estimated by the FBI. 3. All persons 3 years old and over enrolled in nursery school through college. 4. Persons 25 years old and over. 5. Elementary and secondary education expenditures. 6. Based on population estimated by the American Community Survey, 2006–2010.

Table B. States and Counties — **Personal Income**

	Personal income, 2009												
			Per capita[1]					Transfer payments (mil dol)					
									Government payments to individuals				
STATE County	Total (mil dol)	Percent change, 2008–2009	Dollars	Rank	Wages and salaries[2] (mil dol)	Proprietors' income (mil dol)	Dividends, interest, and rent (mil dol)	Total	Total	Social Security	Medical payments	Income mainte-nance	Unemploy-ment insurance
	62	63	64	65	66	67	68	69	70	71	72	73	74
NORTH CAROLINA—Cont'd													
Chowan	468	-1.0	31 666	1 611	207	33	104	132	129	45	56	15	5
Clay	291	0.7	28 119	2 379	69	23	65	96	95	40	39	7	3
Cleveland	2 948	-1.2	29 692	2 051	1 357	133	448	933	915	295	373	104	89
Columbus	1 617	0.4	29 822	2 017	683	126	224	587	577	157	289	72	25
Craven	3 626	2.0	36 798	772	2 881	161	640	771	755	255	321	71	34
Cumberland	13 121	2.8	41 627	355	11 876	398	1 372	2 203	2 154	542	832	307	81
Currituck	861	1.1	35 569	947	220	44	115	142	138	50	55	10	10
Dare	1 287	-1.7	37 526	685	709	136	321	221	214	89	81	12	21
Davidson	5 116	0.0	32 263	1 468	1 724	319	791	1 156	1 127	427	427	117	94
Davie	1 482	-1.2	35 784	915	403	87	331	299	292	118	115	19	25
Duplin	1 550	1.4	29 155	2 153	727	274	186	389	380	112	175	50	17
Durham	10 435	0.6	38 692	566	14 361	811	1 770	1 573	1 524	463	673	181	89
Edgecombe	1 502	1.0	28 973	2 205	919	91	213	521	511	137	228	86	28
Forsyth	12 980	-3.6	36 091	873	9 914	1 033	2 865	2 419	2 354	838	986	232	140
Franklin	1 756	1.2	29 228	2 142	559	107	189	392	381	123	169	42	23
Gaston	6 722	-0.2	32 171	1 493	2 946	360	881	1 665	1 627	533	703	167	138
Gates	314	1.9	26 724	2 607	65	23	41	84	82	29	35	9	3
Graham	209	-1.9	26 089	2 711	81	22	28	78	77	25	36	7	5
Granville	1 604	0.3	27 831	2 430	1 043	63	238	357	347	125	142	39	21
Greene	548	1.2	26 520	2 638	177	70	58	142	138	39	63	21	6
Guilford	18 090	-1.4	37 658	677	14 180	1 406	3 347	3 247	3 159	1 094	1 234	348	237
Halifax	1 538	1.0	28 173	2 369	695	81	217	576	566	164	255	93	22
Harnett	3 185	-0.1	27 514	2 480	933	247	364	688	667	197	273	85	43
Haywood	1 802	-0.3	31 552	1 633	706	124	339	530	519	209	204	40	31
Henderson	3 769	-0.5	36 355	834	1 538	173	1 037	892	873	384	356	49	38
Hertford	668	2.4	28 673	2 265	394	41	86	214	209	59	98	32	5
Hoke	1 309	8.5	28 997	2 199	326	54	96	262	254	63	99	44	10
Hyde	148	-2.0	28 370	2 332	78	16	29	41	40	11	20	5	1
Iredell	5 088	-1.9	32 171	1 493	3 073	227	895	1 085	1 056	376	436	82	104
Jackson	1 095	-1.3	29 674	2 057	630	70	221	258	251	92	96	19	15
Johnston	5 305	-0.3	31 480	1 644	2 000	332	610	993	962	313	402	109	73
Jones	330	4.6	32 724	1 380	70	29	44	92	90	27	43	9	4
Lee	1 845	-0.6	30 505	1 861	1 258	106	298	462	451	140	197	42	36
Lenoir	1 888	0.9	33 476	1 262	1 123	93	314	594	584	166	285	69	23
Lincoln	2 538	1.6	33 375	1 285	857	56	338	536	522	183	216	47	52
McDowell	1 135	0.1	25 797	2 759	592	54	147	370	362	130	144	32	30
Macon	1 020	-1.4	30 699	1 821	435	59	285	306	300	127	122	19	15
Madison	569	0.6	27 823	2 433	160	36	86	173	169	58	76	15	8
Martin	743	2.3	31 833	1 572	359	52	115	241	236	69	114	27	13
Mecklenburg	38 961	-5.3	42 644	290	37 121	4 432	6 621	4 808	4 641	1 461	1 793	598	462
Mitchell	413	1.1	26 418	2 656	211	13	70	144	141	50	62	12	8
Montgomery	732	-2.4	26 375	2 659	356	38	121	219	214	68	96	24	11
Moore	3 359	-1.5	38 539	573	1 381	235	1 020	753	737	318	286	49	27
Nash	3 179	0.7	33 557	1 239	1 874	212	474	753	736	233	308	91	45
New Hanover	7 152	-1.9	36 662	795	4 956	512	1 743	1 384	1 349	485	564	111	83
Northampton	636	1.5	31 598	1 625	227	46	77	216	212	66	100	31	5
Onslow	7 349	7.8	42 463	297	6 411	161	614	883	861	224	331	107	30
Orange	6 186	1.3	47 925	135	3 782	204	1 356	668	644	229	288	50	30
Pamlico	452	0.1	36 348	836	113	24	94	112	109	44	43	9	4
Pasquotank	1 126	-0.8	27 075	2 554	812	68	176	307	300	87	130	34	13
Pender	1 546	2.4	29 520	2 088	424	73	236	375	365	134	148	35	23
Perquimans	382	1.0	29 990	1 980	77	39	68	114	112	44	46	11	4
Person	1 156	1.1	30 688	1 825	444	37	161	301	294	105	119	29	22
Pitt	5 263	0.6	33 089	1 323	3 410	249	856	1 116	1 087	298	479	150	58
Polk	764	-3.4	39 659	472	194	51	254	173	169	78	67	10	6
Randolph	4 082	0.2	28 717	2 255	1 889	185	542	1 019	993	357	407	96	76
Richmond	1 239	1.3	26 959	2 571	592	67	150	466	457	126	200	58	19
Robeson	3 305	1.2	25 511	2 804	1 591	184	346	1 222	1 198	266	609	201	43
Rockingham	2 808	0.4	30 435	1 880	1 196	113	442	809	792	283	343	75	51
Rowan	4 286	-0.4	30 444	1 875	2 433	99	727	1 074	1 049	369	391	97	96
Rutherford	1 701	-1.0	26 820	2 593	760	98	274	574	562	205	219	58	43
Sampson	1 834	-0.2	28 778	2 238	787	208	245	491	479	152	211	64	18
Scotland	1 000	1.2	27 544	2 476	541	64	130	358	352	105	147	60	18
Stanly	1 792	-1.1	29 965	1 988	763	95	293	475	464	168	193	40	35
Stokes	1 373	-0.1	29 751	2 030	292	57	184	329	320	124	129	28	23
Surry	2 212	0.0	30 508	1 860	1 157	123	385	633	620	206	288	56	33

1. Based on the resident population estimated as of July 1 of the year shown.   2. Includes supplements to wages and salaries.

Table B. States and Counties — Earnings, Social Security, and Housing

STATE County	Earnings, 2009 Total (mil dol)	Farm	Goods-related[1] Total	Manufacturing	Information and professional and technical services	Retail trade	Finance, insurance, and real estate	Health care and social services	Government	Social Security beneficiaries, December 2010 Number	Rate[2]	Supplemental Security Income recipients, December 2010	Housing units, 2010 Total	Percent change, 2000–2010
	75	76	77	78	79	80	81	82	83	84	85	86	87	88
NORTH CAROLINA—Cont'd														
Chowan	241	7.4	13.1	7.2	4.8	6.9	3.6	D	18.7	3 910	264	531	7 289	13.1
Clay	93	1.4	D	D	4.5	17.1	3.7	D	26.9	3 330	315	307	7 140	31.6
Cleveland	1 491	1.3	D	21.6	3.8	9.1	3.3	D	18.4	24 100	246	3 102	43 373	7.7
Columbus	809	4.0	21.3	17.6	4.0	7.9	4.2	16.4	22.3	14 160	244	3 307	26 042	8.2
Craven	3 042	0.9	D	6.7	5.7	4.4	2.4	7.7	57.4	21 295	206	2 385	45 002	17.8
Cumberland	12 274	0.1	D	4.6	4.3	3.9	2.1	4.5	66.8	47 960	150	9 242	135 524	14.4
Currituck	264	1.6	D	0.8	D	11.9	10.3	3.2	23.9	4 160	177	271	14 453	35.3
Dare	845	0.0	D	2.8	D	12.4	14.5	5.9	20.2	6 925	204	301	33 492	25.6
Davidson	2 043	0.6	28.0	21.0	5.8	6.9	3.6	11.3	16.5	34 205	210	3 074	72 655	16.4
Davie	490	1.4	21.9	14.9	D	13.2	5.0	8.2	16.8	9 245	224	548	18 238	22.0
Duplin	1 001	16.9	D	22.0	D	4.8	1.9	5.0	16.8	10 340	177	1 907	25 728	25.4
Durham	15 171	0.0	D	27.7	16.0	2.6	6.5	15.1	9.0	35 800	134	5 474	120 217	25.9
Edgecombe	1 009	3.8	D	17.7	5.1	7.9	2.3	D	24.3	12 295	217	2 809	24 838	3.5
Forsyth	10 947	0.0	19.4	15.2	9.9	7.1	9.2	16.9	9.9	63 440	181	6 890	156 872	17.9
Franklin	666	1.5	D	22.2	5.8	5.8	1.9	D	18.7	10 555	174	1 490	26 577	30.5
Gaston	3 305	0.1	D	19.4	5.0	9.1	3.7	18.1	15.7	42 545	206	4 997	88 686	12.4
Gates	88	21.9	D	D	3.3	4.4	2.3	6.1	33.8	2 550	209	320	5 208	18.6
Graham	103	0.5	D	D	2.9	5.7	3.3	D	22.7	2 315	261	300	5 930	16.7
Granville	1 105	1.1	D	27.8	2.0	4.6	1.5	4.3	44.5	10 805	180	1 465	22 827	27.5
Greene	247	10.7	14.5	5.5	D	4.1	3.3	8.7	36.1	3 585	168	745	8 213	11.5
Guilford	15 586	0.1	19.0	14.2	10.0	7.8	8.7	11.9	12.7	83 335	171	9 928	218 017	20.9
Halifax	776	4.7	19.6	15.3	2.5	9.0	3.0	10.8	29.2	14 785	270	4 039	25 781	1.9
Harnett	1 180	3.5	D	5.5	6.6	9.1	4.5	D	23.3	17 880	156	2 805	46 731	21.1
Haywood	830	1.2	D	15.2	7.4	11.4	4.3	10.7	23.8	17 075	289	1 599	34 954	22.0
Henderson	1 711	2.2	D	18.7	5.3	9.2	4.4	14.7	16.5	29 550	277	1 807	54 710	27.2
Hertford	436	5.9	22.1	18.1	2.2	6.8	2.6	D	18.0	5 320	216	1 283	10 635	9.4
Hoke	380	3.5	D	23.4	D	3.7	1.3	8.2	31.3	5 970	127	1 321	18 211	45.4
Hyde	93	16.9	7.5	2.8	D	5.4	3.0	D	36.9	1 070	184	200	3 347	1.4
Iredell	3 300	0.8	D	16.1	5.1	7.7	3.2	10.3	13.9	29 680	186	2 353	69 013	32.9
Jackson	700	1.0	D	2.9	D	6.7	3.2	13.6	40.6	7 715	192	689	25 948	34.5
Johnston	2 332	2.1	32.5	22.9	4.4	8.3	3.1	6.8	19.6	27 505	168	3 865	67 682	34.9
Jones	99	20.1	7.3	1.4	D	5.4	D	15.7	26.5	2 505	247	361	4 838	3.3
Lee	1 364	0.9	43.6	38.8	D	6.9	2.7	9.3	12.1	11 570	200	1 261	24 136	20.8
Lenoir	1 216	2.3	D	14.1	4.7	7.7	3.2	12.1	26.2	14 635	246	2 760	27 437	0.9
Lincoln	913	1.1	D	25.1	3.8	9.3	3.0	5.7	20.9	14 490	185	1 317	33 641	30.9
McDowell	645	1.8	43.4	36.4	D	8.3	2.7	D	18.7	11 165	248	1 272	20 808	13.3
Macon	494	0.5	19.3	7.1	9.3	11.0	5.6	13.2	17.8	10 615	313	819	25 245	21.7
Madison	196	1.1	D	10.5	D	5.1	2.9	D	23.0	5 345	257	810	10 608	9.1
Martin	410	7.9	33.3	28.4	2.7	8.1	2.6	13.0	18.7	5 925	242	1 129	11 704	7.3
Mecklenburg	41 553	0.1	11.9	6.4	16.4	5.2	15.8	7.1	10.8	112 260	122	15 094	398 510	36.1
Mitchell	225	0.6	D	5.3	1.6	9.6	3.0	16.6	24.7	4 405	283	489	8 713	10.1
Montgomery	394	2.9	D	29.1	3.8	6.7	2.3	D	22.2	5 780	208	758	15 914	12.5
Moore	1 616	1.8	D	6.3	9.7	7.7	5.0	27.1	13.9	23 975	272	1 498	43 940	25.0
Nash	2 086	2.7	D	23.7	7.3	7.4	4.4	9.1	15.1	19 765	206	3 384	42 286	14.1
New Hanover	5 468	0.0	D	10.7	14.2	8.3	6.1	11.8	19.8	37 560	185	3 992	101 436	27.4
Northampton	273	12.4	13.4	8.2	D	14.1	D	D	23.7	5 840	264	1 359	11 674	11.7
Onslow	6 571	0.4	D	0.6	1.9	3.3	1.3	2.4	80.6	20 315	114	2 602	68 226	22.4
Orange	3 985	0.4	4.7	2.1	8.9	5.5	4.4	5.7	59.0	16 960	127	1 585	55 597	16.5
Pamlico	137	6.7	11.5	3.1	5.5	8.7	3.4	D	32.2	3 695	281	330	7 534	11.1
Pasquotank	881	1.7	7.7	4.2	5.9	8.4	4.6	9.9	44.0	7 745	190	1 190	16 833	17.8
Pender	496	7.2	17.9	8.8	4.1	7.6	3.1	D	25.9	11 045	212	1 122	26 724	28.6
Perquimans	116	21.3	9.0	1.5	D	5.1	2.6	D	28.1	3 700	275	382	6 986	15.7
Person	481	1.6	D	17.2	3.0	9.2	2.7	9.7	20.9	9 005	228	1 060	18 193	17.3
Pitt	3 659	1.1	D	11.0	4.8	7.2	4.3	13.9	37.3	25 760	153	5 609	74 990	28.5
Polk	245	2.6	18.0	5.7	6.5	6.7	6.7	D	17.4	5 875	286	314	11 432	24.4
Randolph	2 074	2.2	D	32.2	D	6.2	3.1	9.3	15.4	29 175	206	2 803	61 041	12.1
Richmond	660	3.5	25.5	19.7	D	8.8	2.4	13.2	22.0	11 085	238	2 175	20 738	4.3
Robeson	1 775	3.8	20.7	15.4	3.0	7.6	3.3	19.1	24.2	25 245	188	7 312	52 751	10.5
Rockingham	1 309	0.8	D	29.3	D	7.9	2.9	12.9	17.0	23 390	250	2 921	43 696	8.7
Rowan	2 532	0.7	25.5	20.3	D	5.9	1.9	9.5	23.1	29 735	215	2 854	60 211	11.5
Rutherford	858	0.4	D	15.8	5.7	9.0	3.4	15.9	19.6	16 850	248	1 928	33 878	14.7
Sampson	994	22.4	D	14.7	4.0	6.0	1.6	D	21.0	13 335	210	2 272	27 234	8.3
Scotland	606	5.8	23.3	19.5	3.2	7.3	2.7	D	19.9	9 090	251	2 035	15 193	3.4
Stanly	859	1.6	D	19.3	4.0	9.2	3.2	13.6	21.2	13 590	224	1 225	27 110	10.3
Stokes	348	3.7	20.1	11.2	D	7.8	4.4	13.2	25.7	10 125	214	939	21 924	13.8
Surry	1 279	2.5	D	13.8	D	9.3	3.6	10.9	18.4	17 830	242	1 998	33 667	8.5

1. Includes mining, construction, and manufacturing.   2. Per 1,000 resident population enumerated in the 2010 census.

Table B. States and Counties — Housing, Labor Force, and Employment

STATE County	Occupied units Total	Percent	Owner-occupied Median value[1]	Median owner cost as a percent of income With a mortgage	Without a mortgage	Renter-occupied Median rent[2]	Median rent as a percent of income	Sub-standard units[3] (percent)	Civilian labor force, 2010 Total	Percent change, 2009–2010	Unemployment Total	Rate[4]	Civilian employment[5] 2006–2010 Total	Percent Management, business, science and arts	Construction, production, and maintenance occupations
	89	90	91	92	93	94	95	96	97	98	99	100	101	102	103
NORTH CAROLINA—Cont'd															
Chowan	5 904	68.4	137 000	25.2	17.2	622	26.6	1.7	6 298	-9.5	693	11.0	6 008	27.4	30.2
Clay	4 510	83.3	163 000	27.2	10.8	544	35.7	0.9	4 544	-5.4	506	11.1	4 120	29.4	29.9
Cleveland	37 679	68.9	103 300	22.9	11.6	603	29.9	3.8	47 583	-5.5	6 490	13.6	40 619	28.2	31.6
Columbus	21 779	72.0	89 000	24.4	13.0	563	34.2	2.3	24 235	-5.3	3 075	12.7	22 083	24.9	29.5
Craven	40 202	63.5	151 500	24.4	12.4	732	29.2	2.4	41 802	-5.9	4 389	10.5	38 796	29.5	27.1
Cumberland	117 311	58.4	116 900	23.6	12.3	784	28.7	2.4	136 315	1.4	12 811	9.4	117 667	32.2	22.3
Currituck	9 396	82.3	240 000	29.2	12.8	789	31.2	1.0	12 546	1.1	847	6.8	11 393	31.0	26.6
Dare	15 465	71.3	342 100	31.2	13.2	1 010	31.2	0.9	21 423	-5.2	2 286	10.7	17 940	33.8	23.3
Davidson	64 484	73.2	128 200	22.6	10.9	620	26.6	2.0	75 803	-4.4	9 460	12.5	74 623	26.8	32.8
Davie	15 832	83.5	160 900	21.7	11.1	670	24.2	1.7	20 198	-2.8	2 176	10.8	18 336	32.0	28.0
Duplin	20 969	70.6	83 800	24.4	15.9	536	27.4	4.2	24 403	-4.7	2 207	9.0	24 178	22.7	40.4
Durham	105 201	55.6	176 100	23.0	11.2	792	30.0	3.0	141 849	1.8	11 305	8.0	129 486	48.4	15.1
Edgecombe	21 601	62.9	82 600	24.6	16.2	607	33.8	2.7	23 945	-1.6	3 731	15.6	21 804	20.5	37.3
Forsyth	136 612	65.9	149 000	22.7	10.4	668	29.8	3.0	175 845	1.7	17 338	9.9	160 304	37.4	21.0
Franklin	22 765	77.8	121 700	24.8	13.1	636	31.6	4.0	27 447	0.6	2 818	10.3	26 179	30.3	31.5
Gaston	77 363	69.5	120 800	23.4	12.3	678	30.0	2.8	96 874	-1.9	11 842	12.2	90 475	30.5	29.3
Gates	4 406	81.6	120 200	24.0	14.1	673	26.2	2.2	4 749	-4.2	359	7.6	5 048	30.1	37.0
Graham	3 784	77.9	119 000	24.2	10.0	421	33.4	3.4	3 989	2.1	612	15.3	3 345	21.3	32.0
Granville	19 820	75.8	125 200	23.0	13.3	678	27.1	2.4	25 339	-4.0	2 677	10.6	25 907	30.2	28.4
Greene	7 021	70.3	85 100	22.3	14.1	607	25.1	3.4	9 202	0.4	938	10.2	8 423	20.2	35.5
Guilford	189 561	62.9	153 800	23.6	11.0	715	29.9	2.3	246 647	1.7	26 866	10.9	230 715	35.0	21.1
Halifax	21 590	64.0	85 800	25.1	17.0	586	34.4	3.0	23 630	-6.6	3 114	13.2	20 773	27.0	30.0
Harnett	39 111	67.4	123 500	23.8	13.6	701	30.6	3.2	47 640	-3.1	5 338	11.2	44 272	28.3	31.4
Haywood	26 445	75.2	158 200	22.6	11.4	685	29.0	1.2	27 711	2.7	2 677	9.7	26 295	30.7	28.1
Henderson	45 109	76.8	184 200	23.0	10.0	684	29.0	2.9	49 305	2.5	4 140	8.4	45 759	32.8	26.4
Hertford	9 007	65.9	83 000	24.1	17.0	593	30.8	2.1	9 814	-7.4	969	9.9	9 030	27.4	31.2
Hoke	14 232	72.4	116 900	24.9	13.1	705	33.8	3.6	20 783	5.0	1 850	8.9	16 292	25.9	28.5
Hyde	1 921	82.6	95 600	24.2	12.4	602	33.1	0.0	2 914	5.3	243	8.3	1 956	27.6	23.4
Iredell	58 006	74.7	164 300	23.8	10.0	712	28.5	1.6	78 247	-5.1	9 667	12.4	71 592	28.9	31.2
Jackson	15 866	66.3	163 200	22.6	10.0	623	32.9	2.9	20 353	-6.2	1 834	9.0	17 831	31.2	19.9
Johnston	59 093	73.2	136 200	22.9	12.3	745	31.0	2.4	77 842	1.5	7 598	9.8	76 095	32.3	27.4
Jones	4 086	72.1	91 500	22.5	13.4	570	27.5	3.0	4 565	-7.8	499	10.9	4 198	26.3	33.3
Lee	20 986	70.4	127 800	22.5	12.1	621	27.0	4.5	25 888	-4.1	3 357	13.0	25 101	27.8	34.4
Lenoir	24 142	62.3	91 900	23.6	13.9	622	33.7	3.4	26 540	-6.2	3 001	11.3	25 309	27.5	33.2
Lincoln	29 407	76.2	146 700	23.2	10.8	631	30.3	1.1	38 096	-4.7	4 851	12.7	34 829	28.1	33.2
McDowell	17 560	72.6	99 200	19.9	11.1	509	26.2	2.6	19 942	-5.9	2 639	13.2	19 330	27.8	33.9
Macon	15 780	76.8	167 800	25.2	10.0	676	26.3	2.3	15 426	-8.3	1 690	11.0	14 553	29.9	28.1
Madison	8 002	76.8	154 600	22.6	10.2	580	32.0	2.8	9 875	1.9	942	9.5	8 591	27.2	28.7
Martin	9 954	70.0	79 400	23.0	13.5	556	38.1	2.5	11 299	-9.1	1 259	11.1	10 186	27.1	31.5
Mecklenburg	350 392	62.6	185 100	23.3	11.6	829	28.5	2.4	461 879	1.7	50 503	10.9	454 035	40.4	18.1
Mitchell	6 812	75.0	105 000	25.2	10.6	462	24.3	1.8	6 939	-8.5	810	11.7	6 495	23.6	41.9
Montgomery	9 853	74.7	83 100	22.8	13.5	506	29.4	3.7	10 856	-5.7	1 368	12.6	11 026	25.1	41.5
Moore	34 030	76.3	186 900	23.3	10.9	657	27.1	1.9	36 091	-5.7	3 499	9.7	34 055	34.7	20.8
Nash	37 762	63.7	116 300	22.8	12.6	678	27.9	2.7	46 707	1.6	5 752	12.3	43 648	30.6	28.3
New Hanover	83 679	61.4	227 800	25.2	12.2	846	32.4	2.2	103 501	0.8	10 018	9.7	99 334	36.9	17.7
Northampton	8 377	74.8	74 600	24.8	16.7	497	29.4	2.4	8 503	-6.6	1 006	11.8	8 187	23.6	29.2
Onslow	56 633	56.6	137 400	24.0	11.4	802	27.7	2.1	65 982	2.9	5 607	8.5	55 847	28.8	25.1
Orange	50 085	60.6	258 800	22.9	11.1	812	33.2	2.2	68 987	1.0	4 489	6.5	65 485	51.9	12.3
Pamlico	5 463	81.6	133 800	24.7	14.3	642	30.2	2.4	5 229	-8.1	529	10.1	5 257	28.9	32.3
Pasquotank	14 563	66.4	170 700	26.6	12.9	733	30.5	2.1	17 477	-5.9	1 739	10.0	17 547	31.9	24.3
Pender	20 209	80.6	147 200	25.0	13.8	718	30.5	2.2	24 188	0.9	2 612	10.8	21 749	26.0	31.3
Perquimans	5 353	77.2	159 100	26.3	12.7	761	37.6	0.9	5 042	-8.6	488	9.7	5 198	27.8	29.4
Person	15 388	73.9	115 900	21.3	12.6	626	27.0	1.9	18 848	-0.7	2 082	11.0	17 613	27.4	32.5
Pitt	64 005	55.3	125 900	23.7	14.4	672	34.4	2.5	82 080	2.6	8 276	10.1	77 329	36.8	20.4
Polk	9 038	77.9	167 500	24.9	10.4	639	35.4	1.6	9 261	-5.2	812	8.8	8 270	26.0	32.0
Randolph	54 925	73.6	119 100	23.1	12.4	594	30.1	3.3	72 764	-0.1	7 837	10.8	65 793	24.9	38.8
Richmond	17 228	70.7	71 300	23.5	14.3	493	29.3	3.2	19 999	-5.4	2 718	13.6	16 438	23.3	35.1
Robeson	44 504	67.2	69 200	24.0	14.1	539	30.0	5.1	55 233	-6.1	6 957	12.6	48 485	25.4	37.2
Rockingham	37 831	72.1	101 000	21.9	10.7	556	27.6	2.3	43 359	0.1	5 592	12.9	40 941	24.0	36.9
Rowan	52 877	71.4	125 100	22.6	10.8	666	27.9	3.1	68 690	-6.6	8 772	12.8	60 954	26.8	34.0
Rutherford	27 458	71.8	101 100	23.3	12.3	526	27.8	2.4	26 505	-10.8	4 273	16.1	26 484	26.7	33.5
Sampson	23 781	68.5	87 500	23.5	12.5	540	29.4	3.8	31 444	-4.4	2 739	8.7	27 546	27.4	38.4
Scotland	13 236	64.7	77 700	24.1	14.9	561	32.6	2.9	13 414	-7.9	2 248	16.8	11 918	29.9	27.4
Stanly	22 134	76.9	125 600	23.0	11.8	584	24.1	2.7	29 847	-4.8	3 676	12.3	26 314	28.8	31.1
Stokes	18 759	81.8	117 800	20.9	10.0	546	26.1	2.4	23 006	-2.9	2 476	10.8	21 093	23.2	36.6
Surry	29 668	74.3	103 700	21.3	12.1	526	29.0	3.2	32 942	-5.9	3 915	11.9	32 734	26.9	34.5

1. Specified owner-occupied units. 2. Specified renter-occupied units. A value of 10.0 represents 10 percent or less. 3. Overcrowded or lacking complete plumbing facilities. 4. Percent of civilian labor force. 5. Persons 16 years old and over.

Table B. States and Counties — Nonfarm Employment and Agriculture

	Private nonfarm establishments, employment and payroll, 2009								Agriculture, 2007			
	Employment						Annual payroll		Farms			
										Percent with:		
STATE County	Number of establishments	Total	Health care and social assistance	Manufacturing	Retail trade	Finance and insurance	Professional, scientific, and technical services	Total (mil dol)	Average per employee (dollars)	Number	Fewer than 50 acres	500 acres or more	Farm operators whose principal occupation is farming (percent)
	104	105	106	107	108	109	110	111	112	113	114	115	116
NORTH CAROLINA—Cont'd													
Chowan	384	4 022	1 197	671	538	98	112	110	27 422	190	30.0	27.4	68.4
Clay	236	1 541	288	D	377	38	27	33	21 700	137	62.0	1.5	39.4
Cleveland	2 003	27 840	5 203	5 888	3 843	670	750	865	31 083	1 188	44.4	2.4	34.8
Columbus	1 080	12 116	3 416	2 124	2 322	D	198	345	28 504	777	38.7	10.3	50.6
Craven	2 306	28 475	6 460	3 141	4 635	898	1 764	919	32 275	286	46.2	13.6	55.6
Cumberland	5 696	91 510	18 823	7 466	15 703	2 222	5 108	2 776	30 338	500	42.4	10.4	46.6
Currituck	594	4 193	228	D	943	103	D	134	31 902	80	48.8	21.3	51.3
Dare	1 893	13 202	867	415	3 119	436	506	390	29 551	7	57.1	42.9	71.4
Davidson	2 795	34 519	4 748	9 807	4 859	927	849	993	28 760	1 074	53.0	1.7	36.3
Davie	788	9 448	1 057	2 689	1 406	221	244	275	29 061	627	45.9	2.9	44.0
Duplin	879	13 067	2 132	D	1 627	217	204	335	25 644	1 159	38.5	9.4	65.9
Durham	6 532	163 018	23 321	13 587	13 400	5 170	30 405	9 532	58 474	242	63.2	5.0	48.8
Edgecombe	802	15 778	2 542	3 596	1 537	208	D	521	33 045	300	33.3	20.7	56.7
Forsyth	8 430	163 419	31 099	19 797	19 556	11 244	7 142	6 656	40 728	680	67.8	1.6	44.4
Franklin	931	9 464	1 486	2 276	1 227	D	271	332	35 087	593	40.0	7.3	39.3
Gaston	3 979	59 480	11 214	11 637	9 326	1 221	1 429	1 876	31 540	516	59.7	0.8	31.2
Gates	134	910	D	115	153	43	44	23	25 522	181	35.4	14.4	44.2
Graham	182	1 808	320	D	220	42	D	54	30 079	126	67.5	0.0	38.1
Granville	861	13 542	D	4 324	1 292	196	184	435	32 147	673	33.6	6.7	40.1
Greene	243	1 929	763	106	245	42	D	46	23 837	292	35.6	18.8	57.9
Guilford	13 458	239 884	32 113	33 827	28 196	14 009	9 889	9 095	37 916	963	55.1	3.2	45.4
Halifax	1 066	13 571	3 504	1 838	2 718	340	403	350	25 795	365	26.3	26.3	52.1
Harnett	1 627	18 881	3 492	1 857	3 170	529	494	497	26 330	727	51.3	8.9	48.7
Haywood	1 434	13 964	2 982	D	2 877	437	526	417	29 845	707	60.1	1.7	37.2
Henderson	2 626	29 883	6 024	5 770	4 999	901	803	936	31 317	557	67.5	2.3	50.3
Hertford	487	7 312	2 306	906	1 181	D	57	199	27 278	163	28.2	23.3	54.0
Hoke	396	5 259	1 185	2 170	489	D	120	127	24 131	249	47.4	10.8	51.8
Hyde	159	731	D	61	135	D	13	21	28 602	176	38.6	25.6	47.2
Iredell	4 295	57 786	8 809	9 771	8 181	1 222	2 385	2 076	35 934	1 201	48.7	4.7	44.5
Jackson	948	8 905	2 175	248	1 696	211	447	248	27 902	229	70.3	0.9	40.2
Johnston	3 110	35 613	4 895	6 022	7 177	984	1 144	1 069	30 026	1 245	50.1	8.4	48.5
Jones	147	1 001	D	D	D	D	18	30	30 051	159	34.0	21.4	59.1
Lee	1 329	23 496	2 923	8 567	3 124	391	684	775	32 970	272	50.4	3.7	40.8
Lenoir	1 321	21 029	4 715	3 806	3 228	571	511	602	28 613	480	34.4	18.3	61.0
Lincoln	1 557	17 235	2 193	3 864	2 863	387	440	507	29 398	638	53.8	2.4	35.6
McDowell	729	11 892	1 394	5 311	1 603	208	172	304	25 603	383	62.9	1.3	43.9
Macon	1 193	9 512	1 492	861	1 911	384	252	259	27 281	346	65.0	0.6	44.8
Madison	318	2 946	519	375	366	44	D	69	23 470	801	51.8	1.5	40.3
Martin	478	5 894	1 550	905	1 055	164	152	144	24 467	320	24.4	20.0	60.0
Mecklenburg	27 889	531 089	61 298	26 523	52 822	66 714	36 417	25 515	48 042	236	61.0	1.7	47.5
Mitchell	390	4 148	925	601	736	93	D	109	26 371	314	54.1	1.6	37.6
Montgomery	524	6 646	1 011	2 575	805	334	63	190	28 634	289	39.4	6.2	49.5
Moore	2 208	27 815	7 499	1 930	3 965	681	1 481	866	31 118	804	52.9	4.0	48.1
Nash	2 212	37 030	5 689	D	5 701	2 136	995	1 218	32 898	487	42.9	15.6	50.7
New Hanover	6 736	83 846	15 217	5 032	13 961	2 894	5 142	2 884	34 402	73	69.9	1.4	42.5
Northampton	279	4 121	862	443	412	D	33	111	26 973	340	30.6	25.3	47.6
Onslow	2 639	33 956	5 891	884	7 599	1 055	1 495	836	24 616	401	51.1	5.5	59.1
Orange	3 061	39 199	12 293	899	5 891	2 737	2 130	1 486	37 904	604	49.8	3.0	43.5
Pamlico	246	1 835	372	73	327	42	D	42	22 919	85	52.9	29.4	56.5
Pasquotank	991	11 965	2 776	736	2 766	422	326	331	27 642	144	37.5	27.8	66.7
Pender	900	7 172	1 175	1 156	1 160	149	262	196	27 350	357	52.7	9.2	45.7
Perquimans	203	1 375	203	48	219	51	24	36	26 224	171	31.0	28.7	68.4
Person	708	8 051	1 222	1 752	1 464	168	158	234	29 092	403	40.4	12.4	42.2
Pitt	3 542	56 760	15 554	4 813	8 614	1 817	1 864	1 730	30 472	435	37.9	20.0	60.2
Polk	473	3 868	1 511	432	462	143	125	96	24 842	309	60.2	0.6	49.8
Randolph	2 611	38 091	4 618	15 081	4 331	D	666	1 107	29 069	1 501	49.8	3.1	44.4
Richmond	867	11 145	1 905	3 229	2 038	D	202	286	25 626	278	37.8	4.7	44.6
Robeson	1 897	32 802	8 229	8 324	4 872	D	569	848	25 854	1 017	45.6	13.1	54.0
Rockingham	1 769	23 197	3 809	6 568	3 741	553	484	690	29 763	863	42.1	4.2	41.4
Rowan	2 591	41 734	D	9 019	4 587	721	1 184	1 383	33 137	983	54.1	4.4	38.3
Rutherford	1 321	16 329	3 421	3 012	2 572	341	241	488	29 915	705	49.9	2.0	36.5
Sampson	991	12 887	2 466	2 845	2 266	252	194	360	27 897	1 203	34.7	13.7	55.8
Scotland	679	10 883	2 697	2 283	1 639	186	161	310	28 473	190	48.4	13.7	56.3
Stanly	1 335	15 518	3 291	3 537	2 577	370	358	425	27 392	713	48.9	5.5	39.1
Stokes	615	5 642	1 315	1 094	946	D	145	152	27 015	963	46.1	2.0	43.3
Surry	1 693	27 444	4 309	4 826	3 984	598	436	851	31 014	1 258	51.9	2.1	42.0

Table B. States and Counties — **Agriculture**

STATE County	Acreage (1,000) [117]	Percent change, 2002–2007 [118]	Average size of farm [119]	Total irrigated (1,000) [120]	Total cropland (1,000) [121]	Average per farm [122]	Average per acre [123]	Value of machinery and equipment, average per farm (dollars) [124]	Total (mil dol) [125]	Average per farm (dollars) [126]	Crops [127]	Live-stock and poultry products [128]	$10,000 or more [129]	$100,000 or more [130]	Total ($1,000) [131]	Percent of farms [132]
NORTH CAROLINA—Cont'd																
Chowan	75	25.0	393	6.2	53.3	967 227	2 461	191 638	41.1	216 238	83.4	16.6	68.4	42.1	3 441	70.0
Clay	10	-23.1	71	0.0	3.3	502 820	7 131	42 278	1.1	8 131	38.7	61.3	23.4	0.7	71	19.0
Cleveland	116	-0.9	97	0.6	52.6	390 048	4 007	43 728	54.5	45 873	21.2	78.8	24.4	5.6	1 714	34.6
Columbus	152	-5.0	196	2.2	106.6	646 186	3 295	95 387	141.4	181 986	32.2	67.8	43.5	16.1	2 902	48.6
Craven	71	-10.1	248	1.2	49.5	762 422	3 076	102 097	50.5	176 676	48.6	51.4	48.6	25.2	2 218	55.2
Cumberland	88	-2.2	177	3.4	44.6	531 536	3 008	69 974	90.9	181 712	20.8	79.2	38.2	18.0	1 258	38.2
Currituck	28	-20.0	345	0.5	25.1	1 146 012	3 325	126 564	12.2	153 038	98.9	1.1	50.0	25.0	371	38.8
Dare	5	NA	703	0.0	4.7	1 584 429	2 254	132 369	1.1	162 729	100.0	0.0	100.0	100.0	263	42.9
Davidson	91	-13.3	85	1.5	45.3	484 438	5 688	49 149	36.4	33 879	30.1	69.9	23.3	5.0	560	18.6
Davie	70	-7.9	111	0.3	31.2	583 812	5 239	50 271	18.3	29 193	33.1	66.9	30.5	6.1	151	11.2
Duplin	248	5.5	214	25.3	159.3	873 575	4 082	120 938	1 176.3	1 014 902	5.7	94.3	70.1	55.3	3 337	32.2
Durham	26	0.0	108	0.3	8.4	552 803	5 116	42 823	D	D	0.0	D	29.3	5.4	218	26.0
Edgecombe	140	-14.6	466	6.7	103.5	1 162 841	2 495	172 090	146.3	487 781	47.3	52.7	42.3	29.0	5 253	66.3
Forsyth	44	-15.4	64	0.4	24.3	431 497	6 731	44 708	17.1	25 138	83.8	16.2	21.2	4.4	133	13.5
Franklin	113	-11.7	190	5.3	49.2	710 899	3 735	87 830	48.1	81 057	54.6	45.4	29.8	10.3	852	34.2
Gaston	38	-9.5	73	0.1	14.6	405 779	5 574	49 354	11.2	21 745	24.1	75.9	18.8	2.9	198	17.4
Gates	76	18.8	419	2.7	49.8	1 059 067	2 528	137 509	47.9	264 525	47.0	53.0	34.3	23.2	2 359	71.3
Graham	7	-12.5	57	0.0	1.9	250 526	4 395	50 517	1.4	11 254	13.0	87.0	15.9	1.6	6	7.9
Granville	128	-12.9	191	2.7	39.8	637 331	3 341	48 355	19.7	29 344	73.0	27.0	23.9	6.7	705	37.4
Greene	92	-6.1	316	3.6	67.4	1 081 617	3 426	134 917	200.3	685 846	19.2	80.8	65.1	43.5	2 894	65.1
Guilford	97	-12.6	100	2.4	46.0	525 659	5 245	57 354	48.4	50 274	56.5	43.5	27.5	7.8	506	12.3
Halifax	198	1.5	541	2.0	123.9	1 288 434	2 379	141 233	91.5	250 791	48.9	51.1	38.1	25.5	7 578	73.7
Harnett	112	-1.8	154	2.5	72.1	815 320	5 303	83 238	177.2	243 760	21.3	78.7	35.5	21.7	2 812	36.0
Haywood	56	-13.8	80	0.5	14.7	497 582	6 258	49 005	15.5	21 953	38.0	62.0	29.0	4.0	155	10.5
Henderson	38	-22.4	68	1.8	19.0	702 488	10 311	63 616	62.3	111 894	89.9	10.1	31.1	8.1	668	8.8
Hertford	79	-1.3	482	6.0	52.5	990 341	2 053	172 955	84.0	515 491	33.3	66.7	49.1	35.6	2 642	79.8
Hoke	60	-4.8	242	0.5	35.4	818 889	3 386	98 188	67.0	269 257	11.0	89.0	31.3	19.7	1 396	39.4
Hyde	83	-19.4	470	0.6	67.5	1 105 505	2 353	171 764	68.2	387 347	D	D	35.8	22.2	2 578	80.7
Iredell	138	-6.1	115	1.1	69.4	663 938	5 761	65 806	117.6	97 897	10.0	90.0	36.7	16.7	578	13.4
Jackson	13	-18.8	58	0.1	5.4	420 926	7 227	69 679	D	D	0.0	D	29.3	5.7	4	6.6
Johnston	194	0.0	156	5.8	128.2	672 607	4 314	77 828	203.0	163 014	43.8	56.2	35.3	16.9	4 358	41.2
Jones	69	-9.2	434	2.0	51.8	1 213 070	2 792	164 045	101.7	639 766	20.0	80.0	59.7	44.0	2 260	45.9
Lee	36	-21.7	133	1.5	18.6	615 587	4 624	74 273	31.5	115 627	33.3	66.7	32.7	13.6	211	23.5
Lenoir	138	13.1	287	3.6	108.7	969 173	3 382	140 949	236.3	492 282	29.6	70.4	61.9	43.1	7 394	60.6
Lincoln	59	1.7	93	0.5	32.2	429 913	4 621	44 800	20.8	32 662	20.5	79.5	24.1	4.5	441	23.8
McDowell	23	-4.2	60	0.1	6.9	355 761	5 932	44 168	24.4	63 710	64.6	35.4	19.6	5.2	56	4.4
Macon	21	-4.5	61	0.1	6.3	533 897	8 741	42 054	5.6	16 154	40.9	59.1	22.8	2.0	10	4.0
Madison	67	-20.2	83	0.2	17.2	439 656	5 277	34 207	7.9	9 812	47.6	52.4	18.1	1.7	10	10.0
Martin	105	-5.4	330	1.2	74.1	968 779	2 939	136 713	55.2	172 423	79.6	20.4	58.4	30.6	4 889	80.3
Mecklenburg	19	-24.0	81	0.4	8.4	1 256 769	15 500	114 845	D	D	0.0	0.0	30.9	7.2	62	13.1
Mitchell	23	-11.5	73	0.1	6.6	369 209	5 088	40 580	3.6	11 363	84.1	15.9	23.9	1.6	178	8.6
Montgomery	43	2.4	147	1.0	11.6	546 329	3 713	63 578	94.4	326 651	6.7	93.3	43.3	23.5	142	13.1
Moore	80	-20.8	100	2.4	26.5	522 563	5 247	55 297	138.6	172 384	13.3	86.7	30.0	18.2	227	9.0
Nash	154	-3.8	315	6.5	94.7	1 070 817	3 396	106 164	144.5	296 721	49.3	50.7	47.4	30.0	3 133	40.9
New Hanover	4	NA	60	0.1	3.2	484 944	8 017	64 080	5.8	79 515	95.3	4.7	41.1	11.0	36	15.1
Northampton	156	3.3	458	3.0	106.2	1 154 619	2 523	176 598	97.8	287 713	34.7	65.3	51.5	32.9	8 361	80.9
Onslow	55	-14.1	138	5.2	38.1	628 054	4 562	84 654	159.1	396 645	11.8	88.2	46.4	32.4	1 271	34.7
Orange	60	-15.5	99	0.8	26.0	558 040	5 612	56 294	28.1	46 497	44.8	55.2	30.0	8.3	420	21.9
Pamlico	46	-11.5	543	0.9	40.5	1 336 631	2 463	203 616	23.2	272 746	86.4	13.6	52.9	40.0	978	60.0
Pasquotank	86	-13.1	594	0.0	80.0	1 540 302	2 591	203 146	47.9	332 295	98.4	1.6	62.5	34.0	1 263	50.0
Pender	62	-1.6	172	5.4	35.5	694 613	4 027	81 762	165.0	462 179	29.1	70.9	39.8	22.7	555	26.1
Perquimans	68	-27.7	400	1.5	63.6	1 154 491	2 883	208 260	60.2	351 840	49.1	50.9	72.5	45.0	3 042	76.0
Person	99	4.2	244	1.8	52.1	832 271	3 404	87 099	19.3	47 857	73.8	26.2	29.8	12.4	730	26.6
Pitt	172	-7.5	394	4.9	131.4	1 338 293	3 394	154 469	168.4	387 224	46.7	53.3	56.1	32.9	5 130	49.2
Polk	21	-22.2	68	0.2	6.8	506 658	7 455	46 228	D	D	0.0	D	18.1	2.6	83	6.8
Randolph	147	-6.4	98	1.5	63.2	475 393	4 844	58 713	205.9	137 188	5.8	94.2	33.0	16.0	418	13.1
Richmond	41	-16.3	147	0.7	18.5	564 009	3 833	66 819	127.7	459 461	4.2	95.8	35.3	27.7	194	26.6
Robeson	268	-6.6	264	4.7	209.3	759 287	2 881	91 234	268.9	264 438	21.9	78.1	40.7	18.9	5 326	49.0
Rockingham	117	-14.0	136	3.8	44.2	526 286	3 878	61 643	31.9	36 927	67.5	32.5	27.3	8.9	425	23.9
Rowan	116	0.9	118	1.1	63.8	612 721	5 195	70 311	59.9	60 900	55.0	45.0	27.0	7.2	1 012	18.2
Rutherford	66	-2.9	93	0.4	23.5	410 058	4 387	33 735	6.6	9 347	22.0	78.0	18.3	1.1	258	15.3
Sampson	321	7.7	267	29.2	210.7	998 921	3 738	148 397	1 196.3	994 457	12.5	87.5	61.6	43.3	6 793	51.0
Scotland	66	13.8	346	1.0	33.8	1 002 375	2 895	85 969	110.3	580 464	6.1	93.9	43.2	31.1	1 560	26.8
Stanly	105	-2.8	147	0.7	58.2	589 246	4 020	64 731	106.7	149 618	14.1	85.9	29.5	10.7	1 916	27.3
Stokes	91	-15.0	95	0.4	35.2	401 084	4 244	52 049	21.5	22 327	54.2	45.8	23.4	4.2	351	12.7
Surry	114	-11.6	91	1.5	53.5	426 646	4 688	60 597	121.8	96 783	16.6	83.4	33.1	9.2	640	20.0

STATE County	Water use, 2005		Wholesale trade,[1] 2007				Retail trade,[2] 2007				Real estate and rental and leasing,[2] 2007			
	Total water withdrawn (mil gal/day)	Gallons withdrawn per person	Number of establish-ments	Number of employees	Sales (mil dol)	Annual payroll (mil dol)	Number of establish-ments	Number of employees	Sales (mil dol)	Annual payroll (mil dol)	Number of establish-ments	Number of employees	Receipts (mil dol)	Annual payroll (mil dol)
	133	134	135	136	137	138	139	140	141	142	143	144	145	146
NORTH CAROLINA—Cont'd														
Chowan	6.0	416	12	132	38.5	3.7	64	613	136.1	11.8	22	48	7.3	0.8
Clay	1.2	121	1	D	D	D	53	377	133.7	8.6	19	D	D	D
Cleveland	271.6	2 764	92	1 550	1 247.0	52.1	406	3 947	928.8	83.7	66	308	50.5	7.0
Columbus	48.6	887	43	329	234.2	11.1	249	2 318	527.6	46.1	34	111	13.2	2.3
Craven	52.3	576	64	714	827.7	26.5	424	4 538	1 111.7	101.0	118	413	56.0	11.0
Cumberland	41.2	135	161	1 706	920.0	69.8	1 073	15 913	3 897.4	343.3	334	1 700	252.2	48.9
Currituck	3.3	141	15	D	D	D	149	1 102	263.9	23.7	54	676	58.8	20.8
Dare	9.6	282	40	D	D	D	475	3 467	869.1	88.5	159	1 414	127.7	48.6
Davidson	12.0	78	153	D	D	D	507	5 128	1 264.2	110.6	111	337	39.1	7.0
Davie	14.2	363	31	349	139.1	11.9	126	1 475	407.8	34.3	25	64	10.7	1.3
Duplin	43.6	838	41	418	350.2	14.5	192	1 697	412.6	33.5	29	67	6.1	0.9
Durham	40.9	169	215	8 974	7 657.3	842.9	935	14 439	3 135.3	311.5	320	1 941	375.4	76.0
Edgecombe	14.9	275	25	D	D	D	159	1 539	324.7	29.8	34	117	18.9	2.6
Forsyth	54.6	168	424	7 342	4 542.0	312.0	1 442	21 315	5 202.9	479.2	432	D	D	D
Franklin	7.3	135	37	324	178.0	14.6	138	1 245	371.8	29.8	23	65	10.7	1.4
Gaston	1 071.6	5 464	196	2 163	1 178.4	82.7	672	9 557	2 245.3	202.1	162	1 041	167.7	29.2
Gates	3.0	267	10	104	81.1	3.9	22	159	34.0	2.3	1	D	D	D
Graham	42.0	5 200	3	D	D	D	33	209	46.2	3.9	5	D	D	D
Granville	7.2	134	28	286	125.2	9.6	141	1 315	323.9	30.8	31	68	8.1	1.5
Greene	9.1	456	8	31	15.9	0.8	45	376	97.8	6.5	4	D	D	D
Guilford	60.2	136	1 024	14 772	11 295.4	710.0	2 004	30 247	7 252.6	718.7	690	4 564	1 455.5	147.4
Halifax	33.4	596	27	158	77.1	5.9	270	3 023	610.3	58.8	41	134	12.9	2.4
Harnett	14.0	135	46	D	D	D	270	3 148	872.0	65.4	51	D	D	D
Haywood	45.5	805	47	325	174.4	13.1	278	3 010	821.8	69.3	87	204	27.5	4.4
Henderson	13.6	140	115	1 173	709.9	41.9	441	5 353	1 479.2	127.7	120	346	52.3	9.3
Hertford	8.5	362	14	122	61.2	4.8	116	1 213	252.0	24.0	15	53	3.5	0.9
Hoke	5.1	124	10	94	33.1	2.7	67	512	121.7	8.1	16	23	4.3	0.5
Hyde	1.0	188	10	90	23.5	1.9	44	190	26.7	2.8	5	D	D	D
Iredell	19.0	135	228	2 420	1 275.9	116.5	647	8 360	2 288.9	201.7	219	693	119.2	22.8
Jackson	4.5	127	16	148	52.9	5.1	176	1 872	433.7	43.2	65	275	32.1	6.4
Johnston	23.2	159	111	1 055	820.9	49.7	580	7 163	1 971.7	148.1	105	477	77.7	12.2
Jones	5.2	502	10	127	41.2	4.4	29	163	31.8	2.8	1	D	D	D
Lee	14.3	257	56	1 128	672.2	43.6	251	2 966	764.5	65.2	63	197	32.0	6.0
Lenoir	13.5	233	62	D	D	D	276	3 537	842.8	80.8	54	229	28.0	4.7
Lincoln	11.4	163	73	986	436.2	38.6	248	2 683	713.8	60.8	71	181	40.8	6.0
McDowell	8.6	199	82	266	78.2	8.4	144	1 722	482.4	40.0	28	104	9.3	2.2
Macon	323.4	10 058	19	61	14.8	1.8	270	2 136	476.3	48.7	89	196	25.4	4.7
Madison	3.3	161	9	56	26.5	1.3	48	381	76.0	6.3	16	34	3.4	1.0
Martin	160.3	6 505	29	320	111.7	10.2	89	955	227.8	19.9	19	63	6.5	1.2
Mecklenburg	2 664.2	3 345	1 845	27 817	17 104.8	1 537.0	3 525	55 782	14 114.3	1 327.1	1 804	11 907	2 904.8	551.9
Mitchell	4.5	283	16	93	32.3	2.4	65	794	171.9	15.5	20	56	6.2	1.1
Montgomery	7.8	287	25	227	116.6	7.3	96	866	210.2	17.5	12	39	4.0	1.0
Moore	22.6	276	61	410	172.4	16.5	386	4 202	1 001.1	90.2	107	324	56.3	9.4
Nash	22.7	248	106	D	D	D	477	5 773	1 271.2	114.8	89	416	77.2	11.3
New Hanover	39.7	221	295	2 736	1 410.1	113.1	1 107	15 150	3 825.5	355.4	432	1 968	326.8	63.7
Northampton	6.8	316	19	425	256.1	14.5	58	435	102.0	7.6	5	15	1.0	0.2
Onslow	18.6	122	40	259	96.9	10.7	550	7 276	1 913.9	154.2	185	757	108.4	17.2
Orange	15.1	127	77	870	580.5	58.3	390	6 181	1 195.3	142.9	153	502	117.5	17.2
Pamlico	3.3	258	11	79	20.7	1.9	45	328	68.9	6.2	15	D	D	D
Pasquotank	7.2	187	34	447	148.8	13.5	217	2 750	694.3	61.8	50	D	D	D
Pender	9.3	201	34	1 166	583.9	54.7	158	1 271	331.8	26.0	57	172	20.9	5.8
Perquimans	4.5	369	11	84	32.4	2.4	37	242	69.0	5.2	9	D	D	D
Person	1 056.3	28 382	28	383	193.3	13.9	143	1 570	384.2	34.0	21	115	8.8	1.9
Pitt	25.6	180	137	1 700	898.9	70.5	668	8 846	2 176.0	188.8	201	D	D	D
Polk	2.5	128	17	146	65.0	4.9	68	506	110.3	9.5	28	87	10.0	2.2
Randolph	19.9	144	150	1 813	746.4	75.8	438	4 465	1 156.7	95.9	73	292	46.6	7.1
Richmond	12.9	276	33	D	D	D	204	2 076	424.1	40.0	34	93	11.1	1.6
Robeson	33.0	258	73	728	627.1	26.1	431	5 144	1 337.9	103.6	51	259	25.5	4.1
Rockingham	282.0	3 044	59	813	611.5	27.4	340	3 682	839.6	76.3	61	190	15.7	3.5
Rowan	361.0	2 672	111	1 570	628.6	56.4	452	4 755	1 163.8	98.1	98	293	52.2	8.8
Rutherford	13.5	211	45	D	D	D	278	2 767	640.1	59.2	61	218	29.2	6.5
Sampson	42.1	667	52	781	382.0	29.7	226	2 403	575.8	48.7	33	106	16.1	2.6
Scotland	6.5	175	18	D	D	D	153	1 711	361.7	32.9	23	81	9.4	1.9
Stanly	14.5	246	47	D	D	D	237	2 596	610.0	54.4	40	D	D	D
Stokes	1 235.8	26 948	18	73	11.7	2.2	115	893	226.5	18.4	27	D	D	D
Surry	23.9	329	69	D	D	D	350	3 963	1 054.1	82.9	73	272	32.5	6.3

1. Merchant wholesalers, except manufacturers' sales branches and offices. 2. Employer establishments.

Professional Services, Manufacturing, and Accommodation and Food Services

STATE County	Professional, scientific, and technical services,[1] 2007				Manufacturing, 2007				Accommodation and food services, 2007			
	Number of establish-ments	Number of employees	Receipts (mil dol)	Annual payroll (mil dol)	Number of establish-ments	Number of employees	Receipts (mil dol)	Annual payroll (mil dol)	Number of establish-ments	Number of employees	Sales (mil dol)	Annual payroll (mil dol)
	147	148	149	150	151	152	153	154	155	156	157	158
NORTH CAROLINA—Cont'd												
Chowan	23	124	11.6	4.9	25	899	341.7	29.6	28	483	19.5	5.1
Clay	16	49	3.5	1.3	NA	NA	NA	NA	15	217	7.4	2.4
Cleveland	127	752	82.0	28.9	142	7 198	2 229.8	290.6	159	2 277	96.6	25.9
Columbus	56	204	18.0	5.1	41	2 487	887.7	108.8	87	980	41.1	9.4
Craven	223	D	D	D	85	4 745	D	D	178	3 824	142.1	37.9
Cumberland	495	D	D	D	110	8 424	D	391.0	586	D	D	D
Currituck	40	128	20.3	14.7	NA	NA	NA	NA	75	512	34.5	8.5
Dare	131	681	58.9	24.1	45	636	98.4	20.3	301	3 755	248.3	77.0
Davidson	207	778	76.6	26.4	281	11 982	2 696.7	413.6	211	3 621	131.8	39.7
Davie	68	290	21.9	8.1	54	3 503	1 001.6	134.9	59	795	29.0	8.2
Duplin	59	175	14.5	5.3	33	5 747	1 621.4	158.2	76	1 215	42.2	11.1
Durham	970	D	D	D	179	12 930	9 359.6	750.8	617	12 949	729.3	202.7
Edgecombe	43	244	21.7	7.2	43	4 437	1 226.9	152.8	73	954	36.4	9.8
Forsyth	977	D	D	D	350	18 381	16 881.5	858.1	712	14 261	646.8	179.3
Franklin	73	245	28.2	10.7	54	3 150	1 034.1	150.9	46	514	21.4	6.0
Gaston	287	D	D	D	341	14 259	4 158.6	541.2	296	5 638	253.4	67.4
Gates	10	44	4.0	1.3	NA	NA	NA	NA	6	100	2.3	0.7
Graham	7	32	2.4	0.9	NA	NA	NA	NA	22	240	15.4	4.8
Granville	64	184	17.9	5.5	48	4 792	2 252.1	186.8	66	1 132	48.8	11.0
Greene	8	28	2.3	0.8	NA	NA	NA	NA	9	158	6.3	1.8
Guilford	1 533	D	D	D	746	37 752	23 940.4	1 616.0	1 114	22 829	1 044.5	295.5
Halifax	61	404	24.2	9.2	42	2 208	D	D	86	1 899	71.9	20.1
Harnett	126	509	42.7	16.9	71	2 631	464.7	96.3	121	D	D	D
Haywood	107	575	60.3	24.7	45	1 926	D	D	156	2 341	99.1	28.6
Henderson	228	D	D	D	145	6 752	2 129.6	286.6	198	3 449	170.5	47.5
Hertford	19	D	D	D	17	867	D	50.6	43	689	25.4	7.0
Hoke	33	D	D	D	16	2 137	D	59.1	23	D	D	D
Hyde	3	D	D	D	NA	NA	NA	NA	30	233	16.9	4.3
Iredell	378	2 782	321.6	112.2	285	11 898	3 167.1	446.0	332	6 039	246.7	69.9
Jackson	78	D	D	D	NA	NA	NA	NA	96	1 556	74.0	20.1
Johnston	243	1 132	109.7	43.0	125	6 409	2 418.3	284.9	268	4 718	197.2	51.1
Jones	6	D	D	D	NA	NA	NA	NA	8	31	1.2	0.3
Lee	83	742	30.8	39.5	81	9 028	3 521.6	361.8	95	1 796	67.3	17.6
Lenoir	74	459	87.6	21.0	55	4 937	1 229.1	156.0	92	1 811	69.7	19.7
Lincoln	120	601	61.6	20.2	106	5 190	2 106.0	188.7	102	1 705	65.2	17.0
McDowell	37	170	13.2	6.6	65	6 522	1 332.5	196.9	70	1 139	42.0	10.9
Macon	76	272	22.9	9.4	40	821	230.5	26.8	114	1 234	68.2	18.9
Madison	20	43	3.7	1.0	NA	NA	NA	NA	30	282	12.1	3.2
Martin	26	142	7.7	3.6	18	945	362.6	29.7	43	693	26.4	6.9
Mecklenburg	3 689	D	D	D	890	30 349	11 201.0	1 354.0	2 253	47 379	2 550.5	702.9
Mitchell	23	80	5.9	2.0	27	552	71.0	17.1	35	311	12.6	3.4
Montgomery	15	67	6.8	2.0	68	3 307	750.8	108.9	33	282	13.4	3.5
Moore	218	1 452	151.3	60.2	85	2 129	669.6	80.3	174	4 310	227.5	65.9
Nash	179	988	111.3	41.0	102	8 298	2 956.2	347.9	193	4 104	163.8	45.4
New Hanover	832	D	D	D	193	5 743	2 883.6	306.4	615	12 542	525.5	152.3
Northampton	17	39	3.3	0.9	NA	NA	NA	NA	19	142	5.2	1.6
Onslow	210	D	D	D	43	1 016	253.0	31.8	310	6 265	287.9	71.5
Orange	507	D	D	D	73	1 534	D	56.5	304	6 088	275.6	80.1
Pamlico	15	D	D	D	NA	NA	NA	NA	23	355	23.8	6.6
Pasquotank	76	455	50.5	14.9	31	720	D	29.1	93	1 931	64.8	19.0
Pender	74	D	D	D	44	1 416	D	55.4	70	892	35.5	9.3
Perquimans	14	D	D	D	NA	NA	NA	NA	16	167	5.8	1.8
Person	43	D	D	D	39	2 114	D	69.9	50	818	37.4	9.0
Pitt	310	1 750	198.5	77.0	98	6 930	D	265.8	306	7 187	293.5	79.2
Polk	40	138	13.3	4.7	21	605	153.1	17.9	38	436	15.5	4.9
Randolph	167	D	D	D	339	17 982	4 397.7	570.6	175	3 029	131.3	35.1
Richmond	57	215	16.0	5.2	50	3 690	697.3	94.5	67	960	37.7	9.5
Robeson	110	D	D	D	71	8 436	2 792.6	243.8	161	3 476	128.8	31.9
Rockingham	114	D	D	D	109	7 771	3 118.4	274.8	143	2 124	84.6	22.6
Rowan	183	1 213	90.5	35.2	200	12 036	3 724.3	428.4	195	3 283	132.1	37.0
Rutherford	74	294	21.3	6.8	75	3 936	901.9	140.1	110	1 401	60.2	16.7
Sampson	50	182	16.8	5.6	52	3 043	917.6	101.1	81	996	38.6	10.7
Scotland	35	D	D	D	39	3 122	1 061.2	119.9	48	812	32.7	8.8
Stanly	77	329	37.3	12.0	111	3 900	925.8	137.4	103	1 570	55.7	15.7
Stokes	38	147	12.5	4.6	33	1 078	D	37.3	53	775	28.7	8.0
Surry	111	435	39.1	12.2	111	5 478	1 038.0	168.5	153	2 464	84.9	24.9

1. Establishment subject to federal tax.

Table B. States and Counties — Health Care and Social Assistance, Other Services, and Federal Funds

STATE County	Health care and social assistance, 2007				Other services, 2007				Federal funds and grants, 2009–2010 Expenditures (mil dol)			
										Direct payments for individuals[1]		
	Number of establishments	Number of employees	Receipts (mil dol)	Annual payroll (mil dol)	Number of establishments	Number of employees	Receipts (mil dol)	Annual payroll (mil dol)	Total	Social Security and government retirement	Medicare	Food Stamps and Supplemental Security Income
	159	160	161	162	163	164	165	166	167	168	169	170
NORTH CAROLINA—Cont'd												
Chowan	55	1 192	83.8	35.5	22	83	6.3	1.9	149.5	62.2	24.1	9.7
Clay	23	249	13.9	6.1	11	27	2.2	0.6	96.4	48.9	16.2	3.4
Cleveland	234	5 819	490.3	202.6	153	638	53.0	14.4	805.2	354.4	136.2	50.1
Columbus	179	3 658	217.6	90.8	69	229	18.8	4.7	612.3	202.2	121.8	43.2
Craven	270	7 199	648.9	263.3	159	826	66.8	16.7	1 375.4	482.9	124.5	46.5
Cumberland	743	18 732	1 573.8	646.8	411	2 670	176.6	55.2	12 931.5	1 259.5	239.1	170.2
Currituck	27	D	D	D	41	156	13.2	4.0	160.6	93.1	22.4	5.7
Dare	80	D	D	D	104	469	33.4	9.9	228.0	132.2	34.2	5.2
Davidson	199	4 731	325.5	145.4	190	982	67.6	19.2	828.2	428.3	177.2	43.5
Davie	60	1 058	67.1	25.0	58	288	17.0	4.2	292.6	138.7	46.5	6.3
Duplin	100	2 002	108.4	48.0	56	246	19.6	6.0	465.0	148.4	75.2	24.8
Durham	725	22 856	2 828.6	960.5	443	4 038	664.4	153.1	4 398.5	618.5	268.4	96.6
Edgecombe	92	2 468	153.9	63.4	60	290	122.0	6.8	537.8	116.5	122.7	52.6
Forsyth	806	28 766	2 859.9	1 108.0	605	3 859	391.1	95.0	2 593.2	1 071.3	423.0	121.0
Franklin	84	D	D	D	63	191	19.9	4.8	367.4	148.9	63.9	22.9
Gaston	458	10 998	937.0	410.1	287	1 815	186.1	44.0	1 328.2	643.1	286.1	81.3
Gates	10	D	D	D	11	47	3.7	0.8	98.6	43.3	16.9	5.0
Graham	13	355	11.2	6.0	11	36	3.1	0.7	76.6	31.2	13.8	4.7
Granville	93	3 092	230.2	104.3	49	176	20.4	4.8	445.7	148.5	61.8	15.6
Greene	43	D	D	D	13	24	2.1	0.5	136.4	46.4	24.6	8.8
Guilford	1 240	30 287	2 861.8	1 177.0	878	5 437	740.5	148.8	3 543.4	1 401.8	521.0	152.5
Halifax	147	3 611	218.3	96.3	82	566	35.0	12.1	654.1	212.8	110.6	64.2
Harnett	164	3 567	226.1	108.5	107	465	33.0	9.3	646.1	260.0	112.7	39.3
Haywood	143	3 091	230.7	99.3	107	477	37.4	10.5	492.0	250.0	89.4	21.5
Henderson	258	6 122	487.6	204.4	177	1 007	81.9	21.7	828.7	478.5	168.6	24.4
Hertford	92	2 191	124.1	52.4	34	190	10.7	3.3	284.3	80.2	37.2	21.7
Hoke	70	1 927	78.2	35.9	23	117	6.2	2.0	255.0	103.5	26.2	19.2
Hyde	9	118	6.7	2.8	5	D	D	D	70.3	15.5	10.6	4.7
Iredell	424	8 552	821.5	326.2	275	1 666	126.0	37.4	865.3	447.9	182.6	33.0
Jackson	95	1 971	181.1	75.7	50	166	12.4	3.6	257.5	111.6	39.9	13.6
Johnston	273	D	D	D	208	934	80.2	21.0	902.5	373.8	158.3	49.7
Jones	17	340	28.1	12.4	5	16	1.3	0.4	113.8	46.0	20.1	6.6
Lee	163	2 887	196.6	80.7	96	469	32.0	9.7	457.7	227.3	79.5	20.5
Lenoir	199	4 574	298.0	130.7	92	624	44.7	14.6	747.1	224.7	137.2	43.9
Lincoln	133	2 130	166.7	69.0	119	509	39.0	10.1	387.2	214.8	74.0	17.2
McDowell	74	1 529	92.9	42.0	43	273	20.8	6.2	307.6	158.1	51.5	15.9
Macon	91	1 666	120.6	47.7	88	341	29.1	8.4	307.3	162.8	56.7	10.6
Madison	29	602	33.2	15.2	15	43	4.6	1.0	198.6	69.6	31.4	9.8
Martin	78	1 408	83.4	33.9	24	71	5.9	1.7	275.9	89.2	46.0	17.6
Mecklenburg	2 283	55 497	6 082.2	2 453.1	1 613	12 728	2 085.7	371.7	4 900.0	1 882.3	626.8	249.8
Mitchell	33	1 041	61.4	29.9	23	59	5.3	1.2	162.7	58.8	27.4	6.3
Montgomery	60	1 009	52.5	22.7	30	109	8.4	2.2	230.5	81.7	40.7	13.5
Moore	263	7 138	705.1	303.2	139	727	58.8	16.2	751.0	436.3	133.4	23.9
Nash	251	6 815	557.6	243.4	153	908	75.7	23.0	758.4	374.4	97.6	45.9
New Hanover	686	18 139	1 822.5	767.7	468	2 908	234.9	65.3	1 465.8	664.8	215.7	75.9
Northampton	35	782	29.4	14.3	18	44	4.0	0.8	272.8	83.9	40.0	21.7
Onslow	246	5 465	433.8	163.4	213	1 136	68.0	21.4	2 938.6	575.1	92.7	52.6
Orange	346	11 588	1 122.7	491.9	198	1 397	316.4	46.2	1 614.9	300.0	117.3	22.8
Pamlico	20	249	12.5	6.2	16	60	4.7	1.4	121.8	62.3	17.3	5.9
Pasquotank	134	2 919	242.3	101.8	75	459	24.8	7.8	527.7	158.3	56.3	24.5
Pender	75	1 036	69.8	27.3	55	222	16.9	5.4	346.4	178.9	53.9	17.5
Perquimans	17	D	D	D	12	49	2.6	0.9	128.4	66.8	19.1	8.2
Person	75	1 144	90.0	35.7	43	149	15.1	3.8	303.1	109.9	50.8	12.6
Pitt	439	D	D	D	185	1 084	108.0	21.6	1 098.7	401.6	158.8	81.9
Polk	60	1 456	89.9	38.7	30	96	13.7	2.4	156.4	93.5	30.7	3.9
Randolph	223	4 468	325.3	141.7	177	744	66.7	18.5	738.3	366.9	147.6	30.3
Richmond	104	2 119	160.5	62.8	59	D	D	D	439.9	179.3	83.9	33.1
Robeson	296	8 599	561.4	242.8	100	368	30.8	7.8	1 234.5	376.2	188.2	100.7
Rockingham	192	3 997	291.2	118.1	131	503	36.3	9.9	837.6	330.0	161.3	40.9
Rowan	241	7 413	717.6	322.1	164	987	59.9	18.8	1 022.7	451.3	176.7	47.7
Rutherford	140	3 133	214.0	89.4	79	509	34.9	10.2	496.5	231.4	85.4	27.5
Sampson	115	2 686	173.9	74.6	72	D	D	D	509.5	174.4	86.7	29.8
Scotland	120	2 664	202.4	87.2	39	D	D	D	350.6	118.6	48.8	33.0
Stanly	181	3 106	221.3	87.9	94	454	34.3	10.4	395.0	205.0	85.5	17.0
Stokes	54	1 233	69.0	30.2	48	232	17.3	5.0	263.8	143.0	44.0	12.8
Surry	172	3 892	303.4	119.7	103	663	52.0	16.7	574.6	260.6	124.9	24.3

1. State totals may include programs not allocated by county.

Table B. States and Counties — Federal Funds, Residential Construction, and Local Government Finances

	Federal funds and grants, 2009–2010 (cont.)							Value of residential construction authorized by building permits, 2010		Local government finances, 2007				
	Expenditures (mil dol) (cont.)									General revenue				
	Procurement contract awards			Grants[1]								Taxes		
													Per capita[2] (dollars)	
STATE County	Salaries and wages	Defense	Other	Medicaid and other health-related	Nutrition and family welfare	Education	Other	New construction ($1,000)	Number of housing units	Total (mil dol)	Inter-govern-mental (mil dol)	Total (mil dol)	Total	Property
	171	172	173	174	175	176	177	178	179	180	181	182	183	184
NORTH CAROLINA—Cont'd														
Chowan	4.1	0.2	4.0	25.7	6.5	1.3	7.7	5 460	29	45.2	23.4	13.6	932	658
Clay	2.2	0.0	2.1	20.8	1.5	0.7	0.3	7 122	41	25.6	14.1	9.0	881	587
Cleveland	19.6	20.8	3.9	139.6	18.0	10.7	30.5	13 509	92	447.4	160.4	75.9	771	591
Columbus	12.7	0.5	3.6	171.3	15.1	6.3	3.6	3 413	28	187.5	120.9	40.4	747	563
Craven	313.8	208.9	8.9	130.9	15.1	9.6	7.0	47 443	434	304.3	154.3	80.1	828	585
Cumberland	9 417.2	1 227.0	60.3	295.8	65.2	40.4	41.3	302 846	3 054	933.7	488.1	281.0	917	694
Currituck	3.8	11.1	4.1	12.5	3.0	2.0	0.0	34 197	138	88.4	30.2	46.8	1 952	1 232
Dare	19.3	2.6	14.9	9.6	3.7	1.0	0.1	38 203	137	175.9	39.5	105.7	3 129	2 067
Davidson	18.1	4.9	5.5	91.7	20.6	10.9	4.8	49 440	266	363.0	207.3	111.1	709	511
Davie	13.7	24.0	23.5	30.0	4.3	3.0	0.3	10 975	66	106.4	44.6	35.2	868	668
Duplin	17.8	28.3	9.2	112.8	13.4	6.3	5.0	13 222	77	150.9	90.2	38.0	717	525
Durham	362.8	107.7	819.0	1 209.6	37.5	31.8	787.6	181 557	1 230	1 149.4	615.6	365.7	1 426	1 128
Edgecombe	53.8	0.6	7.6	133.8	15.4	4.6	3.7	4 430	37	161.7	99.7	36.6	695	525
Forsyth	127.7	28.7	52.8	528.3	43.6	35.8	71.3	113 297	1 033	1 099.0	503.2	394.7	1 165	908
Franklin	12.7	2.1	5.1	85.6	8.1	3.7	1.9	29 403	158	129.3	63.0	45.1	788	576
Gaston	46.7	0.9	8.3	171.0	32.0	19.6	13.8	103 553	456	649.8	347.4	200.0	987	769
Gates	2.6	0.1	0.6	22.5	2.7	0.8	0.1	5 304	34	29.5	19.4	7.3	622	442
Graham	2.1	0.0	2.3	18.8	1.9	1.3	0.1	4 108	29	29.6	15.7	10.0	1 274	989
Granville	106.7	2.4	12.6	70.1	9.0	4.4	4.5	27 476	202	158.8	68.1	38.0	691	495
Greene	4.6	0.2	0.7	29.3	4.8	1.7	5.7	1 613	9	49.0	31.1	11.7	574	396
Guilford	394.5	103.0	176.2	333.5	68.8	62.4	112.0	172 098	1 480	1 639.0	702.0	602.1	1 292	1 030
Halifax	26.4	0.2	2.6	194.8	17.3	6.8	0.9	11 084	124	187.8	110.9	48.5	880	637
Harnett	29.9	13.5	3.8	124.0	15.7	7.5	2.0	113 621	837	274.5	140.3	72.3	665	463
Haywood	12.1	0.1	12.3	79.7	10.0	3.7	5.3	36 748	172	279.0	102.6	61.6	1 092	809
Henderson	27.6	6.7	5.0	67.4	14.1	6.1	10.4	46 373	226	360.7	113.6	94.5	938	694
Hertford	8.4	0.0	43.0	68.1	7.0	3.3	3.5	2 237	19	77.9	44.8	18.7	808	571
Hoke	21.8	3.4	17.0	43.6	7.8	3.6	0.2	97 705	555	98.1	62.6	24.2	570	386
Hyde	2.3	0.6	5.2	17.7	1.5	0.5	0.3	1 462	9	24.8	13.5	7.6	1 461	1 069
Iredell	27.3	13.7	5.6	88.6	16.8	14.7	6.8	93 115	353	418.9	197.1	146.7	969	718
Jackson	6.4	0.1	2.6	48.5	5.3	7.8	4.6	46 178	155	99.8	48.3	37.7	1 025	700
Johnston	49.1	1.5	6.3	187.5	20.8	7.4	10.8	111 657	641	558.2	231.4	144.9	920	646
Jones	1.5	0.2	0.4	26.2	2.9	1.2	0.0	5 332	51	26.8	17.8	6.8	671	497
Lee	27.9	0.4	2.7	65.4	8.5	4.6	3.2	18 560	114	185.4	98.5	57.2	987	782
Lenoir	64.4	63.7	5.4	142.7	15.2	8.1	6.6	5 348	32	209.4	120.1	49.3	868	648
Lincoln	19.5	3.7	2.6	37.0	8.5	3.9	3.7	46 576	133	188.2	83.6	63.7	871	637
McDowell	8.0	0.0	1.9	55.4	7.8	3.5	0.5	21 780	115	101.0	58.2	29.2	670	434
Macon	14.1	3.3	3.9	42.8	8.5	2.2	0.8	20 246	77	92.4	37.7	38.1	1 169	847
Madison	3.6	0.0	1.0	63.8	4.4	2.8	6.6	9 286	52	47.3	26.7	14.1	696	543
Martin	26.5	0.0	1.0	65.4	10.9	2.1	5.1	3 705	22	92.1	52.2	21.1	894	653
Mecklenburg	571.2	88.9	333.1	406.2	94.0	47.7	433.8	395 799	2 672	5 658.9	1 289.9	1 510.5	1 742	1 297
Mitchell	4.2	0.0	1.6	45.2	7.2	7.8	0.8	6 042	49	51.6	34.8	11.4	720	471
Montgomery	4.5	33.6	1.7	41.7	5.9	2.2	0.7	9 845	40	81.2	49.6	20.2	735	562
Moore	20.8	11.4	3.3	77.7	11.9	7.3	8.1	73 887	366	295.3	171.4	82.0	971	720
Nash	7.3	15.3	2.7	137.3	23.4	8.3	13.5	26 308	175	307.5	170.2	83.5	899	679
New Hanover	104.9	36.2	36.5	180.3	25.8	11.5	64.3	114 122	568	1 251.2	268.4	265.3	1 393	995
Northampton	4.8	0.0	4.9	85.9	12.6	2.2	7.2	4 260	22	65.8	39.8	16.5	790	625
Onslow	1 099.6	920.0	8.7	89.1	25.9	15.1	19.2	245 121	2 375	491.5	204.5	109.0	670	440
Orange	34.7	3.9	69.6	804.5	21.8	29.0	184.2	73 827	352	444.6	174.9	203.8	1 639	1 389
Pamlico	4.0	0.8	1.0	22.0	2.3	1.0	0.1	11 701	48	44.1	25.6	12.2	968	694
Pasquotank	97.6	6.9	90.9	42.1	8.1	11.6	5.3	6 957	45	238.0	73.2	33.7	830	550
Pender	8.3	2.5	2.0	55.7	8.7	4.8	7.9	29 555	183	129.3	59.5	52.1	1 044	801
Perquimans	2.6	-0.2	0.6	22.6	2.7	1.1	0.5	8 674	53	37.4	19.3	10.4	832	619
Person	6.1	29.9	1.0	64.7	6.9	3.8	0.4	12 656	68	121.8	61.8	38.1	1 020	780
Pitt	50.5	13.6	8.7	234.2	24.8	16.7	22.7	75 330	669	467.9	237.2	132.8	873	642
Polk	3.8	0.0	0.9	17.7	2.9	1.3	0.0	10 424	39	51.4	22.8	20.0	1 052	834
Randolph	36.5	17.0	10.1	76.6	19.1	11.7	9.3	45 311	318	317.4	178.5	96.0	685	495
Richmond	19.0	0.1	3.5	92.4	10.8	5.4	1.6	5 998	115	134.3	82.3	35.5	772	554
Robeson	76.6	0.3	7.2	321.7	35.9	19.5	50.4	34 570	206	428.2	262.2	82.2	641	435
Rockingham	16.8	96.2	8.7	140.2	15.3	9.2	1.6	23 225	105	246.0	128.2	75.0	812	621
Rowan	120.9	1.8	57.9	83.5	24.7	15.7	9.9	39 777	207	361.8	189.4	110.3	803	621
Rutherford	11.7	0.7	2.4	101.4	12.0	7.1	8.1	20 596	111	186.9	97.7	48.5	770	534
Sampson	32.6	0.9	1.8	127.9	14.5	6.9	2.0	13 261	93	194.1	120.1	45.5	716	508
Scotland	7.3	0.0	1.2	90.2	18.9	4.8	18.1	8 538	80	121.1	72.4	32.2	886	651
Stanly	13.6	0.8	2.0	45.0	8.1	4.7	1.9	16 887	130	171.4	96.2	48.3	816	615
Stokes	6.7	0.0	1.6	39.2	5.6	3.0	0.0	7 189	40	101.6	57.4	32.2	698	500
Surry	15.3	0.5	3.0	110.2	10.0	6.6	1.8	17 761	88	237.1	138.6	61.3	847	587

1. State totals may include programs not allocated by county.　　2. Based on the resident population estimated as of July 1 of the year shown.

Table B. States and Counties — Local Government Finances, Government Employment, and Voting

STATE County	Total (mil dol)	Per capita¹ (dollars)	Education	Health and hospitals	Police protection	Public welfare	Highways	Total (mil dol)	Per capita¹ (dollars)	Federal civilian	Federal military	State and local	Democratic	Republican	All other
	185	186	187	188	189	190	191	192	193	194	195	196	197	198	199
NORTH CAROLINA—Cont'd															
Chowan	50.5	3 450	46.3	3.6	4.4	8.9	0.7	42.0	2 873	44	37	872	49.1	50.2	0.7
Clay	31.4	3 064	39.4	7.0	2.9	3.0	0.1	13.1	1 278	27	26	523	31.3	66.9	1.8
Cleveland	469.4	4 768	34.1	43.7	3.1	5.6	0.6	204.2	2 074	208	249	5 568	39.6	59.5	0.9
Columbus	177.0	3 275	56.1	4.2	3.6	9.2	1.1	53.8	996	143	136	3 898	45.6	53.5	0.9
Craven	290.3	3 001	46.9	7.3	5.4	8.0	1.6	164.7	1 702	5 627	9 619	7 205	43.4	55.8	0.8
Cumberland	930.3	3 035	51.6	4.5	7.1	8.8	1.6	505.2	1 648	12 670	53 343	23 314	58.5	40.9	0.6
Currituck	81.0	3 382	44.1	4.4	4.8	4.9	0.0	16.8	700	49	62	1 198	33.7	65.2	1.2
Dare	200.8	5 945	36.5	8.2	6.8	3.5	1.4	213.4	6 319	241	197	2 691	44.7	54.0	1.3
Davidson	373.8	2 388	59.0	3.0	5.0	6.8	1.1	193.2	1 234	183	398	6 802	32.7	66.2	1.1
Davie	100.0	2 468	59.9	6.8	3.8	6.0	1.0	61.7	1 522	68	104	1 587	30.3	68.6	1.0
Duplin	148.7	2 807	57.7	4.7	4.4	9.4	1.3	21.8	412	185	134	3 284	45.0	54.4	0.6
Durham	1 159.6	4 521	28.7	4.4	5.3	28.3	2.3	831.0	3 240	5 311	882	14 373	75.6	23.6	0.8
Edgecombe	158.9	3 019	51.9	5.2	4.6	12.1	1.0	31.6	600	388	131	4 514	67.1	32.6	0.3
Forsyth	1 134.6	3 349	44.9	5.7	6.0	5.1	2.4	1 264.1	3 731	1 424	909	18 974	54.8	44.3	0.8
Franklin	137.9	2 409	55.6	6.3	4.4	10.4	0.7	119.4	2 087	85	151	2 475	49.1	49.8	1.1
Gaston	602.9	2 977	46.4	9.7	5.9	6.5	1.7	405.1	2 000	412	527	9 630	37.2	62.2	0.6
Gates	29.6	2 520	67.8	0.8	2.7	12.6	0.0	17.7	1 504	37	30	605	52.2	47.0	0.8
Graham	24.6	3 134	50.6	8.2	3.3	8.2	2.7	5.0	631	40	20	477	30.3	67.7	2.0
Granville	147.0	2 670	45.0	23.5	3.8	6.4	1.0	86.8	1 577	1 437	145	6 582	52.9	46.3	0.8
Greene	48.6	2 381	62.5	4.8	3.8	11.8	0.4	15.7	768	39	52	1 869	46.8	52.7	0.4
Guilford	1 774.8	3 809	43.9	4.9	6.3	5.3	2.9	1 709.2	3 668	4 142	1 261	29 108	58.8	40.4	0.8
Halifax	210.7	3 826	45.2	4.6	3.6	8.6	0.9	130.5	2 369	131	137	4 609	64.0	35.7	0.3
Harnett	253.1	2 328	52.9	4.8	4.9	8.4	1.5	220.3	2 026	130	294	5 275	41.2	57.9	0.8
Haywood	278.6	4 936	34.6	34.6	3.5	4.4	1.4	112.7	1 997	146	145	4 022	45.4	53.1	1.5
Henderson	354.7	3 519	34.7	31.5	3.9	7.1	0.8	165.7	1 644	236	260	5 282	38.9	59.9	1.2
Hertford	78.2	3 368	51.6	8.5	4.4	9.4	1.3	83.0	3 577	72	58	1 649	70.5	29.0	0.5
Hoke	100.8	2 377	59.3	2.8	4.3	8.4	0.8	59.9	1 412	57	113	2 421	59.0	40.3	0.7
Hyde	34.6	6 684	31.4	6.9	2.3	5.6	0.0	3.5	683	42	13	690	50.3	49.1	0.6
Iredell	402.1	2 655	52.5	3.3	5.5	6.9	1.2	322.4	2 129	288	398	8 719	37.3	61.7	1.0
Jackson	99.0	2 693	51.8	4.8	3.4	6.6	0.5	28.2	768	69	94	5 947	52.0	46.6	1.5
Johnston	575.0	3 653	48.4	23.7	2.9	6.0	0.9	389.9	2 476	228	423	8 907	37.7	61.4	0.8
Jones	26.1	2 575	57.8	5.1	3.1	12.1	0.4	3.4	332	23	25	556	45.5	53.9	0.6
Lee	176.7	3 049	60.7	2.4	5.8	6.2	1.5	169.7	2 928	174	152	3 200	45.3	53.7	1.0
Lenoir	199.5	3 515	51.6	3.0	5.8	8.7	1.3	247.7	4 364	290	142	6 218	49.7	49.8	0.4
Lincoln	192.4	2 631	57.0	4.9	4.4	7.4	0.6	167.4	2 289	117	191	3 809	32.7	66.0	1.3
MoDowell	100.2	2 301	61.6	1.7	4.5	10.1	0.9	19.3	443	86	110	2 530	36.7	62.7	1.5
Macon	84.6	2 594	42.4	7.4	5.8	5.6	2.1	20.0	614	180	83	1 648	38.4	59.9	1.7
Madison	46.8	2 305	48.5	6.9	5.4	9.8	1.3	4.9	242	49	51	966	48.4	50.0	1.6
Martin	89.8	3 806	51.8	9.4	4.0	8.4	1.1	29.3	1 242	54	59	1 722	52.1	47.5	0.4
Mecklenburg	5 360.0	6 182	23.3	38.5	3.7	2.2	2.1	7 546.9	8 704	5 763	2 368	62 541	61.8	37.4	0.7
Mitchell	50.3	3 187	68.1	1.9	3.0	7.2	0.7	2.1	133	57	39	1 263	28.5	70.1	1.4
Montgomery	79.5	2 895	61.3	3.7	4.7	8.2	1.8	53.6	1 951	59	70	1 834	43.9	54.9	1.2
Moore	290.3	3 438	43.3	24.6	5.2	4.8	1.9	57.7	684	152	219	4 480	38.9	60.3	0.9
Nash	316.3	3 403	52.3	5.9	5.7	6.1	1.6	56.4	607	113	238	6 314	49.0	50.4	0.6
New Hanover	1 295.2	6 801	21.6	45.7	4.0	3.3	1.0	1 282.9	6 737	953	657	17 477	48.8	50.2	1.0
Northampton	70.7	3 395	47.2	6.4	3.1	11.6	1.4	33.8	1 623	53	51	1 361	65.0	34.6	0.4
Onslow	512.9	3 152	44.1	27.9	3.7	5.4	0.7	286.7	1 762	6 199	50 679	7 985	38.8	60.3	0.8
Orange	455.7	3 666	44.7	7.0	5.5	4.4	1.6	516.8	4 157	267	379	34 980	71.8	27.1	1.1
Pamlico	40.4	3 214	58.6	3.0	2.4	10.4	0.8	8.0	635	32	57	889	42.3	57.0	0.8
Pasquotank	257.5	6 350	28.9	41.4	2.6	4.4	0.9	250.3	6 174	728	837	5 272	56.5	42.8	0.7
Pender	131.7	2 642	53.9	5.2	4.1	7.6	0.7	92.5	1 855	98	132	2 448	41.7	57.3	0.9
Perquimans	36.8	2 944	47.7	2.1	3.6	7.0	0.8	34.6	2 765	33	32	672	42.6	56.6	0.8
Person	123.3	3 301	53.5	5.3	5.3	7.9	0.7	143.1	3 832	58	95	2 132	45.3	53.8	0.8
Pitt	474.8	3 122	47.1	4.9	6.5	7.4	1.5	381.1	2 506	456	413	22 691	54.1	45.3	0.6
Polk	48.5	2 549	49.7	3.2	5.2	7.8	1.7	24.9	1 307	47	48	882	41.6	56.7	1.7
Randolph	325.5	2 323	62.4	2.7	5.3	6.9	1.2	196.3	1 401	249	358	6 476	28.2	70.5	1.3
Richmond	140.2	3 049	59.0	3.2	5.1	7.4	1.0	46.3	1 008	98	115	3 180	50.3	48.8	1.0
Robeson	431.5	3 367	52.6	15.8	4.3	9.6	0.9	75.0	585	292	326	8 669	56.5	42.7	0.8
Rockingham	255.7	2 767	50.9	5.5	6.0	8.4	2.0	96.5	1 044	171	232	4 441	41.5	57.4	1.1
Rowan	366.0	2 664	59.0	2.6	5.2	6.8	1.9	221.8	1 614	2 153	356	6 913	38.0	60.8	1.2
Rutherford	190.8	3 029	54.2	7.0	4.9	7.8	1.5	299.6	4 754	125	159	3 553	33.6	65.4	1.1
Sampson	199.9	3 141	55.7	10.8	4.1	8.0	1.3	220.9	3 471	123	160	4 216	45.5	53.9	0.6
Scotland	118.1	3 246	56.9	2.7	4.6	10.0	0.7	25.0	688	58	91	2 506	57.3	42.2	0.4
Stanly	170.6	2 882	55.4	3.5	6.7	6.5	1.6	50.1	846	161	154	3 645	31.1	67.8	1.0
Stokes	96.4	2 093	60.0	5.0	4.5	8.9	0.6	21.7	471	83	116	1 810	31.6	66.6	1.7
Surry	234.6	3 242	53.8	14.5	3.6	6.0	1.5	87.7	1 212	172	182	4 914	35.5	63.4	1.1

1. Based on the resident population estimated as of July 1 of the year shown.   2. © 2009 Election Data Services, Inc. All rights reserved.

Table B. States and Counties — Land Area and Population

STATE/ County code	CBSA code[1]	County type[2]	STATE County	Land area,[3] (sq km) 2010	Total persons	Rank	Per square kilometer	White	Black	American Indian, Alaska Native	Asian and Pacific Islander	Percent Hispanic or Latino[4]	Under 5 years	5 to 17 years	18 to 24 years	25 to 34 years	35 to 44 years	45 to 54 years
				1	2	3	4	5	6	7	8	9	10	11	12	13	14	15
			NORTH CAROLINA—Cont'd															
37 173	...	8	Swain	1 368	13 981	2 176	10.2	69.2	1.0	29.2	0.7	3.9	6.3	17.1	8.5	10.9	12.1	14.6
37 175	14820	6	Transylvania	980	33 090	1 355	33.8	92.3	4.6	0.9	0.7	2.9	4.6	13.0	8.4	8.9	10.2	13.6
37 177	...	9	Tyrrell	1 008	4 407	2 877	4.4	54.4	38.8	0.4	2.1	5.4	5.3	12.8	8.7	14.9	12.9	16.1
37 179	16740	1	Union	1 636	201 292	305	123.0	75.8	12.2	0.7	2.1	10.4	7.3	23.0	7.3	10.7	16.9	15.1
37 181	25780	4	Vance	657	45 422	1 058	69.1	42.8	50.2	0.5	0.6	6.7	6.8	18.6	9.2	11.1	13.0	14.2
37 183	39580	2	Wake	2 163	900 993	56	416.5	63.7	21.2	0.8	6.2	9.8	7.3	18.8	9.7	15.2	16.2	14.5
37 185	...	8	Warren	1 110	20 972	1 789	18.9	38.8	53.1	5.8	0.4	3.3	5.7	14.6	8.0	10.6	11.2	15.4
37 187	...	7	Washington	902	13 228	2 236	14.7	46.2	50.2	0.7	0.4	3.5	6.5	16.5	7.5	9.6	11.3	14.7
37 189	14380	6	Watauga	810	51 079	965	63.1	93.6	2.0	0.8	1.3	3.4	3.8	10.0	31.8	10.3	9.1	11.2
37 191	24140	3	Wayne	1 432	122 623	493	85.6	57.1	32.1	0.7	1.8	9.9	7.1	17.7	10.0	13.2	12.6	14.5
37 193	35900	6	Wilkes	1 954	69 340	765	35.5	89.8	4.6	0.5	0.6	5.4	5.8	16.7	7.2	10.7	13.3	15.6
37 195	48980	4	Wilson	954	81 234	680	85.2	50.4	39.5	0.6	1.1	9.5	6.7	18.0	8.7	12.0	12.9	14.4
37 197	49180	2	Yadkin	867	38 406	1 210	44.3	86.8	3.5	0.5	0.3	9.8	5.9	17.3	7.4	10.4	14.2	15.3
37 199	...	8	Yancey	810	17 818	1 933	22.0	94.2	0.9	0.7	0.3	4.6	4.8	15.2	6.5	10.0	12.8	14.5
38 000	...	X	NORTH DAKOTA	178 711	672 591	X	3.8	90.3	1.6	6.2	1.4	2.0	6.6	15.7	12.0	13.5	11.2	14.4
38 001	...	9	Adams	2 558	2 343	3 025	0.9	97.7	0.4	1.2	0.8	0.9	5.0	14.0	5.6	9.0	9.2	16.1
38 003	...	6	Barnes	3 863	11 066	2 359	2.9	96.9	1.1	1.2	0.8	1.1	5.3	15.3	9.8	10.1	10.2	15.1
38 005	...	9	Benson	3 597	6 660	2 718	1.9	44.1	0.2	55.7	0.2	1.2	9.8	23.8	8.7	10.9	10.5	12.5
38 007	19860	9	Billings	2 976	783	3 120	0.3	98.6	0.0	0.5	0.5	0.5	5.2	12.4	7.0	10.1	8.2	19.9
38 009	...	9	Bottineau	4 321	6 429	2 733	1.5	96.0	0.7	3.2	0.5	1.3	5.4	13.6	8.4	8.3	10.1	16.0
38 011	...	9	Bowman	3 009	3 151	2 966	1.0	97.0	0.2	0.8	0.1	2.5	6.6	14.9	5.8	11.1	9.3	15.9
38 013	...	9	Burke	2 858	1 968	3 058	0.7	96.6	0.5	0.8	0.8	1.9	5.9	14.9	5.4	9.0	9.9	17.1
38 015	13900	3	Burleigh	4 229	81 308	679	19.2	93.5	0.9	4.8	0.8	1.2	6.6	15.9	10.5	14.2	12.1	14.9
38 017	22020	3	Cass	4 571	149 778	416	32.8	92.0	2.8	1.8	2.9	2.0	7.0	14.9	16.2	17.1	12.3	12.7
38 019	...	9	Cavalier	3 856	3 993	2 908	1.0	98.1	0.2	1.4	0.3	0.6	4.6	15.1	5.1	7.6	9.6	16.5
38 021	...	9	Dickey	2 930	5 289	2 821	1.8	96.4	1.0	1.2	0.7	1.9	6.6	16.4	8.7	9.9	10.6	13.4
38 023	...	9	Divide	3 265	2 071	3 044	0.6	97.5	0.4	0.9	0.3	1.4	4.7	12.4	5.3	9.4	8.2	16.7
38 025	...	9	Dunn	5 202	3 536	2 940	0.7	85.9	0.3	13.5	0.7	1.1	6.0	16.0	7.0	10.5	11.2	16.5
38 027	...	9	Eddy	1 632	2 385	3 020	1.5	94.8	0.3	3.3	0.3	2.2	5.3	15.6	5.2	8.4	9.4	16.1
38 029	...	8	Emmons	3 912	3 550	2 939	0.9	98.4	0.5	0.7	0.3	1.0	4.8	16.6	4.3	6.0	9.6	16.2
38 031	...	9	Foster	1 646	3 343	2 953	2.0	98.4	0.3	0.9	0.1	0.9	5.3	16.5	6.0	8.7	11.2	17.0
38 033	...	9	Golden Valley	2 592	1 680	3 076	0.6	96.5	0.6	1.1	0.3	2.1	5.1	19.0	5.0	9.5	10.0	15.2
38 035	24220	3	Grand Forks	3 720	66 861	786	18.0	90.6	2.6	3.4	2.7	2.9	6.5	13.6	21.6	14.7	10.3	12.6
38 037	...	8	Grant	4 297	2 394	3 018	0.6	98.4	0.4	1.9	0.3	0.3	4.6	14.2	4.2	7.2	9.4	15.8
38 039	...	9	Griggs	1 836	2 420	3 016	1.3	98.6	0.3	0.3	0.2	0.4	5.0	13.9	4.0	8.0	9.3	15.2
38 041	...	9	Hettinger	2 932	2 477	3 010	0.8	96.9	0.7	2.9	0.3	0.5	4.9	14.0	5.6	9.0	10.2	15.6
38 043	...	8	Kidder	3 500	2 435	3 015	0.7	95.8	0.2	0.2	1.0	2.9	5.4	16.1	6.4	9.0	10.5	16.3
38 045	...	9	LaMoure	2 968	4 139	2 894	1.4	98.5	0.5	0.5	0.2	0.8	5.3	15.8	4.6	8.3	9.8	16.7
38 047	...	9	Logan	2 571	1 990	3 055	0.8	98.6	0.2	0.6	0.5	0.6	4.7	16.4	4.5	7.0	9.9	16.0
38 049	33500	9	McHenry	4 854	5 395	2 814	1.1	97.5	0.4	1.1	0.5	1.5	5.4	16.5	5.1	10.0	11.2	16.2
38 051	...	9	McIntosh	2 525	2 809	2 990	1.1	97.7	0.3	0.7	0.5	1.4	5.3	12.9	3.6	8.2	8.6	14.7
38 053	...	9	McKenzie	7 149	6 360	2 740	0.9	76.1	0.3	22.5	0.5	2.2	8.1	18.5	8.2	12.0	10.9	15.3
38 055	...	8	McLean	5 467	8 962	2 529	1.6	92.0	0.2	7.7	0.3	1.2	5.0	14.7	5.1	8.9	10.5	16.3
38 057	...	6	Mercer	2 701	8 424	2 578	3.1	95.8	0.4	2.7	0.6	1.4	5.6	15.8	5.7	10.3	10.4	20.7
38 059	13900	3	Morton	4 989	27 471	1 514	5.5	94.3	0.7	4.4	0.5	1.5	7.0	16.9	7.3	13.7	12.0	15.5
38 061	...	9	Mountrail	4 728	7 673	2 632	1.6	66.3	0.5	31.4	0.5	3.7	6.6	17.2	10.2	13.6	11.2	14.2
38 063	...	8	Nelson	2 543	3 126	2 970	1.2	97.7	0.6	1.7	0.1	1.1	4.3	13.6	5.2	7.9	8.5	16.6
38 065	...	8	Oliver	1 871	1 846	3 067	1.0	97.2	0.3	1.8	0.3	1.0	5.7	16.5	5.0	8.9	9.5	18.7
38 067	...	9	Pembina	2 897	7 413	2 650	2.6	95.0	0.5	3.0	0.3	2.6	5.6	16.0	6.0	9.8	10.3	16.4
38 069	...	7	Pierce	2 638	4 357	2 881	1.7	94.5	0.6	4.4	0.1	1.0	5.5	16.1	5.7	8.8	11.1	15.6
38 071	...	7	Ramsey	3 074	11 451	2 336	3.7	89.5	0.6	10.5	0.6	1.2	6.4	15.6	8.9	11.4	10.4	16.1
38 073	...	8	Ransom	2 233	5 457	2 808	2.4	97.7	0.6	0.8	0.5	1.2	5.6	17.9	5.0	9.5	11.6	15.9
38 075	33500	9	Renville	2 272	2 470	3 012	1.1	98.3	0.6	0.8	0.6	1.0	5.3	16.3	6.0	10.5	11.3	16.2
38 077	47420	6	Richland	3 719	16 321	2 031	4.4	95.2	0.9	2.5	0.9	1.7	6.3	16.1	13.2	10.2	10.4	16.1
38 079	...	9	Rolette	2 339	13 937	2 180	6.0	21.9	0.4	78.6	0.2	1.0	10.1	23.3	9.7	11.9	11.0	13.9
38 081	...	9	Sargent	2 224	3 829	2 917	1.7	97.8	0.2	1.0	0.4	1.3	5.4	17.4	5.0	10.1	10.9	16.5
38 083	...	9	Sheridan	2 518	1 321	3 094	0.5	97.4	0.1	2.0	0.5	1.2	3.3	12.6	4.9	6.8	9.1	16.7
38 085	...	8	Sioux	2 834	4 153	2 892	1.5	14.6	0.5	85.3	0.5	2.0	11.4	25.1	11.7	12.8	12.7	11.7
38 087	...	9	Slope	3 147	727	3 124	0.2	97.4	0.1	1.1	0.0	1.7	5.5	14.6	4.8	10.2	8.9	18.7
38 089	19860	7	Stark	3 457	24 199	1 637	7.0	95.1	1.1	1.5	1.4	1.9	6.2	15.2	12.2	13.0	10.5	15.0
38 091	...	8	Steele	1 845	1 975	3 057	1.1	97.5	0.2	1.5	0.2	1.0	5.1	16.2	4.6	9.4	10.3	17.0
38 093	27420	7	Stutsman	5 754	21 100	1 782	3.7	95.7	0.8	1.9	0.8	1.7	5.6	14.9	10.1	11.7	11.2	15.7
38 095	...	9	Towner	2 654	2 246	3 033	0.8	97.1	0.2	2.7	0.0	0.4	4.7	14.5	5.1	6.6	10.0	18.0
38 097	...	8	Traill	2 232	8 121	2 598	3.6	95.8	0.8	1.3	0.6	2.6	6.3	16.0	9.9	9.7	11.2	15.2
38 099	...	6	Walsh	3 320	11 119	2 356	3.3	89.3	0.4	1.9	0.6	8.7	6.1	16.1	6.5	9.9	10.3	16.5

1. CBSA = Core Based Statistical Area. See Appendix A for explanation. See Appendix B for list of metropolitan areas with component counties.   2. County type code from the Economic Research Service of USDA Rural-Urban Continuum Codes. See Appendix A for definition.   3. Dry land or land partially or temporarily covered by water.   4. May be of any race.

Table B. States and Counties — **Population and Households**

STATE County	55 to 64 years	65 to 74 years	75 years and over	Percent female	Total persons 1990	Total persons 2000	Percent change 1990–2000	Percent change 2000–2010	Births	Deaths	Net migration	Households Number	Percent change 2000–2010	Persons per household	Female family householder[1]	One person
	16	17	18	19	20	21	22	23	24	25	26	27	28	29	30	31
NORTH CAROLINA—Cont'd																
Swain	13.9	9.8	6.8	51.3	11 268	12 968	15.1	7.8	1 679	1 594	424	5 672	10.4	2.42	14.3	27.4
Transylvania	15.5	14.0	11.8	51.7	25 520	29 334	14.9	12.8	2 628	3 377	1 848	14 394	16.8	2.22	9.2	29.1
Tyrrell	12.5	9.4	7.5	44.8	3 856	4 149	7.6	6.2	444	373	-124	1 595	3.8	2.37	16.7	28.2
Union	10.1	6.1	3.6	50.6	84 210	123 677	46.9	62.8	23 753	9 066	60 413	67 864	56.4	2.94	10.7	16.8
Vance	13.0	7.9	6.2	53.1	38 892	42 954	10.4	5.7	6 403	4 378	-1 738	17 395	7.4	2.56	22.2	26.2
Wake	9.8	4.9	3.6	51.3	426 311	627 846	47.3	43.5	111 601	33 984	186 668	345 645	42.8	2.55	11.5	26.3
Warren	15.7	10.6	8.3	49.5	17 265	19 972	15.7	5.0	1 921	2 146	-195	8 321	8.0	2.38	18.0	29.6
Washington	15.6	9.9	8.3	53.0	13 997	13 723	-2.0	-3.6	1 601	1 443	-960	5 526	3.0	2.37	20.2	30.1
Watauga	11.3	7.1	5.3	49.8	36 952	42 695	15.5	19.6	3 433	2 753	2 367	20 403	23.4	2.24	6.6	28.5
Wayne	11.8	7.4	5.7	51.1	104 666	113 329	8.3	8.2	16 239	9 836	-5 293	47 831	12.2	2.50	16.7	27.4
Wilkes	13.9	9.8	7.2	50.6	59 393	65 632	10.5	5.6	7 625	6 260	3	28 360	6.4	2.41	10.5	26.7
Wilson	13.0	8.0	6.2	52.3	66 061	73 814	11.7	10.1	10 072	7 107	2 055	31 962	11.7	2.49	17.9	27.8
Yadkin	13.1	9.3	7.0	50.8	30 488	36 348	19.2	5.7	4 369	3 470	709	15 486	6.8	2.46	10.5	25.9
Yancey	15.6	11.5	9.1	50.9	15 419	17 774	15.3	0.2	1 697	1 856	1 076	7 644	2.3	2.31	8.1	28.4
NORTH DAKOTA	12.2	7.0	7.5	49.5	638 800	642 200	0.5	4.7	76 697	53 637	-15 217	281 192	9.3	2.30	8.2	31.5
Adams	16.7	10.8	13.5	51.7	3 174	2 593	-18.3	-9.6	173	327	-189	1 098	-2.1	2.09	4.8	36.6
Barnes	14.5	9.4	10.3	50.4	12 545	11 775	-6.1	-6.0	1 007	1 324	-643	4 826	-1.2	2.19	6.4	32.9
Benson	11.0	6.9	5.9	49.3	7 198	6 964	-3.3	-4.4	1 350	547	-826	2 233	-4.1	2.98	20.6	23.2
Billings	17.9	10.3	8.9	46.7	1 108	888	-19.9	-11.8	70	35	-95	358	-2.2	2.16	1.7	33.2
Bottineau	16.7	10.5	11.0	48.3	8 011	7 149	-10.8	-10.1	559	828	-491	2 832	-4.4	2.17	5.6	32.2
Bowman	14.4	9.3	12.7	49.9	3 596	3 242	-9.8	-2.8	292	391	-106	1 385	2.0	2.22	4.4	32.9
Burke	16.8	10.1	10.8	47.4	3 002	2 242	-25.3	-12.2	163	208	-355	913	-9.9	2.15	5.4	33.6
Burleigh	12.3	6.7	6.7	50.8	60 131	69 416	15.4	17.1	8 873	5 021	6 950	33 976	22.8	2.31	8.7	30.5
Cass	10.3	4.8	4.9	49.6	102 874	123 138	19.7	21.6	17 514	7 337	10 849	63 899	24.5	2.27	8.3	33.0
Cavalier	15.9	11.9	13.7	48.8	6 064	4 831	-20.3	-17.3	321	525	-927	1 818	-9.9	2.15	4.0	34.2
Dickey	12.4	9.9	12.3	50.3	6 107	5 757	-5.7	-8.1	655	683	-494	2 180	-4.5	2.29	4.4	33.3
Divide	16.9	12.1	14.5	48.8	2 899	2 283	-21.2	-9.3	137	325	-130	977	-2.8	2.05	4.5	36.6
Dunn	15.4	9.0	8.5	47.3	4 005	3 600	-10.1	-1.8	296	312	-199	1 401	1.7	2.43	6.6	26.5
Eddy	15.4	10.1	14.5	51.1	2 951	2 757	-6.6	-13.5	216	409	-264	1 057	-9.2	2.18	7.4	33.9
Emmons	15.1	12.0	15.4	48.7	4 830	4 331	-10.3	-18.0	289	509	-707	1 504	-10.8	2.19	3.8	34.4
Foster	12.6	9.1	13.6	49.9	3 980	3 759	-5.6	-11.1	347	456	-379	1 495	-2.9	2.20	5.5	33.5
Golden Valley	15.0	9.9	11.4	50.5	2 108	1 924	-8.7	-12.7	137	143	-296	774	1.7	2.10	4.3	39.4
Grand Forks	10.4	5.2	5.1	48.6	70 683	66 109	-6.5	1.1	8 388	4 027	-3 729	27 417	7.8	2.28	9.1	32.1
Grant	17.6	13.1	13.8	50.3	3 549	2 841	-19.9	-15.7	161	346	-311	1 128	-5.6	2.10	3.9	36.5
Griggs	18.3	10.8	15.5	49.4	3 303	2 754	-16.6	-12.1	174	371	-200	1 131	-4.0	2.10	4.2	36.3
Hettinger	15.0	11.9	13.8	52.4	3 445	2 715	-21.2	-8.8	164	319	-210	1 056	-8.3	2.19	4.5	33.1
Kidder	15.3	10.3	16.6	49.0	3 332	2 753	-17.4	-11.6	220	298	-454	1 059	-8.5	2.30	5.0	28.1
LaMoure	14.7	11.0	13.7	48.8	5 383	4 701	-12.7	-12.0	404	508	-677	1 825	-6.0	2.23	4.6	32.7
Logan	13.5	13.0	15.0	49.1	2 847	2 308	-18.9	-13.8	160	275	-315	843	-12.5	2.28	3.0	30.8
McHenry	14.9	9.6	11.1	48.2	6 528	5 987	-8.3	-9.9	500	592	-700	2 377	-5.9	2.25	5.8	31.3
McIntosh	12.7	13.8	20.2	51.1	4 021	3 390	-15.7	-17.1	237	588	-441	1 307	-10.9	2.07	3.5	36.2
McKenzie	12.9	7.9	6.3	48.4	6 383	5 737	-10.1	10.9	600	494	-21	2 410	12.0	2.58	10.2	25.3
McLean	17.9	11.5	10.2	49.2	10 457	9 311	-11.0	-3.7	699	1 104	-544	3 897	2.1	2.25	5.1	29.0
Mercer	15.8	8.2	7.5	48.4	9 808	8 644	-11.9	-2.5	696	688	-741	3 625	8.3	2.29	5.0	27.3
Morton	13.0	7.1	7.5	50.1	23 700	25 303	6.8	8.6	3 056	2 162	421	11 289	14.2	2.38	9.3	27.7
Mountrail	13.2	7.1	6.6	45.5	7 021	6 631	-5.6	15.7	941	790	42	2 793	9.1	2.55	11.4	28.3
Nelson	16.4	12.6	14.8	49.0	4 410	3 715	-15.8	-15.9	230	592	-207	1 474	-9.5	2.07	5.4	36.0
Oliver	19.0	9.1	7.6	47.7	2 381	2 065	-13.3	-10.6	148	100	-470	756	-4.4	2.44	4.8	22.6
Pembina	15.8	8.9	11.2	49.0	9 238	8 585	-7.1	-13.7	714	809	-1 067	3 257	-7.9	2.23	5.6	32.4
Pierce	13.7	9.4	14.2	50.0	5 052	4 675	-7.5	-6.8	408	616	-452	1 835	-6.6	2.23	5.9	34.3
Ramsey	13.4	8.4	9.6	50.3	12 681	12 066	-4.8	-5.1	1 348	1 391	-734	4 955	0.0	2.21	9.5	34.5
Ransom	14.6	8.1	11.7	49.2	5 921	5 890	-0.5	-7.4	589	782	-166	2 310	-1.7	2.28	5.4	32.9
Renville	14.2	9.2	11.1	48.6	3 160	2 610	-17.4	-5.4	199	267	-309	1 061	-2.2	2.28	5.1	30.9
Richland	12.8	6.9	8.0	48.3	18 148	17 998	-0.8	-9.3	1 874	1 323	-2 421	6 651	-3.4	2.31	7.1	30.9
Rolette	10.1	5.8	4.3	50.5	12 772	13 674	7.1	1.9	2 758	1 085	-1 492	4 783	5.0	2.89	23.2	25.0
Sargent	15.7	10.5	8.5	46.6	4 549	4 366	-4.0	-12.3	404	335	-468	1 675	-6.2	2.26	4.7	30.2
Sheridan	16.6	15.8	14.2	49.9	2 148	1 710	-20.4	-22.7	70	140	-416	645	-11.8	2.05	5.7	33.0
Sioux	7.5	4.8	2.3	48.7	3 761	4 044	7.5	2.7	944	285	-491	1 158	5.8	3.55	31.6	17.4
Slope	18.7	8.8	9.8	45.5	907	767	-15.4	-5.2	61	29	-151	326	4.2	2.23	4.9	29.4
Stark	11.7	7.0	9.0	50.0	22 832	22 636	-0.9	6.9	2 527	1 950	-234	10 085	12.9	2.31	7.4	30.9
Steele	15.1	11.0	11.3	48.9	2 420	2 258	-6.7	-12.5	148	155	-508	864	-6.4	2.29	4.5	27.8
Stutsman	13.7	7.6	9.9	49.1	22 241	21 908	-1.5	-3.7	1 987	2 136	-1 179	8 931	-0.3	2.17	7.5	35.3
Towner	16.5	11.4	13.2	49.1	3 627	2 876	-20.7	-21.9	165	346	-479	1 048	-14.0	2.10	6.0	36.4
Traill	13.0	8.2	10.6	49.9	8 752	8 477	-3.1	-4.2	807	951	-433	3 394	1.6	2.29	6.2	31.3
Walsh	14.4	9.6	10.5	49.6	13 840	12 389	-10.5	-10.3	1 241	1 400	-1 380	4 746	-5.6	2.27	7.1	32.8

1. No spouse present.

STATE County	Persons in group quarters, 2010	Daytime population, 2006–2010 Number	Employment/residence ratio	Births, average 2006–2008 Total	Rate[1]	Deaths, average 2006–2008 Number	Rate[1]	Persons under 65 with no health insurance, 2009 Number	Percent	Medicare, 2011 Eligible for Medicare	Enrolled in Medicare Advantage	Enrolled in a Medicare prescription drug plan	Serious crimes known to police,[2] 2010 Total Number	Rate[3]
	32	33	34	35	36	37	38	39	40	41	42	43	44	45
NORTH CAROLINA—Cont'd														
Swain	244	15 152	1.2	D	D	183	13.5	2 397	21.7	3 281	237	1 527	397	2 840
Transylvania	1 070	30 813	0.9	D	D	358	11.9	4 151	18.8	8 697	1 310	3 915	669	2 022
Tyrrell	632	4 240	0.9	D	D	39	9.4	984	29.7	750	22	447	68	1 543
Union	2 050	162 628	0.7	2 726	14.8	1 074	5.8	29 020	16.5	23 800	2 028	11 742	3 128	1 856
Vance	846	44 684	1.0	695	16.1	435	10.1	6 583	18.5	9 112	1 970	4 713	3 666	8 071
Wake	20 983	871 817	1.0	13 235	16.0	3 962	4.8	110 038	13.9	97 913	17 181	34 682	24 402	2 708
Warren	1 168	18 160	0.6	D	D	223	11.5	3 458	22.8	4 103	822	2 097	647	3 259
Washington	151	13 371	1.0	D	D	151	11.6	1 780	17.3	2 995	124	1 967	240	1 814
Watauga	5 323	52 243	1.1	395	8.9	297	6.7	7 132	18.6	7 362	708	3 262	1 182	2 322
Wayne	3 219	118 205	1.0	1 783	15.7	1 069	9.4	16 802	17.5	20 566	1 181	10 070	5 601	4 673
Wilkes	967	65 998	0.9	807	12.1	687	10.3	10 594	19.6	15 486	4 422	6 644	1 767	2 548
Wilson	1 593	83 375	1.1	1 133	14.7	790	10.3	13 189	20.3	16 095	771	9 220	3 319	4 133
Yadkin	304	32 290	0.7	478	12.6	376	9.9	6 057	19.5	7 624	3 483	2 331	1 115	3 049
Yancey	165	15 979	0.7	D	D	204	11.0	3 176	21.8	4 721	767	2 148	253	1 420
NORTH DAKOTA	25 056	677 843	1.1	8 800	13.8	5 767	9.0	61 244	11.5	110 341	11 877	69 663	13 408	1 993
Adams	52	2 406	1.1	D	D	35	15.2	223	14.5	623	27	439	12	512
Barnes	492	11 012	1.0	D	D	126	11.7	854	10.3	2 431	222	1 649	102	922
Benson	16	6 672	1.0	D	D	62	8.9	1 011	17.3	1 017	112	673	21	315
Billings	9	883	1.0	NA	NA	NA	NA	119	17.6	137	D	77	4	511
Bottineau	270	5 996	0.9	D	D	92	14.3	649	13.4	1 509	94	980	26	404
Bowman	82	3 238	1.1	D	D	39	13.0	287	12.5	691	32	473	NA	NA
Burke	2	1 949	1.0	D	D	25	13.1	164	11.6	489	25	333	27	1 600
Burleigh	2 763	82 587	1.1	1 033	13.4	567	7.4	6 536	9.7	12 974	1 714	7 867	1 875	2 306
Cass	5 010	156 995	1.1	2 058	15.1	806	5.9	13 419	10.7	17 747	2 361	9 848	3 896	2 601
Cavalier	83	4 096	1.0	D	D	59	15.0	341	12.7	1 042	58	760	38	952
Dickey	299	5 299	1.0	D	D	69	12.9	484	12.4	1 174	78	835	26	492
Divide	66	2 042	1.0	D	D	33	16.3	180	12.5	531	31	358	NA	NA
Dunn	127	3 366	0.9	D	D	36	10.6	430	15.9	647	55	417	NA	NA
Eddy	84	2 263	0.8	D	D	48	19.7	239	14.6	612	45	452	12	503
Emmons	53	3 535	1.0	D	D	59	16.9	399	17.1	991	163	657	NA	NA
Foster	61	3 638	1.1	D	D	46	13.2	262	10.7	795	79	582	NA	NA
Golden Valley	52	1 564	1.0	D	D	16	9.6	173	14.1	402	23	259	12	714
Grand Forks	4 216	70 701	1.1	D	D	440	6.6	6 397	11.2	8 265	907	4 821	1 816	2 716
Grant	25	2 318	0.9	D	D	35	14.2	415	25.4	675	65	465	12	501
Griggs	47	2 380	1.0	D	D	36	15.0	218	13.0	659	30	446	7	289
Hettinger	169	2 331	0.9	D	D	32	13.0	266	16.1	664	53	466	8	323
Kidder	0	2 323	0.8	D	D	34	14.5	301	18.6	571	110	391	6	246
LaMoure	65	4 093	0.9	D	D	54	13.0	422	14.8	1 021	80	742	3	92
Logan	72	1 898	0.9	D	D	33	16.6	275	21.3	542	89	366	14	704
McHenry	48	4 454	0.6	D	D	62	11.7	629	16.0	1 245	146	802	12	222
McIntosh	103	2 983	1.0	D	D	64	22.9	270	17.4	979	107	695	NA	NA
McKenzie	152	6 266	1.1	D	D	54	9.5	705	14.4	955	33	628	46	723
McLean	196	8 324	0.9	D	D	113	13.4	806	12.7	2 082	240	1 288	115	1 283
Mercer	126	9 111	1.2	D	D	69	8.6	601	9.2	1 479	185	832	NA	NA
Morton	597	21 829	0.7	D	D	239	9.2	2 513	11.5	4 737	722	2 996	379	1 380
Mountrail	564	7 919	1.2	D	D	76	11.8	860	15.3	1 281	57	782	79	1 030
Nelson	80	3 028	0.9	D	D	57	17.7	249	11.7	944	33	647	52	1 663
Oliver	2	2 017	1.2	D	D	12	6.7	173	12.8	354	55	233	1	54
Pembina	149	7 877	1.1	D	D	87	11.5	731	12.7	1 600	137	1 059	48	648
Pierce	261	4 474	1.1	D	D	59	14.3	388	13.6	1 042	257	725	45	1 033
Ramsey	492	11 648	1.0	D	D	133	11.8	1 097	12.3	2 339	90	1 585	353	3 083
Ransom	185	5 332	0.9	D	D	81	14.3	494	11.5	1 145	72	795	57	1 045
Renville	54	2 214	0.8	D	D	30	13.0	184	10.9	539	35	362	18	729
Richland	986	16 417	1.0	D	D	129	7.8	1 409	10.6	2 687	387	1 768	244	1 495
Rolette	122	13 611	1.0	D	D	120	8.8	1 835	15.2	1 774	116	1 032	53	390
Sargent	37	4 699	1.4	D	D	41	9.9	257	8.3	802	47	552	33	862
Sheridan	0	1 197	0.8	D	D	15	11.5	165	20.2	410	50	278	18	1 363
Sioux	44	4 821	1.6	D	D	43	10.2	543	14.3	395	27	219	0	0
Slope	0	678	0.9	D	D	D	D	83	16.0	150	D	94	2	275
Stark	909	23 621	1.0	D	D	207	9.2	2 060	11.1	4 199	370	2 935	504	2 083
Steele	0	1 849	0.9	D	D	16	8.6	166	12.2	449	36	294	2	101
Stutsman	1 733	21 526	1.1	D	D	228	11.1	1 879	11.6	4 212	704	2 798	394	1 867
Towner	43	2 214	0.9	D	D	35	15.3	223	13.9	656	34	434	34	1 514
Traill	362	7 585	0.9	D	D	97	12.0	636	10.3	1 564	152	1 059	52	640
Walsh	332	11 383	1.0	D	D	139	12.6	1 026	12.3	2 481	233	1 677	171	1 538

1. Per 1,000 estimated resident population.   2. Data for serious crimes have not been adjusted for underreporting; this may affect comparability between geographic areas and over time.   3. Per 100,000 population estimated by the FBI.

Table B. States and Counties — Crime, Education, Money Income, and Poverty

STATE County	Violent	Property	Enrollment Total	Percent private	High school graduate or less	Bachelor's degree or more	Total current expenditures (mil dol)	Current expenditures per student (dollars)	Per capita income (dollars)	Median income Dollars	Percent change, 2000 to 2006–2010 (constant 2010 dollars)	Percent with income of $200,000 or more	Median household income (dollars)	All persons	Children under 18 years	Children 5 to 17 years in families
	46	47	48	49	50	51	52	53	54	55	56	57	58	59	60	61
NORTH CAROLINA—Cont'd																
Swain	229	2 611	3 275	12.1	53.5	18.6	20.5	9 549	19 297	35 071	-3.2	0.7	36 109	18.5	28.0	25.2
Transylvania	190	1 831	6 234	20.4	43.5	27.0	36.8	9 337	23 939	39 408	-19.3	1.9	40 652	15.9	28.9	27.1
Tyrrell	68	1 475	747	5.6	67.2	8.4	9.2	14 803	15 812	32 215	-0.9	1.1	31 732	28.7	43.3	42.5
Union	138	1 718	55 183	17.7	41.6	29.1	321.3	8 148	28 596	63 386	-1.1	5.5	64 486	9.2	13.1	11.7
Vance	564	7 507	11 786	10.5	62.8	10.7	71.9	8 474	17 622	34 025	-14.2	0.7	34 000	24.3	35.5	33.3
Wake	263	2 445	246 750	19.2	26.0	47.4	1 177.3	8 166	32 592	63 770	-8.4	5.9	61 594	12.0	15.2	13.9
Warren	207	3 052	4 917	7.5	59.9	13.9	29.0	10 551	17 838	30 641	-14.7	1.6	32 574	27.1	36.0	34.3
Washington	484	1 331	3 277	12.5	59.5	11.8	24.5	11 695	16 982	32 716	-10.5	0.7	33 293	22.4	37.3	36.5
Watauga	106	2 215	20 389	4.7	36.0	37.1	45.6	9 769	20 961	31 967	-22.6	2.3	38 923	24.8	21.4	20.2
Wayne	487	4 186	31 873	13.9	49.8	16.2	163.5	8 267	20 446	41 224	-4.1	1.4	40 274	19.7	28.7	28.0
Wilkes	206	2 342	14 599	9.1	60.0	12.3	100.5	8 511	19 406	33 438	-22.9	1.0	34 886	19.9	27.2	24.2
Wilson	468	3 665	21 206	14.6	55.9	17.5	109.1	8 096	20 691	38 596	-8.0	1.4	36 645	22.9	34.5	28.8
Yadkin	243	2 805	8 607	5.5	61.1	11.2	50.9	8 201	20 379	39 807	-14.3	0.8	41 095	15.1	23.6	20.4
Yancey	95	1 325	3 575	11.2	58.1	16.2	23.8	9 615	18 576	35 703	-5.0	0.8	36 934	20.3	31.2	28.7
NORTH DAKOTA	225	1 769	170 195	10.8	38.7	26.3	961.3	10 156	25 803	46 781	6.8	2.3	48 878	12.5	15.7	13.7
Adams	43	469	359	1.9	54.8	18.4	2.8	10 011	20 118	35 968	-2.3	0.8	40 082	10.4	13.5	11.8
Barnes	36	886	2 572	5.8	45.1	25.8	16.0	11 483	26 152	41 773	5.8	2.4	45 884	11.5	13.8	11.6
Benson	60	255	1 782	5.1	65.4	9.8	11.5	13 823	14 545	30 479	-9.8	0.8	32 884	34.9	44.2	37.5
Billings	128	383	161	5.8	48.7	16.8	1.7	40 810	28 666	51 923	25.5	3.4	50 921	12.0	17.7	16.2
Bottineau	0	404	1 327	7.9	40.3	21.6	10.9	12 482	26 277	40 227	6.4	3.1	48 504	11.8	15.0	12.6
Bowman	NA	NA	562	2.1	46.5	19.7	6.0	10 502	27 354	48 063	19.0	2.3	49 656	8.1	9.6	9.0
Burke	178	1 422	300	4.3	48.7	17.6	3.7	14 940	32 347	50 800	58.4	4.6	49 575	9.9	12.4	11.7
Burleigh	263	2 043	19 905	20.4	31.7	32.3	98.0	8 807	28 784	53 465	2.2	2.7	55 565	9.3	11.4	9.8
Cass	244	2 357	42 772	10.6	28.7	36.4	186.8	9 535	28 184	47 600	-1.5	3.2	50 932	12.0	12.7	10.9
Cavalier	0	952	769	14.2	45.7	17.8	5.7	11 723	26 468	48 786	20.9	1.2	47 456	9.7	16.1	13.7
Dickey	76	416	1 326	16.9	44.3	19.1	6.5	7 610	21 824	37 179	0.4	2.3	42 517	11.9	14.5	12.6
Divide	NA	NA	264	12.1	41.6	19.2	3.6	14 480	28 462	48 152	26.4	3.2	48 992	10.5	16.8	15.5
Dunn	NA	NA	714	6.3	52.1	15.1	6.6	14 891	24 832	48 707	28.1	1.7	49 682	12.3	17.0	15.2
Eddy	0	503	577	0.7	47.0	17.8	4.2	11 739	20 302	38 404	5.9	0.7	39 557	12.2	17.0	14.3
Emmons	NA	NA	753	3.7	57.0	13.7	6.3	9 948	21 358	35 615	7.7	1.2	36 823	16.0	21.6	17.9
Foster	NA	NA	691	5.4	46.8	18.2	4.6	8 019	27 945	41 066	1.3	2.5	46 599	8.8	11.2	9.6
Golden Valley	0	714	354	7.3	41.8	19.5	4.9	15 840	21 899	33 333	-12.2	1.1	38 425	13.2	20.9	18.1
Grand Forks	188	2 528	23 368	6.9	31.7	33.3	83.4	9 692	24 276	44 242	-2.4	2.2	45 258	15.8	16.1	13.2
Grant	42	459	498	1.4	51.4	16.4	3.5	13 148	25 840	39 500	34.7	1.6	33 842	18.7	30.2	25.7
Griggs	83	207	378	8.2	50.6	19.0	4.6	11 847	24 122	40 085	7.0	1.4	42 126	9.9	15.2	13.6
Hettinger	0	323	425	2.4	48.2	19.7	4.6	12 646	24 928	38 393	3.8	2.7	42 943	12.1	16.5	14.6
Kidder	41	205	521	4.8	52.5	16.0	4.1	10 174	23 502	34 250	6.5	1.7	34 978	16.7	25.7	23.5
LaMoure	62	31	810	7.3	47.3	20.0	9.4	12 420	27 056	46 098	22.5	1.8	50 019	10.5	13.8	11.9
Logan	0	704	387	2.6	59.1	12.5	3.9	12 231	21 654	41 741	17.8	1.7	38 380	14.4	19.4	16.7
McHenry	0	222	1 157	14.6	52.3	14.3	10.0	11 224	22 911	36 944	7.0	1.2	40 157	12.6	18.9	16.1
McIntosh	NA	NA	412	2.2	59.9	16.1	4.5	11 981	22 608	34 904	4.5	1.5	34 285	15.2	18.7	18.1
McKenzie	31	692	1 446	4.8	40.1	21.2	11.6	14 871	27 605	48 480	30.5	3.5	51 641	13.2	17.5	16.3
McLean	67	1 216	1 651	2.3	45.6	17.4	14.9	10 077	27 029	52 922	29.2	1.3	52 457	10.5	14.8	12.4
Mercer	NA	NA	1 728	1.7	42.3	16.7	13.4	9 871	30 616	60 191	12.5	2.1	63 921	8.2	10.1	8.7
Morton	149	1 230	6 285	18.5	45.1	22.3	38.0	9 414	25 303	50 591	7.9	1.5	49 798	10.6	15.8	14.0
Mountrail	13	1 017	1 680	2.6	41.5	19.9	14.1	10 109	25 762	53 912	57.1	2.1	49 694	13.6	20.5	18.3
Nelson	128	1 536	712	6.9	44.3	21.4	5.2	11 013	22 838	39 071	6.8	0.9	41 291	10.2	13.6	11.6
Oliver	0	54	387	14.5	45.6	19.4	2.8	13 405	29 348	62 308	34.3	1.2	55 742	11.7	20.0	18.2
Pembina	54	594	1 495	7.0	47.0	16.7	12.1	10 880	27 019	48 502	5.1	1.8	48 378	9.9	13.4	11.4
Pierce	0	1 033	854	14.4	53.2	11.1	5.5	8 992	18 575	37 091	10.4	0.9	38 030	13.2	18.1	15.0
Ramsey	262	2 821	2 569	8.2	42.1	20.9	20.3	11 087	24 130	41 792	-7.3	1.3	44 795	13.7	20.4	17.9
Ransom	110	935	1 189	7.1	51.0	17.7	8.0	8 096	21 995	46 044	-3.5	0.2	48 302	9.5	12.0	10.1
Renville	0	729	440	8.6	37.5	20.3	6.2	10 629	26 856	49 583	27.4	2.3	56 123	8.3	11.1	9.3
Richland	98	1 397	4 483	6.8	39.3	22.4	25.6	10 781	24 342	47 131	3.1	1.9	48 821	11.4	13.3	11.2
Rolette	44	346	2 984	2.4	45.1	16.5	35.3	12 127	13 632	28 265	-14.9	0.4	31 725	27.9	36.5	32.6
Sargent	0	862	927	3.5	52.3	15.0	6.7	9 061	26 553	49 318	4.7	1.7	49 830	8.7	11.2	9.9
Sheridan	76	1 287	201	6.5	59.2	14.7	1.9	13 471	24 286	37 727	21.9	1.4	35 771	17.4	31.1	25.6
Sioux	0	0	1 352	8.2	50.1	12.3	7.3	20 338	13 542	30 990	8.9	1.4	28 338	41.3	51.8	49.5
Slope	0	275	130	3.8	38.0	28.1	0.3	18 786	24 824	43 625	39.7	0.9	47 210	12.5	18.5	16.1
Stark	194	1 889	6 097	13.1	44.0	23.1	29.8	9 295	25 282	49 536	20.3	1.7	49 736	10.6	13.8	12.2
Steele	51	51	490	1.0	42.3	18.4	2.9	10 590	27 728	44 191	-2.4	4.4	52 558	7.2	12.2	10.2
Stutsman	209	1 659	4 961	28.6	49.4	22.7	26.2	9 900	23 307	44 620	4.1	1.7	46 466	12.0	14.9	12.3
Towner	0	1 514	517	1.0	42.4	20.2	3.6	11 638	24 203	43 684	5.4	2.2	47 502	10.6	16.2	13.4
Traill	0	640	2 042	2.4	41.4	26.3	14.4	10 311	23 340	44 290	-6.6	0.8	50 061	8.7	9.7	8.4
Walsh	108	1 430	2 176	5.1	51.4	15.8	22.1	11 420	23 829	44 139	3.0	1.6	46 938	11.3	16.1	14.0

1. Data for serious crimes have not been adjusted for underreporting; this may affect comparability between geographic areas and over time. 2. Per 100,000 population estimated by the FBI. 3. All persons 3 years old and over enrolled in nursery school through college. 4. Persons 25 years old and over. 5. Elementary and secondary education expenditures. 6. Based on population estimated by the American Community Survey, 2006–2010.

Table B. States and Counties — **Personal Income**

STATE County	Personal income, 2009 Total (mil dol) [62]	Per capita Percent change, 2008–2009 [63]	Per capita Dollars [64]	Per capita Rank [65]	Wages and salaries[2] (mil dol) [66]	Proprietors' income (mil dol) [67]	Dividends, interest, and rent (mil dol) [68]	Transfer payments (mil dol) Total [69]	Government payments to individuals Total [70]	Social Security [71]	Medical payments [72]	Income maintenance [73]	Unemployment insurance [74]
NORTH CAROLINA—Cont'd													
Swain	380	3.3	28 386	2 328	252	11	63	125	123	41	56	12	7
Transylvania	1 033	-2.0	34 207	1 142	360	64	345	288	282	128	112	17	10
Tyrrell	105	0.4	25 688	2 775	40	9	17	32	31	9	14	5	1
Union	6 603	1.1	33 240	1 302	2 528	312	946	908	872	346	296	82	92
Vance	1 302	1.2	30 236	1 929	631	70	196	421	413	120	180	67	18
Wake	35 728	-1.5	39 821	462	26 289	1 839	5 939	4 143	3 979	1 385	1 569	364	358
Warren	493	2.1	25 383	2 820	147	24	73	172	169	51	77	25	6
Washington	392	2.4	30 483	1 867	118	35	60	140	137	42	60	19	10
Watauga	1 464	-0.1	32 193	1 485	913	103	341	255	247	100	88	17	13
Wayne	3 605	0.3	31 673	1 607	2 274	130	530	912	892	268	397	110	33
Wilkes	2 088	-0.2	31 374	1 673	892	138	341	582	570	202	245	55	35
Wilson	2 556	-0.8	32 628	1 395	1 843	133	396	671	657	212	275	86	39
Yadkin	1 135	0.2	30 107	1 952	364	71	159	292	285	107	125	22	18
Yancey	460	0.5	24 807	2 880	150	24	94	164	160	59	67	16	8
NORTH DAKOTA	26 393	-0.7	40 802	X	17 283	3 524	4 704	4 166	4 049	1 455	1 639	339	124
Adams	92	8.3	41 177	376	37	22	16	22	21	8	11	1	0
Barnes	451	-7.2	41 901	338	202	95	90	82	80	32	33	5	2
Benson	212	-9.5	30 625	1 837	97	54	27	54	53	13	21	11	1
Billings	32	22.6	39 154	520	24	3	8	3	3	2	1	0	0
Bottineau	315	-2.2	49 536	112	105	102	57	53	51	20	22	3	1
Bowman	142	12.2	46 949	150	66	32	34	23	23	9	11	1	0
Burke	102	-1.5	55 596	54	36	40	17	15	14	6	6	1	0
Burleigh	3 238	2.2	40 567	415	2 402	238	576	483	468	173	186	33	15
Cass	6 034	-0.6	42 093	323	4 904	618	1 145	683	657	242	220	59	31
Cavalier	189	-37.8	50 980	88	67	57	40	32	31	14	14	1	0
Dickey	220	-10.9	42 099	322	79	69	36	43	42	14	20	3	2
Divide	110	-2.1	56 320	49	24	53	21	16	15	7	6	1	0
Dunn	119	23.8	35 452	958	46	22	19	21	20	7	9	1	0
Eddy	86	-16.2	37 369	705	26	16	17	22	22	8	11	1	0
Emmons	128	-14.0	37 716	673	40	36	26	31	30	12	14	2	1
Foster	137	-8.1	42 183	315	76	25	29	25	24	10	10	1	0
Golden Valley	42	1.0	25 874	2 751	24	-2	12	11	11	5	5	1	0
Grand Forks	2 401	-0.1	36 147	868	1 916	177	439	347	335	113	127	33	9
Grant	101	6.8	43 208	266	24	34	17	20	20	7	9	2	0
Griggs	96	-9.2	40 772	401	36	19	22	21	21	9	9	1	0
Hettinger	128	45.3	54 563	59	29	57	22	22	21	8	11	1	0
Kidder	74	-8.3	33 819	1 200	28	8	17	19	19	7	9	1	0
LaMoure	192	-10.2	49 201	116	61	65	35	31	31	13	13	2	1
Logan	78	-6.5	41 569	360	22	24	16	17	17	6	9	1	0
McHenry	189	-7.7	36 577	805	56	33	31	43	42	15	18	3	1
McIntosh	108	-0.8	41 936	335	37	24	24	31	31	11	18	1	0
McKenzie	248	14.4	42 838	280	179	33	45	35	33	13	14	3	0
McLean	417	15.1	50 189	98	193	82	63	73	72	28	32	4	2
Mercer	374	13.8	47 529	141	373	25	52	52	51	21	21	3	2
Morton	943	6.7	35 627	938	461	53	144	177	172	60	72	14	7
Mountrail	300	18.3	44 248	228	144	52	43	52	51	16	23	5	1
Nelson	146	-16.3	46 764	153	39	44	27	36	35	13	18	1	1
Oliver	92	31.9	56 011	52	69	17	12	10	10	5	3	1	0
Pembina	334	-10.3	45 169	196	200	61	70	54	52	22	21	3	2
Pierce	149	-6.6	37 343	708	64	33	29	34	33	12	15	2	1
Ramsey	412	-12.3	36 686	789	223	49	83	92	90	31	40	8	2
Ransom	198	-13.1	36 062	876	86	32	36	45	44	14	19	2	4
Renville	131	-17.2	58 816	34	38	51	17	20	19	7	10	1	0
Richland	558	-13.2	34 714	1 062	329	80	109	96	93	36	33	7	4
Rolette	375	-1.2	27 199	2 532	203	46	34	128	126	21	53	32	5
Sargent	178	-14.1	45 150	197	112	41	44	29	28	11	10	1	3
Sheridan	60	-2.4	48 504	127	10	26	10	13	12	5	6	1	0
Sioux	87	1.5	20 717	3 084	81	0	7	35	35	4	15	10	0
Slope	45	189.4	68 720	15	5	28	7	4	4	2	1	0	0
Stark	980	10.4	42 907	274	617	149	150	154	150	54	65	10	4
Steele	78	-21.4	44 504	216	30	18	19	13	12	6	4	1	0
Stutsman	810	-1.4	39 586	479	464	146	146	147	143	54	60	10	3
Towner	114	-23.8	51 484	84	31	40	24	21	21	8	10	1	0
Traill	293	-7.9	37 176	725	135	35	52	56	55	22	23	3	1
Walsh	414	-7.0	38 382	590	216	57	85	86	84	33	38	6	2

1. Based on the resident population estimated as of July 1 of the year shown.   2. Includes supplements to wages and salaries.

Table B. States and Counties — Earnings, Social Security, and Housing

STATE County	Earnings, 2009 Total (mil dol)	Farm	Goods-related[1] Total	Manu-facturing	Information and profes-sional and technical services	Retail trade	Finance, insur-ance, and real estate	Health care and social services	Govern-ment	Social Security beneficiaries, December 2010 Number	Rate[2]	Supple-mental Security Income recipients, December 2010	Housing units, 2010 Total	Percent change, 2000-2010
	75	76	77	78	79	80	81	82	83	84	85	86	87	88
NORTH CAROLINA—Cont'd														
Swain	263	0.4	10.1	4.8	2.8	6.5	1.5	D	46.1	3 835	274	374	8 723	22.8
Transylvania	424	1.3	D	5.0	6.1	10.5	4.6	17.4	17.3	9 610	290	586	19 163	23.3
Tyrrell	49	10.6	D	D	D	7.9	D	1.6	47.9	845	192	139	2 068	1.8
Union	2 840	3.5	D	20.3	5.3	6.8	3.2	4.7	18.5	27 070	134	2 069	72 870	59.4
Vance	701	4.9	D	12.7	D	10.0	2.9	16.1	20.7	10 610	234	2 216	20 082	10.4
Wake	28 128	0.1	12.9	6.4	19.9	6.2	7.3	9.8	17.6	105 880	118	10 839	371 836	43.6
Warren	170	7.6	13.6	8.9	3.1	4.3	1.8	D	40.8	4 680	223	964	11 806	11.9
Washington	153	13.5	6.6	4.6	D	7.3	2.5	12.2	33.1	3 445	260	669	6 491	5.1
Watauga	1 015	0.5	9.4	3.0	5.3	9.1	5.0	16.7	31.6	8 065	158	679	32 137	38.7
Wayne	2 404	2.4	D	11.3	3.4	6.5	3.1	13.2	36.6	23 685	193	4 550	52 949	11.9
Wilkes	1 030	5.5	D	13.8	D	7.4	5.0	7.8	20.9	17 870	258	2 080	33 065	13.0
Wilson	1 976	2.5	D	28.2	5.6	5.8	5.2	6.8	16.8	18 090	223	3 093	35 511	15.6
Yadkin	435	8.3	28.2	19.9	D	6.8	3.9	D	17.9	8 850	230	778	17 341	9.6
Yancey	174	0.8	D	8.5	4.7	8.7	3.4	D	23.6	5 325	299	708	11 032	13.5
NORTH DAKOTA	20 808	9.5	16.5	6.5	6.5	6.3	5.8	12.0	20.6	120 098	179	8 277	317 498	9.6
Adams	59	29.6	6.7	4.3	1.7	6.3	D	27.6	10.7	670	286	16	1 377	-2.8
Barnes	297	21.5	D	11.0	4.9	4.8	4.0	10.3	16.4	2 895	244	148	5 704	1.9
Benson	151	29.8	D	D	D	1.2	2.0	D	48.4	1 235	185	195	2 950	0.6
Billings	27	10.6	D	0.0	D	D	D	0.2	33.7	155	198	0	484	-8.5
Bottineau	208	38.3	16.4	3.4	D	4.6	3.1	D	14.5	1 680	261	52	4 341	-1.5
Bowman	98	24.8	19.7	1.0	4.7	5.6	D	8.8	11.1	755	240	27	1 683	5.5
Burke	78	43.9	9.8	0.3	D	D	2.1	D	24.0	540	274	10	1 340	-5.1
Burleigh	2 641	0.0	11.3	4.2	7.0	7.7	6.4	20.2	22.8	13 975	172	882	35 754	23.3
Cass	5 523	2.9	D	8.0	11.9	7.4	9.6	14.0	14.1	19 100	128	1 567	67 938	26.3
Cavalier	125	33.4	D	D	D	3.6	D	6.2	10.5	1 145	287	23	2 309	-15.3
Dickey	148	39.6	10.4	8.5	D	5.7	D	10.6	9.4	1 255	237	65	2 636	-0.8
Divide	77	63.0	D	D	D	2.6	2.0	D	11.2	585	282	22	1 324	-9.9
Dunn	69	27.8	D	D	D	4.5	1.7	D	17.0	705	199	29	2 132	8.5
Eddy	43	31.5	D	D	D	3.5	D	15.5	17.9	645	270	30	1 323	-6.7
Emmons	76	37.3	7.0	0.6	D	4.2	D	8.8	14.5	1 105	311	43	2 085	-3.8
Foster	101	19.6	21.6	18.2	D	6.4	3.8	12.2	12.7	825	247	33	1 801	0.4
Golden Valley	22	-19.4	D	D	D	7.1	7.2	15.7	30.9	425	253	10	967	-0.6
Grand Forks	2 093	3.1	D	5.3	5.3	8.0	4.0	15.6	33.2	8 875	133	655	29 344	7.2
Grant	58	50.6	D	D	D	2.2	2.6	10.5	13.2	720	301	31	1 690	-1.9
Griggs	55	25.4	D	11.6	D	4.9	2.4	D	14.8	710	293	23	1 461	-3.9
Hettinger	86	59.8	D	2.9	D	1.3	D	4.5	9.7	715	289	21	1 414	-0.4
Kidder	36	14.3	D	D	D	3.9	6.8	2.4	21.6	630	259	27	1 674	4.4
LaMoure	126	46.2	3.7	2.3	D	2.2	D	2.8	12.2	1 075	260	46	2 238	-1.5
Logan	45	40.9	D	D	D	3.3	D	D	14.2	610	307	22	1 144	-4.3
McHenry	89	32.2	D	D	2.8	1.9	4.5	3.4	21.4	1 330	247	56	2 948	-1.2
McIntosh	62	38.9	6.5	5.2	D	4.8	3.4	17.2	13.1	1 030	367	43	1 858	0.3
McKenzie	212	10.4	21.5	0.9	2.3	2.0	3.3	D	32.7	1 085	171	50	3 090	13.6
McLean	275	24.0	D	D	D	2.4	2.3	D	13.7	2 305	257	113	5 590	6.2
Mercer	398	2.3	D	D	2.7	2.6	1.4	D	6.2	1 715	204	78	4 450	1.1
Morton	514	7.8	D	13.2	8.6	7.4	4.2	D	15.5	5 195	189	328	12 079	14.1
Mountrail	196	24.7	D	D	6.5	4.5	D	5.2	18.1	1 400	182	119	4 119	19.9
Nelson	83	46.1	D	D	D	3.3	6.6	D	13.2	1 025	328	31	1 927	-4.3
Oliver	86	18.4	D	1.2	D	D	D	0.6	5.6	415	225	16	905	0.1
Pembina	261	22.9	D	15.6	0.9	3.4	D	3.8	20.0	1 730	233	71	3 859	-6.2
Pierce	97	27.3	8.3	3.3	D	5.5	D	D	13.1	1 110	255	65	2 199	-3.1
Ramsey	272	8.0	D	3.2	4.5	11.2	6.1	D	26.1	2 590	226	186	5 615	-2.0
Ransom	118	22.0	D	9.8	3.0	5.0	4.0	12.1	17.3	1 210	222	61	2 656	2.0
Renville	89	52.6	D	D	D	1.4	D	D	10.9	585	237	13	1 386	-1.9
Richland	409	16.4	D	21.5	D	4.9	2.8	D	22.2	2 930	180	159	7 503	-1.0
Rolette	250	11.0	D	3.5	2.5	5.3	D	D	59.8	2 080	149	806	5 372	6.9
Sargent	153	27.4	D	D	D	2.6	D	1.2	7.9	910	238	33	2 004	-0.6
Sheridan	36	65.8	D	D	D	D	D	D	11.3	425	322	23	894	-3.2
Sioux	81	-2.1	1.3	0.0	D	1.3	0.1	D	95.6	480	116	204	1 311	7.8
Slope	33	84.8	D	0.0	D	0.0	0.0	0.4	2.9	160	220	0	436	-3.3
Stark	766	6.9	28.7	7.8	6.0	6.5	3.6	D	13.7	4 590	190	289	10 735	10.4
Steele	48	35.7	22.9	11.3	D	4.6	D	D	12.9	520	263	0	1 171	-4.9
Stutsman	610	8.1	D	12.7	4.2	6.3	4.1	D	17.1	4 525	214	410	9 862	0.5
Towner	72	50.2	D	D	D	2.4	4.5	D	10.3	675	301	22	1 449	-7.0
Traill	169	20.2	D	12.2	2.0	3.9	5.2	D	19.1	1 720	212	55	3 780	1.9
Walsh	272	13.4	D	10.1	3.9	4.0	4.7	D	20.0	2 730	246	129	5 498	-4.5

1. Includes mining, construction, and manufacturing.   2. Per 1,000 resident population enumerated in the 2010 census.

Table B. States and Counties — Housing, Labor Force, and Employment

STATE County	Total	Percent	Median value[1]	With a mortgage	Without a mortgage	Median rent[2]	Median rent as a percent of income	Substandard units[3] (percent)	Total	Percent change, 2009–2010	Total	Rate[4]	Total	Management, business, science and arts	Construction, production, and maintenance occupations
	89	90	91	92	93	94	95	96	97	98	99	100	101	102	103
NORTH CAROLINA—Cont'd															
Swain	5 772	77.5	114 600	22.9	10.0	651	32.3	0.9	6 754	-6.0	880	13.0	5 590	35.1	19.2
Transylvania	13 847	76.6	169 600	24.3	10.0	649	34.0	1.4	12 720	-8.3	1 243	9.8	13 075	29.2	29.5
Tyrrell	1 663	76.5	112 000	30.1	16.6	461	24.7	1.7	2 238	-4.3	238	10.6	1 522	24.2	36.9
Union	65 635	82.0	194 900	23.3	11.2	787	30.4	2.3	94 115	1.4	9 317	9.9	90 218	36.2	23.3
Vance	16 473	65.2	98 100	26.5	13.1	624	34.3	4.5	19 283	-4.8	2 520	13.1	17 271	24.1	29.4
Wake	325 486	66.2	222 300	22.3	10.0	845	28.5	2.4	456 623	2.2	38 303	8.4	439 524	48.6	14.1
Warren	7 835	75.3	94 700	27.0	15.6	563	34.1	3.2	7 681	-7.5	981	12.8	6 871	29.1	31.7
Washington	4 911	70.4	91 900	24.1	15.9	562	41.1	3.8	7 043	6.6	772	11.0	4 705	28.6	28.8
Watauga	21 153	54.1	215 800	24.0	10.6	740	49.8	1.1	23 548	-3.5	1 892	8.0	25 550	33.4	16.8
Wayne	46 280	64.3	104 800	22.9	12.1	626	28.3	2.5	52 837	-0.4	4 692	8.9	50 504	29.0	30.5
Wilkes	27 814	74.3	109 100	23.5	11.0	512	29.2	3.0	29 475	-7.1	3 966	13.5	29 596	25.0	32.4
Wilson	31 677	61.8	111 100	24.0	14.8	704	30.8	2.2	39 753	-4.3	5 045	12.7	34 074	28.7	31.8
Yadkin	14 908	78.2	109 000	22.5	10.6	526	27.5	2.1	18 296	-3.8	1 884	10.3	17 425	27.8	36.6
Yancey	7 491	78.3	129 700	26.1	10.0	490	24.2	1.9	7 563	-6.4	900	11.9	7 723	20.8	35.9
NORTH DAKOTA	276 642	66.6	111 300	20.3	11.0	555	25.7	1.3	375 728	1.9	14 383	3.8	352 012	34.2	24.1
Adams	1 015	67.8	81 300	23.8	10.3	378	23.9	0.0	1 198	-4.6	35	2.9	1 151	40.7	21.7
Barnes	4 830	68.1	80 600	18.3	11.4	466	22.8	1.2	6 124	-1.1	272	4.4	5 623	34.2	26.9
Benson	2 307	62.1	47 800	19.6	11.5	362	24.4	8.0	2 910	12.4	158	5.4	2 468	30.9	25.6
Billings	354	83.1	79 500	15.6	10.0	444	0.0	4.0	563	8.9	14	2.5	502	51.8	24.9
Bottineau	3 010	77.9	68 300	15.9	11.9	483	26.1	0.9	3 687	1.6	136	3.7	3 030	33.6	24.7
Bowman	1 318	80.2	85 100	16.8	10.0	484	16.9	0.1	1 744	1.7	47	2.7	1 711	26.7	34.4
Burke	982	82.9	45 600	14.3	10.0	386	15.9	1.2	1 137	3.6	32	2.8	976	36.7	27.9
Burleigh	33 001	70.3	152 900	21.6	11.7	569	25.7	0.9	47 181	0.2	1 711	3.6	44 097	37.9	18.5
Cass	62 916	53.6	147 900	21.9	11.4	606	27.6	1.4	86 334	-0.5	3 360	3.9	85 191	36.6	21.3
Cavalier	1 760	83.9	58 800	16.3	10.2	376	22.0	0.6	1 978	1.0	66	3.3	2 002	40.0	23.6
Dickey	2 167	72.9	61 600	19.9	12.4	462	23.3	1.0	2 721	-0.2	96	3.5	2 643	30.8	30.2
Divide	1 012	81.0	56 000	18.6	10.0	346	17.1	0.0	889	2.5	29	3.3	1 187	43.0	23.3
Dunn	1 318	84.9	73 000	16.5	10.0	401	18.9	1.9	2 089	18.4	70	3.4	1 854	37.5	33.6
Eddy	1 036	81.6	48 900	20.2	11.0	379	19.1	0.9	1 187	2.0	61	5.1	1 161	37.2	27.6
Emmons	1 608	84.1	59 600	18.6	13.2	336	14.4	0.9	1 653	-0.7	127	7.7	1 681	45.1	24.3
Foster	1 506	75.8	76 500	20.2	10.8	378	21.4	0.5	1 720	1.0	62	3.6	1 681	41.1	26.2
Golden Valley	730	79.7	56 400	17.3	11.7	422	31.3	2.3	869	-1.9	27	3.1	811	39.3	25.3
Grand Forks	26 514	54.4	139 100	21.7	12.5	628	30.5	0.9	37 298	-0.7	1 461	3.9	36 876	33.1	20.6
Grant	1 152	81.8	59 200	20.4	12.3	408	22.7	1.6	1 214	2.1	54	4.4	1 330	50.8	22.0
Griggs	1 099	79.0	61 200	19.9	11.3	432	23.5	0.6	1 267	0.9	38	3.0	1 240	38.5	26.9
Hettinger	1 177	82.3	58 400	20.5	10.0	377	19.9	1.4	1 195	2.8	47	3.9	1 319	47.2	26.6
Kidder	1 188	71.0	59 400	17.4	10.8	371	28.1	0.8	1 091	-8.0	69	6.3	1 278	44.4	28.7
LaMoure	1 962	83.6	63 400	17.0	10.0	438	22.8	1.0	2 276	1.2	84	3.7	2 151	42.7	26.7
Logan	815	82.8	55 500	19.4	11.5	454	26.3	0.5	970	3.1	36	3.7	899	38.0	26.8
McHenry	2 540	76.9	66 300	19.7	11.4	430	22.6	2.2	2 673	-1.0	133	5.0	2 652	30.2	31.4
McIntosh	1 337	83.2	49 800	18.7	11.4	465	25.0	0.7	1 300	-2.0	58	4.5	1 383	43.8	24.7
McKenzie	2 468	68.4	86 600	14.9	10.0	481	19.4	3.4	3 466	20.9	77	2.2	2 964	34.7	26.4
McLean	3 937	79.3	94 100	17.5	10.0	415	16.4	0.6	4 893	-0.3	246	5.0	4 510	35.9	28.7
Mercer	3 644	78.8	96 100	14.4	10.0	398	19.2	0.7	4 531	-13.8	229	5.1	4 374	24.4	41.5
Morton	10 724	79.2	110 800	21.0	10.8	493	25.1	1.1	14 898	-0.1	706	4.7	14 936	31.0	25.3
Mountrail	2 851	72.4	66 900	14.1	10.0	523	21.4	4.0	4 655	27.4	134	2.9	3 710	31.3	24.1
Nelson	1 448	82.6	51 100	20.5	11.9	366	24.6	0.6	1 645	-2.8	67	4.1	1 449	39.5	25.5
Oliver	762	85.8	92 100	16.8	10.0	389	0.0	1.2	1 411	10.9	51	3.6	928	40.5	26.8
Pembina	3 289	79.6	71 800	18.0	10.0	470	22.3	0.8	3 792	-2.9	258	6.8	3 800	30.1	32.4
Pierce	1 847	70.6	77 100	19.0	11.5	505	28.7	0.0	1 836	-1.3	105	5.7	1 885	27.3	27.3
Ramsey	4 762	65.5	85 300	18.3	10.3	431	22.0	1.6	5 703	1.5	230	4.0	5 942	33.1	21.4
Ransom	2 345	74.7	87 200	20.7	10.2	514	23.8	1.4	2 841	-1.4	135	4.8	2 766	31.6	37.3
Renville	1 097	75.8	64 900	16.0	10.0	477	19.7	1.3	1 230	-2.7	37	3.0	1 264	34.2	30.1
Richland	6 517	73.7	93 400	19.6	11.0	454	24.2	0.8	8 586	0.4	376	4.4	8 445	29.6	31.7
Rolette	4 653	74.0	56 700	17.3	13.3	331	28.0	7.9	5 001	1.6	577	11.5	4 634	36.8	20.5
Sargent	1 770	77.7	74 600	19.3	10.0	450	26.3	0.4	2 003	2.7	90	4.5	2 061	34.7	37.2
Sheridan	638	86.1	48 700	24.0	11.0	325	27.9	0.0	661	2.5	32	4.8	623	39.2	29.4
Sioux	1 060	50.0	71 800	19.0	11.5	406	14.6	14.2	1 265	-0.5	67	5.3	1 182	33.3	21.0
Slope	327	79.5	52 900	25.3	10.0	458	33.0	2.4	628	15.9	10	1.6	403	49.4	25.8
Stark	9 643	72.7	115 300	19.4	11.1	574	24.7	0.6	15 259	7.2	399	2.6	12 872	28.4	30.4
Steele	825	80.7	63 100	17.0	10.1	385	18.0	0.2	1 127	2.9	28	2.5	973	36.9	31.9
Stutsman	8 633	68.7	91 500	19.7	12.0	496	24.4	0.8	11 793	-0.7	472	4.0	10 669	34.2	23.2
Towner	1 056	79.0	48 800	19.3	10.4	412	26.6	1.5	1 096	3.9	37	3.4	1 177	39.2	22.5
Traill	3 425	75.0	89 000	20.8	12.7	504	24.8	0.4	3 967	0.1	168	4.2	4 368	31.0	28.9
Walsh	4 756	74.2	64 300	18.9	11.1	461	20.9	1.8	5 433	-2.2	312	5.7	5 764	30.8	32.3

1. Specified owner-occupied units. 2. Specified renter-occupied units. A value of 10.0 represents 10 percent or less. 3. Overcrowded or lacking complete plumbing facilities. 4. Percent of civilian labor force. 5. Persons 16 years old and over.

Table B. States and Counties — Nonfarm Employment and Agriculture

	Private nonfarm establishments, employment and payroll, 2009									Agriculture, 2007			
		Employment						Annual payroll		Farms			
												Percent with:	
STATE County	Number of establish-ments	Total	Health care and social assistance	Manufac-turing	Retail trade	Finance and insurance	Professional, scientific, and technical services	Total (mil dol)	Average per employee (dollars)	Number	Fewer than 50 acres	500 acres or more	Farm operators whose principal occu-pation is farming (percent)
	104	105	106	107	108	109	110	111	112	113	114	115	116
NORTH CAROLINA—Cont'd													
Swain	397	5 535	D	238	476	69	D	157	28 421	85	50.6	1.2	37.6
Transylvania	837	7 458	1 598	486	1 461	237	206	199	26 694	279	73.5	1.1	35.5
Tyrrell	66	390	D	D	147	D	D	8	20 241	68	35.3	32.4	54.4
Union	4 012	46 657	5 391	10 325	6 598	862	1 239	1 447	31 007	1 107	55.5	5.2	51.5
Vance	878	13 177	2 657	1 766	2 157	251	211	383	29 100	246	28.0	10.6	45.5
Wake	24 619	375 345	50 453	15 749	48 860	19 722	36 039	15 970	42 548	827	56.8	3.5	49.0
Warren	242	1 753	D	289	301	D	44	42	24 087	294	25.2	12.9	44.2
Washington	259	3 179	813	D	430	D	67	101	31 901	187	31.6	21.9	58.3
Watauga	1 641	16 863	3 451	913	3 435	391	644	451	26 743	587	55.5	1.2	34.1
Wayne	2 239	33 986	7 965	5 162	5 611	1 124	745	1 003	29 502	723	42.9	13.4	58.1
Wilkes	1 311	18 983	3 269	3 931	2 442	434	440	575	30 286	1 095	50.7	3.1	49.5
Wilson	1 739	31 014	4 566	7 678	3 860	D	828	1 088	35 075	304	41.4	19.1	53.9
Yadkin	624	7 288	1 305	1 561	823	170	215	197	27 071	990	51.8	3.0	46.0
Yancey	355	2 919	497	367	531	81	92	76	26 038	447	60.0	1.1	40.0
NORTH DAKOTA	21 445	296 083	53 196	24 350	44 573	18 066	10 648	10 046	33 929	31 970	8.3	51.7	57.9
Adams	98	741	D	D	146	D	D	21	27 692	426	8.5	56.3	54.2
Barnes	377	5 509	2 490	717	541	169	93	182	32 955	921	9.0	43.5	56.0
Benson	104	1 071	D	D	D	D	D	29	26 624	591	8.0	56.9	61.9
Billings	44	D	D	0	D	D	D	D	D	243	1.6	61.7	63.8
Bottineau	260	1 812	295	70	456	D	61	49	26 769	899	7.8	50.2	57.2
Bowman	154	1 088	D	D	294	81	D	29	26 979	353	4.5	60.3	55.0
Burke	81	370	D	0	81	34	D	12	33 492	463	2.6	57.7	57.0
Burleigh	2 687	42 751	9 414	1 524	6 678	2 214	1 456	1 477	34 555	1 026	20.6	34.2	43.5
Cass	4 977	95 776	12 858	8 504	12 007	8 037	4 472	3 499	36 535	913	15.9	53.0	68.3
Cavalier	158	1 193	244	D	204	127	10	36	30 396	650	6.5	59.1	64.5
Dickey	213	1 809	353	270	342	66	D	40	22 127	545	5.7	53.0	61.3
Divide	77	494	D	D	62	D	D	12	24 085	503	4.8	60.8	63.0
Dunn	91	961	D	D	117	D	D	26	26 600	563	6.9	62.9	65.5
Eddy	79	571	224	D	104	21	D	13	22 398	366	5.2	52.2	53.8
Emmons	130	765	189	D	117	D	D	20	25 729	694	3.5	62.8	62.8
Foster	142	1 360	311	D	225	59	D	48	34 950	310	8.4	53.2	62.6
Golden Valley	72	405	D	D	135	D	D	8	20 862	243	4.9	64.6	59.7
Grand Forks	1 818	30 760	6 379	2 298	5 789	1 034	1 085	961	31 254	973	11.9	37.8	61.6
Grant	74	414	196	D	50	38	D	10	24 070	528	6.8	66.1	68.9
Griggs	95	704	D	D	D	D	D	19	26 871	479	7.9	45.3	55.1
Hettinger	98	434	D	D	93	46	D	11	26 083	546	6.6	50.4	46.0
Kidder	62	409	45	D	71	D	D	11	27 076	590	6.6	58.3	60.3
LaMoure	149	1 154	151	52	152	109	D	26	22 796	683	5.9	47.1	60.8
Logan	72	406	D	D	43	D	D	9	21 623	426	4.9	54.7	57.5
McHenry	116	867	D	D	132	52	D	19	22 031	928	6.4	52.0	58.2
McIntosh	115	863	312	D	161	56	23	20	23 533	513	3.9	53.8	57.5
McKenzie	182	1 671	203	D	162	108	53	85	50 627	585	6.8	59.5	64.6
McLean	234	2 117	D	D	260	D	16	91	43 055	1 001	7.7	53.6	53.5
Mercer	237	D	400	41	406	117	D	D	D	455	7.7	49.0	45.5
Morton	723	8 245	1 438	877	1 045	343	D	286	34 724	836	11.5	54.4	58.9
Mountrail	214	1 631	295	D	387	110	D	55	33 828	659	2.9	62.2	62.1
Nelson	115	702	232	D	123	71	D	17	24 208	651	7.2	37.3	41.6
Oliver	38	D	D	26	34	D	11	D	D	273	5.1	51.6	55.7
Pembina	295	2 875	D	D	437	125	25	94	32 786	521	10.2	49.9	67.8
Pierce	167	1 452	350	D	292	D	51	38	26 200	530	6.8	55.3	57.7
Ramsey	384	3 974	995	D	895	253	D	101	25 499	629	13.4	47.5	57.6
Ransom	202	1 638	388	312	310	78	41	45	27 377	560	8.2	39.5	46.1
Renville	96	739	D	D	D	D	D	23	31 750	370	10.0	63.8	70.0
Richland	522	5 993	643	D	846	159	118	177	29 527	943	13.6	49.2	68.1
Rolette	194	2 395	545	D	480	91	D	63	26 205	662	8.0	41.7	47.3
Sargent	129	2 128	88	D	146	D	D	60	28 145	493	5.9	50.9	67.7
Sheridan	45	D	D	D	D	D	D	D	D	390	3.6	57.9	57.9
Sioux	29	883	D	0	52	D	D	22	25 155	204	8.3	69.1	68.1
Slope	14	29	0	0	0	D	0	1	26 828	238	2.1	63.9	65.5
Stark	903	10 474	1 797	1 070	1 645	374	283	352	33 578	865	13.1	45.3	50.5
Steele	63	445	D	112	76	48	D	15	34 620	342	7.3	50.9	59.9
Stutsman	652	8 680	2 407	850	1 370	434	271	231	26 651	1 043	7.8	49.9	51.3
Towner	82	577	D	D	38	72	21	15	25 657	496	3.2	59.3	61.7
Traill	295	2 530	577	D	302	175	36	73	28 868	460	13.7	56.5	69.8
Walsh	418	3 560	704	581	564	178	88	90	25 187	968	9.0	40.3	55.9

STATE County	Acreage (1,000) [117]	Percent change, 2002–2007 [118]	Average size of farm [119]	Total irrigated (1,000) [120]	Total cropland (1,000) [121]	Average per farm [122]	Average per acre [123]	Value of machinery and equipment, average per farm (dollars) [124]	Total (mil dol) [125]	Average per farm (dollars) [126]	Crops [127]	Live-stock and poultry products [128]	$10,000 or more [129]	$100,000 or more [130]	Total ($1,000) [131]	Percent of farms [132]
NORTH CAROLINA—Cont'd																
Swain	6	-14.3	66	0.0	1.5	403 101	6 133	50 586	1.4	16 503	86.7	13.3	17.6	3.5	12	15.3
Transylvania	16	-11.1	58	1.0	7.7	422 408	7 345	42 670	12.4	44 310	60.8	39.2	26.9	7.5	228	8.2
Tyrrell	54	-27.0	792	0.0	51.7	1 805 736	2 279	269 674	36.2	531 765	D	D	55.9	36.8	1 026	83.8
Union	178	-6.8	161	0.3	121.1	837 937	5 206	93 151	410.5	370 818	11.4	88.6	43.6	27.0	1 755	19.6
Vance	55	-26.7	224	1.5	20.1	739 950	3 304	62 112	D	D	D	0.0	22.4	6.9	512	50.4
Wake	85	-8.6	103	3.8	45.9	816 154	7 945	58 385	42.3	51 102	86.0	14.0	30.7	5.9	2 196	23.8
Warren	73	-2.7	247	1.4	27.9	607 782	2 458	60 519	22.9	77 832	33.6	66.4	35.0	11.9	661	60.2
Washington	97	-14.9	518	3.2	82.7	1 159 455	2 237	159 949	68.6	366 983	63.5	36.5	44.4	27.3	2 324	73.8
Watauga	46	-11.5	78	0.1	11.7	553 682	7 099	45 254	11.5	19 641	D	D	33.9	2.6	77	7.7
Wayne	175	2.3	242	6.7	131.7	1 008 378	4 160	163 067	501.2	693 190	15.0	85.0	59.2	38.0	3 902	50.5
Wilkes	110	-11.3	100	0.3	37.3	561 362	5 590	76 873	389.8	356 010	1.8	98.2	40.4	24.6	419	3.6
Wilson	105	-8.7	344	2.8	81.8	1 108 122	3 218	168 875	127.8	420 390	77.1	22.9	45.1	25.3	2 997	57.9
Yadkin	105	-10.3	106	0.8	59.7	551 659	5 193	58 570	97.8	98 785	17.9	82.1	30.7	12.8	489	13.2
Yancey	33	-15.4	75	0.1	10.0	364 053	4 868	33 914	5.2	11 573	62.1	37.9	19.5	2.5	123	5.8
NORTH DAKOTA	39 675	1.0	1 241	236.1	27 527.2	957 053	771	174 683	6 084.2	190 310	82.8	17.2	57.9	35.9	359 532	83.5
Adams	627	3.6	1 471	0.0	407.3	856 530	582	144 619	70.5	165 590	55.6	44.4	53.8	32.9	4 711	83.6
Barnes	907	5.8	985	1.8	795.0	925 992	940	183 067	183.3	198 980	94.1	5.9	54.6	36.3	12 066	90.0
Benson	759	3.5	1 285	3.8	603.9	932 327	726	180 433	122.6	207 393	88.1	11.9	60.2	37.7	8 024	84.4
Billings	725	-10.6	2 982	D	120.2	1 404 571	471	103 502	23.8	97 736	30.6	69.4	63.0	30.9	1 130	69.1
Bottineau	1 029	8.5	1 144	D	891.1	839 438	734	168 938	167.9	186 743	94.7	5.3	56.1	35.7	10 514	85.5
Bowman	721	-5.0	2 042	0.9	371.9	1 043 421	511	154 249	77.7	220 062	45.2	54.8	60.6	34.3	4 261	85.8
Burke	571	-4.8	1 232	0.0	425.5	771 723	626	135 643	61.6	133 017	89.7	10.3	55.5	29.8	4 556	89.8
Burleigh	880	1.6	857	5.7	476.9	623 424	727	90 783	82.2	80 152	61.6	38.4	41.2	16.5	6 057	63.2
Cass	1 039	-7.8	1 138	11.7	986.3	1 668 866	1 467	279 562	267.9	293 426	94.1	5.9	67.1	51.3	14 274	84.3
Cavalier	873	6.6	1 344	D	812.3	1 276 743	950	263 511	173.7	267 289	98.6	1.4	64.0	50.9	12 447	92.6
Dickey	698	16.5	1 280	16.4	535.4	1 331 801	1 041	225 365	162.2	297 545	76.7	23.3	62.2	43.1	8 251	86.4
Divide	708	-7.0	1 408	2.3	538.3	880 396	625	172 566	80.9	160 889	91.4	8.6	59.6	40.8	5 998	92.0
Dunn	1 044	-5.6	1 854	0.4	371.2	947 467	511	146 974	68.7	122 046	45.7	54.3	71.0	34.3	2 763	71.6
Eddy	377	8.0	1 029	0.6	272.2	606 782	590	134 760	47.2	129 047	81.8	18.2	50.5	29.8	4 392	83.9
Emmons	872	4.1	1 256	5.0	529.8	852 478	679	145 139	121.0	174 285	71.7	28.3	67.0	42.7	7 122	88.2
Foster	400	4.4	1 290	3.3	336.1	981 190	761	257 515	95.0	306 319	79.6	20.4	65.8	44.8	4 604	81.6
Golden Valley	570	-1.7	2 347	0.9	231.8	1 095 900	467	161 650	43.1	177 374	62.3	37.7	58.0	35.0	2 495	84.8
Grand Forks	826	9.3	848	17.1	753.9	896 590	1 057	216 815	255.6	262 687	91.3	8.7	47.3	33.7	11 583	86.4
Grant	1 058	0.1	2 004	1.9	510.9	1 036 806	517	137 893	79.9	151 270	59.0	41.0	68.4	36.9	5 834	86.9
Griggs	406	7.1	848	4.0	322.5	578 615	682	122 527	63.3	132 160	89.4	10.6	47.2	26.1	5 439	86.0
Hettinger	708	4.0	1 296	0.0	582.8	968 035	747	160 776	93.6	171 356	89.4	10.6	45.1	30.2	8 128	91.2
Kidder	753	-5.2	1 277	18.3	420.2	732 194	573	125 638	78.5	132 977	59.6	40.4	53.4	28.5	5 172	88.3
LaMoure	688	1.6	1 007	6.6	569.0	1 059 157	1 051	198 270	153.4	224 590	80.4	19.6	61.8	40.8	8 024	85.9
Logan	577	-0.2	1 355	2.4	326.0	990 035	731	157 599	84.5	198 452	46.8	53.2	61.0	35.4	4 722	89.9
McHenry	1 083	-3.8	1 167	8.7	692.1	764 603	655	128 138	134.0	144 353	67.4	32.6	56.7	31.5	8 585	81.5
McIntosh	550	-3.3	1 072	D	372.2	777 041	725	131 842	75.9	147 880	65.9	34.1	57.7	33.1	4 133	87.3
McKenzie	1 075	-9.9	1 837	24.8	430.9	948 458	516	159 762	78.1	133 539	64.2	35.8	67.4	34.7	3 543	72.5
McLean	1 163	6.2	1 162	6.7	884.7	905 983	780	168 483	163.4	163 276	89.2	10.8	58.8	37.5	9 673	80.5
Mercer	510	-4.9	1 120	2.3	238.9	673 266	601	101 405	40.1	88 061	61.5	38.5	61.5	20.4	2 609	75.4
Morton	1 165	-8.7	1 394	6.6	548.6	885 436	635	129 538	117.3	140 252	51.9	48.1	64.8	31.3	5 361	71.8
Mountrail	1 037	-2.9	1 573	D	652.4	924 497	588	200 773	108.0	163 888	85.9	14.1	64.8	36.9	7 274	85.1
Nelson	550	3.4	845	0.0	457.1	592 037	701	121 228	85.4	131 135	90.6	9.4	35.3	24.0	7 997	90.8
Oliver	378	-6.4	1 384	5.8	176.1	890 531	643	153 764	53.4	195 563	45.6	54.4	70.7	34.1	1 692	74.4
Pembina	649	5.7	1 246	3.7	601.7	1 685 235	1 352	358 324	235.6	452 248	97.3	2.7	63.3	48.0	7 678	88.5
Pierce	581	9.4	1 097	D	452.1	707 782	645	141 540	72.7	137 195	80.7	19.3	54.0	35.8	6 997	92.8
Ramsey	715	12.4	1 136	D	656.4	800 770	705	202 264	124.6	198 045	98.0	2.0	47.7	34.8	9 947	88.6
Ransom	527	5.2	942	18.5	367.8	967 866	1 028	159 340	93.4	166 710	77.2	22.8	51.4	29.5	7 192	86.4
Renville	554	5.1	1 498	0.0	489.2	1 344 082	897	248 782	106.3	287 218	97.0	3.0	71.4	55.7	5 497	88.4
Richland	906	1.7	961	4.6	833.2	1 325 966	1 380	266 241	261.5	277 305	87.5	12.5	69.5	50.8	11 567	82.9
Rolette	568	11.8	858	D	384.7	573 518	669	104 174	66.6	100 629	79.3	20.7	47.3	23.6	5 423	72.4
Sargent	505	0.0	1 024	13.3	429.6	1 151 242	1 124	217 106	127.7	259 109	81.7	18.3	65.3	44.8	7 187	91.1
Sheridan	500	6.6	1 282	0.0	354.8	752 167	587	125 352	52.5	134 586	83.3	16.7	56.7	30.8	4 779	83.8
Sioux	730	4.0	3 580	D	148.8	1 324 598	370	125 485	32.3	158 425	34.5	65.5	73.0	44.1	1 597	74.5
Slope	769	0.8	3 231	0.5	269.6	1 552 897	481	193 792	47.6	200 188	66.0	34.0	63.4	39.5	2 522	81.5
Stark	837	7.7	968	1.0	529.1	690 697	714	112 700	96.8	111 922	65.8	34.2	50.5	24.4	6 162	76.0
Steele	402	0.2	1 175	1.9	366.7	1 144 258	974	254 960	102.3	299 251	97.7	2.3	63.2	52.3	4 710	88.0
Stutsman	1 193	-1.8	1 144	8.7	931.7	939 366	821	166 881	198.3	190 108	85.0	15.0	49.1	32.1	13 790	84.9
Towner	607	10.6	1 224	0.9	550.5	912 542	745	185 671	107.5	216 678	89.6	10.4	63.5	45.2	7 833	93.3
Traill	544	2.6	1 182	D	530.3	1 623 808	1 374	301 859	182.9	397 543	96.9	3.1	72.8	59.6	7 459	87.2
Walsh	795	4.7	822	2.2	713.6	914 858	1 113	189 962	222.5	229 890	98.0	2.0	48.5	33.3	12 776	90.9

Table B. States and Counties — Water Use, Wholesale Trade, Retail Trade, and Real Estate

STATE County	Water use, 2005		Wholesale trade,[1] 2007				Retail trade,[2] 2007				Real estate and rental and leasing,[2] 2007			
	Total water withdrawn (mil gal/day)	Gallons withdrawn per person	Number of establishments	Number of employees	Sales (mil dol)	Annual payroll (mil dol)	Number of establishments	Number of employees	Sales (mil dol)	Annual payroll (mil dol)	Number of establishments	Number of employees	Receipts (mil dol)	Annual payroll (mil dol)
	133	134	135	136	137	138	139	140	141	142	143	144	145	146
NORTH CAROLINA—Cont'd														
Swain	17.2	1 306	7	23	2.3	0.4	104	619	112.3	10.1	19	45	5.4	0.8
Transylvania	523.2	17 661	11	D	D	D	122	1 331	266.2	27.0	59	173	19.8	4.6
Tyrrell	0.7	159	2	D	D	D	19	143	30.7	2.0	1	D	D	D
Union	66.8	410	264	2 640	1 232.8	112.2	515	6 568	1 699.8	148.6	179	530	100.8	17.6
Vance	10.2	233	30	D	D	D	190	2 242	582.1	48.3	45	164	22.9	3.9
Wake	133.5	178	1 059	15 635	11 334.3	918.8	3 181	49 828	12 598.1	1 162.4	1 374	7 297	1 901.6	324.0
Warren	3.2	164	8	32	17.7	0.9	53	340	62.9	6.2	6	30	3.4	0.6
Washington	5.8	437	13	111	83.2	3.4	52	467	107.7	8.6	5	10	1.1	0.2
Watauga	7.4	174	47	343	169.3	15.6	343	3 588	795.2	79.3	145	505	59.3	11.5
Wayne	45.1	394	102	1 843	1 094.5	71.2	501	5 759	1 388.0	113.7	70	288	35.3	6.6
Wilkes	19.5	290	43	546	260.6	16.6	226	2 503	759.3	50.0	57	229	52.4	8.6
Wilson	16.9	222	93	1 060	728.8	48.9	370	4 130	1 058.6	89.8	70	193	29.9	4.4
Yadkin	5.8	154	24	169	101.2	5.9	127	897	238.6	16.8	13	D	D	D
Yancey	2.2	121	9	32	7.1	0.7	64	592	149.1	12.3	13	30	3.0	0.7
NORTH DAKOTA	1 339.9	2 105	1 332	14 866	13 099.3	627.1	3 361	44 054	10 527.3	891.4	770	3 748	668.8	96.0
Adams	0.5	201	8	46	31.0	1.3	19	147	30.7	2.5	2	D	D	D
Barnes	2.1	189	25	115	142.6	4.5	57	536	147.8	10.6	7	D	D	D
Benson	2.6	367	13	83	125.1	3.1	18	104	20.1	1.2	2	D	D	D
Billings	1.3	1 599	1	D	D	D	10	5	1.2	0.1	NA	NA	NA	NA
Bottineau	1.7	262	16	95	135.0	3.6	47	317	57.0	5.2	10	12	0.6	0.1
Bowman	3.8	1 257	9	66	80.7	2.4	25	197	63.5	4.2	2	D	D	D
Burke	0.6	315	7	39	131.0	1.4	14	51	17.9	0.8	2	D	D	D
Burleigh	15.3	207	132	1 613	889.1	71.9	385	6 713	1 401.0	134.8	110	365	53.8	8.4
Cass	15.9	121	335	D	D	D	663	12 008	2 885.6	256.5	268	1 630	226.4	45.8
Cavalier	0.9	199	13	116	261.5	4.9	33	186	83.2	4.1	1	D	D	D
Dickey	4.5	820	13	109	151.7	3.7	46	308	78.1	6.0	2	D	D	D
Divide	2.6	1 210	5	56	21.3	0.6	12	74	11.8	0.9	5	D	D	D
Dunn	2.0	578	5	22	6.5	0.6	13	106	39.3	2.2	1	D	D	D
Eddy	1.3	503	4	19	21.0	0.7	14	86	32.5	1.8	2	D	D	D
Emmons	5.0	1 311	8	65	46.8	1.7	19	104	26.8	2.3	NA	NA	NA	NA
Foster	2.8	793	15	113	101.7	4.9	27	251	80.7	5.1	2	D	D	NA
Golden Valley	0.7	374	5	120	89.0	5.0	14	86	49.9	1.3	NA	NA	NA	NA
Grand Forks	11.6	176	89	1 169	734.3	49.4	336	5 944	1 238.2	114.6	58	422	58.8	9.2
Grant	13.6	5 205	6	20	27.3	0.5	13	47	12.4	0.9	3	3	0.4	0.0
Griggs	2.3	917	9	62	38.0	2.3	11	48	11.2	1.0	NA	NA	NA	NA
Hettinger	0.4	153	4	D	D	D	16	104	46.9	1.9	3	D	D	D
Kidder	17.8	7 166	3	15	10.5	0.4	10	68	28.0	1.1	4	9	0.8	0.1
LaMoure	4.0	922	14	124	137.8	5.6	24	157	37.2	2.3	2	D	D	D
Logan	2.4	1 175	7	52	62.4	1.8	9	41	21.5	1.0	1	D	D	D
McHenry	20.2	3 667	5	D	D	D	20	128	37.1	2.4	6	D	D	D
McIntosh	0.9	295	9	59	53.3	1.7	26	165	48.5	3.4	3	9	1.0	0.1
McKenzie	13.9	2 476	11	83	94.9	3.7	21	155	36.8	2.7	4	D	D	D
McLean	22.4	2 608	16	123	208.0	5.5	38	290	52.8	4.2	4	8	0.2	0.0
Mercer	500.1	59 788	5	D	D	D	43	393	85.7	7.0	6	6	0.4	0.0
Morton	63.4	2 485	39	283	238.1	9.2	94	1 105	342.1	27.2	33	75	13.6	1.5
Mountrail	1.6	243	11	80	110.9	2.8	39	322	118.9	6.1	3	8	0.3	0.1
Nelson	0.9	275	12	84	138.2	3.5	21	94	24.4	1.5	4	6	0.2	0.0
Oliver	514.4	283 712	1	D	D	D	4	34	10.0	0.7	NA	NA	NA	NA
Pembina	2.0	250	34	286	367.9	9.1	51	480	90.0	8.3	3	2	0.2	0.0
Pierce	1.2	277	11	100	85.9	2.8	28	286	85.7	5.2	2	D	D	D
Ramsey	0.4	34	26	212	266.3	8.0	85	886	234.3	20.1	5	11	0.7	0.1
Ransom	10.3	1 766	8	96	142.5	4.3	33	303	53.9	5.0	3	D	D	D
Renville	0.3	124	13	D	D	D	11	71	23.8	1.4	3	D	D	D
Richland	6.0	344	40	D	D	D	70	718	205.0	14.7	15	49	5.0	0.9
Rolette	2.4	176	10	100	85.8	2.5	45	476	107.1	9.1	1	D	D	D
Sargent	4.1	990	14	101	152.9	3.6	22	141	27.6	2.1	4	9	1.8	0.2
Sheridan	0.5	357	5	21	22.9	0.7	4	11	4.3	0.2	3	3	0.1	0.0
Sioux	0.7	172	NA	NA	NA	NA	7	63	13.2	0.7	NA	NA	NA	NA
Slope	0.9	1 199	NA	NA	NA	NA	NA	NA	NA	NA	NA	NA	NA	NA
Stark	1.9	87	46	D	D	D	160	1 686	403.4	33.8	23	76	11.4	1.9
Steele	1.0	473	6	39	159.8	1.9	9	72	25.9	1.6	2	D	D	D
Stutsman	12.7	609	33	D	D	D	123	1 275	309.7	24.8	23	142	10.6	1.3
Towner	0.4	138	7	D	D	D	13	60	7.2	0.9	2	D	D	D
Traill	1.2	142	31	238	275.7	9.1	41	310	72.5	5.6	9	27	1.4	0.3
Walsh	2.2	190	31	285	296.2	10.6	70	592	98.8	9.2	11	19	0.9	0.2

1. Merchant wholesalers, except manufacturers' sales branches and offices. 2. Employer establishments.

STATE County	Professional, scientific, and technical services,[1] 2007				Manufacturing, 2007				Accommodation and food services, 2007			
	Number of establishments	Number of employees	Receipts (mil dol)	Annual payroll (mil dol)	Number of establishments	Number of employees	Receipts (mil dol)	Annual payroll (mil dol)	Number of establishments	Number of employees	Sales (mil dol)	Annual payroll (mil dol)
	147	148	149	150	151	152	153	154	155	156	157	158
NORTH CAROLINA—Cont'd												
Swain	11	60	2.5	1.6	NA	NA	NA	NA	99	2 857	561.6	68.9
Transylvania	69	D	D	D	32	532	71.9	18.2	84	1 132	62.8	18.4
Tyrrell	3	D	D	D	NA	NA	NA	NA	5	D	D	D
Union	352	1 204	140.3	48.1	249	11 264	D	459.4	246	D	D	D
Vance	45	206	16.7	7.7	42	1 916	639.2	68.4	69	1 363	53.9	15.3
Wake	4 064	34 994	5 389.2	2 217.3	631	17 932	14 091.7	827.9	1 773	36 260	1 726.6	480.0
Warren	17	55	3.7	1.0	NA	NA	NA	NA	18	120	5.7	1.6
Washington	10	85	5.4	1.6	14	1 499	727.9	D	24	376	13.5	3.5
Watauga	160	D	D	D	54	862	129.8	26.6	159	3 289	131.4	41.8
Wayne	143	825	65.7	22.8	84	6 147	1 474.8	221.7	197	3 485	132.1	36.2
Wilkes	92	461	38.9	15.2	98	5 839	1 503.3	173.5	104	1 569	62.1	17.2
Wilson	112	D	D	D	100	8 193	8 357.1	336.3	131	2 582	112.8	28.7
Yadkin	40	247	19.4	7.6	43	1 856	D	65.2	66	883	33.6	9.2
Yancey	25	86	5.6	2.4	17	655	127.4	21.1	22	291	10.5	3.0
NORTH DAKOTA	1 432	9 707	1 110.7	416.9	767	26 361	11 349.8	991.4	1 840	30 307	1 214.2	337.8
Adams	4	D	D	D	NA	NA	NA	NA	9	D	D	D
Barnes	21	94	5.4	3.7	14	691	339.8	22.4	35	439	12.1	3.2
Benson	6	21	1.8	0.8	NA	NA	NA	NA	14	39	2.1	0.4
Billings	1	D	D	D	NA	NA	NA	NA	9	76	13.5	3.2
Bottineau	14	57	4.0	1.7	NA	NA	NA	NA	32	152	6.9	1.5
Bowman	8	28	3.4	1.2	NA	NA	NA	NA	15	95	3.9	0.9
Burke	3	D	D	D	NA	NA	NA	NA	9	59	3.3	0.5
Burleigh	260	D	D	D	73	2 089	D	85.3	173	4 405	170.1	50.3
Cass	412	D	D	D	201	8 266	2 480.1	310.9	363	8 796	341.2	101.0
Cavalier	7	12	1.0	0.4	NA	NA	NA	NA	18	103	3.1	0.7
Dickey	9	36	1.8	0.6	NA	NA	NA	NA	19	168	4.8	1.0
Divide	5	11	1.1	0.2	NA	NA	NA	NA	7	D	D	D
Dunn	1	D	D	D	NA	NA	NA	NA	8	D	D	D
Eddy	5	14	1.3	0.4	NA	NA	NA	NA	8	D	D	D
Emmons	11	148	2.0	1.2	NA	NA	NA	NA	14	D	D	D
Foster	8	12	0.8	0.2	NA	NA	NA	NA	11	130	3.7	1.1
Golden Valley	4	17	1.0	0.3	NA	NA	NA	NA	7	26	1.0	0.2
Grand Forks	118	D	D	D	55	2 762	565.3	85.8	186	4 180	141.1	41.2
Grant	3	7	0.5	0.1	NA	NA	NA	NA	7	D	D	D
Griggs	9	57	3.4	1.2	NA	NA	NA	NA	9	D	D	D
Hettinger	4	D	D	D	NA	NA	NA	NA	6	30	1.2	0.2
Kidder	4	D	D	D	NA	NA	NA	NA	7	D	D	D
LaMoure	3	D	D	D	NA	NA	NA	NA	15	86	2.6	0.6
Logan	2	D	D	D	NA	NA	NA	NA	7	52	1.1	0.2
McHenry	3	D	D	D	NA	NA	NA	NA	10	30	1.0	0.2
McIntosh	9	19	1.5	0.4	NA	NA	NA	NA	12	61	2.1	0.4
McKenzie	13	27	5.0	1.2	NA	NA	NA	NA	17	97	3.5	0.8
McLean	6	18	1.4	0.3	NA	NA	NA	NA	34	160	7.2	1.4
Mercer	11	39	3.5	1.1	NA	NA	NA	NA	34	277	8.2	2.1
Morton	52	D	D	D	39	919	D	43.4	50	717	26.1	7.3
Mountrail	6	D	D	D	NA	NA	NA	NA	21	102	4.8	0.9
Nelson	3	6	0.3	0.1	NA	NA	NA	NA	13	69	2.0	0.5
Oliver	3	D	D	D	NA	NA	NA	NA	2	D	D	D
Pembina	12	23	4.4	0.7	21	707	486.5	28.8	24	177	5.6	1.3
Pierce	11	33	2.5	0.9	NA	NA	NA	NA	15	118	3.0	0.8
Ramsey	19	47	4.5	1.5	NA	NA	NA	NA	45	656	21.7	6.0
Ransom	16	45	3.3	0.9	NA	NA	NA	NA	18	146	4.3	1.1
Renville	6	D	D	D	NA	NA	NA	NA	11	29	1.0	0.2
Richland	24	D	D	D	34	1 788	941.6	73.8	47	1 096	84.6	18.1
Rolette	6	12	0.6	0.2	NA	NA	NA	NA	21	429	36.1	10.5
Sargent	7	15	0.8	0.3	9	D	D	D	14	74	2.2	0.5
Sheridan	1	D	D	D	NA	NA	NA	NA	5	23	0.6	0.2
Sioux	NA	NA	NA	NA	NA	NA	NA	NA	6	D	D	D
Slope	NA	NA	NA	NA	NA	NA	NA	NA	2	D	D	D
Stark	51	D	D	D	33	1 170	270.6	46.9	71	1 089	40.9	11.5
Steele	3	8	0.3	0.1	NA	NA	NA	NA	5	14	0.6	0.1
Stutsman	30	171	12.2	6.1	21	867	230.4	30.4	62	802	30.2	8.6
Towner	6	20	1.7	0.3	NA	NA	NA	NA	8	D	D	D
Traill	10	38	2.4	1.2	NA	NA	NA	NA	30	233	7.0	1.8
Walsh	27	91	6.8	2.0	7	582	D	D	42	281	9.2	2.2

1. Establishment subject to federal tax.

Table B. States and Counties — Health Care and Social Assistance, Other Services, and Federal Funds

STATE County	Health care and social assistance, 2007				Other services, 2007				Federal funds and grants, 2009–2010 Expenditures (mil dol)			
									Total	Direct payments for individuals[1]		
	Number of establishments	Number of employees	Receipts (mil dol)	Annual payroll (mil dol)	Number of establishments	Number of employees	Receipts (mil dol)	Annual payroll (mil dol)		Social Security and government retirement	Medicare	Food Stamps and Supplemental Security Income
	159	160	161	162	163	164	165	166	167	168	169	170
NORTH CAROLINA—Cont'd												
Swain	33	734	66.1	30.1	22	77	14.7	1.9	166.8	54.3	21.7	8.3
Transylvania	75	1 508	129.0	49.3	49	260	19.8	5.8	275.3	154.8	49.7	10.1
Tyrrell	7	D	D	D	8	44	4.0	1.5	42.9	11.2	6.1	3.1
Union	245	5 091	406.8	165.8	279	1 143	102.8	30.0	650.7	361.7	94.7	29.1
Vance	105	2 901	199.7	80.9	52	236	17.8	5.0	419.3	156.6	62.5	35.6
Wake	2 244	46 079	4 446.4	1 865.0	1 598	12 238	1 416.0	382.4	8 348.5	1 895.3	530.2	151.4
Warren	27	313	17.8	7.7	15	D	D	D	188.1	64.1	29.4	12.8
Washington	36	818	36.9	17.9	13	43	4.6	1.3	135.9	50.9	23.1	11.7
Watauga	141	3 151	479.3	119.2	75	395	23.8	7.9	269.8	106.0	43.1	10.9
Wayne	294	7 587	573.0	248.6	159	949	70.0	20.5	1 332.9	419.7	161.2	59.5
Wilkes	149	2 955	184.8	80.4	71	456	24.3	9.3	539.2	225.7	89.9	27.7
Wilson	183	4 655	332.9	143.5	116	660	43.2	14.7	654.2	247.4	119.2	44.3
Yadkin	51	1 200	55.8	25.5	38	170	10.5	2.6	267.2	123.0	50.2	10.9
Yancey	33	527	25.1	11.8	18	78	6.2	1.8	186.5	71.8	26.3	8.6
NORTH DAKOTA	1 748	52 197	3 906.9	1 716.1	1 708	9 261	746.0	199.3	8 696.5	2 159.4	921.1	140.7
Adams	13	330	20.4	11.6	12	24	2.0	0.4	33.4	14.0	5.7	0.3
Barnes	39	1 076	41.5	21.3	33	127	7.2	2.0	137.3	43.2	19.9	2.5
Benson	5	D	D	D	2	D	D	D	135.8	20.0	10.9	4.3
Billings	NA	NA	NA	NA	2	D	D	D	8.0	2.9	0.7	0.0
Bottineau	8	297	13.1	6.3	12	40	3.7	0.6	93.3	29.8	15.8	1.2
Bowman	11	216	12.1	5.9	12	27	2.3	0.4	37.9	16.9	7.5	0.4
Burke	2	D	D	D	4	9	1.1	0.2	42.3	9.7	6.9	0.4
Burleigh	236	8 903	742.0	330.0	256	1 700	150.7	42.5	1 432.4	230.8	81.1	13.9
Cass	427	13 903	1 348.8	549.8	368	D	D	D	1 141.1	336.9	102.5	20.8
Cavalier	11	267	11.8	5.9	17	54	2.7	0.6	110.7	20.4	10.2	0.5
Dickey	23	363	20.2	8.9	18	60	4.2	0.9	93.1	25.3	12.3	1.0
Divide	8	D	D	D	7	D	D	D	39.0	9.3	6.1	0.3
Dunn	6	D	D	D	5	D	D	D	36.5	15.8	5.9	0.5
Eddy	8	199	8.2	4.7	12	32	3.8	0.7	31.5	10.6	6.8	0.4
Emmons	11	200	8.8	3.8	8	D	D	D	54.0	18.3	9.6	0.4
Foster	13	239	18.6	8.7	11	30	1.6	0.4	141.4	13.9	7.6	0.5
Golden Valley	5	D	D	D	8	D	D	D	23.5	10.4	4.1	0.4
Grand Forks	164	9 143	522.1	221.1	153	D	D	D	694.8	153.1	63.1	11.6
Grant	7	212	9.4	4.6	4	D	D	D	40.6	15.0	8.8	0.5
Griggs	3	D	D	D	4	D	D	D	33.5	12.5	6.5	0.4
Hettinger	7	98	5.0	2.1	10	22	1.5	0.3	60.1	26.1	7.6	0.5
Kidder	6	105	3.6	2.0	1	D	D	D	33.7	9.4	6.9	0.3
LaMoure	11	118	4.7	3.0	14	49	3.5	0.7	73.8	18.3	10.5	0.6
Logan	7	97	3.3	1.6	7	D	D	D	32.2	10.6	5.7	0.4
McHenry	6	D	D	D	7	D	D	D	74.0	24.9	14.5	1.3
McIntosh	10	351	15.3	8.5	8	D	D	D	47.8	14.4	13.2	0.4
McKenzie	6	D	D	D	17	43	2.4	0.7	48.9	19.2	7.1	1.8
McLean	14	453	20.2	11.0	23	58	3.7	0.8	165.9	53.8	20.6	1.7
Mercer	17	395	22.9	10.6	14	55	3.3	0.9	63.0	29.5	13.5	1.0
Morton	41	1 197	49.4	28.3	51	265	27.0	7.4	193.5	89.8	38.4	5.6
Mountrail	14	297	11.8	6.5	14	53	4.1	1.4	149.3	27.0	12.9	1.7
Nelson	10	D	D	D	13	34	2.8	0.5	59.5	20.0	11.9	0.6
Oliver	3	D	D	D	2	D	D	D	19.5	7.9	2.6	0.1
Pembina	19	367	15.9	6.6	19	47	3.3	0.7	155.4	27.3	16.6	1.3
Pierce	11	363	18.3	9.2	14	59	3.1	0.7	55.1	18.2	10.3	0.8
Ramsey	48	1 056	49.8	22.6	28	122	7.5	1.8	214.3	48.1	23.3	3.6
Ransom	26	364	21.5	9.6	21	89	5.1	1.2	85.6	21.6	11.8	0.6
Renville	5	D	D	D	3	D	D	D	39.5	12.2	6.1	0.3
Richland	47	D	D	D	35	D	D	D	176.1	48.6	21.8	3.2
Rolette	23	610	56.0	21.9	14	24	2.3	0.5	218.2	34.5	16.2	15.8
Sargent	5	80	3.1	1.8	12	40	4.1	0.7	67.9	21.9	7.7	0.5
Sheridan	1	D	D	D	3	D	D	D	26.3	6.7	4.9	0.6
Sioux	1	D	D	D	3	D	D	D	123.1	8.9	3.5	4.4
Slope	NA	NA	NA	NA	2	D	D	D	43.4	6.1	0.7	0.0
Stark	75	1 879	98.7	47.5	72	D	D	D	190.1	84.2	36.5	5.4
Steele	2	D	D	D	3	5	0.5	0.1	45.0	10.7	4.8	0.3
Stutsman	69	2 315	113.4	58.1	61	318	18.0	5.5	243.4	80.4	32.5	5.8
Towner	3	D	D	D	6	D	D	D	47.3	9.8	7.2	0.4
Traill	21	589	26.2	13.1	22	53	4.9	0.8	91.1	29.9	15.4	1.4
Walsh	31	707	34.7	17.0	34	95	7.0	1.9	129.5	38.9	25.4	2.7

1. State totals may include programs not allocated by county.

STATE County	Federal funds and grants, 2009–2010 (cont.)							Value of residential construction authorized by building permits, 2010		Local government finances, 2007				
	Expenditures (mil dol) (cont.)									General revenue				
	Procurement contract awards			Grants[1]								Taxes		
													Per capita[2] (dollars)	
	Salaries and wages	Defense	Other	Medicaid and other health-related	Nutrition and family welfare	Education	Other	New construction ($1,000)	Number of housing units	Total (mil dol)	Inter-govern-mental (mil dol)	Total (mil dol)	Total	Property
	171	172	173	174	175	176	177	178	179	180	181	182	183	184
NORTH CAROLINA—Cont'd														
Swain	10.2	0.0	2.2	35.2	6.5	3.5	9.2	9 260	46	34.5	21.0	8.2	598	344
Transylvania	11.2	0.1	14.3	24.5	4.1	2.0	1.8	33 284	160	85.1	36.3	36.5	1 218	904
Tyrrell	1.5	0.0	1.0	12.3	1.3	0.6	2.7	950	5	14.8	8.9	4.2	1 007	789
Union	33.7	14.0	11.9	56.6	20.1	8.5	4.6	87 196	520	491.5	226.1	180.6	978	709
Vance	8.0	0.2	12.3	101.9	14.2	5.2	7.6	10 269	83	178.8	110.8	35.7	831	581
Wake	642.7	182.5	193.9	616.7	525.7	1 080.8	2 266.1	768 161	4 414	2 780.6	1 017.2	1 057.8	1 270	953
Warren	3.3	0.0	0.8	63.2	6.1	1.5	2.1	5 942	32	54.3	30.2	16.4	847	655
Washington	2.1	0.0	0.5	32.1	4.1	2.1	0.9	1 637	10	51.8	27.1	10.1	783	559
Watauga	15.2	0.0	3.1	40.8	5.8	4.2	23.3	54 778	271	123.1	47.1	54.0	1 212	863
Wayne	302.7	74.2	4.5	202.6	29.5	13.7	13.4	35 728	279	330.8	188.2	88.4	779	555
Wilkes	24.8	1.1	2.9	122.7	12.5	5.4	16.6	15 063	89	178.1	96.0	51.4	768	519
Wilson	14.2	13.5	3.6	145.5	17.5	8.9	5.0	30 124	181	256.6	128.0	77.9	1 015	784
Yadkin	5.6	0.6	1.4	45.4	7.7	2.6	11.8	10 568	62	85.5	47.1	28.6	756	537
Yancey	3.5	0.4	2.0	48.3	4.1	1.5	19.0	2 715	44	51.6	26.1	13.5	730	492
NORTH DAKOTA	1 083.5	288.2	397.1	630.3	202.8	202.0	1 202.3	481 143	3 833	X	X	X	X	X
Adams	1.5	0.0	0.3	4.0	0.7	0.0	0.1	380	2	6.2	2.3	2.8	1 240	1 153
Barnes	11.6	0.0	1.5	10.5	2.4	0.9	4.9	1 260	6	36.4	14.4	14.6	1 350	1 068
Benson	7.4	1.5	2.2	14.3	4.9	13.8	11.4	180	1	20.8	13.8	4.4	627	626
Billings	1.6	0.0	1.2	0.0	0.1	0.0	0.0	240	4	8.1	4.9	1.2	1 475	1 035
Bottineau	7.4	0.7	2.2	5.8	1.7	0.1	3.8	225	2	24.1	12.7	6.7	1 038	960
Bowman	1.4	0.1	0.7	1.9	0.7	0.1	0.0	750	4	21.8	8.1	5.3	1 799	1 670
Burke	8.7	0.5	2.1	2.3	0.6	0.1	0.0	0	0	6.2	2.6	2.5	1 361	1 357
Burleigh	177.3	5.0	35.0	66.5	46.9	83.9	638.4	84 638	536	231.9	78.5	94.1	1 217	1 004
Cass	186.2	22.0	191.7	84.5	19.8	4.7	96.1	118 880	1 107	448.0	123.5	199.6	1 451	1 178
Cavalier	2.7	12.1	8.7	4.6	1.4	0.1	3.4	300	2	14.2	5.1	6.2	1 576	1 510
Dickey	3.2	0.0	0.5	6.3	1.5	0.2	2.7	0	0	14.1	5.2	6.0	1 116	1 069
Divide	2.1	0.0	2.1	4.6	0.5	0.0	0.0	1 551	14	10.6	3.9	3.1	1 559	1 397
Dunn	1.1	2.3	0.4	2.9	0.8	0.4	0.3	900	5	11.6	5.4	4.2	1 275	1 261
Eddy	1.8	0.0	0.3	2.9	0.7	0.1	0.2	680	5	8.6	3.1	4.4	1 827	1 783
Emmons	1.6	0.1	0.3	6.3	1.6	0.2	0.2	854	6	11.3	5.0	4.0	1 154	1 113
Foster	3.2	0.0	10.1	1.7	0.7	0.1	90.7	275	1	11.8	5.0	4.4	1 258	1 181
Golden Valley	0.7	0.0	0.1	1.7	0.5	0.2	0.2	295	2	8.3	3.9	2.0	1 172	1 122
Grand Forks	159.1	68.7	26.7	58.5	13.7	10.0	80.1	23 808	144	215.4	67.7	85.6	1 278	969
Grant	1.5	0.0	0.4	5.8	1.3	0.1	0.1	0	0	8.2	2.2	4.7	1 911	1 887
Griggs	1.3	0.0	0.3	1.7	0.9	0.0	0.2	300	1	9.9	3.5	4.4	1 847	1 788
Hettinger	2.3	0.0	0.2	7.5	0.9	0.1	0.5	0	0	8.2	3.4	3.7	1 514	1 450
Kidder	1.8	0.0	0.4	3.5	0.9	0.1	2.0	0	0	9.7	3.9	3.5	1 493	1 473
LaMoure	4.5	0.4	0.6	5.8	1.5	0.1	0.4	200	1	31.5	17.4	10.1	2 450	2 393
Logan	1.0	0.0	0.2	4.0	0.7	0.1	0.0	325	1	7.4	3.0	3.5	1 780	1 770
McHenry	3.5	0.0	3.3	6.9	3.7	0.2	0.0	4 264	27	15.2	6.1	6.8	1 306	1 279
McIntosh	2.2	0.0	0.3	5.3	1.0	0.1	0.5	250	1	8.8	3.6	3.5	1 289	1 236
McKenzie	3.7	-0.3	0.8	2.3	1.0	0.3	0.5	2 860	36	29.4	18.0	5.4	954	889
McLean	6.7	25.8	9.4	19.0	2.0	0.3	1.9	5 124	31	25.6	11.0	9.2	1 101	932
Mercer	3.5	0.3	0.8	8.1	1.5	0.1	0.2	1 490	7	29.5	12.3	9.0	1 124	1 067
Morton	8.0	1.7	6.7	18.5	6.9	1.3	4.5	24 478	114	82.3	32.8	29.6	1 142	1 058
Mountrail	4.0	5.5	1.9	9.1	3.4	5.4	51.4	9 354	94	26.9	15.1	5.8	900	858
Nelson	2.2	0.0	0.5	5.9	1.0	0.1	0.1	1 018	7	11.7	4.6	5.3	1 659	1 647
Oliver	0.3	0.0	0.0	2.3	0.3	0.0	2.9	250	1	9.3	2.5	1.7	984	947
Pembina	21.3	13.5	11.5	10.4	1.7	0.3	8.0	0	0	28.0	13.3	11.5	1 524	1 477
Pierce	2.6	0.0	1.9	6.9	1.2	0.2	0.0	350	3	12.7	5.1	4.9	1 188	1 118
Ramsey	35.1	28.1	1.8	14.4	2.8	1.2	1.0	2 477	14	38.0	15.3	13.2	1 180	999
Ransom	3.6	0.1	0.9	4.0	1.2	0.1	18.4	657	4	16.0	5.7	7.3	1 278	1 227
Renville	1.4	0.0	0.2	1.7	0.6	0.1	1.3	50	1	10.3	4.9	3.6	1 564	1 545
Richland	9.4	0.7	1.3	11.5	2.9	0.3	6.2	3 468	24	62.1	25.9	24.0	1 455	1 347
Rolette	35.1	0.2	13.2	36.8	8.0	10.4	21.2	440	3	45.3	36.5	4.1	304	279
Sargent	2.9	0.0	0.9	4.6	1.5	0.1	0.2	359	3	16.2	6.1	6.2	1 509	1 490
Sheridan	0.6	0.0	0.1	5.8	0.7	0.1	0.0	30	2	4.2	1.3	2.3	1 768	1 744
Sioux	9.4	0.1	4.5	9.4	4.8	7.1	48.6	0	0	9.4	6.5	1.3	297	297
Slope	0.1	0.0	0.1	0.6	0.1	0.0	29.0	0	0	2.2	0.9	0.7	1 003	995
Stark	13.3	0.2	2.0	18.7	5.9	1.4	7.9	48 570	310	60.6	24.6	23.5	1 048	848
Steele	0.9	0.0	8.8	0.6	0.5	0.1	0.2	141	2	7.5	2.7	3.5	1 908	1 870
Stutsman	20.4	0.3	12.1	38.6	6.0	0.4	3.3	8 101	83	68.0	22.8	27.5	1 341	1 101
Towner	2.1	1.1	0.3	2.3	0.9	0.0	0.2	0	0	14.2	2.8	9.2	4 005	3 969
Traill	3.3	0.0	1.9	5.2	2.8	0.5	0.3	885	4	30.5	9.7	12.4	1 539	1 486
Walsh	4.8	0.4	1.0	9.9	2.7	0.5	2.0	3 702	48	41.1	17.5	12.5	1 138	1 087

1. State totals may include programs not allocated by county.   2. Based on the resident population estimated as of July 1 of the year shown.

Items 171—184

Table B. States and Counties — **Local Government Finances, Government Employment, and Voting**

	Local government finances, 2007 (cont.)									Government employment, 2009			Presidential election,[2] 2008		
	Direct general expenditure							Debt outstanding					Percent of vote cast:		
			Percent of total for:												
STATE County	Total (mil dol)	Per capita[1] (dollars)	Educa-tion	Health and hospitals	Police protec-tion	Public welfare	High-ways	Total (mil dol)	Per capita[1] (dollars)	Federal civilian	Federal military	State and local	Demo-cratic	Republi-can	All other
	185	186	187	188	189	190	191	192	193	194	195	196	197	198	199
NORTH CAROLINA—Cont'd															
Swain	35.2	2 579	50.9	5.0	3.3	8.0	0.3	13.1	963	194	34	2 237	48.4	50.0	1.6
Transylvania	78.0	2 601	42.2	5.0	7.4	8.4	1.0	36.1	1 203	138	76	1 393	43.0	55.6	1.4
Tyrrell	14.2	3 457	59.8	1.2	5.6	4.8	1.0	0.5	117	26	10	489	48.8	50.3	0.9
Union	573.6	3 106	64.3	2.2	4.2	4.6	0.8	1 370.9	7 424	262	499	10 298	36.2	62.9	0.9
Vance	174.7	4 064	57.0	13.7	3.7	7.2	0.7	48.8	1 136	101	108	3 012	63.1	36.4	0.5
Wake	3 039.8	3 649	42.2	4.3	4.8	4.1	2.9	12 582.4	15 105	5 173	3 050	74 667	56.7	42.3	1.0
Warren	55.2	2 845	47.8	7.5	3.8	11.4	0.4	13.5	696	39	49	1 493	69.5	30.0	0.5
Washington	49.1	3 801	45.3	14.9	4.0	9.9	1.3	13.4	1 037	30	32	1 102	58.1	41.4	0.6
Watauga	114.9	2 580	35.2	6.2	6.5	4.7	3.3	54.1	1 215	113	117	5 949	51.3	47.0	1.7
Wayne	315.2	2 775	55.2	3.9	4.3	8.1	1.0	122.6	1 080	1 254	4 617	8 546	45.4	54.0	0.5
Wilkes	172.4	2 580	63.3	5.5	3.4	8.7	0.6	107.0	1 601	202	167	4 386	30.1	68.3	1.7
Wilson	252.6	3 291	44.8	5.0	6.1	7.0	1.6	214.7	2 797	187	197	6 361	52.8	46.7	0.4
Yadkin	81.8	2 164	62.1	5.9	5.1	10.1	1.1	13.5	358	71	95	1 557	26.4	72.4	1.2
Yancey	49.4	2 676	46.3	18.0	2.8	9.7	0.4	30.6	1 660	47	47	860	46.2	51.9	1.9
NORTH DAKOTA	X	X	X	X	X	X	X	X	X	9 713	11 217	60 878	44.6	53.3	2.1
Adams	6.4	2 828	47.9	0.0	3.6	4.7	15.7	0.4	160	21	17	133	34.2	62.0	3.8
Barnes	38.5	3 572	40.8	2.6	3.6	2.5	12.4	19.7	1 825	96	80	912	48.1	49.6	2.2
Benson	20.5	2 940	62.2	0.4	1.3	4.0	15.6	2.0	288	163	52	1 464	66.1	32.6	1.3
Billings	8.0	9 984	23.2	0.1	4.8	0.0	41.1	0.0	0	68	0	92	22.8	75.2	2.0
Bottineau	24.8	3 864	43.2	0.0	2.4	2.4	19.9	8.3	1 293	81	47	558	69.4	58.6	2.0
Bowman	19.0	6 443	36.0	0.3	1.7	0.0	19.2	0.4	129	24	23	215	29.1	67.5	3.4
Burke	6.6	3 529	55.4	0.0	4.9	1.6	16.8	0.7	369	127	14	164	30.3	67.9	1.8
Burleigh	229.8	2 972	43.1	2.1	5.4	1.5	9.3	141.1	1 825	1 120	600	9 506	37.3	60.9	1.7
Cass	450.0	3 271	46.0	1.6	4.6	2.2	11.6	802.2	5 831	2 004	1 096	10 489	52.7	45.6	1.7
Cavalier	13.6	3 484	40.7	1.2	4.0	7.3	22.3	9.1	2 316	43	28	219	43.7	53.0	3.4
Dickey	13.3	2 479	53.4	0.9	3.7	3.4	18.2	4.6	860	32	39	305	39.8	58.2	1.9
Divide	13.2	6 611	23.0	21.1	2.6	1.5	19.3	2.9	1 466	35	15	132	41.0	55.7	3.3
Dunn	12.0	3 635	56.8	0.4	1.4	3.8	18.1	0.0	4	22	25	232	32.1	65.7	2.3
Eddy	7.4	3 028	62.4	0.4	5.6	2.7	9.5	2.2	886	27	17	152	50.0	47.0	2.9
Emmons	10.9	3 138	58.5	1.8	2.2	2.8	12.3	1.8	521	26	25	217	29.7	67.0	3.3
Foster	11.6	3 324	53.9	1.1	3.4	2.0	14.5	4.5	1 280	26	24	229	41.6	55.4	3.0
Golden Valley	8.3	4 994	54.4	2.2	4.3	3.4	17.1	0.4	243	13	12	173	24.0	73.4	2.6
Grand Forks	204.5	3 054	44.1	0.7	4.4	2.5	4.9	387.1	5 779	1 242	2 231	8 721	51.7	46.6	1.7
Grant	7.4	2 979	47.0	1.5	2.5	0.0	27.3	2.3	940	29	17	153	21.1	44.2	34.8
Griggs	9.8	4 086	49.7	2.1	3.0	3.3	10.6	2.9	1 206	22	17	186	45.5	51.9	2.6
Hettinger	8.5	3 514	65.8	0.0	2.9	0.0	12.3	0.8	314	24	17	167	30.1	66.2	3.6
Kidder	9.5	4 055	51.7	2.4	1.5	0.9	19.8	7.1	3 026	31	16	165	34.4	61.2	4.4
LaMoure	40.9	9 952	24.7	0.3	0.8	0.8	4.6	3.9	960	47	29	281	38.7	58.5	2.8
Logan	6.3	3 238	68.9	1.0	2.6	0.1	12.7	1.5	782	19	14	129	28.3	68.7	3.0
McHenry	15.9	3 042	60.1	1.0	2.8	2.9	14.9	2.0	373	60	39	387	40.6	56.9	2.5
McIntosh	8.3	3 005	57.6	0.1	2.4	3.9	9.0	0.6	215	22	19	175	37.8	59.8	2.4
McKenzie	25.6	4 554	53.1	5.0	2.7	1.9	17.1	0.7	120	56	43	1 411	34.4	64.1	1.5
McLean	25.7	3 077	59.3	0.9	5.0	2.4	7.4	6.5	783	130	62	651	39.4	58.4	2.2
Mercer	32.1	4 029	43.3	0.7	4.5	2.1	11.0	80.8	10 141	48	59	524	33.6	63.4	3.0
Morton	83.3	3 212	48.5	1.1	4.5	2.6	14.5	66.8	2 578	116	197	1 497	38.3	59.3	2.4
Mountrail	24.7	3 817	59.5	1.8	3.2	2.8	7.6	8.4	1 291	71	51	648	50.3	47.9	1.9
Nelson	14.3	4 447	41.9	12.7	1.8	0.2	25.1	5.5	1 698	32	23	237	51.8	45.7	2.6
Oliver	8.8	5 073	32.6	0.8	2.2	0.0	12.0	47.9	27 776	0	12	105	31.9	65.6	2.5
Pembina	29.6	3 934	55.8	0.8	3.1	2.4	8.8	12.3	1 638	277	87	491	45.2	52.1	2.8
Pierce	12.6	3 065	45.5	1.0	4.5	3.1	25.4	0.9	221	27	30	249	37.0	60.8	2.2
Ramsey	39.6	3 543	53.3	0.5	3.1	2.7	12.6	20.6	1 844	195	84	1 273	48.6	49.6	1.8
Ransom	16.0	2 809	53.6	2.0	3.0	2.5	11.5	9.9	1 738	46	41	447	56.4	41.0	2.6
Renville	10.1	4 379	66.8	0.1	2.7	1.8	12.8	1.3	580	24	17	201	37.5	59.4	3.1
Richland	65.3	3 960	48.6	3.2	4.5	1.7	16.0	30.2	1 833	70	126	1 981	46.4	51.6	2.0
Rolette	43.7	3 194	77.8	1.6	1.7	2.5	4.2	9.3	682	864	103	1 979	75.1	23.0	1.9
Sargent	14.8	3 598	45.4	1.7	2.3	2.1	18.9	8.6	2 081	39	29	230	57.9	40.4	1.8
Sheridan	3.4	2 558	58.6	2.2	2.5	0.2	19.7	0.3	216	15	0	95	28.5	69.1	2.4
Sioux	8.7	2 071	80.3	0.2	1.3	9.6	1.7	0.6	133	229	31	1 298	83.1	15.6	1.3
Slope	2.0	3 064	18.4	5.0	2.9	3.3	33.9	0.5	780	0	0	28	25.8	72.3	1.9
Stark	58.2	2 591	49.0	2.5	1.7	4.9	10.4	9.3	416	202	170	2 038	34.3	63.5	2.2
Steele	7.2	3 915	46.6	1.0	2.7	4.2	18.9	4.2	2 264	20	13	119	59.5	39.1	1.4
Stutsman	69.4	3 388	44.0	5.8	5.0	2.4	6.2	51.7	2 523	205	153	1 906	41.5	56.2	2.3
Towner	10.8	4 731	38.7	28.2	2.4	1.3	10.7	6.1	2 655	28	16	125	51.9	44.8	3.3
Traill	29.5	3 659	53.8	2.0	2.9	1.7	11.8	46.4	5 753	41	59	702	52.9	45.7	1.5
Walsh	39.4	3 581	52.6	1.9	5.1	2.1	16.5	10.8	978	70	80	1 248	47.6	49.5	2.9

1. Based on the resident population estimated as of July 1 of the year shown. 2. © 2009 Election Data Services, Inc. All rights reserved.

Table B. States and Counties — **Land Area and Population**

STATE/ County code	CBSA code[1]	County type[2]	STATE County	Land area,[3] (sq km) 2010	Total persons	Rank	Per square kilometer	White	Black	American Indian, Alaska Native	Asian and Pacific Islander	Percent Hispanic or Latino[4]	Under 5 years	5 to 17 years	18 to 24 years	25 to 34 years	35 to 44 years	45 to 54 years
				1	2	3	4	5	6	7	8	9	10	11	12	13	14	15
			NORTH DAKOTA—Cont'd															
38 101	33500	5	Ward	5 214	61 675	843	11.8	90.8	3.3	3.5	1.7	3.0	7.8	15.7	13.8	15.4	11.2	12.8
38 103	...	9	Wells	3 292	4 207	2 891	1.3	99.0	0.3	0.6	0.2	0.5	4.9	13.2	4.4	7.6	9.3	17.1
38 105	48780	7	Williams	5 380	22 398	1 712	4.2	93.4	0.6	6.0	0.7	1.9	6.9	16.2	8.8	14.0	10.7	15.6
39 000	...	X	**OHIO**	105 829	11 536 504	X	109.0	82.7	13.1	0.7	2.1	3.1	6.2	17.4	9.5	12.2	12.8	15.1
39 001	...	6	Adams	1 512	28 550	1 473	18.9	98.3	0.5	1.3	0.2	0.9	6.7	18.3	7.9	11.0	13.4	14.9
39 003	30620	3	Allen	1 042	106 331	556	102.0	84.6	13.5	0.6	1.0	2.4	6.4	17.6	10.7	11.7	11.7	14.6
39 005	11740	4	Ashland	1 095	53 139	932	48.5	97.5	1.1	0.5	0.9	0.9	6.2	17.7	10.3	11.1	11.9	14.3
39 007	11780	4	Ashtabula	1 818	101 497	573	55.8	92.5	4.6	0.8	0.6	3.4	6.2	17.4	7.9	10.9	12.9	15.6
39 009	11900	4	Athens	1 304	64 757	807	49.7	92.6	3.5	1.0	3.3	1.5	4.1	11.7	32.1	11.8	9.5	10.8
39 011	47540	4	Auglaize	1 040	45 949	1 048	44.2	97.9	0.6	0.5	0.6	1.2	6.7	18.7	7.5	11.0	12.6	15.3
39 013	48540	3	Belmont	1 378	70 400	754	51.1	94.8	4.8	0.5	0.5	0.6	5.1	14.6	8.3	11.6	12.4	15.7
39 015	17140	1	Brown	1 269	44 846	1 071	35.3	98.1	1.2	0.7	0.4	0.6	6.3	18.3	7.7	11.3	13.2	15.9
39 017	17140	1	Butler	1 210	368 130	178	304.2	85.9	8.2	0.6	2.9	4.0	6.8	18.3	11.3	12.2	13.3	14.9
39 019	15940	2	Carroll	1 022	28 836	1 457	28.2	98.2	0.8	0.8	0.3	0.8	5.8	17.3	7.1	10.1	12.1	16.4
39 021	46500	6	Champaign	1 110	40 097	1 171	36.1	95.8	3.2	1.0	0.6	1.1	6.3	18.8	8.4	10.8	13.4	15.3
39 023	44220	3	Clark	1 029	138 333	444	134.4	87.4	10.2	0.8	1.0	2.8	6.3	17.3	9.0	11.0	12.1	14.4
39 025	17140	1	Clermont	1 171	197 363	316	168.5	96.1	1.6	0.6	1.3	1.5	6.9	18.8	7.9	12.0	13.9	16.1
39 027	48940	6	Clinton	1 058	42 040	1 129	39.7	95.6	3.2	0.7	0.8	1.3	6.4	18.1	9.6	11.6	12.4	15.7
39 029	20620	4	Columbiana	1 378	107 841	544	78.3	96.0	2.8	0.6	0.5	1.2	5.5	16.3	7.6	11.1	13.0	15.8
39 031	18740	6	Coshocton	1 461	36 901	1 249	25.3	97.6	1.7	0.6	0.4	0.8	6.2	17.9	7.8	11.2	12.3	15.1
39 033	15340	4	Crawford	1 041	43 784	1 091	42.1	97.4	1.3	0.5	0.5	1.2	5.8	17.3	7.5	10.9	12.4	14.8
39 035	17460	1	Cuyahoga	1 184	1 280 122	29	1 081.2	62.8	30.3	0.6	3.1	4.8	5.8	16.8	8.8	12.3	12.4	15.4
39 037	24820	6	Darke	1 549	52 959	933	34.2	97.8	0.9	0.5	0.5	1.2	6.7	18.3	7.4	10.7	12.3	15.0
39 039	19580	4	Defiance	1 066	39 037	1 195	36.6	89.0	2.2	0.6	0.5	8.7	6.4	18.2	8.7	11.5	12.2	14.9
39 041	18140	1	Delaware	1 148	174 214	354	151.8	89.9	4.0	0.5	5.0	2.1	7.5	21.5	6.3	10.9	17.1	15.7
39 043	41780	3	Erie	652	77 079	705	118.2	87.1	10.2	0.8	0.8	3.4	5.4	16.8	7.4	10.3	12.0	15.9
39 045	18140	1	Fairfield	1 306	146 156	428	111.9	90.8	6.8	0.8	1.6	1.7	6.4	19.9	7.8	11.9	14.2	15.4
39 047	47920	6	Fayette	1 052	29 030	1 451	27.6	95.3	3.0	0.6	0.7	1.8	7.1	17.6	7.9	11.8	13.0	14.6
39 049	18140	1	Franklin	1 378	1 163 414	33	844.3	69.5	22.7	0.9	4.6	4.8	7.1	16.8	11.9	16.4	13.6	13.7
39 051	45780	2	Fulton	1 050	42 698	1 112	40.7	91.2	0.6	0.5	0.7	7.8	6.5	19.3	7.5	10.8	12.9	15.9
39 053	38580	6	Gallia	1 208	30 934	1 414	25.6	95.6	3.4	1.0	0.6	0.9	6.3	17.4	8.9	11.4	11.9	15.4
39 055	17460	1	Geauga	1 036	93 389	616	90.1	96.9	1.5	0.3	0.9	1.1	5.6	20.4	6.6	7.7	12.4	17.3
39 057	19380	2	Greene	1 072	161 573	380	150.7	87.2	8.3	0.9	3.8	2.1	5.6	16.1	14.3	11.8	11.4	14.6
39 059	15740	6	Guernsey	1 353	40 087	1 172	29.6	97.0	2.5	0.9	0.5	0.9	6.1	17.8	7.8	11.0	12.4	15.1
39 061	17140	1	Hamilton	1 051	802 374	68	763.4	69.2	26.8	0.6	2.6	2.6	6.6	17.0	10.5	13.5	12.2	14.9
39 063	22300	4	Hancock	1 376	74 782	726	54.3	92.0	2.2	0.5	2.0	4.5	6.4	17.2	10.3	12.1	12.3	15.0
39 065	...	6	Hardin	1 218	32 058	1 391	26.3	97.1	1.3	0.6	0.8	1.3	6.4	17.2	15.7	11.1	11.6	13.1
39 067	...	6	Harrison	1 042	15 864	2 059	15.2	97.1	2.9	0.7	0.3	0.5	5.9	16.0	7.3	9.8	11.8	16.0
39 069	...	6	Henry	1 077	28 215	1 488	26.2	92.4	0.6	0.6	0.5	6.6	6.5	18.7	7.6	11.5	12.4	15.5
39 071	...	6	Highland	1 432	43 589	1 094	30.4	97.3	2.1	0.7	0.4	0.7	6.7	18.8	7.8	11.6	13.1	14.4
39 073	...	6	Hocking	1 091	29 380	1 445	26.9	98.0	1.1	0.9	0.3	0.7	5.9	17.9	7.7	11.0	12.9	15.5
39 075	...	7	Holmes	1 094	42 366	1 118	38.7	98.7	0.5	0.3	0.2	0.8	9.5	24.7	10.0	12.0	11.0	11.7
39 077	35940	4	Huron	1 273	59 626	863	46.8	92.9	1.6	0.7	0.5	5.6	6.8	19.5	7.8	11.8	13.0	15.1
39 079	...	7	Jackson	1 089	33 225	1 344	30.5	97.9	0.9	1.1	0.5	0.8	6.6	18.0	8.3	12.1	13.0	14.5
39 081	44600	3	Jefferson	1 058	69 709	761	65.9	92.6	6.6	0.6	0.6	1.1	5.1	15.1	9.6	9.9	11.7	15.4
39 083	34540	4	Knox	1 361	60 921	849	44.8	97.1	1.3	0.6	0.9	1.2	6.3	17.9	11.8	10.6	11.8	14.5
39 085	17460	1	Lake	589	230 041	277	390.6	92.1	3.8	0.4	1.5	3.4	5.5	16.7	7.5	11.2	13.0	16.4
39 087	26580	2	Lawrence	1 174	62 450	833	53.2	96.6	2.8	0.6	0.6	0.7	6.2	17.3	7.9	11.9	13.4	14.7
39 089	18140	1	Licking	1 768	166 492	369	94.2	94.0	4.3	0.8	1.1	1.4	6.4	18.3	8.8	11.2	13.5	15.9
39 091	13340	4	Logan	1 187	45 858	1 052	38.6	96.3	2.7	0.7	0.8	1.2	6.6	18.8	7.5	11.2	12.6	15.3
39 093	17460	1	Lorain	1 272	301 356	211	236.9	82.2	9.4	0.8	1.3	8.4	6.0	17.9	8.4	11.2	13.4	15.7
39 095	45780	2	Lucas	883	441 815	147	500.4	73.1	20.3	0.8	2.0	6.1	6.7	17.3	11.0	12.7	12.4	14.6
39 097	18140	1	Madison	1 207	43 435	1 100	36.0	91.1	7.3	0.6	0.8	1.4	5.8	16.7	8.4	12.9	15.6	16.3
39 099	49660	2	Mahoning	1 066	238 823	268	224.0	78.9	16.3	0.6	1.0	4.7	5.4	16.1	8.4	10.8	11.9	15.3
39 101	32020	4	Marion	1 046	66 501	788	63.6	91.3	6.6	0.6	0.7	2.3	5.8	16.3	8.9	12.6	13.3	15.7
39 103	17460	1	Medina	1 091	172 332	357	158.0	96.1	1.6	0.5	1.3	1.6	6.0	19.4	6.8	10.4	14.6	16.6
39 105	...	6	Meigs	1 114	23 770	1 653	21.3	98.2	1.3	0.8	0.4	0.5	5.8	17.0	7.9	11.6	13.0	15.2
39 107	16380	7	Mercer	1 198	40 814	1 158	34.1	97.4	0.6	0.5	0.8	1.5	7.1	19.3	7.8	11.0	11.6	15.0
39 109	19380	2	Miami	1 053	102 506	566	97.3	95.1	3.0	0.6	1.5	1.3	6.2	18.0	7.5	11.1	13.1	15.4
39 111	...	8	Monroe	1 180	14 642	2 138	12.4	98.9	0.6	0.9	0.3	0.4	5.5	16.0	6.9	10.0	11.9	15.1
39 113	19380	2	Montgomery	1 195	535 153	118	447.8	74.6	22.1	0.8	2.3	2.3	6.2	16.8	9.6	12.5	12.3	14.7
39 115	...	6	Morgan	1 079	15 054	2 105	14.0	95.8	5.1	1.7	0.3	0.6	5.9	17.5	7.5	10.7	11.6	15.5
39 117	18140	1	Morrow	1 052	34 827	1 307	33.1	98.1	0.7	0.8	0.5	1.1	6.4	19.5	7.3	11.0	13.6	15.9
39 119	49780	4	Muskingum	1 721	86 074	654	50.0	94.7	5.4	0.9	0.6	0.8	6.1	17.9	9.2	11.4	12.7	14.8
39 121	...	6	Noble	1 031	14 645	2 137	14.2	96.6	2.7	0.7	0.3	0.4	5.1	14.0	6.7	9.4	10.1	15.0

1. CBSA = Core Based Statistical Area. See Appendix A for explanation. See Appendix B for list of metropolitan areas with component counties. 2. County type code from the Economic Research Service of USDA Rural-Urban Continuum Codes. See Appendix A for definition. 3. Dry land or land partially or temporarily covered by water. 4. May be of any race.

Table B. States and Counties — **Population and Households**

STATE County	55 to 64 years	65 to 74 years	75 years and over	Percent female	1990	2000	1990–2000	2000–2010	Births	Deaths	Net migration	Number	Percent change, 2000–2010	Persons per house-hold	Female family house-holder[1]	One per-son
	16	17	18	19	20	21	22	23	24	25	26	27	28	29	30	31

Column group headers: **Population, 2010 (cont.)** — Age (percent) (cont.) [16–18], Percent female [19]. **Population change and components of change, 1990–2010** — Total persons [20–21], Percent change [22–23], Components of change, 2000–2009 [24–26]. **Households, 2010** — Number [27], Percent [28–31].

STATE County	55–64	65–74	75+	% fem	1990	2000	90–00	00–10	Births	Deaths	Net migration	Number	% chg 00–10	Per/HH	Fem fam	One person
NORTH DAKOTA—Cont'd																
Ward	10.3	6.3	6.7	49.3	57 921	58 795	1.5	4.9	8 711	4 503	-5 692	25 029	8.6	2.36	8.4	30.0
Wells	14.5	12.8	16.2	50.9	5 864	5 102	-13.0	-17.5	330	646	-678	1 943	-12.3	2.10	5.6	34.3
Williams	12.9	7.1	7.8	48.4	21 129	19 761	-6.5	13.3	2 235	1 854	392	9 293	14.8	2.35	7.7	31.5
OHIO	12.6	7.4	6.7	51.2	10 847 115	11 353 140	4.7	1.6	1 389 016	999 895	-247 751	4 603 435	3.5	2.44	13.1	28.9
Adams	12.9	8.6	6.2	50.6	25 371	27 330	7.7	4.5	3 557	2 779	99	11 147	6.2	2.53	12.1	25.9
Allen	12.6	7.5	7.3	49.6	109 755	108 473	-1.2	-2.0	13 575	9 824	-7 327	40 619	-0.1	2.47	13.8	27.8
Ashland	12.7	8.5	7.3	51.1	47 507	52 523	10.6	1.2	6 371	4 590	1 074	20 196	3.4	2.63	9.4	25.3
Ashtabula	13.4	8.3	7.3	50.1	99 880	102 728	2.9	-1.2	11 728	10 174	-2 889	39 363	-0.1	2.50	12.4	26.9
Athens	9.8	5.7	4.4	49.9	59 549	62 223	4.5	4.1	5 703	4 315	-176	23 578	4.8	2.35	9.2	30.0
Auglaize	12.8	7.6	7.7	50.4	44 585	46 611	4.5	-1.4	5 585	4 302	-941	17 972	3.4	2.53	8.5	25.3
Belmont	14.6	8.8	8.9	49.6	71 074	70 226	-1.2	0.2	6 510	8 351	121	28 679	1.3	2.32	11.4	29.9
Brown	12.9	8.3	6.1	50.4	34 966	42 285	20.9	6.1	5 208	3 836	623	17 014	9.4	2.60	11.2	22.6
Butler	11.7	6.3	5.3	51.1	291 479	332 807	14.2	10.6	45 495	25 574	12 777	135 960	10.5	2.63	12.4	23.5
Carroll	14.6	9.5	7.2	50.1	26 521	28 836	8.7	0.0	2 966	2 473	-626	11 385	2.3	2.50	8.8	24.3
Champaign	12.7	8.4	6.0	50.5	36 019	38 890	8.0	3.1	4 689	3 559	-47	15 329	2.5	2.56	10.2	23.9
Clark	13.6	8.6	7.6	51.6	147 538	144 742	-1.9	-4.4	16 772	15 016	-6 159	55 244	-2.5	2.45	14.1	27.7
Clermont	12.6	6.9	4.9	50.7	150 094	177 977	18.6	10.9	25 590	12 717	6 735	74 828	13.4	2.61	10.9	22.5
Clinton	12.7	7.4	6.1	51.0	35 444	40 543	14.4	3.7	5 379	3 483	898	16 210	5.2	2.52	11.9	25.1
Columbiana	14.1	8.7	7.8	49.8	108 276	112 075	3.5	-3.8	11 368	11 121	-3 952	42 683	-0.7	2.43	11.5	26.8
Coshocton	13.3	8.9	7.3	50.6	35 427	36 655	3.5	0.7	4 276	3 549	-1 399	14 658	2.1	2.49	10.4	26.3
Crawford	13.4	9.4	8.4	51.4	47 870	46 966	-1.9	-6.8	5 082	4 671	-3 751	18 099	-4.5	2.39	11.5	28.4
Cuyahoga	12.8	7.5	8.0	52.6	1 412 140	1 393 978	-1.3	-8.2	156 834	134 376	-134 309	545 056	-4.6	2.29	16.7	35.5
Darke	12.7	8.9	8.0	50.9	53 617	53 309	-0.6	-0.7	6 204	5 134	-2 235	20 929	2.5	2.50	9.0	25.9
Defiance	13.2	8.0	7.0	50.8	39 350	39 500	0.4	-1.2	4 754	3 164	-2 446	15 268	0.9	2.51	10.8	24.6
Delaware	11.4	5.7	3.8	50.7	66 929	109 989	64.3	58.4	21 349	6 764	41 082	62 760	58.2	2.74	7.3	19.0
Erie	14.8	9.1	8.2	51.0	76 781	79 551	3.6	-3.1	8 320	7 682	-2 816	31 860	0.4	2.37	12.9	28.6
Fairfield	12.1	7.1	5.2	50.4	103 468	122 759	18.6	19.1	15 976	9 856	15 316	54 310	19.6	2.64	11.2	21.9
Fayette	13.0	8.3	6.7	50.8	27 466	28 433	3.5	2.1	3 552	3 100	-600	11 438	3.5	2.49	13.5	25.8
Franklin	10.5	5.4	4.6	51.3	961 437	1 068 978	11.2	8.8	162 077	77 106	3 123	477 235	8.8	2.38	14.4	31.9
Fulton	13.1	7.3	6.8	50.9	38 498	42 084	9.3	1.5	4 981	3 328	-1 093	16 188	4.6	2.61	9.3	22.3
Gallia	12.7	9.2	6.8	50.7	30 954	31 069	0.4	-0.4	3 681	3 099	-755	12 062	0.0	2.49	11.6	27.0
Geauga	14.5	8.6	6.9	50.8	81 087	90 895	12.1	2.7	10 052	6 444	1 216	34 264	8.3	2.70	7.7	21.2
Greene	12.5	7.3	6.3	51.0	136 731	147 886	8.2	9.3	16 632	11 124	2 957	62 770	13.5	2.43	10.6	26.5
Guernsey	13.6	8.9	7.1	51.0	39 024	40 792	4.5	-1.7	4 666	8 999	-1 163	16 210	0.7	2.44	12.3	27.7
Hamilton	12.0	6.6	6.7	52.0	866 228	845 303	-2.4	-5.1	108 155	75 325	-77 341	333 945	-3.7	2.34	15.4	33.9
Hancock	12.5	7.5	6.8	51.5	65 536	71 295	8.8	4.9	8 681	5 773	781	30 197	8.2	2.42	10.0	27.9
Hardin	11.5	7.3	6.1	50.4	31 111	31 945	2.7	0.4	3 593	2 889	-635	11 762	-1.7	2.53	10.1	26.7
Harrison	15.0	9.9	8.2	50.4	16 085	15 856	-1.4	0.1	1 591	1 911	-168	6 526	2.0	2.40	9.5	27.1
Henry	12.6	7.7	7.7	50.5	29 108	29 210	0.4	-3.4	3 505	2 433	-1 469	10 934	0.0	2.55	9.3	23.7
Highland	12.4	8.5	6.7	51.0	35 728	40 875	14.4	6.6	5 505	4 031	55	16 693	7.1	2.58	11.9	24.3
Hocking	13.8	9.3	6.0	50.0	25 533	28 241	10.6	4.0	3 318	2 646	168	11 369	4.9	2.52	10.7	24.8
Holmes	9.8	6.0	5.3	50.1	32 849	38 943	18.6	8.8	7 619	2 525	-1 953	12 554	10.7	3.31	6.9	17.2
Huron	12.5	7.4	6.2	50.7	56 238	59 487	5.8	0.2	7 956	4 990	-2 259	22 820	2.3	2.59	12.2	24.4
Jackson	13.4	8.0	6.1	51.1	30 230	32 641	8.0	1.8	4 071	3 412	367	13 010	3.1	2.53	12.7	25.9
Jefferson	14.9	9.4	8.9	52.0	80 298	73 894	-8.0	-5.7	6 691	9 124	-3 342	29 109	-4.3	2.32	12.4	30.5
Knox	12.5	8.0	6.8	51.2	47 473	54 500	14.8	11.8	6 775	5 207	3 867	22 607	13.2	2.54	9.7	25.7
Lake	13.7	8.4	7.6	51.3	215 500	227 511	5.6	1.1	24 024	19 901	2 361	94 156	5.0	2.41	11.2	28.3
Lawrence	13.1	8.9	6.6	51.4	61 834	62 319	0.8	0.2	7 039	6 792	553	24 974	1.0	2.47	13.2	26.1
Licking	12.6	7.6	5.7	51.0	128 300	145 491	13.4	14.4	19 096	12 292	6 970	63 989	15.1	2.55	11.2	23.8
Logan	13.4	8.2	6.5	50.7	42 310	46 005	8.7	-0.3	5 749	4 188	-692	18 111	0.9	2.51	10.5	25.5
Lorain	13.1	7.6	6.7	50.8	271 126	284 664	5.0	5.9	34 107	23 979	7 510	116 274	9.9	2.51	13.5	26.0
Lucas	12.3	6.7	6.4	51.6	462 361	455 054	-1.6	-2.9	58 757	40 322	-31 494	180 267	-1.4	2.39	16.5	31.4
Madison	11.8	7.1	5.3	45.4	37 078	40 213	8.5	8.0	4 531	3 267	1 335	14 734	7.8	2.59	11.3	23.5
Mahoning	14.1	8.3	9.5	51.6	264 806	257 555	-2.7	-7.3	25 051	27 945	-16 529	98 712	-3.8	2.34	15.0	31.8
Marion	13.1	7.5	6.7	47.6	64 274	66 217	3.0	0.4	7 299	6 047	-1 369	24 691	0.5	2.47	13.3	26.3
Medina	13.2	7.4	5.7	50.7	122 354	151 095	23.5	14.1	19 074	10 537	15 201	65 143	19.4	2.63	8.7	21.6
Meigs	13.9	8.8	6.9	50.9	22 987	23 072	0.4	3.0	2 611	2 453	-268	9 557	3.5	2.46	11.5	25.3
Mercer	12.8	7.4	8.0	50.0	39 443	40 924	3.8	-0.3	5 200	3 496	-1 719	15 532	5.3	2.60	7.6	24.5
Miami	13.5	8.5	6.8	50.8	93 184	98 868	6.1	3.7	11 480	8 617	143	40 917	6.5	2.48	10.5	25.3
Monroe	15.1	11.0	8.4	50.2	15 497	15 180	-2.0	-3.5	1 412	1 618	-838	6 065	0.7	2.39	8.6	27.3
Montgomery	12.7	7.7	7.4	52.0	573 809	559 062	-2.6	-4.3	67 215	50 530	-40 229	223 943	-2.3	2.33	15.3	32.2
Morgan	14.0	9.5	7.9	50.2	14 194	14 897	5.0	1.1	1 594	1 481	-645	6 034	2.4	2.46	10.4	26.3
Morrow	12.9	7.9	5.5	49.9	27 749	31 628	14.0	10.1	3 972	2 511	1 711	12 855	11.8	2.68	9.5	20.7
Muskingum	12.6	8.1	7.2	51.6	82 068	84 585	3.1	1.8	9 986	8 017	-1 162	34 271	5.4	2.46	13.2	26.9
Noble	18.9	13.3	7.4	42.2	11 336	14 058	24.0	4.2	1 348	1 132	99	4 852	6.7	2.47	8.6	25.7

1. No spouse present.

Table B. States and Counties — Population, Vital Statistics, Medicare, and Crime

STATE County	Persons in group quarters, 2010	Daytime population, 2006–2010		Births, average 2006–2008		Deaths, average 2006–2008		Persons under 65 with no health insurance, 2009		Medicare, 2011			Serious crimes known to police,[2] 2010 Total	
		Number	Employ-ment/resi-dence ratio	Total	Rate[1]	Number	Rate[1]	Number	Percent	Eligible for Medicare	Enrolled in Medicare Advantage	Enrolled in a Medicare prescription drug plan	Number	Rate[3]
	32	33	34	35	36	37	38	39	40	41	42	43	44	45
NORTH DAKOTA—Cont'd														
Ward	2 685	60 572	1.0	1 004	18.0	495	8.9	4 831	10.3	8 832	774	5 463	1 001	1 623
Wells	119	4 369	1.0	D	D	72	16.8	394	13.9	1 223	69	919	50	1 188
Williams	560	22 240	1.1	D	D	204	10.4	1 971	11.6	3 577	256	2 356	445	1 987
OHIO	306 266	11 526 757	1.0	150 098	13.0	107 709	9.4	1 358 090	14.0	1 955 228	663 844	863 861	410 747	3 560
Adams	338	26 276	0.8	D	D	305	10.8	4 023	17.0	5 691	1 395	3 441	301	1 095
Allen	5 934	113 944	1.2	1 417	13.4	1 040	9.9	13 019	15.0	19 205	4 049	9 829	4 299	4 063
Ashland	2 144	50 229	0.9	682	12.4	506	9.2	7 010	15.3	9 615	3 090	4 465	1 018	1 921
Ashtabula	3 190	93 802	0.8	1 278	12.6	1 108	10.9	13 238	15.7	20 064	4 465	10 925	NA	NA
Athens	9 345	64 963	1.0	569	9.1	471	7.5	9 801	17.6	8 546	2 442	5 586	1 779	2 771
Auglaize	525	43 032	0.9	D	D	489	10.5	4 509	11.7	7 768	1 665	4 371	NA	NA
Belmont	3 834	64 463	0.8	720	10.6	894	13.1	7 902	14.3	14 704	6 449	5 971	719	1 123
Brown	575	35 448	0.5	549	12.4	438	9.9	5 616	15.0	8 254	2 877	3 911	509	1 254
Butler	10 953	341 470	0.9	5 125	14.3	2 812	7.9	42 310	13.5	53 728	19 423	20 778	15 203	4 130
Carroll	405	23 224	0.6	D	D	271	9.4	3 519	14.9	5 530	2 381	2 195	196	680
Champaign	793	34 799	0.7	D	D	387	9.8	4 331	13.0	6 898	2 557	4 140	564	1 407
Clark	2 798	129 736	0.8	1 837	13.1	1 581	11.2	15 775	13.8	26 923	11 657	12 846	6 628	4 802
Clermont	1 717	161 836	0.6	2 791	14.4	1 402	7.2	22 541	13.4	29 568	11 247	11 557	6 350	3 224
Clinton	1 145	46 668	1.2	561	13.0	386	8.9	4 582	12.5	7 251	2 187	3 853	897	2 134
Columbiana	3 944	95 428	0.7	1 219	11.2	1 193	10.9	13 212	14.9	21 469	6 307	9 733	534	651
Coshocton	428	34 525	0.8	441	12.1	376	10.3	5 007	16.8	7 217	1 497	4 261	680	1 843
Crawford	579	41 109	0.8	491	11.1	492	11.1	5 210	14.8	9 508	2 278	5 232	NA	NA
Cuyahoga	29 251	1 429 637	1.2	16 522	12.7	13 960	10.8	154 104	14.7	228 748	79 031	97 081	40 648	3 428
Darke	606	47 775	0.8	693	13.2	556	10.6	6 311	14.9	10 298	2 488	5 190	634	1 246
Defiance	720	38 253	0.9	D	D	355	9.2	3 975	12.5	7 262	1 403	3 706	897	2 298
Delaware	2 368	150 853	0.8	2 377	14.8	772	4.8	11 305	7.7	20 040	7 180	9 180	3 008	1 778
Erie	1 677	78 595	1.0	851	11.0	861	11.1	8 401	13.6	15 802	2 883	7 475	2 240	2 945
Fairfield	2 872	119 219	0.6	1 755	12.4	1 095	7.7	14 153	11.6	22 501	8 948	9 009	4 939	3 415
Fayette	593	28 085	0.9	D	D	333	11.8	3 543	15.0	5 422	2 008	2 803	1 064	3 665
Franklin	25 224	1 255 732	1.2	18 282	16.4	8 375	7.5	158 259	15.7	144 954	54 892	66 302	66 641	5 790
Fulton	391	41 530	0.9	D	D	386	9.1	4 262	12.0	7 339	1 859	4 042	935	2 190
Gallia	921	31 914	1.1	416	13.4	334	10.8	3 841	15.0	6 233	1 330	3 816	1 237	4 016
Geauga	864	84 841	0.8	963	10.1	700	7.4	9 606	11.9	16 237	4 933	7 492	661	796
Greene	8 775	162 470	1.0	1 796	11.6	1 197	7.7	15 756	11.7	25 263	8 683	8 695	4 419	2 735
Guernsey	510	39 373	0.9	D	D	428	10.6	5 025	15.0	8 292	1 808	4 888	1 073	2 708
Hamilton	19 551	923 313	1.3	11 759	14.0	7 937	9.5	99 698	13.9	128 141	44 206	52 050	40 405	5 073
Hancock	1 694	81 616	1.2	952	12.8	631	8.5	7 455	12.0	12 463	2 986	6 381	1 775	2 374
Hardin	2 259	28 264	0.7	D	D	313	9.8	4 117	15.3	5 345	1 098	3 215	820	2 558
Harrison	232	13 543	0.6	D	D	201	12.9	1 760	14.3	3 312	956	1 842	241	1 563
Henry	346	26 116	0.8	D	D	264	9.1	3 200	13.4	5 127	1 175	2 607	691	2 638
Highland	484	39 458	0.8	D	D	439	10.3	5 491	15.4	8 187	2 083	4 500	1 349	3 113
Hocking	718	24 298	0.6	D	D	287	9.9	3 752	15.4	5 503	1 272	2 955	837	2 849
Holmes	765	43 615	1.1	793	19.1	269	6.5	9 564	26.0	4 094	1 575	1 771	315	751
Huron	578	57 015	0.9	861	14.4	543	9.1	7 439	14.7	10 185	1 880	5 406	390	743
Jackson	325	32 481	0.9	434	13.0	379	11.3	4 646	16.4	6 492	1 185	3 975	NA	NA
Jefferson	2 212	68 244	0.9	738	10.7	977	14.1	7 144	13.2	15 472	5 163	7 569	1 644	2 405
Knox	3 485	55 285	0.8	739	12.5	546	9.3	7 196	14.5	10 778	2 959	5 820	NA	NA
Lake	2 786	210 839	0.8	2 532	10.8	2 172	9.3	24 453	12.6	43 290	14 698	18 442	4 342	1 983
Lawrence	669	52 463	0.6	785	12.5	721	11.5	8 032	15.3	13 312	2 282	7 401	1 118	1 861
Licking	3 448	146 692	0.8	2 076	13.2	1 317	8.4	17 241	12.9	27 489	9 287	10 641	4 762	2 985
Logan	450	45 165	1.0	635	13.7	438	9.5	5 293	13.6	8 246	1 975	4 951	1 310	3 002
Lorain	9 332	269 167	0.8	3 637	12.0	2 594	8.6	34 828	13.6	52 361	14 005	21 571	7 809	3 118
Lucas	10 715	462 518	1.1	6 385	14.4	4 277	9.7	59 330	15.1	72 816	24 001	34 059	15 396	3 691
Madison	5 238	39 924	0.8	498	12.0	355	8.5	5 216	14.4	6 502	3 010	2 830	953	2 212
Mahoning	7 925	242 052	1.0	2 634	10.8	3 013	12.4	26 159	13.7	49 825	21 046	19 000	10 428	4 379
Marion	5 457	67 845	1.0	805	12.3	667	10.2	8 458	15.3	12 183	3 538	6 291	2 896	4 355
Medina	1 198	145 237	0.7	1 946	11.4	1 185	7.0	15 325	10.4	26 864	9 673	10 011	1 023	747
Meigs	212	19 113	0.5	D	D	281	12.3	3 206	16.7	4 711	852	2 713	391	1 673
Mercer	439	38 396	0.9	D	D	391	9.5	4 053	12.0	7 246	1 869	4 291	719	1 762
Miami	1 055	96 493	0.9	1 244	12.3	917	9.0	10 897	13.0	18 869	6 040	8 688	1 951	2 519
Monroe	165	14 069	0.9	D	D	156	10.9	1 609	14.3	3 495	1 295	1 544	113	772
Montgomery	14 142	562 959	1.1	7 219	13.4	5 499	10.2	64 808	14.7	96 687	40 940	34 021	22 160	4 213
Morgan	188	12 604	0.6	D	D	160	10.9	1 784	15.3	2 874	712	1 618	201	1 335
Morrow	366	26 327	0.5	D	D	274	8.0	4 555	15.3	5 679	1 653	2 918	549	1 576
Muskingum	1 898	84 914	1.0	1 115	13.0	881	10.3	10 072	14.3	17 139	3 759	9 737	3 153	3 663
Noble	2 672	13 836	0.8	D	D	126	8.9	2 189	18.0	2 268	564	1 379	55	426

1. Per 1,000 estimated resident population.   2. Data for serious crimes have not been adjusted for underreporting; this may affect comparability between geographic areas and over time.   3. Per 100,000 population estimated by the FBI.

Table B. States and Counties — Crime, Education, Money Income, and Poverty

STATE County	Serious crimes known to police,[1] 2010 (cont.) Rate[2] Violent	Property	Education — School enrollment and attainment, 2006–2010 Enrollment[3] Total	Per-cent private	Attainment[4] (percent) High school graduate or less	Bach-elor's degree or more	Local government expenditures,[5] 2008–2009 Total current expendi-tures (mil dol)	Current expendi-tures per student (dollars)	Money income, 2006–2010 Per capita income[6] (dollars)	Households Median income Dollars	Percent change, 2000 to 2006–2010 (constant 2010 dollars)	Percent with income of $200,000 or more	Income and poverty, 2010 Median house-hold income (dollars)	Percent below poverty level All per-sons	Children under 18 years	Children 5 to 17 years in families
	46	47	48	49	50	51	52	53	54	55	56	57	58	59	60	61
NORTH DAKOTA—Cont'd																
Ward	204	1 419	15 148	9.7	36.5	25.8	83.9	9 806	25 326	48 793	14.4	2.1	46 952	12.6	15.9	14.4
Wells	143	1 046	673	10.4	50.5	19.6	6.7	11 759	23 531	40 136	-0.6	2.0	42 540	12.4	14.0	11.9
Williams	214	1 772	4 434	11.5	42.7	19.3	34.3	11 001	29 153	55 396	38.9	2.7	56 689	8.6	11.9	10.8
OHIO	315	3 245	3 043 760	18.3	48.4	24.1	19 031.7	10 490	25 113	47 358	-8.7	2.6	45 151	15.8	23.1	20.8
Adams	18	1 076	6 517	7.7	71.5	10.7	49.6	9 870	17 693	32 791	-11.7	1.0	33 549	22.8	32.2	30.9
Allen	395	3 668	28 738	18.8	54.9	15.8	156.0	9 608	21 713	43 632	-7.0	1.3	41 196	18.7	30.0	27.2
Ashland	51	1 870	13 789	34.8	58.4	17.5	91.7	9 017	20 558	44 542	-10.2	1.1	41 734	15.6	22.9	19.6
Ashtabula	NA	NA	24 795	13.2	61.8	12.9	158.4	9 741	19 898	42 139	-6.5	0.9	38 762	16.1	24.8	24.2
Athens	93	2 678	28 996	2.9	47.7	27.3	96.1	11 831	16 642	31 559	-8.8	1.6	35 557	24.8	25.5	24.6
Auglaize	NA	NA	11 527	9.4	56.8	15.5	79.4	9 497	25 290	52 018	-5.3	1.5	50 103	9.4	13.2	11.7
Belmont	72	1 051	14 789	12.8	58.1	14.1	88.5	9 803	20 266	38 320	1.8	0.6	37 913	16.3	25.4	23.4
Brown	37	1 217	10 763	8.8	67.8	9.8	76.3	9 295	20 167	45 887	-5.4	0.7	41 892	13.0	20.8	19.5
Butler	331	3 799	103 909	13.1	48.0	25.9	589.9	9 781	25 892	54 788	-9.6	2.7	54 359	13.5	17.7	16.6
Carroll	76	603	6 333	13.4	66.1	12.0	31.4	8 013	21 575	43 148	-4.0	1.2	39 414	16.6	26.1	23.2
Champaign	70	1 337	10 194	15.4	59.7	15.3	78.9	9 749	23 438	49 246	-9.8	1.5	48 577	13.1	19.2	16.9
Clark	369	4 432	35 001	19.4	54.3	16.2	216.1	9 456	22 110	44 141	-13.6	1.4	40 524	20.0	29.9	25.9
Clermont	86	3 138	49 841	18.1	48.6	24.8	264.1	9 197	27 900	58 472	-6.5	3.8	56 628	9.6	14.1	13.2
Clinton	69	2 065	10 713	16.8	58.4	14.7	71.7	8 441	22 163	46 261	-9.7	1.5	44 324	15.7	21.1	18.6
Columbiana	15	636	24 519	9.7	61.8	12.4	154.5	9 098	19 635	39 502	-8.9	0.9	36 985	17.7	27.1	25.8
Coshocton	43	1 799	8 660	13.9	64.8	11.6	50.6	9 142	19 635	39 469	-10.2	0.5	37 227	20.4	30.0	26.4
Crawford	NA	NA	10 508	13.1	63.1	10.5	66.3	8 824	20 590	41 228	-10.1	0.7	39 467	16.5	26.1	23.0
Cuyahoga	644	2 884	337 515	26.1	43.8	28.2	2 362.0	12 722	26 263	43 603	-12.1	3.2	41 407	18.2	28.6	25.9
Darke	98	1 148	12 520	12.5	62.2	11.3	79.7	8 708	21 483	44 280	-11.0	1.1	42 023	12.1	17.4	15.9
Defiance	61	2 236	10 243	16.3	57.4	16.3	56.4	8 259	22 139	44 480	-21.8	1.4	45 792	11.5	18.3	16.5
Delaware	77	1 702	48 293	27.2	25.1	49.5	247.3	10 077	40 682	87 908	3.2	10.6	85 628	5.8	6.6	5.8
Erie	289	2 656	17 814	14.8	51.8	20.1	168.0	12 936	25 290	48 593	-13.9	2.1	43 935	14.9	24.4	20.3
Fairfield	158	3 258	38 726	17.0	46.0	24.4	222.9	8 834	26 130	56 796	-6.5	2.1	55 805	11.2	15.7	13.6
Fayette	134	3 531	6 558	10.7	65.4	13.1	42.8	8 883	20 525	39 599	-14.9	1.0	40 250	16.2	23.6	21.9
Franklin	513	5 277	325 484	16.6	38.2	35.0	2 145.6	11 262	26 909	49 087	-9.3	3.3	47 621	18.8	25.5	23.1
Fulton	89	2 101	11 386	9.2	55.1	14.9	100.3	11 727	22 804	50 717	-9.1	0.9	49 909	10.9	15.8	14.7
Gallia	91	3 925	7 699	12.4	62.8	14.3	55.0	11 371	20 199	37 409	-2.1	1.4	37 923	18.2	29.4	28.3
Geauga	39	758	23 779	23.7	38.0	34.0	136.9	10 861	32 735	65 663	+13.9	6.4	63 172	7.8	12.1	10.6
Greene	100	2 635	51 417	22.5	36.3	34.5	239.0	10 278	28 328	56 679	-8.0	2.9	52 056	13.1	16.7	14.0
Guernsey	91	2 617	9 440	12.5	62.7	11.2	58.1	10 019	19 187	37 573	-1.6	0.6	35 684	19.1	32.6	30.4
Hamilton	556	4 517	220 053	26.6	40.5	32.5	1 335.1	11 565	28 799	48 234	-7.0	4.2	46 359	18.5	28.5	25.3
Hancock	127	2 247	19 686	21.4	47.1	24.4	141.2	9 573	25 158	49 070	-11.6	2.0	49 918	11.9	16.5	15.4
Hardin	44	2 514	10 111	36.8	64.8	15.1	42.9	9 082	19 100	41 343	-5.2	1.0	40 710	17.2	20.9	18.0
Harrison	110	1 453	3 445	7.5	67.4	9.0	17.6	9 446	19 318	35 363	-7.9	0.9	36 074	17.8	27.3	24.7
Henry	84	2 564	7 437	15.5	58.2	13.1	58.2	11 659	22 638	48 367	-10.5	1.5	46 136	12.9	17.8	15.7
Highland	196	2 917	10 420	7.8	65.4	9.7	65.6	8 160	18 966	39 844	-10.9	0.9	38 643	18.6	27.5	25.2
Hocking	20	2 828	7 204	8.6	62.7	10.2	36.3	8 826	19 048	39 586	-8.8	0.4	40 017	16.2	24.8	23.1
Holmes	26	725	9 654	33.1	77.4	9.4	39.0	8 693	17 009	43 533	-6.9	1.1	39 917	16.5	27.6	25.9
Huron	25	718	15 180	12.5	63.5	12.1	106.9	8 582	21 743	47 058	-8.4	1.2	44 632	14.0	21.8	19.4
Jackson	NA	NA	7 605	8.5	63.5	12.0	51.0	9 093	18 775	34 044	-12.3	1.3	36 791	22.5	35.4	33.6
Jefferson	193	2 212	16 119	24.0	57.4	14.1	103.1	10 158	20 470	37 527	-3.9	0.9	36 800	18.6	28.3	26.1
Knox	NA	NA	16 200	28.5	56.0	19.0	88.1	10 170	21 204	45 655	-7.3	1.2	46 937	16.5	24.6	21.2
Lake	207	1 776	55 981	18.7	44.6	24.2	369.1	10 748	28 221	54 896	-11.1	2.3	52 854	9.6	14.4	12.7
Lawrence	143	1 718	14 571	5.8	61.0	12.9	109.9	10 318	19 452	36 461	-1.1	1.1	36 551	21.4	31.9	29.8
Licking	172	2 813	43 643	19.6	50.5	22.1	257.4	9 412	25 534	53 291	-4.6	2.3	51 247	12.4	16.7	14.3
Logan	110	2 892	10 864	9.8	60.8	14.3	78.9	10 774	22 974	46 493	-11.5	1.2	44 436	16.9	27.4	24.8
Lorain	267	2 851	78 451	19.6	48.2	20.6	459.7	9 520	25 002	52 066	-8.7	2.3	50 092	14.3	22.3	20.1
Lucas	719	2 973	123 741	17.7	46.0	23.0	791.3	10 777	23 981	42 072	-12.6	2.4	39 200	19.8	29.0	26.7
Madison	67	2 145	10 069	14.4	58.1	15.6	73.2	10 007	23 980	50 533	-9.7	3.0	48 295	15.0	19.5	17.4
Mahoning	356	4 023	59 227	14.5	53.3	20.4	382.0	10 386	22 824	40 123	-10.1	1.7	38 205	17.1	26.0	23.6
Marion	147	4 207	15 000	10.2	61.6	12.0	112.3	9 111	19 849	40 511	-17.4	0.8	41 314	19.3	24.8	22.1
Medina	34	714	46 037	17.6	40.9	29.5	272.8	9 345	29 986	66 193	-6.3	3.9	63 582	7.6	10.3	9.1
Meigs	64	1 608	5 130	12.8	65.3	10.3	34.2	9 465	18 003	33 407	-3.3	0.3	33 194	23.5	35.9	30.0
Mercer	83	1 678	10 565	11.3	58.6	15.4	85.6	9 790	22 348	49 719	-8.1	1.7	48 521	9.6	13.2	11.9
Miami	44	2 475	24 788	16.3	51.6	20.0	169.8	10 262	25 006	51 507	-7.8	1.5	49 195	11.9	18.0	16.8
Monroe	68	703	3 246	8.9	65.9	9.2	24.5	9 315	18 738	37 030	-4.0	0.6	38 015	17.4	27.4	26.3
Montgomery	442	3 772	148 388	21.6	42.6	24.3	880.6	10 987	24 828	43 965	-13.5	2.0	40 885	18.0	27.2	24.5
Morgan	46	1 289	3 662	9.8	63.3	8.7	20.3	9 370	18 777	34 962	-4.4	0.5	35 634	19.6	29.6	27.1
Morrow	34	1 542	8 399	15.9	60.4	13.6	49.6	8 636	20 795	49 891	-3.6	0.2	47 080	13.7	21.9	20.0
Muskingum	144	3 519	22 140	13.6	59.1	14.2	159.9	10 028	20 561	39 538	-11.3	1.1	40 485	17.8	28.6	24.9
Noble	16	411	2 360	3.9	69.2	9.1	16.3	7 914	20 029	39 500	-5.3	0.8	38 013	17.3	23.2	21.5

1. Data for serious crimes have not been adjusted for underreporting; this may affect comparability between geographic areas and over time. 2. Per 100,000 population estimated by the FBI. 3. All persons 3 years old and over enrolled in nursery school through college. 4. Persons 25 years old and over. 5. Elementary and secondary education expenditures. 6. Based on population estimated by the American Community Survey, 2006–2010.

Table B. States and Counties — **Personal Income**

	Personal income, 2009												
		Per capita[1]						Transfer payments (mil dol)					
									Government payments to individuals				
STATE County	Total (mil dol)	Percent change, 2008– 2009	Dollars	Rank	Wages and salaries[2] (mil dol)	Proprietors' income (mil dol)	Dividends, interest, and rent (mil dol)	Total	Total	Social Security	Medical payments	Income mainte- nance	Unemploy- ment insurance
	62	63	64	65	66	67	68	69	70	71	72	73	74
NORTH DAKOTA—Cont'd													
Ward	2 477	1.6	43 438	257	1 688	234	388	357	348	117	139	29	8
Wells	202	-7.8	49 417	113	63	69	39	41	40	15	19	2	1
Williams	961	2.8	46 971	149	765	101	174	136	132	51	55	9	3
OHIO	408 707	-1.4	35 408	X	268 111	25 680	62 910	86 506	84 403	27 064	35 222	8 657	4 768
Adams	716	0.9	25 545	2 802	248	62	85	260	255	68	120	34	15
Allen	3 193	-1.8	30 596	1 843	2 454	282	485	793	774	269	295	80	45
Ashland	1 505	-1.6	27 349	2 508	784	117	229	356	346	135	122	26	27
Ashtabula	2 898	-1.4	28 755	2 246	1 307	137	359	924	905	263	417	88	51
Athens	1 641	4.2	26 041	2 718	991	71	235	449	437	94	176	58	21
Auglaize	1 642	-0.4	35 159	998	845	77	257	343	335	110	156	18	22
Belmont	2 032	-0.3	29 847	2 010	956	108	302	601	588	203	252	54	24
Brown	1 278	0.2	29 044	2 186	348	101	142	342	334	110	139	32	21
Butler	12 586	-1.8	34 654	1 074	7 486	556	1 771	2 338	2 272	773	896	212	140
Carroll	759	-1.1	26 585	2 626	220	78	105	202	197	78	68	18	15
Champaign	1 170	-0.5	29 464	2 101	450	98	142	274	267	98	100	24	19
Clark	4 557	0.3	32 627	1 396	2 217	214	599	1 190	1 164	365	508	124	58
Clermont	6 785	-2.4	34 552	1 084	2 672	498	855	1 176	1 140	431	409	94	79
Clinton	1 417	-2.4	32 900	1 355	1 267	91	185	313	306	95	128	27	24
Columbiana	2 990	-2.2	27 761	2 442	1 236	158	413	919	899	299	385	82	55
Coshocton	1 020	-2.0	28 515	2 297	494	96	152	289	283	98	116	28	18
Crawford	1 249	0.8	28 780	2 236	546	90	181	384	376	133	153	34	25
Cuyahoga	52 803	-2.8	41 391	368	42 341	4 818	9 260	11 152	10 919	3 173	5 032	1 296	462
Darke	1 655	-1.9	31 947	1 540	737	139	263	363	354	143	128	25	24
Defiance	1 216	-2.2	31 642	1 616	743	95	177	289	282	107	103	23	22
Delaware	8 685	2.3	51 479	85	4 167	495	1 154	716	686	277	202	44	49
Erie	2 789	-1.9	36 236	858	1 587	237	474	649	635	229	255	49	39
Fairfield	4 665	-0.6	32 464	1 436	1 701	248	638	887	860	305	331	82	50
Fayette	944	1.1	33 590	1 236	454	96	114	229	224	69	96	24	14
Franklin	43 728	-1.2	38 020	638	39 432	3 229	5 938	7 529	7 320	1 883	3 178	993	405
Fulton	1 433	-0.4	33 786	1 205	779	168	210	306	299	106	119	18	24
Gallia	962	0.5	31 355	1 682	576	45	120	318	312	78	156	39	10
Geauga	4 398	-3.8	44 400	220	1 575	205	919	545	527	237	175	21	29
Greene	5 611	-1.3	35 105	1 004	4 561	289	956	898	869	326	275	74	60
Guernsey	1 119	2.5	27 935	2 412	608	66	136	356	349	107	156	39	18
Hamilton	36 249	-2.7	42 393	298	32 068	2 611	7 320	6 279	6 123	1 790	2 734	685	303
Hancock	2 665	-1.3	35 753	920	2 020	189	415	477	464	180	150	36	32
Hardin	851	0.3	26 736	2 604	357	79	108	211	205	73	79	18	14
Harrison	430	-0.6	28 149	2 373	143	12	54	139	136	44	60	13	7
Henry	931	0.0	32 502	1 426	496	84	137	208	202	73	83	12	16
Highland	1 208	-0.4	28 640	2 271	433	98	154	347	339	105	139	37	24
Hocking	785	0.8	27 167	2 539	270	35	96	234	229	71	99	27	12
Holmes	990	-4.7	23 660	2 985	653	195	148	165	158	54	61	14	11
Huron	1 722	0.0	28 776	2 239	1 019	94	259	463	453	142	182	38	35
Jackson	877	1.1	26 220	2 684	432	45	109	278	271	80	112	39	13
Jefferson	2 154	-0.2	31 822	1 574	1 169	95	294	685	673	224	293	66	32
Knox	1 808	0.3	30 325	1 900	913	106	254	455	444	146	201	36	23
Lake	8 847	-1.8	37 366	706	4 771	322	1 408	1 678	1 634	635	642	95	88
Lawrence	1 783	3.0	28 417	2 319	495	53	178	599	587	172	256	78	20
Licking	5 646	-0.1	35 624	939	2 453	240	776	1 079	1 050	370	398	98	61
Logan	1 478	-1.2	31 729	1 594	964	77	171	339	331	113	132	29	23
Lorain	9 940	-0.9	32 514	1 422	4 621	340	1 384	2 191	2 135	745	825	213	129
Lucas	14 920	-1.4	32 191	1 487	10 764	946	2 125	3 789	3 704	1 001	1 663	488	209
Madison	1 411	-0.5	33 171	1 308	649	144	167	278	270	87	119	24	15
Mahoning	7 805	-2.0	32 970	1 345	4 395	547	1 314	2 219	2 176	702	923	235	118
Marion	2 013	-0.1	30 654	1 832	1 216	126	255	521	509	160	213	56	28
Medina	6 515	-1.3	37 432	697	2 705	259	1 020	1 020	988	391	371	51	61
Meigs	562	3.8	24 592	2 908	140	26	59	197	193	58	80	27	11
Mercer	1 358	-3.6	33 394	1 279	725	110	233	258	251	102	92	16	17
Miami	3 536	-0.1	34 921	1 032	1 759	157	523	729	711	271	268	50	50
Monroe	413	-0.2	29 411	2 115	175	34	51	124	122	47	47	12	6
Montgomery	18 996	-0.9	35 669	932	13 557	874	3 039	4 501	4 405	1 340	1 873	460	238
Morgan	340	2.0	23 778	2 976	100	26	43	115	113	37	46	13	7
Morrow	980	1.0	28 279	2 350	230	66	99	214	208	78	72	21	15
Muskingum	2 550	1.5	30 044	1 969	1 461	113	369	722	706	227	289	87	38
Noble	288	0.9	20 100	3 094	120	18	37	84	81	30	29	8	7

1. Based on the resident population estimated as of July 1 of the year shown.　2. Includes supplements to wages and salaries.

Table B. States and Counties — Earnings, Social Security, and Housing

STATE County	Earnings, 2009									Social Security beneficiaries, December 2010		Supplemental Security Income recipients, December 2010	Housing units, 2010	
	Total (mil dol)	Percent by selected industries								Number	Rate[2]		Total	Percent change, 2000–2010
		Goods-related[1]			Service-related and health				Govern-ment					
		Farm	Total	Manu-facturing	Information and profes-sional and technical services	Retail trade	Finance, insur-ance, and real estate	Health care and social services						
	75	76	77	78	79	80	81	82	83	84	85	86	87	88
NORTH DAKOTA—Cont'd														
Ward	1 923	4.2	11.4	1.7	D	7.1	5.4	12.4	35.4	9 520	154	628	26 744	6.6
Wells	132	45.6	D	1.4	1.0	D	3.7	9.1	9.9	1 295	308	68	2 481	-6.1
Williams	866	7.1	38.6	2.1	D	5.4	5.5	7.4	9.4	3 985	178	234	10 464	8.1
OHIO	293 791	0.7	20.4	15.3	9.9	6.1	7.1	13.2	16.4	2 124 650	184	285 569	5 127 508	7.2
Adams	310	3.1	D	D	2.4	10.5	4.2	D	25.4	6 450	226	1 761	12 978	9.8
Allen	2 737	1.1	D	24.9	4.2	6.8	3.4	19.5	13.8	21 185	199	2 827	44 999	1.7
Ashland	901	1.3	24.0	18.9	8.6	6.2	3.1	D	17.2	10 675	201	709	22 141	6.3
Ashtabula	1 445	1.0	30.6	24.9	3.3	7.5	3.0	16.0	18.4	21 600	213	3 019	46 099	5.3
Athens	1 062	0.1	D	2.3	4.3	8.7	3.4	14.0	51.3	8 810	136	2 265	26 385	6.0
Auglaize	922	3.8	D	38.5	D	5.9	3.2	9.8	13.8	8 465	184	475	19 585	6.0
Belmont	1 065	0.2	23.7	5.7	D	10.7	5.8	15.2	19.1	16 200	230	2 278	32 452	3.9
Brown	449	5.2	D	6.8	3.5	6.4	4.4	D	27.3	9 365	209	1 197	19 301	12.3
Butler	8 042	0.2	D	17.8	4.4	6.6	8.9	10.9	15.5	59 520	162	6 482	148 273	14.3
Carroll	298	6.5	27.1	19.2	D	9.2	4.5	D	16.5	6 320	219	587	13 698	5.2
Champaign	548	6.5	D	32.0	3.5	6.4	4.0	D	18.8	7 755	193	600	16 755	5.4
Clark	2 431	2.0	19.6	16.2	4.1	6.9	6.5	16.4	16.9	29 160	211	3 692	61 419	0.6
Clermont	3 170	0.4	D	10.8	9.7	9.5	13.4	9.4	14.2	33 080	168	2 931	80 656	16.5
Clinton	1 358	2.8	D	15.4	2.4	4.0	3.5	D	14.6	8 100	193	840	18 133	9.4
Columbiana	1 394	1.0	24.2	18.7	2.9	8.6	4.0	15.8	19.9	23 955	222	3 025	47 088	2.2
Coshocton	590	1.8	32.3	25.2	D	6.2	3.8	10.4	13.5	8 115	220	892	16 545	2.7
Crawford	636	5.2	D	24.5	4.2	6.7	7.0	D	16.8	10 530	240	1 078	20 167	-0.1
Cuyahoga	47 159	0.0	D	11.5	13.8	4.4	10.4	14.3	14.8	242 670	189	46 962	621 763	0.8
Darke	876	5.4	D	23.9	6.1	6.6	5.6	10.8	13.2	11 445	216	758	22 730	5.3
Defiance	837	3.5	36.0	32.5	4.1	8.7	5.4	D	13.0	8 325	213	695	16 729	4.3
Delaware	4 662	0.4	11.7	8.4	27.8	7.0	12.6	7.4	9.8	20 870	120	1 085	66 378	56.6
Erie	1 825	0.5	D	21.2	3.7	6.9	3.9	14.8	17.2	17 235	224	1 474	37 845	5.4
Fairfield	1 949	1.0	D	13.9	4.5	9.2	4.6	11.5	24.0	24 740	169	2 320	58 687	22.4
Fayette	550	8.5	24.2	20.4	D	10.9	5.2	D	16.4	6 025	208	893	12 693	6.6
Franklin	42 661	0.0	10.4	6.3	13.9	6.0	10.3	11.5	18.5	152 615	131	28 917	527 186	11.9
Fulton	947	5.7	40.5	34.4	D	4.9	4.5	D	13.9	8 115	190	439	17 407	7.2
Gallia	621	0.5	D	5.5	D	6.7	5.0	D	15.6	6 840	221	1 653	13 925	3.2
Geauga	1 780	0.4	D	25.8	5.4	7.4	4.4	9.9	13.1	16 935	181	666	36 574	11.5
Greene	4 850	0.5	D	4.7	17.4	5.5	2.8	6.0	48.2	26 325	163	2 016	68 241	17.2
Guernsey	674	0.5	D	21.2	5.2	7.9	3.7	14.8	18.3	9 280	231	1 503	19 193	2.2
Hamilton	34 678	0.0	D	12.9	13.0	4.3	7.9	14.3	10.9	137 900	172	22 055	377 364	1.1
Hancock	2 209	1.4	D	27.4	6.6	7.0	2.9	10.7	8.8	13 805	185	1 035	33 174	11.4
Hardin	436	12.2	26.1	23.1	2.8	5.9	3.6	D	16.6	5 975	186	618	13 100	1.5
Harrison	156	0.9	37.4	14.9	2.1	5.4	2.8	D	22.9	3 680	232	514	8 170	6.4
Henry	581	8.1	D	31.8	2.1	5.9	3.8	8.3	17.9	5 640	200	335	11 963	2.9
Highland	530	5.1	23.7	19.3	D	11.8	7.1	D	22.7	9 245	212	1 273	19 380	10.2
Hocking	305	0.5	24.4	15.3	3.0	8.4	3.8	D	33.3	6 195	211	975	13 417	10.5
Holmes	848	2.5	47.3	30.9	D	6.9	2.9	D	10.1	4 470	106	360	13 666	11.3
Huron	1 113	3.9	D	26.8	3.1	5.1	3.1	D	12.4	11 485	193	1 096	25 196	6.8
Jackson	477	0.5	35.7	28.3	2.2	9.2	4.1	12.1	18.1	7 135	215	1 615	14 587	4.9
Jefferson	1 264	0.1	D	10.3	4.1	6.7	2.9	D	14.0	17 400	250	2 589	32 826	-1.4
Knox	1 020	1.4	38.1	30.4	3.7	6.5	3.1	11.6	14.3	11 885	195	1 114	25 118	15.3
Lake	5 093	0.7	D	26.6	6.6	8.2	3.1	10.6	13.9	46 305	201	2 427	101 202	8.3
Lawrence	548	0.2	D	5.8	3.5	11.8	4.2	13.7	27.5	14 680	235	3 728	27 603	1.5
Licking	2 692	1.3	22.7	14.3	6.4	8.4	7.4	11.6	18.0	30 170	181	2 943	69 291	17.8
Logan	1 041	1.9	46.6	43.2	D	5.0	2.7	8.4	12.2	9 065	198	733	23 181	7.5
Lorain	4 961	0.8	D	24.5	4.5	7.9	3.0	12.5	20.0	56 865	189	6 453	127 036	14.1
Lucas	11 710	0.1	19.1	13.2	8.8	6.8	5.2	19.0	16.5	79 260	179	16 527	202 630	3.2
Madison	793	6.9	26.2	22.4	6.2	7.3	2.3	6.5	24.2	7 010	161	628	15 939	10.7
Mahoning	4 942	0.2	16.6	9.1	7.2	9.0	5.3	17.3	17.9	54 950	230	8 284	111 833	0.1
Marion	1 343	2.4	D	28.6	5.5	6.7	3.3	12.1	23.5	13 330	200	2 073	27 834	5.8
Medina	2 964	0.5	24.9	17.1	5.6	8.4	4.3	10.0	14.2	29 195	169	1 232	69 181	21.8
Meigs	167	4.4	18.4	2.5	D	8.7	4.1	D	30.8	5 130	216	1 180	11 191	3.8
Mercer	835	7.2	D	28.0	3.2	7.1	5.2	5.7	16.1	7 860	193	446	17 633	11.1
Miami	1 916	2.1	33.4	28.6	D	7.6	4.1	10.9	15.0	20 900	204	1 516	44 256	9.1
Monroe	209	0.7	D	D	1.6	4.4	D	D	17.3	3 915	267	544	7 567	4.9
Montgomery	14 431	0.1	D	11.6	12.9	5.2	5.9	18.6	17.6	104 785	196	14 837	254 775	2.5
Morgan	126	2.0	D	19.8	3.0	6.6	5.8	D	25.8	3 240	215	520	7 892	1.6
Morrow	296	7.6	25.2	18.6	D	7.1	3.2	D	27.5	6 405	184	607	14 155	16.7
Muskingum	1 575	0.6	19.2	14.1	4.3	9.4	4.0	20.9	16.9	19 410	226	3 090	38 074	8.3
Noble	139	0.7	D	12.4	D	5.3	D	8.9	35.9	2 540	173	306	6 053	10.5

1. Includes mining, construction, and manufacturing.   2. Per 1,000 resident population enumerated in the 2010 census.

STATE County	Housing units, 2006–2010								Civilian labor force, 2010				Civilian employment,[5] 2006–2010		
	Occupied units										Unemployment			Percent	
			Owner-occupied			Renter-occupied									
				Median owner cost as a percent of income											Construction, production, and maintenance occupations
	Total	Percent	Median value[1]	With a mortgage	Without a mortgage	Median rent[2]	Median rent as a percent of income	Substandard units[3] (percent)	Total	Percent change, 2009–2010	Total	Rate[4]	Total	Management, business, science and arts	
	89	90	91	92	93	94	95	96	97	98	99	100	101	102	103
NORTH DAKOTA—Cont'd															
Ward	24 260	64.4	118 200	20.9	10.8	574	24.3	1.0	29 822	1.1	1 088	3.6	29 634	29.4	23.0
Wells	2 059	76.1	55 700	16.9	11.7	381	23.8	1.7	2 012	0.4	93	4.6	2 043	34.3	29.9
Williams	9 192	71.2	93 800	15.2	10.0	515	17.8	1.1	17 402	19.3	301	1.7	11 739	27.8	32.6
OHIO	4 552 270	69.2	136 400	23.4	13.2	678	29.8	1.6	5 864 025	-1.2	585 515	10.0	5 369 857	33.4	24.2
Adams	10 754	72.8	97 600	25.4	13.9	508	31.4	2.5	13 069	-0.3	1 838	14.1	10 551	27.1	36.0
Allen	40 719	71.2	104 800	21.6	12.0	611	30.2	1.2	50 932	-1.8	5 415	10.6	47 826	26.1	28.3
Ashland	20 040	78.8	128 500	24.6	13.2	637	30.7	3.0	27 279	-0.7	3 135	11.5	23 904	28.0	32.8
Ashtabula	38 911	72.8	118 500	24.1	14.3	607	31.0	2.5	48 840	-0.6	6 132	12.6	43 665	25.5	35.8
Athens	22 283	58.6	114 100	22.9	12.9	657	46.2	2.7	31 161	-1.3	2 894	9.3	26 193	35.8	17.8
Auglaize	18 209	77.9	125 000	21.5	11.0	639	25.4	1.8	26 174	-2.3	2 424	9.3	22 951	27.8	36.5
Belmont	29 004	74.4	85 200	20.4	12.1	469	27.1	1.0	34 342	0.9	3 316	9.7	30 084	26.3	27.6
Brown	15 997	79.7	124 100	24.0	13.8	624	28.0	2.0	21 474	-3.2	2 563	11.9	18 752	25.5	35.8
Butler	134 287	70.9	160 600	23.0	13.5	752	31.2	2.1	188 190	-1.8	18 072	9.6	173 206	34.2	22.7
Carroll	11 488	81.7	110 300	24.0	10.4	561	29.0	2.6	13 867	-2.4	1 761	12.7	13 080	24.8	35.5
Champaign	15 161	75.3	124 900	22.8	13.0	605	26.5	1.5	20 037	-2.4	2 238	11.2	18 643	26.3	35.8
Clark	55 145	70.2	109 900	22.5	13.1	632	30.3	1.9	69 991	-2.0	7 312	10.4	62 027	27.5	28.1
Clermont	72 927	77.1	162 000	23.1	13.2	698	27.6	1.3	105 174	-1.8	10 448	9.9	94 434	34.2	24.1
Clinton	16 323	70.2	125 600	23.4	13.7	640	30.9	2.3	19 562	-7.5	3 217	16.4	19 777	26.6	33.8
Columbiana	42 162	74.7	97 400	22.6	12.0	554	31.2	1.4	52 587	-1.7	6 484	12.3	47 216	23.8	35.1
Coshocton	14 582	74.6	94 800	22.0	10.4	514	26.9	1.6	17 291	0.7	2 130	12.3	15 699	25.3	37.3
Crawford	18 105	72.9	93 800	23.6	12.3	613	26.7	1.6	21 142	-6.2	2 620	12.4	19 542	23.4	35.3
Cuyahoga	538 944	62.4	137 200	25.0	15.8	698	31.0	1.5	634 865	-0.8	60 231	9.5	594 551	36.4	18.9
Darke	20 769	77.8	114 600	22.8	12.5	564	26.9	1.5	27 719	-1.4	2 941	10.6	24 868	25.0	37.3
Defiance	15 232	78.6	108 400	22.2	12.5	591	28.4	2.2	19 995	-2.4	2 346	11.7	17 630	26.6	35.9
Delaware	61 203	83.2	252 700	23.0	12.0	781	26.6	0.9	92 273	-0.1	6 592	7.1	85 828	51.3	12.0
Erie	31 855	72.8	138 100	23.0	13.7	641	29.7	1.2	42 747	-0.8	4 426	10.4	36 262	29.6	26.3
Fairfield	53 911	75.8	167 200	23.6	11.6	733	28.7	1.1	75 279	-1.1	6 652	8.8	68 946	35.9	20.8
Fayette	11 597	64.6	112 200	24.2	13.5	658	28.3	1.6	16 374	-3.2	1 885	11.5	13 383	24.2	33.3
Franklin	457 799	57.3	155 300	23.7	13.3	764	29.7	2.5	627 142	-0.4	53 508	8.5	575 696	39.5	16.7
Fulton	16 345	80.9	134 000	23.8	13.4	638	28.2	1.7	21 944	-5.7	2 603	11.9	20 334	26.4	36.3
Gallia	12 246	73.0	98 100	20.7	12.2	523	36.2	1.6	14 141	-0.7	1 493	10.6	12 575	28.7	30.8
Geauga	34 285	87.0	230 900	24.7	14.3	751	27.7	1.9	52 686	4.2	4 014	7.6	44 991	38.2	22.8
Greene	61 962	68.5	160 400	22.1	12.1	766	31.1	0.9	80 142	-0.3	7 998	10.0	76 288	41.2	17.3
Guernsey	16 217	71.9	90 800	22.7	11.8	510	29.3	1.2	19 475	-1.1	2 329	12.0	16 984	25.9	33.9
Hamilton	327 864	61.2	148 200	23.3	13.7	652	30.0	1.8	431 398	-1.7	40 531	9.4	385 734	38.2	18.0
Hancock	30 632	71.1	130 400	22.3	11.8	633	27.1	1.1	40 520	0.8	3 592	8.9	37 473	32.1	30.4
Hardin	11 768	69.6	102 700	22.1	13.5	575	31.5	2.0	15 198	-0.5	1 708	11.2	14 045	24.6	36.9
Harrison	6 377	77.7	81 800	22.6	12.0	518	32.8	2.1	7 257	-1.3	870	12.0	6 701	20.9	34.1
Henry	11 111	79.4	119 800	22.7	14.5	594	23.8	1.0	15 777	-0.8	1 890	12.0	13 413	26.9	36.8
Highland	16 638	73.8	106 200	23.8	12.1	607	29.7	1.9	19 939	-3.6	3 205	16.1	17 822	22.4	38.2
Hocking	11 486	75.5	114 900	23.4	12.1	538	29.4	2.2	14 374	-0.3	1 593	11.1	12 510	25.4	35.1
Holmes	12 120	78.8	154 600	24.0	10.5	533	20.9	4.5	19 537	1.3	1 438	7.4	17 684	22.0	45.1
Huron	22 972	74.6	121 500	22.7	13.0	598	28.2	1.7	28 686	-1.8	3 875	13.5	27 300	22.3	41.0
Jackson	13 105	68.6	88 600	23.7	13.6	549	28.4	2.5	15 265	-1.7	1 742	11.4	12 790	27.0	35.4
Jefferson	29 130	72.9	84 800	21.9	11.7	543	31.4	0.9	32 417	-2.7	4 344	13.4	28 923	25.9	29.0
Knox	22 582	75.1	134 700	23.8	12.0	643	29.8	1.9	30 167	-0.1	2 891	9.6	28 197	30.7	29.6
Lake	94 211	77.0	158 100	24.5	14.1	757	28.6	1.0	133 599	0.6	11 283	8.4	117 690	33.7	23.6
Lawrence	24 631	73.4	92 300	21.9	12.8	556	27.0	1.8	29 154	-1.9	2 486	8.5	24 653	28.1	27.6
Licking	62 569	74.4	152 600	23.4	12.1	682	28.1	1.9	83 122	-1.8	7 894	9.5	78 950	33.2	24.3
Logan	18 398	73.0	124 500	22.3	14.1	641	28.6	2.4	23 970	-4.1	2 702	11.3	21 686	26.7	36.2
Lorain	114 479	74.2	147 400	23.7	13.0	681	30.7	1.4	159 539	-0.6	15 428	9.7	137 811	31.8	26.0
Lucas	179 000	65.0	122 400	23.7	14.3	631	31.7	0.9	220 010	0.1	24 867	11.3	200 711	31.2	24.2
Madison	14 745	71.3	146 800	23.3	15.5	660	28.8	1.8	20 280	-0.7	1 916	9.4	18 877	26.4	29.1
Mahoning	99 024	72.3	98 400	23.4	14.2	586	32.2	1.1	114 828	-1.2	12 996	11.3	105 276	29.8	24.5
Marion	24 863	71.4	98 500	23.0	14.3	641	30.0	1.9	30 968	-3.1	3 335	10.8	28 670	22.7	36.6
Medina	64 202	81.8	184 900	23.4	12.7	784	29.1	1.5	96 650	1.1	7 927	8.2	86 442	37.6	22.3
Meigs	9 675	80.2	80 700	22.5	11.2	498	32.2	1.6	9 542	1.7	1 398	14.7	8 857	24.4	35.9
Mercer	15 606	81.2	125 600	21.6	12.0	606	29.2	1.5	25 006	2.0	1 850	7.4	20 332	27.2	37.4
Miami	41 087	71.3	137 700	22.2	11.7	675	26.4	1.6	54 160	-2.3	5 713	10.5	49 620	31.0	31.2
Monroe	6 174	79.9	86 900	20.8	10.2	459	24.9	2.3	5 721	-0.1	782	13.7	5 697	22.3	40.1
Montgomery	223 660	64.5	119 100	23.3	13.9	684	31.0	1.3	261 944	-2.0	29 016	11.1	243 321	34.6	21.4
Morgan	6 187	79.0	86 000	22.3	11.0	510	27.7	2.1	6 002	-0.9	868	14.5	5 919	23.4	35.2
Morrow	13 037	82.1	131 300	25.3	13.2	671	28.5	1.8	17 862	-2.6	1 848	10.3	16 692	26.2	34.0
Muskingum	34 121	70.1	111 100	23.1	12.8	567	29.9	1.5	38 356	-1.5	5 093	13.3	38 038	26.3	28.8
Noble	4 904	78.2	88 600	19.2	10.0	503	33.3	4.0	5 916	0.2	872	14.7	4 791	27.6	36.8

1. Specified owner-occupied units.　　2. Specified renter-occupied units. A value of 10.0 represents 10 percent or less.　　3. Overcrowded or lacking complete plumbing facilities.　　4. Percent of civilian labor force.　　5. Persons 16 years old and over.

Table B. States and Counties — Nonfarm Employment and Agriculture

STATE County	Private nonfarm establishments, employment and payroll, 2009									Agriculture, 2007			
	Number of establishments	Employment						Annual payroll		Farms			Farm operators whose principal occupation is farming (percent)
		Total	Health care and social assistance	Manufacturing	Retail trade	Finance and insurance	Professional, scientific, and technical services	Total (mil dol)	Average per employee (dollars)	Number	Percent with: Fewer than 50 acres	500 acres or more	
	104	105	106	107	108	109	110	111	112	113	114	115	116
NORTH DAKOTA—Cont'd													
Ward	1 714	23 592	4 297	574	5 013	1 704	608	718	30 443	946	11.8	51.6	60.7
Wells	179	1 350	D	D	216	107	D	31	22 773	618	5.5	50.2	59.5
Williams	909	9 308	1 434	272	1 337	328	240	402	43 194	857	6.2	57.9	56.0
OHIO	256 551	4 460 553	779 678	638 489	560 684	248 027	231 276	171 931	38 545	75 861	42.4	8.9	43.1
Adams	388	4 227	1 177	D	897	160	90	115	27 270	1 379	37.3	5.4	40.6
Allen	2 567	46 048	11 455	7 211	6 496	1 248	896	1 542	33 483	946	40.7	13.1	37.8
Ashland	1 055	16 037	2 370	4 222	2 027	331	D	499	31 119	1 058	42.0	5.6	43.4
Ashtabula	2 033	24 629	5 776	6 225	4 184	578	468	755	30 662	1 127	40.8	5.3	50.3
Athens	1 082	12 862	2 921	240	2 775	417	676	315	24 528	585	32.0	4.6	37.6
Auglaize	1 002	17 205	2 129	6 750	2 434	376	433	562	32 683	1 059	35.9	10.1	40.9
Belmont	1 464	19 314	5 041	1 101	3 916	836	556	538	27 867	681	30.4	5.6	40.1
Brown	535	6 137	1 467	623	1 028	207	120	165	26 931	1 487	41.1	7.8	41.7
Butler	7 019	129 208	16 408	18 271	17 810	8 431	3 388	4 909	37 991	949	56.2	5.3	44.6
Carroll	481	4 815	837	1 248	736	88	95	123	25 451	774	32.6	4.8	44.2
Champaign	640	8 545	910	3 248	1 136	239	135	277	32 361	931	47.8	12.0	41.7
Clark	2 486	41 505	8 608	5 767	6 123	2 563	1 158	1 263	30 431	744	53.5	14.1	42.9
Clermont	3 626	47 231	5 599	4 578	9 736	3 144	2 494	1 592	33 712	898	59.2	4.7	37.4
Clinton	779	17 698	2 137	3 536	1 771	558	D	775	43 768	799	38.7	16.6	51.6
Columbiana	2 155	25 689	5 805	5 460	4 286	651	534	688	26 780	1 056	44.8	4.4	39.7
Coshocton	652	9 433	1 791	2 813	1 281	254	D	304	32 223	1 032	32.6	6.9	40.0
Crawford	883	12 007	2 094	3 756	1 369	652	394	361	30 060	682	35.3	16.7	51.6
Cuyahoga	34 102	648 495	131 299	71 329	61 379	49 480	41 236	28 749	44 332	127	89.0	0.0	52.0
Darke	1 166	14 880	2 261	4 011	2 096	595	284	469	31 523	1 772	42.9	10.8	45.1
Defiance	810	12 766	2 120	2 958	2 330	603	223	447	35 012	1 141	38.5	11.6	35.0
Delaware	3 858	65 879	5 073	5 706	10 527	11 218	3 541	2 828	42 928	726	57.4	11.0	42.3
Erie	1 912	29 155	4 877	5 911	4 496	625	681	973	33 357	403	47.9	11.7	42.7
Fairfield	2 610	32 609	6 218	4 283	6 840	922	1 160	957	29 354	1 112	48.2	7.8	40.6
Fayette	617	9 931	1 379	2 142	2 510	189	84	273	27 469	585	38.3	22.9	53.5
Franklin	27 183	568 889	90 485	30 692	65 087	54 488	37 540	24 492	43 053	429	62.7	7.0	42.2
Fulton	989	15 293	2 233	6 717	1 661	420	237	487	31 842	763	43.9	14.5	41.2
Gallia	554	9 571	D	353	1 519	654	113	335	35 007	993	34.5	2.4	33.4
Geauga	2 749	31 094	3 851	10 612	4 087	755	1 030	1 115	35 866	888	59.6	1.6	47.0
Greene	3 017	48 685	6 060	3 443	9 561	1 269	9 417	1 757	36 085	776	56.7	11.6	43.9
Guernsey	880	12 826	2 608	3 110	1 889	318	D	384	29 934	883	33.0	3.9	44.7
Hamilton	21 750	460 652	84 462	47 609	45 894	31 619	39 963	21 397	46 450	291	67.7	1.7	41.6
Hancock	1 741	37 256	4 800	9 610	4 259	647	901	1 378	36 976	922	36.9	17.1	45.9
Hardin	460	7 064	698	1 755	916	219	96	180	25 446	847	30.7	16.4	47.0
Harrison	284	2 564	D	439	277	67	29	79	30 705	418	21.1	7.7	37.6
Henry	577	7 874	1 286	2 546	1 013	306	95	287	36 404	881	37.1	15.0	41.0
Highland	689	8 603	1 799	1 952	1 767	492	131	240	27 883	1 497	38.9	8.5	41.5
Hocking	495	5 218	970	776	911	174	92	130	24 914	387	40.3	3.1	38.2
Holmes	1 096	15 595	1 501	5 491	1 746	370	280	447	28 643	1 573	39.9	3.2	51.2
Huron	1 213	18 659	2 443	5 706	2 184	437	347	633	33 916	793	43.3	13.6	43.4
Jackson	606	9 507	1 454	3 429	1 427	275	161	256	26 890	462	31.4	6.3	40.7
Jefferson	1 362	20 685	4 182	2 268	3 227	604	360	611	29 555	475	26.1	5.5	45.5
Knox	1 064	18 912	2 672	4 269	2 330	459	265	663	35 038	1 270	45.4	7.6	40.1
Lake	6 237	85 877	10 955	18 994	13 180	2 243	3 513	3 171	36 929	259	75.7	2.3	45.2
Lawrence	837	10 449	2 524	870	2 352	318	243	273	26 089	649	36.1	1.8	39.8
Licking	2 921	47 124	6 933	7 514	6 603	3 786	1 597	1 535	32 576	1 427	50.9	6.2	42.3
Logan	883	16 085	1 897	D	1 784	327	758	576	35 815	956	44.1	10.7	36.9
Lorain	5 723	80 588	13 799	15 295	12 862	2 022	2 426	2 645	32 820	873	58.4	6.5	42.0
Lucas	10 115	189 906	42 728	18 398	23 455	6 267	9 082	6 922	36 451	372	61.3	9.1	44.1
Madison	703	10 328	1 213	2 577	1 813	186	D	325	31 503	718	39.4	22.7	51.8
Mahoning	5 888	84 748	16 882	8 107	12 609	3 214	3 557	2 617	30 874	578	48.3	2.6	45.5
Marion	1 223	21 584	4 321	6 735	2 679	513	296	692	32 056	654	40.2	17.1	43.3
Medina	3 988	50 687	7 204	7 875	8 529	2 549	1 920	1 674	33 036	951	63.7	3.7	44.8
Meigs	316	2 355	505	75	492	140	52	58	24 570	551	25.0	4.0	44.1
Mercer	952	13 307	1 640	3 323	1 976	448	316	398	29 908	1 302	35.6	12.9	51.8
Miami	2 188	32 478	4 331	9 151	4 528	791	791	1 061	32 674	1 048	55.9	11.8	42.9
Monroe	261	3 215	241	D	341	D	D	132	40 957	636	22.5	2.5	46.2
Montgomery	11 855	226 069	51 075	26 760	25 961	8 314	12 294	8 950	39 589	804	64.2	7.5	39.4
Morgan	166	1 867	D	560	D	109	23	48	25 495	524	21.6	6.1	42.0
Morrow	389	3 803	856	D	549	104	155	105	27 608	874	47.9	8.2	38.6
Muskingum	1 829	27 879	6 516	3 747	4 672	771	542	927	33 264	1 162	33.8	5.2	39.7
Noble	206	2 017	448	D	278	66	D	54	26 762	534	20.4	5.8	40.1

Table B. States and Counties — **Agriculture**

STATE County	Land in farms Acreage (1,000) [117]	Percent change, 2002-2007 [118]	Acres Average size of farm [119]	Total irrigated (1,000) [120]	Total cropland (1,000) [121]	Value of land and buildings (dollars) Average per farm [122]	Average per acre [123]	Value of machinery and equipment, average per farm (dollars) [124]	Value of products sold Total (mil dol) [125]	Average per farm (dollars) [126]	Percent from: Crops [127]	Live-stock and poultry products [128]	Percent of farms with sales of: $10,000 or more [129]	$100,000 or more [130]	Government payments Total ($1,000) [131]	Percent of farms [132]
NORTH DAKOTA—Cont'd																
Ward	1 066	-3.9	1 127	0.8	843.8	953 288	846	173 444	167.6	177 164	91.6	8.4	64.6	38.5	8 642	75.6
Wells	757	13.3	1 225	1.0	630.5	1 022 755	835	191 239	144.8	234 236	91.8	8.2	56.5	37.7	7 004	87.4
Williams	1 145	-3.0	1 336	16.5	799.8	881 903	660	157 853	127.3	148 580	91.1	8.9	59.4	31.0	7 339	76.2
OHIO	13 957	-4.3	184	38.0	10 832.8	649 130	3 528	88 352	7 070.2	93 200	58.1	41.9	43.7	15.9	232 184	50.2
Adams	184	-7.1	133	0.1	95.7	380 087	2 849	55 928	29.3	21 216	50.0	50.0	30.3	4.5	2 362	48.8
Allen	187	-0.5	198	0.4	170.4	708 676	3 581	86 747	87.6	92 629	73.7	26.3	54.1	20.6	3 921	79.7
Ashland	151	-6.2	142	0.1	109.3	532 611	3 743	78 117	72.3	68 303	50.2	49.8	48.9	12.0	2 201	52.4
Ashtabula	162	-4.7	143	0.4	106.3	418 008	2 913	79 881	55.2	49 009	51.9	48.1	38.4	10.5	1 284	31.8
Athens	82	-21.9	140	0.0	26.2	364 254	2 593	50 010	8.4	14 407	41.1	58.9	20.2	2.7	204	19.8
Auglaize	213	-2.3	201	D	192.2	767 779	3 812	115 681	138.6	130 885	47.5	52.5	62.0	27.3	5 060	80.3
Belmont	129	-9.2	190	0.0	42.6	399 103	2 105	55 131	14.6	21 370	23.2	76.8	28.2	4.0	140	11.3
Brown	240	8.6	162	0.1	173.2	473 499	2 929	81 338	58.0	39 014	81.1	18.9	36.0	9.9	2 679	52.8
Butler	127	-8.0	134	0.2	96.4	621 828	4 639	81 096	38.8	40 880	67.0	33.0	30.1	8.1	2 415	34.8
Carroll	117	-5.6	151	0.6	62.2	480 676	3 184	68 140	28.7	37 112	43.0	57.0	35.7	8.9	819	31.9
Champaign	205	-1.4	220	2.4	177.1	805 163	3 658	113 332	101.1	108 540	83.5	16.5	46.3	19.8	5 082	59.6
Clark	177	7.3	238	1.5	153.5	911 967	3 826	112 592	137.0	184 200	67.1	32.9	44.9	21.5	3 093	53.4
Clermont	105	-9.5	117	0.1	75.8	483 575	4 148	67 694	24.9	27 702	86.9	13.1	23.2	5.9	1 101	28.5
Clinton	218	-8.8	273	0.1	195.9	985 240	3 603	119 509	85.6	107 126	92.0	8.0	54.7	25.8	4 231	69.3
Columbiana	131	-3.7	124	0.3	87.2	475 649	3 836	75 591	76.4	72 311	28.8	71.2	39.4	12.5	1 384	32.1
Coshocton	171	-5.0	166	0.1	91.9	490 124	2 956	75 986	58.1	56 339	38.2	61.8	35.6	10.8	1 623	38.6
Crawford	220	-6.0	322	0.0	200.8	1 030 121	3 200	141 983	115.6	169 528	72.2	27.8	63.3	31.2	4 134	76.2
Cuyahoga	3	-25.0	23	0.1	1.2	511 801	22 336	48 301	14.5	114 388	94.6	5.4	29.1	8.7	D	1.6
Darke	350	3.2	198	0.4	319.9	829 604	4 195	106 475	479.8	270 741	26.7	73.3	61.9	27.4	7 497	72.6
Defiance	233	11.5	204	D	202.9	609 682	2 983	84 014	87.0	76 271	74.0	26.0	47.4	16.7	5 828	88.1
Delaware	138	-15.3	190	0.3	122.4	851 945	4 477	101 863	85.3	117 556	81.8	18.2	42.8	16.7	2 626	47.4
Erie	84	-11.6	209	0.2	75.3	833 263	3 994	133 276	40.4	100 165	87.1	12.9	55.8	21.1	1 615	55.3
Fairfield	178	-9.2	160	0.3	140.7	676 425	4 231	84 850	71.0	63 813	75.9	24.1	37.5	13.8	4 278	55.1
Fayette	218	7.4	373	0.0	197.6	1 252 824	3 358	130 387	84.0	143 559	94.5	5.5	53.7	30.6	4 295	70.1
Franklin	60	-26.8	139	0.8	50.6	659 530	4 747	94 235	43.7	101 830	93.6	6.4	39.4	15.2	997	37.5
Fulton	184	-6.6	241	0.4	172.0	864 104	3 585	112 682	134.1	175 811	58.0	42.0	58.6	29.2	4 171	72.0
Gallia	117	-0.8	118	0.1	38.1	323 579	2 748	50 056	12.9	13 037	26.3	73.7	19.2	1.7	317	17.4
Geauga	57	-13.6	64	0.4	29.5	383 374	6 019	51 578	26.9	30 246	48.6	51.4	32.7	5.1	428	9.5
Greene	163	-3.6	209	1.7	142.3	821 221	3 921	100 506	77.7	100 161	89.4	10.6	44.6	16.6	2 867	55.2
Guernsey	138	0.7	156	0.0	49.0	406 332	2 608	55 228	17.8	20 199	25.8	74.2	25.7	4.5	277	16.1
Hamilton	21	-30.0	73	0.7	12.3	484 766	6 626	62 046	19.5	66 938	78.0	22.0	34.0	10.7	169	11.3
Hancock	248	-5.3	269	0.1	228.6	874 382	3 251	111 491	101.1	109 639	83.0	17.0	63.6	25.5	4 674	80.2
Hardin	257	4.5	303	D	230.5	982 809	3 241	132 089	181.8	214 668	47.2	52.8	57.9	26.2	5 078	79.0
Harrison	93	-32.6	223	D	38.7	507 665	2 273	62 901	11.8	28 132	39.9	60.1	29.9	6.7	312	24.2
Henry	232	-1.7	264	0.6	218.8	890 427	3 378	110 156	107.4	121 878	87.0	13.0	66.7	26.3	4 400	86.2
Highland	270	-1.1	180	0.2	203.2	563 365	3 126	78 274	67.4	45 006	74.8	25.2	35.8	10.6	5 694	70.2
Hocking	42	-16.0	109	0.0	17.0	366 000	3 373	46 715	4.3	11 213	71.0	29.0	18.9	1.8	300	20.4
Holmes	188	-9.2	119	0.2	103.7	551 698	4 624	57 119	133.8	85 078	16.8	83.2	51.4	20.2	1 328	20.9
Huron	219	-3.9	277	3.0	189.5	956 062	3 456	123 835	113.0	142 501	83.5	16.5	47.8	23.2	4 820	67.1
Jackson	72	-2.7	156	0.0	33.8	394 199	2 534	56 542	8.5	18 317	39.4	60.6	28.6	3.5	449	34.2
Jefferson	69	3.0	146	0.1	31.7	343 595	2 349	59 540	9.3	19 599	37.9	62.1	30.9	5.1	372	26.5
Knox	198	-5.3	156	0.1	142.9	555 208	3 557	75 550	79.6	62 642	59.1	40.9	39.9	13.1	2 563	44.2
Lake	16	-20.0	62	2.2	10.1	476 160	7 677	91 159	88.9	343 113	99.4	0.6	44.8	18.5	D	5.0
Lawrence	66	1.5	101	0.0	18.1	256 391	2 531	46 059	4.6	7 016	38.0	62.0	12.5	0.8	182	15.9
Licking	226	-4.6	158	0.9	169.1	638 358	4 034	81 046	155.7	109 107	42.1	57.9	33.9	10.6	3 738	31.5
Logan	201	-10.7	211	0.0	168.8	661 167	3 140	97 977	88.3	92 387	75.2	24.8	43.2	17.4	4 783	64.7
Lorain	124	-23.5	142	1.3	103.9	639 691	4 500	83 516	131.2	150 292	84.2	15.8	40.9	12.9	1 813	40.0
Lucas	63	-19.2	169	1.2	59.1	735 848	4 351	107 975	47.9	128 731	96.6	3.4	51.3	21.0	1 017	47.8
Madison	248	0.8	345	0.2	225.4	1 337 872	3 875	144 089	122.0	169 972	78.6	21.4	55.8	34.8	5 136	67.0
Mahoning	64	-16.9	111	0.6	46.4	456 868	4 121	76 812	45.1	78 088	35.1	64.9	42.9	11.2	677	36.0
Marion	207	0.5	316	0.0	189.6	975 300	3 084	129 995	100.2	153 257	71.4	28.6	54.3	24.3	4 804	78.9
Medina	95	-22.8	100	0.4	73.7	553 810	5 515	68 862	48.7	51 251	70.4	29.6	37.5	8.6	1 025	20.6
Meigs	78	-13.3	141	0.7	28.3	360 246	2 553	55 840	17.6	31 968	62.1	37.9	29.4	5.3	1 214	24.1
Mercer	293	8.9	225	0.1	265.8	1 098 779	4 882	150 044	535.2	411 051	17.6	82.4	75.7	43.7	6 660	79.5
Miami	197	7.1	188	2.1	179.0	732 444	3 898	93 758	89.8	85 670	83.2	16.8	48.2	19.1	3 545	59.9
Monroe	99	-7.5	156	0.0	29.0	323 906	2 074	47 191	8.7	13 701	18.9	81.1	22.5	2.8	88	12.1
Montgomery	111	8.8	138	0.2	97.5	615 634	4 459	79 936	47.9	59 588	83.6	16.4	36.8	11.6	1 791	48.3
Morgan	102	2.0	195	0.0	31.3	426 845	2 187	58 123	12.5	23 805	24.5	75.5	29.0	4.8	561	28.6
Morrow	165	-7.8	189	0.2	134.9	649 802	3 442	80 480	94.3	107 871	51.3	48.7	41.6	12.5	2 763	49.4
Muskingum	166	-14.0	143	0.0	76.1	401 190	2 801	65 224	35.6	30 649	41.8	58.2	29.8	5.2	1 330	28.1
Noble	89	-16.8	167	0.0	30.3	383 331	2 292	43 986	5.2	9 723	22.0	78.0	22.7	1.1	127	8.6

Table B. States and Counties — Water Use, Wholesale Trade, Retail Trade, and Real Estate

STATE County	Water use, 2005 Total water withdrawn (mil gal/day)	Gallons withdrawn per person	Wholesale trade,[1] 2007 Number of establishments	Number of employees	Sales (mil dol)	Annual payroll (mil dol)	Retail trade,[2] 2007 Number of establishments	Number of employees	Sales (mil dol)	Annual payroll (mil dol)	Real estate and rental and leasing,[2] 2007 Number of establishments	Number of employees	Receipts (mil dol)	Annual payroll (mil dol)
	133	134	135	136	137	138	139	140	141	142	143	144	145	146
NORTH DAKOTA—Cont'd														
Ward	8.3	148	86	1 139	1 379.7	48.4	294	4 738	1 119.0	96.4	70	D	D	D
Wells	1.1	238	18	166	184.6	5.6	35	212	64.0	3.9	3	D	D	D
Williams	29.0	1 505	58	618	442.6	28.2	119	1 400	403.3	30.7	38	223	93.1	12.3
OHIO	11 469.1	1 000	12 591	192 403	135 575.3	8 914.0	40 075	591 237	138 816.0	12 729.5	10 973	67 048	15 011.3	2 339.2
Adams	599.9	21 084	9	62	21.1	1.5	86	941	210.3	18.1	14	52	3.8	1.2
Allen	27.5	259	135	D	D	D	464	6 950	1 677.5	133.6	105	481	67.1	12.2
Ashland	6.2	115	38	494	206.2	20.8	174	2 094	418.6	41.9	33	136	11.8	3.1
Ashtabula	230.1	2 229	59	D	D	D	384	4 298	1 077.6	84.7	82	260	24.1	5.3
Athens	8.5	137	31	D	D	D	210	2 784	563.2	53.8	73	265	35.3	5.5
Auglaize	14.6	308	43	D	D	D	188	2 451	493.8	45.5	43	141	16.0	3.0
Belmont	262.5	3 792	43	D	D	D	331	4 544	888.8	83.4	48	272	29.8	5.5
Brown	5.4	122	20	107	55.0	3.0	104	1 103	262.3	20.4	18	65	5.0	1.1
Butler	190.4	543	453	9 364	7 337.0	461.8	981	16 941	4 876.2	400.2	309	1 717	345.3	53.6
Carroll	3.2	110	18	208	104.2	6.7	79	767	163.6	15.3	11	42	5.0	0.8
Champaign	8.9	225	33	242	146.4	8.3	119	1 204	287.6	23.3	24	71	6.8	1.3
Clark	27.9	196	95	D	D	D	460	6 625	1 398.7	131.7	101	485	64.0	10.9
Clermont	718.8	3 771	151	1 870	1 036.0	96.4	574	10 087	2 439.6	211.8	161	776	99.1	21.4
Clinton	3.5	82	31	D	D	D	142	1 945	450.9	39.6	29	125	12.4	3.2
Columbiana	11.2	101	93	D	D	D	386	4 544	1 064.2	93.7	61	274	29.4	6.6
Coshocton	208.6	5 646	19	D	D	D	121	1 291	259.2	24.1	20	48	3.7	0.7
Crawford	3.6	79	34	D	D	D	150	1 370	338.7	28.8	26	83	8.2	1.5
Cuyahoga	568.6	426	2 116	34 314	18 894.4	1 783.4	4 767	65 431	14 478.9	1 428.9	1 585	15 316	5 925.5	709.0
Darke	7.9	150	58	D	D	D	190	2 166	447.2	44.7	38	200	16.9	6.3
Defiance	5.9	152	41	D	D	D	176	2 624	559.5	50.4	28	115	15.0	2.1
Delaware	25.1	167	145	1 979	998.5	95.4	575	10 155	2 331.4	213.5	168	677	114.1	20.4
Erie	35.2	448	64	D	D	D	351	5 086	1 034.9	101.8	79	360	40.9	8.8
Fairfield	14.3	103	82	D	D	D	441	6 485	1 360.6	129.2	135	493	62.7	11.8
Fayette	3.2	112	26	D	D	D	199	2 495	610.7	45.4	24	102	21.6	2.0
Franklin	205.1	188	1 288	26 610	22 138.4	1 251.1	3 785	71 503	19 403.6	1 758.9	1 558	10 816	2 221.5	414.0
Fulton	4.7	109	44	416	238.8	15.8	168	1 614	405.9	36.5	26	94	8.0	1.6
Gallia	1 188.8	37 906	19	D	D	D	139	1 509	356.0	30.2	21	78	7.6	1.7
Geauga	7.6	80	138	955	424.6	52.7	320	4 005	916.7	88.9	84	347	43.3	9.3
Greene	17.7	116	73	1 126	1 276.6	46.9	540	9 938	2 029.3	193.0	136	540	93.5	13.9
Guernsey	6.7	162	29	D	D	D	169	1 911	468.3	37.2	41	235	22.1	4.5
Hamilton	377.3	468	1 199	19 282	13 030.3	993.2	3 148	49 028	10 629.5	1 082.2	1 066	7 462	1 577.4	296.1
Hancock	46.9	637	71	D	D	D	316	4 752	1 092.8	97.8	68	504	55.9	13.2
Hardin	4.3	135	17	105	112.7	3.7	91	962	193.0	18.7	15	36	4.8	1.0
Harrison	1.6	103	11	117	42.8	5.3	43	323	52.9	4.9	4	102	3.0	1.2
Henry	11.9	404	33	350	317.9	11.9	92	989	268.0	20.0	19	70	14.4	1.7
Highland	3.4	79	15	166	79.8	3.6	143	1 767	370.5	35.3	27	83	8.7	1.7
Hocking	3.0	102	7	D	D	D	85	1 027	218.9	20.2	29	91	7.4	1.7
Holmes	6.2	148	51	658	240.9	18.8	155	1 663	360.3	35.1	16	43	5.3	0.8
Huron	8.0	132	54	D	D	D	203	2 294	550.3	46.2	43	143	18.6	4.1
Jackson	2.3	69	19	131	50.1	4.5	129	1 483	336.1	29.1	26	101	10.0	2.0
Jefferson	2 146.9	30 409	55	D	D	D	271	3 523	721.5	68.3	47	237	27.3	5.0
Knox	9.4	161	38	362	130.8	11.2	192	2 397	541.9	47.6	49	164	16.6	3.6
Lake	884.0	3 803	336	3 443	1 867.8	164.5	866	14 140	3 460.9	314.5	227	1 178	182.9	30.4
Lawrence	8.0	126	20	D	D	D	179	2 312	508.8	44.5	26	87	9.4	1.6
Licking	22.2	143	114	1 769	1 141.4	70.9	466	7 144	1 774.7	145.2	108	536	62.9	13.7
Logan	6.3	135	31	1 117	399.6	41.2	161	1 914	420.7	40.3	38	176	33.1	4.3
Lorain	622.8	2 102	262	2 745	1 822.7	120.2	895	14 057	3 225.5	286.4	222	860	120.8	21.2
Lucas	880.7	1 965	514	7 283	4 943.6	319.4	1 649	25 392	5 830.0	548.2	452	2 854	961.5	103.5
Madison	4.3	105	29	D	D	D	122	1 839	958.6	41.6	33	84	11.5	2.0
Mahoning	7.2	28	278	4 344	1 858.8	172.5	1 026	13 896	3 025.7	281.4	199	1 337	156.7	33.1
Marion	10.2	155	42	598	338.1	21.5	203	2 997	674.8	62.5	59	224	28.5	6.2
Medina	15.0	90	233	2 592	1 303.4	116.6	548	8 390	2 113.4	185.9	140	501	71.5	12.2
Meigs	5.2	224	7	41	11.4	1.0	75	561	124.2	9.5	5	D	D	D
Mercer	10.6	256	56	1 112	655.7	39.5	174	1 876	394.4	40.1	34	187	14.1	2.7
Miami	20.9	206	90	1 551	4 168.9	79.6	354	4 699	1 080.5	101.0	92	323	48.5	8.1
Monroe	7.9	537	9	47	22.8	2.1	51	370	62.6	5.8	1	D	D	D
Montgomery	261.6	478	592	8 419	3 766.7	387.5	1 778	27 154	6 844.6	588.6	576	3 882	564.5	128.9
Morgan	2.0	130	5	D	D	D	28	225	52.3	3.8	4	D	D	D
Morrow	3.2	92	14	D	D	D	58	644	167.9	10.1	13	29	2.6	0.4
Muskingum	18.9	220	55	884	2 222.1	37.7	385	5 125	1 125.7	96.6	71	309	46.8	8.3
Noble	1.4	96	8	36	6.2	0.8	37	324	103.3	6.3	1	D	D	D

1. Merchant wholesalers, except manufacturers' sales branches and offices. 2. Employer establishments.

Table B. States and Counties — Professional Services, Manufacturing, and Accommodation and Food Services

STATE County	Professional, scientific, and technical services,[1] 2007				Manufacturing, 2007				Accommodation and food services, 2007			
	Number of establishments	Number of employees	Receipts (mil dol)	Annual payroll (mil dol)	Number of establishments	Number of employees	Receipts (mil dol)	Annual payroll (mil dol)	Number of establishments	Number of employees	Sales (mil dol)	Annual payroll (mil dol)
	147	148	149	150	151	152	153	154	155	156	157	158
NORTH DAKOTA—Cont'd												
Ward	104	D	D	D	54	623	D	19.9	150	2 891	106.7	30.0
Wells	10	19	0.9	0.3	NA	NA	NA	NA	17	107	3.0	0.8
Williams	61	217	22.9	8.3	NA	NA	NA	NA	66	913	36.6	10.7
OHIO	24 963	224 265	32 285.4	12 304.2	16 237	760 267	295 890.9	35 485.5	23 959	436 598	17 779.9	5 078.5
Adams	27	87	5.8	1.6	35	694	133.9	28.1	43	523	19.0	5.1
Allen	170	D	D	D	136	8 661	10 009.0	475.9	219	4 469	173.2	47.4
Ashland	67	984	128.0	36.1	93	4 140	1 017.4	164.5	101	1 572	55.6	17.7
Ashtabula	114	D	D	D	161	7 218	2 201.4	296.4	219	2 745	110.6	29.7
Athens	70	D	D	D	NA	NA	NA	NA	145	2 712	81.0	23.2
Auglaize	65	400	46.1	14.1	88	7 835	2 550.6	349.6	87	1 193	42.9	11.2
Belmont	103	568	50.3	18.4	53	1 279	500.9	53.0	128	2 517	91.2	26.8
Brown	29	D	D	D	29	736	74.2	27.6	69	794	29.3	7.5
Butler	605	D	D	D	440	21 082	11 362.0	1 035.6	630	13 512	531.1	154.3
Carroll	27	D	D	D	49	1 700	344.6	63.8	43	566	18.9	5.9
Champaign	40	D	D	D	46	3 238	1 050.2	151.4	60	717	25.9	6.5
Clark	163	D	D	D	182	7 164	2 494.3	299.2	241	4 574	173.1	49.6
Clermont	376	D	D	D	183	5 777	1 250.6	258.1	285	6 271	239.5	71.3
Clinton	46	D	D	D	47	3 877	1 025.4	165.6	81	1 390	62.2	15.0
Columbiana	126	D	D	D	197	6 535	1 572.1	239.5	189	2 561	87.5	25.6
Coshocton	35	320	16.5	8.4	52	2 947	1 222.9	129.2	49	633	22.7	6.4
Crawford	44	409	26.8	11.1	93	4 989	1 470.9	182.8	90	1 106	39.1	10.5
Cuyahoga	4 341	41 689	6 487.8	2 543.7	2 172	82 169	23 131.7	4 156.8	3 089	54 151	2 499.2	691.0
Darke	69	313	25.3	8.8	82	4 404	1 517.1	185.6	97	1 088	43.7	11.5
Defiance	50	D	D	D	53	3 940	1 048.4	281.8	81	1 194	41.3	11.2
Delaware	496	D	D	D	133	6 065	2 314.5	282.2	361	8 335	344.2	103.5
Erie	132	D	D	D	110	7 149	2 329.9	344.9	279	5 661	254.7	69.0
Fairfield	187	D	D	D	131	4 804	1 061.6	210.4	228	4 636	169.5	50.3
Fayette	29	D	D	D	33	2 795	975.5	112.5	58	942	38.9	10.7
Franklin	3 545	D	D	D	925	35 625	14 289.4	1 605.8	2 664	56 718	2 596.3	744.2
Fulton	49	313	19.1	6.6	112	9 086	3 330.4	358.4	75	987	34.7	9.3
Gallia	26	90	6.3	1.7	NA	NA	NA	NA	50	883	33.3	9.2
Geauga	332	D	D	D	209	11 444	2 964.4	460.0	190	2 615	94.1	26.5
Greene	428	D	D	D	106	3 881	924.1	176.9	319	7 229	283.3	86.4
Guernsey	45	271	32.0	10.5	61	3 169	1 403.2	119.8	94	1 659	67.0	18.4
Hamilton	2 601	D	D	D	1 155	58 305	25 048.9	3 058.2	1 933	39 897	1 788.4	522.8
Hancock	128	947	81.3	34.7	105	10 975	3 757.2	498.2	172	3 619	130.6	38.4
Hardin	22	95	6.3	2.1	35	2 052	560.5	79.9	51	917	29.5	10.4
Harrison	16	37	2.3	0.6	18	740	165.2	24.3	29	211	6.6	1.5
Henry	20	107	10.5	2.4	46	3 770	2 284.3	162.1	51	609	17.8	5.1
Highland	44	143	10.1	3.2	43	2 879	643.0	102.7	54	958	36.1	9.3
Hocking	24	72	4.3	1.7	23	964	261.5	36.3	66	1 006	40.2	11.2
Holmes	39	291	31.3	10.7	265	6 123	1 366.4	190.0	58	1 057	36.4	12.0
Huron	81	377	27.1	11.0	104	7 206	2 375.8	284.2	108	1 450	51.7	14.4
Jackson	34	185	10.9	3.2	38	4 015	2 083.9	115.7	52	1 087	35.5	10.6
Jefferson	90	D	D	D	37	2 938	D	167.9	157	1 884	66.3	18.1
Knox	66	275	29.5	7.1	75	4 551	1 914.0	244.6	91	1 472	53.0	14.2
Lake	612	D	D	D	688	19 820	5 220.9	887.6	561	9 339	390.8	105.4
Lawrence	44	D	D	D	39	835	D	32.1	68	1 066	41.2	11.1
Licking	252	D	D	D	162	8 610	3 351.8	375.6	284	5 123	194.2	54.7
Logan	50	D	D	D	50	6 042	D	351.6	104	1 333	55.7	14.3
Lorain	469	D	D	D	408	18 330	8 305.3	976.6	565	8 530	326.6	88.0
Lucas	911	D	D	D	560	21 793	20 075.5	1 275.0	1 026	19 773	728.6	211.7
Madison	44	D	D	D	46	2 949	994.6	131.8	66	1 038	38.4	12.0
Mahoning	465	D	D	D	385	9 874	2 475.1	376.4	544	9 489	340.7	96.4
Marion	72	D	D	D	77	7 737	3 409.2	305.4	119	2 051	79.1	22.6
Medina	409	2 246	229.9	91.4	297	9 403	2 558.8	395.6	309	5 106	186.1	53.0
Meigs	20	66	4.6	1.3	NA	NA	NA	NA	31	500	15.3	4.6
Mercer	47	319	31.6	12.5	76	3 926	927.9	149.4	79	1 223	39.4	11.3
Miami	162	D	D	D	241	9 924	2 807.3	420.5	181	3 438	127.6	37.5
Monroe	15	66	5.9	2.4	13	D	D	D	21	123	4.3	1.0
Montgomery	1 213	14 942	2 031.9	829.3	811	34 993	14 049.2	1 607.2	1 112	22 069	882.7	259.0
Morgan	11	29	2.1	0.5	NA	NA	NA	NA	19	264	5.8	2.0
Morrow	32	D	D	D	32	1 150	D	D	36	381	14.0	3.5
Muskingum	103	D	D	D	86	5 131	1 134.2	188.0	194	3 276	124.0	35.9
Noble	11	32	3.5	1.3	NA	NA	NA	NA	23	187	7.3	2.0

1. Establishment subject to federal tax.

Table B. States and Counties — Health Care and Social Assistance, Other Services, and Federal Funds

STATE County	Health care and social assistance, 2007				Other services, 2007				Federal funds and grants, 2009–2010 Expenditures (mil dol)			
										Direct payments for individuals[1]		
	Number of establishments	Number of employees	Receipts (mil dol)	Annual payroll (mil dol)	Number of establishments	Number of employees	Receipts (mil dol)	Annual payroll (mil dol)	Total	Social Security and government retirement	Medicare	Food Stamps and Supplemental Security Income
	159	160	161	162	163	164	165	166	167	168	169	170
NORTH DAKOTA—Cont'd												
Ward	145	4 360	345.9	154.2	142	804	60.2	14.9	799.5	196.7	73.9	11.3
Wells	15	431	17.8	8.2	18	63	3.8	0.8	67.8	21.6	12.1	1.0
Williams	59	1 432	91.6	40.6	67	300	32.1	7.7	171.2	73.2	33.0	5.1
OHIO	27 965	741 194	65 882.5	27 621.4	20 349	135 272	13 047.5	3 463.9	106 448.7	33 289.5	20 459.6	4 587.1
Adams	50	1 037	62.0	25.1	34	90	7.4	1.9	330.0	91.6	64.9	22.5
Allen	330	11 408	999.0	417.5	213	1 448	93.3	27.9	1 079.7	526.6	182.7	48.5
Ashland	120	2 082	157.8	61.9	88	601	40.6	12.3	290.0	150.1	63.9	10.0
Ashtabula	224	5 839	408.3	160.8	165	656	44.9	10.3	776.9	332.9	223.0	46.3
Athens	132	2 593	205.9	84.2	92	453	26.1	7.0	533.4	132.0	92.9	34.2
Auglaize	94	1 995	147.5	53.5	91	583	38.4	11.5	299.8	124.6	82.6	6.4
Belmont	180	4 237	294.3	125.5	134	648	35.1	9.4	592.2	239.3	170.2	35.9
Brown	50	1 563	104.1	41.4	52	182	12.5	3.4	286.9	122.4	63.1	14.0
Butler	720	15 799	1 313.6	535.8	541	3 726	354.1	101.3	2 069.9	918.3	433.9	90.3
Carroll	42	753	37.9	17.0	38	206	12.0	2.9	156.1	72.3	33.8	8.4
Champaign	48	2 077	87.8	43.6	62	335	15.3	4.1	263.0	118.4	53.2	8.1
Clark	319	8 186	619.8	258.2	237	1 402	188.1	38.4	1 247.9	511.9	288.8	64.5
Clermont	299	5 104	392.2	165.2	289	1 734	158.3	44.1	1 010.0	419.7	163.6	36.7
Clinton	95	2 151	205.3	80.6	72	328	34.1	7.9	298.5	133.2	66.5	11.8
Columbiana	288	5 808	384.5	150.6	186	1 007	73.0	18.6	868.6	375.9	227.1	47.8
Coshocton	81	1 979	132.3	52.6	61	253	22.6	4.7	247.3	109.7	58.2	10.2
Crawford	106	2 166	148.3	58.0	80	362	27.6	6.6	337.4	158.2	93.9	16.0
Cuyahoga	3 734	125 281	12 200.2	5 313.6	2 652	19 545	2 112.5	553.2	14 453.1	3 845.3	3 578.0	866.4
Darke	75	2 098	138.9	57.8	102	445	27.1	6.9	340.4	158.3	81.5	9.3
Defiance	84	2 208	196.0	68.9	71	446	31.5	7.6	289.8	129.4	56.2	13.2
Delaware	313	4 655	420.9	171.9	239	1 914	339.1	69.1	1 056.5	282.8	75.5	12.8
Erie	195	4 986	434.3	162.8	155	815	49.6	14.5	666.7	297.9	153.9	23.6
Fairfield	303	5 804	488.6	207.0	181	1 121	102.5	31.8	715.1	381.1	153.4	29.2
Fayette	62	1 289	87.9	36.6	44	213	13.1	3.6	200.9	80.6	46.3	9.7
Franklin	3 020	84 476	8 383.5	3 503.0	2 217	18 766	2 208.7	582.1	14 415.1	2 463.6	1 468.3	462.6
Fulton	96	2 174	147.7	58.5	80	274	25.2	6.2	259.1	128.8	67.8	3.0
Gallia	64	2 853	219.5	89.5	41	180	12.5	3.6	313.7	104.5	67.8	24.5
Geauga	239	3 737	301.3	141.0	204	1 142	105.0	33.0	375.7	228.4	85.3	7.2
Greene	316	5 995	488.2	198.0	221	1 261	95.4	29.9	3 170.8	449.5	138.2	30.7
Guernsey	128	2 427	186.0	69.5	71	304	23.6	4.9	333.6	130.9	82.7	21.6
Hamilton	2 455	80 329	7 905.8	3 420.9	1 585	11 594	1 292.8	325.3	9 881.0	2 328.3	1 759.5	389.4
Hancock	190	4 688	443.2	165.7	146	824	77.7	21.1	394.5	183.3	82.2	13.5
Hardin	38	581	47.0	15.9	40	151	10.5	2.3	175.2	56.0	52.2	8.1
Harrison	32	603	31.4	13.7	18	59	3.1	1.0	142.8	69.1	35.2	8.9
Henry	54	1 190	74.9	32.2	51	312	18.6	5.2	170.3	83.3	44.5	4.5
Highland	87	1 656	120.8	47.8	48	210	13.9	3.0	319.6	119.9	72.0	15.6
Hocking	44	956	62.4	24.2	42	162	14.1	3.2	188.9	83.3	46.3	11.4
Holmes	52	1 317	99.8	34.0	42	198	17.5	4.5	116.4	54.8	21.4	3.1
Huron	103	2 460	202.1	85.0	103	523	39.8	10.3	412.8	208.6	96.1	17.8
Jackson	56	1 099	115.7	43.2	52	179	15.7	3.4	302.1	98.8	59.4	23.1
Jefferson	161	4 454	333.9	139.7	119	627	37.2	10.5	762.6	310.4	217.5	46.0
Knox	124	2 475	191.6	75.8	88	591	37.7	10.9	369.7	172.5	89.5	12.7
Lake	558	10 822	900.8	358.1	527	3 432	252.8	76.9	1 425.4	728.3	380.6	36.0
Lawrence	112	2 226	101.3	48.4	68	271	21.7	6.1	622.7	234.3	133.6	53.1
Licking	243	6 550	476.2	212.4	222	1 766	267.4	63.7	1 072.6	463.5	186.8	42.9
Logan	89	1 988	150.1	60.1	81	516	66.0	10.9	328.4	143.8	81.1	11.9
Lorain	613	13 174	1 097.1	440.0	510	3 049	252.6	68.6	1 999.1	877.7	477.2	103.1
Lucas	1 272	40 299	3 669.6	1 580.7	796	5 652	509.1	131.0	3 758.6	1 193.4	1 009.9	289.3
Madison	67	1 103	78.5	30.0	42	188	9.9	2.8	253.9	115.6	60.8	8.8
Mahoning	792	15 765	1 334.0	516.8	418	2 914	216.6	61.1	2 397.2	863.2	662.5	153.6
Marion	158	4 318	356.2	157.7	115	652	43.2	11.7	490.3	209.8	118.9	28.0
Medina	376	6 790	475.2	207.0	302	1 636	114.7	34.9	796.4	461.0	176.0	16.9
Meigs	41	532	28.4	11.6	15	52	4.5	1.0	200.7	70.1	44.5	19.1
Mercer	79	1 611	102.7	42.0	95	430	37.7	9.3	161.3	41.5	60.4	3.3
Miami	195	D	D	D	177	953	76.1	19.4	690.9	337.4	145.7	21.3
Monroe	18	203	11.5	4.4	24	83	5.5	1.3	132.6	50.8	31.7	7.1
Montgomery	1 505	47 348	4 928.7	1 955.0	954	6 992	738.6	202.7	5 460.1	2 013.2	1 096.3	218.4
Morgan	15	250	14.2	5.5	17	44	2.9	0.8	125.0	42.6	24.7	7.4
Morrow	45	902	60.2	20.7	24	79	7.7	1.9	149.2	75.6	27.3	9.0
Muskingum	220	6 095	498.6	219.4	171	1 233	81.4	23.2	698.8	288.7	147.5	47.6
Noble	19	433	20.2	8.2	15	37	2.5	0.4	75.1	28.0	17.0	4.6

1. State totals may include programs not allocated by county.

Table B. States and Counties — Federal Funds, Residential Construction, and Local Government Finances

	Federal funds and grants, 2009–2010 (cont.)							Value of residential construction authorized by building permits, 2010		Local government finances, 2007				
	Expenditures (mil dol) (cont.)									General revenue				
	Procurement contract awards			Grants[1]								Taxes		
STATE County													Per capita[2] (dollars)	
	Salaries and wages	Defense	Other	Medicaid and other health-related	Nutrition and family welfare	Education	Other	New construction ($1,000)	Number of housing units	Total (mil dol)	Inter-govern-mental (mil dol)	Total (mil dol)	Total	Property
	171	172	173	174	175	176	177	178	179	180	181	182	183	184
NORTH DAKOTA—Cont'd														
Ward	281.4	96.1	20.6	38.5	13.3	15.7	9.6	68 723	692	151.1	65.5	61.0	1 091	851
Wells	2.3	0.0	0.5	6.3	1.2	0.1	1.6	400	2	15.1	5.1	6.4	1 493	1 444
Williams	8.7	0.7	1.6	13.6	4.5	0.9	3.0	57 662	476	65.5	26.6	24.3	1 243	1 029
OHIO	6 974.9	6 064.3	2 765.1	13 659.6	3 021.0	2 193.6	5 524.8	2 297 494	13 710	X	X	X	X	X
Adams	6.1	0.1	1.5	126.5	8.6	2.9	1.5	0	0	99.3	61.1	25.6	910	745
Allen	41.1	87.4	6.3	108.5	24.3	8.3	9.2	13 505	116	397.7	197.7	129.4	1 230	858
Ashland	12.0	6.5	1.9	23.8	8.2	5.1	0.7	5 061	40	149.2	62.2	63.2	1 150	812
Ashtabula	20.1	20.9	5.9	83.9	22.2	7.9	5.1	11 669	81	387.2	210.0	124.0	1 226	954
Athens	22.4	9.0	17.1	111.2	18.2	6.4	28.0	12 570	195	206.8	101.2	68.0	1 075	776
Auglaize	15.8	0.5	2.7	19.9	6.5	2.4	30.7	11 359	69	170.1	69.8	67.8	1 461	868
Belmont	19.5	0.0	4.4	83.5	14.9	5.9	4.9	1 345	13	232.5	127.2	72.2	1 064	626
Brown	7.3	0.0	1.7	50.5	10.7	3.0	4.1	6 750	41	176.2	83.9	32.5	738	550
Butler	83.4	110.0	26.1	255.9	51.8	17.2	40.1	88 135	462	1 364.4	530.9	559.2	1 562	1 130
Carroll	4.2	0.0	1.0	27.5	5.0	1.8	0.6	440	3	60.7	32.7	18.7	655	544
Champaign	6.7	24.1	1.7	34.2	5.7	2.8	0.8	6 337	29	135.7	66.0	44.6	1 129	713
Clark	72.3	22.3	5.4	188.8	27.6	11.8	28.5	9 893	57	580.8	303.3	164.6	1 172	789
Clermont	35.3	180.7	7.8	113.3	25.9	8.8	7.9	60 334	524	602.1	230.6	262.5	1 357	1 158
Clinton	15.5	0.1	2.6	43.0	7.7	5.5	3.2	4 319	33	271.4	76.3	54.6	1 268	822
Columbiana	44.1	8.6	10.8	107.0	25.0	7.2	5.0	2 379	19	301.6	170.5	86.6	797	553
Coshocton	15.1	0.0	2.8	33.2	10.5	2.5	1.7	170	2	117.7	62.2	36.8	1 012	769
Crawford	5.9	2.4	1.5	39.3	8.8	3.4	0.5	2 093	12	170.3	88.3	50.3	1 138	762
Cuyahoga	1 214.1	181.2	811.3	2 549.6	316.0	123.3	613.5	112 848	531	8 286.7	3 091.3	3 445.2	2 658	1 618
Darke	18.7	2.4	4.1	35.6	18.5	3.1	0.2	6 760	30	150.3	71.7	54.1	1 036	610
Defiance	8.8	0.0	1.8	25.4	8.3	2.7	34.0	7 535	55	162.6	79.2	47.6	1 235	775
Delaware	27.0	2.0	4.6	29.1	11.7	424.0	81.3	149 743	577	520.2	107.9	293.3	1 823	1 339
Erie	33.6	25.3	35.8	47.4	16.2	5.5	21.0	11 186	47	382.6	124.9	143.7	1 859	1 381
Fairfield	24.9	0.3	6.0	65.3	18.8	6.7	9.0	39 033	196	457.5	187.2	191.3	1 354	957
Fayette	4.3	0.0	1.7	40.3	6.5	2.0	3.4	3 611	23	125.0	65.7	37.0	1 306	892
Franklin	1 223.8	1 129.9	378.3	1 768.6	822.0	957.1	3 293.4	389 696	3 119	6 008.1	2 164.4	2 783.9	2 490	1 528
Fulton	8.3	10.3	2.4	15.6	6.2	2.4	0.3	6 402	40	181.6	71.0	74.5	1 750	1 203
Gallia	7.1	0.0	1.5	84.2	9.0	3.1	1.1	501	9	119.8	70.0	29.7	964	717
Geauga	10.3	2.7	3.4	17.6	10.3	4.2	3.3	26 082	91	348.9	116.3	186.2	1 960	1 698
Greene	1 140.4	1 074.1	153.5	95.6	19.9	15.0	12.6	106 096	380	559.6	181.3	262.2	1 695	1 202
Guernsey	10.4	0.1	2.2	66.3	9.2	3.1	5.7	1 834	28	129.6	75.6	34.8	860	556
Hamilton	753.8	1 792.2	392.0	1 609.5	176.6	74.0	260.8	90 250	549	4 162.0	1 577.2	1 861.7	2 210	1 381
Hancock	14.1	0.2	2.6	38.3	12.4	3.9	6.0	20 505	86	254.3	99.7	99.5	1 340	907
Hardin	6.5	6.0	1.5	21.7	5.7	5.1	1.0	2 999	22	117.0	58.0	38.0	1 201	788
Harrison	7.9	0.1	1.0	18.4	4.2	1.8	1.3	0	0	50.1	28.1	13.7	884	666
Henry	6.3	0.1	1.5	14.8	4.5	2.8	2.8	2 079	15	118.1	51.4	47.1	1 629	1 129
Highland	9.1	5.2	1.7	66.3	10.2	2.8	0.3	1 832	19	180.3	84.2	36.3	852	475
Hocking	4.3	0.0	1.3	31.7	5.6	2.0	1.7	628	5	125.1	57.5	25.4	876	666
Holmes	6.1	1.6	1.3	16.4	5.1	2.4	2.2	283	3	121.0	46.3	33.8	818	646
Huron	19.1	0.9	2.8	38.3	10.4	4.9	4.1	4 895	35	202.8	100.2	73.4	1 228	716
Jackson	5.7	0.5	1.5	93.5	10.0	2.7	4.4	5 979	40	118.4	70.7	24.3	730	550
Jefferson	19.7	2.8	4.5	116.3	17.1	6.2	9.2	904	4	294.3	164.5	76.4	1 112	744
Knox	9.1	0.0	2.1	53.1	10.1	6.3	4.4	23 987	225	186.6	89.1	72.6	1 231	900
Lake	42.1	40.0	16.4	79.6	31.4	14.9	27.2	60 402	276	985.8	339.1	470.8	2 017	1 478
Lawrence	11.0	1.4	5.7	147.8	20.8	8.6	2.3	1 635	10	210.1	148.6	32.1	513	367
Licking	45.1	114.3	31.5	107.4	24.7	8.5	17.4	46 935	348	540.4	215.6	237.4	1 512	1 047
Logan	15.0	1.2	11.2	40.9	7.4	3.0	2.1	10 602	65	166.5	73.3	63.0	1 362	1 148
Lorain	132.1	10.6	13.0	211.9	54.4	23.1	37.4	103 908	620	1 207.7	500.0	463.9	1 535	1 102
Lucas	192.6	18.3	40.6	656.3	99.5	39.4	116.3	47 719	303	2 140.0	841.8	870.7	1 970	1 200
Madison	6.7	2.7	2.0	39.3	5.9	2.5	1.7	5 212	33	145.3	56.8	62.6	1 508	1 155
Mahoning	116.0	8.3	25.3	394.7	62.2	22.1	38.3	22 803	100	947.0	493.4	324.8	1 351	928
Marion	23.6	0.1	2.4	66.0	18.6	5.1	1.5	12 660	82	229.6	108.2	71.5	1 096	741
Medina	35.3	17.1	7.3	39.9	18.3	7.2	9.4	88 342	423	590.0	215.0	265.0	1 560	1 260
Meigs	5.2	0.1	1.1	47.9	7.2	2.9	1.7	730	5	70.7	45.4	13.2	577	463
Mercer	7.9	0.3	2.6	16.8	7.3	2.4	4.5	6 125	39	195.8	80.5	52.3	1 280	875
Miami	24.8	56.1	4.7	60.1	14.4	5.0	7.1	22 745	108	360.7	134.1	142.3	1 409	934
Monroe	3.7	0.0	0.8	31.6	4.1	1.3	0.3	0	0	53.6	32.6	12.8	899	751
Montgomery	312.7	415.9	168.3	692.6	125.6	48.1	175.0	44 513	243	2 607.2	1 012.6	1 029.5	1 913	1 244
Morgan	19.9	0.1	0.6	22.8	3.9	1.2	1.1	1 665	6	54.3	33.8	13.5	924	500
Morrow	4.8	0.0	1.1	17.3	5.7	2.5	1.9	5 674	33	123.6	54.4	28.1	813	571
Muskingum	25.9	0.4	10.3	123.4	18.6	8.3	9.5	2 762	30	371.8	220.9	93.9	1 100	726
Noble	2.4	0.0	0.7	14.8	5.9	1.0	0.5	1 221	12	35.5	23.5	7.6	539	458

1. State totals may include programs not allocated by county.   2. Based on the resident population estimated as of July 1 of the year shown.

Table B. States and Counties — Local Government Finances, Government Employment, and Voting

STATE County	Local government finances, 2007 (cont.)									Government employment, 2009			Presidential election,[2] 2008		
	Direct general expenditure							Debt outstanding					Percent of vote cast:		
			Percent of total for:												
	Total (mil dol)	Per capita[1] (dollars)	Education	Health and hospitals	Police protection	Public welfare	Highways	Total (mil dol)	Per capita[1] (dollars)	Federal civilian	Federal military	State and local	Democratic	Republican	All other
	185	186	187	188	189	190	191	192	193	194	195	196	197	198	199
NORTH DAKOTA—Cont'd															
Ward	151.1	2 701	64.4	0.3	5.1	2.3	6.5	59.9	1 071	1 338	5 015	3 937	39.6	58.8	1.6
Wells	15.4	3 600	47.0	2.0	3.2	3.2	14.1	2.1	488	34	31	286	35.4	61.8	2.9
Williams	62.6	3 206	54.2	3.4	4.5	2.8	7.3	93.4	4 782	102	152	1 616	31.2	67.1	1.7
OHIO	X	X	X	X	X	X	X	X	X	78 553	36 109	727 034	51.5	46.9	1.6
Adams	90.5	3 213	60.9	2.1	2.0	10.0	5.7	108.5	3 854	75	72	1 626	36.6	60.7	2.7
Allen	390.5	3 711	48.9	3.1	5.8	6.2	4.3	181.4	1 724	404	269	6 343	38.8	59.6	1.6
Ashland	146.2	2 662	46.5	8.2	6.8	1.9	6.7	49.0	892	107	140	2 805	37.0	60.2	2.8
Ashtabula	364.7	3 606	49.3	6.5	4.2	9.8	6.6	198.2	1 959	221	274	5 064	55.8	42.2	2.0
Athens	210.7	3 330	47.0	6.2	2.3	13.2	5.0	97.8	1 545	237	173	10 015	66.6	31.3	2.0
Auglaize	161.7	3 483	51.6	1.5	5.6	6.9	5.6	221.5	4 771	128	119	2 347	28.6	69.8	1.5
Belmont	234.7	3 457	49.7	1.0	2.4	10.6	10.1	90.7	1 335	182	175	4 037	50.3	47.6	2.1
Brown	175.6	3 995	51.8	24.7	3.1	3.2	4.7	68.3	1 553	93	112	2 327	37.3	60.6	2.1
Butler	1 319.4	3 687	47.9	4.9	5.9	5.2	5.4	1 887.2	5 273	607	953	23 008	38.0	60.6	1.4
Carroll	60.3	2 115	46.4	7.5	5.2	9.8	11.6	14.9	524	53	73	1 040	46.0	50.9	3.1
Champaign	149.7	3 787	60.0	4.0	4.2	3.9	5.7	40.9	1 035	79	101	1 966	39.1	59.0	1.9
Clark	533.2	3 795	49.5	6.3	6.0	8.4	3.9	240.3	1 711	717	365	6 651	47.9	50.4	1.8
Clermont	581.4	3 005	47.0	5.4	3.7	7.6	4.3	310.3	1 604	318	501	7 924	33.1	65.5	1.4
Clinton	271.5	6 304	28.1	38.9	3.5	3.2	4.0	411.1	9 545	171	110	3 856	34.0	64.3	1.8
Columbiana	306.2	2 817	52.0	7.1	5.6	7.1	7.2	133.5	1 228	589	276	4 633	45.1	52.8	2.1
Coshocton	113.1	3 113	47.4	7.3	6.1	9.0	8.3	62.6	1 724	90	91	1 580	45.6	51.4	3.0
Crawford	174.6	3 948	59.2	3.0	4.1	6.6	6.3	132.7	3 000	95	111	2 012	39.1	58.2	2.7
Cuyahoga	7 933.8	6 122	35.0	13.4	5.4	4.9	2.8	9 881.7	7 625	16 901	3 839	84 066	68.9	30.0	1.1
Darke	136.5	2 614	56.4	4.7	5.9	5.9	7.4	57.3	1 097	117	132	2 219	30.9	67.0	2.1
Defiance	159.8	4 147	41.0	17.1	3.7	3.0	4.9	64.7	1 678	118	98	1 980	43.8	54.2	2.0
Delaware	531.5	3 304	52.8	3.2	4.6	2.2	7.2	729.1	4 532	257	430	7 329	39.7	59.3	1.1
Erie	363.6	4 702	49.0	2.2	5.8	6.0	4.2	235.3	3 043	238	196	5 471	56.1	42.3	1.6
Fairfield	416.9	2 950	52.1	5.4	2.7	4.5	4.9	545.8	3 862	259	368	8 205	40.7	57.8	1.6
Fayette	114.7	4 051	48.7	6.1	3.8	5.8	7.6	61.0	2 156	56	72	1 719	37.6	60.7	1.6
Franklin	5 819.7	5 205	37.8	5.9	7.0	5.2	3.5	6 882.1	6 155	12 686	3 645	115 557	59.7	39.0	1.3
Fulton	203.0	4 770	53.2	1.1	5.3	6.3	7.5	194.3	4 566	100	108	2 659	45.1	53.2	1.7
Gallia	113.9	3 692	57.1	0.4	4.9	11.0	5.7	110.0	3 568	93	78	1 984	35.9	61.9	2.2
Geauga	338.0	3 557	48.5	6.1	5.2	4.7	7.9	133.9	1 409	162	253	4 129	41.6	56.9	1.5
Greene	550.9	3 562	44.0	3.9	8.3	4.9	3.6	452.6	2 926	11 932	2 479	12 075	40.1	58.5	1.3
Guernsey	130.1	3 221	41.8	4.7	4.1	11.4	6.4	42.2	1 043	122	102	2 313	44.0	53.1	2.9
Hamilton	4 130.4	4 903	38.1	2.7	7.0	11.3	3.0	5 036.1	5 979	9 396	2 289	51 666	53.0	46.0	1.0
Hancock	248.8	3 352	44.6	8.3	4.8	3.7	6.9	203.1	2 737	174	190	3 523	37.5	60.6	1.9
Hardin	111.2	3 515	56.2	6.8	3.8	7.3	8.3	20.7	655	82	81	1 539	38.2	59.1	2.7
Harrison	49.7	3 208	46.8	1.1	3.6	13.9	13.4	63.3	4 082	69	39	783	47.3	49.7	3.0
Henry	125.8	4 347	51.9	1.5	3.0	18.7	6.5	55.8	1 928	78	73	2 080	42.6	55.5	1.9
Highland	162.3	3 804	46.2	22.2	4.7	7.1	2.5	81.1	1 902	111	108	2 273	35.7	62.1	2.2
Hocking	116.9	4 036	42.7	27.5	3.8	7.3	5.3	32.6	1 126	51	74	1 840	48.3	49.1	2.6
Holmes	118.1	2 856	34.3	28.0	2.1	4.8	8.4	38.9	941	72	107	1 679	28.3	69.5	2.3
Huron	194.5	3 253	52.5	1.9	4.2	6.1	6.3	113.8	1 904	148	153	2 606	47.2	50.4	2.4
Jackson	109.1	3 275	52.7	3.7	4.9	7.5	7.3	76.3	2 289	76	85	1 629	38.6	58.7	2.7
Jefferson	272.7	3 968	42.3	8.7	3.5	11.3	5.5	66.6	970	231	174	3 494	49.1	48.9	2.1
Knox	178.0	3 019	52.2	1.6	2.7	7.0	6.5	115.4	1 958	114	152	2 960	39.0	58.9	2.0
Lake	922.8	3 954	49.3	7.2	6.7	2.5	6.1	483.7	2 073	446	632	12 038	49.6	48.7	1.7
Lawrence	207.3	3 312	65.2	3.2	2.3	7.8	4.0	87.1	1 390	135	160	3 165	41.4	56.7	1.9
Licking	555.1	3 536	59.3	2.7	4.6	4.4	3.9	450.9	2 872	515	416	8 037	41.2	57.0	1.8
Logan	156.3	3 378	51.1	1.2	6.5	5.6	8.1	131.8	2 848	146	120	2 317	35.7	62.3	1.9
Lorain	1 153.0	3 815	49.5	6.1	4.5	5.0	4.1	1 861.6	6 159	1 161	801	14 698	58.1	40.2	1.7
Lucas	2 193.6	4 964	39.4	6.3	6.0	5.8	4.4	2 105.6	4 765	1 914	1 252	29 292	65.0	33.5	1.5
Madison	145.3	3 502	53.9	6.4	3.5	5.2	5.3	131.1	3 159	87	109	3 303	37.4	60.8	1.8
Mahoning	934.0	3 885	51.2	5.3	6.6	5.8	3.4	634.0	2 637	1 289	615	15 712	62.2	35.6	2.1
Marion	222.6	3 412	47.0	5.5	5.4	5.3	4.7	318.9	4 887	141	168	5 787	44.4	53.3	2.4
Medina	570.5	3 359	49.6	4.6	5.9	3.4	4.9	367.5	2 164	354	445	7 211	45.2	53.3	1.5
Meigs	65.4	2 857	50.1	2.6	2.2	4.3	22.5	34.8	1 520	80	58	1 054	39.5	58.1	2.4
Mercer	203.5	4 976	44.3	22.0	3.7	5.0	7.0	68.4	1 672	107	104	2 718	27.5	71.0	1.5
Miami	364.8	3 610	52.6	3.2	6.0	3.3	4.3	154.8	1 532	209	259	5 023	34.8	63.3	1.9
Monroe	53.6	3 761	47.3	3.6	3.6	20.8	10.7	6.0	419	56	36	798	53.1	43.9	3.0
Montgomery	2 455.8	4 564	46.5	4.0	6.9	6.7	4.5	2 453.7	4 560	4 909	4 197	29 436	52.4	46.2	1.4
Morgan	47.5	3 254	43.1	4.2	2.2	13.6	11.4	17.7	1 211	45	36	678	44.9	52.1	3.1
Morrow	117.2	3 394	41.8	25.0	2.8	4.7	6.4	35.7	1 035	63	88	1 621	37.1	60.5	2.4
Muskingum	349.6	4 097	55.2	0.9	5.4	8.3	6.6	205.5	2 408	281	218	5 047	45.4	52.6	2.0
Noble	34.8	2 469	48.4	2.6	3.6	13.8	15.4	3.2	227	27	37	1 026	40.1	55.9	4.0

1. Based on the resident population estimated as of July 1 of the year shown. 2. © 2009 Election Data Services, Inc. All rights reserved.

Table B. States and Counties — **Land Area and Population**

STATE/ County code	CBSA code[1]	County type[2]	STATE County	Land area,[3] (sq km) 2010	Total persons	Rank	Per square kilometer	White	Black	American Indian, Alaska Native	Asian and Pacific Islander	Percent Hispanic or Latino[4]	Under 5 years	5 to 17 years	18 to 24 years	25 to 34 years	35 to 44 years	45 to 54 years
				1	2	3	4	5	6	7	8	9	10	11	12	13	14	15
			OHIO—Cont'd															
39 123	45780	2	Ottawa	660	41 428	1 146	62.8	94.5	1.2	0.5	0.5	4.2	4.9	15.8	6.6	9.1	11.6	16.9
39 125	...	6	Paulding	1 079	19 614	1 857	18.2	94.4	1.2	0.7	0.3	4.3	6.9	18.2	7.5	11.2	12.4	15.4
39 127	...	6	Perry	1 057	36 058	1 272	34.1	98.8	0.6	1.0	0.3	0.5	6.6	19.5	8.0	11.5	13.3	15.4
39 129	18140	1	Pickaway	1 298	55 698	899	42.9	94.9	3.9	0.7	0.6	1.1	5.8	17.8	8.7	13.0	14.6	15.3
39 131	...	7	Pike	1 140	28 709	1 466	25.2	97.7	1.4	1.4	0.4	0.7	6.5	18.3	8.2	11.6	13.1	15.1
39 133	10420	2	Portage	1 262	161 419	381	127.9	92.8	4.9	0.7	1.8	1.3	5.1	15.8	15.6	11.0	12.1	15.2
39 135	19380	2	Preble	1 098	42 270	1 120	38.5	98.3	0.8	0.8	0.6	0.6	6.2	18.1	7.6	10.8	12.9	15.5
39 137	...	6	Putnam	1 250	34 499	1 313	27.6	93.9	0.5	0.3	0.3	5.5	7.4	19.2	7.8	11.2	12.1	15.9
39 139	31900	3	Richland	1 283	124 475	487	97.0	88.2	10.4	0.7	0.9	1.4	6.0	16.5	8.4	11.9	12.6	15.0
39 141	17060	4	Ross	1 785	78 064	696	43.7	92.0	7.3	1.0	0.6	1.0	5.9	16.6	7.8	12.9	14.4	16.3
39 143	23380	4	Sandusky	1 058	60 944	848	57.6	87.8	3.8	0.6	0.5	8.9	6.3	18.1	7.6	11.4	12.5	15.6
39 145	39020	4	Scioto	1 580	79 499	687	50.3	95.3	3.4	1.3	0.5	1.1	6.1	16.6	9.8	12.6	12.8	14.1
39 147	45660	4	Seneca	1 427	56 745	888	39.8	92.5	3.1	0.5	0.7	4.4	6.3	17.3	10.8	11.3	11.5	14.9
39 149	43380	4	Shelby	1 056	49 423	988	46.8	95.5	3.0	0.5	1.2	1.3	7.1	20.2	7.6	11.5	13.2	15.3
39 151	15940	2	Stark	1 490	375 586	176	252.1	89.6	8.9	0.8	1.0	1.6	5.8	17.1	8.7	11.0	12.3	15.3
39 153	10420	2	Summit	1 069	541 781	114	506.8	81.4	15.5	0.7	2.7	1.6	5.8	17.0	9.1	11.9	12.8	15.6
39 155	49660	2	Trumbull	1 601	210 312	294	131.4	89.7	9.2	0.6	0.7	1.3	5.5	16.6	7.9	10.6	12.2	15.3
39 157	35420	4	Tuscarawas	1 470	92 582	620	63.0	96.7	1.2	0.6	0.6	1.9	6.1	17.6	7.6	11.5	12.2	15.1
39 159	18140	1	Union	1 118	52 300	945	46.8	93.3	2.8	0.6	3.2	1.3	6.9	20.3	7.1	13.4	16.7	15.7
39 161	46780	6	Van Wert	1 060	28 744	1 463	27.1	96.2	1.5	0.4	0.4	2.6	6.6	18.3	7.4	11.4	12.0	15.1
39 163	...	9	Vinton	1 068	13 435	2 224	12.6	98.6	0.6	1.1	0.4	0.5	6.1	18.8	7.9	11.1	13.5	15.5
39 165	17140	1	Warren	1 039	212 693	291	204.7	90.2	3.7	0.5	4.6	2.2	6.7	20.8	6.7	11.8	15.9	16.2
39 167	37620	3	Washington	1 637	61 778	839	37.7	97.3	1.7	0.9	0.8	0.7	5.2	15.7	8.9	10.6	12.1	15.6
39 169	49300	4	Wayne	1 437	114 520	522	79.7	95.9	2.1	0.5	1.0	1.6	6.8	18.6	9.7	11.1	11.9	14.7
39 171	...	7	Williams	1 090	37 642	1 226	34.5	94.6	1.3	0.5	0.8	3.7	6.0	17.7	7.8	11.6	12.4	15.7
39 173	45780	2	Wood	1 599	125 488	485	78.5	91.3	2.9	0.6	2.0	4.5	5.5	16.3	16.3	11.7	11.9	14.1
39 175	...	7	Wyandot	1 054	22 615	1 703	21.5	96.8	0.5	0.4	0.8	2.2	6.4	18.0	7.3	11.3	12.8	15.0
40 000	...	X	OKLAHOMA	177 660	3 751 351	X	21.1	73.3	8.4	12.2	2.4	8.9	7.0	17.7	10.2	13.5	12.3	14.0
40 001	...	6	Adair	1 485	22 683	1 698	15.3	51.7	0.4	51.6	0.8	5.3	7.2	20.8	8.5	12.0	13.0	14.1
40 003	...	9	Alfalfa	2 244	5 642	2 794	2.5	89.0	4.5	4.1	0.2	4.0	5.0	13.0	5.3	9.5	15.2	18.4
40 005	...	7	Atoka	2 527	14 182	2 162	5.6	79.1	4.7	19.6	0.7	2.9	6.5	17.1	8.3	12.4	12.3	14.2
40 007	...	9	Beaver	4 700	5 636	2 796	1.2	78.1	0.7	2.2	0.4	20.1	6.8	19.3	6.7	11.1	11.7	15.1
40 009	21120	7	Beckham	2 336	22 119	1 732	9.5	80.7	4.4	4.0	1.0	11.8	7.7	16.5	9.8	15.5	12.6	14.4
40 011	...	6	Blaine	2 405	11 943	2 307	5.0	65.4	3.4	9.8	0.4	24.1	6.6	14.7	9.3	17.3	13.2	13.4
40 013	20460	6	Bryan	2 343	42 416	1 115	18.1	80.0	2.2	18.6	0.8	5.0	6.7	16.7	11.7	12.6	11.6	13.0
40 015	...	6	Caddo	3 311	29 600	1 436	8.9	63.8	4.0	26.7	0.6	10.1	6.9	18.4	8.5	13.1	12.2	14.5
40 017	36420	1	Canadian	2 322	115 541	517	49.8	83.0	3.2	7.0	3.6	6.7	7.4	19.5	7.8	14.3	14.1	14.7
40 019	11620	5	Carter	2 129	47 557	1 014	22.3	77.6	8.3	13.5	1.4	5.3	7.1	18.7	7.7	12.6	12.3	14.5
40 021	45140	6	Cherokee	1 941	46 987	1 024	24.2	58.3	2.0	41.3	0.8	6.3	6.7	17.5	13.9	12.5	11.2	13.1
40 023	...	7	Choctaw	1 995	15 205	2 099	7.6	69.1	12.6	21.2	0.5	2.8	7.0	17.2	7.8	10.7	11.1	14.3
40 025	...	9	Cimarron	4 752	2 475	3 011	0.5	77.9	0.2	1.7	0.6	20.8	7.8	17.7	5.9	8.6	10.6	13.3
40 027	36420	1	Cleveland	1 395	255 755	253	183.3	80.2	5.3	7.7	4.7	7.0	6.6	16.6	14.4	15.5	12.6	13.4
40 029	...	9	Coal	1 338	5 925	2 773	4.4	80.4	0.9	23.5	0.3	2.6	6.6	18.9	7.2	11.0	10.8	14.4
40 031	30020	3	Comanche	2 769	124 098	488	44.8	63.2	19.2	7.5	4.2	11.2	7.6	17.5	13.6	16.5	12.3	13.0
40 033	...	6	Cotton	1 639	6 193	2 748	3.8	83.8	2.7	12.2	0.6	5.6	6.5	18.1	7.4	10.7	12.3	14.8
40 035	...	6	Craig	1 972	15 029	2 107	7.6	73.0	4.2	27.7	1.1	2.5	5.7	17.0	7.9	11.1	12.3	15.8
40 037	46140	2	Creek	2 461	69 967	760	28.4	84.2	3.1	15.3	0.7	3.1	6.3	18.6	7.8	11.2	12.5	15.3
40 039	48220	7	Custer	2 561	27 469	1 515	10.7	75.8	3.6	8.0	1.3	13.9	7.0	16.3	17.4	13.3	9.8	12.3
40 041	...	6	Delaware	1 912	41 487	1 143	21.7	73.2	0.4	29.3	1.5	3.0	5.7	16.7	7.0	9.5	10.9	14.5
40 043	...	9	Dewey	2 589	4 810	2 857	1.9	88.6	0.9	7.6	0.9	4.8	6.2	19.1	5.4	11.0	11.0	14.6
40 045	...	9	Ellis	3 190	4 151	2 893	1.3	91.7	0.4	2.4	0.4	6.0	6.4	18.5	5.1	11.1	10.7	13.6
40 047	21420	5	Garfield	2 741	60 580	853	22.1	83.1	3.8	3.8	3.3	8.8	7.6	17.1	9.0	13.7	11.2	14.3
40 049	...	6	Garvin	2 077	27 576	1 512	13.3	83.1	3.3	11.2	0.6	6.2	6.7	17.7	7.7	11.8	12.1	14.2
40 051	36420	1	Grady	2 850	52 431	942	18.4	87.4	3.0	8.3	0.7	4.6	6.8	18.3	8.6	12.2	12.6	15.4
40 053	...	9	Grant	2 592	4 527	2 869	1.7	93.6	1.1	3.4	0.5	3.5	5.8	16.9	6.3	9.2	10.5	16.5
40 055	...	7	Greer	1 656	6 239	2 746	3.8	80.4	7.6	3.9	0.4	9.8	5.1	14.6	8.4	15.4	13.3	14.3
40 057	...	9	Harmon	1 391	2 922	2 985	2.1	65.6	8.2	2.6	0.4	25.9	8.1	17.7	7.6	11.2	11.2	13.7
40 059	...	9	Harper	2 691	3 685	2 932	1.4	81.5	0.2	1.7	0.4	17.5	8.0	17.2	6.5	13.1	10.2	14.2
40 061	...	6	Haskell	1 493	12 769	2 257	8.6	79.9	0.8	21.9	0.8	3.3	7.0	18.4	7.8	11.3	11.5	13.1
40 063	...	7	Hughes	2 084	14 003	2 174	6.7	72.5	6.0	23.5	0.4	3.8	5.7	16.5	7.9	13.2	12.5	14.2
40 065	11060	5	Jackson	2 079	26 446	1 545	12.7	68.5	8.3	3.0	2.2	20.9	7.6	18.5	10.7	13.6	12.1	13.4
40 067	...	8	Jefferson	1 965	6 472	2 729	3.3	84.6	0.9	9.4	0.6	8.5	6.9	17.3	7.5	10.4	11.0	14.4
40 069	...	7	Johnston	1 665	10 957	2 371	6.6	78.8	2.6	21.6	0.5	3.9	7.2	17.3	9.4	10.9	11.6	13.8
40 071	38620	5	Kay	2 382	46 562	1 034	19.5	81.7	2.6	12.8	0.8	6.4	7.2	18.1	8.5	11.8	10.7	14.0
40 073	...	6	Kingfisher	2 326	15 034	2 106	6.5	82.2	1.3	4.9	0.4	13.4	7.5	19.1	7.5	12.0	12.2	15.1

1. CBSA = Core Based Statistical Area. See Appendix A for explanation. See Appendix B for list of metropolitan areas with component counties.   2. County type code from the Economic Research Service of USDA Rural-Urban Continuum Codes. See Appendix A for definition.   3. Dry land or land partially or temporarily covered by water.   4. May be of any race.

Table B. States and Counties — Population and Households

STATE County	55 to 64 years (16)	65 to 74 years (17)	75 years and over (18)	Percent female (19)	Total persons 1990 (20)	Total persons 2000 (21)	Percent change 1990–2000 (22)	Percent change 2000–2010 (23)	Births (24)	Deaths (25)	Net migration (26)	Households Number (27)	Percent change 2000–2010 (28)	Persons per household (29)	Female family householder[1] (30)	One person (31)
OHIO—Cont'd																
Ottawa	16.1	10.6	8.4	50.7	40 029	40 985	2.4	1.1	3 902	4 170	298	17 503	6.2	2.34	8.9	27.4
Paulding	13.5	8.3	6.5	50.5	20 488	20 293	-1.0	-3.3	2 233	1 597	-1 848	7 769	-0.1	2.51	9.2	25.0
Perry	12.8	7.5	5.5	50.1	31 557	34 078	8.0	5.8	4 277	3 010	214	13 576	8.6	2.63	11.6	22.8
Pickaway	12.0	7.5	5.4	47.5	48 248	52 727	9.3	5.6	5 759	4 300	824	19 624	11.5	2.61	10.9	22.2
Pike	12.5	8.0	6.7	50.4	24 249	27 695	14.2	3.7	3 521	2 896	-435	11 012	5.4	2.56	13.1	25.1
Portage	12.3	7.2	5.7	51.2	142 585	152 061	6.6	6.2	15 359	10 910	1 999	62 222	10.2	2.47	10.9	25.4
Preble	13.8	8.6	6.6	50.4	40 113	42 337	5.5	-0.2	4 680	3 673	-1 676	16 341	2.1	2.56	10.1	23.2
Putnam	12.1	7.1	7.2	50.0	33 819	34 726	2.7	-0.7	4 528	2 692	-1 975	12 872	5.5	2.66	7.4	22.5
Richland	13.3	8.5	7.8	49.4	126 137	128 852	2.2	-3.4	14 669	11 456	-6 829	48 921	-1.2	2.40	12.5	28.8
Ross	12.5	7.8	5.7	47.3	69 330	73 345	5.8	6.4	8 403	6 797	1 467	28 919	6.6	2.48	12.6	26.2
Sandusky	13.1	8.0	7.3	50.8	61 963	61 792	-0.3	-1.4	7 510	5 729	-3 178	24 182	2.0	2.48	12.1	26.3
Scioto	12.5	8.4	7.1	50.6	80 327	79 195	-1.4	0.4	9 231	8 596	-3 077	30 870	0.0	2.46	13.7	27.4
Seneca	13.0	7.3	7.5	50.1	59 733	58 683	-1.8	-3.3	6 738	5 208	-3 739	21 774	-2.3	2.49	11.3	26.3
Shelby	12.3	6.9	6.0	50.1	44 915	47 910	6.7	3.2	6 738	3 738	-1 635	18 467	4.7	2.64	10.4	23.0
Stark	13.5	8.2	8.0	51.6	367 585	378 098	2.9	-0.7	42 046	35 913	-6 667	151 089	1.9	2.42	12.7	28.1
Summit	13.2	7.3	7.3	51.6	514 990	542 899	5.4	-0.2	62 327	49 535	-13 609	222 781	2.3	2.39	13.6	30.0
Trumbull	14.3	8.9	8.5	51.4	227 795	225 116	-1.2	-6.6	22 708	22 553	-13 870	86 011	-3.4	2.40	13.7	29.2
Tuscarawas	13.4	8.4	8.0	50.9	84 090	90 914	8.1	1.8	10 966	8 564	-1 577	36 965	3.7	2.47	9.8	26.6
Union	10.4	5.4	4.0	52.8	31 969	40 909	28.0	27.8	6 292	2 805	4 739	18 065	25.9	2.73	8.7	19.5
Van Wert	12.9	8.1	8.2	51.3	30 464	29 659	-2.6	-3.1	3 463	2 854	-1 607	11 439	-1.3	2.48	9.2	26.6
Vinton	13.2	8.4	5.5	50.2	11 098	12 806	15.4	4.9	1 579	1 166	84	5 260	7.5	2.54	12.1	26.1
Warren	11.1	6.2	4.6	49.7	113 973	158 383	39.0	34.3	25 112	11 277	39 025	76 424	36.6	2.70	8.8	20.4
Washington	14.4	9.6	7.9	51.2	62 254	63 251	1.6	-2.3	6 366	6 286	-1 894	25 587	1.8	2.34	10.0	28.1
Wayne	12.6	7.9	6.7	50.6	101 461	111 564	10.0	2.6	14 936	8 951	-2 569	42 638	5.4	2.61	9.2	25.1
Williams	12.9	8.5	7.5	50.4	36 956	39 188	6.0	-3.9	4 242	3 411	-1 998	16 075	-0.2	2.43	9.9	27.0
Wood	12.1	6.4	5.8	51.1	113 269	121 065	6.9	3.7	12 808	8 715	311	49 043	8.6	2.43	9.0	27.5
Wyandot	13.0	8.2	8.1	50.5	22 254	22 908	2.9	-1.3	2 686	2 192	-875	9 091	2.4	2.46	10.2	26.5
OKLAHOMA	11.7	7.5	6.0	50.5	3 145 576	3 450 654	9.7	8.7	481 766	325 299	92 977	1 460 450	8.8	2.49	12.3	27.5
Adair	11.5	7.8	5.1	50.0	18 421	21 038	14.2	7.8	3 430	2 090	-391	8 156	9.2	2.77	14.2	23.0
Alfalfa	13.2	11.0	9.2	41.1	6 416	6 105	-4.8	-7.6	441	625	-407	2 022	-8.0	2.27	6.4	30.2
Atoka	13.0	9.7	6.6	47.9	12 778	13 879	8.6	2.2	1 507	1 343	509	5 391	8.6	2.49	11.2	27.4
Beaver	13.8	8.3	7.2	49.1	6 023	5 857	-2.8	-3.8	610	502	-676	2 192	-2.4	2.55	6.1	23.4
Beckham	10.8	6.6	6.2	46.5	18 812	19 799	5.2	11.7	2 903	2 314	791	8 163	11.0	2.48	11.1	27.6
Blaine	11.0	7.5	6.9	42.0	11 470	11 976	4.4	-0.3	1 355	1 352	694	3 959	-4.8	2.46	10.3	29.4
Bryan	11.9	9.0	9.7	51.1	32 089	36 534	13.9	16.1	4 887	3 912	3 495	16 838	16.8	2.45	12.6	27.6
Caddo	11.8	8.2	6.5	48.3	29 550	30 150	2.0	-1.8	3 923	3 308	-250	10 645	-2.8	2.60	13.7	26.3
Canadian	11.4	6.5	4.4	50.4	74 409	87 697	17.9	31.8	12 315	6 321	16 469	42 434	34.8	2.66	10.6	20.9
Carter	12.2	8.1	6.8	51.2	42 919	45 621	6.3	4.2	6 225	5 460	2 268	18 635	3.6	2.51	13.1	26.5
Cherokee	11.7	7.9	5.5	50.6	34 049	42 521	24.9	10.5	5 829	3 911	1 842	17 836	10.3	2.52	12.4	26.4
Choctaw	13.7	10.6	7.5	51.8	15 302	15 342	0.3	-0.9	2 041	1 941	-481	6 270	0.8	2.40	14.3	30.2
Cimarron	14.7	11.1	10.3	50.2	3 301	3 148	-4.6	-21.4	280	311	-488	1 047	-16.7	2.36	6.6	30.4
Cleveland	10.8	6.0	4.2	50.0	174 253	208 016	19.4	22.9	25 301	13 105	25 488	98 306	24.1	2.49	10.7	25.9
Coal	13.5	9.5	8.3	50.6	5 780	6 031	4.3	-1.8	680	783	-42	2 350	-1.0	2.50	12.1	28.1
Comanche	9.3	5.7	4.5	48.5	111 486	114 996	3.1	7.9	17 846	8 220	-10 848	44 982	13.0	2.53	14.5	27.1
Cotton	13.2	9.7	7.3	50.8	6 651	6 614	-0.6	-6.4	691	734	-264	2 483	-5.0	2.47	11.5	27.2
Craig	12.7	9.7	7.7	49.2	14 104	14 950	6.0	0.5	1 755	1 724	249	5 691	1.3	2.46	11.2	27.3
Creek	13.3	8.7	6.3	50.5	60 915	67 367	10.6	3.9	8 223	6 816	1 897	26 539	4.9	2.60	11.6	23.1
Custer	10.4	6.7	6.7	50.4	26 897	26 142	-2.8	5.1	3 575	2 543	-316	10 698	5.5	2.43	9.8	29.4
Delaware	15.2	12.7	7.9	50.7	28 070	37 077	32.1	11.9	4 200	4 260	3 708	17 093	15.2	2.41	9.8	26.4
Dewey	12.7	11.0	8.9	50.1	5 551	4 743	-14.6	1.4	517	721	-111	1 944	-0.9	2.43	7.9	28.8
Ellis	15.6	10.3	8.8	51.2	4 497	4 075	-9.4	1.9	433	517	-55	1 782	0.7	2.30	7.2	31.3
Garfield	11.8	7.7	7.6	50.7	56 735	57 813	1.9	4.8	8 417	6 324	-617	24 175	4.3	2.43	11.0	28.8
Garvin	12.5	9.3	8.0	51.1	26 605	27 210	2.3	1.3	3 374	3 403	101	11 069	1.9	2.46	11.6	27.1
Grady	12.4	8.1	5.5	50.4	41 747	45 516	9.0	15.2	5 879	4 418	4 934	19 892	14.7	2.58	10.1	22.7
Grant	13.5	10.4	10.9	50.3	5 689	5 144	-9.6	-12.0	404	609	-592	1 910	-8.6	2.33	6.9	29.9
Greer	11.4	8.2	9.2	43.3	6 559	6 061	-7.6	2.9	589	764	-31	2 181	-2.5	2.34	11.1	32.0
Harmon	13.2	8.3	9.0	52.0	3 793	3 283	-13.4	-11.0	378	450	-362	1 112	-12.2	2.54	12.2	26.3
Harper	12.2	8.8	9.8	50.4	4 063	3 562	-12.3	3.5	443	484	-136	1 527	1.2	2.39	7.9	30.8
Haskell	13.3	9.9	7.6	50.3	10 940	11 792	7.8	8.3	1 544	1 451	572	5 044	9.1	2.52	10.1	25.6
Hughes	12.8	9.1	8.1	46.2	13 014	14 154	8.8	-1.1	1 590	1 791	-51	5 050	-5.1	2.46	12.8	28.3
Jackson	11.0	7.1	5.8	50.2	28 764	28 439	-1.1	-7.0	4 143	2 488	-4 640	10 247	-3.2	2.51	11.9	27.0
Jefferson	13.5	10.3	8.9	50.2	7 010	6 818	-2.7	-5.1	761	941	-281	2 634	-3.0	2.40	10.5	29.3
Johnston	13.1	9.5	7.1	50.7	10 032	10 513	4.8	4.2	1 325	1 222	-94	4 312	6.3	2.47	11.6	27.3
Kay	12.7	8.7	8.3	50.7	48 056	48 080	0.0	-3.2	6 393	5 440	-2 664	18 577	-3.0	2.44	11.6	29.2
Kingfisher	11.7	7.9	7.2	50.6	13 212	13 926	5.4	8.0	1 815	1 444	155	5 731	9.2	2.60	9.0	24.3

1. No spouse present.

STATE County	Persons in group quarters, 2010	Daytime population, 2006-2010 Number	Daytime population, 2006-2010 Employment/residence ratio	Births, average 2006-2008 Total	Births, average 2006-2008 Rate[1]	Deaths, average 2006-2008 Number	Deaths, average 2006-2008 Rate[1]	Persons under 65 with no health insurance, 2009 Number	Persons under 65 with no health insurance, 2009 Percent	Medicare, 2011 Eligible for Medicare	Medicare, 2011 Enrolled in Medicare Advantage	Medicare, 2011 Enrolled in a Medicare prescription drug plan	Serious crimes known to police,[2] 2010 Total Number	Serious crimes known to police,[2] 2010 Total Rate[3]
	32	33	34	35	36	37	38	39	40	41	42	43	44	45
OHIO—Cont'd														
Ottawa	489	36 718	0.8	D	D	466	11.4	4 292	13.1	9 358	2 409	4 681	648	1 676
Paulding	85	16 502	0.6	D	D	190	9.9	2 188	13.8	3 648	887	1 918	205	1 067
Perry	307	27 932	0.5	D	D	304	8.7	4 553	15.1	6 269	1 186	3 465	375	1 059
Pickaway	4 455	48 088	0.7	633	11.7	469	8.7	6 668	14.4	9 172	3 512	4 365	2 297	4 184
Pike	496	29 542	1.1	D	D	314	11.2	3 763	16.0	5 702	1 090	3 307	509	1 773
Portage	7 914	141 901	0.8	1 620	10.4	1 200	7.7	17 015	12.7	24 967	10 040	10 006	3 034	2 060
Preble	386	34 999	0.6	D	D	402	9.6	4 816	14.0	7 647	2 823	3 339	712	1 692
Putnam	303	29 095	0.7	D	D	278	8.0	3 238	11.3	5 637	1 159	2 951	135	391
Richland	7 263	127 099	1.0	1 598	12.7	1 258	10.0	14 797	14.5	24 467	4 776	13 086	5 325	4 344
Ross	6 353	75 401	0.9	939	12.4	726	9.6	9 949	15.5	13 634	4 101	6 946	4 403	5 640
Sandusky	901	60 053	1.0	787	12.9	647	10.6	6 739	13.5	11 237	2 478	6 052	1 459	2 725
Scioto	3 642	76 776	0.9	1 006	13.2	934	12.2	9 733	15.2	15 529	2 676	9 374	3 784	4 760
Seneca	2 534	52 049	0.8	720	12.7	582	10.3	6 759	14.3	10 468	1 820	6 329	NA	NA
Shelby	589	55 105	1.3	708	14.5	388	7.9	5 334	12.8	7 840	2 138	4 442	1 326	2 803
Stark	9 264	370 111	1.0	4 499	11.9	3 922	10.3	40 950	13.2	72 646	33 606	25 163	10 801	2 910
Summit	9 967	557 302	1.1	6 550	12.0	5 278	9.7	61 568	13.6	93 481	38 811	31 913	20 282	3 925
Trumbull	3 821	203 365	0.9	2 410	11.3	2 469	11.5	24 679	14.5	44 289	18 793	16 899	7 218	3 432
Tuscarawas	1 250	88 600	0.9	1 188	13.0	921	10.1	12 076	16.1	17 588	6 899	7 421	952	1 078
Union	2 932	55 980	1.2	692	14.6	313	6.6	4 588	10.7	6 281	2 364	2 903	754	1 506
Van Wert	396	27 228	0.9	D	D	303	10.5	2 924	12.4	5 653	1 334	2 969	809	2 815
Vinton	68	10 943	0.5	D	D	127	9.5	1 854	16.3	2 301	488	1 441	394	2 933
Warren	5 985	192 075	0.8	2 696	13.2	1 268	6.2	18 377	10.1	27 761	10 793	10 488	3 550	1 696
Washington	1 781	60 365	0.9	664	10.8	688	11.2	6 803	13.7	12 886	1 799	7 449	871	1 423
Wayne	3 231	110 697	0.9	1 607	14.1	978	8.6	15 626	16.3	19 198	7 073	8 264	2 066	1 889
Williams	990	38 145	1.0	D	D	377	9.8	4 670	15.0	7 268	1 942	4 070	503	1 398
Wood	6 230	127 004	1.0	1 369	11.0	964	7.7	12 408	11.6	18 763	6 577	9 134	2 657	2 205
Wyandot	251	20 592	0.8	D	D	227	10.1	2 574	14.0	4 253	1 121	2 516	39	172
OKLAHOMA	112 017	3 656 436	1.0	54 621	15.1	36 158	10.0	666 731	21.4	621 090	92 542	290 142	146 113	3 895
Adair	92	20 621	0.8	D	D	219	9.9	4 593	24.6	3 917	220	2 285	416	1 834
Alfalfa	1 054	5 195	0.8	D	D	67	11.8	1 060	24.8	1 200	37	785	46	815
Atoka	750	13 334	0.8	D	D	144	9.9	3 127	26.0	2 758	140	1 689	280	1 974
Beaver	43	4 867	0.7	D	D	59	11.2	994	22.9	935	42	544	NA	NA
Beckham	1 907	23 506	1.2	D	D	259	12.9	4 143	23.2	3 455	99	2 230	231	1 044
Blaine	2 190	11 288	0.9	D	D	147	11.6	2 883	27.7	2 015	97	1 232	162	1 356
Bryan	1 134	39 722	0.9	D	D	453	11.5	8 431	25.2	7 795	323	4 221	1 401	3 303
Caddo	1 935	27 307	0.8	D	D	351	11.9	6 691	26.3	5 430	176	3 308	618	2 088
Canadian	2 488	85 468	0.5	1 503	14.5	714	6.9	15 664	16.3	15 292	3 258	5 684	4 574	3 959
Carter	750	49 898	1.1	709	14.9	613	12.8	8 443	21.1	9 236	634	5 227	2 199	4 624
Cherokee	2 008	44 252	0.9	D	D	454	10.0	10 560	26.8	7 848	640	4 160	1 066	2 269
Choctaw	172	14 807	0.9	D	D	219	14.5	2 932	24.8	3 443	143	2 008	245	1 611
Cimarron	7	2 404	0.9	D	D	35	13.2	645	31.3	614	15	379	19	768
Cleveland	10 561	205 960	0.7	2 953	12.6	1 586	6.8	38 042	17.6	32 875	5 020	12 816	10 993	4 298
Coal	61	5 642	0.9	D	D	91	16.0	1 349	28.1	1 117	53	595	108	1 823
Comanche	10 343	123 728	1.1	1 999	17.9	932	8.4	18 866	19.5	15 703	444	6 049	6 558	5 285
Cotton	48	5 431	0.7	D	D	83	13.2	1 139	22.3	1 226	50	625	51	824
Craig	1 050	15 650	1.1	D	D	211	14.0	2 694	22.3	3 312	303	1 937	280	1 863
Creek	1 062	60 079	0.7	882	12.7	790	11.4	12 044	20.6	13 295	4 321	5 011	1 706	2 438
Custer	1 516	27 022	1.0	D	D	271	10.4	5 160	23.0	4 151	174	2 562	687	2 501
Delaware	356	36 448	0.7	D	D	469	11.6	8 318	26.4	8 975	912	4 390	749	1 843
Dewey	93	4 656	1.0	D	D	74	16.8	810	23.9	1 032	26	644	16	333
Ellis	46	3 874	0.9	D	D	52	13.1	667	21.4	860	64	521	51	1 229
Garfield	1 830	59 814	1.0	982	17.0	676	11.7	9 971	20.5	11 054	441	6 710	2 479	4 092
Garvin	317	27 123	1.0	D	D	380	14.0	4 920	22.6	5 904	479	3 460	763	2 767
Grady	1 082	42 679	0.6	664	13.1	483	9.5	8 781	19.9	8 619	796	4 389	1 594	3 040
Grant	73	4 179	0.8	D	D	63	14.0	790	23.7	1 014	36	676	49	1 082
Greer	1 146	5 897	0.8	D	D	86	14.9	1 158	25.3	1 310	61	856	73	1 170
Harmon	100	2 785	0.9	D	D	48	16.6	632	27.9	594	15	412	87	2 977
Harper	41	3 460	0.9	D	D	46	14.0	580	22.0	718	D	476	13	353
Haskell	78	11 986	0.9	D	D	145	12.0	2 541	25.5	2 927	203	1 613	162	1 269
Hughes	1 565	12 748	0.8	D	D	186	13.5	2 907	26.1	3 129	200	1 785	374	2 671
Jackson	687	27 019	1.1	464	18.1	270	10.5	4 309	20.0	3 974	89	2 051	853	3 225
Jefferson	144	5 632	0.7	D	D	98	15.6	1 479	30.1	1 448	64	861	NA	NA
Johnston	292	10 477	0.9	D	D	132	12.7	2 055	24.2	2 284	85	1 370	98	894
Kay	1 273	47 802	1.1	708	15.5	585	12.8	8 112	21.6	9 547	840	5 888	1 787	3 838
Kingfisher	155	14 171	0.9	D	D	158	11.1	2 689	22.5	2 606	212	1 525	153	1 018

1. Per 1,000 estimated resident population.   2. Data for serious crimes have not been adjusted for underreporting; this may affect comparability between geographic areas and over time.   3. Per 100,000 population estimated by the FBI.

Table B. States and Counties — Crime, Education, Money Income, and Poverty

STATE County	Serious crimes known to police,[1] 2010 (cont.) Rate[2] Violent	Property	Education — School enrollment and attainment, 2006-2010 — Enrollment[3] Total	Percent private	Attainment[4] (percent) High school graduate or less	Bachelor's degree or more	Local government expenditures,[5] 2008-2009 Total current expenditures (mil dol)	Current expenditures per student (dollars)	Money income, 2006-2010 Per capita income[6] (dollars)	Households Median income Dollars	Percent change, 2000 to 2006-2010 (constant 2010 dollars)	Percent with income of $200,000 or more	Income and poverty, 2010 Median household income (dollars)	Percent below poverty level All persons	Children under 18 years	Children 5 to 17 years in families
	46	47	48	49	50	51	52	53	54	55	56	57	58	59	60	61
OHIO—Cont'd																
Ottawa	52	1 624	9 198	14.4	46.7	18.9	63.3	10 663	27 809	53 463	-4.5	2.1	50 707	10.2	16.3	14.7
Paulding	36	1 031	4 717	9.3	63.1	10.7	42.4	10 994	20 919	46 459	-9.0	0.3	43 791	13.5	20.5	18.4
Perry	23	1 037	9 242	11.1	67.3	8.9	66.6	10 081	18 916	42 388	-2.6	1.0	39 387	19.1	28.6	27.7
Pickaway	158	4 026	13 320	10.5	63.7	13.5	92.5	9 172	21 432	49 262	-9.2	1.0	49 926	12.7	19.0	17.1
Pike	17	1 756	7 317	5.6	66.7	12.6	61.0	11 232	17 494	35 912	-10.4	0.6	35 051	26.3	36.9	33.3
Portage	63	1 997	48 934	9.6	49.2	24.9	244.6	9 744	25 097	50 447	-10.2	2.2	49 287	15.1	18.1	14.7
Preble	74	1 619	10 298	10.3	60.1	12.0	64.7	9 195	23 290	49 780	-6.6	1.9	47 615	12.1	19.6	17.8
Putnam	17	374	9 142	14.9	55.4	18.1	56.0	9 346	24 023	56 573	-3.8	1.9	53 920	9.0	12.0	10.6
Richland	177	4 167	29 901	17.9	57.6	14.9	200.3	11 543	21 459	42 664	-9.9	1.0	41 462	14.7	23.6	21.9
Ross	365	5 275	18 359	7.1	62.6	13.1	128.1	10 632	20 595	42 626	-9.3	1.7	41 318	19.3	27.7	24.9
Sandusky	183	2 542	15 176	16.8	56.3	13.1	86.8	9 601	22 286	48 056	-6.5	0.4	44 346	12.3	18.2	16.3
Scioto	192	4 567	19 057	8.3	59.1	12.7	132.7	10 183	17 778	32 812	-7.5	0.5	35 860	22.2	31.9	29.1
Seneca	NA	NA	15 534	25.2	56.3	16.1	63.1	10 449	20 976	42 573	-11.6	1.4	42 642	14.6	22.2	19.7
Shelby	159	2 645	13 416	12.0	60.8	14.0	83.9	9 129	21 948	48 475	-14.0	1.2	46 062	12.2	17.2	15.6
Stark	260	2 650	96 333	18.3	52.8	20.4	580.5	9 454	24 015	44 941	-10.9	2.2	42 805	14.6	23.1	20.7
Summit	384	3 540	141 374	17.3	43.2	29.2	858.0	10 705	26 676	47 926	-10.5	3.0	45 768	15.4	22.4	19.4
Trumbull	254	3 178	48 837	11.6	58.9	16.3	334.7	10 161	21 854	42 296	-12.8	1.1	40 389	18.2	31.4	28.8
Tuscarawas	60	1 018	21 469	11.9	64.9	14.3	149.9	9 112	20 536	42 081	-6.4	0.8	39 580	14.7	22.6	20.6
Union	42	1 464	13 679	11.8	47.3	27.3	72.1	9 263	27 389	68 452	4.5	2.9	63 233	8.2	10.1	8.7
Van Wert	129	2 686	7 090	15.7	60.3	14.1	51.4	9 907	20 772	44 415	-11.2	0.5	44 338	12.5	19.1	17.3
Vinton	134	2 799	3 242	2.2	69.7	9.2	24.2	9 651	16 736	34 242	-8.2	0.1	34 977	21.8	35.8	33.2
Warren	71	1 625	56 847	19.0	37.4	35.9	347.3	9 487	31 935	71 274	-2.9	6.2	67 172	5.9	7.7	6.4
Washington	83	1 339	15 002	17.5	56.4	16.0	84.5	8 982	22 786	41 654	-4.0	1.7	41 231	15.7	22.7	20.2
Wayne	74	1 814	28 597	23.8	58.7	19.1	171.8	10 025	22 645	48 375	-8.0	2.2	46 157	12.6	20.4	18.8
Williams	72	1 326	9 178	11.0	59.9	12.9	55.9	8 592	21 381	44 538	-13.7	0.9	41 791	12.2	19.2	17.5
Wood	75	2 130	42 982	11.0	42.0	29.3	219.4	11 396	26 671	53 298	-5.3	2.7	49 344	12.8	13.9	12.8
Wyandot	27	146	5 677	10.9	59.9	13.4	29.4	8 152	22 553	47 216	-4.0	1.0	43 753	9.4	14.3	13.2
OKLAHOMA	479	3 415	962 914	11.2	47.2	22.6	5 082.2	7 885	23 094	42 979	1.6	2.3	42 076	16.8	24.4	22.5
Adair	353	1 481	6 019	4.7	65.0	10.6	42.3	8 690	13 732	29 811	-5.4	0.5	30 190	26.5	37.0	35.7
Alfalfa	89	727	954	4.5	54.0	17.9	8.6	10 364	21 029	42 500	10.9	3.5	35 615	17.6	22.7	20.8
Atoka	141	1 833	3 107	6.2	64.6	14.5	28.9	12 343	15 772	31 179	-0.5	1.3	33 304	22.7	33.6	30.9
Beaver	NA	NA	1 194	4.1	53.5	17.9	12.5	11 266	23 525	49 743	7.0	1.5	48 158	11.6	17.4	16.2
Beckham	172	873	4 872	7.5	56.0	14.7	30.0	8 053	21 144	43 642	25.8	1.9	41 277	17.7	25.0	24.1
Blaine	176	1 181	2 851	5.1	56.0	15.9	18.7	10 040	19 445	41 421	16.4	1.9	44 558	19.9	24.9	24.2
Bryan	455	2 848	10 908	12.2	50.7	20.3	59.0	8 340	19 103	37 230	5.4	1.3	36 925	17.1	25.9	24.9
Caddo	355	1 733	7 270	9.4	59.5	13.7	55.1	9 369	16 787	36 413	5.2	0.4	36 077	21.6	29.1	27.3
Canadian	500	3 459	29 365	8.9	38.5	25.3	153.5	7 094	26 970	60 489	5.1	3.2	57 018	9.3	13.4	12.7
Carter	883	3 741	11 223	10.6	59.0	16.4	74.8	8 151	20 192	38 385	3.1	1.5	37 316	18.4	26.5	25.1
Cherokee	155	2 113	13 776	9.3	47.1	23.8	63.3	8 392	16 084	32 322	-3.8	0.6	33 393	22.0	31.3	28.2
Choctaw	178	1 434	3 475	3.2	64.7	11.5	22.7	8 460	17 231	27 549	-4.3	0.6	29 476	25.5	39.3	36.7
Cimarron	162	606	542	9.0	57.4	16.9	5.5	12 420	18 358	34 096	-12.1	0.4	36 183	17.7	28.1	26.4
Cleveland	330	3 969	77 994	9.4	36.0	31.2	290.7	7 145	25 831	52 688	-0.6	2.6	51 468	13.5	16.1	15.6
Coal	135	1 688	1 296	5.6	68.7	9.1	12.9	10 196	17 338	31 764	5.8	0.2	33 472	21.7	33.0	29.3
Comanche	711	4 574	32 124	7.2	47.1	19.8	169.3	7 750	20 778	44 012	2.6	1.4	43 394	17.4	25.9	24.0
Cotton	129	694	1 526	9.2	57.2	18.6	9.8	8 049	20 948	44 144	28.1	1.1	39 941	15.6	23.4	21.6
Craig	140	1 723	3 296	5.6	59.0	13.5	25.6	8 358	18 784	39 836	1.5	0.8	36 407	15.9	24.4	22.6
Creek	192	2 247	17 595	8.4	56.3	14.9	102.7	7 858	21 891	42 314	0.7	1.6	41 331	15.6	23.0	21.0
Custer	335	2 166	8 384	5.6	45.8	25.0	36.3	7 615	22 003	42 108	16.6	1.9	40 741	17.5	21.6	20.3
Delaware	224	1 619	8 411	7.1	60.5	14.3	61.3	8 883	20 142	34 383	-3.0	1.7	32 878	22.8	35.9	31.5
Dewey	42	291	1 048	1.4	60.3	19.2	11.3	11 578	21 055	39 940	12.0	2.4	39 731	14.1	21.0	18.5
Ellis	193	1 036	876	3.5	50.6	23.3	8.3	10 460	23 767	43 032	21.6	1.7	40 851	13.9	21.6	19.2
Garfield	385	3 707	13 971	13.4	51.1	21.8	76.4	7 618	22 812	40 636	-2.8	1.5	38 827	15.7	24.2	23.8
Garvin	268	2 499	6 308	7.7	64.6	15.4	42.5	7 999	20 176	37 785	6.3	1.7	37 689	16.3	24.1	22.5
Grady	366	2 674	13 247	7.2	52.8	16.8	55.4	7 147	21 687	45 260	9.6	1.1	44 036	16.4	22.2	20.4
Grant	22	1 060	1 113	5.8	46.9	20.8	9.7	11 588	22 204	42 043	14.6	1.5	37 938	12.8	19.2	17.2
Greer	112	1 058	1 039	3.6	63.7	13.0	8.7	9 084	13 241	35 096	7.5	0.3	33 199	21.9	29.4	26.4
Harmon	137	2 841	532	4.1	57.4	15.5	5.1	9 370	17 677	31 679	11.9	1.5	28 914	26.9	36.6	36.5
Harper	54	299	863	7.2	57.8	17.1	6.9	9 428	23 693	39 946	-6.4	0.8	41 437	11.5	17.8	17.4
Haskell	227	1 042	2 837	3.3	61.7	13.4	18.5	7 958	18 735	37 474	20.5	2.0	32 551	17.5	29.3	27.9
Hughes	200	2 471	2 972	2.1	62.5	11.8	21.5	9 053	18 083	32 677	14.1	1.4	30 699	25.9	32.6	28.0
Jackson	185	3 040	6 924	7.0	45.7	21.2	41.3	7 919	21 249	41 437	6.5	1.0	39 565	16.9	25.2	23.3
Jefferson	NA	NA	1 305	6.7	67.5	11.2	11.4	9 578	17 491	32 750	9.2	0.9	29 992	21.6	32.2	30.6
Johnston	283	611	3 534	5.0	49.8	19.0	16.6	8 764	18 451	34 556	11.0	0.9	32 247	22.1	34.3	32.6
Kay	352	3 486	11 564	8.7	50.5	19.9	71.0	8 270	21 167	39 505	1.4	1.4	38 775	17.5	27.3	24.5
Kingfisher	53	964	3 845	6.7	50.7	17.1	27.4	8 366	23 481	49 104	5.7	1.8	48 255	11.9	16.7	15.3

1. Data for serious crimes have not been adjusted for underreporting; this may affect comparability between geographic areas and over time.   2. Per 100,000 population estimated by the FBI.   3. All persons 3 years old and over enrolled in nursery school through college.   4. Persons 25 years old and over.   5. Elementary and secondary education expenditures.   6. Based on population estimated by the American Community Survey, 2006-2010.

STATE County	Total (mil dol)	Percent change, 2008–2009	Per capita¹ Dollars	Per capita¹ Rank	Wages and salaries² (mil dol)	Proprietors' income (mil dol)	Dividends, interest, and rent (mil dol)	Transfer payments (mil dol) Total	Government payments to individuals Total	Social Security	Medical payments	Income mainte-nance	Unemploy-ment insurance
	62	63	64	65	66	67	68	69	70	71	72	73	74
OHIO—Cont'd													
Ottawa	1 519	-0.8	37 094	741	660	80	254	357	349	134	141	19	23
Paulding	588	-0.6	30 946	1 771	200	45	83	142	138	54	49	12	11
Perry	877	2.8	24 796	2 882	268	27	93	288	281	83	125	34	17
Pickaway	1 659	2.1	30 307	1 905	699	103	194	360	350	122	131	37	21
Pike	753	2.5	27 154	2 543	509	41	91	256	251	68	111	39	13
Portage	5 332	-1.0	33 849	1 191	2 528	245	739	1 073	1 044	353	382	76	71
Preble	1 294	0.8	31 240	1 704	441	65	161	304	296	108	118	23	20
Putnam	1 151	-0.7	33 486	1 256	446	90	176	211	205	80	77	12	15
Richland	3 689	-2.2	29 635	2 066	2 349	142	564	999	976	346	388	94	62
Ross	2 199	2.1	28 951	2 212	1 330	105	266	599	585	177	241	74	33
Sandusky	1 847	-0.7	30 754	1 809	1 112	91	254	445	434	158	165	36	31
Scioto	2 174	1.4	28 476	2 303	1 063	85	268	767	753	184	349	106	32
Seneca	1 682	0.2	29 951	1 992	845	88	228	471	461	144	209	34	30
Shelby	1 580	-3.4	32 242	1 477	1 397	95	233	314	305	112	110	26	28
Stark	12 443	-1.7	32 790	1 368	7 102	809	1 900	3 022	2 953	1 028	1 203	273	168
Summit	20 612	-2.4	38 001	639	14 063	840	3 277	4 224	4 125	1 332	1 753	407	226
Trumbull	6 401	-1.3	30 456	1 872	3 281	273	1 012	1 898	1 860	666	772	164	115
Tuscarawas	2 626	-1.9	28 813	2 229	1 363	156	396	678	661	238	259	60	41
Union	1 695	1.1	34 665	1 071	1 825	63	179	243	234	88	80	20	17
Van Wert	906	-2.3	31 789	1 582	431	84	127	196	191	77	63	14	17
Vinton	304	2.3	22 951	3 031	96	9	41	109	106	29	45	16	6
Warren	8 190	-0.2	38 867	549	3 804	358	1 099	1 074	1 036	408	362	59	74
Washington	2 004	0.7	32 828	1 363	1 187	101	286	508	497	177	204	43	24
Wayne	3 405	-2.1	29 808	2 020	2 027	223	591	737	716	267	278	60	45
Williams	1 162	-2.3	30 725	1 815	693	87	184	289	282	101	108	23	26
Wood	4 431	-0.8	35 341	973	2 980	220	658	794	771	259	264	47	58
Wyandot	689	0.3	30 780	1 807	357	67	102	158	154	57	61	10	12
OKLAHOMA	132 132	-1.8	35 837	X	77 994	15 239	21 789	25 988	25 320	8 597	10 619	2 601	869
Adair	491	0.1	22 476	3 051	216	29	47	187	183	49	87	26	7
Alfalfa	137	-13.6	25 074	2 857	54	12	28	40	39	17	17	2	1
Atoka	342	0.1	23 602	2 992	137	43	46	108	105	37	42	13	4
Beaver	173	-5.1	32 774	1 371	69	24	32	32	31	13	13	2	1
Beckham	656	-7.5	31 084	1 732	455	39	133	136	132	45	58	14	5
Blaine	279	-6.0	22 134	3 062	140	21	49	79	77	27	35	8	2
Bryan	1 200	0.8	29 431	2 110	669	61	156	322	314	99	141	32	8
Caddo	743	-1.1	24 455	2 919	335	26	119	224	218	70	95	27	6
Canadian	3 984	1.3	36 325	842	1 257	180	515	573	553	213	200	45	25
Carter	1 678	-1.7	34 717	1 061	1 066	168	295	398	389	130	181	38	12
Cherokee	1 277	3.0	27 739	2 446	672	92	162	350	341	102	140	37	10
Choctaw	399	-0.2	26 826	2 590	176	30	44	153	150	43	71	20	4
Cimarron	81	-12.1	30 942	1 772	30	18	16	17	17	8	6	1	0
Cleveland	8 654	0.1	35 381	968	3 377	516	1 483	1 241	1 196	453	407	112	48
Coal	141	2.9	24 145	2 955	44	6	19	51	49	14	25	5	2
Comanche	4 140	2.9	36 564	807	3 227	130	469	760	741	206	258	90	19
Cotton	199	-13.2	31 646	1 615	74	0	26	47	46	16	19	4	1
Craig	457	0.6	30 123	1 948	265	33	67	146	143	44	73	13	3
Creek	2 139	-0.7	30 451	1 873	804	130	316	526	513	192	217	43	19
Custer	838	-3.1	31 350	1 684	511	43	178	187	182	56	80	17	5
Delaware	1 207	0.2	29 763	2 027	347	61	197	326	318	121	128	32	10
Dewey	140	-12.5	31 790	1 581	59	3	28	36	35	14	17	2	1
Ellis	119	-12.0	30 318	1 901	51	5	26	29	28	11	12	1	1
Garfield	2 167	-2.7	36 772	777	1 300	149	440	474	464	154	226	39	11
Garvin	901	-1.9	33 227	1 303	444	70	143	279	274	81	147	20	7
Grady	1 472	-1.0	28 505	2 298	539	82	215	320	311	116	117	33	13
Grant	157	-11.8	36 273	851	57	18	34	36	35	15	16	2	1
Greer	163	-4.0	27 969	2 406	58	8	24	54	53	16	27	5	1
Harmon	79	-5.2	27 837	2 428	31	7	14	26	26	7	13	3	1
Harper	115	-6.2	33 917	1 185	45	13	31	25	24	10	11	2	1
Haskell	350	-2.2	28 272	2 353	139	20	44	116	114	36	51	11	4
Hughes	336	1.9	24 318	2 933	117	25	49	122	120	38	54	11	4
Jackson	809	-1.3	31 872	1 559	591	33	113	196	192	51	87	22	5
Jefferson	161	-1.1	25 455	2 811	48	15	26	59	58	19	28	5	2
Johnston	272	0.0	26 019	2 725	116	9	28	101	99	30	42	10	3
Kay	1 656	-4.7	35 915	900	954	234	316	373	365	140	142	36	13
Kingfisher	517	-8.5	35 924	898	280	41	106	93	90	36	39	6	3

1. Based on the resident population estimated as of July 1 of the year shown.　　2. Includes supplements to wages and salaries.

Table B. States and Counties — Earnings, Social Security, and Housing

STATE County	Earnings, 2009									Social Security beneficiaries, December 2010			Housing units, 2010	
					Percent by selected industries									
			Goods-related[1]		Service-related and health									
	Total (mil dol)	Farm	Total	Manu-facturing	Infor-mation and profes-sional and technical services	Retail trade	Finance, insur-ance, and real estate	Health care and social services	Govern-ment	Number	Rate[2]	Supple-mental Security Income recipients, December 2010	Total	Percent change, 2000–2010
	75	76	77	78	79	80	81	82	83	84	85	86	87	88
OHIO—Cont'd														
Ottawa	739	2.1	D	18.2	D	6.6	4.7	9.0	17.7	10 095	244	466	27 909	9.3
Paulding	246	17.5	D	22.3	2.3	5.4	3.4	D	21.9	4 170	213	346	8 749	3.2
Perry	295	1.4	35.4	12.3	2.7	5.6	3.1	D	28.7	7 325	203	1 199	15 211	11.4
Pickaway	803	6.5	D	20.9	D	6.3	3.1	9.5	30.0	10 115	182	1 216	21 275	14.4
Pike	550	0.5	D	34.6	D	5.3	2.6	8.2	16.3	6 245	218	1 847	12 481	7.6
Portage	2 773	0.3	27.9	22.3	4.3	6.3	3.5	5.9	29.6	27 065	168	2 284	67 472	12.3
Preble	506	6.8	39.6	35.4	2.0	6.8	3.4	D	18.1	8 540	202	671	17 888	4.1
Putnam	537	9.1	D	29.8	4.1	6.2	4.2	6.6	15.4	6 225	180	307	13 731	7.7
Richland	2 490	0.5	29.0	24.6	5.1	8.0	3.5	15.3	18.9	27 050	217	3 017	54 599	2.9
Ross	1 435	2.1	19.9	17.3	3.3	7.6	3.1	18.1	30.2	14 990	192	2 730	32 148	9.1
Sandusky	1 203	2.3	43.3	39.1	2.5	6.9	3.7	D	13.7	12 365	203	1 095	26 390	4.5
Scioto	1 148	0.8	12.9	8.9	4.5	7.8	3.6	25.1	28.1	16 345	206	5 335	34 142	0.3
Seneca	933	2.4	31.7	24.5	3.3	7.1	D	10.4	16.6	11 600	204	956	24 122	1.8
Shelby	1 492	2.7	D	50.7	2.7	3.9	2.3	D	9.8	8 815	178	751	20 173	8.0
Stark	7 911	0.2	D	19.8	5.5	7.9	6.4	17.9	13.5	79 605	212	8 350	165 215	5.2
Summit	14 902	0.0	19.1	14.3	9.3	6.6	5.3	14.8	13.2	100 665	186	12 760	245 109	6.2
Trumbull	3 555	0.2	29.9	25.6	3.7	8.4	4.4	16.1	15.7	50 410	240	5 788	96 163	1.1
Tuscarawas	1 520	0.8	32.0	23.1	4.2	8.3	4.1	12.9	16.2	19 315	209	1 878	40 206	5.5
Union	1 887	0.8	D	49.9	12.3	3.3	1.7	3.2	9.9	6 840	131	448	19 429	27.7
Van Wert	614	8.3	D	27.6	1.8	6.5	11.4	13.3	14.4	6 170	215	455	12 615	2.0
Vinton	106	1.0	D	21.3	D	4.2	5.4	7.2	34.0	2 550	190	592	6 291	11.3
Warren	4 162	0.4	21.8	17.7	10.0	7.9	9.8	6.7	13.4	30 290	142	1 799	80 750	37.4
Washington	1 288	0.3	31.8	21.8	4.3	6.8	4.9	16.3	12.6	14 435	234	1 784	28 367	2.2
Wayne	2 250	1.5	38.8	30.7	4.8	5.9	4.6	D	16.2	20 865	182	1 679	45 847	8.4
Williams	780	3.9	43.3	39.5	D	5.9	3.3	12.2	14.0	7 815	208	541	16 668	3.3
Wood	3 200	1.5	33.7	28.2	4.1	5.3	3.4	7.6	20.9	19 685	157	1 317	53 376	12.4
Wyandot	424	12.5	41.3	29.3	D	6.3	3.7	D	15.6	4 625	205	266	9 870	5.9
OKLAHOMA	93 233	0.1	25.6	11.7	7.9	6.2	5.2	9.9	22.8	705 364	188	93 855	1 664 378	9.9
Adair	245	2.1	D	29.3	2.0	7.1	2.6	7.8	30.6	4 730	209	972	9 142	9.5
Alfalfa	66	1.1	D	D	D	7.4	D	6.0	32.3	1 330	236	73	2 763	-2.4
Atoka	180	-1.5	D	5.0	4.9	10.5	4.0	D	38.8	3 560	251	645	6 312	11.3
Beaver	93	13.8	D	D	D	3.1	D	0.8	25.3	1 055	187	53	2 670	-1.8
Beckham	493	-2.3	35.6	5.9	D	9.2	7.5	D	11.1	3 875	175	607	9 647	9.7
Blaine	161	1.0	23.2	14.2	D	4.5	5.4	5.1	25.0	2 290	192	290	5 193	-0.3
Bryan	730	0.9	D	7.4	4.0	5.5	4.3	12.0	42.0	8 775	207	1 505	19 586	17.2
Caddo	360	-0.6	9.1	0.9	D	7.8	3.9	D	40.1	6 240	211	970	13 141	0.4
Canadian	1 437	-0.7	29.3	12.6	6.8	7.8	4.6	5.5	25.6	17 020	147	1 169	45 810	34.9
Carter	1 233	-0.4	36.7	17.9	4.7	6.2	4.4	12.5	13.9	10 845	228	1 547	21 148	2.8
Cherokee	763	6.0	4.7	1.0	2.2	6.1	3.4	6.2	55.6	9 095	194	1 542	21 455	10.0
Choctaw	206	-4.1	D	6.5	3.8	8.2	3.4	11.0	34.4	3 980	262	923	7 521	-0.2
Cimarron	49	36.6	D	D	D	7.8	4.3	0.7	24.4	665	269	35	1 587	0.3
Cleveland	3 893	0.1	12.9	4.6	9.6	8.3	4.9	9.9	34.0	36 445	142	3 170	104 821	23.5
Coal	50	-3.4	15.2	2.4	D	8.5	6.0	13.2	38.9	1 270	214	231	2 810	2.4
Comanche	3 357	-0.2	D	7.7	D	5.0	3.3	5.1	60.5	18 040	145	3 002	50 739	11.7
Cotton	74	-10.7	D	D	D	3.7	4.3	4.2	72.5	1 410	228	154	3 016	-2.2
Craig	298	-1.6	D	8.0	D	7.1	5.8	D	35.8	3 810	254	597	6 749	4.5
Creek	934	-0.3	37.7	21.2	3.6	7.0	3.7	7.9	17.4	15 330	219	1 674	29 761	6.3
Custer	554	-1.7	27.3	11.4	4.5	8.9	5.2	D	25.2	4 685	171	565	12 204	4.5
Delaware	409	0.7	17.0	8.5	4.4	9.0	4.1	D	32.4	10 185	245	1 189	24 818	11.3
Dewey	63	-13.1	D	6.4	10.5	8.8	6.1	2.1	32.6	1 175	244	73	2 445	0.8
Ellis	57	-4.6	10.5	0.8	D	6.1	D	8.7	34.9	940	226	44	2 285	6.5
Garfield	1 449	-0.4	22.6	10.1	7.9	6.7	4.5	13.2	24.1	12 370	204	1 386	26 831	3.0
Garvin	514	-0.3	36.8	14.2	3.7	12.3	2.9	6.9	20.8	6 705	243	858	12 827	1.5
Grady	621	0.5	28.1	11.5	4.1	8.8	5.6	7.9	23.0	9 920	189	1 307	22 219	14.3
Grant	75	6.4	15.9	0.6	D	2.5	9.3	3.2	21.6	1 170	258	56	2 486	-5.2
Greer	66	7.4	D	D	D	6.0	D	11.6	57.6	1 475	236	219	2 738	-1.8
Harmon	38	13.5	D	D	D	5.4	D	1.8	38.8	690	236	151	1 544	-6.3
Harper	58	14.7	D	D	D	5.4	D	D	32.1	820	223	37	1 908	2.4
Haskell	159	1.1	20.2	2.6	3.4	8.4	D	22.2	25.7	3 255	255	537	6 028	8.2
Hughes	142	3.3	16.4	7.0	3.1	6.9	D	8.9	30.8	3 445	246	475	6 183	-0.9
Jackson	623	0.9	D	6.8	D	6.6	2.7	3.7	59.8	4 515	171	775	12 077	-2.4
Jefferson	64	6.5	D	2.6	D	7.9	12.6	D	32.7	1 665	257	216	3 378	0.1
Johnston	125	-3.5	24.8	11.7	D	5.3	D	14.3	35.3	2 665	243	467	5 126	7.2
Kay	1 188	0.4	41.3	10.4	6.8	5.6	3.1	7.2	17.9	11 100	238	1 093	21 708	-0.4
Kingfisher	320	-1.8	40.7	15.3	D	7.3	3.1	D	12.6	2 945	196	175	6 409	9.0

1. Includes mining, construction, and manufacturing.   2. Per 1,000 resident population enumerated in the 2010 census.

Items 75—88

Table B. States and Counties — Housing, Labor Force, and Employment

STATE County	Housing units, 2006–2010 Occupied units Owner-occupied Total	Percent	Median value[1]	Median owner cost as a percent of income With a mortgage	Without a mortgage	Renter-occupied Median rent[2]	Median rent as a percent of income	Substandard units[3] (percent)	Civilian labor force, 2010 Total	Percent change, 2009–2010	Unemployment Total	Rate[4]	Civilian employment,[5] 2006–2010 Total	Percent Management, business, science and arts	Construction, production, and maintenance occupations
	89	90	91	92	93	94	95	96	97	98	99	100	101	102	103
OHIO—Cont'd															
Ottawa	17 933	82.1	142 200	22.9	12.7	687	30.8	0.8	20 815	-3.3	2 913	14.0	19 990	30.6	29.4
Paulding	7 661	81.5	89 600	21.2	10.9	534	28.1	2.8	10 281	-2.5	1 178	11.5	9 022	23.2	43.3
Perry	13 554	73.9	100 400	23.2	11.7	549	30.6	3.7	16 795	-0.4	2 151	12.8	15 143	24.1	38.6
Pickaway	19 045	74.6	144 800	24.8	12.8	702	28.1	1.5	24 788	-1.9	2 733	11.0	22 878	28.5	29.0
Pike	10 643	70.8	96 400	23.0	13.8	615	35.6	2.5	11 112	-0.6	1 654	14.9	10 063	27.2	32.7
Portage	61 819	69.1	157 100	23.9	13.6	748	31.7	1.1	91 292	-1.2	8 914	9.8	80 859	30.6	25.7
Preble	16 392	78.7	123 500	23.4	12.7	684	26.6	1.2	21 056	-3.0	2 302	10.9	20 272	25.1	34.9
Putnam	12 891	83.8	130 200	20.2	10.0	598	23.2	1.7	18 098	-2.0	1 751	9.7	17 696	30.0	36.2
Richland	48 557	71.2	112 200	22.4	12.2	587	27.3	1.6	60 490	-3.3	7 112	11.8	54 432	27.2	31.7
Ross	28 107	73.3	111 800	22.1	12.0	616	30.7	1.8	35 096	-0.2	4 049	11.5	30 747	28.9	29.1
Sandusky	24 109	75.7	116 300	22.3	11.7	568	27.2	1.2	33 573	0.4	3 461	10.3	29 616	24.7	39.2
Scioto	30 162	69.5	85 000	22.4	12.6	520	33.1	2.0	32 971	-0.4	4 207	12.8	28 557	29.6	27.1
Seneca	22 138	75.1	101 100	21.5	12.1	577	25.8	1.2	29 623	-3.8	3 426	11.6	26 976	25.7	36.2
Shelby	18 488	75.3	124 500	22.1	12.4	659	29.6	1.8	25 590	-4.1	3 021	11.8	23 679	25.0	38.2
Stark	150 921	71.0	128 000	22.9	12.7	622	28.7	1.2	189 062	-1.6	21 310	11.3	175 433	30.7	25.0
Summit	223 122	69.5	141 200	23.6	14.1	719	30.1	1.2	291 140	-1.8	28 913	9.9	261 590	36.3	20.9
Trumbull	86 463	74.6	102 500	23.2	13.5	582	29.3	1.4	104 779	-2.3	12 337	11.8	89 975	26.4	30.3
Tuscarawas	36 128	74.7	110 900	22.0	12.2	590	28.0	1.4	47 381	-0.2	4 996	10.5	42 187	26.7	34.2
Union	17 826	77.5	174 800	23.5	12.5	762	25.6	1.0	25 904	-1.2	2 164	8.4	24 038	35.4	26.8
Van Wert	11 472	82.8	88 100	21.5	11.0	551	25.3	0.6	14 627	-4.9	1 763	12.1	14 086	23.1	37.1
Vinton	5 349	76.3	87 300	24.6	14.2	535	41.7	4.4	5 734	0.1	746	13.0	5 109	26.5	38.6
Warren	74 144	79.9	194 700	23.2	12.6	890	27.2	1.0	108 294	-0.9	9 692	8.9	100 759	42.1	18.9
Washington	25 373	74.7	110 800	20.8	11.0	554	30.3	1.4	32 312	-3.6	2 942	9.1	27 272	28.4	27.8
Wayne	42 395	75.7	136 800	22.9	11.6	626	26.9	2.6	57 781	-1.1	5 413	9.4	55 125	28.7	32.1
Williams	14 953	76.7	101 900	22.0	12.4	587	27.7	1.4	19 725	-2.4	2 540	12.9	17 672	24.3	39.4
Wood	48 636	69.2	154 600	22.6	13.1	660	27.8	1.2	65 012	-4.8	6 570	10.1	62 776	35.0	24.4
Wyandot	9 169	74.8	107 500	22.0	10.8	559	24.4	0.7	11 172	-0.6	1 314	11.8	11 394	24.5	41.0
OKLAHOMA	1 421 705	68.2	104 300	21.2	11.0	633	28.3	2.9	1 771 234	1.1	122 412	6.9	1 674 765	31.9	25.6
Adair	7 919	71.8	74 100	23.4	10.8	467	28.6	3.3	10 920	-3.0	931	8.5	8 287	24.2	41.1
Alfalfa	2 032	80.6	50 100	16.3	10.0	591	24.3	1.0	2 438	-4.4	136	5.6	2 240	35.8	23.6
Atoka	5 272	76.5	68 300	22.0	11.6	496	26.7	3.5	6 166	-2.0	544	8.8	4 736	32.6	30.1
Beaver	2 213	72.8	66 800	20.2	10.0	551	16.5	3.5	3 243	-3.5	116	3.6	2 818	27.5	37.5
Beckham	7 778	65.1	86 100	19.7	10.0	620	21.3	3.2	11 754	-4.5	626	5.3	9 868	25.2	36.2
Blaine	4 079	73.8	67 900	17.3	12.3	493	23.5	3.8	4 780	-5.1	375	7.8	5 031	24.8	28.6
Bryan	16 060	66.5	85 700	21.4	12.1	582	25.1	3.9	21 036	2.5	1 148	5.5	17 624	28.2	27.9
Caddo	10 410	71.6	64 100	18.4	11.4	491	24.2	5.0	12 980	0.8	882	6.8	10 722	27.7	30.0
Canadian	40 119	77.8	131 600	20.9	10.5	758	26.0	1.5	53 072	0.3	3 127	5.9	54 091	35.7	20.7
Carter	17 648	70.8	88 500	20.5	10.3	563	24.9	2.8	27 822	2.4	1 548	5.6	20 592	25.8	29.5
Cherokee	16 655	66.5	97 100	22.7	10.2	498	27.2	3.8	25 098	1.9	1 519	6.1	17 873	32.8	26.2
Choctaw	6 145	68.1	68 300	21.7	10.4	482	27.5	3.5	7 327	0.9	573	7.8	5 584	25.8	33.5
Cimarron	1 117	76.7	56 400	21.1	10.0	506	23.7	2.7	1 289	-0.4	53	4.1	1 192	32.7	32.6
Cleveland	93 179	68.4	131 800	21.5	10.6	725	29.5	2.3	120 024	-0.6	7 197	6.0	123 556	38.1	18.3
Coal	2 327	70.9	63 100	21.2	10.8	424	25.3	1.8	2 625	-0.9	214	8.2	2 083	21.7	43.5
Comanche	43 757	58.8	99 900	21.1	10.3	660	27.3	3.3	48 413	1.2	3 105	6.4	46 502	30.3	24.4
Cotton	2 442	73.0	72 100	20.0	11.1	533	19.6	3.5	3 704	8.5	208	5.6	2 738	35.8	29.2
Craig	5 682	78.8	87 000	21.7	11.5	551	21.3	1.6	7 248	-4.6	459	6.3	6 528	29.2	27.4
Creek	26 633	74.9	100 600	21.4	11.8	621	25.9	3.4	30 876	-2.3	2 729	8.8	30 481	26.9	30.5
Custer	10 391	65.0	90 000	18.8	10.4	565	27.8	4.7	15 123	-2.2	751	5.0	13 414	30.8	30.1
Delaware	16 070	76.6	92 400	22.9	12.3	535	26.2	4.9	19 382	-1.1	1 398	7.2	15 818	26.1	33.3
Dewey	1 802	82.0	73 200	18.1	12.5	554	28.5	3.1	2 703	-2.4	116	4.3	1 949	35.7	28.5
Ellis	1 688	81.3	66 800	15.7	12.5	450	20.1	2.1	2 421	-3.4	108	4.5	2 011	31.8	33.0
Garfield	23 694	67.5	82 100	19.7	10.2	594	25.0	2.8	32 533	1.8	1 609	4.9	27 530	27.6	30.4
Garvin	10 092	75.2	74 400	19.4	11.8	546	23.2	2.1	14 646	-4.3	937	6.4	11 951	23.7	35.0
Grady	19 391	77.4	104 100	21.1	11.1	581	25.3	2.5	22 952	-2.3	1 601	7.0	23 669	30.4	31.3
Grant	1 885	77.5	60 900	19.6	10.0	500	16.2	0.9	2 654	-1.7	115	4.3	2 175	30.7	27.8
Greer	2 094	69.5	57 800	19.7	11.5	418	26.4	1.3	2 024	-3.8	177	8.7	1 822	34.7	13.7
Harmon	1 128	73.6	44 400	20.2	14.4	494	35.6	5.9	1 358	-1.8	78	5.7	1 260	29.4	30.2
Harper	1 537	79.4	65 700	16.6	10.3	476	21.6	1.1	1 938	-7.2	81	4.2	1 752	31.5	35.5
Haskell	4 640	76.7	72 200	19.8	10.5	493	26.4	2.3	6 039	-3.1	475	7.9	4 524	29.1	36.8
Hughes	5 159	77.9	65 700	19.6	12.0	527	24.8	2.3	5 710	-2.0	625	10.9	4 728	30.2	34.5
Jackson	10 384	62.1	85 100	18.7	10.9	608	26.7	3.2	12 262	-0.3	683	5.6	11 369	29.6	27.5
Jefferson	2 488	77.9	56 100	24.0	13.0	399	24.4	2.9	2 501	-1.2	205	8.2	2 538	22.9	31.7
Johnston	4 261	74.0	64 900	20.7	11.0	505	21.0	3.5	4 971	-4.9	384	7.7	3 668	35.6	33.7
Kay	18 397	71.3	74 700	19.3	11.9	578	26.4	3.3	22 727	-4.7	1 972	8.7	20 282	28.6	29.3
Kingfisher	5 439	77.6	101 800	19.5	10.4	644	24.9	2.4	7 564	-3.5	374	4.9	7 446	30.8	32.6

1. Specified owner-occupied units. 2. Specified renter-occupied units. A value of 10.0 represents 10 percent or less. 3. Overcrowded or lacking complete plumbing facilities. 4. Percent of civilian labor force. 5. Persons 16 years old and over.

Table B. States and Counties — Nonfarm Employment and Agriculture

	Private nonfarm establishments, employment and payroll, 2009									Agriculture, 2007			
		Employment						Annual payroll		Farms			
												Percent with:	
STATE County	Number of establishments	Total	Health care and social assistance	Manufacturing	Retail trade	Finance and insurance	Professional, scientific, and technical services	Total (mil dol)	Average per employee (dollars)	Number	Fewer than 50 acres	500 acres or more	Farm operators whose principal occupation is farming (percent)
	104	105	106	107	108	109	110	111	112	113	114	115	116
OHIO—Cont'd													
Ottawa	1 014	9 812	1 680	2 003	1 440	316	200	371	37 807	589	43.5	10.5	46.2
Paulding	301	3 606	669	1 090	426	96	55	96	26 664	754	32.5	19.4	46.9
Perry	426	3 881	758	819	553	185	D	104	26 745	643	36.2	4.0	37.5
Pickaway	806	10 565	2 327	2 162	1 573	311	195	346	32 750	832	44.6	18.5	48.1
Pike	439	6 639	1 527	1 736	891	201	171	250	37 631	538	28.6	3.3	36.8
Portage	2 970	41 425	5 451	9 500	7 053	820	1 168	1 366	32 969	862	59.0	3.0	41.3
Preble	652	8 429	1 093	3 025	1 439	293	222	265	31 483	1 181	46.0	11.5	46.2
Putnam	722	9 367	986	2 864	1 178	232	226	263	28 063	1 316	29.0	12.9	40.1
Richland	2 798	43 964	7 917	9 176	6 576	1 124	1 032	1 333	30 313	1 009	43.0	4.5	41.8
Ross	1 287	20 715	5 581	3 331	3 695	522	387	757	36 521	1 009	37.0	9.9	43.4
Sandusky	1 353	22 360	3 283	8 563	2 607	519	486	715	31 975	781	42.8	13.8	45.1
Scioto	1 340	17 961	6 498	1 578	3 093	525	568	518	28 838	755	39.3	4.8	38.3
Seneca	1 187	17 684	3 171	4 596	2 058	452	391	503	28 418	1 147	32.2	13.2	40.4
Shelby	1 009	21 985	1 935	10 359	1 917	398	367	891	40 522	1 050	34.5	11.4	39.1
Stark	8 544	136 726	27 576	23 510	20 729	6 224	4 450	4 314	31 553	1 300	56.8	3.5	47.2
Summit	13 886	235 718	42 927	28 068	29 251	9 153	16 005	9 597	40 713	334	74.3	1.2	42.5
Trumbull	4 346	71 852	13 317	13 634	9 793	1 936	1 314	2 308	32 126	970	44.4	5.1	47.3
Tuscarawas	2 208	30 272	5 106	7 835	4 545	754	895	851	28 108	983	40.3	5.5	43.5
Union	1 025	22 692	1 650	6 954	2 092	261	D	1 122	49 434	932	45.6	11.4	45.9
Van Wert	569	9 261	1 742	3 026	1 188	D	177	284	30 694	696	26.1	25.4	48.9
Vinton	138	1 629	287	D	214	D	15	60	36 983	250	27.2	2.8	32.4
Warren	3 930	72 061	6 771	11 219	9 052	7 101	3 682	2 936	40 743	896	65.6	3.9	40.0
Washington	1 464	21 567	4 508	3 677	2 844	768	612	725	33 599	856	23.7	3.9	42.2
Wayne	2 448	36 687	5 404	10 480	4 956	1 218	1 020	1 221	33 279	1 788	45.6	5.5	52.1
Williams	829	13 783	1 908	6 187	1 443	322	218	419	30 415	1 116	39.2	9.9	34.5
Wood	2 784	47 613	4 768	9 729	6 363	946	2 579	1 710	35 914	1 169	43.4	14.3	41.1
Wyandot	524	6 496	764	2 069	817	254	121	209	32 161	632	35.6	21.7	48.4
OKLAHOMA	90 347	1 290 278	206 966	134 603	173 845	62 339	64 443	45 238	35 061	86 565	26.0	17.6	41.6
Adair	227	3 023	481	1 072	528	129	44	76	25 024	1 202	27.5	9.0	43.8
Alfalfa	135	771	D	D	153	72	D	18	23 418	695	8.6	42.4	52.9
Atoka	254	2 240	420	168	540	D	D	48	21 651	1 218	18.4	16.7	47.5
Beaver	169	1 185	D	D	93	61	D	37	31 589	952	6.8	37.2	35.0
Beckham	816	9 172	1 307	D	1 668	305	343	311	33 936	1 053	16.8	23.3	32.1
Blaine	308	2 497	866	D	275	153	73	69	27 462	862	11.5	34.0	47.7
Bryan	751	9 764	2 066	1 086	1 478	527	350	258	26 391	1 701	23.5	11.9	43.6
Caddo	475	4 679	790	50	803	203	288	136	29 005	1 584	12.7	26.5	44.4
Canadian	2 247	22 495	2 813	2 757	3 754	816	644	696	30 923	1 447	31.6	19.8	45.2
Carter	1 485	20 055	3 557	2 913	3 325	694	435	663	33 036	1 426	29.8	11.4	33.2
Cherokee	740	9 100	2 361	208	1 665	341	137	218	23 903	1 375	35.7	6.9	42.0
Choctaw	257	3 358	946	D	502	115	D	79	23 492	1 134	18.6	14.1	45.8
Cimarron	68	373	D	0	111	38	10	7	20 094	557	3.2	50.3	44.0
Cleveland	5 272	65 425	11 449	3 065	10 721	2 212	3 023	2 014	30 786	1 327	54.4	4.6	35.9
Coal	80	770	236	D	148	D	D	17	22 326	634	13.6	21.3	44.5
Comanche	2 218	32 225	6 223	3 354	5 326	2 178	1 353	962	29 852	1 126	24.5	21.0	42.6
Cotton	84	1 390	112	D	108	39	D	39	27 942	517	10.8	34.8	46.8
Craig	348	4 300	1 289	574	653	D	D	124	28 817	1 359	25.2	12.7	44.3
Creek	1 430	15 673	2 008	4 007	2 065	498	306	504	32 132	1 900	41.4	7.6	32.4
Custer	880	9 827	1 595	D	1 812	346	D	282	28 707	907	19.3	30.7	45.8
Delaware	725	7 070	1 282	714	1 341	280	D	181	25 565	1 509	30.0	9.3	46.3
Dewey	133	851	D	D	233	68	67	24	28 052	756	6.5	35.7	43.8
Ellis	114	851	178	D	159	47	D	27	32 148	766	5.6	38.5	38.0
Garfield	1 694	22 749	4 332	2 426	3 566	784	1 208	711	31 254	1 082	20.1	31.1	45.7
Garvin	673	7 957	1 131	923	1 261	257	151	249	31 330	1 666	25.3	14.8	41.1
Grady	1 051	10 711	1 801	1 592	1 621	404	258	295	27 561	1 850	28.1	16.9	44.4
Grant	103	805	74	D	D	65	19	31	38 298	847	7.7	37.3	51.5
Greer	80	622	189	D	D	D	D	14	22 531	571	6.5	28.4	38.7
Harmon	59	463	127	D	D	D	6	11	22 920	400	5.5	40.3	43.0
Harper	105	665	121	D	125	D	35	16	24 660	580	6.9	42.8	39.1
Haskell	233	2 925	990	D	508	66	51	69	23 705	914	18.8	16.0	44.2
Hughes	232	2 529	828	D	436	74	42	54	21 524	1 026	15.8	18.6	45.8
Jackson	531	7 296	D	D	1 452	284	641	193	26 486	745	22.4	32.3	43.0
Jefferson	111	757	79	39	157	81	24	16	21 431	514	12.5	37.4	46.9
Johnston	175	1 810	569	D	221	D	D	46	25 503	706	19.5	16.9	46.9
Kay	1 161	16 336	2 249	3 390	2 441	494	517	516	31 563	1 050	25.7	24.3	46.5
Kingfisher	481	5 231	543	448	641	214	197	175	33 427	1 002	12.8	31.7	48.6

Table B. States and Counties — **Agriculture**

STATE County	Land in farms — Acreage (1,000)	Percent change, 2002–2007	Acres — Average size of farm	Acres — Total irrigated (1,000)	Acres — Total cropland (1,000)	Value of land and buildings (dollars) — Average per farm	Average per acre	Value of machinery and equipment, average per farm (dollars)	Value of products sold — Total (mil dol)	Average per farm (dollars)	Percent from: Crops	Percent from: Live-stock and poultry products	Percent of farms with sales of: $10,000 or more	$100,000 or more	Government payments — Total ($1,000)	Percent of farms
	117	118	119	120	121	122	123	124	125	126	127	128	129	130	131	132
OHIO—Cont'd																
Ottawa	115	0.9	195	0.2	107.1	565 167	2 891	100 476	46.1	78 309	95.1	4.9	56.9	19.2	1 855	78.3
Paulding	256	7.6	339	D	236.6	1 077 646	3 179	133 146	149.0	197 588	54.5	45.5	54.9	24.5	6 257	88.9
Perry	98	6.5	152	0.0	58.5	437 701	2 873	58 127	25.4	39 472	65.5	34.5	27.8	6.2	953	26.7
Pickaway	289	5.1	347	0.8	257.1	1 195 810	3 444	136 102	112.1	134 701	87.8	12.2	45.9	23.8	6 366	64.2
Pike	81	-3.6	150	0.1	38.1	377 217	2 517	56 922	11.3	20 936	69.0	31.0	22.1	4.1	931	43.3
Portage	83	-14.4	96	0.4	57.5	445 918	4 645	65 977	34.0	39 474	68.8	31.2	31.6	7.1	815	20.3
Preble	231	16.7	195	0.2	204.0	709 890	3 635	91 753	109.5	92 739	64.5	35.5	49.7	20.2	4 542	57.4
Putnam	304	-8.4	231	0.5	283.6	804 912	3 487	120 551	146.8	111 517	64.9	35.1	72.8	26.1	5 430	88.4
Richland	147	-7.5	145	0.1	110.2	525 268	3 616	77 684	72.8	72 127	52.6	47.4	41.8	18.3	1 934	41.3
Ross	224	-9.3	222	D	152.6	630 849	2 846	71 947	51.2	50 741	83.5	16.5	29.9	10.3	5 917	55.8
Sandusky	181	-7.7	232	0.5	167.2	717 040	3 088	102 521	79.3	101 533	93.5	6.5	61.8	23.8	3 085	72.6
Scioto	102	6.3	135	0.0	52.3	356 531	2 638	61 696	19.9	26 407	50.4	49.6	22.3	4.0	1 067	27.8
Seneca	269	-3.9	235	0.6	241.7	733 642	3 124	100 325	107.4	93 644	79.0	21.0	61.6	21.4	4 893	81.3
Shelby	218	5.3	208	0.0	192.8	851 633	4 102	110 152	130.5	124 256	52.2	47.8	63.0	27.1	5 430	79.7
Stark	138	-4.8	106	0.8	104.6	505 443	4 759	87 944	135.7	104 363	27.5	72.5	40.9	12.5	1 556	30.0
Summit	15	-28.6	45	0.3	9.8	360 672	7 943	53 977	9.6	28 625	82.9	17.1	35.6	4.8	73	8.1
Trumbull	125	-0.8	129	0.2	87.4	423 502	3 283	74 449	41.6	42 847	63.7	36.3	40.0	9.7	1 128	35.5
Tuscarawas	143	-10.6	145	0.2	81.8	506 516	3 491	70 867	77.0	78 371	20.3	79.7	36.1	14.1	1 151	29.6
Union	219	-14.5	235	0.2	197.9	784 476	3 344	118 940	96.0	103 029	82.7	17.3	49.1	20.9	4 628	65.3
Van Wert	246	-1.6	354	D	235.9	1 268 533	3 582	148 603	110.1	158 160	77.9	22.1	74.4	37.9	5 778	87.2
Vinton	37	-15.9	147	D	14.6	400 253	2 718	43 631	4.0	15 998	82.1	17.9	15.6	1.6	188	30.0
Warren	94	-25.4	105	0.3	72.0	561 696	5 334	62 901	44.2	49 379	89.0	11.0	29.5	6.6	1 095	27.0
Washington	124	-12.1	145	0.2	50.3	371 930	2 566	64 401	24.5	28 590	41.7	58.3	30.5	5.5	572	24.8
Wayne	248	-7.1	139	0.7	192.9	695 790	5 008	99 331	247.3	138 287	23.4	76.6	58.8	25.3	2 999	36.9
Williams	213	0.0	190	0.5	179.1	583 687	3 065	76 702	102.5	91 867	53.5	46.5	36.4	13.7	5 601	80.1
Wood	276	-9.8	236	0.5	259.7	791 826	3 359	112 384	125.4	107 309	86.9	13.1	58.3	21.7	5 160	80.6
Wyandot	220	9.5	348	D	202.0	1 086 393	3 126	144 224	134.9	213 516	54.7	45.3	57.9	30.1	4 417	81.5
OKLAHOMA	35 087	4.2	405	534.8	13 007.6	468 809	1 157	63 642	5 806.1	67 072	20.5	79.5	37.1	8.3	209 465	31.2
Adair	249	4.6	207	0.7	66.8	397 171	1 915	58 705	132.8	110 494	1.9	98.1	36.5	9.4	271	12.5
Alfalfa	543	17.8	781	2.6	358.6	724 520	928	131 468	85.0	122 269	25.4	74.6	61.0	23.6	8 538	81.7
Atoka	408	-17.1	335	0.7	90.8	413 406	1 233	51 851	27.1	22 278	6.6	93.4	38.4	4.5	339	10.8
Beaver	1 129	10.8	1 186	28.5	394.9	747 293	630	94 719	188.5	197 965	19.2	80.8	37.8	15.4	6 993	78.0
Beckham	520	-2.4	493	6.9	187.7	488 747	991	66 942	37.8	35 880	34.5	65.5	37.1	7.2	6 603	63.7
Blaine	586	9.1	680	5.8	286.0	568 359	836	94 624	126.6	146 811	19.8	80.2	57.9	18.0	4 497	68.8
Bryan	491	7.2	288	9.5	167.3	460 275	1 596	55 546	64.2	37 766	24.5	75.5	37.4	5.4	1 208	20.8
Caddo	750	5.5	473	33.2	328.9	516 439	1 091	77 205	102.3	64 571	29.1	70.9	51.8	12.5	9 089	62.4
Canadian	509	1.6	352	4.0	278.8	527 395	1 500	83 751	101.1	69 866	26.8	73.2	45.3	13.0	3 952	44.7
Carter	403	-6.5	282	1.3	96.7	397 835	1 408	46 679	30.9	21 657	11.9	88.1	26.4	3.4	415	10.1
Cherokee	246	11.3	179	1.0	67.3	333 829	1 863	52 880	129.8	94 411	77.1	22.9	30.5	4.3	291	9.2
Choctaw	326	-3.3	288	0.5	83.8	386 496	1 343	53 475	37.9	33 414	11.1	88.9	41.4	4.6	476	16.8
Cimarron	1 045	-6.9	1 875	45.5	413.4	939 651	501	106 426	261.9	470 144	17.9	82.1	46.1	28.0	7 176	83.5
Cleveland	160	-3.0	120	1.1	47.0	289 499	2 404	40 609	15.8	11 873	25.6	74.4	20.4	1.7	390	8.5
Coal	269	2.3	425	0.5	64.2	529 119	1 245	55 875	20.2	31 937	13.5	86.6	43.4	6.8	271	13.6
Comanche	498	17.2	442	1.4	160.7	506 837	1 147	52 948	38.8	34 484	22.7	77.3	36.7	6.0	3 169	40.0
Cotton	367	9.9	709	0.3	196.6	689 734	973	87 679	59.5	115 141	21.5	78.5	52.8	20.7	3 928	74.7
Craig	457	4.8	336	D	133.4	442 031	1 314	56 906	77.5	57 029	9.3	90.7	44.1	8.0	843	19.6
Creek	377	3.0	199	0.3	102.0	315 908	1 590	39 155	19.6	10 303	17.3	82.7	20.6	1.2	136	6.1
Custer	569	4.4	627	4.1	264.5	670 954	1 070	105 101	87.0	95 879	32.6	67.4	53.3	16.2	5 034	68.2
Delaware	309	9.6	205	0.6	93.8	424 988	2 076	50 445	171.1	113 358	2.7	97.3	46.0	13.2	747	13.9
Dewey	589	0.9	779	3.1	173.7	655 115	841	73 903	31.3	41 375	35.0	64.9	48.8	10.1	3 740	69.3
Ellis	718	6.7	937	12.8	167.1	679 751	725	58 832	66.9	87 392	10.1	89.9	42.8	14.5	4 059	70.9
Garfield	663	4.9	613	5.4	443.2	623 900	1 018	98 441	76.2	70 421	38.4	61.6	48.6	15.2	8 754	67.0
Garvin	501	6.8	301	0.8	137.3	399 830	1 330	62 489	42.2	25 330	22.2	77.8	33.5	5.6	1 465	23.5
Grady	608	1.0	329	8.5	208.2	424 959	1 292	64 241	139.2	75 245	11.9	88.1	39.0	8.0	3 296	32.8
Grant	633	6.4	747	1.5	455.1	664 232	889	103 528	48.8	57 590	50.0	50.0	47.9	12.9	7 564	84.9
Greer	375	15.4	658	3.4	146.9	471 410	717	67 968	23.7	41 509	51.1	48.9	42.0	10.0	6 470	80.9
Harmon	322	8.8	806	17.8	152.2	689 885	856	93 830	45.4	113 572	36.1	63.9	46.5	22.0	4 864	81.8
Harper	617	2.7	1 064	6.2	203.4	740 525	696	80 949	122.7	211 622	8.5	91.5	41.0	14.5	4 194	70.2
Haskell	290	5.5	318	1.7	72.3	408 490	1 286	61 540	80.4	87 950	2.4	97.6	44.4	10.1	307	10.3
Hughes	441	17.9	430	2.2	106.7	506 521	1 178	56 718	76.7	74 765	4.4	95.6	36.6	5.0	1 199	28.2
Jackson	475	4.6	637	55.1	301.0	552 780	868	111 981	89.6	120 330	72.2	27.8	45.4	20.8	11 004	66.3
Jefferson	460	13.0	895	0.3	119.1	943 589	1 054	77 038	75.1	146 108	10.2	89.8	58.6	22.4	1 511	55.4
Johnston	334	2.5	473	0.7	57.8	576 144	1 218	52 811	20.3	28 688	9.1	90.9	38.0	6.2	325	18.6
Kay	492	2.5	469	3.6	323.0	484 835	1 034	84 095	50.8	48 354	59.6	40.4	42.2	12.0	5 661	65.1
Kingfisher	566	2.4	565	5.5	337.5	634 845	1 123	117 824	116.6	116 342	21.7	78.3	57.4	20.7	3 920	69.2

STATE County	Total water withdrawn (mil gal/day) 133	Gallons withdrawn per person 134	Number of establishments 135	Number of employees 136	Sales (mil dol) 137	Annual payroll (mil dol) 138	Number of establishments 139	Number of employees 140	Sales (mil dol) 141	Annual payroll (mil dol) 142	Number of establishments 143	Number of employees 144	Receipts (mil dol) 145	Annual payroll (mil dol) 146
OHIO—Cont'd														
Ottawa	46.4	1 115	27	156	71.8	5.3	168	1 623	461.2	40.9	56	175	15.6	4.2
Paulding	2.3	117	17	147	115.5	5.4	53	450	97.3	7.7	6	48	7.0	0.7
Perry	2.7	76	16	134	85.4	3.7	83	644	136.1	11.0	15	39	3.3	0.5
Pickaway	46.7	881	34	D	D	D	136	1 521	416.4	33.0	30	93	12.5	1.8
Pike	7.6	271	17	119	30.1	3.2	86	872	197.0	18.1	14	75	10.7	1.8
Portage	54.8	352	155	3 035	1 875.5	173.6	469	6 734	1 657.4	143.7	128	511	84.6	14.0
Preble	4.7	111	23	240	147.5	7.9	109	1 500	443.1	34.3	26	82	4.8	1.1
Putnam	5.3	152	33	244	172.3	8.5	111	1 225	252.3	22.4	11	33	2.6	0.8
Richland	16.3	128	127	2 113	1 010.6	76.7	497	7 387	1 489.5	145.8	108	571	59.2	12.3
Ross	38.6	514	47	456	226.6	17.5	260	3 640	831.2	73.4	54	165	26.6	3.6
Sandusky	12.9	209	50	D	D	D	220	2 801	598.0	58.8	35	166	13.9	2.6
Scioto	18.4	240	34	D	D	D	277	3 038	700.7	63.1	45	243	20.5	4.8
Seneca	7.3	126	55	D	D	D	184	2 086	458.8	46.8	36	114	9.9	1.8
Shelby	13.7	282	49	D	D	D	147	1 991	432.5	42.7	32	107	17.4	2.9
Stark	50.2	132	373	5 489	2 630.6	232.4	1 384	21 952	4 963.7	474.3	325	1 569	207.8	36.6
Summit	31.4	57	847	13 957	7 063.5	674.3	1 883	30 797	7 384.2	694.2	503	2 855	465.8	85.0
Trumbull	205.6	937	179	D	D	D	771	10 690	2 318.4	204.0	163	1 205	175.7	35.1
Tuscarawas	31.3	340	90	714	251.1	20.2	399	4 730	1 077.4	94.8	73	365	46.8	7.7
Union	10.8	236	67	925	1 881.7	43.8	129	2 022	479.1	49.9	46	148	26.0	4.4
Van Wert	4.9	168	28	229	127.0	9.4	101	1 234	242.8	25.0	13	128	10.5	1.5
Vinton	0.8	62	5	D	D	D	33	223	43.3	3.3	3	3	0.4	0.0
Warren	21.8	111	184	3 170	2 006.8	169.3	566	8 735	1 862.6	178.0	171	800	123.9	25.5
Washington	960.5	15 439	71	D	D	D	256	2 962	658.4	58.4	45	198	34.6	6.4
Wayne	16.5	145	124	D	D	D	409	5 123	1 110.2	109.3	82	279	48.0	7.5
Williams	5.1	131	41	461	229.2	14.7	143	1 575	333.9	29.6	30	97	18.2	2.7
Wood	12.4	100	177	2 923	1 505.1	126.0	434	6 632	1 522.5	125.5	118	657	135.0	21.6
Wyandot	5.6	247	28	295	210.6	9.9	71	922	190.2	15.8	14	37	4.3	1.1
OKLAHOMA	1 727.9	488	3 917	52 262	48 074.7	2 312.2	13 554	170 984	43 095.4	3 610.4	4 003	24 887	3 852.3	806.2
Adair	9.5	433	7	D	D	D	52	528	105.4	8.2	8	D	D	D
Alfalfa	6.7	1 171	10	53	23.3	1.5	25	145	33.3	2.4	2	D	D	D
Atoka	56.4	3 936	10	41	33.1	1.1	51	528	136.9	10.6	8	12	1.3	0.2
Beaver	27.3	5 052	8	13	9.5	0.4	20	103	22.0	1.5	4	D	D	D
Beckham	9.6	512	26	246	146.7	9.2	141	1 480	523.6	30.6	36	248	57.7	13.7
Blaine	8.4	652	13	105	135.3	3.2	53	290	74.6	4.0	7	22	4.0	0.7
Bryan	20.3	538	31	D	D	D	132	1 523	318.8	26.6	24	91	9.2	1.8
Caddo	53.8	1 788	23	237	70.1	5.1	113	970	234.4	15.6	10	22	2.1	0.4
Canadian	14.3	145	88	D	D	D	260	3 385	1 110.7	74.0	119	645	105.4	26.1
Carter	58.7	1 248	67	686	590.4	24.2	248	2 695	686.9	56.1	61	D	D	D
Cherokee	11.0	247	18	D	D	D	137	1 620	332.5	28.5	35	135	20.8	2.0
Chootaw	10.7	696	6	25	15.2	0.7	46	485	118.9	9.5	7	37	1.6	0.5
Cimarron	51.1	18 264	6	20	24.9	0.6	17	91	33.2	1.5	NA	NA	NA	NA
Cleveland	34.9	156	136	1 719	671.5	65.8	723	10 355	2 522.3	217.5	309	1 336	233.5	39.6
Coal	2.2	385	2	D	D	D	24	133	38.1	2.5	NA	NA	NA	NA
Comanche	22.6	204	56	D	D	D	435	5 540	1 206.8	108.0	135	484	66.7	10.9
Cotton	3.1	479	1	D	D	D	15	126	33.5	1.6	1	D	D	D
Craig	2.6	174	14	201	87.0	5.1	60	663	191.7	14.7	8	D	D	D
Creek	24.1	351	66	997	384.5	43.4	179	2 339	518.3	42.5	49	138	18.1	3.2
Custer	11.5	454	33	325	270.9	13.1	155	1 547	407.5	29.1	38	213	45.7	13.9
Delaware	6.0	152	20	80	47.1	2.8	133	1 238	292.6	25.4	26	184	46.5	7.1
Dewey	8.5	1 868	7	25	20.4	0.7	34	216	43.4	2.9	2	D	D	D
Ellis	15.8	3 985	5	D	D	D	24	136	41.2	2.5	1	D	D	D
Garfield	7.8	137	76	D	D	D	259	3 293	737.1	68.1	72	342	43.8	8.7
Garvin	12.4	454	27	179	95.8	6.6	121	1 137	331.6	22.2	15	50	13.6	2.5
Grady	18.1	367	53	550	198.9	19.2	167	1 657	440.1	35.6	40	140	17.7	3.5
Grant	8.0	1 656	11	39	29.6	1.0	12	148	54.7	3.2	NA	NA	NA	NA
Greer	6.3	1 072	3	12	4.0	0.2	16	179	28.1	2.5	3	6	0.8	0.1
Harmon	26.7	8 754	3	D	D	D	15	80	17.7	1.2	3	D	D	D
Harper	15.2	4 560	3	D	D	D	17	117	21.0	1.7	2	D	D	D
Haskell	5.5	455	6	D	D	D	36	425	131.0	9.2	3	11	0.5	0.1
Hughes	9.2	663	7	25	7.9	0.5	52	383	87.5	6.1	7	D	D	D
Jackson	76.3	2 897	23	D	D	D	115	1 365	350.2	28.6	18	83	11.3	1.8
Jefferson	7.7	1 192	1	D	D	D	28	152	34.8	2.6	3	2	0.3	0.1
Johnston	16.2	1 573	8	D	D	D	44	262	74.9	5.3	3	7	0.6	0.1
Kay	31.4	680	49	407	305.1	13.7	205	2 351	576.4	45.6	47	158	20.8	3.0
Kingfisher	10.8	759	27	388	429.2	16.3	64	549	185.2	12.0	9	79	10.9	1.9

1. Merchant wholesalers, except manufacturers' sales branches and offices.   2. Employer establishments.

Table B. States and Counties — Professional Services, Manufacturing, and Accommodation and Food Services

STATE County	Professional, scientific, and technical services,[1] 2007				Manufacturing, 2007				Accommodation and food services, 2007			
	Number of establishments	Number of employees	Receipts (mil dol)	Annual payroll (mil dol)	Number of establishments	Number of employees	Receipts (mil dol)	Annual payroll (mil dol)	Number of establishments	Number of employees	Sales (mil dol)	Annual payroll (mil dol)
	147	148	149	150	151	152	153	154	155	156	157	158
OHIO—Cont'd												
Ottawa	53	D	D	D	52	2 560	762.7	127.2	173	1 635	101.4	27.2
Paulding	12	44	4.4	1.2	37	1 755	388.7	56.9	34	305	7.9	2.1
Perry	27	106	6.8	3.5	25	933	124.5	31.4	45	369	13.8	3.7
Pickaway	59	D	D	D	37	2 342	D	D	73	1 033	40.0	10.8
Pike	21	136	21.4	7.3	30	1 781	620.8	57.6	51	738	31.5	8.4
Portage	253	D	D	D	263	11 370	2 969.6	484.1	297	4 583	187.7	51.5
Preble	45	D	D	D	56	3 248	1 070.3	155.5	65	940	32.2	9.6
Putnam	36	203	20.4	7.3	50	3 304	1 985.0	133.2	67	1 022	23.2	7.2
Richland	194	1 044	110.4	41.0	192	11 080	3 563.7	555.3	277	4 802	178.9	52.5
Ross	82	D	D	D	43	4 135	2 522.2	232.5	121	2 466	90.2	26.1
Sandusky	88	D	D	D	121	9 457	3 373.1	382.1	131	1 853	76.3	19.6
Scioto	81	D	D	D	52	1 874	927.1	65.7	150	2 160	84.8	23.2
Seneca	76	334	21.6	7.6	85	5 777	1 408.8	227.8	111	1 640	46.5	13.9
Shelby	62	339	33.0	16.6	147	15 057	6 238.4	707.2	81	1 351	55.2	14.0
Stark	739	D	D	D	542	27 177	10 387.4	1 175.2	784	13 705	518.0	153.6
Summit	1 618	D	D	D	925	32 483	9 275.5	1 470.3	1 231	22 475	885.0	253.4
Trumbull	300	D	D	D	262	18 808	8 841.0	1 138.4	434	6 588	245.2	68.7
Tuscarawas	142	D	D	D	224	9 223	2 206.5	380.1	215	3 448	114.4	36.4
Union	92	1 863	520.2	149.5	57	8 296	D	559.4	78	1 297	51.4	14.4
Van Wert	42	D	D	D	44	3 604	1 072.3	138.2	48	734	25.5	7.0
Vinton	7	D	D	D	21	592	106.5	19.2	17	69	2.8	0.6
Warren	439	D	D	D	222	13 472	4 111.2	572.2	345	8 227	329.8	99.7
Washington	99	D	D	D	96	4 374	2 563.7	217.1	120	2 065	83.7	22.8
Wayne	155	935	221.8	39.5	250	11 456	2 896.5	467.3	163	3 204	111.0	31.6
Williams	33	192	14.4	4.5	138	7 558	3 376.8	296.4	75	1 012	33.7	9.2
Wood	238	D	D	D	203	16 126	4 416.4	797.4	293	5 767	191.1	57.2
Wyandot	27	142	10.3	3.9	41	2 644	791.2	101.2	52	681	21.8	5.4
OKLAHOMA	9 128	D	D	D	3 964	142 351	60 681.4	5 971.2	6 900	129 159	5 106.6	1 401.3
Adair	13	D	D	D	13	1 314	414.4	41.1	15	269	6.1	1.8
Alfalfa	9	41	3.1	0.9	NA	NA	NA	NA	6	39	1.2	0.3
Atoka	13	46	3.2	0.9	NA	NA	NA	NA	28	317	13.9	2.9
Beaver	17	33	3.1	0.7	NA	NA	NA	NA	7	55	1.2	0.4
Beckham	70	317	32.5	12.1	NA	NA	NA	NA	69	895	39.2	9.7
Blaine	25	72	9.2	2.1	NA	NA	NA	NA	21	190	8.9	1.6
Bryan	61	944	87.3	48.4	38	1 102	238.2	35.2	62	1 089	40.4	10.6
Caddo	40	205	14.1	7.3	NA	NA	NA	NA	43	447	13.1	3.2
Canadian	214	663	67.6	21.1	75	3 234	1 192.9	132.5	146	2 623	102.2	26.3
Carter	118	D	D	D	49	2 993	D	167.2	86	1 979	68.1	20.7
Cherokee	50	134	11.3	3.5	NA	NA	NA	NA	84	1 092	42.1	11.2
Choctaw	19	D	D	D	NA	NA	NA	NA	28	337	10.9	2.7
Cimarron	4	12	1.5	0.2	NA	NA	NA	NA	11	79	3.4	0.7
Cleveland	613	D	D	D	151	3 299	1 223.0	138.1	447	10 104	391.8	108.8
Coal	2	D	D	D	NA	NA	NA	NA	4	70	2.2	0.7
Comanche	175	D	D	D	48	3 549	1 232.4	171.0	204	4 330	154.5	46.4
Cotton	7	12	0.7	0.3	NA	NA	NA	NA	8	D	D	D
Craig	21	83	9.2	3.2	16	783	139.0	26.4	28	374	14.8	4.0
Creek	106	320	25.6	8.0	133	4 257	1 204.4	178.6	83	1 181	43.4	11.0
Custer	72	D	D	D	33	1 346	533.9	45.2	67	1 053	41.5	11.0
Delaware	45	D	D	D	26	540	102.2	18.5	62	738	27.1	7.8
Dewey	9	98	8.2	2.6	NA	NA	NA	NA	4	24	1.2	0.2
Ellis	11	32	4.0	0.7	NA	NA	NA	NA	7	D	D	D
Garfield	128	559	58.4	20.1	68	2 356	1 097.7	75.9	115	1 848	74.4	19.1
Garvin	50	157	11.8	4.1	31	954	D	42.6	40	583	20.3	5.4
Grady	78	D	D	D	59	1 616	419.7	54.6	51	1 092	38.4	9.9
Grant	7	27	1.6	0.5	NA	NA	NA	NA	6	17	0.6	0.1
Greer	5	12	0.6	0.2	NA	NA	NA	NA	5	51	1.7	0.4
Harmon	4	D	D	D	NA	NA	NA	NA	3	D	D	D
Harper	8	30	3.6	1.1	NA	NA	NA	NA	3	D	D	D
Haskell	23	58	4.5	1.3	NA	NA	NA	NA	15	138	6.0	1.1
Hughes	14	40	2.6	0.8	NA	NA	NA	NA	18	237	9.3	2.1
Jackson	41	D	D	D	14	961	357.0	32.6	49	1 106	41.0	10.3
Jefferson	7	28	3.2	0.5	NA	NA	NA	NA	9	D	D	D
Johnston	11	20	1.9	0.8	NA	NA	NA	NA	11	106	3.1	0.9
Kay	96	523	46.1	17.9	72	4 415	D	189.3	100	1 688	61.5	15.4
Kingfisher	25	126	7.4	2.5	NA	NA	NA	NA	28	D	D	D

1. Establishment subject to federal tax.

Table B. States and Counties — Health Care and Social Assistance, Other Services, and Federal Funds

STATE County	Health care and social assistance, 2007				Other services, 2007				Federal funds and grants, 2009–2010 Expenditures (mil dol)			
										Direct payments for individuals[1]		
	Number of establishments	Number of employees	Receipts (mil dol)	Annual payroll (mil dol)	Number of establishments	Number of employees	Receipts (mil dol)	Annual payroll (mil dol)	Total	Social Security and government retirement	Medicare	Food Stamps and Supplemental Security Income
	159	160	161	162	163	164	165	166	167	168	169	170
OHIO—Cont'd												
Ottawa	81	1 637	110.7	45.6	88	343	29.7	8.0	318.1	163.8	81.4	7.1
Paulding	34	698	42.7	15.8	20	74	6.2	1.6	108.2	39.1	28.7	3.5
Perry	54	635	35.1	17.3	36	156	9.1	2.3	260.3	109.2	60.6	19.4
Pickaway	95	2 475	169.4	69.8	52	197	12.7	4.0	325.7	145.7	65.7	14.8
Pike	54	1 517	108.2	38.6	27	92	8.9	1.8	496.2	87.2	47.3	21.9
Portage	241	5 264	393.7	166.5	248	1 440	99.7	32.6	913.6	392.2	192.9	34.4
Preble	56	D	D	D	58	211	17.2	4.8	250.4	128.5	60.8	8.8
Putnam	60	839	39.3	19.8	58	311	21.6	5.9	144.7	53.6	45.1	4.5
Richland	354	7 670	663.5	263.1	238	1 533	109.3	29.3	950.7	414.3	216.4	47.1
Ross	156	5 154	523.2	252.8	96	524	31.0	8.7	753.4	259.0	109.1	36.9
Sandusky	152	3 553	255.6	97.1	115	796	44.3	14.1	394.5	166.3	101.1	18.2
Scioto	227	6 224	459.5	192.9	92	374	31.7	6.9	891.0	269.2	197.4	77.8
Seneca	158	2 914	170.9	73.5	109	500	33.9	8.3	413.2	188.1	109.2	16.8
Shelby	91	1 953	160.7	61.2	71	510	35.2	10.4	245.8	114.8	64.1	10.4
Stark	993	26 783	2 133.6	922.1	734	4 997	421.9	118.4	2 866.5	1 274.8	699.4	138.0
Summit	1 506	40 278	3 667.9	1 497.1	1 137	7 859	748.5	201.0	4 510.6	1 512.6	1 125.9	226.1
Trumbull	581	12 548	1 071.0	422.7	352	2 030	169.6	45.8	1 806.2	815.4	496.5	98.1
Tuscarawas	201	4 721	317.9	130.1	198	1 262	111.7	28.6	606.3	286.8	136.5	26.1
Union	81	1 684	128.4	63.5	75	579	46.8	15.6	230.9	87.9	41.8	6.5
Van Wert	63	1 826	108.9	46.4	52	270	18.6	3.7	160.9	67.6	40.7	4.2
Vinton	15	259	11.0	5.9	8	24	1.9	0.4	98.5	35.9	19.4	7.7
Warren	359	5 727	414.5	179.5	240	1 775	131.8	46.7	800.1	450.1	137.1	21.0
Washington	155	4 309	327.5	129.5	122	575	43.8	11.0	506.5	224.4	115.9	27.0
Wayne	221	5 004	347.5	147.0	168	907	73.3	19.6	717.9	316.9	140.8	23.0
Williams	69	1 680	147.8	63.1	66	337	25.7	5.8	228.8	115.8	62.2	6.4
Wood	249	4 637	338.3	145.9	212	1 461	123.4	36.4	696.2	283.6	150.4	18.3
Wyandot	41	803	50.6	21.0	57	286	21.4	5.4	151.8	71.1	38.1	2.7
OKLAHOMA	10 332	200 777	18 363.2	6 825.0	5 541	31 654	3 318.1	758.8	38 475.0	11 993.7	5 583.6	1 477.4
Adair	20	417	25.7	10.5	16	32	2.8	0.5	235.1	62.3	39.3	10.8
Alfalfa	9	136	4.3	2.0	8	D	D	D	53.6	19.3	14.5	0.8
Atoka	23	400	21.8	8.9	15	60	4.3	0.9	124.2	40.2	26.8	7.8
Beaver	6	77	5.1	1.8	9	D	D	D	37.5	17.1	7.6	1.0
Beckham	94	1 175	97.0	35.4	34	D	D	D	138.8	49.0	37.0	9.6
Blaine	29	397	17.0	7.4	16	25	2.5	0.3	133.0	32.4	25.1	5.1
Bryan	118	2 034	160.5	59.8	41	205	17.1	5.0	424.6	136.7	74.4	18.6
Caddo	44	693	28.0	13.3	25	90	9.8	2.4	330.9	104.2	68.9	19.0
Canadian	197	2 602	171.1	68.3	146	685	65.2	14.4	626.9	320.2	77.9	18.6
Carter	207	D	D	D	86	775	146.3	25.7	431.5	167.6	96.7	22.8
Cherokee	105	2 168	177.3	75.2	45	351	16.9	4.5	432.4	135.7	62.6	24.2
Choctaw	38	995	57.6	21.8	13	71	3.8	0.8	237.9	60.7	41.3	13.6
Cimarron	4	D	D	D	4	D	D	D	39.0	15.4	5.0	0.6
Cleveland	652	10 521	826.9	355.0	284	1 582	299.8	39.2	1 356.4	623.9	160.5	144.6
Coal	9	231	9.2	4.6	5	14	2.2	0.2	64.8	19.8	14.1	3.0
Comanche	274	6 219	580.1	223.7	170	879	63.3	15.2	3 180.5	477.1	114.1	56.3
Cotton	13	116	5.0	2.6	7	26	2.1	0.5	71.3	24.2	15.1	2.8
Craig	57	1 077	57.8	31.0	20	72	9.0	2.5	158.4	68.4	31.8	7.3
Creek	121	1 874	101.1	42.7	82	271	25.8	6.0	476.4	225.6	90.4	27.6
Custer	100	1 416	93.7	42.8	48	328	28.9	8.2	188.4	50.5	50.3	7.1
Delaware	77	1 238	98.6	37.7	52	261	18.3	4.8	304.7	142.1	63.2	15.7
Dewey	6	D	D	D	8	30	3.1	0.4	47.1	18.1	14.1	1.3
Ellis	9	186	14.7	5.1	11	D	D	D	35.1	13.7	11.6	0.9
Garfield	213	3 989	367.5	133.1	129	581	49.7	12.7	628.8	206.7	107.9	22.6
Garvin	65	1 101	61.4	25.3	28	137	17.6	2.3	389.1	110.1	79.1	12.4
Grady	82	1 524	110.5	46.8	67	265	18.5	5.0	337.2	161.1	59.9	20.6
Grant	7	103	4.6	2.0	4	D	D	D	56.7	18.8	14.5	1.4
Greer	13	204	14.8	4.9	6	D	D	D	70.9	22.0	21.8	3.3
Harmon	6	110	8.5	3.0	5	D	D	D	41.8	9.4	12.2	2.3
Harper	7	116	4.7	2.2	9	D	D	D	31.6	13.0	8.9	0.5
Haskell	35	915	48.8	19.5	13	41	3.1	0.7	148.6	50.8	29.3	8.0
Hughes	36	685	24.3	10.8	7	D	D	D	152.1	50.3	36.0	7.1
Jackson	56	1 399	96.7	40.1	40	190	13.1	2.9	449.2	101.0	52.0	12.3
Jefferson	8	70	3.5	1.3	3	D	D	D	75.8	25.6	19.1	3.4
Johnston	24	462	25.9	9.4	6	D	D	D	115.6	38.3	20.4	5.1
Kay	153	2 093	170.2	55.7	86	348	28.7	7.5	563.2	173.4	81.0	16.7
Kingfisher	42	586	29.0	11.3	30	92	8.7	2.0	138.3	43.6	24.2	3.0

1. State totals may include programs not allocated by county.

Table B. States and Counties — Federal Funds, Residential Construction, and Local Government Finances

	Federal funds and grants, 2009–2010 (cont.)							Value of residential construction authorized by building permits, 2010		Local government finances, 2007				
	Expenditures (mil dol) (cont.)									General revenue				
	Procurement contract awards			Grants[1]								Taxes		
													Per capita[2] (dollars)	
STATE County	Salaries and wages	Defense	Other	Medicaid and other health-related	Nutrition and family welfare	Education	Other	New construction ($1,000)	Number of housing units	Total (mil dol)	Inter-govern-mental (mil dol)	Total (mil dol)	Total	Property
	171	172	173	174	175	176	177	178	179	180	181	182	183	184
OHIO—Cont'd														
Ottawa	27.2	8.0	4.5	12.8	5.7	2.2	1.0	27 552	136	174.2	54.8	67.9	1 652	1 345
Paulding	4.1	1.5	1.0	13.3	3.2	1.5	3.9	1 391	12	67.7	37.3	19.4	1 010	671
Perry	5.8	0.2	1.8	48.5	7.6	2.7	1.6	4 182	30	110.8	74.9	20.5	589	488
Pickaway	10.4	0.3	2.0	55.6	10.1	2.9	5.2	4 174	23	238.9	83.8	58.9	1 095	790
Pike	5.9	0.0	238.2	70.3	11.7	2.7	6.3	12 138	75	143.1	72.8	25.0	897	690
Portage	29.0	25.5	5.7	83.1	24.8	12.0	31.1	31 229	175	669.9	217.0	222.5	1 427	1 057
Preble	10.9	0.1	2.0	23.5	6.6	3.1	0.4	5 198	27	132.1	58.3	48.4	1 160	698
Putnam	6.5	0.0	2.0	16.3	5.0	3.6	0.2	7 144	38	121.4	60.9	37.6	1 087	697
Richland	57.7	7.8	8.2	119.8	24.8	10.7	23.4	7 537	45	490.3	239.1	173.6	1 381	907
Ross	65.9	14.1	38.6	118.5	17.1	5.0	73.6	1 194	13	258.7	135.9	79.5	1 054	634
Sandusky	10.9	6.4	14.6	36.6	17.6	4.1	2.9	4 292	33	208.8	97.8	77.5	1 270	806
Scioto	16.6	0.0	4.1	238.9	25.9	9.0	19.9	845	36	274.5	176.1	58.0	764	567
Seneca	18.4	1.3	2.5	41.0	9.7	4.0	1.9	2 626	14	194.1	98.2	62.3	1 098	701
Shelby	7.7	0.5	1.9	27.0	7.0	3.4	1.5	20 728	98	182.3	76.5	72.6	1 488	880
Stark	163.9	9.2	23.1	324.1	69.0	31.1	61.1	73 815	449	1 298.5	606.9	471.2	1 244	941
Summit	210.4	418.2	58.3	540.7	105.1	42.4	157.0	96 501	561	2 354.0	893.1	1 026.1	1 888	1 270
Trumbull	74.4	38.9	8.2	171.4	43.4	21.2	20.1	13 120	73	734.1	362.9	260.6	1 221	898
Tuscarawas	20.3	18.6	4.0	73.0	18.4	10.4	6.3	6 360	43	298.2	139.7	94.8	1 038	779
Union	7.5	1.6	42.4	20.9	5.2	1.9	7.7	22 943	115	262.8	70.0	77.6	1 644	1 234
Van Wert	5.5	1.2	1.4	16.1	4.8	1.5	0.3	3 597	30	111.4	49.5	37.9	1 313	771
Vinton	2.5	0.0	0.6	25.0	4.2	1.2	1.4	0	0	67.1	53.3	7.1	534	445
Warren	42.7	25.9	11.1	68.9	20.8	5.3	6.5	144 708	599	739.7	207.5	387.0	1 894	1 458
Washington	17.0	2.1	6.6	74.5	13.1	7.7	5.7	1 651	13	196.9	96.0	70.1	1 139	792
Wayne	28.5	82.8	5.8	67.6	21.4	7.4	14.1	19 907	132	445.6	155.7	139.9	1 232	929
Williams	9.3	0.7	2.0	16.8	5.3	2.4	0.6	2 653	15	136.8	55.1	48.7	1 269	772
Wood	63.9	1.8	5.4	49.7	15.2	15.5	8.5	35 649	296	495.4	163.1	224.8	1 792	1 219
Wyandot	5.2	0.1	1.5	18.9	3.5	1.2	2.7	8 680	68	100.8	35.0	25.7	1 145	595
OKLAHOMA	5 575.4	2 409.9	964.9	3 961.4	1 023.5	703.9	2 166.0	1 225 761	8 140	X	X	X	X	X
Adair	4.4	12.3	1.0	88.6	5.7	9.0	0.3	2 550	30	64.1	42.1	6.7	304	157
Alfalfa	3.5	0.2	0.6	5.5	0.9	0.2	0.2	0	0	10.6	4.6	4.0	723	500
Atoka	4.2	0.0	0.5	37.8	3.4	1.9	0.8	1 375	17	37.5	20.0	6.7	460	202
Beaver	2.0	0.0	0.5	1.8	1.1	0.3	0.6	0	0	24.7	12.9	6.9	1 280	1 079
Beckham	3.8	0.0	0.8	29.1	4.2	1.5	0.5	1 972	20	69.8	29.1	24.2	1 226	482
Blaine	4.2	36.9	1.0	12.9	7.4	1.9	0.4	555	4	39.4	16.0	8.4	672	363
Bryan	16.3	15.5	28.0	77.5	18.3	8.9	9.3	8 046	80	100.5	53.5	28.1	710	316
Caddo	28.9	12.6	12.4	56.1	11.7	7.6	7.0	2 238	30	95.7	60.2	18.7	637	387
Canadian	129.4	0.7	15.8	22.4	14.6	6.9	2.4	37 633	180	244.6	105.3	91.0	879	574
Carter	34.3	11.4	2.4	67.3	9.1	5.0	11.8	18 166	145	139.7	63.1	48.8	1 025	513
Cherokee	26.5	0.0	8.1	78.1	24.4	11.1	41.0	4 832	38	310.3	154.6	44.3	977	397
Choctaw	3.6	13.7	0.7	74.6	8.3	2.5	17.0	1 503	14	37.0	23.2	8.0	534	196
Cimarron	1.1	0.0	0.2	2.5	0.7	0.3	0.4	0	0	10.8	4.5	3.0	1 118	961
Cleveland	121.5	28.3	70.5	49.6	32.6	22.5	61.9	134 075	1 143	708.8	198.3	199.8	845	520
Coal	1.9	0.0	0.5	22.3	1.7	0.9	0.2	40	1	20.9	11.9	5.8	1 011	516
Comanche	1 851.8	466.2	26.4	87.4	25.3	20.5	22.5	53 879	326	403.3	143.2	85.4	751	385
Cotton	5.5	0.0	0.3	12.0	1.2	3.6	0.2	0	0	14.2	9.0	2.7	436	275
Craig	7.5	0.0	1.0	33.2	2.9	1.8	1.3	160	1	39.6	21.4	11.9	780	378
Creek	20.2	7.6	2.4	60.1	12.3	4.3	22.2	12 415	91	172.8	95.8	49.6	718	440
Custer	24.8	0.1	4.0	18.8	5.1	3.2	9.8	5 670	34	76.1	32.8	27.3	1 046	529
Delaware	6.3	2.6	1.3	54.3	9.8	6.8	0.6	4 934	24	71.1	40.6	21.9	541	364
Dewey	2.6	0.0	0.6	5.4	0.9	0.4	0.5	0	0	25.7	11.3	8.0	1 854	1 348
Ellis	1.9	0.0	0.5	2.5	0.7	0.5	0.7	300	2	14.9	8.3	4.5	1 152	888
Garfield	129.9	84.2	3.6	38.8	10.3	5.4	1.8	16 404	74	144.5	63.8	58.2	1 009	483
Garvin	15.5	105.7	1.8	52.9	5.3	3.4	0.4	600	4	87.6	38.8	17.7	652	330
Grady	19.4	0.1	1.9	52.9	10.6	3.7	0.4	8 962	44	159.1	63.2	37.9	749	368
Grant	2.6	0.0	0.6	3.6	0.9	0.2	0.1	0	0	13.0	5.6	5.4	1 193	899
Greer	1.8	0.0	0.4	15.9	1.3	0.3	0.6	192	4	21.7	10.6	2.5	424	238
Harmon	1.5	0.0	0.2	9.7	1.0	0.3	0.1	NA	NA	7.3	4.3	1.7	588	358
Harper	1.6	0.0	0.3	1.8	0.6	0.2	1.2	0	0	14.2	7.2	4.7	1 451	908
Haskell	3.5	7.0	0.8	36.2	7.7	2.4	1.7	410	3	28.7	17.0	7.9	654	331
Hughes	3.5	0.0	1.0	46.0	3.6	2.2	0.9	3 210	26	40.3	20.5	8.9	648	419
Jackson	144.7	64.4	2.7	41.4	8.1	3.5	0.2	4 912	33	127.3	35.0	16.8	651	292
Jefferson	2.2	0.3	0.4	20.9	1.5	0.7	0.5	0	3	19.6	10.8	2.9	469	206
Johnston	3.8	0.0	0.9	32.4	4.9	1.9	0.5	405	5	20.8	13.4	4.5	433	283
Kay	19.9	185.6	3.5	33.9	10.4	4.8	6.6	829	11	138.4	64.0	40.8	893	505
Kingfisher	4.3	1.1	13.5	4.7	2.8	1.9	27.0	5 437	30	41.8	20.8	14.7	1 026	684

1. State totals may include programs not allocated by county.　　2. Based on the resident population estimated as of July 1 of the year shown.

Table B. States and Counties — **Local Government Finances, Government Employment, and Voting**

STATE County	Local government finances, 2007 (cont.) — Direct general expenditure							Debt outstanding		Government employment, 2009			Presidential election,[2] 2008 — Percent of vote cast:		
			Percent of total for:												
	Total (mil dol)	Per capita[1] (dollars)	Education	Health and hospitals	Police protection	Public welfare	Highways	Total (mil dol)	Per capita[1] (dollars)	Federal civilian	Federal military	State and local	Democratic	Republican	All other
	185	186	187	188	189	190	191	192	193	194	195	196	197	198	199
OHIO—Cont'd															
Ottawa	159.6	3 886	40.1	6.2	5.6	12.0	6.9	117.0	2 847	199	149	2 092	52.2	46.0	1.7
Paulding	68.7	3 582	58.8	3.6	4.1	3.7	10.8	32.8	1 711	54	48	1 111	42.6	54.4	2.9
Perry	115.5	3 316	56.0	3.9	3.5	9.4	7.9	24.3	697	66	90	1 906	47.1	50.1	2.7
Pickaway	213.0	3 958	40.6	30.0	4.4	4.6	3.6	135.0	2 509	96	140	4 233	38.3	60.0	1.8
Pike	137.3	4 917	46.1	21.9	2.1	4.6	5.8	75.6	2 706	75	71	1 726	48.2	49.3	2.5
Portage	642.5	4 122	40.7	24.7	3.7	4.2	3.2	348.5	2 236	304	416	16 196	53.5	44.5	2.0
Preble	127.3	3 049	52.7	3.9	6.0	7.1	7.9	56.1	1 344	90	106	1 856	33.3	64.6	2.1
Putnam	118.2	3 411	53.6	3.5	4.9	6.8	6.2	61.3	1 769	83	88	1 693	28.3	70.0	1.8
Richland	479.8	3 818	47.7	7.1	5.3	5.5	6.8	143.1	1 139	634	319	7 713	42.1	55.7	2.2
Ross	277.1	3 676	54.4	9.5	3.4	6.1	4.5	159.2	2 111	1 524	195	5 100	45.4	52.6	2.0
Sandusky	199.0	3 263	54.1	0.5	7.3	10.8	5.0	93.8	1 537	121	153	3 074	51.4	46.7	1.9
Scioto	266.4	3 507	58.1	4.5	2.5	7.3	3.7	343.9	4 528	170	196	6 219	45.8	52.2	2.0
Seneca	192.9	3 402	50.4	5.6	4.8	5.3	6.8	82.9	1 463	137	144	2 938	47.7	50.4	2.0
Shelby	169.4	3 470	49.5	4.4	4.5	7.6	8.5	103.3	2 115	94	125	2 655	30.9	67.3	1.8
Stark	1 313.0	3 467	52.8	7.2	5.0	5.8	4.8	738.5	1 950	1 114	971	18 293	51.7	46.3	2.0
Summit	2 406.5	4 428	38.5	7.1	6.4	6.2	5.9	2 048.0	3 768	1 949	1 420	32 708	57.6	41.1	1.3
Trumbull	733.6	3 437	54.3	5.6	5.2	5.7	3.8	353.6	1 657	482	545	9 503	60.0	37.6	2.4
Tuscarawas	309.7	3 389	54.0	3.8	4.4	5.6	5.4	154.4	1 690	222	234	4 767	50.1	47.6	2.3
Union	269.3	5 702	34.2	31.1	3.5	2.1	3.7	396.2	8 388	72	125	3 224	35.1	63.2	1.7
Van Wert	111.0	3 843	50.4	0.4	4.7	9.2	11.0	89.5	3 097	68	73	1 461	35.3	62.6	2.1
Vinton	71.8	5 366	62.6	2.1	1.3	8.1	7.9	20.5	1 536	27	34	759	43.6	53.5	2.9
Warren	712.4	3 485	49.6	2.7	4.9	2.8	5.2	1 029.0	5 034	305	538	9 150	31.4	67.5	1.1
Washington	190.2	3 089	50.3	9.1	5.9	6.6	9.3	103.0	1 673	227	156	2 992	41.3	56.9	1.8
Wayne	457.4	4 028	41.7	21.3	3.4	5.4	4.8	252.2	2 221	264	292	6 824	41.6	56.3	2.1
Williams	128.1	3 338	46.3	6.6	4.8	8.8	7.5	66.1	1 773	91	96	2 134	44.4	53.7	1.9
Wood	523.0	4 171	51.3	10.1	3.8	3.8	4.7	393.1	3 135	243	337	13 479	52.7	45.6	1.7
Wyandot	102.4	4 557	37.6	28.1	4.1	4.0	8.0	22.9	1 017	68	57	1 365	40.6	57.1	2.2
OKLAHOMA	X	X	X	X	X	X	X	X	X	46 575	37 856	291 589	34.4	65.6	0.0
Adair	79.1	3 611	55.2	1.1	1.8	0.0	3.1	32.2	1 468	57	95	1 691	30.7	69.3	0.0
Alfalfa	10.8	1 923	66.8	1.9	4.1	0.0	2.3	5.3	956	51	24	427	16.9	83.1	0.0
Atoka	39.6	2 729	49.1	20.0	2.9	0.0	8.4	5.3	362	61	63	1 371	28.1	71.9	0.0
Beaver	22.9	4 263	55.8	2.0	2.0	0.0	27.9	3.2	603	30	23	502	10.8	89.2	0.0
Beckham	60.3	3 058	50.5	2.1	4.6	0.0	7.6	37.4	1 899	83	92	1 082	22.0	78.0	0.0
Blaine	41.3	3 313	48.2	21.8	3.2	0.0	10.0	12.8	1 026	65	55	850	24.6	75.4	0.0
Bryan	97.9	2 474	62.3	1.0	2.7	0.0	6.7	17.5	442	124	179	6 115	32.2	67.8	0.0
Caddo	97.2	3 318	61.8	4.5	4.0	0.2	9.0	22.8	778	509	133	2 407	34.7	65.3	0.0
Canadian	244.8	2 364	68.0	7.1	4.7	0.0	3.7	166.2	1 605	606	900	5 433	23.9	76.1	0.0
Carter	139.9	2 940	57.2	2.5	6.0	0.1	8.1	84.7	1 780	112	212	3 293	29.7	70.3	0.0
Cherokee	291.6	6 424	21.4	28.2	2.5	0.0	36.1	37.9	835	415	201	8 164	43.9	56.1	0.0
Choctaw	33.4	2 226	66.4	6.4	3.9	0.2	7.5	9.0	601	56	65	1 564	33.3	66.7	0.0
Cimarron	10.5	3 927	52.3	28.3	2.5	0.0	6.1	1.8	682	19	15	256	12.0	88.0	0.0
Cleveland	811.1	3 430	41.2	31.7	3.8	0.0	3.6	585.3	2 475	780	1 150	23 474	38.0	62.0	0.0
Coal	19.0	3 332	63.6	4.4	2.3	0.0	8.8	6.5	1 146	24	26	396	26.4	73.6	0.0
Comanche	395.6	3 476	46.6	31.8	4.1	0.0	1.7	141.9	1 247	4 028	12 251	9 980	41.2	58.8	0.0
Cotton	15.3	2 422	60.0	1.0	1.4	0.0	9.9	4.1	659	29	27	1 171	27.8	72.2	0.0
Craig	39.5	2 597	68.5	1.1	5.8	0.0	8.7	9.8	647	68	66	2 038	35.0	65.0	0.0
Creek	171.0	2 476	67.2	0.8	5.2	0.0	8.1	142.7	2 066	106	307	3 080	29.2	70.8	0.0
Custer	65.0	2 489	60.7	0.1	5.3	0.2	8.6	53.2	2 036	185	117	2 721	25.3	74.7	0.0
Delaware	82.5	2 042	74.6	0.6	2.6	0.3	3.2	42.8	1 058	74	177	2 664	33.1	66.9	0.0
Dewey	24.5	5 654	59.3	14.5	2.0	0.0	12.2	3.9	896	37	19	452	15.7	84.3	0.0
Ellis	14.7	3 757	54.6	1.3	2.2	0.0	22.4	1.8	453	28	17	388	14.8	85.2	0.0
Garfield	133.0	2 306	63.0	0.8	6.4	0.1	9.0	65.6	1 138	413	1 539	3 467	24.5	75.5	0.0
Garvin	85.7	3 158	51.7	22.1	3.8	0.1	6.7	29.3	1 080	90	118	2 250	28.2	71.8	0.0
Grady	170.2	3 363	37.7	25.8	4.9	0.1	20.1	55.6	1 098	102	225	2 673	26.6	73.4	0.0
Grant	14.2	3 163	67.6	0.6	3.9	0.0	5.6	2.7	596	40	19	351	21.9	78.1	0.0
Greer	22.0	3 791	35.9	32.7	4.2	0.2	8.3	6.1	1 055	27	25	753	26.8	73.2	0.0
Harmon	7.1	2 512	71.1	3.4	6.5	0.0	0.1	0.3	91	24	12	313	30.6	69.4	0.0
Harper	15.0	4 598	49.1	5.9	3.6	0.0	22.2	0.8	256	26	15	388	14.1	85.9	0.0
Haskell	27.7	2 301	67.4	2.8	4.1	0.0	12.5	1.7	139	58	54	809	31.5	68.5	0.0
Hughes	38.8	2 838	60.7	16.7	2.1	0.0	6.8	17.6	1 286	47	60	957	35.3	64.7	0.0
Jackson	127.2	4 935	32.7	46.3	4.2	0.0	2.3	46.5	1 805	1 553	1 467	2 569	25.2	74.8	0.0
Jefferson	19.4	3 095	63.7	1.0	1.6	0.0	4.7	37.7	6 015	38	28	392	32.8	67.2	0.0
Johnston	20.9	2 005	77.7	2.7	3.9	0.0	2.3	7.2	694	58	46	935	31.6	68.4	0.0
Kay	142.5	3 122	50.2	1.5	6.0	0.0	7.9	81.8	1 793	126	201	4 687	29.2	70.8	0.0
Kingfisher	43.7	3 052	66.4	1.2	4.4	0.0	11.1	15.2	1 063	55	63	843	15.8	84.2	0.0

1. Based on the resident population estimated as of July 1 of the year shown.   2. © 2009 Election Data Services, Inc. All rights reserved.

Table B. States and Counties — Land Area and Population

| | | | | | Population and population characteristics, 2010 | | | | | | | | | | | | | |
| | | | | | | | | Race alone or in combination, not Hispanic or Latino (percent) | | | | | Age (percent) | | | | | |
STATE/ County code	CBSA code[1]	County type[2]	STATE County	Land area,[3] (sq km) 2010	Total persons	Rank	Per square kilometer	White	Black	American Indian, Alaska Native	Asian and Pacific Islander	Percent Hispanic or Latino[4]	Under 5 years	5 to 17 years	18 to 24 years	25 to 34 years	35 to 44 years	45 to 54 years
				1	2	3	4	5	6	7	8	9	10	11	12	13	14	15
			OKLAHOMA—Cont'd															
40 075	...	6	Kiowa	2 629	9 446	2 483	3.6	80.2	5.2	8.5	0.6	8.8	5.8	17.6	7.4	10.8	10.8	15.4
40 077	...	7	Latimer	1 870	11 154	2 354	6.0	76.4	1.2	26.8	0.5	2.6	6.0	17.9	10.0	10.7	11.2	14.0
40 079	22900	2	Le Flore	4 116	50 384	972	12.2	78.3	2.5	16.9	0.8	6.9	6.8	17.9	8.9	12.1	12.2	14.1
40 081	36420	1	Lincoln	2 466	34 273	1 319	13.9	89.0	2.4	10.3	0.5	2.4	6.6	18.9	7.5	10.6	12.2	15.6
40 083	36420	1	Logan	1 927	41 848	1 136	21.7	81.9	10.0	5.8	0.9	5.2	6.7	18.4	10.8	11.6	12.2	15.1
40 085	11620	9	Love	1 331	9 423	2 488	7.1	80.0	2.3	9.1	0.6	11.8	6.5	17.8	7.3	11.3	12.2	14.0
40 087	36420	1	McClain	1 478	34 506	1 312	23.3	85.7	1.1	10.4	0.7	7.0	7.0	19.6	7.0	12.0	13.6	15.4
40 089	...	7	McCurtain	4 791	33 151	1 350	6.9	71.1	9.9	19.7	0.5	4.7	6.9	19.0	8.2	11.3	12.3	13.9
40 091	...	6	McIntosh	1 602	20 252	1 826	12.6	75.6	4.6	24.5	0.6	1.9	5.3	15.7	6.4	9.4	10.6	15.3
40 093	...	9	Major	2 473	7 527	2 641	3.0	89.9	1.0	3.0	0.6	7.5	6.5	16.7	7.0	10.6	10.6	15.9
40 095	...	6	Marshall	961	15 840	2 063	16.5	74.8	2.1	14.1	0.4	14.0	6.7	17.2	6.9	10.2	10.9	14.6
40 097	...	6	Mayes	1 697	41 259	1 149	24.3	75.4	0.7	29.3	0.6	2.7	7.0	18.5	7.9	11.4	12.0	14.6
40 099	...	7	Murray	1 079	13 488	2 220	12.5	81.5	1.8	17.0	0.6	4.9	6.8	17.0	7.3	11.4	11.9	14.6
40 101	34780	4	Muskogee	2 099	70 990	752	33.8	65.0	13.0	23.9	0.8	5.2	6.9	17.8	9.3	13.0	11.9	14.1
40 103	...	6	Noble	1 896	11 561	2 328	6.1	86.9	2.3	11.2	0.9	2.6	7.1	17.6	6.9	11.4	12.5	14.9
40 105	...	6	Nowata	1 465	10 536	2 400	7.2	76.3	3.3	27.1	0.3	2.3	5.9	18.3	7.2	10.7	11.4	15.4
40 107	...	6	Okfuskee	1 602	12 191	2 293	7.6	68.6	9.3	24.8	0.5	2.9	6.3	17.0	7.7	12.1	12.6	15.3
40 109	36420	1	Oklahoma	1 836	718 633	81	391.4	62.8	16.9	5.7	3.8	15.1	7.7	17.5	10.5	15.2	12.4	13.6
40 111	46140	2	Okmulgee	1 806	40 069	1 173	22.2	70.8	10.6	22.5	0.7	3.2	6.6	18.0	9.7	11.4	11.6	14.2
40 113	46140	2	Osage	5 818	47 472	1 016	8.2	70.9	12.4	20.3	0.5	2.9	6.1	18.2	7.3	11.1	11.9	16.1
40 115	33060	6	Ottawa	1 219	31 848	1 398	26.1	74.4	1.1	25.1	1.9	4.7	7.1	17.6	9.8	11.2	11.6	13.3
40 117	46140	2	Pawnee	1 471	16 577	2 012	11.3	85.3	1.3	16.6	0.6	2.0	6.4	18.3	7.4	10.3	12.5	14.9
40 119	44660	4	Payne	1 773	77 350	702	43.6	84.2	4.6	7.9	4.2	3.9	5.8	13.1	26.5	14.7	9.5	10.9
40 121	32540	5	Pittsburg	3 381	45 837	1 053	13.6	78.5	4.3	19.8	0.7	3.9	6.3	15.8	8.0	12.6	11.9	14.4
40 123	10220	7	Pontotoc	1 866	37 492	1 230	20.1	75.4	3.6	22.9	1.0	4.1	6.9	16.5	13.1	12.8	11.1	13.3
40 125	43060	4	Pottawatomie	2 040	69 442	763	34.0	79.6	3.9	17.1	1.1	4.1	6.9	18.1	10.2	12.3	12.3	14.1
40 127	...	9	Pushmataha	3 615	11 572	2 327	3.2	79.1	1.0	22.5	0.4	2.4	6.2	16.2	7.5	10.0	11.0	14.9
40 129	...	9	Roger Mills	2 956	3 647	2 936	1.2	89.1	0.7	7.0	0.6	4.5	7.0	18.1	6.6	11.8	10.4	14.8
40 131	46140	2	Rogers	1 750	86 905	649	49.7	81.1	1.4	20.0	1.5	3.7	6.3	19.8	8.5	11.3	13.4	15.4
40 133	...	7	Seminole	1 639	25 482	1 587	15.5	73.1	6.2	23.4	0.6	3.5	6.6	19.1	8.6	11.2	11.6	14.1
40 135	22900	2	Sequoyah	1 744	42 391	1 116	24.3	73.7	2.4	28.6	0.8	3.4	6.6	19.1	8.0	11.1	13.1	14.5
40 137	20340	4	Stephens	2 254	45 048	1 066	20.0	86.4	2.6	8.1	0.8	6.2	6.6	17.5	7.6	12.0	11.3	14.7
40 139	25100	7	Texas	5 287	20 640	1 812	3.9	53.9	1.7	1.6	1.9	42.0	8.8	20.0	12.1	14.2	12.4	12.4
40 141	...	6	Tillman	2 256	7 992	2 604	3.5	66.9	8.0	4.7	0.4	22.3	6.2	18.5	7.7	10.9	11.6	14.6
40 143	46140	2	Tulsa	1 477	603 403	102	408.5	69.6	12.0	9.5	3.0	11.0	7.4	18.2	9.7	14.4	13.0	13.9
40 145	46140	2	Wagoner	1 454	73 085	740	50.3	80.0	4.7	15.8	1.9	4.8	7.0	19.6	7.4	12.9	13.5	14.4
40 147	12780	4	Washington	1 076	50 976	966	47.4	81.1	3.3	14.7	1.5	5.0	6.5	17.0	8.2	11.4	11.4	14.7
40 149	...	7	Washita	2 598	11 629	2 322	4.5	88.3	1.0	4.6	0.3	8.1	6.9	18.9	7.4	12.4	11.0	14.6
40 151	...	7	Woods	3 332	8 878	2 536	2.7	88.7	3.9	3.8	1.0	4.8	6.0	12.8	18.7	12.8	9.5	12.0
40 153	49260	7	Woodward	3 218	20 081	1 835	6.2	84.5	1.8	3.9	0.8	10.6	7.3	17.0	8.4	14.8	12.4	15.0
41 000	...	X	OREGON	248 608	3 831 074	X	15.4	81.1	2.3	2.3	5.3	11.7	6.2	16.4	9.4	13.7	13.0	14.1
41 001	...	7	Baker	7 947	16 134	2 045	2.0	94.7	0.6	2.7	0.9	3.3	5.3	15.0	6.2	9.5	10.3	15.0
41 003	18700	3	Benton	1 751	85 579	655	48.9	86.5	1.4	1.6	7.2	6.4	4.4	13.4	23.0	12.2	10.0	12.5
41 005	38900	1	Clackamas	4 844	375 992	174	77.6	86.8	1.2	1.5	5.2	7.7	5.7	18.0	7.7	11.4	13.3	15.9
41 007	11820	4	Clatsop	2 147	37 039	1 243	17.3	89.4	0.8	2.0	2.5	7.7	5.6	14.9	8.9	11.5	11.0	14.8
41 009	38900	1	Columbia	1 703	49 351	989	29.0	93.1	0.8	2.9	2.1	4.0	5.7	17.9	7.3	10.9	13.4	16.0
41 011	18300	5	Coos	4 134	63 043	829	15.2	90.5	0.7	5.0	2.1	5.4	5.1	13.8	7.7	10.3	10.1	15.1
41 013	39260	6	Crook	7 716	20 978	1 788	2.7	90.1	0.3	2.5	0.8	7.0	5.4	16.5	6.1	10.2	11.0	14.7
41 015	15060	7	Curry	4 215	22 364	1 715	5.3	91.7	0.7	4.1	1.3	5.4	3.8	11.9	5.4	7.6	8.9	15.0
41 017	13460	3	Deschutes	7 817	157 733	394	20.2	90.3	0.7	1.7	1.9	7.4	6.1	16.9	7.4	12.6	13.5	14.5
41 019	40700	4	Douglas	13 043	107 667	548	8.3	92.1	0.6	3.5	1.8	4.7	5.2	15.3	7.5	10.0	10.5	14.5
41 021	...	9	Gilliam	3 120	1 871	3 066	0.6	93.2	0.3	2.0	1.0	4.7	5.0	13.8	4.7	9.1	10.0	17.6
41 023	...	9	Grant	11 729	7 445	2 646	0.6	95.4	0.5	2.7	0.7	2.8	4.5	14.7	5.6	8.6	9.9	15.0
41 025	...	7	Harney	26 245	7 422	2 648	0.3	92.1	0.4	5.1	1.1	4.0	5.4	17.0	6.7	10.1	10.6	15.5
41 027	26220	6	Hood River	1 352	22 346	1 719	16.5	67.9	0.6	1.5	2.7	29.5	6.7	19.3	7.7	12.4	13.9	15.4
41 029	32780	3	Jackson	7 209	203 206	302	28.2	86.1	1.1	2.3	2.3	10.7	5.9	15.9	8.6	11.5	11.4	14.2
41 031	...	6	Jefferson	4 612	21 720	1 748	4.7	63.8	0.8	17.2	1.1	19.3	7.1	18.1	8.3	11.0	12.4	14.0
41 033	24420	4	Josephine	4 247	82 713	671	19.5	91.0	0.7	2.7	1.7	6.3	5.1	15.3	7.0	9.5	10.3	14.3
41 035	28900	5	Klamath	15 387	66 380	790	4.3	84.1	1.1	5.8	1.7	10.4	6.0	16.3	9.4	10.7	11.5	14.0
41 037	...	7	Lake	21 080	7 895	2 610	0.4	89.8	0.6	4.2	1.5	6.9	4.6	14.7	5.8	9.6	12.1	15.9
41 039	21660	2	Lane	11 793	351 715	183	29.8	87.9	1.6	2.6	3.9	7.4	5.2	14.6	12.6	13.1	11.6	13.7
41 041	...	4	Lincoln	2 538	46 034	1 045	18.1	87.3	0.6	5.3	1.8	7.9	4.9	12.4	6.7	10.0	9.9	15.1
41 043	10540	4	Linn	5 931	116 672	513	19.7	89.4	0.8	2.5	1.9	7.8	6.6	17.6	8.5	12.3	12.1	14.0
41 045	36620	6	Malheur	25 609	31 313	1 408	1.2	64.9	1.3	1.4	2.2	31.5	7.4	18.2	9.8	13.2	12.2	12.8
41 047	41420	2	Marion	3 062	315 335	202	103.0	70.9	1.4	2.1	3.6	24.3	7.5	19.0	9.8	13.6	12.5	13.0

1. CBSA = Core Based Statistical Area. See Appendix A for explanation. See Appendix B for list of metropolitan areas with component counties. 2. County type code from the Economic Research Service of USDA Rural-Urban Continuum Codes. See Appendix A for definition. 3. Dry land or land partially or temporarily covered by water. 4. May be of any race.

Table B. States and Counties — Population and Households

STATE County	Age (percent) (cont.) 55 to 64 years	65 to 74 years	75 years and over	Percent female	Total persons 1990	2000	Percent change 1990–2000	2000–2010	Components of change, 2000–2009 Births	Deaths	Net migration	Households, 2010 Number	Percent change, 2000–2010	Persons per house-hold	Female family house-holder[1]	One per-son
	16	17	18	19	20	21	22	23	24	25	26	27	28	29	30	31
OKLAHOMA—Cont'd																
Kiowa	13.8	10.2	8.1	50.5	11 347	10 227	-9.9	-7.6	1 083	1 493	-661	3 978	-5.5	2.33	11.4	31.1
Latimer	12.7	9.5	7.9	49.4	10 333	10 692	3.5	4.3	1 081	1 153	66	4 208	6.5	2.51	11.8	25.9
Le Flore	12.8	8.9	6.3	49.8	43 270	48 109	11.2	4.7	6 699	5 059	487	18 878	5.7	2.58	12.0	24.8
Lincoln	13.2	9.2	6.1	50.5	29 216	32 080	9.8	6.8	3 724	3 225	-186	13 243	8.7	2.56	10.3	23.5
Logan	12.6	7.6	5.1	50.5	29 011	33 924	16.9	23.4	4 163	2 899	4 259	15 290	23.4	2.60	9.7	22.8
Love	13.6	10.3	6.9	50.9	7 788	8 831	13.4	6.7	1 043	931	232	3 713	7.9	2.51	10.7	24.7
McClain	12.1	8.1	5.1	50.4	22 795	27 740	21.7	24.4	3 839	2 487	4 210	12 891	24.8	2.66	9.9	20.1
McCurtain	12.8	9.0	6.5	51.0	33 433	34 402	2.9	-3.6	4 492	3 606	-1 735	12 958	-2.0	2.52	14.9	27.2
McIntosh	15.3	12.4	9.5	50.6	16 779	19 456	16.0	4.1	2 071	2 556	926	8 460	4.6	2.35	11.6	27.7
Major	13.4	10.1	9.1	50.9	8 055	7 545	-6.3	-0.2	760	932	-148	3 109	2.1	2.40	7.0	26.5
Marshall	13.6	11.9	8.0	49.9	10 829	13 184	21.7	20.1	1 777	1 629	1 756	6 338	18.0	2.45	9.7	27.4
Mayes	12.9	9.3	6.4	50.1	33 366	38 369	15.0	7.5	5 049	3 907	809	16 008	8.0	2.54	10.5	24.9
Murray	13.5	9.6	7.9	50.2	12 042	12 623	4.8	6.9	1 515	1 672	567	5 350	6.9	2.46	10.1	26.9
Muskogee	12.4	7.9	6.8	51.1	68 078	69 451	2.0	2.2	9 406	7 750	752	27 054	2.3	2.49	14.6	27.9
Noble	12.8	9.1	7.6	50.6	11 045	11 411	3.3	1.3	1 356	1 109	-642	4 614	2.4	2.45	10.0	26.6
Nowata	13.1	9.6	8.4	50.6	9 992	10 569	5.8	-0.3	1 150	1 125	-20	4 224	1.9	2.46	10.7	25.9
Okfuskee	12.3	9.8	6.9	46.5	11 551	11 814	2.3	3.2	1 331	1 385	-786	4 354	2.0	2.52	12.0	27.3
Oklahoma	11.1	6.3	5.7	51.1	599 611	660 448	10.1	8.8	109 001	58 955	10 594	287 598	7.8	2.45	14.3	30.7
Okmulgee	12.6	8.7	7.1	50.5	36 490	39 685	8.8	1.0	5 045	4 368	-807	15 362	0.4	2.52	14.6	27.2
Osage	13.9	9.2	6.1	49.7	41 645	44 437	6.7	6.8	4 366	3 634	71	18 205	9.8	2.53	12.0	24.8
Ottawa	12.4	9.1	7.9	51.2	30 561	33 194	8.6	-4.1	4 091	3 972	-1 535	12 345	-4.9	2.50	12.8	27.0
Pawnee	13.8	9.7	6.7	50.2	15 575	16 612	6.7	-0.2	1 909	1 756	-256	6 486	1.6	2.53	10.3	25.5
Payne	9.0	5.6	4.8	49.3	61 507	68 190	10.9	13.4	8 125	4 928	1 969	30 177	13.1	2.31	8.9	30.8
Pittsburg	13.5	9.7	7.8	49.2	40 950	43 953	7.3	4.3	5 027	5 218	1 718	18 012	5.0	2.41	12.1	27.8
Pontotoc	11.5	8.0	6.8	51.5	34 119	35 143	3.0	6.7	4 779	3 800	1 503	14 654	4.8	2.44	12.1	28.4
Pottawatomie	11.8	8.2	6.1	52.1	58 760	65 521	11.5	6.0	8 599	6 661	3 168	25 911	5.6	2.56	13.3	25.1
Pushmataha	14.0	11.7	8.5	50.6	10 997	11 667	6.1	-0.8	1 284	1 456	393	4 809	1.5	2.38	11.8	28.4
Roger Mills	13.7	9.8	7.8	50.3	4 147	3 436	-17.1	6.1	445	341	-128	1 470	2.9	2.47	9.4	26.3
Rogers	11.9	8.0	5.4	50.5	55 170	70 641	28.0	23.0	8 961	6 003	12 411	31 884	23.9	2.69	9.6	20.2
Seminole	12.7	9.0	7.0	51.2	25 412	24 894	-2.0	2.4	3 385	2 996	-846	9 750	1.8	2.55	14.0	26.9
Sequoyah	12.6	9.0	5.9	50.4	33 828	38 972	15.2	8.8	4 947	3 843	1 612	16 208	9.8	2.59	13.1	24.1
Stephens	13.0	9.1	8.2	51.2	42 299	43 182	2.1	4.3	5 110	5 288	790	18 127	3.8	2.46	10.1	26.1
Texas	9.9	5.6	4.7	48.0	16 419	20 107	22.5	2.7	3 562	1 218	-1 290	7 212	0.8	2.78	9.4	23.0
Tillman	12.8	9.8	7.9	50.1	10 384	9 287	-10.6	-13.9	1 041	1 100	-1 416	3 216	-10.5	2.40	12.3	30.3
Tulsa	11.3	6.4	5.7	51.2	503 341	563 299	11.9	7.1	87 429	49 457	4 099	241 737	6.5	2.46	16.3	29.9
Wagoner	12.6	8.0	4.5	50.8	47 883	57 491	20.1	27.1	7 548	3 977	9 527	26 878	27.9	2.71	10.3	18.8
Washington	13.0	8.9	8.9	51.6	48 066	48 996	1.9	4.0	5 726	5 263	1 545	21 036	4.2	2.39	11.0	28.7
Washita	11.7	8.6	8.5	51.2	11 441	11 508	0.6	1.1	1 392	1 293	275	4 599	2.1	2.48	9.5	27.1
Woods	11.0	8.7	8.4	46.5	9 103	9 089	-0.2	-2.3	840	1 092	-385	3 533	-4.1	2.23	7.6	32.3
Woodward	10.9	8.2	6.0	47.6	18 976	18 486	-2.6	8.6	2 593	1 720	704	7 654	7.2	2.46	8.5	28.0
OREGON	13.3	7.6	6.4	50.5	2 842 337	3 421 399	20.4	12.0	433 972	284 372	274 031	1 518 938	13.9	2.47	10.5	27.4
Baker	16.8	12.4	9.5	49.5	15 317	16 741	9.3	-3.6	1 515	1 866	-213	7 040	2.3	2.24	8.3	31.2
Benton	12.4	6.3	5.7	49.9	70 811	78 153	10.4	9.5	7 258	4 578	2 227	34 317	13.8	2.35	7.3	28.2
Clackamas	14.4	7.6	6.1	50.8	278 850	338 391	21.4	11.1	37 655	25 675	37 497	145 790	13.7	2.56	9.8	24.1
Clatsop	16.6	9.4	7.3	50.3	33 301	35 630	7.0	4.0	3 785	3 517	1 579	15 742	7.1	2.29	9.6	31.5
Columbia	15.0	8.2	5.7	49.9	37 557	43 560	16.0	13.3	4 705	3 424	4 965	19 183	17.1	2.55	9.8	23.3
Coos	16.6	12.0	9.4	50.7	60 273	62 779	4.2	0.4	5 899	7 917	2 415	27 133	3.5	2.29	10.2	29.8
Crook	16.1	12.1	8.0	50.4	14 111	19 182	35.9	9.4	2 210	1 851	3 154	8 558	16.4	2.42	9.0	24.1
Curry	19.5	15.9	12.1	50.6	19 327	21 137	9.4	5.8	1 406	2 931	1 628	10 417	9.2	2.12	8.4	32.4
Deschutes	14.2	8.7	6.2	50.6	74 976	115 367	53.9	36.7	16 207	9 603	36 998	64 090	40.6	2.44	9.4	24.1
Douglas	15.9	11.3	9.6	50.6	94 649	100 399	6.1	7.2	10 283	11 273	4 418	44 581	12.0	2.38	10.8	26.6
Gilliam	17.5	11.7	10.5	48.4	1 717	1 915	11.5	-2.3	154	192	-229	864	5.5	2.14	6.4	35.6
Grant	18.1	13.2	10.4	50.3	7 853	7 935	1.0	-6.2	606	832	-885	3 352	3.3	2.19	7.5	30.3
Harney	15.9	10.8	8.1	49.1	7 060	7 609	7.8	-2.5	721	671	-874	3 205	5.6	2.28	8.8	30.0
Hood River	12.1	6.2	6.4	50.0	16 903	20 411	20.8	9.5	2 865	1 640	354	8 173	12.8	2.64	9.3	23.8
Jackson	14.9	9.3	8.4	51.3	146 387	181 269	23.8	12.1	20 549	18 127	18 455	83 076	16.1	2.40	11.0	27.7
Jefferson	13.6	9.6	5.7	48.2	13 676	19 009	39.0	14.3	3 012	1 610	-395	7 790	15.8	2.68	12.6	22.2
Josephine	16.3	12.0	10.3	51.3	62 649	75 726	20.9	9.2	7 547	9 710	7 861	34 646	11.8	2.34	11.0	28.3
Klamath	15.0	9.7	7.4	50.2	57 702	63 775	10.5	4.1	7 589	6 449	1 719	27 280	8.2	2.40	10.7	27.3
Lake	16.9	11.8	8.6	47.3	7 186	7 422	3.3	6.4	672	813	-154	3 378	9.5	2.20	7.4	31.3
Lane	14.2	8.1	6.9	50.8	282 912	322 959	14.2	8.9	33 979	27 501	23 431	145 966	11.9	2.35	10.6	28.9
Lincoln	19.3	12.6	9.0	51.3	38 889	44 479	14.4	3.5	4 187	5 039	2 961	20 550	6.5	2.20	9.6	31.2
Linn	13.5	8.5	6.9	50.6	91 227	103 069	13.0	13.2	13 300	9 860	10 497	45 204	14.3	2.55	11.2	24.4
Malheur	11.4	8.0	7.0	45.9	26 038	31 615	21.4	-1.0	4 304	2 444	-2 582	10 411	1.9	2.69	11.8	26.0
Marion	11.7	6.8	6.1	50.2	228 483	284 834	24.7	10.7	44 027	23 186	14 275	112 957	11.1	2.70	12.4	25.0

1. No spouse present.

Table B. States and Counties — **Population, Vital Statistics, Medicare, and Crime**

STATE County	Persons in group quarters, 2010	Daytime population, 2006–2010 Number	Employment/ residence ratio	Births, average 2006–2008 Total	Rate[1]	Deaths, average 2006–2008 Number	Rate[1]	Persons under 65 with no health insurance, 2009 Number	Percent	Medicare, 2011 Eligible for Medicare	Enrolled in Medicare Advantage	Enrolled in a Medicare prescription drug plan	Serious crimes known to police,[2] 2010 Total Number	Rate[3]
	32	33	34	35	36	37	38	39	40	41	42	43	44	45
OKLAHOMA—Cont'd														
Kiowa	171	8 927	0.8	D	D	169	17.7	1 681	23.7	2 183	81	1 385	201	2 128
Latimer	574	10 969	1.0	D	D	126	11.9	2 027	23.4	2 339	120	1 200	175	1 569
Le Flore	1 616	45 542	0.8	731	14.7	575	11.5	10 481	25.5	9 889	1 205	5 251	1 001	1 987
Lincoln	386	28 650	0.6	406	12.5	366	11.3	5 779	21.7	6 408	845	2 729	593	1 730
Logan	2 161	30 915	0.5	477	12.8	317	8.5	6 519	19.3	6 326	731	3 059	685	1 637
Love	88	9 801	1.1	D	D	107	11.7	1 654	22.5	1 957	80	1 184	126	1 337
McClain	194	27 333	0.6	435	13.7	279	8.8	5 936	21.2	5 702	430	2 603	900	2 608
McCurtain	454	33 072	1.0	502	14.9	393	11.7	6 953	25.3	6 761	530	4 064	1 143	3 448
McIntosh	345	17 990	0.7	229	11.6	297	15.0	3 854	25.6	5 823	410	3 051	485	2 395
Major	77	7 099	0.9	D	D	102	14.1	1 233	21.7	1 597	32	1 012	188	2 498
Marshall	329	14 555	0.9	D	D	188	12.7	3 007	25.3	3 467	146	1 955	231	1 458
Mayes	567	37 440	0.8	588	14.8	422	10.6	7 617	23.1	7 946	887	4 048	873	2 116
Murray	313	12 285	0.8	D	D	180	14.1	2 561	24.6	2 805	201	1 543	261	1 935
Muskogee	3 526	72 505	1.1	1 073	15.1	874	12.3	14 026	23.8	13 797	800	7 204	2 659	3 746
Noble	273	11 142	0.9	D	D	117	10.5	1 780	19.9	2 227	69	1 465	162	1 401
Nowata	157	8 578	0.5	D	D	118	11.0	1 962	23.0	2 339	176	1 281	259	2 458
Okfuskee	1 228	10 813	0.7	D	D	148	13.2	2 212	25.4	2 396	174	1 387	296	2 428
Oklahoma	15 025	802 636	1.3	12 375	17.7	6 356	9.1	133 004	21.8	105 762	20 947	41 741	40 324	5 611
Okmulgee	1 374	35 818	0.8	539	13.7	483	12.3	7 045	21.8	8 164	735	4 171	1 177	2 937
Osage	1 504	37 797	0.5	D	D	439	9.6	8 441	21.9	7 958	1 442	3 533	1 405	2 960
Ottawa	968	31 256	0.9	D	D	452	13.9	6 447	25.1	7 371	480	3 936	821	2 578
Pawnee	194	13 683	0.6	D	D	194	11.7	3 053	22.7	3 402	310	1 736	270	1 629
Payne	7 764	76 498	1.0	921	11.9	542	7.0	13 734	20.1	9 907	147	6 067	2 487	3 215
Pittsburg	2 433	46 959	1.1	580	12.9	619	13.8	8 290	22.7	9 157	540	4 340	1 411	3 078
Pontotoc	1 696	37 842	1.1	544	15.0	413	11.4	7 219	23.0	7 026	299	3 811	1 240	3 307
Pottawatomie	3 053	65 460	0.9	966	14.0	729	10.6	12 345	21.1	12 843	1 779	5 395	3 025	4 356
Pushmataha	110	10 890	0.9	D	D	163	13.9	2 468	26.5	2 870	190	1 571	255	2 204
Roger Mills	11	3 742	1.1	D	D	37	11.1	628	22.8	724	14	461	38	1 042
Rogers	1 216	72 350	0.7	1 004	12.1	726	8.7	13 537	18.3	14 041	4 075	5 007	1 460	1 680
Seminole	581	24 535	0.9	363	14.9	331	13.6	4 420	22.5	5 101	433	2 781	1 101	4 321
Sequoyah	416	36 658	0.7	570	13.9	425	10.3	8 112	23.8	8 507	1 094	4 284	942	2 222
Stephens	540	43 738	1.0	583	13.4	582	13.4	7 570	21.4	9 227	866	5 078	1 700	3 774
Texas	572	19 868	1.0	D	D	141	7.4	4 908	26.3	2 352	103	1 360	406	1 967
Tillman	267	7 405	0.8	D	D	118	14.4	1 513	24.7	1 694	55	1 054	205	2 565
Tulsa	9 817	654 100	1.2	9 682	16.6	5 464	9.3	107 122	20.7	90 656	26 969	33 865	30 632	5 077
Wagoner	319	49 976	0.4	896	13.3	483	7.2	12 175	19.5	10 970	3 399	3 836	1 778	2 433
Washington	798	50 631	1.0	651	13.1	580	11.6	8 059	19.5	10 714	734	6 249	1 677	3 290
Washita	206	10 436	0.8	D	D	139	11.9	2 112	22.2	2 140	76	1 367	120	1 032
Woods	1 005	8 981	1.1	D	D	113	13.5	1 453	21.5	1 608	91	1 089	141	1 588
Woodward	1 240	20 630	1.1	D	D	199	10.2	3 614	21.5	3 322	135	2 015	566	2 819
OREGON	86 642	3 807 437	1.0	49 054	13.1	31 583	8.5	628 573	19.4	646 855	263 226	198 319	125 083	3 265
Baker	373	16 274	1.0	D	D	199	12.4	2 813	22.9	4 164	119	2 403	230	1 426
Benton	5 043	85 394	1.0	D	D	528	6.5	10 964	15.3	11 999	5 342	3 949	1 900	2 220
Clackamas	2 753	343 743	0.8	4 037	10.7	2 905	7.7	51 215	15.5	60 800	34 580	11 612	10 381	2 761
Clatsop	956	37 994	1.1	D	D	379	10.2	6 481	21.3	7 478	1 499	3 279	1 492	4 028
Columbia	499	40 389	0.6	D	D	403	8.2	6 816	16.0	8 791	4 274	2 151	565	1 145
Coos	1 008	63 466	1.0	D	D	841	13.2	10 376	21.3	16 312	922	8 334	1 943	3 210
Crook	245	20 375	0.9	D	D	206	9.0	3 985	21.8	5 017	941	2 109	511	2 436
Curry	318	21 913	0.9	D	D	361	16.5	3 429	22.8	7 250	528	3 358	NA	NA
Deschutes	1 244	156 028	1.0	2 014	13.1	1 125	7.3	26 867	20.2	29 102	8 119	11 106	5 319	3 372
Douglas	1 708	106 471	1.0	1 161	11.1	1 254	12.0	15 946	19.9	27 270	7 178	9 463	2 375	2 206
Gilliam	20	1 944	1.2	D	D	19	11.1	224	18.1	444	13	238	17	909
Grant	105	7 403	1.0	D	D	87	12.3	1 163	22.3	1 879	382	776	49	658
Harney	127	7 335	1.0	D	D	77	11.3	1 302	24.5	1 633	53	985	140	1 886
Hood River	787	22 342	1.1	D	D	171	8.0	4 484	23.9	3 250	754	1 301	139	622
Jackson	3 492	200 815	1.0	2 374	11.9	2 031	10.2	34 768	21.3	43 017	12 623	14 801	6 513	3 205
Jefferson	853	20 688	0.9	346	16.9	179	8.7	4 482	26.2	4 089	964	1 710	582	2 680
Josephine	1 601	80 694	1.0	883	10.8	1 111	13.6	12 721	20.4	21 806	7 797	6 353	2 425	2 932
Klamath	950	66 155	1.0	842	12.7	714	10.7	12 617	23.2	14 115	2 720	5 906	1 739	2 687
Lake	454	7 908	1.0	D	D	93	12.7	1 342	24.3	1 853	122	880	98	1 241
Lane	8 530	348 836	1.0	3 756	11.0	3 075	9.0	58 509	19.8	65 013	29 535	18 652	12 969	3 687
Lincoln	762	46 412	1.0	D	D	540	11.7	8 146	22.4	12 121	2 142	5 324	1 460	3 172
Linn	1 227	109 449	0.9	1 527	13.5	1 129	10.0	18 233	18.9	22 640	10 917	6 208	3 399	2 913
Malheur	3 351	34 065	1.2	D	D	290	9.3	7 266	28.5	5 424	144	3 485	1 013	3 235
Marion	10 429	316 636	1.1	5 066	16.2	2 587	8.3	65 310	23.9	49 444	27 565	11 799	10 490	3 327

1. Per 1,000 estimated resident population. 2. Data for serious crimes have not been adjusted for underreporting; this may affect comparability between geographic areas and over time. 3. Per 100,000 population estimated by the FBI.

Table B. States and Counties — Crime, Education, Money Income, and Poverty

STATE County	Serious crimes known to police,[1] 2010 (cont.) Rate[2] Violent	Property	Education School enrollment and attainment, 2006–2010 Enrollment[3] Total	Percent private	Attainment[4] (percent) High school graduate or less	Bachelor's degree or more	Local government expenditures,[5] 2008–2009 Total current expenditures (mil dol)	Current expenditures per student (dollars)	Money income, 2006–2010 Per capita income[6] (dollars)	Households Median income Dollars	Percent change, 2000 to 2006–2010 (constant 2010 dollars)	Percent with income of $200,000 or more	Income and poverty, 2010 Median household income (dollars)	Percent below poverty level All persons	Children under 18 years	Children 5 to 17 years in families
	46	47	48	49	50	51	52	53	54	55	56	57	58	59	60	61
OKLAHOMA—Cont'd																
Kiowa	191	1 937	2 058	7.1	57.4	16.4	15.2	8 968	18 921	32 565	-1.3	0.8	31 850	23.7	32.8	29.5
Latimer	170	1 399	2 981	6.3	53.6	13.8	16.2	9 358	20 353	42 639	40.5	1.8	35 306	17.8	27.3	24.1
Le Flore	214	1 772	11 818	3.9	59.3	11.4	79.1	7 889	17 357	36 335	5.2	0.6	33 624	22.3	29.9	28.0
Lincoln	166	1 564	8 074	6.0	57.7	13.7	43.7	7 768	20 774	42 282	7.1	1.6	40 076	14.2	22.5	20.8
Logan	179	1 458	11 066	11.1	45.5	23.2	34.0	7 489	25 090	48 683	4.5	3.1	49 006	14.3	19.1	17.0
Love	202	1 136	2 072	6.0	65.5	13.9	12.7	7 775	20 817	41 629	1.0	1.6	41 784	15.6	23.7	21.5
McClain	154	2 455	8 515	5.1	49.2	17.9	57.1	7 086	23 556	53 708	13.8	1.5	51 767	11.3	15.9	14.4
McCurtain	380	3 068	8 159	5.7	62.4	12.3	60.8	8 515	17 456	31 082	1.6	0.9	30 708	23.9	33.6	31.8
McIntosh	222	2 173	4 187	7.1	62.4	11.1	24.2	8 018	16 095	30 620	-6.9	0.2	33 771	20.0	30.9	28.6
Major	13	2 484	1 514	7.6	56.3	16.4	10.8	10 434	24 897	46 748	19.3	2.1	44 736	12.4	18.7	16.9
Marshall	284	1 174	3 284	2.4	61.9	15.9	21.5	7 564	18 794	40 419	20.7	0.9	34 924	17.9	27.3	26.1
Mayes	332	1 784	9 474	3.5	57.5	11.9	56.5	7 625	19 975	41 228	4.6	0.5	40 253	18.1	26.3	24.8
Murray	141	1 794	2 952	7.7	57.6	13.3	16.1	6 960	20 634	40 870	6.5	0.7	39 629	15.1	22.6	20.7
Muskogee	652	3 093	17 644	8.0	50.7	17.5	114.0	8 132	19 161	37 002	2.8	1.5	38 528	20.6	31.1	28.7
Noble	78	1 323	2 778	1.8	51.3	17.5	18.7	8 523	20 032	39 515	-8.1	0.4	41 580	14.3	21.3	19.9
Nowata	579	1 879	2 551	3.8	60.4	12.6	15.7	7 644	20 752	37 500	0.5	0.6	38 040	15.6	24.8	21.5
Okfuskee	262	2 166	2 828	5.2	62.1	10.9	18.9	8 920	15 046	33 286	8.1	0.4	31 423	27.3	32.7	29.8
Oklahoma	704	4 907	185 676	14.7	40.8	28.2	885.6	7 705	25 723	42 916	-3.3	3.3	42 758	17.6	27.6	25.2
Okmulgee	327	2 610	9 929	4.2	55.7	13.5	57.5	8 046	19 071	37 820	8.0	0.6	36 119	21.4	29.1	25.5
Osage	558	2 401	11 862	11.5	51.7	17.8	31.5	8 851	21 446	41 125	-5.8	1.2	41 589	16.5	22.7	19.6
Ottawa	248	2 330	7 850	5.4	54.7	13.1	46.9	7 793	17 638	35 483	1.9	0.9	34 998	20.5	32.3	29.4
Pawnee	157	1 472	3 787	7.8	56.9	16.1	24.9	8 064	19 520	40 059	-0.1	1.5	38 550	16.5	23.9	21.4
Payne	221	2 994	31 216	5.2	37.9	34.0	79.8	7 800	19 540	34 752	-4.5	1.6	36 874	21.7	21.4	19.6
Pittsburg	175	2 904	9 609	11.0	56.4	15.1	65.4	8 104	20 714	39 245	8.1	1.6	38 154	18.8	25.4	23.1
Pontotoc	443	2 866	10 041	7.2	46.8	26.2	59.9	8 704	21 136	37 484	9.8	1.9	38 514	18.0	23.9	21.7
Pottawatomie	490	3 867	18 257	16.5	53.6	16.6	102.9	7 767	19 437	40 085	0.3	1.0	38 259	18.5	26.3	24.5
Pushmataha	242	1 962	2 383	5.6	61.2	11.6	20.5	9 131	15 460	26 742	-4.6	0.2	30 070	23.9	38.3	35.2
Roger Mills	55	987	792	1.5	49.1	20.1	12.0	16 123	28 427	48 917	28.4	5.2	44 595	13.2	19.6	18.5
Rogers	150	1 530	23 521	11.7	45.9	21.2	100.4	6 969	25 358	57 443	2.0	2.4	56 107	9.8	13.2	11.8
Seminole	263	4 058	6 456	6.9	59.6	13.3	41.9	8 166	17 032	32 985	1.9	0.9	33 080	24.1	35.3	32.0
Sequoyah	210	2 012	10 424	3.8	60.8	12.2	68.1	7 631	18 049	36 357	4.0	1.2	35 250	19.7	30.3	28.2
Stephens	235	3 538	9 936	7.7	57.2	16.5	63.6	7 773	22 790	43 524	11.9	1.5	40 996	16.5	24.1	22.3
Texas	141	1 827	5 222	9.3	55.7	20.3	35.2	8 716	21 356	44 623	-1.8	1.8	44 819	12.1	17.6	16.4
Tillman	313	2 252	1 812	2.4	62.2	14.6	22.4	14 090	15 894	29 802	-5.1	0.1	30 364	25.9	38.1	32.1
Tulsa	798	4 278	155 269	18.9	39.3	28.8	863.6	7 727	26 769	45 613	-5.7	3.6	44 231	15.8	23.1	21.8
Wagoner	250	2 182	18 481	11.1	44.4	20.8	46.3	6 867	24 049	55 487	5.0	1.8	56 216	11.5	17.4	15.5
Washington	339	2 950	11 494	12.6	46.2	26.1	63.5	7 758	26 663	44 823	-1.2	3.2	46 957	13.7	21.3	19.0
Washita	241	791	2 594	5.1	59.5	16.4	18.2	8 230	21 511	43 039	15.0	1.4	40 523	15.3	23.2	21.7
Woods	90	1 498	2 421	6.1	44.2	28.5	12.4	9 729	24 292	48 076	31.2	1.7	37 981	16.2	20.9	20.9
Woodward	159	2 659	3 887	9.8	55.5	17.4	28.5	7 851	24 635	49 672	16.8	2.9	48 584	15.1	21.3	20.0
OREGON	252	3 013	932 399	15.1	37.0	28.6	5 510.2	9 827	26 171	49 260	-4.9	3.0	46 536	15.8	21.7	19.5
Baker	25	1 401	3 306	12.0	45.0	20.5	23.8	10 761	21 683	39 704	3.3	1.6	37 868	20.0	31.1	29.3
Benton	112	2 108	31 596	7.6	22.9	47.9	81.5	9 031	26 177	48 012	-9.5	3.5	49 156	19.1	15.2	13.5
Clackamas	110	2 651	93 032	16.2	32.7	31.4	531.8	9 059	31 785	62 007	-6.0	5.2	57 960	10.4	13.2	11.8
Clatsop	121	3 907	8 798	7.1	38.0	21.6	52.6	10 482	25 347	42 223	-8.1	1.8	44 234	14.8	24.6	22.0
Columbia	63	1 082	12 072	9.8	45.6	16.8	72.6	8 460	24 613	55 199	-4.8	1.0	50 707	13.4	18.2	14.7
Coos	251	2 959	12 374	10.5	45.1	18.3	91.4	10 803	21 981	37 491	-6.1	1.6	36 216	19.1	28.5	25.4
Crook	262	2 174	4 345	13.4	50.6	15.4	27.5	8 574	22 275	46 059	3.4	0.9	39 867	17.4	29.3	25.6
Curry	NA	NA	3 556	7.6	43.8	18.5	25.4	9 919	23 842	37 469	-1.8	0.8	36 994	16.0	25.0	22.5
Deschutes	313	3 059	33 758	14.8	32.3	29.1	230.0	9 319	27 920	53 071	0.2	3.0	46 631	14.8	22.2	20.4
Douglas	105	2 101	22 891	11.3	48.0	15.5	156.5	10 330	21 342	39 711	-5.6	1.1	36 991	19.5	30.7	27.4
Gilliam	0	909	278	7.9	40.5	18.8	6.2	26 725	25 559	42 148	-1.0	0.5	45 827	11.4	18.4	17.5
Grant	0	658	1 434	9.4	48.1	17.2	15.6	15 123	22 041	35 974	-12.7	1.7	36 792	16.5	24.8	21.8
Harney	54	1 832	1 540	2.9	53.1	16.2	15.5	13 095	20 849	39 036	-0.4	0.1	36 441	19.1	29.4	26.3
Hood River	13	609	5 367	7.5	43.4	25.9	41.2	10 375	23 930	51 307	5.7	3.3	49 490	13.0	21.2	19.1
Jackson	271	2 934	44 760	11.4	39.7	24.4	274.4	9 674	24 410	44 142	-4.4	2.2	40 603	15.7	23.3	21.0
Jefferson	69	2 610	4 930	9.7	54.1	15.9	39.4	10 692	20 009	41 425	-8.8	1.1	40 888	21.1	33.7	30.3
Josephine	147	2 784	16 658	10.9	46.0	16.5	102.7	9 221	21 539	38 035	-3.8	1.5	36 102	18.8	30.8	28.6
Klamath	267	2 419	16 067	8.7	46.3	18.1	98.2	9 754	22 081	41 818	4.7	1.8	37 370	17.4	26.0	24.7
Lake	329	912	1 427	3.6	49.5	16.4	13.6	12 326	22 586	41 105	10.0	2.0	36 167	20.4	28.7	25.6
Lane	266	3 422	92 457	12.5	35.6	27.7	470.5	10 084	23 869	42 923	-8.2	2.2	40 545	19.1	23.4	20.8
Lincoln	350	2 822	8 061	11.3	38.5	23.8	50.2	9 341	24 354	39 738	-4.2	1.1	38 302	17.0	30.1	28.3
Linn	141	2 772	27 438	10.4	45.6	16.3	179.0	8 414	22 165	45 832	-3.5	1.1	43 019	18.1	29.1	25.0
Malheur	179	3 056	8 405	9.0	54.1	13.8	57.6	11 099	16 335	39 144	2.2	0.5	32 412	39.5	39.9	33.0
Marion	232	3 095	79 170	15.4	44.5	20.9	591.5	10 094	21 915	46 069	-9.8	1.9	44 725	17.9	26.3	23.8

1. Data for serious crimes have not been adjusted for underreporting; this may affect comparability between geographic areas and over time.   2. Per 100,000 population estimated by the FBI.   3. All persons 3 years old and over enrolled in nursery school through college.   4. Persons 25 years old and over.   5. Elementary and secondary education expenditures.   6. Based on population estimated by the American Community Survey, 2006–2010.

STATE County	Total (mil dol)	Percent change, 2008–2009	Per capita¹ Dollars	Per capita¹ Rank	Wages and salaries² (mil dol)	Proprietors' income (mil dol)	Dividends, interest, and rent (mil dol)	Total	Transfer payments (mil dol) Government payments to individuals Total	Social Security	Medical payments	Income maintenance	Unemployment insurance
	62	63	64	65	66	67	68	69	70	71	72	73	74
OKLAHOMA—Cont'd													
Kiowa	259	-12.1	28 452	2 310	96	6	52	86	85	28	39	9	2
Latimer	319	-7.4	30 007	1 975	200	16	40	92	90	30	31	9	4
Le Flore	1 334	0.4	26 725	2 606	518	75	159	441	432	127	197	44	16
Lincoln	937	-0.9	29 093	2 170	291	60	124	218	212	83	81	20	8
Logan	1 378	-3.1	35 052	1 011	282	155	204	241	234	88	84	22	8
Love	327	1.9	35 856	907	165	9	38	72	70	26	29	6	2
McClain	1 267	2.5	38 203	619	328	48	139	217	211	79	86	14	7
McCurtain	864	0.7	25 883	2 749	425	70	111	311	304	88	142	41	12
McIntosh	557	2.4	28 141	2 375	157	36	79	208	204	71	87	18	5
Major	225	-7.9	31 295	1 694	97	29	40	49	48	22	18	3	1
Marshall	403	-2.1	26 858	2 589	169	31	61	131	128	47	55	12	4
Mayes	1 146	-0.1	28 600	2 279	512	54	165	322	315	115	129	32	12
Murray	434	4.1	33 511	1 249	232	19	60	104	102	38	42	8	3
Muskogee	2 112	3.0	29 575	2 076	1 415	115	315	638	625	188	276	68	18
Noble	328	-7.0	29 956	1 991	183	22	61	86	84	31	37	6	4
Nowata	275	0.1	26 161	2 694	72	16	42	85	83	32	33	7	4
Okfuskee	281	0.6	25 703	2 772	95	30	33	110	108	30	55	12	3
Oklahoma	29 856	-2.4	41 657	353	24 278	5 444	4 882	4 824	4 695	1 458	2 017	592	153
Okmulgee	1 136	1.6	28 900	2 218	429	47	142	358	351	112	152	40	11
Osage	1 531	-1.3	33 985	1 171	293	169	184	272	264	119	70	28	16
Ottawa	1 016	2.3	32 107	1 506	483	81	148	307	301	101	136	29	9
Pawnee	493	-1.0	30 012	1 974	155	27	70	135	132	51	55	11	5
Payne	2 315	-1.0	29 030	2 190	1 524	146	428	421	407	140	162	33	16
Pittsburg	1 412	-1.8	31 231	1 705	885	73	225	358	350	125	146	31	11
Pontotoc	1 185	0.5	31 679	1 604	762	56	197	312	306	94	137	30	9
Pottawatomie	2 129	0.2	30 292	1 910	873	150	316	498	485	162	194	61	16
Pushmataha	303	1.0	25 617	2 791	110	25	37	119	117	36	55	12	4
Roger Mills	118	-5.5	34 739	1 055	41	12	37	22	22	8	10	1	1
Rogers	2 974	0.7	34 726	1 057	1 268	179	392	543	527	208	200	38	21
Seminole	703	-0.3	28 955	2 209	323	38	111	234	230	66	104	31	7
Sequoyah	1 131	1.4	27 291	2 518	360	105	127	368	360	113	159	44	13
Stephens	1 475	-3.6	33 929	1 180	720	182	276	333	325	128	125	27	13
Texas	594	-4.3	28 108	2 383	385	53	100	95	91	34	37	9	3
Tillman	193	-10.3	24 790	2 884	81	5	30	68	67	21	31	8	2
Tulsa	27 035	-3.9	44 912	203	18 953	4 951	5 279	4 032	3 922	1 347	1 709	378	146
Wagoner	2 226	1.8	31 626	1 619	325	52	279	380	367	163	112	34	16
Washington	2 025	-1.1	39 940	452	1 101	171	531	389	380	159	147	27	14
Washita	307	-9.9	25 954	2 739	105	9	53	85	83	28	39	6	3
Woods	254	-7.0	30 208	1 933	123	13	70	62	60	22	25	4	1
Woodward	646	-11.0	32 383	1 445	426	68	119	122	119	46	49	9	5
OREGON	138 453	-0.6	36 191	X	87 755	10 102	28 181	26 920	26 223	8 953	9 526	2 525	2 585
Baker	468	2.8	29 098	2 169	223	20	115	138	135	55	50	12	6
Benton	3 133	-0.9	37 922	649	2 037	158	793	429	414	172	108	37	33
Clackamas	16 854	-2.0	43 646	249	7 890	1 137	3 460	2 303	2 233	882	693	161	253
Clatsop	1 249	0.3	33 545	1 242	731	107	259	285	278	108	105	23	18
Columbia	1 653	0.2	33 325	1 290	450	67	264	367	358	133	123	28	40
Coos	1 985	0.8	31 614	1 622	939	137	438	614	603	226	227	57	37
Crook	589	-1.6	26 116	2 706	235	36	152	193	189	69	69	15	22
Curry	733	-0.3	34 683	1 068	262	48	233	230	226	100	81	14	11
Deschutes	5 705	-2.3	35 966	891	2 913	606	1 511	1 127	1 098	409	348	86	157
Douglas	3 270	0.3	31 686	1 600	1 608	162	688	1 038	1 019	377	352	92	86
Gilliam	62	-5.5	37 450	694	52	0	16	14	14	6	5	1	1
Grant	215	2.6	31 669	1 609	104	7	54	63	61	25	22	4	5
Harney	199	0.1	29 447	2 106	104	5	44	59	58	22	20	5	6
Hood River	732	0.3	33 446	1 268	470	39	180	126	122	45	45	12	10
Jackson	6 907	-0.6	34 314	1 123	3 534	666	1 649	1 591	1 555	586	542	149	137
Jefferson	580	0.2	29 059	2 182	265	22	117	171	167	55	65	22	14
Josephine	2 429	1.1	29 981	1 985	963	180	584	791	776	295	276	79	55
Klamath	1 947	-0.5	29 387	2 123	1 009	119	396	580	568	189	210	56	43
Lake	222	-0.2	31 269	1 698	107	22	47	62	61	24	22	6	4
Lane	11 784	-0.8	33 562	1 238	6 659	700	2 650	2 681	2 617	893	920	250	279
Lincoln	1 565	0.5	33 810	1 201	736	125	383	410	402	170	139	35	24
Linn	3 434	-0.8	29 451	2 105	1 949	193	611	983	962	315	376	88	101
Malheur	737	0.0	23 960	2 967	514	36	150	225	219	70	94	27	9
Marion	10 454	0.8	32 876	1 358	6 579	915	1 875	2 326	2 268	681	946	260	188

1. Based on the resident population estimated as of July 1 of the year shown.   2. Includes supplements to wages and salaries.

Table B. States and Counties — **Earnings, Social Security, and Housing**

STATE County	Earnings, 2009									Social Security beneficiaries, December 2010		Supplemental Security Income recipients, December 2010	Housing units, 2010	
	Total (mil dol)	Farm	Percent by selected industries							Number	Rate[2]		Total	Percent change, 2000–2010
			Goods-related[1]		Service-related and health									
			Total	Manu-facturing	Information and professional and technical services	Retail trade	Finance, insurance, and real estate	Health care and social services	Govern-ment					
	75	76	77	78	79	80	81	82	83	84	85	86	87	88
OKLAHOMA—Cont'd														
Kiowa	102	-6.8	D	D	4.5	8.0	6.3	8.3	37.6	2 450	259	365	5 216	-1.7
Latimer	216	-0.7	D	D	1.5	3.2	2.0	2.9	28.2	2 755	247	419	4 979	5.7
Le Flore	593	1.1	26.1	12.8	D	8.3	3.8	D	32.5	11 570	230	2 072	21 448	6.5
Lincoln	351	-1.0	D	7.6	D	6.5	10.4	D	25.9	7 480	218	782	15 208	10.9
Logan	437	-0.7	20.0	3.9	D	7.5	8.2	D	24.3	7 165	171	671	17 195	23.7
Love	174	-0.9	D	D	D	3.9	D	D	70.6	2 185	232	228	4 539	11.6
McClain	376	0.2	27.9	5.5	5.9	13.0	4.6	D	24.0	6 545	190	536	13 996	25.1
McCurtain	495	1.3	28.0	20.8	4.4	7.0	2.8	D	25.6	8 085	244	1 699	15 533	0.7
McIntosh	193	-2.2	9.9	3.9	4.4	16.1	5.1	12.4	26.2	6 090	301	723	13 350	5.6
Major	126	2.8	37.8	6.1	4.0	6.8	5.6	4.3	18.5	1 765	234	92	3 671	3.7
Marshall	199	1.4	D	26.2	D	6.7	5.4	10.5	18.9	3 940	249	455	10 006	17.5
Mayes	566	0.8	32.9	26.3	D	11.3	3.0	6.3	25.4	9 375	227	1 199	19 239	10.4
Murray	252	-1.6	15.1	3.8	D	7.5	3.6	D	49.7	3 240	240	308	6 746	4.1
Muskogee	1 530	0.1	21.5	16.7	3.3	6.8	3.2	D	34.5	15 940	225	2 859	30 908	4.5
Noble	205	3.3	D	D	1.8	3.8	3.8	D	29.7	2 580	223	259	5 341	5.1
Nowata	87	-1.7	D	19.1	D	4.5	5.2	9.2	27.6	2 705	257	259	4 828	2.6
Okfuskee	125	-1.5	23.7	8.1	D	5.8	D	9.0	46.1	2 715	223	580	5 282	3.3
Oklahoma	29 722	0.0	25.7	9.6	9.1	5.3	6.0	11.0	21.7	116 710	162	18 604	319 828	8.4
Okmulgee	476	0.2	24.8	19.6	2.5	8.1	3.8	D	36.3	9 510	237	1 575	17 891	3.3
Osage	462	1.4	33.8	12.7	5.3	5.6	3.5	D	26.6	9 655	203	1 075	21 143	12.3
Ottawa	565	2.9	18.9	14.4	D	6.6	3.6	11.2	38.3	8 645	271	1 324	14 060	-5.3
Pawnee	182	-1.0	D	4.0	D	9.1	5.3	10.9	32.3	4 170	252	423	7 745	3.8
Payne	1 670	-0.3	18.3	8.3	5.1	6.5	4.1	6.5	46.1	11 160	144	1 231	33 991	15.9
Pittsburg	958	-0.1	20.8	12.4	D	7.2	5.9	D	39.0	11 140	243	1 510	22 634	5.2
Pontotoc	817	-0.3	14.5	7.8	6.9	6.4	4.5	D	41.6	8 100	216	1 223	16 595	6.5
Pottawatomie	1 022	-0.1	23.5	15.1	D	8.4	3.8	11.5	25.9	14 435	208	1 945	29 139	6.7
Pushmataha	134	-2.5	12.1	5.8	D	9.5	3.8	18.9	32.6	3 355	290	624	6 110	5.4
Roger Mills	53	-1.3	D	D	D	4.8	3.1	D	39.2	770	211	72	1 905	8.9
Rogers	1 447	0.0	33.6	22.9	D	6.1	4.0	7.2	22.1	16 085	185	1 222	35 160	28.0
Seminole	361	-0.5	D	13.1	2.3	6.6	2.9	D	27.2	5 900	232	1 081	11 642	4.4
Sequoyah	464	1.1	9.6	6.0	9.8	8.9	3.5	13.9	34.1	10 260	242	1 978	18 656	10.1
Stephens	902	-0.6	46.5	13.8	D	7.0	5.3	D	13.0	10 430	232	1 102	20 658	4.0
Texas	438	9.4	32.4	24.4	6.5	5.6	3.3	3.5	19.0	2 635	128	184	8 208	2.4
Tillman	87	-0.7	D	D	D	4.7	D	3.5	40.9	1 915	240	326	4 077	-6.1
Tulsa	23 904	0.0	29.0	15.6	11.0	6.7	5.9	10.6	8.8	101 305	168	18 217	268 426	10.0
Wagoner	378	1.8	30.6	19.4	3.5	8.3	3.9	6.3	25.6	12 955	177	1 176	29 694	28.1
Washington	1 272	0.1	38.2	3.8	4.6	9.2	4.8	D	10.0	12 255	240	1 041	23 451	5.4
Washita	114	-5.7	26.2	2.9	6.8	5.1	7.8	5.7	34.8	2 475	213	222	5 479	0.5
Woods	136	-4.3	16.7	5.0	5.3	10.3	6.2	D	40.1	1 725	194	102	4 478	-0.3
Woodward	495	0.8	35.8	6.3	3.1	7.4	4.6	7.3	15.7	3 700	184	310	8 838	6.0
OREGON	97 857	1.2	18.2	12.4	10.1	6.6	6.3	12.6	18.2	712 216	186	74 860	1 675 562	15.3
Baker	242	1.8	15.5	11.1	4.9	9.0	3.7	14.0	28.0	4 645	288	395	8 826	5.0
Benton	2 196	1.1	19.0	16.1	11.1	4.4	2.9	14.5	30.3	13 030	152	940	36 245	13.3
Clackamas	9 027	1.8	20.7	13.1	11.0	6.7	6.9	13.2	11.8	66 535	177	4 539	156 945	14.6
Clatsop	838	0.4	D	16.6	D	10.2	4.8	12.9	20.8	8 540	231	741	21 546	9.5
Columbia	516	1.5	24.7	19.5	D	8.5	4.7	7.4	23.0	10 240	207	851	20 698	17.8
Coos	1 075	0.1	12.2	7.6	5.2	9.0	3.9	11.9	31.5	18 360	291	2 083	30 593	4.6
Crook	271	-4.1	19.0	12.4	3.6	6.1	3.7	9.9	27.4	5 675	271	374	10 202	23.4
Curry	310	1.5	D	10.5	D	10.7	6.7	7.6	22.8	8 020	359	544	12 613	10.6
Deschutes	3 519	-0.3	15.7	6.7	10.8	9.3	7.9	17.8	14.5	32 570	206	1 890	80 139	46.8
Douglas	1 769	0.0	18.5	13.4	5.0	7.8	3.3	14.1	26.6	30 695	285	2 790	48 915	13.0
Gilliam	53	1.6	D	D	3.7	2.1	D	3.7	20.5	485	259	39	1 156	10.8
Grant	111	-1.6	12.3	5.4	3.6	7.1	3.4	D	51.2	2 115	284	164	4 344	8.5
Harney	109	3.2	4.1	0.5	3.7	8.8	3.4	D	53.3	1 835	247	186	3 835	8.5
Hood River	509	8.4	17.5	12.6	D	7.7	2.5	15.1	14.9	3 710	166	254	9 271	18.6
Jackson	4 200	0.5	15.4	7.0	6.7	11.7	5.3	17.9	16.2	47 270	233	3 912	90 937	20.1
Jefferson	287	5.1	D	14.4	1.6	5.2	2.4	7.6	44.0	4 575	211	463	9 815	18.0
Josephine	1 142	-0.3	16.3	10.1	D	10.7	6.1	20.0	16.7	24 515	296	2 297	38 001	14.3
Klamath	1 129	1.7	D	8.2	D	8.7	4.0	13.7	26.5	15 720	237	1 792	32 774	13.5
Lake	129	7.1	D	7.5	4.9	5.8	3.0	D	44.3	2 060	261	233	4 439	11.0
Lane	7 359	0.5	16.0	10.1	9.5	8.3	5.3	16.5	20.9	71 435	203	7 766	156 112	12.3
Lincoln	861	0.2	D	8.0	4.8	11.8	3.6	12.4	25.5	13 515	294	1 169	30 610	13.8
Linn	2 142	3.3	D	25.1	3.1	6.7	2.5	10.2	16.9	25 415	218	2 906	48 821	14.8
Malheur	550	4.7	D	6.6	3.4	10.9	3.1	12.7	33.2	6 145	196	839	11 692	4.1
Marion	7 494	3.0	12.3	6.4	5.5	6.6	5.1	17.5	29.8	55 440	176	7 025	120 948	11.8

1. Includes mining, construction, and manufacturing. 2. Per 1,000 resident population enumerated in the 2010 census.

Table B. States and Counties — Housing, Labor Force, and Employment

STATE County	Total	Percent	Median value[1]	With a mortgage	Without a mortgage	Median rent[2]	Median rent as a percent of income	Substandard units[3] (percent)	Total	Percent change, 2009–2010	Total	Rate[4]	Total	Management, business, science and arts	Construction, production, and maintenance occupations
	89	90	91	92	93	94	95	96	97	98	99	100	101	102	103
OKLAHOMA—Cont'd															
Kiowa	3 846	66.4	50 100	18.9	11.3	441	27.3	2.2	4 066	-2.2	266	6.5	4 104	27.4	31.1
Latimer	4 130	73.6	65 700	20.0	10.0	477	23.4	5.7	4 450	-2.8	477	10.7	4 597	27.7	35.5
Le Flore	18 651	73.4	72 700	21.0	11.4	529	25.9	3.3	20 683	-1.7	2 069	10.0	19 542	23.2	36.0
Lincoln	12 799	79.3	87 700	19.5	10.6	507	27.3	4.4	13 771	-2.9	993	7.2	14 371	26.4	33.3
Logan	14 468	77.7	116 400	21.5	11.0	578	28.3	2.3	18 090	0.5	1 153	6.4	18 798	32.5	25.7
Love	3 595	76.0	77 200	19.6	10.5	567	20.3	3.8	5 458	1.3	284	5.2	4 330	23.6	30.2
McClain	11 819	81.7	118 200	19.0	11.0	655	24.8	1.9	15 140	-0.3	954	6.3	15 676	31.5	29.1
McCurtain	13 255	67.4	71 500	19.6	10.7	511	29.8	5.1	15 266	2.9	1 696	11.1	12 648	26.0	32.5
McIntosh	7 670	78.3	74 400	22.5	12.7	505	34.8	2.8	8 900	-0.8	828	9.3	6 884	25.4	27.6
Major	3 138	81.0	77 600	17.9	10.0	487	22.3	1.0	4 253	-2.2	202	4.7	3 754	23.7	42.2
Marshall	5 718	76.5	80 800	19.3	11.8	536	21.7	2.5	6 403	-0.9	465	7.3	6 731	24.8	32.2
Mayes	16 073	74.9	89 200	20.7	10.9	581	26.5	3.9	18 143	-1.8	1 634	9.0	17 246	27.6	35.6
Murray	5 232	79.8	77 700	18.8	10.0	562	23.3	2.9	8 956	-2.9	400	4.5	5 838	26.9	28.8
Muskogee	26 927	68.8	84 100	21.8	11.5	561	29.6	2.3	31 181	-0.4	2 579	8.3	28 387	29.9	30.4
Noble	4 493	74.5	74 800	20.9	11.4	563	33.4	2.7	5 684	-3.6	360	6.3	5 340	30.1	29.8
Nowata	4 224	79.2	76 800	20.3	12.3	530	25.7	2.2	5 103	-2.2	469	9.2	4 665	30.9	36.4
Okfuskee	4 321	71.5	70 400	21.7	10.8	526	30.5	2.1	4 685	-3.0	432	9.2	4 297	25.5	28.1
Oklahoma	279 434	61.7	117 500	22.2	11.2	675	29.6	3.0	325 854	-1.0	22 498	6.9	337 313	34.3	21.4
Okmulgee	15 342	71.9	78 000	20.8	11.8	582	30.4	3.2	15 835	-2.1	1 658	10.5	16 445	27.2	30.2
Osage	18 055	79.7	96 100	19.8	11.5	519	27.5	2.8	19 523	-3.6	1 669	8.5	20 635	29.4	29.5
Ottawa	12 164	75.0	78 700	20.5	10.9	520	26.6	3.7	18 573	-0.8	1 214	6.5	13 487	25.7	27.6
Pawnee	6 119	76.2	78 100	19.2	11.4	558	30.0	3.5	7 279	-1.9	711	9.8	7 117	24.8	33.2
Payne	28 735	53.9	116 000	21.2	10.0	599	34.5	1.6	35 466	-0.5	2 224	6.3	37 209	35.4	20.1
Pittsburg	18 623	71.4	83 000	19.1	11.1	588	29.1	2.8	23 610	-0.6	1 605	6.8	17 968	25.7	27.5
Pontotoc	14 782	65.3	92 500	19.9	10.4	522	30.5	3.1	20 245	-3.2	1 118	5.5	17 530	33.5	24.6
Pottawatomie	25 069	73.3	89 300	21.2	10.2	605	29.7	2.9	33 624	-1.2	2 260	6.7	29 636	28.6	29.5
Pushmataha	4 755	74.2	69 400	22.4	13.4	416	28.9	2.5	5 538	-0.6	483	8.7	4 431	28.7	28.8
Roger Mills	1 376	77.6	78 900	16.4	10.0	534	16.5	2.0	1 893	-3.5	79	4.2	1 612	32.3	37.3
Rogers	31 318	78.9	139 200	20.4	10.4	734	25.9	2.3	39 976	-1.6	3 044	7.6	41 329	31.9	29.2
Seminole	9 220	72.4	66 000	20.4	11.2	504	28.3	4.3	11 079	-1.5	968	8.7	9 460	26.4	33.5
Sequoyah	15 328	72.4	80 100	19.5	10.9	544	29.1	3.5	17 646	-0.2	1 853	10.5	16 227	24.0	36.3
Stephens	17 781	75.0	80 900	19.5	10.5	556	24.9	2.0	22 160	-0.8	1 584	7.1	19 034	27.7	31.3
Texas	7 083	68.5	83 600	20.6	10.5	570	21.7	7.1	7 535	-0.9	435	5.8	9 805	25.4	39.7
Tillman	3 039	72.2	51 100	21.4	13.2	466	28.6	3.0	3 443	-4.1	216	6.3	3 184	34.4	31.6
Tulsa	238 715	62.1	126 200	21.9	11.4	689	29.2	2.9	291 837	-1.1	22 317	7.6	289 376	34.8	21.7
Wagoner	25 576	83.1	133 800	21.6	10.1	682	29.6	3.1	33 133	-0.8	2 494	7.5	33 375	30.5	27.3
Washington	21 196	74.3	99 700	19.9	11.2	597	25.5	1.1	27 928	-2.0	1 681	6.0	23 383	33.4	24.2
Washita	4 476	74.8	72 800	18.8	10.0	597	20.9	2.2	6 233	-2.5	343	5.5	4 978	30.5	33.6
Woods	3 549	68.4	80 700	17.3	10.0	529	21.9	1.5	4 430	-3.1	194	4.4	4 254	33.4	22.7
Woodward	7 604	72.6	95 600	18.4	10.0	604	24.6	3.2	11 298	-4.6	676	6.0	9 317	27.5	34.9
OREGON	1 499 267	63.8	252 600	26.7	12.6	795	30.6	3.2	1 983 572	0.2	211 356	10.7	1 763 324	35.1	22.6
Baker	6 902	71.2	142 400	23.5	12.0	580	33.9	2.2	7 693	1.5	783	10.2	6 734	32.3	23.7
Benton	33 471	57.2	263 200	24.3	10.6	740	37.1	2.2	44 203	2.1	3 213	7.3	41 191	46.3	16.6
Clackamas	143 357	70.7	331 100	27.2	13.0	882	29.6	2.6	203 675	1.3	20 655	10.1	180 305	36.4	22.0
Clatsop	16 267	62.0	253 100	28.3	12.3	720	30.3	3.7	21 127	2.1	1 986	9.4	17 346	25.5	25.0
Columbia	19 075	76.8	219 800	25.4	12.0	731	29.4	2.2	24 590	-0.5	3 027	12.3	21 122	27.8	33.2
Coos	27 247	67.0	194 800	25.4	13.6	646	29.3	2.6	28 921	2.0	3 656	12.6	25 557	30.2	23.0
Crook	8 754	72.1	228 700	29.1	12.0	744	26.0	3.0	9 201	-3.0	1 608	17.5	9 252	25.7	30.3
Curry	10 473	70.8	266 800	28.8	10.5	757	36.1	2.3	9 522	1.7	1 211	12.7	8 925	22.2	24.8
Deschutes	63 190	68.0	314 400	28.9	12.3	866	29.6	3.5	80 857	-0.4	11 650	14.4	72 837	33.0	22.7
Douglas	43 916	70.6	185 100	26.3	12.0	693	28.7	2.9	46 775	-0.1	6 834	14.6	43 284	26.1	29.7
Gilliam	851	66.6	99 900	19.3	11.3	707	27.9	1.8	1 237	1.3	83	6.7	906	30.8	37.3
Grant	3 349	72.6	128 500	23.3	12.3	547	23.0	1.8	3 507	2.0	469	13.4	3 135	28.3	26.7
Harney	3 350	63.9	124 300	21.9	12.8	545	26.1	4.6	3 586	2.9	556	15.5	3 313	30.4	26.5
Hood River	7 985	68.3	308 000	27.4	11.8	702	29.1	6.3	14 519	4.1	1 200	8.3	11 282	28.9	30.3
Jackson	83 333	63.3	274 500	29.0	13.9	814	32.7	2.6	102 524	0.9	12 969	12.6	89 412	30.5	22.2
Jefferson	7 795	70.2	184 900	28.3	12.4	644	24.5	5.5	9 457	1.6	1 337	14.1	8 571	23.1	34.0
Josephine	34 325	68.6	253 600	29.0	11.3	692	34.8	3.0	35 171	0.1	4 981	14.2	31 744	26.1	27.0
Klamath	27 663	68.7	170 100	25.0	12.1	681	29.8	3.2	31 038	0.1	4 159	13.4	28 602	28.3	27.9
Lake	3 462	68.4	122 200	21.8	12.2	592	25.3	3.0	3 844	4.9	508	13.2	3 373	36.9	25.2
Lane	143 894	60.8	230 000	26.7	12.6	769	32.8	1.8	182 902	0.3	20 378	11.1	160 946	33.9	22.3
Lincoln	20 652	67.2	246 300	27.6	12.6	691	32.3	2.1	23 428	1.2	2 528	10.8	19 898	28.1	23.1
Linn	44 375	68.2	180 300	26.0	11.5	737	29.3	2.9	56 674	1.5	7 533	13.3	49 426	25.9	32.3
Malheur	10 181	64.6	136 400	23.2	11.5	553	26.9	5.7	13 460	3.7	1 473	10.9	11 487	29.4	29.5
Marion	112 773	62.0	205 100	27.1	13.0	731	30.3	5.1	159 161	1.2	17 786	11.2	135 269	30.3	27.9

1. Specified owner-occupied units.　2. Specified renter-occupied units. A value of 10.0 represents 10 percent or less.　3. Overcrowded or lacking complete plumbing facilities.　4. Percent of civilian labor force.　5. Persons 16 years old and over.

Table B. States and Counties — Nonfarm Employment and Agriculture

	Private nonfarm establishments, employment and payroll, 2009									Agriculture, 2007			
		Employment						Annual payroll		Farms			
												Percent with:	
STATE County	Number of establishments	Total	Health care and social assistance	Manufacturing	Retail trade	Finance and insurance	Professional, scientific, and technical services	Total (mil dol)	Average per employee (dollars)	Number	Fewer than 50 acres	500 acres or more	Farm operators whose principal occupation is farming (percent)
	104	105	106	107	108	109	110	111	112	113	114	115	116

OKLAHOMA—Cont'd

Kiowa	204	1 748	566	D	283	100	41	42	24 020	682	11.7	38.3	47.9
Latimer	177	2 097	417	D	287	58	34	64	30 512	760	26.3	11.8	37.4
Le Flore	789	8 757	2 257	755	1 694	391	300	231	26 352	2 043	31.8	9.1	45.0
Lincoln	583	5 226	685	592	747	418	117	147	28 121	2 300	25.4	8.4	36.3
Logan	737	6 421	1 738	365	955	220	144	152	23 595	1 241	28.0	14.4	36.7
Love	150	3 549	179	210	166	D	D	70	19 856	696	24.0	17.0	41.8
McClain	742	6 923	823	314	1 485	275	256	184	26 516	1 318	38.1	12.9	40.1
McCurtain	562	7 895	1 450	2 076	1 206	259	D	203	25 683	1 796	33.9	7.3	41.9
McIntosh	366	3 403	810	123	989	147	112	77	22 588	1 042	27.1	10.3	41.2
Major	250	2 152	D	95	316	77	D	76	35 485	967	12.0	28.0	43.8
Marshall	279	3 877	D	977	574	D	73	101	26 091	545	28.8	11.7	36.5
Mayes	787	9 394	953	2 811	1 663	330	224	287	30 595	1 640	35.1	8.5	40.9
Murray	270	3 184	642	235	654	137	D	85	26 802	530	23.0	16.6	40.8
Muskogee	1 507	24 809	5 639	4 145	3 538	643	1 051	763	30 772	1 845	33.7	8.5	38.8
Noble	193	3 435	394	D	272	115	30	103	29 926	838	16.8	28.5	41.8
Nowata	154	1 408	309	306	142	82	26	34	24 442	912	22.0	15.9	44.2
Okfuskee	162	1 357	463	D	247	72	D	29	21 106	950	19.4	14.0	40.7
Oklahoma	22 264	347 805	54 280	21 918	41 309	21 060	24 301	13 502	38 819	1 289	55.7	4.8	38.1
Okmulgee	707	8 131	2 714	D	1 403	292	176	227	27 921	1 449	32.4	8.1	37.7
Osage	605	5 922	759	358	811	182	128	171	28 819	1 481	29.4	23.1	43.4
Ottawa	636	9 030	1 420	D	1 269	286	161	231	25 595	1 160	38.4	8.0	42.6
Pawnee	292	2 457	552	929	352	110	75	63	25 654	862	22.4	18.7	40.5
Payne	1 722	22 398	3 574	1 766	4 133	877	1 339	611	27 286	1 567	35.4	11.5	32.8
Pittsburg	979	12 734	2 765	1 264	2 269	408	361	378	29 685	1 761	27.8	13.3	42.3
Pontotoc	987	13 153	3 390	1 204	1 835	1 324	446	346	26 315	1 424	26.9	11.1	41.3
Pottawatomie	1 363	18 778	3 083	2 660	2 929	600	641	471	25 098	1 777	31.2	8.3	40.8
Pushmataha	189	1 954	654	125	412	D	50	44	22 646	833	19.6	13.7	45.5
Roger Mills	98	472	D	D	118	D	10	12	25 631	693	6.2	42.7	45.2
Rogers	1 645	28 108	2 731	8 035	2 634	643	720	1 023	36 388	1 936	47.1	7.6	39.0
Seminole	483	5 482	1 042	581	940	213	88	155	28 197	1 172	24.7	8.4	40.0
Sequoyah	606	6 673	1 902	304	1 347	D	155	144	21 587	1 352	36.3	7.3	40.2
Stephens	1 058	13 129	2 185	2 121	2 104	705	429	387	29 482	1 310	22.8	14.2	37.8
Texas	472	6 858	500	D	991	250	D	221	32 270	1 038	7.8	39.1	42.1
Tillman	145	1 296	263	D	D	D	27	31	23 594	548	7.5	40.1	51.5
Tulsa	18 650	320 789	46 648	37 486	37 386	16 849	19 262	12 990	40 492	1 150	55.9	4.3	36.2
Wagoner	938	7 912	693	1 862	1 176	236	282	236	29 850	1 138	42.6	9.9	39.8
Washington	1 212	18 921	3 192	1 051	2 573	768	892	776	40 995	853	38.8	9.6	39.3
Washita	237	1 643	332	D	271	125	62	42	25 537	975	13.4	34.6	47.9
Woods	274	2 356	D	D	527	151	66	66	28 074	840	13.1	36.2	43.8
Woodward	782	8 040	1 193	426	1 357	375	173	265	32 915	892	15.6	36.2	37.8
OREGON	108 040	1 363 826	202 862	152 428	186 447	62 617	79 963	53 367	39 131	38 553	61.4	10.6	46.2
Baker	548	3 840	735	574	776	129	166	102	26 680	688	33.1	27.2	54.5
Benton	2 077	25 094	4 806	3 717	3 398	613	2 213	993	39 583	906	73.3	4.5	41.1
Clackamas	10 865	124 588	17 145	16 036	17 450	6 052	8 544	5 267	42 276	3 989	82.1	1.2	41.3
Clatsop	1 480	13 640	1 902	D	2 489	299	331	414	30 335	229	60.3	3.1	51.5
Columbia	964	7 284	1 004	1 376	1 396	293	261	205	28 091	805	72.9	1.9	38.5
Coos	1 720	17 007	3 647	1 257	2 946	488	477	500	29 415	746	43.6	7.1	51.7
Crook	501	3 917	470	752	599	108	114	109	27 951	622	51.1	15.1	46.9
Curry	721	4 854	799	588	929	211	112	132	27 258	195	35.9	19.5	61.0
Deschutes	5 951	52 759	8 376	4 197	9 472	2 308	2 741	1 743	33 034	1 405	77.9	2.3	40.8
Douglas	2 621	28 065	5 408	4 424	4 523	935	739	870	31 017	2 095	53.8	8.1	47.5
Gilliam	65	605	D	D	D	D	D	21	34 433	164	2.4	77.4	56.1
Grant	253	1 401	D	118	266	93	58	38	26 840	398	27.1	38.7	53.0
Harney	200	1 323	296	36	297	50	72	35	26 371	523	16.6	43.0	57.7
Hood River	934	8 875	1 544	1 087	1 362	172	434	227	25 574	553	68.7	0.5	59.5
Jackson	5 896	65 112	11 441	5 481	11 175	2 783	2 537	2 094	32 167	1 976	69.5	3.5	45.5
Jefferson	355	3 260	D	740	480	81	66	102	31 248	510	37.5	22.4	52.7
Josephine	2 036	19 520	4 135	2 144	4 161	768	570	546	27 947	675	76.6	1.8	51.1
Klamath	1 700	17 339	2 736	2 346	3 081	1 068	638	554	31 943	1 207	39.4	18.1	57.4
Lake	207	1 247	233	236	218	35	46	35	27 884	417	20.1	41.7	68.8
Lane	9 767	113 703	19 980	14 076	18 506	4 940	5 617	3 720	32 715	3 335	75.5	2.8	37.5
Lincoln	1 638	14 208	1 758	970	2 853	305	349	393	27 677	371	63.6	3.2	49.9
Linn	2 456	32 610	4 403	6 756	4 494	940	1 013	1 105	33 900	2 325	65.1	7.9	44.0
Malheur	724	8 244	1 348	D	2 011	232	230	212	25 721	1 250	34.4	20.6	62.2
Marion	7 777	95 112	17 064	8 937	16 016	3 652	4 038	3 065	32 227	2 670	72.2	5.2	46.4

Table B. States and Counties — **Agriculture**

STATE County	Land in farms Acreage (1,000) [117]	Percent change, 2002–2007 [118]	Average size of farm [119]	Total irrigated (1,000) [120]	Total cropland (1,000) [121]	Value of land and buildings Average per farm [122]	Average per acre [123]	Value of machinery and equipment, average per farm (dollars) [124]	Value of products sold Total (mil dol) [125]	Average per farm (dollars) [126]	Percent from: Crops [127]	Livestock and poultry products [128]	Percent of farms with sales of: $10,000 or more [129]	$100,000 or more [130]	Government payments Total ($1,000) [131]	Percent of farms [132]
OKLAHOMA—Cont'd																
Kiowa	565	-2.6	828	2.6	292.5	762 776	921	103 664	76.2	111 680	46.6	53.4	60.3	20.8	7 485	74.0
Latimer	213	3.4	281	0.4	42.1	353 739	1 260	51 107	20.5	26 932	D	D	26.7	3.4	774	11.6
Le Flore	466	13.4	228	9.4	155.0	380 784	1 668	66 007	213.1	104 288	8.5	91.5	37.4	12.5	2 637	15.7
Lincoln	488	3.4	212	2.2	147.2	346 917	1 636	45 887	37.8	16 442	10.4	89.6	25.4	1.8	512	12.4
Logan	404	10.4	325	1.6	152.4	450 107	1 383	54 289	48.8	39 317	18.2	81.8	31.6	5.0	1 313	33.8
Love	262	7.4	376	1.8	88.0	563 481	1 498	55 450	27.9	40 089	12.2	87.8	41.1	7.5	681	24.6
McClain	337	9.8	256	1.7	110.6	430 232	1 683	64 735	42.0	31 854	25.8	74.2	33.2	5.9	1 331	21.4
McCurtain	340	-5.0	189	0.4	104.5	299 257	1 583	52 109	186.2	103 678	4.8	95.2	35.7	11.7	576	5.8
McIntosh	247	-7.1	237	0.6	70.6	312 954	1 322	45 100	19.2	18 378	14.9	85.1	34.6	2.3	582	17.7
Major	517	1.6	535	8.2	237.4	504 607	943	97 895	113.0	116 863	11.2	88.8	46.8	12.7	4 142	64.8
Marshall	158	-3.7	289	2.3	37.1	438 535	1 515	52 581	16.5	30 240	39.6	60.4	27.9	3.9	230	14.9
Mayes	313	3.6	191	0.8	117.3	375 242	1 965	53 956	73.1	44 564	7.7	92.3	34.7	7.2	773	14.8
Murray	197	-2.5	372	D	38.9	518 378	1 394	57 773	13.9	26 267	D	D	37.4	3.8	312	22.1
Muskogee	374	6.3	203	8.2	145.0	330 688	1 630	53 502	52.7	28 558	27.4	72.6	31.0	4.1	1 467	17.8
Noble	467	18.2	557	0.8	215.8	638 752	1 146	83 646	37.7	45 026	24.5	75.5	43.8	10.0	2 991	55.8
Nowata	355	14.1	389	0.1	76.3	467 676	1 203	53 118	43.9	48 115	4.3	95.7	40.6	6.1	545	21.6
Okfuskee	299	3.1	315	1.3	83.7	373 034	1 186	50 706	33.1	34 809	5.7	94.3	33.6	5.4	357	19.8
Oklahoma	160	-7.0	124	2.9	57.5	319 281	2 575	43 790	28.8	22 376	61.5	38.5	22.0	3.3	371	11.1
Okmulgee	294	1.7	203	0.9	100.0	353 951	1 743	52 121	21.2	14 646	18.1	81.9	27.6	2.1	420	13.6
Osage	1 291	8.9	871	0.4	156.2	818 686	939	55 830	131.2	88 574	3.5	96.5	36.6	8.8	1 107	16.8
Ottawa	238	5.3	205	0.3	108.1	367 647	1 792	71 467	94.0	81 013	47.0	53.0	34.1	6.6	1 217	24.3
Pawnee	298	6.0	345	0.0	60.7	430 043	1 246	49 989	25.0	29 007	8.7	91.3	31.9	6.1	630	28.9
Payne	357	4.7	228	0.9	117.7	377 632	1 659	48 962	38.6	24 621	13.3	86.7	29.7	3.8	998	23.6
Pittsburg	547	8.3	311	1.7	125.8	379 039	1 220	45 799	36.1	20 507	13.9	86.1	30.7	3.5	875	8.9
Pontotoc	379	3.0	266	0.8	112.8	374 161	1 405	47 093	26.6	18 710	14.0	86.0	31.7	2.4	423	15.5
Pottawatomie	395	15.2	222	1.4	127.4	316 605	1 424	42 626	35.1	19 726	19.6	80.4	25.1	2.6	703	15.9
Pushmataha	290	-6.5	349	0.5	47.7	453 298	1 300	51 248	14.9	17 859	D	D	29.4	3.0	149	11.3
Roger Mills	719	-2.7	1 038	4.6	186.4	802 738	773	74 841	36.3	52 372	17.6	82.4	50.2	11.4	2 888	61.6
Rogers	371	19.7	192	0.8	100.7	410 485	2 140	44 152	37.4	19 333	15.5	84.5	26.3	2.7	442	11.3
Seminole	251	-10.0	214	0.8	70.4	296 420	1 385	45 961	19.9	16 958	12.1	87.9	27.9	2.0	436	19.5
Sequoyah	232	4.5	172	1.6	73.5	289 814	1 689	52 559	59.2	43 801	9.3	90.7	30.0	3.6	521	5.9
Stephens	470	11.9	359	1.2	127.8	429 999	1 199	51 054	41.2	31 464	8.9	91.1	33.1	4.9	1 269	28.2
Texas	1 206	2.1	1 162	156.0	656.4	791 501	681	142 789	779.9	751 318	14.7	85.3	45.1	23.4	10 897	73.8
Tillman	464	-4.3	847	13.0	301.0	701 387	828	111 477	86.5	157 764	49.3	50.7	63.3	27.7	8 480	79.9
Tulsa	131	-13.2	114	3.9	59.5	331 281	2 905	44 479	24.5	21 294	67.1	32.9	22.2	2.3	171	9.0
Wagoner	263	1.2	231	5.2	114.3	410 457	1 778	49 621	29.7	26 118	55.7	44.3	32.1	3.9	828	17.6
Washington	227	1.8	266	0.5	67.1	390 140	1 469	50 557	23.2	27 231	15.4	84.6	30.1	4.2	389	17.9
Washita	591	4.0	606	7.3	347.1	606 511	1 001	109 749	104.8	107 531	35.0	65.0	61.1	21.1	8 211	74.5
Woods	834	2.2	993	2.0	303.8	801 448	807	91 804	56.7	67 481	20.8	79.2	45.4	14.6	5 400	69.9
Woodward	783	7.9	878	7.6	183.4	727 483	829	65 327	78.7	88 202	D	D	43.7	13.6	3 233	52.9
OREGON	16 400	-4.0	425	1 845.2	5 010.4	804 145	1 890	79 175	4 386.1	113 769	67.9	32.1	32.5	12.1	76 491	13.3
Baker	712	-18.2	1 035	120.7	115.1	1 201 324	1 161	96 150	62.1	90 316	30.7	69.3	46.8	17.4	1 275	19.0
Benton	115	-11.5	126	23.3	79.2	675 605	5 343	81 023	74.6	82 301	84.4	15.6	23.3	7.8	342	7.7
Clackamas	183	-14.9	46	27.8	104.6	628 848	13 727	55 139	397.3	99 603	84.4	15.6	27.1	8.1	222	2.8
Clatsop	21	-4.5	93	1.0	7.2	564 265	6 096	60 048	9.6	41 801	11.2	88.8	21.0	6.1	35	3.1
Columbia	58	-6.5	72	2.5	21.4	465 382	6 486	39 679	D	D	D	D	14.7	2.2	181	3.6
Coos	146	1.4	195	10.8	26.8	731 998	3 749	59 398	41.3	55 369	43.9	56.1	37.7	11.3	940	10.1
Crook	762	-18.8	1 224	73.2	79.0	1 168 777	955	100 471	31.2	50 219	34.6	65.4	34.6	10.1	264	10.8
Curry	74	5.7	381	2.6	10.7	1 337 378	3 508	65 931	19.7	101 140	69.0	31.1	44.6	14.4	489	19.5
Deschutes	129	-6.5	92	37.8	39.9	633 973	6 885	45 880	19.8	14 063	45.8	54.2	20.4	2.4	135	1.4
Douglas	397	1.8	189	16.4	73.6	644 351	3 400	47 042	50.8	24 243	D	D	24.2	3.7	925	4.8
Gilliam	733	14.0	4 472	7.5	294.6	1 982 107	443	178 524	37.0	225 902	82.4	17.6	53.0	33.5	5 327	76.2
Grant	762	-14.6	1 913	40.8	68.5	1 276 764	667	81 564	18.3	46 085	11.5	88.5	42.5	8.5	284	9.5
Harney	1 462	-7.2	2 794	150.8	244.2	1 461 377	523	104 677	51.7	98 919	25.7	74.3	54.9	22.8	535	14.9
Hood River	27	-6.9	49	16.4	18.4	862 157	17 690	87 283	100.4	181 633	98.2	1.8	55.9	34.2	697	11.6
Jackson	244	-3.2	124	56.4	56.5	721 613	5 843	44 133	79.1	40 042	64.8	35.2	21.3	3.0	458	2.6
Jefferson	709	1.1	1 390	48.4	97.2	1 125 534	810	126 049	56.6	110 887	69.7	30.3	46.9	18.2	1 455	38.6
Josephine	38	18.8	56	8.8	17.4	494 184	8 847	40 143	13.9	20 652	47.0	53.0	19.9	2.2	41	3.0
Klamath	675	-4.0	559	226.3	168.1	883 784	1 580	107 258	149.7	124 038	50.3	49.7	46.6	17.1	2 665	16.1
Lake	693	-7.4	1 661	154.1	169.4	1 542 658	929	141 189	65.1	156 200	42.5	57.5	55.9	30.7	760	18.9
Lane	246	4.7	74	22.4	116.4	547 167	7 432	49 129	131.1	39 307	70.5	29.5	17.5	4.4	759	4.3
Lincoln	31	-6.1	84	0.8	5.7	441 004	5 248	35 662	5.9	15 897	28.8	71.2	17.0	3.5	34	3.2
Linn	376	-2.6	162	32.2	257.3	703 825	4 347	80 435	213.2	91 690	76.3	23.7	27.7	11.1	721	6.2
Malheur	1 171	-0.3	937	198.7	240.1	1 028 826	1 099	133 657	306.8	245 436	37.4	62.6	61.6	25.0	2 113	35.1
Marion	308	-9.7	115	96.4	225.1	795 988	6 908	110 309	586.7	219 754	82.6	17.4	37.1	18.0	1 048	9.0

STATE County	Water use, 2005		Wholesale trade,[1] 2007				Retail trade,[2] 2007				Real estate and rental and leasing,[2] 2007			
	Total water withdrawn (mil gal/day)	Gallons withdrawn per person	Number of establishments	Number of employees	Sales (mil dol)	Annual payroll (mil dol)	Number of establishments	Number of employees	Sales (mil dol)	Annual payroll (mil dol)	Number of establishments	Number of employees	Receipts (mil dol)	Annual payroll (mil dol)
	133	134	135	136	137	138	139	140	141	142	143	144	145	146
OKLAHOMA—Cont'd														
Kiowa	14.6	1 471	11	67	56.8	2.2	44	283	55.4	5.0	7	14	2.0	0.3
Latimer	2.9	276	7	105	90.3	3.6	24	248	40.5	4.0	5	43	17.1	2.7
Le Flore	21.8	441	22	D	D	D	140	1 531	376.3	28.7	15	176	24.6	7.3
Lincoln	10.9	336	22	138	85.5	5.3	87	609	161.9	11.3	14	D	D	D
Logan	11.2	308	22	D	D	D	95	878	275.6	19.9	32	D	D	D
Love	3.9	425	4	24	8.9	0.9	26	181	56.4	4.0	3	D	D	D
McClain	6.3	211	17	D	D	D	108	1 453	413.0	32.3	29	94	19.3	2.7
McCurtain	9.9	291	27	114	95.7	3.8	116	1 075	261.1	20.9	16	78	6.8	1.4
McIntosh	5.0	251	7	30	9.6	0.7	74	820	266.4	14.6	11	28	2.0	0.3
Major	20.3	2 780	9	71	39.5	2.2	40	313	78.8	5.0	7	23	2.3	0.5
Marshall	7.1	497	10	D	D	D	52	567	126.8	11.2	8	25	2.9	0.6
Mayes	107.2	2 719	28	402	301.4	19.2	160	1 490	414.6	31.2	22	46	5.1	0.8
Murray	22.4	1 751	5	87	42.2	3.5	50	627	193.6	13.4	8	119	12.9	4.1
Muskogee	110.2	1 559	65	994	580.7	49.8	287	3 468	904.0	71.7	66	548	45.6	10.3
Noble	5.1	457	6	37	28.0	0.9	30	315	86.8	6.2	6	25	1.7	0.2
Nowata	5.9	542	8	50	16.3	1.6	23	145	24.9	2.6	8	22	1.4	0.5
Okfuskee	4.2	368	4	17	2.8	0.2	29	199	64.6	3.5	2	D	D	D
Oklahoma	108.9	159	1 126	18 070	27 232.3	809.9	2 951	42 806	10 760.0	980.9	1 107	8 218	1 238.5	294.4
Okmulgee	16.9	427	20	125	42.1	4.6	128	1 286	329.5	25.9	19	D	D	D
Osage	19.7	434	17	D	D	D	98	769	172.1	12.9	18	D	D	D
Ottawa	5.8	178	24	D	D	D	98	1 206	287.6	24.9	27	106	9.3	2.3
Pawnee	17.3	1 030	8	D	D	D	45	366	82.5	6.3	10	D	D	D
Payne	7.8	106	41	D	D	D	307	3 890	818.4	74.3	76	247	33.8	5.1
Pittsburg	11.8	264	32	373	230.0	10.5	189	2 198	606.9	43.6	51	202	33.8	5.6
Pontotoc	24.7	701	47	D	D	D	170	1 813	409.0	34.0	38	148	21.8	3.8
Pottawatomie	17.6	259	33	D	D	D	253	2 824	682.3	55.9	47	203	23.7	4.2
Pushmataha	2.1	178	8	62	10.7	1.6	52	385	74.8	5.3	1	D	D	D
Roger Mills	9.0	2 716	1	D	D	D	20	124	42.8	2.4	NA	NA	NA	NA
Rogers	81.9	1 017	59	1 075	921.9	47.3	210	2 575	663.8	58.0	72	392	64.2	6.9
Seminole	31.1	1 262	14	73	85.1	3.1	78	800	192.6	16.7	14	48	5.2	0.9
Sequoyah	11.6	283	13	D	D	D	115	1 258	362.4	23.5	16	43	3.4	0.6
Stephens	20.6	479	42	D	D	D	210	2 076	495.1	40.4	27	107	11.0	1.7
Texas	173.8	8 634	27	D	D	D	80	814	182.6	15.7	12	D	D	D
Tillman	9.4	1 098	8	94	56.8	3.0	30	231	35.8	2.4	1	D	D	D
Tulsa	20.4	36	1 045	16 244	10 026.2	838.5	2 386	37 579	9 580.7	830.1	970	8 195	1 347.7	274.3
Wagoner	9.8	150	34	208	107.8	9.1	106	1 039	276.4	20.7	31	80	17.1	1.5
Washington	6.2	126	28	D	D	D	198	2 531	626.4	53.3	47	D	D	D
Washita	8.9	773	11	113	38.7	3.4	40	249	76.4	4.4	7	77	9.6	2.3
Woods	8.7	787	15	362	69.0	7.1	57	491	99.8	7.9	10	20	1.0	0.1
Woodward	16.8	883	40	330	140.6	9.5	120	1 238	337.4	25.8	28	132	16.8	4.4
OREGON	7 218.2	1 982	4 806	67 040	51 910.8	3 215.5	14 991	204 793	50 870.9	4 916.3	6 391	30 978	5 077.2	950.3
Baker	535.0	32 851	15	81	19.1	2.6	92	747	155.5	15.0	22	45	7.3	1.2
Benton	45.1	573	48	537	387.1	21.2	275	3 559	685.2	73.0	119	543	58.1	11.3
Clackamas	334.7	908	598	8 273	5 292.4	386.7	1 269	19 910	5 095.8	496.5	693	2 795	563.1	98.3
Clatsop	57.8	1 571	24	184	75.5	7.6	303	2 717	604.5	60.4	68	363	38.1	8.2
Columbia	56.8	1 183	25	122	96.8	6.6	132	1 563	357.4	33.8	41	112	15.0	2.5
Coos	28.5	440	41	426	260.8	15.3	290	3 298	716.0	79.5	69	274	33.4	6.2
Crook	262.0	11 873	19	160	100.5	5.1	80	632	139.9	13.3	36	92	6.9	1.7
Curry	19.8	885	15	D	D	D	105	1 188	227.0	23.4	59	107	12.7	2.0
Deschutes	206.6	1 462	234	2 089	1 222.6	93.9	867	10 952	2 809.1	271.9	452	1 782	229.7	48.2
Douglas	54.0	518	69	D	D	D	441	5 113	1 169.2	107.6	150	493	55.4	10.5
Gilliam	14.4	8 010	4	20	31.6	0.8	15	63	13.5	1.0	NA	NA	NA	NA
Grant	175.7	24 078	4	D	D	D	47	286	72.5	6.1	14	D	D	D
Harney	501.2	72 654	4	11	3.0	0.5	31	330	87.6	7.4	16	36	10.7	0.6
Hood River	89.6	4 208	33	754	224.4	25.8	146	1 393	293.7	32.9	36	62	9.3	1.5
Jackson	352.8	1 806	230	2 304	1 047.1	90.9	991	12 243	3 422.4	290.1	360	1 563	205.4	36.5
Jefferson	173.1	8 611	19	154	192.4	6.2	69	667	165.3	15.3	19	D	D	D
Josephine	55.4	686	60	D	D	D	347	4 549	1 024.3	107.4	110	450	47.1	9.5
Klamath	590.4	8 919	62	D	D	D	271	3 311	788.4	73.8	89	356	44.1	7.6
Lake	516.4	70 617	9	92	40.3	3.5	35	235	52.1	4.7	13	D	D	D
Lane	213.9	638	444	5 530	2 889.2	242.0	1 403	20 408	4 452.2	456.9	569	2 554	380.1	59.6
Lincoln	27.5	597	29	171	48.4	6.4	349	3 069	559.6	61.3	96	461	55.9	9.3
Linn	120.6	1 108	126	1 577	956.9	59.9	355	4 708	1 159.0	108.4	114	470	55.0	9.7
Malheur	950.4	30 334	38	D	D	D	143	2 095	484.6	46.7	37	103	10.7	1.7
Marion	277.2	908	312	3 806	3 461.7	161.2	1 109	16 819	4 016.6	399.2	485	2 686	337.4	66.2

1. Merchant wholesalers, except manufacturers' sales branches and offices.   2. Employer establishments.

Table B. States and Counties — **Professional Services, Manufacturing, and Accommodation and Food Services**

STATE County	Professional, scientific, and technical services,[1] 2007				Manufacturing, 2007				Accommodation and food services, 2007			
	Number of establish-ments	Number of employees	Receipts (mil dol)	Annual payroll (mil dol)	Number of establish-ments	Number of employees	Receipts (mil dol)	Annual payroll (mil dol)	Number of establish-ments	Number of employees	Sales (mil dol)	Annual payroll (mil dol)
	147	148	149	150	151	152	153	154	155	156	157	158
OKLAHOMA—Cont'd												
Kiowa	15	32	2.8	0.7	NA	NA	NA	NA	19	192	6.4	2.3
Latimer	15	41	3.0	0.9	NA	NA	NA	NA	10	125	5.1	1.2
Le Flore	56	D	D	D	35	740	147.5	D	49	675	25.8	6.7
Lincoln	46	D	D	D	23	599	198.2	22.1	40	557	19.6	5.4
Logan	43	138	12.9	4.3	NA	NA	NA	NA	53	655	27.9	7.4
Love	16	D	D	D	NA	NA	NA	NA	12	134	5.3	1.4
McClain	59	224	22.8	6.4	NA	NA	NA	NA	53	721	30.8	8.0
McCurtain	30	371	14.1	8.5	27	2 178	1 361.7	89.3	39	577	21.7	5.1
McIntosh	30	114	10.7	4.0	NA	NA	NA	NA	35	366	15.5	3.4
Major	18	38	3.6	1.0	NA	NA	NA	NA	12	120	3.6	0.9
Marshall	21	78	5.0	2.0	21	1 228	207.7	43.7	30	329	12.2	3.4
Mayes	59	277	16.1	6.9	64	3 085	944.0	130.1	70	989	36.0	9.0
Murray	23	83	7.2	2.9	NA	NA	NA	NA	28	278	14.0	3.8
Muskogee	107	D	D	D	69	3 455	1 167.5	153.0	129	2 484	88.1	22.8
Noble	13	35	1.9	0.6	10	D	D	D	17	186	7.1	1.8
Nowata	10	37	4.7	0.8	NA	NA	NA	NA	11	140	4.0	1.2
Okfuskee	7	18	1.2	0.5	NA	NA	NA	NA	11	113	2.3	0.6
Oklahoma	2 783	D	D	D	770	23 255	7 039.4	908.1	1 638	36 363	1 500.9	422.5
Okmulgee	38	166	9.8	3.5	38	971	363.2	43.3	56	829	29.5	7.8
Osage	49	144	12.0	3.4	NA	NA	NA	NA	44	606	18.2	4.8
Ottawa	39	D	D	D	51	1 581	379.1	58.9	59	778	28.0	8.0
Pawnee	25	70	5.9	1.7	NA	NA	NA	NA	21	289	10.4	2.7
Payne	158	D	D	D	69	2 305	1 065.3	84.8	154	3 263	117.8	31.2
Pittsburg	82	D	D	D	24	797	223.8	31.9	85	1 430	64.5	13.5
Pontotoc	88	D	D	D	48	1 648	501.3	52.6	62	1 204	47.1	13.7
Pottawatomie	104	D	D	D	62	3 105	1 024.3	130.3	125	2 706	98.9	26.8
Pushmataha	13	82	10.5	2.1	NA	NA	NA	NA	12	159	4.7	1.2
Roger Mills	6	12	0.5	0.1	NA	NA	NA	NA	9	60	1.9	0.4
Rogers	129	570	49.1	19.3	145	7 179	2 856.0	335.5	96	1 756	62.4	17.1
Seminole	27	89	6.5	1.9	24	679	124.7	24.7	33	536	17.7	4.6
Sequoyah	40	147	12.0	4.1	23	616	272.3	D	61	797	34.9	9.1
Stephens	71	389	31.8	10.8	71	2 625	1 084.9	117.8	84	956	38.8	9.7
Texas	34	D	D	D	12	D	D	D	47	720	24.4	6.1
Tillman	11	35	2.2	1.0	NA	NA	NA	NA	10	81	2.7	0.7
Tulsa	2 398	16 682	2 403.2	894.7	998	39 890	16 400.1	1 834.9	1 452	29 323	1 226.5	347.3
Wagoner	70	199	22.0	6.4	76	2 040	561.4	74.7	57	912	30.7	8.7
Washington	90	D	D	D	51	1 462	353.5	58.1	114	1 889	72.5	17.9
Washita	16	48	7.3	2.0	NA	NA	NA	NA	15	113	3.3	0.9
Woods	24	64	4.1	1.2	NA	NA	NA	NA	23	262	10.4	2.3
Woodward	54	D	D	D	NA	NA	NA	NA	52	797	34.2	8.9
OREGON	11 363	83 190	9 750.4	4 869.5	5 717	183 953	66 880.7	8 138.9	10 241	150 538	7 555.8	2 152.9
Baker	40	D	D	D	27	605	138.0	20.5	58	558	25.7	6.9
Benton	282	D	D	D	92	4 322	590.5	209.8	206	3 197	134.0	37.2
Clackamas	1 234	D	D	D	619	17 625	5 668.2	841.4	775	12 928	607.4	176.9
Clatsop	90	317	22.4	8.1	56	1 868	683.6	92.0	248	3 078	160.6	45.4
Columbia	69	D	D	D	59	2 020	826.2	95.4	97	1 005	44.2	11.8
Coos	117	D	D	D	81	1 652	279.1	53.5	187	2 021	83.5	23.3
Crook	35	D	D	D	41	1 245	209.9	42.5	48	517	22.7	6.4
Curry	39	130	9.5	3.2	21	644	190.7	30.1	113	1 073	56.2	13.7
Deschutes	650	D	D	D	299	5 359	897.4	201.7	504	8 078	416.4	121.1
Douglas	179	D	D	D	132	6 439	1 506.4	236.6	301	4 331	228.4	62.9
Gilliam	1	D	D	D	NA	NA	NA	NA	8	66	1.5	0.5
Grant	19	D	D	D	NA	NA	NA	NA	25	162	6.6	1.9
Harney	11	D	D	D	NA	NA	NA	NA	27	211	11.1	2.6
Hood River	108	401	54.3	17.0	58	1 200	245.7	38.6	88	1 371	55.7	17.7
Jackson	491	D	D	D	324	6 115	2 037.5	228.8	590	7 946	372.9	108.9
Jefferson	24	76	4.7	1.9	20	1 501	242.9	50.7	45	798	45.8	13.3
Josephine	134	D	D	D	127	3 127	471.3	105.0	205	2 493	108.9	33.0
Klamath	118	D	D	D	75	2 360	539.7	92.5	176	2 259	103.0	28.9
Lake	10	D	D	D	NA	NA	NA	NA	27	159	7.2	1.7
Lane	988	5 097	554.6	217.5	606	20 273	6 219.9	853.6	920	13 385	607.7	171.5
Lincoln	102	D	D	D	57	1 108	582.7	58.0	292	4 035	205.4	59.9
Linn	170	D	D	D	198	7 814	2 737.6	393.7	200	2 746	125.4	33.1
Malheur	45	D	D	D	36	1 237	D	42.8	84	1 077	45.3	12.7
Marion	720	3 958	416.3	163.9	380	10 724	2 845.4	367.2	652	D	D	D

1. Establishment subject to federal tax.

Table B. States and Counties — Health Care and Social Assistance, Other Services, and Federal Funds

	Health care and social assistance, 2007				Other services, 2007				Federal funds and grants, 2009–2010 Expenditures (mil dol)	Direct payments for individuals[1]		
STATE County	Number of establishments	Number of employees	Receipts (mil dol)	Annual payroll (mil dol)	Number of establishments	Number of employees	Receipts (mil dol)	Annual payroll (mil dol)	Total	Social Security and government retirement	Medicare	Food Stamps and Supplemental Security Income
	159	160	161	162	163	164	165	166	167	168	169	170
OKLAHOMA—Cont'd												
Kiowa	28	562	24.3	11.9	11	D	D	D	121.2	37.7	30.1	6.0
Latimer	25	368	21.0	8.5	6	D	D	D	97.0	34.3	21.8	6.0
Le Flore	83	2 121	125.4	52.5	47	208	17.8	4.5	498.4	187.1	99.4	27.8
Lincoln	53	679	35.2	14.2	22	74	7.0	1.7	252.2	124.2	44.7	12.2
Logan	52	1 253	69.4	30.4	48	157	13.4	2.9	243.2	97.7	45.4	10.8
Love	10	D	D	D	5	58	2.9	0.9	72.5	31.5	17.4	3.2
McClain	59	802	51.2	21.4	44	124	8.9	2.5	199.5	115.5	39.4	7.3
McCurtain	69	1 380	73.5	30.1	31	202	12.0	3.2	456.2	112.3	82.8	28.7
McIntosh	51	760	36.8	14.8	24	87	8.5	1.6	230.6	103.9	48.6	11.9
Major	14	297	12.9	6.6	11	D	D	D	53.1	23.5	14.2	1.4
Marshall	28	527	35.1	13.9	9	25	2.3	0.6	124.4	59.5	31.5	5.4
Mayes	80	939	60.0	24.5	53	144	9.6	2.7	294.6	137.9	61.5	18.2
Murray	31	735	38.4	17.2	17	50	3.0	0.6	135.4	48.0	27.2	4.8
Muskogee	204	5 438	384.1	180.9	95	525	35.5	10.5	895.8	293.5	143.8	41.8
Noble	18	365	21.0	9.0	11	49	3.4	0.8	85.6	36.6	20.2	3.5
Nowata	17	307	12.4	5.6	12	27	2.2	0.5	85.2	38.8	19.5	3.5
Okfuskee	40	432	28.1	10.9	4	D	D	D	129.5	45.5	27.4	6.9
Oklahoma	2 737	55 697	6 769.4	2 187.6	1 423	10 026	936.1	253.2	9 795.6	2 410.1	1 039.6	225.0
Okmulgee	140	2 352	159.6	68.4	40	147	11.2	2.7	433.2	138.9	84.8	25.7
Osage	50	D	D	D	29	76	5.9	1.3	302.6	84.4	44.0	12.7
Ottawa	77	1 537	101.7	45.9	36	139	9.6	2.2	331.6	125.0	85.0	14.8
Pawnee	32	D	D	D	12	38	2.9	0.6	148.2	61.2	31.3	5.6
Payne	175	3 518	266.5	103.7	128	813	170.0	17.8	547.8	185.1	89.9	20.0
Pittsburg	112	2 647	187.7	81.2	55	272	22.7	6.3	537.0	188.7	87.8	19.6
Pontotoc	142	3 131	253.4	92.6	52	247	17.7	4.4	382.3	128.7	73.2	20.1
Pottawatomie	160	2 846	216.8	79.4	67	322	22.1	6.5	692.2	264.5	89.4	31.8
Pushmataha	22	701	33.9	15.5	6	25	1.8	0.3	152.2	46.4	31.7	8.1
Roger Mills	5	D	D	D	5	D	D	D	32.1	10.3	9.1	0.9
Rogers	172	2 431	186.6	80.4	82	353	36.0	9.0	464.3	233.5	71.6	15.2
Seminole	49	1 081	63.1	22.9	21	81	7.7	1.9	292.9	91.2	59.2	21.1
Sequoyah	77	1 737	70.5	32.7	33	88	6.8	2.0	376.6	148.6	67.9	25.3
Stephens	104	1 988	136.6	52.6	66	530	67.0	11.5	426.4	172.6	85.2	17.6
Texas	44	D	D	D	32	161	11.4	2.3	122.5	39.2	27.6	6.5
Tillman	18	282	15.3	6.2	11	36	1.7	0.5	109.9	27.6	24.2	5.0
Tulsa	2 035	44 983	4 548.0	1 765.5	1 197	7 646	833.4	205.9	4 333.1	1 817.0	890.5	225.8
Wagoner	72	713	45.0	19.9	60	141	11.4	2.8	268.3	132.6	56.1	15.2
Washington	167	3 108	237.6	98.9	90	611	85.0	15.0	350.9	195.9	85.3	15.1
Washita	16	695	18.7	7.5	16	46	3.6	0.8	99.0	36.5	27.0	4.4
Woods	21	357	18.0	8.9	19	64	5.7	1.0	82.2	26.6	19.6	1.8
Woodward	84	1 194	76.0	31.7	43	204	27.2	5.6	118.5	53.3	29.9	6.2
OREGON	11 261	192 233	20 159.6	7 895.9	6 888	39 129	4 462.4	1 090.6	33 974.1	11 620.2	4 615.2	1 531.1
Baker	50	D	D	D	41	108	12.1	2.2	192.3	77.3	28.1	8.3
Benton	229	4 356	504.0	201.1	128	855	158.3	22.7	706.7	202.6	67.9	18.4
Clackamas	963	15 229	1 702.2	665.4	660	3 437	314.4	95.4	2 347.4	1 004.3	361.8	182.6
Clatsop	132	1 627	144.1	62.7	84	522	32.2	9.3	362.8	146.1	60.7	16.3
Columbia	107	826	54.7	20.8	63	218	15.4	4.5	298.0	158.2	58.7	13.9
Coos	236	3 508	329.8	126.1	92	481	59.7	11.1	657.4	301.3	115.1	46.7
Crook	33	540	47.3	18.4	38	168	11.4	3.3	176.8	88.3	28.3	7.9
Curry	98	865	61.8	23.0	34	134	10.3	2.5	236.5	125.6	52.7	12.3
Deschutes	543	8 144	974.3	351.5	322	1 761	169.5	46.5	950.9	535.6	125.8	37.1
Douglas	313	5 280	511.0	215.0	150	757	84.4	17.7	1 059.3	514.9	164.4	61.3
Gilliam	7	D	D	D	4	D	D	D	30.3	11.0	2.9	0.1
Grant	21	D	D	D	20	48	3.4	0.8	101.1	34.0	12.2	4.1
Harney	20	D	D	D	10	35	2.1	0.7	85.6	29.6	9.6	3.5
Hood River	95	1 595	107.6	43.6	47	229	20.7	6.4	160.1	57.6	22.1	6.5
Jackson	627	11 160	1 173.9	434.7	357	2 107	182.0	56.9	1 624.4	769.7	250.3	87.8
Jefferson	21	D	D	D	25	125	8.9	2.4	143.8	67.6	20.9	9.9
Josephine	251	4 055	356.7	128.0	131	605	40.6	12.5	774.4	385.5	129.6	64.9
Klamath	223	3 021	286.0	113.0	119	570	40.2	11.6	663.4	265.2	97.0	42.6
Lake	15	270	18.4	8.1	15	26	2.2	0.5	85.0	35.2	11.8	4.1
Lane	993	18 660	1 947.8	735.6	684	3 684	516.8	95.3	2 802.5	1 158.9	439.6	180.6
Lincoln	106	1 583	155.8	62.7	107	475	30.8	8.8	435.7	209.7	84.7	23.0
Linn	214	3 654	320.4	126.2	149	1 075	112.6	34.9	891.0	423.5	150.2	58.9
Malheur	102	1 403	116.3	45.0	62	D	D	D	245.3	89.1	38.2	21.1
Marion	911	15 212	1 453.0	599.2	514	2 628	214.1	64.3	3 954.1	935.7	377.8	146.3

1. State totals may include programs not allocated by county.

	Federal funds and grants, 2009–2010 (cont.)							Value of residential construction authorized by building permits, 2010		Local government finances, 2007				
	Expenditures (mil dol) (cont.)									General revenue				
		Procurement contract awards		Grants[1]								Taxes		
													Per capita[2] (dollars)	
STATE County	Salaries and wages	Defense	Other	Medicaid and other health-related	Nutrition and family welfare	Education	Other	New construction ($1,000)	Number of housing units	Total (mil dol)	Inter-governmental (mil dol)	Total (mil dol)	Total	Property
	171	172	173	174	175	176	177	178	179	180	181	182	183	184
OKLAHOMA—Cont'd														
Kiowa	5.7	0.1	0.8	25.5	2.8	1.0	1.0	0	0	28.7	18.5	5.8	609	363
Latimer	2.0	0.0	0.5	16.9	2.9	3.5	0.3	125	4	57.7	28.9	20.5	1 952	1 582
Le Flore	23.3	7.8	3.6	110.9	11.4	8.8	6.9	6 980	60	121.0	74.4	21.0	422	230
Lincoln	16.4	1.2	2.9	34.4	6.3	1.8	3.5	2 722	26	58.5	33.5	15.8	490	245
Logan	8.3	0.6	18.1	26.1	5.8	8.6	8.9	1 469	12	67.1	28.5	15.5	424	290
Love	1.5	0.6	0.3	15.1	1.9	0.7	0.1	0	0	17.1	10.7	4.2	459	283
McClain	5.9	0.0	1.3	20.6	4.3	2.3	0.2	25 602	146	90.9	37.4	42.1	1 323	996
McCurtain	10.1	9.1	1.9	127.3	10.6	24.4	42.6	1 145	16	87.2	57.0	19.6	583	321
McIntosh	4.1	2.6	0.8	48.6	5.1	2.8	1.6	3 145	22	50.4	33.7	10.8	550	252
Major	2.7	0.0	0.8	4.3	1.4	0.2	0.1	285	3	25.7	12.2	5.6	780	492
Marshall	2.7	0.0	0.5	19.8	2.5	1.6	0.1	138	2	39.6	25.4	8.9	601	323
Mayes	7.5	0.0	4.3	46.1	6.9	8.7	0.0	1 199	10	82.1	45.4	25.6	645	285
Murray	14.1	0.0	7.4	26.3	2.5	0.7	3.9	1 841	17	29.5	15.6	7.2	565	253
Muskogee	117.8	24.0	35.1	158.4	17.3	10.0	14.0	9 097	62	289.0	90.2	77.8	1 093	574
Noble	3.3	0.0	1.0	8.5	3.0	1.4	1.1	0	0	36.8	13.7	10.8	975	684
Nowata	2.6	0.9	0.5	15.5	1.8	1.0	0.0	95	4	24.1	14.4	5.3	495	286
Okfuskee	3.4	0.0	0.6	36.7	4.8	1.6	1.5	1 126	15	25.8	17.3	5.0	443	253
Oklahoma	1 950.8	956.2	384.9	724.8	301.9	307.0	1 339.3	351 333	2 084	2 322.8	702.5	979.6	1 396	641
Okmulgee	15.7	3.1	2.8	87.4	16.1	5.9	36.5	0	0	86.7	50.4	22.0	560	249
Osage	101.9	0.0	9.1	29.1	9.0	3.9	3.0	15 628	111	57.4	36.7	10.8	238	164
Ottawa	16.4	2.3	1.6	45.2	12.8	5.5	10.4	2 386	31	100.6	50.8	31.4	968	685
Pawnee	9.8	2.3	3.7	15.9	12.9	2.1	1.9	0	0	35.2	20.4	7.2	437	239
Payne	51.6	22.6	17.1	41.2	10.6	26.7	53.5	18 653	108	175.4	67.5	73.5	920	456
Pittsburg	78.3	50.1	6.5	81.4	10.1	7.8	2.7	14 872	178	185.0	55.4	45.1	1 009	432
Pontotoc	31.8	0.0	8.3	59.8	13.7	9.5	18.3	6 348	86	96.6	51.6	27.8	760	327
Pottawatomie	22.7	4.8	3.9	81.1	18.4	7.5	145.6	14 751	119	166.1	94.0	48.3	700	336
Pushmataha	3.2	7.0	0.5	41.4	3.6	5.6	3.3	65	1	34.4	20.9	4.4	381	193
Roger Mills	2.8	0.0	0.6	5.8	0.8	0.3	0.2	0	0	22.2	11.8	4.8	1 463	782
Rogers	32.6	3.1	20.4	37.9	14.3	6.8	11.4	40 094	265	159.1	71.2	57.3	690	401
Seminole	16.6	0.2	3.7	64.6	11.1	6.6	10.8	1 746	21	70.6	40.6	15.4	636	314
Sequoyah	11.5	12.8	2.2	89.4	9.3	6.4	1.6	5 683	56	115.3	63.0	22.0	535	186
Stephens	22.8	0.0	30.4	46.4	9.3	3.0	35.9	4 684	30	106.0	54.5	34.1	787	421
Texas	5.4	0.2	0.9	8.2	3.3	2.4	12.3	353	2	73.3	30.3	17.3	862	493
Tillman	2.5	0.0	0.5	23.0	4.7	1.2	0.9	0	0	31.2	16.2	4.3	530	334
Tulsa	276.4	233.8	170.0	357.0	98.4	48.1	106.7	326 099	1 966	2 023.4	633.7	907.0	1 550	832
Wagoner	5.3	1.8	1.1	40.7	7.8	3.5	0.3	23 445	183	76.6	38.4	27.0	401	200
Washington	2.7	1.1	2.7	25.6	7.0	5.1	5.0	11 977	64	117.6	47.5	47.7	955	572
Washita	3.4	4.6	0.7	9.4	2.4	2.3	1.0	0	0	37.7	19.8	11.7	1 005	762
Woods	11.4	0.0	0.6	4.3	1.6	3.6	2.2	0	0	32.7	9.6	16.3	1 962	1 443
Woodward	7.4	0.4	1.1	9.8	3.5	1.5	1.4	969	19	62.5	25.6	24.8	1 270	567
OREGON	2 568.5	891.5	1 155.6	4 360.1	926.3	608.0	2 800.0	12 966	85	X	X	X	X	X
Baker	18.3	0.0	12.6	39.9	2.8	1.2	0.9	7 089	34	54.0	28.2	14.5	908	819
Benton	57.7	49.4	45.2	85.6	10.1	5.6	129.2	22 735	93	246.0	103.0	88.2	1 083	962
Clackamas	232.4	137.9	59.2	181.6	70.0	19.1	62.5	167 052	665	1 287.1	497.1	519.7	1 381	1 161
Clatsop	52.2	1.5	23.2	42.4	5.5	2.9	8.7	30 399	160	156.1	55.9	60.4	1 616	1 281
Columbia	8.2	6.3	3.7	31.6	6.4	2.8	5.0	12 520	62	154.7	66.0	53.1	1 084	932
Coos	39.7	11.7	21.9	80.2	13.2	6.1	9.8	3 136	24	368.2	120.9	60.4	952	864
Crook	20.1	0.0	7.6	17.4	2.8	1.1	1.6	14 332	61	74.6	24.6	34.6	1 513	1 379
Curry	8.5	0.0	12.1	16.9	3.1	1.4	2.9	7 180	27	91.0	39.2	21.3	977	863
Deschutes	84.9	4.7	24.7	59.4	15.8	6.7	33.8	85 793	377	589.4	201.9	249.0	1 617	1 353
Douglas	79.6	2.9	58.9	115.9	19.5	9.0	14.3	33 214	181	392.1	219.4	79.0	759	686
Gilliam	0.6	0.0	0.1	0.8	0.2	0.2	0.0	NA	NA	18.3	5.0	3.1	1 824	1 751
Grant	13.6	3.0	22.5	7.4	1.3	0.7	1.1	NA	NA	56.8	26.7	7.0	1 016	804
Harney	13.4	0.0	13.8	7.5	1.5	0.7	4.1	2 027	6	45.2	19.6	5.9	873	805
Hood River	10.0	30.2	3.2	18.2	7.5	1.3	0.8	14 997	88	86.6	36.4	21.6	1 014	879
Jackson	132.1	13.7	104.2	176.9	31.5	14.5	25.0	64 241	373	629.4	302.0	211.7	1 062	872
Jefferson	7.6	0.3	3.3	15.4	5.0	4.5	6.4	6 614	32	100.2	40.7	22.7	1 097	904
Josephine	26.8	3.6	19.2	96.9	13.5	6.4	7.7	20 559	106	238.2	124.1	63.4	783	668
Klamath	88.9	10.9	13.3	68.5	14.5	7.8	31.2	12 552	68	245.4	132.8	54.1	814	720
Lake	13.3	0.2	9.7	6.6	1.4	0.7	0.6	2 490	11	43.2	18.3	6.7	921	854
Lane	163.3	29.0	45.5	481.3	53.8	48.9	125.5	108 903	550	1 336.0	563.3	401.7	1 169	991
Lincoln	26.7	0.1	13.0	40.3	9.4	4.8	19.5	25 337	118	180.2	54.6	90.8	1 980	1 660
Linn	46.4	7.9	11.4	124.0	19.3	10.0	18.9	33 406	174	386.2	177.1	124.5	1 099	931
Malheur	18.5	0.0	11.3	37.4	8.7	3.4	3.0	3 997	15	129.3	77.3	18.1	581	500
Marion	240.0	29.2	36.7	429.4	259.4	289.6	1 127.0	107 008	610	1 201.6	620.2	338.7	1 088	944

1. State totals may include programs not allocated by county.   2. Based on the resident population estimated as of July 1 of the year shown.

Table B. States and Counties — Local Government Finances, Government Employment, and Voting

STATE County	\[Direct general expenditure\] Total (mil dol)	Per capita[1] (dollars)	Education	Health and hospitals	Police protection	Public welfare	Highways	\[Debt outstanding\] Total (mil dol)	Per capita[1] (dollars)	Federal civilian	Federal military	State and local	Democratic	Republican	All other
	185	186	187	188	189	190	191	192	193	194	195	196	197	198	199
OKLAHOMA—Cont'd															
Kiowa	26.4	2 794	58.0	1.2	4.2	0.1	15.4	20.6	2 184	59	40	749	32.6	67.4	0.0
Latimer	55.0	5 238	77.3	0.2	1.0	0.0	9.3	16.5	1 573	29	46	1 340	31.5	68.5	0.0
Le Flore	117.3	2 359	66.4	2.1	3.9	0.2	6.6	28.4	571	193	218	4 139	30.7	69.3	0.0
Lincoln	56.7	1 756	72.5	0.1	5.4	0.0	4.2	21.8	674	87	140	1 912	25.1	74.9	0.0
Logan	66.7	1 831	49.6	20.0	3.9	0.0	7.8	26.4	724	76	172	2 027	31.3	68.7	0.0
Love	16.8	1 842	73.3	2.8	3.6	0.0	7.7	8.7	956	28	40	2 740	32.7	67.3	0.0
McClain	88.0	2 762	73.2	1.3	4.5	0.0	5.1	39.9	1 253	76	145	1 746	24.1	75.9	0.0
McCurtain	84.8	2 528	71.3	3.9	2.6	1.1	5.1	38.0	1 134	141	146	2 597	26.5	73.5	0.0
McIntosh	49.6	2 515	52.5	0.8	4.5	0.1	26.6	13.2	672	39	86	1 025	40.4	59.6	0.0
Major	25.1	3 490	42.0	22.6	2.6	0.0	17.7	10.3	1 435	41	31	436	14.8	85.2	0.0
Marshall	37.9	2 553	59.0	1.8	4.9	0.0	13.7	7.5	504	25	66	758	30.6	69.4	0.0
Mayes	83.9	2 117	65.2	0.3	6.1	0.0	5.0	38.3	967	73	175	2 571	36.0	64.0	0.0
Murray	29.0	2 281	57.3	3.2	5.0	0.0	11.6	5.2	412	57	82	2 684	29.8	70.2	0.0
Muskogee	289.6	4 073	40.0	32.5	3.5	0.0	2.9	219.9	3 092	2 518	313	5 975	42.5	57.5	0.0
Noble	36.0	3 238	52.0	18.6	3.6	0.0	10.5	26.7	2 396	43	48	1 378	23.2	76.8	0.0
Nowata	24.5	2 284	70.1	0.0	3.0	0.0	10.8	7.5	698	33	46	500	31.8	68.2	0.0
Okfuskee	25.9	2 307	74.5	1.9	3.6	0.0	8.1	8.9	788	34	48	1 188	35.9	64.1	0.0
Oklahoma	2 306.8	3 287	40.6	0.0	8.0	0.2	5.5	2 413.0	3 438	24 462	9 903	57 069	41.6	58.4	0.0
Okmulgee	85.5	2 176	66.4	0.5	4.8	0.0	6.3	55.2	1 403	143	172	3 448	41.5	58.5	0.0
Osage	57.4	1 262	63.0	6.5	3.0	0.1	8.2	16.5	362	204	223	2 238	38.1	61.9	0.0
Ottawa	100.7	3 100	64.9	1.6	4.6	0.0	4.4	28.5	877	127	138	4 887	38.2	61.8	0.0
Pawnee	32.9	2 001	59.2	13.4	3.9	0.0	5.2	12.8	779	237	72	901	31.3	68.7	0.0
Payne	177.6	2 222	50.5	1.8	7.7	0.2	6.4	98.0	1 226	309	364	14 680	36.5	63.5	0.0
Pittsburg	190.7	4 266	33.6	43.5	2.7	0.0	4.8	97.6	2 184	2 042	200	3 731	31.7	68.3	0.0
Pontotoc	89.2	2 438	66.7	0.4	4.0	0.0	7.2	79.0	2 159	185	163	6 279	31.6	68.4	0.0
Pottawatomie	172.8	2 503	64.6	0.4	4.6	0.0	6.0	78.9	1 142	178	308	5 564	30.8	69.2	0.0
Pushmataha	35.3	3 026	58.1	20.7	2.5	0.0	9.4	15.1	1 293	41	52	916	28.3	71.7	0.0
Roger Mills	20.1	6 068	28.6	15.0	3.3	0.0	38.7	10.4	3 137	53	15	368	16.0	84.0	0.0
Rogers	161.0	1 937	62.8	1.0	2.9	0.0	4.8	98.0	1 179	445	374	5 769	28.0	72.0	0.0
Seminole	64.9	2 684	61.9	10.6	3.0	0.0	4.7	49.6	2 062	151	106	2 021	34.7	65.3	0.0
Sequoyah	94.0	2 291	69.8	1.5	4.3	0.0	5.1	46.5	1 135	145	198	3 248	32.0	68.0	0.0
Stephens	101.5	2 342	66.3	0.8	4.6	0.0	8.9	74.0	1 707	99	190	2 245	24.0	76.0	0.0
Texas	80.5	4 017	43.6	21.2	4.3	0.1	16.8	15.7	782	76	92	1 672	14.7	85.3	0.0
Tillman	32.1	3 936	45.2	19.2	3.1	0.0	6.5	16.5	2 019	82	34	775	32.2	67.8	0.0
Tulsa	2 039.2	3 485	48.4	3.0	5.7	1.3	2.7	3 716.4	6 352	3 617	2 643	33 438	37.8	62.2	0.0
Wagoner	76.2	1 133	59.0	2.7	5.4	0.0	10.7	21.9	326	76	307	1 722	29.1	70.9	0.0
Washington	118.1	2 368	58.8	0.6	5.5	0.1	7.9	98.8	1 981	108	221	2 470	27.7	72.3	0.0
Washita	37.7	3 233	64.6	0.3	4.0	0.4	19.1	5.5	471	48	52	785	22.0	78.0	0.0
Woods	30.0	3 603	55.2	5.3	3.2	0.0	13.5	19.4	2 338	41	37	1 252	22.3	77.7	0.0
Woodward	59.7	3 062	56.1	4.5	5.9	0.0	8.3	32.8	1 681	99	87	1 440	17.4	82.6	0.0
OREGON	X	X	X	X	X	X	X	X	X	29 974	12 465	254 687	56.7	40.4	2.9
Baker	52.2	3 277	46.6	5.8	5.3	2.1	6.1	90.4	5 678	243	46	955	32.0	64.4	3.7
Benton	227.5	2 794	43.3	9.9	8.6	0.0	4.9	279.5	3 432	596	289	13 216	64.3	32.8	2.8
Clackamas	1 355.6	3 603	44.0	4.8	5.9	1.1	4.5	2 190.5	5 822	1 375	1 286	15 443	53.9	43.6	2.5
Clatsop	167.7	4 489	39.2	7.7	4.8	0.4	4.7	283.3	7 581	220	482	2 442	57.7	38.8	3.5
Columbia	157.9	3 222	46.0	4.1	4.9	0.4	5.7	204.3	4 169	83	141	1 949	54.1	42.0	3.9
Coos	337.6	5 316	34.5	41.0	2.5	0.2	4.7	201.1	3 166	358	412	5 168	46.5	49.6	3.9
Crook	76.4	3 335	35.2	0.5	3.5	0.0	33.4	63.3	2 765	319	64	862	35.1	61.5	3.4
Curry	81.8	3 760	33.4	23.4	2.7	4.7	4.2	70.1	3 221	101	99	1 107	42.4	53.9	3.7
Deschutes	590.3	3 832	42.3	3.4	7.3	0.5	6.4	840.1	5 454	916	451	7 385	48.7	49.0	2.4
Douglas	406.4	3 903	44.0	9.5	4.2	0.3	10.6	275.8	2 649	1 562	336	6 384	38.3	58.4	3.2
Gilliam	18.1	10 688	36.8	1.0	3.9	0.0	7.9	66.3	39 212	12	0	202	38.7	58.4	2.9
Grant	57.2	8 285	32.6	26.3	3.1	3.6	9.7	22.8	3 307	271	19	746	25.7	71.2	3.0
Harney	49.2	7 273	36.3	41.6	1.8	0.0	6.5	47.0	6 945	264	19	785	25.8	70.5	3.7
Hood River	86.1	4 044	49.6	2.8	3.9	0.8	9.6	63.9	3 000	119	62	1 187	64.1	33.2	2.7
Jackson	598.7	3 004	44.0	6.5	7.5	0.0	7.3	575.5	2 887	1 739	572	9 563	48.6	48.5	2.9
Jefferson	99.1	4 791	45.3	21.7	3.3	0.0	5.0	88.5	4 277	149	57	2 208	44.3	52.9	2.8
Josephine	233.4	2 880	58.9	5.0	5.2	0.3	3.8	188.1	2 320	310	230	2 988	41.4	54.6	4.0
Klamath	234.7	3 529	47.3	5.1	3.8	0.3	11.0	354.2	5 325	943	203	4 337	31.9	65.0	3.1
Lake	39.9	5 476	32.3	34.8	2.5	0.0	10.4	6.4	881	270	20	721	25.9	71.5	2.5
Lane	1 242.2	3 615	45.9	4.6	6.9	2.5	5.0	1 385.2	4 031	1 743	1 059	27 052	62.3	34.9	2.8
Lincoln	175.6	3 828	33.2	8.5	6.9	0.3	8.4	226.3	4 935	281	209	3 671	59.7	36.8	3.5
Linn	432.9	3 822	48.7	2.4	5.4	1.6	5.2	493.3	4 355	373	332	6 673	42.6	54.0	3.4
Malheur	127.5	4 094	61.9	4.7	1.6	0.2	4.1	70.8	2 274	245	87	3 171	28.3	68.6	3.1
Marion	1 213.3	3 896	55.2	5.7	5.1	0.3	3.9	1 571.6	5 046	1 506	911	33 397	49.6	47.4	3.0

1. Based on the resident population estimated as of July 1 of the year shown.   2. © 2009 Election Data Services, Inc. All rights reserved.

Table B. States and Counties — Land Area and Population

STATE/ County code	CBSA code[1]	County type[2]	STATE County	Land area[3] (sq km) 2010	Total persons	Rank	Per square kilometer	White	Black	American Indian, Alaska Native	Asian and Pacific Islander	Percent Hispanic or Latino[4]	Under 5 years	5 to 17 years	18 to 24 years	25 to 34 years	35 to 44 years	45 to 54 years
				1	2	3	4	5	6	7	8	9	10	11	12	13	14	15
			OREGON—Cont'd															
41 049	37820	6	Morrow	5 262	11 173	2 352	2.1	66.1	0.6	2.1	1.4	31.3	7.1	21.4	8.0	11.4	12.5	13.9
41 051	38900	1	Multnomah	1 117	735 334	79	658.3	75.3	6.7	1.9	8.8	10.9	6.3	14.2	9.7	18.5	15.3	13.5
41 053	41420	2	Polk	1 919	75 403	720	39.3	83.2	1.0	3.2	3.4	12.1	6.5	17.8	11.7	11.7	11.6	13.0
41 055	...	9	Sherman	2 133	1 765	3 070	0.8	92.5	0.3	1.5	0.9	5.6	5.3	14.5	6.3	10.0	9.2	17.8
41 057	...	6	Tillamook	2 856	25 250	1 594	8.8	88.5	0.5	1.9	1.9	9.0	5.4	14.4	6.6	9.8	10.7	14.6
41 059	37820	5	Umatilla	8 328	75 889	714	9.1	71.2	1.0	4.3	1.4	23.9	7.4	19.2	9.3	13.2	12.7	13.4
41 061	29260	7	Union	5 275	25 748	1 576	4.9	92.7	0.8	2.0	2.4	3.9	6.3	16.2	11.1	11.5	10.0	13.6
41 063	...	9	Wallowa	8 149	7 008	2 687	0.9	96.3	0.6	1.6	1.0	2.2	5.3	13.5	5.4	9.1	8.9	15.6
41 065	45520	6	Wasco	6 168	25 213	1 596	4.1	79.3	0.5	5.2	1.9	14.8	6.5	16.7	7.9	11.4	11.1	13.9
41 067	38900	1	Washington	1 876	529 710	120	282.4	72.7	2.4	1.3	11.2	15.7	7.2	18.4	8.3	15.7	15.3	14.1
41 069	...	9	Wheeler	4 441	1 441	3 087	0.3	93.5	0.0	3.3	1.4	4.3	4.8	13.2	4.8	8.4	8.2	13.9
41 071	38900	1	Yamhill	1 854	99 193	584	53.5	81.4	1.2	2.5	2.6	14.7	6.5	18.5	10.4	12.3	12.9	13.9
42 000	...	X	PENNSYLVANIA	115 883	12 702 379	X	109.6	80.7	11.3	0.5	3.2	5.7	5.7	16.2	9.9	11.9	12.7	15.3
42 001	23900	4	Adams	1 343	101 407	575	75.5	91.5	1.9	0.5	1.0	6.0	5.5	16.6	9.7	10.3	13.2	15.6
42 003	38300	1	Allegheny	1 891	1 223 348	31	646.9	82.1	14.2	0.5	3.3	1.6	5.2	14.6	10.1	12.9	11.9	15.3
42 005	38300	1	Armstrong	1 692	68 941	767	40.7	98.4	1.1	0.3	0.4	0.5	5.2	15.4	7.0	10.5	12.6	16.7
42 007	38300	1	Beaver	1 126	170 539	360	151.5	91.9	7.3	0.5	0.7	1.2	5.3	15.2	7.8	10.7	11.9	16.5
42 009	...	6	Bedford	2 622	49 762	981	19.0	98.2	0.8	0.4	0.4	0.9	5.3	16.3	7.0	10.0	13.0	15.8
42 011	39740	2	Berks	2 218	411 442	164	185.5	78.0	4.7	0.4	1.6	16.4	6.1	17.7	10.0	11.2	13.1	15.2
42 013	11020	3	Blair	1 362	127 089	482	93.3	96.7	2.3	0.4	0.8	1.0	5.7	15.5	9.3	11.1	12.2	14.8
42 015	42380	6	Bradford	2 972	62 622	830	21.1	97.6	0.7	0.7	0.8	1.1	6.0	16.7	7.2	10.2	12.1	15.9
42 017	37980	1	Bucks	1 565	625 249	98	399.5	88.0	4.0	0.4	4.4	4.3	5.5	17.5	7.6	10.6	13.4	17.4
42 019	38300	1	Butler	2 042	183 862	335	90.0	96.7	1.4	0.4	1.3	1.1	5.4	17.0	9.1	10.1	13.4	16.4
42 021	27780	3	Cambria	1 783	143 679	432	80.6	94.3	4.3	0.3	0.7	1.4	5.0	14.6	9.3	10.5	12.0	15.3
42 023	...	7	Cameron	1 026	5 085	2 837	5.0	98.9	0.5	0.6	0.4	0.4	4.3	15.1	5.5	9.1	11.0	16.7
42 025	10900	2	Carbon	988	65 249	803	66.0	94.6	1.7	0.5	0.7	3.3	5.3	15.4	6.9	10.5	13.4	16.5
42 027	44300	3	Centre	2 875	153 990	405	53.6	89.2	3.4	0.4	5.9	2.4	4.4	11.5	28.9	12.2	10.4	11.6
42 029	37980	1	Chester	1 944	498 886	129	256.6	83.3	6.6	0.4	4.4	6.5	6.2	18.6	8.9	10.9	13.8	16.4
42 031	...	6	Clarion	1 556	39 988	1 175	25.7	97.5	1.5	0.4	0.7	0.6	5.1	14.3	16.1	9.8	11.5	14.1
42 033	20180	4	Clearfield	2 965	81 642	675	27.5	95.0	2.3	0.3	0.7	2.3	5.0	15.0	7.9	11.4	13.8	16.1
42 035	30820	6	Clinton	2 300	39 238	1 189	17.1	96.6	1.9	0.4	0.7	1.1	5.6	15.1	15.3	10.2	11.3	13.9
42 037	14100	4	Columbia	1 251	67 295	779	53.8	95.2	2.1	0.4	1.1	2.0	4.8	13.9	16.6	9.7	11.8	14.2
42 039	32740	4	Crawford	2 622	88 765	640	33.9	96.7	2.2	0.5	0.7	0.9	5.7	16.7	9.4	10.3	12.3	15.0
42 041	25420	2	Cumberland	1 413	235 406	271	166.6	90.8	3.9	0.4	3.6	2.7	5.4	15.3	10.7	12.0	12.9	15.0
42 043	25420	2	Dauphin	1 360	268 100	243	197.1	72.0	19.0	0.6	3.7	7.0	6.3	16.9	8.5	12.9	12.9	15.5
42 045	37980	1	Delaware	476	558 979	110	1 174.3	72.4	20.3	0.5	5.3	3.0	6.1	17.3	10.5	11.9	12.5	15.4
42 047	41260	7	Elk	2 143	31 946	1 395	14.9	98.7	0.5	0.3	0.5	0.6	4.8	16.0	6.0	9.5	13.6	17.1
42 049	21500	2	Erie	2 070	280 566	230	135.5	88.2	8.1	0.5	1.5	3.4	6.0	16.8	11.6	11.7	12.1	14.7
42 051	38300	1	Fayette	2 047	136 606	452	66.7	94.1	5.5	0.5	0.4	0.8	5.0	15.3	7.6	11.0	13.0	15.6
42 053	...	9	Forest	1 106	7 716	2 628	7.0	76.4	18.0	0.5	0.2	5.4	2.4	10.0	10.6	16.4	13.2	15.0
42 055	16540	4	Franklin	2 000	149 618	417	74.8	91.6	3.8	0.5	1.2	4.3	6.6	17.2	8.0	11.5	13.1	14.5
42 057	...	8	Fulton	1 133	14 845	2 123	13.1	97.8	1.4	0.6	0.2	0.8	6.2	16.9	7.2	10.7	13.8	15.0
42 059	...	6	Greene	1 492	38 686	1 201	25.9	95.0	3.6	0.6	0.5	1.2	5.0	14.8	10.0	11.9	13.6	15.2
42 061	26500	6	Huntingdon	2 265	45 913	1 050	20.3	92.7	5.6	0.4	0.5	1.6	5.4	14.7	9.7	11.9	13.4	15.1
42 063	26860	4	Indiana	2 142	88 880	638	41.5	95.2	3.1	0.4	1.1	1.1	5.1	13.9	17.5	10.4	10.8	13.8
42 065	...	7	Jefferson	1 690	45 200	1 061	26.7	98.7	0.6	0.5	0.4	0.6	5.7	15.8	8.1	10.6	12.2	15.9
42 067	...	6	Juniata	1 014	24 636	1 619	24.3	96.4	0.8	0.4	0.5	2.5	6.3	17.7	7.8	10.9	12.7	15.1
42 069	42540	2	Lackawanna	1 189	214 437	289	180.4	90.7	2.9	0.4	2.0	5.0	5.4	15.1	10.0	11.3	12.3	14.9
42 071	29540	2	Lancaster	2 444	519 445	121	212.5	86.1	3.9	0.4	2.2	8.6	6.8	18.0	9.7	11.7	12.2	14.5
42 073	35260	4	Lawrence	928	91 108	625	98.2	94.6	4.8	0.4	0.6	1.0	5.3	15.9	8.2	10.3	12.0	15.4
42 075	30140	3	Lebanon	937	133 568	463	142.5	87.7	2.1	0.3	1.4	9.3	6.3	16.7	8.3	11.1	12.7	14.8
42 077	10900	2	Lehigh	894	349 497	186	390.9	72.9	5.8	0.4	3.4	18.8	6.1	17.5	8.8	12.1	13.2	15.3
42 079	42540	2	Luzerne	2 306	320 918	198	139.2	89.1	3.5	0.3	1.2	6.7	5.2	15.0	9.3	11.0	12.9	15.2
42 081	48700	3	Lycoming	3 182	116 111	516	36.5	93.4	5.4	0.6	0.8	1.3	5.6	15.3	11.0	11.0	12.1	15.3
42 083	14620	7	McKean	2 536	43 450	1 098	17.1	95.2	2.6	0.6	0.7	1.7	5.5	15.6	9.3	11.2	13.3	15.2
42 085	49660	2	Mercer	1 742	116 638	514	67.0	92.4	6.6	0.5	0.9	1.1	5.1	16.5	9.4	9.9	11.9	15.2
42 087	30380	4	Mifflin	1 065	46 682	1 032	43.8	97.7	1.0	0.3	0.6	1.1	6.3	16.8	7.3	10.4	12.7	14.7
42 089	20700	4	Monroe	1 575	169 842	361	107.8	72.0	13.1	0.7	2.6	13.1	5.1	18.8	10.4	9.4	13.4	17.3
42 091	37980	1	Montgomery	1 251	799 874	70	639.4	80.3	9.3	0.4	7.1	4.3	5.9	17.0	7.7	12.1	13.6	16.0
42 093	14100	6	Montour	337	18 267	1 911	54.2	95.0	1.7	0.3	2.0	1.8	5.7	15.5	7.1	11.3	11.8	16.0
42 095	10900	2	Northampton	957	297 735	213	311.1	82.3	5.2	0.4	2.9	10.5	5.5	16.4	9.9	10.8	13.2	15.7
42 097	44980	4	Northumberland	1 187	94 528	610	79.6	95.1	2.3	0.4	0.5	2.4	5.6	15.0	7.7	11.3	12.5	15.4
42 099	25420	2	Perry	1 428	45 969	1 047	32.2	97.5	1.0	0.5	0.6	1.3	6.0	17.3	7.8	11.0	13.7	16.1
42 101	37980	1	Philadelphia	347	1 526 006	21	4 397.7	38.1	43.4	0.7	7.0	12.3	6.6	15.9	13.3	16.1	12.3	13.0
42 103	35620	1	Pike	1 411	57 369	883	40.7	84.1	6.0	0.8	1.4	9.0	4.9	18.4	7.1	8.5	13.2	17.6

1. CBSA = Core Based Statistical Area. See Appendix A for explanation. See Appendix B for list of metropolitan areas with component counties. 2. County type code from the Economic Research Service of USDA Rural-Urban Continuum Codes. See Appendix A for definition. 3. Dry land or land partially or temporarily covered by water. 4. May be of any race.

Table B. States and Counties — Population and Households

STATE County	55 to 64 years	65 to 74 years	75 years and over	Percent female	1990	2000	1990–2000	2000–2010	Births	Deaths	Net migration	Number	Percent change, 2000–2010	Persons per household	Female family householder[1]	One person
	16	17	18	19	20	21	22	23	24	25	26	27	28	29	30	31
OREGON—Cont'd																
Morrow	12.9	7.6	5.1	48.5	7 625	10 995	44.2	1.6	1 488	671	-224	3 916	3.7	2.85	9.6	19.1
Multnomah	11.9	5.6	5.0	50.5	583 887	660 486	13.1	11.3	89 735	51 803	32 685	304 540	11.9	2.35	10.7	32.6
Polk	13.0	7.8	7.0	51.3	49 541	62 380	25.9	20.9	7 627	5 210	13 520	28 288	22.7	2.60	10.3	23.0
Sherman	15.0	11.5	10.3	49.2	1 918	1 934	0.8	-8.7	142	156	-204	777	-2.5	2.27	7.5	30.5
Tillamook	17.6	12.1	8.8	49.5	21 570	24 262	12.5	4.1	2 418	2 611	954	10 834	6.2	2.29	8.1	29.1
Umatilla	12.1	6.9	5.8	47.9	59 249	70 548	19.1	7.6	9 612	5 182	-1 215	26 904	6.8	2.67	12.0	24.7
Union	14.6	8.8	8.0	50.8	23 598	24 530	3.9	5.0	2 887	2 188	-59	10 501	7.8	2.38	9.5	27.6
Wallowa	19.0	12.6	10.6	50.9	6 911	7 226	4.6	-3.0	578	676	-201	3 133	3.4	2.20	7.1	30.0
Wasco	14.9	9.0	8.7	50.4	21 683	23 791	9.7	6.0	2 669	2 655	471	10 031	6.7	2.44	10.9	28.8
Washington	11.0	5.4	4.6	50.8	311 554	445 342	42.9	18.9	70 962	25 539	49 393	200 934	18.8	2.60	10.1	25.1
Wheeler	17.6	16.5	12.6	50.2	1 396	1 547	10.8	-6.9	71	163	-90	651	-0.3	2.18	7.2	32.4
Yamhill	12.1	7.0	6.4	49.8	65 551	84 992	29.7	16.7	11 348	6 809	9 899	34 726	20.9	2.70	11.1	21.7
PENNSYLVANIA	12.8	7.7	7.7	51.3	11 882 842	12 281 054	3.4	3.4	1 350 244	1 183 448	136 359	5 018 904	5.1	2.45	12.2	28.6
Adams	13.3	8.4	7.3	50.8	78 274	91 292	16.6	11.1	10 124	8 302	9 709	38 013	13.0	2.56	9.2	21.9
Allegheny	13.3	7.8	8.9	52.1	1 336 449	1 281 666	-4.1	-4.6	123 447	135 763	-42 936	533 960	-0.6	2.23	12.2	35.0
Armstrong	14.3	9.2	9.2	50.7	73 478	72 392	-1.5	-4.8	6 561	7 900	-2 771	28 713	-1.0	2.38	9.3	28.0
Beaver	14.1	8.9	9.7	51.8	186 093	181 412	-2.5	-6.0	16 558	19 531	-5 656	71 383	-1.6	2.34	12.1	29.3
Bedford	13.6	10.3	8.8	50.4	47 919	49 984	4.3	-0.4	4 888	4 591	-383	20 233	2.4	2.43	8.2	25.7
Berks	12.1	7.2	7.3	50.9	336 523	373 638	11.0	10.1	46 021	33 196	23 088	154 356	9.0	2.59	12.0	24.5
Blair	13.7	8.7	9.0	51.4	130 542	129 144	-1.1	-1.6	13 442	14 830	-909	52 159	1.2	2.37	11.7	29.6
Bradford	14.1	9.7	8.1	50.8	60 967	62 761	2.9	-0.2	6 847	6 082	-2 017	25 321	3.5	2.45	9.6	26.2
Bucks	13.4	7.6	7.0	51.0	541 174	597 635	10.4	4.6	64 404	47 217	15 080	234 849	7.4	2.63	9.6	23.0
Butler	13.3	7.6	7.5	50.8	152 013	174 083	14.5	5.6	18 965	16 414	9 032	72 835	10.6	2.45	8.4	26.5
Cambria	14.4	8.8	10.0	50.6	163 062	152 598	-6.4	-5.8	13 878	17 463	-4 074	58 950	-2.6	2.30	10.9	31.2
Cameron	16.9	10.2	11.2	50.9	5 913	5 974	1.0	-14.9	496	672	-603	2 273	-7.8	2.20	9.5	32.8
Carbon	14.1	9.4	8.5	50.7	56 803	58 802	3.5	11.0	5 810	7 114	6 677	26 684	12.6	2.42	10.4	26.7
Centre	9.7	5.9	5.3	48.2	124 812	135 758	8.8	13.4	12 056	8 245	7 492	57 573	16.7	2.38	6.4	28.7
Chester	12.3	6.8	6.0	50.9	376 389	433 501	15.2	15.1	56 392	31 254	42 959	182 900	15.8	2.65	8.5	23.0
Clarion	12.8	8.8	7.6	51.6	41 699	41 765	0.2	-4.3	3 691	3 995	-1 733	16 128	0.5	2.37	8.7	28.4
Clearfield	13.4	9.0	8.5	48.4	78 097	83 382	6.8	-2.1	7 441	8 549	591	32 288	-1.5	2.37	10.3	27.7
Clinton	12.4	8.4	7.8	51.0	37 182	37 914	2.0	3.5	3 977	3 776	-1 090	15 151	2.6	2.42	10.3	26.5
Columbia	12.9	8.2	7.9	52.0	63 202	64 151	1.5	4.9	5 803	6 184	1 752	26 479	6.3	2.38	9.3	28.3
Crawford	14.0	8.8	7.7	51.2	86 166	90 366	4.9	-1.8	9 660	8 751	-2 194	35 028	1.0	2.42	9.7	28.0
Cumberland	13.1	7.9	7.7	50.9	195 257	213 674	9.4	10.2	21 725	19 204	17 474	93 943	13.2	2.37	8.8	28.2
Dauphin	13.2	7.1	6.6	51.7	237 813	251 798	5.9	6.5	30 523	22 304	573	110 435	7.6	2.37	13.8	31.2
Delaware	12.1	6.7	7.6	52.1	547 658	550 864	0.6	1.5	62 924	52 010	-1 340	208 700	1.2	2.57	14.6	27.6
Elk	14.0	9.4	9.6	50.3	34 878	35 112	0.7	-9.0	2 985	3 392	-2 523	13 693	-3.1	2.31	8.9	29.8
Erie	12.6	7.3	7.3	50.8	275 575	280 843	1.9	-0.1	31 131	24 747	-9 146	110 413	3.7	2.42	13.2	29.3
Fayette	14.5	8.9	9.1	50.9	145 351	148 644	2.3	-8.1	13 490	16 470	-2 133	55 997	-6.6	2.36	13.1	29.1
Forest	14.0	11.6	6.9	33.1	4 802	4 946	3.0	56.0	341	707	2 248	2 511	25.6	2.08	5.7	36.2
Franklin	12.5	8.6	7.9	51.1	121 082	129 313	6.8	15.7	16 365	12 215	12 346	58 389	15.3	2.52	9.4	24.3
Fulton	13.2	10.2	6.9	49.7	13 837	14 261	3.1	4.1	1 552	1 231	353	6 014	6.3	2.45	8.4	25.0
Greene	14.1	7.9	7.4	48.5	39 550	40 672	2.8	-4.9	3 812	4 031	-953	14 724	-2.2	2.42	10.9	27.0
Huntingdon	13.5	8.9	7.3	47.1	44 164	45 586	3.2	0.7	4 194	3 986	-101	17 280	3.1	2.39	8.7	27.6
Indiana	12.8	8.1	7.6	50.3	89 994	89 605	-0.4	-0.8	8 045	8 191	-1 422	35 005	2.6	2.39	8.4	28.1
Jefferson	13.3	9.1	9.1	50.7	46 083	45 932	-0.3	-1.6	4 657	5 049	-605	18 561	1.0	2.39	9.4	28.2
Juniata	12.7	8.8	8.0	50.1	20 625	22 821	10.6	8.0	2 678	2 025	-217	9 476	10.4	2.57	7.6	23.0
Lackawanna	13.4	8.4	9.3	51.9	219 097	213 295	-2.6	0.5	20 671	25 765	2 065	87 226	1.2	2.37	12.4	31.6
Lancaster	11.9	7.4	7.6	51.1	422 822	470 658	11.3	10.4	63 942	40 627	16 783	193 602	12.2	2.62	9.6	24.2
Lawrence	14.0	8.8	10.0	51.8	96 246	94 643	-1.7	-3.7	9 014	10 691	-2 219	37 126	0.1	2.39	12.3	28.9
Lebanon	13.0	8.5	8.5	51.2	113 744	120 327	5.8	11.0	14 249	12 213	8 808	52 258	12.3	2.49	10.1	25.9
Lehigh	12.2	7.2	7.6	51.6	291 130	312 090	7.2	12.0	37 909	29 139	24 560	133 983	9.9	2.54	12.9	26.3
Luzerne	13.4	8.6	9.4	51.1	328 149	319 250	-2.7	0.5	28 949	39 336	6 034	131 932	1.0	2.34	12.9	31.4
Lycoming	13.2	8.1	8.3	51.0	118 710	120 044	1.1	-3.3	12 366	11 485	-3 329	46 700	-0.6	2.37	10.8	28.2
McKean	13.0	8.5	8.4	49.0	47 131	45 936	-2.5	-5.4	4 440	4 881	-2 058	17 183	-4.7	2.34	11.2	29.5
Mercer	13.5	8.8	9.6	51.0	121 003	120 293	-0.6	-3.0	11 477	12 987	-1 933	46 442	-0.6	2.37	11.6	29.4
Mifflin	13.3	9.7	8.9	51.1	46 197	46 486	0.6	0.4	5 461	4 864	-835	18 743	1.8	2.46	9.3	27.1
Monroe	12.8	7.4	5.3	50.6	95 681	138 687	44.9	22.5	14 663	11 060	24 585	61 091	23.5	2.72	11.5	21.4
Montgomery	12.5	7.3	7.8	51.5	678 193	750 097	10.6	6.6	87 374	65 338	16 369	307 750	7.6	2.53	9.5	26.3
Montour	14.0	8.8	9.8	51.9	17 735	18 236	2.8	0.2	1 968	2 137	-228	7 393	4.3	2.36	9.0	29.4
Northampton	12.9	7.6	8.0	51.2	247 110	267 066	8.1	11.5	28 826	24 143	27 186	113 565	11.8	2.53	11.1	25.0
Northumberland	14.0	9.2	9.4	50.1	96 771	94 556	-2.3	0.0	9 086	10 895	-796	39 242	1.0	2.32	10.3	30.3
Perry	14.5	7.8	5.8	49.8	41 172	43 602	5.9	5.4	5 005	3 609	793	17 903	7.2	2.53	8.7	23.0
Philadelphia	10.5	6.2	5.9	52.8	1 585 577	1 517 550	-4.3	0.6	203 817	147 696	-108 206	599 736	1.6	2.45	22.5	34.1
Pike	14.0	9.8	6.4	50.0	28 032	46 302	65.2	23.9	3 918	3 519	13 882	21 925	25.8	2.59	9.5	22.4

1. No spouse present.

Table B. States and Counties — **Population, Vital Statistics, Medicare, and Crime**

STATE County	Persons in group quarters, 2010	Daytime population, 2006–2010 Number	Daytime population, 2006–2010 Employment/ residence ratio	Births, average 2006–2008 Total	Births, average 2006–2008 Rate[1]	Deaths, average 2006–2008 Number	Deaths, average 2006–2008 Rate[1]	Persons under 65 with no health insurance, 2009 Number	Persons under 65 with no health insurance, 2009 Percent	Medicare, 2011 Eligible for Medicare	Medicare, 2011 Enrolled in Medicare Advantage	Medicare, 2011 Enrolled in a Medicare prescription drug plan	Serious crimes known to police,[2] 2010 Total Number	Serious crimes known to police,[2] 2010 Total Rate[3]
	32	33	34	35	36	37	38	39	40	41	42	43	44	45
OREGON—Cont'd														
Morrow	23	10 780	0.9	D	D	71	6.2	2 291	23.2	1 694	255	799	198	1 772
Multnomah	19 583	808 882	1.3	10 305	14.7	5 495	7.9	120 671	18.9	97 216	51 530	23 742	37 806	5 204
Polk	1 885	61 409	0.6	848	11.3	582	7.7	11 801	18.5	13 172	7 223	3 275	2 078	2 756
Sherman	0	1 934	1.1	D	D	19	11.4	298	22.8	454	77	208	45	2 550
Tillamook	476	25 058	1.0	D	D	282	11.2	4 309	22.0	6 321	1 302	2 679	599	2 372
Umatilla	3 985	74 539	1.0	1 131	15.4	611	8.3	14 802	23.6	11 683	1 689	5 740	2 368	3 207
Union	735	24 987	1.0	D	D	237	9.6	4 013	19.5	5 189	299	3 232	547	2 276
Wallowa	105	6 838	1.0	D	D	79	11.6	1 093	21.2	1 929	45	1 115	68	970
Wasco	741	24 896	1.0	D	D	292	12.3	4 251	21.8	5 093	1 035	2 262	884	3 506
Washington	6 788	514 889	1.0	7 786	14.9	2 817	5.4	78 958	16.5	63 050	33 165	14 646	11 321	2 144
Wheeler	25	1 400	0.9	D	D	21	15.7	327	31.9	451	92	177	NA	NA
Yamhill	5 461	89 096	0.8	1 308	13.6	774	8.0	16 300	19.3	15 692	7 281	4 262	2 294	2 313
PENNSYLVANIA	426 113	12 527 922	1.0	149 692	12.0	126 035	10.1	1 203 026	11.7	2 334 780	890 161	769 168	322 537	2 539
Adams	3 993	85 850	0.7	1 112	11.0	896	8.9	10 508	12.4	19 056	5 110	6 870	1 375	1 356
Allegheny	35 054	1 318 965	1.2	13 225	10.8	14 073	11.5	102 082	10.4	236 187	143 535	36 371	32 696	2 683
Armstrong	650	58 722	0.7	726	10.5	832	12.0	6 347	11.8	15 070	9 363	2 885	774	1 212
Beaver	3 382	149 733	0.7	1 811	10.4	2 134	12.3	13 489	9.9	38 112	24 725	5 524	4 791	2 840
Bedford	551	46 101	0.8	D	D	495	10.0	5 019	12.8	11 503	5 451	3 186	483	971
Berks	12 023	383 311	0.9	5 149	12.8	3 508	8.7	41 909	12.4	71 270	23 081	27 235	10 334	2 512
Blair	3 672	132 563	1.1	1 444	11.5	1 533	12.2	11 821	11.8	27 634	13 321	7 659	2 588	2 036
Bradford	579	60 907	0.9	750	12.2	654	10.6	6 312	12.9	13 349	3 042	6 348	964	1 550
Bucks	8 233	567 085	0.8	6 831	11.0	5 049	8.1	42 105	8.0	109 011	34 278	34 606	12 460	1 993
Butler	5 490	180 658	1.0	1 995	10.9	1 778	9.7	14 927	9.8	33 437	18 697	5 466	2 575	1 401
Cambria	8 092	142 490	1.0	1 490	10.2	1 842	12.7	13 649	12.1	32 937	19 682	7 114	2 842	2 048
Cameron	92	5 300	1.0	D	D	67	12.4	519	13.0	1 364	270	654	135	2 655
Carbon	699	52 571	0.6	668	10.6	766	12.1	6 104	11.9	13 828	2 090	7 106	1 501	2 425
Centre	16 989	158 701	1.1	1 303	9.1	900	6.3	13 929	11.2	19 739	8 452	6 511	2 612	1 696
Chester	13 336	485 246	1.0	6 197	12.7	3 465	7.1	36 080	8.5	73 369	16 463	29 958	7 901	1 608
Clarion	1 841	38 968	0.9	D	D	422	10.5	4 305	13.6	8 150	2 101	3 729	639	1 677
Clearfield	5 115	80 284	0.9	808	9.8	951	11.6	8 813	13.5	17 458	6 025	7 259	1 978	2 423
Clinton	2 623	36 364	0.8	D	D	406	10.9	3 725	12.6	7 659	2 858	3 214	784	1 998
Columbia	4 387	65 730	1.0	D	D	693	10.7	6 214	11.9	12 869	5 156	4 653	1 625	2 614
Crawford	3 875	86 516	0.9	1 023	11.5	983	11.1	10 093	14.1	18 576	4 704	8 868	1 486	1 674
Cumberland	12 830	242 360	1.1	2 500	11.0	2 137	9.4	18 810	9.9	42 267	14 348	12 886	3 891	1 653
Dauphin	6 780	312 545	1.4	3 543	13.9	2 391	9.4	25 548	11.8	44 931	19 606	11 805	8 593	3 222
Delaware	23 055	505 885	0.8	6 969	12.6	5 547	10.0	46 490	10.0	92 847	25 887	34 861	15 614	2 793
Elk	355	31 951	1.0	D	D	351	10.7	2 689	10.7	7 423	1 123	4 260	682	2 135
Erie	12 875	283 770	1.0	3 463	12.4	2 697	9.7	26 010	11.3	50 735	21 644	17 749	7 796	2 779
Fayette	4 216	128 884	0.8	1 388	9.6	1 794	12.4	15 657	13.8	32 068	17 801	6 734	3 043	2 245
Forest	2 500	8 151	1.3	D	D	86	12.7	919	17.3	1 512	419	624	104	1 348
Franklin	2 696	136 857	0.9	2 023	14.3	1 309	9.2	16 102	13.8	29 706	6 031	11 522	2 376	1 588
Fulton	122	13 812	0.9	D	D	132	8.9	1 587	13.3	3 199	564	1 510	227	1 529
Greene	3 076	37 836	0.9	408	10.3	407	10.2	4 187	13.1	7 333	3 440	1 983	789	2 039
Huntingdon	4 570	42 079	0.8	D	D	449	9.8	5 616	15.3	9 220	2 731	4 036	736	1 603
Indiana	5 357	88 046	1.0	873	9.9	859	9.8	9 693	13.7	16 374	9 075	3 286	1 777	2 041
Jefferson	774	42 860	0.9	515	11.4	545	12.0	4 479	12.7	10 077	2 914	4 581	533	1 250
Juniata	292	20 551	0.7	D	D	222	9.6	2 647	14.3	4 719	1 943	1 726	268	1 088
Lackawanna	8 063	216 081	1.0	2 323	11.1	2 718	13.0	18 496	11.1	46 533	11 724	21 302	4 762	2 221
Lancaster	12 638	502 012	1.0	7 215	14.5	4 451	8.9	58 039	13.9	90 498	27 401	36 814	10 511	2 024
Lawrence	2 239	85 667	0.8	962	10.6	1 090	12.0	8 469	11.9	20 686	11 862	4 231	2 802	3 415
Lebanon	3 657	118 798	0.8	1 656	12.9	1 340	10.5	12 316	11.7	26 305	8 396	8 867	2 369	1 812
Lehigh	8 993	357 952	1.1	4 370	12.9	3 083	9.1	33 990	12.0	61 922	17 055	26 705	10 760	3 079
Luzerne	11 791	319 075	1.0	3 232	10.3	4 106	13.1	28 304	11.4	68 643	14 538	32 979	8 446	2 644
Lycoming	5 437	117 555	1.0	1 313	11.2	1 235	10.6	11 658	12.4	23 354	6 197	10 758	2 535	2 183
McKean	3 178	43 226	1.0	D	D	521	11.9	4 472	12.9	9 400	1 517	5 096	797	1 834
Mercer	6 714	118 819	1.0	1 216	10.4	1 431	12.2	10 970	11.9	26 326	10 994	8 985	2 580	2 212
Mifflin	559	44 569	0.9	607	13.1	514	11.1	5 259	14.5	10 399	4 061	4 251	831	1 780
Monroe	3 790	155 347	0.8	1 630	9.9	1 231	7.5	17 628	12.5	26 686	3 857	11 452	5 158	3 037
Montgomery	21 006	857 274	1.2	9 495	12.2	7 031	9.1	51 810	8.0	134 381	38 036	50 361	16 832	2 104
Montour	843	23 233	1.6	217	12.2	233	13.1	1 401	10.0	3 898	1 864	1 204	270	1 478
Northampton	10 620	265 020	0.8	3 269	11.1	2 645	9.0	28 185	11.4	55 465	12 893	24 098	7 022	2 358
Northumberland	3 446	83 851	0.8	1 036	11.4	1 161	12.7	9 509	13.3	20 735	5 842	9 539	1 386	1 466
Perry	657	32 950	0.4	D	D	405	9.0	4 636	12.1	7 984	3 212	2 467	756	1 645
Philadelphia	57 383	1 611 196	1.2	23 473	16.2	15 133	10.4	210 352	16.3	231 102	97 267	73 856	76 339	5 003
Pike	478	46 770	0.6	D	D	412	7.0	5 668	11.5	11 326	809	5 043	1 153	2 010

1. Per 1,000 estimated resident population.   2. Data for serious crimes have not been adjusted for underreporting; this may affect comparability between geographic areas and over time.   3. Per 100,000 population estimated by the FBI.

Table B. States and Counties — Crime, Education, Money Income, and Poverty

STATE County	Serious crimes known to police,[1] 2010 (cont.) Rate[2] Violent	Property	Education School enrollment and attainment, 2006–2010 Enrollment[3] Total	Percent private	Attainment[4] (percent) High school graduate or less	Bachelor's degree or more	Local government expenditures,[5] 2008–2009 Total current expenditures (mil dol)	Current expenditures per student (dollars)	Money income, 2006–2010 Per capita income[6] (dollars)	Households Median income Dollars	Percent change, 2000 to 2006–2010 (constant 2010 dollars)	Percent with income of $200,000 or more	Income and poverty, 2010 Median household income (dollars)	Percent below poverty level All persons	Children under 18 years	Children 5 to 17 years in families
	46	47	48	49	50	51	52	53	54	55	56	57	58	59	60	61
OREGON—Cont'd																
Morrow	179	1 593	2 916	4.9	55.3	11.5	23.7	9 845	20 201	43 902	-7.6	1.3	45 652	16.7	24.8	20.5
Multnomah	498	4 706	175 546	20.9	32.0	37.5	960.7	10 596	28 883	49 618	-5.1	3.9	48 018	18.0	24.6	23.0
Polk	241	2 514	20 557	11.3	37.1	28.1	69.1	8 960	24 345	50 975	-4.9	2.2	49 504	15.7	22.0	18.9
Sherman	0	2 550	373	11.8	39.5	15.4	4.4	15 938	21 688	41 354	-7.1	1.5	49 295	13.7	20.2	18.1
Tillamook	63	2 309	4 718	8.4	44.7	20.0	37.5	11 364	22 824	39 412	-9.2	1.6	40 797	16.0	24.1	21.9
Umatilla	299	2 907	19 110	6.9	49.6	14.6	151.9	11 216	20 035	45 861	-0.1	1.3	43 691	15.5	21.3	19.5
Union	116	2 159	6 676	12.7	47.4	20.3	39.5	10 397	22 947	42 162	-1.3	2.3	41 192	16.7	22.0	19.8
Wallowa	14	956	1 231	13.8	42.4	21.1	13.0	14 944	23 023	41 116	1.1	1.2	38 522	16.6	27.6	25.3
Wasco	63	3 443	5 038	9.1	45.8	21.5	40.3	11 668	21 922	42 133	-7.5	1.5	41 711	15.7	23.5	22.4
Washington	168	1 976	136 192	18.2	28.7	38.9	782.3	9 388	30 522	62 574	-5.2	4.7	60 555	9.7	12.8	11.4
Wheeler	NA	NA	249	17.3	54.0	18.2	3.9	19 924	20 598	33 403	-8.2	1.7	31 983	19.8	34.8	31.8
Yamhill	121	2 192	26 073	24.9	43.1	23.0	135.0	8 605	24 017	52 485	-6.0	2.2	50 288	14.7	18.5	16.3
PENNSYLVANIA	366	2 173	3 172 787	24.6	50.4	26.4	21 984.8	12 493	27 049	50 398	-0.8	3.5	49 245	13.4	18.9	17.5
Adams	192	1 164	25 390	28.2	58.6	18.5	251.2	17 552	25 606	56 529	4.5	2.0	54 415	9.9	15.9	13.6
Allegheny	439	2 244	304 657	26.3	40.7	34.1	2 069.7	13 742	29 549	47 961	-1.2	4.0	47 490	11.9	15.6	14.6
Armstrong	125	1 087	14 196	10.7	64.3	13.9	87.3	13 380	21 828	42 752	7.0	0.7	42 711	13.7	21.8	19.3
Beaver	328	2 513	37 858	18.6	53.2	19.2	356.2	11 139	24 168	46 190	-1.4	1.6	44 020	15.1	21.6	19.4
Bedford	96	874	10 340	10.4	67.4	12.5	78.7	10 055	20 545	40 249	-2.9	1.2	38 548	13.6	20.3	18.7
Berks	332	2 180	105 913	16.4	55.8	21.7	841.7	11 997	25 518	53 470	-5.6	2.4	51 631	13.7	21.6	20.4
Blair	240	1 796	27 979	14.7	59.0	17.3	214.3	11 687	22 880	42 363	1.8	1.6	41 095	13.3	19.6	18.7
Bradford	170	1 380	13 733	11.4	63.0	15.7	100.5	11 625	20 979	40 543	-8.6	1.5	43 060	10.9	17.1	15.9
Bucks	115	1 878	155 984	26.4	39.8	34.5	1 273.2	14 122	35 687	74 828	-1.1	7.5	70 960	6.4	7.8	7.4
Butler	133	1 267	47 272	16.6	45.8	28.8	329.0	9 922	28 446	56 878	6.2	3.3	54 363	9.3	11.6	10.1
Cambria	208	1 840	32 454	18.4	60.4	17.5	201.7	10 534	21 278	39 574	3.6	1.2	40 494	13.7	22.4	20.5
Cameron	79	2 576	1 011	6.0	64.0	14.9	8.6	10 980	21 375	40 733	-0.1	0.3	36 278	14.4	23.7	20.2
Carbon	254	2 171	13 707	16.2	59.9	14.6	100.4	10 920	22 956	47 744	7.4	0.9	45 698	12.2	18.5	16.2
Centre	103	1 594	61 643	7.7	40.1	44.0	167.0	12 174	23 744	47 016	2.7	3.2	45 154	18.9	14.7	13.2
Chester	161	1 447	134 821	28.0	31.7	47.8	1 119.5	14 145	41 251	84 741	2.5	11.8	83 829	6.4	8.0	7.5
Clarion	123	1 554	10 564	9.8	63.5	17.2	83.3	14 184	20 259	40 028	2.7	1.2	37 740	19.0	28.1	25.8
Clearfield	247	2 175	16 638	13.2	65.7	12.3	150.8	12 082	0	37 130	-6.5	1.0	37 025	16.8	24.5	20.9
Clinton	117	1 881	11 104	11.7	61.9	16.7	55.6	14 364	19 261	39 354	0.0	0.6	38 423	16.9	22.7	22.5
Columbia	119	2 495	19 469	6.8	60.3	18.3	76.6	11 809	22 403	42 788	-0.9	1.5	41 898	15.4	16.9	16.1
Crawford	84	1 590	21 118	23.2	60.9	18.3	137.2	10 899	20 383	38 924	-8.4	1.1	38 302	19.7	32.2	28.8
Cumberland	104	1 649	59 583	25.4	44.6	32.3	361.2	12 886	30 119	60 219	1.8	3.4	56 288	7.4	10.2	9.6
Dauphin	500	2 722	63 878	16.9	48.5	27.1	436.7	11 823	27 727	52 371	-0.4	2.7	51 670	13.9	23.1	22.2
Delaware	518	2 275	156 448	35.5	41.7	34.7	1 022.7	14 030	32 067	61 876	-2.5	6.2	59 038	10.0	13.8	12.5
Elk	88	2 047	6 979	26.3	61.7	16.2	41.7	10 249	22 729	43 745	-8.0	1.2	42 750	11.7	17.5	16.2
Erie	271	2 508	75 052	26.9	53.4	23.3	464.0	11 276	22 644	43 595	-6.0	1.8	42 341	17.2	24.4	21.8
Fayette	202	2 043	28 279	10.4	65.9	13.9	199.3	10 789	19 209	34 796	0.1	0.8	35 442	20.7	31.7	29.3
Forest	233	1 115	1 131	13.9	70.1	9.6	15.7	12 796	14 325	35 150	0.6	0.3	34 736	20.4	29.9	24.8
Franklin	131	1 457	32 719	19.7	59.4	18.3	216.3	9 662	25 307	51 035	-0.4	2.0	49 541	9.5	14.8	13.7
Fulton	202	1 327	3 251	10.6	70.0	9.9	26.8	11 317	21 739	45 240	2.4	1.1	43 947	10.5	17.7	17.2
Greene	98	1 941	8 315	16.3	64.1	14.6	68.1	12 138	20 258	40 498	5.4	1.3	41 927	18.0	24.6	22.5
Huntingdon	209	1 394	9 821	26.1	66.5	13.8	60.6	9 941	20 616	41 700	-1.1	1.2	40 947	14.3	20.0	18.3
Indiana	357	1 684	24 522	9.2	59.7	19.2	170.2	14 111	20 587	40 225	5.1	1.3	40 538	18.6	22.6	21.0
Jefferson	206	1 043	9 285	12.7	67.5	12.0	64.1	12 309	20 305	38 406	-4.4	1.2	37 911	16.3	24.8	22.5
Juniata	146	942	5 323	22.6	71.2	10.8	27.6	8 898	20 682	44 276	0.8	0.6	45 810	11.1	18.0	16.9
Lackawanna	220	2 001	51 640	34.2	51.8	23.7	320.4	11 298	24 152	43 673	0.1	2.4	42 081	13.6	20.1	18.1
Lancaster	182	1 841	125 647	26.1	56.5	23.3	847.0	12 313	25 854	54 765	-5.0	2.9	51 784	10.5	15.7	14.9
Lawrence	444	2 971	20 859	18.2	58.4	18.6	138.7	10 293	21 467	42 570	1.4	1.3	39 047	16.2	25.5	23.8
Lebanon	186	1 626	30 174	22.8	61.1	18.3	187.9	9 943	25 525	52 356	1.2	2.1	51 142	11.0	17.0	15.5
Lehigh	284	2 795	87 136	23.2	48.1	27.0	595.0	11 800	27 301	53 541	-2.7	3.7	51 426	13.2	20.6	18.7
Luzerne	255	2 389	72 791	23.4	54.4	20.2	478.0	10 622	23 245	42 224	-1.3	1.8	41 745	15.9	26.6	21.9
Lycoming	171	2 013	27 940	14.7	54.9	18.8	195.9	11 729	21 802	42 689	-0.9	1.4	40 825	17.1	24.3	22.0
McKean	186	1 648	9 985	11.9	61.3	15.6	91.5	13 615	21 022	40 097	-4.2	1.1	39 679	14.9	24.2	22.3
Mercer	195	2 017	28 126	26.7	58.0	19.0	229.7	13 240	21 765	42 573	-3.0	1.5	40 244	16.6	27.2	23.9
Mifflin	111	1 669	9 187	20.3	72.0	11.1	91.3	16 135	19 085	37 539	-7.9	0.7	37 163	16.6	28.1	25.0
Monroe	352	2 685	47 713	14.4	49.4	23.8	406.1	12 620	24 824	56 733	-3.1	2.0	54 111	13.0	16.9	14.9
Montgomery	195	1 909	205 261	33.0	33.7	44.2	1 618.7	15 066	40 076	76 380	-0.8	9.4	75 369	5.8	7.2	6.5
Montour	339	1 139	3 903	18.5	53.7	25.0	27.4	11 607	26 124	45 255	-6.1	4.1	47 518	12.1	19.1	17.2
Northampton	206	2 152	76 164	28.7	48.7	26.3	542.9	11 912	28 362	58 762	2.6	3.4	56 369	10.6	14.6	12.8
Northumberland	304	1 163	18 598	16.4	66.9	13.5	179.1	14 556	20 654	38 387	-3.2	1.0	36 503	15.0	22.4	20.2
Perry	157	1 488	9 658	11.9	65.0	14.0	71.3	10 689	23 701	52 659	-0.8	0.9	51 390	10.1	15.4	14.5
Philadelphia	1 215	3 787	422 271	34.0	56.3	22.2	2 444.2	12 772	21 117	36 251	-6.9	1.9	34 667	26.4	36.4	36.4
Pike	150	1 860	14 226	12.1	46.5	23.3	108.0	11 211	27 564	56 843	0.6	3.1	54 674	9.0	13.2	11.9

1. Data for serious crimes have not been adjusted for underreporting; this may affect comparability between geographic areas and over time.   2. Per 100,000 population estimated by the FBI.   3. All persons 3 years old and over enrolled in nursery school through college.   4. Persons 25 years old and over.   5. Elementary and secondary education expenditures.   6. Based on population estimated by the American Community Survey, 2006–2010.

Table B. States and Counties — **Personal Income**

STATE County	Personal income, 2009 Total (mil dol)	Percent change, 2008–2009	Per capita¹ Dollars	Per capita¹ Rank	Wages and salaries² (mil dol)	Proprietors' income (mil dol)	Dividends, interest, and rent (mil dol)	Transfer payments (mil dol) Total	Government payments to individuals Total	Social Security	Medical payments	Income mainte-nance	Unemploy-ment insurance
	62	63	64	65	66	67	68	69	70	71	72	73	74
OREGON—Cont'd													
Morrow	342	-3.2	29 686	2 053	218	39	46	68	66	23	26	7	4
Multnomah	29 431	-0.8	40 490	420	26 411	3 259	5 767	4 881	4 749	1 307	1 867	556	506
Polk	2 348	0.2	30 056	1 966	752	114	494	503	488	187	173	43	39
Sherman	70	-13.7	41 049	381	53	6	13	16	16	6	7	1	1
Tillamook	816	-1.0	32 773	1 372	367	47	202	219	215	89	79	15	12
Umatilla	2 215	2.5	30 193	1 937	1 375	183	352	503	490	154	195	56	30
Union	780	-1.4	31 163	1 719	427	46	156	210	206	68	77	18	15
Wallowa	225	0.5	32 725	1 379	94	23	62	62	61	26	22	4	4
Wasco	821	1.3	33 979	1 173	456	50	169	195	191	70	75	18	11
Washington	21 205	-0.7	39 465	493	15 787	706	3 634	2 770	2 672	895	915	227	355
Wheeler	37	4.9	27 339	2 509	10	1	11	13	13	6	5	1	0
Yamhill	3 258	1.0	32 894	1 356	1 472	122	607	673	655	219	247	61	70
PENNSYLVANIA	506 397	-0.4	40 175	X	316 721	40 372	82 268	103 317	101 019	33 904	44 030	8 007	7 937
Adams	3 293	1.0	32 184	1 489	1 474	237	526	718	699	271	225	30	128
Allegheny	56 572	-1.5	46 427	159	42 463	6 650	9 288	10 708	10 486	3 512	4 871	775	582
Armstrong	2 311	-0.5	34 067	1 165	863	285	315	657	645	217	280	44	65
Beaver	6 098	0.9	35 518	954	2 731	271	832	1 642	1 610	565	702	107	123
Bedford	1 472	0.9	29 681	2 054	628	159	211	427	418	153	154	27	57
Berks	14 793	-0.4	36 336	839	8 791	912	2 395	3 034	2 960	1 064	1 158	252	282
Blair	4 120	2.2	32 663	1 391	2 701	227	583	1 173	1 150	343	482	95	91
Bradford	1 827	0.2	29 886	2 005	995	142	276	477	466	185	179	41	28
Bucks	31 863	-1.9	50 898	89	14 848	2 399	5 398	4 292	4 178	1 708	1 734	152	283
Butler	7 516	0.3	40 692	406	4 174	360	1 150	1 403	1 370	499	587	69	114
Cambria	4 602	0.8	31 961	1 535	2 547	259	684	1 442	1 415	455	638	95	114
Cameron	159	0.5	30 706	1 818	83	6	31	59	58	19	19	3	13
Carbon	2 007	0.0	31 427	1 658	665	195	306	555	543	205	215	29	54
Centre	4 972	0.9	34 006	1 170	3 756	324	854	809	783	289	265	38	61
Chester	28 454	-1.6	57 033	44	18 651	2 462	5 492	2 898	2 807	1 151	1 097	101	230
Clarion	1 231	0.3	31 174	1 716	600	107	183	369	362	116	152	24	38
Clearfield	2 454	1.9	29 809	2 019	1 277	156	351	773	758	245	311	57	95
Clinton	1 111	2.3	30 181	1 939	573	80	144	307	301	107	111	23	32
Columbia	1 971	-0.1	30 277	1 915	1 111	197	293	526	514	183	203	31	58
Crawford	2 602	0.1	29 394	2 121	1 275	190	380	800	783	260	317	64	85
Cumberland	9 495	0.6	40 843	393	6 975	551	1 722	1 547	1 505	605	586	58	113
Dauphin	10 312	0.4	39 825	461	10 536	587	1 525	1 952	1 904	637	776	164	152
Delaware	27 524	-0.9	49 324	114	12 992	2 047	4 850	4 382	4 281	1 421	1 998	286	253
Elk	1 078	-1.4	33 675	1 224	598	52	189	326	320	113	116	16	59
Erie	9 142	0.3	32 615	1 401	5 836	502	1 392	2 392	2 340	743	933	236	257
Fayette	4 333	0.6	30 383	1 890	1 734	300	575	1 492	1 466	442	660	154	114
Forest	166	3.3	24 435	2 921	111	11	25	65	64	22	31	3	5
Franklin	4 837	-1.1	33 357	1 287	2 628	268	894	997	971	387	359	53	98
Fulton	446	-2.5	30 006	1 976	201	43	66	121	119	41	44	7	20
Greene	1 195	5.9	30 443	1 876	818	42	135	354	347	106	159	35	22
Huntingdon	1 251	1.9	27 566	2 474	555	70	167	381	373	122	142	25	60
Indiana	2 902	1.6	33 189	1 306	1 673	316	435	720	704	235	286	46	65
Jefferson	1 376	1.2	30 825	1 797	646	97	227	429	421	137	175	28	49
Juniata	701	-0.1	30 335	1 898	240	90	113	173	169	61	64	10	22
Lackawanna	7 726	0.1	37 002	751	4 535	525	1 305	1 959	1 921	639	863	133	147
Lancaster	18 450	-1.2	36 336	839	11 047	1 458	3 402	3 425	3 333	1 330	1 257	223	309
Lawrence	2 861	0.1	31 732	1 592	1 362	206	426	897	881	296	391	70	64
Lebanon	4 809	1.4	36 850	765	2 210	227	757	983	959	379	371	58	82
Lehigh	13 587	-0.8	39 551	485	10 015	970	2 323	2 701	2 638	916	1 118	220	225
Luzerne	11 251	1.2	35 964	893	6 520	770	1 775	2 948	2 891	959	1 194	208	248
Lycoming	3 727	1.5	31 900	1 550	2 286	231	616	940	919	332	353	73	92
McKean	1 372	0.6	31 752	1 588	752	91	196	400	392	135	161	34	40
Mercer	3 646	-1.3	31 408	1 664	2 055	173	603	1 104	1 083	383	470	86	79
Mifflin	1 302	1.0	28 334	2 339	639	102	170	413	405	141	169	31	42
Monroe	5 299	0.5	31 852	1 564	2 928	268	728	1 073	1 042	411	397	74	79
Montgomery	49 654	-1.6	63 469	21	35 185	5 042	10 066	5 616	5 473	2 153	2 367	182	428
Montour	699	-0.8	39 448	495	971	73	111	148	144	55	63	8	10
Northampton	11 153	-0.5	37 302	713	5 200	452	1 921	2 200	2 146	839	882	125	151
Northumberland	2 955	2.3	32 366	1 448	1 289	127	437	828	811	283	331	50	91
Perry	1 505	1.4	33 067	1 327	308	75	189	315	307	110	116	18	33
Philadelphia	54 126	0.8	34 981	1 024	45 127	5 878	6 044	15 393	15 111	2 956	8 036	2 431	856
Pike	1 912	0.0	31 583	1 627	432	120	300	372	361	179	117	20	14

1. Based on the resident population estimated as of July 1 of the year shown. 2. Includes supplements to wages and salaries.

Table B. States and Counties — Earnings, Social Security, and Housing

STATE County	Earnings, 2009 Total (mil dol)	Farm	Goods-related[1] Total	Manu-facturing	Information and profes-sional and technical services	Retail trade	Finance, insur-ance, and real estate	Health care and social services	Govern-ment	Social Security beneficiaries, December 2010 Number	Rate[2]	Supple-mental Security Income recipients, December 2010	Housing units, 2010 Total	Percent change, 2000–2010
	75	76	77	78	79	80	81	82	83	84	85	86	87	88
OREGON—Cont'd														
Morrow	257	24.6	D	22.8	D	2.3	2.4	2.4	17.4	1 895	170	183	4 442	3.9
Multnomah	29 670	0.1	D	7.7	14.5	4.8	8.5	11.1	17.8	102 995	140	18 416	324 832	12.6
Polk	865	8.5	17.2	10.8	3.4	5.1	2.3	9.9	33.9	14 860	197	1 270	30 302	23.9
Sherman	60	10.2	D	D	D	5.0	D	0.7	33.1	480	272	26	918	-1.8
Tillamook	413	2.2	23.5	17.9	3.5	7.4	4.1	10.5	24.9	7 135	283	436	18 359	15.4
Umatilla	1 557	7.2	12.0	8.0	D	6.6	3.5	9.5	27.8	12 905	170	1 561	29 693	7.3
Union	473	2.3	D	11.9	4.0	8.9	3.6	15.6	26.9	5 660	220	574	11 489	8.4
Wallowa	117	3.0	11.1	4.5	4.5	10.9	6.4	6.9	31.8	2 190	313	130	4 108	5.3
Wasco	506	7.8	D	5.1	6.0	10.5	3.2	18.5	26.5	5 625	223	617	11 487	7.8
Washington	16 494	0.7	30.5	25.1	10.9	6.1	6.2	9.0	8.3	68 075	129	6 029	212 450	18.7
Wheeler	11	1.0	D	0.0	D	8.4	D	D	44.1	480	333	31	895	6.3
Yamhill	1 595	5.6	28.3	22.5	4.0	6.7	4.3	13.2	16.7	17 370	175	1 395	37 110	22.6
PENNSYLVANIA	357 093	0.2	17.7	11.4	13.0	5.9	8.3	14.2	14.0	2 577 714	203	358 197	5 567 315	6.0
Adams	1 712	1.7	D	20.2	5.5	7.2	3.5	D	16.9	21 160	209	1 108	40 820	13.9
Allegheny	49 113	0.0	15.0	7.7	16.6	5.2	9.6	14.4	10.2	258 140	211	34 928	589 201	1.0
Armstrong	1 148	0.3	34.5	11.6	3.7	8.2	4.1	13.2	14.4	17 400	252	2 193	32 520	0.4
Beaver	3 002	-0.2	21.8	14.8	10.1	7.2	3.3	14.4	15.4	42 695	250	4 831	78 211	0.6
Bedford	787	0.8	D	11.8	D	8.6	3.0	8.7	15.8	12 845	258	1 369	23 954	1.8
Berks	9 703	0.6	25.3	18.7	7.8	7.6	6.0	13.4	14.0	79 760	194	9 684	164 827	9.7
Blair	2 928	0.4	D	13.4	7.1	9.1	4.2	18.8	16.9	28 635	225	4 901	56 276	2.2
Bradford	1 137	1.0	28.7	24.3	3.3	6.9	4.2	22.6	15.1	15 370	245	2 039	29 979	4.6
Bucks	17 247	0.0	22.9	12.5	13.8	7.8	6.3	12.7	10.2	117 500	188	6 616	245 956	9.1
Butler	4 534	-0.1	28.3	20.4	7.1	7.5	3.7	10.4	14.5	37 645	205	3 306	78 167	11.9
Cambria	2 806	0.2	13.5	8.5	9.4	7.7	6.1	19.9	19.8	36 950	257	5 035	65 650	-0.2
Cameron	89	0.7	D	D	1.6	4.5	D	7.3	23.1	1 570	309	149	4 455	-3.0
Carbon	860	0.2	18.4	11.9	16.2	7.1	3.7	14.8	18.1	15 760	242	1 290	34 299	12.5
Centre	4 081	-0.1	10.1	5.2	10.3	5.5	3.8	9.3	47.6	21 625	140	1 587	63 297	19.1
Chester	21 113	0.8	14.0	9.3	21.2	5.5	17.1	8.6	8.1	77 955	156	3 828	192 462	17.5
Clarion	707	0.0	26.5	13.0	3.9	8.3	3.5	13.3	26.8	9 170	229	1 278	19 962	2.8
Clearfield	1 434	-0.1	15.2	8.0	4.2	9.0	3.8	21.9	18.4	19 960	244	2 718	38 644	2.1
Clinton	653	-0.2	30.3	24.9	D	8.1	3.3	9.4	24.7	8 670	221	1 112	19 080	5.0
Columbia	1 308	0.3	31.5	24.6	5.6	8.2	3.3	12.5	20.3	14 630	217	1 443	29 498	6.4
Crawford	1 465	0.8	28.8	23.5	4.1	7.9	3.4	17.0	17.2	20 865	235	3 096	44 686	5.3
Cumberland	7 526	0.3	10.9	6.5	11.0	6.5	11.6	11.6	18.2	45 400	193	2 383	99 988	15.0
Dauphin	11 123	0.1	12.6	8.2	9.3	4.2	8.6	13.7	25.2	49 880	186	6 726	120 406	8.3
Delaware	15 039	0.0	17.1	10.9	12.3	5.9	10.4	14.3	11.4	100 380	180	11 613	222 902	2.7
Elk	650	0.3	D	44.7	2.3	5.6	2.5	13.9	11.6	8 580	269	732	17 585	-2.9
Erie	6 337	0.2	25.5	21.5	5.8	7.1	7.1	17.6	16.2	58 130	207	10 652	119 138	4.2
Fayette	2 034	-0.2	19.7	11.0	6.1	9.2	3.0	16.6	18.7	36 130	264	8 787	62 773	-5.6
Forest	122	3.0	D	D	D	2.0	D	15.7	48.9	1 765	229	166	8 760	0.7
Franklin	2 896	1.6	D	17.4	6.6	7.2	3.3	15.5	19.5	32 040	214	2 463	63 219	17.5
Fulton	244	-1.3	D	37.4	1.6	4.7	2.3	D	16.8	3 585	241	358	7 122	4.9
Greene	859	-0.7	D	2.1	4.1	5.2	2.8	D	17.6	8 445	218	1 917	16 460	-1.3
Huntingdon	625	0.3	D	14.8	3.1	6.5	4.8	D	27.8	10 290	224	1 226	22 365	6.2
Indiana	1 989	0.6	25.4	7.3	4.3	7.6	4.2	11.0	21.3	18 565	209	2 559	38 236	2.6
Jefferson	743	-0.1	38.5	26.4	4.0	7.1	3.1	15.1	14.5	11 255	249	1 504	22 434	1.5
Juniata	331	7.0	D	28.2	D	6.0	4.1	D	13.4	5 270	214	541	10 978	9.5
Lackawanna	5 061	0.2	17.2	12.2	9.5	7.7	7.9	18.4	13.8	51 770	241	6 591	96 832	1.5
Lancaster	12 505	1.1	28.1	18.1	7.7	7.3	5.6	13.9	10.1	98 815	190	9 249	202 952	12.8
Lawrence	1 568	0.0	25.2	14.6	5.5	7.0	6.6	15.0	16.4	23 265	255	3 430	40 975	3.4
Lebanon	2 437	1.8	24.2	19.3	4.2	7.7	2.7	13.2	22.2	29 040	217	2 176	55 592	12.7
Lehigh	10 986	0.1	D	9.9	8.6	5.6	5.5	20.0	9.8	69 230	198	9 480	142 613	10.6
Luzerne	7 290	0.0	17.2	12.0	8.4	7.7	5.5	15.3	16.2	77 420	241	9 717	148 748	2.8
Lycoming	2 517	0.2	27.6	22.1	5.9	7.4	4.4	15.6	19.4	26 325	227	3 465	52 500	0.1
McKean	843	-0.2	35.9	23.2	3.4	6.1	2.3	13.8	18.0	10 720	247	1 681	21 225	-1.9
Mercer	2 228	0.1	26.2	21.0	3.5	8.5	4.9	19.7	13.9	29 530	253	4 194	51 733	3.7
Mifflin	741	1.1	32.8	26.5	2.5	8.2	3.6	17.6	14.4	11 720	251	1 641	21 537	3.8
Monroe	3 196	0.0	20.0	15.1	4.5	8.2	3.4	10.8	29.7	31 360	185	2 739	80 359	18.9
Montgomery	40 227	0.0	18.1	11.3	21.9	5.2	12.4	12.4	6.7	142 935	179	7 460	325 735	9.5
Montour	1 044	0.6	D	1.8	4.2	2.5	3.6	D	7.6	4 320	236	479	7 965	4.4
Northampton	5 652	0.1	D	16.2	8.2	7.3	6.9	10.1	16.0	61 945	208	5 473	120 363	12.8
Northumberland	1 416	1.3	26.0	20.0	4.1	6.3	3.3	11.3	19.1	23 410	248	2 901	45 125	4.5
Perry	384	5.8	D	4.8	4.0	9.3	4.1	7.9	28.8	8 960	195	715	20 424	7.8
Philadelphia	51 004	0.0	D	3.9	18.4	3.0	9.7	16.9	17.3	245 755	161	104 864	670 171	1.2
Pike	552	0.0	8.5	1.4	7.8	10.8	8.4	7.6	30.1	13 165	229	688	38 350	10.6

1. Includes mining, construction, and manufacturing.   2. Per 1,000 resident population enumerated in the 2010 census.

Table B. States and Counties — Housing, Labor Force, and Employment

STATE County	Housing units, 2006–2010 — Occupied units — Owner-occupied: Total	Percent	Median value[1]	Median owner cost as a percent of income: With a mortgage	Without a mortgage	Renter-occupied: Median rent[2]	Median rent as a percent of income	Sub-standard units[3] (percent)	Civilian labor force, 2010: Total	Percent change, 2009–2010	Unemployment: Total	Rate[4]	Civilian employment,[5] 2006–2010: Total	Percent: Management, business, science and arts	Construction, production, and maintenance occupations
	89	90	91	92	93	94	95	96	97	98	99	100	101	102	103
OREGON—Cont'd															
Morrow	3 876	71.2	115 300	23.2	10.4	669	27.2	4.5	5 869	4.5	525	8.9	4 851	23.5	44.0
Multnomah	298 398	56.2	281 600	27.4	14.1	818	31.7	3.6	395 181	1.3	39 858	10.1	367 631	40.6	18.6
Polk	27 690	69.0	227 900	26.0	12.0	731	30.7	2.5	40 373	1.2	3 758	9.3	32 502	34.4	21.2
Sherman	813	67.0	119 500	26.5	11.8	694	19.6	2.2	1 072	-0.2	107	10.0	803	39.2	26.7
Tillamook	11 126	69.2	237 900	27.4	12.0	666	32.0	2.6	13 209	2.0	1 276	9.7	11 168	29.0	29.4
Umatilla	26 545	64.0	137 900	21.9	11.0	608	26.0	5.4	39 422	1.6	3 920	9.9	32 062	26.1	32.7
Union	10 269	66.0	151 200	22.4	11.4	626	29.9	2.4	12 696	1.2	1 322	10.4	11 262	29.2	29.6
Wallowa	3 015	74.7	183 800	25.5	14.9	645	26.0	1.1	3 844	3.0	463	12.0	3 108	36.7	26.8
Wasco	9 801	67.5	188 400	26.3	11.8	633	24.8	3.2	14 320	1.4	1 337	9.3	10 913	29.2	27.5
Washington	196 438	62.7	303 700	25.6	11.8	886	28.5	3.4	292 376	1.2	26 498	9.1	260 391	41.9	17.4
Wheeler	631	77.8	99 100	26.8	12.1	595	26.8	1.1	706	9.3	76	10.8	614	30.5	30.6
Yamhill	34 025	70.3	237 800	26.9	12.6	783	29.8	3.9	48 408	0.2	5 228	10.8	44 102	31.2	26.8
PENNSYLVANIA	4 940 581	71.0	159 300	23.7	13.9	739	29.3	1.6	6 389 595	0.1	540 922	8.5	5 940 972	35.2	22.8
Adams	38 331	77.8	200 700	25.1	13.0	728	27.9	2.5	54 572	-1.1	4 334	7.9	52 028	28.6	32.2
Allegheny	522 703	67.0	115 200	22.1	14.0	688	29.0	1.1	635 184	-0.9	49 013	7.7	596 090	41.0	15.4
Armstrong	28 814	76.4	89 100	22.0	12.8	541	26.9	1.2	32 676	-3.0	3 086	9.4	31 807	26.2	34.0
Beaver	70 350	75.2	112 400	23.0	14.2	584	26.7	1.1	88 530	-2.5	7 214	8.1	81 589	29.9	25.0
Bedford	19 913	79.7	112 800	23.1	13.0	540	27.0	1.9	24 426	0.3	2 618	10.7	22 552	23.1	36.3
Berks	153 307	73.1	170 400	24.2	14.5	743	29.6	1.8	202 918	-0.7	18 689	9.2	196 018	31.1	27.7
Blair	51 651	73.0	97 400	21.2	12.9	557	29.0	0.8	64 246	-1.8	4 942	7.7	58 150	29.6	25.7
Bradford	24 861	74.8	101 700	23.1	13.7	549	27.1	2.3	32 744	4.4	2 265	6.9	27 583	27.4	36.3
Bucks	229 552	78.5	321 500	25.8	14.9	997	30.4	0.9	339 043	-3.4	26 633	7.9	319 595	41.4	18.4
Butler	71 911	77.0	159 000	22.0	12.2	691	29.1	0.8	98 503	-0.7	7 291	7.4	88 703	34.6	23.5
Cambria	58 802	73.8	86 000	20.8	13.3	509	26.2	0.9	68 360	-1.5	6 458	9.4	62 171	30.3	25.4
Cameron	2 181	73.1	74 200	19.8	13.4	488	23.7	0.6	2 326	-1.5	334	14.4	2 363	29.2	37.6
Carbon	26 111	80.2	139 800	24.9	14.4	659	29.0	0.5	31 099	-1.6	3 381	10.9	29 288	25.1	32.1
Centre	54 971	60.1	175 800	23.0	12.0	784	34.7	2.6	75 038	-0.4	4 648	6.2	71 976	42.7	17.8
Chester	181 136	77.1	334 300	24.4	13.8	1 077	27.3	1.5	264 170	-2.7	17 827	6.7	251 250	47.3	15.3
Clarion	15 742	71.3	97 800	20.8	11.0	546	31.1	2.1	20 607	-0.6	2 072	10.1	18 259	28.5	30.3
Clearfield	32 823	76.7	82 900	23.3	14.5	534	29.2	1.4	40 775	0.2	4 107	10.1	34 516	24.1	35.0
Clinton	15 238	72.5	98 400	23.6	15.0	614	30.2	1.2	19 181	-1.1	1 733	9.0	16 881	24.6	32.4
Columbia	25 884	71.5	118 800	22.9	13.4	619	28.1	1.2	36 368	-0.5	3 262	9.0	31 370	26.8	31.5
Crawford	35 456	74.0	97 900	23.5	13.9	553	28.3	2.4	42 806	-0.3	4 073	9.5	38 450	29.2	31.0
Cumberland	93 739	72.4	174 600	22.3	11.7	757	25.4	1.0	122 421	-2.1	8 712	7.1	117 518	38.2	19.8
Dauphin	107 808	65.5	153 100	22.9	12.6	765	27.6	1.4	134 930	-2.1	11 250	8.3	133 638	36.0	20.6
Delaware	206 542	71.8	232 300	24.8	15.8	902	30.9	1.3	277 300	-2.9	23 685	8.5	267 497	41.6	16.6
Elk	13 743	79.9	91 300	21.9	13.4	537	25.6	0.3	17 053	-0.3	1 661	9.7	15 591	22.8	42.5
Erie	108 252	69.2	111 300	22.7	13.1	616	30.4	1.3	138 388	-1.4	12 943	9.4	127 324	31.9	25.0
Fayette	55 363	73.0	82 500	22.6	13.3	521	29.8	1.2	65 572	-2.0	6 595	10.1	54 302	26.1	28.6
Forest	1 996	85.8	79 700	24.0	12.8	445	27.0	2.4	2 347	-1.6	244	10.4	1 956	19.5	35.0
Franklin	58 290	74.3	175 000	23.9	11.4	680	25.6	1.7	79 951	-1.3	6 513	8.1	70 494	30.5	30.8
Fulton	5 848	77.4	157 500	23.7	11.9	548	24.0	2.7	7 773	1.7	928	11.9	6 716	22.5	39.1
Greene	14 010	75.3	81 800	19.3	12.0	505	28.5	1.3	19 381	0.1	1 505	7.8	16 012	27.1	33.4
Huntingdon	16 876	76.8	105 800	22.3	11.9	492	24.5	1.6	22 663	-0.6	2 357	10.4	18 981	27.5	33.2
Indiana	34 375	71.8	98 200	20.9	11.9	594	34.2	2.8	47 428	0.5	3 898	8.2	39 871	26.2	30.9
Jefferson	18 236	76.8	80 100	20.6	12.3	506	27.2	1.6	22 829	-0.2	2 204	9.7	19 786	23.1	38.0
Juniata	9 037	77.0	127 200	23.2	11.7	534	22.7	1.5	12 279	1.0	950	7.7	11 363	24.4	41.2
Lackawanna	86 318	66.1	137 100	23.5	15.4	623	27.4	1.2	105 938	-1.9	9 804	9.3	100 737	31.7	23.5
Lancaster	191 474	70.2	184 400	24.1	12.4	789	28.2	2.2	267 237	-0.9	20 172	7.5	251 165	31.0	29.8
Lawrence	36 587	78.1	92 600	22.7	14.4	597	29.4	1.5	43 092	-1.2	4 098	9.5	40 533	29.8	26.7
Lebanon	51 543	74.6	155 900	22.7	12.4	635	27.6	2.3	72 834	0.3	5 254	7.2	64 176	28.5	28.4
Lehigh	132 879	68.8	203 200	24.4	14.2	822	31.2	1.5	176 343	-1.2	16 639	9.4	164 927	36.2	22.2
Luzerne	130 855	69.9	113 300	22.8	14.8	599	28.4	1.2	159 363	-1.4	15 957	10.0	147 286	29.2	25.8
Lycoming	46 612	69.8	119 200	23.5	14.2	600	29.3	1.5	59 931	-0.6	5 388	9.0	54 610	27.9	30.1
McKean	17 324	74.4	72 300	21.6	12.5	553	29.9	1.3	20 819	-2.3	2 095	10.1	18 774	28.9	31.7
Mercer	46 681	75.3	101 700	22.7	13.4	580	29.3	1.6	53 677	-2.1	5 870	10.9	49 849	28.6	27.5
Mifflin	19 051	73.4	92 500	23.1	14.7	520	25.5	2.5	22 620	0.5	2 206	9.8	19 375	24.5	38.2
Monroe	59 997	81.4	206 400	28.3	16.3	936	29.5	1.6	81 754	-1.9	8 066	9.9	77 192	32.0	23.5
Montgomery	306 661	74.2	297 200	24.4	14.3	1 028	28.1	1.2	419 269	-3.5	31 105	7.4	412 600	47.7	14.9
Montour	7 310	74.4	143 900	22.7	12.9	619	24.9	1.9	9 296	-0.9	625	6.7	8 259	39.1	24.3
Northampton	111 929	75.4	220 800	25.0	14.9	829	29.4	2.2	151 915	-0.8	13 899	9.1	141 297	33.9	24.3
Northumberland	39 234	72.4	93 500	22.5	13.5	524	27.6	0.9	46 557	-2.2	4 570	9.8	42 097	24.6	32.8
Perry	17 943	80.9	144 800	24.2	12.4	631	23.6	2.4	24 282	-2.5	2 063	8.5	22 658	27.2	33.0
Philadelphia	574 488	55.3	135 200	25.8	15.8	819	33.7	3.0	647 411	2.8	70 400	10.9	620 987	33.8	18.3
Pike	22 190	84.3	217 900	28.5	14.6	968	36.5	1.8	27 761	-1.3	2 788	10.0	24 350	30.6	26.1

1. Specified owner-occupied units.   2. Specified renter-occupied units. A value of 10.0 represents 10 percent or less.   3. Overcrowded or lacking complete plumbing facilities.   4. Percent of civilian labor force.   5. Persons 16 years old and over.

Table B. States and Counties — Nonfarm Employment and Agriculture

| | Private nonfarm establishments, employment and payroll, 2009 | | | | | | | | | Agriculture, 2007 | | | |
| | Employment | | | | | | | Annual payroll | | Farms | | | Farm operators whose principal occupation is farming (percent) |
STATE County	Number of establishments	Total	Health care and social assistance	Manufacturing	Retail trade	Finance and insurance	Professional, scientific, and technical services	Total (mil dol)	Average per employee (dollars)	Number	Percent with: Fewer than 50 acres	500 acres or more	
	104	105	106	107	108	109	110	111	112	113	114	115	116
OREGON—Cont'd													
Morrow	178	2 436	185	1 094	98	D	D	98	40 420	421	26.4	53.2	53.4
Multnomah	24 323	381 164	54 337	31 742	36 473	21 840	29 210	16 819	44 125	563	81.3	2.1	45.1
Polk	1 284	11 709	2 431	2 076	1 734	251	313	304	26 005	1 252	62.4	5.8	43.5
Sherman	50	266	D	D	D	D	D	7	25 673	208	5.3	73.6	59.6
Tillamook	713	6 491	D	1 438	939	151	139	180	27 701	302	39.7	3.0	64.2
Umatilla	1 543	21 512	2 707	2 810	3 063	584	D	677	31 477	1 658	51.7	24.9	45.3
Union	783	6 814	1 307	870	1 421	271	233	192	28 171	880	43.6	22.3	44.3
Wallowa	348	1 629	375	72	282	65	74	43	26 264	526	32.3	31.7	47.5
Wasco	724	6 802	1 601	274	1 564	215	224	204	29 964	649	40.5	24.0	47.1
Washington	14 241	227 038	24 670	27 382	28 482	11 291	15 827	11 158	49 146	1 761	74.7	3.1	45.0
Wheeler	32	124	D	0	D	D	0	3	21 073	164	3.7	53.0	52.4
Yamhill	2 243	27 938	4 254	5 790	3 275	763	602	904	32 347	2 115	72.7	3.9	38.7
PENNSYLVANIA	298 432	5 044 648	917 808	574 683	654 782	271 629	313 439	209 778	41 584	63 163	41.0	3.9	45.5
Adams	1 979	28 698	4 377	5 981	3 641	574	537	841	29 322	1 289	49.2	6.6	46.4
Allegheny	33 360	669 057	120 909	39 751	75 540	47 140	57 499	29 530	44 137	534	54.5	0.9	39.3
Armstrong	1 298	13 338	2 878	1 580	2 279	639	345	394	29 516	794	22.8	6.0	43.2
Beaver	3 433	47 878	9 150	7 155	7 580	1 012	2 520	1 587	33 139	824	46.1	0.8	34.2
Bedford	1 098	13 043	1 623	2 193	2 267	319	185	388	29 750	1 173	24.1	7.1	50.0
Berks	8 413	144 462	23 753	28 407	20 339	6 840	6 217	5 704	39 486	1 980	49.5	4.0	54.5
Blair	3 220	49 683	10 382	6 915	8 999	1 338	2 075	1 539	30 977	1 523	33.8	5.9	56.1
Bradford	1 341	17 314	4 322	4 231	2 807	649	453	561	33 559	1 457	25.8	7.1	48.8
Bucks	18 943	248 606	39 855	27 962	38 911	7 967	16 867	9 918	39 896	934	71.2	3.2	46.6
Butler	4 643	74 304	12 632	12 448	10 794	2 322	4 009	2 634	35 455	1 116	41.0	3.3	45.1
Cambria	3 439	50 616	11 709	5 918	7 156	2 299	3 286	1 555	30 719	656	37.0	5.8	38.6
Cameron	122	1 626	207	901	201	D	D	40	24 684	34	17.6	2.9	32.4
Carbon	1 140	13 577	2 652	2 059	2 167	320	281	356	26 205	207	46.9	2.4	37.2
Centre	3 180	42 376	6 567	3 997	8 081	1 748	3 414	1 347	31 798	1 146	40.2	4.3	44.2
Chester	13 860	231 960	31 813	14 997	27 449	23 352	23 191	13 635	58 780	1 733	57.3	3.6	53.8
Clarion	970	11 228	2 470	1 710	1 984	303	207	317	28 234	872	28.1	5.2	32.3
Clearfield	1 973	24 774	5 737	2 556	4 666	677	656	721	29 114	473	33.0	3.2	37.4
Clinton	731	10 699	1 203	3 032	1 940	304	206	310	28 936	537	40.0	2.2	46.9
Columbia	1 438	21 687	3 580	5 372	3 800	583	870	655	30 190	962	36.3	3.6	38.5
Crawford	2 108	26 249	5 192	6 452	3 749	535	651	732	27 886	1 468	29.8	5.5	51.4
Cumberland	6 741	116 406	15 227	9 108	15 927	9 868	7 837	4 473	38 422	1 550	52.0	3.5	44.5
Dauphin	6 866	142 403	30 516	8 095	15 465	11 062	7 287	5 816	40 840	836	49.9	2.9	40.9
Delaware	12 870	206 780	39 507	14 193	25 362	13 543	11 413	10 109	48 886	79	67.1	0.0	36.7
Elk	912	13 425	2 090	6 296	1 516	D	257	416	31 021	376	50.0	0.8	25.8
Erie	6 552	114 158	23 074	23 315	15 550	D	3 639	3 704	32 449	1 609	44.0	2.9	39.7
Fayette	2 746	37 098	7 589	3 649	6 628	676	1 483	1 074	28 958	1 220	40.7	2.5	37.5
Forest	111	1 180	D	258	99	D	D	33	27 726	84	31.0	2.4	32.1
Franklin	3 107	47 245	7 609	7 867	7 550	1 218	1 985	1 503	31 804	1 540	37.5	5.8	54.4
Fulton	284	3 698	D	D	355	80	35	121	32 683	608	25.3	5.3	37.7
Greene	731	12 177	1 377	414	2 616	292	205	514	42 233	1 245	29.3	2.1	31.0
Huntingdon	853	9 533	1 624	2 083	1 527	451	245	274	28 713	930	28.1	4.9	40.8
Indiana	1 982	27 528	4 497	3 063	4 977	D	1 038	948	34 443	1 544	35.6	3.6	38.7
Jefferson	1 159	13 489	2 922	4 023	1 944	308	382	382	28 312	597	26.1	4.2	43.9
Juniata	465	5 033	490	1 831	661	255	D	128	25 470	788	42.0	2.8	45.8
Lackawanna	5 415	98 621	23 107	10 966	13 579	6 247	4 309	3 017	30 589	417	36.9	1.0	31.7
Lancaster	11 981	211 461	34 020	35 813	30 460	7 300	9 924	7 538	35 645	5 462	46.6	1.7	64.1
Lawrence	2 004	26 968	5 908	3 806	3 653	1 296	684	842	31 204	708	34.0	5.4	46.3
Lebanon	2 636	43 082	7 403	8 950	6 536	902	1 047	1 368	31 750	1 193	52.9	1.4	54.8
Lehigh	8 479	153 954	33 833	15 017	19 992	6 814	6 480	7 037	45 706	516	57.9	6.8	50.0
Luzerne	7 379	124 158	23 915	17 153	18 532	4 788	4 527	4 004	32 248	610	39.3	2.8	40.2
Lycoming	2 805	43 559	7 940	9 175	7 070	1 535	1 533	1 332	30 580	1 211	32.6	3.1	41.4
McKean	1 076	13 482	2 931	3 436	1 849	D	235	399	29 564	313	29.7	3.2	36.4
Mercer	2 794	44 087	10 232	7 843	7 335	1 411	857	1 257	28 518	1 210	29.8	4.1	47.1
Mifflin	935	12 736	2 665	3 563	2 222	372	126	390	30 625	1 024	45.2	1.6	46.2
Monroe	3 495	44 554	6 008	5 227	8 678	1 019	1 615	1 451	32 574	349	59.3	2.6	41.8
Montgomery	25 944	468 429	68 507	43 662	56 420	36 187	49 767	25 683	54 829	719	71.2	1.1	42.4
Montour	422	12 965	6 387	D	707	D	594	684	52 766	583	43.2	1.2	35.8
Northampton	6 270	91 604	11 811	11 607	13 021	4 273	4 493	3 401	37 130	486	59.9	7.4	46.5
Northumberland	1 673	23 569	3 934	5 446	3 156	574	565	713	30 245	936	40.4	6.0	44.9
Perry	797	6 269	812	690	1 391	261	235	149	23 829	1 002	36.6	4.5	42.9
Philadelphia	26 787	579 921	143 233	25 615	49 168	37 371	45 780	28 690	49 472	17	82.4	0.0	64.7
Pike	917	7 668	876	D	1 893	155	203	188	24 518	54	50.0	11.1	35.2

STATE County	Agriculture, 2007 (cont.)															
	Land in farms					Value of land and buildings (dollars)		Value of machinery and equipment, average per farm (dollars)	Value of products sold				Percent of farms with sales of:		Government payments	
			Acres								Percent from:					
	Acreage (1,000)	Percent change, 2002–2007	Average size of farm	Total irrigated (1,000)	Total cropland (1,000)	Average per farm	Average per acre		Total (mil dol)	Average per farm (dollars)	Crops	Live-stock and poultry products	$10,000 or more	$100,000 or more	Total ($1,000)	Percent of farms
	117	118	119	120	121	122	123	124	125	126	127	128	129	130	131	132
OREGON—Cont'd																
Morrow	1 104	-1.9	2 623	89.9	485.0	1 938 823	739	207 000	353.5	839 712	35.4	64.6	48.2	30.6	11 482	58.0
Multnomah	29	-14.7	51	7.0	20.0	640 687	12 654	73 682	84.5	150 171	96.6	3.4	34.5	14.9	227	4.1
Polk	167	-1.2	133	16.7	120.1	728 558	5 473	80 988	146.7	117 145	76.8	23.2	29.3	13.4	1 435	17.6
Sherman	514	1.2	2 471	2.8	345.5	1 551 001	628	161 189	31.7	152 639	94.8	5.2	56.3	39.9	6 848	88.9
Tillamook	38	-5.0	125	7.5	17.7	780 085	6 236	134 016	110.9	367 072	1.1	98.9	54.3	39.7	724	33.1
Umatilla	1 447	8.7	873	142.3	804.1	1 010 148	1 157	115 936	320.7	193 413	76.5	23.5	38.1	20.3	18 550	33.3
Union	488	2.1	554	63.3	141.4	833 720	1 505	93 959	58.2	66 186	72.6	27.4	35.9	11.8	3 138	30.8
Wallowa	528	1.9	1 004	44.8	96.0	1 154 495	1 150	75 925	32.3	61 337	37.7	62.3	47.7	16.0	2 879	39.7
Wasco	949	-12.7	1 463	27.7	180.6	1 083 291	740	106 144	89.9	138 462	86.7	13.3	41.4	19.6	6 416	36.1
Washington	128	-2.3	73	26.2	92.6	740 180	10 185	81 575	311.4	176 820	94.7	5.3	35.7	13.7	809	13.0
Wheeler	758	2.7	4 621	14.1	56.3	2 145 451	464	89 715	D	D	D	0.0	42.1	17.1	459	28.7
Yamhill	181	-7.7	86	26.8	114.8	757 162	8 855	76 165	277.6	131 235	83.2	16.8	31.2	10.9	1 818	15.4
PENNSYLVANIA	7 809	0.8	124	37.8	4 870.3	590 376	4 775	72 988	5 808.8	91 965	32.2	67.8	38.5	16.9	75 975	27.6
Adams	175	-3.3	135	1.9	127.5	865 422	6 389	95 911	217.0	168 343	32.4	67.6	44.3	17.1	1 853	31.6
Allegheny	38	11.8	71	0.3	18.4	411 888	5 785	47 397	9.5	17 817	85.7	14.3	18.9	5.6	57	6.6
Armstrong	122	-6.9	154	0.2	69.4	481 854	3 129	75 021	52.0	65 461	66.3	33.7	30.4	9.2	587	22.4
Beaver	67	6.3	81	0.4	35.5	398 130	4 891	47 810	15.2	18 431	44.9	55.1	19.7	4.1	276	12.1
Bedford	211	9.3	180	0.3	118.7	620 452	3 449	78 274	90.9	77 458	18.6	81.4	40.9	20.3	1 861	33.8
Berks	222	2.8	112	1.3	170.8	772 086	6 882	101 016	367.8	185 778	45.0	55.0	52.5	24.8	3 280	33.0
Blair	87	1.2	167	0.2	61.9	690 402	4 130	99 314	85.2	162 904	11.9	88.1	51.6	25.0	1 092	36.3
Bradford	267	-11.6	183	0.1	146.6	558 698	3 053	74 576	121.3	83 261	7.6	92.4	38.4	20.3	4 111	40.5
Bucks	76	-1.3	81	1.4	58.0	808 476	9 951	81 015	70.6	75 560	76.4	23.6	37.0	12.7	713	16.7
Butler	130	-9.7	116	0.7	78.3	530 189	4 557	74 008	38.7	34 645	53.2	46.8	33.8	7.7	860	29.6
Cambria	88	0.0	134	0.0	54.6	466 056	3 477	62 980	23.2	35 316	47.2	52.8	26.1	6.9	756	32.0
Cameron	5	25.0	150	0.0	2.0	298 606	1 994	56 445	0.8	24 356	D	D	44.1	5.9	D	32.4
Carbon	20	5.3	97	0.1	12.7	529 262	5 468	71 656	8.9	43 206	87.5	12.5	38.2	10.1	239	45.4
Centre	148	-10.3	130	0.6	86.1	660 008	5 095	60 906	69.7	60 786	25.1	74.9	39.4	17.2	1 266	26.8
Chester	167	-0.6	96	1.7	117.1	1 034 252	10 740	116 652	553.3	319 267	79.6	20.4	48.8	26.6	2 068	17.5
Clarion	132	21.1	152	0.1	67.5	439 775	2 902	57 045	22.0	25 181	33.7	66.3	23.6	6.4	504	26.3
Clearfield	63	3.3	133	0.1	32.5	334 959	2 526	59 056	11.1	23 472	38.6	61.4	27.5	5.7	240	21.1
Clinton	57	7.5	105	0.6	35.6	445 401	4 224	63 683	43.7	81 305	18.4	81.6	34.6	21.2	559	30.4
Columbia	123	-0.8	127	0.5	88.1	536 605	4 210	69 877	45.9	47 687	59.4	40.7	30.6	10.6	2 138	57.3
Crawford	232	4.5	158	0.6	139.5	455 933	2 884	69 563	101.0	68 826	25.7	74.3	37.8	14.2	2 212	28.8
Cumberland	157	9.8	102	1.2	123.1	644 525	6 347	72 552	132.8	85 680	20.0	80.0	40.9	17.7	2 282	32.3
Dauphin	90	-5.3	107	0.4	66.2	653 346	6 101	71 835	82.9	99 148	19.7	80.3	40.6	17.2	857	34.3
Delaware	4	NA	55	0.0	1.6	718 736	13 020	66 447	9.5	119 681	97.3	2.7	22.8	8.9	5	5.1
Elk	33	50.0	88	0.0	13.7	302 401	3 419	43 126	3.7	9 886	37.4	62.6	12.8	2.9	63	8.5
Erie	173	4.2	108	1.4	101.7	430 926	4 005	62 976	71.3	44 303	69.0	31.0	31.7	11.4	1 348	16.7
Fayette	141	12.8	115	0.1	74.2	420 637	3 648	60 219	26.0	21 290	40.9	59.1	23.2	4.8	556	16.4
Forest	11	83.3	128	D	4.4	422 752	3 310	42 827	3.1	36 979	4.8	95.2	19.0	6.0	49	13.1
Franklin	243	-0.8	158	1.9	185.0	957 792	6 079	107 800	304.5	197 694	11.5	88.5	55.7	35.5	2 746	34.7
Fulton	104	3.0	170	0.1	52.4	594 020	3 489	80 334	38.0	62 562	9.2	90.8	33.7	10.7	1 031	53.8
Greene	150	5.6	121	0.0	66.8	377 350	3 128	40 178	9.3	7 483	35.9	64.1	14.9	1.0	141	5.0
Huntingdon	148	3.5	159	0.2	73.0	583 415	3 659	67 636	62.3	67 011	13.6	86.4	27.8	10.9	1 559	27.7
Indiana	188	19.7	122	2.3	113.0	441 183	3 629	52 313	76.4	49 500	54.1	45.9	24.9	8.0	1 140	19.4
Jefferson	87	0.0	146	0.0	52.1	397 806	2 728	65 476	25.3	42 407	59.1	40.9	30.5	7.2	480	19.3
Juniata	98	14.0	124	0.3	59.1	571 345	4 609	72 986	91.7	116 318	9.1	90.9	44.4	23.7	1 515	45.9
Lackawanna	40	21.2	95	0.3	21.4	470 318	4 933	63 261	16.2	38 886	70.0	30.0	22.3	6.2	166	11.8
Lancaster	425	3.2	78	5.4	326.6	726 059	9 324	83 136	1 072.2	196 293	13.9	86.1	69.5	44.3	4 547	23.0
Lawrence	92	5.7	130	0.1	61.5	495 649	3 798	75 871	35.6	50 338	33.9	66.1	43.9	13.1	841	31.1
Lebanon	113	-9.6	95	1.3	89.6	791 376	8 319	100 682	257.1	215 505	8.6	91.4	51.6	33.4	1 495	29.2
Lehigh	85	-6.6	164	1.2	72.7	963 477	5 874	112 524	72.1	139 650	73.0	27.0	47.9	14.7	984	25.8
Luzerne	67	-8.2	109	0.4	38.6	515 986	4 728	62 107	18.2	29 756	74.0	26.0	27.9	8.4	991	41.1
Lycoming	160	-9.6	132	1.7	88.0	458 300	3 459	61 706	53.4	44 080	38.7	61.3	33.8	11.5	1 832	39.9
McKean	41	-2.4	132	0.0	15.4	280 034	2 114	38 736	5.2	16 564	16.7	83.3	18.2	5.8	228	20.1
Mercer	172	4.9	142	0.2	111.6	453 118	3 190	70 526	60.7	50 128	37.3	62.7	42.6	13.2	1 724	38.4
Mifflin	94	4.4	92	0.1	58.8	425 397	4 628	58 769	86.8	84 783	9.1	90.9	41.5	18.5	897	25.8
Monroe	29	-12.1	84	0.1	14.3	590 756	7 069	53 463	7.8	22 404	58.1	41.9	24.6	5.2	125	9.5
Montgomery	42	-12.5	58	0.7	28.6	584 297	10 025	53 301	30.0	41 764	62.8	37.2	30.0	7.5	238	12.5
Montour	50	25.0	86	0.1	34.3	441 064	5 117	49 379	36.2	62 081	58.4	41.6	28.6	10.5	837	37.2
Northampton	68	-12.8	140	0.2	58.9	854 282	6 083	89 758	31.8	65 355	70.2	29.8	44.9	16.5	849	27.4
Northumberland	148	24.4	158	1.1	110.3	636 980	4 038	76 163	111.0	118 566	35.0	65.0	45.0	19.8	2 390	53.6
Perry	144	11.6	144	0.1	92.3	636 686	4 419	77 512	105.1	104 842	12.9	87.1	34.4	17.1	1 966	37.8
Philadelphia	0	NA	15	D	0.2	539 894	35 031	22 075	0.5	28 629	D	D	29.4	5.9	D	11.8
Pike	28	180.0	511	0.0	2.9	849 318	1 664	55 728	2.5	46 744	92.7	7.3	20.4	9.3	D	1.9

Table B. States and Counties — **Water Use, Wholesale Trade, Retail Trade, and Real Estate**

STATE County	Water use, 2005		Wholesale trade,[1] 2007				Retail trade,[2] 2007				Real estate and rental and leasing,[2] 2007			
	Total water withdrawn (mil gal/day)	Gallons withdrawn per person	Number of establishments	Number of employees	Sales (mil dol)	Annual payroll (mil dol)	Number of establishments	Number of employees	Sales (mil dol)	Annual payroll (mil dol)	Number of establishments	Number of employees	Receipts (mil dol)	Annual payroll (mil dol)
	133	134	135	136	137	138	139	140	141	142	143	144	145	146
OREGON—Cont'd														
Morrow	320.0	27 430	12	67	49.4	2.6	16	80	17.4	1.6	10	12	1.2	0.2
Multnomah	53.8	80	1 271	22 685	22 043.8	1 114.4	2 945	40 269	9 868.5	1 035.5	1 491	9 735	1 770.9	366.4
Polk	50.2	714	33	206	70.3	7.4	150	1 728	375.1	39.0	71	238	21.7	3.6
Sherman	7.2	4 128	4	25	12.0	1.0	10	119	56.0	2.2	1	D	D	D
Tillamook	40.4	1 598	17	134	31.0	3.1	121	1 118	224.9	23.0	34	116	11.0	2.5
Umatilla	405.8	5 493	64	733	284.5	27.6	263	3 024	763.6	71.6	68	224	24.3	4.5
Union	213.9	8 717	20	D	D	D	125	1 483	333.8	32.7	20	86	9.5	1.9
Wallowa	161.8	23 070	2	D	D	D	56	376	82.7	7.5	22	51	5.3	1.0
Wasco	108.6	4 602	23	D	D	D	133	1 749	381.9	39.5	45	85	9.8	1.6
Washington	86.5	173	813	12 907	11 021.8	793.3	1 718	31 456	8 754.4	792.4	843	4 645	992.7	165.9
Wheeler	30.9	21 244	1	D	D	D	7	27	10.4	0.7	2	D	D	D
Yamhill	80.2	869	84	699	396.8	27.5	282	3 509	951.1	84.9	117	331	42.7	7.6
PENNSYLVANIA	9 471.7	762	13 161	200 151	142 859.2	10 100.7	46 532	672 042	166 842.8	14 862.3	9 904	68 954	13 602.6	2 611.8
Adams	17.5	175	62	D	D	D	376	3 798	832.4	79.9	52	230	42.8	5.9
Allegheny	740.8	599	1 600	21 032	18 141.6	1 090.2	4 795	76 658	20 075.4	1 643.2	1 273	9 972	2 000.7	387.3
Armstrong	181.0	2 564	32	D	D	D	221	2 352	532.1	48.4	27	281	29.5	9.7
Beaver	483.3	2 725	107	1 504	1 180.1	64.0	571	7 902	1 555.3	143.4	91	424	74.0	12.5
Bedford	61.1	1 219	41	387	295.5	13.0	209	2 165	581.6	43.1	16	164	45.2	4.8
Berks	61.0	154	375	6 306	4 417.6	306.7	1 327	20 433	4 953.2	466.8	273	1 384	210.2	39.4
Blair	18.4	145	123	2 160	1 511.2	87.6	619	9 366	2 038.7	179.6	82	393	66.7	10.3
Bradford	12.3	197	44	D	D	D	286	2 941	727.8	59.9	26	62	9.3	1.2
Bucks	113.1	182	1 167	14 880	9 859.6	803.5	2 551	41 993	13 089.8	1 020.0	608	3 671	787.7	145.9
Butler	17.6	97	237	3 604	2 580.2	171.0	719	10 950	2 527.3	224.8	141	630	125.2	17.6
Cambria	18.6	125	123	1 362	582.5	44.2	588	7 207	1 626.5	137.9	99	584	65.8	16.7
Cameron	0.8	140	2	D	D	D	18	208	29.6	2.8	NA	NA	NA	NA
Carbon	47.4	765	19	137	35.8	5.7	198	2 301	483.9	48.2	36	117	17.5	3.7
Centre	101.6	723	92	1 091	572.3	70.9	548	8 014	1 604.3	151.0	129	922	184.7	26.2
Chester	253.1	534	769	9 902	8 571.4	771.3	1 610	30 395	11 338.4	923.5	479	D	D	D
Clarion	4.4	107	38	669	287.4	20.4	203	2 147	421.1	42.0	18	50	8.7	1.1
Clearfield	353.8	4 273	66	D	D	D	368	4 677	1 150.1	91.9	39	275	26.4	6.1
Clinton	32.4	866	17	D	D	D	139	1 862	520.7	36.8	26	140	14.6	2.6
Columbia	8.8	135	42	461	109.9	16.0	274	3 692	826.2	71.3	58	206	30.7	5.6
Crawford	17.6	197	76	442	146.7	14.5	329	3 948	977.3	86.8	51	197	24.6	4.2
Cumberland	114.4	513	228	3 165	3 657.8	134.6	907	15 471	3 684.9	333.7	218	1 352	288.3	60.4
Dauphin	100.9	397	277	9 815	6 456.6	493.7	1 064	16 695	3 869.5	361.3	227	2 010	515.1	72.8
Delaware	929.7	1 673	548	7 021	4 220.0	470.4	1 861	26 462	6 358.4	617.2	449	5 011	1 168.9	196.0
Elk	22.2	661	30	226	69.9	7.8	130	1 536	291.2	26.0	13	44	4.2	0.6
Erie	55.7	199	279	3 118	1 157.2	124.0	1 051	15 831	3 428.4	314.5	187	1 115	135.3	25.9
Fayette	42.8	293	106	1 042	528.1	40.6	514	6 849	1 535.5	134.9	79	394	54.6	8.9
Forest	0.2	40	1	D	D	D	20	75	19.3	1.5	2	D	D	D
Franklin	22.3	162	120	D	D	D	503	7 526	1 750.0	160.6	92	485	71.2	13.7
Fulton	1.7	116	14	237	215.3	9.8	48	390	101.4	7.7	4	D	D	D
Greene	21.1	530	20	375	191.1	11.3	134	1 541	432.8	29.6	11	D	D	D
Huntingdon	13.2	288	25	D	D	D	154	1 600	363.2	31.0	17	59	7.7	1.0
Indiana	50.5	569	63	693	492.3	27.0	336	5 039	1 279.0	102.9	49	248	23.9	5.5
Jefferson	6.1	134	46	445	235.4	16.4	183	1 927	477.4	35.0	24	100	14.7	2.4
Juniata	2.9	123	21	169	69.8	7.3	81	785	197.6	14.2	10	D	D	D
Lackawanna	32.1	153	258	4 248	3 127.6	160.5	991	14 196	3 178.8	281.9	158	913	119.1	22.3
Lancaster	102.6	209	604	10 635	6 333.6	435.7	2 000	30 083	6 542.3	644.4	348	2 223	420.1	74.3
Lawrence	161.3	1 738	91	D	D	D	313	4 208	949.6	90.6	46	290	23.1	5.6
Lebanon	124.5	992	104	3 250	2 802.6	122.3	451	6 611	1 488.6	144.1	68	271	43.5	7.3
Lehigh	40.8	124	429	D	D	D	1 273	20 590	5 081.2	466.6	314	1 860	329.1	58.8
Luzerne	113.1	361	309	5 139	2 174.7	206.4	1 279	18 777	5 223.7	389.9	226	1 687	264.5	49.6
Lycoming	14.5	123	116	1 933	701.9	62.0	519	6 968	1 458.4	130.8	94	444	80.7	11.4
McKean	7.5	169	31	D	D	D	176	1 917	422.3	37.9	22	D	D	D
Mercer	32.2	269	91	D	D	D	555	7 229	1 441.6	140.5	85	394	65.8	10.3
Mifflin	11.7	254	48	D	D	D	187	2 415	526.1	48.8	21	78	13.9	1.8
Monroe	64.6	396	98	D	D	D	688	9 091	2 014.9	190.0	166	583	84.7	14.8
Montgomery	122.6	158	1 367	20 029	12 012.4	1 249.2	3 458	58 150	15 151.3	1 443.8	1 062	9 282	2 287.0	478.4
Montour	26.7	1 482	11	131	177.3	5.8	69	690	156.9	14.3	8	29	4.3	0.6
Northampton	399.2	1 387	245	3 915	9 815.9	174.0	908	13 201	3 405.0	302.0	187	D	D	D
Northumberland	25.8	279	47	795	587.5	33.8	318	3 286	797.0	66.7	45	193	19.5	4.7
Perry	4.1	92	20	141	85.1	5.4	154	1 537	393.4	30.1	17	68	4.4	0.7
Philadelphia	395.7	270	1 067	18 338	11 566.1	956.3	4 420	50 225	11 167.8	1 158.1	1 088	9 813	1 956.1	433.9
Pike	26.9	477	22	D	D	D	131	1 946	401.1	43.2	50	D	D	D

1. Merchant wholesalers, except manufacturers' sales branches and offices.   2. Employer establishments.

Table B. States and Counties — **Professional Services, Manufacturing, and Accommodation and Food Services**

STATE County	Professional, scientific, and technical services,[1] 2007				Manufacturing, 2007				Accommodation and food services, 2007			
	Number of establish-ments	Number of employees	Receipts (mil dol)	Annual payroll (mil dol)	Number of establish-ments	Number of employees	Receipts (mil dol)	Annual payroll (mil dol)	Number of establish-ments	Number of employees	Sales (mil dol)	Annual payroll (mil dol)
	147	148	149	150	151	152	153	154	155	156	157	158
OREGON—Cont'd												
Morrow	4	D	D	D	10	774	D	D	18	162	7.1	1.7
Multnomah	3 324	D	D	D	1 153	37 545	10 527.6	1 668.5	2 472	38 415	2 048.6	604.2
Polk	106	312	29.3	8.6	68	2 059	416.7	70.8	121	D	D	D
Sherman	1	D	D	D	NA	NA	NA	NA	8	87	5.9	1.3
Tillamook	38	156	13.0	4.8	29	1 509	633.8	59.1	124	1 033	53.7	15.7
Umatilla	97	D	D	D	69	3 335	D	D	166	2 721	159.4	40.4
Union	60	236	19.3	7.1	33	1 450	337.1	56.4	65	831	32.9	9.0
Wallowa	22	73	6.4	2.1	NA	NA	NA	NA	42	224	7.4	1.9
Wasco	55	196	17.2	6.8	NA	NA	NA	NA	72	896	47.6	13.5
Washington	1 773	D	D	D	770	32 506	24 049.0	1 759.9	1 085	17 125	849.4	249.8
Wheeler	NA	NA	NA	NA	NA	NA	NA	NA	6	14	0.6	0.1
Yamhill	207	D	D	D	205	6 265	1 885.8	291.9	186	2 305	98.9	28.4
PENNSYLVANIA	29 534	292 791	45 888.3	18 184.2	15 406	650 804	234 840.4	29 433.0	26 910	420 209	19 625.4	5 454.0
Adams	135	D	D	D	126	8 038	2 498.3	297.9	206	4 098	160.1	46.1
Allegheny	3 954	D	D	D	1 198	43 118	15 725.2	2 149.5	3 153	56 803	2 540.3	735.1
Armstrong	76	D	D	D	78	2 086	370.9	75.0	103	1 227	39.5	10.1
Beaver	243	D	D	D	191	7 749	4 708.8	344.4	315	4 355	156.3	42.3
Bedford	52	D	D	D	69	2 286	728.7	81.8	104	1 402	70.3	19.4
Berks	735	6 289	1 449.0	389.4	550	32 597	8 461.8	1 487.9	715	11 030	446.0	124.4
Blair	228	D	D	D	139	7 282	1 931.2	285.6	274	4 841	178.9	52.0
Bradford	80	D	D	D	69	4 787	1 772.4	198.6	108	1 206	48.8	13.1
Bucks	2 375	D	D	D	1 129	31 813	9 316.3	1 484.6	1 307	19 756	970.2	258.4
Butler	411	D	D	D	294	14 408	5 362.0	750.1	361	6 949	269.5	74.9
Cambria	221	D	D	D	146	5 409	1 439.8	199.6	307	4 135	156.0	40.9
Cameron	6	17	1.2	0.5	26	1 180	213.8	48.8	14	96	2.8	0.6
Carbon	70	D	D	D	56	2 450	514.3	95.1	127	1 491	104.7	21.7
Centre	376	D	D	D	150	4 341	1 216.5	181.0	301	5 961	240.1	68.8
Chester	2 310	20 064	3 947.2	1 610.7	572	18 981	6 753.0	985.9	907	15 286	783.2	221.0
Clarion	36	D	D	D	46	2 716	586.6	92.7	103	1 315	51.2	13.0
Clearfield	100	D	D	D	112	3 213	D	108.8	177	2 316	88.0	22.5
Clinton	40	182	15.4	4.8	46	2 730	1 215.0	104.5	82	998	43.2	11.5
Columbia	92	843	50.1	27.7	90	6 569	D	245.6	152	2 252	90.6	25.1
Crawford	124	D	D	D	282	7 686	1 632.6	308.8	199	2 438	90.1	26.7
Cumberland	614	D	D	D	200	10 191	3 472.6	404.8	520	9 519	402.7	116.0
Dauphin	720	D	D	D	215	9 794	D	446.3	668	12 489	676.8	194.8
Delaware	1 603	D	D	D	425	16 122	19 060.4	1 158.3	1 028	15 048	779.5	206.2
Elk	36	193	9.0	3.3	139	6 932	1 616.5	280.7	76	634	24.1	5.3
Erie	416	D	D	D	505	24 441	6 890.8	1 190.2	646	10 728	428.1	114.6
Fayette	154	D	D	D	128	3 757	1 161.4	153.0	270	5 432	246.9	78.3
Forest	3	D	D	D	NA	NA	NA	NA	25	145	8.4	2.1
Franklin	227	D	D	D	222	10 149	3 244.4	412.7	278	3 837	164.5	45.5
Fulton	12	41	2.6	0.8	19	D	D	D	23	206	9.9	2.4
Greene	46	D	D	D	25	D	D	D	73	908	36.8	10.2
Huntingdon	49	D	D	D	45	D	D	85.0	86	898	40.4	10.7
Indiana	112	D	D	D	105	3 316	D	120.8	166	2 740	92.4	24.4
Jefferson	66	D	D	D	101	4 415	953.5	171.7	91	908	32.3	8.1
Juniata	20	64	3.2	0.7	54	2 047	392.0	63.6	34	506	14.6	4.5
Lackawanna	472	D	D	D	267	11 834	D	439.1	546	8 601	360.5	99.6
Lancaster	939	D	D	D	920	40 077	13 269.9	1 735.9	935	17 060	763.9	221.2
Lawrence	119	D	D	D	147	3 840	1 745.2	183.6	177	2 325	73.4	21.3
Lebanon	193	D	D	D	213	9 655	2 393.6	363.3	241	3 075	125.3	35.3
Lehigh	763	D	D	D	419	18 331	7 031.6	835.6	740	11 730	546.3	148.6
Luzerne	594	D	D	D	352	17 955	5 708.3	727.4	763	10 586	442.9	119.8
Lycoming	183	1 367	102.9	39.6	183	10 240	3 358.2	408.7	277	3 721	147.9	40.0
McKean	65	D	D	D	56	4 029	1 394.4	160.6	112	1 055	40.9	10.5
Mercer	172	D	D	D	193	8 929	3 463.6	365.1	271	4 434	166.8	48.8
Mifflin	34	D	D	D	91	3 899	950.4	162.2	80	1 055	36.1	10.3
Monroe	340	1 671	198.0	53.9	131	5 322	2 656.5	317.4	386	7 491	394.4	113.0
Montgomery	3 697	45 686	7 015.0	3 370.4	1 110	51 179	20 398.8	2 848.2	1 769	27 834	1 478.0	409.4
Montour	32	444	32.4	25.9	18	950	D	55.4	42	734	27.5	7.5
Northampton	594	D	D	D	340	13 197	3 923.1	608.1	646	8 637	384.8	103.8
Northumberland	99	520	39.6	13.0	105	6 048	1 420.5	226.3	170	1 443	54.5	13.9
Perry	56	D	D	D	35	741	D	25.0	76	490	21.7	5.0
Philadelphia	2 703	44 302	9 243.3	3 533.1	946	32 672	18 069.4	1 396.7	3 396	48 552	3 051.4	837.9
Pike	80	D	D	D	NA	NA	NA	NA	98	1 300	75.8	17.6

1. Establishment subject to federal tax.

Table B. States and Counties — Health Care and Social Assistance, Other Services, and Federal Funds

STATE County	Health care and social assistance, 2007				Other services, 2007				Federal funds and grants, 2009–2010 Expenditures (mil dol)			
										Direct payments for individuals[1]		
	Number of establishments	Number of employees	Receipts (mil dol)	Annual payroll (mil dol)	Number of establishments	Number of employees	Receipts (mil dol)	Annual payroll (mil dol)	Total	Social Security and government retirement	Medicare	Food Stamps and Supplemental Security Income
	159	160	161	162	163	164	165	166	167	168	169	170
OREGON—Cont'd												
Morrow	14	119	11.2	4.8	11	32	2.2	0.7	97.8	36.9	12.7	2.7
Multnomah	2 601	53 379	6 135.2	2 471.3	1 726	11 789	1 748.2	367.3	8 056.3	2 026.5	1 100.6	264.7
Polk	136	2 127	127.1	56.4	82	248	21.8	5.9	449.1	171.0	70.2	13.6
Sherman	3	19	0.2	0.1	1	D	D	D	58.4	11.3	4.2	1.2
Tillamook	57	739	73.7	28.6	46	212	15.6	3.9	219.1	111.3	47.3	9.4
Umatilla	176	2 641	240.9	94.7	103	435	33.4	10.3	729.1	227.8	91.9	39.3
Union	93	1 185	95.8	38.1	51	168	13.3	3.2	234.9	95.6	40.4	13.7
Wallowa	33	345	24.2	10.1	20	72	8.6	1.7	78.3	34.1	13.0	2.8
Wasco	80	1 708	137.4	58.1	43	179	15.2	4.1	259.8	99.7	35.0	11.2
Washington	1 514	23 384	2 575.1	967.1	823	5 172	497.9	165.1	1 908.2	893.5	375.9	84.2
Wheeler	3	D	D	D	2	D	D	D	13.1	6.7	3.5	0.2
Yamhill	241	3 852	342.7	131.0	124	541	45.5	13.4	580.8	269.0	110.3	29.6
PENNSYLVANIA	35 156	874 743	81 977.9	33 431.6	25 316	154 379	17 622.1	3 932.7	145 933.8	41 143.6	31 745.1	4 647.1
Adams	185	3 887	313.4	130.3	165	1 004	81.8	20.2	718.6	339.8	134.9	11.6
Allegheny	4 262	122 200	12 649.6	4 896.5	2 985	19 550	2 504.6	520.9	17 592.4	4 317.2	4 292.2	494.6
Armstrong	187	3 226	201.5	90.4	101	428	33.0	7.2	688.6	284.4	225.6	29.4
Beaver	462	9 722	707.9	319.0	343	1 506	101.6	28.4	1 567.8	688.6	513.8	72.3
Bedford	117	1 558	121.2	45.9	97	373	23.8	5.8	409.4	179.6	114.7	15.2
Berks	799	21 887	2 014.4	848.1	781	4 670	398.8	108.0	2 648.7	1 186.8	686.4	108.4
Blair	403	10 162	909.5	373.1	299	1 686	115.7	33.5	1 300.8	508.9	337.5	63.5
Bradford	151	4 300	465.5	174.1	118	521	31.0	7.9	479.1	216.4	119.8	23.5
Bucks	1 925	37 382	3 395.7	1 381.8	1 395	8 612	709.3	229.6	4 456.9	1 957.7	1 060.1	76.8
Butler	538	11 344	839.5	338.5	370	2 184	230.6	48.0	1 529.0	619.6	392.3	38.3
Cambria	545	11 825	872.0	383.6	320	1 590	114.8	28.9	2 819.4	606.4	492.3	63.8
Cameron	19	D	D	D	12	58	2.6	0.6	54.9	21.9	16.3	1.1
Carbon	153	2 525	180.6	78.6	94	352	26.4	6.6	519.9	248.0	165.6	14.2
Centre	332	6 543	549.7	238.6	228	1 270	100.7	27.6	1 405.5	336.6	165.5	19.1
Chester	1 343	29 982	2 692.4	1 136.2	977	6 655	1 590.1	229.8	5 285.7	1 288.5	639.9	46.6
Clarion	141	2 411	155.7	62.5	85	393	36.9	7.1	349.1	132.8	113.0	18.4
Clearfield	248	5 584	449.8	185.9	162	945	63.1	17.4	696.0	292.4	210.6	32.5
Clinton	80	1 208	90.9	36.0	56	270	23.0	3.8	319.3	117.8	84.3	13.4
Columbia	165	D	D	D	115	683	49.7	14.2	490.3	220.4	142.0	15.4
Crawford	270	5 084	377.9	156.5	177	867	60.3	18.1	740.9	315.1	202.4	36.8
Cumberland	602	14 452	1 308.1	541.9	539	3 906	387.1	102.6	2 421.5	922.8	339.6	21.1
Dauphin	810	28 300	2 611.3	1 119.7	681	4 904	598.9	167.0	9 329.5	858.5	510.0	86.6
Delaware	1 545	38 693	3 531.7	1 521.9	1 055	6 909	1 240.3	197.9	5 548.0	1 719.4	1 479.5	144.4
Elk	124	2 206	134.3	63.1	78	353	23.8	4.9	265.8	122.5	81.4	8.3
Erie	893	21 880	1 847.7	783.0	563	3 529	242.4	70.2	2 238.2	876.3	576.3	134.9
Fayette	410	7 904	526.2	234.4	234	1 061	91.0	21.2	1 753.7	540.1	580.3	118.1
Forest	8	D	D	D	6	18	1.0	0.2	63.3	27.3	18.6	2.4
Franklin	307	7 302	640.1	267.8	297	1 653	121.0	33.1	1 332.9	550.3	208.9	24.2
Fulton	27	542	34.2	15.5	31	103	7.1	1.8	304.2	53.9	27.5	3.1
Greene	109	1 540	121.0	46.4	68	274	22.5	6.0	450.5	133.2	131.9	27.5
Huntingdon	103	1 660	111.2	44.5	69	239	14.8	3.6	358.4	151.0	95.8	13.8
Indiana	259	4 492	319.7	135.2	174	868	76.5	20.1	806.9	288.0	233.4	34.2
Jefferson	161	3 304	179.1	77.6	99	440	28.8	7.1	406.5	166.1	125.3	17.7
Juniata	29	501	29.9	10.8	29	101	11.5	2.9	153.2	72.7	41.7	4.5
Lackawanna	708	18 457	1 560.5	641.5	400	2 264	181.5	52.3	2 449.9	767.7	693.6	67.7
Lancaster	1 062	32 573	2 878.0	1 163.1	1 042	6 812	587.2	157.1	2 993.7	1 497.6	683.1	94.5
Lawrence	256	5 749	392.9	166.1	183	789	56.7	15.6	942.8	374.3	304.9	46.1
Lebanon	266	7 662	626.6	286.9	233	1 059	93.0	25.2	1 398.6	491.7	205.8	22.5
Lehigh	1 111	32 364	3 486.0	1 402.0	715	4 637	451.0	121.5	2 678.2	887.0	678.4	113.3
Luzerne	983	23 418	1 986.6	809.9	582	2 996	231.0	58.1	3 227.1	1 201.7	1 001.1	110.6
Lycoming	285	8 065	675.8	272.5	244	1 521	150.1	33.0	969.5	391.6	250.7	45.6
McKean	165	2 857	191.3	87.7	104	404	26.1	6.1	398.7	152.1	112.2	22.0
Mercer	395	10 499	750.1	314.8	260	1 319	87.8	23.5	1 076.2	454.9	339.1	53.3
Mifflin	115	2 731	210.0	90.3	71	250	19.9	4.7	407.6	162.4	118.5	16.8
Monroe	367	6 064	537.3	221.1	308	1 590	119.9	36.2	2 069.5	498.5	221.3	30.3
Montgomery	2 746	62 216	6 560.8	2 613.6	1 933	12 597	1 506.0	352.9	7 173.0	2 543.6	1 610.3	88.8
Montour	63	D	D	D	33	170	18.8	5.0	146.1	63.0	46.2	4.9
Northampton	749	11 498	979.1	394.3	545	3 094	224.8	70.6	2 482.7	1 084.7	659.9	39.6
Northumberland	199	3 853	241.3	103.8	151	809	44.5	12.4	830.0	343.0	266.7	29.3
Perry	73	565	40.9	13.2	70	241	17.4	4.0	283.5	152.9	73.6	9.2
Philadelphia	3 600	131 738	14 539.8	5 888.7	2 466	17 806	2 843.4	574.6	23 099.4	3 785.4	6 081.5	1 569.2
Pike	89	D	D	D	102	701	56.6	16.3	301.6	184.6	55.6	8.7

1. State totals may include programs not allocated by county.

Federal Funds, Residential Construction, and Local Government Finances

STATE County	Salaries and wages (171)	Defense (172)	Other (173)	Medicaid and other health-related (174)	Nutrition and family welfare (175)	Education (176)	Other (177)	New construction ($1,000) (178)	Number of housing units (179)	Total (mil dol) (180)	Inter-governmental (mil dol) (181)	Total (mil dol) (182)	Total (183)	Property (184)
OREGON—Cont'd														
Morrow	3.7	0.3	4.0	3.8	2.8	0.8	0.6	1 683	5	61.6	25.0	17.3	1 544	1 537
Multnomah	838.7	318.6	481.1	1 707.6	132.1	73.2	878.2	205 591	1 235	4 106.1	1 372.1	1 506.0	2 145	1 328
Polk	24.8	0.1	2.6	71.2	8.6	11.0	62.4	23 085	89	134.8	76.1	37.3	496	402
Sherman	4.4	21.1	0.2	2.4	0.3	0.2	0.0	NA	NA	15.0	5.7	7.3	4 356	4 326
Tillamook	10.6	0.3	4.2	21.2	3.8	2.4	4.0	19 990	90	104.5	42.1	37.3	1 492	1 301
Umatilla	60.4	120.1	11.5	77.1	18.9	7.4	9.9	13 744	78	264.4	149.0	65.8	896	813
Union	25.5	0.2	5.3	25.4	5.4	2.4	6.7	7 724	32	76.6	40.4	20.3	820	729
Wallowa	5.2	0.2	4.1	12.9	1.3	0.5	0.0	NA	NA	43.6	17.5	7.2	1 065	964
Wasco	22.6	22.1	9.1	22.6	4.2	3.3	7.4	NA	NA	91.4	43.5	28.8	1 213	1 099
Washington	126.5	55.7	47.4	173.1	46.9	26.2	52.3	274 396	1 271	1 661.4	649.3	639.3	1 224	1 069
Wheeler	0.4	0.0	0.1	1.4	0.2	0.2	0.1	NA	NA	11.0	4.8	1.2	902	889
Yamhill	42.9	10.4	9.7	59.1	16.9	8.1	11.9	32 312	148	303.3	141.3	87.7	908	773
PENNSYLVANIA	8 802.6	11 900.9	7 451.5	16 147.3	2 976.8	3 813.4	6 473.7	3 293 099	19 740	X	X	X	X	X
Adams	71.5	20.9	19.9	78.1	13.7	1.4	4.5	56 099	306	326.9	140.3	137.2	1 361	1 002
Allegheny	1 201.2	1 885.2	1 430.4	2 592.3	234.4	81.3	591.7	256 876	1 424	6 457.4	2 763.3	2 543.3	2 086	1 470
Armstrong	20.8	4.3	3.7	88.5	14.7	2.1	10.6	9 193	60	220.2	110.1	80.6	1 168	1 005
Beaver	35.8	1.9	10.4	167.9	36.5	6.5	11.3	57 859	337	714.6	310.9	212.6	1 229	991
Bedford	13.4	1.7	2.9	62.8	9.4	1.3	3.8	18 271	108	141.3	65.2	42.2	850	682
Berks	146.1	65.2	29.9	225.9	52.4	11.3	78.4	73 420	415	1 848.0	724.3	738.8	1 838	1 472
Blair	83.3	1.9	63.2	170.2	31.2	4.1	23.9	24 056	159	389.5	217.2	109.2	870	625
Bradford	17.1	0.5	3.5	77.5	12.6	2.2	1.5	26 723	175	247.6	115.3	66.8	1 087	864
Bucks	119.0	778.0	84.7	212.4	67.9	6.1	43.3	80 909	474	2 538.9	654.7	1 357.2	2 185	1 832
Butler	147.3	32.8	90.4	138.7	27.4	2.8	11.5	108 331	523	564.3	233.0	226.5	1 245	955
Cambria	158.9	1 180.9	28.1	180.3	33.8	6.0	41.5	21 744	117	524.9	265.3	128.6	887	691
Cameron	1.3	0.0	0.6	9.6	3.3	0.1	0.0	0	0	16.3	8.4	5.7	1 073	906
Carbon	12.0	12.6	9.2	41.3	8.7	1.7	2.6	25 273	149	228.3	72.4	91.7	1 450	1 180
Centre	72.0	236.8	68.0	179.8	22.9	11.9	192.3	78 299	426	400.8	139.2	181.2	1 253	907
Chester	225.4	1 541.4	1 222.7	175.9	47.5	8.5	49.9	181 395	1 112	1 897.5	491.6	1 084.0	2 229	1 822
Clarion	10.9	0.1	1.9	43.4	8.9	2.3	2.7	7 449	47	148.6	93.3	35.1	878	680
Clearfield	28.4	0.1	5.2	88.7	18.1	2.7	5.8	18 390	124	251.0	134.7	82.4	1 012	823
Clinton	25.9	4.8	12.7	37.5	7.1	1.6	1.0	4 162	31	107.9	44.2	39.3	1 056	804
Columbia	22.2	1.9	4.0	50.5	11.5	2.3	3.9	21 729	123	180.8	77.6	79.6	1 229	914
Crawford	57.2	1.1	5.3	84.9	20.3	3.5	4.6	13 772	108	246.9	126.0	86.8	979	818
Cumberland	438.9	312.2	128.2	79.8	24.5	3.8	118.9	127 742	832	808.9	280.6	382.0	1 675	1 151
Dauphin	266.1	680.8	66.3	566.4	630.2	2 782.6	2 601.4	109 923	691	1 386.8	528.6	466.2	1 823	1 309
Delaware	213.9	1 289.0	35.9	404.4	76.3	19.5	74.6	72 714	363	2 406.7	773.9	1 043.7	1 883	1 679
Elk	18.7	1.5	1.7	20.7	5.5	0.5	3.5	5 580	36	93.6	38.3	33.0	1 013	753
Erie	120.8	41.5	43.0	264.1	59.0	12.5	38.0	73 699	586	1 069.7	529.9	326.3	1 169	941
Fayette	44.1	35.7	10.2	341.9	38.5	7.5	24.3	48 497	240	368.8	225.0	96.3	666	523
Forest	4.3	1.2	0.9	7.0	1.0	0.2	0.3	1 335	10	20.2	11.2	6.5	941	816
Franklin	121.3	295.4	7.8	87.4	19.0	2.8	2.8	70 745	570	384.0	141.5	152.8	1 078	820
Fulton	2.9	190.3	2.5	19.4	3.2	0.4	0.0	3 048	24	42.5	23.3	15.1	1 010	827
Greene	13.9	0.1	42.0	85.2	8.5	1.3	0.8	6 799	41	145.2	72.1	51.4	1 301	1 132
Huntingdon	21.3	0.6	2.1	55.4	9.8	1.0	2.4	18 243	99	112.8	58.2	31.9	700	539
Indiana	32.2	7.2	14.4	130.0	19.5	2.5	7.7	10 446	88	265.3	150.3	81.4	929	720
Jefferson	26.2	0.2	2.3	51.4	10.1	1.3	2.1	12 426	81	119.7	65.5	36.2	801	609
Juniata	6.5	0.0	1.2	18.6	3.5	0.5	0.0	6 128	41	45.3	21.7	19.2	830	656
Lackawanna	113.0	338.4	30.3	249.4	39.3	5.5	32.5	48 885	265	746.7	279.2	308.3	1 473	1 054
Lancaster	177.0	44.0	95.9	238.2	63.5	13.4	51.1	214 507	1 381	1 635.2	540.9	714.1	1 433	1 148
Lawrence	40.4	1.3	17.8	109.6	22.0	3.6	7.1	19 615	105	293.5	166.0	90.5	995	809
Lebanon	423.9	36.7	83.5	61.2	14.6	2.2	45.5	38 916	240	428.2	136.1	157.2	1 229	937
Lehigh	102.5	58.0	37.0	198.1	50.4	12.3	496.9	78 264	589	1 490.9	565.2	590.8	1 751	1 401
Luzerne	259.5	33.9	106.8	346.4	59.4	10.1	45.4	66 034	359	923.2	370.0	391.1	1 253	922
Lycoming	64.5	20.3	16.9	107.0	24.2	4.8	20.0	35 096	207	397.9	173.9	143.6	1 229	892
McKean	37.1	0.0	4.5	53.0	9.3	1.7	4.0	5 688	35	175.0	94.0	42.2	968	768
Mercer	41.3	5.9	9.6	115.5	25.9	4.5	9.7	25 323	152	391.5	214.7	122.6	1 050	807
Mifflin	29.4	1.6	2.1	61.1	8.9	1.5	2.2	10 062	79	130.3	71.5	41.8	891	676
Monroe	153.1	219.6	864.9	40.1	18.4	4.1	7.2	48 176	263	618.0	176.9	356.6	2 165	1 905
Montgomery	458.0	570.0	1 326.0	304.7	78.9	11.4	91.1	209 636	1 061	3 183.4	752.0	1 824.2	2 350	1 887
Montour	3.6	0.0	2.9	19.3	3.3	0.3	0.9	11 138	65	59.8	19.2	22.3	1 254	823
Northampton	132.5	26.2	35.5	180.2	33.0	5.9	246.6	77 210	478	1 249.8	426.7	555.5	1 893	1 521
Northumberland	22.7	3.3	9.2	122.3	14.9	3.2	5.2	21 399	124	274.2	145.3	78.8	866	596
Perry	8.4	0.0	2.0	28.0	5.9	0.8	0.0	18 539	89	116.5	53.9	53.6	1 186	837
Philadelphia	2 201.8	437.7	1 141.7	5 702.6	408.3	149.6	1 204.4	138 790	984	10 578.9	5 544.4	3 600.8	2 484	663
Pike	16.3	2.6	17.9	7.2	5.0	1.4	0.5	43 357	189	121.3	40.4	67.0	1 143	1 056

1. State totals may include programs not allocated by county.   2. Based on the resident population estimated as of July 1 of the year shown.

Table B. States and Counties — Local Government Finances, Government Employment, and Voting

	Local government finances, 2007 (cont.)									Government employment, 2009			Presidential election,[2] 2008		
	Direct general expenditure							Debt outstanding					Percent of vote cast:		
			Percent of total for:												
STATE County	Total (mil dol)	Per capita[1] (dollars)	Education	Health and hospitals	Police protection	Public welfare	Highways	Total (mil dol)	Per capita[1] (dollars)	Federal civilian	Federal military	State and local	Democratic	Republican	All other
	185	186	187	188	189	190	191	192	193	194	195	196	197	198	199
OREGON—Cont'd															
Morrow	60.1	5 366	38.6	12.7	2.4	0.0	2.2	160.7	14 352	70	39	746	34.7	61.8	3.4
Multnomah	3 950.4	5 628	30.8	4.0	5.0	4.7	6.5	7 039.1	10 027	12 649	2 513	58 352	76.7	20.6	2.7
Polk	154.5	2 052	36.8	13.5	6.6	0.8	10.9	165.0	2 192	96	222	5 841	48.4	48.9	2.6
Sherman	15.5	9 236	25.7	4.0	3.3	0.1	7.8	2.1	1 252	94	0	184	36.8	60.6	2.7
Tillamook	102.0	4 073	46.4	5.3	4.2	0.6	6.5	125.6	5 015	137	111	1 697	53.2	43.3	3.5
Umatilla	264.5	3 599	59.0	4.2	4.0	0.1	3.1	258.6	3 519	890	216	6 403	37.2	59.8	3.1
Union	74.5	3 009	50.7	1.9	4.7	0.7	5.8	45.9	1 853	254	71	2 397	36.6	60.2	3.2
Wallowa	53.1	7 859	22.5	48.0	3.2	0.4	9.0	36.9	5 453	116	20	561	33.4	63.5	3.1
Wasco	90.9	3 826	55.4	1.7	5.2	1.8	5.7	149.4	6 289	332	68	1 909	51.9	44.8	3.3
Washington	1 698.0	3 250	45.3	3.9	6.2	0.0	6.7	2 480.0	4 746	858	1 524	20 931	59.8	37.7	2.5
Wheeler	11.5	8 441	35.0	4.1	1.9	0.0	6.7	1.5	1 126	0	0	109	34.6	61.3	4.1
Yamhill	283.6	2 937	48.9	6.8	6.0	0.2	7.2	516.7	5 350	474	281	3 945	47.8	49.1	3.1
PENNSYLVANIA	X	X	X	X	X	X	X	X	X	105 322	36 689	678 653	54.7	44.3	1.0
Adams	389.1	3 861	70.8	3.1	1.3	5.4	2.8	320.4	3 179	735	269	3 734	39.6	59.2	1.1
Allegheny	6 106.5	5 009	43.3	8.4	4.0	6.2	3.4	11 122.6	9 123	14 066	3 683	56 729	57.3	41.8	0.9
Armstrong	224.0	3 243	61.6	0.2	1.1	12.1	3.5	178.3	2 582	223	179	2 836	37.0	61.6	1.3
Beaver	707.9	4 090	50.0	4.7	3.0	12.4	3.1	2 412.0	13 936	362	454	8 206	47.9	50.8	1.3
Bedford	157.4	3 169	58.7	0.0	0.4	1.9	5.1	249.4	5 023	135	132	2 333	27.0	71.8	1.2
Berks	1 817.4	4 521	55.4	4.1	3.6	7.3	2.6	3 268.4	8 131	1 171	1 087	23 006	53.9	44.7	1.4
Blair	382.8	3 050	55.8	0.2	2.5	7.8	5.2	430.7	3 431	1 028	332	8 198	37.3	61.6	1.1
Bradford	267.3	4 349	51.8	3.4	1.4	6.2	3.8	966.8	15 240	210	161	3 112	40.0	58.4	1.6
Bucks	2 564.0	4 128	58.8	3.5	4.8	5.4	2.5	3 298.0	5 310	1 231	1 649	23 969	53.8	45.1	1.1
Butler	585.8	3 220	52.4	3.7	2.2	7.2	3.9	921.2	5 063	1 940	487	9 214	35.7	63.1	1.2
Cambria	556.4	3 838	53.9	5.1	3.3	8.7	4.5	684.2	4 719	1 281	498	8 485	49.4	48.7	1.9
Cameron	16.8	3 132	56.5	0.0	0.9	4.4	6.2	18.5	3 452	17	14	407	39.2	58.9	1.9
Carbon	244.4	3 864	55.6	1.1	1.8	9.1	2.4	378.3	5 982	133	168	2 954	50.0	48.1	1.9
Centre	425.6	2 942	51.8	4.4	3.0	7.7	5.2	425.5	2 942	469	452	44 696	55.4	43.5	1.1
Chester	2 134.3	4 388	56.8	6.1	3.3	2.2	2.7	3 130.1	6 436	3 124	1 316	22 095	54.2	45.0	0.8
Clarion	157.2	3 927	68.2	7.4	0.9	3.0	4.7	80.4	2 008	125	104	3 702	38.0	60.4	1.5
Clearfield	287.9	3 535	55.3	2.2	3.9	2.4	3.7	267.1	3 279	255	218	4 890	43.0	55.2	1.8
Clinton	103.3	2 776	52.9	0.1	1.3	3.4	5.6	92.6	2 488	146	97	3 092	48.0	50.7	1.3
Columbia	182.4	2 819	65.4	0.3	2.9	2.8	4.2	184.2	2 846	172	171	5 241	47.1	51.6	1.3
Crawford	241.8	2 727	53.1	5.4	1.5	8.2	5.9	214.6	2 420	319	234	4 345	44.0	54.4	1.6
Cumberland	800.2	3 509	59.0	5.1	3.3	7.5	3.0	847.9	3 718	4 985	1 233	12 509	42.6	56.3	1.1
Dauphin	1 482.2	5 796	46.4	5.4	3.3	8.5	1.9	3 092.0	12 092	2 702	745	42 888	54.0	45.0	1.0
Delaware	2 470.9	4 457	47.4	3.1	4.3	10.8	2.0	4 574.7	8 252	3 068	1 811	24 118	60.2	38.8	1.0
Elk	79.8	2 448	50.6	0.1	2.5	0.0	11.5	156.6	4 801	114	84	1 370	51.1	46.8	2.1
Erie	1 050.1	3 763	47.5	8.1	2.5	8.8	2.8	1 590.5	5 699	1 653	785	16 003	59.3	39.4	1.2
Fayette	380.8	2 635	56.4	7.8	1.6	2.8	3.4	430.6	2 978	438	376	6 309	49.2	49.6	1.2
Forest	22.9	3 287	55.3	2.8	1.7	5.9	8.4	17.0	2 442	78	18	956	42.5	55.9	1.6
Franklin	410.3	2 896	54.2	4.7	1.6	5.8	5.6	451.6	3 188	2 380	386	6 599	33.3	65.8	0.9
Fulton	40.9	2 738	69.9	0.0	1.9	3.7	3.0	46.8	3 130	38	39	789	25.0	73.6	1.4
Greene	137.8	3 490	54.3	4.5	0.9	3.7	6.1	160.8	4 071	144	103	2 615	49.0	49.4	1.6
Huntingdon	106.0	2 326	58.1	1.8	1.2	6.3	4.1	184.5	4 049	138	120	3 103	35.5	63.0	1.4
Indiana	280.4	3 197	58.5	0.8	1.0	10.8	3.6	346.6	3 952	243	237	7 551	45.7	52.9	1.4
Jefferson	113.2	2 507	62.0	0.1	2.1	0.4	5.9	132.4	2 934	119	118	1 934	34.3	64.1	1.6
Juniata	41.4	1 787	67.1	0.0	0.7	2.7	5.3	9.4	405	80	61	758	31.6	66.8	1.6
Lackawanna	810.6	3 872	41.5	0.3	3.1	5.3	2.8	880.6	4 207	1 081	557	11 109	62.6	36.6	0.8
Lancaster	1 704.0	3 419	57.0	3.5	4.3	3.6	3.2	3 018.1	6 055	1 468	1 338	20 375	43.7	55.5	0.9
Lawrence	306.7	3 370	50.0	0.0	2.9	14.4	4.7	275.2	3 024	398	238	4 137	46.8	51.9	1.3
Lebanon	452.1	3 535	52.0	5.2	2.3	12.1	2.9	710.8	5 558	2 475	407	5 519	40.0	58.9	1.2
Lehigh	1 487.1	4 408	47.9	2.8	2.8	11.6	2.6	3 226.3	9 564	895	937	17 243	57.1	41.6	1.3
Luzerne	954.1	3 055	58.7	0.4	3.1	2.2	5.2	1 177.2	3 770	3 636	853	15 185	53.6	45.2	1.2
Lycoming	377.8	3 234	55.4	0.0	2.6	4.4	4.6	503.7	4 312	477	310	9 265	37.3	61.5	1.2
McKean	183.3	4 201	54.0	3.4	1.7	5.1	5.0	143.5	3 289	463	114	2 118	40.5	57.8	1.6
Mercer	415.3	3 556	64.2	4.5	2.6	2.6	4.8	406.2	3 477	290	307	5 501	49.1	49.4	1.6
Mifflin	141.5	3 014	65.9	0.1	2.0	0.0	2.5	113.8	2 424	102	121	1 908	32.6	66.2	1.2
Monroe	647.0	3 928	72.6	0.1	2.9	3.7	3.1	1 117.5	6 784	4 602	446	9 394	57.6	41.3	1.0
Montgomery	3 308.9	4 263	54.3	1.9	4.5	7.2	3.7	4 577.8	5 898	3 274	2 719	34 581	60.0	39.2	0.8
Montour	61.1	3 430	46.3	0.0	2.4	1.9	4.6	586.6	32 924	41	47	1 435	41.9	57.0	1.1
Northampton	1 355.9	4 619	55.3	3.0	3.4	9.5	2.8	1 935.0	6 592	1 192	787	14 241	55.5	43.2	1.3
Northumberland	270.7	2 974	48.1	0.1	3.5	18.5	3.0	242.0	2 659	234	240	5 051	42.2	56.0	1.7
Perry	107.9	2 389	72.5	0.2	0.9	2.5	5.5	164.4	3 641	94	120	2 109	32.4	66.1	1.5
Philadelphia	9 207.3	6 351	32.8	14.4	5.8	5.4	0.9	18 159.9	12 527	32 052	4 797	73 637	83.1	16.3	0.6
Pike	107.5	1 834	51.7	0.1	8.1	6.7	4.5	60.2	1 027	243	159	2 534	47.3	51.5	1.1

1. Based on the resident population estimated as of July 1 of the year shown.   2. © 2009 Election Data Services, Inc. All rights reserved.

STATE/ County code	CBSA code[1]	County type[2]	STATE County	Land area,[3] (sq km) 2010	Total persons	Rank	Per square kilometer	White	Black	American Indian, Alaska Native	Asian and Pacific Islander	Percent Hispanic or Latino[4]	Under 5 years	5 to 17 years	18 to 24 years	25 to 34 years	35 to 44 years	45 to 54 years
				1	2	3	4	5	6	7	8	9	10	11	12	13	14	15
			PENNSYLVANIA—Cont'd															
42 105	...	9	Potter	2 801	17 457	1 952	6.2	98.1	0.5	0.6	0.5	1.0	5.6	16.8	7.0	9.4	11.4	15.5
42 107	39060	4	Schuylkill	2 017	148 289	420	73.5	94.0	3.0	0.3	0.7	2.8	5.2	14.9	7.3	11.5	13.7	15.6
42 109	42780	7	Snyder	851	39 702	1 178	46.7	96.7	1.2	0.4	0.7	1.7	6.1	16.3	12.5	10.3	12.4	14.3
42 111	43740	4	Somerset	2 783	77 742	697	27.9	96.1	2.6	0.3	0.5	1.1	4.8	14.7	7.4	11.1	13.1	16.0
42 113	...	8	Sullivan	1 165	6 428	2 734	5.5	95.3	2.6	0.8	0.4	1.4	4.0	12.0	9.1	7.9	9.5	16.7
42 115	...	6	Susquehanna	2 133	43 356	1 101	20.3	97.9	0.6	0.4	0.5	1.3	5.0	16.1	7.2	9.6	11.9	17.2
42 117	...	6	Tioga	2 936	41 981	1 131	14.3	97.5	1.1	0.6	0.6	1.0	5.3	15.2	11.4	9.8	11.5	15.2
42 119	30260	4	Union	818	44 947	1 068	54.9	86.2	7.3	0.6	1.7	5.2	4.7	13.8	14.0	12.8	14.3	14.3
42 121	36340	4	Venango	1 746	54 984	911	31.5	97.5	1.6	0.5	0.6	0.9	5.6	15.9	7.3	10.3	11.8	16.3
42 123	47620	6	Warren	2 290	41 815	1 137	18.3	98.3	0.5	0.5	0.6	0.7	5.0	15.9	6.9	9.9	12.1	16.4
42 125	38300	1	Washington	2 220	207 820	297	93.6	94.8	4.1	0.5	0.9	1.1	5.1	15.5	8.9	10.0	12.6	16.1
42 127	...	6	Wayne	1 879	52 822	936	28.1	92.8	3.3	0.5	0.7	3.4	4.1	14.9	6.6	10.1	12.8	16.9
42 129	38300	1	Westmoreland	2 661	365 169	180	137.2	95.9	3.1	0.4	1.0	0.9	4.8	15.0	7.6	9.8	12.6	16.5
42 131	42540	2	Wyoming	1 029	28 276	1 483	27.5	97.2	1.0	0.5	0.5	1.5	5.4	16.4	8.6	10.3	12.7	15.9
42 133	49620	2	York	2 342	434 972	151	185.7	87.6	6.1	0.5	1.6	5.6	6.1	17.3	8.3	11.6	13.9	15.9
44 000	...	X	**RHODE ISLAND**	2 678	1 052 567	X	393.0	78.0	6.2	1.0	3.5	12.4	5.5	15.8	11.4	12.1	13.0	15.4
44 001	39300	1	Bristol	63	49 875	979	791.7	95.5	1.2	0.6	1.9	2.0	4.4	16.0	12.1	8.7	11.7	16.9
44 003	39300	1	Kent	436	166 158	371	381.1	92.9	1.9	0.7	2.5	3.2	4.9	15.7	7.7	11.5	13.7	17.1
44 005	39300	1	Newport	265	82 888	667	312.8	90.0	4.5	1.0	2.5	4.2	4.9	14.9	9.3	10.5	12.9	15.8
44 007	39300	1	Providence	1 061	626 667	97	590.6	67.8	8.8	1.0	4.3	18.8	6.0	16.0	12.2	13.4	13.2	14.5
44 009	39300	1	Washington	853	126 979	483	148.9	93.8	1.8	1.5	2.1	2.4	4.5	15.6	13.2	8.7	11.8	16.8
45 000	...	X	**SOUTH CAROLINA**	77 857	4 625 364	X	59.4	65.2	28.5	0.8	1.7	5.1	6.5	16.8	10.3	12.8	13.0	14.3
45 001	...	6	Abbeville	1 270	25 417	1 590	20.0	70.1	28.8	0.6	0.5	1.0	6.0	16.8	9.5	9.8	12.2	14.4
45 003	12260	2	Aiken	2 774	160 099	386	57.7	69.2	25.2	0.9	1.2	4.9	6.3	16.7	9.1	12.1	12.1	15.0
45 005	...	6	Allendale	1 057	10 419	2 413	9.9	23.5	73.8	0.4	0.5	2.3	5.9	16.4	9.3	13.6	13.3	14.2
45 007	11340	3	Anderson	1 853	187 126	331	101.0	80.0	16.7	0.6	1.0	2.9	6.4	17.5	8.4	11.4	13.3	14.8
45 009	...	7	Bamberg	1 019	15 987	2 050	15.7	36.3	61.7	0.7	0.6	1.6	5.9	16.5	13.8	9.7	10.6	13.6
45 011	...	6	Barnwell	1 420	22 621	1 702	15.9	52.9	44.8	1.0	0.7	1.8	6.6	19.0	8.7	11.2	12.0	15.1
45 013	25940	5	Beaufort	1 493	162 233	379	108.7	67.3	19.7	0.6	1.7	12.1	6.8	14.4	10.1	12.4	10.8	11.5
45 015	16700	2	Berkeley	2 846	177 843	347	62.5	65.8	25.8	1.2	3.2	6.0	7.5	17.8	10.5	14.8	13.7	14.3
45 017	17900	2	Calhoun	987	15 175	2 101	15.4	53.9	42.9	0.7	0.4	3.0	6.0	15.7	7.8	10.5	12.0	15.8
45 019	16700	2	Charleston	2 373	350 209	185	147.6	63.1	30.2	0.6	1.8	5.4	6.5	14.2	12.3	15.8	12.3	13.7
45 021	23500	4	Cherokee	1 017	55 342	906	54.4	75.1	21.0	0.6	0.7	3.7	6.7	17.9	9.5	11.5	13.9	14.2
45 023	16900	6	Chester	1 504	33 140	1 352	22.0	60.3	38.1	0.9	0.5	1.4	6.6	17.3	8.5	10.9	13.2	15.4
45 025	...	6	Chesterfield	2 070	46 734	1 029	22.6	62.8	33.5	1.0	0.5	3.6	6.4	18.3	8.6	11.2	13.7	14.9
45 027	...	6	Clarendon	1 572	34 971	1 301	22.2	46.7	50.2	0.5	0.7	2.6	5.9	16.5	10.3	10.5	11.0	14.5
45 029	47500	6	Colleton	2 736	38 892	1 198	14.2	56.9	39.6	1.3	0.6	2.8	6.6	17.8	8.3	10.7	12.1	14.8
45 031	22500	3	Darlington	1 453	68 681	772	47.3	56.1	42.1	0.6	0.4	1.7	6.3	17.9	8.8	11.1	12.8	14.7
45 033	19900	6	Dillon	1 049	32 062	1 389	30.6	48.4	46.9	3.1	0.4	2.6	7.4	19.3	9.1	12.2	12.2	14.3
45 035	16700	2	Dorchester	1 485	136 555	453	92.0	67.4	26.7	1.3	2.4	4.4	7.1	20.0	8.5	13.6	14.5	14.8
45 037	12260	2	Edgefield	1 296	26 985	1 533	20.8	57.0	37.4	0.6	0.6	5.2	5.2	16.2	8.5	12.8	14.2	16.0
45 039	17900	2	Fairfield	1 777	23 956	1 647	13.5	38.8	59.6	0.5	0.4	1.6	6.0	16.7	8.2	10.4	12.2	16.2
45 041	22500	3	Florence	2 072	136 885	450	66.1	54.9	41.7	0.7	1.4	2.2	6.7	17.9	9.7	12.5	13.0	14.2
45 043	24860	4	Georgetown	2 107	60 158	857	28.6	62.5	33.9	0.5	0.6	3.1	5.6	16.1	6.9	9.7	11.3	14.2
45 045	24860	2	Greenville	2 033	451 225	144	222.0	71.5	18.6	0.6	2.4	8.1	6.9	17.3	9.4	13.4	14.0	14.4
45 047	24860	4	Greenwood	1 178	69 661	762	59.1	62.1	31.7	0.4	1.1	5.4	6.8	16.9	10.7	12.2	12.6	13.5
45 049	...	6	Hampton	1 450	21 090	1 783	14.5	42.0	54.1	0.6	0.7	3.5	6.4	17.8	8.6	12.6	13.8	14.7
45 051	34820	3	Horry	2 937	269 291	240	91.7	78.7	14.1	0.9	1.5	6.2	5.7	14.5	9.7	12.6	12.4	13.8
45 053	25940	6	Jasper	1 697	24 777	1 609	14.6	38.1	46.2	0.5	0.8	15.1	7.5	17.3	10.9	14.9	13.0	14.3
45 055	17900	2	Kershaw	1 882	61 697	842	32.8	70.8	25.1	0.6	0.8	3.7	6.7	17.9	7.8	11.2	12.9	15.5
45 057	29580	4	Lancaster	1 422	76 652	708	53.9	70.7	24.3	0.6	0.8	4.4	6.8	16.5	7.8	12.3	14.1	13.9
45 059	24860	2	Laurens	1 849	66 537	787	36.0	70.0	25.9	0.5	0.5	4.1	6.5	16.7	10.0	10.8	12.9	14.7
45 061	...	6	Lee	1 062	19 220	1 868	18.1	33.3	64.6	0.5	0.6	1.7	5.8	16.4	10.1	13.3	11.8	15.7
45 063	17900	2	Lexington	1 810	262 391	249	145.0	78.2	14.9	0.9	1.8	5.5	6.7	17.8	8.7	13.1	13.9	15.2
45 065	...	8	McCormick	930	10 233	2 425	11.0	49.0	50.1	0.3	0.6	0.8	4.1	10.3	5.9	11.0	11.6	14.9
45 067	...	6	Marion	1 267	33 062	1 357	26.1	40.8	56.2	0.8	0.8	2.4	6.8	17.6	8.4	11.5	11.8	14.3
45 069	13500	6	Marlboro	1 242	28 933	1 454	23.3	41.5	51.4	5.4	0.4	2.8	5.8	16.1	8.4	14.4	14.0	15.1
45 071	35140	6	Newberry	1 632	37 508	1 229	23.0	61.3	31.4	0.5	0.4	7.2	6.5	16.3	10.0	11.2	12.3	14.3
45 073	42860	6	Oconee	1 622	74 273	731	45.8	87.1	8.2	0.6	0.8	4.5	5.6	15.5	8.4	10.4	12.1	14.3
45 075	36700	4	Orangeburg	2 865	92 501	622	32.3	34.5	62.6	0.9	1.1	1.9	6.7	16.5	12.4	11.3	11.0	14.0
45 077	24860	2	Pickens	1 286	119 224	503	92.7	88.4	7.1	0.6	1.9	3.1	5.4	15.0	18.4	11.3	11.7	13.3
45 079	17900	2	Richland	1 961	384 504	171	196.1	46.6	46.5	0.7	2.9	4.8	6.4	16.4	15.3	15.1	13.0	13.4
45 081	17900	2	Saluda	1 173	19 875	1 844	16.9	58.8	26.8	0.5	0.4	14.4	6.9	16.2	8.8	12.4	12.7	13.9
45 083	43900	2	Spartanburg	2 093	284 307	227	135.8	71.2	21.2	0.6	2.4	5.9	6.7	17.8	9.8	11.9	13.7	14.4

1. CBSA = Core Based Statistical Area. See Appendix A for explanation. See Appendix B for list of metropolitan areas with component counties.   2. County type code from the Economic Research Service of USDA Rural-Urban Continuum Codes. See Appendix A for definition.   3. Dry land or land partially or temporarily covered by water.   4. May be of any race.

Table B. States and Counties — **Population and Households**

STATE County	Age (percent) (cont.) 55 to 64 years	65 to 74 years	75 years and over	Percent female	Total persons 1990	Total persons 2000	Percent change 1990–2000	Percent change 2000–2010	Components of change, 2000–2009 Births	Deaths	Net migration	Households, 2010 Number	Percent change, 2000–2010	Persons per house-hold	Female family house-holder[1]	One per-son
	16	17	18	19	20	21	22	23	24	25	26	27	28	29	30	31
PENNSYLVANIA—Cont'd																
Potter	14.9	10.6	8.9	50.0	16 717	18 080	8.2	-3.4	1 921	1 913	-1 284	7 227	3.2	2.39	8.7	27.4
Schuylkill	13.7	8.7	9.4	49.3	152 585	150 336	-1.5	-1.4	13 446	18 820	2 950	60 192	-0.6	2.35	10.9	30.0
Snyder	12.6	8.3	7.2	50.6	36 680	37 546	2.4	5.7	4 346	3 013	-108	14 750	8.0	2.53	8.1	24.1
Somerset	14.4	9.2	9.4	48.5	78 218	80 023	2.3	-2.9	6 968	8 678	-824	31 090	-0.4	2.35	8.7	28.1
Sullivan	16.6	13.0	11.3	48.6	6 104	6 556	7.4	-2.0	472	939	90	2 777	4.4	2.16	6.2	32.3
Susquehanna	14.9	10.3	7.8	49.7	40 380	42 238	4.6	2.6	3 943	4 204	-1 085	17 798	7.7	2.42	8.7	26.4
Tioga	13.7	10.0	8.0	51.0	41 126	41 373	0.6	1.5	3 951	3 851	-329	16 727	5.0	2.39	8.9	26.1
Union	11.3	7.3	7.5	45.0	36 176	41 624	15.1	8.0	3 824	3 385	1 778	14 765	12.0	2.43	7.9	27.6
Venango	14.9	9.3	8.7	51.1	59 381	57 565	-3.1	-4.5	5 539	6 044	-2 510	22 621	-0.6	2.37	11.1	27.5
Warren	15.1	9.8	9.0	50.2	45 050	43 863	-2.6	-4.7	3 840	4 464	-2 353	17 767	0.4	2.31	8.6	30.1
Washington	14.4	8.7	8.8	51.4	204 584	202 897	-0.8	2.4	19 257	22 411	8 867	85 089	4.9	2.37	10.5	28.1
Wayne	15.5	10.8	8.2	47.6	39 944	47 722	19.5	10.7	4 478	5 555	4 920	20 625	12.4	2.38	9.2	27.2
Westmoreland	14.8	9.2	9.6	51.3	370 321	369 993	-0.1	-1.3	31 576	40 359	3 361	153 650	2.6	2.32	10.0	29.0
Wyoming	14.7	9.3	6.7	50.0	28 076	28 080	0.0	0.7	2 861	2 535	-419	11 237	4.4	2.46	9.8	26.1
York	12.8	7.5	6.5	50.7	339 574	381 751	12.4	13.9	45 804	31 498	35 276	168 372	13.6	2.53	10.6	23.7
RHODE ISLAND	12.4	7.0	7.4	51.7	1 003 464	1 048 319	4.5	0.4	115 762	89 989	-14 632	413 600	1.3	2.44	13.5	29.6
Bristol	13.4	7.8	8.9	52.0	48 859	50 648	3.7	-1.5	4 218	4 747	-280	19 150	0.6	2.44	9.8	27.4
Kent	13.7	7.6	8.1	51.9	161 143	167 090	3.7	-0.6	16 570	15 853	1 848	68 645	2.0	2.40	11.1	29.2
Newport	14.7	8.9	8.1	51.2	87 194	85 433	-2.0	-3.0	7 966	6 657	-5 987	34 911	-0.9	2.27	10.2	32.2
Providence	11.2	6.4	7.1	51.7	596 270	621 602	4.2	0.8	75 668	53 766	-11 884	241 717	0.7	2.48	15.8	30.2
Washington	14.5	8.0	7.0	51.4	109 998	123 546	12.3	2.8	11 340	8 966	1 671	49 177	4.8	2.45	9.5	26.1
SOUTH CAROLINA	12.6	8.0	5.7	51.4	3 486 310	4 012 012	15.1	15.3	537 443	355 877	376 441	1 801 181	17.4	2.49	15.6	26.5
Abbeville	14.7	9.4	7.1	51.5	23 862	26 167	9.7	-2.9	2 825	2 331	-1 413	9 990	-1.4	2.45	15.3	27.3
Aiken	13.4	8.8	6.6	51.6	120 991	142 552	17.8	12.3	17 630	13 217	9 834	64 253	15.6	2.45	14.4	26.9
Allendale	14.0	7.6	5.6	46.8	11 727	11 211	-4.4	-7.1	1 439	1 117	-1 290	3 706	-5.3	2.45	26.9	33.7
Anderson	12.9	8.6	6.5	51.8	145 177	165 740	14.2	12.9	21 136	16 888	15 815	73 829	12.5	2.50	14.5	25.4
Bamberg	13.8	8.8	7.2	52.4	16 902	16 658	-1.4	-4.0	1 817	1 625	-1 784	6 048	-1.2	2.44	21.6	31.8
Barnwell	13.3	7.8	6.2	52.2	20 293	23 478	15.7	-3.7	3 041	2 235	-1 455	8 937	-0.9	2.50	20.8	28.4
Beaufort	13.7	12.4	7.9	50.6	86 425	120 937	39.9	34.1	20 077	10 037	24 633	64 945	42.6	2.42	10.7	24.3
Berkeley	11.3	6.5	3.5	50.1	128 658	142 651	10.9	24.7	21 231	9 253	19 731	65 419	31.0	2.66	15.3	22.0
Calhoun	15.8	9.7	6.5	51.3	12 753	15 185	19.1	-0.1	1 585	1 470	-677	6 080	2.8	2.47	15.9	26.8
Charleston	12.3	7.1	5.6	51.5	295 159	309 969	5.0	13.0	44 366	25 940	25 197	144 309	17.0	2.36	14.7	30.1
Cherokee	12.8	7.8	5.6	51.5	44 506	52 537	18.0	5.3	6 533	5 335	1 321	21 519	5.0	2.54	17.4	25.8
Chester	13.6	8.4	6.1	51.7	32 170	34 068	5.9	-2.7	4 139	3 207	-2 400	12 876	0.0	2.56	19.8	25.9
Chesterfield	13.4	8.1	5.4	51.4	38 575	42 768	10.9	9.3	5 170	4 038	-579	18 173	9.8	2.52	18.3	27.4
Clarendon	14.6	10.4	6.4	50.6	28 450	32 502	14.2	7.6	3 852	3 173	11	13 132	11.2	2.54	20.6	26.1
Colleton	14.1	9.3	6.3	51.8	34 377	38 264	11.3	1.6	4 980	3 778	33	15 131	4.6	2.54	18.4	26.8
Darlington	14.0	8.4	5.9	52.6	61 851	67 394	9.0	1.9	8 098	6 757	-1 864	26 531	2.9	2.54	20.5	26.0
Dillon	12.6	7.5	5.5	53.0	29 114	30 722	5.5	4.4	4 537	3 132	-1 032	11 923	6.5	2.65	23.9	26.5
Dorchester	11.3	6.3	3.9	51.4	83 060	96 413	16.1	41.6	14 246	7 176	27 367	50 259	44.8	2.68	16.0	21.6
Edgefield	14.0	8.0	5.1	46.0	18 360	24 595	34.0	9.7	2 420	1 996	909	9 348	13.0	2.56	16.0	24.9
Fairfield	15.5	8.6	6.3	52.1	22 295	23 454	5.2	2.1	2 803	2 636	-142	9 419	7.4	2.50	21.3	26.5
Florence	12.9	7.7	5.5	53.0	114 344	125 761	10.0	8.8	17 728	12 337	3 835	52 653	11.7	2.54	19.6	26.3
Georgetown	16.5	12.2	7.6	52.4	46 302	55 797	20.5	7.8	6 806	5 406	3 806	24 524	13.2	2.43	15.6	25.4
Greenville	11.8	7.2	5.5	51.5	320 127	379 616	18.6	18.9	54 148	31 473	51 339	176 531	18.0	2.49	13.5	27.0
Greenwood	12.1	8.0	7.2	53.1	59 567	66 271	11.3	5.1	8 400	6 364	1 756	27 547	7.1	2.43	17.5	27.9
Hampton	12.8	7.8	5.6	48.8	18 186	21 386	17.6	-1.4	2 695	1 931	-1 004	7 598	2.1	2.57	19.1	28.1
Horry	14.3	10.5	6.6	51.1	144 053	196 629	36.5	37.0	27 141	19 857	60 476	112 225	37.2	2.37	12.5	26.8
Jasper	11.0	6.7	4.4	47.9	15 487	20 678	33.5	19.8	3 128	1 621	1 172	8 517	20.9	2.73	18.6	24.8
Kershaw	13.8	8.3	6.0	51.3	43 599	52 647	20.8	17.2	6 997	4 876	5 548	23 928	18.5	2.56	15.1	24.5
Lancaster	13.4	9.4	5.9	50.7	54 516	61 351	12.5	24.9	7 975	5 584	5 559	29 697	28.1	2.51	15.4	24.7
Laurens	13.4	8.4	6.6	51.5	58 132	69 567	19.7	-4.4	7 632	6 766	65	25 525	-2.9	2.51	17.2	26.1
Lee	13.5	7.6	5.9	48.2	18 437	20 119	9.1	-4.5	2 350	2 021	-609	6 797	-1.3	2.54	24.0	29.3
Lexington	12.4	7.2	5.1	51.2	167 526	216 014	28.9	21.5	29 630	17 031	28 138	102 733	23.4	2.53	13.0	24.9
McCormick	18.2	15.9	8.0	45.7	8 868	9 958	12.3	2.8	785	1 143	594	4 027	13.2	2.22	15.2	27.4
Marion	14.9	8.6	6.1	54.3	33 899	35 466	4.6	-6.8	4 486	3 513	-2 831	13 058	-1.8	2.52	24.9	28.5
Marlboro	13.1	7.8	5.3	47.3	29 716	28 818	-3.0	0.4	3 365	3 048	-187	10 383	-0.9	2.47	24.3	30.0
Newberry	13.6	9.0	6.9	51.3	33 172	36 108	8.9	3.9	4 689	3 761	2 065	14 709	4.9	2.47	17.2	27.0
Oconee	14.7	11.4	7.6	50.6	57 494	66 215	15.2	12.2	7 501	6 455	4 633	30 676	12.4	2.40	11.3	26.2
Orangeburg	13.3	8.6	6.3	53.0	84 804	91 582	8.0	1.0	12 090	9 070	-3 874	35 788	4.9	2.49	22.5	29.0
Pickens	11.5	7.6	5.8	50.0	93 896	110 757	18.0	7.6	12 129	8 606	4 552	45 228	9.5	2.48	10.8	25.2
Richland	10.7	5.5	4.3	51.3	286 321	320 677	12.0	19.9	43 314	24 153	33 720	145 194	20.9	2.43	17.7	30.2
Saluda	13.0	9.2	6.8	49.7	16 441	19 181	16.7	3.6	2 354	1 844	-494	7 527	5.6	2.61	15.0	24.2
Spartanburg	12.4	7.8	5.7	51.5	226 793	253 791	11.9	12.0	32 846	24 070	25 536	109 246	11.8	2.53	15.1	26.2

1. No spouse present.

Table B. States and Counties — Population, Vital Statistics, Medicare, and Crime

STATE County	Persons in group quarters, 2010	Daytime population, 2006–2010 Number	Employ-ment/resi-dence ratio	Births, average 2006–2008 Total	Rate[1]	Deaths, average 2006–2008 Number	Rate[1]	Persons under 65 with no health insurance, 2009 Number	Percent	Medicare, 2011 Eligible for Medicare	Enrolled in Medicare Advantage	Enrolled in a Medicare prescription drug plan	Serious crimes known to police,[2] 2010 Total Number	Rate[3]
	32	33	34	35	36	37	38	39	40	41	42	43	44	45
PENNSYLVANIA—Cont'd														
Potter	217	17 628	1.0	D	D	196	11.5	1 707	13.1	4 040	940	1 783	216	1 237
Schuylkill	6 780	137 011	0.8	1 502	10.2	1 925	13.1	14 039	12.1	32 586	7 915	15 094	2 346	1 587
Snyder	2 317	38 994	1.0	D	D	323	8.5	4 769	15.1	7 214	2 938	2 875	807	2 033
Somerset	4 533	72 977	0.8	723	9.3	930	11.9	8 481	14.1	17 020	9 885	3 893	967	1 292
Sullivan	434	5 768	0.7	D	D	98	15.8	661	14.8	1 739	388	832	160	2 489
Susquehanna	282	36 029	0.6	D	D	472	11.4	4 367	13.4	9 028	1 520	4 144	594	1 370
Tioga	1 951	40 000	0.9	D	D	426	10.4	4 731	14.7	9 331	1 916	4 035	395	977
Union	9 109	47 847	1.2	D	D	362	8.3	5 947	16.7	7 138	2 270	2 920	359	799
Venango	1 297	53 722	0.9	614	11.2	624	11.4	5 342	12.4	12 648	3 709	5 457	842	1 531
Warren	788	39 925	0.9	400	9.7	489	11.9	3 826	11.9	9 287	1 376	4 726	756	1 808
Washington	5 925	194 142	0.9	2 091	10.1	2 407	11.7	16 724	10.1	44 521	27 120	7 386	3 971	1 931
Wayne	3 820	49 319	0.9	D	D	581	11.3	5 290	13.2	11 908	1 204	5 695	652	1 234
Westmoreland	7 962	341 788	0.9	3 361	9.2	4 311	11.9	28 707	10.1	79 294	51 385	11 340	5 802	1 591
Wyoming	602	27 116	0.9	D	D	280	10.0	2 557	11.3	5 682	1 601	2 171	254	928
York	8 430	394 609	0.8	5 238	12.5	3 496	8.3	36 334	10.2	74 712	22 539	26 030	10 034	2 307
RHODE ISLAND	42 663	1 034 585	1.0	12 265	11.6	9 717	9.2	116 176	13.3	187 401	64 869	66 509	29 611	2 813
Bristol	3 242	42 067	0.7	D	D	522	10.3	4 069	10.1	9 937	3 885	3 028	746	1 496
Kent	1 536	160 148	0.9	1 689	10.0	1 706	10.1	13 987	10.0	32 759	12 394	10 318	3 992	2 403
Newport	3 576	86 455	1.1	D	D	767	9.4	6 558	10.1	16 397	3 487	5 795	2 188	2 640
Providence	27 785	629 658	1.0	8 220	13.0	5 670	9.0	81 964	15.7	105 154	38 360	39 378	20 423	3 259
Washington	6 524	116 257	0.8	1 136	9.0	1 052	8.3	9 598	9.1	23 154	6 743	7 990	2 167	1 707
SOUTH CAROLINA	139 154	4 479 214	1.0	62 706	14.2	39 496	8.9	737 955	19.4	811 104	133 521	323 731	208 055	4 498
Abbeville	901	21 640	0.6	299	11.7	275	10.8	4 090	19.8	5 312	1 207	2 129	735	2 892
Aiken	2 439	154 848	1.0	2 021	13.2	1 473	9.6	22 799	17.9	30 313	4 505	11 987	6 706	4 189
Allendale	1 342	10 943	1.1	143	13.5	133	12.6	2 078	24.7	1 806	409	792	509	4 885
Anderson	2 764	171 866	0.8	2 440	13.5	1 859	10.3	29 156	19.1	37 366	8 175	15 420	9 929	5 306
Bamberg	1 241	15 479	0.9	D	D	182	11.7	2 578	21.3	3 049	473	1 424	729	4 560
Barnwell	285	22 119	0.9	D	D	231	10.0	3 646	19.4	3 946	587	1 863	1 129	4 991
Beaufort	5 265	159 981	1.1	2 350	16.0	1 107	7.6	23 363	19.6	35 495	4 111	14 250	6 353	3 916
Berkeley	3 742	145 652	0.7	2 550	15.8	1 019	6.3	30 259	20.0	24 182	3 529	6 996	6 472	3 649
Calhoun	153	12 391	0.6	D	D	155	10.5	2 242	18.8	3 017	629	1 198	457	3 098
Charleston	10 331	395 395	1.3	5 149	15.1	2 820	8.3	55 531	18.7	54 752	6 794	18 326	14 862	4 258
Cherokee	707	53 340	0.9	709	13.1	580	10.7	9 306	20.2	10 739	2 336	4 619	1 728	3 122
Chester	218	30 194	0.8	469	14.4	353	10.8	5 329	19.9	6 545	966	3 180	1 670	5 039
Chesterfield	874	42 724	0.8	601	14.0	463	10.8	7 453	20.7	8 412	797	4 524	1 683	3 601
Clarendon	1 661	32 494	0.8	D	D	353	10.7	5 988	22.8	7 381	1 020	3 376	1 459	4 172
Colleton	388	35 004	0.7	576	14.7	450	11.5	6 617	20.5	8 133	1 456	3 100	2 381	6 122
Darlington	1 345	64 728	0.9	863	12.9	740	11.0	10 852	19.7	13 062	1 248	6 936	3 857	5 616
Dillon	451	29 663	0.8	D	D	333	10.8	5 145	19.7	5 658	567	3 221	2 484	7 747
Dorchester	2 015	105 123	0.6	1 860	15.1	794	6.4	19 888	17.6	18 878	2 578	5 934	6 009	4 465
Edgefield	3 045	22 758	0.6	D	D	220	8.7	4 352	19.9	4 264	769	1 617	625	2 316
Fairfield	397	21 187	0.7	D	D	275	11.7	3 565	18.8	4 510	999	1 770	1 178	4 917
Florence	3 228	143 191	1.1	1 977	15.0	1 363	10.3	20 334	18.2	24 083	1 358	12 979	7 170	5 238
Georgetown	559	59 855	1.0	727	12.0	612	10.1	10 607	21.9	15 252	1 758	6 376	2 808	4 676
Greenville	11 854	467 798	1.2	6 524	15.2	3 530	8.3	75 791	19.8	74 418	17 721	29 157	18 364	4 070
Greenwood	2 640	71 112	1.1	996	14.6	701	10.3	11 833	20.7	13 382	2 324	5 470	4 276	6 138
Hampton	1 531	19 323	0.8	D	D	228	10.8	3 901	22.3	3 843	518	1 721	759	4 131
Horry	2 952	262 633	1.0	3 357	13.5	2 282	9.2	50 690	24.1	57 712	5 904	23 269	17 287	6 427
Jasper	1 488	21 684	0.8	398	18.1	196	8.9	5 513	28.1	3 565	677	1 364	1 173	4 734
Kershaw	526	52 562	0.7	846	14.5	544	9.3	8 993	18.1	11 339	1 351	5 242	2 258	3 660
Lancaster	2 114	64 548	0.7	955	13.5	632	8.9	13 762	21.0	15 154	1 296	7 975	3 038	3 963
Laurens	2 402	60 164	0.7	899	12.9	734	10.5	11 451	19.7	14 120	3 000	5 740	2 861	4 300
Lee	1 975	17 790	0.7	D	D	215	10.7	3 940	23.9	3 500	323	1 975	908	4 724
Lexington	2 320	235 449	0.9	3 404	14.0	1 915	7.9	36 626	16.9	39 716	6 518	13 491	7 824	2 982
McCormick	1 306	9 653	0.8	D	D	126	12.4	1 574	21.4	2 952	638	1 153	219	2 140
Marion	203	30 972	0.8	498	14.6	398	11.6	5 859	21.0	6 573	570	3 708	1 933	5 847
Marlboro	3 291	28 595	0.9	376	13.0	315	10.9	5 637	23.6	5 547	569	3 001	1 700	5 876
Newberry	1 168	35 575	0.9	540	14.3	395	10.5	7 027	22.1	7 463	1 439	2 883	976	2 602
Oconee	795	70 340	0.9	840	11.9	745	10.5	11 074	19.6	17 698	2 592	7 233	2 340	3 151
Orangeburg	3 300	91 540	1.0	1 394	15.4	1 030	11.4	15 867	21.6	17 257	3 256	7 047	5 354	5 984
Pickens	7 053	106 883	0.8	1 367	11.8	969	8.4	18 549	18.8	21 270	5 328	7 910	4 668	3 915
Richland	32 002	415 204	1.2	5 111	14.3	2 640	7.4	50 024	15.6	48 667	7 240	14 990	22 859	5 945
Saluda	239	16 394	0.6	D	D	192	10.2	3 771	24.1	3 755	710	1 503	460	2 314
Spartanburg	7 986	286 042	1.1	3 889	14.1	2 605	9.4	50 204	20.9	52 587	15 532	19 799	11 767	4 146

1. Per 1,000 estimated resident population.   2. Data for serious crimes have not been adjusted for underreporting; this may affect comparability between geographic areas and over time.   3. Per 100,000 population estimated by the FBI.

Table B. States and Counties — Crime, Education, Money Income, and Poverty

STATE County	Serious crimes known to police,[1] 2010 (cont.) Rate[2]		Education						Money income, 2006–2010				Income and poverty, 2010			
			School enrollment and attainment, 2006–2010				Local government expenditures,[5] 2008–2009			Households			Percent below poverty level			
			Enrollment[3]		Attainment[4] (percent)					Median income						
	Violent	Property	Total	Percent private	High school graduate or less	Bachelor's degree or more	Total current expenditures (mil dol)	Current expenditures per student (dollars)	Per capita income[6] (dollars)	Dollars	Percent change, 2000 to 2006–2010 (constant 2010 dollars)	Percent with income of $200,000 or more	Median household income (dollars)	All persons	Children under 18 years	Children 5 to 17 years in families
	46	47	48	49	50	51	52	53	54	55	56	57	58	59	60	61
PENNSYLVANIA—Cont'd																
Potter	246	991	3 692	9.9	64.4	12.4	30.6	11 851	20 594	39 196	-4.0	1.5	40 472	14.8	25.1	22.5
Schuylkill	185	1 402	29 892	14.3	65.0	13.6	220.6	11 517	21 408	42 315	2.2	0.7	40 384	13.0	19.0	17.4
Snyder	393	1 640	9 871	35.4	65.5	15.3	50.5	10 197	21 072	44 713	-1.9	1.5	42 016	13.2	18.3	17.5
Somerset	127	1 165	15 579	14.3	66.3	14.3	112.9	10 713	19 903	39 194	0.1	1.1	39 542	14.9	23.1	21.0
Sullivan	249	2 240	1 067	8.9	65.3	11.4	10.3	15 424	19 718	36 250	-5.5	0.8	34 026	15.2	23.8	22.0
Susquehanna	131	1 239	9 396	14.3	60.3	15.4	90.5	12 573	22 173	43 457	2.1	1.1	43 583	12.8	20.1	17.7
Tioga	99	878	10 069	11.4	56.2	17.7	67.7	11 512	20 358	40 338	-0.5	1.1	40 651	15.8	24.0	22.4
Union	80	719	12 134	49.3	57.0	22.2	46.7	11 466	21 612	45 474	-11.0	3.2	44 997	12.7	16.2	15.1
Venango	122	1 410	11 686	13.1	61.8	14.1	78.2	11 769	20 522	39 812	-2.5	0.8	39 351	15.4	26.6	24.7
Warren	294	1 514	8 566	18.3	58.4	16.9	62.3	11 363	22 170	41 286	-9.6	1.4	41 008	14.1	21.4	19.5
Washington	206	1 725	48 422	16.7	51.7	24.2	346.9	11 907	26 045	49 687	4.3	2.6	47 823	10.6	14.1	13.0
Wayne	115	1 119	11 070	18.3	57.2	17.9	67.8	12 525	22 525	45 930	6.4	1.8	43 627	12.4	18.5	16.2
Westmoreland	168	1 423	80 797	17.6	49.6	24.0	553.0	10 702	25 845	47 689	1.5	2.0	46 468	10.4	15.7	13.6
Wyoming	91	836	6 644	18.9	58.9	16.8	66.4	12 062	22 899	47 403	2.9	1.2	46 899	12.7	19.4	17.9
York	209	2 098	102 191	19.6	54.8	21.5	729.6	10 871	27 196	57 494	0.3	2.5	55 960	9.2	13.5	11.8
RHODE ISLAND	257	2 557	284 670	26.7	44.6	30.3	2 009.4	13 996	28 707	54 902	3.0	3.9	52 053	14.1	19.9	17.7
Bristol	96	1 399	14 425	39.1	36.3	41.1	87.7	12 720	35 588	68 333	6.4	8.2	60 631	8.2	8.3	7.0
Kent	118	2 285	39 231	19.5	42.0	29.2	349.1	14 479	31 221	61 088	1.3	3.5	54 665	10.2	12.8	10.5
Newport	211	2 429	21 487	30.7	32.5	43.4	139.5	13 700	36 994	67 239	5.3	6.1	67 431	8.6	12.4	10.5
Providence	349	2 910	172 210	29.2	50.2	25.6	1 174.4	13 742	25 169	48 500	3.7	2.9	45 572	17.5	25.3	23.2
Washington	74	1 633	37 317	16.0	32.4	41.7	258.8	15 292	34 737	70 285	4.5	6.2	67 195	8.8	9.6	8.3
SOUTH CAROLINA	598	3 900	1 148 054	15.4	48.2	24.0	6 637.7	9 261	23 443	43 939	-6.4	2.4	42 117	18.1	26.0	23.6
Abbeville	456	2 435	6 485	21.1	57.1	15.3	32.0	9 700	16 653	33 143	-19.8	0.2	34 658	19.1	26.6	24.7
Aiken	361	3 828	38 747	11.9	48.1	23.5	198.0	8 021	24 172	44 468	-7.3	2.2	43 196	17.7	25.3	22.1
Allendale	1 190	3 695	2 527	7.4	65.9	13.2	19.0	12 065	14 190	20 081	-24.1	1.4	24 615	40.4	47.1	44.0
Anderson	596	4 710	45 375	15.0	52.8	18.0	264.3	8 489	22 117	42 871	-8.0	1.6	38 851	18.7	28.3	24.0
Bamberg	701	3 859	4 888	24.0	55.6	17.4	25.2	10 455	16 236	32 538	7.0	1.0	29 101	27.6	38.9	36.3
Barnwell	743	4 248	5 941	9.2	63.4	11.5	43.8	10 064	17 592	33 816	-6.6	0.7	30 898	30.4	52.2	34.5
Beaufort	565	3 351	33 466	19.1	33.6	37.4	200.8	10 376	32 731	55 286	-7.1	5.4	55 266	13.0	22.6	21.8
Berkeley	495	3 154	44 742	16.0	49.9	18.3	242.8	8 386	22 865	50 777	0.5	1.6	49 284	15.0	21.2	20.0
Calhoun	461	2 637	3 651	20.3	54.1	20.3	20.3	11 999	20 845	36 790	-11.2	0.4	37 507	18.5	26.8	25.2
Charleston	536	3 721	87 894	18.4	36.1	37.5	414.7	9 803	29 401	48 433	1.2	4.9	46 187	18.7	25.4	22.5
Cherokee	398	2 725	13 500	9.4	65.5	11.7	81.8	8 741	17 862	34 132	-20.2	0.7	35 223	20.6	30.5	26.9
Chester	851	4 188	8 024	10.9	63.7	11.2	55.4	9 643	17 687	32 743	-20.3	1.3	34 908	20.8	30.9	27.7
Chesterfield	518	3 083	11 120	11.5	66.0	11.1	68.1	8 526	17 162	32 979	-11.7	0.6	32 483	23.7	35.2	32.7
Clarendon	540	3 632	8 077	17.4	65.4	13.2	49.8	9 262	16 562	33 066	-3.8	0.7	30 913	27.8	38.5	35.3
Colleton	774	5 348	9 750	13.1	63.7	13.6	59.0	9 395	17 842	33 263	-11.7	0.8	32 446	22.6	35.1	34.1
Darlington	850	4 766	17 528	17.6	60.4	15.9	102.4	9 272	20 096	38 379	-2.5	1.5	33 772	23.2	35.8	31.9
Dillon	1 279	6 469	7 584	7.1	71.6	9.2	53.1	8 744	14 684	26 818	-20.5	0.5	28 665	26.2	37.1	34.6
Dorchester	525	3 941	36 753	20.5	41.6	24.1	205.5	8 525	24 497	55 034	0.3	1.8	51 132	11.7	17.4	16.4
Edgefield	204	2 112	6 202	12.5	58.3	16.3	36.4	8 995	19 901	42 834	-3.8	0.7	41 501	20.6	28.0	24.1
Fairfield	893	4 024	5 864	15.3	60.6	15.9	44.1	13 051	18 877	32 022	-16.8	1.0	32 261	23.4	32.6	29.3
Florence	570	4 668	35 129	13.1	53.4	20.8	215.3	9 315	21 932	40 487	-9.0	1.8	38 914	21.7	29.9	27.7
Georgetown	594	4 081	13 315	8.6	49.2	21.8	98.2	9 752	23 942	42 666	-4.6	3.0	38 340	20.3	30.7	28.0
Greenville	567	3 503	110 215	23.6	43.3	30.0	556.8	7 905	25 931	46 830	-10.1	3.3	45 666	15.4	21.0	18.9
Greenwood	1 057	5 082	17 151	8.3	52.3	22.0	106.3	8 816	21 728	38 797	-11.7	2.1	35 619	22.1	31.9	30.4
Hampton	838	3 293	5 089	9.6	65.1	11.0	42.3	10 796	16 262	34 846	-4.4	0.3	33 367	23.7	33.7	31.5
Horry	663	5 765	53 014	8.9	47.3	21.8	373.6	9 845	24 811	43 142	-6.6	2.1	40 697	19.5	32.4	31.1
Jasper	472	4 262	5 364	18.2	64.7	9.4	38.6	11 472	17 997	37 393	-3.9	2.1	35 533	25.9	37.0	34.9
Kershaw	430	3 230	14 337	10.5	53.2	18.5	92.9	8 848	21 777	44 064	-10.3	1.4	42 174	18.3	26.0	23.2
Lancaster	537	3 426	16 259	8.7	57.9	15.4	103.2	8 743	19 308	38 959	-11.3	1.2	38 312	19.7	28.2	25.5
Laurens	681	3 619	16 350	8.6	60.3	14.5	83.3	8 995	18 757	37 529	-12.7	0.8	36 345	19.5	31.4	28.5
Lee	541	4 183	4 398	14.1	71.3	8.5	25.7	10 194	12 924	23 378	-31.4	0.7	29 756	27.1	37.6	34.7
Lexington	364	2 618	64 081	12.1	41.5	27.6	338.0	9 306	26 393	52 205	-7.7	2.5	51 523	12.9	19.6	17.4
McCormick	469	1 671	1 697	11.0	54.3	16.0	10.9	12 151	19 411	35 858	-10.3	0.9	34 963	21.0	35.7	34.0
Marion	935	4 912	8 025	7.7	65.4	12.9	55.2	9 891	16 653	30 629	-8.8	1.2	27 917	29.5	41.5	36.8
Marlboro	1 192	4 683	6 676	7.0	71.9	8.6	47.0	10 218	13 817	27 688	-17.8	0.6	28 630	33.1	43.2	40.8
Newberry	365	2 237	8 710	15.0	56.9	19.3	61.2	10 235	21 410	41 815	0.5	1.3	39 054	19.0	30.1	27.8
Oconee	516	2 635	16 423	12.1	51.5	21.4	103.8	9 751	24 055	42 266	-9.0	2.4	42 671	13.6	22.7	21.0
Orangeburg	615	5 369	25 276	18.9	60.1	16.7	153.7	10 718	17 579	32 849	-12.3	1.2	32 699	26.7	36.5	34.5
Pickens	346	3 569	39 349	10.3	49.4	23.5	129.8	7 799	20 647	41 898	-8.6	1.7	40 110	17.0	21.5	18.5
Richland	993	4 952	114 268	18.1	34.4	36.5	737.8	10 841	25 805	47 922	-5.3	3.0	45 944	17.0	20.9	18.3
Saluda	538	1 776	4 532	10.0	64.1	12.6	19.0	9 049	18 717	40 508	-10.6	0.7	39 570	19.3	29.1	28.2
Spartanburg	519	3 627	70 065	16.7	51.4	19.9	431.9	9 200	21 924	42 680	-10.3	1.7	41 888	17.2	25.5	23.5

1. Data for serious crimes have not been adjusted for underreporting; this may affect comparability between geographic areas and over time.   2. Per 100,000 population estimated by the FBI.   3. All persons 3 years old and over enrolled in nursery school through college.   4. Persons 25 years old and over.   5. Elementary and secondary education expenditures.   6. Based on population estimated by the American Community Survey, 2006–2010.

Table B. States and Counties — **Personal Income**

STATE County	Total (mil dol)	Percent change, 2008–2009	Per capita[1] Dollars	Per capita[1] Rank	Wages and salaries[2] (mil dol)	Proprietors' income (mil dol)	Dividends, interest, and rent (mil dol)	Transfer payments (mil dol) Total	Government payments to individuals Total	Social Security	Medical payments	Income maintenance	Unemployment insurance
	62	63	64	65	66	67	68	69	70	71	72	73	74
PENNSYLVANIA—Cont'd													
Potter	518	0.7	31 009	1 753	246	77	71	152	149	57	58	11	15
Schuylkill	4 569	1.4	31 094	1 729	2 244	204	672	1 343	1 316	460	526	76	146
Snyder	1 188	-0.6	30 830	1 793	607	102	180	360	353	102	182	15	37
Somerset	2 329	1.2	30 269	1 916	1 074	152	370	677	663	232	268	43	73
Sullivan	182	1.2	29 665	2 059	61	10	37	61	60	24	26	3	4
Susquehanna	1 288	-0.2	31 686	1 600	325	103	209	315	307	128	115	22	20
Tioga	1 089	1.0	26 647	2 616	527	47	175	334	326	130	121	23	25
Union	1 291	0.4	29 635	2 066	794	104	215	269	261	103	100	14	27
Venango	1 717	0.7	31 696	1 598	881	78	242	597	587	182	290	43	44
Warren	1 280	-0.1	31 503	1 640	670	63	199	363	355	138	145	24	28
Washington	8 434	0.5	40 667	408	4 237	473	1 282	1 881	1 844	674	812	111	126
Wayne	1 633	0.9	31 812	1 576	660	77	321	456	447	177	191	25	26
Westmoreland	14 348	0.4	39 607	477	6 328	749	2 236	3 319	3 253	1 193	1 420	176	259
Wyoming	888	1.8	31 932	1 543	478	38	130	228	223	85	89	15	21
York	15 427	-0.2	35 966	891	8 981	709	2 547	2 842	2 764	1 105	1 002	187	276
RHODE ISLAND	43 594	-1.1	41 392	X	26 474	3 006	7 540	8 917	8 725	2 601	3 908	816	696
Bristol	2 590	-3.4	52 275	75	684	168	639	357	348	142	126	17	30
Kent	7 362	-1.0	43 623	250	4 051	397	1 168	1 374	1 344	475	542	83	112
Newport	4 038	-2.4	50 290	97	2 727	201	907	633	619	223	255	40	47
Providence	23 769	-0.4	37 867	658	16 355	1 903	3 675	5 631	5 517	1 417	2 642	630	428
Washington	5 836	-1.8	45 980	169	2 657	337	1 150	921	898	343	342	46	79
SOUTH CAROLINA	148 265	-0.4	32 505	X	91 540	8 830	24 110	33 255	32 430	11 300	12 536	3 545	1 748
Abbeville	665	0.0	26 509	2 641	259	46	81	199	194	73	62	24	12
Aiken	5 329	1.4	34 157	1 145	3 331	329	883	1 232	1 203	439	483	120	51
Allendale	244	2.2	23 949	2 969	177	7	26	93	91	22	39	19	5
Anderson	5 599	-0.5	30 280	1 912	2 583	366	835	1 397	1 364	544	489	137	72
Bamberg	398	1.5	26 505	2 642	181	25	48	149	146	39	60	22	7
Barnwell	561	2.2	24 706	2 892	259	19	67	210	205	55	98	30	11
Beaufort	6 662	-3.0	42 918	272	3 526	402	2 175	1 153	1 127	520	394	72	38
Berkeley	5 304	1.8	30 571	1 848	2 295	319	532	934	903	314	284	108	58
Calhoun	496	0.0	33 930	1 179	216	46	66	113	110	40	40	14	6
Charleston	14 046	-0.9	39 536	488	12 112	1 141	3 002	2 375	2 312	719	1 020	226	108
Cherokee	1 379	-3.9	25 211	2 841	813	48	184	435	425	153	149	55	29
Chester	907	-1.8	28 000	2 399	409	56	95	288	282	94	107	37	22
Chesterfield	1 120	-0.7	26 021	2 724	555	69	136	372	364	116	146	51	22
Clarendon	846	0.5	25 647	2 782	294	59	117	304	298	95	116	49	14
Colleton	1 091	0.8	27 806	2 437	435	64	147	349	342	105	143	50	16
Darlington	1 984	-0.9	29 855	2 009	1 016	85	266	572	560	178	221	87	29
Dillon	766	1.9	24 772	2 887	355	56	76	275	270	70	117	48	15
Dorchester	3 947	-0.6	30 265	1 919	1 287	37	446	801	777	249	304	79	44
Edgefield	807	3.7	31 352	1 683	260	21	102	156	151	58	49	21	8
Fairfield	639	0.5	27 395	2 500	363	21	72	203	199	59	82	28	10
Florence	4 587	0.4	34 178	1 144	3 124	310	658	1 203	1 178	317	541	154	51
Georgetown	2 257	-0.6	37 177	724	1 031	173	527	655	644	222	301	56	26
Greenville	16 235	-1.5	35 963	894	12 318	1 017	2 782	2 921	2 839	1 078	1 077	261	154
Greenwood	2 068	0.9	29 676	2 056	1 402	96	338	562	549	195	202	60	28
Hampton	544	1.9	25 891	2 748	251	24	66	189	185	50	87	26	8
Horry	7 679	-1.0	29 101	2 168	4 390	486	1 548	1 998	1 950	803	680	176	106
Jasper	618	-0.4	26 625	2 619	343	24	49	152	148	43	59	24	7
Kershaw	2 004	0.8	33 382	1 283	799	146	269	453	442	162	170	42	22
Lancaster	1 781	-0.6	22 897	3 035	731	99	239	555	541	216	185	60	37
Laurens	1 887	-3.0	26 945	2 575	848	46	258	583	570	198	235	60	27
Lee	491	-0.5	24 872	2 877	166	41	49	172	168	43	70	32	9
Lexington	9 144	-0.5	35 773	918	4 502	647	1 336	1 575	1 528	567	567	135	95
McCormick	258	2.6	25 440	2 813	74	6	58	103	102	41	38	10	4
Marion	828	-0.1	24 750	2 889	309	62	99	334	328	85	152	52	19
Marlboro	680	-0.4	23 641	2 988	360	27	69	259	254	72	104	43	16
Newberry	1 103	0.4	28 447	2 311	582	39	156	305	298	105	117	33	15
Oconee	2 324	-0.8	32 499	1 428	1 183	132	497	610	597	253	228	43	29
Orangeburg	2 663	2.3	29 550	2 081	1 477	138	335	804	787	228	297	125	45
Pickens	3 247	-1.3	27 487	2 485	1 616	123	526	824	802	307	310	64	42
Richland	13 505	0.1	36 302	846	12 546	814	1 955	2 393	2 327	670	886	262	123
Saluda	629	2.6	32 932	1 350	167	31	70	136	133	51	46	18	6
Spartanburg	8 674	-1.2	30 242	1 927	6 144	499	1 306	2 059	2 006	750	763	188	115

1. Based on the resident population estimated as of July 1 of the year shown. 2. Includes supplements to wages and salaries.

Table B. States and Counties — Earnings, Social Security, and Housing

STATE County	Earnings, 2009									Social Security beneficiaries, December 2010		Supplemental Security Income recipients, December 2010	Housing units, 2010	
			Goods-related[1]		Service-related and health									
	Total (mil dol)	Farm	Total	Manufacturing	Information and professional and technical services	Retail trade	Finance, insurance, and real estate	Health care and social services	Government	Number	Rate[2]		Total	Percent change, 2000–2010
	75	76	77	78	79	80	81	82	83	84	85	86	87	88
PENNSYLVANIA—Cont'd														
Potter	322	0.1	D	10.6	D	6.0	2.1	D	17.2	4 645	266	484	12 932	6.4
Schuylkill	2 448	0.6	27.5	22.1	4.6	7.2	3.2	15.6	17.8	37 145	250	3 655	69 323	2.2
Snyder	709	3.2	D	23.3	D	11.1	2.4	D	18.8	8 290	209	689	16 027	7.6
Somerset	1 226	0.2	25.3	13.2	4.3	7.6	4.1	12.1	20.3	19 285	248	2 359	38 113	2.6
Sullivan	71	-0.7	D	5.8	3.0	8.5	D	D	28.6	1 910	297	140	6 304	4.8
Susquehanna	428	0.6	21.4	4.6	4.6	9.6	3.8	11.9	24.8	10 415	240	941	22 968	5.2
Tioga	574	-1.1	21.8	17.9	3.7	8.4	4.9	D	28.2	10 675	254	1 251	21 364	7.4
Union	898	1.8	D	9.0	2.9	5.7	3.5	D	25.9	7 995	178	599	16 997	15.8
Venango	959	1.0	29.7	26.0	3.1	8.2	4.0	15.8	20.2	14 680	267	2 175	27 464	2.1
Warren	734	-0.3	24.6	18.7	3.0	6.7	5.6	14.7	17.8	10 695	256	971	23 560	2.2
Washington	4 709	-0.2	25.7	11.9	8.8	6.1	5.9	13.4	12.2	50 195	242	5 612	92 977	6.5
Wayne	736	0.0	16.3	3.7	7.4	11.0	4.8	13.9	26.5	13 630	258	1 044	31 653	3.5
Westmoreland	7 077	0.0	22.9	15.7	8.0	8.0	4.2	13.2	13.9	90 015	247	8 705	168 199	4.4
Wyoming	516	-0.6	45.2	37.2	4.1	6.5	2.3	D	12.9	6 630	234	679	13 254	4.3
York	9 690	0.4	30.5	22.7	6.3	6.7	4.3	13.2	15.1	83 805	193	7 811	178 671	14.0
RHODE ISLAND	29 480	0.1	14.7	9.5	11.5	5.8	9.0	14.7	19.0	203 660	193	32 809	463 388	5.4
Bristol	852	0.0	D	11.9	7.4	5.2	5.4	12.1	16.9	10 520	211	687	20 850	4.9
Kent	4 448	0.0	D	12.1	9.8	8.9	9.8	14.0	14.4	36 110	217	3 395	73 701	4.7
Newport	2 928	0.2	D	8.1	12.8	5.2	4.1	7.0	39.3	17 185	207	1 364	41 796	5.6
Providence	18 258	0.0	13.1	7.9	12.5	4.7	10.6	16.5	16.1	114 800	183	25 825	264 835	4.6
Washington	2 994	0.3	20.8	15.6	7.8	8.5	4.3	12.5	24.1	25 045	197	1 537	82 206	9.5
SOUTH CAROLINA	100 370	0.4	19.9	14.1	8.6	7.4	6.5	9.1	23.7	924 726	200	112 094	2 137 683	21.9
Abbeville	305	0.2	D	25.9	3.9	4.3	2.3	4.5	24.9	6 010	236	697	12 079	3.8
Aiken	3 660	0.0	22.8	12.9	8.2	7.0	4.1	7.0	13.2	34 345	215	4 052	72 249	16.6
Allendale	185	1.9	28.5	27.6	D	3.0	D	3.7	30.6	2 080	200	687	4 486	-1.8
Anderson	2 949	-0.1	33.3	25.9	3.8	9.5	3.3	8.7	22.4	43 645	233	4 077	84 774	15.8
Bamberg	206	3.1	17.1	14.7	3.3	10.1	D	7.7	28.9	3 555	222	765	7 716	8.2
Barnwell	278	-0.1	D	28.0	6.6	8.6	2.1	D	27.4	4 780	211	1 122	10 484	2.9
Beaufort	3 928	0.8	7.6	1.3	7.2	7.7	9.0	7.2	38.7	37 655	232	1 839	93 023	53.7
Berkeley	2 613	0.2	D	20.2	18.7	4.8	3.5	3.8	19.9	27 615	155	3 135	73 372	34.2
Calhoun	263	2.3	45.0	33.3	3.2	2.9	2.3	D	15.2	3 440	227	473	7 340	7.0
Charleston	13 253	0.0	12.1	6.6	11.9	7.1	6.4	10.8	29.1	59 255	169	7 251	169 984	20.5
Cherokee	861	0.9	D	33.9	D	7.6	3.2	D	14.8	12 700	229	1 538	23 997	7.1
Chester	465	1.5	40.0	32.3	4.5	5.3	2.7	6.4	19.6	7 835	236	1 054	14 701	2.3
Chesterfield	624	3.0	37.2	33.4	2.1	7.2	2.7	D	17.3	10 025	215	1 671	21 482	14.2
Clarendon	353	6.8	14.6	10.2	3.8	9.8	3.0	D	33.7	8 510	243	1 761	17 467	14.1
Colleton	499	1.2	D	10.5	D	9.2	4.7	12.0	22.8	9 355	241	1 762	19 901	9.8
Darlington	1 101	1.1	D	31.3	2.4	6.2	2.7	D	15.0	15 155	221	2 899	30 297	4.7
Dillon	411	5.7	22.7	20.6	D	11.0	3.6	D	20.0	6 620	206	1 711	13 742	8.4
Dorchester	1 324	0.1	27.1	20.8	D	9.9	3.6	7.9	23.4	21 630	158	2 455	55 186	48.3
Edgefield	281	5.4	D	15.1	1.6	9.8	1.7	D	36.6	4 925	183	664	10 559	14.7
Fairfield	385	1.2	D	6.0	D	4.3	D	D	21.7	5 205	217	884	11 681	12.5
Florence	3 434	0.3	D	15.0	7.4	7.8	12.7	13.0	20.8	27 375	200	5 465	58 666	13.2
Georgetown	1 204	0.2	20.6	12.9	D	8.6	6.0	12.0	24.7	17 500	291	1 639	33 672	19.1
Greenville	13 335	0.0	20.2	14.4	13.0	7.4	6.5	8.4	14.1	84 365	187	8 525	195 462	20.1
Greenwood	1 498	0.3	D	24.8	3.9	6.6	3.3	10.7	26.7	15 495	222	1 740	31 054	9.9
Hampton	275	0.4	16.1	11.6	D	6.6	D	D	34.5	4 460	211	934	9 140	6.5
Horry	4 876	0.1	10.9	3.5	6.8	12.3	10.5	10.6	17.9	65 290	242	5 120	185 992	52.3
Jasper	367	0.6	D	4.6	2.4	9.8	2.5	11.8	22.8	4 020	162	648	10 299	29.9
Kershaw	945	2.8	32.0	23.9	6.4	9.6	6.1	6.0	20.6	13 300	216	1 457	27 478	21.1
Lancaster	830	1.8	D	17.1	6.1	8.1	6.8	12.5	23.0	17 300	226	1 539	32 687	30.9
Laurens	894	0.1	D	31.2	D	5.2	2.0	D	22.6	16 425	247	2 130	30 709	1.6
Lee	206	12.1	17.1	14.3	D	6.6	2.1	9.3	30.8	4 145	216	1 089	7 775	1.4
Lexington	5 149	0.5	19.7	11.7	8.4	9.3	5.7	8.2	20.8	44 655	170	3 911	113 957	25.3
McCormick	81	0.7	D	10.2	D	4.5	2.3	D	53.2	3 270	320	299	5 453	22.3
Marion	371	1.4	17.0	11.8	3.0	11.5	5.3	D	34.3	7 895	239	1 732	14 953	-1.3
Marlboro	387	3.1	D	36.8	D	5.2	1.5	D	30.0	6 615	229	1 513	12 072	1.5
Newberry	621	2.0	44.8	38.8	D	6.5	1.6	D	20.3	8 605	229	963	17 922	6.6
Oconee	1 316	0.8	D	27.1	D	6.5	2.5	7.2	18.2	20 165	271	1 435	38 763	19.7
Orangeburg	1 615	1.6	24.3	21.1	3.0	9.6	3.2	6.9	31.2	20 085	217	3 912	42 504	8.2
Pickens	1 738	0.0	D	17.0	4.2	8.1	3.5	8.6	33.4	24 485	205	1 962	51 244	11.4
Richland	13 360	0.0	9.7	5.7	11.4	5.3	10.3	10.4	33.1	55 170	143	7 776	161 725	24.6
Saluda	198	12.3	36.2	32.4	D	4.7	3.6	3.6	24.2	4 345	219	510	9 289	8.7
Spartanburg	6 643	0.1	30.8	25.5	5.2	6.3	5.2	8.9	17.4	60 455	213	6 763	122 628	14.6

1. Includes mining, construction, and manufacturing.   2. Per 1,000 resident population enumerated in the 2010 census.

Table B. States and Counties — Housing, Labor Force, and Employment

STATE County	Total	Percent	Median value[1]	With a mortgage	Without a mortgage	Median rent[2]	Median rent as a percent of income	Substandard units[3] (percent)	Total	Percent change, 2009-2010	Total	Rate[4]	Total	Management, business, science and arts	Construction, production, and maintenance occupations
	89	90	91	92	93	94	95	96	97	98	99	100	101	102	103
PENNSYLVANIA—Cont'd															
Potter	7 291	76.1	89 600	23.2	14.3	579	30.5	2.1	7 765	0.1	820	10.6	7 238	26.9	35.7
Schuylkill	60 347	77.2	88 400	22.2	14.9	543	26.6	1.2	73 003	-1.6	7 673	10.5	64 730	27.0	33.9
Snyder	14 258	75.1	122 900	23.1	12.2	611	25.5	2.0	19 109	-1.0	1 692	8.9	18 998	23.7	35.0
Somerset	30 319	78.4	92 200	22.2	13.4	512	27.3	1.4	38 973	0.1	3 684	9.5	34 305	27.0	33.6
Sullivan	2 436	82.6	120 600	24.6	12.4	447	28.0	1.5	3 135	4.5	245	7.8	2 623	22.5	41.9
Susquehanna	17 225	79.2	124 400	24.5	14.3	603	26.8	1.5	22 130	1.7	1 878	8.5	19 688	27.2	33.9
Tioga	17 182	74.9	105 700	24.5	14.0	582	28.8	1.8	20 555	0.3	1 700	8.3	18 538	29.6	31.5
Union	14 963	73.7	143 200	23.8	12.4	631	29.3	2.2	17 504	-1.8	1 595	9.1	18 093	35.1	26.2
Venango	22 457	75.0	76 500	21.6	13.0	534	28.8	1.2	26 295	-0.3	2 298	8.7	24 591	26.0	31.2
Warren	17 630	78.3	83 900	21.6	12.9	519	25.7	1.7	21 780	-0.8	1 757	8.1	19 219	26.8	32.5
Washington	83 604	77.3	130 300	21.4	12.4	563	28.4	0.8	105 421	-1.0	8 680	8.2	96 155	32.9	23.6
Wayne	19 678	80.3	173 600	26.1	13.8	691	30.9	1.5	25 644	-0.2	1 978	7.7	22 391	28.7	28.2
Westmoreland	152 640	76.5	126 800	21.5	13.3	578	27.1	0.7	186 704	-1.4	15 518	8.3	171 273	33.6	24.7
Wyoming	11 023	77.1	140 800	23.3	13.4	624	26.0	1.7	14 218	-1.9	1 302	9.2	13 652	25.3	33.9
York	166 600	76.4	175 500	24.3	14.0	748	27.7	1.3	223 818	-1.6	19 731	8.8	216 940	31.8	28.4
RHODE ISLAND	410 305	62.5	279 300	27.5	16.1	882	30.1	2.0	570 301	0.7	66 725	11.7	515 924	36.2	19.9
Bristol	19 236	72.1	363 100	26.9	17.5	890	32.0	0.9	27 323	0.2	2 760	10.1	25 337	44.5	15.5
Kent	69 109	73.8	246 600	27.3	16.3	922	29.2	1.3	98 626	2.1	11 182	11.3	86 160	36.3	19.5
Newport	34 771	63.6	388 800	26.4	14.4	1 087	27.8	0.7	44 274	1.6	4 741	10.7	41 518	43.3	15.0
Providence	238 059	55.5	258 000	28.3	16.8	851	30.7	2.7	331 533	1.5	41 012	12.4	296 788	33.5	21.7
Washington	49 130	76.1	351 100	25.9	14.3	946	29.2	1.0	74 273	1.8	7 261	9.8	66 121	40.9	17.0
SOUTH CAROLINA	1 741 994	69.9	134 100	23.0	11.3	701	29.6	2.4	2 150 576	-1.1	241 162	11.2	2 002 289	31.8	25.7
Abbeville	9 875	77.4	85 900	22.2	13.2	539	37.9	1.7	11 033	-3.4	1 466	13.3	9 993	25.8	36.0
Aiken	62 072	73.3	119 000	20.6	11.0	640	29.3	2.2	77 269	0.3	6 580	8.5	67 980	33.2	27.5
Allendale	3 458	59.1	67 500	27.9	16.4	465	33.6	6.1	3 370	-2.7	647	19.2	2 986	25.0	37.6
Anderson	71 973	74.0	117 700	21.7	10.0	620	31.3	2.4	85 344	-0.8	9 696	11.4	80 545	29.5	29.6
Bamberg	5 658	72.9	84 300	23.1	14.4	569	32.0	2.1	6 448	-1.5	1 008	15.6	5 818	29.9	31.9
Barnwell	8 429	72.9	67 400	19.8	13.1	536	33.4	4.0	8 848	-5.2	1 558	17.6	8 662	25.8	38.6
Beaufort	63 459	70.7	290 900	28.4	12.1	988	29.8	2.6	63 786	-1.6	5 635	8.8	63 988	32.1	19.7
Berkeley	60 472	70.4	149 700	24.3	12.3	844	27.5	2.6	81 258	-0.2	8 159	10.0	77 896	29.4	28.1
Calhoun	6 121	81.9	94 500	20.5	11.7	577	31.6	1.3	6 709	-3.4	790	11.8	6 516	28.9	31.6
Charleston	137 844	61.7	242 100	26.8	13.5	868	31.5	2.0	176 357	0.1	16 027	9.1	167 379	37.7	19.1
Cherokee	20 975	68.5	82 700	22.2	10.0	541	27.0	1.7	24 931	-4.3	3 663	14.7	21 616	22.2	39.0
Chester	12 497	76.3	87 100	23.5	11.9	559	32.9	2.3	14 975	-6.2	2 788	18.6	12 719	21.0	39.6
Chesterfield	17 235	73.6	77 600	20.6	11.7	538	28.6	2.6	18 972	-2.1	2 953	15.6	18 967	22.9	38.5
Clarendon	12 636	74.4	89 100	23.9	10.2	533	28.2	2.7	12 890	-1.3	1 936	15.0	12 504	25.0	35.7
Colleton	15 228	72.5	90 000	25.1	14.1	632	31.3	2.8	17 404	-0.8	2 300	13.2	14 927	24.5	36.0
Darlington	25 805	74.0	81 800	20.9	10.3	556	26.6	3.1	31 000	-2.8	3 903	12.6	28 094	26.6	32.5
Dillon	11 714	61.8	61 400	23.7	12.8	518	31.0	4.5	13 751	-3.2	2 184	15.9	11 913	19.3	40.5
Dorchester	47 622	74.0	171 400	24.6	11.6	868	29.3	1.4	64 493	-0.4	5 980	9.3	60 239	33.0	24.7
Edgefield	9 121	77.3	101 600	19.9	14.0	529	27.7	3.0	11 271	-0.1	1 093	9.7	10 523	28.5	34.0
Fairfield	9 121	75.3	91 500	25.6	13.3	544	30.2	2.5	10 880	-3.1	1 462	13.4	9 763	28.5	31.3
Florence	51 636	66.1	108 400	21.4	10.2	607	27.7	2.4	63 901	-0.5	7 217	11.3	59 400	32.5	23.7
Georgetown	22 406	74.3	174 700	26.8	12.7	720	36.3	3.1	30 376	-2.1	3 740	12.3	23 201	27.4	25.0
Greenville	171 233	68.0	148 100	22.2	10.4	685	28.4	1.8	224 432	0.2	21 088	9.4	205 520	35.4	22.8
Greenwood	26 189	69.8	105 000	21.2	10.3	591	30.0	2.9	30 654	-3.3	3 721	12.1	29 757	27.7	32.6
Hampton	7 196	75.6	79 600	21.9	14.3	580	28.2	4.1	7 975	-1.5	1 130	14.2	7 800	19.5	37.5
Horry	112 057	71.0	170 100	25.6	12.0	788	30.5	5.2	131 995	0.9	15 764	11.9	121 515	27.8	19.8
Jasper	7 695	72.6	118 700	26.7	13.7	759	33.4	4.5	10 183	-1.5	1 011	9.9	10 304	15.5	34.1
Kershaw	23 358	81.0	110 800	21.9	10.6	636	30.0	2.0	29 898	-1.5	3 109	10.4	26 280	28.8	28.8
Lancaster	28 180	74.3	122 300	23.9	11.0	603	30.9	2.1	30 751	-0.7	5 004	16.3	28 858	24.4	31.8
Laurens	25 583	71.0	85 800	21.9	10.4	579	30.9	2.0	32 271	-1.9	3 701	11.5	27 698	23.5	37.4
Lee	6 631	71.6	61 400	24.1	14.3	447	27.9	4.7	8 336	-3.3	1 162	13.9	6 010	22.4	31.2
Lexington	100 793	74.8	136 800	21.4	10.1	745	28.4	1.6	133 449	-0.2	10 848	8.1	126 760	35.6	22.4
McCormick	4 116	77.4	110 800	24.5	12.3	403	31.5	2.2	3 361	-3.7	529	15.7	3 388	22.5	29.7
Marion	12 234	66.5	82 500	21.9	12.5	510	29.9	3.3	12 623	-5.5	2 611	20.7	13 162	24.4	33.2
Marlboro	9 768	66.2	60 300	23.9	14.8	508	31.2	3.7	11 884	-4.3	2 340	19.7	9 484	18.8	45.6
Newberry	14 266	73.1	102 300	21.2	11.9	595	30.1	2.8	18 469	-0.8	2 011	10.9	16 889	27.8	32.6
Oconee	29 910	76.9	126 700	21.4	10.3	584	27.4	1.7	31 186	-2.2	3 678	11.8	30 504	31.9	29.7
Orangeburg	34 725	68.2	81 000	22.6	13.1	585	33.5	3.8	41 043	-3.3	6 260	15.3	35 884	26.4	32.2
Pickens	44 048	70.6	123 500	21.4	10.0	660	33.3	1.7	57 252	-1.6	5 742	10.0	51 924	33.6	26.9
Richland	141 564	61.1	146 300	22.6	11.0	776	30.4	1.4	181 121	-0.6	17 438	9.6	174 875	39.9	16.2
Saluda	6 827	76.4	96 400	21.8	11.1	571	18.9	3.4	8 970	-0.9	835	9.3	8 376	24.5	40.8
Spartanburg	106 397	71.2	116 300	22.4	10.0	621	28.7	1.9	135 287	-1.1	15 488	11.4	122 441	30.0	30.1

1. Specified owner-occupied units.   2. Specified renter-occupied units. A value of 10.0 represents 10 percent or less.   3. Overcrowded or lacking complete plumbing facilities.   4. Percent of civilian labor force.   5. Persons 16 years old and over.

STATE County	Number of establishments	Total	Health care and social assistance	Manufacturing	Retail trade	Finance and insurance	Professional, scientific, and technical services	Total (mil dol)	Average per employee (dollars)	Number	Fewer than 50 acres	500 acres or more	Farm operators whose principal occupation is farming (percent)
	104	105	106	107	108	109	110	111	112	113	114	115	116
PENNSYLVANIA—Cont'd													
Potter	371	4 394	996	791	552	83	D	146	33 291	378	20.9	11.6	46.3
Schuylkill	2 894	40 827	7 976	9 314	6 000	989	969	1 300	31 840	966	45.9	4.7	35.3
Snyder	839	13 853	903	3 629	3 077	D	231	348	25 097	998	45.5	2.6	47.7
Somerset	1 741	20 642	3 038	3 680	2 819	698	710	604	29 245	1 156	28.8	6.8	47.8
Sullivan	165	1 177	414	D	259	D	D	30	25 654	165	26.7	6.1	38.2
Susquehanna	883	6 268	806	611	1 293	175	255	142	22 591	1 008	30.8	5.0	42.2
Tioga	851	9 455	1 944	2 134	1 795	375	241	269	28 469	1 011	23.0	7.2	44.8
Union	898	15 582	3 911	1 700	1 782	376	310	447	28 710	575	36.2	2.8	57.2
Venango	1 186	17 129	3 756	4 419	2 557	514	265	519	30 293	487	36.6	4.3	38.2
Warren	912	13 803	3 074	2 826	2 291	D	244	434	31 413	831	33.0	3.2	33.2
Washington	4 991	80 120	12 819	9 474	8 321	1 671	3 471	3 264	40 744	2 023	39.1	2.1	37.7
Wayne	1 373	12 739	2 302	735	2 793	508	366	361	28 301	603	24.2	4.1	52.1
Westmoreland	8 955	120 610	20 303	19 616	18 081	2 888	4 886	4 057	33 636	1 415	39.6	3.9	41.7
Wyoming	615	8 288	1 118	D	1 149	200	303	292	35 228	649	36.4	2.8	30.0
York	8 647	156 561	22 125	35 366	21 819	4 235	6 287	5 795	37 017	2 370	58.9	5.2	45.2
RHODE ISLAND	28 682	413 584	81 450	44 008	47 032	27 763	23 351	16 776	40 562	1 219	68.7	0.6	50.9
Bristol	1 249	13 602	2 680	2 001	1 282	246	386	388	28 500	51	76.5	0.0	47.1
Kent	4 929	71 108	11 313	8 878	11 103	5 826	2 853	2 658	37 386	143	68.5	0.7	60.8
Newport	2 745	28 620	4 542	D	3 939	740	3 123	1 079	37 705	187	66.3	0.0	58.8
Providence	15 869	258 436	55 477	24 614	23 847	19 836	15 358	11 028	42 671	469	69.9	0.2	46.7
Washington	3 811	40 247	7 424	6 286	6 855	984	1 428	1 554	38 605	369	67.2	1.4	49.1
SOUTH CAROLINA	103 254	1 542 825	212 766	223 092	224 033	67 278	76 487	51 721	33 523	25 867	42.3	7.4	37.7
Abbeville	356	4 713	558	1 995	407	115	51	132	27 945	566	34.8	5.7	33.6
Aiken	2 821	48 735	5 581	6 964	7 193	1 242	2 655	2 008	41 208	1 206	46.7	4.1	38.9
Allendale	130	1 387	D	596	177	D	34	47	34 030	185	22.7	23.2	28.1
Anderson	3 741	52 060	7 975	11 097	8 492	1 135	1 647	1 537	29 530	1 650	48.1	3.2	32.9
Bamberg	305	3 535	844	923	520	106	D	95	26 997	390	18.2	15.9	25.6
Barnwell	369	4 750	774	1 616	903	142	92	125	26 240	412	29.1	11.2	35.9
Beaufort	4 813	48 918	6 406	613	8 983	1 664	2 820	1 528	31 242	125	62.4	14.4	43.2
Berkeley	2 658	38 052	2 060	4 958	6 175	1 023	2 309	1 363	35 821	314	55.1	7.3	40.8
Calhoun	257	3 107	D	1 004	277	74	D	96	30 854	341	26.4	16.4	41.6
Charleston	11 764	172 234	28 796	9 822	26 374	6 555	12 505	6 249	36 284	332	62.0	5.7	45.8
Cherokee	1 014	16 742	1 209	5 302	2 730	335	161	466	27 854	416	37.3	3.6	37.7
Chester	536	6 514	D	2 182	903	155	D	201	30 905	544	31.8	8.5	36.8
Chesterfield	710	11 587	1 863	4 121	1 373	222	73	327	28 248	848	33.5	5.9	32.0
Clarendon	524	5 804	1 532	763	1 232	218	91	143	24 718	491	33.0	14.7	46.6
Colleton	790	8 280	1 297	1 404	1 776	325	241	224	27 088	525	40.4	10.5	34.9
Darlington	1 152	16 911	2 381	3 599	2 383	434	287	619	36 615	369	35.0	21.1	43.1
Dillon	511	8 167	1 052	2 314	1 436	204	D	190	23 321	222	20.3	21.2	52.7
Dorchester	2 173	22 902	2 799	4 407	3 690	705	672	663	28 942	377	50.1	7.2	44.3
Edgefield	341	4 410	510	1 212	441	D	44	118	26 857	407	39.8	7.4	36.9
Fairfield	316	4 438	594	897	651	D	70	180	40 524	187	26.7	12.3	47.6
Florence	3 239	54 201	12 811	6 641	9 036	4 152	2 367	1 809	33 384	675	38.5	12.0	40.9
Georgetown	1 837	18 240	2 256	1 892	2 925	605	808	558	30 596	252	37.7	9.5	35.7
Greenville	12 213	213 246	25 339	28 623	24 464	7 925	13 223	7 784	36 501	1 100	65.5	0.8	30.5
Greenwood	1 415	25 229	5 041	6 708	3 558	620	1 396	812	32 167	493	44.0	4.3	30.6
Hampton	392	3 713	512	620	676	130	107	116	31 232	295	25.8	18.0	37.6
Horry	8 418	97 155	9 824	3 216	20 880	3 813	3 328	2 529	26 035	914	37.1	7.5	46.2
Jasper	549	5 973	817	372	1 193	113	75	178	29 872	109	35.8	16.5	38.5
Kershaw	1 159	14 009	2 275	3 335	2 142	442	474	419	29 924	499	46.5	6.8	42.3
Lancaster	1 215	13 369	2 245	1 697	2 277	1 137	489	434	32 484	573	42.9	3.0	38.2
Laurens	941	16 177	2 077	5 629	1 707	497	198	486	30 057	830	37.2	6.6	35.1
Lee	223	2 161	385	272	427	70	D	55	25 222	476	28.2	12.4	40.8
Lexington	6 101	87 088	12 190	9 070	16 011	3 345	3 172	2 709	31 109	948	55.8	2.5	39.5
McCormick	102	1 007	D	270	161	28	49	24	24 143	79	26.6	17.7	34.2
Marion	555	6 528	1 205	1 305	1 258	260	55	177	27 159	308	43.2	11.0	39.0
Marlboro	358	5 302	976	2 359	752	115	43	155	29 192	233	25.8	25.8	47.6
Newberry	740	12 113	1 196	5 580	1 423	225	150	354	29 200	614	32.4	5.4	40.6
Oconee	1 501	18 461	2 661	4 762	3 001	511	495	678	36 747	804	53.6	2.4	35.3
Orangeburg	1 771	27 410	3 939	7 402	4 524	828	389	774	28 246	1 002	29.8	13.4	36.5
Pickens	2 090	25 521	3 745	5 296	4 191	729	811	699	27 393	829	66.5	1.0	31.5
Richland	9 087	167 702	26 348	16 803	18 071	17 256	12 311	6 172	36 802	364	55.5	3.6	43.4
Saluda	247	3 399	458	1 856	329	55	39	88	25 925	606	29.9	7.4	41.6
Spartanburg	6 396	112 163	13 973	23 852	13 908	2 433	3 479	4 103	36 577	1 242	53.8	2.4	39.7

Table B. States and Counties — **Agriculture**

STATE County	Acreage (1,000) [117]	Percent change, 2002–2007 [118]	Average size of farm [119]	Total irrigated (1,000) [120]	Total cropland (1,000) [121]	Average per farm [122]	Average per acre [123]	Value of machinery and equipment, average per farm (dollars) [124]	Total (mil dol) [125]	Average per farm (dollars) [126]	Crops [127]	Live-stock and poultry products [128]	$10,000 or more [129]	$100,000 or more [130]	Total ($1,000) [131]	Percent of farms [132]
PENNSYLVANIA—Cont'd																
Potter	88	-6.4	234	D	40.4	607 773	2 597	77 189	31.4	83 008	20.2	79.8	31.0	13.2	790	33.6
Schuylkill	119	7.2	123	1.9	81.3	614 809	5 012	80 239	124.8	129 143	45.1	54.9	34.3	15.0	1 917	48.3
Snyder	100	0.0	100	1.0	65.4	500 022	4 981	62 844	109.0	109 259	13.6	86.4	47.0	20.7	1 189	28.7
Somerset	207	-7.2	179	0.2	120.5	511 174	2 859	84 012	83.2	71 931	14.0	86.0	43.1	18.5	1 575	37.5
Sullivan	28	-9.7	169	0.0	14.5	418 154	2 480	64 418	7.2	43 878	12.3	87.7	27.9	10.3	221	37.0
Susquehanna	158	-16.4	157	0.1	75.9	514 686	3 279	61 132	49.3	48 896	9.7	90.3	29.1	11.8	1 447	27.4
Tioga	184	-8.0	182	0.1	96.9	538 400	2 957	69 355	53.8	53 243	11.7	88.3	33.5	14.2	2 735	38.8
Union	64	-7.2	111	0.2	50.2	655 528	5 908	81 201	90.5	157 386	10.4	89.6	58.1	36.5	706	34.6
Venango	65	0.0	133	0.0	31.0	365 006	2 743	55 316	11.8	24 221	46.4	53.6	23.0	6.0	472	20.3
Warren	100	28.2	120	0.1	43.5	315 242	2 631	42 759	18.6	22 387	14.9	85.1	17.9	5.2	440	13.4
Washington	211	-19.2	104	0.4	101.0	460 864	4 418	54 163	28.6	14 161	44.8	55.2	21.7	2.8	836	12.0
Wayne	93	-17.7	154	0.1	42.4	637 576	4 137	70 329	29.4	48 803	10.9	89.1	38.8	14.1	384	21.7
Westmoreland	167	10.6	118	0.4	107.3	533 173	4 504	73 537	58.4	41 298	37.4	62.6	32.2	7.7	1 346	24.5
Wyoming	78	25.8	120	0.1	41.4	417 786	3 478	47 025	13.5	20 796	31.0	69.0	19.3	6.2	557	23.3
York	293	2.8	123	1.0	225.4	701 059	5 680	81 789	212.6	89 719	47.1	52.9	38.4	13.9	2 722	22.7
RHODE ISLAND	68	11.5	56	4.3	24.5	936 229	16 828	65 343	65.9	54 067	84.4	15.6	36.5	9.6	743	8.3
Bristol	2	100.0	33	0.1	1.1	833 282	25 524	42 030	2.8	55 510	88.6	11.4	41.2	11.8	1	5.9
Kent	10	25.0	68	0.2	2.5	904 942	13 378	55 522	3.8	26 320	91.7	8.3	29.4	7.7	37	6.3
Newport	10	-9.1	54	0.6	5.7	1 233 570	22 734	70 050	18.3	97 857	88.2	11.8	51.3	17.1	279	10.7
Providence	22	29.4	46	0.8	5.8	807 987	17 477	56 116	15.1	32 137	76.5	23.5	32.0	6.0	162	8.3
Washington	25	0.0	67	2.6	9.4	974 894	14 593	81 846	25.9	70 301	84.7	15.3	36.9	10.8	264	8.1
SOUTH CAROLINA	4 889	0.9	189	132.4	2 151.2	540 200	2 858	64 977	2 352.7	90 953	33.9	66.1	23.4	7.0	67 253	29.8
Abbeville	91	-4.2	161	1.5	26.4	434 890	2 699	47 588	10.2	18 102	29.2	70.8	25.8	1.6	532	26.0
Aiken	159	10.4	132	3.2	62.2	473 766	3 586	52 149	102.8	85 237	10.1	89.9	22.6	6.7	1 497	21.8
Allendale	125	15.7	677	6.6	49.1	1 233 183	1 822	71 668	15.2	82 427	77.8	22.2	21.6	12.4	1 745	68.6
Anderson	173	-2.3	105	0.7	63.8	413 318	3 939	48 678	50.2	30 443	11.0	89.0	19.2	2.2	941	18.6
Bamberg	125	19.0	320	5.5	53.9	687 030	2 145	81 584	23.5	60 136	69.8	30.2	25.1	9.5	2 168	70.8
Barnwell	93	9.4	225	3.9	46.8	584 928	2 600	62 223	21.0	51 078	43.9	56.1	22.1	9.0	1 689	52.9
Beaufort	49	11.4	395	2.4	7.4	871 559	2 205	72 402	28.3	226 066	97.1	2.9	37.6	7.2	52	12.8
Berkeley	53	-7.0	168	0.6	11.3	577 404	3 439	52 482	D	D	D	D	14.3	2.5	203	19.1
Calhoun	111	16.8	324	10.0	60.9	793 325	2 448	108 715	46.4	136 080	64.7	35.3	29.3	12.3	3 540	47.8
Charleston	42	-12.5	126	1.3	11.3	870 286	6 929	66 426	24.0	72 413	72.9	27.1	24.4	6.9	45	6.6
Cherokee	63	-1.6	151	0.1	18.7	424 703	2 817	55 171	40.4	97 065	3.8	96.2	20.4	3.1	562	19.5
Chester	112	15.5	206	D	29.7	643 186	3 129	56 788	30.1	55 359	6.0	94.0	24.6	5.0	377	11.0
Chesterfield	141	9.3	166	1.1	47.2	392 060	2 364	52 307	80.2	94 563	11.4	88.6	19.2	6.5	1 068	41.0
Clarendon	155	4.7	315	2.8	104.5	623 510	1 978	92 095	82.0	167 021	46.1	53.9	33.0	15.3	2 383	62.1
Colleton	175	27.7	333	2.6	37.5	661 892	1 988	61 236	22.4	42 617	85.1	14.9	19.0	2.9	908	35.2
Darlington	173	7.5	468	4.1	115.4	825 008	1 764	158 230	75.1	203 499	41.7	58.3	41.7	20.3	4 481	56.6
Dillon	105	-6.3	473	1.1	84.5	953 258	2 017	140 889	77.1	347 198	33.6	66.4	47.3	24.3	3 882	66.7
Dorchester	65	12.1	172	1.8	37.4	575 269	3 336	82 312	32.2	85 322	45.0	55.0	26.8	10.3	1 506	31.0
Edgefield	77	4.1	188	5.0	25.8	573 544	3 047	68 039	46.7	114 691	82.8	17.2	23.6	5.9	744	27.5
Fairfield	52	-7.1	277	0.2	10.6	777 047	2 802	58 076	26.8	143 516	5.6	94.4	25.1	8.0	37	5.9
Florence	159	-7.0	235	2.5	111.6	606 692	2 580	77 178	33.8	50 043	89.6	10.4	31.4	8.7	3 189	53.3
Georgetown	58	5.5	229	0.7	17.6	624 429	2 730	53 717	23.5	93 135	88.8	11.2	17.9	8.7	518	54.0
Greenville	73	-16.1	66	1.8	26.7	373 917	5 662	40 844	19.3	17 520	85.4	14.6	14.3	2.0	132	4.9
Greenwood	71	-12.3	143	0.1	18.0	401 827	2 802	51 596	14.1	28 535	43.1	56.9	19.1	1.4	245	14.2
Hampton	127	-0.8	430	2.8	50.2	948 327	2 207	99 976	12.3	41 789	95.8	4.2	32.5	10.2	2 996	64.4
Horry	164	-12.8	179	1.3	97.3	619 386	3 460	77 868	65.9	72 046	65.9	34.1	29.3	10.7	2 240	47.4
Jasper	52	-34.2	478	D	8.6	974 585	2 038	76 466	D	D	D	D	22.0	2.8	100	33.0
Kershaw	86	22.9	171	1.4	23.3	522 010	3 046	62 870	169.5	339 629	2.8	97.2	22.4	10.6	681	28.1
Lancaster	65	-19.8	114	0.3	17.8	418 802	3 680	57 206	67.7	118 174	3.0	97.0	22.3	5.6	284	15.0
Laurens	130	-9.1	157	0.4	38.8	484 696	3 093	46 674	38.1	45 880	6.1	93.9	22.0	3.5	804	17.7
Lee	141	14.6	296	4.3	92.8	626 887	2 116	130 715	69.9	146 807	39.2	60.8	24.4	11.6	5 117	67.9
Lexington	90	-12.6	95	11.1	45.9	419 804	4 406	68 639	166.5	175 586	28.9	71.1	24.6	11.6	1 003	13.6
McCormick	25	8.7	316	D	7.1	800 706	2 537	51 638	D	D	D	0.0	17.7	3.8	175	25.3
Marion	70	-24.7	226	0.9	42.4	541 397	2 398	93 475	21.7	70 544	51.0	49.0	23.4	8.4	1 240	59.7
Marlboro	123	7.0	526	1.6	76.1	961 123	1 828	100 243	37.8	162 233	35.2	64.8	41.6	18.5	3 063	66.1
Newberry	101	-2.9	164	1.4	33.0	479 798	2 923	65 468	99.5	161 999	3.7	96.3	26.4	8.3	607	21.5
Oconee	71	-9.0	88	0.3	21.6	478 112	5 436	52 165	128.6	160 243	2.4	97.6	23.8	8.1	403	11.3
Orangeburg	288	5.1	287	23.6	157.2	647 310	2 256	88 391	149.7	149 446	42.2	57.8	28.9	11.5	5 880	51.1
Pickens	51	8.5	62	0.8	17.9	354 880	5 739	44 376	8.2	9 948	D	D	11.0	1.0	152	5.4
Richland	59	-6.3	162	1.4	23.5	514 598	3 185	63 279	10.2	27 924	66.3	33.7	21.7	5.5	483	10.7
Saluda	110	2.8	181	4.2	35.0	503 974	2 782	61 531	86.0	141 945	7.5	92.5	34.0	10.7	587	25.2
Spartanburg	110	-12.7	89	2.1	41.5	432 985	4 892	41 123	26.3	21 172	57.4	42.6	18.0	2.7	499	10.6

Table B. States and Counties — **Water Use, Wholesale Trade, Retail Trade, and Real Estate**

STATE County	Water use, 2005		Wholesale trade,[1] 2007				Retail trade,[2] 2007				Real estate and rental and leasing,[2] 2007			
	Total water withdrawn (mil gal/day)	Gallons withdrawn per person	Number of establishments	Number of employees	Sales (mil dol)	Annual payroll (mil dol)	Number of establishments	Number of employees	Sales (mil dol)	Annual payroll (mil dol)	Number of establishments	Number of employees	Receipts (mil dol)	Annual payroll (mil dol)
	133	134	135	136	137	138	139	140	141	142	143	144	145	146
PENNSYLVANIA—Cont'd														
Potter	20.1	1 125	8	44	19.0	0.9	77	611	138.4	13.3	9	D	D	D
Schuylkill	58.0	394	111	1 946	1 070.2	69.4	542	6 085	1 317.9	116.0	69	349	52.4	7.6
Snyder	218.1	5 708	33	462	191.2	17.9	197	2 774	566.3	51.9	16	72	8.6	1.8
Somerset	33.8	428	76	D	D	D	288	3 146	764.7	63.1	50	186	21.4	4.7
Sullivan	0.6	94	3	D	D	D	27	234	45.0	3.9	4	D	D	D
Susquehanna	4.2	99	40	385	215.8	11.1	153	1 399	403.6	27.2	17	D	D	D
Tioga	6.3	152	22	362	201.8	11.7	166	1 867	413.5	33.9	22	64	8.6	1.6
Union	6.2	143	29	D	D	D	136	1 658	372.1	32.7	26	158	23.1	4.2
Venango	8.5	151	48	D	D	D	219	2 754	594.2	51.7	27	111	9.8	2.0
Warren	14.5	346	23	D	D	D	156	2 468	485.3	70.4	17	67	8.5	1.5
Washington	806.6	3 908	226	3 427	2 454.7	182.4	688	9 027	2 283.2	192.3	150	1 109	214.6	42.2
Wayne	13.1	261	34	333	112.0	11.7	251	2 925	692.3	64.6	37	132	19.1	3.4
Westmoreland	39.8	108	353	7 050	5 390.5	288.0	1 350	18 320	4 154.7	368.1	255	1 118	178.8	29.9
Wyoming	11.5	407	16	397	95.2	17.2	113	1 156	288.6	22.9	9	28	1.9	0.3
York	2 596.5	6 352	371	6 539	3 822.9	299.4	1 344	21 762	4 942.7	455.6	285	2 158	294.5	75.5
RHODE ISLAND	405.2	376	1 277	18 128	9 182.8	914.9	4 080	50 865	12 286.5	1 215.4	1 233	6 493	1 462.8	227.2
Bristol	0.7	14	52	399	227.4	18.9	154	1 362	295.7	31.8	45	124	24.8	4.2
Kent	3.0	18	251	2 688	1 381.3	132.7	756	12 020	3 242.9	302.7	219	1 573	272.6	57.0
Newport	8.2	98	75	407	264.0	18.4	471	4 251	1 096.2	111.0	126	702	102.1	24.1
Providence	369.6	578	771	12 496	5 856.9	563.2	2 117	25 937	5 994.9	582.2	674	3 676	982.7	130.0
Washington	23.6	184	128	2 138	1 453.2	181.7	582	7 405	1 726.7	187.7	169	418	80.6	11.9
SOUTH CAROLINA	7 845.2	1 844	4 323	58 524	40 498.0	2 599.4	18 886	231 685	54 298.4	4 878.1	5 473	30 417	5 194.1	989.8
Abbeville	4.8	182	9	D	D	D	59	385	71.9	6.1	6	D	D	D
Aiken	209.5	1 395	75	D	D	D	548	7 076	1 599.8	133.8	141	529	92.9	11.6
Allendale	11.6	1 060	6	D	D	D	33	231	32.6	3.3	1	D	D	D
Anderson	163.6	932	183	D	D	D	755	8 901	2 004.7	178.1	140	502	97.1	14.2
Bamberg	5.5	348	7	D	D	D	57	506	102.8	10.6	3	D	D	D
Barnwell	4.1	173	3	D	D	D	85	859	169.1	15.5	13	D	D	D
Beaufort	30.9	224	113	607	298.2	30.7	831	9 776	2 255.1	219.3	458	3 902	452.0	146.7
Berkeley	589.3	3 885	127	2 367	1 766.5	109.9	417	6 328	1 552.3	136.7	145	913	147.3	27.9
Calhoun	75.8	5 022	9	146	144.5	4.9	44	292	66.8	4.1	8	35	7.6	1.0
Charleston	114.7	347	456	6 015	3 267.4	292.6	2 075	27 439	6 321.0	628.8	781	3 982	734.2	133.9
Cherokee	11.7	217	23	D	D	D	249	2 817	718.1	50.5	38	134	19.3	2.5
Chester	5.8	173	13	D	D	D	103	902	210.9	16.0	19	D	D	D
Chesterfield	8.8	202	30	377	150.3	11.9	163	1 354	298.1	26.0	22	70	8.4	1.7
Clarendon	4.7	140	17	191	54.8	5.8	130	1 399	296.4	24.0	14	41	5.9	1.2
Colleton	11.2	284	26	D	D	D	181	1 858	419.7	35.6	55	184	32.6	4.5
Darlington	792.1	11 762	59	426	226.1	15.7	251	2 548	527.5	45.6	31	129	78.6	3.4
Dillon	5.5	179	18	511	300.1	17.6	136	1 331	381.7	22.1	20	55	7.1	1.0
Dorchester	9.8	87	66	467	170.2	19.3	303	4 078	879.5	75.8	118	317	54.4	8.0
Edgefield	6.0	235	10	D	D	D	65	444	120.3	8.7	8	33	2.2	0.6
Fairfield	1 539.2	64 010	10	D	D	D	65	652	216.2	12.6	15	32	4.7	0.8
Florence	43.6	332	162	2 645	1 358.7	102.6	776	9 415	2 237.9	187.5	139	686	104.0	17.8
Georgetown	68.4	1 122	34	D	D	D	331	3 181	702.2	67.4	124	424	60.0	13.1
Greenville	70.3	173	735	10 557	11 581.9	554.2	1 836	25 425	6 036.6	561.9	618	3 268	752.1	121.6
Greenwood	14.6	214	46	476	271.2	17.7	301	3 710	774.3	74.2	64	189	26.3	5.0
Hampton	7.7	362	9	144	92.0	7.4	105	759	150.7	12.7	10	123	3.8	3.1
Horry	171.2	754	256	2 237	907.6	82.2	1 810	21 072	4 967.2	459.4	708	5 839	829.9	187.4
Jasper	22.8	1 067	30	342	145.1	13.4	104	1 489	400.8	38.0	23	73	14.1	3.4
Kershaw	11.7	206	22	D	D	D	199	2 472	577.7	45.4	42	96	13.2	2.5
Lancaster	28.6	453	40	D	D	D	236	2 447	587.9	48.7	39	D	D	D
Laurens	9.7	138	33	225	67.0	9.4	191	1 585	370.1	29.2	31	75	9.4	1.7
Lee	3.6	175	14	98	49.6	3.2	49	416	154.6	6.9	7	18	3.7	0.5
Lexington	220.9	939	289	6 123	3 588.4	280.6	1 057	15 882	3 666.1	330.3	249	1 180	218.4	33.2
McCormick	1.9	192	1	D	D	D	30	144	34.8	2.3	6	D	D	D
Marion	4.7	134	21	144	104.4	4.7	143	1 316	269.9	25.6	15	69	6.4	1.5
Marlboro	25.2	899	14	D	D	D	99	824	159.0	13.1	16	42	3.9	0.6
Newberry	8.9	240	28	D	D	D	155	1 543	369.9	30.4	24	82	20.6	2.2
Oconee	2 607.0	37 470	43	D	D	D	281	3 107	743.5	67.0	86	253	40.0	7.7
Orangeburg	30.8	335	68	801	405.7	25.0	419	4 494	1 007.0	85.1	55	226	24.6	5.4
Pickens	26.3	231	69	588	253.2	23.4	359	4 451	1 153.5	99.3	86	337	60.5	9.1
Richland	543.4	1 598	372	6 129	3 150.7	274.8	1 376	19 518	4 367.7	420.7	467	3 828	845.8	134.4
Saluda	3.6	189	8	D	D	D	49	323	73.4	6.1	5	8	0.6	0.1
Spartanburg	100.7	377	440	6 437	5 482.0	278.5	1 089	13 937	3 638.4	309.0	279	1 279	220.8	45.1

1. Merchant wholesalers, except manufacturers' sales branches and offices.   2. Employer establishments.

Table B. States and Counties — Professional Services, Manufacturing, and Accommodation and Food Services

STATE County	Professional, scientific, and technical services,[1] 2007				Manufacturing, 2007				Accommodation and food services, 2007			
	Number of establishments	Number of employees	Receipts (mil dol)	Annual payroll (mil dol)	Number of establishments	Number of employees	Receipts (mil dol)	Annual payroll (mil dol)	Number of establishments	Number of employees	Sales (mil dol)	Annual payroll (mil dol)
	147	148	149	150	151	152	153	154	155	156	157	158
PENNSYLVANIA—Cont'd												
Potter	27	139	19.5	9.9	24	847	205.9	27.4	44	237	10.6	2.3
Schuylkill	156	D	D	D	199	10 211	3 043.4	397.8	283	2 971	135.8	34.2
Snyder	46	232	20.6	8.3	70	5 014	D	175.0	85	1 423	54.0	15.6
Somerset	99	D	D	D	131	3 933	955.5	146.0	167	2 204	81.4	22.4
Sullivan	9	D	D	D	NA	NA	NA	NA	25	120	6.8	1.4
Susquehanna	51	243	17.2	5.0	68	785	115.7	24.8	84	691	32.1	7.8
Tioga	52	251	20.1	8.4	43	2 220	463.1	75.2	99	1 048	40.0	9.8
Union	78	334	27.5	9.6	37	2 086	D	78.8	95	2 094	80.2	23.4
Venango	63	D	D	D	88	4 097	1 113.0	187.8	105	1 407	44.3	12.6
Warren	52	D	D	D	67	2 932	D	129.5	85	870	35.0	8.8
Washington	401	D	D	D	263	9 565	3 672.9	430.6	384	6 106	233.7	64.3
Wayne	105	D	D	D	66	727	115.0	24.7	172	2 482	187.8	54.9
Westmoreland	751	D	D	D	603	21 064	7 077.0	907.1	762	12 797	454.3	129.6
Wyoming	41	D	D	D	30	2 737	D	71.9	60	571	22.3	6.1
York	726	5 437	620.4	240.9	600	38 016	11 957.4	1 669.8	736	13 112	527.9	146.4
RHODE ISLAND	3 096	22 732	2 777.8	1 173.9	1 831	53 718	12 061.5	2 374.8	2 926	44 426	2 148.7	622.1
Bristol	119	D	D	D	105	2 573	496.5	106.2	126	1 694	68.3	19.2
Kent	521	2 701	336.1	123.1	284	11 531	3 039.1	562.5	459	8 862	398.6	116.0
Newport	321	D	D	D	86	2 796	346.1	181.9	366	5 148	343.0	103.6
Providence	1 780	D	D	D	1 195	29 601	6 422.9	1 177.0	1 527	23 350	1 065.9	303.8
Washington	355	1 442	208.5	75.4	161	7 217	1 757.0	347.3	448	5 372	272.8	79.5
SOUTH CAROLINA	9 459	74 372	9 343.3	3 622.6	4 335	242 153	93 977.5	10 061.5	9 291	182 899	8 383.5	2 311.0
Abbeville	14	D	D	D	31	2 098	657.5	67.3	32	329	11.0	2.9
Aiken	236	D	D	D	96	7 853	3 959.3	375.4	238	4 608	172.9	46.1
Allendale	10	39	4.7	1.6	7	920	385.4	33.0	8	86	2.9	0.6
Anderson	288	D	D	D	222	12 655	4 886.3	495.2	350	6 420	235.8	64.5
Bamberg	19	45	4.7	1.1	22	913	D	28.0	21	286	9.4	2.5
Barnwell	24	157	16.0	4.8	21	2 635	681.3	85.3	28	471	14.7	3.8
Beaufort	563	D	D	D	90	1 092	223.4	35.8	458	9 686	530.5	174.2
Berkeley	206	D	D	D	98	5 794	5 527.3	322.0	208	3 935	161.2	42.2
Calhoun	12	52	4.8	1.3	17	1 057	D	D	9	113	4.1	1.0
Charleston	1 449	D	D	D	302	10 706	5 338.1	479.6	1 045	24 504	1 382.7	377.1
Cherokee	51	D	D	D	62	6 205	2 484.9	208.7	97	1 833	68.2	18.2
Chester	28	D	D	D	51	3 002	1 407.5	132.6	42	616	25.2	6.5
Chesterfield	25	77	7.3	1.8	54	4 663	1 361.0	166.1	76	803	30.5	7.5
Clarendon	22	122	15.9	8.2	18	1 147	291.4	37.0	66	778	29.8	7.2
Colleton	53	250	26.4	7.4	32	1 583	245.2	48.8	71	1 146	56.0	12.1
Darlington	67	D	D	D	66	4 742	2 433.4	212.9	88	1 230	53.9	13.7
Dillon	21	76	5.5	1.5	24	2 687	432.6	65.3	58	867	31.6	8.3
Dorchester	166	D	D	D	93	5 543	2 361.4	240.2	153	2 811	104.0	29.3
Edgefield	15	D	D	D	20	1 112	343.9	37.7	25	262	7.9	2.3
Fairfield	25	70	5.3	2.1	16	D	263.2	42.4	22	261	8.9	2.4
Florence	220	D	D	D	116	7 150	2 885.4	333.4	286	5 943	250.0	68.0
Georgetown	189	D	D	D	47	2 206	1 046.2	116.7	169	2 982	136.6	40.5
Greenville	1 441	13 561	2 034.0	790.8	605	29 758	10 821.4	1 244.5	1 005	19 205	817.8	232.7
Greenwood	118	D	D	D	71	7 950	2 821.1	342.0	124	2 484	86.1	24.2
Hampton	21	D	D	D	15	878	280.3	36.9	43	459	17.6	4.3
Horry	660	D	D	D	168	4 103	894.8	166.8	1 178	25 931	1 483.8	396.2
Jasper	26	D	D	D	23	515	76.4	16.2	56	679	32.4	8.1
Kershaw	90	472	41.7	14.1	68	3 696	1 419.1	161.8	95	1 386	52.2	13.6
Lancaster	73	457	58.8	20.2	68	2 473	1 247.6	103.7	93	1 331	56.3	12.9
Laurens	35	181	11.1	6.4	95	5 523	1 562.3	201.4	80	1 512	53.7	13.2
Lee	9	52	3.4	1.7	NA	NA	NA	NA	19	284	10.7	2.5
Lexington	551	D	D	D	219	9 772	3 465.7	404.4	489	10 726	434.5	123.1
McCormick	6	D	D	D	NA	NA	NA	NA	13	73	2.0	0.6
Marion	28	73	5.9	2.1	29	1 846	367.7	58.0	46	859	31.2	7.8
Marlboro	14	D	D	D	24	2 808	989.8	95.9	31	336	13.4	3.2
Newberry	41	138	11.2	4.7	46	4 931	1 277.5	159.0	61	827	30.4	7.3
Oconee	129	D	D	D	79	4 971	1 546.4	219.7	113	1 581	62.8	15.8
Orangeburg	95	D	D	D	83	6 962	2 597.9	284.9	177	3 686	152.2	36.8
Pickens	135	791	102.7	28.7	125	5 999	1 460.0	226.2	219	3 727	142.9	36.5
Richland	1 207	D	D	D	248	13 434	6 109.8	625.7	779	16 632	733.6	210.8
Saluda	12	43	2.1	1.0	NA	NA	NA	NA	17	95	4.3	1.1
Spartanburg	467	D	D	D	462	26 108	11 731.8	1 204.9	528	10 002	411.5	113.6

1. Establishment subject to federal tax.

Table B. States and Counties — Health Care and Social Assistance, Other Services, and Federal Funds

STATE County	Health care and social assistance, 2007				Other services, 2007				Federal funds and grants, 2009–2010 Expenditures (mil dol)			
										Direct payments for individuals[1]		
	Number of establishments	Number of employees	Receipts (mil dol)	Annual payroll (mil dol)	Number of establishments	Number of employees	Receipts (mil dol)	Annual payroll (mil dol)	Total	Social Security and government retirement	Medicare	Food Stamps and Supplemental Security Income
	159	160	161	162	163	164	165	166	167	168	169	170
PENNSYLVANIA—Cont'd												
Potter	42	959	78.9	36.6	25	112	7.9	1.8	156.0	65.8	38.0	7.2
Schuylkill	329	8 127	582.5	249.2	257	1 183	88.5	22.8	1 338.9	561.7	446.3	39.0
Snyder	71	873	91.6	31.2	68	299	24.2	5.7	234.0	114.8	63.6	6.6
Somerset	190	3 365	255.4	98.5	154	653	44.4	10.6	747.8	282.4	222.0	27.2
Sullivan	16	D	D	D	14	36	2.8	0.5	70.9	28.2	15.5	1.3
Susquehanna	58	1 150	66.1	30.2	71	276	20.3	4.6	303.7	144.9	80.7	12.7
Tioga	102	1 718	120.4	48.4	61	237	17.5	3.5	356.3	153.1	87.0	13.9
Union	127	3 445	295.0	119.2	61	263	20.9	4.1	376.8	124.0	58.4	5.8
Venango	175	3 506	275.1	106.9	118	568	47.7	11.9	504.0	210.9	153.4	26.4
Warren	111	2 982	206.3	94.5	83	528	24.5	6.4	388.3	155.4	99.1	13.9
Washington	667	11 459	1 051.3	428.0	408	2 500	208.2	64.5	1 986.3	814.7	665.6	74.6
Wayne	121	2 206	164.1	62.8	115	734	49.3	15.0	467.8	249.7	108.4	13.4
Westmoreland	1 208	18 721	1 494.6	612.9	838	4 651	586.3	92.4	3 355.8	1 380.8	1 135.4	110.8
Wyoming	70	1 134	74.3	31.2	52	207	17.3	4.3	206.9	102.2	55.5	9.1
York	925	20 265	1 931.3	790.7	746	5 098	582.7	115.6	3 882.1	1 330.7	554.7	77.2
RHODE ISLAND	3 274	81 947	7 161.4	3 091.6	2 382	14 379	1 449.0	373.1	11 759.4	3 139.9	1 988.8	430.8
Bristol	125	2 477	122.6	61.2	109	508	38.2	10.9	410.0	161.1	91.9	14.6
Kent	560	11 848	1 044.5	404.2	404	2 163	261.2	52.9	1 424.9	587.1	333.1	56.5
Newport	248	4 372	328.4	140.2	205	1 192	111.3	33.0	1 694.4	332.7	138.5	27.0
Providence	1 929	55 833	5 104.0	2 241.1	1 377	9 041	908.3	243.3	6 553.7	1 648.0	1 246.2	298.6
Washington	412	7 417	562.0	244.9	287	1 475	130.0	32.9	986.9	410.8	179.0	34.0
SOUTH CAROLINA	9 291	200 216	20 408.6	7 761.4	7 088	45 520	3 901.6	1 127.5	46 578.1	15 285.1	5 203.7	1 896.8
Abbeville	31	662	51.4	20.1	26	67	5.4	1.1	168.9	79.0	27.5	11.7
Aiken	294	5 266	409.6	149.4	199	1 171	94.2	22.0	3 494.6	597.9	199.1	60.8
Allendale	14	D	D	D	12	D	D	D	118.3	27.1	19.2	15.1
Anderson	362	8 112	786.0	301.2	244	1 871	154.5	55.0	1 233.9	629.3	227.6	51.1
Bamberg	38	731	60.2	24.8	24	D	D	D	178.7	48.4	29.8	14.9
Barnwell	45	588	41.2	17.5	26	100	10.4	2.4	218.5	73.6	41.3	20.3
Beaufort	386	6 365	642.3	230.6	308	3 068	238.0	84.7	1 968.8	700.8	146.8	38.9
Berkeley	189	1 837	109.4	42.3	168	880	63.2	18.6	1 787.3	464.3	96.8	56.0
Calhoun	25	D	D	D	14	59	4.4	1.0	98.5	38.7	14.2	8.6
Charleston	1 172	27 107	3 473.9	1 178.0	808	5 844	526.7	158.5	5 819.0	1 300.4	469.9	163.2
Cherokee	81	1 272	123.5	43.5	76	324	31.3	6.6	338.5	163.9	65.7	21.3
Chester	47	D	D	D	37	112	8.0	2.2	257.1	113.1	57.0	21.9
Chesterfield	71	1 480	110.1	45.2	51	169	12.7	3.6	366.3	131.7	60.5	27.6
Clarendon	48	D	D	D	36	163	11.2	3.4	334.5	120.7	50.0	30.7
Colleton	69	1 254	116.6	43.1	45	155	12.7	3.1	373.8	146.5	75.1	30.0
Darlington	91	2 494	206.3	84.5	85	353	28.5	7.1	548.4	209.4	96.0	46.8
Dillon	40	1 072	90.3	34.8	40	94	8.1	1.8	292.7	86.3	57.6	29.9
Dorchester	197	2 586	233.9	88.1	183	831	62.9	19.0	735.5	439.5	94.0	37.1
Edgefield	23	513	24.6	10.7	23	88	10.8	2.4	180.6	55.5	23.8	11.3
Fairfield	38	748	44.5	20.1	13	47	4.2	1.0	191.1	77.9	36.7	17.5
Florence	346	11 564	1 326.6	490.1	206	1 439	126.8	33.5	1 192.9	452.3	203.5	91.0
Georgetown	203	2 044	196.3	80.6	118	628	41.3	12.4	595.2	306.0	116.7	32.6
Greenville	1 015	23 581	2 447.5	997.9	750	5 475	472.2	148.4	2 980.6	1 307.3	474.3	126.3
Greenwood	146	4 589	530.7	197.4	88	619	39.9	10.0	522.9	251.9	84.5	28.4
Hampton	33	486	35.2	14.8	28	134	8.6	2.1	237.4	71.6	36.8	16.9
Horry	611	9 079	976.0	358.7	512	3 110	265.6	65.3	1 722.0	1 023.9	245.0	78.9
Jasper	40	679	58.0	22.5	36	139	10.6	3.0	154.8	52.9	24.0	12.3
Kershaw	93	1 990	179.3	74.3	92	374	26.1	7.0	418.8	229.6	71.7	19.4
Lancaster	114	D	D	D	104	434	55.0	13.9	436.4	212.5	86.5	28.2
Laurens	88	2 025	149.6	58.9	58	416	22.2	9.5	478.7	220.3	81.3	32.4
Lee	32	406	17.5	7.9	17	87	6.0	1.3	171.2	53.8	27.9	21.0
Lexington	498	10 985	869.5	379.9	487	2 989	252.0	79.3	1 540.0	781.4	202.0	54.8
McCormick	7	D	D	D	6	D	D	D	117.7	55.6	12.4	5.1
Marion	72	D	D	D	37	139	9.5	2.5	462.6	111.5	75.6	32.3
Marlboro	51	942	68.5	28.0	20	67	4.1	1.1	311.8	93.4	55.9	22.6
Newberry	55	1 125	84.0	32.3	60	281	21.9	6.3	305.9	137.5	53.9	18.0
Oconee	144	2 853	264.3	105.4	99	613	40.1	11.7	526.8	300.9	97.7	19.6
Orangeburg	225	3 525	326.0	128.6	134	606	44.5	13.3	932.4	308.8	140.0	78.0
Pickens	195	3 134	291.7	105.9	144	767	108.9	18.6	830.3	389.4	120.1	29.9
Richland	919	24 686	2 939.7	1 122.2	701	5 188	511.3	144.2	6 622.7	1 142.5	354.1	147.5
Saluda	23	D	D	D	20	54	5.3	0.9	122.9	47.6	18.1	10.3
Spartanburg	510	13 349	1 287.4	520.8	433	2 920	283.9	69.8	1 826.7	951.9	320.5	93.8

1. State totals may include programs not allocated by county.

Federal Funds, Residential Construction, and Local Government Finances

STATE County	Salaries and wages	Defense	Other	Medicaid and other health-related	Nutrition and family welfare	Education	Other	New construction ($1,000)	Number of housing units	Total (mil dol)	Inter-governmental (mil dol)	Total (mil dol)	Total	Property
	171	172	173	174	175	176	177	178	179	180	181	182	183	184
PENNSYLVANIA—Cont'd														
Potter	4.1	0.6	1.0	25.6	3.8	0.7	7.7	3 555	30	59.2	28.4	21.1	1 243	1 045
Schuylkill	68.6	1.5	11.3	146.9	26.2	3.3	9.4	30 597	188	487.1	237.9	148.6	1 009	738
Snyder	8.4	0.5	2.2	24.6	5.1	1.0	1.8	16 381	89	92.5	35.1	41.8	1 096	749
Somerset	25.0	33.0	26.5	102.3	16.7	2.2	5.0	18 366	112	210.7	109.0	69.2	889	710
Sullivan	2.1	0.0	14.4	7.2	1.2	0.2	0.3	3 413	24	25.5	10.9	10.5	1 691	1 501
Susquehanna	13.7	0.2	2.7	34.8	8.1	1.2	2.0	13 193	73	132.7	70.7	49.3	1 200	1 091
Tioga	18.4	0.7	3.8	50.8	11.2	1.9	4.4	14 153	99	128.5	69.6	45.1	1 109	897
Union	123.8	0.9	20.5	21.6	10.8	0.8	5.4	17 578	91	130.0	65.4	39.8	910	633
Venango	12.8	0.6	2.7	74.1	12.5	2.0	4.9	9 429	68	192.2	105.2	56.3	1 028	831
Warren	14.2	46.3	10.4	35.2	8.2	1.4	1.4	4 287	32	118.4	61.9	43.1	1 052	821
Washington	63.6	16.9	15.9	233.6	38.9	5.9	18.9	93 497	471	726.5	346.0	248.0	1 206	952
Wayne	36.9	0.2	9.7	32.1	8.9	1.3	5.6	33 370	196	169.3	51.0	97.7	1 890	1 783
Westmoreland	102.1	46.5	27.6	343.9	73.3	8.5	84.3	98 848	560	1 224.2	534.1	467.5	1 290	1 050
Wyoming	6.2	1.8	1.4	21.2	5.5	0.6	1.8	9 192	63	90.1	44.9	38.0	1 364	1 152
York	216.5	1 323.7	41.4	211.8	48.0	7.3	31.6	165 330	1 059	1 629.2	579.2	662.4	1 573	1 241
RHODE ISLAND	996.8	776.9	224.5	1 752.5	292.4	269.5	837.6	155 073	934	X	X	X	X	X
Bristol	31.3	2.6	2.5	41.1	7.8	3.5	45.4	8 897	40	185.5	43.7	124.1	2 479	2 435
Kent	145.5	10.5	22.7	133.7	27.8	16.4	37.5	24 129	216	568.3	142.9	357.9	2 122	2 051
Newport	359.5	682.4	23.2	80.2	17.6	8.0	10.4	23 991	93	326.7	90.6	190.3	2 299	2 138
Providence	375.3	53.4	148.4	1 405.3	198.7	234.7	664.1	41 804	297	2 177.8	878.6	1 009.4	1 604	1 566
Washington	85.1	28.0	27.6	91.7	19.1	6.9	72.6	56 251	288	515.3	119.5	338.2	2 665	2 615
SOUTH CAROLINA	4 617.9	4 496.7	3 674.6	4 833.3	853.8	667.4	1 855.9	2 489 139	14 021	X	X	X	X	X
Abbeville	6.1	0.0	1.1	34.6	4.0	2.0	0.8	2 618	19	53.0	25.7	20.2	795	713
Aiken	82.5	6.5	2 325.8	145.8	21.1	10.3	12.1	146 541	697	380.4	163.8	139.7	917	767
Allendale	4.0	0.0	0.5	42.2	3.5	1.4	1.6	174	1	43.7	16.8	12.1	1 153	958
Anderson	86.7	14.6	6.6	132.5	19.3	15.9	25.4	58 869	420	424.3	186.7	168.4	936	819
Bamberg	6.0	0.0	9.4	40.1	4.7	8.6	4.5	1 129	9	39.2	22.2	13.2	857	741
Barnwell	6.4	0.0	0.9	52.2	4.9	2.6	7.9	2 433	15	75.6	46.3	20.8	906	715
Beaufort	200.3	742.3	5.6	69.7	19.2	8.3	12.3	92 080	244	661.2	72.8	303.2	2 058	1 726
Berkeley	95.4	895.7	6.7	79.4	20.3	15.7	11.3	213 346	1 176	362.8	163.8	133.8	818	731
Calhoun	1.9	0.0	0.4	23.7	3.0	1.2	1.8	5 643	32	31.9	14.2	13.8	937	897
Charleston	797.7	1 578.6	713.8	545.4	49.3	24.2	110.2	270 184	1 361	1 355.3	335.2	644.7	1 880	1 389
Cherokee	14.7	0.0	2.2	49.1	7.5	4.6	1.0	8 780	91	145.4	61.9	47.9	887	717
Chester	9.2	0.0	1.2	40.9	6.5	3.5	2.3	4 688	32	123.5	39.8	32.3	992	842
Chesterfield	10.6	0.1	1.6	99.5	11.1	3.7	12.1	5 715	42	121.2	54.2	33.1	773	549
Clarendon	12.5	1.2	4.6	90.9	8.0	3.0	1.3	7 224	70	138.9	44.1	26.3	802	701
Colleton	15.3	0.5	3.3	78.2	10.7	3.5	5.2	11 997	11	98.5	42.3	40.7	1 047	968
Darlington	23.2	0.1	1.7	126.8	14.5	7.1	7.0	18 312	168	162.8	76.3	58.9	881	723
Dillon	7.4	0.1	1.0	84.9	8.0	3.6	4.1	1 525	15	71.5	44.0	18.4	598	396
Dorchester	27.8	17.9	4.3	82.6	12.3	5.4	1.0	122 032	523	289.3	125.9	115.9	938	794
Edgefield	35.7	0.0	6.8	33.2	3.9	2.0	1.3	7 636	40	50.9	27.1	19.6	773	721
Fairfield	5.4	0.0	1.1	39.8	4.9	3.0	1.9	3 640	32	77.5	27.6	42.7	1 832	1 720
Florence	68.1	5.1	15.0	241.7	28.9	14.0	21.1	35 190	308	379.9	174.4	126.8	961	742
Georgetown	31.2	12.7	2.1	67.2	11.1	4.6	4.6	29 696	140	206.5	57.5	110.3	1 823	1 565
Greenville	193.0	303.4	30.1	258.8	53.2	30.0	58.9	277 069	1 304	2 045.9	401.8	436.9	1 020	860
Greenwood	22.8	0.0	2.4	67.2	23.9	7.7	6.7	6 532	50	412.2	79.0	67.3	985	904
Hampton	39.1	0.4	7.0	52.8	5.4	2.1	0.6	2 341	14	59.4	31.6	22.6	1 064	849
Horry	64.1	6.7	8.1	151.2	30.3	14.0	29.6	224 299	1 508	984.4	221.7	404.4	1 618	1 288
Jasper	3.6	11.8	2.0	40.5	4.2	1.9	0.6	33 986	168	66.3	23.8	30.3	1 378	1 095
Kershaw	15.4	0.6	2.1	61.1	7.6	5.6	1.1	31 237	252	207.0	94.4	47.8	821	676
Lancaster	17.7	0.4	6.5	59.3	9.5	6.7	4.1	17 060	120	175.3	75.3	56.8	774	635
Laurens	36.3	0.0	2.0	69.4	8.9	4.6	15.5	9 561	79	180.1	61.5	44.6	640	548
Lee	2.3	0.0	0.4	50.9	5.3	2.1	0.5	1 304	11	44.5	24.3	15.1	758	634
Lexington	75.2	33.3	14.6	93.2	22.5	180.2	55.3	227 687	1 318	1 143.7	299.0	308.1	1 267	1 118
McCormick	5.7	14.0	0.7	21.0	1.8	0.7	0.3	5 089	24	20.5	7.3	9.8	973	906
Marion	35.8	89.6	1.3	87.7	8.5	3.5	7.4	2 214	20	88.5	48.6	24.2	714	592
Marlboro	26.4	5.8	4.9	84.7	7.7	2.9	0.8	895	6	67.3	41.4	16.0	554	482
Newberry	26.6	0.2	2.6	49.8	5.3	2.9	2.6	20 114	69	105.5	43.9	39.1	1 039	946
Oconee	17.6	0.4	3.7	57.8	7.6	5.1	10.6	61 684	186	189.5	66.8	95.4	1 348	1 274
Orangeburg	38.0	6.3	3.6	196.7	26.6	27.4	50.1	12 284	79	389.8	104.1	96.8	1 076	873
Pickens	40.8	34.9	4.6	69.3	11.3	7.3	104.2	47 788	159	235.2	98.6	87.6	755	669
Richland	1 907.3	523.7	359.6	480.8	193.6	109.0	1 166.4	132 430	1 274	984.0	339.5	464.6	1 299	1 124
Saluda	7.3	0.0	0.5	27.0	2.9	2.2	0.4	6 119	34	34.3	16.1	13.1	701	638
Spartanburg	85.6	4.8	10.7	239.6	37.1	19.4	22.2	70 033	562	1 277.3	308.7	290.4	1 054	930

1. State totals may include programs not allocated by county. 2. Based on the resident population estimated as of July 1 of the year shown.

Table B. States and Counties — Local Government Finances, Government Employment, and Voting

STATE County	Local government finances, 2007 (cont.)									Government employment, 2009			Presidential election,[2] 2008		
	Direct general expenditure							Debt outstanding					Percent of vote cast:		
	Total (mil dol)	Per capita[1] (dollars)	Education	Health and hospitals	Police protection	Public welfare	Highways	Total (mil dol)	Per capita[1] (dollars)	Federal civilian	Federal military	State and local	Democratic	Republican	All other
	185	186	187	188	189	190	191	192	193	194	195	196	197	198	199
PENNSYLVANIA—Cont'd															
Potter	56.0	3 295	58.4	0.1	1.4	0.6	9.3	90.4	5 321	57	44	1 087	30.6	68.1	1.3
Schuylkill	504.0	3 422	50.6	4.7	2.0	6.5	4.9	441.8	3 000	661	387	7 295	44.9	53.5	1.6
Snyder	87.6	2 299	58.7	0.0	5.1	2.9	5.8	140.5	3 688	97	102	2 339	34.8	64.0	1.3
Somerset	208.2	2 673	61.1	0.4	1.8	5.5	5.4	345.2	4 434	226	203	4 462	36.6	61.7	1.7
Sullivan	24.5	3 956	45.9	0.4	0.7	3.3	9.3	27.1	4 370	26	16	395	39.5	59.0	1.5
Susquehanna	125.1	3 043	74.0	0.6	0.4	1.9	6.6	80.7	1 962	126	107	1 993	43.5	55.1	1.4
Tioga	119.2	2 931	58.9	0.0	1.0	13.3	5.5	178.1	4 378	171	109	3 186	35.5	63.0	1.5
Union	148.5	3 397	69.8	0.5	1.4	3.2	3.9	126.2	2 887	1 470	118	1 545	42.1	56.7	1.2
Venango	202.6	3 700	57.6	0.0	2.2	10.6	3.5	237.8	4 342	123	143	3 529	39.6	58.9	1.5
Warren	102.1	2 492	58.6	0.4	2.3	2.2	9.8	75.0	1 830	185	108	2 093	46.1	52.3	1.6
Washington	719.2	3 499	51.8	4.4	2.5	10.9	4.8	822.2	4 000	560	569	9 985	47.0	51.8	1.2
Wayne	157.7	3 049	74.2	0.0	0.9	0.0	4.6	257.6	4 982	491	135	2 688	43.3	55.6	1.1
Westmoreland	1 207.4	3 332	54.9	0.1	2.5	9.8	3.4	1 763.3	4 867	1 031	956	15 822	41.1	57.8	1.1
Wyoming	85.6	3 077	58.2	0.1	4.6	6.7	8.8	51.6	1 855	79	73	1 213	45.6	53.2	1.3
York	1 595.0	3 788	45.1	4.3	2.9	10.1	2.6	2 349.1	5 579	4 680	1 601	16 935	42.7	56.3	1.1
RHODE ISLAND	X	X	X	X	X	X	X	X	X	10 299	7 244	55 746	63.3	35.0	1.7
Bristol	182.9	3 653	65.9	0.1	4.4	0.1	4.2	146.5	2 926	101	231	1 910	62.6	35.9	1.5
Kent	570.6	3 383	57.1	0.3	8.1	0.5	2.3	416.9	2 472	855	750	7 556	57.7	40.5	1.8
Newport	312.6	3 776	54.5	0.1	8.7	0.5	2.8	164.3	1 985	4 397	2 795	3 402	60.9	37.6	1.6
Providence	2 190.3	3 480	51.8	0.2	7.2	0.1	2.1	1 393.9	2 215	4 327	2 865	31 008	66.9	31.5	1.6
Washington	505.4	3 983	67.5	0.4	5.6	0.4	4.6	218.7	1 723	619	603	11 870	59.0	39.2	1.8
SOUTH CAROLINA	X	X	X	X	X	X	X	X	X	31 420	55 710	313 948	44.9	53.9	1.2
Abbeville	48.5	1 904	64.6	2.1	5.0	0.0	2.9	23.8	935	47	109	1 482	41.8	56.9	1.3
Aiken	372.9	2 448	55.3	1.4	5.8	0.1	2.5	188.9	1 240	790	680	7 304	37.4	61.4	1.2
Allendale	43.2	4 126	47.0	28.8	4.0	0.0	1.0	27.2	2 596	23	44	1 209	75.3	23.5	1.2
Anderson	416.3	2 313	65.6	1.5	6.3	0.0	2.4	418.4	2 325	353	808	11 404	32.7	66.0	1.3
Bamberg	39.8	2 574	65.6	1.3	4.9	0.0	1.6	14.3	929	34	65	1 250	65.0	33.9	1.2
Barnwell	70.1	3 050	58.9	1.1	5.0	0.1	1.1	51.3	2 234	53	99	1 604	50.3	48.7	1.0
Beaufort	610.6	4 145	36.1	17.6	5.4	0.2	3.5	1 360.5	9 235	2 329	10 665	7 446	44.1	54.9	0.9
Berkeley	432.0	2 640	66.9	0.4	4.4	0.2	1.3	1 187.6	7 258	773	754	7 688	42.8	55.9	1.3
Calhoun	32.5	2 201	63.0	3.3	6.2	1.7	0.9	86.8	5 873	31	64	824	51.3	47.8	0.9
Charleston	1 276.1	3 721	36.1	1.3	8.0	0.4	4.0	3 078.9	8 977	7 685	11 397	35 383	53.5	45.2	1.2
Cherokee	131.6	2 437	69.3	1.6	4.4	0.3	1.6	1 300.2	24 238	97	238	2 195	34.7	64.1	1.2
Chester	115.1	3 538	49.3	29.3	3.6	0.0	0.6	72.1	2 216	70	141	1 688	53.5	45.2	1.3
Chesterfield	111.3	2 603	68.9	0.0	7.3	0.0	2.4	127.2	2 975	95	187	2 036	47.9	50.9	1.2
Clarendon	134.5	4 098	36.9	40.4	4.2	0.0	3.7	83.2	2 534	69	144	2 343	55.8	43.5	0.8
Colleton	105.3	2 705	59.2	1.0	8.7	0.0	3.6	241.5	6 209	117	171	2 202	49.7	49.2	1.0
Darlington	163.1	2 441	68.1	1.9	5.3	0.2	2.0	115.7	1 731	150	289	3 140	49.4	49.6	1.0
Dillon	77.6	2 527	64.3	1.5	5.9	0.2	3.6	55.6	1 811	86	135	1 617	55.2	43.8	1.0
Dorchester	309.3	2 504	72.0	0.1	4.8	0.0	1.3	499.8	4 047	212	565	5 819	41.6	57.1	1.3
Edgefield	48.8	1 919	71.5	2.5	7.6	0.0	1.2	10.2	402	411	112	1 279	44.1	55.0	1.0
Fairfield	75.0	3 213	59.5	4.8	5.9	0.1	1.5	18.6	797	44	102	1 601	65.3	33.7	1.0
Florence	357.4	2 710	58.3	9.3	6.0	0.2	2.3	265.6	2 014	669	585	12 601	48.0	51.2	0.9
Georgetown	192.7	3 185	53.2	1.9	4.7	0.1	1.9	349.9	5 783	134	305	4 857	46.9	52.1	1.0
Greenville	2 189.8	5 113	32.9	38.4	2.9	0.0	2.3	3 759.6	8 779	1 752	2 006	28 011	37.2	61.0	1.8
Greenwood	378.3	5 542	33.1	47.4	2.2	0.0	1.0	448.0	6 564	159	303	7 494	41.6	57.3	1.1
Hampton	58.0	2 736	66.8	3.0	6.4	0.0	1.8	14.7	695	346	91	1 301	62.2	36.8	1.0
Horry	982.5	3 931	45.9	11.4	5.3	0.3	2.6	1 240.3	4 963	568	1 154	14 168	37.1	61.7	1.3
Jasper	82.1	3 741	64.8	0.0	6.1	1.2	3.0	91.2	4 155	44	101	1 541	60.9	38.0	1.1
Kershaw	207.4	3 566	43.0	38.3	2.5	0.0	0.2	257.4	4 424	117	261	3 481	40.1	58.8	1.0
Lancaster	168.5	2 295	66.4	2.2	4.2	0.0	2.7	206.5	2 814	113	339	3 745	42.0	56.8	1.2
Laurens	191.2	2 748	47.4	26.7	3.7	0.1	1.7	159.1	2 286	116	308	4 031	40.2	58.3	1.4
Lee	45.1	2 257	60.7	0.0	5.0	0.0	2.7	47.5	2 374	38	86	1 296	65.1	33.6	1.3
Lexington	1 179.7	4 850	46.8	35.4	3.1	0.0	0.9	975.3	4 009	643	1 113	18 306	30.4	68.4	1.1
McCormick	19.6	1 944	58.0	4.7	6.4	0.3	2.4	25.8	2 553	80	44	795	52.7	46.6	0.8
Marion	86.9	2 563	62.9	1.4	7.9	0.6	2.6	25.6	755	94	150	2 519	63.3	35.7	1.0
Marlboro	73.4	2 547	63.4	1.7	6.2	2.1	1.0	43.0	1 491	381	125	1 595	62.5	36.7	0.8
Newberry	113.0	3 002	65.4	0.9	3.9	0.1	2.3	94.9	2 522	96	169	2 400	40.6	58.2	1.2
Oconee	187.6	2 652	65.0	1.5	5.1	0.3	3.9	165.9	2 344	132	311	4 350	30.5	68.0	1.6
Orangeburg	394.9	4 390	38.0	39.8	3.9	0.1	2.9	387.6	4 309	202	397	7 292	68.6	30.5	0.9
Pickens	224.7	1 937	58.9	0.3	8.6	0.1	3.9	876.5	7 556	206	530	9 128	25.9	72.1	2.0
Richland	1 071.2	2 994	61.3	1.3	5.5	0.1	1.1	1 515.5	4 236	9 377	12 948	44 664	64.0	35.1	0.9
Saluda	32.1	1 710	55.5	1.8	7.1	0.1	2.8	20.3	1 083	48	83	924	38.6	60.3	1.0
Spartanburg	1 311.4	4 760	35.2	42.2	3.2	0.4	1.5	2 196.7	7 973	517	1 254	18 499	38.4	60.0	1.5

1. Based on the resident population estimated as of July 1 of the year shown.   2. © 2009 Election Data Services, Inc. All rights reserved.

Table B. States and Counties — Land Area and Population

STATE/ County code	CBSA code[1]	County type[2]	STATE County	Land area[3] (sq km) 2010	Total persons	Rank	Per square kilometer	White	Black	American Indian, Alaska Native	Asian and Pacific Islander	Percent Hispanic or Latino[4]	Under 5 years	5 to 17 years	18 to 24 years	25 to 34 years	35 to 44 years	45 to 54 years
				1	2	3	4	5	6	7	8	9	10	11	12	13	14	15
			SOUTH CAROLINA—Cont'd															
45 085	44940	3	Sumter	1 723	107 456	549	62.4	48.2	47.5	0.8	1.7	3.3	7.4	18.1	10.8	13.2	12.1	14.1
45 087	46420	6	Union	1 332	28 961	1 452	21.7	67.1	32.0	0.5	0.5	1.0	5.8	17.0	7.9	10.5	12.9	15.5
45 089	...	6	Williamsburg	2 419	34 423	1 315	14.2	31.6	65.9	0.6	0.5	2.0	6.0	17.6	8.4	11.6	12.5	14.6
45 091	16740	1	York	1 763	226 073	279	128.2	74.1	19.7	1.3	1.9	4.5	6.9	18.7	9.2	12.3	14.9	15.1
46 000	...	X	SOUTH DAKOTA	196 350	814 180	X	4.1	86.4	1.7	9.7	1.3	2.7	7.3	17.6	10.0	12.9	11.4	14.4
46 003	...	9	Aurora	1 835	2 710	2 999	1.5	93.9	0.4	1.7	0.8	3.7	7.2	19.6	4.9	9.7	10.8	14.5
46 005	26700	7	Beadle	3 260	17 398	1 957	5.3	86.9	1.3	1.4	3.8	7.7	7.5	16.8	8.0	11.6	10.4	15.5
46 007	...	9	Bennett	3 068	3 431	2 945	1.1	37.0	0.4	64.0	0.5	2.0	10.0	24.6	10.6	11.2	10.1	12.1
46 009	...	9	Bon Homme	1 460	7 070	2 678	4.8	90.0	1.2	7.9	0.2	1.8	5.3	14.5	7.4	12.8	12.6	15.9
46 011	15100	7	Brookings	2 052	31 965	1 393	15.6	93.5	1.1	1.4	3.2	2.0	6.0	12.9	28.6	13.8	9.4	10.5
46 013	10100	5	Brown	4 437	36 531	1 262	8.2	94.0	0.9	3.8	1.4	1.4	6.9	16.3	10.7	12.4	11.0	14.4
46 015	...	9	Brule	2 117	5 255	2 823	2.5	90.1	0.3	10.1	0.3	1.4	7.0	18.8	6.2	11.0	11.4	15.2
46 017	...	9	Buffalo	1 221	1 912	3 062	1.6	15.4	0.4	83.1	0.1	1.8	11.8	27.4	10.8	13.0	11.0	11.8
46 019	...	6	Butte	5 827	10 110	2 438	1.7	94.7	0.5	3.6	0.4	3.0	7.5	17.5	7.7	11.3	10.6	15.5
46 021	...	9	Campbell	1 900	1 466	3 086	0.8	98.0	0.2	0.6	0.3	1.4	4.0	15.1	4.6	7.5	8.3	20.3
46 023	...	9	Charles Mix	2 842	9 129	2 515	3.2	66.5	0.4	33.1	0.6	1.7	8.5	21.2	7.5	9.9	10.0	14.0
46 025	...	9	Clark	2 480	3 691	2 931	1.5	98.0	0.4	0.4	0.1	1.7	6.6	17.1	5.4	10.0	10.1	14.7
46 027	46820	6	Clay	1 068	13 864	2 191	13.0	91.9	1.9	4.0	2.0	2.0	5.2	12.3	32.6	12.6	8.3	9.7
46 029	47980	7	Codington	1 783	27 227	1 523	15.3	95.7	0.6	2.5	0.7	1.6	7.5	17.3	9.5	12.8	11.5	14.8
46 031	...	9	Corson	6 396	4 050	2 902	0.6	31.6	0.3	67.0	0.7	2.6	10.1	24.2	9.7	11.9	10.5	13.6
46 033	...	8	Custer	4 033	8 216	2 594	2.0	94.4	0.3	4.2	0.5	2.2	4.8	15.0	4.4	8.6	9.2	16.6
46 035	33580	7	Davison	1 128	19 504	1 861	17.3	95.1	0.8	3.2	0.8	1.5	7.1	16.4	11.0	12.4	10.3	13.9
46 037	...	9	Day	2 662	5 710	2 790	2.1	89.0	0.5	10.6	0.4	1.1	5.8	16.0	5.8	9.2	9.3	15.7
46 039	...	9	Deuel	1 613	4 364	2 880	2.7	97.3	0.4	0.6	0.3	2.0	6.2	17.4	6.1	10.3	11.3	16.1
46 041	...	9	Dewey	5 963	5 301	2 819	0.9	23.5	0.3	77.0	0.3	1.8	9.5	24.5	10.0	11.7	11.7	13.8
46 043	...	9	Douglas	1 118	3 002	2 979	2.7	96.9	0.4	2.4	0.2	0.8	5.5	17.4	5.6	7.7	9.5	16.1
46 045	10100	9	Edmunds	2 916	4 071	2 901	1.4	97.9	0.3	0.9	0.4	1.4	5.6	18.4	6.0	8.8	9.8	16.5
46 047	...	7	Fall River	4 506	7 094	2 675	1.6	89.9	0.9	8.9	0.6	2.2	4.7	14.1	5.4	8.5	9.3	16.0
46 049	...	9	Faulk	2 543	2 364	3 023	0.9	98.9	0.2	0.5	0.3	0.8	6.1	17.4	6.3	8.5	9.2	15.7
46 051	...	7	Grant	1 765	7 356	2 655	4.2	96.8	0.3	0.7	0.5	2.3	5.9	17.2	6.0	10.3	10.4	17.4
46 053	...	9	Gregory	2 629	4 271	2 884	1.6	91.4	0.5	8.9	0.4	0.9	5.9	16.7	5.1	8.7	9.6	15.1
46 055	...	8	Haakon	4 689	1 937	3 060	0.4	96.5	0.8	3.7	0.6	0.9	6.1	16.2	4.1	10.3	8.8	17.9
46 057	47980	9	Hamlin	1 314	5 903	2 777	4.5	96.7	0.2	0.6	0.4	2.5	9.4	21.2	6.5	11.1	10.6	13.3
46 059	...	9	Hand	3 721	3 431	2 945	0.9	98.7	0.2	0.5	0.5	0.6	5.5	15.4	5.7	9.3	9.5	16.0
46 061	33580	8	Hanson	1 125	3 331	2 954	3.0	98.9	0.1	0.5	0.5	0.5	9.5	23.0	5.7	11.3	12.9	13.3
46 063	...	9	Harding	6 919	1 255	3 096	0.2	96.7	0.4	2.4	0.1	1.6	5.2	18.1	6.6	10.1	12.0	16.7
46 065	38180	7	Hughes	1 921	17 022	1 983	8.9	86.8	0.9	11.7	0.8	1.8	6.8	16.9	7.0	13.4	12.7	16.0
46 067	...	8	Hutchinson	2 105	7 343	2 657	3.5	97.2	0.6	0.9	0.2	1.6	5.7	18.0	5.1	8.7	10.3	14.3
46 069	...	9	Hyde	2 229	1 420	3 088	0.6	90.4	0.1	9.4	0.7	1.1	5.1	17.3	6.4	10.1	9.0	15.2
46 071	...	8	Jackson	4 828	3 031	2 978	0.6	47.1	0.4	55.6	0.1	1.3	9.0	23.9	9.3	11.4	10.1	12.7
46 073	...	9	Jerauld	1 363	2 071	3 044	1.5	95.3	0.1	0.8	0.4	4.1	6.9	14.1	4.8	10.9	9.1	13.3
46 075	...	9	Jones	2 511	1 006	3 108	0.4	96.1	0.3	3.7	0.5	1.3	7.1	15.3	6.4	8.7	10.7	17.4
46 077	...	9	Kingsbury	2 155	5 148	2 833	2.4	97.6	0.2	1.0	0.6	1.4	5.8	16.1	5.4	10.5	9.1	16.5
46 079	...	6	Lake	1 459	11 200	2 351	7.7	96.6	0.7	1.2	1.0	1.6	5.7	15.9	13.0	10.7	9.7	15.0
46 081	43940	6	Lawrence	2 072	24 097	1 642	11.6	94.4	0.6	3.1	1.0	2.5	5.7	13.9	13.3	11.4	9.9	14.6
46 083	43620	3	Lincoln	1 495	44 828	1 192	30.0	96.4	1.2	1.0	1.4	1.2	9.8	19.8	6.9	17.4	14.5	13.0
46 085	...	9	Lyman	4 253	3 755	2 925	0.9	60.3	0.6	40.3	0.4	1.1	7.5	21.9	8.1	11.4	10.6	14.4
46 087	43620	3	McCook	1 487	5 618	2 797	3.8	97.5	0.2	0.6	0.3	1.8	7.3	18.6	4.9	10.6	11.4	15.3
46 089	...	9	McPherson	2 944	2 459	3 013	0.8	98.6	0.2	0.6	0.4	1.0	5.1	16.7	4.2	6.9	9.6	13.6
46 091	...	9	Marshall	2 171	4 656	2 863	2.1	85.5	0.2	8.1	0.3	6.8	5.9	16.3	8.1	11.6	10.2	14.5
46 093	39660	3	Meade	8 990	25 434	1 589	2.8	92.7	1.8	3.8	1.3	3.0	8.1	17.1	10.3	13.2	11.2	15.0
46 095	...	9	Mellette	3 386	2 048	3 050	0.6	44.8	0.2	58.8	0.2	1.5	9.5	22.8	8.4	10.0	10.5	13.1
46 097	...	8	Miner	1 477	2 389	3 019	1.6	97.9	0.6	0.4	0.5	1.3	6.5	17.6	5.5	9.0	9.3	16.5
46 099	43620	3	Minnehaha	2 091	169 468	363	81.0	88.0	4.6	3.1	2.0	4.1	7.6	17.5	10.1	15.5	12.9	14.5
46 101	...	8	Moody	1 345	6 486	2 728	4.8	82.9	0.8	15.5	1.4	1.7	7.6	18.5	7.0	11.0	11.5	15.6
46 103	39660	3	Pennington	7 191	100 948	577	14.0	84.5	1.8	11.2	1.8	4.0	7.3	17.3	9.5	13.8	11.6	14.6
46 105	...	9	Perkins	7 435	2 982	2 981	0.4	97.7	0.3	1.9	0.3	0.7	5.4	16.1	4.8	9.8	9.6	15.9
46 107	...	9	Potter	2 230	2 329	3 028	1.0	97.9	0.3	1.5	0.5	0.7	5.5	14.1	5.2	8.2	8.8	15.6
46 109	...	9	Roberts	2 852	10 149	2 434	3.6	64.0	0.6	36.7	0.5	1.2	8.2	20.2	7.4	9.8	10.8	13.3
46 111	...	9	Sanborn	1 475	2 355	3 024	1.6	98.4	0.2	0.8	0.3	1.2	5.1	16.7	6.3	10.5	9.3	17.1
46 113	...	7	Shannon	5 423	13 586	2 214	2.5	3.3	0.1	94.8	0.3	2.2	11.8	27.5	13.6	12.4	11.2	10.6
46 115	...	7	Spink	3 895	6 415	2 735	1.6	97.3	0.4	1.7	0.2	1.1	6.0	18.9	6.5	9.4	9.8	15.6
46 117	38180	9	Stanley	3 741	2 966	2 983	0.8	92.2	0.5	8.8	0.4	0.7	6.0	18.3	6.2	11.2	12.3	14.9
46 119	...	9	Sully	2 608	1 373	3 092	0.5	97.9	0.3	2.5	0.0	0.9	5.7	16.9	4.2	10.6	9.9	18.4
46 121	...	9	Todd	3 596	9 612	2 469	2.7	10.7	0.4	87.8	0.2	2.4	12.6	27.5	11.5	13.0	10.6	10.4

1. CBSA = Core Based Statistical Area. See Appendix A for explanation. See Appendix B for list of metropolitan areas with component counties. 2. County type code from the Economic Research Service of USDA Rural-Urban Continuum Codes. See Appendix A for definition. 3. Dry land or land partially or temporarily covered by water. 4. May be of any race.

Table B. States and Counties — **Population and Households**

STATE County	Population, 2010 (cont.) Age (percent) (cont.) 55 to 64 years	65 to 74 years	75 years and over	Percent female	Population change and components of change, 1990–2010 Total persons 1990	2000	Percent change 1990–2000	2000–2010	Components of change, 2000–2009 Births	Deaths	Net migration	Households, 2010 Number	Percent change, 2000–2010	Persons per household	Female family householder[1] Percent	One person
	16	17	18	19	20	21	22	23	24	25	26	27	28	29	30	31
SOUTH CAROLINA—Cont'd																
Sumter	11.3	7.3	5.6	51.9	101 276	104 646	3.3	2.7	15 326	8 854	-5 993	40 398	7.1	2.59	20.2	25.8
Union	13.9	9.1	7.4	52.4	30 337	29 881	-1.5	-3.1	3 131	3 385	-2 125	11 974	-0.9	2.38	19.1	29.0
Williamsburg	14.7	8.4	6.2	51.4	36 815	37 217	1.1	-7.5	4 407	3 711	-3 328	13 007	-5.2	2.53	23.0	29.0
York	11.7	6.7	4.6	51.7	131 497	164 614	25.2	37.3	24 465	13 656	51 777	85 864	40.6	2.59	13.9	23.5
SOUTH DAKOTA	12.0	7.1	7.2	50.0	696 004	754 844	8.5	7.9	105 163	64 270	13 367	322 282	11.0	2.42	9.7	29.4
Aurora	13.4	9.4	10.5	49.0	3 135	3 058	-2.5	-11.4	285	334	-129	1 102	-5.4	2.37	5.4	29.9
Beadle	12.9	7.8	9.5	49.7	18 253	17 023	-6.7	2.2	1 825	1 815	-693	7 276	0.9	2.31	8.3	33.0
Bennett	10.1	5.6	5.6	50.9	3 206	3 574	11.5	-4.0	596	240	-579	1 090	-2.9	3.11	20.1	24.3
Bon Homme	12.8	8.2	10.9	41.6	7 089	7 260	2.4	-2.6	552	745	-29	2 457	-6.8	2.24	5.5	32.8
Brookings	8.9	5.1	4.9	48.8	25 207	28 220	12.0	13.3	3 137	1 682	551	12 029	12.8	2.36	6.1	29.6
Brown	12.2	7.3	8.8	51.3	35 580	35 460	-0.3	3.0	4 287	3 250	-1 100	15 489	5.8	2.27	8.1	33.0
Brule	12.9	8.1	9.2	51.4	5 485	5 364	-2.2	-2.0	620	495	-189	2 136	6.9	2.40	8.6	30.5
Buffalo	7.1	5.2	1.9	51.0	1 759	2 032	15.5	-5.9	517	142	-334	532	1.1	3.59	33.1	19.0
Butte	14.3	8.5	7.2	49.7	7 914	9 094	14.9	11.2	1 213	904	218	4 160	18.3	2.40	9.8	28.5
Campbell	14.9	12.4	12.8	49.2	1 965	1 782	-9.3	-17.7	87	125	-403	694	-4.3	2.11	3.0	35.6
Charles Mix	11.2	8.5	9.2	50.5	9 131	9 350	2.4	-2.4	1 423	925	-820	3 249	-2.8	2.63	12.9	29.0
Clark	14.4	9.7	12.1	49.8	4 403	4 143	-5.9	-10.9	374	433	-636	1 445	-9.6	2.22	4.8	32.5
Clay	9.1	5.1	5.1	51.4	13 186	13 537	2.7	2.4	1 445	840	-575	5 110	4.8	2.28	7.3	32.4
Codington	11.7	7.2	7.6	50.2	22 698	25 897	14.1	5.1	3 489	2 143	-930	11 432	10.4	2.35	9.0	30.6
Corson	9.5	6.0	4.4	49.0	4 195	4 181	-0.3	-3.1	822	325	-569	1 260	-0.9	3.21	21.9	22.7
Custer	19.9	13.5	8.0	49.5	6 179	7 275	17.7	12.9	684	705	709	3 636	22.4	2.19	5.5	28.4
Davison	11.9	7.4	9.6	50.5	17 503	18 741	7.1	4.1	2 556	1 746	-510	8 296	9.4	2.26	8.5	34.3
Day	15.2	10.3	12.6	49.8	6 978	6 267	-10.2	-8.9	626	824	-534	2 504	-3.2	2.22	7.8	34.0
Deuel	13.4	9.5	9.8	48.4	4 522	4 498	-0.5	-3.0	498	460	-320	1 819	-1.3	2.37	5.0	29.1
Dewey	9.1	5.7	4.0	50.9	5 523	5 972	8.1	-11.2	1 409	449	-951	1 730	-7.1	3.05	24.2	24.6
Douglas	14.1	10.1	14.2	49.9	3 746	3 458	-7.7	-13.2	300	385	-431	1 210	-8.4	2.33	4.2	29.1
Edmunds	13.1	10.2	11.5	49.2	4 358	4 367	0.3	-6.8	401	471	-338	1 607	-4.4	2.27	4.0	31.0
Fall River	19.0	12.3	10.8	49.2	7 353	7 453	1.4	-4.8	610	1 032	247	3 272	4.6	2.10	8.9	37.6
Faulk	13.0	10.0	13.7	50.5	2 744	2 640	-3.8	-10.5	230	259	-391	869	-14.3	2.15	4.1	36.1
Grant	14.3	9.1	9.4	49.2	8 372	7 847	-6.3	-6.3	718	884	-571	3 089	-0.9	2.35	6.1	29.6
Gregory	15.2	10.4	13.3	49.7	5 359	4 792	-10.6	-10.9	389	622	-535	1 936	-4.3	2.18	7.4	36.6
Haakon	14.9	10.2	11.5	49.4	2 624	2 196	-16.3	-11.8	177	231	-360	850	-2.3	2.24	4.2	33.2
Hamlin	10.6	8.0	9.3	60.0	4 974	5 540	11.4	6.6	892	645	-3	2 108	2.9	2.68	5.6	25.6
Hand	13.4	10.2	15.0	50.4	4 272	3 741	-12.4	-8.3	312	414	-384	1 494	-3.2	2.26	5.3	32.2
Hanson	10.4	8.2	5.9	49.9	2 994	3 139	4.8	8.1	499	172	97	1 045	-6.3	2.69	3.5	21.7
Harding	16.9	8.4	8.1	47.5	1 669	1 353	-18.9	-7.2	119	68	-279	539	2.7	2.27	4.8	32.1
Hughes	13.7	6.8	6.6	51.4	14 817	16 481	11.2	3.3	1 947	1 373	13	7 066	8.5	2.30	9.4	32.3
Hutchinson	12.9	9.4	15.6	51.3	8 262	8 075	-2.3	-9.1	737	1 100	-543	2 930	-8.2	2.22	5.0	33.4
Hyde	14.3	10.1	12.5	48.0	1 696	1 671	-1.5	-15.0	148	206	-219	600	-11.6	2.30	5.5	33.0
Jackson	10.3	7.0	6.5	49.6	2 811	2 930	4.2	3.4	542	242	-567	996	5.4	3.00	16.2	26.2
Jerauld	15.9	10.1	15.0	51.4	2 425	2 295	-5.4	-9.8	211	251	-293	870	-11.9	2.18	6.2	30.9
Jones	13.8	9.8	10.7	50.5	1 324	1 193	-9.9	-15.7	120	67	-210	458	-10.0	2.20	5.2	35.8
Kingsbury	14.8	9.1	12.7	49.3	5 925	5 815	-1.9	-11.5	499	819	-156	2 222	-7.6	2.23	5.0	32.2
Lake	13.0	8.3	8.6	49.2	10 550	11 276	6.9	-0.7	1 229	1 000	519	4 483	2.5	2.30	6.8	30.9
Lawrence	14.6	8.3	8.3	50.5	20 655	21 802	5.6	10.5	2 404	1 874	1 273	10 536	18.6	2.19	8.1	33.2
Lincoln	9.7	4.8	4.2	50.5	15 427	24 131	56.4	85.8	5 690	1 771	12 667	16 649	89.6	2.68	7.3	20.2
Lyman	11.4	8.3	6.3	47.6	3 638	3 895	7.1	-3.6	640	264	-360	1 392	-0.6	2.67	15.2	27.2
McCook	13.0	8.8	10.2	50.0	5 688	5 832	2.5	-3.7	712	639	-252	2 168	-1.6	2.45	6.0	26.2
McPherson	14.1	12.8	17.0	51.1	3 228	2 904	-10.0	-15.3	208	350	-304	1 025	-16.5	2.06	4.3	36.3
Marshall	14.3	9.3	9.8	45.9	4 844	4 576	-5.5	1.7	431	482	-350	1 815	-1.6	2.36	6.0	31.4
Meade	13.0	6.6	5.4	49.0	21 878	24 253	10.9	4.9	3 371	1 844	-1 733	9 903	12.5	2.49	8.8	23.6
Mellette	12.2	6.3	7.2	48.8	2 137	2 083	-2.5	-1.7	346	179	-200	693	-0.1	2.88	19.0	24.7
Miner	13.4	9.0	13.3	49.5	3 272	2 884	-11.9	-17.2	264	328	-392	1 032	-14.9	2.24	5.6	37.6
Minnehaha	10.8	5.6	5.5	50.1	123 809	148 281	19.8	14.3	23 731	10 637	16 032	67 028	15.6	2.43	10.5	29.3
Moody	13.6	8.1	7.0	49.9	6 507	6 595	1.4	-1.7	799	534	-455	2 554	1.1	2.48	8.8	27.4
Pennington	12.4	7.1	6.4	50.2	81 343	88 565	8.9	14.0	14 075	6 409	5 116	41 251	19.1	2.38	11.7	29.0
Perkins	15.5	10.0	13.2	49.8	3 932	3 363	-14.5	-11.3	268	367	-393	1 291	-9.7	2.26	4.9	32.0
Potter	15.8	11.7	15.2	50.5	3 190	2 693	-15.6	-13.5	220	359	-498	1 062	-7.2	2.13	4.2	35.5
Roberts	13.0	8.8	8.5	49.8	9 914	10 016	1.0	1.3	1 456	1 036	-449	3 823	3.8	2.58	13.4	27.3
Sanborn	14.8	8.8	11.4	48.2	2 833	2 675	-5.6	-12.0	251	256	-229	975	-6.5	2.24	6.3	31.1
Shannon	7.0	3.8	2.1	50.7	9 902	12 466	25.9	9.0	3 472	1 132	-1 017	3 144	12.9	4.29	38.0	14.8
Spink	13.7	9.1	11.1	49.7	7 981	7 454	-6.6	-13.9	757	724	-911	2 608	-8.4	2.30	6.4	31.8
Stanley	15.3	10.5	5.3	50.0	2 453	2 772	13.0	7.0	348	145	-172	1 228	10.5	2.42	8.5	26.2
Sully	15.1	10.2	9.0	46.0	1 589	1 556	-2.1	-11.8	204	86	-329	610	-3.2	2.25	4.6	31.6
Todd	8.2	3.6	2.6	50.9	8 352	9 050	8.4	6.2	2 471	652	-737	2 780	12.9	3.45	34.7	21.1

1. No spouse present.

Table B. States and Counties — Population, Vital Statistics, Medicare, and Crime

STATE County	Persons in group quarters, 2010	Daytime population, 2006–2010 Number	Daytime population, 2006–2010 Employment/residence ratio	Births, average 2006–2008 Total	Births, average 2006–2008 Rate[1]	Deaths, average 2006–2008 Number	Deaths, average 2006–2008 Rate[1]	Persons under 65 with no health insurance, 2009 Number	Persons under 65 with no health insurance, 2009 Percent	Medicare, 2011 Eligible for Medicare	Medicare, 2011 Enrolled in Medicare Advantage	Medicare, 2011 Enrolled in a Medicare prescription drug plan	Serious crimes known to police,[2] 2010 Total Number	Serious crimes known to police,[2] 2010 Total Rate[3]
	32	33	34	35	36	37	38	39	40	41	42	43	44	45
SOUTH CAROLINA—Cont'd														
Sumter	2 774	105 774	1.0	1 697	16.3	966	9.3	17 373	20.0	17 984	2 209	7 102	4 830	4 495
Union	503	26 143	0.7	347	12.4	373	13.3	4 410	19.9	6 900	1 429	3 021	1 230	4 247
Williamsburg	1 476	33 682	0.9	463	13.0	416	11.7	6 286	22.4	6 742	985	3 333	1 397	4 119
York	3 905	198 779	0.8	2 993	14.4	1 558	7.5	32 625	16.9	32 805	5 121	13 627	7 509	3 321
SOUTH DAKOTA	34 050	803 159	1.0	12 084	15.2	6 998	8.8	99 891	14.8	140 171	14 902	79 841	17 268	2 121
Aurora	96	2 454	0.8	D	D	29	10.2	416	18.7	592	36	408	2	74
Beadle	620	16 893	1.0	D	D	192	12.2	1 794	14.1	3 363	345	2 073	NA	NA
Bennett	37	3 301	0.9	D	D	30	8.6	628	22.1	443	16	277	22	641
Bon Homme	1 556	6 470	0.8	D	D	83	11.7	1 034	18.9	1 457	108	947	1	14
Brookings	3 588	32 528	1.1	377	13.0	196	6.8	3 035	11.7	3 563	405	2 098	261	817
Brown	1 365	37 185	1.1	D	D	353	10.1	3 620	12.7	6 523	215	4 264	631	1 799
Brule	132	5 256	1.0	D	D	53	10.3	877	20.6	913	68	592	NA	NA
Buffalo	3	1 933	1.0	D	D	18	8.6	366	19.9	198	D	113	NA	NA
Butte	111	8 596	0.7	D	D	103	10.8	1 424	18.3	1 825	336	903	52	514
Campbell	0	1 318	0.8	D	D	14	9.7	172	17.7	396	30	260	3	205
Charles Mix	589	9 331	1.1	D	D	93	10.3	1 487	20.9	1 753	58	1 235	76	962
Clark	489	3 467	0.9	D	D	41	11.7	471	18.6	804	106	574	13	352
Clay	2 237	13 038	0.9	D	D	81	6.1	1 750	15.2	1 672	172	1 099	79	570
Codington	381	28 198	1.1	D	D	242	9.2	2 935	13.6	4 711	876	3 071	707	2 597
Corson	1	3 872	0.9	D	D	40	9.5	795	22.5	500	17	314	10	295
Custer	255	7 089	0.7	D	D	76	9.7	959	15.5	1 885	262	770	68	828
Davison	769	20 682	1.1	D	D	200	10.5	2 223	14.5	3 772	215	2 651	547	2 805
Day	139	5 455	0.9	D	D	80	14.1	863	20.7	1 398	105	934	NA	NA
Deuel	50	3 999	0.8	D	D	60	13.9	517	15.6	973	138	627	21	481
Dewey	19	5 718	1.2	D	D	56	9.3	1 131	21.4	728	27	413	11	208
Douglas	178	3 064	1.0	D	D	40	13.0	402	18.7	731	59	509	6	261
Edmunds	420	3 629	0.8	D	D	50	12.5	515	17.0	888	41	624	2	49
Fall River	235	7 278	1.1	D	D	106	14.7	889	17.1	2 086	217	782	NA	NA
Faulk	497	2 257	0.9	D	D	35	15.1	318	19.5	546	52	371	12	508
Grant	104	7 732	1.1	D	D	86	12.0	796	14.6	1 624	201	1 028	NA	NA
Gregory	44	4 141	0.9	D	D	73	17.6	674	23.4	1 095	93	745	NA	NA
Haakon	36	1 868	1.0	D	D	27	14.7	274	20.6	411	37	280	NA	NA
Hamlin	245	4 823	0.6	D	D	77	13.6	714	15.3	999	142	659	61	1 033
Hand	61	3 325	1.0	D	D	41	12.5	427	18.4	861	37	630	16	466
Hanson	520	2 596	0.5	D	D	22	6.1	506	16.9	1 320	117	597	15	450
Harding	29	1 271	1.0	D	D	D	D	215	23.3	207	16	118	1	80
Hughes	772	17 624	1.1	D	D	144	8.5	1 852	12.9	2 674	235	1 520	522	3 067
Hutchinson	832	7 067	0.9	D	D	108	14.8	834	16.2	1 954	225	1 411	10	136
Hyde	38	1 610	1.1	D	D	23	15.8	178	17.1	313	17	197	NA	NA
Jackson	42	2 999	1.0	D	D	34	12.3	519	23.5	437	43	244	NA	NA
Jerauld	176	2 174	1.1	D	D	28	13.7	237	17.0	637	40	401	1	48
Jones	0	1 070	1.0	D	D	D	D	202	25.4	238	18	144	NA	NA
Kingsbury	203	4 650	0.8	D	D	81	15.0	602	15.0	1 211	105	817	NA	NA
Lake	874	10 385	0.9	D	D	105	9.2	1 207	12.5	2 627	233	1 486	NA	NA
Lawrence	1 071	23 662	1.0	D	D	211	9.1	3 104	16.3	4 569	670	2 164	452	1 876
Lincoln	284	30 513	0.5	765	20.4	208	5.5	3 294	8.6	4 419	556	2 459	1 087	2 494
Lyman	37	3 586	0.9	D	D	25	6.4	728	22.6	628	47	375	NA	NA
McCook	312	4 845	0.7	D	D	72	12.6	635	14.0	1 089	99	724	10	178
McPherson	347	2 415	0.9	D	D	35	14.1	381	23.1	751	44	544	3	122
Marshall	373	4 396	0.9	D	D	48	11.0	651	20.1	968	50	639	61	1 310
Meade	797	21 188	0.7	D	D	214	8.9	2 987	14.7	4 170	612	1 715	223	877
Mellette	49	1 833	0.8	D	D	21	10.5	350	20.8	306	13	194	21	1 025
Miner	80	2 202	0.8	D	D	36	14.3	286	15.5	569	33	381	11	460
Minnehaha	6 291	183 123	1.2	2 735	15.8	1 184	6.9	20 566	13.2	26 016	3 172	13 929	5 113	3 017
Moody	164	5 643	0.8	D	D	57	8.7	822	15.3	1 136	86	705	57	879
Pennington	2 575	102 216	1.1	1 585	16.4	670	6.9	13 898	16.4	18 084	2 526	7 820	3 933	3 896
Perkins	65	3 052	1.1	D	D	47	15.8	524	24.7	747	53	488	11	369
Potter	63	2 384	1.0	D	D	39	17.5	252	17.4	617	12	404	5	215
Roberts	281	9 613	0.9	166	16.7	107	10.8	1 676	20.8	1 963	174	1 162	107	1 054
Sanborn	174	2 172	0.8	D	D	22	9.0	333	17.3	493	36	330	1	42
Shannon	91	14 157	1.2	394	28.8	117	8.6	2 024	16.3	1 114	14	556	0	0
Spink	404	6 512	1.0	D	D	80	11.9	795	15.6	1 493	60	1 064	48	748
Stanley	0	2 445	0.7	D	D	19	7.0	390	16.7	541	52	283	50	1 686
Sully	0	1 207	0.9	D	D	D	D	189	17.2	296	26	172	2	146
Todd	28	9 831	1.1	286	28.2	79	7.8	1 481	16.4	776	14	451	NA	NA

1. Per 1,000 estimated resident population.   2. Data for serious crimes have not been adjusted for underreporting; this may affect comparability between geographic areas and over time.   3. Per 100,000 population estimated by the FBI.

Table B. States and Counties — Crime, Education, Money Income, and Poverty

STATE County	Serious crimes known to police,[1] 2010 (cont.) Rate[2] Violent	Property	Education School enrollment and attainment, 2006–2010 Enrollment[3] Total	Per cent private	Attainment[4] (percent) High school graduate or less	Bach-elor's degree or more	Local government expenditures,[5] 2008–2009 Total current expendi-tures (mil dol)	Current expendi-tures per student (dollars)	Money income, 2006–2010 Per capita income[6] (dollars)	Households Median income Dollars	Percent change, 2000 to 2006–2010 (constant 2010 dollars)	Percent with income of $200,000 or more	Income and poverty, 2010 Median house-hold income (dollars)	Percent below poverty level All per-sons	Children under 18 years	Children 5 to 17 years in families
	46	47	48	49	50	51	52	53	54	55	56	57	58	59	60	61
SOUTH CAROLINA—Cont'd																
Sumter	881	3 614	27 839	16.6	51.6	17.4	146.2	8 323	18 944	39 137	-7.1	1.0	36 554	20.9	31.9	29.4
Union	791	3 456	6 632	7.7	59.5	12.9	41.6	8 987	18 495	33 470	-15.9	0.8	34 125	18.7	29.9	27.4
Williamsburg	551	3 568	8 738	11.2	67.4	11.3	56.7	10 488	13 513	24 191	-21.1	0.1	28 083	32.2	44.2	40.1
York	556	2 766	57 004	11.9	42.8	26.9	351.8	9 058	25 707	51 925	-7.9	2.8	51 403	13.1	17.3	16.0
SOUTH DAKOTA	268	1 852	208 276	13.4	43.5	25.3	1 058.4	8 358	24 110	46 369	3.8	2.3	45 861	14.6	19.4	17.1
Aurora	0	74	616	7.8	59.4	12.2	6.1	10 957	21 291	45 230	19.9	2.0	43 934	11.7	17.4	15.5
Beadle	NA	NA	3 358	21.0	51.9	19.7	19.6	7 937	23 409	40 716	5.4	1.2	39 504	14.6	20.1	18.1
Bennett	117	525	933	14.7	54.8	15.7	5.5	9 856	16 153	32 841	2.5	1.3	31 183	34.2	46.8	42.6
Bon Homme	0	14	1 262	5.8	53.9	15.4	10.0	9 116	20 074	41 107	5.9	1.7	41 580	17.2	19.0	16.2
Brookings	38	779	13 054	4.0	37.7	37.7	33.1	7 994	20 995	45 134	0.6	1.2	48 290	17.2	11.5	10.3
Brown	197	1 602	9 014	12.7	44.0	24.1	39.0	7 701	23 878	45 615	2.9	1.7	47 803	10.3	13.0	11.5
Brule	NA	NA	1 474	12.8	46.5	25.2	11.3	9 823	19 779	48 277	17.8	0.2	42 604	14.2	19.0	16.5
Buffalo	NA	NA	601	13.5	62.2	8.3	NA	NA	11 410	27 926	73.8	0.6	20 577	39.0	47.5	43.6
Butte	59	455	2 326	10.6	49.5	19.2	12.9	7 410	20 418	39 041	6.2	2.0	38 767	15.3	22.5	20.4
Campbell	0	205	300	13.7	50.8	16.9	1.4	10 774	22 338	42 833	17.5	0.0	38 767	12.0	14.8	12.6
Charles Mix	266	696	2 203	17.2	56.3	16.5	16.9	10 086	17 403	35 808	8.5	1.9	35 122	25.7	35.8	34.2
Clark	0	352	787	2.5	58.7	12.5	5.5	9 209	23 909	43 894	14.7	1.9	42 413	14.6	25.5	22.2
Clay	36	534	7 123	4.8	32.8	40.4	10.1	7 866	19 518	37 198	6.7	2.2	40 492	19.7	20.0	16.9
Codington	264	2 332	6 760	15.7	48.6	22.7	32.5	7 158	24 781	43 275	-5.7	2.2	44 999	11.1	14.0	12.3
Corson	0	295	1 262	3.0	52.9	14.3	11.7	12 557	13 359	30 877	18.1	1.3	27 233	40.9	54.1	50.3
Custer	61	767	1 322	11.2	39.8	28.6	9.3	9 301	24 353	46 743	1.7	0.2	46 565	11.2	19.5	17.2
Davison	87	2 717	4 843	23.0	43.7	21.5	23.2	7 846	22 794	41 867	-1.2	1.5	40 972	14.8	17.7	15.8
Day	NA	NA	1 234	19.3	54.2	17.7	7.2	9 037	20 542	36 818	-3.8	1.0	37 186	17.0	24.3	21.3
Deuel	0	481	978	9.8	52.9	17.8	4.0	7 586	22 276	47 000	16.8	1.1	45 772	9.4	14.3	12.5
Dewey	19	189	1 696	3.8	58.3	12.6	10.8	16 934	15 632	33 255	12.8	1.1	31 374	32.0	41.5	36.2
Douglas	0	261	596	26.3	67.1	16.0	3.3	9 737	22 200	42 794	18.7	1.6	42 472	14.2	20.7	17.2
Edmunds	0	49	752	11.4	54.5	20.5	5.9	8 738	24 268	47 026	15.3	3.5	48 588	11.6	16.9	14.4
Fall River	NA	NA	1 245	21.9	46.7	20.2	10.6	8 748	21 574	35 833	-4.5	0.7	36 993	16.7	24.9	21.6
Faulk	0	508	454	10.1	56.2	15.5	2.9	8 735	21 898	38 203	-0.2	1.9	42 633	14.2	24.1	22.5
Grant	NA	NA	1 552	7.4	57.7	15.5	9.9	8 273	22 887	42 625	1.7	1.4	45 436	11.4	15.6	13.5
Gregory	NA	NA	817	6.2	52.7	14.7	7.5	10 365	21 311	33 940	17.9	2.2	31 962	24.4	35.0	29.4
Haakon	NA	NA	288	6.6	49.3	20.0	2.6	8 697	25 877	46 281	22.3	1.2	38 900	13.4	19.7	17.3
Hamlin	152	881	1 463	7.7	54.8	16.7	9.7	7 908	21 558	44 439	3.7	2.5	49 091	10.8	18.8	17.9
Hand	29	437	679	9.0	50.9	17.1	3.8	7 943	23 238	45 895	11.9	0.9	43 683	11.1	15.4	13.1
Hanson	0	450	831	22.4	57.0	18.9	5.2	9 060	21 391	46 556	11.2	2.6	53 987	10.2	16.8	16.1
Harding	0	80	292	7.2	35.7	34.3	2.8	12 593	22 004	34 792	9.9	1.7	37 407	17.6	28.5	25.8
Hughes	317	2 749	3 791	13.2	35.3	33.3	18.8	7 006	28 236	53 501	-1.7	2.2	54 989	10.4	14.1	11.9
Hutchinson	0	136	1 670	10.7	52.2	21.7	14.1	9 255	21 944	39 310	3.4	2.7	41 592	12.3	18.0	15.5
Hyde	NA	NA	287	5.2	58.4	16.8	2.8	9 000	22 995	41 196	4.6	1.5	38 926	13.8	21.0	18.4
Jackson	NA	NA	993	2.9	47.7	19.4	4.3	10 546	14 568	36 354	19.9	1.0	30 499	32.9	49.5	44.8
Jerauld	0	48	303	0.0	61.2	11.0	3.1	10 105	24 942	40 607	4.5	3.4	37 924	15.7	23.4	24.0
Jones	NA	NA	229	21.0	45.4	15.6	1.9	10 599	24 630	49 464	29.0	1.7	38 019	15.5	26.5	26.0
Kingsbury	NA	NA	952	5.4	52.8	20.3	9.6	9 939	24 660	44 948	13.5	0.9	47 775	9.8	14.7	13.1
Lake	NA	NA	3 217	8.0	47.2	22.1	16.1	7 538	22 447	45 606	5.7	0.7	46 388	11.6	15.1	13.2
Lawrence	87	1 789	6 475	15.7	39.6	31.8	22.8	7 939	25 465	42 356	5.3	2.0	45 424	14.0	18.6	15.8
Lincoln	213	2 280	10 885	16.4	30.5	36.9	37.3	7 469	33 261	67 365	10.1	5.0	74 100	4.9	6.1	5.4
Lyman	NA	NA	940	3.8	55.6	19.8	4.5	10 830	16 930	36 323	0.6	0.3	39 774	21.9	32.8	29.0
McCook	0	178	1 354	10.3	47.8	20.4	9.7	9 721	25 502	42 022	-6.2	2.3	44 915	9.7	13.1	11.9
McPherson	0	122	497	5.6	63.4	14.8	4.2	9 522	19 255	31 923	12.6	1.0	35 675	17.8	27.1	23.7
Marshall	129	1 181	1 140	1.3	50.2	16.7	5.8	8 141	22 441	41 023	6.0	1.6	40 437	14.2	22.4	20.3
Meade	39	837	6 126	11.1	43.2	21.0	21.1	7 681	22 045	46 180	-1.4	1.1	48 120	10.6	15.6	15.2
Mellette	391	635	622	2.1	53.6	14.9	5.1	12 086	16 971	34 055	15.8	0.9	30 003	33.5	45.4	42.4
Miner	42	419	499	5.0	54.3	17.5	3.5	9 049	25 450	43 958	17.6	1.7	45 947	13.0	18.4	16.3
Minnehaha	271	2 746	42 429	20.8	38.7	28.9	215.9	7 442	26 392	51 799	-3.9	2.8	49 954	11.7	13.8	11.8
Moody	108	771	1 544	7.1	46.0	21.7	7.7	8 143	24 948	52 354	16.6	2.2	47 162	11.2	15.2	14.0
Pennington	498	3 398	25 421	13.7	36.9	27.8	137.3	8 096	25 894	46 849	-1.3	2.9	45 999	15.2	21.6	18.7
Perkins	0	369	564	13.1	51.9	17.8	4.8	11 481	25 780	33 361	-5.1	2.6	31 033	17.3	26.7	23.2
Potter	43	172	436	17.2	51.6	19.9	4.1	11 003	23 986	42 422	11.4	1.7	44 502	11.7	17.7	15.4
Roberts	158	897	2 518	5.0	52.4	15.0	15.5	9 621	19 825	37 708	5.1	1.9	39 057	20.4	28.8	25.7
Sanborn	42	0	484	12.2	61.6	15.3	3.7	9 426	21 055	44 732	5.8	0.8	43 361	14.5	20.5	17.7
Shannon	0	0	4 761	2.4	53.0	16.1	20.3	14 256	7 772	24 392	-7.9	0.0	27 307	47.3	48.9	43.2
Spink	140	608	1 444	12.7	53.7	15.9	11.9	8 779	25 295	45 000	12.0	3.0	44 272	12.6	14.3	11.7
Stanley	34	1 652	608	17.3	49.2	27.7	4.5	9 339	27 435	51 875	-0.5	3.3	50 944	10.1	15.2	12.2
Sully	73	73	282	8.9	44.3	25.1	3.2	10 322	26 596	48 958	19.0	2.6	48 026	9.0	11.6	10.4
Todd	NA	NA	3 642	5.8	48.5	18.1	27.1	13 951	11 010	25 196	-0.7	1.3	26 393	49.1	58.1	51.6

1. Data for serious crimes have not been adjusted for underreporting; this may affect comparability between geographic areas and over time.   2. Per 100,000 population estimated by the FBI.   3. All persons 3 years old and over enrolled in nursery school through college.   4. Persons 25 years old and over.   5. Elementary and secondary education expenditures.   6. Based on population estimated by the American Community Survey, 2006–2010.

Table B. States and Counties — **Personal Income**

STATE County	Personal income, 2009 Total (mil dol)	Percent change, 2008–2009	Per capita[1] Dollars	Per capita[1] Rank	Wages and salaries[2] (mil dol)	Proprietors' income (mil dol)	Dividends, interest, and rent (mil dol)	Transfer payments (mil dol) Total	Government payments to individuals Total	Social Security	Medical payments	Income maintenance	Unemployment insurance
	62	63	64	65	66	67	68	69	70	71	72	73	74
SOUTH CAROLINA—Cont'd													
Sumter	3 078	-0.1	29 458	2 102	1 985	140	401	824	805	234	303	123	39
Union	772	-0.4	28 223	2 362	291	46	89	268	263	97	101	30	17
Williamsburg	858	1.2	24 904	2 873	416	29	93	321	315	85	131	58	16
York	7 560	1.0	33 302	1 295	3 759	418	984	1 390	1 349	484	484	128	115
SOUTH DAKOTA	31 174	-1.7	38 374	X	17 670	4 564	6 609	4 901	4 754	1 820	1 984	423	85
Aurora	119	-5.0	41 603	357	31	35	31	17	16	7	7	1	0
Beadle	712	-4.1	43 802	246	347	116	171	121	118	42	58	9	1
Bennett	91	-13.0	27 082	2 552	32	9	17	25	24	5	11	5	0
Bon Homme	231	-1.4	33 055	1 332	69	61	52	43	42	17	20	2	1
Brookings	1 084	-1.2	36 060	878	785	96	211	131	125	48	47	7	3
Brown	1 587	-4.2	45 078	198	890	279	358	226	220	86	99	14	3
Brule	209	-3.0	39 540	487	71	65	40	35	34	12	17	2	0
Buffalo	37	-3.5	17 732	3 107	26	5	4	15	15	2	6	4	0
Butte	288	-1.5	30 063	1 962	102	43	68	57	55	22	21	6	1
Campbell	53	-22.6	39 795	464	15	16	12	12	11	4	6	0	0
Charles Mix	326	1.3	36 298	848	124	94	62	69	68	20	33	9	1
Clark	137	-7.1	40 071	445	34	49	27	24	23	10	10	1	0
Clay	547	3.6	40 522	419	248	153	84	71	69	23	27	5	1
Codington	976	-3.0	37 297	715	618	105	224	151	147	63	58	11	4
Corson	112	-4.6	27 484	2 486	39	26	12	32	31	5	16	6	0
Custer	270	0.4	34 078	1 160	100	30	66	55	54	25	19	3	1
Davison	794	-0.9	41 924	336	460	114	202	136	132	48	63	10	2
Day	201	0.8	36 463	822	69	44	47	44	43	17	19	3	1
Deuel	167	-3.7	39 696	470	76	33	30	27	26	12	10	1	1
Dewey	167	3.8	27 924	2 416	90	31	19	46	45	8	20	11	1
Douglas	130	4.7	44 465	217	42	51	19	22	22	8	11	1	0
Edmunds	196	-10.2	49 874	106	48	65	42	26	25	10	12	1	0
Fall River	233	-0.7	32 244	1 475	128	15	55	63	62	24	22	4	1
Faulk	106	-17.1	47 944	134	24	43	23	16	16	6	8	1	0
Grant	285	3.0	40 278	435	158	55	54	50	49	20	22	3	1
Gregory	165	-4.4	41 140	379	50	49	38	34	34	12	16	3	0
Haakon	84	-17.5	47 175	147	28	19	28	12	11	5	5	0	0
Hamlin	202	0.2	35 116	1 002	65	46	36	32	31	13	14	2	1
Hand	149	-13.9	46 102	165	49	48	34	22	22	10	9	1	0
Hanson	167	6.9	47 123	148	21	48	47	31	31	19	9	1	0
Harding	40	-17.2	35 427	963	20	7	11	5	5	3	2	0	0
Hughes	706	-1.9	41 603	357	476	91	150	94	91	36	40	8	1
Hutchinson	312	3.1	43 843	243	92	93	78	53	51	23	23	2	1
Hyde	41	-31.9	29 698	2 049	23	-2	15	10	9	4	4	1	0
Jackson	74	-9.6	27 918	2 417	28	19	11	20	19	5	8	4	0
Jerauld	98	-10.6	50 080	101	51	33	18	16	16	7	7	1	0
Jones	39	-25.1	37 209	722	16	11	7	6	6	3	2	0	0
Kingsbury	236	-1.0	44 508	215	68	75	44	40	39	16	19	1	1
Lake	450	4.0	37 500	690	180	97	94	79	77	34	30	4	2
Lawrence	811	-1.2	34 518	1 089	434	73	229	151	147	62	56	9	2
Lincoln	2 062	7.1	50 022	103	644	201	335	108	101	60	20	7	4
Lyman	127	-17.7	32 615	1 401	54	27	22	25	25	8	10	4	1
McCook	231	4.8	41 152	377	49	72	40	34	33	14	15	2	1
McPherson	87	-4.1	35 744	922	23	22	23	17	16	8	6	1	0
Marshall	141	-14.4	33 823	1 198	58	26	40	28	27	12	12	2	1
Meade	878	-3.4	36 693	788	329	149	160	134	130	53	46	11	2
Mellette	53	-6.4	25 987	2 732	13	10	7	16	15	3	7	3	0
Miner	109	12.1	44 867	204	31	42	19	16	16	7	7	1	0
Minnehaha	6 796	-1.9	37 129	735	5 606	726	1 423	954	921	363	390	79	19
Moody	265	-3.1	41 491	364	100	59	42	34	33	15	12	2	1
Pennington	3 780	0.4	37 481	691	2 580	180	895	651	633	239	243	60	10
Perkins	92	-6.8	31 932	1 543	40	13	25	22	21	9	10	1	0
Potter	121	-15.7	58 882	33	34	36	37	19	19	8	9	1	0
Roberts	326	0.9	32 776	1 370	130	68	56	68	66	24	26	8	1
Sanborn	113	10.1	46 525	157	27	32	26	17	16	6	8	1	0
Shannon	251	3.1	18 260	3 105	194	2	15	109	106	11	44	31	2
Spink	356	-8.7	54 366	60	98	135	61	72	70	18	47	2	1
Stanley	114	-13.3	40 991	383	47	2	30	15	15	8	5	1	0
Sully	79	-46.3	58 412	38	22	27	18	7	7	4	2	0	0
Todd	198	1.4	19 582	3 100	132	15	15	73	71	8	30	21	1

1. Based on the resident population estimated as of July 1 of the year shown.   2. Includes supplements to wages and salaries.

Table B. States and Counties — Earnings, Social Security, and Housing

STATE County	Earnings, 2009									Social Security beneficiaries, December 2010			Housing units, 2010	
				Percent by selected industries										
			Goods-related[1]		Service-related and health							Supple-mental Security Income recipients, December 2010		
	Total (mil dol)	Farm	Total	Manu-facturing	Infor-mation and profes-sional and technical services	Retail trade	Finance, insur-ance, and real estate	Health care and social services	Govern-ment	Number	Rate[2]		Total	Percent change, 2000–2010
	75	76	77	78	79	80	81	82	83	84	85	86	87	88
SOUTH CAROLINA—Cont'd														
Sumter	2 125	1.0	20.8	14.6	3.7	5.7	3.2	11.1	37.8	20 885	194	4 056	46 011	10.2
Union	338	2.3	D	26.0	5.0	7.4	4.1	D	29.9	8 210	283	1 018	14 153	6.0
Williamsburg	445	2.4	D	24.3	D	5.7	4.8	D	29.2	8 065	234	2 099	15 359	-1.2
York	4 176	0.3	20.5	16.0	8.8	8.6	9.3	9.7	15.8	37 805	167	3 362	94 196	42.6
SOUTH DAKOTA	22 234	10.8	14.9	8.9	5.5	6.9	7.9	13.9	18.8	153 508	189	13 812	363 438	12.4
Aurora	66	46.2	D	D	D	3.7	D	11.5	12.6	610	225	27	1 324	2.0
Beadle	463	15.5	D	13.9	3.3	7.6	5.2	D	16.0	3 655	210	368	8 304	1.2
Bennett	41	16.0	D	D	D	6.4	1.7	D	40.5	500	146	153	1 263	-1.2
Bon Homme	130	34.0	D	3.2	2.4	4.7	3.2	10.3	21.7	1 545	219	79	2 931	-2.5
Brookings	881	6.8	D	30.1	3.6	5.2	3.4	4.5	28.0	3 855	121	205	13 137	13.5
Brown	1 170	8.1	D	13.4	5.0	7.9	6.3	16.1	14.0	7 035	193	492	16 706	5.3
Brule	136	37.6	D	0.7	D	7.7	3.0	9.8	13.5	1 035	197	76	2 433	7.2
Buffalo	30	15.6	D	0.2	D	D	D	D	75.5	220	115	123	609	1.2
Butte	145	6.9	D	4.7	4.7	11.8	3.2	D	18.7	1 965	194	188	4 621	13.8
Campbell	30	41.5	D	D	D	3.8	D	2.0	12.0	425	290	17	980	1.9
Charles Mix	219	31.2	6.6	2.4	2.5	5.3	D	D	25.9	1 940	213	242	3 849	-0.1
Clark	83	47.1	10.3	3.0	D	3.8	D	5.1	11.1	865	234	67	1 710	-9.0
Clay	401	22.0	6.1	3.6	3.7	5.4	1.7	8.4	34.4	1 830	132	141	5 639	3.7
Codington	723	3.2	25.0	17.7	3.8	9.9	8.3	15.0	14.5	5 240	192	356	12 397	9.5
Corson	64	38.7	0.8	0.1	D	1.7	D	D	43.8	555	137	217	1 540	0.4
Custer	129	1.5	13.4	1.9	3.7	7.8	3.2	D	34.1	2 085	254	115	4 628	27.7
Davison	573	7.1	D	14.6	7.6	9.8	4.1	16.5	11.5	4 130	212	345	8 852	9.4
Day	113	31.0	13.4	7.0	D	6.0	4.0	8.1	16.8	1 570	275	90	3 630	0.3
Deuel	108	19.6	25.2	16.7	D	4.5	D	D	9.5	1 100	252	48	2 204	1.5
Dewey	121	17.9	D	D	D	8.1	D	D	57.0	850	160	371	2 002	-6.1
Douglas	93	49.9	7.2	3.9	D	2.1	D	D	8.0	760	253	41	1 439	-0.9
Edmunds	113	44.1	7.1	4.4	D	6.4	D	D	12.4	935	230	36	1 966	-2.8
Fall River	143	3.5	4.5	1.2	D	5.3	2.2	D	46.9	2 155	304	174	4 191	9.9
Faulk	67	59.5	D	D	D	D	1.8	D	9.8	550	233	53	1 136	-8.0
Grant	213	20.1	D	14.9	2.0	5.5	7.3	D	7.8	1 790	243	90	3 526	2.0
Gregory	99	36.4	D	0.7	2.9	7.6	4.8	12.0	12.8	1 195	280	105	2 503	4.1
Haakon	47	26.2	D	D	7.2	6.4	4.0	D	12.4	425	219	11	1 013	1.1
Hamlin	112	39.2	D	D	D	4.4	D	4.3	17.9	1 130	191	55	2 760	5.1
Hand	97	45.8	5.3	2.1	D	4.8	D	D	10.2	910	265	48	1 815	-1.4
Hanson	69	64.8	D	3.0	D	1.4	D	D	9.9	1 495	449	65	1 177	-3.4
Harding	27	17.0	D	0.8	D	4.6	D	D	20.6	245	195	0	731	-9.1
Hughes	567	4.9	4.0	0.8	5.8	7.9	6.4	13.4	40.9	2 990	176	269	7 623	8.1
Hutchinson	185	43.0	7.5	4.7	1.3	5.1	D	D	10.6	2 040	278	132	3 351	-4.7
Hyde	21	-10.2	8.4	0.6	D	9.8	D	D	38.8	345	243	17	708	-7.9
Jackson	47	35.6	D	D	D	6.3	D	D	38.4	495	163	134	1 193	1.7
Jerauld	84	30.6	D	D	D	4.0	D	D	6.5	660	319	41	1 070	-8.3
Jones	27	29.0	D	0.0	D	7.0	4.6	2.7	21.9	260	258	0	589	-4.1
Kingsbury	143	46.2	15.0	10.8	D	3.3	D	5.6	9.3	1 325	257	55	2 720	-0.1
Lake	277	23.7	D	9.6	4.6	6.2	2.9	8.4	18.1	2 850	254	135	5 559	5.3
Lawrence	507	0.5	17.5	6.9	4.3	9.1	8.0	14.2	18.2	4 990	207	302	12 756	22.3
Lincoln	845	11.8	D	8.5	6.0	6.3	13.0	14.1	7.0	4 805	107	162	17 875	95.8
Lyman	81	31.9	D	D	D	8.3	D	D	39.7	730	194	84	1 704	4.2
McCook	121	52.0	3.6	0.6	3.5	3.7	2.6	6.8	12.0	1 180	210	56	2 491	4.5
McPherson	46	48.7	10.2	4.9	D	3.1	4.5	7.1	14.9	780	317	61	1 418	-3.2
Marshall	83	25.6	D	16.5	D	5.7	D	D	17.9	1 025	220	81	2 534	-1.1
Meade	478	1.2	D	2.3	D	5.9	6.1	6.3	36.9	4 615	181	325	11 000	8.4
Mellette	24	42.1	D	0.5	D	4.0	D	D	38.0	340	166	112	838	1.7
Miner	73	54.1	D	9.0	D	3.0	1.6	6.3	10.0	615	257	27	1 308	-7.0
Minnehaha	6 332	1.0	D	8.7	8.2	7.5	14.6	19.8	11.0	28 575	169	2 439	71 557	18.8
Moody	159	34.5	17.0	8.4	D	3.1	D	4.9	21.4	1 250	193	54	2 824	2.9
Pennington	2 760	0.2	12.3	4.8	6.6	8.6	6.1	18.5	26.3	19 860	197	1 835	44 949	20.7
Perkins	53	12.7	D	D	2.4	7.5	D	7.8	21.8	805	270	54	1 739	-6.3
Potter	70	47.8	8.6	3.0	D	6.0	4.2	7.7	10.3	680	292	22	1 500	-14.8
Roberts	199	27.2	D	5.0	2.4	5.2	D	7.3	35.2	2 220	219	234	4 905	3.7
Sanborn	59	49.3	D	D	D	1.4	2.6	D	11.5	560	238	24	1 172	-3.9
Shannon	196	-0.5	D	D	D	D	D	D	83.8	1 315	97	1 073	3 593	15.0
Spink	233	55.5	4.2	1.8	D	2.8	3.1	D	19.3	1 605	250	192	3 139	-6.4
Stanley	49	-2.0	D	D	D	8.8	2.4	D	16.6	600	202	30	1 387	8.6
Sully	49	59.7	D	D	D	4.6	D	D	9.9	325	237	0	845	0.1
Todd	146	9.7	D	D	D	3.0	D	D	74.6	920	96	528	3 142	13.6

1. Includes mining, construction, and manufacturing.   2. Per 1,000 resident population enumerated in the 2010 census.

Table B. States and Counties — Housing, Labor Force, and Employment

STATE County	Housing units, 2006–2010								Civilian labor force, 2010				Civilian employment,[5] 2006–2010		
	Occupied units							Sub-stand-ard units[3] (percent)			Unemployment			Percent	
	Owner-occupied					Renter-occupied									
				Median owner cost as a percent of income											Con-struction, produc-tion, and mainte-nance occu-pations
	Total	Percent	Median value[1]	With a mort-gage	Without a mort-gage	Median rent[2]	Median rent as a per-cent of income		Total	Percent change, 2009–2010	Total	Rate[4]	Total	Manage-ment, business, science and arts	
	89	90	91	92	93	94	95	96	97	98	99	100	101	102	103
SOUTH CAROLINA—Cont'd															
Sumter	38 856	66.8	98 800	22.1	12.1	641	27.2	1.9	45 562	1.2	5 416	11.9	40 592	27.6	31.6
Union	12 106	73.2	74 300	21.9	12.7	562	29.9	1.8	11 494	-7.1	2 138	18.6	11 437	25.3	37.4
Williamsburg	11 079	65.2	67 200	26.4	12.7	477	32.3	3.8	16 016	-1.1	2 315	14.5	11 588	20.6	34.0
York	81 826	72.0	158 900	22.6	10.1	737	28.4	2.1	115 101	2.7	17 677	15.4	105 614	35.2	22.6
SOUTH DAKOTA	315 468	68.9	122 200	22.2	11.4	574	25.9	2.3	443 444	-0.1	22 378	5.0	410 156	34.4	24.1
Aurora	1 027	75.9	63 100	17.4	10.0	511	20.1	1.9	1 590	4.2	62	3.9	1 476	32.4	25.8
Beadle	7 205	65.2	83 400	19.3	10.5	443	24.2	2.9	9 799	-0.1	374	3.8	8 833	29.9	34.6
Bennett	1 054	59.9	60 200	16.2	13.0	410	24.0	6.8	1 426	1.5	83	5.8	1 163	36.1	25.8
Bon Homme	2 582	83.1	67 700	19.7	13.3	402	21.7	1.4	3 139	0.5	151	4.8	3 082	38.6	23.7
Brookings	11 405	59.0	138 300	21.7	10.5	575	29.3	1.3	18 781	-1.6	773	4.1	17 401	34.6	27.7
Brown	14 942	69.2	115 700	20.8	12.8	469	24.1	0.8	21 319	0.3	775	3.6	19 878	31.2	25.0
Brule	2 077	72.4	87 300	22.0	10.0	437	24.6	1.6	2 926	3.2	97	3.3	2 665	41.9	19.7
Buffalo	503	28.6	67 500	12.4	15.7	453	20.2	18.7	580	14.2	79	13.6	584	27.7	18.3
Butte	3 977	75.9	114 300	23.5	12.3	467	28.8	3.4	5 418	-0.4	249	4.6	4 697	28.2	30.0
Campbell	612	84.8	40 600	23.5	12.6	419	14.9	0.0	849	-0.8	36	4.2	756	44.7	23.8
Charles Mix	3 236	68.8	67 700	21.2	12.1	410	21.0	5.6	4 227	0.5	196	4.6	3 960	37.7	22.6
Clark	1 387	81.5	64 500	21.7	10.8	299	21.5	2.2	1 895	4.6	97	5.1	1 708	35.8	30.2
Clay	4 936	58.5	116 900	21.5	12.1	574	36.3	0.9	7 578	-1.6	301	4.0	7 212	40.2	16.7
Codington	11 336	69.6	131 000	21.3	12.1	556	26.6	1.0	15 885	-2.8	744	4.7	14 586	32.2	26.6
Corson	1 114	55.5	45 900	19.6	10.4	346	20.3	9.4	1 429	1.1	100	7.0	1 305	40.8	23.8
Custer	3 654	78.4	160 700	23.9	11.3	477	21.8	1.5	4 918	-2.2	222	4.5	3 792	43.9	23.2
Davison	8 086	63.0	108 800	21.9	11.2	534	26.0	1.2	11 155	-0.5	459	4.1	10 391	29.5	24.9
Day	2 504	69.2	64 800	20.8	12.5	450	20.0	1.9	2 864	-2.4	195	6.8	2 817	33.8	26.0
Deuel	1 802	81.9	87 200	22.1	10.0	411	21.9	2.2	2 607	-5.2	157	6.0	2 331	30.6	35.0
Dewey	1 699	56.9	56 900	17.8	10.0	374	26.0	7.9	2 801	6.8	318	11.4	2 020	47.1	20.4
Douglas	1 224	77.1	58 300	20.8	10.0	474	24.5	2.5	1 838	3.8	75	4.1	1 528	42.4	26.2
Edmunds	1 587	80.7	70 300	20.9	10.0	475	24.6	1.2	2 019	-2.3	71	3.5	1 956	36.4	26.6
Fall River	3 014	64.8	86 800	21.2	10.9	508	27.9	1.8	3 852	0.6	201	5.2	3 010	38.2	19.9
Faulk	913	80.1	51 300	19.4	11.1	413	33.3	4.5	1 163	0.5	42	3.6	1 051	41.7	23.6
Grant	3 183	74.7	99 800	25.4	10.8	484	24.2	2.1	4 227	0.4	209	4.9	4 269	31.2	25.7
Gregory	1 973	77.4	56 100	19.0	12.4	423	26.4	1.7	2 405	1.7	91	3.8	2 095	44.1	20.6
Haakon	769	81.4	74 800	20.9	10.0	486	16.5	2.3	1 168	-0.1	35	3.0	1 000	37.4	27.5
Hamlin	2 025	83.1	83 700	20.5	12.5	440	23.0	3.0	2 936	0.4	147	5.0	2 739	29.6	36.6
Hand	1 483	72.7	74 900	21.3	10.0	444	27.5	0.8	1 915	-1.4	59	3.1	1 844	36.8	28.3
Hanson	1 156	84.5	87 300	22.6	12.9	554	20.3	1.5	1 935	-0.8	98	5.1	1 541	35.8	31.1
Harding	526	74.3	67 000	18.2	12.1	409	20.8	1.0	835	5.6	25	3.0	650	52.3	23.7
Hughes	7 111	69.1	133 200	22.0	10.0	500	25.8	2.5	10 541	0.6	348	3.3	9 669	40.9	14.8
Hutchinson	2 961	79.0	68 700	18.9	12.7	394	25.3	0.6	3 872	1.6	148	3.8	3 500	38.4	31.0
Hyde	588	76.4	66 600	22.3	10.9	408	25.5	1.0	767	0.4	29	3.8	690	41.4	29.3
Jackson	964	64.7	54 600	22.4	11.8	430	24.4	16.8	1 251	-2.8	80	6.4	1 125	37.3	18.3
Jerauld	903	69.8	62 200	23.3	10.2	421	23.4	1.0	1 439	3.3	42	2.9	1 024	30.6	34.6
Jones	471	73.0	75 000	14.9	10.9	397	13.3	0.6	727	1.1	19	2.6	647	37.6	20.9
Kingsbury	2 332	77.9	70 300	19.2	11.2	398	17.6	0.7	2 991	-1.2	156	5.2	2 660	33.2	33.7
Lake	4 533	71.0	108 800	21.4	12.7	475	28.4	0.6	6 528	-2.8	354	5.4	5 780	29.8	30.8
Lawrence	10 651	64.7	155 100	24.0	12.1	543	28.4	1.0	13 584	-0.5	600	4.4	12 182	31.4	20.2
Lincoln	15 782	76.1	169 700	22.6	10.0	814	25.7	1.0	22 122	0.6	980	4.4	23 327	41.0	19.0
Lyman	1 449	60.5	64 900	22.2	11.2	383	15.2	6.6	2 059	2.1	122	5.9	1 725	37.8	25.4
McCook	2 171	80.0	91 900	19.9	11.9	502	24.2	2.3	2 620	-3.9	143	5.5	2 879	36.6	23.1
McPherson	1 048	80.0	45 100	16.1	14.4	236	43.8	2.6	1 171	0.1	58	5.0	1 086	42.6	26.0
Marshall	1 737	70.2	81 700	20.7	10.6	446	23.3	3.7	2 127	-0.7	123	5.8	2 254	33.2	32.7
Meade	9 714	72.6	145 800	26.4	12.9	612	27.1	1.4	12 020	-2.5	673	5.6	12 058	28.0	26.5
Mellette	677	66.6	49 800	21.6	11.8	409	23.9	7.5	919	5.0	53	5.8	809	45.9	19.9
Miner	1 089	81.2	58 400	19.5	11.9	437	21.4	0.3	1 236	-2.8	68	5.5	1 226	38.9	32.3
Minnehaha	65 462	65.9	144 900	22.1	10.9	648	26.1	1.7	99 700	-1.0	5 072	5.1	92 826	32.5	23.3
Moody	2 595	78.1	102 800	22.4	10.2	496	18.3	2.9	3 963	0.4	278	7.0	3 676	33.0	30.1
Pennington	39 939	66.6	149 700	24.4	12.3	671	28.3	1.9	54 746	-0.7	2 691	4.9	49 340	35.1	21.3
Perkins	1 371	69.4	50 800	22.0	11.0	389	19.4	3.6	1 652	0.1	64	3.9	1 489	45.7	22.8
Potter	1 019	82.0	55 600	18.1	12.4	500	32.1	0.2	1 334	1.0	57	4.3	1 231	33.8	26.2
Roberts	3 766	70.7	73 200	22.2	11.3	413	20.9	3.6	4 890	1.7	278	5.7	4 411	32.1	26.7
Sanborn	966	76.6	62 700	18.9	10.1	450	19.0	4.0	1 392	-2.2	55	4.0	1 203	29.3	31.9
Shannon	2 828	51.3	18 600	25.9	13.0	376	16.5	36.5	3 901	-0.8	464	11.9	3 345	43.2	14.1
Spink	2 640	77.7	62 700	17.3	10.0	457	24.2	1.4	3 523	1.3	135	3.8	2 989	35.5	25.5
Stanley	1 160	76.1	113 700	17.5	12.3	821	32.8	0.9	1 982	2.6	68	3.4	1 702	32.7	26.4
Sully	587	78.5	72 200	21.7	10.0	560	18.9	0.0	1 020	1.0	30	2.9	831	41.3	22.6
Todd	2 553	40.6	53 800	26.6	10.0	431	17.0	16.7	3 725	6.6	256	6.9	2 929	37.8	22.4

1. Specified owner-occupied units.   2. Specified renter-occupied units. A value of 10.0 represents 10 percent or less.   3. Overcrowded or lacking complete plumbing facilities.   4. Percent of civilian labor force.   5. Persons 16 years old and over.

Table B. States and Counties — **Nonfarm Employment and Agriculture**

STATE County	Private nonfarm establishments, employment and payroll, 2009									Agriculture, 2007			
		Employment						Annual payroll		Farms			
												Percent with:	
	Number of establishments	Total	Health care and social assistance	Manufacturing	Retail trade	Finance and insurance	Professional, scientific, and technical services	Total (mil dol)	Average per employee (dollars)	Number	Fewer than 50 acres	500 acres or more	Farm operators whose principal occupation is farming (percent)
	104	105	106	107	108	109	110	111	112	113	114	115	116
SOUTH CAROLINA—Cont'd													
Sumter	1 842	28 652	4 526	6 892	4 324	820	796	832	29 055	554	43.0	12.8	49.6
Union	467	6 265	788	1 836	1 057	D	162	157	24 983	262	30.2	5.0	30.5
Williamsburg	534	7 159	844	D	891	241	559	209	29 140	861	33.0	12.1	34.7
York	4 441	65 053	8 379	8 569	8 684	5 350	2 353	2 244	34 488	1 038	47.4	3.8	33.5
SOUTH DAKOTA	25 483	330 517	60 812	40 477	50 335	27 542	11 048	10 454	31 628	31 169	15.5	46.7	60.2
Aurora	86	628	219	D	75	D	D	23	35 873	379	14.5	43.8	61.7
Beadle	583	7 055	1 453	1 342	1 274	416	129	185	26 221	750	19.2	47.6	61.2
Bennett	65	577	138	0	123	D	13	14	24 390	265	6.8	69.1	70.9
Bon Homme	189	1 326	485	73	232	D	D	28	21 398	563	12.4	40.3	70.0
Brookings	853	14 397	1 341	5 875	1 817	470	390	437	30 375	986	25.5	26.6	48.8
Brown	1 315	18 296	3 244	2 354	3 041	1 229	455	571	31 232	1 036	16.5	46.1	56.9
Brule	218	1 773	443	27	284	69	42	41	23 302	370	11.6	64.3	66.5
Buffalo	8	135	D	D	D	0	D	3	22 356	86	16.3	66.3	70.9
Butte	305	1 978	270	174	389	84	79	53	26 877	584	20.0	40.4	50.7
Campbell	50	273	24	D	D	D	7	7	24 414	318	8.8	56.9	53.1
Charles Mix	287	2 340	521	84	414	109	48	54	23 026	693	13.1	47.6	68.3
Clark	113	524	D	D	77	D	D	14	26 710	577	10.6	44.2	62.9
Clay	308	3 732	674	D	924	104	57	69	18 541	484	21.5	42.1	61.0
Codington	1 074	13 509	1 671	3 027	2 501	965	274	371	27 480	663	24.7	29.6	45.6
Corson	36	213	33	0	64	D	0	5	22 183	392	5.1	71.7	70.7
Custer	268	1 341	238	D	257	D	36	40	30 022	359	20.9	35.7	48.5
Davison	735	10 896	1 836	1 609	1 960	346	292	307	28 185	406	24.4	35.7	51.7
Day	189	1 475	312	191	269	68	D	37	25 047	675	8.0	43.6	59.2
Deuel	132	1 442	177	414	D	D	D	44	30 760	583	15.4	34.8	55.4
Dewey	105	694	184	D	150	42	D	20	29 131	410	5.4	72.9	65.1
Douglas	112	889	D	118	123	D	D	21	23 929	363	15.4	44.1	67.5
Edmunds	119	796	211	D	140	48	D	22	27 330	425	6.4	56.7	60.7
Fall River	214	2 096	1 046	26	260	D	47	90	43 014	330	13.0	49.7	53.9
Faulk	72	396	D	D	88	D	D	11	26 730	294	6.8	72.8	74.8
Grant	287	3 197	378	554	481	D	54	98	30 533	555	12.4	39.6	62.5
Gregory	178	1 063	290	42	238	D	24	24	22 707	511	10.0	54.6	64.4
Haakon	83	581	D	D	92	D	D	14	24 817	284	2.5	79.6	71.8
Hamlin	158	1 002	178	D	139	55	D	29	28 773	449	24.5	36.7	50.1
Hand	134	990	216	67	169	D	25	27	26 974	484	7.2	61.6	75.0
Hanson	56	205	D	17	D	30	D	5	26 498	308	17.2	40.9	61.4
Harding	30	D	D	0	25	D	D	D	D	252	2.0	82.1	75.4
Hughes	687	6 418	1 060	D	1 417	D	281	177	27 622	305	18.0	43.9	53.8
Hutchinson	235	2 080	636	197	397	D	27	51	24 622	723	13.1	46.5	67.5
Hyde	42	478	D	0	69	D	D	14	28 523	181	7.2	68.5	68.0
Jackson	46	253	D	D	111	D	D	5	21 664	297	6.7	76.1	77.1
Jerauld	75	D	D	D	D	28	D	D	D	239	6.7	49.4	57.3
Jones	54	278	D	D	106	D	D	7	25 255	163	4.9	73.0	68.1
Kingsbury	170	1 316	212	337	160	102	D	39	29 312	551	14.9	43.2	58.6
Lake	364	3 515	624	761	501	107	122	93	26 385	514	24.5	37.7	54.7
Lawrence	979	9 888	D	228	1 445	D	273	255	25 779	301	26.9	19.3	42.9
Lincoln	1 076	10 980	1 926	1 727	1 341	892	387	379	34 531	855	29.2	24.0	54.6
Lyman	72	639	D	0	266	38	D	13	19 977	443	6.5	59.8	54.4
McCook	187	968	245	D	211	45	50	21	21 414	545	20.2	39.8	63.7
McPherson	75	348	D	53	D	52	12	7	20 862	398	6.3	50.8	55.3
Marshall	151	965	D	260	172	56	28	27	27 951	523	11.3	49.9	59.3
Meade	672	5 115	1 487	284	615	193	166	196	38 393	879	17.3	55.9	58.7
Mellette	28	D	D	0	D	6	D	D	D	216	2.3	83.8	75.5
Miner	77	562	140	D	D	D	D	16	29 119	356	11.5	46.9	61.0
Minnehaha	5 469	110 148	22 042	11 292	14 224	14 274	4 754	3 969	36 037	1 194	34.5	24.5	51.3
Moody	165	1 665	D	D	201	22	22	52	31 172	556	22.3	28.2	53.4
Pennington	3 559	44 419	8 302	2 495	8 368	2 598	1 820	1 395	31 408	655	20.8	40.0	51.5
Perkins	132	798	180	D	118	55	8	19	23 452	432	4.2	78.2	74.3
Potter	103	812	169	D	157	D	D	23	28 602	238	7.1	60.1	65.5
Roberts	231	2 130	506	D	368	111	26	49	22 790	887	13.5	39.1	63.7
Sanborn	59	345	D	0	43	D	20	8	22 455	354	8.8	45.8	61.6
Shannon	68	1 856	340	D	165	D	D	52	28 142	250	6.8	60.0	61.6
Spink	178	1 235	285	113	196	72	25	35	28 729	624	6.9	62.7	69.7
Stanley	103	999	D	D	D	D	24	27	27 392	165	10.9	74.5	52.1
Sully	59	294	D	D	79	D	D	8	27 942	195	4.1	71.8	76.9
Todd	53	1 887	D	D	225	D	D	36	19 331	258	6.6	55.8	64.7

Table B. States and Counties — **Agriculture**

STATE County	Acreage (1,000)	Percent change, 2002–2007	Acres: Average size of farm	Total irrigated (1,000)	Total cropland (1,000)	Value of land and buildings (dollars): Average per farm	Average per acre	Value of machinery and equipment, average per farm (dollars)	Total (mil dol)	Average per farm (dollars)	Crops	Live-stock and poultry products	$10,000 or more	$100,000 or more	Government payments: Total ($1,000)	Percent of farms
	117	118	119	120	121	122	123	124	125	126	127	128	129	130	131	132
SOUTH CAROLINA—Cont'd																
Sumter	153	12.5	277	9.5	88.8	552 862	1 996	91 687	88.8	160 337	37.3	62.7	25.6	11.0	4 016	54.0
Union	46	-9.8	174	0.1	9.5	446 475	2 570	48 427	D	D	D	0.0	16.0	0.8	133	10.3
Williamsburg	209	1.5	243	0.9	105.6	592 524	2 436	66 117	42.4	49 302	70.8	29.2	23.9	7.8	3 738	58.5
York	124	4.2	120	1.0	39.3	477 437	3 991	47 917	92.5	89 082	D	D	17.2	2.7	609	13.9
SOUTH DAKOTA	43 666	-0.3	1 401	373.8	19 094.3	1 255 332	896	155 652	6 570.5	210 801	51.5	48.5	65.4	38.3	270 748	73.5
Aurora	365	4.0	962	0.0	228.8	1 316 163	1 368	144 420	102.7	271 018	46.0	54.0	68.6	38.5	3 133	84.7
Beadle	770	-4.9	1 026	20.0	492.4	1 338 462	1 304	185 877	195.4	260 566	50.9	49.1	66.7	43.5	7 087	73.5
Bennett	753	3.6	2 843	6.7	257.2	1 053 384	371	162 231	38.1	143 879	46.6	53.4	76.2	41.1	2 561	73.6
Bon Homme	309	-10.4	548	8.2	219.8	804 317	1 467	126 226	109.2	193 914	40.0	60.0	79.0	42.3	2 953	88.6
Brookings	463	10.8	469	15.9	351.3	1 001 355	2 134	134 499	186.7	189 376	46.7	53.3	54.0	30.1	6 565	71.0
Brown	1 085	-6.1	1 047	7.5	827.6	1 656 624	1 582	213 411	248.8	240 121	74.5	25.5	59.6	38.0	12 461	72.8
Brule	518	15.9	1 401	5.5	287.6	1 471 816	1 050	218 093	99.7	269 491	45.2	54.8	76.8	49.7	3 704	77.8
Buffalo	312	9.5	3 629	1.5	73.8	1 990 955	549	219 024	25.0	291 226	43.2	56.8	68.6	47.7	1 525	73.3
Butte	1 140	-9.7	1 953	47.7	163.4	956 959	490	84 311	55.4	94 936	16.1	83.9	56.2	20.5	2 310	42.3
Campbell	401	2.6	1 261	1.1	205.6	924 190	733	152 437	49.4	155 318	59.9	40.1	52.5	31.8	3 362	87.4
Charles Mix	661	-10.2	953	9.8	403.4	1 196 875	1 256	172 826	176.2	254 293	43.8	56.2	72.4	45.3	4 812	84.1
Clark	509	-3.2	882	6.6	335.7	1 285 162	1 458	164 048	146.5	253 893	43.8	56.2	67.1	41.8	5 639	87.2
Clay	267	-28.4	551	12.5	237.3	1 281 632	2 326	184 260	80.8	166 986	80.2	19.8	70.9	45.5	3 874	83.5
Codington	367	-5.2	554	4.6	247.7	867 278	1 566	125 614	107.8	162 581	49.9	50.1	54.4	28.5	4 054	70.9
Corson	1 283	-7.6	3 273	1.2	372.9	1 231 837	376	139 259	65.5	167 027	45.5	54.5	74.2	41.6	3 704	76.5
Custer	601	2.0	1 674	3.6	87.2	962 135	575	67 814	14.4	40 048	4.0	96.0	39.8	11.4	1 075	25.9
Davison	280	0.4	688	1.6	214.9	1 174 521	1 706	133 167	78.1	192 467	59.4	40.6	62.8	35.0	2 368	65.5
Day	567	6.8	840	0.3	387.0	1 035 545	1 232	137 370	97.8	144 910	70.7	29.3	54.5	32.0	8 133	84.1
Deuel	317	-3.4	544	0.6	199.6	855 693	1 573	124 117	105.1	180 261	40.4	59.6	59.3	30.4	4 440	82.0
Dewey	1 450	6.0	3 536	D	250.0	1 239 985	351	125 059	49.1	119 731	34.8	65.2	72.4	37.3	3 573	60.0
Douglas	225	-5.1	620	2.5	157.3	910 819	1 468	130 148	107.1	294 948	34.1	65.9	81.3	54.0	1 933	80.7
Edmunds	657	12.3	1 545	1.1	454.3	1 586 042	1 026	222 248	162.5	382 407	56.5	43.5	65.4	45.9	4 594	81.6
Fall River	950	-3.3	2 878	8.1	97.1	1 162 239	404	83 397	96.9	293 719	1.4	98.6	45.8	19.1	1 527	40.9
Faulk	615	15.0	2 091	D	373.4	2 027 335	970	273 805	109.7	372 986	63.2	36.8	78.2	57.5	5 840	88.1
Grant	364	4.0	655	4.0	263.7	1 042 232	1 590	168 499	133.5	240 587	50.3	49.7	70.1	41.1	3 704	80.7
Gregory	654	0.5	1 281	1.7	256.3	932 875	728	124 613	73.4	143 689	42.2	57.8	76.3	34.8	1 932	73.0
Haakon	1 151	-5.8	4 053	0.0	324.7	1 722 236	425	154 974	53.0	186 751	38.6	61.4	77.5	50.4	4 459	79.4
Hamlin	310	1.0	690	8.7	244.8	1 289 702	1 870	183 276	111.0	247 164	56.3	43.7	63.3	39.9	3 877	79.1
Hand	899	3.6	1 857	2.4	506.2	1 724 861	929	207 910	163.9	338 738	59.7	40.3	71.1	48.8	6 471	81.8
Hanson	219	-12.0	711	2.7	174.4	1 390 310	1 955	196 282	67.3	218 569	54.9	45.1	67.9	42.2	2 319	76.0
Harding	1 596	-4.7	6 334	1.0	207.6	2 304 456	364	155 526	41.3	163 669	18.5	81.5	79.0	48.8	2 661	72.6
Hughes	411	11.7	1 348	9.2	235.1	1 124 494	834	169 567	60.8	199 253	65.7	34.3	62.6	34.8	3 091	69.2
Hutchinson	510	0.8	705	3.3	394.7	1 291 838	1 832	169 124	192.4	266 048	53.9	46.1	71.9	49.5	5 499	86.4
Hyde	481	2.6	2 657	D	207.2	1 694 362	638	191 459	47.2	260 600	59.4	40.6	71.8	45.9	2 813	76.8
Jackson	1 184	-0.6	3 987	1.3	229.0	1 426 638	358	127 970	36.9	124 182	31.5	68.5	75.1	42.4	2 881	65.3
Jerauld	329	-2.1	1 375	1.3	185.6	1 259 237	916	179 222	68.7	287 599	49.3	50.7	68.2	40.2	1 932	79.5
Jones	519	0.6	3 186	0.7	190.5	1 244 663	391	143 369	28.8	176 753	50.5	49.5	74.8	46.6	2 514	84.0
Kingsbury	477	-8.1	867	1.8	356.9	1 314 692	1 517	176 214	172.5	313 044	52.8	47.2	69.9	44.1	5 771	79.5
Lake	315	-3.1	613	2.8	260.0	1 478 016	2 412	181 240	131.8	256 512	62.1	37.9	63.2	42.6	3 953	75.3
Lawrence	134	-5.0	444	3.8	30.5	640 919	1 445	55 318	11.6	38 605	21.5	78.5	39.9	8.3	115	10.3
Lincoln	333	7.4	389	2.1	303.4	1 194 710	3 070	130 819	158.1	184 923	64.2	35.8	69.5	34.3	4 690	73.9
Lyman	976	10.3	2 204	9.8	467.7	1 379 745	626	157 717	84.4	190 620	60.6	39.4	58.9	37.7	6 744	80.4
McCook	363	5.2	667	0.0	289.2	1 396 692	2 095	157 585	129.2	237 076	62.1	37.9	67.2	45.9	4 422	81.5
McPherson	518	-3.5	1 302	0.5	250.3	975 939	750	131 359	84.9	213 210	33.3	66.7	55.5	33.4	3 206	84.7
Marshall	534	1.7	1 021	0.6	328.2	1 190 237	1 165	186 355	161.3	308 394	34.6	65.4	62.9	38.2	7 791	83.7
Meade	2 209	-0.9	2 513	6.6	520.4	1 264 860	503	107 585	78.4	89 201	25.9	74.1	57.2	25.9	5 967	48.7
Mellette	730	10.6	3 379	1.0	127.3	1 221 424	362	123 889	53.3	246 611	12.6	87.4	87.5	48.1	1 447	68.5
Miner	300	3.1	843	0.0	201.7	1 271 442	1 508	163 285	75.0	210 594	54.7	45.3	62.4	42.1	3 065	80.3
Minnehaha	421	-0.2	353	2.7	326.4	973 600	2 759	135 251	190.3	159 415	57.5	42.5	60.7	33.8	5 630	67.2
Moody	293	3.5	528	2.4	235.5	1 322 921	2 507	158 890	158.1	284 378	49.4	50.6	61.5	37.2	4 864	83.1
Pennington	1 185	-2.1	1 809	7.9	280.3	1 240 492	686	100 796	56.0	85 554	33.0	67.0	46.7	18.2	3 274	37.3
Perkins	1 829	2.6	4 234	0.6	427.3	1 735 967	410	135 386	59.5	137 696	23.1	76.9	78.0	43.8	5 362	79.4
Potter	517	14.1	2 171	D	355.9	2 022 031	931	253 542	90.4	379 730	84.2	15.8	68.1	51.3	3 916	81.5
Roberts	593	0.0	668	1.3	412.4	982 539	1 470	156 315	135.3	152 589	67.3	32.7	61.7	35.2	7 806	82.1
Sanborn	318	-16.3	899	D	175.1	1 105 508	1 230	144 063	63.6	179 623	43.0	57.0	66.7	39.0	3 005	83.9
Shannon	1 334	5.3	5 335	D	104.9	1 138 819	213	86 381	19.8	79 214	20.3	79.7	56.8	24.8	1 229	40.8
Spink	908	-0.3	1 455	19.1	686.9	1 997 548	1 373	274 523	229.1	367 210	65.6	34.4	75.2	53.0	10 508	89.3
Stanley	921	6.4	5 582	0.0	233.6	2 211 090	396	165 522	35.2	213 384	66.0	34.0	65.5	38.2	2 890	62.4
Sully	609	6.3	3 123	15.4	488.9	2 819 856	903	310 864	116.5	597 224	80.0	20.0	77.4	60.0	5 482	87.7
Todd	869	-5.2	3 370	8.5	139.6	983 601	292	125 329	35.8	138 783	26.8	73.2	68.2	30.6	488	33.7

Table B. States and Counties — Water Use, Wholesale Trade, Retail Trade, and Real Estate

STATE County	Water use, 2005		Wholesale trade,[1] 2007				Retail trade,[2] 2007				Real estate and rental and leasing,[2] 2007			
	Total water withdrawn (mil gal/day)	Gallons withdrawn per person	Number of establishments	Number of employees	Sales (mil dol)	Annual payroll (mil dol)	Number of establishments	Number of employees	Sales (mil dol)	Annual payroll (mil dol)	Number of establishments	Number of employees	Receipts (mil dol)	Annual payroll (mil dol)
	133	134	135	136	137	138	139	140	141	142	143	144	145	146
SOUTH CAROLINA—Cont'd														
Sumter	24.9	236	73	D	D	D	417	4 919	1 021.5	91.8	87	308	36.7	6.8
Union	6.5	227	15	D	D	D	107	885	192.2	16.9	14	37	3.7	0.7
Williamsburg	6.2	174	19	237	102.5	7.5	124	995	224.6	16.9	14	46	3.9	0.9
York	177.7	935	222	2 949	2 150.1	141.9	689	8 200	2 172.7	179.1	229	825	113.7	21.4
SOUTH DAKOTA	500.4	645	1 248	13 402	11 400.5	550.8	4 172	50 842	12 266.2	1 045.3	888	3 844	523.9	90.3
Aurora	0.8	283	5	22	19.2	0.6	15	86	38.1	1.3	2	D	D	D
Beadle	12.0	757	25	D	D	D	97	1 262	245.8	23.2	31	108	12.4	1.3
Bennett	9.8	2 728	1	D	D	D	15	118	24.0	1.9	NA	NA	NA	NA
Bon Homme	6.4	897	11	87	43.2	2.0	38	231	40.7	3.4	3	6	0.2	0.0
Brookings	15.1	535	30	D	D	D	118	1 729	338.2	30.7	38	151	14.4	3.4
Brown	7.9	227	78	863	1 471.6	34.6	209	2 980	692.2	65.4	55	264	39.3	5.8
Brule	2.7	526	11	70	46.8	2.7	42	320	78.5	5.0	2	D	D	D
Buffalo	5.3	2 529	NA	NA	NA	NA	2	D	D	D	1	D	D	D
Butte	51.3	5 501	9	67	29.1	2.2	46	386	108.9	8.9	11	D	D	D
Campbell	2.5	1 610	5	D	D	D	5	21	3.9	0.2	1	D	D	D
Charles Mix	14.2	1 543	15	113	73.1	3.2	60	428	82.1	6.2	3	5	1.0	0.1
Clark	6.3	1 648	8	50	64.3	2.0	16	82	21.0	1.6	1	D	D	D
Clay	7.0	536	10	D	D	D	45	772	140.1	12.2	14	75	5.3	0.6
Codington	8.5	328	62	536	344.0	22.7	201	2 602	560.7	51.7	40	D	D	D
Corson	1.6	355	4	D	D	D	7	59	10.6	0.9	NA	NA	NA	NA
Custer	7.8	988	4	D	D	D	30	228	51.5	5.1	9	17	2.8	0.3
Davison	1.6	84	33	393	407.0	17.7	135	2 055	436.2	38.6	27	D	D	D
Day	4.0	693	11	128	97.1	4.4	35	245	51.0	3.9	5	D	D	D
Deuel	1.8	412	3	D	D	D	24	142	36.4	2.6	1	D	D	D
Dewey	1.2	192	7	39	12.5	1.1	20	132	23.8	1.5	2	D	D	D
Douglas	3.2	961	6	D	D	D	16	113	22.5	1.9	2	D	D	D
Edmunds	1.3	323	12	119	196.3	4.5	24	159	89.7	2.7	3	10	0.1	0.0
Fall River	26.5	3 608	3	20	3.6	0.4	40	338	68.7	5.4	6	32	3.0	0.2
Faulk	0.8	339	8	49	72.7	1.2	13	75	20.3	1.7	1	D	D	D
Grant	9.0	1 216	11	114	122.8	5.2	48	500	99.8	9.3	10	29	2.7	0.3
Gregory	2.5	576	10	41	27.3	0.8	38	277	53.0	4.5	1	D	D	D
Haakon	1.9	1 004	6	31	54.6	1.0	15	106	23.9	1.7	1	D	D	D
Hamlin	6.2	1 085	8	90	80.7	4.5	24	147	49.1	3.1	1	D	D	D
Hand	2.2	665	11	107	76.5	3.7	24	150	30.3	2.7	NA	NA	NA	NA
Hanson	1.4	382	6	D	D	D	5	45	6.0	0.5	2	D	D	D
Harding	1.7	1 388	NA	NA	NA	NA	6	36	8.7	0.5	NA	NA	NA	NA
Hughes	25.3	1 499	22	227	250.1	6.9	120	1 409	262.3	27.8	31	134	6.8	1.1
Hutchinson	2.8	369	24	237	321.5	7.2	48	338	74.0	5.7	3	4	0.4	0.1
Hyde	0.8	489	NA	NA	NA	NA	10	116	37.5	2.0	2	D	D	D
Jackson	3.2	1 106	2	D	D	D	15	114	29.1	2.0	NA	NA	NA	NA
Jerauld	2.1	988	8	D	D	D	11	79	20.5	1.5	2	D	D	D
Jones	0.8	726	2	D	D	D	13	99	23.0	1.9	NA	NA	NA	NA
Kingsbury	4.5	813	6	82	103.3	3.6	30	155	34.1	2.6	2	D	D	D
Lake	1.8	160	12	215	225.0	8.6	54	516	134.7	10.4	15	44	2.3	0.5
Lawrence	12.9	575	23	D	D	D	148	1 532	435.1	35.0	61	197	19.8	4.4
Lincoln	4.3	129	47	355	337.8	14.4	115	1 241	444.4	33.9	34	D	D	D
Lyman	2.5	630	5	D	D	D	19	278	69.0	4.3	1	D	D	D
McCook	1.5	256	10	59	41.4	1.7	26	152	43.5	3.0	5	D	D	D
McPherson	3.2	1 207	3	D	D	D	16	60	15.7	1.0	3	3	0.2	0.0
Marshall	2.3	518	11	75	38.1	2.1	27	177	48.2	3.1	1	D	D	D
Meade	9.3	379	21	88	39.2	3.6	86	702	194.3	15.1	29	94	15.6	1.5
Mellette	2.5	1 193	2	D	D	D	6	47	9.3	0.7	NA	NA	NA	NA
Miner	0.7	263	5	D	D	D	13	64	10.7	0.9	NA	NA	NA	NA
Minnehaha	32.2	201	322	4 798	3 023.5	224.1	851	14 984	3 823.8	329.4	205	1 263	204.2	36.8
Moody	3.1	467	7	32	16.5	1.0	20	180	38.3	3.2	2	D	D	D
Pennington	35.3	378	155	1 934	1 007.2	75.1	600	7 902	1 967.8	178.9	158	677	112.7	16.5
Perkins	1.5	490	4	D	D	D	26	144	28.2	2.7	1	D	D	D
Potter	1.4	608	7	59	52.0	2.3	21	169	26.8	2.0	2	D	D	D
Roberts	3.2	322	16	108	211.1	3.4	51	384	81.0	6.0	1	D	D	D
Sanborn	0.8	299	7	75	51.0	3.4	7	65	6.7	0.5	NA	NA	NA	NA
Shannon	1.4	104	NA	NA	NA	NA	15	194	39.2	2.4	1	D	D	D
Spink	21.9	3 173	10	127	248.3	5.6	30	199	41.1	3.6	3	7	0.4	0.0
Stanley	0.9	325	4	D	D	D	19	114	30.7	2.3	3	3	0.3	0.1
Sully	10.0	7 000	2	D	D	D	13	86	31.3	1.7	1	D	D	D
Todd	11.4	1 158	1	D	D	D	21	241	39.5	2.9	NA	NA	NA	NA

1. Merchant wholesalers, except manufacturers' sales branches and offices.   2. Employer establishments.

Table B. States and Counties — Professional Services, Manufacturing, and Accommodation and Food Services

STATE County	Professional, scientific, and technical services,[1] 2007				Manufacturing, 2007				Accommodation and food services, 2007			
	Number of establishments	Number of employees	Receipts (mil dol)	Annual payroll (mil dol)	Number of establishments	Number of employees	Receipts (mil dol)	Annual payroll (mil dol)	Number of establishments	Number of employees	Sales (mil dol)	Annual payroll (mil dol)
	147	148	149	150	151	152	153	154	155	156	157	158
SOUTH CAROLINA—Cont'd												
Sumter	139	D	D	D	82	7 707	1 922.0	253.3	149	3 173	109.4	29.8
Union	25	192	6.9	2.2	31	2 062	488.4	72.4	32	554	18.5	4.9
Williamsburg	31	117	10.1	3.9	35	2 811	1 398.1	93.0	29	404	12.8	3.1
York	403	D	D	D	233	10 096	3 621.2	457.8	365	6 983	285.8	78.0
SOUTH DAKOTA	1 735	10 073	1 093.4	385.9	1 052	40 961	13 051.1	1 539.3	2 426	36 710	1 622.8	436.2
Aurora	5	25	2.2	0.4	NA	NA	NA	NA	11	D	D	D
Beadle	24	D	D	D	32	1 140	298.6	32.3	54	609	20.8	5.4
Bennett	4	9	0.3	0.1	NA	NA	NA	NA	8	57	1.8	0.4
Bon Homme	8	13	1.5	0.3	NA	NA	NA	NA	15	80	2.3	0.5
Brookings	64	350	33.7	12.4	42	5 104	2 265.7	210.4	76	1 636	53.2	14.1
Brown	85	419	41.1	15.3	37	D	D	D	116	1 989	74.1	19.8
Brule	13	33	2.3	0.8	NA	NA	NA	NA	26	252	9.9	2.4
Buffalo	NA	NA	NA	NA	NA	NA	NA	NA	1	D	D	D
Butte	23	67	5.7	1.9	NA	NA	NA	NA	32	261	8.5	2.2
Campbell	3	7	0.2	0.1	NA	NA	NA	NA	7	D	D	D
Charles Mix	13	47	4.3	1.0	NA	NA	NA	NA	26	453	18.2	6.7
Clark	6	19	1.6	0.3	NA	NA	NA	NA	7	47	1.6	0.4
Clay	18	D	D	D	NA	NA	NA	NA	44	703	19.3	5.2
Codington	64	D	D	D	73	D	D	D	88	1 873	75.6	22.1
Corson	NA	NA	NA	NA	NA	NA	NA	NA	3	5	0.1	0.0
Custer	15	40	2.4	0.9	NA	NA	NA	NA	58	281	27.8	7.3
Davison	44	D	D	D	45	1 717	D	68.7	69	1 211	45.6	13.5
Day	8	31	1.9	0.7	NA	NA	NA	NA	21	146	4.3	1.2
Deuel	4	D	D	D	NA	NA	NA	NA	15	60	2.5	0.5
Dewey	4	D	D	D	NA	NA	NA	NA	7	D	D	D
Douglas	6	13	0.9	0.2	NA	NA	NA	NA	10	D	D	D
Edmunds	6	19	2.2	0.7	NA	NA	NA	NA	15	81	1.9	0.4
Fall River	19	72	3.7	1.2	NA	NA	NA	NA	41	248	10.0	2.6
Faulk	2	D	D	D	NA	NA	NA	NA	9	D	D	D
Grant	18	64	4.5	1.4	13	531	634.2	20.6	30	297	9.1	2.4
Gregory	8	25	2.3	0.5	NA	NA	NA	NA	19	102	2.8	0.7
Haakon	7	12	1.2	0.4	NA	NA	NA	NA	9	D	D	D
Hamlin	2	D	D	D	NA	NA	NA	NA	15	77	2.3	0.5
Hand	11	23	2.3	0.8	NA	NA	NA	NA	14	56	2.7	0.5
Hanson	3	D	D	D	NA	NA	NA	NA	3	23	0.4	0.1
Harding	1	D	D	D	NA	NA	NA	NA	3	15	0.9	0.1
Hughes	61	248	29.9	9.5	NA	NA	NA	NA	55	935	35.1	9.4
Hutchinson	10	28	1.8	0.7	NA	NA	NA	NA	17	135	3.9	0.8
Hyde	3	D	D	D	NA	NA	NA	NA	1	D	D	D
Jackson	1	D	D	D	NA	NA	NA	NA	13	30	1.9	0.5
Jerauld	6	10	1.2	0.2	1	D	D	D	7	D	D	D
Jones	3	D	D	D	NA	NA	NA	NA	13	70	3.7	1.1
Kingsbury	9	21	2.7	0.5	NA	NA	NA	NA	17	106	3.7	0.9
Lake	30	143	22.1	4.4	26	935	342.9	35.0	45	471	14.3	3.7
Lawrence	62	250	21.7	7.4	44	D	D	17.3	140	2 623	221.7	42.6
Lincoln	64	D	D	D	67	1 630	D	59.2	45	840	27.6	8.0
Lyman	2	D	D	D	NA	NA	NA	NA	19	249	15.9	3.4
McCook	12	D	D	D	NA	NA	NA	NA	21	91	3.4	0.6
McPherson	4	7	0.4	0.1	NA	NA	NA	NA	7	D	D	D
Marshall	13	28	2.1	0.6	NA	NA	NA	NA	17	90	4.4	1.1
Meade	38	D	D	D	NA	NA	NA	NA	71	557	33.4	8.2
Mellette	2	D	D	D	NA	NA	NA	NA	4	D	D	D
Miner	3	19	0.9	0.4	NA	NA	NA	NA	8	D	D	D
Minnehaha	469	D	D	D	184	11 483	3 518.8	475.0	426	9 651	389.9	118.4
Moody	10	21	1.1	0.4	NA	NA	NA	NA	17	D	D	D
Pennington	288	D	D	D	119	2 893	678.3	D	341	5 981	286.5	80.6
Perkins	4	12	0.6	0.1	NA	NA	NA	NA	7	D	D	D
Potter	3	9	0.5	0.1	NA	NA	NA	NA	12	81	4.2	0.8
Roberts	12	D	D	D	NA	NA	NA	NA	28	221	7.2	1.7
Sanborn	5	13	1.6	0.4	NA	NA	NA	NA	7	28	1.1	0.2
Shannon	2	D	D	D	NA	NA	NA	NA	8	343	18.1	6.1
Spink	4	21	2.0	0.6	NA	NA	NA	NA	16	143	4.6	1.4
Stanley	4	36	2.2	0.7	NA	NA	NA	NA	12	166	5.4	1.3
Sully	2	D	D	D	NA	NA	NA	NA	9	54	2.0	0.5
Todd	NA	NA	NA	NA	NA	NA	NA	NA	4	24	1.7	0.4

1. Establishment subject to federal tax.

Table B. States and Counties — Health Care and Social Assistance, Other Services, and Federal Funds

STATE County	Health care and social assistance, 2007				Other services, 2007				Federal funds and grants, 2009–2010 Expenditures (mil dol)			
										Direct payments for individuals[1]		
	Number of establishments	Number of employees	Receipts (mil dol)	Annual payroll (mil dol)	Number of establishments	Number of employees	Receipts (mil dol)	Annual payroll (mil dol)	Total	Social Security and government retirement	Medicare	Food Stamps and Supplemental Security Income
	159	160	161	162	163	164	165	166	167	168	169	170
SOUTH CAROLINA—Cont'd												
Sumter	180	4 812	469.3	172.7	152	1 141	69.7	21.7	1 422.2	401.7	121.4	78.0
Union	38	843	67.2	27.3	36	130	7.0	2.4	245.3	110.4	51.1	14.4
Williamsburg	51	827	49.6	20.3	47	216	9.9	3.1	388.3	103.5	57.4	37.7
York	341	7 680	718.6	271.7	285	1 897	155.7	47.3	1 138.6	661.8	182.8	52.8
SOUTH DAKOTA	2 241	56 480	4 767.2	2 038.8	1 815	8 518	749.6	181.9	9 506.6	2 544.7	994.9	232.9
Aurora	9	D	D	D	5	D	D	D	29.1	8.3	5.9	0.3
Beadle	55	1 392	77.8	34.6	54	230	14.4	3.9	208.0	63.6	32.2	3.3
Bennett	5	D	D	D	4	D	D	D	34.6	7.6	3.8	4.2
Bon Homme	22	454	20.9	9.1	11	27	1.9	0.4	56.3	22.7	15.0	0.9
Brookings	67	1 209	62.3	28.9	69	307	49.5	7.2	214.7	62.3	26.8	4.3
Brown	153	3 178	275.0	99.1	89	467	31.6	8.1	439.8	123.4	59.9	7.4
Brule	21	378	21.3	9.1	17	61	6.6	1.3	62.2	16.7	10.1	2.8
Buffalo	3	D	D	D	NA	NA	NA	NA	39.8	2.8	2.4	0.5
Butte	21	137	9.2	3.9	25	79	6.2	1.6	67.5	34.2	10.0	3.1
Campbell	4	D	D	D	2	D	D	D	25.5	9.3	5.2	0.2
Charles Mix	25	495	22.8	10.2	26	81	7.8	1.7	125.2	26.2	16.7	4.4
Clark	8	114	5.0	2.1	7	D	D	D	48.9	13.0	7.6	0.8
Clay	30	D	D	D	24	155	31.3	2.6	112.4	27.6	13.3	3.7
Codington	85	1 592	157.0	49.1	86	386	29.0	6.7	178.5	79.0	26.8	5.4
Corson	5	16	0.8	0.3	NA	NA	NA	NA	56.1	13.4	8.4	4.0
Custer	15	52	3.1	1.4	13	75	5.6	1.7	76.8	40.8	7.8	1.6
Davison	92	D	D	D	55	D	D	D	162.7	57.7	34.0	5.4
Day	21	327	13.6	5.6	13	37	2.7	0.6	92.4	28.7	14.6	2.3
Deuel	7	210	8.8	4.1	5	22	1.2	0.3	39.2	14.1	7.7	0.8
Dewey	14	176	21.1	7.7	6	12	1.0	0.4	109.6	13.5	5.0	6.1
Douglas	8	231	10.8	5.1	7	D	D	D	30.3	11.1	7.0	0.6
Edmunds	12	199	9.7	4.0	7	19	1.9	0.3	52.0	13.2	9.3	0.4
Fall River	21	593	65.4	34.0	20	62	4.5	1.0	114.0	50.1	12.0	2.4
Faulk	5	D	D	D	8	D	D	D	34.1	7.9	6.0	0.3
Grant	21	260	13.5	4.9	21	75	6.2	1.4	67.7	28.1	14.1	1.4
Gregory	17	266	17.2	7.6	12	D	D	D	46.2	16.6	11.1	1.7
Haakon	6	D	D	D	3	D	D	D	21.2	8.0	3.5	0.2
Hamlin	11	182	5.6	2.4	7	17	1.0	0.3	42.2	15.2	7.3	0.8
Hand	8	208	8.5	4.2	10	D	D	D	48.5	10.7	6.8	0.6
Hanson	2	D	D	D	3	D	D	D	38.5	24.8	2.9	0.5
Harding	5	D	D	D	2	D	D	D	12.2	5.6	1.6	0.2
Hughes	52	D	D	D	92	382	55.6	11.0	846.1	47.0	18.1	3.6
Hutchinson	19	684	33.3	15.0	14	40	3.7	0.7	85.3	30.2	16.9	1.3
Hyde	4	D	D	D	2	D	D	D	57.2	4.7	2.9	0.3
Jackson	1	D	D	D	1	D	D	D	27.7	6.6	1.8	2.2
Jerauld	6	D	D	D	6	D	D	D	22.6	6.9	6.3	0.3
Jones	3	D	D	D	1	D	D	D	14.5	3.4	2.1	0.1
Kingsbury	16	274	12.2	6.0	10	33	3.4	0.7	61.4	22.0	13.4	0.9
Lake	34	623	34.1	15.3	23	126	5.5	3.2	109.4	47.3	18.6	2.1
Lawrence	68	1 002	71.9	30.2	67	233	17.2	4.5	170.2	86.0	27.0	4.6
Lincoln	95	1 906	189.0	75.1	53	223	21.5	5.9	92.6	48.2	15.4	1.7
Lyman	3	D	D	D	1	D	D	D	55.4	10.5	4.7	1.7
McCook	22	240	11.9	5.1	9	D	D	D	68.6	19.0	10.3	0.9
McPherson	8	58	3.0	1.0	7	33	1.5	0.3	31.8	9.2	5.2	0.4
Marshall	13	177	9.4	3.8	8	28	2.5	0.5	67.5	18.4	9.2	0.9
Meade	37	D	D	D	45	128	18.0	3.2	260.5	87.8	24.3	4.2
Mellette	3	D	D	D	1	D	D	D	21.4	4.2	3.1	2.5
Miner	8	D	D	D	5	D	D	D	33.3	10.1	7.3	0.8
Minnehaha	459	19 818	1 859.2	861.9	380	2 417	200.5	55.5	1 667.9	512.0	150.7	34.5
Moody	15	184	9.5	4.2	6	40	4.4	1.5	72.7	17.4	10.1	0.8
Pennington	328	D	D	D	259	1 546	127.6	34.5	1 134.0	384.3	91.1	36.3
Perkins	13	D	D	D	18	42	3.0	0.9	46.3	14.7	7.7	0.6
Potter	13	168	8.1	3.5	10	27	1.7	0.3	34.5	9.7	7.3	0.4
Roberts	21	472	24.2	10.8	18	53	2.7	0.8	118.7	29.9	15.2	5.3
Sanborn	5	D	D	D	4	D	D	D	28.0	8.3	6.1	0.5
Shannon	12	320	27.4	10.6	7	D	D	D	315.0	21.6	10.1	22.4
Spink	16	274	14.9	7.1	9	16	1.2	0.3	102.2	24.9	17.6	1.3
Stanley	3	D	D	D	7	21	1.0	0.2	22.7	9.8	2.7	0.4
Sully	2	D	D	D	3	0	0.2	0.1	24.1	4.1	2.1	0.1
Todd	8	D	D	D	NA	NA	NA	NA	165.0	13.2	7.3	15.1

1. State totals may include programs not allocated by county.

Table B. States and Counties — Federal Funds, Residential Construction, and Local Government Finances

	Federal funds and grants, 2009–2010 (cont.)							Value of residential construction authorized by building permits, 2010		Local government finances, 2007				
	Expenditures (mil dol) (cont.)									General revenue				
		Procurement contract awards		Grants[1]								Taxes		
STATE County	Salaries and wages	Defense	Other	Medicaid and other health-related	Nutrition and family welfare	Education	Other	New construction ($1,000)	Number of housing units	Total (mil dol)	Inter-governmental (mil dol)	Total (mil dol)	Per capita[2] (dollars) Total	Property
	171	172	173	174	175	176	177	178	179	180	181	182	183	184
SOUTH CAROLINA—Cont'd														
Sumter	294.5	176.0	76.3	180.0	28.4	13.9	15.1	37 677	353	256.0	124.9	98.3	946	684
Union	19.7	0.0	1.2	37.0	5.1	2.3	2.0	1 964	17	111.2	43.0	19.3	695	649
Williamsburg	33.4	1.6	3.5	108.7	9.9	4.9	11.8	4 054	30	81.6	47.5	24.0	678	642
York	61.5	7.2	10.6	88.5	24.4	13.0	14.9	206 268	938	564.7	201.0	252.5	1 209	1 112
SOUTH DAKOTA	1 030.6	560.7	352.2	761.9	216.0	251.0	1 021.2	403 140	2 946	X	X	X	X	X
Aurora	1.5	0.0	0.3	1.6	0.6	0.1	0.1	922	7	8.8	2.8	5.0	1 738	1 457
Beadle	30.4	12.3	7.4	24.9	2.3	0.4	1.6	4 424	31	47.9	13.9	22.9	1 460	1 068
Bennett	1.2	0.0	0.2	5.3	0.5	2.8	1.5	87	1	9.4	5.2	2.8	816	677
Bon Homme	2.3	0.0	0.5	6.4	1.2	0.3	0.0	1 334	8	17.9	7.4	8.5	1 200	985
Brookings	20.7	6.5	3.2	15.9	2.7	1.1	45.6	15 245	117	137.4	18.8	38.7	1 324	935
Brown	42.3	57.4	10.6	33.1	6.8	1.2	3.6	12 844	170	102.4	31.6	52.2	1 487	1 021
Brule	3.9	3.4	0.5	6.9	0.9	1.2	6.7	1 465	7	19.3	7.6	8.1	1 565	1 191
Buffalo	6.4	1.0	10.8	3.3	1.0	0.2	2.9	NA	NA	0.6	0.2	0.3	157	151
Butte	5.7	0.0	1.1	5.8	3.1	0.3	0.5	3 224	25	27.7	10.7	9.9	1 050	762
Campbell	0.8	0.0	0.2	3.7	0.3	0.0	0.1	500	4	5.1	1.8	2.4	1 728	1 561
Charles Mix	12.4	4.8	6.1	16.0	5.0	10.6	6.1	930	5	35.1	16.8	14.3	1 598	1 358
Clark	2.1	0.0	0.5	5.8	0.8	0.1	0.2	2 614	24	11.0	3.3	5.8	1 664	1 496
Clay	8.8	0.0	0.8	20.1	3.9	2.3	13.2	3 938	40	31.5	11.0	14.6	1 093	862
Codington	20.4	1.0	3.3	19.2	3.1	1.0	3.4	9 379	59	85.9	28.0	36.7	1 394	908
Corson	3.6	0.0	0.7	7.9	1.2	9.6	0.6	0	0	15.9	11.8	2.1	492	427
Custer	16.6	0.0	2.6	4.8	0.9	0.4	0.4	4 536	34	22.7	7.0	11.9	1 522	1 249
Davison	27.9	0.3	1.3	18.6	2.6	0.6	1.2	8 353	87	64.0	19.5	28.9	1 520	961
Day	5.2	0.0	2.4	11.7	1.5	0.4	0.6	4 099	28	14.6	5.1	7.6	1 336	1 086
Deuel	2.1	2.2	0.5	4.8	0.7	0.1	0.1	1 650	8	9.6	2.7	5.4	1 261	1 088
Dewey	18.1	2.8	8.3	10.9	3.7	10.6	17.8	0	0	13.5	10.2	2.5	418	326
Douglas	1.9	0.0	0.5	2.1	0.6	0.1	0.7	730	5	8.0	2.7	4.0	1 325	1 126
Edmunds	1.6	0.0	0.5	3.7	0.6	0.1	0.0	2 365	21	15.3	3.3	6.8	1 705	1 530
Fall River	17.4	3.5	13.4	8.5	1.2	1.5	2.4	158	2	22.1	7.6	9.8	1 358	1 079
Faulk	1.5	0.0	0.4	2.1	0.4	0.1	0.0	615	3	10.3	2.5	3.8	1 667	1 468
Grant	6.3	0.0	0.6	7.9	1.2	0.1	0.4	1 612	12	22.3	6.5	11.2	1 560	1 260
Gregory	2.8	0.0	0.6	5.8	1.0	1.2	0.6	1 260	6	15.4	6.8	6.0	1 463	1 224
Haakon	1.0	0.1	0.4	0.0	0.4	0.1	0.3	70	1	10.1	2.7	3.2	1 750	1 443
Hamlin	2.3	0.0	1.8	3.2	1.1	0.2	1.2	4 107	24	19.9	6.6	8.4	1 499	1 348
Hand	1.9	0.0	0.5	3.2	0.5	0.0	0.3	1 380	5	9.2	2.5	5.5	1 687	1 489
Hanson	0.8	0.0	0.2	1.1	0.5	0.1	0.0	0	0	7.5	3.0	3.8	1 059	973
Harding	1.4	0.0	0.5	0.0	0.2	0.0	0.0	0	0	6.0	2.8	2.5	2 141	1 925
Hughes	25.0	9.3	14.6	46.0	34.1	83.3	541.3	5 380	29	47.3	13.6	22.1	1 309	903
Hutchinson	5.3	0.0	1.1	8.6	1.3	0.3	0.2	1 100	14	25.8	9.2	12.7	1 731	1 536
Hyde	0.2	0.0	37.0	1.1	0.3	0.2	2.7	0	0	8.8	1.5	3.4	2 322	2 070
Jackson	4.3	0.0	2.2	1.1	0.3	0.7	0.6	0	0	6.4	3.7	2.1	755	606
Jerauld	1.0	0.0	0.2	1.6	0.4	0.1	0.5	1 705	8	6.2	1.6	3.3	1 649	1 387
Jones	0.6	0.0	0.1	1.1	0.1	0.0	2.0	222	6	4.2	1.4	2.2	2 054	1 868
Kingsbury	4.2	0.0	1.1	3.2	0.9	0.1	3.6	1 048	9	16.7	5.8	8.5	1 573	1 406
Lake	14.0	0.1	0.7	8.0	4.6	0.2	3.2	4 370	26	31.6	8.8	15.4	1 350	1 068
Lawrence	14.3	0.1	2.6	16.0	2.4	1.0	8.3	30 722	162	72.9	18.4	37.7	1 616	1 115
Lincoln	4.1	0.0	1.0	6.9	1.8	0.4	3.1	21 626	145	56.4	15.4	31.9	844	751
Lyman	4.5	0.0	1.1	5.1	1.0	1.5	7.0	1 490	8	8.7	2.9	4.4	1 132	861
McCook	14.1	0.0	0.6	4.2	0.9	0.1	8.7	2 931	14	17.0	5.8	9.2	1 598	1 403
McPherson	0.6	0.0	0.1	4.2	0.5	0.1	0.1	960	5	8.5	2.8	4.7	1 881	1 685
Marshall	2.2	0.0	0.5	5.3	0.9	0.1	3.1	147	4	12.4	4.0	6.1	1 420	1 202
Meade	37.6	58.1	18.4	9.6	2.8	2.9	6.1	12 251	87	66.4	21.8	26.9	1 120	925
Mellette	0.8	0.0	0.2	5.3	0.7	1.6	0.0	254	2	7.5	4.8	1.8	871	777
Miner	1.5	0.0	0.3	5.4	0.5	0.0	0.5	485	3	8.4	2.4	4.8	1 939	1 708
Minnehaha	198.3	43.2	103.6	117.9	17.3	3.7	121.7	109 316	894	524.1	143.6	281.6	1 607	1 007
Moody	7.6	0.0	19.1	3.5	1.0	0.6	5.1	2 845	15	15.8	4.8	8.3	1 280	1 039
Pennington	312.8	76.7	22.2	71.7	18.8	13.5	57.8	69 556	555	314.3	95.0	159.0	1 651	1 140
Perkins	2.1	0.0	0.7	6.4	0.6	0.2	6.6	0	0	11.7	5.6	4.6	1 568	1 308
Potter	1.3	0.0	0.2	2.6	0.5	0.1	1.2	75	1	11.8	2.7	7.9	3 632	3 375
Roberts	11.2	0.1	4.6	19.0	4.6	4.1	7.6	2 743	18	29.7	11.6	10.0	1 016	815
Sanborn	1.2	0.0	0.3	2.6	0.5	0.1	0.0	591	1	7.8	2.5	4.0	1 653	1 486
Shannon	30.0	0.1	18.3	44.7	13.9	22.7	83.7	NA	NA	20.8	19.1	0.7	55	30
Spink	6.1	0.0	1.0	8.5	0.9	0.1	0.9	5 377	22	28.0	6.8	11.5	1 712	1 419
Stanley	0.8	0.1	0.2	0.5	0.5	0.3	0.2	2 662	13	10.3	4.4	4.6	1 667	1 358
Sully	0.5	0.0	0.1	0.0	0.2	0.0	0.1	375	2	10.9	1.8	4.3	3 039	2 763
Todd	15.9	0.0	9.0	28.9	6.8	16.4	17.6	0	0	31.5	27.0	2.4	231	156

1. State totals may include programs not allocated by county.   2. Based on the resident population estimated as of July 1 of the year shown.

Table B. States and Counties — **Local Government Finances, Government Employment, and Voting**

STATE County	Local government finances, 2007 (cont.)									Government employment, 2009			Presidential election,[2] 2008		
	Direct general expenditure							Debt outstanding					Percent of vote cast:		
			Percent of total for:												
	Total (mil dol)	Per capita[1] (dollars)	Education	Health and hospitals	Police protection	Public welfare	Highways	Total (mil dol)	Per capita[1] (dollars)	Federal civilian	Federal military	State and local	Democratic	Republican	All other
	185	186	187	188	189	190	191	192	193	194	195	196	197	198	199
SOUTH CAROLINA—Cont'd															
Sumter	251.4	2 418	60.8	1.6	6.9	0.0	2.4	433.8	4 174	1 310	5 020	5 956	57.3	41.9	0.8
Union	114.7	4 129	36.8	33.1	3.6	0.0	1.1	122.2	4 399	81	119	1 911	43.8	55.0	1.2
Williamsburg	82.7	2 333	65.1	3.4	6.5	0.2	1.7	78.6	2 218	381	150	2 074	68.6	30.4	1.0
York	583.0	2 792	66.0	0.5	5.1	0.0	2.5	875.1	4 191	447	989	11 495	40.5	58.2	1.4
SOUTH DAKOTA	X	X	X	X	X	X	X	X	X	11 676	8 452	63 408	44.7	53.2	2.1
Aurora	8.5	2 973	60.4	0.5	2.6	0.2	16.8	2.0	709	24	18	184	43.8	53.1	3.1
Beadle	43.2	2 756	44.3	0.3	3.8	0.7	8.0	24.6	1 570	330	102	936	45.3	52.6	2.2
Bennett	8.7	2 516	58.1	0.2	8.0	0.0	5.6	1.6	456	34	21	367	46.1	50.8	3.1
Bon Homme	16.2	2 294	60.8	1.5	3.1	0.0	15.5	27.3	3 855	37	44	621	43.1	53.9	3.0
Brookings	123.8	4 232	24.7	19.3	2.5	0.2	5.8	71.2	2 435	160	195	5 342	51.7	46.1	2.2
Brown	112.2	3 196	35.3	0.9	4.6	0.8	10.9	104.1	2 965	528	222	2 569	51.9	46.3	1.8
Brule	20.2	3 894	66.5	2.4	2.7	0.3	8.3	8.8	1 691	45	33	360	39.6	57.7	2.7
Buffalo	0.6	261	0.0	2.5	13.1	0.0	31.9	0.0	0	140	13	285	73.3	25.2	1.5
Butte	26.3	2 776	48.3	0.5	3.8	0.3	7.1	18.5	1 953	60	60	599	30.7	66.3	3.0
Campbell	5.4	3 886	43.5	0.6	3.0	0.1	19.5	0.3	188	14	0	86	28.5	69.2	2.3
Charles Mix	29.8	3 333	63.7	2.0	2.6	0.1	6.4	9.1	1 018	181	57	1 108	45.4	53.0	1.6
Clark	10.9	3 138	47.7	8.7	2.5	0.1	19.6	4.4	1 274	27	22	230	42.8	54.9	2.3
Clay	29.2	2 183	42.8	0.4	6.4	0.2	13.7	27.1	2 025	44	89	3 049	61.0	36.8	2.2
Codington	81.5	3 092	58.1	0.2	4.3	0.3	8.6	40.5	1 537	182	165	1 867	45.9	52.3	1.8
Corson	14.2	3 369	82.1	0.1	2.3	0.0	6.2	0.0	7	77	26	588	59.5	38.1	2.4
Custer	20.9	2 675	46.2	4.0	4.6	1.9	9.8	17.4	2 219	214	50	614	32.7	64.5	2.7
Davison	59.3	3 116	51.1	0.5	5.6	1.0	9.7	40.8	2 144	123	119	1 252	42.0	56.0	2.0
Day	13.7	2 409	49.1	0.8	4.0	0.2	19.5	4.4	769	71	35	394	55.7	42.8	1.5
Deuel	10.5	2 465	39.3	2.8	4.5	0.6	19.6	6.0	1 403	32	26	244	47.5	49.1	3.4
Dewey	12.9	2 144	81.5	0.5	2.5	0.0	7.3	2.1	344	332	38	1 128	65.8	32.6	1.6
Douglas	7.7	2 536	43.8	0.8	2.6	0.1	19.3	1.5	505	28	18	154	24.1	73.6	2.2
Edmunds	14.7	3 667	40.1	17.5	2.1	7.7	14.4	2.1	517	25	25	366	39.5	58.4	2.1
Fall River	23.6	3 277	42.8	7.6	4.4	0.1	13.6	5.0	691	538	46	541	35.1	61.6	3.2
Faulk	13.0	5 726	23.2	53.1	2.5	0.1	10.0	7.7	3 386	22	14	137	35.7	62.0	2.3
Grant	21.4	2 988	49.8	1.0	3.3	0.2	13.6	51.5	7 194	39	44	347	46.6	50.9	2.4
Gregory	16.2	3 935	60.1	0.8	2.4	0.2	14.6	4.4	1 069	38	25	278	34.3	63.3	2.4
Haakon	10.5	5 694	26.3	0.4	2.1	0.2	17.5	2.6	1 389	18	11	105	16.2	81.4	2.8
Hamlin	19.1	3 402	50.9	1.0	1.8	12.9	15.0	10.7	1 901	36	36	472	37.4	59.6	3.0
Hand	8.6	2 627	46.9	0.5	4.5	0.2	22.0	2.9	875	24	20	203	35.7	62.0	2.3
Hanson	7.1	1 973	65.6	0.4	2.7	2.4	12.6	1.9	520	11	22	168	39.5	58.7	1.8
Harding	5.8	4 873	49.5	0.7	3.3	0.0	26.2	0.0	0	33	0	87	18.4	78.3	3.3
Hughes	43.9	2 600	44.9	0.7	6.7	0.2	7.0	58.2	3 446	305	108	3 674	35.9	62.6	1.6
Hutchinson	23.3	3 177	58.0	3.6	2.6	0.2	17.5	8.4	1 142	46	45	443	34.4	63.3	2.2
Hyde	8.2	5 592	26.2	0.1	1.7	0.1	11.8	2.7	1 821	0	0	201	28.8	69.7	1.5
Jackson	5.8	2 078	65.4	0.9	3.2	0.1	11.2	0.2	74	124	17	254	38.4	59.0	2.6
Jerauld	6.4	3 209	47.9	3.4	3.9	0.1	15.1	10.0	5 012	18	12	129	49.0	49.4	1.5
Jones	3.9	3 668	54.2	0.3	4.1	0.1	15.9	0.0	29	13	0	145	23.4	73.8	2.7
Kingsbury	15.9	2 946	57.6	0.5	2.9	0.0	15.0	10.1	1 869	46	33	268	45.9	51.5	2.6
Lake	29.4	2 587	55.3	0.6	4.5	0.4	14.4	80.4	7 068	72	75	1 024	49.3	48.6	2.1
Lawrence	63.7	2 730	37.7	0.5	6.2	0.1	9.3	111.2	4 764	192	148	1 749	40.9	56.3	2.8
Lincoln	57.9	1 534	60.6	0.6	3.8	0.2	9.9	195.7	5 183	54	260	1 149	41.6	56.8	1.6
Lyman	7.6	1 936	53.5	1.8	4.0	0.0	13.7	0.9	219	89	24	650	43.3	54.5	2.3
McCook	17.4	3 016	56.5	1.4	3.3	0.5	14.2	10.5	1 828	39	35	316	41.4	55.9	2.7
McPherson	8.8	3 514	53.0	0.6	1.7	0.6	20.8	0.6	238	18	15	170	32.1	66.5	1.4
Marshall	13.2	3 053	51.3	1.2	4.3	0.2	17.0	4.4	1 027	32	26	320	57.6	41.1	1.4
Meade	60.5	2 522	54.5	2.6	5.0	0.0	10.5	22.0	916	1 387	150	1 437	32.3	64.8	2.9
Mellette	7.7	3 833	64.6	5.1	4.0	0.0	5.9	0.4	218	21	13	215	44.2	52.8	3.0
Miner	8.9	3 594	46.1	1.3	3.9	0.2	27.6	0.1	46	24	15	149	49.7	47.4	3.0
Minnehaha	538.1	3 070	45.1	2.0	5.5	0.7	6.3	446.1	2 545	2 484	1 179	8 075	49.5	48.7	1.8
Moody	15.2	2 331	51.5	1.9	6.8	0.1	13.7	15.5	2 381	122	40	642	51.1	46.3	2.6
Pennington	307.9	3 198	44.6	2.1	6.6	0.3	6.8	217.5	2 259	1 527	3 940	5 949	38.5	59.6	1.9
Perkins	12.3	4 228	37.8	1.6	3.3	1.6	12.0	1.5	500	33	18	254	29.6	65.4	5.0
Potter	10.3	4 703	38.2	0.5	2.6	0.0	17.0	1.3	616	22	13	157	33.5	65.1	1.5
Roberts	33.3	3 371	57.7	0.7	2.2	0.3	10.8	16.9	1 714	191	62	1 331	58.9	39.3	1.8
Sanborn	8.3	3 377	61.9	0.9	3.2	0.4	14.1	3.5	1 428	21	15	162	41.4	55.4	3.1
Shannon	19.1	1 406	96.9	0.1	0.6	0.0	1.0	0.0	1	573	86	2 653	88.7	9.9	1.4
Spink	28.1	4 163	44.6	27.0	3.8	0.4	11.8	2.3	338	51	41	1 021	47.4	50.8	1.8
Stanley	9.9	3 565	42.4	1.1	2.1	0.2	21.1	6.9	2 464	0	18	202	32.8	65.5	1.7
Sully	10.1	7 172	29.8	0.2	1.9	0.0	13.4	0.1	57	14	0	113	28.0	69.7	2.3
Todd	30.7	3 020	90.3	0.1	0.5	0.0	2.9	0.1	12	289	63	2 110	78.1	20.2	1.7

1. Based on the resident population estimated as of July 1 of the year shown.   2. © 2009 Election Data Services, Inc. All rights reserved.

Table B. States and Counties — **Land Area and Population**

STATE/ County code	CBSA code[1]	County type[2]	STATE County	Land area,[3] (sq km) 2010	Total persons	Rank	Per square kilometer	White	Black	American Indian, Alaska Native	Asian and Pacific Islander	Percent Hispanic or Latino[4]	Under 5 years	5 to 17 years	18 to 24 years	25 to 34 years	35 to 44 years	45 to 54 years
				1	2	3	4	5	6	7	8	9	10	11	12	13	14	15
			SOUTH DAKOTA—Cont'd															
46 123	...	7	Tripp	4 176	5 644	2 793	1.4	84.9	0.3	15.5	0.2	1.1	6.1	17.3	6.7	9.3	10.2	16.0
46 125	43620	3	Turner	1 598	8 347	2 584	5.2	97.5	0.4	1.1	0.4	1.3	6.4	17.4	6.0	10.6	11.1	15.8
46 127	43580	3	Union	1 193	14 399	2 149	12.1	95.7	1.0	1.1	1.3	2.1	6.8	19.4	5.9	11.5	13.2	15.4
46 129	...	7	Walworth	1 835	5 438	2 810	3.0	84.6	0.4	16.3	0.5	0.7	6.3	15.8	6.1	9.6	9.7	13.9
46 135	49460	7	Yankton	1 350	22 438	1 711	16.6	92.7	1.9	3.1	0.7	2.7	5.9	16.3	8.1	12.5	12.3	16.1
46 137	...	9	Ziebach	5 080	2 801	2 991	0.6	23.8	0.6	74.9	0.2	3.1	12.6	26.5	10.4	13.1	10.6	12.6
47 000	...	X	**TENNESSEE**	106 798	6 346 105	X	59.4	76.9	17.2	0.8	1.8	4.6	6.4	17.1	9.6	13.0	13.5	14.6
47 001	28940	2	Anderson	873	75 129	723	86.1	92.4	4.6	1.0	1.4	2.4	5.6	16.3	7.7	11.0	12.5	15.4
47 003	43180	6	Bedford	1 227	45 058	1 064	36.7	79.9	8.5	0.6	1.0	11.3	7.6	19.1	8.5	12.9	13.7	13.7
47 005	...	7	Benton	1 021	16 489	2 020	16.1	95.3	2.3	0.9	0.6	1.8	5.1	15.4	6.6	9.6	12.6	15.1
47 007	...	8	Bledsoe	1 053	12 876	2 252	12.2	93.7	4.0	1.0	0.4	2.0	5.0	16.5	7.5	11.2	14.1	16.0
47 009	28940	2	Blount	1 447	123 010	491	85.0	93.3	3.3	0.9	1.0	2.8	5.6	16.7	8.1	11.1	13.7	15.2
47 011	17420	3	Bradley	851	98 963	587	116.3	89.8	4.8	0.8	1.1	4.7	6.1	16.9	10.6	12.3	13.5	14.4
47 013	29220	6	Campbell	1 244	40 716	1 160	32.7	98.0	0.5	0.9	0.4	1.2	5.7	16.3	7.7	11.1	13.8	14.3
47 015	34980	1	Cannon	688	13 801	2 198	20.1	96.8	1.6	0.9	0.3	1.5	5.8	16.7	8.0	11.1	13.7	15.9
47 017	...	6	Carroll	1 552	28 522	1 476	18.4	87.1	10.9	0.8	0.3	2.1	5.8	16.1	9.6	10.0	12.6	14.3
47 019	27740	3	Carter	884	57 424	882	65.0	96.5	1.7	0.7	0.5	1.5	5.3	14.8	9.5	10.8	13.4	15.1
47 021	34980	1	Cheatham	783	39 105	1 194	49.9	95.5	1.8	0.8	0.7	2.3	6.3	18.7	7.6	11.4	15.1	17.2
47 023	27180	3	Chester	740	17 131	1 976	23.2	87.9	10.0	0.9	0.5	2.0	5.7	17.6	14.1	11.0	12.3	13.2
47 025	...	6	Claiborne	1 126	32 213	1 386	28.6	97.4	1.1	0.9	0.7	0.8	5.1	15.9	9.9	11.2	13.5	14.3
47 027	...	8	Clay	613	7 861	2 615	12.8	96.8	1.7	0.8	0.2	1.6	6.1	14.8	7.1	9.4	12.5	15.4
47 029	35460	6	Cocke	1 126	35 662	1 280	31.7	95.7	2.5	1.1	0.5	1.8	5.6	15.8	7.5	10.7	13.2	15.6
47 031	46100	4	Coffee	1 111	52 796	937	47.5	91.5	4.3	0.8	1.1	3.8	6.6	17.7	8.1	11.6	12.8	14.8
47 033	...	8	Crockett	688	14 586	2 141	21.2	78.2	13.4	0.4	0.3	8.7	6.6	17.9	8.2	11.6	12.4	14.9
47 035	18900	7	Cumberland	1 764	56 053	895	31.8	96.6	0.4	0.8	0.6	2.3	5.0	14.1	6.6	9.1	10.9	13.3
47 037	34980	1	Davidson	1 305	626 681	96	480.2	59.0	28.5	0.7	3.8	9.8	7.1	14.6	11.7	18.1	13.7	13.6
47 039	...	9	Decatur	865	11 757	2 313	13.6	94.0	3.2	0.7	0.4	2.6	5.7	15.8	6.8	10.6	11.9	14.2
47 041	...	6	DeKalb	788	18 723	1 889	23.8	91.5	1.6	0.7	0.4	6.6	6.1	16.8	7.9	11.5	13.2	15.1
47 043	34980	1	Dickson	1 269	49 666	984	39.1	91.8	4.9	0.9	0.6	3.2	6.6	18.4	8.0	12.1	14.0	15.5
47 045	20540	5	Dyer	1 327	38 335	1 211	28.9	82.4	15.1	0.7	0.6	2.6	6.4	18.5	7.9	11.6	13.3	15.0
47 047	32820	1	Fayette	1 825	38 413	1 209	21.0	68.9	28.3	0.6	0.8	2.2	6.5	16.6	6.7	11.6	12.3	16.2
47 049	...	9	Fentress	1 291	17 959	1 924	13.9	98.3	0.3	0.8	0.3	1.1	5.8	17.4	7.1	10.3	13.1	14.6
47 051	46100	6	Franklin	1 436	41 052	1 153	28.6	91.2	5.7	1.1	1.0	2.5	5.3	16.6	10.0	10.3	12.2	14.6
47 053	26480	4	Gibson	1 561	49 683	983	31.8	78.7	19.5	0.6	0.3	2.0	6.5	18.5	7.4	11.5	12.6	14.6
47 055	...	6	Giles	1 582	29 485	1 439	18.6	87.3	11.2	1.0	0.7	1.6	5.8	16.3	8.9	10.6	12.2	15.7
47 057	34100	3	Grainger	727	22 657	1 700	31.2	96.9	0.7	0.7	0.2	2.3	5.9	16.4	7.5	10.4	14.1	15.2
47 059	24620	6	Greene	1 611	68 831	770	42.7	94.9	2.4	0.7	0.5	2.5	5.3	15.9	8.1	10.6	13.4	15.0
47 061	...	8	Grundy	934	13 703	2 205	14.7	98.2	0.4	1.3	0.3	0.8	5.8	17.3	7.5	11.1	12.6	14.3
47 063	34100	3	Hamblen	417	62 544	831	150.0	84.3	4.8	0.6	1.1	10.7	6.5	17.1	8.2	12.1	13.6	14.1
47 065	16860	2	Hamilton	1 405	336 463	191	239.5	73.2	20.7	0.7	2.1	4.5	6.1	15.5	10.2	12.9	12.8	14.6
47 067	...	8	Hancock	576	6 819	2 703	11.8	98.9	0.8	1.0	0.3	0.2	5.6	16.3	7.0	11.6	12.3	15.3
47 069	...	6	Hardeman	1 730	27 253	1 521	15.8	56.5	41.7	0.5	0.7	1.4	5.5	15.7	9.2	14.3	13.2	15.3
47 071	...	6	Hardin	1 495	26 026	1 562	17.4	93.9	4.1	0.9	0.5	1.9	5.4	16.2	7.5	10.1	12.7	14.8
47 073	28700	3	Hawkins	1 261	56 833	886	45.1	96.8	1.6	0.7	0.6	1.2	5.6	16.8	7.1	10.7	14.2	15.1
47 075	15140	6	Haywood	1 381	18 787	1 886	13.6	45.4	50.8	0.4	0.2	3.8	6.5	19.1	8.3	11.7	11.8	15.4
47 077	...	6	Henderson	1 347	27 769	1 505	20.6	89.7	9.0	0.5	0.4	1.9	6.6	17.8	7.8	12.0	13.3	14.8
47 079	37540	7	Henry	1 456	32 330	1 382	22.2	89.6	8.9	0.7	0.5	1.7	5.9	15.8	6.9	10.3	12.0	14.8
47 081	34980	1	Hickman	1 586	24 690	1 615	15.6	92.9	4.9	1.1	0.4	1.8	5.6	16.9	8.5	12.0	14.4	15.8
47 083	...	8	Houston	519	8 426	2 577	16.2	95.6	2.8	1.1	0.5	1.5	5.6	18.0	7.7	10.3	12.5	14.1
47 085	...	6	Humphreys	1 375	18 538	1 897	13.5	95.4	2.9	0.8	0.4	1.5	5.6	17.5	7.4	10.6	12.8	14.7
47 087	18260	8	Jackson	799	11 638	2 321	14.6	97.8	0.5	1.1	0.2	1.4	4.8	15.6	7.1	9.8	13.2	16.3
47 089	34100	3	Jefferson	710	51 407	959	72.4	94.0	2.5	0.8	0.7	3.1	5.8	16.3	9.9	10.4	13.3	14.7
47 091	...	6	Johnson	773	18 244	1 913	23.6	96.1	2.3	0.7	0.4	1.5	4.9	13.5	7.9	12.1	14.3	15.5
47 093	28940	2	Knox	1 316	432 226	153	328.4	85.4	9.6	0.8	2.3	3.5	6.1	15.8	11.6	13.7	13.3	14.4
47 095	...	9	Lake	429	7 832	2 620	18.3	70.1	28.4	0.6	0.2	1.7	4.5	12.2	10.6	17.7	15.1	14.4
47 097	...	6	Lauderdale	1 222	27 815	1 502	22.8	62.2	35.5	0.9	0.4	2.0	6.7	17.6	9.3	14.6	13.7	14.4
47 099	29980	6	Lawrence	1 598	41 869	1 135	26.2	96.1	2.0	1.0	0.5	1.6	6.7	18.4	8.0	11.0	13.1	14.2
47 101	...	6	Lewis	731	12 161	2 296	16.6	95.8	2.1	0.8	0.6	1.8	6.0	17.9	7.4	10.8	12.3	15.1
47 103	...	6	Lincoln	1 477	33 361	1 341	22.6	89.6	7.4	1.3	0.6	2.7	6.5	16.9	7.8	10.7	12.3	15.8
47 105	28940	2	Loudon	594	48 556	1 001	81.7	91.0	1.4	0.6	0.8	7.0	5.3	15.1	6.6	9.6	12.2	14.1
47 107	11940	4	McMinn	1 114	52 266	948	46.9	92.1	4.6	1.1	1.0	2.8	5.7	16.9	8.1	10.9	13.1	14.9
47 109	...	6	McNairy	1 458	26 075	1 561	17.9	92.1	6.5	0.8	0.3	1.5	5.9	17.6	7.5	11.0	12.5	14.4
47 111	34980	1	Macon	795	22 248	1 725	28.0	95.0	0.5	0.8	0.4	4.1	6.8	18.2	8.4	11.8	14.0	14.1
47 113	27180	3	Madison	1 443	98 294	592	68.1	59.1	36.9	0.5	1.2	3.4	6.8	17.3	11.3	12.5	12.3	14.5
47 115	16860	6	Marion	1 290	28 237	1 487	21.9	94.3	4.0	1.0	0.5	1.3	5.6	16.3	7.8	11.1	13.0	15.5

1. CBSA = Core Based Statistical Area. See Appendix A for explanation. See Appendix B for list of metropolitan areas with component counties.   2. County type code from the Economic Research Service of USDA Rural-Urban Continuum Codes. See Appendix A for definition.   3. Dry land or land partially or temporarily covered by water.   4. May be of any race.

Table B. States and Counties — **Population and Households**

	Population, 2010 (cont.) Age (percent) (cont.)				Population change and components of change, 1990–2010							Households, 2010				
					Total persons		Percent change		Components of change, 2000–2009						Percent	
STATE County	55 to 64 years	65 to 74 years	75 years and over	Percent female	1990	2000	1990–2000	2000–2010	Births	Deaths	Net migration	Number	Percent change, 2000–2010	Persons per house-hold	Female family house-holder[1]	One per-son
	16	17	18	19	20	21	22	23	24	25	26	27	28	29	30	31
SOUTH DAKOTA—Cont'd																
Tripp	13.4	9.3	11.7	50.7	6 924	6 430	-7.1	-12.2	667	729	-802	2 419	-5.1	2.28	8.4	34.6
Turner	13.8	8.5	10.4	49.8	8 576	8 849	3.2	-5.7	820	1 010	-372	3 452	-1.7	2.37	5.9	27.4
Union	13.9	7.2	6.9	49.9	10 189	12 584	23.5	14.4	1 633	924	1 365	5 756	16.8	2.49	7.5	25.1
Walworth	14.6	10.9	13.0	51.2	6 087	5 974	-1.9	-9.0	623	787	-554	2 392	-4.5	2.21	8.9	32.8
Yankton	12.6	8.0	8.4	48.5	19 252	21 652	12.5	3.6	2 386	1 831	-96	8 770	7.1	2.30	8.8	32.0
Ziebach	7.3	4.1	2.9	51.5	2 220	2 519	13.5	11.2	391	98	-254	836	12.8	3.35	29.3	20.9
TENNESSEE	12.4	7.7	5.8	51.3	4 877 203	5 689 283	16.7	11.5	754 589	525 554	356 078	2 493 552	11.7	2.48	13.9	26.9
Anderson	14.1	8.9	8.5	51.7	68 250	71 330	4.5	5.3	7 832	7 681	3 845	31 253	4.9	2.37	12.5	29.0
Bedford	11.4	7.7	5.3	50.4	30 411	37 586	23.6	19.9	6 084	3 681	6 187	16 530	18.9	2.69	13.1	23.0
Benton	15.7	11.9	8.0	51.0	14 524	16 537	13.9	-0.3	1 540	2 113	166	7 063	2.9	2.31	11.3	29.1
Bledsoe	14.3	9.6	5.8	45.9	9 669	12 367	27.9	4.1	1 214	1 042	498	4 697	6.0	2.51	9.1	24.0
Blount	13.7	9.3	6.8	51.6	85 962	105 823	23.1	16.2	12 316	10 743	15 872	49 265	15.5	2.46	11.2	24.9
Bradley	12.1	8.3	5.8	51.3	73 712	87 965	19.3	12.5	11 124	7 684	6 875	37 947	10.7	2.54	12.4	23.8
Campbell	13.9	10.4	6.9	51.2	35 079	39 854	13.6	2.2	4 488	4 438	1 384	16 354	1.4	2.46	13.0	26.0
Cannon	12.8	9.3	6.8	50.5	10 467	12 826	22.5	7.6	1 412	1 303	993	5 472	9.5	2.49	10.6	26.0
Carroll	13.8	9.7	8.2	51.7	27 514	29 475	7.1	-3.2	3 266	3 943	-120	11 507	-2.3	2.39	12.6	27.7
Carter	14.0	10.0	7.1	51.1	51 505	56 742	10.2	1.2	5 568	6 020	3 013	24 197	3.0	2.31	11.9	28.6
Cheatham	12.9	6.8	4.0	50.0	27 140	35 912	32.3	8.9	4 516	2 660	2 338	14 520	12.8	2.67	10.8	20.1
Chester	11.5	8.0	6.6	51.7	12 819	15 540	21.2	10.2	1 691	1 396	552	6 208	9.7	2.56	12.7	23.6
Claiborne	14.2	9.7	6.3	51.0	26 137	29 862	14.3	7.9	3 288	3 324	1 632	12 853	8.9	2.41	11.4	26.4
Clay	14.7	12.3	7.8	50.4	7 298	7 976	10.2	-1.4	818	919	71	3 358	-0.6	2.31	10.6	29.7
Cocke	14.8	10.2	6.6	51.5	29 141	33 565	15.2	6.2	3 894	3 878	2 624	14 788	7.5	2.39	14.0	27.5
Coffee	12.5	8.8	7.0	51.4	40 343	48 014	19.0	10.0	6 408	5 191	3 587	20 926	10.8	2.50	12.6	25.9
Crockett	11.9	9.1	7.3	52.0	13 378	14 532	8.6	0.4	1 775	1 689	-36	5 709	1.4	2.52	14.8	25.8
Cumberland	15.1	15.4	10.5	51.2	34 736	46 802	34.7	19.8	4 877	5 456	8 136	23 791	22.0	2.33	9.7	24.4
Davidson	10.7	5.6	4.9	51.6	510 786	569 891	11.6	10.0	86 411	46 643	5 609	259 499	9.3	2.32	14.7	34.5
Decatur	14.3	11.6	9.0	50.7	10 472	11 731	12.0	0.2	1 201	1 510	174	4 927	0.4	2.34	10.9	29.7
DeKalb	13.7	9.2	6.6	50.5	14 360	17 423	21.3	7.5	2 235	1 913	1 315	7 420	6.2	2.48	12.1	26.0
Dickson	12.0	7.8	5.4	50.9	35 061	43 156	23.1	15.1	6 132	3 996	3 166	19 107	16.0	2.57	13.1	23.9
Dyer	12.9	8.2	6.1	51.8	34 854	37 279	7.0	2.8	4 710	3 908	-45	15 183	2.9	2.49	15.7	26.1
Fayette	15.3	9.2	5.7	50.4	25 559	28 806	12.7	33.4	4 148	2 900	8 834	14 505	38.6	2.62	13.2	20.8
Fentress	14.7	10.8	6.2	50.7	14 669	16 625	13.3	8.0	1 888	2 039	1 293	7 250	8.3	2.46	12.1	26.6
Franklin	13.7	9.8	7.6	51.2	34 923	39 270	12.4	4.5	4 127	3 899	2 053	16 011	6.7	2.45	11.6	24.6
Gibson	12.4	8.5	8.0	52.4	46 315	48 152	4.0	3.2	5 772	6 392	2 235	19 690	0.9	2.47	15.7	27.1
Giles	13.9	9.7	6.9	51.2	25 741	29 447	14.4	0.1	3 120	3 208	-99	11 875	1.4	2.43	12.6	27.4
Grainger	14.4	10.1	5.9	50.2	17 095	20 659	20.8	9.7	2 450	2 122	1 965	9 029	9.2	2.49	9.9	23.3
Greene	14.3	10.4	7.1	50.9	55 832	62 909	12.7	9.4	6 750	7 006	4 024	28 018	8.8	2.39	11.6	26.8
Grundy	13.8	10.7	6.8	50.5	13 362	14 332	7.3	-4.4	1 757	1 682	-188	5 405	-2.8	2.50	12.4	26.4
Hamblen	12.6	9.2	6.6	51.3	50 480	58 128	15.2	7.6	7 944	5 899	3 255	24 560	5.8	2.51	13.1	25.7
Hamilton	13.2	7.8	6.9	51.9	285 536	307 896	7.8	9.3	37 922	29 545	8 209	136 682	9.8	2.39	13.9	29.3
Hancock	14.9	9.8	7.2	50.6	6 739	6 786	0.7	0.5	724	809	-68	2 825	2.0	2.36	12.7	29.0
Hardeman	12.8	8.0	6.0	45.6	23 377	28 105	20.2	-3.0	3 078	2 667	-737	9 301	-1.2	2.52	18.7	27.1
Hardin	14.7	10.6	7.9	51.3	22 633	25 578	13.0	1.8	2 615	3 052	1 286	10 643	2.1	2.41	12.0	26.7
Hawkins	14.2	10.0	6.5	51.0	44 565	53 563	20.2	6.1	5 906	5 334	3 969	23 343	6.4	2.42	11.3	25.8
Haywood	13.5	7.6	6.2	52.9	19 437	19 797	1.9	-5.1	2 529	2 039	-1 310	7 459	-1.3	2.50	23.0	27.6
Henderson	13.0	8.5	6.3	51.9	21 844	25 522	16.8	8.8	3 368	2 858	1 161	11 224	8.9	2.45	13.1	27.1
Henry	14.6	11.4	8.3	51.6	27 888	31 115	11.6	3.9	3 410	4 062	1 610	13 604	4.5	2.34	12.0	28.4
Hickman	12.9	8.4	5.6	47.5	16 754	22 295	33.1	10.7	2 585	2 156	1 224	8 976	11.1	2.58	12.1	24.5
Houston	14.0	10.3	7.5	50.8	7 018	8 088	15.2	4.2	934	995	182	3 349	4.1	2.46	11.0	28.1
Humphreys	14.1	10.2	7.1	50.8	15 813	17 929	13.4	3.4	1 981	1 959	423	7 454	3.0	2.46	11.5	26.4
Jackson	15.5	10.8	6.8	50.1	9 297	10 984	18.1	6.0	981	1 321	292	4 789	7.2	2.39	10.5	27.3
Jefferson	13.3	10.2	6.0	50.9	33 016	44 294	34.2	16.1	5 159	4 425	6 903	19 864	15.8	2.51	11.0	23.1
Johnson	14.2	10.7	7.0	46.1	13 766	17 499	27.1	4.3	1 545	1 914	958	7 195	5.4	2.28	11.0	29.7
Knox	12.1	7.1	6.0	51.4	335 749	382 032	13.8	13.1	47 344	33 911	35 895	177 249	12.3	2.37	11.5	29.7
Lake	11.8	7.7	6.0	36.3	7 129	7 954	11.6	-1.5	667	883	-387	2 270	-5.8	2.35	17.8	32.0
Lauderdale	11.4	7.3	5.0	47.5	23 491	27 101	15.4	2.6	3 543	2 591	-1 427	9 795	2.4	2.56	20.5	25.6
Lawrence	12.4	9.0	7.1	51.2	35 303	39 926	13.1	4.9	5 371	4 185	449	16 275	5.1	2.55	11.5	25.6
Lewis	14.3	9.2	7.0	51.0	9 247	11 367	22.9	7.0	1 398	1 252	87	4 781	9.1	2.50	12.9	25.6
Lincoln	13.4	9.5	7.2	51.2	28 157	31 340	11.3	6.4	3 815	3 489	1 904	13 382	7.0	2.47	12.0	25.7
Loudon	15.7	13.2	8.3	50.9	31 255	39 086	25.1	24.2	4 713	4 442	7 548	19 826	24.3	2.42	8.8	23.2
McMinn	13.6	9.7	7.1	51.4	42 383	49 015	15.6	6.6	5 662	5 165	3 508	20 865	5.8	2.46	11.4	26.0
McNairy	13.9	10.1	7.2	50.9	22 422	24 653	10.0	5.8	3 004	2 955	1 225	10 326	3.5	2.49	12.1	26.1
Macon	12.7	8.3	5.8	50.7	15 906	20 386	28.2	9.1	2 583	2 116	1 323	8 561	8.1	2.57	11.3	24.3
Madison	12.1	7.2	6.0	52.5	77 982	91 837	17.8	7.0	12 639	8 191	1 590	38 073	7.1	2.47	17.9	27.7
Marion	14.9	9.5	6.4	50.9	24 683	27 776	12.5	1.7	3 124	2 895	226	11 403	3.3	2.45	12.3	25.5

1. No spouse present.

Items 16—31

Table B. States and Counties — Population, Vital Statistics, Medicare, and Crime

STATE County	Daytime population, 2006–2010			Births, average 2006–2008		Deaths, average 2006–2008		Persons under 65 with no health insurance, 2009		Medicare, 2011			Serious crimes known to police,[2] 2010 Total	
	Persons in group quarters, 2010	Number	Employ-ment/ resi-dence ratio	Total	Rate[1]	Number	Rate[1]	Number	Percent	Eligible for Medicare	Enrolled in Medicare Advantage	Enrolled in a Medicare prescription drug plan	Number	Rate[3]
	32	33	34	35	36	37	38	39	40	41	42	43	44	45
SOUTH DAKOTA—Cont'd														
Tripp	131	5 738	1.0	D	D	72	12.2	953	22.5	1 267	33	865	42	744
Turner	153	6 742	0.6	D	D	102	12.1	930	14.4	1 647	190	1 135	54	647
Union	89	15 706	1.2	D	D	107	7.7	1 220	9.7	2 454	346	1 406	NA	NA
Walworth	152	5 300	1.0	D	D	71	13.3	688	18.2	1 419	90	900	63	1 159
Yankton	2 296	23 808	1.1	D	D	194	8.9	2 330	13.1	4 157	431	2 695	544	2 424
Ziebach	0	2 524	0.7	D	D	14	5.4	547	23.9	154	D	95	2	71
TENNESSEE	153 472	6 274 792	1.0	85 542	13.9	57 582	9.3	867 718	16.3	1 098 695	281 861	449 481	271 053	4 271
Anderson	1 183	86 994	1.4	876	11.9	839	11.4	8 544	14.0	16 119	4 781	4 506	3 020	4 020
Bedford	545	41 624	0.9	699	15.9	416	9.4	8 239	20.8	7 550	1 437	3 376	1 154	2 561
Benton	162	14 789	0.7	D	D	255	15.7	2 333	18.6	4 301	405	2 585	487	2 953
Bledsoe	1 101	11 589	0.6	D	D	113	8.6	2 238	20.4	2 327	371	1 242	154	1 196
Blount	2 027	113 822	0.9	1 361	11.4	1 173	9.8	15 325	15.1	24 672	8 388	7 133	3 522	2 863
Bradley	2 744	95 544	1.0	1 226	12.9	863	9.1	14 432	17.6	18 979	5 149	7 853	3 492	3 529
Campbell	519	37 490	0.8	D	D	495	12.1	6 367	19.1	9 776	3 539	3 748	2 399	5 892
Cannon	164	10 580	0.5	D	D	133	9.8	2 063	17.9	2 762	714	1 200	243	1 761
Carroll	974	25 618	0.7	362	12.5	444	15.3	3 920	17.1	6 752	558	4 106	539	1 890
Carter	1 491	47 785	0.6	605	10.2	648	10.9	9 368	19.2	12 975	4 573	4 713	1 546	2 692
Cheatham	283	30 075	0.5	D	D	296	7.5	5 584	16.0	5 816	2 097	1 763	1 090	2 787
Chester	1 262	14 210	0.6	D	D	156	9.7	2 295	16.8	3 233	230	1 976	454	2 650
Claiborne	1 257	30 023	0.8	343	10.9	358	11.4	4 940	19.0	7 612	2 583	3 170	1 181	3 666
Clay	96	6 797	0.6	D	D	92	11.7	1 303	20.3	1 889	194	1 088	135	1 717
Cocke	294	32 314	0.8	441	12.5	409	11.6	5 833	19.6	8 501	3 037	3 231	2 093	5 869
Coffee	557	55 486	1.1	754	14.5	563	10.9	7 066	16.4	10 865	1 713	5 232	2 052	3 887
Crockett	194	12 278	0.6	D	D	175	12.3	2 457	20.6	3 027	168	2 039	290	1 988
Cumberland	636	54 255	1.0	D	D	609	11.5	7 281	18.5	17 757	1 754	8 543	2 288	4 082
Davidson	25 870	723 432	1.4	10 023	16.5	5 056	8.3	96 450	17.5	81 626	29 002	23 841	39 622	6 323
Decatur	213	10 959	0.8	D	D	153	13.5	1 749	19.4	3 180	255	1 922	256	2 177
DeKalb	298	18 241	1.0	D	D	210	11.4	3 073	19.3	3 791	1 419	1 339	653	3 488
Dickson	617	43 985	0.8	691	14.6	456	9.6	6 961	16.9	8 396	2 342	3 277	1 596	3 213
Dyer	516	39 504	1.1	535	14.2	421	11.2	5 285	16.7	7 584	534	4 818	2 158	5 629
Fayette	421	29 724	0.5	D	D	322	8.7	5 216	16.0	7 341	1 251	3 298	1 135	2 955
Fentress	132	16 863	0.9	D	D	224	12.8	2 766	18.9	4 563	473	2 831	468	2 606
Franklin	1 776	37 358	0.8	D	D	430	10.4	5 442	16.1	8 937	1 400	4 329	1 115	2 716
Gibson	991	46 282	0.9	637	13.1	694	14.2	6 535	16.2	10 565	825	6 629	1 794	3 611
Giles	678	27 709	0.8	D	D	331	11.4	3 927	16.3	6 239	626	3 151	759	2 574
Grainger	151	17 524	0.5	D	D	237	10.5	3 668	19.2	4 958	2 085	1 684	459	2 026
Greene	1 752	67 698	1.0	D	D	787	11.9	9 272	17.1	16 500	5 230	6 267	2 663	3 869
Grundy	180	12 498	0.7	D	D	186	13.0	2 235	19.3	3 331	563	1 840	225	1 642
Hamblen	918	66 505	1.2	890	14.4	663	10.8	9 786	18.7	12 964	3 982	5 249	3 440	5 500
Hamilton	9 778	366 823	1.2	4 316	13.3	3 176	9.8	42 756	15.3	60 008	15 012	26 593	17 321	5 148
Hancock	149	6 003	0.6	D	D	86	12.9	994	18.1	1 226	393	586	234	3 432
Hardeman	3 825	26 615	0.9	D	D	278	10.0	4 347	18.5	5 235	385	3 255	1 010	3 706
Hardin	371	24 866	0.9	D	D	317	12.1	3 896	18.4	6 420	502	4 052	1 233	4 738
Hawkins	456	47 384	0.6	629	11.0	606	10.6	7 635	16.0	13 360	6 717	3 791	2 218	3 903
Haywood	174	18 012	0.9	262	13.7	211	11.0	2 864	18.1	3 420	334	2 155	947	5 041
Henderson	218	25 264	0.8	D	D	294	11.0	3 747	16.6	5 174	408	3 208	1 059	3 814
Henry	491	31 595	1.0	D	D	436	13.7	4 490	17.8	7 954	782	4 481	1 078	3 334
Hickman	1 513	19 522	0.5	280	11.8	228	9.6	3 888	19.4	4 426	1 298	1 883	388	1 571
Houston	177	7 256	0.6	D	D	106	13.1	1 218	18.5	1 661	215	930	215	2 552
Humphreys	205	18 083	1.0	D	D	212	11.6	2 479	16.6	4 039	413	2 350	303	1 634
Jackson	177	9 232	0.5	D	D	137	12.6	1 678	19.0	2 715	391	1 531	259	2 225
Jefferson	1 594	43 439	0.7	601	12.0	508	10.1	7 423	17.3	11 039	3 754	3 884	1 726	3 358
Johnson	1 827	16 815	0.8	D	D	210	11.6	3 162	21.6	4 518	1 249	1 847	359	1 968
Knox	12 348	455 109	1.2	5 408	12.8	3 720	8.8	49 852	13.5	70 661	24 580	23 313	21 365	4 943
Lake	2 506	7 976	1.1	D	D	88	11.9	1 507	25.1	1 217	65	886	94	1 200
Lauderdale	2 734	26 008	0.8	376	14.1	279	10.4	4 355	19.4	4 733	523	2 801	1 219	4 383
Lawrence	407	38 291	0.8	D	D	460	11.2	6 157	18.1	8 992	926	5 319	1 503	3 590
Lewis	217	10 689	0.7	D	D	137	11.8	1 824	18.9	2 393	355	1 263	312	2 566
Lincoln	283	29 140	0.7	431	13.1	387	11.8	4 472	16.4	6 940	964	3 255	1 013	3 036
Loudon	480	44 659	0.9	D	D	505	11.1	5 321	14.7	12 576	4 538	3 608	1 553	3 198
McMinn	942	50 828	0.9	D	D	577	11.0	7 485	17.2	11 325	2 410	5 362	2 284	4 370
McNairy	313	24 561	0.9	D	D	328	12.8	3 565	17.2	6 196	447	3 896	700	2 685
Macon	269	19 167	0.7	D	D	230	10.6	3 761	20.0	4 279	1 063	2 165	326	1 465
Madison	4 418	111 368	1.3	1 413	14.7	866	9.0	12 844	15.6	16 624	1 518	9 459	5 658	5 756
Marion	250	24 920	0.7	340	12.1	323	11.5	4 098	17.4	6 134	1 401	3 182	847	3 000

1. Per 1,000 estimated resident population.   2. Data for serious crimes have not been adjusted for underreporting; this may affect comparability between geographic areas and over time.   3. Per 100,000 population estimated by the FBI.

Table B. States and Counties — Crime, Education, Money Income, and Poverty

STATE County	Serious crimes known to police,[1] 2010 (cont.) Rate[2] Violent	Property	School enrollment and attainment, 2006-2010 Enrollment[3] Total	Percent private	Attainment[4] (percent) High school graduate or less	Bachelor's degree or more	Local government expenditures,[5] 2008-2009 Total current expenditures (mil dol)	Current expenditures per student (dollars)	Money income, 2006-2010 Per capita income[6] (dollars)	Households Median income Dollars	Percent change, 2000 to 2006-2010 (constant 2010 dollars)	Percent with income of $200,000 or more	Income and poverty, 2010 Median household income (dollars)	Percent below poverty level All persons	Children under 18 years	Children 5 to 17 years in families
	46	47	48	49	50	51	52	53	54	55	56	57	58	59	60	61
SOUTH DAKOTA—Cont'd																
Tripp	89	656	1 212	6.6	51.8	16.0	8.4	8 284	21 192	40 221	12.1	1.0	36 390	21.3	29.5	24.9
Turner	60	587	1 970	9.9	49.6	21.5	14.1	8 872	22 871	48 068	5.3	1.3	47 912	10.9	12.0	10.2
Union	NA	NA	3 538	13.1	41.6	29.1	24.3	8 568	33 783	59 889	5.6	4.7	65 142	7.0	9.0	7.1
Walworth	147	1 011	1 070	10.4	48.8	21.3	8.1	9 384	23 716	39 517	12.1	4.4	37 506	16.3	24.8	22.1
Yankton	165	2 260	5 315	26.4	45.3	26.8	24.8	7 845	24 776	47 124	5.2	2.8	45 297	12.3	15.6	13.0
Ziebach	0	71	943	11.9	55.8	12.0	3.9	11 455	11 069	27 578	20.6	0.0	25 669	50.1	52.2	49.5
TENNESSEE	613	3 658	1 549 717	16.9	50.9	22.7	7 667.5	7 893	23 722	43 314	-5.9	2.7	41 461	17.8	25.9	23.9
Anderson	379	3 640	15 970	11.8	52.0	22.1	114.6	9 190	24 242	44 650	-0.6	2.1	45 917	16.2	25.4	23.2
Bedford	388	2 173	10 250	9.9	67.4	12.8	49.9	6 367	18 471	38 550	-17.1	1.2	39 057	23.5	33.9	29.4
Benton	303	2 650	3 069	8.5	65.1	12.6	19.5	7 862	19 114	33 953	-6.5	0.4	32 346	19.9	33.9	31.1
Bledsoe	54	1 142	3 004	8.1	71.5	8.8	15.0	7 680	12 907	29 729	-19.0	0.2	33 366	22.4	34.3	30.7
Blount	303	2 560	27 108	14.4	50.2	20.6	150.3	8 089	24 071	47 322	-1.3	2.1	41 736	14.0	20.4	18.6
Bradley	603	2 925	24 787	24.4	52.0	19.2	110.0	7 174	21 444	40 032	-9.8	2.0	38 558	19.1	25.2	24.6
Campbell	413	5 479	8 311	12.1	72.0	9.2	40.8	6 791	16 426	30 686	-4.2	0.8	31 699	24.3	34.8	33.1
Cannon	217	1 543	2 757	10.3	70.8	11.1	16.6	7 158	18 076	38 733	-6.8	0.8	36 246	16.7	26.2	23.9
Carroll	245	1 644	6 425	14.4	63.9	15.5	35.4	7 200	19 712	36 160	-6.3	1.6	34 566	20.3	29.7	27.6
Carter	219	2 473	12 896	14.8	62.3	14.9	63.1	7 816	17 601	31 173	-10.1	0.7	31 145	26.0	40.6	34.4
Cheatham	258	2 529	9 416	14.5	55.7	17.9	48.9	7 116	24 392	52 585	-9.4	1.8	51 106	12.2	18.9	16.8
Chester	315	2 335	4 665	34.7	61.8	13.8	17.2	6 222	17 343	39 915	-8.2	0.2	39 492	19.1	26.3	24.6
Claiborne	404	3 263	7 281	18.5	69.7	11.1	35.2	7 261	17 128	31 353	-4.0	0.7	29 227	25.1	33.9	32.2
Clay	254	1 463	1 242	1.0	71.2	11.0	9.3	8 496	18 367	32 106	5.8	1.3	28 014	22.9	37.8	36.6
Cocke	620	5 249	6 765	7.1	71.4	7.8	41.8	7 254	16 957	28 809	-11.0	0.7	28 832	31.9	48.9	45.6
Coffee	492	3 394	12 838	10.0	56.6	19.0	75.4	8 087	20 737	40 078	-9.3	1.1	39 321	22.1	33.0	30.9
Crockett	446	1 543	3 253	5.8	66.8	12.2	20.2	7 090	19 742	36 556	-3.8	1.5	37 945	19.8	29.6	27.3
Cumberland	364	3 718	9 826	8.8	59.5	15.6	51.0	6 768	20 544	36 813	-5.9	1.3	36 214	17.9	30.4	28.6
Davidson	1 124	5 199	153 774	31.4	40.0	34.0	719.7	9 685	27 780	45 668	-9.4	4.0	43 825	20.0	30.7	29.1
Decatur	196	1 982	2 368	15.2	68.2	10.4	11.1	6 612	19 757	30 445	-16.3	1.0	35 134	20.4	30.9	27.9
DeKalb	288	3 199	4 308	10.2	71.7	11.7	20.1	6 774	17 976	34 863	-9.3	1.8	35 726	20.8	31.9	30.4
Dickson	377	2 837	11 423	11.3	61.4	14.9	60.9	7 154	21 415	44 554	-9.9	1.2	43 353	14.0	22.6	20.9
Dyer	590	5 040	9 138	6.4	63.4	14.5	54.2	7 760	19 169	36 856	-11.2	1.0	36 735	20.5	30.4	28.6
Fayette	500	2 455	8 038	35.7	53.3	18.9	30.9	8 070	26 898	56 729	11.2	4.2	53 935	12.8	19.7	18.7
Fentress	150	2 456	3 317	3.6	73.4	10.1	17.9	7 225	17 291	29 642	0.7	0.3	29 088	24.4	37.9	35.2
Franklin	370	2 346	9 855	22.2	58.7	16.5	46.2	7 531	20 817	40 983	-10.2	1.3	40 247	14.8	24.2	22.1
Gibson	650	2 961	11 624	10.8	59.1	14.8	63.7	7 031	20 065	35 947	-8.7	1.0	35 711	18.6	27.2	26.2
Giles	271	2 303	6 761	12.5	64.9	12.1	34.3	7 712	19 778	37 860	-14.1	1.4	35 466	17.5	26.1	24.5
Grainger	128	1 898	4 517	7.7	74.8	7.3	24.5	7 851	16 783	30 623	-13.6	0.8	33 291	20.1	31.3	28.7
Greene	378	3 491	12 847	9.5	64.9	14.0	75.6	7 206	18 782	36 867	-4.2	1.2	34 649	22.6	31.1	27.4
Grundy	299	1 343	2 995	4.8	77.0	8.0	18.2	7 802	14 000	26 529	-8.7	0.1	27 494	30.3	42.8	39.2
Hamblen	585	4 915	13 844	10.0	58.1	15.6	70.1	6 937	21 162	39 807	-2.8	1.7	38 711	20.6	33.7	28.3
Hamilton	631	4 517	79 258	22.9	43.4	27.0	357.9	8 613	26 588	45 408	-7.9	3.6	44 132	15.6	24.7	24.1
Hancock	396	3 036	1 323	3.3	79.0	7.4	9.0	8 189	13 717	23 125	-7.6	0.0	24 891	30.9	45.2	41.7
Hardeman	598	3 108	5 832	15.5	68.2	10.7	33.1	7 617	15 838	32 539	-11.7	0.7	31 747	26.6	34.3	30.0
Hardin	569	4 169	5 636	8.5	70.6	9.4	29.9	7 692	18 122	30 732	-12.8	2.1	31 883	23.3	36.8	31.7
Hawkins	292	3 611	12 126	9.0	62.4	12.4	60.9	7 180	19 600	35 392	-10.7	1.0	37 164	18.8	30.2	27.1
Haywood	1 107	3 934	4 508	8.5	66.3	12.9	26.3	7 930	17 047	32 414	-7.5	0.8	34 310	23.6	34.2	30.0
Henderson	709	3 104	6 277	9.2	64.3	11.8	32.8	6 884	19 988	38 887	-4.2	0.8	36 347	17.5	25.7	23.2
Henry	322	3 013	6 347	8.0	62.3	14.8	36.5	7 495	20 687	36 836	-3.6	0.9	36 247	20.3	31.9	29.9
Hickman	178	1 393	5 648	9.3	66.5	10.6	30.1	7 594	18 447	42 075	7.1	0.7	35 948	19.7	31.3	28.1
Houston	368	2 184	1 927	4.2	70.6	7.5	10.7	7 100	17 791	33 738	-11.1	0.8	38 300	19.7	29.3	26.5
Humphreys	178	1 456	4 215	7.2	61.8	13.2	23.1	7 132	20 874	41 486	-8.5	1.1	38 300	16.6	27.8	24.7
Jackson	232	1 993	2 067	7.2	73.6	9.4	12.8	7 966	17 452	32 722	-2.5	1.3	31 093	21.7	33.7	30.2
Jefferson	265	3 093	12 120	22.0	57.9	13.5	53.0	6 986	19 680	38 239	-8.0	1.8	37 279	16.7	25.0	23.8
Johnson	411	1 557	2 912	6.9	70.3	10.1	19.2	8 333	16 638	29 949	2.5	0.8	29 219	26.4	37.3	35.0
Knox	560	4 383	112 030	17.5	38.6	33.8	440.1	7 924	27 349	46 759	-1.4	3.7	44 074	12.9	17.0	15.1
Lake	192	1 009	1 354	13.5	77.0	5.2	8.0	8 334	11 813	24 700	-11.3	0.9	27 142	40.4	46.8	41.3
Lauderdale	726	3 656	6 504	4.8	72.0	9.9	34.1	7 194	16 006	32 894	-12.7	1.3	32 741	23.9	32.3	30.5
Lawrence	516	3 074	9 969	10.4	66.7	11.0	50.9	7 355	18 086	34 985	-9.4	0.8	34 637	18.2	27.5	26.3
Lewis	452	2 113	2 661	6.7	65.1	11.2	12.8	6 357	17 473	35 000	-9.2	1.2	33 495	20.5	32.4	30.0
Lincoln	444	2 593	7 472	14.6	60.5	15.8	37.2	7 075	22 811	42 962	1.5	1.7	41 022	17.1	25.9	23.7
Loudon	375	2 824	8 842	10.9	49.6	22.6	55.3	7 418	27 046	49 343	-3.6	2.7	47 206	14.3	23.6	21.8
McMinn	549	3 821	11 340	12.6	62.6	13.9	59.5	7 057	19 796	37 146	-8.1	1.1	38 183	18.6	28.3	26.1
McNairy	249	2 435	5 896	15.8	68.3	10.9	31.6	7 036	18 488	34 777	-8.9	1.3	33 139	21.9	30.3	27.6
Macon	234	1 232	5 126	6.2	73.6	7.6	23.3	6 069	16 518	33 087	-12.5	0.5	33 036	22.7	36.5	34.4
Madison	713	5 043	26 000	25.3	47.6	24.5	112.2	8 204	22 948	40 178	-14.2	2.8	40 670	19.5	29.9	26.8
Marion	439	2 560	6 153	18.2	62.0	13.3	33.6	7 296	20 811	38 785	-2.5	1.7	37 672	21.9	33.2	30.2

1. Data for serious crimes have not been adjusted for underreporting; this may affect comparability between geographic areas and over time.   2. Per 100,000 population estimated by the FBI.   3. All persons 3 years old and over enrolled in nursery school through college.   4. Persons 25 years old and over.   5. Elementary and secondary education expenditures.   6. Based on population estimated by the American Community Survey, 2006-2010.

Table B. States and Counties — **Personal Income**

STATE County	Total (mil dol) 62	Percent change, 2008–2009 63	Dollars 64	Rank 65	Wages and salaries[2] (mil dol) 66	Proprietors' income (mil dol) 67	Dividends, interest, and rent (mil dol) 68	Total 69	Total 70	Social Security 71	Medical payments 72	Income maintenance 73	Unemployment insurance 74
SOUTH DAKOTA—Cont'd													
Tripp	197	-9.9	35 583	943	78	47	40	43	42	15	20	4	0
Turner	377	5.2	45 738	180	119	103	53	50	49	21	21	3	1
Union	765	-2.7	52 435	72	443	110	215	78	75	35	29	4	3
Walworth	181	-3.5	34 609	1 079	78	26	48	39	38	17	14	4	1
Yankton	792	0.7	36 028	883	504	80	185	140	136	55	60	10	2
Ziebach	52	-13.2	20 549	3 086	15	13	5	14	13	2	6	4	0
TENNESSEE	215 819	-1.5	34 277	X	134 879	24 061	29 655	45 426	44 281	15 228	18 292	5 439	1 902
Anderson	2 534	-0.4	33 851	1 190	2 207	290	402	589	575	232	227	60	22
Bedford	1 298	-1.5	28 256	2 357	721	104	186	297	289	104	108	38	20
Benton	421	1.3	26 247	2 680	143	23	70	164	161	60	68	16	6
Bledsoe	296	-0.5	22 806	3 041	75	14	32	95	93	29	40	13	5
Blount	3 728	-0.8	30 362	1 895	2 107	284	545	846	823	350	298	76	43
Bradley	2 964	-0.7	30 335	1 898	1 663	414	373	716	698	266	281	73	24
Campbell	1 072	-0.6	26 174	2 692	385	66	132	409	402	126	178	54	13
Cannon	398	-2.3	28 708	2 258	72	34	50	120	118	38	56	11	7
Carroll	805	1.4	28 216	2 363	292	71	98	297	292	90	130	28	18
Carter	1 514	-1.1	25 640	2 785	414	112	209	465	454	171	175	53	16
Cheatham	1 256	-5.7	31 498	1 642	374	165	115	224	216	85	82	21	13
Chester	431	-0.4	26 442	2 653	130	42	48	117	115	43	42	14	6
Claiborne	846	0.2	27 092	2 549	330	45	119	304	298	98	129	40	8
Clay	184	-0.8	23 272	3 021	58	19	25	69	68	23	29	9	3
Cocke	851	2.3	23 602	2 992	318	41	97	329	323	106	132	46	18
Coffee	1 676	-1.2	31 918	1 545	1 103	219	238	442	433	152	190	44	17
Crockett	422	1.2	29 132	2 162	161	59	51	132	129	39	63	14	6
Cumberland	1 558	-0.5	28 794	2 233	621	134	328	534	524	247	188	44	14
Davidson	27 626	-2.6	43 457	256	24 160	6 762	3 675	4 013	3 897	1 176	1 719	522	179
Decatur	341	0.6	29 582	2 074	166	28	36	126	124	40	60	12	5
DeKalb	521	-0.8	27 467	2 489	220	52	76	155	152	50	69	18	7
Dickson	1 417	-2.0	29 377	2 125	581	106	171	340	331	117	137	35	18
Dyer	1 175	-2.0	31 070	1 740	683	141	144	330	323	106	136	43	14
Fayette	1 366	-1.8	35 223	993	345	167	171	234	227	97	71	32	11
Fentress	462	0.2	26 110	2 707	159	53	54	187	184	55	90	24	6
Franklin	1 145	-0.8	27 722	2 449	389	80	185	325	317	122	129	30	13
Gibson	1 414	0.5	28 590	2 282	594	163	167	485	476	147	237	50	21
Giles	828	-1.8	28 458	2 306	358	52	134	253	248	86	104	26	15
Grainger	596	1.7	26 091	2 710	128	26	66	190	186	63	81	21	10
Greene	2 086	-4.5	31 476	1 646	1 030	131	276	799	787	214	446	57	31
Grundy	334	0.8	23 644	2 987	75	32	33	140	137	40	64	20	6
Hamblen	1 801	0.4	28 579	2 284	1 308	135	243	489	477	181	177	53	25
Hamilton	12 466	-2.4	36 971	754	9 543	1 447	1 871	2 534	2 473	865	1 068	263	78
Hancock	126	2.5	19 186	3 103	36	3	14	59	57	13	29	10	3
Hardeman	692	-0.4	25 061	2 860	343	51	78	228	223	69	99	35	8
Hardin	767	-0.2	29 225	2 143	341	83	107	256	251	84	113	31	9
Hawkins	1 535	-0.3	26 572	2 628	507	63	189	478	467	189	172	55	21
Haywood	579	9.0	30 679	1 827	288	71	61	156	153	43	64	28	10
Henderson	693	-1.7	25 623	2 789	302	44	94	232	227	70	103	25	17
Henry	924	1.3	28 990	2 202	423	100	153	299	294	112	120	31	11
Hickman	561	-1.1	23 584	2 994	137	25	61	180	176	60	77	21	9
Houston	218	0.9	26 689	2 610	52	10	24	80	79	23	40	7	3
Humphreys	526	-0.9	28 784	2 235	294	20	82	159	155	58	66	15	7
Jackson	291	-0.9	26 735	2 605	63	47	33	102	100	34	44	12	5
Jefferson	1 395	-0.8	26 965	2 569	494	97	177	435	426	152	183	42	20
Johnson	404	2.8	22 459	3 052	159	17	56	162	159	54	72	19	4
Knox	15 372	-2.2	35 278	984	11 288	1 508	2 333	2 742	2 663	993	1 057	280	104
Lake	147	0.0	20 150	3 093	56	4	19	71	70	15	42	9	1
Lauderdale	604	-0.1	22 824	3 039	260	47	68	218	213	61	95	34	12
Lawrence	1 029	0.5	24 898	2 874	401	96	130	362	354	123	163	36	15
Lewis	273	-0.8	23 712	2 980	84	22	29	105	103	32	46	12	6
Lincoln	992	0.7	29 726	2 039	374	58	145	249	243	90	105	26	6
Loudon	1 630	-1.9	34 888	1 036	622	60	327	431	422	185	171	27	16
McMinn	1 413	-0.5	26 787	2 599	773	91	193	440	431	153	172	44	24
McNairy	672	-0.8	26 037	2 720	232	60	65	255	251	81	117	29	10
Macon	565	-3.1	25 608	2 794	158	62	68	170	166	55	70	22	10
Madison	3 214	-1.7	33 023	1 338	2 519	256	471	740	722	229	292	100	29
Marion	834	-1.1	29 715	2 044	277	42	96	246	241	85	99	29	11

1. Based on the resident population estimated as of July 1 of the year shown.   2. Includes supplements to wages and salaries.

Table B. States and Counties — Earnings, Social Security, and Housing

STATE County	Earnings, 2009									Social Security beneficiaries, December 2010		Supplemental Security Income recipients, December 2010	Housing units, 2010	
			Percent by selected industries											
			Goods-related[1]		Service-related and health									
	Total (mil dol)	Farm	Total	Manufacturing	Information and professional and technical services	Retail trade	Finance, insurance, and real estate	Health care and social services	Government	Number	Rate[2]		Total	Percent change, 2000– 2010
	75	76	77	78	79	80	81	82	83	84	85	86	87	88
SOUTH DAKOTA—Cont'd														
Tripp	125	25.2	6.3	1.7	4.3	10.7	D	D	14.6	1 370	243	138	3 072	1.2
Turner	222	40.9	D	4.1	2.3	2.3	D	5.6	8.4	1 800	216	86	3 939	2.3
Union	553	13.7	14.8	12.4	4.7	2.2	9.4	13.0	6.4	2 725	189	86	6 280	17.5
Walworth	105	11.9	D	D	D	9.2	4.2	13.5	17.1	1 505	277	141	3 003	-4.5
Yankton	584	10.1	D	20.7	3.8	6.4	4.8	15.4	17.3	4 575	204	357	9 652	9.2
Ziebach	28	48.5	D	D	D	2.0	D	D	28.6	175	62	83	987	12.3
TENNESSEE	158 940	0.2	18.2	13.1	9.4	7.1	7.7	14.0	15.4	1 251 947	197	174 486	2 812 133	15.3
Anderson	2 497	-0.1	32.2	27.3	22.6	4.5	3.7	9.3	14.0	18 380	245	2 309	34 717	7.0
Bedford	826	-0.6	D	35.5	D	6.5	5.1	D	11.8	8 795	195	1 002	18 360	22.5
Benton	166	-1.4	D	13.6	3.1	11.2	4.5	D	25.8	5 070	307	532	8 975	4.4
Bledsoe	89	-2.4	D	3.0	D	5.2	6.2	6.5	49.1	2 685	209	428	5 718	11.2
Blount	2 391	-0.1	D	19.4	4.4	9.1	5.8	8.1	16.2	28 000	228	2 649	55 266	17.4
Bradley	2 077	-0.1	D	25.3	4.1	6.5	10.7	16.1	11.9	21 985	222	2 527	41 395	12.4
Campbell	451	-0.6	D	16.9	3.4	9.9	6.0	D	20.4	11 380	279	2 802	19 966	7.9
Cannon	106	-2.5	D	6.3	3.4	9.0	3.3	18.3	23.2	3 265	237	392	6 037	11.4
Carroll	363	6.0	18.0	14.7	D	7.4	6.2	D	18.8	7 730	271	905	13 184	0.9
Carter	526	-0.6	D	9.4	D	10.3	6.6	14.0	22.2	15 070	262	2 272	27 746	7.0
Cheatham	539	0.1	D	30.4	D	5.6	3.7	D	14.2	6 895	176	621	15 663	16.0
Chester	172	0.9	D	10.4	D	8.6	6.8	D	24.6	3 745	219	459	6 980	13.0
Claiborne	374	-1.4	28.0	17.9	D	7.6	4.9	D	23.4	8 990	279	2 062	14 850	11.8
Clay	77	-2.8	D	9.8	D	10.9	2.9	14.9	24.5	2 250	286	389	4 282	8.2
Cocke	359	0.2	D	22.9	D	9.9	4.4	D	23.4	9 865	277	1 950	17 459	10.2
Coffee	1 322	0.0	21.0	17.7	29.2	7.2	4.5	10.2	14.2	12 550	238	1 448	23 434	13.0
Crockett	220	8.0	35.7	30.4	D	4.6	3.0	D	18.4	3 450	237	453	6 425	4.7
Cumberland	755	-2.3	22.5	11.2	7.6	11.0	5.0	15.8	14.9	19 755	352	1 661	28 151	25.4
Davidson	30 922	0.0	9.8	5.4	14.4	5.7	7.7	23.3	11.0	89 620	148	13 941	283 978	12.3
Decatur	193	-0.2	D	13.2	3.5	5.9	D	25.0	15.9	3 630	309	428	6 873	6.6
DeKalb	272	4.7	30.5	27.4	D	6.5	2.8	D	13.9	4 435	237	690	9 405	11.9
Dickson	687	-1.6	D	16.6	D	10.8	5.5	14.5	17.9	9 745	196	1 083	20 820	18.2
Dyer	824	3.6	32.0	26.6	D	6.8	6.4	11.4	15.1	9 025	235	1 536	16 703	3.6
Fayette	513	4.3	29.2	25.2	3.4	6.0	14.0	3.7	14.9	8 105	211	1 326	15 669	39.8
Fentress	212	0.4	D	5.6	4.4	11.9	6.9	D	18.3	5 295	295	1 171	8 961	17.9
Franklin	468	1.8	20.0	15.7	4.8	9.4	4.8	D	18.1	10 070	245	1 014	18 697	11.2
Gibson	757	5.3	26.7	22.0	3.3	9.3	7.4	7.2	18.0	12 340	248	1 520	21 999	4.5
Giles	409	-2.5	D	28.4	D	8.6	6.2	D	16.2	7 240	246	818	13 844	5.6
Grainger	155	-2.7	D	26.7	D	7.2	D	5.1	25.3	5 745	254	1 052	10 894	11.9
Greene	1 161	-1.4	D	27.1	D	9.8	7.2	D	16.9	18 965	276	2 447	32 025	13.9
Grundy	107	-0.5	D	7.0	D	10.4	4.2	11.2	27.3	3 965	289	837	6 397	1.8
Hamblen	1 443	0.4	D	29.5	3.2	7.9	3.5	12.8	12.8	16 035	240	1 899	26 963	9.2
Hamilton	10 990	-0.1	D	11.6	9.3	7.8	13.3	12.4	15.9	66 570	198	8 107	151 107	12.2
Hancock	39	-0.2	11.3	7.6	D	9.2	D	16.3	45.2	1 415	208	538	3 624	10.6
Hardeman	394	2.8	D	30.4	D	4.5	2.7	D	23.4	6 100	224	1 443	10 851	1.5
Hardin	425	1.3	32.3	26.0	6.8	9.1	7.3	D	18.7	7 430	285	1 235	13 946	8.9
Hawkins	570	-0.9	D	38.2	D	7.1	3.5	5.3	21.6	15 925	280	2 154	26 870	10.1
Haywood	359	13.7	26.4	24.4	14.9	5.1	4.7	5.3	15.2	3 950	210	1 025	8 315	2.8
Henderson	347	1.2	32.5	28.4	D	9.1	8.2	8.6	18.4	6 125	221	840	12 776	11.6
Henry	523	4.9	D	15.7	4.1	10.0	5.3	D	23.2	9 190	284	938	17 054	8.1
Hickman	161	-1.3	D	14.4	3.2	6.4	2.7	7.6	33.9	5 200	211	668	10 311	15.8
Houston	62	-3.3	D	13.2	D	8.3	4.6	18.7	32.2	1 950	231	257	4 188	7.4
Humphreys	315	-2.5	D	34.1	3.4	5.9	2.7	D	24.8	4 745	256	518	8 865	4.5
Jackson	110	-1.1	16.4	10.9	D	6.4	D	7.9	19.9	3 215	276	541	5 843	13.2
Jefferson	591	-0.4	D	26.7	3.2	8.8	3.7	D	18.6	12 825	249	1 354	23 499	21.6
Johnson	176	-0.5	D	23.3	3.5	9.2	4.1	8.8	23.1	5 140	282	885	8 956	13.7
Knox	12 796	0.0	11.6	5.5	12.7	8.0	7.4	16.1	16.2	77 615	180	9 489	194 949	13.7
Lake	60	6.5	D	D	D	6.7	1.6	10.2	55.4	1 400	179	357	2 598	-4.3
Lauderdale	307	9.4	22.7	21.2	D	6.2	5.1	7.3	28.8	5 500	198	1 191	11 256	6.5
Lawrence	496	1.4	D	19.0	4.7	9.7	4.2	D	19.3	10 610	253	1 290	18 177	8.1
Lewis	106	-1.7	15.1	8.9	3.1	15.3	2.7	D	25.7	2 880	237	355	5 470	13.5
Lincoln	432	-0.8	D	28.7	D	9.2	4.0	5.1	24.2	7 830	235	876	15 241	8.9
Loudon	682	2.6	D	21.9	D	7.5	4.9	7.5	16.1	13 905	286	898	21 725	25.7
McMinn	865	-1.2	D	35.2	D	8.1	5.6	D	12.9	12 980	248	1 696	23 341	7.9
McNairy	292	-0.6	D	34.1	2.0	8.2	2.7	D	18.2	7 190	276	1 117	11 933	6.4
Macon	220	3.4	16.2	11.4	7.5	11.3	8.8	D	20.3	5 100	229	787	9 861	10.9
Madison	2 775	0.7	D	18.2	4.7	7.5	4.5	14.0	22.7	18 800	191	3 001	41 877	9.6
Marion	318	-0.3	D	24.4	D	11.6	4.5	D	18.0	7 035	249	1 065	12 954	6.7

1. Includes mining, construction, and manufacturing. 2. Per 1,000 resident population enumerated in the 2010 census.

Table B. States and Counties — Housing, Labor Force, and Employment

STATE County	Total (89)	Percent (90)	Median value[1] (91)	With a mortgage (92)	Without a mortgage (93)	Median rent[2] (94)	Median rent as a percent of income (95)	Substandard units[3] (percent) (96)	Total (97)	Percent change, 2009–2010 (98)	Unemployment Total (99)	Rate[4] (100)	Total (101)	Management, business, science and arts (102)	Construction, production, and maintenance occupations (103)
SOUTH DAKOTA—Cont'd															
Tripp	2 542	73.6	69 400	19.9	10.0	471	30.5	3.9	2 966	-0.5	113	3.8	2 953	42.6	25.8
Turner	3 403	79.8	85 600	22.5	12.4	520	19.8	1.4	4 039	-4.8	199	4.9	4 546	29.5	30.2
Union	5 799	75.1	132 200	19.3	10.9	671	21.5	0.6	8 321	0.0	443	5.3	7 485	35.4	25.0
Walworth	2 208	76.8	62 500	20.2	11.1	448	25.8	1.5	2 762	1.2	157	5.7	2 341	39.3	23.1
Yankton	8 688	70.2	115 500	21.5	10.0	509	28.5	2.3	11 773	-2.3	568	4.8	11 065	31.4	26.5
Ziebach	770	52.6	62 200	21.5	13.2	440	24.7	12.5	923	5.6	59	6.4	813	49.8	21.4
TENNESSEE	2 443 475	69.6	134 100	23.3	10.9	678	29.7	2.3	3 084 127	1.1	301 100	9.8	2 816 637	32.1	25.7
Anderson	30 939	71.8	116 400	21.2	10.5	612	27.6	1.9	36 211	1.0	3 250	9.0	31 564	33.3	24.8
Bedford	16 005	68.6	114 400	22.9	12.1	602	30.1	4.6	22 945	4.0	2 660	11.6	18 654	23.3	42.2
Benton	6 980	83.2	77 900	22.6	12.1	470	28.1	2.8	7 076	0.7	884	12.5	6 407	24.9	38.8
Bledsoe	4 430	76.7	99 700	26.8	10.0	517	30.6	4.3	4 896	0.0	627	12.8	3 952	22.6	36.0
Blount	48 151	76.1	157 200	23.1	10.1	639	27.8	1.6	63 591	0.5	5 313	8.4	56 309	30.5	26.1
Bradley	37 476	67.7	133 800	23.4	10.6	631	30.0	2.8	47 906	1.9	4 301	9.0	43 224	29.3	30.1
Campbell	15 791	72.0	86 400	23.4	12.0	447	30.5	1.6	16 718	-1.2	2 026	12.1	14 156	24.6	36.8
Cannon	5 321	76.2	112 100	25.9	12.2	530	24.1	2.9	6 533	-1.1	622	9.5	5 625	20.2	41.0
Carroll	11 090	77.3	77 400	21.8	11.4	488	27.5	2.8	13 883	1.6	2 037	14.7	11 867	27.0	38.1
Carter	23 933	73.3	92 700	22.8	11.3	484	28.4	1.4	29 619	0.3	2 925	9.9	23 849	27.2	29.6
Cheatham	14 198	80.9	155 900	23.6	10.0	763	32.6	1.9	20 669	1.9	1 858	9.0	19 066	31.6	26.5
Chester	5 987	74.2	102 500	24.0	11.5	610	26.5	2.3	7 824	-0.1	801	10.2	7 149	28.0	32.2
Claiborne	12 512	77.3	89 300	23.5	10.0	470	31.7	2.3	12 995	-0.7	1 446	11.1	12 172	24.6	36.2
Clay	3 621	77.9	88 600	20.3	13.4	334	27.5	3.1	3 335	0.2	407	12.2	3 135	22.8	38.8
Cocke	14 757	73.0	95 900	24.6	11.2	481	27.0	4.3	16 518	0.7	2 176	13.2	13 771	19.3	34.5
Coffee	20 869	72.3	119 200	23.4	12.0	600	29.3	3.0	25 549	1.3	2 575	10.1	22 254	29.7	32.3
Crockett	5 549	68.5	84 100	23.0	11.5	558	25.3	2.8	6 664	3.0	851	12.8	6 402	24.7	36.0
Cumberland	23 035	79.1	133 900	24.2	10.6	566	28.8	2.0	22 900	0.1	2 449	10.7	20 903	27.3	29.5
Davidson	252 477	57.6	164 700	24.9	11.5	776	30.1	2.5	328 687	2.5	28 805	8.8	312 839	37.3	18.3
Decatur	4 985	78.1	66 500	22.5	11.3	472	31.3	2.8	5 683	0.2	700	12.3	4 636	27.6	33.6
DeKalb	7 165	72.3	98 000	22.0	12.8	507	24.4	1.5	9 892	-0.1	961	9.7	7 630	27.5	37.2
Dickson	18 889	74.1	128 700	23.8	10.0	671	28.8	1.8	23 651	0.6	2 337	9.9	22 724	27.4	31.9
Dyer	15 079	65.0	91 900	22.4	12.8	594	30.2	2.9	17 161	-1.8	2 156	12.6	16 168	26.6	34.4
Fayette	13 498	83.3	170 400	23.6	10.0	662	24.6	2.3	17 906	-0.6	1 908	10.7	16 664	30.8	26.8
Fentress	7 331	77.1	101 000	24.5	12.7	475	29.7	3.5	7 873	-0.8	922	11.7	6 662	28.4	39.5
Franklin	15 750	77.3	110 700	22.0	11.9	580	25.2	1.4	19 637	0.9	2 007	10.2	17 295	30.6	34.0
Gibson	19 548	72.0	86 900	22.0	12.2	537	31.0	2.3	21 659	1.3	2 874	13.3	20 463	26.7	33.7
Giles	11 697	74.7	98 700	20.9	12.2	543	36.6	1.7	13 458	1.3	1 719	12.8	12 104	25.5	35.7
Grainger	8 623	82.5	89 900	24.3	11.1	525	28.7	3.5	10 059	0.0	1 288	12.8	9 374	21.3	43.8
Greene	28 134	74.2	104 200	22.9	10.3	527	27.7	1.7	29 788	1.0	3 938	13.2	28 640	25.5	35.7
Grundy	5 258	80.7	80 100	28.0	12.5	537	32.6	3.5	5 984	0.2	724	12.1	4 919	22.4	41.0
Hamblen	24 451	71.3	118 900	22.9	10.0	574	27.8	1.6	29 586	0.1	3 200	10.8	26 771	23.6	36.6
Hamilton	133 953	65.5	147 200	22.5	10.7	671	28.8	2.2	165 563	2.2	13 982	8.4	158 958	35.7	20.6
Hancock	3 008	71.5	76 200	26.5	10.5	392	26.2	7.6	2 623	0.5	403	15.4	2 160	18.3	39.4
Hardeman	8 993	73.2	88 700	26.6	11.7	490	31.5	3.1	11 038	-2.1	1 464	13.3	9 422	26.4	32.7
Hardin	10 505	77.2	86 600	23.7	12.2	559	29.7	2.0	12 055	1.5	1 384	11.5	9 995	22.3	38.3
Hawkins	23 669	76.1	104 900	23.0	10.3	508	28.2	2.2	26 944	-0.6	2 515	9.3	23 040	28.3	34.6
Haywood	7 445	65.3	87 100	25.5	12.8	598	33.4	6.4	9 246	1.2	1 407	15.2	7 711	22.9	36.4
Henderson	10 850	77.6	90 700	22.1	10.2	560	29.4	1.9	11 743	-1.9	1 846	15.7	11 538	26.3	35.9
Henry	13 534	77.3	85 000	21.9	10.2	534	27.3	1.7	13 710	1.4	1 649	12.0	12 964	25.4	33.7
Hickman	9 020	78.0	102 800	22.2	10.0	576	27.4	3.7	10 132	-0.3	1 189	11.7	10 568	23.0	37.2
Houston	3 392	73.6	87 900	21.3	13.7	539	27.4	2.5	4 002	3.3	418	10.4	3 020	21.7	41.5
Humphreys	7 555	75.6	104 900	22.9	10.3	514	22.3	1.0	9 219	2.9	992	10.8	7 795	23.8	36.4
Jackson	4 648	76.3	89 200	24.2	12.8	493	30.4	2.0	4 956	-0.8	567	11.4	4 327	22.3	40.9
Jefferson	19 597	74.8	122 600	22.9	10.9	604	30.4	2.1	24 332	1.4	2 928	12.0	22 346	25.4	30.6
Johnson	7 376	76.4	92 800	24.8	11.6	487	26.4	2.1	7 332	-2.8	976	13.3	6 596	24.9	38.8
Knox	177 855	67.2	152 300	22.2	10.0	689	29.7	1.6	232 390	1.9	17 593	7.6	209 556	39.2	17.1
Lake	2 300	61.7	65 400	20.2	13.1	403	33.2	1.6	2 735	3.6	292	10.7	1 919	17.4	34.4
Lauderdale	9 365	66.5	77 100	22.9	12.7	537	28.5	3.2	9 965	-3.8	1 568	15.7	9 839	23.7	37.5
Lawrence	15 786	77.9	91 600	23.7	12.2	494	29.3	2.3	16 542	-1.1	2 375	14.4	16 738	24.4	36.4
Lewis	4 546	78.6	90 400	22.8	10.8	490	28.1	1.2	5 481	-1.2	805	14.7	4 488	28.9	30.3
Lincoln	13 452	76.2	113 600	20.8	11.7	512	27.7	1.0	17 347	2.9	1 128	6.5	14 639	29.2	33.8
Loudon	19 441	77.9	166 400	22.8	10.0	644	25.6	1.9	23 640	0.3	1 966	8.3	20 122	28.1	29.4
McMinn	20 810	75.2	105 600	21.5	10.6	558	27.6	1.4	23 198	-0.9	2 886	12.4	21 693	26.4	37.4
McNairy	10 113	76.9	84 200	22.1	12.2	493	27.2	2.5	10 969	-1.1	1 342	12.2	9 707	24.7	39.2
Macon	8 204	75.4	93 500	24.3	11.4	517	28.6	2.7	10 552	-0.4	1 055	10.0	8 713	23.8	41.9
Madison	37 020	67.1	112 100	23.5	11.8	685	35.6	2.1	48 373	1.2	4 838	10.0	43 976	32.8	24.5
Marion	11 305	77.0	107 400	24.1	10.7	579	29.4	2.3	12 637	-1.0	1 332	10.5	11 521	23.7	36.9

1. Specified owner-occupied units.   2. Specified renter-occupied units. A value of 10.0 represents 10 percent or less.   3. Overcrowded or lacking complete plumbing facilities.   4. Percent of civilian labor force.   5. Persons 16 years old and over.

Table B. States and Counties — Nonfarm Employment and Agriculture

	Private nonfarm establishments, employment and payroll, 2009								Agriculture, 2007			
		Employment					Annual payroll		Farms			
										Percent with:		
STATE County	Number of establishments	Total	Health care and social assistance	Manufacturing	Retail trade	Finance and insurance	Professional, scientific, and technical services	Total (mil dol)	Average per employee (dollars)	Number	Fewer than 50 acres	500 acres or more	Farm operators whose principal occupation is farming (percent)
	104	105	106	107	108	109	110	111	112	113	114	115	116

SOUTH DAKOTA—Cont'd													
Tripp	222	1 619	512	44	398	D	38	38	23 345	624	8.8	61.9	62.8
Turner	246	1 680	442	152	265	D	44	45	26 624	722	22.2	34.1	60.9
Union	466	8 814	833	1 700	481	1 324	191	310	35 118	521	21.9	36.5	62.4
Walworth	223	1 811	357	D	360	D	92	46	25 368	279	19.0	48.4	56.3
Yankton	726	10 230	1 872	2 697	1 599	558	225	298	29 165	658	18.8	34.2	58.7
Ziebach	17	70	D	D	12	D	0	2	26 729	234	7.3	77.4	71.8
TENNESSEE	132 901	2 317 986	362 000	311 239	307 847	114 742	100 676	86 220	37 196	79 280	44.4	4.6	38.9
Anderson	1 618	39 623	3 839	8 738	3 851	1 274	9 131	2 048	51 689	538	54.8	0.4	29.7
Bedford	739	11 770	971	4 390	1 545	360	215	351	29 826	1 554	43.4	5.8	43.6
Benton	290	3 174	674	592	610	149	64	77	24 295	500	32.2	3.6	35.8
Bledsoe	91	536	144	46	D	47	D	13	24 634	580	29.0	4.8	37.9
Blount	2 355	37 831	6 159	D	5 823	1 744	2 039	1 289	34 072	1 154	54.5	1.9	42.5
Bradley	1 919	35 307	4 532	6 941	4 690	1 418	902	1 130	31 993	959	55.3	3.2	40.9
Campbell	594	7 177	1 699	1 634	1 446	292	108	206	28 758	404	43.8	2.2	37.6
Cannon	173	1 364	415	155	241	47	26	34	25 055	880	37.4	4.4	40.0
Carroll	456	6 254	1 565	1 542	824	248	106	153	24 479	971	39.1	6.0	36.5
Carter	736	9 252	1 794	1 164	1 877	370	171	235	25 408	516	59.1	1.9	36.8
Cheatham	542	5 783	496	2 030	913	144	190	185	31 969	554	43.3	3.1	43.3
Chester	237	2 837	417	321	384	117	52	65	22 907	484	30.2	4.5	36.6
Claiborne	429	6 912	1 260	1 981	829	301	80	196	28 331	1 090	41.3	3.0	40.9
Clay	103	894	D	D	138	D	D	12	25 225	462	26.2	7.8	40.9
Cocke	487	5 919	767	1 435	1 392	228	D	164	27 673	705	46.1	1.3	38.4
Coffee	1 239	20 489	2 895	4 123	2 961	720	613	696	33 981	1 008	48.6	6.3	41.0
Crockett	219	1 934	528	288	289	94	47	58	30 132	470	40.6	15.5	35.1
Cumberland	1 059	13 430	3 041	2 027	2 475	391	361	357	26 610	842	46.4	5.5	37.3
Davidson	18 338	377 596	65 986	19 259	38 433	19 704	21 745	16 574	43 893	515	57.3	1.6	25.2
Decatur	259	3 226	1 087	594	334	136	D	107	33 020	455	26.6	6.4	37.1
DeKalb	296	4 981	715	2 570	525	104	79	142	28 546	722	39.6	4.3	39.9
Dickson	945	11 800	2 054	3 052	2 241	441	238	345	29 227	1 285	45.1	2.3	30.0
Dyer	835	13 147	1 933	4 702	2 027	485	176	389	29 597	584	37.5	20.7	39.6
Fayette	590	6 314	557	2 082	921	254	112	219	34 640	952	38.3	9.7	36.0
Fentress	268	3 211	1 075	327	660	134	47	82	25 690	628	40.7	5.8	40.1
Franklin	684	9 772	1 422	3 088	1 375	254	161	305	31 204	1 104	50.0	5.8	40.9
Gibson	943	12 866	1 875	3 486	2 203	389	246	355	27 577	1 049	36.7	10.5	40.2
Giles	570	7 258	859	2 438	1 262	274	D	210	28 975	1 789	34.3	4.4	40.6
Grainger	226	2 026	D	739	330	D	D	50	24 900	1 008	45.6	0.8	41.5
Greene	1 154	20 513	4 063	5 460	2 764	761	299	583	28 428	3 061	56.8	1.1	42.5
Grundy	161	1 298	331	132	258	D	D	30	23 146	328	47.0	6.4	39.9
Hamblen	1 338	27 283	4 153	9 276	3 942	577	336	837	30 667	715	48.3	2.2	40.1
Hamilton	8 756	170 950	25 575	24 258	19 605	13 445	7 643	6 058	35 438	669	57.1	2.2	39.3
Hancock	54	665	200	D	194	D	D	15	21 914	462	31.6	2.6	43.1
Hardeman	374	5 988	1 439	1 821	648	205	46	166	27 719	624	23.7	9.6	30.4
Hardin	509	6 070	1 065	1 587	1 167	199	105	195	32 202	623	37.6	8.2	31.8
Hawkins	611	9 610	1 336	4 065	1 414	254	95	254	26 472	1 683	48.1	1.5	43.7
Haywood	337	5 152	444	2 261	711	195	D	187	36 320	491	33.4	18.9	43.2
Henderson	521	6 265	886	1 746	1 093	D	127	158	25 157	1 017	28.9	4.8	29.0
Henry	711	7 951	1 445	1 190	1 576	311	242	214	26 954	958	30.7	7.4	40.9
Hickman	275	2 394	D	567	338	D	38	64	26 756	651	30.1	7.4	39.9
Houston	100	925	D	107	146	55	D	23	24 392	382	37.2	3.4	42.1
Humphreys	335	3 998	610	1 233	597	D	126	152	38 133	638	35.1	9.2	31.2
Jackson	92	919	D	253	109	D	D	27	29 086	587	38.8	4.4	37.0
Jefferson	701	10 810	1 081	2 273	1 763	272	151	294	27 184	1 211	53.6	1.6	40.7
Johnson	245	2 570	490	548	418	105	D	80	31 206	513	49.3	1.2	37.0
Knox	11 248	200 624	32 348	11 286	31 989	10 972	10 245	7 159	35 682	1 224	61.0	1.1	40.8
Lake	83	589	D	0	101	17	D	11	18 520	59	6.8	59.3	67.8
Lauderdale	320	4 609	605	1 140	770	190	40	126	27 387	602	42.2	12.3	34.2
Lawrence	704	7 743	1 147	1 584	1 503	255	225	203	26 251	1 842	40.6	4.2	40.4
Lewis	213	1 783	443	176	427	D	D	38	21 185	260	39.2	5.4	36.9
Lincoln	613	6 754	864	2 073	1 349	239	159	202	29 838	1 782	40.8	4.7	39.2
Loudon	868	11 654	1 388	3 055	1 735	399	361	372	31 957	768	56.4	4.3	41.3
McMinn	911	14 876	2 178	5 185	2 271	611	284	483	32 501	1 204	50.9	2.3	41.3
McNairy	443	5 030	816	1 684	741	149	D	139	27 585	763	29.0	5.9	28.4
Macon	340	3 484	543	885	788	D	D	91	26 255	1 066	40.8	3.4	39.6
Madison	2 561	49 204	10 930	8 158	6 847	1 303	1 241	1 622	32 969	706	35.3	11.2	37.3
Marion	445	5 140	874	1 096	1 132	171	83	142	27 532	392	42.1	3.6	42.3

Table B. States and Counties — **Agriculture**

STATE County	Acreage (1,000)	Percent change, 2002–2007	Average size of farm	Total irrigated (1,000)	Total cropland (1,000)	Average per farm	Average per acre	Value of machinery and equipment, average per farm (dollars)	Total (mil dol)	Average per farm (dollars)	Crops	Live-stock and poultry products	$10,000 or more	$100,000 or more	Total ($1,000)	Percent of farms
	117	118	119	120	121	122	123	124	125	126	127	128	129	130	131	132
SOUTH DAKOTA—Cont'd																
Tripp	1 014	-3.8	1 626	3.5	440.9	1 183 311	728	150 856	136.7	219 033	32.3	67.7	76.6	42.6	3 930	77.9
Turner	371	6.6	514	25.6	308.3	1 154 468	2 244	153 032	173.4	240 225	51.3	48.7	70.6	42.8	5 054	78.4
Union	279	0.7	535	39.9	251.4	1 382 073	2 582	182 970	128.2	246 075	61.7	38.3	71.8	46.4	4 762	83.7
Walworth	444	4.0	1 592	2.5	238.3	1 154 542	725	163 187	54.6	195 742	65.0	35.0	55.6	38.7	3 485	68.1
Yankton	322	-5.8	490	10.7	249.3	965 996	1 973	140 192	123.6	187 828	55.4	44.6	68.7	40.9	3 961	79.2
Ziebach	1 058	-9.8	4 523	0.0	258.6	1 351 815	299	132 937	37.5	160 176	46.3	53.7	73.5	41.9	2 524	61.5
TENNESSEE	10 970	-6.1	138	81.4	6 047.3	467 420	3 378	58 882	2 617.4	33 015	43.9	56.1	25.2	4.8	95 744	21.8
Anderson	40	-16.7	75	0.1	17.0	398 508	5 342	58 265	4.4	8 224	26.1	73.9	15.8	1.1	20	4.8
Bedford	231	5.5	149	0.3	106.9	550 239	3 698	55 372	113.6	73 078	4.2	95.8	33.3	10.0	563	16.7
Benton	73	-6.4	145	0.0	37.6	324 173	2 235	47 759	4.6	9 207	45.4	54.6	18.2	1.2	572	40.4
Bledsoe	92	-1.1	159	0.7	43.0	505 425	3 185	77 922	27.7	47 692	19.7	80.3	40.0	7.6	161	18.1
Blount	98	-6.7	85	0.5	51.5	474 105	5 560	49 673	17.4	15 052	D	D	20.5	2.3	103	9.9
Bradley	96	1.1	100	0.1	40.5	478 879	4 804	54 985	98.5	102 671	4.2	95.8	28.5	12.2	140	7.4
Campbell	34	0.0	85	D	14.9	293 806	3 473	53 708	2.9	7 121	23.8	76.2	15.6	0.5	10	5.9
Cannon	117	-4.1	133	0.1	48.6	428 757	3 233	50 431	13.5	15 391	36.3	63.7	24.8	3.3	361	18.8
Carroll	180	-1.6	185	0.7	122.0	470 286	2 541	56 702	27.9	28 749	86.9	13.1	19.5	4.8	3 200	56.7
Carter	39	5.4	76	0.1	18.3	308 364	4 041	47 616	6.0	11 632	25.3	74.7	21.9	1.4	34	8.7
Cheatham	63	-12.5	114	0.3	30.3	467 056	4 099	54 389	8.4	15 211	64.3	35.7	24.9	3.4	43	7.9
Chester	72	-8.9	148	0.1	36.4	361 531	2 441	50 367	5.0	10 262	58.6	41.4	18.6	2.5	834	58.9
Claiborne	125	-7.4	114	0.0	44.0	355 675	3 108	45 003	13.1	11 981	12.2	87.8	21.1	1.3	81	13.7
Clay	78	11.4	168	D	31.5	415 764	2 470	59 611	34.7	75 080	2.9	97.1	33.8	7.6	267	23.4
Cocke	64	-12.3	91	0.5	27.6	343 441	3 774	54 145	22.2	31 541	29.5	70.5	22.4	3.3	154	8.1
Coffee	140	-3.4	139	D	83.8	486 522	3 504	64 689	37.4	37 092	39.2	60.8	27.0	6.9	712	17.4
Crockett	149	2.8	318	3.3	134.0	742 358	2 338	113 304	31.1	66 064	93.8	6.2	32.8	14.9	6 749	79.6
Cumberland	123	11.8	146	0.4	54.3	510 586	3 508	72 559	42.0	49 916	22.2	77.8	26.5	3.0	165	11.9
Davidson	41	-19.6	80	0.5	17.4	499 368	6 219	46 450	11.6	22 464	84.2	15.8	12.4	1.6	18	3.1
Decatur	76	-13.6	168	0.4	33.1	353 247	2 104	46 646	5.9	13 017	22.2	77.8	25.3	2.0	223	31.0
DeKalb	95	-5.0	132	1.1	38.7	419 666	3 179	51 939	72.0	99 752	91.7	8.3	28.9	4.4	147	19.3
Dickson	139	-12.0	108	0.3	55.3	367 318	3 391	47 953	13.5	10 470	25.3	74.7	20.2	1.3	112	10.4
Dyer	239	12.2	409	10.6	218.9	1 124 138	2 751	119 717	61.8	105 847	95.4	4.6	42.6	18.5	5 688	67.6
Fayette	227	-17.2	239	2.2	154.6	771 945	3 231	78 232	35.2	36 975	77.1	22.9	22.9	7.4	5 812	48.9
Fentress	84	5.0	135	0.0	34.3	473 001	3 493	65 409	49.8	79 914	6.0	94.0	33.1	10.1	214	23.6
Franklin	144	-5.9	131	1.7	93.1	487 683	3 732	73 098	78.7	71 312	24.4	75.6	34.1	10.8	1 422	26.4
Gibson	287	-7.7	273	2.2	250.3	699 824	2 560	87 456	71.7	68 329	88.8	11.2	31.8	11.2	7 852	68.8
Giles	261	-3.7	146	1.3	104.0	462 339	3 164	52 670	32.1	17 917	20.0	80.0	27.7	2.7	1 165	27.6
Grainger	92	-10.7	91	0.4	39.8	345 012	3 786	45 819	17.3	17 175	43.9	56.2	25.3	2.2	64	7.6
Greene	229	-7.3	75	0.4	118.6	319 705	4 270	52 619	76.7	25 065	10.1	89.9	20.8	3.5	557	12.6
Grundy	43	2.4	130	0.7	22.1	421 717	3 242	65 141	34.4	104 769	26.7	73.3	35.7	17.7	75	5.5
Hamblen	69	19.0	97	D	38.9	370 033	3 813	51 491	29.4	41 173	D	D	20.6	3.6	61	7.6
Hamilton	55	-12.7	82	0.1	22.5	443 871	5 439	53 761	9.2	13 825	24.6	75.4	15.2	1.9	32	3.6
Hancock	61	-4.7	131	0.0	23.1	387 894	2 955	42 371	7.0	15 110	10.3	89.7	27.1	1.9	42	13.2
Hardeman	148	-3.9	237	D	78.7	587 967	2 480	49 151	14.0	22 471	68.4	31.6	19.7	5.0	3 145	61.5
Hardin	110	-1.8	176	1.0	63.5	449 058	2 549	50 904	11.2	17 898	67.2	32.8	21.7	4.5	1 156	42.4
Hawkins	151	-10.1	90	0.2	56.3	326 463	3 638	45 112	18.7	11 084	22.5	77.5	20.0	1.2	194	13.3
Haywood	214	1.4	437	5.2	196.3	1 056 476	2 420	143 687	46.0	93 765	96.6	3.4	33.0	17.7	8 558	77.6
Henderson	165	-4.6	163	0.2	86.2	380 482	2 339	50 442	19.5	19 160	43.8	56.2	24.9	3.4	1 762	55.2
Henry	193	-0.5	202	1.7	126.5	547 644	2 713	70 034	54.7	57 113	48.6	51.4	29.6	8.9	1 885	52.9
Hickman	112	-13.2	172	0.1	43.7	471 801	2 738	48 760	9.8	15 105	24.6	75.4	28.1	2.0	173	17.2
Houston	47	-4.1	124	D	18.4	298 207	2 414	40 494	4.4	11 557	7.8	92.2	18.1	1.6	24	11.3
Humphreys	118	-12.6	186	0.0	52.7	477 999	2 575	69 275	9.6	15 034	39.2	60.8	27.4	3.0	243	12.5
Jackson	76	-3.8	129	0.1	27.9	350 839	2 723	45 516	5.1	8 664	25.9	74.1	21.1	0.5	64	12.3
Jefferson	102	-5.6	84	D	49.2	392 469	4 679	50 058	29.3	24 214	19.9	80.1	21.2	2.3	123	8.5
Johnson	44	-10.2	85	0.0	18.1	370 818	4 369	51 716	5.6	10 997	34.1	65.9	18.7	1.6	32	6.6
Knox	83	-11.7	68	0.5	35.1	438 547	6 472	49 922	19.4	15 832	61.8	38.2	13.2	1.1	102	4.2
Lake	84	-6.7	1 425	5.5	81.1	3 936 558	2 762	355 817	25.8	437 818	99.8	0.2	96.6	61.0	2 169	91.5
Lauderdale	192	-10.7	319	4.9	162.7	696 984	2 183	85 066	44.0	73 126	94.7	5.3	24.4	10.6	5 356	68.4
Lawrence	238	0.8	129	0.5	120.9	401 150	3 101	51 422	45.5	24 726	25.8	74.2	29.6	4.5	2 059	35.0
Lewis	36	-2.7	137	D	14.0	391 603	2 863	42 361	2.6	10 031	12.3	87.7	22.3	1.2	27	16.5
Lincoln	261	-8.1	146	3.1	117.9	503 358	3 438	60 944	57.8	32 439	29.1	70.9	30.8	4.3	1 400	17.5
Loudon	77	-7.2	100	0.2	39.3	495 878	4 943	86 645	60.2	78 427	D	D	21.9	3.0	159	15.2
McMinn	123	-3.9	102	0.3	56.4	409 461	4 024	54 646	48.4	40 237	4.8	95.2	24.5	5.8	177	8.7
McNairy	123	-8.2	161	0.7	68.3	355 340	2 209	51 034	12.0	15 771	73.6	26.4	18.2	3.5	1 587	62.8
Macon	128	-11.7	120	0.1	55.4	391 972	3 269	47 359	22.8	21 374	45.7	54.3	25.9	4.1	228	18.0
Madison	177	9.3	251	1.5	134.4	702 495	2 801	80 584	28.2	39 885	81.2	18.8	21.7	7.9	5 548	65.3
Marion	51	0.0	129	0.1	24.7	468 342	3 629	61 859	20.3	51 762	11.4	88.6	23.0	7.1	115	10.2

Table B. States and Counties — Water Use, Wholesale Trade, Retail Trade, and Real Estate

STATE County	Water use, 2005		Wholesale trade,[1] 2007				Retail trade,[2] 2007				Real estate and rental and leasing,[2] 2007			
	Total water withdrawn (mil gal/day)	Gallons withdrawn per person	Number of establishments	Number of employees	Sales (mil dol)	Annual payroll (mil dol)	Number of establishments	Number of employees	Sales (mil dol)	Annual payroll (mil dol)	Number of establishments	Number of employees	Receipts (mil dol)	Annual payroll (mil dol)
	133	134	135	136	137	138	139	140	141	142	143	144	145	146
SOUTH DAKOTA—Cont'd														
Tripp	6.1	999	12	142	70.4	4.2	48	411	88.4	7.3	5	4	0.7	0.1
Turner	20.7	2 434	17	119	166.6	4.1	43	302	52.4	4.4	1	D	D	D
Union	18.6	1 383	24	D	D	D	46	541	304.2	12.4	17	36	8.0	1.6
Walworth	7.3	1 321	9	69	107.0	2.6	49	411	74.8	6.0	4	13	0.8	0.1
Yankton	19.4	891	32	D	D	D	138	1 559	293.0	29.5	22	87	8.3	1.5
Ziebach	0.5	182	3	D	D	D	4	D	D	D	NA	NA	NA	NA
TENNESSEE	10 838.3	1 818	6 282	99 238	80 116.5	4 593.4	24 234	320 739	77 547.3	7 244.6	6 087	37 737	6 950.4	1 243.0
Anderson	570.2	7 873	37	269	208.3	11.8	268	3 457	907.8	78.4	64	309	42.3	7.3
Bedford	26.3	623	25	D	D	D	156	1 508	340.6	31.6	29	156	23.1	4.7
Benton	2.5	152	10	82	35.2	2.5	69	644	136.8	12.0	9	25	2.4	0.4
Bledsoe	1.9	145	3	9	3.4	0.2	21	134	30.5	2.0	2	D	D	D
Blount	14.6	127	80	1 069	898.0	49.1	407	6 236	1 551.1	152.4	93	354	70.0	9.9
Bradley	18.2	197	60	D	D	D	396	4 673	1 164.6	107.3	82	461	88.0	12.4
Campbell	4.6	114	20	329	134.4	8.7	147	1 562	361.8	31.5	18	123	11.1	2.2
Cannon	1.8	138	4	D	D	D	33	268	53.6	5.6	7	22	2.6	0.2
Carroll	5.4	187	15	280	71.8	7.0	104	950	188.9	16.7	16	44	7.1	0.9
Carter	21.7	369	13	76	35.0	3.3	154	1 806	461.3	37.4	29	100	12.5	1.9
Cheatham	3.4	88	17	59	33.8	2.0	80	1 010	238.8	20.1	19	49	8.7	1.1
Chester	2.0	127	12	66	24.4	1.7	55	450	117.7	9.9	7	22	1.6	0.3
Claiborne	4.4	140	11	77	26.0	2.0	93	820	155.9	14.4	24	75	16.5	1.6
Clay	13.7	1 709	3	D	D	D	25	149	37.3	2.9	7	28	2.3	0.9
Cocke	5.4	154	9	D	D	D	122	1 430	326.9	28.0	24	119	8.5	2.0
Coffee	32.1	632	41	425	196.6	17.4	272	3 148	790.8	68.5	45	184	21.3	3.8
Crockett	3.5	242	11	158	112.1	5.9	48	262	65.0	4.2	3	6	1.0	0.1
Cumberland	6.5	126	37	D	D	D	252	2 531	597.0	51.9	56	279	32.5	6.2
Davidson	160.7	279	1 009	20 028	11 942.6	983.6	2 795	42 241	10 581.8	1 046.2	934	6 617	1 588.0	252.2
Decatur	2.2	189	3	D	D	D	56	433	98.9	9.8	5	6	0.4	0.1
DeKalb	2.2	123	7	47	8.5	1.5	63	551	119.4	10.8	10	22	2.5	0.4
Dickson	5.7	125	26	413	327.9	17.1	198	2 394	605.9	51.8	36	130	18.7	2.3
Dyer	15.8	417	41	315	252.5	11.1	191	2 187	514.1	47.7	36	89	15.1	3.2
Fayette	5.6	162	27	161	74.4	6.3	82	580	126.6	11.8	23	49	5.8	0.8
Fentress	2.2	126	3	D	D	D	68	687	140.5	13.0	6	101	15.2	3.1
Franklin	7.8	178	18	D	D	D	156	1 471	343.6	31.4	21	98	11.4	2.0
Gibson	10.4	215	39	D	D	D	207	2 054	439.0	38.8	32	101	11.5	2.5
Giles	4.7	160	22	311	112.9	13.4	126	1 300	313.3	27.1	15	73	6.4	1.4
Grainger	4.6	204	5	37	8.6	0.5	53	371	79.5	5.9	6	13	1.1	0.2
Greene	12.5	191	42	D	D	D	217	2 900	682.0	61.1	41	156	23.6	3.4
Grundy	2.3	154	3	D	D	D	49	324	67.5	5.5	3	17	1.0	0.1
Hamblen	9.9	165	59	1 370	591.7	57.0	307	4 199	1 055.0	91.8	57	268	41.6	6.3
Hamilton	1 648.6	5 302	497	5 989	2 958.5	268.0	1 500	20 722	4 865.7	467.7	403	2 354	367.5	100.3
Hancock	0.8	112	1	D	D	D	18	182	24.4	2.9	2	D	D	D
Hardeman	3.9	137	19	148	42.1	3.6	80	723	158.8	13.7	6	32	2.7	0.6
Hardin	27.7	1 067	22	124	79.7	4.7	130	1 129	313.7	25.9	24	59	8.4	1.7
Hawkins	700.7	12 469	14	D	D	D	124	1 356	286.9	24.7	26	75	6.8	1.5
Haywood	3.9	198	18	91	74.2	2.7	61	676	180.6	12.6	10	29	2.4	0.7
Henderson	3.8	143	19	135	31.8	3.6	116	1 082	279.6	21.7	11	24	3.6	0.5
Henry	5.8	182	32	D	D	D	163	1 658	404.2	35.9	26	83	10.0	1.7
Hickman	3.2	136	10	D	D	D	52	296	76.9	6.1	10	D	D	D
Houston	1.3	166	NA	NA	NA	NA	26	156	33.4	2.7	3	8	0.9	0.2
Humphreys	1 292.7	70 979	12	138	57.2	4.4	69	635	181.9	12.6	10	37	2.0	0.6
Jackson	1.0	90	5	37	7.2	0.9	26	116	27.8	1.7	1	D	D	D
Jefferson	6.9	142	17	101	35.3	3.9	145	1 650	554.3	35.6	34	106	11.2	1.5
Johnson	2.8	152	3	D	D	D	56	453	93.2	7.9	17	39	3.9	0.4
Knox	68.6	169	699	10 084	7 402.5	474.4	1 904	33 315	8 209.4	794.3	542	3 195	624.4	103.4
Lake	5.2	688	4	D	D	D	23	103	19.5	1.9	3	9	0.8	0.1
Lauderdale	6.6	247	19	520	829.7	23.5	82	809	151.8	14.3	16	34	4.5	1.0
Lawrence	7.5	183	39	D	D	D	181	1 587	381.0	33.5	26	95	9.3	1.7
Lewis	1.8	158	5	D	D	D	49	460	132.8	9.2	7	21	2.1	0.4
Lincoln	7.9	245	22	244	147.5	8.7	148	1 396	366.5	31.8	22	110	10.6	2.6
Loudon	16.9	390	44	610	360.6	17.1	141	1 714	435.6	35.3	36	104	15.8	2.4
McMinn	71.5	1 393	33	D	D	D	201	2 334	561.3	49.6	30	106	15.9	2.2
McNairy	4.3	170	13	99	45.7	5.2	107	788	194.7	14.0	11	54	10.3	1.4
Macon	3.2	149	10	111	30.4	2.5	72	738	167.3	15.0	20	39	4.4	0.5
Madison	20.0	211	154	2 008	1 160.4	84.0	509	7 057	1 696.5	153.0	108	765	101.1	19.3
Marion	5.3	190	23	D	D	D	109	1 194	286.6	24.1	14	32	2.8	0.5

1. Merchant wholesalers, except manufacturers' sales branches and offices.   2. Employer establishments.

Table B. States and Counties — Professional Services, Manufacturing, and Accommodation and Food Services

STATE County	Professional, scientific, and technical services,[1] 2007				Manufacturing, 2007				Accommodation and food services, 2007			
	Number of establish-ments	Number of employees	Receipts (mil dol)	Annual payroll (mil dol)	Number of establish-ments	Number of employees	Receipts (mil dol)	Annual payroll (mil dol)	Number of establish-ments	Number of employees	Sales (mil dol)	Annual payroll (mil dol)
	147	148	149	150	151	152	153	154	155	156	157	158
SOUTH DAKOTA—Cont'd												
Tripp	16	53	6.1	1.5	NA	NA	NA	NA	25	208	8.1	2.0
Turner	11	D	D	D	NA	NA	NA	NA	18	90	2.2	0.5
Union	36	D	D	D	26	D	D	55.7	40	459	19.7	4.2
Walworth	16	101	7.1	2.2	NA	NA	NA	NA	31	370	19.8	5.3
Yankton	42	205	23.2	7.8	30	2 710	635.2	91.7	71	1 068	34.5	9.2
Ziebach	NA	NA	NA	NA	NA	NA	NA	NA	2	D	D	D
TENNESSEE	11 278	D	D	D	6 752	369 165	140 447.8	15 165.6	11 592	239 379	10 626.8	3 009.2
Anderson	219	D	D	D	114	9 827	1 911.2	543.9	126	3 030	126.6	35.9
Bedford	49	252	21.3	6.7	54	4 805	1 047.3	177.0	58	863	35.3	9.5
Benton	20	55	4.2	1.2	21	629	82.3	17.3	30	395	13.3	3.0
Bledsoe	5	D	D	D	NA	NA	NA	NA	10	107	3.5	0.8
Blount	186	D	D	D	125	7 527	5 312.3	375.7	209	4 739	208.5	63.7
Bradley	151	D	D	D	131	9 540	D	D	164	3 211	130.5	35.7
Campbell	28	120	10.9	4.0	39	1 737	333.9	64.2	54	901	35.4	9.3
Cannon	11	D	D	D	NA	NA	NA	NA	10	190	7.1	1.6
Carroll	28	D	D	D	37	1 640	767.0	58.6	39	448	15.4	3.6
Carter	41	D	D	D	42	1 880	296.7	D	67	1 151	41.9	12.1
Cheatham	47	161	18.8	5.3	37	2 198	754.9	86.3	44	580	23.3	5.6
Chester	16	D	D	D	NA	NA	NA	NA	21	293	11.6	3.3
Claiborne	22	83	6.0	2.1	35	2 880	436.2	79.4	27	576	21.6	5.9
Clay	5	D	D	D	NA	NA	NA	NA	11	73	4.0	1.0
Cocke	28	D	D	D	38	1 542	601.3	64.8	67	998	44.3	12.4
Coffee	87	D	D	D	77	5 036	D	201.5	102	2 204	79.3	23.3
Crockett	10	35	6.6	1.3	NA	NA	NA	NA	10	122	7.0	1.2
Cumberland	74	307	26.5	8.8	56	2 163	468.9	80.9	91	1 297	61.7	16.0
Davidson	1 912	23 798	2 943.3	1 285.4	633	23 715	7 347.2	999.0	1 605	38 979	2 203.0	626.4
Decatur	18	84	9.2	1.5	27	765	D	24.0	21	176	6.0	1.5
DeKalb	26	97	6.8	2.7	29	2 873	743.8	97.4	28	307	12.1	3.1
Dickson	59	244	23.9	8.7	56	3 805	876.6	141.8	95	1 527	60.5	17.7
Dyer	48	D	D	D	45	5 251	1 647.0	189.0	70	1 107	42.8	11.4
Fayette	40	261	17.2	8.0	49	2 337	889.8	92.7	39	355	12.6	3.3
Fentress	17	75	4.8	1.0	NA	NA	NA	NA	23	272	8.2	2.2
Franklin	43	D	D	D	46	D	3 187.1	D	51	971	28.0	8.7
Gibson	53	247	17.7	5.6	68	3 910	977.4	147.6	71	879	30.8	7.8
Giles	32	130	10.7	3.6	48	2 710	1 004.2	99.5	49	632	24.9	5.8
Grainger	10	D	D	D	29	912	171.3	28.5	13	150	6.1	1.1
Greene	83	D	D	D	109	6 613	1 814.0	225.1	100	1 681	62.0	18.0
Grundy	10	D	D	D	NA	NA	NA	NA	15	262	9.8	2.4
Hamblen	80	D	D	D	117	12 923	3 214.0	453.8	107	2 342	91.3	26.3
Hamilton	783	D	D	D	478	26 947	8 040.6	1 125.0	763	15 719	663.3	196.0
Hancock	3	D	D	D	NA	NA	NA	NA	3	42	1.4	0.3
Hardeman	11	42	4.2	0.8	27	1 913	423.7	54.8	32	370	15.6	3.7
Hardin	33	96	7.0	2.4	43	1 678	691.8	80.9	52	626	28.7	7.6
Hawkins	35	103	9.6	2.5	49	4 154	1 148.7	144.2	62	852	31.7	8.9
Haywood	19	D	D	D	21	2 761	631.5	89.4	35	414	13.9	3.6
Henderson	31	222	8.7	2.8	42	1 588	566.7	59.5	38	579	20.9	5.6
Henry	42	239	16.0	7.0	46	1 695	D	D	64	1 054	29.4	8.4
Hickman	10	37	3.3	1.0	35	666	D	21.0	27	219	7.1	1.8
Houston	5	D	D	D	NA	NA	NA	NA	13	93	2.7	0.7
Humphreys	18	73	6.7	3.0	23	1 301	1 052.9	81.1	40	441	17.8	4.1
Jackson	6	D	D	D	NA	NA	NA	NA	11	78	2.6	0.7
Jefferson	40	264	14.6	6.1	48	2 682	862.9	84.0	72	1 329	48.3	13.6
Johnson	15	36	3.9	1.1	18	603	118.2	22.4	25	210	6.6	1.9
Knox	1 265	D	D	D	452	14 456	4 470.9	601.7	890	21 308	919.2	273.6
Lake	4	D	D	D	NA	NA	NA	NA	13	174	5.9	1.6
Lauderdale	18	30	3.4	0.9	16	2 281	372.9	70.0	20	318	9.7	3.0
Lawrence	45	231	18.3	6.1	55	2 015	D	67.9	51	1 007	37.4	9.1
Lewis	16	D	D	D	NA	NA	NA	NA	18	232	8.0	2.2
Lincoln	41	148	15.9	4.1	42	2 680	D	87.5	45	649	26.2	5.6
Loudon	57	D	D	D	57	3 361	1 502.3	144.5	71	1 325	50.8	16.1
McMinn	53	D	D	D	73	6 792	2 381.0	317.2	83	1 499	57.5	16.4
McNairy	19	D	D	D	44	1 903	420.9	68.5	37	472	13.1	3.9
Macon	23	67	5.6	1.7	34	917	D	29.6	23	282	11.9	2.7
Madison	190	D	D	D	116	9 613	D	D	214	5 487	204.9	55.2
Marion	27	D	D	D	26	1 089	D	37.0	57	786	32.7	9.1

1. Establishment subject to federal tax.

Table B. States and Counties — Health Care and Social Assistance, Other Services, and Federal Funds

STATE County	Health care and social assistance, 2007				Other services, 2007				Federal funds and grants, 2009–2010 Expenditures (mil dol)			
										Direct payments for individuals[1]		
	Number of establishments	Number of employees	Receipts (mil dol)	Annual payroll (mil dol)	Number of establishments	Number of employees	Receipts (mil dol)	Annual payroll (mil dol)	Total	Social Security and government retirement	Medicare	Food Stamps and Supplemental Security Income
	159	160	161	162	163	164	165	166	167	168	169	170
SOUTH DAKOTA—Cont'd												
Tripp	24	416	23.8	10.0	14	35	3.0	0.7	54.1	18.6	10.1	2.9
Turner	23	456	19.7	10.0	14	D	D	D	65.1	28.8	14.1	1.4
Union	49	D	D	D	32	147	8.4	2.8	362.9	42.4	20.2	1.9
Walworth	11	363	21.1	9.1	19	82	4.9	1.4	53.5	17.2	7.8	2.6
Yankton	67	1 777	158.2	65.2	57	231	16.6	3.9	171.0	67.1	31.9	4.5
Ziebach	2	D	D	D	1	D	D	D	20.8	3.0	1.3	2.8
TENNESSEE	14 267	337 741	33 799.9	13 093.2	8 811	62 425	6 338.7	1 681.0	68 865.5	20 061.6	13 284.1	3 020.5
Anderson	189	4 039	374.3	150.2	130	683	158.7	17.7	4 611.2	334.0	191.0	40.0
Bedford	86	1 078	72.8	28.3	46	196	17.7	4.6	276.0	127.0	71.7	11.9
Benton	40	784	38.6	14.9	21	80	6.0	2.0	176.0	78.0	52.2	8.5
Bledsoe	11	126	6.5	2.8	2	D	D	D	109.3	34.0	32.2	8.2
Blount	219	5 817	466.8	199.2	182	962	84.2	27.1	894.6	453.6	202.8	41.0
Bradley	229	4 355	364.9	139.7	112	D	D	D	676.0	315.0	174.0	36.0
Campbell	55	1 720	121.5	49.7	36	159	13.6	3.1	465.6	168.4	137.1	38.6
Cannon	15	D	D	D	14	D	D	D	117.1	47.6	41.0	5.3
Carroll	63	1 482	92.8	36.8	32	106	9.0	2.8	363.2	118.7	105.6	14.4
Carter	83	1 825	125.0	48.0	51	D	D	D	465.4	191.7	126.5	32.2
Cheatham	44	D	D	D	27	70	5.6	1.5	218.9	103.2	46.7	9.6
Chester	24	377	24.3	12.7	17	45	4.5	0.9	133.6	44.2	36.1	5.4
Claiborne	39	1 367	72.7	34.4	31	138	13.2	4.3	355.2	122.8	101.2	29.2
Clay	11	D	D	D	7	13	1.3	0.3	99.8	22.3	33.2	3.8
Cocke	37	655	54.5	24.5	20	D	D	D	385.7	135.0	108.8	27.6
Coffee	202	2 650	246.7	85.2	82	600	60.4	18.3	956.7	212.8	120.6	21.1
Crockett	28	462	28.4	11.9	17	37	3.4	0.6	169.3	46.7	51.6	6.0
Cumberland	128	2 705	202.3	82.7	58	614	37.3	10.2	426.4	283.7	116.1	21.2
Davidson	1 805	55 849	7 038.6	2 486.9	1 351	13 834	1 315.2	434.2	9 471.1	1 524.1	1 217.1	307.6
Decatur	22	945	64.5	29.9	19	68	7.8	1.9	127.9	41.2	50.1	5.7
DeKalb	34	560	43.4	15.6	23	124	10.7	3.3	169.7	60.8	56.6	9.9
Dickson	118	1 857	190.8	69.2	54	291	27.0	7.9	335.7	151.8	88.0	18.4
Dyer	116	1 698	162.5	56.8	52	209	15.3	4.3	402.3	131.8	113.7	25.5
Fayette	51	649	48.4	18.8	43	150	11.8	3.4	291.2	93.7	82.7	17.6
Fentress	31	839	60.7	24.8	18	47	5.3	0.9	223.4	66.4	74.8	15.3
Franklin	90	D	D	D	38	D	D	D	355.2	146.2	104.6	14.8
Gibson	109	1 808	115.3	43.3	54	262	19.6	5.7	574.5	176.9	173.0	24.5
Giles	70	862	69.5	25.0	31	129	10.5	2.3	280.3	106.4	85.9	11.4
Grainger	12	D	D	D	16	72	5.9	1.4	216.5	81.9	64.2	14.3
Greene	142	3 580	255.9	100.8	75	451	32.0	8.8	664.5	263.5	150.6	34.9
Grundy	15	288	15.9	7.7	11	18	2.2	0.4	152.6	52.1	46.5	14.0
Hamblen	177	4 036	343.4	131.7	82	406	28.0	7.5	568.2	221.4	140.4	30.3
Hamilton	1 040	24 700	2 639.2	1 019.6	624	5 007	487.4	130.9	3 591.5	1 224.3	800.6	173.8
Hancock	6	154	9.1	3.7	5	D	D	D	99.7	17.7	35.2	8.3
Hardeman	41	1 453	77.6	38.1	25	50	5.0	1.2	465.2	84.1	99.4	22.1
Hardin	52	961	62.3	25.5	21	80	6.6	1.8	285.4	92.9	89.6	18.1
Hawkins	50	1 350	87.7	35.9	41	D	D	D	502.8	227.1	123.4	30.0
Haywood	29	D	D	D	27	D	D	D	248.8	46.4	83.9	17.6
Henderson	45	651	50.1	18.2	39	139	11.2	3.0	248.2	90.9	82.3	12.3
Henry	78	1 536	123.0	47.8	52	257	12.4	3.9	349.1	144.6	93.0	14.5
Hickman	35	580	41.6	16.2	22	D	D	D	193.7	76.3	46.2	9.8
Houston	15	361	22.4	9.2	7	D	D	D	90.9	37.9	24.7	4.0
Humphreys	31	560	34.4	13.0	27	118	8.0	2.9	398.8	74.5	48.8	6.6
Jackson	7	D	D	D	3	D	D	D	127.8	32.6	38.9	6.2
Jefferson	56	D	D	D	50	173	13.6	4.3	416.8	220.1	99.4	21.4
Johnson	20	371	22.5	10.1	16	34	2.6	0.6	197.5	71.3	59.8	11.4
Knox	1 200	30 846	3 184.9	1 259.7	760	5 638	513.6	159.1	3 928.4	1 363.2	814.7	171.3
Lake	9	D	D	D	7	D	D	D	95.8	19.8	30.3	5.9
Lauderdale	31	845	36.7	15.2	16	82	6.1	1.9	312.0	76.6	94.7	20.9
Lawrence	78	1 133	90.6	31.6	41	129	8.8	2.5	403.5	174.6	114.1	18.9
Lewis	27	445	22.0	8.7	15	57	3.5	1.0	110.3	37.4	33.5	5.6
Lincoln	69	933	63.6	25.0	47	155	12.3	3.4	287.4	121.9	75.7	12.8
Loudon	85	D	D	D	54	D	D	D	385.0	248.0	99.3	15.2
McMinn	100	1 932	158.2	56.3	52	258	16.0	4.6	490.1	198.4	119.7	24.3
McNairy	43	758	52.9	21.8	27	76	8.0	1.9	360.0	113.6	103.9	19.2
Macon	36	521	33.0	12.7	23	89	7.4	2.2	207.9	58.3	55.5	8.9
Madison	304	10 656	1 030.8	435.5	143	948	71.3	26.0	878.2	291.6	232.4	49.0
Marion	48	D	D	D	31	D	D	D	258.1	105.2	85.0	16.6

1. State totals may include programs not allocated by county.

Table B. States and Counties — Federal Funds, Residential Construction, and Local Government Finances

	Federal funds and grants, 2009–2010 (cont.)							Value of residential construction authorized by building permits, 2010		Local government finances, 2007				
	Expenditures (mil dol) (cont.)										General revenue			
	Procurement contract awards			Grants[1]								Taxes		
													Per capita[2] (dollars)	
STATE County	Salaries and wages	Defense	Other	Medicaid and other health-related	Nutrition and family welfare	Education	Other	New construction ($1,000)	Number of housing units	Total (mil dol)	Inter-govern-mental (mil dol)	Total (mil dol)	Total	Property
	171	172	173	174	175	176	177	178	179	180	181	182	183	184
SOUTH DAKOTA—Cont'd														
Tripp	3.3	0.0	0.7	7.4	1.1	0.8	0.1	0	0	20.4	8.1	8.3	1 428	1 102
Turner	2.6	0.0	0.7	7.4	1.1	0.2	0.1	4 639	28	24.2	8.0	11.3	1 348	1 123
Union	3.8	272.3	5.0	8.4	1.8	0.1	0.4	20 531	74	52.4	10.1	25.2	1 805	1 494
Walworth	4.2	0.0	0.8	6.9	1.1	4.8	1.2	1 705	11	16.1	7.0	6.4	1 217	836
Yankton	22.6	5.3	3.1	19.9	2.6	0.4	1.3	10 192	56	60.4	16.9	31.8	1 467	1 106
Ziebach	0.3	0.0	0.0	3.7	0.4	1.5	0.4	NA	NA	5.3	3.7	1.1	420	353
TENNESSEE	3 837.3	3 100.9	7 039.8	8 035.9	1 360.7	1 441.1	3 256.8	2 344 869	16 475	X	X	X	X	X
Anderson	74.0	107.4	3 681.9	130.3	13.0	7.3	15.3	17 647	146	209.6	76.5	99.2	1 350	809
Bedford	10.4	0.2	1.3	35.8	5.1	4.4	1.7	15 234	127	117.8	44.4	49.2	1 117	505
Benton	5.6	1.4	1.0	23.6	2.9	1.8	0.0	0	0	41.6	21.8	10.5	646	352
Bledsoe	1.3	0.0	0.3	20.0	4.9	2.6	4.2	NA	NA	25.6	18.1	4.3	331	246
Blount	52.6	11.7	12.4	84.0	12.6	8.0	6.2	35 145	207	602.9	125.8	136.8	1 142	821
Bradley	16.6	0.1	4.9	69.3	22.7	10.1	2.3	40 222	449	205.5	83.8	71.6	750	475
Campbell	12.3	3.3	2.8	80.0	7.8	4.2	3.7	14 002	135	80.7	45.7	22.3	548	337
Cannon	2.3	0.0	0.5	16.4	1.8	1.1	0.2	678	7	26.2	15.8	6.3	469	342
Carroll	15.0	3.4	1.6	57.4	4.9	4.5	3.8	2 391	59	55.7	35.0	9.2	318	162
Carter	13.5	0.0	2.1	76.0	8.9	4.7	3.0	12 634	143	104.0	55.0	30.6	516	282
Cheatham	10.6	2.5	1.7	16.9	4.1	2.4	0.2	8 929	50	86.2	42.9	29.5	753	445
Chester	13.0	0.0	0.4	22.7	6.0	1.1	0.3	2 242	27	28.0	15.8	8.6	535	263
Claiborne	9.1	0.8	2.2	67.1	9.9	3.9	0.9	10 283	108	137.9	35.6	15.6	498	342
Clay	2.4	3.2	2.3	26.2	1.6	0.9	2.0	NA	NA	17.1	11.0	4.2	539	319
Cocke	11.0	0.0	3.8	85.0	6.7	3.3	1.2	152	2	66.9	36.3	23.7	670	379
Coffee	51.1	471.9	4.7	48.4	6.7	4.3	2.3	10 385	70	119.7	48.1	50.9	983	487
Crockett	4.7	11.0	0.8	32.5	2.7	1.3	0.0	75	1	33.7	19.7	9.2	647	367
Cumberland	9.1	3.1	-71.3	46.4	6.7	3.2	3.6	6 483	69	94.8	39.4	38.5	727	328
Davidson	786.7	83.2	560.2	1 385.5	348.3	971.9	1 955.4	268 646	1 608	2 386.1	563.2	1 174.7	1 896	1 237
Decatur	5.7	0.0	0.7	20.4	1.9	1.1	0.3	0	0	33.7	12.7	6.7	589	248
DeKalb	3.2	4.8	0.8	27.4	2.6	1.6	0.4	706	6	36.7	20.9	9.5	517	384
Dickson	19.0	0.3	1.8	37.8	6.3	3.2	3.7	18 859	109	120.6	44.2	56.6	1 194	604
Dyer	20.8	0.0	2.3	71.2	5.4	4.5	1.5	6 129	58	103.4	42.6	40.1	1 064	535
Fayette	5.3	0.0	1.2	74.6	6.3	2.1	0.1	135 034	159	44.1	26.6	11.0	296	148
Fentress	13.9	0.2	0.7	46.0	3.5	1.3	0.7	0	0	32.3	18.6	8.4	485	219
Franklin	18.1	5.3	2.7	44.6	5.3	3.3	2.1	12 335	85	78.2	39.3	26.1	633	478
Gibson	45.2	27.7	5.7	86.8	8.3	4.4	3.0	17 045	132	126.1	65.7	33.8	697	392
Giles	6.7	1.9	3.4	49.2	4.1	2.1	0.9	400	5	62.9	27.8	24.4	840	561
Grainger	3.6	0.0	0.8	44.5	3.4	1.8	0.3	360	2	38.2	25.4	8.0	355	257
Greene	24.2	12.3	38.9	89.4	8.9	25.3	5.8	12 062	136	140.5	60.4	55.6	843	563
Grundy	9.8	0.0	0.5	24.3	2.8	1.7	0.3	0	0	27.2	19.3	5.9	412	294
Hamblen	17.4	25.4	7.2	75.3	15.9	6.3	5.5	9 670	80	127.1	47.7	53.2	861	375
Hamilton	182.9	41.7	507.5	338.3	48.4	28.9	164.3	118 873	817	1 549.8	288.0	418.6	1 268	886
Hancock	0.8	0.0	0.4	33.2	1.9	0.9	0.5	0	0	16.8	11.8	2.4	357	246
Hardeman	8.5	160.8	2.2	74.9	6.0	2.9	0.5	4 349	41	55.2	30.8	16.1	578	319
Hardin	9.7	0.0	2.1	60.1	4.2	2.4	2.0	685	15	83.0	27.7	19.3	739	336
Hawkins	8.0	0.0	13.0	83.0	7.6	4.4	0.8	2 761	25	102.5	51.8	35.7	625	385
Haywood	9.7	0.0	1.6	68.6	5.5	1.6	1.3	1 618	17	50.2	25.5	15.1	787	526
Henderson	7.6	0.0	0.9	45.3	3.7	2.1	0.4	5 482	53	57.7	27.4	20.4	763	363
Henry	14.7	0.0	13.4	45.2	4.9	4.0	8.0	1 059	12	141.6	40.8	23.1	732	376
Hickman	14.7	13.0	1.1	24.2	2.9	1.6	1.4	0	0	48.7	26.9	13.8	582	352
Houston	4.2	0.0	0.7	13.7	3.3	0.7	0.3	354	3	19.7	11.4	5.3	657	402
Humphreys	4.2	0.2	232.4	24.9	2.6	1.4	0.3	4 688	58	44.2	19.9	13.8	758	432
Jackson	2.0	0.0	0.5	26.0	1.8	0.9	16.8	NA	NA	21.2	14.5	4.6	430	335
Jefferson	12.2	0.0	2.4	45.1	5.5	3.3	1.0	24 287	124	91.0	42.6	34.3	683	379
Johnson	3.2	4.2	0.9	39.7	3.0	1.5	0.6	309	2	34.5	21.4	7.2	400	280
Knox	277.9	71.7	399.6	400.3	53.8	34.2	167.2	186 874	1 606	1 168.8	322.6	585.6	1 382	753
Lake	8.8	2.1	0.3	21.3	1.7	0.7	0.1	591	7	19.5	10.3	3.5	476	294
Lauderdale	7.2	8.2	7.8	70.3	6.2	2.9	4.9	2 854	33	61.5	33.9	16.6	622	371
Lawrence	16.7	0.0	2.0	59.2	6.2	3.4	1.6	392	4	95.5	40.3	34.3	839	430
Lewis	6.1	0.0	3.5	16.7	1.8	1.0	2.3	317	4	26.0	14.4	6.5	564	270
Lincoln	5.9	0.3	1.5	46.3	11.1	2.6	2.8	3 444	23	102.9	31.3	16.6	507	315
Loudon	15.0	4.2	-50.2	39.6	5.4	2.8	1.7	39 036	238	98.1	40.1	35.0	771	504
McMinn	27.3	39.8	2.2	56.5	6.7	4.2	3.5	0	0	124.2	50.2	33.3	638	489
McNairy	10.7	0.6	1.8	73.0	3.9	2.6	27.9	4 660	72	51.4	28.2	13.7	536	362
Macon	8.8	0.0	0.6	30.1	2.8	1.9	25.2	1 010	28	43.6	24.0	13.6	629	357
Madison	72.2	0.1	8.5	138.3	14.2	10.9	13.2	38 871	222	842.2	102.3	134.7	1 396	706
Marion	4.1	0.0	1.0	36.2	4.3	2.7	1.1	8 030	49	55.5	28.1	17.9	636	346

1. State totals may include programs not allocated by county. 2. Based on the resident population estimated as of July 1 of the year shown.

Table B. States and Counties — Local Government Finances, Government Employment, and Voting

STATE County	Total (mil dol) [185]	Per capita[1] (dollars) [186]	Education [187]	Health and hospitals [188]	Police protection [189]	Public welfare [190]	Highways [191]	Total (mil dol) [192]	Per capita[1] (dollars) [193]	Federal civilian [194]	Federal military [195]	State and local [196]	Democratic [197]	Republican [198]	All other [199]
SOUTH DAKOTA—Cont'd															
Tripp	18.0	3 094	51.1	0.9	4.2	0.0	17.2	17.3	2 986	39	35	378	32.2	65.5	2.3
Turner	19.9	2 378	53.4	0.7	4.4	0.2	15.8	25.1	2 996	42	52	431	38.6	58.3	3.1
Union	46.3	3 317	49.9	0.3	5.8	0.1	10.6	39.4	2 826	49	92	706	42.1	56.0	1.9
Walworth	15.8	3 001	42.9	0.6	5.3	0.3	16.4	2.3	446	34	33	394	34.8	62.9	2.2
Yankton	58.3	2 692	46.1	1.3	5.1	0.3	9.4	45.2	2 087	216	138	1 705	47.7	49.7	2.5
Ziebach	5.6	2 102	71.6	0.4	2.4	0.1	15.9	0.4	132	10	16	161	62.2	35.0	2.8
TENNESSEE	X	X	X	X	X	X	X	X	X	50 222	23 766	380 346	41.8	56.9	1.3
Anderson	227.2	3 092	49.6	2.5	4.8	0.0	3.2	272.6	3 711	1 019	256	4 165	36.1	62.3	1.6
Bedford	119.0	2 700	59.2	2.7	4.4	5.9	5.1	165.1	3 747	75	155	2 134	32.4	65.9	1.7
Benton	38.5	2 364	50.4	1.4	5.6	0.0	5.6	32.3	1 983	54	54	916	40.8	57.0	2.1
Bledsoe	26.4	2 017	55.7	3.2	2.7	0.0	6.0	16.7	1 273	21	44	1 095	31.7	66.2	2.1
Blount	580.7	4 845	24.7	27.5	3.1	0.1	2.3	2 169.6	18 101	259	423	7 386	29.5	68.9	1.6
Bradley	222.2	2 328	48.7	12.7	8.3	0.2	5.2	227.3	2 381	226	330	4 633	24.5	74.2	1.3
Campbell	78.8	1 934	62.4	1.7	5.9	0.4	5.8	89.8	2 202	87	138	2 196	30.6	67.6	1.8
Cannon	24.9	1 855	62.1	3.6	5.9	0.8	8.4	17.2	1 283	39	47	551	36.9	60.9	2.3
Carroll	60.6	2 095	59.0	0.3	5.3	0.2	7.2	32.8	1 133	92	96	1 451	34.2	64.0	1.8
Carter	101.4	1 714	65.5	0.6	4.7	0.0	5.1	45.7	772	80	199	2 445	25.7	72.8	1.5
Cheatham	75.8	1 937	66.0	2.9	4.8	0.1	5.3	66.3	1 695	83	134	1 573	33.5	65.1	1.4
Chester	26.2	1 621	61.5	0.9	9.6	0.6	7.5	17.6	1 093	29	55	981	27.8	71.0	1.2
Claiborne	88.7	2 837	41.6	38.4	2.7	0.0	5.1	78.4	2 506	71	105	2 194	29.5	68.9	1.6
Clay	17.4	2 208	56.6	1.4	5.8	0.2	9.7	15.4	1 954	48	27	436	41.7	56.0	2.3
Cocke	64.2	1 816	64.0	0.5	6.5	0.0	6.6	37.2	1 053	73	121	1 803	26.8	71.7	1.6
Coffee	111.6	2 156	64.8	2.6	8.4	0.1	2.9	82.1	1 588	420	238	3 159	34.3	63.7	2.0
Crockett	32.0	2 249	60.2	2.9	3.6	0.6	7.3	32.2	2 262	41	49	725	32.6	66.2	1.3
Cumberland	93.1	1 754	56.3	3.3	6.2	0.3	3.6	97.0	1 828	112	182	2 283	30.7	67.8	1.5
Davidson	2 353.5	3 798	29.1	7.7	7.6	1.3	2.3	4 619.2	7 455	8 288	2 880	42 209	59.9	38.9	1.2
Decatur	34.1	3 004	35.9	31.1	5.6	0.0	5.2	37.4	3 298	32	39	779	32.9	65.1	2.0
DeKalb	30.4	1 649	61.6	1.6	5.3	0.2	7.2	43.5	2 358	46	64	768	40.1	57.8	2.1
Dickson	106.4	2 246	55.4	3.0	8.1	0.0	5.2	158.1	3 337	98	163	2 500	38.5	59.8	1.7
Dyer	101.3	2 689	54.6	2.1	6.5	0.6	7.4	76.2	2 021	111	127	2 822	30.5	68.2	1.2
Fayette	64.3	1 729	47.3	2.6	6.7	0.0	7.4	56.8	1 527	63	131	1 734	35.8	63.2	1.0
Fentress	30.4	1 746	57.5	3.9	4.4	0.0	9.3	20.0	1 149	43	59	845	27.2	71.1	1.8
Franklin	79.9	1 939	57.8	0.4	8.8	0.1	7.7	108.7	2 638	148	139	1 719	37.9	60.5	1.6
Gibson	149.0	3 069	52.1	1.7	6.4	0.0	4.8	183.4	3 776	161	167	2 820	34.8	63.6	1.6
Giles	60.5	2 085	55.7	2.8	6.5	0.1	7.9	21.4	736	78	98	1 445	39.5	59.0	1.6
Grainger	47.7	2 114	72.7	2.3	3.2	0.1	4.1	52.0	2 305	55	77	868	27.5	70.6	1.9
Greene	131.0	1 985	57.8	4.7	4.9	0.0	5.7	125.8	1 907	236	223	3 930	28.8	69.5	1.7
Grundy	25.8	1 805	71.4	0.7	3.6	0.0	7.5	15.5	1 086	25	48	763	42.6	55.3	2.1
Hamblen	117.4	1 899	60.2	1.4	5.4	0.1	1.8	90.9	1 469	189	213	3 670	30.0	68.4	1.6
Hamilton	1 378.8	4 176	24.7	33.5	5.7	1.5	2.8	1 502.7	4 551	5 562	1 175	21 622	43.6	55.4	1.1
Hancock	16.5	2 449	53.3	9.2	2.8	0.0	10.3	20.1	2 988	10	22	480	27.0	70.9	2.2
Hardeman	49.9	1 793	63.2	3.3	7.7	0.1	6.5	16.8	605	61	93	2 008	52.7	46.5	0.8
Hardin	81.5	3 127	38.0	32.9	2.6	3.2	4.6	37.0	1 418	125	88	1 659	27.8	70.5	1.6
Hawkins	91.8	1 609	65.5	0.7	5.4	0.2	5.7	80.3	1 407	277	194	2 166	28.2	70.1	1.7
Haywood	51.5	2 693	54.0	3.2	7.6	0.0	6.7	12.8	671	76	64	1 104	60.3	39.0	0.8
Henderson	51.7	1 932	62.8	0.4	6.2	0.4	6.7	39.6	1 479	68	91	1 302	27.9	70.8	1.3
Henry	127.6	4 033	28.3	48.0	3.3	0.0	4.6	59.1	1 868	140	139	2 375	38.0	60.4	1.6
Hickman	50.6	2 128	59.6	2.9	4.5	0.2	4.2	64.1	2 698	59	80	1 199	41.9	56.3	1.8
Houston	19.3	2 385	53.4	3.2	6.8	0.0	8.0	16.7	2 072	21	27	533	50.0	47.9	2.0
Humphreys	43.6	2 402	49.6	0.8	4.2	0.0	10.3	84.4	4 646	378	62	1 006	47.5	50.4	2.1
Jackson	20.7	1 918	62.3	3.0	4.8	0.3	10.5	19.0	1 757	34	37	504	49.4	48.5	2.0
Jefferson	93.7	1 866	56.8	4.6	6.1	0.2	5.7	56.4	1 122	126	174	2 339	27.9	70.6	1.4
Johnson	35.3	1 947	60.8	0.8	4.0	0.2	6.8	20.8	1 147	45	61	989	27.9	70.1	2.0
Knox	1 118.5	2 639	39.4	2.5	7.1	0.4	2.1	1 826.1	4 308	3 707	1 530	33 293	37.7	60.7	1.5
Lake	18.5	2 496	39.6	3.5	5.6	0.5	10.1	23.7	3 200	16	25	819	45.8	52.5	1.7
Lauderdale	57.3	2 145	58.5	2.5	7.3	0.3	4.9	43.8	1 639	60	89	2 003	46.3	52.8	0.9
Lawrence	83.9	2 051	55.5	1.7	5.9	0.2	8.0	443.8	10 854	128	139	1 936	32.2	66.0	1.8
Lewis	24.6	2 119	53.8	0.6	5.6	0.0	6.7	12.3	1 059	31	39	653	37.3	61.0	1.6
Lincoln	80.7	2 464	45.0	28.1	3.7	0.1	4.9	63.2	1 931	66	112	2 557	28.1	70.3	1.6
Loudon	103.2	2 271	53.7	0.6	7.1	0.3	3.4	1 504.0	33 094	157	157	1 943	27.3	71.3	1.4
McMinn	124.9	2 396	47.2	21.1	3.9	0.0	4.2	41.2	791	120	177	2 139	29.5	69.1	1.4
McNairy	48.7	1 904	61.2	1.1	5.4	0.0	4.8	36.5	1 426	87	87	1 193	30.0	68.5	1.5
Macon	40.6	1 882	61.9	3.9	7.1	0.6	4.0	21.4	991	35	74	1 071	28.0	69.9	2.1
Madison	944.7	9 788	12.8	70.7	2.0	0.0	0.8	1 397.2	14 476	468	332	11 544	46.1	53.1	0.8
Marion	57.5	2 043	59.4	0.8	4.9	0.0	4.7	76.2	2 708	69	94	1 230	39.4	59.0	1.6

1. Based on the resident population estimated as of July 1 of the year shown.   2. © 2009 Election Data Services, Inc. All rights reserved.

Table B. States and Counties — Land Area and Population

STATE/ County code	CBSA code[1]	County type[2]	STATE County	Land area,[3] (sq km) 2010	Total persons	Rank	Per square kilometer	White	Black	American Indian, Alaska Native	Asian and Pacific Islander	Percent Hispanic or Latino[4]	Under 5 years	5 to 17 years	18 to 24 years	25 to 34 years	35 to 44 years	45 to 54 years
				1	2	3	4	5	6	7	8	9	10	11	12	13	14	15
			TENNESSEE—Cont'd															
47 117	30280	6	Marshall	972	30 617	1 420	31.5	88.1	7.2	0.8	0.7	4.5	6.4	18.2	7.9	12.3	13.7	15.1
47 119	17940	4	Maury	1 588	80 956	681	51.0	81.7	13.4	0.7	0.9	4.8	7.2	17.1	8.2	13.3	12.7	15.5
47 121	...	8	Meigs	505	11 753	2 314	23.3	96.8	1.2	1.2	0.2	1.5	5.1	16.4	7.1	10.6	13.8	15.4
47 123	...	6	Monroe	1 646	44 519	1 076	27.0	93.9	2.5	1.3	0.5	3.3	6.0	16.9	7.7	10.9	13.3	14.3
47 125	17300	3	Montgomery	1 396	172 331	358	123.4	70.0	20.5	1.3	3.7	8.0	8.9	19.1	12.5	17.2	13.5	12.4
47 127	46100	9	Moore	335	6 362	2 739	19.0	95.9	2.7	0.8	0.5	1.1	4.7	17.4	6.8	10.1	13.3	15.3
47 129	...	6	Morgan	1 352	21 987	1 739	16.3	95.0	3.9	1.1	0.3	0.9	5.2	15.9	8.2	13.6	15.0	15.4
47 131	46460	7	Obion	1 411	31 807	1 400	22.5	85.8	11.2	0.5	0.3	3.1	5.5	17.3	7.5	11.2	13.3	14.6
47 133	18260	7	Overton	1 123	22 083	1 737	19.7	98.1	0.7	0.9	0.3	0.9	6.0	17.3	7.4	10.8	13.3	14.2
47 135	...	8	Perry	1 074	7 915	2 608	7.4	96.1	1.9	1.3	0.3	1.7	5.8	16.7	7.7	10.3	11.6	14.2
47 137	...	9	Pickett	422	5 077	2 838	12.0	98.3	0.2	0.6	0.1	1.3	4.6	14.6	6.6	9.5	11.6	14.2
47 139	17420	3	Polk	1 126	16 825	1 995	14.9	97.8	0.5	1.3	0.3	1.4	5.4	16.8	7.3	10.2	14.0	15.0
47 141	18260	4	Putnam	1 039	72 321	743	69.6	91.1	2.5	0.7	1.5	5.3	6.0	15.5	15.0	12.4	11.9	12.9
47 143	...	6	Rhea	817	31 809	1 399	38.9	93.4	2.5	1.0	0.6	3.7	6.3	17.2	9.3	11.2	13.0	14.0
47 145	25340	4	Roane	934	54 181	921	58.0	95.1	3.2	1.1	0.8	1.3	5.0	15.8	6.9	9.7	12.7	15.6
47 147	34980	1	Robertson	1 234	66 283	792	53.7	85.8	7.9	0.7	0.7	5.9	7.0	18.7	7.9	13.0	13.9	15.7
47 149	34980	1	Rutherford	1 604	262 604	248	163.7	77.3	13.5	0.7	3.6	6.7	7.3	18.8	12.4	15.6	14.7	13.6
47 151	...	6	Scott	1 379	22 228	1 727	16.1	98.9	0.2	0.8	0.3	0.5	6.6	18.7	8.2	12.6	13.6	14.3
47 153	16860	2	Sequatchie	689	14 112	2 165	20.5	95.9	0.4	1.0	0.4	3.3	6.1	17.4	7.7	11.0	13.7	14.7
47 155	42940	4	Sevier	1 535	89 889	630	58.6	92.6	1.0	0.8	1.2	5.3	5.9	16.3	8.3	11.6	13.5	15.2
47 157	32820	1	Shelby	1 977	927 644	47	469.2	39.6	52.6	0.5	2.7	5.6	7.2	19.2	10.2	14.0	13.5	14.3
47 159	34980	1	Smith	814	19 166	1 871	23.5	95.1	2.6	1.1	0.3	2.2	6.1	18.1	7.9	11.7	13.5	16.2
47 161	17300	3	Stewart	1 190	13 324	2 230	11.2	95.1	1.8	1.4	1.4	1.9	5.2	17.7	7.5	9.9	12.9	15.9
47 163	28700	3	Sullivan	1 071	156 823	398	146.4	95.5	2.6	0.7	0.8	1.5	5.2	15.3	7.5	10.4	13.4	15.3
47 165	34980	1	Sumner	1 371	160 645	383	117.2	88.2	7.0	0.7	1.4	3.9	6.5	18.8	7.6	12.1	14.5	15.5
47 167	32820	1	Tipton	1 187	61 081	846	51.5	78.0	19.3	1.0	1.0	2.1	6.7	20.5	8.7	12.1	14.0	15.4
47 169	34980	1	Trousdale	296	7 870	2 614	26.6	87.4	10.4	0.8	0.3	2.5	6.3	18.3	8.2	11.6	13.3	15.3
47 171	27740	3	Unicoi	482	18 313	1 908	38.0	95.6	0.4	0.8	0.3	3.8	5.1	15.1	6.8	10.4	12.6	15.2
47 173	28940	2	Union	579	19 109	1 874	33.0	98.2	0.3	1.1	0.2	1.3	6.7	17.2	8.4	11.3	13.3	16.0
47 175	...	9	Van Buren	708	5 548	2 804	7.8	98.3	0.5	1.0	0.1	0.9	5.1	15.7	6.7	10.4	12.5	15.7
47 177	32660	6	Warren	1 121	39 839	1 176	35.5	88.3	3.3	0.7	0.7	8.1	6.5	17.8	7.7	12.2	13.5	14.5
47 179	27740	3	Washington	846	122 979	492	145.4	91.6	4.6	0.7	1.5	3.0	5.4	14.8	11.6	12.6	13.3	14.3
47 181	...	8	Wayne	1 901	17 021	1 984	9.0	92.0	6.0	0.8	0.3	1.6	5.0	14.6	8.4	13.7	14.4	15.2
47 183	32280	7	Weakley	1 503	35 021	1 298	23.3	88.8	8.4	0.7	1.3	2.0	5.4	14.7	17.3	10.7	11.4	13.1
47 185	...	7	White	976	25 841	1 573	26.5	95.9	2.3	0.9	0.5	1.6	5.8	16.6	7.7	10.9	12.9	14.5
47 187	34980	1	Williamson	1 509	183 182	336	121.4	87.8	4.7	0.5	3.6	4.5	6.7	22.5	5.8	9.9	16.1	17.2
47 189	34980	1	Wilson	1 478	113 993	523	77.1	88.8	7.0	0.8	1.5	3.2	6.4	18.6	7.3	11.5	15.0	16.3
48 000	...	X	**TEXAS**	676 587	25 145 561	X	37.2	46.4	12.0	0.7	4.4	37.6	7.7	19.6	10.2	14.4	13.8	13.7
48 001	37300	5	Anderson	2 752	58 458	875	21.2	62.2	21.4	0.8	0.7	15.9	5.4	14.3	8.0	15.8	16.3	16.1
48 003	11380	6	Andrews	3 887	14 786	2 128	3.8	48.6	1.6	1.0	0.7	48.7	8.3	20.9	9.6	13.3	12.0	14.6
48 005	31260	5	Angelina	2 066	86 771	651	42.0	64.1	15.3	0.6	1.1	19.8	7.5	19.2	9.2	12.5	12.8	13.6
48 007	18580	2	Aransas	653	23 158	1 682	35.5	71.7	1.4	1.2	2.2	24.6	5.1	14.4	6.6	8.5	10.0	14.6
48 009	48660	3	Archer	2 339	9 054	2 521	3.9	91.4	0.6	1.2	0.4	7.5	5.2	18.9	7.6	9.2	12.1	17.8
48 011	11100	3	Armstrong	2 355	1 901	3 063	0.8	91.6	0.8	1.3	0.1	6.5	5.6	16.6	5.3	10.6	10.6	14.8
48 013	41700	1	Atascosa	3 159	44 911	1 069	14.2	36.8	0.7	0.7	0.4	61.9	7.4	21.2	8.6	11.3	12.6	13.9
48 015	26420	1	Austin	1 674	28 417	1 480	17.0	66.5	9.7	0.7	0.6	23.4	6.5	18.6	7.4	10.7	12.1	15.5
48 017	...	7	Bailey	2 141	7 165	2 669	3.3	38.7	1.0	0.4	0.4	59.8	9.5	21.4	9.1	12.8	11.2	12.0
48 019	41700	1	Bandera	2 049	20 485	1 820	10.0	81.9	0.6	1.2	0.5	16.7	4.5	15.1	5.5	7.7	10.8	18.3
48 021	12420	1	Bastrop	2 300	74 171	732	32.2	58.6	8.1	1.0	1.0	32.6	6.8	19.5	7.7	11.6	13.7	16.0
48 023	...	6	Baylor	2 247	3 726	2 927	1.7	85.4	2.3	0.7	0.3	12.2	6.1	14.5	6.7	9.6	10.1	15.1
48 025	13300	4	Bee	2 280	31 861	1 397	14.0	34.9	8.1	0.5	0.7	56.2	6.1	15.9	11.2	16.3	14.7	14.8
48 027	28660	2	Bell	2 722	310 235	206	114.0	53.3	22.3	1.2	4.8	21.6	9.1	19.6	12.6	17.0	12.6	12.0
48 029	41700	1	Bexar	3 211	1 714 773	19	534.0	31.3	7.5	0.5	3.1	58.7	7.6	19.5	11.0	14.8	13.5	13.2
48 031	...	8	Blanco	1 837	10 497	2 404	5.7	80.2	0.8	0.9	0.6	18.2	5.2	16.6	5.9	8.5	11.5	16.3
48 033	...	9	Borden	2 324	641	3 133	0.3	84.7	0.0	0.9	0.2	14.8	4.4	17.2	6.6	8.1	12.3	16.4
48 035	...	6	Bosque	2 546	18 212	1 915	7.2	81.7	2.0	0.9	0.3	16.1	5.6	17.3	6.4	9.3	11.1	14.6
48 037	45500	3	Bowie	2 292	92 565	621	40.4	67.7	24.9	1.3	1.1	6.5	6.4	17.9	8.7	13.3	13.2	14.4
48 039	26420	1	Brazoria	3 516	313 166	203	89.1	54.5	12.4	0.8	6.0	27.7	7.9	19.9	8.2	13.9	15.1	14.9
48 041	17780	3	Brazos	1 516	194 851	322	128.5	60.3	11.2	0.6	5.8	23.3	6.4	14.0	30.9	15.3	9.8	9.3
48 043	...	7	Brewster	16 016	9 232	2 507	0.6	55.4	1.1	1.1	1.0	42.4	5.9	14.5	9.5	13.1	11.0	14.0
48 045	...	9	Briscoe	2 331	1 637	3 078	0.7	72.3	2.6	0.6	0.7	25.1	6.3	15.8	6.2	9.8	10.5	14.7
48 047	...	6	Brooks	2 443	7 223	2 666	3.0	8.1	0.3	0.1	0.2	91.2	8.6	19.2	9.7	10.2	9.5	13.2
48 049	15220	5	Brown	2 446	38 106	1 214	15.6	76.0	4.0	1.1	0.6	19.6	6.2	17.7	9.1	11.2	11.5	13.9
48 051	17780	3	Burleson	1 707	17 187	1 972	10.1	69.0	12.5	0.8	0.3	18.4	6.2	17.3	7.4	9.9	11.8	15.6
48 053	31920	6	Burnet	2 575	42 750	1 110	16.6	77.1	1.9	1.0	0.7	20.2	5.8	17.4	7.1	10.5	11.2	15.0

1. CBSA = Core Based Statistical Area. See Appendix A for explanation. See Appendix B for list of metropolitan areas with component counties. 2. County type code from the Economic Research Service of USDA Rural-Urban Continuum Codes. See Appendix A for definition. 3. Dry land or land partially or temporarily covered by water. 4. May be of any race.

Table B. States and Counties — Population and Households

STATE County	Population, 2010 (cont.) Age (percent) (cont.) 55 to 64 years	65 to 74 years	75 years and over	Percent female	Population change and components of change, 1990–2010 Total persons 1990	2000	Percent change 1990–2000	2000–2010	Components of change, 2000–2009 Births	Deaths	Net migration	Households, 2010 Number	Percent change, 2000–2010	Persons per household	Percent Female family householder[1]	One person
	16	17	18	19	20	21	22	23	24	25	26	27	28	29	30	31
TENNESSEE—Cont'd																
Marshall	13.2	7.6	5.5	51.1	21 539	26 767	24.3	14.4	3 552	2 534	2 651	11 850	15.0	2.55	13.0	24.4
Maury	13.1	7.2	5.7	51.6	54 812	69 498	26.8	16.5	9 882	6 589	11 779	31 663	19.7	2.52	14.1	24.3
Meigs	15.6	10.3	5.7	50.3	8 033	11 086	38.0	6.0	1 254	1 104	942	4 686	8.9	2.48	10.8	23.2
Monroe	14.5	10.3	6.1	50.5	30 541	38 961	27.6	14.3	5 022	3 980	5 992	17 711	15.6	2.49	11.3	24.9
Montgomery	8.5	4.7	3.3	51.0	100 498	134 768	34.1	27.9	23 974	8 467	11 262	63 673	31.7	2.65	15.0	22.5
Moore	14.0	10.8	7.6	50.8	4 696	5 740	22.2	10.8	519	482	349	2 492	12.7	2.51	8.1	22.6
Morgan	13.2	8.3	5.4	44.9	17 300	19 757	14.2	11.3	2 063	1 815	-1 173	7 692	10.0	2.53	11.5	24.3
Obion	13.8	9.5	7.2	51.8	31 717	32 450	2.3	-2.0	3 668	3 596	-902	13 077	-0.8	2.40	12.9	27.3
Overton	14.2	10.1	6.7	50.6	17 636	20 118	14.1	9.8	2 277	2 348	1 143	8 820	8.8	2.47	11.0	25.7
Perry	14.8	10.9	7.8	49.8	6 612	7 631	15.4	3.7	854	893	266	3 160	4.5	2.47	10.1	26.6
Pickett	16.4	13.5	9.0	49.8	4 548	4 945	8.7	2.7	489	603	-26	2 177	4.1	2.30	8.2	29.0
Polk	14.3	10.4	6.6	50.2	13 643	16 050	17.6	4.8	1 781	1 835	-266	6 653	3.2	2.49	10.3	25.0
Putnam	11.6	8.2	6.4	50.5	51 373	62 315	21.3	16.1	8 413	6 049	8 046	28 930	16.3	2.41	10.9	28.0
Rhea	13.4	9.4	6.3	51.1	24 344	28 400	16.7	12.0	3 782	3 064	2 543	12 276	9.8	2.52	12.9	24.6
Roane	15.7	10.4	8.1	50.9	47 227	51 910	9.9	4.4	5 072	5 725	2 569	22 376	5.5	2.39	10.9	26.9
Robertson	12.0	6.9	4.8	50.8	41 492	54 433	31.2	21.8	8 978	4 922	8 408	24 197	21.6	2.71	11.9	19.9
Rutherford	9.4	4.9	3.3	50.6	118 570	182 023	53.5	44.3	31 760	11 764	55 711	96 232	44.8	2.68	12.8	22.1
Scott	12.3	8.3	5.5	50.9	18 358	21 127	15.1	5.2	2 924	1 990	-85	8 671	5.7	2.53	13.2	25.6
Sequatchie	13.7	10.0	5.6	50.4	8 863	11 370	28.3	24.1	1 506	1 093	2 173	5 519	23.7	2.52	11.8	23.4
Sevier	13.8	9.5	8.0	50.7	51 050	71 170	39.4	26.3	9 413	6 592	12 641	35 343	24.2	2.52	11.4	23.4
Shelby	11.4	5.7	4.6	52.3	826 330	897 472	8.6	3.4	135 219	71 293	-44 373	350 971	3.7	2.59	21.7	28.3
Smith	13.0	8.0	5.6	50.8	14 143	17 712	25.2	8.2	2 108	1 883	1 357	7 410	7.7	2.57	11.0	24.5
Stewart	14.2	10.0	6.6	50.1	9 479	12 370	30.5	7.7	1 329	1 362	1 066	5 386	9.2	2.46	9.6	26.5
Sullivan	14.2	10.4	8.3	51.6	143 596	153 048	6.6	2.5	15 398	16 606	3 706	66 298	4.3	2.33	11.4	28.8
Sumner	12.4	7.5	5.1	51.2	103 281	130 449	26.3	23.1	17 916	10 637	21 673	60 975	24.6	2.61	11.7	22.1
Tipton	11.4	6.7	4.3	51.0	37 568	51 271	36.5	19.1	6 968	4 492	6 029	21 617	19.4	2.78	15.7	19.7
Trousdale	13.5	7.9	5.6	50.3	5 920	7 259	22.6	8.4	841	834	702	2 976	7.1	2.60	12.6	23.5
Unicoi	15.0	10.8	8.9	51.1	16 549	17 667	6.8	9.7	1 674	2 332	834	7 726	2.8	2.32	10.7	28.5
Union	13.3	8.9	4.9	50.2	13 694	17 808	30.0	7.3	2 254	1 529	710	7 391	9.6	2.56	10.9	23.1
Van Buren	16.8	10.8	6.1	50.1	4 846	5 508	13.7	0.7	531	504	-27	2 246	3.0	2.43	11.7	24.3
Warren	12.6	8.6	6.5	50.7	32 992	38 276	16.0	4.1	5 043	3 957	1 358	15 850	4.4	2.48	12.6	27.0
Washington	12.8	8.6	6.7	51.1	92 336	107 198	16.1	14.7	12 478	10 952	12 369	51 322	16.1	2.31	10.7	29.9
Wayne	12.9	9.1	6.8	44.8	13 935	16 842	20.9	1.1	1 529	1 656	-113	6 136	3.4	2.43	10.4	26.5
Weakley	12.1	8.2	7.1	51.0	31 972	34 895	9.1	0.4	3 313	3 420	-1 186	13 898	2.2	2.36	11.4	28.2
White	13.9	9.9	7.6	51.1	20 090	23 102	15.0	11.9	2 834	2 758	2 398	10 272	11.3	2.48	12.1	24.9
Williamson	12.1	5.7	4.0	51.2	81 021	126 638	56.3	44.7	18 264	7 332	39 745	64 886	45.1	2.81	8.2	17.7
Wilson	12.7	7.6	4.6	51.0	67 675	88 809	31.2	28.4	12 351	7 073	18 606	42 563	29.8	2.65	11.2	19.9
TEXAS	10.3	5.9	4.5	50.4	16 986 335	20 851 820	22.8	20.6	3 568 617	1 444 493	1 781 785	8 922 933	20.7	2.75	14.1	24.2
Anderson	11.6	7.2	5.4	39.2	48 024	55 109	14.8	6.1	6 106	5 544	1 534	17 218	9.8	2.57	13.8	25.7
Andrews	10.1	6.1	5.2	50.2	14 338	13 004	-9.3	13.7	2 050	1 048	97	5 259	14.3	2.80	11.6	21.3
Angelina	11.5	7.5	6.2	51.0	69 884	80 130	14.7	8.3	12 124	7 300	-765	31 090	8.4	2.70	15.4	23.9
Aransas	16.6	14.5	9.7	50.4	17 892	22 497	25.7	2.9	2 442	2 664	2 646	9 795	7.3	2.32	9.8	27.8
Archer	13.1	9.3	6.7	49.6	7 973	8 854	11.0	2.3	918	697	-120	3 538	5.8	2.54	8.1	23.4
Armstrong	15.7	11.4	9.4	51.2	2 021	2 148	6.3	-11.5	223	216	-88	751	-6.4	2.46	6.1	23.4
Atascosa	12.2	7.2	5.5	50.7	30 533	38 628	26.5	16.3	6 159	2 991	3 092	15 246	19.0	2.92	14.2	20.7
Austin	13.6	8.7	6.9	50.5	19 832	23 590	18.9	20.5	3 229	2 549	3 116	10 837	23.9	2.60	10.5	23.4
Bailey	9.9	7.5	6.6	49.5	7 064	6 594	-6.7	8.7	1 160	555	-911	2 468	5.1	2.86	10.7	22.9
Bandera	18.0	12.4	7.7	50.3	10 562	17 645	67.1	16.1	1 728	1 563	2 819	8 564	22.2	2.35	8.1	26.1
Bastrop	13.2	6.8	4.7	48.8	38 263	57 733	50.9	28.5	8 537	4 547	13 335	25 840	28.6	2.78	11.8	22.4
Baylor	12.9	13.0	12.1	51.8	4 385	4 093	-6.7	-9.0	444	576	-273	1 669	-6.8	2.19	8.3	34.3
Bee	10.3	5.9	4.9	40.2	25 135	32 359	28.7	-1.5	3 540	2 076	-1 226	9 042	-0.2	2.69	16.1	25.4
Bell	8.7	4.8	3.9	50.5	191 073	237 974	24.5	30.4	52 002	15 527	10 122	114 035	33.4	2.65	14.9	24.0
Bexar	10.1	5.6	4.6	51.0	1 185 394	1 392 931	17.5	23.1	238 092	97 206	126 324	608 931	24.5	2.75	16.6	25.3
Blanco	17.8	10.9	7.3	49.5	5 972	8 418	41.0	24.7	1 007	901	717	4 309	30.5	2.41	7.6	26.2
Borden	14.4	11.5	9.2	47.7	799	729	-8.8	-12.1	26	31	-126	264	-9.6	2.43	4.9	22.0
Bosque	14.5	12.1	9.0	50.3	15 125	17 204	13.7	5.9	1 932	2 318	917	7 254	7.9	2.47	9.1	26.5
Bowie	12.0	7.6	6.6	49.5	81 665	89 306	9.4	3.6	10 851	8 857	3 153	34 669	4.9	2.49	16.7	27.7
Brazoria	10.6	5.7	3.9	49.2	191 707	241 767	26.1	29.5	41 377	16 568	43 889	106 589	30.1	2.84	12.1	19.9
Brazos	7.0	4.0	3.2	49.4	121 862	152 415	25.1	27.8	22 531	7 325	13 336	71 739	30.0	2.53	10.7	26.6
Brewster	15.5	9.6	7.0	49.8	8 653	8 866	2.5	4.1	1 111	672	233	4 207	14.7	2.18	9.3	37.0
Briscoe	14.8	10.9	11.0	50.2	1 971	1 790	-9.2	-8.5	166	162	-364	692	-4.4	2.37	6.5	28.3
Brooks	12.7	9.3	7.7	50.4	8 204	7 976	-2.8	-9.4	1 277	656	-1 199	2 642	-2.5	2.71	20.6	26.1
Brown	13.1	9.7	7.6	50.6	34 371	37 674	9.6	1.1	4 552	4 377	460	14 778	3.3	2.47	11.8	26.9
Burleson	14.2	9.0	8.5	50.5	13 625	16 470	20.9	4.4	2 072	1 469	-422	6 822	7.2	2.50	11.2	26.5
Burnet	14.5	10.5	8.1	50.9	22 677	34 147	50.6	25.2	4 584	3 752	10 260	16 511	25.7	2.53	9.7	23.7

1. No spouse present.

Table B. States and Counties — Population, Vital Statistics, Medicare, and Crime

STATE County	Persons in group quarters, 2010	Daytime population, 2006–2010 Number	Daytime population, 2006–2010 Employment/residence ratio	Births, average 2006–2008 Total	Births, average 2006–2008 Rate[1]	Deaths, average 2006–2008 Number	Deaths, average 2006–2008 Rate[1]	Persons under 65 with no health insurance, 2009 Number	Persons under 65 with no health insurance, 2009 Percent	Medicare, 2011 Eligible for Medicare	Medicare, 2011 Enrolled in Medicare Advantage	Medicare, 2011 Enrolled in a Medicare prescription drug plan	Serious crimes known to police,[2] 2010 Total Number	Serious crimes known to police,[2] 2010 Total Rate[3]
	32	33	34	35	36	37	38	39	40	41	42	43	44	45
TENNESSEE—Cont'd														
Marshall	359	27 646	0.8	411	14.0	289	9.9	4 357	16.8	5 314	1 087	2 196	525	1 715
Maury	1 009	74 075	0.9	1 164	14.5	721	9.0	11 887	16.6	13 976	2 595	6 108	2 866	3 540
Meigs	128	9 643	0.5	D	D	125	10.7	1 746	17.2	2 607	615	1 230	374	3 182
Monroe	500	41 174	0.8	553	12.3	457	10.2	7 118	18.8	10 075	3 156	3 927	1 581	3 551
Montgomery	3 416	143 471	0.7	2 854	18.8	987	6.5	21 162	14.7	18 056	2 757	6 389	5 876	3 410
Moore	104	5 362	0.7	D	D	55	9.0	762	15.3	1 206	99	505	115	1 808
Morgan	2 527	17 938	0.5	D	D	202	10.0	2 772	17.6	4 613	1 739	1 581	599	2 724
Obion	461	33 420	1.1	377	11.9	394	12.4	4 092	16.1	6 983	406	3 676	1 104	3 471
Overton	286	19 109	0.7	D	D	241	11.5	3 089	18.0	4 958	450	2 877	334	1 512
Perry	123	7 476	0.9	D	D	94	12.3	1 210	19.3	1 834	343	976	167	2 110
Pickett	74	4 357	0.7	D	D	62	12.9	755	20.7	1 394	120	836	26	512
Polk	244	13 673	0.5	D	D	193	12.2	2 427	19.1	3 707	612	1 948	333	1 979
Putnam	2 715	78 104	1.3	950	13.6	679	9.7	11 656	19.3	13 958	1 506	7 389	3 118	4 311
Rhea	924	32 379	1.1	420	13.8	363	11.9	4 673	17.9	6 443	913	3 632	798	2 509
Roane	646	47 846	0.7	560	10.5	619	11.6	6 185	14.3	12 753	3 887	4 091	1 797	3 317
Robertson	703	53 692	0.6	1 067	16.8	576	9.1	9 441	16.3	10 222	3 327	3 781	1 708	2 577
Rutherford	5 109	234 259	0.9	3 899	16.3	1 365	5.7	33 006	14.4	28 592	8 708	9 051	9 335	3 555
Scott	264	21 418	0.9	D	D	212	9.6	3 566	19.0	4 706	943	2 688	949	4 269
Sequatchie	188	12 087	0.7	D	D	130	9.8	2 150	18.5	3 103	567	1 674	371	2 629
Sevier	982	87 056	1.0	1 138	13.7	738	8.9	14 625	20.5	18 019	6 757	5 579	4 437	4 936
Shelby	18 329	995 660	1.2	15 170	16.7	7 565	8.3	132 941	16.7	121 197	21 714	52 159	59 879	6 455
Smith	159	16 862	0.7	D	D	213	11.3	2 732	16.6	3 339	774	1 542	254	1 325
Stewart	92	11 558	0.7	D	D	147	11.2	1 715	15.5	2 831	325	1 290	259	1 944
Sullivan	2 631	164 165	1.1	1 693	11.0	1 798	11.7	19 086	15.4	37 554	19 161	9 850	6 200	3 954
Sumner	1 252	132 322	0.7	2 089	13.7	1 215	8.0	19 606	14.4	25 446	9 365	8 328	3 516	2 189
Tipton	962	46 302	0.5	802	13.8	493	8.5	8 126	15.8	8 853	1 305	3 976	2 099	3 436
Trousdale	130	6 118	0.5	D	D	93	12.0	1 301	19.5	1 476	439	651	320	4 066
Unicoi	405	17 060	0.8	D	D	254	14.3	2 295	16.4	4 644	1 478	1 854	244	1 332
Union	152	15 583	0.5	D	D	163	8.6	3 374	20.7	3 908	1 759	1 278	524	2 742
Van Buren	94	4 750	0.6	D	D	54	9.9	878	19.2	1 358	144	808	132	2 379
Warren	580	38 831	1.0	536	13.5	443	11.1	7 182	21.3	8 025	1 450	4 203	1 068	2 681
Washington	4 649	129 242	1.2	1 386	11.9	1 220	10.5	16 709	16.8	24 287	8 193	8 215	4 850	3 944
Wayne	2 140	15 921	0.8	D	D	180	10.8	3 014	22.1	3 534	335	2 111	153	899
Weakley	2 244	31 407	0.8	D	D	368	11.0	5 070	18.2	6 629	444	3 967	946	2 701
White	382	23 097	0.8	D	D	287	11.6	3 772	18.1	5 906	752	3 202	923	3 572
Williamson	1 153	184 555	1.1	2 153	13.0	883	5.3	12 668	8.1	21 125	5 908	6 585	2 759	1 506
Wilson	1 232	93 994	0.7	1 391	13.0	789	7.4	12 800	13.2	17 911	5 407	6 294	3 362	2 949
TEXAS	581 139	24 294 705	1.0	404 261	17.0	160 871	6.7	5 710 171	26.3	3 151 825	636 330	1 219 709	1 064 477	4 233
Anderson	14 217	57 855	1.0	665	11.7	590	10.4	14 489	30.5	8 910	1 007	4 057	1 328	2 272
Andrews	82	13 758	1.0	239	18.0	127	9.6	3 338	27.2	1 917	196	961	386	2 611
Angelina	2 953	85 398	1.0	1 335	16.1	801	9.7	17 862	25.5	15 009	2 056	7 108	3 185	3 671
Aransas	459	21 638	0.8	D	D	311	12.5	5 313	28.4	6 221	1 727	2 015	785	3 390
Archer	56	7 368	0.6	D	D	71	7.7	1 810	24.0	1 634	48	798	104	1 149
Armstrong	54	1 534	0.5	D	D	24	11.6	402	24.6	409	20	196	22	1 157
Atascosa	384	36 036	0.5	D	D	338	7.7	10 850	28.2	7 039	2 064	2 395	1 118	2 489
Austin	212	26 619	0.9	D	D	256	9.6	5 404	23.9	4 910	457	2 247	520	1 830
Bailey	106	6 862	0.9	D	D	58	9.1	1 896	36.2	1 058	45	715	188	2 624
Bandera	320	16 010	0.5	D	D	184	9.1	4 259	26.2	4 508	619	1 387	221	1 079
Bastrop	2 337	56 715	0.5	981	13.5	525	7.2	17 496	26.9	10 624	937	3 912	2 371	3 197
Baylor	65	3 743	1.0	D	D	56	14.7	771	27.8	1 054	37	556	76	2 040
Bee	7 499	31 753	1.0	D	D	228	6.9	7 982	28.5	4 015	753	1 794	576	1 808
Bell	8 049	309 327	1.1	6 232	22.8	1 803	6.6	49 852	19.8	34 485	8 637	8 288	12 167	3 922
Bexar	42 001	1 698 886	1.1	27 135	17.1	10 710	6.7	342 381	23.6	225 051	77 098	51 939	110 587	6 449
Blanco	106	9 084	0.8	D	D	102	11.1	2 161	26.7	2 017	150	746	163	1 553
Borden	0	NA	NA	D	D	D	D	117	24.6	125	D	49	2	312
Bosque	329	15 608	0.7	D	D	255	14.2	3 736	27.0	4 183	932	1 562	210	1 208
Bowie	6 206	98 026	1.2	1 237	13.5	910	9.9	18 914	24.1	16 701	1 820	6 763	4 181	4 517
Brazoria	10 559	258 012	0.7	4 864	16.5	1 887	6.4	61 108	22.2	36 095	6 015	12 451	7 136	2 279
Brazos	13 512	189 516	1.0	2 629	15.6	791	4.7	34 867	21.8	16 886	1 505	5 940	7 945	4 077
Brewster	75	8 997	1.0	D	D	72	7.9	2 443	30.8	1 678	118	662	127	1 376
Briscoe	0	1 496	0.7	D	D	21	14.1	386	35.5	413	20	226	10	611
Brooks	67	7 951	1.2	D	D	85	11.2	1 667	27.4	1 574	280	939	210	2 907
Brown	1 668	39 675	1.1	492	12.7	479	12.4	8 049	26.1	8 032	584	3 986	1 194	3 133
Burleson	163	14 530	0.6	D	D	168	10.1	3 320	24.8	3 526	561	1 404	213	1 239
Burnet	1 059	40 101	0.9	D	D	382	8.7	9 613	28.7	9 501	1 110	3 700	965	2 257

1. Per 1,000 estimated resident population. 2. Data for serious crimes have not been adjusted for underreporting; this may affect comparability between geographic areas and over time. 3. Per 100,000 population estimated by the FBI.

Table B. States and Counties — Crime, Education, Money Income, and Poverty

STATE County	Serious crimes known to police,[1] 2010 (cont.) Rate[2] Violent	Property	Education — Enrollment[3] Total	Percent private	Attainment[4] (percent) High school graduate or less	Bachelor's degree or more	Local government expenditures,[5] 2008–2009 Total current expenditures (mil dol)	Current expenditures per student (dollars)	Money income, 2006–2010 Per capita income[6] (dollars)	Households Median income Dollars	Percent change, 2000 to 2006–2010 (constant 2010 dollars)	Percent with income of $200,000 or more	Income and poverty, 2010 Median household income (dollars)	Percent below poverty level All persons	Children under 18 years	Children 5 to 17 years in families
	46	47	48	49	50	51	52	53	54	55	56	57	58	59	60	61
TENNESSEE—Cont'd																
Marshall	245	1 470	6 669	5.8	63.4	11.5	39.1	7 343	20 157	40 435	-17.0	0.8	40 052	14.7	23.4	21.8
Maury	566	2 974	18 360	20.2	53.8	16.1	89.0	7 547	23 136	46 278	-12.1	1.8	45 445	14.3	20.7	19.8
Meigs	357	2 825	2 384	8.3	67.9	9.0	13.3	7 146	18 768	33 506	-9.9	0.4	36 584	22.1	37.3	33.0
Monroe	389	3 163	9 502	10.6	67.7	10.4	50.0	6 957	18 651	36 209	-5.7	1.5	35 833	19.4	31.0	29.7
Montgomery	519	2 890	47 924	12.5	41.9	22.3	203.5	7 081	22 092	48 930	-0.9	1.1	47 258	15.7	21.5	20.2
Moore	79	1 729	1 507	6.1	63.6	12.6	8.0	7 967	26 678	44 433	-4.1	4.3	45 066	13.6	21.4	19.1
Morgan	141	2 583	4 034	9.0	73.2	6.3	26.0	7 619	17 883	36 772	4.8	1.3	35 322	20.3	28.9	25.2
Obion	305	3 166	7 299	6.6	64.8	11.9	41.0	7 450	21 235	39 543	-4.7	1.4	38 530	16.0	26.3	23.5
Overton	231	1 282	4 605	3.3	69.7	10.5	23.5	6 811	17 720	34 347	0.8	1.6	33 230	19.3	30.6	28.4
Perry	316	1 794	1 672	7.9	69.1	10.6	9.4	7 974	17 028	31 776	-10.6	0.3	31 486	21.4	33.6	31.1
Pickett	20	492	947	2.3	70.3	12.0	5.7	8 268	19 327	30 193	-3.4	1.8	30 016	20.3	33.0	29.6
Polk	214	1 765	3 649	10.6	67.6	10.1	20.2	7 316	17 481	34 027	-9.4	0.7	35 083	20.0	30.6	28.1
Putnam	303	4 009	19 242	5.9	54.5	21.7	75.5	6 927	19 434	35 185	-10.1	1.7	35 225	21.5	28.3	24.7
Rhea	368	2 141	7 306	16.2	63.0	11.2	35.0	6 893	17 655	36 761	-4.6	0.8	36 308	20.6	32.2	30.9
Roane	308	3 008	10 475	9.3	54.6	16.7	59.9	7 933	23 196	42 698	1.5	1.5	42 620	15.2	24.9	22.5
Robertson	510	2 067	15 549	15.1	59.7	14.2	75.7	6 824	22 668	50 820	-7.0	1.5	51 074	12.7	20.3	19.0
Rutherford	409	3 145	75 263	11.0	43.4	26.3	321.4	7 252	24 390	53 770	-8.3	1.8	51 815	14.4	18.4	15.8
Scott	427	3 842	5 151	2.6	69.9	9.9	32.2	7 431	15 087	28 728	-5.8	0.0	29 792	27.0	36.0	34.2
Sequatchie	368	2 260	3 294	7.9	68.6	13.3	15.1	6 626	18 094	33 850	-13.7	1.0	38 082	22.0	34.0	31.1
Sevier	358	4 578	18 331	11.6	57.7	15.2	115.0	7 961	22 047	41 476	-5.7	1.7	39 349	16.5	26.5	25.1
Shelby	1 206	5 249	262 221	18.3	43.2	27.8	1 388.1	8 708	25 002	44 705	-10.8	3.9	43 859	20.4	29.2	27.3
Smith	188	1 137	4 516	8.5	65.2	12.8	22.7	6 840	21 026	43 200	-4.2	1.1	39 330	20.3	26.8	25.2
Stewart	188	1 766	3 190	11.5	60.2	11.5	17.5	7 532	20 670	40 214	-1.7	0.8	40 329	15.3	24.3	22.0
Sullivan	499	3 454	34 663	14.1	51.9	20.0	190.3	8 431	23 263	39 957	-5.9	2.3	36 337	18.0	27.8	26.3
Sumner	288	1 900	38 846	14.9	47.1	23.0	202.2	7 561	26 014	54 916	-5.8	2.9	52 334	13.3	19.0	15.9
Tipton	761	2 675	16 074	14.8	55.2	13.8	83.7	6 942	21 585	49 378	-6.8	1.1	47 824	13.6	19.5	17.9
Trousdale	584	3 482	1 970	10.1	69.3	10.0	9.1	7 365	19 996	44 205	8.4	2.1	35 824	16.9	26.7	23.7
Unicoi	137	1 196	3 821	6.0	63.5	12.2	19.0	7 189	20 540	34 387	-9.1	1.2	35 976	17.3	27.4	25.0
Union	204	2 538	4 155	10.2	75.7	6.3	24.5	8 026	16 155	30 143	-12.9	0.7	32 533	26.4	40.0	40.4
Van Buren	360	2 019	1 134	17.5	79.9	9.0	6.3	7 729	17 160	29 087	-18.4	1.1	31 455	22.1	33.2	30.5
Warren	326	2 354	8 753	10.0	68.3	10.9	46.7	7 070	18 508	34 946	-10.7	1.4	33 265	26.4	37.7	32.7
Washington	444	3 500	30 925	10.5	45.4	27.9	123.5	7 409	24 114	41 256	-1.6	3.1	41 702	17.8	22.6	22.1
Wayne	170	729	3 476	7.4	71.9	8.7	20.9	8 130	15 814	34 993	4.0	0.4	32 334	22.1	31.7	29.2
Weakley	331	2 370	10 169	4.6	58.1	18.4	34.9	7 225	18 895	32 358	-14.8	1.7	34 782	21.6	28.5	26.5
White	279	3 293	5 464	6.1	71.3	11.0	26.8	6 598	17 880	33 865	-9.0	1.1	33 251	21.0	32.9	28.3
Williamson	122	1 384	50 735	26.0	23.0	51.8	269.4	8 000	41 220	87 832	0.4	12.3	82 273	6.4	7.4	6.5
Wilson	461	2 488	27 625	21.1	47.3	24.0	128.0	7 072	27 814	60 678	-4.4	3.7	56 270	10.0	15.1	13.0
TEXAS	450	3 783	6 836 694	11.2	46.0	25.8	40 538.2	8 536	24 870	49 646	-1.8	4.0	48 622	17.9	25.7	24.2
Anderson	257	2 015	12 949	5.5	61.6	11.3	71.0	8 342	17 465	40 378	-0.2	2.3	40 482	20.9	27.2	24.7
Andrews	365	2 245	3 716	6.6	58.0	12.4	31.4	10 074	29 605	48 699	13.0	4.1	51 339	13.5	19.4	18.1
Angelina	311	3 359	22 050	6.0	52.3	15.9	134.4	7 878	20 104	39 148	-8.6	1.5	38 954	19.0	27.0	25.6
Aransas	168	3 221	4 826	10.9	46.5	23.9	30.2	9 950	25 610	42 179	8.5	3.4	38 516	22.3	41.2	35.7
Archer	133	1 016	2 176	5.0	53.6	18.8	15.3	8 467	23 882	50 891	4.3	2.0	51 895	11.1	15.2	13.3
Armstrong	0	1 157	461	2.4	35.4	25.9	3.7	11 443	24 195	60 530	25.2	0.7	48 733	8.8	11.6	11.3
Atascosa	200	2 289	11 763	7.3	63.4	11.0	76.2	8 794	18 461	42 927	2.5	2.0	42 439	20.4	30.5	28.4
Austin	215	1 615	6 455	17.4	53.7	17.9	49.2	8 763	26 959	53 263	8.9	3.7	50 154	12.5	18.3	16.4
Bailey	279	2 345	2 045	2.2	57.7	18.5	13.3	9 053	18 275	42 375	19.9	2.1	35 476	18.8	30.2	30.0
Bandera	63	1 015	4 075	10.2	41.8	24.0	27.1	9 474	24 249	44 352	-10.2	2.9	46 678	16.5	27.3	23.4
Bastrop	516	2 680	17 439	12.3	52.4	17.9	118.7	8 133	22 918	51 829	-6.1	2.0	49 812	15.5	24.4	22.5
Baylor	644	1 396	837	1.6	48.9	24.5	5.7	10 335	22 884	33 459	7.3	3.6	32 131	19.3	31.9	29.3
Bee	273	1 535	7 369	10.0	60.9	9.2	43.4	8 479	14 188	40 278	12.0	2.0	36 462	27.3	34.6	32.8
Bell	450	3 472	83 251	10.6	40.7	21.2	500.3	8 113	22 722	48 618	4.1	2.2	49 338	13.2	20.2	18.0
Bexar	543	5 906	485 015	13.5	44.3	25.3	2 654.9	8 444	23 225	47 048	-3.1	3.1	47 724	17.0	24.6	23.2
Blanco	200	1 353	2 108	5.4	45.2	25.4	17.2	10 466	27 010	46 128	-7.5	4.4	46 981	12.7	20.0	18.3
Borden	0	312	127	4.7	64.4	19.1	4.0	20 911	40 916	58 409	57.9	11.9	47 938	11.9	15.5	14.8
Bosque	52	1 156	4 044	2.3	56.1	14.8	23.6	9 372	21 269	45 288	4.6	1.3	40 732	17.5	27.4	24.8
Bowie	725	3 792	23 650	7.0	49.6	18.1	152.0	8 609	22 293	42 550	1.8	2.4	42 272	18.7	27.8	25.2
Brazoria	192	2 087	83 482	11.5	41.3	26.1	447.6	7 576	27 529	65 607	6.5	4.3	64 242	12.1	15.3	15.1
Brazos	350	3 727	82 929	5.6	38.1	39.3	209.9	8 170	21 018	37 898	2.8	3.1	37 468	30.8	26.0	23.4
Brewster	162	1 213	2 352	6.1	43.3	30.4	14.8	11 989	23 577	35 799	3.2	2.6	37 200	14.7	23.3	22.1
Briscoe	122	489	330	1.5	54.1	15.0	4.4	11 071	17 652	34 196	-9.7	0.3	35 931	16.4	28.6	27.1
Brooks	277	2 630	1 884	4.6	74.1	12.5	19.7	12 088	14 728	19 959	-15.4	0.0	26 027	33.0	49.5	48.9
Brown	451	2 682	8 933	13.4	58.4	15.0	59.2	8 796	20 586	38 832	-1.0	2.0	37 512	18.8	28.5	24.8
Burleson	209	1 030	4 014	9.3	63.9	10.5	28.1	10 044	21 379	43 185	3.3	0.8	41 273	15.2	24.9	23.4
Burnet	152	2 105	9 302	10.3	46.9	21.4	67.5	9 207	25 245	48 187	0.3	2.9	49 195	14.6	24.4	22.3

1. Data for serious crimes have not been adjusted for underreporting; this may affect comparability between geographic areas and over time.   2. Per 100,000 population estimated by the FBI.   3. All persons 3 years old and over enrolled in nursery school through college.   4. Persons 25 years old and over.   5. Elementary and secondary education expenditures.   6. Based on population estimated by the American Community Survey, 2006–2010.

Table B. States and Counties — **Personal Income**

STATE County	Total (mil dol)	Percent change, 2008–2009	Per capita[1] Dollars	Per capita[1] Rank	Wages and salaries[2] (mil dol)	Proprietors' income (mil dol)	Dividends, interest, and rent (mil dol)	Transfer payments (mil dol) Total	Government payments to individuals Total	Social Security	Medical payments	Income mainte-nance	Unemploy-ment insurance
	62	63	64	65	66	67	68	69	70	71	72	73	74
TENNESSEE—Cont'd													
Marshall	766	-3.2	25 299	2 827	312	67	126	214	209	76	83	22	16
Maury	2 395	-2.1	28 415	2 321	1 525	233	303	593	578	200	245	62	32
Meigs	308	1.0	25 404	2 818	79	37	35	101	99	35	39	13	5
Monroe	1 080	-1.9	23 567	2 998	484	70	166	362	354	133	136	41	21
Montgomery	6 295	1.7	39 104	527	1 881	300	587	898	871	242	286	116	25
Moore	192	1.4	31 514	1 639	78	2	24	39	38	17	14	3	1
Morgan	486	-0.5	25 929	2 743	126	39	49	157	153	61	52	22	6
Obion	1 036	1.8	32 968	1 346	654	106	160	269	264	100	111	29	8
Overton	523	-0.4	24 811	2 879	174	47	63	185	182	63	78	21	9
Perry	204	-1.5	26 031	2 723	59	18	28	83	82	25	42	7	4
Pickett	120	-0.6	25 137	2 855	31	6	20	49	48	18	21	5	1
Polk	430	-2.3	27 468	2 488	99	12	51	151	148	51	69	14	7
Putnam	2 154	1.0	29 739	2 034	1 366	197	381	575	561	190	251	58	17
Rhea	795	0.2	25 228	2 837	510	34	84	276	270	88	122	32	12
Roane	1 767	0.5	33 015	1 340	1 153	46	238	493	483	180	206	43	15
Robertson	2 035	-4.3	30 570	1 849	773	201	207	414	402	146	162	42	23
Rutherford	7 811	-1.2	30 386	1 888	5 184	791	841	1 193	1 147	408	395	133	83
Scott	489	1.3	22 341	3 058	209	29	49	206	202	56	88	34	8
Sequatchie	397	1.1	28 547	2 289	86	17	45	115	112	39	47	13	5
Sevier	2 755	0.0	31 949	1 538	1 309	287	411	606	590	244	211	61	33
Shelby	37 313	-2.5	40 547	417	29 319	4 654	5 165	6 145	5 977	1 676	2 385	1 223	231
Smith	520	-6.9	27 065	2 558	203	26	79	148	144	46	65	15	11
Stewart	377	1.9	28 296	2 346	141	11	47	109	107	38	41	11	3
Sullivan	5 267	-1.3	34 081	1 157	3 566	351	899	1 334	1 306	540	515	114	35
Sumner	5 328	-1.8	33 557	1 239	1 898	312	675	972	943	371	365	87	52
Tipton	1 931	1.8	32 451	1 438	441	97	156	390	379	123	149	54	21
Trousdale	204	-2.5	25 752	2 766	59	21	27	64	63	20	29	7	3
Unicoi	534	-0.8	30 116	1 950	278	21	63	190	187	55	89	15	6
Union	449	0.4	23 447	3 007	124	11	46	136	133	50	48	21	6
Van Buren	148	2.4	26 951	2 573	55	10	16	50	49	17	21	6	3
Warren	1 042	-1.2	25 740	2 768	510	78	163	359	351	108	173	39	14
Washington	4 027	-0.3	33 391	1 281	2 780	238	627	924	902	332	373	80	28
Wayne	351	0.6	21 281	3 076	142	14	48	136	133	46	61	15	5
Weakley	970	2.0	28 998	2 197	446	92	142	275	269	90	113	28	11
White	589	0.1	23 149	3 027	236	39	78	224	219	77	97	24	9
Williamson	9 442	-1.8	53 392	65	5 523	819	1 568	720	688	322	245	36	33
Wilson	4 002	-2.7	35 612	942	1 670	282	493	664	643	259	252	52	33
TEXAS	956 808	-1.2	38 609	X	600 279	127 857	158 860	140 968	136 469	41 299	61 045	16 665	6 069
Anderson	1 497	0.4	26 264	2 675	845	159	221	402	392	116	194	33	13
Andrews	507	-2.1	36 062	876	298	56	72	86	84	27	41	8	3
Angelina	2 911	-0.5	34 787	1 048	1 556	389	519	708	692	206	340	76	22
Aransas	951	0.5	38 289	604	221	54	294	217	212	86	89	18	5
Archer	373	-1.4	41 857	340	83	55	63	50	49	23	16	3	2
Armstrong	78	-2.3	37 819	664	17	4	18	16	16	6	8	1	0
Atascosa	1 265	1.9	28 333	2 340	403	103	156	301	292	83	134	42	10
Austin	1 061	0.1	38 954	544	676	59	234	193	188	69	90	14	6
Bailey	209	-5.0	33 307	1 293	104	25	44	48	47	13	26	5	1
Bandera	735	0.8	35 729	925	111	41	176	138	134	59	47	9	4
Bastrop	2 028	-0.2	27 083	2 551	632	97	285	402	388	140	157	41	18
Baylor	119	-5.7	32 494	1 430	45	12	23	39	38	14	20	3	1
Bee	760	0.6	23 397	3 012	342	70	117	212	206	49	106	25	7
Bell	11 386	2.8	39 839	458	10 606	419	1 379	1 684	1 638	428	573	197	71
Bexar	60 220	1.0	36 465	821	41 137	6 963	10 815	10 441	10 145	2 681	4 522	1 300	352
Blanco	405	1.3	44 063	235	122	40	113	78	76	26	40	3	2
Borden	25	13.8	41 808	344	6	5	7	3	3	2	0	0	0
Bosque	563	0.4	31 947	1 540	155	39	122	147	144	56	63	10	5
Bowie	3 184	1.2	33 886	1 187	2 088	185	654	715	698	204	329	80	21
Brazoria	11 602	1.3	37 523	687	4 651	543	1 577	1 541	1 484	522	650	133	78
Brazos	5 247	3.1	29 151	2 155	3 781	279	1 112	728	695	225	259	94	35
Brewster	317	5.6	33 485	1 258	186	21	70	60	58	21	20	5	2
Briscoe	49	3.1	34 048	1 168	14	6	9	15	14	5	7	1	0
Brooks	192	0.9	25 985	2 734	112	4	25	82	80	16	46	13	2
Brown	1 151	2.4	30 218	1 931	631	79	185	356	349	105	183	27	9
Burleson	551	0.3	33 257	1 300	171	34	92	126	123	44	53	11	4
Burnet	1 675	-1.0	37 098	739	536	195	553	310	302	134	120	19	9

1. Based on the resident population estimated as of July 1 of the year shown. 2. Includes supplements to wages and salaries.

Table B. States and Counties — Earnings, Social Security, and Housing

STATE County	Total (mil dol)	Farm	Goods-related[1] Total	Manufacturing	Information and professional and technical services	Retail trade	Finance, insurance, and real estate	Health care and social services	Government	Social Security beneficiaries, December 2010 Number	Rate[2]	Supplemental Security Income recipients, December 2010	Housing units, 2010 Total	Percent change, 2000–2010
	75	76	77	78	79	80	81	82	83	84	85	86	87	88
TENNESSEE—Cont'd														
Marshall	379	-1.6	D	31.2	D	8.2	8.5	4.2	21.2	6 260	204	612	13 119	17.3
Maury	1 758	-0.7	D	24.1	6.2	8.7	7.0	11.9	19.4	16 115	199	1 654	35 254	22.9
Meigs	116	-2.9	D	29.2	D	5.4	D	4.1	18.9	3 130	266	472	5 628	8.5
Monroe	553	-0.6	D	34.8	2.3	8.7	3.6	8.4	15.2	11 650	262	1 688	20 787	20.2
Montgomery	2 181	0.4	D	14.9	6.1	10.3	5.0	11.1	22.4	21 485	125	2 978	70 098	34.4
Moore	80	-3.8	D	41.5	D	3.5	D	5.7	39.0	1 380	217	84	2 915	15.9
Morgan	165	-1.6	D	10.1	D	5.9	D	D	35.5	5 475	249	896	8 920	15.6
Obion	761	4.6	45.0	42.0	3.4	7.8	5.4	D	11.2	8 110	255	974	14 659	1.2
Overton	221	-1.3	D	16.2	3.5	7.8	6.8	13.6	23.4	5 860	265	809	10 295	12.3
Perry	76	-2.6	D	17.6	D	7.2	D	22.3	22.9	2 110	267	216	4 599	11.8
Pickett	37	-3.1	D	5.5	D	13.3	D	15.7	30.0	1 615	318	201	3 462	17.1
Polk	111	0.3	D	8.4	2.6	12.1	4.4	D	37.0	4 390	261	608	7 991	8.4
Putnam	1 562	-0.4	24.1	18.3	6.4	9.1	5.6	9.4	25.1	15 985	221	1 848	31 882	18.5
Rhea	544	-0.2	38.8	30.9	D	5.4	2.4	D	34.6	7 410	233	1 142	14 365	14.3
Roane	1 199	-0.3	D	4.9	43.9	5.4	1.4	6.0	15.8	14 425	266	1 757	25 716	10.0
Robertson	974	3.1	37.0	30.4	D	9.4	4.3	4.8	17.6	11 945	180	1 272	26 086	24.2
Rutherford	5 974	-0.1	D	24.9	7.3	6.3	6.8	11.1	15.9	32 880	125	3 300	102 968	45.8
Scott	238	-0.9	29.7	22.9	2.6	8.6	2.7	D	24.4	5 480	247	1 543	9 910	11.2
Sequatchie	103	0.4	D	7.9	D	11.9	6.9	7.9	26.9	3 525	250	531	6 368	29.6
Sevier	1 595	-0.1	D	3.7	4.1	14.3	8.0	4.7	18.8	20 745	231	1 794	55 918	50.1
Shelby	33 973	0.0	13.2	9.4	6.9	6.1	8.7	11.1	15.5	137 350	148	31 766	398 274	9.7
Smith	229	-1.8	D	25.1	2.3	9.9	6.0	D	19.9	4 060	212	527	8 529	11.3
Stewart	152	0.2	19.5	14.1	D	5.3	2.5	5.5	52.0	3 365	253	426	6 778	13.4
Sullivan	3 917	-0.2	33.5	25.7	6.7	7.0	4.7	18.2	9.7	42 985	274	4 700	73 760	6.8
Sumner	2 210	-0.2	D	15.1	6.4	7.2	5.7	12.0	17.3	29 150	181	2 528	65 968	27.7
Tipton	538	5.6	D	14.0	D	8.4	4.2	D	23.6	10 365	170	1 602	23 199	21.7
Trousdale	81	0.3	16.5	12.9	D	7.0	D	10.2	28.1	1 770	225	235	3 368	8.8
Unicoi	300	0.1	D	37.1	D	4.4	3.5	5.8	17.3	4 865	266	623	8 830	7.5
Union	135	-2.8	D	32.7	D	9.1	D	5.9	27.7	4 590	240	913	8 958	13.2
Van Buren	65	-3.3	D	D	D	3.0	D	D	23.7	1 540	278	237	2 663	8.6
Warren	588	2.1	31.8	27.6	D	8.1	3.9	12.3	16.0	9 400	236	1 467	17 821	6.8
Washington	3 018	0.0	14.9	11.6	7.6	7.3	6.0	20.9	24.2	27 240	222	2 979	57 254	19.8
Wayne	156	-0.3	D	13.0	D	8.1	5.8	6.8	33.8	4 125	242	508	7 287	8.7
Weakley	538	6.7	D	8.2	D	6.6	11.1	D	29.2	7 610	217	903	15 495	3.8
White	275	-2.2	D	27.3	D	9.8	4.2	11.0	19.3	6 910	207	889	11 511	12.9
Williamson	6 342	0.0	8.6	3.2	17.3	7.8	16.0	13.0	7.6	22 785	124	994	68 498	45.7
Wilson	1 952	-0.8	D	17.9	D	13.2	5.2	8.8	11.6	20 160	177	1 562	45 569	30.5
TEXAS	728 136	0.2	24.4	10.2	11.9	5.6	7.8	9.3	16.1	3 440 442	137	616 968	9 977 436	22.3
Anderson	1 004	0.6	11.7	2.7	5.5	6.5	4.5	14.6	27.0	9 735	167	1 354	20 116	9.1
Andrews	354	1.2	46.2	1.6	D	3.4	6.0	D	18.0	2 150	145	311	5 814	7.7
Angelina	1 945	0.1	28.1	18.6	5.7	9.3	4.7	15.7	16.5	17 185	198	3 099	35 589	9.7
Aransas	275	-0.5	15.3	1.0	7.0	12.9	8.5	D	18.6	6 845	296	709	15 355	19.5
Archer	138	3.3	43.6	2.7	D	5.7	2.9	1.7	16.7	1 760	194	143	4 107	6.1
Armstrong	21	3.7	D	D	6.8	2.3	D	D	28.6	445	234	20	904	-1.7
Atascosa	506	0.5	19.9	3.0	4.6	9.3	4.6	D	21.9	7 995	178	1 742	17 631	18.5
Austin	735	0.4	44.4	35.4	6.9	8.6	3.8	4.8	12.7	5 430	191	462	12 926	26.7
Bailey	129	15.2	D	D	D	5.0	D	3.2	20.3	1 165	163	154	2 784	1.7
Bandera	152	1.2	14.0	0.5	6.2	7.3	8.2	D	24.9	4 940	241	363	11 561	21.7
Bastrop	730	-0.5	19.6	7.5	6.9	9.9	4.4	6.2	32.3	11 855	160	1 551	29 316	31.8
Baylor	57	1.7	16.2	2.0	D	6.0	D	21.2	21.1	1 125	302	123	2 665	-5.5
Bee	412	-0.9	22.0	1.6	4.1	7.5	3.3	D	37.8	4 510	142	1 148	10 649	-2.7
Bell	11 024	-0.1	D	3.1	4.6	3.6	2.1	8.1	65.2	39 135	126	6 452	125 470	35.2
Bexar	48 100	0.0	12.7	5.1	10.5	6.1	10.6	11.6	25.2	247 600	144	52 545	662 872	27.1
Blanco	162	3.6	D	2.2	5.7	4.5	8.9	D	17.6	2 140	204	126	5 532	37.2
Borden	11	40.9	5.8	0.0	2.2	D	0.9	0.0	37.3	145	226	0	385	-11.5
Bosque	194	3.3	D	12.4	D	7.0	5.1	D	26.2	4 460	245	395	9 623	11.3
Bowie	2 273	0.1	7.9	4.6	4.3	8.2	6.9	18.3	33.8	18 340	198	3 950	38 493	5.6
Brazoria	5 194	0.3	40.2	24.1	6.3	7.3	3.9	6.3	16.9	40 060	128	4 795	118 336	30.6
Brazos	4 059	0.1	14.5	6.0	8.4	6.7	3.8	11.8	39.7	18 190	93	3 048	77 700	31.7
Brewster	207	1.4	D	1.6	8.9	11.0	7.3	8.1	36.1	1 790	194	212	5 383	16.7
Briscoe	20	13.4	D	D	D	5.7	D	D	23.7	440	269	40	953	-5.3
Brooks	116	-0.4	D	D	D	6.4	D	D	46.6	1 745	242	636	3 239	1.1
Brown	710	0.0	30.7	24.7	D	10.0	4.4	D	19.2	8 930	234	1 250	18 287	2.2
Burleson	206	-1.1	35.9	6.6	4.4	8.3	4.7	D	19.9	3 845	224	476	8 832	7.7
Burnet	731	-0.2	21.9	7.3	10.5	10.1	7.4	9.9	17.4	10 375	243	629	20 870	30.8

1. Includes mining, construction, and manufacturing.   2. Per 1,000 resident population enumerated in the 2010 census.

Table B. States and Counties — Housing, Labor Force, and Employment

STATE County	Housing units, 2006–2010 Total	Owner-occupied Percent	Median value[1]	Median owner cost as a percent of income — With a mortgage	Without a mortgage	Renter-occupied Median rent[2]	Median rent as a percent of income	Substandard units[3] (percent)	Civilian labor force, 2010 Total	Percent change, 2009–2010	Unemployment Total	Rate[4]	Civilian employment[5] 2006–2010 Total	Percent — Management, business, science and arts	Construction, production, and maintenance occupations
	89	90	91	92	93	94	95	96	97	98	99	100	101	102	103
TENNESSEE—Cont'd															
Marshall	11 707	74.7	107 900	24.0	11.6	628	28.0	2.4	12 353	-0.4	2 029	16.4	13 281	23.4	36.5
Maury	31 745	72.7	137 100	22.7	11.3	640	28.0	2.1	36 061	-2.4	5 195	14.4	37 020	28.8	28.7
Meigs	4 558	75.6	107 000	23.9	11.6	567	19.7	4.1	5 171	1.5	658	12.7	4 411	21.4	46.1
Monroe	17 546	74.5	107 900	23.5	10.4	532	27.7	1.2	18 417	-1.6	2 534	13.8	17 665	20.5	41.5
Montgomery	60 412	65.1	129 400	22.4	10.0	726	28.2	1.9	71 488	5.5	6 512	9.1	66 660	29.3	25.6
Moore	2 396	80.4	135 500	21.2	10.5	607	27.4	4.0	3 079	0.0	296	9.6	2 927	31.8	33.0
Morgan	7 954	81.8	79 600	22.5	11.2	560	23.1	4.3	8 837	0.8	943	10.7	8 210	23.4	38.4
Obion	12 662	69.7	87 700	21.2	11.4	511	24.8	1.9	15 119	0.3	1 468	9.7	14 320	22.7	36.6
Overton	8 830	80.4	87 700	21.6	11.9	457	27.6	2.2	9 945	-1.3	1 053	10.6	8 949	26.5	39.0
Perry	3 293	76.4	71 600	23.4	11.4	490	24.8	6.4	2 680	-4.8	426	15.9	2 867	21.5	38.6
Pickett	2 174	76.1	94 900	27.2	10.0	412	21.7	1.1	1 851	2.8	264	14.3	2 321	29.3	42.2
Polk	6 311	80.7	96 300	28.3	10.0	546	26.4	4.8	7 072	0.0	820	11.6	6 490	22.5	46.1
Putnam	27 560	64.1	124 000	23.3	11.3	568	30.8	2.2	36 299	2.5	3 265	9.0	29 972	32.5	25.2
Rhea	11 861	74.5	102 600	25.6	10.4	537	30.3	2.5	13 279	0.6	1 678	12.6	12 238	22.6	41.7
Roane	22 572	76.9	118 900	22.9	10.5	569	28.9	1.7	27 738	1.6	2 223	8.0	22 816	30.4	29.1
Robertson	23 793	77.5	149 100	23.9	10.8	711	27.8	2.6	34 045	1.9	2 962	8.7	30 373	27.8	33.0
Rutherford	92 343	69.0	157 100	22.9	10.0	801	29.3	2.4	136 961	3.0	11 883	8.7	125 225	32.8	25.7
Scott	8 617	74.0	76 600	22.7	11.6	413	29.8	2.3	8 302	-2.0	1 567	18.9	8 303	25.2	39.1
Sequatchie	5 083	77.8	105 800	23.8	10.0	535	26.3	3.9	6 269	1.8	660	10.5	5 265	29.0	34.2
Sevier	37 583	68.7	155 500	23.2	10.0	669	27.1	2.5	49 191	2.1	5 048	10.3	43 684	24.4	22.8
Shelby	340 443	61.7	135 300	24.9	13.3	782	33.2	3.2	432 370	-0.4	43 294	10.0	418 387	33.5	21.4
Smith	6 837	76.6	117 400	21.4	10.0	523	30.1	2.5	9 199	-1.8	959	10.4	8 277	26.7	33.1
Stewart	5 383	81.0	105 900	21.0	10.0	582	35.2	3.1	6 077	2.3	717	11.8	4 712	25.0	36.8
Sullivan	66 584	75.8	110 500	21.2	10.0	544	27.7	1.5	74 835	1.1	6 319	8.4	67 789	31.0	25.9
Sumner	59 503	74.7	169 100	23.5	10.1	748	28.4	1.6	81 144	1.9	7 094	8.7	74 499	33.7	22.7
Tipton	21 235	74.2	135 100	22.6	11.2	688	29.7	2.6	28 190	-2.1	3 080	10.9	26 340	27.8	30.7
Trousdale	2 814	79.6	109 300	23.0	10.8	548	25.8	0.5	3 719	0.8	389	10.5	3 636	22.2	36.2
Unicoi	7 600	71.8	111 900	21.0	10.0	487	26.2	1.1	8 455	0.2	878	10.4	7 658	30.4	32.3
Union	7 390	80.4	91 300	24.8	11.1	502	31.9	2.2	8 888	0.3	826	9.3	7 595	17.3	40.8
Van Buren	2 096	84.2	73 800	24.2	13.2	409	42.3	3.7	2 337	-8.1	311	13.3	2 170	22.6	36.9
Warren	14 994	73.0	90 400	24.1	10.7	536	24.6	1.8	17 100	0.5	1 961	11.5	16 294	24.2	38.3
Washington	49 111	67.9	136 700	23.0	10.2	596	28.0	1.1	63 044	2.5	5 207	8.3	54 929	35.0	20.0
Wayne	5 877	85.1	74 500	22.9	10.5	489	28.1	1.8	6 627	0.0	834	12.6	6 023	23.6	35.4
Weakley	13 781	66.1	82 100	20.2	11.8	513	33.1	1.4	15 808	0.9	1 828	11.6	14 657	28.5	29.1
White	9 827	76.6	94 600	23.3	11.4	549	28.3	3.3	10 897	3.9	1 297	11.9	10 840	23.4	41.6
Williamson	62 508	82.9	335 800	22.4	10.0	1 045	27.9	0.8	90 915	3.6	6 420	7.1	85 210	51.6	10.0
Wilson	41 221	82.0	187 500	23.0	10.0	750	29.2	2.0	59 362	2.6	4 916	8.3	53 925	34.2	24.2
TEXAS	8 539 206	64.8	123 500	23.3	12.6	786	29.5	5.3	12 269 727	3.1	1 004 979	8.2	11 125 616	33.7	23.7
Anderson	15 904	73.7	81 000	21.0	14.0	647	29.4	4.1	21 134	1.2	2 001	9.5	19 500	23.5	26.9
Andrews	5 205	79.9	86 600	20.0	11.2	621	22.7	6.4	7 108	1.4	426	6.0	6 523	20.3	38.7
Angelina	31 100	69.2	81 300	21.0	12.5	695	30.8	3.8	40 283	0.6	3 233	8.0	35 933	27.9	30.5
Aransas	10 056	74.3	129 900	26.9	14.9	788	35.8	4.8	11 850	2.1	955	8.1	9 218	31.8	24.0
Archer	3 363	81.1	93 500	19.8	12.7	531	26.1	2.8	5 021	-2.3	302	6.0	4 204	27.7	32.0
Armstrong	706	82.0	90 700	19.1	10.0	653	25.9	2.0	1 064	-3.5	50	4.7	895	33.4	21.5
Atascosa	14 521	75.8	80 400	20.0	12.9	665	28.4	7.1	19 842	2.0	1 570	7.9	18 478	25.0	34.4
Austin	10 447	77.5	146 500	22.0	11.5	638	23.2	3.3	13 433	0.4	1 073	8.0	13 493	30.0	29.0
Bailey	2 380	74.6	65 000	21.2	12.7	565	33.8	6.3	3 345	-0.7	236	7.1	3 060	29.4	35.3
Bandera	8 419	78.5	147 100	23.1	11.3	703	30.7	1.1	10 036	1.7	710	7.1	8 878	38.7	20.8
Bastrop	25 214	79.0	119 800	23.8	13.1	848	31.2	4.8	35 184	1.6	2 948	8.4	33 193	32.2	29.7
Baylor	1 657	71.5	64 700	17.3	13.3	500	29.8	2.7	1 889	-4.0	124	6.6	1 596	33.6	24.8
Bee	8 485	67.0	73 200	19.3	13.8	688	26.7	5.1	12 415	4.3	1 126	9.1	8 849	24.5	20.2
Bell	101 433	58.2	113 800	22.9	11.9	820	27.9	3.1	131 715	4.2	9 823	7.5	114 976	31.7	21.8
Bexar	580 224	62.5	117 100	23.1	11.8	761	29.5	4.5	782 191	2.2	58 145	7.4	738 564	33.7	20.3
Blanco	3 935	82.6	165 600	22.6	13.5	720	30.8	5.7	5 092	0.0	302	5.9	4 854	35.1	26.1
Borden	244	62.7	75 200	0.0	10.0	668	12.0	0.0	462	9.7	23	5.0	298	39.9	29.9
Bosque	6 732	75.4	88 800	21.9	12.4	604	24.3	4.1	8 371	-3.0	728	8.7	7 506	29.8	29.2
Bowie	33 573	66.6	88 600	19.8	10.8	632	28.4	2.5	45 241	2.5	3 756	8.3	39 533	30.2	26.9
Brazoria	101 656	75.8	140 300	21.9	11.9	821	27.5	4.0	148 943	1.9	13 384	9.0	138 962	38.7	24.4
Brazos	66 105	47.1	141 700	22.2	11.4	750	41.1	3.9	99 119	2.5	6 018	6.1	87 908	39.3	19.0
Brewster	4 151	60.6	101 200	22.4	10.0	539	25.1	6.1	5 337	0.8	294	5.5	4 526	29.8	24.9
Briscoe	679	80.9	43 000	24.5	12.8	535	37.1	2.1	695	-3.2	41	5.9	702	33.9	27.4
Brooks	2 588	67.1	46 800	17.1	12.7	426	32.1	4.1	3 245	-3.5	322	9.9	2 534	26.3	20.1
Brown	13 559	72.5	76 900	21.3	13.6	582	28.8	2.1	18 841	-2.3	1 377	7.3	15 424	27.0	31.6
Burleson	6 750	80.2	80 200	20.0	10.0	576	25.5	4.9	8 304	-1.0	576	6.9	7 312	24.3	36.2
Burnet	16 315	75.0	137 800	26.2	12.5	683	28.5	4.7	22 505	1.0	1 453	6.5	19 017	28.6	25.4

1. Specified owner-occupied units. 2. Specified renter-occupied units. A value of 10.0 represents 10 percent or less. 3. Overcrowded or lacking complete plumbing facilities. 4. Percent of civilian labor force. 5. Persons 16 years old and over.

Table B. States and Counties — **Nonfarm Employment and Agriculture**

	Private nonfarm establishments, employment and payroll, 2009									Agriculture, 2007			
		Employment						Annual payroll		Farms			
											Percent with:		
STATE County	Number of establish-ments	Total	Health care and social assistance	Manufac-turing	Retail trade	Finance and insurance	Professional, scientific, and technical services	Total (mil dol)	Average per employee (dollars)	Number	Fewer than 50 acres	500 acres or more	Farm operators whose principal occu-pation is farming (percent)
	104	105	106	107	108	109	110	111	112	113	114	115	116
TENNESSEE—Cont'd													
Marshall	494	7 398	690	3 342	1 112	208	96	209	28 226	1 078	38.0	5.0	42.4
Maury	1 653	26 216	4 866	D	4 040	1 697	592	902	34 412	1 696	42.5	4.4	37.9
Meigs	100	1 459	D	850	271	D	D	46	31 239	367	43.3	4.1	46.0
Monroe	715	9 654	1 222	3 592	1 556	329	195	275	28 457	935	49.5	2.4	39.8
Montgomery	2 547	37 864	6 491	5 610	7 455	1 227	1 301	1 080	28 517	862	38.1	7.8	45.0
Moore	70	D	171	D	D	D	D	D	D	346	31.5	4.6	43.4
Morgan	177	1 688	407	D	274	D	D	48	28 683	407	37.3	2.5	42.5
Obion	696	11 810	1 257	4 983	1 666	334	161	375	31 721	693	39.4	15.2	41.0
Overton	293	3 380	788	852	409	D	98	96	28 528	1 009	44.1	3.2	33.0
Perry	127	1 076	371	253	142	D	D	29	26 565	257	21.4	7.8	39.7
Pickett	88	531	106	77	121	D	11	13	24 684	365	41.1	1.6	31.5
Polk	233	1 518	385	D	271	74	22	40	26 194	305	50.2	2.0	51.5
Putnam	1 759	28 204	5 176	5 736	4 647	1 649	706	811	28 758	1 069	48.4	2.6	33.1
Rhea	496	8 697	981	3 755	1 126	231	112	240	27 588	449	40.1	4.7	36.1
Roane	737	8 899	1 934	1 301	1 805	275	213	229	25 764	580	45.2	1.2	37.2
Robertson	1 075	16 038	1 851	5 034	2 413	408	211	463	28 845	1 408	46.0	6.6	41.4
Rutherford	4 500	84 899	9 715	13 341	11 890	D	2 802	3 127	36 837	1 525	52.7	3.7	35.3
Scott	323	3 833	779	978	729	144	54	101	26 227	261	41.0	3.1	26.4
Sequatchie	195	1 945	471	218	429	D	50	46	23 868	232	50.0	4.7	31.9
Sevier	2 605	32 140	1 747	919	7 533	1 093	701	771	23 998	707	50.5	0.7	38.0
Shelby	20 262	428 357	64 457	27 295	45 033	19 422	16 732	17 928	41 852	600	58.2	5.2	41.5
Smith	285	3 791	657	1 169	660	D	D	105	27 733	981	39.2	2.8	36.6
Stewart	156	1 205	197	149	277	D	27	30	25 004	353	28.9	5.9	39.4
Sullivan	3 433	67 415	13 203	D	9 007	1 906	1 723	2 435	36 126	1 280	66.6	1.6	33.5
Sumner	2 895	36 688	5 151	5 537	6 480	1 422	1 412	1 137	30 984	1 673	51.8	3.2	34.7
Tipton	768	8 408	1 255	1 472	1 826	314	124	221	26 316	610	44.6	9.7	47.4
Trousdale	122	1 100	284	D	209	61	40	26	23 677	338	39.1	3.6	36.7
Unicoi	257	4 299	D	1 710	498	78	40	147	34 090	86	65.8	1.2	38.4
Union	205	1 769	165	607	390	63	D	45	25 401	494	45.1	1.2	38.5
Van Buren	48	510	D	D	43	D	0	13	25 225	213	34.3	8.5	39.9
Warren	756	9 079	1 819	2 584	1 607	324	D	271	29 803	1 331	48.3	4.3	47.0
Washington	2 846	50 044	11 480	5 551	8 362	3 396	2 405	1 529	30 559	1 660	60.2	1.8	39.9
Wayne	211	2 629	D	740	357	161	40	60	22 978	646	25.5	6.8	37.8
Weakley	570	7 664	1 859	1 592	1 193	216	95	182	23 749	1 214	39.5	8.6	39.3
White	381	4 895	797	1 892	756	112	65	145	29 699	1 035	41.4	4.2	44.2
Williamson	6 069	93 418	10 425	2 842	12 535	10 716	8 531	4 855	51 976	1 442	60.2	3.1	36.9
Wilson	2 324	30 807	3 488	D	4 585	849	964	1 302	42 253	1 745	45.1	2.8	39.7
TEXAS	519 028	8 925 096	1 216 496	784 367	1 149 349	460 870	568 061	376 647	42 201	247 437	37.9	16.2	39.9
Anderson	919	11 897	2 035	D	2 095	455	253	372	31 309	1 771	36.3	7.1	36.9
Andrews	321	4 355	D	D	362	108	74	172	39 497	175	36.0	36.0	36.0
Angelina	1 856	29 415	7 364	4 533	5 148	905	836	883	30 004	1 109	55.9	2.2	38.9
Aransas	483	4 163	525	33	1 185	177	129	97	23 282	94	61.7	11.7	23.4
Archer	189	1 208	129	D	115	D	D	40	32 776	513	17.3	38.8	46.4
Armstrong	30	199	D	0	D	D	D	4	19 060	291	4.1	54.6	44.7
Atascosa	623	6 499	1 262	210	1 547	D	279	178	27 435	1 810	33.3	16.1	38.6
Austin	576	9 925	646	3 615	1 018	301	276	392	39 473	2 112	39.3	5.9	34.5
Bailey	167	1 394	D	D	251	63	43	35	24 765	564	9.4	41.8	45.4
Bandera	374	2 073	214	D	359	81	87	46	22 388	972	36.8	15.7	42.2
Bastrop	1 029	10 883	1 694	1 009	2 267	369	366	297	27 310	2 207	44.4	7.1	38.0
Baylor	119	1 050	D	55	91	D	D	17	16 610	268	13.8	44.0	47.8
Bee	449	4 906	1 245	D	1 101	189	180	124	25 284	952	31.3	20.0	39.8
Bell	4 698	81 198	19 210	5 848	13 318	3 575	3 496	2 717	33 466	2 384	50.8	8.1	36.2
Bexar	32 411	633 667	101 993	33 438	81 615	51 487	36 181	23 209	36 627	2 496	61.4	5.3	43.5
Blanco	257	1 786	147	100	223	92	89	61	33 965	888	31.6	22.0	42.0
Borden	3	6	0	0	D	0	D	0	14 167	116	8.6	64.7	44.8
Bosque	299	2 586	572	494	435	119	67	73	28 041	1 399	25.9	16.7	39.0
Bowie	2 179	32 288	6 987	2 202	6 321	1 334	962	951	29 444	1 610	48.8	7.9	38.4
Brazoria	4 752	75 335	7 060	12 719	13 781	2 043	2 368	2 892	38 387	2 580	61.9	7.1	33.7
Brazos	3 754	54 808	7 936	4 639	9 567	1 609	2 810	1 565	28 553	1 350	44.9	8.1	35.0
Brewster	299	2 766	571	49	448	180	60	60	21 662	158	20.9	60.1	47.5
Briscoe	36	132	D	D	D	D	0	3	23 727	333	7.5	49.2	47.4
Brooks	132	1 543	D	0	322	D	27	39	25 336	494	22.3	17.2	45.3
Brown	905	12 755	3 024	2 796	2 001	384	174	344	26 939	1 726	32.5	16.4	37.4
Burleson	305	2 479	D	277	487	122	112	80	32 231	1 582	30.8	9.8	38.7
Burnet	1 074	9 623	1 276	811	2 220	367	297	290	30 148	1 531	37.4	13.1	36.4

Table B. States and Counties — **Agriculture**

STATE County	Acreage (1,000)	Percent change, 2002–2007	Average size of farm	Total irrigated (1,000)	Total cropland (1,000)	Average per farm	Average per acre	Value of machinery and equipment, average per farm (dollars)	Total (mil dol)	Average per farm (dollars)	Crops	Live-stock and poultry products	$10,000 or more	$100,000 or more	Total ($1,000)	Percent of farms
	117	118	119	120	121	122	123	124	125	126	127	128	129	130	131	132
TENNESSEE—Cont'd																
Marshall	152	-13.1	141	0.1	63.1	459 053	3 265	48 755	25.8	23 941	6.7	93.3	31.2	4.0	213	15.2
Maury	226	-6.2	133	0.4	107.3	505 101	3 784	51 885	28.5	16 808	19.3	80.7	24.4	2.6	470	15.6
Meigs	49	0.0	134	0.2	21.3	479 098	3 580	56 582	6.4	17 396	3.9	96.1	29.4	2.7	145	12.8
Monroe	93	-6.1	99	0.0	43.6	404 826	4 089	51 427	23.5	25 139	6.8	93.2	23.4	3.6	133	11.1
Montgomery	151	-9.6	176	0.8	87.8	568 924	3 238	72 512	27.8	32 277	66.1	33.9	32.7	6.5	690	20.8
Moore	52	-17.5	150	0.0	21.2	491 455	3 282	79 392	18.3	52 795	3.2	96.8	35.5	7.5	34	5.2
Morgan	53	-7.0	131	0.0	20.6	378 576	2 889	58 942	12.8	31 352	3.8	96.2	20.9	4.4	23	7.1
Obion	252	-4.5	363	0.8	211.7	926 419	2 549	115 722	85.6	123 497	68.3	31.7	38.2	17.5	4 467	66.5
Overton	115	-7.3	114	0.2	49.7	369 485	3 247	53 260	15.1	14 921	10.8	89.2	25.4	2.1	67	8.2
Perry	51	2.0	198	0.1	19.4	419 021	2 116	47 295	2.9	11 283	28.5	71.5	27.6	2.3	138	30.7
Pickett	38	-9.5	104	D	17.6	361 120	3 476	44 107	11.7	32 027	4.7	95.3	31.0	3.8	19	10.4
Polk	32	0.0	106	0.1	17.8	495 514	4 665	67 210	25.1	82 213	7.0	93.0	26.9	10.2	148	17.0
Putnam	104	-12.6	97	0.1	41.2	403 524	4 161	49 621	11.5	10 804	20.2	79.8	19.9	1.9	98	9.6
Rhea	56	-8.2	125	0.4	26.5	449 752	3 594	53 202	11.9	26 600	41.5	58.5	24.3	4.2	160	14.9
Roane	53	-15.9	91	0.0	18.8	385 280	4 250	43 203	5.1	8 858	28.0	71.9	21.7	0.9	21	6.2
Robertson	227	-2.6	161	2.1	160.1	620 415	3 843	76 736	82.0	58 259	71.8	28.2	35.2	10.9	1 771	34.4
Rutherford	164	-22.3	108	1.4	77.9	493 027	4 573	47 070	24.5	16 039	42.5	57.5	20.6	2.3	660	11.1
Scott	31	-11.4	119	D	12.0	373 615	3 137	50 265	5.0	19 077	4.2	95.8	10.7	2.3	D	8.8
Sequatchie	29	3.6	124	0.0	12.6	418 376	3 385	50 649	4.9	21 307	10.0	90.0	18.5	3.4	75	16.8
Sevier	56	-25.3	80	0.1	22.3	441 378	5 528	48 410	6.8	9 593	15.2	84.8	19.0	1.4	16	4.4
Shelby	92	-20.7	154	1.7	68.7	716 648	4 659	64 056	23.5	39 232	89.4	10.6	17.8	5.3	2 279	21.5
Smith	127	-9.9	130	0.2	49.3	408 529	3 153	52 143	14.1	14 399	34.1	65.9	23.9	1.9	197	16.0
Stewart	55	0.0	157	0.3	19.4	425 012	2 710	51 950	6.0	17 071	D	D	26.3	4.0	82	11.0
Sullivan	82	-18.8	64	0.1	36.8	326 716	5 094	56 038	17.1	13 394	17.3	82.7	17.6	2.3	47	7.9
Sumner	183	-5.2	110	0.3	89.5	443 513	4 045	60 727	32.4	19 342	42.1	57.9	22.5	2.8	283	13.0
Tipton	170	0.6	279	2.6	145.0	655 800	2 351	90 326	37.0	60 699	92.8	7.2	28.9	9.3	4 502	47.0
Trousdale	44	-6.4	130	0.1	19.8	421 195	3 235	45 920	4.3	12 647	25.4	74.6	26.9	2.1	22	6.2
Unicoi	5	-44.4	55	0.0	1.8	398 631	7 230	38 391	1.3	15 073	5.9	94.1	10.5	3.5	D	1.2
Union	46	-4.2	93	0.0	19.8	340 540	3 664	50 606	4.1	8 293	11.6	88.4	18.2	0.6	10	6.3
Van Buren	35	9.4	164	D	14.3	465 800	2 847	63 970	4.2	19 709	6.9	93.1	35.7	2.8	D	1.9
Warren	161	-6.9	121	6.8	91.4	426 095	3 532	70 573	108.6	81 569	81.8	18.2	42.8	12.4	410	13.9
Washington	119	-11.2	72	0.9	62.6	396 345	5 514	56 808	38.9	23 601	24.7	75.3	22.8	3.5	195	15.5
Wayne	115	-8.0	178	0.2	41.3	393 113	2 202	51 363	12.6	19 429	10.7	89.3	27.1	2.8	235	26.0
Weakley	256	6.7	211	0.5	204.7	532 829	2 531	74 806	75.0	61 797	61.5	38.5	27.3	11.0	3 614	58.7
White	132	-3.6	127	0.1	56.8	417 998	3 286	55 475	23.2	22 412	7.5	92.5	33.5	4.2	116	10.7
Williamson	162	-19.8	112	0.9	69.8	602 384	5 367	52 188	26.9	18 621	29.9	70.1	21.6	2.5	180	8.9
Wilson	193	-17.9	111	0.1	69.1	452 626	4 094	52 680	21.3	12 230	9.2	90.8	23.6	1.5	241	11.8
TEXAS	130 399	0.4	527	5 010.4	33 667.2	669 154	1 270	64 350	21 001.1	84 874	31.3	68.7	29.0	7.1	720 903	19.4
Anderson	346	-5.2	195	2.3	74.9	436 160	2 232	51 164	39.4	22 225	32.7	67.3	28.4	2.0	172	2.9
Andrews	808	0.5	4 620	12.2	62.2	1 572 018	340	90 734	15.9	90 965	71.4	28.6	24.6	14.9	1 634	36.6
Angelina	115	-1.7	104	0.5	43.3	290 792	2 798	44 485	29.4	26 545	6.9	93.1	18.2	2.1	145	2.2
Aransas	51	2.0	542	0.0	D	747 807	1 380	36 197	1.7	17 757	2.7	97.3	10.6	2.1	D	2.1
Archer	508	-5.2	989	1.0	110.4	963 189	973	89 155	61.0	118 877	8.6	91.4	53.8	21.6	1 229	42.7
Armstrong	516	2.0	1 774	5.9	159.4	1 533 026	864	94 828	37.4	128 435	42.0	58.0	48.5	20.6	3 041	75.9
Atascosa	644	-3.9	356	22.6	139.1	584 079	1 643	52 911	50.3	27 764	33.0	67.0	22.6	3.3	1 855	12.8
Austin	334	-9.0	158	1.6	96.6	539 487	3 412	48 817	30.9	14 649	31.6	68.4	28.2	2.3	688	6.9
Bailey	476	20.8	844	69.7	326.0	766 537	908	102 476	234.0	414 872	16.8	83.2	42.6	23.8	8 612	77.0
Bandera	329	-10.4	339	0.6	21.4	776 642	2 292	42 876	7.0	7 175	13.6	86.4	11.9	0.6	260	3.8
Bastrop	402	-5.0	182	2.5	76.1	499 654	2 743	46 194	38.2	17 303	28.5	71.5	23.7	1.7	428	6.3
Baylor	547	66.8	2 041	3.3	141.7	1 198 087	587	107 654	42.9	160 238	21.6	78.4	56.7	22.0	2 121	67.5
Bee	548	7.5	576	5.7	104.9	820 945	1 425	57 604	39.2	41 180	48.7	51.3	25.4	5.9	1 571	15.4
Bell	432	-4.2	181	2.7	183.8	427 359	2 359	50 594	61.7	25 901	51.8	48.2	24.4	3.6	2 176	17.8
Bexar	426	-3.4	171	14.1	125.0	467 393	2 739	42 868	84.2	33 743	76.5	23.5	15.3	2.2	573	7.7
Blanco	396	1.8	446	1.0	43.6	443 459	2 505	43 459	18.2	20 459	51.7	48.3	20.6	1.7	286	5.5
Borden	435	-9.4	3 751	2.2	93.8	2 171 362	579	126 920	13.2	114 081	60.7	39.3	49.1	30.2	1 987	62.9
Bosque	551	-2.1	394	1.0	96.2	849 731	2 158	50 349	42.8	30 591	29.0	71.0	26.2	3.0	552	12.9
Bowie	292	-5.2	181	3.4	96.2	335 490	1 852	52 632	48.4	30 062	19.5	80.5	26.5	3.8	1 270	10.5
Brazoria	529	-13.8	205	12.0	186.2	448 494	2 188	48 795	55.1	21 365	54.7	45.3	19.2	3.0	2 697	6.1
Brazos	276	-10.7	204	9.0	62.7	563 474	2 759	62 995	54.5	40 378	23.0	77.0	28.2	4.1	1 356	5.0
Brewster	1 747	4.2	11 058	0.5	50.1	3 797 111	343	81 828	9.6	60 517	12.8	87.2	42.4	13.9	202	13.9
Briscoe	547	28.4	1 642	31.7	166.7	1 016 703	619	99 624	27.9	83 905	71.4	28.6	39.9	19.8	6 290	85.3
Brooks	549	24.8	1 111	1.5	58.4	1 153 983	1 039	44 947	19.1	38 686	4.8	95.2	20.2	2.6	524	16.2
Brown	560	16.2	324	3.7	95.3	585 658	1 805	39 183	35.9	20 791	16.4	83.6	25.3	2.8	917	16.2
Burleson	361	-7.2	228	14.5	92.3	515 165	2 257	56 109	56.4	35 651	33.6	66.4	34.1	4.7	1 559	6.3
Burnet	482	-14.7	315	1.3	57.6	712 764	2 263	40 614	12.3	8 030	18.3	81.7	18.2	1.1	111	3.6

— **Water Use, Wholesale Trade, Retail Trade, and Real Estate**

STATE County	Water use, 2005		Wholesale trade,[1] 2007				Retail trade,[2] 2007				Real estate and rental and leasing,[2] 2007			
	Total water withdrawn (mil gal/day)	Gallons withdrawn per person	Number of establish-ments	Number of employees	Sales (mil dol)	Annual payroll (mil dol)	Number of establish-ments	Number of employees	Sales (mil dol)	Annual payroll (mil dol)	Number of establish-ments	Number of employees	Receipts (mil dol)	Annual payroll (mil dol)
	133	134	135	136	137	138	139	140	141	142	143	144	145	146
TENNESSEE—Cont'd														
Marshall	4.0	141	10	D	D	D	122	1 176	269.7	24.3	19	53	5.9	0.7
Maury	14.3	187	58	649	245.1	29.4	333	3 824	898.3	81.1	89	355	56.8	9.8
Meigs	1.5	125	2	D	D	D	22	149	29.8	2.7	2	D	D	D
Monroe	9.6	222	28	315	173.4	8.6	150	1 695	453.0	37.9	28	88	9.6	1.5
Montgomery	24.3	165	72	629	345.5	26.3	522	8 016	1 877.6	180.3	145	577	110.7	15.3
Moore	1.7	281	1	D	D	D	11	85	16.3	1.2	NA	NA	NA	NA
Morgan	2.2	109	6	D	D	D	40	300	58.5	4.6	3	D	D	D
Obion	12.8	399	39	D	D	D	158	1 767	403.5	37.0	24	76	8.2	1.5
Overton	3.3	158	9	70	46.7	2.6	66	457	110.7	8.0	7	D	D	D
Perry	1.5	194	2	D	D	D	24	144	24.3	1.9	5	D	D	D
Pickett	0.9	185	2	D	D	D	24	115	23.6	2.1	1	D	D	D
Polk	6.0	375	3	D	D	D	48	297	67.7	6.1	8	17	1.7	0.4
Putnam	14.7	220	70	745	465.7	30.8	379	4 766	1 193.0	106.6	72	241	40.3	5.5
Rhea	192.8	6 446	10	73	17.9	2.0	108	1 097	250.8	21.0	20	89	8.2	1.3
Roane	1 291.6	24 422	20	D	D	D	157	1 852	436.4	39.2	33	487	36.0	11.4
Robertson	8.0	133	52	742	779.4	20.7	183	2 433	627.8	53.8	52	148	19.9	2.9
Rutherford	35.2	161	232	5 472	6 226.3	256.0	758	11 262	2 804.3	250.1	212	1 110	381.8	29.8
Scott	2.9	131	8	54	28.4	1.1	83	771	159.6	14.5	8	24	3.9	0.5
Sequatchie	1.3	101	11	D	D	D	47	441	105.3	8.1	15	59	5.9	0.8
Sevier	12.3	155	40	D	D	D	750	8 050	1 641.1	170.8	198	2 343	462.4	77.6
Shelby	626.5	689	1 271	26 595	29 636.0	1 384.8	3 300	49 554	11 932.9	1 177.7	1 044	8 375	1 532.0	329.3
Smith	2.5	132	12	66	52.5	1.6	66	598	117.8	13.9	11	34	3.6	0.6
Stewart	2 082.9	160 605	4	D	D	D	34	233	63.7	5.6	4	33	1.8	0.2
Sullivan	534.4	3 500	183	2 207	1 055.3	99.4	622	8 148	2 026.3	183.8	132	649	108.4	17.1
Sumner	966.5	6 665	134	2 007	1 634.9	81.8	428	5 565	1 300.1	121.9	152	801	182.0	30.0
Tipton	5.5	98	24	253	241.9	7.3	164	1 690	404.2	33.0	27	115	11.8	2.1
Trousdale	1.2	155	2	D	D	D	27	203	41.7	3.4	1	D	D	D
Unicoi	6.2	355	8	D	D	D	44	514	119.5	10.1	6	22	2.2	0.7
Union	2.0	103	11	40	6.6	0.8	37	297	60.5	5.0	9	54	3.6	0.9
Van Buren	1.1	192	NA	NA	NA	NA	7	35	9.2	0.4	6	26	1.2	0.5
Warren	7.8	196	36	D	D	D	179	1 834	373.7	38.8	22	59	8.3	1.3
Washington	22.4	199	135	2 000	1 090.8	70.6	551	8 257	1 869.1	169.3	127	967	114.1	17.8
Wayne	2.2	132	7	52	38.0	1.8	50	347	66.6	5.4	5	D	D	D
Weakley	5.5	162	32	D	D	D	120	1 256	265.4	22.5	20	68	7.8	1.4
White	4.1	168	11	88	28.9	2.8	81	793	195.4	17.7	11	52	3.5	0.9
Williamson	5.6	36	211	2 340	2 756.0	151.2	783	13 038	3 307.0	306.4	277	2 658	406.2	84.2
Wilson	15.5	154	80	1 298	967.9	62.5	394	4 621	1 165.0	103.4	115	541	85.9	16.1
TEXAS	26 747.0	1 170	27 066	386 370	424 238.2	20 260.6	78 795	1 138 440	311 334.8	28 395.2	26 593	173 745	36 399.2	7 067.2
Anderson	16.0	284	33	409	365.3	16.8	183	1 958	495.5	42.5	36	149	53.3	6.1
Andrews	53.4	4 185	12	D	D	D	36	314	98.3	7.5	12	70	12.9	4.7
Angelina	22.8	280	63	D	D	D	356	5 086	1 174.1	106.3	75	359	49.1	9.6
Aransas	3.5	142	10	32	13.5	1.0	95	1 125	241.5	23.5	37	152	14.3	2.7
Archer	56.8	6 240	13	52	43.4	2.3	23	91	39.4	2.0	4	D	D	D
Armstrong	7.7	3 520	1	D	D	D	4	24	2.4	0.2	NA	NA	NA	NA
Atascosa	35.8	827	22	187	69.4	6.3	124	1 499	362.9	30.4	25	86	11.9	1.6
Austin	12.9	495	18	D	D	D	95	878	234.2	19.8	22	54	9.1	1.7
Bailey	147.2	21 882	20	137	69.9	4.4	27	229	41.7	3.6	1	D	D	D
Bandera	3.2	159	5	18	1.4	0.5	56	359	76.5	6.4	14	38	5.8	0.8
Bastrop	250.9	3 588	33	198	51.6	8.0	167	2 069	684.7	48.1	52	173	18.6	4.1
Baylor	6.6	1 717	8	48	33.8	1.7	16	107	27.1	1.3	3	D	D	D
Bee	10.1	306	7	D	D	D	82	1 071	247.1	23.4	25	87	10.8	2.6
Bell	105.7	413	125	2 933	4 202.7	125.3	924	12 506	3 350.0	283.0	308	1 501	209.4	40.3
Bexar	784.8	517	1 427	22 636	12 232.1	1 042.4	4 737	81 409	22 815.3	1 891.9	1 793	12 057	2 215.6	425.7
Blanco	2.2	238	10	D	D	D	30	213	50.6	3.6	7	D	D	D
Borden	8.2	12 623	NA	NA	NA	NA	1	D	D	D	NA	NA	NA	NA
Bosque	7.9	438	12	70	28.4	2.7	55	457	106.5	9.2	10	13	2.0	0.3
Bowie	121.5	1 341	104	D	D	D	487	6 447	1 535.4	141.3	102	483	67.3	11.5
Brazoria	970.1	3 483	181	1 572	841.9	74.6	743	11 791	2 958.8	265.3	252	1 604	366.6	61.3
Brazos	39.8	255	111	1 498	779.6	56.5	646	9 149	2 119.1	189.9	226	1 192	196.3	32.4
Brewster	8.6	948	9	58	20.3	1.4	60	470	86.8	8.9	23	61	5.6	1.1
Briscoe	29.5	17 920	3	20	5.4	0.3	8	27	6.7	0.4	NA	NA	NA	NA
Brooks	2.9	377	2	D	D	D	25	345	81.6	6.9	1	D	D	D
Brown	14.8	383	40	392	171.0	13.0	196	1 973	512.5	41.0	40	116	16.1	2.8
Burleson	29.0	1 684	17	D	D	D	49	501	183.8	12.0	5	16	2.2	0.5
Burnet	10.8	258	31	163	81.9	7.4	195	2 139	639.5	51.6	57	295	26.6	6.9

1. Merchant wholesalers, except manufacturers' sales branches and offices. 2. Employer establishments.

Professional Services, Manufacturing, and Accommodation and Food Services

STATE County	Professional, scientific, and technical services,[1] 2007				Manufacturing, 2007				Accommodation and food services, 2007			
	Number of establish- ments	Number of employees	Receipts (mil dol)	Annual payroll (mil dol)	Number of establish- ments	Number of employees	Receipts (mil dol)	Annual payroll (mil dol)	Number of establish- ments	Number of employees	Sales (mil dol)	Annual payroll (mil dol)
	147	148	149	150	151	152	153	154	155	156	157	158
TENNESSEE—Cont'd												
Marshall	28	93	6.8	1.9	52	3 821	1 490.1	145.0	37	518	21.1	5.2
Maury	108	D	D	D	82	4 575	D	312.3	144	2 835	97.3	28.3
Meigs	3	D	D	D	14	770	253.0	28.8	6	46	2.0	0.6
Monroe	48	160	12.2	5.7	72	5 246	1 386.2	189.2	81	1 224	41.0	11.3
Montgomery	160	D	D	D	70	6 052	D	D	300	6 151	245.2	64.7
Moore	2	D	D	D	NA	NA	NA	NA	8	48	1.4	0.5
Morgan	10	D	D	D	NA	NA	NA	NA	8	105	3.5	1.1
Obion	34	D	D	D	43	5 506	D	D	65	D	D	D
Overton	22	D	D	D	35	1 101	D	32.3	25	317	13.3	3.3
Perry	3	D	D	D	12	1 042	170.0	30.1	6	D	D	D
Pickett	5	D	D	D	NA	NA	NA	NA	9	67	3.1	0.5
Polk	11	D	D	D	NA	NA	NA	NA	23	175	8.8	2.4
Putnam	139	D	D	D	112	6 106	1 384.0	203.1	154	3 387	138.0	38.5
Rhea	38	97	8.6	3.1	33	4 705	894.7	149.7	45	761	26.9	6.9
Roane	60	182	19.6	6.9	23	1 440	369.7	54.9	66	1 304	46.0	12.7
Robertson	56	D	D	D	84	6 281	1 667.5	211.8	83	1 669	60.7	17.3
Rutherford	325	D	D	D	203	18 166	11 304.8	901.6	417	9 745	387.0	111.2
Scott	16	68	6.4	4.3	44	1 499	401.7	46.8	29	410	14.6	3.9
Sequatchie	12	D	D	D	13	749	D	19.2	23	244	9.4	2.5
Sevier	162	703	65.8	24.1	82	1 448	341.5	50.4	517	10 254	611.9	169.6
Shelby	1 913	16 716	2 230.2	920.2	704	31 108	17 969.7	1 490.7	1 724	39 318	1 788.0	501.5
Smith	16	47	5.2	1.5	27	1 387	D	49.2	20	347	12.4	3.2
Stewart	7	D	D	D	NA	NA	NA	NA	19	164	6.1	1.6
Sullivan	252	1 726	214.8	68.6	157	15 632	5 463.6	742.7	312	6 590	255.1	70.1
Sumner	219	D	D	D	213	7 023	1 741.4	273.0	217	4 053	155.5	45.0
Tipton	39	D	D	D	36	2 080	774.2	81.5	61	846	29.8	7.5
Trousdale	8	44	2.7	1.1	NA	NA	NA	NA	10	114	4.6	1.3
Unicoi	13	D	D	D	25	2 100	348.6	D	27	361	13.0	3.3
Union	9	D	D	D	23	615	125.6	20.5	12	198	5.7	1.2
Van Buren	2	D	D	D	NA	NA	NA	NA	1	D	D	D
Warren	38	121	12.7	3.1	67	3 140	852.3	144.5	52	803	28.8	7.8
Washington	231	D	D	D	145	6 166	1 577.7	214.1	254	6 361	247.1	74.9
Wayne	8	D	D	D	27	736	109.9	20.5	20	193	8.5	2.1
Weakley	25	D	D	D	36	1 680	D	D	58	D	D	D
White	22	64	4.9	1.5	45	2 118	552.2	66.4	28	398	16.8	5.2
Williamson	782	D	D	D	126	3 524	1 106.8	129.5	366	8 329	383.5	109.9
Wilson	185	D	D	D	111	6 274	D	273.8	179	3 640	147.3	43.5
TEXAS	57 373	534 386	90 668.7	35 376.4	21 115	893 842	593 541.5	42 835.7	43 509	866 189	42 054.6	11 502.3
Anderson	79	258	25.1	7.2	NA	NA	NA	NA	69	1 046	48.6	11.9
Andrews	19	62	9.1	2.5	NA	NA	NA	NA	23	340	14.9	3.3
Angelina	155	688	81.9	28.9	75	6 343	1 291.4	217.7	133	2 748	112.6	31.5
Aransas	39	D	D	D	NA	NA	NA	NA	84	1 089	48.8	13.4
Archer	6	D	D	D	NA	NA	NA	NA	7	38	1.4	0.4
Armstrong	1	D	D	D	NA	NA	NA	NA	6	16	0.6	0.2
Atascosa	34	264	25.9	5.5	NA	NA	NA	NA	66	904	32.2	8.5
Austin	57	D	D	D	39	2 222	D	D	46	568	25.0	6.2
Bailey	12	45	4.5	1.4	NA	NA	NA	NA	10	185	7.0	1.9
Bandera	32	D	D	D	NA	NA	NA	NA	55	499	23.2	5.8
Bastrop	84	340	33.8	11.9	64	1 068	238.6	37.7	97	2 015	115.1	33.1
Baylor	6	26	1.2	0.5	NA	NA	NA	NA	7	95	3.2	0.9
Bee	40	D	D	D	NA	NA	NA	NA	52	711	25.5	7.0
Bell	342	D	D	D	136	7 028	1 925.0	246.6	500	9 329	401.4	104.9
Bexar	3 625	D	D	D	986	35 502	12 305.1	1 366.0	3 207	75 006	3 829.0	1 073.1
Blanco	27	103	9.3	3.6	NA	NA	NA	NA	32	225	9.4	2.9
Borden	1	D	D	D	NA	NA	NA	NA	NA	NA	NA	NA
Bosque	22	84	7.7	2.5	NA	NA	NA	NA	20	104	5.3	1.2
Bowie	169	D	D	D	65	2 579	1 729.2	103.9	166	3 668	166.5	49.4
Brazoria	411	D	D	D	225	13 787	31 048.1	1 020.4	383	7 330	313.5	85.2
Brazos	388	D	D	D	111	4 881	979.4	167.5	368	8 497	340.3	91.4
Brewster	22	59	5.8	1.3	NA	NA	NA	NA	48	630	25.4	7.1
Briscoe	NA	NA	NA	NA	NA	NA	NA	NA	4	17	0.3	0.1
Brooks	12	23	2.0	0.5	NA	NA	NA	NA	28	326	14.2	4.1
Brown	54	184	16.8	4.9	41	3 100	1 249.4	125.4	87	1 374	49.9	13.7
Burleson	19	D	D	D	NA	NA	NA	NA	36	338	12.8	3.2
Burnet	82	335	31.5	12.5	57	924	D	49.7	102	1 386	74.4	21.6

1. Establishment subject to federal tax.

Table B. States and Counties — **Health Care and Social Assistance, Other Services, and Federal Funds**

STATE County	Health care and social assistance, 2007				Other services, 2007				Federal funds and grants, 2009–2010			
									Expenditures (mil dol)			
										Direct payments for individuals[1]		
	Number of establishments	Number of employees	Receipts (mil dol)	Annual payroll (mil dol)	Number of establishments	Number of employees	Receipts (mil dol)	Annual payroll (mil dol)	Total	Social Security and government retirement	Medicare	Food Stamps and Supplemental Security Income
	159	160	161	162	163	164	165	166	167	168	169	170
TENNESSEE—Cont'd												
Marshall	61	725	48.0	17.6	29	D	D	D	216.8	88.7	65.9	9.5
Maury	205	5 346	450.4	191.8	105	631	55.6	15.6	593.2	268.3	152.2	31.0
Meigs	7	D	D	D	5	8	0.7	0.2	110.4	48.7	24.3	7.1
Monroe	61	1 200	82.6	31.9	39	147	10.0	2.9	382.0	165.6	91.2	22.4
Montgomery	270	D	D	D	189	1 066	72.9	20.9	1 075.2	555.2	152.8	51.3
Moore	11	D	D	D	4	D	D	D	29.7	15.1	9.0	1.3
Morgan	17	399	21.9	9.4	10	21	4.3	1.0	224.2	66.1	47.8	12.9
Obion	89	D	D	D	47	D	D	D	319.1	127.5	93.3	15.8
Overton	34	D	D	D	15	D	D	D	224.7	70.9	77.8	10.6
Perry	17	367	20.0	8.1	6	46	1.0	0.3	84.6	29.9	30.6	3.5
Pickett	5	D	D	D	5	D	D	D	59.7	17.0	21.5	2.5
Polk	20	395	28.7	11.6	9	D	D	D	174.7	69.7	54.3	8.5
Putnam	214	4 527	428.2	151.4	117	591	47.0	13.3	690.5	277.4	157.2	26.5
Rhea	65	831	49.5	22.4	24	90	6.5	1.8	298.4	127.5	81.0	19.3
Roane	88	1 812	118.1	51.2	43	172	14.9	4.0	608.3	244.2	154.5	27.9
Robertson	107	1 606	145.3	52.0	79	297	24.3	6.1	398.7	188.4	101.3	18.3
Rutherford	447	9 041	1 019.4	424.6	285	2 300	227.1	69.6	1 642.8	563.8	199.2	44.4
Scott	42	719	52.3	22.0	21	107	8.3	2.5	286.3	71.0	84.3	22.3
Sequatchie	22	D	D	D	12	D	D	D	116.5	40.1	25.7	7.4
Sevier	134	1 672	136.2	46.3	152	884	72.3	19.5	620.2	309.3	109.9	26.6
Shelby	2 166	62 091	6 542.5	2 623.9	1 349	12 280	1 807.9	356.1	10 393.2	2 345.3	1 990.9	697.4
Smith	33	632	55.0	21.1	22	69	5.0	1.6	207.4	54.8	58.7	6.4
Stewart	15	D	D	D	8	22	2.0	0.5	145.4	66.3	30.7	5.7
Sullivan	446	12 705	1 354.3	507.3	253	D	D	D	1 642.8	669.5	374.0	77.7
Sumner	313	5 031	518.5	196.1	202	1 110	96.1	22.8	971.9	446.2	220.2	40.3
Tipton	85	1 224	96.6	35.4	45	198	14.0	3.8	437.8	184.3	105.0	25.5
Trousdale	21	254	19.7	6.7	7	D	D	D	63.6	21.5	23.7	3.5
Unicoi	27	681	41.5	17.4	21	D	D	D	224.2	84.9	56.2	9.8
Union	12	D	D	D	17	D	D	D	126.3	51.6	62.7	9.3
Van Buren	4	D	D	D	2	D	D	D	49.7	14.5	14.3	2.6
Warren	92	1 571	137.2	44.4	52	194	14.0	4.5	367.8	138.0	126.6	18.9
Washington	319	10 712	1 168.4	459.6	195	1 042	73.8	22.8	1 173.2	488.0	245.0	50.1
Wayne	29	236	12.8	5.1	10	28	4.6	0.7	160.4	49.9	46.2	9.7
Weakley	74	1 527	111.8	46.0	38	D	D	D	307.0	100.2	87.1	13.0
White	39	740	61.0	22.1	24	71	6.9	1.9	228.0	95.1	69.2	11.6
Williamson	616	10 109	1 089.7	493.9	312	2 111	177.7	52.9	734.6	398.3	128.3	16.6
Wilson	230	3 596	306.6	114.5	131	616	48.4	13.2	645.7	301.8	160.9	24.2
TEXAS	54 991	1 166 613	113 830.2	43 118.2	34 462	253 503	25 778.5	6 993.6	225 724.9	56 814.1	27 711.9	9 056.0
Anderson	135	2 083	188.4	67.2	53	319	17.2	7.4	433.7	169.4	107.5	19.5
Andrews	20	433	35.3	14.6	22	277	40.5	10.7	77.5	31.6	21.1	5.7
Angelina	270	7 552	517.1	207.1	129	732	120.8	17.8	693.4	276.8	159.8	36.6
Aransas	42	522	42.3	12.7	49	153	11.9	3.1	174.9	102.2	38.6	11.0
Archer	12	D	D	D	10	22	1.4	0.4	88.9	23.7	11.3	22.0
Armstrong	4	D	D	D	2	D	D	D	18.1	8.5	4.3	0.1
Atascosa	85	1 000	93.5	32.8	44	222	18.3	4.9	283.3	117.8	51.6	22.8
Austin	32	590	31.3	14.6	33	110	9.8	2.4	830.6	86.8	47.6	6.2
Bailey	16	199	13.5	5.0	19	62	3.8	0.9	63.0	16.5	14.6	3.0
Bandera	20	247	17.7	5.9	30	92	8.1	1.8	139.8	91.4	19.8	4.1
Bastrop	89	1 648	97.1	43.5	81	332	30.4	7.6	419.4	205.3	66.6	17.9
Baylor	14	535	13.2	6.7	17	39	4.3	0.6	50.0	17.8	14.2	1.2
Bee	49	868	63.7	28.0	41	178	13.6	3.2	241.5	70.4	56.0	16.4
Bell	476	18 504	1 979.2	802.1	401	2 418	173.8	50.9	11 820.3	1 045.2	220.7	89.4
Bexar	4 094	99 461	9 820.8	3 564.2	2 505	18 260	1 516.2	428.4	20 014.5	5 248.5	2 064.1	758.3
Blanco	18	128	6.6	2.9	19	58	5.1	1.1	94.5	50.6	27.0	1.1
Borden	NA	NA	NA	NA	NA	NA	NA	NA	7.5	1.3	0.8	0.0
Bosque	19	588	43.2	18.1	26	97	9.6	1.7	163.1	71.0	37.8	4.6
Bowie	304	6 810	654.9	261.4	153	940	72.8	20.8	1 123.7	370.9	186.6	46.5
Brazoria	501	7 074	500.6	206.8	341	2 203	207.4	65.3	1 269.0	673.7	261.9	70.4
Brazos	389	7 161	872.8	287.0	260	1 859	359.3	42.4	1 175.4	313.8	104.6	43.0
Brewster	20	434	33.5	14.0	20	83	5.4	1.4	104.5	27.2	11.8	2.8
Briscoe	1	D	D	D	2	D	D	D	26.0	6.1	6.5	0.5
Brooks	18	707	15.2	8.1	12	D	D	D	125.3	20.1	19.9	10.3
Brown	124	3 034	194.7	73.1	72	417	25.9	7.4	337.5	137.2	94.8	17.3
Burleson	18	258	21.6	9.0	24	100	8.3	1.8	154.9	57.6	29.7	7.0
Burnet	113	1 250	102.6	37.7	72	286	21.1	6.0	294.8	185.5	48.1	9.4

1. State totals may include programs not allocated by county.

Table B. States and Counties — Federal Funds, Residential Construction, and Local Government Finances

STATE County	Federal funds and grants, 2009–2010 (cont.)							Value of residential construction authorized by building permits, 2010		Local government finances, 2007				
	Expenditures (mil dol) (cont.)									General revenue				
	Procurement contract awards			Grants[1]									Taxes	
														Per capita[2] (dollars)
	Salaries and wages	Defense	Other	Medicaid and other health-related	Nutrition and family welfare	Education	Other	New construction ($1,000)	Number of housing units	Total (mil dol)	Inter-govern-mental (mil dol)	Total (mil dol)	Total	Property
	171	172	173	174	175	176	177	178	179	180	181	182	183	184
TENNESSEE—Cont'd														
Marshall	11.5	1.8	1.2	29.5	3.4	2.9	0.4	10 557	66	62.8	24.8	24.6	844	525
Maury	23.2	0.5	17.0	69.8	9.0	5.5	1.1	35 646	341	375.7	67.0	68.2	853	533
Meigs	12.9	0.0	0.4	13.5	1.8	0.9	0.1	5 969	34	22.4	14.9	4.9	419	312
Monroe	13.5	10.6	2.9	59.5	6.0	3.6	3.9	7 208	110	82.7	44.1	26.0	579	297
Montgomery	104.7	20.4	7.3	74.7	20.9	11.8	9.7	155 955	1 800	387.2	154.6	148.2	959	614
Moore	0.6	0.0	0.1	2.2	0.7	0.4	0.0	3 012	22	13.5	7.3	4.0	659	537
Morgan	2.9	0.3	0.8	30.3	5.3	1.4	52.8	178	2	37.0	23.2	9.0	440	348
Obion	14.5	0.0	2.3	46.3	5.2	3.2	0.6	3 760	32	72.2	33.4	26.2	828	386
Overton	7.7	0.0	0.9	48.2	3.2	1.8	1.6	437	4	39.0	23.7	10.8	514	281
Perry	1.6	0.0	0.3	15.3	1.2	0.7	0.4	125	1	20.8	11.4	6.0	781	590
Pickett	1.0	0.0	0.2	15.1	1.0	0.4	0.2	NA	NA	12.0	7.1	3.0	637	316
Polk	4.6	0.0	4.9	28.1	2.4	1.4	0.2	18 193	101	30.8	18.8	8.4	535	353
Putnam	33.7	2.3	60.5	74.7	17.0	5.3	14.1	37 273	282	321.0	56.7	70.2	1 004	502
Rhea	7.9	0.0	4.4	43.9	4.4	2.7	3.2	3 375	52	83.5	33.2	19.1	629	339
Roane	18.0	0.0	45.2	75.1	9.5	4.5	2.0	1 507	15	137.2	45.1	42.7	799	479
Robertson	13.9	0.4	7.2	43.9	6.8	3.6	0.7	20 138	159	142.1	55.2	60.7	959	531
Rutherford	192.5	6.5	443.1	82.7	18.5	14.9	15.8	159 123	1 123	635.2	190.0	319.2	1 322	582
Scott	9.3	1.0	27.6	61.1	5.2	2.2	0.8	354	3	42.0	26.0	8.2	372	203
Sequatchie	3.8	0.0	19.9	12.9	2.0	1.7	2.4	1 320	21	26.4	13.0	10.5	787	350
Sevier	27.2	0.3	77.6	49.4	9.0	4.4	3.3	10 564	120	307.7	65.3	178.1	2 133	558
Shelby	909.3	1 627.9	593.9	1 431.4	243.5	81.7	265.2	235 515	1 548	3 929.4	1 243.7	1 718.7	1 888	1 323
Smith	9.2	42.4	0.9	23.6	2.5	1.0	0.1	8 286	47	39.0	19.8	13.0	691	378
Stewart	4.7	0.1	14.6	17.8	1.8	1.3	0.1	870	4	28.6	17.4	7.8	593	395
Sullivan	50.8	205.4	10.3	173.1	28.4	12.2	17.2	42 991	294	378.1	124.5	176.4	1 149	738
Sumner	30.7	3.3	98.2	79.2	13.2	6.7	2.2	64 824	454	360.7	138.1	134.3	879	642
Tipton	15.3	7.0	2.1	67.9	8.6	3.1	2.7	14 966	100	138.8	76.0	41.3	716	464
Trousdale	0.9	0.0	0.3	9.4	1.1	0.4	0.2	1 109	10	16.1	9.8	3.9	502	310
Unicoi	7.8	1.1	27.9	29.8	2.8	1.5	1.6	0	0	61.1	19.6	8.3	472	347
Union	2.1	0.3	0.5	24.0	3.0	1.4	0.4	9 951	76	35.1	23.4	6.1	325	202
Van Buren	0.5	0.0	8.4	7.7	0.9	0.5	0.4	NA	NA	15.1	10.4	2.8	523	333
Warren	16.1	0.8	2.7	49.7	5.4	3.5	1.3	981	9	88.3	38.6	31.8	802	420
Washington	116.8	10.9	65.6	119.3	13.7	12.4	13.8	68 201	598	286.5	93.0	132.8	1 138	551
Wayne	7.5	0.0	0.6	30.7	2.7	1.2	0.4	700	8	44.2	24.3	8.3	498	279
Weakley	27.4	0.1	2.0	35.4	15.6	2.3	1.9	8 210	58	69.3	33.9	18.6	559	310
White	4.8	0.0	1.0	38.7	3.5	2.0	0.6	4 766	51	44.4	25.7	11.3	456	283
Williamson	35.5	28.1	37.7	42.7	9.6	5.3	1.5	185 059	569	605.4	133.8	279.1	1 680	837
Wilson	55.8	1.5	11.0	54.2	15.3	4.9	2.1	115 456	928	235.8	78.6	109.6	1 030	512
TEXAS	29 926.4	30 331.5	10 263.0	23 603.8	5 505.0	3 710.8	11 804.5	13 739 563	88 461	X	X	X	X	X
Anderson	18.7	0.0	2.4	102.5	5.8	1.5	3.7	2 831	16	112.0	41.0	54.0	951	766
Andrews	1.4	-0.2	2.9	9.4	2.3	0.3	0.0	7 715	71	102.4	7.9	65.3	4 972	4 694
Angelina	39.2	10.9	9.3	124.6	12.2	3.5	0.9	11 699	123	279.1	113.9	86.3	1 042	772
Aransas	2.2	0.1	0.7	13.8	3.8	0.8	0.3	14 024	100	66.2	11.3	43.8	1 771	1 534
Archer	20.8	0.0	0.3	7.4	0.8	0.2	0.0	1 209	12	25.1	10.5	10.9	1 216	1 043
Armstrong	0.3	0.0	0.1	2.0	0.2	0.1	0.0	0	0	5.8	2.8	2.0	981	864
Atascosa	4.2	0.0	1.0	65.7	8.1	4.1	2.9	4 779	36	120.4	64.8	35.6	816	677
Austin	8.5	640.6	1.7	33.3	2.5	0.4	0.3	2 564	21	86.6	23.5	44.0	1 654	1 475
Bailey	1.7	0.0	0.3	9.6	1.7	0.2	2.5	0	0	28.9	10.7	7.4	1 170	1 033
Bandera	12.1	0.0	0.6	8.3	1.6	0.5	0.3	0	0	42.3	11.6	24.7	1 222	1 092
Bastrop	32.5	2.0	8.0	71.1	9.0	1.8	1.7	3 556	33	206.2	64.3	90.4	1 251	1 113
Baylor	1.4	0.0	0.2	9.9	1.0	0.1	0.3	0	0	18.3	5.3	4.1	1 078	927
Bee	3.7	1.7	0.7	58.4	10.8	3.3	4.0	1 039	9	103.8	57.0	24.9	760	618
Bell	8 698.5	1 281.2	91.4	153.7	32.7	67.0	36.0	265 211	1 914	1 034.5	481.0	303.9	1 097	838
Bexar	4 388.8	3 693.9	582.7	2 025.9	319.3	117.0	331.7	651 596	4 653	6 200.6	2 179.4	2 329.0	1 461	1 212
Blanco	8.1	0.0	1.1	5.1	0.6	0.2	0.2	2 211	21	26.5	6.4	17.4	1 924	1 748
Borden	0.2	0.0	0.0	0.0	0.2	1.8	0.0	NA	NA	11.3	0.8	9.6	16 426	16 357
Bosque	4.8	18.3	1.2	21.7	2.0	0.5	0.1	664	6	47.6	19.2	20.2	1 126	997
Bowie	161.6	131.5	9.8	157.1	15.7	3.8	16.5	13 016	192	287.0	133.2	99.2	1 084	844
Brazoria	53.5	11.4	22.3	115.2	22.2	5.8	8.5	319 967	1 979	973.1	219.1	530.2	1 802	1 569
Brazos	123.3	47.9	30.8	190.7	23.2	10.5	229.2	116 068	978	454.6	109.1	248.8	1 455	1 132
Brewster	17.3	0.7	16.1	11.6	1.6	4.4	2.1	2 700	18	28.9	11.8	11.3	1 222	978
Briscoe	0.6	0.0	0.1	6.6	0.1	0.1	0.0	NA	NA	4.4	1.6	2.2	1 510	1 371
Brooks	17.6	0.1	1.3	49.5	2.9	0.6	1.3	285	3	38.8	10.7	21.0	2 767	2 565
Brown	10.8	1.0	2.0	58.3	6.4	1.3	2.6	2 376	21	117.2	48.2	45.7	1 185	903
Burleson	3.4	10.9	0.8	37.4	2.7	0.5	0.6	1 210	11	43.5	15.0	22.2	1 336	1 183
Burnet	7.4	0.5	2.8	26.8	1.9	0.9	3.1	36 861	189	118.5	20.6	78.0	1 785	1 545

1. State totals may include programs not allocated by county.   2. Based on the resident population estimated as of July 1 of the year shown.

Local Government Finances, Government Employment, and Voting

	Local government finances, 2007 (cont.)									Government employment, 2009			Presidential election,[2] 2008		
	Direct general expenditure							Debt outstanding					Percent of vote cast:		
			Percent of total for:												
STATE County	Total (mil dol)	Per capita[1] (dollars)	Educa-tion	Health and hospitals	Police protec-tion	Public welfare	High-ways	Total (mil dol)	Per capita[1] (dollars)	Federal civilian	Federal military	State and local	Demo-cratic	Republi-can	All other
	185	186	187	188	189	190	191	192	193	194	195	196	197	198	199
TENNESSEE—Cont'd															
Marshall	56.1	1 923	63.4	4.6	6.0	0.2	6.5	60.0	2 056	69	102	1 587	38.3	59.8	1.9
Maury	378.8	4 736	22.7	51.9	4.1	0.0	2.7	277.9	3 475	195	285	6 280	38.7	60.1	1.2
Meigs	20.7	1 774	63.5	2.1	3.5	0.0	9.8	7.4	636	32	41	440	32.4	66.0	1.6
Monroe	84.7	1 888	56.7	4.0	5.6	0.1	4.9	59.9	1 336	96	154	1 738	30.1	68.5	1.4
Montgomery	381.6	2 471	50.9	1.9	6.6	0.1	4.3	7 887.6	51 066	913	502	8 152	45.5	53.4	1.1
Moore	13.8	2 257	54.3	2.1	5.0	0.0	9.0	0.8	136	0	21	740	29.8	68.1	2.1
Morgan	39.5	1 939	64.0	2.9	2.8	0.2	7.8	21.6	1 061	40	63	1 408	28.9	69.1	2.0
Obion	71.7	2 266	58.5	0.2	6.1	2.8	5.8	33.4	1 055	120	106	1 732	32.2	66.3	1.6
Overton	38.1	1 814	60.8	3.0	2.6	0.2	6.8	27.5	1 311	52	71	1 282	42.3	55.6	2.2
Perry	18.8	2 457	45.8	3.8	7.6	0.0	13.0	10.3	1 341	19	26	400	44.3	53.2	2.5
Pickett	12.1	2 533	47.3	4.8	3.8	0.0	10.2	12.1	2 541	10	16	291	32.0	66.9	1.2
Polk	34.0	2 168	56.9	2.9	3.5	0.3	6.9	23.1	1 475	82	53	810	32.7	65.6	1.7
Putnam	302.0	4 320	24.9	54.1	3.8	0.0	1.6	257.6	3 684	264	249	7 563	35.7	62.6	1.7
Rhea	75.0	2 475	46.5	23.0	3.9	0.0	4.2	30.4	1 004	1 021	106	1 601	26.2	72.4	1.4
Roane	141.4	2 648	39.8	26.7	3.6	0.1	4.2	102.1	1 912	468	180	3 253	31.0	67.3	1.7
Robertson	130.7	2 064	52.4	2.7	8.5	0.0	3.9	230.8	3 644	103	224	3 456	33.7	64.8	1.4
Rutherford	622.8	2 579	50.7	2.2	8.8	1.4	7.7	887.7	3 676	2 483	870	14 229	39.8	58.9	1.4
Scott	45.6	2 073	66.4	0.8	4.7	1.8	6.2	62.6	2 849	97	74	1 338	25.4	72.7	1.9
Sequatchie	27.9	2 090	66.7	2.8	3.3	0.0	4.5	17.7	1 326	12	47	622	31.6	66.4	2.0
Sevier	321.2	3 846	34.9	1.2	5.3	0.2	5.1	507.7	6 078	372	290	4 389	25.3	73.4	1.2
Shelby	4 041.0	4 440	47.3	9.7	8.2	1.0	2.3	6 595.8	7 247	14 235	4 717	59 953	63.4	36.0	0.6
Smith	38.3	2 035	56.7	2.4	7.1	0.1	7.1	27.3	1 448	119	65	840	38.7	58.9	2.4
Stewart	30.7	2 347	53.4	3.7	5.4	0.2	6.7	44.4	3 394	498	45	598	44.9	53.7	1.5
Sullivan	358.0	2 332	51.8	1.7	7.0	0.0	5.1	328.2	2 138	452	522	7 045	28.7	70.0	1.3
Sumner	333.5	2 184	54.0	2.0	5.9	0.1	3.7	439.4	2 877	494	534	7 207	32.0	66.9	1.2
Tipton	122.0	2 114	70.1	0.5	3.9	0.2	4.7	72.5	1 257	108	200	2 444	31.3	67.8	0.9
Trousdale	16.3	2 107	56.6	0.4	7.3	0.3	10.3	10.4	1 346	40	27	442	45.5	52.1	2.3
Unicoi	63.6	3 591	30.2	43.1	3.2	0.3	5.1	25.0	1 411	90	60	1 044	29.2	69.4	1.5
Union	37.8	2 003	65.8	4.0	2.9	0.0	5.6	19.9	1 053	26	64	871	28.6	69.8	1.6
Van Buren	10.6	1 948	60.2	3.1	4.9	0.0	10.1	10.4	1 904	0	18	371	38.5	58.7	2.9
Warren	84.5	2 129	51.7	2.2	4.6	0.8	3.6	55.4	1 395	109	136	1 831	38.3	59.5	2.2
Washington	242.4	2 078	49.2	1.3	6.5	0.7	5.8	927.7	7 952	2 427	423	10 639	32.5	66.0	1.4
Wayne	46.2	2 774	50.9	0.7	2.9	14.5	8.2	38.0	2 282	28	56	1 412	24.5	73.7	1.7
Weakley	63.5	1 911	51.5	2.1	5.7	10.4	8.8	59.5	1 791	142	117	3 609	33.6	64.7	1.7
White	43.2	1 737	67.8	1.7	2.7	0.0	6.5	17.9	718	59	86	1 313	35.0	63.3	1.8
Williamson	666.4	3 831	46.4	20.7	4.2	0.2	4.7	772.2	4 648	405	595	8 524	29.8	69.3	1.0
Wilson	245.8	2 311	58.7	0.5	10.0	0.0	4.6	313.6	2 948	203	378	4 228	31.1	67.6	1.3
TEXAS	X	X	X	X	X	X	X	X	X	198 042	189 348	1 594 903	43.7	55.5	0.9
Anderson	108.4	1 910	62.1	0.2	4.2	0.1	4.2	54.6	961	132	134	5 656	27.8	71.4	0.8
Andrews	106.2	8 081	56.3	24.5	3.2	0.0	2.1	45.4	3 458	18	33	1 221	17.1	82.4	0.5
Angelina	260.0	3 140	60.2	10.2	4.7	0.3	3.1	196.3	2 370	369	198	6 796	32.2	67.1	0.7
Aransas	60.3	2 438	56.2	1.5	7.0	1.0	6.0	41.4	1 673	24	58	1 042	30.7	68.4	0.8
Archer	22.8	2 528	66.0	1.7	4.7	0.0	8.0	15.0	1 661	22	43	482	17.0	82.4	0.7
Armstrong	5.4	2 615	61.4	0.0	3.7	0.0	11.4	2.6	1 274	0	0	134	12.9	86.5	0.6
Atascosa	123.7	2 839	59.5	13.4	3.4	1.1	3.6	95.3	2 187	55	105	2 379	44.4	55.0	0.6
Austin	88.1	3 310	59.8	10.8	4.0	0.2	4.7	98.0	3 682	102	65	1 844	24.1	75.0	1.0
Bailey	26.2	4 125	49.5	28.0	5.2	0.0	4.2	48.5	7 625	29	15	616	29.4	69.9	0.7
Bandera	37.2	1 843	66.6	1.2	4.4	4.9	5.0	37.6	1 861	19	48	795	24.2	74.6	1.2
Bastrop	218.9	3 030	57.6	11.8	5.4	0.8	3.6	455.6	6 307	396	176	4 047	45.1	53.3	1.6
Baylor	17.7	4 611	31.7	40.5	4.1	0.3	3.7	2.7	711	21	0	265	22.3	76.8	0.9
Bee	102.0	3 119	70.4	1.0	3.0	1.0	3.1	53.5	1 637	47	76	3 563	44.7	54.8	0.5
Bell	996.8	3 599	60.1	2.3	3.9	0.4	2.4	1 580.9	5 708	9 843	54 300	18 662	44.7	54.5	0.8
Bexar	6 277.8	3 937	50.4	12.3	5.0	1.1	2.4	14 684.7	9 210	31 664	35 753	104 843	52.4	46.8	0.7
Blanco	21.5	2 374	68.9	0.0	4.2	0.6	3.1	29.0	3 198	71	22	507	29.7	69.2	1.1
Borden	10.5	18 022	88.4	0.0	0.7	0.0	5.9	0.0	0	0	0	90	11.1	87.5	1.4
Bosque	45.8	2 550	65.6	0.1	3.7	6.4	3.4	51.4	2 865	77	42	1 105	23.5	75.4	1.1
Bowie	266.1	2 907	67.3	0.7	4.5	0.3	3.6	320.2	3 498	5 228	235	6 370	30.7	68.7	0.6
Brazoria	1 101.8	3 745	55.7	5.0	3.8	0.2	6.7	2 869.0	9 751	507	797	17 185	34.8	64.3	0.9
Brazos	480.7	2 812	49.0	2.2	5.6	0.3	4.3	778.8	4 556	896	509	31 499	34.9	63.9	1.2
Brewster	26.2	2 835	59.5	3.4	5.0	0.4	5.0	11.2	1 216	297	22	984	50.5	47.6	1.9
Briscoe	3.2	2 185	64.5	0.1	3.9	0.0	8.3	6.6	4 450	15	0	106	24.7	74.3	1.0
Brooks	37.5	4 939	52.3	2.1	9.1	0.2	4.7	10.4	1 366	276	17	563	75.7	24.1	0.3
Brown	132.1	3 424	56.9	6.2	4.0	0.4	4.0	142.9	3 703	128	90	2 808	18.8	80.3	0.9
Burleson	43.4	2 615	64.9	1.0	4.7	0.0	8.6	31.5	1 899	53	39	886	30.8	68.2	1.0
Burnet	118.7	2 716	54.7	1.6	7.0	0.4	3.7	184.0	4 213	87	106	2 468	27.3	71.4	1.3

1. Based on the resident population estimated as of July 1 of the year shown.   2. © 2009 Election Data Services, Inc. All rights reserved.

Table B. States and Counties — **Land Area and Population**

					Population and population characteristics, 2010													
								Race alone or in combination, not Hispanic or Latino (percent)					Age (percent)					
STATE/ County code	CBSA code[1]	County type[2]	STATE County	Land area,[3] (sq km) 2010	Total persons	Rank	Per square kilometer	White	Black	American Indian, Alaska Native	Asian and Pacific Islander[4]	Percent Hispanic or Latino[4]	Under 5 years	5 to 17 years	18 to 24 years	25 to 34 years	35 to 44 years	45 to 54 years
				1	2	3	4	5	6	7	8	9	10	11	12	13	14	15
			TEXAS—Cont'd															
48 055	12420	1	Caldwell	1 412	38 066	1 216	27.0	45.1	6.9	0.6	1.1	47.1	6.9	19.6	11.6	12.2	12.9	13.8
48 057	47020	3	Calhoun	1 313	21 381	1 768	16.3	46.4	2.6	0.5	4.6	46.4	7.1	19.4	8.5	11.4	11.8	14.4
48 059	10180	3	Callahan	2 329	13 544	2 215	5.8	90.4	1.4	1.2	0.8	7.6	5.8	18.1	6.8	10.5	11.2	15.4
48 061	15180	2	Cameron	2 307	406 220	165	176.1	10.8	0.3	0.2	0.7	88.1	8.8	24.2	9.8	12.8	12.7	11.3
48 063	...	6	Camp	507	12 401	2 281	24.5	60.4	18.2	0.9	0.9	21.4	7.2	19.8	8.1	11.6	10.8	13.2
48 065	11100	3	Carson	2 383	6 182	2 749	2.6	89.7	0.9	1.7	0.5	8.5	5.9	19.8	5.9	9.9	11.9	15.6
48 067	...	6	Cass	2 427	30 464	1 421	12.6	78.2	17.9	1.0	0.5	3.5	5.8	17.3	7.1	10.3	11.8	14.6
48 069	...	6	Castro	2 317	8 062	2 602	3.5	37.5	1.9	0.5	0.4	59.9	8.7	22.6	8.2	12.0	11.1	12.8
48 071	26420	1	Chambers	1 547	35 096	1 296	22.7	71.6	8.5	0.8	1.2	18.9	6.9	21.6	7.9	12.2	15.0	15.1
48 073	27380	6	Cherokee	2 727	50 845	968	18.6	64.0	15.2	0.8	0.6	20.6	7.1	18.8	9.4	11.8	12.2	13.5
48 075	...	7	Childress	1 804	7 041	2 683	3.9	62.3	10.0	0.9	0.8	26.8	6.0	15.4	11.3	19.0	11.3	11.7
48 077	48660	3	Clay	2 820	10 752	2 386	3.8	93.8	0.7	2.0	0.6	4.3	5.6	17.1	6.3	9.7	11.6	16.7
48 079	...	9	Cochran	2 008	3 127	2 969	1.6	43.0	3.7	0.6	0.3	52.9	7.9	21.4	9.3	10.8	10.5	14.1
48 081	...	8	Coke	2 361	3 320	2 955	1.4	80.9	0.3	1.4	0.3	18.1	5.0	16.1	5.3	8.8	9.4	15.0
48 083	...	6	Coleman	3 268	8 895	2 534	2.7	81.1	2.5	1.1	0.4	16.0	5.6	16.6	6.4	8.7	11.1	14.8
48 085	19100	1	Collin	2 179	782 341	74	359.0	64.9	8.9	0.9	12.4	14.7	7.5	21.2	7.2	14.0	17.4	15.2
48 087	...	9	Collingsworth	2 379	3 057	2 975	1.3	64.4	4.3	2.1	0.1	30.0	8.4	19.3	7.3	11.5	10.3	13.6
48 089	...	6	Colorado	2 487	20 874	1 796	8.4	60.5	13.0	0.4	0.6	26.1	6.4	17.4	7.2	10.0	10.5	14.9
48 091	41700	1	Comal	1 449	108 472	541	74.9	72.4	1.7	0.8	1.2	24.9	5.7	18.0	6.9	10.0	12.8	16.2
48 093	...	7	Comanche	2 429	13 974	2 178	5.8	73.4	0.3	0.8	0.4	25.8	6.7	17.5	7.3	9.2	11.5	13.7
48 095	...	8	Concho	2 548	4 087	2 899	1.6	44.5	1.4	0.5	0.6	53.2	3.9	10.2	6.7	17.1	19.8	16.4
48 097	23620	6	Cooke	2 266	38 437	1 207	17.0	80.0	3.2	1.6	0.9	15.6	7.0	18.6	8.7	11.0	11.5	14.3
48 099	28660	2	Coryell	2 725	75 388	721	27.7	65.0	17.1	1.4	4.0	15.9	8.9	19.0	12.6	18.3	14.3	11.9
48 101	...	9	Cottle	2 332	1 505	3 083	0.6	69.9	8.9	0.4	0.2	21.0	5.2	18.1	5.8	8.6	9.3	14.4
48 103	...	6	Crane	2 033	4 375	2 878	2.2	40.8	2.9	1.1	0.4	55.1	7.7	21.8	8.9	11.5	13.0	15.3
48 105	...	7	Crockett	7 271	3 719	2 929	0.5	35.7	0.4	0.6	0.4	63.2	8.0	18.7	6.5	11.9	12.0	15.1
48 107	31180	3	Crosby	2 332	6 059	2 761	2.6	43.9	3.6	0.5	0.2	52.3	8.3	20.5	7.2	10.9	11.0	13.0
48 109	...	9	Culberson	9 875	2 398	3 017	0.2	22.0	0.5	1.0	1.3	76.2	7.5	20.4	8.7	10.2	12.1	13.7
48 111	...	7	Dallam	3 893	6 703	2 712	1.7	56.8	1.4	1.5	0.7	40.5	9.3	20.6	9.4	14.0	13.9	13.0
48 113	19100	1	Dallas	2 257	2 368 139	9	1 049.2	34.1	22.5	0.7	5.5	38.3	8.1	19.5	10.0	16.3	14.5	13.4
48 115	29500	7	Dawson	2 332	13 833	2 194	5.9	39.6	6.6	0.4	0.5	53.4	7.6	17.1	10.2	17.0	11.8	12.5
48 117	25820	6	Deaf Smith	3 877	19 372	1 862	5.0	31.1	1.0	0.5	0.4	67.3	9.5	22.7	9.6	13.3	11.8	11.9
48 119	19100	1	Delta	665	5 231	2 825	7.9	85.3	8.0	2.4	0.8	5.5	5.9	16.7	7.5	9.6	11.6	14.9
48 121	19100	1	Denton	2 275	662 614	91	291.3	66.1	8.9	1.1	7.4	18.2	7.5	20.0	10.6	15.1	16.3	14.5
48 123	...	6	DeWitt	2 354	20 097	1 833	8.5	57.8	9.3	0.5	0.3	32.4	6.2	16.2	6.9	11.1	12.5	15.3
48 125	...	8	Dickens	2 335	2 444	3 014	1.0	65.7	3.8	1.3	0.8	29.0	5.4	14.7	7.4	13.7	11.6	15.1
48 127	...	6	Dimmit	3 442	9 996	2 447	2.9	12.3	0.8	0.1	0.5	86.2	8.2	21.8	8.7	10.5	11.4	12.6
48 129	...	8	Donley	2 401	3 677	2 933	1.5	86.4	4.9	1.0	0.5	8.4	5.5	15.1	12.6	9.8	9.6	13.3
48 131	...	7	Duval	4 645	11 782	2 312	2.5	10.4	0.7	0.2	0.2	88.5	7.2	18.9	9.7	11.6	11.6	13.8
48 133	...	6	Eastland	2 400	18 583	1 892	7.7	82.9	2.0	0.9	0.5	14.4	6.0	16.4	10.0	10.4	9.6	14.4
48 135	36220	3	Ector	2 325	137 130	449	59.0	41.8	4.4	0.8	1.0	52.7	8.8	20.2	11.2	14.4	12.0	13.3
48 137	...	9	Edwards	5 485	2 002	3 054	0.4	47.5	0.5	0.7	0.1	51.3	5.7	15.1	7.3	8.4	9.6	14.7
48 139	19100	1	Ellis	2 423	149 610	418	61.7	66.5	9.2	0.9	0.9	23.5	7.3	21.6	8.9	12.2	14.0	14.8
48 141	21340	2	El Paso	2 623	800 647	69	305.2	13.7	2.9	0.4	1.4	82.2	8.1	22.0	11.2	13.3	13.1	12.7
48 143	44500	7	Erath	2 805	37 890	1 219	13.5	78.5	1.3	1.0	0.9	19.2	6.3	16.0	19.4	12.4	10.7	12.3
48 145	...	6	Falls	1 983	17 866	1 929	9.0	53.3	25.4	0.8	0.4	20.8	6.0	15.7	9.3	12.9	13.0	14.8
48 147	14300	6	Fannin	2 307	33 915	1 328	14.7	82.4	7.2	1.8	0.6	9.5	5.8	16.3	8.3	12.1	12.7	15.1
48 149	...	6	Fayette	2 461	24 554	1 622	10.0	74.1	6.9	0.5	0.4	18.7	5.6	16.3	6.3	9.5	10.3	15.4
48 151	...	8	Fisher	2 328	3 974	2 912	1.7	71.0	3.3	0.8	0.2	25.1	5.5	17.1	6.5	8.6	11.5	14.7
48 153	...	6	Floyd	2 570	6 446	2 732	2.5	43.4	3.4	0.3	0.2	52.9	7.6	21.2	7.2	10.4	11.1	13.1
48 155	...	9	Foard	1 824	1 336	3 093	0.7	81.7	4.0	0.3	0.3	14.0	4.3	16.5	7.2	8.2	11.1	15.8
48 157	26420	1	Fort Bend	2 231	585 375	107	262.4	37.4	21.7	0.5	18.0	23.7	7.5	22.2	7.9	12.5	15.9	15.8
48 159	...	8	Franklin	737	10 605	2 393	14.4	82.3	4.4	1.3	0.6	12.6	6.6	17.9	7.8	9.9	11.1	14.0
48 161	...	7	Freestone	2 273	19 816	1 850	8.7	69.7	16.3	0.7	0.5	13.6	6.2	17.2	6.9	12.1	13.0	14.9
48 163	...	6	Frio	2 936	17 217	1 959	5.9	16.6	3.2	0.4	2.2	77.8	7.0	17.7	12.2	17.2	12.9	11.9
48 165	...	7	Gaines	3 891	17 526	1 949	4.5	61.3	1.7	0.5	0.3	36.6	10.4	24.5	10.3	13.6	11.5	12.6
48 167	26420	1	Galveston	980	291 309	222	297.3	60.5	14.0	0.8	3.5	22.4	6.9	18.6	8.8	12.9	13.5	15.8
48 169	...	6	Garza	2 314	6 461	2 731	2.8	46.2	6.3	0.5	0.2	47.1	5.9	13.8	13.9	18.5	11.6	15.0
48 171	23240	7	Gillespie	2 741	24 837	1 607	9.1	79.0	0.3	0.6	0.5	20.0	5.0	15.3	5.6	8.2	9.8	13.9
48 173	...	8	Glasscock	2 332	1 226	3 098	0.5	67.5	1.4	0.3	0.2	30.8	6.4	22.3	5.4	12.3	12.4	15.5
48 175	47020	3	Goliad	2 207	7 210	2 667	3.3	60.8	4.6	0.7	0.3	34.1	5.3	17.5	6.3	8.3	11.7	15.6
48 177	...	6	Gonzales	2 763	19 807	1 851	7.2	45.2	7.1	0.4	0.5	47.2	7.7	19.4	8.7	11.6	11.6	14.1
48 179	37420	6	Gray	2 398	22 535	1 710	9.4	70.4	5.1	1.4	0.6	23.8	7.3	17.5	7.6	12.9	12.9	14.3
48 181	43300	3	Grayson	2 416	120 877	500	50.0	80.5	6.4	2.4	1.2	11.3	6.5	17.6	9.3	11.4	12.2	14.9
48 183	30980	3	Gregg	708	121 730	497	171.9	62.0	20.6	0.9	1.4	16.4	7.5	18.0	10.5	13.7	12.0	13.7
48 185	...	6	Grimes	2 040	26 604	1 541	13.0	61.8	16.8	0.9	0.4	21.2	5.9	16.8	8.2	12.5	13.1	16.2

1. CBSA = Core Based Statistical Area. See Appendix A for explanation. See Appendix B for list of metropolitan areas with component counties.   2. County type code from the Economic Research Service of USDA Rural-Urban Continuum Codes. See Appendix A for definition.   3. Dry land or land partially or temporarily covered by water.   4. May be of any race.

Table B. States and Counties — **Population and Households**

	Population, 2010 (cont.)				Population change and components of change, 1990–2010							Households, 2010				
	Age (percent) (cont.)				Total persons		Percent change		Components of change, 2000–2009						Percent	
STATE County	55 to 64 years	65 to 74 years	75 years and over	Percent female	1990	2000	1990– 2000	2000– 2010	Births	Deaths	Net migration	Number	Percent change, 2000– 2010	Persons per house- hold	Female family house- holder[1]	One per- son
	16	17	18	19	20	21	22	23	24	25	26	27	28	29	30	31
TEXAS—Cont'd																
Caldwell	11.3	6.4	5.4	49.6	26 392	32 194	22.0	18.2	4 891	2 590	3 473	12 301	13.7	2.82	14.5	23.1
Calhoun	12.3	8.5	6.7	49.3	19 053	20 647	8.4	3.6	2 884	1 702	-1 177	7 766	4.4	2.72	11.7	23.2
Callahan	14.2	10.4	7.8	51.2	11 859	12 905	8.8	5.0	1 326	1 366	630	5 447	7.6	2.47	10.0	24.7
Cameron	9.3	6.1	5.0	51.9	260 120	335 227	28.9	21.2	79 503	19 083	3 050	119 631	23.0	3.36	20.0	16.4
Camp	13.1	9.1	7.0	50.9	9 904	11 549	16.6	7.4	1 832	1 283	772	4 678	7.9	2.64	14.5	24.9
Carson	13.9	9.0	8.2	50.8	6 576	6 516	-0.9	-5.1	677	590	-476	2 452	-0.7	2.49	7.9	23.7
Cass	13.9	10.8	8.3	51.5	29 982	30 438	1.5	0.1	3 150	3 567	-631	12 429	2.0	2.42	13.8	27.3
Castro	11.2	6.9	6.5	49.3	9 070	8 285	-8.7	-2.7	1 199	560	-1 778	2 744	-0.6	2.91	10.5	21.5
Chambers	11.9	5.7	3.7	49.7	20 088	26 031	29.6	34.8	3 383	1 808	3 951	11 952	30.8	2.92	9.9	16.7
Cherokee	12.3	8.3	6.7	49.2	41 049	46 659	13.7	9.0	6 870	4 700	-77	17 894	7.5	2.68	14.1	24.1
Childress	10.1	7.7	7.4	41.5	5 953	7 688	29.1	-8.4	797	738	-160	2 326	-6.0	2.42	11.0	30.8
Clay	15.2	10.5	7.3	50.9	10 024	11 006	9.8	-2.3	907	961	-16	4 319	-0.1	2.47	8.3	23.9
Cochran	11.1	8.8	6.1	50.9	4 377	3 730	-14.8	-16.2	520	306	-1 026	1 113	-15.0	2.74	13.7	24.0
Coke	14.4	14.4	11.6	51.0	3 424	3 864	12.9	-14.1	275	507	-304	1 466	-5.1	2.24	8.0	31.2
Coleman	15.0	11.9	9.9	50.4	9 710	9 235	-4.9	-3.7	942	1 392	-252	3 857	-0.8	2.30	10.9	31.0
Collin	9.7	4.9	2.8	50.9	264 036	491 675	86.2	59.1	96 314	21 836	221 337	283 759	55.9	2.74	9.6	22.0
Collingsworth	11.8	8.5	9.4	51.0	3 573	3 206	-10.3	-4.6	403	396	-139	1 179	-8.9	2.55	10.9	26.5
Colorado	14.2	10.2	9.2	50.4	18 383	20 390	10.9	2.4	2 483	2 243	158	8 182	7.1	2.51	10.9	27.1
Comal	14.9	9.1	6.5	50.9	51 832	78 021	50.5	39.0	11 514	7 041	32 148	41 363	42.3	2.60	9.6	21.4
Comanche	13.2	11.9	9.0	50.7	13 381	14 026	4.8	-0.4	1 612	1 717	-290	5 580	1.1	2.48	9.2	27.8
Concho	12.3	8.3	5.4	31.7	3 044	3 966	30.3	3.1	274	281	-362	1 041	-1.6	2.40	10.2	26.5
Cooke	13.2	8.8	7.1	50.4	30 777	36 363	18.1	5.7	5 074	3 560	995	14 513	6.4	2.60	11.1	24.1
Coryell	7.6	4.6	2.9	51.1	64 226	74 978	16.7	0.5	8 609	3 235	-7 574	22 545	13.0	2.84	13.8	20.4
Cottle	15.0	12.8	11.0	52.6	2 247	1 904	-15.3	-21.0	176	201	-308	677	-17.4	2.22	11.5	33.1
Crane	10.7	6.3	5.0	51.0	4 652	3 996	-14.1	9.5	540	341	-19	1 471	8.2	2.92	10.7	19.2
Crockett	13.1	8.5	6.2	50.8	4 078	4 099	0.5	-9.3	523	289	-585	1 422	-6.7	2.58	9.6	24.4
Crosby	11.8	9.5	8.0	51.9	7 304	7 072	-3.2	-14.3	1 003	667	-1 284	2 237	-10.9	2.68	12.4	25.0
Culberson	12.8	8.5	6.3	51.3	3 407	2 975	-12.7	-19.4	350	163	-869	908	-13.7	2.63	17.0	27.0
Dallam	10.4	5.7	3.7	48.1	5 461	6 222	13.9	7.7	1 016	466	-460	2 448	5.7	2.72	11.3	24.4
Dallas	9.4	4.9	3.9	50.6	1 852 691	2 218 899	19.8	6.7	395 761	129 399	-59 446	855 960	6.0	2.73	16.0	28.0
Dawson	9.8	7.1	6.9	43.5	14 349	14 985	4.4	-7.7	1 875	1 298	-1 843	4 385	-7.2	2.67	13.3	26.1
Deaf Smith	8.7	6.0	5.5	50.2	19 153	18 561	-3.1	4.4	3 366	1 380	-2 133	6 365	3.0	2.99	14.2	20.2
Delta	14.0	11.9	8.0	51.0	4 857	5 327	9.7	-1.8	552	619	178	2 088	-0.3	2.47	11.7	25.8
Denton	9.1	4.4	2.5	50.8	273 644	432 976	58.2	53.0	82 618	19 350	159 464	240 289	51.2	2.71	10.2	22.7
DeWitt	13.5	9.0	9.3	48.0	18 840	20 013	6.2	0.4	2 204	2 348	-33	7 407	2.8	2.47	12.5	28.3
Dickens	12.4	11.3	8.4	43.4	2 571	2 762	7.4	-11.5	220	292	-247	930	-5.1	2.29	7.5	30.3
Dimmit	12.5	7.4	6.8	51.6	10 433	10 248	-1.8	-2.5	1 603	751	-1 278	3 421	3.4	2.89	19.8	22.0
Donley	13.0	11.3	9.9	50.4	3 696	3 828	3.6	-3.9	335	434	-69	1 517	-3.9	2.27	9.7	31.3
Duval	11.1	8.9	7.2	48.4	12 918	13 120	1.6	-10.2	1 810	1 139	-1 736	4 090	-6.0	2.74	17.6	25.0
Eastland	13.4	10.7	9.2	51.2	18 488	18 297	-1.0	1.6	2 130	2 497	350	7 465	2.0	2.37	11.2	29.9
Ector	10.0	5.6	4.6	50.6	118 934	121 123	1.8	13.2	21 870	9 969	2 232	48 688	11.0	2.77	15.4	24.5
Edwards	17.2	13.1	8.7	49.0	2 266	2 162	-4.6	-7.4	228	147	-381	839	4.7	2.38	8.6	28.0
Ellis	11.1	6.0	4.0	50.6	85 167	111 360	30.8	34.3	19 112	8 480	30 084	50 503	36.4	2.93	12.4	17.5
El Paso	9.3	5.5	4.7	51.6	591 610	679 622	14.9	17.8	133 078	39 858	-17 748	256 557	22.2	3.06	20.3	19.8
Erath	10.3	6.8	5.9	50.0	27 991	33 001	17.9	14.8	4 410	2 967	1 969	14 569	15.9	2.47	8.4	27.0
Falls	12.2	8.5	7.6	52.5	17 712	18 576	4.9	-3.8	1 891	2 034	-1 567	6 302	-3.0	2.51	15.1	28.9
Fannin	12.7	9.4	7.6	47.0	24 804	31 242	26.0	8.6	3 573	3 962	2 331	12 149	9.4	2.53	10.9	25.1
Fayette	15.1	11.2	10.3	50.8	20 095	21 804	8.5	12.6	2 389	2 932	1 735	10 078	15.5	2.39	8.9	27.3
Fisher	13.9	11.4	10.8	50.7	4 842	4 344	-10.3	-8.5	326	512	-275	1 668	-6.6	2.37	9.5	29.0
Floyd	11.5	8.8	8.9	50.7	8 497	7 771	-8.5	-17.1	1 002	691	-1 587	2 402	-12.0	2.67	12.0	23.5
Foard	13.0	12.4	11.5	52.3	1 794	1 622	-9.6	-17.6	118	153	-249	573	-13.7	2.28	8.9	30.0
Fort Bend	11.0	4.6	2.7	50.8	225 421	354 452	57.2	65.1	59 898	16 516	156 096	187 384	68.9	3.09	12.9	14.9
Franklin	13.9	10.5	8.1	50.8	7 802	9 458	21.2	12.1	1 121	1 015	1 327	4 159	10.8	2.52	11.5	24.8
Freestone	13.2	9.4	7.1	47.3	15 818	17 867	13.0	10.9	2 126	1 954	1 454	7 259	10.2	2.51	10.5	27.0
Frio	9.8	6.2	5.1	41.7	13 472	16 252	20.6	5.9	2 356	1 094	-1 295	4 854	2.3	2.87	18.4	23.5
Gaines	8.2	5.0	4.0	49.8	14 123	14 467	2.4	21.1	2 749	894	-894	5 606	19.8	3.11	9.5	18.2
Galveston	12.3	6.5	4.8	50.5	217 396	250 158	15.1	16.5	37 219	21 491	22 127	108 969	15.0	2.63	13.5	24.7
Garza	10.5	6.1	4.8	36.7	5 143	4 872	-5.3	32.6	620	461	-368	1 671	0.5	2.60	12.7	25.5
Gillespie	15.6	13.2	13.3	51.8	17 204	20 814	21.0	19.3	2 252	2 686	3 886	10 572	24.1	2.31	8.0	28.4
Glasscock	12.6	8.3	4.7	47.1	1 447	1 406	-2.8	-12.8	116	38	-264	441	-8.7	2.78	3.9	18.8
Goliad	16.2	10.7	8.3	50.1	5 980	6 928	15.9	4.1	715	653	86	2 868	8.5	2.48	11.0	24.8
Gonzales	11.7	8.1	7.0	49.7	17 205	18 628	8.3	6.3	3 154	1 840	-221	7 120	5.0	2.74	13.8	24.9
Gray	11.5	8.2	7.8	48.1	23 967	22 744	-5.1	-0.9	2 832	2 551	-826	8 443	-4.0	2.48	10.1	27.5
Grayson	12.6	8.5	7.0	51.3	95 019	110 595	16.4	9.3	14 731	11 608	6 936	46 905	9.5	2.53	12.2	25.5
Gregg	11.1	6.9	6.6	51.1	104 948	111 379	6.1	9.3	17 488	11 001	2 519	45 798	7.3	2.56	14.8	27.0
Grimes	13.5	8.2	5.6	45.5	18 843	23 552	25.0	13.0	3 131	2 156	1 613	8 902	14.8	2.65	12.5	24.1

1. No spouse present.

Table B. States and Counties — Population, Vital Statistics, Medicare, and Crime

STATE County	Daytime population, 2006–2010 — Persons in group quarters, 2010	Number	Employment/residence ratio	Births, average 2006–2008 — Total	Rate[1]	Deaths, average 2006–2008 — Number	Rate[1]	Persons under 65 with no health insurance, 2009 — Number	Percent	Medicare, 2011 — Eligible for Medicare	Enrolled in Medicare Advantage	Enrolled in a Medicare prescription drug plan	Serious crimes known to police,[2] 2010 Total — Number	Rate[3]
	32	33	34	35	36	37	38	39	40	41	42	43	44	45
TEXAS—Cont'd														
Caldwell	3 376	30 812	0.6	D	D	293	8.0	8 692	26.9	5 533	526	2 399	955	2 509
Calhoun	249	24 195	1.3	D	D	197	9.6	4 757	27.5	3 694	214	1 533	652	3 049
Callahan	75	10 233	0.4	D	D	156	11.5	2 745	25.2	2 877	245	1 227	201	1 484
Cameron	3 730	391 084	1.0	8 428	21.7	2 182	5.6	125 976	36.6	49 386	10 300	24 557	19 823	4 880
Camp	67	11 554	0.9	D	D	151	12.1	2 970	28.2	2 456	363	1 166	316	2 548
Carson	71	5 189	0.6	D	D	68	10.7	838	16.7	1 117	93	516	78	1 262
Cass	354	27 494	0.8	D	D	390	13.2	5 162	22.5	6 977	822	3 129	830	2 725
Castro	64	7 218	0.8	D	D	59	8.1	2 062	34.6	1 138	44	655	300	3 721
Chambers	229	28 198	0.7	D	D	204	7.1	5 521	19.6	4 497	720	1 638	996	2 838
Cherokee	2 851	47 491	0.9	758	15.7	510	10.6	11 224	27.9	9 145	1 011	4 206	1 767	3 489
Childress	1 418	7 336	1.1	D	D	81	10.6	2 182	34.9	1 241	56	606	112	1 591
Clay	70	8 135	0.4	D	D	107	9.7	2 093	23.1	2 243	90	1 070	140	1 302
Cochran	78	3 009	0.9	D	D	28	9.1	798	32.9	563	43	328	73	2 335
Coke	35	3 044	0.8	D	D	54	15.3	736	30.8	844	51	398	17	512
Coleman	40	8 361	0.8	D	D	142	16.5	1 981	31.0	2 256	144	1 173	296	3 328
Collin	3 914	689 864	0.9	10 996	15.1	2 689	3.7	118 558	16.5	72 334	12 703	28 308	20 201	2 582
Collingsworth	52	2 921	0.9	D	D	44	15.0	800	33.2	603	27	343	0	0
Colorado	328	19 729	0.9	D	D	248	11.9	4 913	29.9	4 462	161	2 452	408	1 955
Comal	1 060	97 105	0.9	1 286	12.2	814	7.7	18 832	19.6	20 958	4 184	6 180	2 974	2 742
Comanche	161	12 900	0.8	D	D	185	13.6	3 562	33.8	3 226	199	1 616	406	2 905
Concho	1 588	4 217	1.2	D	D	33	9.1	1 251	42.5	597	30	292	46	1 126
Cooke	686	36 161	0.9	584	15.1	395	10.2	8 705	27.0	6 918	632	3 267	1 106	2 877
Coryell	11 444	60 917	0.6	1 012	14.0	372	5.1	16 043	24.7	7 356	1 330	1 559	1 592	2 112
Cottle	0	1 508	0.8	D	D	30	18.3	423	36.9	459	15	264	25	1 661
Crane	86	3 961	0.9	D	D	37	9.4	989	27.2	585	53	262	66	1 509
Crockett	49	3 987	1.1	D	D	39	10.2	1 014	32.2	605	22	342	NA	NA
Crosby	62	5 603	0.8	D	D	70	11.1	1 454	29.2	1 195	138	653	81	1 337
Culberson	12	2 692	1.2	D	D	15	6.0	729	38.3	431	17	279	15	626
Dallam	39	6 776	1.1	D	D	56	9.1	1 968	35.9	890	48	473	129	1 925
Dallas	30 398	2 654 575	1.3	43 844	18.5	13 937	5.9	695 939	31.9	255 861	51 808	108 599	117 842	4 976
Dawson	2 146	14 258	1.1	D	D	128	9.2	3 536	30.9	2 258	141	1 342	285	2 060
Deaf Smith	371	19 427	1.0	375	20.2	147	7.9	5 314	33.7	2 583	261	1 420	551	2 844
Delta	69	3 960	0.4	D	D	67	12.2	1 087	25.3	1 212	68	576	121	2 313
Denton	10 344	499 825	0.6	9 409	15.4	2 397	3.9	107 194	17.7	57 531	10 319	21 203	16 904	2 551
DeWitt	1 790	19 512	0.9	D	D	252	12.7	4 293	27.0	4 120	142	2 313	317	1 577
Dickens	315	2 463	1.0	D	D	26	10.2	678	35.3	499	26	304	6	245
Dimmit	104	10 335	1.1	D	D	81	8.1	2 437	29.3	1 689	269	1 049	204	2 041
Donley	240	3 444	0.9	D	D	54	13.9	921	32.6	841	34	427	49	1 333
Duval	578	11 339	0.9	D	D	115	9.4	2 590	25.9	2 227	447	1 238	372	3 157
Eastland	885	18 051	0.9	D	D	247	13.5	4 212	29.5	4 176	419	1 985	305	1 641
Ector	2 175	131 222	1.0	2 625	20.2	1 133	8.7	34 540	29.2	17 153	1 892	8 688	5 706	4 161
Edwards	5	2 016	1.0	D	D	15	7.7	614	36.8	474	20	219	34	1 698
Ellis	1 610	121 981	0.7	2 166	15.1	919	6.4	30 707	23.0	19 115	2 266	8 243	3 741	2 501
El Paso	15 792	770 090	1.0	14 233	19.3	4 364	5.9	207 206	31.5	102 200	35 310	33 006	24 099	3 010
Erath	1 888	37 013	1.0	D	D	314	8.9	9 309	30.2	5 410	539	2 326	834	2 201
Falls	2 068	15 818	0.7	D	D	217	12.6	4 007	29.2	3 195	632	1 281	301	1 685
Fannin	3 145	28 955	0.6	D	D	440	13.3	7 245	27.1	6 696	496	3 036	610	1 799
Fayette	455	22 994	0.9	D	D	319	14.1	4 441	25.4	5 682	309	2 679	425	1 731
Fisher	22	3 570	0.7	D	D	58	14.5	819	27.7	928	50	476	64	1 610
Floyd	35	5 976	0.8	D	D	74	11.1	1 612	31.0	1 228	129	672	165	2 560
Foard	30	1 307	0.9	D	D	21	14.9	331	33.1	355	D	183	7	524
Fort Bend	5 936	421 014	0.5	7 468	14.6	2 007	3.9	95 641	18.7	50 774	11 261	18 384	13 784	2 356
Franklin	114	10 421	0.9	D	D	112	10.4	2 262	26.1	2 130	241	1 044	138	1 301
Freestone	1 581	19 261	1.0	D	D	202	10.7	4 113	25.9	3 451	231	1 541	344	1 736
Frio	3 271	16 814	1.0	D	D	115	7.1	4 352	31.6	2 243	369	1 383	361	2 097
Gaines	87	15 967	0.9	D	D	107	7.2	4 980	37.0	1 750	89	1 011	174	993
Galveston	4 297	255 690	0.8	4 211	14.8	2 373	8.3	54 462	21.8	40 084	6 102	14 270	11 121	3 818
Garza	2 109	6 433	1.1	D	D	48	10.1	1 209	31.0	783	110	389	38	588
Gillespie	390	24 063	1.0	D	D	291	12.3	4 828	27.5	6 835	390	2 934	339	1 365
Glasscock	0	1 363	1.1	D	D	D	D	303	28.7	176	D	99	14	1 142
Goliad	93	5 819	0.6	D	D	69	9.7	1 470	25.8	1 439	75	737	70	971
Gonzales	311	19 129	0.9	337	17.5	198	10.3	5 196	32.0	3 462	221	1 911	536	2 706
Gray	1 610	22 690	1.0	353	16.0	277	12.6	4 976	27.9	4 076	307	1 998	1 027	4 557
Grayson	2 214	115 080	0.9	1 583	13.3	1 285	10.8	25 202	25.4	22 967	1 818	9 986	3 944	3 263
Gregg	4 414	138 204	1.3	2 038	17.4	1 221	10.4	24 695	24.6	20 499	2 695	9 634	6 400	5 258
Grimes	3 012	24 664	0.8	D	D	223	8.7	6 075	28.2	4 267	519	1 853	615	2 312

1. Per 1,000 estimated resident population.   2. Data for serious crimes have not been adjusted for underreporting; this may affect comparability between geographic areas and over time.   3. Per 100,000 population estimated by the FBI.

Table B. States and Counties — Crime, Education, Money Income, and Poverty

STATE County	Serious crimes known to police,[1] 2010 (cont.) Rate[2]		Education School enrollment and attainment, 2006–2010				Local government expenditures,[5] 2008–2009		Money income, 2006–2010	Households Median income			Income and poverty, 2010 Percent below poverty level		
			Enrollment[3]		Attainment[4] (percent)										
	Violent	Property	Total	Percent private	High school graduate or less	Bachelor's degree or more	Total current expenditures (mil dol)	Current expenditures per student (dollars)	Per capita income[6] (dollars)	Dollars	Percent change, 2000 to 2006–2010 (constant 2010 dollars)	Percent with income of $200,000 or more	Median household income (dollars)	All persons	Children under 18 years	Children 5 to 17 years in families
	46	47	48	49	50	51	52	53	54	55	56	57	58	59	60	61
TEXAS—Cont'd																
Caldwell	342	2 167	9 352	7.8	62.7	14.3	52.1	8 340	18 106	41 594	-10.2	1.2	41 749	17.3	25.7	25.1
Calhoun	650	2 399	5 195	9.2	55.8	14.7	38.9	8 846	22 835	43 258	-4.7	1.7	42 745	19.4	30.7	26.4
Callahan	103	1 381	3 392	13.6	49.4	17.1	35.6	13 870	22 300	44 596	8.5	1.5	40 614	15.4	24.9	22.0
Cameron	331	4 549	124 095	5.0	62.0	14.5	872.7	8 877	13 695	31 264	-5.6	1.5	31 624	35.8	48.5	44.9
Camp	185	2 363	3 046	4.2	58.2	14.9	22.0	9 334	18 710	36 029	-8.7	1.4	37 704	21.3	33.7	31.2
Carson	146	1 116	1 601	4.8	44.9	23.6	13.4	10 172	24 977	56 106	10.0	1.7	51 311	8.4	10.6	9.2
Cass	295	2 429	7 072	8.0	57.4	12.9	49.7	8 794	20 137	36 360	1.0	1.6	34 556	20.4	32.4	28.2
Castro	136	3 585	2 186	4.1	63.1	14.9	14.9	8 968	16 073	35 087	-9.5	0.6	35 973	20.2	29.9	27.7
Chambers	228	2 610	9 139	6.9	45.2	16.2	72.7	11 162	26 453	66 764	9.9	2.1	69 491	10.6	14.2	12.9
Cherokee	357	3 132	11 956	6.5	63.0	11.8	83.3	8 144	17 230	36 966	-0.4	1.1	34 910	24.7	35.4	32.7
Childress	383	1 207	1 441	10.3	59.5	15.7	11.5	10 407	16 338	42 004	20.8	3.6	35 171	22.8	32.8	30.6
Clay	93	1 209	2 399	6.6	49.7	19.3	17.8	9 791	24 565	50 881	12.4	1.7	47 434	12.5	18.3	16.7
Cochran	0	2 335	837	3.6	64.7	11.7	19.4	14 835	16 018	37 446	7.4	0.2	35 496	20.5	33.8	31.6
Coke	30	482	748	5.7	53.1	11.8	6.4	11 600	18 384	38 702	5.1	0.9	35 754	13.2	22.4	20.0
Coleman	124	3 204	1 723	3.3	60.7	13.7	15.2	9 920	16 494	26 951	-17.0	1.5	30 637	21.1	36.0	33.2
Collin	185	2 397	214 257	15.6	23.0	48.3	1 261.6	8 134	37 362	80 504	-10.2	9.1	77 862	7.7	9.6	8.2
Collingsworth	0	0	721	1.7	56.7	18.3	6.5	10 171	21 726	39 712	23.3	5.0	32 949	18.9	31.2	30.1
Colorado	206	1 749	4 470	16.5	60.1	15.3	31.1	9 131	22 676	41 145	0.2	3.3	41 395	17.3	27.6	24.6
Comal	311	2 431	24 151	16.1	36.5	32.6	186.6	7 872	31 862	64 752	10.8	5.8	61 573	11.9	16.5	14.2
Comanche	293	2 612	2 962	5.6	57.8	18.1	21.4	9 469	18 086	35 218	-2.1	0.7	34 878	20.7	30.1	28.2
Concho	98	1 028	509	3.7	67.1	10.5	4.7	11 309	17 731	49 063	23.7	0.3	33 711	28.4	32.2	30.6
Cooke	216	2 661	9 360	11.2	49.2	19.5	54.5	8 845	23 598	48 899	2.6	2.2	45 428	15.1	24.4	22.5
Coryell	236	1 876	20 340	6.9	44.8	15.4	89.8	8 121	18 936	47 374	3.9	1.1	45 431	12.4	15.4	15.1
Cottle	0	1 661	421	3.6	59.2	15.9	2.6	10 266	17 385	33 859	5.1	0.8	31 892	20.4	32.9	28.2
Crane	137	1 371	1 174	0.0	58.1	13.1	13.2	12 910	20 185	50 425	23.7	0.6	50 356	9.9	15.3	14.3
Crockett	NA	NA	857	4.6	60.2	9.1	10.0	13 195	24 194	50 653	36.3	6.6	42 329	15.8	26.3	23.2
Crosby	149	1 188	1 560	2.9	63.3	13.3	16.0	12 831	17 940	36 301	11.2	1.9	33 332	27.1	40.0	38.1
Culberson	209	417	781	0.0	72.0	13.8	6.2	12 427	16 000	35 500	8.3	7.7	30 666	26.2	39.3	35.7
Dallam	269	1 656	1 711	22.6	64.2	8.4	15.9	9 019	18 940	47 073	33.0	2.3	37 454	15.1	22.5	21.8
Dallas	498	4 479	623 383	13.8	46.8	28.0	3 810.0	8 480	26 185	47 974	-12.6	4.8	46 909	19.0	29.3	28.7
Dawson	195	1 865	3 411	5.9	67.4	8.7	25.5	10 119	15 288	33 623	-5.9	1.0	33 938	25.7	35.5	35.9
Deaf Smith	356	2 488	5 145	7.0	64.8	13.2	36.6	8 470	16 687	41 127	9.7	0.6	36 638	20.6	30.4	29.6
Delta	96	2 218	1 259	3.7	54.8	16.0	7.3	8 594	20 837	37 908	2.9	1.5	36 193	17.7	27.8	26.1
Denton	189	2 362	194 186	12.6	28.4	39.5	938.8	8 521	32 538	70 622	-4.2	6.6	68 671	8.1	9.4	8.9
DeWitt	189	1 388	4 233	6.1	61.1	12.1	40.8	9 383	20 020	40 668	11.8	2.4	36 611	21.3	32.3	30.6
Dickens	82	164	406	4.7	61.3	12.7	5.8	14 979	18 642	33 813	3.1	2.1	32 669	21.4	30.5	27.7
Dimmit	470	1 571	2 490	5.6	71.1	12.6	23.5	9 885	14 045	25 882	-6.7	0.0	29 685	31.0	44.8	41.3
Donley	245	1 088	1 133	5.5	52.7	16.6	7.5	11 171	20 137	46 130	25.6	1.0	34 967	17.0	26.8	25.1
Duval	654	2 504	3 014	3.2	60.7	8.5	28.1	10 587	15 134	30 493	7.4	0.7	30 365	26.9	38.5	35.9
Eastland	145	1 496	4 643	5.9	56.6	15.5	31.0	9 866	17 973	32 452	-4.5	1.5	32 913	22.4	32.5	30.1
Ector	650	3 511	36 721	7.9	57.2	13.1	212.3	7 584	22 859	45 815	16.1	2.9	42 339	19.6	28.3	26.0
Edwards	150	1 548	394	2.8	57.7	22.1	8.3	13 671	31 109	40 163	25.4	4.7	32 643	25.3	39.8	38.3
Ellis	203	2 298	41 442	14.0	47.7	21.0	264.4	7 809	25 346	60 877	-4.5	3.4	57 929	11.5	17.1	15.6
El Paso	421	2 589	255 330	6.8	53.1	19.3	1 505.8	8 636	16 768	36 333	-7.6	1.6	36 064	24.6	33.8	33.1
Erath	203	1 998	12 293	2.1	47.5	24.0	47.9	8 204	20 903	39 200	0.8	2.3	38 068	18.5	23.7	22.4
Falls	185	1 500	4 374	4.5	62.4	9.8	25.9	9 905	14 979	31 083	-7.7	0.1	30 576	25.3	32.4	31.6
Fannin	147	1 651	7 512	10.9	57.9	14.7	50.9	8 993	20 221	44 551	2.0	1.5	40 891	16.2	24.1	22.2
Fayette	114	1 617	4 906	7.9	56.4	17.6	32.8	9 058	26 898	45 450	4.0	2.7	45 123	13.0	19.7	18.1
Fisher	252	1 359	961	4.1	60.9	15.2	6.7	10 306	20 516	41 458	18.4	1.6	35 794	14.6	23.5	21.8
Floyd	372	2 187	1 794	3.9	57.2	17.1	16.2	11 200	18 093	35 240	3.6	0.0	33 345	21.0	34.5	32.2
Foard	75	449	249	0.0	60.0	15.6	3.0	12 381	18 368	30 417	-6.9	0.5	31 479	18.2	29.1	25.8
Fort Bend	319	2 037	167 482	14.4	31.7	40.4	1 188.7	7 691	32 016	79 845	-1.2	9.7	76 758	9.0	12.5	11.2
Franklin	207	1 094	2 718	5.0	49.1	23.6	12.7	8 406	23 821	45 625	12.8	3.2	40 579	15.9	25.3	23.5
Freestone	232	1 504	4 641	3.4	56.2	14.0	37.9	10 320	23 235	44 560	12.5	4.7	42 266	18.1	23.7	21.8
Frio	203	1 893	4 706	6.2	72.9	8.1	32.6	10 359	15 036	35 940	15.8	1.3	30 820	35.3	42.7	40.1
Gaines	80	913	4 151	16.2	69.0	12.9	38.3	12 343	22 785	46 393	20.4	4.3	39 111	18.8	26.6	26.5
Galveston	348	3 470	78 735	10.6	41.2	26.3	637.3	8 577	28 959	58 317	8.6	4.4	57 124	13.0	19.5	18.4
Garza	31	557	1 508	6.0	68.0	8.6	12.1	12 068	16 185	35 750	3.8	1.8	38 400	27.4	30.0	28.6
Gillespie	36	1 329	4 446	18.2	43.0	26.8	32.1	9 319	28 072	52 682	9.2	3.2	47 216	12.1	20.1	17.9
Glasscock	82	1 060	425	9.4	48.4	16.4	4.6	17 737	26 104	61 184	35.5	2.1	54 354	11.2	18.2	16.1
Goliad	250	721	1 583	11.7	52.3	18.0	13.5	10 252	28 120	51 786	19.6	3.5	42 646	15.5	25.3	22.5
Gonzales	545	2 161	4 397	9.9	65.5	13.9	33.0	8 676	18 716	37 094	3.3	1.8	34 166	20.8	31.7	30.2
Gray	541	4 016	4 981	8.7	55.6	12.2	30.8	8 078	20 567	40 442	1.8	2.1	42 701	15.4	21.6	20.9
Grayson	280	2 982	29 604	11.7	47.7	19.2	182.1	8 665	23 242	46 875	-0.4	2.0	44 356	14.9	21.4	19.8
Gregg	603	4 655	30 410	13.1	46.9	20.3	206.2	8 756	23 024	43 367	-2.2	2.4	41 623	20.5	29.8	28.1
Grimes	320	1 992	5 745	6.3	63.7	11.3	38.2	9 045	17 365	39 429	-3.5	0.5	39 959	19.7	27.5	25.5

1. Data for serious crimes have not been adjusted for underreporting; this may affect comparability between geographic areas and over time.   2. Per 100,000 population estimated by the FBI.   3. All persons 3 years old and over enrolled in nursery school through college.   4. Persons 25 years old and over.   5. Elementary and secondary education expenditures.   6. Based on population estimated by the American Community Survey, 2006–2010.

Table B. States and Counties — **Personal Income**

	Personal income, 2009												
			Per capita[1]					Transfer payments (mil dol)					
									Government payments to individuals				
STATE County	Total (mil dol)	Percent change, 2008–2009	Dollars	Rank	Wages and salaries[2] (mil dol)	Proprietors' income (mil dol)	Dividends, interest, and rent (mil dol)	Total	Total	Social Security	Medical payments	Income mainte-nance	Unemploy-ment insurance
	62	63	64	65	66	67	68	69	70	71	72	73	74

TEXAS—Cont'd

STATE County	62	63	64	65	66	67	68	69	70	71	72	73	74
Caldwell	958	-0.8	25 328	2 825	266	56	141	240	233	71	112	26	9
Calhoun	648	0.3	31 479	1 645	614	61	104	151	147	51	66	15	5
Callahan	419	-0.8	31 209	1 710	99	23	73	102	100	37	45	7	3
Cameron	8 874	3.2	22 388	3 055	4 747	711	1 202	2 722	2 650	504	1 291	578	99
Camp	402	0.3	31 421	1 660	152	30	88	108	106	34	51	11	3
Carson	227	-1.0	37 163	729	429	14	37	39	38	16	17	2	1
Cass	935	2.1	32 017	1 529	325	88	146	297	292	93	144	26	10
Castro	239	-14.8	33 542	1 245	99	52	32	51	50	15	26	7	1
Chambers	1 422	5.4	45 257	194	592	35	169	161	155	67	57	12	9
Cherokee	1 417	0.6	29 225	2 143	599	133	263	391	382	121	183	40	12
Childress	166	7.2	21 943	3 070	96	15	30	50	49	15	24	5	1
Clay	422	1.4	38 764	558	74	62	63	72	70	31	25	4	3
Cochran	105	-8.0	35 980	889	36	25	19	27	26	7	14	3	1
Coke	96	0.2	29 006	2 195	29	7	20	31	30	12	15	2	1
Coleman	264	-0.7	31 081	1 733	81	22	49	99	97	29	53	7	2
Collin	36 323	-3.8	45 884	175	19 224	3 236	5 879	2 529	2 385	1 013	793	180	197
Collingsworth	93	0.3	30 402	1 886	33	8	21	26	26	8	14	2	1
Colorado	754	-0.4	36 525	812	279	68	174	167	163	60	76	13	5
Comal	4 241	2.0	37 028	749	1 765	280	946	700	679	284	263	40	24
Comanche	413	-2.3	30 474	1 869	145	47	82	125	122	41	61	9	3
Concho	83	1.4	23 152	3 026	37	6	15	25	25	7	14	2	1
Cooke	1 578	-5.1	40 819	395	708	248	327	264	257	95	107	20	10
Coryell	2 651	0.6	36 547	808	650	64	259	356	346	93	124	39	17
Cottle	62	7.9	39 863	456	20	11	15	16	16	5	8	1	0
Crane	133	-4.1	31 813	1 575	95	11	15	24	23	8	11	2	1
Crockett	119	-1.7	31 764	1 587	54	9	29	24	23	8	11	2	1
Crosby	208	0.8	34 095	1 154	64	22	32	63	62	15	37	6	1
Culberson	69	10.0	29 979	1 986	43	6	8	19	19	5	10	3	1
Dallam	221	-2.1	35 142	1 000	162	58	37	45	44	11	25	4	1
Dallas	111 323	-3.0	45 406	188	99 692	23 607	21 031	12 393	11 946	3 493	5 405	1 643	626
Dawson	374	2.4	27 409	2 498	166	41	79	117	115	29	67	12	3
Deaf Smith	516	-0.9	28 132	2 378	290	40	102	126	122	32	66	17	3
Delta	141	-0.4	26 126	2 702	43	8	17	48	47	16	23	4	1
Denton	25 774	0.0	39 133	525	8 699	1 200	3 561	2 199	2 078	811	726	164	164
DeWitt	599	-0.7	30 364	1 894	263	48	128	171	167	52	87	16	5
Dickens	62	7.1	25 593	2 796	25	5	8	25	25	7	16	1	1
Dimmit	252	2.9	25 836	2 755	131	15	34	86	85	17	46	15	3
Donley	118	4.1	32 200	1 482	35	12	20	32	32	11	14	2	1
Duval	342	-1.2	28 454	2 308	138	21	31	130	128	24	80	14	4
Eastland	679	-2.3	37 381	703	246	101	166	182	178	55	89	13	4
Ector	4 516	-4.6	33 544	1 243	3 139	383	599	850	825	235	399	105	39
Edwards	56	3.1	30 181	1 939	20	5	16	17	16	6	7	2	1
Ellis	4 865	0.4	32 059	1 515	1 788	204	622	799	771	269	334	76	37
El Paso	22 073	3.6	29 381	2 124	13 642	2 658	2 927	4 914	4 781	1 052	2 099	884	195
Erath	1 079	-1.7	29 830	2 015	561	67	205	241	234	69	114	16	8
Falls	436	0.5	25 998	2 730	149	17	66	142	139	39	70	15	4
Fannin	936	0.6	28 370	2 332	310	60	156	271	265	90	127	19	8
Fayette	896	-0.7	39 147	522	367	52	261	202	197	75	97	11	5
Fisher	116	-3.8	29 979	1 986	38	8	19	36	35	12	17	2	1
Floyd	212	-1.6	32 738	1 377	72	34	42	57	56	17	29	6	1
Foard	41	-2.9	30 956	1 769	12	2	9	15	15	4	9	1	0
Fort Bend	25 503	2.4	45 798	179	7 957	1 610	3 546	1 839	1 738	664	580	221	129
Franklin	330	-2.6	30 484	1 866	124	45	72	74	72	30	30	6	2
Freestone	575	1.1	29 669	2 058	286	48	116	131	127	46	54	11	4
Frio	393	5.1	24 333	2 931	181	30	47	119	116	24	65	18	4
Gaines	418	-6.4	27 178	2 536	224	50	61	86	83	21	48	8	3
Galveston	11 937	-1.1	41 621	356	5 384	606	2 047	1 800	1 748	573	818	162	78
Garza	172	-0.1	36 939	756	75	34	40	40	39	10	23	4	1
Gillespie	1 081	0.6	44 723	210	359	80	448	210	205	92	90	8	4
Glasscock	47	2.1	38 371	592	15	9	13	5	5	2	1	1	0
Goliad	204	-2.4	29 071	2 179	58	7	49	56	54	18	26	4	2
Gonzales	551	-0.2	28 092	2 386	250	36	108	147	144	44	72	17	4
Gray	869	-4.1	39 357	501	444	122	172	180	176	58	91	12	7
Grayson	3 849	1.2	32 066	1 513	1 978	198	743	931	909	318	414	68	30
Gregg	5 052	-2.0	42 228	311	3 604	880	941	981	960	289	492	87	31
Grimes	723	0.1	27 815	2 436	343	45	132	166	161	57	71	17	7

1. Based on the resident population estimated as of July 1 of the year shown.　2. Includes supplements to wages and salaries.

Table B. States and Counties — **Earnings, Social Security, and Housing**

STATE County	Total (mil dol)	Farm	Goods-related[1] Total	Manu-facturing	Information and profes-sional and technical services	Retail trade	Finance, insur-ance, and real estate	Health care and social services	Govern-ment	Number	Rate[2]	Supple-mental Security Income recipients, December 2010	Total	Percent change, 2000-2010
	75	76	77	78	79	80	81	82	83	84	85	86	87	88
TEXAS—Cont'd														
Caldwell	323	0.1	16.1	3.0	3.2	9.7	5.0	14.5	26.4	6 185	162	958	13 759	15.6
Calhoun	676	0.6	64.0	43.5	D	4.7	2.3	D	11.2	4 165	195	525	11 410	11.4
Callahan	122	-2.5	35.2	5.5	D	10.4	6.5	D	26.3	3 145	232	317	6 549	10.5
Cameron	5 458	0.5	9.2	5.5	5.3	7.9	4.4	22.4	29.4	54 575	134	21 426	141 924	18.6
Camp	181	3.8	D	D	D	9.0	7.2	10.3	15.7	2 785	225	454	5 656	8.2
Carson	444	0.8	D	D	D	1.3	0.6	D	11.7	1 220	197	71	2 784	-1.1
Cass	413	2.4	31.1	22.5	3.1	7.5	5.1	D	21.2	7 980	262	1 115	14 379	3.5
Castro	151	37.8	D	1.6	D	3.5	3.6	D	17.2	1 265	157	162	3 166	-1.0
Chambers	627	0.1	41.0	28.6	D	5.0	7.2	D	14.9	5 255	150	515	13 291	28.6
Cherokee	732	6.2	19.1	12.1	4.2	6.1	5.7	10.3	26.0	10 200	201	1 592	20 859	8.8
Childress	111	5.9	D	D	3.5	9.9	3.6	6.5	48.5	1 335	190	189	2 883	-5.8
Clay	136	2.7	32.9	3.5	D	6.3	4.1	D	18.2	2 490	232	209	5 150	3.2
Cochran	60	17.7	D	0.0	D	3.8	1.9	D	25.0	645	206	131	1 360	-14.3
Coke	36	3.2	D	D	D	5.4	D	2.4	37.2	955	288	67	2 667	-6.2
Coleman	104	-2.2	19.3	2.9	D	10.2	7.1	D	31.1	2 525	284	305	5 543	5.6
Collin	22 460	0.0	17.4	9.4	23.0	6.4	11.2	8.2	9.9	74 830	96	6 514	300 960	54.4
Collingsworth	41	12.7	D	D	D	4.4	5.9	D	26.9	665	218	84	1 616	-6.2
Colorado	346	2.2	28.1	14.6	3.6	7.4	7.5	12.1	14.1	4 800	230	526	10 527	11.7
Comal	2 045	0.1	23.8	10.1	6.5	9.1	3.9	9.7	14.2	22 495	207	1 259	47 108	44.0
Comanche	192	2.3	D	3.8	7.7	8.4	5.9	6.8	23.5	3 520	252	388	7 223	1.7
Concho	42	4.1	D	D	D	3.5	D	4.8	26.3	685	168	67	1 637	10.0
Cooke	956	0.1	46.0	16.8	D	6.1	4.2	D	14.7	7 520	196	650	16 606	10.3
Coryell	714	-1.1	D	3.4	8.5	7.2	5.4	D	40.0	8 690	115	1 103	25 178	15.6
Cottle	30	28.1	D	D	D	6.1	D	3.7	20.3	475	316	55	968	-11.0
Crane	106	0.4	D	D	D	3.6	D	4.0	16.5	655	150	108	1 632	2.3
Crockett	63	1.9	D	D	4.5	6.2	4.2	1.4	28.3	680	183	64	1 866	-8.9
Crosby	86	14.7	D	D	D	4.4	D	D	24.4	1 290	213	199	2 902	-9.4
Culberson	49	9.2	11.9	3.2	D	11.1	D	D	38.8	500	209	117	1 137	-13.9
Dallam	219	15.5	16.8	9.3	5.6	3.9	6.7	2.1	11.3	060	140	110	2 827	4.8
Dallas	123 298	0.0	19.0	9.7	17.4	4.4	13.1	9.5	9.4	275 140	116	56 215	943 257	10.4
Dawson	207	13.1	13.2	1.8	2.6	8.5	3.9	3.5	33.9	2 480	179	475	5 220	-5.1
Deaf Smith	930	11.3	D	16.6	3.4	6.7	3.8	3.0	18.1	2 770	143	468	7 077	2.4
Delta	51	5.9	D	D	D	4.8	D	18.6	26.4	1 365	261	188	2 458	2.0
Denton	9 898	0.2	17.7	10.1	11.8	7.6	7.4	10.0	18.8	61 890	93	5 486	256 139	52.4
DeWitt	311	-1.7	24.8	14.7	3.8	6.9	9.2	D	31.1	4 545	226	675	9 176	4.9
Dickens	30	11.4	5.3	0.0	D	6.2	D	1.7	26.3	575	235	59	1 282	-6.3
Dimmit	146	1.1	18.9	0.7	D	7.0	2.4	D	45.9	1 910	191	733	4 350	5.8
Donley	47	11.5	D	D	4.4	9.1	D	7.0	35.6	900	245	78	2 142	-9.9
Duval	159	0.2	39.3	0.2	D	2.7	1.7	4.6	38.2	2 480	210	747	5 523	-0.4
Eastland	347	-1.7	40.8	8.1	3.3	6.4	5.5	D	18.6	4 640	250	611	10 258	7.4
Ector	3 522	0.0	34.8	7.4	5.7	6.9	4.8	8.0	14.5	19 285	141	3 845	53 027	7.1
Edwards	24	5.4	6.1	0.0	D	9.7	D	3.9	42.0	490	245	97	1 606	32.0
Ellis	1 993	0.1	35.2	27.6	4.0	7.8	3.8	7.2	17.5	21 280	142	2 495	54 365	39.1
El Paso	16 301	0.1	13.2	7.5	5.3	6.3	7.5	10.2	35.9	109 255	136	28 797	270 307	20.4
Erath	628	3.4	21.0	13.0	5.5	8.1	4.6	10.3	22.9	5 800	153	607	16 987	17.8
Falls	166	-1.8	D	4.1	2.5	8.4	3.3	10.3	46.6	3 525	197	808	7 724	0.9
Fannin	370	1.2	14.0	6.8	4.0	8.7	3.8	8.8	38.9	7 440	219	872	14 191	10.1
Fayette	419	-1.0	22.4	9.7	5.1	9.1	7.5	D	22.3	5 975	243	453	13 868	24.8
Fisher	46	7.0	D	D	D	3.7	6.6	4.9	31.5	1 030	259	117	2 212	-2.9
Floyd	107	29.4	4.8	2.7	D	3.6	3.9	5.1	24.7	1 380	214	185	3 004	-6.7
Foard	14	10.1	D	D	D	6.1	D	D	31.7	385	288	37	789	-7.2
Fort Bend	9 567	0.3	33.4	13.4	9.1	6.3	6.3	7.8	13.9	52 640	90	9 008	197 030	69.9
Franklin	169	-0.4	D	D	D	7.0	D	22.2	11.4	2 400	226	231	5 770	12.4
Freestone	334	-1.3	28.6	3.0	3.3	7.4	4.3	D	20.1	3 795	192	409	9 265	13.9
Frio	211	5.7	14.8	0.4	D	5.8	3.2	D	27.7	2 570	149	781	5 846	3.3
Gaines	274	6.9	28.9	1.0	D	6.4	2.8	1.4	21.3	1 950	111	344	6 301	16.5
Galveston	5 990	0.0	26.5	15.0	6.3	6.5	7.4	7.1	27.4	43 990	151	5 966	132 492	18.6
Garza	109	-0.6	37.0	1.7	D	4.2	3.3	2.6	18.3	900	139	119	2 237	16.0
Gillespie	439	1.1	21.9	8.4	5.7	10.9	4.9	19.6	12.8	7 175	289	263	12 778	29.0
Glasscock	24	17.9	D	0.0	D	D	D	D	20.8	180	147	10	580	-12.1
Goliad	65	-8.8	D	2.4	D	6.9	D	D	32.9	1 625	225	203	3 710	8.3
Gonzales	286	8.5	D	15.7	3.9	7.4	4.2	D	22.4	3 860	195	620	8 794	7.3
Gray	566	2.0	48.0	20.2	D	6.5	3.9	D	12.7	4 495	199	426	10 158	-3.9
Grayson	2 176	0.3	26.4	18.7	4.5	9.0	6.6	17.7	14.7	25 345	210	2 824	53 727	11.2
Gregg	4 484	0.0	34.9	14.3	9.0	8.3	4.4	12.7	8.4	22 940	188	3 993	49 514	6.8
Grimes	388	1.0	29.6	22.6	3.6	4.6	4.5	5.1	25.3	4 780	180	704	10 917	15.0

1. Includes mining, construction, and manufacturing. 2. Per 1,000 resident population enumerated in the 2010 census.

Table B. States and Counties — Housing, Labor Force, and Employment

STATE County	Housing units, 2006–2010 Total	Occupied units Owner-occupied Percent	Median value[1]	Median owner cost as a percent of income With a mortgage	Without a mortgage	Renter-occupied Median rent[2]	Median rent as a percent of income	Sub-standard units[3] (percent)	Civilian labor force, 2010 Total	Percent change, 2009–2010	Unemployment Total	Rate[4]	Civilian employment,[5] 2006–2010 Total	Percent Management, business, science and arts	Construction, production, and mainte-nance occupations
	89	90	91	92	93	94	95	96	97	98	99	100	101	102	103
TEXAS—Cont'd															
Caldwell	11 408	69.2	99 600	23.5	13.7	695	27.6	7.2	16 139	2.0	1 391	8.6	14 884	27.1	28.5
Calhoun	7 971	69.6	89 800	23.4	11.7	649	25.2	5.2	9 579	1.2	865	9.0	9 377	27.8	33.8
Callahan	5 133	82.8	73 700	20.6	12.9	660	23.3	2.6	7 108	-1.2	426	6.0	6 006	24.9	32.9
Cameron	113 547	69.2	74 000	26.7	13.9	584	32.8	12.1	158 000	4.3	17 650	11.2	139 195	26.7	23.3
Camp	4 588	66.8	93 700	23.0	11.7	563	26.2	7.4	5 910	2.8	521	8.8	5 056	24.8	37.7
Carson	2 415	85.3	82 800	16.6	10.6	594	14.8	0.7	3 246	-3.6	170	5.2	2 877	33.5	34.4
Cass	12 099	72.1	68 700	21.4	11.2	481	26.1	4.3	13 495	0.5	1 484	11.0	12 143	24.2	35.6
Castro	2 677	77.0	68 300	23.7	12.9	574	31.2	6.8	3 633	-0.9	203	5.6	3 527	28.6	37.1
Chambers	11 080	86.2	136 600	21.5	12.8	715	22.2	4.0	15 624	5.8	1 542	9.9	14 842	31.2	35.4
Cherokee	16 799	74.1	68 100	22.2	13.4	583	29.6	5.6	20 914	-0.4	1 910	9.1	19 759	23.2	35.5
Childress	2 177	73.1	54 800	15.4	13.4	582	29.6	2.4	3 292	-1.5	235	7.1	2 774	26.8	19.8
Clay	4 451	86.0	77 300	20.6	11.5	591	22.7	4.6	6 072	-0.5	398	6.6	5 069	34.5	27.7
Cochran	1 099	77.3	40 100	18.9	10.0	563	19.0	9.8	1 408	-7.5	116	8.2	1 245	23.1	42.4
Coke	1 287	73.7	58 000	19.4	11.7	518	26.5	2.8	1 328	-0.2	105	7.9	1 351	31.5	29.5
Coleman	3 514	71.0	59 000	26.2	14.9	449	28.5	0.7	4 419	-0.1	307	6.9	3 144	30.8	31.9
Collin	268 042	70.8	199 000	23.1	12.1	968	27.3	2.3	421 754	2.9	31 648	7.5	383 069	50.2	11.3
Collingsworth	1 188	75.4	58 900	21.2	10.0	502	22.1	3.5	1 454	-3.2	78	5.4	1 274	38.1	26.7
Colorado	8 205	77.1	97 000	23.0	13.2	602	24.1	4.1	10 630	-1.9	794	7.5	9 045	28.2	34.3
Comal	38 984	75.9	187 400	22.1	11.0	860	26.3	4.2	58 523	4.7	3 887	6.6	48 439	37.8	21.6
Comanche	5 243	78.4	83 900	22.9	13.8	492	28.0	5.5	6 843	-0.4	456	6.7	5 367	28.7	33.7
Concho	996	78.4	70 300	15.6	11.7	554	21.1	5.6	1 315	-3.2	109	8.3	1 119	32.4	28.7
Cooke	14 547	70.3	111 400	22.4	13.6	739	29.1	5.3	22 060	0.2	1 445	6.6	18 285	28.0	31.9
Coryell	20 762	59.5	92 000	21.8	11.3	821	26.9	2.6	25 150	3.3	2 213	8.8	25 479	28.1	25.8
Cottle	617	79.9	42 400	23.4	12.5	298	29.8	3.2	763	-6.5	48	6.3	623	25.4	28.7
Crane	1 426	75.8	54 200	18.6	10.0	740	26.4	4.5	1 662	-8.0	135	8.1	1 756	21.5	38.2
Crockett	1 259	61.2	60 800	23.0	10.0	556	14.0	8.2	2 152	-7.5	147	6.8	1 716	21.2	41.8
Crosby	2 144	71.9	51 200	20.8	11.4	516	28.8	5.1	2 623	-2.0	208	7.9	2 593	29.5	31.1
Culberson	724	76.4	39 900	20.2	13.4	500	32.4	4.7	1 700	-6.1	75	4.4	976	27.6	14.3
Dallam	2 154	66.2	70 200	21.9	10.0	672	21.0	4.7	3 792	2.5	197	5.2	3 504	18.6	44.0
Dallas	832 360	54.7	129 700	25.6	13.6	831	29.7	6.5	1 166 085	1.1	102 781	8.8	1 109 206	32.1	25.3
Dawson	4 424	75.7	48 000	21.4	12.5	441	21.8	3.8	5 394	-0.4	442	8.2	4 624	26.9	27.1
Deaf Smith	6 053	65.0	73 600	21.0	12.9	640	23.9	7.4	9 194	-0.4	523	5.7	8 006	23.4	40.1
Delta	2 045	80.4	62 700	19.5	12.7	687	36.4	1.4	2 297	-1.2	210	9.1	2 301	25.6	36.6
Denton	224 840	66.2	178 300	23.2	12.3	878	28.7	2.3	356 748	2.6	26 626	7.5	332 090	42.0	15.8
DeWitt	7 361	76.5	68 700	20.6	10.1	526	25.9	4.0	9 332	1.9	737	7.9	8 247	24.0	34.8
Dickens	841	80.4	44 000	17.0	13.9	433	19.1	2.0	990	-4.5	102	10.3	849	27.2	30.5
Dimmit	3 600	69.5	49 000	20.9	17.0	510	26.7	5.3	4 271	0.9	409	9.6	3 702	22.4	29.7
Donley	1 279	73.3	58 300	19.2	11.2	545	21.2	2.9	1 937	0.8	124	6.4	1 587	34.2	27.0
Duval	4 138	73.3	53 300	22.9	14.7	533	19.7	6.4	5 318	-0.2	596	11.2	4 718	18.4	38.4
Eastland	7 273	75.4	58 400	21.2	13.4	484	25.7	5.1	8 778	0.3	695	7.9	7 240	27.0	29.6
Ector	47 653	67.5	75 500	19.2	11.1	651	24.9	6.2	72 680	2.4	5 660	7.8	61 256	22.4	33.8
Edwards	858	81.2	61 500	19.1	12.9	567	28.3	2.8	1 029	-4.3	74	7.2	901	31.1	33.0
Ellis	48 503	76.3	136 100	23.0	13.4	855	29.0	4.6	72 330	1.8	6 143	8.5	68 585	31.8	26.7
El Paso	242 943	63.9	101 800	24.4	12.1	618	30.9	7.2	318 108	3.7	30 262	9.5	304 211	28.5	23.9
Erath	13 877	62.0	110 900	21.4	13.5	599	30.9	4.3	19 342	0.4	1 253	6.5	17 916	30.8	30.6
Falls	5 700	72.9	59 500	22.7	14.4	543	28.2	4.0	6 749	0.8	647	9.6	6 547	23.9	28.3
Fannin	11 676	74.7	81 500	21.7	13.3	645	28.6	3.5	13 918	2.5	1 295	9.3	14 211	27.2	33.7
Fayette	10 658	74.1	133 500	22.6	11.5	615	23.0	3.2	12 151	-1.6	715	5.9	11 503	29.4	31.7
Fisher	1 673	74.0	52 000	18.6	13.9	507	27.2	3.0	2 015	-0.1	130	6.5	1 718	31.8	37.9
Floyd	2 612	71.7	56 000	19.8	12.6	543	33.5	7.9	3 105	-2.6	263	8.5	3 057	30.2	30.1
Foard	563	61.5	29 700	22.4	13.3	407	23.5	1.8	713	-0.7	45	6.3	665	29.9	29.8
Fort Bend	167 620	80.8	171 500	23.9	11.8	1 062	28.2	3.5	282 100	3.7	22 670	8.0	259 598	45.7	15.3
Franklin	3 734	80.8	94 600	22.8	12.2	624	29.5	4.7	5 417	-2.2	419	7.7	4 341	29.7	28.7
Freestone	7 107	78.8	89 900	19.8	12.4	678	35.2	3.9	10 416	1.7	687	6.6	7 460	34.9	30.6
Frio	4 748	66.5	49 500	20.9	13.5	560	19.9	9.2	7 619	2.3	580	7.6	6 146	17.4	32.4
Gaines	5 348	73.0	77 600	16.3	10.0	501	21.8	10.4	7 024	0.1	437	6.2	7 318	25.1	43.2
Galveston	106 617	69.5	141 400	22.8	13.3	839	30.1	3.9	143 307	-1.1	13 170	9.2	137 205	38.1	22.3
Garza	1 649	72.7	57 000	17.0	13.4	446	24.5	1.9	2 499	2.5	136	5.4	1 855	30.8	34.4
Gillespie	10 413	75.5	191 100	23.8	12.6	787	28.2	1.8	13 707	-0.2	661	4.8	11 547	34.2	25.2
Glasscock	430	73.5	90 800	20.0	10.0	1 031	0.0	6.0	628	-4.0	35	5.6	592	29.7	43.8
Goliad	2 920	82.8	99 100	16.1	10.0	609	32.0	5.0	3 426	-1.3	251	7.3	3 338	27.6	28.4
Gonzales	7 036	68.4	69 500	22.5	12.3	495	26.2	11.1	10 010	-1.3	619	6.2	8 210	25.5	37.0
Gray	8 221	76.9	65 500	19.4	12.4	596	25.0	2.5	10 978	-4.3	822	7.5	8 659	24.8	34.3
Grayson	45 545	70.4	99 600	23.3	13.3	716	27.8	3.0	57 431	1.0	4 838	8.4	54 436	30.2	26.1
Gregg	44 873	63.1	109 800	20.6	11.3	686	26.7	4.3	66 583	2.6	4 814	7.2	55 339	29.2	28.1
Grimes	8 366	74.9	89 400	23.7	12.6	630	26.2	5.2	11 909	2.5	1 045	8.8	9 991	22.9	31.1

1. Specified owner-occupied units.   2. Specified renter-occupied units. A value of 10.0 represents 10 percent or less.   3. Overcrowded or lacking complete plumbing facilities.   4. Percent of civilian labor force.   5. Persons 16 years old and over.

Table B. States and Counties — Nonfarm Employment and Agriculture

STATE County	Number of establishments	Employment Total	Health care and social assistance	Manufacturing	Retail trade	Finance and insurance	Professional, scientific, and technical services	Annual payroll Total (mil dol)	Average per employee (dollars)	Farms Number	Fewer than 50 acres	500 acres or more	Farm operators whose principal occupation is farming (percent)
	104	105	106	107	108	109	110	111	112	113	114	115	116
TEXAS—Cont'd													
Caldwell	524	5 430	1 098	720	1 120	169	133	135	24 915	1 421	41.3	9.3	39.8
Calhoun	408	8 527	575	2 893	919	191	291	359	42 122	291	31.6	36.4	46.4
Callahan	224	1 923	115	143	327	71	D	57	29 667	1 058	31.9	19.3	38.3
Cameron	6 320	99 750	28 556	6 078	17 819	2 954	2 614	2 379	23 854	1 241	63.1	13.7	43.3
Camp	227	3 368	418	D	382	113	D	143	42 446	482	40.7	3.7	44.2
Carson	113	4 077	D	D	129	D	37	297	72 948	422	13.0	57.1	53.8
Cass	517	5 557	1 158	1 121	944	245	116	171	30 786	1 067	36.0	7.0	37.8
Castro	179	1 093	D	40	203	61	94	28	25 361	485	7.8	59.4	67.0
Chambers	493	8 876	542	1 705	718	156	276	416	46 820	650	47.7	17.5	37.7
Cherokee	788	10 744	2 337	2 725	1 508	339	158	304	28 296	1 625	39.6	5.7	35.2
Childress	166	1 566	425	D	425	D	35	37	23 688	374	11.2	32.6	39.0
Clay	133	1 006	186	D	247	D	19	27	27 212	931	18.3	28.5	44.9
Cochran	61	378	D	D	82	D	D	12	30 929	341	1.8	56.9	46.0
Coke	68	273	0	D	69	D	D	6	22 484	430	7.9	45.1	45.1
Coleman	219	1 579	326	222	246	82	D	37	23 419	1 003	9.7	35.1	40.9
Collin	17 253	286 458	27 925	19 238	41 456	33 627	22 000	15 087	52 666	2 235	66.0	4.6	32.8
Collingsworth	67	478	D	D	90	D	D	12	24 954	442	6.3	41.6	43.9
Colorado	551	5 845	871	1 373	912	163	131	165	28 286	1 790	29.9	13.5	41.8
Comal	2 789	34 543	4 013	3 571	5 125	819	1 013	1 131	32 748	939	43.5	9.2	34.8
Comanche	278	2 462	570	D	476	154	86	64	26 120	1 451	25.6	19.9	48.0
Concho	50	680	135	D	85	D	D	20	29 065	418	4.8	50.0	50.7
Cooke	872	12 000	1 156	3 249	1 919	322	311	394	32 841	1 956	44.1	10.2	34.2
Coryell	736	10 553	1 171	471	1 794	365	1 589	274	25 927	1 339	31.2	18.6	39.7
Cottle	36	160	D	0	48	D	D	3	18 281	299	5.7	42.1	41.1
Crane	78	1 171	D	D	111	D	D	46	38 943	37	21.6	59.5	32.4
Crockett	133	1 041	D	D	268	D	D	28	27 258	183	3.8	73.2	57.4
Crosby	112	725	162	48	D	D	D	27	37 408	371	4.9	49.9	52.6
Culberson	52	570	D	D	229	0	D	11	19 935	55	5.5	85.5	63.6
Dallam	222	1 780	D	61	216	99	63	51	28 669	452	2.9	64.4	50.7
Dallas	61 359	1 253 122	138 877	104 397	115 042	96 870	113 040	63 706	50 838	755	64.9	4.4	38.0
Dawson	285	2 743	370	134	518	131	61	74	26 954	555	9.7	45.0	51.0
Deaf Smith	408	5 197	511	1 398	797	184	152	155	29 874	637	14.6	52.6	54.0
Delta	57	533	349	D	29	D	10	8	15 417	538	37.2	10.4	38.3
Denton	11 225	157 762	19 490	9 741	25 761	8 775	7 607	5 761	36 519	2 575	69.8	4.5	32.7
DeWitt	425	4 219	1 040	762	700	248	107	114	27 060	1 811	24.3	15.1	43.1
Dickens	48	373	30	0	84	D	D	10	27 962	446	5.8	32.1	37.4
Dimmit	164	1 780	446	D	D	40	24	47	26 220	388	25.0	32.7	35.3
Donley	82	442	D	D	141	D	D	8	18 559	392	7.1	29.8	40.8
Duval	135	1 888	515	D	209	57	D	50	26 715	1 607	11.3	22.6	36.6
Eastland	463	6 282	1 013	648	904	125	100	198	31 579	1 324	18.0	19.0	38.1
Ector	3 248	50 980	7 600	3 878	7 167	1 422	2 099	1 945	38 152	301	74.4	13.0	29.2
Edwards	35	194	D	0	59	D	D	4	22 624	480	11.0	41.9	38.8
Ellis	2 446	33 190	3 261	8 420	5 259	800	727	1 048	31 582	2 415	53.4	7.0	35.3
El Paso	13 179	205 190	35 665	14 235	33 671	6 704	9 709	5 699	27 773	590	78.3	7.5	47.6
Erath	927	11 414	1 780	1 965	1 956	348	372	330	28 901	2 189	31.1	13.9	39.2
Falls	230	1 785	498	D	D	101	28	44	24 543	1 295	27.2	15.5	47.7
Fannin	490	4 812	1 381	587	851	166	131	142	29 508	2 110	36.9	9.1	39.7
Fayette	745	6 361	1 117	902	1 100	247	190	179	28 153	2 991	32.2	7.3	38.4
Fisher	63	544	132	D	D	46	D	18	32 754	661	10.1	37.5	44.3
Floyd	160	983	D	D	118	57	D	27	27 733	650	8.0	40.2	43.8
Foard	33	193	55	D	D	D	D	3	17 171	212	9.0	43.4	47.2
Fort Bend	8 932	111 961	13 233	11 484	21 117	3 610	7 411	4 359	38 937	1 404	51.6	10.8	38.2
Franklin	184	5 913	D	D	D	69	D	104	17 507	564	30.3	14.2	47.5
Freestone	357	4 279	656	D	623	153	D	148	34 472	1 473	35.5	12.0	40.9
Frio	243	2 788	521	D	497	100	D	76	27 119	724	18.9	33.0	41.9
Gaines	338	3 051	D	D	465	91	55	104	34 081	825	7.2	49.8	57.9
Galveston	5 073	71 738	14 072	6 230	11 249	3 956	2 642	2 650	36 936	692	74.9	7.2	32.4
Garza	125	1 199	D	D	161	D	D	36	30 111	300	15.3	49.0	44.3
Gillespie	890	8 061	1 460	606	1 599	285	256	219	27 157	1 853	32.3	16.7	40.7
Glasscock	15	94	0	D	D	D	D	3	36 096	185	7.0	67.6	60.5
Goliad	115	831	D	D	161	21	24	23	27 596	1 083	23.7	17.4	41.2
Gonzales	388	4 632	743	1 353	729	159	122	131	28 268	1 861	24.7	17.4	43.4
Gray	633	6 401	853	D	1 142	199	D	215	33 662	391	12.5	43.7	39.9
Grayson	2 582	38 107	7 555	6 699	6 233	2 501	911	1 200	31 491	2 723	55.3	4.9	35.1
Gregg	3 991	66 079	10 035	9 343	9 516	2 197	2 122	2 275	34 432	486	63.0	3.5	31.3
Grimes	362	5 180	391	2 046	601	176	91	184	35 518	1 853	40.0	9.9	40.2

STATE County	Land in farms					Value of land and buildings (dollars)		Value of machinery and equipment, average per farm (dollars)	Value of products sold				Percent of farms with sales of:		Government payments	
			Acres								Percent from:					
	Acreage (1,000)	Percent change, 2002–2007	Average size of farm	Total irrigated (1,000)	Total cropland (1,000)	Average per farm	Average per acre		Total (mil dol)	Average per farm (dollars)	Crops	Live-stock and poultry products	$10,000 or more	$100,000 or more	Total ($1,000)	Percent of farms
	117	118	119	120	121	122	123	124	125	126	127	128	129	130	131	132
TEXAS—Cont'd																
Caldwell	305	0.0	214	0.9	71.5	496 921	2 317	47 346	47.0	33 098	15.9	84.1	23.6	3.0	791	6.5
Calhoun	230	-7.3	792	3.6	88.9	1 261 479	1 593	123 615	29.0	99 525	69.3	30.7	48.1	21.6	2 770	39.2
Callahan	533	3.5	503	0.6	104.3	640 488	1 272	48 345	25.4	24 012	16.0	84.0	29.0	4.8	876	22.0
Cameron	349	-0.3	282	101.1	226.1	544 393	1 933	73 172	112.4	90 532	93.5	6.5	33.1	11.9	7 614	41.6
Camp	69	0.0	142	2.1	23.4	387 269	2 723	61 878	143.1	296 803	2.1	97.9	35.7	8.3	140	6.8
Carson	537	18.8	1 274	41.5	331.0	1 039 725	816	146 348	93.7	221 930	56.2	43.8	49.8	30.6	6 625	73.7
Cass	177	-8.3	166	0.3	51.6	356 841	2 155	46 284	68.8	64 518	8.2	91.8	27.9	5.4	152	3.3
Castro	567	0.5	1 170	213.3	434.6	1 209 915	1 034	276 986	973.4	2 006 911	15.1	84.9	66.0	52.2	11 405	77.9
Chambers	267	-2.9	411	11.5	115.6	596 789	1 451	68 100	17.6	27 088	50.1	49.9	23.2	6.0	2 338	17.1
Cherokee	294	2.8	181	1.1	76.6	421 476	2 327	61 321	140.3	86 312	63.5	36.5	31.9	5.2	269	4.0
Childress	399	8.1	1 068	14.0	143.2	761 909	713	82 171	25.9	69 248	72.7	27.3	35.6	16.0	4 360	76.2
Clay	662	1.2	711	1.0	117.0	939 178	1 322	69 857	56.9	61 098	9.3	90.7	44.3	10.6	988	27.4
Cochran	489	11.4	1 434	82.5	305.3	1 251 971	873	157 465	91.7	268 802	D	D	41.6	30.2	8 875	85.9
Coke	491	1.2	1 142	D	45.9	894 646	783	43 258	13.6	31 719	4.4	95.6	28.6	5.6	486	28.8
Coleman	699	8.9	697	1.2	188.4	897 473	1 287	60 942	20.0	19 975	27.2	72.8	35.2	4.0	1 648	38.7
Collin	291	-6.1	130	0.7	150.2	450 519	3 462	46 504	61.2	27 366	57.1	42.9	17.0	2.9	1 492	8.5
Collingsworth	513	1.2	1 160	29.7	193.5	999 653	862	106 334	50.3	113 822	71.9	28.1	42.8	18.3	6 775	76.0
Colorado	527	-2.2	295	31.5	169.0	695 995	2 362	57 933	72.0	40 221	49.2	50.8	33.7	6.3	4 503	11.8
Comal	192	-5.4	205	0.5	37.5	616 173	3 006	34 985	6.6	6 982	44.5	55.5	14.4	1.0	219	6.2
Comanche	579	6.6	399	12.6	170.3	785 609	1 969	71 389	144.9	99 881	14.9	85.1	45.8	7.2	1 482	20.6
Concho	551	1.3	1 319	4.5	106.0	1 346 320	1 021	85 095	21.2	50 699	48.2	51.8	51.9	12.2	2 874	68.4
Cooke	455	-0.9	233	0.5	136.6	579 478	2 489	55 791	58.3	29 802	19.6	80.4	30.2	5.1	815	14.4
Coryell	488	-1.0	365	0.8	120.9	730 994	2 004	59 922	40.1	29 984	16.8	83.2	28.2	4.8	759	18.1
Cottle	535	-6.8	1 788	1.6	153.1	1 151 133	644	68 300	17.5	58 665	45.2	54.8	30.1	11.0	3 995	79.9
Crane	375	NA	10 140	0.0	15.3	3 877 193	382	31 050	1.7	45 237	0.4	99.6	48.6	18.9	117	24.3
Crockett	1 602	-7.7	8 757	0.5	18.6	3 560 877	407	68 139	13.6	74 515	D	D	53.6	18.6	614	28.4
Crosby	553	12.9	1 490	110.0	289.0	1 027 919	690	192 112	92.7	249 975	94.5	5.5	48.5	39.4	11 537	85.4
Culberson	1 374	-18.9	24 982	32.8	47.2	7 549 126	302	221 613	15.1	274 175	46.7	53.3	63.6	40.0	611	30.9
Dallam	937	6.0	2 073	230.9	534.2	1 751 802	845	254 557	552.9	1 223 139	27.6	72.4	56.6	44.2	7 856	71.5
Dallas	88	-1.1	117	0.9	43.5	385 282	3 305	46 240	35.2	46 588	88.5	11.5	18.9	3.7	220	5.6
Dawson	568	-0.7	1 023	77.7	462.4	871 403	851	160 721	112.3	202 418	96.7	3.3	49.2	38.2	18 924	85.2
Deaf Smith	946	-1.9	1 485	131.6	524.2	1 356 340	913	190 751	1 148.4	1 802 762	7.7	92.3	54.6	38.9	12 593	69.7
Delta	133	-6.3	247	D	67.4	398 611	1 614	60 070	17.2	32 031	51.8	48.2	30.1	6.3	735	29.2
Denton	350	0.3	136	1.3	140.9	486 155	3 574	50 899	79.2	30 772	23.4	76.6	19.6	3.0	848	8.8
DeWitt	549	-4.9	303	1.2	78.6	563 032	1 856	45 578	41.0	22 630	16.2	83.8	35.3	3.5	396	6.5
Dickens	574	1.2	1 288	4.6	143.3	1 061 647	825	65 532	21.1	47 351	52.3	47.7	30.7	10.3	4 035	77.8
Dimmit	708	24.0	1 825	5.5	29.1	1 838 263	1 007	64 983	21.7	55 905	12.1	87.9	21.4	5.9	304	5.9
Donley	589	0.9	1 502	16.9	83.7	964 711	642	80 416	85.8	218 916	15.3	84.7	35.2	12.0	3 802	66.3
Duval	1 021	20.1	678	4.6	120.3	690 308	1 019	38 885	14.8	9 802	26.7	73.3	13.5	1.3	1 931	27.3
Eastland	520	4.4	393	5.1	118.4	679 600	1 730	53 202	28.0	21 168	25.7	74.3	33.5	4.3	1 533	21.4
Ector	424	-15.9	1 408	1.1	7.0	560 521	398	43 889	3.6	11 824	27.5	72.5	15.3	3.3	109	4.3
Edwards	996	2.3	2 076	0.9	24.9	1 663 356	801	54 390	8.8	18 354	6.1	93.8	28.1	5.6	1 169	18.5
Ellis	443	-4.5	183	0.8	204.6	448 222	2 445	50 017	49.4	20 448	67.6	32.4	20.4	3.1	3 435	21.0
El Paso	169	48.2	286	37.8	54.1	418 167	1 464	78 916	47.5	80 447	86.2	13.8	26.1	11.4	894	10.3
Erath	623	7.2	285	12.1	165.0	683 811	2 403	69 014	250.2	114 295	5.1	94.9	32.3	7.1	1 087	8.9
Falls	445	8.8	344	4.4	218.6	546 113	1 588	73 854	126.8	97 928	24.6	75.4	45.5	12.6	2 117	24.7
Fannin	474	-1.9	225	5.3	207.5	435 434	1 939	53 890	48.7	23 090	49.2	50.8	25.3	3.3	2 086	21.3
Fayette	566	2.5	189	1.3	122.5	521 538	2 757	45 517	52.8	17 652	20.0	80.0	29.3	2.3	557	10.4
Fisher	545	13.8	824	4.6	239.4	746 880	906	76 973	50.5	76 392	57.2	42.8	38.3	13.0	7 961	81.7
Floyd	628	9.4	966	129.8	420.7	974 761	1 009	142 624	263.0	404 673	D	D	38.3	27.7	16 505	84.2
Foard	376	31.5	1 773	2.4	120.5	1 241 100	700	96 036	17.6	83 141	64.2	35.8	49.5	17.0	1 825	77.8
Fort Bend	383	-7.7	273	8.3	152.1	630 401	2 312	72 989	94.5	67 304	85.0	15.0	29.8	7.8	4 237	23.4
Franklin	134	1.5	237	2.1	34.7	534 117	2 256	66 542	85.8	152 198	4.4	95.6	44.5	14.9	229	12.4
Freestone	400	-6.8	271	0.3	80.1	473 115	1 744	53 438	33.9	23 031	9.5	90.5	31.1	3.1	188	4.3
Frio	645	7.0	891	42.9	151.3	1 203 065	1 350	76 282	70.3	97 069	56.4	43.6	28.5	9.8	2 541	17.1
Gaines	948	24.9	1 149	242.6	641.7	1 092 377	951	236 962	193.2	234 175	96.8	3.2	53.0	41.9	28 297	78.3
Galveston	103	-18.9	149	0.6	21.8	365 699	2 448	40 300	8.3	11 923	60.4	39.6	14.2	1.3	353	2.6
Garza	512	2.4	1 708	17.1	99.8	1 049 034	614	72 113	27.4	91 479	82.2	17.8	38.3	19.7	4 024	68.0
Gillespie	653	1.2	352	1.9	90.4	916 819	2 602	41 962	28.6	15 427	26.1	73.9	26.0	2.2	684	15.1
Glasscock	480	-2.6	2 593	29.5	126.7	1 910 119	737	243 043	46.3	250 041	95.3	4.7	64.9	45.4	5 262	70.8
Goliad	470	-7.1	434	0.9	58.9	705 897	1 628	52 833	20.0	18 477	23.5	76.5	30.6	2.8	356	6.6
Gonzales	654	-6.0	351	5.3	99.0	745 355	2 121	61 318	404.0	217 098	3.8	96.2	38.1	9.0	441	5.8
Gray	509	12.4	1 303	23.9	180.6	950 279	729	88 232	191.5	489 715	10.8	89.2	34.5	14.8	3 237	59.3
Grayson	400	-9.3	147	3.1	166.5	446 159	3 034	48 025	52.8	19 405	56.5	43.5	21.0	3.0	1 251	11.1
Gregg	45	-4.3	93	0.3	11.6	318 554	3 426	40 183	3.8	7 731	41.9	58.1	16.3	1.4	17	1.9
Grimes	437	5.3	236	2.0	87.0	575 760	2 441	61 013	49.9	26 938	15.0	85.0	30.3	3.1	80	1.1

Table B. States and Counties — Water Use, Wholesale Trade, Retail Trade, and Real Estate

STATE County	Water use, 2005		Wholesale trade,[1] 2007				Retail trade,[2] 2007				Real estate and rental and leasing,[2] 2007			
	Total water withdrawn (mil gal/day)	Gallons withdrawn per person	Number of establishments	Number of employees	Sales (mil dol)	Annual payroll (mil dol)	Number of establishments	Number of employees	Sales (mil dol)	Annual payroll (mil dol)	Number of establishments	Number of employees	Receipts (mil dol)	Annual payroll (mil dol)
	133	134	135	136	137	138	139	140	141	142	143	144	145	146
TEXAS—Cont'd														
Caldwell	18.6	508	18	89	26.4	2.8	84	997	298.3	21.3	26	135	15.4	2.9
Calhoun	41.2	1 997	16	D	D	D	69	972	322.2	26.1	14	D	D	D
Callahan	2.6	190	16	61	20.5	1.5	39	340	118.9	6.6	10	33	3.1	0.7
Cameron	210.1	555	341	3 704	1 516.6	96.3	1 230	17 667	3 911.7	340.0	341	1 593	169.4	30.0
Camp	4.1	331	8	62	33.5	2.3	46	389	96.9	7.4	8	D	D	D
Carson	54.0	8 198	5	D	D	D	23	130	49.7	2.9	1	D	D	D
Cass	3.1	103	20	184	155.0	7.2	98	888	216.8	17.7	20	51	6.6	0.9
Castro	360.6	47 200	14	109	154.6	3.7	36	196	40.0	2.9	3	D	D	D
Chambers	533.3	18 770	30	308	137.2	11.8	81	757	274.9	15.0	16	102	44.4	4.1
Cherokee	209.4	4 321	31	D	D	D	143	1 468	363.2	28.7	36	141	10.5	2.0
Childress	10.1	1 318	7	68	31.4	2.2	28	361	75.5	6.6	8	18	1.8	0.3
Clay	16.8	1 488	8	26	5.4	0.6	29	226	77.6	6.0	6	D	D	D
Cochran	126.4	38 440	4	17	12.0	0.6	13	68	26.9	1.4	NA	NA	NA	NA
Coke	60.3	16 705	1	D	D	D	12	71	24.5	1.3	NA	NA	NA	NA
Coleman	48.0	5 535	7	38	16.2	1.2	34	230	47.9	4.1	11	21	3.4	0.4
Collin	593.8	900	735	10 505	9 374.9	733.2	2 287	41 634	12 350.8	1 038.1	886	5 430	1 054.0	228.6
Collingsworth	51.8	17 463	3	D	D	D	13	77	17.2	1.7	1	D	D	D
Colorado	125.8	6 068	32	254	136.8	7.7	108	942	226.8	19.0	21	D	D	D
Comal	30.4	317	103	1 045	960.6	48.9	379	5 003	1 539.7	123.8	143	643	89.4	15.8
Comanche	28.0	2 039	24	157	83.1	4.6	54	457	117.8	8.7	8	27	2.3	0.4
Concho	4.3	1 138	2	D	D	D	13	100	17.7	1.2	2	D	D	D
Cooke	9.8	252	38	365	99.8	12.2	181	1 935	499.7	42.9	31	99	24.1	2.3
Coryell	8.8	116	17	80	34.3	3.5	140	1 752	442.6	36.7	51	153	16.9	2.7
Cottle	4.7	2 703	NA	NA	NA	NA	7	50	12.7	0.9	NA	NA	NA	NA
Crane	21.2	5 533	4	17	23.2	0.8	14	109	47.8	2.5	NA	NA	NA	NA
Crockett	9.5	2 410	4	D	D	D	27	262	58.9	4.2	3	D	D	D
Crosby	126.1	18 860	11	149	119.4	8.4	21	126	23.8	2.2	3	D	D	D
Culberson	18.8	7 164	2	D	D	D	19	221	106.2	3.6	2	D	D	D
Dallam	368.1	59 624	18	281	311.1	9.8	33	178	85.4	4.6	9	21	3.0	0.3
Dallas	979.4	425	3 935	72 986	58 165.1	4 220.6	7 719	118 275	33 177.2	3 063.0	3 505	36 320	8 668.9	1 992.1
Dawson	108.2	7 588	19	110	91.3	3.1	48	583	148.4	11.4	8	19	1.4	0.2
Deaf Smith	218.1	11 764	34	D	D	D	66	744	224.2	15.9	18	71	5.4	1.0
Delta	1.9	338	2	D	D	D	14	57	26.4	1.4	3	14	2.2	0.6
Denton	87.1	157	472	9 066	12 359.0	466.0	1 619	25 683	7 668.3	600.8	564	2 757	519.2	93.1
DeWitt	4.7	228	15	83	30.5	2.7	71	692	159.9	14.0	12	87	10.6	2.9
Dickens	9.4	3 556	NA	NA	NA	NA	11	73	11.3	0.9	1	D	D	D
Dimmit	6.3	605	4	D	D	D	26	330	74.8	6.6	6	D	D	D
Donley	34.2	8 791	2	D	D	D	23	123	29.2	2.2	3	D	D	D
Duval	14.1	1 110	8	64	17.5	2.6	27	188	49.6	2.8	4	D	D	D
Eastland	13.0	706	12	153	180.8	8.8	99	895	259.7	18.1	17	39	6.1	1.0
Ector	64.0	511	286	4 048	2 004.3	219.0	476	6 660	2 090.6	167.6	157	1 383	338.4	74.3
Edwards	1.0	513	1	D	D	D	6	53	11.7	0.6	1	D	D	D
Ellis	23.5	176	100	716	279.2	30.4	376	4 725	1 323.1	107.3	114	374	58.7	9.4
El Paso	267.3	370	911	8 442	5 002.5	303.1	2 334	33 948	8 460.9	683.1	672	3 599	629.2	106.8
Erath	17.1	501	38	D	D	D	156	1 912	445.0	39.7	43	124	17.7	3.3
Falls	15.8	893	13	79	53.1	2.3	44	330	71.6	6.0	12	32	5.3	0.5
Fannin	9.3	281	11	D	D	D	85	874	297.3	25.3	16	97	7.7	2.6
Fayette	767.4	34 048	29	376	158.7	15.8	133	1 041	262.0	23.8	33	94	20.3	2.4
Fisher	6.1	1 497	1	D	D	D	14	64	12.0	1.0	1	D	D	D
Floyd	156.8	21 855	15	113	65.6	4.1	24	137	40.0	2.6	3	D	D	D
Foard	4.7	3 109	5	D	D	D	6	25	7.0	0.5	NA	NA	NA	NA
Fort Bend	1 396.8	3 013	526	5 754	6 615.3	275.2	1 213	19 344	5 306.2	442.9	392	1 546	337.8	56.0
Franklin	6.0	584	4	21	4.8	0.8	32	304	87.9	5.7	9	24	4.3	1.1
Freestone	513.1	27 291	11	71	41.6	3.1	66	605	254.3	14.3	16	122	23.9	4.5
Frio	84.8	5 177	11	66	31.5	3.2	50	472	107.6	9.2	9	65	6.0	2.0
Gaines	23.9	1 621	18	290	169.3	12.8	46	393	82.6	7.7	9	28	4.8	1.0
Galveston	129.7	467	191	1 715	1 761.6	69.2	860	10 790	2 750.3	246.1	265	1 197	221.1	33.8
Garza	18.2	3 635	5	23	10.0	1.3	20	152	35.0	2.0	4	D	D	D
Gillespie	4.5	196	35	224	100.4	6.1	170	1 592	311.1	33.5	35	109	14.0	2.3
Glasscock	43.1	32 509	2	D	D	D	2	D	D	D	NA	NA	NA	NA
Goliad	9.0	1 267	3	D	D	D	24	149	37.3	2.2	4	D	D	D
Gonzales	12.9	657	21	188	90.2	7.3	83	682	179.2	13.4	16	33	3.4	0.5
Gray	39.4	1 833	31	D	D	D	104	D	D	D	29	192	29.1	7.8
Grayson	23.6	202	103	1 004	651.7	33.1	497	6 333	1 594.7	140.4	114	456	69.9	11.1
Gregg	257.5	2 226	239	3 138	1 401.5	129.5	701	9 168	2 405.2	220.9	182	1 333	290.8	56.4
Grimes	33.5	1 330	20	216	142.5	9.1	60	597	157.3	11.3	14	41	9.8	1.3

1. Merchant wholesalers, except manufacturers' sales branches and offices.   2. Employer establishments.

Professional Services, Manufacturing, and Accommodation and Food Services

STATE County	Professional, scientific, and technical services,[1] 2007				Manufacturing, 2007				Accommodation and food services, 2007			
	Number of establish- ments	Number of employees	Receipts (mil dol)	Annual payroll (mil dol)	Number of establish- ments	Number of employees	Receipts (mil dol)	Annual payroll (mil dol)	Number of establish- ments	Number of employees	Sales (mil dol)	Annual payroll (mil dol)
	147	148	149	150	151	152	153	154	155	156	157	158
TEXAS—Cont'd												
Caldwell	27	D	D	D	18	615	89.8	13.9	54	672	28.2	7.2
Calhoun	31	D	D	D	17	D	D	D	60	514	21.1	5.3
Callahan	13	D	D	D	NA	NA	NA	NA	16	220	7.6	2.1
Cameron	474	D	D	D	221	D	D	D	643	12 287	503.1	131.4
Camp	16	39	4.9	1.6	NA	NA	NA	NA	15	202	7.5	1.9
Carson	6	D	D	D	NA	NA	NA	NA	12	65	1.8	0.5
Cass	26	97	8.8	2.8	30	1 339	644.7	68.9	37	432	17.5	4.2
Castro	10	29	3.5	1.0	NA	NA	NA	NA	11	76	2.4	0.6
Chambers	37	349	30.1	14.6	23	D	D	131.2	50	804	31.4	8.4
Cherokee	45	170	14.8	4.0	75	3 431	552.5	90.1	66	959	36.5	9.9
Childress	9	32	4.9	1.3	NA	NA	NA	NA	24	358	11.7	3.2
Clay	9	D	D	D	NA	NA	NA	NA	9	111	2.6	0.9
Cochran	3	4	0.2	0.1	NA	NA	NA	NA	4	15	0.3	0.1
Coke	3	D	D	D	NA	NA	NA	NA	6	D	D	D
Coleman	14	39	3.0	0.7	NA	NA	NA	NA	21	166	5.1	1.3
Collin	2 581	D	D	D	420	20 823	7 433.8	1 175.1	1 290	27 578	1 380.4	392.5
Collingsworth	6	D	D	D	NA	NA	NA	NA	8	41	1.4	0.4
Colorado	46	144	13.4	4.4	28	1 155	307.3	38.3	43	570	21.7	5.9
Comal	251	1 268	112.1	38.3	106	3 475	1 093.7	128.6	255	4 362	184.4	48.5
Comanche	22	67	6.1	1.3	NA	NA	NA	NA	17	D	D	D
Concho	2	D	D	D	NA	NA	NA	NA	6	50	4.3	0.9
Cooke	65	290	37.4	14.7	75	3 439	579.7	128.9	84	1 322	52.6	13.9
Coryell	56	D	D	D	19	504	D	D	74	1 231	45.4	11.3
Cottle	1	D	D	D	NA	NA	NA	NA	4	D	D	D
Crane	2	D	D	D	NA	NA	NA	NA	5	33	1.0	0.2
Crockett	6	13	1.0	0.3	NA	NA	NA	NA	18	153	8.3	1.7
Crosby	4	8	0.5	0.2	NA	NA	NA	NA	5	D	D	D
Culberson	1	D	D	D	NA	NA	NA	NA	19	239	10.3	2.4
Dallam	14	56	6.7	1.8	NA	NA	NA	NA	26	295	12.5	2.7
Dallas	8 664	110 830	21 051.4	8 025.1	2 706	133 063	39 047.0	6 512.8	4 753	102 354	5 705.1	1 600.9
Dawson	19	58	7.0	2.3	NA	NA	NA	NA	26	279	12.5	3.2
Deaf Smith	22	93	11.4	2.5	31	1 104	470.8	35.7	33	377	17.3	3.8
Delta	2	D	D	D	NA	NA	NA	NA	3	D	D	D
Denton	1 372	6 160	1 012.6	306.7	363	11 406	4 008.3	476.3	909	17 865	797.9	219.5
DeWitt	29	113	8.4	3.1	28	835	110.4	25.5	43	464	14.9	3.9
Dickens	2	D	D	D	NA	NA	NA	NA	6	27	0.9	0.3
Dimmit	7	20	1.6	0.3	NA	NA	NA	NA	19	253	8.3	2.9
Donley	6	20	2.3	0.4	NA	NA	NA	NA	12	105	3.7	0.8
Duval	6	10	1.0	0.3	NA	NA	NA	NA	13	55	3.7	0.7
Eastland	29	109	9.1	3.3	22	608	135.5	22.6	44	427	17.7	4.3
Ector	224	D	D	D	240	4 814	2 049.7	222.0	245	5 213	228.6	59.4
Edwards	2	D	D	D	NA	NA	NA	NA	5	D	D	D
Ellis	164	D	D	D	178	9 369	4 080.6	416.0	185	2 828	126.6	34.4
El Paso	1 151	D	D	D	588	16 091	14 423.5	617.6	1 269	24 563	1 031.3	268.5
Erath	68	355	31.3	11.9	40	2 577	849.3	108.1	81	1 489	55.4	15.9
Falls	8	26	4.1	0.7	NA	NA	NA	NA	20	D	D	D
Fannin	30	120	8.6	2.9	37	531	135.9	17.2	37	464	18.5	5.3
Fayette	60	205	17.1	5.6	40	1 024	277.8	36.3	67	782	32.0	8.4
Fisher	4	D	D	D	NA	NA	NA	NA	2	D	D	D
Floyd	10	19	1.3	0.4	NA	NA	NA	NA	11	42	1.8	0.4
Foard	2	D	D	D	NA	NA	NA	NA	3	D	D	D
Fort Bend	1 154	D	D	D	344	15 306	4 986.6	771.0	657	12 354	583.4	158.9
Franklin	13	28	2.8	1.0	NA	NA	NA	NA	18	180	6.5	2.2
Freestone	30	118	9.7	3.4	NA	NA	NA	NA	25	480	22.5	5.8
Frio	11	46	2.4	1.1	NA	NA	NA	NA	24	232	7.4	2.1
Gaines	10	53	4.1	2.0	NA	NA	NA	NA	27	249	9.5	2.1
Galveston	502	2 262	319.0	122.0	158	6 061	23 480.8	519.4	589	12 643	591.0	160.0
Garza	4	7	0.5	0.2	NA	NA	NA	NA	15	157	6.2	1.7
Gillespie	79	253	25.6	7.9	50	620	88.3	20.7	88	1 220	52.2	15.9
Glasscock	2	D	D	D	NA	NA	NA	NA	NA	NA	NA	NA
Goliad	12	D	D	D	NA	NA	NA	NA	12	97	3.9	1.1
Gonzales	38	109	10.4	2.9	22	1 416	444.7	48.1	38	399	17.4	4.5
Gray	46	D	D	D	22	D	683.7	74.3	41	D	D	D
Grayson	220	1 086	92.5	34.5	132	6 148	2 542.8	293.7	226	4 001	167.7	48.6
Gregg	340	D	D	D	184	10 510	4 234.0	456.9	294	6 063	246.7	71.9
Grimes	24	134	13.2	3.4	28	2 194	892.6	93.9	31	259	12.5	3.0

1. Establishment subject to federal tax.

Table B. States and Counties — Health Care and Social Assistance, Other Services, and Federal Funds

STATE County	Health care and social assistance, 2007				Other services, 2007				Federal funds and grants, 2009–2010 Expenditures (mil dol)			
										Direct payments for individuals[1]		
	Number of establish-ments	Number of employees	Receipts (mil dol)	Annual payroll (mil dol)	Number of establish-ments	Number of employees	Receipts (mil dol)	Annual payroll (mil dol)	Total	Social Security and government retirement	Medicare	Food Stamps and Supplemental Security Income
	159	160	161	162	163	164	165	166	167	168	169	170
TEXAS—Cont'd												
Caldwell	60	1 137	75.1	31.8	33	104	7.4	1.8	244.8	96.7	54.1	13.2
Calhoun	30	634	42.4	16.8	38	192	20.2	5.4	159.6	61.6	29.4	8.4
Callahan	10	115	4.0	1.8	12	45	3.5	0.9	117.5	48.2	23.8	4.1
Cameron	925	27 384	1 711.7	686.6	424	2 214	140.9	36.3	2 895.6	668.7	441.3	326.4
Camp	31	401	31.8	10.7	12	37	5.4	0.9	121.5	46.5	31.0	5.6
Carson	3	D	D	D	9	D	D	D	49.1	22.8	12.9	0.7
Cass	49	1 305	70.8	29.2	38	303	31.2	5.6	315.8	129.8	74.9	16.5
Castro	8	D	D	D	16	50	5.5	1.1	62.4	17.5	12.4	3.9
Chambers	34	638	36.5	15.8	30	182	16.3	5.6	220.0	52.5	37.3	5.8
Cherokee	88	2 576	163.2	77.3	53	188	13.4	3.9	355.9	130.1	97.3	18.7
Childress	20	363	28.5	10.8	9	25	2.2	0.5	58.5	19.9	14.9	3.0
Clay	13	D	D	D	10	36	1.6	0.4	66.7	32.8	17.9	1.9
Cochran	7	D	D	D	3	D	D	D	44.5	10.3	7.4	2.5
Coke	NA	NA	NA	NA	6	D	D	D	27.5	13.5	7.7	0.7
Coleman	20	357	17.6	8.7	14	43	3.2	0.7	112.2	36.4	37.0	4.1
Collin	2 014	24 679	3 179.0	1 127.8	878	6 502	493.2	154.1	3 155.0	1 274.4	242.2	59.0
Collingsworth	8	177	8.2	3.7	6	17	1.0	0.1	49.8	9.7	10.0	1.8
Colorado	34	837	60.1	24.0	33	151	10.5	2.9	186.7	66.5	44.1	7.2
Comal	271	3 624	323.2	130.3	197	1 392	78.5	44.0	1 068.3	444.6	104.2	15.1
Comanche	24	555	33.9	13.9	17	57	4.0	0.9	138.8	48.2	41.4	4.2
Concho	6	107	5.8	2.6	1	D	D	D	33.7	9.5	8.5	0.6
Cooke	85	1 158	90.7	35.2	62	417	29.3	8.7	238.7	110.2	62.0	11.0
Coryell	56	D	D	D	76	516	52.9	13.2	418.8	236.3	46.8	13.4
Cottle	4	44	1.6	0.7	2	D	D	D	23.0	6.7	5.6	1.1
Crane	8	159	9.5	4.5	2	D	D	D	21.4	8.8	8.0	1.3
Crockett	4	24	0.9	0.5	8	20	1.0	0.2	25.4	9.7	5.0	1.2
Crosby	11	D	D	D	8	D	D	D	75.5	16.8	23.4	4.7
Culberson	4	D	D	D	1	D	D	D	24.4	6.0	5.3	2.0
Dallam	12	D	D	D	21	47	9.2	1.2	65.0	23.8	14.1	2.2
Dallas	6 140	127 611	15 499.3	6 007.4	3 633	32 949	4 299.4	1 068.5	18 044.2	4 578.2	2 656.6	853.9
Dawson	20	352	35.8	9.6	19	77	5.2	1.5	157.8	40.4	46.3	8.7
Deaf Smith	24	492	31.4	11.6	37	168	14.2	3.3	136.3	43.3	28.3	9.7
Delta	6	289	6.4	3.1	5	D	D	D	61.7	19.3	14.9	2.3
Denton	1 199	16 986	1 795.5	641.2	674	4 360	369.5	112.8	1 841.9	907.3	235.7	50.6
DeWitt	41	1 007	62.0	25.3	39	159	12.5	3.2	185.6	55.9	48.4	9.0
Dickens	6	28	0.7	0.4	2	D	D	D	33.6	8.6	13.7	1.0
Dimmit	29	403	23.4	11.1	11	D	D	D	130.4	21.2	20.7	11.7
Donley	7	37	4.7	1.4	5	14	1.4	0.3	36.8	13.1	9.8	1.3
Duval	10	520	16.5	9.3	6	45	7.2	1.7	179.0	32.9	41.5	11.1
Eastland	38	1 038	42.7	22.7	34	156	10.9	3.1	187.5	68.3	54.4	7.0
Ector	300	6 988	644.3	248.5	246	2 115	283.6	64.3	749.5	287.9	194.9	70.3
Edwards	3	D	D	D	4	D	D	D	30.4	8.6	11.5	1.7
Ellis	214	3 320	254.6	99.6	157	863	55.1	16.6	703.8	368.6	149.4	32.4
El Paso	1 345	34 489	3 057.1	1 096.2	916	6 163	402.6	125.2	9 449.6	1 712.4	810.7	497.2
Erath	75	1 916	150.0	53.5	70	405	33.5	8.2	227.3	89.4	55.9	7.7
Falls	24	484	31.1	12.4	18	48	2.8	0.8	189.8	52.4	40.1	11.3
Fannin	55	1 291	117.6	48.0	36	D	D	D	542.8	118.5	68.0	10.4
Fayette	62	1 053	78.5	30.5	56	237	15.7	4.0	220.7	92.0	56.7	5.7
Fisher	6	151	10.0	4.0	7	17	1.1	0.2	52.6	14.2	12.9	1.2
Floyd	22	273	16.8	6.7	15	47	2.4	0.6	84.4	18.6	17.8	4.1
Foard	5	49	2.0	0.8	4	D	D	D	25.7	5.9	5.1	0.7
Fort Bend	993	12 302	1 197.4	443.3	518	3 251	318.1	89.4	1 338.5	719.9	163.0	70.4
Franklin	21	4 888	83.1	46.0	19	75	6.2	1.5	66.3	30.2	18.6	2.4
Freestone	31	550	37.6	13.2	29	117	9.8	1.7	136.2	57.8	28.5	6.4
Frio	29	474	27.9	10.6	15	45	2.9	0.7	183.5	32.1	23.6	11.9
Gaines	13	D	D	D	34	186	36.3	4.9	115.8	27.7	24.2	5.2
Galveston	526	14 414	1 219.8	484.8	422	2 658	336.9	70.9	2 443.9	755.1	424.3	106.5
Garza	13	D	D	D	5	D	D	D	43.7	12.5	13.9	2.4
Gillespie	86	1 533	119.2	51.8	54	249	25.6	5.9	195.0	116.7	44.5	2.7
Glasscock	NA	NA	NA	NA	NA	NA	NA	NA	20.2	6.1	1.1	0.1
Goliad	12	129	6.3	3.0	8	23	1.8	0.3	62.0	22.6	14.7	2.9
Gonzales	24	648	37.8	16.9	25	106	8.5	2.2	360.1	55.7	37.8	9.5
Gray	59	929	73.7	27.2	48	198	17.6	4.5	183.1	72.4	68.3	7.6
Grayson	382	8 254	706.2	279.6	165	820	59.1	16.6	868.6	401.2	214.3	37.4
Gregg	426	9 705	943.9	336.1	261	1 827	189.8	52.1	948.9	410.1	223.3	53.3
Grimes	22	266	19.3	9.9	23	80	7.0	1.9	185.2	69.6	38.7	10.0

1. State totals may include programs not allocated by county.

Table B. States and Counties — Federal Funds, Residential Construction, and Local Government Finances

STATE County	Federal funds and grants, 2009–2010 (cont.)							Value of residential construction authorized by building permits, 2010		Local government finances, 2007				
	Expenditures (mil dol) (cont.)									General revenue				
	Procurement contract awards			Grants[1]								Taxes		
													Per capita[2] (dollars)	
	Salaries and wages	Defense	Other	Medicaid and other health-related	Nutrition and family welfare	Education	Other	New construction ($1,000)	Number of housing units	Total (mil dol)	Inter-govern-mental (mil dol)	Total (mil dol)	Total	Property
	171	172	173	174	175	176	177	178	179	180	181	182	183	184
TEXAS—Cont'd														
Caldwell	5.0	0.0	2.3	63.9	2.4	1.1	1.2	2 946	39	86.7	37.9	31.8	867	743
Calhoun	5.8	16.7	1.1	23.5	4.0	0.6	0.6	7 393	56	123.8	10.3	72.3	3 553	3 347
Callahan	2.1	3.5	0.5	14.5	1.2	0.9	0.9	329	2	32.2	16.8	10.4	773	644
Cameron	234.8	17.6	103.1	761.1	155.1	35.2	63.4	179 568	1 258	1 402.5	780.0	367.1	948	734
Camp	2.7	0.0	0.6	33.1	0.7	0.5	0.2	280	4	29.8	12.8	13.2	1 050	894
Carson	1.0	0.0	0.2	3.3	0.6	0.2	0.0	30	1	21.9	4.3	14.9	2 336	2 272
Cass	5.7	0.0	1.4	73.8	10.0	1.0	0.5	0	0	92.2	38.7	27.6	941	850
Castro	1.2	0.0	0.2	8.6	3.5	0.4	0.1	0	0	35.8	13.0	8.9	1 228	1 076
Chambers	4.1	53.4	32.5	16.8	2.6	1.1	0.4	38 901	226	137.8	25.8	91.7	3 187	2 996
Cherokee	7.0	0.1	1.6	82.9	7.7	1.8	2.3	1 923	30	110.2	60.5	36.9	766	637
Childress	1.9	0.0	0.6	11.6	1.5	0.2	0.1	375	3	39.2	10.0	5.1	671	505
Clay	2.1	0.0	0.5	7.8	1.1	0.3	0.1	0	0	43.4	11.9	13.2	1 185	1 062
Cochran	0.6	0.0	0.1	6.1	0.6	0.3	0.0	0	0	21.5	6.6	12.6	4 093	4 001
Coke	1.3	0.0	0.2	2.6	0.4	0.1	0.1	0	0	19.4	8.1	5.7	1 590	1 468
Coleman	3.3	0.6	0.7	22.2	5.1	0.4	0.3	12	1	32.4	14.8	8.5	992	762
Collin	134.5	1 046.7	184.4	95.8	35.8	6.6	19.0	1 149 407	4 533	2 925.7	413.4	1 736.2	2 376	2 008
Collingsworth	13.5	0.0	0.3	8.6	0.7	0.1	0.1	180	1	11.4	5.3	4.0	1 333	1 174
Colorado	4.2	0.0	5.7	45.2	3.5	0.6	0.6	814	7	62.9	15.1	30.9	1 494	1 317
Comal	175.0	254.3	4.1	37.9	9.2	3.3	3.0	180 615	846	325.8	52.2	212.2	2 017	1 685
Comanche	3.8	7.2	0.8	28.1	1.8	0.4	0.2	150	1	51.7	17.2	11.4	842	751
Concho	2.1	0.0	1.0	7.0	0.7	0.1	0.1	NA	NA	42.3	33.1	5.1	1 430	1 288
Cooke	5.6	0.8	1.5	22.6	4.1	1.5	6.4	3 427	26	175.9	48.1	57.8	1 503	1 250
Coryell	28.6	24.5	2.1	31.4	8.1	16.1	0.4	74 515	313	156.0	71.8	43.3	600	487
Cottle	0.6	0.0	0.1	5.1	0.2	0.1	0.1	0	0	7.1	3.4	2.9	1 829	1 678
Crane	0.5	0.0	0.1	2.0	0.3	0.1	0.0	2 893	26	42.0	4.6	31.6	8 195	7 934
Crockett	0.4	0.0	0.2	6.1	1.0	0.1	0.0	NA	NA	48.1	4.1	38.4	10 130	10 033
Crosby	1.3	0.0	0.3	11.5	1.7	0.4	0.3	0	0	31.4	17.9	5.7	905	809
Culberson	4.9	0.0	1.2	3.4	0.2	0.2	0.2	160	3	19.6	3.7	7.6	3 061	2 687
Dallam	1.0	0.0	0.2	4.0	1.2	0.2	5.2	7 793	83	22.7	7.2	11.6	1 897	1 564
Dallas	2 323.5	3 142.1	1 165.9	1 874.2	339.8	105.8	663.4	1 082 245	5 485	11 121.0	2 421.7	5 443.7	2 300	1 772
Dawson	3.9	0.0	0.6	27.3	7.8	0.7	0.5	300	1	76.8	33.2	23.6	1 700	1 502
Deaf Smith	2.7	0.0	1.8	24.8	5.2	0.8	0.0	140	1	176.4	65.8	18.9	1 026	869
Delta	1.7	0.0	0.4	16.4	1.7	0.2	0.1	534	3	16.3	9.5	5.2	958	850
Denton	153.1	130.1	55.6	74.6	29.7	13.0	60.6	495 461	2 096	1 636.7	270.9	1 070.2	1 748	1 513
DeWitt	6.1	0.0	0.7	54.6	6.1	1.7	0.7	879	7	92.1	46.7	21.9	1 109	994
Dickens	1.0	0.0	0.2	6.6	0.7	0.1	0.1	NA	NA	9.2	2.6	4.8	1 919	1 572
Dimmit	16.9	0.0	0.4	44.8	10.6	0.8	1.9	1 301	5	44.1	27.2	11.3	1 149	929
Donley	1.0	0.0	0.1	5.6	0.8	0.1	0.1	176	1	21.4	8.2	4.3	1 103	941
Duval	9.6	0.8	0.2	76.3	3.8	0.7	0.8	NA	NA	66.9	21.4	22.7	1 862	1 698
Eastland	4.8	0.1	2.2	35.4	2.6	0.8	0.6	180	1	76.2	29.3	17.3	946	784
Ector	28.1	0.0	3.8	92.7	28.4	8.5	16.4	79 163	708	609.9	162.7	189.3	1 461	1 149
Edwards	1.6	0.0	0.2	4.0	0.6	0.1	1.4	NA	NA	12.4	2.9	8.0	4 150	4 014
Ellis	23.9	4.0	9.0	85.7	10.0	2.7	0.7	71 444	497	413.0	112.4	231.8	1 616	1 377
El Paso	3 576.5	958.0	360.1	892.5	190.6	57.3	171.8	617 294	4 549	2 916.2	1 424.5	895.6	1 219	955
Erath	13.8	0.4	1.2	32.3	3.8	2.3	1.8	5 321	45	84.1	29.5	41.6	1 166	931
Falls	3.5	0.0	0.7	67.8	2.7	0.8	0.9	371	5	44.6	24.5	10.9	636	531
Fannin	254.5	1.0	3.3	67.8	5.4	0.8	2.5	300	1	73.4	35.1	25.8	782	672
Fayette	6.1	0.0	2.4	51.8	2.8	0.4	0.7	798	5	62.3	12.1	37.2	1 651	1 437
Fisher	1.6	0.0	0.3	10.1	0.6	0.1	0.2	0	0	24.5	11.1	6.2	1 570	1 476
Floyd	2.0	0.0	0.4	16.4	2.8	0.4	0.7	0	0	28.4	13.5	6.1	915	806
Foard	0.4	3.6	0.1	4.5	2.0	0.1	0.1	NA	NA	5.6	2.6	2.4	1 724	1 575
Fort Bend	90.5	67.7	50.8	78.8	31.0	7.1	22.4	894 774	4 954	1 337.9	321.4	798.6	1 566	1 390
Franklin	1.8	0.0	0.4	9.6	1.8	0.3	0.7	226	2	23.7	4.4	14.3	1 291	1 213
Freestone	3.2	0.1	0.7	34.9	2.5	0.5	0.2	902	9	98.4	11.3	73.9	3 934	3 836
Frio	7.3	0.1	49.2	44.3	5.9	0.9	4.1	275	11	59.3	31.4	13.6	846	695
Gaines	1.4	0.0	0.3	12.1	3.3	0.7	0.1	1 184	7	98.2	12.6	57.4	3 844	3 729
Galveston	115.6	432.3	51.6	400.5	38.5	17.5	51.2	349 314	1 971	1 247.5	280.4	735.9	2 591	2 267
Garza	1.0	0.0	2.2	7.1	1.4	0.2	0.1	161	1	17.8	5.0	10.4	2 220	2 146
Gillespie	14.3	1.1	1.3	8.6	2.9	0.4	0.4	6 746	34	62.5	9.5	42.0	1 785	1 472
Glasscock	0.3	0.0	0.1	1.5	0.3	0.0	0.0	NA	NA	13.4	1.2	10.5	8 920	8 861
Goliad	1.7	0.0	0.3	16.2	1.2	0.2	0.1	NA	NA	27.1	5.3	19.8	2 772	2 612
Gonzales	191.2	0.0	1.3	55.3	4.2	1.2	0.7	90	1	67.5	24.1	18.4	957	774
Gray	4.5	0.0	1.0	24.1	1.6	0.5	0.0	482	3	57.0	15.1	32.2	1 461	1 224
Grayson	25.3	6.5	10.0	123.9	16.0	2.7	7.8	21 820	327	363.4	126.4	155.6	1 311	1 087
Gregg	40.0	0.7	7.0	145.3	28.2	3.9	12.2	45 301	476	474.8	179.5	207.5	1 771	1 273
Grimes	4.4	0.5	2.0	53.6	3.5	1.1	0.6	450	3	58.0	18.1	32.2	1 258	1 120

1. State totals may include programs not allocated by county.   2. Based on the resident population estimated as of July 1 of the year shown.

STATE County	Direct general expenditure							Debt outstanding		Government employment, 2009			Presidential election,[2] 2008 Percent of vote cast:		
	Total (mil dol)	Per capita[1] (dollars)	Educa-tion	Health and hospitals	Police protec-tion	Public welfare	High-ways	Total (mil dol)	Per capita[1] (dollars)	Federal civilian	Federal military	State and local	Demo-cratic	Republi-can	All other
	185	186	187	188	189	190	191	192	193	194	195	196	197	198	199
TEXAS—Cont'd															
Caldwell	82.6	2 251	59.8	2.1	5.2	0.4	4.4	76.0	2 072	54	89	1 739	46.4	52.4	1.2
Calhoun	127.2	6 252	46.9	18.7	2.7	1.4	3.7	75.9	3 731	39	102	1 496	39.7	59.7	0.6
Callahan	31.9	2 361	72.5	0.1	3.5	0.3	1.7	16.6	1 226	46	32	674	18.6	80.3	1.1
Cameron	1 380.8	3 566	64.6	1.2	4.1	0.4	2.2	2 023.2	5 225	2 728	1 045	26 937	64.1	35.3	0.7
Camp	26.1	2 080	73.3	0.3	5.3	0.1	4.4	25.6	2 039	33	30	613	38.0	61.3	0.8
Carson	21.0	3 300	69.9	1.9	2.6	0.1	3.8	3.3	524	244	14	445	13.6	85.5	0.9
Cass	84.8	2 888	58.3	18.9	5.1	0.2	2.7	46.3	1 578	68	69	1 919	29.5	69.9	0.7
Castro	28.6	3 972	55.7	26.6	4.2	0.0	4.0	40.0	5 550	25	17	631	31.4	68.2	0.4
Chambers	136.5	4 745	61.7	5.7	3.8	0.3	3.7	201.2	6 992	59	74	1 809	24.0	75.1	0.9
Cherokee	99.8	2 071	63.7	8.3	6.6	0.3	3.9	49.7	1 031	81	114	4 129	28.1	71.2	0.7
Childress	41.7	5 516	34.8	50.0	1.9	0.0	1.2	8.0	1 064	31	18	1 170	21.6	77.6	0.7
Clay	42.0	3 774	46.6	15.8	2.6	0.1	4.9	306.9	27 605	30	26	568	20.3	78.9	0.8
Cochran	21.3	6 909	68.5	13.2	3.0	0.0	3.9	0.2	66	15	0	318	26.9	71.7	1.4
Coke	17.1	4 799	50.1	0.0	2.6	24.0	3.0	0.1	31	19	0	347	19.1	79.8	1.1
Coleman	29.5	3 452	53.7	18.9	3.1	0.0	3.6	16.1	1 885	45	20	727	17.4	81.3	1.3
Collin	3 278.1	4 486	51.8	0.5	3.7	0.0	4.1	8 428.6	11 535	1 442	1 870	38 095	36.8	62.3	0.9
Collingsworth	11.4	3 849	57.2	9.4	4.6	0.0	4.6	4.7	1 585	20	0	259	19.6	78.9	1.5
Colorado	59.4	2 873	52.7	13.9	4.6	0.1	6.3	94.3	4 564	63	49	955	30.0	69.4	0.6
Comal	354.7	3 372	64.4	0.4	5.2	0.5	4.0	693.7	6 595	176	270	5 096	25.7	73.2	1.1
Comanche	47.7	3 521	41.2	34.6	2.6	0.0	4.1	33.9	2 504	52	32	1 051	25.6	73.1	1.3
Concho	40.8	11 339	11.9	7.0	1.5	0.0	1.0	8.2	2 275	31	0	220	23.9	74.9	1.2
Cooke	170.0	4 418	52.4	20.7	4.7	0.1	2.9	166.4	4 324	73	91	2 910	20.3	79.0	0.7
Coryell	153.5	2 127	63.3	12.4	4.2	0.0	2.8	125.4	1 738	191	128	5 876	36.1	63.0	0.9
Cottle	5.9	3 648	43.1	1.7	1.9	0.1	5.3	0.7	457	15	0	138	26.5	72.2	1.3
Crane	36.0	9 332	70.4	9.7	2.4	0.1	1.4	4.1	1 067	0	10	358	21.9	77.0	1.1
Crockett	43.5	11 467	65.8	2.0	2.0	7.1	4.5	2.9	772	0	0	449	33.1	66.4	0.5
Crosby	27.4	4 340	60.2	0.1	2.6	0.8	2.9	0.7	108	22	14	494	35.7	63.8	0.5
Culberson	17.6	7 069	46.4	26.4	3.3	0.0	2.1	3.6	1 443	83	0	283	64.8	33.9	1.3
Dallam	24.6	4 010	64.6	0.0	4.7	0.0	4.7	26.0	4 239	19	15	530	19.0	79.9	1.1
Dallas	10 545.4	4 456	40.0	12.2	5.9	0.2	5.1	20 793.0	8 786	27 318	7 331	140 925	57.3	42.0	0.7
Dawson	54.8	3 953	58.8	16.6	4.1	0.9	2.6	154.1	11 112	64	32	1 530	28.1	70.9	0.9
Deaf Smith	160.0	8 672	21.0	7.8	1.7	0.0	1.7	1 888.1	102 327	42	43	1 303	26.3	73.1	0.7
Delta	19.0	2 419	68.3	0.0	6.4	0.3	4.7	12.8	2 382	21	13	317	26.9	72.2	0.8
Denton	1 666.0	2 721	58.0	1.4	4.9	0.1	5.1	4 761.3	7 775	1 787	1 564	30 611	37.5	61.6	0.9
DeWitt	86.0	4 359	47.5	30.7	2.7	0.2	2.7	63.9	3 240	41	46	2 186	25.9	73.8	0.3
Dickens	10.1	4 006	73.6	0.1	1.0	0.4	3.3	8.0	3 198	15	0	169	24.1	75.1	0.8
Dimmit	40.0	4 084	52.3	25.6	2.5	0.0	2.8	15.1	1 538	262	23	870	75.0	24.4	0.6
Donley	21.0	5 380	72.9	0.2	2.4	9.6	3.5	18.4	4 714	17	0	420	17.2	81.3	1.5
Duval	70.0	5 741	45.6	31.6	3.7	0.5	3.0	102.2	8 390	160	28	1 146	74.8	24.4	0.8
Eastland	76.2	4 158	69.2	14.9	1.7	0.1	2.0	46.7	2 546	58	43	1 510	19.5	79.4	1.1
Ector	554.0	4 275	41.9	34.4	3.8	0.0	2.2	306.9	2 369	178	319	9 479	25.6	73.6	0.8
Edwards	10.6	5 489	75.6	1.5	2.4	0.1	4.4	0.4	231	25	0	187	33.4	65.0	1.5
Ellis	450.0	3 136	66.4	0.3	4.6	0.6	3.9	1 154.7	8 049	245	357	6 745	28.5	70.7	0.8
El Paso	2 885.0	3 927	57.2	12.5	4.4	0.3	2.0	3 658.4	4 980	11 664	20 802	53 546	65.9	33.4	0.8
Erath	83.2	2 336	51.6	12.1	8.2	0.3	5.3	73.8	2 070	74	85	3 542	22.3	76.8	0.9
Falls	41.4	2 411	68.0	0.9	3.9	0.6	4.9	36.2	2 111	404	40	1 322	39.7	59.4	0.8
Fannin	74.7	2 259	65.8	2.2	6.0	0.5	5.1	87.8	2 656	503	78	1 986	29.6	69.2	1.2
Fayette	58.0	2 573	58.6	2.6	5.2	0.1	9.8	21.9	972	76	54	1 626	28.1	70.8	1.1
Fisher	20.8	5 266	32.0	23.3	2.8	0.1	4.6	53.2	13 443	23	0	320	38.5	60.7	0.8
Floyd	29.2	4 389	59.6	24.5	3.7	0.0	1.0	19.6	2 942	34	15	538	29.0	70.8	0.3
Foard	4.6	3 228	63.0	3.8	5.0	0.0	8.9	1.6	1 094	10	0	111	36.8	60.8	2.4
Fort Bend	1 343.3	2 635	58.9	0.7	4.6	0.5	3.8	3 071.3	6 024	1 250	1 312	22 222	48.5	50.9	0.6
Franklin	22.1	1 988	61.1	0.0	4.7	0.1	9.0	12.2	1 099	19	26	388	23.1	75.5	1.4
Freestone	92.7	4 930	79.5	7.5	3.7	0.0	0.8	101.9	5 422	37	46	1 473	27.9	71.4	0.7
Frio	55.0	3 412	58.0	2.0	4.3	0.0	2.9	259.6	16 093	29	38	1 314	59.2	40.5	0.3
Gaines	99.6	6 674	56.1	27.6	2.5	0.1	4.6	226.5	15 174	31	36	1 322	16.0	83.2	0.8
Galveston	1 237.2	4 357	58.4	5.5	4.8	0.6	3.0	2 036.6	7 172	919	1 078	24 825	39.8	59.3	0.9
Garza	16.6	3 541	68.6	1.9	5.9	0.0	4.1	9.7	2 073	15	11	375	21.4	77.5	1.1
Gillespie	59.5	2 533	60.4	3.6	8.1	0.0	6.3	38.3	1 630	65	57	1 089	20.9	77.5	1.6
Glasscock	14.5	12 371	86.1	8.0	0.4	0.0	0.8	8.1	6 897	0	0	115	9.3	90.1	0.5
Goliad	26.4	3 690	74.9	3.1	5.3	0.6	5.0	14.9	2 085	20	17	466	36.4	62.9	0.8
Gonzales	70.1	3 648	48.7	26.7	3.9	0.0	5.6	29.3	1 528	75	46	1 397	34.5	64.8	0.7
Gray	54.7	2 482	59.7	0.7	5.8	0.2	5.7	137.3	6 230	56	52	1 522	14.2	85.1	0.7
Grayson	365.4	3 079	62.8	2.5	4.5	0.1	3.3	392.7	3 309	358	284	5 997	30.6	68.5	1.0
Gregg	419.7	3 584	59.9	5.8	5.1	0.0	2.4	428.1	3 655	330	284	7 427	30.9	68.5	0.6
Grimes	67.4	2 634	71.6	0.1	4.2	0.1	6.4	53.5	2 089	47	61	1 960	32.5	66.8	0.7

1. Based on the resident population estimated as of July 1 of the year shown.   2. © 2009 Election Data Services, Inc. All rights reserved.

Table B. States and Counties — **Land Area and Population**

STATE/ County code	CBSA code[1]	County type[2]	STATE County	Land area,[3] (sq km) 2010	Total persons	Rank	Per square kilometer	White	Black	American Indian, Alaska Native	Asian and Pacific Islander	Percent Hispanic or Latino[4]	Under 5 years	5 to 17 years	18 to 24 years	25 to 34 years	35 to 44 years	45 to 54 years
				1	2	3	4	5	6	7	8	9	10	11	12	13	14	15
			TEXAS—Cont'd															
48 187	41700	1	Guadalupe	1 842	131 533	469	71.4	56.2	6.7	0.8	2.2	35.6	7.0	20.7	8.4	12.0	14.4	14.8
48 189	38380	4	Hale	2 602	36 273	1 268	13.9	38.3	5.3	0.6	0.6	55.9	8.3	20.5	11.2	13.2	12.3	12.8
48 191	...	9	Hall	2 288	3 353	2 952	1.5	60.0	7.2	0.6	0.1	32.4	6.5	19.4	6.7	9.1	9.8	13.2
48 193	...	6	Hamilton	2 165	8 517	2 567	3.9	88.6	0.6	0.6	0.5	10.1	5.5	15.8	6.5	9.5	10.6	14.0
48 195	...	7	Hansford	2 382	5 613	2 798	2.4	55.6	0.7	0.6	0.3	43.3	8.3	22.0	7.5	11.6	12.3	13.7
48 197	...	7	Hardeman	1 800	4 139	2 894	2.3	72.5	5.8	1.2	0.4	21.5	6.5	18.1	6.4	10.4	11.1	13.9
48 199	13140	2	Hardin	2 307	54 635	916	23.7	88.6	6.1	0.8	0.7	4.4	6.7	19.1	8.3	12.1	12.8	15.1
48 201	26420	1	Harris	4 412	4 092 459	3	927.6	33.9	18.9	0.5	6.8	40.8	8.2	19.8	10.1	16.2	14.4	13.4
48 203	32220	4	Harrison	2 331	65 631	798	28.2	66.0	22.4	0.9	0.7	11.1	7.1	18.7	9.2	12.2	12.0	14.8
48 205	...	9	Hartley	3 787	6 062	2 760	1.6	68.3	7.0	0.6	0.5	23.9	5.8	16.8	4.2	15.6	18.5	16.6
48 207	...	6	Haskell	2 339	5 899	2 778	2.5	71.5	4.0	0.9	0.8	24.0	5.3	15.5	7.1	11.4	11.1	14.5
48 209	12420	1	Hays	1 756	157 107	396	89.5	59.9	3.6	0.8	1.7	35.3	6.7	17.9	17.8	13.5	12.8	12.7
48 211	...	9	Hemphill	2 347	3 807	2 922	1.6	70.5	0.2	0.8	0.7	28.5	8.6	20.8	6.7	12.9	13.0	13.1
48 213	11980	4	Henderson	2 263	78 532	690	34.7	82.0	6.6	1.1	0.6	10.8	5.9	16.8	7.9	10.4	11.6	14.3
48 215	32580	2	Hidalgo	4 069	774 769	75	190.4	7.9	0.4	0.1	1.0	90.6	9.6	25.0	10.7	14.0	13.2	10.3
48 217	...	6	Hill	2 483	35 089	1 297	14.1	74.7	6.8	0.8	0.5	18.3	6.5	17.8	8.4	10.6	11.4	13.7
48 219	30220	6	Hockley	2 353	22 935	1 692	9.7	52.1	3.8	0.6	0.3	43.6	7.6	19.5	12.2	12.2	10.7	13.9
48 221	24180	4	Hood	1 089	51 182	962	47.0	88.0	0.6	1.1	0.8	10.2	5.7	15.6	6.6	10.0	10.9	14.8
48 223	44860	6	Hopkins	1 987	35 161	1 295	17.7	76.7	7.6	0.9	0.8	15.3	6.9	18.7	8.4	11.4	12.5	14.2
48 225	...	7	Houston	3 188	23 732	1 655	7.4	63.3	26.3	0.8	0.5	10.0	5.7	15.0	6.9	11.4	12.9	15.6
48 227	13700	5	Howard	2 333	35 012	1 299	15.0	54.5	6.3	0.9	1.0	37.9	6.5	16.0	10.5	13.4	11.9	17.4
48 229	...	8	Hudspeth	11 839	3 476	2 942	0.3	18.8	1.2	0.7	0.5	79.6	7.0	23.2	7.7	10.6	11.1	14.7
48 231	19100	1	Hunt	2 176	86 129	653	39.6	76.2	8.7	1.5	1.5	13.6	6.6	18.2	10.0	11.8	12.6	14.8
48 233	14420	6	Hutchinson	2 298	22 150	1 729	9.6	76.0	2.8	2.3	0.6	19.8	7.2	19.1	7.8	12.4	11.6	14.4
48 235	41660	3	Irion	2 724	1 599	3 080	0.6	73.2	0.8	1.4	0.8	25.5	4.3	18.8	6.8	8.3	11.7	18.6
48 237	...	6	Jack	2 359	9 044	2 523	3.8	81.2	4.0	0.8	0.4	14.2	5.4	16.7	9.6	12.6	13.6	15.4
48 239	...	6	Jackson	2 148	14 075	2 168	6.6	63.6	7.0	0.6	0.5	29.0	7.3	18.1	7.9	11.7	11.1	14.6
48 241	...	6	Jasper	2 432	35 710	1 279	14.7	76.5	17.3	0.9	0.8	5.6	6.8	18.1	7.5	11.4	11.8	14.6
48 243	...	9	Jeff Davis	5 865	2 342	3 026	0.4	65.1	1.1	1.2	0.5	33.7	3.8	16.0	4.6	6.6	8.5	15.9
48 245	13140	2	Jefferson	2 270	252 273	257	111.1	45.5	34.1	0.6	3.7	17.0	6.8	17.1	10.6	14.2	12.5	14.7
48 247	...	6	Jim Hogg	2 943	5 300	2 820	1.8	6.5	0.4	0.3	0.4	92.6	8.7	20.3	8.3	11.9	11.7	12.0
48 249	10860	4	Jim Wells	2 240	40 838	1 157	18.2	20.0	0.4	0.4	0.4	79.0	8.2	20.6	9.4	12.0	11.9	13.4
48 251	19100	1	Johnson	1 877	150 934	413	80.4	77.8	2.9	1.1	1.3	18.1	7.1	20.1	8.5	12.6	13.7	15.0
48 253	10180	3	Jones	2 405	20 202	1 828	8.4	63.0	11.8	0.6	0.5	24.8	4.7	13.8	9.5	15.8	15.4	15.7
48 255	...	6	Karnes	1 936	14 824	2 125	7.7	40.5	9.2	0.3	0.3	49.8	5.6	14.4	10.3	16.6	13.5	14.5
48 257	19100	1	Kaufman	2 022	103 350	564	51.1	71.2	10.8	1.1	1.2	17.0	7.5	21.3	7.8	12.9	14.5	14.7
48 259	41700	1	Kendall	1 716	33 410	1 338	19.5	78.0	0.6	0.9	1.0	20.4	5.3	19.0	6.7	8.4	11.9	16.7
48 261	28780	9	Kenedy	3 777	416	3 140	0.1	20.9	0.5	1.4	0.2	76.7	6.5	18.0	9.9	10.3	11.1	15.6
48 263	...	9	Kent	2 337	808	3 119	0.3	83.7	1.0	1.5	0.1	14.9	4.7	18.2	4.7	7.5	10.4	15.0
48 265	28500	4	Kerr	2 858	49 625	985	17.4	73.2	1.8	1.0	1.0	24.0	5.2	15.0	7.9	9.1	9.9	13.7
48 267	...	7	Kimble	3 240	4 607	2 864	1.4	75.3	0.4	0.6	0.5	23.4	5.1	15.3	5.3	9.1	10.4	14.4
48 269	...	9	King	2 359	286	3 141	0.1	86.0	0.0	1.7	0.0	13.6	3.8	19.9	6.6	8.0	15.0	21.0
48 271	...	9	Kinney	3 523	3 598	2 937	1.0	42.2	1.2	1.0	0.3	55.7	5.3	14.8	7.9	9.9	11.8	12.5
48 273	28780	4	Kleberg	2 283	32 061	1 390	14.0	23.9	3.6	0.3	2.5	70.2	7.7	17.4	18.1	13.6	10.7	11.2
48 275	...	9	Knox	2 203	3 719	2 929	1.7	64.1	6.2	0.7	0.3	29.6	7.5	17.9	6.5	11.0	10.9	13.7
48 277	37580	4	Lamar	2 350	49 793	980	21.2	78.1	14.2	2.6	0.9	6.5	6.4	17.9	9.1	11.1	12.6	14.0
48 279	...	6	Lamb	2 632	13 977	2 177	5.3	43.7	4.3	0.5	0.2	51.7	8.1	21.1	8.1	11.3	11.1	13.6
48 281	28660	2	Lampasas	1 846	19 677	1 856	10.7	77.5	3.6	1.6	2.0	17.5	6.2	18.5	7.4	10.3	12.9	15.7
48 283	...	6	La Salle	3 851	6 886	2 695	1.8	13.2	0.3	0.5	0.2	86.0	6.0	15.7	17.9	16.0	11.3	10.6
48 285	...	6	Lavaca	2 512	19 263	1 866	7.7	76.9	6.9	0.4	0.5	16.0	6.4	16.7	6.3	9.5	10.8	14.5
48 287	...	6	Lee	1 629	16 612	2 009	10.2	66.1	11.4	0.7	0.6	22.4	6.5	19.7	8.0	10.7	11.7	15.4
48 289	...	8	Leon	2 779	16 801	1 996	6.0	78.6	7.3	0.8	0.6	13.5	6.1	16.2	6.7	9.7	10.2	15.1
48 291	26420	1	Liberty	3 000	75 643	716	25.2	70.2	11.2	0.9	0.7	18.0	6.9	18.7	9.3	13.4	13.6	15.0
48 293	...	6	Limestone	2 345	23 384	1 671	10.0	62.8	18.0	0.8	0.5	19.1	6.5	17.1	9.1	12.6	11.7	14.1
48 295	...	9	Lipscomb	2 414	3 302	2 959	1.4	68.2	0.4	1.8	0.5	30.5	7.7	19.9	8.1	12.4	10.9	14.5
48 297	...	6	Live Oak	2 693	11 531	2 333	4.3	59.6	4.1	0.8	0.7	35.2	5.0	15.4	7.1	11.9	12.1	15.4
48 299	...	7	Llano	2 419	19 301	1 864	8.0	90.5	0.7	1.0	0.6	8.0	4.3	11.7	4.6	7.4	8.4	13.7
48 301	...	9	Loving	1 733	82	3 143	0.0	73.2	0.0	4.9	0.0	22.0	3.7	7.3	13.4	4.9	11.0	17.1
48 303	31180	3	Lubbock	2 320	278 831	231	120.2	58.3	7.6	0.7	2.5	31.9	7.2	17.1	16.9	14.6	11.0	12.4
48 305	...	6	Lynn	2 310	5 915	2 776	2.6	51.0	2.1	0.8	0.2	46.4	7.4	20.4	6.8	10.8	11.4	15.4
48 307	...	7	McCulloch	2 760	8 283	2 588	3.0	67.7	1.8	0.5	0.4	29.9	6.5	18.1	6.4	9.7	11.1	13.7
48 309	47380	3	McLennan	2 686	234 906	272	87.5	60.1	15.1	0.7	1.7	23.6	7.1	18.3	14.3	12.9	11.4	12.9
48 311	...	8	McMullen	2 951	707	3 127	0.2	61.5	1.1	0.4	0.4	36.9	4.0	12.9	7.2	9.2	10.0	16.5
48 313	...	6	Madison	1 207	13 664	2 209	11.3	59.8	20.2	0.7	0.7	19.7	6.0	16.0	11.5	17.2	13.3	11.4
48 315	...	8	Marion	986	10 546	2 399	10.7	73.3	22.8	1.8	0.8	3.1	5.2	13.9	6.5	8.8	10.6	16.4
48 317	...	6	Martin	2 370	4 799	2 858	2.0	54.4	1.7	0.6	0.3	43.5	8.2	22.2	8.8	11.2	12.7	14.0

1. CBSA = Core Based Statistical Area. See Appendix A for explanation. See Appendix B for list of metropolitan areas with component counties. 2. County type code from the Economic Research Service of USDA Rural-Urban Continuum Codes. See Appendix A for definition. 3. Dry land or land partially or temporarily covered by water. 4. May be of any race.

Table B. States and Counties — **Population and Households**

STATE County	55 to 64 years	65 to 74 years	75 years and over	Percent female	1990	2000	1990– 2000	2000– 2010	Births	Deaths	Net migration	Number	Percent change, 2000– 2010	Persons per house-hold	Female family house-holder[1]	One per-son
	16	17	18	19	20	21	22	23	24	25	26	27	28	29	30	31
TEXAS—Cont'd																
Guadalupe	11.0	6.8	4.8	50.8	64 873	89 023	37.2	47.8	12 861	6 577	26 420	45 762	48.1	2.83	12.3	19.3
Hale	9.5	6.2	6.0	48.3	34 671	36 602	5.6	-0.9	5 822	2 759	-4 142	11 846	-1.1	2.83	14.3	22.2
Hall	12.7	12.1	10.6	50.6	3 905	3 782	-3.1	-11.3	442	489	-398	1 372	-11.4	2.41	9.7	31.6
Hamilton	13.4	12.5	12.2	50.7	7 733	8 229	6.4	3.5	836	1 235	249	3 442	2.0	2.40	9.0	27.6
Hansford	11.0	7.2	6.5	50.1	5 848	5 369	-8.2	4.5	910	506	-349	2 006	0.0	2.77	6.8	22.1
Hardeman	14.0	11.0	8.6	50.4	5 283	4 724	-10.6	-12.4	490	466	-876	1 722	-11.4	2.39	12.6	29.3
Hardin	12.3	7.8	5.7	50.7	41 320	48 073	16.3	13.7	6 149	4 533	4 035	20 462	14.9	2.65	11.6	21.3
Harris	9.8	4.8	3.4	50.2	2 818 101	3 400 578	20.7	20.3	622 264	192 381	184 991	1 435 155	19.0	2.82	15.3	25.2
Harrison	12.6	7.6	5.7	50.9	57 483	62 110	8.0	5.7	7 762	5 547	838	24 523	6.2	2.62	14.8	24.3
Hartley	10.0	6.6	5.9	39.0	3 634	5 537	52.4	9.5	684	407	-867	1 771	10.4	2.63	5.3	22.8
Haskell	13.3	10.5	11.3	47.4	6 820	6 093	-10.7	-3.2	564	800	-834	2 297	-10.6	2.33	10.0	30.3
Hays	10.1	5.1	3.3	50.2	65 614	97 589	48.7	61.0	16 616	5 711	47 048	55 245	65.4	2.72	9.8	21.7
Hemphill	12.1	6.8	6.1	49.4	3 720	3 351	-9.9	13.6	499	281	-94	1 382	8.0	2.73	7.2	22.1
Henderson	13.9	11.1	8.1	51.0	58 543	73 277	25.2	7.2	8 955	8 321	5 365	31 020	7.7	2.49	11.8	25.6
Hidalgo	7.8	5.1	4.2	51.3	383 545	569 463	48.5	36.1	152 574	29 453	52 865	216 471	38.0	3.55	18.8	14.0
Hill	13.3	10.2	8.1	51.0	27 146	32 321	19.1	8.6	4 464	3 844	3 097	13 238	8.5	2.59	11.6	24.1
Hockley	11.1	7.2	5.6	50.7	24 199	22 716	-6.1	1.0	3 296	1 865	-1 760	8 242	3.1	2.70	12.9	22.7
Hood	15.2	12.5	8.8	50.8	28 981	41 100	41.8	24.5	4 986	4 771	10 296	20 795	28.6	2.43	8.6	24.0
Hopkins	12.4	8.6	6.9	50.5	28 833	31 960	10.8	10.0	4 331	3 260	1 763	13 308	8.3	2.61	11.5	24.2
Houston	13.3	10.4	8.9	46.2	21 375	23 185	8.5	2.4	2 379	2 782	-278	8 656	4.8	2.41	14.1	28.9
Howard	11.3	7.0	6.2	43.7	32 343	33 627	4.0	4.1	4 310	3 417	-1 423	11 333	-0.5	2.55	14.4	27.1
Hudspeth	12.1	8.4	5.2	49.7	2 915	3 344	14.7	3.9	429	134	-524	1 174	7.5	2.89	12.9	23.8
Hunt	12.0	8.2	5.7	50.4	64 343	76 596	19.0	12.4	10 373	7 091	3 447	32 076	11.6	2.63	12.2	24.0
Hutchinson	12.8	7.5	7.2	50.0	25 689	23 857	-7.1	-7.2	2 876	2 325	-2 836	8 812	-5.1	2.50	10.5	26.6
Irion	13.4	10.5	7.7	49.5	1 629	1 771	8.7	-9.7	98	95	-25	653	-5.9	2.45	8.6	25.0
Jack	11.8	8.7	6.3	44.4	6 981	8 763	25.5	3.2	858	842	-253	3 136	2.9	2.52	9.1	25.7
Jackson	12.9	8.8	7.6	50.6	13 039	14 391	10.4	-2.2	1 920	1 434	-524	5 284	-1.0	2.62	11.0	24.6
Jasper	13.2	9.5	7.2	50.9	31 102	35 604	14.5	0.3	4 408	3 672	-1 763	13 770	2.4	2.52	13.8	24.9
Jeff Davis	21.4	14.7	8.5	49.3	1 946	2 207	13.4	6.1	162	156	56	1 034	15.4	2.18	5.8	30.2
Jefferson	11.3	6.4	6.3	48.9	239 389	252 051	5.3	0.1	31 624	23 581	-15 531	93 441	0.6	2.53	16.9	28.6
Jim Hogg	12.2	8.6	6.3	50.6	5 109	5 281	3.4	0.4	805	436	-646	1 902	4.8	2.78	15.8	26.4
Jim Wells	11.5	7.2	5.9	50.8	37 679	39 326	4.4	3.8	6 135	3 248	-996	13 961	7.7	2.90	16.9	21.1
Johnson	11.5	7.0	4.6	50.0	97 165	126 811	30.5	19.0	18 813	10 040	21 953	52 193	19.6	2.84	11.5	18.6
Jones	11.5	7.7	6.0	38.7	16 490	20 785	26.0	-2.8	1 735	1 841	-1 647	6 034	-1.7	2.52	10.5	25.4
Karnes	11.2	6.9	7.1	40.4	12 455	15 446	24.0	-4.0	1 660	1 400	-596	4 463	0.2	2.57	14.3	27.1
Kaufman	11.1	6.2	4.1	50.8	52 220	71 313	36.6	44.9	12 557	6 882	25 716	34 964	43.5	2.92	12.4	17.5
Kendall	15.3	9.5	7.2	51.2	14 589	23 743	62.7	40.7	3 220	2 498	9 530	12 617	46.5	2.61	8.2	21.7
Kenedy	14.4	6.7	7.5	49.0	460	414	-10.0	0.5	50	29	-66	147	6.5	2.83	11.6	25.2
Kent	13.7	10.6	15.1	51.5	1 010	859	-15.0	-5.9	58	139	-72	350	-0.8	2.16	9.4	37.1
Kerr	14.4	12.5	12.3	51.5	36 304	43 653	20.2	13.7	5 101	6 012	5 888	20 550	15.4	2.32	10.2	29.1
Kimble	17.7	13.0	9.9	50.5	4 122	4 468	8.4	3.1	458	570	204	2 016	8.0	2.26	8.6	31.4
King	12.2	7.0	6.3	50.7	354	356	0.6	-19.7	24	13	-83	113	4.6	2.53	4.4	20.4
Kinney	13.5	12.7	11.6	45.7	3 119	3 379	8.3	6.5	317	301	-111	1 350	2.7	2.42	6.8	28.3
Kleberg	9.7	6.5	5.0	49.0	30 274	31 549	4.2	1.6	4 731	2 048	-3 461	11 097	1.8	2.71	16.1	23.7
Knox	11.4	10.1	11.2	50.7	4 837	4 253	-12.1	-12.6	427	546	-806	1 506	-10.9	2.40	11.0	30.6
Lamar	12.3	9.3	7.3	51.7	43 949	48 499	10.4	2.7	6 049	5 326	48	19 829	3.9	2.48	14.5	27.3
Lamb	10.7	8.1	7.8	50.2	15 072	14 709	-2.4	-5.0	2 159	1 591	-2 071	5 081	-5.2	2.71	12.4	24.1
Lampasas	13.1	9.2	6.6	50.7	13 521	17 762	31.4	10.8	2 279	1 782	2 759	7 539	15.0	2.58	10.0	23.0
La Salle	10.0	7.4	5.1	40.6	5 254	5 866	11.6	17.4	852	415	-467	1 931	6.2	2.75	16.4	26.6
Lavaca	14.6	10.5	10.7	51.1	18 690	19 210	2.8	0.3	2 255	2 498	-312	7 808	1.8	2.41	9.5	27.8
Lee	12.3	8.7	7.1	49.4	12 854	15 657	21.8	6.1	1 959	1 363	79	6 151	8.6	2.62	9.6	23.9
Leon	14.4	12.7	8.8	50.1	12 665	15 335	21.1	9.6	1 863	1 832	1 645	6 896	11.4	2.42	9.9	25.8
Liberty	11.9	6.6	4.6	50.8	52 726	70 154	33.1	7.8	9 847	6 310	2 524	25 073	7.9	2.81	12.8	21.8
Limestone	12.8	9.1	7.1	48.2	20 946	22 051	5.3	6.0	2 727	2 617	262	8 499	7.5	2.56	13.7	26.3
Lipscomb	11.9	7.5	7.2	49.7	3 143	3 057	-2.7	8.0	385	300	-34	1 263	4.8	2.59	8.2	26.7
Live Oak	13.8	10.8	8.4	46.3	9 556	12 309	28.8	-6.3	1 039	868	-1 408	4 257	0.6	2.44	9.5	26.9
Llano	18.9	17.3	13.8	51.7	11 631	17 044	46.5	13.2	1 452	2 518	2 324	9 008	14.3	2.12	6.9	31.5
Loving	28.0	9.8	4.9	43.9	107	67	-37.4	22.4	5	2	-28	39	25.8	2.10	10.3	30.8
Lubbock	9.8	5.9	5.1	50.6	222 636	242 628	9.0	14.9	37 577	18 725	9 310	105 781	14.3	2.53	13.5	27.5
Lynn	11.9	8.8	7.0	50.2	6 758	6 550	-3.1	-9.7	831	530	-1 173	2 246	-4.6	2.61	11.2	24.7
McCulloch	14.6	10.4	9.5	51.0	8 778	8 205	-6.5	1.0	954	1 023	-122	3 338	1.9	2.45	10.4	28.4
McLennan	10.7	6.5	6.0	51.4	189 123	213 517	12.9	10.0	31 310	18 546	8 593	86 892	10.2	2.60	14.7	26.2
McMullen	13.7	16.0	10.5	48.1	817	851	4.2	-16.9	62	56	-41	310	-12.7	2.28	7.1	28.1
Madison	10.8	7.9	6.0	42.4	10 931	12 940	18.4	5.6	1 456	1 224	183	4 187	7.0	2.65	13.6	24.6
Marion	17.1	12.8	8.7	51.0	9 984	10 941	9.6	-3.6	1 006	1 358	-281	4 595	-0.3	2.26	12.5	31.3
Martin	10.7	7.0	5.3	49.8	4 956	4 746	-4.2	1.1	652	431	-368	1 649	1.5	2.88	12.4	21.2

1. No spouse present.

Table B. States and Counties — **Population, Vital Statistics, Medicare, and Crime**

STATE County	Persons in group quarters, 2010	Daytime population, 2006–2010 Number	Daytime population, 2006–2010 Employment/residence ratio	Births, average 2006–2008 Total	Births, average 2006–2008 Rate[1]	Deaths, average 2006–2008 Number	Deaths, average 2006–2008 Rate[1]	Persons under 65 with no health insurance, 2009 Number	Persons under 65 with no health insurance, 2009 Percent	Medicare, 2011 Eligible for Medicare	Medicare, 2011 Enrolled in Medicare Advantage	Medicare, 2011 Enrolled in a Medicare prescription drug plan	Serious crimes known to police,[2] 2010 Total Number	Serious crimes known to police,[2] 2010 Total Rate[3]
	32	33	34	35	36	37	38	39	40	41	42	43	44	45
TEXAS—Cont'd														
Guadalupe	1 888	100 648	0.6	1 585	14.1	798	7.1	23 128	22.1	18 356	3 447	5 414	3 419	2 599
Hale	2 802	36 733	1.0	D	D	290	8.1	8 664	28.7	5 081	442	2 663	1 156	3 187
Hall	44	3 291	0.9	D	D	46	13.0	941	36.9	797	40	449	74	2 207
Hamilton	254	8 309	1.0	D	D	125	15.3	1 878	31.2	2 091	467	837	208	2 914
Hansford	60	5 137	0.9	D	D	55	10.5	1 501	33.2	865	40	498	58	1 033
Hardeman	21	3 909	0.8	D	D	31	7.6	838	27.5	909	24	452	139	3 358
Hardin	380	43 139	0.6	703	13.6	503	9.7	9 605	21.2	9 072	2 139	3 319	960	1 757
Harris	44 524	4 231 088	1.2	71 085	18.1	21 421	5.4	1 046 478	28.6	401 744	116 739	137 539	221 632	5 216
Harrison	1 363	60 724	0.9	881	13.8	618	9.7	13 796	25.1	10 752	1 523	4 676	2 111	3 216
Hartley	1 406	6 076	1.0	D	D	53	10.1	1 277	29.9	619	32	359	96	1 584
Haskell	544	5 325	0.8	D	D	93	17.5	1 168	31.7	1 391	78	790	61	1 034
Hays	7 017	126 978	0.7	2 010	14.3	704	5.0	31 005	22.2	16 991	1 753	6 165	3 933	2 503
Hemphill	40	4 025	1.2	D	D	32	9.3	700	23.7	508	15	294	56	1 471
Henderson	1 242	69 283	0.7	1 026	12.9	929	11.7	17 379	27.8	17 663	2 315	7 691	2 636	3 366
Hidalgo	6 982	726 811	1.0	17 152	24.1	3 339	4.7	247 348	37.9	80 452	11 604	47 325	38 800	5 008
Hill	829	30 764	0.7	480	13.5	423	11.9	8 474	29.1	7 424	725	3 355	790	2 251
Hockley	641	21 597	0.9	D	D	197	8.8	5 145	27.1	3 504	332	1 617	694	3 026
Hood	701	43 531	0.7	596	12.0	554	11.2	8 836	21.8	12 265	1 791	4 797	1 274	2 489
Hopkins	431	34 239	1.0	D	D	335	9.9	8 261	28.7	6 465	333	3 403	481	1 368
Houston	2 908	23 073	0.9	D	D	310	13.6	5 188	29.6	4 754	343	2 291	483	2 035
Howard	6 080	34 578	1.0	477	14.7	367	11.3	7 503	27.3	5 213	351	2 220	1 768	5 050
Hudspeth	86	3 487	1.0	D	D	20	6.1	1 132	42.8	505	60	273	54	1 554
Hunt	1 869	79 827	0.9	1 161	14.0	802	9.7	18 615	26.6	14 815	1 240	7 110	3 565	4 139
Hutchinson	161	22 274	1.0	D	D	258	11.8	4 435	24.3	3 785	258	2 016	970	4 786
Irion	0	1 405	0.7	D	D	12	7.0	409	28.8	311	22	141	19	1 188
Jack	1 140	9 193	1.0	D	D	90	10.1	1 968	28.1	1 570	136	760	126	1 393
Jackson	217	13 957	1.0	D	D	155	10.9	3 008	25.4	2 585	209	1 180	232	1 648
Jasper	941	34 476	0.9	479	13.8	392	11.3	6 728	24.0	7 267	909	3 456	779	2 181
Jeff Davis	88	2 453	1.1	D	D	15	6.4	594	33.8	546	32	200	14	598
Jefferson	15 983	275 058	1.3	3 589	14.8	2 531	10.4	51 524	25.2	39 074	8 835	16 730	12 149	4 816
Jim Hogg	16	5 314	1.1	D	D	48	9.5	1 207	29.1	933	111	528	35	660
Jim Wells	357	40 661	1.0	719	17.5	340	8.3	9 037	25.7	6 904	1 989	3 105	1 911	4 679
Johnson	2 644	124 885	0.7	2 121	14.1	1 111	7.4	32 488	23.7	22 328	7 080	7 068	3 857	2 555
Jones	5 007	19 262	0.9	D	D	185	9.5	4 893	31.0	3 087	228	1 568	577	2 856
Karnes	3 336	14 988	1.0	D	D	149	9.9	4 194	33.7	2 542	148	1 471	437	2 948
Kaufman	1 336	81 576	0.6	1 502	15.5	779	8.1	22 127	24.2	14 200	2 551	5 816	3 144	3 042
Kendall	519	30 423	0.9	D	D	284	9.0	5 461	19.5	6 607	1 088	2 091	511	1 529
Kenedy	0	NA	NA	NA	NA	NA	NA	113	35.3	51	11	29	4	962
Kent	52	838	1.2	D	D	12	16.1	138	27.0	185	13	92	23	2 847
Kerr	1 910	49 302	1.0	D	D	667	14.0	9 935	28.1	13 488	759	5 122	1 157	2 331
Kimble	43	4 222	0.8	D	D	62	13.7	1 214	34.8	1 097	50	527	131	2 843
King	0	NA	NA	NA	NA	NA	NA	71	27.3	28	D	12	5	1 748
Kinney	332	3 673	1.1	D	D	32	9.7	738	31.7	890	134	329	21	584
Kleberg	1 974	31 206	1.0	D	D	218	7.1	6 947	26.3	4 423	1 038	1 477	1 847	5 761
Knox	104	3 884	1.1	D	D	52	14.7	859	33.9	850	32	488	35	941
Lamar	713	50 358	1.0	D	D	591	12.0	9 812	24.6	10 185	285	5 194	2 262	4 543
Lamb	184	13 754	0.9	D	D	161	11.6	3 208	29.9	2 562	257	1 455	454	3 248
Lampasas	222	16 230	0.6	D	D	204	9.8	4 708	27.4	3 895	651	1 104	333	1 692
La Salle	1 583	6 728	1.0	D	D	44	7.5	1 576	31.9	1 010	201	560	73	1 060
Lavaca	409	17 804	0.8	D	D	253	13.5	3 440	24.1	4 559	197	2 475	251	1 303
Lee	525	15 138	0.8	D	D	167	10.2	3 655	27.3	2 905	312	1 175	357	2 149
Leon	104	16 906	1.0	D	D	201	12.1	3 564	27.2	4 411	476	1 921	196	1 167
Liberty	5 144	65 137	0.7	1 074	14.2	700	9.3	17 944	27.3	10 827	2 743	4 091	3 032	4 008
Limestone	1 592	23 217	1.0	D	D	282	12.6	5 121	28.0	4 564	394	2 074	964	4 122
Lipscomb	37	3 231	1.0	D	D	33	11.0	753	29.1	537	17	290	16	485
Live Oak	1 164	11 028	0.9	D	D	106	9.3	2 577	29.3	1 775	273	816	103	893
Llano	184	18 420	0.9	NA	NA	281	15.3	3 059	24.2	5 685	643	2 285	481	2 492
Loving	0	NA	NA	NA	NA	NA	NA	11	26.2	12	D	0	0	0
Lubbock	11 037	273 725	1.0	4 279	16.5	2 104	8.1	54 967	23.6	37 180	5 318	16 127	15 924	5 711
Lynn	42	5 320	0.7	D	D	56	9.3	1 443	30.7	1 076	105	630	68	1 150
McCulloch	109	8 254	1.0	D	D	107	13.5	1 908	29.8	1 850	54	989	158	1 908
McLennan	9 085	235 065	1.1	3 499	15.3	2 031	8.9	45 794	23.1	35 661	6 498	14 412	10 887	4 635
McMullen	0	1 040	1.3	D	D	D	D	164	26.9	179	24	62	8	1 132
Madison	2 554	13 597	1.0	D	D	132	9.9	3 697	33.7	2 136	205	957	376	2 752
Marion	167	9 777	0.7	D	D	162	15.0	2 173	27.5	2 620	376	1 226	348	3 300
Martin	48	4 276	0.8	D	D	41	9.2	1 155	29.3	695	30	381	84	1 750

1. Per 1,000 estimated resident population.   2. Data for serious crimes have not been adjusted for underreporting; this may affect comparability between geographic areas and over time.   3. Per 100,000 population estimated by the FBI.

Table B. States and Counties — Crime, Education, Money Income, and Poverty

STATE County	Serious crimes known to police,[1] 2010 (cont.) Rate[2] Violent	Property	School enrollment and attainment, 2006–2010 Enrollment[3] Total	Per cent private	Attainment[4] (percent) High school grad-uate or less	Bach-elor's degree or more	Local government expenditures,[5] 2008–2009 Total current expendi-tures (mil dol)	Current expendi-tures per student (dollars)	Money income, 2006–2010 Per capita income[6] (dollars)	Households Median income Dollars	Percent change, 2000 to 2006–2010 (constant 2010 dollars)	Percent with income of $200,000 or more	Income and poverty, 2010 Percent below poverty level Median house-hold income (dollars)	All per-sons	Children under 18 years	Children 5 to 17 years in families
	46	47	48	49	50	51	52	53	54	55	56	57	58	59	60	61
TEXAS—Cont'd																
Guadalupe	210	2 390	35 088	13.0	44.2	24.0	163.3	7 572	25 218	61 274	10.1	2.2	58 799	11.4	17.3	16.1
Hale	215	2 972	10 364	16.0	62.0	14.1	61.6	8 185	16 322	36 509	-7.8	1.6	35 640	20.3	28.9	27.9
Hall	447	1 760	839	2.9	60.6	15.2	5.8	10 323	20 126	29 219	0.3	1.9	29 302	24.1	40.3	37.4
Hamilton	336	2 578	1 746	5.8	49.1	23.4	16.3	8 992	22 429	40 808	3.5	2.6	38 179	16.2	27.3	25.8
Hansford	71	962	1 480	3.6	56.5	20.2	15.3	11 411	21 095	52 239	16.4	1.5	43 338	14.3	20.4	18.9
Hardeman	266	3 093	878	10.4	59.6	14.7	9.6	12 954	17 401	36 295	1.2	0.8	33 640	22.9	35.2	31.0
Hardin	141	1 616	13 207	10.2	54.6	15.4	95.7	8 804	23 965	52 755	10.8	1.8	49 556	13.0	17.6	16.0
Harris	777	4 639	1 105 964	11.1	46.5	27.7	6 219.7	8 507	26 788	51 444	-4.6	5.2	50 437	18.7	27.1	25.6
Harrison	419	2 797	17 605	17.7	52.6	16.2	110.9	8 765	22 019	44 425	4.7	2.4	44 506	17.3	25.6	24.1
Hartley	297	1 287	1 323	23.9	57.8	19.8	3.8	10 659	24 616	66 583	13.5	5.6	57 589	11.9	12.7	11.9
Haskell	102	932	1 031	3.3	65.9	11.7	10.6	11 881	22 734	35 295	17.7	3.1	30 845	25.5	39.4	35.8
Hays	208	2 296	50 069	8.7	35.0	35.0	226.1	8 177	25 998	56 353	-1.1	4.0	57 051	14.4	14.4	13.7
Hemphill	368	1 103	842	18.1	48.4	16.3	9.1	11 256	29 343	62 159	38.4	3.2	55 391	9.2	13.3	12.8
Henderson	359	3 007	17 965	6.7	55.6	14.2	101.8	8 552	21 580	39 779	-3.4	1.8	37 137	19.3	30.7	26.7
Hidalgo	314	4 694	242 120	4.1	64.3	15.1	1 826.4	9 082	13 480	31 879	1.3	1.6	33 070	33.4	44.8	44.6
Hill	105	2 146	8 524	9.4	51.8	15.3	60.0	9 302	20 554	39 293	-1.8	1.3	38 583	17.1	27.1	25.0
Hockley	432	2 594	6 882	5.5	52.8	18.0	49.6	10 250	20 255	46 430	18.0	1.8	40 334	19.1	26.1	25.1
Hood	191	2 298	9 944	10.1	42.4	23.9	72.0	9 213	30 687	54 882	-0.7	4.6	52 633	11.9	19.8	19.1
Hopkins	162	1 206	8 238	5.5	54.4	16.7	56.3	8 548	21 163	41 642	2.3	1.6	40 446	18.0	28.4	26.9
Houston	202	1 833	5 387	9.0	62.7	13.4	32.3	9 528	18 813	31 929	-10.3	1.3	33 198	23.7	32.7	31.2
Howard	571	4 478	7 368	5.3	57.1	10.1	43.8	8 150	17 832	39 574	1.5	1.4	39 022	22.9	30.6	28.5
Hudspeth	288	1 266	1 097	1.3	72.6	10.5	9.3	12 376	11 485	22 647	-15.0	0.5	26 993	29.5	41.7	37.6
Hunt	423	3 717	22 395	7.4	54.6	17.0	123.8	8 572	21 646	43 101	-7.4	2.1	41 841	20.0	28.0	25.6
Hutchinson	997	3 789	5 810	5.0	52.6	13.0	37.5	8 797	21 075	42 213	-8.9	0.9	46 035	13.4	19.9	17.8
Irion	63	1 126	368	7.0	57.7	12.3	4.1	12 208	31 857	48 833	2.8	3.7	52 857	9.6	14.5	12.2
Jack	199	1 194	2 064	9.8	61.8	10.5	16.7	10 443	21 349	46 801	13.7	3.1	41 510	15.5	20.4	17.9
Jackson	242	1 407	3 236	6.9	55.5	16.9	28.2	8 671	24 337	47 483	6.4	2.8	42 007	16.2	25.3	25.3
Jasper	308	1 873	8 239	12.9	59.6	14.0	54.6	8 818	19 182	38 062	-2.7	1.1	37 495	19.5	29.2	27.1
Jeff Davis	213	384	486	30.2	38.3	34.3	6.3	15 788	22 007	43 750	7.3	1.4	46 122	12.1	18.5	16.5
Jefferson	593	4 223	63 915	9.7	51.8	17.8	410.2	9 842	22 095	42 293	-3.8	2.6	39 756	22.6	33.5	29.3
Jim Hogg	189	472	1 233	0.5	73.4	12.4	12.0	10 589	17 163	40 000	22.3	1.2	34 077	24.8	36.8	36.2
Jim Wells	634	4 045	11 127	6.5	63.2	10.6	70.5	8 380	16 976	37 020	1.4	1.3	36 404	21.6	32.5	31.3
Johnson	231	2 324	37 599	11.7	53.3	16.1	251.5	8 218	23 669	54 954	-2.7	2.6	52 360	12.8	18.2	17.4
Jones	416	2 440	3 847	11.9	65.4	9.3	27.9	10 096	15 880	39 568	5.7	1.2	35 193	24.3	29.9	28.1
Karnes	250	2 698	1 687	10.2	68.0	8.4	22.6	9 955	15 949	39 611	17.9	0.6	34 970	26.3	33.3	31.4
Kaufman	357	2 685	26 820	12.1	51.0	17.2	175.4	7 893	23 909	58 555	3.3	2.9	56 899	11.9	17.3	15.7
Kendall	114	1 416	7 849	20.0	31.5	35.5	69.1	9 193	36 418	66 655	6.3	8.8	68 301	10.0	14.2	12.3
Kenedy	0	962	38	0.0	48.4	17.9	1.4	15 557	16 655	48 333	52.7	0.0	33 502	12.5	17.6	16.0
Kent	248	2 599	171	1.2	48.0	19.4	2.8	19 727	27 021	47 750	23.9	1.6	37 318	11.2	16.8	14.7
Kerr	177	2 154	9 823	22.8	42.5	27.0	60.2	8 718	25 454	43 072	-0.8	3.0	42 064	15.6	28.1	26.3
Kimble	412	2 431	823	5.6	51.2	20.3	6.2	9 231	27 118	43 429	16.7	2.5	36 126	18.6	33.7	31.1
King	350	1 399	28	0.0	29.3	36.8	3.0	31 579	39 511	61 563	36.5	13.7	48 003	12.5	15.3	14.8
Kinney	195	389	652	7.2	58.0	14.5	5.8	9 842	14 207	24 388	-32.0	0.5	35 725	24.7	36.8	33.9
Kleberg	861	4 900	11 478	5.2	50.5	20.4	51.8	9 420	18 580	36 571	-1.5	2.4	37 418	24.6	32.8	32.8
Knox	27	914	750	3.2	62.7	12.9	8.7	11 360	20 375	32 055	-0.5	0.7	31 054	22.3	35.7	35.0
Lamar	370	4 173	12 250	6.0	52.2	17.4	74.9	8 290	20 588	38 015	-5.0	1.5	38 852	18.4	27.4	25.6
Lamb	401	2 848	3 775	7.2	61.2	13.8	29.8	9 480	17 553	35 458	0.4	1.0	34 251	21.6	32.7	29.8
Lampasas	117	1 575	4 807	5.8	49.3	17.3	30.0	8 190	22 943	46 378	1.2	2.6	47 772	15.3	26.7	24.9
La Salle	189	871	1 620	5.3	69.1	8.1	13.3	11 102	13 542	30 144	8.9	1.5	28 834	34.4	44.9	43.0
Lavaca	88	1 215	4 018	16.2	61.9	14.0	18.4	9 003	23 168	41 429	12.3	2.0	39 468	14.5	20.9	20.1
Lee	391	1 758	4 063	13.1	57.3	14.5	27.6	9 122	23 074	46 986	2.3	1.8	45 661	13.1	18.3	16.7
Leon	113	1 054	3 206	6.2	59.2	12.6	30.3	10 025	22 484	40 355	2.9	1.7	40 847	14.4	25.1	24.3
Liberty	412	3 596	18 365	6.9	63.0	8.8	124.1	8 554	18 807	45 929	-5.4	1.2	46 770	18.8	25.7	23.9
Limestone	569	3 554	4 793	2.9	60.8	12.0	40.7	10 067	18 420	42 140	13.3	0.6	37 438	19.0	28.8	27.3
Lipscomb	0	485	758	1.8	48.5	22.5	10.7	13 340	24 839	52 566	29.9	2.8	46 347	13.3	20.6	19.7
Live Oak	69	824	2 480	8.8	55.7	14.0	17.0	9 886	21 540	43 719	7.7	1.8	39 091	18.6	27.8	25.5
Llano	124	2 368	2 828	8.4	42.4	26.0	18.1	9 208	29 027	41 969	-4.8	4.1	40 102	15.8	30.4	27.6
Loving	0	0	2	0.0	82.1	17.9	NA	NA	42 220	83 889	65.6	0.0	50 188	14.5	33.3	75.0
Lubbock	804	4 907	88 312	9.0	43.5	27.5	378.2	8 278	22 831	42 562	4.4	2.9	41 757	20.8	27.6	24.5
Lynn	85	1 065	1 502	8.0	63.0	15.9	14.2	11 002	19 752	43 672	29.2	0.6	36 145	19.7	30.4	28.7
McCulloch	241	1 666	1 803	7.3	58.0	20.4	16.7	10 116	20 116	34 459	5.9	2.2	32 469	22.2	37.8	34.4
McLennan	542	4 092	71 102	24.9	48.5	20.6	362.8	8 702	20 652	40 672	-4.3	2.0	39 620	21.3	29.4	26.9
McMullen	283	849	170	13.5	59.3	10.5	2.9	17 539	21 358	41 453	0.7	4.9	44 541	11.9	19.2	17.4
Madison	322	2 430	3 367	9.4	64.4	11.5	21.1	8 200	14 245	37 207	-0.1	1.8	35 189	23.3	30.2	29.0
Marion	512	2 788	1 784	10.7	60.2	11.2	12.6	10 207	20 125	29 943	-6.7	1.6	32 173	23.7	35.4	33.2
Martin	125	1 625	1 172	4.4	62.5	12.6	12.2	12 906	19 695	38 111	-5.5	0.7	44 863	16.2	24.0	22.3

1. Data for serious crimes have not been adjusted for underreporting; this may affect comparability between geographic areas and over time. 2. Per 100,000 population estimated by the FBI. 3. All persons 3 years old and over enrolled in nursery school through college. 4. Persons 25 years old and over. 5. Elementary and secondary education expenditures. 6. Based on population estimated by the American Community Survey, 2006–2010.

Table B. States and Counties — **Personal Income**

STATE County	Personal income, 2009 Total (mil dol)	Per capita Percent change, 2008–2009	Per capita Dollars	Per capita Rank	Wages and salaries[2] (mil dol)	Proprietors' income (mil dol)	Dividends, interest, and rent (mil dol)	Transfer payments (mil dol) Total	Government payments to individuals Total	Social Security	Medical payments	Income mainte-nance	Unemploy-ment insurance
	62	63	64	65	66	67	68	69	70	71	72	73	74
TEXAS—Cont'd													
Guadalupe	4 370	4.7	35 988	887	1 319	116	611	693	671	236	250	63	25
Hale	942	0.7	26 602	2 623	559	68	160	255	248	66	130	32	7
Hall	91	8.3	27 283	2 519	32	15	18	32	32	10	17	3	1
Hamilton	276	-0.6	34 371	1 117	106	11	75	76	74	27	36	4	2
Hansford	186	-11.8	34 373	1 115	95	32	40	31	30	12	14	2	1
Hardeman	122	-5.5	31 376	1 672	48	3	22	38	37	12	19	3	1
Hardin	1 948	1.4	36 468	820	554	114	282	411	401	135	194	31	16
Harris	196 779	-4.0	48 337	130	147 151	47 252	29 001	20 191	19 448	5 403	9 115	2 537	991
Harrison	2 382	-0.8	36 763	779	1 131	218	369	437	425	145	175	52	18
Hartley	201	0.0	40 469	422	75	35	34	13	12	8	1	1	1
Haskell	173	-5.3	34 576	1 082	78	16	33	56	55	19	27	5	1
Hays	4 623	0.7	29 721	2 040	1 961	364	857	652	623	225	221	59	34
Hemphill	181	-18.2	52 387	73	105	31	42	19	18	7	9	1	1
Henderson	2 414	-1.4	30 593	1 844	639	165	476	602	587	245	226	53	19
Hidalgo	15 200	3.6	20 509	3 087	8 394	1 485	1 731	4 617	4 481	757	2 060	1 131	208
Hill	1 043	0.4	29 089	2 171	350	79	191	294	288	101	129	24	9
Hockley	748	-3.4	33 567	1 237	389	62	109	178	173	47	84	17	6
Hood	2 022	-0.6	39 293	509	547	64	534	396	387	174	154	21	13
Hopkins	1 058	1.7	30 598	1 842	501	78	207	252	245	87	117	22	7
Houston	652	2.2	29 143	2 158	298	33	137	210	206	64	107	19	5
Howard	1 032	1.4	31 339	1 687	605	83	164	262	256	69	130	24	7
Hudspeth	86	7.8	27 681	2 454	66	10	10	20	20	4	8	4	1
Hunt	2 613	-1.3	31 641	1 636	1 487	145	359	594	579	208	247	56	20
Hutchinson	786	1.3	36 491	818	527	62	136	150	146	58	63	11	5
Irion	83	1.7	47 608	139	30	12	15	11	10	5	4	0	0
Jack	308	-5.7	36 300	847	145	41	53	57	56	21	26	3	2
Jackson	436	-3.0	30 515	1 859	217	23	92	111	108	35	55	9	3
Jasper	1 093	0.8	31 800	1 579	459	99	161	324	317	101	159	31	11
Jeff Davis	78	1.8	34 693	1 066	33	4	24	14	14	7	5	1	0
Jefferson	9 034	0.5	37 139	732	7 208	687	1 582	2 064	2 020	569	1 056	205	75
Jim Hogg	173	4.5	34 642	1 076	85	7	36	46	45	10	25	6	2
Jim Wells	1 342	-4.0	32 740	1 376	738	119	157	384	376	85	217	45	13
Johnson	4 850	-0.8	30 891	1 779	1 815	291	644	927	898	303	402	76	42
Jones	502	-1.1	26 462	2 647	158	32	63	142	139	43	72	11	4
Karnes	355	0.4	23 631	2 989	150	27	61	117	115	30	64	12	3
Kaufman	3 306	1.7	32 082	1 508	1 148	202	374	664	645	203	324	57	25
Kendall	1 720	1.6	50 495	92	513	81	487	214	207	90	85	9	6
Kenedy	19	-4.4	50 333	96	21	2	6	2	2	1	1	0	0
Kent	25	7.8	35 253	989	11	2	7	7	7	2	4	0	0
Kerr	2 105	-0.4	43 508	254	786	175	846	416	407	182	155	26	9
Kimble	142	1.7	31 384	1 669	51	16	42	38	37	15	16	3	1
King	12	9.4	42 483	296	7	2	3	1	1	0	0	0	0
Kinney	97	4.8	29 728	2 038	40	2	22	28	27	11	11	3	1
Kleberg	982	1.9	32 036	1 521	598	38	133	230	225	52	106	30	8
Knox	107	-9.2	32 117	1 503	55	1	18	38	37	10	22	3	1
Lamar	1 522	-0.1	31 079	1 734	854	139	268	425	416	136	193	43	12
Lamb	380	-2.8	28 876	2 221	174	32	61	118	115	32	63	12	3
Lampasas	884	4.0	42 280	308	184	28	135	176	173	48	79	12	4
La Salle	138	-0.7	23 670	2 983	85	11	18	45	44	11	22	7	2
Lavaca	681	0.0	36 736	782	224	49	173	183	180	60	97	10	4
Lee	551	-1.4	33 919	1 184	252	27	102	107	104	39	47	7	4
Leon	547	2.3	32 325	1 453	309	25	108	158	155	62	69	10	4
Liberty	2 556	0.0	33 729	1 212	745	251	259	577	563	156	306	52	21
Limestone	688	2.6	30 868	1 785	335	58	98	203	199	60	105	18	5
Lipscomb	114	-3.0	36 753	781	51	16	27	18	17	7	8	1	1
Live Oak	314	-3.0	28 447	2 311	141	29	55	73	71	23	35	6	2
Llano	669	-0.3	36 634	797	175	22	225	171	168	78	66	8	4
Loving	7	2.0	150 933	1	1	1	4	0	0	0	0	0	0
Lubbock	9 220	1.6	34 079	1 158	5 461	898	1 778	1 815	1 766	501	902	189	50
Lynn	162	5.2	28 608	2 277	59	11	30	49	48	15	24	5	1
McCulloch	247	-1.7	30 924	1 774	106	24	50	78	76	23	42	7	2
McLennan	7 530	2.2	32 265	1 466	4 902	473	1 328	1 502	1 460	472	576	175	51
McMullen	31	-1.7	37 723	672	10	3	11	5	5	2	2	0	0
Madison	336	2.3	25 228	2 837	151	30	66	89	87	29	41	10	3
Marion	294	0.5	28 546	2 290	72	27	51	95	93	35	39	9	4
Martin	151	3.5	32 996	1 342	64	19	25	32	31	9	17	3	1

1. Based on the resident population estimated as of July 1 of the year shown. 2. Includes supplements to wages and salaries.

Table B. States and Counties — Earnings, Social Security, and Housing

STATE County	Earnings, 2009 Total (mil dol)	Farm	Goods-related[1] Total	Manu-facturing	Service-related and health — Information and profesional and technical services	Retail trade	Finance, insurance, and real estate	Health care and social services	Govern-ment	Social Security beneficiaries, December 2010 — Number	Rate[2]	Supplemental Security Income recipients, December 2010	Housing units, 2010 — Total	Percent change, 2000–2010
	75	76	77	78	79	80	81	82	83	84	85	86	87	88
TEXAS—Cont'd														
Guadalupe	1 434	0.1	30.9	20.8	4.6	8.5	3.6	7.3	21.2	20 365	155	2 028	50 015	48.9
Hale	628	4.6	21.7	18.2	2.9	7.3	4.1	D	18.9	5 590	154	943	13 541	0.1
Hall	48	22.0	5.2	3.5	D	8.3	D	5.9	25.0	875	261	95	1 943	-2.3
Hamilton	116	-0.6	D	9.5	4.5	9.4	3.4	8.9	27.2	2 270	267	172	4 566	2.5
Hansford	127	18.8	28.8	2.6	D	4.2	D	1.6	19.6	910	162	64	2 338	0.4
Hardeman	52	-10.8	D	D	D	8.4	D	D	41.2	1 025	248	129	2 417	2.5
Hardin	668	-0.4	24.9	7.2	5.3	9.6	4.3	17.0	16.7	10 495	192	1 223	22 597	13.9
Harris	194 403	0.0	33.8	10.5	13.6	3.9	6.8	6.7	8.9	429 760	105	94 081	1 598 698	23.2
Harrison	1 349	-0.3	41.8	15.9	D	6.0	6.2	D	12.6	12 175	186	2 180	27 704	5.5
Hartley	110	41.4	D	D	D	3.4	1.7	D	25.3	585	97	27	1 946	10.6
Haskell	94	2.6	D	D	D	9.7	4.6	8.3	20.4	1 515	257	209	3 443	-3.2
Hays	2 325	0.0	20.2	9.0	7.6	11.4	4.9	10.0	24.9	18 305	117	1 599	59 417	66.7
Hemphill	136	6.3	40.7	0.8	1.8	3.7	6.3	2.0	13.8	520	137	21	1 629	5.2
Henderson	803	0.7	20.0	9.9	6.5	10.7	4.9	D	19.9	19 665	250	2 275	39 595	10.2
Hidalgo	9 879	0.6	8.4	2.6	5.1	9.5	4.1	21.5	28.0	89 745	116	40 227	248 287	28.9
Hill	428	-0.4	26.9	9.9	3.6	11.8	4.5	9.5	24.7	8 235	235	894	16 118	10.2
Hockley	452	1.9	37.2	3.0	2.2	5.1	3.4	D	19.3	3 800	166	528	9 293	1.6
Hood	611	-0.1	25.4	5.3	6.3	12.1	6.8	9.6	17.9	13 030	255	659	24 951	30.6
Hopkins	579	0.7	23.5	12.5	5.5	9.7	4.7	D	18.4	7 240	206	908	15 029	7.2
Houston	331	0.4	19.9	11.9	8.5	6.3	5.5	D	30.2	5 315	224	941	11 532	7.5
Howard	688	0.7	28.6	10.4	D	5.9	3.0	D	31.9	5 845	167	922	13 124	-3.4
Hudspeth	76	14.1	D	D	D	1.2	D	D	67.6	570	164	157	1 527	3.8
Hunt	1 632	0.0	D	38.7	4.0	7.0	3.6	6.6	20.0	16 785	195	2 433	38 704	13.0
Hutchinson	589	0.2	63.9	19.3	2.4	4.0	2.0	3.8	12.4	4 290	194	426	10 629	-2.2
Irion	42	4.1	60.7	2.4	D	3.4	D	D	13.0	355	222	20	856	-6.3
Jack	186	-1.5	53.9	1.5	D	2.9	6.9	3.7	14.7	1 715	190	147	4 095	11.6
Jackson	240	-2.0	D	D	5.4	5.4	3.2	2.8	19.5	2 830	201	320	6 590	0.7
Jasper	558	-0.2	31.2	23.4	4.4	9.1	4.5	11.0	17.8	8 325	233	1 345	16 798	1.3
Jeff Davis	36	4.5	D	D	D	3.1	D	D	40.9	600	256	41	1 613	13.6
Jefferson	7 895	0.1	35.6	21.4	10.2	6.8	3.0	11.4	13.9	44 565	177	8 821	104 424	2.3
Jim Hogg	92	1.1	13.3	2.4	D	5.3	D	10.4	53.5	1 005	190	319	2 441	5.8
Jim Wells	857	-0.3	35.6	2.0	3.4	5.8	6.9	D	13.0	7 865	193	2 049	16 147	9.0
Johnson	2 105	0.1	30.5	14.4	5.1	8.0	4.7	8.6	17.7	24 250	161	2 720	56 719	22.6
Jones	190	-2.7	27.8	8.6	D	6.3	7.8	D	30.3	3 465	172	461	7 422	2.6
Karnes	177	-2.4	21.3	7.8	D	5.8	4.7	5.1	40.4	2 765	187	581	5 650	3.1
Kaufman	1 351	-0.4	27.2	14.2	D	8.4	6.4	7.4	22.6	16 290	158	1 974	38 322	46.7
Kendall	595	0.2	19.9	7.2	9.8	13.8	8.0	9.6	16.7	7 010	210	262	14 055	46.2
Kenedy	23	17.2	D	0.0	D	0.0	0.0	D	14.2	55	132	0	233	-17.1
Kent	13	13.2	D	0.0	D	D	D	10.4	50.5	205	254	18	552	0.2
Kerr	962	0.5	15.6	4.8	8.4	10.5	6.0	D	20.4	14 315	288	906	23 831	17.8
Kimble	67	7.9	D	5.8	D	10.5	4.9	2.8	23.4	1 210	263	116	3 371	12.5
King	9	26.7	8.6	0.0	D	0.0	0.0	1.7	37.2	30	105	0	186	6.9
Kinney	41	1.7	D	D	D	3.1	D	1.6	67.2	965	268	133	1 940	1.7
Kleberg	636	1.5	9.9	3.0	D	7.9	4.1	D	45.7	4 840	151	1 206	12 787	0.3
Knox	56	-8.7	D	D	D	7.6	3.6	5.7	30.6	895	241	148	2 044	-4.0
Lamar	994	-0.4	D	26.3	D	8.3	4.9	15.7	14.7	11 475	230	1 999	22 481	6.5
Lamb	206	14.1	D	11.1	D	5.8	D	6.0	22.0	2 810	201	457	6 128	-2.6
Lampasas	212	-0.1	31.2	12.1	3.9	11.3	5.7	D	22.3	4 180	212	438	8 718	14.7
La Salle	96	3.3	D	0.0	D	3.1	D	D	38.7	1 185	172	369	2 746	12.7
Lavaca	273	-1.8	35.3	25.6	2.3	8.4	5.0	D	15.5	5 060	263	434	10 344	7.1
Lee	279	-1.0	37.9	8.6	4.9	6.2	6.5	D	22.1	3 215	194	332	7 499	9.5
Leon	334	-0.4	48.1	13.4	1.9	4.4	4.9	1.3	12.4	4 805	286	435	9 509	14.6
Liberty	995	0.1	27.7	15.4	D	10.2	6.4	10.3	21.0	12 680	168	2 095	28 759	9.1
Limestone	393	-0.6	18.5	9.2	D	6.9	4.4	14.0	32.5	5 145	220	854	10 536	8.3
Lipscomb	67	16.9	D	D	D	2.1	D	0.6	24.5	560	170	26	1 512	-1.9
Live Oak	169	-1.4	D	D	D	6.4	3.8	3.2	32.6	1 940	168	278	6 065	-2.1
Llano	198	-2.3	14.4	2.4	4.1	7.1	7.2	D	28.5	5 995	311	363	14 280	20.9
Loving	2	5.1	D	D	D	0.0	0.0	0.0	38.3	20	244	0	50	-28.6
Lubbock	6 359	0.5	10.5	3.7	8.2	8.4	8.5	16.4	23.6	40 750	146	6 135	115 064	14.4
Lynn	70	19.0	3.4	1.5	6.3	2.2	4.3	2.3	31.2	1 155	195	164	2 676	0.2
McCulloch	131	2.8	D	19.0	3.6	12.7	4.6	6.6	22.9	2 040	246	347	4 302	2.8
McLennan	5 375	0.0	26.7	19.6	5.9	6.0	7.6	11.6	17.6	39 755	169	6 930	95 124	12.2
McMullen	13	10.5	D	0.0	D	D	5.1	D	38.1	185	262	21	485	-18.1
Madison	182	14.2	D	1.7	4.1	11.1	7.1	6.8	30.6	2 425	177	320	5 096	6.2
Marion	99	-0.6	D	11.4	D	7.5	2.8	D	21.0	2 995	284	479	6 218	-2.6
Martin	82	11.8	D	D	D	5.7	D	4.9	24.4	750	156	102	1 852	-2.4

1. Includes mining, construction, and manufacturing.   2. Per 1,000 resident population enumerated in the 2010 census.

Table B. States and Counties — Housing, Labor Force, and Employment

STATE County	Housing units, 2006–2010 Occupied units Owner-occupied Total	Percent	Median value[1]	Median owner cost as a percent of income With a mortgage	Without a mortgage	Renter-occupied Median rent[2]	Median rent as a percent of income	Substandard units[3] (percent)	Civilian labor force, 2010 Total	Percent change, 2009–2010	Unemployment Total	Rate[4]	Civilian employment,[5] 2006–2010 Total	Percent Management, business, science and arts	Construction, production, and maintenance occupations
	89	90	91	92	93	94	95	96	97	98	99	100	101	102	103
TEXAS—Cont'd															
Guadalupe	42 738	78.6	142 400	21.5	11.1	795	28.4	4.3	61 341	3.9	4 243	6.9	57 879	33.9	23.5
Hale	11 444	65.3	73 500	21.5	11.5	550	26.7	5.4	17 480	0.9	1 228	7.0	14 184	25.1	33.7
Hall	1 440	67.0	44 300	18.5	14.7	594	32.8	5.3	1 415	-3.5	130	9.2	1 285	33.2	28.6
Hamilton	3 064	80.9	82 900	22.8	15.0	567	23.1	2.6	4 438	2.3	270	6.1	3 637	28.3	29.8
Hansford	1 948	75.8	64 900	16.6	10.1	586	23.8	8.0	2 769	-1.1	132	4.8	2 595	30.1	35.8
Hardeman	1 672	78.8	46 900	23.7	11.8	634	33.3	4.5	2 272	-0.8	157	6.9	1 676	34.5	26.2
Hardin	19 711	78.2	95 500	19.1	10.3	677	24.5	3.0	27 602	3.6	2 567	9.3	23 561	28.6	31.6
Harris	1 372 163	57.8	131 700	24.0	12.6	820	29.7	6.8	2 009 311	1.4	170 211	8.5	1 889 211	33.2	25.4
Harrison	22 997	74.7	94 400	20.1	11.2	627	27.2	3.3	33 043	-0.1	2 909	8.8	28 200	25.5	33.1
Hartley	1 715	73.3	128 500	18.5	10.0	660	29.4	3.6	2 482	-2.1	120	4.8	2 335	43.3	23.4
Haskell	2 549	76.0	39 200	15.6	13.4	347	15.0	2.4	3 122	-5.1	155	5.0	2 599	28.8	29.4
Hays	50 479	67.8	173 300	23.9	12.9	807	36.5	3.4	81 115	3.7	5 725	7.1	71 433	38.6	18.1
Hemphill	1 533	77.3	90 700	14.5	10.2	609	22.3	5.5	2 538	-6.4	82	3.2	1 980	29.4	38.8
Henderson	30 540	77.5	86 400	24.0	14.5	636	28.9	3.8	35 926	2.0	3 080	8.6	31 868	25.8	30.4
Hidalgo	205 971	70.8	73 000	26.2	13.7	601	34.0	14.6	305 786	3.0	36 133	11.8	268 488	25.9	24.3
Hill	12 988	76.5	85 000	23.4	14.0	648	28.6	3.9	16 377	-1.0	1 352	8.3	14 619	25.2	35.9
Hockley	8 100	74.4	71 200	18.4	10.6	608	26.6	4.6	12 222	-0.1	768	6.3	10 018	28.5	30.3
Hood	20 240	78.5	152 200	23.0	12.5	832	27.0	1.9	26 231	-1.6	1 977	7.5	22 538	34.9	25.7
Hopkins	13 045	71.1	95 300	22.3	13.6	642	27.8	4.5	18 001	0.6	1 228	6.8	15 305	28.5	34.0
Houston	7 872	74.3	67 600	22.2	14.3	559	33.6	4.7	8 542	3.6	840	9.8	9 319	22.2	27.2
Howard	11 080	68.9	57 200	19.8	10.6	618	30.2	2.9	14 218	-1.1	1 020	7.2	12 234	25.0	29.8
Hudspeth	1 066	79.4	43 900	31.9	17.0	629	21.7	6.4	1 817	5.2	105	5.8	1 063	21.9	39.9
Hunt	30 391	70.5	90 700	22.8	13.1	696	33.6	4.8	37 170	-0.3	3 275	8.8	36 849	29.8	28.9
Hutchinson	8 390	80.6	56 400	17.9	11.6	612	25.5	3.9	11 321	-1.0	825	7.3	9 426	24.9	32.2
Irion	620	83.2	74 700	15.9	10.7	594	30.3	1.5	935	4.0	45	4.8	940	25.6	36.1
Jack	2 984	77.6	67 500	19.1	10.9	604	20.1	3.5	5 087	-6.2	310	6.1	3 413	24.5	35.4
Jackson	5 030	74.1	77 500	18.3	11.2	602	21.1	5.3	6 947	-0.4	505	7.3	6 616	30.4	34.3
Jasper	13 466	79.3	76 600	21.1	11.1	579	29.2	4.2	15 903	-0.5	1 821	11.5	13 285	26.7	32.7
Jeff Davis	999	78.8	101 300	24.3	10.0	442	23.0	2.6	1 212	2.5	64	5.3	1 086	37.3	23.6
Jefferson	90 671	65.2	88 400	20.6	12.6	681	28.3	3.7	117 865	2.0	12 869	10.9	103 135	29.8	27.1
Jim Hogg	1 738	72.0	65 000	23.4	10.0	488	50.0	4.0	2 998	-1.4	237	7.9	2 036	20.0	38.1
Jim Wells	13 441	73.3	67 800	23.1	13.3	645	31.9	6.7	21 358	-4.1	1 842	8.6	16 365	25.1	28.8
Johnson	50 425	76.6	111 800	22.7	12.7	830	28.2	3.6	75 597	0.6	6 290	8.3	66 967	28.7	31.5
Jones	6 022	78.8	51 700	19.7	11.6	505	19.9	2.7	7 799	-1.5	625	8.0	6 135	26.0	31.9
Karnes	4 657	68.8	69 700	19.2	11.6	579	29.8	7.6	5 531	1.2	520	9.4	4 675	30.8	28.3
Kaufman	33 131	77.6	130 000	23.3	14.1	830	30.6	4.7	47 877	2.1	4 292	9.0	47 102	33.3	25.3
Kendall	12 055	75.4	243 900	23.8	10.7	891	32.5	3.4	17 046	3.7	1 022	6.0	15 034	43.9	19.2
Kenedy	92	38.0	71 000	0.0	10.0	666	13.9	0.0	237	-4.4	13	5.5	115	26.1	62.6
Kent	365	80.8	48 900	18.6	10.0	446	0.0	0.0	441	-5.4	26	5.9	431	35.7	31.3
Kerr	20 285	73.6	129 600	23.9	12.8	728	28.3	4.1	23 189	-1.5	1 443	6.2	20 705	32.8	21.4
Kimble	1 897	71.7	89 500	20.4	10.3	563	25.4	3.3	2 055	-3.9	134	6.5	2 221	27.0	33.1
King	95	38.9	325 000	19.4	12.5	530	30.4	4.2	193	-0.5	13	6.7	152	67.1	13.8
Kinney	1 150	79.7	46 400	16.8	16.4	495	34.2	3.7	1 497	2.6	135	9.0	960	12.7	31.9
Kleberg	10 924	59.7	74 500	24.2	11.7	635	29.2	6.5	17 278	0.3	1 211	7.0	12 935	32.8	22.9
Knox	1 625	67.8	42 900	20.0	13.1	449	27.1	3.3	1 813	-1.5	106	5.8	1 649	31.8	30.0
Lamar	19 053	68.8	81 100	19.9	14.1	587	28.7	3.5	23 910	1.4	2 140	9.0	21 524	28.4	29.1
Lamb	4 804	75.1	50 100	20.9	11.6	590	24.7	3.6	6 939	-2.5	492	7.1	6 191	23.3	34.2
Lampasas	7 031	76.2	121 300	21.8	14.1	686	28.6	5.1	10 841	2.1	670	6.2	8 365	26.2	30.1
La Salle	1 872	61.2	39 600	19.9	12.4	399	24.7	9.8	3 152	10.1	248	7.9	2 249	19.9	37.9
Lavaca	7 974	78.3	83 100	21.5	10.2	522	21.8	5.3	10 084	1.1	661	6.6	8 900	28.6	36.2
Lee	6 022	76.8	115 300	21.5	13.1	593	23.0	4.9	9 290	0.5	622	6.7	7 532	28.1	32.6
Leon	6 569	83.7	78 100	24.6	13.4	616	22.4	4.6	8 169	-4.2	639	7.8	6 500	22.9	37.5
Liberty	24 034	78.9	79 200	21.4	11.5	690	26.4	6.5	32 067	-0.1	3 542	11.0	29 201	23.4	36.8
Limestone	7 856	78.8	78 600	19.9	13.9	659	24.9	3.8	11 725	3.5	797	6.8	8 473	30.5	28.2
Lipscomb	1 127	77.6	73 700	18.2	10.0	563	14.9	4.2	1 696	-2.6	95	5.6	1 656	32.4	38.9
Live Oak	3 856	80.4	83 500	19.0	11.4	659	25.9	4.7	5 310	2.5	358	6.7	4 065	30.3	24.5
Llano	8 463	77.9	150 700	25.6	13.6	601	28.6	1.8	8 344	-2.7	628	7.5	7 698	32.7	22.6
Loving	22	45.5	66 700	15.6	10.0	0	0.0	0.0	50	25.0	4	8.0	36	58.3	41.7
Lubbock	102 170	59.7	103 100	22.0	11.4	731	33.2	4.6	143 869	1.4	8 874	6.2	131 152	32.0	20.3
Lynn	2 165	73.9	66 900	19.6	10.9	504	24.6	3.2	2 818	-1.7	199	7.1	2 784	25.1	28.9
McCulloch	3 098	71.6	71 200	18.8	12.8	511	29.2	4.8	3 955	0.6	282	7.1	3 498	30.4	27.1
McLennan	82 998	60.1	101 000	22.7	12.8	737	33.5	3.6	115 706	1.1	8 507	7.4	104 084	31.1	24.3
McMullen	307	83.1	83 100	19.0	10.0	463	28.2	3.9	373	3.3	25	6.7	496	25.2	49.4
Madison	3 592	79.4	84 700	19.6	13.5	528	26.1	5.2	5 638	5.1	447	7.9	4 093	25.1	29.6
Marion	4 744	79.8	58 700	22.2	12.1	552	28.5	3.4	5 166	0.5	533	10.3	4 003	20.5	38.2
Martin	1 492	75.4	75 200	19.4	14.5	395	20.8	4.2	2 248	-0.7	128	5.7	2 160	34.3	30.5

1. Specified owner-occupied units.   2. Specified renter-occupied units. A value of 10.0 represents 10 percent or less.   3. Overcrowded or lacking complete plumbing facilities.   4. Percent of civilian labor force.   5. Persons 16 years old and over.

Table B. States and Counties — Nonfarm Employment and Agriculture

STATE County	Private nonfarm establishments, employment and payroll, 2009									Agriculture, 2007			
	Number of establishments	Employment						Annual payroll		Farms			
		Total	Health care and social assistance	Manufacturing	Retail trade	Finance and insurance	Professional, scientific, and technical services	Total (mil dol)	Average per employee (dollars)	Number	Percent with:		Farm operators whose principal occupation is farming (percent)
											Fewer than 50 acres	500 acres or more	
	104	105	106	107	108	109	110	111	112	113	114	115	116

TEXAS—Cont'd

Guadalupe	1 784	25 976	3 009	5 118	4 179	619	506	818	31 480	2 462	50.5	5.2	39.9
Hale	738	11 293	1 098	2 509	1 555	336	192	319	28 278	957	12.2	36.4	46.4
Hall	90	550	93	54	D	46	D	11	20 351	382	3.7	44.2	44.5
Hamilton	229	2 070	476	172	355	62	45	61	29 294	1 045	14.7	20.9	42.3
Hansford	148	1 119	D	D	D	D	41	37	33 467	242	6.6	69.0	63.6
Hardeman	87	774	204	D	138	42	D	22	27 802	332	6.3	46.4	44.9
Hardin	777	8 915	1 574	670	2 169	200	182	273	30 662	699	67.2	2.7	33.2
Harris	91 082	1 809 432	206 808	159 891	183 144	77 077	163 758	97 475	53 870	2 210	69.8	4.3	38.4
Harrison	1 295	18 896	1 549	3 927	2 373	1 031	729	691	36 545	1 205	45.8	7.5	38.3
Hartley	89	1 083	D	D	188	D	D	31	28 283	282	3.9	65.2	62.4
Haskell	130	886	139	D	291	58	33	21	23 735	553	9.2	40.3	49.4
Hays	3 106	36 031	4 586	3 683	8 961	918	1 329	1 036	28 744	1 136	46.8	8.0	34.1
Hemphill	160	1 340	170	D	151	D	16	49	36 322	233	8.2	54.9	46.4
Henderson	1 244	12 923	2 410	1 878	2 652	455	339	363	28 097	2 109	48.5	5.5	38.1
Hidalgo	10 660	164 066	49 556	5 242	33 562	6 058	5 003	4 108	25 037	2 151	61.6	14.9	44.1
Hill	679	6 976	1 136	919	1 627	212	115	184	26 370	2 113	37.2	10.3	38.7
Hockley	505	5 633	1 034	243	923	213	142	172	30 520	842	15.4	33.5	39.0
Hood	1 220	12 266	1 969	500	2 594	436	377	378	30 811	1 076	58.6	7.5	34.8
Hopkins	741	10 052	1 186	D	1 688	455	233	319	31 717	1 955	35.4	9.7	44.1
Houston	367	3 636	705	680	733	162	93	105	28 835	1 562	27.4	12.5	46.7
Howard	690	9 490	2 233	669	1 391	329	194	321	33 793	519	26.6	32.8	37.4
Hudspeth	32	171	D	D	D	D	D	5	27 754	169	21.9	49.7	53.3
Hunt	1 395	21 830	2 972	7 626	3 620	486	941	847	38 794	3 139	52.9	3.9	37.1
Hutchinson	493	6 297	454	1 707	902	171	170	283	44 892	259	29.3	35.5	42.1
Irion	45	282	D	0	D	D	D	9	30 652	156	28.8	49.4	42.9
Jack	233	2 863	D	D	193	25	40	125	43 505	902	18.1	22.4	34.3
Jackson	279	3 896	262	D	529	D	D	133	34 198	847	28.1	26.9	46.6
Jasper	650	8 963	2 379	D	1 603	293	154	261	29 170	920	66.8	2.3	29.1
Jeff Davis	59	330	D	0	40	D	22	8	25 576	105	12.4	61.9	41.0
Jefferson	5 721	106 468	17 196	13 703	14 616	2 619	6 030	4 547	42 704	793	52.1	16.6	47.2
Jim Hogg	101	1 293	D	D	225	90	D	25	19 148	240	10.8	48.8	36.3
Jim Wells	846	13 644	4 451	360	1 670	368	302	404	29 586	1 109	31.4	15.6	44.0
Johnson	2 559	38 159	4 345	5 061	5 180	805	682	1 205	31 582	2 746	62.3	4.4	33.5
Jones	301	2 468	799	D	269	115	28	77	31 221	1 053	21.6	22.3	40.6
Karnes	241	2 311	D	251	479	81	66	63	27 181	1 208	16.0	17.5	44.0
Kaufman	1 692	20 779	3 100	3 607	3 603	655	481	604	29 064	2 563	59.1	5.0	36.9
Kendall	1 083	9 844	1 302	1 012	2 065	D	535	361	36 642	1 164	43.0	13.9	34.4
Kenedy	12	71	0	D	0	0	D	3	42 014	25	4.0	76.0	72.0
Kent	10	D	0	0	D	D	0	D	D	212	3.8	44.8	36.3
Kerr	1 421	15 346	3 528	545	2 919	D	687	478	31 156	1 226	33.0	16.6	36.0
Kimble	150	1 080	D	197	280	D	D	26	24 228	639	16.6	40.2	42.9
King	NA	NA	NA	NA	NA	NA	NA	NA	NA	64	3.1	56.3	34.4
Kinney	36	347	D	0	D	0	0	8	21 876	220	5.5	55.0	40.5
Kleberg	558	7 000	1 366	D	1 773	293	152	193	27 508	349	52.4	12.3	45.8
Knox	113	832	209	0	141	54	D	22	26 519	219	11.0	52.1	56.6
Lamar	1 170	17 650	3 412	4 318	2 603	527	323	537	30 450	1 817	29.4	12.5	38.5
Lamb	274	2 921	528	D	392	D	43	81	27 772	987	6.3	37.9	47.1
Lampasas	396	3 598	455	575	639	115	90	94	26 213	966	32.1	21.7	37.9
La Salle	83	1 289	94	0	178	D	D	31	23 905	399	10.3	45.1	46.6
Lavaca	453	5 322	968	1 413	748	269	69	141	26 452	2 747	32.0	7.1	38.4
Lee	408	3 966	297	399	699	233	80	124	31 349	1 844	33.7	7.5	36.0
Leon	361	4 343	96	573	550	118	66	186	42 925	2 066	34.8	11.9	45.8
Liberty	1 027	12 610	1 939	D	2 839	374	283	400	31 731	1 589	56.4	8.3	36.2
Limestone	402	5 444	1 039	961	1 250	252	D	146	26 769	1 494	25.2	16.2	47.1
Lipscomb	99	D	D	D	D	43	D	D	D	294	2.7	60.2	49.3
Live Oak	229	1 926	D	D	396	103	D	72	37 576	896	19.0	25.6	39.8
Llano	434	3 710	796	106	475	202	125	94	25 310	791	26.8	32.0	38.8
Loving	1	D	0	0	0	0	0	D	D	9	11.1	77.8	66.7
Lubbock	6 813	103 866	21 737	5 676	16 672	5 079	3 492	3 109	29 933	1 205	40.1	23.2	41.2
Lynn	95	704	D	D	87	67	D	20	28 276	506	12.6	48.0	61.1
McCulloch	218	2 098	287	D	484	105	64	53	25 353	694	13.4	32.6	42.8
McLennan	4 955	94 548	15 234	14 618	11 752	5 011	2 537	2 936	31 058	2 798	52.9	7.0	34.8
McMullen	14	100	D	0	D	D	D	4	43 780	225	6.2	64.0	37.3
Madison	205	1 893	D	51	497	102	85	49	25 725	1 057	33.9	10.8	40.2
Marion	158	1 439	349	348	228	D	D	36	24 918	258	32.2	7.0	35.3
Martin	93	815	147	0	D	D	D	28	34 952	464	15.1	42.2	53.0

Table B. States and Counties — **Agriculture**

STATE County	Land in farms Acreage (1,000)	Land in farms Percent change, 2002–2007	Acres Average size of farm	Acres Total irrigated (1,000)	Acres Total cropland (1,000)	Value of land and buildings (dollars) Average per farm	Value of land and buildings (dollars) Average per acre	Value of machinery and equipment, average per farm (dollars)	Value of products sold Total (mil dol)	Value of products sold Average per farm (dollars)	Percent from: Crops	Percent from: Livestock and poultry products	Percent of farms with sales of: $10,000 or more	Percent of farms with sales of: $100,000 or more	Government payments Total ($1,000)	Government payments Percent of farms
	117	118	119	120	121	122	123	124	125	126	127	128	129	130	131	132
TEXAS—Cont'd																
Guadalupe	385	0.0	156	1.1	126.0	406 933	2 602	43 017	41.2	16 725	45.7	54.3	22.0	2.6	1 263	11.8
Hale	589	-2.6	615	243.5	462.3	712 744	1 159	170 015	364.4	380 811	43.8	56.2	44.4	30.3	21 470	81.4
Hall	534	23.6	1 398	27.9	219.0	1 165 765	834	104 525	43.5	113 802	85.3	14.7	44.2	22.8	7 509	85.6
Hamilton	471	4.7	451	0.8	97.6	770 944	1 711	56 406	51.4	49 163	8.5	91.5	37.0	5.3	458	17.7
Hansford	585	-1.3	2 419	100.7	331.5	1 949 295	806	293 887	589.8	2 437 187	14.7	85.3	69.8	57.0	4 932	75.2
Hardeman	370	6.9	1 115	11.5	162.4	904 259	811	86 255	24.0	72 195	41.9	58.1	49.4	15.7	2 685	75.6
Hardin	91	31.9	130	1.0	22.1	296 543	2 273	49 252	6.3	9 033	54.3	45.7	14.6	2.3	231	2.3
Harris	259	-15.1	117	7.0	91.4	395 227	3 372	50 849	62.5	28 295	62.8	37.2	17.5	3.1	723	2.9
Harrison	201	-12.2	167	0.8	52.3	367 952	2 207	50 846	14.1	11 708	20.3	79.7	20.6	1.4	200	4.1
Hartley	911	15.5	3 230	171.7	345.2	2 184 140	676	361 687	724.5	2 569 176	20.3	79.7	63.8	56.4	5 096	74.8
Haskell	495	0.6	895	35.1	290.9	794 365	888	112 606	67.7	122 430	65.1	34.9	51.0	18.8	9 853	80.8
Hays	236	-15.1	207	0.9	39.3	585 716	2 825	33 253	11.5	10 081	41.8	58.2	13.2	1.6	248	3.6
Hemphill	549	0.5	2 355	5.3	75.6	1 715 338	728	105 978	117.7	505 163	1.6	98.4	50.2	25.8	1 156	48.1
Henderson	318	-6.7	151	1.3	86.5	369 324	2 446	48 910	44.5	21 106	43.0	57.0	27.4	2.3	124	3.9
Hidalgo	723	21.9	336	169.3	404.3	732 730	2 181	88 682	314.3	146 098	91.8	8.2	35.1	11.0	10 723	19.6
Hill	525	4.2	248	1.2	253.9	457 258	1 841	61 171	74.2	35 095	58.4	41.6	29.1	4.9	3 662	25.0
Hockley	484	-1.4	575	132.3	411.4	614 787	1 069	129 960	107.7	127 921	94.1	5.9	37.4	25.4	14 237	76.4
Hood	206	2.0	191	4.3	80.8	521 853	2 730	52 883	18.9	17 590	38.1	61.9	24.0	3.1	290	10.9
Hopkins	390	-9.5	200	11.6	143.0	456 522	2 286	67 748	208.3	106 522	7.9	92.1	40.4	9.8	636	8.8
Houston	440	-5.4	282	4.6	109.2	578 277	2 051	61 623	40.7	26 027	22.3	77.7	36.6	3.6	410	4.4
Howard	523	1.0	1 007	8.4	228.0	773 530	768	81 064	40.9	78 714	81.4	18.5	30.6	15.4	7 075	61.8
Hudspeth	2 258	6.4	13 358	27.3	106.5	3 776 355	283	157 771	31.1	183 861	64.9	35.1	52.1	23.7	766	24.9
Hunt	388	-3.0	124	2.1	171.6	305 177	2 466	45 239	40.5	12 905	55.7	44.3	17.3	1.6	1 144	10.4
Hutchinson	557	0.7	2 152	33.0	144.1	1 436 458	668	116 890	49.6	191 338	53.3	46.7	35.1	22.8	2 154	33.2
Irion	625	16.6	4 004	1.3	7.5	2 492 999	623	54 142	6.1	38 959	11.6	88.4	42.3	10.3	509	22.4
Jack	576	-3.4	639	0.7	72.0	950 445	1 488	51 512	18.3	20 259	10.3	89.7	30.2	4.3	233	11.0
Jackson	493	4.7	582	8.9	198.8	793 028	1 364	106 143	64.6	76 294	72.8	27.2	42.3	14.6	6 455	30.8
Jasper	96	0.0	104	0.3	20.2	292 057	2 801	44 807	6.7	7 243	43.7	56.3	16.8	1.0	644	10.8
Jeff Davis	1 391	-6.6	13 247	0.3	44.0	3 697 058	279	90 527	10.4	99 458	1.4	98.6	44.8	20.0	179	9.5
Jefferson	333	-14.2	420	16.9	153.6	584 497	1 391	61 295	26.8	33 755	49.2	50.8	27.1	6.7	3 061	17.4
Jim Hogg	640	6.0	2 668	D	9.8	1 722 887	646	58 337	7.4	31 035	D	D	37.1	4.2	314	12.9
Jim Wells	463	-7.0	417	1.8	150.9	609 575	1 461	54 010	61.0	55 035	40.7	59.3	20.5	4.1	2 862	20.6
Johnson	331	-8.6	121	1.9	116.7	411 185	3 408	48 534	62.0	22 562	21.3	78.7	20.3	2.0	977	7.0
Jones	573	10.8	544	3.9	334.8	597 255	1 097	72 611	59.2	56 265	68.8	31.2	29.3	11.5	10 566	58.3
Karnes	417	-12.2	346	1.4	104.5	596 572	1 726	49 042	24.6	20 334	43.3	56.7	33.9	3.5	1 180	21.8
Kaufman	422	0.5	165	1.6	155.1	430 143	2 614	46 495	43.7	17 031	32.1	67.9	17.6	2.2	480	3.4
Kendall	343	4.9	294	0.7	34.1	799 738	2 718	35 979	7.6	6 557	12.9	87.1	15.8	0.6	280	7.1
Kenedy	909	91.8	36 362	0.4	2.8	21 107 929	580	327 043	19.0	758 441	D	D	64.0	28.0	34	20.0
Kent	568	1.2	2 677	0.8	53.6	1 612 444	602	54 334	6.8	31 928	22.2	77.8	34.9	9.9	1 672	63.2
Kerr	614	8.9	500	2.3	40.2	892 896	1 784	44 264	13.4	10 948	8.9	91.1	15.1	1.3	344	5.5
Kimble	620	0.6	970	2.5	35.9	1 447 847	1 492	43 088	8.4	13 196	16.0	84.0	23.0	2.3	523	11.7
King	542	-0.9	8 471	D	29.4	3 211 985	379	132 974	17.9	279 617	8.7	91.3	40.6	15.6	750	82.8
Kinney	601	-2.1	2 733	2.6	11.6	2 473 089	905	60 734	6.4	29 276	12.1	87.9	30.5	7.3	515	14.5
Kleberg	498	NA	1 428	0.0	82.6	1 689 955	1 183	61 633	65.0	186 222	38.6	61.4	28.4	6.0	1 755	27.5
Knox	493	-12.6	2 253	21.9	212.7	1 924 489	854	188 199	38.4	175 549	61.8	38.2	61.2	36.5	5 030	81.7
Lamar	521	10.9	287	4.0	218.6	472 031	1 646	62 669	60.4	33 234	44.0	56.0	33.1	4.8	3 768	27.4
Lamb	635	1.0	643	234.8	515.0	667 082	1 037	159 305	406.3	411 642	35.2	64.8	42.1	30.8	17 326	83.7
Lampasas	416	1.0	431	0.4	70.6	800 073	1 858	55 974	14.0	14 464	15.2	84.8	26.9	2.4	208	8.5
La Salle	649	16.1	1 627	8.8	76.3	1 814 392	1 115	62 863	31.0	77 818	25.1	74.9	29.3	8.0	981	16.3
Lavaca	567	-5.8	206	3.2	113.1	438 979	2 128	44 220	58.9	21 454	12.7	87.3	32.6	2.4	714	9.9
Lee	326	-10.9	177	1.4	68.3	458 300	2 595	49 848	40.9	22 191	20.1	79.9	32.5	2.1	267	8.6
Leon	569	1.1	275	2.8	121.1	556 154	2 019	53 192	85.8	41 530	9.9	90.1	29.2	3.6	197	2.5
Liberty	298	-2.3	187	5.3	127.7	374 776	1 999	52 280	25.1	15 781	40.4	59.6	19.1	2.8	1 603	5.8
Limestone	506	-4.5	339	0.8	141.9	530 153	1 566	51 422	45.7	30 591	20.1	79.9	35.1	4.1	1 190	12.0
Lipscomb	571	-1.2	1 942	19.4	127.0	1 411 816	727	133 035	80.5	273 900	14.7	85.3	50.7	24.5	2 436	76.9
Live Oak	501	-4.6	559	2.1	90.6	834 010	1 491	56 075	21.0	23 402	25.5	74.5	29.6	4.8	1 222	17.5
Llano	539	1.1	681	0.3	27.3	1 283 993	1 885	43 574	11.8	14 904	2.2	97.8	29.6	2.4	240	8.0
Loving	427	-17.1	47 421	0.0	D	6 220 443	131	66 219	0.5	55 217	0.0	100.0	66.7	33.3	47	44.4
Lubbock	516	-7.4	428	159.5	415.8	513 145	1 199	128 861	209.0	173 453	D	D	37.4	21.9	17 900	57.8
Lynn	494	-6.8	976	73.7	408.8	863 702	885	210 645	98.9	195 388	97.9	2.1	54.5	36.8	17 028	86.0
McCulloch	613	12.3	883	0.9	108.5	1 172 811	1 329	63 892	18.1	26 081	30.6	69.4	35.4	6.2	1 629	37.8
McLennan	530	-1.5	189	2.9	241.6	390 384	2 062	49 514	104.7	37 431	39.8	60.2	21.9	3.7	2 612	16.0
McMullen	506	-15.2	2 251	D	38.5	2 366 821	1 051	81 980	8.8	39 012	3.4	96.6	37.8	5.8	177	12.4
Madison	273	11.4	258	0.5	39.6	542 272	2 099	61 512	83.3	78 813	D	D	34.3	3.4	88	2.4
Marion	42	-30.0	164	0.2	11.0	332 071	2 027	51 191	4.2	16 085	26.5	73.5	19.8	1.9	31	3.1
Martin	458	-12.9	987	16.9	276.0	637 030	645	124 129	52.9	114 009	96.8	3.2	41.8	28.4	10 662	82.3

Table B. States and Counties — Water Use, Wholesale Trade, Retail Trade, and Real Estate

STATE County	Water use, 2005		Wholesale trade,[1] 2007				Retail trade,[2] 2007				Real estate and rental and leasing,[2] 2007			
	Total water withdrawn (mil gal/day)	Gallons withdrawn per person	Number of establishments	Number of employees	Sales (mil dol)	Annual payroll (mil dol)	Number of establishments	Number of employees	Sales (mil dol)	Annual payroll (mil dol)	Number of establishments	Number of employees	Receipts (mil dol)	Annual payroll (mil dol)
	133	134	135	136	137	138	139	140	141	142	143	144	145	146
TEXAS—Cont'd														
Guadalupe	34.3	333	85	1 519	822.1	66.5	281	3 718	1 026.1	83.1	88	401	53.9	10.2
Hale	325.3	8 978	55	D	D	D	129	1 490	325.1	26.8	29	77	10.7	1.8
Hall	25.6	6 905	3	D	D	D	17	88	23.2	1.3	1	D	D	D
Hamilton	2.7	328	8	85	44.8	3.3	59	365	78.6	7.0	3	D	D	D
Hansford	211.4	40 428	18	101	89.3	3.5	23	188	60.1	3.5	2	D	D	D
Hardeman	5.8	1 342	4	16	18.6	0.6	16	116	22.2	1.7	1	D	D	D
Hardin	19.9	390	17	115	35.9	3.9	147	2 170	612.4	51.5	26	70	5.5	0.9
Harris	764.3	207	6 086	98 893	205 478.8	5 991.8	12 342	183 618	51 899.1	4 543.5	5 047	40 175	9 714.3	1 786.5
Harrison	39.8	627	56	469	303.6	22.7	207	2 144	603.9	48.9	46	170	24.3	4.7
Hartley	365.4	67 048	5	39	41.9	2.0	9	176	34.1	2.6	5	20	1.8	0.5
Haskell	35.3	6 376	2	D	D	D	29	212	59.2	3.8	3	D	D	D
Hays	15.9	128	110	925	451.2	37.4	556	8 797	1 954.7	171.3	178	666	124.9	20.0
Hemphill	3.9	1 151	16	88	63.5	4.1	21	119	39.2	2.9	4	28	4.2	0.9
Henderson	117.0	1 463	38	D	D	D	245	2 819	657.4	59.7	55	206	28.4	4.5
Hidalgo	394.4	581	670	7 808	4 301.1	257.5	2 132	32 803	7 898.8	635.3	491	2 289	366.9	53.2
Hill	11.7	330	17	82	41.6	2.3	197	1 742	400.3	31.4	29	110	17.3	1.9
Hockley	175.6	7 707	28	D	D	D	73	971	201.7	16.3	13	41	2.9	0.9
Hood	66.7	1 391	40	278	95.5	11.5	214	2 513	730.0	60.2	64	D	D	D
Hopkins	18.9	416	37	D	D	D	155	1 702	447.7	35.3	30	86	12.6	1.8
Houston	8.3	357	13	119	39.1	3.4	67	707	159.3	13.2	9	39	4.9	0.8
Howard	23.5	722	23	173	88.5	6.9	121	1 297	341.2	27.6	39	183	36.5	3.5
Hudspeth	149.5	45 363	1	D	D	D	13	53	12.5	0.5	2	D	D	D
Hunt	123.2	1 492	45	463	263.4	15.0	262	3 554	931.3	85.6	82	328	40.0	8.5
Hutchinson	110.2	4 902	22	D	D	D	78	835	210.8	16.0	13	83	32.3	3.5
Irion	2.8	1 617	1	D	D	D	4	D	D	D	NA	NA	NA	NA
Jack	2.8	306	8	80	112.3	4.1	32	200	34.1	3.2	10	21	2.9	0.6
Jackson	69.6	4 853	16	113	67.0	4.0	52	508	133.5	9.7	10	D	D	D
Jasper	51.2	1 439	31	215	123.3	7.0	153	1 563	371.0	32.2	20	59	6.5	1.0
Jeff Davis	3.9	1 709	1	D	D	D	6	39	7.1	0.8	2	D	D	D
Jefferson	263.4	1 064	267	4 147	2 852.5	196.1	1 050	14 764	3 973.1	339.4	289	1 562	333.1	54.7
Jim Hogg	2.0	396	3	D	D	D	30	262	61.6	3.8	2	D	D	D
Jim Wells	8.8	216	36	422	193.4	20.3	148	1 645	462.4	34.7	42	389	85.1	21.3
Johnson	18.7	127	117	1 210	536.2	50.2	355	4 679	1 269.6	108.0	109	369	70.7	12.4
Jones	4.5	228	19	111	379.0	4.0	51	446	163.3	9.8	9	21	1.4	0.2
Karnes	4.7	307	7	57	40.7	2.3	50	443	101.8	8.8	6	18	3.9	0.2
Kaufman	7.0	78	89	690	443.1	25.8	305	3 493	943.8	79.6	57	199	26.0	4.3
Kendall	4.2	148	46	284	285.3	12.3	152	1 977	808.1	55.7	60	222	46.4	8.6
Kenedy	1.0	2 326	NA	NA	NA	NA	NA	NA	NA	NA	NA	NA	NA	NA
Kent	15.9	20 307	NA	NA	NA	NA	4	D	D	D	NA	NA	NA	NA
Kerr	10.1	217	39	D	D	D	227	2 888	719.9	68.4	89	279	39.5	6.4
Kimble	3.2	690	3	14	0.1	0.0	37	267	78.7	4.6	5	D	D	D
King	3.2	10 358	NA	NA	NA	NA	NA	NA	NA	NA	NA	NA	NA	NA
Kinney	5.3	1 578	2	D	D	D	8	59	8.1	0.7	1	D	D	D
Kleberg	16.0	520	3	D	D	D	116	1 985	657.1	47.9	32	111	10.7	1.8
Knox	37.3	9 873	15	89	41.6	2.5	18	193	34.3	1.9	1	D	D	D
Lamar	25.9	521	42	D	D	D	230	2 627	637.6	55.5	44	148	20.8	3.3
Lamb	351.9	24 322	18	152	84.2	6.2	51	350	95.8	6.5	4	D	D	D
Lampasas	1.2	61	5	25	11.5	0.9	61	644	207.1	14.4	18	50	5.7	2.0
La Salle	5.7	949	NA	NA	NA	NA	19	162	79.9	2.5	5	D	D	D
Lavaca	10.6	562	21	627	221.2	16.5	89	789	172.0	15.7	12	D	D	D
Lee	5.4	326	21	210	58.2	6.7	77	760	162.6	14.4	17	90	21.0	3.6
Leon	7.7	468	15	244	92.3	8.3	76	593	159.9	10.1	18	54	12.4	1.8
Liberty	379.9	5 055	36	293	151.5	9.6	207	2 602	653.0	58.1	40	279	50.5	9.2
Limestone	23.8	1 043	12	66	27.4	2.4	90	1 043	268.3	21.4	10	42	2.6	0.6
Lipscomb	23.0	7 401	5	66	47.2	2.1	18	65	24.5	0.9	1	D	D	D
Live Oak	12.1	1 034	9	52	25.3	1.6	41	378	112.7	6.9	7	D	D	D
Llano	165.4	9 070	12	235	94.9	8.9	81	459	113.0	9.1	28	82	42.2	7.2
Loving	1.5	23 710	NA	NA	NA	NA	NA	NA	NA	NA	NA	NA	NA	NA
Lubbock	204.0	809	376	4 888	3 707.4	212.8	1 043	16 793	3 924.9	346.3	380	D	D	D
Lynn	83.0	13 314	6	D	D	D	14	88	19.7	1.7	4	6	0.4	0.1
McCulloch	6.6	835	8	53	31.1	1.4	40	391	104.3	7.7	7	D	D	D
McLennan	198.4	883	243	3 197	4 606.2	123.3	872	11 703	2 942.6	248.7	211	1 408	281.7	54.3
McMullen	2.0	2 276	NA	NA	NA	NA	4	D	D	D	NA	NA	NA	NA
Madison	13.6	1 034	7	32	31.9	0.9	35	477	178.9	11.2	13	35	14.2	0.9
Marion	16.4	1 499	4	9	5.5	0.3	38	221	66.3	5.0	5	D	D	D
Martin	18.0	4 092	4	28	24.4	1.2	18	135	45.4	2.9	NA	NA	NA	NA

1. Merchant wholesalers, except manufacturers' sales branches and offices.   2. Employer establishments.

Items 133—146

TX(Guadalupe)—TX(Martin)   655

Table B. States and Counties — Professional Services, Manufacturing, and Accommodation and Food Services

STATE County	Professional, scientific, and technical services,[1] 2007				Manufacturing, 2007				Accommodation and food services, 2007			
	Number of establishments	Number of employees	Receipts (mil dol)	Annual payroll (mil dol)	Number of establishments	Number of employees	Receipts (mil dol)	Annual payroll (mil dol)	Number of establishments	Number of employees	Sales (mil dol)	Annual payroll (mil dol)
	147	148	149	150	151	152	153	154	155	156	157	158
TEXAS—Cont'd												
Guadalupe	126	411	33.7	13.0	119	7 311	2 154.1	312.4	158	2 690	116.5	33.1
Hale	49	D	D	D	25	2 720	D	83.0	71	1 050	40.3	10.9
Hall	3	D	D	D	NA	NA	NA	NA	8	79	1.8	0.5
Hamilton	16	45	4.2	0.8	NA	NA	NA	NA	18	160	6.0	1.8
Hansford	8	36	6.0	1.7	NA	NA	NA	NA	13	95	3.1	0.6
Hardeman	3	6	0.4	0.1	NA	NA	NA	NA	14	128	3.4	1.1
Hardin	53	D	D	D	34	795	D	32.4	63	1 023	37.2	10.3
Harris	12 246	D	D	D	4 215	168 354	169 275.1	8 937.2	7 132	147 118	7 874.7	2 104.9
Harrison	113	671	90.9	34.0	85	4 505	1 564.3	150.9	91	1 579	64.0	16.7
Hartley	5	D	D	D	NA	NA	NA	NA	4	32	1.0	0.2
Haskell	7	25	0.8	0.2	NA	NA	NA	NA	14	115	4.7	1.1
Hays	310	1 899	141.7	53.4	135	3 692	1 081.8	154.0	286	5 739	235.3	66.8
Hemphill	10	19	4.0	1.0	NA	NA	NA	NA	10	98	4.1	1.1
Henderson	101	343	42.2	12.1	55	1 411	201.9	48.1	124	1 632	63.1	18.0
Hidalgo	793	D	D	D	276	6 007	1 503.2	183.5	896	17 219	758.0	186.5
Hill	39	142	14.4	4.4	42	832	153.6	25.9	67	1 053	44.3	12.1
Hockley	24	185	8.4	9.2	NA	NA	NA	NA	40	559	19.8	5.6
Hood	113	383	43.0	15.1	40	D	D	D	91	1 564	61.9	17.5
Hopkins	53	258	28.0	9.9	39	1 564	923.1	60.2	53	865	29.2	8.6
Houston	29	103	8.9	2.5	19	840	265.4	32.0	35	413	18.7	4.8
Howard	48	193	15.1	5.4	22	890	2 449.6	44.9	70	1 022	42.5	10.8
Hudspeth	1	D	D	D	NA	NA	NA	NA	5	34	2.0	0.4
Hunt	91	D	D	D	85	14 100	3 134.4	D	115	D	D	D
Hutchinson	29	117	14.6	4.5	23	1 832	D	145.2	46	539	21.1	5.4
Irion	3	D	D	D	NA	NA	NA	NA	1	D	D	D
Jack	13	48	5.3	2.2	NA	NA	NA	NA	16	144	6.5	1.9
Jackson	23	64	5.9	1.9	10	D	D	D	21	219	9.9	2.3
Jasper	45	170	18.7	4.2	21	1 708	725.6	104.7	54	794	32.6	7.7
Jeff Davis	1	D	D	D	NA	NA	NA	NA	10	148	7.1	1.9
Jefferson	527	D	D	D	215	15 460	D	997.3	419	9 143	387.5	110.1
Jim Hogg	3	11	0.3	0.2	NA	NA	NA	NA	9	102	3.6	1.1
Jim Wells	40	155	18.2	5.6	NA	NA	NA	NA	76	1 177	46.1	12.0
Johnson	190	749	78.9	25.0	173	5 314	1 441.4	230.2	189	3 086	126.4	33.3
Jones	10	D	D	D	NA	NA	NA	NA	15	137	4.6	1.3
Karnes	16	63	4.4	1.1	NA	NA	NA	NA	25	235	8.6	2.3
Kaufman	122	D	D	D	108	D	1 172.6	148.1	142	2 240	93.7	26.5
Kendall	121	551	59.7	24.7	32	814	180.9	27.3	83	1 229	55.8	17.1
Kenedy	1	D	D	D	NA	NA	NA	NA	NA	NA	NA	NA
Kent	NA	NA	NA	NA	NA	NA	NA	NA	2	D	D	D
Kerr	150	685	58.2	24.1	44	784	161.8	31.8	122	1 958	97.6	28.3
Kimble	10	16	1.0	0.3	NA	NA	NA	NA	22	184	8.2	2.2
King	NA	NA	NA	NA	NA	NA	NA	NA	NA	NA	NA	NA
Kinney	NA	NA	NA	NA	NA	NA	NA	NA	4	19	1.1	0.2
Kleberg	35	D	D	D	NA	NA	NA	NA	70	1 160	43.2	11.9
Knox	4	D	D	D	NA	NA	NA	NA	6	33	1.4	0.3
Lamar	62	D	D	D	59	4 501	2 411.6	192.5	87	1 413	61.1	16.8
Lamb	18	41	3.1	1.0	10	D	D	D	25	188	7.0	1.8
Lampasas	29	D	D	D	NA	NA	NA	NA	36	380	16.1	4.0
La Salle	NA	NA	NA	NA	NA	NA	NA	NA	11	127	5.3	1.3
Lavaca	32	74	6.5	1.6	35	1 701	238.2	45.2	25	249	9.1	2.4
Lee	23	102	7.8	2.9	19	503	128.5	17.8	28	283	13.2	3.0
Leon	29	76	7.7	1.8	20	501	D	34.8	25	263	13.1	2.8
Liberty	83	D	D	D	33	D	D	D	88	1 294	48.9	13.1
Limestone	33	147	11.0	5.2	18	1 073	210.8	35.3	40	395	18.2	4.1
Lipscomb	5	21	2.1	0.7	NA	NA	NA	NA	5	D	D	D
Live Oak	24	59	6.4	2.4	NA	NA	NA	NA	24	345	11.7	2.8
Llano	40	148	14.6	5.1	NA	NA	NA	NA	50	1 017	61.1	21.3
Loving	NA	NA	NA	NA	NA	NA	NA	NA	1	D	D	D
Lubbock	581	3 402	374.1	128.5	255	D	D	D	582	D	D	D
Lynn	6	17	0.8	0.3	NA	NA	NA	NA	5	27	0.8	0.2
McCulloch	18	76	5.6	2.2	NA	NA	NA	NA	22	243	8.8	2.1
McLennan	352	D	D	D	255	13 971	5 888.9	550.4	468	9 123	375.3	100.9
McMullen	1	D	D	D	NA	NA	NA	NA	1	D	D	D
Madison	16	242	12.5	3.3	NA	NA	NA	NA	26	326	13.1	3.2
Marion	8	18	1.3	0.7	NA	NA	NA	NA	22	154	5.8	1.5
Martin	6	12	0.9	0.4	NA	NA	NA	NA	3	D	D	D

1. Establishment subject to federal tax.

Table B. States and Counties — Health Care and Social Assistance, Other Services, and Federal Funds

STATE County	Health care and social assistance, 2007				Other services, 2007				Federal funds and grants, 2009–2010 Expenditures (mil dol)			
										Direct payments for individuals[1]		
	Number of establishments	Number of employees	Receipts (mil dol)	Annual payroll (mil dol)	Number of establishments	Number of employees	Receipts (mil dol)	Annual payroll (mil dol)	Total	Social Security and government retirement	Medicare	Food Stamps and Supplemental Security Income
	159	160	161	162	163	164	165	166	167	168	169	170
TEXAS—Cont'd												
Guadalupe	169	2 773	207.8	83.7	135	739	55.0	15.6	783.2	483.7	94.4	25.3
Hale	78	1 101	81.5	28.9	56	329	19.2	6.7	295.7	82.0	73.8	17.5
Hall	7	31	1.6	0.7	6	11	3.3	0.5	44.9	11.5	12.2	1.8
Hamilton	23	447	28.3	12.7	18	42	3.7	0.9	76.1	29.5	26.4	2.1
Hansford	5	D	D	D	16	75	5.8	1.8	47.4	22.2	8.5	0.8
Hardeman	14	231	14.9	6.0	11	39	3.1	0.7	47.7	14.7	13.7	1.9
Hardin	76	1 426	62.9	32.3	47	291	27.0	7.7	338.0	163.0	93.1	16.5
Harris	9 464	205 171	23 069.3	8 823.8	5 961	54 568	6 434.3	1 777.1	27 347.6	6 861.6	3 878.8	1 583.2
Harrison	107	1 714	133.0	46.3	91	754	71.9	27.3	497.3	163.6	101.5	27.9
Hartley	5	D	D	D	8	32	3.8	0.7	16.8	4.1	1.6	0.1
Haskell	15	224	11.5	4.5	12	28	2.2	0.5	72.9	21.9	18.7	3.0
Hays	267	4 674	354.5	138.2	183	973	95.1	25.5	696.2	322.8	76.0	21.4
Hemphill	8	177	10.4	4.1	12	D	D	D	17.2	7.4	6.6	0.3
Henderson	134	2 665	222.5	80.9	81	360	26.5	7.1	485.2	216.7	120.4	24.8
Hidalgo	1 655	44 931	2 877.2	1 137.1	573	3 257	238.5	61.9	4 297.2	973.0	654.8	575.5
Hill	48	951	66.8	24.6	43	155	21.0	4.0	312.9	130.8	69.0	13.5
Hockley	37	839	73.4	20.1	24	133	15.7	3.2	197.4	54.3	43.2	9.7
Hood	116	1 591	141.8	54.4	85	503	26.3	8.8	331.8	227.6	65.8	8.8
Hopkins	64	1 136	82.6	31.8	46	177	14.9	3.8	244.2	98.7	65.8	7.0
Houston	37	613	44.6	15.9	28	139	13.8	3.8	245.5	79.9	58.6	11.9
Howard	80	2 276	215.7	93.4	50	266	18.8	5.5	350.5	112.2	81.4	14.6
Hudspeth	1	D	D	D	2	D	D	D	62.3	6.5	3.9	1.5
Hunt	161	2 871	245.4	102.5	97	D	D	D	2 001.6	250.9	138.0	32.2
Hutchinson	45	481	32.0	14.6	38	240	25.4	6.6	154.7	68.9	44.8	7.1
Irion	1	D	D	D	2	D	D	D	12.1	5.7	2.7	0.3
Jack	11	184	10.4	4.4	8	15	2.9	0.4	51.4	23.2	15.3	2.5
Jackson	18	309	18.1	7.8	25	90	6.2	1.3	132.2	44.1	33.7	4.9
Jasper	78	3 505	149.9	51.2	45	158	12.5	3.1	336.6	114.0	88.5	16.6
Jeff Davis	5	D	D	D	7	D	D	D	18.0	8.8	3.2	0.4
Jefferson	849	17 840	1 618.2	580.6	404	3 012	265.8	73.0	2 284.4	711.0	624.6	141.3
Jim Hogg	8	488	8.4	4.6	4	D	D	D	80.1	12.2	15.3	3.7
Jim Wells	105	3 981	170.6	84.9	74	480	41.5	12.9	410.1	118.7	93.3	24.6
Johnson	190	3 530	234.8	93.3	173	1 046	82.0	29.2	780.5	442.5	168.2	30.7
Jones	27	675	29.9	14.8	21	65	4.1	1.2	157.8	49.7	39.7	9.0
Karnes	32	386	24.5	10.7	15	53	2.6	0.6	157.2	40.3	34.7	7.9
Kaufman	139	3 213	198.6	86.8	113	747	50.3	23.5	630.6	308.1	156.2	25.4
Kendall	101	975	72.6	29.4	65	358	27.6	9.0	274.7	172.6	33.8	3.2
Kenedy	NA	NA	NA	NA	1	D	D	D	3.0	0.8	0.6	0.1
Kent	1	D	D	D	NA	NA	NA	NA	9.5	3.0	2.2	0.1
Kerr	173	3 825	305.3	143.8	106	654	53.8	14.3	446.1	259.2	96.0	13.6
Kimble	10	144	8.4	3.8	6	32	1.5	0.5	36.0	17.4	9.1	1.6
King	NA	NA	NA	NA	NA	NA	NA	NA	2.9	0.4	0.3	0.0
Kinney	2	D	D	D	4	D	D	D	46.3	17.4	7.3	1.8
Kleberg	69	1 466	78.0	37.6	51	D	D	D	436.4	77.8	48.3	22.4
Knox	8	147	7.8	3.2	13	D	D	D	51.7	12.3	14.1	2.2
Lamar	180	3 332	297.7	102.7	84	390	27.3	7.3	481.8	168.5	97.9	25.1
Lamb	26	383	22.5	10.6	14	42	2.9	0.6	140.3	36.6	37.8	7.8
Lampasas	26	D	D	D	27	149	13.0	2.9	174.5	102.6	36.4	6.0
La Salle	11	99	6.1	2.5	6	D	D	D	73.5	13.4	11.7	5.0
Lavaca	50	900	57.6	21.7	44	162	11.5	2.2	218.1	80.6	58.9	5.1
Lee	29	309	17.4	7.7	29	99	8.9	2.4	96.6	44.7	21.9	3.4
Leon	18	146	8.0	3.3	22	127	8.8	2.3	185.7	78.0	41.8	6.6
Liberty	101	1 881	154.1	52.9	69	293	27.5	5.9	524.4	216.4	152.4	34.2
Limestone	45	893	66.9	25.1	18	87	7.1	1.5	209.6	74.9	46.3	10.9
Lipscomb	1	D	D	D	4	D	D	D	20.4	8.2	6.0	0.3
Live Oak	12	D	D	D	21	66	5.6	1.1	90.1	26.7	19.8	3.8
Llano	34	791	49.5	23.8	31	79	8.2	1.7	152.8	91.2	41.6	3.1
Loving	NA	NA	NA	NA	NA	NA	NA	NA	0.9	0.3	0.0	0.0
Lubbock	813	D	D	D	473	D	D	D	1 892.2	644.2	457.1	105.1
Lynn	7	124	5.7	2.7	4	19	1.0	0.2	72.3	17.5	15.7	3.2
McCulloch	22	290	19.5	7.7	17	58	4.0	0.9	86.4	28.5	24.0	4.0
McLennan	525	15 510	1 219.3	504.2	394	2 615	244.7	64.2	2 019.0	701.0	261.8	104.5
McMullen	1	D	D	D	NA	NA	NA	NA	6.4	2.8	1.0	0.2
Madison	17	265	20.5	7.6	16	71	6.2	1.6	81.7	32.3	18.1	5.3
Marion	15	D	D	D	14	30	2.3	0.5	114.9	36.1	20.6	6.7
Martin	10	168	9.5	5.1	7	17	2.0	0.4	81.5	16.2	9.0	2.2

1. State totals may include programs not allocated by county.

Table B. States and Counties — Federal Funds, Residential Construction, and Local Government Finances

	Federal funds and grants, 2009–2010 (cont.)							Value of residential construction authorized by building permits, 2010		Local government finances, 2007					
	Expenditures (mil dol) (cont.)									General revenue					
	Procurement contract awards			Grants[1]								Taxes			
STATE County	Salaries and wages	Defense	Other	Medicaid and other health-related	Nutrition and family welfare	Education	Other	New construction ($1,000)	Number of housing units	Total (mil dol)	Inter-govern-mental (mil dol)	Total (mil dol)		Per capita[2] (dollars)	
													Total	Property
	171	172	173	174	175	176	177	178	179	180	181	182	183	184

TEXAS—Cont'd

	171	172	173	174	175	176	177	178	179	180	181	182	183	184
Guadalupe	24.7	25.5	3.6	81.9	11.1	2.9	3.1	172 398	1 055	264.6	85.6	131.0	1 162	988
Hale	9.2	0.1	-0.3	60.4	9.7	1.3	1.4	1 538	13	102.5	48.9	38.4	1 075	875
Hall	1.3	0.0	0.2	11.2	0.7	0.2	0.1	0	0	13.4	6.9	4.5	1 290	1 059
Hamilton	2.3	0.0	0.5	12.6	0.7	0.2	0.2	0	0	58.2	12.1	10.0	1 231	1 017
Hansford	1.0	0.0	0.2	2.5	0.6	0.2	0.0	0	0	25.9	4.2	18.8	3 587	3 392
Hardeman	1.2	0.0	0.2	11.1	1.0	0.1	0.5	0	0	30.4	5.4	9.8	2 374	2 136
Hardin	6.3	0.0	1.5	49.3	5.2	1.2	0.0	10 008	87	143.4	71.1	54.1	1 049	905
Harris	2 397.3	2 658.4	4 427.2	3 288.1	512.6	196.3	944.0	1 880 531	15 039	16 357.1	4 096.2	7 980.7	2 028	1 652
Harrison	15.5	9.5	2.2	143.4	10.9	4.8	3.6	8 571	87	169.9	43.8	101.7	1 602	1 421
Hartley	0.3	0.0	0.0	0.5	0.4	0.1	0.0	NA	NA	6.2	1.1	4.5	869	810
Haskell	2.1	0.0	0.4	12.6	1.0	0.3	0.2	75	2	20.4	8.6	6.3	1 208	1 057
Hays	39.8	7.3	62.2	77.7	17.0	6.1	11.2	250 846	2 380	440.1	109.5	236.3	1 670	1 325
Hemphill	0.6	0.0	0.1	1.0	0.5	0.1	0.0	0	0	30.3	1.5	23.2	6 903	6 568
Henderson	9.6	0.0	2.5	86.3	7.3	2.1	1.2	8 898	60	186.4	63.6	90.2	1 143	986
Hidalgo	296.2	-35.5	207.6	1 025.4	205.3	97.6	84.4	421 852	3 552	2 583.5	1 512.6	687.4	968	774
Hill	8.0	0.6	2.9	59.7	3.8	1.6	0.4	532	9	105.2	47.5	39.2	1 108	885
Hockley	3.9	0.1	0.9	25.6	16.5	2.0	3.4	1 230	8	140.2	48.3	58.0	2 608	2 458
Hood	9.2	0.9	-2.6	14.3	4.1	0.9	0.1	15 119	76	113.7	22.1	72.7	1 479	1 232
Hopkins	7.2	1.1	1.6	53.1	6.3	1.2	0.3	1 682	14	125.1	38.5	38.5	1 141	899
Houston	6.8	0.0	1.2	77.0	2.0	1.8	3.5	173	2	51.8	22.0	21.3	936	768
Howard	41.8	0.6	14.0	56.1	5.8	1.6	3.5	385	2	182.9	106.9	42.1	1 304	1 011
Hudspeth	23.1	4.5	18.5	1.0	0.9	0.3	0.5	NA	NA	17.7	9.6	5.5	1 656	1 587
Hunt	34.4	1 391.0	3.7	107.3	9.3	3.8	8.3	5 665	47	309.9	91.5	93.3	1 125	932
Hutchinson	4.8	0.0	1.9	16.7	2.0	0.7	0.4	0	0	103.2	29.6	41.6	1 905	1 673
Irion	0.4	0.0	0.1	1.5	0.1	0.1	0.0	NA	NA	9.3	1.2	7.2	4 145	4 004
Jack	1.8	0.0	0.4	6.6	0.9	0.2	0.0	140	4	28.1	6.4	17.3	1 960	1 741
Jackson	2.3	0.0	0.5	22.3	2.6	0.7	1.2	1 367	12	61.7	15.6	29.8	2 113	1 921
Jasper	6.3	15.7	1.3	73.4	6.4	1.2	11.4	6 172	40	97.1	49.4	36.1	1 045	889
Jeff Davis	1.3	0.1	0.8	3.0	0.2	0.1	0.0	NA	NA	8.5	4.8	3.0	1 345	1 170
Jefferson	197.1	49.8	38.6	359.9	47.2	12.0	43.0	104 442	1 111	977.4	265.4	471.5	1 948	1 561
Jim Hogg	18.0	0.4	0.2	26.4	1.7	0.2	0.4	NA	NA	18.9	5.4	12.1	2 438	2 305
Jim Wells	7.5	5.3	1.4	125.6	22.0	1.9	1.5	1 974	18	192.1	67.0	65.9	1 603	1 309
Johnson	22.9	0.1	16.9	73.6	11.7	2.5	3.2	84 446	833	394.2	134.7	187.7	1 253	1 059
Jones	13.5	0.0	0.7	28.3	3.5	0.6	0.4	0	0	47.0	22.4	12.4	644	526
Karnes	2.8	0.0	1.9	58.2	6.1	1.0	0.6	4 151	25	38.5	21.7	11.5	761	636
Kaufman	46.5	0.1	4.0	65.2	11.4	3.3	3.4	38 421	189	310.3	113.3	154.7	1 605	1 382
Kendall	4.9	41.0	7.6	6.6	1.6	0.8	0.7	40 732	202	107.3	15.4	77.8	2 482	2 196
Kenedy	0.2	0.0	0.1	0.5	0.0	0.0	0.2	NA	NA	7.9	0.2	7.3	18 434	18 348
Kent	0.8	0.0	0.1	1.7	0.2	0.0	0.1	NA	NA	9.2	0.9	7.4	10 116	10 023
Kerr	23.7	0.5	6.5	23.3	4.8	1.4	12.1	8 672	41	114.0	26.6	70.9	1 481	1 174
Kimble	0.9	0.0	0.2	4.6	0.9	0.1	0.2	127	1	16.6	3.4	5.7	1 273	967
King	0.3	0.0	0.0	0.5	0.0	0.0	0.0	NA	NA	7.0	0.4	6.1	20 873	20 869
Kinney	10.2	0.0	0.1	6.6	0.8	0.1	0.3	0	0	10.8	5.3	3.4	1 024	922
Kleberg	110.0	76.5	1.1	57.6	7.2	4.6	6.8	2 154	19	87.0	37.2	35.8	1 177	919
Knox	1.6	0.0	0.3	12.1	1.2	0.2	0.2	NA	NA	17.7	6.9	4.8	1 362	1 159
Lamar	14.8	1.3	2.9	133.5	7.1	2.4	4.4	3 626	46	156.5	64.4	60.9	1 235	953
Lamb	2.7	0.0	0.6	28.8	2.5	0.6	0.3	0	0	68.0	26.4	19.9	1 433	1 308
Lampasas	4.0	0.9	0.8	17.2	3.1	0.8	0.2	2 030	14	45.0	19.0	17.8	851	727
La Salle	9.2	0.0	1.0	28.5	2.1	0.3	0.9	283	6	20.6	9.8	9.0	1 506	1 332
Lavaca	4.6	0.3	1.2	62.7	2.4	0.5	0.4	580	9	55.2	8.5	21.9	1 169	1 066
Lee	2.7	0.0	0.8	19.7	2.1	0.4	0.4	1 245	20	41.8	13.7	21.6	1 323	1 138
Leon	4.0	0.0	0.9	51.2	1.8	0.5	0.2	NA	NA	49.1	13.9	29.7	1 806	1 665
Liberty	11.2	3.5	2.5	83.1	10.2	2.2	1.7	27 698	269	201.0	79.7	94.7	1 256	1 112
Limestone	4.6	0.0	1.0	60.7	3.8	0.7	0.6	599	4	81.6	28.3	38.2	1 705	1 506
Lipscomb	1.5	0.0	0.3	2.0	0.5	0.2	0.0	351	2	19.5	3.2	14.5	4 795	4 628
Live Oak	20.0	0.0	0.9	14.7	1.2	0.3	0.2	518	8	28.8	6.6	18.5	1 626	1 450
Llano	2.5	0.0	0.5	11.1	0.9	0.4	0.2	38 188	197	48.9	4.9	36.6	1 990	1 910
Loving	0.1	0.0	0.0	0.0	0.0	0.0	0.0	NA	NA	2.8	0.0	2.4	44 055	43 800
Lubbock	155.5	13.8	17.3	246.8	42.4	9.9	111.4	219 523	1 451	991.2	278.9	342.3	1 312	991
Lynn	1.3	0.0	0.2	13.1	1.8	0.3	0.1	51	1	34.5	14.0	10.1	1 719	1 632
McCulloch	2.2	0.0	0.4	21.7	1.9	0.4	0.6	0	0	36.4	13.7	8.8	1 118	859
McLennan	190.6	256.7	34.8	300.0	33.5	11.5	35.7	82 962	602	1 359.6	479.5	300.6	1 318	1 012
McMullen	0.4	0.5	0.1	0.5	0.3	0.0	0.1	NA	NA	10.5	0.8	8.8	10 059	9 875
Madison	1.9	0.0	0.4	21.2	1.7	0.4	0.2	491	19	36.6	17.3	13.3	997	814
Marion	2.3	7.2	0.4	37.9	2.4	0.4	0.1	322	5	19.9	6.0	11.6	1 083	955
Martin	0.8	0.0	0.2	9.6	2.6	0.2	29.6	1 305	9	25.9	4.8	13.9	3 115	2 982

1. State totals may include programs not allocated by county.   2. Based on the resident population estimated as of July 1 of the year shown.

STATE County	Total (mil dol) [185]	Per capita[1] (dollars) [186]	Education [187]	Health and hospitals [188]	Police protection [189]	Public welfare [190]	Highways [191]	Total (mil dol) [192]	Per capita[1] (dollars) [193]	Federal civilian [194]	Federal military [195]	State and local [196]	Democratic [197]	Republican [198]	All other [199]
TEXAS—Cont'd															
Guadalupe	287.3	2 548	63.7	1.2	5.7	0.8	4.6	529.0	4 691	208	286	5 698	34.0	65.0	0.9
Hale	94.9	2 657	63.7	7.5	6.7	0.9	2.5	38.4	1 075	125	83	2 441	27.2	72.1	0.6
Hall	12.6	3 605	64.9	2.9	3.1	0.1	3.7	0.8	222	28	0	285	25.6	73.6	0.8
Hamilton	48.4	5 943	27.3	25.4	1.8	28.7	1.5	26.0	3 190	31	19	675	22.8	76.1	1.0
Hansford	25.7	4 915	78.5	1.3	2.5	0.0	2.5	27.9	5 327	17	13	555	11.4	87.9	0.7
Hardeman	28.4	6 891	31.4	44.9	2.4	0.0	4.2	4.9	1 191	19	0	488	23.4	75.2	1.4
Hardin	143.0	2 771	65.0	0.5	3.8	0.3	3.3	118.2	2 291	79	126	2 469	19.0	80.2	0.8
Harris	16 565.0	4 209	43.9	9.5	6.2	0.3	3.2	44 270.4	11 248	25 382	10 820	234 997	50.4	48.8	0.7
Harrison	160.2	2 522	66.7	0.6	5.5	1.1	2.1	208.6	3 285	148	153	3 529	34.0	65.4	0.6
Hartley	5.9	1 137	67.5	0.2	6.8	0.0	7.6	0.5	97	10	12	658	12.6	86.2	1.2
Haskell	20.1	3 836	50.4	23.3	3.3	0.0	6.3	10.9	2 068	35	12	439	33.0	65.6	1.4
Hays	515.2	3 642	58.2	5.4	4.4	0.2	2.1	1 136.7	8 034	193	374	10 968	48.1	50.2	1.7
Hemphill	27.6	8 211	69.7	17.2	0.7	0.0	2.6	20.5	6 091	11	0	387	13.8	85.7	0.6
Henderson	199.4	2 527	73.0	0.3	5.8	0.0	3.5	122.2	1 548	107	187	3 329	27.3	71.9	0.8
Hidalgo	2 724.7	3 836	70.2	1.7	3.5	0.8	2.3	2 783.8	3 918	3 287	1 749	49 704	69.0	30.3	0.7
Hill	100.2	2 835	73.3	0.4	3.4	0.0	3.2	140.1	3 962	104	84	2 293	28.9	70.2	0.9
Hockley	139.9	6 294	80.6	0.3	1.9	0.3	2.5	150.7	6 780	52	52	1 921	23.5	75.8	0.7
Hood	102.2	2 079	63.4	0.2	5.3	0.2	4.6	162.9	3 314	104	121	2 078	22.5	76.6	0.9
Hopkins	129.2	3 825	45.8	29.7	4.1	0.1	4.6	63.1	1 870	82	81	2 299	27.3	72.0	0.7
Houston	60.2	2 643	72.3	0.3	4.1	0.0	4.3	35.3	1 549	91	53	2 113	30.8	68.1	1.1
Howard	173.8	5 383	40.1	10.4	3.0	0.2	2.0	292.8	9 065	933	78	2 857	26.3	72.5	1.2
Hudspeth	17.1	5 200	55.4	0.2	6.5	0.1	6.7	3.4	1 034	340	0	332	47.9	51.0	1.1
Hunt	298.2	3 595	38.8	26.0	5.3	0.2	2.8	436.5	5 262	246	263	6 757	29.1	69.7	1.2
Hutchinson	100.3	4 592	61.1	14.7	3.3	0.1	2.0	120.9	5 534	79	51	1 565	15.1	84.0	0.9
Irion	8.3	4 782	69.7	0.2	4.2	0.0	5.2	19.4	11 155	0	0	122	20.1	78.8	1.1
Jack	27.4	3 100	69.6	0.0	4.9	0.0	3.4	45.0	5 090	18	20	604	15.5	83.6	0.8
Jackson	57.8	4 103	57.5	17.5	3.2	0.0	4.7	128.1	9 089	33	34	1 083	25.7	73.6	0.7
Jasper	87.5	2 533	65.5	2.3	5.1	0.6	4.6	123.8	3 583	86	81	2 170	28.6	70.6	0.8
Jeff Davis	7.3	3 204	83.9	1.7	2.9	0.3	0.4	1.3	559	26	0	268	37.9	60.6	1.5
Jefferson	895.5	3 701	44.2	5.1	6.5	0.6	3.3	1 676.5	6 928	1 942	772	16 669	50.8	48.6	0.6
Jim Hogg	17.8	3 570	64.4	0.8	8.8	0.9	10.7	3.9	783	274	12	416	73.6	26.0	0.4
Jim Wells	195.3	4 750	37.9	31.7	1.5	0.0	11.1	118.5	2 883	91	124	2 225	57.8	41.7	0.6
Johnson	409.6	2 735	63.1	0.4	4.7	0.2	5.5	843.1	5 628	254	371	7 098	25.8	73.3	0.9
Jones	46.3	2 398	58.5	21.7	4.0	0.0	4.2	52.4	2 715	85	49	1 346	26.3	72.4	1.3
Karnes	35.4	2 347	66.3	1.1	4.1	0.0	4.7	16.2	1 073	38	36	1 667	38.9	60.4	0.7
Kaufman	335.8	3 484	63.0	5.5	3.9	0.3	3.2	646.8	6 711	202	244	6 010	31.8	67.5	0.7
Kendall	123.5	3 939	76.4	1.1	5.1	0.0	2.4	180.4	5 756	62	80	1 838	21.5	77.5	1.1
Kenedy	8.6	21 766	92.3	0.0	0.7	0.1	1.2	3.3	8 368	0	0	79	53.5	46.5	0.0
Kent	7.8	10 601	93.4	0.3	0.9	0.0	0.6	0.9	1 165	10	0	196	22.1	76.3	1.6
Kerr	104.4	2 181	56.6	0.6	8.6	0.8	4.6	90.3	1 887	537	115	2 799	24.7	74.3	1.0
Kimble	14.4	3 232	43.0	33.0	2.3	0.0	2.5	29.4	6 583	16	11	345	18.6	80.7	0.8
King	4.5	15 351	74.9	0.0	1.5	0.0	9.9	0.0	0	0	0	69	4.9	92.6	2.5
Kinney	9.2	2 762	63.7	1.2	9.3	0.9	2.8	0.5	141	148	0	281	40.8	58.5	0.7
Kleberg	79.8	2 624	64.2	0.3	9.0	0.3	3.4	104.9	3 451	895	470	3 848	53.2	46.0	0.8
Knox	18.0	5 106	58.9	21.9	2.8	0.2	3.2	4.1	1 165	31	0	383	26.8	72.1	1.1
Lamar	146.9	2 983	65.3	1.9	7.4	1.3	4.6	187.6	3 808	158	116	3 050	28.6	70.5	0.9
Lamb	62.2	4 474	50.5	17.6	5.1	0.0	3.7	229.1	16 480	41	31	998	25.5	73.9	0.6
Lampasas	44.1	2 113	64.7	2.1	6.9	0.2	5.8	114.0	5 459	49	49	986	24.9	74.0	1.0
La Salle	20.4	3 393	67.6	0.2	1.4	0.0	2.8	43.2	7 183	121	14	575	59.2	40.2	0.6
Lavaca	55.4	2 952	49.9	19.3	4.2	0.1	6.3	25.1	1 338	56	44	922	22.7	76.5	0.7
Lee	39.4	2 408	66.0	1.0	5.7	0.1	7.5	102.8	6 282	32	38	1 308	31.4	67.6	1.0
Leon	43.2	2 621	74.4	0.1	2.4	0.4	5.8	39.8	2 419	48	40	888	20.1	79.1	0.8
Liberty	194.5	2 579	63.0	0.5	4.2	0.5	5.2	185.1	2 454	131	178	4 427	27.7	71.4	0.9
Limestone	74.4	3 317	61.4	11.9	3.9	0.0	2.9	29.6	1 318	53	52	2 966	32.9	66.4	0.7
Lipscomb	18.2	5 985	74.4	0.7	2.4	0.1	5.0	5.1	1 671	24	0	424	12.3	87.0	0.6
Live Oak	26.1	2 297	65.4	0.1	6.2	0.6	5.7	23.2	2 040	290	26	589	25.1	74.1	0.8
Llano	45.7	2 484	62.3	0.0	7.2	0.1	4.9	63.5	3 454	30	43	1 137	23.4	75.6	1.0
Loving	1.5	26 600	0.0	0.0	13.7	0.0	18.6	0.0	0	0	0	17	15.2	84.8	0.0
Lubbock	1 034.7	3 966	39.5	30.6	4.8	0.1	3.0	1 365.1	5 232	1 335	664	24 589	31.3	68.0	0.8
Lynn	30.3	5 159	50.2	24.5	2.7	0.0	3.7	7.5	1 271	29	13	532	29.6	69.6	0.8
McCulloch	33.2	4 225	48.3	23.3	2.8	0.0	2.1	51.3	6 521	31	19	677	24.2	75.2	0.6
McLennan	1 351.0	5 922	29.1	1.9	3.4	0.3	1.4	15 878.1	69 603	3 584	616	14 010	37.7	61.6	0.8
McMullen	8.5	9 737	76.7	0.7	4.3	0.3	6.6	1.7	1 951	0	0	116	24.6	74.5	0.9
Madison	30.9	2 311	71.0	0.2	4.4	0.2	3.5	35.2	2 632	23	31	1 229	28.1	71.0	0.9
Marion	19.6	1 826	67.4	1.0	7.4	0.0	4.4	9.3	867	36	24	432	38.7	60.4	1.0
Martin	25.5	5 712	53.5	28.8	2.1	0.1	3.1	2.4	536	17	11	386	18.3	81.0	0.7

1. Based on the resident population estimated as of July 1 of the year shown.   2. © 2009 Election Data Services, Inc. All rights reserved.

Table B. States and Counties — Land Area and Population

STATE/ County code	CBSA code[1]	County type[2]	STATE County	Population and population characteristics, 2010														
								Race alone or in combination, not Hispanic or Latino (percent)					Age (percent)					
				Land area,[3] (sq km) 2010	Total persons	Rank	Per square kilometer	White	Black	American Indian, Alaska Native	Asian and Pacific Islander	Percent Hispanic or Latino[4]	Under 5 years	5 to 17 years	18 to 24 years	25 to 34 years	35 to 44 years	45 to 54 years
				1	2	3	4	5	6	7	8	9	10	11	12	13	14	15
			TEXAS—Cont'd															
48 319	...	9	Mason	2 406	4 012	2 906	1.7	77.5	0.5	0.5	0.2	21.5	5.0	16.2	5.1	8.0	10.1	14.4
48 321	13060	4	Matagorda	2 850	36 702	1 256	12.9	48.2	11.5	0.6	2.2	38.3	7.0	19.3	8.7	11.5	11.1	15.3
48 323	20580	5	Maverick	3 313	54 258	920	16.4	2.9	0.2	1.0	0.3	95.7	8.8	25.0	10.2	11.9	12.7	11.3
48 325	41700	1	Medina	3 433	46 006	1 046	13.4	47.2	2.2	0.7	0.9	49.7	6.5	19.3	9.2	11.0	12.5	15.3
48 327	...	8	Menard	2 336	2 242	3 034	1.0	63.8	0.5	0.4	0.2	35.2	5.7	13.9	5.7	8.6	8.5	15.2
48 329	33260	3	Midland	2 332	136 872	451	58.7	54.1	6.7	0.8	1.5	37.7	8.0	19.4	10.0	14.4	11.9	14.4
48 331	...	6	Milam	2 634	24 757	1 610	9.4	66.2	10.0	0.7	0.5	23.3	6.9	19.6	7.2	10.3	11.3	14.2
48 333	...	9	Mills	1 938	4 936	2 844	2.5	82.4	0.7	0.7	0.3	16.6	6.0	18.2	5.6	8.5	10.6	13.2
48 335	...	7	Mitchell	2 360	9 403	2 491	4.0	51.0	11.3	0.7	0.3	37.0	5.2	14.1	12.1	18.1	13.7	12.7
48 337	...	6	Montague	2 411	19 719	1 854	8.2	89.0	0.4	1.4	0.5	9.8	6.3	16.7	7.2	10.0	11.8	14.4
48 339	26420	1	Montgomery	2 698	455 746	143	168.9	72.4	4.5	0.9	2.6	20.8	7.3	20.4	7.9	13.0	14.4	15.1
48 341	20300	6	Moore	2 330	21 904	1 741	9.4	38.8	1.4	0.9	6.6	52.7	9.3	22.7	9.8	14.1	12.8	12.5
48 343	...	6	Morris	653	12 934	2 245	19.8	68.1	23.8	1.1	0.7	7.8	6.5	16.8	7.5	10.9	11.0	14.4
48 345	...	8	Motley	2 563	1 210	3 099	0.5	83.9	2.0	0.8	0.0	13.5	5.2	16.6	5.6	8.8	8.3	13.5
48 347	34860	5	Nacogdoches	2 452	64 524	810	26.3	62.7	18.6	0.8	1.5	17.6	6.9	16.5	20.1	12.3	10.3	11.7
48 349	18620	4	Navarro	2 615	47 735	1 011	18.3	60.8	14.1	0.7	1.5	23.8	7.3	19.8	8.9	11.4	12.4	13.9
48 351	...	8	Newton	2 418	14 445	2 147	6.0	76.2	20.6	1.1	0.6	2.8	5.8	17.4	8.7	11.0	12.6	14.7
48 353	45020	6	Nolan	2 362	15 216	2 098	6.4	61.3	4.9	0.6	0.5	33.5	7.4	18.4	8.7	10.9	11.8	13.2
48 355	18580	2	Nueces	2 172	340 223	190	156.6	33.6	3.9	0.5	2.0	60.6	7.1	18.9	10.3	13.6	12.2	14.3
48 357	...	7	Ochiltree	2 377	10 223	2 426	4.3	50.2	0.3	1.0	0.3	48.7	9.3	22.3	8.9	14.1	12.5	13.1
48 359	...	8	Oldham	3 886	2 052	3 048	0.5	83.9	3.3	1.2	0.9	11.8	4.9	29.1	5.8	10.8	10.7	14.0
48 361	13140	2	Orange	864	81 837	674	94.7	84.1	8.8	1.0	1.3	5.8	6.6	18.5	8.6	11.9	12.8	15.3
48 363	33420	6	Palo Pinto	2 465	28 111	1 494	11.4	79.1	2.5	0.9	0.7	17.7	6.8	18.2	7.9	10.9	11.6	15.0
48 365	...	6	Panola	2 077	23 796	1 650	11.5	74.6	16.7	0.9	0.5	8.3	6.5	18.2	8.5	12.3	11.3	14.2
48 367	19100	1	Parker	2 340	116 927	510	50.0	86.5	1.9	1.4	0.9	10.6	6.3	19.3	8.3	11.2	13.8	16.4
48 369	...	7	Parmer	2 281	10 269	2 419	4.5	38.7	1.0	0.3	0.3	60.0	8.9	22.4	9.4	12.7	12.1	13.1
48 371	...	7	Pecos	12 338	15 507	2 081	1.3	28.2	3.5	0.6	0.7	67.3	7.6	17.1	8.9	14.2	14.2	15.2
48 373	...	6	Polk	2 738	45 413	1 059	16.6	73.3	11.8	2.3	0.5	13.1	5.8	15.3	7.8	11.4	12.4	14.6
48 375	11100	3	Potter	2 353	121 073	499	51.5	50.3	10.5	1.0	4.3	35.3	8.5	19.3	10.0	14.9	12.8	13.6
48 377	...	7	Presidio	9 985	7 818	2 623	0.8	14.9	0.5	0.5	1.0	83.4	7.3	21.7	7.6	9.4	12.2	12.0
48 379	...	8	Rains	594	10 914	2 376	18.4	88.6	2.6	1.5	0.8	7.7	5.3	16.4	6.6	9.2	11.6	15.0
48 381	11100	3	Randall	2 361	120 725	501	51.1	79.4	2.7	1.0	1.7	16.4	6.8	18.1	10.8	13.8	12.2	14.0
48 383	...	6	Reagan	3 044	3 367	2 950	1.1	36.9	2.2	0.5	0.1	60.9	8.2	21.8	8.5	13.4	12.3	14.6
48 385	...	9	Real	1 811	3 309	2 956	1.8	73.6	0.8	1.6	0.5	24.6	4.9	15.0	5.3	7.3	9.5	14.5
48 387	...	6	Red River	2 685	12 860	2 254	4.8	75.2	17.8	1.5	0.3	6.6	5.6	15.7	7.0	9.9	11.5	14.4
48 389	37780	7	Reeves	6 826	13 783	2 202	2.0	19.7	5.0	0.2	0.9	74.2	6.6	16.2	11.3	15.4	14.7	14.2
48 391	...	6	Refugio	1 995	7 383	2 651	3.7	45.9	6.4	0.6	0.4	47.2	6.0	18.1	7.7	8.9	11.7	14.7
48 393	37420	9	Roberts	2 393	929	3 114	0.4	91.5	0.0	1.3	0.2	8.0	7.9	17.5	6.5	12.3	11.1	14.9
48 395	17780	3	Robertson	2 216	16 622	2 008	7.5	59.9	21.5	0.7	0.7	18.0	7.0	18.4	7.9	10.9	11.6	14.2
48 397	19100	1	Rockwall	329	78 337	692	238.1	75.3	6.1	0.9	3.0	15.9	7.3	22.7	6.4	12.3	15.8	15.5
48 399	...	6	Runnels	2 722	10 501	2 403	3.9	65.6	1.8	0.6	0.3	32.0	6.7	18.4	7.2	9.7	11.2	14.0
48 401	30980	3	Rusk	2 393	53 330	930	22.3	67.2	18.2	0.9	0.6	14.3	6.4	16.8	9.0	13.3	12.9	15.1
48 403	...	9	Sabine	1 273	10 834	2 382	8.5	88.8	7.7	1.0	0.5	3.2	5.0	14.6	6.0	7.6	9.3	14.6
48 405	...	9	San Augustine	1 374	8 865	2 538	6.5	70.6	23.2	0.7	0.4	6.0	5.4	15.7	7.2	8.6	10.2	15.0
48 407	26420	1	San Jacinto	1 474	26 384	1 548	17.9	77.9	10.6	1.2	0.8	10.9	6.1	17.9	7.4	9.7	11.2	15.5
48 409	18580	2	San Patricio	1 796	64 804	806	36.1	42.9	1.7	0.6	1.2	54.4	7.3	20.9	8.7	11.9	12.4	14.2
48 411	...	7	San Saba	2 940	6 131	2 752	2.1	68.1	3.3	0.9	0.4	28.0	5.8	15.2	10.0	13.5	10.0	12.2
48 413	...	8	Schleicher	3 395	3 461	2 943	1.0	54.5	1.0	0.3	0.3	44.4	9.9	21.9	7.7	11.8	11.4	11.9
48 415	43660	7	Scurry	2 345	16 921	1 989	7.2	58.5	4.9	0.6	0.4	36.3	7.5	17.5	9.7	13.3	12.1	14.1
48 417	...	8	Shackelford	2 368	3 378	2 949	1.4	88.9	1.0	0.7	0.4	10.1	6.5	18.1	7.2	8.9	12.0	15.9
48 419	...	6	Shelby	2 061	25 448	1 588	12.3	65.6	17.7	0.5	0.4	16.4	7.5	18.9	8.8	11.6	12.2	13.5
48 421	...	9	Sherman	2 391	3 034	2 977	1.3	58.6	0.4	0.8	0.2	40.4	7.1	23.1	7.0	10.4	14.3	14.6
48 423	46340	3	Smith	2 387	209 714	295	87.9	63.2	18.4	0.8	1.5	17.2	7.1	18.5	10.8	12.8	12.2	13.1
48 425	24180	8	Somervell	483	8 490	2 569	17.6	78.9	0.8	1.3	0.8	19.2	5.8	20.6	7.4	9.9	12.7	15.1
48 427	40100	4	Starr	3 168	60 968	847	19.2	4.1	0.0	0.0	0.2	95.7	9.0	24.9	10.8	12.8	13.0	10.7
48 429	...	7	Stephens	2 322	9 630	2 467	4.1	76.3	2.3	0.7	0.5	20.9	6.5	17.4	8.7	11.8	10.9	13.6
48 431	...	8	Sterling	2 392	1 143	3 104	0.5	65.6	1.8	1.8	0.0	31.9	7.7	16.7	7.6	12.2	10.1	16.1
48 433	...	8	Stonewall	2 373	1 490	3 084	0.6	82.1	3.1	0.9	1.1	14.0	5.5	17.2	5.3	9.6	10.6	14.5
48 435	...	7	Sutton	3 766	4 128	2 897	1.1	39.9	0.3	0.1	0.1	59.6	7.5	20.0	7.3	10.9	12.5	14.8
48 437	...	6	Swisher	2 306	7 854	2 617	3.4	52.1	7.5	1.0	0.1	40.1	7.8	18.3	9.1	12.9	10.8	12.9
48 439	19100	1	Tarrant	2 237	1 809 034	16	808.7	53.2	15.2	0.9	5.5	26.7	7.9	20.1	9.6	14.7	14.6	14.3
48 441	10180	3	Taylor	2 371	131 506	470	55.5	68.7	7.8	1.0	2.2	22.1	7.5	17.0	14.2	13.8	11.0	13.0
48 443	...	9	Terrell	6 107	984	3 110	0.2	50.8	0.8	1.0	0.4	47.5	6.6	15.5	5.6	10.3	12.5	13.2
48 445	...	6	Terry	2 302	12 651	2 266	5.5	46.0	4.7	0.4	0.3	49.1	7.9	18.0	10.8	13.2	11.3	13.9
48 447	...	9	Throckmorton	2 363	1 641	3 077	0.7	89.1	0.6	1.0	0.6	9.3	5.7	16.6	5.7	9.3	10.0	15.0
48 449	34420	7	Titus	1 052	32 334	1 381	30.7	49.9	9.6	0.7	0.9	39.6	9.1	21.5	9.8	12.8	13.0	12.2

1. CBSA = Core Based Statistical Area. See Appendix A for explanation. See Appendix B for list of metropolitan areas with component counties.   2. County type code from the Economic Research Service of USDA Rural-Urban Continuum Codes. See Appendix A for definition.   3. Dry land or land partially or temporarily covered by water.   4. May be of any race.

Table B. States and Counties — **Population and Households**

STATE County	55 to 64 years (16)	65 to 74 years (17)	75 years and over (18)	Percent female (19)	1990 (20)	2000 (21)	1990–2000 (22)	2000–2010 (23)	Births (24)	Deaths (25)	Net migration (26)	Number (27)	Percent change, 2000–2010 (28)	Persons per household (29)	Female family householder[1] (30)	One person (31)
TEXAS—Cont'd																
Mason	16.8	14.1	10.3	50.7	3 423	3 738	9.2	7.3	330	446	369	1 754	9.1	2.29	8.6	29.2
Matagorda	12.8	8.1	6.2	50.0	36 928	37 957	2.8	-3.3	5 081	3 214	-2 677	13 894	-0.1	2.61	13.4	26.4
Maverick	9.5	5.9	4.6	51.2	36 378	47 297	30.0	14.7	9 766	2 608	-948	15 563	18.9	3.42	18.4	15.5
Medina	12.6	7.6	5.9	48.6	27 312	39 304	43.9	17.1	5 288	3 161	3 527	15 530	20.6	2.81	12.6	20.0
Menard	15.7	14.3	12.5	49.5	2 252	2 360	4.8	-5.0	209	310	-120	994	0.4	2.22	8.4	32.3
Midland	10.8	5.6	5.4	50.9	106 611	116 009	8.8	18.0	18 512	8 634	7 106	50 845	18.9	2.66	12.8	24.8
Milam	13.2	9.1	8.2	50.6	22 946	24 238	5.6	2.1	3 336	2 751	-72	9 408	2.3	2.59	12.7	26.5
Mills	14.4	12.5	11.0	50.5	4 531	5 151	13.7	-4.2	432	654	90	1 975	-1.3	2.42	9.4	26.7
Mitchell	11.0	6.9	6.2	38.9	8 016	9 698	21.0	-3.0	886	970	-222	2 809	-1.0	2.49	12.0	28.2
Montague	13.9	11.0	8.7	51.0	17 274	19 117	10.7	3.1	2 323	2 586	839	7 989	2.8	2.43	9.3	26.9
Montgomery	11.6	6.4	4.0	50.4	182 201	293 768	61.2	55.1	51 533	22 008	122 645	162 530	57.3	2.78	10.6	20.6
Moore	9.3	5.1	4.5	48.3	17 865	20 121	12.6	8.9	3 868	1 237	-1 956	7 197	6.2	3.02	11.3	19.3
Morris	13.4	10.5	8.9	51.8	13 200	13 048	-1.2	-0.9	1 498	1 660	-195	5 226	0.2	2.45	15.0	27.5
Motley	15.0	15.2	11.9	49.3	1 532	1 426	-6.9	-15.1	143	165	-115	542	-10.6	2.23	7.4	32.3
Nacogdoches	10.4	6.4	5.4	52.3	54 753	59 203	8.1	9.0	8 711	5 109	1 684	23 861	8.4	2.49	13.6	28.7
Navarro	12.0	8.1	6.3	50.4	39 926	45 124	13.0	6.8	6 503	4 766	2 860	17 380	5.4	2.70	13.8	23.8
Newton	13.5	9.6	6.6	48.5	13 569	15 072	11.1	-4.2	1 281	1 423	-1 179	5 476	-1.9	2.51	13.4	26.2
Nolan	13.0	8.9	7.6	50.3	16 594	15 802	-4.8	-3.7	2 155	1 701	-1 280	5 999	-2.8	2.47	13.4	28.8
Nueces	11.7	6.5	5.6	50.9	291 145	313 645	7.7	8.5	46 808	23 015	-12 561	124 587	12.9	2.68	16.6	25.1
Ochiltree	9.5	5.5	4.8	48.8	9 128	9 006	-1.3	13.5	1 617	668	-145	3 617	10.9	2.81	10.2	21.8
Oldham	12.3	7.3	5.2	49.6	2 278	2 185	-4.1	-6.1	209	128	-141	691	-6.0	2.56	8.7	21.6
Orange	12.3	7.9	6.2	50.3	80 509	84 966	5.5	-3.7	10 050	8 124	-4 754	31 031	-1.9	2.62	13.5	23.0
Palo Pinto	13.2	9.6	6.7	50.9	25 055	27 026	7.9	4.0	3 619	3 077	133	10 871	2.6	2.56	11.5	25.4
Panola	13.4	8.8	6.8	50.4	22 035	22 756	3.3	4.6	2 761	2 344	269	9 271	5.1	2.53	12.3	25.4
Parker	12.7	7.5	4.7	49.3	64 785	88 495	36.6	32.1	11 465	7 277	22 537	42 069	35.1	2.71	9.4	19.7
Parmer	9.5	6.5	5.4	48.8	9 863	10 016	1.6	2.5	1 505	712	-1 496	3 413	2.7	2.99	9.4	19.3
Pecos	11.1	6.8	4.9	43.6	14 675	16 809	14.5	-7.7	2 149	1 121	-1 535	4 894	-5.0	2.75	13.2	22.8
Polk	13.6	11.3	7.7	46.5	30 687	41 133	34.0	10.4	4 781	5 467	6 212	16 503	9.2	2.49	12.4	26.3
Potter	10.0	5.6	5.2	48.9	97 841	113 546	16.1	6.6	20 737	11 088	-738	42 933	6.3	2.66	16.3	27.8
Presidio	12.1	9.4	8.4	51.2	6 637	7 304	10.0	7.0	1 448	353	-917	2 906	14.9	2.69	14.3	27.3
Rains	15.6	13.0	7.4	49.7	6 715	9 139	36.1	19.4	1 021	1 030	2 199	4 377	21.0	2.48	10.3	23.3
Randall	11.7	6.9	5.6	51.3	89 673	104 312	16.3	15.7	13 221	7 236	6 696	47 975	16.3	2.47	10.2	26.0
Reagan	10.8	5.9	4.5	48.1	4 514	3 326	-26.3	1.2	471	219	-574	1 156	4.4	2.89	9.3	20.7
Real	17.6	15.9	9.9	50.5	2 412	3 047	26.3	8.6	286	347	-66	1 374	10.4	2.36	8.8	26.3
Red River	14.7	11.8	9.3	51.3	14 317	14 314	0.0	-10.2	1 423	1 966	-945	5 469	-6.1	2.32	13.7	30.2
Reeves	9.5	6.5	5.5	39.9	15 852	13 137	-17.1	4.9	1 714	992	-2 803	3 839	-6.2	2.78	15.6	24.9
Refugio	13.4	10.9	8.6	50.3	7 976	7 828	-1.9	-5.7	880	789	-670	2 841	-4.8	2.55	13.3	25.7
Roberts	13.9	10.3	5.7	49.5	1 025	887	-13.5	4.7	98	83	-26	359	-0.8	2.59	4.5	17.5
Robertson	13.4	9.2	7.5	50.8	15 511	16 000	3.2	3.9	2 121	1 808	-544	6 541	5.9	2.61	15.2	27.2
Rockwall	10.4	5.8	3.8	50.8	25 604	43 080	68.3	81.8	8 638	3 252	32 374	26 448	82.0	2.94	9.3	16.0
Runnels	13.4	10.1	9.4	50.5	11 294	11 495	1.8	-8.6	1 325	1 391	-1 218	4 165	-5.9	2.47	11.8	27.3
Rusk	12.5	7.6	6.4	47.4	43 735	47 372	8.3	12.6	5 912	4 799	1 014	18 476	6.4	2.60	12.6	24.6
Sabine	16.2	16.0	10.8	51.1	9 586	10 469	9.2	3.5	937	1 497	358	4 738	5.6	2.27	10.7	28.2
San Augustine	14.9	12.6	10.5	50.8	7 999	8 946	11.8	-0.9	978	1 168	-137	3 625	1.4	2.38	13.1	28.7
San Jacinto	14.9	10.9	6.4	50.0	16 372	22 246	35.9	18.6	2 448	2 187	2 512	10 096	16.7	2.60	11.4	24.2
San Patricio	11.8	7.3	5.6	50.4	58 749	67 138	14.3	-3.5	10 561	4 842	-4 423	22 637	2.5	2.83	14.6	21.0
San Saba	14.1	9.9	9.3	45.1	5 401	6 186	14.5	-0.9	620	731	-171	2 257	-1.4	2.41	9.4	27.4
Schleicher	12.5	7.5	5.2	50.1	2 990	2 935	-1.8	17.9	387	290	-300	1 182	6.0	2.93	9.1	22.8
Scurry	11.6	7.2	6.8	46.6	18 634	16 361	-12.2	3.4	2 148	1 506	-707	5 838	1.4	2.60	11.8	25.5
Shackelford	13.9	9.0	8.5	51.7	3 316	3 302	-0.4	2.3	320	361	-204	1 367	5.2	2.44	9.4	28.3
Shelby	11.8	8.9	6.8	50.5	22 034	25 224	14.5	0.9	3 646	2 754	845	9 648	0.6	2.62	13.0	25.9
Sherman	10.2	6.6	6.8	49.0	2 858	3 186	11.5	-4.8	381	235	-406	1 081	-3.8	2.78	6.3	21.6
Smith	11.3	7.6	6.6	51.6	151 309	174 706	15.5	20.0	26 991	15 869	19 952	79 055	20.3	2.60	13.3	25.3
Somervell	13.6	8.3	6.5	50.7	5 360	6 809	27.0	24.7	881	702	1 077	3 078	26.3	2.67	8.8	21.8
Starr	8.4	6.0	4.4	51.7	40 518	53 597	32.3	13.8	13 657	2 755	-1 548	17 001	18.0	3.54	19.2	13.6
Stephens	12.9	9.6	8.5	48.3	9 010	9 674	7.4	-0.5	1 244	1 037	-193	3 665	0.1	2.47	10.8	28.3
Sterling	13.1	7.4	8.9	49.6	1 438	1 393	-3.1	-17.9	111	105	-137	440	-14.2	2.52	7.5	24.1
Stonewall	13.6	11.0	12.7	51.9	2 013	1 693	-15.9	-12.0	181	200	-319	642	-10.0	2.28	10.1	31.2
Sutton	13.2	7.5	6.3	50.8	4 135	4 077	-1.4	1.3	581	271	-90	1 550	2.3	2.65	10.7	24.6
Swisher	11.0	8.4	8.7	47.3	8 133	8 378	3.0	-6.3	1 202	725	-1 409	2 762	-5.6	2.61	11.9	24.9
Tarrant	9.9	5.3	3.8	51.0	1 170 103	1 446 219	23.6	25.1	258 671	92 106	186 365	657 134	23.1	2.72	13.8	24.9
Taylor	10.4	6.8	6.4	51.3	119 655	126 555	5.8	3.9	19 054	10 922	-6 257	50 725	7.3	2.49	12.9	27.4
Terrell	15.4	11.3	9.6	48.3	1 410	1 081	-23.3	-9.0	78	85	-101	430	-2.9	2.29	6.3	37.2
Terry	10.5	7.8	6.6	46.9	13 218	12 761	-3.5	-0.9	1 802	1 045	-1 339	4 200	-1.8	2.73	13.3	23.5
Throckmorton	13.2	13.3	11.3	50.8	1 880	1 850	-1.6	-11.3	117	180	-193	721	-5.8	2.26	6.9	31.8
Titus	10.1	6.4	5.1	50.6	24 009	28 118	17.1	15.0	5 202	2 321	-633	10 813	13.2	2.96	13.5	21.6

1. No spouse present.

Table B. States and Counties — Population, Vital Statistics, Medicare, and Crime

STATE County	Daytime population, 2006–2010 Persons in group quarters, 2010	Number	Employ-ment/resi-dence ratio	Births, average 2006–2008 Total	Rate¹	Deaths, average 2006–2008 Number	Rate¹	Persons under 65 with no health insurance, 2009 Number	Percent	Medicare, 2011 Eligible for Medicare	Enrolled in Medicare Advantage	Enrolled in a Medicare prescription drug plan	Serious crimes known to police,² 2010 Total Number	Rate³
	32	33	34	35	36	37	38	39	40	41	42	43	44	45
TEXAS—Cont'd														
Mason	3	3 797	0.9	D	D	53	13.6	1 063	35.2	1 079	34	531	37	922
Matagorda	400	35 303	0.9	D	D	344	9.2	9 153	29.2	6 005	723	2 677	1 399	3 812
Maverick	969	50 902	0.9	1 058	20.3	304	5.8	16 140	35.0	8 193	1 436	5 096	1 681	3 098
Medina	2 309	37 811	0.6	572	13.0	364	8.3	10 173	26.8	7 276	1 479	2 419	848	1 889
Menard	38	2 194	1.0	D	D	39	17.9	598	38.2	594	23	286	9	401
Midland	1 678	136 214	1.1	2 217	17.5	952	7.5	27 449	23.8	16 955	1 557	8 171	4 699	3 433
Milam	405	23 264	0.8	D	D	313	12.5	5 421	27.0	5 039	1 567	1 515	642	2 593
Mills	151	4 729	0.9	D	D	65	12.8	1 158	30.5	1 190	271	458	55	1 114
Mitchell	2 406	9 292	1.0	D	D	96	10.4	2 410	30.5	1 385	53	725	203	2 159
Montague	266	17 831	0.8	D	D	266	13.5	4 039	26.3	4 581	269	2 303	524	2 806
Montgomery	3 224	380 392	0.8	6 262	15.1	2 558	6.2	82 638	21.0	58 024	14 962	19 648	12 674	2 781
Moore	154	21 880	1.1	D	D	146	7.2	5 884	32.0	2 251	110	1 171	479	2 187
Morris	145	12 929	1.0	D	D	175	13.5	2 318	23.3	3 278	512	1 492	421	3 255
Motley	0	1 129	1.0	D	D	20	15.7	332	35.5	338	D	162	21	1 736
Nacogdoches	5 144	63 165	1.0	996	16.0	558	9.0	15 593	28.5	9 469	782	4 470	2 583	4 003
Navarro	736	45 508	0.9	734	14.8	508	10.3	11 626	28.0	8 719	635	4 281	2 110	4 420
Newton	724	11 669	0.5	D	D	162	11.7	2 918	26.0	2 377	313	1 216	149	1 031
Nolan	410	15 210	1.0	239	16.2	182	12.3	3 187	25.9	2 940	212	1 533	655	4 305
Nueces	5 792	344 570	1.1	4 997	15.5	2 520	7.8	72 710	26.0	48 735	19 383	12 589	18 896	5 554
Ochiltree	54	10 628	1.2	D	D	72	7.5	2 713	31.3	1 185	37	612	179	1 751
Oldham	282	2 220	1.2	D	D	15	7.0	464	25.4	346	20	150	19	926
Orange	639	74 564	0.8	1 139	13.7	903	10.8	14 729	21.4	14 962	3 308	6 223	3 331	4 070
Palo Pinto	263	25 855	0.8	429	15.6	323	11.7	6 748	29.6	5 267	355	2 455	969	3 447
Panola	358	23 786	1.0	D	D	266	11.5	4 323	22.6	4 287	386	1 954	467	1 963
Parker	3 121	94 745	0.7	1 375	12.6	855	7.8	22 025	22.1	17 271	2 017	6 548	2 376	2 032
Parmer	73	10 943	1.2	D	D	87	9.2	2 678	33.9	1 344	36	802	147	1 431
Pecos	2 025	16 086	1.1	D	D	119	7.4	4 534	32.2	2 049	152	1 089	422	2 721
Polk	4 241	44 626	0.9	539	11.6	624	13.4	10 830	29.9	16 562	2 443	6 063	1 173	2 583
Potter	6 919	143 626	1.4	2 222	18.4	1 183	9.8	32 242	31.0	16 344	1 758	8 127	7 086	5 853
Presidio	0	7 577	1.0	D	D	46	6.1	2 456	40.2	1 727	138	1 090	NA	NA
Rains	66	8 466	0.5	D	D	114	10.1	2 549	29.1	2 461	241	1 193	136	1 246
Randall	2 000	93 402	0.6	1 558	13.8	845	7.5	18 619	18.1	17 449	1 687	7 370	6 050	5 011
Reagan	27	3 429	1.1	D	D	25	8.3	876	32.9	415	20	235	9	267
Real	70	3 344	1.1	D	D	42	14.2	715	33.7	1 020	78	442	17	514
Red River	189	11 277	0.7	D	D	206	15.6	2 789	27.9	3 228	131	1 741	221	1 719
Reeves	3 110	13 166	1.0	D	D	110	9.8	3 263	35.6	2 004	80	1 307	340	2 467
Refugio	129	7 005	0.8	D	D	87	11.7	1 560	26.9	1 645	142	817	82	1 111
Roberts	0	853	0.9	D	D	D	D	124	17.1	156	11	78	28	3 014
Robertson	193	16 328	1.0	D	D	191	12.0	3 388	26.5	3 141	391	1 358	439	2 641
Rockwall	659	61 263	0.7	984	13.4	378	5.1	13 599	18.8	9 197	1 429	3 718	1 626	2 076
Runnels	194	9 832	0.8	D	D	150	14.3	2 319	29.0	2 353	93	1 343	209	1 990
Rusk	5 210	46 292	0.7	691	14.2	498	10.3	10 372	25.4	8 553	1 000	3 909	1 470	2 756
Sabine	79	10 190	0.9	D	D	168	16.4	1 798	24.6	3 262	304	1 500	132	1 322
San Augustine	223	8 554	0.8	D	D	132	15.2	1 594	25.2	2 263	261	1 133	148	1 669
San Jacinto	128	20 167	0.4	D	D	267	10.7	5 604	27.7	5 054	1 153	1 940	843	3 195
San Patricio	680	59 914	0.8	1 126	16.4	529	7.7	14 635	25.1	10 915	4 142	3 087	2 218	3 423
San Saba	684	5 718	0.9	D	D	68	11.4	1 599	34.5	1 265	140	533	83	1 354
Schleicher	0	3 078	0.8	D	D	36	13.0	729	32.2	500	30	243	12	347
Scurry	1 724	17 245	1.1	D	D	150	9.3	3 581	26.3	2 734	159	1 534	588	3 475
Shackelford	36	3 063	0.9	D	D	38	11.9	699	28.6	632	48	343	40	1 184
Shelby	172	25 089	1.0	D	D	287	10.8	6 425	29.1	4 867	508	2 421	639	2 511
Sherman	31	2 885	0.9	D	D	23	7.8	866	34.8	352	15	198	18	593
Smith	4 127	212 556	1.1	3 074	15.5	1 767	8.9	42 660	25.1	36 208	4 098	16 222	8 538	4 107
Somervell	287	9 282	1.3	D	D	75	9.5	1 641	24.5	1 346	206	543	102	1 201
Starr	810	58 787	0.9	1 387	22.4	331	5.3	18 904	34.6	8 076	548	5 942	1 320	2 165
Stephens	591	9 681	1.0	D	D	111	11.6	2 543	32.5	1 896	157	978	148	1 537
Sterling	35	1 249	1.2	D	D	10	8.3	266	26.2	202	12	115	18	1 575
Stonewall	27	1 449	1.0	D	D	26	18.6	348	34.2	368	D	212	15	1 007
Sutton	13	5 131	1.4	D	D	34	7.9	1 101	30.1	630	16	390	41	993
Swisher	645	7 247	0.8	D	D	78	10.1	1 993	33.3	1 488	66	911	179	2 279
Tarrant	20 634	1 722 802	1.0	29 380	17.2	10 422	6.1	393 513	24.6	197 760	60 680	58 593	86 225	4 766
Taylor	5 287	134 078	1.1	2 135	16.9	1 183	9.4	24 096	22.3	20 872	1 529	9 221	5 669	4 311
Terrell	0	922	1.2	D	D	12	12.7	259	33.4	237	19	116	34	3 455
Terry	1 166	11 607	0.8	D	D	126	10.3	3 259	32.1	2 052	300	1 003	249	1 968
Throckmorton	13	1 660	0.8	D	D	20	12.2	383	32.0	398	22	224	5	305
Titus	357	33 790	1.2	623	20.9	259	8.7	7 899	30.4	4 356	380	2 023	1 056	3 266

1. Per 1,000 estimated resident population.　2. Data for serious crimes have not been adjusted for underreporting; this may affect comparability between geographic areas and over time.　3. Per 100,000 population estimated by the FBI.

Table B. States and Counties — Crime, Education, Money Income, and Poverty

STATE County	Rate[2] Violent	Rate[2] Property	Enrollment[3] Total	Enrollment[3] Percent private	Attainment[4] (percent) High school graduate or less	Attainment[4] (percent) Bachelor's degree or more	Local government expenditures[5] 2008–2009 Total current expenditures (mil dol)	Current expenditures per student (dollars)	Per capita income[6] (dollars)	Median income Dollars	Percent change, 2000 to 2006–2010 (constant 2010 dollars)	Percent with income of $200,000 or more	Median household income (dollars)	Percent below poverty level All persons	Children under 18 years	Children 5 to 17 years in families
	46	47	48	49	50	51	52	53	54	55	56	57	58	59	60	61
TEXAS—Cont'd																
Mason	50	872	907	11.5	52.4	28.9	6.6	10 405	23 555	38 702	-1.2	4.1	38 802	16.2	30.6	28.0
Matagorda	262	3 550	8 832	5.3	58.1	14.1	70.9	9 726	22 623	43 205	6.0	2.0	39 874	19.9	28.4	25.8
Maverick	241	2 857	17 919	2.7	67.1	13.7	124.0	8 776	12 444	28 813	7.2	1.5	27 710	39.9	53.2	48.9
Medina	194	1 695	12 375	10.8	50.7	19.3	75.0	8 400	20 604	49 138	7.6	1.8	47 099	17.5	27.1	24.6
Menard	45	357	397	0.5	58.3	13.9	5.0	14 364	23 362	40 996	30.7	4.1	30 277	24.0	40.9	40.9
Midland	330	3 104	35 468	13.4	44.1	23.9	191.2	8 099	30 956	54 945	11.0	6.6	53 482	14.4	22.3	21.6
Milam	149	2 444	6 014	7.4	60.3	13.5	38.6	8 262	21 509	39 035	-7.1	2.4	36 799	19.8	29.8	27.7
Mills	41	1 074	871	6.4	58.6	18.7	11.1	13 213	20 438	31 895	-17.6	1.8	36 108	17.2	27.8	26.8
Mitchell	149	2 010	1 974	1.9	60.2	9.4	14.8	10 361	13 358	37 260	15.8	0.8	34 877	23.3	28.3	26.6
Montague	166	2 640	4 257	9.1	53.7	16.7	31.2	9 467	22 328	42 482	8.1	2.3	42 415	16.1	24.8	22.9
Montgomery	266	2 515	114 163	13.0	39.7	29.7	634.6	7 508	31 959	65 620	1.9	8.1	65 483	11.5	16.0	14.0
Moore	265	1 922	6 274	4.1	60.7	13.7	39.4	8 118	18 239	44 216	0.2	1.1	44 680	15.0	23.2	21.5
Morris	518	2 737	2 914	5.3	52.2	17.3	22.5	9 835	20 292	38 843	5.7	1.1	34 451	19.2	31.7	29.4
Motley	165	1 570	198	17.7	52.6	18.5	2.5	14 299	19 754	34 081	-5.1	0.7	35 672	16.7	25.2	23.4
Nacogdoches	625	3 379	21 241	5.9	49.6	24.0	85.3	8 260	18 180	33 189	-7.4	1.4	35 854	25.5	33.3	30.2
Navarro	354	4 066	13 109	5.5	55.8	15.7	78.2	8 240	20 539	41 654	5.2	2.3	37 864	21.5	33.1	29.9
Newton	69	962	3 274	6.5	68.6	8.6	22.9	10 459	17 721	37 452	3.8	1.0	36 429	23.3	31.6	28.7
Nolan	979	3 325	3 678	4.6	55.9	17.1	31.1	10 137	19 973	37 102	11.8	1.6	33 981	20.1	32.7	29.7
Nueces	674	4 880	92 138	8.2	48.8	19.9	514.6	8 400	22 558	43 280	-5.0	2.4	41 899	20.0	31.1	28.2
Ochiltree	235	1 516	2 641	5.3	63.8	17.9	18.1	8 088	21 143	49 309	2.4	1.9	50 979	12.7	19.1	18.4
Oldham	97	828	666	6.3	42.7	29.8	12.5	15 123	22 504	51 111	19.7	2.4	43 739	13.4	25.5	19.0
Orange	371	3 699	20 180	7.6	56.6	12.5	132.2	8 723	23 155	47 914	0.7	1.4	45 264	15.1	23.0	21.3
Palo Pinto	402	3 045	6 313	4.6	57.8	13.7	44.7	9 075	21 551	41 095	4.0	2.3	39 595	16.8	27.2	25.9
Panola	273	1 689	5 700	7.1	55.9	11.4	37.8	9 692	22 846	45 622	12.9	1.8	48 621	13.8	20.5	19.4
Parker	168	1 864	28 822	12.1	43.6	22.4	158.5	8 236	28 539	61 340	6.5	4.7	57 092	12.0	17.7	15.9
Parmer	234	1 198	2 817	6.9	59.7	15.7	22.6	9 490	16 926	39 753	1.9	1.0	38 619	14.9	21.3	20.8
Pecos	451	2 270	3 168	2.6	66.7	11.3	33.9	11 156	16 717	38 125	7.4	2.1	39 118	22.1	27.8	27.9
Polk	227	2 356	8 707	9.5	62.8	10.6	61.1	8 793	16 961	33 325	-13.7	1.0	38 747	19.6	31.4	29.8
Potter	575	5 278	32 228	7.8	52.7	15.0	275.2	7 966	18 725	36 766	-1.6	1.6	35 323	24.5	36.0	34.8
Presidio	NA	NA	2 014	1.8	68.5	17.8	18.4	10 710	15 635	29 613	17.4	2.1	30 357	23.6	37.3	34.5
Rains	156	1 090	2 252	6.2	59.5	12.1	22.0	8 904	20 855	42 491	-0.5	0.3	40 966	16.7	28.1	25.7
Randall	482	4 529	33 597	10.1	33.2	30.1	78.4	8 887	28 668	56 041	3.6	3.7	57 862	8.7	11.2	10.4
Reagan	59	208	877	2.1	66.2	10.0	9.7	12 015	23 028	54 224	28.9	0.8	48 667	11.7	15.6	15.0
Real	151	363	700	8.7	49.4	19.4	6.6	18 000	15 074	29 186	-8.2	0.5	31 490	24.1	45.1	43.6
Red River	179	1 540	2 923	5.3	64.7	8.6	26.2	10 566	18 105	37 047	6.2	0.5	32 128	19.2	31.7	30.1
Reeves	368	2 195	3 092	0.3	76.3	7.6	24.7	10 361	13 112	32 593	10.4	0.5	32 623	32.2	36.2	34.7
Refugio	176	935	1 613	0.6	60.2	11.2	18.6	12 558	18 638	42 949	13.1	1.6	39 582	17.8	26.5	23.9
Roberts	323	2 691	161	2.5	33.8	34.1	2.4	14 901	29 291	52 500	-7.4	4.0	58 372	6.9	8.9	9.2
Robertson	295	2 346	4 159	11.1	60.0	15.8	36.8	11 198	21 113	38 393	5.0	2.4	36 935	21.6	33.9	31.7
Rockwall	133	1 943	21 732	14.6	32.2	35.6	146.0	8 191	33 274	78 032	-5.4	6.9	81 113	6.4	9.1	8.2
Runnels	181	1 809	2 217	2.2	61.6	16.4	20.5	9 690	20 056	37 823	7.4	1.1	32 628	23.1	34.5	32.8
Rusk	330	2 426	12 131	8.7	55.1	14.8	69.0	8 963	22 392	46 574	11.8	2.9	43 318	15.3	23.6	22.4
Sabine	300	1 022	1 998	0.8	61.7	12.2	19.3	9 202	18 155	33 589	-2.5	0.1	34 034	18.5	30.6	28.5
San Augustine	259	1 410	2 047	4.8	69.4	11.9	12.0	9 078	17 184	25 974	-24.1	1.6	31 729	21.2	34.9	32.2
San Jacinto	311	2 884	5 432	6.8	61.9	9.6	31.3	9 072	21 453	46 285	13.4	1.9	42 770	19.1	31.4	28.8
San Patricio	292	3 131	17 866	5.7	54.7	15.1	125.6	8 444	20 766	45 189	2.4	2.1	44 307	21.1	31.7	29.2
San Saba	359	995	1 213	4.5	54.9	18.1	10.7	10 932	19 721	36 308	-4.8	2.6	34 264	21.0	34.2	32.8
Schleicher	29	318	928	3.6	60.6	17.4	6.2	9 910	21 299	55 186	46.5	2.7	32 831	17.5	24.7	24.7
Scurry	804	2 671	4 512	1.2	55.9	16.3	28.3	9 010	22 424	42 401	5.8	2.5	44 063	17.4	24.0	23.3
Shackelford	118	1 066	755	10.3	44.8	27.6	7.1	10 496	22 346	46 629	20.8	1.2	42 685	13.5	20.7	19.3
Shelby	303	2 208	6 037	5.6	63.9	13.5	48.5	9 347	20 103	32 425	-12.0	2.3	34 490	21.9	33.1	28.8
Sherman	0	593	801	9.0	54.6	19.1	8.0	9 060	21 587	50 069	19.2	2.3	41 518	12.5	16.9	15.5
Smith	418	3 689	55 363	13.7	42.4	24.5	271.3	8 301	25 374	46 139	-1.9	3.7	44 249	15.0	21.7	20.3
Somervell	82	1 119	2 262	6.4	42.0	28.4	20.7	11 107	26 314	52 135	4.5	3.7	49 582	10.7	17.1	15.5
Starr	294	1 871	19 067	3.8	74.0	9.8	163.0	9 772	11 659	24 441	16.9	1.3	24 497	39.2	54.7	54.7
Stephens	187	1 350	1 962	4.7	55.1	12.2	14.8	9 641	19 573	35 691	-4.7	1.7	38 002	20.0	31.0	29.1
Sterling	262	1 312	280	9.3	54.3	22.7	3.1	15 542	20 640	41 548	-6.6	0.0	49 064	12.4	19.0	18.9
Stonewall	336	671	313	8.3	47.6	22.4	3.0	12 831	25 177	52 222	47.6	2.0	36 687	17.2	26.3	24.5
Sutton	170	824	1 305	6.3	44.3	11.8	11.5	11 385	23 325	56 146	28.9	2.0	51 386	13.4	22.0	20.8
Swisher	369	1 910	1 935	4.2	59.4	14.6	14.1	9 628	16 513	37 907	0.3	1.4	33 786	20.9	30.0	29.1
Tarrant	446	4 321	490 565	15.1	40.8	28.7	2 635.5	8 015	27 333	55 306	-5.4	4.2	52 482	14.4	20.7	19.4
Taylor	439	3 872	36 621	27.8	43.6	24.2	177.9	8 082	22 606	42 403	-1.6	1.8	41 558	17.9	24.3	21.9
Terrell	407	3 049	165	0.0	60.1	20.7	3.4	20 048	18 871	35 403	15.4	0.0	35 683	15.2	23.1	22.6
Terry	174	1 794	3 074	4.0	66.0	14.3	23.3	10 376	22 306	39 498	11.0	2.8	34 495	21.9	34.8	34.4
Throckmorton	0	305	353	5.1	57.2	16.7	4.1	12 150	20 677	36 339	1.5	1.3	37 273	14.7	25.3	23.2
Titus	312	2 954	8 843	6.0	58.1	13.7	69.5	10 276	17 520	39 423	-4.1	2.0	37 818	20.7	29.5	27.7

1. Data for serious crimes have not been adjusted for underreporting; this may affect comparability between geographic areas and over time. 2. Per 100,000 population estimated by the FBI. 3. All persons 3 years old and over enrolled in nursery school through college. 4. Persons 25 years old and over. 5. Elementary and secondary education expenditures. 6. Based on population estimated by the American Community Survey, 2006–2010.

Table B. States and Counties — **Personal Income**

STATE County	Total (mil dol) [62]	Percent change, 2008–2009 [63]	Per capita¹ Dollars [64]	Rank [65]	Wages and salaries² (mil dol) [66]	Proprietors' income (mil dol) [67]	Dividends, interest, and rent (mil dol) [68]	Transfer payments Total [69]	Gov. payments Total [70]	Social Security [71]	Medical payments [72]	Income mainte-nance [73]	Unemploy-ment insurance [74]
TEXAS—Cont'd													
Mason	122	1.7	30 680	1 826	39	12	39	32	31	13	14	2	1
Matagorda	1 124	1.5	30 409	1 883	618	84	188	268	261	83	121	31	12
Maverick	1 050	6.3	19 740	3 096	593	69	74	405	396	66	208	83	22
Medina	1 330	2.6	29 735	2 037	307	58	195	298	290	86	138	30	9
Menard	68	0.7	31 992	1 530	17	7	20	21	20	7	10	1	0
Midland	7 167	-7.0	54 164	62	3 908	1 557	1 403	755	731	243	315	102	28
Milam	737	-2.6	29 910	2 000	297	50	134	201	196	67	88	19	8
Mills	153	-2.1	30 552	1 852	51	8	38	47	46	15	24	3	1
Mitchell	214	1.4	22 846	3 037	103	24	36	63	61	19	33	5	2
Montague	742	-3.1	37 905	652	203	98	151	178	174	63	87	10	5
Montgomery	20 366	2.0	45 490	186	6 833	948	3 541	2 231	2 149	835	894	180	100
Moore	611	-2.6	29 479	2 096	441	47	81	102	98	32	45	12	4
Morris	397	-1.5	31 447	1 651	215	21	66	136	134	44	63	12	6
Motley	38	-0.5	29 738	2 036	15	3	8	11	11	4	5	1	0
Nacogdoches	1 804	2.3	28 141	2 375	915	140	368	455	443	130	208	48	13
Navarro	1 410	0.9	28 516	2 296	627	86	261	385	376	116	173	39	11
Newton	360	2.9	26 377	2 658	72	11	38	110	108	32	53	13	5
Nolan	472	2.4	31 621	1 620	260	37	82	137	134	38	69	13	3
Nueces	12 005	-1.5	37 162	730	8 002	1 369	1 913	2 398	2 339	610	1 161	304	80
Ochiltree	373	-9.8	38 118	624	214	77	65	45	43	16	19	4	2
Oldham	62	-7.4	29 139	2 160	35	4	10	12	11	5	5	1	0
Orange	2 869	0.1	35 070	1 008	1 150	117	388	739	724	228	363	58	28
Palo Pinto	930	-1.2	33 746	1 210	390	61	165	208	203	71	94	18	7
Panola	838	-2.6	35 959	895	411	94	156	178	173	59	80	15	6
Parker	4 093	-2.6	35 617	940	1 146	277	690	596	576	245	204	43	28
Parmer	281	-4.4	30 260	1 923	204	19	61	53	52	17	25	6	1
Pecos	405	-10.9	24 941	2 869	268	37	47	92	90	24	47	10	5
Polk	1 726	2.0	37 098	739	449	85	536	594	585	251	253	36	11
Potter	3 878	-1.0	31 835	1 570	3 793	824	587	903	881	213	465	105	24
Presidio	180	3.6	24 113	2 958	108	2	29	56	55	13	22	12	4
Rains	305	0.5	27 032	2 560	62	24	53	85	83	35	34	6	3
Randall	4 564	1.8	39 182	516	1 194	124	943	462	440	238	75	41	21
Reagan	105	-11.3	34 731	1 056	90	13	13	18	17	6	8	2	1
Real	95	3.7	32 406	1 444	24	6	28	32	32	12	15	2	1
Red River	366	2.0	28 679	2 264	104	15	59	136	134	39	73	11	4
Reeves	296	3.7	26 779	2 602	159	23	36	91	89	23	47	12	4
Refugio	267	-2.5	36 937	757	92	8	77	68	67	22	34	6	2
Roberts	29	-14.3	33 218	1 304	9	-3	7	5	4	2	2	0	0
Robertson	537	0.6	34 222	1 139	183	49	103	133	130	41	61	15	4
Rockwall	3 500	2.6	42 999	270	895	165	548	329	314	134	119	21	18
Runnels	290	-1.5	28 488	2 301	117	22	58	93	91	30	47	7	2
Rusk	1 516	-1.5	30 827	1 795	712	106	279	336	327	119	145	31	13
Sabine	341	1.9	33 425	1 275	117	17	81	136	135	48	67	8	4
San Augustine	236	1.4	27 567	2 473	64	15	37	99	97	31	51	8	2
San Jacinto	783	2.1	31 443	1 653	90	28	109	185	180	71	71	21	6
San Patricio	2 256	-1.5	33 068	1 326	1 066	62	301	519	507	141	256	58	18
San Saba	160	2.1	27 331	2 511	63	8	36	50	49	16	26	4	1
Schleicher	85	-2.6	31 073	1 737	39	7	16	19	19	6	9	2	1
Scurry	559	-7.6	34 488	1 094	318	65	104	113	110	35	56	9	4
Shackelford	137	-4.5	44 846	205	47	30	31	25	24	9	12	1	1
Shelby	750	1.3	27 960	2 408	322	66	132	227	222	64	120	22	6
Sherman	109	-13.1	37 312	711	32	32	18	15	15	5	8	1	0
Smith	7 843	-0.6	38 319	597	4 560	1 019	1 709	1 467	1 430	504	631	128	51
Somervell	290	-4.4	36 159	863	315	18	42	53	51	18	24	4	2
Starr	1 030	6.3	16 433	3 111	482	55	79	460	449	62	234	109	27
Stephens	332	-3.0	34 442	1 104	133	60	68	81	80	27	41	7	2
Sterling	42	-6.8	33 053	1 333	26	2	11	8	8	3	4	0	0
Stonewall	55	1.9	40 777	400	22	4	16	14	14	5	8	1	0
Sutton	213	-5.2	49 731	108	180	13	36	26	25	8	12	2	2
Swisher	212	-4.6	28 521	2 295	84	21	47	56	54	19	26	6	1
Tarrant	70 486	-1.4	39 380	500	44 441	8 085	10 837	8 639	8 313	2 737	3 422	971	473
Taylor	4 712	-0.3	36 902	760	2 933	499	930	928	906	273	435	89	26
Terrell	38	8.6	39 461	494	19	0	9	8	8	2	3	0	0
Terry	365	-2.9	30 072	1 960	172	27	63	106	104	27	60	11	3
Throckmorton	72	-3.8	44 949	201	19	18	14	15	14	5	7	1	0
Titus	916	2.4	30 312	1 904	703	61	150	210	205	59	102	22	7

1. Based on the resident population estimated as of July 1 of the year shown.   2. Includes supplements to wages and salaries.

Table B. States and Counties — Earnings, Social Security, and Housing

STATE County	Earnings, 2009									Social Security beneficiaries, December 2010		Supplemental Security Income recipients, December 2010	Housing units, 2010	
			Goods-related[1]		Service-related and health									
	Total (mil dol)	Farm	Total	Manu-facturing	Infor-mation and profes-sional and technical services	Retail trade	Finance, insur-ance, and real estate	Health care and social services	Govern-ment	Number	Rate[2]		Total	Percent change, 2000–2010
	75	76	77	78	79	80	81	82	83	84	85	86	87	88
TEXAS—Cont'd														
Mason	51	3.8	7.4	0.9	D	6.0	13.4	7.0	23.8	1 110	277	79	2 733	15.2
Matagorda	702	4.3	10.7	5.6	5.1	5.3	3.4	D	16.9	6 710	183	1 091	18 801	1.0
Maverick	661	-0.6	5.8	3.3	3.0	9.2	3.4	15.0	45.3	9 000	166	4 135	17 462	17.3
Medina	365	-0.3	11.9	2.3	4.8	9.4	6.5	D	36.4	8 000	174	1 211	17 991	21.4
Menard	23	3.5	D	0.0	D	9.0	6.9	2.7	34.4	665	297	70	1 702	5.9
Midland	5 465	0.0	51.1	3.7	6.7	4.6	4.7	5.1	9.0	18 750	137	2 356	54 351	13.1
Milam	348	0.0	37.1	17.5	D	6.2	4.5	10.3	16.6	5 525	223	838	11 305	4.0
Mills	59	-3.1	9.0	4.3	D	11.3	6.0	14.7	27.3	1 290	261	120	2 846	5.8
Mitchell	126	5.4	20.4	2.2	D	5.7	D	4.3	43.5	1 570	167	222	4 064	-2.5
Montague	302	0.6	35.3	5.2	4.3	7.2	6.8	D	20.4	5 110	259	448	10 131	2.7
Montgomery	7 782	0.1	24.8	8.8	10.2	8.8	6.2	9.9	14.7	63 700	140	6 798	177 647	57.5
Moore	488	2.2	50.2	38.7	D	6.7	1.9	D	15.7	2 540	116	293	7 881	5.4
Morris	236	0.9	D	46.3	8.3	3.1	3.0	4.0	13.3	3 610	279	569	6 024	0.1
Motley	18	9.3	15.8	8.1	D	5.8	D	5.7	25.8	350	289	37	779	-7.2
Nacogdoches	1 055	1.0	20.9	13.2	4.0	8.6	4.5	15.4	26.6	10 645	165	2 022	27 406	9.4
Navarro	713	-0.4	24.4	16.7	2.7	7.9	5.1	11.8	23.4	9 860	207	1 680	20 234	9.7
Newton	83	-4.0	D	9.1	D	5.0	D	10.5	34.8	2 765	191	594	7 142	-2.6
Nolan	297	0.1	25.2	15.0	5.9	9.1	4.3	5.7	27.4	3 230	212	530	7 152	0.6
Nueces	9 371	0.1	25.1	8.2	7.4	6.3	4.5	13.9	22.0	54 130	159	12 675	141 033	14.7
Ochiltree	291	8.7	47.9	0.8	2.4	5.0	3.2	D	11.5	1 310	128	113	4 062	7.8
Oldham	38	18.3	D	D	D	2.6	D	D	35.1	385	188	29	841	3.2
Orange	1 267	1.2	40.5	31.8	3.0	7.7	4.2	6.5	17.0	17 290	211	2 385	35 313	1.5
Palo Pinto	451	0.2	40.0	23.1	2.8	7.6	3.7	4.3	19.8	5 890	210	735	15 214	7.9
Panola	506	0.9	48.5	7.4	3.4	4.6	2.8	4.9	12.7	4 815	202	673	10 920	3.8
Parker	1 423	0.2	23.8	8.6	7.1	10.1	4.7	9.8	18.0	19 155	164	1 381	46 628	36.8
Parmer	223	17.4	D	D	D	3.3	D	2.2	15.6	1 480	144	142	3 799	1.8
Pecos	306	3.8	35.9	0.6	D	5.9	3.6	3.0	28.9	2 255	145	433	5 585	-11.9
Polk	534	-0.2	20.4	12.4	6.1	11.1	4.3	9.0	25.4	18 945	417	1 700	22 683	7.1
Potter	4 617	0.1	19.3	7.9	8.2	6.5	7.0	16.6	16.8	17 985	149	3 181	47 271	6.0
Presidio	110	19.3	D	D	D	4.3	D	D	55.7	1 695	217	757	3 825	15.9
Rains	86	0.5	D	4.2	D	12.4	5.3	4.9	24.6	2 765	253	262	5 269	16.5
Randall	1 318	1.4	15.5	6.3	6.9	10.8	8.3	9.8	18.3	18 145	150	1 130	51 587	19.2
Reagan	103	1.5	96.4	0.0	D	2.8	0.9	0.4	15.3	440	131	45	1 372	-5.5
Real	30	7.0	D	D	3.0	6.4	D	13.3	30.6	1 080	326	146	2 599	29.4
Red River	119	2.6	22.3	13.6	D	5.9	4.8	17.3	29.5	3 600	280	564	6 826	-1.6
Reeves	182	5.0	18.0	1.8	2.0	8.5	3.9	4.0	42.8	2 215	161	537	4 640	-8.0
Refugio	101	-2.9	D	D	D	6.3	11.7	6.1	30.7	1 835	249	242	3 726	1.6
Roberts	7	-46.9	D	0.0	D	D	D	0.0	58.8	160	172	0	439	-2.2
Robertson	232	0.8	86.4	9.6	2.2	4.1	4.0	5.5	20.9	3 515	211	657	8 484	7.7
Rockwall	1 060	-0.2	D	6.0	11.1	9.0	7.2	16.7	17.7	10 035	128	657	27 939	82.0
Runnels	140	-1.5	34.4	22.4	D	6.7	D	5.8	25.5	2 595	247	322	5 298	-1.9
Rusk	817	1.2	39.5	6.7	D	5.5	4.9	7.0	14.2	9 700	182	1 349	21 191	6.7
Sabine	135	-0.3	D	D	D	5.7	3.8	6.7	17.0	3 735	345	382	7 988	4.3
San Augustine	78	3.4	D	3.9	D	7.8	3.8	21.1	23.7	2 570	290	486	5 342	-0.3
San Jacinto	118	-1.3	D	2.4	7.0	5.9	6.1	4.8	35.9	5 665	215	895	13 187	14.5
San Patricio	1 128	0.2	39.2	13.2	3.5	5.1	2.2	4.1	31.6	12 345	190	2 415	26 521	6.4
San Saba	71	-3.6	D	2.1	D	9.0	5.4	8.0	32.0	1 400	228	165	3 177	7.7
Schleicher	46	5.8	D	D	D	2.8	2.6	5.1	23.7	545	157	73	1 489	8.6
Scurry	384	-1.0	42.8	2.4	3.0	5.1	3.4	D	19.9	3 000	177	369	6 963	-2.1
Shackelford	77	2.3	D	D	4.4	3.0	3.9	D	13.3	700	207	59	1 754	8.7
Shelby	388	3.6	34.0	25.3	4.1	9.2	5.7	6.4	16.4	5 520	217	1 052	11 873	-0.7
Sherman	64	43.7	D	D	D	2.9	5.0	1.2	20.1	365	120	16	1 252	-1.8
Smith	5 579	0.2	21.8	8.3	9.3	7.6	7.4	21.6	12.4	39 520	188	5 105	87 309	21.8
Somervell	333	0.2	D	0.6	D	2.0	1.7	D	10.6	1 455	171	129	3 674	33.6
Starr	537	0.5	4.5	0.7	1.8	8.1	2.1	D	50.7	9 125	150	5 056	19 526	11.0
Stephens	193	0.3	49.5	7.8	D	4.9	8.1	5.1	18.2	2 110	219	237	4 938	0.9
Sterling	29	0.5	D	D	D	8.8	D	D	21.3	225	197	26	615	-2.8
Stonewall	26	-9.3	D	D	D	7.4	D	1.8	38.0	395	265	30	928	-0.9
Sutton	192	-0.1	D	D	1.2	2.3	2.5	1.0	10.9	695	168	80	2 031	1.7
Swisher	106	19.7	D	4.0	D	3.8	D	D	30.7	1 605	204	161	3 221	-2.8
Tarrant	52 526	0.1	25.9	14.0	9.6	6.3	7.3	9.6	13.0	213 695	118	31 087	714 803	26.3
Taylor	3 432	-0.2	16.2	3.3	5.9	6.6	5.3	15.8	28.5	22 885	174	3 546	55 750	7.1
Terrell	19	-1.7	D	0.0	D	1.0	2.0	D	62.3	230	234	28	700	-29.4
Terry	199	7.5	24.3	4.1	D	9.4	3.3	D	25.0	2 275	180	385	4 828	-5.1
Throckmorton	37	20.5	D	D	D	1.4	D	5.8	21.2	445	271	23	1 079	1.2
Titus	763	0.6	44.2	35.8	2.3	8.5	3.5	D	19.3	4 905	152	762	12 054	12.9

1. Includes mining, construction, and manufacturing.   2. Per 1,000 resident population enumerated in the 2010 census.

Table B. States and Counties — **Housing, Labor Force, and Employment**

STATE County	Housing units, 2006–2010 Occupied units Owner-occupied Total	Percent	Median value[1]	Median owner cost as a percent of income With a mortgage	Without a mortgage	Renter-occupied Median rent[2]	Median rent as a percent of income	Substandard units[3] (percent)	Civilian labor force, 2010 Total	Percent change, 2009–2010	Unemployment Total	Rate[4]	Civilian employment,[5] 2006–2010 Percent Total	Management, business, science and arts	Construction, production, and maintenance occupations
	89	90	91	92	93	94	95	96	97	98	99	100	101	102	103
TEXAS—Cont'd															
Mason	1 553	79.8	131 400	20.2	14.1	533	29.0	6.3	2 405	-0.3	122	5.1	1 647	36.9	18.0
Matagorda	13 786	71.6	83 400	18.1	12.4	609	30.5	6.4	18 352	3.3	2 073	11.3	15 472	27.3	34.4
Maverick	14 552	69.7	77 700	28.9	14.4	524	29.6	14.0	23 306	1.2	3 535	15.2	19 098	21.7	28.0
Medina	15 106	76.8	102 900	20.9	12.0	645	27.3	5.0	20 358	1.5	1 502	7.4	18 412	32.9	27.3
Menard	927	74.9	66 600	22.0	12.0	520	21.2	0.9	1 062	-4.7	74	7.0	1 050	28.5	25.7
Midland	49 122	69.7	121 200	19.9	11.0	768	28.1	3.9	77 066	3.3	4 076	5.3	65 586	31.5	25.9
Milam	9 575	73.0	81 600	22.3	13.0	617	28.1	4.3	11 295	-1.7	1 171	10.4	10 258	27.4	32.3
Mills	1 974	78.5	95 000	22.8	13.1	379	24.1	3.3	2 383	-3.1	144	6.0	2 085	33.7	28.1
Mitchell	2 711	77.8	55 300	22.7	11.0	562	25.2	2.2	3 604	3.8	309	8.6	2 713	26.2	25.4
Montague	7 978	78.1	83 900	20.9	13.2	607	30.8	4.5	10 428	-3.7	753	7.2	8 708	27.5	32.9
Montgomery	150 546	75.6	157 100	22.4	12.0	879	27.2	4.2	223 875	3.0	16 968	7.6	202 290	36.8	23.1
Moore	6 724	66.7	83 100	18.9	11.0	608	22.5	11.1	11 732	1.5	580	4.9	9 711	22.4	41.8
Morris	5 131	78.9	75 500	18.9	11.4	498	33.4	2.8	6 077	-2.5	787	13.0	5 267	28.9	30.4
Motley	435	74.9	60 500	19.7	15.0	371	35.0	1.8	711	4.3	40	5.6	467	39.2	30.4
Nacogdoches	23 082	59.9	88 600	22.1	11.7	641	37.3	4.8	32 122	0.5	2 203	6.9	28 029	31.1	26.5
Navarro	17 313	71.5	79 300	24.0	13.3	670	29.1	6.0	21 849	2.6	1 980	9.1	20 814	26.8	33.3
Newton	5 164	83.2	67 600	19.9	12.9	420	25.4	5.1	5 889	-0.5	767	13.0	5 403	23.6	38.6
Nolan	5 836	68.1	51 600	19.4	12.1	478	26.7	2.8	7 883	-0.3	546	6.9	6 944	28.0	28.5
Nueces	121 056	61.6	103 900	24.0	13.8	792	32.3	5.6	169 000	2.2	12 857	7.6	148 104	30.5	24.3
Ochiltree	3 533	69.5	82 100	16.8	12.2	571	21.6	6.3	5 600	0.7	287	5.1	4 401	26.8	40.1
Oldham	710	71.0	86 900	21.9	13.2	853	29.3	3.7	927	1.8	56	6.0	1 079	37.5	20.5
Orange	31 271	77.1	81 500	19.5	11.0	648	28.1	3.4	42 059	0.1	4 529	10.8	34 012	27.1	35.0
Palo Pinto	10 513	68.3	80 500	22.4	12.4	717	30.8	4.2	14 242	-0.7	1 130	7.9	11 901	23.3	34.9
Panola	8 632	81.0	81 900	20.7	11.0	565	23.9	2.9	13 835	3.4	1 012	7.3	9 742	25.3	42.2
Parker	40 489	80.3	147 100	23.7	13.1	813	27.3	2.9	55 098	1.2	4 256	7.7	51 014	34.1	26.5
Parmer	3 299	72.7	88 500	22.0	11.5	599	28.2	8.0	4 673	0.7	220	4.7	4 610	25.6	44.4
Pecos	4 912	70.0	50 900	17.0	11.4	539	24.2	2.3	9 067	10.2	610	6.7	5 787	20.6	33.5
Polk	16 789	78.9	67 700	24.0	13.6	626	32.5	5.2	18 402	2.5	1 828	9.9	15 369	23.4	32.3
Potter	41 422	59.4	80 600	22.8	11.5	637	30.6	5.0	58 035	0.5	3 783	6.5	55 050	23.7	29.9
Presidio	2 617	67.5	56 200	31.7	10.4	354	23.9	10.5	3 960	8.0	687	17.3	2 936	27.6	19.2
Rains	4 069	83.3	82 000	21.0	14.5	617	21.7	4.1	5 134	0.6	471	9.2	4 955	26.1	35.2
Randall	46 018	70.1	130 400	20.5	10.9	717	28.6	2.2	69 539	1.3	3 450	5.0	61 329	35.6	20.8
Reagan	1 142	70.9	63 100	14.8	10.8	616	14.4	6.2	2 536	20.0	104	4.1	1 630	22.6	46.0
Real	1 335	75.5	75 300	25.6	16.0	538	32.2	3.7	1 559	1.8	91	5.8	1 102	28.8	29.3
Red River	5 108	71.2	59 700	19.4	12.9	548	26.8	3.8	5 968	-1.9	657	11.0	5 201	25.8	36.6
Reeves	3 628	74.3	31 400	15.5	13.0	447	23.9	8.3	4 777	2.5	520	10.9	4 956	21.3	30.3
Refugio	2 786	77.9	67 800	19.3	12.3	592	30.5	4.4	4 219	0.9	290	6.9	2 708	26.3	25.5
Roberts	328	75.9	111 400	18.0	12.0	662	0.0	0.6	571	1.8	27	4.7	424	42.7	16.7
Robertson	6 232	66.9	77 300	23.9	11.9	528	29.6	6.0	7 424	0.1	642	8.6	6 873	27.4	28.7
Rockwall	24 790	84.3	189 000	25.2	13.7	1 134	28.5	2.5	40 033	4.0	3 026	7.6	35 856	42.8	16.4
Runnels	3 953	72.0	60 100	19.8	13.5	478	22.3	1.8	4 605	-0.3	415	9.0	4 386	26.6	30.6
Rusk	18 102	78.6	86 700	18.6	10.8	614	23.6	3.4	24 765	1.0	1 871	7.6	21 396	25.2	34.9
Sabine	4 430	83.0	68 000	23.8	11.9	503	23.4	4.5	3 591	0.3	586	16.3	3 245	25.9	36.2
San Augustine	3 691	79.1	65 000	19.9	14.5	402	31.5	3.0	3 728	3.6	415	11.1	2 940	25.3	36.9
San Jacinto	9 184	82.5	75 600	20.7	11.7	651	22.7	3.9	10 358	-0.4	1 076	10.4	9 781	24.8	34.9
San Patricio	22 592	66.2	88 300	21.7	13.1	726	29.3	5.8	31 569	2.7	3 253	10.3	27 527	28.4	27.8
San Saba	2 122	77.7	71 200	22.1	12.7	469	24.5	2.4	2 303	-5.5	190	8.3	2 500	26.2	38.7
Schleicher	989	80.7	67 900	14.7	10.0	581	22.7	3.8	1 478	-3.9	118	8.0	1 536	38.1	32.7
Scurry	6 181	71.0	71 100	17.9	12.2	609	28.5	5.6	7 990	2.9	512	6.4	6 500	29.9	35.4
Shackelford	1 195	77.8	69 000	19.9	11.3	424	18.6	2.2	2 229	5.0	102	4.6	1 535	35.2	30.0
Shelby	9 705	76.2	64 400	19.2	11.8	482	29.5	7.3	13 043	4.7	1 026	7.9	10 433	26.8	40.0
Sherman	971	78.7	80 800	20.5	12.0	618	22.6	4.5	1 452	0.5	69	4.8	1 406	34.2	37.3
Smith	76 427	69.4	118 000	21.8	12.8	752	32.3	4.2	101 403	0.8	7 974	7.9	93 658	32.1	23.6
Somervell	2 923	77.0	144 300	20.3	13.2	580	26.5	4.5	4 246	-1.7	336	7.9	3 717	41.4	22.4
Starr	15 569	79.4	57 000	23.1	14.4	454	34.3	12.9	25 306	3.3	4 526	17.9	20 412	24.3	25.7
Stephens	3 624	74.2	57 600	24.3	12.8	602	31.5	2.7	4 630	-1.5	330	7.1	4 042	22.5	34.1
Sterling	446	78.0	68 700	21.4	11.7	615	32.9	6.3	779	-11.5	36	4.6	521	34.9	37.8
Stonewall	592	80.6	55 300	18.0	11.0	457	26.0	5.1	823	-4.2	40	4.9	745	45.1	24.7
Sutton	1 375	71.4	77 700	18.2	10.3	546	12.9	6.7	3 020	-17.1	196	6.5	2 036	29.6	36.6
Swisher	2 689	69.3	59 500	19.3	13.2	542	28.2	4.9	3 590	-1.4	222	6.2	2 933	30.4	30.8
Tarrant	632 518	63.4	134 900	23.5	13.4	833	29.3	4.1	908 651	1.2	75 124	8.3	850 459	34.8	23.0
Taylor	49 757	61.9	89 900	21.2	12.6	723	30.5	3.3	68 397	0.9	4 345	6.4	59 688	31.9	21.0
Terrell	372	69.9	42 600	21.7	12.1	534	14.7	1.1	388	0.3	33	8.5	386	36.5	23.6
Terry	4 043	72.6	63 000	18.9	10.9	499	30.5	5.5	5 843	-3.7	433	7.4	4 971	30.6	30.1
Throckmorton	795	81.0	46 700	21.8	15.3	342	26.5	2.6	1 055	2.5	51	4.8	753	20.1	36.5
Titus	10 693	70.2	86 800	22.0	12.1	585	27.1	10.0	14 578	1.6	1 134	7.8	12 702	22.4	39.9

1. Specified owner-occupied units. 2. Specified renter-occupied units. A value of 10.0 represents 10 percent or less. 3. Overcrowded or lacking complete plumbing facilities. 4. Percent of civilian labor force. 5. Persons 16 years old and over.

Table B. States and Counties — Nonfarm Employment and Agriculture

STATE County	Private nonfarm establishments, employment and payroll, 2009									Agriculture, 2007			
	Number of establish- ments	Employment						Annual payroll		Farms			
		Total	Health care and social assistance	Manufac- turing	Retail trade	Finance and insurance	Professional, scientific, and technical services	Total (mil dol)	Average per employee (dollars)	Number	Percent with: Fewer than 50 acres	500 acres or more	Farm operators whose principal occu- pation is farming (percent)
	104	105	106	107	108	109	110	111	112	113	114	115	116
TEXAS—Cont'd													
Mason	141	769	192	D	144	45	D	16	20 713	647	14.4	40.6	48.5
Matagorda	729	7 882	1 176	576	1 428	231	182	346	43 950	903	29.1	25.2	50.1
Maverick	770	10 939	3 809	338	2 519	402	187	231	21 153	312	49.0	19.2	42.0
Medina	637	5 220	814	D	1 216	253	302	129	24 726	2 139	35.9	15.2	39.5
Menard	53	283	D	D	85	D	D	4	15 417	356	14.0	41.3	51.4
Midland	4 496	61 008	6 448	2 154	7 822	1 957	3 364	2 711	44 441	601	51.1	16.5	28.6
Milam	416	4 221	734	406	712	D	121	123	29 222	2 045	32.2	11.9	42.5
Mills	126	821	200	59	204	52	D	19	23 048	921	19.0	23.9	41.3
Mitchell	126	1 143	D	26	265	47	D	29	25 591	519	14.5	26.0	29.5
Montague	457	4 111	749	278	848	184	157	113	27 547	1 545	24.7	15.0	38.1
Montgomery	8 743	121 158	13 872	10 083	20 473	4 470	8 058	5 517	45 537	1 886	69.1	3.2	31.8
Moore	447	8 069	602	4 130	968	156	87	263	32 581	283	8.8	67.1	60.1
Morris	226	4 442	236	D	319	141	95	125	28 195	457	41.1	7.9	36.8
Motley	36	D	D	D	D	D	D	D	D	229	1.7	59.8	42.8
Nacogdoches	1 263	18 883	3 501	3 582	2 961	536	394	483	25 588	1 277	34.5	8.0	43.6
Navarro	925	12 743	1 867	2 957	2 144	409	342	339	26 594	2 078	37.4	12.0	42.2
Newton	138	1 237	327	82	157	D	D	29	23 369	403	61.8	1.2	38.7
Nolan	345	4 509	642	935	819	147	90	130	28 941	580	15.5	32.1	30.3
Nueces	7 798	124 249	24 561	8 111	16 648	3 927	5 410	4 259	34 282	712	42.7	22.9	42.1
Ochiltree	341	3 573	D	41	447	140	185	134	37 388	382	5.2	53.7	61.3
Oldham	34	D	D	D	44	D	0	D	D	150	4.7	68.7	58.0
Orange	1 374	19 849	1 517	5 845	3 319	541	426	803	40 452	675	77.2	3.3	33.5
Palo Pinto	612	6 351	842	1 176	1 222	199	172	184	28 942	1 194	39.4	16.0	34.2
Panola	492	7 238	696	909	873	170	201	265	36 585	1 042	35.4	10.7	41.7
Parker	2 176	23 367	2 788	2 471	4 846	673	789	702	30 040	3 677	66.9	3.8	34.0
Parmer	205	D	D	D	163	93	40	D	D	555	10.8	53.3	61.8
Pecos	317	4 078	442	D	744	141	D	145	35 602	287	11.5	63.8	42.5
Polk	698	8 640	1 275	D	1 841	299	315	240	27 751	812	48.4	6.8	38.9
Potter	3 573	59 573	12 747	D	8 952	3 744	1 798	1 988	33 364	279	40.5	26.5	29.4
Presidio	129	714	D	D	241	61	D	15	20 587	148	14.2	60.8	37.8
Rains	143	1 118	D	63	414	D	140	26	21 928	657	48.6	6.4	37.1
Randall	2 295	26 879	2 955	1 481	4 954	1 462	679	751	29 003	887	36.1	27.3	34.0
Reagan	106	912	D	0	88	D	D	35	37 986	137	5.8	71.5	51.1
Real	84	539	194	D	60	D	D	12	21 725	301	19.9	37.5	40.5
Red River	187	1 682	454	455	244	93	D	44	26 297	1 206	23.7	17.1	44.9
Reeves	196	1 926	D	D	536	D	45	52	26 775	221	19.5	43.9	32.6
Refugio	137	1 394	230	D	215	120	D	50	36 040	295	26.1	30.5	55.3
Roberts	12	93	0	D	D	0	D	3	28 763	108	4.6	69.4	46.3
Robertson	253	2 469	380	144	410	106	33	90	36 328	1 552	30.3	12.7	45.6
Rockwall	1 650	19 020	3 032	1 231	3 567	637	1 021	564	29 663	347	65.1	4.6	32.0
Runnels	251	2 379	330	695	491	121	D	63	26 660	953	12.3	27.7	42.4
Rusk	811	10 614	1 516	1 312	1 332	D	707	369	34 796	1 521	32.8	8.0	35.8
Sabine	151	1 359	215	301	270	61	D	41	30 441	223	39.9	4.9	29.1
San Augustine	130	1 317	511	D	237	54	D	33	25 267	346	32.4	10.4	43.6
San Jacinto	182	1 047	104	35	217	D	71	30	28 758	688	52.5	3.5	33.1
San Patricio	1 043	13 371	1 602	D	2 427	384	438	442	33 040	652	45.7	22.9	44.3
San Saba	149	826	D	31	226	35	28	18	22 231	725	15.7	33.9	40.3
Schleicher	58	499	D	D	72	22	13	17	34 160	332	10.5	59.9	55.1
Scurry	422	5 611	D	219	705	166	135	216	38 569	681	18.9	31.1	36.0
Shackelford	129	947	D	126	113	D	D	30	31 634	254	12.2	48.0	53.5
Shelby	483	6 426	600	2 135	1 127	303	123	176	27 408	1 123	29.3	7.2	47.8
Sherman	56	263	D	D	D	D	D	8	28 620	362	6.4	61.3	54.7
Smith	5 363	85 043	19 379	8 169	11 880	3 082	3 944	3 016	35 464	2 514	53.1	4.5	35.0
Somervell	199	2 943	482	D	256	44	48	138	46 802	366	43.7	9.3	37.2
Starr	500	8 302	4 376	D	1 799	294	81	160	19 267	1 104	13.2	26.0	44.5
Stephens	250	2 388	364	371	351	102	D	74	31 074	487	9.7	36.1	34.3
Sterling	28	238	D	D	D	D	D	18	77 651	74	10.8	64.9	59.5
Stonewall	51	399	D	0	45	D	D	10	25 637	376	4.8	40.7	39.4
Sutton	151	1 278	D	D	136	74	D	44	34 703	234	8.5	72.2	47.9
Swisher	147	1 072	214	123	156	52	D	26	24 058	527	8.3	46.3	52.6
Tarrant	36 935	677 390	79 031	75 860	89 377	38 712	37 083	27 626	40 783	1 248	73.2	4.8	34.9
Taylor	3 357	52 178	10 953	2 034	8 150	2 967	1 820	1 525	29 232	1 292	30.0	19.3	29.7
Terrell	17	86	D	0	D	D	D	2	27 535	107	4.7	70.1	44.9
Terry	257	2 246	375	D	485	99	D	66	29 296	624	13.8	44.7	54.2
Throckmorton	50	289	96	D	21	D	D	7	24 886	264	4.5	43.9	48.9
Titus	660	13 796	2 077	5 541	1 926	426	188	418	30 305	810	37.0	6.5	35.1

Table B. States and Counties — **Agriculture**

STATE County	Land in farms Acreage (1,000)	Percent change, 2002–2007	Acres Average size of farm	Total irrigated (1,000)	Total cropland (1,000)	Value of land and buildings (dollars) Average per farm	Average per acre	Value of machinery and equipment, average per farm (dollars)	Value of products sold Total (mil dol)	Average per farm (dollars)	Percent from: Crops	Live-stock and poultry products	Percent of farms with sales of: $10,000 or more	$100,000 or more	Government payments Total ($1,000)	Percent of farms
	117	118	119	120	121	122	123	124	125	126	127	128	129	130	131	132
TEXAS—Cont'd																
Mason	536	-3.6	829	4.2	57.1	1 518 909	1 832	50 104	48.0	74 256	3.8	96.2	44.8	7.0	720	22.7
Matagorda	578	-6.6	640	35.8	234.7	882 948	1 380	105 674	106.8	118 224	57.0	43.0	46.7	17.4	5 890	30.6
Maverick	474	-0.4	1 518	13.0	30.8	1 371 322	903	45 793	26.1	83 629	7.4	92.6	23.7	5.1	392	5.8
Medina	748	-7.1	350	41.2	173.5	689 884	1 972	52 028	80.9	37 798	53.5	46.5	22.3	4.0	2 526	15.3
Menard	491	-10.6	1 380	2.1	22.7	1 502 957	1 089	50 239	7.9	22 275	7.7	92.3	36.8	6.2	592	28.1
Midland	457	26.2	760	8.3	90.0	660 020	869	59 919	15.4	25 621	77.7	22.3	18.5	5.5	2 750	29.8
Milam	539	-6.6	263	2.8	205.1	504 079	1 914	61 152	105.3	51 509	27.5	72.5	35.0	6.9	2 675	15.6
Mills	474	11.0	515	4.9	74.6	867 829	1 685	53 750	37.6	40 873	14.1	85.9	37.5	4.8	349	16.7
Mitchell	575	17.8	1 108	4.1	163.8	910 923	822	77 643	27.3	52 571	63.8	36.2	23.5	10.0	5 546	73.6
Montague	508	0.8	329	0.6	120.1	676 962	2 060	51 734	36.6	23 716	19.5	80.5	31.5	4.1	599	13.2
Montgomery	170	-14.1	90	2.3	33.8	341 332	3 789	45 703	42.6	22 607	58.9	41.1	15.5	1.5	47	1.0
Moore	553	0.5	1 955	105.1	297.7	1 677 878	858	230 886	463.2	1 636 750	17.0	83.0	63.6	47.3	5 402	66.1
Morris	86	-14.0	187	0.1	19.8	424 709	2 266	52 656	38.6	84 570	3.1	96.9	32.2	8.5	148	8.1
Motley	575	18.1	2 510	3.3	105.3	1 493 116	595	73 206	16.4	71 724	44.1	55.9	48.9	17.9	3 172	75.1
Nacogdoches	265	-3.3	208	0.5	59.4	502 706	2 421	65 918	317.3	248 463	1.7	98.3	40.3	15.3	135	2.7
Navarro	587	9.3	282	1.1	164.2	455 317	1 612	58 640	52.4	25 220	41.6	58.4	27.9	3.8	2 578	18.7
Newton	59	-14.5	147	0.1	8.1	275 975	1 878	55 735	2.1	5 200	29.5	70.5	12.7	0.7	150	6.2
Nolan	540	12.3	931	5.2	132.6	956 626	1 027	71 333	37.1	64 008	56.0	44.0	23.6	8.1	5 288	54.7
Nueces	509	-2.9	715	4.3	369.4	922 672	1 290	118 802	110.9	155 766	97.4	2.6	35.3	18.7	9 869	37.5
Ochiltree	579	3.6	1 517	66.1	355.4	1 232 313	812	209 240	395.1	1 034 196	65.7	39.3	65.7	39.3	5 450	75.7
Oldham	880	-6.0	5 870	2.3	105.3	1 915 816	326	119 270	119.4	795 699	7.1	92.9	62.7	42.0	2 206	85.3
Orange	64	-12.3	94	0.6	15.2	239 279	2 534	39 998	D	D	D	0.0	12.3	1.2	460	4.1
Palo Pinto	551	13.6	462	0.6	84.9	895 335	1 938	47 812	23.5	19 669	16.0	84.0	22.9	3.8	209	6.4
Panola	218	-2.2	209	0.4	50.7	415 045	1 986	58 408	63.4	60 886	4.3	95.7	29.8	6.0	202	4.1
Parker	442	-9.2	120	1.5	103.8	438 074	3 648	44 533	60.0	16 327	24.7	75.3	17.8	2.0	232	3.1
Parmer	561	-2.6	1 010	175.0	437.2	1 029 842	1 019	237 005	937.7	1 689 485	13.3	86.7	65.8	49.7	12 236	76.9
Pecos	2 908	-0.3	10 132	17.3	101.4	2 747 518	271	114 819	27.5	95 974	42.7	57.3	40.1	16.0	1 543	25.4
Polk	132	1.5	162	1.4	23.7	372 410	2 297	53 217	9.9	12 236	39.5	60.5	22.0	1.7	162	2.7
Potter	573	9.8	2 054	7.0	74.4	1 359 920	662	56 973	29.9	107 002	17.5	82.5	31.9	12.5	1 191	27.6
Presidio	1 560	3.7	10 539	2.0	28.1	4 379 252	416	75 093	D	D	D	D	39.2	14.9	389	13.5
Rains	98	4.3	149	0.6	32.7	359 804	2 422	41 527	13.9	21 180	33.5	66.5	27.7	4.3	121	5.6
Randall	575	12.3	648	19.8	270.1	742 860	1 146	71 915	393.4	443 484	6.1	93.9	31.9	12.6	6 386	45.7
Reagan	684	27.1	4 991	8.5	57.9	2 507 427	502	188 481	16.5	120 227	75.2	24.8	54.7	28.5	1 940	54.0
Real	372	-7.0	1 237	0.5	26.1	1 336 437	1 080	43 939	2.8	9 149	14.0	86.0	13.3	2.3	110	5.6
Red River	450	6.4	373	2.8	104.5	495 457	1 329	53 657	35.9	29 743	20.6	79.4	34.7	5.7	1 816	18.5
Reeves	1 040	3.0	4 707	8.0	136.7	1 482 120	315	58 257	17.2	77 733	24.9	75.1	28.5	10.4	2 835	54.3
Refugio	491	-3.0	1 663	D	94.3	1 217 943	732	81 772	29.4	99 582	68.2	31.8	39.3	16.6	2 739	28.1
Roberts	485	-2.0	4 493	8.5	61.4	3 024 216	673	123 863	16.7	154 816	40.3	59.7	55.6	31.5	1 271	57.4
Robertson	455	-11.7	291	21.5	117.4	587 284	2 015	65 850	116.0	74 295	16.2	83.8	36.6	6.2	2 137	10.2
Rockwall	37	-19.6	108	0.1	14.5	486 897	4 513	49 077	3.9	11 129	47.6	52.4	15.9	1.2	97	5.2
Runnels	656	12.1	689	3.5	264.8	775 878	1 127	82 243	53.8	56 495	57.2	42.8	39.9	12.1	5 788	65.4
Rusk	301	10.7	198	0.8	67.3	405 054	2 047	56 959	56.1	36 897	31.1	68.9	26.8	3.1	94	1.8
Sabine	32	3.2	142	0.0	7.8	364 379	2 561	50 738	8.5	37 918	3.5	96.5	21.1	2.2	97	3.6
San Augustine	73	23.7	210	0.1	12.8	417 017	1 986	63 482	55.6	160 807	2.5	97.5	37.3	10.1	191	6.4
San Jacinto	95	2.2	139	0.9	21.0	364 629	2 627	47 812	6.9	10 002	33.9	66.1	17.9	1.2	73	2.3
San Patricio	370	7.2	567	14.2	258.7	702 535	1 239	126 104	109.2	167 486	82.1	17.9	35.3	20.6	8 744	35.4
San Saba	718	1.3	990	3.8	80.2	1 609 135	1 625	68 399	28.6	39 422	23.6	76.4	45.2	9.5	523	16.8
Schleicher	801	3.0	2 411	0.6	49.9	2 180 436	904	68 855	13.6	40 982	24.0	76.0	46.7	10.5	1 719	40.7
Scurry	520	-8.0	763	2.9	214.3	684 653	897	75 845	43.4	63 780	65.0	35.0	28.3	11.0	6 440	67.1
Shackelford	552	-0.9	2 175	D	71.5	1 823 967	839	66 055	16.1	63 327	12.9	87.1	45.3	15.4	1 049	44.1
Shelby	198	3.1	176	0.6	45.5	494 931	2 810	77 590	403.1	358 963	1.0	99.0	47.6	23.1	163	2.7
Sherman	584	7.0	1 614	157.6	392.7	1 313 201	814	231 515	448.9	1 239 944	23.2	76.8	50.0	39.0	8 146	82.9
Smith	302	5.2	120	2.7	91.8	377 217	3 136	53 392	68.0	27 049	62.5	37.5	23.3	2.8	68	1.7
Somervell	83	-1.2	226	0.5	20.0	715 789	3 171	46 090	D	D	D	D	19.9	1.4	57	7.1
Starr	653	14.6	591	6.5	173.2	731 696	1 237	45 665	64.4	58 290	19.5	80.5	20.2	4.1	2 409	19.5
Stephens	429	0.2	881	0.2	67.1	1 086 812	1 233	49 688	12.4	25 468	8.3	91.7	33.7	3.1	374	25.3
Sterling	578	-8.7	7 815	0.3	9.5	2 869 436	367	91 979	D	D	D	D	51.4	23.0	549	37.8
Stonewall	486	-7.3	1 292	2.4	101.7	864 088	669	47 892	13.7	36 546	29.4	70.6	36.2	9.6	2 550	77.7
Sutton	895	1.7	3 823	0.9	21.6	3 044 106	796	75 347	9.6	41 082	3.5	96.5	47.4	15.0	641	26.1
Swisher	563	-0.5	1 068	83.8	380.1	775 406	726	142 939	453.7	860 821	14.6	85.4	46.7	28.8	10 979	80.6
Tarrant	154	-11.0	124	1.4	46.1	448 616	3 627	43 657	61.4	49 173	87.4	12.6	16.9	3.5	145	4.2
Taylor	579	8.4	449	5.1	204.3	554 558	1 236	52 849	50.6	39 178	31.0	69.0	20.4	4.4	4 438	44.0
Terrell	1 302	-7.9	12 170	D	15.1	2 734 256	225	62 635	4.0	37 669	D	D	30.8	7.5	313	16.8
Terry	497	11.7	796	142.0	419.3	704 407	885	198 671	124.8	199 992	90.1	9.9	49.4	33.7	17 287	83.2
Throckmorton	574	2.3	2 174	1.4	94.5	1 894 914	872	71 772	21.9	82 946	21.7	78.2	50.4	11.7	1 383	48.9
Titus	166	-6.7	205	0.5	42.1	421 723	2 053	50 812	79.5	98 170	4.0	96.0	34.1	5.8	140	8.8

Table B. States and Counties — Water Use, Wholesale Trade, Retail Trade, and Real Estate

STATE County	Water use, 2005		Wholesale trade,[1] 2007				Retail trade,[2] 2007				Real estate and rental and leasing,[2] 2007			
	Total water withdrawn (mil gal/day)	Gallons withdrawn per person	Number of establishments	Number of employees	Sales (mil dol)	Annual payroll (mil dol)	Number of establishments	Number of employees	Sales (mil dol)	Annual payroll (mil dol)	Number of establishments	Number of employees	Receipts (mil dol)	Annual payroll (mil dol)
	133	134	135	136	137	138	139	140	141	142	143	144	145	146
TEXAS—Cont'd														
Mason	10.2	2 621	9	65	41.3	1.6	27	137	29.0	2.1	5	6	2.7	0.2
Matagorda	223.0	5 892	31	D	D	D	157	1 428	313.9	26.8	36	286	30.2	10.8
Maverick	52.0	1 017	32	D	D	D	184	2 327	504.8	41.7	34	84	15.1	1.9
Medina	55.1	1 280	19	170	189.9	5.1	110	1 179	360.1	25.6	28	66	6.6	1.0
Menard	1.9	845	4	40	6.7	0.6	11	56	16.3	0.8	1	D	D	D
Midland	31.1	256	259	3 334	2 411.7	162.2	551	7 744	2 276.7	183.9	227	1 418	270.7	56.8
Milam	55.6	2 192	25	171	87.3	6.6	72	705	181.4	14.3	16	66	9.3	2.1
Mills	2.7	517	5	D	D	D	29	235	70.4	4.7	2	D	D	D
Mitchell	11.9	1 266	4	14	3.4	0.4	31	266	55.8	4.6	2	D	D	D
Montague	8.3	421	26	91	38.6	3.5	73	782	213.7	15.9	14	32	2.9	0.4
Montgomery	67.9	180	426	4 234	6 399.3	198.6	1 263	19 489	5 260.1	433.1	390	2 045	340.9	63.9
Moore	276.2	13 573	22	D	D	D	72	889	217.9	17.5	13	49	5.9	0.9
Morris	50.9	3 936	11	332	138.9	13.6	41	339	70.3	5.8	7	22	2.9	0.5
Motley	9.7	7 452	3	D	D	D	6	28	5.2	0.5	NA	NA	NA	NA
Nacogdoches	24.6	407	44	D	D	D	244	2 819	691.2	61.4	44	142	19.4	3.2
Navarro	7.9	161	26	415	285.7	13.8	184	2 168	471.8	41.1	45	139	19.8	3.3
Newton	3.9	274	6	46	10.0	1.1	23	174	50.9	2.5	2	D	D	D
Nolan	7.0	468	17	D	D	D	64	804	179.7	13.7	10	34	4.7	0.6
Nueces	349.5	1 093	399	4 448	2 978.5	207.0	1 174	16 877	4 314.5	365.5	432	2 613	415.5	79.1
Ochiltree	69.8	7 440	27	295	139.2	14.9	49	442	97.4	7.5	14	105	28.6	5.2
Oldham	6.2	2 946	1	D	D	D	9	50	16.8	0.9	NA	NA	NA	NA
Orange	1 181.8	13 906	39	235	114.4	12.1	270	3 207	852.0	62.9	58	179	36.3	4.4
Palo Pinto	118.1	4 298	18	D	D	D	124	1 135	272.7	23.0	29	102	14.0	2.4
Panola	12.6	547	22	152	80.0	4.0	89	825	222.0	15.3	27	122	21.3	3.0
Parker	10.9	106	95	692	524.2	25.3	309	4 566	1 517.8	113.9	95	312	55.9	8.3
Parmer	424.7	43 542	30	181	224.9	5.3	29	167	39.5	3.0	6	D	D	D
Pecos	60.1	3 789	9	108	117.0	4.2	68	702	154.0	11.8	9	24	3.8	0.6
Polk	18.9	405	22	101	51.1	3.7	120	1 721	445.4	37.0	32	100	9.2	2.3
Potter	14.6	122	179	2 786	2 064.1	117.3	579	8 658	2 490.0	183.4	159	D	D	D
Presidio	8.0	1 040	3	9	3.2	0.2	34	229	42.5	3.1	3	D	D	D
Rains	3.2	287	4	D	D	D	33	289	93.9	6.5	5	88	1.7	0.6
Randall	53.7	488	76	D	D	D	346	5 080	1 465.5	122.4	133	D	D	D
Reagan	16.6	5 549	3	25	4.4	1.0	18	98	23.7	1.8	1	D	D	D
Real	0.8	247	4	D	D	D	15	38	9.4	0.7	4	10	1.0	0.1
Red River	8.6	636	7	32	15.1	0.9	43	297	61.2	5.3	8	10	2.3	0.2
Reeves	83.8	7 201	8	D	D	D	34	446	113.2	7.8	6	17	1.4	0.3
Refugio	11.6	1 515	5	32	18.0	1.3	24	231	62.0	3.8	9	61	5.6	1.4
Roberts	13.6	16 610	NA	NA	NA	NA	2	D	D	D	NA	NA	NA	NA
Robertson	35.0	2 163	2	D	D	D	53	420	115.2	7.8	10	32	9.7	1.6
Rockwall	1.9	29	63	D	D	D	222	3 272	946.3	73.8	61	218	38.9	6.6
Runnels	5.3	483	8	41	24.6	1.2	51	480	128.4	11.5	3	D	D	D
Rusk	2 248.1	46 863	21	205	99.8	7.8	141	1 423	354.3	28.4	24	81	10.1	1.8
Sabine	3.5	334	NA	NA	NA	NA	35	237	51.9	4.0	4	D	D	D
San Augustine	3.2	354	5	36	6.4	0.9	28	247	70.1	4.1	3	D	D	D
San Jacinto	5.4	216	3	D	D	D	31	230	54.7	4.4	8	29	5.1	0.5
San Patricio	35.8	517	32	232	135.2	8.8	180	2 265	621.6	51.6	72	247	31.5	4.8
San Saba	11.5	1 896	12	96	18.1	2.9	38	232	60.5	4.3	4	D	D	D
Schleicher	1.9	682	6	30	13.1	0.9	10	71	10.4	1.0	NA	NA	NA	NA
Scurry	34.4	2 118	28	D	D	D	59	674	199.6	13.7	21	139	19.4	4.2
Shackelford	2.0	628	5	16	4.1	0.3	18	103	14.8	1.5	3	14	0.5	0.2
Shelby	12.2	462	12	81	97.6	4.8	95	1 106	246.5	21.2	13	38	4.0	0.6
Sherman	352.1	117 288	8	D	D	D	10	49	10.1	0.8	NA	NA	NA	NA
Smith	45.5	239	242	2 216	922.1	97.5	855	12 347	3 110.1	287.8	229	1 447	204.5	41.3
Somervell	63.2	8 333	7	32	14.8	1.3	37	259	55.2	4.7	8	D	D	D
Starr	17.2	282	14	D	D	D	134	1 878	445.3	31.2	10	32	3.2	0.7
Stephens	30.2	3 154	9	28	21.4	0.9	36	369	78.8	7.9	6	26	3.5	0.5
Sterling	1.8	1 389	2	D	D	D	5	D	D	D	NA	NA	NA	NA
Stonewall	3.3	2 434	2	D	D	D	10	42	8.6	0.6	2	D	D	D
Sutton	2.1	491	6	53	29.3	3.3	25	147	41.9	2.6	6	47	7.1	1.5
Swisher	154.1	19 686	14	130	42.4	3.1	22	164	35.2	2.6	6	D	D	D
Tarrant	522.3	322	1 932	32 231	25 801.5	1 571.5	5 539	89 503	24 931.4	2 192.6	1 827	11 203	2 770.6	432.7
Taylor	25.0	200	135	1 540	1 079.7	58.0	579	8 333	2 063.3	181.8	160	637	133.6	19.4
Terrell	1.1	1 054	1	D	D	D	4	12	3.9	0.3	NA	NA	NA	NA
Terry	108.5	8 736	18	187	87.3	7.7	42	478	133.7	9.3	12	73	7.6	3.1
Throckmorton	2.2	1 384	4	11	3.4	0.4	6	22	6.8	0.4	NA	NA	NA	NA
Titus	1 427.7	48 488	29	D	D	D	148	1 782	425.1	39.1	29	84	11.6	1.8

1. Merchant wholesalers, except manufacturers' sales branches and offices.   2. Employer establishments.

Table B. States and Counties — Professional Services, Manufacturing, and Accommodation and Food Services

STATE County	Professional, scientific, and technical services,[1] 2007				Manufacturing, 2007				Accommodation and food services, 2007			
	Number of establish-ments	Number of employees	Receipts (mil dol)	Annual payroll (mil dol)	Number of establish-ments	Number of employees	Receipts (mil dol)	Annual payroll (mil dol)	Number of establish-ments	Number of employees	Sales (mil dol)	Annual payroll (mil dol)
	147	148	149	150	151	152	153	154	155	156	157	158
TEXAS—Cont'd												
Mason	12	43	3.2	0.9	NA	NA	NA	NA	11	147	3.7	1.4
Matagorda	51	177	15.6	4.8	27	604	D	43.6	77	1 023	38.8	10.0
Maverick	39	D	D	D	NA	NA	NA	NA	64	1 126	48.5	11.3
Medina	58	320	20.0	7.3	30	554	75.3	12.2	73	771	29.8	8.4
Menard	3	4	0.6	0.1	NA	NA	NA	NA	5	D	D	D
Midland	436	D	D	D	140	2 366	533.8	95.2	254	5 324	259.2	69.3
Milam	32	200	14.8	6.8	15	1 521	D	D	38	481	17.7	4.4
Mills	8	20	2.1	0.4	NA	NA	NA	NA	10	64	2.1	0.6
Mitchell	7	25	4.3	0.7	NA	NA	NA	NA	13	140	3.7	0.9
Montague	44	131	12.5	4.0	NA	NA	NA	NA	24	323	10.9	3.0
Montgomery	1 101	D	D	D	373	11 265	3 667.0	522.7	621	14 471	728.6	196.7
Moore	24	90	10.1	3.3	17	D	D	D	43	548	23.0	5.1
Morris	11	95	9.3	3.9	18	2 675	1 140.4	125.1	21	229	8.8	2.2
Motley	NA	NA	NA	NA	NA	NA	NA	NA	3	9	0.3	0.0
Nacogdoches	92	D	D	D	64	4 034	1 418.9	126.1	108	2 253	87.8	23.2
Navarro	60	370	19.1	7.0	57	3 149	758.5	103.4	64	932	42.7	11.2
Newton	4	7	1.4	0.4	NA	NA	NA	NA	6	40	1.9	0.4
Nolan	27	97	10.6	3.0	13	866	224.9	35.0	39	537	16.8	4.3
Nueces	785	D	D	D	215	8 284	D	508.2	811	15 167	662.0	186.1
Ochiltree	21	169	18.6	9.2	NA	NA	NA	NA	19	217	9.2	2.1
Oldham	2	D	D	D	NA	NA	NA	NA	11	39	2.9	0.8
Orange	89	D	D	D	85	5 308	D	339.7	128	2 060	85.3	21.6
Palo Pinto	44	178	16.7	4.6	36	1 283	307.2	44.0	70	891	44.9	11.5
Panola	39	211	21.2	5.9	19	947	264.0	29.0	31	461	18.3	4.8
Parker	173	D	D	D	135	2 814	550.4	104.1	156	2 502	110.4	29.7
Parmer	14	37	3.1	0.7	4	D	D	D	9	56	1.8	0.4
Pecos	17	123	3.7	4.6	NA	NA	NA	NA	34	529	24.3	5.3
Polk	56	268	30.2	8.2	23	D	98.5	17.2	54	833	33.4	8.1
Potter	291	D	D	D	134	D	D	D	338	6 829	326.0	85.8
Presidio	4	10	0.7	0.2	NA	NA	NA	NA	27	153	5.0	1.3
Rains	8	180	4.5	2.3	NA	NA	NA	NA	15	163	6.2	1.7
Randall	187	D	D	D	73	D	D	D	171	3 442	131.9	35.3
Reagan	6	7	0.6	0.1	NA	NA	NA	NA	8	58	2.2	0.4
Real	7	21	2.0	0.7	NA	NA	NA	NA	13	41	3.7	0.7
Red River	7	20	2.2	0.7	16	634	101.8	18.3	14	D	D	D
Reeves	15	D	D	D	NA	NA	NA	NA	26	297	12.4	3.4
Refugio	7	11	1.2	0.3	NA	NA	NA	NA	16	D	D	D
Roberts	2	D	D	D	NA	NA	NA	NA	2	D	D	D
Robertson	11	D	D	D	NA	NA	NA	NA	23	303	15.2	3.4
Rockwall	185	D	D	D	68	D	301.3	D	124	2 500	105.9	30.4
Runnels	12	72	10.6	3.4	17	959	207.0	35.9	21	168	5.6	1.4
Rusk	58	D	D	D	35	1 484	D	46.9	55	666	29.7	7.8
Sabine	8	20	1.7	0.4	NA	NA	NA	NA	12	89	3.3	0.8
San Augustine	10	23	1.6	0.5	NA	NA	NA	NA	6	41	1.4	0.3
San Jacinto	17	D	D	D	NA	NA	NA	NA	9	115	4.0	1.4
San Patricio	83	D	D	D	33	1 586	D	D	135	2 042	77.6	19.2
San Saba	15	33	2.4	0.6	NA	NA	NA	NA	17	94	4.1	0.9
Schleicher	3	8	0.8	0.1	NA	NA	NA	NA	3	21	0.3	0.1
Scurry	25	137	13.6	4.9	NA	NA	NA	NA	47	517	20.6	5.9
Shackelford	6	10	1.5	0.3	NA	NA	NA	NA	7	61	1.9	0.6
Shelby	29	102	15.8	2.9	25	2 242	552.0	69.2	24	304	14.9	3.4
Sherman	2	D	D	D	NA	NA	NA	NA	3	D	D	D
Smith	548	D	D	D	224	10 737	5 423.5	474.5	339	7 563	337.3	93.6
Somervell	15	26	4.2	1.2	NA	NA	NA	NA	27	437	23.1	7.1
Starr	20	75	5.1	1.6	NA	NA	NA	NA	44	578	26.2	6.0
Stephens	22	101	20.7	3.0	NA	NA	NA	NA	20	193	6.2	1.8
Sterling	2	D	D	D	NA	NA	NA	NA	3	D	D	D
Stonewall	2	D	D	D	NA	NA	NA	NA	2	D	D	D
Sutton	10	24	2.1	0.6	NA	NA	NA	NA	18	229	9.7	2.5
Swisher	7	24	1.3	0.6	NA	NA	NA	NA	13	142	4.0	1.1
Tarrant	4 064	D	D	D	1 789	100 996	43 337.5	5 192.3	3 141	73 070	3 763.5	1 035.3
Taylor	276	D	D	D	99	2 341	D	D	286	6 524	246.2	69.0
Terrell	2	D	D	D	NA	NA	NA	NA	2	D	D	D
Terry	14	60	4.1	1.1	NA	NA	NA	NA	25	237	9.9	2.6
Throckmorton	2	D	D	D	NA	NA	NA	NA	4	D	D	D
Titus	33	135	11.8	3.8	41	5 696	1 291.5	164.4	56	1 030	40.7	11.6

1. Establishment subject to federal tax.

Table B. States and Counties — **Health Care and Social Assistance, Other Services, and Federal Funds**

STATE County	Health care and social assistance, 2007				Other services, 2007				Federal funds and grants, 2009–2010 Expenditures (mil dol)			
										Direct payments for individuals[1]		
	Number of establishments	Number of employees	Receipts (mil dol)	Annual payroll (mil dol)	Number of establishments	Number of employees	Receipts (mil dol)	Annual payroll (mil dol)	Total	Social Security and government retirement	Medicare	Food Stamps and Supplemental Security Income
	159	160	161	162	163	164	165	166	167	168	169	170
TEXAS—Cont'd												
Mason	10	119	5.4	2.7	9	24	1.2	0.2	36.5	16.4	9.3	1.1
Matagorda	65	1 248	111.1	37.0	69	331	35.5	12.4	255.8	103.2	58.3	18.4
Maverick	85	D	D	D	31	116	8.7	1.8	445.3	86.8	70.5	58.5
Medina	58	655	45.5	17.9	45	187	15.3	4.2	309.5	136.7	51.8	12.6
Menard	1	D	D	D	3	D	D	D	24.8	9.0	7.1	1.1
Midland	359	5 999	697.2	241.4	255	2 469	287.0	65.5	638.5	281.9	156.8	40.0
Milam	43	901	46.0	22.8	35	145	12.5	2.6	219.5	85.0	41.8	11.8
Mills	13	238	9.4	5.0	10	D	D	D	47.2	18.4	14.4	1.8
Mitchell	7	D	D	D	11	31	2.0	0.4	72.5	23.4	20.4	2.9
Montague	35	747	45.4	19.6	34	102	8.0	1.9	171.4	79.4	47.9	6.2
Montgomery	771	12 641	1 617.6	531.2	515	4 034	322.1	102.0	1 780.5	1 040.1	342.8	84.3
Moore	43	592	40.8	17.6	40	127	9.1	2.1	86.3	38.2	19.8	4.0
Morris	21	D	D	D	22	76	10.5	2.6	135.0	54.6	34.6	7.0
Motley	3	D	D	D	5	D	D	D	16.8	5.5	4.8	0.5
Nacogdoches	196	3 849	361.3	125.5	95	469	31.8	8.4	495.9	161.2	107.6	23.5
Navarro	87	1 687	111.9	46.7	60	220	18.5	4.3	415.3	145.5	82.7	22.2
Newton	10	301	11.6	5.7	5	D	D	D	117.0	40.0	28.2	8.5
Nolan	38	645	40.2	17.7	21	93	9.3	2.3	163.6	48.7	37.8	7.8
Nueces	1 014	24 413	2 103.8	808.8	671	4 159	454.4	120.5	3 257.7	939.8	518.2	195.1
Ochiltree	19	287	22.3	6.7	21	100	7.4	1.9	48.0	21.4	10.7	2.0
Oldham	2	D	D	D	3	D	D	D	18.9	8.9	3.6	0.2
Orange	142	1 666	146.0	54.4	95	755	115.9	20.8	636.6	276.6	186.3	38.0
Palo Pinto	52	D	D	D	40	D	D	D	202.3	85.9	55.6	12.7
Panola	47	710	52.6	17.5	32	164	17.7	3.3	182.0	67.7	47.0	8.0
Parker	171	D	D	D	137	773	59.9	15.7	518.5	310.9	93.1	15.3
Parmer	9	94	7.8	3.2	16	45	4.0	0.9	79.0	26.7	13.6	2.6
Pecos	17	464	35.1	13.7	26	171	9.2	2.4	85.6	28.0	18.0	7.7
Polk	59	1 013	81.4	29.3	55	338	21.9	5.7	515.5	297.0	113.0	21.9
Potter	469	12 140	1 391.8	482.7	258	1 942	218.0	44.0	4 241.0	515.7	229.2	65.4
Presidio	2	D	D	D	7	D	D	D	113.6	17.0	9.8	8.9
Rains	6	22	1.2	0.4	10	D	D	D	71.4	41.5	14.4	1.8
Randall	220	2 528	233.1	73.0	161	918	75.5	18.9	224.7	94.5	59.1	8.1
Reagan	4	D	D	D	8	D	D	D	18.6	7.5	3.9	0.8
Real	11	146	6.3	3.2	1	D	D	D	33.7	16.4	6.8	1.9
Red River	21	437	34.5	12.0	15	44	2.6	0.7	188.7	50.6	42.6	6.2
Reeves	15	271	21.0	8.4	12	D	D	D	106.6	26.3	22.6	8.5
Refugio	9	235	17.8	6.2	8	31	1.6	0.4	80.2	27.4	19.7	3.7
Roberts	NA	NA	NA	NA	NA	NA	NA	NA	5.7	2.1	1.7	0.0
Robertson	23	331	14.9	6.9	27	74	6.4	1.4	174.9	49.5	33.5	11.2
Rockwall	175	2 455	238.8	100.4	83	607	44.0	14.7	332.2	163.4	34.3	6.6
Runnels	18	327	17.7	7.2	14	31	2.7	0.7	113.0	38.0	28.0	4.8
Rusk	65	1 145	95.5	34.2	46	266	19.7	6.0	320.1	122.0	82.2	16.1
Sabine	13	171	11.8	5.1	13	40	2.8	0.9	144.3	66.2	38.7	5.3
San Augustine	19	472	21.1	9.1	9	23	1.3	0.3	103.9	33.9	25.3	4.2
San Jacinto	12	111	6.0	2.6	15	40	3.4	0.7	151.2	65.6	37.4	10.0
San Patricio	96	1 415	95.9	38.1	78	391	25.7	7.1	557.6	206.9	113.4	40.0
San Saba	13	227	8.9	4.6	9	30	2.2	0.5	76.3	19.6	17.4	2.4
Schleicher	4	D	D	D	5	D	D	D	22.5	8.4	5.7	1.0
Scurry	23	503	38.7	14.3	34	226	25.8	6.2	126.4	42.5	34.4	6.4
Shackelford	5	71	3.8	1.8	5	D	D	D	28.1	11.0	6.9	0.8
Shelby	36	637	39.4	16.5	31	D	D	D	264.5	77.6	65.5	12.4
Sherman	1	D	D	D	4	D	D	D	26.8	9.1	4.8	0.2
Smith	636	19 044	2 002.7	784.8	334	2 556	192.7	71.9	1 498.6	640.5	307.9	66.0
Somervell	21	449	31.2	13.2	11	28	2.6	0.7	43.3	21.9	10.1	2.1
Starr	67	4 455	134.6	68.3	26	90	4.0	0.9	442.6	76.7	59.7	76.8
Stephens	24	358	18.1	8.4	15	57	3.6	1.2	78.5	28.4	24.4	3.2
Sterling	3	D	D	D	1	D	D	D	8.0	3.1	2.2	0.2
Stonewall	4	130	6.4	2.9	5	D	D	D	17.1	5.8	4.7	0.6
Sutton	4	82	8.6	2.3	10	35	3.6	0.6	22.2	10.0	5.6	1.0
Swisher	13	249	12.2	5.5	10	30	1.7	0.5	84.8	25.9	17.1	2.9
Tarrant	3 999	75 845	8 750.6	3 062.5	2 408	19 973	1 777.8	505.0	18 312.5	3 714.9	1 585.2	422.3
Taylor	377	11 521	833.6	333.5	249	1 554	147.9	31.0	1 246.9	420.0	195.8	49.2
Terrell	1	D	D	D	2	D	D	D	16.4	4.3	2.2	0.5
Terry	20	601	28.0	11.0	19	79	4.5	1.4	130.4	33.6	32.4	7.1
Throckmorton	4	69	3.2	1.6	3	D	D	D	19.6	6.3	4.9	0.4
Titus	86	1 907	144.5	62.0	39	227	16.5	6.7	208.8	75.2	54.3	9.6

1. State totals may include programs not allocated by county.

Table B. States and Counties — Federal Funds, Residential Construction, and Local Government Finances

	Federal funds and grants, 2009–2010 (cont.)							Value of residential construction authorized by building permits, 2010		Local government finances, 2007				
	Expenditures (mil dol) (cont.)									General revenue				
	Procurement contract awards			Grants[1]								Taxes		
													Per capita[2] (dollars)	
STATE County	Salaries and wages	Defense	Other	Medicaid and other health-related	Nutrition and family welfare	Education	Other	New construction ($1,000)	Number of housing units	Total (mil dol)	Inter-govern-mental (mil dol)	Total (mil dol)	Total	Property
	171	172	173	174	175	176	177	178	179	180	181	182	183	184
TEXAS—Cont'd														
Mason	1.4	0.0	0.4	6.6	0.5	0.1	0.2	810	9	12.4	6.1	4.5	1 161	1 032
Matagorda	6.5	-16.8	2.4	48.5	18.3	1.3	2.4	10 533	68	194.4	33.8	71.7	1 937	1 770
Maverick	64.0	2.7	4.0	131.1	13.7	5.0	4.7	9 711	205	177.0	115.8	35.4	685	515
Medina	32.0	0.1	8.0	51.6	6.4	1.5	0.8	1 881	12	115.9	52.2	37.0	843	751
Menard	0.5	0.0	0.1	6.1	0.2	0.1	0.1	NA	NA	12.2	6.1	3.2	1 512	1 299
Midland	57.0	0.2	10.5	53.0	9.0	4.2	10.7	54 595	394	587.8	144.8	231.6	1 832	1 400
Milam	4.6	0.0	1.1	62.2	3.2	0.9	1.2	561	3	81.2	27.4	29.6	1 189	1 025
Mills	1.4	0.0	0.3	9.1	0.6	0.4	0.1	NA	NA	15.5	9.6	4.6	913	773
Mitchell	1.8	0.0	0.4	17.2	0.8	0.3	0.2	91	1	41.5	9.9	14.7	1 583	1 416
Montague	4.7	0.0	1.1	27.8	2.6	0.5	0.2	0	0	86.6	42.9	21.6	1 101	969
Montgomery	102.6	2.7	17.8	116.5	24.7	6.2	22.2	658 784	2 932	1 080.2	277.7	641.4	1 554	1 378
Moore	4.0	0.0	0.3	6.6	1.0	0.6	0.1	1 967	12	85.0	13.0	41.5	2 065	1 920
Morris	2.4	0.0	0.6	31.9	2.5	0.4	0.4	0	0	30.7	9.6	16.9	1 292	1 155
Motley	0.6	0.0	0.1	3.5	0.1	0.0	0.0	NA	NA	4.0	1.7	1.8	1 364	1 226
Nacogdoches	26.3	0.0	2.6	110.9	13.5	4.2	9.1	22 268	250	235.6	68.3	63.1	1 010	865
Navarro	22.1	2.4	3.5	97.2	7.5	2.1	1.4	5 819	109	177.9	75.0	57.4	1 163	935
Newton	2.5	0.0	0.7	32.9	2.7	0.5	0.2	0	0	34.4	14.9	15.9	1 149	1 079
Nolan	3.5	0.8	0.8	26.4	3.0	0.7	12.8	400	1	73.5	19.0	24.8	1 695	1 392
Nueces	326.5	477.9	75.8	486.9	83.4	18.5	46.9	114 369	999	1 198.6	393.8	537.4	1 673	1 295
Ochiltree	1.7	0.0	0.3	2.5	0.5	0.2	0.1	225	1	38.6	7.9	18.5	1 930	1 619
Oldham	0.6	0.0	0.1	1.0	0.3	0.3	0.0	512	4	15.0	6.6	3.5	1 668	1 465
Orange	11.1	0.0	2.7	85.5	12.6	2.2	7.8	28 355	226	262.4	87.2	109.0	1 318	1 094
Palo Pinto	4.7	1.1	1.1	33.9	3.9	0.9	1.0	6 379	96	116.9	33.5	45.3	1 660	1 365
Panola	5.7	0.0	1.1	45.0	1.9	0.6	1.0	1 159	10	113.3	17.0	78.0	3 389	3 277
Parker	20.2	3.1	10.0	33.8	13.8	2.9	2.9	25 357	147	330.3	83.4	153.2	1 409	1 211
Parmer	3.8	0.0	0.3	8.1	1.5	0.4	0.0	0	0	32.4	16.5	10.9	1 160	963
Pecos	3.8	0.0	0.4	17.2	5.2	0.6	0.7	645	6	104.4	13.9	67.0	4 195	4 061
Polk	8.9	0.0	1.4	60.8	6.6	1.9	2.5	59 746	346	100.1	37.7	44.8	968	809
Potter	138.1	2 428.4	637.6	103.3	30.2	8.5	50.7	176 825	855	641.0	244.4	260.4	2 156	1 553
Presidio	24.1	1.5	21.2	27.6	1.9	0.9	0.3	341	2	31.3	22.9	5.2	686	575
Rains	1.5	0.0	0.4	10.1	1.0	0.3	0.0	0	0	22.3	7.3	10.7	956	754
Randall	4.2	0.5	1.0	14.7	5.1	3.6	0.1	12 929	71	103.7	27.1	60.4	535	491
Reagan	0.5	0.0	0.1	1.0	1.0	0.1	0.0	0	0	30.9	3.3	22.1	7 223	6 821
Real	0.4	0.0	0.4	7.1	0.4	0.2	0.0	0	0	8.0	1.2	6.3	2 112	2 043
Red River	3.4	0.0	0.8	76.3	3.1	0.5	0.3	846	11	39.3	23.2	10.5	802	686
Reeves	4.9	0.0	3.2	33.9	4.4	0.7	0.5	180	1	113.5	12.0	18.7	1 670	1 427
Refugio	2.9	0.0	1.0	14.7	1.2	0.3	0.3	381	3	34.9	6.7	22.7	3 083	2 914
Roberts	0.4	0.0	0.1	0.5	0.1	0.0	0.0	NA	NA	10.9	0.6	9.7	11 650	11 496
Robertson	3.4	0.0	0.8	67.2	1.4	0.7	1.4	696	6	76.1	20.2	45.8	2 895	2 709
Rockwall	9.1	100.1	2.9	8.1	2.4	0.6	0.4	107 347	613	217.4	46.3	140.5	1 903	1 676
Runnels	3.2	0.0	0.7	25.3	1.8	0.4	0.2	200	1	43.4	18.9	13.5	1 301	1 063
Rusk	7.7	0.2	3.8	79.9	4.7	1.3	0.6	0	0	125.5	33.2	75.8	1 560	1 405
Sabine	3.9	0.0	0.7	26.8	1.2	1.1	0.2	310	5	28.1	12.6	7.9	782	651
San Augustine	1.5	0.0	0.4	36.9	0.6	0.5	0.3	0	0	19.6	11.4	5.5	631	518
San Jacinto	2.9	0.0	0.7	31.9	1.2	0.8	0.0	70	2	44.0	18.6	21.2	853	797
San Patricio	19.7	9.7	1.9	117.8	15.7	2.5	5.0	15 674	126	223.6	100.2	89.9	1 312	1 146
San Saba	1.5	0.0	0.3	19.2	9.2	0.3	4.9	0	0	20.5	12.9	5.4	909	760
Schleicher	0.5	0.0	0.1	4.0	0.7	0.1	0.1	0	0	14.6	2.3	7.8	2 769	2 549
Scurry	3.0	0.0	0.6	21.7	4.3	2.5	0.0	7 450	84	103.7	19.3	48.3	3 018	2 603
Shackelford	1.0	0.2	0.2	3.8	0.7	0.1	2.4	NA	NA	11.9	4.5	5.7	1 807	1 576
Shelby	5.6	0.9	1.0	91.0	7.4	1.2	0.4	1 285	8	67.6	35.0	23.9	903	750
Sherman	0.3	0.0	0.0	0.5	0.4	0.1	0.0	751	8	16.3	2.4	11.2	3 846	3 677
Smith	80.8	56.3	30.8	223.4	25.1	8.5	17.5	37 614	266	557.5	164.4	281.6	1 417	1 075
Somervell	1.5	0.0	0.3	6.6	0.3	0.1	0.1	1 404	8	43.2	5.1	32.0	4 122	4 047
Starr	41.6	3.7	3.5	139.1	24.7	5.7	5.8	NA	NA	234.2	147.0	46.0	744	664
Stephens	1.5	0.1	0.4	12.6	1.5	0.3	5.4	420	3	32.6	6.6	15.3	1 608	1 366
Sterling	0.1	0.0	0.0	1.0	0.2	0.0	0.0	NA	NA	13.3	1.1	10.1	8 145	7 994
Stonewall	0.8	0.0	0.2	2.0	0.4	0.1	0.0	NA	NA	9.4	2.0	4.2	2 958	2 843
Sutton	0.3	0.0	0.4	4.0	0.3	0.1	0.3	0	0	33.9	3.3	25.7	5 979	5 668
Swisher	1.9	0.0	0.3	10.2	2.9	0.3	1.7	0	0	34.8	12.4	7.0	913	794
Tarrant	1 257.2	9 369.9	531.6	805.9	168.8	62.4	205.1	805 271	5 089	6 450.0	1 550.5	3 416.9	1 990	1 600
Taylor	303.6	71.2	8.5	125.6	24.0	5.4	16.2	43 254	388	391.1	163.7	163.1	1 289	927
Terrell	4.6	0.1	0.1	2.9	0.3	0.1	0.1	NA	NA	15.1	0.6	13.3	14 267	13 931
Terry	2.3	0.0	0.5	25.8	3.1	0.6	0.0	3 000	48	54.3	16.1	20.1	1 646	1 457
Throckmorton	0.7	0.8	0.9	3.0	0.1	0.1	0.0	NA	NA	8.2	2.3	3.5	2 116	1 992
Titus	8.7	0.1	2.9	43.0	5.7	1.9	0.2	560	4	183.7	44.7	52.0	1 769	1 480

1. State totals may include programs not allocated by county.   2. Based on the resident population estimated as of July 1 of the year shown.

Table B. States and Counties — Local Government Finances, Government Employment, and Voting

STATE County	Direct general expenditure Total (mil dol)	Per capita[1] (dollars)	Education	Health and hospitals	Police protection	Public welfare	Highways	Debt outstanding Total (mil dol)	Per capita[1] (dollars)	Federal civilian	Federal military	State and local	Demo-cratic	Republican	All other
	185	186	187	188	189	190	191	192	193	194	195	196	197	198	199
TEXAS—Cont'd															
Mason	9.6	2 465	61.0	1.9	6.6	0.4	6.7	2.8	720	21	0	284	25.7	72.8	1.5
Matagorda	189.8	5 126	38.8	39.4	3.2	0.1	3.6	119.2	3 219	93	87	2 507	35.9	63.3	0.8
Maverick	171.7	3 323	65.0	1.7	4.3	0.0	2.7	123.3	2 388	910	125	4 696	78.2	21.2	0.6
Medina	116.2	2 650	61.1	10.4	4.0	0.2	4.5	178.7	4 078	59	105	2 924	32.7	66.6	0.7
Menard	12.1	5 672	40.2	0.0	2.5	15.1	2.2	2.3	1 074	0	0	212	29.0	69.9	1.1
Midland	564.0	4 462	39.4	32.9	4.4	0.0	1.9	394.8	3 123	641	311	8 069	21.0	78.2	0.8
Milam	81.6	3 282	51.5	19.7	3.0	0.5	4.6	114.7	4 613	59	58	1 200	36.4	62.4	1.1
Mills	15.4	3 066	73.7	2.0	2.5	0.4	3.8	4.1	806	21	12	386	18.3	80.5	1.2
Mitchell	36.6	3 950	42.8	34.8	3.1	0.2	5.4	17.2	1 855	26	22	1 247	24.1	74.7	1.2
Montague	86.1	4 381	34.3	45.6	3.3	0.3	3.6	39.2	1 995	59	46	1 423	20.1	78.6	1.4
Montgomery	1 143.6	2 772	60.9	4.3	4.7	0.1	5.5	2 844.3	6 893	806	1 059	21 800	23.3	75.9	0.8
Moore	79.3	3 948	49.0	27.9	6.1	0.1	3.4	19.5	972	72	49	1 568	20.7	78.8	0.6
Morris	28.6	2 193	70.8	0.1	4.8	0.5	3.0	19.3	1 477	25	30	701	39.2	60.2	0.7
Motley	3.6	2 789	71.1	3.3	4.4	0.1	5.4	0.9	667	14	0	104	11.3	87.9	0.8
Nacogdoches	226.8	3 633	35.4	36.3	3.6	0.2	2.0	208.2	3 335	161	156	5 209	35.9	63.4	0.7
Navarro	169.3	3 428	65.8	3.5	5.5	0.3	3.6	220.4	4 461	115	116	3 714	33.1	66.2	0.7
Newton	30.8	2 231	76.9	0.0	3.9	0.6	3.8	27.7	2 005	28	32	654	33.3	65.5	1.2
Nolan	68.8	4 708	44.9	29.4	4.6	0.0	2.9	59.2	4 051	48	35	1 779	30.0	68.8	1.1
Nueces	1 247.9	3 886	50.5	5.3	5.8	0.1	4.0	1 480.1	4 609	6 429	3 287	22 144	47.3	51.8	0.9
Ochiltree	39.9	4 163	46.5	25.7	4.5	0.0	5.4	8.0	832	27	23	757	7.8	91.7	0.5
Oldham	14.5	7 004	80.5	0.0	3.6	0.0	2.2	1.4	664	10	0	296	11.1	88.4	0.5
Orange	240.6	2 911	53.9	0.8	6.3	0.2	2.9	611.0	7 390	111	194	4 413	26.0	73.1	0.9
Palo Pinto	118.3	4 331	49.1	27.0	2.2	0.0	3.3	96.2	3 520	47	66	1 840	25.3	73.4	1.3
Panola	106.3	4 620	77.2	0.0	2.5	0.2	4.8	57.8	2 513	79	55	1 271	25.3	74.2	0.5
Parker	322.4	2 966	56.1	16.2	3.7	0.1	4.3	662.6	6 096	197	271	4 943	21.9	77.1	1.0
Parmer	29.4	3 118	71.6	2.4	3.4	5.4	4.4	10.7	1 132	63	22	845	19.4	80.0	0.7
Pecos	92.6	5 797	56.5	18.9	2.6	0.2	2.7	38.1	2 386	59	38	1 835	36.8	61.8	1.3
Polk	93.5	2 017	65.0	0.1	5.9	0.4	7.2	221.3	4 776	83	110	3 011	30.9	68.1	0.9
Potter	664.3	5 501	56.2	6.0	5.1	0.1	3.2	459.6	3 805	2 044	331	11 852	29.8	69.2	1.0
Presidio	24.1	3 182	65.9	1.0	2.7	0.0	2.0	33.4	4 413	332	18	623	71.3	27.8	0.9
Rains	20.3	1 810	64.1	0.0	2.1	0.2	5.0	10.2	910	22	27	449	24.7	74.3	1.0
Randall	99.7	882	51.1	1.2	6.7	0.0	2.8	251.5	2 225	87	274	4 915	18.3	80.9	0.8
Reagan	34.0	11 137	60.0	11.1	1.6	0.0	3.3	49.6	16 247	15	0	350	19.8	80.0	0.2
Real	5.4	1 809	61.4	0.6	4.2	1.9	3.3	16.9	5 712	0	0	249	23.0	76.0	0.9
Red River	36.1	2 757	77.4	0.0	4.5	0.5	6.0	18.4	1 404	44	30	802	30.5	68.5	1.0
Reeves	109.1	9 671	22.7	11.9	4.1	0.1	1.2	82.0	7 332	88	26	1 496	52.2	47.0	0.8
Refugio	39.7	5 389	73.8	1.8	3.5	0.0	4.0	18.9	2 573	54	17	680	42.4	56.9	0.7
Roberts	10.6	12 699	87.7	0.5	0.9	2.5	2.0	3.0	3 564	0	0	97	7.9	92.1	0.0
Robertson	87.1	5 508	74.8	0.5	3.8	1.0	3.8	61.9	3 911	51	37	1 034	39.9	59.3	0.8
Rockwall	281.2	3 810	63.2	0.4	4.6	0.1	6.0	680.7	9 222	107	192	3 510	26.5	72.7	0.9
Runnels	35.9	3 469	53.9	18.0	3.5	1.0	2.8	57.9	5 592	43	24	816	18.6	80.6	0.7
Rusk	120.9	2 490	71.1	0.1	4.9	0.4	5.2	117.0	2 410	90	116	2 458	26.6	72.9	0.5
Sabine	27.3	2 695	58.1	18.4	4.5	0.0	5.6	23.8	2 344	57	24	484	22.1	76.9	1.0
San Augustine	17.8	2 059	71.3	2.7	3.7	0.1	4.7	22.0	2 542	19	20	398	35.7	63.0	1.2
San Jacinto	41.1	1 658	72.7	0.0	3.7	0.8	8.2	44.5	1 792	27	59	981	30.4	68.7	1.0
San Patricio	223.6	3 263	61.7	6.4	4.8	0.5	3.2	222.1	3 241	269	1 651	4 066	41.4	58.0	0.6
San Saba	16.8	2 817	60.1	1.4	3.6	1.0	6.0	6.1	1 023	23	14	500	19.8	79.0	1.2
Schleicher	12.2	4 355	46.6	22.3	4.6	0.7	7.2	0.9	323	12	0	257	24.8	74.4	0.8
Scurry	101.3	6 327	62.3	18.3	1.8	0.2	2.8	39.4	2 462	40	38	1 589	19.5	79.3	1.2
Shackelford	10.5	3 336	65.8	4.5	5.6	0.0	4.9	2.3	724	15	0	225	13.8	85.3	0.9
Shelby	60.7	2 288	73.1	0.6	5.1	0.0	6.3	50.3	1 897	82	63	1 301	27.6	71.9	0.5
Sherman	15.5	5 352	64.2	2.2	3.7	13.5	6.6	4.1	1 425	13	0	309	12.5	86.7	0.9
Smith	599.0	3 015	63.3	5.0	4.6	0.4	3.7	786.9	3 960	919	485	11 812	29.8	69.4	0.8
Somervell	38.8	4 997	69.4	1.7	6.6	0.0	1.3	11.7	1 514	15	19	699	22.6	75.8	1.6
Starr	236.2	3 820	71.4	9.5	2.4	0.0	2.8	244.4	3 952	598	148	4 850	84.5	15.2	0.3
Stephens	36.8	3 861	48.8	24.3	2.9	0.0	3.8	25.5	2 674	22	23	774	17.8	81.4	0.9
Sterling	13.0	10 439	64.7	2.0	2.2	16.4	2.5	24.3	19 556	0	0	167	15.7	84.0	0.3
Stonewall	8.8	6 238	31.4	48.9	2.1	0.0	5.3	1.1	811	13	0	236	28.0	71.3	0.7
Sutton	27.8	6 458	73.2	10.2	2.3	0.0	2.8	6.5	1 506	0	10	467	24.1	75.3	0.5
Swisher	29.4	3 823	46.9	27.3	4.5	0.1	3.7	10.4	1 349	34	17	740	32.1	66.4	1.5
Tarrant	6 134.2	3 572	46.0	10.5	6.4	0.1	4.1	14 177.4	8 255	14 214	5 173	90 030	43.7	55.4	0.8
Taylor	405.0	3 200	56.5	4.2	6.7	0.4	2.6	256.2	2 025	1 230	5 056	9 725	26.8	72.3	0.9
Terrell	13.6	14 604	82.1	1.5	1.3	0.0	3.0	1.1	1 151	60	0	135	35.8	62.2	1.9
Terry	49.9	4 094	44.3	24.0	4.0	0.1	4.0	13.5	1 104	34	29	1 119	32.2	67.3	0.5
Throckmorton	8.4	5 067	44.8	30.0	0.5	0.0	11.3	1.6	990	12	0	210	19.8	80.1	0.1
Titus	180.2	6 131	53.5	30.7	1.9	0.0	2.0	169.8	5 778	116	71	2 996	34.0	65.2	0.8

1. Based on the resident population estimated as of July 1 of the year shown.   2. © 2009 Election Data Services, Inc. All rights reserved.

Table B. States and Counties — **Land Area and Population**

STATE/ County code	CBSA code[1]	County type[2]	STATE County	Land area,[3] (sq km) 2010	Total persons	Rank	Per square kilometer	White	Black	American Indian, Alaska Native	Asian and Pacific Islander	Percent Hispanic or Latino[4]	Under 5 years	5 to 17 years	18 to 24 years	25 to 34 years	35 to 44 years	45 to 54 years
				1	2	3	4	5	6	7	8	9	10	11	12	13	14	15
			TEXAS—Cont'd															
48 451	41660	3	Tom Green	3 942	110 224	537	28.0	59.1	4.1	0.8	1.5	35.7	7.0	16.5	13.9	13.4	11.0	13.1
48 453	12420	1	Travis	2 565	1 024 266	39	399.3	52.1	8.7	0.7	6.6	33.5	7.4	16.5	12.7	18.8	15.1	12.9
48 455	...	8	Trinity	1 796	14 585	2 142	8.1	82.1	9.8	0.9	0.5	7.7	5.6	15.2	6.7	9.1	10.4	14.7
48 457	...	6	Tyler	2 394	21 766	1 745	9.1	81.4	11.4	1.0	0.3	6.8	5.2	14.8	8.4	13.3	12.1	13.9
48 459	30980	3	Upshur	1 510	39 309	1 187	26.0	83.6	9.3	1.4	0.6	6.6	6.4	18.3	7.7	11.2	11.8	15.4
48 461	...	8	Upton	3 215	3 355	2 951	1.0	48.6	1.5	1.2	0.1	49.0	7.4	19.9	7.6	13.7	10.3	14.6
48 463	46620	7	Uvalde	4 020	26 405	1 547	6.6	29.4	0.5	0.4	0.6	69.3	7.7	21.2	9.8	11.0	11.7	12.4
48 465	19620	5	Val Verde	8 145	48 879	997	6.0	17.9	1.3	0.3	0.7	80.2	8.3	21.5	10.4	13.1	12.9	11.6
48 467	...	6	Van Zandt	2 182	52 579	940	24.1	86.9	3.1	1.5	0.5	9.2	6.0	18.1	7.3	10.3	11.9	14.7
48 469	47020	3	Victoria	2 285	86 793	650	38.0	48.7	6.4	0.5	1.2	43.9	7.5	19.2	8.9	12.8	11.8	14.3
48 471	26660	4	Walker	2 031	67 861	775	33.4	59.5	22.9	0.7	1.2	16.8	4.8	11.9	19.9	14.1	13.7	14.7
48 473	26420	1	Waller	1 330	43 205	1 102	32.5	45.5	25.0	0.7	0.7	29.0	7.3	17.4	17.8	10.8	11.6	13.6
48 475	...	6	Ward	2 164	10 658	2 390	4.9	47.0	4.8	0.9	0.4	47.6	7.6	19.8	8.4	12.2	11.3	14.2
48 477	14780	6	Washington	1 564	33 718	1 330	21.6	67.1	17.9	0.5	1.5	13.8	6.0	16.1	10.6	10.3	10.9	14.3
48 479	29700	3	Webb	8 706	250 304	261	28.8	3.4	0.2	0.1	0.6	95.7	9.8	25.5	10.9	14.0	13.7	10.9
48 481	20900	4	Wharton	2 813	41 280	1 147	14.7	48.2	14.0	0.4	0.5	37.4	7.3	19.5	8.7	12.2	11.5	14.2
48 483	...	9	Wheeler	2 369	5 410	2 812	2.3	72.2	2.5	0.9	0.6	24.8	7.2	18.1	7.1	11.2	11.2	13.8
48 485	48660	3	Wichita	1 626	131 500	471	80.9	70.1	11.0	1.4	2.7	16.6	6.8	16.3	14.1	14.0	11.5	13.6
48 487	46900	6	Wilbarger	2 514	13 535	2 216	5.4	64.6	8.3	1.4	1.0	25.9	7.1	18.5	9.5	11.8	10.9	14.3
48 489	39700	6	Willacy	1 530	22 134	1 731	14.5	10.3	1.8	0.2	0.7	87.2	7.1	19.7	12.3	15.1	12.7	11.7
48 491	12420	1	Williamson	2 896	422 679	159	146.0	65.4	6.6	0.8	5.8	23.2	7.9	20.8	7.5	15.0	16.6	13.7
48 493	41700	1	Wilson	2 082	42 918	1 106	20.6	59.5	1.7	0.7	0.5	38.2	6.2	20.3	7.1	10.1	13.8	16.6
48 495	...	6	Winkler	2 178	7 110	2 674	3.3	43.1	2.0	0.8	0.3	53.8	8.9	20.8	8.3	12.5	11.7	15.0
48 497	19100	1	Wise	2 342	59 127	867	25.2	80.9	1.2	1.3	0.7	17.1	6.7	19.3	8.3	11.6	13.4	16.2
48 499	...	6	Wood	1 671	41 964	1 132	25.1	85.9	5.1	1.1	0.6	8.5	5.2	15.1	7.3	8.9	10.3	13.6
48 501	...	7	Yoakum	2 071	7 879	2 613	3.8	39.9	1.0	0.7	0.4	58.7	9.3	22.5	8.4	12.7	11.8	13.9
48 503	...	6	Young	2 368	18 550	1 895	7.8	81.5	1.5	0.9	0.5	16.4	6.5	17.5	7.6	10.7	11.3	14.9
48 505	...	6	Zapata	2 586	14 018	2 173	5.4	6.2	0.1	0.2	0.2	93.3	10.4	23.8	11.1	13.2	11.8	10.3
48 507	...	7	Zavala	3 360	11 677	2 318	3.5	5.7	0.4	0.2	0.1	93.9	9.0	22.4	11.2	11.9	11.4	11.3
49 000	...	X	**UTAH**	212 818	2 763 885	X	13.0	82.0	1.3	1.4	3.9	13.0	9.5	22.0	11.5	16.1	12.0	11.1
49 001	...	9	Beaver	6 708	6 629	2 721	1.0	86.8	0.3	1.2	1.7	10.8	9.3	24.6	7.1	13.2	10.9	12.2
49 003	14940	4	Box Elder	14 881	49 975	977	3.4	89.6	0.5	1.3	1.6	8.3	9.9	24.0	8.2	14.1	11.2	12.3
49 005	30860	3	Cache	3 017	112 656	528	37.3	86.7	0.8	0.8	3.0	10.0	10.2	21.4	17.3	16.9	10.1	9.3
49 007	39220	7	Carbon	3 829	21 403	1 767	5.6	85.5	0.7	1.6	1.0	12.4	8.0	18.7	10.5	13.5	10.3	13.0
49 009	...	8	Daggett	1 805	1 059	3 106	0.6	95.1	0.7	0.8	0.9	3.1	6.3	16.6	4.4	13.9	11.0	12.7
49 011	36260	2	Davis	774	306 479	209	396.0	87.6	1.6	0.7	3.5	8.4	10.2	24.1	9.4	15.6	12.5	11.5
49 013	...	6	Duchesne	8 394	18 607	1 891	2.2	89.0	0.4	5.7	0.8	6.0	10.7	23.2	9.1	14.8	10.6	11.7
49 015	...	9	Emery	11 557	10 976	2 367	0.9	92.7	0.4	1.0	0.6	6.0	9.3	22.4	7.9	13.1	9.9	12.9
49 017	...	9	Garfield	13 404	5 172	2 832	0.4	92.3	0.4	1.8	1.7	4.5	7.3	19.4	7.6	11.3	10.0	13.3
49 019	...	7	Grand	9 509	9 225	2 508	1.0	85.3	0.7	4.4	1.3	9.6	6.5	16.5	7.1	13.3	12.8	15.3
49 021	16260	4	Iron	8 538	46 163	1 040	5.4	88.7	0.7	2.6	1.9	7.7	9.3	20.9	16.7	14.6	9.9	10.0
49 023	39340	2	Juab	8 786	10 246	2 424	1.2	94.9	0.4	1.3	0.6	3.7	10.3	27.1	7.6	13.1	11.7	10.9
49 025	...	6	Kane	10 335	7 125	2 673	0.7	94.1	0.4	2.0	0.7	3.7	7.0	17.3	6.6	10.5	9.3	13.3
49 027	...	7	Millard	17 023	12 503	2 274	0.7	85.5	0.2	1.2	1.0	12.8	8.8	23.6	7.2	11.7	10.1	13.0
49 029	36260	2	Morgan	1 578	9 469	2 482	6.0	96.8	0.4	0.4	0.7	2.4	9.5	25.8	7.5	11.0	12.3	13.2
49 031	...	9	Piute	1 963	1 556	3 081	0.8	92.0	0.6	0.8	0.5	7.0	7.1	23.0	5.1	9.5	8.8	11.8
49 033	...	8	Rich	2 665	2 264	3 032	0.8	94.8	0.3	1.1	0.2	4.2	9.6	21.5	6.7	12.5	10.2	11.9
49 035	41620	2	Salt Lake	1 923	1 029 655	38	535.4	75.7	1.9	1.0	6.0	17.1	8.8	20.4	10.6	17.2	13.1	12.0
49 037	...	7	San Juan	20 254	14 746	2 131	0.7	45.3	0.4	51.1	0.6	4.4	9.1	24.9	10.1	11.8	11.3	12.2
49 039	...	6	Sanpete	4 118	27 822	1 501	6.8	87.7	0.9	1.3	1.8	9.4	8.0	22.0	15.9	12.4	10.6	10.3
49 041	...	7	Sevier	4 948	20 802	1 803	4.2	93.9	0.4	1.5	0.8	4.5	8.7	23.0	7.8	13.5	10.2	11.8
49 043	41620	2	Summit	4 848	36 324	1 263	7.5	86.4	0.5	0.5	2.1	11.5	6.8	20.9	7.2	12.2	15.0	17.7
49 045	41620	2	Tooele	17 978	58 218	876	3.2	86.0	1.0	1.4	1.8	11.4	10.2	25.9	7.7	15.0	14.1	11.4
49 047	46860	7	Uintah	11 602	32 588	1 375	2.8	84.4	0.5	8.3	1.3	7.1	10.6	22.7	9.6	16.3	11.0	11.7
49 049	39340	2	Utah	5 189	516 564	123	99.5	85.9	0.8	0.9	3.5	10.8	11.3	23.9	15.8	17.1	10.9	8.4
49 051	25720	6	Wasatch	3 045	23 530	1 663	7.7	85.1	0.3	0.6	1.3	13.5	9.9	24.0	7.6	14.0	14.0	12.4
49 053	41100	3	Washington	6 284	138 115	445	22.0	87.1	0.8	1.6	2.4	9.8	9.0	21.2	9.7	13.0	10.0	9.7
49 055	...	9	Wayne	6 373	2 778	2 994	0.4	94.6	0.2	0.7	1.6	4.2	7.2	23.0	5.8	11.6	10.8	13.0
49 057	36260	2	Weber	1 492	231 236	276	155.0	79.8	1.7	1.1	2.4	16.7	9.0	21.0	10.6	15.8	11.9	12.2
50 000	...	X	**VERMONT**	23 871	625 741	X	26.2	95.8	1.4	1.1	1.7	1.5	5.1	15.5	10.4	11.1	12.5	16.4
50 001	...	6	Addison	1 985	36 821	1 253	18.5	95.6	1.1	1.0	1.9	1.9	4.8	15.6	13.0	9.2	12.4	16.4
50 003	13540	6	Bennington	1 748	37 125	1 237	21.2	96.8	1.1	0.7	1.1	1.4	5.1	15.4	8.7	9.1	11.5	16.3
50 005	...	7	Caledonia	1 681	31 227	1 411	18.6	97.1	0.8	1.3	1.0	1.1	5.5	16.2	9.7	10.3	11.8	15.7

1. CBSA = Core Based Statistical Area. See Appendix A for explanation. See Appendix B for list of metropolitan areas with component counties. 2. County type code from the Economic Research Service of USDA Rural-Urban Continuum Codes. See Appendix A for definition. 3. Dry land or land partially or temporarily covered by water. 4. May be of any race.

Table B. States and Counties — Population and Households

STATE County	55 to 64 years	65 to 74 years	75 years and over	Percent female	Total persons 1990	Total persons 2000	Percent change 1990–2000	Percent change 2000–2010	Births	Deaths	Net migration	Number	Percent change, 2000–2010	Persons per household	Female family householder[1]	One person
	16	17	18	19	20	21	22	23	24	25	26	27	28	29	30	31
TEXAS—Cont'd																
Tom Green	11.3	7.2	6.7	51.0	98 458	104 010	5.6	6.0	15 029	9 176	-819	42 331	7.2	2.48	13.3	28.1
Travis	9.3	4.2	3.1	49.6	576 407	812 280	40.9	26.1	141 567	38 914	115 762	404 467	26.1	2.48	11.0	30.8
Trinity	15.9	13.0	9.4	51.3	11 445	13 779	20.4	5.8	1 520	1 891	555	6 142	7.3	2.37	12.2	28.7
Tyler	13.4	10.9	8.1	46.1	16 646	20 871	25.4	4.3	2 156	2 247	-117	8 007	3.0	2.41	10.4	27.1
Upshur	13.4	9.1	6.6	50.5	31 370	35 291	12.5	11.4	4 484	3 783	2 197	14 925	12.3	2.60	11.7	23.4
Upton	11.9	7.8	6.9	50.1	4 447	3 404	-23.5	-1.4	449	248	-480	1 256	0.0	2.62	9.9	25.4
Uvalde	11.4	7.7	7.0	51.1	23 340	25 926	11.1	1.8	4 231	2 118	-1 084	9 025	5.4	2.86	15.9	21.7
Val Verde	9.9	6.9	5.4	49.8	38 721	44 856	15.8	9.0	8 629	2 891	-2 184	15 654	10.6	3.00	16.3	20.2
Van Zandt	13.8	10.4	7.6	50.8	37 944	48 140	26.9	9.2	5 696	5 423	3 860	20 047	10.2	2.59	10.3	23.6
Victoria	12.1	7.2	6.3	51.2	74 361	84 088	13.1	3.2	12 705	6 659	-1 832	32 187	7.0	2.65	14.5	24.5
Walker	10.6	6.0	4.2	41.0	50 917	61 758	21.3	9.9	5 733	3 943	877	20 969	14.6	2.44	12.6	27.9
Waller	11.2	6.2	4.0	50.5	23 374	32 663	39.7	32.3	5 056	2 369	1 351	14 040	33.0	2.81	13.1	21.1
Ward	11.7	7.6	7.2	51.7	13 115	10 909	-16.8	-2.3	1 503	972	-897	3 995	0.8	2.64	13.6	25.4
Washington	13.5	9.3	9.1	50.8	26 154	30 373	16.1	11.0	3 849	3 240	2 056	13 037	15.1	2.45	11.7	27.6
Webb	7.4	4.4	3.4	51.5	133 239	193 117	44.9	29.6	55 432	9 634	3 855	67 106	32.3	3.68	20.9	13.4
Wharton	12.0	7.6	7.0	50.8	39 955	41 188	3.1	0.2	6 003	3 759	-2 223	15 132	2.3	2.70	14.4	24.6
Wheeler	12.9	10.4	8.0	50.8	5 879	5 284	-10.1	2.4	595	683	-298	2 181	1.3	2.46	9.0	26.8
Wichita	10.6	6.7	6.4	48.7	122 378	131 664	7.6	-0.1	17 585	11 881	-9 116	49 016	1.2	2.44	13.6	29.3
Wilbarger	12.3	8.0	7.5	50.2	15 121	14 676	-2.9	-7.8	1 947	1 656	-1 359	5 289	-4.5	2.44	13.1	29.9
Willacy	9.7	6.3	5.4	45.6	17 705	20 082	13.4	10.2	3 603	1 066	-2 149	5 764	3.2	3.28	19.3	18.0
Williamson	9.4	5.4	3.5	50.8	139 551	249 967	79.1	69.1	61 293	13 588	122 942	152 606	75.9	2.74	10.8	21.2
Wilson	13.4	7.2	5.4	50.2	22 650	32 408	43.1	32.4	4 348	2 727	6 848	15 009	36.0	2.82	10.0	17.4
Winkler	11.1	6.5	5.3	50.1	8 626	7 173	-16.8	-0.9	1 013	677	-737	2 578	-0.2	2.72	13.2	23.2
Wise	12.1	7.7	4.6	49.6	34 679	48 793	40.7	21.2	6 625	4 026	8 255	21 015	22.3	2.77	9.5	19.4
Wood	15.4	14.4	9.8	50.9	29 380	36 752	25.1	14.2	4 151	4 949	7 260	17 118	17.4	2.39	8.9	25.2
Yoakum	10.1	6.1	5.2	50.5	8 786	7 322	-16.7	7.6	1 219	478	-337	2 643	7.0	2.96	9.5	18.2
Young	13.0	9.1	9.3	50.7	18 126	17 943	-1.0	3.4	2 154	2 394	169	7 343	2.5	2.49	11.1	25.3
Zapata	8.9	6.1	4.3	49.8	9 279	12 182	31.3	15.1	2 693	730	-40	4 297	9.6	3.26	15.9	18.1
Zavala	10.7	6.5	5.6	50.7	12 162	11 600	-4.6	0.7	2 021	829	-1 162	3 573	4.2	3.15	24.0	19.8
UTAH	8.7	5.0	4.0	49.8	1 722 850	2 233 169	29.6	23.8	479 519	124 262	118 543	877 692	25.2	3.10	9.7	18.7
Beaver	10.2	7.0	5.5	48.6	4 765	6 005	26.0	10.4	1 116	536	-287	2 265	14.3	2.92	7.2	22.1
Box Elder	9.0	6.0	5.1	49.6	36 485	42 745	17.2	16.9	8 037	2 749	760	16 058	22.2	3.09	8.7	17.2
Cache	7.2	4.2	3.6	50.3	70 183	91 391	30.2	23.3	22 314	3 934	242	34 722	26.1	3.14	7.7	16.3
Carbon	12.5	7.1	6.5	50.4	20 228	20 422	1.0	4.8	2 891	1 885	-1 349	7 978	7.6	2.61	10.7	25.5
Daggett	16.1	12.0	7.0	43.6	690	921	33.5	15.0	95	31	-45	426	25.3	2.34	4.9	29.1
Davis	8.4	4.5	3.6	49.8	187 941	238 994	27.2	28.2	52 427	11 570	18 620	93 545	31.4	3.24	9.6	15.2
Duchesne	9.2	6.3	4.4	49.2	12 645	14 371	13.6	29.5	3 077	1 071	1 634	6 003	31.7	3.05	8.6	17.7
Emery	11.9	7.6	4.9	49.1	10 332	10 860	5.1	1.1	1 631	757	-1 163	3 732	7.6	2.93	7.4	18.4
Garfield	15.1	8.7	7.4	48.3	3 980	4 735	19.0	9.2	645	370	-370	1 930	22.5	2.59	6.2	26.2
Grand	15.0	7.6	5.9	49.6	6 620	8 485	28.2	8.7	1 084	635	349	3 889	13.2	2.34	10.2	30.7
Iron	8.8	5.9	3.9	50.3	20 789	33 779	62.5	36.7	8 107	2 019	5 606	15 022	41.4	3.00	8.9	18.3
Juab	9.2	6.7	4.5	49.0	5 817	8 238	41.6	24.4	1 726	581	896	3 093	25.9	3.27	8.8	17.3
Kane	16.6	12.2	7.2	50.6	5 169	6 046	17.0	17.8	820	540	309	2 900	29.6	2.42	6.2	29.6
Millard	11.4	7.6	6.6	49.1	11 333	12 405	9.5	0.8	1 827	980	-924	4 201	9.4	2.95	6.3	19.8
Morgan	10.1	6.4	4.1	49.6	5 528	7 129	29.0	32.8	1 183	329	957	2 820	37.8	3.36	5.2	12.1
Piute	13.3	12.9	8.4	48.8	1 277	1 435	12.4	8.4	175	145	-32	576	13.2	2.64	5.6	24.8
Rich	12.5	9.0	6.1	48.3	1 725	1 961	13.7	15.5	297	113	20	805	24.8	2.81	5.2	18.4
Salt Lake	9.3	4.8	3.9	49.7	725 956	898 387	23.8	14.6	174 015	48 967	-5 329	342 622	16.1	2.96	10.9	21.9
San Juan	9.7	6.4	4.4	49.8	12 621	14 413	14.2	2.3	2 269	668	-921	4 505	10.2	3.21	14.7	20.7
Sanpete	9.4	6.8	4.6	47.7	16 259	22 763	40.0	22.2	3 813	1 599	1 090	7 952	21.5	3.19	8.1	17.4
Sevier	10.4	8.1	6.4	49.6	15 431	18 842	22.1	10.4	3 250	1 609	-418	7 094	16.7	2.89	8.0	20.1
Summit	12.5	5.4	2.3	48.5	15 518	29 736	91.6	22.2	4 884	992	3 528	12 990	25.7	2.79	6.6	20.1
Tooele	8.3	4.4	3.1	49.6	26 601	40 735	53.1	42.9	9 929	2 327	10 144	17 971	41.8	3.22	10.0	16.8
Uintah	8.8	5.1	4.1	49.2	22 211	25 224	13.6	29.2	5 205	1 722	2 919	10 563	29.0	3.07	10.2	18.1
Utah	6.1	3.6	2.9	49.9	263 590	368 536	39.8	40.2	105 082	16 389	38 195	140 602	40.7	3.57	8.0	11.6
Wasatch	9.5	5.3	3.3	49.2	10 089	15 215	50.8	54.7	3 539	898	3 771	7 287	53.6	3.19	7.4	15.5
Washington	10.1	9.3	8.0	50.6	48 560	90 354	86.1	52.9	21 799	7 547	33 149	46 334	54.8	2.94	8.4	18.8
Wayne	13.5	8.6	6.7	49.5	2 177	2 509	15.3	10.7	362	169	-93	1 059	19.0	2.61	5.9	26.3
Weber	9.4	5.3	4.8	49.8	158 330	196 533	24.1	17.7	37 921	13 130	7 285	78 748	19.9	2.90	11.5	21.4
VERMONT	14.4	7.9	6.6	50.7	562 758	608 827	8.2	2.8	59 886	47 266	3 877	256 442	6.6	2.34	9.6	28.2
Addison	14.8	7.7	6.2	50.1	32 953	35 974	9.2	2.4	3 321	2 433	104	14 084	7.8	2.41	8.6	25.5
Bennington	15.1	9.6	9.2	51.6	35 845	36 994	3.2	0.4	3 421	3 673	-98	15 470	4.2	2.30	10.6	29.9
Caledonia	15.4	8.1	7.2	50.3	27 846	29 702	6.7	5.1	3 149	2 576	184	12 553	7.6	2.38	10.1	27.5

1. No spouse present.

Table B. States and Counties — Population, Vital Statistics, Medicare, and Crime

STATE County	Daytime population, 2006–2010 Persons in group quarters, 2010	Daytime population, 2006–2010 Number	Daytime population, 2006–2010 Employment/residence ratio	Births, average 2006–2008 Total	Births, average 2006–2008 Rate[1]	Deaths, average 2006–2008 Number	Deaths, average 2006–2008 Rate[1]	Persons under 65 with no health insurance, 2009 Number	Persons under 65 with no health insurance, 2009 Percent	Medicare, 2011 Eligible for Medicare	Medicare, 2011 Enrolled in Medicare Advantage	Medicare, 2011 Enrolled in a Medicare prescription drug plan	Serious crimes known to police,[2] 2010 Total Number	Serious crimes known to police,[2] 2010 Total Rate[3]
	32	33	34	35	36	37	38	39	40	41	42	43	44	45
TEXAS—Cont'd														
Tom Green	5 165	107 604	1.0	1 667	15.7	996	9.4	23 417	25.7	18 435	1 296	7 682	4 914	4 458
Travis	23 046	1 086 572	1.2	16 469	17.1	4 455	4.6	220 429	23.6	95 301	11 353	34 617	55 135	5 383
Trinity	48	12 971	0.7	D	D	218	15.4	2 870	27.3	3 873	387	1 695	404	2 770
Tyler	2 448	19 803	0.7	D	D	239	11.7	4 204	26.0	4 452	565	1 998	520	2 389
Upshur	516	30 981	0.5	D	D	409	10.8	7 844	24.5	7 331	1 062	3 365	948	2 484
Upton	61	3 295	1.0	D	D	33	10.7	837	31.8	551	52	291	22	656
Uvalde	564	26 259	1.0	D	D	220	8.2	7 122	31.7	4 672	559	2 352	842	3 189
Val Verde	1 945	47 232	1.0	946	19.7	331	6.9	12 810	32.5	7 232	794	3 549	985	2 015
Van Zandt	667	43 639	0.6	633	12.1	629	12.0	12 422	29.7	10 650	1 297	5 018	1 139	2 166
Victoria	1 508	85 745	1.0	1 439	16.7	760	8.8	18 289	24.5	14 438	1 254	7 245	4 372	5 037
Walker	16 708	68 439	1.1	625	9.8	444	7.0	15 904	28.9	7 826	713	2 841	1 887	2 781
Waller	3 703	35 642	0.7	608	17.0	264	7.4	8 502	26.8	4 933	922	1 822	1 111	2 571
Ward	125	10 155	0.9	D	D	115	11.1	2 398	27.0	1 856	167	924	304	2 852
Washington	1 816	33 852	1.1	D	D	358	11.2	6 543	25.0	6 878	375	3 346	921	2 731
Webb	3 479	241 568	1.0	6 020	25.7	1 085	4.6	77 572	35.8	25 195	1 534	14 652	13 217	5 280
Wharton	449	38 464	0.9	640	15.6	380	9.3	9 494	27.6	6 952	552	3 618	1 246	3 018
Wheeler	46	5 844	1.3	D	D	65	13.6	1 138	28.8	1 034	40	560	85	1 571
Wichita	12 017	135 980	1.1	1 913	15.1	1 278	10.1	25 660	23.8	21 058	821	9 218	6 426	4 887
Wilbarger	615	13 969	1.1	D	D	178	12.7	3 025	26.6	2 543	90	1 178	444	3 280
Willacy	3 254	20 991	0.9	D	D	126	6.1	5 651	32.4	3 144	534	1 750	1 150	5 196
Williamson	5 097	336 465	0.7	6 210	16.6	1 647	4.4	60 438	16.5	46 309	8 354	14 905	9 806	2 320
Wilson	551	30 264	0.4	482	12.2	313	7.9	7 832	22.3	6 194	1 422	1 836	610	1 421
Winkler	97	6 869	1.0	D	D	76	11.5	1 735	29.9	1 063	86	531	99	1 392
Wise	980	52 991	0.8	795	13.7	462	8.0	13 107	25.4	8 630	1 290	3 525	932	1 576
Wood	1 103	39 011	0.8	D	D	546	13.0	8 781	27.2	11 739	1 481	5 374	807	1 923
Yoakum	53	8 215	1.2	D	D	50	6.6	1 994	29.7	1 093	34	653	120	1 523
Young	279	18 226	1.0	D	D	263	14.8	3 946	27.7	3 967	131	2 254	490	2 642
Zapata	30	13 965	1.1	D	D	73	5.4	4 176	34.8	1 657	83	943	316	2 254
Zavala	409	11 348	0.9	D	D	87	7.4	2 972	29.9	1 851	408	1 082	187	1 601
UTAH	46 152	2 656 569	1.0	54 756	20.6	13 982	5.3	397 794	15.9	296 116	103 791	83 263	93 759	3 392
Beaver	24	6 422	1.0	D	D	56	9.0	1 066	20.0	994	223	497	36	629
Box Elder	339	47 686	1.0	944	19.7	293	6.1	6 456	14.7	6 485	2 244	2 009	906	2 008
Cache	3 594	105 997	1.0	2 449	22.9	429	4.0	15 469	14.9	10 171	4 281	2 739	1 479	1 313
Carbon	544	21 293	1.1	D	D	211	10.8	2 312	13.6	3 684	454	1 906	653	3 248
Daggett	63	863	1.1	D	D	D	D	156	20.4	201	47	56	19	1 794
Davis	3 293	265 801	0.8	6 134	21.4	1 351	4.7	31 206	11.4	29 990	10 312	6 076	7 622	2 487
Duchesne	297	17 560	1.0	D	D	114	7.0	2 943	18.4	2 545	480	1 105	338	1 817
Emery	43	10 541	1.0	D	D	89	8.4	1 353	14.9	1 644	359	608	88	802
Garfield	171	4 947	1.0	D	D	39	8.5	666	17.7	884	192	296	NA	NA
Grand	143	9 461	1.1	D	D	72	7.9	1 838	22.4	1 510	211	615	375	4 065
Iron	1 050	44 218	1.0	964	22.5	267	6.2	7 331	18.4	5 673	1 657	1 859	1 183	2 728
Juab	122	8 925	0.8	D	D	66	6.8	1 425	15.9	1 255	272	497	250	2 440
Kane	100	6 707	0.9	D	D	70	10.7	1 066	20.3	1 504	301	584	59	828
Millard	122	12 181	1.0	D	D	96	7.9	2 095	20.1	1 965	472	687	251	2 008
Morgan	0	7 163	0.5	D	D	42	5.0	1 039	13.0	1 130	359	231	77	813
Piute	37	1 588	0.9	D	D	17	12.7	242	22.2	368	105	118	NA	NA
Rich	1	2 177	1.0	D	D	16	7.4	371	20.3	322	69	122	48	2 120
Salt Lake	14 006	1 069 175	1.1	19 444	19.4	5 413	5.4	158 989	17.0	108 290	42 376	31 196	51 186	4 973
San Juan	289	14 301	1.0	D	D	82	5.6	3 136	23.3	1 676	240	962	150	1 017
Sanpete	2 417	25 320	0.9	D	D	164	6.6	4 380	19.7	3 709	965	1 358	NA	NA
Sevier	301	20 534	1.0	355	17.9	194	9.8	2 667	15.8	3 430	962	1 363	548	2 634
Summit	116	38 988	1.2	D	D	125	3.5	4 942	14.4	3 526	1 055	1 017	946	2 604
Tooele	355	47 789	0.7	1 114	20.2	264	4.8	7 582	14.2	5 395	1 051	1 430	1 692	2 906
Uintah	192	31 396	1.0	642	22.2	195	6.7	6 037	21.2	3 319	714	1 327	849	2 605
Utah	13 912	466 991	0.9	12 181	24.7	1 874	3.8	70 493	14.1	40 293	16 773	10 037	12 017	2 326
Wasatch	250	19 190	0.7	413	20.0	94	4.5	3 570	18.8	2 345	805	670	242	1 028
Washington	1 853	134 117	1.0	2 744	20.7	889	6.7	21 684	19.6	24 973	7 805	7 432	2 824	2 045
Wayne	9	2 786	1.1	D	D	23	9.0	366	17.2	491	86	185	22	792
Weber	2 509	212 452	0.9	4 217	19.1	1 432	6.5	36 912	18.1	28 344	8 921	6 281	9 328	4 034
VERMONT	25 329	620 416	1.0	6 454	10.4	5 146	8.3	53 420	10.4	116 452	6 618	62 462	15 096	2 412
Addison	2 852	33 862	0.8	D	D	258	7.0	3 463	11.2	6 111	398	3 262	791	2 148
Bennington	1 475	39 223	1.1	D	D	405	11.1	3 009	10.5	8 328	465	4 827	817	2 201
Caledonia	1 345	29 628	0.9	D	D	275	9.0	2 888	11.6	6 058	351	3 310	599	1 918

1. Per 1,000 estimated resident population.   2. Data for serious crimes have not been adjusted for underreporting; this may affect comparability between geographic areas and over time.   3. Per 100,000 population estimated by the FBI.

Table B. States and Counties — Crime, Education, Money Income, and Poverty

STATE County	Serious crimes known to police,[1] 2010 (cont.) Rate[2] Violent	Property	Education: School enrollment and attainment, 2006–2010 Enrollment[3] Total	Per-cent private	Attainment[4] (percent) High school grad-uate or less	Bach-elor's degree or more	Local government expenditures,[5] 2008–2009 Total current expendi-tures (mil dol)	Current expendi-tures per student (dollars)	Money income, 2006–2010 Per capita income[6] (dollars)	Households Median income Dollars	Percent change, 2000 to 2006–2010 (constant 2010 dollars)	Percent with income of $200,000 or more	Income and poverty, 2010 Median house-hold income (dollars)	Percent below poverty level All per-sons	Children under 18 years	Children 5 to 17 years in families
	46	47	48	49	50	51	52	53	54	55	56	57	58	59	60	61
TEXAS—Cont'd																
Tom Green	277	4 181	28 269	8.4	48.6	21.6	154.4	8 544	22 292	41 398	-1.4	2.2	39 004	19.2	27.0	25.8
Travis	420	4 963	276 992	12.8	31.3	43.5	1 310.2	9 327	31 785	54 074	-8.7	6.2	51 905	18.8	24.5	22.9
Trinity	206	2 564	2 698	3.6	65.6	11.2	22.3	9 775	19 828	36 814	7.4	1.5	34 045	18.2	32.0	30.4
Tyler	436	1 953	4 027	5.9	57.5	12.2	34.6	9 566	19 450	35 346	-6.4	1.4	37 914	19.9	28.3	26.0
Upshur	183	2 301	8 926	12.7	51.7	15.1	61.0	8 620	21 946	44 403	5.2	1.8	42 508	16.3	25.5	23.0
Upton	60	596	584	0.9	62.6	12.7	11.8	17 014	23 112	49 234	34.2	1.3	47 407	15.7	23.2	22.1
Uvalde	273	2 916	7 949	5.8	54.7	16.1	55.2	9 051	17 842	35 087	2.0	2.0	31 941	26.4	42.3	36.7
Val Verde	178	1 837	13 285	6.8	61.6	15.8	81.1	7 834	16 615	36 993	3.0	0.5	36 647	26.8	39.8	36.4
Van Zandt	219	1 948	11 828	7.9	58.2	12.1	82.3	8 293	20 989	43 074	-2.9	1.1	41 476	16.8	23.6	21.5
Victoria	573	4 465	21 332	12.8	50.2	16.9	122.8	8 214	24 146	48 767	-0.6	3.0	46 566	18.2	28.0	25.8
Walker	363	2 418	20 954	4.3	53.7	17.1	64.5	9 353	13 920	34 259	-14.0	1.1	37 160	25.9	27.0	24.4
Waller	222	2 349	12 311	15.8	57.1	19.6	74.2	8 648	21 621	47 324	-2.0	3.2	46 313	20.4	28.1	26.4
Ward	582	2 271	2 537	2.2	63.2	10.0	19.7	9 245	20 055	41 117	10.5	1.6	41 625	20.1	27.4	24.9
Washington	276	2 456	8 379	15.0	50.7	25.8	44.4	8 404	25 464	43 159	-7.3	3.8	44 245	14.8	23.3	22.1
Webb	509	4 772	84 447	5.0	58.8	16.7	566.7	8 558	14 163	36 684	3.1	1.6	34 878	31.5	41.7	38.9
Wharton	414	2 604	10 919	8.1	58.5	15.4	74.5	9 302	21 049	41 148	0.9	1.5	36 097	19.1	26.6	23.9
Wheeler	259	1 312	1 138	1.7	58.2	15.1	13.5	13 195	27 282	42 909	9.2	4.0	41 228	13.6	21.1	20.1
Wichita	386	4 500	33 676	7.7	50.9	20.0	183.6	8 487	22 837	42 971	0.5	2.7	39 299	17.1	22.9	23.4
Wilbarger	458	2 822	3 318	3.2	59.8	15.9	22.1	8 852	19 916	40 105	7.4	1.5	38 913	17.1	25.6	24.1
Willacy	1 170	4 025	5 989	2.5	71.9	8.6	45.6	10 170	10 800	22 881	-18.3	0.6	28 307	36.9	46.8	45.4
Williamson	144	2 176	108 981	13.0	29.3	37.8	773.7	8 208	29 663	68 780	-10.4	3.4	66 152	7.9	11.0	9.8
Wilson	91	1 330	10 736	10.3	51.5	18.2	67.0	8 153	25 149	60 493	19.4	2.5	55 992	12.1	17.8	15.4
Winkler	183	1 210	1 807	5.0	65.3	9.8	20.3	12 600	19 309	41 828	8.0	1.0	45 237	16.4	22.9	22.1
Wise	238	1 338	14 507	7.8	54.1	15.6	81.6	9 118	24 075	55 207	4.0	2.6	52 117	12.5	17.8	16.0
Wood	117	1 806	9 081	17.9	54.8	16.5	47.6	9 075	21 682	41 277	-0.9	1.9	40 149	18.3	33.9	28.8
Yoakum	152	1 371	1 913	4.8	57.8	15.0	21.7	10 897	19 937	49 146	18.8	2.7	48 953	14.8	21.1	20.8
Young	178	2 464	4 013	7.1	56.8	13.6	28.6	8 264	24 656	36 900	-4.6	2.9	40 490	17.6	26.2	24.2
Zapata	264	1 990	3 932	1.7	72.4	9.6	35.2	9 549	13 915	24 496	-21.5	1.1	29 915	32.3	46.6	44.9
Zavala	377	1 225	3 341	1.0	61.5	7.7	28.8	11 483	10 180	21 707	1.8	0.0	22 948	36.9	51.2	48.3
UTAH	213	3 180	859 875	14.5	34.2	29.4	3 540.4	6 327	23 139	56 330	-2.7	3.0	54 740	13.3	15.9	14.9
Beaver	70	559	1 805	2.7	52.6	10.4	10.5	6 659	16 131	41 514	-5.1	1.2	44 077	13.4	18.2	15.3
Box Elder	135	1 873	15 220	8.5	41.5	22.7	70.3	6 241	20 465	55 135	-2.4	1.2	55 534	9.4	12.9	11.6
Cache	61	1 252	41 649	6.9	29.6	35.1	145.6	6 521	19 670	47 013	-6.6	2.0	47 367	15.8	16.4	15.4
Carbon	164	3 084	5 939	7.5	44.8	14.2	32.7	7 950	20 260	41 967	-2.6	1.0	45 244	15.1	19.2	17.6
Daggett	0	1 794	115	6.1	51.7	18.8	2.8	15 317	22 862	36 390	-6.8	1.1	41 248	6.3	5.6	5.1
Davis	110	2 377	97 831	9.0	27.7	33.8	425.0	6 126	25 244	66 866	-1.7	3.5	64 840	8.0	10.4	9.6
Duchesne	156	1 661	4 824	4.3	52.1	16.0	30.8	6 928	21 767	52 895	33.5	2.3	53 196	12.5	15.4	14.8
Emery	9	793	2 813	5.9	48.9	13.2	20.2	8 739	19 968	49 237	-2.4	0.4	51 205	11.6	16.2	15.4
Garfield	NA	NA	1 228	3.7	40.1	19.6	11.3	11 893	23 187	44 745	0.4	2.4	42 668	11.2	20.1	18.5
Grand	238	3 827	1 623	10.5	44.0	24.3	12.3	7 962	20 611	41 396	0.9	0.4	39 726	14.9	25.5	23.7
Iron	166	2 562	16 037	13.1	36.0	28.2	57.9	6 162	16 898	42 247	0.8	0.7	39 980	20.9	27.0	27.0
Juab	68	2 372	3 324	8.5	48.2	13.1	17.2	6 965	18 193	53 225	10.2	1.3	51 917	12.2	17.4	16.5
Kane	28	800	1 402	4.6	38.5	23.7	11.7	9 783	25 155	43 540	0.4	0.8	43 939	12.8	20.4	19.5
Millard	128	1 880	3 400	2.3	44.2	19.3	25.0	8 248	18 839	44 594	-2.7	1.2	45 810	13.9	20.1	18.6
Morgan	74	739	2 977	6.6	32.9	27.1	13.8	5 976	24 276	70 152	10.2	3.9	71 484	5.4	6.7	6.3
Piute	NA	NA	564	29.8	50.3	16.2	4.1	11 440	16 140	37 708	0.5	0.6	35 233	20.1	32.5	30.0
Rich	88	2 032	566	8.5	39.4	22.2	5.3	11 668	25 376	54 737	8.7	2.2	51 902	11.2	16.3	16.4
Salt Lake	374	4 599	300 269	13.1	35.6	30.1	1 203.7	6 285	25 041	58 004	-5.3	3.6	56 664	13.7	17.8	16.3
San Juan	75	943	4 552	5.9	51.1	17.2	36.1	12 142	15 150	38 076	6.9	0.7	37 259	25.2	27.5	25.3
Sanpete	NA	NA	9 491	11.0	42.7	18.7	40.4	7 507	15 731	42 395	1.3	1.5	39 999	18.4	21.6	20.7
Sevier	163	2 471	6 096	5.6	44.1	16.9	29.7	6 281	18 856	45 622	0.6	1.2	44 830	14.7	20.5	18.4
Summit	85	2 519	9 118	11.1	24.7	50.8	62.1	8 913	40 270	79 461	-3.4	10.8	74 535	7.6	11.9	10.7
Tooele	189	2 717	17 406	7.8	39.1	18.6	80.0	5 921	22 020	60 590	4.5	1.7	60 541	9.0	11.6	10.6
Uintah	181	2 424	8 527	7.1	52.6	14.7	41.9	6 535	24 160	59 730	36.7	3.1	54 090	14.3	17.2	17.0
Utah	88	2 239	192 153	27.4	24.8	35.5	655.1	5 770	20 210	56 927	-1.9	3.0	54 385	14.7	13.1	12.5
Wasatch	38	990	6 703	10.7	31.7	31.1	34.5	6 887	26 873	65 204	3.8	7.1	61 593	7.9	13.1	12.4
Washington	109	1 935	38 057	11.0	37.7	24.0	170.5	6 369	21 378	50 050	6.2	2.3	48 247	14.7	22.1	21.6
Wayne	180	612	645	3.9	41.0	22.7	5.3	9 176	19 829	49 414	21.9	1.1	42 456	15.1	22.0	19.4
Weber	203	3 831	65 541	9.8	40.7	22.5	284.5	6 344	22 849	54 086	-3.0	1.8	53 612	13.7	17.7	16.6
VERMONT	130	2 282	156 943	20.3	41.5	33.3	1 350.9	15 449	27 478	51 841	0.2	2.8	49 393	12.4	15.9	13.6
Addison	79	2 069	10 021	32.5	44.5	32.6	79.6	16 121	26 599	55 800	2.1	2.5	51 967	12.0	14.6	12.0
Bennington	172	2 028	8 544	25.3	43.2	31.1	70.3	16 661	27 962	47 396	-6.3	3.2	47 161	13.8	21.2	16.9
Caledonia	134	1 784	7 681	24.5	46.5	27.5	51.1	16 189	22 504	42 706	-3.1	1.2	40 219	16.1	21.8	19.0

1. Data for serious crimes have not been adjusted for underreporting; this may affect comparability between geographic areas and over time.   2. Per 100,000 population estimated by the FBI.   3. All persons 3 years old and over enrolled in nursery school through college.   4. Persons 25 years old and over.   5. Elementary and secondary education expenditures.   6. Based on population estimated by the American Community Survey, 2006–2010.

Table B. States and Counties — **Personal Income**

STATE County	Total (mil dol)	Percent change, 2008–2009	Per capita¹ Dollars	Per capita¹ Rank	Wages and salaries² (mil dol)	Proprietors' income (mil dol)	Dividends, interest, and rent (mil dol)	Transfer payments (mil dol) Total	Government payments to individuals Total	Social Security	Medical payments	Income mainte-nance	Unemploy-ment insurance
	62	63	64	65	66	67	68	69	70	71	72	73	74
TEXAS—Cont'd													
Tom Green	3 870	0.6	35 704	929	2 141	345	867	762	743	243	342	72	23
Travis	41 605	-0.9	40 544	418	35 593	4 451	8 413	4 076	3 889	1 274	1 494	462	243
Trinity	393	2.9	28 271	2 354	81	20	66	143	140	55	60	13	3
Tyler	609	2.0	29 623	2 071	161	34	85	184	180	64	85	15	6
Upshur	1 214	-0.7	31 891	1 553	279	59	173	300	293	102	136	26	10
Upton	123	-5.6	39 336	502	74	8	19	23	23	8	11	2	1
Uvalde	788	2.7	29 401	2 118	352	48	199	223	218	53	104	33	6
Val Verde	1 358	2.6	28 202	2 366	910	66	164	310	301	68	138	55	14
Van Zandt	1 725	-0.7	33 165	1 310	403	90	270	423	413	152	196	29	12
Victoria	3 349	-3.1	38 151	623	1 741	389	691	645	629	199	300	67	21
Walker	1 608	3.9	25 072	2 858	1 007	70	292	339	327	107	135	34	13
Waller	1 235	0.0	33 798	1 204	688	81	182	229	222	68	90	24	9
Ward	354	-5.4	33 632	1 231	193	43	51	77	75	26	35	8	3
Washington	1 322	0.9	40 185	438	621	98	380	275	269	93	122	20	7
Webb	5 624	1.0	23 294	3 020	3 424	593	655	1 418	1 374	243	630	339	54
Wharton	1 369	-0.5	33 400	1 278	574	130	256	307	300	94	147	30	10
Wheeler	193	-9.7	39 532	490	90	28	34	48	47	14	28	2	1
Wichita	4 837	-2.1	37 899	656	2 920	743	923	911	889	278	412	84	31
Wilbarger	464	3.1	34 287	1 129	292	33	80	117	115	33	59	10	3
Willacy	481	0.7	23 584	2 994	149	25	46	174	170	31	92	33	7
Williamson	14 801	-0.2	36 040	881	6 804	671	2 368	1 562	1 487	629	502	118	100
Wilson	1 307	1.8	32 067	1 512	241	42	177	242	234	77	102	21	8
Winkler	247	-8.2	36 425	825	134	38	27	52	50	15	27	5	2
Wise	2 008	-3.6	33 802	1 203	908	164	277	307	296	121	112	23	16
Wood	1 268	1.8	29 398	2 120	372	57	297	407	399	165	175	22	10
Yoakum	283	-9.4	36 793	774	181	52	44	46	45	14	22	4	2
Young	760	-2.4	42 742	283	314	156	168	161	158	55	82	11	4
Zapata	276	-0.8	19 638	3 099	169	13	45	89	87	17	44	18	4
Zavala	207	3.9	17 892	3 106	92	16	19	97	95	18	49	21	4
UTAH	87 947	-1.0	31 584	X	61 578	6 209	16 027	11 986	11 479	3 994	4 284	1 197	678
Beaver	184	9.4	29 359	2 128	129	7	32	39	38	13	16	3	2
Box Elder	1 407	-1.4	28 186	2 368	1 050	55	230	229	220	88	82	20	13
Cache	2 890	-0.5	25 071	2 859	1 967	125	524	434	413	140	147	44	22
Carbon	681	2.4	34 063	1 166	473	33	96	156	152	53	62	14	6
Daggett	24	2.1	25 211	2 841	17	1	6	6	6	3	2	0	0
Davis	9 959	-0.3	33 104	1 322	5 576	512	1 652	1 102	1 047	383	366	97	66
Duchesne	612	-8.0	34 107	1 153	418	22	77	98	95	33	39	10	6
Emery	283	5.3	26 599	2 624	221	6	34	60	58	25	22	5	3
Garfield	132	2.0	28 443	2 313	84	1	21	31	30	12	11	2	2
Grand	288	0.2	29 844	2 011	173	16	81	54	52	20	19	6	4
Iron	1 075	0.3	23 738	2 979	621	58	222	233	225	77	82	26	12
Juab	251	1.9	24 500	2 917	148	11	32	53	51	17	23	5	3
Kane	224	1.5	33 907	1 186	110	11	49	48	46	21	18	3	2
Millard	333	-7.6	27 112	2 546	208	24	56	66	64	26	25	6	3
Morgan	276	0.3	31 031	1 746	91	6	57	33	31	14	10	1	2
Piute	36	0.8	25 138	2 854	13	1	6	12	12	5	5	1	0
Rich	67	-1.8	31 231	1 705	27	1	17	10	10	4	3	1	1
Salt Lake	38 581	-1.1	37 276	716	32 315	3 317	7 011	4 643	4 455	1 514	1 711	472	263
San Juan	307	6.7	20 404	3 090	179	6	46	90	88	19	30	29	4
Sanpete	544	-1.8	20 963	3 082	276	8	85	144	140	51	55	14	6
Sevier	536	0.7	26 816	2 595	326	21	98	128	125	48	52	12	5
Summit	2 282	-2.8	61 719	26	922	150	652	119	112	51	30	6	10
Tooele	1 524	2.1	26 126	2 702	862	46	183	215	204	63	76	25	15
Uintah	916	-10.3	29 034	2 189	717	42	127	138	132	47	50	14	10
Utah	12 775	-1.1	23 428	3 008	8 118	1 181	2 112	1 826	1 727	561	646	190	103
Wasatch	618	-2.9	28 605	2 278	251	28	153	84	80	34	28	6	6
Washington	3 595	-1.7	26 147	2 696	1 903	206	930	798	773	339	268	60	39
Wayne	68	1.1	26 146	2 697	41	1	16	14	14	6	5	1	1
Weber	7 482	0.3	32 273	1 463	4 340	311	1 421	1 122	1 080	325	400	124	70
VERMONT	24 376	-0.3	39 205	X	14 815	1 808	4 447	4 990	4 876	1 580	2 204	490	265
Addison	1 311	-2.2	35 675	931	689	123	246	227	220	82	87	22	15
Bennington	1 508	-2.3	41 427	367	805	131	375	325	319	116	132	33	17
Caledonia	989	-0.3	32 701	1 384	504	104	154	240	234	78	94	30	15

1. Based on the resident population estimated as of July 1 of the year shown. 2. Includes supplements to wages and salaries.

Table B. States and Counties — Earnings, Social Security, and Housing

STATE County	Earnings, 2009 Total (mil dol)	Goods-related[1] Farm	Goods-related[1] Total	Goods-related[1] Manufacturing	Service-related and health: Information and professional and technical services	Retail trade	Finance, insurance, and real estate	Health care and social services	Government	Social Security beneficiaries, Dec 2010 Number	Rate[2]	Supplemental Security Income recipients, December 2010	Housing units, 2010 Total	Percent change, 2000–2010
	75	76	77	78	79	80	81	82	83	84	85	86	87	88
TEXAS—Cont'd														
Tom Green	2 486	0.0	19.5	8.3	7.2	6.8	6.2	15.2	28.0	20 470	186	2 863	46 571	6.0
Travis	40 044	0.0	17.7	11.1	19.6	5.0	7.6	9.4	19.3	100 250	98	16 162	441 240	31.4
Trinity	101	-0.5	D	8.5	D	7.1	D	D	26.8	4 380	300	618	8 713	7.0
Tyler	195	2.9	D	4.6	4.1	7.9	3.8	6.5	40.3	5 000	230	679	10 579	1.5
Upshur	338	0.0	18.5	5.1	9.9	7.6	4.4	D	24.6	8 430	214	1 158	16 613	11.3
Upton	82	1.6	D	D	D	1.9	0.9	0.9	25.5	625	186	84	1 548	-3.8
Uvalde	401	1.4	10.2	3.5	D	9.9	3.4	D	35.1	5 180	196	1 229	10 811	6.3
Val Verde	976	0.2	D	7.2	D	6.6	3.1	8.4	50.0	7 760	159	2 459	18 651	14.5
Van Zandt	493	5.8	21.0	4.6	D	7.8	4.1	10.6	22.2	12 030	229	1 177	22 817	9.2
Victoria	2 130	-0.1	28.1	9.9	5.1	9.8	5.3	15.8	15.1	16 235	187	2 559	35 417	7.5
Walker	1 077	0.7	8.0	5.3	4.0	6.4	2.9	D	58.0	8 460	125	1 192	24 058	14.0
Waller	769	1.8	34.2	25.2	5.7	8.8	2.2	3.1	24.1	5 380	125	770	15 839	32.5
Ward	236	-0.3	49.1	2.2	4.3	3.9	4.5	2.7	18.1	2 135	200	341	4 694	-2.9
Washington	719	0.6	30.5	20.1	5.7	8.7	8.7	9.1	19.2	7 355	218	888	15 514	17.2
Webb	4 018	0.2	10.1	0.8	4.3	8.3	4.6	10.8	31.2	27 860	111	11 656	73 496	33.1
Wharton	704	5.0	24.9	11.2	3.3	9.3	6.5	D	19.6	7 595	184	1 104	17 127	3.1
Wheeler	117	8.0	34.8	0.9	D	5.4	D	D	19.6	1 180	218	80	2 730	1.6
Wichita	3 663	0.0	27.7	11.4	4.7	6.0	4.5	12.6	30.5	23 335	177	3 699	55 566	4.2
Wilbarger	325	2.1	23.1	18.9	2.7	6.0	3.8	D	42.4	2 830	209	428	6 318	-0.8
Willacy	174	3.6	D	D	D	7.9	4.5	10.1	31.9	3 485	157	1 424	7 040	4.7
Williamson	7 474	0.2	14.2	5.4	9.0	8.2	7.7	8.8	15.3	49 360	117	3 521	162 773	80.2
Wilson	282	-1.4	D	5.2	5.2	10.4	5.6	D	34.6	6 895	161	783	16 766	38.4
Winkler	172	0.1	D	D	D	3.0	8.0	0.6	16.9	1 225	172	246	3 027	-5.8
Wise	1 072	-0.2	33.2	7.3	D	7.4	3.3	7.1	16.4	9 655	163	733	23 781	23.6
Wood	429	1.3	22.0	9.7	6.2	9.3	6.0	D	21.0	12 785	305	952	20 861	16.3
Yoakum	233	6.4	49.7	3.8	1.1	2.9	2.7	0.6	16.1	1 205	153	143	2 978	0.1
Young	470	-0.9	53.1	15.2	5.1	4.9	3.9	5.4	13.3	4 415	238	537	8 622	1.4
Zapata	182	-0.2	38.0	1.4	D	4.9	2.8	4.0	35.3	1 850	132	632	6 203	0.6
Zavala	107	9.6	D	D	D	5.1	D	12.3	92.5	2 165	185	929	4 283	5.1
UTAH	67 787	0.2	19.5	11.1	11.5	7.3	7.5	8.9	19.6	324 136	117	28 106	979 709	27.5
Beaver	136	20.1	18.8	2.4	D	5.8	1.6	2.9	22.9	1 085	164	63	2 908	9.3
Box Elder	1 105	1.6	57.6	52.0	1.6	6.7	1.6	4.6	11.6	7 250	145	421	17 326	21.9
Cache	2 092	0.6	29.9	25.0	7.0	7.1	3.4	9.0	25.1	11 225	100	756	37 024	27.5
Carbon	506	-0.2	D	4.1	D	7.4	2.3	D	20.2	4 205	196	446	9 551	9.3
Daggett	19	-0.5	D	D	D	D	D	D	0.9	220	208	0	1 141	5.3
Davis	8 088	0.2	D	9.0	9.9	6.4	3.8	7.5	35.9	32 055	105	2 126	97 570	31.6
Duchesne	440	-2.2	40.3	2.0	3.8	5.2	2.0	6.0	18.4	2 955	159	326	9 493	35.8
Emery	227	-2.2	D	0.5	4.6	4.8	1.0	D	17.9	1 920	175	140	4 489	8.4
Garfield	86	-2.8	D	1.5	D	4.7	D	D	36.7	1 005	194	40	3 726	34.7
Grand	189	-1.3	D	0.7	5.5	11.5	3.4	6.6	26.2	1 675	182	150	4 816	20.0
Iron	679	2.6	D	11.3	3.9	9.5	6.8	8.4	30.6	6 410	139	529	19 667	44.4
Juab	159	2.0	40.9	16.3	D	5.0	2.0	D	19.0	1 450	142	105	3 502	24.6
Kane	122	0.3	D	5.5	1.9	7.3	4.1	D	28.8	1 680	236	65	5 815	54.4
Millard	233	10.2	D	4.1	D	6.4	D	D	21.9	2 205	176	131	4 939	9.2
Morgan	97	-1.5	D	13.3	D	6.6	3.4	D	18.6	1 160	123	35	3 006	39.3
Piute	15	12.3	D	0.0	D	D	D	D	39.6	420	270	20	898	20.5
Rich	28	3.4	D	D	D	6.3	D	D	32.7	360	159	14	2 834	17.7
Salt Lake	35 632	0.0	18.0	10.3	12.6	7.1	10.2	8.4	16.5	118 000	115	12 089	364 031	17.1
San Juan	185	-1.6	20.4	2.5	D	3.9	1.1	D	42.8	1 865	126	608	5 734	5.2
Sanpete	285	-2.2	17.6	9.5	D	9.1	3.5	D	40.6	4 325	155	311	10 379	31.7
Sevier	347	-0.8	18.7	4.7	4.5	11.9	3.0	D	23.2	3 970	191	282	8 449	20.4
Summit	1 073	0.3	14.7	3.9	9.3	9.9	9.8	6.4	12.9	3 745	103	94	26 545	51.8
Tooele	908	0.7	14.6	9.9	D	5.1	1.8	5.2	35.6	5 945	102	594	19 455	40.9
Uintah	759	0.1	36.0	1.0	4.1	7.0	4.5	4.9	18.9	3 860	118	313	11 972	32.4
Utah	9 299	0.3	17.5	11.0	19.2	7.7	4.7	10.1	14.3	45 590	88	4 021	148 350	42.2
Wasatch	279	-1.1	19.7	4.3	9.9	7.8	5.5	7.7	24.5	2 695	115	96	10 577	61.1
Washington	2 109	-0.2	15.2	5.1	D	11.4	5.3	17.9	17.5	27 245	197	1 083	57 734	58.3
Wayne	42	1.5	D	0.7	D	4.8	D	D	34.1	540	194	0	1 591	19.7
Weber	4 651	0.0	D	15.7	5.2	8.1	5.8	12.5	25.5	29 075	126	3 231	86 187	22.3
VERMONT	16 623	0.7	19.7	12.9	9.8	7.9	5.6	14.7	19.3	128 619	206	15 265	322 539	9.6
Addison	812	3.7	21.3	14.8	7.2	9.1	3.4	D	12.6	6 735	183	631	16 760	9.4
Bennington	936	0.1	D	18.4	8.3	12.0	4.1	18.4	12.4	9 255	249	1 126	20 922	7.8
Caledonia	608	0.5	D	14.3	9.9	8.6	3.5	14.4	17.8	6 680	214	942	15 942	9.9

1. Includes mining, construction, and manufacturing.   2. Per 1,000 resident population enumerated in the 2010 census.

Table B. States and Counties — Housing, Labor Force, and Employment

STATE County	Housing units, 2006–2010								Civilian labor force, 2010				Civilian employment,[5] 2006–2010		
	Occupied units										Unemployment			Percent	
	Owner-occupied					Renter-occupied									
				Median owner cost as a percent of income											
	Total	Percent	Median value[1]	With a mort-gage	Without a mort-gage	Median rent[2]	Median rent as a per-cent of income	Sub-stand-ard units[3] (percent)	Total	Percent change, 2009–2010	Total	Rate[4]	Total	Manage-ment, business, science and arts	Con-struction, produc-tion, and mainte-nance occu-pations
	89	90	91	92	93	94	95	96	97	98	99	100	101	102	103
TEXAS—Cont'd															
Tom Green	41 464	67.9	88 600	21.5	12.4	655	29.7	3.3	53 884	2.3	3 448	6.4	48 386	29.1	23.3
Travis	390 862	52.6	200 300	24.2	12.4	891	30.2	4.4	560 967	2.1	38 797	6.9	522 183	43.8	16.3
Trinity	5 124	81.1	73 800	20.9	13.2	510	29.7	2.0	5 920	-0.6	522	8.8	5 003	22.3	28.7
Tyler	8 113	81.7	71 100	20.2	11.9	568	28.9	4.2	8 610	0.8	915	10.6	6 844	30.2	33.6
Upshur	14 668	77.8	86 100	20.4	10.3	597	24.8	5.2	20 160	0.2	1 577	7.8	16 830	25.8	33.4
Upton	1 179	78.8	42 800	17.7	10.0	502	14.8	3.6	1 856	2.2	93	5.0	1 307	26.9	33.7
Uvalde	8 824	73.5	64 400	22.3	13.7	663	24.6	12.3	11 720	2.2	1 065	9.1	10 760	26.2	30.6
Val Verde	15 042	65.7	81 000	21.6	13.5	584	29.5	6.6	21 248	0.1	1 933	9.1	18 779	26.1	27.6
Van Zandt	19 559	78.1	95 900	22.6	13.3	677	29.1	4.6	25 960	-1.3	1 978	7.6	21 880	28.0	30.7
Victoria	31 917	66.2	98 200	21.0	11.9	677	29.2	4.3	45 957	1.4	3 366	7.3	40 372	29.8	29.1
Walker	19 902	58.0	106 100	22.4	13.7	699	36.2	2.2	28 132	0.7	2 138	7.6	21 051	30.6	19.2
Waller	13 499	68.6	117 900	26.3	13.1	743	29.8	5.1	16 719	0.5	1 494	8.9	18 996	29.3	31.9
Ward	3 790	74.0	45 200	18.1	10.6	531	23.9	2.0	5 015	-1.7	401	8.0	4 393	24.2	34.4
Washington	12 855	69.4	135 500	24.6	11.7	725	32.2	2.6	17 106	-0.4	1 101	6.4	14 268	30.3	26.3
Webb	64 714	64.6	104 000	28.3	14.8	690	33.9	17.1	95 694	1.3	8 273	8.6	96 301	24.9	23.0
Wharton	14 808	69.3	85 800	19.9	13.8	616	30.3	5.0	21 225	-0.7	1 829	8.6	19 308	27.7	34.6
Wheeler	2 113	79.0	65 300	21.6	10.0	587	34.0	2.8	3 264	0.2	153	4.7	2 351	28.1	37.9
Wichita	48 601	64.1	87 400	22.1	12.7	681	30.0	3.0	61 884	0.6	4 938	8.0	56 578	28.1	25.1
Wilbarger	5 201	60.9	57 500	19.2	13.1	609	28.4	3.7	7 941	0.8	485	6.1	5 702	27.1	28.9
Willacy	5 485	71.1	46 200	24.4	16.8	585	26.3	11.2	9 187	10.9	1 141	12.4	5 848	22.6	18.4
Williamson	142 110	70.3	172 200	23.6	12.5	977	27.7	2.6	214 801	3.3	15 931	7.4	197 039	44.7	15.6
Wilson	14 455	84.5	124 100	20.5	10.5	703	24.9	3.8	19 388	1.6	1 426	7.4	20 026	35.0	27.3
Winkler	2 521	81.7	38 900	16.7	10.2	573	18.9	2.9	3 362	-3.1	263	7.8	2 649	21.6	45.1
Wise	19 712	81.0	119 900	22.5	12.8	814	24.5	2.9	28 288	-0.7	2 306	8.2	26 947	26.6	33.9
Wood	16 026	81.4	94 800	21.9	12.6	643	24.5	2.6	18 416	-1.7	1 578	8.6	15 848	25.6	31.5
Yoakum	2 596	85.2	61 000	15.9	11.0	576	18.3	5.5	4 008	-3.0	253	6.3	3 392	25.0	46.0
Young	7 484	69.1	69 400	20.0	14.0	620	26.1	4.0	9 727	-0.3	655	6.7	8 237	21.0	35.7
Zapata	4 341	75.9	47 100	18.1	14.1	518	36.5	16.5	5 514	2.5	604	11.0	4 750	25.0	35.2
Zavala	3 558	67.8	36 900	23.4	16.9	376	34.3	9.1	4 039	3.2	630	15.6	3 863	16.6	31.5
UTAH	859 158	71.2	218 100	24.5	10.0	781	28.2	3.9	1 361 756	-1.6	109 041	8.0	1 236 803	34.7	22.7
Beaver	2 091	76.7	150 200	21.1	13.4	677	37.3	5.6	3 343	-6.7	319	9.5	2 467	24.4	32.2
Box Elder	15 612	81.5	162 000	22.6	10.0	593	22.4	2.4	22 185	-4.0	2 005	9.0	21 028	32.0	31.0
Cache	33 820	63.9	180 300	24.1	10.0	656	28.1	4.5	62 689	1.5	3 569	5.7	52 061	34.8	24.1
Carbon	7 966	70.8	109 200	21.3	11.5	542	27.9	2.5	10 400	-1.3	848	8.2	8 776	27.2	33.8
Daggett	352	64.2	181 800	24.2	10.0	718	25.0	0.9	486	2.3	34	7.0	356	31.2	17.4
Davis	90 607	78.3	224 400	23.7	10.0	820	26.5	2.3	145 411	0.3	10 275	7.1	134 025	39.1	19.9
Duchesne	6 521	74.4	162 600	22.1	10.0	663	27.7	4.9	9 784	-6.0	786	8.0	7 241	27.9	35.0
Emery	3 779	80.9	105 500	18.0	10.0	594	18.8	5.6	5 279	0.7	411	7.8	4 750	26.8	40.0
Garfield	2 136	79.5	129 900	21.4	10.0	449	10.9	3.9	2 991	4.3	307	10.3	2 643	38.1	21.1
Grand	3 719	69.0	194 100	23.8	10.0	729	27.7	4.5	5 422	0.8	586	10.8	4 486	28.7	23.0
Iron	15 155	63.2	204 600	28.5	10.6	643	28.6	6.5	20 434	-1.7	1 964	9.6	19 016	31.1	23.5
Juab	3 045	82.7	163 300	22.0	10.0	699	25.3	5.4	3 982	0.7	418	10.5	4 192	24.2	36.4
Kane	3 065	76.2	174 500	21.4	10.0	551	20.8	2.0	3 527	0.1	289	8.2	3 260	32.3	22.8
Millard	4 046	76.6	121 100	20.6	10.0	502	25.7	4.4	6 431	-0.7	419	6.5	5 103	25.8	35.7
Morgan	2 714	88.2	260 600	26.0	10.0	600	16.7	0.4	4 111	1.7	305	7.4	4 092	35.3	26.1
Piute	539	89.1	163 500	21.0	12.4	580	21.0	5.4	804	-10.0	61	7.6	569	36.2	26.9
Rich	762	88.3	120 300	22.0	10.0	820	23.3	2.8	1 316	-11.1	75	5.7	1 101	34.9	34.4
Salt Lake	335 075	68.5	237 500	24.7	10.0	818	28.8	4.0	556 793	0.5	41 312	7.4	499 497	34.6	21.7
San Juan	4 331	78.2	108 000	21.8	10.0	568	24.2	17.5	5 419	2.9	720	13.3	5 076	29.2	29.3
Sanpete	7 870	77.2	148 700	24.7	10.5	524	27.0	5.4	10 950	-3.1	1 032	9.4	10 435	29.1	30.7
Sevier	6 937	81.3	148 300	21.5	10.0	609	23.9	4.0	9 881	0.3	818	8.3	8 539	29.3	30.2
Summit	13 600	74.4	492 100	24.8	10.0	957	29.0	2.5	22 379	1.8	1 688	7.5	19 066	44.0	16.2
Tooele	17 718	75.6	183 000	22.6	10.0	752	26.5	3.1	28 325	1.7	2 308	8.1	24 724	30.4	26.5
Uintah	10 474	75.1	183 100	21.3	10.0	911	25.0	3.8	17 316	-1.9	1 250	7.2	14 091	25.2	36.2
Utah	135 620	69.4	233 800	25.7	10.0	773	29.3	4.7	223 128	0.8	17 231	7.7	211 786	37.9	19.3
Wasatch	7 154	77.9	317 900	27.0	10.0	888	27.0	4.6	10 065	0.7	924	9.2	10 718	36.6	23.1
Washington	45 895	70.9	240 900	28.5	10.0	880	30.1	4.7	58 965	-1.7	5 962	10.1	53 472	30.9	25.0
Wayne	899	78.4	167 500	21.4	10.0	625	18.6	6.0	1 460	-1.3	136	9.3	1 327	34.9	23.7
Weber	77 656	72.6	168 300	23.7	10.0	702	26.5	2.7	114 776	0.3	9 917	8.6	102 906	30.7	27.0
VERMONT	256 612	71.4	208 400	25.7	16.4	809	30.8	2.0	359 844	-0.1	23 059	6.4	329 676	39.0	21.2
Addison	14 080	75.6	219 000	25.1	15.3	831	30.2	2.3	21 786	-0.2	1 291	5.9	19 717	39.3	25.5
Bennington	15 559	72.6	198 800	25.6	16.2	720	30.1	2.3	20 656	-0.4	1 439	7.0	18 898	35.6	23.4
Caledonia	12 581	71.4	154 200	24.3	16.5	601	28.6	2.8	16 675	-1.0	1 183	7.1	15 574	34.9	24.0

1. Specified owner-occupied units. 2. Specified renter-occupied units. A value of 10.0 represents 10 percent or less. 3. Overcrowded or lacking complete plumbing facilities. 4. Percent of civilian labor force. 5. Persons 16 years old and over.

Table B. States and Counties — Nonfarm Employment and Agriculture

STATE County	Private nonfarm establishments, employment and payroll, 2009									Agriculture, 2007			
		Employment						Annual payroll		Farms			
												Percent with:	
	Number of establishments	Total	Health care and social assistance	Manufacturing	Retail trade	Finance and insurance	Professional, scientific, and technical services	Total (mil dol)	Average per employee (dollars)	Number	Fewer than 50 acres	500 acres or more	Farm operators whose principal occupation is farming (percent)
	104	105	106	107	108	109	110	111	112	113	114	115	116
TEXAS—Cont'd													
Tom Green	2 600	36 046	7 021	2 967	6 176	1 509	1 188	1 050	29 116	1 180	45.2	24.7	37.5
Travis	27 776	473 672	53 744	30 396	53 878	24 209	57 031	22 486	47 472	1 214	51.4	8.9	36.0
Trinity	190	1 876	342	214	D	D	41	43	22 869	576	35.4	8.7	43.8
Tyler	261	2 397	561	86	653	D	D	55	22 964	792	55.6	4.4	37.1
Upshur	474	4 176	567	D	791	224	186	117	27 983	1 507	48.6	4.8	38.0
Upton	80	760	D	0	72	D	D	31	40 763	110	19.1	49.1	43.6
Uvalde	575	6 561	1 394	787	1 284	266	161	161	24 602	690	22.9	34.8	48.4
Val Verde	772	9 989	2 944	273	2 126	547	160	213	21 324	402	46.8	34.1	40.5
Van Zandt	818	7 484	1 191	827	1 501	258	218	211	28 245	3 253	51.6	5.1	40.3
Victoria	2 243	31 855	6 473	2 116	5 804	1 205	831	1 041	32 675	1 351	41.7	14.4	38.3
Walker	904	11 544	2 139	1 143	2 266	368	518	296	25 601	1 188	51.7	7.3	42.1
Waller	680	9 734	979	2 839	1 344	D	341	381	39 155	1 640	58.4	7.4	38.7
Ward	268	2 474	238	D	287	87	43	92	37 336	119	37.8	29.4	31.1
Washington	861	12 243	1 703	2 680	2 107	760	270	369	30 161	2 399	42.8	4.8	39.2
Webb	4 695	64 376	12 699	687	12 649	2 618	1 485	1 574	24 451	663	15.7	41.3	34.1
Wharton	946	11 361	1 946	1 697	2 049	447	363	324	28 541	1 506	39.0	21.0	47.3
Wheeler	184	1 538	377	D	237	D	D	43	27 883	507	8.5	41.4	39.6
Wichita	3 226	46 441	10 209	5 133	7 728	1 881	1 281	1 366	29 422	658	42.6	13.8	36.8
Wilbarger	305	3 759	536	D	685	133	D	105	27 949	461	13.4	35.4	51.0
Willacy	203	2 864	1 265	D	D	83	D	69	24 157	352	39.5	27.3	51.7
Williamson	7 846	120 066	11 778	6 470	21 914	7 993	5 284	5 410	45 061	2 728	51.4	8.5	37.0
Wilson	500	4 647	1 247	345	884	D	146	113	24 338	2 570	38.5	7.4	39.6
Winkler	156	1 348	D	0	166	D	D	52	38 363	53	35.8	39.6	49.1
Wise	1 230	16 439	2 274	1 405	2 243	408	338	615	37 390	3 164	58.0	5.0	35.0
Wood	831	7 425	963	D	1 361	387	194	212	28 503	1 718	46.7	5.4	40.7
Yoakum	177	2 116	D	34	184	60	20	88	41 412	348	6.6	54.0	53.7
Young	599	6 008	951	910	890	227	218	198	32 965	806	17.7	25.3	35.7
Zapata	178	2 194	290	29	302	88	14	59	26 684	459	8.9	46.8	41.0
Zavala	102	1 846	D	D	D	52	20	34	18 305	311	11.6	48.2	41.2
UTAH	69 464	1 059 722	117 747	110 538	139 792	63 831	66 916	37 848	35 715	16 700	55.8	13.2	38.0
Beaver	174	1 447	D	D	309	44	D	38	26 294	229	37.6	22.8	52.0
Box Elder	1 031	16 635	1 238	D	1 789	305	262	707	42 512	1 113	45.6	22.4	42.6
Cache	3 037	37 432	4 916	11 078	5 327	1 125	2 175	1 074	28 696	1 195	50.5	8.4	36.1
Carbon	519	7 234	951	539	1 275	171	221	240	33 177	294	58.5	16.7	35.4
Daggett	22	98	D	D	D	0	D	3	30 429	48	33.3	22.9	37.5
Davis	6 257	74 246	9 258	8 350	13 029	3 433	6 372	2 321	31 261	496	83.1	1.4	38.5
Duchesne	635	6 045	D	165	765	107	105	236	39 112	879	38.5	13.4	37.8
Emery	216	2 696	113	D	520	57	112	127	46 934	545	42.9	17.1	32.8
Garfield	142	1 122	209	D	123	D	13	35	31 035	275	43.3	13.5	45.8
Grand	430	3 378	D	46	641	58	137	91	26 806	90	55.6	17.8	54.4
Iron	1 273	11 624	1 687	1 291	2 253	414	507	283	24 385	487	40.9	22.8	41.7
Juab	182	2 251	D	560	377	43	D	59	26 383	335	27.2	27.2	30.4
Kane	264	2 156	192	88	366	46	D	62	28 912	145	33.1	30.3	37.2
Millard	241	2 723	228	395	577	80	D	102	37 493	703	26.2	31.7	47.8
Morgan	233	1 441	63	D	D	48	62	49	34 143	316	53.5	15.2	30.7
Piute	23	101	D	0	D	D	0	2	17 079	113	21.2	26.5	59.3
Rich	75	354	D	D	43	D	D	13	36 520	167	28.1	45.5	53.9
Salt Lake	29 003	503 630	55 992	47 620	59 840	38 011	33 461	20 511	40 727	587	79.6	6.0	32.7
San Juan	279	2 548	467	110	425	98	97	65	25 661	758	70.3	14.8	60.9
Sanpete	425	4 552	884	858	1 011	134	60	105	23 046	879	45.4	14.3	43.1
Sevier	507	5 845	648	D	1 389	140	157	171	29 227	655	57.9	9.2	34.5
Summit	2 045	23 908	771	D	3 751	657	822	602	25 172	629	57.7	11.0	29.9
Tooele	753	10 174	1 112	1 466	1 780	225	1 593	372	36 575	379	59.4	17.2	34.3
Uintah	1 146	10 111	673	D	1 819	215	389	381	37 665	981	51.6	12.0	30.5
Utah	10 624	155 202	18 673	15 130	22 599	4 533	12 816	5 150	33 181	2 175	75.9	5.3	34.0
Wasatch	720	4 707	541	201	719	148	384	118	25 093	432	71.8	4.9	28.2
Washington	3 974	39 405	6 949	2 150	7 689	1 334	1 852	1 083	27 480	593	60.4	13.2	31.0
Wayne	82	717	D	D	127	D	17	17	24 247	201	23.4	11.9	53.7
Weber	4 994	71 286	10 128	11 073	11 040	4 400	4 111	2 306	32 354	1 001	78.3	2.3	33.8
VERMONT	21 567	264 766	48 986	32 504	38 752	12 531	20 779	9 085	34 314	6 984	35.8	7.6	49.6
Addison	1 177	12 252	2 100	1 858	1 987	316	470	408	33 316	773	35.3	12.8	52.8
Bennington	1 496	14 006	2 071	2 369	3 032	336	387	437	31 186	226	42.9	6.6	44.2
Caledonia	922	9 248	1 775	1 647	1 743	338	457	297	32 146	531	35.0	5.5	48.4

STATE County	Agriculture, 2007 (cont.)															
	Land in farms					Value of land and buildings (dollars)		Value of machinery and equipment, average per farm (dollars)	Value of products sold				Percent of farms with sales of:		Government payments	
			Acres								Percent from:					
	Acreage (1,000)	Percent change, 2002–2007	Average size of farm	Total irrigated (1,000)	Total cropland (1,000)	Average per farm	Average per acre		Total (mil dol)	Average per farm (dollars)	Crops	Live-stock and poultry products	$10,000 or more	$100,000 or more	Total ($1,000)	Percent of farms
	117	118	119	120	121	122	123	124	125	126	127	128	129	130	131	132
TEXAS—Cont'd																
Tom Green	924	9.3	783	33.7	228.0	844 202	1 079	79 066	133.0	112 704	37.6	62.4	26.9	12.5	5 800	25.8
Travis	262	-12.1	216	1.6	76.0	612 252	2 832	46 601	22.8	18 808	67.5	32.5	20.7	4.0	1 036	14.3
Trinity	109	3.8	189	0.3	27.3	363 908	1 923	58 355	9.2	16 026	13.7	86.3	34.4	2.1	D	0.7
Tyler	84	5.0	106	0.4	19.7	298 244	2 804	49 342	21.8	27 479	D	D	14.9	0.5	217	5.3
Upshur	198	1.0	131	1.5	60.2	339 710	2 584	44 425	48.9	32 481	9.9	90.1	20.0	3.6	182	2.3
Upton	635	-12.2	5 768	7.3	32.0	2 956 855	513	103 983	8.6	77 940	72.7	27.3	38.2	19.1	1 325	34.5
Uvalde	990	2.2	1 482	45.3	131.4	1 558 967	1 087	100 482	77.7	112 588	40.9	59.1	28.1	10.9	2 749	22.0
Val Verde	1 494	-10.1	3 716	2.3	24.8	1 697 190	457	54 411	12.0	29 791	3.4	96.6	19.9	5.5	737	10.9
Van Zandt	416	-1.4	128	5.5	141.8	389 067	3 043	49 569	95.2	29 253	51.3	48.7	27.5	2.7	219	3.2
Victoria	494	-3.9	366	2.8	134.1	566 841	1 551	63 405	43.4	32 142	54.1	45.9	29.2	5.6	2 645	17.7
Walker	224	8.7	189	0.9	37.1	462 208	2 451	57 851	26.9	22 651	52.5	47.5	20.8	1.7	32	0.7
Waller	271	-2.2	165	9.9	103.5	545 765	3 303	59 849	55.1	33 611	66.3	33.7	24.4	4.5	1 696	9.1
Ward	433	-7.1	3 638	1.6	22.9	1 347 150	370	46 873	1.5	12 852	31.3	68.7	28.6	2.5	243	12.6
Washington	338	-4.8	141	1.4	90.4	523 071	3 708	51 773	44.8	18 679	23.0	77.0	28.8	2.3	110	4.1
Webb	1 856	-9.2	2 799	5.1	58.8	2 090 515	747	57 689	24.7	37 298	1.2	98.8	26.4	5.4	298	5.0
Wharton	616	-3.4	409	61.7	376.0	721 807	1 765	108 858	240.2	159 493	60.8	39.2	44.2	18.9	12 968	44.1
Wheeler	584	9.4	1 151	14.1	151.1	782 659	680	65 934	129.5	255 380	6.1	93.9	39.6	10.1	3 608	60.9
Wichita	331	9.6	503	6.7	129.5	487 974	971	59 809	27.2	41 407	57.9	42.1	30.9	7.9	1 853	29.3
Wilbarger	614	-29.6	1 332	15.5	237.3	982 831	738	95 736	42.9	93 102	66.6	33.4	54.4	23.2	5 072	69.0
Willacy	338	-8.6	960	18.5	196.4	1 146 610	1 194	144 505	51.2	145 453	90.2	9.8	44.9	25.6	6 422	58.8
Williamson	542	-7.0	199	1.0	229.7	559 150	2 816	48 657	190.4	69 792	28.6	71.4	23.6	5.1	5 108	25.7
Wilson	467	4.7	182	13.5	153.9	429 236	2 361	45 025	52.9	20 590	29.4	70.6	22.6	2.4	1 699	16.6
Winkler	533	8.3	10 054	0.2	D	2 637 615	262	64 310	3.3	61 545	D	D	37.7	13.2	67	9.4
Wise	443	-10.1	140	2.5	134.0	441 108	3 152	43 677	41.1	12 983	33.1	66.9	21.7	2.1	344	5.9
Wood	234	2.6	136	1.9	71.7	394 364	2 898	51 757	104.0	60 550	13.3	86.7	29.1	5.2	171	5.0
Yoakum	444	-2.4	1 275	101.1	281.9	1 077 712	846	198 120	90.1	258 995	90.1	9.9	46.6	36.8	11 394	78.7
Young	527	3.3	654	D	127.8	822 775	1 258	59 948	21.2	26 321	26.4	73.6	33.0	5.6	1 367	25.7
Zapata	459	15.3	1 001	2.0	45.8	920 368	919	63 172	13.1	28 541	D	D	27.0	2.2	149	4.8
Zavala	752	6.4	2 418	26.1	101.5	2 544 549	1 052	84 687	59.8	192 187	30.9	69.1	36.0	16.4	1 206	19.6
UTAH	11 095	-5.4	664	1 134.1	1 837.9	829 816	1 249	75 365	1 415.7	84 771	26.3	73.7	34.9	9.7	22 759	17.7
Beaver	158	13.7	691	29.9	35.4	1 608 052	2 326	137 667	210.6	919 807	4.0	96.0	60.3	31.9	233	26.2
Box Elder	1 320	-5.8	1 186	112.1	327.7	1 087 702	917	106 044	141.2	126 903	35.8	64.2	49.6	19.3	6 343	42.1
Cache	252	2.0	211	80.2	143.7	661 074	3 140	92 952	136.1	113 861	17.9	82.1	44.5	14.3	2 537	36.2
Carbon	216	8.5	733	14.8	22.8	784 277	1 070	52 777	5.1	17 364	16.5	83.5	24.8	5.4	242	7.8
Daggett	D	D	D	9.2	8.6	690 141	1 578	95 709	1.7	35 530	27.0	73.1	45.8	6.3	12	8.3
Davis	49	-25.8	99	12.2	12.4	533 777	5 373	65 164	37.2	75 093	84.0	16.0	27.2	8.1	78	10.1
Duchesne	1 076	-17.5	1 225	102.0	93.4	809 965	661	78 236	34.4	39 166	18.7	81.3	43.1	8.2	469	10.2
Emery	205	NA	376	41.8	58.6	484 195	1 289	63 677	11.3	20 778	19.4	80.6	37.4	3.9	376	18.7
Garfield	82	2.5	298	22.3	17.4	782 863	2 630	77 121	6.1	22 310	18.3	81.7	31.3	5.5	111	5.8
Grand	D	D	D	4.7	8.0	1 022 079	419	69 638	2.6	28 362	37.0	63.0	36.7	7.8	57	7.8
Iron	492	2.7	1 011	59.1	87.6	1 622 977	1 606	105 129	70.5	144 831	59.9	40.1	41.9	14.6	460	15.0
Juab	260	-3.7	777	27.1	65.7	913 824	1 175	92 017	19.8	59 152	42.5	57.5	35.8	8.4	1 098	47.8
Kane	113	-27.6	782	4.3	8.7	1 167 784	1 493	51 145	9.4	65 080	3.0	97.0	33.8	4.8	193	11.0
Millard	567	27.4	806	103.3	153.7	952 187	1 181	116 556	137.8	196 024	30.5	69.5	58.9	20.8	2 114	40.7
Morgan	301	NA	953	13.8	23.4	1 305 632	1 370	57 621	11.9	37 573	11.9	88.1	30.4	7.3	285	7.3
Piute	42	NA	375	16.9	19.5	1 055 538	2 814	159 699	12.3	108 566	2.5	97.5	61.9	15.9	153	26.5
Rich	364	-28.5	2 177	51.8	76.5	1 761 002	809	115 904	17.0	101 628	4.6	95.4	63.5	31.1	403	16.2
Salt Lake	107	30.5	183	9.9	29.1	594 651	3 248	48 495	21.4	36 423	83.6	16.4	18.6	3.7	81	1.9
San Juan	1 547	-0.8	2 041	5.2	143.2	736 197	361	35 193	10.3	13 588	42.6	57.4	12.4	3.8	2 033	26.6
Sanpete	312	-12.6	354	70.8	98.2	778 418	2 196	95 990	129.3	147 047	8.6	91.4	42.5	14.4	1 728	20.1
Sevier	186	12.7	284	52.5	42.6	562 086	1 983	74 184	50.7	77 439	24.8	75.2	35.1	10.8	367	14.0
Summit	415	10.4	660	24.0	30.7	948 930	1 439	53 954	25.4	40 415	6.2	93.8	31.2	8.7	207	6.2
Tooele	253	-39.0	667	24.5	23.4	1 093 601	1 639	68 992	32.7	86 156	23.3	76.7	27.7	7.1	106	6.9
Uintah	1 800	NA	1 835	84.5	83.2	977 970	533	67 209	33.1	33 789	25.3	74.7	32.4	6.1	620	8.4
Utah	346	0.9	159	77.5	117.8	679 389	4 275	62 282	181.7	83 554	37.9	62.1	27.8	6.0	1 452	9.3
Wasatch	66	-5.7	153	17.4	13.5	731 866	4 795	59 413	8.0	18 578	16.9	83.1	19.9	4.2	61	3.0
Washington	174	-19.8	294	13.8	42.8	915 375	3 116	56 838	9.8	16 587	39.0	61.0	26.1	3.4	268	10.3
Wayne	45	7.1	225	18.9	19.2	614 413	2 731	98 590	15.4	76 551	6.7	93.3	63.2	13.4	254	49.8
Weber	106	21.8	106	29.6	31.3	525 416	4 950	58 846	32.7	32 648	36.4	63.6	22.2	5.2	418	8.5
VERMONT	1 233	-1.0	177	2.3	516.9	512 684	2 903	74 500	673.7	96 465	14.7	85.3	41.1	15.4	6 773	19.3
Addison	187	-3.1	243	0.4	116.1	636 913	2 626	111 549	161.4	208 819	9.1	90.9	51.4	24.7	1 059	33.1
Bennington	37	-9.8	162	0.2	13.2	596 966	3 688	70 462	10.5	46 542	30.2	69.8	35.4	6.6	63	8.4
Caledonia	82	-2.4	154	0.0	30.8	407 288	2 639	66 406	31.5	59 401	11.8	88.2	36.7	13.0	328	16.2

Table B. States and Counties — Water Use, Wholesale Trade, Retail Trade, and Real Estate

STATE County	Water use, 2005 Total water withdrawn (mil gal/day)	Gallons withdrawn per person	Wholesale trade,[1] 2007 Number of establishments	Number of employees	Sales (mil dol)	Annual payroll (mil dol)	Retail trade,[2] 2007 Number of establishments	Number of employees	Sales (mil dol)	Annual payroll (mil dol)	Real estate and rental and leasing,[2] 2007 Number of establishments	Number of employees	Receipts (mil dol)	Annual payroll (mil dol)
	133	134	135	136	137	138	139	140	141	142	143	144	145	146
TEXAS—Cont'd														
Tom Green	42.0	406	119	D	D	D	448	D	D	D	135	631	76.0	15.8
Travis	563.1	634	1 129	19 691	14 119.8	1 362.7	3 352	52 883	13 879.5	1 341.0	1 776	12 622	2 423.6	501.6
Trinity	3.5	244	4	93	34.0	3.8	44	316	57.0	4.4	6	29	1.4	0.3
Tyler	5.3	256	7	55	70.5	4.5	56	596	115.0	10.2	3	D	D	D
Upshur	21.5	567	12	171	58.4	3.5	100	835	216.7	15.5	11	23	1.9	0.2
Upton	16.8	5 504	5	29	21.8	1.4	10	69	16.7	0.9	2	D	D	D
Uvalde	65.0	2 411	27	214	120.7	7.3	109	1 350	322.2	27.1	32	88	10.6	1.8
Val Verde	17.4	365	23	127	39.3	3.7	169	2 172	524.4	41.4	26	92	11.3	2.1
Van Zandt	15.5	296	29	209	50.1	7.4	150	1 543	410.5	30.7	35	101	26.9	1.6
Victoria	27.1	316	104	1 284	651.1	54.6	403	5 951	1 434.3	129.2	124	869	162.2	36.1
Walker	7.5	119	32	D	D	D	155	2 300	626.3	47.2	51	261	68.1	8.6
Waller	27.3	784	43	788	451.6	30.6	103	1 589	593.1	46.2	23	70	8.5	1.6
Ward	24.3	2 373	9	305	52.0	8.3	37	291	94.6	6.1	11	79	20.9	4.2
Washington	8.1	255	28	D	D	D	148	1 964	509.9	44.2	46	202	35.2	5.8
Webb	88.8	395	351	2 519	1 472.1	79.2	819	12 864	2 913.5	235.4	205	724	119.6	18.9
Wharton	291.7	7 020	53	808	541.1	32.6	179	1 961	466.7	43.6	40	169	37.9	6.8
Wheeler	11.9	2 482	8	55	25.8	1.4	30	200	46.1	3.2	5	12	0.7	0.1
Wichita	42.2	335	155	1 396	548.0	52.3	537	7 577	1 715.9	156.9	179	832	99.2	19.2
Wilbarger	32.1	2 309	15	D	D	D	55	674	170.2	12.8	9	28	2.6	0.5
Willacy	35.0	1 718	6	D	D	D	38	468	122.9	9.2	12	32	2.4	0.5
Williamson	54.1	182	307	2 913	1 525.2	153.3	1 188	21 116	9 918.0	525.2	399	1 732	363.2	60.2
Wilson	21.6	575	18	98	49.0	2.5	74	820	180.5	16.9	13	43	4.2	0.6
Winkler	15.1	2 253	7	42	29.1	2.0	25	167	40.3	3.0	5	50	7.6	1.7
Wise	12.8	225	55	506	418.4	23.8	162	2 002	565.3	49.6	39	365	63.5	17.4
Wood	20.6	504	38	268	137.0	7.4	142	1 448	383.5	30.7	36	154	21.6	3.2
Yoakum	131.2	17 713	17	160	51.2	6.8	27	169	37.0	3.3	5	D	D	D
Young	161.9	8 996	25	198	86.2	9.1	74	834	185.2	17.0	22	60	45.4	1.9
Zapata	5.6	421	3	D	D	D	37	318	62.1	4.3	7	18	2.8	0.5
Zavala	53.2	4 507	2	D	D	D	19	202	33.3	3.1	NA	NA	NA	NA
UTAH	5 115.2	2 008	3 043	43 900	25 417.4	2 012.0	8 984	142 266	36 574.2	3 240.7	4 886	20 413	3 390.8	617.4
Beaver	91.4	14 411	NA	NA	NA	NA	32	312	89.7	4.7	3	3	0.3	0.1
Box Elder	435.9	9 621	30	D	D	D	135	1 790	447.4	34.5	48	88	12.0	1.7
Cache	280.4	2 708	110	796	361.6	29.3	398	5 347	1 095.1	96.9	191	D	D	D
Carbon	54.4	2 811	29	D	D	D	98	1 271	298.9	25.4	17	63	13.1	1.5
Daggett	34.7	36 064	NA	NA	NA	NA	5	D	D	D	NA	NA	NA	NA
Davis	123.9	445	218	D	D	D	780	13 393	3 217.7	286.7	404	1 120	174.1	27.5
Duchesne	334.5	21 954	18	138	54.7	4.7	69	795	216.0	16.7	25	87	27.8	3.4
Emery	224.7	21 421	3	3	1.0	0.1	44	503	128.6	8.0	3	D	D	D
Garfield	87.7	18 648	2	D	D	D	22	134	22.9	1.8	10	13	1.9	0.4
Grand	22.5	2 550	12	84	19.7	3.2	76	661	159.9	14.7	36	106	16.2	2.6
Iron	275.2	6 648	40	D	D	D	191	2 274	652.2	48.4	96	203	35.0	4.5
Juab	74.0	8 240	5	43	19.3	1.3	34	318	112.2	4.8	2	D	D	D
Kane	31.7	5 109	5	10	3.8	0.3	49	351	72.1	6.2	22	53	6.8	1.0
Millard	425.5	32 304	11	62	23.2	1.9	65	566	125.1	9.1	3	5	0.5	0.1
Morgan	40.2	4 716	6	D	D	D	23	184	42.7	3.4	9	D	D	D
Piute	59.2	43 253	1	D	D	D	7	D	D	D	NA	NA	NA	NA
Rich	184.6	89 544	NA	NA	NA	NA	9	56	11.5	0.9	11	67	6.8	1.8
Salt Lake	344.4	352	1 649	28 039	16 956.4	1 350.3	3 424	60 133	16 758.7	1 510.5	2 085	11 470	2 022.2	384.1
San Juan	29.3	2 011	4	D	D	D	37	378	44.6	4.4	2	D	D	D
Sanpete	273.0	10 723	12	58	31.2	1.4	88	956	196.9	16.9	22	274	14.3	5.5
Sevier	189.9	9 666	14	126	112.0	4.2	108	1 312	324.6	27.4	10	65	5.2	1.4
Summit	94.8	2 613	57	322	165.8	11.7	294	3 224	659.9	64.7	270	1 214	221.5	41.6
Tooele	212.5	4 076	14	71	73.6	5.1	100	1 773	503.6	37.1	35	91	13.5	1.8
Uintah	287.8	10 704	44	D	D	D	135	1 703	461.4	37.0	75	364	138.5	19.2
Utah	402.3	882	406	6 033	2 425.0	275.6	1 357	23 988	5 772.2	518.3	753	D	D	D
Wasatch	60.6	3 029	12	D	D	D	80	1 253	228.4	27.1	46	134	12.3	2.5
Washington	98.9	778	146	1 260	510.8	48.3	593	8 035	2 087.8	185.9	367	856	122.0	20.0
Wayne	68.1	27 177	NA	NA	NA	NA	17	101	27.8	1.5	2	D	D	D
Weber	273.4	1 279	195	2 790	2 218.2	111.3	714	11 422	2 810.6	247.5	339	D	D	D
VERMONT	522.5	839	762	9 852	5 121.7	424.8	3 852	40 416	9 310.1	938.7	797	3 395	497.3	95.9
Addison	13.6	367	32	216	101.4	8.0	212	2 139	464.8	53.2	38	D	D	D
Bennington	6.7	180	31	D	D	D	338	3 415	833.0	82.6	64	230	35.2	6.8
Caledonia	4.9	162	26	212	66.2	10.1	188	1 743	412.7	39.7	26	81	14.2	2.6

1. Merchant wholesalers, except manufacturers' sales branches and offices.   2. Employer establishments.

Table B. States and Counties — **Professional Services, Manufacturing, and Accommodation and Food Services**

STATE County	Professional, scientific, and technical services,[1] 2007				Manufacturing, 2007				Accommodation and food services, 2007			
	Number of establish-ments	Number of employees	Receipts (mil dol)	Annual payroll (mil dol)	Number of establish-ments	Number of employees	Receipts (mil dol)	Annual payroll (mil dol)	Number of establish-ments	Number of employees	Sales (mil dol)	Annual payroll (mil dol)
	147	148	149	150	151	152	153	154	155	156	157	158
TEXAS—Cont'd												
Tom Green	185	D	D	D	120	D	D	D	209	D	D	D
Travis	4 745	D	D	D	768	35 731	28 294.7	1 827.7	2 277	52 877	2 833.7	797.8
Trinity	11	42	2.8	0.9	NA	NA	NA	NA	16	195	11.9	2.0
Tyler	16	60	5.0	1.4	NA	NA	NA	NA	21	225	9.8	2.1
Upshur	38	D	D	D	31	512	D	18.5	31	587	20.2	6.6
Upton	3	D	D	D	NA	NA	NA	NA	9	D	D	D
Uvalde	43	149	13.1	4.3	23	630	203.7	23.2	75	1 014	39.9	10.9
Val Verde	44	D	D	D	NA	NA	NA	NA	88	1 436	59.0	15.5
Van Zandt	52	212	25.6	8.0	35	645	119.9	24.8	64	839	32.9	9.4
Victoria	155	D	D	D	78	D	D	D	170	3 166	130.8	35.4
Walker	84	499	35.3	10.8	39	1 043	D	40.5	95	1 960	73.8	19.9
Waller	54	285	52.7	17.7	65	2 352	D	111.0	41	642	24.7	5.9
Ward	13	40	3.1	1.2	NA	NA	NA	NA	20	218	8.9	1.8
Washington	59	265	32.5	9.2	46	2 782	762.8	108.0	76	1 024	41.3	11.9
Webb	309	D	D	D	89	914	242.4	30.7	360	7 489	317.3	86.5
Wharton	59	304	34.8	13.6	47	3 941	464.0	56.6	76	1 160	45.9	12.1
Wheeler	10	30	2.7	0.9	NA	NA	NA	NA	19	197	9.3	2.3
Wichita	237	D	D	D	142	6 047	1 492.5	262.7	290	6 626	254.8	79.7
Wilbarger	22	85	5.4	1.5	9	D	D	31.9	33	368	16.1	4.2
Willacy	9	D	D	D	NA	NA	NA	NA	26	287	13.2	2.6
Williamson	886	D	D	D	269	6 524	1 647.6	312.5	636	12 187	583.6	156.5
Wilson	37	D	D	D	NA	NA	NA	NA	47	553	20.8	5.6
Winkler	9	15	4.0	0.5	NA	NA	NA	NA	9	85	4.7	1.0
Wise	78	D	D	D	76	1 728	376.5	72.3	93	1 356	59.3	16.6
Wood	66	221	20.2	6.2	44	1 026	708.0	41.2	66	761	30.4	8.3
Yoakum	6	14	1.5	0.4	NA	NA	NA	NA	18	147	6.0	1.4
Young	34	117	11.4	4.1	23	973	301.4	41.1	40	481	17.7	5.0
Zapata	6	19	1.4	0.3	NA	NA	NA	NA	22	212	9.4	2.0
Zavala	5	19	1.4	0.3	NA	NA	NA	NA	16	108	4.6	1.1
UTAH	8 203	67 426	8 197.7	3 157.3	3 368	123 249	42 431.7	5 508.5	4 541	91 808	3 980.6	1 148.6
Beaver	5	11	1.3	0.3	NA	NA	NA	NA	25	310	12.8	3.2
Box Elder	63	D	D	D	78	10 869	3 150.9	D	70	1 171	36.8	11.9
Cache	351	D	D	D	214	10 326	D	405.8	135	2 727	95.2	29.5
Carbon	39	D	D	D	NA	NA	NA	NA	40	763	26.2	6.8
Daggett	3	D	D	D	NA	NA	NA	NA	8	67	6.4	1.8
Davis	791	D	D	D	273	9 914	4 985.2	D	368	7 425	274.3	76.9
Duchesne	37	88	11.4	3.5	NA	NA	NA	NA	30	374	13.6	3.8
Emery	11	71	5.0	1.8	NA	NA	NA	NA	25	245	10.8	2.7
Garfield	5	D	D	D	NA	NA	NA	NA	43	460	49.3	12.1
Grand	33	157	14.3	5.3	NA	NA	NA	NA	80	1 369	68.2	19.9
Iron	116	D	D	D	72	1 665	736.0	59.4	101	1 618	59.6	16.9
Juab	14	277	25.2	9.7	NA	NA	NA	NA	21	223	7.2	1.8
Kane	18	27	2.9	0.9	NA	NA	NA	NA	42	404	20.9	6.1
Millard	5	D	D	D	NA	NA	NA	NA	26	342	11.6	3.2
Morgan	25	D	D	D	NA	NA	NA	NA	11	142	5.7	1.3
Piute	1	D	D	D	NA	NA	NA	NA	7	D	D	D
Rich	3	D	D	D	NA	NA	NA	NA	12	65	3.7	0.9
Salt Lake	3 763	D	D	D	1 483	51 595	18 860.5	2 351.7	1 826	40 212	1 874.6	556.6
San Juan	10	D	D	D	NA	NA	NA	NA	61	D	D	D
Sanpete	20	224	8.7	3.1	NA	NA	NA	NA	32	363	8.3	2.4
Sevier	37	134	14.3	5.8	NA	NA	NA	NA	45	828	24.7	7.2
Summit	293	896	130.5	44.8	NA	NA	NA	NA	167	4 907	228.9	70.4
Tooele	55	D	D	D	39	D	D	D	55	931	35.2	8.8
Uintah	104	324	44.6	14.3	NA	NA	NA	NA	64	1 005	46.5	11.1
Utah	1 428	16 469	1 328.9	499.4	522	D	D	D	543	11 712	451.7	128.4
Wasatch	76	346	37.0	12.8	NA	NA	NA	NA	43	722	38.8	9.1
Washington	432	D	D	D	154	3 225	609.6	117.4	279	5 631	254.5	74.5
Wayne	3	D	D	D	NA	NA	NA	NA	24	117	7.7	1.8
Weber	462	D	D	D	244	12 066	D	494.1	358	7 107	261.2	70.9
VERMONT	2 100	16 346	1 615.6	649.5	1 108	35 571	10 751.5	1 650.1	1 942	31 176	1 367.6	427.9
Addison	115	390	42.5	17.3	57	1 948	539.0	93.0	83	971	48.2	16.2
Bennington	125	407	53.7	16.5	75	2 443	571.6	97.4	152	2 316	106.7	33.0
Caledonia	66	D	D	D	60	2 120	339.1	70.8	73	712	29.9	8.4

1. Establishment subject to federal tax.

Table B. States and Counties — Health Care and Social Assistance, Other Services, and Federal Funds

STATE County	Health care and social assistance, 2007				Other services, 2007				Federal funds and grants, 2009–2010 Expenditures (mil dol)			
										Direct payments for individuals[1]		
	Number of establishments	Number of employees	Receipts (mil dol)	Annual payroll (mil dol)	Number of establishments	Number of employees	Receipts (mil dol)	Annual payroll (mil dol)	Total	Social Security and government retirement	Medicare	Food Stamps and Supplemental Security Income
	159	160	161	162	163	164	165	166	167	168	169	170
TEXAS—Cont'd												
Tom Green	259	D	D	D	212	D	D	D	1 004.2	349.5	150.3	39.6
Travis	2 549	48 334	5 562.7	2 156.3	1 930	18 213	2 025.4	609.7	16 359.5	1 800.2	625.1	235.7
Trinity	22	314	20.8	8.4	20	85	5.2	1.1	155.9	64.4	42.9	7.7
Tyler	22	479	27.0	11.8	11	42	3.6	0.9	175.3	74.7	50.3	9.3
Upshur	43	602	41.1	16.9	31	96	11.6	2.4	268.8	119.4	70.3	12.7
Upton	7	D	D	D	1	D	D	D	26.8	9.6	7.3	1.9
Uvalde	58	1 392	90.5	40.0	35	208	14.2	4.1	232.1	66.6	38.3	19.6
Val Verde	83	2 891	127.5	53.8	49	257	16.5	3.4	567.1	119.3	45.0	34.7
Van Zandt	82	1 209	67.2	29.5	57	255	22.6	6.0	359.7	173.4	103.3	14.4
Victoria	322	6 266	586.9	233.1	166	1 202	112.2	33.1	625.0	256.1	134.2	37.9
Walker	101	2 028	133.5	56.2	64	384	23.1	6.3	359.4	130.1	65.3	18.1
Waller	43	678	38.4	17.4	50	185	16.9	4.3	239.9	70.1	37.7	13.4
Ward	13	242	14.8	7.2	17	74	8.9	2.1	78.8	30.1	20.2	5.7
Washington	81	1 825	104.7	42.6	52	281	17.9	5.1	287.5	116.5	50.9	10.6
Webb	441	12 142	723.4	284.3	257	1 465	124.3	28.6	1 613.9	325.1	210.5	164.0
Wharton	63	2 282	165.5	56.7	74	291	20.7	5.3	382.7	112.8	84.1	17.0
Wheeler	14	227	13.3	6.2	8	19	1.8	0.4	52.6	16.7	20.0	1.8
Wichita	374	10 412	823.4	329.8	264	1 486	141.7	34.9	1 486.8	488.6	210.5	33.0
Wilbarger	35	D	D	D	23	126	6.1	1.8	128.3	40.6	38.4	5.4
Willacy	32	1 199	53.1	27.9	17	D	D	D	249.6	39.1	34.0	20.3
Williamson	748	9 836	926.3	368.7	518	3 892	305.6	101.9	2 047.8	847.6	145.0	32.0
Wilson	51	1 206	65.5	28.8	42	112	13.3	1.9	237.5	126.5	35.2	9.1
Winkler	11	139	9.2	3.7	11	D	D	D	49.0	17.0	17.9	3.4
Wise	104	D	D	D	70	383	30.9	8.5	261.5	146.5	51.2	9.2
Wood	73	1 004	76.3	27.4	53	245	16.4	4.4	398.5	199.1	84.5	11.8
Yoakum	5	D	D	D	9	48	4.5	1.0	53.8	17.9	11.8	2.3
Young	59	950	65.9	26.9	39	126	9.4	2.7	155.3	64.2	45.6	7.0
Zapata	14	325	8.6	3.8	6	D	D	D	103.8	21.8	25.1	10.2
Zavala	12	542	14.4	6.9	3	D	D	D	112.3	20.9	21.0	15.3
UTAH	6 392	112 646	10 860.4	4 156.2	4 141	26 236	2 356.1	653.1	23 545.2	5 855.1	3 539.1	538.1
Beaver	16	232	17.8	5.8	8	D	D	D	65.9	18.1	25.0	1.1
Box Elder	109	1 128	93.0	31.2	59	D	D	D	948.9	132.6	61.5	8.0
Cache	299	D	D	D	161	D	D	D	687.3	177.6	99.0	14.0
Carbon	76	933	82.1	24.3	52	D	D	D	181.0	69.9	59.7	11.7
Daggett	1	D	D	D	NA	NA	NA	NA	21.1	4.6	2.3	0.1
Davis	584	8 030	679.7	262.5	363	2 225	161.9	47.1	2 964.4	745.0	212.4	39.4
Duchesne	46	1 048	87.8	31.9	34	137	13.5	3.3	129.3	43.2	31.6	11.1
Emery	14	D	D	D	10	D	D	D	79.3	29.6	20.3	3.7
Garfield	7	170	13.1	4.8	2	D	D	D	60.6	17.2	12.0	1.3
Grand	22	249	21.4	8.5	21	55	4.5	1.2	112.1	28.2	14.3	3.9
Iron	108	1 434	123.3	42.3	69	394	25.3	6.8	244.3	107.6	37.6	10.2
Juab	21	D	D	D	8	D	D	D	49.6	22.1	15.9	1.7
Kane	15	166	15.5	3.9	14	D	D	D	56.8	27.4	9.9	1.9
Millard	24	D	D	D	14	46	9.6	1.2	91.5	32.3	23.9	4.1
Morgan	10	49	3.0	0.8	9	61	3.4	1.2	42.1	28.9	7.0	0.4
Piute	1	D	D	D	1	D	D	D	23.2	6.2	8.9	0.6
Rich	2	D	D	D	8	D	D	D	12.8	6.0	2.7	0.3
Salt Lake	2 644	53 465	5 733.1	2 203.6	1 907	13 222	1 262.1	355.0	8 889.3	1 975.0	1 518.8	218.8
San Juan	27	D	D	D	8	D	D	D	248.8	25.2	95.6	14.8
Sanpete	47	830	54.2	22.9	27	D	D	D	176.0	61.3	48.9	6.6
Sevier	48	694	51.0	19.5	25	133	13.4	4.9	161.0	60.1	46.2	7.3
Summit	108	D	D	D	95	868	98.8	22.3	127.8	66.7	11.9	1.8
Tooele	92	D	D	D	57	269	20.7	6.0	679.6	145.5	48.6	9.9
Uintah	57	598	62.7	18.5	64	297	39.7	9.0	174.8	58.2	40.3	8.3
Utah	1 014	D	D	D	539	D	D	D	2 526.1	727.1	480.6	65.9
Wasatch	43	464	39.7	13.6	42	D	D	D	78.0	41.3	17.8	1.9
Washington	393	6 648	628.5	250.2	198	1 116	95.0	27.4	1 063.0	435.9	120.4	18.5
Wayne	4	D	D	D	3	D	D	D	25.3	7.8	5.4	0.3
Weber	560	10 314	914.5	357.4	343	2 171	160.9	48.8	2 115.7	750.9	460.4	70.6
VERMONT	2 176	41 917	3 537.1	1 495.3	1 629	7 269	798.6	182.9	7 404.8	1 929.1	756.7	205.9
Addison	125	1 840	126.7	55.6	88	344	55.3	8.5	366.4	94.5	37.0	9.4
Bennington	166	2 867	238.3	103.6	97	441	29.7	8.0	303.4	130.2	57.2	13.4
Caledonia	105	1 763	124.0	55.5	72	252	20.3	5.1	248.5	95.6	40.4	13.5

1. State totals may include programs not allocated by county.

Table B. States and Counties — Federal Funds, Residential Construction, and Local Government Finances

	Federal funds and grants, 2009–2010 (cont.)							Value of residential construction authorized by building permits, 2010		Local government finances, 2007				
	Expenditures (mil dol) (cont.)									General revenue				
	Procurement contract awards			Grants[1]								Taxes		
													Per capita[2] (dollars)	
STATE County	Salaries and wages	Defense	Other	Medicaid and other health-related	Nutrition and family welfare	Education	Other	New construction ($1,000)	Number of housing units	Total (mil dol)	Inter-govern-mental (mil dol)	Total (mil dol)	Total	Property
	171	172	173	174	175	176	177	178	179	180	181	182	183	184
TEXAS—Cont'd														
Tom Green	205.1	64.0	5.4	111.2	22.7	3.7	16.8	24 682	177	289.4	126.4	115.4	1 085	797
Travis	914.4	473.2	697.7	1 200.0	1 079.3	1 315.3	7 734.6	663 461	4 397	3 808.7	655.4	2 194.7	2 252	1 820
Trinity	2.5	0.0	0.6	34.5	1.0	0.5	1.1	112	4	30.3	16.5	10.2	719	614
Tyler	3.6	0.3	0.7	30.8	3.0	0.8	0.2	235	4	67.1	26.7	23.4	1 149	1 066
Upshur	5.7	0.5	1.2	53.1	3.2	1.1	0.3	1 115	15	84.2	34.6	39.9	1 051	960
Upton	0.6	0.0	0.2	3.5	0.7	0.1	0.0	50	1	48.5	2.0	39.8	13 028	12 849
Uvalde	17.5	0.3	1.5	51.8	7.2	2.9	5.0	777	12	141.3	54.3	28.8	1 083	850
Val Verde	190.0	51.9	12.9	83.9	17.5	2.7	3.9	4 270	38	156.5	95.3	39.0	811	597
Van Zandt	7.5	0.1	2.9	47.5	5.6	1.4	1.3	899	9	117.7	54.4	44.5	855	737
Victoria	34.1	0.2	4.6	98.8	17.5	3.9	5.7	7 305	47	401.0	96.8	116.6	1 351	1 031
Walker	29.4	10.4	2.3	60.9	7.2	3.9	5.1	54 805	629	258.5	58.0	54.7	855	668
Waller	7.1	17.0	8.0	27.7	3.9	8.5	17.0	2 274	59	113.2	42.3	57.9	1 611	1 369
Ward	1.6	0.0	0.4	18.7	1.0	0.3	0.3	1 375	7	48.9	6.0	30.9	3 011	2 840
Washington	7.6	3.7	1.3	74.3	1.9	0.7	1.7	6 388	54	149.2	42.3	53.3	1 665	1 346
Webb	205.4	2.8	40.7	421.4	132.8	21.3	39.6	93 949	663	1 057.5	514.3	342.7	1 470	1 182
Wharton	27.2	0.1	1.8	85.7	7.1	2.0	0.8	2 101	12	167.0	52.1	67.9	1 660	1 428
Wheeler	2.2	0.0	1.2	8.1	0.7	0.2	0.0	0	0	40.4	5.0	26.7	5 574	5 337
Wichita	357.2	181.1	8.9	129.8	26.2	5.5	16.7	31 657	175	352.8	118.3	165.0	1 289	967
Wilbarger	2.9	0.1	0.5	22.8	2.9	0.5	0.3	180	2	69.8	19.9	24.0	1 707	1 506
Willacy	9.7	0.0	0.7	68.8	5.5	1.5	54.7	1 482	16	73.7	43.3	20.1	979	797
Williamson	70.7	442.1	226.7	87.8	21.9	13.7	118.6	364 721	1 937	1 329.7	229.3	866.0	2 319	1 958
Wilson	5.7	0.0	1.5	41.5	2.7	0.8	10.5	7 633	61	102.7	42.9	33.1	843	776
Winkler	0.9	0.0	0.2	8.1	0.6	0.2	0.2	90	1	48.6	6.9	32.1	4 904	4 553
Wise	22.8	0.4	1.9	22.8	3.7	0.8	0.2	4 040	26	148.3	29.8	99.2	1 722	1 529
Wood	11.8	0.1	1.9	48.5	4.8	3.0	29.0	195	3	85.9	27.3	46.4	1 105	992
Yoakum	0.8	0.0	0.2	5.6	2.1	0.2	0.0	907	6	84.9	6.2	59.8	8 028	7 870
Young	4.1	0.0	3.0	25.8	2.4	0.5	0.3	530	5	78.1	23.2	22.6	1 278	976
Zapata	10.8	0.1	0.3	30.3	1.1	0.9	2.3	NA	NA	66.6	10.8	52.0	3 823	3 781
Zavala	1.0	0.0	0.2	46.6	1.7	1.1	1.2	359	4	36.8	25.8	7.1	608	531
UTAH	3 194.8	2 521.6	1 236.8	2 083.8	491.2	447.5	1 964.2	1 672 395	9 171	X	X	X	X	X
Beaver	3.3	0.0	0.6	14.6	1.1	0.1	1.2	2 824	19	39.6	12.9	9.1	1 490	1 110
Box Elder	19.1	105.2	572.9	23.9	6.7	0.5	8.7	35 812	264	140.9	71.5	43.8	916	660
Cache	37.4	52.6	24.2	48.1	18.7	23.8	150.4	71 393	603	263.3	116.5	85.0	780	461
Carbon	13.4	0.0	-14.2	24.3	8.3	0.9	1.8	6 722	39	89.4	40.7	30.0	1 526	1 139
Daggett	2.9	0.0	1.0	1.1	0.1	0.0	8.7	1 442	13	10.1	4.1	2.1	2 303	1 916
Davis	815.2	854.0	146.9	76.1	34.8	3.7	20.9	203 551	960	780.0	331.1	247.1	857	564
Duchesne	5.2	0.0	12.8	14.7	3.7	0.5	3.5	14 508	64	62.4	30.0	20.9	1 290	968
Emery	3.4	0.0	1.1	9.4	2.5	0.2	5.8	3 212	19	61.5	21.6	23.1	2 222	1 883
Garfield	7.5	0.0	4.4	5.7	1.2	0.1	11.3	5 302	30	36.3	13.4	7.7	1 698	1 017
Grand	11.5	0.5	42.1	6.8	1.6	0.4	1.8	11 279	41	56.4	14.9	15.5	1 716	901
Iron	25.2	3.1	13.9	13.4	8.7	2.3	5.6	24 986	147	134.3	45.5	49.7	1 141	810
Juab	1.9	-1.7	1.6	5.7	1.3	0.2	0.1	5 371	36	34.6	18.6	10.3	1 069	843
Kane	4.6	0.0	8.5	1.2	1.2	0.1	1.3	7 210	33	43.9	12.1	14.3	2 190	1 403
Millard	6.6	0.0	9.4	9.1	3.5	0.3	0.6	1 983	11	54.9	22.3	22.8	1 909	1 703
Morgan	1.0	0.2	0.8	2.3	0.9	0.0	0.0	14 755	43	22.7	9.7	8.2	985	773
Piute	0.6	0.0	0.2	5.6	0.5	0.1	0.2	290	4	7.7	5.9	1.1	839	630
Rich	0.7	0.0	0.2	2.0	0.4	0.1	0.1	6 011	36	11.0	5.1	4.0	1 911	1 578
Salt Lake	1 212.6	564.2	304.1	1 124.2	227.6	228.6	1 316.5	430 810	2 472	3 181.0	979.6	1 290.8	1 279	869
San Juan	8.5	0.0	2.2	80.3	3.9	9.5	4.8	5 013	34	73.3	41.7	12.1	837	615
Sanpete	14.0	0.1	1.2	25.0	5.6	1.9	4.4	5 409	44	81.0	37.4	17.3	701	467
Sevier	15.1	1.0	2.9	18.2	4.3	0.4	3.5	8 516	44	74.0	40.9	19.2	972	639
Summit	6.3	8.4	1.1	2.6	2.7	0.3	23.3	50 540	243	220.6	26.3	143.3	4 032	2 784
Tooele	61.1	372.4	2.9	19.5	5.9	1.8	10.1	34 930	274	173.2	75.6	45.5	828	602
Uintah	24.6	0.0	5.4	17.7	8.8	1.6	7.4	15 621	71	157.7	76.7	50.2	1 728	1 092
Utah	165.0	498.8	26.1	239.0	55.1	13.5	130.9	395 832	1 949	1 294.5	535.9	423.4	875	571
Wasatch	3.7	0.4	1.3	8.0	2.0	0.2	0.5	50 042	269	96.8	25.4	36.8	1 792	1 280
Washington	377.3	0.4	27.3	27.9	11.5	4.2	17.9	168 923	893	442.8	162.8	155.0	1 158	767
Wayne	4.8	0.0	2.4	2.7	0.7	0.1	0.5	1 703	10	11.1	7.9	2.1	841	622
Weber	342.5	61.8	33.5	254.6	36.1	9.7	15.0	88 405	506	629.8	249.9	227.5	1 026	678
VERMONT	724.0	711.3	220.4	1 088.4	192.4	140.1	959.0	227 617	1 319	X	X	X	X	X
Addison	12.7	138.4	10.1	42.7	7.0	0.8	4.6	15 363	84	114.3	86.0	16.9	460	453
Bennington	16.6	9.3	2.0	48.7	7.7	2.4	7.6	12 728	49	120.4	85.3	23.1	633	583
Caledonia	16.1	5.1	2.0	54.2	7.1	2.8	6.8	11 249	86	87.7	64.0	17.1	556	550

1. State totals may include programs not allocated by county.   2. Based on the resident population estimated as of July 1 of the year shown.

Table B. States and Counties — Local Government Finances, Government Employment, and Voting

	Local government finances, 2007 (cont.)									Government employment, 2009			Presidential election,[2] 2008		
	Direct general expenditure							Debt outstanding					Percent of vote cast:		
			Percent of total for:												
STATE County	Total (mil dol)	Per capita[1] (dollars)	Educa-tion	Health and hospitals	Police protec-tion	Public welfare	High-ways	Total (mil dol)	Per capita[1] (dollars)	Federal civilian	Federal military	State and local	Demo-cratic	Republi-can	All other
	185	186	187	188	189	190	191	192	193	194	195	196	197	198	199
TEXAS—Cont'd															
Tom Green	278.9	2 623	53.3	4.0	6.3	0.3	2.9	198.6	1 868	1 351	3 267	7 549	28.7	70.4	0.9
Travis	3 653.4	3 749	46.1	4.9	6.8	0.5	2.9	11 856.4	12 168	9 560	2 684	119 200	63.9	34.4	1.7
Trinity	29.2	2 058	71.4	1.9	4.2	0.3	5.3	12.6	888	32	33	632	31.7	67.4	0.9
Tyler	61.6	3 017	55.8	17.0	3.4	0.0	3.2	26.3	1 290	53	48	1 759	27.4	71.4	1.3
Upshur	78.0	2 056	75.2	0.0	3.3	0.1	3.8	66.6	1 756	65	90	1 785	25.0	74.0	1.0
Upton	44.0	14 424	77.7	17.4	0.2	0.0	0.8	6.0	1 956	0	0	449	24.1	75.0	0.9
Uvalde	136.8	5 145	61.1	24.7	3.1	0.2	1.5	65.8	2 475	246	63	2 526	47.1	52.4	0.6
Val Verde	138.6	2 885	56.0	0.6	5.1	0.4	4.5	147.5	3 072	2 208	1 608	2 853	54.5	44.9	0.7
Van Zandt	119.2	2 289	72.9	0.4	3.2	0.2	3.0	191.9	3 687	97	122	2 374	22.1	77.1	0.8
Victoria	362.6	4 202	41.8	30.5	5.4	0.0	2.6	485.6	5 628	265	214	6 330	32.8	66.4	0.7
Walker	273.4	4 278	24.0	2.1	2.4	0.0	2.0	976.6	15 283	156	154	12 713	38.3	60.7	1.0
Waller	99.9	2 779	70.4	0.1	4.0	0.4	4.2	134.0	3 728	60	93	3 878	46.1	53.3	0.6
Ward	49.9	4 857	56.1	10.8	3.5	0.0	4.7	34.3	3 337	19	25	891	25.0	74.0	1.0
Washington	141.6	4 420	72.8	1.3	3.5	0.7	3.5	118.5	3 698	84	77	2 977	28.1	70.8	1.2
Webb	1 026.5	4 402	63.3	1.1	5.2	0.5	0.9	1 283.2	5 504	3 092	569	18 738	71.4	28.0	0.5
Wharton	169.4	4 141	64.3	9.7	4.0	0.3	5.7	97.8	2 392	98	97	2 996	34.2	65.4	0.3
Wheeler	36.9	7 703	63.4	24.6	2.5	0.0	1.9	7.3	1 519	29	12	541	14.0	85.4	0.6
Wichita	328.3	2 564	54.1	4.1	7.1	0.7	4.4	381.0	2 976	2 297	7 841	9 132	30.2	69.0	0.8
Wilbarger	67.8	4 831	62.2	15.3	2.7	0.1	3.3	29.3	2 086	49	32	3 217	26.5	72.8	0.7
Willacy	67.3	3 281	69.5	1.1	3.4	0.3	4.6	90.3	4 402	36	52	1 207	69.5	29.7	0.8
Williamson	1 392.3	3 729	61.6	3.3	3.7	0.1	6.7	3 211.8	8 602	1 655	968	19 622	42.7	55.8	1.5
Wilson	102.6	2 613	62.6	18.7	2.7	0.0	3.3	237.8	6 055	65	96	2 141	32.8	66.6	0.6
Winkler	47.5	7 260	64.7	10.5	1.8	0.3	2.0	74.4	11 370	10	16	614	23.5	75.2	1.3
Wise	132.0	2 292	61.8	1.6	4.7	1.0	9.8	162.0	2 813	117	140	3 454	21.7	77.4	0.9
Wood	90.8	2 161	70.4	0.4	5.0	0.2	5.6	89.4	2 127	96	102	1 873	22.5	76.8	0.7
Yoakum	72.2	9 692	63.1	20.0	2.4	0.0	2.9	16.4	2 198	18	18	814	18.3	80.9	0.8
Young	77.8	4 402	40.2	31.0	3.7	0.1	3.2	163.3	9 237	62	42	1 380	17.8	81.3	0.8
Zapata	54.8	4 031	89.3	0.1	1.5	0.1	2.3	25.6	1 879	164	33	1 106	67.7	32.1	0.3
Zavala	39.3	3 371	73.7	0.7	3.9	0.0	0.8	44.7	3 835	12	27	895	84.2	15.4	0.4
UTAH	X	X	X	X	X	X	X	X	X	36 395	16 959	178 543	34.4	62.6	3.0
Beaver	35.4	5 810	29.7	29.4	5.2	0.0	5.5	46.2	7 585	47	28	649	21.6	75.8	2.6
Box Elder	129.8	2 714	50.3	1.5	5.6	0.1	6.0	121.8	2 545	237	221	2 334	17.4	79.9	2.7
Cache	249.4	2 290	50.8	4.0	5.2	0.2	5.1	220.9	2 028	674	515	9 887	24.9	70.8	4.6
Carbon	78.1	3 978	43.0	6.0	6.7	0.0	10.8	100.7	5 131	163	88	1 967	44.6	52.6	2.8
Daggett	8.4	9 026	33.6	0.8	13.5	0.0	5.1	6.0	6 472	54	0	163	29.8	67.7	2.5
Davis	820.0	2 846	53.4	3.5	5.4	0.3	4.6	606.1	2 103	12 555	5 464	12 008	27.5	69.7	2.8
Duchesne	64.8	3 995	34.5	1.5	3.7	0.0	10.8	49.4	2 813	88	79	1 715	16.9	81.6	2.5
Emery	61.1	5 878	37.6	4.5	5.5	0.0	6.7	249.1	23 950	64	47	817	21.9	75.5	2.6
Garfield	29.2	6 441	34.7	26.2	2.9	0.1	7.8	19.7	4 359	177	20	411	18.8	79.2	2.0
Grand	52.5	5 816	21.5	32.9	5.3	0.3	6.0	91.2	10 102	243	43	647	50.7	45.9	3.4
Iron	127.9	2 939	45.2	0.4	6.4	0.0	7.5	133.3	3 063	348	200	3 802	19.8	76.1	4.1
Juab	34.0	3 540	54.0	1.2	7.3	0.0	8.9	39.8	4 144	43	45	627	20.5	74.2	5.3
Kane	37.0	5 676	35.6	26.8	12.1	0.0	6.1	27.6	4 225	103	29	617	27.1	70.1	2.7
Millard	51.5	4 306	50.4	3.4	6.8	0.0	8.8	7.6	639	103	54	956	16.0	77.1	6.9
Morgan	24.4	2 917	68.7	0.6	5.6	0.0	4.3	56.4	6 750	12	39	399	16.6	79.6	3.9
Piute	6.6	4 942	62.4	1.0	7.1	0.0	8.9	2.5	1 886	0	0	136	17.7	79.6	2.8
Rich	9.6	4 570	54.6	0.8	5.7	3.0	7.5	7.5	3 587	14	10	177	15.3	82.6	2.1
Salt Lake	2 909.0	2 882	39.8	1.5	6.6	1.7	4.4	6 051.5	5 994	10 562	4 955	81 008	48.7	48.6	2.8
San Juan	69.1	4 769	50.1	15.2	2.9	0.0	14.1	21.3	1 473	166	66	1 474	46.9	51.4	1.7
Sanpete	80.8	3 280	49.3	22.2	4.3	0.0	4.5	63.7	2 587	84	115	2 467	18.6	76.0	5.4
Sevier	70.3	3 567	46.0	6.2	5.5	0.0	16.9	61.1	3 100	206	88	1 438	17.0	79.9	3.2
Summit	200.7	5 646	35.3	1.6	6.8	0.0	10.4	137.4	3 867	74	245	2 407	56.7	41.4	1.9
Tooele	172.0	3 132	48.3	1.8	6.7	2.0	3.5	163.9	2 985	1 881	286	2 642	33.6	63.4	2.9
Uintah	140.3	4 832	47.5	6.5	5.2	3.3	16.3	75.2	2 591	421	139	2 332	14.4	83.2	2.4
Utah	1 203.3	2 488	51.4	3.6	5.9	0.3	4.2	1 998.2	4 131	1 045	2 427	25 701	18.8	77.7	3.5
Wasatch	81.5	3 971	47.7	3.0	5.2	0.0	4.9	149.3	7 270	57	95	1 162	33.9	63.7	2.4
Washington	406.0	3 035	48.1	2.7	6.5	0.0	5.3	645.9	4 828	548	608	6 424	21.9	75.3	2.8
Wayne	10.7	4 229	53.7	0.3	8.8	0.0	14.4	1.9	736	101	11	182	25.5	71.5	3.0
Weber	626.3	2 823	47.0	1.4	6.7	4.3	2.9	545.6	2 459	6 618	1 032	13 994	35.0	62.5	2.5
VERMONT	X	X	X	X	X	X	X	X	X	6 570	4 166	46 310	67.5	30.4	2.1
Addison	151.9	4 134	80.3	0.3	1.6	0.1	6.6	48.1	1 308	119	240	1 812	68.6	29.5	1.9
Bennington	149.5	4 101	74.3	0.1	2.6	0.0	6.0	43.2	1 186	130	237	2 084	65.5	32.1	2.5
Caledonia	91.1	2 971	73.2	0.2	1.7	0.0	10.2	30.2	987	124	197	2 000	60.4	37.2	2.4

1. Based on the resident population estimated as of July 1 of the year shown.   2. © 2009 Election Data Services, Inc. All rights reserved.

Table B. States and Counties — **Land Area and Population**

					Population and population characteristics, 2010													
								Race alone or in combination, not Hispanic or Latino (percent)						Age (percent)				
STATE/ County code	CBSA code[1]	County type[2]	STATE County	Land area,[3] (sq km) 2010	Total persons	Rank	Per square kilometer	White	Black	American Indian, Alaska Native	Asian and Pacific Islander	Percent Hispanic or Latino[4]	Under 5 years	5 to 17 years	18 to 24 years	25 to 34 years	35 to 44 years	45 to 54 years
				1	2	3	4	5	6	7	8	9	10	11	12	13	14	15
			VERMONT—Cont'd															
50 007	15540	3	Chittenden	1 390	156 545	400	112.6	92.9	2.6	0.8	3.5	1.8	5.0	15.0	15.4	13.2	12.7	15.5
50 009	13620	9	Essex	1 719	6 306	2 742	3.7	97.9	0.4	1.5	0.5	0.9	4.0	15.0	6.3	8.3	12.5	17.4
50 011	15540	3	Franklin	1 641	47 746	1 010	29.1	96.8	0.8	2.5	0.7	1.2	6.3	18.4	7.1	12.0	14.4	16.8
50 013	15540	3	Grand Isle	212	6 970	2 689	32.9	97.2	0.5	3.1	0.6	1.1	4.6	15.8	6.2	9.7	13.0	18.6
50 015	...	8	Lamoille	1 188	24 475	1 629	20.6	97.1	0.9	1.2	0.8	1.3	6.1	16.2	9.6	11.9	13.4	16.2
50 017	30100	9	Orange	1 779	28 936	1 453	16.3	97.8	0.7	1.1	0.8	1.0	5.1	15.8	8.2	10.3	12.4	17.6
50 019	...	7	Orleans	1 796	27 231	1 522	15.2	97.4	0.9	1.3	0.6	1.1	5.2	16.1	7.2	10.8	12.3	15.4
50 021	40860	5	Rutland	2 408	61 642	844	25.6	97.5	0.9	0.8	0.9	1.1	4.6	14.7	9.8	9.9	12.0	16.9
50 023	12740	4	Washington	1 780	59 534	864	33.4	96.4	1.2	1.0	1.3	1.7	5.2	15.5	9.1	10.8	13.3	16.6
50 025	...	6	Windham	2 034	44 513	1 077	21.9	95.8	1.4	1.1	1.4	1.8	4.8	15.0	8.2	10.4	11.6	17.3
50 027	30100	7	Windsor	2 511	56 670	889	22.6	96.9	0.9	1.1	1.4	1.2	4.7	15.1	6.4	10.8	11.8	17.2
51 000	...	X	**VIRGINIA**	102 279	8 001 024	X	78.2	66.8	20.1	0.8	6.6	7.9	6.4	16.8	10.0	13.6	13.9	15.2
51 001	...	7	Accomack	1 164	33 164	1 348	28.5	62.3	28.6	0.9	0.9	8.6	5.9	15.0	7.5	10.7	11.4	15.3
51 003	16820	3	Albemarle	1 867	98 970	586	53.0	79.8	10.6	0.6	5.5	5.5	5.6	15.9	12.4	12.7	12.0	14.7
51 005	...	6	Alleghany	1 154	16 250	2 037	14.1	93.7	5.4	0.5	0.4	1.1	4.8	16.4	6.3	8.8	12.6	15.3
51 007	40060	1	Amelia	920	12 690	2 262	13.8	73.9	23.7	1.0	0.4	2.3	5.9	16.4	7.5	10.5	12.7	17.2
51 009	31340	3	Amherst	1 227	32 353	1 380	26.4	77.5	20.1	1.7	0.8	1.9	5.4	16.0	10.1	10.0	12.5	15.7
51 011	31340	3	Appomattox	864	14 973	2 111	17.3	78.1	21.2	0.6	0.4	1.1	5.4	16.8	7.5	10.8	12.3	15.9
51 013	47900	1	Arlington	67	207 627	298	3 098.9	66.2	8.9	0.6	11.4	15.1	5.7	10.0	9.8	27.6	15.8	12.4
51 015	44420	4	Augusta	2 505	73 750	734	29.4	93.2	4.4	0.6	0.7	2.1	5.2	16.2	7.4	10.7	13.4	16.6
51 017	...	9	Bath	1 371	4 731	2 861	3.5	92.9	4.9	0.4	0.4	2.1	3.3	13.7	7.0	8.6	13.0	16.4
51 019	31340	3	Bedford	1 950	68 676	773	35.2	91.3	6.1	0.6	1.3	1.6	4.9	17.4	6.6	8.7	13.4	17.5
51 021	...	8	Bland	927	6 824	2 702	7.4	95.8	3.6	0.3	0.3	0.6	4.2	13.7	6.5	11.8	16.1	15.0
51 023	40220	2	Botetourt	1 402	33 148	1 351	23.6	95.1	3.3	0.6	0.8	1.1	4.9	17.5	6.1	8.2	13.5	17.4
51 025	...	6	Brunswick	1 466	17 434	1 954	11.9	40.5	57.7	0.6	0.4	1.7	4.7	14.6	10.1	12.9	12.3	14.9
51 027	...	9	Buchanan	1 302	24 098	1 641	18.5	96.7	2.7	0.3	0.4	0.4	4.6	14.1	7.7	11.9	13.5	16.9
51 029	...	8	Buckingham	1 501	17 146	1 975	11.4	62.5	36.0	0.7	0.5	1.7	5.4	13.8	8.6	13.0	14.4	16.6
51 031	31340	3	Campbell	1 305	54 842	913	42.0	82.7	15.0	0.8	1.3	1.7	5.5	16.5	9.2	11.1	13.0	15.5
51 033	40060	1	Caroline	1 366	28 545	1 474	20.9	65.7	30.8	1.7	1.2	3.4	7.0	16.9	7.5	13.4	13.6	15.7
51 035	...	6	Carroll	1 229	30 042	1 427	24.4	96.4	0.8	0.4	0.3	2.6	5.3	15.4	6.6	9.7	13.4	15.1
51 036	40060	1	Charles City	473	7 256	2 664	15.3	42.3	50.0	8.4	0.6	1.2	4.2	13.7	6.8	9.9	12.4	19.0
51 037	...	8	Charlotte	1 231	12 586	2 270	10.2	67.7	30.4	0.8	0.3	1.9	5.5	17.5	7.8	9.3	11.4	16.0
51 041	40060	1	Chesterfield	1 096	316 236	201	288.5	67.1	22.7	0.8	4.1	7.2	6.3	19.8	8.5	12.0	14.6	15.9
51 043	47900	1	Clarke	456	14 034	2 171	30.8	89.9	6.0	0.8	1.5	3.5	5.2	17.7	5.9	8.4	12.8	18.7
51 045	40220	2	Craig	853	5 190	2 829	6.1	98.9	0.3	0.3	0.5	0.7	5.0	16.4	6.6	9.3	12.9	17.1
51 047	19020	6	Culpeper	982	46 689	1 030	47.5	73.7	16.9	0.8	1.8	8.9	7.0	18.9	7.8	12.3	14.3	15.7
51 049	40060	1	Cumberland	770	10 052	2 443	13.1	64.7	33.6	1.1	0.6	1.8	6.2	16.5	8.8	10.8	12.3	15.0
51 051	...	9	Dickenson	856	15 903	2 056	18.6	98.8	0.4	0.4	0.2	0.5	5.5	15.4	7.2	11.8	12.6	15.9
51 053	40060	1	Dinwiddie	1 305	28 001	1 497	21.5	64.0	33.3	0.7	0.7	2.4	5.7	17.1	8.7	11.2	13.6	17.0
51 057	...	8	Essex	666	11 151	2 355	16.7	57.4	39.1	1.0	1.0	3.1	5.8	16.2	8.2	10.4	12.1	15.2
51 059	47900	1	Fairfax	1 013	1 081 726	36	1 067.8	57.1	9.7	0.5	19.6	15.6	6.7	17.5	7.7	14.7	15.3	16.2
51 061	47900	1	Fauquier	1 677	65 203	804	38.9	83.7	9.1	0.8	1.9	6.4	5.8	19.4	7.1	9.7	13.8	18.1
51 063	...	8	Floyd	985	15 279	2 094	15.5	95.0	2.1	0.5	0.5	2.7	5.5	16.4	6.3	10.5	13.2	15.3
51 065	16820	3	Fluvanna	741	25 691	1 580	34.7	80.8	16.4	0.7	1.0	3.0	6.2	16.8	6.0	12.2	14.9	15.6
51 067	40220	2	Franklin	1 788	56 159	894	31.4	88.4	8.7	0.5	0.6	2.5	5.6	15.2	8.7	9.5	12.4	15.8
51 069	49020	3	Frederick	1 071	78 305	693	73.1	87.8	4.8	0.7	1.7	6.6	6.3	18.8	7.9	11.7	14.6	16.0
51 071	13980	3	Giles	921	17 286	1 965	18.8	96.8	1.8	0.6	0.5	1.2	5.3	16.4	7.0	10.1	13.8	14.9
51 073	47260	1	Gloucester	564	36 858	1 250	65.4	87.5	9.5	1.1	1.3	2.5	5.0	17.1	7.6	10.5	13.3	17.9
51 075	40060	1	Goochland	729	21 717	1 751	29.8	77.3	19.6	0.6	1.4	2.1	4.7	15.6	5.4	9.2	14.9	18.9
51 077	...	9	Grayson	1 145	15 533	2 080	13.6	94.9	2.4	0.6	0.1	2.7	4.5	14.5	6.8	9.1	12.6	15.4
51 079	16820	3	Greene	405	18 403	1 904	45.4	87.6	7.4	0.6	1.8	4.2	7.1	17.8	7.1	12.0	14.2	16.2
51 081	...	6	Greensville	765	12 243	2 289	16.0	38.3	60.0	0.4	0.5	1.4	4.1	12.3	8.7	15.5	16.5	17.1
51 083	...	6	Halifax	2 118	36 241	1 269	17.1	61.0	37.2	0.6	0.5	1.6	5.5	16.5	6.9	9.7	11.9	14.9
51 085	40060	1	Hanover	1 214	99 863	581	82.3	86.7	9.8	0.8	1.8	2.1	5.5	19.6	7.8	8.9	14.3	17.6
51 087	40060	1	Henrico	605	306 935	208	507.3	58.5	30.2	0.8	7.3	4.9	6.7	17.6	8.1	14.3	14.3	15.1
51 089	32300	4	Henry	990	54 151	923	54.7	72.8	22.7	0.5	0.6	4.7	5.4	15.1	7.2	9.9	12.9	15.8
51 091	...	9	Highland	1 075	2 321	3 029	2.2	98.6	0.3	0.3	0.2	0.8	2.8	12.1	5.4	7.0	9.7	18.1
51 093	47260	1	Isle of Wight	817	35 270	1 292	43.2	72.2	25.3	0.9	1.3	1.9	5.2	17.5	6.8	9.4	12.9	18.8
51 095	47260	1	James City	369	67 009	785	181.6	79.5	14.0	0.9	3.2	4.5	5.2	16.3	7.0	9.5	12.1	14.9
51 097	40060	1	King and Queen	816	6 945	2 692	8.5	66.9	29.3	2.2	0.5	2.6	5.2	15.6	7.2	9.9	11.9	17.1
51 099	...	8	King George	465	23 584	1 660	50.7	76.9	19.1	1.1	2.1	3.3	7.6	20.1	7.6	12.4	14.9	16.5
51 101	40060	1	King William	710	15 935	2 053	22.4	77.9	18.7	2.6	1.1	2.0	6.3	18.4	7.2	12.1	14.4	16.6
51 103	...	9	Lancaster	345	11 391	2 339	33.0	70.4	28.3	0.4	0.7	1.0	4.0	12.1	5.8	6.9	8.5	14.1
51 105	...	8	Lee	1 128	25 587	1 582	22.7	94.0	3.8	0.8	0.4	1.6	5.2	15.1	7.8	12.9	14.3	14.9
51 107	47900	1	Loudoun	1 335	312 311	204	233.9	65.1	8.0	0.6	16.8	12.4	8.8	21.7	5.9	13.9	18.9	15.6

1. CBSA = Core Based Statistical Area. See Appendix A for explanation. See Appendix B for list of metropolitan areas with component counties.   2. County type code from the Economic Research Service of USDA Rural-Urban Continuum Codes. See Appendix A for definition.   3. Dry land or land partially or temporarily covered by water.   4. May be of any race.

Table B. States and Counties — **Population and Households**

STATE County	Population, 2010 (cont.) Age (percent) (cont.) 55 to 64 years	65 to 74 years	75 years and over	Percent female	Population change and components of change, 1990–2010 Total persons 1990	2000	Percent change 1990–2000	2000–2010	Components of change, 2000–2009 Births	Deaths	Net migration	Households, 2010 Number	Percent change, 2000–2010	Persons per house-hold	Percent Female family house-holder[1]	One per-son
	16	17	18	19	20	21	22	23	24	25	26	27	28	29	30	31
VERMONT—Cont'd																
Chittenden	11.9	6.0	5.3	51.3	131 761	146 571	11.2	6.8	15 082	8 844	438	61 827	9.5	2.37	9.1	27.7
Essex	17.1	11.1	8.2	49.4	6 405	6 459	0.8	-2.4	502	565	36	2 818	8.3	2.23	8.7	29.3
Franklin	12.8	6.7	5.4	50.4	39 980	45 417	13.6	5.1	5 563	3 351	828	18 513	10.4	2.55	10.7	22.7
Grand Isle	18.2	9.0	5.0	50.1	5 318	6 901	29.8	1.0	646	469	509	2 902	5.1	2.40	8.6	22.5
Lamoille	13.2	7.7	5.7	50.0	19 735	23 233	17.7	5.3	2 634	1 664	1 784	10 014	8.6	2.37	9.4	27.3
Orange	15.9	8.4	6.4	50.2	26 149	28 226	7.9	2.5	2 677	2 152	295	11 887	8.7	2.37	9.3	25.9
Orleans	15.3	9.8	7.9	50.0	24 053	26 277	9.2	3.6	2 576	2 488	1 062	11 320	8.4	2.33	9.6	27.8
Rutland	15.5	9.0	7.6	50.7	62 142	63 400	2.0	-2.8	5 611	5 763	119	25 984	1.2	2.28	9.9	30.2
Washington	15.1	7.7	6.7	50.6	54 928	58 039	5.7	2.6	5 650	4 488	-143	25 027	5.8	2.28	10.0	29.7
Windham	16.5	8.9	7.2	50.9	41 588	44 216	6.3	0.7	4 037	3 709	-812	19 290	5.0	2.23	10.1	31.8
Windsor	16.2	9.8	8.0	51.0	54 055	57 418	6.2	-1.3	5 017	5 091	-429	24 753	2.4	2.25	9.0	30.0
VIRGINIA	11.9	6.9	5.3	50.9	6 189 197	7 078 515	14.4	13.0	957 904	532 166	375 639	3 056 058	13.2	2.54	12.4	26.0
Accomack	15.2	10.6	8.5	51.3	31 703	38 305	20.8	-13.4	4 446	4 135	93	13 798	-9.8	2.37	13.5	28.8
Albemarle	12.5	7.4	6.9	51.9	68 177	79 236	16.2	24.9	9 723	5 833	7 389	38 157	19.7	2.41	9.6	28.0
Alleghany	15.4	11.6	8.7	51.1	17 494	17 215	-1.6	25.7	1 682	2 198	-373	6 891	33.8	2.32	9.6	28.9
Amelia	14.1	9.6	6.2	50.9	8 787	11 400	29.7	11.3	1 366	1 167	1 357	4 821	13.7	2.61	11.3	21.2
Amherst	13.8	9.4	7.1	52.2	28 578	31 894	11.6	1.4	3 024	2 890	646	12 560	5.2	2.45	13.4	25.4
Appomattox	13.9	10.1	7.3	51.3	12 300	13 705	11.4	9.3	1 427	1 305	805	6 033	13.4	2.47	12.6	24.3
Arlington	9.9	4.9	3.8	50.2	170 895	189 453	10.9	9.6	25 711	9 376	3 807	98 050	13.5	2.09	5.9	41.3
Augusta	14.4	9.3	6.7	49.3	54 557	65 615	20.3	12.4	6 937	5 404	5 260	28 516	14.9	2.49	9.2	22.5
Bath	15.6	12.9	9.3	49.5	4 799	5 048	5.2	-6.3	303	535	-314	2 162	5.3	2.16	6.8	32.9
Bedford	15.3	9.9	6.3	50.4	45 553	60 371	32.5	13.8	5 787	4 644	5 986	27 465	15.2	2.49	8.1	21.9
Bland	15.4	10.5	6.9	44.8	6 514	6 871	5.5	-0.7	528	715	143	2 566	-0.1	2.39	8.7	24.7
Botetourt	16.0	9.6	6.8	50.5	24 992	30 496	22.0	8.7	2 623	2 468	2 009	13 126	12.2	2.50	7.7	21.6
Brunswick	13.9	9.3	7.2	47.5	15 987	18 419	15.2	-5.3	1 663	1 883	-596	6 366	1.4	2.40	19.2	29.2
Buchanan	16.3	10.2	5.8	48.9	31 333	26 978	-13.9	-10.7	2 151	2 756	-3 461	9 968	-4.7	2.30	10.6	27.9
Buckingham	13.9	8.4	5.9	44.6	12 873	15 623	21.4	9.7	1 436	1 575	677	5 965	12.0	2.48	16.3	20.3
Campbell	13.4	9.0	6.8	51.3	47 499	51 078	7.5	7.4	5 405	4 262	1 080	22 441	8.7	2.42	12.4	26.2
Caroline	12.7	7.7	5.4	50.8	19 217	22 121	15.1	29.0	3 133	2 146	4 880	10 456	30.4	2.68	14.0	22.0
Carroll	15.1	11.0	8.4	50.7	26 519	29 245	10.3	2.7	2 653	3 085	402	12 831	5.3	2.32	9.6	28.1
Charles City	17.2	10.1	6.6	50.8	6 282	6 926	10.3	4.8	642	596	284	2 955	10.7	2.46	15.5	23.6
Charlotte	13.8	10.2	8.5	50.9	11 688	12 472	6.7	0.9	1 335	1 451	-256	5 109	3.2	2.43	14.2	28.5
Chesterfield	12.6	6.2	4.2	51.8	209 599	259 903	24.0	21.7	33 875	15 291	29 836	115 690	20.4	2.69	13.2	20.7
Clarke	14.9	8.9	7.4	50.2	12 101	12 652	4.6	10.9	1 208	1 218	2 018	5 509	11.5	2.50	8.9	24.9
Craig	15.5	10.3	6.8	50.6	4 372	5 091	16.4	1.9	439	455	-71	2 183	6.0	2.37	8.2	26.6
Culpeper	11.8	7.2	5.0	49.3	27 791	34 262	23.3	36.3	5 424	3 136	10 066	16 231	33.7	2.77	11.9	21.1
Cumberland	14.3	9.5	6.6	51.6	7 825	9 017	15.2	11.5	971	758	584	3 980	12.8	2.52	14.6	26.1
Dickenson	14.8	9.8	6.9	50.0	17 620	16 395	-7.0	-3.0	1 575	1 785	2	6 590	-2.1	2.36	10.1	27.2
Dinwiddie	13.1	8.4	5.3	50.9	22 279	24 533	10.1	14.1	2 418	2 152	1 647	10 504	15.3	2.58	15.3	23.0
Essex	14.8	9.7	7.7	52.7	8 689	9 989	15.0	11.6	1 166	1 197	1 276	4 517	13.1	2.43	15.5	27.3
Fairfax	12.2	5.8	4.0	50.6	818 310	969 749	18.5	11.5	137 141	39 825	-24 878	391 627	11.7	2.74	9.2	22.7
Fauquier	13.3	7.6	5.1	50.7	48 700	55 139	13.2	18.3	7 095	4 173	10 169	23 658	19.2	2.74	9.2	20.4
Floyd	15.2	10.4	7.2	49.8	11 965	13 874	16.0	10.1	1 465	1 391	1 145	6 415	10.8	2.37	7.9	27.2
Fluvanna	12.6	9.3	6.4	54.1	12 429	20 047	61.3	28.2	2 901	1 563	4 397	9 449	27.9	2.58	10.4	20.2
Franklin	15.3	10.6	6.9	50.7	39 549	47 286	19.6	18.8	5 130	4 387	4 189	22 780	20.1	2.40	10.5	24.7
Frederick	11.9	7.5	5.2	50.3	45 723	59 209	29.5	32.3	8 316	4 315	12 049	28 864	30.6	2.68	10.0	20.5
Giles	14.5	10.0	8.0	51.0	16 366	16 657	1.8	3.8	1 766	1 956	977	7 215	3.2	2.38	10.5	27.9
Gloucester	13.9	8.7	5.9	50.5	30 131	34 780	15.4	6.0	3 699	2 907	3 765	14 293	8.9	2.55	10.3	21.3
Goochland	16.5	9.3	5.6	50.4	14 163	16 863	19.1	28.8	1 824	1 421	4 126	7 998	29.9	2.54	8.1	18.7
Grayson	16.1	11.3	9.7	51.0	16 278	17 917	10.1	-13.3	1 432	2 006	-420	6 846	-5.7	2.24	9.5	29.3
Greene	12.8	7.8	5.0	50.8	10 297	15 244	48.0	20.7	2 379	1 130	1 981	6 780	21.6	2.69	10.9	20.1
Greensville	13.1	7.4	5.1	37.4	8 553	11 560	35.2	5.9	1 237	917	239	3 566	5.7	2.44	19.5	26.7
Halifax	15.3	10.6	8.8	52.3	36 030	37 355	3.7	-3.0	3 845	4 365	-1 351	15 085	0.4	2.35	15.6	30.1
Hanover	13.2	7.4	5.7	50.9	63 306	86 320	36.4	15.7	9 957	6 384	10 512	36 589	17.6	2.68	10.4	19.2
Henrico	11.6	6.2	6.1	53.0	217 878	262 300	20.4	17.0	36 180	21 837	21 479	124 601	15.2	2.44	14.8	28.9
Henry	14.1	11.1	8.5	51.8	56 942	57 930	1.7	-6.5	5 797	5 883	-2 656	23 151	-3.2	2.31	13.9	29.2
Highland	19.9	14.6	10.3	50.1	2 635	2 536	-3.8	-8.5	136	260	-70	1 081	-4.4	2.15	6.1	29.0
Isle of Wight	14.7	8.7	5.9	51.3	25 053	29 728	18.7	18.6	3 323	2 732	5 694	13 718	21.2	2.55	12.6	21.4
James City	14.3	11.5	9.2	51.7	34 779	48 102	38.3	39.3	4 934	4 128	15 022	26 860	41.3	2.45	9.5	21.9
King and Queen	15.9	9.6	7.7	50.3	6 289	6 630	5.4	4.8	664	727	286	2 882	7.8	2.41	13.1	26.5
King George	10.9	6.4	3.7	49.7	13 527	16 803	24.2	40.4	2 854	1 221	5 177	8 376	37.5	2.78	10.7	19.8
King William	12.7	7.2	5.2	51.3	10 913	13 146	20.5	21.2	1 812	1 151	2 479	5 979	23.4	2.65	11.3	19.8
Lancaster	17.4	15.8	15.4	53.0	10 896	11 567	6.2	-1.5	969	1 871	627	5 265	5.2	2.13	11.0	31.6
Lee	13.9	9.6	6.4	47.8	24 496	23 589	-3.7	8.5	2 268	2 814	2 203	10 159	4.7	2.35	12.0	29.1
Loudoun	8.6	3.9	2.6	50.7	86 185	169 599	96.8	84.1	43 650	7 459	95 450	104 583	74.6	2.98	8.3	17.8

1. No spouse present.

Table B. States and Counties — Population, Vital Statistics, Medicare, and Crime

STATE County	Persons in group quarters, 2010	Daytime population, 2006–2010 Number	Daytime population Employment/residence ratio	Births, average 2006–2008 Total	Births Rate[1]	Deaths, average 2006–2008 Number	Deaths Rate[1]	Persons under 65 with no health insurance, 2009 Number	Persons under 65 Percent	Medicare, 2011 Eligible for Medicare	Enrolled in Medicare Advantage	Enrolled in a Medicare prescription drug plan	Serious crimes known to police,[2] 2010 Total Number	Total Rate[3]
	32	33	34	35	36	37	38	39	40	41	42	43	44	45
VERMONT—Cont'd														
Chittenden	9 795	168 951	1.2	1 606	10.6	962	6.3	11 969	9.1	23 256	1 341	11 111	4 958	3 167
Essex	16	5 161	0.6	D	D	63	9.7	709	14.0	1 711	96	946	NA	NA
Franklin	529	41 202	0.7	596	12.4	365	7.6	4 128	10.1	7 043	371	4 006	1 113	2 331
Grand Isle	0	5 083	0.5	D	D	55	7.1	717	11.4	1 475	112	688	71	1 019
Lamoille	694	23 289	0.9	D	D	186	7.5	2 457	11.9	4 159	202	2 398	367	1 499
Orange	715	23 423	0.6	D	D	235	8.1	2 621	11.0	5 366	256	2 811	369	1 275
Orleans	818	26 193	0.9	D	D	254	9.3	2 827	12.9	6 274	402	3 690	517	1 899
Rutland	2 318	61 355	1.0	591	9.3	641	10.1	5 458	10.8	13 775	708	8 299	1 686	2 941
Washington	2 410	63 163	1.1	609	10.3	496	8.4	4 754	9.8	11 066	731	5 660	1 420	2 385
Windham	1 464	46 014	1.1	D	D	390	9.0	4 015	11.3	9 073	448	5 039	1 154	2 593
Windsor	898	53 869	0.9	547	9.6	560	9.8	4 403	9.7	12 757	737	6 415	844	1 489
VIRGINIA	239 834	7 761 262	1.0	107 796	14.0	58 338	7.6	908 234	13.6	1 190 827	169 483	492 015	203 283	2 541
Accomack	428	33 108	0.9	498	12.9	446	11.5	6 258	20.3	7 687	854	3 643	671	2 023
Albemarle	6 864	103 908	1.2	1 117	12.0	679	7.3	9 545	11.9	15 118	1 137	7 572	2 280	2 304
Alleghany	281	16 815	1.1	D	D	241	14.7	1 743	13.6	4 148	559	2 642	280	1 723
Amelia	128	9 952	0.5	D	D	135	10.7	1 894	17.9	2 511	454	1 171	182	1 434
Amherst	1 538	26 882	0.6	D	D	324	10.0	4 200	16.0	6 678	1 124	3 560	501	1 549
Appomattox	56	11 918	0.6	D	D	155	10.8	1 961	16.6	3 312	502	1 884	119	795
Arlington	2 892	249 979	1.4	2 866	14.0	950	4.6	22 651	11.8	19 486	1 806	5 970	5 076	2 445
Augusta	2 708	66 830	0.8	809	11.4	626	8.8	8 695	14.5	14 568	1 825	7 942	833	1 129
Bath	53	4 657	0.9	D	D	55	11.8	611	17.9	1 190	80	735	48	1 015
Bedford	287	50 327	0.5	641	9.6	555	8.3	7 716	13.6	14 266	2 443	6 679	1 008	1 468
Bland	686	6 357	0.8	D	D	83	12.0	885	16.1	1 599	236	835	43	630
Botetourt	275	26 806	0.6	284	8.8	296	9.2	3 126	11.7	6 913	1 188	3 173	383	1 155
Brunswick	2 184	15 587	0.6	D	D	192	10.8	2 806	20.0	3 532	522	1 951	213	1 222
Buchanan	1 173	25 150	1.1	D	D	287	12.0	3 530	18.5	7 398	2 020	3 580	495	2 054
Buckingham	2 326	16 003	0.8	D	D	170	10.6	2 774	20.7	2 960	324	1 494	232	1 353
Campbell	468	48 089	0.8	D	D	479	9.1	6 590	15.1	11 039	2 056	5 660	971	1 771
Caroline	513	21 219	0.5	D	D	246	9.0	3 807	16.2	4 591	580	1 912	495	1 734
Carroll	337	27 392	0.8	D	D	347	11.9	4 180	18.1	7 173	838	4 333	539	1 794
Charles City	0	5 812	0.6	D	D	65	9.1	1 088	19.0	1 499	343	632	43	593
Charlotte	175	10 879	0.6	D	D	157	12.7	1 834	19.4	3 091	448	1 725	131	1 041
Chesterfield	4 651	267 692	0.7	3 863	12.9	1 787	6.0	31 243	11.4	42 558	7 168	16 271	7 575	2 395
Clarke	255	11 763	0.7	D	D	136	9.4	1 518	12.8	2 512	221	1 055	206	1 468
Craig	9	3 360	0.3	D	D	48	9.3	701	17.2	1 170	203	571	22	424
Culpeper	1 761	40 970	0.8	697	15.3	364	8.0	6 229	15.7	7 166	746	3 128	794	1 701
Cumberland	37	7 394	0.4	D	D	88	9.2	1 449	18.3	1 950	326	958	69	686
Dickenson	335	15 034	0.8	D	D	191	11.8	2 246	17.1	4 555	1 285	1 882	244	1 534
Dinwiddie	919	22 271	0.6	D	D	245	9.5	3 336	14.9	4 886	765	2 135	525	1 875
Essex	190	9 948	0.8	D	D	131	12.1	1 393	15.7	2 442	305	1 203	167	1 498
Fairfax	9 290	1 054 022	1.0	15 055	14.9	4 384	4.3	99 958	10.9	115 011	11 292	30 704	17 949	1 659
Fauquier	389	55 497	0.7	813	12.2	466	7.0	6 910	11.8	9 397	804	3 454	945	1 449
Floyd	85	11 922	0.6	D	D	153	10.4	2 358	19.4	3 302	480	1 803	174	1 139
Fluvanna	1 272	18 386	0.4	D	D	185	7.3	2 940	13.8	4 579	422	1 958	296	1 152
Franklin	1 472	46 713	0.7	592	11.6	503	9.8	6 875	16.3	12 185	2 508	5 858	845	1 505
Frederick	967	68 008	0.8	972	13.4	485	6.7	8 790	13.6	11 863	1 182	5 102	1 680	2 145
Giles	136	16 036	0.8	D	D	211	12.2	1 988	14.1	4 164	758	1 869	272	1 574
Gloucester	368	28 776	0.6	D	D	342	8.9	4 659	14.2	6 668	851	2 297	613	1 663
Goochland	1 405	23 827	1.4	D	D	155	7.5	1 904	10.6	4 086	650	1 823	210	967
Grayson	178	12 369	0.5	D	D	211	13.2	2 240	18.3	4 208	341	2 559	152	979
Greene	137	12 504	0.4	D	D	121	6.8	2 469	15.8	2 853	270	1 405	292	1 587
Greensville	3 527	11 586	0.9	D	D	108	9.3	1 863	18.5	2 153	678	1 465	166	1 356
Halifax	738	35 323	0.9	400	11.2	477	13.4	4 565	16.7	8 808	1 580	5 118	925	2 552
Hanover	1 980	91 607	0.9	1 046	10.5	717	7.2	8 233	9.7	15 654	2 706	6 521	1 212	1 214
Henrico	2 494	310 236	1.1	4 078	14.1	2 370	8.2	32 124	12.9	44 230	7 753	18 466	8 272	2 695
Henry	561	51 501	0.8	639	11.5	678	12.2	8 130	18.5	14 323	3 891	7 962	1 219	2 251
Highland	0	2 180	0.8	D	D	28	11.5	426	24.4	669	62	371	15	646
Isle of Wight	310	28 578	0.6	D	D	307	8.7	3 844	12.8	6 403	1 105	2 353	675	1 914
James City	1 100	59 981	0.9	D	D	486	8.0	5 000	10.0	15 365	1 369	5 192	1 031	1 539
King and Queen	0	5 190	0.4	D	D	81	11.7	959	17.5	1 435	185	758	77	1 109
King George	301	24 095	1.1	352	15.6	142	6.3	2 434	11.8	2 843	181	890	426	1 806
King William	72	12 381	0.6	D	D	128	8.2	1 799	12.9	2 587	319	1 361	152	954
Lancaster	183	12 666	1.2	D	D	204	17.7	1 243	16.6	3 886	343	1 824	163	1 431
Lee	1 706	22 185	0.6	D	D	293	12.4	3 746	18.0	6 022	1 562	2 763	307	1 200
Loudoun	1 172	266 018	0.8	5 191	18.6	891	3.2	19 621	7.1	23 100	2 708	7 222	3 869	1 239

1. Per 1,000 estimated resident population.   2. Data for serious crimes have not been adjusted for underreporting; this may affect comparability between geographic areas and over time.   3. Per 100,000 population estimated by the FBI.

Table B. States and Counties — Crime, Education, Money Income, and Poverty

STATE County	Serious crimes known to police,[1] 2010 (cont.) Rate[2] Violent	Property	Education — School enrollment and attainment, 2006–2010 Enrollment[3] Total	Per-cent private	Attainment[4] (percent) High school graduate or less	Bach-elor's degree or more	Local government expenditures,[5] 2008–2009 Total current expenditures (mil dol)	Current expenditures per student (dollars)	Money income, 2006–2010 Per capita income[6] (dollars)	Households Median income Dollars	Percent change, 2000 to 2006–2010 (constant 2010 dollars)	Percent with income of $200,000 or more	Income and poverty, 2010 Median household income (dollars)	Percent below poverty level All persons	Children under 18 years	Children 5 to 17 years in families
	46	47	48	49	50	51	52	53	54	55	56	57	58	59	60	61
VERMONT—Cont'd																
Chittenden	152	3 015	46 424	20.1	29.9	44.8	322.9	14 807	31 095	59 878	-0.8	4.2	56 016	11.8	11.9	10.0
Essex	NA	NA	1 235	12.3	61.6	15.9	11.5	15 682	20 040	37 734	-2.3	1.0	34 947	17.2	26.5	22.3
Franklin	147	2 184	11 598	9.1	52.7	21.2	113.5	13 495	24 767	53 623	1.6	1.3	51 296	11.9	15.5	13.7
Grand Isle	0	1 019	1 568	12.6	43.3	28.6	11.4	17 863	30 499	57 436	5.4	3.2	54 907	8.1	14.8	12.9
Lamoille	53	1 446	5 877	10.2	38.9	34.6	52.7	14 514	27 164	52 232	4.8	3.2	47 994	13.3	16.6	15.1
Orange	55	1 220	7 084	19.8	44.8	29.2	71.7	16 729	25 951	52 079	3.2	1.8	48 008	12.5	17.3	14.9
Orleans	125	1 774	5 452	10.3	56.4	19.9	64.8	15 811	20 652	40 202	2.1	1.1	36 515	17.0	24.4	21.6
Rutland	133	2 808	14 774	15.3	48.5	26.3	138.6	15 539	25 426	47 027	1.1	2.1	43 600	13.2	16.7	15.2
Washington	123	2 263	14 179	24.5	37.8	37.4	126.2	14 281	28 337	55 313	6.6	2.6	51 334	10.8	14.0	11.5
Windham	173	2 420	10 297	28.1	40.8	33.8	103.4	17 357	27 247	46 714	-3.4	2.4	43 045	12.8	18.1	15.6
Windsor	132	1 357	12 209	21.2	42.0	32.8	133.2	17 056	29 053	50 893	-1.2	3.3	48 804	10.2	14.0	12.3
VIRGINIA	214	2 327	2 071 067	17.2	39.9	33.8	13 499.0	10 930	32 145	61 406	3.9	6.3	60 665	11.1	14.6	13.1
Accomack	187	1 836	6 964	11.4	59.0	18.0	50.1	9 652	22 766	41 372	8.0	1.7	37 312	20.5	28.7	25.4
Albemarle	134	2 169	29 395	17.8	28.0	51.6	[7]216.9	[7]12 860	36 685	64 847	0.9	8.3	61 845	9.1	10.0	9.0
Alleghany	92	1 631	3 724	8.3	56.5	14.9	29.3	10 132	22 013	43 160	NA	0.7	43 110	13.1	20.4	17.3
Amelia	165	1 269	2 412	10.7	62.0	13.1	17.6	9 444	24 197	50 135	-1.6	2.3	49 057	11.4	16.8	15.2
Amherst	90	1 459	8 129	29.6	56.7	15.6	45.7	9 578	21 097	44 757	-5.5	0.9	42 063	13.6	18.9	16.5
Appomattox	140	855	3 375	16.7	62.1	11.8	21.0	9 356	22 388	49 224	6.5	0.4	44 479	14.1	21.8	18.9
Arlington	157	2 288	41 128	30.4	17.0	70.1	361.6	18 452	57 724	94 880	18.9	15.1	93 231	7.2	10.4	10.6
Augusta	100	1 029	15 525	16.4	58.4	19.1	104.0	9 454	23 571	50 612	-7.1	1.4	50 534	9.5	13.2	11.0
Bath	21	993	829	15.8	68.2	11.5	9.4	12 825	22 083	50 589	14.1	0.0	41 266	11.2	15.7	12.7
Bedford	360	1 108	16 040	21.8	47.8	24.2	[8]95.4	[8]8 731	27 732	54 110	-0.9	3.1	51 656	9.8	12.9	10.6
Bland	73	557	1 191	10.2	57.5	12.0	8.5	9 099	20 468	41 552	8.0	1.2	39 975	15.0	18.0	15.4
Botetourt	91	1 065	7 502	19.3	46.7	22.9	48.7	9 852	29 540	64 724	4.9	4.2	63 528	6.5	8.8	7.6
Brunswick	132	1 090	3 929	28.6	65.1	11.9	24.5	11 289	16 739	35 184	-11.2	0.3	36 806	20.5	26.9	24.0
Buchanan	141	1 913	4 769	12.8	67.8	8.9	37.1	10 911	16 742	29 183	3.7	0.5	29 712	24.8	34.9	32.6
Buckingham	163	1 190	1 552	31.6	74.0	12.4	22.1	10 664	16 752	34 720	-8.2	0.6	37 568	20.5	25.2	23.8
Campbell	148	1 623	13 110	24.9	53.2	16.3	78.5	8 983	22 044	43 478	-7.9	0.9	42 158	14.3	18.6	16.2
Caroline	158	1 576	6 197	11.4	57.7	15.6	38.2	8 992	25 024	57 690	14.3	1.3	52 779	11.2	16.6	15.6
Carroll	110	1 684	6 140	8.2	63.1	11.7	39.5	9 692	18 670	36 142	-6.7	0.0	34 796	17.6	24.9	21.9
Charles City	96	496	1 418	10.7	66.1	10.9	11.1	12 925	23 955	46 337	-14.4	1.5	45 916	11.9	18.4	16.2
Charlotte	111	930	3 297	8.7	58.4	15.1	21.8	9 980	17 348	34 881	-4.8	0.5	33 899	18.6	28.1	25.1
Chesterfield	157	2 238	88 773	14.0	35.4	35.7	547.0	9 259	31 711	71 321	-3.8	5.2	69 190	6.9	9.0	7.7
Clarke	164	1 304	3 145	23.4	43.8	29.2	20.6	9 494	34 630	73 244	12.1	6.4	67 982	8.3	10.1	8.4
Craig	0	424	1 081	14.9	66.3	13.6	6.8	9 735	23 461	51 291	8.6	0.9	44 882	11.6	17.9	15.8
Culpeper	201	1 499	11 238	18.6	51.5	21.6	71.2	9 635	27 507	65 132	13.6	3.2	56 897	10.5	14.8	13.8
Cumberland	149	537	2 290	14.8	64.0	12.5	16.5	10 668	19 691	40 143	-0.4	2.0	39 394	17.2	26.0	23.1
Dickenson	113	1 421	3 065	1.9	72.4	8.8	26.9	10 607	16 278	29 080	-2.0	0.6	32 955	23.0	26.6	23.8
Dinwiddie	179	1 696	6 125	9.7	62.4	13.1	44.5	9 510	23 423	51 459	-2.3	1.3	50 535	11.9	16.6	14.6
Essex	108	1 390	2 117	19.3	56.4	16.6	16.8	10 343	23 795	46 235	-2.4	0.6	43 125	14.1	23.6	22.5
Fairfax	99	1 560	288 530	21.2	22.0	58.0	[9]2 233.7	[9]13 215	49 001	105 416	2.7	17.4	102 726	5.9	7.3	6.7
Fauquier	106	1 343	17 338	18.1	39.4	30.8	125.3	11 126	38 710	83 877	6.8	10.1	83 176	7.5	9.1	7.4
Floyd	65	1 073	3 007	20.9	55.0	19.3	19.4	9 382	21 425	42 044	5.1	0.9	44 188	13.6	19.6	17.6
Fluvanna	74	1 078	5 535	13.7	44.5	25.8	37.5	10 120	29 407	68 223	16.2	2.8	63 869	7.3	9.2	8.2
Franklin	91	1 414	12 133	18.3	57.0	15.2	72.2	9 723	23 527	45 555	-5.5	1.8	40 931	14.4	21.6	20.7
Frederick	126	2 019	19 118	15.7	50.2	23.1	[10]177.3	[10]10 526	27 977	61 973	4.3	3.2	62 173	7.4	11.0	9.4
Giles	81	1 493	3 948	13.9	57.1	16.1	23.3	9 014	20 985	41 186	-6.9	1.3	40 773	13.4	18.9	16.4
Gloucester	49	1 614	8 554	11.4	48.0	19.2	59.1	9 803	27 395	59 331	3.2	2.3	58 893	9.9	14.1	12.0
Goochland	101	866	3 696	29.8	47.3	30.7	26.6	10 996	38 553	79 574	11.6	12.5	81 938	7.7	9.8	8.4
Grayson	135	843	2 830	1.8	62.0	10.3	22.4	10 875	19 499	32 178	-11.4	0.9	31 930	17.1	27.4	24.9
Greene	272	1 315	3 866	14.7	55.9	20.0	28.3	9 920	24 969	54 307	-6.6	1.2	57 592	9.7	13.3	12.2
Greensville	147	1 209	1 963	9.6	75.6	5.5	[11]27.2	[11]9 971	17 631	38 574	-4.8	0.9	38 702	23.9	25.8	22.5
Halifax	193	2 359	8 253	9.8	61.5	13.2	61.1	10 152	19 909	34 705	-8.4	1.9	35 879	19.3	28.3	23.0
Hanover	82	1 132	27 337	17.7	37.6	33.0	179.2	9 445	34 201	76 425	1.9	6.1	72 319	5.3	6.4	5.5
Henrico	163	2 532	77 738	17.0	34.1	38.9	444.9	9 081	33 001	60 114	-3.5	5.2	59 128	9.8	13.4	11.4
Henry	292	1 959	11 435	7.8	61.2	10.9	70.2	9 280	19 206	34 086	-15.4	1.2	32 669	17.7	27.2	24.3
Highland	86	560	318	9.7	63.2	21.4	3.7	13 370	25 690	43 481	15.5	1.1	35 793	14.4	22.8	18.9
Isle of Wight	125	1 789	9 061	23.1	44.7	25.1	56.3	10 241	29 547	62 242	8.3	3.7	62 224	8.8	12.3	10.3
James City	93	1 446	15 157	15.9	28.0	45.0	[12]120.1	[12]11 393	38 162	73 903	5.0	7.6	74 241	7.7	10.3	8.9
King and Queen	202	907	1 155	20.1	66.8	9.9	10.7	13 319	21 777	44 442	-2.4	1.5	44 277	12.8	19.4	17.2
King George	110	1 696	5 721	16.7	40.1	30.5	34.0	8 366	32 630	76 241	20.7	5.9	77 200	6.9	9.0	8.0
King William	63	891	3 778	15.0	53.2	19.8	30.4	10 174	26 853	64 946	2.8	1.2	64 205	7.7	11.0	9.6
Lancaster	70	1 361	1 854	11.4	45.3	27.7	14.9	10 792	29 275	45 209	7.4	2.3	44 296	13.9	26.1	24.0
Lee	125	1 075	5 384	7.2	60.7	12.0	39.9	10 789	16 513	31 352	7.8	0.4	31 116	25.5	33.1	28.3
Loudoun	79	1 160	87 353	20.3	21.0	57.2	740.4	13 013	45 356	115 574	13.2	17.4	119 075	3.7	4.2	3.8

1. Data for serious crimes have not been adjusted for underreporting; this may affect comparability between geographic areas and over time. 2. Per 100,000 population estimated by the FBI. 3. All persons 3 years old and over enrolled in nursery school through college. 4. Persons 25 years old and over. 5. Elementary and secondary education expenditures. 6. Based on population estimated by the American Community Survey, 2006–2010. 7. Charlottesville city is included with Albemarle county. 8. Bedford city is included with Bedford county. 9. Fairfax city is included with Fairfax county. 10. Winchester city is included with Frederick county. 11. Emporia city is included with Greensville county. 12. Williamsburg city is included with James City county.

Table B. States and Counties — **Personal Income**

STATE County	Personal income, 2009 Total (mil dol)	Percent change, 2008–2009	Per capita[1] Dollars	Per capita[1] Rank	Wages and salaries[2] (mil dol)	Proprietors' income (mil dol)	Dividends, interest, and rent (mil dol)	Transfer payments (mil dol) Total	Government payments to individuals Total	Social Security	Medical payments	Income maintenance	Unemployment insurance
	62	63	64	65	66	67	68	69	70	71	72	73	74
VERMONT—Cont'd													
Chittenden	6 623	-0.5	43 483	255	5 475	444	1 244	1 007	979	327	430	97	56
Essex	152	0.7	23 787	2 973	51	10	21	53	52	22	14	7	3
Franklin	1 759	1.1	36 518	814	839	121	192	317	309	89	133	43	19
Grand Isle	281	0.8	37 168	728	49	16	56	47	45	21	12	5	4
Lamoille	952	-0.2	36 669	793	458	89	190	197	192	55	95	19	13
Orange	973	0.0	33 677	1 222	339	82	153	202	196	70	77	21	11
Orleans	892	0.8	32 668	1 390	413	100	144	271	266	78	123	33	15
Rutland	2 415	0.4	38 320	596	1 306	101	402	735	724	188	409	61	32
Washington	2 477	0.5	42 208	313	1 692	176	413	529	519	152	260	42	24
Windham	1 684	-0.7	38 730	563	1 048	135	346	385	377	125	163	36	19
Windsor	2 359	-0.8	41 706	350	1 147	174	513	455	445	175	176	40	21
VIRGINIA	347 284	-0.3	44 057	X	242 599	20 655	57 238	44 806	43 390	16 061	17 114	4 339	1 662
Accomack	1 099	1.1	28 584	2 283	593	73	222	276	269	101	112	35	5
Albemarle	(3)6 330	(3)-2.0	(3)46 163	(3)163	(3)5 117	(3)506	(3)1 708	(3)745	(3)720	(3)291	(3)305	(3)60	(3)18
Alleghany	(4)688	(4)-0.7	(4)30 724	(4)1 816	(4)396	(4)32	(4)110	(4)216	(4)211	(4)77	(4)86	(4)18	(4)7
Amelia	422	-1.1	32 782	1 369	112	32	58	88	85	35	32	9	4
Amherst	954	0.8	29 372	2 126	432	35	130	225	219	93	84	21	7
Appomattox	448	1.0	30 782	1 805	138	20	60	110	108	44	39	12	4
Arlington	15 917	1.6	73 187	7	18 340	945	2 727	734	695	231	280	48	20
Augusta	(5)3 912	(5)-1.6	(5)33 114	(5)1 318	(5)2 114	(5)319	(5)761	(5)830	(5)808	(5)348	(5)310	(5)68	(5)31
Bath	173	-3.8	38 495	578	90	6	48	42	41	16	19	2	1
Bedford	(6)2 772	(6)-1.7	(6)37 715	(6)674	(6)818	(6)168	(6)497	(6)503	(6)490	(6)221	(6)168	(6)34	(6)15
Bland	195	1.7	28 773	2 240	101	6	27	54	52	22	20	4	2
Botetourt	1 366	-1.2	41 950	333	476	80	215	210	204	95	66	11	7
Brunswick	460	0.9	26 274	2 672	198	21	62	150	147	45	61	20	5
Buchanan	707	0.1	30 915	1 778	435	50	88	266	262	109	98	31	5
Buckingham	389	-0.3	24 198	2 948	145	28	55	107	104	37	41	14	4
Campbell	(7)4 068	(7)-0.4	(7)32 052	(7)1 516	(7)3 481	(7)205	(7)757	(7)1 017	(7)994	(7)343	(7)439	(7)100	(7)27
Caroline	940	0.0	33 729	1 212	270	51	109	168	163	61	62	18	9
Carroll	(8)1 047	(8)2.0	(8)29 162	(8)2 152	(8)478	(8)72	(8)148	(8)351	(8)345	(8)119	(8)166	(8)32	(8)12
Charles City	235	-3.4	32 527	1 418	73	13	38	56	54	21	22	5	3
Charlotte	337	0.3	28 012	2 397	113	23	58	113	111	40	48	13	3
Chesterfield	12 713	-3.4	41 454	365	6 514	616	1 905	1 477	1 421	633	463	125	76
Clarke	558	-2.1	38 231	612	211	19	133	78	75	33	29	4	4
Craig	151	-2.1	30 296	1 907	27	8	21	35	34	15	10	3	1
Culpeper	1 536	-0.9	33 035	1 336	727	89	239	254	246	95	102	23	11
Cumberland	280	-0.3	28 747	2 249	55	9	37	67	65	26	24	9	2
Dickenson	431	3.6	26 779	2 602	187	14	51	171	168	66	65	19	3
Dinwiddie	(9)2 704	(9)1.9	(9)35 052	(9)1 011	(9)1 508	(9)71	(9)366	(9)769	(9)755	(9)208	(9)379	(9)82	(9)27
Essex	352	-1.2	31 432	1 655	153	21	63	93	90	34	39	10	3
Fairfax	(10)74 381	(10)-1.3	(10)69 241	(10)12	(10)58 212	(10)6 412	(10)13 118	(10)3 946	(10)3 752	(10)1 465	(10)1 454	(10)267	(10)129
Fauquier	3 320	-1.8	48 822	123	1 139	182	649	308	295	130	113	19	13
Floyd	401	1.0	26 683	2 611	109	27	67	106	104	43	40	9	4
Fluvanna	896	1.4	34 811	1 040	191	21	142	150	146	66	57	9	5
Franklin	1 720	-0.9	33 116	1 317	541	59	335	386	376	166	128	35	15
Frederick	(11)3 683	(11)-0.4	(11)36 360	(11)832	(11)2 546	(11)188	(11)670	(11)561	(11)543	(11)224	(11)200	(11)47	(11)33
Giles	492	2.8	28 350	2 334	241	12	72	148	144	58	59	12	6
Gloucester	1 361	0.2	34 724	1 058	395	47	197	227	220	90	82	19	7
Goochland	1 300	-2.2	61 005	28	875	113	370	126	122	60	33	6	6
Grayson	371	-0.8	23 481	3 004	95	6	64	132	129	54	49	13	5
Greene	645	1.7	35 012	1 017	130	32	79	97	93	39	36	8	4
Greensville	(12)412	(12)-1.2	(12)23 272	(12)3 021	(12)333	(12)13	(12)60	(12)136	(12)133	(12)44	(12)57	(12)20	(12)4
Halifax	1 024	0.9	29 047	2 185	538	58	169	310	304	116	123	39	9
Hanover	4 300	-2.3	43 030	268	2 270	176	692	550	531	238	206	27	27
Henrico	13 168	-2.7	44 423	219	10 703	616	2 564	1 564	1 510	664	517	151	84
Henry	(13)2 000	(13)-1.2	(13)28 773	(13)2 240	(13)1 016	(13)106	(13)400	(13)645	(13)632	(13)256	(13)240	(13)73	(13)29
Highland	74	-1.1	31 673	1 607	20	1	25	20	20	9	9	1	1
Isle of Wight	1 403	1.5	39 113	526	591	64	187	230	224	90	90	19	6
James City	(14)3 789	(14)-0.8	(14)49 551	(14)111	(14)1 884	(14)240	(14)998	(14)518	(14)504	(14)252	(14)171	(14)26	(14)13
King and Queen	206	-2.8	30 268	1 917	66	14	28	50	48	19	20	4	2
King George	862	2.1	36 586	802	982	60	131	98	94	33	38	10	4
King William	593	-0.5	36 532	810	179	19	87	93	91	39	34	7	5
Lancaster	537	-3.7	47 854	136	195	33	214	123	121	56	49	8	3
Lee	656	3.3	26 054	2 715	246	34	77	239	235	78	104	33	2
Loudoun	15 576	4.2	51 717	81	9 532	549	2 083	784	729	297	261	50	45

1. Based on the resident population estimated as of July 1 of the year shown.   2. Includes supplements to wages and salaries.   3. Charlottesville city is included with Albemarle county.   4. Covington city is included with Alleghany county.   5. Staunton and Waynesboro cities are included with Augusta county.   6. Bedford city is included with Bedford county.   7. Lynchburg city is included with Campbell county.   8. Galax city is included with Carroll county.   9. Petersburg and Colonial Heights cities are included with Dinwiddie county.   10. Fairfax city and Falls Church city are included with Fairfax county.   11. Winchester city is included with Frederick county.   12. Emporia city is included with Greensville county.   13. Martinsville city is included with Henry county.   14. Williamsburg city is included with James City county.

STATE County	Earnings, 2009									Social Security beneficiaries, December 2010		Supplemental Security Income recipients, December 2010	Housing units, 2010	
			Goods-related[1]		Service-related and health									
	Total (mil dol)	Farm	Total	Manufacturing	Information and professional and technical services	Retail trade	Finance, insurance, and real estate	Health care and social services	Government	Number	Rate[2]		Total	Percent change, 2000–2010
	75	76	77	78	79	80	81	82	83	84	85	86	87	88
VERMONT—Cont'd														
Chittenden	5 920	0.2	21.5	15.5	12.9	7.2	6.3	15.9	17.8	25 315	162	2 749	65 722	11.6
Essex	61	1.6	D	D	D	5.1	D	D	37.1	1 955	310	239	5 019	5.4
Franklin	960	3.0	D	17.8	D	8.1	2.5	13.1	28.0	7 890	165	1 284	21 588	12.5
Grand Isle	65	3.0	D	D	D	7.2	D	5.9	22.8	1 635	235	143	5 048	8.3
Lamoille	547	1.1	14.8	6.2	10.5	8.3	4.1	14.2	16.3	4 610	188	498	12 969	17.8
Orange	421	1.6	18.0	5.8	7.7	6.8	3.3	16.0	22.9	6 000	207	701	14 845	10.9
Orleans	513	2.3	D	10.2	4.0	8.8	4.6	18.5	21.9	7 025	258	1 080	16 162	10.1
Rutland	1 408	0.4	21.9	13.5	5.5	9.4	3.7	16.3	17.5	15 440	250	2 013	33 768	4.5
Washington	1 869	0.3	12.4	7.6	8.3	7.4	12.2	11.9	25.8	12 370	208	1 486	29 941	8.3
Windham	1 183	0.5	D	10.0	D	7.2	4.5	12.7	13.2	9 995	225	1 153	29 735	10.0
Windsor	1 322	0.3	D	7.6	13.8	6.1	3.6	12.2	25.2	13 715	242	1 220	34 118	7.9
VIRGINIA	263 254	0.1	11.8	6.1	20.3	5.1	6.7	8.1	25.9	1 284 823	161	148 501	3 364 939	15.9
Accomack	666	5.1	D	20.5	7.9	4.6	3.4	6.4	28.4	8 640	261	1 161	21 002	7.4
Albemarle	(3)5 624	(3)-0.1	(3)11.2	(3)4.5	(3)12.9	(3)5.5	(3)6.9	(3)10.0	(3)35.9	15 790	160	858	42 122	24.8
Alleghany	(4)428	(4)-0.4	(4)D	(4)D	(4)D	(4)7.2	(4)D	(4)D	(4)19.5	4 425	272	497	8 074	2.4
Amelia	145	1.9	D	8.1	3.5	7.0	3.7	D	20.9	2 935	231	309	5 359	16.3
Amherst	467	-0.8	26.8	19.4	D	6.8	3.3	D	31.1	7 645	236	786	13 976	7.9
Appomattox	158	-3.2	D	11.7	4.8	9.3	5.2	D	28.7	3 770	252	532	6 921	18.8
Arlington	19 285	0.0	D	D	27.6	D	5.0	2.8	40.0	17 125	82	1 906	105 404	16.6
Augusta	(5)2 433	(5)0.4	(5)D	(5)D	(5)6.7	(5)7.2	(5)5.7	(5)11.6	(5)19.1	16 770	227	993	31 194	16.7
Bath	96	-0.5	8.7	1.3	D	2.6	3.9	D	16.2	1 340	283	80	3 270	13.0
Bedford	(6)986	(6)-1.2	(6)D	(6)13.7	(6)D	(6)6.8	(6)8.5	(6)9.3	(6)16.1	15 680	228	1 026	31 937	19.0
Bland	107	-2.2	D	34.4	D	2.6	D	8.7	28.2	1 850	271	138	3 265	3.3
Botetourt	556	-0.6	D	22.0	4.5	8.5	5.7	5.8	14.3	7 395	223	445	14 562	15.8
Brunswick	218	3.1	D	7.1	D	4.1	3.1	D	31.5	4 035	231	682	8 166	8.3
Buchanan	485	-0.2	49.2	5.4	2.8	4.2	2.7	6.0	16.3	8 890	369	1 886	11 576	-2.6
Buckingham	173	-0.1	D	3.6	4.8	6.1	2.3	D	38.5	3 335	195	490	7 244	15.2
Campbell	(7)3 686	(7)-0.1	(7)D	(7)21.4	(7)10.6	(7)6.6	(7)6.0	(7)15.1	(7)11.2	12 670	231	1 280	24 769	12.1
Caroline	321	-0.4	D	4.7	D	6.2	7.8	D	33.7	5 130	180	447	11 729	31.9
Carroll	(8)551	(8)-0.5	(8)D	(8)17.0	(8)D	(8)11.5	(8)3.8	(8)D	(8)22.1	8 215	273	788	16 569	12.9
Charles City	87	5.7	D	12.0	D	3.6	D	1.7	19.5	1 700	234	162	3 229	11.5
Charlotte	136	2.4	D	11.8	D	6.6	D	D	32.9	3 570	284	602	6 273	9.4
Chesterfield	7 130	0.0	D	10.0	11.3	7.8	7.9	9.7	19.1	47 370	150	3 700	122 555	25.5
Clarke	230	-1.9	D	20.9	9.3	4.3	5.1	D	16.9	2 665	190	131	6 235	15.7
Craig	36	-3.1	D	D	D	9.8	12.0	4.2	32.5	1 325	255	116	2 809	10.0
Culpeper	816	-0.2	18.3	8.5	11.6	8.1	5.1	13.9	22.5	7 855	168	748	17 657	37.2
Cumberland	64	8.9	16.6	7.7	D	7.9	D	D	37.5	2 260	225	303	4 626	13.2
Dickenson	201	-0.9	44.0	1.7	2.2	6.6	D	5.4	23.1	5 530	348	1 075	7 579	-1.4
Dinwiddie	(9)1 579	(9)0.1	(9)D	(9)12.8	(9)D	(9)10.4	(9)D	(9)D	(9)25.8	5 595	200	781	11 422	17.7
Essex	174	4.2	12.1	7.0	6.0	14.1	6.4	D	16.3	2 785	250	290	5 757	16.9
Fairfax	(10)64 624	(10)0.0	(10)5.6	(10)1.2	(10)41.1	3.6	(10)7.2	(10)5.8	(10)15.9	104 835	97	10 465	407 998	13.5
Fauquier	1 321	-1.1	18.0	3.6	14.2	7.6	6.5	11.0	20.9	9 865	151	541	25 600	21.5
Floyd	136	0.7	D	12.0	6.9	5.8	6.6	D	22.4	3 670	240	314	7 790	15.2
Fluvanna	212	-0.9	D	2.4	D	3.8	4.8	D	35.7	5 120	199	253	10 383	29.5
Franklin	600	0.2	28.0	18.4	3.7	9.4	4.5	D	19.3	13 670	243	1 148	29 315	29.1
Frederick	(11)2 735	(11)-0.1	(11)D	(11)16.5	(11)15.9	(11)5.9		(11)18.5	(11)16.6	12 885	165	873	31 346	34.4
Giles	253	-1.1	D	33.4	4.5	8.4	2.7	D	16.1	4 750	275	557	8 319	7.6
Gloucester	442	0.7	D	2.1	5.1	12.4	4.8	12.2	29.9	7 375	200	593	15 852	9.4
Goochland	988	-0.3	D	2.3	3.9	2.5	D	D	9.0	4 380	202	220	8 618	31.5
Grayson	101	-4.1	27.9	23.0	D	5.2	9.0	D	32.5	4 880	314	510	9 156	0.4
Greene	163	0.2	D	3.8	8.3	11.2	2.7	D	27.4	3 120	170	243	7 509	25.4
Greensville	(12)346	(12)0.9	(12)D	(12)24.5	(12)D	(12)7.7	(12)D	(12)14.9	(12)27.3	2 525	206	407	4 090	8.6
Halifax	596	2.5	D	18.7	2.5	6.8	3.1	D	18.9	10 190	281	1 710	18 004	6.2
Hanover	2 445	0.2	20.8	7.1	6.4	9.1	4.3	11.8	13.0	17 155	172	767	38 360	19.1
Henrico	11 319	0.0	D	4.4	14.6	6.4	17.6	12.7	9.2	48 385	158	4 552	132 778	18.0
Henry	(13)1 122	(13)0.0	(13)D	(13)22.6	(13)3.7	(13)10.6	(13)4.6	(13)D	(13)18.3	16 510	305	1 455	26 268	1.3
Highland	21	-12.3	16.6	4.8	D	4.8	D	8.2	31.3	765	330	30	1 837	0.8
Isle of Wight	656	1.6	D	5.9	4.9	4.0	D		13.8	7 135	202	618	14 633	21.3
James City	(14)2 124	(14)0.0	(14)13.1	(14)7.6	(14)D	(14)6.6	(14)8.2	(14)8.7	(14)25.2	15 970	238	508	29 797	43.4
King and Queen	81	4.0	17.9	8.4	D	3.5	D	D	38.1	1 640	236	151	3 414	13.6
King George	1 042	-0.1	3.5	0.6	25.3	1.2	1.5	D	59.5	2 925	124	232	9 477	39.0
King William	198	2.9	D	33.1	4.2	5.6	6.3	D	20.1	3 030	190	215	6 522	25.7
Lancaster	228	0.1	D	2.3	9.4	10.8	10.1	20.6	11.9	4 185	367	257	7 402	13.9
Lee	279	-1.2	18.5	3.0	2.7	9.0	3.0	12.1	35.9	7 075	277	1 866	11 745	5.9
Loudoun	10 081	0.0	14.8	4.1	30.2	5.5	4.2	5.5	15.9	22 595	72	1 632	109 442	76.1

1. Includes mining, construction, and manufacturing.   2. Per 1,000 resident population enumerated in the 2010 census.   3. Charlottesville city is included with Albemarle county.   4. Covington city is included with Alleghany county.   5. Staunton and Waynesboro cities are included with Augusta county.   6. Bedford city is included with Bedford county.   7. Lynchburg city is included with Campbell county.   8. Galax city is included with Carroll county.   9. Petersburg and Colonial Heights cities are included with Dinwiddie county.   10. Fairfax city and Falls Church city are included with Fairfax county.   11. Winchester city is included with Frederick county.   12. Emporia city is included with Greensville county.   13. Martinsville city is included with Henry county.   14. Williamsburg city is included with James City county.

Table B. States and Counties — Housing, Labor Force, and Employment

STATE County	Total	Percent	Median value[1]	With a mortgage	Without a mortgage	Median rent[2]	Median rent as a percent of income	Sub-standard units[3] (percent)	Total	Percent change, 2009–2010	Total	Rate[4]	Total	Management, business, science and arts	Construction, production, and mainte-nance occu-pations
	89	90	91	92	93	94	95	96	97	98	99	100	101	102	103
VERMONT—Cont'd															
Chittenden	61 581	65.9	254 700	25.6	15.3	959	33.1	1.5	91 059	1.0	4 592	5.0	86 572	44.5	14.4
Essex	2 842	83.9	124 300	24.5	16.2	581	33.5	1.8	3 303	-1.6	299	9.1	2 977	27.5	35.6
Franklin	18 482	74.8	202 800	26.3	16.5	822	30.7	1.7	26 855	1.8	1 642	6.1	24 613	32.5	28.4
Grand Isle	3 077	81.6	235 600	28.6	14.9	787	29.0	0.8	4 287	-1.1	304	7.1	3 880	34.8	22.1
Lamoille	10 345	69.0	211 100	27.0	17.3	867	28.8	2.7	15 741	2.0	1 156	7.3	13 024	39.8	20.5
Orange	11 967	81.2	182 700	25.3	15.7	766	30.6	2.1	16 728	0.2	1 023	6.1	15 456	38.8	23.1
Orleans	10 785	76.6	149 200	25.2	18.4	647	32.4	1.6	14 689	-0.5	1 316	9.0	12 590	30.0	31.3
Rutland	26 405	70.0	172 100	24.8	16.6	727	29.0	1.6	35 381	-0.8	2 587	7.3	31 580	33.3	25.8
Washington	24 621	72.6	197 600	24.6	16.1	780	28.5	2.1	34 987	0.1	2 115	6.0	32 114	44.4	17.4
Windham	19 483	69.6	204 600	27.1	16.9	731	29.0	1.9	25 670	1.7	1 571	6.1	23 474	38.8	22.8
Windsor	24 804	72.1	209 900	26.6	17.4	839	31.8	2.7	32 945	-1.1	1 949	5.9	29 207	38.8	20.8
VIRGINIA	2 974 481	68.9	255 100	24.5	10.9	970	29.2	2.1	4 255 162	1.8	294 746	6.9	3 824 131	41.1	19.7
Accomack	14 085	74.1	149 800	24.1	12.0	709	24.7	3.9	20 117	3.8	1 450	7.2	14 972	28.7	32.0
Albemarle	37 459	65.4	349 800	23.7	10.3	1 031	28.5	1.5	52 677	-0.5	2 852	5.4	47 910	52.6	13.8
Alleghany	6 964	82.7	104 000	19.0	10.6	504	28.6	1.2	7 122	2.2	641	9.0	7 331	28.7	32.0
Amelia	4 901	83.2	189 800	24.0	12.2	672	23.5	2.1	6 716	-1.0	520	7.7	5 670	27.1	34.5
Amherst	12 706	75.4	142 200	21.9	10.0	582	24.9	0.9	15 848	-1.1	1 345	8.5	15 271	27.3	31.0
Appomattox	5 976	76.0	132 200	20.6	10.0	540	24.2	1.2	7 266	-0.2	650	8.9	6 903	25.0	34.1
Arlington	91 892	47.0	571 700	23.3	11.3	1 519	25.8	2.7	140 416	1.3	5 936	4.2	125 922	67.3	7.1
Augusta	27 909	81.3	187 800	23.8	10.0	658	26.3	1.5	38 393	1.2	2 565	6.7	34 224	29.4	31.5
Bath	2 025	87.0	129 700	21.5	10.0	712	28.8	2.2	2 739	3.2	172	6.3	2 404	11.9	40.6
Bedford	27 150	84.5	187 200	22.7	10.0	643	26.6	1.4	35 315	-1.1	2 387	6.8	33 191	34.5	27.4
Bland	2 580	84.8	88 600	22.1	10.0	429	19.2	1.5	3 583	0.6	241	6.7	2 742	25.5	31.8
Botetourt	12 918	87.2	202 500	21.5	10.0	732	21.1	2.5	17 629	-0.7	1 112	6.3	16 387	35.4	25.4
Brunswick	6 086	70.0	97 500	24.0	11.9	608	31.0	2.2	7 047	-1.7	825	11.7	6 161	22.7	32.3
Buchanan	9 123	79.5	62 000	19.2	10.0	501	36.4	1.5	9 470	3.7	780	8.2	7 320	23.3	39.5
Buckingham	4 859	74.7	99 300	24.4	10.0	630	23.4	4.5	7 547	2.8	706	9.4	3 833	26.5	28.5
Campbell	22 005	75.7	134 000	22.1	10.0	570	26.5	2.2	27 317	-1.8	1 993	7.3	26 014	29.8	29.2
Caroline	10 270	82.9	218 800	25.6	11.7	943	31.1	2.7	14 375	0.1	1 303	9.1	13 098	31.3	28.9
Carroll	12 818	76.2	97 400	22.7	10.0	493	25.8	1.5	14 550	1.3	1 604	11.0	12 788	20.2	41.3
Charles City	2 713	85.0	146 000	25.0	10.0	708	24.9	2.2	3 893	-0.9	370	9.5	3 432	21.2	39.3
Charlotte	4 415	77.9	103 200	25.8	12.5	499	28.2	3.7	5 495	-0.4	506	9.2	4 964	25.6	40.3
Chesterfield	112 404	78.4	235 600	23.5	10.0	988	29.1	1.4	169 486	-0.4	11 696	6.9	157 224	41.0	18.3
Clarke	5 535	75.8	366 900	23.5	10.6	954	28.8	1.6	8 242	-1.9	471	5.7	7 065	40.4	22.9
Craig	1 989	85.7	142 100	20.6	10.0	497	14.3	0.6	2 473	-3.2	193	7.8	2 730	28.8	29.7
Culpeper	15 834	72.6	309 000	27.4	11.2	963	30.6	2.3	21 552	2.6	1 696	7.9	22 201	34.0	23.3
Cumberland	3 969	77.8	149 700	30.2	10.0	750	30.7	6.1	4 668	-0.2	363	7.8	4 189	22.7	32.1
Dickenson	6 170	80.6	71 300	21.3	11.9	441	34.8	1.5	6 680	4.5	563	8.4	4 738	20.3	36.4
Dinwiddie	9 800	75.8	163 800	24.2	11.1	817	26.7	2.3	13 145	-0.9	1 014	7.7	12 501	26.6	30.8
Essex	4 466	74.8	185 400	27.3	13.2	766	26.2	2.9	5 930	2.6	522	8.8	5 316	29.1	23.1
Fairfax	381 768	71.9	507 800	24.0	10.0	1 492	27.8	2.6	602 551	0.1	29 600	4.9	571 268	56.2	10.6
Fauquier	22 369	78.8	390 900	24.3	10.2	1 140	30.2	1.9	38 360	-0.3	2 160	5.6	33 392	43.3	18.7
Floyd	6 334	78.5	138 800	23.6	10.0	486	22.0	3.0	7 530	2.5	567	7.5	7 172	31.5	29.4
Fluvanna	9 128	87.2	246 100	22.1	11.5	829	24.6	1.1	14 155	-0.9	816	5.8	11 844	35.1	19.2
Franklin	23 355	78.5	156 100	24.3	10.0	619	21.9	2.0	26 946	-0.9	2 147	8.0	24 702	26.8	33.2
Frederick	28 558	78.8	248 600	25.4	11.8	1 021	28.3	2.0	41 729	0.6	2 934	7.0	37 824	33.8	27.4
Giles	7 100	77.8	97 800	21.3	10.0	545	28.0	1.3	8 367	-1.8	769	9.2	7 261	30.4	32.2
Gloucester	14 014	82.4	228 100	23.9	10.1	728	26.5	1.4	21 059	-0.3	1 345	6.4	17 929	32.2	28.1
Goochland	6 831	91.2	338 000	23.3	10.0	965	24.6	0.7	11 482	0.0	731	6.4	7 497	46.2	15.3
Grayson	6 858	81.3	92 200	22.1	10.0	424	22.6	1.4	7 408	1.2	843	11.4	6 779	24.2	40.1
Greene	6 709	79.8	223 100	24.5	10.6	965	36.2	1.1	10 885	0.9	638	5.9	9 048	29.8	22.0
Greensville	3 385	74.6	94 600	20.8	13.6	680	25.3	3.4	4 506	3.9	414	9.2	4 339	20.4	35.6
Halifax	14 650	75.9	96 000	23.1	13.4	534	29.4	1.8	16 914	3.7	1 975	11.7	14 471	28.6	32.1
Hanover	36 114	83.9	281 600	22.9	10.8	977	26.9	0.8	55 089	-1.5	3 560	6.5	51 754	42.8	17.9
Henrico	121 767	66.9	230 000	24.2	10.5	940	29.6	1.5	165 959	-0.4	11 377	6.9	155 559	42.0	15.8
Henry	22 909	75.9	91 200	22.9	10.8	530	28.6	2.9	25 477	1.2	3 422	13.4	22 864	24.4	36.9
Highland	1 130	76.6	177 400	27.1	10.0	538	23.2	0.0	1 177	3.6	92	7.8	1 149	25.2	41.9
Isle of Wight	13 553	81.1	256 600	24.0	11.6	710	27.7	2.8	19 148	0.0	1 355	7.1	17 295	35.4	26.1
James City	25 851	76.5	348 600	24.2	10.3	1 066	28.7	0.8	32 494	0.4	1 835	5.6	30 254	45.5	13.7
King and Queen	2 815	80.4	171 500	27.0	12.1	812	23.4	3.6	3 319	-1.4	287	8.6	3 213	18.9	43.1
King George	8 194	76.4	305 200	23.0	10.0	982	27.7	1.9	10 569	3.7	854	8.1	10 280	46.4	17.9
King William	5 909	85.4	198 100	23.6	10.0	771	26.2	0.9	8 761	-0.3	625	7.1	7 744	25.4	36.1
Lancaster	5 421	77.1	254 500	25.9	11.8	796	24.8	2.5	5 717	1.6	535	9.4	5 228	31.4	24.6
Lee	9 836	73.8	77 600	22.3	10.0	443	25.9	2.3	10 280	2.3	817	7.9	9 475	25.8	31.4
Loudoun	95 330	80.8	495 000	26.6	10.8	1 531	29.4	1.6	178 615	1.7	8 553	4.8	155 907	56.0	10.3

1. Specified owner-occupied units. 2. Specified renter-occupied units. A value of 10.0 represents 10 percent or less. 3. Overcrowded or lacking complete plumbing facilities. 4. Percent of civilian labor force. 5. Persons 16 years old and over.

Table B. States and Counties — Nonfarm Employment and Agriculture

STATE County	Private nonfarm establishments, employment and payroll, 2009									Agriculture, 2007			
	Number of establishments	Employment						Annual payroll		Farms			Farm operators whose principal occupation is farming (percent)
		Total	Health care and social assistance	Manufacturing	Retail trade	Finance and insurance	Professional, scientific, and technical services	Total (mil dol)	Average per employee (dollars)	Number	Percent with:		
											Fewer than 50 acres	500 acres or more	
	104	105	106	107	108	109	110	111	112	113	114	115	116

VERMONT—Cont'd

County	104	105	106	107	108	109	110	111	112	113	114	115	116
Chittenden	5 513	85 937	14 833	11 018	12 194	3 425	8 872	3 675	42 765	591	43.8	6.1	45.9
Essex	126	761	D	D	78	D	D	17	22 351	94	13.8	25.5	55.3
Franklin	1 028	11 745	2 537	2 838	2 010	309	540	402	34 213	740	27.0	12.0	52.4
Grand Isle	203	610	61	D	130	D	42	19	31 341	114	34.2	6.1	52.6
Lamoille	1 001	9 974	1 434	413	1 562	228	374	268	26 823	300	31.3	7.3	43.3
Orange	787	6 074	1 322	557	1 016	D	348	200	32 915	683	30.9	5.1	45.7
Orleans	821	7 624	1 663	D	1 373	217	149	206	26 981	635	30.6	9.8	55.0
Rutland	2 265	24 516	4 625	3 149	4 328	655	701	782	31 910	658	34.3	9.0	51.7
Washington	2 258	25 982	4 074	2 925	3 831	2 275	1 096	927	35 675	444	39.6	3.2	49.5
Windham	1 811	21 295	2 965	1 938	2 642	582	647	664	31 169	428	46.5	3.7	48.6
Windsor	2 106	28 924	D	1 912	2 824	D	1 101	703	24 311	767	43.0	3.5	47.7
VIRGINIA	194 018	3 061 186	384 352	252 213	412 600	158 692	407 365	137 138	44 799	47 383	39.5	7.0	42.8
Accomack	818	9 424	1 209	D	1 148	217	762	241	25 567	248	46.0	18.1	54.8
Albemarle	2 486	35 959	4 562	2 699	6 088	D	3 026	1 514	42 100	895	38.1	7.7	41.6
Alleghany	250	2 756	823	307	565	50	32	73	26 453	209	32.5	3.8	39.2
Amelia	295	1 969	D	288	260	D	44	52	26 262	455	29.7	10.8	37.4
Amherst	618	7 051	768	D	1 195	127	139	202	28 580	424	31.4	9.4	42.2
Appomattox	297	2 723	368	D	504	87	D	66	24 144	323	18.3	9.3	44.9
Arlington	5 856	122 173	8 197	333	9 196	2 823	36 191	8 534	69 851	6	100.0	0.0	16.7
Augusta	1 388	18 923	3 891	4 155	2 111	329	434	673	35 554	1 729	44.9	6.9	49.4
Bath	137	1 764	D	41	89	D	21	53	30 274	120	30.8	20.0	49.2
Bedford	1 413	11 967	948	1 934	2 209	297	726	373	31 191	1 428	35.7	4.9	38.7
Bland	79	1 177	D	509	87	D	D	45	38 641	387	21.7	7.8	46.5
Botetourt	756	10 279	743	2 496	736	200	256	332	32 344	638	40.0	5.3	35.9
Brunswick	289	2 948	43	389	352	D	D	72	24 386	367	21.3	11.2	36.0
Buchanan	459	6 110	686	322	691	D	217	258	42 172	107	49.5	0.9	21.5
Buckingham	268	1 868	D	89	291	38	77	55	29 577	411	27.5	7.5	41.6
Campbell	1 190	15 221	965	3 708	1 879	398	658	524	34 401	722	25.1	8.4	35.8
Caroline	406	4 238	D	264	717	92	206	136	32 175	225	43.6	12.0	34.2
Carroll	429	4 226	622	878	794	D	123	100	23 569	1 001	39.1	3.9	41.4
Charles City	139	1 165	D	D	D	D	D	39	33 134	80	43.8	16.3	51.3
Charlotte	233	1 868	379	422	245	56	44	44	23 313	489	21.9	10.8	44.2
Chesterfield	6 918	100 727	9 822	10 278	17 335	5 281	6 693	3 866	38 384	220	57.3	3.2	44.5
Clarke	387	3 451	224	1 200	284	D	159	123	35 529	496	51.2	6.0	47.4
Craig	60	377	D	D	118	28	D	10	25 533	193	29.5	9.8	46.6
Culpeper	958	11 792	1 976	1 342	2 192	D	624	440	37 336	667	43.6	6.7	47.8
Cumberland	148	995	123	87	230	D	D	24	24 158	285	23.9	7.4	46.0
Dickenson	233	2 844	447	D	454	76	216	117	41 204	170	45.9	1.8	38.8
Dinwiddie	354	4 454	300	830	546	113	46	155	34 741	374	35.6	8.8	42.8
Essex	319	3 506	543	458	974	156	97	92	26 338	102	40.2	28.4	51.0
Fairfax	28 736	564 426	49 792	8 248	48 821	26 469	185 478	37 259	66 012	166	75.3	0.0	34.3
Fauquier	1 776	15 293	1 486	715	2 817	597	1 676	556	36 335	1 222	44.5	7.1	46.5
Floyd	306	1 966	287	D	362	D	61	47	23 769	864	33.6	5.1	46.9
Fluvanna	403	2 691	228	D	341	42	D	77	28 711	327	36.7	5.2	45.0
Franklin	1 195	11 631	1 239	2 358	1 916	304	289	309	26 547	1 043	31.4	7.0	46.4
Frederick	1 424	20 381	1 447	4 483	3 629	D	691	732	35 895	676	43.3	5.6	35.9
Giles	310	3 868	546	1 124	677	78	D	145	37 363	344	26.5	6.1	43.0
Gloucester	902	7 254	1 153	261	1 949	312	298	179	24 727	159	70.4	8.8	57.9
Goochland	635	11 275	422	194	518	4 863	276	815	72 244	379	55.7	6.1	36.9
Grayson	182	1 493	162	376	182	D	29	38	25 362	852	37.6	7.5	40.0
Greene	339	2 225	D	61	491	D	D	68	30 341	222	33.8	5.0	38.3
Greensville	114	2 576	D	959	307	D	D	71	27 490	143	27.3	18.2	37.1
Halifax	753	9 890	1 784	1 866	1 460	195	179	301	30 455	908	22.9	7.8	45.2
Hanover	3 012	39 978	4 829	2 985	6 199	584	1 545	1 359	33 984	625	51.8	6.7	41.9
Henrico	8 809	165 889	22 507	8 109	23 575	25 918	9 558	7 612	45 884	178	61.2	2.2	43.3
Henry	907	12 965	788	4 380	1 602	286	289	341	26 309	340	34.7	3.8	46.2
Highland	95	360	D	D	D	D	D	8	22 706	239	15.1	18.4	50.2
Isle of Wight	644	9 318	586	D	988	184	289	263	28 206	195	44.6	22.1	49.2
James City	1 657	24 181	2 218	2 992	3 852	661	1 393	773	31 962	74	67.6	1.4	51.4
King and Queen	120	799	D	44	D	D	33	32	39 865	153	24.2	19.0	42.5
King George	457	5 620	271	D	435	111	2 901	275	48 941	180	31.7	8.9	44.4
King William	326	2 815	304	D	465	100	D	106	37 779	136	40.4	14.0	41.9
Lancaster	527	4 212	1 015	D	850	320	D	127	30 265	64	56.3	14.1	53.1
Lee	292	3 259	614	112	884	213	52	80	24 430	1 044	34.8	2.1	39.8
Loudoun	7 861	114 986	8 303	4 503	16 338	D	14 895	6 076	52 843	1 427	68.9	3.9	44.0

Table B. States and Counties — **Agriculture**

STATE County	Land in farms — Acreage (1,000) [117]	Percent change, 2002–2007 [118]	Acres — Average size of farm [119]	Acres — Total irrigated (1,000) [120]	Acres — Total cropland (1,000) [121]	Value of land and buildings — Average per farm [122]	Value of land and buildings — Average per acre [123]	Value of machinery and equipment, average per farm (dollars) [124]	Value of products sold — Total (mil dol) [125]	Value of products sold — Average per farm (dollars) [126]	Percent from: Crops [127]	Percent from: Livestock and poultry products [128]	Percent of farms with sales of: $10,000 or more [129]	Percent of farms with sales of: $100,000 or more [130]	Government payments — Total ($1,000) [131]	Government payments — Percent of farms [132]
VERMONT—Cont'd																
Chittenden	83	7.8	141	0.4	31.2	535 965	3 799	59 871	33.7	56 958	41.0	59.0	37.9	9.8	200	10.5
Essex	27	35.0	284	0.0	11.6	443 431	1 559	98 230	12.1	129 222	8.3	91.7	40.4	25.5	111	28.7
Franklin	180	-5.3	243	0.2	85.1	605 808	2 490	111 550	160.6	217 052	6.2	93.8	54.6	30.4	2 143	33.1
Grand Isle	17	6.3	150	0.0	11.3	541 859	3 604	78 410	13.4	117 463	10.2	89.8	46.5	13.2	220	30.7
Lamoille	50	-7.4	166	0.1	17.3	517 751	3 122	72 059	21.6	71 980	34.0	66.0	39.3	15.0	326	21.7
Orange	102	-7.3	149	0.2	35.6	440 724	2 961	59 124	43.3	63 385	21.4	78.6	37.5	13.0	516	17.7
Orleans	130	-1.5	205	0.1	55.2	474 493	2 312	74 048	82.3	129 682	5.6	94.4	49.1	19.7	603	22.4
Rutland	131	8.3	198	0.3	46.3	495 992	2 499	69 361	35.3	53 626	24.7	75.3	40.1	14.6	571	20.5
Washington	61	13.0	137	0.2	20.7	475 291	3 458	63 371	21.5	48 448	24.0	76.0	36.3	7.2	302	10.4
Windham	51	-17.7	119	0.3	15.0	439 951	3 709	50 866	21.4	50 018	39.7	60.3	29.2	9.1	157	8.6
Windsor	96	6.7	125	0.1	27.6	502 248	4 014	55 055	25.0	32 566	31.6	68.4	31.3	7.2	173	9.8
VIRGINIA	8 104	-6.0	171	82.2	3 274.1	720 538	4 213	65 870	2 906.2	61 334	29.5	70.5	32.9	7.9	54 940	20.8
Accomack	94	3.3	378	6.5	76.6	1 143 944	3 026	138 683	153.0	617 096	34.7	65.3	66.5	43.5	1 618	42.3
Albemarle	158	-10.7	177	1.0	46.2	1 029 626	5 821	59 279	24.2	27 010	40.1	59.9	29.1	3.8	225	7.9
Alleghany	29	-12.1	138	D	8.0	392 728	2 842	46 550	2.1	10 092	13.4	86.6	17.2	0.5	34	12.4
Amelia	91	0.0	201	0.6	33.5	720 230	3 583	106 026	68.7	151 086	11.3	88.7	33.0	11.6	458	35.4
Amherst	88	-12.0	209	0.1	21.0	638 897	3 063	53 647	7.6	18 030	17.8	82.2	32.3	3.1	89	14.9
Appomattox	76	-10.6	235	0.0	26.9	655 944	2 792	64 148	7.5	23 099	16.3	83.7	39.6	4.6	209	27.9
Arlington	0	NA	6	0.0	0.0	355 896	59 316	16 833	0.0	3 431	D	D	16.7	0.0	0	0.0
Augusta	286	-6.5	166	3.8	107.8	810 635	4 897	72 873	194.8	112 675	10.3	89.7	44.2	14.4	1 364	20.1
Bath	38	-26.9	320	0.0	11.8	1 191 441	3 722	63 386	3.9	32 242	28.7	71.3	37.5	5.8	42	15.8
Bedford	212	6.5	149	0.6	68.9	702 581	4 727	60 495	23.6	16 560	16.5	83.5	28.7	3.2	342	11.9
Bland	81	-13.8	209	0.0	19.6	614 260	2 943	63 023	8.6	22 186	4.9	95.1	38.0	2.8	68	21.7
Botetourt	88	-9.3	138	0.1	27.7	584 921	4 245	56 887	13.5	21 234	18.4	81.6	24.5	3.4	241	12.2
Brunswick	87	10.1	236	1.3	26.8	589 501	2 495	54 693	12.1	33 023	57.9	42.1	24.3	5.4	1 300	47.4
Buchanan	9	0.0	87	D	2.0	234 924	2 694	29 908	0.4	3 392	28.9	71.1	9.3	0.0	4	3.7
Buckingham	77	-4.9	188	0.0	28.7	579 314	3 080	62 002	32.6	79 359	4.3	95.7	34.8	9.7	311	24.1
Campbell	140	0.7	194	0.8	49.9	652 029	3 354	66 627	25.3	35 104	12.7	87.3	28.7	3.6	751	32.5
Caroline	56	-5.1	247	2.1	36.0	1 150 906	4 662	109 969	10.8	47 822	76.4	23.6	28.0	10.7	627	27.6
Carroll	124	1.6	124	0.6	41.7	507 488	4 107	47 358	34.4	34 413	25.0	75.0	39.0	5.3	380	12.8
Charles City	27	-6.9	344	0.7	18.4	1 238 678	3 605	104 058	10.5	131 610	D	D	37.5	13.8	458	17.5
Charlotte	126	-6.0	257	0.7	40.7	684 892	2 668	62 044	19.4	39 645	34.4	65.6	34.6	7.6	578	31.3
Chesterfield	22	-4.3	98	0.2	6.6	551 410	5 635	68 307	4.5	20 397	48.3	51.7	18.6	2.7	65	12.3
Clarke	68	-8.1	137	0.5	32.5	934 785	6 827	66 704	21.9	44 156	23.9	76.1	27.8	7.1	350	12.5
Craig	42	-12.5	216	0.0	11.1	765 895	3 551	68 201	5.5	28 530	8.7	91.3	39.4	4.1	82	16.6
Culpeper	111	-11.2	167	1.3	56.1	990 792	5 934	73 158	27.1	40 685	47.2	52.8	31.9	6.1	376	17.4
Cumberland	57	-9.5	199	D	17.1	778 053	3 903	61 355	42.0	147 222	4.6	95.4	33.3	11.9	216	30.9
Dickenson	14	16.7	84	D	3.1	269 312	3 192	34 795	0.6	3 645	23.9	76.1	12.4	0.0	2	3.5
Dinwiddie	79	-14.1	211	1.9	35.3	670 930	3 183	66 683	12.6	33 663	65.6	34.4	25.9	6.1	1 688	42.2
Essex	53	-8.6	523	D	38.3	1 696 251	3 243	148 984	9.9	96 717	93.6	6.4	40.2	23.5	808	53.9
Fairfax	7	-30.0	42	0.0	2.9	543 876	12 841	27 898	2.0	12 006	85.9	14.1	22.9	0.6	12	9.0
Fauquier	222	-6.7	182	0.9	85.1	1 052 419	5 780	73 883	48.0	39 264	21.3	78.7	30.6	5.0	628	11.5
Floyd	129	-4.4	149	0.1	45.0	619 915	4 156	58 108	43.4	50 186	43.2	56.8	37.4	5.2	182	11.1
Fluvanna	49	-18.3	149	0.3	18.1	743 771	4 975	64 086	5.6	17 110	47.5	52.5	23.9	1.8	79	11.6
Franklin	167	-3.5	160	0.9	66.8	665 563	4 167	82 567	54.0	51 743	13.0	87.0	33.1	8.2	684	20.1
Frederick	98	-13.3	145	0.3	37.9	849 880	5 846	65 281	28.0	41 356	71.1	28.9	25.1	5.0	228	7.2
Giles	65	-4.4	190	0.0	16.0	595 734	3 129	53 207	5.0	14 626	15.6	84.4	33.4	2.3	78	11.6
Gloucester	23	-11.5	144	0.1	16.4	811 941	5 623	77 321	9.0	56 298	D	D	31.4	13.2	318	19.5
Goochland	59	13.5	156	0.0	22.8	827 846	5 292	63 826	11.2	29 647	32.5	67.6	19.3	5.5	122	11.9
Grayson	137	-9.3	161	0.1	40.3	740 517	4 614	59 445	23.4	27 452	15.3	84.7	36.0	4.2	274	17.0
Greene	31	-6.1	140	0.2	12.6	915 588	6 554	69 142	7.7	34 669	22.4	77.6	38.7	4.1	61	25.7
Greensville	49	16.7	341	D	29.6	944 097	2 770	81 771	7.2	50 028	93.6	6.4	33.6	12.6	2 511	74.8
Halifax	194	-12.6	213	1.5	70.6	590 848	2 770	49 469	29.3	32 227	45.9	54.1	27.9	5.3	1 039	43.0
Hanover	92	-8.9	147	3.2	56.0	832 305	5 667	81 120	43.9	70 247	81.1	18.9	31.2	8.2	859	13.6
Henrico	20	-28.6	113	D	12.2	612 368	5 424	47 849	8.5	47 653	96.5	3.5	26.4	5.1	85	10.7
Henry	51	-3.8	149	0.5	15.3	466 656	3 125	42 383	11.0	32 228	11.0	89.0	17.4	2.1	125	10.3
Highland	77	-19.8	321	0.0	12.6	974 901	3 035	55 259	13.1	54 921	1.8	98.2	55.6	8.8	48	25.9
Isle of Wight	73	-16.1	377	0.7	50.6	1 191 659	3 163	141 306	23.0	118 020	60.0	40.0	49.2	22.6	2 808	53.8
James City	6	-33.3	79	0.0	3.0	661 643	8 397	69 119	2.9	38 735	51.3	48.8	31.1	12.2	62	23.0
King and Queen	53	-10.2	347	D	32.3	1 255 077	3 615	100 445	11.9	77 761	61.0	39.0	47.1	14.4	709	48.4
King George	37	15.6	204	0.7	15.4	856 220	4 197	69 653	4.5	24 781	84.6	15.4	36.7	3.3	389	39.4
King William	46	-24.6	339	2.7	25.6	1 302 697	3 846	122 914	16.3	119 749	86.4	13.6	36.8	15.4	543	20.6
Lancaster	14	16.7	220	D	10.4	934 311	4 242	76 187	2.9	44 629	95.9	4.1	29.7	12.5	322	48.4
Lee	118	-7.8	113	0.3	37.7	309 252	2 741	40 225	14.3	13 659	29.6	70.4	26.3	1.8	408	30.7
Loudoun	142	-13.9	100	3.5	73.6	737 428	7 387	53 042	33.8	23 691	57.7	42.3	22.9	4.1	277	6.9

Table B. States and Counties — **Water Use, Wholesale Trade, Retail Trade, and Real Estate**

STATE County	Water use, 2005		Wholesale trade,[1] 2007				Retail trade,[2] 2007				Real estate and rental and leasing,[2] 2007			
	Total water withdrawn (mil gal/day)	Gallons withdrawn per person	Number of establishments	Number of employees	Sales (mil dol)	Annual payroll (mil dol)	Number of establishments	Number of employees	Sales (mil dol)	Annual payroll (mil dol)	Number of establishments	Number of employees	Receipts (mil dol)	Annual payroll (mil dol)
	133	134	135	136	137	138	139	140	141	142	143	144	145	146
VERMONT—Cont'd														
Chittenden	19.0	127	260	3 812	2 392.5	192.8	907	12 646	2 740.9	292.5	244	1 548	256.4	46.4
Essex	2.3	352	2	D	D	D	19	86	15.0	1.0	1	D	D	D
Franklin	8.0	168	42	667	413.3	23.2	222	2 022	545.3	42.6	30	111	10.1	2.0
Grand Isle	5.1	668	6	15	9.1	0.3	32	176	39.5	3.4	6	15	2.0	0.4
Lamoille	2.9	118	28	D	D	D	185	1 532	313.5	32.2	35	106	24.4	4.2
Orange	4.5	155	25	D	D	D	115	1 019	237.2	22.3	23	D	D	D
Orleans	4.5	161	31	299	73.4	9.4	157	1 351	324.1	31.3	23	89	12.7	2.3
Rutland	10.8	169	79	800	267.6	29.2	450	4 556	1 084.9	103.3	80	303	33.4	6.9
Washington	7.2	121	88	D	D	D	390	3 974	946.6	95.2	68	242	27.4	6.4
Windham	426.8	9 669	52	1 541	867.1	63.9	300	2 896	660.7	69.0	71	246	28.4	5.7
Windsor	6.2	106	60	749	327.7	31.0	337	2 861	691.7	70.3	88	D	D	D
VIRGINIA	10 618.8	1 403	6 502	98 304	60 513.4	4 787.4	29 633	431 634	105 663.3	9 991.9	9 475	60 502	12 636.8	2 408.7
Accomack	11.6	293	30	135	59.4	4.4	184	1 288	298.0	25.6	37	126	15.6	2.8
Albemarle	15.5	170	72	1 329	530.6	68.3	367	6 496	1 689.3	168.6	163	1 023	136.3	29.6
Alleghany	47.2	2 825	4	26	2.2	0.6	50	597	123.1	11.5	6	17	1.7	0.3
Amelia	1.4	117	5	150	55.4	6.2	30	236	68.0	4.8	10	17	1.6	0.3
Amherst	19.1	595	14	306	161.9	10.1	104	1 319	311.8	26.7	21	52	5.2	0.9
Appomattox	2.3	168	8	70	16.8	2.7	61	529	107.2	9.7	11	35	5.7	0.7
Arlington	0.1	1	89	1 289	453.2	94.4	641	10 702	2 482.9	275.4	326	3 620	1 333.9	243.0
Augusta	44.1	633	45	899	306.3	32.9	205	2 310	636.3	51.5	58	178	26.9	4.1
Bath	259.2	52 508	3	6	1.5	0.1	25	123	21.0	1.6	10	43	8.0	1.8
Bedford	18.5	283	48	393	369.0	13.3	182	2 048	466.5	44.9	77	160	20.8	5.1
Bland	1.0	141	5	D	D	D	20	114	38.4	1.8	1	D	D	D
Botetourt	19.0	594	34	D	D	D	87	833	247.8	16.2	23	D	D	D
Brunswick	27.6	1 542	7	46	42.0	1.9	51	377	74.6	6.3	4	11	0.9	0.1
Buchanan	8.0	322	23	229	189.8	9.3	93	750	143.9	12.6	10	30	4.4	0.8
Buckingham	2.5	154	11	76	21.5	2.1	41	284	68.7	5.5	6	10	1.0	0.1
Campbell	10.7	203	40	584	249.4	23.3	217	2 060	511.8	43.0	58	151	19.2	2.9
Caroline	5.6	220	10	59	21.2	1.9	61	760	365.9	13.7	15	43	5.5	0.6
Carroll	3.1	105	19	113	33.6	2.4	97	775	203.0	13.7	18	43	3.7	1.0
Charles City	1.1	152	7	D	D	D	10	58	10.9	2.0	4	31	5.3	1.1
Charlotte	1.7	135	6	29	10.1	1.0	36	261	62.1	4.8	6	16	0.5	0.2
Chesterfield	1 016.6	3 519	297	3 719	1 561.2	189.2	987	19 119	4 615.9	423.1	327	1 563	307.5	56.4
Clarke	1.8	126	14	D	D	D	41	299	91.6	5.5	15	38	3.6	0.6
Craig	0.5	101	1	D	D	D	10	116	15.8	1.7	2	D	D	D
Culpeper	4.7	111	32	D	D	D	170	2 282	547.4	50.9	38	D	D	D
Cumberland	2.1	225	5	D	D	D	31	260	46.1	5.2	3	8	0.5	0.1
Dickenson	5.5	340	6	18	8.3	0.5	61	519	122.8	9.0	4	6	0.7	0.2
Dinwiddie	2.0	79	14	335	267.0	15.4	63	529	114.9	9.7	6	18	1.9	0.5
Essex	1.1	101	5	33	8.5	1.1	65	1 007	224.6	23.0	10	37	4.9	1.2
Fairfax	313.8	312	837	14 481	13 299.5	1 136.9	2 976	53 158	14 002.4	1 444.8	1 461	11 691	3 549.6	644.9
Fauquier	26.4	407	39	D	D	D	248	2 989	853.1	78.8	84	270	36.8	9.5
Floyd	1.9	126	9	29	25.9	1.0	46	355	72.4	6.3	5	15	2.9	0.2
Fluvanna	223.5	9 031	9	61	10.4	2.3	37	326	79.4	6.8	25	39	7.0	1.3
Franklin	5.2	103	42	558	473.6	29.6	204	2 047	444.5	43.4	75	215	27.2	5.7
Frederick	7.3	106	85	1 746	632.2	78.3	193	3 291	1 120.7	83.0	53	D	D	D
Giles	333.6	19 512	7	37	18.9	1.9	74	742	172.4	14.4	8	22	4.5	0.6
Gloucester	3.6	94	23	D	D	D	145	2 107	500.1	45.9	51	162	15.9	2.8
Goochland	2.8	143	31	215	97.4	9.3	64	593	184.0	15.3	22	117	14.5	4.2
Grayson	2.2	134	5	D	D	D	34	230	47.5	3.6	7	11	1.0	0.2
Greene	0.8	48	9	79	24.6	4.2	48	371	96.0	9.6	8	30	2.5	0.6
Greensville	4.6	410	4	D	D	D	27	187	101.9	3.1	2	D	D	D
Halifax	15.6	430	21	260	133.7	8.7	141	1 474	324.1	29.4	31	143	11.8	2.1
Hanover	155.3	1 594	232	4 834	3 405.9	219.4	373	5 829	1 706.4	150.8	137	579	114.8	20.2
Henrico	45.7	163	377	7 248	6 197.3	368.7	1 321	23 829	6 737.2	565.7	449	3 800	724.7	135.6
Henry	13.6	240	40	714	527.7	19.9	199	1 623	437.0	33.7	26	116	13.3	2.5
Highland	15.5	6 263	1	D	D	D	24	54	8.9	0.7	1	D	D	D
Isle of Wight	97.7	2 925	20	192	148.2	9.6	109	1 034	212.7	19.0	37	118	16.5	3.1
James City	13.1	227	40	422	140.1	17.4	297	3 636	658.8	77.2	94	554	101.2	19.1
King and Queen	0.8	110	4	32	22.0	1.3	11	36	16.2	0.8	3	3	0.4	0.1
King George	5.9	285	9	43	8.2	1.3	50	464	155.0	10.4	19	69	11.2	1.5
King William	65.6	4 450	12	57	30.7	2.0	51	497	126.0	10.0	15	50	4.9	0.9
Lancaster	1.1	91	17	116	49.3	3.1	97	782	166.6	16.7	27	52	8.2	2.3
Lee	3.8	160	13	60	27.5	1.4	82	905	171.6	15.2	12	19	2.2	0.4
Loudoun	10.7	42	227	2 901	1 492.0	175.2	954	16 811	4 469.5	432.0	328	1 621	401.1	67.2

1. Merchant wholesalers, except manufacturers' sales branches and offices.　　2. Employer establishments.

Professional Services, Manufacturing, and Accommodation and Food Services

STATE County	Professional, scientific, and technical services,¹ 2007				Manufacturing, 2007				Accommodation and food services, 2007			
	Number of establish-ments	Number of employees	Receipts (mil dol)	Annual payroll (mil dol)	Number of establish-ments	Number of employees	Receipts (mil dol)	Annual payroll (mil dol)	Number of establish-ments	Number of employees	Sales (mil dol)	Annual payroll (mil dol)
	147	148	149	150	151	152	153	154	155	156	157	158
VERMONT—Cont'd												
Chittenden	713	5 579	920.1	347.2	207	12 224	4 823.5	713.8	421	7 330	360.8	104.9
Essex	5	D	D	D	12	574	62.8	17.7	18	128	3.1	1.0
Franklin	60	637	39.6	15.7	54	D	D	111.2	104	903	39.6	11.4
Grand Isle	23	38	4.0	1.4	NA	NA	NA	NA	23	52	6.5	1.8
Lamoille	96	367	42.8	16.8	NA	NA	NA	NA	113	3 837	174.2	59.5
Orange	79	D	D	D	56	846	161.9	29.2	54	556	26.2	8.1
Orleans	50	D	D	D	36	1 199	D	D	68	1 002	36.3	11.3
Rutland	185	D	D	D	111	3 885	640.8	178.5	235	3 190	124.4	37.1
Washington	244	D	D	D	131	2 690	1 011.9	103.5	172	2 907	119.0	38.2
Windham	140	667	65.4	25.1	111	2 163	375.1	89.2	232	3 861	138.4	47.5
Windsor	199	D	D	D	138	2 306	406.5	89.2	194	3 411	154.4	49.4
VIRGINIA	27 078	376 172	66 543.7	26 936.8	5 777	277 456	92 417.8	12 169.6	15 765	302 446	15 340.5	4 273.0
Accomack	71	955	187.0	50.7	28	D	526.2	67.4	105	1 005	48.1	13.0
Albemarle	288	D	D	D	64	1 487	307.1	60.2	148	2 454	120.2	36.1
Alleghany	12	26	3.4	0.4	10	642	D	21.5	22	302	11.0	3.5
Amelia	14	47	3.2	1.0	NA	NA	NA	NA	9	122	3.8	0.8
Amherst	37	153	11.1	3.8	41	1 573	554.2	68.2	40	583	23.8	6.6
Appomattox	15	D	D	D	15	572	D	16.0	15	195	7.3	1.9
Arlington	1 585	34 964	7 990.5	2 819.1	NA	NA	NA	NA	596	14 421	1 164.0	304.7
Augusta	71	D	D	D	68	4 655	1 582.6	195.5	80	1 271	57.1	14.5
Bath	11	D	D	D	NA	NA	NA	NA	17	D	D	D
Bedford	152	810	82.7	28.1	60	2 098	785.4	102.7	59	585	27.9	8.6
Bland	3	D	D	D	9	589	192.1	23.5	4	D	D	D
Botetourt	62	284	27.3	10.9	33	2 444	883.9	D	47	D	D	D
Brunswick	20	60	3.9	1.5	19	578	96.5	16.3	16	258	8.8	2.8
Buchanan	30	250	12.4	4.8	NA	NA	NA	NA	21	337	12.1	3.3
Buckingham	12	72	11.4	3.4	NA	NA	NA	NA	7	D	D	D
Campbell	80	713	79.1	39.0	67	3 798	1 527.6	170.8	57	901	32.7	9.0
Caroline	34	175	10.9	5.0	NA	NA	NA	NA	24	271	14.7	3.5
Carroll	27	D	D	D	22	1 190	236.8	27.7	37	532	23.3	5.2
Charles City	5	23	4.4	1.0	NA	NA	NA	NA	5	D	D	D
Charlotte	12	D	D	D	16	615	91.9	19.8	7	81	2.7	0.9
Chesterfield	758	7 220	726.3	357.6	189	10 511	3 850.0	574.4	510	10 924	491.5	133.5
Clarke	50	D	D	D	20	1 223	228.3	47.0	20	160	9.0	2.4
Craig	4	D	D	D	NA	NA	NA	NA	4	D	D	D
Culpeper	94	D	D	D	40	D	D	D	65	942	45.3	12.3
Cumberland	4	D	D	D	NA	NA	NA	NA	5	50	1.2	0.4
Dickenson	13	D	D	D	NA	NA	NA	NA	18	181	5.2	1.4
Dinwiddie	15	47	3.0	1.2	16	934	645.7	52.6	17	315	13.8	3.1
Essex	23	D	D	D	15	530	56.9	12.7	31	522	19.4	5.9
Fairfax	7 447	169 544	32 423.1	13 770.6	440	9 872	2 052.7	454.7	2 035	38 874	2 705.7	718.7
Fauquier	269	D	D	D	50	854	159.6	36.8	117	2 144	104.4	33.6
Floyd	22	D	D	D	NA	NA	NA	NA	23	209	6.6	2.0
Fluvanna	42	99	9.7	3.9	NA	NA	NA	NA	17	349	11.9	3.9
Franklin	93	286	21.4	8.0	59	3 462	D	118.9	68	961	40.3	10.8
Frederick	103	D	D	D	86	5 423	2 578.7	214.0	103	2 074	86.7	25.0
Giles	9	D	D	D	15	959	D	47.8	24	289	12.5	3.7
Gloucester	70	D	D	D	NA	NA	NA	NA	63	1 070	40.1	11.9
Goochland	68	233	26.8	11.5	NA	NA	NA	NA	36	280	15.8	4.8
Grayson	5	D	D	D	17	557	93.4	18.2	14	D	D	D
Greene	23	D	D	D	NA	NA	NA	NA	18	209	10.0	2.9
Greensville	1	D	D	D	7	D	248.7	29.9	15	243	14.1	3.3
Halifax	44	D	D	D	40	1 985	620.1	79.1	62	839	31.2	8.4
Hanover	284	1 672	216.1	84.1	143	3 702	926.3	149.8	170	2 915	137.0	39.1
Henrico	1 060	D	D	D	209	9 569	3 265.0	458.3	656	14 769	685.8	192.0
Henry	36	D	D	D	79	5 479	1 097.9	169.8	70	984	38.4	10.0
Highland	5	D	D	D	NA	NA	NA	NA	6	D	D	D
Isle of Wight	47	248	19.7	7.5	21	D	D	D	48	795	33.0	9.3
James City	226	D	D	D	34	2 364	1 567.2	117.0	118	3 273	164.4	47.8
King and Queen	6	19	1.4	0.5	NA	NA	NA	NA	2	D	D	D
King George	93	D	D	D	NA	NA	NA	NA	36	339	14.7	3.7
King William	27	155	11.2	4.5	NA	NA	NA	NA	15	216	7.5	1.9
Lancaster	59	242	23.7	9.5	NA	NA	NA	NA	43	461	16.0	4.9
Lee	19	D	D	D	NA	NA	NA	NA	19	336	8.6	2.3
Loudoun	1 765	D	D	D	157	5 266	1 400.2	322.6	526	10 275	610.2	173.3

1. Establishment subject to federal tax.

Table B. States and Counties — Health Care and Social Assistance, Other Services, and Federal Funds

STATE County	Health care and social assistance, 2007				Other services, 2007				Federal funds and grants, 2009–2010 Expenditures (mil dol)			
										Direct payments for individuals[1]		
	Number of establishments	Number of employees	Receipts (mil dol)	Annual payroll (mil dol)	Number of establishments	Number of employees	Receipts (mil dol)	Annual payroll (mil dol)	Total	Social Security and government retirement	Medicare	Food Stamps and Supplemental Security Income
	159	160	161	162	163	164	165	166	167	168	169	170
VERMONT—Cont'd												
Chittenden	558	13 272	1 316.5	514.9	402	2 035	174.5	54.8	1 877.5	365.3	135.3	36.7
Essex	10	D	D	D	8	39	6.0	0.5	66.0	28.4	10.3	3.1
Franklin	113	2 413	169.5	74.0	71	289	19.0	5.2	490.8	124.4	51.4	15.4
Grand Isle	12	69	2.9	1.2	12	15	2.2	0.5	46.5	24.3	7.9	2.3
Lamoille	81	D	D	D	75	317	125.7	7.8	194.2	97.6	26.4	8.1
Orange	76	1 188	89.8	41.5	56	219	23.4	5.7	221.2	89.9	32.8	10.1
Orleans	73	1 705	129.5	51.4	70	230	21.0	4.4	253.8	98.0	36.7	14.1
Rutland	226	4 434	370.4	155.8	176	773	60.8	16.3	688.9	234.2	100.4	27.0
Washington	236	4 379	318.6	143.2	226	1 030	120.0	32.5	1 251.8	192.5	73.3	19.7
Windham	197	2 850	214.3	93.1	129	576	55.2	14.0	365.5	140.4	61.8	15.9
Windsor	198	3 736	327.4	158.4	147	709	85.5	19.8	654.7	212.5	85.7	17.2
VIRGINIA	17 540	371 067	37 522.0	14 962.4	15 072	111 129	16 498.2	3 915.1	136 082.9	27 413.1	8 408.4	2 104.8
Accomack	60	1 229	63.6	26.3	60	368	25.8	8.0	495.5	140.2	64.8	17.1
Albemarle	262	4 140	493.7	194.5	144	1 431	299.4	59.9	658.3	196.0	90.9	10.2
Alleghany	45	864	82.1	28.9	19	89	7.3	1.6	100.4	41.3	23.2	5.2
Amelia	22	314	17.3	8.1	22	62	4.5	1.5	80.8	44.5	11.6	2.9
Amherst	42	D	D	D	63	166	12.4	3.3	204.7	109.7	34.8	9.1
Appomattox	22	D	D	D	17	56	4.2	1.1	92.4	47.1	14.9	5.0
Arlington	451	6 844	1 089.9	314.5	612	10 109	2 803.2	629.2	15 854.6	594.2	214.1	29.5
Augusta	103	3 817	394.1	139.2	85	479	39.7	12.1	315.4	170.4	60.5	8.4
Bath	7	D	D	D	7	D	D	D	46.3	22.4	12.9	0.9
Bedford	87	D	D	D	83	378	22.9	7.3	403.0	271.8	55.2	10.8
Bland	7	57	8.0	2.2	7	20	3.3	0.5	104.4	26.8	12.9	1.1
Botetourt	43	D	D	D	52	D	D	D	252.3	123.6	32.5	3.7
Brunswick	13	190	8.7	4.4	20	D	D	D	168.7	59.2	30.5	9.3
Buchanan	45	762	57.7	22.2	29	139	10.6	2.9	266.8	117.6	61.3	21.0
Buckingham	16	354	12.1	8.9	12	59	8.8	1.9	108.7	39.6	21.5	5.9
Campbell	76	913	40.8	18.5	84	428	34.3	9.7	378.9	160.1	43.6	19.0
Caroline	20	271	19.5	9.5	31	193	15.1	4.3	246.1	101.4	30.1	7.0
Carroll	35	586	30.9	13.7	26	76	8.1	2.2	190.8	86.9	40.3	7.8
Charles City	4	D	D	D	12	34	3.1	0.7	58.0	32.6	9.0	3.0
Charlotte	22	232	13.9	6.1	15	29	3.2	0.5	129.7	61.1	24.5	9.0
Chesterfield	668	9 348	867.4	385.7	471	3 356	329.6	81.4	1 303.1	660.8	141.6	47.4
Clarke	20	D	D	D	31	98	11.2	2.6	127.4	48.4	15.0	1.5
Craig	4	D	D	D	2	D	D	D	31.3	18.2	5.7	1.0
Culpeper	63	1 703	163.2	68.6	77	558	50.3	16.8	260.5	147.8	46.3	8.9
Cumberland	14	D	D	D	6	24	1.3	0.4	56.8	22.6	9.3	3.7
Dickenson	25	387	23.9	9.8	17	D	D	D	168.5	78.1	37.0	13.8
Dinwiddie	21	314	14.3	6.2	36	177	13.7	7.3	159.6	82.2	30.1	7.0
Essex	33	621	54.1	18.3	22	D	D	D	89.4	43.4	24.3	4.2
Fairfax	2 599	41 062	4 494.5	1 837.0	1 879	17 014	2 856.0	738.2	31 238.1	3 049.1	448.3	118.5
Fauquier	135	2 365	241.9	98.8	128	858	70.5	24.1	465.1	226.2	54.2	9.0
Floyd	18	D	D	D	21	65	6.3	1.5	102.2	49.0	19.4	4.0
Fluvanna	21	D	D	D	24	D	D	D	142.0	89.7	24.7	2.7
Franklin	62	D	D	D	94	282	22.8	5.7	302.4	169.8	53.8	12.1
Frederick	76	1 364	100.9	45.9	90	518	53.5	15.2	264.5	167.9	36.0	10.4
Giles	30	542	48.4	17.5	27	D	D	D	144.0	72.9	34.0	6.6
Gloucester	64	1 201	82.8	33.1	75	320	24.0	6.6	258.2	163.2	41.9	9.4
Goochland	33	D	D	D	38	378	38.0	17.6	113.7	60.2	16.1	2.9
Grayson	12	D	D	D	13	D	D	D	120.5	50.4	26.7	4.0
Greene	10	D	D	D	27	D	D	D	85.1	50.3	15.1	2.6
Greensville	3	D	D	D	6	D	D	D	41.6	13.7	6.2	3.2
Halifax	83	1 562	140.4	57.7	69	284	24.8	4.8	378.9	142.5	65.9	15.3
Hanover	218	4 557	531.6	184.8	253	1 493	138.0	43.1	897.8	333.5	93.6	12.8
Henrico	904	21 906	2 351.1	905.8	657	4 832	750.1	151.6	1 256.7	464.5	271.6	39.4
Henry	46	798	41.8	17.7	66	316	24.0	6.7	322.2	173.2	71.8	16.4
Highland	6	D	D	D	9	D	D	D	23.4	11.1	6.4	0.5
Isle of Wight	44	463	34.4	14.6	53	212	14.6	4.9	265.8	152.6	40.2	8.2
James City	151	2 000	194.7	75.0	98	475	33.2	10.5	222.0	161.5	22.4	6.5
King and Queen	5	D	D	D	8	13	1.5	0.3	51.5	25.7	10.4	2.1
King George	20	242	17.6	7.0	33	123	9.2	2.7	939.2	89.9	16.2	3.7
King William	23	307	16.4	7.9	37	110	11.0	2.6	94.3	48.6	18.9	2.4
Lancaster	41	1 063	84.9	37.9	44	169	12.6	4.1	170.6	82.8	33.5	4.1
Lee	33	640	53.1	21.8	21	78	5.8	1.5	505.4	93.7	58.5	23.5
Loudoun	596	7 622	813.8	330.8	480	3 824	485.0	126.6	4 776.5	600.3	73.9	14.6

1. State totals may include programs not allocated by county.

STATE County	Federal funds and grants, 2009–2010 (cont.) Expenditures (mil dol) (cont.) Procurement contract awards — Salaries and wages	Defense	Other	Grants[1] — Medicaid and other health-related	Nutrition and family welfare	Education	Other	Value of residential construction authorized by building permits, 2010 — New construction ($1,000)	Number of housing units	Local government finances, 2007 — General revenue — Total (mil dol)	Inter-govern-mental (mil dol)	Taxes — Total (mil dol)	Taxes Per capita[2] (dollars) — Total	Property
	171	172	173	174	175	176	177	178	179	180	181	182	183	184
VERMONT—Cont'd														
Chittenden	310.7	475.0	61.6	276.6	26.5	13.7	114.7	66 699	411	530.7	336.2	97.2	640	528
Essex	7.0	0.0	0.6	12.1	1.7	0.3	1.4	942	10	18.5	14.5	3.0	468	462
Franklin	107.2	28.0	53.9	86.7	10.3	1.7	5.9	23 116	161	146.9	114.8	17.5	365	351
Grand Isle	1.8	0.0	0.5	7.6	1.3	0.2	0.0	2 182	13	21.4	16.0	3.9	511	501
Lamoille	11.5	0.4	1.4	38.6	4.8	0.7	1.5	26 200	73	86.9	58.1	17.4	705	702
Orange	13.6	11.2	2.8	46.1	6.3	1.2	2.2	4 495	28	97.5	76.2	14.6	503	501
Orleans	23.0	0.1	3.4	58.7	10.3	1.2	3.9	9 278	88	87.1	67.2	13.3	487	477
Rutland	40.6	29.2	12.0	140.0	14.3	2.3	77.1	9 211	56	203.9	139.3	38.2	603	580
Washington	63.3	8.4	6.0	138.1	54.7	69.3	583.6	18 426	105	183.6	124.2	32.8	556	553
Windham	22.9	0.7	3.8	54.2	11.9	2.4	35.1	12 649	77	170.6	118.8	34.2	786	772
Windsor	77.0	5.3	60.5	78.6	10.5	1.2	101.0	15 079	78	197.8	130.6	42.2	742	733
VIRGINIA	21 112.2	40 377.7	17 960.0	5 483.9	1 142.6	1 214.5	4 386.5	3 246 376	20 992	X	X	X	X	X
Accomack	58.7	16.7	114.0	54.6	9.0	2.4	7.4	14 707	89	101.0	56.8	32.3	838	579
Albemarle	94.5	150.2	22.3	73.2	4.7	4.6	5.3	118 717	631	326.1	125.7	165.6	1 778	1 268
Alleghany	2.4	0.0	0.5	17.8	3.3	2.1	0.1	1 835	17	58.8	32.6	18.3	1 119	892
Amelia	2.3	0.4	0.8	13.4	1.5	0.9	0.0	7 768	44	28.1	18.3	7.6	601	420
Amherst	6.8	0.1	10.8	25.9	2.9	2.0	0.9	9 811	66	72.4	42.6	23.5	731	490
Appomattox	3.7	0.0	0.8	16.8	1.5	1.0	0.8	8 381	61	33.4	20.6	10.6	747	542
Arlington	4 304.0	4 901.8	4 849.9	69.3	22.5	55.7	637.8	95 918	875	1 827.6	380.0	705.0	3 446	2 575
Augusta	11.5	3.6	6.1	34.0	7.3	3.7	0.2	31 976	300	162.5	88.1	59.9	844	577
Bath	2.4	0.0	0.5	5.6	0.7	0.4	0.3	3 877	25	16.4	4.4	10.9	2 361	2 169
Bedford	9.1	17.3	2.3	25.0	5.3	3.0	0.7	62 057	317	181.4	87.9	67.5	1 011	830
Bland	53.4	0.0	0.4	8.1	0.9	0.6	0.0	1 126	11	21.4	9.8	3.8	552	413
Botetourt	4.5	67.9	2.8	12.5	2.2	1.5	0.0	11 470	66	83.5	38.3	34.2	1 069	830
Brunswick	4.5	7.1	1.0	31.2	3.9	3.8	0.2	2 915	17	43.6	28.5	10.5	592	454
Buchanan	5.6	0.1	1.1	48.4	8.6	2.8	0.1	1 240	21	77.6	44.1	28.7	1 202	607
Buckingham	2.0	0.5	0.6	27.9	2.8	1.1	6.3	3 500	31	41.8	30.9	9.2	576	450
Campbell	27.5	74.9	1.4	37.7	5.5	3.9	0.9	20 161	111	127.7	74.3	39.8	754	543
Caroline	32.4	48.1	2.7	16.2	2.8	1.6	0.0	13 965	96	53.5	32.6	17.9	658	418
Carroll	4.3	0.5	1.2	39.3	4.0	2.8	1.5	13 013	75	67.5	36.1	19.9	684	501
Charles City	1.5	0.7	0.3	8.1	1.1	0.5	0.1	6 176	43	19.4	8.4	7.0	973	878
Charlotte	4.3	0.0	0.9	22.5	2.5	1.0	0.1	2 935	24	34.3	23.5	8.6	696	545
Chesterfield	156.3	184.9	18.6	27.1	16.5	15.6	8.4	115 836	871	1 060.4	422.7	441.0	1 472	1 118
Clarke	4.7	0.7	42.7	8.1	0.8	0.6	3.7	6 408	23	58.2	24.9	19.7	1 373	1 128
Craig	1.3	0.0	0.2	3.1	0.6	0.4	0.0	2 859	19	11.2	6.3	3.1	601	480
Culpeper	12.3	0.2	6.7	28.7	4.3	2.1	0.8	19 869	93	163.4	61.1	63.8	1 396	1 027
Cumberland	1.2	0.0	0.3	14.4	4.1	0.7	0.0	3 610	20	27.2	18.9	7.9	823	687
Dickenson	2.8	0.4	0.6	28.2	3.0	1.5	1.7	1 153	12	51.5	28.0	19.5	1 205	491
Dinwiddie	3.4	0.0	0.8	27.8	2.6	1.6	0.0	10 926	72	74.3	40.1	27.1	1 052	827
Essex	1.8	0.0	0.3	11.0	1.1	0.9	0.2	4 465	25	29.6	14.5	13.2	1 216	774
Fairfax	2 789.1	16 145.7	8 126.3	163.6	64.4	50.8	91.2	156 264	896	4 579.8	1 059.6	2 848.4	2 820	2 253
Fauquier	47.3	2.1	89.4	19.9	4.7	2.7	6.2	30 441	151	227.3	72.8	126.5	1 908	1 541
Floyd	3.7	0.0	0.9	12.2	1.5	0.9	9.3	7 417	49	26.0	15.5	9.6	659	506
Fluvanna	4.1	0.0	1.0	14.4	1.6	1.0	1.5	16 767	95	43.7	21.5	20.3	803	694
Franklin	10.1	0.4	2.0	36.3	5.6	3.3	0.8	28 737	117	126.9	66.1	51.3	1 003	647
Frederick	4.8	5.7	3.6	18.7	4.3	3.3	0.3	45 318	247	215.9	88.9	105.6	1 450	1 051
Giles	3.6	0.5	1.0	20.6	2.1	1.3	0.6	2 997	25	44.2	24.1	15.6	903	710
Gloucester	9.2	1.6	2.2	12.8	3.3	1.8	7.5	17 531	102	94.1	46.8	40.5	1 057	759
Goochland	2.8	0.4	1.3	9.4	1.3	1.0	0.1	14 065	60	60.9	16.9	39.1	1 895	1 624
Grayson	2.6	0.0	0.7	29.3	2.4	1.3	2.0	4 447	31	32.4	21.2	8.8	545	396
Greene	2.7	0.5	0.6	10.3	1.3	1.0	0.0	24 664	235	50.6	24.1	17.1	957	739
Greensville	0.2	1.7	0.2	10.3	2.8	1.2	0.0	2 841	27	39.8	26.0	7.0	587	401
Halifax	10.4	0.3	1.8	85.2	7.9	3.0	36.9	8 508	54	109.9	65.5	30.4	856	567
Hanover	16.6	401.0	4.7	19.3	4.6	3.4	1.1	46 616	283	317.8	132.7	149.9	1 515	1 191
Henrico	74.0	33.0	121.7	81.7	120.6	12.0	20.3	111 035	635	1 039.7	380.5	480.9	1 659	1 195
Henry	5.7	4.0	2.5	34.0	6.5	5.0	1.3	5 033	36	124.9	70.5	42.2	760	393
Highland	1.0	0.0	0.2	3.5	0.3	0.3	0.0	2 206	12	9.3	4.1	4.5	1 840	1 595
Isle of Wight	8.3	19.8	1.3	24.0	3.9	1.3	0.2	25 809	256	92.8	43.4	43.2	1 234	997
James City	1.8	3.7	4.7	11.2	4.0	0.5	0.1	107 667	496	224.3	50.8	128.7	2 103	1 586
King and Queen	1.3	1.2	2.1	5.3	1.0	0.5	0.4	3 242	25	25.6	13.8	6.3	913	759
King George	269.1	545.7	2.3	7.2	1.5	1.0	0.0	15 142	86	63.0	27.0	21.2	938	671
King William	10.7	0.0	0.8	6.9	2.8	0.8	0.0	6 819	45	43.1	19.9	20.2	1 290	1 108
Lancaster	3.6	31.9	1.0	10.0	1.6	0.6	0.3	18 087	93	23.1	8.0	13.2	1 145	913
Lee	27.1	0.3	212.2	73.3	8.1	2.6	3.2	5 321	49	59.5	43.9	11.1	475	317
Loudoun	415.7	2 972.3	491.3	138.1	8.7	7.0	39.1	326 652	2 041	1 240.1	276.2	831.9	2 984	2 406

1. State totals may include programs not allocated by county. 2. Based on the resident population estimated as of July 1 of the year shown.

Table B. States and Counties — Local Government Finances, Government Employment, and Voting

STATE County	Direct general expenditure — Total (mil dol)	Per capita[1] (dollars)	Percent of total for: Education	Health and hospitals	Police protection	Public welfare	Highways	Debt outstanding — Total (mil dol)	Per capita[1] (dollars)	Federal civilian	Federal military	State and local	Demo-cratic	Republi-can	All other
	185	186	187	188	189	190	191	192	193	194	195	196	197	198	199
VERMONT—Cont'd															
Chittenden	605.4	3 988	62.5	0.3	4.7	0.0	4.5	428.9	2 825	2 248	1 045	13 372	71.4	26.7	1.9
Essex	20.1	3 099	79.6	0.2	0.5	0.0	8.6	1.9	300	105	42	318	55.9	41.4	2.7
Franklin	159.6	3 330	78.0	0.5	1.7	0.0	6.4	57.4	1 198	1 164	314	2 872	61.4	36.6	2.0
Grand Isle	20.3	2 673	76.7	0.0	0.9	0.0	8.8	13.5	1 774	22	49	294	63.1	34.9	2.0
Lamoille	102.0	4 135	71.1	1.3	3.4	0.0	8.2	78.0	3 159	75	169	1 591	70.4	27.7	1.9
Orange	124.9	4 305	81.3	0.4	1.4	0.1	6.1	46.0	1 587	100	188	1 859	64.6	33.2	2.2
Orleans	108.9	3 987	79.3	0.1	1.3	0.0	7.6	36.0	1 318	267	178	1 842	62.6	35.1	2.3
Rutland	242.7	3 836	74.9	0.1	2.5	0.1	6.5	76.5	1 209	330	412	4 317	61.2	36.6	2.1
Washington	218.7	3 711	71.2	0.9	2.8	0.0	6.7	90.9	1 543	300	435	7 540	69.3	28.4	2.3
Windham	213.6	4 912	74.6	0.2	2.2	0.2	7.1	57.9	1 333	176	283	2 794	73.0	24.9	2.1
Windsor	233.8	4 110	68.6	0.5	3.5	0.0	9.4	84.2	1 480	1 410	377	3 615	68.8	29.1	2.0
VIRGINIA	X	X	X	X	X	X	X	X	X	182 831	154 739	537 350	52.6	46.3	1.0
Accomack	116.0	3 015	59.9	0.9	4.5	6.3	0.8	68.1	1 770	614	319	2 159	48.7	50.1	1.2
Albemarle	304.5	3 270	54.3	2.4	4.8	4.3	0.3	317.7	3 412	[3]1 356	[3]749	[3]28 023	58.4	40.4	1.2
Alleghany	55.7	3 398	57.1	0.3	4.4	7.2	1.2	45.0	2 748	[4]81	[4]76	[4]1 657	48.2	50.4	1.4
Amelia	29.0	2 283	57.5	0.6	6.8	4.6	0.0	6.6	518	30	44	533	38.1	60.8	1.1
Amherst	73.1	2 270	63.4	1.5	7.1	3.7	0.1	34.1	1 057	54	110	2 954	41.5	57.6	0.9
Appomattox	33.0	2 322	60.6	2.4	5.9	5.7	0.0	25.3	1 782	63	49	878	34.6	64.3	1.1
Arlington	2 264.3	11 069	20.3	1.6	2.4	2.7	2.5	6 059.5	29 621	31 121	12 073	11 177	71.7	27.1	1.2
Augusta	198.4	2 798	68.5	7.5	3.5	6.0	0.1	132.5	1 869	[5]304	[5]401	[5]8 804	29.5	69.4	1.2
Bath	15.1	3 258	66.6	0.5	6.0	4.6	0.1	0.0	0	20	15	334	42.9	55.5	1.6
Bedford	196.5	2 943	58.4	0.3	3.2	9.5	0.5	130.1	1 949	[6]154	[6]249	[6]3 105	30.7	68.2	1.1
Bland	14.3	2 078	59.5	1.6	5.1	7.7	0.0	24.2	3 511	16	23	614	29.2	68.6	2.2
Botetourt	108.9	3 401	58.0	0.3	4.5	2.5	0.1	88.2	2 755	58	110	1 416	32.7	65.9	1.4
Brunswick	42.4	2 381	59.3	0.7	6.5	6.6	0.1	26.5	1 487	68	59	1 471	62.8	36.4	0.8
Buchanan	77.2	3 232	47.4	0.9	4.0	10.5	4.3	12.5	525	57	77	1 626	46.5	52.0	1.5
Buckingham	43.0	2 696	54.3	1.4	3.9	3.2	0.0	21.5	1 352	32	54	1 330	49.9	49.0	1.1
Campbell	125.0	2 366	64.8	1.3	3.9	8.3	1.4	107.0	2 024	[7]517	[7]444	[7]7 800	31.3	67.6	1.1
Caroline	53.3	1 952	68.4	0.0	3.1	8.7	0.6	58.2	2 134	502	100	1 265	55.4	43.5	1.1
Carroll	62.3	2 138	62.3	7.3	4.6	6.5	0.4	101.2	3 474	[8]110	[8]121	[8]2 573	32.7	65.1	2.2
Charles City	24.0	3 351	57.4	1.2	5.4	11.4	0.0	2.8	387	19	24	328	68.3	31.0	0.7
Charlotte	31.7	2 574	65.0	0.8	5.1	4.1	0.1	31.8	2 575	50	41	1 001	43.9	54.8	1.3
Chesterfield	977.9	3 263	57.6	4.7	6.0	3.7	2.3	781.7	2 608	2 989	1 042	18 455	45.9	53.3	0.8
Clarke	47.8	3 327	47.7	0.7	5.0	4.9	0.3	161.5	11 248	41	49	706	46.5	51.7	1.8
Craig	11.6	2 263	57.9	0.5	6.1	7.5	0.3	5.0	978	18	17	227	33.5	64.7	1.9
Culpeper	180.4	3 945	52.9	10.7	6.0	6.7	1.4	134.7	2 945	122	158	3 259	44.6	54.3	1.2
Cumberland	30.8	3 199	75.1	0.3	4.7	3.1	0.0	27.6	2 864	14	33	458	47.7	51.2	1.1
Dickenson	51.1	3 161	51.2	4.4	6.2	5.8	5.7	13.0	804	39	54	1 021	48.5	49.2	2.2
Dinwiddie	96.5	3 708	73.9	1.9	4.8	3.1	0.0	99.4	3 860	[9]259	[9]264	[9]7 458	48.4	50.6	0.9
Essex	33.8	3 116	53.8	0.1	4.4	4.2	1.0	37.2	3 422	30	38	505	54.7	44.4	1.0
Fairfax	4 458.6	4 413	52.1	4.3	5.0	5.2	1.1	4 786.8	4 738	[10]41 352	[10]7 385	[10]59 724	60.1	38.9	0.9
Fauquier	217.7	3 283	55.8	1.4	5.5	3.8	0.9	144.1	2 172	438	230	3 727	42.7	56.2	1.1
Floyd	28.4	1 943	63.7	2.2	4.5	2.0	0.0	34.1	2 328	53	51	597	39.1	59.1	1.8
Fluvanna	46.7	1 845	73.2	0.2	4.7	9.4	0.0	2.8	111	36	87	1 307	48.6	50.4	1.0
Franklin	120.1	2 348	60.1	0.4	5.0	7.8	1.1	57.9	1 132	114	176	2 036	37.9	60.7	1.5
Frederick	202.3	2 776	71.3	1.2	4.8	2.5	0.2	156.6	2 149	[11]1 306	[11]351	[11]5 796	38.6	59.9	1.5
Giles	41.8	2 428	58.7	1.7	6.4	4.7	2.8	29.9	1 736	40	59	925	40.9	57.2	1.8
Gloucester	89.4	2 331	67.6	0.9	5.2	3.8	0.0	81.8	2 134	96	133	2 485	36.0	62.9	1.1
Goochland	58.3	2 827	54.9	10.2	2.9	3.3	1.4	34.5	1 674	41	72	1 663	38.3	60.8	0.8
Grayson	33.2	2 069	68.3	0.8	5.3	6.5	0.3	4.8	297	28	53	714	34.3	62.9	2.8
Greene	50.8	2 843	58.1	1.3	5.3	5.9	1.3	51.8	2 898	36	62	857	38.4	60.3	1.3
Greensville	42.9	3 606	54.1	0.2	8.4	7.4	0.4	29.1	2 447	[12]39	[12]60	[12]1 929	63.9	35.4	0.7
Halifax	111.2	3 197	57.8	8.9	4.8	5.4	1.0	29.6	832	96	119	2 263	48.2	51.0	0.7
Hanover	299.2	3 024	59.7	0.0	8.2	2.3	3.0	233.9	2 364	176	338	5 351	32.8	66.4	0.8
Henrico	1 035.5	3 573	45.5	2.8	6.0	2.8	4.5	1 005.1	3 468	1 030	1 005	16 434	55.7	43.5	0.8
Henry	124.6	2 243	64.0	0.4	4.7	5.7	0.0	68.2	1 228	[13]145	[13]236	[13]3 845	44.1	54.6	1.3
Highland	7.9	3 244	50.0	4.5	7.2	3.7	1.3	2.1	847	11	0	146	38.0	59.8	2.2
Isle of Wight	82.1	2 344	62.8	5.8	5.0	0.0	1.9	86.1	2 457	104	122	1 548	42.9	56.3	0.8
James City	229.5	3 751	48.9	6.3	4.2	2.3	0.0	379.8	6 206	[14]267	[14]682	[14]8 762	44.9	54.2	0.9
King and Queen	26.5	3 844	46.6	2.0	3.1	3.5	0.0	12.7	1 842	13	162	283	51.8	47.6	0.6
King George	52.6	2 325	58.3	0.6	7.2	6.1	0.3	157.5	6 958	3 599	647	944	42.7	56.2	1.1
King William	42.1	2 680	66.8	0.9	5.9	3.8	0.6	54.5	3 473	24	55	763	39.9	59.2	0.9
Lancaster	27.5	2 381	58.1	3.0	5.2	4.5	3.1	9.2	801	44	38	518	46.6	52.6	0.8
Lee	61.8	2 635	64.9	0.7	4.5	11.7	0.5	13.4	571	422	85	1 302	34.9	63.1	2.0
Loudoun	1 242.7	4 457	58.3	2.7	4.6	3.5	1.8	2 076.3	7 447	4 158	1 022	16 877	53.7	45.4	0.9

1. Based on the resident population estimated as of July 1 of the year shown. 2. © 2009 Election Data Services, Inc. All rights reserved. 3. Charlottesville city is included with Albemarle county. 4. Covington city is included with Alleghany county. 5. Staunton and Waynesboro cities are included with Augusta county. 6. Bedford city is included with Bedford county. 7. Lynchburg city is included with Campbell county. 8. Galax city is included with Carroll county. 9. Petersburg and Colonial Heights cities are included with Dinwiddie county. 10. Fairfax city and Falls Church city are included with Fairfax county. 11. Winchester city is included with Frederick county. 12. Emporia city is included with Greensville county. 13. Martinsville city is included with Henry county. 14. Williamsburg city is included with James City county.

STATE/County code	CBSA code[1]	County type[2]	STATE County	Population and population characteristics, 2010				Race alone or in combination, not Hispanic or Latino (percent)					Age (percent)					
				Land area,[3] (sq km) 2010	Total persons	Rank	Per square kilometer	White	Black	American Indian, Alaska Native	Asian and Pacific Islander	Percent Hispanic or Latino[4]	Under 5 years	5 to 17 years	18 to 24 years	25 to 34 years	35 to 44 years	45 to 54 years
				1	2	3	4	5	6	7	8	9	10	11	12	13	14	15
			VIRGINIA—Cont'd															
51 109	40060	1	Louisa	1 285	33 153	1 349	25.8	79.0	19.0	1.0	0.8	2.3	6.1	16.0	6.8	11.5	13.1	17.1
51 111	...	9	Lunenburg	1 118	12 914	2 248	11.6	61.1	35.4	0.8	0.4	3.6	5.3	14.0	8.0	11.7	12.9	15.7
51 113	...	8	Madison	831	13 308	2 232	16.0	87.6	11.0	0.9	0.9	1.8	5.7	16.6	7.1	9.8	11.9	16.4
51 115	47260	1	Mathews	223	8 978	2 527	40.3	88.9	9.9	1.2	0.7	1.2	3.9	14.3	5.8	7.0	11.2	15.4
51 117	...	7	Mecklenburg	1 620	32 727	1 370	20.2	59.8	37.4	0.7	0.9	2.5	4.8	14.7	7.3	10.4	11.7	15.4
51 119	...	8	Middlesex	337	10 959	2 370	32.5	79.7	18.7	0.9	0.5	1.5	4.0	12.1	6.4	8.1	10.0	16.6
51 121	13980	3	Montgomery	1 002	94 392	611	94.2	87.6	4.5	0.5	6.4	2.7	4.7	11.4	31.2	13.0	10.5	10.4
51 125	16820	3	Nelson	1 220	15 020	2 108	12.3	83.0	13.7	0.8	0.7	3.1	4.8	14.4	6.2	9.5	11.0	16.0
51 127	40060	1	New Kent	543	18 429	1 902	33.9	82.2	14.2	2.2	1.5	2.1	5.3	17.0	6.6	10.3	14.7	18.4
51 131	...	9	Northampton	548	12 389	2 283	22.6	55.6	37.0	0.6	0.8	7.1	5.5	14.2	7.2	9.8	9.6	15.5
51 133	...	9	Northumberland	495	12 330	2 286	24.9	71.0	25.9	0.8	0.4	3.1	4.3	12.1	6.0	7.3	8.3	14.2
51 135	...	6	Nottoway	814	15 853	2 062	19.5	56.3	39.5	0.7	0.5	3.8	5.6	15.0	8.6	13.1	12.7	15.5
51 137	...	6	Orange	883	33 481	1 335	37.9	82.7	13.8	0.9	1.3	3.4	6.0	16.9	6.7	10.7	13.1	15.2
51 139	...	6	Page	805	24 042	1 644	29.9	96.0	2.3	0.5	0.6	1.6	5.5	16.1	7.2	10.9	13.2	15.6
51 141	...	8	Patrick	1 251	18 490	1 901	14.8	91.1	6.4	0.6	0.4	2.4	5.0	14.3	6.1	9.1	13.0	15.7
51 143	19260	3	Pittsylvania	2 510	63 506	819	25.3	75.2	22.5	0.6	0.5	2.1	5.2	16.1	7.1	10.0	12.9	16.7
51 145	40060	1	Powhatan	674	28 046	1 496	41.6	83.7	14.1	0.7	0.7	1.8	5.1	18.0	7.1	10.0	15.8	17.8
51 147	...	6	Prince Edward	906	23 368	1 674	25.8	63.4	33.8	0.7	1.2	2.2	4.3	13.0	26.5	9.7	10.1	11.9
51 149	40060	1	Prince George	687	35 725	1 278	52.0	60.1	32.7	1.2	2.5	5.8	5.5	17.0	9.0	14.1	15.6	16.2
51 153	47900	1	Prince William	871	402 002	166	461.5	51.6	21.2	0.9	9.3	20.3	8.3	20.6	8.5	14.8	16.3	15.2
51 155	13980	3	Pulaski	828	34 872	1 304	42.1	92.9	5.8	0.6	0.7	1.2	4.9	14.6	7.2	10.4	14.2	15.3
51 157	...	8	Rappahannock	690	7 373	2 652	10.7	91.6	5.2	0.9	0.7	3.1	4.5	15.4	6.4	8.3	11.5	17.2
51 159	...	9	Richmond	496	9 254	2 503	18.7	63.3	31.1	0.7	0.8	5.5	4.3	12.9	7.5	13.5	14.4	16.9
51 161	40220	2	Roanoke	649	92 376	623	142.3	89.9	5.6	0.5	3.2	2.1	5.0	16.8	7.1	10.0	13.5	15.8
51 163	...	6	Rockbridge	1 548	22 307	1 723	14.4	95.0	3.1	1.2	0.7	1.3	4.7	14.4	7.5	9.2	11.9	15.7
51 165	25500	3	Rockingham	2 199	76 314	710	34.7	92.2	2.1	0.4	0.8	5.3	6.1	17.6	8.7	10.8	12.9	15.4
51 167	...	6	Russell	1 227	28 897	1 455	23.6	97.9	0.9	0.4	0.3	1.0	5.4	15.1	7.6	11.2	13.4	16.3
51 169	28700	3	Scott	1 387	23 177	1 681	16.7	98.0	0.7	0.5	0.3	1.0	5.1	14.3	7.1	10.6	13.4	15.2
51 171	...	6	Shenandoah	1 318	41 993	1 130	31.9	91.4	2.2	0.7	0.7	6.1	5.9	16.1	7.3	10.5	12.8	15.0
51 173	...	6	Smyth	1 168	32 208	1 387	27.6	95.9	2.3	0.6	0.4	1.6	5.4	15.4	8.0	10.3	13.5	14.9
51 175	...	6	Southampton	1 552	18 570	1 894	12.0	60.9	37.9	0.8	0.4	1.1	5.1	16.0	7.3	9.9	12.8	19.3
51 177	47900	1	Spotsylvania	1 040	122 397	494	117.7	74.3	16.4	0.9	3.3	7.6	6.7	21.1	8.3	12.1	14.9	15.9
51 179	47900	1	Stafford	697	128 961	478	185.0	70.4	18.1	1.0	4.2	9.2	6.8	22.1	9.3	12.3	15.4	17.0
51 181	47260	1	Surry	722	7 058	2 679	9.8	51.9	46.8	0.9	0.6	1.2	5.3	15.8	8.1	9.1	11.6	19.2
51 183	40060	1	Sussex	1 270	12 087	2 300	9.5	39.2	58.3	0.4	0.6	2.2	4.3	12.4	9.5	16.0	14.2	15.8
51 185	14140	7	Tazewell	1 344	45 078	1 063	33.5	95.5	3.4	0.5	0.8	0.7	5.2	15.2	7.6	11.6	12.7	15.4
51 187	47900	1	Warren	553	37 575	1 227	67.9	90.6	5.5	1.0	1.4	3.5	6.5	17.7	8.6	11.1	14.0	17.0
51 191	28700	3	Washington	1 453	54 876	912	37.8	96.8	1.5	0.4	0.5	1.3	5.0	14.7	7.9	10.9	13.3	15.7
51 193	...	7	Westmoreland	594	17 454	1 953	29.4	65.2	29.1	1.1	0.9	5.7	5.3	14.7	7.4	9.8	10.7	15.3
51 195	...	7	Wise	1 044	41 452	1 146	39.7	93.2	5.5	0.5	0.5	1.1	5.6	15.2	10.7	13.2	13.6	14.2
51 197	...	6	Wythe	1 196	29 235	1 447	24.4	95.6	3.4	0.5	0.6	1.0	5.4	15.5	6.9	10.9	13.9	15.2
51 199	47260	1	York	271	65 464	800	241.6	76.5	14.4	1.0	6.5	4.4	5.8	20.6	8.1	10.4	13.3	17.7
	...		**Independent cities**															
51 510	47900	1	Alexandria city	39	139 966	438	3 588.9	55.5	22.3	0.7	7.5	16.1	7.1	10.0	7.2	24.4	17.7	13.4
51 515	31340	3	Bedford city	18	6 222	2 747	345.7	76.7	21.4	0.6	0.9	2.2	6.4	14.1	9.5	11.0	11.1	14.1
51 520	28700	3	Bristol city	34	17 835	1 932	524.6	92.0	6.8	0.8	0.9	1.2	6.2	14.6	9.5	12.2	12.2	13.7
51 530	...	6	Buena Vista city	17	6 650	2 719	391.2	91.4	5.9	1.7	1.0	1.5	6.2	15.2	14.3	11.7	11.3	12.6
51 540	16820	3	Charlottesville city	27	43 475	1 096	1 610.2	68.7	20.4	0.7	7.7	5.1	5.3	9.6	28.1	18.7	10.2	10.0
51 550	47260	1	Chesapeake city	883	222 209	280	251.7	62.6	30.6	1.0	4.1	4.4	6.5	19.4	9.1	12.6	13.9	16.8
51 570	40060	1	Colonial Heights city	19	17 411	1 956	916.4	82.2	10.9	0.8	4.1	3.9	5.4	16.9	8.2	11.3	12.0	14.3
51 580	...	6	Covington city	14	5 961	2 771	425.8	84.7	13.9	0.8	0.8	1.5	5.8	15.5	8.1	11.1	12.5	15.3
51 590	19260	3	Danville city	111	43 055	1 104	387.9	47.6	48.9	0.5	1.2	2.9	6.3	15.2	9.5	10.8	10.9	14.2
51 595	...	6	Emporia city	18	5 927	2 772	329.3	32.0	63.2	0.4	1.0	4.4	6.9	18.9	8.9	11.9	11.6	13.4
51 600	47900	1	Fairfax city	16	22 565	1 709	1 410.3	63.7	5.3	0.6	17.0	15.8	5.7	14.7	10.0	14.5	13.8	15.2
51 610	47900	1	Falls Church city	5	12 332	2 285	2 466.4	76.9	5.0	0.7	11.8	9.0	6.3	18.4	6.1	13.5	14.9	16.5
51 620	...	6	Franklin city	21	8 582	2 561	408.7	40.1	58.0	1.0	1.1	1.6	7.4	16.5	9.4	10.7	11.3	14.6
51 630	47900	1	Fredericksburg city	27	24 286	1 632	899.5	63.3	24.0	1.0	4.0	10.7	6.5	13.1	23.3	15.7	11.2	11.3
51 640	...	6	Galax city	21	7 042	2 681	335.3	79.3	6.7	0.5	0.8	14.0	5.9	16.0	8.2	10.6	12.8	13.6
51 650	47260	1	Hampton city	133	137 436	448	1 033.4	43.1	50.8	1.4	3.3	4.5	6.5	16.3	12.8	13.9	11.7	15.2
51 660	25500	3	Harrisonburg city	45	48 914	996	1 087.0	74.3	6.9	0.4	4.6	15.7	5.0	10.1	41.8	12.7	8.2	7.8
51 670	40060	1	Hopewell city	27	22 591	1 706	836.7	55.4	38.1	0.9	1.5	6.6	7.7	17.4	9.3	13.8	12.3	13.5
51 678	...	6	Lexington city	6	7 042	2 681	1 173.7	83.9	10.2	0.5	3.2	3.8	2.6	7.5	44.4	8.4	5.9	7.1
51 680	31340	3	Lynchburg city	127	75 568	717	595.0	64.3	30.5	0.8	2.9	3.0	6.1	13.5	22.9	12.5	9.8	11.3
51 683	47900	1	Manassas city	26	37 821	1 220	1 454.7	49.7	14.5	0.7	5.9	31.4	8.4	20.0	9.6	16.5	14.5	14.4

1. CBSA = Core Based Statistical Area. See Appendix A for explanation. See Appendix B for list of metropolitan areas with component counties. 2. County type code from the Economic Research Service of USDA Rural-Urban Continuum Codes. See Appendix A for definition. 3. Dry land or land partially or temporarily covered by water. 4. May be of any race.

Table B. States and Counties — Population and Households

STATE County	Age (percent) (cont.)				Total persons		Percent change		Components of change, 2000-2009			Households, 2010			Percent	
	55 to 64 years	65 to 74 years	75 years and over	Percent female	1990	2000	1990–2000	2000–2010	Births	Deaths	Net migration	Number	Percent change, 2000–2010	Persons per house-hold	Female family house-holder[1]	One per-son
	16	17	18	19	20	21	22	23	24	25	26	27	28	29	30	31

VIRGINIA—Cont'd

Louisa	14.9	9.1	5.4	50.7	20 325	25 627	26.1	29.4	3 378	2 490	6 648	12 944	30.2	2.54	10.5	21.9
Lunenburg	15.3	9.8	7.4	46.9	11 419	13 146	15.1	-1.8	1 191	1 420	-39	4 957	-0.8	2.36	14.2	29.9
Madison	15.0	10.0	7.6	51.2	11 949	12 520	4.8	6.3	1 333	1 154	1 073	5 083	7.3	2.58	9.7	21.2
Mathews	16.8	14.7	10.8	51.4	8 348	9 207	10.3	-2.5	647	1 182	362	3 858	-1.9	2.30	8.7	26.5
Mecklenburg	15.1	11.7	9.1	50.4	29 241	32 380	10.7	1.1	3 139	3 907	575	13 495	4.2	2.30	14.9	30.4
Middlesex	17.7	14.7	10.5	50.1	8 653	9 932	14.8	10.3	740	1 305	1 407	4 708	10.7	2.24	9.3	27.6
Montgomery	9.1	5.4	4.4	48.3	73 913	83 629	13.1	12.9	7 898	4 819	4 866	35 767	15.4	2.38	7.9	26.4
Nelson	18.1	12.1	7.8	51.4	12 778	14 445	13.0	4.0	1 445	1 503	1 165	6 396	8.6	2.33	11.1	27.4
New Kent	15.7	8.1	4.0	49.1	10 466	13 462	28.6	36.9	1 531	1 010	4 159	6 813	38.3	2.62	8.7	17.0
Northampton	15.8	11.5	10.9	52.1	13 061	13 093	0.2	-5.4	1 510	1 807	775	5 323	0.0	2.27	14.8	32.0
Northumberland	17.7	17.6	12.5	51.3	10 524	12 259	16.5	0.6	1 007	1 599	1 364	5 540	1.3	2.23	9.9	27.4
Nottoway	12.4	9.1	7.9	47.2	14 993	15 725	4.9	0.8	1 652	1 812	453	5 706	0.7	2.46	16.2	29.7
Orange	13.3	10.5	7.6	51.0	21 421	25 881	20.8	29.4	3 328	2 788	7 296	12 895	27.0	2.55	10.9	22.5
Page	13.8	10.0	7.6	50.8	21 690	23 177	6.9	3.7	2 467	2 324	894	9 746	4.7	2.45	11.1	25.7
Patrick	15.3	12.4	9.1	50.8	17 473	19 407	11.1	-4.7	1 566	2 071	-159	8 081	-0.7	2.26	9.3	29.4
Pittsylvania	14.9	10.1	7.1	50.8	55 672	61 745	10.9	2.9	6 246	5 786	-426	26 183	6.1	2.39	13.2	26.5
Powhatan	14.1	7.9	4.2	46.1	15 328	22 377	46.0	25.3	2 476	1 410	4 609	9 494	30.8	2.70	8.4	16.4
Prince Edward	10.6	7.2	6.8	50.3	17 320	19 720	13.9	18.5	1 893	2 013	2 843	7 916	20.7	2.41	15.0	29.4
Prince George	12.1	6.5	3.9	45.4	27 390	33 047	20.7	8.1	3 426	1 584	2 183	11 451	12.7	2.70	13.3	18.9
Prince William	9.6	4.4	2.3	50.3	214 954	280 813	30.6	43.2	57 518	11 783	53 569	130 785	38.3	3.05	12.1	17.7
Pulaski	15.6	10.4	7.5	50.6	34 496	35 127	1.8	-0.7	3 258	3 853	716	14 821	1.2	2.29	11.7	29.3
Rappahannock	17.7	11.8	7.3	50.0	6 622	6 983	5.5	5.6	693	633	-89	3 072	10.2	2.39	8.6	26.3
Richmond	12.4	9.0	9.1	43.5	7 273	8 809	21.1	5.1	843	1 093	455	3 159	7.6	2.36	12.9	31.2
Roanoke	14.6	9.0	8.2	52.3	79 278	85 778	8.2	7.7	9 569	8 191	4 419	37 608	8.4	2.39	9.9	26.7
Rockbridge	16.8	11.6	9.1	50.7	18 350	20 808	13.4	7.2	2 224	2 012	401	9 555	12.6	2.32	9.8	27.3
Rockingham	12.7	8.3	7.3	50.9	57 482	67 725	17.8	12.7	8 150	5 527	4 111	29 177	15.1	2.57	9.2	22.8
Russell	14.7	9.6	6.8	51.0	28 667	30 308	5.7	-4.7	2 781	3 154	535	11 943	1.3	2.38	10.1	26.3
Scott	14.7	11.2	8.6	50.4	23 204	23 403	0.9	-1.0	2 085	2 821	66	9 775	-0.2	2.30	9.8	28.7
Shenandoah	13.8	10.2	8.3	51.1	31 636	35 075	10.9	19.7	4 415	3 868	5 605	17 076	19.4	2.43	10.5	25.8
Smyth	14.2	10.0	8.1	51.2	32 370	33 081	2.2	-2.6	3 198	3 874	-468	13 319	-1.3	2.36	12.3	27.7
Southampton	14.4	9.0	6.3	47.9	17 022	17 482	2.7	6.2	1 606	1 750	1 225	6 719	7.0	2.53	14.5	23.9
Spotsylvania	11.1	5.9	4.0	51.0	57 397	90 395	57.5	35.4	15 040	5 770	21 602	41 942	34.0	2.91	11.7	17.5
Stafford	9.7	4.6	2.8	49.7	62 255	92 446	48.5	39.5	14 842	4 625	21 683	41 769	38.4	3.00	11.3	15.7
Surry	15.0	9.4	6.5	50.6	6 145	6 829	11.1	3.4	643	589	247	2 826	7.9	2.50	13.9	25.7
Sussex	13.1	8.0	6.4	41.4	10 248	12 504	22.0	-3.3	1 107	1 277	-154	3 994	-3.2	2.38	18.3	29.5
Tazewell	15.2	9.5	7.7	50.6	45 960	44 598	-3.0	1.1	4 607	5 231	1 515	18 449	0.9	2.35	10.7	27.3
Warren	12.4	7.4	5.3	50.3	26 142	31 584	20.8	19.0	4 437	2 903	3 908	14 085	16.5	2.62	11.2	24.1
Washington	14.8	10.3	7.4	50.7	45 887	51 103	11.4	7.4	4 887	5 253	2 629	22 843	8.5	2.33	9.1	27.6
Westmoreland	15.9	12.4	8.5	51.2	15 480	16 718	8.0	4.4	1 741	1 991	1 297	7 310	6.8	2.38	13.4	28.5
Wise	13.5	7.9	6.2	48.3	39 573	40 123	1.4	3.3	4 550	4 417	-294	15 968	-0.3	2.40	12.6	27.4
Wythe	14.4	10.1	7.7	51.1	25 471	27 599	8.4	5.9	2 993	3 040	1 449	12 472	8.3	2.32	10.7	28.7
York	12.0	7.3	4.9	51.1	42 434	56 297	32.7	16.3	5 520	3 193	2 470	24 006	20.0	2.70	10.6	18.4

Independent cities

Alexandria city	11.0	5.2	3.9	51.9	111 183	128 283	15.4	9.1	23 149	7 102	-1 721	68 082	10.0	2.03	8.6	43.4
Bedford city	12.2	8.4	13.1	53.8	6 176	6 299	2.0	-1.2	696	1 018	403	2 627	4.3	2.23	17.2	33.0
Bristol city	12.8	9.4	9.5	53.0	18 426	17 367	-5.7	2.7	1 809	2 298	881	7 879	2.6	2.21	14.5	34.6
Buena Vista city	12.7	9.0	7.0	53.5	6 406	6 349	-0.9	4.7	563	742	83	2 603	2.2	2.40	14.4	28.9
Charlottesville city	8.8	4.9	4.4	52.3	40 470	45 049	11.3	-3.5	4 839	2 847	-2 492	17 778	5.5	2.31	11.3	34.1
Chesapeake city	11.3	6.0	4.4	51.4	151 982	199 184	31.1	11.6	26 780	13 389	11 080	79 574	13.8	2.75	15.6	19.8
Colonial Heights city	12.3	9.1	10.5	53.7	16 064	16 897	5.2	3.0	2 041	1 998	992	7 275	3.5	2.37	14.5	30.4
Covington city	13.1	9.7	9.0	51.6	7 352	6 303	-14.3	-5.4	510	784	151	2 632	-7.2	2.23	13.7	36.1
Danville city	13.9	8.9	10.1	54.4	53 056	48 411	-8.8	-11.1	5 406	6 701	-2 460	18 831	-8.6	2.21	21.4	36.5
Emporia city	11.6	7.8	9.1	53.9	5 556	5 665	2.0	4.6	608	883	269	2 316	4.0	2.45	24.9	32.6
Fairfax city	12.4	7.2	6.5	50.7	19 945	21 498	7.8	5.0	2 956	1 769	2 020	8 347	3.9	2.64	9.6	24.0
Falls Church city	13.8	5.8	4.7	51.0	9 464	10 377	9.6	18.8	1 279	710	1 048	5 101	14.1	2.41	8.3	31.0
Franklin city	13.0	8.6	8.7	55.5	8 392	8 346	-0.5	2.8	1 345	1 221	380	3 530	4.3	2.39	24.0	30.1
Fredericksburg city	8.9	4.9	5.1	54.1	19 033	19 279	1.3	26.0	3 601	1 892	2 303	9 505	17.3	2.28	14.6	36.0
Galax city	12.7	9.2	11.0	52.9	6 745	6 837	1.4	3.0	853	928	152	2 922	-0.9	2.28	15.2	33.7
Hampton city	11.4	6.8	5.4	52.2	133 773	146 437	9.5	-6.1	18 363	10 370	-9 502	55 031	2.1	2.42	18.1	29.2
Harrisonburg city	6.2	3.7	4.5	53.4	30 707	40 468	31.8	20.9	4 818	2 388	2 447	15 988	21.7	2.59	10.1	27.3
Hopewell city	11.1	7.6	7.3	53.6	23 101	22 354	-3.2	1.1	3 331	2 469	97	9 129	0.8	2.45	23.1	30.1
Lexington city	8.8	6.6	8.7	44.3	6 959	6 867	-1.3	2.5	352	576	301	2 237	0.2	2.00	8.4	43.0
Lynchburg city	10.0	6.5	7.5	53.1	66 120	65 269	-1.3	15.8	8 624	7 202	7 543	28 476	11.8	2.30	16.3	33.3
Manassas city	9.6	4.1	2.8	49.9	27 757	35 135	26.6	7.6	6 305	1 738	-2 621	12 527	6.5	3.02	13.8	22.1

1. No spouse present.

Table B. States and Counties — Population, Vital Statistics, Medicare, and Crime

STATE County	Persons in group quarters, 2010	Daytime population, 2006–2010 Number	Daytime population, 2006–2010 Employment/residence ratio	Births, average 2006–2008 Total	Births, average 2006–2008 Rate[1]	Deaths, average 2006–2008 Number	Deaths, average 2006–2008 Rate[1]	Persons under 65 with no health insurance, 2009 Number	Persons under 65 with no health insurance, 2009 Percent	Medicare, 2011 Eligible for Medicare	Medicare, 2011 Enrolled in Medicare Advantage	Medicare, 2011 Enrolled in a Medicare prescription drug plan	Serious crimes known to police,[2] 2010 Total Number	Serious crimes known to police,[2] 2010 Total Rate[3]
	32	33	34	35	36	37	38	39	40	41	42	43	44	45
VIRGINIA—Cont'd														
Louisa	211	25 911	0.6	D	D	270	8.5	4 255	15.6	5 945	747	2 631	386	1 164
Lunenburg	1 203	11 307	0.6	D	D	156	12.0	1 954	19.4	2 707	320	1 433	166	1 285
Madison	193	10 821	0.6	D	D	131	9.6	1 949	17.7	2 494	265	1 236	119	894
Mathews	94	7 337	0.5	D	D	114	12.6	992	14.9	2 498	282	958	98	1 092
Mecklenburg	1 740	33 961	1.1	D	D	425	13.2	4 452	18.2	8 241	1 363	4 256	724	2 212
Middlesex	393	9 763	0.8	D	D	135	12.7	1 405	18.1	3 138	411	1 507	176	1 606
Montgomery	9 237	97 374	1.1	917	10.4	528	6.0	11 156	14.1	11 479	1 300	6 419	2 366	2 507
Nelson	102	12 288	0.6	D	D	158	10.4	2 113	17.6	3 658	321	1 818	232	1 545
New Kent	551	12 722	0.4	D	D	108	6.3	2 092	13.3	2 955	420	1 150	301	1 633
Northampton	326	12 794	1.0	D	D	181	13.4	2 056	19.9	3 224	333	1 862	263	2 123
Northumberland	0	10 869	0.7	D	D	176	13.6	1 520	17.3	4 216	362	1 726	132	1 071
Nottoway	1 836	15 534	1.0	D	D	185	11.8	2 497	20.0	3 368	456	1 864	270	1 703
Orange	601	27 006	0.6	D	D	301	9.3	4 192	15.6	7 268	572	2 972	366	1 093
Page	194	20 373	0.6	D	D	250	10.3	3 520	18.2	5 299	694	2 539	496	2 063
Patrick	203	16 969	0.8	D	D	238	12.5	2 696	18.7	4 695	954	2 558	317	1 714
Pittsylvania	839	51 440	0.6	658	10.8	634	10.4	8 661	17.0	14 062	2 947	7 400	836	1 316
Powhatan	2 395	23 733	0.6	D	D	169	6.1	3 353	14.0	4 311	761	1 824	273	973
Prince Edward	4 318	23 734	1.1	D	D	210	9.9	3 456	18.9	4 001	559	2 136	393	1 682
Prince George	4 772	37 834	1.2	D	D	191	5.3	4 621	14.0	4 631	484	1 652	518	1 450
Prince William	2 520	300 738	0.6	6 775	18.8	1 414	3.9	43 883	12.8	32 521	3 735	9 393	8 204	2 041
Pulaski	960	34 024	0.9	D	D	431	12.3	4 214	15.0	8 149	1 073	4 439	1 129	3 238
Rappahannock	35	6 711	0.8	D	D	66	9.2	981	17.3	1 633	114	742	68	922
Richmond	1 792	9 055	0.9	D	D	126	13.8	1 540	22.2	1 775	241	826	70	756
Roanoke	2 328	81 914	0.8	944	10.4	911	10.1	7 683	10.3	19 404	2 874	9 103	1 617	1 750
Rockbridge	175	20 817	0.9	D	D	231	10.8	2 857	16.8	5 082	945	2 509	323	1 448
Rockingham	1 471	68 329	0.8	880	12.0	626	8.5	10 713	17.1	14 053	2 256	7 255	695	911
Russell	434	26 025	0.7	D	D	338	11.7	4 040	17.0	7 309	1 617	3 493	479	1 658
Scott	652	19 966	0.6	D	D	310	13.6	3 077	17.4	6 197	2 704	2 185	521	2 248
Shenandoah	427	37 206	0.8	D	D	428	10.6	5 289	16.1	8 872	1 020	4 053	734	1 748
Smyth	774	32 204	1.0	364	11.3	425	13.2	4 219	16.6	8 228	1 285	4 594	712	2 211
Southampton	1 567	14 440	0.5	D	D	190	10.6	2 756	18.2	3 530	385	1 836	337	1 815
Spotsylvania	524	93 851	0.5	1 711	14.3	653	5.5	12 870	12.1	14 698	1 286	5 226	2 644	2 160
Stafford	3 593	99 242	0.6	1 720	14.2	544	4.5	11 390	10.1	11 569	739	3 508	2 292	1 777
Surry	0	6 112	0.7	D	D	65	9.1	869	14.9	1 369	281	503	80	1 133
Sussex	2 593	12 036	1.0	D	D	139	11.4	2 119	21.8	2 161	327	1 096	235	1 944
Tazewell	1 645	44 391	1.0	D	D	570	12.9	6 311	17.3	11 171	2 137	5 663	1 251	2 775
Warren	725	32 200	0.7	D	D	340	9.3	4 730	15.2	5 897	518	2 612	894	2 379
Washington	1 627	54 892	1.0	540	10.3	589	11.4	6 931	16.2	13 033	3 368	5 581	1 355	2 469
Westmoreland	70	14 020	0.6	D	D	217	12.5	2 600	18.9	4 156	327	1 727	167	957
Wise	3 131	42 670	1.1	493	11.8	480	11.5	5 848	16.8	9 732	2 810	3 993	876	2 113
Wythe	260	28 549	1.0	D	D	321	11.2	3 793	16.5	6 853	1 106	3 733	524	1 792
York	648	56 352	0.7	D	D	361	5.9	4 895	9.4	9 161	795	2 433	1 292	1 974
Independent cities														
Alexandria city	1 827	144 393	1.1	2 782	19.8	735	5.2	16 849	13.1	13 870	1 092	4 329	3 535	2 526
Bedford city	368	9 064	2.0	D	D	100	15.9	845	18.2	1 587	268	830	237	3 809
Bristol city	431	21 240	1.5	D	D	225	12.9	2 128	16.2	4 384	1 441	1 766	662	3 712
Buena Vista city	400	5 721	0.7	D	D	85	13.1	804	16.6	1 326	269	770	45	677
Charlottesville city	2 438	58 069	1.8	548	13.4	277	6.8	5 513	15.9	5 358	348	3 176	1 894	4 357
Chesapeake city	3 721	202 603	0.8	2 937	13.4	1 505	6.8	23 217	12.1	28 887	3 823	8 780	8 447	3 801
Colonial Heights city	171	19 314	1.2	D	D	222	12.5	1 971	14.1	3 856	344	1 456	838	4 813
Covington city	87	5 102	0.6	D	D	75	12.2	837	17.9	1 604	146	978	214	3 590
Danville city	1 483	51 901	1.5	594	13.2	698	15.5	5 358	16.0	10 745	1 660	6 044	2 362	5 486
Emporia city	246	6 961	1.5	D	D	86	15.2	794	18.3	1 202	94	294	364	6 141
Fairfax city	521	45 376	3.0	432	18.6	200	8.6	2 937	14.2	3 167	321	791	589	2 610
Falls Church city	42	15 406	1.6	D	D	83	7.5	713	7.1	1 523	149	431	323	2 619
Franklin city	129	10 057	1.5	D	D	136	15.3	1 190	17.0	1 740	185	878	561	6 537
Fredericksburg city	2 596	36 451	2.3	409	18.5	189	8.5	3 316	17.7	3 208	204	1 494	1 180	4 859
Galax city	377	8 393	1.5	D	D	100	14.8	1 054	19.8	1 954	91	1 281	325	4 615
Hampton city	4 454	139 689	1.0	2 082	14.3	1 122	7.7	16 559	13.6	21 159	3 042	6 403	5 753	4 186
Harrisonburg city	7 583	59 924	1.6	521	12.1	258	6.0	7 384	19.0	4 484	469	2 566	1 167	2 386
Hopewell city	237	21 479	0.9	394	17.2	255	11.1	3 304	17.4	4 086	429	1 720	1 249	5 529
Lexington city	2 567	9 467	2.2	D	D	54	7.8	939	17.7	1 537	245	814	50	710
Lynchburg city	10 198	96 824	1.7	1 038	14.7	759	10.8	9 038	15.3	13 427	2 069	7 392	2 931	3 879
Manassas city	46	40 240	1.2	684	19.1	178	5.0	5 707	17.8	3 280	332	1 304	1 142	3 019

1. Per 1,000 estimated resident population.   2. Data for serious crimes have not been adjusted for underreporting; this may affect comparability between geographic areas and over time.   3. Per 100,000 population estimated by the FBI.

Table B. States and Counties — Crime, Education, Money Income, and Poverty

STATE County	Serious crimes known to police,[1] 2010 (cont.) Rate[2] Violent	Property	Education — Enrollment[3] Total	Percent private	High school graduate or less	Bachelor's degree or more	Local government expenditures,[5] 2008–2009 Total current expenditures (mil dol)	Current expenditures per student (dollars)	Money income, 2006–2010 Per capita income[6] (dollars)	Households Median income Dollars	Percent change, 2000 to 2006–2010 (constant 2010 dollars)	Percent with income of $200,000 or more	Income and poverty, 2010 Median household income (dollars)	Percent below poverty level All persons	Children under 18 years	Children 5 to 17 years in families
	46	47	48	49	50	51	52	53	54	55	56	57	58	59	60	61
VIRGINIA—Cont'd																
Louisa	139	1 026	6 624	14.5	57.3	17.9	46.7	9 861	27 562	54 257	8.7	3.7	50 101	9.9	15.6	14.6
Lunenburg	209	1 076	2 698	12.5	67.2	10.0	17.1	10 138	17 744	37 424	5.9	0.1	35 260	20.5	28.4	25.5
Madison	75	819	3 054	8.1	54.5	20.7	17.4	9 283	26 081	56 608	12.2	1.4	49 389	11.7	17.4	14.9
Mathews	67	1 025	1 586	7.1	53.1	20.6	12.2	9 673	27 011	47 435	-13.3	3.0	53 418	10.2	17.1	14.4
Mecklenburg	208	2 004	6 586	10.6	61.5	13.4	43.8	9 053	20 162	36 431	-8.3	1.3	35 196	20.2	28.4	25.3
Middlesex	128	1 478	1 830	17.8	46.0	27.5	12.5	9 726	28 539	50 207	7.5	2.8	45 686	13.6	22.3	19.7
Montgomery	127	2 379	41 692	5.4	36.1	39.4	98.3	10 111	22 040	43 229	5.6	2.4	42 827	20.5	17.2	15.3
Nelson	73	1 471	2 867	14.2	54.7	22.9	22.5	11 630	26 996	48 118	3.3	2.3	47 368	13.1	20.9	18.8
New Kent	92	1 541	4 024	8.4	49.0	22.6	25.5	9 169	31 741	70 590	4.0	3.2	67 979	5.8	8.4	7.3
Northampton	129	1 994	2 220	17.6	58.0	18.8	20.5	11 150	23 233	35 760	-0.1	4.3	35 308	18.7	31.6	29.0
Northumberland	114	957	1 859	11.1	46.8	22.3	14.8	10 035	28 646	51 944	7.6	2.9	46 320	14.4	28.2	25.1
Nottoway	132	1 571	3 441	11.7	65.0	11.6	23.0	9 453	20 318	37 344	-4.5	1.5	36 975	20.8	27.9	26.4
Orange	81	1 013	7 251	13.0	50.7	21.5	46.9	8 809	26 447	54 916	1.1	2.5	53 837	10.7	14.8	13.1
Page	121	1 942	5 096	11.7	69.6	11.1	35.1	9 529	22 969	41 617	-1.5	1.2	37 970	15.7	22.7	20.1
Patrick	130	1 585	3 874	9.2	62.7	9.5	24.2	9 147	18 396	35 813	-1.5	0.7	33 678	18.7	28.1	19.4
Pittsylvania	79	1 238	14 580	16.4	59.9	12.8	83.5	9 027	20 652	39 224	-11.9	0.8	41 031	15.9	22.4	19.1
Powhatan	89	884	5 838	15.9	52.2	21.9	44.8	10 019	25 851	73 593	7.6	5.2	70 025	7.1	9.2	7.7
Prince Edward	154	1 528	8 508	18.4	62.2	18.5	27.4	10 488	18 192	36 191	-8.7	1.7	36 100	22.8	27.0	24.9
Prince George	76	1 374	8 599	9.8	51.0	17.2	59.1	9 420	25 769	64 171	1.6	2.3	59 346	9.7	12.7	11.6
Prince William	159	1 882	110 065	15.8	33.8	37.5	773.1	10 459	35 737	91 098	9.1	9.8	91 290	6.1	8.5	8.0
Pulaski	212	3 025	6 986	5.0	54.6	13.9	46.5	9 583	20 976	41 163	-4.0	0.3	41 184	15.8	23.4	20.1
Rappahannock	68	854	1 651	26.3	43.0	37.4	11.1	12 100	37 149	62 117	6.8	7.9	57 499	9.8	15.5	13.8
Richmond	97	659	1 658	7.4	66.6	9.8	12.9	10 641	19 965	42 182	0.9	1.1	40 596	18.5	23.8	21.1
Roanoke	141	1 610	21 925	17.5	36.3	32.6	140.6	9 410	31 046	59 446	-1.6	3.3	57 720	7.0	9.4	7.9
Rockbridge	54	1 394	4 906	16.3	55.6	21.8	28.9	9 147	23 753	44 417	-2.7	1.6	44 502	12.2	17.1	14.9
Rockingham	66	845	17 873	21.8	58.7	21.9	(7)170.2	(7)10 343	25 274	49 930	-3.2	2.7	49 158	10.8	15.3	13.2
Russell	87	1 571	6 053	6.3	64.0	10.7	41.1	9 499	17 909	32 780	-3.5	0.6	34 460	18.1	25.2	22.6
Scott	116	2 131	4 435	3.9	65.8	10.3	37.8	9 544	18 667	34 250	-1.1	0.5	33 797	18.9	25.0	22.2
Shenandoah	64	1 684	8 826	11.0	57.3	17.5	63.3	10 012	24 502	50 171	1.1	1.4	46 016	11.7	17.2	16.1
Smyth	199	2 012	6 996	7.5	60.7	14.6	47.5	9 414	19 906	34 864	-8.5	1.4	35 437	18.7	28.0	23.8
Southampton	151	1 664	4 066	12.0	58.7	12.6	29.6	10 371	21 201	45 426	5.5	0.8	43 232	16.4	20.0	17.2
Spotsylvania	215	1 945	35 184	12.0	41.0	29.9	232.2	9 630	31 012	76 574	5.1	4.6	72 463	7.9	10.5	8.9
Stafford	161	1 617	38 138	13.6	35.1	35.4	253.2	9 429	34 691	93 065	10.0	8.1	93 185	5.2	6.8	5.6
Surry	298	836	1 679	28.2	60.6	13.6	15.2	14 577	23 835	55 030	15.7	0.9	46 112	12.3	19.7	17.6
Sussex	232	1 713	2 739	10.5	70.7	10.0	19.4	15 947	10 795	37 878	-3.3	0.4	37 019	22.5	24.0	22.1
Tazewell	120	2 655	9 619	11.9	57.6	14.3	57.9	8 447	19 016	35 215	1.9	0.8	35 485	18.5	23.5	21.3
Warren	112	2 267	8 913	21.5	53.4	21.4	47.4	8 729	29 098	60 522	12.7	3.5	55 758	10.3	14.4	12.7
Washington	106	2 364	11 579	24.1	52.2	20.5	70.0	9 318	23 488	40 422	-2.5	1.9	39 690	14.1	19.3	17.0
Westmoreland	80	877	3 566	10.2	58.7	15.9	24.5	10 227	27 501	52 990	16.9	2.4	45 291	14.7	26.2	23.8
Wise	142	1 971	8 764	5.7	64.1	11.3	66.1	9 742	17 944	33 608	1.5	0.9	36 789	22.2	27.5	25.0
Wythe	99	1 693	6 181	7.4	56.2	14.0	40.0	9 045	20 589	38 948	-4.6	1.2	37 624	15.8	22.9	20.7
York	130	1 844	19 359	10.5	25.5	41.5	118.9	9 222	35 823	81 055	10.4	5.8	77 070	5.3	6.8	5.6
Independent cities																
Alexandria city	194	2 331	25 790	30.3	21.8	60.4	203.0	18 092	54 345	80 847	13.9	11.2	78 023	9.3	14.2	15.9
Bedford city	289	3 520	1 357	12.1	47.8	20.8	(8)	(8)	20 092	32 262	-11.5	0.3	35 664	17.4	27.9	26.6
Bristol city	342	3 370	4 196	16.6	50.1	19.7	23.6	9 768	19 700	32 079	-7.5	0.6	33 149	21.5	33.9	30.6
Buena Vista city	15	662	1 830	18.0	61.6	16.5	11.4	9 900	19 030	39 955	-2.6	0.0	37 629	15.5	22.6	20.8
Charlottesville city	449	3 908	17 401	6.7	34.7	46.7	(9)	(9)	24 578	42 240	7.6	2.9	42 686	20.2	22.7	22.4
Chesapeake city	395	3 407	61 948	17.2	38.1	27.9	433.0	10 851	29 306	67 855	5.6	3.7	67 674	8.0	11.4	10.0
Colonial Heights city	258	4 555	3 950	8.4	50.0	20.0	32.7	11 271	26 115	50 571	-7.6	0.9	48 883	9.4	15.1	13.5
Covington city	185	3 405	1 247	1.4	58.3	10.4	10.4	11 365	20 781	35 277	-8.1	1.3	33 962	15.9	24.4	21.3
Danville city	399	5 087	10 773	17.5	54.0	16.2	70.0	10 676	18 840	29 936	-12.1	1.0	31 153	26.6	41.7	36.8
Emporia city	540	5 601	1 174	12.4	65.3	15.4	(10)	(10)	19 245	32 788	-14.6	1.9	33 255	22.8	31.5	30.0
Fairfax city	133	2 477	5 532	19.9	22.1	53.2	(11)	(11)	44 008	97 900	14.3	12.6	83 413	7.1	8.1	7.2
Falls Church city	105	2 514	3 308	20.9	15.7	71.0	35.6	18 089	55 389	114 409	20.6	19.6	105 124	3.1	2.7	2.2
Franklin city	408	6 129	2 111	8.9	53.3	19.0	15.9	12 215	19 453	33 174	-17.3	0.9	36 454	21.6	33.2	32.0
Fredericksburg city	404	4 455	7 398	11.5	43.6	31.9	36.2	12 734	27 870	43 558	-0.5	4.5	43 460	19.8	23.4	23.5
Galax city	355	4 260	1 335	6.7	56.6	12.7	12.5	9 186	19 609	22 333	-37.5	1.1	32 061	22.3	35.9	33.0
Hampton city	287	3 899	38 876	20.2	42.1	21.8	231.3	10 607	24 051	49 815	-0.5	1.3	50 923	13.1	20.3	18.6
Harrisonburg city	186	2 200	23 337	9.8	46.8	33.3	(7)	(7)	16 750	37 235	-1.8	2.0	37 179	30.1	21.9	20.7
Hopewell city	907	4 621	5 107	4.7	62.7	10.9	42.2	10 070	19 148	37 789	-10.1	0.8	37 226	17.3	27.5	25.4
Lexington city	43	667	3 684	48.2	39.7	44.4	4.6	9 330	17 022	31 571	-14.0	1.0	41 298	21.4	15.0	11.9
Lynchburg city	427	3 451	25 514	53.1	45.6	28.3	93.8	10 861	21 586	37 058	-9.2	3.0	36 397	22.8	29.6	26.1
Manassas city	362	2 657	9 672	16.0	44.7	28.3	83.4	12 707	28 941	75 173	-1.7	5.2	64 274	11.7	17.9	16.2

1. Data for serious crimes have not been adjusted for underreporting; this may affect comparability between geographic areas and over time.   2. Per 100,000 population estimated by the FBI.   3. All persons 3 years old and over enrolled in nursery school through college.   4. Persons 25 years old and over.   5. Elementary and secondary education expenditures.   6. Based on population estimated by the American Community Survey, 2006–2010.   7. Harrisonburg city is included with Rockingham county.   8. Bedford city is included with Bedford county.   9. Charlottesville city is included with Albemarle county.   10. Emporia city is included with Greensville county.   11. Fairfax city is included with Fairfax county.

Table B. States and Counties — **Personal Income**

STATE County	Total (mil dol)	Percent change, 2008–2009	Per capita[1] Dollars	Per capita[1] Rank	Wages and salaries[2] (mil dol)	Proprietors' income (mil dol)	Dividends, interest, and rent (mil dol)	Transfer payments (mil dol) Total	Government payments to individuals Total	Social Security	Medical payments	Income maintenance	Unemployment insurance
	62	63	64	65	66	67	68	69	70	71	72	73	74
VIRGINIA—Cont'd													
Louisa	1 200	0.0	36 283	850	451	118	153	213	207	80	88	18	9
Lunenburg	328	1.6	25 630	2 787	117	10	56	95	92	33	35	12	3
Madison	440	-1.7	32 114	1 505	127	27	88	80	78	33	31	6	3
Mathews	441	-2.2	49 032	120	63	29	109	77	75	34	30	4	1
Mecklenburg	962	0.8	30 093	1 956	498	52	170	287	281	111	115	32	9
Middlesex	424	-1.9	39 524	491	135	18	124	100	98	45	38	6	2
Montgomery	(3)2 928	(3)0.0	(3)27 308	(3)2 514	(3)2 369	(3)116	(3)537	(3)521	(3)501	(3)189	(3)189	(3)54	(3)18
Nelson	574	1.0	37 093	742	137	22	113	129	126	50	55	10	4
New Kent	629	-0.7	34 747	1 054	179	19	93	101	98	45	34	5	6
Northampton	453	-0.4	33 548	1 241	223	65	89	113	111	41	47	15	2
Northumberland	481	-2.6	36 982	753	109	23	169	120	118	57	45	8	3
Nottoway	464	-1.3	29 153	2 154	244	15	74	143	140	41	68	16	3
Orange	1 113	-0.2	33 124	1 315	400	32	226	242	236	100	96	15	8
Page	665	-1.1	27 645	2 460	223	41	111	177	173	68	67	17	10
Patrick	466	-0.3	25 027	2 862	180	23	78	159	156	63	63	16	5
Pittsylvania	(4)3 184	(4)0.1	(4)30 092	(4)1 957	(4)1 640	(4)214	(4)524	(4)905	(4)886	(4)342	(4)338	(4)115	(4)36
Powhatan	1 135	-0.7	40 592	412	316	42	165	135	130	63	45	7	6
Prince Edward	498	1.0	22 281	3 059	363	11	88	153	149	52	60	20	4
Prince George	(5)2 019	(5)1.7	(5)33 523	(5)1 248	(5)1 972	(5)73	(5)253	(5)352	(5)352	(5)125	(5)130	(5)45	(5)15
Prince William	(6)18 746	(6)2.7	(6)43 827	(6)244	(6)8 305	(6)736	(6)2 121	(6)1 480	(6)1 404	(6)473	(6)525	(6)154	(6)75
Pulaski	1 110	0.2	31 695	1 599	528	43	149	303	296	114	117	26	19
Rappahannock	297	-2.1	42 214	312	81	17	87	52	50	22	22	3	2
Richmond	235	-1.0	26 257	2 678	128	11	51	64	63	23	27	6	2
Roanoke	(7)4 562	(7)-1.9	(7)39 166	(7)518	(7)3 314	(7)328	(7)868	(7)724	(7)703	(7)343	(7)211	(7)44	(7)22
Rockbridge	(8)1 123	(8)-1.6	(8)32 617	(8)1 399	(8)583	(8)63	(8)270	(8)255	(8)248	(8)109	(8)95	(8)20	(8)8
Rockingham	(9)3 689	(9)-0.9	(9)30 673	(9)1 828	(9)2 772	(9)274	(9)675	(9)599	(9)577	(9)254	(9)202	(9)60	(9)20
Russell	776	1.9	26 543	2 634	337	16	93	288	282	101	123	30	9
Scott	609	0.0	26 953	2 572	207	12	83	216	211	82	93	22	2
Shenandoah	1 310	-1.8	31 917	1 547	547	84	271	275	267	119	98	21	12
Smyth	886	0.3	27 917	2 418	515	36	123	286	280	109	112	32	12
Southampton	(10)856	(10)-0.2	(10)31 367	(10)1 678	(10)365	(10)26	(10)161	(10)217	(10)212	(10)72	(10)93	(10)27	(10)7
Spotsylvania	(11)5 660	(11)0.4	(11)39 262	(11)513	(11)2 676	(11)372	(11)812	(11)678	(11)651	(11)233	(11)256	(11)64	(11)33
Stafford	4 970	1.2	40 027	448	2 549	111	586	459	438	153	159	38	17
Surry	232	2.8	32 693	1 385	221	7	27	47	46	18	19	5	2
Sussex	346	-0.1	28 592	2 281	160	6	45	97	95	31	45	11	3
Tazewell	1 415	0.5	31 516	1 638	738	58	224	438	430	158	173	41	9
Warren	1 392	0.6	37 917	650	529	47	185	208	202	82	73	20	13
Washington	(12)2 298	(12)0.7	(12)32 506	(12)1 424	(12)1 502	(12)126	(12)415	(12)597	(12)584	(12)241	(12)225	(12)59	(12)15
Westmoreland	592	0.3	33 494	1 254	139	26	106	140	137	52	59	13	4
Wise	(13)1 392	(13)-4.5	(13)30 613	(13)1 839	(13)945	(13)102	(13)163	(13)454	(13)445	(13)153	(13)190	(13)53	(13)16
Wythe	826	0.4	28 615	2 275	464	43	120	248	242	92	97	21	16
York	(14)3 456	(14)-0.7	(14)47 380	(14)145	(14)1 225	(14)146	(14)597	(14)395	(14)382	(14)152	(14)154	(14)19	(14)9
Independent cities													
Alexandria city	10 627	1.6	70 846	9	9 257	547	1 626	602	575	168	265	51	26
Bedford city	(15)	(15)	(15)	(15)	(15)	(15)	(15)	(15)	(15)	(15)	(15)	(15)	(15)
Bristol city	(12)	(12)	(12)	(12)	(12)	(12)	(12)	(12)	(12)	(12)	(12)	(12)	(12)
Buena Vista city	(8)	(8)	(8)	(8)	(8)	(8)	(8)	(8)	(8)	(8)	(8)	(8)	(8)
Charlottesville city	(16)	(16)	(16)	(16)	(16)	(16)	(16)	(16)	(16)	(16)	(16)	(16)	(16)
Chesapeake city	8 891	0.3	39 966	451	4 821	345	1 021	1 155	1 115	384	429	117	44
Colonial Heights city	(17)	(17)	(17)	(17)	(17)	(17)	(17)	(17)	(17)	(17)	(17)	(17)	(17)
Covington city	(18)	(18)	(18)	(18)	(18)	(18)	(18)	(18)	(18)	(18)	(18)	(18)	(18)
Danville city	(4)	(4)	(4)	(4)	(4)	(4)	(4)	(4)	(4)	(4)	(4)	(4)	(4)
Emporia city	(19)	(19)	(19)	(19)	(19)	(19)	(19)	(19)	(19)	(19)	(19)	(19)	(19)
Fairfax city	(20)	(20)	(20)	(20)	(20)	(20)	(20)	(20)	(20)	(20)	(20)	(20)	(20)
Falls Church city	(20)	(20)	(20)	(20)	(20)	(20)	(20)	(20)	(20)	(20)	(20)	(20)	(20)
Franklin city	(10)	(10)	(10)	(10)	(10)	(10)	(10)	(10)	(10)	(10)	(10)	(10)	(10)
Fredericksburg city	(11)	(11)	(11)	(11)	(11)	(11)	(11)	(11)	(11)	(11)	(11)	(11)	(11)
Galax city	(21)	(21)	(21)	(21)	(21)	(21)	(21)	(21)	(21)	(21)	(21)	(21)	(21)
Hampton city	5 229	0.3	36 252	854	4 291	157	596	921	896	279	346	109	33
Harrisonburg city	(9)	(9)	(9)	(9)	(9)	(9)	(9)	(9)	(9)	(9)	(9)	(9)	(9)
Hopewell city	(5)	(5)	(5)	(5)	(5)	(5)	(5)	(5)	(5)	(5)	(5)	(5)	(5)
Lexington city	(8)	(8)	(8)	(8)	(8)	(8)	(8)	(8)	(8)	(8)	(8)	(8)	(8)
Lynchburg city	(22)	(22)	(22)	(22)	(22)	(22)	(22)	(22)	(22)	(22)	(22)	(22)	(22)
Manassas city	(6)	(6)	(6)	(6)	(6)	(6)	(6)	(6)	(6)	(6)	(6)	(6)	(6)

1. Based on the resident population estimated as of July 1 of the year shown. 2. Includes supplements to wages and salaries. 3. Radford city is included with Montgomery county. 4. Danville city is included with Pittsylvania county. 5. Hopewell city is included with Prince George county. 6. Manassas and Manassas Park cities are included with Prince William county. 7. Salem city is included with Roanoke county. 8. Buena Vista and Lexington cities are included with Rockbridge county. 9. Harrisonburg city is included with Rockingham county. 10. Franklin city is included with Southhampton county. 11. Fredericksburg city is included with Spotsylvania county. 12. Bristol city included with Washington county. 13. Norton city is included with Wise county. 14. Poquoson city is included with York county. 15. Bedford city is included with Bedford county. 16. Charlottesville city is included with Albemarle county. 17. Petersburg and Colonial Heights cities are included with Dinwiddie county. 18. Covington city is included with Alleghany county. 19. Emporia city is included with Greensville county. 20. Fairfax city and Falls Church city are included with Fairfax county. 21. Galax city is included with Carroll county. 22. Lynchburg city is included with Campbell county.

Table B. States and Counties — Earnings, Social Security, and Housing

STATE County	Earnings, 2009									Social Security beneficiaries, December 2010			Housing units, 2010	
				Percent by selected industries										
			Goods-related[1]		Service-related and health							Supplemental Security Income recipients, December 2010		
	Total (mil dol)	Farm	Total	Manufacturing	Information and professional and technical services	Retail trade	Finance, insurance, and real estate	Health care and social services	Government	Number	Rate[2]		Total	Percent change, 2000–2010
	75	76	77	78	79	80	81	82	83	84	85	86	87	88
VIRGINIA—Cont'd														
Louisa	569	-0.7	D	15.7	D	3.7	5.1	3.5	14.2	6 715	203	614	16 319	37.7
Lunenburg	127	1.6	22.4	11.8	D	6.3	D	6.5	31.3	3 010	233	484	5 935	3.5
Madison	154	-2.2	18.1	8.0	5.2	17.7	2.5	D	19.7	2 750	207	200	5 932	13.2
Mathews	93	0.1	14.9	3.5	D	9.8	D	D	23.7	2 665	297	124	5 669	6.3
Mecklenburg	549	2.1	D	9.2	D	8.0	4.2	D	21.7	9 450	289	1 320	18 591	6.8
Middlesex	153	1.9	16.2	6.0	D	8.4	5.8	7.2	30.7	3 415	312	213	7 133	12.0
Montgomery	[3]2 484	[3]0.0	[3]D	[3]15.6	[3]8.4	[3]6.0	[3]3.4	[3]8.7	[3]38.6	12 615	134	1 187	38 569	18.6
Nelson	159	0.4	D	4.7	7.3	5.5	6.3	7.0	22.0	4 100	273	358	9 931	16.1
New Kent	198	0.3	24.3	4.2	D	7.1	2.2	D	26.4	3 395	184	158	7 295	40.2
Northampton	288	18.5	10.6	6.9	D	5.5	5.1	17.5	17.8	3 520	284	664	7 301	11.5
Northumberland	132	3.4	D	18.8	9.0	7.4	4.0	2.6	20.1	4 385	356	239	8 995	11.5
Nottoway	259	1.0	D	5.6	2.8	6.7	3.0	D	48.1	3 580	226	570	6 650	4.3
Orange	432	4.0	D	11.2	5.4	7.8	4.5	2.5	24.0	7 895	236	535	14 616	28.7
Page	263	5.8	21.9	14.6	4.3	8.0	3.3	D	28.9	5 985	249	567	11 600	9.9
Patrick	203	0.5	33.5	29.3	6.2	8.0	2.6	9.3	19.2	5 395	292	530	10 083	2.6
Pittsylvania	[4]1 855	[4]0.7	[4]D	[4]21.8	[4]3.8	[4]8.7	[4]4.0	[4]13.1	[4]19.0	16 590	261	2 047	31 307	11.8
Powhatan	357	0.6	D	2.5	D	4.0	9.7	3.8	34.8	4 710	168	245	10 043	33.7
Prince Edward	374	0.6	5.4	1.8	2.7	11.0	4.3	D	31.6	4 555	195	921	9 149	21.5
Prince George	[5]2 045	[5]0.0	[5]D	[5]11.2	[5]D	[5]2.0	[5]1.6	[5]4.3	[5]61.7	5 290	148	462	12 056	12.4
Prince William	[6]9 041	[6]0.0	[6]D	[6]3.3	[6]D	[6]D	[6]D	[6]8.0	[6]30.2	33 418	83	3 407	137 115	39.8
Pulaski	570	0.0	D	34.4	D	8.5	2.5	D	19.8	9 325	267	930	17 235	5.6
Rappahannock	98	-5.7	17.7	2.9	30.7	5.5	6.8	D	18.0	1 750	237	93	3 839	14.4
Richmond	139	3.1	11.2	4.5	8.7	5.4	3.9	D	36.4	1 960	212	218	3 850	9.8
Roanoke	[7]3 642	[7]0.0	[7]D	[7]19.7	[7]8.2	[7]6.0	[7]8.8	[7]D	[7]16.6	19 985	216	1 141	40 016	10.8
Rockbridge	[8]647	[8]-0.6	[8]D	[8]D	[8]D	[8]7.2	[8]4.7	[8]D	[8]23.3	6 570	250	459	11 152	16.8
Rockingham	[9]3 046	[9]2.0	[9]D	[9]20.1	[9]8.1	[9]8.2	[9]3.7	[9]11.1	[9]17.9	15 580	204	934	33 660	23.2
Russell	352	-1.4	23.2	7.0	8.5	8.7	4.2	D	22.5	8 620	298	1 553	13 484	2.2
Scott	219	-2.9	D	17.4	D	9.4	D	13.3	28.6	7 130	308	1 337	11 916	4.9
Shenandoah	631	0.1	D	24.3	6.3	7.6	4.4	8.9	17.3	9 716	231	617	20 876	24.9
Smyth	551	-0.6	D	31.6	D	6.4	3.4	12.0	25.5	9 555	297	1 342	16 427	2.1
Southampton	[10]392	[10]3.8	[10]D	[10]9.2	[10]3.9	[10]8.7	[10]5.1	[10]D	[10]31.9	4 010	216	481	7 473	5.9
Spotsylvania	[11]3 048	[11]-0.1	[11]D	[11]D	[11]9.2	[11]11.6	[11]18.9	[11]18.9	[11]18.1	15 960	130	1 163	45 185	35.6
Stafford	2 660	-0.1	D	1.2	11.4	4.6	18.6	4.1	39.2	12 225	95	821	43 978	40.0
Surry	229	1.4	4.6	2.1	2.2	0.5	D	0.1	10.5	1 545	219	164	3 444	4.6
Sussex	166	3.8	D	D	D	8.6	D	D	43.9	2 470	204	454	4 696	0.9
Tazewell	795	-0.4	26.8	11.7	5.0	10.7	4.7	D	20.1	12 915	287	1 978	20 826	2.1
Warren	576	-0.9	D	12.0	4.0	8.4	4.5	10.8	18.6	6 535	174	534	16 034	21.2
Washington	[12]1 628	[12]-0.3	[12]D	[12]16.7	[12]D	[12]8.9	[12]4.0	[12]D	[12]16.7	15 010	274	1 613	25 601	11.4
Westmoreland	165	4.9	23.4	16.4	D	7.5	5.2	D	25.2	4 410	253	422	10 618	14.3
Wise	[13]1 047	[13]-0.1	[13]D	[13]1.9	[13]6.0	[13]7.8	[13]1.8	[13]D	[13]22.5	11 625	280	2 517	17 940	0.8
Wythe	507	-0.4	27.9	22.7	D	11.6	4.3	11.1	22.1	7 830	268	803	14 079	10.5
York	[14]1 372	[14]0.1	[14]D	[14]D	[14]D	[14]8.1	[14]D	[14]5.1	[14]35.1	9 665	148	404	26 849	29.7
Independent cities														
Alexandria city	9 804	0.0	D	D	25.6	3.4	5.6	4.2	34.6	12 400	89	1 597	72 376	12.6
Bedford city	(15)	(15)	(15)	(15)	(15)	(15)	(15)	(15)	(15)	1 735	279	226	2 920	8.1
Bristol city	(12)	(12)	(12)	(12)	(12)	(12)	(12)	(12)	(12)	5 035	282	860	8 831	4.3
Buena Vista city	(8)	(8)	(8)	(8)	(8)	(8)	(8)	(8)	(8)	1 615	243	206	2 936	8.1
Charlottesville city	(16)	(16)	(16)	(16)	(16)	(16)	(16)	(16)	(16)	5 655	130	852	19 189	9.2
Chesapeake city	5 166	0.2	16.4	5.5	15.2	8.7	5.5	6.3	20.2	31 680	143	3 356	83 196	14.5
Colonial Heights city	(17)	(17)	(17)	(17)	(17)	(17)	(17)	(17)	(17)	4 175	240	256	7 831	6.7
Covington city	(18)	(18)	(18)	(18)	(18)	(18)	(18)	(18)	(18)	1 845	310	291	3 067	-4.0
Danville city	(4)	(4)	(4)	(4)	(4)	(4)	(4)	(4)	(4)	12 255	285	2 465	22 438	-2.9
Emporia city	(19)	(19)	(19)	(19)	(19)	(19)	(19)	(19)	(19)	1 290	218	401	2 565	6.3
Fairfax city	(20)	(20)	(20)	(20)	(20)	(20)	(20)	(20)	(20)	2 840	126	229	8 680	5.8
Falls Church city	(20)	(20)	(20)	(20)	(20)	(20)	(20)	(20)	(20)	1 300	105	94	5 489	16.2
Franklin city	(10)	(10)	(10)	(10)	(10)	(10)	(10)	(10)	(10)	2 050	239	527	3 901	3.6
Fredericksburg city	(11)	(11)	(11)	(11)	(11)	(11)	(11)	(11)	(11)	3 285	135	417	10 467	17.8
Galax city	(21)	(21)	(21)	(21)	(21)	(21)	(21)	(21)	(21)	2 170	308	366	3 252	1.1
Hampton city	4 448	0.0	7.0	4.1	13.5	4.6	2.3	7.2	52.4	23 395	170	3 119	59 566	3.9
Harrisonburg city	(9)	(9)	(9)	(9)	(9)	(9)	(9)	(9)	(9)	4 935	101	642	17 444	27.5
Hopewell city	(5)	(5)	(5)	(5)	(5)	(5)	(5)	(5)	(5)	4 765	211	926	10 121	3.8
Lexington city	(8)	(8)	(8)	(8)	(8)	(8)	(8)	(8)	(8)	1 600	227	126	2 546	7.2
Lynchburg city	(22)	(22)	(22)	(22)	(22)	(22)	(22)	(22)	(22)	14 980	198	2 335	31 992	15.7
Manassas city	(6)	(6)	(6)	(6)	(6)	(6)	(6)	(6)	(6)	3 435	91	376	13 123	8.3

1. Includes mining, construction, and manufacturing.   2. Per 1,000 resident population enumerated in the 2010 census.   3. Radford city is included with Montgomery county.   4. Danville city is included with Pittsylvania county.   5. Hopewell city is included with Prince George county.   6. Manassas and Manassas Park cities are included with Prince William county.   7. Salem city is included with Roanoke county.   8. Buena Vista and Lexington cities are included with Rockbridge county.   9. Harrisonburg city is included with Rockingham county.   10. Franklin city is included with Southampton county.   11. Fredericksburg city is included with Spotsylvania county.   12. Bristol city included with Washington county.   13. Norton city is included with Wise county.   14. Poquoson city is included with York county.   15. Bedford city is included with Bedford county.   16. Charlottesville city is included with Albemarle county.   17. Petersburg and Colonial Heights cities are included with Dinwiddie county.   18. Covington city is included with Alleghany county.   19. Emporia city is included with Greensville county.   20. Fairfax city and Falls Church city are included with Fairfax county.   21. Galax city is included with Carroll county.   22. Lynchburg city is included with Campbell county.

Table B. States and Counties — Housing, Labor Force, and Employment

STATE County	Housing units, 2006–2010								Civilian labor force, 2010				Civilian employment,[5] 2006–2010		
	Occupied units						Sub-stand-ard units[3] (percent)			Percent change, 2009–2010	Unemployment			Percent	
	Owner-occupied					Renter-occupied									Manage-ment, business, science and arts	Con-struction, produc-tion, and mainte-nance occu-pations
				Median owner cost as a percent of income												
	Total	Percent	Median value[1]	With a mort-gage	Without a mort-gage	Median rent[2]	Median rent as a per-cent of income		Total		Total	Rate[4]	Total		
	89	90	91	92	93	94	95	96	97	98	99	100	101	102	103

VIRGINIA—Cont'd

STATE County	89	90	91	92	93	94	95	96	97	98	99	100	101	102	103
Louisa	13 253	78.2	218 600	24.1	11.4	812	27.9	1.7	16 864	-0.3	1 351	8.0	15 651	30.1	30.8
Lunenburg	4 515	74.4	101 500	24.7	13.1	619	29.0	2.3	5 564	1.1	557	10.0	4 953	21.4	30.8
Madison	5 213	81.0	250 900	26.3	11.4	809	17.6	2.2	7 421	1.1	460	6.2	6 566	32.8	29.9
Mathews	3 773	83.0	207 900	23.3	10.0	849	31.4	2.0	4 390	-2.1	265	6.0	3 699	28.6	35.4
Mecklenburg	12 594	75.1	115 000	25.4	12.5	593	28.2	2.4	14 022	0.8	1 612	11.5	12 850	28.8	31.1
Middlesex	4 303	81.1	248 100	23.7	10.0	806	27.3	0.6	5 167	0.1	375	7.3	4 790	37.1	26.8
Montgomery	34 369	56.4	187 600	22.4	10.0	727	36.6	1.1	45 831	-0.9	3 397	7.4	44 283	44.8	16.9
Nelson	6 534	77.8	174 100	22.2	10.0	655	24.0	4.1	8 115	-0.8	504	6.2	7 201	32.7	28.0
New Kent	6 513	90.1	251 000	23.6	10.3	974	29.6	1.2	10 021	0.5	742	7.4	8 884	34.9	23.1
Northampton	5 088	71.1	199 600	24.5	14.7	642	28.5	3.2	6 495	3.2	525	8.1	5 613	31.3	26.6
Northumberland	5 478	84.3	251 600	26.0	10.3	772	29.5	1.1	6 250	3.3	543	8.7	5 518	31.4	27.5
Nottoway	5 607	64.3	126 100	24.8	13.1	700	32.0	2.7	6 629	0.9	553	8.3	6 721	21.8	31.0
Orange	12 669	78.4	249 100	26.9	10.0	879	28.4	1.3	16 044	2.0	1 235	7.7	14 269	32.7	27.2
Page	9 629	75.6	168 700	24.1	12.8	637	28.2	2.7	12 189	1.1	1 409	11.6	10 827	20.9	36.3
Patrick	7 344	81.3	102 000	21.7	10.0	440	25.2	1.1	9 400	2.9	1 055	11.2	7 481	23.8	36.5
Pittsylvania	26 563	79.4	102 000	23.7	12.3	552	28.3	2.3	31 684	-1.6	3 288	10.4	27 834	23.4	35.6
Powhatan	8 637	89.6	279 300	23.4	11.5	844	28.7	1.1	14 354	-1.4	947	6.6	10 331	42.4	18.1
Prince Edward	7 314	63.4	155 400	23.3	10.9	713	31.2	3.6	10 223	4.0	1 002	9.8	9 808	27.3	22.3
Prince George	10 474	75.4	202 700	22.1	10.9	992	27.8	1.3	15 268	2.0	1 118	7.3	13 371	31.0	30.0
Prince William	124 879	74.8	377 700	27.0	10.0	1 338	29.5	2.5	214 106	2.1	12 361	5.8	195 593	42.8	17.8
Pulaski	14 898	73.1	121 100	21.3	10.1	541	24.9	1.4	17 872	-4.0	1 668	9.3	15 520	26.6	32.5
Rappahannock	3 163	72.5	428 700	24.4	13.9	898	26.3	3.5	4 269	1.9	241	5.6	3 712	42.7	22.1
Richmond	3 007	79.9	148 700	22.2	11.9	675	26.3	2.1	4 183	2.7	336	8.0	3 783	21.4	29.8
Roanoke	37 833	77.7	189 500	22.1	10.2	763	24.6	0.8	49 057	-1.0	3 052	6.2	47 742	40.9	19.9
Rockbridge	9 372	76.4	180 900	25.9	11.6	634	32.9	1.9	11 528	0.4	804	7.0	10 747	30.5	31.2
Rockingham	29 701	74.7	192 900	23.5	10.0	730	26.6	2.7	42 703	0.3	2 596	6.1	37 240	29.0	33.3
Russell	11 529	77.0	85 200	22.1	10.0	448	32.1	2.0	12 249	0.1	1 237	10.1	11 450	24.6	35.5
Scott	9 610	77.0	85 000	19.3	10.0	445	27.2	2.0	9 947	-2.1	947	9.5	9 382	24.7	34.2
Shenandoah	17 316	69.5	216 200	24.7	10.0	700	28.0	2.4	20 340	1.4	1 654	8.1	20 013	27.2	32.1
Smyth	12 992	72.9	86 900	20.3	10.0	496	24.9	1.7	15 226	1.8	1 596	10.5	13 025	30.3	35.5
Southampton	6 571	76.2	149 200	24.4	11.8	693	31.2	3.2	8 231	2.2	794	9.6	8 481	22.4	37.8
Spotsylvania	41 009	79.9	305 000	25.0	10.0	1 178	31.3	1.6	66 618	-1.1	3 894	5.8	57 987	39.6	18.5
Stafford	40 183	78.4	355 300	24.9	10.0	1 280	28.7	1.6	67 313	0.2	3 914	5.8	57 814	44.4	16.9
Surry	2 481	74.2	171 800	22.4	10.1	607	22.3	5.0	3 767	-2.0	302	8.0	3 280	20.5	38.4
Sussex	3 796	67.0	119 300	23.8	13.3	635	30.7	3.2	4 504	-1.5	473	10.5	5 269	19.1	33.6
Tazewell	18 015	73.4	80 200	21.0	10.0	511	28.6	1.3	21 403	0.2	1 455	6.8	17 278	28.4	29.0
Warren	14 160	74.8	254 400	24.6	10.6	849	29.9	2.1	20 122	-2.3	1 431	7.1	18 981	29.6	28.3
Washington	22 711	74.2	126 100	22.3	10.0	591	26.1	2.1	27 326	-0.7	2 402	8.8	24 152	31.1	27.2
Westmoreland	7 135	76.1	202 300	24.1	10.8	888	23.5	4.0	9 256	2.0	732	7.9	7 992	26.4	30.9
Wise	15 750	69.7	77 100	20.7	10.0	504	25.1	2.7	20 298	7.6	1 450	7.1	15 265	25.4	30.8
Wythe	11 665	77.0	104 500	20.7	10.0	507	25.6	3.0	16 304	0.2	1 558	9.6	13 164	26.0	33.0
York	24 002	78.6	324 800	22.7	10.0	1 165	27.0	1.1	30 779	-1.5	1 758	5.7	29 058	50.6	14.2

Independent cities

STATE County	89	90	91	92	93	94	95	96	97	98	99	100	101	102	103
Alexandria city	63 738	45.7	486 800	24.2	12.3	1 330	26.8	2.2	96 701	2.1	4 674	4.8	83 338	58.5	9.2
Bedford city	2 782	66.6	139 100	23.6	13.6	656	31.3	0.9	2 671	-1.0	253	9.5	2 995	28.7	25.8
Bristol city	7 948	61.8	94 100	23.1	12.2	529	28.3	2.0	8 156	0.0	775	9.5	7 314	27.8	25.1
Buena Vista city	2 693	64.8	126 000	19.7	12.0	625	28.0	2.6	3 415	-2.2	316	9.3	3 208	27.8	34.7
Charlottesville city	17 290	41.3	279 700	24.7	13.6	895	33.0	1.8	22 070	0.6	1 523	6.9	20 911	46.1	12.1
Chesapeake city	78 778	74.9	272 800	27.1	12.6	1 005	31.4	1.7	116 385	-0.4	8 015	6.9	106 845	39.3	20.8
Colonial Heights city	7 075	65.8	187 700	24.2	11.8	834	26.9	1.3	9 281	-1.0	756	8.1	8 083	30.7	22.0
Covington city	2 641	68.7	65 900	22.7	12.0	599	28.8	0.2	2 785	3.4	298	10.7	2 577	18.6	29.9
Danville city	19 448	54.6	89 100	24.9	13.2	573	33.9	1.8	20 044	-2.5	2 678	13.4	17 821	26.9	29.5
Emporia city	2 406	48.4	97 700	26.6	17.6	584	28.7	3.7	2 629	4.0	353	13.4	2 297	36.8	20.4
Fairfax city	8 524	72.1	488 900	24.7	10.0	1 484	29.8	2.1	14 894	1.4	845	5.7	11 580	54.8	11.1
Falls Church city	4 706	63.9	641 900	23.7	12.7	1 453	29.0	2.6	7 386	3.9	468	6.3	6 173	64.0	5.5
Franklin city	3 524	46.3	184 900	25.2	13.8	710	36.0	3.1	4 016	1.6	476	11.9	3 187	29.7	26.2
Fredericksburg city	9 206	39.0	335 800	23.9	11.1	1 030	36.4	1.6	13 310	-0.3	1 262	9.5	10 598	38.4	19.3
Galax city	3 326	63.3	90 600	21.8	15.0	470	34.3	0.8	3 278	3.1	335	10.2	2 852	31.6	31.1
Hampton city	53 283	59.3	191 500	25.9	13.7	923	31.3	5.2	68 240	-2.2	5 765	8.4	63 198	31.5	25.0
Harrisonburg city	14 965	38.6	213 400	22.0	10.0	778	32.9	4.8	23 756	2.6	1 795	7.6	19 895	29.5	27.5
Hopewell city	8 914	51.7	130 700	25.6	11.6	756	28.2	2.6	10 695	-1.4	1 146	10.7	8 755	21.6	30.5
Lexington city	2 108	51.2	244 300	22.0	10.9	670	38.9	4.5	2 489	1.6	289	11.6	2 039	41.5	9.9
Lynchburg city	27 875	56.3	139 100	23.5	12.1	668	29.5	1.6	35 233	0.6	3 003	8.5	32 664	32.5	18.8
Manassas city	11 732	68.2	325 800	24.4	13.5	1 232	37.2	6.3	21 002	1.7	1 579	7.5	19 015	32.8	23.5

1. Specified owner-occupied units.   2. Specified renter-occupied units. A value of 10.0 represents 10 percent or less.   3. Overcrowded or lacking complete plumbing facilities.   4. Percent of civilian labor force.   5. Persons 16 years old and over.

	Private nonfarm establishments, employment and payroll, 2009								Agriculture, 2007			
	Employment						Annual payroll		Farms			
										Percent with:		
STATE County	Number of establishments	Total	Health care and social assistance	Manufacturing	Retail trade	Finance and insurance	Professional, scientific, and technical services	Total (mil dol)	Average per employee (dollars)	Number	Fewer than 50 acres	500 acres or more	Farm operators whose principal occupation is farming (percent)
	104	105	106	107	108	109	110	111	112	113	114	115	116
VIRGINIA—Cont'd												
Louisa	555	6 697	309	1 366	725	D	149	271	40 402	534	39.0	5.8	40.3
Lunenburg	191	1 765	214	D	265	83	D	48	26 981	371	21.0	10.5	39.4
Madison	285	2 747	322	205	1 082	D	76	71	25 976	564	43.6	8.0	44.9
Mathews	193	1 044	119	D	265	26	D	22	21 252	50	72.0	4.0	34.0
Mecklenburg	831	10 700	1 779	1 602	1 868	289	318	271	25 287	580	20.2	13.4	48.3
Middlesex	383	2 340	493	159	437	D	133	58	24 774	76	44.7	9.2	43.4
Montgomery	1 999	26 297	3 980	3 558	4 950	752	1 956	778	29 585	628	42.2	5.7	43.6
Nelson	392	3 156	228	132	304	D	144	75	23 612	462	35.3	5.0	32.7
New Kent	353	2 615	467	123	475	28	60	77	29 299	121	52.1	8.3	40.5
Northampton	338	3 211	D	D	625	D	46	92	28 759	151	41.7	22.5	62.3
Northumberland	383	1 789	39	370	363	76	73	55	30 662	129	42.6	21.7	54.3
Nottoway	324	3 655	D	351	745	127	184	95	25 987	394	29.7	5.1	43.9
Orange	662	5 513	316	871	991	142	274	176	31 853	518	35.9	9.5	38.8
Page	444	4 610	538	685	761	D	169	112	24 370	530	49.2	4.2	49.2
Patrick	318	4 156	541	1 787	576	83	D	95	22 823	613	35.9	3.6	66.5
Pittsylvania	859	7 887	888	2 019	981	139	144	209	26 454	1 356	22.4	8.8	44.8
Powhatan	676	4 143	222	162	555	155	172	125	30 291	228	49.6	5.7	38.6
Prince Edward	545	6 771	1 778	160	1 584	204	132	175	25 857	446	23.1	6.7	39.9
Prince George	438	5 952	180	651	701	86	229	201	33 809	186	37.6	10.8	39.8
Prince William	6 876	81 776	7 364	1 985	19 284	2 054	10 301	3 022	36 954	345	60.9	2.0	34.5
Pulaski	657	10 785	1 095	D	1 676	163	127	345	31 972	415	39.3	7.2	34.9
Rappahannock	192	856	37	28	119	25	98	26	30 329	416	46.6	5.8	44.7
Richmond	208	2 031	D	113	303	62	42	51	25 071	124	28.2	18.5	53.2
Roanoke	2 126	34 318	4 949	4 633	3 649	6 377	1 724	1 146	33 385	345	55.1	2.6	40.9
Rockbridge	454	4 746	202	1 305	1 230	D	94	125	26 285	805	36.8	7.1	41.1
Rockingham	1 418	23 844	1 633	7 181	1 908	D	369	765	32 065	1 970	43.3	3.3	51.3
Russell	503	6 361	897	893	1 114	274	192	195	30 692	1 019	38.2	4.7	35.9
Scott	308	3 688	834	D	752	92	104	107	29 035	1 396	36.4	2.5	38.0
Shenandoah	930	11 565	1 252	3 437	1 799	313	338	319	27 555	1 043	46.9	5.1	43.6
Smyth	574	9 296	2 041	3 075	1 292	148	231	282	30 359	761	45.6	7.4	40.7
Southampton	238	3 153	148	D	280	D	D	125	39 573	342	23.1	25.4	50.0
Spotsylvania	2 306	26 010	2 541	1 692	6 886	749	1 517	805	30 933	359	50.4	6.7	42.6
Stafford	2 104	27 491	2 463	719	3 928	D	3 229	967	35 165	233	55.4	2.6	48.1
Surry	81	D	D	D	D	D	D	D	D	121	38.8	20.7	52.1
Sussex	187	2 271	457	209	320	D	D	62	27 101	151	24.5	23.8	55.6
Tazewell	1 142	14 494	2 559	1 619	3 403	527	404	426	29 365	576	30.6	14.1	42.2
Warren	810	9 892	1 266	1 121	1 647	249	517	289	29 181	387	48.3	4.9	33.6
Washington	1 213	17 365	2 618	3 880	3 034	537	780	575	33 114	1 791	49.7	3.5	37.9
Westmoreland	347	2 742	240	730	439	D	143	73	26 599	171	28.1	22.2	50.3
Wise	854	11 101	1 786	220	2 030	255	416	404	36 391	178	55.1	5.1	28.7
Wythe	704	9 340	1 285	2 175	2 055	247	148	244	26 117	946	30.9	6.1	41.2
York	1 462	18 384	1 639	D	4 162	436	1 122	522	28 394	45	84.4	0.0	60.0
Independent cities												
Alexandria city	4 512	79 423	7 071	1 585	7 184	2 975	17 785	4 384	55 204	NA	NA	NA	NA
Bedford city	319	3 961	953	941	443	124	128	104	26 294	NA	NA	NA	NA
Bristol city	649	11 113	517	1 703	1 846	341	257	295	26 505	NA	NA	NA	NA
Buena Vista city	119	1 862	293	751	110	31	D	56	30 267	NA	NA	NA	NA
Charlottesville city	2 015	31 301	10 181	542	3 455	861	2 293	1 263	40 338	NA	NA	NA	NA
Chesapeake city	5 364	84 983	8 711	3 962	16 078	3 857	7 310	2 945	34 651	291	70.4	7.9	54.3
Colonial Heights city	691	9 544	1 503	D	3 677	263	507	216	22 633	NA	NA	NA	NA
Covington city	248	3 536	213	D	472	103	88	144	40 798	NA	NA	NA	NA
Danville city	1 414	22 888	4 932	4 030	4 471	1 060	463	672	29 350	NA	NA	NA	NA
Emporia city	242	3 954	1 071	D	631	79	88	107	27 013	NA	NA	NA	NA
Fairfax city	2 320	28 629	3 204	212	5 841	1 417	6 401	1 342	46 892	NA	NA	NA	NA
Falls Church city	814	9 091	1 625	D	915	170	1 801	399	43 864	NA	NA	NA	NA
Franklin city	301	3 692	1 073	D	1 118	211	92	93	25 075	NA	NA	NA	NA
Fredericksburg city	1 394	20 710	6 357	322	3 734	654	1 053	784	37 845	NA	NA	NA	NA
Galax city	325	5 676	1 553	1 109	1 275	118	150	145	25 600	NA	NA	NA	NA
Hampton city	2 405	41 202	6 321	2 751	6 519	1 062	5 212	1 458	35 376	NA	NA	NA	NA
Harrisonburg city	1 574	27 359	5 247	2 214	6 399	900	907	810	29 622	NA	NA	NA	NA
Hopewell city	460	6 922	1 285	1 370	673	131	598	280	40 517	NA	NA	NA	NA
Lexington city	308	4 108	700	D	466	96	112	129	31 371	NA	NA	NA	NA
Lynchburg city	2 255	54 809	9 577	8 584	7 644	3 238	3 653	2 006	36 604	NA	NA	NA	NA
Manassas city	1 410	23 077	3 819	4 052	2 589	598	3 961	1 288	55 831	NA	NA	NA	NA

Table B. States and Counties — **Agriculture**

STATE County	Land in farms — Acreage (1,000)	Percent change, 2002–2007	Acres — Average size of farm	Acres — Total irrigated (1,000)	Acres — Total cropland (1,000)	Value of land and buildings (dollars) — Average per farm	Value of land and buildings (dollars) — Average per acre	Value of machinery and equipment, average per farm (dollars)	Value of products sold — Total (mil dol)	Value of products sold — Average per farm (dollars)	Percent from: Crops	Percent from: Livestock and poultry products	Percent of farms with sales of: $10,000 or more	Percent of farms with sales of: $100,000 or more	Government payments — Total ($1,000)	Government payments — Percent of farms
	117	118	119	120	121	122	123	124	125	126	127	128	129	130	131	132
VIRGINIA—Cont'd																
Louisa	79	-9.2	147	0.3	30.1	720 509	4 901	51 235	12.2	22 816	29.3	70.7	25.7	4.1	258	21.5
Lunenburg	83	-9.8	224	0.8	31.6	660 098	2 942	58 144	9.7	26 064	45.8	54.2	31.0	3.8	439	34.8
Madison	103	0.0	182	0.1	42.0	1 052 790	5 778	68 641	20.2	35 857	28.3	71.7	34.9	7.1	310	19.1
Mathews	4	NA	88	0.1	3.2	503 398	5 705	41 862	3.0	60 390	86.1	13.9	38.0	12.0	54	18.0
Mecklenburg	157	-6.5	271	3.2	66.1	858 108	3 164	74 587	32.3	55 628	65.8	34.2	34.3	9.8	587	24.8
Middlesex	18	-14.3	233	0.5	13.7	1 172 720	5 033	108 046	6.2	82 077	89.9	10.1	48.7	10.5	373	42.1
Montgomery	89	-11.0	142	0.4	30.2	587 681	4 128	57 023	19.0	30 219	27.6	72.4	34.9	4.8	327	12.9
Nelson	73	-14.1	158	0.8	22.9	741 745	4 685	49 064	12.4	26 937	69.2	30.8	34.4	3.2	76	10.2
New Kent	20	5.3	168	0.5	14.1	898 236	5 338	59 461	4.6	38 132	93.5	6.5	27.3	9.1	214	19.8
Northampton	64	23.1	422	9.3	58.2	1 662 991	3 938	222 557	90.1	596 486	65.9	34.1	74.8	51.0	1 181	43.7
Northumberland	44	10.0	344	0.1	36.9	1 305 871	3 796	161 323	11.9	92 047	95.4	4.6	47.3	19.4	971	47.3
Nottoway	65	-8.5	166	0.4	24.9	579 671	3 496	59 078	37.3	94 656	6.5	93.5	34.3	6.1	125	20.3
Orange	105	0.0	202	0.6	45.2	1 119 940	5 546	84 145	76.1	146 877	66.6	33.4	33.4	10.0	341	19.3
Page	64	0.0	121	0.3	27.7	747 898	6 156	59 891	148.3	279 895	1.4	98.6	46.8	25.7	239	15.1
Patrick	80	-12.1	131	0.4	25.4	453 225	3 472	49 869	15.9	25 959	47.3	52.7	28.1	3.4	358	22.2
Pittsylvania	274	-5.2	202	4.2	103.6	638 676	3 157	73 087	62.6	46 198	37.4	62.6	32.1	7.9	1 494	34.1
Powhatan	30	-45.5	131	0.0	11.6	839 981	6 428	57 175	8.7	38 305	30.8	69.2	22.8	4.4	77	11.8
Prince Edward	82	3.8	185	0.1	25.0	568 244	3 078	55 372	15.5	34 750	12.7	87.3	27.6	5.2	239	32.7
Prince George	45	-18.2	241	D	22.3	906 129	3 762	80 713	5.5	29 504	91.1	8.9	27.4	6.5	625	39.2
Prince William	33	0.0	95	0.7	18.2	697 825	7 336	68 245	9.4	27 330	51.6	48.4	21.4	1.7	107	6.1
Pulaski	75	-7.4	182	0.2	21.1	663 148	3 647	66 549	13.3	32 142	4.6	95.4	32.3	4.8	185	12.5
Rappahannock	65	-16.7	156	0.1	20.9	972 016	6 213	46 567	7.5	18 122	32.7	67.3	30.3	3.8	110	11.1
Richmond	37	-17.8	301	0.2	24.2	1 108 946	3 681	104 507	10.6	85 176	90.9	9.1	43.5	13.7	704	56.5
Roanoke	29	-6.5	85	0.1	8.8	428 456	5 060	40 485	4.9	14 195	70.2	29.8	26.1	2.0	12	7.5
Rockbridge	138	-12.1	172	0.1	40.5	747 890	4 353	56 686	19.7	24 447	19.2	80.8	36.4	3.6	292	13.9
Rockingham	233	-6.4	118	4.8	114.5	727 644	6 150	84 927	534.1	271 138	3.8	96.2	54.7	31.6	1 356	16.1
Russell	152	-10.1	149	0.1	35.4	421 070	2 831	46 379	20.7	20 321	7.4	92.6	30.5	2.8	255	15.8
Scott	154	-2.5	110	0.2	41.9	325 065	2 949	46 321	13.1	9 413	36.5	63.5	21.7	1.1	243	18.6
Shenandoah	141	6.0	135	0.8	60.2	730 823	5 395	67 444	101.6	97 389	11.1	88.9	36.5	11.0	907	16.5
Smyth	127	1.6	167	0.2	30.3	553 385	3 308	52 255	26.1	34 307	8.1	91.9	35.6	6.6	279	20.8
Southampton	162	-4.1	473	3.5	91.3	1 224 543	2 591	121 365	35.7	104 335	77.1	22.9	42.1	21.9	6 288	74.6
Spotsylvania	52	-7.1	145	0.1	23.8	738 592	5 077	61 026	8.2	22 893	29.4	70.6	25.1	4.2	350	21.7
Stafford	20	-23.1	85	0.2	10.6	750 722	8 827	57 439	2.8	12 011	61.5	38.5	17.6	3.0	158	17.2
Surry	41	-14.6	340	1.0	29.3	1 122 105	3 303	104 126	13.9	114 603	59.4	40.6	47.1	16.5	1 375	43.8
Sussex	74	0.0	492	1.6	38.3	1 554 000	3 161	154 396	16.9	112 235	D	D	40.4	13.9	1 942	55.6
Tazewell	154	10.8	267	0.3	31.5	609 596	2 285	56 491	21.5	37 308	4.7	95.3	34.2	7.6	137	14.1
Warren	48	-2.0	123	0.1	13.4	781 852	6 352	51 288	5.6	14 365	21.7	78.3	24.5	2.1	11	3.9
Washington	199	1.0	111	0.4	64.2	487 860	4 394	45 394	44.0	24 546	11.1	88.9	27.1	3.7	960	23.8
Westmoreland	64	-5.9	374	1.7	44.7	1 346 860	3 600	196 964	25.4	148 442	95.6	4.4	53.2	25.7	888	55.6
Wise	22	15.8	125	0.1	3.8	347 538	2 790	39 902	1.2	6 680	17.7	82.3	15.2	1.1	50	3.9
Wythe	159	5.3	168	0.2	52.0	660 726	3 928	66 160	38.2	40 350	6.5	93.5	42.6	7.1	485	21.7
York	1	0.0	29	0.0	0.3	510 872	17 684	44 240	4.0	88 372	D	D	35.6	13.3	3	8.9
Independent cities																
Alexandria city	NA	NA	NA	NA	NA	NA	NA	NA	NA	NA	NA	NA	NA	NA	NA	NA
Bedford city	NA	NA	NA	NA	NA	NA	NA	NA	NA	NA	NA	NA	NA	NA	NA	NA
Bristol city	NA	NA	NA	NA	NA	NA	NA	NA	NA	NA	NA	NA	NA	NA	NA	NA
Buena Vista city	NA	NA	NA	NA	NA	NA	NA	NA	NA	NA	NA	NA	NA	NA	NA	NA
Charlottesville city	NA	NA	NA	NA	NA	NA	NA	NA	NA	NA	NA	NA	NA	NA	NA	NA
Chesapeake city	51	-16.4	176	0.2	43.2	945 593	5 382	104 082	35.6	122 430	86.9	13.1	28.2	12.7	750	23.7
Colonial Heights city	NA	NA	NA	NA	NA	NA	NA	NA	NA	NA	NA	NA	NA	NA	NA	NA
Covington city	NA	NA	NA	NA	NA	NA	NA	NA	NA	NA	NA	NA	NA	NA	NA	NA
Danville city	NA	NA	NA	NA	NA	NA	NA	NA	NA	NA	NA	NA	NA	NA	NA	NA
Emporia city	NA	NA	NA	NA	NA	NA	NA	NA	NA	NA	NA	NA	NA	NA	NA	NA
Fairfax city	NA	NA	NA	NA	NA	NA	NA	NA	NA	NA	NA	NA	NA	NA	NA	NA
Falls Church city	NA	NA	NA	NA	NA	NA	NA	NA	NA	NA	NA	NA	NA	NA	NA	NA
Franklin city	NA	NA	NA	NA	NA	NA	NA	NA	NA	NA	NA	NA	NA	NA	NA	NA
Fredericksburg city	NA	NA	NA	NA	NA	NA	NA	NA	NA	NA	NA	NA	NA	NA	NA	NA
Galax city	NA	NA	NA	NA	NA	NA	NA	NA	NA	NA	NA	NA	NA	NA	NA	NA
Hampton city	NA	NA	NA	NA	NA	NA	NA	NA	NA	NA	NA	NA	NA	NA	NA	NA
Harrisonburg city	NA	NA	NA	NA	NA	NA	NA	NA	NA	NA	NA	NA	NA	NA	NA	NA
Hopewell city	NA	NA	NA	NA	NA	NA	NA	NA	NA	NA	NA	NA	NA	NA	NA	NA
Lexington city	NA	NA	NA	NA	NA	NA	NA	NA	NA	NA	NA	NA	NA	NA	NA	NA
Lynchburg city	NA	NA	NA	NA	NA	NA	NA	NA	NA	NA	NA	NA	NA	NA	NA	NA
Manassas city	NA	NA	NA	NA	NA	NA	NA	NA	NA	NA	NA	NA	NA	NA	NA	NA

Table B. States and Counties — Water Use, Wholesale Trade, Retail Trade, and Real Estate

STATE County	Water use, 2005		Wholesale trade,[1] 2007				Retail trade,[2] 2007				Real estate and rental and leasing,[2] 2007			
	Total water withdrawn (mil gal/day)	Gallons withdrawn per person	Number of establishments	Number of employees	Sales (mil dol)	Annual payroll (mil dol)	Number of establishments	Number of employees	Sales (mil dol)	Annual payroll (mil dol)	Number of establishments	Number of employees	Receipts (mil dol)	Annual payroll (mil dol)
	133	134	135	136	137	138	139	140	141	142	143	144	145	146
VIRGINIA—Cont'd														
Louisa	2 281.4	75 997	13	216	102.9	10.4	71	601	153.8	11.4	22	106	25.1	4.8
Lunenburg	2.0	151	5	144	45.7	3.1	43	300	54.7	5.4	4	6	1.2	0.1
Madison	3.2	237	9	32	8.7	0.9	52	504	112.9	11.3	6	21	1.9	0.2
Mathews	0.7	74	6	D	D	D	35	268	59.4	5.3	16	D	D	D
Mecklenburg	61.1	1 879	36	256	74.7	6.0	180	1 822	406.3	34.1	39	155	15.9	3.7
Middlesex	1.0	96	19	162	31.5	5.7	65	460	94.5	9.9	23	50	5.4	1.0
Montgomery	35.3	419	49	368	97.3	14.2	357	5 195	1 102.6	109.8	96	499	83.4	13.8
Nelson	4.8	317	5	7	6.7	0.2	58	345	75.6	6.1	17	51	6.6	1.6
New Kent	31.3	1 943	6	D	D	D	37	395	135.2	7.9	20	36	4.5	0.9
Northampton	4.7	350	16	149	59.3	3.4	80	681	135.1	11.7	16	41	5.9	0.8
Northumberland	3.7	289	13	76	29.7	2.1	52	421	90.2	7.9	18	44	6.0	0.6
Nottoway	1.7	107	12	125	80.2	3.2	65	754	137.3	14.5	8	25	2.1	0.5
Orange	3.3	109	12	219	212.2	12.1	112	1 031	280.3	23.4	29	59	6.7	1.7
Page	3.7	154	8	60	9.6	1.6	78	773	167.4	15.0	14	53	9.4	1.6
Patrick	2.6	137	6	46	19.0	1.7	49	559	148.6	11.5	11	18	2.2	0.2
Pittsylvania	60.1	971	33	648	247.6	15.6	157	1 088	269.3	19.5	20	84	5.7	1.2
Powhatan	2.9	109	28	158	46.6	6.1	75	604	159.3	15.5	26	76	11.2	2.3
Prince Edward	1.5	71	20	148	43.1	4.6	121	1 473	350.6	30.3	21	88	9.7	1.6
Prince George	58.1	1 583	20	718	502.6	24.1	61	559	197.8	13.5	19	68	5.3	1.2
Prince William	254.9	731	159	2 119	1 750.6	112.7	1 119	19 373	4 948.9	465.4	334	1 417	284.8	46.3
Pulaski	6.8	192	15	136	39.2	4.5	122	1 498	317.3	30.7	25	81	8.8	1.4
Rappahannock	1.0	138	2	D	D	D	30	142	21.9	3.0	10	10	1.2	0.2
Richmond	1.1	123	12	D	D	D	43	301	75.6	6.3	10	40	1.5	0.4
Roanoke	20.1	228	99	1 023	504.7	43.5	293	3 973	835.7	86.9	110	491	70.0	13.9
Rockbridge	37.1	1 746	11	92	32.7	3.0	82	1 253	338.4	25.3	15	33	2.8	0.5
Rockingham	44.2	620	61	990	539.9	41.6	225	1 985	455.5	42.0	47	939	104.3	28.7
Russell	22.0	761	21	82	36.5	2.0	94	966	255.6	20.6	10	39	3.5	0.7
Scott	2.5	108	8	D	D	D	90	837	197.2	14.4	9	D	D	D
Shenandoah	18.8	479	22	312	347.2	11.6	164	1 875	494.2	37.6	32	169	15.3	2.6
Smyth	25.8	791	14	130	52.7	4.2	127	1 337	300.3	28.4	18	88	7.9	2.4
Southampton	39.9	2 271	14	117	70.5	4.2	37	267	57.9	4.8	8	21	2.3	0.5
Spotsylvania	9.6	82	66	845	430.4	38.0	416	7 219	2 148.5	177.8	106	645	73.8	19.8
Stafford	20.2	172	60	1 370	1 249.9	60.4	267	3 787	930.3	84.8	95	376	69.5	11.0
Surry	2 062.9	294 151	1	D	D	D	14	56	12.6	1.0	3	D	D	D
Sussex	2.2	182	10	D	D	D	50	314	68.9	6.0	6	13	1.7	0.3
Tazewell	8.4	188	63	D	D	D	240	3 396	811.8	67.0	57	265	23.2	5.4
Warren	11.2	315	13	88	18.7	2.5	134	1 311	369.6	30.2	31	136	12.5	2.7
Washington	82.5	1 584	43	417	279.6	20.7	280	2 940	701.6	59.0	48	131	15.4	3.1
Westmoreland	1.8	103	13	79	38.9	2.8	47	479	100.4	9.3	21	57	4.7	1.2
Wise	7.4	177	35	512	496.1	22.6	205	2 077	438.6	38.0	26	80	23.0	2.6
Wythe	12.5	440	19	318	105.5	10.8	160	2 130	908.1	45.4	32	235	21.4	4.8
York	1 011.0	16 371	49	262	149.7	8.9	243	3 759	852.2	84.2	71	267	36.0	7.1
Independent cities														
Alexandria city	249.9	1 846	91	1 262	525.7	65.2	528	8 052	2 353.8	232.5	229	2 484	811.8	127.1
Bedford city	0.0	0	4	85	28.9	2.7	56	553	124.9	10.7	14	44	5.1	1.0
Bristol city	0.1	3	34	883	318.8	28.8	172	1 884	343.5	34.2	27	D	D	D
Buena Vista city	1.4	217	1	D	D	D	25	162	30.6	3.1	6	18	0.7	0.2
Charlottesville city	0.0	0	55	473	203.4	20.4	349	3 880	699.4	78.1	98	557	86.5	19.7
Chesapeake city	553.3	2 527	239	3 428	2 123.3	156.1	869	16 523	3 977.8	345.5	273	1 355	274.7	49.0
Colonial Heights city	0.0	0	8	86	28.4	2.6	204	4 064	761.1	71.4	26	134	22.6	4.5
Covington city	39.8	6 421	5	38	13.0	1.1	70	491	104.6	9.5	10	21	1.8	0.4
Danville city	3.7	81	55	462	204.1	18.8	330	4 395	892.2	81.8	66	332	41.4	8.8
Emporia city	1.0	184	4	D	D	D	64	705	131.6	13.2	15	50	5.0	0.9
Fairfax city	0.1	4	48	265	192.3	13.0	289	6 460	1 884.0	178.4	80	241	36.0	9.8
Falls Church city	0.0	0	16	D	D	D	104	1 129	288.0	35.4	30	195	58.1	6.3
Franklin city	1.2	135	6	50	25.5	1.4	63	900	186.3	19.5	17	65	8.0	1.6
Fredericksburg city	0.0	0	32	D	D	D	280	4 436	1 052.1	94.6	77	403	70.0	15.4
Galax city	1.7	261	5	48	36.9	1.6	78	1 085	227.5	22.5	13	62	10.3	1.5
Hampton city	0.3	2	60	800	288.9	33.5	436	7 295	1 805.7	162.3	115	873	113.9	24.2
Harrisonburg city	0.1	2	55	1 033	378.5	42.7	376	6 265	1 465.3	158.1	80	346	68.3	8.8
Hopewell city	186.1	8 203	12	130	58.1	8.8	84	696	173.9	15.1	22	98	19.3	3.2
Lexington city	0.0	0	3	6	1.9	0.2	48	447	86.8	9.8	21	50	6.1	1.2
Lynchburg city	0.1	2	82	1 125	541.5	43.2	419	7 266	1 665.1	151.2	107	466	72.4	15.3
Manassas city	0.1	3	44	D	D	D	187	2 635	921.2	85.3	59	230	41.7	8.3

1. Merchant wholesalers, except manufacturers' sales branches and offices.   2. Employer establishments.

STATE County	Professional, scientific, and technical services,[1] 2007				Manufacturing, 2007				Accommodation and food services, 2007			
	Number of establish-ments	Number of employees	Receipts (mil dol)	Annual payroll (mil dol)	Number of establish-ments	Number of employees	Receipts (mil dol)	Annual payroll (mil dol)	Number of establish-ments	Number of employees	Sales (mil dol)	Annual payroll (mil dol)
	147	148	149	150	151	152	153	154	155	156	157	158
VIRGINIA—Cont'd												
Louisa	55	188	19.2	7.0	34	1 377	435.9	62.1	22	357	13.9	3.8
Lunenburg	10	D	D	D	8	778	D	21.6	10	D	D	D
Madison	31	D	D	D	NA	NA	NA	NA	16	210	10.1	3.0
Mathews	22	54	3.7	1.6	NA	NA	NA	NA	15	D	D	D
Mecklenburg	48	295	21.7	8.1	31	1 847	281.0	47.7	76	1 111	43.5	12.5
Middlesex	30	130	7.8	3.8	NA	NA	NA	NA	23	255	8.7	2.6
Montgomery	234	D	D	D	55	3 097	838.1	141.9	187	4 037	148.3	44.8
Nelson	39	D	D	D	NA	NA	NA	NA	20	152	6.2	1.6
New Kent	20	52	3.0	1.1	NA	NA	NA	NA	23	211	9.7	2.2
Northampton	22	D	D	D	9	D	D	D	37	494	23.6	7.3
Northumberland	29	D	D	D	23	595	D	17.5	20	116	5.2	1.4
Nottoway	23	125	7.5	2.7	NA	NA	NA	NA	27	379	11.1	3.0
Orange	70	311	34.0	13.0	21	947	222.2	36.0	51	668	26.0	7.1
Page	27	194	11.4	4.9	15	868	204.1	23.2	57	679	35.4	9.2
Patrick	17	D	D	D	42	1 823	248.5	51.1	22	152	6.6	1.5
Pittsylvania	49	D	D	D	53	2 441	752.1	81.3	43	449	15.3	4.3
Powhatan	56	185	20.1	8.9	NA	NA	NA	NA	29	384	17.6	4.0
Prince Edward	30	D	D	D	NA	NA	NA	NA	51	994	40.0	11.1
Prince George	36	144	18.4	7.2	22	1 330	783.8	61.0	28	426	23.1	4.9
Prince William	918	D	D	D	120	2 548	563.6	121.6	568	10 617	537.9	148.4
Pulaski	47	D	D	D	49	6 611	2 797.1	305.5	70	917	40.7	10.0
Rappahannock	31	D	D	D	NA	NA	NA	NA	16	253	20.0	5.5
Richmond	13	D	D	D	NA	NA	NA	NA	11	D	D	D
Roanoke	190	D	D	D	67	3 769	896.1	155.4	128	2 668	112.7	32.7
Rockbridge	26	93	8.2	2.9	27	1 221	326.0	39.0	59	875	49.2	13.7
Rockingham	83	D	D	D	87	7 288	5 437.5	296.8	82	2 042	62.1	27.0
Russell	34	D	D	D	15	1 219	192.9	28.0	34	420	15.6	4.2
Scott	23	94	5.6	1.7	8	768	451.5	30.0	21	315	11.6	3.4
Shenandoah	77	D	D	D	39	5 034	1 058.1	160.9	71	1 157	50.1	15.0
Smyth	34	D	D	D	47	3 870	777.2	138.7	53	679	24.1	6.6
Southampton	11	D	D	D	14	1 917	831.4	112.2	9	D	D	D
Spotsylvania	217	1 387	228.3	78.2	64	2 164	496.4	88.8	190	3 542	169.8	47.9
Stafford	284	D	D	D	46	727	140.8	25.3	179	3 324	140.3	38.8
Surry	5	20	1.9	0.5	NA	NA	NA	NA	2	D	D	D
Sussex	8	D	D	D	NA	NA	NA	NA	14	284	15.7	4.0
Tazewell	71	D	D	D	61	1 485	354.5	D	59	1 368	52.2	15.0
Warren	77	477	36.6	17.4	24	1 002	D	41.2	67	837	41.3	11.4
Washington	110	742	49.6	24.7	74	4 862	1 359.5	171.4	91	1 505	59.2	16.7
Westmoreland	28	130	13.7	7.1	14	573	199.6	19.1	35	426	14.2	4.1
Wise	50	383	39.3	13.7	NA	NA	NA	NA	58	1 040	40.1	10.4
Wythe	42	149	16.8	6.2	44	2 009	567.4	73.2	76	1 385	63.2	17.5
York	153	1 461	184.8	74.2	39	592	D	31.7	134	3 614	187.4	50.9
Independent cities												
Alexandria city	1 166	D	D	D	88	1 483	284.5	56.3	355	6 961	471.7	135.1
Bedford city	31	D	D	D	23	1 204	D	40.3	26	442	15.4	4.7
Bristol city	43	276	21.2	11.6	32	1 673	659.8	62.1	82	2 053	76.6	23.1
Buena Vista city	8	D	D	D	15	988	202.8	37.4	13	D	D	D
Charlottesville city	290	D	D	D	51	1 589	677.1	79.1	261	5 617	303.6	85.8
Chesapeake city	485	D	D	D	139	4 487	1 437.1	200.1	431	8 991	369.8	105.5
Colonial Heights city	56	466	31.4	12.6	NA	NA	NA	NA	81	1 768	76.1	19.5
Covington city	21	D	D	D	8	D	D	D	21	D	D	D
Danville city	76	D	D	D	43	4 485	1 275.9	212.7	140	2 741	110.3	30.0
Emporia city	17	D	D	D	11	1 074	311.5	34.5	25	566	24.2	7.0
Fairfax city	655	D	D	D	NA	NA	NA	NA	150	2 521	140.3	36.8
Falls Church city	158	D	D	D	14	D	D	D	101	872	56.3	14.6
Franklin city	16	D	D	D	NA	NA	NA	NA	27	802	22.6	6.7
Fredericksburg city	166	D	D	D	NA	NA	NA	NA	178	4 003	171.6	53.4
Galax city	23	157	12.2	4.7	17	1 935	204.1	40.4	38	632	22.5	6.9
Hampton city	280	D	D	D	77	2 790	522.4	122.0	233	5 888	233.6	69.2
Harrisonburg city	150	D	D	D	47	2 824	746.3	103.1	175	4 284	168.6	46.7
Hopewell city	34	328	27.8	15.8	14	1 297	1 496.0	98.0	56	923	47.8	11.9
Lexington city	28	D	D	D	NA	NA	NA	NA	52	655	31.3	7.8
Lynchburg city	203	D	D	D	96	9 486	2 801.6	500.1	234	5 226	190.0	58.3
Manassas city	218	D	D	D	41	4 038	1 408.7	340.5	101	1 307	75.6	19.0

1. Establishment subject to federal tax.

Table B. States and Counties — Health Care and Social Assistance, Other Services, and Federal Funds

| STATE County | Health care and social assistance, 2007 | | | | Other services, 2007 | | | | Federal funds and grants, 2009–2010 Expenditures (mil dol) | | | |
| | | | | | | | | | | Direct payments for individuals[1] | | |
	Number of establishments	Number of employees	Receipts (mil dol)	Annual payroll (mil dol)	Number of establishments	Number of employees	Receipts (mil dol)	Annual payroll (mil dol)	Total	Social Security and government retirement	Medicare	Food Stamps and Supplemental Security Income
	159	160	161	162	163	164	165	166	167	168	169	170
VIRGINIA—Cont'd												
Louisa	23	D	D	D	45	232	16.8	4.8	210.4	120.7	36.7	6.4
Lunenburg	17	237	9.3	4.2	16	D	D	D	93.4	39.4	19.9	7.4
Madison	23	318	13.8	6.0	19	64	7.6	2.6	86.6	41.1	18.9	2.7
Mathews	11	D	D	D	12	D	D	D	94.7	53.5	22.2	2.1
Mecklenburg	75	1 807	149.4	58.5	71	328	21.1	5.8	433.3	138.4	63.4	9.6
Middlesex	20	D	D	D	36	108	7.5	2.2	101.1	61.1	20.7	3.0
Montgomery	213	4 007	427.0	162.2	159	816	249.3	18.0	660.2	206.1	71.8	17.4
Nelson	19	230	13.3	6.2	24	135	10.0	3.8	147.9	76.8	26.5	5.8
New Kent	18	D	D	D	28	103	8.9	3.3	96.9	63.7	17.4	1.9
Northampton	42	1 041	83.2	34.6	24	60	5.1	1.1	147.1	53.0	25.7	9.5
Northumberland	10	47	2.3	0.8	29	94	5.9	1.5	134.6	79.5	28.2	3.5
Nottoway	24	826	39.6	22.0	39	131	10.9	3.3	281.5	65.1	30.2	7.2
Orange	42	283	17.9	6.9	54	332	35.2	10.4	267.7	166.0	46.9	6.4
Page	34	522	36.3	15.9	38	118	8.4	2.4	200.6	92.2	37.6	6.1
Patrick	25	602	29.2	13.4	17	49	4.1	1.2	147.0	72.1	27.8	6.9
Pittsylvania	57	655	30.7	13.9	67	300	19.0	5.0	395.7	171.2	71.5	17.2
Powhatan	28	250	15.3	6.9	44	153	17.7	6.0	139.7	81.3	17.0	2.6
Prince Edward	78	1 677	106.9	48.8	38	157	18.5	3.3	170.4	78.9	30.1	9.5
Prince George	15	D	D	D	33	125	9.1	3.4	1 648.2	102.9	17.4	4.7
Prince William	530	7 037	690.9	267.2	500	3 204	512.8	96.7	4 426.5	998.8	87.8	44.8
Pulaski	67	1 356	89.9	40.0	50	210	17.7	5.1	275.8	126.3	68.9	12.0
Rappahannock	8	D	D	D	11	37	3.0	0.9	66.3	40.7	12.5	1.2
Richmond	19	797	27.3	13.6	12	66	6.6	2.1	70.4	33.6	19.0	2.4
Roanoke	238	4 618	340.9	163.7	163	824	68.4	21.3	290.3	167.0	48.8	9.9
Rockbridge	32	197	15.0	5.4	29	93	8.5	2.0	114.3	54.9	19.3	3.9
Rockingham	85	1 625	86.1	36.1	104	508	39.3	12.2	343.9	189.5	70.7	10.2
Russell	50	865	61.3	25.5	30	91	6.7	2.1	272.1	119.8	64.3	19.5
Scott	40	D	D	D	18	D	D	D	305.1	98.3	51.7	12.0
Shenandoah	69	D	D	D	90	363	31.5	7.6	284.7	166.6	51.1	7.0
Smyth	62	2 205	141.3	70.6	44	183	17.0	4.3	295.2	126.2	58.6	14.6
Southampton	9	D	D	D	18	D	D	D	128.4	49.0	28.2	6.3
Spotsylvania	176	2 198	135.5	58.7	177	1 020	91.7	27.7	566.3	270.4	31.1	12.9
Stafford	146	1 939	129.0	59.4	193	1 203	99.5	32.9	837.1	406.1	36.1	10.4
Surry	3	D	D	D	1	D	D	D	52.4	26.8	10.6	2.6
Sussex	14	D	D	D	16	94	6.0	1.8	111.5	44.1	27.1	6.7
Tazewell	149	2 424	187.5	77.1	92	595	55.8	15.6	438.7	219.0	105.3	26.7
Warren	55	D	D	D	77	525	36.1	11.9	211.1	120.3	35.4	8.8
Washington	143	2 092	197.7	76.1	73	357	22.1	7.6	390.9	185.5	64.5	14.7
Westmoreland	18	287	10.5	5.4	32	109	6.2	1.5	189.7	112.0	39.3	7.2
Wise	82	1 601	101.3	38.9	70	D	D	D	508.1	186.8	90.4	35.6
Wythe	70	1 283	92.5	37.2	51	275	21.2	5.3	263.0	126.4	52.4	11.0
York	94	1 620	176.7	67.1	138	702	47.5	16.3	682.6	391.8	40.6	6.1
Independent cities												
Alexandria city	397	6 347	909.3	332.6	591	9 336	2 436.1	524.5	5 465.0	659.2	230.2	31.7
Bedford city	44	D	D	D	36	268	21.3	7.3	105.4	65.8	16.8	4.9
Bristol city	47	D	D	D	48	D	D	D	268.4	111.7	50.7	10.9
Buena Vista city	15	318	15.9	8.6	7	D	D	D	61.1	28.5	12.4	3.6
Charlottesville city	190	10 090	1 339.7	449.4	165	1 389	295.9	42.8	842.8	195.7	73.1	18.0
Chesapeake city	469	7 730	746.9	298.5	404	3 023	333.8	91.6	1 748.9	847.9	194.7	52.2
Colonial Heights city	84	1 275	94.0	46.2	55	361	26.9	8.8	163.8	102.4	33.3	3.7
Covington city	20	232	8.0	3.6	19	D	D	D	120.9	67.3	30.5	5.0
Danville city	208	4 620	407.1	161.8	126	620	53.0	13.4	503.8	225.6	108.7	31.9
Emporia city	35	923	70.3	27.7	21	78	6.7	1.7	92.9	36.4	24.8	7.2
Fairfax city	221	3 303	269.8	121.2	181	1 155	132.0	39.9	1 031.5	388.9	69.6	7.8
Falls Church city	101	D	D	D	86	536	68.2	19.7	1 196.5	80.6	66.7	1.8
Franklin city	53	933	76.1	29.4	32	205	14.5	3.8	118.6	46.5	25.0	8.0
Fredericksburg city	212	5 813	824.6	293.8	106	947	60.1	21.3	440.1	252.0	74.5	7.9
Galax city	49	1 451	115.3	49.9	22	84	7.0	2.0	109.5	54.6	26.1	5.3
Hampton city	243	6 619	660.4	300.7	191	1 177	96.6	29.1	3 200.3	615.3	171.6	55.2
Harrisonburg city	160	4 724	463.1	193.2	133	725	79.2	18.1	232.7	84.2	40.7	7.6
Hopewell city	61	D	D	D	42	303	42.2	6.9	214.2	101.0	43.5	16.8
Lexington city	47	759	69.7	24.1	30	228	29.2	6.5	121.6	55.7	15.3	1.3
Lynchburg city	261	8 776	828.1	355.5	175	1 058	80.3	24.4	979.1	278.1	124.2	28.2
Manassas city	179	3 373	357.5	175.1	132	803	75.2	22.1	1 231.8	261.8	44.9	9.5

1. State totals may include programs not allocated by county.

Table B. States and Counties — Federal Funds, Residential Construction, and Local Government Finances

	Federal funds and grants, 2009–2010 (cont.)							Value of residential construction authorized by building permits, 2010		Local government finances, 2007				
	Expenditures (mil dol) (cont.)									General revenue				
	Procurement contract awards			Grants[1]									Taxes	
STATE County														Per capita[2] (dollars)
	Salaries and wages	Defense	Other	Medicaid and other health-related	Nutrition and family welfare	Education	Other	New construction ($1,000)	Number of housing units	Total (mil dol)	Inter-govern-mental (mil dol)	Total (mil dol)	Total	Property
	171	172	173	174	175	176	177	178	179	180	181	182	183	184
VIRGINIA—Cont'd														
Louisa	5.0	7.1	1.8	26.2	2.9	1.5	0.7	29 372	163	91.2	29.2	50.3	1 573	1 373
Lunenburg	1.9	0.0	0.5	18.0	2.5	0.8	0.1	2 533	15	32.0	21.7	7.5	572	401
Madison	3.7	0.9	1.0	14.4	2.4	0.8	0.1	5 580	27	30.9	14.5	13.3	966	723
Mathews	4.4	1.1	1.6	5.3	0.9	0.5	0.0	7 780	30	22.9	10.4	11.0	1 220	1 047
Mecklenburg	9.3	21.8	97.9	59.7	4.7	2.1	19.2	15 214	100	84.6	46.6	31.1	970	664
Middlesex	3.6	0.4	0.5	5.6	1.3	1.3	0.1	7 766	60	25.9	11.1	13.3	1 250	988
Montgomery	33.7	46.0	31.1	80.0	6.9	5.3	135.7	27 510	169	214.6	95.2	84.7	949	621
Nelson	5.5	0.0	1.4	21.4	1.8	0.8	7.4	11 918	51	39.7	18.8	18.6	1 221	926
New Kent	3.9	0.1	0.9	5.9	1.0	0.9	0.2	23 285	146	40.1	20.1	16.9	990	810
Northampton	4.5	9.9	2.3	32.7	3.6	1.1	0.1	6 416	26	102.0	24.9	17.6	1 315	960
Northumberland	2.7	7.0	0.7	8.1	1.6	0.8	0.2	14 094	48	30.4	12.2	16.5	1 276	1 081
Nottoway	116.2	5.0	1.2	20.3	3.0	1.6	30.1	4 650	57	38.9	24.6	9.6	607	398
Orange	5.5	0.0	4.7	25.0	3.7	1.5	0.5	8 744	54	82.0	38.8	34.5	1 061	817
Page	10.2	0.0	27.4	20.6	2.5	1.9	1.7	3 988	37	60.9	39.7	14.1	585	431
Patrick	3.7	8.5	1.5	20.0	2.3	1.4	0.7	5 497	47	37.1	23.3	10.6	561	409
Pittsylvania	8.2	0.5	2.5	95.1	9.1	4.5	0.4	9 548	90	141.5	91.2	44.8	737	627
Powhatan	28.4	0.0	1.1	5.9	1.3	0.9	0.0	16 340	70	66.6	33.3	25.3	908	724
Prince Edward	9.0	3.4	1.3	25.6	2.9	1.9	1.2	8 075	74	67.2	34.4	17.9	838	452
Prince George	1 131.5	353.8	18.4	7.8	2.4	4.8	0.0	7 374	42	107.0	65.3	30.2	842	658
Prince William	762.7	2 205.3	168.3	30.0	16.5	13.4	56.6	285 706	2 092	1 505.3	562.4	700.8	1 944	1 490
Pulaski	10.5	1.7	1.8	32.4	4.5	2.9	5.5	7 454	44	100.2	46.9	28.2	804	606
Rappahannock	1.8	0.1	0.9	7.2	0.6	0.4	0.5	3 834	16	18.5	6.8	10.6	1 474	1 251
Richmond	2.9	0.0	0.9	8.7	1.1	0.5	0.1	5 677	28	29.1	14.6	10.0	1 085	794
Roanoke	4.9	27.0	2.6	18.1	5.3	4.2	0.0	24 533	137	291.4	125.3	145.1	1 605	1 170
Rockbridge	3.9	3.7	3.3	16.2	2.5	1.3	3.4	10 365	52	65.0	27.2	26.0	1 208	807
Rockingham	13.3	0.4	8.8	35.6	4.8	3.7	0.0	42 458	261	202.3	106.5	69.1	939	752
Russell	5.0	0.0	1.5	49.6	5.4	2.6	0.9	5 288	43	64.9	42.1	20.2	700	403
Scott	15.2	0.3	1.1	58.8	5.7	2.1	57.2	3 627	29	69.4	48.3	15.8	693	463
Shenandoah	20.8	0.6	8.8	20.7	2.9	2.5	1.3	15 393	90	112.6	50.4	44.2	1 095	808
Smyth	10.1	8.2	6.5	53.6	8.1	2.2	3.1	6 295	37	90.1	56.9	24.3	759	493
Southampton	4.0	0.0	0.8	29.8	2.8	1.4	0.1	8 137	47	51.6	27.3	17.8	1 010	760
Spotsylvania	5.5	202.8	9.3	13.7	6.6	3.9	0.1	59 011	254	361.3	163.4	154.3	1 295	923
Stafford	59.5	124.6	155.9	11.5	6.9	4.9	0.7	105 210	530	401.5	172.6	179.9	1 490	1 127
Surry	1.6	0.1	0.3	6.6	1.1	0.4	0.0	3 403	33	31.3	7.7	21.6	3 052	2 961
Sussex	5.9	0.0	0.7	21.2	2.3	0.8	0.0	2 040	15	44.4	17.7	19.6	1 605	704
Tazewell	8.6	0.0	1.5	51.7	8.0	5.7	0.6	3 591	25	122.4	69.8	34.8	793	574
Warren	16.8	1.0	7.7	14.9	2.6	2.0	0.4	9 288	50	97.0	41.3	45.0	1 240	920
Washington	14.0	0.1	4.2	72.1	9.8	4.1	7.0	11 272	111	190.0	121.9	41.5	787	564
Westmoreland	4.5	6.0	1.1	12.5	3.3	1.3	0.1	9 407	52	46.8	21.3	21.2	1 228	832
Wise	12.8	1.4	65.3	65.5	8.1	4.8	26.1	3 258	26	136.2	80.0	44.8	1 075	501
Wythe	8.8	0.0	1.7	36.2	3.9	4.8	9.5	6 816	71	86.0	45.8	22.7	797	452
York	110.9	57.0	24.4	9.7	5.4	10.5	0.2	27 236	160	224.8	95.1	99.5	1 624	1 137
Independent cities														
Alexandria city	1 997.9	922.9	1 128.3	86.0	13.7	12.5	348.9	48 784	468	559.1	66.4	429.0	3 064	2 220
Bedford city	9.8	0.9	2.3	4.1	0.2	0.2	0.3	219	1	16.8	7.3	6.6	1 057	612
Bristol city	20.5	0.1	4.8	35.3	2.7	1.7	26.0	449	5	98.2	32.0	28.3	1 609	940
Buena Vista city	1.7	0.4	1.6	9.7	0.7	0.5	0.0	433	4	19.6	10.2	6.0	922	664
Charlottesville city	71.4	48.5	31.1	276.5	5.3	15.4	88.8	15 546	93	183.3	68.7	86.6	2 100	1 259
Chesapeake city	102.3	299.2	73.7	77.7	16.7	12.2	17.3	200 957	1 085	1 117.3	369.5	418.2	1 908	1 343
Colonial Heights city	5.9	8.3	0.8	5.6	1.0	1.3	0.1	548	6	57.2	16.5	35.6	1 999	1 045
Covington city	5.7	0.6	0.8	9.4	0.7	0.7	0.2	131	2	25.6	10.8	11.5	1 864	1 214
Danville city	15.2	0.5	6.1	76.2	9.3	4.4	11.4	7 894	70	165.3	85.6	47.9	1 066	577
Emporia city	4.1	0.0	0.5	18.4	0.2	0.6	0.4	565	13	16.0	3.4	9.2	1 641	739
Fairfax city	107.7	124.6	104.3	34.6	8.0	36.5	120.4	4 756	22	106.6	9.9	82.6	3 537	2 149
Falls Church city	402.3	561.6	30.7	32.6	0.6	2.0	2.4	7 189	24	71.7	9.7	46.9	4 284	3 252
Franklin city	3.2	-0.1	0.5	23.7	3.5	1.4	2.4	60	1	48.1	26.3	13.8	1 551	793
Fredericksburg city	28.6	17.3	14.6	15.3	2.3	1.3	19.6	37 349	346	150.3	48.2	59.2	2 639	1 232
Galax city	6.4	0.4	0.6	11.6	2.8	0.7	0.6	593	6	27.6	12.1	10.1	1 480	746
Hampton city	1 087.7	483.9	498.1	61.1	15.3	19.2	120.4	29 944	134	550.7	234.8	218.3	1 491	1 014
Harrisonburg city	21.9	22.8	5.8	13.1	3.3	2.3	15.8	17 804	201	119.7	38.5	56.9	1 293	539
Hopewell city	3.2	8.7	5.2	20.8	4.2	2.8	4.7	3 050	36	88.4	40.7	28.1	1 222	967
Lexington city	22.9	4.1	0.8	10.4	0.6	0.2	7.7	0	0	21.2	6.3	6.9	987	546
Lynchburg city	36.9	22.2	296.0	68.6	10.9	6.4	15.7	23 149	144	262.8	103.6	103.9	1 457	803
Manassas city	56.1	756.4	57.4	22.3	4.1	3.4	11.2	5 601	52	164.4	50.2	80.4	2 271	1 676

1. State totals may include programs not allocated by county.   2. Based on the resident population estimated as of July 1 of the year shown.

Table B. States and Counties — Local Government Finances, Government Employment, and Voting

STATE County	Local government finances, 2007 (cont.)									Government employment, 2009			Presidential election,[2] 2008		
	Direct general expenditure							Debt outstanding					Percent of vote cast:		
			Percent of total for:												
	Total (mil dol)	Per capita[1] (dollars)	Educa-tion	Health and hospitals	Police protec-tion	Public welfare	High-ways	Total (mil dol)	Per capita[1] (dollars)	Federal civilian	Federal military	State and local	Demo-cratic	Republi-can	All other
	185	186	187	188	189	190	191	192	193	194	195	196	197	198	199
VIRGINIA—Cont'd															
Louisa	79.8	2 497	60.6	2.8	5.4	6.4	0.2	38.6	1 206	65	112	1 483	45.5	53.3	1.3
Lunenburg	37.2	2 860	52.8	1.2	8.0	5.6	1.4	27.9	2 142	24	43	799	47.8	51.3	0.8
Madison	27.8	2 024	66.1	3.3	5.8	5.7	0.0	85.3	6 221	69	46	520	42.7	56.1	1.2
Mathews	20.6	2 276	58.7	0.8	6.5	8.7	0.1	15.5	1 715	27	68	381	35.6	63.5	0.9
Mecklenburg	88.3	2 750	60.3	0.9	7.6	2.4	2.2	97.7	3 043	143	108	2 285	47.3	51.8	0.9
Middlesex	36.1	3 389	61.6	0.8	3.7	4.5	1.0	39.7	3 730	23	36	993	39.8	59.0	1.2
Montgomery	201.9	2 264	45.3	2.1	6.7	3.0	6.4	294.7	3 304	(3)386	(3)412	(3)16 665	51.7	46.8	1.5
Nelson	42.9	2 817	75.4	1.0	1.7	4.2	0.0	0.0	0	50	52	635	54.0	44.8	1.2
New Kent	36.9	2 158	58.6	1.2	6.1	4.4	0.0	31.2	1 822	45	61	922	35.0	63.9	1.1
Northampton	79.7	5 950	27.6	1.2	2.7	4.2	0.1	244.1	18 218	42	73	928	57.7	41.2	1.1
Northumberland	25.8	2 001	60.9	1.0	3.4	6.0	0.2	2.1	163	30	44	466	44.7	54.6	0.7
Nottoway	39.6	2 511	65.2	0.3	6.5	6.1	2.9	17.3	1 100	396	56	2 109	48.8	50.1	1.1
Orange	78.3	2 410	55.5	1.3	5.7	3.0	0.7	74.1	2 281	67	114	2 019	45.0	53.8	1.2
Page	63.8	2 641	65.3	0.0	5.9	4.3	1.7	27.0	1 119	200	82	1 330	40.8	58.1	1.1
Patrick	39.8	2 110	73.2	0.9	4.1	4.8	0.0	5.6	298	48	63	821	33.7	64.4	1.9
Pittsylvania	135.9	2 235	59.5	0.5	5.1	13.0	1.3	65.6	1 079	(4)253	(4)360	(4)6 733	37.5	61.5	0.9
Powhatan	62.8	2 259	67.5	0.3	3.9	5.9	0.0	105.0	3 775	44	95	2 265	29.3	69.8	0.9
Prince Edward	64.4	3 013	45.7	5.9	5.9	5.3	5.7	47.3	2 213	83	76	2 247	54.3	44.5	1.2
Prince George	126.4	3 524	44.8	0.4	4.2	1.8	0.2	146.8	4 091	(5)4 275	(5)6 746	(5)3 127	44.6	54.7	0.8
Prince William	1 469.9	4 078	56.0	3.7	6.2	2.9	1.5	1 542.2	4 279	(6)6 236	(6)6 865	(6)21 631	57.5	41.6	0.9
Pulaski	95.8	2 732	46.1	2.7	5.3	8.5	1.4	65.1	1 856	55	119	2 416	39.3	58.9	1.8
Rappahannock	17.7	2 464	64.5	1.2	3.2	3.0	1.1	17.6	2 442	27	24	307	47.8	50.6	1.7
Richmond	26.2	2 857	51.6	0.7	1.1	4.3	0.2	21.1	2 305	38	30	932	43.2	55.9	0.9
Roanoke	267.0	2 952	53.5	0.3	8.0	6.0	0.7	370.9	4 102	(7)2 182	(7)394	(7)6 716	38.9	60.0	1.2
Rockbridge	68.4	3 180	41.8	0.7	3.1	7.1	0.1	72.7	3 384	(8)107	(8)148	(8)2 693	42.6	56.2	1.1
Rockingham	231.4	3 147	55.3	3.7	4.7	8.9	2.1	151.0	2 054	(9)349	(9)412	(9)10 141	31.4	67.4	1.2
Russell	56.7	1 967	66.7	0.0	3.0	8.8	0.6	67.6	2 346	67	99	1 440	42.9	55.6	1.5
Scott	80.1	3 515	54.2	1.1	6.3	9.8	1.2	16.7	734	70	77	1 197	27.6	70.7	1.7
Shenandoah	110.0	2 724	55.9	0.3	7.8	5.8	2.6	100.7	2 493	143	139	1 988	36.0	62.5	1.6
Smyth	84.8	2 646	60.1	1.3	6.1	6.4	2.5	110.6	3 452	86	108	2 887	34.5	63.5	2.0
Southampton	53.0	3 000	56.0	0.7	0.5	4.2	0.3	73.3	4 151	(10)99	(10)93	(10)2 512	48.5	50.5	0.9
Spotsylvania	386.4	3 242	60.2	0.5	3.8	3.7	2.7	501.9	4 210	(11)331	(11)489	(11)8 857	46.0	53.0	1.0
Stafford	416.4	3 449	68.9	0.4	7.7	2.8	0.1	398.5	3 301	2 631	2 761	5 910	46.4	52.7	0.9
Surry	27.1	3 819	63.4	1.8	4.1	8.2	0.0	31.9	4 501	19	24	452	60.7	38.5	0.8
Sussex	36.2	2 964	58.1	0.6	7.1	6.0	0.2	17.5	1 433	53	41	1 302	61.6	37.8	0.7
Tazewell	114.1	2 602	52.6	13.7	4.8	4.8	2.7	40.9	932	83	162	3 525	32.8	65.7	1.5
Warren	93.8	2 585	48.0	0.9	8.2	7.2	2.3	120.8	3 327	199	124	1 644	43.4	55.1	1.6
Washington	150.4	2 853	45.0	9.2	4.2	3.9	1.6	108.0	2 048	(18)364	(12)243	(12)4 770	32.9	65.6	1.5
Westmoreland	40.7	2 362	62.8	1.3	6.6	4.1	0.5	9.0	523	68	60	791	54.6	44.4	1.0
Wise	130.2	3 124	56.5	3.7	4.7	6.7	2.0	72.6	1 742	(13)254	(13)154	(13)4 443	35.3	63.0	1.6
Wythe	93.0	3 258	42.7	0.1	5.2	5.4	2.7	97.7	3 424	103	98	2 370	32.9	65.7	1.4
York	219.1	3 576	59.7	1.1	3.5	2.5	0.1	162.2	2 647	(14)1 154	(14)1 936	(14)3 963	40.4	58.5	1.1
Independent cities															
Alexandria city	593.3	4 237	33.9	6.3	8.9	8.0	3.5	435.5	3 110	14 976	4 428	8 817	71.7	27.3	1.0
Bedford city	19.9	3 171	33.3	2.0	13.3	1.0	11.1	18.8	2 998	(15)	(15)	(15)	44.2	54.8	1.1
Bristol city	90.9	5 167	25.6	0.7	6.8	5.0	4.3	121.3	6 897	(12)	(12)	(12)	36.2	62.2	1.6
Buena Vista city	21.6	3 326	48.4	0.0	7.4	4.4	4.6	25.9	3 998	(8)	(8)	(8)	45.7	52.9	1.4
Charlottesville city	181.0	4 391	35.6	6.2	6.7	10.5	3.1	103.9	2 520	(16)	(16)	(16)	78.4	20.3	1.3
Chesapeake city	993.3	4 532	45.2	21.2	4.1	2.3	4.4	821.8	3 750	1 023	1 704	15 281	50.2	48.9	0.8
Colonial Heights city	58.2	3 272	53.6	0.3	4.9	1.0	6.0	23.4	1 315	(17)	(17)	(17)	29.0	69.6	1.4
Covington city	27.2	4 411	41.9	1.2	5.5	7.0	5.7	29.7	4 810	(18)	(18)	(18)	55.4	43.3	1.3
Danville city	157.1	3 495	44.9	0.4	5.8	5.3	4.7	193.3	4 301	(4)	(4)	(4)	59.1	40.0	0.8
Emporia city	15.9	2 833	24.5	1.3	19.5	3.4	5.2	17.9	3 180	(19)	(19)	(19)	65.0	34.3	0.7
Fairfax city	137.4	5 883	55.5	0.6	7.6	0.0	3.9	206.2	8 830	(20)	(20)	(20)	57.7	41.2	1.2
Falls Church city	100.1	9 143	35.1	0.0	5.3	1.6	2.0	66.8	6 104	(20)	(20)	(20)	69.6	29.2	1.3
Franklin city	48.1	5 400	35.4	0.4	6.5	3.6	3.3	29.2	3 280	(10)	(10)	(10)	63.7	35.6	0.7
Fredericksburg city	162.4	7 246	22.0	13.3	10.4	0.4	4.2	646.0	28 826	(11)	(11)	(11)	63.6	35.3	1.1
Galax city	26.4	3 867	44.7	0.9	7.1	6.9	7.1	17.6	2 585	(21)	(21)	(21)	43.8	54.8	1.4
Hampton city	519.1	3 545	45.1	0.7	5.4	5.5	0.9	336.2	2 296	8 471	8 492	8 654	69.1	30.1	0.8
Harrisonburg city	143.3	3 255	54.2	0.7	4.8	1.8	7.1	404.6	9 186	(9)	(9)	(9)	57.5	41.2	1.2
Hopewell city	95.8	4 158	41.3	0.2	5.7	4.2	6.4	45.6	1 981	(5)	(5)	(5)	55.5	43.6	0.9
Lexington city	26.4	3 763	20.4	2.2	10.1	0.0	12.5	27.7	3 944	(8)	(8)	(8)	62.2	36.9	0.9
Lynchburg city	246.4	3 457	38.5	6.1	7.6	3.2	4.7	67.6	949	(22)	(22)	(22)	47.4	51.4	1.3
Manassas city	163.6	4 621	58.1	3.4	8.1	0.2	8.0	152.7	4 312	(6)	(6)	(6)	55.2	43.8	1.0

1. Based on the resident population estimated as of July 1 of the year shown.   2. © 2009 Election Data Services, Inc. All rights reserved.   3. Radford city is included with Montgomery county.   4. Danville city is included with Pittsylvania county.   5. Hopewell city is included with Prince George county.   6. Manassas and Manassas Park cities are included with Prince William county.   7. Salem city is included with Roanoke county.   8. Buena Vista and Lexington cities are included with Rockbridge county.   9. Harrisonburg city is included with Rockingham county.   10. Franklin city is included with Southhampton county.   11. Fredericksburg city is included with Spotsylvania county.   12. Bristol city included with Washington county.   13. Norton city is included with Wise county.   14. Poquoson city is included with York county.   15. Bedford city is included with Bedford county.   16. Charlottesville city is included with Albemarle county.   17. Petersburg and Colonial Heights cities are included with Dinwiddie county.   18. Covington city is included with Alleghany county.   19. Emporia city is included with Greensville county.   20. Fairfax city and Falls Church city are included with Fairfax county.   21. Galax city is included with Carroll county.   22. Lynchburg city is included with Campbell county.

STATE/ County code	CBSA code[1]	County type[2]	STATE County	Land area,[3] (sq km) 2010	Total persons	Rank	Per square kilometer	White	Black	American Indian, Alaska Native	Asian and Pacific Islander	Percent Hispanic or Latino[4]	Under 5 years	5 to 17 years	18 to 24 years	25 to 34 years	35 to 44 years	45 to 54 years
				1	2	3	4	5	6	7	8	9	10	11	12	13	14	15
			VIRGINIA—Cont'd															
51 685	47900	1	Manassas Park city	7	14 273	2 157	2 039.0	45.1	13.9	0.7	10.4	32.5	9.1	19.4	9.5	19.3	17.0	12.7
51 690	32300	4	Martinsville city	28	13 821	2 196	493.6	49.9	46.1	0.4	1.1	4.0	6.2	15.2	7.9	10.6	12.1	15.6
51 700	47260	1	Newport News city	178	180 719	342	1 015.3	48.6	41.9	1.3	4.1	7.5	7.4	16.9	13.4	15.6	12.2	14.0
51 710	47260	1	Norfolk city	140	242 803	267	1 734.3	46.6	43.9	1.2	4.6	6.6	6.8	14.1	19.8	17.1	11.4	12.3
51 720	...	7	Norton city	19	3 958	2 914	208.3	90.0	8.0	0.7	1.7	1.7	6.1	15.7	10.1	12.4	12.3	14.7
51 730	40060	1	Petersburg city	59	32 420	1 379	549.5	16.2	79.7	0.8	1.2	3.8	6.5	14.2	11.6	12.9	11.6	15.4
51 735	47260	1	Poquoson city	40	12 150	2 298	303.8	95.0	0.9	0.7	2.8	1.8	4.4	20.0	7.0	8.1	13.0	18.1
51 740	47260	1	Portsmouth city	87	95 535	606	1 098.1	42.1	54.2	1.2	1.8	3.1	7.4	16.3	10.4	15.0	12.0	14.1
51 750	13980	3	Radford city	26	16 408	2 025	631.1	87.9	9.2	0.7	2.2	2.3	3.6	9.4	46.7	9.8	7.7	7.7
51 760	40060	1	Richmond city	155	204 214	300	1 317.5	40.4	51.2	0.8	3.0	6.3	6.3	12.3	18.1	17.2	11.5	12.6
51 770	40220	2	Roanoke city	110	97 032	596	882.1	63.9	29.8	0.7	2.2	5.5	7.2	14.6	8.9	14.9	13.1	14.4
51 775	40220	2	Salem city	37	24 802	1 608	670.3	88.5	7.8	0.5	1.9	2.4	4.8	15.1	13.6	10.1	11.8	14.5
51 790	44420	4	Staunton city	52	23 746	1 654	456.7	84.4	13.6	0.6	1.2	2.2	5.7	13.8	9.6	12.7	11.4	13.7
51 800	47260	1	Suffolk city	1 036	84 585	657	81.6	52.4	43.5	0.8	2.3	2.9	7.0	19.1	7.9	12.0	14.9	16.2
51 810	47260	1	Virginia Beach city	645	437 994	150	679.1	67.2	20.6	1.0	7.8	6.6	6.7	17.4	10.7	15.4	13.6	14.8
51 820	44420	4	Waynesboro city	39	21 006	1 786	538.6	81.9	12.2	0.9	1.2	6.4	7.3	16.0	8.3	14.1	11.7	13.9
51 830	47260	1	Williamsburg city	23	14 068	2 170	611.7	73.3	14.9	0.7	7.1	6.7	3.1	6.9	42.5	11.5	6.6	7.5
51 840	49020	3	Winchester city	24	26 203	1 551	1 091.8	71.1	12.2	0.5	2.8	15.4	6.8	15.4	12.9	14.8	11.8	13.4
53 000	...	X	**WASHINGTON**	172 119	6 724 540	X	39.1	75.8	4.5	2.5	9.7	11.2	6.5	17.0	9.7	13.9	13.5	14.7
53 001	...	6	Adams	4 986	18 728	1 888	3.8	39.4	0.4	0.7	0.8	59.3	10.8	24.0	10.0	13.3	11.7	10.9
53 003	30300	3	Asotin	1 648	21 623	1 757	13.1	94.5	0.9	2.4	1.2	3.0	5.8	15.9	8.1	11.2	10.7	14.7
53 005	28420	3	Benton	4 404	175 177	352	39.8	76.4	1.7	1.5	3.7	18.7	7.5	19.7	9.0	13.2	12.4	14.3
53 007	48300	3	Chelan	7 564	72 453	742	9.6	72.1	0.5	1.5	1.5	25.8	6.8	18.1	8.6	11.6	11.6	14.6
53 009	38820	5	Clallam	4 502	71 404	748	15.9	87.6	1.2	6.7	2.6	5.1	4.7	13.5	7.3	9.9	9.7	14.0
53 011	38900	1	Clark	1 629	425 363	156	261.1	84.8	2.8	1.8	6.4	7.6	6.9	19.5	8.3	12.9	14.0	14.6
53 013	...	6	Columbia	2 250	4 078	2 900	1.8	91.2	0.5	2.2	1.3	6.2	5.3	14.9	5.5	8.5	10.3	15.4
53 015	31020	3	Cowlitz	2 953	102 410	567	34.7	88.5	1.1	3.0	2.6	7.8	6.4	17.7	8.2	11.4	12.3	14.7
53 017	48300	3	Douglas	4 712	38 431	1 208	8.2	69.3	0.5	1.5	1.5	28.7	7.3	20.0	8.3	12.2	12.1	13.7
53 019	...	9	Ferry	5 706	7 551	2 638	1.3	79.2	0.7	19.7	1.6	3.4	5.1	14.7	8.5	8.6	9.8	15.3
53 021	28420	3	Franklin	3 217	78 163	695	24.3	44.5	2.1	0.9	2.5	51.2	10.6	23.6	10.3	16.2	13.0	10.7
53 023	...	8	Garfield	1 841	2 266	3 031	1.2	93.9	0.3	0.7	2.3	4.0	4.2	15.8	5.8	8.6	9.8	15.4
53 025	34180	4	Grant	6 940	89 120	635	12.8	58.9	1.2	1.7	1.4	38.3	9.1	21.5	10.0	13.1	12.0	12.1
53 027	10140	4	Grays Harbor	4 926	72 797	741	14.8	84.3	1.5	6.1	2.6	8.6	5.9	15.7	8.6	11.8	11.8	14.9
53 029	36020	4	Island	540	78 506	691	145.4	86.4	3.1	1.9	7.0	5.5	5.8	15.0	8.8	11.6	10.8	14.0
53 031	...	6	Jefferson	4 672	29 872	1 431	6.4	92.1	1.2	3.9	2.8	2.8	3.6	11.3	5.3	7.8	9.1	15.1
53 033	42660	1	King	5 479	1 931 249	14	352.5	68.3	7.3	1.7	17.9	8.9	6.2	15.2	9.2	16.2	15.4	15.1
53 035	14740	3	Kitsap	1 023	251 133	259	245.5	83.5	3.7	3.0	8.7	6.2	5.9	16.6	10.1	12.5	12.2	15.4
53 037	21260	6	Kittitas	5 950	40 915	1 155	6.9	88.4	1.3	1.9	3.2	7.6	5.0	13.3	23.1	11.7	10.0	12.4
53 039	...	6	Klickitat	4 847	20 318	1 823	4.2	86.1	0.5	3.7	1.5	10.7	5.5	16.6	6.1	9.6	11.8	15.1
53 041	16500	4	Lewis	6 223	75 455	718	12.1	88.4	0.9	2.8	1.7	8.7	6.1	17.1	8.4	11.2	11.4	14.5
53 043	...	8	Lincoln	5 984	10 570	2 398	1.8	95.4	0.5	2.9	0.9	2.3	5.2	17.5	5.8	8.2	9.9	15.8
53 045	43220	6	Mason	2 485	60 699	850	24.4	86.1	1.5	5.0	2.7	8.0	5.4	15.0	7.6	11.4	11.5	15.1
53 047	...	6	Okanogan	13 644	41 120	1 152	3.0	70.6	0.7	12.5	1.0	17.6	6.8	16.7	7.2	10.5	11.1	14.6
53 049	...	7	Pacific	2 416	20 920	1 793	8.7	87.3	0.6	4.1	2.9	8.0	4.8	13.2	6.2	8.7	9.5	14.1
53 051	...	8	Pend Oreille	3 626	13 001	2 243	3.6	92.0	0.8	5.2	1.2	3.0	5.4	16.2	5.6	8.0	10.6	16.4
53 053	42660	1	Pierce	4 324	795 225	72	183.9	75.2	8.8	2.7	10.2	9.2	7.0	17.9	9.9	14.1	13.6	15.0
53 055	...	9	San Juan	450	15 769	2 064	35.0	92.2	0.5	1.7	2.0	5.4	3.4	12.4	4.6	8.0	10.0	16.0
53 057	34580	3	Skagit	4 484	116 901	511	26.1	78.7	1.0	2.8	2.7	16.9	6.5	17.2	8.2	12.1	11.8	14.1
53 059	38900	1	Skamania	4 288	11 066	2 359	2.6	92.1	0.7	3.0	1.7	5.0	5.5	16.8	6.3	10.3	12.5	17.7
53 061	42660	1	Snohomish	5 406	713 335	83	132.0	77.6	3.4	2.3	11.5	9.0	6.6	17.8	8.8	13.9	14.6	16.0
53 063	44060	2	Spokane	4 568	471 221	138	103.2	89.7	2.7	2.7	3.7	4.5	6.4	16.8	11.4	13.2	12.3	14.4
53 065	...	6	Stevens	6 417	43 531	1 095	6.8	90.8	0.7	7.3	1.5	2.7	5.3	18.8	6.2	8.5	11.1	16.0
53 067	36500	3	Thurston	1 870	252 264	258	134.9	82.8	3.8	2.6	8.2	7.1	6.1	16.9	9.1	13.5	13.1	14.7
53 069	...	8	Wahkiakum	682	3 978	2 909	5.8	95.1	0.5	3.3	1.3	2.7	4.0	14.5	4.3	7.6	9.7	14.2
53 071	47460	4	Walla Walla	3 290	58 781	871	17.9	76.0	2.2	1.6	2.5	19.7	6.0	16.5	13.2	12.4	11.5	13.4
53 073	13380	3	Whatcom	5 457	201 140	306	36.9	84.6	1.6	3.7	5.3	7.8	5.6	15.3	14.2	13.0	11.9	13.6
53 075	39420	4	Whitman	5 592	44 776	1 073	8.0	85.0	2.2	1.6	9.8	4.6	4.4	10.6	36.4	13.3	8.2	9.4
53 077	49420	3	Yakima	11 125	243 231	266	21.9	49.2	1.1	4.7	1.6	45.0	8.8	21.6	9.9	13.1	12.1	12.5
54 000	...	X	**WEST VIRGINIA**	62 259	1 852 994	X	29.8	94.4	4.1	0.7	0.9	1.2	5.6	15.3	9.1	11.9	12.8	14.9
54 001	...	7	Barbour	883	16 589	2 010	18.8	97.8	1.4	1.3	0.3	0.6	5.7	16.0	9.4	10.6	12.8	14.9
54 003	25180	3	Berkeley	832	104 169	562	125.2	87.9	8.4	0.8	1.3	3.8	7.0	18.2	7.7	13.6	14.6	15.1
54 005	16620	2	Boone	1 299	24 629	1 620	19.0	98.9	0.7	0.4	0.1	0.4	6.2	16.6	7.2	11.6	13.9	14.9
54 007	...	8	Braxton	1 323	14 523	2 145	11.0	98.6	0.7	0.7	0.3	0.5	5.4	15.3	7.5	10.7	12.7	15.3

1. CBSA = Core Based Statistical Area. See Appendix A for explanation. See Appendix B for list of metropolitan areas with component counties.   2. County type code from the Economic Research Service of USDA Rural-Urban Continuum Codes. See Appendix A for definition.   3. Dry land or land partially or temporarily covered by water.   4. May be of any race.

Table B. States and Counties — **Population and Households**

STATE County	Age (percent) (cont.)				Population change and components of change, 1990–2010							Households, 2010				
	55 to 64 years	65 to 74 years	75 years and over	Percent female	Total persons		Percent change		Components of change, 2000–2009				Percent change, 2000–2010	Persons per house-hold	Female family house-holder[1]	One per-son
					1990	2000	1990–2000	2000–2010	Births	Deaths	Net migration	Number				
	16	17	18	19	20	21	22	23	24	25	26	27	28	29	30	31

VIRGINIA—Cont'd																
Manassas Park city	7.4	3.5	2.1	49.3	6 798	10 290	51.4	38.7	2 277	307	-182	4 507	38.5	3.17	13.1	21.3
Martinsville city	13.2	9.2	9.9	54.5	16 162	15 416	-4.6	-10.3	1 627	2 254	-72	6 084	-6.4	2.21	21.5	37.5
Newport News city	9.9	5.7	4.9	51.7	171 477	180 150	5.1	0.3	29 641	12 825	-16 789	70 664	1.4	2.45	18.9	29.1
Norfolk city	9.1	4.7	4.7	48.2	261 250	234 403	-10.3	3.6	37 622	18 534	-21 482	86 485	0.3	2.43	19.3	31.1
Norton city	13.9	7.9	6.8	53.9	4 247	3 904	-8.1	1.4	365	417	-121	1 750	1.2	2.22	15.4	37.4
Petersburg city	12.8	7.9	7.0	53.3	37 071	33 740	-9.0	-3.9	5 133	4 322	-1 354	13 634	-1.2	2.30	25.9	36.0
Poquoson city	13.9	9.3	6.2	50.6	11 005	11 566	5.1	5.0	812	839	308	4 525	8.6	2.67	8.7	17.5
Portsmouth city	11.6	6.7	6.6	51.9	103 910	100 565	-3.2	-5.0	14 882	9 768	-5 868	37 324	-2.2	2.47	21.7	29.4
Radford city	6.7	4.3	4.1	52.6	15 940	15 859	-0.5	3.5	1 247	1 045	162	5 990	3.1	2.30	9.3	31.4
Richmond city	10.9	5.6	5.5	52.3	202 713	197 790	-2.4	3.2	28 852	20 278	-1 052	87 151	3.1	2.20	18.9	37.9
Roanoke city	12.7	6.8	7.4	52.2	96 487	94 911	-1.6	2.2	11 943	11 347	-630	42 712	1.7	2.22	17.3	37.1
Salem city	13.0	8.6	8.5	52.6	23 835	24 747	3.8	0.2	2 157	2 755	1 459	10 045	0.9	2.30	13.1	30.9
Staunton city	13.3	9.8	10.0	54.7	24 581	23 853	-3.0	-0.4	2 452	2 772	421	10 480	8.3	2.15	13.1	36.3
Suffolk city	11.4	6.7	4.8	52.0	52 143	63 677	22.1	32.8	10 349	6 141	15 874	30 868	32.6	2.70	16.2	20.9
Virginia Beach city	10.8	5.9	4.7	51.0	393 089	425 257	8.2	3.0	59 209	23 852	-24 973	165 089	6.9	2.60	13.9	23.3
Waynesboro city	11.7	8.6	8.4	52.4	18 549	19 520	5.2	7.6	2 726	2 185	2 291	8 903	6.9	2.34	15.3	30.8
Williamsburg city	8.6	7.6	5.7	52.9	11 600	11 998	3.4	17.3	1 504	1 055	325	4 571	26.3	2.17	9.4	31.4
Winchester city	10.9	6.7	7.3	50.8	21 947	23 585	7.5	11.1	3 776	2 384	1 453	10 607	6.1	2.38	13.0	34.3
WASHINGTON	12.4	6.8	5.5	50.2	4 866 669	5 894 121	21.1	14.1	772 324	424 029	440 988	2 620 076	15.4	2.51	10.5	27.2
Adams	9.0	5.6	4.6	49.0	13 603	16 428	20.8	14.0	3 506	962	-1 185	5 720	9.4	3.25	11.8	18.8
Asotin	14.3	10.7	8.6	51.7	17 605	20 551	16.7	5.2	2 330	1 918	593	9 236	10.4	2.32	12.1	29.4
Benton	12.2	6.6	5.2	50.1	112 560	142 475	26.6	23.0	20 841	9 699	15 340	65 304	23.5	2.66	11.1	24.3
Chelan	13.3	8.0	7.4	50.1	52 250	66 616	27.5	8.8	8 773	5 402	2 744	27 827	11.2	2.57	9.7	26.3
Clallam	16.9	12.9	11.2	50.4	56 210	64 525	14.8	10.7	5 846	7 759	9 466	31 329	15.3	2.22	9.2	30.4
Clark	12.3	6.6	4.8	50.6	238 053	345 238	45.0	23.2	51 962	23 977	60 423	158 099	24.3	2.67	11.3	23.1
Columbia	17.0	12.9	10.1	50.4	4 024	4 064	1.0	0.3	330	444	107	1 762	4.4	2.27	9.2	29.3
Cowlitz	13.8	8.6	6.8	50.6	82 119	92 948	13.2	10.2	11 793	9 000	6 806	40 244	12.3	2.51	11.8	25.8
Douglas	12.2	7.9	6.3	50.0	26 205	32 603	24.4	17.9	4 572	2 410	3 021	13 894	18.5	2.75	10.7	20.8
Ferry	19.1	11.9	7.0	48.3	6 295	7 260	15.3	4.0	669	619	242	3 190	13.0	2.29	9.2	28.5
Franklin	8.4	4.2	3.1	48.3	37 473	49 347	31.7	58.4	13 098	2 738	17 804	23 245	56.6	3.28	13.4	16.4
Garfield	18.1	9.8	12.6	50.7	2 248	2 397	6.6	-5.5	158	231	-213	989	0.2	2.25	6.1	30.2
Grant	10.4	6.6	5.3	49.0	54 798	74 698	36.3	19.3	13 642	5 271	5 529	30 041	19.2	2.93	11.5	22.0
Grays Harbor	15.0	9.4	6.8	48.7	64 175	67 194	4.7	8.3	7 805	7 248	4 443	28 579	6.6	2.45	11.8	27.6
Island	15.7	10.8	7.6	50.5	60 195	71 558	18.9	9.7	8 765	5 709	6 484	32 746	17.9	2.35	7.9	28.9
Jefferson	21.6	15.8	10.4	50.5	20 406	25 953	27.2	15.1	1 984	2 757	4 268	14 049	20.6	2.08	7.3	32.2
King	11.8	5.8	5.1	50.2	1 507 305	1 737 034	15.2	11.2	212 511	106 885	70 745	789 232	11.0	2.40	9.1	31.0
Kitsap	14.1	7.6	5.6	49.4	189 731	231 969	22.3	8.3	27 437	16 612	-897	97 220	12.5	2.49	10.2	25.2
Kittitas	11.8	7.6	5.2	49.2	26 725	33 362	24.8	22.6	3 467	2 318	5 222	16 595	24.0	2.32	7.3	28.7
Klickitat	17.4	11.0	6.8	49.5	16 616	19 161	15.3	6.0	2 115	1 575	968	8 327	11.4	2.42	8.5	26.4
Lewis	14.0	9.7	7.7	50.0	59 358	68 600	15.6	10.0	8 337	7 128	5 302	29 743	13.1	2.51	10.9	25.7
Lincoln	16.9	11.7	9.1	50.1	8 864	10 184	14.9	3.8	914	1 033	229	4 422	6.5	2.37	7.7	27.1
Mason	15.8	10.8	7.5	48.3	38 341	49 405	28.9	22.9	5 553	5 073	8 411	23 832	26.0	2.45	9.5	25.3
Okanogan	15.9	10.2	7.0	49.5	33 350	39 564	18.6	3.9	4 883	3 420	-276	16 519	9.9	2.45	10.7	28.0
Pacific	18.8	14.4	10.4	49.9	18 882	20 984	11.1	-0.3	1 888	2 740	1 241	9 499	4.4	2.17	8.1	33.0
Pend Oreille	18.6	11.9	7.3	49.3	8 915	11 732	31.6	10.8	1 135	1 208	1 361	5 479	18.1	2.35	9.1	28.2
Pierce	11.5	6.2	4.9	50.6	586 203	700 820	19.6	13.5	97 668	50 675	53 118	299 918	15.0	2.59	13.0	25.1
San Juan	22.5	14.4	8.8	51.4	10 035	14 077	40.3	12.0	945	1 108	1 653	7 613	17.7	2.05	6.6	34.0
Skagit	13.9	8.8	7.4	50.4	79 545	102 979	29.5	13.5	13 550	9 372	12 884	45 557	17.3	2.53	10.1	25.6
Skamania	16.6	8.9	5.6	49.7	8 289	9 872	19.1	12.1	962	676	792	4 522	20.4	2.44	8.9	25.6
Snohomish	11.9	5.8	4.6	50.0	465 628	606 024	30.2	17.7	82 473	38 302	48 244	268 325	19.3	2.62	10.4	24.3
Spokane	12.5	6.8	6.1	50.6	361 333	417 939	15.7	12.7	53 083	34 345	34 266	187 167	14.4	2.44	11.2	28.6
Stevens	16.7	10.8	6.4	50.0	30 948	40 066	29.5	8.6	4 402	3 660	1 785	17 316	15.3	2.50	9.0	24.6
Thurston	13.6	7.2	5.7	51.3	161 238	207 355	28.6	21.7	25 107	15 894	35 240	100 650	23.3	2.46	11.4	25.9
Wahkiakum	20.3	16.1	9.4	49.7	3 327	3 824	14.9	4.0	285	451	415	1 737	11.8	2.26	6.2	26.8
Walla Walla	12.0	7.1	7.9	49.2	48 439	55 180	13.9	6.5	6 570	4 943	2 565	21 719	10.5	2.50	10.5	28.2
Whatcom	13.0	7.3	6.0	50.5	127 780	166 814	30.5	20.6	19 800	12 286	26 920	80 370	24.7	2.43	8.8	27.8
Whitman	8.1	5.0	4.5	49.1	38 775	40 740	5.1	9.9	3 839	2 038	327	17 468	14.5	2.22	5.4	32.7
Yakima	10.4	6.2	5.3	50.0	188 823	222 581	17.9	9.3	39 326	16 143	-5 419	80 592	8.9	2.97	14.7	21.6
WEST VIRGINIA	14.3	8.8	7.2	50.7	1 793 477	1 808 344	0.8	2.5	192 926	193 308	21 653	763 831	3.7	2.36	11.2	28.4
Barbour	13.9	9.4	7.2	50.6	15 699	15 557	-0.9	6.6	1 583	1 760	466	6 548	6.9	2.46	10.9	24.2
Berkeley	12.4	6.9	4.5	50.4	59 253	75 905	28.1	37.2	11 660	6 719	23 220	39 855	34.8	2.59	12.0	23.4
Boone	15.3	8.2	6.0	50.3	25 870	25 535	-1.3	-3.5	2 977	2 857	-831	9 928	-3.5	2.47	11.3	25.7
Braxton	15.5	10.0	7.5	49.6	12 998	14 702	13.1	-1.2	1 399	1 601	25	6 000	4.0	2.36	9.5	27.9

1. No spouse present.

STATE County	Persons in group quarters, 2010	Daytime population, 2006–2010 Number	Daytime population, 2006–2010 Employment/residence ratio	Births, average 2006–2008 Total	Births, average 2006–2008 Rate[1]	Deaths, average 2006–2008 Number	Deaths, average 2006–2008 Rate[1]	Persons under 65 with no health insurance, 2009 Number	Persons under 65 with no health insurance, 2009 Percent	Medicare, 2011 Eligible for Medicare	Medicare, 2011 Enrolled in Medicare Advantage	Medicare, 2011 Enrolled in a Medicare prescription drug plan	Serious crimes known to police,[2] 2010 Total Number	Serious crimes known to police,[2] 2010 Total Rate[3]
	32	33	34	35	36	37	38	39	40	41	42	43	44	45
VIRGINIA—Cont'd														
Manassas Park city	6	9 099	0.4	D	D	41	3.6	2 129	19.6	898	115	352	220	1 541
Martinsville city	377	17 791	1.7	D	D	233	15.9	1 898	17.6	3 713	793	2 454	491	3 553
Newport News city	7 499	198 891	1.2	3 244	18.1	1 351	7.5	24 418	14.8	23 829	3 683	8 061	7 621	4 217
Norfolk city	32 780	309 689	1.6	4 130	17.7	2 005	8.6	35 435	17.7	28 564	4 514	10 785	14 651	6 034
Norton city	68	7 016	2.8	D	D	32	8.8	456	15.2	1 136	240	556	245	6 190
Petersburg city	1 058	34 409	1.2	609	18.6	429	13.1	4 374	16.7	6 695	789	3 323	1 694	5 225
Poquoson city	51	8 971	0.5	D	D	99	8.4	934	9.8	2 167	157	544	144	1 185
Portsmouth city	3 416	108 212	1.3	1 648	16.3	1 025	10.1	12 945	15.6	16 152	2 528	5 650	6 120	6 406
Radford city	2 652	16 971	1.1	D	D	112	7.2	2 097	15.3	1 919	242	1 143	527	3 212
Richmond city	12 725	268 594	1.7	3 217	16.2	2 026	10.2	29 584	17.8	29 076	5 997	13 506	10 109	4 950
Roanoke city	2 126	124 032	1.6	1 530	16.6	1 206	13.1	13 522	17.9	18 242	3 062	9 079	5 424	5 590
Salem city	1 718	34 848	1.9	D	D	281	11.2	2 621	12.8	5 443	686	2 754	717	2 891
Staunton city	1 185	24 565	1.1	D	D	300	12.6	2 936	16.1	5 633	479	3 087	564	2 375
Suffolk city	1 128	72 495	0.7	1 162	14.2	686	8.4	9 599	13.5	12 676	1 959	5 010	2 334	2 759
Virginia Beach city	9 253	401 154	0.8	6 482	14.9	2 627	6.0	46 918	12.5	54 768	6 402	16 709	14 156	3 232
Waynesboro city	192	21 406	1.1	D	D	237	10.9	2 903	16.5	4 377	413	2 594	725	3 451
Williamsburg city	4 171	22 732	2.6	D	D	101	8.3	1 208	11.9	2 158	209	875	285	2 026
Winchester city	976	37 510	1.9	445	17.4	264	10.3	4 166	19.9	4 462	342	2 198	1 183	4 515
WASHINGTON	139 375	6 510 949	1.0	88 725	13.7	47 357	7.3	865 282	15.0	1 017 567	265 711	363 475	270 354	4 020
Adams	162	17 711	1.0	410	24.0	109	6.4	3 408	21.7	2 186	292	1 112	927	4 950
Asotin	174	18 545	0.7	D	D	218	10.2	2 549	15.0	5 206	664	2 322	611	2 826
Benton	1 428	165 070	1.0	2 414	15.0	1 145	7.1	20 734	14.3	25 370	3 195	11 786	4 739	2 705
Chelan	928	76 785	1.2	1 026	14.4	606	8.5	11 826	19.8	13 500	1 775	6 119	2 165	2 988
Clallam	1 899	70 073	1.0	644	9.1	910	12.9	9 940	18.4	20 504	1 457	9 348	2 277	3 189
Clark	3 210	369 764	0.8	5 855	14.0	2 700	6.5	55 039	14.6	61 550	30 125	13 729	13 105	3 081
Columbia	75	3 804	0.9	D	D	49	12.2	540	17.2	1 062	24	571	197	4 831
Cowlitz	1 207	98 538	0.9	1 350	13.4	1 011	10.1	13 873	16.1	20 639	8 346	6 135	3 923	3 831
Douglas	190	30 479	0.6	561	15.5	267	7.4	6 560	20.5	6 185	749	2 856	714	1 858
Ferry	252	7 478	1.0	D	D	78	10.5	1 244	20.1	1 781	198	778	50	662
Franklin	1 846	71 725	1.0	1 592	22.9	323	4.6	16 995	24.2	7 432	909	3 734	1 878	2 403
Garfield	36	2 141	0.9	D	D	27	12.9	265	17.0	553	58	318	57	2 515
Grant	1 245	86 564	1.0	1 584	19.0	592	7.1	16 374	21.5	12 831	1 433	6 389	4 572	5 435
Grays Harbor	2 731	70 079	0.9	889	12.4	778	10.9	11 726	19.7	15 273	668	8 196	2 806	3 855
Island	1 466	71 623	0.8	959	11.8	622	7.6	7 950	12.6	16 467	4 326	4 811	1 265	1 611
Jefferson	631	28 455	0.9	D	D	317	10.8	3 375	15.4	9 175	609	4 233	773	2 588
King	37 131	2 044 829	1.2	24 803	13.4	11 774	6.4	217 449	12.9	249 602	71 140	92 097	84 865	4 394
Kitsap	8 722	237 117	0.9	2 995	12.5	1 854	7.8	27 146	13.2	40 623	6 763	12 141	7 455	2 969
Kittitas	2 417	38 385	0.9	D	D	260	6.8	6 220	18.4	6 245	216	2 970	1 847	4 514
Klickitat	198	19 071	0.9	D	D	164	8.1	3 353	20.0	4 622	164	2 456	431	2 121
Lewis	941	72 384	0.9	D	D	730	9.9	9 932	16.3	16 377	3 940	6 353	2 897	3 904
Lincoln	94	9 795	0.8	D	D	115	11.1	1 193	14.9	2 545	272	1 397	171	1 618
Mason	2 332	53 251	0.7	635	11.2	589	10.4	8 362	17.7	13 513	2 624	5 174	2 741	4 516
Okanogan	640	40 497	1.0	D	D	377	9.5	8 158	24.5	8 756	807	4 177	856	2 094
Pacific	292	19 948	0.8	D	D	296	13.8	3 141	19.9	6 240	578	3 149	681	3 255
Pend Oreille	98	12 107	0.8	D	D	145	11.3	1 551	14.7	3 129	464	1 345	438	3 369
Pierce	17 945	738 576	0.9	11 362	14.7	5 644	7.3	102 493	14.7	112 378	27 432	35 744	35 919	4 517
San Juan	187	15 462	1.0	D	D	128	8.4	1 977	16.9	4 045	733	1 642	201	1 275
Skagit	1 624	114 200	1.0	1 564	13.4	1 051	9.0	17 408	17.5	22 715	6 888	7 558	6 063	5 186
Skamania	25	9 319	0.7	D	D	75	7.0	1 357	14.6	1 826	214	812	232	2 295
Snohomish	10 397	619 473	0.8	9 484	14.0	4 281	6.3	83 593	13.5	90 997	33 961	26 794	24 448	3 427
Spokane	14 692	470 479	1.0	6 045	13.3	3 876	8.5	59 673	14.9	78 258	21 884	27 348	25 447	5 400
Stevens	266	38 845	0.7	465	11.0	403	9.6	5 969	17.1	9 453	1 226	4 075	1 199	2 773
Thurston	4 222	230 553	0.9	2 929	12.2	1 846	7.7	28 758	13.3	41 373	12 732	10 700	8 714	3 454
Wahkiakum	48	3 608	0.7	D	D	52	12.8	463	15.2	1 103	213	423	33	830
Walla Walla	4 489	59 805	1.1	702	12.2	560	9.7	9 167	18.7	10 584	1 074	4 669	1 980	3 368
Whatcom	5 704	191 746	1.0	2 200	11.5	1 385	7.2	29 077	17.0	33 362	10 885	11 474	6 362	3 163
Whitman	5 948	46 064	1.1	D	D	223	5.4	5 554	14.7	4 893	271	2 227	995	2 237
Yakima	3 485	236 601	1.0	4 438	19.0	1 778	7.6	50 892	24.6	35 214	6 402	16 313	11 959	4 917
WEST VIRGINIA	49 382	1 820 041	1.0	21 475	11.9	21 105	11.7	250 222	16.8	389 822	87 043	204 545	47 330	2 554
Barbour	469	13 878	0.6	D	D	181	11.6	2 393	18.7	3 525	649	1 948	135	814
Berkeley	910	85 465	0.7	1 423	14.3	762	7.6	13 856	15.4	15 983	2 346	6 123	2 542	2 440
Boone	131	26 593	1.2	334	13.2	349	13.8	3 325	15.9	5 414	1 110	3 288	491	2 432
Braxton	335	13 705	0.8	D	D	183	12.4	2 305	19.6	3 190	842	1 744	158	1 305

1. Per 1,000 estimated resident population.   2. Data for serious crimes have not been adjusted for underreporting; this may affect comparability between geographic areas and over time.   3. Per 100,000 population estimated by the FBI.

STATE County	Serious crimes known to police,[1] 2010 (cont.) Rate[2]		Education School enrollment and attainment, 2006-2010				Local government expenditures,[5] 2008-2009		Money income, 2006-2010	Households			Income and poverty, 2010 Percent below poverty level		
			Enrollment[3]		Attainment[4] (percent)					Median income					
	Violent	Property	Total	Per-cent private	High school grad-uate or less	Bach-elor's degree or more	Total current expendi-tures (mil dol)	Current expendi-tures per student (dollars)	Per capita income[6] (dollars)	Dollars	Percent change, 2000 to 2006-2010 (constant 2010 dollars)	Percent with income of $200,000 or more	Median house-hold income (dollars)	All per-sons	Children under 18 years	Children 5 to 17 years in families
	46	47	48	49	50	51	52	53	54	55	56	57	58	59	60	61

STATE County	46	47	48	49	50	51	52	53	54	55	56	57	58	59	60	61
VIRGINIA—Cont'd																
Manassas Park city	126	1 415	3 606	13.7	52.5	21.9	28.7	11 664	27 335	70 299	-8.7	3.2	67 948	8.6	13.6	12.5
Martinsville city	282	3 270	3 246	13.5	52.1	20.4	27.2	10 673	19 766	32 408	-6.7	2.2	29 887	24.0	36.1	34.1
Newport News city	544	3 673	52 502	14.2	40.4	23.5	321.7	10 277	24 249	49 562	6.9	1.9	49 228	15.1	23.3	21.2
Norfolk city	597	5 437	66 489	14.7	45.9	23.7	359.7	10 447	23 773	42 677	5.9	2.2	41 015	19.0	25.5	24.5
Norton city	126	6 064	953	3.6	46.1	20.6	7.2	8 883	24 145	33 944	17.6	1.8	33 662	19.5	31.6	29.0
Petersburg city	583	4 642	6 834	4.7	61.6	15.2	50.1	10 713	19 142	36 449	-0.2	0.8	32 435	25.2	41.4	34.8
Poquoson city	66	1 119	3 403	10.1	31.1	36.0	22.5	9 024	36 840	84 315	9.3	7.6	79 229	5.4	6.6	5.3
Portsmouth city	639	5 768	24 929	16.2	49.1	18.7	159.6	10 413	22 302	45 488	6.5	1.1	42 740	18.3	28.5	26.1
Radford city	390	2 822	9 006	1.9	35.9	35.1	14.6	9 739	16 496	29 155	-6.6	1.0	34 009	25.6	19.3	16.9
Richmond city	741	4 209	57 255	19.9	44.1	32.6	311.1	13 423	26 034	38 266	-2.9	3.5	39 214	25.3	35.0	33.8
Roanoke city	697	4 893	21 928	12.3	49.6	21.9	147.9	11 189	22 530	36 422	-6.4	1.5	37 486	22.4	33.9	31.7
Salem city	137	2 754	7 049	36.1	43.8	29.1	39.8	10 135	27 081	48 828	-1.1	3.8	46 636	9.7	13.2	11.9
Staunton city	126	2 249	5 326	25.3	49.4	28.5	32.1	11 738	24 077	42 724	2.4	1.3	40 855	15.2	23.7	22.1
Suffolk city	316	2 444	22 334	19.0	44.4	25.1	139.3	9 885	28 441	65 104	25.0	2.8	62 419	11.9	17.2	15.4
Virginia Beach city	190	3 042	120 421	17.4	32.1	31.9	755.5	10 559	30 873	64 618	4.8	3.9	63 354	8.0	11.0	10.2
Waynesboro city	343	3 109	4 494	11.1	56.8	21.8	31.0	9 733	23 190	40 977	-1.0	2.2	40 256	17.5	27.3	27.9
Williamsburg city	128	1 898	6 878	2.8	28.3	43.3	(7)	(7)	22 851	50 794	8.1	6.3	46 285	18.5	22.7	21.5
Winchester city	214	4 301	5 964	16.5	48.2	29.7	(8)	(8)	26 341	44 873	3.2	2.9	41 008	19.3	24.7	22.6
WASHINGTON	314	3 707	1 661 690	14.9	34.7	31.0	9 894.8	9 552	29 733	57 244	-1.2	4.1	55 584	13.5	18.2	16.1
Adams	331	4 619	4 542	7.7	61.2	13.4	40.5	9 720	16 689	40 829	-4.9	1.6	41 099	20.4	30.4	27.9
Asotin	185	2 641	4 645	12.9	46.4	18.2	33.2	10 048	23 731	41 665	-1.9	2.4	39 340	15.8	25.5	22.4
Benton	218	2 487	44 036	10.1	37.6	27.6	284.3	9 027	27 161	57 354	-3.7	3.0	59 409	12.8	18.4	15.6
Chelan	161	2 827	16 551	10.1	45.0	23.2	127.1	9 879	24 378	48 674	3.0	2.4	45 561	14.2	21.7	19.8
Clallam	269	2 920	13 644	12.1	37.1	23.3	94.9	8 937	24 449	44 398	-3.8	1.4	42 111	15.5	23.3	19.3
Clark	233	2 848	109 800	12.2	35.8	25.7	718.8	9 381	27 828	58 262	-4.9	3.2	55 144	12.7	17.6	15.5
Columbia	98	4 733	810	5.2	39.7	20.0	6.0	11 048	25 810	43 611	2.8	2.6	41 244	14.6	21.0	18.6
Cowlitz	319	3 511	25 054	12.1	44.7	14.7	161.1	9 091	22 948	45 877	-9.0	1.3	43 031	20.6	28.7	22.3
Douglas	109	1 749	9 632	7.1	47.2	17.3	67.1	9 773	22 359	48 708	0.0	1.6	48 113	14.2	21.5	18.9
Ferry	106	556	1 690	0.4	50.7	16.7	12.4	11 806	18 021	35 485	-7.8	1.6	35 721	21.0	27.9	24.7
Franklin	270	2 133	20 893	10.0	58.0	14.6	148.8	9 382	18 660	47 749	-3.3	2.0	49 873	18.8	24.9	24.1
Garfield	132	2 383	453	2.8	42.9	17.7	4.2	12 613	22 825	42 269	-0.1	0.7	41 482	18.9	19.6	16.3
Grant	294	5 141	23 009	6.0	54.6	14.4	175.2	9 593	19 718	42 572	-4.7	2.1	42 514	21.7	30.1	25.4
Grays Harbor	181	3 673	16 076	7.3	48.5	14.5	114.2	10 159	21 656	41 899	-3.1	1.2	40 281	17.9	28.6	25.6
Island	130	1 481	16 857	14.3	29.9	29.8	76.1	8 732	29 079	57 190	-0.8	2.4	54 714	9.7	14.6	12.3
Jefferson	204	2 384	4 909	12.7	30.7	34.8	30.3	10 353	28 528	46 048	-4.0	2.3	45 600	12.0	22.0	19.6
King	340	4 054	461 310	19.8	25.8	45.2	2 331.1	9 759	38 211	68 065	1.1	7.4	66 147	12.2	15.3	13.3
Kitsap	398	2 571	59 581	14.6	31.4	28.0	369.6	9 716	29 755	59 549	0.4	3.6	57 107	11.3	14.9	13.2
Kittitas	139	4 375	14 311	4.4	39.1	31.9	48.4	9 003	23 467	41 232	0.0	1.5	40 376	20.9	18.7	16.9
Klickitat	79	2 043	4 418	9.6	48.1	17.9	35.2	10 804	21 553	37 398	-13.8	1.8	42 510	17.4	29.0	25.5
Lewis	236	3 668	17 172	10.7	47.9	15.0	115.3	9 418	21 695	43 874	-2.4	1.1	40 109	16.5	22.2	19.2
Lincoln	66	1 552	2 251	13.1	39.9	20.3	28.2	13 117	24 757	45 582	2.1	2.5	48 746	11.7	18.1	16.3
Mason	308	4 208	12 674	9.0	45.2	17.9	79.2	9 620	22 530	48 104	-4.0	1.4	46 062	16.0	22.3	19.1
Okanogan	159	1 935	8 661	8.6	48.7	17.7	66.8	10 731	20 093	38 551	2.4	1.4	35 682	22.0	31.9	30.1
Pacific	163	3 093	3 818	8.0	46.3	16.8	33.2	11 681	23 326	39 642	0.3	1.3	37 832	17.9	26.7	24.2
Pend Oreille	123	3 246	2 549	8.5	46.2	17.9	18.9	10 661	22 546	38 896	-3.0	1.8	39 035	18.9	29.2	26.4
Pierce	480	4 037	201 178	15.7	39.7	23.4	1 231.2	9 417	27 446	57 869	1.1	2.8	56 446	12.3	17.1	15.7
San Juan	89	1 186	2 289	15.0	24.3	44.9	18.9	11 564	35 487	50 726	-7.9	4.9	50 836	11.8	20.1	17.5
Skagit	211	4 975	26 262	9.2	37.7	23.2	196.6	10 187	26 925	54 811	2.1	2.5	54 600	13.0	20.5	18.9
Skamania	99	2 196	2 435	4.3	37.3	19.7	14.5	11 185	24 140	48 704	-2.2	0.8	47 804	13.8	19.5	17.2
Snohomish	225	3 202	174 667	14.3	34.9	28.2	1 158.8	9 085	30 635	66 300	-1.3	3.7	63 391	10.0	12.9	11.3
Spokane	347	5 053	123 841	17.8	33.3	27.9	721.1	9 542	25 127	47 250	0.0	2.7	46 881	14.7	17.7	15.9
Stevens	127	2 645	10 178	12.3	42.9	19.2	70.9	10 331	21 773	42 845	-2.4	1.1	41 147	17.4	26.9	23.0
Thurston	249	3 205	61 363	11.8	31.6	31.6	379.6	9 201	29 707	60 930	2.4	2.8	60 672	10.7	14.2	12.1
Wahkiakum	50	779	746	7.6	40.3	15.3	4.4	9 373	23 115	40 372	-19.2	1.4	44 740	13.8	26.1	22.5
Walla Walla	259	3 110	16 829	26.3	38.7	24.2	87.8	9 990	23 027	45 575	0.3	2.3	43 119	15.7	22.2	19.5
Whatcom	220	2 943	56 173	13.1	33.8	31.7	247.5	9 358	25 407	49 031	-3.2	2.4	49 999	14.4	16.3	14.3
Whitman	139	2 097	22 496	3.3	23.5	47.4	52.6	11 580	19 506	36 368	0.5	2.0	39 251	24.4	15.7	13.9
Yakima	340	4 577	64 077	8.6	56.7	15.6	490.9	9 844	19 325	42 877	-2.8	1.8	40 503	23.9	35.4	32.4
WEST VIRGINIA	315	2 240	421 148	10.7	59.4	17.3	2 922.5	10 367	21 232	38 380	2.1	1.5	38 241	18.2	25.7	23.4
Barbour	175	639	3 810	18.1	68.5	13.3	24.3	9 744	17 304	31 212	-0.3	0.9	31 634	17.6	29.8	27.6
Berkeley	194	2 246	24 940	14.5	54.6	19.7	172.0	9 994	25 460	52 857	7.7	1.7	50 923	12.7	18.2	16.1
Boone	287	2 145	4 935	4.0	73.4	8.2	53.2	11 500	20 457	39 783	22.4	0.9	38 126	18.9	26.0	23.3
Braxton	215	1 090	2 753	5.2	72.5	9.5	24.0	10 485	17 469	32 158	4.0	0.5	32 606	23.6	33.9	31.4

1. Data for serious crimes have not been adjusted for underreporting; this may affect comparability between geographic areas and over time.   2. Per 100,000 population estimated by the FBI.   3. All persons 3 years old and over enrolled in nursery school through college.   4. Persons 25 years old and over.   5. Elementary and secondary education expenditures.   6. Based on population estimated by the American Community Survey, 2006-2010.   7. Williamsburg city is included with James City county.   8. Winchester city is included with Frederick county.

STATE County	Personal income, 2009												
	Total (mil dol)	Per capita[1]			Wages and salaries[2] (mil dol)	Proprietors' income (mil dol)	Dividends, interest, and rent (mil dol)	Transfer payments (mil dol)					
		Percent change, 2008–2009	Dollars	Rank				Total	Government payments to individuals				
									Total	Social Security	Medical payments	Income mainte-nance	Unemploy-ment insurance
	62	63	64	65	66	67	68	69	70	71	72	73	74

VIRGINIA—Cont'd													
Manassas Park city	(3)	(3)	(3)	(3)	(3)	(3)	(3)	(3)	(3)	(3)	(3)	(3)	(3)
Martinsville city	(4)	(4)	(4)	(4)	(4)	(4)	(4)	(4)	(4)	(4)	(4)	(4)	(4)
Newport News city	6 011	0.0	31 120	1 726	6 200	199	857	1 118	1 084	321	423	163	41
Norfolk city	8 595	-0.6	36 838	768	13 937	571	1 284	1 555	1 519	362	633	241	58
Norton city	(5)	(5)	(5)	(5)	(5)	(5)	(5)	(5)	(5)	(5)	(5)	(5)	(5)
Petersburg city	(6)	(6)	(6)	(6)	(6)	(6)	(6)	(6)	(6)	(6)	(6)	(6)	(6)
Poquoson city	(7)	(7)	(7)	(7)	(7)	(7)	(7)	(7)	(7)	(7)	(7)	(7)	(7)
Portsmouth city	3 341	0.4	33 637	1 229	3 359	138	415	750	733	192	316	113	25
Radford city	(8)	(8)	(8)	(8)	(8)	(8)	(8)	(8)	(8)	(8)	(8)	(8)	(8)
Richmond city	8 774	-1.5	42 916	273	10 542	960	1 702	1 758	1 720	397	891	242	78
Roanoke city	3 715	1.1	39 315	504	3 625	191	670	887	870	235	391	100	25
Salem city	(9)	(9)	(9)	(9)	(9)	(9)	(9)	(9)	(9)	(9)	(9)	(9)	(9)
Staunton city	(10)	(10)	(10)	(10)	(10)	(10)	(10)	(10)	(10)	(10)	(10)	(10)	(10)
Suffolk city	3 053	1.2	36 494	816	1 380	99	433	489	474	168	176	63	15
Virginia Beach city	19 510	-1.5	44 999	200	10 278	1 192	3 013	2 192	2 119	759	766	189	74
Waynesboro city	(10)	(10)	(10)	(10)	(10)	(10)	(10)	(10)	(10)	(10)	(10)	(10)	(10)
Williamsburg city	(11)	(11)	(11)	(11)	(11)	(11)	(11)	(11)	(11)	(11)	(11)	(11)	(11)
Winchester city	(12)	(12)	(12)	(12)	(12)	(12)	(12)	(12)	(12)	(12)	(12)	(12)	(12)
WASHINGTON	285 696	-0.5	42 870	X	183 679	21 665	57 741	44 837	43 630	14 013	15 593	4 818	3 708
Adams	516	-2.1	29 119	2 166	276	44	118	120	116	30	54	19	5
Asotin	730	0.5	34 077	1 163	219	63	150	200	196	73	79	24	5
Benton	6 447	4.6	38 307	601	4 748	344	1 016	1 071	1 040	368	373	125	58
Chelan	2 550	0.7	35 237	991	1 699	192	543	526	513	184	181	60	33
Clallam	2 560	1.1	35 852	908	1 053	177	764	701	688	285	252	58	31
Clark	15 132	-2.5	35 027	1 016	7 064	1 050	2 984	2 667	2 588	858	899	312	197
Columbia	141	-6.5	34 971	1 025	63	7	30	38	37	14	15	3	1
Cowlitz	3 147	1.1	30 859	1 787	1 830	171	558	889	870	307	306	116	65
Douglas	1 111	1.2	29 565	2 078	423	13	218	285	278	85	131	24	17
Ferry	190	7.1	25 284	2 830	81	7	34	71	69	24	25	9	4
Franklin	2 038	6.6	26 342	2 663	1 243	220	266	439	425	96	181	75	25
Garfield	68	-6.9	32 470	1 435	39	-2	16	19	19	7	8	2	0
Grant	2 557	1.4	29 025	2 192	1 506	272	410	623	607	172	245	91	47
Grays Harbor	2 117	1.2	29 479	2 096	1 058	106	382	683	670	219	263	81	53
Island	2 942	-4.0	36 293	849	1 387	152	844	554	540	235	167	35	30
Jefferson	1 279	-0.5	43 100	267	365	58	464	289	284	129	99	19	12
King	109 053	-2.4	56 904	45	86 944	11 235	25 440	11 466	11 116	3 452	3 850	1 080	1 202
Kitsap	10 454	-0.6	43 404	259	5 938	503	2 251	1 628	1 586	501	574	152	108
Kittitas	1 271	1.0	32 149	1 496	593	127	275	255	248	87	80	23	19
Klickitat	717	4.5	34 872	1 037	338	44	163	179	175	63	67	21	8
Lewis	2 255	1.8	30 169	1 941	1 104	111	413	700	686	231	267	77	51
Lincoln	321	0.0	31 364	1 679	125	20	75	89	87	36	32	7	4
Mason	1 822	1.3	31 411	1 662	620	96	386	514	504	190	182	51	32
Okanogan	1 303	-0.1	32 136	1 498	622	148	230	363	356	115	145	46	20
Pacific	647	2.0	30 403	1 885	247	29	152	227	223	91	83	21	11
Pend Oreille	374	4.8	28 923	2 215	144	18	64	129	126	44	47	16	8
Pierce	32 333	1.5	40 577	414	18 454	1 917	4 835	5 398	5 259	1 549	1 828	623	488
San Juan	881	-3.9	56 873	46	230	45	480	116	113	56	38	5	5
Skagit	4 569	-0.6	38 225	615	2 346	396	1 099	929	907	320	336	92	71
Skamania	362	0.1	33 241	1 301	92	5	73	70	68	26	20	8	6
Snohomish	30 294	1.7	43 616	251	15 766	1 242	4 265	4 104	3 978	1 274	1 283	374	516
Spokane	16 216	0.8	34 599	1 080	10 730	901	3 080	3 523	3 438	1 044	1 311	420	223
Stevens	1 190	1.7	28 109	2 382	435	68	236	369	361	127	132	41	26
Thurston	10 240	1.4	40 801	398	5 453	549	1 771	1 726	1 681	589	555	160	113
Wahkiakum	122	-0.4	30 000	1 978	32	4	32	38	37	17	13	2	2
Walla Walla	1 952	0.3	33 059	1 331	1 263	130	408	421	411	138	156	51	14
Whatcom	7 111	-0.5	35 478	956	4 013	499	1 705	1 309	1 272	448	438	139	99
Whitman	1 209	-1.8	28 320	2 342	880	84	235	223	216	70	71	24	4
Yakima	7 474	0.6	31 265	1 699	4 255	619	1 277	1 886	1 842	456	806	333	98
WEST VIRGINIA	58 378	2.0	32 080	X	34 466	3 962	7 553	15 987	15 655	5 617	6 489	1 568	518
Barbour	400	2.9	25 361	2 822	136	24	50	138	136	47	56	16	5
Berkeley	3 122	2.6	30 059	1 964	1 577	199	353	579	560	225	179	59	31
Boone	681	3.1	27 558	2 475	595	34	53	225	220	86	80	28	6
Braxton	354	3.6	24 522	2 912	165	24	34	119	116	41	45	15	4

1. Based on the resident population estimated as of July 1 of the year shown.   2. Includes supplements to wages and salaries.   3. Manassas and Manassas Park cities are included with Prince William county.   4. Martinsville city is included with Henry county.   5. Norton city is included with Wise county.   6. Petersburg and Colonial Heights cities are included with Dinwiddie county.   7. Poquoson city is included with York county.   8. Radford city is included with Montgomery county.   9. Salem city is included with Roanoke county.   10. Staunton and Waynesboro cities are included with Augusta county.   11. Williamsburg city is included with James City county.   12. Winchester city is included with Frederick county.

Table B. States and Counties — Earnings, Social Security, and Housing

STATE County	Earnings, 2009									Social Security beneficiaries, December 2010		Supplemental Security Income recipients, December 2010	Housing units, 2010	
	Total (mil dol)	Percent by selected industries								Number	Rate²		Total	Percent change, 2000–2010
		Farm	Goods-related¹		Service-related and health				Govern-ment					
			Total	Manu-facturing	Infor-mation and profes-sional and technical services	Retail trade	Finance, insur-ance, and real estate	Health care and social services						
	75	76	77	78	79	80	81	82	83	84	85	86	87	88
VIRGINIA—Cont'd														
Manassas Park city	(3)	(3)	(3)	(3)	(3)	(3)	(3)	(3)	(3)	1 010	71	121	4 904	45.7
Martinsville city	(4)	(4)	(4)	(4)	(4)	(4)	(4)	(4)	(4)	4 580	331	679	7 205	-0.6
Newport News city	6 399	0.0	D	28.3	8.6	4.4	3.9	8.0	28.8	26 635	147	4 461	76 198	2.5
Norfolk city	14 508	0.0	D	3.0	8.5	2.7	4.7	8.0	55.3	31 650	130	7 266	95 018	0.6
Norton city	(5)	(5)	(5)	(5)	(5)	(5)	(5)	(5)	(5)	1 365	345	340	1 945	-0.1
Petersburg city	(6)	(6)	(6)	(6)	(6)	(6)	(6)	(6)	(6)	7 485	231	2 188	16 326	2.3
Poquoson city	(7)	(7)	(7)	(7)	(7)	(7)	(7)	(7)	(7)	2 230	184	58	4 726	9.9
Portsmouth city	3 498	0.0	7.9	3.8	3.9	2.6	1.7	8.3	59.8	17 560	184	3 799	40 806	-1.9
Radford city	(8)	(8)	(8)	(8)	(8)	(8)	(8)	(8)	(8)	2 190	133	258	6 427	4.7
Richmond city	11 501	0.0	D	5.8	16.8	2.5	8.5	10.7	26.3	32 255	158	8 872	98 349	6.5
Roanoke city	3 816	0.0	D	6.3	7.8	6.8	6.4	20.6	14.3	19 930	205	4 069	47 453	4.8
Salem city	(9)	(9)	(9)	(9)	(9)	(9)	(9)	(9)	(9)	5 845	236	403	10 832	4.1
Staunton city	(10)	(10)	(10)	(10)	(10)	(10)	(10)	(10)	(10)	5 900	248	507	11 738	12.6
Suffolk city	1 479	1.1	D	9.8	D	6.6	3.8	12.7	28.7	14 280	169	2 286	33 035	33.7
Virginia Beach city	11 470	0.0	D	2.7	11.0	6.1	10.2	9.3	32.5	59 535	136	5 113	177 879	9.6
Waynesboro city	(10)	(10)	(10)	(10)	(10)	(10)	(10)	(10)	(10)	5 020	239	538	9 717	9.6
Williamsburg city	(11)	(11)	(11)	(11)	(11)	(11)	(11)	(11)	(11)	2 240	159	149	5 176	33.4
Winchester city	(12)	(12)	(12)	(12)	(12)	(12)	(12)	(12)	(12)	4 920	188	575	11 872	12.1
WASHINGTON	205 345	1.1	17.4	10.9	16.0	6.2	6.7	10.2	20.8	1 089 887	162	137 546	2 885 677	17.7
Adams	320	13.9	18.3	15.7	1.7	5.3	2.3	D	23.3	2 460	131	319	6 242	8.1
Asotin	282	0.7	15.5	5.9	4.2	11.8	7.0	15.1	20.6	5 825	269	673	9 872	8.4
Benton	5 092	2.6	D	5.2	24.3	5.6	3.4	9.2	17.2	27 460	157	3 277	68 618	22.6
Chelan	1 891	6.1	D	5.4	5.1	7.9	4.7	19.3	21.6	14 765	204	1 423	35 465	16.6
Clallam	1 230	-0.1	14.8	7.8	5.3	10.2	3.9	9.7	36.5	22 265	312	1 780	35 582	16.0
Clark	8 114	0.0	19.0	10.0	11.2	6.5	8.0	14.2	19.1	67 135	158	7 726	167 413	24.9
Columbia	70	10.2	D	D	2.8	D	1.9	D	35.7	1 200	294	152	2 136	5.8
Cowlitz	2 001	-0.1	32.7	21.4	4.2	7.2	3.5	13.8	16.4	23 515	230	3 271	43 450	12.6
Douglas	437	9.7	11.6	4.6	D	10.8	3.2	7.9	30.8	6 765	176	531	16 004	23.6
Ferry	87	-2.9	D	D	1.8	6.0	1.1	3.0	57.1	2 100	278	293	4 400	16.6
Franklin	1 463	15.4	D	9.5	3.6	6.7	2.8	7.5	21.3	8 095	104	1 587	24 423	51.8
Garfield	37	-5.0	D	D	D	5.8	2.6	D	75.2	615	271	35	1 233	-4.3
Grant	1 778	19.5	19.9	14.3	2.1	6.0	2.9	5.6	26.5	14 420	162	2 022	35 083	20.6
Grays Harbor	1 164	1.0	21.7	15.8	3.6	8.3	4.4	10.5	29.3	17 410	239	2 581	35 166	8.2
Island	1 539	0.2	D	2.2	4.6	5.4	3.8	4.6	62.8	18 135	231	919	40 234	24.3
Jefferson	423	0.1	18.8	10.6	6.9	7.6	6.8	9.0	30.3	10 000	335	564	17 767	25.6
King	98 180	0.0	16.0	10.4	25.5	5.5	8.2	8.3	12.5	251 040	130	36 229	851 261	14.7
Kitsap	6 441	0.1	6.7	1.7	7.2	6.2	3.5	10.1	54.7	42 700	170	4 838	107 367	15.9
Kittitas	719	7.4	D	4.0	6.0	7.8	3.3	5.3	36.3	6 795	166	485	21 900	32.9
Klickitat	382	5.5	D	6.0	21.9	7.6	2.3	3.5	25.0	5 220	257	590	9 786	13.4
Lewis	1 215	1.6	20.6	14.1	3.8	9.4	3.0	12.9	22.4	18 665	247	2 322	34 050	15.1
Lincoln	145	8.8	7.0	0.7	4.9	6.7	5.1	D	43.2	2 845	269	210	5 776	9.0
Mason	716	1.1	D	10.6	D	7.1	5.6	6.2	40.6	15 155	250	1 470	32 518	27.4
Okanogan	770	15.8	7.8	1.5	3.1	11.1	3.7	7.1	34.1	9 945	242	1 326	22 245	16.6
Pacific	277	1.2	14.7	10.7	3.1	7.0	6.8	5.2	41.3	7 010	335	658	15 547	11.1
Pend Oreille	162	0.3	23.4	19.6	3.4	3.9	4.1	D	51.0	3 625	279	512	7 936	20.1
Pierce	20 371	0.1	13.6	6.0	5.4	5.7	5.5	13.6	37.4	122 775	154	17 773	325 375	17.4
San Juan	275	-0.5	D	3.5	D	10.2	5.7	5.8	19.9	4 235	269	134	13 313	36.5
Skagit	2 742	2.5	25.6	16.8	4.7	10.5	6.1	9.7	22.5	24 655	211	2 258	51 473	20.6
Skamania	97	-1.9	D	11.0	D	4.0	D	D	48.1	2 090	189	208	5 628	23.0
Snohomish	17 009	0.1	38.0	30.1	7.6	6.5	6.3	8.3	17.8	97 130	136	11 065	286 659	21.4
Spokane	11 631	0.2	15.2	8.3	7.7	8.0	7.5	17.3	21.1	84 400	179	12 511	201 434	15.1
Stevens	502	1.0	18.3	11.4	3.1	8.8	2.5	14.4	31.6	10 740	247	1 248	21 156	20.2
Thurston	6 002	0.3	8.5	3.1	6.2	6.6	5.2	12.5	41.7	46 365	184	4 755	108 182	24.8
Wahkiakum	36	-2.8	9.5	4.6	D	D	D	D	36.7	1 265	318	88	2 067	15.3
Walla Walla	1 393	7.6	D	14.1	4.1	6.2	4.6	14.6	27.8	11 075	188	1 300	23 451	10.9
Whatcom	4 513	1.4	24.0	13.0	8.3	8.4	4.9	11.6	19.8	35 880	178	4 013	90 665	22.7
Whitman	964	4.6	D	12.2	2.6	3.8	2.6	6.7	52.7	5 315	119	384	19 323	15.9
Yakima	4 874	12.8	12.6	8.1	3.4	7.1	3.6	15.8	20.6	38 795	159	7 016	85 474	8.0
WEST VIRGINIA	38 427	-0.2	23.2	8.7	7.2	7.1	4.0	14.4	23.1	443 911	240	80 367	881 917	4.4
Barbour	160	-1.8	D	2.8	4.3	6.1	3.2	D	25.5	4 040	244	913	7 849	6.8
Berkeley	1 775	0.4	D	5.3	10.6	6.2	3.2	11.3	39.5	18 070	173	1 946	44 762	36.0
Boone	629	0.0	58.2	0.2	D	3.9	1.3	3.0	13.6	6 530	265	1 522	11 070	-4.4
Braxton	189	-0.9	23.2	10.3	2.4	11.6	3.0	D	24.3	3 555	245	835	7 415	0.6

1. Includes mining, construction, and manufacturing. 2. Per 1,000 resident population enumerated in the 2010 census. 3. Manassas and Manassas Park cities are included with Prince William county. 4. Martinsville city is included with Henry county. 5. Norton city is included with Wise county. 6. Petersburg and Colonial Heights cities are included with Dinwiddie county. 7. Poquoson city is included with York county. 8. Radford city is included with Montgomery county. 9. Salem city is included with Roanoke county. 10. Staunton and Waynesboro cities are included with Augusta county. 11. Williamsburg city is included with James City county. 12. Winchester city is included with Frederick county.

Table B. States and Counties — Housing, Labor Force, and Employment

STATE County	Housing units, 2006–2010								Civilian labor force, 2010				Civilian employment,[5] 2006–2010		
	Occupied units										Unemployment			Percent	
			Owner-occupied			Renter-occupied									
				Median owner cost as a percent of income			Median rent as a per-cent of income	Sub-stand-ard units[3] (percent)		Percent change, 2009–2010				Manage-ment, business, science and arts	Con-struction, produc-tion, and mainte-nance occu-pations
	Total	Percent	Median value[1]	With a mort-gage	Without a mort-gage	Median rent[2]			Total		Total	Rate[4]	Total		
	89	90	91	92	93	94	95	96	97	98	99	100	101	102	103
VIRGINIA—Cont'd															
Manassas Park city	4 206	71.2	303 400	33.4	12.9	1 344	31.7	1.9	7 039	4.1	431	6.1	7 109	31.2	27.9
Martinsville city	5 922	59.4	89 200	23.6	12.9	547	35.5	3.5	6 179	2.1	1 177	19.0	5 610	26.8	23.9
Newport News city	70 653	52.1	198 500	25.1	12.8	881	30.2	2.0	95 526	6.0	7 490	7.8	82 883	31.8	23.5
Norfolk city	85 061	46.6	208 400	27.7	14.3	845	31.6	3.4	100 213	-1.6	9 265	9.2	103 262	30.9	23.2
Norton city	1 764	54.0	75 200	18.9	10.0	551	28.8	1.7	1 806	8.1	128	7.1	1 878	24.8	26.8
Petersburg city	12 305	50.8	115 900	24.7	12.5	770	31.0	2.5	14 521	-1.9	1 862	12.8	13 005	25.7	24.5
Poquoson city	4 524	84.8	326 200	22.9	12.6	1 132	32.6	0.8	6 295	-1.5	378	6.0	5 897	45.4	17.4
Portsmouth city	37 325	61.5	180 400	29.1	14.5	880	31.8	2.2	45 787	-2.6	4 174	9.1	42 579	30.8	23.8
Radford city	5 667	51.6	154 700	21.2	10.0	641	42.4	0.5	7 993	-1.6	753	9.4	6 796	34.8	16.0
Richmond city	83 498	44.9	201 800	26.9	15.2	805	33.5	3.1	102 718	0.1	10 383	10.1	96 569	36.6	17.5
Roanoke city	42 833	56.0	128 700	25.8	13.3	636	29.9	1.9	47 733	0.3	4 208	8.8	45 228	29.0	24.5
Salem city	9 890	68.8	165 700	23.0	11.6	710	26.7	0.9	13 469	-0.9	933	6.9	11 794	33.8	16.0
Staunton city	10 408	60.4	164 400	24.0	10.9	642	31.0	2.2	11 892	0.0	905	7.6	11 294	32.4	21.2
Suffolk city	30 126	75.1	252 200	27.0	12.4	855	32.5	1.6	41 302	0.7	3 184	7.7	37 419	35.4	25.2
Virginia Beach city	163 944	66.5	277 400	27.0	12.5	1 143	29.9	1.3	222 159	-1.7	14 133	6.4	210 964	38.2	17.6
Waynesboro city	8 546	58.7	169 700	23.4	12.3	662	30.8	3.0	10 682	1.4	933	8.7	8 913	28.5	28.3
Williamsburg city	4 069	49.5	344 800	24.1	10.7	988	29.5	0.0	5 605	0.3	851	15.2	5 708	39.4	9.3
Winchester city	10 221	50.6	267 000	25.3	13.5	860	29.3	1.6	14 450	0.3	1 045	7.2	13 551	34.0	25.9
WASHINGTON	2 577 375	64.8	285 400	26.7	12.0	882	29.6	3.0	3 516 463	-0.5	349 065	9.9	3 124 821	37.9	21.5
Adams	5 599	63.9	131 100	26.2	10.3	530	24.6	11.6	8 589	2.0	808	9.4	7 176	26.5	43.5
Asotin	8 977	71.3	157 600	24.8	10.0	622	28.1	1.6	10 412	0.3	931	8.9	9 452	28.4	25.9
Benton	62 038	69.7	169 500	20.8	10.0	729	28.5	3.0	96 556	3.3	6 950	7.2	78 211	38.2	24.0
Chelan	26 676	68.0	245 500	25.1	10.1	674	27.1	2.9	41 891	-1.3	3 610	8.6	32 096	31.1	27.6
Clallam	30 987	71.1	241 500	27.5	11.6	766	31.8	2.2	30 261	-0.1	3 133	10.4	27 861	30.8	24.5
Clark	155 042	67.8	260 800	27.1	11.9	859	30.0	2.6	220 472	1.3	30 245	13.7	191 355	34.5	24.2
Columbia	1 732	72.3	146 800	19.3	10.0	529	33.2	3.2	1 550	-2.9	174	11.2	1 730	37.3	22.0
Cowlitz	39 441	67.3	191 500	25.6	11.4	681	32.7	2.4	44 695	-0.2	5 704	12.8	41 511	28.0	31.6
Douglas	13 802	71.9	204 800	23.8	10.5	705	28.5	6.0	21 957	-0.5	1 793	8.2	17 282	23.7	32.2
Ferry	2 706	71.6	146 100	24.2	10.0	534	28.1	3.0	3 059	-0.5	440	14.4	2 374	30.2	32.1
Franklin	21 422	66.8	147 000	23.4	10.0	672	29.1	7.8	38 215	6.2	3 182	8.3	30 034	23.2	36.5
Garfield	903	72.8	115 700	22.7	10.8	518	28.1	1.4	1 047	1.6	82	7.8	867	37.0	28.5
Grant	29 427	62.6	141 100	23.3	10.0	606	26.0	7.9	42 251	-0.3	4 445	10.5	35 503	26.1	36.9
Grays Harbor	28 191	68.7	158 200	25.6	11.7	655	27.2	4.0	31 102	-1.2	4 139	13.3	28 601	24.0	31.3
Island	32 976	73.9	307 100	29.3	12.1	941	28.2	1.2	32 872	-0.3	3 081	9.4	31 334	34.4	22.5
Jefferson	14 194	73.8	308 500	28.2	12.2	769	34.8	2.7	12 929	-1.7	1 252	9.7	12 088	37.2	23.0
King	781 977	59.9	407 700	27.0	12.9	999	28.6	3.0	1 111 470	0.1	97 373	8.8	1 005 216	47.2	15.6
Kitsap	95 758	68.4	284 700	26.4	12.0	914	30.3	2.2	125 057	-0.3	9 847	7.9	109 244	37.3	21.7
Kittitas	16 619	56.5	265 600	27.8	12.5	757	42.8	2.8	21 225	1.6	1 955	9.2	18 375	34.0	22.3
Klickitat	8 405	69.9	200 200	26.2	11.2	661	32.7	4.3	11 015	1.4	1 189	10.8	8 058	31.9	34.1
Lewis	29 290	72.2	188 600	25.2	11.9	704	29.5	3.3	31 356	-1.4	4 231	13.5	30 815	27.1	32.8
Lincoln	4 649	78.5	145 000	21.7	10.7	608	26.2	3.4	4 880	0.7	420	8.6	4 753	37.1	23.4
Mason	21 808	80.9	216 000	27.4	10.9	789	28.8	2.6	25 380	-0.2	2 817	11.1	22 481	28.8	29.5
Okanogan	15 747	68.6	161 600	22.6	10.4	554	29.7	4.1	22 152	-0.1	2 284	10.3	16 411	32.4	26.5
Pacific	9 667	74.2	165 400	24.4	12.1	627	30.7	4.6	9 244	-0.3	1 184	12.8	8 312	29.7	28.8
Pend Oreille	5 511	79.3	200 400	25.4	10.0	491	33.9	3.7	5 472	-1.2	751	13.7	4 609	30.5	32.3
Pierce	295 554	63.3	269 300	27.8	13.0	902	30.6	2.6	396 507	0.1	39 414	9.9	352 708	32.3	24.0
San Juan	7 986	70.4	495 600	31.6	12.1	853	28.2	5.5	8 344	-1.7	585	7.0	7 870	36.5	22.7
Skagit	45 253	70.1	278 300	28.5	12.7	872	30.0	4.0	58 833	0.6	6 141	10.4	51 839	29.9	28.8
Skamania	4 514	76.2	244 600	29.4	10.0	693	26.2	4.3	5 126	0.2	676	13.2	4 873	33.6	27.0
Snohomish	263 931	68.1	338 600	28.5	13.4	994	29.6	2.5	381 552	-0.4	39 110	10.3	350 071	35.8	22.5
Spokane	184 590	65.0	187 900	24.8	11.3	705	30.9	1.8	237 502	-1.0	22 807	9.6	212 417	34.5	19.3
Stevens	17 404	80.6	174 800	26.3	10.2	576	27.9	3.7	18 735	-0.9	2 354	12.6	16 843	30.6	26.7
Thurston	98 491	67.4	257 800	25.9	11.6	928	29.6	2.6	130 969	-0.6	10 793	8.2	113 729	40.7	17.4
Wahkiakum	1 763	72.3	206 800	23.5	11.1	584	30.5	2.5	1 570	-3.4	216	13.8	1 475	26.0	32.5
Walla Walla	21 367	61.8	195 200	24.4	11.4	657	30.4	3.4	31 747	1.4	2 361	7.4	24 711	34.2	21.4
Whatcom	78 186	62.3	293 500	28.0	12.3	798	32.7	2.9	106 627	-1.0	9 379	8.8	94 761	33.2	22.1
Whitman	15 717	49.0	182 500	21.4	10.0	639	43.7	1.3	21 982	2.6	1 342	6.1	20 246	45.5	12.2
Yakima	79 075	64.1	149 700	24.8	11.2	644	29.3	7.2	127 027	0.5	12 313	9.7	97 529	25.5	35.2
WEST VIRGINIA	740 874	74.6	94 500	19.9	10.0	549	29.0	1.7	801 895	0.7	68 126	8.5	763 691	30.0	27.0
Barbour	6 219	76.3	80 300	21.2	10.0	480	31.6	1.4	6 755	-0.3	688	10.2	6 400	22.8	38.5
Berkeley	38 730	75.6	193 700	23.6	10.1	703	30.4	2.3	44 737	-1.1	4 235	9.5	48 045	30.4	29.0
Boone	10 023	76.2	76 400	16.2	10.0	439	26.2	1.6	8 821	-5.1	708	8.0	8 624	28.5	35.9
Braxton	6 028	78.6	76 200	19.3	10.0	496	24.8	4.2	5 785	-1.0	606	10.5	5 237	21.2	36.9

1. Specified owner-occupied units.   2. Specified renter-occupied units. A value of 10.0 represents 10 percent or less.   3. Overcrowded or lacking complete plumbing facilities.   4. Percent of civilian labor force.   5. Persons 16 years old and over.

Table B. States and Counties — Nonfarm Employment and Agriculture

STATE County	Private nonfarm establishments, employment and payroll, 2009									Agriculture, 2007			
	Number of establish-ments	Employment						Annual payroll		Farms			
		Total	Health care and social assistance	Manufac-turing	Retail trade	Finance and insurance	Professional, scientific, and technical services	Total (mil dol)	Average per employee (dollars)	Number	Fewer than 50 acres	500 acres or more	Farm operators whose principal occu-pation is farming (percent)
	104	105	106	107	108	109	110	111	112	113	114	115	116
VIRGINIA—Cont'd													
Manassas Park city	280	2 836	D	D	257	D	86	127	44 685	NA	NA	NA	NA
Martinsville city	606	8 437	1 337	644	1 573	329	303	225	26 696	NA	NA	NA	NA
Newport News city	3 808	86 385	11 998	D	9 847	1 690	5 629	3 508	40 613	NA	NA	NA	NA
Norfolk city	5 888	119 653	19 219	7 035	12 498	7 139	13 000	4 987	41 680	NA	NA	NA	NA
Norton city	259	4 722	D	D	904	D	165	170	36 061	NA	NA	NA	NA
Petersburg city	752	12 798	4 791	D	1 533	204	331	432	33 736	NA	NA	NA	NA
Poquoson city	222	1 436	201	D	323	D	93	33	22 635	NA	NA	NA	NA
Portsmouth city	1 812	28 124	7 158	2 224	3 214	590	1 936	938	33 348	NA	NA	NA	NA
Radford city	324	5 337	538	2 161	583	168	235	220	41 167	NA	NA	NA	NA
Richmond city	6 105	120 753	23 494	8 462	8 913	10 711	11 468	5 823	48 224	NA	NA	NA	NA
Roanoke city	3 227	66 413	12 730	4 685	9 687	3 508	3 672	2 507	37 749	NA	NA	NA	NA
Salem city	989	18 775	4 567	3 359	2 028	703	616	757	40 346	NA	NA	NA	NA
Staunton city	800	10 552	1 894	393	2 030	493	312	280	26 579	NA	NA	NA	NA
Suffolk city	1 488	20 945	3 328	2 138	3 443	620	1 672	744	35 524	311	54.3	11.9	53.4
Virginia Beach city	10 906	145 524	15 942	6 318	22 820	11 646	13 466	4 995	34 324	174	70.1	5.7	43.1
Waynesboro city	610	9 431	738	2 006	2 024	368	267	290	30 774	NA	NA	NA	NA
Williamsburg city	481	9 636	D	D	1 648	156	200	263	27 317	NA	NA	NA	NA
Winchester city	1 329	22 060	5 812	2 294	3 979	635	1 076	842	38 185	NA	NA	NA	NA
WASHINGTON	177 276	2 385 282	360 487	234 232	309 936	104 647	163 100	110 390	46 279	39 284	61.1	11.4	45.9
Adams	367	4 202	D	D	588	79	62	140	33 396	782	17.6	44.6	57.8
Asotin	444	4 394	917	334	1 065	138	189	128	29 023	192	41.1	41.7	53.1
Benton	3 906	56 298	8 840	3 224	8 744	1 709	8 518	2 600	46 185	1 630	73.5	8.9	40.1
Chelan	2 441	25 939	5 205	1 736	4 257	817	1 137	937	36 132	979	70.8	2.8	55.4
Clallam	2 174	17 371	3 906	1 472	3 393	612	783	543	31 248	512	80.1	0.8	41.2
Clark	9 525	110 009	18 125	12 774	16 110	4 818	6 234	4 372	39 741	2 101	83.4	0.6	38.8
Columbia	129	762	169	60	D	22	D	22	28 408	283	27.9	36.0	51.9
Cowlitz	2 240	30 640	5 466	5 910	4 540	897	921	1 177	38 424	481	67.8	1.9	44.3
Douglas	684	5 862	634	282	1 476	210	182	169	28 897	955	45.4	26.3	55.9
Ferry	133	737	260	D	D	22	D	19	25 623	232	21.6	16.4	44.8
Franklin	1 336	16 301	1 676	2 058	2 775	399	384	543	33 305	891	35.8	28.7	62.0
Garfield	44	800	D	0	60	15	6	9	29 813	239	17.2	45.6	48.1
Grant	1 740	18 640	2 992	3 092	3 226	580	406	629	33 733	1 858	34.1	26.0	55.9
Grays Harbor	1 774	16 278	2 751	2 556	2 938	D	409	526	32 310	628	62.4	3.0	43.9
Island	1 825	11 836	2 384	587	2 272	537	568	348	29 407	458	81.7	0.4	46.5
Jefferson	1 071	6 753	1 309	785	1 037	D	272	203	29 988	211	70.6	0.9	48.8
King	63 244	1 032 598	127 792	77 335	99 244	47 187	95 455	59 568	57 687	1 790	89.8	0.4	42.1
Kitsap	5 741	57 587	12 894	1 998	10 967	2 342	4 411	1 964	34 112	664	91.3	0.3	45.5
Kittitas	1 161	10 409	1 438	D	1 620	205	265	260	24 930	1 038	59.5	8.1	42.5
Klickitat	540	3 530	609	D	299	80	277	151	42 643	893	47.4	18.8	42.6
Lewis	1 886	19 031	2 915	3 357	3 632	432	509	602	31 656	1 717	63.5	1.4	41.4
Lincoln	281	1 495	421	D	280	70	D	50	33 381	798	14.4	54.4	62.3
Mason	1 055	9 832	1 595	1 288	1 755	358	231	300	30 515	471	79.8	1.3	35.0
Okanogan	1 190	8 440	2 167	D	1 826	D	255	225	26 641	1 662	48.3	14.1	44.7
Pacific	648	4 167	771	764	595	158	D	110	26 499	390	54.1	6.4	49.7
Pend Oreille	239	1 828	417	D	249	55	60	62	33 856	316	43.4	6.6	35.4
Pierce	16 768	228 905	41 704	15 876	33 143	11 720	8 481	8 669	37 872	1 448	84.6	0.4	41.9
San Juan	1 007	4 089	428	183	648	133	232	131	32 055	291	67.7	1.7	38.8
Skagit	3 485	37 356	6 893	5 363	6 967	1 543	1 443	1 325	35 467	1 215	74.7	4.4	39.4
Skamania	202	1 281	90	D	133	D	D	35	27 169	123	76.4	1.6	43.9
Snohomish	17 281	220 362	26 782	50 671	32 781	8 845	9 941	9 584	43 493	1 670	81.6	1.7	39.5
Spokane	12 515	177 847	35 391	14 361	25 492	11 083	8 782	6 493	36 507	2 502	54.8	10.6	36.3
Stevens	905	7 347	1 710	1 125	1 232	232	200	207	28 159	1 258	40.4	10.5	47.6
Thurston	5 858	64 807	11 285	2 628	11 841	2 710	5 357	2 222	34 286	1 288	76.9	2.0	40.5
Wahkiakum	89	617	D	39	58	10	13	15	23 548	119	45.4	1.7	52.9
Walla Walla	1 413	19 272	4 123	D	2 689	D	480	630	32 715	929	50.5	26.0	48.4
Whatcom	6 281	70 390	10 415	8 823	10 537	2 228	3 647	2 494	35 434	1 483	71.2	2.2	45.2
Whitman	818	8 784	1 693	1 468	1 218	267	221	264	30 041	1 247	19.6	47.8	56.2
Yakima	4 681	62 674	12 820	7 423	9 961	1 622	1 996	2 178	34 755	3 540	69.8	6.0	51.6
WEST VIRGINIA	38 990	572 960	122 596	55 357	89 919	20 027	24 670	18 864	32 924	23 618	29.5	5.3	41.5
Barbour	247	2 910	728	103	358	82	106	66	22 705	539	21.5	6.7	42.5
Berkeley	1 592	20 726	5 075	2 437	3 802	632	1 010	691	33 318	833	57.0	2.5	35.1
Boone	313	7 251	685	49	835	D	139	373	51 409	22	54.5	4.5	45.5
Braxton	283	3 007	848	336	661	82	44	75	24 803	381	19.4	9.2	42.8

Table B. States and Counties — **Agriculture**

STATE County	Land in farms Acreage (1,000)	Percent change, 2002–2007	Acres Average size of farm	Total irrigated (1,000)	Total cropland (1,000)	Value of land and buildings (dollars) Average per farm	Average per acre	Value of machinery and equipment, average per farm (dollars)	Value of products sold Total (mil dol)	Average per farm (dollars)	Percent from: Crops	Live-stock and poultry products	Percent of farms with sales of: $10,000 or more	$100,000 or more	Government payments Total ($1,000)	Percent of farms
	117	118	119	120	121	122	123	124	125	126	127	128	129	130	131	132
VIRGINIA—Cont'd																
Manassas Park city	NA	NA	NA	NA	NA	NA	NA	NA	NA	NA	NA	NA	NA	NA	NA	NA
Martinsville city	NA	NA	NA	NA	NA	NA	NA	NA	NA	NA	NA	NA	NA	NA	NA	NA
Newport News city	NA	NA	NA	NA	NA	NA	NA	NA	NA	NA	NA	NA	NA	NA	NA	NA
Norfolk city	NA	NA	NA	NA	NA	NA	NA	NA	NA	NA	NA	NA	NA	NA	NA	NA
Norton city	NA	NA	NA	NA	NA	NA	NA	NA	NA	NA	NA	NA	NA	NA	NA	NA
Petersburg city	NA	NA	NA	NA	NA	NA	NA	NA	NA	NA	NA	NA	NA	NA	NA	NA
Poquoson city	NA	NA	NA	NA	NA	NA	NA	NA	NA	NA	NA	NA	NA	NA	NA	NA
Portsmouth city	NA	NA	NA	NA	NA	NA	NA	NA	NA	NA	NA	NA	NA	NA	NA	NA
Radford city	NA	NA	NA	NA	NA	NA	NA	NA	NA	NA	NA	NA	NA	NA	NA	NA
Richmond city	NA	NA	NA	NA	NA	NA	NA	NA	NA	NA	NA	NA	NA	NA	NA	NA
Roanoke city	NA	NA	NA	NA	NA	NA	NA	NA	NA	NA	NA	NA	NA	NA	NA	NA
Salem city	NA	NA	NA	NA	NA	NA	NA	NA	NA	NA	NA	NA	NA	NA	NA	NA
Staunton city	NA	NA	NA	NA	NA	NA	NA	NA	NA	NA	NA	NA	NA	NA	NA	NA
Suffolk city	71	0.0	230	0.6	53.8	1 045 364	4 554	117 887	51.3	164 859	82.4	17.6	41.5	20.6	2 913	45.7
Virginia Beach city	27	-3.6	153	0.2	21.5	954 463	6 227	93 578	12.6	72 240	D	D	31.6	13.2	354	25.9
Waynesboro city	NA	NA	NA	NA	NA	NA	NA	NA	NA	NA	NA	NA	NA	NA	NA	NA
Williamsburg city	NA	NA	NA	NA	NA	NA	NA	NA	NA	NA	NA	NA	NA	NA	NA	NA
Winchester city	NA	NA	NA	NA	NA	NA	NA	NA	NA	NA	NA	NA	NA	NA	NA	NA
WASHINGTON	14 973	-2.3	381	1 735.9	7 609.2	759 146	1 992	83 468	6 792.9	172 917	70.0	30.0	33.9	15.2	138 272	17.6
Adams	1 098	2.9	1 405	124.5	825.9	1 438 309	1 024	191 192	344.1	440 064	71.7	28.3	46.3	32.9	14 454	69.7
Asotin	274	-2.1	1 426	0.3	80.4	1 185 136	831	99 164	13.4	69 668	D	D	37.5	18.2	2 339	43.2
Benton	633	4.1	388	181.6	476.5	901 747	2 323	104 430	525.9	322 649	89.4	10.6	33.0	14.5	6 064	9.6
Chelan	94	-16.1	96	28.2	43.5	698 166	7 280	63 054	208.8	213 278	98.2	1.8	69.5	33.3	292	3.4
Clallam	23	4.5	45	4.5	8.8	467 520	10 489	45 634	10.8	21 030	D	D	23.8	3.7	59	3.1
Clark	78	9.9	37	4.4	34.3	493 410	13 230	36 479	52.7	25 079	42.4	57.6	14.7	2.5	115	1.6
Columbia	313	6.1	1 107	4.2	184.1	1 104 813	998	119 009	39.8	140 702	91.0	9.0	38.2	22.3	5 257	73.5
Cowlitz	31	-22.5	64	3.0	10.9	485 875	7 612	51 689	26.5	55 007	40.2	59.8	18.3	5.6	29	1.9
Douglas	883	0.5	925	19.4	539.5	1 020 277	1 103	100 225	193.4	202 479	96.7	3.3	53.2	29.0	11 647	39.7
Ferry	749	-6.3	3 230	3.4	14.8	1 423 137	441	42 795	2.9	12 555	22.3	77.7	24.1	3.9	73	9.5
Franklin	609	-8.4	684	217.2	467.9	1 477 309	2 161	202 364	467.0	524 145	82.1	17.9	62.3	47.4	7 238	33.4
Garfield	308	-1.3	1 290	0.5	174.6	1 043 703	809	111 192	26.4	110 629	87.8	12.2	38.1	25.9	5 086	72.8
Grant	1 088	1.3	586	469.8	771.8	1 460 726	2 495	204 775	1 190.2	640 576	71.2	28.8	58.2	41.5	11 192	34.1
Grays Harbor	119	120.4	190	4.9	24.1	508 492	2 677	42 517	32.8	52 263	53.4	46.6	22.9	5.1	326	6.8
Island	18	20.0	39	1.8	8.6	475 138	12 295	35 920	14.3	31 319	25.5	74.5	18.3	2.8	161	3.9
Jefferson	13	8.3	60	0.6	3.8	439 708	7 296	50 482	8.7	41 179	12.9	87.1	27.0	4.7	59	5.2
King	49	16.7	28	3.3	18.0	489 767	17 788	43 236	127.3	71 100	35.9	64.1	25.1	5.5	316	2.9
Kitsap	15	-6.3	23	0.9	3.7	429 990	18 668	31 903	7.0	10 520	75.5	24.6	17.2	1.2	88	2.6
Kittitas	191	-17.3	184	82.1	69.7	719 491	3 908	72 666	60.9	58 717	63.6	36.4	34.9	11.3	435	7.7
Klickitat	601	-1.0	673	21.3	191.4	839 128	1 246	67 202	57.3	64 163	76.6	23.4	28.4	9.1	4 400	34.2
Lewis	132	0.8	77	7.3	54.4	453 053	5 913	48 925	110.0	64 063	26.2	73.8	20.3	5.4	255	5.1
Lincoln	1 090	-11.6	1 366	32.1	743.2	1 360 226	996	142 374	126.2	158 165	93.3	6.7	49.2	34.8	15 371	74.6
Mason	25	13.6	53	1.2	6.1	439 720	8 223	52 101	37.0	78 478	4.3	95.7	24.8	7.4	39	2.3
Okanogan	1 205	-2.9	725	51.6	127.1	879 713	1 213	58 180	208.8	125 606	88.2	11.8	38.0	15.3	1 065	4.5
Pacific	62	19.2	158	2.3	15.0	525 009	3 316	78 099	35.0	89 734	20.6	79.4	37.9	14.4	173	6.9
Pend Oreille	55	-9.8	174	1.1	19.0	526 951	3 022	50 271	2.8	8 917	44.9	55.1	12.3	1.3	50	2.8
Pierce	48	-15.8	33	4.5	17.3	485 594	14 748	42 222	83.4	57 598	38.8	61.2	16.1	4.5	68	1.2
San Juan	21	23.5	74	0.4	9.0	641 253	8 691	30 459	3.6	12 431	46.7	53.3	26.8	0.7	165	4.1
Skagit	109	-4.4	89	16.3	69.8	602 607	6 746	80 332	256.2	210 904	68.0	32.0	26.5	10.8	630	8.9
Skamania	5	-16.7	44	0.3	1.6	392 013	8 812	41 944	2.7	21 635	38.1	61.9	23.6	4.9	15	2.4
Snohomish	77	11.6	46	5.5	37.0	497 509	10 813	44 159	125.6	75 221	46.9	53.1	22.6	6.6	630	4.0
Spokane	626	-2.6	250	13.5	394.9	588 545	2 351	65 660	117.1	46 789	84.2	15.8	23.6	8.3	5 929	24.5
Stevens	531	0.6	422	15.0	88.3	588 494	1 394	55 880	24.5	19 499	47.6	52.4	26.6	3.7	846	14.2
Thurston	81	9.5	63	6.9	26.3	535 414	8 554	56 688	117.9	91 525	36.5	63.5	18.9	4.7	297	2.8
Wahkiakum	12	0.0	101	0.2	4.7	402 743	3 986	49 220	3.1	25 773	7.2	92.8	26.9	4.2	142	17.6
Walla Walla	682	-2.7	734	92.4	567.2	1 266 236	1 724	145 553	344.5	370 818	D	D	36.0	22.9	11 909	43.3
Whatcom	103	-30.4	69	35.0	73.7	773 740	11 186	95 287	326.5	220 128	30.6	69.4	36.2	16.8	1 050	19.7
Whitman	1 271	-4.3	1 019	6.9	1 057.6	1 137 925	1 116	153 010	254.0	203 714	95.9	4.1	49.9	37.0	25 305	72.4
Yakima	1 649	-1.8	466	267.6	344.5	712 970	1 530	97 908	1 203.8	340 058	65.4	34.6	52.6	21.8	4 705	9.2
WEST VIRGINIA	3 698	3.2	157	2.2	942.1	373 435	2 385	38 871	591.7	25 051	13.2	86.8	20.1	3.2	2 929	9.2
Barbour	91	15.2	169	0.0	23.1	277 451	1 643	36 250	7.2	13 275	19.1	80.9	26.3	2.6	15	5.6
Berkeley	75	-1.3	90	0.2	38.3	603 895	6 698	39 635	21.7	26 069	64.6	35.4	20.0	3.8	176	16.7
Boone	2	-33.3	105	0.0	0.2	161 392	1 544	9 033	0.1	2 545	12.5	87.5	0.0	0.0	0	0.0
Braxton	79	19.7	208	D	12.9	336 083	1 612	35 120	3.1	8 040	10.1	89.9	23.4	0.3	14	4.7

Table B. States and Counties — Water Use, Wholesale Trade, Retail Trade, and Real Estate

STATE County	Water use, 2005		Wholesale trade,[1] 2007				Retail trade,[2] 2007				Real estate and rental and leasing,[2] 2007			
	Total water withdrawn (mil gal/day)	Gallons withdrawn per person	Number of establishments	Number of employees	Sales (mil dol)	Annual payroll (mil dol)	Number of establishments	Number of employees	Sales (mil dol)	Annual payroll (mil dol)	Number of establishments	Number of employees	Receipts (mil dol)	Annual payroll (mil dol)
	133	134	135	136	137	138	139	140	141	142	143	144	145	146
VIRGINIA—Cont'd														
Manassas Park city	0.4	35	17	D	D	D	33	403	158.0	12.2	5	63	8.9	1.7
Martinsville city	0.0	0	22	D	D	D	117	1 748	316.9	34.0	36	141	22.5	3.3
Newport News city	38.0	211	116	1 470	902.0	68.5	727	10 894	2 431.3	233.8	273	2 884	374.2	84.2
Norfolk city	2.4	10	250	8 577	3 280.4	247.2	975	13 764	2 724.1	293.5	324	2 898	385.8	98.3
Norton city	0.9	242	8	54	94.2	2.5	61	886	283.8	20.0	9	15	3.8	0.6
Petersburg city	0.0	0	29	647	356.1	19.0	155	1 569	324.2	37.5	36	192	21.4	4.6
Poquoson city	0.0	0	4	D	D	D	23	331	54.7	5.5	14	34	4.6	0.7
Portsmouth city	19.2	191	48	611	173.6	27.4	296	3 428	682.1	75.7	93	383	48.6	8.5
Radford city	2.3	156	9	57	30.3	2.3	47	575	109.7	11.7	24	90	10.6	2.3
Richmond city	225.0	1 161	289	4 408	2 843.3	231.1	883	9 029	1 922.8	211.6	302	2 361	636.4	126.2
Roanoke city	5.6	60	198	3 098	2 233.6	130.4	588	9 765	2 039.8	215.4	161	1 274	188.6	33.5
Salem city	3.9	158	65	1 074	621.2	54.0	156	2 163	537.8	50.3	40	210	31.9	5.2
Staunton city	0.1	6	20	238	68.3	7.3	165	2 026	447.5	43.9	45	222	23.9	8.0
Suffolk city	98.7	1 249	50	1 105	715.8	55.7	228	3 174	820.3	70.4	74	287	44.5	10.6
Virginia Beach city	4.1	9	374	5 069	2 835.1	207.4	1 625	25 639	5 579.9	568.5	717	6 190	830.7	197.8
Waynesboro city	7.1	334	17	327	113.2	15.8	127	1 842	386.6	38.7	36	111	11.4	2.3
Williamsburg city	1.7	144	4	D	D	D	114	1 913	323.0	39.5	28	150	49.1	5.4
Winchester city	0.2	6	30	D	D	D	307	4 695	998.7	101.1	76	329	63.3	12.0
WASHINGTON	5 637.1	897	8 181	111 294	76 791.0	5 557.6	23 075	328 053	92 968.5	8 585.3	10 480	51 196	10 467.3	1 818.7
Adams	158.3	9 420	32	530	574.2	19.1	60	587	144.8	12.0	12	D	D	D
Asotin	5.2	245	12	D	D	D	57	764	208.9	20.6	24	81	6.7	1.2
Benton	842.6	5 334	103	1 062	755.4	42.6	579	8 702	2 122.0	205.5	211	1 020	197.8	30.5
Chelan	91.1	1 306	98	2 025	788.3	71.4	399	4 401	1 022.0	107.1	122	536	71.6	13.5
Clallam	20.2	290	53	D	D	D	306	3 678	838.3	92.9	118	356	39.9	8.4
Clark	165.5	410	398	3 778	4 238.1	213.4	1 036	16 868	4 170.0	401.5	509	2 600	386.6	88.1
Columbia	4.7	1 129	20	48	30.8	1.4	23	136	28.9	2.3	5	5	0.8	0.1
Cowlitz	147.8	1 518	78	1 136	1 415.8	51.8	360	5 018	1 219.7	117.1	117	442	54.3	9.7
Douglas	39.0	1 114	39	469	127.4	13.6	106	1 583	413.6	38.3	24	93	14.8	2.1
Ferry	6.0	794	1	D	D	D	25	213	35.0	3.7	3	D	D	D
Franklin	551.9	8 759	100	1 291	1 028.0	51.2	183	2 775	788.5	74.8	59	256	46.9	6.7
Garfield	1.2	520	8	120	70.5	3.7	12	56	11.7	1.0	NA	NA	NA	NA
Grant	1 161.2	14 296	107	1 415	599.6	49.9	306	3 137	777.5	73.9	88	180	29.6	3.9
Grays Harbor	67.7	955	64	D	D	D	293	3 214	768.6	79.2	93	332	35.6	7.1
Island	9.5	120	42	D	D	D	246	2 411	519.9	58.4	123	349	51.4	8.4
Jefferson	22.6	790	22	119	51.1	4.9	159	1 201	210.9	24.7	55	159	21.5	3.2
King	227.9	127	3 444	53 288	41 042.7	3 092.0	6 976	106 600	37 153.9	2 985.0	4 090	24 282	5 961.1	1 049.6
Kitsap	28.0	116	150	1 011	553.1	41.7	840	11 918	2 936.2	301.3	392	1 332	224.2	37.3
Kittitas	280.8	7 622	37	D	D	D	168	1 817	472.7	41.0	63	240	26.7	5.2
Klickitat	40.6	2 044	14	91	25.8	2.8	55	370	65.7	6.6	21	37	5.4	0.7
Lewis	47.1	651	71	D	D	D	355	3 853	910.6	92.6	86	380	40.6	8.8
Lincoln	36.8	3 547	40	160	133.2	6.7	48	292	91.6	8.0	9	11	1.8	0.2
Mason	19.5	359	33	D	D	D	153	1 846	420.2	44.5	58	299	32.0	6.7
Okanogan	92.6	2 328	40	590	224.4	15.7	205	1 780	417.2	39.9	59	143	15.9	2.6
Pacific	7.6	351	7	D	D	D	116	620	114.5	14.8	27	82	7.2	1.4
Pend Oreille	4.3	340	5	6	1.7	0.2	38	296	66.6	5.3	13	D	D	D
Pierce	198.5	263	704	11 348	6 090.5	468.5	2 306	35 815	9 741.6	952.3	1 094	5 695	970.6	161.2
San Juan	1.9	127	19	D	D	D	119	777	155.3	21.6	71	148	20.8	3.2
Skagit	44.2	390	124	1 557	698.0	61.2	616	7 788	2 134.8	200.4	181	653	105.5	18.3
Skamania	9.7	905	4	7	2.4	0.3	22	161	26.0	2.6	8	8	1.3	0.2
Snohomish	127.7	195	783	7 873	6 708.4	400.3	2 267	34 313	9 057.1	930.4	1 003	3 977	766.8	134.1
Spokane	191.7	435	655	9 341	5 354.3	394.8	1 712	26 853	6 741.2	697.7	662	3 426	630.3	105.1
Stevens	29.6	705	25	205	47.2	5.6	137	1 230	281.6	27.9	36	125	16.6	2.3
Thurston	46.2	202	177	1 766	1 003.4	78.8	822	12 136	3 103.0	313.2	323	1 234	238.8	31.6
Wahkiakum	1.3	333	NA	NA	NA	NA	14	50	11.7	0.9	5	D	D	D
Walla Walla	156.4	2 717	55	555	257.5	18.8	212	2 551	534.1	59.7	64	215	26.3	5.3
Whatcom	81.3	443	306	3 294	1 373.6	144.5	851	11 100	2 556.0	263.5	352	1 254	240.2	33.3
Whitman	10.8	269	70	520	388.9	21.4	113	1 243	271.1	23.6	45	205	19.6	3.4
Yakima	658.3	2 843	251	D	D	D	780	9 900	2 425.6	239.5	255	977	151.6	23.7
WEST VIRGINIA	4 811.8	2 648	1 372	16 790	11 036.5	656.0	7 047	92 227	20 538.8	1 776.5	1 586	7 055	1 171.0	175.3
Barbour	1.9	118	7	D	D	D	43	340	75.0	5.8	4	8	1.2	0.2
Berkeley	19.7	211	42	878	573.5	42.7	278	3 536	886.4	74.2	93	339	40.3	6.8
Boone	5.1	200	10	D	D	D	81	959	190.6	16.3	8	16	1.8	0.4
Braxton	8.6	580	10	120	57.4	4.9	83	687	219.6	14.2	6	29	3.2	0.7

1. Merchant wholesalers, except manufacturers' sales branches and offices.   2. Employer establishments.

Table B. States and Counties — Professional Services, Manufacturing, and Accommodation and Food Services

STATE County	Professional, scientific, and technical services,[1] 2007				Manufacturing, 2007				Accommodation and food services, 2007			
	Number of establish-ments	Number of employees	Receipts (mil dol)	Annual payroll (mil dol)	Number of establish-ments	Number of employees	Receipts (mil dol)	Annual payroll (mil dol)	Number of establish-ments	Number of employees	Sales (mil dol)	Annual payroll (mil dol)
	147	148	149	150	151	152	153	154	155	156	157	158
VIRGINIA—Cont'd												
Manassas Park city	19	D	D	D	NA	NA	NA	NA	14	91	5.3	1.6
Martinsville city	45	200	16.5	8.0	24	1 157	201.4	36.7	51	875	28.7	7.9
Newport News city	345	D	D	D	107	24 155	4 702.7	1 216.0	384	7 660	329.1	89.9
Norfolk city	653	D	D	D	166	7 448	1 280.8	300.0	551	11 667	505.0	140.2
Norton city	22	D	D	D	9	D	D	D	25	464	17.3	4.9
Petersburg city	35	D	D	D	42	2 114	595.9	102.1	70	864	36.6	9.7
Poquoson city	21	95	6.7	2.2	NA	NA	NA	NA	19	290	9.2	2.6
Portsmouth city	144	D	D	D	63	2 360	652.9	105.2	169	2 513	106.2	28.8
Radford city	28	D	D	D	25	1 610	D	68.6	39	923	36.2	8.8
Richmond city	826	10 582	1 682.7	785.0	224	9 341	10 192.1	545.8	547	10 136	476.8	143.5
Roanoke city	321	D	D	D	115	4 544	1 582.4	182.7	294	6 162	267.2	83.3
Salem city	74	D	D	D	69	3 736	984.0	170.7	87	1 897	67.9	20.7
Staunton city	60	342	33.5	14.2	27	546	101.4	20.7	85	1 706	65.5	20.7
Suffolk city	122	D	D	D	48	2 362	1 307.8	109.7	121	1 981	72.8	20.2
Virginia Beach city	1 310	D	D	D	243	6 544	1 806.5	236.9	1 134	21 694	1 074.2	294.9
Waynesboro city	43	D	D	D	35	2 218	759.9	86.0	64	1 148	48.9	13.5
Williamsburg city	34	168	13.7	6.8	NA	NA	NA	NA	134	3 984	239.6	72.7
Winchester city	147	D	D	D	30	D	D	D	123	2 343	104.6	29.5
WASHINGTON	19 242	150 367	23 394.7	9 778.0	7 650	269 851	112 053.3	13 274.5	15 893	233 235	12 389.4	3 618.1
Adams	15	D	D	D	13	1 042	442.2	D	29	322	14.8	4.1
Asotin	31	D	D	D	NA	NA	NA	NA	39	591	23.0	7.4
Benton	397	D	D	D	139	3 740	D	166.4	338	5 248	238.0	69.6
Chelan	190	D	D	D	103	1 870	D	D	271	3 245	171.2	51.0
Clallam	163	D	D	D	76	1 491	470.4	72.7	227	2 376	105.7	31.6
Clark	1 066	D	D	D	457	14 492	D	D	701	10 681	493.3	143.2
Columbia	8	D	D	D	NA	NA	NA	NA	13	67	2.7	0.5
Cowlitz	150	D	D	D	128	7 001	2 914.7	356.7	215	2 782	124.0	36.2
Douglas	36	D	D	D	NA	NA	NA	NA	56	835	30.4	9.4
Ferry	11	D	D	D	NA	NA	NA	NA	13	67	2.1	0.5
Franklin	73	D	D	D	51	2 235	D	75.3	109	1 386	67.7	19.5
Garfield	3	D	D	D	NA	NA	NA	NA	3	19	0.5	0.1
Grant	113	460	43.7	14.7	68	3 528	993.0	139.9	187	1 942	95.8	27.4
Grays Harbor	94	D	D	D	84	3 158	1 056.9	132.5	238	2 234	111.0	31.7
Island	191	D	D	D	51	710	D	27.9	176	1 980	77.6	22.8
Jefferson	95	D	D	D	82	770	209.5	33.6	114	1 110	48.7	15.1
King	9 050	D	D	D	2 485	95 136	37 390.8	5 067.7	5 516	90 130	5 478.9	1 611.9
Kitsap	716	D	D	D	163	2 154	D	78.3	505	7 483	392.8	117.4
Kittitas	73	D	D	D	26	892	81.1	21.8	160	2 165	84.4	28.0
Klickitat	55	D	D	D	31	740	D	37.2	51	332	16.1	4.8
Lewis	123	D	D	D	132	3 757	1 109.1	153.6	192	2 040	96.2	26.6
Lincoln	13	86	7.6	4.3	NA	NA	NA	NA	24	88	4.0	1.0
Mason	76	D	D	D	57	1 695	D	59.0	111	1 684	115.4	33.9
Okanogan	74	D	D	D	NA	NA	NA	NA	128	1 122	49.0	14.5
Pacific	37	131	11.2	4.0	35	941	138.7	24.5	114	737	37.2	8.8
Pend Oreille	16	72	6.7	2.5	14	606	D	D	32	192	9.2	2.5
Pierce	1 386	D	D	D	668	20 326	4 958.6	894.2	1 578	24 076	1 172.5	332.7
San Juan	112	D	D	D	NA	NA	NA	NA	97	735	63.3	17.9
Skagit	305	D	D	D	205	6 387	8 918.2	294.5	347	4 734	251.0	74.1
Skamania	25	D	D	D	NA	NA	NA	NA	24	644	28.5	12.5
Snohomish	1 503	D	D	D	871	50 214	22 552.3	2 847.5	1 521	19 961	1 049.8	294.9
Spokane	1 231	8 631	1 157.2	432.4	589	17 412	3 895.4	730.7	993	17 046	780.2	232.2
Stevens	57	180	17.0	6.4	46	1 374	383.6	52.6	89	689	27.7	7.6
Thurston	598	D	D	D	189	3 118	870.1	120.7	497	7 612	346.7	102.7
Wahkiakum	6	D	D	D	NA	NA	NA	NA	12	60	1.8	0.7
Walla Walla	105	D	D	D	114	3 094	2 155.5	138.4	120	1 723	75.8	22.9
Whatcom	670	3 562	419.2	163.4	334	10 165	11 809.7	467.2	505	8 461	407.9	116.2
Whitman	55	246	20.9	7.6	27	1 248	D	D	121	1 349	49.0	13.5
Yakima	320	D	D	D	255	8 696	2 686.1	304.4	427	5 287	245.6	70.8
WEST VIRGINIA	2 906	20 766	2 341.1	857.5	1 413	59 981	25 080.6	2 645.8	3 650	61 711	2 553.3	712.8
Barbour	19	85	7.0	2.5	NA	NA	NA	NA	25	289	9.9	2.8
Berkeley	131	D	D	D	45	D	D	D	179	2 777	156.4	35.9
Boone	19	D	D	D	NA	NA	NA	NA	24	349	13.2	3.8
Braxton	12	39	2.6	0.9	NA	NA	NA	NA	37	495	16.8	4.8

1. Establishment subject to federal tax.

STATE County	Health care and social assistance, 2007				Other services, 2007				Federal funds and grants, 2009–2010 Expenditures (mil dol)			
										Direct payments for individuals[1]		
	Number of establishments	Number of employees	Receipts (mil dol)	Annual payroll (mil dol)	Number of establishments	Number of employees	Receipts (mil dol)	Annual payroll (mil dol)	Total	Social Security and government retirement	Medicare	Food Stamps and Supplemental Security Income
	159	160	161	162	163	164	165	166	167	168	169	170
VIRGINIA—Cont'd												
Manassas Park city	3	D	D	D	45	223	25.0	7.7	36.4	5.8	0.3	2.0
Martinsville city	120	1 182	115.8	42.8	50	190	16.9	3.4	230.9	121.8	47.9	10.5
Newport News city	384	12 477	1 114.9	486.6	316	2 165	161.4	52.0	5 698.8	638.8	215.2	93.0
Norfolk city	543	19 046	2 097.9	833.8	448	3 670	470.1	117.0	6 285.5	706.2	351.9	157.6
Norton city	41	1 305	129.3	51.7	21	108	5.2	3.5	70.9	25.3	13.8	4.2
Petersburg city	121	3 782	324.7	136.8	85	562	46.0	13.3	449.9	164.7	105.0	24.8
Poquoson city	13	D	D	D	26	D	D	D	62.0	36.7	7.8	0.7
Portsmouth city	218	7 247	635.9	271.9	175	1 535	122.3	41.0	2 334.9	389.4	202.1	66.8
Radford city	42	520	36.8	16.3	25	D	D	D	212.3	48.3	22.9	4.7
Richmond city	641	24 371	2 530.9	1 052.8	577	4 024	535.3	122.0	6 277.3	1 306.2	542.8	187.8
Roanoke city	318	11 059	1 301.2	448.7	271	2 009	155.7	45.9	1 295.2	518.6	236.7	53.8
Salem city	98	5 127	596.1	259.9	103	657	37.9	15.0	381.7	136.2	50.7	3.2
Staunton city	97	2 054	140.2	69.9	68	387	26.9	8.9	279.5	137.1	60.4	7.6
Suffolk city	142	3 165	347.0	128.6	97	586	116.2	11.4	943.0	329.4	91.9	31.4
Virginia Beach city	933	15 592	1 547.4	617.9	897	5 832	633.2	125.9	5 534.8	1 712.0	327.6	96.1
Waynesboro city	52	715	44.0	16.4	60	397	38.4	11.5	193.9	108.1	40.5	9.2
Williamsburg city	46	1 580	118.5	77.4	26	335	65.0	11.7	347.1	193.8	60.4	1.4
Winchester city	236	5 527	637.1	278.1	86	576	43.9	14.6	386.6	158.4	51.1	6.9
WASHINGTON	18 474	345 161	35 886.4	14 349.6	12 324	71 213	8 920.8	2 030.0	70 437.5	19 564.4	6 975.9	2 305.3
Adams	26	636	59.9	25.3	25	85	6.3	1.3	161.7	33.8	15.9	9.8
Asotin	50	835	84.3	26.7	30	123	8.2	2.1	179.2	90.7	34.1	13.6
Benton	498	8 313	812.5	315.2	238	1 300	103.9	30.9	4 220.9	525.1	137.5	65.7
Chelan	208	D	D	D	165	663	60.2	14.1	564.2	243.0	79.6	26.9
Clallam	258	3 757	291.6	122.1	155	672	50.2	15.5	783.1	385.4	127.0	24.3
Clark	933	D	D	D	635	3 111	362.0	80.8	2 433.2	1 205.0	317.1	128.6
Columbia	12	183	11.9	5.6	14	56	7.1	2.0	58.5	19.7	7.6	2.0
Cowlitz	249	5 122	487.3	198.6	146	894	75.9	22.8	779.0	356.7	134.8	53.8
Douglas	53	D	D	D	39	143	9.6	2.5	236.3	98.4	49.1	7.8
Ferry	15	D	D	D	7	D	D	D	64.9	29.9	7.7	4.6
Franklin	115	1 477	140.0	59.3	87	508	47.4	13.6	393.2	135.5	48.6	29.5
Garfield	6	D	D	D	1	D	D	D	42.4	13.5	4.9	1.5
Grant	133	2 721	236.8	99.9	128	526	36.1	9.4	590.7	225.6	77.4	31.3
Grays Harbor	205	2 691	236.1	90.8	121	575	38.2	10.5	639.6	279.2	133.5	46.3
Island	199	2 273	176.6	76.6	99	432	33.2	10.7	821.9	393.9	69.8	14.4
Jefferson	104	1 284	103.5	44.2	93	342	27.7	8.7	286.8	168.4	48.3	9.6
King	6 535	122 486	14 324.2	5 614.7	4 508	28 932	5 137.7	935.6	18 153.0	4 438.3	2 112.0	576.6
Kitsap	659	12 424	1 169.6	482.9	392	2 004	157.5	48.0	4 004.4	1 088.8	231.7	79.6
Kittitas	98	1 407	99.1	41.4	77	327	26.7	7.3	239.4	105.7	38.4	9.4
Klickitat	35	575	45.3	20.5	33	116	8.8	2.2	237.9	86.2	24.4	10.9
Lewis	178	3 000	271.4	115.9	126	521	44.5	11.5	649.1	302.5	124.8	37.1
Lincoln	17	443	31.8	14.3	19	50	5.5	1.2	158.3	54.3	19.1	3.3
Mason	101	1 611	141.5	51.2	85	353	23.5	7.0	465.0	275.2	82.3	26.2
Okanogan	122	1 971	133.9	59.4	77	246	26.7	4.7	412.1	154.5	50.6	22.6
Pacific	50	748	51.5	21.8	46	149	10.8	2.7	223.2	108.0	47.2	11.4
Pend Oreille	22	D	D	D	14	34	3.3	0.6	140.1	57.8	14.7	9.4
Pierce	1 880	42 047	4 395.2	1 781.3	1 301	8 493	803.1	251.2	11 944.2	2 496.4	737.4	314.3
San Juan	62	410	26.2	10.2	56	172	27.7	4.6	101.5	65.2	18.3	2.0
Skagit	342	6 346	614.5	241.6	237	1 158	94.1	27.6	846.6	417.2	158.3	40.4
Skamania	15	D	D	D	10	18	1.6	0.4	64.1	29.2	6.7	4.1
Snohomish	1 656	24 552	2 423.9	980.0	1 144	6 150	523.3	170.6	3 752.7	1 585.6	562.4	171.4
Spokane	1 424	33 424	3 273.7	1 325.9	863	5 436	479.1	132.2	4 074.6	1 547.5	616.2	199.1
Stevens	84	1 452	109.5	47.3	60	176	15.7	4.1	346.8	162.8	46.4	17.8
Thurston	710	11 596	1 238.4	447.6	464	2 812	273.7	88.2	4 306.4	924.1	232.8	71.1
Wahkiakum	8	D	D	D	4	D	D	D	34.0	19.2	7.8	1.1
Walla Walla	164	3 939	387.3	160.0	79	454	34.6	7.9	562.1	198.9	77.2	22.3
Whatcom	636	9 730	862.9	348.7	390	2 155	207.5	59.0	1 279.8	567.6	165.5	57.7
Whitman	86	1 633	127.4	53.4	59	221	13.7	3.9	445.6	97.5	39.7	7.7
Yakima	537	11 636	1 119.8	441.2	297	1 767	132.9	33.9	1 822.9	574.3	269.3	140.3
WEST VIRGINIA	4 860	114 663	9 874.7	3 828.9	2 927	16 527	1 550.2	388.3	21 510.6	7 227.8	3 417.0	1 000.0
Barbour	29	736	36.3	14.3	14	34	2.7	0.5	149.3	56.4	30.5	9.8
Berkeley	194	D	D	D	133	643	51.0	15.1	1 012.8	347.9	86.2	23.0
Boone	41	693	35.4	14.5	22	145	10.4	4.2	216.3	101.2	44.6	19.0
Braxton	20	918	36.1	14.3	17	74	8.3	2.2	138.9	49.9	22.4	10.0

1. State totals may include programs not allocated by county.

STATE County	Federal funds and grants, 2009–2010 (cont.)							Value of residential construction authorized by building permits, 2010		Local government finances, 2007				
	Expenditures (mil dol) (cont.)									General revenue				
		Procurement contract awards		Grants[1]									Taxes	
														Per capita[2] (dollars)
	Salaries and wages	Defense	Other	Medicaid and other health-related	Nutrition and family welfare	Education	Other	New construction ($1,000)	Number of housing units	Total (mil dol)	Inter-governmental (mil dol)	Total (mil dol)	Total	Property
	171	172	173	174	175	176	177	178	179	180	181	182	183	184
VIRGINIA—Cont'd														
Manassas Park city	7.5	3.2	0.5	15.0	0.6	0.8	0.0	0	0	54.7	20.4	29.1	2 550	2 043
Martinsville city	8.1	0.1	1.2	24.9	1.9	2.6	3.7	419	7	53.1	28.7	17.1	1 171	602
Newport News city	1 284.3	3 013.8	198.7	116.7	25.3	16.9	39.7	11 230	188	777.0	333.3	301.9	1 685	1 162
Norfolk city	2 195.3	2 126.5	79.0	301.4	53.1	38.9	77.8	46 320	304	1 361.6	550.3	396.5	1 682	1 005
Norton city	8.8	0.0	0.3	7.8	4.3	0.5	5.0	573	6	16.8	8.1	7.0	1 876	637
Petersburg city	11.6	0.9	5.6	75.9	7.0	9.9	20.5	13 548	177	125.8	73.7	40.3	1 227	806
Poquoson city	11.7	1.7	0.1	0.9	0.5	0.8	0.0	3 970	14	42.0	18.7	18.3	1 547	1 312
Portsmouth city	691.9	664.0	93.6	149.4	17.1	13.6	22.9	10 576	66	447.3	230.3	143.6	1 408	977
Radford city	8.8	100.7	1.6	8.3	4.0	0.7	3.0	3 542	30	32.5	14.4	10.8	666	393
Richmond city	586.2	48.1	139.5	677.9	167.0	545.1	1 948.0	42 637	607	1 013.8	400.9	395.9	1 978	1 311
Roanoke city	129.4	30.1	84.1	137.3	22.1	8.9	34.0	14 155	77	425.3	194.0	166.5	1 798	1 008
Salem city	78.3	3.9	51.3	17.2	2.1	1.6	0.1	3 070	20	81.6	24.6	46.3	1 835	1 097
Staunton city	27.7	0.1	3.9	27.1	2.2	1.5	3.1	5 497	41	79.9	36.2	30.4	1 276	754
Suffolk city	93.7	252.5	17.0	86.1	10.0	4.4	8.9	52 143	297	306.9	134.4	141.0	1 733	1 324
Virginia Beach city	760.4	2 086.2	150.1	73.6	32.2	31.9	59.8	106 513	629	1 817.7	634.2	844.0	1 941	1 349
Waynesboro city	3.7	0.3	1.8	11.4	2.3	1.2	14.3	3 663	35	56.7	24.3	26.3	1 214	675
Williamsburg city	35.3	4.8	11.3	7.1	1.5	3.3	23.0	6 810	34	48.0	11.3	30.8	2 476	841
Winchester city	117.2	3.5	14.6	22.9	1.9	2.7	4.1	11 405	37	122.6	34.6	60.7	2 360	1 154
WASHINGTON	11 538.6	5 150.5	4 890.3	7 161.4	1 608.2	1 188.1	4 767.7	3 891 040	20 691	X	X	X	X	X
Adams	2.4	0.0	4.0	45.0	5.7	1.0	0.5	4 743	33	108.4	57.5	17.6	1 039	765
Asotin	3.4	1.7	1.2	21.0	4.0	1.7	1.8	4 822	27	62.4	36.7	14.6	692	529
Benton	74.3	15.3	3 127.6	93.0	25.6	7.5	116.8	269 713	1 259	767.4	352.2	190.3	1 194	672
Chelan	44.2	0.1	13.7	66.8	16.4	4.7	43.6	37 928	206	323.2	121.0	99.6	1 402	840
Clallam	50.2	20.9	61.0	52.3	13.8	6.1	19.6	30 708	169	346.1	98.8	76.9	1 091	650
Clark	288.8	30.7	77.8	209.1	56.1	22.6	43.3	253 756	1 070	1 400.6	617.9	511.7	1 224	787
Columbia	2.9	2.7	0.6	7.7	1.2	0.1	0.1	772	4	25.6	11.0	4.2	1 065	770
Cowlitz	46.3	17.2	6.0	92.5	19.4	18.2	16.7	28 222	131	372.1	160.5	105.3	1 048	664
Douglas	8.8	15.2	0.4	18.4	6.3	1.0	1.8	23 369	114	130.6	75.7	29.8	823	615
Ferry	10.4	0.0	2.7	4.7	2.5	1.6	0.2	1 947	22	35.5	24.4	4.6	620	496
Franklin	48.7	20.8	12.1	37.5	17.1	5.9	6.1	153 897	763	238.2	124.3	63.4	911	542
Garfield	5.2	4.5	1.1	1.2	0.6	0.1	0.0	220	4	11.5	7.9	2.2	1 085	847
Grant	63.8	5.0	31.3	59.4	19.5	8.6	4.1	42 322	228	453.5	194.1	84.9	1 023	700
Grays Harbor	23.2	5.6	6.3	86.8	18.0	6.7	11.2	24 624	166	296.9	142.4	87.0	1 219	714
Island	199.0	95.5	2.8	19.1	9.3	6.4	3.4	40 308	219	250.9	85.7	74.3	914	557
Jefferson	12.9	13.7	3.1	18.5	6.6	2.2	2.3	19 848	97	134.0	32.5	40.0	1 370	886
King	1 927.4	2 723.5	828.5	3 419.0	300.1	100.8	1 398.9	1 031 097	6 020	10 357.4	2 943.2	4 126.9	2 220	1 144
Kitsap	969.1	598.8	59.3	132.3	45.2	26.1	709.1	110 936	623	945.8	465.9	310.5	1 312	828
Kittitas	13.4	0.2	3.1	26.7	7.4	4.4	10.1	35 752	183	152.8	55.6	43.8	1 137	642
Klickitat	6.6	73.0	5.0	17.4	4.5	0.8	0.4	11 001	77	114.5	43.4	20.4	1 017	682
Lewis	34.7	3.2	9.4	86.0	16.1	10.1	16.7	28 741	204	249.3	118.1	74.0	1 005	609
Lincoln	4.6	0.0	1.8	4.2	2.1	0.4	1.0	7 251	43	73.5	43.5	11.3	1 103	929
Mason	6.4	1.6	3.4	32.1	11.0	4.1	14.6	28 394	140	216.0	73.1	64.2	1 138	719
Okanogan	28.4	14.8	21.4	43.3	14.5	5.8	21.7	19 617	123	187.5	84.2	32.4	816	550
Pacific	11.2	0.0	2.7	22.8	5.0	1.1	11.6	7 196	125	109.0	37.8	29.6	1 377	980
Pend Oreille	7.2	0.2	1.4	13.9	3.2	0.6	30.4	10 665	52	67.6	25.4	12.9	1 007	777
Pierce	6 284.9	644.9	143.8	724.3	134.3	56.9	277.0	420 684	1 900	2 957.3	1 201.4	1 093.9	1 415	896
San Juan	5.0	0.4	3.5	2.1	2.0	0.2	2.0	41 583	189	72.5	22.0	33.3	2 189	1 353
Skagit	29.4	19.2	34.2	69.5	23.5	15.8	19.7	40 141	207	655.4	196.6	178.4	1 533	973
Skamania	9.0	3.7	4.2	4.6	1.9	0.2	0.1	5 669	25	35.4	16.7	8.4	787	556
Snohomish	291.6	344.3	108.3	355.8	87.9	27.3	154.9	448 929	2 120	2 605.7	907.9	921.4	1 361	841
Spokane	486.6	237.7	134.2	482.5	91.6	32.6	129.8	238 193	1 609	1 575.8	697.5	548.2	1 202	709
Stevens	22.1	12.5	24.2	33.6	10.7	4.9	4.4	14 265	72	129.4	80.5	31.3	749	537
Thurston	122.2	119.1	24.2	287.1	340.4	673.5	1 437.6	232 869	1 156	882.4	347.7	334.2	1 401	841
Wahkiakum	1.2	0.1	0.8	2.8	0.5	0.1	0.4	1 654	11	30.0	18.4	3.7	914	611
Walla Walla	80.8	16.7	39.7	48.6	13.2	5.8	6.6	18 599	128	207.3	95.1	68.6	1 189	802
Whatcom	120.9	22.1	48.4	128.8	33.0	12.1	69.1	92 775	458	612.9	225.3	248.7	1 288	756
Whitman	25.8	3.2	6.4	57.8	8.5	10.8	75.8	17 432	90	164.7	52.8	41.2	1 000	705
Yakima	134.0	62.6	30.9	333.3	103.9	48.1	58.2	90 398	624	808.0	483.0	196.6	844	524
WEST VIRGINIA	1 936.4	344.6	1 437.9	2 463.2	510.8	338.2	1 658.0	345 589	2 395	X	X	X	X	X
Barbour	3.5	0.1	0.8	32.5	2.8	1.4	8.5	736	8	36.6	20.2	6.9	445	242
Berkeley	217.2	17.7	246.7	39.4	12.0	3.7	3.8	63 925	400	205.4	94.6	79.1	794	638
Boone	7.3	0.0	1.3	32.1	4.4	2.1	2.2	3 825	54	104.1	33.0	32.5	1 291	1 247
Braxton	12.0	1.6	0.8	35.5	3.5	1.6	0.9	2 100	1	31.3	18.4	5.1	347	303

1. State totals may include programs not allocated by county.   2. Based on the resident population estimated as of July 1 of the year shown.

Table B. States and Counties — **Local Government Finances, Government Employment, and Voting**

STATE County	Direct general expenditure — Total (mil dol)	Per capita[1] (dollars)	Education	Health and hospitals	Police protection	Public welfare	Highways	Debt outstanding — Total (mil dol)	Per capita[1] (dollars)	Federal civilian	Federal military	State and local	Democratic	Republican	All other
	185	186	187	188	189	190	191	192	193	194	195	196	197	198	199
VIRGINIA—Cont'd															
Manassas Park city	60.3	5 280	65.0	0.0	6.4	6.2	1.1	151.2	13 237	(3)	(3)	(3)	59.5	39.5	1.0
Martinsville city	56.2	3 857	47.6	0.0	6.8	3.6	5.2	25.1	1 722	(4)	(4)	(4)	63.5	35.4	1.1
Newport News city	742.7	4 146	44.2	10.3	5.8	6.5	4.1	1 027.6	5 736	5 226	7 164	12 897	63.9	35.3	0.8
Norfolk city	1 408.2	5 973	38.4	4.4	4.4	5.7	3.3	1 971.4	8 362	15 258	50 847	21 749	71.0	28.1	0.9
Norton city	17.5	4 712	43.4	0.4	8.9	8.4	9.2	10.1	2 706	(5)	(5)	(5)	49.1	49.2	1.7
Petersburg city	124.4	3 782	45.7	0.9	12.1	6.5	3.5	86.6	2 634	(6)	(6)	(6)	88.6	10.2	1.2
Poquoson city	38.7	3 261	56.6	0.8	6.0	1.3	4.5	51.7	4 361	(7)	(7)	(7)	24.7	74.0	1.2
Portsmouth city	423.3	4 151	40.6	2.6	6.6	6.5	1.4	473.9	4 647	10 989	6 069	5 782	69.3	30.0	0.8
Radford city	32.4	2 009	44.6	0.7	10.3	1.5	6.6	11.2	697	(8)	(8)	(8)	54.0	44.5	1.5
Richmond city	1 028.4	5 139	31.1	5.0	10.9	7.3	3.8	1 724.5	8 617	6 065	1 316	37 337	79.1	20.0	0.9
Roanoke city	423.6	4 574	39.1	0.5	4.8	9.0	3.3	394.7	4 263	1 682	345	7 143	61.2	37.8	1.1
Salem city	99.9	3 960	40.8	1.2	8.6	0.0	9.8	100.1	3 965	(9)	(9)	(9)	41.6	57.1	1.2
Staunton city	88.5	3 711	37.0	8.4	5.9	6.7	3.5	67.4	2 827	(10)	(10)	(10)	50.6	48.4	1.1
Suffolk city	298.4	3 669	48.6	0.4	4.5	3.5	4.9	531.1	6 531	516	475	5 554	56.2	43.0	0.7
Virginia Beach city	1 719.3	3 955	48.5	3.5	5.0	2.4	3.5	1 697.0	3 903	5 251	20 631	23 088	49.1	49.8	1.0
Waynesboro city	70.2	3 242	62.2	0.9	5.4	0.0	5.8	60.0	2 771	(10)	(10)	(10)	44.1	54.3	1.6
Williamsburg city	59.7	4 803	19.4	0.8	6.8	2.8	11.6	32.6	2 620	(11)	(11)	(11)	63.8	34.7	1.6
Winchester city	142.5	5 536	46.2	0.4	4.6	5.2	3.4	231.0	8 978	(12)	(12)	(12)	52.0	46.7	1.3
WASHINGTON	X	X	X	X	X	X	X	X	X	72 866	81 107	476 307	57.7	40.5	1.9
Adams	98.4	5 793	37.0	21.9	3.2	0.0	8.9	107.7	6 344	48	55	1 519	31.9	66.3	1.7
Asotin	59.7	2 829	49.9	5.8	4.0	0.0	10.0	37.9	1 795	64	66	1 148	42.3	55.7	1.9
Benton	696.0	3 886	43.8	24.4	3.7	0.0	4.7	7 452.6	46 750	812	533	11 339	36.1	62.2	1.8
Chelan	275.9	3 886	44.2	12.8	4.4	0.0	5.5	1 441.3	20 303	687	225	6 003	43.1	55.1	1.8
Clallam	372.2	5 281	23.1	40.1	2.7	0.0	3.3	168.1	2 386	477	575	6 726	50.5	47.2	2.2
Clark	1 361.4	3 256	49.4	3.4	4.1	0.4	6.1	2 008.5	4 804	2 981	1 341	21 406	52.2	46.1	1.7
Columbia	27.0	6 770	21.2	43.5	4.6	0.0	9.8	31.0	7 765	61	12	388	30.8	67.3	1.9
Cowlitz	352.0	3 503	42.9	4.2	5.1	0.0	6.6	638.1	6 351	238	316	5 588	54.4	43.2	2.4
Douglas	108.7	3 004	57.3	6.3	4.4	0.0	12.9	301.5	8 335	202	122	1 971	38.5	59.8	1.7
Ferry	37.2	5 043	32.7	34.6	2.4	0.3	10.3	6.3	859	180	23	781	41.9	54.7	3.4
Franklin	230.6	3 314	55.6	1.0	3.8	0.0	6.7	243.2	3 496	512	239	4 923	37.4	61.1	1.5
Garfield	11.1	5 398	36.5	5.2	6.8	0.0	16.2	5.2	2 546	123	0	357	28.0	70.5	1.5
Grant	406.4	4 894	38.1	25.7	3.2	0.6	6.3	1 439.4	17 332	656	272	7 111	35.0	62.5	2.5
Grays Harbor	284.7	3 992	45.4	6.6	5.1	0.0	6.0	341.5	4 787	244	266	6 174	56.0	41.5	2.5
Island	233.4	2 870	43.4	23.2	3.8	0.0	5.2	411.2	5 058	1 339	6 524	3 294	52.3	46.1	1.6
Jefferson	129.5	4 433	22.4	37.1	3.2	0.0	4.4	142.2	4 871	175	104	1 988	66.3	31.7	2.0
King	9 655.6	5 193	27.8	11.0	5.0	0.8	4.4	18 860.4	10 144	22 136	7 440	146 775	70.3	28.2	1.5
Kitsap	934.1	3 946	41.1	3.4	4.0	0.0	4.0	820.7	3 467	15 563	11 232	13 393	55.2	42.9	1.9
Kittitas	145.4	3 772	30.8	27.5	4.5	0.0	8.0	110.5	2 867	160	132	4 711	44.9	53.0	2.1
Klickitat	106.2	5 286	33.8	30.7	3.8	0.0	8.9	254.9	12 683	107	63	1 681	48.8	48.6	2.5
Lewis	265.1	3 600	42.6	7.1	4.3	0.0	6.6	322.2	4 375	242	231	4 807	39.3	58.4	2.3
Lincoln	69.4	6 769	37.1	33.2	3.2	0.0	9.0	19.9	1 939	80	32	1 238	34.0	63.6	2.4
Mason	201.1	3 566	41.5	24.1	3.5	0.0	7.3	117.9	2 090	82	179	5 330	53.2	44.5	2.3
Okanogan	189.8	4 787	44.0	24.8	3.7	0.2	4.8	92.0	2 320	506	125	4 447	45.1	52.2	2.7
Pacific	105.5	4 911	35.9	29.1	3.7	0.0	5.7	88.5	4 116	67	173	1 812	55.7	41.6	2.6
Pend Oreille	61.5	4 821	28.5	32.2	3.6	0.0	9.5	42.7	3 350	124	40	1 344	39.1	56.7	4.2
Pierce	3 026.4	3 914	45.2	3.8	5.1	0.4	5.5	4 196.0	5 427	11 748	36 606	46 703	55.2	43.0	1.8
San Juan	74.4	4 891	23.8	6.9	3.1	0.2	6.5	62.7	4 121	69	48	970	70.0	28.1	1.9
Skagit	668.9	5 747	25.6	41.8	3.1	0.0	3.7	488.5	4 197	430	369	10 402	53.8	44.2	2.1
Skamania	35.3	3 294	36.4	5.6	5.6	0.1	7.6	99.1	9 244	169	34	634	51.3	46.0	2.7
Snohomish	2 481.6	3 666	45.4	9.9	4.4	0.5	4.8	3 324.1	4 911	2 348	6 750	37 044	58.5	39.6	2.0
Spokane	1 516.3	3 324	49.0	4.6	5.4	0.1	5.0	957.6	2 099	4 807	4 164	30 962	48.2	49.3	2.5
Stevens	130.5	3 120	51.2	5.7	3.5	0.0	6.5	53.7	1 283	346	131	2 732	38.0	58.8	3.2
Thurston	845.2	3 543	48.3	5.0	3.8	0.0	5.0	708.9	2 972	960	801	36 202	59.9	38.2	1.9
Wahkiakum	27.5	6 813	16.1	41.3	3.3	0.1	9.5	4.3	1 061	17	13	256	48.9	48.2	3.0
Walla Walla	188.3	3 263	43.6	5.8	7.1	0.0	10.0	204.0	3 536	1 232	185	4 484	40.8	57.4	1.9
Whatcom	575.8	2 984	41.1	3.0	5.3	0.0	6.1	473.4	2 453	1 309	690	14 077	58.0	40.1	1.9
Whitman	158.6	3 847	31.1	32.9	3.8	1.3	5.2	86.9	2 109	274	147	9 334	51.6	46.1	2.4
Yakima	822.6	3 529	56.3	1.4	4.6	1.2	5.4	518.4	2 224	1 291	843	16 253	43.9	54.4	1.7
WEST VIRGINIA	X	X	X	X	X	X	X	X	X	23 631	10 182	124 967	42.6	55.7	1.7
Barbour	33.7	2 172	59.6	0.1	4.5	0.0	3.2	32.6	2 102	44	83	758	38.8	59.1	2.1
Berkeley	229.5	2 302	65.4	0.2	3.9	0.0	0.8	280.6	2 814	3 732	588	4 627	42.9	55.9	1.2
Boone	102.2	4 054	43.2	33.2	3.7	0.0	0.4	11.6	461	88	129	1 591	54.1	43.4	2.5
Braxton	29.1	1 987	73.0	0.1	2.0	0.5	0.1	88.7	6 059	62	76	958	50.0	48.6	1.4

1. Based on the resident population estimated as of July 1 of the year shown.   2. © 2009 Election Data Services, Inc. All rights reserved.   3. Manassas and Manassas Park cities are included with Prince William county.   4. Martinsville city is included with Henry county.   5. Norton city is included with Wise county.   6. Petersburg and Colonial Heights cities are included with Dinwiddie county.   7. Poquoson city is included with York county.   8. Radford city is included with Montgomery county.   9. Salem city is included with Roanoke county.   10. Staunton and Waynesboro cities are included with Augusta county.   11. Williamsburg city is included with James City county.   12. Winchester city is included with Frederick county.

Table B. States and Counties — **Land Area and Population**

STATE/ County code	CBSA code[1]	County type[2]	STATE County	Land area,[3] (sq km) 2010	Total persons	Rank	Per square kilometer	White	Black	American Indian, Alaska Native	Asian and Pacific Islander	Percent Hispanic or Latino[4]	Under 5 years	5 to 17 years	18 to 24 years	25 to 34 years	35 to 44 years	45 to 54 years
				1	2	3	4	5	6	7	8	9	10	11	12	13	14	15
			WEST VIRGINIA—Cont'd															
54 009	44600	3	Brooke	231	24 069	1 643	104.2	97.6	1.7	0.4	0.6	0.7	4.7	14.4	9.4	9.8	12.0	14.9
54 011	26580	2	Cabell	728	96 319	599	132.3	92.6	6.0	0.8	1.3	1.1	5.8	13.9	12.3	13.6	12.2	13.3
54 013	...	8	Calhoun	723	7 627	2 634	10.5	98.6	0.4	0.7	0.3	0.7	5.4	14.4	7.0	11.1	11.9	15.7
54 015	16620	2	Clay	886	9 386	2 492	10.6	99.3	0.2	0.7	0.2	0.4	6.1	17.6	7.1	11.0	13.1	15.0
54 017	17220	9	Doddridge	828	8 202	2 595	9.9	97.7	1.6	1.0	0.3	0.5	4.8	15.7	8.5	11.9	12.6	15.6
54 019	36060	6	Fayette	1 713	46 039	1 044	26.9	94.1	5.2	0.7	0.3	0.9	5.7	14.8	7.8	11.6	12.7	15.0
54 021	...	9	Gilmer	877	8 693	2 555	9.9	81.1	12.6	1.2	0.7	5.7	4.2	10.3	13.9	16.5	15.5	14.3
54 023	...	6	Grant	1 236	11 937	2 308	9.7	98.0	0.9	0.4	0.2	1.0	5.3	16.1	6.8	10.2	13.1	14.8
54 025	...	7	Greenbrier	2 641	35 480	1 288	13.4	95.3	3.5	0.8	0.6	1.2	5.2	14.9	7.6	10.8	11.6	15.2
54 027	49020	3	Hampshire	1 658	23 964	1 646	14.5	97.5	1.4	0.6	0.5	1.0	5.3	17.1	6.8	10.6	13.3	15.6
54 029	44600	3	Hancock	214	30 676	1 419	143.3	96.2	3.1	0.5	0.5	1.0	5.0	15.1	6.2	10.5	12.8	16.0
54 031	...	8	Hardy	1 508	14 025	2 172	9.3	93.0	2.7	0.5	1.1	3.4	5.7	15.8	7.2	11.0	13.8	15.5
54 033	17220	5	Harrison	1 077	69 099	766	64.2	96.4	2.2	0.8	0.7	1.3	5.8	16.1	7.3	11.9	13.0	15.4
54 035	...	6	Jackson	1 203	29 211	1 448	24.3	98.6	0.6	0.6	0.4	0.6	5.8	16.8	7.3	10.9	12.9	15.3
54 037	47900	1	Jefferson	543	53 498	928	98.5	87.2	7.7	0.9	1.8	4.7	6.3	17.4	9.8	11.3	14.6	15.8
54 039	16620	2	Kanawha	2 335	193 063	324	82.7	90.4	8.4	0.8	1.4	0.9	5.6	15.0	7.8	12.4	12.3	15.4
54 041	...	7	Lewis	997	16 372	2 027	16.4	98.4	0.7	0.7	0.5	0.6	5.7	15.0	7.1	11.1	13.1	15.2
54 043	16620	2	Lincoln	1 132	21 720	1 748	19.2	99.3	0.2	0.4	0.2	0.4	6.0	16.7	7.2	11.7	13.6	15.4
54 045	...	6	Logan	1 175	36 743	1 255	31.3	96.8	2.5	0.4	0.4	0.7	5.1	15.3	7.1	12.3	13.5	15.4
54 047	...	7	McDowell	1 382	22 113	1 733	16.0	89.8	10.1	0.6	0.2	0.4	5.4	14.5	7.7	11.5	12.6	15.8
54 049	21900	4	Marion	800	56 418	892	70.5	95.0	4.1	0.6	0.7	0.9	5.5	14.3	10.1	12.4	12.8	14.0
54 051	48540	3	Marshall	791	33 107	1 354	41.9	98.1	0.8	0.4	0.5	0.8	5.3	15.6	7.2	10.5	12.4	15.3
54 053	38580	6	Mason	1 116	27 324	1 519	24.5	98.4	1.0	0.6	0.5	0.4	5.8	16.0	7.0	11.9	12.4	15.8
54 055	14140	5	Mercer	1 085	62 264	835	57.4	92.4	6.8	0.6	0.7	0.8	5.7	14.8	9.1	11.3	12.1	13.8
54 057	19060	3	Mineral	849	28 212	1 489	33.2	95.9	3.5	0.5	0.5	0.7	6.4	15.4	9.6	10.3	13.0	14.5
54 059	...	6	Mingo	1 096	26 839	1 536	24.5	97.5	2.2	0.4	0.3	0.4	6.0	16.0	7.6	12.4	13.4	15.8
54 061	34060	3	Monongalia	933	96 189	602	103.1	91.2	4.4	0.5	3.6	1.8	4.6	11.2	26.7	14.9	10.7	11.3
54 063	...	8	Monroe	1 224	13 502	2 218	11.0	98.3	1.0	1.0	0.3	0.6	5.6	15.4	6.7	10.0	12.3	15.0
54 065	25180	3	Morgan	593	17 541	1 946	29.6	97.7	1.0	0.9	0.5	1.0	4.8	15.7	6.4	9.6	13.5	16.0
54 067	...	6	Nicholas	1 675	26 233	1 550	15.7	98.8	0.3	0.8	0.4	0.6	6.0	15.2	7.3	10.8	12.9	15.2
54 069	48540	3	Ohio	274	44 443	1 078	162.2	94.4	4.9	0.6	1.1	0.8	5.1	14.0	11.0	10.6	11.1	15.0
54 071	...	8	Pendleton	1 803	7 695	2 629	4.3	96.6	2.5	0.6	0.5	0.9	5.0	14.0	7.2	9.4	11.1	15.6
54 073	37620	3	Pleasants	337	7 605	2 635	22.6	97.6	1.5	0.8	0.2	0.8	4.7	15.7	7.4	11.5	14.3	16.3
54 075	...	9	Pocahontas	2 435	8 719	2 551	3.6	98.2	0.9	0.9	0.2	0.8	4.5	13.4	6.3	10.9	11.6	17.0
54 077	34060	3	Preston	1 680	33 520	1 333	20.0	97.8	1.3	0.6	0.3	0.7	5.4	14.2	7.4	13.8	13.8	15.3
54 079	16620	2	Putnam	895	55 486	903	62.0	97.2	1.3	0.6	1.0	0.9	6.0	17.7	6.5	11.6	14.1	15.8
54 081	13220	4	Raleigh	1 568	78 859	689	50.3	89.3	8.9	0.9	1.2	1.3	6.0	14.7	8.0	12.8	13.1	14.2
54 083	...	7	Randolph	2 693	29 405	1 443	10.9	97.6	1.4	0.5	0.5	0.7	5.1	14.3	8.4	11.5	12.9	15.4
54 085	...	8	Ritchie	1 171	10 449	2 407	8.9	99.0	0.3	0.6	0.2	0.5	5.5	15.7	6.9	10.5	12.6	16.6
54 087	...	6	Roane	1 252	14 926	2 115	11.9	98.7	0.4	0.6	0.5	0.7	5.5	16.2	6.7	10.7	12.8	15.6
54 089	...	7	Summers	934	13 927	2 183	14.9	93.4	5.2	0.9	0.4	1.4	4.5	13.6	6.1	11.9	12.9	15.9
54 091	17220	6	Taylor	447	16 895	1 991	37.8	97.8	1.1	0.6	0.5	0.8	5.7	15.1	7.3	12.1	13.7	15.5
54 093	...	9	Tucker	1 085	7 141	2 670	6.6	98.9	0.3	0.5	0.3	0.6	4.6	14.5	6.7	9.6	12.4	15.3
54 095	...	6	Tyler	664	9 208	2 509	13.9	99.0	0.2	0.5	0.3	0.5	5.1	15.8	6.6	9.0	13.2	16.0
54 097	...	7	Upshur	919	24 254	1 635	26.4	97.8	0.9	0.6	0.5	1.0	5.9	14.8	11.6	10.6	12.1	14.4
54 099	26580	2	Wayne	1 310	42 481	1 113	32.4	98.9	0.4	0.6	0.3	0.5	5.7	16.7	7.8	11.3	13.5	14.5
54 101	...	9	Webster	1 433	9 154	2 513	6.4	99.2	0.3	0.7	0.2	0.5	5.9	15.6	6.8	10.1	13.0	15.3
54 103	...	6	Wetzel	927	16 583	2 011	17.9	99.0	0.3	0.4	0.4	0.5	5.1	15.8	7.2	9.8	12.4	15.4
54 105	37620	3	Wirt	602	5 717	2 788	9.5	99.0	0.4	0.8	0.2	0.5	5.3	15.7	7.0	10.3	12.6	18.0
54 107	37620	3	Wood	949	86 956	648	91.6	97.1	1.8	0.7	0.8	0.9	5.8	16.0	7.6	11.5	12.9	15.4
54 109	...	7	Wyoming	1 294	23 796	1 650	18.4	98.8	0.8	0.7	0.2	0.4	5.6	15.9	7.5	11.1	12.9	15.4
55 000	...	X	**WISCONSIN**	140 268	5 686 986	X	40.5	84.6	6.8	1.3	2.7	5.9	6.3	17.3	9.7	12.7	12.8	15.4
55 001	...	8	Adams	1 672	20 875	1 795	12.5	91.9	3.3	1.3	0.6	3.8	4.1	12.3	5.9	9.8	11.4	16.2
55 003	...	7	Ashland	2 707	16 157	2 044	6.0	86.6	0.7	13.3	0.7	1.9	6.2	17.0	10.0	11.5	10.8	15.4
55 005	...	6	Barron	2 234	45 870	1 051	20.5	95.9	1.2	1.3	0.7	1.9	6.0	16.2	7.4	11.2	11.5	15.6
55 007	...	8	Bayfield	3 828	15 014	2 109	3.9	88.9	0.5	11.6	0.6	1.1	4.4	14.6	5.0	8.4	10.6	17.6
55 009	24580	2	Brown	1 372	248 007	262	180.8	85.3	2.8	3.2	3.1	7.3	6.9	18.0	9.9	13.7	13.3	15.3
55 011	...	8	Buffalo	1 740	13 587	2 213	7.8	97.3	0.4	0.6	0.4	1.7	5.7	16.5	6.9	10.1	12.1	16.2
55 013	...	8	Burnett	2 129	15 457	2 084	7.3	93.2	0.9	6.4	0.6	1.3	5.1	14.8	5.4	8.3	10.5	15.9
55 015	11540	3	Calumet	824	48 971	994	59.4	93.5	0.9	0.7	2.4	3.5	7.0	20.1	6.5	12.0	14.9	16.6
55 017	20740	3	Chippewa	2 612	62 415	834	23.9	95.4	1.9	0.8	1.5	1.3	6.6	17.0	7.6	12.6	13.0	16.0
55 019	...	8	Clark	3 133	34 690	1 310	11.1	95.2	0.4	0.7	0.5	3.7	8.4	20.7	7.7	10.9	11.2	14.1
55 021	31540	2	Columbia	1 983	56 833	886	28.7	95.2	1.5	0.7	0.8	2.5	6.0	17.3	6.8	12.0	13.6	16.5
55 023	...	7	Crawford	1 478	16 644	2 006	11.3	96.7	1.9	0.5	0.6	0.9	5.7	16.7	6.6	10.5	11.0	15.9
55 025	31540	2	Dane	3 101	488 073	136	157.4	83.7	6.1	0.7	5.5	5.9	6.2	15.5	12.9	16.2	13.3	14.1

1. CBSA = Core Based Statistical Area. See Appendix A for explanation. See Appendix B for list of metropolitan areas with component counties. 2. County type code from the Economic Research Service of USDA Rural-Urban Continuum Codes. See Appendix A for definition. 3. Dry land or land partially or temporarily covered by water. 4. May be of any race.

Table B. States and Counties — **Population and Households**

STATE County	Population, 2010 (cont.) Age (percent) (cont.)				Population change and components of change, 1990–2010							Households, 2010				
					Total persons		Percent change		Components of change, 2000–2009						Percent	
	55 to 64 years	65 to 74 years	75 years and over	Percent female	1990	2000	1990–2000	2000–2010	Births	Deaths	Net migration	Number	Percent change, 2000–2010	Persons per house-hold	Female family house-holder[1]	One per-son
	16	17	18	19	20	21	22	23	24	25	26	27	28	29	30	31
WEST VIRGINIA—Cont'd																
Brooke	15.8	9.4	9.7	51.5	26 992	25 447	-5.7	-5.4	2 105	2 985	-1 001	10 020	-3.6	2.32	10.7	29.2
Cabell	13.0	8.3	7.6	51.2	96 827	96 784	0.0	-0.5	10 780	10 919	-801	41 223	0.1	2.24	12.3	33.5
Calhoun	16.3	10.1	8.1	49.9	7 885	7 582	-3.8	0.6	718	823	-330	3 268	6.4	2.33	9.7	28.5
Clay	14.4	8.7	7.0	50.3	9 983	10 330	3.5	-9.1	1 231	1 108	-372	3 728	-7.3	2.50	9.7	26.2
Doddridge	14.8	9.8	6.4	46.5	6 994	7 403	5.8	10.8	637	746	-45	3 099	8.9	2.41	9.1	26.1
Fayette	15.4	8.9	8.1	49.9	47 952	47 579	-0.8	-3.2	5 307	5 612	-890	18 813	-0.7	2.35	12.5	29.1
Gilmer	11.7	7.5	6.2	39.5	7 669	7 160	-6.6	21.4	612	775	-139	2 753	-0.5	2.34	10.1	27.6
Grant	15.4	10.7	7.6	50.3	10 428	11 299	8.4	5.6	1 174	1 134	553	4 941	7.6	2.39	8.3	25.7
Greenbrier	15.5	10.6	8.7	51.3	34 693	34 453	-0.7	3.0	3 480	4 116	907	15 443	6.0	2.26	10.8	30.6
Hampshire	14.9	9.8	6.5	49.4	16 498	20 203	22.5	18.6	2 204	1 939	2 344	9 595	20.6	2.44	9.1	25.8
Hancock	15.6	9.3	9.5	51.6	35 233	32 667	-7.3	-6.1	3 078	3 915	-1 866	13 297	-2.8	2.29	12.2	29.5
Hardy	14.4	10.0	6.6	49.5	10 977	12 669	15.4	10.7	1 392	1 290	896	5 818	11.8	2.40	10.0	27.0
Harrison	13.9	8.6	7.9	51.3	69 371	68 652	-1.0	0.7	7 584	7 866	958	28 533	2.4	2.39	11.9	28.3
Jackson	13.3	9.8	7.9	50.6	25 938	28 000	7.9	4.3	2 980	2 843	64	11 931	7.9	2.43	10.3	25.0
Jefferson	13.0	7.2	4.6	50.6	35 926	42 190	17.4	26.8	5 866	3 681	8 525	19 931	23.3	2.61	10.1	22.7
Kanawha	14.7	8.7	8.0	52.0	207 619	200 073	-3.6	-3.5	21 609	22 660	-6 124	84 201	-2.3	2.26	13.1	32.5
Lewis	14.7	10.0	7.8	50.7	17 223	16 919	-1.8	-3.2	1 812	2 101	848	6 863	-1.2	2.35	10.9	28.5
Lincoln	14.3	9.0	6.2	50.3	21 382	22 108	3.4	-1.8	2 630	2 403	-59	8 783	1.4	2.47	10.7	25.6
Logan	16.0	8.4	6.8	50.7	43 032	37 710	-12.4	-2.6	4 075	4 506	-1 565	14 907	0.2	2.43	12.5	26.1
McDowell	15.8	9.2	7.4	50.5	35 233	27 329	-22.4	-19.1	2 666	3 448	-4 069	9 176	-17.8	2.36	13.9	28.8
Marion	14.0	8.9	8.0	51.2	57 249	56 598	-1.1	-0.3	5 746	6 629	1 342	23 786	0.6	2.32	11.1	29.3
Marshall	16.1	9.3	8.3	51.2	37 356	35 519	-4.9	-6.8	3 108	3 559	-2 349	13 869	-2.4	2.35	11.5	28.0
Mason	14.2	9.6	7.4	51.9	25 178	25 957	3.1	5.3	2 770	2 790	-224	11 149	5.3	2.39	11.6	27.4
Mercer	15.2	9.5	8.5	52.2	64 980	62 980	-3.1	-1.1	6 704	7 621	243	26 603	0.4	2.30	12.9	30.1
Mineral	14.4	10.3	7.1	50.4	26 697	27 078	1.4	4.2	2 791	2 855	351	11 550	7.1	2.39	10.0	27.0
Mingo	15.4	7.8	5.7	51.0	33 739	28 253	-16.3	-5.0	3 378	3 169	-1 945	11 125	-1.6	2.40	11.8	27.7
Monongalia	10.2	5.5	4.7	48.4	75 509	81 866	8.4	17.5	8 428	5 803	6 037	39 777	18.9	2.24	8.2	31.7
Monroe	15.3	11.2	8.4	50.5	12 406	14 583	17.5	-7.4	1 218	1 409	782	5 655	3.8	2.38	9.3	26.9
Morgan	16.7	10.7	7.6	50.1	12 128	14 943	23.2	17.4	1 422	1 696	1 787	7 303	18.8	2.39	8.9	25.7
Nicholas	15.5	10.0	7.1	50.8	26 775	26 562	-0.8	-1.2	2 696	2 818	-59	10 938	2.0	2.38	10.7	26.5
Ohio	14.8	8.7	9.8	52.4	50 871	47 427	-6.8	-6.3	4 430	5 450	-2 149	18 914	-4.2	2.21	11.7	35.3
Pendleton	15.9	11.3	10.5	49.4	8 054	8 196	1.8	-6.1	750	836	-678	3 285	-1.9	2.28	7.1	29.0
Pleasants	13.9	9.3	6.9	46.4	7 546	7 514	-0.4	1.2	638	802	56	2 861	-0.9	2.44	9.8	24.9
Pocahontas	16.9	11.1	8.2	48.7	9 008	9 131	1.4	-4.5	789	1 105	-350	3 758	-2.0	2.24	9.1	31.3
Preston	14.6	9.1	6.6	48.4	29 037	29 334	1.0	14.3	2 943	3 055	1 212	12 895	11.7	2.42	9.1	24.6
Putnam	13.9	8.5	5.9	50.9	42 835	51 589	20.4	7.6	5 961	4 329	2 750	21 981	9.8	2.51	9.5	22.3
Raleigh	15.1	8.5	7.5	50.1	76 819	79 220	3.1	-0.5	8 247	8 513	711	31 831	0.1	2.36	12.2	28.6
Randolph	14.6	10.2	7.6	48.5	27 803	28 262	1.7	4.0	2 983	3 174	472	11 695	5.6	2.32	10.5	28.4
Ritchie	15.1	10.1	7.1	50.0	10 233	10 343	1.1	1.0	1 046	1 157	35	4 367	4.4	2.37	9.8	28.2
Roane	15.4	10.0	7.2	50.5	15 120	15 446	2.2	-3.4	1 533	1 645	-409	6 195	0.6	2.39	9.9	27.2
Summers	15.9	10.3	8.9	55.1	14 204	12 999	-8.5	7.1	1 065	1 490	-819	5 572	0.8	2.26	10.9	30.8
Taylor	14.4	8.8	7.4	49.4	15 144	16 089	6.2	5.0	1 463	1 731	599	6 778	7.2	2.42	10.6	26.1
Tucker	15.8	12.2	8.8	49.9	7 728	7 321	-5.3	-2.5	589	791	-264	3 057	0.2	2.29	7.5	28.3
Tyler	15.8	10.3	8.2	51.0	9 796	9 592	-2.1	-4.0	829	1 060	-642	3 858	0.6	2.37	8.7	27.2
Upshur	14.0	9.6	7.1	50.8	22 867	23 404	2.3	3.6	2 580	2 436	395	9 619	7.2	2.40	9.6	26.9
Wayne	13.9	9.2	7.3	51.2	41 636	42 903	3.0	-1.0	4 291	4 323	-1 526	17 347	0.6	2.43	11.7	26.4
Webster	15.8	10.1	7.4	50.5	10 729	9 719	-9.4	-5.8	898	1 094	-21	3 792	-5.4	2.40	11.2	26.5
Wetzel	14.7	10.9	8.6	50.9	19 258	17 693	-8.1	-6.3	1 769	1 943	-1 220	6 968	-2.7	2.36	10.4	27.4
Wirt	15.4	10.1	5.5	49.8	5 192	5 873	13.1	-2.7	521	530	-234	2 391	4.7	2.39	9.5	25.2
Wood	13.9	9.5	7.4	51.8	86 915	87 986	1.2	-1.2	9 326	8 986	-897	36 571	0.8	2.35	11.6	28.4
Wyoming	16.4	8.6	6.5	50.4	28 990	25 708	-11.3	-7.4	2 455	2 702	-2 047	9 687	-7.3	2.45	10.3	25.1
WISCONSIN	12.3	7.0	6.6	50.4	4 891 954	5 363 675	9.6	6.0	654 879	429 869	59 904	2 279 768	9.4	2.43	10.3	28.2
Adams	16.8	14.3	9.1	46.2	15 682	18 643	18.9	12.0	1 520	2 132	848	8 666	9.7	2.24	8.1	27.7
Ashland	13.2	8.1	7.8	50.0	16 307	16 866	3.4	-4.2	1 877	1 816	-646	6 736	0.3	2.31	11.6	32.4
Barron	13.9	9.4	8.8	50.3	40 750	44 963	10.3	2.0	4 848	4 401	428	19 173	7.4	2.36	8.7	27.7
Bayfield	18.7	12.4	8.3	48.6	14 008	15 013	7.2	0.0	1 216	1 369	8	6 686	7.7	2.23	7.1	29.2
Brown	11.4	6.1	5.5	50.5	194 594	226 778	16.5	9.4	30 990	14 903	6 135	98 383	12.7	2.45	10.2	27.7
Buffalo	14.4	9.5	8.6	49.5	13 584	13 804	1.6	-1.6	1 389	1 174	-517	5 708	3.6	2.36	7.1	27.5
Burnett	16.9	13.8	9.3	49.5	13 084	15 674	19.8	-1.4	1 387	1 700	572	6 807	2.9	2.25	7.9	28.4
Calumet	11.5	6.1	5.4	49.9	34 291	40 631	18.5	20.5	5 876	2 401	801	18 575	24.6	2.63	6.8	21.1
Chippewa	13.0	7.5	6.8	48.1	52 360	55 195	5.4	13.1	6 798	4 704	3 669	24 410	14.3	2.45	8.9	25.8
Clark	11.4	7.4	8.2	49.3	31 647	33 557	6.0	3.4	5 074	3 046	-1 962	12 679	5.2	2.69	6.9	25.3
Columbia	13.2	7.7	6.9	49.1	45 088	52 468	16.4	8.3	5 995	4 671	1 706	22 735	11.2	2.43	8.4	26.0
Crawford	15.2	10.1	8.3	48.5	15 940	17 243	8.2	-3.5	1 801	1 601	-613	6 812	2.0	2.33	9.1	29.3
Dane	11.6	5.4	4.8	50.5	367 085	426 526	16.2	14.4	54 809	24 654	37 354	203 750	17.4	2.33	8.6	30.5

1. No spouse present.

Table B. States and Counties — Population, Vital Statistics, Medicare, and Crime

STATE County	Persons in group quarters, 2010	Daytime population, 2006–2010 Number	Daytime population Employment/ residence ratio	Births, average 2006–2008 Total	Births Rate[1]	Deaths, average 2006–2008 Number	Deaths Rate[1]	Persons under 65 with no health insurance, 2009 Number	Percent	Medicare, 2011 Eligible for Medicare	Enrolled in Medicare Advantage	Enrolled in a Medicare prescription drug plan	Serious crimes known to police,[2] 2010 Total Number	Rate[3]
	32	33	34	35	36	37	38	39	40	41	42	43	44	45
WEST VIRGINIA—Cont'd														
Brooke	872	22 444	0.8	D	D	331	13.9	2 627	14.2	5 279	1 844	2 553	264	1 146
Cabell	3 936	108 088	1.3	1 232	13.1	1 213	12.9	13 333	17.2	19 997	5 262	10 101	4 292	4 456
Calhoun	22	6 660	0.6	D	D	85	11.7	1 159	20.2	1 890	301	1 100	NA	NA
Clay	74	8 715	0.7	D	D	126	12.4	1 503	18.4	2 287	655	1 270	NA	NA
Doddridge	722	6 151	0.4	D	D	74	10.2	1 107	18.7	1 194	277	544	NA	NA
Fayette	1 840	42 589	0.8	587	12.6	626	13.5	7 084	18.8	10 196	2 386	5 427	621	1 596
Gilmer	2 239	8 662	1.1	D	D	91	13.2	1 173	21.2	1 397	332	830	80	920
Grant	126	10 951	0.8	D	D	117	9.8	1 630	18.0	2 696	425	1 559	91	991
Greenbrier	616	36 080	1.1	D	D	456	13.2	5 219	19.1	8 658	1 658	4 958	265	803
Hampshire	508	19 158	0.5	D	D	202	9.0	3 541	19.1	4 719	626	2 575	298	1 262
Hancock	226	28 985	0.9	D	D	404	13.3	3 372	14.3	7 027	1 695	3 817	195	723
Hardy	58	15 050	1.2	D	D	133	9.8	1 972	17.8	2 896	544	1 544	166	1 184
Harrison	885	73 402	1.2	838	12.2	835	12.2	9 798	17.3	14 782	2 719	7 907	1 984	2 931
Jackson	180	26 950	0.8	D	D	323	11.4	3 579	15.9	6 500	1 156	3 121	214	733
Jefferson	1 391	45 066	0.7	684	13.4	405	7.9	6 526	14.2	8 074	1 218	3 112	816	1 525
Kanawha	3 163	213 735	1.2	2 401	12.5	2 475	12.9	24 573	15.7	41 983	11 262	20 909	6 688	3 592
Lewis	248	17 180	1.1	D	D	231	13.5	2 648	18.7	4 020	1 075	2 214	140	855
Lincoln	65	18 062	0.4	D	D	262	11.7	3 466	18.9	4 803	1 282	2 655	454	2 090
Logan	464	37 770	1.1	D	D	496	13.9	5 171	17.5	8 575	2 106	4 744	1 139	3 194
McDowell	471	23 036	1.1	298	12.8	376	16.2	3 652	20.2	5 911	1 392	3 450	248	1 371
Marion	1 340	53 171	0.9	628	11.1	698	12.3	7 964	17.4	12 086	2 156	7 325	732	1 443
Marshall	447	31 168	0.8	D	D	389	11.7	3 756	14.2	6 449	2 303	2 762	675	2 165
Mason	635	25 178	0.8	318	12.4	309	12.0	2 979	14.5	6 004	963	2 972	452	1 710
Mercer	1 188	61 396	1.0	762	12.4	857	14.0	9 364	18.9	15 227	2 877	8 968	1 843	3 029
Mineral	646	24 135	0.7	D	D	295	11.0	3 401	15.1	5 871	694	3 365	529	1 984
Mingo	85	26 134	0.9	357	13.4	374	14.0	4 205	18.9	6 735	1 767	3 783	328	1 317
Monongalia	7 262	104 801	1.3	921	10.6	621	7.2	11 314	14.4	11 440	2 570	6 725	2 510	2 660
Monroe	57	10 872	0.5	D	D	158	11.6	2 153	19.7	3 291	574	1 753	91	684
Morgan	123	14 385	0.6	D	D	187	11.4	2 329	17.7	3 744	466	1 647	296	1 804
Nicholas	162	25 785	1.0	309	11.8	323	12.3	3 800	17.9	6 417	1 685	3 098	653	2 700
Ohio	2 618	53 483	1.4	486	10.9	577	13.0	4 931	14.2	10 289	4 205	4 090	903	2 145
Pendleton	196	6 696	0.7	D	D	99	13.0	1 146	20.3	1 923	360	1 098	NA	NA
Pleasants	623	7 706	1.0	D	D	77	10.6	987	16.1	1 541	371	822	NA	NA
Pocahontas	318	8 852	1.0	D	D	116	13.5	1 344	20.3	2 092	425	1 203	71	926
Preston	2 378	27 709	0.6	D	D	324	10.7	4 546	18.4	6 516	1 152	3 740	465	1 549
Putnam	225	50 215	0.8	D	D	487	8.8	6 015	12.7	10 345	2 807	4 725	738	1 413
Raleigh	3 857	80 537	1.1	938	11.8	928	11.7	11 912	18.4	18 117	3 836	9 630	2 930	3 859
Randolph	2 273	29 792	1.0	D	D	327	11.6	4 310	18.8	6 522	1 143	3 859	646	2 197
Ritchie	106	10 591	1.0	D	D	127	12.2	1 564	18.8	2 628	502	1 484	138	1 487
Roane	98	13 653	0.7	D	D	189	12.3	2 368	19.5	3 731	917	1 975	106	710
Summers	1 329	12 639	0.7	D	D	165	12.5	2 170	21.2	3 252	695	1 965	269	1 931
Taylor	511	13 083	0.5	D	D	177	10.9	2 391	18.0	3 389	529	1 967	35	207
Tucker	142	7 016	1.0	D	D	83	12.0	962	18.3	1 630	376	999	72	1 273
Tyler	67	8 279	0.7	D	D	109	12.1	1 090	15.8	2 115	639	985	24	261
Upshur	1 215	23 672	1.0	D	D	257	10.9	3 576	18.5	4 988	1 263	2 445	190	783
Wayne	246	37 191	0.7	455	11.0	450	10.9	5 894	17.5	9 257	2 139	4 607	1 039	2 487
Webster	58	8 397	0.7	D	D	120	12.6	1 536	20.2	2 396	573	1 438	NA	NA
Wetzel	124	16 693	1.0	D	D	210	12.8	2 053	15.9	3 898	1 365	1 587	NA	NA
Wirt	0	4 535	0.5	D	D	59	10.0	835	18.2	1 349	248	809	89	1 557
Wood	1 046	91 323	1.1	994	11.5	968	11.2	10 940	15.6	19 664	2 927	11 769	1 967	2 262
Wyoming	56	22 579	0.8	D	D	306	12.9	3 376	17.4	5 920	1 354	3 457	546	2 361
WISCONSIN	150 214	5 585 211	1.0	72 462	12.9	46 403	8.3	506 363	10.6	940 936	286 948	318 762	156 754	2 756
Adams	1 432	18 003	0.6	D	D	224	10.9	2 039	13.2	5 694	980	2 256	499	2 390
Ashland	623	17 881	1.2	D	D	185	11.3	1 686	12.5	3 421	794	1 304	431	2 668
Barron	681	45 648	1.0	D	D	469	10.3	4 173	11.4	9 966	2 936	3 534	656	1 545
Bayfield	126	12 903	0.7	D	D	145	9.7	1 513	12.8	3 802	1 019	1 224	313	2 085
Brown	6 629	263 640	1.2	3 472	14.3	1 649	6.8	22 738	10.7	35 787	14 307	10 071	5 099	2 056
Buffalo	107	11 434	0.7	D	D	125	9.0	1 152	10.6	2 879	508	1 166	110	810
Burnett	139	14 647	0.8	D	D	168	10.3	1 536	12.6	4 434	1 204	1 580	289	1 870
Calumet	198	36 449	0.5	668	15.0	273	6.1	3 083	7.9	6 355	3 559	1 363	919	1 877
Chippewa	2 542	57 715	0.9	803	13.3	492	8.1	5 404	10.6	10 983	2 902	3 564	1 067	1 710
Clark	536	32 066	0.8	D	D	316	9.4	4 227	15.3	5 984	2 642	1 449	457	1 317
Columbia	1 526	49 313	0.8	656	11.9	491	8.9	4 052	8.9	9 968	2 152	4 135	1 083	1 906
Crawford	785	17 592	1.1	D	D	172	10.1	1 671	12.3	3 720	1 070	1 433	NA	NA
Dane	12 775	514 156	1.1	6 176	13.0	2 721	5.7	36 149	8.4	62 294	12 171	24 186	15 101	3 094

1. Per 1,000 estimated resident population. 2. Data for serious crimes have not been adjusted for underreporting; this may affect comparability between geographic areas and over time. 3. Per 100,000 population estimated by the FBI.

Table B. States and Counties — Crime, Education, Money Income, and Poverty

STATE County	Serious crimes known to police,[1] 2010 (cont.) Rate[2] Violent	Property	Education — School enrollment and attainment, 2006–2010 — Enrollment[3] Total	Per cent private	Attainment[4] (percent) High school graduate or less	Bachelor's degree or more	Local government expenditures,[5] 2008–2009 Total current expenditures (mil dol)	Current expenditures per student (dollars)	Money income, 2006–2010 Per capita income[6] (dollars)	Households Median income Dollars	Percent change, 2000 to 2006–2010 (constant 2010 dollars)	Percent with income of $200,000 or more	Income and poverty, 2010 Median household income (dollars)	Percent below poverty level All persons	Children under 18 years	Children 5 to 17 years in families
	46	47	48	49	50	51	52	53	54	55	56	57	58	59	60	61
WEST VIRGINIA—Cont'd																
Brooke	74	1 072	5 179	16.8	58.2	15.6	36.9	10 775	22 377	39 475	-5.5	0.7	38 197	14.7	22.1	18.8
Cabell	296	4 160	24 972	11.2	49.3	23.0	129.3	10 322	21 907	34 492	-4.4	1.6	36 274	23.3	35.3	32.9
Calhoun	NA	NA	1 487	4.4	72.6	8.0	11.2	9 955	17 121	26 922	-1.5	0.6	29 084	24.2	36.4	33.3
Clay	NA	NA	2 162	3.1	73.5	8.3	21.0	10 354	16 205	30 789	9.9	1.2	31 232	26.0	37.6	34.1
Doddridge	NA	NA	1 799	6.1	72.1	8.0	14.3	11 879	14 658	30 019	-11.4	0.8	34 444	20.6	29.7	25.9
Fayette	206	1 391	10 060	11.3	68.5	10.7	71.0	10 433	17 082	31 912	1.7	0.4	30 856	22.6	32.4	29.3
Gilmer	196	725	2 476	10.7	65.9	12.2	10.9	11 613	13 899	29 706	2.6	2.0	31 558	29.1	30.6	29.3
Grant	229	763	2 440	6.4	71.6	11.5	18.1	9 185	19 358	35 593	-2.8	0.5	36 487	17.6	26.2	22.9
Greenbrier	39	764	7 265	13.0	61.0	17.2	55.7	10 620	20 044	33 732	-1.1	1.1	35 456	20.8	29.4	25.3
Hampshire	250	1 012	5 300	7.7	74.6	9.4	33.6	9 027	17 752	31 792	-20.7	0.3	33 991	18.4	25.6	23.4
Hancock	59	663	6 229	11.9	57.2	15.3	43.8	10 119	23 118	38 565	-9.8	1.8	38 501	13.6	20.7	18.3
Hardy	193	991	3 482	3.7	70.6	9.5	20.5	8 710	16 944	31 347	-22.3	0.4	37 002	16.3	24.7	22.4
Harrison	309	2 622	14 613	10.0	55.9	17.6	117.4	10 492	21 010	39 191	1.3	1.2	40 441	17.3	24.8	22.1
Jackson	75	657	6 555	4.3	58.6	14.5	51.4	10 145	20 633	41 406	0.8	0.7	38 600	20.2	29.7	28.2
Jefferson	131	1 394	14 553	13.8	47.9	27.7	89.7	10 682	29 733	65 603	16.8	4.7	63 156	11.1	15.4	13.8
Kanawha	444	3 149	41 417	14.1	52.2	23.4	290.1	10 191	25 439	42 669	-0.2	2.8	43 110	14.8	22.1	20.4
Lewis	153	702	3 086	9.6	68.6	12.0	29.9	11 114	18 240	33 293	-2.9	1.1	34 734	19.2	27.5	25.8
Lincoln	244	1 846	4 202	4.8	73.9	7.7	39.6	10 989	16 439	30 868	7.6	1.1	34 119	24.2	33.6	29.7
Logan	379	2 815	7 151	2.9	69.7	8.9	63.9	9 814	18 614	35 465	13.8	1.0	33 202	22.3	30.1	26.0
McDowell	343	1 028	4 162	7.6	78.5	6.3	42.9	11 666	12 955	22 154	3.3	0.2	24 133	33.6	45.4	42.6
Marion	211	1 232	13 228	10.6	55.4	19.2	86.3	10 620	20 752	38 115	5.1	0.8	38 856	16.8	24.5	23.1
Marshall	106	2 059	7 372	10.4	61.1	12.2	57.6	11 788	21 064	34 419	-12.3	0.7	37 206	17.0	25.7	22.8
Mason	91	1 619	5 755	8.0	65.4	10.3	47.4	11 023	19 609	36 027	4.9	1.1	36 279	18.4	27.2	24.9
Mercer	320	2 708	13 341	9.3	62.1	16.4	97.1	10 182	18 431	32 131	-4.7	1.2	32 366	21.6	31.4	30.3
Mineral	289	1 695	6 538	8.2	62.7	13.0	48.0	10 553	20 805	36 571	-7.3	0.9	38 629	16.7	24.6	21.8
Mingo	237	1 080	5 518	4.9	70.4	9.0	51.2	10 922	17 629	32 902	21.7	0.5	31 915	23.7	31.6	28.5
Monongalia	394	2 266	35 079	5.3	44.3	35.8	108.0	10 490	23 116	39 167	8.1	3.1	42 247	22.2	17.0	15.8
Monroe	45	639	2 524	13.1	66.5	13.3	20.3	10 401	18 927	39 574	13.8	0.0	34 637	17.9	26.1	23.4
Morgan	134	1 670	3 477	6.4	66.8	12.7	27.1	10 066	20 732	37 281	-15.9	0.5	40 636	13.5	20.9	18.2
Nicholas	748	1 952	5 259	3.7	67.6	13.0	42.9	10 511	19 359	38 457	12.6	1.1	35 945	18.6	27.6	26.5
Ohio	409	1 737	10 653	24.3	47.9	25.9	59.1	11 192	23 950	39 669	1.6	2.4	38 997	16.6	24.5	22.2
Pendleton	NA	NA	1 286	2.8	64.7	13.1	12.2	11 045	19 401	33 323	-13.5	0.0	36 733	15.3	24.5	21.7
Pleasants	NA	NA	1 827	1.6	61.0	10.4	16.6	12 341	18 770	38 882	-6.2	0.0	40 416	15.1	20.5	17.3
Pocahontas	300	626	1 511	2.8	67.0	13.5	13.5	11 165	19 763	32 161	-3.8	0.8	31 289	19.9	30.5	27.7
Preston	183	1 366	6 230	6.5	67.8	11.6	45.7	10 001	19 329	40 753	15.2	1.0	42 528	15.8	23.6	21.9
Putnam	136	1 278	11 783	10.3	48.9	23.8	94.8	10 147	25 857	52 618	-0.8	2.5	52 942	10.4	14.0	12.2
Raleigh	452	3 407	16 667	19.1	61.3	15.4	120.1	9 754	20 457	38 006	6.6	1.4	37 915	18.0	25.8	25.3
Randolph	439	1 758	6 158	18.4	65.4	17.6	42.5	9 595	18 472	36 176	4.6	1.6	35 176	18.7	29.0	26.8
Ritchie	183	1 304	2 216	4.7	61.7	10.3	17.5	11 007	18 255	32 619	-5.8	1.4	35 170	19.9	27.5	25.6
Roane	121	590	2 982	2.2	74.1	9.1	24.1	9 498	15 103	27 428	-11.6	0.1	31 362	23.2	33.4	29.8
Summers	215	1 716	2 794	8.5	67.7	11.2	16.0	10 470	15 190	27 720	3.5	0.5	29 261	23.0	34.0	31.6
Taylor	12	195	3 627	9.3	64.3	14.5	23.8	9 797	18 562	36 956	7.6	0.3	36 846	20.3	28.2	25.5
Tucker	354	919	1 290	8.8	66.2	13.7	12.3	10 883	20 020	32 712	-1.6	0.5	33 915	19.2	25.7	22.2
Tyler	11	250	1 750	0.5	70.9	8.3	17.2	11 628	18 245	33 496	-9.7	1.0	36 122	16.2	25.6	23.1
Upshur	62	722	6 007	27.3	67.0	15.2	38.3	9 914	18 823	36 114	5.7	1.6	35 893	21.9	30.5	26.3
Wayne	141	2 346	9 909	8.3	64.2	12.7	75.1	9 720	18 410	35 079	1.3	1.0	36 360	20.2	27.9	25.5
Webster	NA	NA	1 551	1.7	76.6	8.0	15.7	10 148	17 268	28 025	5.1	0.7	29 083	26.5	40.3	37.7
Wetzel	NA	NA	3 568	5.1	64.7	12.6	32.8	11 229	19 899	36 636	-6.5	0.1	36 390	18.3	27.8	24.3
Wirt	245	1 312	1 226	7.7	68.5	11.0	10.0	10 528	18 438	36 705	-5.7	0.0	36 037	22.1	34.1	31.1
Wood	408	1 854	19 912	11.0	49.2	19.1	138.5	10 274	22 890	42 146	0.0	1.7	39 456	15.5	25.3	22.4
Wyoming	285	2 075	5 082	5.9	73.1	9.3	46.1	11 128	17 662	36 343	19.9	0.1	35 872	20.0	30.0	27.0
WISCONSIN	249	2 508	1 479 601	17.1	44.6	25.8	9 605.4	11 078	26 624	51 598	-7.0	2.6	48 974	13.2	19.0	17.0
Adams	149	2 242	3 626	7.6	58.7	10.8	21.4	11 655	21 917	39 885	-5.7	0.8	42 347	14.9	28.7	27.3
Ashland	179	2 488	4 093	20.4	46.6	20.7	33.9	11 822	19 730	38 111	-4.8	0.8	36 651	18.9	28.2	25.7
Barron	97	1 449	9 914	9.5	53.4	17.6	85.2	10 770	22 666	42 601	-9.7	1.7	42 805	13.6	22.0	20.4
Bayfield	180	1 905	2 890	13.5	40.3	26.8	21.9	14 115	24 028	43 176	2.1	1.0	40 155	14.8	25.1	21.7
Brown	181	1 875	66 037	18.2	44.5	25.6	433.1	10 294	26 816	52 553	-10.6	2.8	51 330	10.3	14.8	13.0
Buffalo	66	743	2 991	7.3	55.5	15.5	23.4	10 464	22 579	45 302	-3.8	1.0	44 088	12.0	16.8	14.9
Burnett	142	1 727	2 980	11.7	52.4	16.0	25.8	9 892	22 767	39 626	-8.5	1.4	38 774	15.3	26.6	24.9
Calumet	114	1 762	12 396	15.4	45.7	25.3	38.3	9 519	27 567	61 685	-7.3	2.3	62 173	5.4	7.8	6.9
Chippewa	123	1 586	14 146	13.1	54.0	17.5	91.6	10 362	23 952	48 672	-2.9	1.4	46 479	12.3	18.8	17.0
Clark	274	1 044	7 985	21.5	63.3	11.3	54.2	10 476	19 797	42 777	-2.3	1.6	40 136	14.8	23.9	22.9
Columbia	165	1 740	12 776	12.2	48.1	19.9	94.9	10 633	26 993	55 910	-2.0	2.1	54 304	9.5	13.6	12.1
Crawford	NA	NA	4 040	13.7	56.7	15.9	26.7	11 612	21 346	39 486	-8.7	1.5	37 649	14.3	21.2	19.6
Dane	260	2 834	143 191	12.4	26.6	45.4	765.6	11 517	32 392	60 519	-2.9	4.3	58 958	12.3	12.5	11.3

1. Data for serious crimes have not been adjusted for underreporting; this may affect comparability between geographic areas and over time. 2. Per 100,000 population estimated by the FBI. 3. All persons 3 years old and over enrolled in nursery school through college. 4. Persons 25 years old and over. 5. Elementary and secondary education expenditures. 6. Based on population estimated by the American Community Survey, 2006–2010.

Table B. States and Counties — **Personal Income**

STATE County	Personal income, 2009 Total (mil dol)	Per capita Percent change, 2008–2009	Per capita Dollars	Per capita Rank	Wages and salaries[2] (mil dol)	Proprietors' income (mil dol)	Dividends, interest, and rent (mil dol)	Transfer payments (mil dol) Total	Government payments to individuals Total	Social Security	Medical payments	Income mainte-nance	Unemploy-ment insurance
	62	63	64	65	66	67	68	69	70	71	72	73	74
WEST VIRGINIA—Cont'd													
Brooke	728	0.0	30 971	1 763	367	59	102	203	199	84	79	15	10
Cabell	3 221	1.2	33 834	1 193	2 596	217	494	903	886	280	390	86	24
Calhoun	167	2.4	23 414	3 010	58	19	18	71	69	25	28	9	3
Clay	214	3.6	21 351	3 074	108	13	16	83	82	30	28	13	3
Doddridge	160	1.3	22 165	3 061	44	13	18	39	38	17	10	6	2
Fayette	1 269	2.7	27 523	2 478	558	64	120	470	461	148	208	50	13
Gilmer	194	3.2	28 437	2 314	104	23	23	61	60	18	27	6	2
Grant	355	1.9	29 985	1 982	219	30	49	108	106	35	50	8	4
Greenbrier	1 045	0.6	30 279	1 914	535	78	163	344	337	119	155	27	11
Hampshire	544	0.5	23 978	2 965	165	35	73	157	153	64	54	17	6
Hancock	947	0.9	31 839	1 568	487	38	139	309	303	113	140	21	15
Hardy	343	0.5	25 166	2 849	220	11	49	85	83	38	24	9	5
Harrison	2 498	2.1	36 257	853	1 796	276	340	604	591	210	252	60	16
Jackson	775	-0.9	27 599	2 468	363	45	101	244	239	94	91	23	17
Jefferson	1 920	1.9	36 390	830	645	94	251	286	276	111	92	22	13
Kanawha	7 985	0.8	41 663	352	5 885	912	1 087	1 878	1 843	636	856	163	47
Lewis	531	2.5	30 541	1 854	283	64	73	148	145	54	58	18	5
Lincoln	543	3.5	24 517	2 913	153	30	45	178	174	67	54	29	6
Logan	1 141	5.3	32 145	1 497	584	32	102	449	443	134	192	44	9
McDowell	544	5.1	24 305	2 934	312	14	52	263	258	85	98	45	7
Marion	1 898	3.6	33 463	1 265	1 045	119	241	490	479	182	187	41	13
Marshall	1 020	0.7	31 330	1 689	615	68	125	260	254	99	104	25	10
Mason	702	3.0	27 453	2 494	365	25	79	240	236	85	98	26	12
Mercer	1 910	3.5	30 840	1 790	961	104	262	694	683	210	312	71	14
Mineral	824	3.5	30 293	1 909	371	37	94	235	230	81	94	20	8
Mingo	771	2.3	29 222	2 145	530	33	72	298	293	102	114	43	7
Monongalia	3 312	3.6	36 767	778	2 757	286	468	580	564	171	271	40	17
Monroe	341	2.5	24 842	2 878	98	17	40	114	111	45	43	9	3
Morgan	553	0.5	33 769	1 207	119	40	75	133	130	53	52	9	5
Nicholas	756	4.0	28 833	2 225	388	37	88	249	244	93	97	26	8
Ohio	1 623	-0.5	36 869	762	1 290	34	383	444	436	154	202	32	13
Pendleton	227	-1.3	30 693	1 823	88	13	38	64	63	24	28	4	2
Pleasants	219	-2.0	29 689	2 052	153	16	23	75	74	23	40	5	3
Pocahontas	248	1.6	29 433	2 108	118	19	34	96	94	28	52	6	3
Preston	877	3.7	28 994	2 201	324	50	96	239	233	88	92	23	9
Putnam	2 042	1.8	36 674	790	1 153	103	219	350	340	157	113	29	14
Raleigh	2 647	2.6	33 429	1 272	1 615	165	304	769	754	269	309	70	19
Randolph	867	1.9	30 532	1 856	466	75	108	285	280	85	140	23	9
Ritchie	289	0.1	28 273	2 352	136	20	34	91	89	37	32	10	3
Roane	368	0.4	24 764	2 888	127	29	43	136	133	50	51	17	6
Summers	321	3.0	24 507	2 916	99	10	39	140	138	38	64	14	3
Taylor	423	3.5	25 916	2 745	123	12	52	126	123	43	47	14	4
Tucker	193	1.8	28 399	2 325	84	9	28	67	66	24	31	4	3
Tyler	221	1.6	25 471	2 808	114	9	30	73	71	33	23	8	3
Upshur	639	2.1	26 863	2 588	352	51	91	183	179	68	65	20	7
Wayne	1 154	5.1	28 070	2 389	552	33	115	285	277	122	62	46	11
Webster	222	4.7	23 478	3 006	110	10	27	90	89	32	32	13	3
Wetzel	497	1.5	30 659	1 831	155	18	69	167	164	59	75	16	6
Wirt	123	2.5	21 948	3 069	27	6	12	45	44	17	15	6	2
Wood	2 782	1.5	32 019	1 527	1 918	149	408	790	774	289	323	75	29
Wyoming	630	1.6	27 026	2 561	258	16	51	233	229	95	75	31	7
WISCONSIN	211 337	-0.9	37 373	X	138 798	11 883	36 423	38 912	37 882	13 693	15 543	3 346	2 898
Adams	613	0.7	30 516	1 858	191	71	95	172	168	83	53	13	6
Ashland	519	3.8	32 079	1 509	393	34	74	151	148	46	70	12	11
Barron	1 425	0.2	31 249	1 700	834	95	241	362	353	135	149	25	23
Bayfield	474	1.6	32 020	1 526	137	35	97	126	123	53	47	9	6
Brown	9 234	-0.2	37 338	709	7 820	503	1 594	1 405	1 360	520	498	114	122
Buffalo	502	-2.9	37 400	699	257	44	81	99	97	38	43	6	4
Burnett	481	0.7	30 281	1 911	170	46	84	143	140	63	53	9	6
Calumet	1 749	-2.6	39 093	529	481	131	252	211	203	95	56	12	26
Chippewa	1 953	0.7	32 231	1 478	941	158	319	431	420	150	180	32	33
Clark	940	-2.3	28 111	2 381	429	73	147	243	237	79	109	13	21
Columbia	2 195	0.5	39 778	465	936	121	354	390	380	145	160	18	35
Crawford	483	-0.6	28 860	2 224	292	28	76	125	121	47	50	8	9
Dane	21 533	-1.1	43 824	245	17 149	1 353	4 077	2 566	2 477	920	962	242	170

1. Based on the resident population estimated as of July 1 of the year shown.   2. Includes supplements to wages and salaries.

Table B. States and Counties — Earnings, Social Security, and Housing

STATE County	Earnings, 2009									Social Security beneficiaries, December 2010		Supplemental Security Income recipients, December 2010	Housing units, 2010	
			Percent by selected industries											
			Goods-related[1]		Service-related and health									
	Total (mil dol)	Farm	Total	Manu-facturing	Infor-mation and profes-sional and technical services	Retail trade	Finance, insur-ance, and real estate	Health care and social services	Govern-ment	Number	Rate[2]		Total	Percent change, 2000-2010
	75	76	77	78	79	80	81	82	83	84	85	86	87	88
WEST VIRGINIA—Cont'd														
Brooke	426	-0.1	D	31.3	D	5.1	3.5	D	11.8	6 105	254	605	10 967	-2.0
Cabell	2 813	-0.1	D	11.2	6.8	7.5	4.2	24.5	17.8	21 625	225	4 250	46 169	1.2
Calhoun	77	-2.3	D	1.7	2.6	8.7	2.8	17.3	21.9	2 170	285	687	3 963	3.0
Clay	121	-0.7	44.9	2.8	D	4.3	D	8.3	21.6	2 610	278	770	4 572	-5.5
Doddridge	58	-3.0	D	D	D	7.6	D	7.3	41.9	1 400	171	261	3 946	7.8
Fayette	622	-0.1	22.7	5.7	3.8	9.2	3.5	D	27.4	12 000	261	2 718	21 618	0.0
Gilmer	127	-2.2	D	6.7	D	3.8	D	4.5	47.8	1 575	181	348	3 448	-4.8
Grant	250	-0.1	D	6.9	D	4.5	2.6	6.6	18.3	3 095	259	423	6 366	4.3
Greenbrier	613	0.4	12.2	5.9	D	10.7	3.5	D	20.3	9 820	277	1 436	18 980	7.6
Hampshire	199	-1.6	D	5.9	D	7.9	5.6	D	34.3	5 505	230	764	13 688	22.4
Hancock	525	-0.1	D	34.5	4.6	6.5	3.3	6.5	13.9	8 165	266	811	14 541	-1.0
Hardy	231	-2.7	D	D	D	7.8	3.3	D	16.4	3 260	232	456	8 078	13.5
Harrison	2 072	-0.3	19.0	5.9	9.7	6.7	3.0	12.4	29.6	16 840	244	3 087	31 431	1.0
Jackson	408	-1.7	D	28.8	4.9	9.4	3.5	D	18.3	7 520	257	1 269	13 305	8.7
Jefferson	739	0.5	D	5.6	9.0	7.2	3.8	8.5	31.2	8 755	164	789	22 037	25.0
Kanawha	6 797	0.0	17.2	4.5	12.4	6.1	6.5	16.8	19.4	47 660	247	7 463	92 618	-1.2
Lewis	347	-1.0	37.4	2.6	1.8	6.8	2.9	10.5	22.2	4 540	277	985	7 958	0.2
Lincoln	182	-0.5	D	0.7	4.0	4.9	1.2	7.9	26.2	5 660	261	1 862	9 887	0.4
Logan	615	0.0	D	5.8	4.3	9.6	2.2	D	18.6	10 290	280	2 446	16 743	-0.4
McDowell	327	0.0	D	0.6	2.7	5.6	1.6	4.1	26.0	7 120	322	3 138	11 322	-16.6
Marion	1 164	-0.1	D	5.9	11.9	7.7	4.1	9.1	19.8	13 770	244	2 031	26 463	-0.7
Marshall	683	-0.7	D	20.2	D	5.2	2.5	D	14.5	7 425	224	981	15 918	0.7
Mason	391	1.6	D	10.9	5.8	5.1	1.7	13.6	20.8	6 940	254	1 307	13 006	7.9
Mercer	1 064	-0.3	13.0	6.4	5.0	10.0	3.7	16.9	25.3	17 005	273	3 736	30 115	-0.1
Mineral	408	-0.3	42.1	36.3	6.9	8.1	2.5	D	20.4	6 340	225	748	13 039	7.8
Mingo	563	0.0	53.9	3.1	D	3.4	1.6	7.3	12.7	7 995	298	2 872	12 699	-1.5
Monongalia	3 043	-0.1	17.1	8.3	6.9	5.4	3.0	19.5	31.7	12 770	133	1 711	43 238	17.8
Monroe	115	-4.9	D	18.2	D	5.1	D	5.6	42.2	3 775	280	514	7 601	4.6
Morgan	159	-0.9	D	16.1	D	11.0	4.4	D	29.3	4 160	237	329	9 753	20.8
Nicholas	425	-0.5	30.8	9.2	2.9	10.5	2.7	7.9	22.8	7 445	284	1 381	13 064	5.3
Ohio	1 324	-0.1	D	5.3	10.1	8.0	5.5	22.5	16.0	11 485	258	1 369	21 172	-4.5
Pendleton	102	1.8	D	2.2	3.3	5.5	D	9.0	47.9	2 165	281	231	5 132	0.6
Pleasants	169	-0.4	D	D	D	3.9	D	6.2	19.5	1 840	242	267	3 390	5.5
Pocahontas	137	-1.3	D	D	D	7.5	3.0	D	27.8	2 385	274	325	8 847	16.5
Preston	374	-1.0	25.3	9.4	3.3	7.5	2.8	7.2	36.5	7 285	217	1 255	15 097	12.3
Putnam	1 255	0.3	30.9	13.1	7.6	5.8	5.2	7.9	10.9	11 725	211	1 287	23 438	8.4
Raleigh	1 780	-0.1	20.9	3.3	5.7	8.9	3.5	16.2	22.8	20 935	265	3 630	35 931	0.7
Randolph	541	-0.1	19.4	10.5	2.6	10.1	3.9	D	22.0	7 325	249	1 400	14 189	5.3
Ritchie	156	-2.0	D	24.3	D	5.4	2.8	D	16.8	3 120	299	630	5 843	6.0
Roane	156	-3.9	33.7	5.3	2.9	11.2	4.4	D	21.9	4 290	287	1 106	7 351	-0.1
Summers	110	0.4	5.2	1.2	12.0	7.6	2.7	14.4	30.9	3 300	237	901	7 680	4.8
Taylor	135	0.1	D	D	D	10.6	1.2	D	40.6	3 635	215	740	7 541	5.8
Tucker	93	-0.7	D	14.6	D	6.7	4.9	10.2	31.7	1 925	270	239	5 346	15.4
Tyler	123	-0.8	49.6	44.5	D	4.2	D	8.1	23.6	2 570	279	356	5 000	4.6
Upshur	403	-0.3	34.7	12.0	4.0	10.1	2.7	D	16.6	5 740	237	1 129	11 099	3.2
Wayne	585	0.0	25.5	6.6	1.7	4.6	1.0	D	42.2	10 275	242	2 591	19 227	0.6
Webster	121	-0.2	D	4.9	D	4.2	1.6	7.3	24.4	2 785	304	832	5 428	2.9
Wetzel	173	-0.2	12.2	2.3	3.8	15.6	4.5	D	34.7	4 505	272	852	8 173	-1.7
Wirt	33	-3.1	D	D	D	6.1	D	11.1	40.0	1 555	272	346	3 231	-1.1
Wood	2 066	-0.2	24.8	12.7	4.6	9.5	5.8	15.9	21.6	22 390	257	3 635	40 215	1.1
Wyoming	273	-0.1	42.8	1.7	1.3	6.7	1.8	D	23.0	7 150	300	1 852	10 958	-6.3
WISCONSIN	150 682	0.7	24.6	19.0	8.4	6.2	7.3	13.1	15.3	1 061 501	187	107 571	2 624 358	13.1
Adams	262	5.9	15.1	8.2	D	6.4	2.0	5.9	26.2	6 515	312	493	17 436	23.5
Ashland	427	0.6	27.7	13.6	3.4	6.6	2.3	D	22.6	3 915	242	404	9 656	8.7
Barron	929	1.6	D	26.1	3.5	9.4	3.5	12.4	20.3	11 305	246	898	23 614	12.6
Bayfield	172	1.6	11.9	2.8	D	8.2	3.5	D	35.1	4 210	280	260	12 999	11.7
Brown	8 323	0.4	23.1	17.6	7.1	5.4	8.8	13.6	11.6	40 770	164	4 352	104 371	15.7
Buffalo	301	2.5	10.7	5.8	D	3.3	2.6	4.7	14.9	3 225	237	208	6 664	9.3
Burnett	216	0.8	D	21.3	4.3	7.6	2.9	D	23.5	5 040	326	277	15 278	21.4
Calumet	612	3.0	D	26.0	7.6	5.7	7.1	D	11.5	7 385	151	417	19 695	25.0
Chippewa	1 100	1.8	D	26.2	3.5	9.7	2.9	10.4	15.9	12 485	200	1 111	27 185	19.1
Clark	502	2.0	D	26.7	2.8	6.5	2.5	7.2	17.5	6 825	197	480	15 076	11.4
Columbia	1 058	1.0	33.0	26.0	3.4	7.3	3.6	11.4	18.1	11 345	200	569	26 137	15.2
Crawford	320	1.2	D	21.8	D	18.7	D	D	14.8	4 085	245	332	8 802	3.8
Dane	18 502	0.4	14.1	8.9	14.0	5.6	10.9	9.8	24.9	68 255	140	6 989	216 022	19.7

1. Includes mining, construction, and manufacturing.   2. Per 1,000 resident population enumerated in the 2010 census.

Table B. States and Counties — Housing, Labor Force, and Employment

STATE County	Housing units, 2006–2010								Civilian labor force, 2010				Civilian employment,[5] 2006–2010		
	Occupied units										Unemployment			Percent	
			Owner-occupied			Renter-occupied									
				Median owner cost as a percent of income			Median rent as a percent of income	Sub-stand-ard units[3] (percent)		Percent change, 2009–2010				Manage-ment, business, science and arts	Con-struction, produc-tion, and mainte-nance occu-pations
	Total	Percent	Median value[1]	With a mort-gage	Without a mort-gage	Median rent[2]			Total		Total	Rate[4]	Total		
	89	90	91	92	93	94	95	96	97	98	99	100	101	102	103
WEST VIRGINIA—Cont'd															
Brooke	9 824	79.2	85 300	19.2	10.5	513	23.8	1.0	10 474	-3.9	1 371	13.1	10 779	26.9	25.3
Cabell	40 564	64.2	97 500	19.8	10.0	590	31.4	1.1	42 623	-3.6	3 453	8.1	42 044	33.5	18.2
Calhoun	3 030	77.6	71 200	18.4	10.0	358	29.1	3.3	2 775	-1.3	406	14.6	2 699	19.2	40.3
Clay	3 530	79.7	76 400	17.8	10.0	385	30.1	2.9	3 482	-0.8	521	15.0	3 136	24.7	36.7
Doddridge	2 860	81.9	75 900	23.5	10.3	535	22.3	3.9	2 770	-1.5	248	9.0	3 021	18.0	39.2
Fayette	18 140	76.9	67 800	19.4	11.0	480	28.6	1.3	17 667	-0.9	1 776	10.1	16 417	26.0	28.1
Gilmer	2 460	71.5	69 000	19.8	10.0	552	33.5	3.0	3 157	0.1	246	7.8	2 499	20.0	29.2
Grant	4 899	79.7	105 300	20.7	10.8	484	28.3	0.9	4 846	-3.1	603	12.4	5 866	22.3	40.5
Greenbrier	15 302	75.0	93 900	21.7	10.0	571	29.5	2.2	14 671	0.8	1 371	9.3	14 340	28.4	29.4
Hampshire	9 755	67.6	134 100	22.1	10.4	486	28.9	2.6	9 046	-1.3	907	10.0	9 716	18.9	44.4
Hancock	13 296	75.2	85 300	19.5	11.2	540	28.6	1.1	13 767	-4.4	1 862	13.5	13 271	27.7	27.5
Hardy	4 877	78.4	130 600	20.8	10.2	488	23.8	0.6	6 437	-2.6	666	10.3	5 606	18.9	48.4
Harrison	27 740	73.3	95 500	19.7	11.1	558	31.7	2.1	30 534	-1.3	2 393	7.8	29 120	30.5	24.2
Jackson	11 634	79.6	102 100	18.4	10.0	523	29.1	2.6	10 998	-4.4	1 370	12.5	11 860	31.5	29.0
Jefferson	19 164	77.8	255 800	24.8	10.3	815	25.6	3.3	23 878	-1.3	1 688	7.1	25 646	37.5	20.4
Kanawha	82 501	71.3	98 500	19.0	10.0	589	25.7	1.2	88 238	-2.4	6 916	7.8	88 264	35.0	18.9
Lewis	6 527	72.5	87 400	19.4	10.0	471	25.2	2.3	7 694	2.4	634	8.2	6 380	24.6	30.4
Lincoln	8 711	77.9	65 100	21.1	10.0	485	32.3	3.1	7 794	-3.6	883	11.3	6 731	18.6	39.2
Logan	14 740	72.8	79 700	19.1	10.0	477	22.7	2.5	12 783	-2.7	1 264	9.9	11 803	26.0	30.0
McDowell	8 338	78.5	32 800	21.8	10.0	386	33.8	2.5	7 136	-3.4	848	11.9	5 451	28.3	33.3
Marion	22 744	75.1	87 500	19.2	11.6	574	29.5	1.9	25 576	-1.6	1 958	7.7	25 099	29.3	26.4
Marshall	13 997	78.0	77 900	19.5	10.0	483	29.2	1.5	14 449	-1.5	1 551	10.7	13 125	26.5	29.0
Mason	10 932	78.1	79 400	18.3	10.0	490	30.7	3.0	9 748	-3.1	1 315	13.5	10 360	21.6	35.4
Mercer	25 344	73.9	73 500	19.7	10.0	509	30.9	2.2	24 139	-2.3	2 019	8.4	22 698	30.2	26.3
Mineral	11 308	76.9	114 700	20.1	10.4	485	31.4	1.5	13 259	-0.8	1 155	8.7	11 883	24.9	32.3
Mingo	10 936	77.1	63 900	19.5	10.0	429	23.6	2.5	8 640	-1.7	909	10.5	8 284	25.2	35.5
Monongalia	35 073	59.2	145 400	19.3	10.0	644	35.8	1.3	48 828	1.4	2 703	5.5	44 075	40.6	18.7
Monroe	5 594	84.9	95 200	20.0	10.0	453	23.1	2.5	5 531	-2.4	419	7.6	5 552	28.4	33.5
Morgan	7 068	71.2	167 100	22.5	11.2	680	29.5	2.2	6 634	-2.1	667	10.1	7 153	25.2	36.2
Nicholas	10 304	82.0	73 400	18.7	10.0	472	27.8	1.5	10 411	-1.5	1 086	10.4	10 250	26.4	33.9
Ohio	18 850	70.0	94 800	18.7	10.0	503	29.0	1.3	20 590	-1.3	1 913	9.3	20 975	33.3	20.1
Pendleton	3 516	78.0	95 300	22.3	10.0	608	28.5	1.5	3 418	-4.3	291	8.5	3 838	22.3	36.8
Pleasants	2 591	79.7	89 400	19.7	10.0	462	27.7	2.9	3 024	-2.2	332	11.0	2 830	27.3	30.1
Pocahontas	3 812	80.4	100 000	23.6	10.0	465	24.9	1.1	3 473	-2.2	441	12.7	3 584	24.9	35.9
Preston	12 850	82.7	87 700	19.1	10.0	457	25.6	2.8	15 089	-1.0	1 221	8.1	13 717	22.0	37.5
Putnam	20 975	85.9	135 200	19.1	10.0	626	26.5	0.7	26 602	-2.5	2 012	7.6	24 886	39.0	22.2
Raleigh	31 196	76.6	88 000	19.2	10.0	510	25.5	0.6	31 664	-1.9	2 697	8.5	30 266	29.4	25.5
Randolph	11 319	77.9	94 100	21.9	10.0	461	31.4	1.1	11 933	-4.6	1 302	10.9	11 705	29.0	27.6
Ritchie	4 213	77.7	70 000	21.6	10.0	496	24.6	0.3	4 243	-2.1	411	9.7	4 271	25.5	35.1
Roane	6 015	76.1	75 000	21.9	10.0	436	31.1	2.4	5 369	-1.5	744	13.9	4 954	20.0	39.8
Summers	5 075	81.5	74 100	20.3	11.0	433	28.3	1.0	4 572	-0.1	443	9.7	4 316	23.7	31.0
Taylor	6 579	78.5	77 000	19.4	10.0	465	29.5	1.2	6 907	-0.6	567	8.2	6 931	27.9	29.9
Tucker	3 132	79.5	87 900	22.4	11.5	461	29.8	0.9	2 719	-4.3	359	13.2	3 197	29.3	31.8
Tyler	3 792	82.6	77 700	18.9	10.5	480	29.1	1.8	3 523	-1.1	397	11.3	3 284	21.2	36.9
Upshur	9 291	79.2	99 700	20.9	10.0	506	25.1	1.9	10 451	-1.0	948	9.1	9 724	28.5	29.5
Wayne	16 751	76.6	85 500	20.3	10.0	525	33.5	2.3	16 562	-3.7	1 593	9.6	16 339	25.8	26.9
Webster	4 116	79.1	58 500	22.2	10.0	437	29.9	3.2	3 109	-3.3	380	12.2	3 389	16.6	40.9
Wetzel	6 897	80.0	82 200	18.6	10.0	482	32.5	2.6	6 114	-1.5	827	13.5	6 443	25.1	33.7
Wirt	2 364	81.4	61 800	15.6	10.0	471	28.9	3.5	2 286	-7.0	296	12.9	2 334	24.0	41.5
Wood	36 222	73.4	102 500	19.9	10.0	569	31.4	1.2	38 643	-3.6	3 780	9.8	37 484	30.7	25.4
Wyoming	9 126	81.4	59 300	18.3	10.0	461	27.5	1.3	7 969	-1.3	875	11.0	7 790	26.5	40.3
WISCONSIN	2 274 611	69.5	169 000	24.5	13.9	713	28.7	2.0	3 082 676	-0.6	260 873	8.5	2 869 310	33.0	26.4
Adams	9 341	82.2	130 700	26.7	16.8	589	27.0	1.9	9 873	-1.1	1 093	11.1	8 354	20.3	33.9
Ashland	6 967	70.7	103 000	24.1	13.8	510	27.1	3.2	8 867	-2.3	887	10.0	7 815	27.2	28.6
Barron	19 421	74.1	134 500	25.2	14.8	595	29.2	1.8	24 474	-2.7	2 112	8.6	22 532	27.9	33.6
Bayfield	6 990	81.8	157 300	24.1	14.9	528	26.2	4.1	7 905	-1.1	825	10.4	6 932	35.4	26.2
Brown	96 937	66.6	159 100	23.5	13.1	665	27.3	2.2	141 097	1.6	10 472	7.4	125 775	32.1	25.0
Buffalo	5 775	77.9	130 600	24.7	14.3	656	27.2	1.7	7 864	-5.6	533	6.8	7 104	27.2	36.2
Burnett	7 414	80.4	156 100	29.4	15.7	687	33.3	2.8	8 026	2.2	812	10.1	6 647	27.0	32.3
Calumet	18 265	83.6	158 700	23.2	12.8	643	24.8	1.5	25 356	-1.1	1 705	6.7	25 580	33.9	32.9
Chippewa	24 223	74.2	146 300	24.1	13.2	616	25.8	1.4	33 178	0.8	2 628	7.9	31 120	27.0	32.8
Clark	13 031	79.0	110 900	24.6	14.1	543	24.5	5.2	17 241	-2.8	1 689	9.8	16 024	27.0	39.1
Columbia	22 945	75.5	177 500	25.9	13.8	695	26.6	1.4	31 142	-0.3	2 528	8.1	29 655	28.8	30.6
Crawford	6 891	77.0	113 900	23.9	14.1	526	28.2	2.2	9 142	-2.0	860	9.4	8 014	26.0	34.5
Dane	196 383	62.1	230 800	25.1	12.5	832	29.7	1.9	299 149	1.5	16 843	5.6	272 016	46.6	14.8

1. Specified owner-occupied units. 2. Specified renter-occupied units. A value of 10.0 represents 10 percent or less. 3. Overcrowded or lacking complete plumbing facilities. 4. Percent of civilian labor force. 5. Persons 16 years old and over.

Table B. States and Counties — Nonfarm Employment and Agriculture

	Private nonfarm establishments, employment and payroll, 2009								Agriculture, 2007			
		Employment					Annual payroll		Farms			
										Percent with:		
STATE County	Number of establishments	Total	Health care and social assistance	Manufacturing	Retail trade	Finance and insurance	Professional, scientific, and technical services	Total (mil dol)	Average per employee (dollars)	Number	Fewer than 50 acres	500 acres or more	Farm operators whose principal occupation is farming (percent)
	104	105	106	107	108	109	110	111	112	113	114	115	116
WEST VIRGINIA—Cont'd												
Brooke	411	7 531	2 097	1 926	863	160	D	232	30 777	104	28.8	3.8	56.7
Cabell	2 584	47 641	12 876	5 194	7 200	1 366	2 085	1 534	32 201	462	27.9	1.3	33.3
Calhoun	124	1 088	D	D	161	D	D	31	28 385	287	22.0	7.7	35.5
Clay	118	1 487	348	D	150	D	D	64	43 123	145	20.7	1.4	40.7
Doddridge	73	528	170	D	96	31	D	11	20 877	490	23.5	4.9	38.6
Fayette	837	8 916	2 074	D	1 833	D	219	255	28 630	265	33.2	2.3	41.9
Gilmer	134	1 218	208	D	167	D	48	30	24 383	263	13.3	12.9	40.7
Grant	234	2 521	620	334	366	97	58	84	33 190	471	24.0	11.9	45.0
Greenbrier	1 001	10 228	2 870	753	2 142	D	288	291	28 447	881	29.6	9.1	43.7
Hampshire	349	2 731	850	165	450	187	67	66	24 310	677	38.8	9.0	41.9
Hancock	612	10 127	1 238	2 909	968	320	362	294	29 024	109	40.4	0.9	56.9
Hardy	262	5 356	486	D	633	148	D	134	25 036	514	33.7	11.1	49.8
Harrison	1 793	27 598	6 302	1 992	4 978	575	1 304	911	33 012	774	28.0	4.3	42.1
Jackson	538	6 811	1 065	D	1 295	225	146	219	32 123	950	24.3	2.6	37.4
Jefferson	881	10 217	1 188	929	1 993	351	342	262	25 598	546	54.4	6.6	51.3
Kanawha	5 489	90 493	17 093	3 419	12 643	5 450	6 806	3 344	36 955	256	46.9	0.4	41.4
Lewis	428	5 118	D	164	811	115	50	160	31 295	507	23.5	6.1	34.5
Lincoln	237	2 275	D	D	295	D	D	72	31 853	215	17.7	2.8	31.6
Logan	707	10 992	1 862	1 109	2 025	221	263	397	36 117	34	76.5	0.0	55.9
McDowell	291	3 148	881	D	648	D	103	94	29 792	15	53.3	6.7	40.0
Marion	1 264	17 942	2 956	1 400	2 371	631	1 234	599	33 375	550	31.6	0.9	40.0
Marshall	482	7 849	1 593	450	1 285	D	151	297	37 857	752	21.0	1.7	36.6
Mason	339	4 670	D	D	669	130	D	180	38 621	946	30.1	4.7	41.2
Mercer	1 377	19 375	4 791	1 884	3 396	615	511	557	28 773	445	32.6	3.1	44.3
Mineral	475	6 600	1 275	D	1 074	D	136	209	31 723	493	33.9	4.9	39.8
Mingo	467	6 287	857	228	463	164	323	237	37 645	37	64.9	8.1	27.0
Monongalia	2 168	39 982	11 834	3 227	6 289	847	2 392	1 366	34 164	457	28.4	2.6	36.3
Monroe	207	1 440	257	D	175	47	28	37	25 747	707	22.8	7.9	46.1
Morgan	263	2 302	545	D	429	106	D	61	26 645	212	43.9	2.8	51.4
Nicholas	585	8 346	1 374	791	1 518	125	275	266	31 914	434	35.7	3.0	40.3
Ohio	1 472	27 574	6 735	1 514	3 314	D	1 698	829	30 071	241	27.8	2.9	38.6
Pendleton	147	1 161	297	136	201	D	13	29	24 570	600	20.0	15.5	47.3
Pleasants	121	2 048	D	469	158	65	D	81	39 775	246	28.9	1.2	32.1
Pocahontas	221	3 243	433	336	315	54	D	60	18 397	390	19.2	16.2	47.4
Preston	573	5 063	1 135	582	927	175	181	142	28 123	1 048	27.6	4.3	45.8
Putnam	1 204	16 468	1 631	2 034	2 677	529	599	622	37 783	625	35.0	1.1	39.4
Raleigh	1 914	28 080	6 799	1 270	5 466	621	974	1 031	34 730	351	42.5	4.0	37.0
Randolph	710	9 204	2 316	1 266	1 563	279	181	237	25 770	484	30.0	10.1	43.8
Ritchie	215	2 468	D	D	287	118	D	77	31 210	441	14.3	7.5	38.3
Roane	265	2 618	D	221	563	134	D	72	27 354	674	16.6	6.4	45.4
Summers	168	1 537	458	40	D	D	121	38	24 452	383	23.5	4.4	47.0
Taylor	226	1 957	549	D	427	41	D	54	27 498	471	41.8	2.8	34.2
Tucker	184	2 038	273	D	225	D	D	49	23 887	197	24.9	7.1	46.2
Tyler	121	1 439	457	D	175	D	D	61	42 258	277	17.3	4.7	45.8
Upshur	544	7 084	1 719	950	1 152	141	200	202	28 454	503	27.4	3.2	36.8
Wayne	587	7 724	D	608	1 050	D	153	295	38 169	261	23.8	5.0	49.8
Webster	144	1 473	393	98	191	D	15	45	30 471	123	39.0	0.0	52.8
Wetzel	376	4 432	D	D	929	133	D	153	34 525	353	19.0	2.8	41.1
Wirt	69	396	D	D	77	D	D	8	20 432	238	17.2	5.5	37.4
Wood	2 130	34 000	6 814	3 849	6 331	1 808	928	992	29 191	902	35.6	0.6	38.7
Wyoming	335	3 851	822	73	689	107	58	116	30 118	37	43.2	5.4	54.1
WISCONSIN	140 861	2 355 879	377 578	431 014	301 908	145 343	101 541	89 374	37 937	78 463	31.6	7.8	47.2
Adams	333	3 074	488	447	465	D	62	78	25 447	408	26.7	11.8	43.1
Ashland	552	6 835	1 447	1 265	982	189	141	233	34 127	203	22.7	13.8	40.4
Barron	1 304	16 017	2 781	4 590	3 018	497	329	483	30 180	1 484	26.5	9.4	48.1
Bayfield	438	2 261	D	D	398	87	D	52	22 952	383	19.8	10.4	44.6
Brown	6 447	133 583	18 111	24 066	15 152	D	5 419	5 465	40 912	1 053	44.0	6.8	54.7
Buffalo	321	4 352	322	407	290	150	159	149	34 215	1 229	20.5	11.5	46.3
Burnett	432	3 165	565	631	522	111	86	88	27 899	531	27.9	7.7	39.4
Calumet	867	11 939	1 032	3 327	1 844	633	207	349	29 264	732	29.9	9.6	55.7
Chippewa	1 490	19 200	3 024	5 279	3 564	496	520	637	33 153	1 575	19.8	8.7	53.6
Clark	724	8 181	1 292	2 886	985	D	138	242	29 573	2 170	19.7	6.3	65.5
Columbia	1 408	19 605	2 600	4 719	3 142	414	391	576	29 405	1 585	35.5	9.4	48.7
Crawford	419	5 904	1 107	1 506	1 043	123	158	155	26 273	1 347	26.5	5.8	40.5
Dane	13 265	247 333	41 285	23 898	30 917	23 219	18 426	10 092	40 802	3 331	46.2	6.9	44.3

Table B. States and Counties — Agriculture

STATE County	Land in farms Acreage (1,000)	Percent change, 2002–2007	Acres Average size of farm	Total irrigated (1,000)	Total cropland (1,000)	Value of land and buildings (dollars) Average per farm	Average per acre	Value of machinery and equipment, average per farm (dollars)	Value of products sold Total (mil dol)	Average per farm (dollars)	Percent from: Crops	Live-stock and poultry products	Percent of farms with sales of: $10,000 or more	$100,000 or more	Government payments Total ($1,000)	Percent of farms
	117	118	119	120	121	122	123	124	125	126	127	128	129	130	131	132
WEST VIRGINIA—Cont'd																
Brooke	15	7.1	148	D	5.1	243 010	1 640	37 970	1.0	9 475	23.1	76.9	21.2	1.0	4	5.8
Cabell	48	14.3	103	0.0	9.2	260 208	2 524	32 911	1.5	3 340	45.4	54.6	5.4	0.4	10	5.8
Calhoun	56	12.0	195	D	9.3	302 156	1 548	28 348	1.6	5 409	8.2	91.8	9.8	0.3	3	1.0
Clay	20	5.3	138	0.0	4.2	228 220	1 659	23 174	0.7	4 537	12.5	87.4	11.0	0.0	14	10.3
Doddridge	81	-14.7	166	0.1	16.4	244 177	1 471	25 662	1.7	3 550	29.7	70.3	7.8	0.0	2	1.0
Fayette	27	12.5	101	D	7.9	206 292	2 049	32 691	1.7	6 507	20.6	79.5	14.3	0.0	7	6.4
Gilmer	64	-3.0	243	D	12.1	355 692	1 461	38 203	2.2	8 478	9.8	90.2	22.8	0.4	14	4.6
Grant	109	0.9	231	0.1	20.6	537 679	2 327	45 431	42.1	89 434	1.5	98.5	34.4	13.0	212	17.0
Greenbrier	177	-8.3	201	0.1	38.5	484 704	2 413	50 458	43.0	48 781	4.0	96.0	35.9	6.8	130	14.2
Hampshire	129	-7.2	191	0.0	33.5	911 704	4 778	55 484	32.5	48 078	10.4	89.6	31.2	7.1	365	20.7
Hancock	10	42.9	89	D	3.1	241 981	2 734	28 811	0.4	3 358	50.5	49.5	5.5	0.0	0	9.2
Hardy	134	4.7	261	0.0	28.3	797 092	3 049	66 109	148.0	287 994	1.3	98.7	44.4	28.0	218	15.4
Harrison	112	-6.7	144	0.0	26.8	300 421	2 082	34 693	6.9	8 889	22.3	77.7	15.8	0.8	38	3.7
Jackson	129	0.0	136	0.1	36.8	269 258	1 976	33 387	6.1	6 389	20.8	79.2	13.7	0.9	65	6.8
Jefferson	72	0.0	132	0.2	43.0	896 621	6 791	64 102	19.5	35 639	41.2	58.8	27.8	7.9	476	22.7
Kanawha	24	20.0	93	0.0	4.0	253 222	2 729	24 408	0.9	3 558	33.2	66.8	6.6	0.4	9	5.9
Lewis	92	16.5	182	D	22.1	308 072	1 695	41 362	7.2	14 248	5.2	94.8	24.3	0.8	5	3.4
Lincoln	32	-8.6	151	0.0	6.7	223 448	1 483	38 793	0.7	3 205	19.7	80.3	9.3	0.0	8	7.9
Logan	1	-50.0	41	D	0.3	116 296	2 839	42 212	D	D	0.0	D	5.9	2.9	D	2.9
McDowell	1	0.0	99	D	0.5	219 419	2 222	42 871	0.1	5 514	9.6	90.4	6.7	0.0	0	0.0
Marion	58	16.0	105	0.0	16.0	223 716	2 121	28 220	2.7	4 870	41.1	58.8	10.0	0.9	8	3.6
Marshall	96	5.5	127	0.1	30.3	237 948	1 868	33 433	3.0	4 036	25.5	74.5	9.6	0.3	25	5.1
Mason	132	-7.0	140	0.4	40.4	311 226	2 227	38 471	18.8	19 837	61.5	38.5	18.7	3.0	243	14.5
Mercer	54	-3.6	121	0.0	11.6	267 233	2 203	30 255	3.7	8 354	25.8	74.2	17.8	1.3	13	3.1
Mineral	78	-3.7	158	0.2	19.6	438 363	2 772	36 194	15.5	31 379	8.2	91.8	18.1	4.7	63	13.0
Mingo	4	100.0	108	0.0	0.3	106 359	986	10 762	0.1	2 778	1.9	97.1	8.1	0.0	0	0.0
Monongalia	59	-1.7	130	0.0	16.7	357 613	2 758	41 183	3.1	6 734	22.5	77.5	17.3	0.4	20	5.3
Monroe	133	-8.3	188	0.0	31.4	431 149	2 294	50 221	16.4	23 204	7.0	93.0	34.8	4.5	140	19.9
Morgan	22	-4.3	106	0.0	7.8	458 846	4 335	33 576	1.9	8 733	55.8	44.2	19.8	1.4	32	17.9
Nicholas	51	15.9	118	D	15.3	239 319	2 023	36 259	2.7	6 252	15.5	84.5	16.6	0.7	18	8.5
Ohio	31	40.9	128	0.0	10.7	270 831	2 119	31 697	2.5	10 179	22.8	77.2	14.5	2.9	46	17.4
Pendleton	170	-0.6	283	0.0	29.6	602 289	2 127	60 443	91.8	152 980	1.5	98.5	52.5	18.5	131	21.3
Pleasants	26	13.0	105	D	7.6	218 584	2 086	25 439	D	D	0.0	D	8.5	0.4	D	0.4
Pocahontas	122	-0.8	313	0.0	23.7	633 940	2 029	60 712	8.2	20 935	6.1	93.9	33.1	3.8	88	28.5
Preston	152	7.0	145	0.0	46.3	347 363	2 391	44 699	13.6	13 019	18.2	81.8	26.4	1.4	72	6.6
Putnam	66	15.8	106	0.2	15.0	253 355	2 384	33 068	7.4	11 892	76.8	23.2	8.6	0.5	23	6.7
Raleigh	43	30.3	124	0.0	14.1	284 192	2 298	35 459	2.5	6 985	27.6	72.4	17.1	1.4	16	6.6
Randolph	104	3.0	216	0.0	25.6	431 626	2 000	41 657	8.2	16 938	11.1	88.9	26.0	2.3	62	14.7
Ritchie	91	12.3	206	0.0	21.8	344 698	1 673	37 744	4.1	9 250	18.2	81.8	15.6	1.1	3	1.4
Roane	118	19.2	174	0.0	29.5	302 235	1 733	34 460	5.0	7 459	19.8	80.3	19.7	0.6	27	5.0
Summers	60	9.1	156	0.0	13.6	312 136	2 005	43 382	5.3	13 965	30.9	69.1	19.8	1.8	21	5.7
Taylor	54	25.6	114	0.0	14.0	250 911	2 196	32 974	6.3	13 293	31.4	68.6	15.3	2.8	11	2.1
Tucker	35	0.0	177	0.0	8.6	341 698	1 930	35 345	1.7	8 834	22.8	77.2	25.9	0.0	11	13.7
Tyler	48	-9.4	172	0.0	12.0	322 560	1 880	36 274	1.9	6 801	22.9	77.0	11.9	0.7	22	9.7
Upshur	71	2.9	141	0.0	19.5	299 677	2 127	35 035	4.1	8 217	18.5	81.5	19.3	1.0	15	3.6
Wayne	40	11.1	153	0.0	7.2	276 589	1 812	25 133	1.6	5 954	31.0	69.0	12.6	0.8	7	3.1
Webster	12	9.1	94	0.0	2.8	184 900	1 972	17 239	0.2	1 969	22.3	77.7	2.4	0.0	6	6.5
Wetzel	52	6.1	147	0.0	10.0	226 386	1 541	25 293	1.0	2 755	31.4	68.6	2.8	0.3	4	3.4
Wirt	41	2.5	173	D	9.9	280 691	1 621	40 644	3.5	14 776	8.9	91.1	16.8	2.5	2	2.5
Wood	89	15.6	99	0.0	27.4	225 326	2 284	26 009	3.5	3 920	32.1	67.9	8.4	0.3	13	2.0
Wyoming	4	0.0	109	D	0.8	148 664	1 361	25 604	0.1	3 572	34.8	65.2	5.4	0.0	0	8.1
WISCONSIN	15 191	-3.5	194	377.3	10 116.3	624 428	3 225	96 278	8 967.4	114 288	29.8	70.2	45.2	21.2	195 787	60.5
Adams	115	-7.3	283	37.6	79.6	895 606	3 168	119 690	74.8	183 276	89.6	10.4	38.2	15.9	781	61.8
Ashland	55	-6.8	273	0.0	26.5	584 484	2 143	63 121	11.9	58 855	10.7	89.3	36.0	7.9	179	23.2
Barron	324	-8.0	218	10.3	207.2	541 130	2 477	106 042	206.4	139 109	19.7	80.3	48.0	24.2	3 388	62.3
Bayfield	89	-20.5	233	0.2	47.6	505 901	2 170	63 949	16.2	42 310	27.5	72.5	38.6	9.4	213	22.5
Brown	187	-5.1	178	0.5	160.6	697 205	3 922	131 817	253.8	240 985	12.2	87.8	54.0	31.2	2 774	59.6
Buffalo	307	-2.8	250	3.2	159.1	641 667	2 568	104 653	159.1	129 487	16.6	83.4	48.0	21.7	3 169	69.5
Burnett	96	-2.0	181	0.2	48.5	463 610	2 560	52 790	22.8	42 891	24.1	75.9	31.8	8.7	546	45.8
Calumet	152	1.3	207	0.1	128.5	791 675	3 821	130 933	167.0	228 080	17.3	82.7	68.3	32.5	1 978	72.5
Chippewa	353	-5.6	224	3.0	226.3	558 659	2 489	98 921	165.6	105 150	15.5	84.5	52.1	26.9	4 181	63.3
Clark	440	-4.6	203	0.2	291.6	507 601	2 501	101 342	278.9	128 516	9.5	90.5	62.9	37.2	3 880	50.6
Columbia	316	-9.2	199	1.4	241.9	747 274	3 746	101 916	166.7	105 156	45.8	54.2	50.1	19.9	5 505	64.2
Crawford	238	-6.7	177	0.1	105.4	459 109	2 596	56 927	61.1	45 369	34.2	65.8	33.5	12.3	2 286	62.5
Dane	536	4.1	161	6.0	417.2	696 424	4 330	106 389	470.6	141 277	28.6	71.4	42.3	19.1	10 441	57.5

Table B. States and Counties — Water Use, Wholesale Trade, Retail Trade, and Real Estate

STATE County	Water use, 2005		Wholesale trade,[1] 2007				Retail trade,[2] 2007				Real estate and rental and leasing,[2] 2007			
	Total water withdrawn (mil gal/day)	Gallons withdrawn per person	Number of establishments	Number of employees	Sales (mil dol)	Annual payroll (mil dol)	Number of establishments	Number of employees	Sales (mil dol)	Annual payroll (mil dol)	Number of establishments	Number of employees	Receipts (mil dol)	Annual payroll (mil dol)
	133	134	135	136	137	138	139	140	141	142	143	144	145	146
WEST VIRGINIA—Cont'd														
Brooke	81.3	3 314	11	D	D	D	63	651	158.1	14.4	6	21	4.8	0.5
Cabell	58.8	625	112	1 698	778.9	66.7	486	7 531	1 496.1	142.7	113	413	68.4	10.8
Calhoun	0.8	104	1	D	D	D	25	147	34.1	2.2	5	11	0.6	0.2
Clay	1.5	147	NA	NA	NA	NA	24	148	41.3	2.5	1	D	D	D
Doddridge	0.8	104	2	D	D	D	16	105	19.3	1.2	2	D	D	D
Fayette	40.3	860	27	D	D	D	165	1 860	345.7	34.4	24	58	7.5	0.8
Gilmer	1.5	216	3	D	D	D	24	153	34.3	2.9	3	4	0.3	0.0
Grant	1 165.9	99 877	2	D	D	D	44	394	118.3	7.8	8	18	1.4	0.1
Greenbrier	9.3	266	30	256	59.1	7.3	198	2 133	490.2	43.1	43	150	21.4	3.5
Hampshire	3.5	161	7	D	D	D	57	442	112.2	8.3	14	D	D	D
Hancock	185.3	5 911	10	157	118.0	4.7	109	1 247	238.5	22.6	29	93	10.0	1.9
Hardy	23.4	1 763	3	31	7.2	0.9	54	660	132.1	12.5	8	23	2.2	0.5
Harrison	56.4	826	72	858	322.8	30.5	334	4 909	1 148.5	96.0	61	337	107.7	8.5
Jackson	31.8	1 119	15	171	77.4	5.5	110	1 467	325.2	28.2	16	43	5.3	1.0
Jefferson	16.4	332	20	D	D	D	138	2 356	455.7	49.9	52	172	23.3	4.1
Kanawha	502.2	2 595	270	3 829	1 727.0	163.6	853	13 517	2 947.3	259.8	277	1 799	367.7	54.8
Lewis	4.1	239	15	93	54.8	3.4	78	843	212.9	14.5	12	33	4.6	0.8
Lincoln	1.8	81	3	D	D	D	47	359	73.4	5.9	7	D	D	D
Logan	6.6	181	36	354	155.7	15.7	151	2 006	494.7	41.2	30	109	13.0	3.1
McDowell	5.6	229	6	20	20.0	0.6	66	711	129.4	11.7	10	35	4.3	0.9
Marion	46.3	820	43	D	D	D	189	2 277	614.9	48.1	43	197	25.3	4.0
Marshall	723.2	21 062	14	D	D	D	96	1 341	272.4	25.4	12	41	3.2	0.9
Mason	1 094.0	42 468	5	D	D	D	62	675	135.4	11.2	18	58	5.7	1.0
Mercer	12.4	201	48	D	D	D	281	3 612	765.6	74.5	45	183	58.1	4.6
Mineral	4.4	164	13	D	D	D	87	1 009	223.6	18.5	12	D	D	D
Mingo	7.0	256	13	165	50.5	6.0	68	481	108.2	10.1	17	45	12.1	0.8
Monongalia	168.8	2 000	47	413	370.3	16.8	383	6 453	1 289.7	112.7	130	589	78.5	14.7
Monroe	5.0	372	7	29	3.7	0.5	35	190	31.6	3.2	5	10	0.5	0.1
Morgan	4.8	298	5	26	5.7	0.6	48	458	94.8	8.8	15	45	2.9	0.7
Nicholas	5.1	192	20	173	136.7	6.1	111	1 460	345.9	28.6	19	42	5.8	1.1
Ohio	18.4	408	74	1 578	3 117.0	54.3	213	3 045	649.9	62.4	66	368	37.0	8.2
Pendleton	11.8	1 504	4	12	4.2	0.1	28	215	39.4	3.5	2	D	D	D
Pleasants	100.7	13 646	2	D	D	D	18	152	40.4	3.0	3	D	D	D
Pocahontas	6.1	688	2	D	D	D	39	332	60.2	5.2	7	49	9.8	0.7
Preston	111.2	3 691	16	D	D	D	104	912	221.1	15.3	21	36	4.2	0.8
Putnam	57.0	1 046	67	904	541.7	41.2	185	2 366	589.8	42.8	48	225	42.0	6.6
Raleigh	15.4	195	94	D	D	D	376	5 507	1 260.8	114.0	76	328	43.8	8.5
Randolph	18.4	643	24	309	366.9	10.5	135	1 513	319.2	28.2	24	81	12.7	1.8
Ritchie	2.8	245	6	54	23.3	1.6	35	259	60.4	4.0	5	12	1.1	0.2
Roane	2.3	149	9	57	40.7	1.8	56	613	142.0	11.7	10	21	2.0	0.4
Summers	3.8	276	6	D	D	D	28	274	53.7	5.1	4	6	0.6	0.2
Taylor	11.1	680	5	D	D	D	30	435	91.7	8.7	2	D	D	D
Tucker	17.6	2 533	2	D	D	D	32	239	53.4	4.3	11	78	4.3	1.0
Tyler	20.1	2 148	1	D	D	D	29	248	45.5	3.5	1	D	D	D
Upshur	6.5	275	12	216	179.3	7.4	90	1 202	297.1	24.4	21	104	6.4	1.4
Wayne	20.0	475	18	288	77.4	10.1	123	1 112	232.8	19.1	21	83	5.7	1.0
Webster	1.6	167	3	D	D	D	31	176	40.1	3.5	5	D	D	D
Wetzel	25.6	1 497	8	43	14.4	1.2	80	967	206.4	19.6	15	76	9.1	1.4
Wirt	0.8	131	1	D	D	D	15	76	14.4	0.9	2	D	D	D
Wood	51.6	593	84	760	330.7	26.1	422	6 796	1 712.2	131.8	85	D	D	D
Wyoming	5.9	242	5	31	5.9	0.6	91	671	147.0	12.3	9	41	5.7	0.8
WISCONSIN	8 597.4	1 553	6 215	99 773	59 996.2	4 639.0	21 205	320 140	72 283.3	6 778.3	5 119	27 226	4 043.5	788.9
Adams	45.8	2 200	6	27	12.6	0.8	50	440	130.4	9.0	13	38	3.9	0.9
Ashland	55.2	3 317	13	105	30.2	3.6	90	846	193.6	19.4	20	74	7.6	1.4
Barron	19.6	427	51	433	126.6	14.8	256	3 268	670.8	65.2	41	100	15.8	2.1
Bayfield	13.8	912	9	62	29.6	1.7	78	520	107.6	9.0	12	38	2.9	0.5
Brown	519.7	2 174	349	5 907	3 388.3	270.8	984	15 914	3 538.4	327.1	236	1 594	229.9	45.4
Buffalo	538.2	38 533	7	75	24.2	2.7	51	311	74.0	5.5	7	19	0.9	0.1
Burnett	2.5	154	9	24	5.5	0.7	78	622	118.7	10.8	19	38	3.6	0.7
Calumet	7.3	166	33	401	149.0	14.6	116	1 801	390.1	36.6	23	89	8.7	1.2
Chippewa	16.0	266	43	464	206.0	16.7	246	3 712	1 059.6	83.8	28	107	13.9	2.9
Clark	6.5	191	34	252	107.2	9.7	119	1 014	263.9	20.3	10	24	1.3	0.2
Columbia	28.3	510	45	435	203.4	17.9	217	2 819	631.3	54.9	48	D	D	D
Crawford	3.7	215	15	368	101.0	8.4	88	1 159	218.3	22.7	12	23	2.5	0.3
Dane	298.1	651	600	11 205	6 043.0	529.6	1 788	32 582	7 132.4	715.1	683	4 691	638.1	144.2

1. Merchant wholesalers, except manufacturers' sales branches and offices. 2. Employer establishments.

Table B. States and Counties — Professional Services, Manufacturing, and Accommodation and Food Services

STATE County	Professional, scientific, and technical services,[1] 2007				Manufacturing, 2007				Accommodation and food services, 2007			
	Number of establishments	Number of employees	Receipts (mil dol)	Annual payroll (mil dol)	Number of establishments	Number of employees	Receipts (mil dol)	Annual payroll (mil dol)	Number of establishments	Number of employees	Sales (mil dol)	Annual payroll (mil dol)
	147	148	149	150	151	152	153	154	155	156	157	158
WEST VIRGINIA—Cont'd												
Brooke	17	D	D	D	24	3 217	2 645.1	181.0	58	711	31.3	8.0
Cabell	195	D	D	D	97	5 623	D	D	279	5 340	205.2	57.9
Calhoun	6	D	D	D	NA	NA	NA	NA	7	42	1.3	0.4
Clay	1	D	D	D	NA	NA	NA	NA	7	39	1.3	0.3
Doddridge	3	D	D	D	NA	NA	NA	NA	2	D	D	D
Fayette	57	D	D	D	31	694	D	30.0	69	803	35.7	9.3
Gilmer	9	43	4.7	0.9	NA	NA	NA	NA	13	190	5.2	1.3
Grant	14	66	4.5	1.4	NA	NA	NA	NA	20	176	6.1	1.5
Greenbrier	65	D	D	D	33	886	148.3	31.9	85	2 595	139.5	47.9
Hampshire	24	D	D	D	NA	NA	NA	NA	41	373	17.4	4.6
Hancock	54	D	D	D	22	2 278	D	79.4	93	851	34.0	8.1
Hardy	17	40	4.5	0.8	13	D	D	D	27	447	10.8	3.7
Harrison	115	D	D	D	58	D	D	D	162	2 911	117.6	32.3
Jackson	33	135	12.0	3.6	21	2 211	1 296.6	124.8	49	815	31.8	8.3
Jefferson	81	D	D	D	22	D	D	D	112	1 463	71.9	20.7
Kanawha	587	D	D	D	133	3 450	D	193.4	480	9 058	414.9	115.0
Lewis	19	D	D	D	NA	NA	NA	NA	34	559	27.3	9.3
Lincoln	18	104	8.4	3.0	NA	NA	NA	NA	13	84	2.8	0.7
Logan	35	D	D	D	38	706	124.9	26.4	67	1 134	39.6	10.3
McDowell	16	D	D	D	NA	NA	NA	NA	19	166	6.9	1.7
Marion	112	D	D	D	53	1 285	546.4	49.3	111	1 692	67.2	17.2
Marshall	27	D	D	D	NA	NA	NA	NA	57	793	26.3	7.0
Mason	23	67	6.0	1.6	21	707	D	D	29	319	12.1	3.6
Mercer	80	D	D	D	63	1 741	252.5	D	108	2 299	88.4	24.1
Mineral	32	D	D	D	14	1 620	D	86.7	53	538	21.4	5.3
Mingo	55	D	D	D	NA	NA	NA	NA	38	281	10.0	2.9
Monongalia	195	D	D	D	66	3 099	D	151.7	229	5 085	192.8	53.3
Monroe	11	31	2.2	0.6	NA	NA	NA	NA	14	87	2.8	0.8
Morgan	16	D	D	D	NA	NA	NA	NA	25	309	11.5	4.1
Nicholas	42	D	D	D	32	800	192.6	27.8	51	756	30.5	8.2
Ohio	141	D	D	D	59	1 329	D	D	131	2 403	98.3	27.5
Pendleton	8	D	D	D	NA	NA	NA	NA	12	83	3.1	0.7
Pleasants	7	D	D	D	10	D	D	D	11	191	6.6	1.8
Pocahontas	10	D	D	D	NA	NA	NA	NA	23	1 760	60.4	22.2
Preston	36	D	D	D	32	819	D	22.1	37	316	12.2	3.0
Putnam	92	652	67.2	24.8	37	2 156	D	119.9	87	1 441	61.6	15.2
Raleigh	125	D	D	D	65	1 284	D	49.9	151	3 402	144.3	40.8
Randolph	42	D	D	D	29	1 873	321.5	55.4	61	965	30.7	8.6
Ritchie	10	40	2.4	0.8	17	1 116	D	33.5	17	94	3.6	0.7
Roane	15	52	4.5	1.3	NA	NA	NA	NA	9	201	7.3	1.7
Summers	11	94	13.5	5.3	NA	NA	NA	NA	20	243	9.1	2.5
Taylor	8	D	D	D	NA	NA	NA	NA	18	D	D	D
Tucker	9	25	1.3	0.4	NA	NA	NA	NA	30	358	12.1	3.0
Tyler	5	D	D	D	7	D	218.6	35.3	8	39	1.8	0.3
Upshur	37	162	9.5	3.4	23	1 314	264.8	55.7	50	609	24.5	6.1
Wayne	23	D	D	D	29	791	D	D	50	457	18.4	5.0
Webster	7	28	1.6	0.5	NA	NA	NA	NA	12	74	2.0	0.6
Wetzel	20	95	5.0	1.7	16	1 394	D	92.1	46	522	21.0	5.4
Wirt	5	D	D	D	NA	NA	NA	NA	5	34	0.9	0.3
Wood	138	D	D	D	69	D	D	D	228	4 173	157.9	47.7
Wyoming	17	79	3.8	1.4	NA	NA	NA	NA	27	286	9.9	2.8
WISCONSIN	11 255	97 445	12 797.3	4 999.0	9 659	487 573	163 563.2	21 850.3	14 439	227 475	9 247.3	2 535.2
Adams	19	71	5.0	2.2	NA	NA	NA	NA	60	928	42.0	12.3
Ashland	26	155	11.7	5.0	35	1 411	222.4	50.6	78	730	29.5	8.2
Barron	71	316	38.3	11.9	95	5 176	1 207.4	182.5	139	1 425	50.4	13.8
Bayfield	16	42	2.7	1.0	NA	NA	NA	NA	111	700	34.2	9.0
Brown	511	D	D	D	446	25 490	9 321.9	1 099.3	613	12 801	464.6	135.1
Buffalo	22	76	4.5	1.4	NA	NA	NA	NA	44	D	D	D
Burnett	25	85	9.2	2.7	28	856	227.0	34.0	69	D	D	D
Calumet	55	210	16.4	7.1	66	3 946	1 355.2	169.0	86	1 515	40.1	11.1
Chippewa	86	555	71.1	30.9	131	5 184	1 575.0	202.3	158	1 512	56.3	13.6
Clark	32	150	22.2	5.8	75	3 001	1 475.2	106.3	64	D	D	D
Columbia	83	D	D	D	100	4 853	1 744.1	D	194	4 000	164.2	45.8
Crawford	19	75	5.9	2.3	24	2 048	820.8	69.8	49	629	22.6	6.1
Dane	1 584	D	D	D	590	27 640	6 968.1	1 295.0	1 204	23 413	916.7	268.9

1. Establishment subject to federal tax.

Table B. States and Counties — Health Care and Social Assistance, Other Services, and Federal Funds

STATE County	Health care and social assistance, 2007				Other services, 2007				Federal funds and grants, 2009–2010 Expenditures (mil dol)			
										Direct payments for individuals[1]		
	Number of establishments	Number of employees	Receipts (mil dol)	Annual payroll (mil dol)	Number of establishments	Number of employees	Receipts (mil dol)	Annual payroll (mil dol)	Total	Social Security and government retirement	Medicare	Food Stamps and Supplemental Security Income
	159	160	161	162	163	164	165	166	167	168	169	170
WEST VIRGINIA—Cont'd												
Brooke	62	1 774	153.3	62.5	36	155	8.8	2.4	206.6	106.7	54.0	10.8
Cabell	370	D	D	D	193	1 104	96.4	23.8	1 021.2	419.8	185.4	58.7
Calhoun	9	D	D	D	8	D	D	D	81.5	26.6	15.9	7.6
Clay	20	344	14.4	7.0	5	D	D	D	100.8	38.7	18.2	10.2
Doddridge	10	D	D	D	4	D	D	D	47.4	19.5	8.8	3.9
Fayette	93	1 811	135.4	49.3	59	288	34.7	6.9	534.9	202.0	123.2	34.6
Gilmer	16	209	9.9	4.4	7	19	1.1	0.3	94.6	22.4	12.8	5.9
Grant	24	627	36.1	15.3	19	64	5.3	1.3	113.9	55.1	16.2	7.3
Greenbrier	141	2 482	208.1	80.7	68	212	18.9	3.8	337.2	147.5	72.1	14.9
Hampshire	40	789	37.7	17.1	26	87	6.9	1.7	154.6	80.4	28.1	8.0
Hancock	83	1 193	60.1	23.8	52	234	15.2	3.8	317.8	172.4	98.5	8.8
Hardy	35	420	19.4	7.8	19	61	4.7	1.0	128.4	46.7	15.5	3.8
Harrison	222	D	D	D	136	643	57.4	12.2	1 152.8	280.9	144.3	41.0
Jackson	60	946	60.2	23.7	33	139	12.8	3.1	227.5	113.7	43.5	14.1
Jefferson	73	1 041	87.0	34.9	71	411	47.8	10.2	542.4	191.2	47.0	9.3
Kanawha	739	16 612	1 720.2	627.3	419	3 169	299.7	77.6	3 516.9	775.2	428.7	99.6
Lewis	32	1 112	86.2	33.9	37	117	8.8	1.8	170.0	68.0	35.7	12.2
Lincoln	26	461	20.9	9.5	17	D	D	D	214.8	83.9	35.3	21.4
Logan	90	1 758	151.6	48.5	58	458	77.8	18.3	443.3	173.5	94.7	32.8
McDowell	41	812	55.8	19.7	22	106	12.3	5.1	371.0	112.9	79.2	40.8
Marion	158	2 944	233.3	89.6	107	747	51.5	19.4	636.1	229.7	116.9	29.8
Marshall	69	1 475	89.7	36.2	45	216	14.3	4.0	236.4	109.2	62.5	13.7
Mason	35	1 052	91.3	38.3	33	98	5.9	1.4	218.4	100.2	45.0	14.8
Mercer	225	4 790	399.6	147.9	102	805	71.5	22.0	679.6	286.0	155.8	45.4
Mineral	62	1 083	54.1	22.5	42	221	13.4	3.3	301.5	101.4	59.8	8.1
Mingo	46	727	65.4	23.8	25	D	D	D	343.6	129.4	59.5	33.6
Monongalia	221	D	D	D	143	990	163.0	23.8	1 075.0	214.8	104.3	24.1
Monroe	18	D	D	D	13	38	2.5	0.6	146.9	61.2	28.9	5.5
Morgan	16	D	D	D	30	178	19.5	7.2	112.4	71.6	20.6	4.1
Nicholas	53	1 339	86.8	35.8	41	189	18.0	4.9	234.1	113.7	48.2	16.8
Ohio	236	6 249	558.5	210.2	131	923	75.3	20.8	498.3	184.3	114.9	21.1
Pendleton	17	271	13.7	5.6	13	61	6.5	1.5	95.4	31.4	14.5	2.1
Pleasants	15	D	D	D	11	D	D	D	51.8	25.5	13.1	3.1
Pocahontas	23	369	21.0	8.6	25	171	7.2	2.1	85.3	64.8	20.5	3.0
Preston	51	D	D	D	43	200	14.2	3.5	343.0	113.3	48.9	16.0
Putnam	125	1 624	138.5	45.7	61	380	37.6	10.8	325.6	172.2	54.8	13.7
Raleigh	274	6 168	560.5	224.8	138	820	70.6	19.7	850.8	351.3	161.8	45.3
Randolph	110	2 418	164.4	65.5	43	156	15.5	3.4	282.4	116.8	55.1	14.4
Ritchie	16	179	8.7	3.8	12	42	3.8	0.7	86.8	39.7	17.7	5.8
Roane	29	671	37.2	17.8	12	D	D	D	132.8	53.0	27.0	9.8
Summers	26	485	30.1	12.2	17	49	2.7	0.8	198.0	54.6	26.9	10.7
Taylor	28	D	D	D	20	D	D	D	126.4	53.5	24.4	9.2
Tucker	12	259	11.7	5.3	15	123	12.7	3.0	69.5	28.1	11.8	2.6
Tyler	14	467	21.0	10.3	11	30	2.4	0.5	65.6	32.5	14.5	4.5
Upshur	75	1 593	75.8	35.8	32	134	9.7	3.3	184.5	84.5	31.9	14.4
Wayne	61	D	D	D	46	187	18.6	5.6	442.6	127.1	53.8	26.1
Webster	12	401	20.3	8.7	9	D	D	D	111.5	38.1	20.5	10.2
Wetzel	42	609	46.3	17.4	41	121	7.0	1.8	158.1	76.1	32.9	11.4
Wirt	4	D	D	D	4	D	D	D	52.0	22.6	8.8	3.9
Wood	286	D	D	D	170	943	81.1	17.2	911.1	360.3	168.0	45.7
Wyoming	31	793	34.2	16.1	17	69	5.6	1.5	253.2	111.5	52.8	23.5
WISCONSIN	14 417	369 289	33 841.3	14 082.9	10 724	66 392	6 359.6	1 678.7	54 866.1	16 179.8	7 536.0	1 653.2
Adams	29	519	35.1	14.0	25	124	11.0	3.2	159.6	63.1	28.6	6.1
Ashland	66	1 484	112.1	52.3	36	D	D	D	177.2	60.0	34.5	6.0
Barron	128	2 608	234.9	96.3	101	345	25.7	7.1	367.3	163.6	66.0	11.9
Bayfield	17	207	9.2	4.7	25	57	6.4	1.7	151.8	55.3	24.2	3.3
Brown	586	19 287	2 001.9	777.2	480	3 089	233.0	66.2	1 443.2	635.1	221.0	55.7
Buffalo	26	401	17.1	8.2	22	D	D	D	109.6	48.0	20.1	3.6
Burnett	31	587	30.1	15.3	22	75	6.6	1.6	141.7	67.7	24.4	4.2
Calumet	66	920	62.5	26.3	70	250	15.8	4.0	175.4	76.8	32.6	3.0
Chippewa	126	3 053	236.3	97.9	102	566	56.6	15.8	431.5	176.3	81.5	14.2
Clark	60	1 295	53.3	27.1	63	179	14.3	3.3	242.6	96.1	60.7	5.5
Columbia	113	2 602	189.6	80.0	99	395	35.9	8.9	446.1	197.6	86.2	7.4
Crawford	51	1 212	69.5	31.9	31	109	7.3	1.8	135.5	52.6	25.6	3.7
Dane	1 188	39 141	4 098.2	1 670.0	1 054	8 466	1 352.9	263.8	6 407.9	1 095.7	406.8	82.1

1. State totals may include programs not allocated by county.

Table B. States and Counties — Federal Funds, Residential Construction, and Local Government Finances

	Federal funds and grants, 2009–2010 (cont.)							Value of residential construction authorized by building permits, 2010		Local government finances, 2007				
	Expenditures (mil dol) (cont.)									General revenue				
		Procurement contract awards		Grants[1]								Taxes		
													Per capita[2] (dollars)	
STATE County	Salaries and wages	Defense	Other	Medicaid and other health-related	Nutrition and family welfare	Education	Other	New construction ($1,000)	Number of housing units	Total (mil dol)	Inter-govern-mental (mil dol)	Total (mil dol)	Total	Property
	171	172	173	174	175	176	177	178	179	180	181	182	183	184
WEST VIRGINIA—Cont'd														
Brooke	6.3	0.0	0.8	14.9	3.2	1.7	4.9	2 224	12	46.1	23.1	18.0	761	707
Cabell	71.0	2.8	33.2	137.5	19.7	8.4	46.7	16 692	124	258.8	104.5	94.6	1 001	772
Calhoun	2.3	0.1	0.4	25.9	1.5	0.9	0.0	NA	NA	13.1	10.1	2.4	328	308
Clay	2.3	0.0	0.6	27.1	2.4	0.9	0.2	935	24	30.8	25.3	4.1	403	391
Doddridge	1.2	0.0	0.3	11.6	1.3	0.6	0.0	NA	NA	19.6	11.9	6.6	909	902
Fayette	47.8	0.0	10.0	82.6	9.4	3.4	17.3	4 890	39	145.6	61.0	53.3	1 150	557
Gilmer	21.7	0.0	6.2	17.8	1.5	0.9	1.3	0	0	19.9	6.3	4.2	615	591
Grant	5.0	0.0	2.1	19.7	3.5	0.7	1.4	2 568	28	56.1	16.2	8.1	678	626
Greenbrier	17.2	1.7	2.9	53.9	6.6	2.2	6.8	24 104	102	86.7	39.2	28.6	826	566
Hampshire	6.5	0.0	0.8	24.5	3.1	1.3	0.3	7 551	62	45.8	25.7	14.4	640	585
Hancock	5.6	2.5	2.2	17.4	3.9	1.7	2.8	1 336	9	90.9	29.9	25.6	848	696
Hardy	5.6	0.3	1.3	24.6	1.8	0.9	25.4	5 112	41	25.1	14.5	7.3	532	482
Harrison	281.9	42.8	248.1	72.7	13.2	7.0	8.7	22 072	116	181.2	82.5	70.1	1 026	726
Jackson	10.2	0.1	3.0	29.4	4.2	1.9	6.3	81	2	70.9	38.4	22.5	796	726
Jefferson	62.1	17.7	156.2	21.1	5.1	1.9	4.2	33 906	159	122.3	40.9	56.3	1 107	835
Kanawha	251.1	17.9	54.6	247.5	140.4	172.3	1 237.6	27 199	148	528.1	217.8	219.7	1 149	781
Lewis	11.8	0.9	1.1	35.2	2.9	1.3	0.5	0	0	34.2	17.7	14.4	838	656
Lincoln	3.4	0.0	0.8	62.1	4.2	2.7	0.1	1 437	13	44.3	32.8	8.7	389	364
Logan	13.0	5.8	7.6	65.5	8.7	3.8	11.2	450	13	76.6	44.0	23.6	663	628
McDowell	8.9	0.3	11.5	99.1	6.5	3.6	7.9	0	0	58.8	32.9	15.8	689	612
Marion	29.7	22.5	91.8	56.0	14.1	8.7	18.0	409	5	143.1	66.4	44.3	781	581
Marshall	11.0	0.1	1.2	26.3	5.0	2.6	2.8	342	3	100.7	38.4	30.5	921	789
Mason	7.2	7.4	1.3	33.3	3.8	2.0	1.5	365	2	60.5	31.0	19.2	751	684
Mercer	43.8	1.5	6.4	100.4	12.2	9.4	4.7	1 358	8	213.9	123.4	31.8	518	396
Mineral	4.8	65.6	23.9	23.1	5.0	2.6	4.8	6 199	39	56.7	36.4	13.6	508	457
Mingo	7.7	0.5	4.4	74.7	9.9	2.8	19.8	0	0	67.7	40.7	20.8	779	720
Monongalia	119.6	19.7	326.4	124.6	11.4	7.5	80.0	30 000	300	201.5	73.5	75.4	862	642
Monroe	14.4	0.0	4.3	28.4	2.6	1.1	0.0	0	0	26.2	20.6	3.8	283	269
Morgan	2.8	0.1	1.3	8.3	1.9	1.0	0.0	5 890	43	45.2	14.1	12.0	737	679
Nicholas	8.9	3.2	1.4	32.7	5.6	2.1	0.9	561	4	95.2	33.9	15.4	590	449
Ohio	46.8	9.3	13.3	48.0	11.1	2.9	27.5	3 852	22	173.1	69.3	50.1	1 129	648
Pendleton	10.8	7.5	0.7	16.8	1.2	0.9	8.8	3 378	26	13.7	9.4	3.1	410	371
Pleasants	1.0	0.0	0.3	7.0	1.1	0.4	0.0	1 396	9	38.4	9.2	11.2	1 558	1 471
Pocahontas	4.0	0.2	3.3	15.5	1.6	0.6	0.4	0	0	25.6	9.0	7.1	829	678
Preston	85.8	3.7	25.8	37.8	5.0	2.6	1.9	76	1	53.0	33.1	8.5	279	261
Putnam	34.7	6.9	2.6	29.8	6.5	2.2	0.5	18 412	119	116.0	49.4	42.5	773	705
Raleigh	107.3	0.2	45.9	88.7	15.0	5.2	9.2	17 340	110	193.2	100.3	61.6	778	602
Randolph	19.1	0.0	6.4	50.7	5.0	3.7	7.3	2 395	12	59.1	39.3	10.8	381	302
Ritchie	2.5	0.0	0.5	16.6	1.8	0.9	0.7	0	0	22.3	11.9	7.0	679	635
Roane	7.4	0.0	0.6	27.7	3.0	1.5	2.1	1 999	30	25.7	19.1	4.6	299	215
Summers	3.1	61.1	0.5	36.9	2.2	1.1	0.3	1 871	20	18.4	11.8	4.7	353	242
Taylor	10.7	0.4	2.7	20.2	2.6	1.4	0.3	202	1	30.0	17.3	8.9	554	484
Tucker	4.0	0.0	1.2	13.0	1.3	0.6	6.8	900	12	19.9	8.8	4.8	704	625
Tyler	1.7	0.0	0.4	9.3	1.5	0.8	0.2	0	0	28.8	11.7	5.7	639	619
Upshur	9.5	1.8	1.8	27.0	5.2	1.8	1.9	5 375	42	50.3	28.7	12.7	542	450
Wayne	87.5	5.9	39.7	79.3	6.1	2.7	11.2	5 782	85	83.4	55.1	22.3	540	495
Webster	1.3	0.0	0.3	31.7	1.9	1.3	5.2	0	0	18.6	12.6	3.7	395	310
Wetzel	4.6	0.1	0.8	28.2	2.7	1.4	0.0	483	10	65.6	23.8	12.2	741	584
Wirt	1.2	3.5	0.3	10.1	1.0	0.5	0.0	669	11	10.1	7.3	1.9	321	306
Wood	161.6	10.8	33.5	78.4	12.2	6.4	14.1	15 192	126	205.4	90.2	69.4	807	626
Wyoming	6.8	0.0	1.8	44.5	7.5	2.5	1.1	0	0	55.7	32.2	17.7	748	640
WISCONSIN	2 926.4	8 469.0	1 336.1	6 592.2	1 312.1	860.1	3 227.7	1 793 681	10 864	X	X	X	X	X
Adams	21.6	0.0	1.5	29.8	3.6	0.9	1.0	9 846	62	68.5	28.2	29.2	1 412	1 312
Ashland	11.2	0.1	5.3	34.0	5.1	4.2	5.3	2 720	19	82.0	50.2	19.8	1 216	1 107
Barron	13.1	0.0	2.4	80.0	15.4	3.1	1.5	12 209	80	182.1	86.8	66.3	1 454	1 317
Bayfield	10.6	1.9	5.8	24.7	5.4	2.3	17.5	7 998	59	69.4	28.9	30.4	2 023	1 887
Brown	109.4	49.8	58.2	174.4	37.8	16.7	35.5	115 703	988	1 061.0	468.5	389.7	1 603	1 467
Buffalo	6.6	1.4	3.2	19.3	3.0	0.8	0.0	3 913	25	52.4	31.0	15.6	1 133	1 073
Burnett	2.5	4.7	0.6	25.3	4.0	1.2	3.8	9 986	62	58.2	22.9	28.2	1 728	1 651
Calumet	34.8	2.3	1.2	13.9	4.5	1.9	0.1	10 905	57	109.4	49.9	36.5	824	806
Chippewa	53.1	5.8	3.1	66.3	10.7	4.1	5.4	20 503	130	210.1	108.4	62.3	1 032	946
Clark	12.1	0.0	3.0	47.0	6.3	2.5	0.2	5 309	39	137.6	78.4	30.4	909	897
Columbia	25.0	0.0	55.0	46.8	12.1	3.1	3.3	18 697	102	240.1	102.6	99.0	1 792	1 670
Crawford	7.6	0.3	1.2	31.9	3.5	1.1	5.7	4 625	48	66.8	38.3	20.5	1 208	1 099
Dane	438.3	166.7	182.8	965.7	283.4	450.2	2 189.6	206 845	1 060	2 063.7	709.8	953.7	2 000	1 842

1. State totals may include programs not allocated by county.   2. Based on the resident population estimated as of July 1 of the year shown.

Table B. States and Counties — **Local Government Finances, Government Employment, and Voting**

STATE County	Total (mil dol)	Per capita[1] (dollars)	Education	Health and hospitals	Police protection	Public welfare	Highways	Total (mil dol)	Per capita[1] (dollars)	Federal civilian	Federal military	State and local	Democratic	Republican	All other
	185	186	187	188	189	190	191	192	193	194	195	196	197	198	199
WEST VIRGINIA—Cont'd															
Brooke	41.8	1 765	72.5	0.3	7.4	0.1	1.1	18.6	787	38	123	976	47.9	50.3	1.8
Cabell	241.6	2 558	48.5	2.4	6.0	0.4	0.9	161.8	1 714	1 127	540	6 901	44.2	54.3	1.5
Calhoun	13.9	1 932	86.0	0.2	1.1	0.0	0.3	2.9	399	23	37	316	40.9	56.2	2.9
Clay	30.1	2 974	84.5	7.5	2.0	0.0	0.1	1.4	134	23	53	527	43.5	53.8	2.7
Doddridge	23.5	3 242	83.8	2.0	2.8	0.0	0.1	7.6	1 048	14	38	475	24.4	73.5	2.2
Fayette	128.7	2 777	48.6	0.7	4.1	0.2	6.6	75.1	1 621	321	242	2 765	47.7	50.4	1.9
Gilmer	15.9	2 308	56.7	0.2	2.3	0.0	0.6	5.3	766	324	36	621	39.8	57.3	2.9
Grant	55.1	4 617	32.5	49.5	2.3	0.0	0.6	13.6	1 138	42	62	929	23.6	75.1	1.3
Greenbrier	76.4	2 209	61.8	1.7	3.5	0.1	1.4	60.6	1 753	110	181	2 186	42.8	55.1	2.1
Hampshire	46.6	2 064	72.2	2.3	1.6	0.0	0.5	20.0	886	52	119	1 368	35.7	62.6	1.7
Hancock	87.1	2 886	43.8	11.9	5.6	0.0	4.3	65.1	2 155	69	156	1 323	41.6	56.9	1.5
Hardy	25.7	1 883	70.0	2.0	5.5	0.0	1.3	6.9	508	53	71	741	35.2	62.4	2.4
Harrison	171.2	2 506	61.4	0.9	5.6	0.0	3.6	137.4	2 012	4 020	362	4 061	42.6	55.9	1.5
Jackson	68.1	2 412	67.6	3.7	5.2	0.0	0.7	29.5	1 046	81	147	1 369	39.7	58.4	1.9
Jefferson	135.5	2 666	66.9	1.5	5.0	0.1	1.3	58.9	1 158	754	276	3 076	51.8	47.0	1.1
Kanawha	547.1	2 860	51.1	0.4	5.7	0.0	3.4	304.1	1 590	2 246	1 119	19 747	49.2	49.6	1.1
Lewis	32.0	1 865	77.8	2.2	2.9	0.3	1.5	0.6	34	59	91	1 476	31.9	65.6	2.5
Lincoln	44.4	1 990	88.9	0.6	0.5	0.0	0.0	6.0	270	42	116	889	44.3	53.2	2.5
Logan	84.3	2 365	77.7	1.4	1.2	0.1	0.5	24.5	688	118	186	2 100	43.6	54.4	2.0
McDowell	52.3	2 276	75.7	0.1	2.5	0.0	0.7	7.7	334	81	117	1 766	53.3	44.8	1.8
Marion	151.7	2 675	61.1	0.2	3.6	0.2	0.9	282.1	4 974	212	298	4 286	49.2	48.7	2.1
Marshall	94.9	2 863	53.9	3.9	4.9	0.2	1.3	212.4	6 407	64	181	1 843	42.8	55.4	1.8
Mason	76.0	2 974	73.7	0.2	2.3	0.0	3.0	59.0	2 309	121	134	1 504	42.3	55.2	2.5
Mercer	208.1	3 393	40.4	39.1	2.6	0.0	1.7	147.3	2 401	245	325	4 782	35.4	63.0	1.6
Mineral	54.4	2 036	74.4	1.9	2.9	0.1	1.0	25.2	945	69	143	1 568	32.5	66.0	1.6
Mingo	67.7	2 530	64.5	2.1	2.4	0.0	0.7	27.6	1 033	77	138	1 336	43.0	55.0	2.0
Monongalia	209.8	2 397	55.7	3.4	5.6	0.3	1.8	226.6	2 589	1 313	480	14 686	51.1	47.3	1.6
Monroe	24.8	1 830	76.4	0.0	3.9	0.0	0.2	64.5	4 765	216	72	552	36.1	60.9	2.9
Morgan	47.4	2 898	50.4	23.5	4.1	0.0	0.0	12.3	751	31	86	969	37.4	60.9	1.7
Nicholas	97.3	3 719	42.3	37.8	4.4	0.0	0.8	22.4	858	107	137	1 731	46.5	51.3	2.1
Ohio	164.5	3 704	33.3	0.8	8.9	0.1	3.6	139.1	3 132	465	232	3 777	44.0	54.7	1.3
Pendleton	13.5	1 770	76.8	2.7	0.9	0.0	0.2	3.8	436	170	231	333	38.6	59.9	1.5
Pleasants	37.8	5 265	44.5	0.3	2.7	0.7	0.5	171.4	23 860	14	39	680	38.4	59.6	2.1
Pocahontas	26.5	3 094	47.1	27.6	2.2	0.1	0.2	5.4	626	62	44	767	42.5	55.2	2.3
Preston	51.7	1 708	73.2	0.9	2.2	0.0	0.8	35.8	1 184	601	159	1 681	35.6	62.1	2.3
Putnam	123.4	2 243	68.6	3.2	4.0	0.0	0.6	218.1	3 966	237	293	2 240	37.7	61.2	1.1
Raleigh	196.1	2 477	58.3	1.3	7.0	0.6	1.4	128.6	1 624	1 776	637	3 742	36.2	62.1	1.7
Randolph	56.9	2 012	65.1	3.4	2.9	0.2	1.7	29.2	1 031	197	149	2 053	41.9	55.9	2.2
Ritchie	21.2	2 049	69.3	4.7	3.8	0.0	0.5	1.9	183	32	53	529	25.9	72.3	1.7
Roane	25.1	1 644	85.6	0.1	1.1	0.0	1.7	8.8	576	38	78	633	45.1	52.9	2.0
Summers	18.7	1 419	77.5	1.5	4.4	0.0	1.7	3.1	238	45	69	740	43.1	54.4	2.5
Taylor	27.7	1 717	73.3	0.0	2.1	0.0	2.2	15.9	989	45	86	1 096	39.7	58.1	2.2
Tucker	21.4	3 119	50.0	3.9	3.3	0.0	1.3	23.3	3 388	57	36	618	36.7	60.5	2.7
Tyler	25.5	2 851	60.0	24.0	1.8	0.1	0.7	18.3	2 043	22	45	590	33.2	64.6	2.3
Upshur	51.4	2 186	66.8	0.6	3.6	0.3	1.4	17.7	752	123	125	1 215	32.6	65.9	1.5
Wayne	83.6	2 028	81.1	1.0	3.5	0.4	0.7	25.3	615	1 375	223	1 956	39.8	58.0	2.2
Webster	18.5	1 963	78.7	1.1	1.1	0.0	0.1	2.7	288	19	49	567	50.8	45.3	3.9
Wetzel	63.3	3 854	45.3	38.6	3.1	0.0	0.9	29.0	1 765	45	85	1 158	45.6	51.8	2.6
Wirt	10.5	1 804	85.8	0.0	0.1	0.0	0.2	1.1	188	15	29	259	33.6	64.3	2.1
Wood	219.0	2 544	65.9	1.0	5.3	0.1	2.8	217.5	2 526	2 227	456	4 484	34.9	63.6	1.5
Wyoming	53.9	2 276	76.4	0.7	4.6	0.0	0.5	30.2	1 275	88	122	1 146	36.3	61.4	2.3
WISCONSIN	X	X	X	X	X	X	X	X	X	30 223	17 138	386 166	56.2	42.3	1.5
Adams	72.5	3 505	30.8	6.7	6.6	4.7	19.6	69.8	3 377	320	58	886	58.1	39.8	2.1
Ashland	83.0	5 096	41.7	2.8	5.2	10.3	13.9	40.5	2 484	187	47	1 963	67.9	30.7	1.4
Barron	192.4	4 219	46.4	0.8	4.1	11.5	14.1	137.7	3 018	145	132	4 369	52.8	45.7	1.5
Bayfield	74.1	4 930	31.7	11.6	3.9	3.1	20.8	48.4	3 221	131	57	1 223	63.1	35.5	1.4
Brown	1 085.3	4 464	50.3	3.8	5.1	6.0	7.5	1 603.5	6 595	1 000	739	16 843	53.9	44.8	1.3
Buffalo	59.3	4 296	43.7	0.9	2.3	8.2	22.8	39.7	2 871	159	39	713	56.4	41.8	1.8
Burnett	60.3	3 692	40.8	6.4	3.9	5.3	19.9	45.0	2 756	39	46	1 158	49.9	48.3	1.7
Calumet	110.0	2 482	39.4	5.9	5.0	6.4	13.7	117.0	2 639	128	129	1 267	50.2	48.1	1.7
Chippewa	205.1	3 395	47.6	3.2	4.0	8.5	14.5	674.3	11 163	168	176	3 258	53.7	44.6	1.7
Clark	140.1	4 184	43.2	7.8	3.3	15.9	10.5	57.2	1 709	116	96	1 878	52.5	45.0	2.5
Columbia	248.1	4 488	47.8	1.2	4.4	10.1	9.6	218.9	3 960	208	159	3 660	56.9	41.7	1.4
Crawford	64.4	3 790	41.2	2.7	4.7	10.7	15.0	46.8	2 754	67	48	956	62.5	35.5	2.1
Dane	2 082.0	4 367	45.1	2.2	5.8	8.6	5.9	2 406.9	5 048	4 939	1 480	74 561	72.8	25.8	1.4

1. Based on the resident population estimated as of July 1 of the year shown.   2. © 2009 Election Data Services, Inc. All rights reserved.

Table B. States and Counties — Land Area and Population

STATE/ County code	CBSA code[1]	County type[2]	STATE County	Land area,[3] (sq km) 2010	Total persons	Rank	Per square kilometer	White	Black	American Indian, Alaska Native	Asian and Pacific Islander	Percent Hispanic or Latino[4]	Under 5 years	5 to 17 years	18 to 24 years	25 to 34 years	35 to 44 years	45 to 54 years
				1	2	3	4	5	6	7	8	9	10	11	12	13	14	15
			WISCONSIN—Cont'd															
55 027	13180	4	Dodge	2 268	88 759	641	39.1	92.3	2.9	0.7	0.8	4.0	5.7	16.4	7.7	12.9	13.7	16.7
55 029	...	6	Door	1 248	27 785	1 504	22.3	96.1	0.8	1.0	0.5	2.4	4.6	13.7	5.6	9.1	10.4	16.6
55 031	20260	2	Douglas	3 378	44 159	1 083	13.1	94.9	1.8	3.5	1.2	1.1	5.9	15.6	10.4	12.6	12.0	15.6
55 033	32860	6	Dunn	2 202	43 857	1 088	19.9	95.0	0.8	0.8	3.1	1.4	5.5	15.1	19.6	11.4	11.3	13.4
55 035	20740	3	Eau Claire	1 652	98 736	590	59.8	93.4	1.4	0.9	3.9	1.8	5.9	15.2	17.2	13.3	11.0	13.1
55 037	27020	9	Florence	1 264	4 423	2 876	3.5	97.9	0.3	1.4	0.6	0.8	4.2	13.3	5.4	8.2	11.2	19.7
55 039	22540	3	Fond du Lac	1 864	101 633	570	54.5	92.9	1.7	0.8	1.4	4.3	5.9	16.8	9.1	12.1	12.7	15.6
55 041	...	9	Forest	2 626	9 304	2 497	3.5	84.3	1.0	15.0	0.5	1.5	5.4	16.6	8.7	9.3	11.1	14.7
55 043	38420	6	Grant	2 970	51 208	961	17.2	96.8	1.3	0.4	0.8	1.3	5.8	15.4	17.0	10.5	10.2	13.8
55 045	33820	6	Green	1 512	36 842	1 251	24.4	96.1	0.7	0.4	0.8	2.8	6.4	17.9	6.5	11.2	13.3	16.5
55 047	...	6	Green Lake	905	19 051	1 877	21.1	94.9	0.6	0.5	0.6	3.9	5.8	17.2	6.4	10.0	11.3	15.8
55 049	31540	2	Iowa	1 975	23 687	1 657	12.0	97.5	0.7	0.4	0.8	1.4	6.8	18.1	6.3	11.2	13.1	17.0
55 051	...	9	Iron	1 964	5 916	2 775	3.0	98.4	0.3	1.3	0.4	0.6	3.6	13.0	4.9	7.7	10.8	17.3
55 053	...	6	Jackson	2 558	20 449	1 821	8.0	89.2	2.1	6.7	0.7	2.5	6.1	16.5	7.4	12.1	12.9	15.6
55 055	48020	4	Jefferson	1 441	83 686	660	58.1	91.6	1.1	0.6	1.0	6.6	6.3	17.5	10.3	12.0	13.2	15.2
55 057	...	7	Juneau	1 986	26 664	1 539	13.4	93.5	2.3	1.8	0.6	2.6	5.5	15.8	6.9	11.2	12.7	16.7
55 059	16980	1	Kenosha	704	166 426	370	236.4	79.8	7.5	0.8	2.0	11.8	6.6	19.1	10.0	12.5	13.9	15.7
55 061	24580	2	Kewaunee	887	20 574	1 815	23.2	96.7	0.5	0.9	0.5	2.3	5.7	17.9	6.7	11.0	12.8	16.1
55 063	29100	3	La Crosse	1 170	114 638	521	98.0	92.4	2.0	0.8	4.6	1.5	5.9	15.5	15.6	12.9	11.4	13.8
55 065	...	8	Lafayette	1 641	16 836	1 993	10.3	96.1	0.3	0.5	0.5	3.1	7.1	18.8	7.8	10.7	11.5	16.2
55 067	...	6	Langlade	2 255	19 977	1 841	8.9	96.8	0.7	1.6	0.5	1.6	5.2	15.9	6.7	9.8	11.4	16.7
55 069	32980	6	Lincoln	2 277	28 743	1 464	12.6	97.4	0.8	0.7	0.7	1.2	5.1	16.8	6.3	9.7	12.4	17.7
55 071	31820	4	Manitowoc	1 526	81 442	677	53.4	93.2	0.8	0.9	2.8	3.1	5.6	16.8	7.3	10.9	12.2	16.7
55 073	48140	3	Marathon	4 001	134 063	461	33.5	91.2	1.0	0.8	5.8	2.2	6.5	18.0	7.8	12.2	13.2	15.6
55 075	31940	6	Marinette	3 624	41 749	1 138	11.5	97.4	0.5	1.0	0.8	1.3	5.0	15.5	7.7	9.9	10.9	16.7
55 077	...	8	Marquette	1 180	15 404	2 089	13.1	96.0	0.7	0.8	0.5	2.5	5.2	14.8	6.3	8.8	11.0	17.2
55 078	...	8	Menominee	926	4 232	2 889	4.6	11.6	0.6	84.7	0.0	4.2	9.7	22.9	10.2	10.4	11.6	14.1
55 079	33340	1	Milwaukee	625	947 735	45	1 516.4	56.1	27.6	1.1	3.9	13.3	7.3	17.6	11.4	15.4	12.6	13.4
55 081	...	6	Monroe	2 333	44 673	1 075	19.1	93.4	1.5	1.5	1.0	3.7	7.2	18.9	7.3	11.9	12.2	15.5
55 083	24580	2	Oconto	2 585	37 660	1 225	14.6	96.9	0.4	1.8	0.5	1.4	5.6	16.8	6.5	10.1	13.2	17.8
55 085	...	7	Oneida	2 883	35 998	1 275	12.5	97.1	0.6	1.6	0.8	1.1	4.7	13.8	6.3	9.0	11.3	17.4
55 087	11540	3	Outagamie	1 651	176 695	350	107.0	90.8	1.4	2.0	3.4	3.6	6.6	18.5	8.7	13.5	13.7	15.9
55 089	33340	1	Ozaukee	604	86 395	652	143.0	94.3	1.7	0.5	2.2	2.3	5.3	18.3	7.4	9.4	12.8	17.4
55 091	...	8	Pepin	601	7 469	2 644	12.4	98.3	0.3	0.5	0.4	1.0	6.3	16.5	6.5	10.0	12.0	16.1
55 093	33460	1	Pierce	1 486	41 019	1 154	27.6	96.8	0.9	0.8	1.1	1.5	5.9	16.4	16.7	11.5	12.3	15.2
55 095	...	6	Polk	2 367	44 205	1 082	18.7	96.9	0.5	1.4	0.6	1.5	6.1	17.6	6.4	10.6	12.7	16.5
55 097	44620	4	Portage	2 074	70 019	758	33.8	93.6	0.9	0.6	3.2	2.6	5.6	15.2	16.4	12.0	11.4	14.5
55 099	...	9	Price	3 249	14 159	2 163	4.4	97.4	0.4	1.0	1.0	1.1	4.4	14.7	5.3	8.4	11.4	18.2
55 101	39540	3	Racine	861	195 408	320	227.0	76.0	12.0	0.7	1.4	11.5	6.5	18.3	8.1	12.2	13.2	16.3
55 103	...	6	Richland	1 518	18 021	1 921	11.9	96.7	0.7	0.5	0.7	2.0	6.5	16.8	7.6	10.4	11.2	15.0
55 105	27500	3	Rock	1 860	160 331	384	86.2	86.2	5.9	0.7	1.4	7.6	6.5	18.5	8.6	12.6	13.3	15.0
55 107	...	6	Rusk	2 366	14 755	2 130	6.2	97.6	0.6	1.0	0.5	1.2	5.5	17.0	6.1	9.0	11.2	16.2
55 109	33460	1	St. Croix	1 871	84 345	658	45.1	95.9	1.1	0.7	1.5	2.0	7.3	19.8	6.7	13.7	15.0	16.1
55 111	12660	4	Sauk	2 152	61 976	837	28.8	93.4	0.9	1.5	0.8	4.3	6.4	17.4	7.5	12.5	13.0	15.4
55 113	...	9	Sawyer	3 256	16 557	2 014	5.1	81.4	0.7	18.7	0.5	1.6	5.9	15.0	6.4	8.8	10.8	16.0
55 115	...	6	Shawano	2 313	41 949	1 133	18.1	89.7	0.5	8.7	0.7	2.2	5.8	17.0	7.1	10.4	12.6	15.7
55 117	43100	3	Sheboygan	1 324	115 507	518	87.2	88.0	1.9	0.7	5.0	5.5	6.2	17.7	7.7	12.0	13.0	16.1
55 119	...	6	Taylor	2 525	20 689	1 810	8.2	97.7	0.4	0.4	0.5	1.5	6.6	18.0	6.8	10.7	12.5	17.0
55 121	...	8	Trempealeau	1 898	28 816	1 449	15.2	93.4	0.4	0.4	0.5	5.8	6.5	17.7	6.9	11.7	13.0	15.4
55 123	...	6	Vernon	2 050	29 773	1 432	14.5	97.7	0.7	0.5	0.5	1.3	7.1	19.3	6.6	10.0	11.2	15.8
55 125	...	9	Vilas	2 219	21 430	1 764	9.7	87.6	0.3	11.4	0.5	1.3	4.5	13.3	5.3	7.6	10.3	16.2
55 127	48580	4	Walworth	1 438	102 228	568	71.1	87.6	1.3	0.5	1.1	10.3	6.1	17.4	11.8	11.2	12.4	15.2
55 129	...	6	Washburn	2 065	15 911	2 055	7.7	97.0	0.4	2.1	0.5	1.3	5.5	14.8	5.5	9.2	10.9	16.2
55 131	33340	1	Washington	1 116	131 887	465	118.2	95.2	1.2	0.5	1.4	2.6	6.2	18.3	6.6	11.2	14.1	17.3
55 133	33340	1	Waukesha	1 423	389 891	170	274.0	91.5	1.6	0.5	3.3	4.1	5.5	18.6	6.9	10.3	13.3	17.5
55 135	...	6	Waupaca	1 937	52 410	943	27.1	96.4	0.4	0.8	0.5	2.5	5.6	17.1	6.6	10.6	12.3	16.4
55 137	...	8	Waushara	1 622	24 496	1 627	15.1	91.9	2.1	0.8	0.6	5.4	4.8	15.0	6.3	10.3	11.7	16.7
55 139	36780	3	Winnebago	1 125	166 994	368	148.4	91.8	2.2	0.9	2.7	3.5	5.9	15.7	11.9	13.1	12.8	15.3
55 141	32270	4	Wood	2 054	74 749	727	36.4	94.7	0.9	1.0	2.0	2.2	6.0	16.8	7.5	11.0	12.0	16.4
56 000	...	X	**WYOMING**	251 470	563 626	X	2.2	87.3	1.1	2.8	1.3	8.9	7.1	16.9	10.0	13.8	11.9	14.8
56 001	29660	4	Albany	11 069	36 299	1 266	3.3	86.6	1.4	1.2	3.6	8.8	5.6	11.0	28.9	16.4	9.2	10.2
56 003	...	9	Big Horn	8 125	11 668	2 320	1.4	90.2	0.3	1.3	0.5	8.4	6.7	19.1	7.0	10.1	10.7	14.0
56 005	23940	5	Campbell	12 439	46 133	1 042	3.7	90.3	0.5	1.7	1.0	7.8	8.8	19.3	9.8	16.6	12.9	16.2
56 007	...	7	Carbon	20 455	15 885	2 058	0.8	80.9	1.0	1.4	0.9	16.8	7.1	16.5	7.7	14.1	12.1	15.7
56 009	...	6	Converse	11 020	13 833	2 194	1.3	92.4	0.5	1.3	0.6	6.3	7.0	18.4	7.4	12.4	12.4	15.9

1. CBSA = Core Based Statistical Area. See Appendix A for explanation. See Appendix B for list of metropolitan areas with component counties.   2. County type code from the Economic Research Service of USDA Rural-Urban Continuum Codes. See Appendix A for definition.   3. Dry land or land partially or temporarily covered by water.   4. May be of any race.

Table B. States and Counties — **Population and Households**

STATE County	55 to 64 years (16)	65 to 74 years (17)	75 years and over (18)	Percent female (19)	1990 (20)	2000 (21)	1990–2000 (22)	2000–2010 (23)	Births (24)	Deaths (25)	Net migration (26)	Number (27)	Percent change, 2000–2010 (28)	Persons per house-hold (29)	Female family house-holder[1] (30)	One person (31)
WISCONSIN—Cont'd																
Dodge	12.0	7.4	7.5	47.4	76 559	85 897	12.2	3.3	8 907	8 008	1 092	33 840	7.7	2.44	8.4	26.5
Door	17.6	12.2	10.2	50.8	25 690	27 961	8.8	-0.6	2 299	2 822	558	12 548	6.1	2.19	6.5	29.9
Douglas	13.6	7.7	6.7	50.0	41 758	43 287	3.7	2.0	4 551	4 055	739	18 555	4.2	2.31	10.9	30.2
Dunn	11.5	6.3	5.9	49.5	35 909	39 858	11.0	10.0	4 379	2 594	1 570	16 373	14.2	2.47	7.1	25.7
Eau Claire	11.6	6.3	6.3	51.0	85 183	93 142	9.3	6.0	10 720	6 626	2 725	39 493	10.2	2.38	8.9	28.4
Florence	17.0	12.5	8.5	48.9	4 590	5 088	10.8	-13.1	324	466	-382	1 987	-6.8	2.20	5.0	28.1
Fond du Lac	12.9	7.4	7.6	50.9	90 083	97 296	8.0	4.5	10 853	8 492	1 036	40 697	10.2	2.41	8.5	27.6
Forest	13.9	10.9	9.4	49.2	8 776	10 024	14.2	-7.2	1 011	1 056	-333	3 836	-5.1	2.33	11.3	28.5
Grant	11.7	7.6	7.9	48.0	49 266	49 597	0.7	3.2	5 320	4 644	-976	19 396	5.0	2.44	7.7	27.1
Green	13.3	7.5	7.4	50.5	30 339	33 647	10.9	9.5	3 861	2 996	1 811	14 866	12.5	2.45	8.1	25.7
Green Lake	14.4	9.6	9.5	50.1	18 651	19 105	2.4	-0.3	2 064	2 186	-404	7 919	2.8	2.38	7.9	29.0
Iowa	13.8	7.2	6.6	49.9	20 150	22 780	13.1	4.0	2 872	1 788	-220	9 547	8.9	2.46	7.8	26.0
Iron	17.4	12.1	13.3	50.0	6 153	6 861	11.5	-13.8	391	815	-330	2 822	-8.5	2.06	7.2	34.3
Jackson	13.2	9.0	7.2	46.8	16 588	19 100	15.1	7.1	2 187	1 826	544	7 843	10.9	2.44	9.4	26.9
Jefferson	12.3	7.3	5.9	50.2	67 783	74 021	9.2	13.1	9 252	5 558	1 908	32 117	13.9	2.49	8.7	25.2
Juneau	13.8	9.8	7.7	47.4	21 650	24 316	12.3	9.7	2 657	2 584	2 212	10 527	8.6	2.38	9.4	28.5
Kenosha	10.8	5.9	5.4	50.6	128 181	149 577	16.7	11.3	20 067	11 672	8 370	62 650	11.8	2.58	13.0	26.2
Kewaunee	13.3	8.2	8.3	49.2	18 878	20 187	6.9	1.9	2 145	1 711	-193	8 239	8.1	2.48	6.8	25.8
La Crosse	11.8	6.5	6.7	51.2	97 904	107 120	9.4	7.0	11 891	8 341	3 677	46 137	10.9	2.37	8.7	29.6
Lafayette	12.5	7.8	7.6	49.0	16 074	16 137	0.4	4.3	1 868	1 313	-887	6 609	6.4	2.53	7.6	25.7
Langlade	14.4	10.6	9.4	49.8	19 505	20 740	6.3	-3.7	1 986	2 176	-427	8 587	1.6	2.29	8.7	29.0
Lincoln	13.6	9.5	8.8	49.9	26 993	29 641	9.8	-3.0	2 878	2 885	-32	12 094	3.2	2.33	8.3	27.3
Manitowoc	13.6	8.3	8.5	50.3	80 421	82 887	3.1	-1.7	8 219	7 362	-2 657	34 013	3.9	2.36	7.7	29.1
Marathon	12.4	7.2	6.9	49.8	115 400	125 834	9.0	6.5	14 783	9 077	886	53 176	11.5	2.49	8.5	25.8
Marinette	14.6	10.5	9.2	50.3	40 548	43 384	7.0	-3.8	3 952	4 609	-497	17 974	2.2	2.26	8.4	29.9
Marquette	16.5	12.0	9.0	49.3	12 321	15 832	28.5	-2.7	1 488	1 590	348	6 571	9.8	2.32	7.1	27.3
Menominee	9.6	7.5	3.9	50.4	4 075	4 562	12.0	-7.2	951	298	-700	1 318	-2.0	3.17	26.6	18.3
Milwaukee	10.7	5.5	6.0	51.7	959 212	940 164	-2.0	0.8	137 965	78 995	-68 822	383 591	1.6	2.41	17.4	33.7
Monroe	12.9	7.4	6.5	49.3	36 633	40 899	11.6	9.2	5 758	3 747	1 141	17 376	12.8	2.52	9.7	26.8
Oconto	14.1	9.1	6.8	49.0	30 226	35 634	17.9	5.7	3 617	3 077	1 159	15 415	10.3	2.42	7.0	24.5
Oneida	15.8	11.9	9.8	50.0	31 679	36 776	16.1	-2.1	2 921	3 726	176	16 003	4.4	2.21	7.5	28.9
Outagamie	11.3	6.2	5.6	50.1	140 510	160 971	14.6	9.8	21 358	10 639	6 374	69 648	15.1	2.49	8.8	25.8
Ozaukee	14.1	8.0	7.3	51.0	72 894	82 317	12.9	5.0	8 046	5 856	2 376	34 228	10.9	2.47	6.9	24.8
Pepin	14.8	9.0	8.9	49.4	7 107	7 213	1.5	3.5	813	669	-19	3 051	10.6	2.40	6.7	26.8
Pierce	11.5	5.8	4.7	50.2	32 765	36 804	12.3	11.5	4 069	2 179	1 611	15 002	15.3	2.55	7.7	22.1
Polk	14.0	8.7	7.3	49.8	34 773	41 319	18.8	7.0	4 635	3 819	2 371	18 004	10.8	2.43	8.3	26.3
Portage	12.1	6.7	6.0	50.0	61 405	67 182	9.4	4.2	6 939	4 230	-289	27 814	11.1	2.39	7.5	27.2
Price	16.7	10.9	10.0	49.3	15 600	15 822	1.4	-10.5	1 176	1 799	-903	6 829	-3.6	2.20	6.7	31.0
Racine	12.3	6.9	6.3	50.5	175 034	188 831	7.9	3.5	24 129	14 364	-1 079	75 651	6.8	2.52	13.0	26.4
Richland	14.4	9.0	9.0	49.8	17 521	17 924	2.3	0.5	2 022	1 600	-330	7 349	3.2	2.41	8.1	28.3
Rock	11.8	7.2	6.4	50.8	139 510	152 307	9.2	5.3	19 132	12 368	2 074	62 905	7.3	2.50	12.3	26.3
Rusk	14.9	10.3	9.8	50.0	15 079	15 347	1.8	-3.9	1 494	1 632	-769	6 232	2.2	2.34	8.0	30.2
St. Croix	11.3	5.5	4.5	49.9	50 251	63 155	25.7	33.6	9 971	4 212	14 674	31 799	35.8	2.63	8.1	21.4
Sauk	12.8	7.7	7.3	50.2	46 975	55 225	17.6	12.2	6 845	4 843	2 071	25 192	16.4	2.43	9.2	27.3
Sawyer	16.3	12.3	8.4	49.3	14 181	16 196	14.2	2.2	1 748	1 761	848	7 038	6.0	2.31	10.7	27.9
Shawano	13.0	9.8	8.5	50.1	37 157	40 664	9.4	3.2	4 419	4 063	441	17 019	7.6	2.42	8.7	26.6
Sheboygan	12.7	7.3	7.3	49.8	103 877	112 646	8.4	2.5	12 630	9 702	-320	46 390	6.5	2.42	8.6	27.9
Taylor	12.4	8.0	8.1	49.0	18 901	19 680	4.1	5.1	2 262	1 673	-958	8 388	11.4	2.44	6.8	26.8
Trempealeau	12.9	8.1	7.7	49.2	25 263	27 010	6.9	6.7	3 186	2 718	457	11 524	7.2	2.46	7.9	26.7
Vernon	13.4	8.5	8.2	50.1	25 617	28 056	9.5	6.1	3 825	2 804	453	11 616	7.3	2.53	7.2	27.3
Vilas	16.9	14.6	11.3	49.3	17 707	21 033	18.8	1.9	1 710	2 403	1 193	9 658	6.5	2.20	8.0	28.7
Walworth	12.4	7.2	6.3	49.9	75 000	93 759	25.0	9.0	10 972	7 698	5 874	39 699	15.0	2.51	9.1	26.6
Washburn	16.6	12.1	9.2	50.2	13 772	16 036	16.4	-0.8	1 618	1 675	794	6 916	4.7	2.27	7.5	28.3
Washington	12.8	7.2	6.3	50.4	95 328	117 493	23.3	12.3	13 971	8 119	8 042	51 605	17.7	2.53	7.4	22.9
Waukesha	13.6	7.4	6.9	50.9	304 715	360 767	18.4	8.1	39 231	26 283	11 783	152 663	12.9	2.52	7.1	23.8
Waupaca	13.4	8.7	9.4	49.5	46 104	51 731	12.2	1.3	5 330	6 266	1 059	21 387	7.7	2.37	8.1	28.0
Waushara	15.3	11.0	9.0	47.4	19 385	23 154	19.4	5.8	2 246	2 420	1 783	9 949	6.6	2.34	6.9	27.5
Winnebago	11.8	6.7	6.7	49.7	140 320	156 763	11.7	6.5	17 328	11 856	2 183	67 875	11.0	2.34	9.1	29.9
Wood	13.2	8.4	8.7	50.8	73 605	75 555	2.6	-1.1	8 057	6 491	-2 765	31 598	4.9	2.34	8.9	29.5
WYOMING	13.0	7.0	5.4	49.0	453 589	493 782	8.9	14.1	65 633	38 277	25 660	226 879	17.2	2.42	8.9	28.0
Albany	9.9	4.9	3.8	47.9	30 797	32 014	4.0	13.4	3 721	1 673	90	15 691	18.3	2.17	6.7	34.9
Big Horn	14.4	10.2	7.9	49.6	10 525	11 461	8.9	1.8	1 325	1 260	119	4 561	5.8	2.52	7.6	26.2
Campbell	10.6	3.5	2.2	47.4	29 370	33 698	14.7	36.9	5 698	1 699	6 426	17 172	40.7	2.66	8.6	22.4
Carbon	14.0	7.7	5.1	46.2	16 659	15 639	-6.1	1.6	1 828	1 271	-407	6 388	4.2	2.36	7.8	29.6
Converse	13.6	7.3	5.6	49.3	11 128	12 052	8.3	14.8	1 454	828	962	5 673	20.9	2.42	8.2	26.5

1. No spouse present.

STATE County	Persons in group quarters, 2010	Daytime population, 2006–2010 Number	Employ-ment/resi-dence ratio	Births, average 2006–2008 Total	Rate[1]	Deaths, average 2006–2008 Number	Rate[1]	Persons under 65 with no health insurance, 2009 Number	Percent	Medicare, 2011 Eligible for Medicare	Enrolled in Medicare Advantage	Enrolled in a Medicare prescription drug plan	Serious crimes known to police,[2] 2010 Total Number	Rate[3]
	32	33	34	35	36	37	38	39	40	41	42	43	44	45
WISCONSIN—Cont'd														
Dodge	6 192	80 105	0.8	965	10.9	863	9.8	6 959	9.6	14 736	3 826	5 223	1 642	1 850
Door	348	27 715	1.0	D	D	291	10.4	2 394	11.3	7 479	1 570	3 140	275	990
Douglas	1 372	40 033	0.8	519	11.8	434	9.9	4 253	11.5	8 247	2 554	3 005	2 101	4 758
Dunn	3 415	40 139	0.8	D	D	297	7.0	4 019	10.9	7 200	1 795	2 903	637	1 452
Eau Claire	4 796	103 267	1.1	1 200	12.4	735	7.6	8 914	10.5	16 078	4 226	5 261	2 472	2 504
Florence	59	3 709	0.6	D	D	53	11.0	448	12.5	1 166	220	397	136	3 075
Fond du Lac	3 589	96 172	0.9	1 203	12.1	931	9.4	7 762	9.3	17 770	6 935	5 479	1 922	1 891
Forest	379	9 477	1.0	D	D	124	12.6	1 147	15.4	2 368	513	830	257	2 762
Grant	3 897	46 539	0.8	D	D	504	10.3	5 005	12.5	9 181	3 182	4 135	960	1 875
Green	405	33 085	0.8	D	D	317	8.8	2 918	9.7	6 377	893	2 485	728	1 976
Green Lake	212	17 480	0.8	D	D	227	12.1	1 752	12.0	4 227	1 822	1 129	336	1 884
Iowa	214	22 505	0.9	D	D	196	8.3	2 073	10.5	4 031	1 021	1 751	327	1 391
Iron	96	5 681	0.8	D	D	81	12.7	599	13.3	1 797	630	535	161	2 721
Jackson	1 333	19 305	0.9	D	D	180	9.1	2 375	14.3	3 873	1 386	1 089	388	1 897
Jefferson	3 678	73 102	0.8	1 028	12.8	598	7.4	7 605	11.1	13 381	2 631	6 016	1 585	1 935
Juneau	1 651	24 734	0.8	D	D	273	10.2	2 810	13.0	5 602	942	2 022	535	2 006
Kenosha	4 601	144 320	0.7	2 222	13.6	1 294	7.9	16 054	11.2	23 374	4 649	9 572	4 625	2 779
Kewaunee	178	18 126	0.8	D	D	181	8.8	1 601	9.6	3 754	1 358	1 200	251	1 220
La Crosse	5 195	120 881	1.1	1 321	11.9	918	8.3	9 091	9.4	18 256	7 840	5 307	3 007	2 623
Lafayette	120	13 571	0.6	D	D	144	9.0	1 647	12.6	2 962	731	1 300	207	1 279
Langlade	281	19 696	0.9	D	D	237	11.6	1 855	11.8	4 818	1 455	1 584	804	4 025
Lincoln	560	26 627	0.8	D	D	304	10.2	2 462	10.5	6 363	2 115	1 868	695	2 418
Manitowoc	1 100	76 881	0.9	900	11.1	811	10.0	6 570	10.0	16 240	5 482	5 040	1 148	1 410
Marathon	1 655	135 041	1.0	1 692	13.0	1 023	7.8	11 274	10.2	22 183	8 416	6 137	2 518	1 878
Marinette	1 073	43 608	1.1	D	D	490	11.6	3 735	11.3	10 141	2 855	3 560	1 050	2 515
Marquette	153	13 336	0.7	D	D	165	10.9	1 416	12.3	3 891	942	1 317	278	1 805
Menominee	59	4 986	1.5	D	D	35	7.6	555	13.2	685	166	264	62	1 465
Milwaukee	24 490	980 581	1.1	15 299	16.3	8 161	8.7	114 434	13.9	136 061	40 139	48 228	51 120	5 394
Monroe	859	45 638	1.1	656	15.2	396	9.2	4 306	11.7	7 329	2 431	1 826	1 097	2 482
Oconto	281	29 631	0.6	D	D	330	8.8	3 290	10.7	7 551	3 065	2 116	746	1 981
Oneida	610	36 965	1.0	D	D	412	11.3	2 928	10.7	9 751	2 641	3 286	994	2 761
Outagamie	3 039	180 993	1.1	2 307	13.3	1 177	6.8	14 507	9.6	25 449	13 039	5 731	4 226	2 392
Ozaukee	1 804	81 597	0.9	843	9.8	684	8.0	4 652	6.5	15 255	4 226	5 420	891	1 031
Pepin	136	6 417	0.7	D	D	67	9.2	742	12.5	1 747	327	758	47	629
Pierce	2 766	28 872	0.5	D	D	232	5.8	3 119	8.9	5 485	1 654	1 989	776	1 892
Polk	461	39 246	0.8	D	D	422	9.5	3 925	10.7	8 567	2 586	2 963	695	1 572
Portage	3 509	69 487	1.0	749	11.0	467	6.9	5 904	9.9	10 920	3 603	3 344	1 336	1 908
Price	204	14 481	1.0	D	D	186	12.8	1 113	10.0	3 608	1 210	1 142	246	1 737
Racine	4 995	182 201	0.9	2 653	13.5	1 574	8.0	19 191	11.3	32 636	9 041	10 599	5 922	3 031
Richland	336	16 962	0.9	D	D	179	9.9	1 754	12.1	3 448	509	1 398	145	805
Rock	2 934	150 355	0.9	2 121	13.3	1 343	8.4	15 403	11.4	27 113	4 844	11 704	5 134	3 202
Rusk	174	14 637	1.0	D	D	158	10.7	1 510	13.2	3 470	1 219	1 034	281	1 904
St. Croix	850	70 851	0.7	1 187	14.6	450	5.5	5 817	8.0	10 288	3 248	3 487	1 514	1 795
Sauk	858	62 729	1.1	795	13.6	554	9.5	5 364	11.0	11 116	3 232	4 547	2 208	3 659
Sawyer	325	17 259	1.1	D	D	189	11.1	1 974	14.6	4 447	1 026	1 599	565	3 412
Shawano	794	36 852	0.7	491	11.9	432	10.5	4 094	12.3	8 651	4 099	2 039	694	1 654
Sheboygan	3 023	115 225	1.0	1 410	12.3	1 036	9.0	9 479	9.9	19 811	6 627	5 731	2 428	2 102
Taylor	231	20 144	1.0	D	D	173	8.9	1 883	11.9	3 553	1 431	969	361	1 745
Trempealeau	512	28 390	1.0	D	D	305	10.9	2 566	11.3	5 360	2 012	1 624	400	1 388
Vernon	390	26 600	0.8	D	D	290	10.0	3 625	15.1	5 886	2 812	1 378	240	859
Vilas	190	21 372	1.0	D	D	281	12.7	2 334	14.8	7 150	1 614	2 634	356	1 661
Walworth	2 709	95 744	0.9	1 228	12.2	822	8.2	10 493	12.4	16 087	2 060	6 960	2 120	2 074
Washburn	205	15 696	1.0	D	D	173	10.3	1 481	11.5	4 348	1 202	1 512	311	1 955
Washington	1 143	112 879	0.8	1 500	11.7	904	7.0	8 302	7.5	20 803	6 050	7 167	1 972	1 495
Waukesha	5 650	408 338	1.1	4 055	10.7	2 905	7.6	19 057	6.0	65 336	18 724	22 449	5 469	1 403
Waupaca	1 635	49 625	0.9	D	D	692	13.3	4 248	10.1	10 966	4 812	3 046	1 191	2 272
Waushara	1 261	21 340	0.7	D	D	257	10.3	2 560	13.1	5 638	2 388	1 396	461	1 882
Winnebago	8 239	173 535	1.1	1 925	11.9	1 312	8.1	14 081	10.2	26 615	12 231	6 429	3 547	2 124
Wood	891	79 001	1.1	925	12.5	707	9.5	5 509	9.3	14 964	6 447	4 443	1 550	2 074
WYOMING	13 712	552 983	1.0	7 868	15.0	4 268	8.2	80 707	17.3	83 284	4 755	41 871	14 978	2 657
Albany	2 248	34 668	1.0	D	D	182	5.7	5 175	17.3	3 758	213	1 746	1 010	2 782
Big Horn	183	11 017	0.9	D	D	149	13.2	1 921	20.9	2 270	46	1 309	149	1 277
Campbell	422	47 088	1.2	718	17.8	207	5.1	5 830	14.2	3 373	165	1 806	1 224	2 653
Carbon	780	15 731	1.0	215	13.9	140	9.1	2 594	19.5	2 378	110	1 373	372	2 409
Converse	103	12 754	0.9	D	D	94	7.2	1 893	16.3	2 056	174	1 136	308	2 227

1. Per 1,000 estimated resident population.   2. Data for serious crimes have not been adjusted for underreporting; this may affect comparability between geographic areas and over time.   3. Per 100,000 population estimated by the FBI.

Table B. States and Counties — Crime, Education, Money Income, and Poverty

STATE County	Serious crimes known to police,[1] 2010 (cont.) Rate[2] Violent	Property	Education — School enrollment and attainment, 2006–2010 Enrollment[3] Total	Percent private	Attainment[4] (percent) High school graduate or less	Bachelor's degree or more	Local government expenditures,[5] 2008–2009 Total current expenditures (mil dol)	Current expenditures per student (dollars)	Money income, 2006–2010 Per capita income[6] (dollars)	Households Median income Dollars	Percent change, 2000 to 2006–2010 (constant 2010 dollars)	Percent with income of $200,000 or more	Income and poverty, 2010 Median household income (dollars)	Percent below poverty level All persons	Children under 18 years	Children 5 to 17 years in families
	46	47	48	49	50	51	52	53	54	55	56	57	58	59	60	61
WISCONSIN—Cont'd																
Dodge	101	1 749	19 474	19.1	55.2	15.2	118.1	10 804	23 663	52 571	-8.1	1.1	50 996	9.2	12.7	10.8
Door	29	961	4 826	12.7	44.3	27.5	44.9	12 080	29 154	47 775	-2.8	2.1	45 990	11.2	17.2	15.0
Douglas	186	4 572	10 762	10.8	42.9	22.0	70.1	10 446	24 552	43 127	-3.3	1.4	40 930	14.2	19.9	17.4
Dunn	59	1 393	14 699	8.6	46.3	24.9	61.3	10 253	21 624	48 376	-1.4	0.9	47 442	15.2	19.3	18.5
Eau Claire	170	2 333	30 061	9.9	38.0	30.2	147.6	10 741	24 826	45 846	-7.7	2.1	43 901	16.7	18.1	15.6
Florence	203	2 871	963	11.0	57.5	12.1	6.5	12 589	20 283	40 180	-8.7	0.1	41 928	13.6	22.2	19.0
Fond du Lac	171	1 720	25 495	20.1	51.6	18.0	140.1	10 283	25 360	51 549	-10.7	1.8	50 327	11.6	15.7	13.6
Forest	86	2 676	2 097	7.4	58.4	12.0	20.5	11 813	20 578	37 627	-7.2	0.8	38 735	16.9	27.2	24.9
Grant	160	1 715	14 822	10.3	51.6	19.2	82.2	11 502	20 758	43 889	-4.4	1.1	42 256	16.0	20.6	19.5
Green	128	1 848	8 639	8.1	49.1	18.8	63.7	10 542	26 721	53 088	-3.0	2.2	51 019	10.0	14.4	13.1
Green Lake	50	1 833	4 124	14.6	55.2	16.5	34.1	11 224	24 973	47 624	-4.7	1.9	43 571	13.1	24.3	21.2
Iowa	89	1 302	5 351	12.8	44.7	22.3	41.0	11 182	25 156	54 737	1.7	1.7	51 738	9.2	13.2	12.4
Iron	304	2 417	950	3.2	49.3	17.9	9.8	12 012	21 286	35 618	-4.9	0.6	35 532	17.5	26.4	22.6
Jackson	59	1 839	4 271	8.2	56.6	14.8	33.4	10 352	20 778	43 191	-7.9	1.2	38 812	18.2	27.4	23.5
Jefferson	209	1 726	22 649	18.7	47.3	22.7	144.2	10 634	24 729	54 769	-7.8	1.7	50 963	10.9	18.3	13.7
Juneau	251	1 755	5 834	10.1	58.3	12.1	43.6	11 101	23 026	45 664	2.1	1.1	40 228	15.5	25.7	23.9
Kenosha	192	2 587	47 886	16.2	46.6	22.5	333.4	11 127	26 168	54 430	-8.5	2.8	52 028	13.2	19.5	17.2
Kewaunee	58	1 162	4 914	17.8	56.9	13.6	36.1	10 137	24 574	54 152	-2.4	1.3	50 099	10.0	12.9	11.0
La Crosse	180	2 443	33 737	14.2	37.2	28.8	186.5	11 676	24 917	49 328	-1.3	2.2	47 271	12.9	14.2	12.7
Lafayette	19	1 260	3 917	9.3	56.8	15.9	34.0	11 577	22 026	48 114	2.1	1.0	46 595	11.9	20.4	19.2
Langlade	195	3 829	4 271	18.2	60.4	12.9	36.8	11 724	22 025	41 034	-2.3	1.5	37 762	13.5	22.5	20.0
Lincoln	184	2 234	6 006	14.9	55.1	14.7	47.9	10 539	23 793	46 625	-5.9	1.2	45 092	11.4	16.9	14.7
Manitowoc	113	1 297	19 417	19.5	52.3	17.5	121.0	10 347	25 161	49 354	-10.0	1.7	48 059	11.5	17.1	14.8
Marathon	127	1 751	33 607	12.6	49.4	20.8	221.9	11 110	25 893	53 471	-6.5	2.1	50 192	11.9	18.7	16.1
Marinette	65	2 450	9 033	16.8	56.0	14.2	67.3	10 474	22 999	39 698	-11.1	1.0	38 099	14.6	21.4	19.6
Marquette	58	1 746	2 843	11.3	60.3	12.8	22.1	11 363	22 895	46 012	-0.6	0.7	43 976	11.9	21.4	19.5
Menominee	71	1 394	1 172	7.8	54.7	10.5	15.6	19 274	14 794	31 076	-16.6	0.0	31 509	29.8	47.9	47.7
Milwaukee	727	4 667	265 325	24.1	45.5	26.7	1 707.4	12 463	23 740	43 215	-10.4	2.0	40 582	21.9	34.6	32.5
Monroe	172	2 310	9 893	16.9	52.7	16.4	73.2	10 622	23 052	47 333	0.6	1.3	44 941	15.4	24.1	21.4
Oconto	53	1 928	8 365	8.3	58.6	13.2	46.4	10 381	24 521	46 633	-10.6	1.1	44 421	12.5	18.3	16.3
Oneida	92	2 670	6 977	12.3	42.4	22.4	59.2	12 471	28 085	45 857	-3.7	2.5	44 038	11.4	18.5	15.9
Outagamie	168	2 224	45 618	16.4	43.9	25.8	336.4	10 082	26 965	51 914	-11.0	2.1	55 556	9.1	12.3	10.8
Ozaukee	43	988	23 492	30.2	27.3	43.1	143.8	10 590	39 778	74 996	-6.6	8.7	73 471	5.7	6.0	5.1
Pepin	27	602	1 716	14.9	53.0	17.2	16.7	12 392	24 233	48 446	1.7	1.8	43 912	12.3	20.7	19.4
Pierce	112	1 780	12 902	8.9	40.7	25.4	76.3	10 238	26 313	60 181	-4.1	2.3	57 111	10.8	11.1	9.3
Polk	285	1 287	10 330	8.3	49.0	18.4	83.1	10 491	24 704	49 806	-4.5	1.5	46 871	12.5	18.2	16.1
Portage	96	1 812	21 943	12.2	45.5	27.1	99.9	10 427	24 873	51 456	-6.6	2.5	49 652	11.6	13.5	12.1
Price	85	1 653	2 834	12.8	55.5	15.3	23.2	10 975	23 125	41 026	-8.1	1.1	41 116	13.6	21.7	18.9
Racine	262	2 769	50 595	18.6	46.8	23.1	338.0	11 081	26 321	53 855	-11.5	2.6	51 712	14.5	20.5	18.6
Richland	11	794	3 964	15.9	57.8	14.4	20.2	11 472	21 301	43 900	2.0	1.0	40 685	14.8	24.4	22.9
Rock	248	2 955	41 572	14.0	50.9	19.8	303.1	10 686	23 926	49 716	-13.7	1.6	47 128	14.0	21.0	18.5
Rusk	95	1 810	2 969	6.8	59.6	14.8	28.2	12 166	20 573	38 352	-3.4	0.8	35 757	19.6	32.1	27.4
St. Croix	53	1 742	22 087	15.0	34.6	32.5	133.2	9 870	31 377	67 446	-3.0	4.0	64 990	6.8	8.2	7.3
Sauk	202	3 457	13 704	10.7	50.5	20.0	123.8	10 690	25 452	50 390	-5.1	1.6	47 531	11.4	16.9	15.1
Sawyer	169	3 243	3 001	18.3	48.5	20.5	25.9	11 315	23 527	37 091	-9.3	2.0	37 858	18.0	32.4	29.9
Shawano	86	1 569	9 384	10.8	59.9	14.4	62.6	10 961	22 539	45 841	-4.9	1.2	45 139	13.6	20.4	17.1
Sheboygan	145	1 957	28 947	17.8	49.2	20.5	215.8	10 938	24 976	51 127	-12.7	1.5	50 397	9.9	14.6	12.2
Taylor	58	1 687	4 636	12.8	61.1	13.6	32.7	10 542	22 639	44 489	-8.7	1.3	43 942	13.8	21.5	20.0
Trempealeau	52	1 336	6 535	10.1	55.3	17.1	62.7	10 596	23 224	46 582	-2.9	1.4	43 425	13.6	19.4	16.5
Vernon	32	827	6 591	23.0	51.3	18.8	45.4	10 856	21 618	43 632	3.9	1.3	45 059	14.7	26.4	24.5
Vilas	56	1 605	3 904	11.4	43.5	25.0	39.0	14 114	27 128	41 631	-2.6	2.4	37 154	14.4	24.6	22.2
Walworth	97	1 977	28 049	11.4	45.6	25.1	178.4	10 880	26 769	54 487	-7.0	3.1	52 823	12.8	17.0	14.5
Washburn	107	1 848	3 055	9.0	49.6	18.7	30.6	11 585	23 221	41 641	-2.5	1.2	38 474	14.5	25.7	24.4
Washington	52	1 444	32 344	22.2	41.9	26.0	207.4	10 292	30 580	64 434	-10.8	3.1	61 955	6.3	8.5	7.0
Waukesha	67	1 336	101 035	23.9	31.4	39.2	677.4	10 822	36 752	75 064	-5.7	6.6	71 176	6.1	7.2	6.0
Waupaca	99	2 173	12 161	13.7	57.6	16.1	100.5	10 589	23 293	46 876	-9.5	1.0	47 121	11.2	17.3	15.5
Waushara	86	1 796	4 963	15.7	59.7	13.3	31.6	10 861	22 002	42 540	-9.2	1.0	42 590	14.6	23.2	20.3
Winnebago	206	1 918	44 872	12.2	46.3	23.7	240.6	10 382	26 383	50 974	-9.4	2.4	49 166	12.0	13.1	11.4
Wood	31	2 043	16 953	11.5	49.1	19.2	140.8	10 751	24 893	47 204	-10.4	1.9	45 226	11.7	17.8	15.9
WYOMING	196	2 462	137 655	9.2	39.9	23.6	1 267.4	14 573	27 860	53 802	12.1	2.6	53 757	11.4	14.9	12.8
Albany	138	2 645	14 940	8.7	23.6	47.4	49.9	13 873	25 622	42 890	17.6	2.4	40 430	20.7	15.5	14.2
Big Horn	197	1 080	2 819	7.0	41.3	20.3	34.9	16 667	24 486	48 270	16.6	2.2	44 137	13.0	17.7	15.0
Campbell	102	2 551	10 585	4.5	44.8	17.6	104.7	13 117	31 968	76 576	22.1	2.9	76 441	6.8	8.9	7.9
Carbon	194	2 214	3 212	7.8	48.4	17.9	38.8	15 933	26 122	56 565	23.9	1.8	52 935	12.4	16.3	13.8
Converse	267	1 959	3 061	13.4	45.1	17.6	34.6	14 512	27 656	54 599	8.9	2.9	58 599	10.4	14.4	11.8

1. Data for serious crimes have not been adjusted for underreporting; this may affect comparability between geographic areas and over time.   2. Per 100,000 population estimated by the FBI.   3. All persons 3 years old and over enrolled in nursery school through college.   4. Persons 25 years old and over.   5. Elementary and secondary education expenditures.   6. Based on population estimated by the American Community Survey, 2006–2010.

Table B. States and Counties — Personal Income

STATE County	Personal income, 2009												
			Per capita[1]					Transfer payments (mil dol)					
									Government payments to individuals				
	Total (mil dol)	Percent change, 2008–2009	Dollars	Rank	Wages and salaries[2] (mil dol)	Proprietors' income (mil dol)	Dividends, interest, and rent (mil dol)	Total	Total	Social Security	Medical payments	Income mainte-nance	Unemploy-ment insurance
	62	63	64	65	66	67	68	69	70	71	72	73	74
WISCONSIN—Cont'd													
Dodge	2 818	-2.4	32 271	1 464	1 611	192	452	516	501	214	175	28	58
Door	1 116	-1.7	40 124	441	505	72	320	244	239	110	91	9	18
Douglas	1 346	2.4	30 404	1 884	756	48	193	369	361	109	158	35	13
Dunn	1 265	0.5	29 432	2 109	741	51	196	261	253	94	95	22	18
Eau Claire	3 433	0.6	34 530	1 087	2 590	253	586	647	629	222	266	48	38
Florence	144	0.6	31 620	1 621	32	3	27	38	37	17	13	2	2
Fond du Lac	3 541	-2.3	35 389	966	2 120	218	580	719	701	254	300	36	60
Forest	273	2.8	28 386	2 328	125	27	41	87	86	32	35	6	5
Grant	1 511	-0.7	30 861	1 786	731	100	278	356	347	125	159	18	19
Green	1 264	-2.0	34 997	1 020	631	84	247	239	232	91	91	18	21
Green Lake	646	-2.7	34 958	1 029	276	45	149	151	147	60	60	7	13
Iowa	844	-0.2	35 934	897	498	46	135	134	130	53	48	9	12
Iron	185	2.5	30 377	1 891	65	16	37	62	61	25	26	4	3
Jackson	634	0.1	31 880	1 555	375	52	97	137	134	51	53	10	9
Jefferson	2 790	-0.5	34 512	1 090	1 544	194	427	547	532	199	236	25	45
Juneau	739	0.2	27 930	2 414	349	53	113	211	207	77	87	14	15
Kenosha	5 462	-3.3	33 027	1 337	2 615	250	747	1 050	1 020	357	415	102	67
Kewaunee	707	-2.7	34 805	1 041	398	6	123	132	128	53	51	6	10
La Crosse	4 056	2.0	35 682	930	3 162	194	720	746	725	252	312	48	41
Lafayette	480	-5.3	30 486	1 865	158	33	103	99	96	39	39	6	7
Langlade	644	0.1	32 196	1 484	311	59	109	180	176	67	72	13	12
Lincoln	940	0.6	31 961	1 535	482	60	147	248	242	91	100	13	24
Manitowoc	2 874	-1.4	35 669	932	1 708	109	468	608	593	236	232	30	61
Marathon	4 746	-1.4	36 058	879	3 296	280	760	832	808	313	298	60	87
Marinette	1 316	-0.8	31 368	1 677	803	66	201	388	381	145	158	22	30
Marquette	442	1.0	30 033	1 971	141	19	77	138	136	56	53	8	11
Menominee	106	9.0	23 417	3 009	86	3	10	40	40	9	16	8	2
Milwaukee	35 587	0.5	37 088	743	29 116	2 671	5 328	8 119	7 944	1 972	3 774	1 314	480
Monroe	1 338	1.6	30 577	1 847	921	64	213	279	271	91	103	22	21
Oconto	1 257	0.5	33 834	1 193	339	60	176	261	254	107	86	16	28
Oneida	1 321	-0.1	36 755	780	695	116	285	350	343	143	144	16	19
Outagamie	6 417	-2.5	36 222	861	5 193	363	1 021	991	958	384	350	63	99
Ozaukee	5 001	-3.4	57 946	39	1 973	169	1 325	524	508	248	178	14	40
Pepin	237	-0.2	32 525	1 419	92	11	43	57	55	22	25	3	3
Pierce	1 292	-2.7	32 226	1 480	446	64	207	209	201	78	82	10	10
Polk	1 371	0.1	30 980	1 760	645	64	226	310	302	121	120	21	20
Portage	2 374	0.8	34 314	1 123	1 586	94	398	433	421	154	165	29	32
Price	462	-0.4	32 486	1 432	243	22	86	140	137	51	59	8	12
Racine	7 364	-0.8	36 708	785	3 956	307	1 239	1 380	1 344	502	539	122	117
Richland	524	-0.5	29 372	2 126	252	28	89	133	130	45	59	10	10
Rock	5 012	-2.5	31 294	1 695	2 981	183	794	1 160	1 131	411	432	100	126
Rusk	373	1.0	25 970	2 738	193	18	61	128	125	46	49	9	12
St. Croix	3 077	-1.7	36 911	759	1 239	147	462	373	357	153	132	20	23
Sauk	2 130	-1.2	36 155	865	1 522	142	363	401	390	157	153	24	33
Sawyer	537	2.1	31 677	1 606	268	37	111	160	157	62	61	13	9
Shawano	1 277	-1.0	31 014	1 750	523	68	217	300	292	119	113	18	23
Sheboygan	4 328	-1.9	37 783	667	2 966	285	763	743	722	299	264	47	76
Taylor	562	-0.5	29 243	2 140	339	42	85	138	135	47	53	10	17
Trempealeau	904	0.9	32 589	1 407	569	26	136	213	207	71	100	12	14
Vernon	819	1.3	27 934	2 413	347	54	138	203	197	77	82	14	12
Vilas	722	-0.3	33 607	1 233	272	44	210	212	208	101	75	10	10
Walworth	3 333	-2.4	33 136	1 313	1 684	181	627	614	596	245	224	38	46
Washburn	492	1.2	29 543	2 083	221	9	96	172	169	59	74	10	8
Washington	5 336	-4.4	40 834	394	2 464	195	903	755	731	323	258	34	79
Waukesha	20 054	-2.2	52 339	74	13 315	821	4 015	2 294	2 224	1 031	807	87	180
Waupaca	1 835	0.7	35 526	953	844	55	317	451	441	154	203	20	33
Waushara	692	-0.4	28 117	2 380	223	28	135	185	180	80	64	11	13
Winnebago	6 059	0.0	37 088	743	4 920	216	1 067	1 012	982	397	382	60	78
Wood	2 828	-0.5	38 248	611	2 317	78	457	612	599	218	266	41	40
WYOMING	26 289	-2.7	48 302	X	15 468	2 326	7 360	3 357	3 259	1 148	1 269	199	191
Albany	1 271	3.0	37 404	698	781	37	361	176	170	50	64	9	5
Big Horn	335	-1.1	28 936	2 214	200	15	66	81	79	31	31	4	5
Campbell	2 128	-1.2	48 398	129	2 040	106	304	172	164	50	59	10	16
Carbon	622	-7.4	39 556	484	382	38	164	97	94	33	36	6	6
Converse	601	-2.1	44 283	226	341	55	111	80	77	29	30	5	4

1. Based on the resident population estimated as of July 1 of the year shown.　2. Includes supplements to wages and salaries.

Table B. States and Counties — Earnings, Social Security, and Housing

STATE County	Earnings, 2009 Total (mil dol)	Farm	Goods-related[1] Total	Manu-facturing	Information and professional and technical services	Retail trade	Finance, insurance, and real estate	Health care and social services	Government	Social Security beneficiaries, December 2010 Number	Rate[2]	Supplemental Security Income recipients, December 2010	Housing units, 2010 Total	Percent change, 2000–2010
	75	76	77	78	79	80	81	82	83	84	85	86	87	88
WISCONSIN—Cont'd														
Dodge	1 802	1.6	D	29.1	3.1	5.7	2.1	10.9	15.0	16 575	187	788	37 005	9.9
Door	577	1.0	D	20.2	4.7	9.4	5.0	12.1	16.0	8 245	297	245	23 966	22.4
Douglas	804	0.2	D	10.6	3.3	7.4	2.8	8.4	20.1	8 950	203	1 173	22 825	12.1
Dunn	792	3.1	D	19.3	D	6.8	3.6	D	24.7	8 230	188	705	17 964	17.6
Eau Claire	2 844	0.2	15.6	10.3	7.2	7.3	8.3	20.4	15.1	17 965	182	1 947	42 151	12.5
Florence	35	0.5	D	D	D	D	5.7	6.2	35.4	1 410	319	99	4 780	12.8
Fond du Lac	2 337	0.9	34.9	25.9	4.7	6.8	4.6	13.6	13.1	19 525	192	1 317	43 910	11.8
Forest	152	0.3	D	8.1	D	4.8	2.0	D	50.6	2 660	286	220	8 970	7.8
Grant	831	3.0	D	13.8	5.5	7.8	5.9	D	26.8	10 440	204	778	21 581	8.2
Green	715	2.7	D	20.7	D	14.8	3.0	14.5	13.9	7 245	197	397	15 856	14.3
Green Lake	321	1.4	27.5	17.2	D	7.1	5.4	15.7	16.6	4 760	250	250	10 616	8.0
Iowa	544	2.1	D	9.7	2.7	40.4	2.3	D	12.6	4 460	188	300	10 719	11.9
Iron	81	0.9	D	11.8	D	12.1	3.5	12.1	22.1	2 020	341	135	5 999	5.1
Jackson	427	5.3	D	9.8	2.3	5.8	2.5	8.9	24.5	4 415	216	403	9 727	21.1
Jefferson	1 738	1.9	D	32.5	4.9	6.8	3.2	9.8	12.4	15 120	181	912	35 147	16.7
Juneau	401	3.5	31.1	26.2	1.7	6.6	2.3	D	20.9	6 475	243	537	14 669	18.6
Kenosha	2 864	0.5	D	17.7	4.3	7.2	3.1	14.1	19.6	27 245	164	3 314	69 288	15.5
Kewaunee	403	3.7	D	24.7	D	4.0	2.7	3.4	15.3	4 235	206	204	9 304	13.2
La Crosse	3 356	0.1	18.6	13.8	5.8	6.9	6.5	23.1	14.6	20 180	176	2 159	48 402	11.3
Lafayette	190	8.0	D	17.3	D	5.2	4.6	3.2	25.5	3 400	202	216	7 230	8.3
Langlade	371	3.6	D	21.1	2.6	11.8	3.0	D	14.3	5 490	275	435	12 360	10.5
Lincoln	541	0.8	D	29.2	2.2	7.4	10.3	7.7	18.2	7 280	253	432	16 784	14.3
Manitowoc	1 816	1.5	36.3	32.2	4.8	5.5	2.4	12.9	12.5	18 325	225	1 208	37 189	7.3
Marathon	3 576	0.8	29.7	24.2	6.6	7.1	10.1	13.4	11.8	24 925	186	2 030	67 734	14.6
Marinette	870	0.6	D	34.3	3.3	7.1	2.8	D	12.2	11 675	280	780	30 379	15.7
Marquette	160	5.6	D	32.9	D	5.9	3.5	D	22.5	4 420	287	233	9 896	14.2
Menominee	89	0.0	D	D	0.1	D	D	D	94.2	845	200	239	2 253	7.4
Milwaukee	31 787	0.0	D	13.5	12.0	4.4	9.9	15.1	13.7	154 235	163	38 843	418 053	4.5
Monroe	985	2.2	D	16.0	3.2	5.9	2.6	7.2	32.0	8 300	186	819	19 204	15.2
Oconto	399	3.6	28.2	20.9	3.2	8.2	3.1	D	22.1	8 700	231	567	23 537	18.8
Oneida	810	0.6	19.7	10.0	5.0	14.8	4.0	18.2	17.4	11 055	307	568	30 125	13.1
Outagamie	5 556	0.3	D	21.8	7.2	7.0	8.4	11.6	11.0	29 435	167	2 038	73 149	16.8
Ozaukee	2 141	0.4	D	27.4	9.1	6.7	7.4	11.6	10.6	16 575	192	436	36 267	13.2
Pepin	103	8.5	14.4	6.0	D	9.2	3.2	11.6	21.0	1 915	256	99	3 579	17.8
Pierce	510	2.8	D	11.1	6.4	5.4	3.7	10.0	34.4	6 130	149	302	16 132	19.6
Polk	709	1.4	D	26.1	D	7.1	4.4	D	17.9	9 855	223	556	24 248	14.8
Portage	1 680	2.1	D	13.8	5.0	7.4	18.6	9.8	16.6	12 225	175	895	30 054	13.0
Price	265	1.2	D	39.2	5.4	6.4	2.5	9.4	17.5	4 150	293	306	11 120	16.2
Racine	4 263	0.5	D	34.0	6.1	5.9	4.3	12.7	13.6	37 635	193	4 639	82 164	10.0
Richland	280	1.6	D	32.0	D	9.0	2.6	13.3	17.8	3 945	219	397	8 868	8.6
Rock	3 164	1.0	24.6	18.8	4.8	9.5	3.1	15.9	15.5	31 450	196	3 439	68 422	10.0
Rusk	211	2.0	D	30.1	D	7.6	3.0	5.0	24.1	3 980	270	359	8 883	16.7
St. Croix	1 386	1.6	29.5	22.4	6.6	8.7	5.0	12.3	14.9	11 750	139	605	33 983	40.0
Sauk	1 664	0.8	D	18.9	4.4	9.2	5.6	10.9	15.4	12 495	202	800	29 708	22.3
Sawyer	305	0.9	16.3	10.1	4.7	9.8	5.6	12.0	28.5	5 020	303	389	15 975	16.4
Shawano	591	3.2	D	19.5	D	7.5	3.8	10.1	21.7	9 710	231	645	20 720	13.1
Sheboygan	3 251	0.5	D	39.9	3.5	5.4	5.2	12.9	10.4	22 500	195	1 628	50 766	10.5
Taylor	381	3.7	D	24.9	D	6.5	3.4	D	12.3	4 055	196	273	10 582	23.1
Trempealeau	595	2.6	D	43.3	2.7	4.0	3.1	D	16.7	6 010	209	406	12 619	9.9
Vernon	400	5.8	12.9	8.7	4.1	7.6	5.8	D	19.7	6 715	226	580	13 720	10.5
Vilas	316	0.9	D	3.9	D	11.7	4.8	D	29.3	7 850	366	351	25 116	12.1
Walworth	1 865	1.3	D	24.7	4.2	7.2	3.3	7.6	19.4	18 210	178	1 026	51 531	17.8
Washburn	230	0.7	20.3	16.8	D	9.9	3.2	13.5	27.0	4 890	307	378	12 979	20.0
Washington	2 659	0.6	32.7	26.8	4.4	7.9	6.3	11.9	11.5	23 425	178	817	54 695	19.4
Waukesha	14 136	0.1	D	21.7	11.4	5.8	8.3	10.5	7.5	71 530	183	2 496	160 864	14.7
Waupaca	899	0.8	32.4	28.5	5.1	6.1	3.6	D	19.8	12 240	234	730	25 396	12.8
Waushara	251	7.9	D	16.0	3.3	7.9	3.2	10.1	22.0	6 475	264	416	14 843	8.6
Winnebago	5 135	0.2	D	33.0	7.2	4.4	3.9	10.8	12.5	30 360	182	2 264	73 329	13.3
Wood	2 395	1.2	D	14.0	4.2	5.3	2.0	39.8	11.2	16 805	225	1 258	34 088	7.6
WYOMING	17 794	0.3	30.2	3.9	5.9	5.9	4.2	7.7	24.3	91 019	161	6 337	261 868	17.0
Albany	818	-0.1	9.4	2.6	8.1	5.9	4.2	9.3	49.3	3 860	106	282	17 939	17.9
Big Horn	215	1.7	28.6	5.2	D	D	2.4	D	34.7	2 480	213	164	5 379	5.4
Campbell	2 146	-0.3	53.6	2.5	3.7	4.2	2.0	2.9	12.4	3 925	85	243	18 955	42.6
Carbon	420	0.8	D	D	3.9	6.3	2.5	D	29.2	2 550	161	140	8 576	3.2
Converse	396	-0.3	43.9	1.3	D	3.4	2.1	D	20.2	2 315	167	135	6 403	12.9

1. Includes mining, construction, and manufacturing.   2. Per 1,000 resident population enumerated in the 2010 census.

Table B. States and Counties — **Housing, Labor Force, and Employment**

STATE County	Housing units, 2006–2010								Civilian labor force, 2010		Unemployment		Civilian employment,[5] 2006–2010		
	Occupied units												Percent		
			Owner-occupied			Renter-occupied									
				Median owner cost as a percent of income											Construction, production, and maintenance occupations
	Total	Percent	Median value[1]	With a mortgage	Without a mortgage	Median rent[2]	Median rent as a percent of income	Sub-standard units[3] (percent)	Total	Percent change, 2009–2010	Total	Rate[4]	Total	Management, business, science and arts	
	89	90	91	92	93	94	95	96	97	98	99	100	101	102	103
WISCONSIN—Cont'd															
Dodge	33 929	73.9	155 900	25.4	14.5	704	25.8	1.6	46 134	-4.2	4 118	8.9	44 047	26.6	36.0
Door	13 684	77.6	189 500	27.4	14.7	695	28.1	0.9	16 992	-2.1	1 709	10.1	14 620	30.5	27.4
Douglas	19 138	69.8	130 200	23.1	13.6	605	28.4	1.5	23 416	1.0	1 875	8.0	22 130	30.3	25.6
Dunn	15 862	71.4	152 700	24.3	13.8	653	28.9	1.3	25 608	-0.5	1 752	6.8	21 794	30.4	29.5
Eau Claire	39 240	64.8	147 200	22.9	13.2	657	30.9	1.8	57 159	2.2	3 843	6.7	53 220	31.5	22.7
Florence	2 048	85.2	123 700	26.5	14.2	450	30.1	2.1	2 412	-1.1	241	10.0	2 147	22.8	32.7
Fond du Lac	40 484	72.5	143 000	23.7	13.7	635	28.1	1.8	55 523	-1.0	4 578	8.2	53 122	25.9	33.5
Forest	4 182	75.4	117 900	23.9	14.8	495	23.6	2.0	4 783	-1.6	481	10.1	3 879	24.8	31.1
Grant	19 157	74.7	118 300	23.4	13.9	535	27.3	1.8	28 347	-1.0	1 985	7.0	25 654	29.8	30.2
Green	14 541	77.5	150 300	25.6	14.3	644	25.0	1.1	19 700	-3.7	1 619	8.2	19 543	33.2	29.5
Green Lake	7 940	76.3	137 500	23.9	13.6	564	24.6	2.0	9 807	-4.0	913	9.3	9 780	25.1	36.0
Iowa	9 705	77.8	155 500	25.0	14.4	665	25.0	0.9	14 033	-0.7	1 070	7.6	12 799	31.7	28.7
Iron	3 016	76.1	106 700	24.0	15.0	463	26.9	4.4	2 956	-1.1	338	11.4	2 695	26.2	30.4
Jackson	8 269	74.5	121 400	25.1	14.4	547	28.3	3.9	9 596	-3.9	859	9.0	9 481	28.2	31.9
Jefferson	31 442	71.8	182 500	26.1	14.6	729	27.6	1.5	41 787	-1.9	3 824	9.2	43 742	28.3	30.2
Juneau	11 012	79.1	115 500	24.8	14.5	612	25.3	2.5	13 281	-2.4	1 312	9.9	12 745	22.7	34.2
Kenosha	62 226	68.0	182 400	25.8	15.3	787	29.6	2.3	85 037	-0.5	9 162	10.8	79 640	31.7	25.5
Kewaunee	8 274	81.7	144 400	23.6	14.0	619	25.8	1.3	11 638	0.8	934	8.0	10 597	25.5	40.0
La Crosse	45 501	66.1	148 700	23.2	13.2	655	28.9	1.7	65 652	0.9	4 136	6.3	60 930	32.9	23.0
Lafayette	6 533	79.2	117 700	25.5	14.5	556	25.0	1.5	9 319	0.2	635	6.8	8 798	28.8	35.3
Langlade	8 805	80.5	107 500	23.7	13.6	509	30.6	4.4	10 747	-1.2	1 076	10.0	9 622	24.6	37.1
Lincoln	13 113	74.7	131 300	22.2	12.7	548	26.4	2.3	14 991	-4.2	1 722	11.5	14 707	24.9	37.3
Manitowoc	34 171	76.8	124 000	22.7	13.6	547	24.7	1.5	44 446	-4.5	4 196	9.4	41 873	26.0	36.8
Marathon	52 708	75.5	139 500	22.7	12.9	639	25.0	2.1	73 551	-0.9	6 491	8.8	69 980	30.3	31.1
Marinette	19 171	76.2	109 700	23.4	14.4	530	26.9	2.0	22 154	-0.3	2 357	10.6	19 783	25.0	38.0
Marquette	6 754	80.0	141 000	26.2	16.1	668	24.7	1.5	7 604	-2.9	783	10.3	7 113	23.6	36.0
Menominee	1 521	70.3	92 600	26.0	13.7	336	19.1	4.9	1 629	-1.5	253	15.5	1 413	19.0	33.3
Milwaukee	379 372	53.4	165 700	25.8	16.4	752	31.4	3.0	463 595	-0.2	44 618	9.6	442 542	33.7	22.4
Monroe	17 322	72.3	126 800	23.7	13.8	634	25.6	3.8	24 526	-0.5	1 763	7.2	21 534	28.4	32.5
Oconto	16 442	81.9	146 300	25.5	14.9	561	26.4	1.3	20 307	-1.6	1 990	9.8	18 964	27.5	37.0
Oneida	17 475	77.8	172 800	25.0	13.8	618	28.5	1.0	18 594	-2.0	1 866	10.0	17 802	29.3	26.5
Outagamie	69 062	72.7	153 500	23.1	12.8	664	25.1	1.8	98 792	0.6	7 821	7.9	93 197	31.6	27.7
Ozaukee	33 856	78.3	255 600	23.9	12.4	769	26.0	0.7	46 751	-1.2	3 199	6.8	45 616	43.1	17.7
Pepin	3 092	76.2	138 500	24.1	15.8	540	24.8	1.9	4 068	-1.2	288	7.1	3 831	28.8	34.4
Pierce	14 817	76.7	200 500	26.2	14.1	724	31.4	1.4	23 012	-2.9	1 576	6.8	23 202	30.9	29.4
Polk	18 170	82.0	170 300	27.7	15.0	659	29.1	1.8	23 699	-3.6	2 292	9.7	21 939	26.2	35.0
Portage	27 573	70.1	143 100	22.1	12.2	617	27.9	1.9	42 279	-1.8	3 037	7.2	36 395	30.8	26.4
Price	6 825	80.6	111 500	24.0	14.0	545	26.8	4.7	7 866	-9.4	788	10.0	7 073	26.4	41.0
Racine	75 546	69.9	175 700	25.0	14.1	708	30.4	1.7	98 046	-0.8	9 790	10.0	92 665	31.5	28.8
Richland	7 530	74.7	123 000	25.9	14.3	568	29.8	2.9	9 900	-5.9	827	8.4	9 201	24.4	38.5
Rock	62 598	73.5	138 000	24.1	14.1	698	30.5	1.3	80 327	-1.8	8 898	11.1	77 427	28.4	30.8
Rusk	6 660	76.1	110 200	24.5	14.6	546	27.8	3.2	7 083	-5.7	837	11.8	6 682	27.0	41.6
St. Croix	31 824	77.8	225 700	25.1	12.7	808	28.2	1.5	46 364	-1.6	3 380	7.3	44 484	37.7	24.7
Sauk	25 438	72.8	166 400	25.7	13.3	700	28.1	1.5	35 116	-1.4	2 839	8.1	33 210	27.8	29.2
Sawyer	7 982	71.7	168 200	26.1	13.7	518	28.2	3.2	8 991	-1.0	908	10.1	7 673	27.7	27.4
Shawano	17 174	76.7	125 100	24.1	14.1	574	26.0	2.0	22 173	-1.5	2 115	9.5	20 038	27.2	33.5
Sheboygan	46 572	72.3	151 100	23.2	14.1	620	26.1	1.8	63 307	-2.1	5 483	8.7	59 611	27.4	33.7
Taylor	8 821	79.0	120 100	25.0	13.8	528	25.0	2.9	10 556	-1.6	1 104	10.5	10 311	26.1	44.8
Trempealeau	11 502	75.6	132 800	24.5	14.4	555	24.9	2.7	16 324	0.4	1 140	7.0	14 611	28.0	38.0
Vernon	11 905	79.0	131 700	25.3	13.9	549	24.3	4.6	15 067	0.2	1 141	7.6	13 816	30.2	33.1
Vilas	10 560	79.4	194 900	26.9	14.4	630	27.7	1.2	10 674	-2.5	1 126	10.5	9 764	34.3	22.0
Walworth	39 082	71.2	198 000	26.5	14.1	761	31.5	2.5	54 913	-1.9	4 855	8.8	52 480	30.5	27.5
Washburn	7 254	82.1	148 400	26.6	15.1	586	34.8	2.9	7 865	0.2	756	9.6	7 139	31.4	30.2
Washington	51 458	78.2	228 000	24.7	14.2	770	26.6	1.2	73 465	-0.9	5 857	8.0	70 787	34.3	26.8
Waukesha	151 161	77.7	262 200	23.8	13.2	869	27.7	0.9	210 548	-0.5	15 651	7.4	205 653	43.0	18.3
Waupaca	21 526	75.4	137 100	24.8	15.0	617	27.6	2.0	27 980	-1.0	2 485	8.9	25 549	23.9	38.9
Waushara	10 330	81.9	136 600	26.4	14.5	594	28.2	2.6	12 636	-1.6	1 265	10.0	10 887	23.7	37.8
Winnebago	66 694	68.4	140 500	23.2	13.6	623	26.8	1.2	95 331	1.2	6 876	7.2	84 881	29.5	26.9
Wood	31 979	76.4	116 500	21.9	12.4	559	28.9	1.2	40 864	-2.3	3 514	8.6	36 924	27.7	31.2
WYOMING	217 688	70.2	174 000	21.7	10.0	666	24.4	2.6	303 215	2.1	21 220	7.0	284 148	31.0	29.5
Albany	14 591	53.5	189 500	23.2	10.0	646	33.8	1.2	19 272	-0.6	981	5.1	20 029	44.0	14.9
Big Horn	4 547	77.4	116 100	20.5	10.0	526	22.8	2.8	5 016	0.7	395	7.9	5 346	31.8	36.3
Campbell	16 039	75.7	197 700	19.8	10.0	795	20.6	4.6	27 531	-2.5	1 643	6.0	24 597	24.4	43.8
Carbon	6 205	71.3	129 100	18.7	10.0	702	19.1	3.3	7 707	-0.8	587	7.6	7 788	27.5	31.3
Converse	5 564	71.6	167 500	19.9	10.0	637	25.3	1.8	7 529	1.2	436	5.8	7 022	26.9	41.6

1. Specified owner-occupied units.   2. Specified renter-occupied units. A value of 10.0 represents 10 percent or less.   3. Overcrowded or lacking complete plumbing facilities.   4. Percent of civilian labor force.   5. Persons 16 years old and over.

Table B. States and Counties — Nonfarm Employment and Agriculture

STATE County	Private nonfarm establishments, employment and payroll, 2009									Agriculture, 2007			
		Employment						Annual payroll		Farms			
												Percent with:	
	Number of establishments	Total	Health care and social assistance	Manufacturing	Retail trade	Finance and insurance	Professional, scientific, and technical services	Total (mil dol)	Average per employee (dollars)	Number	Fewer than 50 acres	500 acres or more	Farm operators whose principal occupation is farming (percent)
	104	105	106	107	108	109	110	111	112	113	114	115	116
WISCONSIN—Cont'd													
Dodge	1 801	27 906	4 519	10 015	3 258	674	506	950	34 042	1 979	30.8	9.7	53.9
Door	1 305	10 437	1 456	2 205	1 603	396	239	319	30 526	854	37.4	4.8	41.1
Douglas	1 064	13 516	2 063	1 399	2 050	362	327	428	31 679	333	21.3	9.9	44.7
Dunn	911	12 425	2 427	2 254	1 733	524	373	388	31 260	1 690	26.9	9.8	39.9
Eau Claire	2 617	47 040	10 424	4 411	7 229	3 431	1 605	1 601	34 038	1 223	28.6	4.4	41.3
Florence	117	592	D	D	D	D	D	12	19 586	115	27.0	5.2	44.3
Fond du Lac	2 460	39 419	5 846	7 522	5 770	1 750	1 316	1 313	33 311	1 643	30.3	8.9	51.6
Forest	243	1 815	295	301	271	D	D	42	23 317	173	28.9	4.6	37.0
Grant	1 243	12 964	2 374	1 865	2 406	787	479	345	26 577	2 866	27.2	8.6	49.3
Green	939	11 602	2 088	2 530	2 159	345	263	366	31 584	1 534	33.9	8.0	48.8
Green Lake	516	5 810	1 100	1 407	944	291	116	181	31 193	723	30.7	7.9	46.6
Iowa	565	8 738	1 023	D	D	191	123	312	35 684	1 813	25.9	8.9	41.5
Iron	216	1 543	308	216	D	D	22	35	22 453	54	20.4	11.1	42.6
Jackson	420	6 120	1 069	D	940	190	139	221	36 064	945	21.6	11.1	48.9
Jefferson	1 995	30 438	3 759	8 994	4 086	712	667	989	32 505	1 434	39.6	6.3	44.3
Juneau	555	6 148	1 043	1 528	1 048	D	D	192	31 187	797	26.5	8.7	42.8
Kenosha	3 077	45 219	8 769	6 416	6 954	1 223	1 222	1 503	33 234	460	52.0	7.4	47.0
Kewaunee	488	5 521	543	1 899	585	164	140	215	38 969	893	29.5	6.5	51.6
La Crosse	2 969	56 501	11 124	6 816	8 237	2 772	2 011	1 874	33 173	845	23.3	7.7	49.5
Lafayette	350	2 597	266	646	432	146	49	66	25 253	1 342	31.1	10.8	55.8
Langlade	602	6 595	1 061	1 564	1 344	239	99	199	30 189	487	24.6	12.1	49.3
Lincoln	710	8 750	1 039	2 473	1 416	862	135	270	30 892	575	31.1	5.4	42.6
Manitowoc	1 842	30 225	4 953	10 536	3 925	793	666	1 007	33 331	1 444	38.8	7.5	45.5
Marathon	3 425	63 576	9 892	16 802	7 901	4 977	2 220	2 230	35 070	2 545	25.3	6.4	53.8
Marinette	1 141	17 281	2 914	6 067	2 360	475	211	519	30 055	746	34.5	7.4	40.8
Marquette	313	3 046	266	1 165	359	D	91	88	28 883	626	32.3	8.9	42.0
Menominee	15	D	0	D	35	0	D	D	D	4	75.0	0	0.0
Milwaukee	20 309	453 280	85 970	53 489	42 688	39 877	25 556	20 186	44 533	96	71.9	1.0	68.8
Monroe	933	14 283	2 245	3 436	1 960	426	423	441	30 881	2 115	27.7	5.2	44.4
Oconto	789	6 765	1 489	D	928	192	202	175	25 800	1 244	36.7	6.8	44.1
Oneida	1 369	13 672	3 258	1 382	3 334	339	390	441	32 219	179	33.5	8.4	36.3
Outagamie	5 009	92 898	11 441	16 355	12 507	6 021	4 378	3 446	37 092	1 362	40.9	8.6	51.6
Ozaukee	2 786	35 836	4 325	8 053	4 626	2 049	2 065	1 315	36 701	513	45.6	5.8	45.0
Pepin	217	1 614	299	116	294	78	D	52	31 993	503	24.1	9.1	49.5
Pierce	777	6 109	977	1 054	975	288	255	171	27 965	1 531	33.8	7.4	41.9
Polk	1 120	12 445	2 416	3 866	1 913	374	312	357	28 689	1 582	30.6	7.1	42.9
Portage	1 629	29 247	3 882	4 172	3 816	5 225	734	993	33 987	1 066	26.1	9.8	49.3
Price	455	4 869	1 029	1 802	593	167	106	143	29 312	545	21.7	7.2	37.2
Racine	4 094	65 755	10 657	13 607	8 560	2 486	2 364	2 463	37 461	652	53.7	7.5	44.6
Richland	392	4 602	D	1 376	1 026	D	D	132	28 729	1 645	27.4	5.9	36.7
Rock	3 347	51 757	8 503	8 619	8 918	1 794	1 131	1 811	34 987	1 556	45.5	9.6	47.6
Rusk	312	4 075	927	1 362	650	132	45	111	27 158	651	16.3	10.4	55.6
St. Croix	2 076	24 439	3 898	5 202	3 769	874	1 208	778	31 820	1 808	35.7	6.2	41.3
Sauk	1 815	29 955	3 781	5 164	4 086	895	1 063	912	30 439	1 923	31.4	7.4	41.3
Sawyer	707	4 940	633	607	985	227	135	141	28 578	231	34.2	10.0	51.5
Shawano	915	10 433	1 569	2 060	1 639	314	207	296	28 378	1 450	26.5	7.3	54.6
Sheboygan	2 699	51 338	6 873	16 816	6 194	2 019	1 549	1 742	33 933	1 059	42.0	9.4	53.7
Taylor	458	6 477	948	2 296	749	265	111	206	31 849	1 208	28.4	7.8	47.6
Trempealeau	662	11 140	1 366	5 609	998	393	197	375	33 637	1 721	21.2	7.4	41.6
Vernon	644	6 729	1 641	858	1 193	D	163	200	29 649	2 492	32.6	3.6	46.7
Vilas	977	5 936	739	264	1 162	229	111	148	24 950	71	52.1	7.0	40.8
Walworth	2 662	32 657	3 896	7 478	4 688	847	971	1 024	31 344	1 000	41.4	10.7	49.1
Washburn	531	4 487	869	1 017	761	117	D	126	28 063	558	28.1	6.8	37.3
Washington	3 192	47 741	5 614	11 995	7 139	2 331	1 525	1 686	35 326	831	43.3	7.0	52.6
Waukesha	12 702	218 305	24 797	42 452	26 721	12 748	11 970	9 539	43 694	675	59.7	5.5	47.3
Waupaca	1 277	15 975	2 328	5 707	2 274	490	324	479	30 010	1 330	30.5	8.2	47.4
Waushara	489	4 526	814	786	743	136	107	97	21 440	677	27.8	9.7	42.7
Winnebago	3 628	82 414	13 919	22 501	7 645	2 948	2 304	3 408	41 348	1 001	39.6	8.1	44.5
Wood	1 844	34 875	10 012	5 496	4 145	1 314	571	1 363	39 078	1 114	26.7	8.3	54.3
WYOMING	20 360	214 715	30 963	10 453	31 960	7 176	9 322	8 244	38 397	11 069	24.0	38.3	49.2
Albany	1 026	10 122	1 979	383	1 768	442	1 036	285	28 188	448	18.5	41.1	36.4
Big Horn	292	2 506	D	D	410	81	67	84	33 651	621	28.2	23.5	52.3
Campbell	1 466	23 006	D	675	2 587	398	780	1 158	50 325	633	24.3	49.3	38.7
Carbon	543	4 883	615	D	780	148	94	190	38 860	287	16.4	54.0	54.4
Converse	444	3 966	601	D	448	D	82	148	37 397	435	17.0	48.0	48.0

Table B. States and Counties — **Agriculture**

STATE County	Land in farms		Acres			Value of land and buildings (dollars)		Value of machinery and equipment, average per farm (dollars)	Value of products sold		Percent from:		Percent of farms with sales of:		Government payments	
	Acreage (1,000)	Percent change, 2002–2007	Average size of farm	Total irrigated (1,000)	Total cropland (1,000)	Average per farm	Average per acre		Total (mil dol)	Average per farm (dollars)	Crops	Live-stock and poultry products	$10,000 or more	$100,000 or more	Total ($1,000)	Percent of farms
	117	118	119	120	121	122	123	124	125	126	127	128	129	130	131	132
WISCONSIN—Cont'd																
Dodge	413	2.2	209	0.6	342.9	765 236	3 667	130 875	294.8	148 980	34.4	65.6	59.0	29.9	7 462	71.4
Door	134	-0.7	157	0.8	99.0	530 569	3 370	89 005	60.5	70 849	40.9	59.1	43.6	16.7	1 960	59.5
Douglas	73	-14.1	218	0.1	29.8	448 195	2 053	48 152	6.1	18 321	29.4	70.6	29.4	5.1	43	9.9
Dunn	383	-4.0	226	29.3	250.8	633 800	2 800	90 324	173.6	102 723	29.6	70.4	36.6	18.2	4 699	66.6
Eau Claire	205	0.5	168	3.7	131.6	469 888	2 798	70 746	84.0	68 653	33.6	66.4	39.6	15.5	3 036	69.1
Florence	20	-4.8	176	D	9.4	416 398	2 363	62 220	2.5	21 610	17.5	82.5	22.6	6.1	34	28.7
Fond du Lac	336	-2.3	204	0.9	279.9	721 664	3 532	127 243	290.4	176 760	24.0	76.0	56.1	30.6	5 413	77.6
Forest	34	0.0	195	D	11.0	376 172	1 925	42 069	2.5	14 282	35.8	64.2	27.7	2.9	41	29.5
Grant	611	0.8	213	0.5	354.6	671 204	3 149	106 736	329.7	115 041	23.8	76.2	51.8	26.6	10 445	69.7
Green	307	0.0	200	2.6	240.0	714 250	3 571	111 791	188.1	122 610	29.4	70.6	49.4	29.1	5 726	74.4
Green Lake	143	-3.4	197	3.4	108.5	686 818	3 478	95 370	74.1	102 436	47.2	52.8	46.3	21.0	2 023	62.5
Iowa	365	-0.5	201	6.7	201.8	662 634	3 292	86 696	157.9	87 119	24.9	75.1	39.3	20.2	6 966	80.5
Iron	10	-23.1	187	0.2	4.1	355 729	1 900	55 451	D	D	D	D	24.1	11.1	D	11.1
Jackson	239	-7.4	253	4.2	127.1	654 119	2 587	99 927	121.0	128 055	45.6	54.4	45.6	24.2	2 273	63.4
Jefferson	244	-1.6	170	7.5	190.2	688 346	4 042	98 958	209.3	145 951	41.3	58.7	48.1	19.0	4 095	72.3
Juneau	181	0.6	227	8.8	111.6	649 950	2 861	92 326	90.3	113 260	54.5	45.5	40.9	18.2	2 279	66.8
Kenosha	84	-5.6	183	0.2	71.7	933 034	5 089	105 704	59.7	129 839	70.9	29.1	42.8	21.5	1 245	44.1
Kewaunee	175	0.6	196	0.1	142.2	686 411	3 494	139 521	194.9	218 270	18.5	81.5	51.4	28.7	2 654	76.0
La Crosse	165	-5.2	196	0.9	87.7	566 874	2 897	90 238	60.8	71 947	29.4	70.6	43.4	18.2	1 725	64.9
Lafayette	343	0.0	255	0.1	249.9	898 536	3 519	131 055	219.3	163 391	32.4	67.6	56.8	34.9	7 134	76.6
Langlade	123	-12.8	252	17.5	78.3	644 726	2 555	115 616	74.0	152 051	55.9	44.1	45.8	23.4	767	47.8
Lincoln	87	-11.2	151	0.3	42.6	385 627	2 555	70 177	30.1	52 294	37.5	62.5	31.1	11.8	397	29.0
Manitowoc	248	-3.5	172	0.7	199.7	600 456	3 493	105 670	257.2	178 096	14.7	85.3	46.2	24.9	3 662	65.4
Marathon	491	-7.5	193	7.1	323.6	526 977	2 734	100 135	307.4	120 800	14.8	85.2	54.9	29.0	4 727	50.3
Marinette	144	-3.4	193	2.1	86.6	520 600	2 691	81 884	66.9	89 684	19.6	80.4	32.0	14.1	1 249	39.3
Marquette	136	-6.8	217	6.5	90.3	666 068	3 068	80 159	55.7	88 955	43.2	56.8	33.4	12.6	1 506	54.2
Menominee	0	NA	80	0.0	0.3	93 333	1 174	13 283	D	D	D	D	25.0	0.0	D	50.0
Milwaukee	5	-16.7	57	0.1	4.6	410 021	7 212	47 954	9.9	103 411	97.5	2.5	60.4	16.7	78	21.9
Monroe	351	-0.3	166	4.0	167.2	492 944	2 968	77 892	165.1	78 058	36.4	63.6	40.3	15.8	3 188	54.4
Oconto	206	-5.9	166	1.3	146.8	492 990	2 978	78 199	115.8	93 111	20.0	80.0	39.9	19.0	2 388	50.0
Oneida	39	-23.5	219	2.7	13.9	622 980	2 847	58 245	17.5	97 892	83.0	17.0	21.8	11.7	15	11.2
Outagamie	247	-6.1	182	0.2	207.5	671 959	3 698	128 126	236.7	173 791	22.8	77.2	54.3	28.5	4 370	66.4
Ozaukee	71	-5.3	138	0.4	57.7	659 419	4 785	87 055	59.1	115 120	35.4	64.6	43.9	19.3	1 058	63.4
Pepin	108	-2.7	216	1.5	67.5	589 201	2 733	92 461	53.2	105 795	25.1	74.9	49.9	21.3	1 539	82.3
Pierce	271	1.5	177	0.3	178.0	591 718	3 341	86 651	115.2	75 241	33.5	66.5	39.8	16.7	4 235	67.1
Polk	289	-1.4	183	1.0	172.2	527 048	2 885	71 601	103.7	65 524	19.7	80.3	33.9	13.1	2 875	61.7
Portage	282	-3.4	264	91.7	206.8	908 590	3 440	128 456	196.1	183 914	68.2	31.8	47.7	21.7	1 860	53.6
Price	102	-1.9	188	D	40.4	366 093	1 948	51 180	22.3	40 900	31.2	68.8	28.6	7.7	293	20.9
Racine	120	-3.2	185	3.5	105.0	883 553	4 782	131 796	101.9	156 324	61.3	38.7	45.1	18.3	2 081	52.8
Richland	254	-1.6	164	1.5	118.4	462 704	2 817	62 546	84.0	54 348	17.2	82.8	30.2	12.1	2 710	63.7
Rock	344	0.0	221	15.6	298.2	891 333	4 028	113 908	195.6	125 720	62.2	37.8	46.9	21.7	7 095	71.7
Rusk	161	-6.9	247	0.1	81.6	572 272	2 321	85 830	53.0	81 348	11.9	88.1	45.3	20.9	1 000	49.5
St. Croix	308	-0.6	171	4.8	222.4	650 052	3 812	80 560	142.5	78 828	22.6	77.4	33.6	13.4	4 957	66.7
Sauk	359	1.7	187	15.6	209.6	633 243	3 393	92 570	179.8	93 510	23.0	77.0	42.2	17.6	4 034	60.5
Sawyer	47	-13.0	204	0.6	22.5	606 685	2 976	64 633	17.4	75 148	40.6	59.4	37.2	12.1	330	22.9
Shawano	272	0.4	187	0.3	189.1	577 079	3 080	106 084	199.1	137 314	11.0	89.0	52.5	26.6	3 097	64.8
Sheboygan	192	-1.5	181	0.1	157.6	700 484	3 869	124 039	166.9	157 569	20.3	79.7	54.3	26.3	2 134	59.2
Taylor	243	-5.4	201	0.1	129.8	467 348	2 324	80 630	92.4	76 489	14.6	85.4	42.7	20.9	1 561	42.9
Trempealeau	341	-7.3	198	5.8	192.3	518 480	2 614	82 079	192.4	111 818	16.5	83.5	39.7	18.4	4 715	75.2
Vernon	357	-6.5	143	0.2	187.9	425 193	2 967	59 654	167.5	67 211	18.1	81.9	40.9	13.6	3 162	47.2
Vilas	10	0.0	140	1.0	3.6	696 398	4 973	87 651	8.6	120 532	D	D	38.0	12.7	1	8.5
Walworth	218	-0.9	218	2.5	182.3	942 876	4 333	105 261	145.5	145 520	45.1	54.9	51.0	24.2	4 258	65.9
Washburn	102	-2.9	183	1.1	45.6	498 360	2 730	51 420	19.8	35 412	25.6	74.4	22.8	8.4	483	30.1
Washington	130	0.0	156	0.5	104.3	795 218	5 092	117 770	107.8	129 684	37.1	62.9	50.4	24.1	1 740	51.5
Waukesha	87	-11.2	128	1.4	69.4	703 625	5 484	83 027	45.2	67 027	67.2	32.8	36.6	14.7	1 568	36.6
Waupaca	234	-5.3	176	8.6	159.8	569 244	3 230	89 366	137.0	102 973	23.1	76.9	43.2	20.0	2 580	59.3
Waushara	149	-22.8	220	35.6	108.9	777 250	3 532	119 149	97.5	143 982	74.4	25.6	41.4	16.1	1 071	50.4
Winnebago	164	-3.5	164	0.3	133.3	563 264	3 438	93 394	107.8	107 655	28.6	71.4	45.2	19.2	2 690	69.9
Wood	222	-2.6	199	6.9	127.0	599 051	3 007	101 330	143.9	129 201	45.6	54.4	52.3	26.6	1 727	52.8
WYOMING	30 170	-12.3	2 726	1 550.7	2 576.0	1 397 691	513	97 356	1 157.5	104 575	18.5	81.5	47.7	19.2	28 157	25.2
Albany	1 856	-22.1	4 143	148.8	104.9	1 950 763	471	71 595	35.9	80 232	10.2	89.8	41.1	19.4	487	7.1
Big Horn	438	6.3	705	111.0	116.5	618 696	877	103 028	51.8	83 377	47.5	52.5	45.1	17.4	1 365	32.2
Campbell	2 346	-21.4	3 706	4.0	170.4	1 446 525	390	96 333	41.1	64 994	8.2	91.8	42.3	17.4	1 643	23.5
Carbon	2 173	-6.7	7 570	146.5	123.5	2 377 318	314	138 927	59.8	208 509	3.3	96.7	55.4	30.3	478	9.8
Converse	2 366	-6.0	5 439	37.8	60.9	1 868 944	344	94 379	34.8	79 891	8.6	91.4	44.1	18.9	1 001	14.7

Table B. States and Counties — Water Use, Wholesale Trade, Retail Trade, and Real Estate

STATE County	Water use, 2005		Wholesale trade,[1] 2007				Retail trade,[2] 2007				Real estate and rental and leasing,[2] 2007			
	Total water withdrawn (mil gal/day)	Gallons withdrawn per person	Number of establish-ments	Number of employees	Sales (mil dol)	Annual payroll (mil dol)	Number of establish-ments	Number of employees	Sales (mil dol)	Annual payroll (mil dol)	Number of establish-ments	Number of employees	Receipts (mil dol)	Annual payroll (mil dol)
	133	134	135	136	137	138	139	140	141	142	143	144	145	146
WISCONSIN—Cont'd														
Dodge	15.6	177	68	1 064	557.8	35.5	238	3 387	735.7	68.5	50	136	14.0	2.6
Door	6.7	237	27	112	40.5	4.5	284	1 771	406.3	38.7	53	201	19.2	3.9
Douglas	9.2	208	48	D	D	D	163	2 174	504.5	48.9	34	96	10.8	1.8
Dunn	31.9	764	39	D	D	D	125	1 640	381.8	33.0	25	75	6.6	1.3
Eau Claire	18.9	200	104	1 899	909.8	72.6	442	7 608	1 512.5	144.2	109	683	76.8	14.4
Florence	0.4	72	6	D	D	D	17	77	21.4	1.3	2	D	D	D
Fond du Lac	13.5	136	104	1 330	993.6	59.5	407	5 999	1 277.7	118.3	77	305	34.3	5.3
Forest	1.8	181	7	40	10.4	1.3	35	301	56.6	4.5	6	29	3.4	0.3
Grant	264.4	5 322	62	481	210.6	16.3	204	2 190	480.1	41.5	50	148	9.6	2.3
Green	11.0	313	48	D	D	D	155	2 338	766.6	72.2	18	63	7.2	1.3
Green Lake	9.4	492	16	95	30.6	2.8	91	1 180	252.9	23.0	13	51	4.7	0.6
Iowa	10.5	446	28	252	150.6	12.5	108	4 385	1 707.9	164.1	13	D	D	D
Iron	1.0	152	7	90	16.3	1.9	34	318	74.6	6.5	9	26	3.8	0.4
Jackson	7.5	378	12	133	31.2	3.5	74	966	251.0	17.4	16	30	5.7	0.5
Jefferson	30.8	388	74	D	D	D	296	4 179	857.2	76.4	74	292	33.2	5.8
Juneau	12.4	465	21	154	51.9	3.8	95	983	284.5	19.9	15	66	3.8	0.8
Kenosha	30.6	191	108	1 805	1 547.8	89.0	526	7 504	1 800.6	165.7	148	629	87.3	12.9
Kewaunee	828.7	39 765	10	73	15.1	2.0	80	640	152.9	12.1	7	9	0.6	0.1
La Crosse	69.9	642	129	D	D	D	449	8 876	1 799.7	166.7	125	604	82.5	14.9
Lafayette	3.7	226	16	209	88.8	7.9	51	452	96.8	8.8	7	11	0.8	0.1
Langlade	34.8	1 679	28	310	438.8	14.0	109	1 350	309.2	30.6	18	56	6.6	1.6
Lincoln	12.5	413	19	D	D	D	133	1 395	289.5	25.9	19	73	7.1	2.4
Manitowoc	2 142.7	26 147	65	D	D	D	302	3 808	815.5	74.5	49	346	21.6	5.4
Marathon	232.9	1 806	184	2 965	1 146.4	122.1	505	10 000	2 139.1	196.5	99	473	75.4	11.9
Marinette	48.5	1 116	32	D	D	D	214	2 616	526.9	47.4	19	44	8.9	0.7
Marquette	10.4	681	9	47	12.2	1.3	45	352	79.7	6.4	13	27	2.2	0.3
Menominee	1.2	251	NA	NA	NA	NA	3	33	5.2	0.4	1	D	D	D
Milwaukee	1 224.2	1 328	904	17 503	10 955.3	871.9	2 889	46 027	10 207.3	1 006.5	808	5 418	1 080.4	205.4
Monroe	10.3	240	38	432	306.1	18.2	161	1 985	502.2	41.5	29	141	16.9	2.8
Oconto	8.4	224	25	98	28.4	2.6	123	969	257.5	18.8	30	94	7.6	1.6
Oneida	33.6	909	34	465	186.7	20.5	254	3 527	921.2	81.3	56	256	45.9	5.2
Outagamie	100.7	589	272	4 467	3 528.1	222.3	794	13 406	2 903.0	272.2	147	793	152.3	24.0
Ozaukee	301.7	3 506	160	1 751	707.6	84.4	331	4 584	976.5	99.3	111	362	57.4	9.1
Pepin	3.0	412	9	250	134.7	7.8	40	320	90.0	6.9	4	4	1.3	0.2
Pierce	4.9	125	21	D	D	D	99	959	208.5	18.2	35	51	5.1	1.3
Polk	11.6	261	26	355	134.3	12.9	197	2 069	423.2	39.7	40	82	7.7	1.1
Portage	139.1	2 059	71	D	D	D	257	4 518	937.9	86.4	56	268	31.6	6.9
Price	13.0	856	16	100	31.0	3.8	86	622	121.1	12.8	10	43	3.2	0.6
Racine	42.3	216	186	D	D	D	654	10 082	2 230.0	198.7	140	596	64.5	13.4
Richland	5.5	297	12	55	73.6	1.5	80	1 037	223.3	22.0	11	36	3.1	0.6
Rock	96.0	609	132	3 075	2 700.1	151.1	579	9 269	2 439.8	216.8	126	432	92.6	10.3
Rusk	3.9	259	7	108	12.5	2.6	59	889	198.4	15.5	11	33	1.4	0.3
St. Croix	17.7	229	83	919	1 987.0	44.7	258	3 919	933.4	87.8	87	244	27.2	4.5
Sauk	25.7	445	61	D	D	D	343	4 506	1 050.9	95.8	68	429	80.5	16.1
Sawyer	2.8	162	16	155	50.2	7.2	117	1 040	224.1	21.7	37	108	9.7	1.9
Shawano	8.5	206	40	467	256.4	18.1	144	1 636	414.0	34.6	19	83	6.3	1.6
Sheboygan	402.3	3 510	88	1 206	503.5	58.1	427	6 386	1 398.7	131.5	80	372	73.8	12.1
Taylor	3.3	164	12	83	26.0	2.7	82	827	189.1	14.7	11	31	2.2	0.4
Trempealeau	11.3	405	31	237	114.7	9.0	106	1 025	251.8	21.6	8	23	2.4	0.4
Vernon	215.2	7 406	21	273	153.8	15.3	111	1 194	250.5	24.2	17	34	3.1	0.7
Vilas	8.3	372	13	102	29.4	3.2	198	1 381	312.2	28.5	39	79	15.9	3.1
Walworth	17.4	174	104	1 678	1 124.6	86.8	396	4 746	1 091.2	103.5	104	405	50.8	8.5
Washburn	4.6	276	13	146	27.9	3.6	98	762	178.1	15.5	21	65	10.7	1.8
Washington	13.8	110	156	2 852	2 800.5	144.1	389	7 320	1 760.0	151.4	90	323	56.1	8.5
Waukesha	36.4	96	913	14 527	6 882.1	788.2	1 403	27 197	5 955.0	596.1	465	3 554	480.0	114.7
Waupaca	19.3	368	33	289	86.2	10.9	221	2 371	516.6	49.2	33	111	12.3	1.9
Waushara	52.0	2 098	16	150	49.8	5.9	86	768	203.0	15.2	15	36	3.1	0.7
Winnebago	76.6	480	160	2 536	1 109.2	102.8	540	8 027	1 796.5	162.1	125	756	97.5	19.6
Wood	268.8	3 573	57	1 591	893.2	90.5	337	4 542	1 002.9	95.7	65	238	39.5	5.3
WYOMING	4 591.9	9 016	705	6 347	6 352.9	306.6	2 951	32 033	8 957.6	758.1	1 121	4 651	991.6	159.7
Albany	275.1	8 906	21	149	113.5	4.7	170	1 927	468.8	38.6	56	158	23.8	3.4
Big Horn	385.4	34 004	7	D	D	D	53	377	71.0	6.3	13	27	2.0	0.3
Campbell	109.1	2 917	93	1 219	917.3	68.7	191	2 490	775.1	63.3	71	375	90.1	11.7
Carbon	366.9	23 932	9	47	51.5	1.5	96	819	295.3	18.5	28	92	28.2	1.6
Converse	305.5	23 928	10	D	D	D	65	511	134.3	10.0	22	53	5.0	0.8

1. Merchant wholesalers, except manufacturers' sales branches and offices.   2. Employer establishments.

Table B. States and Counties — Professional Services, Manufacturing, and Accommodation and Food Services

STATE County	Professional, scientific, and technical services,[1] 2007				Manufacturing, 2007				Accommodation and food services, 2007			
	Number of establish-ments	Number of employees	Receipts (mil dol)	Annual payroll (mil dol)	Number of establish-ments	Number of employees	Receipts (mil dol)	Annual payroll (mil dol)	Number of establish-ments	Number of employees	Sales (mil dol)	Annual payroll (mil dol)
	147	148	149	150	151	152	153	154	155	156	157	158
WISCONSIN—Cont'd												
Dodge	79	558	63.1	25.1	155	9 924	3 094.4	429.8	179	2 148	66.1	18.1
Door	78	324	30.5	12.0	59	2 204	432.8	85.8	250	2 120	130.1	35.4
Douglas	65	D	D	D	49	1 246	1 311.6	57.9	167	2 126	76.6	20.5
Dunn	56	349	32.7	13.4	56	2 768	1 613.5	117.1	98	1 425	42.6	11.9
Eau Claire	179	1 205	124.3	54.4	97	5 578	1 534.0	221.9	260	4 893	170.3	49.5
Florence	7	D	D	D	NA	NA	NA	NA	27	165	4.6	1.1
Fond du Lac	157	1 320	101.9	65.4	151	9 745	2 903.2	392.3	242	4 001	131.5	37.5
Forest	9	81	8.9	2.8	NA	NA	NA	NA	39	D	D	D
Grant	75	458	43.5	18.2	73	2 390	D	82.0	139	1 297	40.9	10.3
Green	64	D	D	D	80	2 722	925.8	95.9	89	956	33.5	8.8
Green Lake	29	112	9.1	3.1	41	1 636	321.5	58.2	58	655	22.4	7.3
Iowa	48	D	D	D	37	874	395.5	D	61	609	25.9	7.1
Iron	9	D	D	D	NA	NA	NA	NA	57	D	D	D
Jackson	28	119	8.0	3.4	27	947	229.1	28.6	59	659	23.2	6.1
Jefferson	123	645	82.7	23.7	154	9 430	3 674.3	387.6	204	2 475	86.4	22.8
Juneau	21	85	6.5	3.3	46	1 720	374.9	63.7	81	666	28.3	7.5
Kenosha	208	D	D	D	197	7 716	3 093.7	353.0	362	5 419	214.0	59.3
Kewaunee	27	D	D	D	44	1 923	408.1	79.1	51	513	14.4	3.9
La Crosse	225	D	D	D	166	7 109	D	254.6	313	6 067	214.4	63.0
Lafayette	15	52	5.5	1.5	21	525	209.7	17.4	37	D	D	D
Langlade	21	126	7.4	3.8	54	1 684	372.3	60.5	69	625	25.3	6.5
Lincoln	29	124	9.1	3.8	53	3 135	D	121.1	97	780	27.2	6.9
Manitowoc	98	596	66.4	21.4	197	11 319	3 018.8	459.1	177	2 699	82.4	23.4
Marathon	235	D	D	D	250	18 678	D	765.6	321	4 813	173.7	48.8
Marinette	49	217	19.3	8.2	90	6 520	1 784.2	276.9	153	1 466	54.4	14.4
Marquette	16	50	4.3	1.3	25	1 260	254.8	49.1	48	D	D	D
Menominee	2	D	D	D	NA	NA	NA	NA	1	D	D	D
Milwaukee	2 024	24 421	3 245.0	1 426.3	1 164	60 678	19 065.4	3 148.4	1 913	35 759	1 570.6	442.9
Monroe	53	278	23.4	8.8	65	3 644	1 055.8	124.8	116	1 791	71.4	20.3
Oconto	50	D	D	D	62	2 069	400.5	66.5	105	793	28.2	7.5
Oneida	89	351	33.5	12.9	55	1 439	494.2	64.9	200	1 796	84.1	21.3
Outagamie	357	4 411	478.4	188.3	349	18 954	6 802.6	875.2	438	8 070	296.1	82.4
Ozaukee	357	D	D	D	222	10 712	3 161.9	540.1	203	3 558	124.9	38.4
Pepin	11	38	2.9	1.1	NA	NA	NA	NA	29	D	D	D
Pierce	71	D	D	D	54	1 217	529.0	53.4	92	972	32.9	8.4
Polk	73	D	D	D	116	4 143	958.5	149.4	129	1 158	41.8	11.2
Portage	107	D	D	D	86	4 636	1 449.5	185.3	187	2 908	97.0	27.1
Price	26	101	7.9	2.9	49	2 317	529.4	82.5	45	D	D	D
Racine	346	D	D	D	345	17 183	7 863.3	890.8	388	6 239	242.7	66.1
Richland	23	66	4.9	1.6	32	1 827	613.1	73.6	38	D	D	D
Rock	199	D	D	D	236	13 527	12 381.6	720.3	383	5 673	211.7	58.6
Rusk	14	48	3.2	1.0	24	1 735	301.2	54.2	26	D	D	D
St. Croix	206	D	D	D	169	5 973	1 347.3	245.7	198	3 239	110.9	32.4
Sauk	123	D	D	D	92	5 942	1 638.3	224.0	258	7 494	462.1	122.5
Sawyer	37	148	13.6	5.3	46	621	180.9	28.6	128	1 222	74.7	20.6
Shawano	37	236	15.5	6.0	74	2 252	582.0	87.3	120	1 290	42.7	11.0
Sheboygan	176	1 743	209.1	70.5	246	18 774	6 126.1	816.0	271	4 869	193.0	54.8
Taylor	16	89	8.9	3.6	44	3 142	630.7	106.0	44	D	D	D
Trempealeau	37	199	13.8	5.9	66	6 224	1 438.9	234.4	80	D	D	D
Vernon	44	161	12.4	4.1	36	778	178.4	28.0	60	D	D	D
Vilas	44	138	18.0	5.7	NA	NA	NA	NA	231	2 691	161.6	47.3
Walworth	187	924	85.4	34.9	212	8 944	2 247.4	381.9	293	5 925	267.2	76.4
Washburn	34	157	14.5	5.6	33	1 005	D	40.1	88	681	25.3	6.7
Washington	225	D	D	D	331	14 138	3 393.4	615.3	259	4 495	152.9	42.5
Waukesha	1 361	D	D	D	1 023	45 147	15 663.5	2 286.8	819	15 832	616.6	177.5
Waupaca	61	337	25.5	9.6	97	6 303	2 133.6	275.0	145	1 645	55.6	14.9
Waushara	19	103	6.1	2.6	35	772	111.3	25.3	75	787	25.1	7.3
Winnebago	250	D	D	D	319	23 777	9 198.9	1 149.8	377	6 071	212.1	58.4
Wood	97	D	D	D	126	6 990	2 562.6	311.7	193	2 373	84.3	24.2
WYOMING	1 890	8 711	1 079.3	387.5	596	11 904	8 834.8	573.7	1 768	26 992	1 469.0	411.9
Albany	114	D	D	D	NA	NA	NA	NA	105	1 608	65.8	18.1
Big Horn	20	83	4.5	1.9	NA	NA	NA	NA	28	202	5.6	1.5
Campbell	116	711	70.9	28.9	36	716	262.5	36.6	79	1 713	89.2	23.3
Carbon	34	92	10.9	4.3	NA	NA	NA	NA	80	791	42.9	11.2
Converse	23	74	10.8	2.1	NA	NA	NA	NA	36	490	20.9	5.2

1. Establishment subject to federal tax.

Table B. States and Counties — Health Care and Social Assistance, Other Services, and Federal Funds

STATE County	Health care and social assistance, 2007				Other services, 2007				Federal funds and grants, 2009–2010 Expenditures (mil dol)			
									Total	Direct payments for individuals[1]		
	Number of establishments	Number of employees	Receipts (mil dol)	Annual payroll (mil dol)	Number of establishments	Number of employees	Receipts (mil dol)	Annual payroll (mil dol)		Social Security and government retirement	Medicare	Food Stamps and Supplemental Security Income
	159	160	161	162	163	164	165	166	167	168	169	170
WISCONSIN—Cont'd												
Dodge	207	4 080	318.3	138.0	146	1 209	39.1	32.6	406.6	138.6	88.9	9.1
Door	68	1 360	99.9	44.0	91	736	42.9	11.1	309.4	117.8	53.5	4.0
Douglas	114	2 153	143.6	57.9	81	518	28.1	8.8	395.4	166.7	74.7	18.9
Dunn	93	2 327	143.8	64.6	72	330	19.7	7.7	257.2	107.7	38.6	11.0
Eau Claire	315	9 957	981.7	441.6	211	1 181	94.2	27.0	669.7	285.7	120.5	28.6
Florence	3	D	D	D	5	D	D	D	36.1	16.3	8.0	1.0
Fond du Lac	266	6 180	607.2	223.9	193	1 206	88.4	24.4	626.2	314.9	134.3	14.8
Forest	18	310	10.6	5.7	14	45	3.4	0.7	107.8	39.4	16.9	2.9
Grant	103	2 299	130.7	58.4	117	409	38.7	7.7	371.0	154.9	80.2	7.4
Green	70	1 988	166.1	71.1	78	D	D	D	210.8	103.6	48.4	5.3
Green Lake	50	1 086	84.4	36.9	39	147	9.0	2.7	157.7	69.2	34.9	3.1
Iowa	56	1 043	67.5	27.5	36	130	9.6	2.5	137.6	58.8	24.3	3.3
Iron	12	279	10.9	6.7	13	D	D	D	62.5	26.6	15.0	1.5
Jackson	37	918	61.4	28.4	29	127	7.3	2.0	150.6	63.4	26.1	5.6
Jefferson	208	3 809	268.8	118.9	145	774	45.7	13.8	519.1	247.0	112.2	8.8
Juneau	48	1 115	86.5	37.3	48	199	18.8	4.7	254.0	99.7	41.8	7.7
Kenosha	401	8 243	692.6	291.2	252	1 578	92.5	29.7	1 009.8	420.4	207.9	48.7
Kewaunee	37	486	18.0	8.7	33	65	7.5	1.5	129.0	63.3	29.0	2.1
La Crosse	271	D	D	D	233	D	D	D	781.3	321.0	123.6	31.7
Lafayette	21	283	18.4	5.7	22	146	15.7	4.1	117.0	42.9	24.3	2.2
Langlade	53	943	95.3	34.4	55	216	12.2	3.6	180.9	76.2	39.5	4.7
Lincoln	64	D	D	D	54	D	D	D	263.0	114.7	51.6	6.1
Manitowoc	191	4 811	358.8	171.3	140	621	46.6	12.5	551.1	263.9	128.8	14.0
Marathon	345	9 438	926.4	379.0	253	1 591	139.1	36.2	828.7	350.2	152.5	30.7
Marinette	115	2 700	208.5	93.3	82	D	D	D	536.7	182.1	74.8	10.2
Marquette	29	311	13.3	6.4	32	384	32.9	11.3	147.9	73.6	29.7	3.4
Menominee	NA	NA	NA	NA	2	D	D	D	68.4	10.5	6.2	4.5
Milwaukee	3 129	84 815	8 090.0	3 381.2	1 613	12 259	1 464.3	359.9	9 118.4	2 362.8	1 859.7	763.1
Monroe	77	2 387	181.4	95.4	66	371	25.7	7.5	774.6	168.8	48.9	9.5
Oconto	72	1 279	84.6	35.5	41	114	10.4	2.2	233.5	113.8	46.6	6.6
Oneida	118	2 972	298.8	119.9	99	388	31.2	8.8	332.8	172.8	68.9	8.9
Outagamie	467	11 774	1 169.2	491.3	358	2 530	217.6	59.7	937.9	480.1	148.3	21.8
Ozaukee	278	4 369	395.2	165.7	202	1 286	78.0	25.1	436.9	270.7	94.6	4.1
Pepin	16	230	19.8	7.5	16	D	D	D	57.9	24.7	13.4	1.0
Pierce	64	738	41.6	18.6	66	D	D	D	248.9	104.4	38.5	4.2
Polk	102	2 090	163.3	69.8	77	281	20.4	4.7	285.6	136.4	58.6	8.3
Portage	151	3 874	299.9	126.6	131	817	63.1	17.5	403.9	176.0	67.9	14.4
Price	46	978	47.3	22.8	34	94	6.6	1.8	139.2	61.3	29.4	4.2
Racine	417	11 897	946.4	478.0	343	2 167	162.7	49.1	1 319.4	599.0	262.3	65.9
Richland	43	810	61.3	24.3	26	113	7.8	2.0	129.1	50.8	26.8	4.3
Rock	330	9 276	878.5	337.0	285	1 578	108.7	30.6	1 258.0	478.3	210.7	48.9
Rusk	28	899	66.8	24.5	20	D	D	D	138.2	52.3	24.9	6.3
St. Croix	157	3 042	282.0	108.2	145	D	D	D	321.2	177.5	52.4	7.0
Sauk	143	3 776	286.8	124.6	144	492	42.9	13.4	420.6	178.4	80.2	8.6
Sawyer	38	642	50.0	21.8	46	190	12.9	3.6	173.2	67.4	28.8	7.1
Shawano	79	1 482	115.5	42.6	71	247	16.3	4.8	297.1	134.1	59.5	7.3
Sheboygan	292	6 709	501.4	242.7	217	1 093	76.8	20.2	765.1	334.6	141.0	18.9
Taylor	40	1 005	64.3	28.6	36	122	9.4	2.2	134.3	51.3	27.7	3.8
Trempealeau	53	1 344	80.2	33.5	42	133	12.0	3.1	229.4	90.3	44.2	6.4
Vernon	58	1 540	106.9	44.4	47	113	7.7	1.7	224.9	91.5	39.9	5.7
Vilas	45	685	40.7	16.0	64	329	26.5	13.8	205.1	105.0	43.5	3.1
Walworth	216	4 082	284.3	120.9	209	1 025	68.6	20.2	524.1	269.3	113.6	11.8
Washburn	40	862	45.8	20.5	32	122	9.2	2.7	191.4	89.9	28.8	4.4
Washington	253	5 876	470.4	203.1	263	1 421	102.1	31.4	618.1	366.1	119.7	9.8
Waukesha	1 219	23 720	2 271.3	960.5	848	6 424	610.5	199.0	2 157.8	1 185.3	399.3	28.6
Waupaca	112	2 526	151.6	67.5	102	339	28.3	7.0	430.8	202.6	85.5	8.6
Waushara	40	803	42.3	18.0	39	93	7.6	1.7	176.9	85.4	36.9	6.4
Winnebago	430	12 589	1 344.9	476.6	290	2 355	199.8	61.9	8 060.3	447.7	214.4	25.8
Wood	182	9 246	1 105.4	432.7	146	731	84.9	16.6	635.7	283.5	123.7	20.9
WYOMING	1 710	29 242	2 576.3	1 072.8	1 385	6 526	766.2	179.3	6 210.6	1 607.9	567.4	87.8
Albany	112	1 936	157.5	64.9	89	453	93.0	9.9	281.2	69.5	32.3	4.7
Big Horn	21	305	18.6	8.7	22	45	3.4	0.7	103.5	40.7	19.3	1.4
Campbell	85	1 583	154.8	71.9	135	873	118.0	32.7	132.9	61.9	17.9	3.5
Carbon	56	619	55.0	19.5	39	143	15.3	3.6	234.8	43.1	21.3	2.1
Converse	25	538	45.3	18.7	33	102	9.0	2.1	67.6	36.7	11.3	2.1

1. State totals may include programs not allocated by county.

Table B. States and Counties — Federal Funds, Residential Construction, and Local Government Finances

STATE County	Federal funds and grants, 2009–2010 (cont.) Expenditures (mil dol) (cont.)							Value of residential construction authorized by building permits, 2010		Local government finances, 2007 General revenue				
	Procurement contract awards		Other	Grants[1]								Taxes		
													Per capita[2] (dollars)	
	Salaries and wages	Defense	Other	Medicaid and other health-related	Nutrition and family welfare	Education	Other	New construction ($1,000)	Number of housing units	Total (mil dol)	Inter-govern-mental (mil dol)	Total (mil dol)	Total	Property
	171	172	173	174	175	176	177	178	179	180	181	182	183	184
WISCONSIN—Cont'd														
Dodge	36.5	0.2	5.3	44.5	9.9	5.9	5.4	20 390	144	258.5	130.8	89.0	1 014	930
Door	87.0	3.4	4.3	25.6	4.0	1.4	2.5	26 551	145	127.8	42.0	67.0	2 409	2 246
Douglas	18.0	0.5	3.3	75.1	13.2	4.1	10.2	11 129	92	228.6	106.8	84.5	1 933	1 795
Dunn	17.8	0.5	3.5	46.4	7.3	3.9	1.9	11 012	74	154.6	76.0	49.2	1 163	1 084
Eau Claire	32.0	16.1	8.3	115.7	15.2	6.7	10.0	33 131	227	385.1	174.6	149.6	1 536	1 409
Florence	1.4	0.0	1.7	5.9	1.3	0.2	0.1	3 692	24	20.5	8.9	9.2	1 936	1 890
Fond du Lac	23.2	7.1	5.1	78.8	14.5	6.4	4.9	28 206	229	412.3	176.1	143.4	1 447	1 409
Forest	6.4	0.0	2.6	24.7	3.4	1.7	7.8	7 066	54	43.0	20.7	18.7	1 906	1 849
Grant	16.0	0.1	3.2	65.6	8.1	4.3	3.2	12 178	93	199.8	103.5	57.5	1 179	1 118
Green	8.9	0.0	2.4	25.6	4.8	2.6	0.2	12 039	54	139.6	67.5	45.4	1 271	1 180
Green Lake	8.3	3.9	9.3	21.4	3.0	1.0	0.1	6 513	40	78.2	32.4	35.5	1 897	1 790
Iowa	12.2	0.1	1.6	21.4	5.2	1.2	2.7	6 879	36	85.6	40.1	32.0	1 359	1 272
Iron	2.4	0.0	0.4	14.2	1.7	0.4	0.1	2 869	18	32.4	16.3	12.1	1 922	1 790
Jackson	4.3	0.0	1.0	37.8	5.0	1.6	0.8	8 450	58	78.6	44.8	20.8	1 045	962
Jefferson	29.6	21.8	5.8	68.4	9.7	4.5	0.6	31 411	194	297.9	129.3	110.8	1 381	1 275
Juneau	43.3	8.4	2.5	37.7	5.0	1.9	1.8	13 564	87	99.4	53.1	34.5	1 298	1 211
Kenosha	39.6	65.7	14.4	121.4	24.9	10.1	22.9	40 408	248	753.1	346.2	295.4	1 813	1 702
Kewaunee	4.6	1.4	1.0	15.1	2.9	1.1	2.7	6 589	37	79.3	40.9	24.6	1 196	1 176
La Crosse	52.8	39.0	31.3	110.9	19.9	7.4	13.2	36 752	287	517.1	238.8	175.8	1 578	1 447
Lafayette	4.8	0.0	1.1	19.7	2.9	1.2	1.8	3 645	26	83.9	41.2	18.8	1 189	1 137
Langlade	6.4	2.4	1.2	39.4	5.1	1.7	1.0	6 424	55	81.7	40.8	28.0	1 381	1 289
Lincoln	20.7	16.0	1.4	38.9	5.8	1.7	4.3	9 496	72	117.5	54.4	38.2	1 287	1 211
Manitowoc	23.1	0.3	10.7	79.0	10.9	4.6	2.1	17 212	88	293.9	151.0	86.5	1 069	1 040
Marathon	72.1	2.2	42.5	122.5	19.4	6.0	6.0	45 568	262	538.7	241.1	193.6	1 489	1 374
Marinette	18.3	2.7	163.0	65.5	8.1	2.3	1.3	13 789	109	160.9	75.3	57.3	1 345	1 250
Marquette	4.4	0.1	1.8	14.4	2.7	0.7	13.9	3 289	22	49.3	22.0	22.5	1 502	1 428
Menominee	0.7	0.0	0.4	11.7	4.9	8.7	7.1	406	4	26.6	20.4	5.3	1 139	1 133
Milwaukee	637.2	142.9	377.9	1 845.2	278.2	104.3	552.7	127 068	1 006	4 546.0	2 114.9	1 522.4	1 600	1 476
Monroe	241.8	204.5	21.8	57.4	7.2	2.8	5.8	18 136	174	162.4	90.1	46.7	1 084	989
Oconto	8.2	0.0	2.0	38.7	6.3	2.0	1.1	14 535	109	122.9	62.4	43.9	1 172	1 107
Oneida	16.2	0.6	5.4	41.5	10.4	2.8	1.3	24 428	136	168.5	44.4	102.9	2 839	2 683
Outagamie	37.3	48.2	21.6	101.5	18.2	8.6	22.9	85 316	530	781.1	360.3	279.2	1 607	1 568
Ozaukee	13.6	2.4	4.3	20.9	7.8	3.3	4.9	35 998	121	314.2	89.2	167.3	1 954	1 818
Pepin	2.0	0.0	0.5	11.7	1.6	0.5	0.5	2 650	18	33.6	18.9	11.1	1 500	1 431
Pierce	20.6	19.9	2.2	34.8	5.9	3.6	0.4	17 685	121	160.3	76.1	59.2	1 495	1 413
Polk	10.7	4.6	3.7	45.2	8.2	2.0	0.5	14 351	91	178.6	78.9	71.2	1 609	1 515
Portage	33.1	0.6	3.4	53.5	13.0	4.2	7.8	29 233	138	250.3	126.0	81.8	1 199	1 091
Price	7.3	0.0	2.0	29.3	3.6	0.7	0.2	7 453	48	61.5	32.1	22.2	1 533	1 460
Racine	53.3	54.5	10.7	196.2	34.6	13.0	18.6	39 605	240	724.8	359.2	255.6	1 310	1 266
Richland	6.0	0.1	1.0	31.9	3.1	1.0	1.3	3 885	41	73.4	31.3	17.7	976	905
Rock	40.5	204.4	16.2	176.1	29.3	13.4	15.9	20 602	111	656.4	360.8	202.7	1 270	1 232
Rusk	6.9	0.1	2.1	32.8	6.5	1.2	2.2	7 752	50	89.4	40.5	17.0	1 163	1 079
St. Croix	23.3	0.7	4.8	30.3	7.7	2.1	5.9	26 465	150	266.1	115.8	109.1	1 345	1 229
Sauk	32.1	28.1	11.0	53.7	8.1	2.8	11.0	23 923	119	246.4	104.9	105.8	1 809	1 491
Sawyer	11.5	0.1	1.0	29.4	5.3	4.2	6.3	13 053	101	67.4	24.9	34.8	2 038	1 891
Shawano	10.6	0.0	2.3	60.2	6.9	3.2	3.0	9 159	64	140.7	74.1	42.4	1 033	962
Sheboygan	28.1	38.1	90.0	78.4	16.4	5.6	4.7	17 112	69	493.2	225.5	180.9	1 580	1 523
Taylor	13.6	2.2	1.1	20.5	3.8	1.1	2.6	4 907	25	70.5	41.6	21.1	1 090	1 029
Trempealeau	17.0	0.3	1.9	51.7	9.2	1.7	0.9	12 025	92	142.6	75.2	36.6	1 314	1 235
Vernon	9.5	3.7	2.0	55.4	5.4	2.4	3.1	11 175	77	106.6	55.5	30.1	1 039	975
Vilas	5.4	0.1	2.9	26.4	5.3	3.9	6.5	24 776	131	84.7	20.2	54.4	2 463	2 309
Walworth	24.6	0.7	4.6	56.2	11.6	5.3	5.9	40 703	111	387.8	128.2	198.0	1 964	1 812
Washburn	9.9	9.7	2.2	31.3	3.8	1.2	1.1	10 998	59	72.9	25.2	36.3	2 174	2 035
Washington	34.6	1.2	8.1	50.7	13.6	4.9	4.1	58 484	328	432.5	161.7	201.1	1 569	1 448
Waukesha	97.2	146.4	54.5	120.9	37.8	15.3	42.7	151 984	486	1 415.4	404.5	788.3	2 078	2 010
Waupaca	22.8	29.3	2.8	54.1	8.5	2.8	8.3	12 267	72	212.4	109.5	73.1	1 404	1 329
Waushara	5.0	0.1	1.2	31.9	4.4	1.0	0.0	10 401	68	79.7	37.2	33.2	1 340	1 269
Winnebago	82.1	7 100.1	11.7	112.5	23.6	7.7	10.5	55 905	359	566.0	263.6	202.6	1 249	1 209
Wood	24.0	0.4	6.7	100.0	13.2	4.7	44.9	13 729	109	323.0	161.2	112.3	1 519	1 426
WYOMING	709.3	155.4	414.0	441.9	114.6	134.2	1 563.4	435 190	2 298	X	X	X	X	X
Albany	24.7	7.7	5.4	41.2	5.6	10.5	50.2	24 527	172	169.4	60.7	32.2	1 001	544
Big Horn	7.9	9.1	2.3	15.1	1.9	0.7	-0.2	2 326	14	98.1	59.8	15.3	1 361	1 145
Campbell	15.8	0.0	15.2	5.9	4.7	2.6	3.1	96 132	317	453.7	82.5	217.4	5 378	4 185
Carbon	13.1	0.0	131.0	17.4	3.4	0.8	1.0	2 998	18	126.7	39.3	55.2	3 562	2 496
Converse	5.7	0.0	0.5	7.0	1.7	0.5	0.3	2 768	23	88.4	36.0	26.6	2 064	1 706

1. State totals may include programs not allocated by county.　　2. Based on the resident population estimated as of July 1 of the year shown.

Table B. States and Counties — **Local Government Finances, Government Employment, and Voting**

STATE County	Total (mil dol)	Per capita[1] (dollars)	Education	Health and hospitals	Police protection	Public welfare	Highways	Total (mil dol)	Per capita[1] (dollars)	Federal civilian	Federal military	State and local	Democratic	Republican	All other
	185	186	187	188	189	190	191	192	193	194	195	196	197	198	199
WISCONSIN—Cont'd															
Dodge	256.8	2 925	33.9	6.1	6.0	12.6	12.8	205.8	2 344	201	253	4 855	44.8	53.7	1.5
Door	135.0	4 855	34.1	7.1	5.2	3.3	13.1	143.8	5 169	92	149	1 643	58.0	40.7	1.3
Douglas	227.4	5 202	53.5	5.9	4.8	4.6	8.5	263.5	6 027	109	130	3 141	65.8	32.6	1.7
Dunn	158.9	3 754	38.9	1.9	5.2	16.9	12.8	108.2	2 557	98	125	4 172	56.6	41.6	1.8
Eau Claire	398.1	4 087	53.9	6.0	5.3	4.5	8.1	218.8	2 246	432	286	7 766	60.3	38.1	1.6
Florence	18.7	3 925	37.9	9.7	5.4	0.5	16.9	11.1	2 320	20	13	267	42.2	56.3	1.5
Fond du Lac	425.1	4 289	50.7	12.4	4.9	4.6	6.8	370.8	3 740	246	289	5 535	44.8	53.8	1.3
Forest	41.4	4 222	52.4	3.2	4.6	4.5	15.2	12.5	1 270	105	28	1 602	57.1	41.9	1.0
Grant	204.7	4 195	52.0	6.5	3.8	8.3	11.4	104.5	2 142	167	141	4 870	61.2	37.3	1.6
Green	144.0	4 030	43.5	3.6	5.8	12.1	13.3	102.1	2 858	88	104	2 002	62.1	36.3	1.6
Green Lake	78.6	4 198	45.7	6.6	5.6	4.7	11.2	53.6	2 860	62	53	1 108	41.9	56.6	1.5
Iowa	85.7	3 637	51.0	1.0	5.0	9.3	14.3	50.7	2 151	96	68	1 306	66.7	32.0	1.3
Iron	33.6	5 320	31.4	9.3	6.5	0.4	18.3	27.9	4 427	20	18	352	55.8	42.7	1.6
Jackson	79.7	4 013	42.9	10.1	3.7	10.9	13.0	36.4	1 836	57	57	2 410	60.2	38.4	1.4
Jefferson	296.9	3 701	45.4	11.2	6.0	4.8	8.8	297.7	3 712	193	233	4 104	49.7	48.9	1.4
Juneau	101.2	3 811	46.3	5.7	4.7	4.7	10.8	121.1	4 562	236	76	1 498	53.7	44.6	1.7
Kenosha	762.0	4 677	54.6	4.9	5.6	6.2	3.5	712.6	4 374	281	502	9 529	58.2	40.1	1.7
Kewaunee	85.2	4 151	43.1	7.0	3.9	7.1	18.3	41.2	2 008	74	60	1 167	54.7	43.7	1.6
La Crosse	520.5	4 672	47.9	2.7	4.4	15.5	5.7	400.1	3 591	458	331	9 296	60.9	37.5	1.6
Lafayette	82.3	5 200	42.6	13.0	2.6	13.9	11.6	48.1	3 043	66	45	1 033	60.4	38.1	1.5
Langlade	81.5	4 012	47.8	4.3	4.5	5.2	15.0	69.6	3 428	50	58	1 079	49.8	48.8	1.3
Lincoln	119.6	4 033	41.3	7.6	5.5	11.0	13.0	67.6	2 280	79	85	1 822	55.2	42.7	2.1
Manitowoc	313.6	3 875	39.4	1.1	5.2	13.4	10.9	352.8	4 359	181	257	3 883	52.9	45.3	1.8
Marathon	586.2	4 511	46.6	14.1	4.0	3.7	9.8	477.0	3 670	533	381	7 249	53.5	44.7	1.8
Marinette	159.2	3 739	44.0	5.2	5.4	6.6	13.5	153.8	3 613	128	124	2 081	52.7	45.8	1.6
Marquette	53.1	3 546	44.9	7.3	6.6	4.9	16.9	35.7	2 385	63	42	740	51.8	46.6	1.6
Menominee	27.7	6 010	62.5	0.0	4.8	15.2	6.8	7.9	1 702	0	13	2 047	86.8	12.8	0.4
Milwaukee	4 664.5	4 904	40.9	8.6	7.7	4.9	4.4	5 285.0	5 556	10 115	3 272	54 238	67.3	31.4	1.2
Monroe	159.0	3 687	45.3	1.3	4.4	18.9	13.8	148.7	3 449	2 500	184	2 434	53.2	45.2	1.5
Oconto	130.7	3 489	39.1	8.6	6.5	5.1	18.8	95.8	2 557	111	107	1 778	52.3	46.2	1.5
Oneida	162.7	4 488	55.3	2.4	6.0	3.9	10.2	81.3	2 243	218	104	2 304	54.3	43.9	1.8
Outagamie	841.8	4 846	55.6	4.0	4.4	4.8	8.2	817.0	4 704	439	510	10 146	54.9	43.3	1.7
Ozaukee	326.3	3 812	43.1	4.9	6.8	6.8	12.1	306.4	3 580	157	249	3 881	38.6	60.3	1.2
Pepin	35.7	4 838	46.5	7.2	3.7	6.5	17.1	16.1	2 178	29	21	495	55.7	42.9	1.4
Pierce	161.0	4 069	48.4	8.2	4.4	2.9	14.7	137.0	3 461	112	117	3 800	53.4	44.4	2.2
Polk	190.0	4 293	48.2	5.7	3.6	6.5	12.5	180.7	4 081	157	128	2 526	48.0	49.8	2.1
Portage	244.4	3 579	39.8	14.0	5.1	5.7	12.5	141.5	2 073	205	203	5 637	63.0	35.0	2.0
Price	62.8	4 344	40.4	2.1	4.5	11.7	15.8	26.5	1 830	106	41	917	55.6	42.2	2.1
Racine	733.5	3 760	46.9	4.9	8.3	6.0	7.2	719.6	3 688	377	579	8 991	53.1	45.7	1.3
Richland	69.8	3 845	29.6	14.7	4.2	17.9	11.9	26.5	1 460	63	51	1 093	59.7	39.0	1.3
Rock	655.8	4 109	49.7	6.8	6.1	7.0	6.4	520.8	3 262	323	462	8 648	63.8	34.6	1.6
Rusk	87.9	5 999	35.2	21.7	3.2	10.6	12.1	44.1	3 012	53	41	1 130	53.0	44.7	2.3
St. Croix	270.2	3 330	47.6	3.0	5.3	10.8	13.6	339.8	4 189	177	240	4 054	47.2	51.0	1.8
Sauk	260.6	4 456	40.4	8.9	5.9	4.4	9.1	235.3	4 024	155	171	5 335	60.8	37.8	1.5
Sawyer	70.8	4 145	38.6	6.5	4.3	6.7	20.0	29.8	1 744	87	49	2 006	52.4	46.2	1.3
Shawano	147.3	3 586	43.5	5.7	5.0	7.3	14.4	89.3	2 175	132	119	2 849	51.1	47.5	1.5
Sheboygan	509.8	4 452	52.0	6.2	5.0	8.7	7.4	481.1	4 202	223	349	5 865	48.9	49.6	1.5
Taylor	70.1	3 629	47.2	3.3	4.2	8.7	15.1	43.7	2 262	71	55	951	48.8	49.1	2.1
Trempealeau	148.6	5 342	42.8	2.0	3.5	19.1	11.4	102.0	3 668	131	80	2 071	62.5	36.1	1.4
Vernon	107.4	3 702	45.4	1.5	3.6	16.0	13.4	86.9	2 997	115	84	1 758	60.1	38.1	1.7
Vilas	88.6	4 011	45.5	1.7	6.8	5.6	13.2	91.0	4 122	75	62	2 017	47.2	51.3	1.5
Walworth	391.6	3 885	45.8	6.6	7.7	5.6	7.8	504.9	5 009	201	290	7 072	47.9	50.5	1.5
Washburn	78.3	4 693	41.7	1.6	3.4	10.4	20.0	40.3	2 417	115	48	1 117	51.5	47.2	1.3
Washington	452.8	3 532	45.8	5.5	6.0	5.8	10.5	440.9	3 439	283	380	5 225	34.6	64.1	1.3
Waukesha	1 411.4	3 721	54.9	3.0	6.2	3.5	6.3	1 455.4	3 837	854	1 104	16 928	36.6	62.3	1.0
Waupaca	217.4	4 178	47.0	2.6	4.6	10.5	11.8	218.9	4 205	138	149	3 640	50.8	47.9	1.3
Waushara	79.7	3 218	42.7	2.9	4.8	12.4	13.9	29.6	1 196	52	71	1 151	49.5	48.7	1.8
Winnebago	592.7	3 655	40.8	2.6	5.6	11.6	8.2	694.9	4 285	501	478	11 972	54.9	43.3	1.8
Wood	345.7	4 675	54.8	7.9	5.0	6.1	8.2	289.7	3 917	198	213	4 845	55.6	42.5	1.9
WYOMING	X	X	X	X	X	X	X	X	X	7 794	6 252	59 870	32.5	64.8	2.7
Albany	164.6	5 107	29.1	39.0	5.3	0.3	3.2	41.8	1 297	210	215	7 644	50.5	46.4	3.1
Big Horn	88.5	7 858	52.9	18.2	3.8	0.2	2.6	25.0	2 222	112	70	1 398	20.9	76.2	3.0
Campbell	392.0	9 694	35.0	24.5	3.6	0.5	6.7	123.7	3 059	90	268	3 991	18.3	79.7	2.0
Carbon	122.4	7 902	36.4	19.3	4.4	0.0	7.4	8.2	528	245	96	1 913	34.1	63.2	2.7
Converse	88.0	6 836	48.7	24.1	3.9	0.1	4.4	22.2	1 724	67	83	1 334	21.4	76.3	2.3

1. Based on the resident population estimated as of July 1 of the year shown.   2. © 2009 Election Data Services, Inc. All rights reserved.

STATE/ County code	CBSA code[1]	County type[2]	STATE County	Land area,[3] (sq km) 2010	Total persons	Rank	Per square kilometer	White	Black	American Indian, Alaska Native	Asian and Pacific Islander	Percent Hispanic or Latino[4]	Under 5 years	5 to 17 years	18 to 24 years	25 to 34 years	35 to 44 years	45 to 54 years
				1	2	3	4	5	6	7	8	9	10	11	12	13	14	15
			WYOMING—Cont'd															
56 011	...	9	Crook	7 393	7 083	2 677	1.0	97.0	0.3	1.3	0.3	2.0	7.1	16.8	6.4	10.7	10.9	16.4
56 013	40180	7	Fremont	23 786	40 123	1 169	1.7	73.6	0.4	21.9	0.7	5.6	7.8	17.6	8.8	12.1	11.2	14.3
56 015	...	7	Goshen	5 764	13 249	2 233	2.3	88.7	0.7	1.1	0.5	9.7	5.3	15.1	10.1	10.3	11.0	15.2
56 017	...	7	Hot Springs	5 191	4 812	2 856	0.9	95.8	0.5	2.2	0.6	2.2	5.2	14.8	6.5	9.3	9.3	16.3
56 019	...	7	Johnson	10 759	8 569	2 562	0.8	95.2	0.3	1.4	0.6	3.2	6.7	15.4	5.8	11.1	11.2	15.1
56 021	16940	3	Laramie	6 956	91 738	624	13.2	82.6	3.0	1.4	1.8	13.1	7.3	17.1	9.7	13.5	12.4	14.8
56 023	...	7	Lincoln	10 557	18 106	1 920	1.7	94.4	0.3	1.2	0.7	4.3	8.0	20.2	6.3	12.7	12.2	14.9
56 025	16220	3	Natrona	13 831	75 450	719	5.5	90.6	1.4	1.5	1.1	6.9	7.1	16.8	9.6	14.2	12.1	15.0
56 027	...	9	Niobrara	6 801	2 484	3 009	0.4	96.4	0.5	1.7	0.6	2.1	3.9	15.1	5.8	11.3	12.5	16.2
56 029	...	7	Park	17 980	28 205	1 490	1.6	93.7	0.4	1.2	1.1	4.8	5.8	15.1	8.8	11.1	10.6	15.1
56 031	...	7	Platte	5 398	8 667	2 557	1.6	92.2	0.5	0.8	0.7	6.7	4.9	15.4	6.2	9.1	10.9	16.0
56 033	43260	7	Sheridan	6 537	29 116	1 450	4.5	94.3	0.5	1.8	1.1	3.5	6.4	15.9	7.9	11.7	11.5	15.5
56 035	...	9	Sublette	12 656	10 247	2 423	0.8	91.4	0.5	1.4	0.8	6.9	7.0	16.7	7.3	14.6	13.5	16.9
56 037	40540	5	Sweetwater	27 005	43 806	1 090	1.6	82.1	1.3	1.3	1.3	15.3	8.4	18.7	9.9	16.0	12.1	14.8
56 039	27220	7	Teton	10 348	21 294	1 774	2.1	83.1	0.3	0.7	1.8	15.0	6.0	13.1	8.0	19.9	15.5	14.6
56 041	21740	7	Uinta	5 390	21 118	1 781	3.9	89.9	0.5	1.4	1.0	8.8	8.4	21.7	7.6	13.7	12.4	15.1
56 043	...	7	Washakie	5 798	8 533	2 566	1.5	85.0	0.5	1.3	0.7	13.6	7.0	18.4	6.0	11.4	10.8	14.7
56 045	...	7	Weston	6 211	7 208	2 668	1.2	95.2	0.5	2.2	0.5	3.0	5.7	16.1	7.5	12.3	11.5	16.3

1. CBSA = Core Based Statistical Area. See Appendix A for explanation. See Appendix B for list of metropolitan areas with component counties. 2. County type code from the Economic Research Service of USDA Rural-Urban Continuum Codes. See Appendix A for definition. 3. Dry land or land partially or temporarily covered by water. 4. May be of any race.

STATE County	55 to 64 years	65 to 74 years	75 years and over	Percent female	1990	2000	1990–2000	2000–2010	Births	Deaths	Net migration	Number	Percent change, 2000–2010	Persons per house-hold	Female family house-holder[1]	One per-son
	16	17	18	19	20	21	22	23	24	25	26	27	28	29	30	31
WYOMING—Cont'd																
Crook	15.5	10.0	6.3	48.5	5 294	5 887	11.2	20.3	691	462	563	2 921	26.6	2.41	6.5	25.0
Fremont	13.7	8.1	6.4	50.1	33 662	35 804	6.4	12.1	5 178	3 411	1 355	15 455	14.1	2.54	12.2	27.0
Goshen	14.2	10.3	8.5	47.9	12 373	12 538	1.3	5.7	1 257	1 215	-198	5 311	4.9	2.29	7.9	30.0
Hot Springs	16.0	12.9	9.7	50.6	4 809	4 882	1.5	-1.4	398	585	-88	2 185	3.7	2.16	8.3	32.6
Johnson	16.1	10.3	8.2	49.1	6 145	7 075	15.1	21.1	758	719	1 433	3 782	27.8	2.25	6.7	31.8
Laramie	12.7	7.0	5.5	50.0	73 142	81 607	11.6	12.4	11 666	6 399	2 445	37 576	17.7	2.40	10.7	29.1
Lincoln	13.4	7.6	4.8	48.6	12 625	14 573	15.4	24.2	2 245	1 068	1 327	6 861	30.3	2.63	5.3	22.8
Natrona	12.7	6.4	6.1	49.7	61 226	66 533	8.7	13.4	9 175	5 547	4 734	30 616	14.2	2.41	10.9	28.5
Niobrara	14.7	11.8	8.9	53.3	2 499	2 407	-3.7	3.2	181	249	39	1 069	5.7	2.12	7.4	34.5
Park	15.9	9.8	7.7	50.3	23 178	25 786	11.3	9.4	2 697	2 219	1 863	11 885	15.3	2.29	7.2	28.5
Platte	16.8	11.8	8.9	50.4	8 145	8 807	8.1	-1.6	782	887	-469	3 838	5.9	2.23	6.9	30.6
Sheridan	15.6	8.5	7.1	50.0	23 562	26 560	12.7	9.6	3 067	2 730	2 407	12 360	10.7	2.27	8.4	30.9
Sublette	13.8	6.4	3.7	45.8	4 843	5 920	22.2	73.1	859	458	2 472	3 906	64.7	2.48	5.1	25.6
Sweetwater	11.8	4.9	3.4	47.8	38 823	37 613	-3.1	16.5	5 812	2 371	327	16 475	16.8	2.62	9.0	24.0
Teton	13.1	6.3	3.5	47.4	11 173	18 251	63.3	16.7	2 363	692	907	8 973	16.7	2.34	5.6	29.2
Uinta	12.1	5.3	3.6	49.5	18 705	19 742	5.5	7.0	2 908	1 130	-513	7 668	12.4	2.72	9.7	22.6
Washakie	13.9	9.6	8.1	50.1	8 388	8 289	-1.2	2.9	924	786	-484	3 492	6.5	2.40	7.9	27.7
Weston	14.7	8.5	7.4	47.4	6 518	6 644	1.9	8.5	646	618	350	3 021	15.1	2.28	6.9	29.9

1. No spouse present.

Table B. States and Counties — **Population, Vital Statistics, Medicare, and Crime**

STATE County	Persons in group quarters, 2010	Daytime population, 2006–2010		Births, average 2006–2008		Deaths, average 2006–2008		Persons under 65 with no health insurance, 2009		Medicare, 2011			Serious crimes known to police,[2] 2010 Total	
		Number	Employ-ment/resi-dence ratio	Total	Rate[1]	Number	Rate[1]	Number	Percent	Eligible for Medicare	Enrolled in Medicare Advantage	Enrolled in a Medicare prescription drug plan	Number	Rate[3]
	32	33	34	35	36	37	38	39	40	41	42	43	44	45
WYOMING—Cont'd														
Crook	34	6 335	0.9	D	D	46	7.2	1 118	21.0	1 270	79	613	93	1 313
Fremont	864	38 423	1.0	628	16.7	387	10.3	7 227	22.3	6 976	464	3 522	1 051	2 619
Goshen	1 070	12 117	0.9	D	D	126	10.4	1 796	18.8	2 727	46	1 658	255	1 925
Hot Springs	86	4 529	0.9	D	D	61	13.4	702	20.8	1 272	16	744	81	1 683
Johnson	71	8 408	1.0	D	D	81	9.8	1 326	19.4	1 737	184	836	152	1 774
Laramie	1 644	90 721	1.0	1 343	15.5	721	8.3	12 516	16.6	14 346	1 096	6 318	2 972	3 240
Lincoln	71	16 423	0.9	D	D	115	7.0	2 499	17.3	2 609	154	1 253	206	1 210
Natrona	1 645	73 924	1.0	1 074	15.0	611	8.5	10 163	15.9	11 338	547	6 138	2 993	3 967
Niobrara	214	2 427	1.0	D	D	29	12.5	419	23.1	544	D	335	23	926
Park	942	28 053	1.0	D	D	248	9.1	4 161	18.5	5 863	102	3 061	629	2 230
Platte	103	8 846	1.0	D	D	92	11.0	1 283	20.1	1 974	43	1 069	216	2 492
Sheridan	1 009	27 329	0.9	D	D	303	10.8	4 147	17.2	5 440	220	2 629	554	1 903
Sublette	550	10 995	1.4	D	D	52	6.5	1 217	15.3	1 110	71	500	157	1 532
Sweetwater	679	44 492	1.1	726	18.5	259	6.6	5 868	15.8	4 565	594	1 799	1 204	2 748
Teton	271	24 132	1.3	D	D	72	3.6	3 364	18.0	2 344	88	1 231	389	1 827
Uinta	270	19 697	0.9	D	D	137	6.7	3 160	16.9	2 361	225	1 163	481	2 531
Washakie	140	8 406	1.0	D	D	84	10.7	1 280	20.2	1 692	24	954	44	516
Weston	313	6 468	0.8	D	D	72	10.5	1 047	18.3	1 281	94	678	129	2 112

1. Per 1,000 estimated resident population.   2. Data for serious crimes have not been adjusted for underreporting; this may affect comparability between geographic areas and over time.   3. Per 100,000 population estimated by the FBI.

Table B. States and Counties — Crime, Education, Money Income, and Poverty

STATE County	Serious crimes known to police,[1] 2010 (cont.) Rate[2] — Violent	Property	Education — School enrollment and attainment, 2006–2010 — Enrollment[3] Total	Percent private	Attainment[4] (percent) High school graduate or less	Bachelor's degree or more	Local government expenditures,[5] 2008–2009 — Total current expenditures (mil dol)	Current expenditures per student (dollars)	Money income, 2006–2010 — Per capita income[6] (dollars)	Households — Median income — Dollars	Percent change, 2000 to 2006–2010 (constant 2010 dollars)	Percent with income of $200,000 or more	Income and poverty, 2010 — Median household income (dollars)	Percent below poverty level — All persons	Children under 18 years	Children 5 to 17 years in families
	46	47	48	49	50	51	52	53	54	55	56	57	58	59	60	61
WYOMING—Cont'd																
Crook	71	1 242	1 478	10.8	46.2	22.8	16.9	15 559	24 520	49 890	10.7	0.9	53 961	8.2	11.3	10.4
Fremont	167	2 452	9 520	8.0	39.6	22.8	120.5	18 858	24 173	46 397	12.7	1.3	45 998	13.8	20.4	18.8
Goshen	234	1 691	3 163	18.2	45.1	19.6	28.7	15 823	23 753	42 590	4.4	2.4	41 226	17.0	23.5	19.3
Hot Springs	42	1 642	670	4.5	45.9	19.3	10.5	16 098	25 269	42 469	12.2	0.3	40 126	11.7	15.6	13.2
Johnson	210	1 564	1 649	6.5	40.5	25.3	19.7	16 151	26 753	45 638	6.0	3.5	56 475	9.8	13.6	12.1
Laramie	199	3 040	23 060	11.1	37.5	22.9	191.5	13 905	27 406	52 824	5.3	2.0	50 278	12.0	16.2	13.2
Lincoln	123	1 087	4 276	7.2	46.1	19.3	44.7	13 629	24 421	57 794	11.9	1.5	58 175	9.4	13.4	11.7
Natrona	192	3 775	18 475	9.2	39.4	20.9	165.6	13 810	28 235	50 936	9.8	3.0	52 101	10.3	15.1	13.1
Niobrara	322	604	556	7.6	41.7	19.7	6.4	16 965	22 885	45 813	21.8	0.5	40 683	14.8	20.5	15.4
Park	234	1 996	6 538	7.5	36.2	27.7	55.1	13 942	26 203	46 637	2.8	2.2	50 058	12.0	17.3	14.7
Platte	69	2 423	1 998	11.4	48.0	17.3	22.7	17 528	24 185	42 947	0.1	1.6	44 288	12.0	18.0	14.7
Sheridan	86	1 817	6 303	7.5	38.5	23.1	60.2	14 512	26 756	48 141	10.1	2.2	51 926	10.2	13.8	12.4
Sublette	78	1 454	2 021	11.6	38.7	22.8	25.6	15 227	31 433	70 147	41.9	3.6	73 855	6.0	7.8	7.1
Sweetwater	473	2 276	10 946	11.0	44.9	17.1	100.8	13 214	30 961	69 828	18.5	3.2	67 508	9.1	13.2	11.1
Teton	254	1 573	3 448	16.7	26.9	49.7	36.0	15 704	42 224	70 271	1.6	9.1	68 358	9.0	14.0	11.6
Uinta	37	2 494	5 637	5.4	45.3	17.4	60.0	13 724	24 460	58 346	3.4	1.9	60 532	11.2	14.1	11.7
Washakie	117	398	1 906	10.7	44.7	24.5	22.1	15 761	28 557	48 379	9.3	2.5	47 831	12.1	15.6	13.7
Weston	98	2 014	1 394	4.2	49.7	17.9	17.3	15 564	28 463	53 853	31.5	2.9	48 653	9.9	12.8	10.4

1. Data for serious crimes have not been adjusted for underreporting; this may affect comparability between geographic areas and over time.   2. Per 100,000 population estimated by the FBI.   3. All persons 3 years old and over enrolled in nursery school through college.   4. Persons 25 years old and over.   5. Elementary and secondary education expenditures.   6. Based on population estimated by the American Community Survey, 2006–2010.

Table B. States and Counties — **Personal Income**

STATE County	Total (mil dol)	Percent change, 2008–2009	Per capita[1] Dollars	Rank	Wages and salaries[2] (mil dol)	Proprietors' income (mil dol)	Dividends, interest, and rent (mil dol)	Total	Transfer payments (mil dol) Total	Government payments to individuals Social Security	Medical payments	Income mainte-nance	Unemploy-ment insurance
	62	63	64	65	66	67	68	69	70	71	72	73	74
WYOMING—Cont'd													
Crook	295	-1.2	44 386	221	112	32	64	39	38	17	13	1	2
Fremont	1 475	-0.2	38 105	627	795	81	372	313	306	95	145	23	17
Goshen	440	0.0	35 719	927	187	37	116	96	94	35	39	7	2
Hot Springs	193	-0.4	41 966	330	87	20	46	46	45	18	20	2	2
Johnson	364	-3.8	42 681	286	156	34	134	52	50	23	17	2	3
Laramie	4 083	0.7	45 950	170	2 616	252	992	604	588	187	232	41	26
Lincoln	630	-4.6	37 062	745	334	48	160	94	90	37	33	4	7
Natrona	3 976	-5.0	53 361	66	2 163	724	937	476	462	163	183	35	30
Niobrara	100	-1.3	42 125	320	43	10	28	19	19	7	9	1	1
Park	1 252	-0.7	44 745	208	645	116	405	199	194	83	75	10	8
Platte	333	0.3	40 689	407	183	21	85	67	66	27	27	3	2
Sheridan	1 555	-2.6	53 334	68	699	120	591	193	188	69	67	10	12
Sublette	555	-4.4	63 081	22	402	42	136	37	35	15	10	1	4
Sweetwater	1 900	-6.6	46 096	166	1 594	133	319	209	202	70	69	11	18
Teton	2 647	-5.7	127 823	2	884	247	1 669	89	85	34	26	2	11
Uinta	876	-4.9	41 880	339	521	73	127	112	108	33	44	8	8
Washakie	358	-0.9	45 274	192	193	30	108	59	58	24	24	3	2
Weston	299	-4.9	42 647	288	110	53	64	46	45	18	18	2	2

1. Based on the resident population estimated as of July 1 of the year shown.   2. Includes supplements to wages and salaries.

STATE County	Earnings, 2009									Social Security beneficiaries, December 2010			Housing units, 2010	
	Total (mil dol)	Farm	Percent by selected industries									Supple-mental Security Income recipients, December 2010		
			Goods-related[1]		Service-related and health									
			Total	Manu-facturing	Infor-mation and profes-sional and technical services	Retail trade	Finance, insur-ance, and real estate	Health care and social services	Govern-ment	Number	Rate[2]		Total	Percent change, 2000–2010
	75	76	77	78	79	80	81	82	83	84	85	86	87	88

WYOMING—Cont'd

STATE County	75	76	77	78	79	80	81	82	83	84	85	86	87	88
Crook	145	-0.5	38.6	6.5	D	5.9	D	D	26.0	1 385	196	39	3 595	22.5
Fremont	877	-0.2	17.5	1.8	5.3	7.8	4.2	D	35.7	7 800	194	860	17 796	14.5
Goshen	224	2.9	D	5.6	4.2	9.2	5.2	D	27.9	2 925	221	222	5 972	1.5
Hot Springs	107	1.0	D	3.3	4.2	4.6	2.6	10.8	27.1	1 390	289	89	2 582	1.8
Johnson	190	-0.7	27.8	0.8	4.5	5.7	4.8	D	29.2	1 850	216	35	4 553	30.0
Laramie	2 868	0.8	D	4.6	7.0	6.2	4.9	8.3	42.3	15 255	166	1 339	40 462	18.3
Lincoln	382	0.3	36.9	2.0	4.5	5.7	2.9	3.6	25.9	2 925	162	113	8 946	31.0
Natrona	2 887	0.0	34.4	4.0	5.5	6.4	4.6	13.1	13.1	12 615	167	1 136	33 807	13.1
Niobrara	53	3.2	D	D	D	D	D	4.5	41.2	600	242	30	1 338	0.0
Park	761	1.1	22.9	3.4	6.6	8.1	4.1	10.2	26.9	6 485	230	267	13 562	14.3
Platte	204	2.3	D	1.6	2.7	6.1	3.8	D	23.8	2 140	247	104	4 667	3.1
Sheridan	819	-0.4	19.0	2.0	8.8	7.2	4.7	9.7	28.4	5 720	196	281	13 939	10.8
Sublette	444	0.4	54.4	0.8	D	3.6	1.9	D	15.6	1 185	116	30	5 770	62.4
Sweetwater	1 727	0.0	49.9	7.7	3.4	4.8	3.5	3.2	15.0	5 305	121	343	18 735	17.7
Teton	1 131	0.3	14.4	0.5	12.2	6.7	10.5	6.2	13.1	2 385	112	50	12 813	24.8
Uinta	594	-0.3	38.3	4.2	6.6	6.3	3.6	D	19.1	2 625	124	274	8 713	8.8
Washakie	223	4.1	31.8	12.4	5.8	5.2	4.4	10.9	21.7	1 875	220	93	3 833	4.9
Weston	163	-2.0	34.4	8.2	6.9	6.1	3.4	D	25.5	1 425	198	67	3 533	9.3

1. Includes mining, construction, and manufacturing.   2. Per 1,000 resident population enumerated in the 2010 census.

Table B. States and Counties — **Housing, Labor Force, and Employment**

STATE County	Housing units, 2006–2010								Civilian labor force, 2010				Civilian employment,[5] 2006–2010		
	Occupied units										Unemployment			Percent	
		Owner-occupied				Renter-occupied									
				Median owner cost as a percent of income											Con-struction, produc-tion, and mainte-nance occu-pations
	Total	Percent	Median value[1]	With a mort-gage	Without a mort-gage	Median rent[2]	Median rent as a per-cent of income	Sub-stand-ard units[3] (percent)	Total	Percent change, 2009–2010	Total	Rate[4]	Total	Manage-ment, business, science and arts	
	89	90	91	92	93	94	95	96	97	98	99	100	101	102	103
WYOMING—Cont'd															
Crook	2 769	75.5	151 100	21.3	10.0	612	14.7	3.6	3 486	-1.0	202	5.8	3 215	33.2	35.5
Fremont	15 541	72.2	154 400	20.6	10.5	567	23.2	4.5	19 094	1.3	1 532	8.0	18 907	34.3	24.0
Goshen	5 241	70.6	123 100	23.5	10.0	550	26.6	3.6	6 294	2.1	382	6.1	6 543	32.4	33.2
Hot Springs	2 201	64.1	117 800	18.1	10.0	493	25.6	0.7	2 539	2.3	139	5.5	2 283	29.6	25.3
Johnson	3 731	73.0	208 400	25.7	10.0	642	20.5	4.9	3 908	-2.6	326	8.3	4 315	36.7	27.0
Laramie	35 790	69.0	169 900	23.5	10.0	668	25.4	1.6	43 188	0.7	3 247	7.5	44 165	33.3	24.3
Lincoln	6 474	76.8	196 400	22.3	10.0	781	20.8	2.0	8 121	-1.3	750	9.2	8 663	27.2	34.7
Natrona	29 597	70.4	173 300	20.7	10.0	648	27.0	1.2	40 739	0.8	2 934	7.2	38 058	29.0	27.7
Niobrara	939	63.8	107 500	17.3	10.0	473	19.5	1.3	1 259	-0.2	69	5.5	1 178	40.7	26.4
Park	11 742	68.7	191 500	24.0	11.7	652	23.6	1.5	14 839	1.3	1 024	6.9	14 498	32.4	26.4
Platte	3 737	77.5	127 600	21.1	10.0	557	26.1	2.1	4 153	2.5	286	6.9	4 260	29.3	29.7
Sheridan	12 172	70.4	211 900	24.4	10.0	670	27.0	2.2	16 032	-0.8	1 245	7.8	14 836	31.9	29.0
Sublette	3 148	73.6	278 300	21.0	10.0	964	22.2	5.9	7 163	0.9	329	4.6	4 909	32.3	39.6
Sweetwater	16 415	73.7	169 500	19.4	10.0	801	19.2	3.7	23 703	-0.4	1 584	6.7	22 517	22.9	38.8
Teton	7 470	60.8	723 700	26.5	11.1	915	23.4	4.6	13 376	-2.3	1 093	8.2	12 915	34.7	16.9
Uinta	7 279	73.7	171 600	19.6	10.0	601	25.6	4.7	11 213	-1.0	782	7.0	10 220	26.7	34.4
Washakie	3 399	70.9	130 000	22.0	10.0	504	17.0	0.9	4 337	0.4	282	6.5	4 177	30.3	32.6
Weston	3 097	77.9	115 200	18.1	10.0	605	19.2	0.8	NA	NA	NA	NA	3 707	27.2	42.2

1. Specified owner-occupied units. 2. Specified renter-occupied units. A value of 10.0 represents 10 percent or less. 3. Overcrowded or lacking complete plumbing facilities. 4. Percent of civilian labor force. 5. Persons 16 years old and over.

STATE County	Private nonfarm establishments, employment and payroll, 2009									Agriculture, 2007			
		Employment						Annual payroll		Farms			
												Percent with:	
	Number of establishments	Total	Health care and social assistance	Manufacturing	Retail trade	Finance and insurance	Professional, scientific, and technical services	Total (mil dol)	Average per employee (dollars)	Number	Fewer than 50 acres	500 acres or more	Farm operators whose principal occupation is farming (percent)
	104	105	106	107	108	109	110	111	112	113	114	115	116
WYOMING—Cont'd													
Crook	231	1 513	241	143	201	D	25	50	32 773	457	7.0	64.8	65.2
Fremont	1 362	11 972	1 995	373	2 278	322	445	383	31 955	1 394	32.6	21.4	48.8
Goshen	341	3 219	774	398	448	D	156	75	23 432	815	14.6	41.2	54.0
Hot Springs	206	1 824	421	D	187	60	43	49	26 860	180	29.4	33.9	51.1
Johnson	405	2 535	432	55	379	D	138	74	29 008	319	8.5	58.3	59.6
Laramie	2 641	31 678	6 323	1 435	5 464	1 811	1 525	1 062	33 532	844	20.9	39.7	39.6
Lincoln	630	4 607	700	D	670	128	143	185	40 069	535	37.0	21.1	51.0
Natrona	2 962	34 720	5 106	2 419	5 551	1 086	1 709	1 352	38 952	413	28.8	41.4	46.2
Niobrara	86	390	58	D	100	33	D	8	19 921	235	3.8	80.0	73.6
Park	1 208	10 081	1 824	461	1 714	403	424	337	33 451	782	35.9	22.0	49.4
Platte	276	2 218	390	D	406	99	51	71	32 204	487	16.2	49.9	58.3
Sheridan	1 171	10 561	2 553	300	1 798	394	725	356	33 662	599	25.9	39.7	46.4
Sublette	503	3 696	195	80	386	D	122	195	52 774	366	31.4	34.4	40.4
Sweetwater	1 352	16 785	1 089	1 704	2 648	366	474	807	48 082	244	14.8	33.2	38.9
Teton	1 897	15 977	1 037	D	1 867	493	868	548	34 320	180	43.9	12.8	39.4
Uinta	634	8 026	1 469	D	1 188	164	234	322	40 169	344	36.0	33.4	50.9
Washakie	378	3 332	811	373	405	116	116	100	29 967	214	26.2	43.0	62.6
Weston	215	1 564	375	D	277	D	33	41	26 303	237	4.2	67.1	44.3

Table B. States and Counties — **Agriculture**

STATE County	Land in farms					Value of land and buildings (dollars)		Value of machinery and equipment, average per farm (dollars)	Value of products sold				Percent of farms with sales of:		Government payments	
			Acres								Percent from:					
	Acreage (1,000)	Percent change, 2002–2007	Average size of farm	Total irrigated (1,000)	Total cropland (1,000)	Average per farm	Average per acre		Total (mil dol)	Average per farm (dollars)	Crops	Live-stock and poultry products	$10,000 or more	$100,000 or more	Total ($1,000)	Percent of farms
	117	118	119	120	121	122	123	124	125	126	127	128	129	130	131	132
WYOMING—Cont'd																
Crook	1 570	3.1	3 435	4.6	166.6	2 054 086	598	122 506	44.0	96 243	10.0	90.0	56.5	23.6	972	45.5
Fremont	1 801	-28.1	1 292	164.3	170.1	1 182 494	916	83 180	86.7	62 196	25.8	74.2	42.8	14.5	2 330	13.0
Goshen	1 368	8.7	1 679	111.5	286.2	1 002 457	597	105 641	157.5	193 266	20.3	79.7	58.2	24.5	4 291	56.3
Hot Springs	547	-37.6	3 039	21.4	40.5	2 230 236	734	74 689	13.4	74 526	11.3	88.7	52.8	19.4	181	17.8
Johnson	1 946	-9.7	6 101	40.3	45.0	2 357 058	386	109 274	28.0	87 734	7.3	92.7	58.6	26.3	837	24.5
Laramie	1 692	-3.6	2 004	53.0	345.6	971 638	485	88 824	124.1	147 031	17.5	82.5	37.3	14.5	4 352	38.7
Lincoln	343	-6.0	640	65.3	93.9	734 860	1 147	96 088	30.1	56 197	22.7	77.3	43.6	14.6	570	32.5
Natrona	2 181	-24.0	5 282	40.3	49.6	1 762 052	334	92 949	32.7	79 187	16.5	83.5	47.0	17.4	1 623	19.4
Niobrara	1 449	-9.4	6 166	12.3	52.8	2 326 340	377	120 272	37.1	157 690	8.1	91.9	74.5	38.7	743	36.2
Park	882	8.9	1 128	111.9	113.5	935 351	830	102 491	81.8	104 571	41.1	58.9	44.4	18.8	996	24.7
Platte	1 308	-2.7	2 686	75.7	196.2	1 643 815	612	109 962	97.1	199 324	11.8	88.2	52.4	21.6	3 037	40.9
Sheridan	1 225	-25.2	2 044	56.3	91.4	1 606 503	786	86 611	48.7	81 239	12.0	88.0	48.6	15.2	621	14.4
Sublette	599	2.2	1 637	141.4	117.9	1 657 964	1 013	91 670	36.3	99 085	8.6	91.4	39.3	20.5	157	3.6
Sweetwater	1 486	0.4	6 092	30.3	46.1	1 087 499	179	75 900	14.5	59 451	29.9	70.1	54.5	14.3	281	14.3
Teton	53	-7.0	294	18.2	18.5	536 771	1 825	71 552	9.2	50 929	25.1	74.9	26.7	11.1	60	5.0
Uinta	743	-19.1	2 159	104.8	70.2	1 270 517	588	95 624	27.1	78 667	3.3	96.7	52.9	16.0	80	7.0
Washakie	470	10.1	2 195	44.4	46.6	1 252 034	570	154 625	39.6	184 819	39.6	60.4	65.0	36.0	994	25.7
Weston	1 328	-17.3	5 605	6.6	49.3	2 484 428	443	100 407	26.5	111 818	2.8	97.2	56.5	23.2	1 058	33.3

STATE County	Water use, 2005		Wholesale trade,[1] 2007				Retail trade,[2] 2007				Real estate and rental and leasing,[2] 2007			
	Total water withdrawn (mil gal/day)	Gallons withdrawn per person	Number of establish-ments	Number of employees	Sales (mil dol)	Annual payroll (mil dol)	Number of establish-ments	Number of employees	Sales (mil dol)	Annual payroll (mil dol)	Number of establish-ments	Number of employees	Receipts (mil dol)	Annual payroll (mil dol)
	133	134	135	136	137	138	139	140	141	142	143	144	145	146
WYOMING—Cont'd														
Crook	42.6	6 897	6	29	14.1	1.4	29	177	56.4	3.6	5	6	0.6	0.2
Fremont	413.6	11 335	36	254	76.2	8.0	203	2 145	558.4	53.8	78	439	116.1	19.0
Goshen	312.3	25 507	20	131	52.4	4.7	61	517	116.1	9.1	22	35	4.4	0.7
Hot Springs	90.7	19 987	3	D	D	D	34	228	38.3	3.4	7	9	0.9	0.1
Johnson	121.4	15 725	5	D	D	D	55	407	71.8	7.3	27	56	9.4	2.1
Laramie	272.5	3 200	98	800	628.1	35.2	360	5 603	1 720.5	133.4	134	519	94.2	14.3
Lincoln	201.9	12 616	9	103	26.8	2.7	92	699	221.7	14.7	24	62	4.5	0.8
Natrona	119.5	1 712	158	1 765	2 889.4	90.0	406	5 138	1 377.0	130.4	164	1 076	263.3	45.7
Niobrara	84.5	36 942	3	D	D	D	12	86	19.6	1.5	5	5	1.2	0.0
Park	340.5	12 769	37	200	155.5	8.5	213	1 588	388.4	37.4	67	161	19.0	2.7
Platte	229.4	26 616	5	63	34.1	2.1	47	413	93.4	7.9	15	32	3.8	0.6
Sheridan	198.8	7 259	40	D	D	D	176	1 769	478.2	43.7	66	234	32.3	6.2
Sublette	170.6	24 633	7	D	D	D	43	364	82.8	8.9	32	143	23.0	3.5
Sweetwater	156.8	4 130	62	573	437.5	32.0	202	2 753	898.2	69.7	74	426	105.3	18.8
Teton	67.5	3 547	32	D	D	D	261	2 043	515.6	57.9	150	528	138.7	22.1
Uinta	114.1	5 724	28	225	159.4	12.3	101	1 262	414.0	25.7	33	138	14.2	3.1
Washakie	181.3	22 850	10	69	12.1	2.0	51	476	98.3	8.9	19	68	10.1	1.7
Weston	31.9	4 788	6	51	11.5	2.1	30	241	64.3	4.3	9	9	1.5	0.2

1. Merchant wholesalers, except manufacturers' sales branches and offices.　　2. Employer establishments.

Professional Services, Manufacturing, and Accommodation and Food Services

STATE County	Professional, scientific, and technical services,[1] 2007				Manufacturing, 2007				Accommodation and food services, 2007			
	Number of establish-ments	Number of employees	Receipts (mil dol)	Annual payroll (mil dol)	Number of establish-ments	Number of employees	Receipts (mil dol)	Annual payroll (mil dol)	Number of establish-ments	Number of employees	Sales (mil dol)	Annual payroll (mil dol)
	147	148	149	150	151	152	153	154	155	156	157	158
WYOMING—Cont'd												
Crook	12	22	3.2	0.8	NA	NA	NA	NA	31	147	6.1	1.5
Fremont	118	406	55.5	14.8	NA	NA	NA	NA	133	1 495	67.0	18.4
Goshen	20	D	D	D	19	500	147.9	14.2	31	362	11.8	2.7
Hot Springs	18	46	3.3	1.3	NA	NA	NA	NA	24	309	10.4	3.0
Johnson	45	147	15.2	5.3	NA	NA	NA	NA	43	400	20.7	5.8
Laramie	312	1 402	182.0	65.2	61	1 710	2 420.2	80.9	185	3 938	173.7	52.1
Lincoln	46	124	11.6	4.1	22	539	D	29.4	61	435	21.1	4.3
Natrona	271	D	D	D	94	2 525	1 230.6	114.9	185	3 853	168.0	50.0
Niobrara	4	D	D	D	NA	NA	NA	NA	13	69	3.1	0.7
Park	93	374	40.3	15.5	54	541	62.7	20.0	157	1 363	133.0	32.8
Platte	22	56	5.2	1.2	NA	NA	NA	NA	34	347	12.1	3.2
Sheridan	119	D	D	D	NA	NA	NA	NA	96	1 398	66.8	19.0
Sublette	54	125	14.3	4.6	NA	NA	NA	NA	46	225	19.7	3.9
Sweetwater	104	447	64.5	22.2	34	2 122	D	145.8	108	2 040	150.4	30.1
Teton	253	D	D	D	NA	NA	NA	NA	180	4 525	327.4	112.2
Uinta	51	D	D	D	NA	NA	NA	NA	51	773	35.5	8.1
Washakie	28	115	10.8	3.5	NA	NA	NA	NA	33	299	10.2	2.8
Weston	13	D	D	D	NA	NA	NA	NA	29	210	7.5	1.8

1. Establishment subject to federal tax.

Table B. States and Counties — **Health Care and Social Assistance, Other Services, and Federal Funds**

STATE County	Health care and social assistance, 2007				Other services, 2007				Federal funds and grants, 2009–2010			
									Expenditures (mil dol)			
										Direct payments for individuals[1]		
	Number of establishments	Number of employees	Receipts (mil dol)	Annual payroll (mil dol)	Number of establishments	Number of employees	Receipts (mil dol)	Annual payroll (mil dol)	Total	Social Security and government retirement	Medicare	Food Stamps and Supplemental Security Income
	159	160	161	162	163	164	165	166	167	168	169	170
WYOMING—Cont'd												
Crook	16	D	D	D	12	D	D	D	45.9	22.3	6.9	0.4
Fremont	129	1 842	148.8	58.2	85	340	32.4	8.8	331.3	122.4	54.8	12.6
Goshen	24	763	39.2	19.3	26	86	6.8	1.6	112.8	46.5	18.8	1.4
Hot Springs	16	358	26.5	10.9	16	63	4.0	1.0	46.0	22.2	10.4	0.9
Johnson	24	428	30.0	13.1	23	84	6.9	2.2	58.3	29.5	8.6	0.9
Laramie	281	6 040	563.1	232.9	180	947	83.0	25.0	1 699.6	348.0	94.1	16.7
Lincoln	52	635	44.9	18.2	37	94	11.4	2.0	100.8	48.0	14.2	1.7
Natrona	283	4 819	482.2	203.0	202	1 200	141.1	34.1	499.4	205.5	84.1	15.6
Niobrara	6	D	D	D	8	D	D	D	21.2	8.9	4.2	2.1
Park	108	1 569	144.9	58.6	81	296	23.6	5.3	264.6	105.4	33.0	4.4
Platte	23	403	25.7	10.9	19	58	5.0	0.8	115.1	36.8	14.6	1.7
Sheridan	106	2 320	219.6	100.3	72	346	39.4	7.4	288.9	113.1	33.2	4.1
Sublette	20	192	13.2	5.7	29	150	25.8	6.6	40.7	19.1	4.9	0.5
Sweetwater	98	1 091	115.3	36.8	94	448	54.2	14.5	191.1	93.0	35.2	3.3
Teton	114	D	D	D	94	461	67.4	14.5	132.2	37.6	10.8	0.5
Uinta	69	1 403	97.1	39.5	47	143	13.3	2.9	78.9	44.8	11.7	5.2
Washakie	25	675	47.6	19.9	30	112	6.9	1.9	81.9	29.0	15.6	1.1
Weston	17	382	20.2	8.4	12	41	3.7	0.8	74.1	23.7	10.2	0.9

1. State totals may Include programs not allocated by county.

Table B. States and Counties — **Federal Funds, Residential Construction, and Local Government Finances**

STATE County	Federal funds and grants, 2009–2010 (cont.)							Value of residential construction authorized by building permits, 2010		Local government finances, 2007				
	Expenditures (mil dol) (cont.)									General revenue				
	Procurement contract awards			Grants[1]								Taxes		
													Per capita[2] (dollars)	
	Salaries and wages	Defense	Other	Medicaid and other health-related	Nutrition and family welfare	Education	Other	New con-struction ($1,000)	Number of housing units	Total (mil dol)	Inter-govern-mental (mil dol)	Total (mil dol)	Total	Property
	171	172	173	174	175	176	177	178	179	180	181	182	183	184
WYOMING—Cont'd														
Crook....................................	4.3	0.0	1.6	4.7	0.8	0.4	3.1	850	4	46.2	28.3	9.7	1 543	1 147
Fremont...............................	29.8	0.7	10.6	40.3	9.6	22.7	11.6	3 080	21	235.5	150.8	58.9	1 572	1 458
Goshen................................	11.2	0.0	1.0	23.1	2.3	0.9	0.1	795	6	70.5	51.5	9.9	826	564
Hot Springs	1.0	0.0	0.2	8.1	0.7	0.3	1.8	74	1	45.5	18.4	11.5	2 519	2 140
Johnson..............................	8.0	0.0	0.9	4.6	0.8	1.4	1.4	1 075	12	77.7	26.5	32.1	3 940	3 393
Laramie	342.8	87.9	58.5	123.4	32.6	51.0	504.2	39 460	238	582.4	242.9	90.9	1 052	576
Lincoln	8.9	0.0	3.4	5.8	2.0	0.7	13.9	10 281	49	132.3	54.4	46.1	2 848	2 451
Natrona...............................	60.4	6.7	26.2	43.2	9.6	5.5	33.5	85 998	807	354.6	203.8	86.7	1 209	798
Niobrara..............................	1.1	0.0	0.7	2.3	0.4	0.2	0.1	320	4	18.6	9.4	4.5	1 975	1 494
Park....................................	39.0	0.0	47.6	19.7	3.2	1.6	1.7	21 496	118	203.2	87.4	42.3	1 562	1 381
Platte	15.4	10.5	18.0	8.1	5.7	0.6	0.4	3 032	19	49.0	31.2	10.2	1 215	959
Sheridan..............................	50.5	3.7	27.3	31.3	4.2	1.1	6.9	20 947	121	198.3	80.8	45.2	1 615	1 076
Sublette...............................	7.5	0.0	3.0	1.2	0.7	0.4	0.6	8 223	42	167.7	35.9	118.2	14 919	14 764
Sweetwater..........................	19.7	0.7	4.3	16.4	5.7	1.6	5.9	20 146	147	358.3	89.5	164.7	4 192	2 944
Teton	19.1	1.6	49.8	3.7	2.2	0.9	3.5	82 079	115	212.3	35.0	70.4	3 520	2 230
Uinta	5.7	0.0	1.0	3.6	4.2	1.1	1.1	7 853	45	118.2	49.4	54.9	2 717	2 309
Washakie..............................	14.9	0.1	5.2	9.6	3.9	0.6	0.6	130	1	49.8	34.1	10.1	1 286	990
Weston	2.9	26.7	0.5	5.8	0.9	0.4	0.5	600	4	42.6	23.7	8.8	1 287	1 029

1. State totals may include programs not allocated by county.   2. Based on the resident population estimated as of July 1 of the year shown.

Table B. States and Counties — **Local Government Finances, Government Employment, and Voting**

STATE County	Local government finances, 2007 (cont.)							Debt outstanding		Government employment, 2009			Presidential election,[2] 2008		
	Direct general expenditure												Percent of vote cast:		
			Percent of total for:												
	Total (mil dol)	Per capita[1] (dollars)	Educa-tion	Health and hospitals	Police protec-tion	Public welfare	High-ways	Total (mil dol)	Per capita[1] (dollars)	Federal civilian	Federal military	State and local	Demo-cratic	Republi-can	All other
	185	186	187	188	189	190	191	192	193	194	195	196	197	198	199
WYOMING—Cont'd															
Crook..............................	45.4	7 218	54.0	14.6	2.9	0.1	5.0	2.8	442	94	40	629	16.6	80.6	2.8
Fremont.............................	209.7	5 594	68.5	1.3	4.0	0.3	2.2	31.1	831	462	235	5 350	34.2	63.0	2.8
Goshen.............................	64.6	5 389	67.6	2.2	4.3	0.3	4.0	11.7	974	102	75	1 148	31.0	66.7	2.3
Hot Springs	47.0	10 315	42.9	31.7	2.5	0.3	2.7	17.5	3 852	16	28	573	24.3	72.0	3.7
Johnson............................	74.4	9 140	48.2	21.6	2.9	0.1	10.5	19.5	2 395	148	52	832	20.9	76.6	2.6
Laramie	565.4	6 548	41.9	29.9	2.9	0.3	4.0	169.5	1 963	2 692	3 468	11 230	38.6	59.0	2.4
Lincoln.............................	126.1	7 797	50.0	21.1	3.3	0.1	4.0	57.6	3 564	129	103	1 710	21.3	75.7	3.0
Natrona............................	342.8	4 778	60.3	1.0	4.9	0.4	3.5	80.2	1 118	684	454	5 074	31.5	65.8	2.7
Niobrara............................	17.9	7 903	38.1	26.9	3.0	0.1	10.4	14.0	6 175	17	14	424	18.9	78.7	2.5
Park.................................	199.8	7 379	50.8	22.8	2.6	0.0	4.0	45.4	1 675	796	171	2 687	25.1	72.3	2.6
Platte...............................	51.9	6 182	46.2	2.7	2.7	0.1	3.2	60.8	7 239	139	50	783	30.9	65.8	3.3
Sheridan...........................	188.7	6 739	47.2	27.4	3.0	0.1	3.6	37.3	1 334	735	177	2 635	29.8	67.9	2.3
Sublette	176.7	22 302	51.4	5.5	2.4	1.5	13.1	12.0	1 511	139	53	897	21.5	76.1	2.4
Sweetwater........................	334.9	8 521	41.6	21.8	4.4	0.4	6.4	239.5	6 094	241	251	4 182	34.5	62.0	3.5
Teton...............................	179.5	8 976	23.0	32.2	4.6	0.7	4.5	45.3	2 267	413	126	1 817	60.7	37.1	2.3
UInta	128.7	6 374	59.9	1.2	4.7	0.1	4.5	82.5	4 083	78	127	2 092	27.6	68.7	3.6
Washakie...........................	38.7	4 951	59.3	1.6	4.7	1.8	3.1	10.3	1 322	130	48	758	25.5	72.3	2.2
Weston	41.0	5 979	40.8	28.1	3.6	0.5	8.3	4.7	685	55	48	769	19.4	77.2	3.4

1. Based on the resident population estimated as of July 1 of the year shown.   2. © 2009 Election Data Services, Inc. All rights reserved.

Metropolitan Areas

(For explanation of symbols, see page viii)

Page

Metropolitan Area Highlights and Rankings

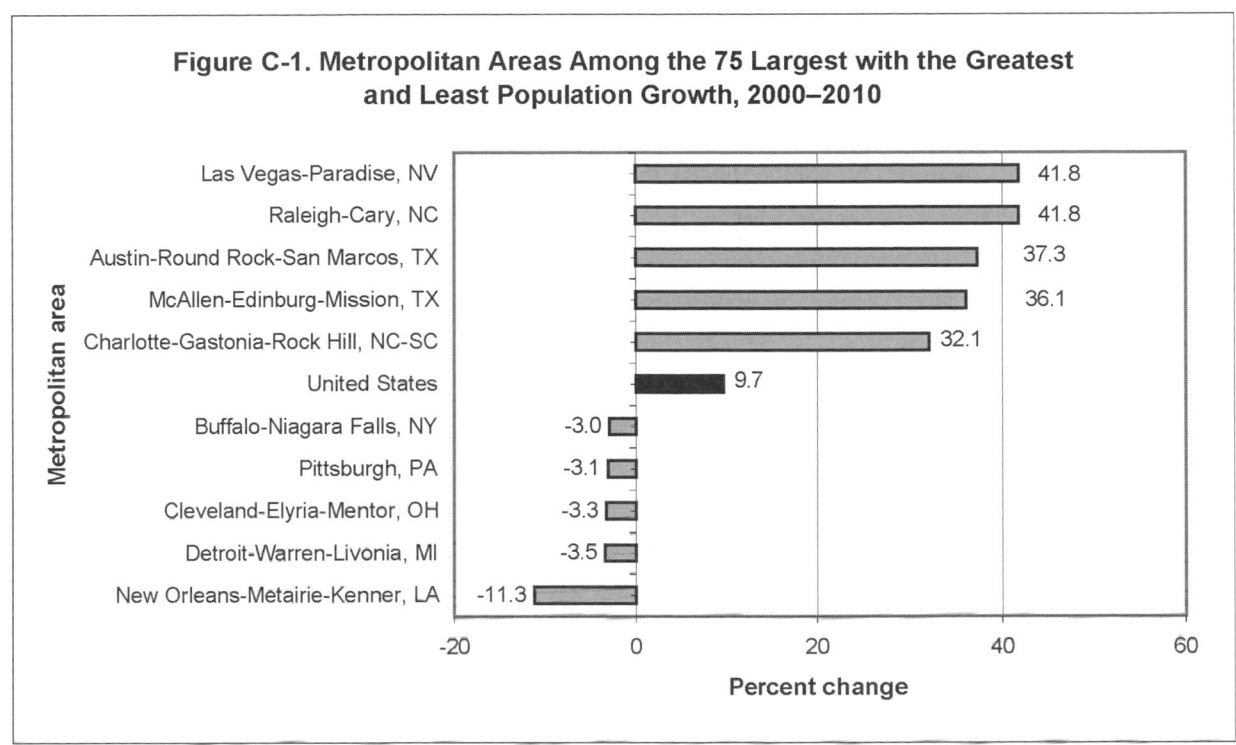

Figure C-1. Metropolitan Areas Among the 75 Largest with the Greatest and Least Population Growth, 2000–2010

In 2010, 82.9 percent of Americans lived in metropolitan areas, but these metropolitan areas made up a mere 26 percent of the nation's land area. After nearly a decade of research and development, the Office of Management and Budget (OMB) first established new rules for defining metropolitan areas and issued a completely new list after the 2000 census. This scheme defines a variety of areas called "Core Based Statistical Areas" (CBSAs). Along with the new definition of metropolitan areas, OMB defined a new type of area—called a micropolitan area—that defines the many American communities with population clusters that are too small to meet the 50,000 minimum that defines a metropolitan area. Appendix C lists these micropolitan areas as of December 2009 but, because of size constraints, *County and City Extra* continues to include only metropolitan area data in Table C. In 2013, the Census Bureau expects to release data for new metropolitan and micropolitan areas based on the 2010 census.

With nearly 19 million people, the New York metropolitan area was the largest, followed by Los Angeles with a population of 12.8 million. Chicago ranked third with 9.5 million people. Another 11 metropolitan areas had more than 4 million residents (Dallas, Philadelphia, Houston, Miami, Washington, Atlanta, Boston, San Francisco, Detroit, Riverside-San Bernardino-Ontario, and Phoenix), while 37 other metropolitan areas had between 1 million and 4 million people. Nearly 54 percent of the U.S. population lived in these 51 metropolitan areas with one million or more residents.

Sixty-five metropolitan areas grew by 20 percent or more between 2000 and 2010. Palm Coast, Fl, had by far the highest growth rate, increasing by 92.0 percent to a 2010 population of 95,696 residents. Phoenix, Atlanta, Dallas, and Houston all ranked near the top for both population size and population growth. Among the 75 largest metropolitan areas, Raleigh, NC and Las Vegas, NV had the highest proportional increase, at 41.8 percent. Six of the most populous metropolitan areas lost population since 2000. All but New Orleans, LA, were areas located in the Great Lakes region (Dayton, OH; Buffalo, NY; Pittsburgh, PA; Cleveland, OH; and Detroit, MI).

Among metropolitan areas, New York and Los Angeles shared the top spots for density as well as for total population. With 1,091.1 persons per square kilometer, the New York metropolitan area is only slightly more densely populated than the Los Angeles metropolitan area, which had nearly 1,021.6 persons per square kilometer. At the other extreme, 4 of the largest metropolitan areas had fewer than 50 persons per square kilometer. All 4 of these had large land areas and were located in western states (Albuquerque, NM; Bakersfield, CA; Tucson, AZ; and Salt Lake City, UT).

In 2010, 131 metropolitan areas had an unemployment rate at 10 percent or higher. In contrast, only 11 metropolitan areas had an unemployment rate at 10 percent or higher in 2008. Topping the list are El Centro, CA and Yuma, AZ, two metropolitan areas with large agricultural workforces and unemployment rates over 25 percent. Nine of the 10 metropolitan areas with the highest unemployment were in California. Twenty-seven of the 75 most populous metropolitan areas had unemployment rates higher than 10 percent and three had unemployment rates over 15 percent. Six metropolitan areas had unemployment rates below 5 percent in 2010. All of them were relatively small areas. Bismark, ND had the lowest unemployment rate among all metropolitan areas at 3.9 percent, followed by Fargo, ND at 4.1 percent.

75 Largest Metropolitan Areas by 2010 Population
Selected Rankings

Popu-lation rank	Metropolitan area	Population [col 2]	Popu-lation rank	Land area rank	Metropolitan area	Land area (square kilometers) [col 1]
1	New York-Northern New Jersey-Long Island, NY-NJ-PA	18 897 109	13	1	Riverside-San Bernardino-Ontario, CA	1 091
2	Los Angeles-Long Beach-Santa Ana, CA	12 828 837	14	2	Phoenix-Mesa-Glendale, AZ	1 022
3	Chicago-Joliet-Naperville, IL-IN-WI	9 461 105	50	3	Salt Lake City, UT	678
4	Dallas-Fort Worth-Arlington, TX	6 371 773	57	4	Albuquerque, NM	613
5	Philadelphia-Camden-Wilmington, PA-NJ-DE-MD	5 965 343	52	5	Tucson, AZ	567
6	Houston-Sugar Land-Baytown, TX	5 946 800	4	6	Dallas-Fort Worth-Arlington, TX	551
7	Washington-Arlington-Alexandria, DC-VA-MD-WV	5 582 170	6	7	Houston-Sugar Land-Baytown, TX	508
8	Miami-Fort Lauderdale-Pompano Beach, FL	5 564 635	18	8	St. Louis, MO-IL	504
9	Atlanta-Sandy Springs-Marietta, GA	5 268 860	21	9	Denver-Aurora-Broomfield, CO	501
10	Boston-Cambridge-Quincy, MA-NH	4 552 402	9	10	Atlanta-Sandy Springs-Marietta, GA	428
11	San Francisco-Oakland-Fremont, CA	4 335 391	62	11	Bakersfield-Delano, CA	427
12	Detroit-Warren-Livonia, MI	4 296 250	30	12	Las Vegas-Paradise, NV	423
13	Riverside-San Bernardino-Ontario, CA	4 224 851	29	13	Kansas City, MO-KS	413
14	Phoenix-Mesa-Glendale, AZ	4 192 887	25	14	San Antonio-New Braunfels, TX	402
15	Seattle-Tacoma-Bellevue, WA	3 439 809	3	14	Chicago-Joliet-Naperville, IL-IN-WI	402
16	Minneapolis-St. Paul-Bloomington, MN	3 279 833	1	16	New York-Northern New Jersey-Long Island, NY-NJ-PA	390
17	San Diego-Carlsbad-San Marcos, CA	3 095 313	23	17	Portland-Vancouver-Hillsboro, OR-WA	385
18	St. Louis, MO-IL	2 812 896	54	18	Tulsa, OK	309
19	Tampa-St. Petersburg-Clearwater, FL	2 783 243	16	19	Minneapolis-St. Paul-Bloomington, MN	305
20	Baltimore-Towson, MD	2 710 489	55	20	Fresno, CA	302
21	Denver-Aurora-Broomfield, CO	2 543 482	15	21	Seattle-Tacoma-Bellevue, WA	284
22	Pittsburgh, PA	2 356 285	38	22	Nashville-Davidson—Murfreesboro—Franklin, TN	280
23	Portland-Vancouver-Hillsboro, OR-WA	2 226 009	43	23	Richmond, VA	276
24	Sacramento—Arden-Arcade—Roseville, CA	2 149 127	7	24	Washington-Arlington-Alexandria, DC-VA-MD-WV	265
25	San Antonio-New Braunfels, TX	2 142 508	44	25	Oklahoma City, OK	260
26	Orlando-Kissimmee-Sanford, FL	2 134 411	22	26	Pittsburgh, PA	245
27	Cincinnati-Middletown, OH-KY-IN	2 130 151	49	27	Birmingham-Hoover, AL	244
28	Cleveland-Elyria-Mentor, OH	2 077 240	24	28	Sacramento—Arden-Arcade—Roseville, CA	237
29	Kansas City, MO-KS	2 035 334	8	29	Miami-Fort Lauderdale-Pompano Beach, FL	226
30	Las Vegas-Paradise, NV	1 951 269	2	30	Los Angeles-Long Beach-Santa Ana, CA	220
31	San Jose-Sunnyvale-Santa Clara, CA	1 836 911	5	31	Philadelphia-Camden-Wilmington, PA-NJ-DE-MD	218
32	Columbus, OH	1 836 536	41	32	Memphis, TN-MS-AR	210
33	Charlotte-Gastonia-Rock Hill, NC-SC	1 758 038	27	33	Cincinnati-Middletown, OH-KY-IN	209
34	Indianapolis-Carmel, IN	1 756 241	59	34	Omaha-Council Bluffs, NE-IA	206
35	Austin-Round Rock-San Marcos, TX	1 716 289	35	35	Austin-Round Rock-San Marcos, TX	204
36	Virginia Beach-Norfolk-Newport News, VA-NC	1 671 683	17	36	San Diego-Carlsbad-San Marcos, CA	191
37	Providence-New Bedford-Fall River, RI-MA	1 600 852	42	37	Louisville-Jefferson County, KY-IN	190
38	Nashville-Davidson—Murfreesboro—Franklin, TN	1 589 934	74	38	Little Rock-North Little Rock-Conway, AR	187
39	Milwaukee-Waukesha-West Allis, WI	1 555 908	65	39	Baton Rouge, LA	179
40	Jacksonville, FL	1 345 596	32	40	Columbus, OH	176
41	Memphis, TN-MS-AR	1 316 100	12	41	Detroit-Warren-Livonia, MI	173
42	Louisville-Jefferson County, KY-IN	1 283 566	34	42	Indianapolis-Carmel, IN	172
43	Richmond, VA	1 258 251	70	43	Columbia, SC	163
44	Oklahoma City, OK	1 252 987	10	44	Boston-Cambridge-Quincy, MA-NH	162
45	Hartford-West Hartford-East Hartford, CT	1 212 381	26	45	Orlando-Kissimmee-Sanford, FL	157
46	New Orleans-Metairie-Kenner, LA	1 167 764	40	46	Jacksonville, FL	152
47	Buffalo-Niagara Falls, NY	1 135 509	33	47	Charlotte-Gastonia-Rock Hill, NC-SC	145
48	Raleigh-Cary, NC	1 130 490	46	48	New Orleans-Metairie-Kenner, LA	140
49	Birmingham-Hoover, AL	1 128 047	51	49	Rochester, NY	139
50	Salt Lake City, UT	1 124 197	58	50	Albany-Schenectady-Troy, NY	129
51	Rochester, NY	1 054 323	69	51	Grand Rapids-Wyoming, MI	126
52	Tucson, AZ	980 263	31	52	San Jose-Sunnyvale-Santa Clara, CA	121
53	Honolulu, HI	953 207	36	53	Virginia Beach-Norfolk-Newport News, VA-NC	120
54	Tulsa, OK	937 478	20	54	Baltimore-Towson, MD	118
55	Fresno, CA	930 450	19	55	Tampa-St. Petersburg-Clearwater, FL	113
56	Bridgeport-Stamford-Norwalk, CT	916 829	11	56	San Francisco-Oakland-Fremont, CA	111
57	Albuquerque, NM	887 077	48	56	Raleigh-Cary, NC	111
58	Albany-Schenectady-Troy, NY	870 716	28	58	Cleveland-Elyria-Mentor, OH	108
59	Omaha-Council Bluffs, NE-IA	865 350	71	59	Greensboro-High Point, NC	107
60	New Haven-Milford, CT	862 477	75	60	Knoxville, TN	100
61	Dayton, OH	841 502	63	61	Oxnard-Thousand Oaks-Ventura, CA	96
62	Bakersfield-Delano, CA	839 631	61	62	Dayton, OH	88
63	Oxnard-Thousand Oaks-Ventura, CA	823 318	37	63	Providence-New Bedford-Fall River, RI-MA	86
64	Allentown-Bethlehem-Easton, PA-NJ	821 173	68	64	McAllen-Edinburg-Mission, TX	83
65	Baton Rouge, LA	802 484	47	65	Buffalo-Niagara Falls, NY	80
66	El Paso, TX	800 647	45	66	Hartford-West Hartford-East Hartford, CT	77
67	Worcester, MA	798 552	67	66	Worcester, MA	77
68	McAllen-Edinburg-Mission, TX	774 769	39	68	Milwaukee-Waukesha-West Allis, WI	66
69	Grand Rapids-Wyoming, MI	774 160	64	69	Allentown-Bethlehem-Easton, PA-NJ	60
70	Columbia, SC	767 598	73	69	North Port-Bradenton-Sarasota, FL	60
71	Greensboro-High Point, NC	723 801	66	71	El Paso, TX	58
72	Akron, OH	703 200	72	72	Akron, OH	45
73	North Port-Bradenton-Sarasota, FL	702 281	56	73	Bridgeport-Stamford-Norwalk, CT	41
74	Little Rock-North Little Rock-Conway, AR	699 757	60	74	New Haven-Milford, CT	40
75	Knoxville, TN	698 030	53	75	Honolulu, HI	37

75 Largest Metropolitan Areas by 2010 Population
Selected Rankings

Population density, 2010				Percent population change, 2000–2010			
Population rank	Density rank	Metropolitan area	Density (per square kilometer) [col 4]	Population rank	Percent change rank	Metropolitan area	Percent change [col 23]
1	1	New York-Northern New Jersey-Long Island, NY-NJ-PA	1 091.10	30	1	Las Vegas-Paradise, NV	41.8
2	2	Los Angeles-Long Beach-Santa Ana, CA	1 021.60	48	1	Raleigh-Cary, NC	41.8
11	3	San Francisco-Oakland-Fremont, CA	677.50	35	3	Austin-Round Rock-San Marcos, TX	37.3
53	4	Honolulu, HI	612.60	68	4	McAllen-Edinburg-Mission, TX	36.1
56	5	Bridgeport-Stamford-Norwalk, CT	566.60	33	5	Charlotte-Gastonia-Rock Hill, NC-SC	32.1
60	6	New Haven-Milford, CT	550.80	13	6	Riverside-San Bernardino-Ontario, CA	29.8
3	7	Chicago-Joliet-Naperville, IL-IN-WI	507.60	26	6	Orlando-Kissimmee-Sanford, FL	29.8
10	8	Boston-Cambridge-Quincy, MA-NH	504	14	8	Phoenix-Mesa-Glendale, AZ	28.9
5	9	Philadelphia-Camden-Wilmington, PA-NJ-DE-MD	500.50	62	9	Bakersfield-Delano, CA	26.9
19	10	Tampa-St. Petersburg-Clearwater, FL	427.50	6	10	Houston-Sugar Land-Baytown, TX	26.1
12	11	Detroit-Warren-Livonia, MI	426.60	25	11	San Antonio-New Braunfels, TX	25.2
8	12	Miami-Fort Lauderdale-Pompano Beach, FL	423.20	9	12	Atlanta-Sandy Springs-Marietta, GA	24.0
39	13	Milwaukee-Waukesha-West Allis, WI	412.90	4	13	Dallas-Fort Worth-Arlington, TX	23.4
20	14	Baltimore-Towson, MD	402.30	57	14	Albuquerque, NM	21.6
28	15	Cleveland-Elyria-Mentor, OH	401.60	38	15	Nashville-Davidson—Murfreesboro—Franklin, TN	21.2
37	16	Providence-New Bedford-Fall River, RI-MA	389.50	40	16	Jacksonville, FL	19.8
7	17	Washington-Arlington-Alexandria, DC-VA-MD-WV	385	24	17	Sacramento—Arden-Arcade—Roseville, CA	19.6
45	18	Hartford-West Hartford-East Hartford, CT	309	73	18	North Port-Bradenton-Sarasota, FL	19.0
66	19	El Paso, TX	305.20	70	19	Columbia, SC	18.6
72	20	Akron, OH	301.70	21	20	Denver-Aurora-Broomfield, CO	17.9
17	21	San Diego-Carlsbad-San Marcos, CA	284.10	66	21	El Paso, TX	17.8
47	22	Buffalo-Niagara Falls, NY	280.20	7	22	Washington-Arlington-Alexandria, DC-VA-MD-WV	16.4
4	23	Dallas-Fort Worth-Arlington, TX	275.60	55	22	Fresno, CA	16.4
31	24	San Jose-Sunnyvale-Santa Clara, CA	264.80	19	24	Tampa-St. Petersburg-Clearwater, FL	16.2
6	25	Houston-Sugar Land-Baytown, TX	260.10	52	24	Tucson, AZ	16.2
36	26	Virginia Beach-Norfolk-Newport News, VA-NC	248.40	50	26	Salt Lake City, UT	16.0
9	27	Atlanta-Sandy Springs-Marietta, GA	244	23	27	Portland-Vancouver-Hillsboro, OR-WA	15.5
26	28	Orlando-Kissimmee-Sanford, FL	236.90	34	28	Indianapolis-Carmel, IN	15.2
15	29	Seattle-Tacoma-Bellevue, WA	226.20	43	29	Richmond, VA	14.7
33	30	Charlotte-Gastonia-Rock Hill, NC-SC	220	74	30	Little Rock-North Little Rock-Conway, AR	14.6
64	31	Allentown-Bethlehem-Easton, PA-NJ	218.20	44	31	Oklahoma City, OK	14.4
16	32	Minneapolis-St. Paul-Bloomington, MN	210.10	32	32	Columbus, OH	13.9
73	33	North Port-Bradenton-Sarasota, FL	208.80	65	33	Baton Rouge, LA	13.7
48	34	Raleigh-Cary, NC	206.10	75	34	Knoxville, TN	13.3
67	35	Worcester, MA	204.10	15	35	Seattle-Tacoma-Bellevue, WA	13.0
61	36	Dayton, OH	190.50	59	36	Omaha-Council Bluffs, NE-IA	12.8
68	37	McAllen-Edinburg-Mission, TX	190.40	71	37	Greensboro-High Point, NC	12.5
27	38	Cincinnati-Middletown, OH-KY-IN	187.30	8	38	Miami-Fort Lauderdale-Pompano Beach, FL	11.1
32	39	Columbus, OH	178.70	29	39	Kansas City, MO-KS	10.9
34	40	Indianapolis-Carmel, IN	175.90	64	39	Allentown-Bethlehem-Easton, PA-NJ	10.9
63	41	Oxnard-Thousand Oaks-Ventura, CA	172.50	16	41	Minneapolis-St. Paul-Bloomington, MN	10.5
22	42	Pittsburgh, PA	172.30	42	41	Louisville-Jefferson County, KY-IN	10.5
24	43	Sacramento—Arden-Arcade—Roseville, CA	162.90	17	43	San Diego-Carlsbad-San Marcos, CA	10.0
40	44	Jacksonville, FL	162.30	63	44	Oxnard-Thousand Oaks-Ventura, CA	9.3
35	45	Austin-Round Rock-San Marcos, TX	157	41	45	Memphis, TN-MS-AR	9.2
46	46	New Orleans-Metairie-Kenner, LA	152.30	54	46	Tulsa, OK	9.1
75	47	Knoxville, TN	145.20	53	47	Honolulu, HI	8.8
71	48	Greensboro-High Point, NC	140.20	49	48	Birmingham-Hoover, AL	7.2
51	49	Rochester, NY	139	67	49	Worcester, MA	6.3
23	50	Portland-Vancouver-Hillsboro, OR-WA	128.60	20	50	Baltimore-Towson, MD	6.2
18	51	St. Louis, MO-IL	125.90	27	51	Cincinnati-Middletown, OH-KY-IN	6.0
42	52	Louisville-Jefferson County, KY-IN	120.60	36	51	Virginia Beach-Norfolk-Newport News, VA-NC	6.0
58	53	Albany-Schenectady-Troy, NY	119.60	31	53	San Jose-Sunnyvale-Santa Clara, CA	5.8
21	54	Denver-Aurora-Broomfield, CO	117.70	45	54	Hartford-West Hartford-East Hartford, CT	5.6
25	55	San Antonio-New Braunfels, TX	113.10	58	55	Albany-Schenectady-Troy, NY	5.4
14	56	Phoenix-Mesa-Glendale, AZ	111.10	11	56	San Francisco-Oakland-Fremont, CA	5.1
41	57	Memphis, TN-MS-AR	111	5	57	Philadelphia-Camden-Wilmington, PA-NJ-DE-MD	4.9
38	58	Nashville-Davidson—Murfreesboro—Franklin, TN	107.90	60	58	New Haven-Milford, CT	4.7
69	59	Grand Rapids-Wyoming, MI	107.30	69	59	Grand Rapids-Wyoming, MI	4.5
29	60	Kansas City, MO-KS	100.40	18	60	St. Louis, MO-IL	4.2
30	61	Las Vegas-Paradise, NV	95.50	3	61	Chicago-Joliet-Naperville, IL-IN-WI	4.0
44	62	Oklahoma City, OK	87.80	56	62	Bridgeport-Stamford-Norwalk, CT	3.9
43	63	Richmond, VA	85.50	2	63	Los Angeles-Long Beach-Santa Ana, CA	3.7
49	64	Birmingham-Hoover, AL	82.50	10	63	Boston-Cambridge-Quincy, MA-NH	3.7
70	65	Columbia, SC	80	39	63	Milwaukee-Waukesha-West Allis, WI	3.7
65	66	Baton Rouge, LA	76.90	1	66	New York-Northern New Jersey-Long Island, NY-NJ-PA	3.1
59	67	Omaha-Council Bluffs, NE-IA	76.80	51	67	Rochester, NY	1.6
74	68	Little Rock-North Little Rock-Conway, AR	66.10	72	68	Akron, OH	1.2
55	69	Fresno, CA	60.30	37	69	Providence-New Bedford-Fall River, RI-MA	1.1
13	70	Riverside-San Bernardino-Ontario, CA	59.80	61	70	Dayton, OH	-0.8
54	71	Tulsa, OK	57.70	47	71	Buffalo-Niagara Falls, NY	-3.0
50	72	Salt Lake City, UT	45.40	22	72	Pittsburgh, PA	-3.1
52	73	Tucson, AZ	41.20	28	73	Cleveland-Elyria-Mentor, OH	-3.3
62	74	Bakersfield-Delano, CA	39.90	12	74	Detroit-Warren-Livonia, MI	-3.5
57	75	Albuquerque, NM	36.90	46	75	New Orleans-Metairie-Kenner, LA	-11.3

75 Largest Metropolitan Areas by 2010 Population
Selected Rankings

	Percent White, not Hispanic or Latino, alone or in combination, 2010				Percent Black, not Hispanic or Latino, alone or in combination, 2010		
Popu-lation rank	White rank	Metropolitan area	Percent White [col 5]	Popu-lation rank	Black rank	Metropolitan area	Percent Black [col 6]
22	1	Pittsburgh, PA	88.3	41	1	Memphis, TN-MS-AR	46.1
75	1	Knoxville, TN	88.3	65	2	Baton Rouge, LA	36.0
58	3	Albany-Schenectady-Troy, NY	84.6	46	3	New Orleans-Metairie-Kenner, LA	34.3
72	4	Akron, OH	84.0	70	4	Columbia, SC	33.8
27	5	Cincinnati-Middletown, OH-KY-IN	83.1	9	5	Atlanta-Sandy Springs-Marietta, GA	32.9
67	6	Worcester, MA	82.2	36	6	Virginia Beach-Norfolk-Newport News, VA-NC	32.2
69	7	Grand Rapids-Wyoming, MI	81.3	43	7	Richmond, VA	30.6
37	8	Providence-New Bedford-Fall River, RI-MA	81.1	20	8	Baltimore-Towson, MD	29.6
47	9	Buffalo-Niagara Falls, NY	80.9	49	9	Birmingham-Hoover, AL	28.6
61	10	Dayton, OH	80.7	7	10	Washington-Arlington-Alexandria, DC-VA-MD-WV	26.5
73	10	North Port-Bradenton-Sarasota, FL	80.7	71	11	Greensboro-High Point, NC	26.3
16	12	Minneapolis-St. Paul-Bloomington, MN	80.6	33	12	Charlotte-Gastonia-Rock Hill, NC-SC	24.6
42	13	Louisville-Jefferson County, KY-IN	80.4	12	13	Detroit-Warren-Livonia, MI	23.6
59	13	Omaha-Council Bluffs, NE-IA	80.4	74	14	Little Rock-North Little Rock-Conway, AR	22.8
64	15	Allentown-Bethlehem-Easton, PA-NJ	79.9	40	15	Jacksonville, FL	22.2
51	16	Rochester, NY	79.7	5	16	Philadelphia-Camden-Wilmington, PA-NJ-DE-MD	21.2
23	17	Portland-Vancouver-Hillsboro, OR-WA	79.2	28	17	Cleveland-Elyria-Mentor, OH	20.7
32	18	Columbus, OH	77.9	48	17	Raleigh-Cary, NC	20.7
50	19	Salt Lake City, UT	76.6	8	19	Miami-Fort Lauderdale-Pompano Beach, FL	20.4
18	20	St. Louis, MO-IL	76.5	18	20	St. Louis, MO-IL	19.1
10	21	Boston-Cambridge-Quincy, MA-NH	76.3	3	21	Chicago-Joliet-Naperville, IL-IN-WI	17.6
29	21	Kansas City, MO-KS	76.3	39	22	Milwaukee-Waukesha-West Allis, WI	17.4
34	23	Indianapolis-Carmel, IN	76.2	6	23	Houston-Sugar Land-Baytown, TX	17.3
38	24	Nashville-Davidson—Murfreesboro—Franklin, TN	75.4	1	24	New York-Northern New Jersey-Long Island, NY-NJ-PA	16.8
28	25	Cleveland-Elyria-Mentor, OH	73.1	32	25	Columbus, OH	16.1
54	26	Tulsa, OK	73.0	61	25	Dayton, OH	16.1
45	27	Hartford-West Hartford-East Hartford, CT	72.9	26	27	Orlando-Kissimmee-Sanford, FL	15.9
15	28	Seattle-Tacoma-Bellevue, WA	71.8	34	27	Indianapolis-Carmel, IN	15.9
44	29	Oklahoma City, OK	71.2	38	27	Nashville-Davidson—Murfreesboro—Franklin, TN	15.9
74	30	Little Rock-North Little Rock-Conway, AR	70.9	4	30	Dallas-Fort Worth-Arlington, TX	15.4
39	31	Milwaukee-Waukesha-West Allis, WI	70.4	42	31	Louisville-Jefferson County, KY-IN	14.6
12	32	Detroit-Warren-Livonia, MI	69.5	29	32	Kansas City, MO-KS	13.4
19	33	Tampa-St. Petersburg-Clearwater, FL	69.0	72	33	Akron, OH	13.0
60	34	New Haven-Milford, CT	68.9	27	34	Cincinnati-Middletown, OH-KY-IN	12.8
21	35	Denver-Aurora-Broomfield, CO	67.6	60	34	New Haven-Milford, CT	12.8
40	36	Jacksonville, FL	67.5	47	36	Buffalo-Niagara Falls, NY	12.7
56	37	Bridgeport-Stamford-Norwalk, CT	67.4	19	37	Tampa-St. Petersburg-Clearwater, FL	12.0
5	38	Philadelphia-Camden-Wilmington, PA-NJ-DE-MD	66.3	51	37	Rochester, NY	12.0
49	39	Birmingham-Hoover, AL	65.9	44	39	Oklahoma City, OK	11.6
48	40	Raleigh-Cary, NC	64.9	30	40	Las Vegas-Paradise, NV	11.2
71	41	Greensboro-High Point, NC	63.4	45	41	Hartford-West Hartford-East Hartford, CT	10.9
33	42	Charlotte-Gastonia-Rock Hill, NC-SC	62.6	56	42	Bridgeport-Stamford-Norwalk, CT	10.8
20	43	Baltimore-Towson, MD	61.7	54	43	Tulsa, OK	9.5
43	44	Richmond, VA	61.5	22	44	Pittsburgh, PA	9.2
14	45	Phoenix-Mesa-Glendale, AZ	60.3	11	45	San Francisco-Oakland-Fremont, CA	9.1
70	46	Columbia, SC	59.6	69	46	Grand Rapids-Wyoming, MI	8.9
36	47	Virginia Beach-Norfolk-Newport News, VA-NC	59.5	59	47	Omaha-Council Bluffs, NE-IA	8.8
24	48	Sacramento—Arden-Arcade—Roseville, CA	58.9	16	48	Minneapolis-St. Paul-Bloomington, MN	8.4
65	49	Baton Rouge, LA	58.8	24	49	Sacramento—Arden-Arcade—Roseville, CA	8.3
52	50	Tucson, AZ	56.8	58	49	Albany-Schenectady-Troy, NY	8.3
35	51	Austin-Round Rock-San Marcos, TX	56.2	13	51	Riverside-San Bernardino-Ontario, CA	8.0
3	52	Chicago-Joliet-Naperville, IL-IN-WI	56.1	35	52	Austin-Round Rock-San Marcos, TX	7.6
46	53	New Orleans-Metairie-Kenner, LA	54.9	10	53	Boston-Cambridge-Quincy, MA-NH	7.4
26	54	Orlando-Kissimmee-Sanford, FL	54.6	2	54	Los Angeles-Long Beach-Santa Ana, CA	7.3
9	55	Atlanta-Sandy Springs-Marietta, GA	52.0	75	55	Knoxville, TN	7.1
4	56	Dallas-Fort Worth-Arlington, TX	51.6	73	56	North Port-Bradenton-Sarasota, FL	6.9
17	57	San Diego-Carlsbad-San Marcos, CA	51.1	15	57	Seattle-Tacoma-Bellevue, WA	6.8
7	58	Washington-Arlington-Alexandria, DC-VA-MD-WV	50.7	25	58	San Antonio-New Braunfels, TX	6.6
63	58	Oxnard-Thousand Oaks-Ventura, CA	50.7	21	59	Denver-Aurora-Broomfield, CO	6.1
30	60	Las Vegas-Paradise, NV	50.5	62	60	Bakersfield-Delano, CA	6.0
1	61	New York-Northern New Jersey-Long Island, NY-NJ-PA	49.9	17	61	San Diego-Carlsbad-San Marcos, CA	5.6
41	62	Memphis, TN-MS-AR	47.1	14	62	Phoenix-Mesa-Glendale, AZ	5.4
11	63	San Francisco-Oakland-Fremont, CA	45.4	37	62	Providence-New Bedford-Fall River, RI-MA	5.4
57	64	Albuquerque, NM	43.6	55	62	Fresno, CA	5.4
6	65	Houston-Sugar Land-Baytown, TX	40.7	64	65	Allentown-Bethlehem-Easton, PA-NJ	5.0
62	66	Bakersfield-Delano, CA	40.2	67	66	Worcester, MA	4.3
13	67	Riverside-San Bernardino-Ontario, CA	38.4	52	67	Tucson, AZ	3.8
31	68	San Jose-Sunnyvale-Santa Clara, CA	37.8	23	68	Portland-Vancouver-Hillsboro, OR-WA	3.6
25	69	San Antonio-New Braunfels, TX	37.2	53	69	Honolulu, HI	3.0
8	70	Miami-Fort Lauderdale-Pompano Beach, FL	35.6	66	70	El Paso, TX	2.9
55	71	Fresno, CA	34.2	31	71	San Jose-Sunnyvale-Santa Clara, CA	2.8
2	72	Los Angeles-Long Beach-Santa Ana, CA	33.3	57	71	Albuquerque, NM	2.8
53	73	Honolulu, HI	32.3	63	73	Oxnard-Thousand Oaks-Ventura, CA	2.1
66	74	El Paso, TX	13.7	50	74	Salt Lake City, UT	1.8
68	75	McAllen-Edinburg-Mission, TX	7.9	68	75	McAllen-Edinburg-Mission, TX	0.4

75 Largest Metropolitan Areas by 2010 Population
Selected Rankings

Percent American Indian, Alaska Native, alone or in combination, 2010				Percent Asian and Pacific Islander, alone or in combination, 2010			
Population rank	American Indian Alaska native rank	Metropolitan area	Percent American Indian, Alaska Native [col 7]	Population rank	Asian and Pacific Islander rank	Metropolitan area	Percent Asian and Pacific Islander [col 8]
54	1	Tulsa, OK	12.6	53	1	Honolulu, HI	79.7
44	2	Oklahoma City, OK	6.6	31	2	San Jose-Sunnyvale-Santa Clara, CA	33.7
57	3	Albuquerque, NM	5.7	11	3	San Francisco-Oakland-Fremont, CA	26.4
52	4	Tucson, AZ	3.0	2	4	Los Angeles-Long Beach-Santa Ana, CA	16.2
14	5	Phoenix-Mesa-Glendale, AZ	2.3	15	5	Seattle-Tacoma-Bellevue, WA	14.8
15	6	Seattle-Tacoma-Bellevue, WA	2.0	24	5	Sacramento—Arden-Arcade—Roseville, CA	14.8
23	7	Portland-Vancouver-Hillsboro, OR-WA	1.7	17	7	San Diego-Carlsbad-San Marcos, CA	13.3
24	8	Sacramento—Arden-Arcade—Roseville, CA	1.6	30	8	Las Vegas-Paradise, NV	11.3
53	9	Honolulu, HI	1.5	1	9	New York-Northern New Jersey-Long Island, NY-NJ-PA	10.8
62	9	Bakersfield-Delano, CA	1.5	7	10	Washington-Arlington-Alexandria, DC-VA-MD-WV	10.7
16	11	Minneapolis-St. Paul-Bloomington, MN	1.2	55	11	Fresno, CA	10.4
29	11	Kansas City, MO-KS	1.2	63	12	Oxnard-Thousand Oaks-Ventura, CA	8.3
55	11	Fresno, CA	1.2	23	13	Portland-Vancouver-Hillsboro, OR-WA	7.8
21	14	Denver-Aurora-Broomfield, CO	1.1	13	14	Riverside-San Bernardino-Ontario, CA	7.4
36	14	Virginia Beach-Norfolk-Newport News, VA-NC	1.1	10	15	Boston-Cambridge-Quincy, MA-NH	7.2
47	14	Buffalo-Niagara Falls, NY	1.1	6	16	Houston-Sugar Land-Baytown, TX	7.1
13	17	Riverside-San Bernardino-Ontario, CA	1.0	16	17	Minneapolis-St. Paul-Bloomington, MN	6.6
17	17	San Diego-Carlsbad-San Marcos, CA	1.0	3	18	Chicago-Joliet-Naperville, IL-IN-WI	6.3
30	17	Las Vegas-Paradise, NV	1.0	4	19	Dallas-Fort Worth-Arlington, TX	6.0
50	17	Salt Lake City, UT	1.0	5	20	Philadelphia-Camden-Wilmington, PA-NJ-DE-MD	5.6
59	17	Omaha-Council Bluffs, NE-IA	1.0	35	20	Austin-Round Rock-San Marcos, TX	5.6
69	17	Grand Rapids-Wyoming, MI	1.0	50	20	Salt Lake City, UT	5.6
71	17	Greensboro-High Point, NC	1.0	9	23	Atlanta-Sandy Springs-Marietta, GA	5.5
74	17	Little Rock-North Little Rock-Conway, AR	1.0	20	24	Baltimore-Towson, MD	5.4
4	25	Dallas-Fort Worth-Arlington, TX	0.9	56	25	Bridgeport-Stamford-Norwalk, CT	5.3
11	25	San Francisco-Oakland-Fremont, CA	0.9	48	26	Raleigh-Cary, NC	5.1
12	25	Detroit-Warren-Livonia, MI	0.9	26	27	Orlando-Kissimmee-Sanford, FL	4.8
33	25	Charlotte-Gastonia-Rock Hill, NC-SC	0.9	62	27	Bakersfield-Delano, CA	4.8
37	25	Providence-New Bedford-Fall River, RI-MA	0.9	21	29	Denver-Aurora-Broomfield, CO	4.7
39	25	Milwaukee-Waukesha-West Allis, WI	0.9	36	29	Virginia Beach-Norfolk-Newport News, VA-NC	4.7
43	25	Richmond, VA	0.9	67	31	Worcester, MA	4.6
20	32	Baltimore-Towson, MD	0.8	45	32	Hartford-West Hartford-East Hartford, CT	4.5
32	32	Columbus, OH	0.8	40	33	Jacksonville, FL	4.4
35	32	Austin-Round Rock-San Marcos, TX	0.8	14	34	Phoenix-Mesa-Glendale, AZ	4.3
40	32	Jacksonville, FL	0.8	12	35	Detroit-Warren-Livonia, MI	4.0
46	32	New Orleans-Metairie-Kenner, LA	0.8	60	35	New Haven-Milford, CT	4.0
48	32	Raleigh-Cary, NC	0.8	32	37	Columbus, OH	3.8
61	32	Dayton, OH	0.8	43	37	Richmond, VA	3.8
63	32	Oxnard-Thousand Oaks-Ventura, CA	0.8	58	37	Albany-Schenectady-Troy, NY	3.8
70	32	Columbia, SC	0.8	33	40	Charlotte-Gastonia-Rock Hill, NC-SC	3.7
75	32	Knoxville, TN	0.8	19	41	Tampa-St. Petersburg-Clearwater, FL	3.6
7	42	Washington-Arlington-Alexandria, DC-VA-MD-WV	0.7	44	41	Oklahoma City, OK	3.6
9	42	Atlanta-Sandy Springs-Marietta, GA	0.7	39	43	Milwaukee-Waukesha-West Allis, WI	3.5
18	42	St. Louis, MO-IL	0.7	52	43	Tucson, AZ	3.5
19	42	Tampa-St. Petersburg-Clearwater, FL	0.7	71	45	Greensboro-High Point, NC	3.4
38	42	Nashville-Davidson—Murfreesboro—Franklin, TN	0.7	46	46	New Orleans-Metairie-Kenner, LA	3.2
42	42	Louisville-Jefferson County, KY-IN	0.7	37	47	Providence-New Bedford-Fall River, RI-MA	3.1
51	42	Rochester, NY	0.7	51	47	Rochester, NY	3.1
58	42	Albany-Schenectady-Troy, NY	0.7	29	49	Kansas City, MO-KS	3.0
72	42	Akron, OH	0.7	64	50	Allentown-Bethlehem-Easton, PA-NJ	2.9
2	51	Los Angeles-Long Beach-Santa Ana, CA	0.6	8	51	Miami-Fort Lauderdale-Pompano Beach, FL	2.8
5	51	Philadelphia-Camden-Wilmington, PA-NJ-DE-MD	0.6	34	51	Indianapolis-Carmel, IN	2.8
6	51	Houston-Sugar Land-Baytown, TX	0.6	38	51	Nashville-Davidson—Murfreesboro—Franklin, TN	2.8
25	51	San Antonio-New Braunfels, TX	0.6	18	54	St. Louis, MO-IL	2.7
26	51	Orlando-Kissimmee-Sanford, FL	0.6	25	54	San Antonio-New Braunfels, TX	2.7
27	51	Cincinnati-Middletown, OH-KY-IN	0.6	47	54	Buffalo-Niagara Falls, NY	2.7
28	51	Cleveland-Elyria-Mentor, OH	0.6	59	54	Omaha-Council Bluffs, NE-IA	2.7
31	51	San Jose-Sunnyvale-Santa Clara, CA	0.6	57	58	Albuquerque, NM	2.6
34	51	Indianapolis-Carmel, IN	0.6	72	59	Akron, OH	2.5
41	51	Memphis, TN-MS-AR	0.6	27	60	Cincinnati-Middletown, OH-KY-IN	2.4
49	51	Birmingham-Hoover, AL	0.6	28	60	Cleveland-Elyria-Mentor, OH	2.4
60	51	New Haven-Milford, CT	0.6	61	60	Dayton, OH	2.4
65	51	Baton Rouge, LA	0.6	69	60	Grand Rapids-Wyoming, MI	2.4
67	51	Worcester, MA	0.6	41	64	Memphis, TN-MS-AR	2.3
1	65	New York-Northern New Jersey-Long Island, NY-NJ-PA	0.5	54	64	Tulsa, OK	2.3
10	65	Boston-Cambridge-Quincy, MA-NH	0.5	70	66	Columbia, SC	2.2
22	65	Pittsburgh, PA	0.5	22	67	Pittsburgh, PA	2.1
45	65	Hartford-West Hartford-East Hartford, CT	0.5	65	67	Baton Rouge, LA	2.1
73	65	North Port-Bradenton-Sarasota, FL	0.5	42	69	Louisville-Jefferson County, KY-IN	2.0
3	70	Chicago-Joliet-Naperville, IL-IN-WI	0.4	73	70	North Port-Bradenton-Sarasota, FL	1.9
56	70	Bridgeport-Stamford-Norwalk, CT	0.4	74	70	Little Rock-North Little Rock-Conway, AR	1.9
64	70	Allentown-Bethlehem-Easton, PA-NJ	0.4	75	72	Knoxville, TN	1.8
66	70	El Paso, TX	0.4	49	73	Birmingham-Hoover, AL	1.5
8	74	Miami-Fort Lauderdale-Pompano Beach, FL	0.3	66	74	El Paso, TX	1.4
68	75	McAllen-Edinburg-Mission, TX	0.1	68	75	McAllen-Edinburg-Mission, TX	1.0

75 Largest Metropolitan Areas by 2010 Population
Selected Rankings

Percent Hispanic or Latino,[1] 2010				Percent under 18 years old, 2010			
Population rank	Hispanic or Latino rank	Metropolitan area	Percent Hispanic or Latino [col 9]	Population rank	Under 18 years old rank	Metropolitan area	Percent Under 18 years old [cols 10 and 11]
68	1	McAllen-Edinburg-Mission, TX	90.6	68	1	McAllen-Edinburg-Mission, TX	34.6
66	2	El Paso, TX	82.2	62	2	Bakersfield-Delano, CA	30.3
25	3	San Antonio-New Braunfels, TX	54.1	66	3	El Paso, TX	30.1
55	4	Fresno, CA	50.3	55	4	Fresno, CA	29.8
62	5	Bakersfield-Delano, CA	49.2	50	5	Salt Lake City, UT	29.5
13	6	Riverside-San Bernardino-Ontario, CA	47.3	13	6	Riverside-San Bernardino-Ontario, CA	28.7
57	7	Albuquerque, NM	46.7	6	7	Houston-Sugar Land-Baytown, TX	27.9
2	8	Los Angeles-Long Beach-Santa Ana, CA	44.4	4	8	Dallas-Fort Worth-Arlington, TX	27.8
8	9	Miami-Fort Lauderdale-Pompano Beach, FL	41.6	25	9	San Antonio-New Braunfels, TX	26.8
63	10	Oxnard-Thousand Oaks-Ventura, CA	40.3	41	10	Memphis, TN-MS-AR	26.6
6	11	Houston-Sugar Land-Baytown, TX	35.3	9	11	Atlanta-Sandy Springs-Marietta, GA	26.5
52	12	Tucson, AZ	34.6	14	11	Phoenix-Mesa-Glendale, AZ	26.5
17	13	San Diego-Carlsbad-San Marcos, CA	32.0	59	13	Omaha-Council Bluffs, NE-IA	26.2
35	14	Austin-Round Rock-San Marcos, TX	31.4	34	14	Indianapolis-Carmel, IN	26.2
14	15	Phoenix-Mesa-Glendale, AZ	29.5	48	14	Raleigh-Cary, NC	26.2
30	16	Las Vegas-Paradise, NV	29.1	33	16	Charlotte-Gastonia-Rock Hill, NC-SC	25.9
31	17	San Jose-Sunnyvale-Santa Clara, CA	27.8	69	16	Grand Rapids-Wyoming, MI	25.9
4	18	Dallas-Fort Worth-Arlington, TX	27.5	29	18	Kansas City, MO-KS	25.7
26	19	Orlando-Kissimmee-Sanford, FL	25.2	63	18	Oxnard-Thousand Oaks-Ventura, CA	25.7
1	20	New York-Northern New Jersey-Long Island, NY-NJ-PA	22.9	54	20	Tulsa, OK	25.6
21	21	Denver-Aurora-Broomfield, CO	22.5	35	21	Austin-Round Rock-San Marcos, TX	25.3
11	22	San Francisco-Oakland-Fremont, CA	21.7	3	22	Chicago-Joliet-Naperville, IL-IN-WI	25.1
3	23	Chicago-Joliet-Naperville, IL-IN-WI	20.7	16	23	Minneapolis-St. Paul-Bloomington, MN	25.0
24	24	Sacramento—Arden-Arcade—Roseville, CA	20.2	27	23	Cincinnati-Middletown, OH-KY-IN	25.0
56	25	Bridgeport-Stamford-Norwalk, CT	16.9	30	23	Las Vegas-Paradise, NV	25.0
50	26	Salt Lake City, UT	16.6	44	23	Oklahoma City, OK	25.0
19	27	Tampa-St. Petersburg-Clearwater, FL	16.2	21	27	Denver-Aurora-Broomfield, CO	24.9
60	28	New Haven-Milford, CT	15.0	24	27	Sacramento—Arden-Arcade—Roseville, CA	24.9
7	29	Washington-Arlington-Alexandria, DC-VA-MD-WV	13.8	56	29	Bridgeport-Stamford-Norwalk, CT	24.8
64	30	Allentown-Bethlehem-Easton, PA-NJ	13.0	32	30	Columbus, OH	24.7
45	31	Hartford-West Hartford-East Hartford, CT	12.5	65	30	Baton Rouge, LA	24.7
44	32	Oklahoma City, OK	11.3	39	32	Milwaukee-Waukesha-West Allis, WI	24.7
73	33	North Port-Bradenton-Sarasota, FL	11.1	57	33	Albuquerque, NM	24.6
23	34	Portland-Vancouver-Hillsboro, OR-WA	10.9	74	34	Little Rock-North Little Rock-Conway, AR	24.5
9	35	Atlanta-Sandy Springs-Marietta, GA	10.4	2	35	Los Angeles-Long Beach-Santa Ana, CA	24.4
37	36	Providence-New Bedford-Fall River, RI-MA	10.2	38	35	Nashville-Davidson—Murfreesboro—Franklin, TN	24.4
48	37	Raleigh-Cary, NC	10.1	12	37	Detroit-Warren-Livonia, MI	24.3
33	38	Charlotte-Gastonia-Rock Hill, NC-SC	9.8	31	37	San Jose-Sunnyvale-Santa Clara, CA	24.3
39	39	Milwaukee-Waukesha-West Allis, WI	9.5	42	39	Louisville-Jefferson County, KY-IN	24.0
67	40	Worcester, MA	9.4	49	40	Birmingham-Hoover, AL	23.9
10	41	Boston-Cambridge-Quincy, MA-NH	9.0	7	41	Washington-Arlington-Alexandria, DC-VA-MD-WV	23.8
15	41	Seattle-Tacoma-Bellevue, WA	9.0	18	41	St. Louis, MO-IL	23.8
59	41	Omaha-Council Bluffs, NE-IA	9.0	40	41	Jacksonville, FL	23.8
54	44	Tulsa, OK	8.4	23	44	Portland-Vancouver-Hillsboro, OR-WA	23.7
69	44	Grand Rapids-Wyoming, MI	8.4	36	45	Virginia Beach-Norfolk-Newport News, VA-NC	23.5
29	46	Kansas City, MO-KS	8.2	67	45	Worcester, MA	23.5
53	47	Honolulu, HI	8.1	70	45	Columbia, SC	23.5
46	48	New Orleans-Metairie-Kenner, LA	7.9	71	45	Greensboro-High Point, NC	23.5
5	49	Philadelphia-Camden-Wilmington, PA-NJ-DE-MD	7.8	17	49	San Diego-Carlsbad-San Marcos, CA	23.4
71	50	Greensboro-High Point, NC	7.6	26	49	Orlando-Kissimmee-Sanford, FL	23.4
40	51	Jacksonville, FL	6.9	46	49	New Orleans-Metairie-Kenner, LA	23.4
38	52	Nashville-Davidson—Murfreesboro—Franklin, TN	6.6	5	52	Philadelphia-Camden-Wilmington, PA-NJ-DE-MD	23.3
34	53	Indianapolis-Carmel, IN	6.2	43	52	Richmond, VA	23.3
51	54	Rochester, NY	6.1	28	54	Cleveland-Elyria-Mentor, OH	23.1
16	55	Minneapolis-St. Paul-Bloomington, MN	5.4	20	55	Baltimore-Towson, MD	23.0
36	55	Virginia Beach-Norfolk-Newport News, VA-NC	5.4	52	55	Tucson, AZ	23.0
70	57	Columbia, SC	5.1	61	55	Dayton, OH	23.0
41	58	Memphis, TN-MS-AR	5.0	15	58	Seattle-Tacoma-Bellevue, WA	22.9
43	58	Richmond, VA	5.0	1	59	New York-Northern New Jersey-Long Island, NY-NJ-PA	22.8
74	60	Little Rock-North Little Rock-Conway, AR	4.8	64	60	Allentown-Bethlehem-Easton, PA-NJ	22.7
28	61	Cleveland-Elyria-Mentor, OH	4.7	51	61	Rochester, NY	22.6
20	62	Baltimore-Towson, MD	4.6	60	62	New Haven-Milford, CT	22.3
49	63	Birmingham-Hoover, AL	4.3	72	62	Akron, OH	22.3
47	64	Buffalo-Niagara Falls, NY	4.1	45	64	Hartford-West Hartford-East Hartford, CT	22.2
58	64	Albany-Schenectady-Troy, NY	4.1	53	65	Honolulu, HI	22.1
12	66	Detroit-Warren-Livonia, MI	3.9	75	66	Knoxville, TN	21.9
42	66	Louisville-Jefferson County, KY-IN	3.9	8	67	Miami-Fort Lauderdale-Pompano Beach, FL	21.6
32	68	Columbus, OH	3.6	10	67	Boston-Cambridge-Quincy, MA-NH	21.6
65	69	Baton Rouge, LA	3.4	37	67	Providence-New Bedford-Fall River, RI-MA	21.6
75	69	Knoxville, TN	3.4	47	67	Buffalo-Niagara Falls, NY	21.6
18	71	St. Louis, MO-IL	2.6	58	71	Albany-Schenectady-Troy, NY	21.4
27	71	Cincinnati-Middletown, OH-KY-IN	2.6	11	72	San Francisco-Oakland-Fremont, CA	21.2
61	73	Dayton, OH	2.0	19	72	Tampa-St. Petersburg-Clearwater, FL	21.2
72	74	Akron, OH	1.5	22	74	Pittsburgh, PA	20.1
22	75	Pittsburgh, PA	1.3	73	75	North Port-Bradenton-Sarasota, FL	18.0

1. May be of any race.

75 Largest Metropolitan Areas by 2010 Population
Selected Rankings

Percent 65 years old and over, 2010				Percent female-headed family households, 2010			
Population rank	65 years old and over rank	Metropolitan area	Percent 65 years old and over [cols 17 + 18]	Population rank	Female households rank	Metropolitan area	Percent female households [col 30]
73	1	North Port-Bradenton-Sarasota, FL	27.6	41	1	Memphis, TN-MS-AR	20.3
19	2	Tampa-St. Petersburg-Clearwater, FL	17.3	66	1	El Paso, TX	20.3
22	2	Pittsburgh, PA	17.3	68	3	McAllen-Edinburg-Mission, TX	18.8
8	4	Miami-Fort Lauderdale-Pompano Beach, FL	16.0	46	4	New Orleans-Metairie-Kenner, LA	17.4
47	5	Buffalo-Niagara Falls, NY	15.8	65	5	Baton Rouge, LA	17.0
52	6	Tucson, AZ	15.4	55	6	Fresno, CA	16.9
28	7	Cleveland-Elyria-Mentor, OH	15.2	8	7	Miami-Fort Lauderdale-Pompano Beach, FL	15.8
64	7	Allentown-Bethlehem-Easton, PA-NJ	15.2	36	7	Virginia Beach-Norfolk-Newport News, VA-NC	15.8
61	9	Dayton, OH	14.9	70	7	Columbia, SC	15.8
75	10	Knoxville, TN	14.7	62	10	Bakersfield-Delano, CA	15.7
53	11	Honolulu, HI	14.5	25	11	San Antonio-New Braunfels, TX	15.5
37	12	Providence-New Bedford-Fall River, RI-MA	14.4	1	12	New York-Northern New Jersey-Long Island, NY-NJ-PA	15.3
45	13	Hartford-West Hartford-East Hartford, CT	14.3	9	12	Atlanta-Sandy Springs-Marietta, GA	15.3
60	13	New Haven-Milford, CT	14.3	12	12	Detroit-Warren-Livonia, MI	15.3
72	15	Akron, OH	14.2	49	12	Birmingham-Hoover, AL	15.3
51	16	Rochester, NY	14.1	20	16	Baltimore-Towson, MD	15.2
58	17	Albany-Schenectady-Troy, NY	14.0	5	17	Philadelphia-Camden-Wilmington, PA-NJ-DE-MD	14.8
56	18	Bridgeport-Stamford-Norwalk, CT	13.5	40	17	Jacksonville, FL	14.8
18	19	St. Louis, MO-IL	13.4	13	19	Riverside-San Bernardino-Ontario, CA	14.7
5	20	Philadelphia-Camden-Wilmington, PA-NJ-DE-MD	13.3	28	19	Cleveland-Elyria-Mentor, OH	14.7
12	21	Detroit-Warren-Livonia, MI	13.2	43	19	Richmond, VA	14.7
71	21	Greensboro-High Point, NC	13.2	26	22	Orlando-Kissimmee-Sanford, FL	14.6
10	23	Boston-Cambridge-Quincy, MA-NH	13.1	2	23	Los Angeles-Long Beach-Santa Ana, CA	14.5
1	24	New York-Northern New Jersey-Long Island, NY-NJ-PA	13.1	60	23	New Haven-Milford, CT	14.5
49	25	Birmingham-Hoover, AL	13.0	71	25	Greensboro-High Point, NC	14.4
42	26	Louisville-Jefferson County, KY-IN	12.8	74	25	Little Rock-North Little Rock-Conway, AR	14.4
54	26	Tulsa, OK	12.8	6	27	Houston-Sugar Land-Baytown, TX	14.3
20	28	Baltimore-Towson, MD	12.7	33	28	Charlotte-Gastonia-Rock Hill, NC-SC	14.1
67	28	Worcester, MA	12.7	42	29	Louisville-Jefferson County, KY-IN	13.9
11	30	San Francisco-Oakland-Fremont, CA	12.6	57	30	Albuquerque, NM	13.8
39	31	Milwaukee-Waukesha-West Allis, WI	12.5	3	31	Chicago-Joliet-Naperville, IL-IN-WI	13.7
26	32	Orlando-Kissimmee-Sanford, FL	12.4	18	31	St. Louis, MO-IL	13.7
14	33	Phoenix-Mesa-Glendale, AZ	12.3	37	31	Providence-New Bedford-Fall River, RI-MA	13.7
27	33	Cincinnati-Middletown, OH-KY-IN	12.3	61	34	Dayton, OH	13.6
57	33	Albuquerque, NM	12.3	30	35	Las Vegas-Paradise, NV	13.5
74	36	Little Rock-North Little Rock-Conway, AR	12.2	34	35	Indianapolis-Carmel, IN	13.5
40	37	Jacksonville, FL	12.1	47	35	Buffalo-Niagara Falls, NY	13.5
43	37	Richmond, VA	12.1	4	38	Dallas-Fort Worth-Arlington, TX	13.4
46	37	New Orleans-Metairie-Kenner, LA	12.1	39	38	Milwaukee-Waukesha-West Allis, WI	13.4
24	40	Sacramento—Arden-Arcade—Roseville, CA	12.0	51	40	Rochester, NY	13.2
29	40	Kansas City, MO-KS	12.0	45	41	Hartford-West Hartford-East Hartford, CT	13.1
44	42	Oklahoma City, OK	11.7	24	42	Sacramento—Arden-Arcade—Roseville, CA	13.0
63	42	Oxnard-Thousand Oaks-Ventura, CA	11.7	27	42	Cincinnati-Middletown, OH-KY-IN	13.0
69	44	Grand Rapids-Wyoming, MI	11.6	72	42	Akron, OH	13.0
36	45	Virginia Beach-Norfolk-Newport News, VA-NC	11.5	19	45	Tampa-St. Petersburg-Clearwater, FL	12.9
70	45	Columbia, SC	11.5	32	45	Columbus, OH	12.9
3	47	Chicago-Joliet-Naperville, IL-IN-WI	11.4	38	47	Nashville-Davidson—Murfreesboro—Franklin, TN	12.8
17	48	San Diego-Carlsbad-San Marcos, CA	11.3	52	47	Tucson, AZ	12.8
23	48	Portland-Vancouver-Hillsboro, OR-WA	11.3	44	49	Oklahoma City, OK	12.7
30	48	Las Vegas-Paradise, NV	11.3	53	49	Honolulu, HI	12.7
59	51	Omaha-Council Bluffs, NE-IA	11.1	54	51	Tulsa, OK	12.6
31	52	San Jose-Sunnyvale-Santa Clara, CA	11.1	7	52	Washington-Arlington-Alexandria, DC-VA-MD-WV	12.5
2	53	Los Angeles-Long Beach-Santa Ana, CA	11.0	14	53	Phoenix-Mesa-Glendale, AZ	12.4
25	53	San Antonio-New Braunfels, TX	11.0	29	53	Kansas City, MO-KS	12.4
34	55	Indianapolis-Carmel, IN	10.9	56	55	Bridgeport-Stamford-Norwalk, CT	12.3
15	56	Seattle-Tacoma-Bellevue, WA	10.8	67	56	Worcester, MA	12.2
65	56	Baton Rouge, LA	10.8	17	57	San Diego-Carlsbad-San Marcos, CA	12.1
38	58	Nashville-Davidson—Murfreesboro—Franklin, TN	10.7	69	58	Grand Rapids-Wyoming, MI	12.0
16	59	Minneapolis-St. Paul-Bloomington, MN	10.6	10	59	Boston-Cambridge-Quincy, MA-NH	11.9
32	59	Columbus, OH	10.6	63	60	Oxnard-Thousand Oaks-Ventura, CA	11.8
41	61	Memphis, TN-MS-AR	10.6	48	61	Raleigh-Cary, NC	11.7
13	62	Riverside-San Bernardino-Ontario, CA	10.4	58	61	Albany-Schenectady-Troy, NY	11.7
66	63	El Paso, TX	10.2	59	61	Omaha-Council Bluffs, NE-IA	11.7
21	64	Denver-Aurora-Broomfield, CO	10.1	64	61	Allentown-Bethlehem-Easton, PA-NJ	11.7
33	65	Charlotte-Gastonia-Rock Hill, NC-SC	10.1	22	65	Pittsburgh, PA	11.4
7	66	Washington-Arlington-Alexandria, DC-VA-MD-WV	10.0	75	66	Knoxville, TN	11.3
55	66	Fresno, CA	10.0	11	67	San Francisco-Oakland-Fremont, CA	11.2
68	68	McAllen-Edinburg-Mission, TX	9.3	35	68	Austin-Round Rock-San Marcos, TX	10.9
9	69	Atlanta-Sandy Springs-Marietta, GA	9.0	31	69	San Jose-Sunnyvale-Santa Clara, CA	10.8
48	69	Raleigh-Cary, NC	9.0	50	70	Salt Lake City, UT	10.7
62	69	Bakersfield-Delano, CA	9.0	21	71	Denver-Aurora-Broomfield, CO	10.6
4	72	Dallas-Fort Worth-Arlington, TX	8.8	23	72	Portland-Vancouver-Hillsboro, OR-WA	10.5
6	73	Houston-Sugar Land-Baytown, TX	8.6	15	73	Seattle-Tacoma-Bellevue, WA	10.2
50	73	Salt Lake City, UT	8.6	16	73	Minneapolis-St. Paul-Bloomington, MN	10.2
35	75	Austin-Round Rock-San Marcos, TX	8.1	73	75	North Port-Bradenton-Sarasota, FL	9.6

75 Largest Metropolitan Areas by 2010 Population
Selected Rankings

Birth rate, average 2006–2008				Percent under 65 who have no health insurance, 2009			
Population rank	Birth rate rank	Metropolitan area	Births (per 1,000 population) [col 36]	Population rank	No health insurance rank	Metropolitan area	Percent with no health insurance [col 40]
68	1	McAllen-Edinburg-Mission, TX	24.1	68	1	McAllen-Edinburg-Mission, TX	37.9
62	2	Bakersfield-Delano, CA	19.3	66	2	El Paso, TX	31.5
66	2	El Paso, TX	19.3	8	3	Miami-Fort Lauderdale-Pompano Beach, FL	29.7
55	4	Fresno, CA	18.9	6	4	Houston-Sugar Land-Baytown, TX	26.3
50	5	Salt Lake City, UT	18.8	4	5	Dallas-Fort Worth-Arlington, TX	25.5
6	6	Houston-Sugar Land-Baytown, TX	17.0	30	6	Las Vegas-Paradise, NV	24.9
4	7	Dallas-Fort Worth-Arlington, TX	16.9	26	7	Orlando-Kissimmee-Sanford, FL	24.2
13	8	Riverside-San Bernardino-Ontario, CA	16.8	73	8	North Port-Bradenton-Sarasota, FL	23.9
14	8	Phoenix-Mesa-Glendale, AZ	16.8	2	9	Los Angeles-Long Beach-Santa Ana, CA	23.6
30	10	Las Vegas-Paradise, NV	16.5	25	10	San Antonio-New Braunfels, TX	23.4
35	11	Austin-Round Rock-San Marcos, TX	16.2	19	11	Tampa-St. Petersburg-Clearwater, FL	22.2
17	12	San Diego-Carlsbad-San Marcos, CA	15.8	13	12	Riverside-San Bernardino-Ontario, CA	22.0
44	12	Oklahoma City, OK	15.8	35	12	Austin-Round Rock-San Marcos, TX	22.0
33	14	Charlotte-Gastonia-Rock Hill, NC-SC	15.7	62	14	Bakersfield-Delano, CA	21.9
48	14	Raleigh-Cary, NC	15.7	46	15	New Orleans-Metairie-Kenner, LA	21.8
25	16	San Antonio-New Braunfels, TX	15.6	55	16	Fresno, CA	21.7
41	16	Memphis, TN-MS-AR	15.6	9	17	Atlanta-Sandy Springs-Marietta, GA	20.9
31	18	San Jose-Sunnyvale-Santa Clara, CA	15.5	54	18	Tulsa, OK	20.5
34	19	Indianapolis-Carmel, IN	15.4	44	19	Oklahoma City, OK	20.3
9	20	Atlanta-Sandy Springs-Marietta, GA	15.3	14	20	Phoenix-Mesa-Glendale, AZ	20.1
63	20	Oxnard-Thousand Oaks-Ventura, CA	15.3	57	21	Albuquerque, NM	20.0
7	22	Washington-Arlington-Alexandria, DC-VA-MD-WV	15.1	40	22	Jacksonville, FL	19.2
21	22	Denver-Aurora-Broomfield, CO	15.1	71	23	Greensboro-High Point, NC	19.0
53	22	Honolulu, HI	15.1	17	24	San Diego-Carlsbad-San Marcos, CA	18.8
2	25	Los Angeles-Long Beach-Santa Ana, CA	15.0	52	25	Tucson, AZ	18.2
32	25	Columbus, OH	15.0	63	26	Oxnard-Thousand Oaks-Ventura, CA	18.1
69	27	Grand Rapids-Wyoming, MI	14.9	65	27	Baton Rouge, LA	17.6
57	28	Albuquerque, NM	14.7	33	28	Charlotte-Gastonia-Rock Hill, NC-SC	17.1
16	29	Minneapolis-St. Paul-Bloomington, MN	14.6	41	28	Memphis, TN-MS-AR	17.1
40	29	Jacksonville, FL	14.6	23	30	Portland-Vancouver-Hillsboro, OR-WA	16.9
24	31	Sacramento—Arden-Arcade—Roseville, CA	14.5	50	31	Salt Lake City, UT	16.8
74	31	Little Rock-North Little Rock-Conway, AR	14.5	21	32	Denver-Aurora-Broomfield, CO	16.7
3	33	Chicago-Joliet-Naperville, IL-IN-WI	14.4	70	33	Columbia, SC	16.6
26	33	Orlando-Kissimmee-Sanford, FL	14.4	74	34	Little Rock-North Little Rock-Conway, AR	16.1
29	35	Kansas City, MO-KS	14.3	3	35	Chicago-Joliet-Naperville, IL-IN-WI	15.9
38	35	Nashville-Davidson—Murfreesboro—Franklin, TN	14.3	38	36	Nashville-Davidson—Murfreesboro—Franklin, TN	15.3
49	35	Birmingham-Hoover, AL	14.3	34	37	Indianapolis-Carmel, IN	15.2
54	35	Tulsa, OK	14.3	24	38	Sacramento—Arden-Arcade—Roseville, CA	14.9
65	35	Baton Rouge, LA	14.3	48	38	Raleigh-Cary, NC	14.9
39	40	Milwaukee-Waukesha-West Allis, WI	14.1	42	40	Louisville-Jefferson County, KY-IN	14.6
52	40	Tucson, AZ	14.1	1	41	New York-Northern New Jersey-Long Island, NY-NJ-PA	14.5
15	42	Seattle-Tacoma-Bellevue, WA	13.8	49	42	Birmingham-Hoover, AL	14.4
1	43	New York-Northern New Jersey-Long Island, NY-NJ-PA	13.6	12	43	Detroit-Warren-Livonia, MI	14.3
27	43	Cincinnati-Middletown, OH-KY-IN	13.6	32	44	Columbus, OH	14.2
23	45	Portland-Vancouver-Hillsboro, OR-WA	13.5	75	45	Knoxville, TN	14.1
5	46	Philadelphia-Camden-Wilmington, PA-NJ-DE-MD	13.4	29	46	Kansas City, MO-KS	14.0
46	46	New Orleans-Metairie-Kenner, LA	13.4	11	47	San Francisco-Oakland-Fremont, CA	13.9
8	48	Miami-Fort Lauderdale-Pompano Beach, FL	13.3	31	47	San Jose-Sunnyvale-Santa Clara, CA	13.9
11	48	San Francisco-Oakland-Fremont, CA	13.3	61	47	Dayton, OH	13.9
20	48	Baltimore-Towson, MD	13.3	69	47	Grand Rapids-Wyoming, MI	13.9
71	51	Greensboro-High Point, NC	13.2	28	51	Cleveland-Elyria-Mentor, OH	13.8
70	52	Columbia, SC	13.1	36	52	Virginia Beach-Norfolk-Newport News, VA-NC	13.7
56	53	Bridgeport-Stamford-Norwalk, CT	12.8	43	52	Richmond, VA	13.7
19	54	Tampa-St. Petersburg-Clearwater, FL	12.5	15	54	Seattle-Tacoma-Bellevue, WA	13.4
12	55	Detroit-Warren-Livonia, MI	12.4	27	54	Cincinnati-Middletown, OH-KY-IN	13.4
18	55	St. Louis, MO-IL	12.4	72	54	Akron, OH	13.4
67	55	Worcester, MA	12.4	18	57	St. Louis, MO-IL	12.5
61	58	Dayton, OH	12.3	59	58	Omaha-Council Bluffs, NE-IA	12.1
28	59	Cleveland-Elyria-Mentor, OH	12.2	20	59	Baltimore-Towson, MD	12.0
10	60	Boston-Cambridge-Quincy, MA-NH	12.1	7	60	Washington-Arlington-Alexandria, DC-VA-MD-WV	11.8
60	60	New Haven-Milford, CT	12.1	5	61	Philadelphia-Camden-Wilmington, PA-NJ-DE-MD	11.7
64	62	Allentown-Bethlehem-Easton, PA-NJ	11.9	64	61	Allentown-Bethlehem-Easton, PA-NJ	11.7
72	63	Akron, OH	11.7	56	63	Bridgeport-Stamford-Norwalk, CT	11.4
45	64	Hartford-West Hartford-East Hartford, CT	11.3	39	64	Milwaukee-Waukesha-West Allis, WI	11.1
51	65	Rochester, NY	11.2	37	65	Providence-New Bedford-Fall River, RI-MA	10.6
75	65	Knoxville, TN	11.2	22	66	Pittsburgh, PA	10.5
37	67	Providence-New Bedford-Fall River, RI-MA	10.9	60	67	New Haven-Milford, CT	10.3
47	68	Buffalo-Niagara Falls, NY	10.7	47	68	Buffalo-Niagara Falls, NY	9.9
58	68	Albany-Schenectady-Troy, NY	10.7	51	68	Rochester, NY	9.9
73	70	North Port-Bradenton-Sarasota, FL	10.5	58	70	Albany-Schenectady-Troy, NY	9.7
22	71	Pittsburgh, PA	10.4	16	71	Minneapolis-St. Paul-Bloomington, MN	9.6
36	X	Virginia Beach-Norfolk-Newport News, VA-NC	D	45	72	Hartford-West Hartford-East Hartford, CT	9.3
42	X	Louisville-Jefferson County, KY-IN	D	53	73	Honolulu, HI	7.4
43	X	Richmond, VA	D	10	74	Boston-Cambridge-Quincy, MA-NH	5.4
59	X	Omaha-Council Bluffs, NE-IA	D	67	75	Worcester, MA	4.6

75 Largest Metropolitan Areas by 2010 Population
Selected Rankings

Percent college graduates (bachelor's degree or more), 2010

Population rank	Percent college graduates rank	Metropolitan area	Percent college graduates [col 51]
7	1	Washington-Arlington-Alexandria, DC-VA-MD-WV	46.8
31	2	San Jose-Sunnyvale-Santa Clara, CA	45.3
56	3	Bridgeport-Stamford-Norwalk, CT	44.0
11	4	San Francisco-Oakland-Fremont, CA	43.4
10	5	Boston-Cambridge-Quincy, MA-NH	43.0
48	6	Raleigh-Cary, NC	41.0
35	7	Austin-Round Rock-San Marcos, TX	39.4
21	8	Denver-Aurora-Broomfield, CO	38.2
16	9	Minneapolis-St. Paul-Bloomington, MN	37.9
15	10	Seattle-Tacoma-Bellevue, WA	37.0
1	11	New York-Northern New Jersey-Long Island, NY-NJ-PA	36.0
20	12	Baltimore-Towson, MD	35.1
45	13	Hartford-West Hartford-East Hartford, CT	34.6
9	14	Atlanta-Sandy Springs-Marietta, GA	34.1
3	15	Chicago-Joliet-Naperville, IL-IN-WI	34.0
17	16	San Diego-Carlsbad-San Marcos, CA	33.7
58	17	Albany-Schenectady-Troy, NY	33.2
5	18	Philadelphia-Camden-Wilmington, PA-NJ-DE-MD	33.1
23	19	Portland-Vancouver-Hillsboro, OR-WA	33.0
51	19	Rochester, NY	33.0
59	19	Omaha-Council Bluffs, NE-IA	33.0
67	22	Worcester, MA	32.7
29	23	Kansas City, MO-KS	32.5
32	23	Columbus, OH	32.5
33	25	Charlotte-Gastonia-Rock Hill, NC-SC	32.2
53	26	Honolulu, HI	31.9
60	27	New Haven-Milford, CT	31.8
39	28	Milwaukee-Waukesha-West Allis, WI	31.7
43	28	Richmond, VA	31.7
4	30	Dallas-Fort Worth-Arlington, TX	31.1
2	31	Los Angeles-Long Beach-Santa Ana, CA	31.0
63	32	Oxnard-Thousand Oaks-Ventura, CA	30.8
34	33	Indianapolis-Carmel, IN	30.7
52	34	Tucson, AZ	30.0
18	35	St. Louis, MO-IL	29.9
70	36	Columbia, SC	29.8
38	37	Nashville-Davidson—Murfreesboro—Franklin, TN	29.7
24	38	Sacramento—Arden-Arcade—Roseville, CA	29.4
27	39	Cincinnati-Middletown, OH-KY-IN	29.3
57	39	Albuquerque, NM	29.3
22	41	Pittsburgh, PA	29.1
50	42	Salt Lake City, UT	29.0
75	43	Knoxville, TN	28.8
36	44	Virginia Beach-Norfolk-Newport News, VA-NC	28.5
37	44	Providence-New Bedford-Fall River, RI-MA	28.5
72	44	Akron, OH	28.5
6	47	Houston-Sugar Land-Baytown, TX	28.4
47	48	Buffalo-Niagara Falls, NY	28.3
8	49	Miami-Fort Lauderdale-Pompano Beach, FL	28.1
26	49	Orlando-Kissimmee-Sanford, FL	28.1
28	51	Cleveland-Elyria-Mentor, OH	27.7
44	52	Oklahoma City, OK	27.6
12	53	Detroit-Warren-Livonia, MI	27.3
14	54	Phoenix-Mesa-Glendale, AZ	27.2
40	55	Jacksonville, FL	26.9
73	55	North Port-Bradenton-Sarasota, FL	26.9
46	57	New Orleans-Metairie-Kenner, LA	26.8
64	58	Allentown-Bethlehem-Easton, PA-NJ	26.6
65	58	Baton Rouge, LA	26.6
49	60	Birmingham-Hoover, AL	26.3
19	61	Tampa-St. Petersburg-Clearwater, FL	26.2
69	61	Grand Rapids-Wyoming, MI	26.2
74	61	Little Rock-North Little Rock-Conway, AR	26.2
42	64	Louisville-Jefferson County, KY-IN	25.8
71	65	Greensboro-High Point, NC	25.6
25	66	San Antonio-New Braunfels, TX	25.4
41	67	Memphis, TN-MS-AR	25.1
54	68	Tulsa, OK	24.8
61	69	Dayton, OH	24.4
30	70	Las Vegas-Paradise, NV	21.6
55	71	Fresno, CA	20.1
66	72	El Paso, TX	19.6
13	73	Riverside-San Bernardino-Ontario, CA	19.5
68	74	McAllen-Edinburg-Mission, TX	15.8
62	75	Bakersfield-Delano, CA	15.0

Median household income, 2010

Population rank	Median income rank	Metropolitan area	Median income (dollars) [col 55]
7	1	Washington-Arlington-Alexandria, DC-VA-MD-WV	84 523
31	2	San Jose-Sunnyvale-Santa Clara, CA	83 944
56	3	Bridgeport-Stamford-Norwalk, CT	74 831
11	4	San Francisco-Oakland-Fremont, CA	73 027
63	5	Oxnard-Thousand Oaks-Ventura, CA	71 864
53	6	Honolulu, HI	68 537
10	7	Boston-Cambridge-Quincy, MA-NH	68 020
20	8	Baltimore-Towson, MD	64 812
45	9	Hartford-West Hartford-East Hartford, CT	63 104
15	10	Seattle-Tacoma-Bellevue, WA	63 088
16	11	Minneapolis-St. Paul-Bloomington, MN	62 352
1	12	New York-Northern New Jersey-Long Island, NY-NJ-PA	61 927
67	13	Worcester, MA	61 212
17	14	San Diego-Carlsbad-San Marcos, CA	59 923
21	15	Denver-Aurora-Broomfield, CO	58 732
5	16	Philadelphia-Camden-Wilmington, PA-NJ-DE-MD	58 095
48	17	Raleigh-Cary, NC	57 840
50	18	Salt Lake City, UT	57 419
36	19	Virginia Beach-Norfolk-Newport News, VA-NC	57 315
3	20	Chicago-Joliet-Naperville, IL-IN-WI	57 104
60	21	New Haven-Milford, CT	57 056
2	22	Los Angeles-Long Beach-Santa Ana, CA	56 691
24	23	Sacramento—Arden-Arcade—Roseville, CA	56 233
58	24	Albany-Schenectady-Troy, NY	55 796
35	25	Austin-Round Rock-San Marcos, TX	55 744
64	26	Allentown-Bethlehem-Easton, PA-NJ	55 630
43	27	Richmond, VA	55 325
4	28	Dallas-Fort Worth-Arlington, TX	54 449
59	29	Omaha-Council Bluffs, NE-IA	54 060
6	30	Houston-Sugar Land-Baytown, TX	53 942
29	31	Kansas City, MO-KS	53 919
13	32	Riverside-San Bernardino-Ontario, CA	53 548
9	33	Atlanta-Sandy Springs-Marietta, GA	53 182
23	34	Portland-Vancouver-Hillsboro, OR-WA	53 078
37	35	Providence-New Bedford-Fall River, RI-MA	51 935
27	36	Cincinnati-Middletown, OH-KY-IN	51 572
30	37	Las Vegas-Paradise, NV	51 437
32	38	Columbus, OH	51 039
18	39	St. Louis, MO-IL	50 912
33	40	Charlotte-Gastonia-Rock Hill, NC-SC	50 449
14	41	Phoenix-Mesa-Glendale, AZ	50 385
40	42	Jacksonville, FL	50 324
25	43	San Antonio-New Braunfels, TX	50 225
51	44	Rochester, NY	50 211
39	45	Milwaukee-Waukesha-West Allis, WI	49 774
34	46	Indianapolis-Carmel, IN	48 867
65	47	Baton Rouge, LA	48 294
12	48	Detroit-Warren-Livonia, MI	48 198
38	49	Nashville-Davidson—Murfreesboro—Franklin, TN	47 975
57	50	Albuquerque, NM	47 383
69	51	Grand Rapids-Wyoming, MI	47 040
22	52	Pittsburgh, PA	46 700
72	53	Akron, OH	46 521
26	54	Orlando-Kissimmee-Sanford, FL	46 478
47	55	Buffalo-Niagara Falls, NY	46 420
44	56	Oklahoma City, OK	46 238
28	57	Cleveland-Elyria-Mentor, OH	46 231
46	58	New Orleans-Metairie-Kenner, LA	46 134
74	59	Little Rock-North Little Rock-Conway, AR	45 991
70	60	Columbia, SC	45 929
62	61	Bakersfield-Delano, CA	45 524
41	62	Memphis, TN-MS-AR	45 377
8	63	Miami-Fort Lauderdale-Pompano Beach, FL	45 352
73	64	North Port-Bradenton-Sarasota, FL	45 283
55	65	Fresno, CA	45 221
42	66	Louisville-Jefferson County, KY-IN	44 678
54	67	Tulsa, OK	44 519
52	68	Tucson, AZ	44 274
49	69	Birmingham-Hoover, AL	44 216
61	70	Dayton, OH	43 832
19	71	Tampa-St. Petersburg-Clearwater, FL	43 547
75	72	Knoxville, TN	43 114
71	73	Greensboro-High Point, NC	41 120
66	74	El Paso, TX	36 015
68	75	McAllen-Edinburg-Mission, TX	33 732

75 Largest Metropolitan Areas by 2010 Population
Selected Rankings

Percent of population below the poverty level, 2010				Percent of children under 18 years old below the poverty level, 2010			
Population rank	Poverty rate rank	Metropolitan area	Poverty rate [col 59]	Population rank	Poverty rate rank	Metropolitan area	Poverty rate [col 60]
68	1	McAllen-Edinburg-Mission, TX	33.4	68	1	McAllen-Edinburg-Mission, TX	45.3
55	2	Fresno, CA	26.8	55	2	Fresno, CA	38.7
66	3	El Paso, TX	24.3	66	3	El Paso, TX	33.4
62	4	Bakersfield-Delano, CA	21.2	62	4	Bakersfield-Delano, CA	30.5
41	5	Memphis, TN-MS-AR	19.1	41	5	Memphis, TN-MS-AR	27.6
71	6	Greensboro-High Point, NC	18.1	71	6	Greensboro-High Point, NC	27.4
52	7	Tucson, AZ	17.8	49	7	Birmingham-Hoover, AL	26.0
46	8	New Orleans-Metairie-Kenner, LA	17.4	57	8	Albuquerque, NM	25.9
57	9	Albuquerque, NM	17.2	46	9	New Orleans-Metairie-Kenner, LA	25.8
8	10	Miami-Fort Lauderdale-Pompano Beach, FL	17.1	61	10	Dayton, OH	25.0
13	10	Riverside-San Bernardino-Ontario, CA	17.1	52	11	Tucson, AZ	24.7
49	12	Birmingham-Hoover, AL	17.0	39	12	Milwaukee-Waukesha-West Allis, WI	24.2
12	13	Detroit-Warren-Livonia, MI	16.6	13	13	Riverside-San Bernardino-Ontario, CA	24.1
6	14	Houston-Sugar Land-Baytown, TX	16.5	6	14	Houston-Sugar Land-Baytown, TX	23.9
69	15	Grand Rapids-Wyoming, MI	16.4	28	14	Cleveland-Elyria-Mentor, OH	23.9
2	16	Los Angeles-Long Beach-Santa Ana, CA	16.3	65	14	Baton Rouge, LA	23.9
14	16	Phoenix-Mesa-Glendale, AZ	16.3	12	17	Detroit-Warren-Livonia, MI	23.8
25	16	San Antonio-New Braunfels, TX	16.3	25	17	San Antonio-New Braunfels, TX	23.8
61	16	Dayton, OH	16.3	44	17	Oklahoma City, OK	23.8
70	20	Columbia, SC	16.2	69	17	Grand Rapids-Wyoming, MI	23.8
65	21	Baton Rouge, LA	16.1	8	21	Miami-Fort Lauderdale-Pompano Beach, FL	22.9
35	22	Austin-Round Rock-San Marcos, TX	15.9	30	22	Las Vegas-Paradise, NV	22.8
44	22	Oklahoma City, OK	15.9	38	22	Nashville-Davidson—Murfreesboro—Franklin, TN	22.8
32	24	Columbus, OH	15.7	14	24	Phoenix-Mesa-Glendale, AZ	22.7
39	25	Milwaukee-Waukesha-West Allis, WI	15.5	54	24	Tulsa, OK	22.7
54	25	Tulsa, OK	15.5	2	26	Los Angeles-Long Beach-Santa Ana, CA	22.6
72	25	Akron, OH	15.5	73	27	North Port-Bradenton-Sarasota, FL	22.5
19	28	Tampa-St. Petersburg-Clearwater, FL	15.4	42	28	Louisville-Jefferson County, KY-IN	22.4
38	28	Nashville-Davidson—Murfreesboro—Franklin, TN	15.4	72	29	Akron, OH	22.1
40	30	Jacksonville, FL	15.3	19	30	Tampa-St. Petersburg-Clearwater, FL	21.6
42	30	Louisville-Jefferson County, KY-IN	15.3	40	31	Jacksonville, FL	21.5
74	32	Little Rock-North Little Rock-Conway, AR	15.2	70	31	Columbia, SC	21.5
24	33	Sacramento—Arden-Arcade—Roseville, CA	15.1	47	33	Buffalo-Niagara Falls, NY	21.4
28	33	Cleveland-Elyria-Mentor, OH	15.1	4	34	Dallas-Fort Worth-Arlington, TX	21.2
30	33	Las Vegas-Paradise, NV	15.1	34	35	Indianapolis-Carmel, IN	21.1
9	36	Atlanta-Sandy Springs-Marietta, GA	14.8	74	35	Little Rock-North Little Rock-Conway, AR	21.1
17	36	San Diego-Carlsbad-San Marcos, CA	14.8	51	37	Rochester, NY	20.8
34	36	Indianapolis-Carmel, IN	14.8	32	38	Columbus, OH	20.7
26	39	Orlando-Kissimmee-Sanford, FL	14.7	9	39	Atlanta-Sandy Springs-Marietta, GA	20.5
4	40	Dallas-Fort Worth-Arlington, TX	14.6	24	39	Sacramento—Arden-Arcade—Roseville, CA	20.5
33	41	Charlotte-Gastonia-Rock Hill, NC-SC	14.5	26	41	Orlando-Kissimmee-Sanford, FL	20.4
47	42	Buffalo-Niagara Falls, NY	14.4	35	42	Austin-Round Rock-San Marcos, TX	20.1
51	43	Rochester, NY	14.2	27	43	Cincinnati-Middletown, OH-KY-IN	19.7
27	44	Cincinnati-Middletown, OH-KY-IN	14.0	1	44	New York-Northern New Jersey-Long Island, NY-NJ-PA	19.5
1	45	New York-Northern New Jersey-Long Island, NY-NJ-PA	13.8	33	45	Charlotte-Gastonia-Rock Hill, NC-SC	19.4
75	45	Knoxville, TN	13.8	3	46	Chicago-Joliet-Naperville, IL-IN-WI	19.3
37	47	Providence-New Bedford-Fall River, RI-MA	13.7	17	47	San Diego-Carlsbad-San Marcos, CA	19.2
3	48	Chicago-Joliet-Naperville, IL-IN-WI	13.6	18	48	St. Louis, MO-IL	18.8
73	48	North Port-Bradenton-Sarasota, FL	13.6	75	49	Knoxville, TN	18.4
23	50	Portland-Vancouver-Hillsboro, OR-WA	13.4	37	50	Providence-New Bedford-Fall River, RI-MA	18.3
18	51	St. Louis, MO-IL	13.3	29	51	Kansas City, MO-KS	17.7
50	52	Salt Lake City, UT	13.1	59	51	Omaha-Council Bluffs, NE-IA	17.7
48	53	Raleigh-Cary, NC	12.9	23	53	Portland-Vancouver-Hillsboro, OR-WA	17.6
5	54	Philadelphia-Camden-Wilmington, PA-NJ-DE-MD	12.7	64	54	Allentown-Bethlehem-Easton, PA-NJ	17.5
21	55	Denver-Aurora-Broomfield, CO	12.5	48	55	Raleigh-Cary, NC	17.2
29	56	Kansas City, MO-KS	12.4	5	56	Philadelphia-Camden-Wilmington, PA-NJ-DE-MD	17.1
59	56	Omaha-Council Bluffs, NE-IA	12.4	50	56	Salt Lake City, UT	17.1
22	58	Pittsburgh, PA	12.2	22	58	Pittsburgh, PA	16.8
15	59	Seattle-Tacoma-Bellevue, WA	11.7	21	59	Denver-Aurora-Broomfield, CO	16.7
60	59	New Haven-Milford, CT	11.7	60	60	New Haven-Milford, CT	16.5
64	59	Allentown-Bethlehem-Easton, PA-NJ	11.7	58	61	Albany-Schenectady-Troy, NY	16.1
43	62	Richmond, VA	11.6	36	62	Virginia Beach-Norfolk-Newport News, VA-NC	16.0
58	63	Albany-Schenectady-Troy, NY	11.5	15	63	Seattle-Tacoma-Bellevue, WA	15.6
20	64	Baltimore-Towson, MD	11.0	20	64	Baltimore-Towson, MD	14.9
11	65	San Francisco-Oakland-Fremont, CA	10.9	16	65	Minneapolis-St. Paul-Bloomington, MN	14.8
16	65	Minneapolis-St. Paul-Bloomington, MN	10.9	43	66	Richmond, VA	14.6
67	67	Worcester, MA	10.8	63	67	Oxnard-Thousand Oaks-Ventura, CA	14.3
63	68	Oxnard-Thousand Oaks-Ventura, CA	10.7	67	68	Worcester, MA	14.1
31	69	San Jose-Sunnyvale-Santa Clara, CA	10.6	31	69	San Jose-Sunnyvale-Santa Clara, CA	13.5
36	69	Virginia Beach-Norfolk-Newport News, VA-NC	10.6	11	70	San Francisco-Oakland-Fremont, CA	13.3
10	71	Boston-Cambridge-Quincy, MA-NH	10.3	45	71	Hartford-West Hartford-East Hartford, CT	12.7
45	72	Hartford-West Hartford-East Hartford, CT	10.1	10	72	Boston-Cambridge-Quincy, MA-NH	11.9
56	73	Bridgeport-Stamford-Norwalk, CT	9.4	53	73	Honolulu, HI	11.0
53	74	Honolulu, HI	9.1	56	74	Bridgeport-Stamford-Norwalk, CT	10.9
7	75	Washington-Arlington-Alexandria, DC-VA-MD-WV	8.4	7	75	Washington-Arlington-Alexandria, DC-VA-MD-WV	10.7

75 Largest Metropolitan Areas by 2010 Population
Selected Rankings

		Median value of owner-occupied housing units, 2010				Median gross rent of renter-occupied housing units, 2010	
Popu-lation rank	Median value rank	Metropolitan area	Median value (dollars) [col 91]	Popu-lation rank	Median gross rent	Metropolitan area	Median rent (dollars) [col 94]
31	1	San Jose-Sunnyvale-Santa Clara, CA	631 400	31	1	San Jose-Sunnyvale-Santa Clara, CA	1 412
11	2	San Francisco-Oakland-Fremont, CA	588 300	63	2	Oxnard-Thousand Oaks-Ventura, CA	1 381
53	3	Honolulu, HI	560 500	53	3	Honolulu, HI	1 363
63	4	Oxnard-Thousand Oaks-Ventura, CA	458 200	7	4	Washington-Arlington-Alexandria, DC-VA-MD-WV	1 351
2	5	Los Angeles-Long Beach-Santa Ana, CA	455 900	11	5	San Francisco-Oakland-Fremont, CA	1 314
56	6	Bridgeport-Stamford-Norwalk, CT	441 400	17	6	San Diego-Carlsbad-San Marcos, CA	1 249
1	7	New York-Northern New Jersey-Long Island, NY-NJ-PA	426 500	56	7	Bridgeport-Stamford-Norwalk, CT	1 233
17	8	San Diego-Carlsbad-San Marcos, CA	407 000	2	8	Los Angeles-Long Beach-Santa Ana, CA	1 196
7	9	Washington-Arlington-Alexandria, DC-VA-MD-WV	376 200	1	9	New York-Northern New Jersey-Long Island, NY-NJ-PA	1 150
10	10	Boston-Cambridge-Quincy, MA-NH	365 200	10	10	Boston-Cambridge-Quincy, MA-NH	1 141
15	11	Seattle-Tacoma-Bellevue, WA	333 100	13	11	Riverside-San Bernardino-Ontario, CA	1 078
20	12	Baltimore-Towson, MD	288 700	8	12	Miami-Fort Lauderdale-Pompano Beach, FL	1 063
24	13	Sacramento—Arden-Arcade—Roseville, CA	279 100	20	13	Baltimore-Towson, MD	1 048
23	14	Portland-Vancouver-Hillsboro, OR-WA	271 700	36	14	Virginia Beach-Norfolk-Newport News, VA-NC	1 022
60	15	New Haven-Milford, CT	269 200	15	15	Seattle-Tacoma-Bellevue, WA	1 017
67	16	Worcester, MA	268 100	60	16	New Haven-Milford, CT	1 015
37	17	Providence-New Bedford-Fall River, RI-MA	266 700	24	17	Sacramento—Arden-Arcade—Roseville, CA	1 005
45	18	Hartford-West Hartford-East Hartford, CT	258 300	30	18	Las Vegas-Paradise, NV	986
5	19	Philadelphia-Camden-Wilmington, PA-NJ-DE-MD	246 300	26	19	Orlando-Kissimmee-Sanford, FL	976
36	20	Virginia Beach-Norfolk-Newport News, VA-NC	246 200	5	20	Philadelphia-Camden-Wilmington, PA-NJ-DE-MD	945
21	21	Denver-Aurora-Broomfield, CO	245 900	35	21	Austin-Round Rock-San Marcos, TX	919
50	22	Salt Lake City, UT	236 800	45	21	Hartford-West Hartford-East Hartford, CT	919
3	23	Chicago-Joliet-Naperville, IL-IN-WI	236 000	3	23	Chicago-Joliet-Naperville, IL-IN-WI	913
43	24	Richmond, VA	227 400	73	23	North Port-Bradenton-Sarasota, FL	913
13	25	Riverside-San Bernardino-Ontario, CA	225 600	9	25	Atlanta-Sandy Springs-Marietta, GA	910
16	26	Minneapolis-St. Paul-Bloomington, MN	225 500	40	26	Jacksonville, FL	908
64	27	Allentown-Bethlehem-Easton, PA-NJ	218 700	43	27	Richmond, VA	903
55	28	Fresno, CA	212 500	19	28	Tampa-St. Petersburg-Clearwater, FL	900
48	29	Raleigh-Cary, NC	207 800	46	29	New Orleans-Metairie-Kenner, LA	884
39	30	Milwaukee-Waukesha-West Allis, WI	203 600	14	30	Phoenix-Mesa-Glendale, AZ	883
58	31	Albany-Schenectady-Troy, NY	199 000	21	31	Denver-Aurora-Broomfield, CO	879
8	32	Miami-Fort Lauderdale-Pompano Beach, FL	195 700	23	32	Portland-Vancouver-Hillsboro, OR-WA	867
35	33	Austin-Round Rock-San Marcos, TX	187 600	67	32	Worcester, MA	867
57	34	Albuquerque, NM	183 300	4	34	Dallas-Fort Worth-Arlington, TX	855
46	35	New Orleans-Metairie-Kenner, LA	176 900	48	35	Raleigh-Cary, NC	851
9	36	Atlanta-Sandy Springs-Marietta, GA	175 900	64	36	Allentown-Bethlehem-Easton, PA-NJ	848
38	37	Nashville-Davidson—Murfreesboro—Franklin, TN	173 500	6	37	Houston-Sugar Land-Baytown, TX	846
52	38	Tucson, AZ	173 200	58	37	Albany-Schenectady-Troy, NY	846
73	39	North Port-Bradenton-Sarasota, FL	173 000	16	39	Minneapolis-St. Paul-Bloomington, MN	845
14	40	Phoenix-Mesa-Glendale, AZ	172 900	50	40	Salt Lake City, UT	835
33	41	Charlotte-Gastonia-Rock Hill, NC-SC	172 500	37	41	Providence-New Bedford-Fall River, RI-MA	831
40	42	Jacksonville, FL	170 900	55	42	Fresno, CA	825
30	43	Las Vegas-Paradise, NV	170 100	62	43	Bakersfield-Delano, CA	821
26	44	Orlando-Kissimmee-Sanford, FL	169 000	12	44	Detroit-Warren-Livonia, MI	793
62	45	Bakersfield-Delano, CA	164 200	41	44	Memphis, TN-MS-AR	793
32	46	Columbus, OH	163 500	25	46	San Antonio-New Braunfels, TX	788
18	47	St. Louis, MO-IL	161 400	33	47	Charlotte-Gastonia-Rock Hill, NC-SC	787
29	48	Kansas City, MO-KS	159 200	38	48	Nashville-Davidson—Murfreesboro—Franklin, TN	783
65	49	Baton Rouge, LA	158 300	52	49	Tucson, AZ	768
27	50	Cincinnati-Middletown, OH-KY-IN	155 500	29	50	Kansas City, MO-KS	766
19	51	Tampa-St. Petersburg-Clearwater, FL	152 200	39	51	Milwaukee-Waukesha-West Allis, WI	764
75	52	Knoxville, TN	151 400	75	52	Columbia, SC	763
4	53	Dallas-Fort Worth-Arlington, TX	150 400	32	53	Columbus, OH	758
42	54	Louisville-Jefferson County, KY-IN	148 100	65	54	Baton Rouge, LA	756
28	55	Cleveland-Elyria-Mentor, OH	146 700	59	55	Omaha-Council Bluffs, NE-IA	753
49	56	Birmingham-Hoover, AL	146 600	49	56	Birmingham-Hoover, AL	749
59	57	Omaha-Council Bluffs, NE-IA	146 100	57	57	Albuquerque, NM	748
72	58	Akron, OH	145 000	34	58	Indianapolis-Carmel, IN	746
34	59	Indianapolis-Carmel, IN	143 600	51	59	Rochester, NY	735
71	60	Greensboro-High Point, NC	141 100	18	60	St. Louis, MO-IL	734
6	61	Houston-Sugar Land-Baytown, TX	140 800	74	61	Little Rock-North Little Rock-Conway, AR	731
41	62	Memphis, TN-MS-AR	138 700	28	62	Cleveland-Elyria-Mentor, OH	714
70	63	Columbia, SC	137 100	44	63	Oklahoma City, OK	713
69	64	Grand Rapids-Wyoming, MI	136 800	27	64	Cincinnati-Middletown, OH-KY-IN	710
74	65	Little Rock-North Little Rock-Conway, AR	132 700	61	65	Dayton, OH	705
25	66	San Antonio-New Braunfels, TX	131 700	72	66	Akron, OH	702
54	67	Tulsa, OK	128 400	69	67	Grand Rapids-Wyoming, MI	698
44	68	Oklahoma City, OK	127 400	75	68	Knoxville, TN	690
51	68	Rochester, NY	127 400	54	69	Tulsa, OK	688
61	70	Dayton, OH	125 600	71	70	Greensboro-High Point, NC	680
12	71	Detroit-Warren-Livonia, MI	124 400	47	71	Buffalo-Niagara Falls, NY	672
22	72	Pittsburgh, PA	122 200	42	72	Louisville-Jefferson County, KY-IN	671
47	73	Buffalo-Niagara Falls, NY	120 700	66	73	El Paso, TX	666
66	74	El Paso, TX	108 200	22	74	Pittsburgh, PA	656
68	75	McAllen-Edinburg-Mission, TX	80 400	68	75	McAllen-Edinburg-Mission, TX	608

75 Largest Metropolitan Areas by 2010 Population
Selected Rankings

Unemployment rate, 2010

Population rank	Unemployment rate rank	Metropolitan area	Unemployment rate [col 100]
55	1	Fresno, CA	16.8
62	2	Bakersfield-Delano, CA	15.9
30	3	Las Vegas-Paradise, NV	15.2
13	4	Riverside-San Bernardino-Ontario, CA	14.5
12	5	Detroit-Warren-Livonia, MI	13.5
24	6	Sacramento—Arden-Arcade—Roseville, CA	12.6
73	7	North Port-Bradenton-Sarasota, FL	12.2
19	8	Tampa-St. Petersburg-Clearwater, FL	12.1
2	9	Los Angeles-Long Beach-Santa Ana, CA	11.9
68	10	McAllen-Edinburg-Mission, TX	11.8
33	11	Charlotte-Gastonia-Rock Hill, NC-SC	11.6
8	12	Miami-Fort Lauderdale-Pompano Beach, FL	11.5
37	12	Providence-New Bedford-Fall River, RI-MA	11.5
26	14	Orlando-Kissimmee-Sanford, FL	11.4
31	15	San Jose-Sunnyvale-Santa Clara, CA	11.3
40	16	Jacksonville, FL	11.2
71	17	Greensboro-High Point, NC	11.1
61	18	Dayton, OH	10.8
63	18	Oxnard-Thousand Oaks-Ventura, CA	10.8
23	20	Portland-Vancouver-Hillsboro, OR-WA	10.6
17	21	San Diego-Carlsbad-San Marcos, CA	10.5
69	21	Grand Rapids-Wyoming, MI	10.5
11	23	San Francisco-Oakland-Fremont, CA	10.3
42	23	Louisville-Jefferson County, KY-IN	10.3
3	25	Chicago-Joliet-Naperville, IL-IN-WI	10.2
9	25	Atlanta-Sandy Springs-Marietta, GA	10.2
60	27	New Haven-Milford, CT	10.1
18	28	St. Louis, MO-IL	10.0
41	28	Memphis, TN-MS-AR	10.0
72	30	Akron, OH	9.9
27	31	Cincinnati-Middletown, OH-KY-IN	9.7
66	32	El Paso, TX	9.5
64	33	Allentown-Bethlehem-Easton, PA-NJ	9.4
15	34	Seattle-Tacoma-Bellevue, WA	9.3
67	34	Worcester, MA	9.3
70	34	Columbia, SC	9.3
14	37	Phoenix-Mesa-Glendale, AZ	9.2
28	37	Cleveland-Elyria-Mentor, OH	9.2
34	37	Indianapolis-Carmel, IN	9.2
29	40	Kansas City, MO-KS	9.1
45	40	Hartford-West Hartford-East Hartford, CT	9.1
5	42	Philadelphia-Camden-Wilmington, PA-NJ-DE-MD	9.0
21	42	Denver-Aurora-Broomfield, CO	9.0
49	42	Birmingham-Hoover, AL	9.0
52	42	Tucson, AZ	9.0
1	46	New York-Northern New Jersey-Long Island, NY-NJ-PA	8.9
57	47	Albuquerque, NM	8.8
39	48	Milwaukee-Waukesha-West Allis, WI	8.7
48	48	Raleigh-Cary, NC	8.7
32	50	Columbus, OH	8.6
38	50	Nashville-Davidson—Murfreesboro—Franklin, TN	8.6
6	52	Houston-Sugar Land-Baytown, TX	8.5
47	53	Buffalo-Niagara Falls, NY	8.4
4	54	Dallas-Fort Worth-Arlington, TX	8.3
56	54	Bridgeport-Stamford-Norwalk, CT	8.3
51	56	Rochester, NY	8.1
22	57	Pittsburgh, PA	8.0
20	58	Baltimore-Towson, MD	7.9
54	58	Tulsa, OK	7.9
75	58	Knoxville, TN	7.9
10	61	Boston-Cambridge-Quincy, MA-NH	7.7
43	61	Richmond, VA	7.7
50	63	Salt Lake City, UT	7.5
65	63	Baton Rouge, LA	7.5
36	65	Virginia Beach-Norfolk-Newport News, VA-NC	7.4
46	65	New Orleans-Metairie-Kenner, LA	7.4
25	67	San Antonio-New Braunfels, TX	7.3
58	67	Albany-Schenectady-Troy, NY	7.3
16	69	Minneapolis-St. Paul-Bloomington, MN	7.2
35	70	Austin-Round Rock-San Marcos, TX	7.1
74	71	Little Rock-North Little Rock-Conway, AR	7.0
44	72	Oklahoma City, OK	6.6
7	73	Washington-Arlington-Alexandria, DC-VA-MD-WV	6.2
53	74	Honolulu, HI	5.6
59	75	Omaha-Council Bluffs, NE-IA	5.2

Percent of Votes for Barack Obama, 2008

Population Rank	Vote for Obama rank	Metropolitan area	Percent of votes for Obama [col 197]
11	1	San Francisco-Oakland-Fremont, CA	76.4
53	2	Honolulu, HI	69.8
31	3	San Jose-Sunnyvale-Santa Clara, CA	69.2
68	4	McAllen-Edinburg-Mission, TX	69.0
7	5	Washington-Arlington-Alexandria, DC-VA-MD-WV	68.3
3	6	Chicago-Joliet-Naperville, IL-IN-WI	67.2
66	7	El Paso, TX	65.9
5	8	Philadelphia-Camden-Wilmington, PA-NJ-DE-MD	65.2
15	9	Seattle-Tacoma-Bellevue, WA	64.7
1	10	New York-Northern New Jersey-Long Island, NY-NJ-PA	64.2
45	11	Hartford-West Hartford-East Hartford, CT	63.8
2	12	Los Angeles-Long Beach-Santa Ana, CA	63.6
23	13	Portland-Vancouver-Hillsboro, OR-WA	62.6
37	14	Providence-New Bedford-Fall River, RI-MA	62.4
12	15	Detroit-Warren-Livonia, MI	62.0
8	16	Miami-Fort Lauderdale-Pompano Beach, FL	61.9
28	16	Cleveland-Elyria-Mentor, OH	61.9
10	18	Boston-Cambridge-Quincy, MA-NH	61.6
60	19	New Haven-Milford, CT	61.0
56	20	Bridgeport-Stamford-Norwalk, CT	58.6
57	20	Albuquerque, NM	58.6
30	22	Las Vegas-Paradise, NV	58.5
21	23	Denver-Aurora-Broomfield, CO	57.7
18	24	St. Louis, MO-IL	57.5
20	25	Baltimore-Towson, MD	57.4
72	26	Akron, OH	56.7
41	27	Memphis, TN-MS-AR	56.5
47	27	Buffalo-Niagara Falls, NY	56.5
58	29	Albany-Schenectady-Troy, NY	56.4
35	30	Austin-Round Rock-San Marcos, TX	56.3
16	31	Minneapolis-St. Paul-Bloomington, MN	56.1
67	32	Worcester, MA	55.8
36	33	Virginia Beach-Norfolk-Newport News, VA-NC	55.2
63	33	Oxnard-Thousand Oaks-Ventura, CA	55.2
24	35	Sacramento—Arden-Arcade—Roseville, CA	54.8
51	35	Rochester, NY	54.8
17	37	San Diego-Carlsbad-San Marcos, CA	54.1
26	37	Orlando-Kissimmee-Sanford, FL	54.1
39	39	Milwaukee-Waukesha-West Allis, WI	54.0
64	39	Allentown-Bethlehem-Easton, PA-NJ	54.0
48	41	Raleigh-Cary, NC	53.9
43	42	Richmond, VA	52.7
52	43	Tucson, AZ	52.4
32	44	Columbus, OH	52.3
19	45	Tampa-St. Petersburg-Clearwater, FL	52.0
29	45	Kansas City, MO-KS	52.0
71	47	Greensboro-High Point, NC	51.5
9	48	Atlanta-Sandy Springs-Marietta, GA	51.4
33	48	Charlotte-Gastonia-Rock Hill, NC-SC	51.4
13	50	Riverside-San Bernardino-Ontario, CA	51.1
22	51	Pittsburgh, PA	50.8
34	51	Indianapolis-Carmel, IN	50.8
55	53	Fresno, CA	50.2
70	54	Columbia, SC	49.9
42	55	Louisville-Jefferson County, KY-IN	49.2
69	56	Grand Rapids-Wyoming, MI	48.6
50	57	Salt Lake City, UT	48.3
73	58	North Port-Bradenton-Sarasota, FL	48.1
59	59	Omaha-Council Bluffs, NE-IA	47.9
25	60	San Antonio-New Braunfels, TX	47.1
61	61	Dayton, OH	47.0
46	62	New Orleans-Metairie-Kenner, LA	46.1
6	63	Houston-Sugar Land-Baytown, TX	45.6
4	64	Dallas-Fort Worth-Arlington, TX	44.5
74	64	Little Rock-North Little Rock-Conway, AR	44.5
38	66	Nashville-Davidson—Murfreesboro—Franklin, TN	44.3
14	67	Phoenix-Mesa-Glendale, AZ	44.0
27	68	Cincinnati-Middletown, OH-KY-IN	42.6
65	69	Baton Rouge, LA	42.2
40	70	Jacksonville, FL	41.8
49	71	Birmingham-Hoover, AL	40.1
62	71	Bakersfield-Delano, CA	40.1
44	73	Oklahoma City, OK	37.2
54	74	Tulsa, OK	35.6
75	75	Knoxville, TN	35.2

75 Largest Metropolitan Areas by 2010 Population
Selected Rankings

Employment in manufacturing as a percent of total nonfarm employment, 2009				Employment in professional, scientific, and technical services as a percent of total nonfarm employment, 2009			
Population rank	Manufacturing rank	Metropolitan area	Percent employed in manufacturing [col 107/col 105]	Population rank	Professional services rank	Metropolitan area	Percent employed in services [col 110/col 105]
71	1	Greensboro-High Point, NC	18.4	7	1	Washington-Arlington-Alexandria, DC-VA-MD-WV	20.0
69	2	Grand Rapids-Wyoming, MI	17.4	31	2	San Jose-Sunnyvale-Santa Clara, CA	13.5
39	3	Milwaukee-Waukesha-West Allis, WI	15.4	11	3	San Francisco-Oakland-Fremont, CA	12.0
28	4	Cleveland-Elyria-Mentor, OH	13.8	17	4	San Diego-Carlsbad-San Marcos, CA	10.6
51	4	Rochester, NY	13.8	12	5	Detroit-Warren-Livonia, MI	10.0
54	6	Tulsa, OK	13.7	10	6	Boston-Cambridge-Quincy, MA-NH	9.9
72	7	Akron, OH	13.6	35	7	Austin-Round Rock-San Marcos, TX	9.9
61	8	Dayton, OH	13.4	20	8	Baltimore-Towson, MD	9.8
37	9	Providence-New Bedford-Fall River, RI-MA	12.2	56	9	Bridgeport-Stamford-Norwalk, CT	9.3
42	9	Louisville-Jefferson County, KY-IN	12.2	1	10	New York-Northern New Jersey-Long Island, NY-NJ-PA	9.2
45	11	Hartford-West Hartford-East Hartford, CT	12.1	2	11	Los Angeles-Long Beach-Santa Ana, CA	9.2
67	11	Worcester, MA	12.1	9	12	Atlanta-Sandy Springs-Marietta, GA	9.1
70	13	Columbia, SC	11.8	21	13	Denver-Aurora-Broomfield, CO	8.9
12	14	Detroit-Warren-Livonia, MI	11.6	48	14	Raleigh-Cary, NC	8.9
47	14	Buffalo-Niagara Falls, NY	11.6	58	15	Albany-Schenectady-Troy, NY	8.8
27	16	Cincinnati-Middletown, OH-KY-IN	11.5	59	16	Omaha-Council Bluffs, NE-IA	8.7
2	17	Los Angeles-Long Beach-Santa Ana, CA	11.4	63	17	Oxnard-Thousand Oaks-Ventura, CA	8.6
64	18	Allentown-Bethlehem-Easton, PA-NJ	11.3	36	18	Virginia Beach-Norfolk-Newport News, VA-NC	8.6
60	19	New Haven-Milford, CT	11.1	57	19	Albuquerque, NM	8.4
16	20	Minneapolis-St. Paul-Bloomington, MN	11.0	6	20	Houston-Sugar Land-Baytown, TX	8.3
23	21	Portland-Vancouver-Hillsboro, OR-WA	10.8	5	21	Philadelphia-Camden-Wilmington, PA-NJ-DE-MD	8.3
31	22	San Jose-Sunnyvale-Santa Clara, CA	10.6	3	22	Chicago-Joliet-Naperville, IL-IN-WI	8.0
3	23	Chicago-Joliet-Naperville, IL-IN-WI	10.4	19	23	Tampa-St. Petersburg-Clearwater, FL	8.0
55	23	Fresno, CA	10.4	29	24	Kansas City, MO-KS	7.9
75	25	Knoxville, TN	10.2	15	25	Seattle-Tacoma-Bellevue, WA	7.7
34	26	Indianapolis-Carmel, IN	10.1	75	26	Knoxville, TN	7.5
63	26	Oxnard-Thousand Oaks-Ventura, CA	10.1	8	27	Miami-Fort Lauderdale-Pompano Beach, FL	7.4
13	28	Riverside-San Bernardino-Ontario, CA	9.9	26	28	Orlando-Kissimmee-Sanford, FL	7.4
15	29	Seattle-Tacoma-Bellevue, WA	9.7	40	29	Jacksonville, FL	7.3
36	30	Virginia Beach-Norfolk-Newport News, VA-NC	9.6	4	30	Dallas-Fort Worth-Arlington, TX	7.2
4	31	Dallas-Fort Worth-Arlington, TX	9.4	61	31	Dayton, OH	7.2
6	31	Houston-Sugar Land-Baytown, TX	9.4	16	32	Minneapolis-St. Paul-Bloomington, MN	7.2
56	33	Bridgeport-Stamford-Norwalk, CT	9.3	22	33	Pittsburgh, PA	7.1
50	34	Salt Lake City, UT	9.2	24	34	Sacramento—Arden-Arcade—Roseville, CA	7.0
29	35	Kansas City, MO-KS	9.1	18	35	St. Louis, MO-IL	7.0
22	36	Pittsburgh, PA	9.0	23	36	Portland-Vancouver-Hillsboro, OR-WA	6.9
38	37	Nashville-Davidson—Murfreesboro—Franklin, TN	8.9	46	37	New Orleans-Metairie-Kenner, LA	6.8
18	38	St. Louis, MO-IL	8.8	50	38	Salt Lake City, UT	6.7
49	38	Birmingham-Hoover, AL	8.8	65	39	Baton Rouge, LA	6.6
52	40	Tucson, AZ	8.7	43	40	Richmond, VA	6.3
33	41	Charlotte-Gastonia-Rock Hill, NC-SC	8.6	62	41	Bakersfield-Delano, CA	6.3
17	42	San Diego-Carlsbad-San Marcos, CA	8.4	27	42	Cincinnati-Middletown, OH-KY-IN	6.2
74	43	Little Rock-North Little Rock-Conway, AR	8.3	72	43	Akron, OH	6.2
59	44	Omaha-Council Bluffs, NE-IA	8.2	44	44	Oklahoma City, OK	6.2
32	45	Columbus, OH	8.0	34	45	Indianapolis-Carmel, IN	6.1
5	46	Philadelphia-Camden-Wilmington, PA-NJ-DE-MD	7.6	32	46	Columbus, OH	6.1
43	47	Richmond, VA	7.5	45	47	Hartford-West Hartford-East Hartford, CT	6.1
41	48	Memphis, TN-MS-AR	7.4	14	48	Phoenix-Mesa-Glendale, AZ	6.1
65	49	Baton Rouge, LA	7.3	73	49	North Port-Bradenton-Sarasota, FL	5.9
10	50	Boston-Cambridge-Quincy, MA-NH	7.1	70	50	Columbia, SC	5.8
11	51	San Francisco-Oakland-Fremont, CA	7.0	33	51	Charlotte-Gastonia-Rock Hill, NC-SC	5.7
66	52	El Paso, TX	6.9	47	52	Buffalo-Niagara Falls, NY	5.7
14	53	Phoenix-Mesa-Glendale, AZ	6.8	28	53	Cleveland-Elyria-Mentor, OH	5.6
46	54	New Orleans-Metairie-Kenner, LA	6.7	51	54	Rochester, NY	5.6
62	54	Bakersfield-Delano, CA	6.7	53	55	Honolulu, HI	5.5
44	56	Oklahoma City, OK	6.6	49	56	Birmingham-Hoover, AL	5.5
9	57	Atlanta-Sandy Springs-Marietta, GA	6.5	67	57	Worcester, MA	5.5
35	57	Austin-Round Rock-San Marcos, TX	6.5	39	58	Milwaukee-Waukesha-West Allis, WI	5.4
73	59	North Port-Bradenton-Sarasota, FL	6.4	38	59	Nashville-Davidson—Murfreesboro—Franklin, TN	5.4
25	60	San Antonio-New Braunfels, TX	6.1	25	60	San Antonio-New Braunfels, TX	5.4
57	60	Albuquerque, NM	6.1	54	61	Tulsa, OK	5.4
58	62	Albany-Schenectady-Troy, NY	5.8	55	62	Fresno, CA	5.3
20	63	Baltimore-Towson, MD	5.7	42	63	Louisville-Jefferson County, KY-IN	5.2
24	63	Sacramento—Arden-Arcade—Roseville, CA	5.7	52	64	Tucson, AZ	5.1
48	63	Raleigh-Cary, NC	5.7	30	65	Las Vegas-Paradise, NV	5.0
19	66	Tampa-St. Petersburg-Clearwater, FL	5.6	60	66	New Haven-Milford, CT	4.9
21	67	Denver-Aurora-Broomfield, CO	5.5	74	67	Little Rock-North Little Rock-Conway, AR	4.8
40	68	Jacksonville, FL	5.0	37	68	Providence-New Bedford-Fall River, RI-MA	4.8
1	69	New York-Northern New Jersey-Long Island, NY-NJ-PA	4.9	66	69	El Paso, TX	4.7
26	70	Orlando-Kissimmee-Sanford, FL	4.3	69	70	Grand Rapids-Wyoming, MI	4.5
8	71	Miami-Fort Lauderdale-Pompano Beach, FL	3.7	64	71	Allentown-Bethlehem-Easton, PA-NJ	4.2
68	72	McAllen-Edinburg-Mission, TX	3.2	71	72	Greensboro-High Point, NC	3.7
53	73	Honolulu, HI	3.0	41	73	Memphis, TN-MS-AR	3.5
30	74	Las Vegas-Paradise, NV	2.7	13	74	Riverside-San Bernardino-Ontario, CA	3.4
7	75	Washington-Arlington-Alexandria, DC-VA-MD-WV	2.3	68	75	McAllen-Edinburg-Mission, TX	3.0

75 Largest Metropolitan Areas by 2010 Population
Selected Rankings

Popu-lation rank	Local taxes rank	Metropolitan area	Local per capita taxes (dollars) [col 183]	Popu-lation rank	Crime rate rank	Metropolitan area	Crime rate (per 100,000 population) [col 46]
		Per capita local government taxes, 2007				**Violent crime rate, 2010 (violent crimes known to police)**	
1	1	New York-Northern New Jersey-Long Island, NY-NJ-PA............	3 848	41	1	Memphis, TN-MS-AR	1 027
7	2	Washington-Arlington-Alexandria, DC-VA-MD-WV	3 239	74	2	Little Rock-North Little Rock-Conway, AR	791
56	3	Bridgeport-Stamford-Norwalk, CT	3 019	30	3	Las Vegas-Paradise, NV	777
11	4	San Francisco-Oakland-Fremont, CA	2 530	70	4	Columbia, SC	708
31	5	San Jose-Sunnyvale-Santa Clara, CA	2 453	20	5	Baltimore-Towson, MD	688
58	6	Albany-Schenectady-Troy, NY	2 386	34	6	Indianapolis-Carmel, IN	683
8	7	Miami-Fort Lauderdale-Pompano Beach, FL	2 343	57	7	Albuquerque, NM	658
28	8	Cleveland-Elyria-Mentor, OH	2 304	12	8	Detroit-Warren-Livonia, MI	645
3	9	Chicago-Joliet-Naperville, IL-IN-WI	2 250	38	9	Nashville-Davidson—Murfreesboro—Franklin, TN	639
45	10	Hartford-West Hartford-East Hartford, CT	2 216	6	10	Houston-Sugar Land-Baytown, TX	624
51	11	Rochester, NY	2 189	26	11	Orlando-Kissimmee-Sanford, FL	613
35	12	Austin-Round Rock-San Marcos, TX	2 139	8	12	Miami-Fort Lauderdale-Pompano Beach, FL	611
32	13	Columbus, OH	2 128	54	13	Tulsa, OK	607
5	14	Philadelphia-Camden-Wilmington, PA-NJ-DE-MD	2 126	62	14	Bakersfield-Delano, CA	581
73	15	North Port-Bradenton-Sarasota, FL	2 125	65	15	Baton Rouge, LA	576
60	16	New Haven-Milford, CT	2 086	40	16	Jacksonville, FL	559
21	17	Denver-Aurora-Broomfield, CO	2 077	5	17	Philadelphia-Camden-Wilmington, PA-NJ-DE-MD	558
4	18	Dallas-Fort Worth-Arlington, TX	2 072	44	18	Oklahoma City, OK	547
46	19	New Orleans-Metairie-Kenner, LA	2 019	55	19	Fresno, CA	535
47	20	Buffalo-Niagara Falls, NY	1 983	11	20	San Francisco-Oakland-Fremont, CA	529
6	21	Houston-Sugar Land-Baytown, TX	1 954	18	21	St. Louis, MO-IL	519
10	22	Boston-Cambridge-Quincy, MA-NH	1 947	73	22	North Port-Bradenton-Sarasota, FL	508
20	23	Baltimore-Towson, MD	1 938	19	23	Tampa-St. Petersburg-Clearwater, FL	500
29	24	Kansas City, MO-KS	1 918	24	24	Sacramento—Arden-Arcade—Roseville, CA	481
15	25	Seattle-Tacoma-Bellevue, WA	1 856	46	25	New Orleans-Metairie-Kenner, LA	480
64	26	Allentown-Bethlehem-Easton, PA-NJ	1 844	29	26	Kansas City, MO-KS	478
17	27	San Diego-Carlsbad-San Marcos, CA	1 831	25	27	San Antonio-New Braunfels, TX	476
72	28	Akron, OH	1 785	75	28	Knoxville, TN	473
61	29	Dayton, OH	1 774	47	29	Buffalo-Niagara Falls, NY	471
9	30	Atlanta-Sandy Springs-Marietta, GA	1 757	39	30	Milwaukee-Waukesha-West Allis, WI	466
2	31	Los Angeles-Long Beach-Santa Ana, CA	1 755	67	31	Worcester, MA	465
36	32	Virginia Beach-Norfolk-Newport News, VA-NC	1 751	33	32	Charlotte-Gastonia-Rock Hill, NC-SC	450
26	33	Orlando-Kissimmee-Sanford, FL	1 744	2	33	Los Angeles-Long Beach-Santa Ana, CA	445
39	34	Milwaukee-Waukesha-West Allis, WI	1 735	3	33	Chicago-Joliet-Naperville, IL-IN-WI	445
27	35	Cincinnati-Middletown, OH-KY-IN	1 722	52	35	Tucson, AZ	429
30	36	Las Vegas-Paradise, NV	1 720	9	36	Atlanta-Sandy Springs-Marietta, GA	427
24	37	Sacramento—Arden-Arcade—Roseville, CA	1 718	66	37	El Paso, TX	421
59	38	Omaha-Council Bluffs, NE-IA	1 711	60	38	New Haven-Milford, CT	416
37	39	Providence-New Bedford-Fall River, RI-MA	1 695	10	39	Boston-Cambridge-Quincy, MA-NH	411
19	40	Tampa-St. Petersburg-Clearwater, FL	1 686	28	40	Cleveland-Elyria-Mentor, OH	408
22	41	Pittsburgh, PA	1 645	42	41	Louisville-Jefferson County, KY-IN	396
63	42	Oxnard-Thousand Oaks-Ventura, CA	1 642	1	42	New York-Northern New Jersey-Long Island, NY-NJ-PA	395
41	43	Memphis, TN-MS-AR	1 567	59	43	Omaha-Council Bluffs, NE-IA	386
18	44	St. Louis, MO-IL	1 565	69	44	Grand Rapids-Wyoming, MI	385
65	44	Baton Rouge, LA	1 565	4	45	Dallas-Fort Worth-Arlington, TX	382
12	46	Detroit-Warren-Livonia, MI	1 533	71	46	Greensboro-High Point, NC	381
23	47	Portland-Vancouver-Hillsboro, OR-WA	1 529	7	47	Washington-Arlington-Alexandria, DC-VA-MD-WV	380
43	48	Richmond, VA	1 523	17	48	San Diego-Carlsbad-San Marcos, CA	376
49	49	Birmingham-Hoover, AL	1 502	14	49	Phoenix-Mesa-Glendale, AZ	371
14	50	Phoenix-Mesa-Glendale, AZ	1 490	37	49	Providence-New Bedford-Fall River, RI-MA	371
13	51	Riverside-San Bernardino-Ontario, CA	1 486	13	51	Riverside-San Bernardino-Ontario, CA	370
38	52	Nashville-Davidson—Murfreesboro—Franklin, TN	1 455	32	51	Columbus, OH	370
25	53	San Antonio-New Braunfels, TX	1 447	21	53	Denver-Aurora-Broomfield, CO	368
33	54	Charlotte-Gastonia-Rock Hill, NC-SC	1 426	50	54	Salt Lake City, UT	355
40	55	Jacksonville, FL	1 415	15	55	Seattle-Tacoma-Bellevue, WA	349
34	56	Indianapolis-Carmel, IN	1 380	36	56	Virginia Beach-Norfolk-Newport News, VA-NC	342
67	57	Worcester, MA	1 374	35	57	Austin-Round Rock-San Marcos, TX	335
50	58	Salt Lake City, UT	1 345	27	58	Cincinnati-Middletown, OH-KY-IN	328
52	59	Tucson, AZ	1 333	22	59	Pittsburgh, PA	322
16	60	Minneapolis-St. Paul-Bloomington, MN	1 299	61	60	Dayton, OH	316
62	61	Bakersfield-Delano, CA	1 292	68	61	McAllen-Edinburg-Mission, TX	314
75	62	Knoxville, TN	1 266	72	62	Akron, OH	313
70	63	Columbia, SC	1 243	49	63	Birmingham-Hoover, AL	308
66	64	El Paso, TX	1 219	51	64	Rochester, NY	307
54	65	Tulsa, OK	1 193	58	65	Albany-Schenectady-Troy, NY	303
48	66	Raleigh-Cary, NC	1 191	45	66	Hartford-West Hartford-East Hartford, CT	300
55	67	Fresno, CA	1 189	16	67	Minneapolis-St. Paul-Bloomington, MN	287
69	68	Grand Rapids-Wyoming, MI	1 170	56	68	Bridgeport-Stamford-Norwalk, CT	282
44	69	Oklahoma City, OK	1 158	23	69	Portland-Vancouver-Hillsboro, OR-WA	274
42	70	Louisville-Jefferson County, KY-IN	1 130	43	70	Richmond, VA	267
71	71	Greensboro-High Point, NC	1 107	53	70	Honolulu, HI	267
57	72	Albuquerque, NM	1 072	31	72	San Jose-Sunnyvale-Santa Clara, CA	266
53	73	Honolulu, HI	1 000	48	73	Raleigh-Cary, NC	250
68	74	McAllen-Edinburg-Mission, TX	968	64	74	Allentown-Bethlehem-Easton, PA-NJ	229
74	75	Little Rock-North Little Rock-Conway, AR	762	63	75	Oxnard-Thousand Oaks-Ventura, CA	212

All Metropolitan Areas
Selected Rankings

		Defense contracts, 2009–2010				Non-defense contracts, 2009–2010	
Popu-lation rank	Defense contracts rank	Metropolitan area	Defense contracts (millions of dollars) [col 172]	Popu-lation rank	Non-defense contracts rank	Metropolitan area	Non-defense contracts (millions of dollars) [col 173]
7	1	Washington-Arlington-Alexandria, DC-VA-MD-WV	37 778.4	7	1	Washington-Arlington-Alexandria, DC-VA-MD-WV	43 558.9
4	2	Dallas-Fort Worth-Arlington, TX	15 187.7	2	2	Los Angeles-Long Beach-Santa Ana, CA	6 235.7
2	3	Los Angeles-Long Beach-Santa Ana, CA	12 663.2	1	3	New York-Northern New Jersey-Long Island, NY-NJ-PA	5 053.8
17	4	San Diego-Carlsbad-San Marcos, CA	11 593.0	11	4	San Francisco-Oakland-Fremont, CA	4 836.0
10	5	Boston-Cambridge-Quincy, MA-NH	10 905.4	5	5	Philadelphia-Camden-Wilmington, PA-NJ-DE-MD	4 627.6
18	6	St. Louis, MO-IL	9 200.0	6	6	Houston-Sugar Land-Baytown, TX	4 615.0
36	7	Virginia Beach-Norfolk-Newport News, VA-NC	9 027.1	75	7	Knoxville, TN	4 044.3
1	8	New York-Northern New Jersey-Long Island, NY-NJ-PA	8 653.9	3	8	Chicago-Joliet-Naperville, IL-IN-WI	3 872.4
5	9	Philadelphia-Camden-Wilmington, PA-NJ-DE-MD	6 849.6	21	9	Denver-Aurora-Broomfield, CO	3 473.8
20	10	Baltimore-Towson, MD	5 598.5	9	10	Atlanta-Sandy Springs-Marietta, GA	3 094.4
52	11	Tucson, AZ	5 268.8	57	11	Albuquerque, NM	2 911.8
3	12	Chicago-Joliet-Naperville, IL-IN-WI	5 106.0	10	12	Boston-Cambridge-Quincy, MA-NH	2 895.5
9	13	Atlanta-Sandy Springs-Marietta, GA	4 883.8	20	13	Baltimore-Towson, MD	2 795.0
31	14	San Jose-Sunnyvale-Santa Clara, CA	4 727.3	29	14	Kansas City, MO-KS	2 234.4
24	15	Sacramento—Arden-Arcade—Roseville, CA	4 694.0	4	15	Dallas-Fort Worth-Arlington, TX	1 986.3
46	16	New Orleans-Metairie-Kenner, LA	4 493.1	22	16	Pittsburgh, PA	1 588.6
14	17	Phoenix-Mesa-Glendale, AZ	4 444.2	12	17	Detroit-Warren-Livonia, MI	1 375.8
56	18	Bridgeport-Stamford-Norwalk, CT	4 045.9	17	18	San Diego-Carlsbad-San Marcos, CA	1 288.7
25	19	San Antonio-New Braunfels, TX	4 014.7	38	19	Nashville-Davidson—Murfreesboro—Franklin, TN	1 164.5
6	20	Houston-Sugar Land-Baytown, TX	3 886.9	36	20	Virginia Beach-Norfolk-Newport News, VA-NC	1 160.6
15	21	Seattle-Tacoma-Bellevue, WA	3 712.7	16	21	Minneapolis-St. Paul-Bloomington, MN	1 118.0
26	22	Orlando-Kissimmee-Sanford, FL	3 485.6	15	22	Seattle-Tacoma-Bellevue, WA	1 080.6
45	23	Hartford-West Hartford-East Hartford, CT	3 420.8	31	23	San Jose-Sunnyvale-Santa Clara, CA	1 076.4
42	24	Louisville-Jefferson County, KY-IN	3 130.3	8	24	Miami-Fort Lauderdale-Pompano Beach, FL	1 068.1
12	25	Detroit-Warren-Livonia, MI	2 718.6	19	25	Tampa-St. Petersburg-Clearwater, FL	1 042.0
13	26	Riverside-San Bernardino-Ontario, CA	2 713.9	18	26	St. Louis, MO-IL	1 003.6
21	27	Denver-Aurora-Broomfield, CO	2 410.9	35	27	Austin-Round Rock-San Marcos, TX	996.8
37	28	Providence-New Bedford-Fall River, RI-MA	2 362.0	14	28	Phoenix-Mesa-Glendale, AZ	933.6
53	29	Honolulu, HI	2 218.2	30	29	Las Vegas-Paradise, NV	893.0
27	30	Cincinnati-Middletown, OH-KY-IN	2 211.5	28	30	Cleveland-Elyria-Mentor, OH	851.4
19	31	Tampa-St. Petersburg-Clearwater, FL	2 146.8	46	31	New Orleans-Metairie-Kenner, LA	801.8
22	32	Pittsburgh, PA	2 023.4	23	32	Portland-Vancouver-Hillsboro, OR-WA	683.2
51	33	Rochester, NY	1 939.3	26	33	Orlando-Kissimmee-Sanford, FL	630.6
41	34	Memphis, TN-MS-AR	1 645.7	41	34	Memphis, TN-MS-AR	609.7
11	35	San Francisco-Oakland-Fremont, CA	1 586.8	25	35	San Antonio-New Braunfels, TX	609.1
61	36	Dayton, OH	1 546.3	34	36	Indianapolis-Carmel, IN	552.5
29	37	Kansas City, MO-KS	1 385.0	44	37	Oklahoma City, OK	495.3
34	38	Indianapolis-Carmel, IN	1 374.2	24	38	Sacramento—Arden-Arcade—Roseville, CA	488.7
16	39	Minneapolis-St. Paul-Bloomington, MN	1 360.4	27	39	Cincinnati-Middletown, OH-KY-IN	486.1
32	40	Columbus, OH	1 251.1	32	40	Columbus, OH	468.0
43	41	Richmond, VA	1 096.7	13	41	Riverside-San Bernardino-Ontario, CA	448.8
8	42	Miami-Fort Lauderdale-Pompano Beach, FL	1 045.7	39	42	Milwaukee-Waukesha-West Allis, WI	444.9
44	43	Oklahoma City, OK	987.1	52	43	Tucson, AZ	388.9
40	44	Jacksonville, FL	970.7	37	44	Providence-New Bedford-Fall River, RI-MA	383.6
66	45	El Paso, TX	958.0	70	45	Columbia, SC	378.4
50	46	Salt Lake City, UT	944.9	40	46	Jacksonville, FL	376.4
35	47	Austin-Round Rock-San Marcos, TX	924.6	33	47	Charlotte-Gastonia-Rock Hill, NC-SC	374.8
57	48	Albuquerque, NM	770.5	49	48	Birmingham-Hoover, AL	373.3
59	49	Omaha-Council Bluffs, NE-IA	735.9	66	49	El Paso, TX	360.1
63	50	Oxnard-Thousand Oaks-Ventura, CA	681.1	53	50	Honolulu, HI	350.0
23	51	Portland-Vancouver-Hillsboro, OR-WA	563.3	56	51	Bridgeport-Stamford-Norwalk, CT	346.9
70	52	Columbia, SC	557.6	61	52	Dayton, OH	328.5
62	53	Bakersfield-Delano, CA	484.6	43	53	Richmond, VA	328.0
74	54	Little Rock-North Little Rock-Conway, AR	450.3	50	54	Salt Lake City, UT	308.1
72	55	Akron, OH	443.7	59	55	Omaha-Council Bluffs, NE-IA	278.9
30	56	Las Vegas-Paradise, NV	443.1	42	56	Louisville-Jefferson County, KY-IN	262.0
58	57	Albany-Schenectady-Troy, NY	383.8	58	57	Albany-Schenectady-Troy, NY	258.0
65	58	Baton Rouge, LA	326.2	51	58	Rochester, NY	253.2
39	59	Milwaukee-Waukesha-West Allis, WI	292.8	74	59	Little Rock-North Little Rock-Conway, AR	248.2
49	60	Birmingham-Hoover, AL	291.3	45	60	Hartford-West Hartford-East Hartford, CT	245.8
47	61	Buffalo-Niagara Falls, NY	285.9	62	61	Bakersfield-Delano, CA	233.1
54	62	Tulsa, OK	251.7	47	62	Buffalo-Niagara Falls, NY	226.9
28	63	Cleveland-Elyria-Mentor, OH	251.6	54	63	Tulsa, OK	209.3
73	64	North Port-Bradenton-Sarasota, FL	224.2	68	64	McAllen-Edinburg-Mission, TX	207.6
71	65	Greensboro-High Point, NC	216.2	48	65	Raleigh-Cary, NC	205.3
75	66	Knoxville, TN	195.2	71	66	Greensboro-High Point, NC	195.0
48	67	Raleigh-Cary, NC	186.1	60	67	New Haven-Milford, CT	179.4
38	68	Nashville-Davidson—Murfreesboro—Franklin, TN	181.3	63	68	Oxnard-Thousand Oaks-Ventura, CA	175.4
67	69	Worcester, MA	165.3	55	69	Fresno, CA	167.6
64	70	Allentown-Bethlehem-Easton, PA-NJ	129.3	67	70	Worcester, MA	113.1
33	71	Charlotte-Gastonia-Rock Hill, NC-SC	113.0	69	71	Grand Rapids-Wyoming, MI	103.8
69	72	Grand Rapids-Wyoming, MI	89.0	64	72	Allentown-Bethlehem-Easton, PA-NJ	87.0
60	73	New Haven-Milford, CT	79.2	72	73	Akron, OH	64.0
55	74	Fresno, CA	72.9	73	74	North Port-Bradenton-Sarasota, FL	38.9
68	75	McAllen-Edinburg-Mission, TX	-35.5	65	75	Baton Rouge, LA	-77.6

75 Metropolitan Areas with Highest Agricultural Sales
Selected Rankings

	Value of agricultural products sold, 2007			Number of farms, 2007		
Value of sales rank	Metropolitan area	Value of sales (millions of dollars) [col 125]	Value of sales rank	Number of farms rank	Metropolitan area	Number of farms [col 113]
1	Fresno, CA	3 730.5	55	1	Dallas-Fort Worth-Arlington, TX	25 402
2	Visalia-Porterville, CA	3 335	28	2	Kansas City, MO-KS	15 529
3	Bakersfield, CA	3 204.1	20	3	St. Louis, MO-IL	12 686
4	Merced, CA	2 330.4	73	4	Oklahoma City, OK	10 772
5	Salinas, CA	2 178.5	8	5	Chicago-Naperville-Joliet, IL-IN-WI	7 714
6	Modesto, CA	1 820.6	18	6	Fayetteville-Springdale-Rogers, AR-MO	7 401
7	Riverside-San Bernardino-Ontario, CA	1 755.7	32	7	Columbus, OH	7 050
8	Chicago-Naperville-Joliet, IL-IN-WI	1 715.6	21	8	Philadelphia-Camden-Wilmington, PA-NJ-DE-MD	6 987
9	Miami-Fort Lauderdale-Pompano Beach, FL	1 643.1	30	9	Madison, WI	6 729
10	Phoenix-Mesa-Scottsdale, AZ	1 613.3	23	10	San Diego-Carlsbad-San Marcos, CA	6 687
11	Stockton, CA	1 564.4	58	11	Fort Smith, AR-OK	6 111
12	Greeley, CO	1 539.1	47	12	New York-Northern New Jersey-Long Island, NY-NJ-PA	6 110
13	Hanford-Corcoran, CA	1 358.4	1	13	Fresno, CA	6 081
14	Oxnard-Thousand Oaks-Ventura, CA	1 316.3	19	14	Omaha-Council Bluffs, NE-IA	5 783
15	El Centro, CA	1 290.3	34	15	Indianapolis-Carmel, IN	5 756
16	Lexington-Fayette, KY	1 248.5	22	16	Lancaster, PA	5 462
17	Yakima, WA	1 203.8	2	17	Visalia-Porterville, CA	5 240
18	Fayetteville-Springdale-Rogers, AR-MO	1 123	29	18	Boise City-Nampa, ID	5 238
19	Omaha-Council Bluffs, NE-IA	1 102.6	31	19	Sacramento—Arden-Arcade—Roseville, CA	5 132
20	St. Louis, MO-IL	1 084.7	16	20	Lexington-Fayette, KY	4 988
21	Philadelphia-Camden-Wilmington, PA-NJ-DE-MD	1 084.2	42	21	Tampa-St. Petersburg-Clearwater, FL	4 955
22	Lancaster, PA	1 072.2	7	22	Riverside-San Bernardino-Ontario, CA	4 868
23	San Diego-Carlsbad-San Marcos, CA	1 054.2	35	23	Des Moines-West Des Moines, IA	4 782
24	Kennewick-Pasco-Richland, WA	992.9	61	24	Wichita, KS	4 774
25	Madera-Chowchilla, CA	990.1	48	25	Grand Rapids-Wyoming, MI	4 491
26	Yuma, AZ	960	9	26	Miami-Fort Lauderdale-Pompano Beach, FL	4 308
27	Santa Barbara-Santa Maria-Goleta, CA	951.3	43	27	St. Cloud, MN	4 287
28	Kansas City, MO-KS	818.6	6	28	Modesto, CA	4 114
29	Boise City-Nampa, ID	814.8	67	29	Jackson, MS	3 969
30	Madison, WI	795.2	33	30	Salem, OR	3 922
30	Sacramento—Arden-Arcade—Roseville, CA	795.2	12	31	Greeley, CO	3 921
32	Columbus, OH	780.1	36	32	Davenport-Moline-Rock Island, IA-IL	3 819
33	Salem, OR	733.4	44	33	Cedar Rapids, IA	3 781
34	Indianapolis-Carmel, IN	697.1	40	34	Rochester, NY	3 728
35	Des Moines-West Des Moines, IA	690.8	37	35	Peoria, IL	3 679
36	Davenport-Moline-Rock Island, IA-IL	686.2	11	36	Stockton, CA	3 624
37	Peoria, IL	676.2	17	37	Yakima, WA	3 540
38	Los Angeles-Long Beach-Santa Ana, CA	662.3	41	38	Santa Rosa-Petaluma, CA	3 429
39	Sioux Falls, SD	651	51	39	Orlando-Kissimmee, FL	3 415
40	Rochester, NY	649.8	39	40	Sioux Falls, SD	3 316
41	Santa Rosa-Petaluma, CA	647.6	52	41	Green Bay, WI	3 190
42	Tampa-St. Petersburg-Clearwater, FL	637.6	62	42	Rochester, MN	3 083
43	St. Cloud, MN	633.3	59	43	Columbia, SC	2 945
44	Cedar Rapids, IA	628.8	69	44	Evansville, IN-KY	2 841
45	Champaign-Urbana, IL	603.9	54	45	San Luis Obispo-Paso Robles, CA	2 784
46	Grand Forks, ND-MN	597	50	46	Waterloo-Cedar Falls, IA	2 737
47	New York-Northern New Jersey-Long Island, NY-NJ-PA	594.2	4	47	Merced, CA	2 607
48	Grand Rapids-Wyoming, MI	591.5	46	48	Grand Forks, ND-MN	2 582
49	Sioux City, IA-NE-SD	579.5	10	49	Phoenix-Mesa-Scottsdale, AZ	2 578
50	Waterloo-Cedar Falls, IA	573.3	64	50	Iowa City, IA	2 550
51	Orlando-Kissimmee, FL	570.1	24	51	Kennewick-Pasco-Richland, WA	2 521
52	Green Bay, WI	564.5	49	52	Sioux City, IA-NE-SD	2 516
53	Mankato, North Mankato, MN	564.3	14	53	Oxnard-Thousand Oaks-Ventura, CA	2 437
54	San Luis Obispo-Paso Robles, CA	560.6	45	54	Champaign-Urbana, IL	2 393
55	Dallas-Fort Worth-Arlington, TX	554.8	3	55	Bakersfield, CA	2 117
56	Amarillo, TX	554.4	74	56	Appleton, WI	2 094
57	Harrisonburg, VA	534.1	70	57	Yuba City, CA	2 091
58	Fort Smith, AR-OK	510.4	53	58	Mankato, North Mankato, MN	2 074
59	Columbia, SC	505.4	38	59	Los Angeles-Long Beach-Santa Ana, CA	2 059
60	Goldsboro, NC	501.2	57	60	Harrisonburg, VA	1 970
61	Wichita, KS	498.6	56	61	Amarillo, TX	1 879
62	Rochester, MN	472.1	63	62	Fargo, ND-MN	1 834
63	Fargo, ND-MN	469.7	71	63	Athens-Clarke County, GA	1 784
64	Iowa City, IA	458.8	72	64	Idaho Falls, ID	1 752
64	San Jose-Sunnyvale-Santa Clara, CA	458.8	75	65	Lafayette, IN	1 737
66	Pine Bluff, AR	455.3	25	66	Madera-Chowchilla, CA	1 708
67	Jackson, MS	450.1	65	67	San Jose-Sunnyvale-Santa Clara, CA	1 693
68	Santa Cruz-Watsonville, CA	447.4	27	68	Santa Barbara-Santa Maria-Goleta, CA	1 597
69	Evansville, IN-KY	437.2	5	69	Salinas, CA	1 199
70	Yuba City, CA	430.5	13	70	Hanford-Corcoran, CA	1 129
71	Athens-Clarke County, GA	426.9	66	71	Pine Bluff, AR	1 114
72	Idaho Falls, ID	422.4	60	72	Goldsboro, NC	723
73	Oklahoma City, OK	413.5	68	73	Santa Cruz-Watsonville, CA	682
74	Appleton, WI	403.7	15	74	El Centro, CA	452
75	Lafayette, IN	402.6	26	74	Yuma, AZ	452

75 Metropolitan Areas with Highest Agricultural Sales
Selected Rankings

Land in farms, 2007				Average value of agricultural land and buildings per acre, 2007			
Value of sales rank	Land in farms rank	Metropolitan area	Land in farms (1,000 acres) [col 117]	Value of sales rank	Value per Acre rank	Metropolitan area	Value per acre (1,000 acres) [col 123]
28	1	Kansas City, MO-KS	3 607	14	1	Oxnard-Thousand Oaks-Ventura, CA	22 782
55	2	Dallas-Fort Worth-Arlington, TX	3 522	68	2	Santa Cruz-Watsonville, CA	22 423
20	3	St. Louis, MO-IL	3 076	23	3	San Diego-Carlsbad-San Marcos, CA	19 247
73	4	Oklahoma City, OK	2 665	41	4	Santa Rosa-Petaluma, CA	15 887
3	5	Bakersfield, CA	2 362	38	5	Los Angeles-Long Beach-Santa Ana, CA	13 165
61	6	Wichita, KS	2 346	21	6	Philadelphia-Camden-Wilmington, PA-NJ-DE-MD	10 868
8	7	Chicago-Naperville-Joliet, IL-IN-WI	2 291	11	7	Stockton, CA	10 168
56	8	Amarillo, TX	2 202	6	8	Modesto, CA	9 476
19	9	Omaha-Council Bluffs, NE-IA	2 159	22	9	Lancaster, PA	9 324
12	10	Greeley, CO	2 089	42	10	Tampa-St. Petersburg-Clearwater, FL	9 310
46	11	Grand Forks, ND-MN	1 925	26	11	Yuma, AZ	8 361
63	12	Fargo, ND-MN	1 653	7	12	Riverside-San Bernardino-Ontario, CA	8 310
17	13	Yakima, WA	1 649	2	13	Visalia-Porterville, CA	8 266
1	14	Fresno, CA	1 636	1	14	Fresno, CA	7 927
10	15	Phoenix-Mesa-Scottsdale, AZ	1 533	4	15	Merced, CA	7 210
32	16	Columbus, OH	1 522	27	16	Santa Barbara-Santa Maria-Goleta, CA	7 081
39	17	Sioux Falls, SD	1 489	9	17	Miami-Fort Lauderdale-Pompano Beach, FL	7 064
35	18	Des Moines-West Des Moines, IA	1 426	31	18	Sacramento—Arden-Arcade—Roseville, CA	6 933
54	19	San Luis Obispo-Paso Robles, CA	1 370	25	19	Madera-Chowchilla, CA	6 783
34	20	Indianapolis-Carmel, IN	1 354	33	20	Salem, OR	6 404
5	21	Salinas, CA	1 328	70	21	Yuba City, CA	6 365
29	22	Boise City-Nampa, ID	1 255	57	22	Harrisonburg, VA	6 150
37	23	Peoria, IL	1 251	13	23	Hanford-Corcoran, CA	5 465
24	24	Kennewick-Pasco-Richland, WA	1 242	15	24	El Centro, CA	5 290
36	25	Davenport-Moline-Rock Island, IA-IL	1 223	10	25	Phoenix-Mesa-Scottsdale, AZ	5 177
30	26	Madison, WI	1 217	16	26	Lexington-Fayette, KY	4 958
2	27	Visalia-Porterville, CA	1 169	5	27	Salinas, CA	4 645
49	28	Sioux City, IA-NE-SD	1 140	8	28	Bakersfield, CA	4 626
45	29	Champaign-Urbana, IL	1 088	71	29	Athens-Clarke County, GA	4 591
58	30	Fort Smith, AR-OK	1 075	54	30	San Luis Obispo-Paso Robles, CA	4 546
44	31	Cedar Rapids, IA	1 060	8	31	Chicago-Naperville-Joliet, IL-IN-WI	4 455
31	32	Sacramento—Arden-Arcade—Roseville, CA	1 048	51	32	Orlando-Kissimmee, FL	4 397
18	33	Fayetteville-Springdale-Rogers, AR-MO	1 041	45	33	Champaign-Urbana, IL	4 262
4	33	Merced, CA	1 041	60	34	Goldsboro, NC	4 160
69	35	Evansville, IN-KY	968	37	35	Peoria, IL	4 064
51	36	Orlando-Kissimmee, FL	939	34	36	Indianapolis-Carmel, IN	4 048
43	37	St. Cloud, MN	894	36	37	Davenport-Moline-Rock Island, IA-IL	3 957
65	38	San Jose-Sunnyvale-Santa Clara, CA	880	50	38	Waterloo-Cedar Falls, IA	3 926
67	39	Jackson, MS	872	30	39	Madison, WI	3 867
7	40	Riverside-San Bernardino-Ontario, CA	869	32	40	Columbus, OH	3 824
40	41	Rochester, NY	863	65	41	San Jose-Sunnyvale-Santa Clara, CA	3 786
50	42	Waterloo-Cedar Falls, IA	841	48	42	Grand Rapids-Wyoming, MI	3 781
16	43	Lexington-Fayette, KY	808	75	43	Lafayette, IN	3 772
62	44	Rochester, MN	806	74	44	Appleton, WI	3 745
6	45	Modesto, CA	789	64	45	Iowa City, IA	3 719
72	46	Idaho Falls, ID	778	18	46	Fayetteville-Springdale-Rogers, AR-MO	3 695
11	47	Stockton, CA	738	44	47	Cedar Rapids, IA	3 623
27	48	Santa Barbara-Santa Maria-Goleta, CA	727	53	48	Mankato, North Mankato, MN	3 480
48	49	Grand Rapids-Wyoming, MI	710	20	49	St. Louis, MO-IL	3 477
53	50	Mankato, North Mankato, MN	689	52	50	Green Bay, WI	3 448
13	51	Hanford-Corcoran, CA	681	62	51	Rochester, MN	3 407
75	51	Lafayette, IN	681	35	52	Des Moines-West Des Moines, IA	3 231
25	53	Madera-Chowchilla, CA	680	19	53	Omaha-Council Bluffs, NE-IA	3 094
21	54	Philadelphia-Camden-Wilmington, PA-NJ-DE-MD	679	59	54	Columbia, SC	3 092
64	55	Iowa City, IA	647	55	55	Dallas-Fort Worth-Arlington, TX	3 058
9	56	Miami-Fort Lauderdale-Pompano Beach, FL	601	69	56	Evansville, IN-KY	2 933
52	57	Green Bay, WI	569	29	57	Boise City-Nampa, ID	2 925
41	58	Santa Rosa-Petaluma, CA	531	43	58	St. Cloud, MN	2 875
70	59	Yuba City, CA	521	39	59	Sioux Falls, SD	2 538
66	60	Pine Bluff, AR	520	49	60	Sioux City, IA-NE-SD	2 457
59	61	Columbia, SC	507	24	61	Kennewick-Pasco-Richland, WA	2 244
33	62	Salem, OR	474	28	62	Kansas City, MO-KS	2 227
15	63	El Centro, CA	427	66	63	Pine Bluff, AR	2 221
42	63	Tampa-St. Petersburg-Clearwater, FL	427	40	64	Rochester, NY	2 151
22	65	Lancaster, PA	425	58	65	Fort Smith, AR-OK	2 089
74	66	Appleton, WI	399	67	66	Jackson, MS	2 075
47	67	New York-Northern New Jersey-Long Island, NY-NJ-PA	369	72	67	Idaho Falls, ID	2 047
23	68	San Diego-Carlsbad-San Marcos, CA	304	63	68	Fargo, ND-MN	1 609
14	69	Oxnard-Thousand Oaks-Ventura, CA	259	73	69	Oklahoma City, OK	1 601
57	70	Harrisonburg, VA	233	12	70	Greeley, CO	1 550
71	71	Athens-Clarke County, GA	222	17	71	Yakima, WA	1 530
26	72	Yuma, AZ	210	46	72	Grand Forks, ND-MN	1 311
38	73	Los Angeles-Long Beach-Santa Ana, CA	196	61	73	Wichita, KS	1 161
60	74	Goldsboro, NC	175	56	74	Amarillo, TX	873
68	75	Santa Cruz-Watsonville, CA	47	47	X	New York-Northern New Jersey-Long Island, NY-NJ-PA	D

Table C. Metropolitan Areas — **Land Area and Population**

CBSA code[1]	Area name	Land area,[2] 2010 (sq km)	Population and population characteristics, 2010												
			Total persons	Rank	Per square kilometer	Race alone or in combination, not Hispanic or Latino (percent)				Percent Hispanic or Latino[3]	Age (percent)					
						White	Black	American Indian, Alaska Native	Asian and Pacific Islander		Under 5 years	5 to 17 years	18 to 24 years	25 to 34 years	35 to 44 years	45 to 54 years
		1	2	3	4	5	6	7	8	9	10	11	12	13	14	15

1. CBSA = Core Based Statistical Area. DIV = Metropolitan Division. See Appendix A for explanation. See Appendix B for list of metropolitan areas identified by type. 2. Dry land or land partially or temporarily covered by water. 3. May be of any race.

Table C. Metropolitan Areas — **Population and Households**

Area name	Population, 2010 (cont.)			Population change and components of change, 1990–2010							Households, 2010				
	Age (percent) (cont.)			Total persons		Percent change		Components of change, 2000–2009						Percent	
	55 to 64 years	65 to 74 years	75 years and over	Percent female	1990	2000	1990–2000	2000–2010	Births	Deaths	Net migration	Number	Percent change, 2000–2010	Persons per house-hold	Female family house-holder[1]	One person
	16	17	18	19	20	21	22	23	24	25	26	27	28	29	30	31

1. No spouse present.

Table C. Metropolitan Areas — **Population, Vital Statistics, Medicare, and Crime**

Area name	Persons in group quarters, 2010	Daytime population, 2010		Births, average 2006–2008		Deaths, average 2006–2008		Persons under 65 with no health insurance 2009		Medicare, 2011			Serious crimes known to police,[2] 2010	
		Number	Employ-ment/ residence ratio	Total	Rate[1]	Number	Rate[1]	Number	Percent	Enrolled in original Medicare	Enrolled in Medicare Advantage	Enrolled in a Medicare prescription drug plan	Total	
													Number	Rate[3]
	32	33	34	35	36	37	38	39	40	41	42	43	44	45

1. Per 1,000 estimated resident population. 2. Data for serious crimes have not been adjusted for underreporting; this may affect comparability between geographic areas and over time. 3. Per 100,000 population estimated by the FBI.

Table C. Metropolitan Areas — **Crime, Education, Money Income, and Poverty**

Area name	Serious crimes known to police,[1] 2010 (cont.)		Education							Income and Poverty, 2010							
	Rate[2]		School enrollment and attainment, 2010				Local government expenditures,[5] 2008–2009								Percent below poverty level		
			Enrollment[3]		Attainment[4] (percent)									Percent of house-holds with in-come of $200,000 or more			
	Violent	Property	Total	Percent private	High school grad-uate or less	Bach-elor's degree or more	Total current expendi-tures (mil dol)	Current expendi-tures per student (dollars)	Per capita income[6] (dollars)	Median house-hold income (dollars)	Percent of households with income of less than $25,000	Percent of house-holds with income of $100,000 or more		All persons	Children under 18 years	Children under 5
	46	47	48	49	50	51	52	53	54	55	56	57	58	59	60	61

1. Data for serious crimes have not been adjusted for underreporting; this may affect comparability between geographic areas and over time. 2. Per 100,000 population estimated by the FBI. 3. All persons 3 years old and over enrolled in nursery school through college. 4. Persons 25 years old and over. 5. Elementary and secondary education expenditures. 6. Based on resident population estimated as of July 1, 2009.

Table C. Metropolitan Areas — **Personal Income**

Area name	Personal income, 2009												
			Per capita[1]						Transfer payments				
										Government payments to individuals			
	Total (mil dol)	Percent change, 2008–2009	Dollars	Rank	Wages and salaries[2] (mil dol)	Proprietors' income (mil dol)	Dividends, interest, and rent (mil dol)	Total (mil dol)	Total (mil dol)	Social Security (mil dol)	Medical payments (mil dol)	Income mainte-nance (mil dol)	Unemploy-ment insurance (mil dol)
	62	63	64	65	66	67	68	69	70	71	72	73	74

1. Based on the resident population estimated as of July 1 of the year shown.   2. Includes other labor income.

Table C. Metropolitan Areas — **Earnings, Social Security, and Housing**

Area name	Earnings, 2009								Social Security beneficiaries, December 2010		Housing units, 2010		
		Percent by selected industries											
			Goods-related[1]		Service-related and health								
	Total (mil dol)	Farm	Total	Manu-facturing	Infor-mation, profes-sional, and technical services	Retail trade	Finance, insur-ance, and real estate	Health care and social services	Govern-ment	Number	Rate[2]	Supple-mental Security Income recipients, December 2009	Total	Percent change, 2000–2010
	75	76	77	78	79	80	81	82	83	84	85	86	87	88

1. Includes mining, construction, and manufacturing.   2. Per 1,000 resident population enumerated in the 2010 census.

Table C. Metropolitan Areas — **Housing, Labor Force, and Employment**

Area name	Housing units, 2010								Civilian labor force, 2010				Civilian employment,[5] 2010		
		Occupied units									Unemployment			Percent	
			Owner-occupied				Renter-occupied								
				Median owner cost as a percent of income											
	Total	Percent	Median value[1]	With a mort-gage	Without a mort-gage	Median rent[2]	Median rent as a percent of in-come	Sub-stand-ard units[3] (percent)	Total	Percent change, 2009–2010	Total	Rate[4]	Total	Management, business, science, and arts occupations	Construction, production, and maintenance occupations
	89	90	91	92	93	94	95	96	97	98	99	100	101	102	103

1. Specified owner-occupied units.   2. Specified renter-occupied units. A value of 10.0 represents 10 percent or less.   3. Overcrowded or lacking complete plumbing facilities.   4. Percent of civilian labor force.   5. Persons 16 years old and over.

Table C. Metropolitan Areas — **Nonfarm Employment and Agriculture**

Area name	Private nonfarm establishments, employment and payroll, 2009								Agriculture, 2007			
		Employment						Annual payroll		Farms		
											Percent with:	
	Number of establish-ments	Total	Health care and social assistance	Manufac-turing	Retail trade	Finance and insurance	Professional, scientific, and technical services	Total (mil dol)	Average per employee (dollars)	Number	Fewer than 50 acres	500 acres or more	Farm operators whose principal occu-pation is farming (percent)
	104	105	106	107	108	109	110	111	112	113	114	115	116

Table C. Metropolitan Areas — Agriculture

Area name	Agriculture, 2007 (cont.)															
	Land in farms					Value of land and buildings (dollars)			Value of products sold				Percent of farms with sales of:		Government payments	
			Acres					Value of machinery and equipment, average per farm (dollars)			Percent from:					
	Acreage (1,000)	Percent change, 2002–2007	Average size of farm	Total irrigated (1,000)	Total cropland (1,000)	Average per farm	Average per acre		Total (mil dol)	Average per farm (dollars)	Crops	Live-stock and poultry products	$10,000 or more	$100,000 or more	Total ($1,000)	Percent of farms
	117	118	119	120	121	122	123	124	125	126	127	128	129	130	131	132

Table C. Metropolitan Areas — Water Use, Wholesale Trade, Retail Trade, and Real Estate

Area name	Water use, 2005		Wholesale trade,[1] 2007				Retail trade, 2007				Real estate and rental and leasing, 2007			
	Total water withdrawn (mil gal/day)	Gallons withdrawn per person	Number of establish-ments	Number of employees	Sales (mil dol)	Annual payroll (mil dol)	Number of establish-ments	Number of employees	Sales (mil dol)	Annual payroll (mil dol)	Number of establish-ments	Number of employees	Receipts (mil dol)	Annual payroll (mil dol)
	133	134	135	136	137	138	139	140	141	142	143	144	145	146

1. Merchant wholesalers, except manufacturers' sales branches and offices.

Table C. Metropolitan Areas — Professional Services, Manufacturing, and Accommodation and Food Services

Area name	Professional, scientific, and technical services,[1] 2007				Manufacturing, 2007				Accommodation and food services, 2007			
	Number of establish-ments	Number of employees	Sales (mil dol)	Annual payroll (mil dol)	Number of establish-ments	Number of employees	Sales (mil dol)	Annual payroll (mil dol)	Number of establish-ments	Number of employees	Sales (mil dol)	Annual payroll (mil dol)
	147	148	149	150	151	152	153	154	155	156	157	158

1. Establishments subject to federal tax.

Table C. Metropolitan Areas — Health Care and Social Assistance, Other Services, and Federal Funds

Area name	Health care and social assistance,[1] 2007				Other services,[1] 2007				Federal funds and grants, 2009–2010			
									Expenditures (mil dol)			
										Direct payments for individuals		
	Number of establish-ments	Number of employees	Receipts (mil dol)	Annual payroll (mil dol)	Number of establish-ments	Number of employees	Receipts (mil dol)	Annual payroll (mil dol)	Total	Social Security and government retirement	Medicare	Food stamps and Supplemental Security Income
	159	160	161	162	163	164	165	166	167	168	169	170

1. Establishments subject to federal tax.

Table C. Metropolitan Areas — Federal Funds, Residential Construction and Local Government Finances

Area name	Federal funds and grants, 2009–2010 (cont.)							Value of residential construction authorized by building permits, 2010		Local government finances, 2007					
	Expenditures (mil dol) (cont.)									General revenue					
	Procurement contract awards			Grants								Taxes			
														Per capita[1] (dollars)	
	Salaries and wages	Defense	Other	Medicaid and other health-related	Nutrition and family welfare	Education	Other	New construction ($1,000)	Number of housing units	Total (mil dol)	Inter-govern-mental (mil dol)	Total (mil dol)	Total	Property
	171	172	173	174	175	176	177	178	179	180	181	182	183	184

1. Based on the resident population estimated as of July 1 of the year shown.

Table C. Metropolitan Areas — Local Government Finances, Government Employment, and Voting

Area name	Local government finances, 2007 (cont.)									Government employment, 2009			Presidential election,[2] 2008		
	Direct general expenditure							Debt outstanding					Percent of vote cast:		
			Percent of total for:												
	Total (mil dol)	Per capita[1] (dollars)	Educa-tion	Health and hospitals	Police protec-tion	Public welfare	High-ways	Total (mil dol)	Per capita[1] (dollars)	Federal civilian	Federal military	State and local	Demo-cratic	Republi-can	All other
	185	186	187	188	189	190	191	192	193	194	195	196	197	198	199

1. Based on the resident population estimated as of July 1 of the year shown.   2. © 2009 Election Data Services, Inc. All rights reserved.

Table C. Metropolitan Areas — Land Area and Population

CBSA code[1]	Area name	Land area,[2] 2010 (sq km)	Total persons	Rank	Per square kilometer	White	Black	American Indian, Alaska Native	Asian and Pacific Islander	Percent Hispanic or Latino[3]	Under 5 years	5 to 17 years	18 to 24 years	25 to 34 years	35 to 44 years	45 to 54 years
		1	2	3	4	5	6	7	8	9	10	11	12	13	14	15
10180	Abilene, TX	7 106	165 252	240	23.3	69.8	7.8	0.9	1.9	21.2	7.0	16.7	13.0	13.8	11.5	13.5
10420	Akron, OH	2 331	703 200	72	301.7	84.0	13.0	0.7	2.5	1.5	5.6	16.7	10.6	11.7	12.7	15.5
10500	Albany, GA	5 005	157 308	252	31.4	44.5	52.6	0.6	1.3	2.1	7.2	18.7	11.3	12.6	12.3	13.8
10580	Albany-Schenectady-Troy, NY	7 282	870 716	58	119.6	84.6	8.3	0.7	3.8	4.1	5.4	16.0	10.8	12.1	13.0	15.6
10740	Albuquerque, NM	24 042	887 077	57	36.9	43.6	2.8	5.7	2.6	46.7	6.8	17.8	9.8	13.8	12.8	14.5
10780	Alexandria, LA	5 079	153 922	257	30.3	65.6	30.2	1.4	1.4	2.8	6.9	18.6	8.8	13.4	12.6	14.4
10900	Allentown-Bethlehem-Easton, PA-NJ	3 764	821 173	64	218.2	79.9	5.0	0.4	2.9	13.0	5.7	17.0	8.9	11.2	13.4	15.8
11020	Altoona, PA	1 362	127 089	301	93.3	96.7	2.3	0.4	0.8	1.0	5.7	15.5	9.3	11.1	12.2	14.8
11100	Amarillo, TX	9 451	249 881	185	26.4	65.6	6.5	1.0	2.9	25.3	7.6	18.7	10.3	14.2	12.5	13.9
11180	Ames, IA	1 484	89 542	356	60.3	88.2	2.9	0.5	6.7	3.0	5.4	12.5	29.0	14.3	9.3	10.4
11260	Anchorage, AK	68 149	380 821	133	5.6	73.1	5.8	11.1	10.3	6.7	7.6	19.1	10.6	15.0	13.5	15.5
11300	Anderson, IN	1 170	131 636	293	112.5	87.7	9.2	0.6	0.7	3.2	6.2	16.9	9.0	12.4	13.2	14.3
11340	Anderson, SC	1 853	187 126	222	101.0	80.0	16.7	0.6	1.0	2.9	6.4	17.5	8.4	11.4	13.3	14.8
11460	Ann Arbor, MI	1 828	344 791	146	188.6	74.7	14.0	1.0	9.1	4.0	5.6	15.3	16.9	14.3	12.7	13.7
11500	Anniston-Oxford, AL	1 569	118 572	315	75.6	74.9	21.1	0.9	1.1	3.3	6.1	16.8	10.9	12.5	12.3	14.3
11540	Appleton, WI	2 475	225 666	194	91.2	91.4	1.3	1.8	3.1	3.6	6.7	18.9	8.2	13.2	14.0	16.0
11700	Asheville, NC	5 265	424 858	117	80.7	87.6	5.2	0.9	1.3	6.4	5.5	14.9	7.8	12.0	12.9	14.4
12020	Athens-Clarke County, GA	2 654	192 541	219	72.5	69.0	20.0	0.5	3.8	8.0	6.0	14.9	21.4	14.3	11.7	11.8
12060	Atlanta-Sandy Springs-Marietta, GA	21 597	5 268 860	9	244.0	52.0	32.9	0.7	5.5	10.4	7.2	19.3	9.2	14.5	15.8	14.7
12100	Atlantic City-Hammonton, NJ	1 439	274 549	166	190.8	60.0	15.9	0.7	8.2	16.8	6.0	17.3	9.3	11.4	13.2	16.3
12220	Auburn-Opelika, AL	1 574	140 247	276	89.1	70.9	23.2	0.7	3.1	3.3	6.2	16.3	20.5	13.8	12.3	12.2
12260	Augusta-Richmond County, GA-SC	8 470	556 877	92	65.7	58.1	36.0	0.8	2.5	4.4	6.8	18.0	10.1	13.2	12.6	14.7
12420	Austin-Round Rock-San Marcos, TX	10 929	1 716 289	35	157.0	56.2	7.6	0.8	5.6	31.4	7.4	17.9	11.7	16.9	15.1	13.3
12540	Bakersfield-Delano, CA	21 062	839 631	62	39.9	40.2	6.0	1.5	4.8	49.2	8.7	21.6	11.2	14.5	12.9	12.9
12580	Baltimore-Towson, MD	6 738	2 710 489	20	402.3	61.7	29.6	0.8	5.4	4.6	6.2	16.8	9.9	13.4	13.4	15.6
12620	Bangor, ME	8 799	153 923	256	17.5	96.0	1.1	2.0	1.3	1.1	5.2	14.5	13.2	11.5	12.3	15.7
12700	Barnstable Town, MA	1 020	215 888	197	211.7	93.0	2.6	1.2	1.5	2.2	4.1	13.2	6.5	8.2	10.6	15.9
12940	Baton Rouge, LA	10 430	802 484	65	76.9	58.8	36.0	0.6	2.1	3.4	6.9	17.8	11.7	14.6	12.8	14.1
12980	Battle Creek, MI	1 829	136 146	287	74.4	82.3	12.4	1.4	2.1	4.5	6.4	17.8	9.3	11.5	12.4	14.8
13020	Bay City, MI	1 146	107 771	333	94.0	92.7	2.3	1.1	0.7	4.7	5.8	16.4	8.5	11.4	12.2	15.6
13140	Beaumont-Port Arthur, TX	5 440	388 745	132	71.5	59.7	24.9	0.7	2.8	12.9	6.7	17.7	9.9	13.4	12.6	14.9
13380	Bellingham, WA	5 457	201 140	210	36.9	84.6	1.6	3.7	5.3	7.8	5.6	15.3	14.2	13.0	11.9	13.6
13460	Bend, OR	7 817	157 733	251	20.2	90.3	0.7	1.7	1.9	7.4	6.1	16.9	7.4	12.6	13.5	14.5
13740	Billings, MT	12 127	158 050	250	13.0	90.7	1.1	4.7	1.2	4.5	6.7	16.8	8.7	13.3	12.0	15.2
13780	Binghamton, NY	3 171	251 725	182	79.4	90.0	4.7	0.7	3.5	3.0	5.3	15.5	11.8	11.2	11.3	15.8
13820	Birmingham-Hoover, AL	13 674	1 128 047	49	82.5	65.9	28.6	0.6	1.5	4.3	6.6	17.3	9.1	13.8	13.4	14.6
13900	Bismarck, ND	9 218	108 779	332	11.8	93.7	0.9	4.7	0.7	1.3	6.7	16.2	9.7	14.1	12.1	15.0
13980	Blacksburg-Christiansburg-Radford, VA	2 778	162 958	241	58.7	89.8	5.0	0.6	4.1	2.2	4.7	12.4	25.1	11.8	11.3	11.6
14020	Bloomington, IN	3 425	192 714	218	56.3	91.0	3.0	0.7	4.6	2.4	5.0	13.3	22.8	13.4	10.8	12.2
14060	Bloomington-Normal, IL	3 065	169 572	235	55.3	83.7	8.4	0.6	4.8	4.4	6.3	16.4	17.3	13.8	12.4	13.3
14260	Boise City-Nampa, ID	30 473	616 561	86	20.2	83.8	1.2	1.3	2.9	12.6	7.8	20.2	9.1	14.2	13.7	13.4
14460	Boston-Cambridge-Quincy, MA-NH	9 032	4 552 402	10	504.0	76.3	7.4	0.5	7.2	9.0	5.6	16.0	10.4	13.6	13.8	15.5
14460	Boston-Quincy, MA Div	2 884	1 887 792	X	654.6	70.3	12.4	0.6	7.3	9.6	5.6	15.5	11.9	14.5	13.6	14.6
14460	Cambridge-Newton-Framingham, MA Div	2 118	1 503 085	X	709.7	78.3	5.0	0.4	10.3	6.5	5.7	15.6	9.5	14.5	14.2	15.5
14460	Peabody, MA Div	1 276	743 159	X	582.4	77.2	3.2	0.4	3.6	16.5	5.9	17.3	8.8	11.3	13.5	16.3
14460	Rockingham County-Strafford County, NH Div	2 755	418 366	X	151.9	95.0	1.1	0.6	2.5	2.0	5.2	17.0	9.6	10.5	14.1	17.9
14500	Boulder, CO	1 881	294 567	160	156.6	81.1	1.2	0.9	5.3	13.3	5.6	15.7	14.2	13.4	13.9	15.1
14540	Bowling Green, KY	2 187	125 953	304	57.6	84.5	9.2	0.6	3.0	4.2	6.3	16.4	15.5	13.7	12.4	13.3
14740	Bremerton-Silverdale, WA	1 023	251 133	183	245.5	83.5	3.7	3.0	8.7	6.2	5.9	16.6	10.1	12.5	12.2	15.4
14860	Bridgeport-Stamford-Norwalk, CT	1 618	916 829	56	566.6	67.4	10.8	0.4	5.3	16.9	6.2	18.6	7.9	11.6	14.3	16.3
15180	Brownsville-Harlingen, TX	2 307	406 220	126	176.1	10.8	0.3	0.2	0.7	88.1	8.8	24.2	9.8	12.8	12.7	11.3
15260	Brunswick, GA	3 332	112 370	325	33.7	70.2	24.0	0.7	1.3	5.1	6.6	17.6	8.4	11.5	12.7	14.8
15380	Buffalo-Niagara Falls, NY	4 053	1 135 509	47	280.2	80.9	12.7	1.1	2.7	4.1	5.3	16.3	10.3	11.6	12.3	15.6
15500	Burlington, NC	1 098	151 131	264	137.6	68.5	19.5	0.8	1.5	11.0	6.3	17.2	10.6	11.4	13.7	14.5
15540	Burlington-South Burlington, VT	3 243	211 261	199	65.1	93.9	2.1	1.2	2.8	1.7	5.3	15.8	13.3	12.8	13.1	15.9
15940	Canton-Massillon, OH	2 512	404 422	128	161.0	90.3	8.3	0.8	1.0	1.5	5.8	17.1	8.6	11.0	12.3	15.4
15980	Cape Coral-Fort Myers, FL	2 032	618 754	85	304.5	72.0	8.3	0.5	1.8	18.3	5.3	14.2	7.7	10.6	11.4	13.2
16020	Cape Girardeau-Jackson, MO-IL	3 709	96 275	350	26.0	88.2	9.4	0.8	1.3	1.8	6.3	15.9	12.7	12.2	11.7	14.1
16180	Carson City, NV	375	55 274	366	147.4	72.4	2.2	2.8	3.1	21.3	5.8	15.5	8.5	12.0	12.6	15.2
16220	Casper, WY	13 831	75 450	364	5.5	90.6	1.4	1.5	1.1	6.9	7.1	16.8	9.6	14.2	12.1	15.0
16300	Cedar Rapids, IA	5 203	257 940	176	49.6	92.3	4.5	0.6	2.1	2.4	6.6	17.9	9.2	13.3	13.0	14.7
16580	Champaign-Urbana, IL	4 976	231 891	191	46.6	76.2	11.7	0.6	8.7	4.8	5.8	14.2	21.5	14.4	10.8	12.2

1. CBSA = Core Based Statistical Area. DIV = Metropolitan Division. See Appendix A for explanation. See Appendix B for list of metropolitan areas identified by type.   2. Dry land or land partially or temporarily covered by water.   3. May be of any race.

Table C. Metropolitan Areas — **Population and Households**

Area name	Population, 2010 (cont.) Age (percent) (cont.) 55 to 64 years	65 to 74 years	75 years and over	Percent female	Population change and components of change, 1990–2010 Total persons 1990	2000	Percent change 1990–2000	2000–2010	Components of change, 2000–2009 Births	Deaths	Net migration	Households, 2010 Number	Percent change, 2000–2010	Persons per house-hold	Percent Female family house-holder[1]	One person
	16	17	18	19	20	21	22	23	24	25	26	27	28	29	30	31
Abilene, TX	10.8	7.2	6.5	49.8	148 004	160 245	8.3	3.1	22 115	14 129	-7 274	62 206	6.4	2.49	12.4	26.9
Akron, OH	13.0	7.3	6.9	51.5	657 575	694 960	5.7	1.2	77 686	60 445	-11 610	285 003	3.9	2.40	13.0	29.0
Albany, GA	12.1	6.8	5.2	52.6	146 583	157 833	7.7	-0.3	21 802	12 766	-3 258	59 319	3.3	2.56	22.2	26.8
Albany-Schenectady-Troy, NY	13.0	7.1	6.9	51.2	809 642	825 875	2.0	5.4	87 732	69 924	18 883	355 301	7.6	2.36	11.7	30.3
Albuquerque, NM	12.2	6.9	5.4	50.9	599 416	729 649	21.7	21.6	108 220	54 737	79 082	347 366	23.6	2.51	13.8	28.5
Alexandria, LA	11.9	7.6	5.9	50.6	149 082	145 035	-2.7	6.1	20 339	14 217	894	57 897	6.8	2.53	17.7	26.8
Allentown-Bethlehem-Easton, PA-NJ	12.7	7.5	7.7	51.3	686 718	740 395	7.8	10.9	84 386	68 582	62 530	315 712	10.5	2.53	11.7	25.7
Altoona, PA	13.7	8.7	9.0	51.4	130 542	129 144	-1.1	-1.6	13 442	14 830	-909	52 159	1.2	2.37	11.7	29.6
Amarillo, TX	11.0	6.3	5.5	50.1	196 111	226 522	15.5	10.3	34 858	19 130	5 394	94 111	10.4	2.56	12.9	26.7
Ames, IA	9.2	5.0	5.0	48.2	74 252	79 981	7.7	12.0	8 914	4 398	3 142	34 736	18.2	2.34	6.2	28.3
Anchorage, AK	11.5	4.7	2.7	49.0	266 021	319 605	20.1	19.2	50 142	14 765	21 100	139 156	20.6	2.67	11.0	24.3
Anderson, IN	12.6	8.1	7.2	50.0	130 669	133 358	2.1	-1.3	15 110	13 311	-2 927	51 927	-2.1	2.41	13.6	28.3
Anderson, SC	12.9	8.6	6.5	51.8	145 177	165 740	14.2	12.9	21 136	16 888	15 815	73 829	12.5	2.50	14.5	25.4
Ann Arbor, MI	11.4	5.6	4.5	50.7	282 937	322 895	14.1	6.8	38 579	17 347	5 434	137 193	9.5	2.38	9.8	30.6
Anniston-Oxford, AL	12.7	8.0	6.4	51.8	116 032	112 249	-3.3	5.6	13 946	12 201	795	47 331	4.5	2.44	15.2	27.7
Appleton, WI	11.3	6.1	5.6	50.1	174 801	201 602	15.3	11.9	27 234	13 040	7 175	88 223	16.9	2.52	8.4	24.9
Asheville, NC	14.1	9.8	8.6	51.7	308 005	369 171	19.9	15.1	42 511	40 118	43 056	179 917	16.6	2.30	10.4	29.5
Athens-Clarke County, GA	9.9	5.8	4.3	51.9	136 025	166 079	22.1	15.9	21 714	10 920	16 334	73 191	15.4	2.50	12.5	26.5
Atlanta-Sandy Springs-Marietta, GA	10.5	5.4	3.6	51.3	3 068 976	4 247 981	38.4	24.0	723 568	265 101	643 228	1 937 225	24.6	2.68	15.3	25.3
Atlantic City-Hammonton, NJ	12.4	7.7	6.5	51.5	224 327	252 552	12.6	8.7	32 749	24 188	12 152	102 847	8.2	2.61	15.5	26.9
Auburn-Opelika, AL	9.5	5.4	3.7	50.7	87 146	115 092	32.1	21.9	13 824	7 455	15 088	55 682	21.8	2.44	13.0	27.9
Augusta-Richmond County, GA-SC	12.3	7.2	5.3	51.4	435 799	499 684	14.7	11.4	69 338	42 918	15 872	212 245	14.9	2.54	17.7	26.1
Austin-Round Rock-San Marcos, TX	9.6	4.7	3.4	49.9	846 227	1 249 763	47.7	37.3	222 904	65 350	302 560	650 459	37.9	2.58	10.9	27.3
Bakersfield-Delano, CA	9.2	5.2	3.8	48.4	544 981	661 645	21.4	26.9	126 951	48 438	71 540	254 610	22.0	3.15	15.7	19.3
Baltimore-Towson, MD	12.2	6.8	5.9	51.9	2 382 172	2 552 994	7.2	6.2	322 155	215 971	9 396	1 038 765	6.6	2.54	15.2	27.4
Bangor, ME	13.2	7.6	6.9	50.7	146 601	144 919	-1.1	6.2	14 718	12 774	3 491	62 966	8.4	2.33	10.3	28.0
Barnstable Town, MA	16.5	12.4	12.6	52.4	186 605	222 230	19.1	-2.9	18 189	25 467	7 503	95 755	1.0	2.21	9.6	31.8
Baton Rouge, LA	11.4	6.2	4.6	50.9	623 850	705 973	13.2	13.7	99 353	54 884	39 924	300 022	16.9	2.59	17.0	25.7
Battle Creek, MI	12.9	7.6	7.2	51.1	135 982	137 985	1.5	-1.3	17 334	13 195	-5 694	54 016	-0.2	2.44	14.6	28.8
Bay City, MI	13.9	8.5	7.7	51.1	111 723	110 157	-1.4	-2.2	11 791	10 262	-3 583	44 603	1.5	2.38	11.8	29.3
Beaumont-Port Arthur, TX	11.7	6.9	6.2	49.4	361 218	385 090	6.6	0.9	47 823	36 238	-16 250	144 934	1.8	2.56	15.4	26.4
Bellingham, WA	13.0	7.3	6.0	50.5	127 780	166 814	30.5	20.6	19 800	12 286	26 920	80 370	24.7	2.43	8.8	27.8
Bend, OR	14.2	8.7	6.2	50.6	74 976	115 367	53.9	36.7	16 207	9 603	36 998	64 090	40.6	2.44	9.4	24.1
Billings, MT	13.0	7.5	6.9	51.0	121 499	138 904	14.3	13.8	18 076	12 020	10 373	65 243	16.2	2.37	10.2	29.8
Binghamton, NY	12.7	8.0	8.3	50.9	264 497	252 320	-4.6	-0.2	24 938	23 106	-7 976	102 517	2.0	2.35	11.7	30.9
Birmingham-Hoover, AL	12.3	7.1	5.9	51.8	956 668	1 052 238	10.0	7.2	139 887	101 637	41 832	441 924	7.2	2.50	15.3	27.4
Bismarck, ND	12.5	6.8	6.9	50.6	83 831	94 719	13.0	14.8	11 929	7 183	7 371	45 265	20.5	2.33	8.8	29.8
Blacksburg-Christiansburg-Radford, VA	10.8	6.9	5.4	49.5	140 715	151 272	7.5	7.7	14 169	11 673	6 721	63 793	9.2	2.35	9.2	27.7
Bloomington, IN	10.6	6.3	6.4	50.1	156 669	175 506	12.0	9.8	18 076	12 382	5 439	76 837	12.1	2.31	8.4	30.6
Bloomington-Normal, IL	10.3	5.3	4.9	51.4	129 180	150 433	16.5	12.7	20 116	9 583	7 620	65 104	14.7	2.44	9.6	28.1
Boise City-Nampa, ID	10.8	6.1	4.8	50.1	319 596	464 840	45.4	32.6	82 980	31 976	92 620	225 594	32.5	2.67	10.6	23.6
Boston-Cambridge-Quincy, MA-NH	12.0	6.7	6.4	51.6	4 133 895	4 391 344	6.2	3.7	515 962	326 004	-38 453	1 760 584	4.8	2.50	11.9	28.5
Boston-Quincy, MA Div	11.5	6.6	6.2	51.8	1 715 269	1 812 937	5.7	4.1	218 254	136 991	-28 950	731 807	5.2	2.47	13.2	30.1
Cambridge-Newton-Framingham, MA Div	11.8	6.6	6.5	51.4	1 398 468	1 465 396	4.8	2.6	167 999	103 765	-24 296	580 688	3.5	2.49	10.1	27.8
Peabody, MA Div	12.8	7.0	7.1	52.0	670 080	723 419	8.0	2.7	86 145	59 276	-3 304	285 956	3.8	2.54	13.5	28.1
Rockingham County-Strafford County, NH Div	13.2	6.9	5.5	50.8	350 078	389 592	11.3	7.4	43 564	25 972	18 097	162 133	10.2	2.51	9.3	24.3
Boulder, CO	12.0	5.7	4.3	49.8	225 339	291 288	29.3	1.1	32 395	13 271	9 349	119 300	4.0	2.39	7.7	29.0
Bowling Green, KY	11.0	6.5	5.0	51.0	88 077	104 166	18.3	20.9	13 801	8 370	11 563	48 531	21.3	2.46	11.7	27.4
Bremerton-Silverdale, WA	14.1	7.6	5.6	49.4	189 731	231 969	22.3	8.3	27 437	16 612	-897	97 220	12.5	2.49	10.2	25.2
Bridgeport-Stamford-Norwalk, CT	11.7	6.8	6.7	51.4	827 645	882 567	6.6	3.9	108 655	62 364	-22 755	335 545	3.5	2.68	12.3	24.9
Brownsville-Harlingen, TX	9.3	6.1	5.0	51.9	260 120	335 227	28.9	21.2	79 503	19 083	3 050	119 631	23.0	3.36	20.0	16.4
Brunswick, GA	13.5	8.8	6.1	51.9	82 207	93 044	13.2	20.8	12 505	9 256	8 026	44 630	21.1	2.48	15.5	26.8
Buffalo-Niagara Falls, NY	12.8	7.7	8.1	51.7	1 189 340	1 170 111	-1.6	-3.0	117 578	111 673	-45 070	473 720	1.1	2.33	13.5	32.7
Burlington, NC	11.9	7.6	7.0	52.4	108 213	130 800	20.9	15.5	17 491	12 555	15 422	59 960	16.2	2.45	14.5	27.8
Burlington-South Burlington, VT	12.3	6.3	5.3	51.0	177 059	198 889	12.3	6.2	21 291	12 664	1 775	83 242	9.6	2.41	9.5	26.4
Canton-Massillon, OH	13.6	8.3	7.9	51.5	394 106	406 934	3.3	-0.6	45 012	38 386	-7 293	162 474	1.9	2.43	12.4	27.8
Cape Coral-Fort Myers, FL	14.1	13.1	10.4	50.9	335 113	440 888	31.6	40.3	58 943	52 082	141 120	259 818	37.8	2.35	10.3	26.7
Cape Girardeau-Jackson, MO-IL	12.2	7.7	7.1	51.2	82 878	90 312	9.0	6.6	11 012	8 740	1 605	38 024	7.5	2.41	11.4	27.6
Carson City, NV	13.8	8.7	7.8	48.1	40 443	52 457	29.7	5.4	6 931	5 924	2 024	21 427	6.2	2.41	12.0	30.4
Casper, WY	12.7	6.4	6.1	49.7	61 226	66 533	8.7	13.4	9 175	5 547	4 734	30 616	14.2	2.41	10.9	28.5
Cedar Rapids, IA	11.7	7.0	6.6	50.5	210 640	237 230	12.6	8.7	30 943	17 852	6 202	104 617	11.2	2.40	9.6	28.6
Champaign-Urbana, IL	10.1	5.6	5.4	50.2	202 848	210 275	3.7	10.3	25 382	14 219	6 046	93 123	12.6	2.31	9.7	32.3

1. No spouse present.

Table C. Metropolitan Areas — **Population, Vital Statistics, Medicare, and Crime**

Area name	Daytime population, 2010			Births, average 2006–2008		Deaths, average 2006–2008		Persons under 65 with no health insurance 2009		Medicare, 2011			Serious crimes known to police,[2] 2010 Total	
	Persons in group quarters, 2010	Number	Employment/ residence ratio	Total	Rate[1]	Number	Rate[1]	Number	Percent	Enrolled in original Medicare	Enrolled in Medicare Advantage	Enrolled in a Medicare prescription drug plan	Number	Rate[3]
	32	33	34	35	36	37	38	39	40	41	42	43	44	45
Abilene, TX	10 369	165 428	1.01	D	D	1 524	9.6	31 734	23.6	26 836	2 002	12 016	6 447	3 901
Akron, OH	17 881	697 259	0.98	8 170	11.7	6 478	9.3	78 583	13.4	118 448	48 851	41 919	23 316	3 511
Albany, GA	5 578	163 588	1.02	2 299	14.0	1 418	8.6	28 565	20.3	24 548	4 497	10 759	7 483	4 787
Albany-Schenectady-Troy, NY	32 571	882 054	1.03	9 086	10.7	7 367	8.6	69 844	9.7	148 011	51 447	38 178	25 528	2 932
Albuquerque, NM	14 850	886 089	0.99	12 204	14.7	6 425	7.7	148 582	20.0	132 886	59 580	32 464	40 121	4 523
Alexandria, LA	7 438	D	D	2 291	15.2	1 491	9.9	24 271	18.8	27 957	2 663	12 430	7 715	5 298
Allentown-Bethlehem-Easton, PA-NJ	22 280	780 213	0.89	9 572	11.9	7 411	9.2	79 007	11.7	149 270	33 247	66 058	20 859	2 551
Altoona, PA	3 672	D	D	1 444	11.5	1 533	12.2	11 821	11.8	27 634	13 321	7 659	2 588	2 036
Amarillo, TX	9 044	250 445	0.99	3 780	15.6	2 120	8.7	52 101	24.4	35 319	3 558	16 209	13 236	5 297
Ames, IA	8 174	90 309	1.02	1 014	12.1	499	5.9	5 837	7.7	10 418	972	6 130	2 514	2 808
Anchorage, AK	9 820	381 672	0.99	5 846	16.1	1 743	4.8	71 095	20.8	37 120	263	13 957	NA	NA
Anderson, IN	6 277	D	D	1 623	12.4	1 410	10.8	18 942	17.6	25 617	3 451	9 362	4 688	3 561
Anderson, SC	2 764	D	D	2 440	13.5	1 859	10.3	29 156	19.1	37 366	8 175	15 420	9 929	5 306
Ann Arbor, MI	17 812	377 510	1.20	4 028	11.6	1 936	5.6	31 502	10.4	44 137	9 355	13 708	10 607	3 076
Anniston-Oxford, AL	2 919	D	D	1 535	13.6	1 320	11.7	14 673	15.5	24 180	2 381	9 781	5 163	4 354
Appleton, WI	3 237	220 614	0.95	2 975	13.6	1 450	6.6	17 590	9.3	31 804	16 598	7 094	5 145	2 280
Asheville, NC	10 813	427 662	1.03	4 607	11.4	4 465	11.1	61 840	18.8	93 728	15 316	40 212	11 050	2 614
Athens-Clarke County, GA	9 681	199 360	1.08	D	D	1 184	6.3	36 027	21.6	24 994	5 432	9 275	7 902	4 128
Atlanta-Sandy Springs-Marietta, GA	84 370	5 294 495	1.00	80 719	15.3	29 796	5.7	1 013 092	20.9	592 487	147 262	222 169	209 402	3 988
Atlantic City-Hammonton, NJ	6 046	284 152	1.08	3 641	13.4	2 521	9.3	35 494	15.5	46 504	4 150	21 678	11 236	4 093
Auburn-Opelika, AL	4 410	132 095	0.86	1 702	13.1	822	6.3	18 579	15.5	17 048	1 656	6 799	3 781	2 696
Augusta-Richmond County, GA-SC	17 233	563 925	1.02	7 225	13.7	4 724	8.9	82 642	18.1	88 586	18 451	30 461	27 487	4 945
Austin-Round Rock-San Marcos, TX	40 873	1 736 398	1.01	25 670	16.2	7 624	4.8	338 060	22.0	174 758	22 923	61 998	72 200	4 207
Bakersfield-Delano, CA	36 757	844 168	1.01	15 254	19.3	5 327	6.7	156 590	21.9	95 872	32 969	36 161	35 429	4 220
Baltimore-Towson, MD	68 923	2 681 782	0.98	35 392	13.3	23 121	8.7	276 265	12.0	403 490	36 564	169 077	102 715	3 790
Bangor, ME	7 318	157 411	1.05	1 597	10.8	1 379	9.3	15 168	12.2	30 630	4 265	15 957	4 767	3 097
Barnstable Town, MA	3 961	210 308	0.94	1 909	8.6	2 661	11.9	8 026	4.9	63 183	5 424	26 581	7 540	3 493
Baton Rouge, LA	25 547	807 343	1.01	11 050	14.3	6 237	8.1	120 076	17.6	110 185	40 223	30 709	35 418	4 463
Battle Creek, MI	4 275	D	D	1 831	13.4	1 415	10.3	16 249	14.3	26 559	4 303	9 517	5 853	4 352
Bay City, MI	1 438	D	D	1 233	11.4	1 141	10.6	11 309	12.8	22 583	4 251	8 079	2 971	2 757
Beaumont-Port Arthur, TX	17 002	399 830	1.07	5 431	14.4	3 937	10.4	75 858	23.8	63 108	14 282	26 272	16 440	4 229
Bellingham, WA	5 704	197 908	0.96	2 200	11.5	1 385	7.2	29 077	17.0	33 362	10 885	11 474	6 362	3 163
Bend, OR	1 244	158 440	1.01	2 014	13.1	1 125	7.3	26 867	20.2	29 102	8 119	11 106	5 319	3 372
Billings, MT	3 748	157 898	1.01	1 979	13.2	1 382	9.2	26 077	19.9	26 641	5 501	12 371	6 334	4 008
Binghamton, NY	10 664	251 527	1.00	2 699	11.0	2 494	10.1	22 167	11.1	50 569	13 563	18 540	6 567	2 609
Birmingham-Hoover, AL	24 287	1 133 319	1.01	15 832	14.3	11 026	9.9	137 443	14.4	193 839	73 187	47 916	38 440	3 482
Bismarck, ND	3 360	D	D	D	D	806	7.8	9 049	10.1	17 711	2 436	10 863	2 254	2 072
Blacksburg-Christiansburg-Radford, VA	12 985	163 549	1.02	D	D	1 282	8.2	19 455	14.4	25 711	3 373	13 870	4 294	2 635
Bloomington, IN	15 454	193 376	1.01	D	D	1 361	7.5	26 794	16.8	27 482	3 435	13 297	5 681	3 363
Bloomington-Normal, IL	10 676	174 938	1.06	2 213	13.5	1 075	6.6	14 560	9.9	20 841	2 895	7 634	4 531	2 733
Boise City-Nampa, ID	13 394	616 772	0.99	9 300	15.9	3 761	6.4	97 390	18.3	84 660	35 411	21 260	14 175	2 301
Boston-Cambridge-Quincy, MA-NH	159 463	4 700 283	1.06	54 488	12.1	34 000	7.6	209 655	5.4	712 146	111 772	298 544	117 849	2 604
Boston-Quincy, MA Div	76 660	2 048 803	1.17	23 079	12.4	14 124	7.6	81 392	5.0	288 699	41 580	124 891	56 750	3 019
Cambridge-Newton-Framingham, MA Div	55 412	1 565 893	1.08	18 170	12.3	10 726	7.3	58 888	4.6	227 874	46 952	85 726	33 092	2 206
Peabody, MA Div	16 472	692 480	0.85	8 978	12.2	6 275	8.5	30 050	4.8	127 930	18 977	58 886	18 786	2 528
Rockingham County-Strafford County, NH Div	10 919	D	D	4 261	10.2	2 875	6.9	39 325	10.9	67 643	4 263	29 041	9 221	2 293
Boulder, CO	8 949	320 674	1.17	3 374	11.7	1 510	5.2	37 861	14.0	35 488	11 949	9 859	7 507	2 548
Bowling Green, KY	6 533	D	D	D	D	908	7.8	18 005	17.4	19 013	2 615	11 001	3 611	2 867
Bremerton-Silverdale, WA	8 722	242 068	0.91	2 995	12.5	1 854	7.8	27 146	13.2	40 623	6 763	12 141	7 455	2 969
Bridgeport-Stamford-Norwalk, CT	19 168	945 694	1.06	11 507	12.8	6 512	7.3	86 933	11.4	136 463	26 598	55 233	18 552	2 063
Brownsville-Harlingen, TX	3 730	406 207	0.99	8 428	21.7	2 182	5.6	125 976	36.6	49 386	10 300	24 557	19 823	4 880
Brunswick, GA	1 590	D	D	D	D	1 032	10.1	18 619	21.5	19 615	3 432	8 798	5 946	5 291
Buffalo-Niagara Falls, NY	32 706	1 139 604	1.01	12 146	10.7	11 741	10.4	91 307	9.9	220 264	112 791	37 700	39 588	3 486
Burlington, NC	4 229	D	D	1 984	13.6	1 405	9.7	23 815	19.0	26 857	10 729	9 009	6 368	4 214
Burlington-South Burlington, VT	10 324	217 347	1.06	2 202	10.6	1 382	6.7	16 814	9.4	31 774	1 824	15 805	6 142	2 907
Canton-Massillon, OH	9 669	394 711	0.95	4 499	11.0	4 193	10.3	44 469	13.3	78 176	35 987	27 358	10 997	2 749
Cape Coral-Fort Myers, FL	8 488	611 658	0.96	7 412	12.7	5 842	10.0	113 656	25.6	136 497	32 817	50 272	18 535	2 996
Cape Girardeau-Jackson, MO-IL	4 529	D	D	D	D	954	10.2	11 742	15.1	17 461	1 164	9 336	3 975	4 129
Carson City, NV	3 625	D	D	D	D	655	11.9	11 339	24.9	10 743	685	4 955	1 295	2 343
Casper, WY	1 645	D	D	1 074	15.0	611	8.5	10 163	15.9	11 338	547	6 138	2 993	3 967
Cedar Rapids, IA	6 783	261 441	1.02	D	D	1 983	7.9	18 108	8.4	41 263	9 802	20 131	7 109	2 783
Champaign-Urbana, IL	16 611	238 631	1.04	D	D	1 490	6.8	23 561	12.0	29 454	5 398	9 549	6 828	3 033

1. Per 1,000 estimated resident population.   2. Data for serious crimes have not been adjusted for underreporting; this may affect comparability between geographic areas and over time.   3. Per 100,000 population estimated by the FBI.

Table C. Metropolitan Areas — Crime, Education, Money Income, and Poverty

Area name	Serious crimes known to police,[1] 2010 (cont.) Rate[2] Violent	Property	Education — School enrollment and attainment, 2010 — Enrollment[3] Total	Percent private	Attainment[4] (percent) High school graduate or less	Bachelor's degree or more	Local government expenditures,[5] 2008–2009 Total current expenditures (mil dol)	Current expenditures per student (dollars)	Income and Poverty, 2010 Per capita income[6] (dollars)	Median household income (dollars)	Percent of households with income of less than $25,000 or more	Percent of households with income of $100,000 or more	Percent of households with income of $200,000 or more	Percent below poverty level All persons	Children under 18 years	Children under 5
	46	47	48	49	50	51	52	53	54	55	56	57	58	59	60	61
Abilene, TX	408	3 493	43 252	23.9	45.4	20.9	241.4	8 829	20 877	40 630	29.9	13.1	1.3	18.0	22.0	30.6
Akron, OH	313	3 198	192 564	16.9	44.3	28.5	1 102.6	10 476	24 961	46 521	26.7	16.4	2.5	15.5	22.1	30.9
Albany, GA	541	4 247	48 653	7.8	52.3	15.8	259.4	9 236	18 187	34 002	38.6	10.4	1.5	27.7	38.1	47.7
Albany-Schenectady-Troy, NY	303	2 628	226 718	21.3	37.5	33.2	1 797.8	15 207	29 528	55 796	22.5	23.7	3.2	11.5	16.1	22.7
Albuquerque, NM	658	3 865	243 728	13.6	37.8	29.3	1 202.3	8 856	25 044	47 383	25.7	17.8	2.9	17.2	25.9	28.7
Alexandria, LA	651	4 647	39 496	16.4	55.5	16.8	240.4	8 890	21 636	40 017	34.5	11.6	1.2	19.5	28.6	38.8
Allentown-Bethlehem-Easton, PA-NJ	229	2 322	209 869	26.3	47.4	26.6	1 518.4	12 273	27 253	55 630	22.0	21.9	3.6	11.7	17.5	22.0
Altoona, PA	240	1 796	27 408	15.1	60.8	16.1	214.3	11 687	23 083	42 990	28.8	10.8	2.0	12.3	14.8	14.2
Amarillo, TX	515	4 782	69 870	6.1	41.7	24.7	370.7	8 236	23 112	46 390	25.8	13.3	2.5	16.3	24.6	26.4
Ames, IA	297	2 511	37 857	3.5	23.7	48.4	98.6	9 068	25 639	48 034	27.4	16.1	2.5	19.8	12.1	11.6
Anchorage, AK	NA	NA	106 336	15.9	30.8	30.8	863.5	13 165	33 211	71 490	15.7	33.6	7.0	9.4	12.3	18.4
Anderson, IN	206	3 355	29 325	15.2	54.0	17.1	182.5	9 370	20 407	38 772	29.3	11.1	1.2	18.5	31.5	31.1
Anderson, SC	596	4 710	48 080	18.2	51.6	17.7	264.3	8 489	20 496	36 770	37.0	10.3	1.6	19.7	30.7	41.6
Ann Arbor, MI	341	2 735	126 145	10.8	22.7	50.4	544.3	11 405	30 670	55 880	21.2	25.1	5.1	12.9	12.6	21.1
Anniston-Oxford, AL	431	3 923	30 222	12.5	55.9	14.7	155.2	8 369	19 245	36 675	37.2	11.1	1.5	25.0	34.0	30.2
Appleton, WI	156	2 124	58 128	16.3	41.1	26.1	374.7	10 021	26 409	55 883	19.3	18.7	1.7	8.1	11.5	14.5
Asheville, NC	224	2 390	89 730	17.2	38.2	29.4	475.9	8 717	23 741	42 168	28.1	11.2	1.9	16.3	23.4	28.9
Athens-Clarke County, GA	367	3 761	70 143	9.6	44.1	35.0	284.6	10 959	21 070	40 391	34.0	17.0	2.8	27.3	27.7	30.3
Atlanta-Sandy Springs-Marietta, GA	427	3 561	1 520 639	17.9	37.7	34.1	8 883.9	9 731	26 333	53 182	22.3	22.3	4.4	14.8	20.5	24.1
Atlantic City-Hammonton, NJ	531	3 561	70 466	14.2	49.5	23.0	756.3	16 212	24 783	52 571	23.1	19.2	2.9	14.3	20.1	31.3
Auburn-Opelika, AL	185	2 511	62 509	11.5	40.4	31.2	176.1	8 847	21 184	39 381	35.0	14.0	1.6	22.3	20.1	26.5
Augusta-Richmond County, GA-SC	388	4 557	151 126	13.1	48.4	24.5	828.4	8 893	22 516	44 477	29.8	14.5	2.4	19.9	28.4	37.0
Austin-Round Rock-San Marcos, TX	335	3 872	507 385	12.0	32.5	39.4	2 480.8	8 759	28 435	55 744	21.5	23.5	5.0	15.9	20.1	22.1
Bakersfield-Delano, CA	581	3 639	251 802	9.0	54.4	15.0	1 663.9	9 565	19 077	45 524	27.1	17.8	2.2	21.2	30.5	34.5
Baltimore-Towson, MD	688	3 102	734 834	21.7	38.5	35.1	5 029.7	13 118	32 568	64 812	18.0	30.3	6.5	11.0	14.9	19.1
Bangor, ME	67	3 030	43 262	15.1	45.5	24.1	259.4	11 432	22 262	42 964	29.3	13.8	1.1	16.6	22.8	35.2
Barnstable Town, MA	475	3 017	39 914	19.9	31.0	39.1	406.4	14 728	33 435	55 294	20.1	22.2	4.3	11.3	17.8	13.7
Baton Rouge, LA	576	3 887	223 534	19.0	46.1	26.6	1 251.4	10 683	24 792	48 294	26.8	19.2	3.1	16.1	23.9	29.0
Battle Creek, MI	691	3 662	35 898	11.3	47.9	17.2	245.0	10 868	20 661	42 921	27.9	12.1	1.0	16.2	23.9	26.9
Bay City, MI	339	2 418	25 555	10.9	45.4	20.3	158.4	10 179	22 378	45 451	27.7	12.1	0.7	16.2	23.7	31.0
Beaumont-Port Arthur, TX	483	3 746	96 383	9.1	53.7	15.0	638.1	9 425	20 599	41 291	32.7	14.3	1.6	19.6	29.0	37.8
Bellingham, WA	220	2 943	56 996	14.4	31.0	32.1	247.5	9 358	24 768	49 938	24.3	15.7	1.9	14.3	14.5	19.9
Bend, OR	313	3 059	37 104	12.7	29.3	30.3	230.0	9 319	25 131	44 680	27.2	15.5	2.6	15.4	24.5	24.5
Billings, MT	221	3 787	37 207	14.6	38.2	31.6	210.2	9 139	25 631	47 968	23.0	15.2	1.9	13.5	20.1	31.0
Binghamton, NY	212	2 397	64 883	7.9	44.4	23.5	569.5	15 150	23 513	45 959	26.5	13.6	2.3	15.0	21.9	23.2
Birmingham-Hoover, AL	308	3 173	284 469	16.5	44.3	26.3	1 602.6	9 069	24 474	44 216	28.5	16.9	2.6	17.0	26.0	28.1
Bismarck, ND	234	1 838	28 431	18.7	32.2	32.2	136.0	8 968	27 287	53 403	22.3	18.0	2.6	9.5	11.0	14.1
Blacksburg-Christiansburg-Radford, VA	167	2 468	61 905	5.2	42.2	30.0	182.7	9 792	20 141	40 127	35.0	12.1	1.4	22.2	22.6	26.8
Bloomington, IN	267	3 098	72 343	6.3	42.7	32.7	207.7	9 286	21 276	38 143	35.3	12.1	1.9	21.5	16.7	17.6
Bloomington-Normal, IL	367	2 367	57 236	15.8	32.2	40.4	232.5	9 534	29 332	59 588	20.6	25.5	4.3	11.8	5.8	9.9
Boise City-Nampa, ID	219	2 081	178 204	12.4	36.8	28.3	761.1	6 873	22 830	47 237	24.5	15.4	2.6	16.2	21.2	25.8
Boston-Cambridge-Quincy, MA-NH	411	2 193	1 231 746	30.8	34.3	43.0	9 142.0	14 082	35 999	68 020	19.1	33.0	8.2	10.3	11.9	14.5
Boston-Quincy, MA Div	580	2 439	528 843	35.8	35.9	41.6	3 709.2	14 339	35 229	65 129	21.6	31.6	8.1	12.9	15.3	18.2
Cambridge-Newton-Framingham, MA Div	296	1 910	403 279	31.4	30.7	50.0	3 153.3	14 796	39 194	75 534	16.2	36.9	9.6	8.1	8.2	9.9
Peabody, MA Div	360	2 168	192 287	22.6	36.8	36.9	1 550.4	13 649	33 337	61 789	21.4	30.3	7.0	10.3	14.1	16.9
Rockingham County-Strafford County, NH Div	149	2 144	107 337	19.1	35.4	34.7	729.1	11 431	32 720	67 285	14.8	29.7	5.5	6.6	6.5	10.3
Boulder, CO	203	2 346	92 027	12.6	19.6	57.5	481.0	8 783	35 988	61 859	20.9	30.0	8.0	14.7	16.6	18.2
Bowling Green, KY	146	2 721	38 935	5.9	47.9	24.7	150.2	7 884	21 895	39 092	33.0	11.7	1.9	20.5	26.5	30.2
Bremerton-Silverdale, WA	398	2 571	59 238	15.2	31.0	28.7	369.6	9 716	28 808	56 303	17.6	20.5	3.3	11.3	15.7	15.9
Bridgeport-Stamford-Norwalk, CT	282	1 781	249 019	23.1	35.2	44.0	2 256.4	15 467	44 024	74 831	17.1	38.2	14.3	9.4	10.9	12.5
Brownsville-Harlingen, TX	331	4 549	126 316	4.3	61.7	14.3	872.7	8 877	13 450	31 736	42.2	9.7	1.1	36.3	49.8	59.3
Brunswick, GA	513	4 778	NA	NA	50.9	20.6	180.9	9 910	25 002	39 066	30.4	15.4	3.0	19.8	34.1	49.1
Buffalo-Niagara Falls, NY	471	3 015	293 108	17.0	41.6	28.3	2 316.3	14 516	25 178	46 420	27.8	16.2	2.2	14.4	21.4	25.2
Burlington, NC	405	3 809	39 196	18.1	47.6	20.9	184.1	7 782	21 185	41 058	29.2	11.5	1.7	18.9	31.6	46.1
Burlington-South Burlington, VT	146	2 762	58 873	16.9	34.4	40.2	447.8	14 513	29 862	54 738	22.3	22.1	4.2	12.5	15.0	15.0
Canton-Massillon, OH	247	2 502	103 298	16.7	51.5	19.8	611.9	9 367	22 361	42 365	26.9	12.8	1.9	14.7	23.9	30.6
Cape Coral-Fort Myers, FL	376	2 619	129 278	12.7	46.2	23.4	717.9	9 037	24 699	43 936	26.1	15.5	3.4	17.4	29.2	33.9
Cape Girardeau-Jackson, MO-IL	530	3 599	26 986	11.3	52.6	23.7	110.0	8 581	21 153	41 288	29.9	11.4	2.4	19.1	32.0	41.8
Carson City, NV	293	2 050	NA	NA	41.5	20.8	73.4	9 105	26 011	52 414	22.7	18.1	0.7	16.7	26.0	36.1
Casper, WY	192	3 775	18 944	7.0	42.0	18.0	165.6	13 810	26 860	51 735	17.9	18.3	3.2	6.8	9.9	12.9
Cedar Rapids, IA	198	2 585	68 237	19.7	37.8	28.1	436.1	10 341	27 553	53 755	19.8	18.8	2.0	9.2	11.2	14.2
Champaign-Urbana, IL	590	2 443	89 836	7.4	33.4	37.7	296.0	9 839	24 768	45 845	28.8	17.9	3.2	19.4	19.2	18.0

1. Data for serious crimes have not been adjusted for underreporting; this may affect comparability between geographic areas and over time. 2. Per 100,000 population estimated by the FBI. 3. All persons 3 years old and over enrolled in nursery school through college. 4. Persons 25 years old and over. 5. Elementary and secondary education expenditures. 6. Based on resident population estimated as of July 1, 2009.

Table C. Metropolitan Areas — **Personal Income**

Area name	Total (mil dol)	Percent change, 2008–2009	Per capita¹ Dollars	Per capita¹ Rank	Wages and salaries² (mil dol)	Proprietors' income (mil dol)	Dividends, interest, and rent (mil dol)	Transfer payments Total (mil dol)	Govt payments to individuals Total (mil dol)	Social Security (mil dol)	Medical payments (mil dol)	Income mainte-nance (mil dol)	Unemploy-ment insurance (mil dol)
	62	63	64	65	66	67	68	69	70	71	72	73	74
Abilene, TX	5 632	-0.4	35 188	186	3 189	554	1 066	1 172	1 144	353	551	107	33
Akron, OH	25 944	-2.1	37 066	137	16 590	1 085	4 016	5 297	5 169	1 685	2 135	484	298
Albany, GA..............................	4 834	0.5	29 220	340	3 025	369	755	1 179	1 149	323	435	219	54
Albany-Schenectady-Troy, NY	36 195	0.5	42 206	50	25 337	2 242	6 322	6 545	6 389	2 196	2 572	571	324
Albuquerque, NM	30 309	0.5	35 329	181	20 500	1 677	4 903	5 736	5 580	1 740	2 389	611	237
Alexandria, LA........................	5 530	0.6	35 885	168	3 132	458	885	1 423	1 395	331	781	155	23
Allentown-Bethlehem-Easton, PA-NJ	31 420	-0.7	38 505	101	17 960	1 803	5 252	6 257	6 108	2 240	2 540	412	515
Altoona, PA............................	4 120	2.2	32 663	252	2 701	227	583	1 173	1 150	343	482	95	91
Amarillo, TX	8 747	0.4	35 489	175	5 434	966	1 585	1 420	1 375	473	565	148	46
Ames, IA	3 106	0.6	35 616	174	2 236	254	568	410	394	151	145	32	19
Anchorage, AK.......................	17 311	-1.2	46 217	26	12 130	1 812	2 620	2 370	2 304	477	861	248	104
Anderson, IN	4 025	-3.5	30 627	313	1 716	319	501	1 097	1 073	406	436	96	74
Anderson, SC	5 599	-0.5	30 280	316	2 583	366	835	1 397	1 364	544	489	137	72
Ann Arbor, MI	13 159	-4.4	37 859	119	11 194	845	2 549	1 909	1 846	700	684	144	156
Anniston-Oxford, AL...............	3 656	-0.8	32 045	271	2 439	173	610	939	919	316	376	104	29
Appleton, WI	8 166	-2.5	36 800	140	5 674	494	1 273	1 201	1 161	479	406	75	125
Asheville, NC	14 188	-1.2	34 381	204	7 701	808	3 410	3 365	3 290	1 286	1 374	252	165
Athens-Clarke County, GA ...	5 722	-1.6	29 770	329	3 980	294	1 104	1 005	970	342	359	123	57
Atlanta-Sandy Springs-Marietta, GA........................	203 138	-3.1	37 101	135	143 529	20 725	32 168	25 747	24 750	8 311	8 942	3 290	1 892
Atlantic City-Hammonton, NJ	10 639	-1.5	39 156	88	7 255	1 182	1 619	2 313	2 264	679	967	205	267
Auburn-Opelika, AL................	3 756	0.0	27 643	352	2 190	180	621	671	646	244	214	92	17
Augusta-Richmond County, GA-SC.............................	18 122	0.9	33 613	228	11 965	849	2 845	3 930	3 834	1 228	1 465	505	203
Austin-Round Rock-San Marcos, TX...........................	64 015	-0.6	37 544	128	45 256	5 639	12 064	6 932	6 621	2 339	2 486	705	404
Bakersfield-Delano, CA........	23 924	-0.2	29 630	332	15 206	2 561	3 379	4 934	4 787	1 229	1 820	862	398
Baltimore-Towson, MD	129 704	0.3	48 201	18	86 050	7 457	21 369	19 006	18 518	5 648	8 717	1 931	910
Bangor, ME............................	5 045	1.6	33 767	222	3 341	369	630	1 302	1 274	385	594	133	46
Barnstable Town, MA	11 086	-2.4	50 128	14	4 572	908	3 040	2 205	2 165	892	882	117	167
Baton Rouge, LA	29 989	1.6	38 107	111	20 703	1 675	4 849	5 190	5 047	1 470	2 411	682	119
Battle Creek, MI	4 370	0.4	32 227	266	3 135	170	606	1 165	1 140	384	444	144	79
Bay City, MI	3 348	-0.4	31 165	297	1 765	137	558	952	933	343	361	90	64
Beaumont-Port Arthur, TX	13 851	0.6	36 597	145	8 912	918	2 252	3 213	3 144	932	1 612	294	118
Bellingham, WA	7 111	-0.5	35 478	176	4 013	499	1 705	1 309	1 272	448	438	139	99
Bend, OR	5 705	-2.3	35 966	164	2 913	606	1 511	1 127	1 098	409	348	86	157
Billings, MT	6 060	-0.4	39 212	85	3 902	534	1 241	973	945	357	361	72	37
Binghamton, NY	8 408	0.7	34 360	205	5 424	394	1 401	2 072	2 027	736	840	224	103
Birmingham-Hoover, AL........	43 650	-2.7	38 592	99	27 652	4 430	7 466	7 981	7 775	2 841	3 133	849	258
Bismarck, ND	4 181	3.2	39 337	84	2 863	292	721	660	641	233	258	47	22
Blacksburg-Christiansburg-Radford, VA	4 530	0.3	28 384	347	3 137	170	757	971	942	361	364	92	43
Bloomington, IN	5 744	1.6	30 950	301	3 626	285	972	1 077	1 043	390	412	84	67
Bloomington-Normal, IL	6 489	0.5	38 695	96	5 222	459	963	784	753	298	237	75	67
Boise City-Nampa, ID	20 587	-2.8	33 950	216	12 851	2 207	3 934	3 382	3 271	1 138	1 201	289	301
Boston-Cambridge-Quincy, MA-NH	245 736	-2.4	53 553	8	179 722	22 188	43 857	34 004	33 168	9 578	15 870	3 126	2 877
Boston-Quincy, MA Div	102 126	-2.2	53 240	X	85 266	11 460	16 829	15 601	15 252	3 760	7 898	1 552	1 274
Cambridge-Newton-Framingham, MA Div	88 410	-2.8	58 744	X	66 102	6 609	18 029	9 983	9 709	3 144	4 307	815	935
Peabody, MA Div	36 599	-1.8	49 286	X	18 073	2 418	6 234	6 045	5 910	1 713	2 746	635	543
Rockingham County-Strafford County, NH Div	18 601	-2.8	43 988	X	10 280	1 700	2 765	2 374	2 297	961	919	124	124
Boulder, CO	14 584	-4.3	48 056	19	10 511	1 201	3 644	1 169	1 113	466	375	73	92
Bowling Green, KY	3 728	-0.7	30 912	302	2 582	209	557	854	832	257	347	88	52
Bremerton-Silverdale, WA	10 454	-0.6	43 404	36	5 938	503	2 251	1 628	1 586	501	574	152	108
Bridgeport-Stamford-Norwalk, CT	67 380	-5.4	74 767	1	40 229	6 919	15 952	6 588	6 423	2 090	3 110	455	489
Brownsville-Harlingen, TX.....	8 874	3.2	22 388	365	4 747	711	1 202	2 722	2 650	504	1 291	578	99
Brunswick, GA	3 650	-2.4	35 149	188	1 985	165	888	775	756	273	304	84	34
Buffalo-Niagara Falls, NY	42 108	0.3	37 469	130	27 086	2 387	6 671	9 686	9 481	3 294	3 938	1 045	508
Burlington, NC........................	4 612	-2.2	30 671	311	2 530	273	831	1 097	1 070	388	433	97	91
Burlington-South Burlington, VT	8 664	-0.2	41 641	57	6 363	582	1 491	1 371	1 333	437	575	146	79
Canton-Massillon, OH..........	13 201	-1.6	32 356	258	7 322	886	2 006	3 224	3 150	1 106	1 271	291	183
Cape Coral-Fort Myers, FL...	23 916	-4.3	40 750	63	10 069	1 291	9 140	4 658	4 551	1 933	1 739	328	237
Cape Girardeau-Jackson, MO-IL..............................	3 073	1.9	32 795	248	2 034	231	518	689	672	233	283	69	26
Carson City, NV	2 219	-4.2	40 218	70	1 649	166	533	416	406	137	177	26	37
Casper, WY	3 976	-5.0	53 361	9	2 163	724	937	476	462	163	183	35	30
Cedar Rapids, IA	10 002	-0.7	39 022	91	7 322	612	1 680	1 587	1 541	612	569	138	101
Champaign-Urbana, IL..........	7 830	-0.2	34 624	198	5 401	544	1 439	1 127	1 085	367	379	123	104

1. Based on the resident population estimated as of July 1 of the year shown.   2. Includes other labor income.

Table C. Metropolitan Areas — **Earnings, Social Security, and Housing**

Area name	Total (mil dol)	Farm	Goods-related[1] Total	Manufacturing	Information, professional, and technical services	Retail trade	Finance, insurance, and real estate	Health care and social services	Government	Social Security beneficiaries Number	Rate[2]	Supplemental Security Income recipients, December 2009	Housing units Total	Percent change, 2000–2010
	75	76	77	78	79	80	81	82	83	84	85	86	87	88
Abilene, TX	3 743	-0.4	17.4	3.6	D	6.7	5.4	NA	28.5	29 495	178	4 324	69 721	6.9
Akron, OH	17 675	0.1	20.5	15.5	8.5	6.6	5.0	13.4	15.8	127 730	182	15 044	312 581	7.4
Albany, GA	3 395	3.5	D	NA	D	6.8	D	NA	26.4	28 055	178	6 922	66 060	3.6
Albany-Schenectady-Troy, NY	27 579	0.1	D	6.1	14.6	5.9	7.4	11.9	27.5	165 145	190	19 886	393 297	8.1
Albuquerque, NM	22 178	0.2	D	6.1	D	6.6	5.3	NA	26.0	145 380	164	21 189	374 404	22.4
Alexandria, LA	3 590	0.9	18.8	8.6	5.9	6.9	D	NA	26.7	30 595	199	7 694	64 570	6.6
Allentown-Bethlehem-Easton, PA-NJ	19 763	0.1	D	13.5	8.4	6.6	5.5	16.1	12.8	166 910	203	17 535	342 200	11.4
Altoona, PA	2 928	0.4	D	13.4	7.1	9.1	4.2	18.8	16.9	28 635	225	4 901	56 276	2.2
Amarillo, TX	6 399	0.4	D	D	D	7.0	D	NA	16.8	37 795	151	4 402	102 546	12.0
Ames, IA	2 489	3.3	D	12.4	5.6	5.3	3.0	8.2	42.7	11 145	124	644	36 789	20.1
Anchorage, AK	13 942	0.0	14.8	1.1	12.2	6.0	5.4	11.0	28.5	40 330	106	6 989	154 361	20.9
Anderson, IN	2 035	1.9	D	18.1	4.3	7.0	4.0	15.8	18.1	30 275	230	3 055	59 068	3.7
Anderson, SC	2 949	-0.1	33.3	25.9	3.8	9.5	3.3	8.7	22.4	43 645	233	4 077	84 774	15.8
Ann Arbor, MI	12 039	0.1	12.6	10.0	14.5	4.7	4.2	11.2	35.2	48 455	141	4 869	147 573	12.7
Anniston-Oxford, AL	2 612	0.4	D	14.4	6.3	6.6	2.5	9.0	37.3	27 935	236	4 671	53 289	3.8
Appleton, WI	6 168	0.6	D	22.2	7.3	6.9	8.3	NA	11.1	36 820	163	2 455	92 844	18.5
Asheville, NC	8 508	0.8	D	13.6	D	8.5	4.8	NA	18.2	103 300	243	9 561	213 637	21.8
Athens-Clarke County, GA	4 274	1.8	D	12.0	D	6.5	4.7	NA	34.5	28 115	146	4 343	81 719	21.0
Atlanta-Sandy Springs-Marietta, GA	164 254	0.1	D	7.1	D	5.7	D	NA	13.2	660 480	125	93 165	2 165 495	31.7
Atlantic City-Hammonton, NJ	8 437	0.9	D	2.0	6.7	7.6	3.7	13.0	21.2	51 835	189	6 246	126 647	11.0
Auburn-Opelika, AL	2 370	0.3	19.8	14.0	4.6	7.2	4.1	6.9	37.8	19 975	142	3 205	62 391	24.0
Augusta-Richmond County, GA-SC	12 814	0.5	D	10.8	D	6.2	4.0	NA	31.3	100 970	181	15 698	236 949	15.8
Austin-Round Rock-San Marcos, TX	50 896	0.0	17.3	10.1	17.3	5.9	7.4	9.3	19.2	185 955	108	23 791	706 505	42.4
Bakersfield-Delano, CA	17 766	6.6	18.9	5.3	6.2	5.8	3.3	8.7	25.6	107 095	128	33 005	284 367	22.8
Baltimore-Towson, MD	93 508	0.1	D	6.0	D	5.3	7.5	12.5	24.0	428 800	158	62 260	1 132 251	8.0
Bangor, ME	3 710	0.2	D	7.6	6.3	9.9	4.0	21.7	21.2	33 585	218	5 190	73 860	10.5
Barnstable Town, MA	5 479	0.1	D	2.4	10.7	10.3	6.1	17.7	18.6	65 730	304	3 645	160 281	9.0
Baton Rouge, LA	22 378	0.3	D	11.1	D	6.0	D	NA	21.0	122 430	153	25 189	329 729	16.7
Battle Creek, MI	3 305	0.5	D	22.9	D	5.5	2.7	12.5	21.0	30 320	223	4 592	61 042	4.0
Bay City, MI	1 902	1.3	16.9	13.5	14.0	8.7	4.0	16.3	18.3	26 365	245	2 992	48 220	3.9
Beaumont-Port Arthur, TX	9 830	0.2	35.5	21.7	9.0	7.1	3.2	11.1	14.5	72 350	186	12 429	162 334	3.6
Bellingham, WA	4 513	1.4	24.0	13.0	8.3	8.4	4.9	11.6	19.8	35 880	178	4 013	90 665	22.7
Bend, OR	3 519	-0.3	15.7	6.7	10.8	9.3	7.9	17.8	14.5	32 570	206	1 890	80 139	46.8
Billings, MT	4 436	0.0	18.2	6.6	8.9	8.3	6.6	17.5	14.1	28 940	183	2 474	70 384	17.2
Binghamton, NY	5 818	0.1	27.4	22.0	6.2	6.3	4.5	14.2	23.1	57 420	228	7 915	112 766	2.3
Birmingham-Hoover, AL	32 082	0.1	D	7.0	11.3	6.3	10.1	NA	16.0	224 770	199	36 494	500 025	10.1
Bismarck, ND	3 155	1.2	D	5.6	7.3	7.6	6.1	NA	21.6	19 170	176	1 210	47 833	20.8
Blacksburg-Christiansburg-Radford, VA	3 307	-0.1	D	20.2	D	6.6	3.2	D	33.6	28 880	177	2 932	70 550	12.5
Bloomington, IN	3 910	0.8	D	13.8	D	6.0	3.6	NA	30.5	30 770	160	2 712	84 409	11.4
Bloomington-Normal, IL	5 681	2.8	D	5.0	D	4.9	22.7	9.1	13.8	22 795	134	1 743	69 656	16.1
Boise City-Nampa, ID	15 059	1.5	D	12.2	D	7.6	D	NA	16.8	94 255	153	10 469	246 052	35.8
Boston-Cambridge-Quincy, MA-NH	201 909	0.0	D	8.8	21.1	4.4	13.2	12.5	10.9	731 400	161	111 852	1 883 206	7.5
Boston-Quincy, MA Div	96 726	0.0	D	3.6	17.2	3.8	21.8	14.7	11.7	294 495	156	57 743	786 042	7.8
Cambridge-Newton-Framingham, MA Div	72 711	0.0	17.2	12.4	29.6	3.9	4.7	8.9	9.1	229 325	153	27 085	612 004	6.1
Peabody, MA Div	20 492	0.0	24.2	18.6	14.2	6.7	5.3	15.3	12.4	132 945	179	23 007	306 754	6.8
Rockingham County-Strafford County, NH Div	11 981	0.1	18.8	11.5	11.8	8.8	8.8	10.9	12.9	74 635	178	4 017	178 406	12.5
Boulder, CO	11 712	0.1	17.0	12.5	30.7	4.9	5.5	9.9	15.7	35 790	122	2 313	127 071	14.0
Bowling Green, KY	2 791	0.6	D	NA	D	7.2	D	13.4	18.2	21 520	171	3 964	53 690	20.8
Bremerton-Silverdale, WA	6 441	0.1	6.7	1.7	7.2	6.2	3.5	10.1	54.7	42 700	170	4 838	107 367	15.9
Bridgeport-Stamford-Norwalk, CT	47 148	0.0	D	10.2	15.6	5.6	23.4	8.9	8.8	142 295	155	11 329	361 221	6.4
Brownsville-Harlingen, TX	5 458	0.5	9.2	5.5	5.3	7.9	4.4	22.4	29.4	54 575	134	21 426	141 924	18.6
Brunswick, GA	2 150	0.1	D	8.4	D	7.8	5.0	9.5	32.4	22 235	198	2 775	58 022	29.3
Buffalo-Niagara Falls, NY	29 474	0.2	D	14.0	9.5	6.1	6.9	13.1	20.8	247 800	218	34 643	519 094	1.5
Burlington, NC	2 803	0.4	D	16.5	5.7	8.4	4.8	15.5	12.5	30 590	202	2 934	66 576	20.0
Burlington-South Burlington, VT	6 945	0.6	D	NA	D	7.4	D	15.4	19.3	34 840	165	4 176	92 358	11.7
Canton-Massillon, OH	8 208	0.4	D	19.8	D	7.9	6.3	NA	13.6	85 925	212	8 937	178 913	5.2
Cape Coral-Fort Myers, FL	11 360	0.1	12.3	2.1	10.7	10.2	7.1	11.7	20.4	147 530	238	9 953	371 099	51.2
Cape Girardeau-Jackson, MO-IL	2 265	0.7	D	10.4	5.9	7.8	D	NA	15.9	19 665	204	2 585	42 500	7.5
Carson City, NV	1 815	0.0	D	8.6	6.6	6.8	4.6	9.7	41.8	11 400	206	806	23 534	10.6
Casper, WY	2 887	0.0	34.4	4.0	5.5	6.4	4.6	13.1	13.1	12 615	167	1 136	33 807	13.1
Cedar Rapids, IA	7 934	2.0	D	21.8	D	7.0	9.6	NA	11.8	46 185	179	3 567	112 257	13.3
Champaign-Urbana, IL	5 945	4.2	D	7.9	8.4	5.2	4.4	NA	35.4	30 805	133	3 159	101 120	14.7

1. Includes mining, construction, and manufacturing. 2. Per 1,000 resident population enumerated in the 2010 census.

Table C. Metropolitan Areas — Housing, Labor Force, and Employment

Area name	Housing units, 2010								Civilian labor force, 2010		Unemployment		Civilian employment,[5] 2010		
	Occupied units													Percent	
			Owner-occupied			Renter-occupied									
				Median owner cost as a percent of income											
	Total	Percent	Median value[1]	With a mortgage	Without a mortgage	Median rent[2]	Median rent as a percent of income	Sub-stand-ard units[3] (percent)	Total	Percent change, 2009–2010	Total	Rate[4]	Total	Management, business, science, and arts occupations	Construction, production, and maintenance occupations
	89	90	91	92	93	94	95	96	97	98	99	100	101	102	103
Abilene, TX	59 857	62.7	90 900	20.3	12.3	751	31.1	2.6	83 304	0.8	5 396	6.5	69 596	31.3	19.4
Akron, OH	281 523	69.0	145 000	23.0	14.0	702	31.1	1.3	382 432	-1.0	37 827	9.9	327 285	36.1	19.8
Albany, GA	60 263	59.2	98 400	26.2	12.4	715	37.4	4.0	75 223	-1.3	8 222	10.9	60 004	29.5	26.9
Albany-Schenectady-Troy, NY	348 634	64.8	199 000	23.4	13.9	846	30.1	1.7	448 510	-1.7	32 925	7.3	433 323	41.9	14.7
Albuquerque, NM	344 800	66.8	183 300	25.0	10.0	748	29.6	3.3	408 526	0.9	35 751	8.8	402 636	39.8	17.1
Alexandria, LA	54 774	67.2	113 900	20.6	10.2	661	37.6	3.6	69 337	-0.1	4 922	7.1	59 763	34.3	22.1
Allentown-Bethlehem-Easton, PA-NJ	311 470	71.9	218 700	25.2	15.0	848	33.0	1.8	418 714	-0.7	39 325	9.4	377 341	35.5	22.3
Altoona, PA	52 111	71.6	105 400	20.0	11.3	586	28.3	0.8	64 246	-1.0	4 942	7.7	58 564	30.1	25.9
Amarillo, TX	94 287	63.8	114 900	21.6	11.0	682	27.5	4.3	131 884	0.6	7 453	5.7	122 286	31.2	23.3
Ames, IA	35 851	52.1	159 000	20.2	10.0	686	33.6	1.7	48 905	0.2	2 268	4.6	47 928	47.6	17.5
Anchorage, AK	135 320	65.2	261 800	22.9	10.8	981	29.8	6.1	197 048	0.7	14 516	7.4	183 528	37.2	18.7
Anderson, IN	50 641	70.5	91 600	20.6	12.5	658	31.3	2.3	61 538	-1.0	7 035	11.4	55 285	29.6	25.5
Anderson, SC	73 794	72.7	113 500	21.7	10.0	628	37.7	2.5	85 344	-0.8	9 696	11.4	77 245	25.9	30.0
Ann Arbor, MI	132 028	62.4	190 600	24.4	14.0	839	30.3	0.9	182 223	-0.3	14 782	8.1	167 616	51.3	11.9
Anniston-Oxford, AL..............	45 862	67.5	102 500	22.7	11.3	607	31.1	1.9	52 565	-2.9	5 017	9.5	42 768	29.2	30.2
Appleton, WI	88 085	75.7	161 000	23.6	13.3	676	24.7	2.7	124 148	-0.7	9 526	7.7	116 286	34.5	27.3
Asheville, NC	181 239	69.9	183 800	24.9	11.6	730	31.6	2.3	208 338	-0.1	17 945	8.6	186 384	36.5	18.7
Athens-Clarke County, GA ...	64 210	59.1	160 200	23.3	10.8	749	36.7	2.6	104 822	-1.0	8 162	7.8	79 703	39.9	21.1
Atlanta-Sandy Springs-Marietta, GA	1 879 479	66.5	175 900	25.7	12.1	910	32.1	3.3	2 662 876	-1.4	272 391	10.2	2 422 146	38.8	19.2
Atlantic City-Hammonton, NJ	100 096	73.4	238 400	32.2	19.5	993	36.5	2.6	136 064	-0.2	16 930	12.4	126 545	28.8	15.9
Auburn-Opelika, AL..............	55 073	63.6	151 900	24.1	13.0	696	39.3	1.5	64 873	-0.6	5 301	8.2	63 718	36.7	23.0
Augusta-Richmond County, GA-SC...................................	206 641	67.6	126 200	22.5	12.5	704	29.5	2.1	260 516	-0.1	23 444	9.0	224 054	34.0	25.2
Austin-Round Rock-San Marcos, TX...............................	647 500	57.4	187 600	24.1	13.0	919	31.8	4.5	908 206	2.5	64 792	7.1	860 254	43.2	16.1
Bakersfield-Delano, CA........	252 284	59.0	164 200	27.0	11.0	821	33.5	8.9	368 546	1.5	58 554	15.9	310 764	27.4	31.4
Baltimore-Towson, MD	1 022 553	66.0	288 700	24.8	13.1	1 048	30.7	2.2	1 394 877	-0.8	109 951	7.9	1 326 838	43.7	15.5
Bangor, ME	60 428	69.3	140 600	22.2	12.7	662	31.9	2.5	78 205	-0.7	6 462	8.3	74 367	34.3	21.3
Barnstable Town, MA	93 576	77.5	369 900	30.7	16.2	1 104	34.0	1.7	123 046	0.6	11 283	9.2	96 547	36.9	18.7
Baton Rouge, LA	291 692	69.2	158 300	20.8	10.0	756	31.1	3.0	379 430	0.6	28 278	7.5	370 025	33.6	22.8
Battle Creek, MI	52 600	72.2	103 100	24.7	13.8	624	29.1	1.5	66 989	-0.8	7 334	10.9	56 454	25.0	28.9
Bay City, MI	44 064	77.9	95 800	21.8	13.0	556	30.0	0.9	53 266	-1.5	6 209	11.7	47 467	31.8	21.7
Beaumont-Port Arthur, TX	140 356	67.6	92 400	21.5	11.9	717	29.9	3.8	187 526	1.9	19 965	10.6	157 409	27.0	29.0
Bellingham, WA	80 288	61.2	284 100	27.8	12.1	826	32.4	3.2	106 627	-1.1	9 379	8.8	94 053	38.7	20.4
Bend, OR	64 120	64.9	260 700	29.2	12.8	870	37.4	1.3	80 857	-1.2	11 650	14.4	66 715	38.1	17.5
Billings, MT	65 861	69.8	179 800	22.1	10.6	671	26.6	2.1	86 306	-0.2	4 791	5.6	80 512	35.4	21.0
Binghamton, NY	100 830	70.2	106 100	21.6	13.3	652	31.3	2.0	121 255	-1.8	10 523	8.7	112 946	35.2	20.9
Birmingham-Hoover, AL........	430 441	70.7	146 600	24.2	12.6	749	32.3	1.7	516 227	-2.4	46 411	9.0	491 276	35.4	21.3
Bismarck, ND	44 857	75.7	158 900	21.4	10.6	575	26.9	NA	62 079	-0.7	2 417	3.9	59 745	36.5	21.2
Blacksburg-Christiansburg-Radford, VA	62 446	64.3	156 800	22.7	10.0	750	44.2	1.1	80 063	-1.2	6 587	8.2	72 814	39.2	21.2
Bloomington, IN	74 442	61.9	132 700	21.6	10.9	669	34.6	2.1	96 500	-1.2	7 666	7.9	85 589	38.5	22.0
Bloomington-Normal, IL	61 576	68.6	159 600	20.5	13.0	702	26.9	NA	93 167	2.3	7 201	7.7	87 438	41.8	13.2
Boise City-Nampa, ID	225 007	68.2	173 200	24.4	10.5	743	32.3	3.6	294 281	0.3	28 355	9.6	274 248	37.8	20.1
Boston-Cambridge-Quincy, MA-NH	1 745 690	61.7	365 200	26.2	15.6	1 141	30.0	1.9	2 467 286	0.6	190 033	7.7	2 321 659	46.3	14.0
Boston-Quincy, MA Div	722 233	57.2	367 300	26.6	15.0	1 189	30.6	2.2	1 005 085	0.7	82 166	8.2	943 321	44.8	13.7
Cambridge-Newton-Framingham, MA Div	576 710	62.5	403 500	25.4	15.1	1 210	28.6	1.8	830 943	0.4	58 318	7.0	789 816	52.0	12.1
Peabody, MA Div	285 158	64.0	352 900	26.7	16.3	970	32.2	1.7	385 253	0.9	34 429	8.9	364 731	42.2	15.7
Rockingham County-Strafford County, NH Div	161 589	74.4	261 600	26.5	17.7	984	30.2	1.5	246 005	0.6	15 120	6.1	223 791	39.0	18.8
Boulder, CO	119 774	62.3	352 800	24.1	10.0	996	34.6	2.8	173 234	-1.3	12 269	7.1	153 738	53.7	10.4
Bowling Green, KY	47 972	59.5	136 300	22.5	10.0	622	33.5	NA	64 972	0.8	6 060	9.3	56 565	33.6	22.1
Bremerton-Silverdale, WA ...	99 150	65.3	268 000	26.0	11.3	936	32.0	2.7	125 057	-0.2	9 847	7.9	105 492	37.6	20.3
Bridgeport-Stamford-Norwalk, CT	329 091	69.0	441 400	29.1	18.6	1 233	34.3	2.7	473 538	0.6	39 379	8.3	432 039	42.4	14.7
Brownsville-Harlingen, TX.....	115 579	67.6	75 400	25.1	12.4	632	35.9	11.9	158 000	4.4	17 650	11.2	142 057	27.3	22.7
Brunswick, GA	43 625	66.0	120 600	26.4	12.0	733	27.2	6.5	51 023	-3.7	5 074	9.9	46 771	30.4	23.1
Buffalo-Niagara Falls, NY	464 581	65.5	120 700	22.1	14.0	672	30.8	1.1	578 343	-0.8	48 597	8.4	525 026	36.0	18.3
Burlington, NC	59 811	65.3	132 900	24.4	12.9	663	31.3	3.6	69 940	-1.7	7 971	11.4	66 788	29.2	27.9
Burlington-South Burlington, VT	84 093	66.4	253 500	25.4	14.9	904	33.2	NA	122 201	0.7	6 538	5.4	116 010	41.7	17.2
Canton-Massillon, OH..........	159 421	72.5	123 300	23.5	12.3	635	30.4	1.4	202 929	-1.1	23 071	11.4	178 954	29.9	24.8
Cape Coral-Fort Myers, FL...	233 693	71.0	149 500	29.2	14.7	873	34.4	2.8	277 533	-0.7	35 441	12.8	233 140	28.3	17.0
Cape Girardeau-Jackson, MO-IL	36 922	66.6	123 700	20.4	10.0	658	30.7	3.1	46 844	-1.0	3 828	8.2	44 548	33.6	26.4
Carson City, NV	20 564	58.8	218 500	25.2	13.3	851	27.7	NA	28 632	-1.1	4 024	14.1	NA	NA	NA
Casper, WY	30 763	71.6	177 000	22.2	10.0	760	28.1	NA	40 739	-0.2	2 934	7.2	39 196	26.5	26.8
Cedar Rapids, IA	105 963	73.6	137 100	21.0	11.7	659	26.3	1.6	147 992	0.8	8 993	6.1	135 453	35.5	22.9
Champaign-Urbana, IL..........	90 783	57.9	147 100	20.6	11.6	742	35.1	1.2	122 475	1.5	11 038	9.0	111 462	42.5	16.5

1. Specified owner-occupied units.   2. Specified renter-occupied units. A value of 10.0 represents 10 percent or less.   3. Overcrowded or lacking complete plumbing facilities.   4. Percent of civilian labor force.   5. Persons 16 years old and over.

Table C. Metropolitan Areas — **Nonfarm Employment and Agriculture**

Area name	Private nonfarm establishments, employment and payroll, 2009									Agriculture, 2007			
	Number of establishments	Employment						Annual payroll		Farms			
		Total	Health care and social assistance	Manufacturing	Retail trade	Finance and insurance	Professional, scientific, and technical services	Total (mil dol)	Average per employee (dollars)	Number	Percent with:		Farm operators whose principal occupation is farming (percent)
											Fewer than 50 acres	500 acres or more	
	104	105	106	107	108	109	110	111	112	113	114	115	116
Abilene, TX	3 882	56 559	11 867	2 371	8 746	3 153	1 875	1 659	29 334	3 403	28.0	20.2	35.7
Akron, OH	16 856	277 143	48 378	37 568	36 304	9 973	17 173	10 962	39 555	1 196	63.3	2.5	41.6
Albany, GA	3 384	47 847	9 041	6 087	7 953	1 699	1 903	1 449	30 278	1 253	29.8	25.7	48.6
Albany-Schenectady-Troy, NY	20 945	327 687	60 284	18 951	47 563	20 944	28 704	13 075	39 900	2 364	39.3	5.1	52.3
Albuquerque, NM	19 077	288 559	46 854	17 616	41 908	13 509	24 251	10 440	36 180	2 749	65.7	13.7	43.0
Alexandria, LA	3 455	50 898	13 901	4 455	7 875	1 752	1 685	1 589	31 219	1 227	53.2	7.7	43.0
Allentown-Bethlehem-Easton, PA-NJ	18 472	288 826	54 070	32 721	41 085	12 005	12 267	12 083	41 836	2 142	62.1	4.9	46.9
Altoona, PA	3 220	49 683	10 382	6 915	8 999	1 338	2 075	1 539	30 977	523	33.8	5.9	58.1
Amarillo, TX	6 011	89 728	15 855	7 614	14 082	5 246	2 515	3 039	33 873	1 879	26.6	38.1	39.4
Ames, IA	1 998	28 999	4 881	4 350	4 903	895	1 241	887	30 575	1 077	36.1	20.1	50.7
Anchorage, AK	10 371	159 525	23 749	2 770	18 380	5 589	11 670	8 417	52 765	278	50.4	6.1	52.5
Anderson, IN	2 366	33 639	6 641	2 971	5 088	1 137	952	983	29 211	870	55.3	14.3	49.8
Anderson, SC	3 741	52 060	7 975	11 097	8 492	1 135	1 647	1 537	29 530	1 650	48.1	3.2	32.9
Ann Arbor, MI	7 932	135 600	34 129	12 536	15 783	4 163	12 779	6 356	46 876	1 300	54.9	6.1	45.2
Anniston-Oxford, AL	2 444	38 324	6 617	6 581	6 406	932	1 671	1 155	30 150	735	51.6	2.0	40.7
Appleton, WI	5 876	104 837	12 473	19 682	14 351	6 654	4 585	3 795	36 200	2 094	37.1	8.9	53.1
Asheville, NC	11 639	145 790	30 515	17 627	22 987	4 040	5 379	4 604	31 579	3 142	61.7	1.6	40.0
Athens-Clarke County, GA	4 452	55 540	10 641	7 022	9 616	1 813	2 488	1 707	30 733	1 784	47.1	4.4	39.0
Atlanta-Sandy Springs-Marietta, GA	130 408	2 073 320	221 946	135 117	243 980	110 700	188 238	94 449	45 554	8 518	56.1	2.9	40.8
Atlantic City-Hammonton, NJ	6 630	115 605	17 539	2 040	15 934	3 167	5 164	4 080	35 289	499	75.2	1.6	45.3
Auburn-Opelika, AL	2 431	37 367	6 025	5 771	6 646	851	1 042	1 011	27 061	356	40.4	7.3	46.3
Augusta-Richmond County, GA-SC	10 426	172 789	32 203	21 693	25 251	4 523	7 379	6 187	35 806	2 634	42.2	7.6	38.2
Austin-Round Rock-San Marcos, TX	40 281	646 082	72 900	42 278	88 140	33 658	64 143	29 364	45 450	8 706	47.4	8.3	37.2
Bakersfield-Delano, CA	12 111	179 606	26 613	11 970	26 922	6 166	11 317	6 848	38 130	2 117	43.0	24.7	57.4
Baltimore-Towson, MD	65 746	1 074 425	181 561	61 515	133 001	59 014	105 160	49 462	46 036	3 836	55.4	5.9	47.1
Bangor, ME	4 219	59 622	14 516	4 629	10 872	2 228	1 941	1 974	33 104	706	41.4	9.1	49.9
Barnstable Town, MA	8 301	70 322	16 250	2 119	14 118	2 385	4 598	2 687	38 205	406	93.3	0.0	53.4
Baton Rouge, LA	17 769	315 532	45 698	23 051	43 151	14 927	20 682	12 468	39 513	2 987	51.1	10.1	38.9
Battle Creek, MI	2 723	48 904	9 165	11 438	6 211	D	1 119	1 988	40 650	1 178	37.6	9.3	45.3
Bay City, MI	2 315	30 816	6 434	3 051	5 370	1 057	1 243	1 057	34 300	851	40.2	12.1	48.3
Beaumont-Port Arthur, TX	7 872	135 232	20 287	20 218	20 104	3 360	6 638	5 623	41 580	2 167	64.8	8.0	38.4
Bellingham, WA	6 281	70 390	10 415	8 823	10 837	2 228	3 647	2 494	35 434	1 483	71.2	2.2	45.2
Bend, OR	5 951	52 759	8 376	4 197	9 472	2 308	2 741	1 743	33 034	1 405	77.9	2.3	40.8
Billings, MT	5 872	69 419	12 619	3 768	10 724	4 493	3 644	2 461	35 306	2 122	36.4	25.5	41.1
Binghamton, NY	5 083	87 675	16 041	11 383	13 295	3 185	9 866	3 220	36 726	1 145	27.5	5.5	43.5
Birmingham-Hoover, AL	26 087	447 536	66 972	39 209	58 572	34 023	24 653	18 081	40 402	4 464	47.0	3.8	41.7
Bismarck, ND	3 410	50 996	10 852	2 401	7 723	2 557	2 456	1 764	34 583	1 862	16.4	43.3	50.4
Blacksburg-Christiansburg-Radford, VA	3 290	46 287	6 159	11 670	7 886	1 161	2 523	1 487	32 126	1 387	37.4	6.3	40.9
Bloomington, IN	3 910	58 163	10 054	8 637	8 951	1 877	3 198	1 801	30 972	1 850	43.4	6.3	40.8
Bloomington-Normal, IL	3 691	78 693	9 375	4 814	9 593	22 997	2 749	3 469	44 089	1 513	35.1	30.5	53.7
Boise City-Nampa, ID	16 724	212 943	33 605	24 695	28 135	10 805	10 983	7 697	36 145	5 238	70.9	7.1	41.4
Boston-Cambridge-Quincy, MA-NH	122 467	2 251 076	386 611	159 618	244 844	178 630	223 575	126 753	56 308	3 281	72.3	1.2	48.8
Boston-Quincy, MA Div	NA	NA	NA	NA	NA	NA	NA	NA	NA	1 153	75.9	1.5	51.6
Cambridge-Newton-Framingham, MA Div	NA	NA	NA	NA	NA	NA	NA	NA	NA	700	75.0	0.6	48.7
Peabody, MA Div	NA	NA	NA	NA	NA	NA	NA	NA	NA	531	75.7	1.9	45.2
Rockingham County-Strafford County, NH Div	NA	NA	NA	NA	NA	NA	NA	NA	NA	897	63.5	0.9	47.4
Boulder, CO	11 352	134 041	18 318	14 284	16 474	4 457	25 169	6 484	48 372	746	67.2	6.4	38.6
Bowling Green, KY	2 768	47 283	7 468	8 324	7 216	1 444	2 172	1 498	31 687	2 536	42.7	4.5	35.3
Bremerton-Silverdale, WA	5 741	57 587	12 894	1 998	10 967	2 342	4 411	1 964	34 112	664	91.3	0.3	45.5
Bridgeport-Stamford-Norwalk, CT	27 291	407 342	60 274	37 795	48 617	39 793	37 828	28 989	71 166	310	71.0	2.6	47.4
Brownsville-Harlingen, TX	6 320	99 750	28 556	6 078	17 819	2 954	2 614	2 379	23 854	1 241	63.1	13.7	43.3
Brunswick, GA	2 945	34 240	5 020	2 597	5 671	1 039	1 117	1 009	29 463	333	52.9	3.9	40.8
Buffalo-Niagara Falls, NY	26 839	458 110	82 144	53 065	62 934	29 170	25 895	16 479	35 973	2 080	47.4	5.0	51.7
Burlington, NC	3 212	49 711	7 341	10 201	7 861	1 563	1 295	1 469	29 541	753	42.6	3.9	43.0
Burlington-South Burlington, VT	6 744	98 292	17 431	13 913	14 334	3 749	9 454	4 096	41 672	1 445	34.5	9.1	49.8
Canton-Massillon, OH	9 025	141 541	28 413	24 758	21 465	6 312	4 545	4 437	31 345	2 074	47.8	4.0	46.0
Cape Coral-Fort Myers, FL	15 593	169 998	26 724	4 164	33 374	5 935	9 199	5 602	32 954	944	86.4	4.1	37.7
Cape Girardeau-Jackson, MO-IL	3 048	40 635	10 193	4 234	6 378	1 420	1 028	1 221	30 037	2 445	25.8	10.5	43.8
Carson City, NV	2 178	22 258	3 549	3 101	3 627	1 227	1 453	833	37 425	21	66.7	9.5	42.9
Casper, WY	2 962	34 720	5 106	2 419	5 551	1 086	1 709	1 352	38 952	413	28.8	41.4	46.2
Cedar Rapids, IA	6 518	123 684	16 090	18 337	16 214	9 361	5 686	4 726	38 208	3 781	30.9	17.8	50.5
Champaign-Urbana, IL	4 913	75 508	13 643	8 282	11 692	2 871	3 202	2 494	33 023	2 393	30.8	30.1	55.9

Table C. Metropolitan Areas — **Agriculture**

Area name	Land in farms — Acreage (1,000)	Percent change, 2002–2007	Acres — Average size of farm	Acres — Total irrigated (1,000)	Acres — Total cropland (1,000)	Value of land and buildings (dollars) — Average per farm	Value of land and buildings (dollars) — Average per acre	Value of machinery and equipment, average per farm (dollars)	Value of products sold — Total (mil dol)	Value of products sold — Average per farm (dollars)	Percent from: Crops	Percent from: Livestock and poultry products	Percent of farms with sales of: $10,000 or more	Percent of farms with sales of: $100,000 or more	Government payments — Total ($1,000)	Government payments — Percent of farms
	117	118	119	120	121	122	123	124	125	126	127	128	129	130	131	132
Abilene, TX	1 685	7.5	495	9.6	643.4	594 486	1 200	57 564	135.2	39 750	44.7	55.3	25.9	6.7	15 880	41.6
Akron, OH	98	-16.9	82	0.7	67.4	422 112	5 156	62 626	43.6	36 444	71.9	28.2	32.7	6.4	888	16.9
Albany, GA	678	0.7	541	112.3	326.1	1 333 707	2 464	154 585	208.2	166 136	77.1	22.9	39.7	23.7	22 792	60.5
Albany-Schenectady-Troy, NY	336	-9.4	142	2.8	183.7	451 426	3 173	79 550	156.8	66 329	33.9	66.1	39.6	10.5	D	21.5
Albuquerque, NM	3 131	D	1 139	67.6	151.9	528 636	464	45 368	103.7	37 722	33.5	66.5	19.6	4.2	980	4.8
Alexandria, LA	229	-3.4	187	10.3	128.5	440 346	2 359	77 519	90.5	73 821	85.8	14.2	32.9	10.4	4 489	17.6
Allentown-Bethlehem-Easton, PA-NJ	248	-6.8	116	4.0	195.8	909 370	7 857	82 210	188.3	87 881	67.1	32.9	38.0	12.8	3 021	22.6
Altoona, PA	87	1.2	167	0.2	61.9	690 402	4 130	99 314	85.2	162 904	11.9	88.1	51.6	25.0	1 092	36.3
Amarillo, TX	2 202	10.5	1 172	74.2	834.9	1 023 528	873	89 962	554.4	294 973	17.6	82.4	38.5	17.9	17 243	54.0
Ames, IA	352	-2.2	327	0.3	328.1	1 163 987	3 559	162 630	200.6	186 271	80.6	19.4	64.2	34.2	7 792	73.9
Anchorage, AK	38	NA	138	1.7	17.0	488 278	3 536	72 515	31.8	114 216	49.6	50.4	41.0	14.4	110	6.1
Anderson, IN	217	-11.1	250	1.5	204.1	933 308	3 736	115 455	115.5	132 730	87.5	12.5	50.9	21.6	4 441	61.0
Anderson, SC	173	-2.3	105	0.7	63.8	413 318	3 939	48 678	50.2	30 443	11.0	89.0	19.2	2.2	941	18.6
Ann Arbor, MI	167	-4.6	128	2.7	133.1	642 197	5 003	83 247	73.2	56 305	74.9	25.1	37.3	12.4	2 193	32.6
Anniston-Oxford, AL	76	1.3	104	1.7	26.0	329 225	3 176	56 359	69.1	93 961	14.8	85.2	25.3	7.8	391	13.3
Appleton, WI	399	-3.6	191	0.3	336.1	713 808	3 745	129 107	403.7	192 768	20.5	79.5	59.2	29.9	6 348	68.6
Asheville, NC	233	-20.2	74	3.1	71.2	511 435	6 897	49 059	122.9	39 130	76.3	23.7	23.0	3.7	1 146	9.6
Athens-Clarke County, GA	222	10.4	125	2.1	65.6	572 301	4 591	63 550	426.9	239 316	D	D	32.7	15.8	1 164	18.6
Atlanta-Sandy Springs-Marietta, GA	871	-15.2	102	D	256.4	512 802	5 013	51 117	D	D	11.3	D	23.4	7.5	D	11.1
Atlantic City-Hammonton, NJ	30	0.0	61	11.7	18.6	902 470	14 827	113 651	128.3	257 192	98.0	2.0	44.9	20.6	349	5.0
Auburn-Opelika, AL	63	-14.9	177	0.8	13.9	534 602	3 012	57 383	D	D	D	D	28.7	2.8	497	16.3
Augusta-Richmond County, GA-SC	495	-4.8	188	26.5	219.6	569 763	3 031	62 451	228.1	86 595	D	D	25.8	6.5	6 623	23.6
Austin-Round Rock-San Marcos, TX	1 746	-7.5	201	6.9	492.5	544 782	2 716	45 522	309.9	35 596	30.0	70.0	21.9	3.3	7 611	13.2
Bakersfield-Delano, CA	2 362	-13.5	1 116	786.3	942.8	5 160 784	4 626	253 255	3 204.1	1 513 532	79.6	20.4	59.6	40.3	27 346	17.1
Baltimore-Towson, MD	501	-5.1	131	15.8	358.7	1 093 432	8 373	94 420	353.8	92 231	59.8	40.2	38.1	13.1	8 525	29.7
Bangor, ME	115	7.5	162	1.8	47.1	370 924	2 285	67 340	42.5	60 231	30.2	69.8	32.7	9.1	889	11.5
Barnstable Town, MA	5	-16.7	13	1.3	2.0	457 980	35 532	44 526	17.7	43 475	57.5	42.5	46.6	10.3	282	9.6
Baton Rouge, LA	697	-1.1	233	D	359.8	645 966	2 769	79 310	217.0	72 646	69.8	30.2	30.0	7.6	5 342	15.9
Battle Creek, MI	228	-5.0	194	9.3	175.1	583 048	3 012	81 935	89.8	76 244	60.6	39.4	37.4	13.1	3 170	49.6
Bay City, MI	186	0.0	219	4.1	166.7	616 830	2 818	117 055	77.2	90 744	89.2	10.8	49.9	20.7	2 424	67.0
Beaumont-Port Arthur, TX	488	-7.9	225	18.4	190.9	384 081	1 705	50 777	D	D	D	59.0	18.5	3.6	3 752	8.4
Bellingham, WA	103	-30.4	69	35.0	73.7	773 740	11 186	95 287	326.5	220 128	30.6	69.4	36.2	16.8	1 050	19.7
Bend, OR	129	-6.5	92	37.8	39.9	633 973	6 885	45 880	19.8	14 063	45.8	54.2	20.4	2.4	135	1.4
Billings, MT	2 409	3.7	1 135	150.9	482.2	1 126 609	992	77 324	209.9	98 922	26.2	73.8	39.0	13.1	5 338	32.3
Binghamton, NY	193	-15.0	169	0.5	97.4	303 050	1 794	66 246	66.6	58 122	15.7	84.3	30.9	11.3	1 807	27.9
Birmingham-Hoover, AL	527	-4.4	118	6.1	159.4	362 781	3 074	55 331	D	D	D	D	28.9	7.3	1 828	11.3
Bismarck, ND	2 045	-4.5	1 098	12.3	1 025.5	741 062	675	108 183	199.5	107 136	55.9	44.1	51.8	23.1	11 418	67.0
Blacksburg-Christiansburg-Radford, VA	230	-7.6	166	0.7	67.3	612 259	3 686	58 927	37.3	26 927	17.8	82.2	33.7	4.2	590	12.5
Bloomington, IN	311	-5.8	168	1.4	199.7	524 496	3 119	66 246	109.0	58 895	58.1	41.9	34.5	7.9	3 825	40.6
Bloomington-Normal, IL	676	-1.7	447	2.9	647.4	1 868 207	4 181	175 125	366.5	242 265	89.5	10.5	65.1	44.7	12 275	77.9
Boise City-Nampa, ID	1 255	-6.2	240	406.6	433.5	701 088	2 925	78 774	814.8	155 557	35.1	64.9	33.9	11.9	4 227	19.4
Boston-Cambridge-Quincy, MA-NH	182	D	56	15.0	71.7	793 133	14 266	59 302	235.2	71 717	D	D	37.0	11.4	D	5.9
Boston-Quincy, MA Div	61	D	53	12.1	21.6	841 609	15 813	60 468	92.6	80 334	D	D	46.3	15.4	D	8.1
Cambridge-Newton-Framingham, MA Div	34	3.0	48	1.5	15.4	907 619	18 745	56 824	81.7	116 726	84.2	15.8	34.3	11.7	D	2.0
Peabody, MA Div	28	0.0	52	0.9	12.2	971 091	18 526	59 475	25.0	47 122	75.9	24.1	33.9	10.0	276	4.0
Rockingham County-Strafford County, NH Div	59	-9.2	66	0.5	22.6	536 131	8 108	59 634	35.9	40 075	71.1	28.9	29.0	6.9	342	7.2
Boulder, CO	138	27.8	185	33.9	54.4	588 686	3 190	66 628	34.0	45 626	76.4	23.6	31.2	6.8	376	11.1
Bowling Green, KY	362	3.7	143	0.4	193.0	410 520	2 878	56 921	92.2	36 342	27.0	73.0	32.1	5.2	2 896	33.4
Bremerton-Silverdale, WA	15	-6.3	23	0.9	3.7	429 990	18 668	31 903	7.0	10 520	75.5	24.6	17.2	1.2	88	2.6
Bridgeport-Stamford-Norwalk, CT	40	207.7	128	0.2	6.6	1 850 189	14 505	64 999	37.3	120 274	77.7	22.3	39.4	11.3	19	2.6
Brownsville-Harlingen, TX	349	-0.3	282	101.1	226.1	544 393	1 933	73 172	112.4	90 532	93.5	6.5	33.1	11.9	7 614	41.6
Brunswick, GA	40	-21.6	121	0.5	13.8	331 124	2 737	59 737	9.2	27 658	35.8	64.2	19.5	3.3	D	16.2
Buffalo-Niagara Falls, NY	292	-5.8	140	5.5	212.2	359 197	2 559	98 364	220.6	106 094	46.4	53.6	38.7	14.4	2 935	24.6
Burlington, NC	88	-10.2	117	1.6	35.9	538 124	4 610	60 524	42.6	56 598	19.2	80.8	34.3	10.5	459	18.2
Burlington-South Burlington, VT	281	-0.7	194	0.6	127.6	572 197	2 947	87 799	207.7	143 718	12.1	87.9	47.1	20.6	2 563	23.7
Canton-Massillon, OH	255	-5.2	123	1.5	166.8	496 200	4 037	80 553	164.4	79 265	30.2	69.8	39.0	11.2	2 375	30.7
Cape Coral-Fort Myers, FL	86	-31.7	91	14.6	22.0	982 569	10 818	39 788	116.1	122 945	97.1	2.9	26.2	6.1	142	1.2
Cape Girardeau-Jackson, MO-IL	558	-1.6	228	D	333.7	533 823	2 339	65 475	117.4	48 002	59.1	40.9	40.6	8.8	5 674	52.1
Carson City, NV	3	-25.0	131	D	1.2	408 435	3 112	67 740	1.1	54 143	D	D	23.8	14.3	0	0.0
Casper, WY	2 181	-24.0	5 282	40.3	49.6	1 762 052	334	92 949	32.7	79 186	16.5	83.5	47.0	17.4	1 623	19.4
Cedar Rapids, IA	1 060	-0.1	280	1.2	922.6	1 015 910	3 623	129 041	628.8	166 313	60.0	40.0	63.0	33.2	25 307	80.1
Champaign-Urbana, IL	1 088	-2.9	455	7.6	1 054.3	1 938 330	4 262	182 960	603.9	252 333	93.2	6.8	72.4	45.4	20 145	86.4

Table C. Metropolitan Areas — Water Use, Wholesale Trade, Retail Trade, and Real Estate

Area name	Water use, 2005		Wholesale trade,[1] 2007				Retail trade, 2007				Real estate and rental and leasing, 2007			
	Total water withdrawn (mil gal/day)	Gallons withdrawn per person	Number of establishments	Number of employees	Sales (mil dol)	Annual payroll (mil dol)	Number of establishments	Number of employees	Sales (mil dol)	Annual payroll (mil dol)	Number of establishments	Number of employees	Receipts (mil dol)	Annual payroll (mil dol)
	133	134	135	136	137	138	139	140	141	142	143	144	145	146
Abilene, TX	32.1	202	193	1 967	2 268.2	73.8	669	9 119	2 345.6	198.3	179	691	138.2	20.3
Akron, OH	86.2	123	1 219	20 568	16 631.7	1 019.7	2 352	37 531	9 041.6	837.9	631	3 366	550.4	99.0
Albany, GA	230.7	1 417	215	2 662	1 564.5	101.7	713	8 401	1 873.5	169.0	191	816	105.1	20.8
Albany-Schenectady-Troy, NY	378.8	446	982	13 583	11 573.9	698.0	3 171	49 200	13 228.5	1 093.6	837	5 299	996.5	172.8
Albuquerque, NM	433.6	543	1 076	14 486	9 054.4	627.5	2 639	43 054	11 242.4	1 044.5	1 142	5 807	964.0	165.4
Alexandria, LA	531.4	3 591	160	1 971	871.4	72.0	632	8 233	1 984.9	175.8	142	742	93.3	18.7
Allentown-Bethlehem-Easton, PA-NJ	515.2	652	964	20 599	25 205.8	1 139.1	2 820	42 384	10 520.7	957.2	609	3 073	646.9	95.0
Altoona, PA	18.4	145	143	2 326	1 655.2	94.4	619	9 366	2 038.7	179.6	82	393	66.7	10.3
Amarillo, TX	129.9	544	295	5 106	4 256.4	208.3	952	13 887	4 007.6	308.9	293	1 331	220.1	38.7
Ames, IA	11.9	149	93	1 178	752.6	61.9	320	4 611	968.3	91.7	96	371	38.1	10.1
Anchorage, AK	114.4	325	444	6 534	5 323.2	318.7	1 156	19 042	5 336.6	528.6	450	2 688	490.9	100.8
Anderson, IN	15.6	119	89	1 535	848.2	73.7	431	5 542	1 234.9	108.0	103	434	61.5	10.2
Anderson, SC	163.6	932	204	2 685	2 839.5	111.1	755	8 901	2 004.7	178.1	140	502	97.1	14.2
Ann Arbor, MI	37.9	111	346	4 097	4 021.3	224.6	1 148	16 403	3 681.1	355.3	368	2 595	712.4	98.3
Anniston-Oxford, AL	29.0	258	114	2 074	2 821.7	80.5	552	6 854	1 543.0	139.1	93	459	66.3	10.2
Appleton, WI	108.1	502	356	5 551	4 551.6	275.0	910	15 207	3 293.1	308.8	170	882	161.0	25.2
Asheville, NC	366.2	932	502	5 464	3 758.5	222.2	1 972	24 609	5 974.9	545.7	650	2 118	361.0	66.0
Athens-Clarke County, GA	15.1	86	188	2 661	2 082.7	109.0	750	10 066	2 184.3	208.0	299	975	144.9	28.2
Atlanta-Sandy Springs-Marietta, GA	1 137.4	231	9 593	158 372	208 828.5	9 408.4	17 974	270 206	68 892.2	6 431.2	8 188	47 362	11 310.7	2 418.0
Atlantic City-Hammonton, NJ	51.4	190	222	3 376	1 707.0	153.3	1 291	17 258	4 429.4	428.6	287	1 887	378.7	56.9
Auburn-Opelika, AL	21.5	175	74	D	D	D	472	6 391	1 451.6	125.3	122	636	79.4	15.0
Augusta-Richmond County, GA-SC	436.4	839	433	4 840	6 428.9	222.6	1 989	25 509	6 159.3	545.1	508	2 512	401.4	64.3
Austin-Round Rock-San Marcos, TX	902.6	621	1 902	49 950	67 697.7	3 260.9	5 347	85 862	26 735.1	2 106.9	2 431	15 328	2 945.6	588.7
Bakersfield-Delano, CA	2 663.6	3 519	654	9 008	6 890.3	442.1	1 993	30 123	7 876.0	725.6	627	3 414	565.5	112.8
Baltimore-Towson, MD	1 521.7	573	3 400	56 795	45 872.4	3 139.0	9 536	141 052	36 583.9	3 462.3	3 126	22 029	5 938.1	951.3
Bangor, ME	45.1	307	179	2 391	1 551.7	91.7	777	10 842	2 983.9	241.6	172	782	124.9	21.8
Barnstable Town, MA	529.6	2 338	220	1 393	951.9	64.9	1 628	16 213	3 973.2	427.7	385	1 632	270.6	50.3
Baton Rouge, LA	1 711.4	2 332	1 018	D	D	D	2 955	42 265	10 269.6	925.2	790	4 107	773.4	129.2
Battle Creek, MI	35.6	255	117	1 177	862.9	48.4	531	7 074	1 571.3	136.0	95	475	62.7	11.7
Bay City, MI	629.6	5 774	108	1 326	1 255.5	55.1	430	5 580	1 301.0	115.5	77	316	39.9	6.0
Beaumont-Port Arthur, TX	1 465.0	3 820	390	5 724	6 727.5	279.7	1 467	20 141	5 437.5	453.8	373	1 811	374.9	60.0
Bellingham, WA	81.3	443	343	3 433	1 563.8	151.4	851	11 100	2 556.0	263.5	352	1 254	240.2	33.3
Bend, OR	206.6	1 462	264	2 142	1 372.8	96.6	867	10 952	2 809.1	271.9	452	1 782	229.7	48.2
Billings, MT	765.3	5 221	377	5 080	4 229.0	228.5	816	10 481	2 901.4	255.0	283	938	147.3	27.2
Binghamton, NY	125.5	505	243	4 513	2 868.2	176.0	904	13 259	2 875.2	264.9	169	1 138	195.2	31.5
Birmingham-Hoover, AL	1 934.9	1 775	1 946	30 000	29 323.4	1 528.0	4 676	62 472	15 876.1	1 402.5	1 167	9 929	1 714.4	357.8
Bismarck, ND	78.7	792	202	2 233	1 477.7	91.5	479	7 818	1 743.1	162.0	143	440	67.3	9.8
Blacksburg-Christiansburg-Radford, VA	377.9	2 502	98	834	412.3	29.2	600	8 010	1 702.0	166.6	153	692	107.3	18.1
Bloomington, IN	24.2	136	124	2 308	1 891.9	106.7	670	8 993	1 863.2	174.4	212	1 206	149.0	30.2
Bloomington-Normal, IL	16.0	100	195	3 322	5 883.8	180.4	608	9 660	2 231.4	197.0	153	934	139.2	24.9
Boise City-Nampa, ID	3 330.0	6 119	921	12 110	11 570.5	632.6	2 086	31 707	8 214.7	755.8	1 166	4 330	626.0	134.3
Boston-Cambridge-Quincy, MA-NH	2 211.5	501	6 813	119 540	117 889.5	8 202.0	17 098	252 997	62 993.3	6 370.9	5 163	38 734	12 365.6	1 975.4
Boston-Quincy, MA Div	380.8	212	2 667	45 484	40 858.2	2 896.0	6 996	101 159	25 422.3	2 592.9	2 351	21 098	7 628.9	1 225.5
Cambridge-Newton-Framingham, MA Div	388.9	267	2 464	51 935	54 648.1	3 879.8	5 306	80 413	19 661.1	2 036.6	1 690	12 621	3 802.7	571.3
Peabody, MA Div	505.2	684	963	13 443	14 341.3	890.2	2 690	38 874	9 822.1	962.0	647	3 045	584.1	109.8
Rockingham County-Strafford County, NH Div	936.7	2 262	719	8 678	8 041.9	536.0	2 106	32 551	8 087.8	779.4	475	1 970	349.9	68.8
Boulder, CO	203.7	726	493	6 003	5 023.0	503.9	1 244	17 620	4 039.3	444.5	669	2 365	441.7	83.2
Bowling Green, KY	20.9	189	151	2 199	2 357.6	84.1	562	7 706	1 723.7	153.7	133	1 113	114.4	28.7
Bremerton-Silverdale, WA	28.0	116	184	1 178	765.1	49.0	840	11 918	2 936.2	301.3	392	1 332	224.2	37.3
Bridgeport-Stamford-Norwalk, CT	652.0	722	1 514	26 495	102 548.3	2 145.5	3 770	53 738	15 702.2	1 648.8	1 174	7 465	2 283.4	450.7
Brownsville-Harlingen, TX	210.1	555	369	3 911	1 687.8	103.8	1 230	17 667	3 911.7	340.0	341	1 593	169.4	30.0
Brunswick, GA	116.0	1 178	117	841	712.8	37.2	613	5 777	1 528.2	131.0	210	746	98.2	20.8
Buffalo-Niagara Falls, NY	1 093.4	953	1 537	27 236	28 529.7	1 362.0	4 106	63 093	13 292.3	1 288.6	962	6 639	1 001.2	187.0
Burlington, NC	24.3	173	170	1 941	729.4	79.1	631	8 251	1 968.8	168.1	135	523	83.0	14.7
Burlington-South Burlington, VT	32.2	157	352	5 012	3 160.1	252.4	1 161	14 844	3 325.7	338.6	280	1 674	268.5	48.9
Canton-Massillon, OH	53.4	130	462	6 462	6 803.2	283.7	1 463	22 719	5 127.3	489.7	336	1 611	212.8	37.3
Cape Coral-Fort Myers, FL	709.1	1 291	722	6 704	3 136.0	278.9	2 624	38 417	9 193.1	923.2	1 307	5 643	1 000.1	171.3
Cape Girardeau-Jackson, MO-IL	48.9	529	161	2 392	1 944.1	89.0	502	6 629	1 435.4	130.8	123	447	65.0	10.2
Carson City, NV	9.9	177	110	628	466.6	34.9	262	3 698	991.5	99.5	147	569	73.4	16.0
Casper, WY	119.5	1 712	195	2 240	3 159.9	117.2	406	5 138	1 377.0	130.4	164	1 076	263.3	45.7
Cedar Rapids, IA	276.8	1 123	434	5 479	3 412.3	249.5	971	16 000	4 026.9	346.6	264	1 765	363.2	93.1
Champaign-Urbana, IL	47.9	222	249	4 262	4 179.3	174.1	773	12 055	2 578.2	232.8	246	1 707	352.3	51.7

1. Merchant wholesalers, except manufacturers' sales branches and offices.

Table C. Metropolitan Areas — **Professional Services, Manufacturing, and Accommodation and Food Services**

Area name	Professional, scientific, and technical services,[1] 2007				Manufacturing, 2007				Accommodation and food services, 2007			
	Number of establishments	Number of employees	Sales (mil dol)	Annual payroll (mil dol)	Number of establishments	Number of employees	Sales (mil dol)	Annual payroll (mil dol)	Number of establishments	Number of employees	Sales (mil dol)	Annual payroll (mil dol)
	147	148	149	150	151	152	153	154	155	156	157	158
Abilene, TX	299	D	D	D	122	2 733	872.6	98.4	317	6 881	258.4	72.4
Akron, OH	1 871	D	D	D	1 188	43 853	12 245.1	1 954.4	1 528	27 058	1 072.7	304.9
Albany, GA	257	1 638	184.3	66.3	121	6 359	3 634.3	293.1	261	4 659	190.0	47.7
Albany-Schenectady-Troy, NY	2 360	D	D	D	644	21 188	7 638.7	1 042.7	2 110	29 445	1 417.6	404.0
Albuquerque, NM	2 517	D	D	D	772	23 520	8 364.1	1 084.6	1 584	35 110	1 617.4	473.8
Alexandria, LA	289	1 767	208.0	69.4	90	4 781	4 348.7	203.9	228	4 326	176.7	45.0
Allentown-Bethlehem-Easton, PA-NJ	1 687	D	D	D	951	38 581	13 681.2	1 779.0	1 763	24 480	1 153.7	305.4
Altoona, PA	228	D	D	D	139	7 282	1 931.2	285.6	274	4 841	178.9	52.0
Amarillo, TX	485	D	D	D	209	8 141	4 404.5	316.3	527	10 352	460.4	121.7
Ames, IA	193	D	D	D	75	4 668	1 970.8	213.4	224	4 388	151.0	43.4
Anchorage, AK	1 224	9 898	1 669.9	623.5	230	2 522	527.6	99.9	905	15 805	1 047.0	314.1
Anderson, IN	202	D	D	D	118	4 652	1 046.9	191.8	246	4 343	155.1	43.6
Anderson, SC	288	D	D	D	222	12 655	4 886.3	495.2	350	6 420	235.8	64.5
Ann Arbor, MI	1 215	14 248	1 788.8	1 017.4	324	15 543	5 331.8	881.4	679	13 734	613.5	180.4
Anniston-Oxford, AL	171	D	D	D	141	6 961	2 680.0	279.3	224	5 129	186.5	51.5
Appleton, WI	412	4 621	494.8	195.4	415	22 900	8 157.8	1 044.1	524	9 585	336.2	93.5
Asheville, NC	1 181	5 910	636.1	259.1	517	21 057	6 271.5	863.5	1 042	20 002	966.0	282.4
Athens-Clarke County, GA	476	D	D	D	165	7 971	2 219.7	300.5	421	8 235	341.3	92.1
Atlanta-Sandy Springs-Marietta, GA	20 442	D	D	D	4 312	161 018	58 521.5	6 922.0	10 511	207 366	10 689.7	2 961.9
Atlantic City-Hammonton, NJ	648	D	D	D	140	2 974	D	113.8	862	56 370	6 093.0	1 505.4
Auburn-Opelika, AL	189	D	D	D	123	D	D	D	271	5 515	201.2	55.8
Augusta-Richmond County, GA-SC	939	7 751	952.3	400.6	348	24 428	12 650.6	1 145.3	921	18 737	730.0	197.2
Austin-Round Rock-San Marcos, TX	6 052	D	D	D	1 254	47 630	31 352.5	2 345.7	3 350	73 490	3 796.0	1 061.5
Bakersfield-Delano, CA	1 123	D	D	D	390	12 789	9 456.2	583.7	1 203	19 344	940.3	252.2
Baltimore-Towson, MD	9 266	D	D	D	1 923	70 099	24 306.5	3 738.1	5 326	97 405	5 371.3	1 450.1
Bangor, ME	333	D	D	D	155	4 795	1 088.5	171.9	320	5 179	224.2	68.1
Barnstable Town, MA	753	D	D	D	210	2 461	533.3	110.3	1 100	12 721	891.0	261.6
Baton Rouge, LA	2 098	21 316	3 219.4	1 140.7	593	24 773	D	1 555.1	1 330	29 936	1 290.3	354.2
Battle Creek, MI	209	D	D	D	179	11 532	4 954.0	537.5	284	4 558	182.0	54.1
Bay City, MI	174	D	D	D	126	3 532	1 107.2	191.2	238	3 973	134.7	41.3
Beaumont-Port Arthur, TX	669	D	D	D	334	21 563	55 089.6	1 369.4	610	12 226	510.0	142.0
Bellingham, WA	670	3 562	419.2	163.4	334	10 165	11 809.7	467.2	505	8 461	407.9	116.2
Bend, OR	650	D	D	D	299	5 359	897.4	201.7	504	8 078	416.4	121.1
Billings, MT	597	3 280	381.0	140.5	199	4 019	5 749.0	192.4	418	8 244	380.3	102.9
Binghamton, NY	386	D	D	D	248	12 807	3 061.1	547.3	590	8 663	359.2	102.8
Birmingham-Hoover, AL	2 807	D	D	D	1 124	43 380	14 083.7	1 858.2	1 941	37 945	1 780.0	490.8
Bismarck, ND	312	D	D	D	112	3 008	2 444.2	128.7	223	5 122	196.2	57.5
Blacksburg-Christiansburg-Radford, VA	318	D	D	D	144	12 277	4 578.7	563.8	320	6 166	237.7	67.2
Bloomington, IN	345	3 106	341.1	119.1	165	8 676	2 098.3	358.6	407	8 252	317.8	87.3
Bloomington-Normal, IL	338	D	D	D	115	5 497	2 578.8	270.5	375	8 558	336.1	97.4
Boise City-Nampa, ID	1 896	D	D	D	686	31 240	7 792.3	1 593.2	1 214	22 484	955.9	263.5
Boston-Cambridge-Quincy, MA-NH	17 498	217 147	44 853.7	19 181.6	5 111	195 861	61 691.3	11 207.1	10 883	185 188	11 243.7	3 263.0
Boston-Quincy, MA Div	7 059	87 301	19 961.7	7 896.4	1 634	52 290	16 621.4	2 675.9	4 715	90 155	5 884.4	1 711.7
Cambridge-Newton-Framingham, MA Div	6 883	106 332	21 264.5	9 828.5	1 853	72 842	22 482.6	4 609.2	3 372	54 344	3 250.2	932.3
Peabody, MA Div	2 221	D	D	D	997	47 909	17 488.7	2 877.4	1 708	23 927	1 301.5	377.7
Rockingham County-Strafford County, NH Div	1 335	D	D	D	627	22 820	5 098.6	1 044.6	1 088	16 762	807.6	241.3
Boulder, CO	2 447	23 459	5 054.5	1 781.8	534	16 791	3 855.9	896.9	815	14 563	668.9	208.4
Bowling Green, KY	214	D	D	D	123	9 585	4 553.4	420.7	230	5 598	237.5	65.3
Bremerton-Silverdale, WA	716	D	D	D	163	2 154	D	78.3	505	7 483	392.8	117.4
Bridgeport-Stamford-Norwalk, CT	3 778	38 942	7 103.5	3 058.3	1 029	42 123	20 028.4	2 455.4	2 094	27 883	1 861.9	523.1
Brownsville-Harlingen, TX	474	D	D	D	221	D	D	D	643	12 287	503.1	131.4
Brunswick, GA	288	D	D	D	90	2 703	1 039.9	128.0	301	8 019	422.4	168.9
Buffalo-Niagara Falls, NY	2 438	D	D	D	1 381	58 267	19 306.9	2 971.5	2 602	45 852	2 125.2	585.3
Burlington, NC	233	D	D	D	236	11 733	3 163.1	445.0	281	5 080	219.4	62.8
Burlington-South Burlington, VT	796	6 254	963.7	364.3	267	14 916	6 278.4	825.9	548	8 285	406.9	118.1
Canton-Massillon, OH	766	D	D	D	591	28 877	10 732.0	1 239.0	827	14 271	536.8	159.5
Cape Coral-Fort Myers, FL	1 848	10 115	1 305.2	511.3	403	5 988	1 181.8	222.6	1 095	23 070	1 192.0	344.2
Cape Girardeau-Jackson, MO-IL	173	D	D	D	117	D	3 422.7		210	4 772	153.9	44.6
Carson City, NV	381	D	D	D	143	3 528	621.6	141.7	167	2 664	127.7	37.8
Casper, WY	271	D	D	D	94	2 525	1 230.6	114.9	185	3 853	168.0	50.0
Cedar Rapids, IA	568	4 799	591.8	251.1	297	19 479	8 586.7	1 183.3	564	10 050	373.0	108.5
Champaign-Urbana, IL	513	3 125	317.1	134.5	178	10 029	3 636.3	375.3	569	10 437	395.9	110.4

1. Establishments subject to federal tax.

Area name	Health care and social assistance,[1] 2007				Other services,[1] 2007				Federal funds and grants, 2009–2010 Expenditures (mil dol)			
									Total	Direct payments for individuals		
	Number of establishments	Number of employees	Receipts (mil dol)	Annual payroll (mil dol)	Number of establishments	Number of employees	Receipts (mil dol)	Annual payroll (mil dol)		Social Security and government retirement	Medicare	Food stamps and Supplemental Security Income
	159	160	161	162	163	164	165	166	167	168	169	170
Abilene, TX	414	12 311	867.5	349.6	282	1 664	155.5	33.1	1 522.1	517.9	259.3	62.4
Akron, OH	1 747	45 542	4 061.5	1 663.5	1 385	9 299	848.2	233.6	5 424.2	1 904.7	1 318.8	260.5
Albany, GA	381	9 322	901.4	336.0	261	1 363	108.3	31.5	1 593.7	466.2	223.1	137.2
Albany-Schenectady-Troy, NY	2 387	59 709	5 105.9	2 166.3	1 562	11 148	1 149.1	327.4	15 440.0	2 615.5	1 260.0	237.9
Albuquerque, NM	1 980	47 563	4 218.4	1 840.5	1 252	8 778	735.2	228.6	10 866.1	2 763.5	828.3	308.1
Alexandria, LA	504	13 319	1 227.1	490.7	234	1 217	103.1	28.2	1 612.5	501.6	309.4	85.6
Allentown-Bethlehem-Easton, PA-NJ	2 303	52 271	5 144.4	2 080.5	1 597	9 216	808.4	228.4	6 417.2	2 552.6	1 716.2	181.3
Altoona, PA	403	10 162	909.5	373.1	299	1 686	115.7	33.5	1 300.8	508.9	337.5	63.5
Amarillo, TX	696	14 808	1 630.0	558.6	430	2 890	296.8	63.7	4 532.8	641.5	305.5	74.3
Ames, IA	172	5 026	415.3	172.4	148	1 096	212.9	28.7	1 268.6	195.3	80.6	12.0
Anchorage, AK	1 265	23 414	2 932.2	1 066.8	693	4 558	498.1	139.1	5 174.2	871.7	168.0	93.3
Anderson, IN	266	6 713	556.4	223.6	201	1 239	83.4	24.0	1 214.0	561.7	257.3	55.3
Anderson, SC	362	8 112	786.0	301.2	244	1 871	154.5	55.0	1 233.9	629.3	227.6	51.1
Ann Arbor, MI	958	34 745	3 715.8	1 627.0	557	3 917	443.2	122.6	3 527.0	780.4	357.0	71.1
Anniston-Oxford, AL	283	6 307	545.7	206.7	186	944	81.3	22.1	1 726.3	565.6	229.3	61.1
Appleton, WI	533	12 694	1 231.7	517.6	428	2 780	233.4	63.7	1 113.3	556.9	180.9	24.8
Asheville, NC	1 187	30 282	2 822.7	1 140.5	736	4 230	346.8	97.5	3 486.0	1 639.3	616.9	147.1
Athens-Clarke County, GA	502	9 685	949.3	406.1	288	2 216	236.0	46.0	1 291.2	448.1	174.0	68.2
Atlanta-Sandy Springs-Marietta, GA	11 642	213 216	23 772.3	8 863.9	8 707	63 724	7 448.4	2 039.4	40 616.0	11 173.4	4 215.5	1 600.6
Atlantic City-Hammonton, NJ	821	16 172	1 780.0	702.6	547	3 496	270.1	81.7	2 365.5	831.2	563.0	79.3
Auburn-Opelika, AL	221	6 157	469.5	191.8	152	748	49.7	14.2	762.5	321.6	107.1	38.7
Augusta-Richmond County, GA-SC	1 202	30 349	3 176.8	1 186.0	715	4 312	403.1	97.3	8 423.1	1 929.1	643.9	292.8
Austin-Round Rock-San Marcos, TX	3 713	65 629	7 015.6	2 738.4	2 745	23 514	2 463.8	746.5	19 767.6	3 272.5	966.8	320.3
Bakersfield-Delano, CA	1 456	25 119	2 746.4	1 042.9	857	5 637	569.1	145.0	5 744.5	1 632.6	1 074.6	328.6
Baltimore-Towson, MD	7 208	173 557	19 053.3	7 171.0	4 997	36 876	4 149.0	1 100.5	42 393.2	8 445.7	8 890.6	968.5
Bangor, ME	563	14 538	1 318.9	561.5	276	1 350	139.8	33.6	1 644.1	537.9	207.0	75.8
Barnstable Town, MA	807	15 247	1 466.2	620.7	601	3 279	334.9	88.2	2 650.7	1 059.0	647.7	45.7
Baton Rouge, LA	1 846	44 467	3 987.1	1 469.8	1 286	8 991	1 020.9	274.9	11 347.0	1 776.3	1 142.6	316.9
Battle Creek, MI	341	8 967	898.1	372.5	225	1 249	503.8	42.5	1 481.8	503.1	252.8	76.8
Bay City, MI	315	5 902	513.3	209.5	196	1 068	75.9	21.8	897.4	401.0	203.4	50.5
Beaumont-Port Arthur, TX	1 067	20 932	1 827.1	667.3	546	4 058	408.7	101.5	3 258.9	1 150.7	904.1	195.8
Bellingham, WA	636	9 730	862.0	348.7	390	2 155	207.5	59.0	1 279.8	567.6	165.5	57.7
Bend, OR	543	8 144	974.3	351.5	322	1 761	169.5	46.5	950.9	535.6	125.8	37.1
Billings, MT	530	11 746	1 181.9	481.4	396	2 015	200.9	49.3	1 203.6	486.3	179.4	34.3
Binghamton, NY	509	14 884	1 302.9	525.8	393	2 253	180.7	49.2	2 815.9	834.7	420.9	100.2
Birmingham-Hoover, AL	2 532	67 157	7 562.2	2 841.0	1 808	12 646	1 451.4	387.1	10 252.3	3 661.4	2 153.4	475.9
Bismarck, ND	277	10 100	791.4	358.3	307	1 965	177.7	49.9	1 625.9	320.6	119.5	19.5
Blacksburg-Christiansburg-Radford, VA	352	6 425	602.1	236.0	261	1 258	286.9	29.4	1 292.2	453.5	197.6	40.7
Bloomington, IN	398	9 059	775.2	333.4	292	2 362	632.3	60.8	1 461.9	495.9	186.9	41.7
Bloomington-Normal, IL	333	8 693	875.8	354.5	260	2 362	187.8	59.7	758.0	353.8	140.8	25.7
Boise City-Nampa, ID	1 697	31 482	2 897.6	1 212.9	1 042	5 975	489.1	149.9	4 516.3	1 573.1	405.9	151.6
Boston-Cambridge-Quincy, MA-NH	12 525	363 736	38 593.4	16 468.8	9 748	68 801	7 926.9	2 151.1	57 692.9	11 465.4	9 038.9	1 325.8
Boston-Quincy, MA Div	4 996	196 332	22 166.2	9 425.4	4 172	31 341	3 772.0	965.8	25 223.8	4 550.7	4 100.1	703.5
Cambridge-Newton-Framingham, MA Div	4 386	99 055	10 192.8	4 326.2	3 202	23 744	2 577.2	790.2	20 144.1	3 615.4	3 012.9	287.1
Peabody, MA Div	2 030	47 584	4 272.0	1 909.5	1 470	8 644	1 096.7	254.2	9 423.9	2 019.7	1 518.0	274.1
Rockingham County-Strafford County, NH Div	1 113	20 765	1 962.4	807.6	904	5 072	481.0	140.9	2 901.1	1 279.6	407.9	61.2
Boulder, CO	1 158	17 109	1 712.5	716.4	711	4 509	794.5	161.0	3 118.2	722.8	256.8	37.7
Bowling Green, KY	330	7 655	723.8	248.3	170	1 195	85.2	25.0	960.1	327.7	250.2	47.8
Bremerton-Silverdale, WA	659	12 424	1 169.6	482.9	392	2 004	157.5	48.0	4 004.4	1 088.8	231.7	79.6
Bridgeport-Stamford-Norwalk, CT	2 739	60 497	6 923.5	2 604.2	2 056	13 357	1 722.7	431.1	13 539.9	2 248.1	4 982.5	184.7
Brownsville-Harlingen, TX	925	27 384	1 711.7	686.6	424	2 214	140.9	36.3	2 895.6	668.7	441.3	326.4
Brunswick, GA	288	4 943	911.7	189.7	180	984	79.4	22.4	1 113.1	380.2	183.4	51.5
Buffalo-Niagara Falls, NY	3 234	83 751	7 057.8	2 815.2	2 120	14 710	1 200.3	353.0	10 696.4	4 017.3	2 172.2	485.5
Burlington, NC	335	6 483	549.1	227.9	201	1 165	93.5	27.7	925.3	465.3	191.6	35.2
Burlington-South Burlington, VT	683	15 754	1 488.8	590.1	485	2 339	195.7	60.4	2 414.8	514.0	194.6	54.4
Canton-Massillon, OH	1 035	27 536	2 171.5	939.1	772	5 203	433.8	121.3	3 022.6	1 347.1	733.2	146.4
Cape Coral-Fort Myers, FL	1 389	25 867	3 068.2	1 115.8	1 206	6 552	589.9	162.5	4 275.2	2 289.1	1 205.1	133.0
Cape Girardeau-Jackson, MO-IL	307	10 119	997.5	366.8	184	820	69.0	17.4	771.9	289.0	131.1	37.9
Carson City, NV	220	3 407	453.3	164.1	149	948	83.3	25.4	1 497.0	208.9	85.3	13.9
Casper, WY	283	4 819	482.2	203.0	202	1 200	141.1	34.1	499.4	205.5	84.1	15.6
Cedar Rapids, IA	636	14 920	1 253.2	527.7	494	2 818	266.2	68.4	2 861.1	713.8	293.0	59.9
Champaign-Urbana, IL	425	12 236	1 340.7	527.4	334	2 303	437.5	58.5	1 707.6	478.9	205.3	48.8

1. Establishments subject to federal tax.

Area name	Federal funds and grants, 2009–2010 (cont.)							Value of residential construction authorized by building permits, 2010		Local government finances, 2007				
	Expenditures (mil dol) (cont.)									General revenue				
	Procurement contract awards			Grants									Taxes	
													Per capita[1] (dollars)	
	Salaries and wages	Defense	Other	Medicaid and other health-related	Nutrition and family welfare	Education	Other	New construction ($1,000)	Number of housing units	Total (mil dol)	Inter-governmental (mil dol)	Total (mil dol)	Total	Property
	171	172	173	174	175	176	177	178	179	180	181	182	183	184
Abilene, TX	319.2	74.7	9.7	168.4	28.6	6.8	17.5	43 583	390	470.3	202.9	186.0	1 167	854
Akron, OH	239.3	443.7	64.0	623.8	129.8	54.4	188.1	127 731	736	3 024.0	1 110.1	1 248.6	1 785	1 223
Albany, GA	176.9	112.3	64.4	231.4	51.4	23.1	18.1	27 796	248	550.1	247.8	204.8	1 248	771
Albany-Schenectady-Troy, NY	728.8	383.8	258.0	1 647.8	1 313.6	2 357.6	4 085.2	279 849	1 429	4 338.0	1 520.4	2 036.1	2 386	1 696
Albuquerque, NM	1 275.3	770.5	2 911.8	1 248.6	152.1	93.8	273.1	304 216	1 764	2 999.5	1 585.5	895.0	1 072	551
Alexandria, LA	276.2	11.0	90.0	217.3	35.6	14.0	45.7	62 051	434	476.7	234.0	178.8	1 194	433
Allentown-Bethlehem-Easton, PA-NJ	290.1	129.3	87.0	475.1	109.6	23.7	755.1	203 837	1 388	3 470.1	1 251.1	1 482.4	1 844	1 536
Altoona, PA	83.3	1.9	63.2	170.2	31.2	4.1	23.9	24 055	159	389.5	217.2	109.2	870	625
Amarillo, TX	143.6	2 428.8	638.8	123.3	36.1	12.4	50.9	189 784	927	772.5	278.6	337.7	1 394	1 070
Ames, IA	85.6	15.0	63.0	61.0	8.3	2.6	699.8	34 489	167	394.2	77.8	112.0	1 321	1 045
Anchorage, AK	1 152.4	964.8	317.7	347.8	96.0	52.1	1 036.5	125 839	533	1 504.4	673.5	577.6	1 594	1 354
Anderson, IN	33.7	4.5	13.0	160.5	19.5	3.3	93.3	17 237	80	356.2	165.7	101.0	769	650
Anderson, SC	86.7	14.6	6.6	132.5	19.3	15.9	25.4	58 869	420	424.3	186.7	168.4	936	819
Ann Arbor, MI	231.6	107.4	209.4	1 191.4	49.9	31.5	388.9	56 891	368	1 351.8	485.7	589.1	1 683	1 660
Anniston-Oxford, AL	233.1	415.3	58.5	104.4	16.3	9.1	7.4	15 959	107	507.7	186.6	103.4	915	334
Appleton, WI	72.0	50.5	22.8	115.4	22.7	10.6	23.0	96 221	587	890.5	410.2	315.7	1 448	1 413
Asheville, NC	257.4	34.7	134.3	437.0	65.4	31.7	48.2	278 780	2 038	1 444.9	558.6	469.0	1 160	845
Athens-Clarke County, GA	130.5	5.7	34.6	209.7	37.7	19.7	109.9	45 137	226	947.2	205.0	237.4	1 267	877
Atlanta-Sandy Springs-Marietta, GA	5 338.8	4 883.8	3 094.4	3 008.9	1 054.1	1 467.7	3 707.8	1 277 838	7 575	19 722.7	5 897.8	9 275.4	1 757	1 171
Atlantic City-Hammonton, NJ.	301.1	40.6	95.9	278.6	51.5	10.0	40.2	79 406	512	1 515.6	456.0	828.2	3 060	2 999
Auburn-Opelika, AL	70.4	22.7	10.2	66.3	18.2	7.9	59.1	150 616	971	728.3	134.9	132.6	1 016	470
Augusta-Richmond County, GA-SC	1 841.2	308.0	2 426.2	622.2	107.1	46.4	88.9	431 228	2 474	1 604.4	689.3	568.4	1 075	726
Austin-Round Rock-San Marcos, TX	1 062.5	924.6	996.8	1 500.5	1 129.7	1 338.0	7 867.2	1 285 530	8 786	5 871.3	1 096.4	3 419.2	2 139	1 751
Bakersfield-Delano, CA	772.0	484.6	233.1	712.0	203.4	69.5	80.2	256 977	1 656	5 502.3	2 722.3	1 021.3	1 292	1 083
Baltimore-Towson, MD	5 294.7	5 598.5	2 795.0	5 324.4	670.0	800.7	3 035.1	826 668	5 594	10 299.2	3 623.0	5 170.4	1 938	979
Bangor, ME	173.7	131.4	69.6	254.0	28.6	10.5	90.0	38 001	272	413.1	167.1	177.0	1 190	1 173
Barnstable Town, MA	250.1	84.7	75.5	189.4	35.0	11.3	233.0	139 122	418	915.3	212.8	541.7	2 438	2 298
Baton Rouge, LA	395.4	326.2	-77.6	764.4	331.9	475.7	5 723.7	474 085	2 962	2 588.1	848.0	1 205.4	1 565	592
Battle Creek, MI	156.6	156.0	60.6	190.7	37.0	11.3	11.6	5 066	33	634.9	350.7	166.3	1 217	1 073
Bay City, MI	40.3	1.8	13.8	103.8	22.2	5.9	6.3	8 410	54	514.5	250.3	131.3	1 221	1 199
Beaumont-Port Arthur, TX	214.5	49.8	42.8	494.6	65.0	15.3	50.9	142 805	1 424	1 383.2	423.7	634.6	1 687	1 368
Bellingham, WA	120.9	22.1	48.4	128.8	33.0	12.1	69.1	92 775	458	612.9	225.3	248.7	1 288	756
Bend, OR	84.9	4.7	24.7	59.4	15.8	6.7	33.8	85 793	377	589.4	201.9	249.0	1 617	1 353
Billings, MT	162.4	3.5	112.1	134.9	33.5	10.7	13.7	73 001	457	487.6	170.6	139.3	931	856
Binghamton, NY	78.3	902.7	21.3	268.4	68.8	22.7	70.9	18 851	108	1 283.1	575.4	516.8	2 097	1 385
Birmingham-Hoover, AL	970.2	291.3	373.3	1 229.2	154.1	84.7	470.7	312 409	1 924	4 025.7	1 389.6	1 664.7	1 502	599
Bismarck, ND	185.3	6.7	41.7	85.0	53.8	85.2	642.9	109 117	650	314.1	111.3	123.7	1 198	1 018
Blacksburg-Christiansburg-Radford, VA	56.6	148.9	35.6	141.3	17.5	10.2	144.8	41 503	268	391.6	180.6	139.2	883	604
Bloomington, IN	94.9	9.1	16.4	443.8	22.0	13.7	88.9	37 442	263	428.6	173.5	142.3	774	676
Bloomington-Normal, IL	67.4	0.3	18.6	56.5	18.9	5.3	21.8	62 284	427	542.8	157.7	275.3	1 676	1 372
Boise City-Nampa, ID	524.3	45.0	165.4	502.1	111.2	134.3	785.3	349 090	1 693	1 650.3	728.4	519.6	884	806
Boston-Cambridge-Quincy, MA-NH	3 497.6	10 905.4	2 895.5	10 529.5	976.2	1 129.9	4 630.0	1 253 961	6 672	19 175.6	7 604.7	8 730.3	1 947	1 885
Boston-Quincy, MA Div	1 700.4	924.2	1 218.4	6 916.5	589.5	684.0	2 868.1	NA	NA	8 898.4	4 131.0	3 591.8	1 933	1 848
Cambridge-Newton-Framingham, MA Div	1 248.1	5 847.4	1 415.4	2 508.9	213.3	356.0	1 452.4	NA	NA	6 250.8	1 991.3	3 083.9	2 093	2 040
Peabody, MA Div	269.8	3 843.8	150.9	900.1	132.3	59.5	163.4	NA	NA	2 602.3	1 061.9	1 210.2	1 651	1 609
Rockingham County-Strafford County, NH Div	279.4	290.0	110.8	204.0	41.1	30.4	146.1	NA	NA	1 424.2	420.5	844.3	2 019	1 990
Boulder, CO	317.0	183.9	532.6	216.3	30.3	21.4	757.2	126 880	657	1 187.5	282.9	670.7	2 311	1 403
Bowling Green, KY	64.9	1.9	22.2	94.7	20.5	11.0	60.5	124 400	573	258.0	112.2	111.8	963	444
Bremerton-Silverdale, WA	969.1	598.8	59.3	132.3	45.2	26.1	709.1	110 936	623	945.8	465.9	310.5	1 312	828
Bridgeport-Stamford-Norwalk, CT	303.9	4 045.9	346.9	869.6	127.7	52.2	278.3	325 062	926	4 018.8	884.0	2 701.7	3 019	2 940
Brownsville-Harlingen, TX	234.8	17.6	103.1	761.1	155.1	35.2	63.4	179 568	1 258	1 402.5	780.0	367.1	948	734
Brunswick, GA	209.9	12.0	123.1	79.7	27.1	9.4	18.8	90 407	404	582.6	107.4	194.1	1 907	1 222
Buffalo-Niagara Falls, NY	753.4	285.9	226.9	1 795.3	331.4	103.0	275.7	251 660	1 498	5 642.4	2 660.4	2 237.6	1 983	1 360
Burlington, NC	28.0	5.2	9.0	128.2	19.4	10.3	9.6	79 991	847	402.1	208.0	128.4	883	667
Burlington-South Burlington, VT	419.8	503.0	115.9	371.0	38.0	15.6	120.6	91 997	585	699.0	467.0	118.5	572	486
Canton-Massillon, OH	168.2	9.2	24.1	351.7	74.1	33.0	61.7	74 255	452	1 359.3	639.7	489.8	1 203	913
Cape Coral-Fort Myers, FL	190.7	4.9	41.8	138.2	62.1	27.1	94.8	239 579	1 276	3 868.3	890.3	1 485.2	2 515	2 088
Cape Girardeau-Jackson, MO-IL	61.4	11.5	9.7	147.6	12.4	6.6	30.0	12 810	99	214.6	87.5	90.2	966	537
Carson City, NV	66.8	14.4	10.5	71.7	107.2	177.7	730.6	9 963	71	198.2	99.8	49.3	897	577
Casper, WY	60.4	6.7	26.2	43.2	9.6	5.5	33.5	85 998	807	354.6	203.8	86.7	1 209	798
Cedar Rapids, IA	107.1	1 128.7	254.2	153.2	35.3	6.4	37.3	83 762	855	942.6	364.3	357.6	1 415	1 268
Champaign-Urbana, IL	140.1	32.8	47.5	253.8	30.2	19.8	377.6	76 634	529	716.8	278.6	307.3	1 391	1 167

1. Based on the resident population estimated as of July 1 of the year shown.

Table C. Metropolitan Areas — Local Government Finances, Government Employment, and Voting

Area name	Local government finances, 2007 (cont.)									Government employment, 2009			Presidential election,[2] 2008		
	Direct general expenditure							Debt outstanding					Percent of vote cast:		
	Total (mil dol)	Per capita[1] (dollars)	Education	Health and hospitals	Police protection	Public welfare	Highways	Total (mil dol)	Per capita[1] (dollars)	Federal civilian	Federal military	State and local	Democratic	Republican	All other
					Percent of total for:										
	185	186	187	188	189	190	191	192	193	194	195	196	197	198	199
Abilene, TX	483.1	3 032	57.7	5.6	6.2	0.4	2.7	325.2	2 041	1 361	5 137	11 745	25.9	73.1	1.0
Akron, OH	3 049.0	4 360	38.9	10.8	5.8	5.8	5.3	2 396.6	3 427	2 253	1 836	48 904	56.7	41.8	1.4
Albany, GA	533.4	3 251	54.1	5.5	5.8	0.1	3.8	484.6	2 954	3 411	926	10 383	52.9	46.6	0.5
Albany-Schenectady-Troy, NY	4 414.1	5 173	47.6	3.3	3.7	11.9	4.2	4 465.8	5 233	7 025	3 113	98 691	56.4	41.8	1.8
Albuquerque, NM	2 712.4	3 248	50.0	0.6	8.2	2.0	6.4	2 515.3	3 012	15 266	5 827	66 847	58.6	40.1	1.3
Alexandria, LA	453.6	3 028	50.6	0.2	9.0	0.0	5.2	371.5	2 480	3 009	658	12 378	32.7	65.9	1.5
Allentown-Bethlehem-Easton, PA-NJ	3 616.8	4 499	52.6	2.7	3.1	9.4	2.8	5 776.8	7 186	2 493	2 117	40 322	54.0	44.6	1.4
Altoona, PA	382.8	3 050	55.8	0.2	2.5	7.8	5.2	430.7	3 431	1 028	332	8 196	37.3	61.6	1.1
Amarillo, TX	790.4	3 263	55.9	5.2	5.2	0.0	3.2	717.0	2 960	2 382	624	17 346	22.1	77.0	0.9
Ames, IA	363.8	4 292	28.6	44.0	3.1	0.7	3.6	190.7	2 251	1 116	397	18 488	57.0	40.8	2.2
Anchorage, AK	1 455.5	4 017	53.2	2.3	6.4	0.0	8.0	2 093.7	5 778	9 790	14 752	24 636	NA	NA	NA
Anderson, IN	426.4	3 247	50.8	0.3	4.1	3.0	3.4	373.2	2 842	283	443	6 481	52.6	46.0	1.4
Anderson, SC	416.3	2 313	65.6	1.5	6.3	0.0	2.4	418.4	2 325	353	808	11 404	32.7	66.0	1.3
Ann Arbor, MI	1 453.7	4 153	53.1	3.4	5.9	0.9	5.5	1 701.4	4 861	2 917	690	67 464	69.8	28.8	1.4
Anniston-Oxford, AL	494.3	4 370	38.2	35.3	3.6	0.2	4.0	141.5	1 251	5 539	606	8 068	33.2	65.7	1.1
Appleton, WI	951.8	4 365	53.8	4.3	4.5	4.9	8.9	934.0	4 284	567	639	11 413	53.9	44.4	1.7
Asheville, NC	1 464.8	3 623	38.3	18.5	4.1	6.0	1.3	696.1	1 722	3 403	1 085	23 809	50.3	48.4	1.3
Athens-Clarke County, GA	938.0	5 005	30.7	42.5	3.1	0.2	2.3	476.4	2 542	1 608	905	25 242	49.3	49.5	1.2
Atlanta-Sandy Springs-Marietta, GA	19 476.8	3 690	49.4	5.6	5.8	0.7	4.1	30 295.4	5 739	45 328	19 914	285 810	51.4	47.8	0.8
Atlantic City-Hammonton, NJ	1 447.7	5 349	53.0	0.9	7.2	2.0	2.4	1 176.7	4 348	2 700	882	20 516	57.0	41.9	1.1
Auburn-Opelika, AL	542.0	4 153	36.5	35.4	3.4	0.1	4.0	632.6	4 847	315	724	15 418	39.6	59.3	1.1
Augusta-Richmond County, GA-SC	1 685.7	3 190	51.5	9.8	4.8	0.2	2.8	2 485.7	4 703	8 352	12 760	39 212	46.0	53.2	0.7
Austin-Round Rock-San Marcos, TX	5 862.5	3 668	51.5	4.8	5.7	0.4	3.8	16 736.5	10 472	11 858	4 291	155 576	56.3	42.1	1.6
Bakersfield-Delano, CA	5 086.6	6 433	43.2	8.2	3.5	7.3	1.6	2 907.0	3 676	10 347	3 663	48 495	40.1	57.9	2.0
Baltimore-Towson, MD	10 472.5	3 925	51.2	2.3	7.3	0.6	4.3	8 728.9	3 272	73 020	24 595	175 340	57.4	40.7	1.9
Bangor, ME	434.5	2 920	52.8	0.4	4.1	0.5	4.6	271.7	1 828	1 385	509	13 376	51.7	46.6	1.7
Barnstable Town, MA	979.9	4 411	46.8	1.1	6.2	0.3	3.2	860.0	3 871	1 765	1 234	12 443	56.1	42.4	1.5
Baton Rouge, LA	2 346.3	3 047	45.4	5.2	6.7	0.2	5.6	3 202.0	4 158	3 411	3 701	74 823	42.2	56.4	1.4
Battle Creek, MI	649.8	4 756	50.9	14.2	3.9	2.4	4.3	580.6	4 250	3 068	283	6 912	53.8	44.5	1.7
Bay City, MI	497.3	4 625	48.5	16.6	3.8	4.2	5.0	312.7	2 909	282	225	5 827	56.7	41.4	1.8
Beaumont-Port Arthur, TX	1 279.1	3 400	48.4	3.8	6.2	0.5	3.2	2 405.7	6 394	2 132	1 092	23 551	40.8	58.5	0.7
Bellingham, WA	575.8	2 984	41.1	3.0	5.3	0.0	6.1	473.4	2 453	1 309	690	14 077	58.0	40.1	1.9
Bend, OR	590.3	3 832	42.3	3.4	7.3	0.5	6.4	840.1	5 454	916	451	7 385	48.7	49.0	2.4
Billings, MT	478.1	3 195	47.5	5.7	5.8	0.2	6.5	239.3	1 599	1 979	791	7 652	45.3	52.0	2.7
Binghamton, NY	1 347.2	5 467	47.6	2.9	2.6	10.8	4.6	1 079.9	4 382	850	419	22 937	51.3	47.1	1.6
Birmingham-Hoover, AL	4 040.7	3 646	46.0	4.2	6.0	0.1	5.3	9 265.7	8 361	8 903	5 658	72 343	40.1	58.9	0.9
Bismarck, ND	313.0	3 032	44.5	1.9	5.1	1.8	10.7	207.9	2 014	1 236	797	11 003	37.6	60.5	1.9
Blacksburg-Christiansburg-Radford, VA	371.9	2 360	47.0	2.1	6.6	4.5	4.7	401.0	2 544	481	590	20 006	48.0	50.4	1.6
Bloomington, IN	437.4	2 381	49.8	5.5	3.2	3.8	4.6	408.9	2 226	523	637	24 951	59.7	39.1	1.2
Bloomington-Normal, IL	563.9	3 434	44.5	1.2	5.4	1.4	5.2	651.5	3 968	728	341	14 407	49.8	48.5	1.7
Boise City-Nampa, ID	1 550.9	2 639	46.4	2.0	7.3	0.5	6.7	1 297.5	2 208	6 344	2 420	36 863	41.1	56.7	2.1
Boston-Cambridge-Quincy, MA-NH	17 835.4	3 979	50.4	5.2	5.7	1.0	2.7	16 972.0	3 786	38 669	14 514	260 658	61.6	36.9	1.6
Boston-Quincy, MA Div	7 572.1	4 075	46.6	2.5	7.0	1.3	2.5	10 257.6	5 520	20 057	6 070	126 148	62.7	35.8	1.5
Cambridge-Newton-Framingham, MA Div	6 127.7	4 159	50.3	11.8	4.4	0.3	2.7	3 686.3	2 502	13 360	4 989	73 520	64.2	34.1	1.7
Peabody, MA Div	2 691.9	3 672	57.7	0.4	4.9	0.1	2.6	2 237.1	3 052	3 660	1 919	36 337	59.4	39.0	1.6
Rockingham County-Strafford County, NH Div	1 443.7	3 453	56.5	0.4	5.8	4.6	3.8	790.9	1 892	1 592	1 536	24 653	52.5	46.2	1.3
Boulder, CO	1 157.4	3 987	40.7	0.9	7.7	2.8	6.3	2 072.2	7 139	2 298	890	27 370	72.3	26.1	1.6
Bowling Green, KY	257.4	2 219	52.4	0.9	6.6	0.1	4.5	849.4	7 322	682	385	9 775	39.1	59.8	1.1
Bremerton-Silverdale, WA	934.1	3 946	41.1	3.4	4.0	0.0	4.0	820.7	3 467	15 563	11 232	13 393	55.2	42.9	1.9
Bridgeport-Stamford-Norwalk, CT	3 883.2	4 339	56.0	0.9	5.8	0.7	2.3	3 327.6	3 718	3 329	1 721	44 684	58.6	40.6	0.7
Brownsville-Harlingen, TX	1 380.8	3 566	64.6	1.2	4.1	0.4	2.2	2 023.2	5 225	2 728	1 045	26 937	64.1	35.3	0.7
Brunswick, GA	549.2	5 864	32.4	37.6	4.0	0.1	2.0	467.0	4 588	1 953	387	8 449	36.4	62.9	0.7
Buffalo-Niagara Falls, NY	5 723.0	5 073	48.5	3.1	4.0	11.0	3.3	5 124.0	4 542	10 189	2 099	81 693	56.5	41.9	1.6
Burlington, NC	417.6	2 873	49.4	8.4	5.8	6.2	2.8	191.4	1 317	258	379	6 952	44.9	54.2	0.9
Burlington-South Burlington, VT	785.4	3 787	66.0	0.3	4.0	0.0	5.0	499.8	2 410	3 434	1 408	16 538	69.1	28.9	1.9
Canton-Massillon, OH	1 373.3	3 373	52.6	7.2	5.0	6.0	5.1	753.4	1 850	1 167	1 044	19 333	51.3	46.6	2.1
Cape Coral-Fort Myers, FL	3 524.7	5 968	29.1	19.2	4.5	0.4	5.9	4 370.1	7 400	2 483	1 223	33 380	44.5	54.8	0.7
Cape Girardeau-Jackson, MO-IL	229.4	2 459	61.1	1.2	4.3	0.1	7.4	185.6	1 989	491	369	7 228	34.2	64.6	1.2
Carson City, NV	199.1	3 625	39.8	3.2	11.6	1.0	5.7	200.1	3 642	592	133	10 093	49.1	48.2	2.7
Casper, WY	342.8	4 778	60.3	1.0	4.9	0.4	3.5	80.2	1 118	684	454	5 074	31.5	65.8	2.7
Cedar Rapids, IA	928.6	3 673	57.3	3.8	4.5	1.3	6.2	956.0	3 782	1 290	1 082	15 333	58.7	39.7	1.5
Champaign-Urbana, IL	689.4	3 120	49.3	2.5	5.6	3.9	6.0	375.4	1 699	1 361	487	36 736	54.9	43.1	1.9

1. Based on the resident population estimated as of July 1 of the year shown.   2. © 2009 Election Data Services, Inc. All rights reserved.

Table C. Metropolitan Areas — **Land Area and Population**

						Population and population characteristics, 2010								
						Race alone or in combination, not Hispanic or Latino (percent)					Age (percent)				
CBSA code[1]	Area name	Land area,[2] 2010 (sq km)	Total persons	Rank	Per square kilometer	White	Black	American Indian, Alaska Native	Asian and Pacific Islander	Percent Hispanic or Latino[3]	Under 5 years	5 to 17 years	18 to 24 years	25 to 34 years	35 to 44 years	45 to 54 years
		1	2	3	4	5	6	7	8	9	10	11	12	13	14	15
16620	Charleston, WV..................	6 547	304 284	154	46.5	93.2	5.7	0.7	1.1	0.8	5.8	15.8	7.5	12.1	12.9	15.4
16700	Charleston-North Charleston-Summerville, SC.....	6 703	664 607	79	99.2	64.7	28.3	0.9	2.3	5.4	6.9	16.4	11.1	15.1	13.1	14.1
16740	Charlotte-Gastonia-Rock Hill, NC-SC	7 991	1 758 038	33	220.0	62.6	24.6	0.9	3.7	9.8	7.2	18.7	8.9	14.5	15.7	14.4
16820	Charlottesville, VA	4 258	201 559	209	47.3	78.5	13.4	0.6	4.7	4.8	5.7	14.7	14.0	13.6	12.1	14.0
16860	Chattanooga, TN-GA	5 410	528 143	97	97.6	80.8	14.4	0.8	1.7	3.5	6.1	16.3	9.5	12.5	13.1	14.7
16940	Cheyenne, WY	6 956	91 738	354	13.2	82.6	3.0	1.4	1.8	13.1	7.3	17.1	9.7	13.5	12.4	14.8
16980	Chicago-Joliet-Naperville, IL-IN-WI	18 640	9 461 105	3	507.6	56.1	17.6	0.4	6.3	20.7	6.7	18.4	9.4	14.4	14.0	14.6
16980	Chicago-Joliet-Naperville, IL Div	11 921	7 883 147	X	661.3	53.8	18.7	0.4	6.7	21.5	6.7	18.2	9.5	14.9	14.0	14.4
16980	Gary, IN Div	4 865	708 070	X	145.5	66.0	19.1	0.6	1.5	14.0	6.5	18.8	8.8	12.5	12.8	15.0
16980	Lake County-Kenosha County, IL-WI Div	1 854	869 888	X	469.2	69.1	7.3	0.5	6.2	18.3	6.7	20.4	9.2	11.7	14.1	16.1
17020	Chico, CA...........................	4 238	220 000	195	51.9	78.3	2.2	3.3	5.4	14.1	5.6	15.3	14.7	12.1	10.6	13.1
17140	Cincinnati-Middletown, OH-KY-IN	11 375	2 130 151	27	187.3	83.1	12.8	0.6	2.4	2.6	6.8	18.2	9.5	12.9	13.3	15.3
17300	Clarksville, TN-KY.............	5 588	273 949	168	49.0	72.5	19.5	1.2	3.0	6.8	8.8	18.8	12.3	16.2	12.8	12.2
17420	Cleveland, TN	1 977	115 788	319	58.6	91.0	4.2	0.9	1.0	4.2	6.0	16.9	10.1	12.0	13.6	14.5
17460	Cleveland-Elyria-Mentor, OH	5 173	2 077 240	28	401.6	73.1	20.7	0.6	2.4	4.7	5.8	17.3	8.4	11.7	12.8	15.7
17660	Coeur d'Alene, ID	3 222	138 494	279	43.0	93.9	0.6	2.2	1.5	3.8	6.5	18.3	8.7	12.1	12.5	14.3
17780	College Station-Bryan, TX ...	5 439	228 660	192	42.0	60.9	12.0	0.6	5.0	22.5	6.4	14.6	27.4	14.6	10.1	10.2
17820	Colorado Springs, CO	6 951	645 613	82	92.9	75.7	7.0	1.6	4.5	14.7	7.2	18.8	10.7	13.8	13.1	15.1
17860	Columbia, MO	2 977	172 786	232	58.0	83.8	10.3	1.0	4.3	2.9	6.2	14.9	20.5	14.9	11.4	12.4
17900	Columbia, SC......................	9 590	767 598	70	80.0	59.6	33.8	0.8	2.2	5.1	6.5	17.0	11.9	13.8	13.2	14.3
17980	Columbus, GA-AL...............	5 015	294 865	159	58.8	51.7	41.0	0.9	2.6	5.7	7.3	18.1	11.2	14.2	12.5	13.8
18020	Columbus, IN	1 054	76 794	363	72.9	88.2	2.4	0.5	3.8	6.2	6.8	18.4	7.9	12.7	13.6	14.3
18140	Columbus, OH	10 275	1 836 536	32	178.7	77.9	16.1	0.8	3.8	3.6	6.9	17.8	10.4	14.7	14.1	14.5
18580	Corpus Christi, TX	4 621	428 185	114	92.7	37.1	3.4	0.6	1.9	57.7	7.0	18.9	9.9	13.0	12.1	14.3
18700	Corvallis, OR	1 751	85 579	358	48.9	86.5	1.4	1.6	7.2	6.4	4.4	13.4	23.0	12.2	10.0	12.5
18880	Crestview-Fort Walton Beach-Destin, FL..........	2 409	180 822	225	75.1	80.1	10.3	1.3	4.7	6.8	6.4	15.9	10.2	13.8	12.0	15.9
19060	Cumberland, MD-WV...........	1 948	103 299	339	53.0	91.3	7.4	0.5	0.9	1.2	4.9	13.9	11.9	11.6	12.6	14.3
19100	Dallas-Fort Worth-Arlington, TX...............................	23 122	6 371 773	4	275.6	51.6	15.4	0.9	6.0	27.5	7.8	20.0	9.4	14.9	15.0	14.2
19100	Dallas-Plano-Irving, TX Div..............................	14 326	4 235 751	X	295.7	48.5	16.5	0.8	6.7	28.8	7.8	20.0	9.4	15.3	15.3	14.1
19100	Fort Worth-Arlington, TX Div..............................	8 796	2 136 022	X	242.8	57.6	13.3	0.9	4.8	24.9	7.7	20.1	9.4	14.3	14.4	14.5
19140	Dalton, GA	1 644	142 227	275	86.5	69.5	3.2	0.5	1.2	26.5	7.7	20.4	9.4	13.0	14.3	13.7
19180	Danville, IL	2 327	81 625	359	35.1	82.0	13.9	0.7	0.9	4.2	6.7	17.7	8.1	11.9	11.8	14.5
19260	Danville, VA	2 621	106 561	336	40.7	64.1	33.2	0.5	0.7	2.4	5.6	15.7	8.1	10.3	12.1	15.7
19340	Davenport-Moline-Rock Island, IA-IL	5 879	379 690	134	64.6	83.7	7.9	0.7	2.0	7.6	6.5	17.1	8.7	12.6	12.2	14.8
19380	Dayton, OH........................	4 418	841 502	61	190.5	80.7	16.1	0.8	2.4	2.0	6.1	16.9	10.1	12.1	12.2	14.8
19460	Decatur, AL........................	3 289	153 829	258	46.8	79.5	12.3	3.3	0.7	6.3	6.3	17.5	8.4	12.3	13.5	15.3
19500	Decatur, IL	1 504	110 768	330	73.6	80.5	17.8	0.6	1.3	1.9	6.3	16.6	9.3	11.7	11.6	14.7
19660	Deltona-Daytona Beach-Ormond Beach, FL	2 852	494 593	103	173.4	76.7	10.7	0.8	2.0	11.2	4.9	13.9	9.0	10.3	11.4	15.0
19740	Denver-Aurora-Broomfield, CO	21 616	2 543 482	21	117.7	67.6	6.1	1.1	4.7	22.5	7.1	17.8	8.6	15.3	14.8	14.8
19780	Des Moines-West Des Moines, IA......................	7 469	569 633	88	76.3	85.1	5.6	0.6	3.6	6.7	7.6	18.4	8.7	15.1	14.0	14.1
19820	Detroit-Warren-Livonia, MI...	10 071	4 296 250	12	426.6	69.5	23.6	0.9	4.0	3.9	6.0	18.3	8.6	11.8	13.8	15.7
19820	Detroit-Livonia-Dearborn, MI Div	1 585	1 820 584	X	1 148.6	51.2	41.4	0.9	3.2	5.2	6.5	18.9	9.7	12.0	13.5	14.8
19820	Warren-Troy-Farmington Hills, MI Div	8 486	2 475 666	X	291.7	82.9	10.5	0.8	4.5	2.9	5.7	17.8	7.9	11.6	14.1	16.4
20020	Dothan, AL.........................	4 444	145 639	270	32.8	72.7	23.7	1.0	0.9	3.0	6.3	17.6	8.1	12.1	12.9	14.6
20100	Dover, DE	1 518	162 310	242	106.9	67.6	25.2	1.4	2.8	5.8	6.9	18.0	11.0	12.3	12.7	14.3
20220	Dubuque, IA	1 576	93 653	353	59.4	94.0	3.2	0.4	1.6	1.9	6.4	17.4	10.6	11.9	11.7	14.6
20260	Duluth, MN-WI	21 789	279 771	165	12.8	94.0	2.0	3.8	1.2	1.2	5.7	14.9	11.5	11.8	11.3	15.3
20500	Durham-Chapel Hill, NC	4 554	504 357	102	110.8	56.7	27.7	0.8	5.0	11.3	6.5	15.5	12.6	15.3	13.6	13.7
20740	Eau Claire, WI	4 264	161 151	245	37.8	94.2	1.6	0.9	2.9	1.6	6.2	15.9	13.5	13.0	11.8	14.2
20940	El Centro, CA......................	10 817	174 528	231	16.1	14.2	3.1	1.2	1.6	80.4	7.8	21.5	10.9	13.9	13.1	12.9
21060	Elizabethtown, KY...............	2 292	119 736	314	52.2	82.0	11.8	1.1	3.1	4.8	7.4	18.3	9.7	13.9	13.2	14.9
21140	Elkhart-Goshen, IN	1 200	197 559	215	164.6	78.9	6.7	0.7	1.3	14.1	8.1	20.3	8.9	12.8	13.1	13.5
21300	Elmira, NY..........................	1 055	88 830	357	84.2	89.6	7.8	0.8	1.5	2.5	5.9	16.4	8.9	11.8	12.3	15.7
21340	El Paso, TX........................	2 623	800 647	66	305.2	13.7	2.9	0.4	1.4	82.2	8.1	22.0	11.2	13.3	13.1	12.7
21500	Erie, PA.............................	2 070	280 566	164	135.5	88.2	8.1	0.5	1.5	3.4	6.0	16.8	11.6	11.7	12.1	14.7
21660	Eugene-Springfield, OR.......	11 793	351 715	143	29.8	87.9	1.6	2.6	3.9	7.4	5.2	14.6	12.6	13.1	11.6	13.7
21780	Evansville, IN-KY................	5 915	358 676	142	60.6	90.5	7.2	0.6	1.3	1.9	6.5	16.9	9.7	12.3	12.3	15.3
21820	Fairbanks, AK	19 006	97 581	346	5.1	79.5	5.5	10.5	4.7	5.8	8.1	17.5	13.4	16.6	12.8	13.9
22020	Fargo, ND-MN	7 279	208 777	204	28.7	92.0	2.6	1.9	2.7	2.4	6.9	15.3	16.6	16.0	11.9	12.7
22140	Farmington, NM..................	14 279	130 044	296	9.1	44.1	0.8	37.1	0.7	19.1	8.4	20.6	9.8	13.8	11.7	14.0
22180	Fayetteville, NC	2 702	366 383	139	135.6	49.1	37.4	3.7	3.6	9.8	8.5	18.7	12.2	16.1	12.8	13.0
22220	Fayetteville-Springdale-Rogers, AR-MO..................	8 192	463 204	109	56.5	78.2	2.3	2.6	4.0	14.9	7.7	19.0	11.2	14.9	13.3	12.7

1. CBSA = Core Based Statistical Area. DIV = Metropolitan Division. See Appendix A for explanation. See Appendix B for list of metropolitan areas identified by type. 2. Dry land or land partially or temporarily covered by water. 3. May be of any race.

Table C. Metropolitan Areas — **Population and Households**

Area name	Population, 2010 (cont.) Age (percent) (cont.)				Population change and components of change, 1990–2010							Households, 2010				
					Total persons		Percent change		Components of change, 2000–2009						Percent	
	55 to 64 years	65 to 74 years	75 years and over	Percent female	1990	2000	1990–2000	2000–2010	Births	Deaths	Net migration	Number	Percent change, 2000–2010	Persons per house-hold	Female family house-holder[1]	One person
	16	17	18	19	20	21	22	23	24	25	26	27	28	29	30	31
Charleston, WV	14.6	8.7	7.3	51.5	307 689	309 635	0.6	-1.7	34 408	33 357	-4 636	128 621	-0.5	2.34	12.1	29.6
Charleston-North Charleston-Summerville, SC	11.8	6.8	4.7	51.1	506 877	549 033	8.3	21.1	79 843	42 369	72 295	259 987	25.0	2.49	15.1	26.4
Charlotte-Gastonia-Rock Hill, NC-SC	10.5	5.8	4.3	51.4	1 024 096	1 330 448	29.9	32.1	222 058	99 316	298 363	671 229	31.5	2.58	14.1	25.9
Charlottesville, VA	12.2	7.5	6.2	52.1	144 151	174 021	20.7	15.8	21 287	12 876	12 440	78 560	16.3	2.43	10.3	27.7
Chattanooga, TN-GA	13.1	8.1	6.6	51.6	433 039	476 531	10.0	10.8	58 319	45 580	23 224	210 867	11.2	2.44	13.4	27.6
Cheyenne, WY	12.7	7.0	5.5	50.0	73 142	81 607	11.6	12.4	11 666	6 399	2 445	37 576	17.7	2.40	10.7	29.1
Chicago-Joliet-Naperville, IL-IN-WI	11.1	6.1	5.3	51.1	8 181 939	9 098 316	11.2	4.0	1 300 208	638 482	-183 711	3 475 726	6.0	2.68	13.7	27.2
Chicago-Joliet-Naperville, IL Div	11.0	6.1	5.3	51.2	6 894 440	7 628 412	10.6	3.3	1 098 745	532 467	-205 040	2 903 474	5.4	2.67	13.8	27.9
Gary, IN Div	12.4	7.1	6.1	51.4	642 900	675 971	5.1	4.7	86 739	58 387	4 247	267 890	6.2	2.60	15.3	26.1
Lake County-Kenosha County, IL-WI Div	11.2	5.8	4.8	50.2	644 599	793 933	23.2	9.6	114 724	47 628	17 082	304 362	11.8	2.77	10.9	22.4
Chico, CA	13.1	7.8	7.6	50.5	182 120	203 171	11.6	8.3	22 583	20 493	16 458	87 618	10.1	2.45	11.6	27.9
Cincinnati-Middletown, OH-KY-IN	11.9	6.6	5.7	51.1	1 844 888	2 009 632	8.9	6.0	273 994	164 600	5 477	830 608	6.6	2.51	13.0	27.7
Clarksville, TN-KY	9.2	5.6	4.0	50.5	189 279	232 000	22.6	18.1	40 724	16 803	5 648	101 086	21.3	2.62	14.8	23.6
Cleveland, TN	12.4	8.6	5.9	51.2	87 355	104 015	19.1	11.3	12 905	9 519	6 609	44 600	9.5	2.53	12.1	24.0
Cleveland-Elyria-Mentor, OH	13.1	7.6	7.6	51.9	2 102 207	2 148 143	2.2	-3.3	244 091	195 237	-108 021	854 893	0.2	2.38	14.7	31.8
Coeur d'Alene, ID	13.2	8.3	6.2	50.7	69 795	108 685	55.7	27.4	15 031	8 820	24 974	54 200	31.2	2.53	10.0	24.3
College Station-Bryan, TX	8.0	4.7	3.9	49.5	150 998	184 885	22.4	23.7	26 724	10 602	12 370	85 102	25.6	2.52	11.1	26.6
Colorado Springs, CO	11.2	5.8	4.3	50.1	409 482	537 484	31.3	20.1	82 028	31 659	35 444	245 764	22.6	2.55	11.1	25.9
Columbia, MO	10.1	5.2	4.5	51.4	122 010	145 666	19.4	18.6	19 047	9 136	11 572	68 058	19.5	2.40	10.6	28.7
Columbia, SC	11.8	6.6	4.9	51.2	548 935	647 158	17.9	18.6	86 683	52 010	66 193	294 881	20.2	2.48	15.8	27.5
Columbus, GA-AL	11.2	6.5	5.3	51.3	266 452	281 768	5.7	4.6	40 385	24 933	-3 394	113 239	8.9	2.50	19.9	28.2
Columbus, IN	12.2	7.8	6.2	50.6	63 657	71 435	12.2	7.6	9 688	6 069	1 413	29 860	6.9	2.53	10.7	25.3
Columbus, OH	11.0	5.9	4.7	50.9	1 405 178	1 612 694	14.8	13.9	239 052	118 901	75 100	723 572	13.7	2.47	12.9	28.4
Corpus Christi, TX	12.0	7.0	5.8	50.8	367 786	403 280	9.7	6.2	59 811	30 521	-14 338	157 019	10.9	2.68	15.9	24.7
Corvallis, OR	12.4	6.3	5.7	49.9	70 811	78 153	10.4	9.5	7 258	4 578	2 227	34 317	13.8	2.35	7.3	28.2
Crestview-Fort Walton Beach-Destin, FL	11.8	7.8	6.2	49.8	143 777	170 498	18.6	6.1	24 131	13 120	-2 606	72 379	9.2	2.43	11.8	26.1
Cumberland, MD-WV	13.2	9.4	8.3	48.9	101 643	102 008	0.4	1.3	9 265	11 194	295	40 727	1.5	2.38	10.7	30.3
Dallas-Fort Worth-Arlington, TX	9.8	5.1	3.7	50.7	3 989 294	5 161 544	29.4	23.4	921 499	310 358	652 264	2 298 498	22.2	2.74	13.4	24.8
Dallas-Plano-Irving, TX Div	9.6	5.0	3.5	50.7	2 622 562	3 451 226	31.6	22.7	625 925	196 909	413 154	1 526 087	21.6	2.74	13.5	25.2
Fort Worth-Arlington, TX Div	10.3	5.4	4.0	50.8	1 366 732	1 710 318	25.1	24.9	295 574	113 449	239 110	772 411	23.4	2.73	13.3	24.0
Dalton, GA	10.5	6.6	4.4	50.2	98 609	120 031	21.7	18.5	22 582	9 174	1 463	49 260	15.4	2.86	13.3	21.0
Danville, IL	13.0	8.5	7.8	50.4	88 257	83 919	-4.9	-2.7	10 275	8 782	-4 898	32 655	-2.2	2.41	14.7	29.8
Danville, VA	14.5	9.6	8.3	52.3	108 728	110 156	1.3	-3.3	11 652	12 487	-2 886	45 014	-0.6	2.32	16.7	30.7
Davenport-Moline-Rock Island, IA-IL	13.1	7.8	7.2	50.9	368 145	376 019	2.1	1.0	46 120	31 842	-9 522	155 175	3.6	2.39	11.7	29.4
Dayton, OH	12.8	7.8	7.1	51.6	843 837	848 153	0.5	-0.8	100 007	73 944	-38 805	343 971	1.5	2.38	13.6	29.9
Decatur, AL	12.6	8.3	6.0	50.8	131 556	145 867	10.9	5.5	17 837	13 282	1 864	60 684	6.2	2.50	12.8	25.5
Decatur, IL	13.5	8.2	8.2	52.2	117 206	114 706	-2.1	-3.4	13 075	10 972	-8 040	45 855	-1.5	2.33	14.1	30.9
Deltona-Daytona Beach-Ormond Beach, FL	14.3	10.9	10.2	51.1	370 737	443 343	19.6	11.6	45 857	55 622	64 614	208 236	12.7	2.31	12.1	29.5
Denver-Aurora-Broomfield, CO	11.4	5.7	4.4	50.3	1 650 489	2 157 756	30.7	17.9	345 305	130 716	164 083	1 004 696	19.0	2.50	10.6	29.1
Des Moines-West Des Moines, IA	11.0	5.9	5.2	51.0	416 346	481 394	15.6	18.3	74 957	35 063	40 545	223 268	17.9	2.50	10.4	27.1
Detroit-Warren-Livonia, MI	12.6	6.9	6.3	51.5	4 248 699	4 452 557	4.8	-3.5	539 008	359 037	-269 835	1 682 111	-0.9	2.53	15.3	28.8
Detroit-Livonia-Dearborn, MI Div	12.0	6.5	6.2	52.0	2 111 687	2 061 162	-2.4	-11.7	260 776	177 768	-267 576	702 749	-8.5	2.56	20.7	30.7
Warren-Troy-Farmington Hills, MI Div	13.0	7.2	6.4	51.2	2 137 012	2 391 395	11.9	3.5	278 232	181 269	-2 259	979 362	5.5	2.50	11.4	27.4
Dothan, AL	13.0	8.7	6.7	51.8	120 352	130 861	8.7	11.3	16 847	13 269	8 922	58 883	11.4	2.44	15.4	26.9
Dover, DE	11.3	7.8	5.7	51.9	110 993	126 697	14.1	28.1	19 478	10 966	23 051	60 278	27.6	2.62	14.9	23.6
Dubuque, IA	12.2	7.6	7.7	50.7	86 403	89 143	3.2	5.1	11 108	7 771	625	36 815	9.3	2.43	9.2	28.4
Duluth, MN-WI	14.0	7.8	7.7	49.7	269 249	275 486	2.3	1.6	27 810	26 744	1 518	116 876	3.9	2.28	9.7	31.8
Durham-Chapel Hill, NC	11.6	6.2	5.0	52.1	344 665	426 493	23.7	18.3	61 039	30 703	49 417	202 476	20.0	2.39	12.9	29.8
Eau Claire, WI	12.2	6.8	6.5	49.9	137 543	148 337	7.8	8.6	17 518	11 330	6 394	63 903	11.8	2.41	8.9	27.4
El Centro, CA	9.5	5.6	4.8	48.6	109 303	142 361	30.2	22.6	27 286	8 568	6 736	49 126	24.7	3.34	19.6	17.0
Elizabethtown, KY	11.0	6.5	5.0	50.1	100 919	107 547	6.6	11.3	15 682	7 974	-1 098	45 468	14.3	2.55	12.8	24.7
Elkhart-Goshen, IN	11.1	6.4	5.7	50.7	156 198	182 791	17.0	8.1	30 789	13 222	1 188	70 244	6.2	2.76	12.6	22.7
Elmira, NY	13.2	7.7	8.0	50.3	95 195	91 070	-4.3	-4.9	9 812	8 603	-3 424	35 462	1.2	2.37	13.0	30.3
El Paso, TX	9.3	5.5	4.7	51.6	591 610	679 622	14.9	17.8	133 078	39 858	-17 748	256 557	22.2	3.06	20.3	19.8
Erie, PA	12.6	7.3	7.3	50.8	275 575	280 843	1.9	-0.1	31 131	24 747	-9 146	110 413	3.7	2.42	13.2	29.3
Eugene-Springfield, OR	14.2	8.1	6.9	50.8	282 912	322 959	14.2	8.9	33 979	27 501	23 431	145 966	11.9	2.35	10.6	28.9
Evansville, IN-KY	12.8	7.5	6.8	51.3	324 858	342 815	5.5	4.6	41 946	32 177	1 394	144 362	5.6	2.41	11.8	28.5
Fairbanks, AK	11.1	4.3	2.3	47.2	77 720	82 840	6.6	17.8	14 991	3 184	-2 173	36 441	22.4	2.56	8.8	26.7
Fargo, ND-MN	10.2	5.1	5.3	49.9	153 296	174 367	13.7	19.7	23 724	10 977	14 165	86 178	23.1	2.32	8.6	31.4
Farmington, NM	11.0	6.1	4.7	50.4	91 605	113 801	24.2	14.3	18 809	7 409	-491	44 404	17.7	2.89	15.6	21.9
Fayetteville, NC	9.6	5.4	3.8	51.6	297 569	336 609	13.1	8.8	57 706	21 428	-11 016	138 963	17.0	2.56	19.0	25.8
Fayetteville-Springdale-Rogers, AR-MO	9.9	6.3	5.0	50.3	239 495	347 045	44.9	33.5	60 698	26 732	74 357	173 054	31.2	2.62	10.2	24.8

1. No spouse present.

Area name	Daytime population, 2010 Persons in group quarters, 2010	Daytime population, 2010 Number	Daytime population, 2010 Employment/residence ratio	Births, average 2006–2008 Total	Births, average 2006–2008 Rate¹	Deaths, average 2006–2008 Number	Deaths, average 2006–2008 Rate¹	Persons under 65 with no health insurance 2009 Number	Persons under 65 with no health insurance 2009 Percent	Medicare, 2011 Enrolled in original Medicare	Medicare, 2011 Enrolled in Medicare Advantage	Medicare, 2011 Enrolled in a Medicare prescription drug plan	Serious crimes known to police,² 2010 Total Number	Serious crimes known to police,² 2010 Total Rate³
	32	33	34	35	36	37	38	39	40	41	42	43	44	45
Charleston, WV	3 658	314 374	1.08	D	D	3 699	12.1	38 882	15.5	64 832	17 116	32 847	8 441	3 012
Charleston-North Charleston-Summerville, SC	16 088	671 248	1.01	9 559	15.3	4 633	7.4	105 678	18.8	97 812	12 901	31 256	27 343	4 137
Charlotte-Gastonia-Rock Hill, NC-SC	29 251	1 818 034	1.07	25 815	15.7	11 179	6.8	260 279	17.1	224 685	35 926	101 315	66 900	3 898
Charlottesville, VA	10 813	208 691	1.10	D	D	1 420	7.4	22 580	13.8	31 566	2 498	15 929	4 994	2 478
Chattanooga, TN-GA	12 993	537 519	1.03	6 268	12.3	5 011	9.8	73 397	16.8	95 990	22 366	44 922	22 769	4 311
Cheyenne, WY	1 644	D	D	1 343	15.5	721	8.3	12 516	16.6	14 346	1 096	6 318	2 972	3 240
Chicago-Joliet-Naperville, IL-IN-WI	162 698	9 513 792	1.01	137 673	14.4	67 610	7.1	1 321 494	15.9	1 268 449	99 529	612 786	304 046	3 305
Chicago-Joliet-Naperville, IL Div	126 538	7 977 701	1.02	116 618	14.7	56 070	7.0	1 139 160	16.4	1 045 879	86 027	510 469	260 856	3 379
Gary, IN Div	10 850	669 015	0.87	9 100	13.0	6 298	9.0	91 528	15.5	113 061	6 008	50 734	26 186	3 871
Lake County-Kenosha County, IL-WI Div	25 310	D	D	11 955	13.7	5 242	6.0	90 806	11.8	109 509	7 494	51 583	17 004	2 111
Chico, CA	4 942	219 110	0.99	2 560	11.7	2 299	10.5	32 858	17.9	42 738	2 438	22 282	6 702	3 046
Cincinnati-Middletown, OH-KY-IN	46 438	2 135 551	1.00	28 953	13.6	17 781	8.3	247 555	13.4	323 554	107 383	132 289	79 008	3 814
Clarksville, TN-KY	8 975	D	D	D	D	1 884	7.4	37 294	15.9	34 074	4 647	15 097	8 409	3 088
Cleveland, TN	2 988	D	D	D	D	1 056	9.5	16 859	17.8	22 686	5 761	9 801	3 825	3 303
Cleveland-Elyria-Mentor, OH	43 431	2 123 270	1.05	25 600	12.2	20 611	9.8	238 316	13.8	367 500	122 340	154 597	54 483	2 906
Coeur d'Alene, ID	1 488	D	D	1 756	13.1	1 001	7.4	22 178	19.0	25 892	7 453	9 101	3 953	2 854
College Station-Bryan, TX	13 868	229 030	0.99	D	D	1 150	5.7	41 575	22.3	23 553	2 457	8 702	8 597	3 760
Colorado Springs, CO	19 273	644 432	0.99	8 868	14.6	3 546	5.8	84 192	15.2	80 585	19 211	19 475	22 384	3 630
Columbia, MO	9 712	176 375	1.05	2 083	12.9	1 027	6.4	19 017	13.0	21 486	2 027	11 484	5 674	3 284
Columbia, SC	35 637	780 994	1.03	9 361	13.1	5 721	8.0	105 221	16.6	111 004	17 447	38 194	35 036	4 567
Columbus, GA-AL	11 379	302 173	1.08	4 383	15.3	2 738	9.6	45 068	18.0	44 832	9 093	16 138	17 315	6 286
Columbus, IN	1 147	D	D	1 090	14.6	666	8.9	9 762	15.4	13 183	1 777	5 886	2 890	3 782
Columbus, OH	46 903	1 881 478	1.05	26 313	15.0	12 970	7.4	221 985	14.2	242 618	90 846	108 148	83 903	4 643
Corpus Christi, TX	6 931	433 826	1.03	6 123	14.7	3 360	8.1	92 658	26.0	65 871	25 252	17 691	21 899	5 114
Corvallis, OR	5 043	89 286	1.10	D	D	528	6.5	10 964	15.3	11 999	5 342	3 949	1 900	2 220
Crestview-Fort Walton Beach-Destin, FL	4 883	D	D	2 738	15.2	1 445	8.0	28 277	18.8	30 673	2 272	8 848	5 907	3 267
Cumberland, MD-WV	8 570	D	D	D	D	1 185	11.9	12 076	15.0	21 769	1 251	11 535	3 407	3 348
Dallas-Fort Worth-Arlington, TX	77 578	6 428 835	1.01	103 733	16.9	34 818	5.7	1 468 959	25.5	690 254	153 451	259 307	260 534	4 089
Dallas-Plano-Irving, TX Div	50 199	4 361 262	1.05	70 062	17.0	21 968	5.3	1 007 826	26.0	444 265	82 384	183 573	167 144	3 946
Fort Worth-Arlington, TX Div	27 379	2 067 573	0.92	33 671	16.6	12 850	6.3	461 133	24.4	245 989	71 067	75 734	93 390	4 372
Dalton, GA	1 256	D	D	2 492	18.6	1 050	7.8	31 761	27.0	20 509	2 214	12 173	4 238	3 031
Danville, IL	2 903	D	D	1 130	13.9	940	11.6	8 539	13.1	16 505	3 927	6 274	3 551	4 422
Danville, VA	2 322	D	D	1 252	11.8	1 332	12.5	14 019	16.6	24 807	4 607	13 444	3 198	3 001
Davenport-Moline-Rock Island, IA-IL	8 556	386 892	1.03	D	D	3 438	9.1	36 668	11.6	67 719	10 151	27 714	12 613	3 378
Dayton, OH	24 358	856 163	1.04	10 259	12.3	8 015	9.6	96 277	13.9	148 466	58 486	54 743	29 242	3 623
Decatur, AL	2 362	D	D	1 987	13.3	1 528	10.2	20 481	16.1	28 878	2 216	13 441	4 307	2 800
Decatur, IL	4 059	116 866	1.14	1 426	13.1	1 188	10.9	11 144	12.6	21 843	1 564	12 466	4 250	3 837
Deltona-Daytona Beach-Ormond Beach, FL	12 809	471 520	0.88	5 308	10.7	5 968	12.0	93 013	24.3	114 994	43 769	31 004	21 115	4 269
Denver-Aurora-Broomfield, CO	33 586	2 555 732	1.00	37 222	15.1	14 494	5.9	375 694	16.7	306 502	139 651	67 940	79 907	3 169
Des Moines-West Des Moines, IA	11 976	587 320	1.06	D	D	3 908	7.2	44 471	9.2	77 994	12 299	37 819	18 156	3 187
Detroit-Warren-Livonia, MI	48 644	4 304 125	1.01	55 198	12.4	38 775	8.7	535 341	14.3	707 699	171 608	253 202	156 289	3 638
Detroit-Livonia-Dearborn, MI Div	23 849	1 869 995	1.08	26 541	13.5	18 694	9.5	277 663	16.8	295 568	71 554	106 196	99 845	5 484
Warren-Troy-Farmington Hills, MI Div	24 795	2 434 130	0.96	28 657	11.5	20 081	8.1	257 678	12.4	412 131	100 054	147 006	56 444	2 280
Dothan, AL	1 844	143 493	0.96	D	D	1 447	10.4	20 141	17.3	29 961	3 483	13 828	5 106	3 560
Dover, DE	4 322	155 738	0.90	2 257	14.9	1 284	8.5	17 180	12.9	27 402	883	11 325	6 419	3 955
Dubuque, IA	4 268	D	D	1 225	13.2	868	9.4	6 850	9.0	16 781	6 492	9 978	2 214	2 364
Duluth, MN-WI	12 789	281 743	1.01	D	D	2 843	10.4	25 715	11.3	54 520	19 845	21 236	9 887	3 534
Durham-Chapel Hill, NC	20 898	547 644	1.18	6 964	14.6	3 394	7.1	71 898	16.7	69 699	12 519	25 090	21 131	4 190
Eau Claire, WI	7 338	164 538	1.04	2 003	12.7	1 227	7.8	14 318	10.6	27 061	7 128	8 825	3 539	2 196
El Centro, CA	10 684	D	D	3 172	19.6	912	5.6	35 351	24.3	24 259	1 414	15 267	6 390	3 661
Elizabethtown, KY	3 569	D	D	D	D	891	8.0	14 658	15.2	18 048	2 287	7 579	2 136	1 784
Elkhart-Goshen, IN	3 804	214 855	1.20	3 501	17.6	1 469	7.4	36 316	20.9	28 684	6 222	13 054	5 428	2 748
Elmira, NY	4 916	D	D	1 025	11.6	951	10.8	8 268	11.4	18 079	4 391	6 317	2 080	2 342
El Paso, TX	15 792	803 824	1.00	14 233	19.3	4 364	5.9	207 206	31.5	102 200	35 310	33 006	24 099	3 010
Erie, PA	12 875	287 401	1.05	3 463	12.4	2 697	9.7	26 010	11.3	50 735	21 644	17 749	7 796	2 779
Eugene-Springfield, OR	8 530	352 292	1.00	3 756	11.0	3 075	9.0	58 509	19.8	65 013	29 535	18 652	12 969	3 687
Evansville, IN-KY	10 795	369 824	1.07	D	D	3 469	9.9	42 805	14.6	64 191	14 630	29 136	10 164	3 008
Fairbanks, AK	4 313	D	D	1 726	18.3	370	3.9	18 922	20.9	8 046	38	2 483	NA	NA
Fargo, ND-MN	8 753	212 103	1.02	2 831	14.8	1 198	6.2	18 512	10.7	26 091	5 365	13 816	5 079	2 433
Farmington, NM	1 754	D	D	2 253	18.2	862	7.0	30 070	27.1	16 202	404	8 759	3 604	2 771
Fayetteville, NC	10 827	384 283	1.10	6 504	18.6	2 373	6.8	53 722	17.0	45 881	6 620	15 469	20 177	5 507
Fayetteville-Springdale-Rogers, AR-MO	9 860	469 007	1.02	6 686	15.4	3 022	7.0	81 929	20.3	65 696	14 795	25 994	12 166	2 643

1. Per 1,000 estimated resident population.   2. Data for serious crimes have not been adjusted for underreporting; this may affect comparability between geographic areas and over time.   3. Per 100,000 population estimated by the FBI.

Table C. Metropolitan Areas — Crime, Education, Money Income, and Poverty

Area name	Serious crimes known to police,[1] 2010 (cont.) Rate[2] Violent	Serious crimes known to police,[1] 2010 (cont.) Rate[2] Property	Education — Enrollment[3] Total	Education — Enrollment[3] Percent private	Education — Attainment[4] (percent) High school graduate or less	Education — Attainment[4] (percent) Bachelor's degree or more	Local government expenditures,[5] 2008–2009 Total current expenditures (mil dol)	Local government expenditures,[5] 2008–2009 Current expenditures per student (dollars)	Per capita income[6] (dollars)	Median household income (dollars)	Percent of households with income of less than $25,000	Percent of households with income of $100,000 or more	Percent of households with income of $200,000 or more	Percent below poverty level All persons	Percent below poverty level Children under 18 years	Percent below poverty level Children under 5
	46	47	48	49	50	51	52	53	54	55	56	57	58	59	60	61
Charleston, WV	365	2 647	62 988	10.2	57.1	19.5	498.7	10 375	24 086	43 922	28.6	12.6	2.5	14.6	19.8	23.9
Charleston-North Charleston-Summerville, SC	523	3 614	179 949	18.3	38.6	31.9	863.0	9 050	25 350	48 062	26.0	18.0	3.3	16.2	22.1	26.9
Charlotte-Gastonia-Rock Hill, NC-SC	450	3 448	483 489	17.3	38.1	32.2	2 441.3	8 434	26 657	50 449	23.4	19.8	3.9	14.5	19.4	23.6
Charlottesville, VA	202	2 275	63 533	11.2	33.8	42.2	305.2	12 035	31 854	56 808	21.7	22.8	5.1	12.3	9.5	12.5
Chattanooga, TN-GA	522	3 790	129 072	20.0	47.1	23.2	623.1	8 611	23 381	42 288	29.4	15.2	2.4	16.0	25.4	24.6
Cheyenne, WY	199	3 040	21 639	6.5	37.2	22.6	191.5	13 905	26 608	48 784	25.9	18.4	2.1	13.1	18.3	28.9
Chicago-Joliet-Naperville, IL-IN-WI	445	2 860	2 630 708	20.6	39.0	34.0	18 065.9	11 244	28 630	57 104	21.5	24.8	5.2	13.6	19.3	20.7
Chicago-Joliet-Naperville, IL Div	487	2 893	2 184 992	21.3	38.6	34.7	14 911.5	11 339	28 716	57 108	21.7	24.9	5.3	13.9	19.7	21.0
Gary, IN Div	339	3 532	193 990	15.9	47.7	21.5	1 126.7	9 321	22 737	48 094	25.5	15.7	1.6	15.2	22.1	21.7
Lake County-Kenosha County, IL-WI Div	135	1 976	251 726	18.3	35.7	37.8	2 027.7	11 872	32 645	67 845	16.3	31.9	8.2	9.5	13.3	17.0
Chico, CA	346	2 700	65 593	7.5	38.0	22.5	319.5	9 963	22 263	41 657	29.0	13.0	1.9	20.3	24.2	27.0
Cincinnati-Middletown, OH-KY-IN	328	3 485	578 860	20.2	43.3	29.3	3 280.1	9 981	26 639	51 572	23.9	19.6	3.5	14.0	19.7	24.9
Clarksville, TN-KY	406	2 682	76 330	13.1	46.6	18.8	315.6	7 453	20 534	42 262	26.9	10.5	1.2	16.5	23.3	28.1
Cleveland, TN	547	2 757	29 360	23.6	55.3	16.7	130.2	7 195	19 212	37 193	34.3	9.8	2.0	20.5	27.7	21.3
Cleveland-Elyria-Mentor, OH	408	2 497	535 997	23.2	42.2	27.7	3 600.5	11 611	25 668	46 231	26.7	16.7	2.9	15.1	23.9	28.9
Coeur d'Alene, ID	295	2 560	36 037	11.0	38.4	22.9	136.1	6 463	22 652	42 316	24.9	11.1	2.1	14.4	16.5	20.4
College Station-Bryan, TX	335	3 424	96 410	8.3	42.6	32.1	274.8	8 648	19 570	35 961	39.2	13.0	2.4	30.0	28.5	34.5
Colorado Springs, CO	463	3 167	186 323	15.3	29.3	34.1	932.9	8 540	26 194	51 683	23.0	21.4	3.0	13.3	18.9	24.3
Columbia, MO	395	2 889	64 573	15.3	28.4	49.0	215.5	9 015	24 293	40 853	32.3	15.5	3.0	20.5	16.8	17.3
Columbia, SC	708	3 859	220 068	16.5	39.6	29.8	1 252.1	10 259	23 774	45 929	26.8	15.1	2.4	16.2	21.5	27.8
Columbus, GA-AL	472	5 814	87 178	9.9	47.1	21.0	464.6	9 424	22 308	36 553	34.6	13.4	2.7	19.5	27.7	34.0
Columbus, IN	141	3 641	19 438	15.6	47.7	24.0	125.3	10 293	24 635	47 192	25.7	16.7	2.5	13.3	24.2	34.6
Columbus, OH	370	4 273	509 607	17.5	39.6	32.5	3 160.6	10 586	26 527	51 039	24.4	20.0	3.5	15.7	20.7	26.5
Corpus Christi, TX	589	4 525	118 087	8.0	47.1	20.0	670.4	8 468	21 673	41 994	29.7	15.8	2.2	20.5	33.2	41.4
Corvallis, OR	112	2 108	32 287	7.0	22.3	48.0	81.5	9 031	25 302	45 913	32.2	21.4	4.0	21.2	13.9	11.4
Crestview-Fort Walton Beach-Destin, FL	367	2 900	41 485	10.1	37.8	25.6	236.6	8 123	27 527	51 529	20.5	18.7	3.3	12.4	19.7	21.7
Cumberland, MD-WV	382	2 966	24 445	12.5	62.1	14.8	178.0	12 920	18 996	34 847	34.9	10.0	0.6	17.7	27.6	32.8
Dallas-Fort Worth-Arlington, TX	382	3 706	1 829 180	13.3	39.7	31.1	9 854.4	8 271	27 016	54 449	21.0	23.3	4.7	14.6	21.2	23.0
Dallas-Plano-Irving, TX Div	369	3 577	1 218 574	12.8	38.8	33.2	6 727.3	8 370	27 707	55 572	20.7	24.5	5.2	14.7	21.5	23.1
Fort Worth-Arlington, TX Div	410	3 963	610 606	14.3	41.6	26.9	3 127.1	8 067	25 643	52 879	21.4	21.0	3.6	14.3	20.6	22.9
Dalton, GA	229	2 802	38 001	6.6	64.1	13.2	257.0	9 188	18 007	39 476	30.9	9.8	1.6	21.0	27.7	37.3
Danville, IL	592	3 831	19 188	11.0	56.2	13.5	134.5	9 713	19 294	38 167	33.1	6.9	0.5	21.4	33.6	40.7
Danville, VA	208	2 793	25 057	16.3	56.7	14.5	153.5	9 711	19 020	35 964	35.7	7.1	0.7	21.2	36.9	50.1
Davenport-Moline-Rock Island, IA-IL	462	2 915	95 669	16.0	41.4	25.1	589.7	9 621	25 597	46 310	24.9	15.7	2.7	13.3	19.6	22.5
Dayton, OH	316	3 307	238 980	19.1	43.3	24.4	1 354.1	10 664	23 586	43 832	28.2	13.5	1.7	16.3	25.0	30.4
Decatur, AL	189	2 611	39 749	10.6	55.4	14.9	234.4	9 300	21 293	42 172	28.1	12.4	1.1	14.1	17.9	22.6
Decatur, IL	502	3 335	28 061	23.1	45.7	22.1	168.6	9 936	22 688	40 919	31.0	11.0	1.9	18.3	28.4	44.5
Deltona-Daytona Beach-Ormond Beach, FL	551	3 719	112 653	20.5	44.8	20.9	518.5	8 227	22 459	41 556	28.7	12.8	2.0	16.3	26.7	33.5
Denver-Aurora-Broomfield, CO	368	2 802	670 866	16.6	33.2	38.2	3 667.8	8 750	30 891	58 732	20.1	25.6	5.2	12.5	16.7	20.9
Des Moines-West Des Moines, IA	295	2 893	150 764	20.7	37.2	32.0	948.2	9 975	27 830	54 685	19.2	21.4	3.1	9.9	13.5	18.3
Detroit-Warren-Livonia, MI	645	2 992	1 166 627	13.0	40.2	27.3	7 915.9	10 683	25 403	48 198	26.5	18.6	3.0	16.6	23.8	27.6
Detroit-Livonia-Dearborn, MI Div	1 157	4 327	511 438	11.5	46.7	20.9	3 524.2	10 727	20 948	39 408	33.9	13.6	1.9	23.7	34.8	39.0
Warren-Troy-Farmington Hills, MI Div	269	2 011	655 189	14.3	35.8	31.7	4 391.7	10 648	28 670	54 476	21.4	22.0	3.7	11.3	15.1	18.0
Dothan, AL	425	3 135	32 389	15.7	54.3	16.4	185.4	8 362	20 512	38 638	32.9	11.0	1.1	17.1	25.2	29.1
Dover, DE	553	3 402	45 229	18.4	48.4	21.1	280.9	11 343	23 170	54 617	21.5	16.2	1.5	11.2	18.9	24.9
Dubuque, IA	202	2 162	27 085	39.6	44.0	28.1	130.3	9 233	24 937	49 776	19.5	15.3	2.1	10.1	12.0	13.5
Duluth, MN-WI	212	3 322	70 675	15.4	37.8	24.9	429.8	11 110	24 179	42 083	29.7	13.1	1.7	16.2	20.5	29.3
Durham-Chapel Hill, NC	429	3 761	152 848	20.1	34.4	42.9	684.6	9 885	27 180	47 982	25.6	19.8	4.3	18.9	24.9	27.8
Eau Claire, WI	152	2 044	46 074	11.2	40.8	26.2	239.2	10 593	23 509	44 086	27.1	13.4	1.2	15.4	18.3	27.4
El Centro, CA	354	3 307	54 503	3.8	58.4	13.2	370.8	10 223	15 886	41 802	32.5	13.0	1.8	21.5	30.8	33.6
Elizabethtown, KY	191	1 593	33 010	9.1	47.4	18.9	151.7	8 083	22 808	42 363	29.8	14.6	2.0	16.7	27.9	32.9
Elkhart-Goshen, IN	118	2 629	51 336	14.5	57.1	16.6	340.5	9 490	19 497	41 748	25.3	11.0	1.8	17.5	27.7	30.8
Elmira, NY	229	2 113	21 312	16.1	44.0	21.6	186.4	14 942	24 437	47 643	27.2	15.3	2.7	14.8	21.6	28.6
El Paso, TX	421	2 589	268 599	7.6	51.4	19.6	1 505.8	8 636	16 835	36 015	35.6	12.3	1.8	24.3	33.4	33.9
Erie, PA	271	2 508	75 565	25.7	52.0	23.4	464.0	11 276	22 192	42 519	31.6	13.6	1.9	17.4	24.7	33.7
Eugene-Springfield, OR	266	3 422	93 757	10.9	34.5	27.9	470.5	10 084	22 967	40 276	31.1	13.2	2.0	19.3	23.4	26.0
Evansville, IN-KY	227	2 781	87 646	16.2	48.2	20.1	456.7	9 037	23 412	44 319	26.9	13.5	1.6	13.6	18.2	24.5
Fairbanks, AK	NA	NA	27 941	11.9	34.8	27.9	227.3	14 440	28 677	60 785	14.6	24.3	2.2	7.0	7.9	14.6
Fargo, ND-MN	210	2 223	62 122	15.0	29.3	35.6	276.4	9 720	27 048	50 088	23.9	16.8	2.5	12.7	13.2	16.6
Farmington, NM	631	2 141	33 514	5.2	51.6	15.1	219.5	9 285	19 265	45 127	28.1	15.1	2.1	27.1	41.6	49.5
Fayetteville, NC	469	5 038	114 291	17.1	39.2	23.7	525.0	8 408	21 637	43 458	25.9	13.4	1.6	18.2	25.1	27.6
Fayetteville-Springdale-Rogers, AR-MO	335	2 308	131 725	9.7	48.1	25.1	639.7	8 257	22 005	45 101	27.0	15.3	2.2	15.0	18.6	22.9

1. Data for serious crimes have not been adjusted for underreporting; this may affect comparability between geographic areas and over time. 2. Per 100,000 population estimated by the FBI. 3. All persons 3 years old and over enrolled in nursery school through college. 4. Persons 25 years old and over. 5. Elementary and secondary education expenditures. 6. Based on resident population estimated as of July 1, 2009.

Table C. Metropolitan Areas — **Personal Income**

Area name	Total (mil dol) [62]	Per capita: Percent change, 2008–2009 [63]	Per capita: Dollars [64]	Per capita: Rank [65]	Wages and salaries[2] (mil dol) [66]	Proprietors' income (mil dol) [67]	Dividends, interest, and rent (mil dol) [68]	Transfer payments Total (mil dol) [69]	Gov't payments to individuals Total (mil dol) [70]	Social Security (mil dol) [71]	Medical payments (mil dol) [72]	Income maintenance (mil dol) [73]	Unemployment insurance (mil dol) [74]
Charleston, WV	11 465	1.3	37 687	123	7 894	1 091	1 421	2 714	2 659	976	1 131	263	76
Charleston-North Charleston-Summerville, SC	23 297	-0.2	35 342	180	15 694	1 497	3 980	4 110	3 992	1 282	1 608	414	209
Charlotte-Gastonia-Rock Hill, NC-SC	66 389	-3.3	38 034	112	49 670	5 916	10 324	10 104	9 785	3 256	3 831	1 104	913
Charlottesville, VA	8 445	-1.1	42 921	39	5 576	582	2 041	1 121	1 085	445	453	87	31
Chattanooga, TN-GA	17 701	-1.9	33 760	223	11 174	1 737	2 491	3 887	3 791	1 361	1 593	399	145
Cheyenne, WY	4 083	0.7	45 950	28	2 616	252	992	604	588	187	232	41	26
Chicago-Joliet-Naperville, IL-IN-WI	425 178	-3.1	44 379	34	285 404	36 308	78 839	61 183	59 440	18 201	25 793	6 548	5 024
Chicago-Joliet-Naperville, IL Div	357 741	-3.0	44 727	X	243 502	32 956	66 624	51 556	50 099	14 747	22 194	5 649	4 252
Gary, IN Div	24 758	-2.6	35 149	X	13 518	1 234	3 319	5 078	4 949	1 786	1 967	535	337
Lake County-Kenosha County, IL-WI Div	42 680	-4.3	48 613	X	28 383	2 118	8 896	4 549	4 392	1 668	1 631	364	435
Chico, CA	7 189	0.6	32 593	256	3 448	746	1 484	1 813	1 773	564	701	219	102
Cincinnati-Middletown, OH-KY-IN	82 460	-1.9	37 967	115	56 351	4 856	13 677	14 305	13 909	4 609	5 651	1 349	836
Clarksville, TN-KY	9 484	1.0	35 318	182	7 026	455	997	1 593	1 550	456	553	202	66
Cleveland, TN	3 394	-0.9	29 939	325	1 763	426	424	867	847	317	350	87	31
Cleveland-Elyria-Mentor, OH	82 503	-2.4	39 451	80	56 011	5 945	13 992	16 586	16 205	5 183	7 045	1 676	771
Coeur d'Alene, ID	4 428	-0.5	31 770	283	2 265	333	917	912	886	358	315	64	64
College Station-Bryan, TX	6 335	2.6	29 847	326	4 135	362	1 308	987	948	310	373	121	42
Colorado Springs, CO	24 048	1.2	38 401	102	16 823	1 562	3 910	3 397	3 288	1 031	1 168	307	214
Columbia, MO	6 079	1.7	36 568	147	4 223	428	1 027	995	965	296	442	84	37
Columbia, SC	26 418	0.0	35 473	177	18 595	1 705	3 768	4 874	4 740	1 550	1 791	500	262
Columbus, GA-AL	10 709	0.6	36 577	146	7 677	479	1 797	2 064	2 013	595	723	336	78
Columbus, IN	2 859	-4.5	37 589	127	2 321	227	455	513	499	204	197	35	35
Columbus, OH	68 469	-0.4	37 999	114	51 155	4 588	9 144	11 306	10 977	3 209	4 510	1 317	634
Corpus Christi, TX	15 212	-1.4	36 558	149	9 289	1 485	2 508	3 133	3 058	838	1 506	380	103
Corvallis, OR	3 133	-0.9	37 922	117	2 037	158	793	429	414	172	108	37	33
Crestview-Fort Walton Beach-Destin, FL	7 497	-1.2	42 007	53	5 540	376	1 714	1 228	1 198	400	490	94	36
Cumberland, MD-WV	3 135	3.8	31 432	292	1 775	138	460	997	978	292	470	79	35
Dallas-Fort Worth-Arlington, TX	269 280	-2.2	41 764	54	181 285	37 583	44 839	30 023	28 847	9 551	12 111	3 313	1 647
Dallas-Plano-Irving, TX Div	187 843	-2.5	43 418	X	132 975	28 767	32 391	19 554	18 765	6 145	7 971	2 200	1 089
Fort Worth-Arlington, TX Div	81 437	-1.5	38 391	X	48 310	8 817	12 448	10 469	10 082	3 406	4 140	1 113	559
Dalton, GA	3 765	-3.0	28 027	349	3 048	228	577	831	806	279	319	96	57
Danville, IL	2 459	0.0	30 713	308	1 429	171	371	672	657	231	241	86	46
Danville, VA	3 184	0.1	30 092	321	1 640	214	524	905	886	342	338	115	36
Davenport-Moline-Rock Island, IA-IL	14 659	-0.8	38 670	97	9 692	1 011	2 542	2 785	2 716	968	910	264	164
Dayton, OH	29 436	-0.8	35 251	185	20 318	1 385	4 679	6 432	6 281	2 045	2 534	606	368
Decatur, AL	4 841	0.1	31 974	272	2 599	319	713	1 083	1 055	424	418	101	45
Decatur, IL	4 239	-1.2	39 174	87	2 928	359	710	889	869	315	327	94	65
Deltona-Daytona Beach-Ormond Beach, FL	15 995	-1.9	32 255	265	6 933	507	4 427	4 194	4 104	1 620	1 638	311	170
Denver-Aurora-Broomfield, CO	118 961	-2.1	46 611	22	81 238	15 797	19 806	12 422	11 956	4 040	4 677	1 071	907
Des Moines-West Des Moines, IA	23 649	-0.7	42 012	52	17 791	2 150	3 533	3 194	3 091	1 138	1 193	307	210
Detroit-Warren-Livonia, MI	167 009	-4.6	37 927	116	107 407	13 834	26 675	34 523	33 720	11 157	13 795	3 698	3 153
Detroit-Livonia-Dearborn, MI Div	61 411	-2.5	31 888	X	44 215	4 166	8 087	17 366	17 015	4 577	7 530	2 577	1 420
Warren-Troy-Farmington Hills, MI Div	105 597	-5.7	42 621	X	63 191	9 668	18 588	17 157	16 705	6 580	6 265	1 121	1 732
Dothan, AL	4 713	-0.4	33 028	245	2 581	302	815	1 084	1 058	400	405	132	24
Dover, DE	4 910	1.0	31 127	298	3 291	284	702	1 113	1 085	383	442	102	52
Dubuque, IA	3 317	-0.8	35 635	173	2 412	201	689	633	616	240	245	49	38
Duluth, MN-WI	9 633	-0.6	34 855	193	5 899	597	1 665	2 416	2 366	745	1 034	211	141
Durham-Chapel Hill, NC	20 554	0.8	41 008	60	19 227	1 279	3 957	2 946	2 855	984	1 214	287	163
Eau Claire, WI	5 386	0.7	33 659	227	3 532	412	905	1 078	1 049	372	445	80	71
El Centro, CA	4 786	2.5	28 681	345	2 718	618	509	1 248	1 217	248	461	231	169
Elizabethtown, KY	3 984	2.3	35 126	190	3 050	235	514	834	815	233	339	75	48
Elkhart-Goshen, IN	6 028	-7.8	30 064	323	4 745	551	982	1 218	1 182	429	404	114	155
Elmira, NY	2 904	-0.7	32 881	246	1 843	116	458	778	762	262	325	85	37
El Paso, TX	22 073	3.6	29 381	338	13 642	2 658	2 927	4 914	4 781	1 052	2 099	884	195
Erie, PA	9 142	0.3	32 615	254	5 836	502	1 392	2 392	2 340	743	933	236	257
Eugene-Springfield, OR	11 784	-0.8	33 562	230	6 659	700	2 650	2 681	2 617	893	920	250	279
Evansville, IN-KY	12 836	-1.1	36 475	151	8 628	1 024	2 072	2 601	2 537	948	1 043	217	144
Fairbanks, AK	3 837	-1.3	38 895	94	3 181	202	577	578	562	105	225	52	25
Fargo, ND-MN	7 981	-0.6	39 883	74	5 716	735	1 441	1 064	1 027	351	389	95	49
Farmington, NM	3 811	-2.4	30 702	309	2 683	255	497	779	756	214	344	90	34
Fayetteville, NC	14 430	3.3	40 045	72	12 202	452	1 468	2 465	2 408	605	931	351	91
Fayetteville-Springdale-Rogers, AR-MO	14 764	-0.4	31 776	282	10 496	688	2 909	2 355	2 270	902	819	211	131

1. Based on the resident population estimated as of July 1 of the year shown. 2. Includes other labor income.

Table C. Metropolitan Areas — **Earnings, Social Security, and Housing**

Area name	Earnings, 2009									Social Security beneficiaries, December 2010			Housing units, 2010	
			Percent by selected industries											
			Goods-related[1]		Service-related and health							Supplemental Security Income recipients, December 2009		
	Total (mil dol)	Farm	Total	Manufacturing	Information, professional, and technical services	Retail trade	Finance, insurance, and real estate	Health care and social services	Government	Number	Rate[2]		Total	Percent change, 2000–2010
	75	76	77	78	79	80	81	82	83	84	85	86	87	88
Charleston, WV	8 985	0.0	D	5.3	D	5.8	D	14.3	18.0	74 185	244	12 904	141 585	-0.1
Charleston-North Charleston-Summerville, SC	17 191	0.1	D	9.8	D	7.0	5.8	9.5	27.3	108 500	163	12 841	298 542	28.2
Charlotte-Gastonia-Rock Hill, NC-SC	55 586	0.3	D	9.1	D	6.1	13.1	NA	12.6	254 185	145	29 178	737 775	35.0
Charlottesville, VA	6 158	-0.1	D	4.4	D	5.6	6.7	NA	35.3	33 785	168	2 564	89 134	20.7
Chattanooga, TN-GA	12 911	0.1	D	12.9	D	8.1	12.0	NA	16.6	107 830	204	13 128	234 440	14.2
Cheyenne, WY	2 868	0.8	D	4.6	7.0	6.2	4.9	8.3	42.3	15 255	166	1 339	40 462	18.3
Chicago-Joliet-Naperville, IL-IN-WI	321 712	0.1	D	10.6	D	5.0	11.0	NA	13.0	1 349 410	143	205 185	3 797 247	9.7
Chicago-Joliet-Naperville, IL Div	276 458	0.1	14.8	9.0	18.0	4.7	11.7	NA	12.6	1 100 205	140	179 750	3 173 522	9.2
Gary, IN Div	14 752	1.0	D	20.8	D	7.3	3.5	NA	13.6	130 530	184	14 941	294 127	9.1
Lake County-Kenosha County, IL-WI Div	30 501	0.1	D	20.4	8.6	6.9	7.8	7.7	16.7	118 675	136	10 494	329 598	15.2
Chico, CA	4 194	4.9	11.0	4.5	6.9	8.6	8.0	18.6	21.3	46 520	211	11 421	95 835	12.1
Cincinnati-Middletown, OH-KY-IN	61 207	0.1	D	NA	D	5.5	D	NA	13.0	355 810	167	44 757	917 396	10.1
Clarksville, TN-KY	7 481	0.9	D	8.1	D	4.5	2.2	NA	60.1	40 160	147	6 411	114 145	24.0
Cleveland, TN	2 188	-0.1	D	24.5	4.0	6.8	10.4	NA	13.2	26 375	228	3 135	49 386	11.8
Cleveland-Elyria-Mentor, OH	61 957	0.2	D	14.4	11.8	5.2	8.8	13.5	15.1	391 870	189	57 740	955 756	4.9
Coeur d'Alene, ID	2 598	0.4	18.2	8.1	8.8	10.7	6.6	12.6	20.6	29 290	211	2 315	63 177	35.6
College Station-Bryan, TX	4 497	0.1	16.6	6.2	7.9	6.7	3.9	NA	37.9	25 550	112	4 181	95 016	26.5
Colorado Springs, CO	18 385	0.0	D	NA	D	5.6	6.0	8.0	34.9	87 905	136	7 602	265 495	24.8
Columbia, MO	4 651	0.6	D	4.6	6.0	7.6	D	NA	37.6	23 975	139	2 791	74 133	21.5
Columbia, SC	20 300	0.4	D	8.7	D	6.4	D	NA	28.8	126 115	164	15 011	331 470	23.1
Columbus, GA-AL	8 156	0.2	D	NA	D	NA	D	NA	41.5	51 530	175	9 628	128 214	10.8
Columbus, IN	2 548	1.0	D	42.5	4.4	4.7	4.8	8.3	12.5	15 250	199	1 153	33 098	10.9
Columbus, OH	55 743	0.4	D	9.1	D	6.3	9.6	NA	17.9	258 765	141	38 164	792 340	16.4
Corpus Christi, TX	10 774	0.1	26.3	8.5	7.0	6.4	4.4	NA	22.9	73 320	171	15 699	182 909	13.8
Corvallis, OR	2 196	1.1	19.0	16.1	11.1	4.4	2.9	14.6	30.3	13 030	152	940	36 245	13.3
Crestview-Fort Walton Beach-Destin, FL	5 916	0.0	9.0	5.0	12.3	6.1	5.9	7.0	44.1	33 805	187	2 690	92 407	17.6
Cumberland, MD-WV	1 913	0.0	20.6	15.1	4.6	7.3	2.9	D	26.1	23 305	226	2 962	46 350	2.8
Dallas-Fort Worth-Arlington, TX	218 868	0.0	D	NA	D	5.4	D	9.4	11.2	744 370	117	111 883	2 502 075	25.2
Dallas-Plano-Irving, TX Div	161 742	0.0	D	NA	D	5.0	D	9.3	10.4	477 615	113	75 962	1 660 144	24.6
Fort Worth-Arlington, TX Div	57 127	0.1	26.2	13.7	D	6.5	7.0	9.5	13.4	266 755	125	35 921	841 931	26.5
Dalton, GA	3 276	0.3	D	38.1	D	7.4	2.3	NA	11.7	23 410	165	3 178	55 878	24.0
Danville, IL	1 600	5.2	D	20.0	D	5.9	4.9	10.1	23.2	18 625	228	2 797	36 318	-0.1
Danville, VA	1 855	0.7	D	21.8	3.8	8.7	4.0	13.1	19.0	28 845	271	4 512	53 745	5.1
Davenport-Moline-Rock Island, IA-IL	10 703	1.5	D	15.3	7.6	6.6	5.1	11.2	17.6	74 465	196	7 175	167 110	5.4
Dayton, OH	21 703	0.5	D	12.1	D	5.5	5.0	NA	24.2	160 550	191	19 040	385 160	5.7
Decatur, AL	2 918	2.0	D	33.8	D	6.6	3.6	7.9	16.1	33 735	219	4 665	66 422	6.4
Decatur, IL	3 287	2.1	35.5	27.5	5.4	5.5	3.4	13.1	10.7	23 855	215	3 137	50 475	0.5
Deltona-Daytona Beach-Ormond Beach, FL	7 440	0.6	12.5	6.1	7.4	9.9	5.6	18.8	17.8	128 415	260	10 249	254 226	20.0
Denver-Aurora-Broomfield, CO	97 034	0.1	D	NA	D	4.8	9.8	NA	13.3	319 070	125	32 812	1 078 837	21.1
Des Moines-West Des Moines, IA	19 941	1.3	D	5.8	9.4	5.9	23.0	NA	14.1	85 740	151	7 929	240 203	20.5
Detroit-Warren-Livonia, MI	121 241	0.1	D	14.5	D	5.8	7.5	12.5	13.0	806 380	188	120 289	1 886 537	5.0
Detroit-Livonia-Dearborn, MI Div	48 382	0.0	17.2	13.3	13.9	4.9	4.9	13.3	16.7	344 625	189	79 513	821 693	-0.5
Warren-Troy-Farmington Hills, MI Div	72 859	0.1	D	15.3	D	6.4	9.2	12.1	10.6	461 755	187	40 776	1 064 844	9.7
Dothan, AL	2 884	1.8	D	10.4	D	9.4	4.5	NA	19.4	34 230	235	5 735	66 897	12.0
Dover, DE	3 575	1.5	D	D	4.2	7.9	3.5	11.3	41.5	31 040	191	3 541	65 338	29.4
Dubuque, IA	2 612	0.8	D	18.9	8.2	7.4	7.9	15.9	9.5	18 820	201	1 472	38 951	9.7
Duluth, MN-WI	6 496	0.1	D	6.7	5.8	6.7	7.3	19.9	21.7	59 935	214	6 989	141 539	9.0
Durham-Chapel Hill, NC	20 505	0.3	D	22.1	14.1	3.6	5.9	13.0	19.3	75 670	150	8 851	222 760	23.7
Eau Claire, WI	3 943	0.7	D	14.8	6.2	8.0	6.8	17.6	15.3	30 450	189	3 058	69 336	15.0
El Centro, CA	3 336	15.1	D	3.8	2.5	7.1	2.5	4.6	38.6	26 290	151	10 373	56 067	27.7
Elizabethtown, KY	3 285	0.2	D	9.0	D	5.7	3.4	6.7	52.7	20 750	173	3 409	49 433	13.6
Elkhart-Goshen, IN	5 295	0.5	D	42.2	3.9	5.3	3.2	9.9	9.0	32 225	163	2 965	77 767	11.4
Elmira, NY	1 958	0.0	24.9	18.7	4.4	7.9	4.1	17.2	23.3	20 820	234	3 500	38 369	1.7
El Paso, TX	16 301	0.1	13.2	7.5	5.3	6.3	7.5	10.2	35.9	109 255	136	28 797	270 307	20.4
Erie, PA	6 337	0.2	25.5	21.5	5.8	7.1	7.1	17.6	16.2	58 130	207	10 652	119 138	4.2
Eugene-Springfield, OR	7 359	0.5	16.0	10.1	9.5	8.3	5.3	16.5	20.9	71 435	203	7 766	156 112	12.3
Evansville, IN-KY	9 652	1.7	34.3	22.1	D	5.8	3.5	NA	10.2	73 350	205	8 192	159 314	7.8
Fairbanks, AK	3 383	0.2	12.9	1.5	4.1	5.5	2.9	7.8	51.7	8 790	90	1 086	41 783	25.5
Fargo, ND-MN	6 451	3.3	D	7.6	10.8	7.4	8.8	13.5	15.7	28 115	135	2 533	91 897	25.0
Farmington, NM	2 938	0.3	30.0	2.8	3.2	7.2	3.0	10.3	21.3	18 805	145	4 025	49 341	14.2
Fayetteville, NC	12 653	0.2	D	5.2	D	3.9	2.0	4.6	65.7	53 930	147	10 563	153 735	17.4
Fayetteville-Springdale-Rogers, AR-MO	11 184	0.6	D	11.8	D	5.9	4.7	NA	14.9	75 230	162	7 960	198 298	37.3

1. Includes mining, construction, and manufacturing. 2. Per 1,000 resident population enumerated in the 2010 census.

Table C. Metropolitan Areas — Housing, Labor Force, and Employment

Area name	Housing units, 2010 Occupied units Total	Owner-occupied Percent	Median value[1]	Median owner cost as a percent of income With a mortgage	Without a mortgage	Renter-occupied Median rent[2]	Median rent as a percent of income	Sub-standard units[3] (percent)	Civilian labor force, 2010 Total	Percent change, 2009–2010	Unemployment Total	Rate[4]	Civilian employment,[5] 2010 Total	Percent Management, business, science, and arts occupations	Construction, production, and maintenance occupations
	89	90	91	92	93	94	95	96	97	98	99	100	101	102	103
Charleston, WV....................	125 628	74.7	99 600	19.3	10.0	604	25.7	1.6	134 937	-2.6	11 040	8.2	130 860	33.6	21.8
Charleston-North Charleston-Summerville, SC......	252 574	65.4	192 900	26.3	13.9	890	34.2	2.3	322 108	0.3	30 166	9.4	303 968	35.6	20.0
Charlotte-Gastonia-Rock Hill, NC-SC........	663 300	67.2	172 500	24.0	12.2	787	31.1	2.9	861 984	-0.6	100 232	11.6	814 367	37.3	20.0
Charlottesville, VA................	76 764	63.7	281 900	22.5	12.6	1 043	28.9	1.2	107 902	-0.1	6 333	5.9	93 820	47.5	14.6
Chattanooga, TN-GA	208 995	68.8	142 000	22.7	11.5	688	29.6	2.8	258 497	0.3	22 506	8.7	238 061	33.4	23.1
Cheyenne, WY	38 389	66.7	178 000	22.8	10.0	642	28.3	NA	43 188	-0.4	3 247	7.5	43 950	35.2	21.6
Chicago-Joliet-Naperville, IL-IN-WI	3 415 317	66.2	236 000	27.8	14.9	913	32.3	3.8	4 870 140	0.3	496 038	10.2	4 378 486	37.4	20.0
Chicago-Joliet-Naperville, IL Div..................	2 852 322	64.8	245 300	28.4	15.3	928	32.4	4.0	4 095 625	0.4	414 594	10.1	3 667 547	37.7	19.5
Gary, IN Div..................	261 367	71.6	150 200	22.5	11.2	758	32.6	3.0	323 795	-2.4	33 887	10.5	302 150	31.1	28.0
Lake County-Kenosha County, IL-WI Div	301 628	74.4	242 200	27.0	15.4	890	30.8	2.9	450 720	0.7	47 557	10.6	408 789	39.2	19.1
Chico, CA........................	84 629	59.5	233 800	28.7	14.2	862	34.1	3.9	104 580	0.8	14 587	13.9	88 041	34.0	19.4
Cincinnati-Middletown, OH-KY-IN	811 494	68.9	155 500	23.2	13.5	710	30.9	2.1	1 118 961	-0.6	109 045	9.7	989 443	37.1	19.4
Clarksville, TN-KY................	99 039	65.4	130 900	23.2	11.7	740	29.1	2.8	114 088	2.4	11 458	10.0	100 722	29.2	28.0
Cleveland, TN	43 805	71.5	131 600	24.7	11.0	701	36.0	NA	54 978	0.4	5 121	9.3	47 668	29.0	28.8
Cleveland-Elyria-Mentor, OH	840 929	67.6	146 700	24.4	14.4	714	31.4	1.5	1 077 339	-0.1	98 883	9.2	954 731	36.5	19.7
Coeur d'Alene, ID	55 456	69.9	195 600	27.7	12.0	753	34.4	NA	71 444	1.7	7 862	11.0	59 952	33.1	20.9
College Station-Bryan, TX	81 720	51.8	129 500	22.6	12.1	795	46.0	5.4	114 847	2.6	7 236	6.3	101 956	38.3	19.3
Colorado Springs, CO..........	244 194	64.2	214 300	25.1	10.0	807	30.8	2.7	310 216	-0.9	29 913	9.6	286 840	39.4	18.5
Columbia, MO	67 997	58.5	155 800	21.8	10.4	726	34.2	2.6	94 216	1.1	6 091	6.5	86 041	45.2	13.1
Columbia, SC.....................	293 357	67.4	137 100	22.6	11.6	763	32.7	1.3	371 065	-0.5	34 482	9.3	347 265	36.5	20.7
Columbus, GA-AL................	108 930	58.3	131 300	23.9	12.7	756	33.4	2.2	129 018	-0.4	12 252	9.5	114 013	35.2	19.6
Columbus, IN	31 046	67.2	138 600	21.3	13.5	751	25.3	NA	37 652	-1.7	3 491	9.3	36 534	39.9	23.5
Columbus, OH	707 956	63.0	163 500	23.6	12.5	758	30.6	2.4	966 650	-0.1	83 307	8.6	888 589	38.6	18.1
Corpus Christi, TX	154 206	60.8	109 400	25.5	13.4	794	32.2	6.4	212 419	2.3	17 065	8.0	184 319	31.6	22.8
Corvallis, OR......................	32 888	59.1	255 900	25.3	10.0	730	40.4	NA	44 203	1.0	3 213	7.3	40 325	48.5	13.4
Crestview-Fort Walton Beach-Destin, FL..........	70 407	66.8	180 800	26.3	10.0	991	32.4	3.5	96 350	-0.5	7 789	8.1	81 612	33.0	19.7
Cumberland, MD-WV...........	40 076	73.4	123 800	22.4	13.0	591	33.4	NA	48 898	-0.9	4 432	9.1	39 195	29.5	29.8
Dallas-Fort Worth-Arlington, TX...................	2 274 493	61.7	150 400	23.7	13.1	855	29.7	5.1	3 211 928	1.7	265 977	8.3	3 055 170	37.0	21.4
Dallas-Plano-Irving, TX Div..................	1 504 306	60.3	158 700	23.8	13.0	859	29.6	5.5	2 144 294	1.9	178 001	8.3	2 048 462	38.2	20.3
Fort Worth-Arlington, TX Div..................	770 187	64.2	135 700	23.5	13.1	848	30.0	4.4	1 067 634	1.3	87 976	8.2	1 006 708	34.7	23.7
Dalton, GA	48 349	68.1	117 000	26.0	10.0	689	30.3	8.7	62 338	-1.8	7 484	12.0	58 439	22.6	43.7
Danville, IL	31 332	69.8	74 000	21.6	12.5	608	33.3	NA	37 494	1.5	4 547	12.1	32 082	28.9	28.6
Danville, VA........................	45 278	70.4	95 500	24.9	12.5	557	35.5	NA	51 728	-1.9	5 966	11.5	43 656	26.2	29.4
Davenport-Moline-Rock Island, IA-IL..................	154 889	72.5	125 400	21.8	12.2	636	27.6	1.6	204 442	1.2	17 127	8.4	180 123	33.8	24.5
Dayton, OH	342 919	65.8	125 600	23.6	13.7	705	31.3	1.2	417 302	-1.2	45 029	10.8	368 137	34.6	21.8
Decatur, AL........................	57 902	74.8	120 500	21.1	10.5	586	27.9	NA	71 231	-1.6	7 076	9.9	64 976	26.6	32.1
Decatur, IL.........................	45 624	67.7	91 800	21.3	12.5	618	31.5	1.4	55 274	1.3	6 502	11.8	46 390	31.2	21.5
Deltona-Daytona Beach-Ormond Beach, FL	190 757	74.7	151 600	28.0	14.6	876	33.8	1.8	253 470	0.1	30 403	12.0	193 104	28.8	20.1
Denver-Aurora-Broomfield, CO................................	1 001 253	64.8	245 900	24.8	10.9	879	30.9	3.3	1 380 902	-1.0	124 036	9.0	1 277 834	40.7	17.5
Des Moines-West Des Moines, IA.................	223 767	72.2	151 900	22.2	12.1	718	28.4	1.9	315 869	0.3	19 110	6.0	300 812	38.3	18.7
Detroit-Warren-Livonia, MI....	1 655 395	71.2	124 400	25.0	14.9	793	33.7	2.3	2 069 920	-1.8	280 044	13.5	1 773 943	36.7	19.4
Detroit-Livonia-Dearborn, MI Div..................	675 079	65.4	89 500	25.8	15.6	758	37.6	3.6	850 005	-2.2	123 597	14.5	661 178	31.7	22.0
Warren-Troy-Farmington Hills, MI Div..................	980 316	75.2	151 300	24.7	14.5	827	30.8	1.5	1 219 915	-1.6	156 447	12.8	1 112 765	39.7	17.9
Dothan, AL.........................	58 581	65.7	111 400	21.7	11.4	610	27.2	2.0	62 780	-2.7	5 406	8.6	63 295	27.6	26.5
Dover, DE	54 896	75.4	206 200	25.3	13.0	959	30.9	2.0	72 499	-1.2	6 107	8.4	68 808	31.0	23.2
Dubuque, IA........................	37 177	74.3	150 100	20.1	12.3	629	28.9	NA	53 627	2.7	3 231	6.0	48 745	34.6	24.3
Duluth, MN-WI	121 010	71.2	142 400	23.2	11.6	630	33.0	1.9	147 529	0.3	11 837	8.0	129 567	34.0	20.3
Durham-Chapel Hill, NC	198 793	60.7	199 000	23.2	10.9	787	32.0	2.9	263 298	-1.1	20 350	7.7	235 712	48.0	15.4
Eau Claire, WI.....................	63 436	67.6	147 500	23.1	12.7	614	31.2	1.7	90 337	0.4	6 471	7.2	82 801	30.9	24.6
El Centro, CA......................	48 206	58.0	154 100	28.5	13.6	733	31.5	10.4	77 099	1.5	22 860	29.7	56 573	22.6	28.0
Elizabethtown, KY...............	44 911	66.5	136 800	20.5	10.0	646	29.3	NA	56 343	1.8	5 361	9.5	44 972	34.3	22.4
Elkhart-Goshen, IN	67 959	71.7	126 200	23.0	12.0	669	31.5	3.7	90 354	-0.2	12 325	13.6	86 514	24.8	36.0
Elmira, NY..........................	35 534	67.1	92 100	18.8	11.8	624	28.9	2.0	40 742	-0.5	3 478	8.5	40 394	30.5	22.6
El Paso, TX.........................	248 770	63.0	108 200	25.1	11.9	666	30.6	7.8	318 108	3.5	30 262	9.5	304 833	28.4	22.7
Erie, PA.............................	109 388	66.7	117 500	21.7	11.7	626	31.6	1.1	138 388	-0.8	12 943	9.4	125 071	31.0	25.6
Eugene-Springfield, OR........	144 923	60.2	229 400	27.7	12.8	773	35.0	2.0	182 902	-0.7	20 378	11.1	155 311	34.9	20.3
Evansville, IN-KY	142 984	71.5	116 300	21.3	11.7	646	30.8	2.6	182 308	0.7	15 720	8.6	168 210	28.1	28.5
Fairbanks, AK	37 413	57.8	212 200	24.9	11.5	1 124	29.8	11.5	46 563	1.5	3 295	7.1	45 393	36.2	26.8
Fargo, ND-MN.....................	86 373	55.9	154 600	20.9	11.1	616	26.6	1.5	119 797	-0.7	4 950	4.1	121 241	36.8	20.7
Farmington, NM	41 703	70.3	153 200	21.2	10.0	742	26.6	13.3	56 513	0.0	5 406	9.6	50 157	28.4	27.8
Fayetteville, NC..................	133 054	58.8	127 500	23.9	11.6	823	28.4	2.4	157 098	-0.1	14 661	9.3	135 617	32.0	22.5
Fayetteville-Springdale-Rogers, AR-MO..................	170 006	63.8	146 300	22.0	10.0	675	28.6	4.5	226 358	0.6	14 650	6.5	213 890	33.9	24.8

1. Specified owner-occupied units.   2. Specified renter-occupied units. A value of 10.0 represents 10 percent or less.   3. Overcrowded or lacking complete plumbing facilities.   4. Percent of civilian labor force.   5. Persons 16 years old and over.

Table C. Metropolitan Areas — Nonfarm Employment and Agriculture

	Private nonfarm establishments, employment and payroll, 2009									Agriculture, 2007			
		Employment						Annual payroll		Farms			
											Percent with:		
Area name	Number of establishments	Total	Health care and social assistance	Manufacturing	Retail trade	Finance and insurance	Professional, scientific, and technical services	Total (mil dol)	Average per employee (dollars)	Number	Fewer than 50 acres	500 acres or more	Farm operators whose principal occupation is farming (percent)
	104	105	106	107	108	109	110	111	112	113	114	115	116
Charleston, WV	7 361	117 974	20 241	5 574	16 500	6 200	7 639	4 476	37 938	1 263	33.2	1.3	38.7
Charleston-North Charleston-Summerville, SC	16 595	233 188	33 645	19 187	36 239	8 283	15 486	8 275	35 487	1 023	55.5	6.7	43.7
Charlotte-Gastonia-Rock Hill, NC-SC	44 698	765 726	96 922	65 557	88 797	75 163	43 310	33 181	43 333	3 995	50.8	4.2	40.5
Charlottesville, VA	5 635	75 332	15 390	3 775	10 679	4 181	5 849	2 996	39 768	1 906	36.7	6.3	39.6
Chattanooga, TN-GA	11 280	203 529	30 410	32 049	25 729	14 725	8 305	6 951	34 150	2 358	49.7	3.1	38.8
Cheyenne, WY	2 641	31 678	6 323	1 435	5 464	1 811	1 525	1 062	33 532	844	20.9	39.7	39.6
Chicago-Joliet-Naperville, IL-IN-WI	237 245	3 918 027	533 839	408 017	438 683	251 130	312 688	192 308	49 083	7 714	51.5	17.5	49.8
Chicago-Joliet-Naperville, IL Div	NA	NA	NA	NA	NA	NA	NA	NA	NA	4 732	52.5	17.5	51.8
Gary, IN Div	NA	NA	NA	NA	NA	NA	NA	NA	NA	2 126	44.5	22.2	46.3
Lake County-Kenosha County, IL-WI Div	NA	NA	NA	NA	NA	NA	NA	NA	NA	856	63.8	6.0	47.2
Chico, CA	4 794	55 308	13 069	3 744	9 776	2 407	2 528	1 727	31 228	2 048	64.5	7.9	51.6
Cincinnati-Middletown, OH-KY-IN	46 858	904 386	136 330	104 332	121 085	57 338	56 305	37 738	41 728	10 376	43.9	4.3	39.7
Clarksville, TN-KY	4 284	63 607	10 890	10 737	11 318	2 064	2 220	1 824	28 677	2 997	31.5	9.1	43.9
Cleveland, TN	2 152	36 825	4 917	7 141	4 961	1 492	924	1 169	31 754	1 264	54.0	2.9	43.4
Cleveland-Elyria-Mentor, OH	52 799	896 741	167 108	124 105	100 037	57 049	50 125	37 355	41 656	3 098	63.1	3.6	45.0
Coeur d'Alene, ID	4 510	44 289	7 881	3 926	7 406	2 088	3 114	1 380	31 155	826	57.9	8.0	40.0
College Station-Bryan, TX	4 312	59 756	8 565	5 060	10 464	1 837	2 955	1 735	29 027	4 494	34.9	10.3	40.0
Colorado Springs, CO	16 453	221 446	29 904	11 285	29 690	10 694	21 091	8 602	38 846	1 655	46.8	17.6	34.3
Columbia, MO	4 500	66 465	15 353	4 401	11 447	5 548	3 014	2 140	32 204	2 189	30.4	11.4	32.9
Columbia, SC	17 167	279 743	42 241	32 965	37 481	21 253	16 108	9 664	34 646	2 945	43.6	6.6	41.6
Columbus, GA-AL	5 818	95 183	14 780	10 756	13 929	12 707	4 231	3 209	33 718	924	39.7	10.6	37.4
Columbus, IN	1 893	40 133	5 349	11 132	4 771	1 208	2 946	1 561	38 898	668	46.0	13.6	39.7
Columbus, OH	39 495	761 889	114 695	60 811	95 084	71 276	46 829	31 711	41 621	7 050	49.0	11.0	43.7
Corpus Christi, TX	9 324	141 783	26 688	9 410	20 260	4 488	5 977	4 798	33 842	1 458	45.3	22.2	41.9
Corvallis, OR	2 077	25 094	4 806	3 717	3 398	613	2 213	993	39 583	906	73.3	4.5	41.1
Crestview-Fort Walton Beach-Destin, FL	5 005	57 415	8 337	3 419	11 194	2 857	6 196	1 949	33 950	567	47.6	3.5	36.3
Cumberland, MD-WV	2 166	30 825	7 346	4 629	4 920	991	716	909	29 985	795	32.1	3.5	38.6
Dallas-Fort Worth-Arlington, TX	139 977	2 548 049	287 444	239 058	299 983	182 468	184 699	117 774	46 221	25 402	61.3	4.8	34.9
Dallas-Plano-Irving, TX Div	NA	NA	NA	NA	NA	NA	NA	NA	NA	14 567	59.4	5.1	35.3
Fort Worth-Arlington, TX Div	NA	NA	NA	NA	NA	NA	NA	NA	NA	10 835	63.8	4.4	34.3
Dalton, GA	2 757	56 530	4 590	23 140	5 738	989	1 321	1 902	33 654	788	48.1	1.5	34.6
Danville, IL	1 537	24 945	4 795	5 059	3 435	1 343	387	852	34 162	1 014	38.7	27.3	52.4
Danville, VA	2 273	30 775	5 820	6 049	5 452	1 199	607	880	28 608	1 356	22.4	8.8	44.8
Davenport-Moline-Rock Island, IA-IL	9 265	157 820	23 425	24 104	21 870	6 253	6 453	5 877	37 236	3 819	36.6	20.5	51.8
Dayton, OH	17 712	315 661	62 559	42 379	41 489	10 667	22 724	12 033	38 121	3 809	54.7	10.8	43.4
Decatur, AL	3 144	48 062	6 942	13 449	6 606	1 586	2 041	1 622	33 750	3 058	46.9	3.9	38.9
Decatur, IL	2 548	46 139	7 782	7 924	5 485	1 516	1 257	1 696	36 748	708	44.1	27.0	54.5
Deltona-Daytona Beach-Ormond Beach, FL	11 881	129 006	25 359	7 644	22 893	4 450	6 566	3 809	29 529	1 243	84.5	2.4	46.7
Denver-Aurora-Broomfield, CO	73 916	1 062 780	129 559	58 325	122 119	64 038	94 952	51 185	48 162	4 928	50.0	16.0	33.1
Des Moines-West Des Moines, IA	14 889	283 733	35 907	18 035	34 917	49 815	15 421	11 639	41 020	4 782	37.0	16.3	42.1
Detroit-Warren-Livonia, MI	98 486	1 565 724	248 175	181 310	195 155	80 284	155 805	70 873	45 265	4 560	59.4	5.2	46.8
Detroit-Livonia-Dearborn, MI Div	NA	NA	NA	NA	NA	NA	NA	NA	NA	313	78.0	1.9	46.6
Warren-Troy-Farmington Hills, MI Div	NA	NA	NA	NA	NA	NA	NA	NA	NA	4 247	58.0	5.4	46.8
Dothan, AL	3 572	50 646	10 674	5 969	9 051	1 417	1 416	1 653	32 648	2 427	30.5	10.6	41.3
Dover, DE	3 169	48 947	8 129	4 918	9 072	1 339	1 918	1 580	32 286	825	57.0	9.3	58.4
Dubuque, IA	2 745	52 354	7 666	8 499	7 280	2 793	1 851	1 721	32 879	1 483	26.0	11.1	53.1
Duluth, MN-WI	7 331	103 467	25 761	7 186	16 102	4 491	3 783	3 394	32 807	1 579	21.8	8.2	43.8
Durham-Chapel Hill, NC	11 570	224 500	39 570	20 239	22 892	8 318	33 243	11 642	51 857	2 338	48.4	4.1	44.4
Eau Claire, WI	4 107	66 240	13 448	9 690	10 793	3 927	2 125	2 238	33 781	2 798	23.7	6.8	48.2
El Centro, CA	2 441	30 887	4 335	3 324	7 647	993	923	855	27 676	452	28.1	39.4	71.0
Elizabethtown, KY	2 352	35 692	6 039	5 807	6 149	1 471	2 151	1 024	28 703	2 399	40.7	5.3	40.3
Elkhart-Goshen, IN	4 972	92 665	9 642	41 093	9 043	2 087	2 258	3 187	34 388	1 617	64.1	4.5	37.3
Elmira, NY	1 869	32 016	6 936	5 986	5 385	1 085	754	1 071	33 460	373	22.3	7.8	49.1
El Paso, TX	13 179	205 190	35 665	14 235	33 671	6 704	9 709	5 699	27 773	590	78.3	7.5	47.6
Erie, PA	6 552	114 158	23 074	23 315	15 550	D	3 639	3 704	32 449	1 609	44.0	2.9	39.7
Eugene-Springfield, OR	9 767	113 703	19 980	14 076	18 506	4 940	5 617	3 720	32 715	3 335	75.5	2.8	37.5
Evansville, IN-KY	8 656	162 632	25 979	27 884	19 658	6 749	5 464	5 750	35 353	2 841	40.3	17.3	44.2
Fairbanks, AK	2 445	26 479	4 978	557	4 935	824	1 315	1 171	44 230	212	34.0	22.2	56.1
Fargo, ND-MN	6 256	112 499	15 989	9 390	15 093	8 511	5 010	3 918	34 823	1 834	17.7	41.8	59.5
Farmington, NM	2 852	40 754	6 117	1 470	6 982	1 091	1 386	1 547	37 963	1 897	85.7	2.2	55.4
Fayetteville, NC	6 092	96 769	20 008	9 636	16 192	2 302	5 228	2 903	30 001	749	44.1	10.5	48.3
Fayetteville-Springdale-Rogers, AR-MO	10 676	178 827	20 033	25 974	22 416	5 423	8 428	7 231	40 436	7 401	43.3	5.3	42.2

Table C. Metropolitan Areas — **Agriculture**

Table C. Metropolitan Areas — **Agriculture**

Area name	Land in farms					Value of land and buildings (dollars)		Value of machinery and equipment, average per farm (dollars)	Value of products sold				Percent of farms with sales of:		Government payments	
			Acres								Percent from:					
	Acreage (1,000)	Percent change, 2002–2007	Average size of farm	Total irrigated (1,000)	Total cropland (1,000)	Average per farm	Average per acre		Total (mil dol)	Average per farm (dollars)	Crops	Live-stock and poultry products	$10,000 or more	$100,000 or more	Total ($1,000)	Percent of farms
	117	118	119	120	121	122	123	124	125	126	127	128	129	130	131	132
Charleston, WV	145	9.0	115	0.2	30.0	243 749	2 126	30 733	9.8	7 717	64.0	36.0	8.5	0.3	54	7.0
Charleston-North Charleston-Summerville, SC	159	-1.9	156	3.8	60.0	671 668	4 310	68 000	D	D	D	D	22.2	6.8	1 754	19.5
Charlotte-Gastonia-Rock Hill, NC-SC	517	-6.2	129	2.6	245.7	657 897	5 088	67 692	D	D	D	D	28.9	12.8	4 250	20.9
Charlottesville, VA	311	-12.4	163	2.2	99.8	897 521	5 494	58 776	49.9	26 186	45.5	54.5	30.6	3.4	441	11.2
Chattanooga, TN-GA	261	-6.5	111	0.5	98.3	471 016	4 258	57 563	168.7	71 593	D	D	22.2	6.0	529	9.5
Cheyenne, WY	1 692	-3.6	2 004	53.0	345.6	971 638	485	88 824	124.1	147 031	17.5	82.5	37.3	14.5	4 352	38.7
Chicago-Joliet-Naperville, IL-IN-WI	2 291	-1.8	297	D	2 144.9	1 323 210	4 455	144 387	1 715.6	222 402	72.1	27.9	53.0	30.5	44 684	53.1
Chicago-Joliet-Naperville, IL Div	1 398	-4.9	295	D	1 325.3	1 425 731	4 826	151 220	1 022.5	216 069	81.9	18.1	54.2	31.9	29 017	50.9
Gary, IN Div	774	5.3	364	46.9	719.4	1 323 186	3 633	151 441	602.6	283 454	55.2	44.8	55.8	32.5	13 978	67.5
Lake County-Kenosha County, IL-WI Div	119	-7.0	139	0.8	100.2	756 535	5 448	89 089	90.5	105 783	73.2	26.8	39.1	17.3	1 689	30.1
Chico, CA	374	-2.1	183	202.2	222.7	1 371 244	7 513	108 816	342.8	167 366	96.5	3.5	53.6	25.5	14 780	14.3
Cincinnati-Middletown, OH-KY-IN	1 342	-5.6	129	3.9	804.8	468 425	3 622	62 166	300.6	28 977	71.6	28.4	28.5	6.0	11 530	30.5
Clarksville, TN-KY	689	0.3	230	4.6	420.6	628 879	2 736	78 467	163.8	54 658	D	D	37.2	11.3	8 210	40.4
Cleveland, TN	128	1.6	101	0.3	58.3	482 893	4 769	57 935	123.6	97 734	4.8	95.2	28.1	11.7	288	9.7
Cleveland-Elyria-Mentor, OH	295	-21.3	95	4.2	218.6	520 944	5 468	69 058	310.2	100 128	83.8	16.2	37.3	9.7	D	20.8
Coeur d'Alene, ID	131	-14.9	158	11.0	71.2	642 680	4 057	52 170	16.4	19 834	75.1	24.9	18.8	3.6	869	17.4
College Station-Bryan, TX	1 092	-10.0	243	45.0	272.5	554 744	2 283	61 563	226.9	50 502	22.1	77.9	33.2	5.0	5 052	7.3
Colorado Springs, CO	690	-22.1	417	17.3	97.5	554 050	1 329	53 758	40.5	24 466	49.3	50.7	20.7	3.1	D	8.2
Columbia, MO	535	-0.9	245	15.6	324.8	598 049	2 445	61 636	90.6	41 381	70.2	29.8	37.8	9.0	5 523	43.8
Columbia, SC	507	2.6	172	28.4	199.2	532 092	3 092	69 506	505.4	171 597	19.3	80.7	26.4	10.4	6 331	21.6
Columbus, GA-AL	214	-12.3	231	D	54.2	607 141	2 627	54 032	D	D	27.4	D	21.0	4.7	D	18.3
Columbus, IN	166	3.1	249	10.2	148.3	945 855	3 798	108 015	69.5	104 009	87.5	12.5	48.4	19.3	3 817	64.7
Columbus, OH	1 522	-6.9	216	3.7	1 298.1	825 409	3 824	102 450	780.1	110 652	70.8	29.2	42.4	17.6	30 532	51.4
Corpus Christi, TX	930	1.2	638	18.6	D	812 956	1 275	116 742	221.8	152 109	89.2	10.8	33.7	18.4	D	34.3
Corvallis, OR	115	-11.5	126	23.3	79.2	675 605	5 343	81 023	74.6	82 301	84.4	15.6	23.3	7.8	342	7.7
Crestview-Fort Walton Beach-Destin, FL	66	20.0	116	0.4	24.3	628 564	5 410	38 958	D	D	D	D	13.1	3.4	1 641	36.2
Cumberland, MD-WV	115	-4.2	144	0.5	32.1	474 725	3 293	37 716	18.7	23 433	16.7	83.3	22.0	3.3	254	17.4
Dallas-Fort Worth-Arlington, TX	3 522	-5.7	139	D	1 348.2	424 036	3 058	46 883	554.8	21 835	47.0	53.0	19.1	2.5	10 149	8.3
Dallas-Plano-Irving, TX Div	2 152	-3.1	148	D	947.7	417 101	2 823	48 138	330.3	22 668	50.1	49.9	18.7	2.7	8 451	10.7
Fort Worth-Arlington, TX Div	1 370	-9.6	126	7.3	400.5	433 360	3 427	45 196	224.5	20 714	42.4	57.6	19.5	2.2	1 698	5.0
Dalton, GA	83	-2.4	105	0.5	29.1	457 636	4 362	55 960	159.9	202 869	1.5	98.5	32.2	13.1	207	7.7
Danville, IL	457	1.6	451	0.7	428.1	1 781 695	3 950	178 307	224.0	220 876	95.5	4.5	61.3	37.7	8 500	78.9
Danville, VA	274	NA	202	4.2	103.6	638 676	3 157	73 087	62.6	46 198	37.4	62.6	32.1	7.9	1 494	34.1
Davenport-Moline-Rock Island, IA-IL	1 223	4.4	320	21.6	1 090.8	1 267 848	3 957	130 651	686.2	179 693	75.3	24.7	59.2	34.4	27 720	75.7
Dayton, OH	701	7.4	184	4.1	622.8	718 881	3 906	91 594	324.9	85 309	78.5	21.5	45.5	17.4	12 745	55.7
Decatur, AL	384	0.3	126	4.4	188.9	340 474	2 712	57 567	241.9	79 098	9.8	90.2	28.6	8.2	7 743	31.8
Decatur, IL	291	-9.3	410	0.0	280.7	1 831 072	4 461	177 853	156.8	221 463	96.8	3.2	58.9	37.3	5 131	74.2
Deltona-Daytona Beach-Ormond Beach, FL	83	-11.7	67	9.1	18.3	662 001	9 881	38 989	125.5	101 002	94.9	5.1	36.7	10.2	47	1.3
Denver-Aurora-Broomfield, CO	2 726	D	553	D	1 035.4	735 672	1 330	64 519	257.2	52 208	D	D	22.1	6.1	D	17.5
Des Moines-West Des Moines, IA	1 426	-2.6	298	5.5	1 124.0	963 853	3 231	117 099	690.8	144 456	62.0	38.0	47.9	21.3	29 631	71.1
Detroit-Warren-Livonia, MI	545	-8.9	120	9.6	427.9	560 530	4 688	81 252	261.8	57 401	78.2	21.8	31.8	10.9	4 843	21.5
Detroit-Livonia-Dearborn, MI Div	17	-19.0	56	0.8	13.1	431 377	7 741	73 184	28.8	91 875	97.1	2.9	35.8	11.2	93	10.9
Warren-Troy-Farmington Hills, MI Div	528	-8.5	124	8.7	414.8	570 048	4 587	81 846	233.0	54 860	75.9	24.1	31.5	10.9	4 750	22.3
Dothan, AL	591	4.2	244	21.3	284.6	490 989	2 016	67 033	225.9	93 065	27.9	72.1	34.0	11.3	19 609	59.8
Dover, DE	174	-5.9	211	29.1	146.5	2 091 092	9 926	122 692	188.4	228 352	D	D	46.7	26.1	3 285	37.3
Dubuque, IA	311	-1.6	210	D	237.4	711 542	3 395	119 819	271.1	182 789	23.6	76.4	65.3	37.2	7 841	81.2
Duluth, MN-WI	319	-14.7	202	2.4	144.4	408 519	2 020	48 794	27.7	17 541	37.4	62.6	26.2	4.5	286	8.7
Durham-Chapel Hill, NC	289	-7.1	124	3.7	119.3	594 313	4 809	57 227	D	D	18.3	D	32.7	11.8	1 898	18.6
Eau Claire, WI	559	-3.3	200	6.6	357.9	519 857	2 603	86 606	249.6	89 197	21.6	78.4	46.6	21.9	7 217	65.8
El Centro, CA	427	-16.9	945	376.5	396.7	5 001 024	5 290	413 760	1 290.3	2 854 542	54.5	45.5	83.2	61.9	4 885	29.2
Elizabethtown, KY	348	-7.0	145	0.8	193.8	409 608	2 826	57 110	73.5	30 632	55.2	44.8	33.8	6.0	2 528	34.8
Elkhart-Goshen, IN	163	-18.9	101	22.0	141.6	560 281	5 548	72 668	205.8	127 245	26.1	73.9	49.7	26.2	1 909	26.3
Elmira, NY	65	-5.8	175	0.2	32.9	319 539	1 830	69 729	16.6	44 525	18.9	81.1	29.2	9.4	394	27.9
El Paso, TX	169	48.2	286	37.8	54.1	418 167	1 464	78 916	47.5	80 447	86.2	13.8	26.1	11.4	894	10.3
Erie, PA	173	4.2	108	1.4	101.7	430 926	4 005	62 976	71.3	44 303	69.0	31.0	31.7	11.4	1 348	16.7
Eugene-Springfield, OR	246	4.7	74	22.4	116.4	547 167	7 432	49 129	131.1	39 307	70.5	29.5	17.5	4.4	759	4.3
Evansville, IN-KY	968	4.0	341	D	826.2	998 966	2 933	130 927	437.2	153 889	76.0	24.0	47.4	23.7	15 625	68.4
Fairbanks, AK	111	NA	523	2.0	63.6	406 163	777	74 337	7.1	33 373	83.2	16.8	42.5	7.5	1 356	23.6
Fargo, ND-MN	1 653	-4.3	901	17.6	1 535.9	1 449 652	1 609	228 729	469.7	256 095	89.9	10.1	57.9	41.1	24 398	81.0
Farmington, NM	1 631	D	860	78.4	107.4	268 195	312	37 574	57.2	30 152	82.6	17.4	8.9	1.3	900	4.6
Fayetteville, NC	149	-3.2	198	3.9	80.0	627 065	3 161	79 354	157.9	210 816	16.7	83.3	35.9	18.6	2 654	38.6
Fayetteville-Springdale-Rogers, AR-MO	1 041	-12.6	141	2.1	341.1	519 753	3 695	59 940	1 123.0	151 730	1.8	98.2	38.8	13.2	1 278	6.3

Table C. Metropolitan Areas — Water Use, Wholesale Trade, Retail Trade, and Real Estate

Area name	Water use, 2005		Wholesale trade,[1] 2007				Retail trade, 2007				Real estate and rental and leasing, 2007			
	Total water withdrawn (mil gal/day)	Gallons withdrawn per person	Number of establishments	Number of employees	Sales (mil dol)	Annual payroll (mil dol)	Number of establishments	Number of employees	Sales (mil dol)	Annual payroll (mil dol)	Number of establishments	Number of employees	Receipts (mil dol)	Annual payroll (mil dol)
	133	134	135	136	137	138	139	140	141	142	143	144	145	146
Charleston, WV	567.6	1 852	432	6 150	4 160.1	294.4	1 190	17 349	3 842.5	327.3	341	2 055	412.3	61.9
Charleston-North Charleston-Summerville, SC	713.8	1 200	760	11 530	8 645.0	556.3	2 799	37 845	8 752.8	841.3	1 044	5 212	936.0	169.8
Charlotte-Gastonia-Rock Hill, NC-SC	4 008.8	2 635	3 489	55 343	52 134.4	3 081.9	6 225	91 990	23 219.9	2 112.7	2 596	15 084	3 396.6	642.2
Charlottesville, VA	244.6	1 298	180	2 108	925.7	102.3	859	11 418	2 639.8	269.2	311	1 700	239.0	52.8
Chattanooga, TN-GA	1 674.6	3 403	708	8 176	4 895.3	357.8	2 094	27 398	6 586.1	607.2	501	2 682	410.3	107.2
Cheyenne, WY	272.5	3 200	116	1 017	828.8	46.2	360	5 603	1 720.5	133.4	134	519	94.2	14.3
Chicago-Joliet-Naperville, IL-IN-WI	9 495.4	1 006	16 000	265 925	346 250.0	16 552.3	30 234	475 144	129 111.8	11 514.3	11 251	75 220	19 819.5	3 666.0
Chicago-Joliet-Naperville, IL Div	6 106.4	775	13 725	219 797	282 205.5	13 219.7	24 781	387 591	97 414.1	9 183.2	9 612	67 343	18 193.2	3 353.8
Gary, IN Div	2 502.8	3 589	697	8 772	8 406.2	431.8	2 397	35 715	9 560.9	758.3	645	3 292	456.8	86.2
Lake County-Kenosha County, IL-WI Div	886.2	1 027	1 578	37 356	55 638.4	2 900.7	3 056	51 838	22 136.9	1 572.8	994	4 585	1 169.4	226.0
Chico, CA	789.9	3 688	182	1 934	868.1	76.0	798	11 316	2 400.7	256.8	264	1 462	158.8	32.6
Cincinnati-Middletown, OH-KY-IN	2 131.1	1 029	3 110	57 817	90 116.2	3 373.3	6 977	110 110	25 842.3	2 395.2	2 142	13 389	2 615.8	470.2
Clarksville, TN-KY	2 127.7	8 732	159	1 861	1 433.9	73.1	866	11 876	2 948.3	262.5	230	949	147.3	22.4
Cleveland, TN	24.1	223	79	D	D	D	444	4 970	1 232.3	113.5	90	478	89.7	12.8
Cleveland-Elyria-Mentor, OH	2 097.9	987	3 869	55 061	48 609.8	2 933.9	7 396	106 023	24 195.3	2 304.4	2 258	18 202	6 344.0	782.1
Coeur d'Alene, ID	73.2	573	163	1 625	915.7	67.8	609	7 398	2 175.2	187.5	249	876	155.3	27.4
College Station-Bryan, TX	103.9	548	155	1 882	1 013.5	70.2	748	10 070	2 418.2	209.7	241	1 240	208.1	34.5
Colorado Springs, CO	163.5	278	559	9 150	6 385.6	592.9	2 158	31 970	8 119.2	787.7	1 183	4 028	603.3	117.2
Columbia, MO	23.8	155	153	1 878	960.2	75.4	689	11 629	3 100.3	245.4	245	1 045	149.9	25.5
Columbia, SC	2 394.6	3 471	885	15 623	10 539.6	760.4	2 790	39 139	8 967.8	819.2	786	5 179	1 090.3	172.1
Columbus, GA-AL	94.5	333	235	3 163	1 999.3	132.6	1 097	15 393	3 468.3	313.1	321	1 822	321.8	60.6
Columbus, IN	21.2	289	95	1 166	891.8	61.2	375	5 133	1 075.2	106.7	74	319	50.1	8.9
Columbus, OH	331.6	194	2 220	45 650	57 654.2	2 373.1	5 712	101 313	26 892.3	2 381.3	2 091	12 876	2 513.7	468.5
Corpus Christi, TX	388.7	940	509	5 792	4 541.3	276.3	1 449	20 267	5 177.6	440.5	541	3 012	461.3	86.7
Corvallis, OR	45.1	573	57	585	430.5	24.0	275	3 559	685.2	73.0	119	543	58.1	11.3
Crestview-Fort Walton Beach-Destin, FL	26.4	140	130	710	702.4	34.8	903	12 427	3 031.0	272.4	398	1 772	260.5	57.0
Cumberland, MD-WV	48.8	484	64	D	D	D	391	5 051	1 088.8	91.1	70	266	38.1	6.3
Dallas-Fort Worth-Arlington, TX	2 382.2	409	9 458	167 324	206 962.4	9 823.0	19 069	301 443	85 651.3	7 513.7	7 342	57 889	13 368.4	2 812.1
Dallas-Plano-Irving, TX Div	1 817.6	467	6 819	120 653	161 092.6	7 061.1	12 704	200 693	57 367.2	5 049.6	5 272	45 640	10 407.7	2 341.2
Fort Worth-Arlington, TX Div	564.7	293	2 639	46 671	45 869.8	2 761.9	6 365	100 750	28 284.1	2 464.1	2 070	12 249	2 960.7	470.8
Dalton, GA	43.2	328	297	5 190	4 943.3	208.6	605	6 525	1 659.1	146.9	100	412	61.5	12.0
Danville, IL	17.1	208	81	D	D	D	281	3 443	757.9	68.5	59	254	34.3	6.6
Danville, VA	63.8	591	101	1 463	614.1	48.0	487	5 478	1 161.5	101.3	86	416	47.1	10.1
Davenport-Moline-Rock Island, IA-IL	1 214.1	3 226	597	8 829	9 543.2	377.1	1 492	22 567	5 127.2	480.3	357	2 521	378.9	62.4
Dayton, OH	304.9	361	947	14 608	12 999.4	702.0	2 781	43 291	10 397.4	916.9	830	4 827	711.2	152.0
Decatur, AL	192.2	1 296	194	2 297	1 356.1	94.0	631	6 676	1 804.6	144.0	109	448	63.1	11.4
Decatur, IL	40.4	366	123	1 251	738.5	57.2	432	6 231	1 450.6	132.5	91	454	64.6	12.6
Deltona-Daytona Beach-Ormond Beach, FL	171.2	346	516	5 110	2 897.3	188.5	1 970	26 205	6 099.9	575.9	842	3 978	531.8	101.5
Denver-Aurora-Broomfield, CO	703.0	298	4 366	69 932	75 213.8	4 051.4	8 476	129 655	34 016.1	3 309.8	4 608	25 955	5 102.5	1 132.5
Des Moines-West Des Moines, IA	69.6	133	1 007	15 770	12 947.7	773.9	2 118	35 904	8 120.5	790.2	655	3 810	754.6	137.3
Detroit-Warren-Livonia, MI	3 636.2	810	6 291	90 203	152 004.0	5 301.9	15 985	204 938	49 928.3	4 590.6	4 085	29 503	9 253.9	1 012.8
Detroit-Livonia-Dearborn, MI Div	1 858.7	930	1 974	34 186	64 988.9	1 867.3	6 361	68 272	17 275.8	1 451.0	1 276	7 929	5 528.0	241.0
Warren-Troy-Farmington Hills, MI Div	1 777.4	714	4 317	56 017	87 015.1	3 434.6	9 624	136 666	32 652.6	3 139.6	2 809	21 574	3 725.9	771.8
Dothan, AL	145.2	1 063	221	3 607	9 466.8	151.1	780	9 231	2 172.2	202.2	143	601	85.1	17.9
Dover, DE	37.6	261	113	D	D	D	632	9 614	2 589.2	224.6	127	604	91.0	22.0
Dubuque, IA	86.8	947	170	2 664	2 452.9	100.5	467	7 056	1 433.5	135.0	103	446	73.6	16.6
Duluth, MN-WI	306.6	1 113	296	4 396	3 324.6	176.0	1 313	16 792	3 622.4	344.6	266	1 146	180.9	25.6
Durham-Chapel Hill, NC	1 271.6	2 788	451	12 129	11 159.7	1 102.3	1 658	24 387	5 274.3	536.1	536	2 686	514.3	98.2
Eau Claire, WI	34.8	226	171	2 760	1 505.0	107.5	688	11 320	2 572.1	227.9	137	790	90.7	17.3
El Centro, CA	2 144.9	13 765	236	2 040	1 364.8	71.7	534	8 052	1 727.3	170.2	134	555	73.4	12.5
Elizabethtown, KY	15.2	137	72	661	375.2	20.3	464	6 229	1 498.7	136.1	106	459	57.1	9.3
Elkhart-Goshen, IN	36.5	187	418	6 711	4 123.4	293.6	727	9 710	2 416.9	219.0	180	813	109.4	20.4
Elmira, NY	15.7	175	95	1 221	425.6	48.6	388	5 580	1 207.2	111.0	79	410	65.6	10.7
El Paso, TX	267.3	370	1 012	9 918	7 291.8	362.0	2 334	33 948	8 460.9	683.1	672	3 599	629.2	106.8
Erie, PA	55.7	199	308	3 575	1 371.9	141.6	1 051	15 831	3 428.4	314.5	187	1 115	135.3	25.9
Eugene-Springfield, OR	213.9	638	515	6 214	3 806.1	269.5	1 403	20 408	4 452.2	456.9	569	2 554	380.1	59.6
Evansville, IN-KY	981.6	2 808	463	8 450	5 344.0	400.5	1 421	20 550	4 797.5	435.3	326	1 923	282.5	49.6
Fairbanks, AK	38.3	437	81	924	839.9	43.3	339	5 236	1 574.3	146.7	136	745	152.5	29.9
Fargo, ND-MN	25.4	137	480	7 639	5 309.3	354.9	843	14 809	3 515.8	311.1	308	1 809	243.8	49.0
Farmington, NM	332.7	2 636	167	1 684	1 253.7	84.8	482	6 671	1 742.0	155.5	120	879	211.5	45.2
Fayetteville, NC	46.2	134	187	2 362	1 180.6	96.3	1 140	16 425	4 019.1	351.4	350	1 723	256.5	49.4
Fayetteville-Springdale-Rogers, AR-MO	454.1	1 121	618	9 579	25 120.0	449.5	1 658	22 909	5 451.8	497.6	609	3 481	362.7	93.6

1. Merchant wholesalers, except manufacturers' sales branches and offices.

Area name	Professional, scientific, and technical services,[1] 2007				Manufacturing, 2007				Accommodation and food services, 2007			
	Number of establishments	Number of employees	Sales (mil dol)	Annual payroll (mil dol)	Number of establishments	Number of employees	Sales (mil dol)	Annual payroll (mil dol)	Number of establishments	Number of employees	Sales (mil dol)	Annual payroll (mil dol)
	147	148	149	150	151	152	153	154	155	156	157	158
Charleston, WV	717	6 459	781.4	312.8	184	5 767	4 491.5	318.7	611	10 971	493.9	135.0
Charleston-North Charleston-Summerville, SC	1 821	D	D	D	493	22 043	13 226.8	1 041.9	1 406	31 250	1 647.9	448.6
Charlotte-Gastonia-Rock Hill, NC-SC	5 109	D	D	D	1 926	75 520	37 009.7	3 256.2	3 511	70 733	3 599.1	983.2
Charlottesville, VA	682	D	D	D	167	3 650	1 087.3	D	464	8 781	451.9	130.3
Chattanooga, TN-GA	947	D	D	D	653	37 654	11 406.2	1 484.4	1 014	19 768	823.0	238.8
Cheyenne, WY	312	1 402	182.0	65.2	61	1 710	2 420.2	80.9	185	3 938	173.7	52.1
Chicago-Joliet-Naperville, IL-IN-WI	32 985	D	D	D	12 022	482 380	177 305.4	24 319.0	19 142	351 200	20 892.1	5 611.5
Chicago-Joliet-Naperville, IL Div	28 421	D	D	D	10 275	386 223	127 798.4	18 049.7	15 897	294 630	18 056.4	4 851.0
Gary, IN Div	1 335	D	D	D	628	39 027	30 031.8	2 198.6	1 391	26 183	1 322.4	335.4
Lake County-Kenosha County, IL-WI Div	3 229	D	D	D	1 119	57 130	19 475.2	4 070.7	1 854	30 387	1 513.3	425.1
Chico, CA	426	D	D	D	224	4 404	987.4	150.6	429	7 708	355.8	96.7
Cincinnati-Middletown, OH-KY-IN	4 956	D	D	D	2 531	125 573	50 675.7	6 169.7	4 240	92 094	4 413.7	1 211.4
Clarksville, TN-KY	267	D	D	D	169	12 535	4 357.3	496.6	453	8 714	342.7	91.6
Cleveland, TN	162	D	D	D	144	9 807	4 730.9	340.2	187	3 386	139.2	38.1
Cleveland-Elyria-Mentor, OH	6 163	51 027	7 535.8	2 959.6	3 774	141 166	42 181.1	6 876.6	4 714	79 741	3 496.7	963.9
Coeur d'Alene, ID	438	D	D	D	246	4 401	992.2	163.3	363	6 773	303.7	96.0
College Station-Bryan, TX	418	D	D	D	134	5 316	1 059.6	181.9	427	9 138	368.3	98.0
Colorado Springs, CO	2 423	D	D	D	516	14 448	5 075.3	693.2	1 316	25 914	1 281.8	388.6
Columbia, MO	394	D	D	D	107	4 831	1 605.9	192.9	437	8 615	318.6	94.0
Columbia, SC	1 897	19 364	1 922.4	763.5	574	29 335	11 562.5	1 282.6	1 411	29 213	1 237.5	352.0
Columbus, GA-AL	453	D	D	D	201	10 451	3 354.4	404.7	551	12 099	529.9	150.0
Columbus, IN	157	D	D	D	143	11 711	4 843.9	502.9	160	3 416	139.7	39.9
Columbus, OH	4 707	D	D	D	1 523	69 841	34 330.4	3 346.4	3 790	78 561	3 448.1	993.4
Corpus Christi, TX	907	D	D	D	255	9 899	D	D	1 030	18 298	788.4	218.7
Corvallis, OR	282	D	D	D	92	4 322	590.5	209.8	206	3 197	134.0	37.2
Crestview-Fort Walton Beach-Destin, FL	637	D	D	D	98	3 858	656.7	166.4	431	10 619	491.9	148.9
Cumberland, MD-WV	140	D	D	D	74	4 299	1 123.9	195.6	227	3 386	146.1	39.7
Dallas-Fort Worth-Arlington, TX	17 686	176 361	32 628.1	12 124.7	6 102	304 809	104 883.8	15 172.3	11 100	237 408	12 349.0	3 442.0
Dallas-Plano-Irving, TX Div	13 181	142 565	27 891.2	10 170.3	3 929	193 957	59 178.0	9 573.4	7 521	157 394	8 289.5	2 327.1
Fort Worth-Arlington, TX Div	4 505	33 796	4 736.9	1 954.3	2 173	110 852	45 705.8	5 598.8	3 579	80 014	4 059.5	1 114.9
Dalton, GA	187	D	D	D	399	27 729	9 130.6	863.7	232	4 001	169.4	45.4
Danville, IL	93	396	44.7	12.9	100	5 458	2 576.4	239.7	156	2 370	85.0	24.6
Danville, VA	125	D	D	D	96	6 926	2 028.1	294.0	183	3 190	125.5	34.3
Davenport-Moline-Rock Island, IA-IL	766	5 999	759.2	267.7	423	25 175	11 531.2	1 137.5	902	16 365	695.8	189.7
Dayton, OH	1 848	D	D	D	1 214	52 046	18 851.0	2 360.1	1 677	33 676	1 325.8	392.4
Decatur, AL	262	1 563	124.4	50.4	223	13 563	9 505.9	668.3	249	4 299	177.4	47.5
Decatur, IL	181	1 185	125.8	51.1	112	8 762	9 590.8	409.4	219	4 733	170.9	52.0
Deltona-Daytona Beach-Ormond Beach, FL	1 353	D	D	D	369	9 491	1 948.6	366.2	1 006	19 359	899.2	245.8
Denver-Aurora-Broomfield, CO	12 019	91 413	17 642.7	6 530.9	2 443	67 646	24 222.8	3 445.5	5 380	108 481	5 759.1	1 667.2
Des Moines-West Des Moines, IA	1 616	13 296	1 965.3	705.0	471	21 153	8 439.5	919.1	1 307	23 794	976.7	285.2
Detroit-Warren-Livonia, MI	11 820	164 820	20 494.6	11 254.7	5 987	234 520	112 084.5	13 174.3	8 135	146 138	6 949.9	1 976.0
Detroit-Livonia-Dearborn, MI Div	2 880	D	D	D	1 729	87 991	55 896.9	5 545.3	3 215	57 836	3 112.4	857.5
Warren-Troy-Farmington Hills, MI Div	8 940	D	D	D	4 258	146 529	56 187.5	7 629.0	4 920	88 302	3 837.5	1 118.5
Dothan, AL	292	D	D	D	170	7 348	1 889.8	253.6	282	5 007	195.0	53.1
Dover, DE	248	D	D	D	87	5 253	2 361.8	213.8	236	5 352	447.9	76.2
Dubuque, IA	168	D	D	D	150	9 378	4 711.2	380.3	253	4 502	145.7	42.5
Duluth, MN-WI	529	D	D	D	310	8 551	3 487.9	370.8	812	12 944	607.7	148.9
Durham-Chapel Hill, NC	1 655	34 201	4 881.9	2 788.6	373	21 560	11 749.3	1 044.7	1 045	20 891	1 081.9	304.6
Eau Claire, WI	265	1 760	195.3	85.3	228	10 762	3 109.0	424.2	418	6 405	226.5	63.2
El Centro, CA	153	D	D	D	58	2 846	1 207.9	96.9	261	3 719	167.8	46.2
Elizabethtown, KY	156	D	D	D	99	6 206	1 882.3	245.1	194	4 712	174.5	54.5
Elkhart-Goshen, IN	338	D	D	D	852	64 309	15 779.8	2 508.4	385	7 395	272.4	76.0
Elmira, NY	115	D	D	D	93	6 348	1 280.8	285.8	198	3 151	123.1	35.2
El Paso, TX	1 151	D	D	D	588	16 091	14 423.5	617.6	1 269	24 563	1 031.3	268.5
Erie, PA	416	D	D	D	505	24 441	6 890.8	1 190.2	646	10 728	428.1	114.6
Eugene-Springfield, OR	988	5 097	554.6	217.5	606	20 273	6 219.9	853.6	920	13 385	607.7	171.5
Evansville, IN-KY	731	D	D	D	478	33 017	21 220.2	1 619.5	746	15 457	668.7	190.4
Fairbanks, AK	228	1 329	174.9	64.7	78	745	D	37.3	220	3 430	221.6	60.9
Fargo, ND-MN	483	D	D	D	249	9 191	2 797.2	346.6	452	10 382	399.7	117.5
Farmington, NM	239	D	D	D	91	1 649	668.7	64.3	192	4 108	173.2	45.8
Fayetteville, NC	528	D	D	D	126	10 561	3 758.8	450.1	609	13 292	526.3	144.2
Fayetteville-Springdale-Rogers, AR-MO	1 134	D	D	D	457	30 601	7 300.6	1 007.3	858	17 438	664.7	191.7

1. Establishments subject to federal tax.

Table C. Metropolitan Areas — Health Care and Social Assistance, Other Services, and Federal Funds

Area name	Health care and social assistance,[1] 2007				Other services,[1] 2007				Federal funds and grants, 2009–2010 Expenditures (mil dol)			
										Direct payments for individuals		
	Number of establishments	Number of employees	Receipts (mil dol)	Annual payroll (mil dol)	Number of establishments	Number of employees	Receipts (mil dol)	Annual payroll (mil dol)	Total	Social Security and government retirement	Medicare	Food stamps and Supplemental Security Income
	159	160	161	162	163	164	165	166	167	168	169	170
Charleston, WV	951	19 734	1 929.5	704.0	524	3 801	356.9	95.5	4 374.4	1 171.2	581.5	163.9
Charleston-North Charleston-Summerville, SC	1 558	31 530	3 817.1	1 308.4	1 159	7 555	652.9	196.0	8 341.7	2 204.2	660.7	256.3
Charlotte-Gastonia-Rock Hill, NC-SC	3 703	89 158	8 873.9	3 640.6	2 734	18 931	2 657.5	525.1	9 160.6	4 103.5	1 442.0	472.4
Charlottesville, VA	502	14 902	1 872.9	662.2	384	3 223	623.6	112.0	1 876.0	608.5	230.4	39.3
Chattanooga, TN-GA	1 272	29 256	3 004.0	1 159.3	789	5 942	552.4	150.0	4 819.9	1 809.8	1 114.5	245.4
Cheyenne, WY	281	6 040	563.1	232.9	180	947	83.0	25.0	1 699.6	348.0	94.1	16.7
Chicago-Joliet-Naperville, IL-IN-WI	23 636	518 516	54 052.7	21 616.2	17 377	133 283	17 239.0	4 354.1	70 771.9	21 338.2	14 345.8	3 584.0
Chicago-Joliet-Naperville, IL Div	19 763	438 790	46 146.8	18 456.8	14 619	114 385	15 632.8	3 889.5	60 361.8	17 168.7	12 306.7	3 123.2
Gary, IN Div	1 654	40 530	3 833.0	1 495.6	1 260	8 871	726.0	216.3	5 168.5	2 173.9	1 213.4	322.5
Lake County-Kenosha County, IL-WI Div	2 219	39 196	4 072.9	1 663.8	1 498	10 027	880.2	248.3	5 241.6	1 995.6	825.7	138.3
Chico, CA	737	12 120	1 179.3	427.5	321	2 168	173.6	49.9	1 788.2	699.6	453.6	104.9
Cincinnati-Middletown, OH-KY-IN	4 833	129 504	12 087.4	5 143.1	3 426	24 021	2 390.8	645.9	17 400.1	5 605.3	3 371.5	700.1
Clarksville, TN-KY	481	10 538	859.8	317.0	316	1 915	135.1	39.2	7 603.2	881.1	381.0	95.5
Cleveland, TN	249	4 750	393.6	151.3	121	1 045	92.3	21.0	850.6	384.7	228.2	44.5
Cleveland-Elyria-Mentor, OH	5 520	159 804	14 974.6	6 459.7	4 195	28 804	2 837.6	766.6	19 049.7	6 140.7	4 697.2	1 029.6
Coeur d'Alene, ID	458	7 004	573.4	238.0	240	1 242	82.8	24.6	1 486.4	487.5	118.9	38.9
College Station-Bryan, TX	430	7 750	909.3	303.0	311	2 033	374.0	45.6	1 505.2	420.9	167.7	61.1
Colorado Springs, CO	1 796	27 724	2 934.4	1 110.6	1 127	8 222	1 328.2	259.3	11 194.6	2 150.8	478.3	140.3
Columbia, MO	593	16 310	1 710.0	622.4	334	2 107	185.0	52.6	1 272.5	389.5	184.1	47.2
Columbia, SC	1 596	39 169	4 070.4	1 614.8	1 327	8 711	803.3	233.4	8 993.9	2 317.7	696.9	258.1
Columbus, GA-AL	665	15 093	1 456.2	569.0	452	2 820	212.2	65.9	6 317.7	1 088.8	378.8	191.2
Columbus, IN	228	5 095	439.1	178.5	120	857	82.8	19.5	709.5	247.2	97.4	15.8
Columbus, OH	4 167	107 649	10 205.8	4 268.1	3 052	24 610	2 994.8	771.0	18 219.0	4 015.7	2 079.5	586.7
Corpus Christi, TX	1 152	26 350	2 241.9	859.7	698	4 703	492.1	130.7	3 990.3	1 248.9	670.1	246.1
Corvallis, OR	229	4 356	504.0	201.1	128	855	158.3	22.7	706.7	202.6	67.9	18.4
Crestview-Fort Walton Beach-Destin, FL	499	8 357	845.8	312.4	393	2 053	166.4	46.1	3 812.1	1 006.3	281.1	43.9
Cumberland, MD-WV	318	6 931	612.8	232.2	201	1 079	76.8	20.6	1 263.2	393.7	439.5	41.4
Dallas-Fort Worth-Arlington, TX	14 512	265 112	30 774.9	11 459.6	8 428	68 607	7 289.1	1 956.1	46 644.0	12 484.9	5 525.1	1 540.0
Dallas-Plano-Irving, TX Div	10 048	181 424	21 417.7	8 168.7	5 640	46 432	5 338.5	1 397.7	26 771.0	7 870.1	3 627.4	1 062.4
Fort Worth-Arlington, TX Div	4 464	83 688	9 357.2	3 290.9	2 788	22 175	1 950.6	558.4	19 873.0	4 614.8	1 897.8	477.6
Dalton, GA	228	4 281	480.5	183.3	166	839	77.6	24.0	696.4	326.3	145.8	40.2
Danville, IL	149	4 729	437.7	203.4	138	780	54.8	14.5	774.1	302.8	150.8	44.4
Danville, VA	265	5 275	437.9	175.7	193	920	72.0	18.3	899.5	396.9	180.1	49.1
Davenport-Moline-Rock Island, IA-IL	967	21 784	1 824.2	791.5	724	4 533	376.3	104.8	3 590.3	1 291.2	555.9	142.1
Dayton, OH	2 072	58 768	5 776.5	2 310.8	1 410	9 417	927.3	256.7	9 572.2	2 928.6	1 441.0	279.2
Decatur, AL	384	6 863	547.9	220.1	212	1 159	99.7	28.5	1 109.8	555.6	231.0	48.7
Decatur, IL	282	7 449	750.1	281.3	197	1 526	222.4	33.5	1 043.4	382.0	189.1	51.9
Deltona-Daytona Beach-Ormond Beach, FL	1 246	24 171	2 513.9	949.0	1 028	5 409	499.6	119.4	4 310.1	2 079.7	1 282.7	171.3
Denver-Aurora-Broomfield, CO	6 481	122 406	13 292.8	5 288.1	5 126	33 777	4 179.6	1 015.3	22 522.1	5 519.4	2 340.6	530.5
Des Moines-West Des Moines, IA	1 302	36 966	3 416.4	1 483.0	1 157	8 289	893.7	260.2	5 273.3	1 398.0	641.2	141.9
Detroit-Warren-Livonia, MI	12 227	241 649	24 485.3	10 037.1	7 434	46 504	5 094.0	1 259.1	38 663.6	13 116.2	8 958.2	2 311.2
Detroit-Livonia-Dearborn, MI Div	4 200	99 597	10 640.0	4 241.8	2 859	18 419	2 068.3	511.0	19 605.8	5 484.5	4 914.9	1 781.8
Warren-Troy-Farmington Hills, MI Div	8 027	142 052	13 845.3	5 795.3	4 575	28 085	3 025.7	748.1	19 057.8	7 631.7	4 043.3	529.4
Dothan, AL	390	10 440	987.5	395.0	238	1 230	115.9	27.3	1 173.3	554.3	232.7	67.0
Dover, DE	354	7 773	672.8	269.3	249	1 460	100.8	32.3	2 016.4	584.1	142.1	46.2
Dubuque, IA	242	7 056	592.0	264.0	208	1 505	102.2	27.4	640.7	284.2	148.6	20.4
Duluth, MN-WI	887	26 320	2 359.8	1 087.0	574	3 348	266.5	68.8	2 734.6	1 024.5	584.2	93.6
Durham-Chapel Hill, NC	1 263	39 491	4 277.7	1 577.9	769	5 961	1 025.2	213.4	6 636.7	1 195.1	501.1	143.4
Eau Claire, WI	441	13 010	1 218.0	539.6	313	1 747	150.7	42.7	1 101.3	461.9	202.0	42.7
El Centro, CA	265	4 257	394.1	142.6	163	1 046	83.2	25.1	1 240.1	314.4	226.8	84.2
Elizabethtown, KY	323	6 123	600.9	217.9	169	1 136	82.5	25.7	2 914.9	521.5	203.1	43.6
Elkhart-Goshen, IN	347	9 746	1 024.6	358.1	374	2 298	195.7	60.1	913.7	486.1	182.1	45.9
Elmira, NY	221	6 722	587.1	247.0	129	786	59.9	15.7	754.7	306.1	159.0	39.0
El Paso, TX	1 345	34 489	3 057.1	1 096.2	916	6 163	402.6	125.2	9 449.6	1 712.4	810.7	497.2
Erie, PA	893	21 880	1 847.7	783.0	563	3 529	242.4	70.2	2 238.2	876.3	576.3	134.9
Eugene-Springfield, OR	993	18 660	1 947.8	735.6	684	3 684	516.8	95.3	2 802.5	1 158.9	439.6	180.6
Evansville, IN-KY	971	24 277	2 270.7	859.5	646	4 383	377.5	110.8	2 764.7	1 122.3	636.0	128.2
Fairbanks, AK	267	4 867	570.5	223.9	195	1 081	106.8	31.3	1 546.6	196.7	45.0	19.0
Fargo, ND-MN	575	16 573	1 464.0	604.3	481	3 152	263.7	75.3	1 566.4	481.3	176.6	38.3
Farmington, NM	265	6 274	534.2	226.2	192	1 363	170.4	37.1	995.9	299.9	102.4	51.5
Fayetteville, NC	813	20 659	1 652.0	682.6	434	2 787	182.7	57.2	13 186.5	1 363.0	265.3	189.4
Fayetteville-Springdale-Rogers, AR-MO	945	18 182	1 764.3	701.8	617	4 171	425.2	104.0	2 474.5	1 130.6	367.0	85.8

1. Establishments subject to federal tax.

Area name	Federal funds and grants, 2009–2010 (cont.)							Value of residential construction authorized by building permits, 2010		Local government finances, 2007				
	Expenditures (mil dol) (cont.)									General revenue				
	Procurement contract awards			Grants								Taxes		
													Per capita[1] (dollars)	
	Salaries and wages	Defense	Other	Medicaid and other health-related	Nutrition and family welfare	Education	Other	New construction ($1,000)	Number of housing units	Total (mil dol)	Inter-govern-mental (mil dol)	Total (mil dol)	Total	Property
	171	172	173	174	175	176	177	178	179	180	181	182	183	184
Charleston, WV	298.8	24.7	59.9	398.7	158.0	180.3	1 240.5	51 807	358	823.4	358.3	307.6	1 012	762
Charleston-North Charleston-Summerville, SC	920.9	2 492.1	724.9	707.3	81.9	45.4	122.5	605 563	3 060	2 007.4	624.9	894.4	1 419	1 101
Charlotte-Gastonia-Rock Hill, NC-SC	766.7	113.0	374.8	869.0	195.7	101.8	477.8	881 518	5 288	7 982.4	2 334.7	2 355.2	1 426	1 095
Charlottesville, VA	178.2	199.2	56.3	395.8	14.7	22.8	103.0	187 611	1 105	643.4	258.7	308.2	1 599	1 115
Chattanooga, TN-GA	210.2	42.3	533.9	480.1	77.4	43.2	168.8	155 272	1 086	1 988.8	507.3	576.5	1 120	723
Cheyenne, WY	342.8	87.9	58.5	123.4	32.6	51.0	504.2	39 460	238	582.4	242.9	90.9	1 052	576
Chicago-Joliet-Naperville, IL-IN-WI	5 222.5	5 106.0	3 872.4	9 562.0	1 752.2	483.3	3 369.3	1 653 551	7 267	44 952.9	14 135.7	21 434.7	2 250	1 816
Chicago-Joliet-Naperville, IL Div	4 436.8	4 317.4	3 499.0	8 481.7	1 535.2	425.6	3 166.5	NA	NA	37 931.2	11 869.0	18 150.9	2 282	1 788
Gary, IN Div	210.2	36.9	42.1	787.3	123.7	21.8	125.2	NA	NA	2 974.2	1 124.2	1 038.6	1 486	1 411
Lake County-Kenosha County, IL-WI Div	575.4	751.7	331.3	293.1	93.3	36.0	77.6	NA	NA	4 047.5	1 142.5	2 245.2	2 571	2 400
Chico, CA	47.0	0.5	36.4	263.4	44.7	22.7	34.9	61 182	512	1 116.2	653.8	247.0	1 129	888
Cincinnati-Middletown, OH-KY-IN	1 308.5	2 211.5	486.1	2 376.1	347.8	131.5	381.8	537 783	3 206	8 511.5	3 081.7	3 674.7	1 722	1 165
Clarksville, TN-KY	5 297.1	557.0	38.9	177.9	39.1	21.3	15.7	166 545	1 921	565.5	255.1	201.0	768	474
Cleveland, TN	21.2	0.1	9.7	97.5	25.1	11.5	2.4	58 415	550	236.3	102.6	80.0	720	458
Cleveland-Elyria-Mentor, OH	1 434.0	251.6	851.4	2 898.7	430.4	172.6	690.8	391 583	1 941	11 419.1	4 261.7	4 831.1	2 304	1 502
Coeur d'Alene, ID	61.7	13.4	618.3	103.5	13.6	2.4	6.8	102 367	627	567.8	168.3	115.8	862	708
College Station-Bryan, TX	130.1	58.8	32.3	295.4	27.3	11.7	231.2	117 974	995	574.2	144.4	316.8	1 558	1 259
Colorado Springs, CO	4 748.0	2 889.0	109.3	235.8	70.4	62.1	68.2	525 095	1 760	2 475.6	754.9	790.1	1 297	720
Columbia, MO	113.9	8.9	49.9	202.3	20.2	29.0	144.1	98 012	607	467.8	146.6	209.0	1 288	755
Columbia, SC	2 012.5	557.6	378.4	725.7	234.5	301.2	1 226.8	406 756	2 942	2 478.4	790.7	890.3	1 243	1 088
Columbus, GA-AL	3 054.4	1 079.5	24.5	294.9	70.8	28.8	38.8	177 077	1 384	953.6	446.5	327.8	1 159	786
Columbus, IN	185.4	19.5	4.0	68.4	12.8	1.3	49.9	23 921	131	398.0	87.4	73.8	988	791
Columbus, OH	1 350.1	1 251.1	468.0	2 103.5	904.0	1 406.1	3 417.6	663 411	4 444	8 296.9	2 940.2	3 733.2	2 128	1 364
Corpus Christi, TX	348.3	487.8	78.3	618.6	102.9	19.9	52.3	144 067	1 225	1 488.4	505.3	671.1	1 619	1 285
Corvallis, OR	57.7	49.4	45.2	85.6	10.1	5.6	129.2	22 735	93	246.0	103.0	88.2	1 083	962
Crestview-Fort Walton Beach-Destin, FL	868.9	1 397.5	25.3	84.9	28.9	14.3	25.7	122 079	547	652.5	245.8	266.4	1 468	1 264
Cumberland, MD-WV	58.3	67.2	36.1	149.3	23.8	7.2	22.4	22 636	161	350.9	187.1	87.3	879	556
Dallas-Fort Worth-Arlington, TX	4 049.8	15 187.7	1 986.3	3 263.5	638.0	204.5	967.4	3 869 637	19 558	24 273.0	5 277.3	12 732.6	2 072	1 668
Dallas-Plano-Irving, TX Div	2 726.7	5 814.2	1 425.9	2 327.4	440.0	135.9	756.0	NA	NA	16 950.2	3 478.9	8 875.6	2 159	1 732
Fort Worth-Arlington, TX Div	1 323.1	9 373.6	560.4	936.1	198.0	68.6	211.4	NA	NA	7 322.8	1 798.4	3 857.0	1 897	1 538
Dalton, GA	31.9	13.1	10.1	75.1	22.7	11.8	0.9	12 379	101	458.4	197.7	150.6	1 124	582
Danville, IL	56.9	14.7	69.5	79.2	19.3	3.6	9.5	1 384	13	277.9	144.2	79.7	981	836
Danville, VA	23.4	0.9	8.6	171.4	18.4	8.8	11.8	17 442	160	306.8	176.9	92.7	877	606
Davenport-Moline-Rock Island, IA-IL	452.5	363.7	29.9	235.2	63.4	12.3	68.4	96 753	702	1 382.8	549.3	536.5	1 426	1 210
Dayton, OH	1 488.9	1 546.3	328.5	871.8	166.5	71.2	195.1	178 552	758	3 659.6	1 386.3	1 482.4	1 774	1 172
Decatur, AL	50.4	16.5	7.6	127.8	28.8	10.5	9.4	26 375	165	509.0	191.9	104.5	700	339
Decatur, IL	63.7	2.0	18.1	111.7	20.3	4.3	179.3	28 243	101	391.1	180.1	140.6	1 293	1 103
Deltona-Daytona Beach-Ormond Beach, FL	119.4	115.2	49.7	230.3	58.2	31.4	57.5	158 948	715	2 373.1	574.3	864.5	1 728	1 379
Denver-Aurora-Broomfield, CO	2 642.9	2 410.9	3 473.8	1 946.2	565.6	555.2	1 928.3	1 010 751	5 042	11 468.2	2 949.0	5 120.6	2 077	1 204
Des Moines-West Des Moines, IA	643.9	83.3	183.2	454.1	195.5	241.3	1 133.5	501 247	2 815	2 213.9	729.9	959.8	1 756	1 480
Detroit-Warren-Livonia, MI	2 388.3	2 718.6	1 375.8	4 764.8	915.4	348.0	1 126.4	595 845	3 210	20 217.9	8 914.1	6 850.1	1 533	1 368
Detroit-Livonia-Dearborn, MI Div	1 265.6	104.6	779.9	3 645.7	580.9	207.1	501.2	NA	NA	10 286.1	4 751.5	3 099.1	1 561	1 241
Warren-Troy-Farmington Hills, MI Div	1 122.7	2 614.0	595.9	1 119.0	334.5	140.9	625.3	NA	NA	9 931.8	4 162.6	3 751.0	1 511	1 469
Dothan, AL	45.3	12.9	10.0	151.4	26.7	12.7	12.5	53 401	321	601.3	168.0	106.8	766	243
Dover, DE	309.0	144.0	10.1	177.8	24.9	223.7	297.7	95 156	813	410.9	241.0	85.8	564	439
Dubuque, IA	35.9	3.8	5.3	77.2	14.0	3.3	28.3	69 095	548	300.1	111.3	128.9	1 395	1 009
Duluth, MN-WI	188.0	28.5	47.9	495.7	72.5	28.2	101.7	71 475	486	1 330.0	643.6	306.1	1 116	1 007
Durham-Chapel Hill, NC	417.5	142.6	891.2	2 120.9	73.3	67.3	977.5	327 475	1 913	1 863.9	910.1	672.6	1 402	1 125
Eau Claire, WI	85.0	21.9	11.4	182.0	25.8	10.8	15.4	53 634	357	595.2	283.0	211.9	1 343	1 232
El Centro, CA	178.5	47.7	59.2	199.4	50.0	23.2	20.8	17 870	102	1 139.1	670.3	166.9	1 031	684
Elizabethtown, KY	1 614.7	316.7	93.7	72.9	17.9	6.7	2.1	122 644	1 242	434.7	129.0	72.4	649	371
Elkhart-Goshen, IN	27.9	21.1	-6.4	103.4	21.7	5.2	14.1	35 051	234	585.9	266.7	200.5	1 013	835
Elmira, NY	36.0	2.0	7.9	143.0	26.0	6.1	19.8	11 868	76	422.5	199.0	150.5	1 710	1 109
El Paso, TX	3 576.5	958.0	360.1	892.5	190.6	57.3	171.8	617 293	4 549	2 916.2	1 424.5	895.6	1 219	955
Erie, PA	120.8	41.5	43.0	264.1	59.0	12.5	38.0	73 698	586	1 069.7	529.9	326.3	1 169	941
Eugene-Springfield, OR	163.3	29.0	45.5	481.3	53.8	48.9	125.5	108 902	550	1 336.0	563.3	401.7	1 169	991
Evansville, IN-KY	147.1	145.7	26.9	358.1	57.3	14.2	47.5	93 738	644	1 027.7	399.3	357.8	1 023	867
Fairbanks, AK	343.6	493.1	116.7	114.0	33.8	18.3	135.5	8 443	42	327.0	164.7	114.5	1 174	1 041
Fargo, ND-MN	211.1	72.0	194.5	134.8	31.2	8.1	103.0	152 811	1 318	687.5	252.6	234.1	1 217	1 010
Farmington, NM	106.8	1.2	79.4	196.6	23.1	38.8	10.4	43 935	273	501.8	314.6	117.3	958	569
Fayetteville, NC	9 438.9	1 230.5	77.3	339.3	73.0	44.0	41.5	400 551	3 609	1 031.7	550.7	305.2	875	656
Fayetteville-Springdale-Rogers, AR-MO	208.5	159.6	125.3	185.1	42.9	26.3	83.7	251 646	1 221	1 154.1	594.6	330.8	759	275

1. Based on the resident population estimated as of July 1 of the year shown.

	Local government finances, 2007 (cont.)									Government employment, 2009			Presidential election,[2] 2008		
	Direct general expenditure							Debt outstanding					Percent of vote cast:		
Area name			Percent of total for:												
	Total (mil dol)	Per capita[1] (dollars)	Educa-tion	Health and hospitals	Police protec-tion	Public welfare	High-ways	Total (mil dol)	Per capita[1] (dollars)	Federal civilian	Federal military	State and local	Demo-cratic	Republi-can	All other
	185	186	187	188	189	190	191	192	193	194	195	196	197	198	199
Charleston, WV	847.2	2 787	55.8	5.0	4.8	0.0	2.3	541.3	1 781	2 636	1 710	24 994	46.9	51.8	1.3
Charleston-North Charles-ton-Summerville, SC	2 017.4	3 202	48.2	0.9	6.7	0.3	3.0	4 766.3	7 564	8 570	12 716	48 890	48.7	50.1	1.3
Charlotte-Gastonia-Rock Hill, NC-SC	7 764.6	4 701	33.6	27.9	4.2	2.8	2.0	10 865.6	6 579	7 232	4 879	109 698	51.4	47.8	0.8
Charlottesville, VA	625.9	3 247	52.0	3.2	5.2	6.6	1.1	476.2	2 470	1 478	950	30 822	59.2	39.6	1.2
Chattanooga, TN-GA	1 815.0	3 527	35.2	26.7	5.4	1.3	2.8	1 825.0	3 547	5 886	1 764	30 009	38.5	60.4	1.2
Cheyenne, WY	565.4	6 548	41.9	29.9	2.9	0.3	4.0	169.5	1 963	2 692	3 468	11 230	38.6	59.0	2.4
Chicago-Joliet-Naperville, IL-IN-WI	44 542.0	4 676	42.7	3.8	7.0	1.4	4.2	64 743.2	6 797	58 673	37 407	519 027	67.2	31.7	1.1
Chicago-Joliet-Naperville, IL Div	37 373.2	4 700	41.3	3.6	7.3	1.1	4.3	58 210.7	7 320	50 600	16 349	436 166	68.7	30.2	1.1
Gary, IN Div	3 159.2	4 520	43.8	7.6	5.2	4.4	2.3	2 856.6	4 087	2 024	2 366	36 223	61.7	37.3	1.0
Lake County-Kenosha County, IL-WI Div	4 009.6	4 592	54.7	2.4	5.8	1.9	4.3	3 675.9	4 210	6 049	18 692	46 638	59.0	39.7	1.2
Chico, CA	1 112.9	5 087	41.0	5.4	4.3	12.0	2.7	441.7	2 019	571	363	14 417	49.8	47.5	2.7
Cincinnati-Middletown, OH-KY-IN	8 496.8	3 982	42.4	4.2	5.8	7.3	3.9	12 281.8	5 756	17 086	5 993	119 174	42.6	56.2	1.2
Clarksville, TN-KY	565.4	2 159	52.4	1.6	6.2	0.1	4.4	8 398.1	32 076	6 232	32 818	13 089	43.0	55.9	1.1
Cleveland, TN	266.2	2 306	49.8	11.4	7.6	0.2	5.5	250.4	2 253	308	383	5 443	25.7	72.9	1.4
Cleveland-Elyria-Mentor, OH	10 918.1	5 208	38.9	11.4	5.4	4.6	3.5	12 728.5	6 071	19 024	5 970	122 142	61.9	36.8	1.3
Coeur d'Alene, ID	541.9	4 031	32.3	34.0	3.6	0.5	4.0	219.9	1 636	594	546	9 198	35.7	62.0	2.3
College Station-Bryan, TX	611.2	3 005	53.8	1.9	5.3	0.4	4.6	872.2	4 289	1 000	585	33 419	35.0	60.8	1.1
Colorado Springs, CO	2 508.2	4 118	43.3	16.5	5.4	1.8	4.4	3 894.9	6 395	12 009	35 353	36 299	39.6	58.9	1.5
Columbia, MO	495.0	3 050	48.1	2.2	4.3	1.5	7.1	543.3	3 347	2 236	719	28 981	54.5	43.9	1.6
Columbia, SC	2 597.8	3 628	53.2	19.9	4.2	0.1	1.0	2 873.8	4 014	10 260	14 571	69 800	49.9	49.1	1.0
Columbus, GA-AL	928.5	3 284	52.8	6.0	5.2	1.7	3.7	879.4	3 110	5 885	22 327	17 849	53.8	45.7	0.5
Columbus, IN	413.6	5 533	28.0	41.7	2.3	1.9	2.1	184.1	2 463	208	256	6 253	43.7	55.0	1.3
Columbus, OH	8 067.9	4 599	41.3	7.3	6.2	4.8	3.9	9 305.9	5 305	14 035	5 321	151 599	52.3	46.3	1.4
Corpus Christi, TX	1 531.8	3 697	52.3	5.3	5.7	0.2	4.0	1 743.5	4 208	6 722	4 996	27 252	45.1	54.0	0.9
Corvallis, OR	227.5	2 794	43.3	9.9	8.6	0.0	4.9	279.5	3 432	596	289	13 216	64.3	32.8	2.8
Crestview-Fort Walton Beach-Destin, FL	652.0	3 592	50.0	1.8	7.1	0.3	4.7	355.6	1 959	7 149	15 029	8 050	27.1	72.0	0.9
Cumberland, MD-WV	356.2	3 586	58.7	1.8	2.8	6.1	3.4	185.0	1 863	624	356	7 788	35.0	63.0	2.0
Dallas-Fort Worth-Arlington, TX	23 865.9	3 884	46.8	8.9	5.5	0.2	4.7	52 759.4	8 586	46 150	17 789	338 495	44.5	54.6	0.8
Dallas-Plano-Irving, TX Div	16 867.6	4 103	45.6	8.5	5.3	0.2	4.9	36 914.4	8 978	31 368	11 834	232 970	46.6	52.6	0.8
Fort Worth-Arlington, TX Div	6 998.3	3 441	47.8	10.0	6.2	0.1	4.3	15 845.1	7 792	14 782	5 955	105 525	40.5	58.6	0.9
Dalton, GA	471.5	3 618	53.5	9.6	3.7	0.2	4.6	316.0	2 358	295	414	6 959	28.7	70.2	1.2
Danville, IL	256.8	3 163	54.1	1.5	6.1	3.3	6.8	94.9	1 168	1 540	160	4 550	49.4	48.8	1.7
Danville, VA	293.0	2 770	51.7	0.5	5.4	8.9	3.1	259.0	2 448	253	360	6 733	46.3	52.8	0.9
Davenport-Moline-Rock Island, IA-IL	1 368.0	3 637	49.8	4.7	6.2	1.4	5.2	928.7	2 469	6 997	1 396	20 164	58.0	40.8	1.3
Dayton, OH	3 498.8	4 187	47.0	3.9	7.0	6.0	4.5	3 117.3	3 731	17 140	7 041	48 390	47.0	51.5	1.5
Decatur, AL	533.1	3 571	43.9	19.2	5.2	0.4	3.2	637.0	4 267	387	734	8 355	29.2	69.4	1.3
Decatur, IL	379.7	3 492	50.8	2.2	6.6	0.3	7.8	200.6	1 845	318	226	5 963	49.8	48.7	1.5
Deltona-Daytona Beach-Ormond Beach, FL	2 294.2	4 585	36.0	21.7	6.6	0.5	3.7	3 233.2	6 461	1 432	1 021	20 929	52.4	46.7	0.9
Denver-Aurora-Broomfield, CO	11 502.8	4 667	33.5	6.9	5.7	3.1	4.5	24 034.4	9 751	28 298	9 337	154 526	57.7	40.7	1.6
Des Moines-West Des Moines, IA	2 310.0	4 226	49.8	7.5	4.4	1.1	5.6	2 610.0	4 775	5 666	2 503	37 265	54.1	44.2	1.8
Detroit-Warren-Livonia, MI	20 226.1	4 527	46.8	4.7	6.1	2.9	4.5	28 206.6	6 314	29 187	9 072	190 677	62.0	36.5	1.5
Detroit-Livonia-Dearborn, MI Div	10 151.2	5 114	39.6	3.2	6.4	4.6	3.5	17 567.5	8 850	15 921	4 023	94 406	74.1	24.7	1.2
Warren-Troy-Farmington Hills, MI Div	10 074.8	4 058	54.1	6.2	5.8	1.1	5.4	10 639.1	4 286	13 266	5 049	96 271	53.7	44.6	1.7
Dothan, AL	602.5	4 319	31.7	40.5	4.4	1.6	4.3	441.8	3 167	458	693	10 413	28.0	71.3	0.7
Dover, DE	421.6	2 769	68.9	0.9	5.1	0.0	1.8	243.8	1 601	1 721	4 275	16 860	54.4	44.6	1.1
Dubuque, IA	294.8	3 192	47.5	4.1	5.2	2.1	9.1	144.0	1 559	263	410	4 326	59.7	38.9	1.5
Duluth, MN-WI	1 357.6	4 949	34.9	9.3	5.2	8.0	9.0	1 399.6	5 102	1 723	1 126	23 540	64.9	32.9	2.2
Durham-Chapel Hill, NC	1 883.6	3 927	36.3	5.0	5.3	19.6	1.9	1 603.3	3 343	5 784	1 519	53 908	69.7	29.4	0.9
Eau Claire, WI	603.2	3 822	51.8	5.0	4.8	5.9	10.3	893.1	5 659	600	462	11 024	57.9	40.4	1.6
El Centro, CA	1 068.8	6 603	47.6	16.7	3.8	7.4	2.8	843.5	5 211	2 474	517	15 525	62.2	36.1	1.7
Elizabethtown, KY	419.1	3 755	34.9	45.8	2.1	0.1	2.1	357.2	3 200	5 419	9 216	7 000	38.0	60.8	1.2
Elkhart-Goshen, IN	815.9	4 122	53.1	1.4	3.8	2.4	2.6	702.5	3 549	295	674	8 353	43.9	55.1	0.9
Elmira, NY	429.2	4 877	43.9	2.8	3.2	18.3	6.8	316.2	3 593	309	144	6 909	48.8	50.0	1.1
El Paso, TX	2 885.0	3 927	57.2	12.5	4.4	0.3	2.0	3 658.4	4 980	11 664	20 802	53 546	65.9	33.4	0.8
Erie, PA	1 050.1	3 763	47.5	8.1	2.5	8.8	2.8	1 590.5	5 699	1 653	785	16 003	59.3	39.4	1.2
Eugene-Springfield, OR	1 242.2	3 615	45.9	4.6	6.9	2.5	5.0	1 385.2	4 031	1 743	1 059	27 052	62.3	34.9	2.8
Evansville, IN-KY	1 134.3	3 243	43.5	1.4	4.9	2.1	3.7	1 566.4	4 479	1 455	1 176	16 963	47.9	51.0	1.1
Fairbanks, AK	291.2	2 987	60.0	1.2	2.8	0.0	3.6	185.0	1 898	3 477	9 411	8 000	0.0	0.0	0.0
Fargo, ND-MN	707.0	3 674	41.0	1.8	4.4	4.0	11.2	1 269.6	6 598	2 125	1 309	14 587	53.9	44.2	1.8
Farmington, NM	519.0	4 239	59.6	0.9	5.4	1.2	4.5	941.0	7 686	1 548	334	9 931	38.8	59.9	1.3
Fayetteville, NC	1 031.1	2 955	52.4	4.3	6.8	8.7	1.5	565.1	1 620	12 727	53 456	25 735	58.6	40.8	0.6
Fayetteville-Springdale-Rog-ers, AR-MO	1 243.2	2 853	57.0	1.9	4.8	0.0	7.2	1 666.4	3 824	2 547	2 222	25 519	35.8	62.0	2.1

1. Based on the resident population estimated as of July 1 of the year shown.   2. © 2009 Election Data Services, Inc. All rights reserved.

Table C. Metropolitan Areas — Land Area and Population

CBSA code[1]	Area name	Land area,[2] 2010 (sq km)	Total persons	Rank	Per square kilometer	White	Black	American Indian, Alaska Native	Asian and Pacific Islander	Percent Hispanic or Latino[3]	Under 5 years	5 to 17 years	18 to 24 years	25 to 34 years	35 to 44 years	45 to 54 years
		1	2	3	4	5	6	7	8	9	10	11	12	13	14	15
22380	Flagstaff, AZ	48 223	134 421	289	2.8	57.1	1.6	27.7	2.1	13.5	6.7	17.0	17.7	13.5	11.5	13.4
22420	Flint, MI...............................	1 650	425 790	115	258.1	74.7	21.8	1.3	1.3	3.0	6.4	18.6	8.9	11.8	12.9	15.3
22500	Florence, SC.........................	3 525	205 566	206	58.3	55.3	41.8	0.7	1.1	2.0	6.6	17.9	9.4	12.0	12.9	14.4
22520	Florence-Muscle Shoals, AL	3 264	147 137	268	45.1	84.5	12.8	1.0	0.8	2.2	5.6	16.1	9.9	11.1	12.5	14.6
22540	Fond du Lac, WI..................	1 864	101 633	341	54.5	92.9	1.7	0.8	1.4	4.3	5.9	16.8	9.1	12.1	12.7	15.6
22660	Fort Collins-Loveland, CO ...	6 724	299 630	156	44.6	86.1	1.2	1.0	2.8	10.6	5.9	15.5	13.9	14.1	12.2	14.2
22900	Fort Smith, AR-OK..............	10 350	298 592	158	28.8	79.7	4.2	9.2	2.7	8.2	7.0	18.5	9.0	12.2	12.8	14.4
23060	Fort Wayne, IN	3 525	416 257	121	118.1	81.3	11.2	0.8	2.9	5.8	7.3	19.4	9.2	12.9	12.8	14.4
23420	Fresno, CA...........................	15 431	930 450	55	60.3	34.2	5.4	1.2	10.4	50.3	8.5	21.3	11.7	14.3	12.3	12.4
23460	Gadsden, AL.........................	1 386	104 430	338	75.3	80.5	15.6	0.9	0.8	3.3	5.9	17.1	8.5	11.5	13.4	14.3
23540	Gainesville, FL......................	3 172	264 275	173	83.3	67.0	20.0	0.7	5.9	8.2	5.3	12.8	22.5	14.6	10.4	12.1
23580	Gainesville, GA....................	1 017	179 684	226	176.7	64.6	7.6	0.5	2.1	26.1	7.9	20.1	9.3	13.4	14.3	13.5
24020	Glens Falls, NY....................	4 398	128 923	298	29.3	95.3	2.2	0.7	0.8	2.0	5.1	15.7	8.1	11.1	13.1	16.4
24140	Goldsboro, NC......................	1 432	122 623	311	85.6	57.1	32.1	0.7	1.8	9.9	7.1	17.7	10.0	13.2	12.6	14.5
24220	Grand Forks, ND-MN..........	8 825	98 461	345	11.2	90.9	2.1	3.0	2.1	3.7	6.5	14.7	17.9	13.5	10.5	13.3
24300	Grand Junction, CO............	8 622	146 723	269	17.0	84.6	0.9	1.3	1.3	13.3	6.8	16.7	9.9	13.1	11.4	14.3
24340	Grand Rapids-Wyoming, MI	7 212	774 160	69	107.3	81.3	8.9	1.0	2.4	8.4	7.1	18.8	10.1	13.4	12.8	14.8
24500	Great Falls, MT....................	6 988	81 327	360	11.6	90.3	1.9	6.0	1.7	3.3	6.8	16.1	10.1	12.8	11.1	14.7
24540	Greeley, CO.........................	10 327	252 825	179	24.5	68.9	1.1	1.1	1.7	28.4	7.9	19.9	11.0	13.8	13.7	13.5
24580	Green Bay, WI.....................	4 844	306 241	153	63.2	87.5	2.4	2.8	2.6	6.2	6.7	17.9	9.2	13.1	13.2	15.6
24660	Greensboro-High Point, NC.	5 164	723 801	71	140.2	63.4	26.3	1.0	3.4	7.6	6.2	17.3	10.4	12.5	13.9	14.6
24780	Greenville, NC.....................	2 377	189 510	220	79.7	57.2	35.1	0.7	1.9	6.5	6.7	15.9	17.3	14.4	12.4	12.8
24860	Greenville-Mauldin-Easley, SC..	5 168	636 986	83	123.3	74.5	17.3	0.6	2.1	6.7	6.6	16.8	11.2	12.8	13.4	14.3
25060	Gulfport-Biloxi, MS.............	3 867	248 820	186	64.3	73.1	20.0	1.1	3.1	4.7	7.1	17.2	10.4	13.6	12.6	14.8
25180	Hagerstown-Martinsburg, MD-WV	2 611	269 140	172	103.1	87.1	9.2	0.7	1.6	3.4	6.3	17.3	8.0	12.8	14.3	15.4
25260	Hanford-Corcoran, CA.........	3 599	152 982	259	42.5	37.1	7.5	1.3	4.9	50.9	8.4	19.4	11.6	16.7	14.3	13.3
25420	Harrisburg-Carlisle, PA........	4 201	549 475	93	130.8	82.2	11.0	0.5	3.4	4.7	5.9	16.3	9.4	12.4	13.0	15.4
25500	Harrisonburg, VA	2 244	125 228	306	55.8	85.2	4.0	0.4	2.3	9.4	5.6	14.7	21.6	11.6	11.1	12.5
25540	Hartford-West Hartford-East Hartford, CT.................	3 923	1 212 381	45	309.0	72.9	10.9	0.5	4.5	12.5	5.4	16.8	9.6	11.7	13.3	16.1
25620	Hattiesburg, MS...................	4 171	142 842	274	34.2	67.8	28.8	0.6	1.1	2.8	7.3	17.5	13.4	15.0	12.4	12.8
25860	Hickory-Lenoir-Morganton, NC...	4 241	365 497	140	86.2	83.9	7.6	0.6	2.8	6.3	5.9	17.1	8.2	11.2	14.1	15.2
25980	Hinesville-Fort Stewart, GA.	2 305	77 917	361	33.8	48.4	40.1	1.2	3.4	10.2	10.1	20.2	13.3	16.4	12.5	12.6
26100	Holland-Grand Haven, MI....	1 459	263 801	174	180.8	87.1	1.9	0.7	3.1	8.6	6.7	19.3	12.8	11.7	12.6	14.2
26180	Honolulu, HI.........................	1 556	953 207	53	612.6	32.3	3.0	1.5	79.7	8.1	6.4	15.7	10.3	14.1	13.1	13.8
26300	Hot Springs, AR...................	1 755	96 024	351	54.7	85.8	8.7	1.4	1.1	4.8	5.6	15.3	7.6	10.8	11.4	14.0
26380	Houma-Bayou Cane-Thibo-daux, LA..........................	5 957	208 178	205	34.9	74.4	16.9	5.3	1.2	3.9	7.2	18.2	10.3	13.6	12.9	14.9
26420	Houston-Sugar Land-Bay-town, TX.............................	22 863	5 946 800	6	260.1	40.7	17.3	0.6	7.1	35.3	7.9	20.0	9.6	15.1	14.5	14.0
26580	Huntington-Ashland, WV-KY-OH	4 519	287 702	161	63.7	95.5	3.4	0.7	0.8	0.9	5.9	15.7	9.2	12.4	13.0	14.4
26620	Huntsville, AL......................	3 526	417 593	120	118.4	70.4	22.4	1.5	2.9	4.8	6.3	17.5	9.9	13.2	13.5	16.0
26820	Idaho Falls, ID	7 665	130 374	295	17.0	87.0	0.8	1.0	1.3	11.2	9.8	22.5	8.4	14.5	11.5	12.6
26900	Indianapolis-Carmel, IN	9 983	1 756 241	34	175.9	76.2	15.9	0.6	2.8	6.2	7.3	18.9	8.9	14.2	14.1	14.8
26980	Iowa City, IA	3 064	152 586	260	49.8	86.1	4.9	0.6	5.2	4.8	6.2	14.4	19.4	16.3	11.5	12.0
27060	Ithaca, NY...........................	1 229	101 564	342	82.6	82.7	4.9	0.9	9.8	4.2	4.3	12.1	26.2	13.5	10.2	11.8
27100	Jackson, MI..........................	1 817	160 248	247	88.2	87.9	9.2	1.0	1.0	3.0	5.9	17.3	9.3	11.6	13.2	15.6
27140	Jackson, MS.........................	9 651	539 057	96	55.9	48.9	48.0	0.4	1.3	2.1	7.2	18.9	10.0	14.0	13.0	14.2
27180	Jackson, TN.........................	2 183	115 425	321	52.9	63.4	32.9	0.5	1.1	3.2	6.6	17.3	11.7	12.3	12.3	14.3
27260	Jacksonville, FL	8 291	1 345 596	40	162.3	67.5	22.2	0.8	4.4	6.9	6.5	17.3	9.6	13.4	13.6	15.2
27340	Jacksonville, NC...................	1 975	177 772	227	90.0	71.8	16.7	1.3	3.4	10.1	9.6	15.7	23.0	16.3	10.5	10.2
27500	Janesville, WI.......................	1 860	160 331	246	86.2	86.2	5.9	0.7	1.4	7.6	6.5	18.5	8.6	12.6	13.3	15.0
27620	Jefferson City, MO...............	5 822	149 807	266	25.7	89.1	8.1	0.9	1.2	2.1	6.4	17.1	9.7	13.1	13.3	15.3
27740	Johnson City, TN.................	2 211	198 716	214	89.9	93.4	3.4	0.7	1.1	2.6	5.4	14.8	10.5	11.9	13.2	14.6
27780	Johnstown, PA......................	1 783	143 679	272	80.6	94.3	4.3	0.3	0.7	1.4	5.0	14.6	9.3	10.5	12.0	15.3
27860	Jonesboro, AR......................	3 796	121 026	312	31.9	82.8	12.6	0.8	1.2	4.0	7.1	17.7	12.1	13.8	12.5	12.9
27900	Joplin, MO...........................	3 272	175 518	230	53.6	89.2	2.2	3.3	1.9	6.0	7.3	18.3	9.9	12.9	12.3	13.8
28020	Kalamazoo-Portage, MI........	3 028	326 589	148	107.9	83.0	10.7	1.3	2.3	5.4	6.3	17.1	13.3	12.8	12.0	14.0
28100	Kankakee-Bradley, IL	1 752	113 449	324	64.8	74.7	16.0	0.6	1.2	9.0	6.8	18.6	10.2	12.5	12.5	14.3
28140	Kansas City, MO-KS............	20 273	2 035 334	29	100.4	76.3	13.4	1.2	3.0	8.2	7.2	18.5	8.3	14.0	13.5	14.9
28420	Kennewick-Pasco-Richland, WA...............	7 621	253 340	178	33.2	66.6	1.9	1.3	3.3	28.7	8.4	20.9	9.4	14.1	12.6	13.2
28660	Killeen-Temple-Fort Hood, TX..	7 293	405 300	127	55.6	56.7	20.4	1.3	4.5	20.3	9.0	19.2	12.3	16.9	12.9	12.2
28700	Kingsport-Bristol-Bristol, TN-VA..................................	5 206	309 544	151	59.5	96.0	2.3	0.7	0.7	1.3	5.3	15.4	7.6	10.7	13.4	15.2
28740	Kingston, NY........................	2 912	182 493	224	62.7	83.5	6.6	0.9	2.2	8.7	4.9	15.2	10.0	10.9	13.2	16.8
28940	Knoxville, TN........................	4 809	698 030	75	145.2	88.3	7.1	0.8	1.8	3.4	5.9	16.0	10.1	12.6	13.2	14.6

1. CBSA = Core Based Statistical Area. DIV = Metropolitan Division. See Appendix A for explanation. See Appendix B for list of metropolitan areas identified by type. 2. Dry land or land partially or temporarily covered by water. 3. May be of any race.

Table C. Metropolitan Areas — **Population and Households**

Area name	Population, 2010 (cont.) Age (percent) (cont.)				Population change and components of change, 1990–2010							Households, 2010				
					Total persons		Percent change		Components of change, 2000–2009						Percent	
	55 to 64 years	65 to 74 years	75 years and over	Percent female	1990	2000	1990–2000	2000–2010	Births	Deaths	Net migration	Number	Percent change, 2000–2010	Persons per household	Female family householder[1]	One person
	16	17	18	19	20	21	22	23	24	25	26	27	28	29	30	31
Flagstaff, AZ	11.4	5.5	3.3	50.4	96 591	116 320	20.4	15.6	18 473	5 751	1 515	46 711	15.5	2.69	12.7	24.5
Flint, MI	12.4	7.3	6.4	51.8	430 459	436 141	1.3	-2.4	56 689	36 619	-29 759	169 202	-0.4	2.48	17.2	28.4
Florence, SC	13.3	7.9	5.6	52.9	176 195	193 155	9.6	6.4	25 826	19 094	1 971	79 184	8.6	2.54	19.9	26.2
Florence-Muscle Shoals, AL	13.1	9.4	7.6	52.1	131 327	142 950	8.9	2.9	14 757	14 528	1 977	61 453	5.0	2.36	12.7	28.9
Fond du Lac, WI	12.9	7.4	7.6	50.9	90 083	97 296	8.0	4.5	10 853	8 492	1 036	40 697	10.2	2.41	8.5	27.6
Fort Collins-Loveland, CO	12.3	6.6	5.2	50.4	186 136	251 494	35.1	19.1	31 991	14 535	30 632	120 295	23.8	2.42	8.2	25.9
Fort Smith, AR-OK	12.1	8.0	6.0	50.6	234 078	273 170	16.7	9.3	38 232	25 896	9 343	115 169	10.2	2.55	12.5	25.9
Fort Wayne, IN	11.8	6.4	5.9	51.1	354 435	390 156	10.1	6.7	56 366	29 234	-483	161 632	7.1	2.53	12.5	27.5
Fresno, CA	9.5	5.3	4.7	50.0	667 479	799 407	19.8	16.4	146 819	54 132	29 307	289 391	14.4	3.15	16.9	19.8
Gadsden, AL	13.5	8.7	7.1	51.5	99 840	103 459	3.6	0.9	11 815	12 376	1 411	42 036	1.0	2.43	14.3	28.1
Gainesville, FL	11.1	6.1	5.0	51.3	191 263	232 392	21.5	13.7	26 494	16 163	19 343	106 637	15.2	2.34	12.7	29.8
Gainesville, GA	10.5	6.4	4.7	50.1	95 434	139 277	45.9	29.0	28 238	10 211	30 157	60 691	28.1	2.91	12.4	20.3
Glens Falls, NY	14.2	8.7	7.6	49.7	118 539	124 345	4.9	3.7	11 884	11 189	4 474	52 132	8.2	2.40	10.9	27.4
Goldsboro, NC	11.8	7.4	5.7	51.1	104 666	113 329	8.3	8.2	16 239	9 836	-5 293	47 831	12.2	2.50	16.7	27.4
Grand Forks, ND-MN	11.1	6.1	6.3	49.0	103 272	97 478	-5.6	1.0	11 833	7 311	-4 295	40 121	7.0	2.32	9.1	31.5
Grand Junction, CO	12.9	7.8	7.1	50.3	93 145	116 255	24.8	26.2	16 500	11 505	24 757	58 095	26.8	2.46	10.0	26.5
Grand Rapids-Wyoming, MI	11.3	6.1	5.5	50.5	645 918	740 482	14.6	4.5	107 069	50 831	-14 389	290 340	6.7	2.60	12.0	25.3
Great Falls, MT	12.7	8.2	7.4	50.1	77 691	80 357	3.4	1.2	10 392	7 008	-3 770	33 809	3.9	2.33	10.2	30.5
Greeley, CO	10.6	5.6	4.0	50.0	131 821	180 936	37.3	39.7	35 157	11 616	51 045	89 349	41.3	2.76	9.9	21.5
Green Bay, WI	11.9	6.6	5.9	50.3	243 698	282 599	16.0	8.4	36 752	19 691	7 101	122 037	12.1	2.45	9.5	27.2
Greensboro-High Point, NC	12.0	7.2	6.0	52.0	540 041	643 430	19.1	12.5	83 177	53 780	46 084	290 694	13.4	2.43	14.4	28.6
Greenville, NC	10.5	5.7	4.5	52.1	123 864	152 772	23.3	24.0	21 945	11 783	17 712	74 890	26.4	2.41	15.8	29.6
Greenville-Mauldin-Easley, SC	11.9	7.4	5.7	51.2	472 155	559 940	18.6	13.8	73 909	46 845	55 956	247 284	13.9	2.49	13.4	26.6
Gulfport-Biloxi, MS	11.8	7.3	5.1	50.3	207 875	246 190	18.4	1.1	33 202	21 143	-18 654	95 021	2.0	2.54	16.3	26.1
Hagerstown-Martinsburg, MD-WV	12.5	7.4	6.0	49.7	192 774	222 771	15.6	20.8	29 379	20 663	35 740	102 845	20.4	2.52	11.8	25.3
Hanford-Corcoran, CA	8.4	4.5	3.4	43.8	101 469	129 461	27.6	18.2	23 111	7 167	4 022	41 233	19.8	3.19	15.9	17.5
Harrisburg-Carlisle, PA	13.2	7.6	7.0	51.2	474 242	509 074	7.3	7.9	57 253	45 117	18 840	222 281	9.8	2.38	11.3	29.3
Harrisonburg, VA	10.2	6.5	6.2	51.9	88 189	108 193	22.7	15.7	12 968	7 915	6 558	45 165	17.3	2.57	9.5	24.4
Hartford-West Hartford-East Hartford, CT	12.6	7.2	7.1	51.3	1 123 678	1 148 618	2.2	5.6	126 416	93 499	21 963	472 533	6.0	2.46	13.1	28.1
Hattiesburg, MS	10.2	6.5	5.0	51.9	109 603	123 812	13.0	15.4	18 890	10 689	11 740	54 962	19.5	2.53	16.3	26.9
Hickory-Lenoir-Morganton, NC	13.2	8.6	6.4	50.5	292 405	341 851	16.9	6.9	41 159	30 597	14 376	144 504	7.9	2.47	12.2	26.1
Hinesville-Fort Stewart, GA	8.5	4.2	2.2	51.1	58 947	71 914	22.0	8.3	14 148	3 281	-8 113	27 178	18.4	2.76	20.9	21.0
Holland-Grand Haven, MI	10.9	6.3	5.5	51.0	187 768	238 314	26.9	10.7	38 235	14 084	6 089	90 775	14.8	2.73	8.4	20.9
Honolulu, HI	12.0	7.2	7.3	49.9	836 231	876 156	4.8	8.8	122 222	59 029	-26 320	311 047	8.6	2.95	12.7	22.8
Hot Springs, AR	14.3	11.3	9.6	51.5	76 897	88 068	20.0	9.0	10 300	11 827	12 329	40 994	8.4	2.29	11.9	29.6
Houma-Bayou Cane-Thibodaux, LA	11.1	6.7	5.1	50.6	182 842	194 477	6.4	7.0	27 059	15 048	-2 341	75 577	11.1	2.71	14.8	22.0
Houston-Sugar Land-Baytown, TX	10.3	5.1	3.5	50.3	3 767 218	4 715 407	25.2	26.1	836 254	284 187	543 202	2 072 625	25.1	2.83	14.3	23.5
Huntington-Ashland, WV-KY-OH	13.4	8.9	7.3	51.1	288 189	288 649	0.2	-0.3	31 446	31 325	-1 507	118 002	0.3	2.37	12.3	28.9
Huntsville, AL	11.4	7.0	5.2	50.6	293 047	342 376	16.8	22.0	43 836	27 093	46 719	166 146	23.4	2.45	12.5	27.8
Idaho Falls, ID	10.1	5.8	4.8	50.1	88 750	101 677	14.6	28.2	20 440	7 114	11 725	44 775	29.2	2.88	9.6	21.1
Indianapolis-Carmel, IN	10.9	6.0	4.9	51.2	1 294 217	1 525 104	17.8	15.2	234 754	117 029	101 123	680 257	14.4	2.53	13.5	27.0
Iowa City, IA	10.4	5.2	4.7	50.1	115 731	131 676	13.8	15.9	17 017	7 135	10 261	61 456	17.9	2.35	7.6	30.0
Ithaca, NY	11.1	5.6	5.1	50.7	94 097	96 501	2.6	5.2	8 394	5 464	2 986	38 967	7.0	2.27	8.7	33.3
Jackson, MI	12.9	7.4	6.7	49.0	149 756	158 422	5.8	1.2	19 051	14 022	-2 727	60 771	4.5	2.48	13.3	27.1
Jackson, MS	11.4	6.3	5.0	52.3	446 941	497 197	11.2	8.4	74 387	41 467	13 184	201 054	11.4	2.60	19.8	26.4
Jackson, TN	12.0	7.3	6.1	52.4	90 801	107 377	18.3	7.5	14 330	9 587	2 142	44 281	7.4	2.48	17.2	27.1
Jacksonville, FL	12.2	6.9	5.2	51.3	925 213	1 122 750	21.4	19.8	164 281	96 090	142 734	524 146	21.2	2.52	14.8	26.0
Jacksonville, NC	7.3	4.5	3.0	46.4	149 838	150 355	0.3	18.2	30 997	7 500	-537	60 092	24.9	2.66	13.1	20.3
Janesville, WI	11.8	7.2	6.4	50.8	139 510	152 307	9.2	5.3	19 132	12 368	2 074	62 905	7.3	2.50	12.3	26.3
Jefferson City, MO	12.4	6.8	5.9	48.9	120 704	140 052	16.0	7.0	17 303	11 045	2 013	56 915	10.2	2.45	10.5	27.7
Johnson City, TN	13.4	9.2	7.0	51.1	160 390	181 607	13.2	9.4	19 720	19 304	16 216	83 245	10.7	2.31	11.1	29.4
Johnstown, PA	14.4	8.8	10.0	50.6	163 062	152 598	-6.4	-5.8	13 878	17 463	-4 074	58 950	-2.6	2.30	10.9	31.2
Jonesboro, AR	11.0	7.2	5.7	51.2	93 620	107 762	15.1	12.3	15 161	10 365	8 155	47 045	11.1	2.49	14.2	26.5
Joplin, MO	11.5	7.6	6.4	50.9	134 910	157 322	16.6	11.6	23 406	15 109	9 645	67 660	9.9	2.54	11.7	26.0
Kalamazoo-Portage, MI	11.9	6.7	5.9	50.9	293 471	314 866	7.3	3.7	38 988	24 089	-1 017	129 538	6.6	2.45	11.9	28.3
Kankakee-Bradley, IL	11.8	7.0	6.4	50.9	96 255	103 833	7.9	9.3	14 630	9 961	3 934	41 511	8.7	2.61	14.7	25.5
Kansas City, MO-KS	11.6	6.4	5.6	51.0	1 636 527	1 836 038	12.2	10.9	269 663	142 839	67 416	799 637	11.4	2.51	12.4	27.8
Kennewick-Pasco-Richland, WA	11.0	5.8	4.5	49.5	150 033	191 822	27.9	32.1	33 939	12 437	33 174	88 549	30.8	2.82	11.7	22.2
Killeen-Temple-Fort Hood, TX	8.7	5.0	3.8	50.6	268 820	330 714	23.0	22.6	62 890	20 544	5 307	144 119	28.7	2.68	14.4	23.4
Kingsport-Bristol-Bristol, TN-VA	14.3	10.3	7.9	51.3	275 678	298 484	8.3	3.7	30 085	32 312	11 251	130 138	4.9	2.33	11.1	28.4
Kingston, NY	14.0	7.9	6.9	50.2	165 380	177 749	7.5	2.7	16 887	14 309	2 250	71 049	5.3	2.40	11.4	29.0
Knoxville, TN	12.9	8.2	6.5	51.4	534 910	616 079	15.2	13.3	74 459	58 306	63 870	284 984	12.6	2.39	11.3	28.1

1. No spouse present.

Items 16—31

Table C. Metropolitan Areas — Population, Vital Statistics, Medicare, and Crime

Area name	Persons in group quarters, 2010	Daytime population, 2010 Number	Employ-ment/ residence ratio	Births, average 2006–2008 Total	Rate[1]	Deaths, average 2006–2008 Number	Rate[1]	Persons under 65 with no health insurance 2009 Number	Percent	Medicare, 2011 Enrolled in original Medicare	Enrolled in Medicare Advantage	Enrolled in a Medicare prescription drug plan	Serious crimes known to police,[2] 2010 Total Number	Rate[3]
	32	33	34	35	36	37	38	39	40	41	42	43	44	45
Flagstaff, AZ..................	8 834	136 096	1.03	2 061	16.2	663	5.2	23 124	19.5	14 479	1 759	6 701	4 924	3 663
Flint, MI	5 973	411 950	0.91	5 936	13.6	3 973	9.1	43 547	12.1	77 596	20 529	22 788	18 447	4 413
Florence, SC	4 573	D	D	2 840	14.3	2 103	10.6	31 186	18.7	37 145	2 606	19 915	11 027	5 364
Florence-Muscle Shoals, AL.	2 365	D	D	1 659	11.6	1 632	11.4	18 928	16.2	31 779	2 625	14 902	3 808	2 588
Fond du Lac, WI	3 589	96 706	0.90	1 203	12.1	931	9.4	7 762	9.3	17 770	6 935	5 479	1 922	1 891
Fort Collins-Loveland, CO ...	8 530	293 587	0.95	3 485	12.2	1 611	5.6	40 094	15.5	42 554	10 156	14 283	8 435	2 815
Fort Smith, AR-OK..............	5 254	300 115	1.00	4 024	13.9	2 886	10.0	54 547	22.1	55 788	12 385	24 520	10 174	3 416
Fort Wayne, IN.................	7 015	424 267	1.05	D	D	3 192	7.8	57 386	16.2	63 781	24 789	25 683	11 792	2 997
Fresno, CA......................	17 523	940 473	1.02	16 978	18.9	6 014	6.7	175 794	21.7	112 620	29 175	48 856	44 374	4 769
Gadsden, AL	2 085	D	D	1 272	12.3	1 373	13.3	14 486	17.1	22 745	3 571	8 503	4 581	4 387
Gainesville, FL	15 048	278 306	1.10	2 887	11.4	1 800	7.1	45 610	20.3	36 101	3 474	14 779	10 940	4 187
Gainesville, GA	3 141	D	D	3 128	17.4	1 153	6.4	42 755	25.9	25 665	6 164	10 352	4 841	2 694
Glens Falls, NY	3 902	D	D	1 273	9.9	1 187	9.2	13 224	12.6	26 021	8 582	7 204	2 160	1 675
Goldsboro, NC	3 219	D	D	1 783	15.7	1 069	9.4	16 802	17.5	20 566	1 181	10 070	5 601	4 673
Grand Forks, ND-MN...........	5 546	101 617	1.04	D	D	800	8.2	9 214	11.2	14 252	3 078	7 846	2 389	2 426
Grand Junction, CO	3 631	D	D	1 997	14.4	1 289	9.3	22 255	18.1	25 715	9 745	7 691	4 091	2 802
Grand Rapids-Wyoming, MI .	18 037	801 342	1.08	11 522	14.9	5 467	7.0	93 572	13.9	115 661	45 226	33 662	22 465	2 920
Great Falls, MT	2 562	D	D	1 186	14.6	741	9.1	13 370	19.8	15 227	3 371	6 256	3 194	3 927
Greeley, CO	5 895	D	D	4 018	16.5	1 296	5.3	43 497	19.0	29 727	6 742	11 612	6 223	2 508
Green Bay, WI	7 088	314 703	1.05	D	D	2 160	7.2	27 629	10.6	47 092	18 730	13 387	6 096	1 991
Greensboro-High Point, NC..	17 845	757 881	1.10	9 172	13.2	5 969	8.6	113 965	19.0	120 107	44 921	39 977	31 615	4 369
Greenville, NC	8 846	186 130	0.95	2 533	14.8	1 292	7.5	30 458	19.7	25 270	996	13 774	NA	NA
Greenville-Mauldin-Easley, SC......	21 309	650 353	1.04	8 790	14.3	5 233	8.5	105 791	19.6	109 808	26 049	42 807	25 893	4 065
Gulfport-Biloxi, MS	7 287	262 058	1.11	3 587	15.5	2 125	9.2	43 732	21.6	40 079	4 083	16 970	10 105	4 581
Hagerstown-Martinsburg, MD-WV	9 458	246 813	0.83	3 318	12.7	2 280	8.7	32 674	14.5	45 127	5 193	19 680	6 312	2 355
Hanford-Corcoran, CA	21 580	151 274	0.97	2 726	18.4	795	5.4	31 296	23.5	14 144	1 613	7 358	3 489	2 281
Harrisburg-Carlisle, PA	20 267	599 561	1.18	6 043	11.4	4 933	9.3	48 994	11.0	95 182	37 166	27 158	13 240	2 416
Harrisonburg, VA	9 054	D	D	1 401	12.0	884	7.6	18 097	17.8	18 537	2 725	9 821	1 862	1 487
Hartford-West Hartford-East Hartford, CT	49 429	1 246 599	1.06	13 407	11.3	10 019	8.4	92 911	9.3	202 428	42 296	74 942	29 077	2 850
Hattiesburg, MS	4 041	D	D	2 083	15.1	1 159	8.4	24 725	20.2	21 501	2 656	11 296	3 695	2 829
Hickory-Lenoir-Morganton, NC........	7 889	361 793	0.98	D	D	3 427	9.5	61 165	20.1	70 207	12 495	35 492	12 317	3 388
Hinesville-Fort Stewart, GA ..	2 907	D	D	1 586	22.1	376	5.2	14 660	21.7	6 036	975	2 042	2 513	3 225
Holland-Grand Haven, MI.....	8 261	246 237	0.85	3 490	13.5	1 594	6.2	25 851	11.5	38 257	19 238	8 970	5 112	1 938
Honolulu, HI	35 300	957 077	1.00	13 689	15.1	6 611	7.3	57 090	7.4	151 641	66 911	38 177	34 216	3 589
Hot Springs, AR	2 166	D	D	1 183	12.3	1 264	13.1	15 944	21.2	25 009	3 500	11 083	6 163	6 418
Houma-Bayou Cane-Thibo-daux, LA..................	3 104	210 807	1.03	3 111	15.4	1 757	8.7	34 997	19.9	32 507	5 688	16 391	7 871	3 781
Houston-Sugar Land-Bay-town, TX...................	77 956	5 984 157	1.00	95 572	17.0	31 937	5.7	1 383 302	26.3	616 942	161 074	214 030	272 849	4 588
Huntington-Ashland, WV-KY-OH..................	7 643	D	D	D	D	3 408	12.0	38 494	16.5	62 580	12 779	32 072	8 570	3 022
Huntsville, AL	10 949	448 546	1.15	5 171	13.4	3 088	8.0	46 157	13.3	63 841	6 921	21 487	16 233	3 918
Idaho Falls, ID...................	1 283	132 575	1.00	D	D	821	6.9	19 608	17.7	17 089	3 028	7 712	2 859	2 193
Indianapolis-Carmel, IN	32 080	1 792 464	1.04	25 995	15.4	12 742	7.5	227 200	15.2	238 476	45 592	99 181	69 750	4 591
Iowa City, IA.....................	8 167	161 466	1.10	D	D	798	5.5	12 055	9.0	18 189	2 131	8 874	3 037	1 990
Ithaca, NY	13 232	110 486	1.19	D	D	600	5.9	9 274	10.5	13 128	1 993	4 030	2 487	2 449
Jackson, MI	9 672	D	D	1 989	12.3	1 497	9.2	18 035	13.4	28 926	5 879	10 631	4 049	2 561
Jackson, MS	16 906	548 252	1.03	8 459	15.9	4 546	8.5	81 407	17.7	81 044	13 779	39 133	21 177	4 389
Jackson, TN	5 680	D	D	D	D	1 022	9.1	15 139	15.8	19 857	1 748	11 435	6 112	5 295
Jacksonville, FL	26 921	1 355 299	1.01	19 005	14.6	10 644	8.2	218 503	19.2	204 243	37 550	77 283	58 447	4 344
Jacksonville, NC	17 805	D	D	3 640	22.8	847	5.3	24 555	15.9	17 545	868	6 711	5 178	2 913
Janesville, WI	2 934	D	D	2 121	13.3	1 343	8.4	15 403	11.4	27 173	4 844	11 704	5 134	3 202
Jefferson City, MO..............	10 596	D	D	D	D	1 202	8.3	18 001	14.3	23 757	1 526	11 568	4 098	2 736
Johnson City, TN	6 545	D	D	1 991	10.3	2 122	11.0	28 372	17.5	41 906	14 244	14 782	6 640	3 341
Johnstown, PA	8 092	141 185	0.96	1 490	10.2	1 842	12.7	13 649	12.1	32 937	19 682	7 114	2 842	2 048
Jonesboro, AR	3 920	D	D	1 768	15.3	1 131	9.8	20 496	20.1	21 091	2 295	12 359	4 665	3 896
Joplin, MO	3 358	180 247	1.05	2 628	15.4	1 668	9.8	26 259	17.8	30 689	4 510	15 608	7 206	4 106
Kalamazoo-Portage, MI	9 332	327 886	1.01	4 214	13.1	2 623	8.1	38 095	13.6	53 060	13 145	18 235	11 375	3 483
Kankakee-Bradley, IL...........	5 107	D	D	1 596	14.4	1 055	9.5	14 200	14.8	19 209	462	10 636	3 216	3 176
Kansas City, MO-KS.............	32 031	2 049 942	1.01	28 345	14.3	15 841	8.0	248 381	14.0	297 414	72 668	109 648	82 011	4 030
Kennewick-Pasco-Richland, WA..................	3 272	253 009	0.98	4 006	17.4	1 468	6.4	37 729	17.5	32 802	4 104	15 520	6 617	2 612
Killeen-Temple-Fort Hood, TX..................	19 745	408 482	1.00	7 244	19.8	2 379	6.5	70 603	21.1	45 736	10 618	10 951	14 092	3 477
Kingsport-Bristol-Bristol, TN-VA..................	5 797	311 196	1.00	D	D	3 528	11.6	38 857	15.8	74 528	33 391	23 173	10 956	3 539
Kingston, NY	11 773	D	D	1 839	10.1	1 510	8.3	20 641	13.6	33 637	5 800	11 817	3 836	2 102
Knoxville, TN....................	16 190	726 001	1.09	7 645	11.2	6 400	9.4	82 416	14.1	127 936	44 046	39 838	29 984	4 296

1. Per 1,000 estimated resident population. 2. Data for serious crimes have not been adjusted for underreporting; this may affect comparability between geographic areas and over time. 3. Per 100,000 population estimated by the FBI.

Table C. Metropolitan Areas — **Crime, Education, Money Income, and Poverty**

Area name	Serious crimes known to police,[1] 2010 (cont.) Rate[2]		School enrollment and attainment, 2010				Local government expenditures,[5] 2008–2009		Income and Poverty, 2010							
			Enrollment[3]		Attainment[4] (percent)									Percent below poverty level		
	Violent	Property	Total	Percent private	High school graduate or less	Bachelor's degree or more	Total current expenditures (mil dol)	Current expenditures per student (dollars)	Per capita income[6] (dollars)	Median household income (dollars)	Percent of households with income of less than $25,000	Percent of households with income of $100,000 or more	Percent of households with income of $200,000 or more	All persons	Children under 18 years	Children under 5
	46	47	48	49	50	51	52	53	54	55	56	57	58	59	60	61
Flagstaff, AZ	377	3 286	42 813	7.6	37.0	31.3	191.6	9 298	19 703	42 130	27.9	13.6	1.6	25.9	29.7	33.7
Flint, MI	813	3 600	120 045	13.2	44.6	19.2	796.4	10 292	19 860	38 819	33.2	10.9	1.0	21.0	31.0	38.5
Florence, SC	664	4 701	52 137	12.0	54.6	17.7	317.7	9 301	20 035	37 590	34.7	9.9	1.4	21.8	32.5	39.4
Florence-Muscle Shoals, AL	181	2 407	38 420	9.9	49.7	19.9	199.0	9 191	20 608	37 638	34.9	10.5	1.3	19.1	30.9	34.7
Fond du Lac, WI	171	1 720	25 552	20.3	50.3	18.1	140.1	10 283	24 455	49 718	21.7	12.1	1.3	12.5	18.8	22.8
Fort Collins-Loveland, CO	239	2 576	91 519	10.3	23.7	45.8	362.6	8 535	28 622	54 154	21.6	21.5	3.8	14.3	12.9	23.1
Fort Smith, AR-OK	417	2 999	76 695	4.5	54.0	15.2	428.7	8 141	19 869	37 992	30.7	10.1	1.8	18.9	29.3	32.9
Fort Wayne, IN	219	2 778	114 953	18.6	44.6	24.1	602.7	9 336	24 276	47 004	22.7	14.2	2.3	12.8	17.7	16.9
Fresno, CA	535	4 234	294 405	6.8	48.6	20.1	1 821.6	9 398	19 083	45 221	30.0	17.0	2.4	26.8	38.7	42.5
Gadsden, AL	461	3 926	23 691	12.6	52.8	12.9	135.2	8 299	18 665	35 897	35.6	8.2	1.0	18.0	27.7	36.1
Gainesville, FL	624	3 564	97 079	9.7	34.1	37.6	260.5	8 598	22 571	40 274	35.2	16.2	3.0	27.0	29.8	28.0
Gainesville, GA	181	2 513	45 417	11.4	52.9	23.5	295.5	9 238	21 642	47 002	24.0	16.0	2.5	18.5	26.5	24.7
Glens Falls, NY	144	1 531	27 071	13.5	49.1	23.4	312.3	15 745	25 224	50 936	20.8	16.3	1.3	9.4	13.3	22.6
Goldsboro, NC	487	4 186	34 216	12.4	47.5	15.4	163.5	8 267	21 581	40 787	32.3	9.9	2.2	19.7	29.5	30.4
Grand Forks, ND-MN	195	2 231	30 591	9.0	35.0	28.8	134.4	9 797	24 542	46 057	26.5	15.7	2.2	14.4	12.9	18.8
Grand Junction, CO	266	2 535	39 153	12.4	39.8	25.0	182.5	7 988	25 117	46 231	28.7	16.2	2.0	16.4	20.4	24.7
Grand Rapids-Wyoming, MI	385	2 534	214 375	19.0	41.8	26.2	1 403.0	10 142	22 682	47 040	25.3	14.3	2.1	16.4	23.8	27.8
Great Falls, MT	205	3 722	18 860	11.0	36.2	25.3	105.2	8 940	23 429	41 871	24.6	12.1	1.4	11.9	20.1	19.7
Greeley, CO	277	2 231	74 391	9.0	41.9	25.1	303.9	8 353	22 920	51 956	24.6	18.1	1.8	14.9	20.1	24.6
Green Bay, WI	157	1 833	83 448	18.1	45.9	23.6	518.6	10 291	24 814	49 016	22.9	15.7	2.1	10.7	15.5	20.3
Greensboro-High Point, NC	381	3 988	193 304	11.3	45.0	25.6	964.2	8 702	22 427	41 120	29.5	12.7	2.3	18.1	27.4	31.5
Greenville, NC	NA	NA	68 591	10.0	41.9	26.7	228.2	8 505	21 795	39 664	34.1	14.4	2.9	21.4	27.2	28.2
Greenville-Mauldin-Easley, SC	538	3 527	167 966	19.8	44.6	26.9	769.9	7 991	23 163	42 640	29.0	14.8	2.4	15.8	22.0	27.9
Gulfport-Biloxi, MS	219	4 362	59 652	16.0	45.0	21.8	331.2	9 054	21 183	41 875	28.3	11.3	1.1	18.7	31.0	41.5
Hagerstown-Martinsburg, MD-WV	250	2 105	64 149	12.4	53.4	20.1	468.4	11 010	24 930	50 529	24.3	17.0	1.9	12.1	18.3	22.9
Hanford-Corcoran, CA	348	1 932	38 801	8.4	57.7	10.9	259.1	9 137	17 129	44 609	26.2	17.6	1.3	22.2	32.9	37.5
Harrisburg-Carlisle, PA	301	2 115	137 708	21.1	46.8	28.7	869.2	12 134	27 963	54 009	20.2	19.9	2.7	10.9	17.6	17.7
Harrisonburg, VA	113	1 374	42 668	11.6	54.9	26.4	170.2	10 343	23 016	45 188	26.2	14.4	3.0	19.9	17.5	22.0
Hartford-West Hartford-East Hartford, CT	300	2 550	329 812	18.3	39.1	34.6	2 698.3	14 420	32 739	63 104	19.3	28.4	6.0	10.1	12.7	18.3
Hattiesburg, MS	145	2 685	41 835	13.9	43.9	25.2	190.5	8 459	19 764	38 538	35.4	12.2	1.4	24.4	30.7	34.5
Hickory-Lenoir-Morganton, NC	215	3 172	86 239	11.6	52.7	17.6	474.8	7 947	20 189	39 381	31.5	9.1	1.5	16.4	24.9	30.2
Hinesville-Fort Stewart, GA	318	2 907	23 900	8.8	46.7	18.6	120.3	8 915	18 316	37 536	33.8	10.5	1.2	22.6	34.4	34.0
Holland-Grand Haven, MI	179	1 759	80 489	19.1	40.4	29.5	427.4	9 812	24 047	53 056	19.3	17.1	3.0	11.9	14.7	18.3
Honolulu, HI	267	3 322	241 679	26.3	37.1	31.9	2 225.4	12 399	28 629	68 537	16.2	30.9	5.8	9.1	11.0	13.8
Hot Springs, AR	595	5 824	20 472	12.0	47.0	20.8	118.9	8 375	21 028	36 482	34.7	9.7	1.9	23.8	45.7	48.7
Houma-Bayou Cane-Thibodaux, LA	378	3 403	49 878	16.6	66.7	13.0	325.4	9 682	23 229	48 185	27.3	17.7	3.0	15.3	21.5	30.6
Houston-Sugar Land-Baytown, TX	624	3 965	1 691 725	10.8	43.3	28.4	9 479.4	8 299	26 440	53 942	22.0	24.1	5.5	16.5	23.9	27.3
Huntington-Ashland, WV-KY-OH	193	2 828	69 567	8.2	56.0	16.1	432.6	9 649	19 564	36 022	35.8	8.7	1.1	21.7	34.4	36.0
Huntsville, AL	398	3 521	112 741	16.9	36.4	34.4	573.7	9 074	28 734	52 384	23.4	23.8	4.6	13.0	18.0	21.4
Idaho Falls, ID	223	1 970	38 228	14.8	39.3	23.6	165.2	6 191	20 436	50 113	23.7	13.7	1.6	12.2	14.2	21.1
Indianapolis-Carmel, IN	683	3 908	470 434	18.8	42.2	30.7	2 749.1	9 545	25 944	48 867	24.4	18.9	3.4	14.8	21.1	26.5
Iowa City, IA	241	1 750	56 169	9.9	28.0	45.6	173.1	9 338	27 202	48 425	26.1	18.3	3.9	16.4	10.3	13.2
Ithaca, NY	117	2 332	42 983	62.3	27.4	53.4	201.0	16 716	25 041	52 064	26.2	21.8	2.0	21.8	13.5	17.6
Jackson, MI	382	2 179	42 520	15.8	44.1	17.8	269.2	10 524	20 803	42 862	31.4	12.2	1.8	19.8	33.1	37.9
Jackson, MS	445	3 944	157 210	18.1	39.3	28.3	679.0	7 729	22 525	42 501	29.5	15.4	3.2	17.9	26.5	27.3
Jackson, TN	654	4 641	31 306	23.1	52.0	21.9	129.4	7 871	22 039	40 464	29.2	12.9	2.7	19.1	30.4	39.6
Jacksonville, FL	559	3 785	369 327	20.9	39.5	26.9	1 716.0	8 428	25 758	50 324	24.0	17.8	3.0	15.3	21.5	24.3
Jacksonville, NC	237	2 675	43 683	11.9	40.0	18.1	193.5	8 056	20 503	41 787	23.7	10.3	1.2	14.6	19.7	18.7
Janesville, WI	248	2 955	42 359	15.1	49.5	19.7	303.1	10 686	23 072	46 758	24.4	14.1	2.2	14.1	20.8	24.4
Jefferson City, MO	287	2 448	41 698	23.8	47.4	24.9	164.7	8 316	23 040	51 742	23.6	14.6	1.0	12.1	16.7	19.1
Johnson City, TN	351	2 991	48 130	12.2	48.1	25.3	205.6	7 508	22 438	36 791	33.8	11.8	2.8	20.5	29.2	30.7
Johnstown, PA	208	1 840	32 702	16.7	58.6	19.7	201.7	10 534	21 472	41 220	30.6	8.9	1.2	12.9	23.7	23.9
Jonesboro, AR	398	3 498	31 457	5.6	53.9	18.9	170.1	8 117	20 555	35 526	36.0	12.0	2.8	25.5	34.9	44.0
Joplin, MO	378	3 727	45 705	12.3	48.7	18.9	218.2	7 410	20 259	38 448	31.7	11.0	0.8	16.7	23.1	31.8
Kalamazoo-Portage, MI	413	3 070	102 135	10.1	37.0	30.5	538.5	10 280	24 226	43 634	27.6	16.2	3.0	19.1	25.3	31.8
Kankakee-Bradley, IL	382	2 794	31 876	15.4	51.5	16.1	185.2	9 401	21 771	44 784	25.9	14.4	1.7	14.4	17.4	19.8
Kansas City, MO-KS	478	3 552	538 624	17.3	36.7	32.5	3 342.6	9 972	27 377	53 919	21.9	20.8	3.3	12.4	17.7	20.9
Kennewick-Pasco-Richland, WA	234	2 378	67 444	10.1	43.2	24.1	433.1	9 146	23 991	56 407	21.1	21.6	2.2	15.1	21.0	22.8
Killeen-Temple-Fort Hood, TX	394	3 083	117 303	10.2	42.1	19.9	620.1	8 118	21 440	49 778	20.0	13.3	1.5	12.5	18.9	23.5
Kingsport-Bristol-Bristol, TN-VA	354	3 186	67 246	19.0	55.1	18.6	382.6	8 513	21 423	34 741	36.7	9.7	2.1	17.3	25.8	27.7
Kingston, NY	224	1 878	47 949	12.7	41.6	29.0	492.2	18 768	26 701	51 301	23.1	20.9	3.2	12.3	13.0	14.8
Knoxville, TN	473	3 823	171 046	14.8	43.0	28.8	784.8	8 083	24 654	43 114	27.6	14.6	2.7	13.8	18.4	25.9

1. Data for serious crimes have not been adjusted for underreporting; this may affect comparability between geographic areas and over time. 2. Per 100,000 population estimated by the FBI. 3. All persons 3 years old and over enrolled in nursery school through college. 4. Persons 25 years old and over. 5. Elementary and secondary education expenditures. 6. Based on resident population estimated as of July 1, 2009.

Table C. Metropolitan Areas — **Personal Income**

Area name	Personal income, 2009 Total (mil dol)	Percent change, 2008–2009	Per capita[1] Dollars	Rank	Wages and salaries[2] (mil dol)	Proprietors' income (mil dol)	Dividends, interest, and rent (mil dol)	Transfer payments Total (mil dol)	Government payments to individuals Total (mil dol)	Social Security (mil dol)	Medical payments (mil dol)	Income mainte-nance (mil dol)	Unemploy-ment insurance (mil dol)
	62	63	64	65	66	67	68	69	70	71	72	73	74
Flagstaff, AZ	4 481	0.3	34 510	201	2 802	309	817	906	883	191	463	99	33
Flint, MI	12 520	-0.8	29 526	334	6 674	719	1 724	3 949	3 871	1 248	1 512	516	300
Florence, SC	6 571	0.0	32 747	249	4 140	395	924	1 774	1 738	496	761	241	80
Florence-Muscle Shoals, AL.	4 441	0.2	30 792	306	2 315	283	789	1 164	1 138	466	433	102	38
Fond du Lac, WI	3 541	-2.3	35 389	179	2 120	218	580	719	701	254	300	36	60
Fort Collins-Loveland, CO	11 292	-1.9	37 844	120	6 833	832	2 367	1 429	1 375	546	494	95	95
Fort Smith, AR-OK	9 054	-1.5	30 896	303	5 128	847	1 506	2 283	2 230	753	940	231	99
Fort Wayne, IN	13 949	-2.1	33 669	226	9 840	1 079	2 306	2 643	2 568	964	959	243	214
Fresno, CA	28 050	-0.2	30 646	312	16 621	3 094	4 212	6 397	6 230	1 351	2 610	1 167	501
Gadsden, AL	3 108	-0.4	29 984	324	1 492	184	463	898	880	328	369	88	22
Gainesville, FL	9 163	0.0	35 149	188	6 536	357	1 948	1 598	1 551	490	671	163	42
Gainesville, GA	5 452	-3.2	29 038	344	3 560	398	1 020	968	934	362	343	97	59
Glens Falls, NY	4 263	0.7	33 106	243	2 481	192	720	1 022	998	375	412	90	54
Goldsboro, NC	3 605	0.3	31 673	288	2 274	130	530	912	892	268	397	110	33
Grand Forks, ND-MN	3 511	-1.3	36 126	161	2 439	251	616	607	590	189	252	56	21
Grand Junction, CO	5 083	-4.1	34 791	195	3 108	307	1 025	935	908	326	354	76	59
Grand Rapids-Wyoming, MI .	25 242	-2.9	32 445	257	18 344	2 341	3 812	4 854	4 712	1 712	1 664	559	433
Great Falls, MT	3 077	1.0	37 437	132	1 860	272	636	592	577	202	232	44	19
Greeley, CO	6 926	-3.2	27 186	355	4 071	661	1 059	1 148	1 101	374	440	102	86
Green Bay, WI	11 198	-0.3	36 742	142	8 557	569	1 893	1 798	1 742	679	635	135	160
Greensboro-High Point, NC..	24 980	-0.9	34 948	192	17 265	1 705	4 331	5 075	4 944	1 734	1 983	520	364
Greenville, NC	5 811	0.7	32 334	260	3 588	318	914	1 258	1 226	338	542	171	64
Greenville-Mauldin-Easley, SC	21 370	-1.6	33 410	234	14 781	1 186	3 566	4 328	4 211	1 582	1 622	387	223
Gulfport-Biloxi, MS	8 567	0.4	35 879	170	6 185	428	1 558	1 758	1 716	526	817	178	43
Hagerstown-Martinsburg, MD-WV	8 819	1.8	33 137	240	4 833	414	1 228	1 736	1 687	632	655	151	93
Hanford-Corcoran, CA	3 931	-3.2	26 426	357	2 583	406	468	791	765	172	320	129	61
Harrisburg-Carlisle, PA	21 312	0.6	39 693	77	17 819	1 213	3 436	3 814	3 716	1 352	1 478	240	298
Harrisonburg, VA	3 689	-0.9	30 673	310	2 772	274	675	599	577	254	202	60	20
Hartford-West Hartford-East Hartford, CT	60 607	-1.7	50 675	12	43 557	5 387	10 590	9 294	9 076	2 989	4 200	700	704
Hattiesburg, MS	4 189	0.8	29 274	339	2 637	318	608	985	959	301	435	110	24
Hickory-Lenoir-Morganton, NC	10 902	-1.8	29 840	327	6 294	713	1 891	2 824	2 757	1 001	1 083	261	254
Hinesville-Fort Stewart, GA ..	1 963	-1.4	26 372	358	2 661	56	203	368	358	77	127	69	21
Holland-Grand Haven, MI	8 470	-1.1	32 334	260	4 907	406	1 485	1 419	1 371	582	436	89	159
Honolulu, HI	41 291	0.3	45 496	32	29 472	2 404	7 191	5 539	5 381	1 954	2 053	667	328
Hot Springs, AR	3 320	0.4	33 715	224	1 469	143	954	962	944	354	422	66	30
Houma-Bayou Cane-Thibodaux, LA	8 222	-1.3	40 506	65	5 421	545	1 376	1 413	1 376	454	662	159	24
Houston-Sugar Land-Baytown, TX	273 247	-2.5	46 570	23	174 768	51 413	40 665	28 947	27 876	8 430	12 670	3 358	1 428
Huntington-Ashland, WV-KY-OH	9 025	2.5	31 597	291	5 566	435	1 146	2 607	2 555	839	1 039	287	86
Huntsville, AL	15 588	1.3	38 364	103	13 415	825	2 532	2 293	2 219	850	827	216	74
Idaho Falls, ID	4 113	-1.1	32 606	255	2 082	434	755	702	679	238	291	64	34
Indianapolis-Carmel, IN	67 187	-2.0	38 532	100	49 000	5 933	9 411	10 555	10 237	3 600	3 831	1 017	748
Iowa City, IA	5 831	0.3	38 299	108	4 462	389	1 025	691	663	261	238	68	35
Ithaca, NY	3 428	0.1	33 684	225	2 795	149	688	563	544	198	201	56	33
Jackson, MI	4 713	-1.2	29 488	335	2 696	249	702	1 239	1 210	442	458	123	101
Jackson, MS	19 468	-0.8	35 994	163	12 705	2 116	2 903	3 680	3 582	1 145	1 538	516	96
Jackson, TN	3 645	-1.6	32 078	268	2 650	298	519	857	836	272	335	114	35
Jacksonville, FL	52 297	-2.0	39 376	82	34 279	2 629	10 907	8 611	8 371	2 763	3 355	891	420
Jacksonville, NC	7 349	7.8	42 463	45	6 411	161	614	883	861	224	331	107	30
Janesville, WI	5 012	-2.5	31 294	293	2 981	183	794	1 160	1 131	411	432	100	126
Jefferson City, MO	5 115	0.5	34 691	197	3 715	373	794	944	917	339	398	73	36
Johnson City, TN	6 075	-0.5	30 778	307	3 473	371	898	1 579	1 543	558	636	148	50
Johnstown, PA	4 602	0.8	31 961	274	2 547	259	684	1 442	1 415	455	638	95	114
Jonesboro, AR	3 627	0.3	30 192	319	2 092	372	546	914	892	286	383	101	39
Joplin, MO	5 200	0.5	29 836	328	3 534	316	758	1 265	1 233	418	557	124	44
Kalamazoo-Portage, MI	10 804	-1.5	33 075	244	7 029	529	1 805	2 306	2 246	803	857	254	180
Kankakee-Bradley, IL	3 598	0.6	31 780	281	1 984	174	516	871	850	273	358	90	71
Kansas City, MO-KS	83 610	-1.2	40 438	67	58 576	6 946	13 590	12 700	12 324	4 327	5 349	1 029	692
Kennewick-Pasco-Richland, WA	8 484	5.1	34 539	200	5 990	564	1 282	1 510	1 465	465	554	200	83
Killeen-Temple-Fort Hood, TX	14 921	2.5	39 344	83	11 440	511	1 772	2 216	2 156	569	776	247	92
Kingsport-Bristol-Bristol, TN-VA	9 710	-0.6	31 770	283	5 782	552	1 585	2 625	2 569	1 052	1 006	250	73
Kingston, NY	6 626	-0.2	36 519	150	2 948	297	1 192	1 413	1 379	495	609	123	71
Knoxville, TN	23 713	-1.7	33 912	219	16 348	2 154	3 654	4 743	4 616	1 810	1 801	464	191

1. Based on the resident population estimated as of July 1 of the year shown. 2. Includes other labor income.

Table C. Metropolitan Areas — **Earnings, Social Security, and Housing**

Area name	Total (mil dol)	Farm	Goods-related[1] Total	Manu-facturing	Infor-mation, profes-sional, and technical services	Retail trade	Finance, insur-ance, and real estate	Health care and social services	Govern-ment	Number	Rate[2]	Supple-mental Security Income recipients, December 2009	Total	Percent change, 2000–2010
	75	76	77	78	79	80	81	82	83	84	85	86	87	88
Flagstaff, AZ	3 110	0.0	14.3	9.5	4.6	7.6	3.5	15.7	32.9	16 315	121	2 920	63 321	18.5
Flint, MI	7 393	0.1	15.7	11.2	8.2	8.4	6.6	18.4	20.1	91 680	215	15 387	192 180	4.7
Florence, SC	4 535	0.5	D	18.9	6.1	7.4	10.2	D	19.4	42 530	207	8 364	88 963	10.1
Florence-Muscle Shoals, AL.	2 597	2.2	21.7	14.1	4.5	9.4	4.5	10.3	26.9	36 950	251	4 919	69 549	6.3
Fond du Lac, WI	2 337	0.9	34.9	25.9	4.7	6.8	4.6	13.6	13.1	19 525	192	1 317	43 910	11.8
Fort Collins-Loveland, CO	7 665	0.2	22.1	12.6	14.2	6.9	4.9	12.6	20.5	44 200	148	2 380	132 722	25.9
Fort Smith, AR-OK	5 975	0.5	27.9	17.1	D	6.8	3.9	NA	16.8	65 970	221	10 686	128 891	11.7
Fort Wayne, IN	10 919	0.7	D	19.0	D	5.9	7.1	NA	11.5	72 885	175	7 501	178 124	9.7
Fresno, CA	19 715	6.5	13.7	7.7	6.8	6.7	5.3	13.0	22.7	118 240	127	41 602	315 531	16.6
Gadsden, AL	1 676	0.1	21.3	16.6	4.8	8.0	5.3	20.7	17.6	26 905	258	4 634	47 454	3.3
Gainesville, FL	6 893	0.2	D	3.8	D	6.0	5.4	NA	39.6	39 900	151	5 687	120 073	18.9
Gainesville, GA	3 958	0.7	26.5	20.0	4.6	6.9	6.0	14.8	14.0	28 775	160	2 549	68 825	34.8
Glens Falls, NY	2 673	0.3	D	15.4	D	8.8	4.8	14.6	22.9	29 915	232	3 260	67 570	9.6
Goldsboro, NC	2 404	2.4	D	11.3	3.4	6.5	3.1	13.2	36.6	23 685	193	4 550	52 949	11.9
Grand Forks, ND-MN	2 690	4.8	D	7.3	5.0	7.5	3.8	D	30.9	15 470	157	1 253	43 954	6.2
Grand Junction, CO	3 416	0.2	22.8	4.2	6.7	8.0	5.8	14.7	17.5	27 295	186	2 205	62 644	28.6
Grand Rapids-Wyoming, MI .	20 685	0.5	D	20.3	D	6.6	6.9	NA	10.9	132 220	171	17 553	323 764	10.5
Great Falls, MT	2 132	0.4	9.9	2.7	6.8	7.8	7.3	17.2	30.0	16 785	206	1 789	37 276	5.8
Greeley, CO	4 732	3.4	29.3	12.7	4.7	6.0	7.4	9.5	15.7	32 020	127	3 065	96 281	45.5
Green Bay, WI	9 126	0.7	D	18.1	D	5.4	8.3	NA	12.2	53 705	175	5 123	137 212	16.0
Greensboro-High Point, NC..	18 969	0.4	D	17.2	D	7.6	7.7	11.7	13.3	135 900	188	15 652	322 754	17.4
Greenville, NC	3 906	1.7	D	10.7	D	7.0	4.2	13.5	37.2	29 345	155	6 354	83 203	26.6
Greenville-Mauldin-Easley, SC	15 967	0.0	D	15.7	D	7.4	5.9	NA	16.7	125 275	197	12 617	277 415	16.1
Gulfport-Biloxi, MS	6 613	0.0	D	D	7.0	6.4	3.5	NA	39.4	45 540	183	7 138	114 182	7.7
Hagerstown-Martinsburg, MD-WV	5 247	0.5	D	10.9	D	8.9	7.7	NA	24.6	50 240	187	5 197	115 329	22.7
Hanford-Corcoran, CA	2 989	9.9	D	9.3	2.0	5.7	2.0	8.4	46.3	15 815	103	4 624	43 867	20.0
Harrisburg-Carlisle, PA	19 032	0.3	D	7.5	9.9	5.2	9.7	12.7	22.5	104 240	190	9 824	240 818	11.0
Harrisonburg, VA	3 046	2.0	D	20.1	8.1	8.2	3.7	11.1	17.9	20 515	164	1 576	51 104	24.6
Hartford-West Hartford-East Hartford, CT	48 944	0.1	D	12.3	11.1	4.9	17.6	12.1	17.0	216 750	179	21 857	507 049	7.5
Hattiesburg, MS	2 955	0.7	D	7.7	D	9.2	D	17.5	27.7	24 860	174	4 529	61 878	22.6
Hickory-Lenoir-Morganton, NC	7 007	1.1	D	26.0	4.0	7.3	3.2	12.0	17.3	80 810	221	7 011	162 613	12.2
Hinesville-Fort Stewart, GA ..	2 717	0.1	D	NA	D	2.2	D	1.4	80.4	7 285	93	1 352	32 770	25.0
Holland-Grand Haven, MI	5 313	1.9	38.8	33.2	5.3	5.5	4.6	7.0	15.3	43 250	164	2 535	102 495	18.0
Honolulu, HI	31 876	0.2	8.4	2.0	8.9	5.3	5.1	9.6	38.5	166 280	164	17 024	336 899	6.6
Hot Springs, AR	1 611	0.4	12.8	6.1	6.2	10.7	4.8	23.4	17.4	28 235	204	3 451	50 548	12.4
Houma-Bayou Cane-Thibo-daux, LA	5 966	0.6	29.1	11.3	3.9	6.1	5.5	7.8	12.9	37 695	181	7 882	82 469	10.0
Houston-Sugar Land-Bay-town, TX	226 181	0.0	D	11.2	D	4.4	6.7	NA	10.2	664 560	112	125 385	2 308 205	28.3
Huntington-Ashland, WV-KY-OH	6 000	-0.1	D	11.7	D	7.4	3.5	NA	19.4	67 785	236	14 707	131 132	1.0
Huntsville, AL	14 240	0.6	D	14.7	24.7	5.0	3.0	6.4	29.3	69 520	166	8 547	181 424	23.2
Idaho Falls, ID	2 516	4.0	D	5.3	D	9.5	4.6	15.0	15.1	19 525	150	2 138	48 453	31.8
Indianapolis-Carmel, IN	54 934	0.5	D	14.7	D	5.8	8.3	NA	14.4	270 780	154	29 507	757 441	17.5
Iowa City, IA	4 851	2.1	D	7.1	6.8	5.8	3.9	7.7	43.4	19 500	128	1 720	65 483	20.4
Ithaca, NY	2 943	0.4	11.2	8.1	6.8	4.8	3.1	D	13.7	14 600	144	1 783	41 674	7.9
Jackson, MI	2 945	0.2	21.0	16.8	4.4	7.3	3.6	15.0	19.7	33 420	209	4 119	69 458	10.4
Jackson, MS	14 821	0.6	D	6.5	D	6.3	7.9	NA	23.0	92 855	172	18 655	222 584	13.2
Jackson, TN	2 947	0.7	D	17.7	D	7.5	4.6	NA	22.8	22 545	195	3 460	48 857	10.1
Jacksonville, FL	36 908	0.1	D	5.8	D	6.9	11.4	NA	18.9	226 105	168	27 881	598 490	26.0
Jacksonville, NC	6 571	0.4	D	0.6	1.9	3.3	1.3	2.4	80.6	20 315	114	2 602	68 226	22.4
Janesville, WI	3 164	1.0	24.6	18.8	4.8	9.5	3.1	15.9	15.5	31 450	196	3 439	68 422	10.0
Jefferson City, MO	4 088	1.2	D	7.4	D	6.3	4.7	D	35.4	27 945	187	2 558	63 555	12.0
Johnson City, TN	3 844	0.0	D	13.3	D	7.5	5.9	18.8	23.4	47 175	237	5 874	93 830	14.5
Johnstown, PA	2 806	0.2	13.5	8.5	9.4	7.7	6.1	19.9	19.8	36 950	257	5 035	65 650	-0.2
Jonesboro, AR	2 464	5.6	D	13.3	4.4	7.5	4.9	19.3	18.6	24 905	206	5 349	51 438	11.4
Joplin, MO	3 849	0.9	23.3	19.2	4.4	8.3	3.9	15.8	12.6	36 120	206	4 580	74 981	11.1
Kalamazoo-Portage, MI	7 559	1.1	25.4	20.5	6.8	6.3	7.2	14.8	16.5	60 890	186	7 873	146 792	10.2
Kankakee-Bradley, IL	2 159	4.2	D	16.6	D	8.2	4.4	17.6	17.2	21 225	187	2 714	45 246	11.4
Kansas City, MO-KS	65 522	0.3	D	8.5	D	5.7	D	NA	16.3	328 215	161	31 289	883 099	15.0
Kennewick-Pasco-Richland, WA	6 555	5.4	D	6.2	19.7	5.9	3.1	8.8	18.2	35 555	140	4 864	93 041	29.1
Killeen-Temple-Fort Hood, TX	11 950	-0.1	D	3.3	4.9	3.9	2.3	NA	63.0	52 005	128	7 993	159 366	30.5
Kingsport-Bristol-Bristol, TN-VA	6 334	-0.4	D	24.2	D	7.6	D	D	13.2	86 085	278	10 664	146 978	7.9
Kingston, NY	3 245	0.6	11.7	6.4	5.5	10.2	4.4	13.8	31.6	37 585	206	4 428	83 638	7.8
Knoxville, TN	18 502	0.0	D	11.1	D	7.7	D	13.7	16.0	142 490	204	16 258	315 615	14.3

1. Includes mining, construction, and manufacturing.   2. Per 1,000 resident population enumerated in the 2010 census.

Table C. Metropolitan Areas — **Housing, Labor Force, and Employment**

Area name	Housing units, 2010 Total	Percent	Owner-occupied Median value[1]	Median owner cost as a percent of income With a mortgage	Without a mortgage	Renter-occupied Median rent[2]	Median rent as a percent of income	Sub-standard units[3] (percent)	Civilian labor force, 2010 Total	Percent change, 2009–2010	Unemployment Total	Rate[4]	Civilian employment,[5] 2010 Total	Percent Management, business, science, and arts occupations	Construction, production, and maintenance occupations
	89	90	91	92	93	94	95	96	97	98	99	100	101	102	103
Flagstaff, AZ	44 276	61.6	233 800	28.3	10.0	958	33.5	10.6	76 599	1.4	6 819	8.9	59 481	33.5	16.9
Flint, MI	166 539	69.9	94 100	25.0	15.2	681	40.5	2.0	190 785	-2.8	26 142	13.7	151 813	30.2	22.6
Florence, SC	79 218	66.1	100 800	20.0	11.3	600	30.3	2.1	94 901	-0.8	11 120	11.7	80 413	31.8	22.1
Florence-Muscle Shoals, AL	60 910	71.2	107 300	23.3	12.5	595	33.2	1.0	68 013	-1.6	6 230	9.2	61 029	28.7	26.5
Fond du Lac, WI	40 736	71.6	147 700	23.7	13.1	638	27.8	2.3	55 523	-1.3	4 578	8.2	52 211	27.8	33.0
Fort Collins-Loveland, CO	117 812	66.7	247 600	25.5	10.0	894	32.3	1.9	175 823	-0.6	13 058	7.4	151 483	45.3	15.0
Fort Smith, AR-OK	112 468	70.3	99 800	21.1	10.6	589	27.1	3.4	134 066	-0.5	11 024	8.2	124 590	27.7	29.1
Fort Wayne, IN	160 275	71.2	113 200	20.2	10.0	610	26.0	1.8	206 210	-1.6	21 540	10.4	185 426	33.8	23.6
Fresno, CA	284 690	54.2	212 500	26.9	11.0	825	34.6	11.6	438 606	0.9	73 601	16.8	363 891	28.3	27.2
Gadsden, AL	39 731	74.0	91 700	25.3	13.3	609	28.8	2.7	44 377	-1.7	4 191	9.4	38 584	25.5	31.0
Gainesville, FL	100 329	57.4	170 600	24.5	12.9	883	40.5	2.5	139 016	0.7	11 545	8.3	118 346	43.2	11.6
Gainesville, GA	60 969	66.1	180 600	27.4	12.0	806	31.8	5.7	89 018	-0.3	8 119	9.1	75 227	31.9	28.9
Glens Falls, NY	52 974	72.0	170 900	23.6	13.6	764	29.0	2.7	68 253	-0.8	5 578	8.2	60 564	31.2	24.0
Goldsboro, NC	47 759	63.0	106 900	23.3	12.6	621	28.4	2.5	52 837	-1.7	4 692	8.9	51 470	27.7	30.4
Grand Forks, ND-MN	39 993	60.2	141 000	20.6	10.6	639	30.1	0.5	54 773	-0.6	2 454	4.5	51 593	36.2	20.6
Grand Junction, CO	57 311	72.5	219 500	26.8	10.9	834	36.2	3.4	78 853	-4.2	8 330	10.6	64 449	33.0	21.2
Grand Rapids-Wyoming, MI	292 388	73.0	136 800	24.4	13.4	698	31.1	2.2	387 533	-0.4	40 529	10.5	347 175	33.4	24.4
Great Falls, MT	33 053	67.5	158 300	22.2	11.8	582	25.9	3.9	40 712	1.0	2 476	6.1	36 653	32.5	22.2
Greeley, CO	89 056	71.7	182 500	24.8	10.8	725	33.1	5.1	119 689	-1.3	12 188	10.2	118 678	32.0	25.9
Green Bay, WI	121 806	69.5	157 900	23.4	13.5	659	27.2	2.4	173 042	-0.1	13 396	7.7	150 604	31.1	26.6
Greensboro-High Point, NC	282 554	65.1	141 100	24.5	12.3	680	31.2	3.2	362 770	-1.0	40 295	11.1	325 631	31.5	24.2
Greenville, NC	70 345	58.5	126 100	23.1	17.7	680	32.7	2.8	91 282	0.0	9 214	10.1	88 384	37.0	21.1
Greenville-Mauldin-Easley, SC	241 533	68.2	142 600	22.9	10.5	692	30.1	2.0	313 955	-0.5	30 531	9.7	280 335	34.7	23.7
Gulfport-Biloxi, MS	93 746	68.3	142 000	25.0	11.1	822	32.1	4.3	114 695	1.6	10 269	9.0	107 456	30.1	24.3
Hagerstown-Martinsburg, MD-WV	101 783	69.4	196 500	23.8	11.6	710	30.6	1.7	118 897	-0.8	11 839	10.0	120 491	32.7	24.7
Hanford-Corcoran, CA	40 818	51.3	184 600	26.2	10.0	824	30.1	10.8	61 350	1.3	10 126	16.5	52 477	23.5	33.1
Harrisburg-Carlisle, PA	221 667	70.2	168 100	23.3	12.4	788	27.6	1.5	281 633	-1.5	22 025	7.8	270 114	37.0	20.9
Harrisonburg, VA	43 840	60.1	200 100	22.1	10.5	738	30.4	3.4	66 459	1.1	4 391	6.6	56 177	30.9	29.9
Hartford-West Hartford-East Hartford, CT	472 161	68.2	258 300	25.1	16.6	919	30.9	2.1	647 507	0.4	59 122	9.1	595 596	41.6	16.7
Hattiesburg, MS	53 532	64.0	129 100	22.6	11.8	701	35.1	4.3	67 349	2.0	6 004	8.9	61 691	34.2	22.9
Hickory-Lenoir-Morganton, NC	140 327	73.4	118 500	22.2	11.3	623	30.4	1.9	168 960	-2.0	22 716	13.4	156 213	28.2	32.5
Hinesville-Fort Stewart, GA	26 902	59.3	124 700	24.7	10.0	890	39.3	NA	32 828	0.9	2 893	8.8	NA	NA	NA
Holland-Grand Haven, MI	91 334	80.0	156 000	23.6	12.4	718	34.6	1.7	129 037	0.0	14 232	11.0	124 574	31.7	26.2
Honolulu, HI	309 154	56.1	560 500	29.0	10.4	1 363	33.5	8.4	438 993	-0.2	24 478	5.6	452 669	34.9	17.7
Hot Springs, AR	38 369	68.1	133 900	24.0	11.0	682	29.1	NA	42 151	-0.8	3 405	8.1	37 505	29.9	28.0
Houma-Bayou Cane-Thibodaux, LA	73 829	75.9	127 500	20.6	10.0	685	30.1	6.0	103 581	1.0	5 568	5.4	91 468	25.8	34.8
Houston-Sugar Land-Baytown, TX	2 022 402	62.8	140 800	23.8	12.6	846	29.8	6.5	2 895 737	1.9	245 130	8.5	2 765 449	35.6	23.8
Huntington-Ashland, WV-KY-OH	113 825	68.3	95 700	20.7	10.9	570	32.4	1.8	129 535	-1.1	11 392	8.8	110 785	32.0	20.7
Huntsville, AL	160 762	72.7	161 400	19.2	10.0	689	30.2	2.0	206 722	-0.9	15 569	7.5	190 789	44.0	19.3
Idaho Falls, ID	43 751	75.6	157 700	23.0	10.0	647	27.9	NA	62 148	1.5	4 411	7.1	58 405	34.3	24.4
Indianapolis-Carmel, IN	669 860	67.2	143 600	21.9	11.1	746	32.3	2.0	888 932	-0.9	81 365	9.2	820 792	37.5	19.6
Iowa City, IA	61 883	60.8	177 100	22.0	11.3	807	40.2	1.3	92 161	0.5	4 129	4.5	83 246	42.5	16.7
Ithaca, NY	37 812	56.0	167 600	23.2	10.6	890	31.2	NA	56 653	0.2	3 431	6.1	48 498	56.0	11.2
Jackson, MI	58 388	74.9	116 600	25.3	13.2	658	31.0	2.2	73 313	-2.7	9 250	12.6	62 770	29.9	24.1
Jackson, MS	197 941	68.2	128 200	22.3	10.0	779	32.6	4.3	264 172	1.6	22 213	8.4	239 089	36.0	20.8
Jackson, TN	39 618	64.9	111 900	22.6	10.9	701	32.5	NA	56 197	0.0	5 639	10.0	47 096	34.3	24.3
Jacksonville, FL	503 541	66.8	170 900	27.0	12.3	908	32.2	1.8	687 829	0.7	76 916	11.2	602 028	34.9	18.0
Jacksonville, NC	60 242	53.1	149 600	25.3	11.9	938	31.6	2.3	65 982	0.7	5 607	8.5	55 285	25.6	23.3
Janesville, WI	62 555	72.7	137 000	24.4	13.4	698	33.2	NA	80 327	-2.6	8 898	11.1	76 879	28.4	28.1
Jefferson City, MO	56 355	71.3	133 900	19.9	10.0	590	25.5	NA	77 772	-0.6	5 738	7.4	72 157	35.6	21.4
Johnson City, TN	82 383	70.5	128 100	23.7	10.6	596	29.9	NA	101 118	0.6	9 010	8.9	84 914	36.2	19.1
Johnstown, PA	59 030	73.1	86 200	20.1	12.6	550	27.9	NA	68 360	-0.8	6 458	9.4	62 467	31.0	24.5
Jonesboro, AR	46 614	59.3	105 000	19.5	10.0	597	29.5	2.9	57 872	1.1	4 352	7.5	51 561	31.1	29.3
Joplin, MO	66 336	69.9	97 000	22.7	11.6	592	27.9	NA	85 840	0.2	7 349	8.6	80 556	29.0	25.7
Kalamazoo-Portage, MI	127 035	68.0	139 600	22.4	13.2	683	36.0	1.3	168 320	-1.5	18 055	10.7	146 958	34.4	21.5
Kankakee-Bradley, IL	42 046	67.0	157 500	24.5	12.9	707	31.6	1.8	57 222	2.4	7 511	13.1	48 535	26.7	26.6
Kansas City, MO-KS	785 477	67.8	159 200	22.8	12.6	766	29.3	2.0	1 037 453	-1.0	94 264	9.1	991 303	38.0	19.1
Kennewick-Pasco-Richland, WA	86 626	67.6	168 900	20.5	10.0	717	27.2	4.8	134 771	4.2	10 132	7.5	114 292	33.6	28.6
Killeen-Temple-Fort Hood, TX	131 062	57.9	112 900	22.0	11.3	810	27.0	2.6	167 706	3.8	12 706	7.6	152 541	32.8	21.6
Kingsport-Bristol-Bristol, TN-VA	130 117	72.5	119 100	22.4	11.4	553	29.1	1.7	147 208	-0.6	12 958	8.8	124 732	29.7	25.9
Kingston, NY	68 581	69.4	234 300	28.9	20.0	979	33.6	1.1	88 883	-1.0	7 273	8.2	84 462	36.9	18.3
Knoxville, TN	285 762	69.1	151 400	22.8	10.7	690	30.4	1.3	364 720	0.6	28 948	7.9	314 632	37.0	19.8

1. Specified owner-occupied units.   2. Specified renter-occupied units. A value of 10.0 represents 10 percent or less.   3. Overcrowded or lacking complete plumbing facilities.   4. Percent of civilian labor force.   5. Persons 16 years old and over.

Table C. Metropolitan Areas — Nonfarm Employment and Agriculture

Area name	Private nonfarm establishments, employment and payroll, 2009									Agriculture, 2007			
	Number of establishments	Employment						Annual payroll		Farms			Farm operators whose principal occupation is farming (percent)
		Total	Health care and social assistance	Manufacturing	Retail trade	Finance and insurance	Professional, scientific, and technical services	Total (mil dol)	Average per employee (dollars)	Number	Percent with:		
											Fewer than 50 acres	500 acres or more	
	104	105	106	107	108	109	110	111	112	113	114	115	116
Flagstaff, AZ	3 634	44 916	7 328	D	7 784	834	1 749	1 452	32 330	1 597	94.3	2.8	67.3
Flint, MI	7 992	114 954	25 626	9 952	19 613	5 301	4 648	4 014	34 922	988	61.3	5.3	47.5
Florence, SC	4 391	71 112	15 192	10 240	11 419	4 586	2 654	2 429	34 152	1 044	37.3	15.2	41.7
Florence-Muscle Shoals, AL.	3 308	45 430	7 306	8 290	7 852	1 484	1 905	1 250	27 507	2 433	47.1	5.3	33.9
Fond du Lac, WI	2 460	39 419	5 846	7 522	5 770	1 750	1 316	1 313	33 311	1 643	30.3	8.9	51.6
Fort Collins-Loveland, CO	9 361	104 597	16 756	11 148	16 643	3 569	8 144	3 847	36 780	1 757	60.8	9.2	34.1
Fort Smith, AR-OK	6 269	103 625	18 116	21 567	13 686	3 170	2 473	3 218	31 055	6 111	38.8	7.0	41.6
Fort Wayne, IN	10 530	183 363	32 938	33 168	22 680	9 708	7 250	6 453	35 195	3 159	54.8	9.5	36.9
Fresno, CA	15 971	233 208	38 365	24 357	34 040	10 222	12 362	8 277	35 491	6 081	61.3	10.8	57.1
Gadsden, AL	2 079	29 773	6 907	4 611	4 725	1 019	775	865	29 057	1 004	52.7	2.1	33.5
Gainesville, FL	6 009	84 207	21 031	3 828	13 746	4 182	4 991	2 810	33 370	2 101	69.9	5.1	40.9
Gainesville, GA	4 007	59 965	10 152	15 239	7 832	2 073	1 629	2 152	35 896	799	60.6	1.6	40.3
Glens Falls, NY	3 453	41 035	8 214	6 924	7 469	D	1 084	1 411	34 377	929	32.6	12.4	48.5
Goldsboro, NC	2 239	33 986	7 965	5 162	5 611	1 124	745	1 003	29 502	723	42.9	13.4	58.1
Grand Forks, ND-MN	2 591	40 206	8 737	4 052	7 176	1 304	1 307	1 239	30 829	2 582	12.9	35.4	49.3
Grand Junction, CO	4 816	53 464	9 381	2 593	8 734	2 225	2 947	1 828	34 192	1 767	71.0	6.6	36.6
Grand Rapids-Wyoming, MI .	18 143	326 328	47 285	56 728	37 671	15 225	14 707	12 409	38 026	4 491	45.4	6.9	42.6
Great Falls, MT	2 498	29 975	6 041	1 006	5 389	2 170	1 373	887	29 586	1 112	30.5	33.3	44.6
Greeley, CO	5 193	66 870	7 992	11 496	8 049	4 019	1 886	2 533	37 873	3 921	34.4	18.1	40.9
Green Bay, WI	7 724	145 869	20 148	27 930	16 665	10 306	5 761	5 855	40 138	3 190	37.1	6.7	49.7
Greensboro-High Point, NC..	17 838	301 172	40 540	55 476	36 268	15 559	11 039	10 893	36 169	3 327	49.3	3.4	43.9
Greenville, NC	3 785	58 689	16 317	4 919	8 859	1 859	1 897	1 776	30 254	727	37.0	19.5	59.3
Greenville-Mauldin-Easley, SC	15 244	254 944	31 161	39 548	30 362	9 151	14 232	8 969	35 181	2 759	57.3	2.6	32.1
Gulfport-Biloxi, MS	5 184	83 310	14 277	4 782	13 030	3 296	4 858	2 792	33 515	976	54.6	3.2	37.3
Hagerstown-Martinsburg, MD-WV	5 352	79 593	15 134	8 637	13 981	5 911	3 022	2 625	32 982	1 889	51.0	3.4	44.4
Hanford-Corcoran, CA	1 638	23 220	4 546	3 666	4 146	582	501	760	32 739	1 129	53.3	17.7	57.8
Harrisburg-Carlisle, PA	13 404	266 078	46 555	17 891	32 783	21 191	15 359	10 438	39 376	3 388	46.9	3.7	43.2
Harrisonburg, VA	2 992	51 203	6 880	9 395	8 307	1 240	1 276	1 575	30 760	1 970	46.3	3.3	51.3
Hartford-West Hartford-East Hartford, CT	29 648	540 720	95 692	65 318	62 040	67 917	33 057	26 699	49 377	1 667	68.0	1.6	45.7
Hattiesburg, MS	3 369	50 576	11 174	5 440	9 338	1 901	1 800	1 513	29 909	1 238	42.6	3.1	37.8
Hickory-Lenoir-Morganton, NC	7 813	126 473	18 549	41 760	16 127	2 492	2 786	3 930	31 070	2 304	57.8	2.1	39.5
Hinesville-Fort Stewart, GA ..	898	13 434	1 881	1 323	2 318	279	526	424	31 535	135	45.9	10.4	40.7
Holland-Grand Haven, MI	5 748	90 843	10 543	27 905	9 893	2 191	4 125	3 232	35 574	1 451	59.4	4.9	43.2
Honolulu, HI	21 748	338 594	48 340	10 135	44 004	16 747	18 718	12 917	38 150	967	90.6	1.6	71.5
Hot Springs, AR	2 738	31 558	6 823	2 338	6 035	976	1 162	848	26 859	439	56.9	2.1	38.3
Houma-Bayou Cane-Thibo-daux, LA	4 888	79 330	10 141	8 244	11 797	1 982	3 185	3 134	39 501	609	46.6	12.0	44.7
Houston-Sugar Land-Bay-town, TX	121 540	2 231 816	259 255	209 879	255 900	92 132	185 484	114 512	51 309	15 451	58.5	6.8	35.5
Huntington-Ashland, WV-KY-OH	5 946	95 955	25 068	9 880	15 832	2 736	3 706	3 243	33 799	2 330	32.1	2.5	37.2
Huntsville, AL	9 417	170 137	21 321	25 376	21 413	3 890	33 710	7 379	43 370	2 539	50.1	6.5	39.2
Idaho Falls, ID	3 701	46 088	7 446	3 255	7 500	1 296	D	1 673	36 310	1 752	53.6	17.4	40.9
Indianapolis-Carmel, IN	42 643	762 105	111 842	77 202	89 872	44 325	46 852	31 493	41 323	5 756	58.1	12.0	42.9
Iowa City, IA	3 720	65 803	17 562	6 113	9 593	2 371	1 971	2 164	32 893	2 550	28.5	15.8	52.8
Ithaca, NY	2 297	45 542	5 178	2 867	5 115	1 081	2 537	1 563	34 320	588	40.5	9.0	45.9
Jackson, MI	3 077	45 403	9 248	7 504	7 059	1 536	2 257	1 737	38 263	1 184	50.3	6.1	40.2
Jackson, MS	12 845	205 638	40 639	17 260	27 937	12 510	11 470	7 297	35 483	3 969	33.1	8.0	37.1
Jackson, TN	2 798	52 041	11 347	8 479	7 231	1 420	1 293	1 687	32 421	1 190	32.8	8.5	37.0
Jacksonville, FL	34 400	508 838	73 895	25 291	67 530	48 131	37 100	19 942	39 191	1 732	76.0	3.3	43.0
Jacksonville, NC	2 639	33 956	5 891	884	7 599	1 055	1 495	836	24 616	401	51.1	5.5	59.1
Janesville, WI	3 347	51 757	8 503	8 619	8 918	1 794	1 131	1 811	34 987	1 556	45.5	9.6	47.6
Jefferson City, MO	3 610	50 339	9 030	5 375	7 710	2 519	2 001	1 693	33 630	4 925	23.3	8.7	39.6
Johnson City, TN	3 839	63 595	14 103	8 425	10 737	3 844	2 616	1 911	30 048	2 252	59.8	1.8	39.1
Johnstown, PA	3 439	50 616	11 709	5 918	7 156	2 299	3 286	1 555	30 719	656	37.0	5.6	38.6
Jonesboro, AR	2 780	39 957	8 375	6 498	7 139	1 358	1 023	1 169	29 247	1 154	34.9	34.3	55.4
Joplin, MO	4 312	72 838	12 781	12 589	10 220	1 856	1 473	2 274	31 216	2 959	35.6	6.5	42.5
Kalamazoo-Portage, MI	7 017	117 250	20 645	19 179	15 771	5 104	7 450	4 238	36 148	2 086	51.6	5.5	46.7
Kankakee-Bradley, IL	2 424	35 858	6 651	5 021	5 748	1 639	774	1 130	31 507	835	34.9	26.6	51.0
Kansas City, MO-KS	50 729	893 093	121 704	80 978	106 473	63 304	70 745	37 409	41 887	15 529	37.0	10.1	38.7
Kennewick-Pasco-Richland, WA	5 242	72 599	10 516	5 282	11 519	2 108	8 902	3 143	43 293	2 521	60.2	15.9	47.8
Killeen-Temple-Fort Hood, TX	5 830	95 349	20 836	6 894	15 751	4 055	5 175	3 085	32 358	4 689	41.4	13.9	37.5
Kingsport-Bristol-Bristol, TN-VA	6 214	109 191	18 508	26 068	16 053	3 130	2 959	3 666	33 579	6 150	49.8	2.3	38.6
Kingston, NY	4 682	45 021	8 572	3 557	8 731	2 763	1 921	1 417	31 468	501	42.1	5.0	57.1
Knoxville, TN	16 294	291 501	43 899	29 662	43 788	14 452	21 810	10 913	37 438	4 178	55.7	1.8	39.7

Table C. Metropolitan Areas — **Agriculture**

	Agriculture, 2007 (cont.)														
Area name	Land in farms					Value of land and buildings (dollars)		Value of machinery and equipment, average per farm (dollars)	Value of products sold				Percent of farms with sales of:		Government payments	
	Acreage (1,000)	Percent change, 2002–2007	Acres			Average per farm	Average per acre		Total (mil dol)	Average per farm (dollars)	Percent from:		$10,000 or more	$100,000 or more	Total ($1,000)	Percent of farms
			Average size of farm	Total irrigated (1,000)	Total cropland (1,000)						Crops	Live-stock and poultry products				
	117	118	119	120	121	122	123	124	125	126	127	128	129	130	131	132
Flagstaff, AZ	6 102	D	3 821	2.2	20.5	752 116	197	22 738	D	D	D	D	7.4	1.9	372	3.0
Flint, MI	129	-9.8	131	1.1	106.6	488 344	3 733	82 249	58.8	59 489	81.3	18.7	31.4	9.2	1 569	31.6
Florence, SC	331	-0.6	317	6.6	227.0	683 855	2 155	105 826	108.9	104 282	56.6	43.4	35.1	12.8	7 670	54.5
Florence-Muscle Shoals, AL.	357	5.0	147	3.5	168.3	332 283	2 267	52 669	87.4	35 921	29.0	71.0	26.6	5.1	7 242	34.6
Fond du Lac, WI	336	-2.3	204	0.9	279.9	721 664	3 532	127 243	290.4	176 760	24.0	76.0	56.1	30.6	5 413	77.6
Fort Collins-Loveland, CO	490	-6.1	279	63.4	120.0	695 145	2 494	63 923	128.1	72 921	38.9	61.1	26.0	6.8	803	9.0
Fort Smith, AR-OK	1 075	-0.6	176	14.6	369.7	367 435	2 089	58 848	510.4	83 515	7.7	92.3	34.4	9.2	3 595	8.6
Fort Wayne, IN	586	-14.2	185	1.8	532.9	702 875	3 790	87 713	314.6	99 583	68.4	31.6	45.2	18.7	11 658	65.5
Fresno, CA	1 636	-15.2	269	984.5	1 102.2	2 132 914	7 927	147 707	3 730.5	613 476	67.0	33.0	71.6	33.6	24 737	9.2
Gadsden, AL	94	4.4	94	0.6	29.6	282 306	3 009	44 457	66.2	65 893	5.3	94.7	23.2	7.0	518	11.2
Gainesville, FL	244	-19.7	116	21.2	98.5	825 789	7 113	49 698	168.8	80 317	48.1	51.9	27.3	5.4	1 777	8.2
Gainesville, GA	57	-8.1	72	0.2	15.4	532 486	7 426	53 349	181.5	227 193	0.6	99.4	31.0	19.3	213	11.3
Glens Falls, NY	211	-0.9	228	0.5	113.3	497 142	2 184	99 374	D	D	D	D	47.4	19.6	2 189	25.0
Goldsboro, NC	175	2.3	242	6.7	131.7	1 008 378	4 160	163 067	501.2	693 189	15.0	85.0	59.2	38.0	3 902	50.5
Grand Forks, ND-MN	1 925	3.1	746	27.5	1 730.3	977 778	1 311	202 134	597.0	231 221	92.3	7.7	45.9	30.7	31 811	85.2
Grand Junction, CO	373	-3.1	211	64.3	131.2	703 108	3 335	57 102	61.2	34 652	49.4	50.6	28.1	5.7	476	7.9
Grand Rapids-Wyoming, MI .	710	-1.5	158	27.7	534.3	597 908	3 781	85 735	591.5	131 710	42.1	57.9	36.0	13.4	7 836	38.5
Great Falls, MT	1 380	-0.6	1 241	35.6	506.6	1 130 619	911	85 783	83.6	75 148	49.0	51.0	37.5	15.3	5 971	52.2
Greeley, CO	2 089	15.3	533	327.8	987.9	825 561	1 550	123 541	1 539.1	392 520	17.7	82.3	39.8	16.4	15 403	39.4
Green Bay, WI	569	-3.6	178	1.9	449.5	614 546	3 448	113 064	564.5	176 960	16.0	84.0	47.8	25.7	7 816	60.5
Greensboro-High Point, NC..	361	-10.6	108	7.7	153.4	503 144	4 638	59 080	286.2	86 024	21.3	78.7	29.9	11.8	1 349	15.6
Greenville, NC	264	-7.0	363	8.5	198.8	1 235 199	3 405	146 616	368.7	507 165	31.8	68.2	59.7	37.1	8 024	55.6
Greenville-Mauldin-Easley, SC	254	-8.0	92	3.0	83.3	401 523	4 362	43 659	65.6	23 776	D	D	15.6	2.1	1 088	8.9
Gulfport-Biloxi, MS	116	-3.3	118	0.6	26.7	380 352	3 212	49 307	14.0	14 340	D	D	19.3	1.9	969	13.2
Hagerstown-Martinsburg, MD-WV	212	-5.8	112	1.1	127.8	775 919	6 927	64 246	107.3	56 780	33.1	66.9	31.8	12.4	1 194	21.3
Hanford-Corcoran, CA	681	5.4	603	421.6	512.9	3 295 061	5 465	245 730	1 358.4	1 203 198	48.0	52.0	63.7	41.9	23 258	35.5
Harrisburg-Carlisle, PA	391	6.5	115	1.7	281.6	644 383	5 579	73 842	320.8	94 670	17.6	82.4	38.9	17.4	5 105	34.4
Harrisonburg, VA	233	NA	118	4.8	114.5	727 644	6 150	84 927	534.1	271 138	3.8	96.2	54.7	31.6	1 356	16.1
Hartford-West Hartford-East Hartford, CT	109	3.8	66	7.0	53.8	926 360	14 108	73 912	227.0	136 118	88.4	11.6	35.6	11.1	836	4.7
Hattiesburg, MS	160	3.2	129	1.8	42.3	352 911	2 736	55 212	61.8	49 899	18.6	81.4	26.6	5.7	2 742	24.7
Hickory-Lenoir-Morganton, NC	189	-7.4	82	5.3	83.9	441 797	5 399	55 330	198.9	86 295	24.3	75.7	28.9	12.2	835	10.2
Hinesville-Fort Stewart, GA ..	23	-42.5	167	0.5	6.1	355 065	2 129	71 386	5.5	40 978	15.4	84.6	18.5	3.7	154	15.6
Holland-Grand Haven, MI	171	3.6	118	15.2	130.0	683 668	5 817	97 890	391.1	269 533	59.3	40.7	51.8	24.7	1 463	24.9
Honolulu, HI	60	-15.5	62	8.4	18.9	1 106 333	17 710	61 269	126.6	130 897	84.4	15.6	48.2	15.1	294	1.8
Hot Springs, AR	39	-15.2	90	0.1	11.4	329 321	3 662	37 905	12.2	27 886	19.4	80.6	19.1	3.4	41	3.2
Houma-Bayou Cane-Thibodaux, LA	285	39.7	467	3.6	85.2	772 453	1 653	105 878	69.9	114 755	44.9	55.1	39.6	10.0	192	5.4
Houston-Sugar Land-Baytown, TX	2 710	-9.0	175	59.5	949.7	458 301	2 613	52 832	398.6	25 802	62.1	37.9	21.1	3.3	14 455	7.1
Huntington-Ashland, WV-KY-OH	274	-2.1	118	0.1	71.2	264 161	2 248	40 040	13.8	5 878	35.4	64.6	11.7	0.5	392	14.1
Huntsville, AL	436	2.8	172	13.9	272.8	458 553	2 667	64 462	108.3	42 646	56.1	43.9	28.4	6.6	13 226	34.3
Idaho Falls, ID	778	-0.6	444	366.3	523.7	909 499	2 047	125 875	422.4	241 055	55.7	44.3	43.1	18.4	8 152	43.4
Indianapolis-Carmel, IN	1 354	-2.0	235	D	1 210.5	952 245	4 048	100 975	697.1	121 101	D	D	40.9	17.8	22 173	48.8
Iowa City, IA	647	1.9	254	3.2	550.8	943 716	3 719	118 547	458.8	179 906	43.8	56.2	60.2	33.9	18 196	77.6
Ithaca, NY	109	7.9	185	0.3	67.3	418 353	2 262	94 081	60.2	102 355	25.4	74.6	39.6	17.0	955	30.4
Jackson, MI	182	-5.7	154	3.8	135.1	534 327	3 469	73 640	56.9	48 039	55.8	44.2	31.0	8.6	2 030	32.3
Jackson, MS	872	1.0	220	4.4	257.1	455 853	2 075	59 209	450.1	113 423	9.4	90.6	25.8	8.2	11 269	30.2
Jackson, TN	249	3.3	209	1.6	170.8	563 817	2 697	68 294	33.2	27 837	77.8	22.2	20.4	5.7	6 382	62.7
Jacksonville, FL	160	D	92	18.3	39.9	647 007	7 010	41 530	61.8	35 693	D	D	17.6	4.5	108	2.7
Jacksonville, NC	55	-14.1	138	5.2	38.1	628 054	4 562	84 654	159.1	396 646	11.8	88.2	46.4	32.4	1 271	34.7
Janesville, WI	344	0.0	221	15.6	298.2	891 333	4 028	113 908	195.6	125 720	62.2	37.8	46.9	21.7	7 095	71.7
Jefferson City, MO	1 044	-6.5	212	5.3	468.7	489 787	2 310	59 835	293.2	59 531	21.4	78.6	45.7	8.2	5 979	35.3
Johnson City, TN	163	-9.4	72	1.0	82.7	376 273	5 208	53 999	46.2	20 533	24.2	75.8	22.1	3.0	D	13.4
Johnstown, PA	88	0.0	134	0.0	54.6	466 056	3 477	62 980	23.2	35 317	47.2	52.8	26.1	6.9	756	32.0
Jonesboro, AR	678	-7.4	587	506.5	624.7	1 375 169	2 342	221 904	313.1	271 313	98.0	2.0	53.6	37.1	30 648	59.9
Joplin, MO	505	-9.3	171	6.3	243.7	411 304	2 411	59 052	328.3	110 931	14.8	85.2	39.8	8.7	3 847	23.5
Kalamazoo-Portage, MI	330	1.9	158	61.8	251.0	670 849	4 238	105 030	352.8	169 093	77.0	23.0	41.0	17.0	3 410	25.3
Kankakee-Bradley, IL	386	11.2	462	16.0	376.2	2 000 617	4 330	187 468	244.1	292 277	88.8	11.2	70.2	41.8	5 988	75.0
Kansas City, MO-KS	3 607	-2.0	232	D	2 182.2	517 348	2 227	63 988	818.6	52 715	D	D	36.2	8.7	35 030	43.3
Kennewick-Pasco-Richland, WA	1 242	-2.4	493	398.8	944.4	1 105 169	2 244	139 043	992.9	393 864	85.9	14.1	43.4	26.1	13 302	18.0
Killeen-Temple-Fort Hood, TX	1 336	-1.5	285	4.0	375.4	590 850	2 073	54 366	115.8	24 711	35.2	64.8	26.0	3.7	3 143	16.0
Kingsport-Bristol-Bristol, TN-VA	586	-6.1	95	0.9	199.3	373 200	3 918	47 743	92.9	15 106	18.1	81.9	22.0	2.2	1 444	16.4
Kingston, NY	75	-9.6	150	4.7	31.7	598 130	3 985	92 909	65.6	130 928	89.7	10.3	42.9	15.8	284	11.0
Knoxville, TN	344	-8.8	82	1.4	162.8	442 163	5 363	57 759	105.5	25 252	D	D	17.7	1.7	394	8.1

Table C. Metropolitan Areas — Water Use, Wholesale Trade, Retail Trade, and Real Estate

Area name	Water use, 2005 Total water withdrawn (mil gal/day)	Gallons withdrawn per person	Wholesale trade,[1] 2007 Number of establishments	Number of employees	Sales (mil dol)	Annual payroll (mil dol)	Retail trade, 2007 Number of establishments	Number of employees	Sales (mil dol)	Annual payroll (mil dol)	Real estate and rental and leasing, 2007 Number of establishments	Number of employees	Receipts (mil dol)	Annual payroll (mil dol)
	133	134	135	136	137	138	139	140	141	142	143	144	145	146
Flagstaff, AZ......................	48.0	387	110	1 422	604.8	49.4	674	7 861	1 691.7	169.3	237	754	187.5	24.2
Flint, MI	20.4	46	351	7 069	4 820.8	427.9	1 614	21 531	4 836.7	440.5	339	1 813	270.2	47.7
Florence, SC	835.7	4 211	248	3 648	2 359.2	136.4	1 027	11 963	2 765.4	233.1	170	815	182.6	21.2
Florence-Muscle Shoals, AL.	1 380.3	9 697	178	2 425	1 138.6	77.1	683	8 102	1 952.9	167.1	124	556	68.1	12.5
Fond du Lac, WI	13.5	136	115	1 827	1 577.9	88.3	407	5 999	1 277.7	118.3	77	305	34.3	5.3
Fort Collins-Loveland, CO	504.4	1 855	359	5 978	4 107.4	407.8	1 306	17 510	3 922.9	402.7	562	2 181	327.1	63.6
Fort Smith, AR-OK..............	85.2	299	333	4 053	2 385.7	146.1	1 072	13 267	3 157.1	268.5	268	1 326	212.0	40.6
Fort Wayne, IN....................	63.8	158	719	11 763	14 384.5	465.5	1 569	24 077	5 339.0	493.8	466	2 102	343.2	58.9
Fresno, CA..........................	3 260.2	3 715	941	14 594	9 307.3	671.5	2 579	38 046	9 808.3	905.0	755	4 478	695.2	132.1
Gadsden, AL........................	173.9	1 685	102	1 288	588.0	43.9	453	4 786	1 114.8	92.7	79	428	68.7	12.1
Gainesville, FL	74.8	291	217	2 742	1 510.4	110.2	1 010	14 849	3 204.7	304.8	405	2 086	316.2	60.0
Gainesville, GA	108.6	655	317	4 112	5 520.4	189.9	630	8 134	2 220.7	206.5	229	558	125.5	18.4
Glens Falls, NY	22.2	173	114	1 081	686.6	43.9	658	7 833	1 867.8	182.4	106	435	72.7	11.5
Goldsboro, NC	45.1	394	117	2 092	1 268.6	81.9	501	5 759	1 388.0	113.7	70	288	35.3	6.6
Grand Forks, ND-MN...........	36.3	374	154	1 840	1 302.3	71.5	458	7 262	1 536.0	141.6	75	511	62.7	10.7
Grand Junction, CO.............	926.3	7 132	254	2 766	1 385.8	117.9	693	8 856	2 389.5	223.8	323	1 101	246.9	40.1
Grand Rapids-Wyoming, MI .	118.9	154	1 267	26 437	19 901.8	1 391.8	2 698	38 265	9 136.1	811.4	729	D	D	D
Great Falls, MT	189.2	2 378	132	1 225	758.4	47.8	388	5 507	1 302.3	121.0	137	378	56.3	8.3
Greeley, CO........................	773.0	3 377	275	3 811	3 471.5	167.5	650	8 735	2 246.1	212.9	227	838	115.6	23.7
Green Bay, WI	1 356.8	4 561	459	6 744	4 622.3	312.9	1 187	17 523	3 948.8	358.1	273	1 697	238.1	47.1
Greensboro-High Point, NC..	362.1	537	1 555	23 166	20 428.2	1 158.6	2 782	38 394	9 248.9	890.9	824	5 046	1 517.8	158.0
Greenville, NC.....................	34.8	214	165	1 845	1 003.8	76.7	713	9 221	2 273.8	185.3	205	860	129.8	27.2
Greenville-Mauldin-Easley, SC.,,,,,,,,,,,	106.2	180	986	13 098	14 081.9	664.8	2 386	31 461	7 560.2	690.4	735	3 680	822.0	132.3
Gulfport-Biloxi, MS	209.3	820	213	2 013	1 042.5	86.9	1 002	13 198	3 477.1	302.9	295	1 075	191.1	31.4
Hagerstown-Martinsburg, MD-WV	95.4	380	208	3 151	1 990.0	135.4	999	14 220	3 444.5	302.5	239	1 016	180.2	25.4
Hanford-Corcoran, CA	1 380.4	9 625	67	D	D	D	326	4 267	1 035.9	93.9	95	343	55.4	7.2
Harrisburg-Carlisle, PA	219.4	420	627	15 518	14 070.1	784.1	2 125	33 703	7 947.8	725.1	462	3 430	807.8	123.9
Harrisonburg, VA	44.3	397	129	2 364	1 562.3	92.4	601	8 250	1 920.8	200.1	127	1 285	172.7	37.5
Hartford-West Hartford-East Hartford, CT	387.4	326	1 515	27 480	25 182.0	1 561.2	4 578	66 748	17 156.2	1 646.9	1 188	7 661	1 500.4	298.6
Hattiesburg, MS	75.2	570	131	1 692	1 410.5	54.7	739	9 647	3 173.8	199.3	166	609	82.4	16.4
Hickory-Lenoir-Morganton, NC	1 217.8	3 424	471	9 323	6 434.0	395.2	1 441	18 856	4 209.6	366.9	320	1 098	190.5	29.5
Hinesville-Fort Stewart, GA ..	17.0	247	13	D	D	D	204	2 004	556.7	42.0	55	238	29.4	5.9
Holland-Grand Haven, MI	854.5	3 346	372	3 682	2 973.4	164.1	830	10 670	2 367.8	220.4	186	891	107.9	23.9
Honolulu, HI	1 593.3	1 760	1 419	16 288	10 152.0	879.6	3 058	46 613	11 518.8	1 144.1	1 294	9 867	2 660.2	399.9
Hot Springs, AR..................	19.9	212	107	1 402	1 176.0	55.9	523	5 898	1 443.4	126.9	158	614	88.0	14.6
Houma-Bayou Cane-Thibodaux, LA	67.9	340	298	4 019	2 119.2	180.6	796	11 724	2 832.9	259.9	256	2 290	487.9	103.0
Houston-Sugar Land-Baytown, TX	4 287.5	812	8 790	138 496	283 564.2	8 341.6	16 938	251 088	69 984.2	6 074.4	6 455	47 101	11 098.2	2 018.8
Huntington-Ashland, WV-KY-OH...............................	150.1	525	257	3 409	3 931.5	136.9	1 179	16 402	3 527.9	306.9	233	888	132.8	20.9
Huntsville, AL	2 084.4	5 654	496	6 679	4 298.8	350.3	1 594	21 451	5 161.9	479.9	487	2 247	369.3	69.3
Idaho Falls, ID....................	2 990.0	26 358	196	3 945	2 780.6	145.9	568	7 849	1 963.8	167.4	155	548	91.8	12.2
Indianapolis-Carmel, IN	666.8	406	2 817	44 273	39 808.4	2 236.5	5 955	94 406	22 908.2	2 182.8	2 163	14 833	2 732.4	557.0
Iowa City, IA.......................	49.5	357	151	1 665	1 156.8	66.9	639	9 417	1 848.1	185.7	157	720	143.4	21.7
Ithaca, NY	254.2	2 541	60	498	256.7	19.8	372	5 068	1 018.3	106.1	95	748	116.2	19.8
Jackson, MI	22.6	138	168	2 011	2 085.7	90.1	582	7 462	1 690.9	153.6	118	608	64.9	12.5
Jackson, MS	92.9	178	805	13 008	10 469.1	588.3	2 125	28 700	6 842.9	630.8	594	3 156	700.8	106.6
Jackson, TN	22.0	199	186	2 313	1 442.9	96.3	564	7 507	1 814.1	162.9	115	787	102.8	19.6
Jacksonville, FL	891.1	697	1 813	28 131	29 028.3	1 440.2	5 190	74 132	18 173.6	1 692.3	2 141	10 977	2 447.5	444.5
Jacksonville, NC	18.6	122	47	281	113.6	11.5	550	7 276	1 913.9	154.2	185	757	108.4	17.2
Janesville, WI	96.0	609	150	3 305	2 902.1	161.6	579	9 269	2 439.8	216.8	126	432	92.6	10.3
Jefferson City, MO..............	110.5	768	133	3 192	1 023.1	97.7	606	7 808	1 827.3	158.6	116	360	53.0	8.1
Johnson City, TN	50.4	267	170	2 294	1 353.5	82.3	749	10 577	2 449.9	216.8	162	1 079	128.8	20.4
Johnstown, PA....................	18.6	125	139	1 641	656.9	53.3	588	7 207	1 626.5	137.9	99	584	65.8	16.7
Jonesboro, AR	1 182.3	10 548	163	1 921	1 206.1	77.8	587	7 419	1 634.1	139.8	115	545	79.7	13.2
Joplin, MO...........................	39.5	238	207	3 128	1 709.4	106.4	799	10 096	2 573.1	208.2	182	835	95.0	19.2
Kalamazoo-Portage, MI	226.9	710	358	5 456	3 870.0	340.7	1 180	16 579	3 365.5	327.5	271	2 701	239.3	72.0
Kankakee-Bradley, IL...........	35.3	327	129	2 274	1 410.4	94.0	389	5 737	1 258.5	118.1	105	342	63.5	9.5
Kansas City, MO-KS............	1 615.9	830	3 403	64 263	66 226.3	2 953.3	6 840	110 941	27 215.8	2 521.7	2 726	15 815	3 167.4	531.1
Kennewick-Pasco-Richland, WA	1 394.5	6 311	231	2 843	2 702.3	127.9	762	11 477	2 910.5	280.3	270	1 276	244.8	37.2
Killeen-Temple-Fort Hood, TX	115.7	329	168	3 345	4 520.1	143.8	1 125	14 902	3 999.7	334.1	377	1 704	232.0	44.9
Kingsport-Bristol-Bristol, TN-VA	1 320.1	4 382	329	5 782	5 204.9	272.3	1 238	15 165	3 555.5	316.0	242	997	198.3	26.6
Kingston, NY	472.5	2 586	160	D	D	D	794	9 242	2 241.1	216.3	209	676	125.2	18.4
Knoxville, TN	672.4	1 026	1 042	15 943	17 370.7	853.9	2 757	45 019	11 164.5	1 065.4	744	4 016	756.1	124.0

1. Merchant wholesalers, except manufacturers' sales branches and offices.

Table C. Metropolitan Areas — Professional Services, Manufacturing, and Accommodation and Food Services

Area name	Professional, scientific, and technical services,[1] 2007				Manufacturing, 2007				Accommodation and food services, 2007			
	Number of establishments	Number of employees	Sales (mil dol)	Annual payroll (mil dol)	Number of establishments	Number of employees	Sales (mil dol)	Annual payroll (mil dol)	Number of establishments	Number of employees	Sales (mil dol)	Annual payroll (mil dol)
	147	148	149	150	151	152	153	154	155	156	157	158
Flagstaff, AZ	322	D	D	D	109	4 219	1 526.8	240.5	531	11 181	717.7	181.9
Flint, MI	694	D	D	D	309	14 878	12 579.5	1 099.6	762	13 583	528.7	151.9
Florence, SC	287	D	D	D	182	11 892	5 318.7	546.2	374	7 173	303.9	81.7
Florence-Muscle Shoals, AL.	270	D	D	D	203	7 312	3 166.8	301.3	249	5 128	198.5	56.3
Fond du Lac, WI	157	1 320	101.9	65.4	151	9 745	2 903.2	392.3	242	4 001	131.5	37.5
Fort Collins-Loveland, CO	1 327	7 876	867.5	387.3	420	11 764	3 226.8	664.5	807	14 244	604.4	181.9
Fort Smith, AR-OK	498	D	D	D	337	25 540	7 272.0	816.0	477	8 222	332.1	90.5
Fort Wayne, IN	978	7 253	753.3	346.6	694	38 250	22 548.5	1 837.4	803	16 997	598.0	182.2
Fresno, CA	1 564	D	D	D	646	26 898	7 827.3	1 018.0	1 460	25 553	1 147.2	320.9
Gadsden, AL	156	876	76.6	26.8	118	5 430	1 253.0	203.7	177	3 381	138.0	38.1
Gainesville, FL	810	5 326	629.8	265.2	154	4 028	1 068.9	178.6	543	11 333	502.1	135.7
Gainesville, GA	419	D	D	D	265	17 296	6 069.0	602.5	272	4 930	224.1	62.5
Glens Falls, NY	250	1 196	113.7	43.9	176	7 263	1 962.7	302.9	529	5 579	325.0	97.8
Goldsboro, NC	143	825	65.7	22.8	84	6 147	1 474.8	221.7	197	3 485	132.1	36.2
Grand Forks, ND-MN	157	D	D	D	94	4 495	1 519.4	152.9	247	5 190	177.8	51.3
Grand Junction, CO	547	D	D	D	177	2 691	539.6	104.9	301	6 307	268.8	77.6
Grand Rapids-Wyoming, MI .	1 821	D	D	D	1 344	69 520	18 393.9	3 337.5	1 382	27 437	1 027.0	312.3
Great Falls, MT	199	D	D	D	81	1 094	670.9	44.8	247	3 997	174.3	48.6
Greeley, CO	462	D	D	D	284	10 186	4 193.7	451.8	379	6 099	217.2	63.8
Green Bay, WI	588	D	D	D	552	29 482	10 130.5	1 245.0	769	14 107	507.2	146.5
Greensboro-High Point, NC..	1 814	D	D	D	1 194	63 505	31 456.5	2 461.3	1 432	27 982	1 260.5	353.3
Greenville, NC	318	1 778	200.8	77.8	107	7 017	2 053.5	268.5	315	7 345	299.9	81.0
Greenville-Mauldin-Easley, SC	1 611	14 533	2 147.8	825.9	825	41 280	13 843.6	1 672.0	1 304	24 444	1 014.4	282.4
Gulfport-Biloxi, MS	504	D	D	D	165	4 713	D	219.0	458	20 051	1 771.6	473.7
Hagerstown-Martinsburg, MD-WV	382	D	D	D	201	10 289	3 522.3	464.8	494	8 122	397.6	105.1
Hanford-Corcoran, CA	101	535	52.9	16.9	73	4 291	2 107.7	148.7	171	4 209	360.1	77.5
Harrisburg-Carlisle, PA	1 390	14 474	2 081.9	808.0	450	20 726	7 695.4	876.1	1 264	22 498	1 101.3	315.8
Harrisonburg, VA	233	D	D	D	134	10 112	6 183.8	399.8	257	6 326	230.7	73.8
Hartford-West Hartford-East Hartford, CT	2 900	D	D	D	1 813	77 946	19 374.0	4 299.5	2 577	41 547	2 104.5	622.3
Hattiesburg, MS	292	D	D	D	110	5 737	1 282.6	198.1	281	6 813	263.6	73.3
Hickory-Lenoir-Morganton, NC	584	D	D	D	845	50 686	10 725.5	1 618.2	645	11 611	466.1	127.1
Hinesville-Fort Stewart, GA ..	57	D	D	D	19	1 183	704.0	58.3	101	1 767	64.7	16.5
Holland-Grand Haven, MI	515	D	D	D	584	31 912	9 210.9	1 395.5	381	7 551	277.2	83.8
Honolulu, HI	2 433	18 508	2 686.9	1 056.8	684	10 996	8 201.9	398.9	2 347	57 064	4 123.8	1 126.5
Hot Springs, AR	218	D	D	D	119	2 786	661.7	99.9	265	5 080	203.3	62.2
Houma-Bayou Cane-Thibodaux, LA	441	D	D	D	185	8 372	1 729.9	360.7	397	7 226	339.8	95.2
Houston-Sugar Land-Baytown, TX	15 662	181 596	34 284.2	13 772.5	5 484	222 142	238 606.5	12 175.3	9 616	197 339	10 225.1	2 740.7
Huntington-Ashland, WV-KY-OH	400	D	D	D	213	10 799	15 159.1	562.3	537	10 187	386.3	107.4
Huntsville, AL	1 374	32 363	5 761.6	2 244.1	391	27 771	9 598.0	1 303.6	739	15 537	664.5	184.8
Idaho Falls, ID	426	D	D	D	177	3 649	796.3	119.1	224	4 062	160.9	43.1
Indianapolis-Carmel, IN	4 907	43 194	6 898.8	2 701.5	1 803	88 795	35 647.6	4 407.4	3 598	75 084	3 413.5	1 004.1
Iowa City, IA	293	D	D	D	122	6 712	8 945.4	263.8	370	8 130	373.5	97.1
Ithaca, NY	273	D	D	D	92	3 152	742.8	137.3	308	3 742	177.7	51.9
Jackson, MI	235	D	D	D	284	9 250	2 783.0	403.6	300	4 999	185.4	53.5
Jackson, MS	1 398	10 281	1 536.4	535.8	403	19 953	10 509.1	813.4	990	19 771	818.4	218.5
Jackson, TN	206	D	D	D	137	10 111	4 567.9	452.1	235	5 780	216.4	58.5
Jacksonville, FL	4 453	33 141	4 168.3	1 671.0	869	31 029	13 029.4	1 460.0	2 713	53 981	2 747.5	786.4
Jacksonville, NC	210	D	D	D	43	1 016	253.0	31.8	310	6 265	287.9	71.5
Janesville, WI	199	D	D	D	236	13 527	12 381.6	720.3	383	5 673	211.7	58.6
Jefferson City, MO	303	1 653	192.6	69.2	160	5 992	2 357.6	239.2	267	4 426	173.1	50.2
Johnson City, TN	285	D	D	D	212	10 146	2 222.9	367.4	348	7 873	302.0	90.3
Johnstown, PA	221	D	D	D	146	5 409	1 439.8	199.6	307	4 135	156.0	40.9
Jonesboro, AR	194	D	D	D	139	7 289	2 002.3	259.0	215	4 324	158.3	44.2
Joplin, MO	269	D	D	D	269	13 785	3 983.2	490.7	352	6 754	251.9	73.1
Kalamazoo-Portage, MI	647	D	D	D	434	21 099	8 458.8	1 065.0	675	13 767	495.2	153.7
Kankakee-Bradley, IL	169	D	D	D	115	5 633	3 418.9	280.8	229	D	D	D
Kansas City, MO-KS	6 155	D	D	D	2 033	82 421	38 876.0	4 091.7	3 882	84 322	4 368.5	1 184.5
Kennewick-Pasco-Richland, WA	470	D	D	D	190	5 975	2 049.7	241.7	447	6 634	305.7	89.1
Killeen-Temple-Fort Hood, TX	427	D	D	D	179	7 848	2 146.6	278.0	610	10 940	462.9	120.2
Kingsport-Bristol-Bristol, TN-VA	463	2 941	300.8	109.1	320	27 089	9 083.1	1 150.5	568	11 315	434.2	122.1
Kingston, NY	455	D	D	D	202	D	D	165.3	533	6 542	321.4	103.9
Knoxville, TN	1 736	D	D	D	771	35 786	13 322.3	1 686.2	1 308	30 600	1 310.9	390.5

1. Establishments subject to federal tax.

Table C. Metropolitan Areas — Health Care and Social Assistance, Other Services, and Federal Funds

Area name	Health care and social assistance,[1] 2007				Other services,[1] 2007				Federal funds and grants, 2009–2010 — Expenditures (mil dol)			
										Direct payments for individuals		
	Number of establishments	Number of employees	Receipts (mil dol)	Annual payroll (mil dol)	Number of establishments	Number of employees	Receipts (mil dol)	Annual payroll (mil dol)	Total	Social Security and government retirement	Medicare	Food stamps and Supplemental Security Income
	159	160	161	162	163	164	165	166	167	168	169	170
Flagstaff, AZ	389	6 628	878.6	305.9	247	1 493	100.8	32.2	1 357.4	341.8	109.5	63.7
Flint, MI	1 261	25 790	2 505.1	1 005.4	648	3 695	418.1	103.4	3 751.3	1 495.5	857.8	303.7
Florence, SC	437	14 058	1 532.9	574.6	291	1 792	155.3	40.5	1 741.4	661.7	299.5	137.8
Florence-Muscle Shoals, AL.	405	7 284	660.9	251.0	219	1 393	120.9	31.9	1 276.6	647.5	269.2	53.4
Fond du Lac, WI	266	6 180	607.2	223.9	193	1 206	88.4	24.4	626.2	314.9	134.3	14.8
Fort Collins-Loveland, CO	908	15 177	1 400.5	610.6	612	3 123	286.8	77.2	1 879.7	719.3	236.7	38.7
Fort Smith, AR-OK	683	17 336	1 343.8	568.0	363	1 756	145.1	39.7	2 326.1	997.8	443.1	128.6
Fort Wayne, IN	1 114	31 151	2 944.2	1 142.1	825	5 686	457.1	140.9	3 457.0	1 110.1	468.8	125.3
Fresno, CA	2 099	36 707	4 150.8	1 713.0	1 069	7 309	704.7	191.7	5 953.8	1 736.7	991.7	468.5
Gadsden, AL	302	6 515	626.7	229.8	121	691	54.0	15.8	966.6	420.9	248.2	51.1
Gainesville, FL	729	20 958	2 363.5	926.2	390	2 806	658.1	88.3	2 490.7	709.9	467.3	111.2
Gainesville, GA	398	8 599	1 046.7	384.6	272	1 384	136.1	36.5	1 157.9	440.8	154.3	39.2
Glens Falls, NY	365	7 916	610.9	283.2	220	1 029	97.8	27.8	927.4	452.4	183.3	33.8
Goldsboro, NC	294	7 587	573.0	248.6	159	949	70.0	20.5	1 332.9	419.7	161.2	59.5
Grand Forks, ND-MN	244	8 510	646.2	281.6	215	1 471	98.5	28.9	1 009.3	247.1	135.8	22.5
Grand Junction, CO	425	8 480	847.4	336.2	317	1 599	160.1	42.3	1 064.5	462.6	163.9	33.6
Grand Rapids-Wyoming, MI .	1 755	44 696	4 274.2	1 694.3	1 354	8 877	832.6	219.4	4 504.9	1 946.7	827.8	239.2
Great Falls, MT	269	6 050	517.8	206.6	166	845	65.4	18.8	1 022.7	329.7	119.7	23.9
Greeley, CO	429	8 538	763.1	292.3	340	1 513	161.2	40.0	1 076.8	454.9	177.6	43.9
Green Bay, WI	695	21 052	2 104.4	821.4	554	3 268	251.0	70.0	1 805.7	812.2	296.5	64.4
Greensboro-High Point, NC..	1 655	38 752	3 478.4	1 436.9	1 186	6 684	843.5	177.2	5 119.3	2 098.7	829.8	223.7
Greenville, NC	482	15 787	1 448.3	594.0	198	1 108	110.0	22.0	1 235.2	448.0	183.4	90.7
Greenville-Mauldin-Easley, SC	1 298	28 740	2 888.9	1 162.6	952	6 658	603.3	176.5	4 289.6	1 916.9	675.7	188.5
Gulfport-Biloxi, MS	515	14 123	1 610.8	615.9	349	1 983	201.4	52.9	3 461.0	905.3	418.3	107.2
Hagerstown-Martinsburg, MD-WV	617	14 608	1 323.3	582.3	431	2 659	229.8	65.5	2 296.6	887.3	459.1	62.0
Hanford-Corcoran, CA	204	4 106	433.8	153.1	105	582	57.6	13.4	994.5	260.9	141.1	49.3
Harrisburg-Carlisle, PA	1 485	43 317	3 960.3	1 674.8	1 290	9 051	1 003.3	273.6	12 034.5	1 934.0	923.3	116.9
Harrisonburg, VA	245	6 349	549.2	229.3	237	1 233	118.5	30.4	576.5	273.7	111.4	17.8
Hartford-West Hartford-East Hartford, CT	3 459	91 507	8 632.4	3 847.9	2 515	18 825	1 935.7	541.0	19 348.8	3 326.8	7 193.4	350.2
Hattiesburg, MS	329	10 401	1 074.6	453.7	167	1 033	73.2	20.9	1 387.3	420.5	184.6	64.4
Hickory-Lenoir-Morganton, NC	761	17 609	1 598.0	630.1	483	2 583	257.5	67.2	2 224.3	1 148.6	427.1	100.2
Hinesville-Fort Stewart, GA ..	70	D	D	D	72	438	61.4	9.2	526.0	203.4	98.6	32.6
Holland-Grand Haven, MI	500	9 536	761.6	294.0	425	2 575	240.6	67.4	1 266.2	660.2	197.4	28.4
Honolulu, HI	2 473	47 727	5 055.4	2 047.9	2 083	15 228	1 462.7	388.7	17 392.9	3 117.6	1 100.2	333.7
Hot Springs, AR	278	6 590	613.4	244.4	179	1 309	80.6	26.6	1 017.6	513.5	231.6	44.9
Houma-Bayou Cane-Thibo-daux, LA	440	9 563	954.4	373.8	288	2 161	280.2	78.5	1 780.1	533.5	330.2	99.6
Houston-Sugar Land-Bay-town, TX	12 477	255 500	27 871.1	10 593.2	7 954	67 524	7 692.8	2 123.5	36 145.6	10 541.6	5 383.2	1 984.7
Huntington-Ashland, WV-KY-OH	868	23 995	2 299.4	929.8	447	2 666	274.7	69.0	3 042.9	1 164.2	666.4	191.4
Huntsville, AL	1 001	20 402	2 020.2	828.1	569	4 019	619.4	103.1	10 321.0	1 562.5	387.8	120.4
Idaho Falls, ID	497	7 331	626.0	235.0	183	978	87.0	23.0	2 103.3	312.1	100.4	38.8
Indianapolis-Carmel, IN	4 211	106 787	11 177.8	4 309.3	3 135	24 557	3 592.7	713.3	16 770.2	4 427.5	2 079.9	519.9
Iowa City, IA	423	16 714	1 562.4	607.3	263	1 529	193.2	38.7	1 203.5	313.8	114.4	20.8
Ithaca, NY	250	4 919	388.7	152.9	149	945	129.2	21.6	939.3	220.0	84.8	21.6
Jackson, MI	379	8 711	810.5	346.6	241	1 528	147.0	41.2	1 149.7	513.5	248.9	66.6
Jackson, MS	1 282	38 253	3 760.2	1 403.3	875	5 548	542.3	151.7	6 208.0	1 464.1	675.3	265.8
Jackson, TN	328	11 033	1 055.1	448.2	160	993	75.7	26.9	1 011.8	335.9	268.4	54.4
Jacksonville, FL	3 270	69 014	7 365.5	2 800.4	2 485	15 941	2 498.5	501.2	12 558.3	4 491.2	2 326.4	464.7
Jacksonville, NC	246	5 465	433.8	163.4	213	1 136	68.0	21.4	2 938.6	575.1	92.7	52.6
Janesville, WI	330	9 276	878.5	337.0	285	1 578	108.7	30.6	1 258.0	478.3	210.7	48.9
Jefferson City, MO	374	9 056	781.7	308.8	341	1 987	199.9	56.9	3 845.0	431.2	215.2	32.7
Johnson City, TN	429	13 218	1 334.8	525.0	267	1 476	101.5	31.8	1 862.8	764.6	427.8	92.1
Johnstown, PA	545	11 825	872.0	383.6	320	1 590	114.3	28.9	2 819.4	606.4	492.3	63.8
Jonesboro, AR	346	8 212	792.6	294.5	161	887	71.6	18.0	953.8	358.2	156.0	58.1
Joplin, MO	507	12 259	1 089.4	435.8	344	1 675	117.3	34.6	1 283.1	512.7	258.5	60.8
Kalamazoo-Portage, MI	754	20 517	1 978.8	776.7	523	3 982	511.7	103.0	2 745.9	926.9	419.8	125.9
Kankakee-Bradley, IL	290	6 260	618.8	228.6	193	1 080	105.7	26.6	794.0	326.4	202.6	42.4
Kansas City, MO-KS	4 880	116 844	11 601.6	4 734.2	3 655	24 541	3 112.4	683.1	18 387.4	5 715.0	2 909.5	538.7
Kennewick-Pasco-Richland, WA	613	9 790	952.5	374.4	325	1 808	151.3	44.5	4 614.1	660.7	186.0	95.1
Killeen-Temple-Fort Hood, TX	558	19 898	2 047.3	834.3	504	3 083	239.7	66.9	12 413.6	1 384.1	303.9	108.9
Kingsport-Bristol-Bristol, TN-VA	726	17 368	1 714.0	650.5	433	2 909	354.4	66.8	3 110.1	1 292.0	664.2	145.3
Kingston, NY	520	D	D	D	316	1 559	117.0	30.2	1 284.7	551.4	269.0	46.9
Knoxville, TN	1 705	42 022	4 132.4	1 651.0	1 143	7 707	793.7	215.5	9 945.5	2 450.3	1 340.5	276.8

1. Establishments subject to federal tax.

Table C. Metropolitan Areas —

Federal Funds, Residential Construction and Local Government Finances

Area name	Federal funds and grants, 2009–2010 (cont.)							Value of residential construction authorized by building permits, 2010		Local government finances, 2007				
	Expenditures (mil dol) (cont.)									General revenue				
	Procurement contract awards			Grants								Taxes		
													Per capita[1] (dollars)	
	Salaries and wages	Defense	Other	Medicaid and other health-related	Nutrition and family welfare	Education	Other	New construction ($1,000)	Number of housing units	Total (mil dol)	Inter-govern-mental (mil dol)	Total (mil dol)	Total	Property
	171	172	173	174	175	176	177	178	179	180	181	182	183	184
Flagstaff, AZ	171.0	6.3	128.3	330.2	40.9	50.2	48.2	40 707	315	557.6	231.7	219.0	1 718	965
Flint, MI	129.6	8.1	36.2	510.6	112.4	40.8	46.5	13 006	78	2 037.0	976.1	403.5	928	864
Florence, SC	91.3	5.2	16.8	368.5	43.4	21.2	28.1	53 502	476	542.7	250.7	185.6	934	735
Florence-Muscle Shoals, AL..	49.8	8.0	30.9	125.0	18.9	12.5	19.4	22 173	232	814.4	194.3	115.9	810	344
Fond du Lac, WI	23.2	7.1	5.1	78.8	14.5	6.4	4.9	28 206	229	412.3	176.1	143.4	1 447	1 409
Fort Collins-Loveland, CO	212.8	26.2	223.3	157.5	30.1	13.6	166.3	182 920	1 153	1 133.2	287.5	531.6	1 848	1 167
Fort Smith, AR-OK	189.4	42.1	36.0	332.0	48.7	29.4	26.3	94 983	690	781.9	449.3	193.3	667	243
Fort Wayne, IN	220.6	905.2	172.3	268.8	58.0	12.6	-46.7	147 270	885	1 213.8	451.0	429.4	1 047	853
Fresno, CA	601.7	72.9	167.6	992.0	274.8	96.6	252.1	398 560	2 248	4 901.8	2 877.0	1 069.3	1 189	832
Gadsden, AL	42.2	4.3	15.2	119.3	15.8	11.8	10.7	12 408	105	268.4	133.0	101.5	983	266
Gainesville, FL	225.4	16.6	159.3	454.4	42.2	25.1	173.7	63 708	490	922.3	333.5	315.3	1 226	950
Gainesville, GA	62.2	264.1	41.1	74.7	41.3	9.3	3.2	29 977	184	1 091.0	200.0	285.5	1 585	843
Glens Falls, NY	34.9	1.6	8.3	144.7	36.5	8.9	8.6	40 733	279	680.5	266.1	307.3	2 384	1 757
Goldsboro, NC	302.7	74.2	4.5	202.6	29.5	13.7	13.4	35 728	279	330.8	188.2	88.4	779	555
Grand Forks, ND-MN	172.8	69.5	29.0	118.7	29.0	12.2	86.1	34 971	200	381.6	163.9	114.7	1 174	940
Grand Junction, CO	89.3	38.4	99.1	98.5	13.1	8.5	20.1	83 016	408	480.7	186.9	192.8	1 387	752
Grand Rapids-Wyoming, MI...	327.2	89.0	103.8	550.7	124.2	47.0	108.0	140 940	843	2 911.5	1 413.0	909.1	1 170	1 052
Great Falls, MT	238.8	90.2	17.2	136.8	15.5	7.4	11.5	28 243	150	227.1	110.8	63.8	781	755
Greeley, CO	57.0	27.5	23.5	135.0	20.5	17.0	66.4	166 578	863	851.6	256.5	359.0	1 473	1 074
Green Bay, WI	122.1	51.1	61.2	228.2	46.9	19.8	39.2	136 827	1 134	1 263.2	571.8	458.2	1 522	1 402
Greensboro-High Point, NC...	447.9	216.2	195.0	550.3	103.2	83.3	122.8	240 634	1 903	2 202.4	1 008.7	773.2	1 107	868
Greenville, NC	55.1	13.8	9.4	263.5	29.6	18.4	28.3	76 944	678	516.9	268.3	144.5	838	612
Greenville-Mauldin-Easley, SC	270.1	338.4	36.7	397.4	73.3	41.9	178.6	334 418	1 542	2 461.3	561.9	569.1	927	788
Gulfport-Biloxi, MS	787.5	344.6	527.2	159.7	47.4	10.5	100.6	189 611	1 744	1 611.7	774.5	264.0	1 140	955
Hagerstown-Martinsburg, MD-WV	278.7	36.5	294.8	168.0	37.3	11.6	23.9	116 742	699	759.6	303.4	298.4	1 143	755
Hanford-Corcoran, CA	195.1	28.9	66.6	129.2	37.8	20.1	11.0	39 838	265	632.3	386.7	115.8	778	616
Harrisburg-Carlisle, PA	713.5	993.0	196.5	674.2	660.6	2 787.2	2 720.3	256 204	1 612	2 312.2	863.1	901.8	1 705	1 200
Harrisonburg, VA	35.3	23.2	14.6	48.7	8.2	6.0	15.8	60 261	462	322.0	145.0	126.0	1 072	672
Hartford-West Hartford-East Hartford, CT	703.2	3 420.8	245.8	1 592.4	345.7	315.6	1 586.1	214 583	1 279	4 648.4	1 604.0	2 635.0	2 216	2 179
Hattiesburg, MS	317.7	88.2	14.3	128.8	26.3	9.8	74.5	10 078	74	710.9	196.5	120.0	869	796
Hickory-Lenoir-Morganton, NC	104.1	8.7	25.1	255.0	52.7	34.5	19.3	95 989	448	1 152.9	543.0	273.7	759	554
Hinesville-Fort Stewart, GA....	121.4	34.9	2.0	34.1	16.8	15.0	11.1	22 215	111	230.2	110.9	70.7	984	534
Holland-Grand Haven, MI	41.7	105.5	62.4	68.2	32.7	11.3	12.0	75 699	434	809.0	388.8	287.7	1 110	1 090
Honolulu, HI	7 676.7	2 218.2	350.0	983.8	208.1	288.2	929.3	409 780	1 891	1 503.1	212.0	905.8	1 000	754
Hot Springs, AR	42.3	22.1	39.0	77.7	12.8	8.8	7.4	4 175	38	219.2	115.5	56.9	591	174
Houma-Bayou Cane-Thibo-daux, LA	50.7	123.7	369.0	161.3	38.4	18.9	31.2	85 827	365	953.3	312.6	273.7	1 361	458
Houston-Sugar Land-Bay-town, TX	2 793.3	3 886.9	4 615.0	4 191.9	649.4	245.9	1 067.8	4 174 877	27 452	21 578.3	5 384.7	10 996.2	1 954	1 628
Huntington-Ashland, WV-KY-OH	231.9	16.5	95.0	464.8	62.1	26.7	69.0	30 795	248	755.9	408.5	217.7	766	552
Huntsville, AL	1 360.8	5 254.2	1 129.8	207.8	35.0	35.6	106.2	296 428	2 275	1 841.8	755.2	363.9	941	411
Idaho Falls, ID	69.2	66.5	1 362.0	97.5	19.8	1.9	5.4	44 506	390	312.2	168.7	78.2	655	628
Indianapolis-Carmel, IN	1 921.8	1 374.2	552.5	1 448.4	507.1	513.8	2 464.1	837 383	5 921	6 662.6	2 171.5	2 338.9	1 380	1 160
Iowa City, IA	133.2	11.9	66.3	427.3	14.5	13.0	42.8	109 304	553	436.9	136.4	202.0	1 373	1 223
Ithaca, NY	39.8	18.9	15.5	210.4	23.7	11.1	260.2	22 337	153	478.3	175.8	213.9	2 117	1 557
Jackson, MI	65.1	17.2	7.3	140.0	36.5	10.9	9.0	10 457	63	577.7	311.0	149.1	915	851
Jackson, MS	552.5	355.4	182.9	696.7	255.0	328.5	1 232.7	256 378	1 391	1 530.0	760.6	488.4	914	859
Jackson, TN	85.2	0.1	8.9	161.1	20.2	12.0	13.5	41 113	249	870.2	118.1	143.4	1 273	643
Jacksonville, FL	1 747.8	970.7	376.4	912.4	195.3	112.9	276.8	717 904	3 606	5 029.7	1 751.1	1 840.9	1 415	1 070
Jacksonville, NC	1 099.6	920.0	8.7	89.1	25.9	15.1	19.2	245 122	2 375	491.5	204.5	109.0	670	440
Janesville, WI	40.5	204.4	16.2	176.1	29.3	13.4	15.9	20 602	111	656.4	360.8	202.7	1 270	1 232
Jefferson City, MO	214.4	10.2	19.7	248.6	250.4	407.1	1 971.0	35 981	222	297.6	99.9	142.1	976	633
Johnson City, TN	138.1	11.9	95.6	225.1	25.4	18.6	18.4	80 835	741	451.5	167.7	171.7	887	450
Johnstown, PA	158.9	1 180.9	28.1	180.3	33.8	6.0	41.5	21 744	117	524.9	265.3	128.6	887	691
Jonesboro, AR	64.8	11.5	11.4	152.9	16.6	10.6	17.4	60 330	611	298.5	174.8	73.3	630	299
Joplin, MO	87.9	37.8	31.3	189.0	27.0	16.7	24.8	21 191	202	411.9	157.3	155.2	906	487
Kalamazoo-Portage, MI	163.3	39.0	32.9	344.9	70.7	24.7	504.2	72 366	367	1 302.3	629.0	384.4	1 189	1 162
Kankakee-Bradley, IL	53.7	0.2	4.7	96.5	20.0	5.2	18.9	12 972	71	374.3	178.8	129.3	1 168	1 106
Kansas City, MO-KS	2 972.4	1 385.0	2 234.4	1 524.5	244.3	112.0	358.3	532 344	2 714	8 632.1	2 284.3	3 808.5	1 918	1 190
Kennewick-Pasco-Richland, WA	122.9	36.1	3 139.6	130.5	42.7	13.4	122.8	423 610	2 022	1 005.6	476.4	253.7	1 108	632
Killeen-Temple-Fort Hood, TX	8 731.2	1 306.7	94.3	202.2	43.8	83.8	36.5	341 756	2 241	1 235.5	571.8	365.0	986	763
Kingsport-Bristol-Bristol, TN-VA	108.5	205.9	33.2	422.3	54.2	24.5	108.2	61 100	464	838.2	378.5	297.7	980	632
Kingston, NY	54.7	6.1	10.4	260.8	43.2	12.7	10.8	43 306	334	984.4	317.9	535.2	2 943	2 321
Knoxville, TN	421.6	195.2	4 044.3	678.1	87.9	53.8	190.8	288 653	2 273	2 114.5	588.5	862.9	1 266	739

1. Based on the resident population estimated as of July 1 of the year shown.

Area name	Total (mil dol)	Per capita[1] (dollars)	Education	Health and hospitals	Police protection	Public welfare	Highways	Total (mil dol)	Per capita[1] (dollars)	Federal civilian	Federal military	State and local	Democratic	Republican	All other
	Local government finances, 2007 (cont.)									Government employment, 2009			Presidential election,[2] 2008		
	Direct general expenditure							Debt outstanding					Percent of vote cast:		
			Percent of total for:												
	185	186	187	188	189	190	191	192	193	194	195	196	197	198	199
Flagstaff, AZ..................	485.8	3 812	39.5	2.6	9.4	1.2	10.3	462.9	3 632	3 049	289	13 690	57.8	40.8	1.3
Flint, MI	2 071.2	4 764	47.7	24.0	4.0	0.9	3.3	1 026.1	2 360	1 431	776	23 133	65.5	32.9	1.6
Florence, SC..................	520.5	2 619	61.4	7.0	5.8	0.2	2.2	381.2	1 918	819	874	15 741	48.5	50.6	0.9
Florence-Muscle Shoals, AL.	550.8	3 847	42.0	30.7	3.5	0.1	4.3	459.8	3 212	1 439	703	10 703	36.6	61.7	1.8
Fond du Lac, WI	425.1	4 289	50.7	12.4	4.9	4.6	6.8	370.8	3 740	246	289	5 535	44.8	53.8	1.3
Fort Collins-Loveland, CO	1 068.3	3 715	36.2	4.8	7.0	2.5	11.5	1 529.2	5 317	2 514	789	24 724	54.0	44.3	1.7
Fort Smith, AR-OK..................	750.1	2 589	62.5	0.7	4.3	0.1	7.1	771.8	2 664	1 641	1 447	17 241	30.1	68.2	1.7
Fort Wayne, IN..................	1 349.4	3 291	50.4	0.8	4.4	2.7	3.2	996.9	2 431	2 158	1 392	20 107	45.7	53.4	0.9
Fresno, CA..................	4 984.7	5 543	47.6	6.2	5.4	9.9	3.3	3 891.0	4 326	9 903	1 794	56 953	50.2	48.1	1.7
Gadsden, AL..................	274.7	2 661	50.8	1.8	7.6	0.2	3.9	247.2	2 395	360	503	5 178	30.2	68.4	1.4
Gainesville, FL..................	906.1	3 524	42.3	2.6	8.4	0.7	3.4	1 732.8	6 740	4 251	596	39 591	58.2	40.6	1.2
Gainesville, GA..................	1 105.6	6 136	27.0	44.1	2.1	0.6	1.6	1 620.4	8 994	534	580	9 989	24.1	75.0	0.8
Glens Falls, NY..................	688.4	5 341	50.1	3.7	2.1	10.4	7.1	503.6	3 907	379	210	10 324	50.1	48.3	1.6
Goldsboro, NC..................	315.2	2 775	55.2	3.9	4.3	8.1	1.0	122.6	1 080	1 254	4 617	8 546	45.4	54.0	0.5
Grand Forks, ND-MN..........	380.7	3 897	37.4	0.8	4.1	5.7	9.4	558.3	5 715	1 381	2 346	11 278	51.5	46.6	1.9
Grand Junction, CO	515.5	3 707	37.5	1.5	9.2	4.5	14.9	409.8	2 946	1 383	376	8 192	34.5	64.0	1.5
Grand Rapids-Wyoming, MI .	3 051.8	3 929	55.2	5.6	3.9	2.1	5.1	4 164.6	5 362	3 397	1 446	31 398	48.6	49.7	1.8
Great Falls, MT..................	225.3	2 755	48.3	2.4	8.2	0.6	3.2	95.4	1 166	1 734	3 477	4 221	49.9	47.6	2.4
Greeley, CO..................	813.1	3 336	41.4	2.0	5.9	2.3	7.6	908.7	3 728	614	655	14 373	44.7	53.4	1.9
Green Bay, WI	1 301.3	4 321	48.7	4.5	5.2	6.0	9.3	1 740.6	5 780	1 185	906	19 788	53.8	44.9	1.4
Greensboro-High Point, NC..	2 356.0	3 373	47.2	4.7	6.1	5.8	2.5	2 002.0	2 866	4 562	1 851	40 025	51.5	47.6	0.9
Greenville, NC..................	523.4	3 035	48.5	4.9	6.2	7.8	1.4	396.8	2 300	495	465	24 560	53.4	46.0	0.6
Greenville-Mauldin-Easley, SC	2 605.7	4 245	36.3	34.3	3.4	0.1	2.4	4 795.1	7 812	2 074	2 844	41 170	35.5	62.7	1.8
Gulfport-Biloxi, MS	1 506.0	6 505	32.5	19.8	4.3	0.1	3.5	1 124.6	4 857	8 458	11 232	16 024	33.0	66.0	1.0
Hagerstown-Martinsburg, MD-WV	730.9	2 798	59.4	2.1	4.1	0.5	3.5	630.4	2 413	4 483	1 117	14 046	42.3	56.0	1.7
Hanford-Corcoran, CA	609.8	4 096	45.4	5.7	5.8	8.7	3.3	264.9	1 780	1 219	5 675	12 100	42.0	56.1	1.9
Harrisburg-Carlisle, PA	2 390.2	4 519	51.8	5.0	3.2	7.9	2.4	4 104.3	7 760	7 781	2 098	57 506	47.5	51.4	1.1
Harrisonburg, VA..................	374.7	3 188	54.9	2.5	4.7	6.2	4.0	555.6	4 726	349	412	10 141	39.4	59.4	1.2
Hartford-West Hartford-East Hartford, CT..................	4 694.5	3 948	58.9	0.7	5.0	0.8	3.5	2 515.2	2 115	6 672	2 308	92 739	63.8	35.0	1.2
Hattiesburg, MS	704.5	5 100	31.2	47.6	2.9	0.1	4.2	523.9	3 792	895	1 075	14 170	32.3	66.7	1.0
Hickory-Lenoir-Morganton, NC..................	1 148.6	3 186	46.7	19.9	4.0	7.8	1.3	490.0	1 359	870	920	23 972	36.3	62.4	1.3
Hinesville-Fort Stewart, GA ..	234.3	3 264	54.1	14.0	4.6	0.3	3.7	46.3	645	3 896	17 214	3 688	59.3	40.1	0.6
Holland-Grand Haven, MI ,,,,,	823.2	3 176	56.8	5.0	3.3	1.0	7.2	1 132.8	4 370	459	546	13 567	37.3	61.2	1.5
Honolulu, HI	1 403.3	1 550	0.0	2.0	13.7	0.0	9.7	4 105.7	4 534	30 601	52 528	67 775	69.8	28.7	1.4
Hot Springs, AR..................	214.2	2 223	58.7	0.3	6.5	0.0	3.5	179.2	1 860	586	472	4 352	36.4	61.4	2.3
Houma-Bayou Cane-Thibodaux, LA..................	891.5	4 432	34.7	33.0	3.9	0.3	2.6	379.5	1 887	447	894	13 754	27.0	70.4	2.6
Houston-Sugar Land-Baytown, TX..................	21 951.1	3 900	47.7	8.1	5.7	0.3	3.6	55 754.3	9 906	29 243	15 535	333 968	45.6	53.7	0.7
Huntington-Ashland, WV-KY-OH..................	728.0	2 563	59.0	2.5	4.1	2.4	2.7	582.5	2 051	3 217	1 196	16 757	42.4	55.8	1.8
Huntsville, AL..................	1 656.3	4 284	33.6	38.0	4.1	0.1	3.1	2 142.7	5 542	17 440	3 505	28 689	39.5	59.3	1.2
Idaho Falls, ID..................	298.3	2 498	55.1	1.3	5.0	0.4	6.2	186.7	1 564	893	494	6 379	25.0	72.6	2.3
Indianapolis-Carmel, IN	7 797.8	4 600	41.1	15.5	3.5	1.8	2.2	11 019.6	6 501	16 169	6 401	110 207	50.8	48.3	0.9
Iowa City, IA..................	508.5	3 458	33.2	7.3	3.9	0.5	5.1	753.4	5 124	1 878	658	32 559	67.2	31.1	1.7
Ithaca, NY..................	492.8	4 876	48.5	4.3	2.7	7.5	7.6	461.8	4 570	300	182	6 596	70.2	28.1	1.7
Jackson, MI..................	646.7	3 968	55.8	6.7	2.6	3.5	7.1	487.5	2 991	391	293	9 094	50.3	47.9	1.8
Jackson, MS..................	1 529.8	2 865	54.4	1.5	6.3	0.4	6.5	1 746.0	3 269	6 213	3 340	52 775	49.6	49.8	0.7
Jackson, TN..................	970.9	8 618	14.1	68.8	2.2	0.0	1.0	1 414.9	12 559	497	387	12 525	43.7	55.4	0.8
Jacksonville, FL	4 872.0	3 745	44.3	1.1	5.8	2.0	3.6	15 196.7	11 682	17 563	18 941	59 322	41.8	57.6	0.7
Jacksonville, NC	512.9	3 152	44.1	27.9	3.7	5.4	0.7	286.7	1 762	6 199	50 679	7 985	38.8	60.3	0.8
Janesville, WI..................	655.8	4 109	49.7	6.8	6.1	7.0	6.4	520.8	3 262	323	462	8 648	63.8	34.6	1.6
Jefferson City, MO	308.9	2 120	56.3	2.6	6.0	0.0	6.9	301.3	2 068	890	633	27 804	35.6	63.1	1.4
Johnson City, TN	407.4	2 105	50.3	7.6	5.6	0.5	5.5	998.4	5 158	2 597	682	14 128	30.3	68.2	1.5
Johnstown, PA..................	556.4	3 838	53.9	5.1	3.3	8.7	4.5	684.2	4 719	1 281	498	8 485	49.4	48.7	1.9
Jonesboro, AR..................	298.1	2 561	59.8	0.6	5.3	0.0	6.2	479.6	4 120	448	579	8 753	36.1	61.1	2.8
Joplin, MO..................	432.5	2 525	58.0	6.7	5.8	0.1	7.2	359.1	2 096	486	716	9 274	31.6	67.1	1.3
Kalamazoo-Portage, MI	1 304.4	4 035	49.8	17.1	5.7	0.9	5.4	1 509.8	4 670	1 176	602	19 185	57.8	40.5	1.7
Kankakee-Bradley, IL..........	395.4	3 571	54.9	1.0	6.0	0.1	5.7	256.7	2 319	254	227	6 227	51.5	46.9	1.5
Kansas City, MO-KS............	8 688.9	4 376	42.2	8.6	6.7	0.4	4.5	15 122.7	7 617	27 557	12 252	130 316	52.0	46.7	1.3
Kennewick-Pasco-Richland, WA	926.6	4 046	46.7	18.5	3.7	0.0	5.2	7 695.8	33 607	1 324	772	16 262	36.3	62.0	1.7
Killeen-Temple-Fort Hood, TX	1 194.4	3 228	60.7	3.6	4.1	0.4	2.6	1 820.3	4 920	10 083	54 477	25 524	42.1	57.1	0.8
Kingsport-Bristol-Bristol, TN-VA	771.3	2 540	49.3	2.9	6.1	2.4	4.0	654.6	2 155	1 163	1 036	15 178	29.8	68.8	1.4
Kingston, NY..................	971.0	5 340	51.6	2.6	3.4	12.6	4.9	738.4	4 060	460	314	14 005	61.0	37.4	1.7
Knoxville, TN..................	2 067.5	3 034	37.6	9.4	5.7	0.3	2.4	5 792.1	8 499	5 168	2 430	47 658	35.2	63.3	1.5

1. Based on the resident population estimated as of July 1 of the year shown.   2. © 2009 Election Data Services, Inc. All rights reserved.

Table C. Metropolitan Areas — **Land Area and Population**

CBSA code[1]	Area name	Land area,[2] 2010 (sq km)	Total persons	Rank	Per square kilometer	White	Black	American Indian, Alaska Native	Asian and Pacific Islander	Percent Hispanic or Latino[3]	Under 5 years	5 to 17 years	18 to 24 years	25 to 34 years	35 to 44 years	45 to 54 years
		1	2	3	4	5	6	7	8	9	10	11	12	13	14	15
29020	Kokomo, IN	1 434	98 688	344	68.8	90.4	6.9	0.8	1.2	2.6	6.1	17.5	7.8	11.2	12.5	15.2
29100	La Crosse, WI-MN	2 600	133 665	291	51.4	93.2	1.9	0.7	4.1	1.4	5.9	15.7	14.3	12.5	11.4	14.2
29140	Lafayette, IN	3 311	201 789	208	60.9	83.9	4.1	0.6	5.9	7.0	6.4	14.9	22.1	13.9	11.0	11.6
29180	Lafayette, LA	2 606	273 738	169	105.0	67.9	27.2	0.7	1.7	3.5	7.1	17.7	11.8	14.9	12.6	14.4
29340	Lake Charles, LA	6 083	199 607	213	32.8	71.5	24.8	1.0	1.4	2.6	7.1	18.3	10.1	13.4	12.0	14.6
29420	Lake Havasu City-Kingman, AZ	34 476	200 186	211	5.8	81.1	1.2	2.7	1.8	14.8	5.5	15.1	6.8	9.1	10.0	14.3
29460	Lakeland-Winter Haven, FL.	4 656	602 095	87	129.3	65.8	15.0	0.7	2.1	17.7	6.5	17.1	8.8	11.8	12.2	13.3
29540	Lancaster, PA	2 444	519 445	99	212.5	86.1	3.9	0.4	2.2	8.6	6.8	18.0	9.7	11.7	12.2	14.5
29620	Lansing-East Lansing, MI	4 397	464 036	108	105.5	80.6	10.1	1.2	4.4	6.2	5.8	16.3	15.7	12.9	11.7	13.9
29700	Laredo, TX	8 706	250 304	184	28.8	3.4	0.2	0.1	0.6	95.7	9.8	25.5	10.9	14.0	13.7	10.9
29740	Las Cruces, NM	9 861	209 233	203	21.2	30.9	1.7	1.1	1.4	65.7	7.4	19.3	13.1	13.2	11.2	12.7
29820	Las Vegas-Paradise, NV	20 439	1 951 269	30	95.5	50.5	11.2	1.0	11.3	29.1	7.1	17.9	9.2	15.1	14.8	13.6
29940	Lawrence, KS	1 181	110 826	329	93.8	84.6	5.1	3.6	4.8	5.1	5.6	13.5	24.6	15.8	10.8	11.2
30020	Lawton, OK	2 769	124 098	310	44.8	63.2	19.2	7.5	4.2	11.2	7.6	17.5	13.6	16.5	12.3	13.0
30140	Lebanon, PA	937	133 568	292	142.5	87.7	2.1	0.3	1.4	9.3	6.3	16.7	8.3	11.1	12.7	14.8
30300	Lewiston, ID-WA	3 844	60 888	365	15.8	92.0	0.7	5.2	1.3	2.9	5.7	16.0	9.3	11.6	11.2	14.3
30340	Lewiston-Auburn, ME	1 212	107 702	334	88.9	93.6	4.3	1.1	1.1	1.5	6.4	16.2	9.3	12.0	13.4	15.8
30460	Lexington-Fayette, KY	3 803	472 099	106	124.1	80.7	11.8	0.6	2.8	5.9	6.6	16.1	12.0	15.1	13.6	14.1
30620	Lima, OH	1 042	106 331	337	102.0	84.6	13.5	0.6	1.0	2.4	6.4	17.6	10.7	11.7	11.7	14.6
30700	Lincoln, NE	3 649	302 157	155	82.8	87.0	4.4	1.1	4.0	5.6	7.0	16.1	14.6	15.1	12.0	13.0
30780	Little Rock-North Little Rock-Conway, AR	10 581	699 757	74	66.1	70.9	22.8	1.0	1.9	4.8	6.9	17.6	9.8	14.4	13.2	14.1
30860	Logan, UT-ID	4 736	125 442	305	26.5	87.3	0.7	0.8	2.7	9.6	10.2	21.8	16.3	16.4	10.2	9.5
30980	Longview, TX	4 611	214 369	198	46.5	67.3	17.9	1.0	1.0	14.1	7.0	17.8	9.6	13.1	12.2	14.3
31020	Longview, WA	2 953	102 410	340	34.7	88.5	1.1	3.0	2.6	7.8	6.4	17.7	8.2	11.4	12.3	14.7
31100	Los Angeles-Long Beach-Santa Ana, CA	12 557	12 828 837	2	1 021.6	33.3	7.3	0.6	16.2	44.4	6.5	17.9	10.7	14.7	14.6	14.1
31100	Los Angeles-Long Beach-Glendale, CA Div	10 510	9 818 605	X	934.2	29.4	8.9	0.5	15.1	47.7	6.6	17.9	10.8	15.0	14.6	13.9
31100	Santa Ana-Anaheim-Irvine, CA Div	2 048	3 010 232	X	1 469.8	46.2	1.9	0.6	19.9	33.7	6.4	18.1	10.1	13.7	14.6	14.8
31140	Louisville-Jefferson County, KY-IN	10 647	1 283 566	42	120.6	80.4	14.6	0.7	2.0	3.9	6.5	17.5	8.6	13.4	13.5	15.3
31180	Lubbock, TX	4 651	284 890	162	61.3	57.9	7.5	0.7	2.4	32.3	7.3	17.2	16.7	14.5	11.0	12.4
31340	Lynchburg, VA	5 492	252 634	180	46.0	78.5	18.4	0.9	1.6	2.1	5.5	15.7	12.6	10.7	12.0	14.8
31420	Macon, GA	4 462	232 293	190	52.1	52.5	43.9	0.6	1.6	2.4	6.9	18.2	9.8	12.3	12.6	14.8
31460	Madera-Chowchilla, CA	5 535	150 865	265	27.3	39.5	3.6	2.1	2.3	53.7	7.9	20.5	10.5	13.6	12.7	12.8
31540	Madison, WI	7 059	568 593	89	80.5	85.4	5.5	0.7	4.8	5.4	6.2	15.8	12.0	15.5	13.3	14.5
31700	Manchester-Nashua, NH	2 269	400 721	129	176.6	89.1	2.4	0.6	3.8	5.3	5.9	17.5	8.6	12.3	14.4	17.1
31740	Manhattan, KS	4 754	127 081	302	26.7	79.3	10.0	1.5	5.0	7.7	8.3	15.5	23.8	16.9	9.8	9.7
31860	Mankato, North Mankato, MN	3 098	96 740	348	31.2	92.5	3.0	0.6	2.2	2.9	6.2	14.3	20.3	13.8	10.3	12.5
31900	Mansfield, OH	1 283	124 475	308	97.0	88.2	10.4	0.7	0.9	1.4	6.0	16.5	8.4	11.9	12.6	15.0
32580	McAllen-Edinburg-Mission, TX	4 069	774 769	68	190.4	7.9	0.4	0.1	1.0	90.6	9.6	25.0	10.7	14.0	13.2	10.3
32780	Medford, OR	7 209	203 206	207	28.2	86.1	1.1	2.3	2.3	10.7	5.9	15.9	8.6	11.5	11.4	14.2
32820	Memphis, TN-MS-AR	11 857	1 316 100	41	111.0	47.1	46.1	0.6	2.3	5.0	7.2	19.4	9.7	13.7	13.6	14.4
32900	Merced, CA	5 012	255 793	177	51.0	33.4	4.0	1.0	8.3	54.9	8.7	22.9	11.9	13.7	12.5	12.1
33100	Miami-Fort Lauderdale-Pompano Beach, FL	13 150	5 564 635	8	423.2	35.6	20.4	0.3	2.8	41.6	5.8	15.8	9.0	12.8	14.2	14.9
33100	Fort Lauderdale-Pompano Beach-Deerfield Beach, FL Div	3 133	1 748 066	X	558.0	44.6	26.8	0.4	4.1	25.1	5.9	16.5	8.4	12.8	14.4	15.8
33100	Miami-Miami Beach-Kendall, FL Div	4 915	2 496 435	X	507.9	15.8	17.5	0.2	1.9	65.0	6.0	15.9	9.9	13.6	14.9	14.7
33100	West Palm Beach-Boca Raton-Boynton Beach, FL Div	5 102	1 320 134	X	258.7	61.1	17.5	0.4	3.0	19.0	5.4	15.0	8.0	11.1	12.5	14.3
33140	Michigan City-La Porte, IN	1 550	111 467	327	71.9	83.0	11.7	0.7	0.8	5.5	5.9	16.8	8.4	12.9	13.2	15.3
33260	Midland, TX	2 332	136 872	284	58.7	54.1	6.7	0.8	1.5	37.7	8.0	19.4	10.0	14.4	11.9	14.4
33340	Milwaukee-Waukesha-West Allis, WI	3 768	1 555 908	39	412.9	70.4	17.4	0.9	3.5	9.5	6.7	18.0	9.7	13.5	12.9	15.0
33460	Minneapolis-St. Paul-Bloomington, MN	15 610	3 279 833	16	210.1	80.6	8.4	1.2	6.6	5.4	6.9	18.1	9.1	14.6	13.9	15.5
33540	Missoula, MT	6 717	109 299	331	16.3	93.2	0.8	3.7	1.9	2.6	5.8	14.2	15.0	15.9	11.6	13.5
33660	Mobile, AL	3 184	412 992	124	129.7	60.1	35.1	1.4	2.2	2.4	6.8	18.3	10.0	13.0	12.4	14.5
33700	Modesto, CA	3 872	514 453	100	132.9	48.9	3.2	1.4	7.0	41.9	7.7	20.9	10.5	13.6	13.0	13.5
33740	Monroe, LA	3 852	176 441	229	45.8	61.4	35.7	0.6	1.1	2.1	7.2	18.7	11.0	13.3	12.1	13.5
33780	Monroe, MI	1 423	152 021	262	106.8	93.9	2.8	0.9	0.8	3.1	5.7	18.4	8.4	10.9	13.3	16.6
33860	Montgomery, AL	7 027	374 536	136	53.3	52.3	43.0	0.7	2.0	3.2	6.7	17.9	10.4	13.6	13.5	14.4
34060	Morgantown, WV	2 613	129 709	297	49.6	92.9	3.6	0.5	2.8	1.5	4.8	12.0	21.7	14.6	11.5	12.4
34100	Morristown, TN	1 854	136 608	285	73.7	90.0	3.2	0.7	0.8	6.5	6.1	16.7	8.7	11.2	13.6	14.5
34580	Mount Vernon-Anacortes, WA	4 484	116 901	317	26.1	78.7	1.0	2.8	2.7	16.9	6.5	17.0	8.2	12.1	11.8	14.1
34620	Muncie, IN	1 016	117 671	316	115.8	89.9	7.9	0.7	1.5	1.8	5.4	14.6	19.2	10.9	11.0	12.7
34740	Muskegon-Norton Shores, MI	1 293	172 188	234	133.2	79.4	15.6	1.6	0.9	4.8	6.6	18.3	9.0	12.4	12.4	15.2
34820	Myrtle Beach-North Myrtle Beach-Conway, SC	2 937	269 291	171	91.7	78.7	14.1	0.9	1.5	6.2	5.7	14.5	9.7	12.6	12.4	13.8
34900	Napa, CA	1 938	136 484	286	70.4	58.3	2.2	1.1	8.2	32.2	6.0	17.1	8.8	12.3	13.1	14.6

1. CBSA = Core Based Statistical Area. DIV = Metropolitan Division. See Appendix A for explanation. See Appendix B for list of metropolitan areas identified by type. 2. Dry land or land partially or temporarily covered by water. 3. May be of any race.

Table C. Metropolitan Areas — **Population and Households**

Area name	Population, 2010 (cont.) Age (percent) (cont.)				Population change and components of change, 1990–2010							Households, 2010				
					Total persons		Percent change		Components of change, 2000–2009						Percent	
	55 to 64 years	65 to 74 years	75 years and over	Percent female	1990	2000	1990–2000	2000–2010	Births	Deaths	Net migration	Number	Percent change, 2000–2010	Persons per household	Female family householder[1]	One person
	16	17	18	19	20	21	22	23	24	25	26	27	28	29	30	31
Kokomo, IN	13.4	8.9	7.5	51.7	96 946	101 541	4.7	-2.8	12 302	9 597	-4 927	40 677	-1.4	2.39	12.6	28.8
La Crosse, WI-MN	12.1	6.8	7.1	51.1	116 401	126 838	9.0	5.4	13 912	10 046	3 005	53 986	9.7	2.37	8.6	29.2
Lafayette, IN	9.8	5.6	4.8	49.2	158 848	178 541	12.4	13.0	22 599	11 792	8 043	76 911	15.7	2.43	9.5	28.6
Lafayette, LA	10.9	5.9	4.6	51.1	208 859	239 086	14.5	14.5	34 785	17 593	8 557	106 243	18.7	2.52	15.4	26.9
Lake Charles, LA	11.8	7.0	5.6	51.2	177 394	193 568	9.1	3.1	26 276	16 923	-7 670	76 571	6.0	2.56	15.7	25.9
Lake Havasu City-Kingman, AZ	15.7	14.1	9.2	50.0	93 497	155 032	65.8	29.1	20 655	21 291	41 241	82 539	31.4	2.39	10.4	26.7
Lakeland-Winter Haven, FL	12.3	10.1	7.9	51.0	405 382	483 924	19.4	24.4	70 065	50 723	83 146	227 485	21.5	2.59	13.7	23.8
Lancaster, PA	11.9	7.4	7.6	51.1	422 822	470 658	11.3	10.4	63 942	40 627	16 783	193 602	12.2	2.62	9.6	24.2
Lansing-East Lansing, MI	12.0	6.4	5.3	51.2	432 684	447 728	3.5	3.6	52 544	29 676	-14 832	183 422	6.4	2.42	11.7	28.9
Laredo, TX	7.4	4.4	3.4	51.5	133 239	193 117	44.9	29.6	55 432	9 634	3 855	67 106	32.3	3.68	20.9	13.4
Las Cruces, NM	10.7	7.0	5.4	51.0	135 510	174 682	28.9	19.8	30 311	11 251	13 752	75 532	26.8	2.71	16.0	24.2
Las Vegas-Paradise, NV	11.0	6.9	4.4	49.7	741 368	1 375 765	85.6	41.8	246 666	111 822	399 902	715 365	39.7	2.70	13.5	25.3
Lawrence, KS	9.6	4.7	4.2	49.9	81 798	99 962	22.2	10.9	11 606	5 286	5 836	43 576	13.2	2.34	8.6	29.8
Lawton, OK	9.3	5.7	4.5	48.5	111 486	114 996	3.1	7.9	17 846	8 220	-10 848	44 982	13.0	2.53	14.5	27.1
Lebanon, PA	13.0	8.5	8.5	51.2	113 744	120 327	5.8	11.0	14 249	12 213	8 808	52 258	12.3	2.49	10.1	25.9
Lewiston, ID-WA	13.4	9.5	9.0	50.9	51 359	57 961	12.9	5.0	6 548	5 772	2 178	25 477	7.7	2.35	10.9	28.9
Lewiston-Auburn, ME	12.8	7.3	6.8	51.1	105 259	103 793	-1.4	3.8	12 088	9 615	871	44 315	5.4	2.37	12.0	28.3
Lexington-Fayette, KY	11.3	6.2	4.9	50.9	348 428	408 326	17.2	15.6	56 321	30 383	29 926	190 142	16.0	2.39	12.4	29.3
Lima, OH	12.6	7.5	7.3	49.6	109 755	108 473	-1.2	-2.0	13 576	9 824	-7 327	40 619	-0.1	2.47	13.8	27.8
Lincoln, NE	11.0	5.7	5.4	49.8	229 091	266 787	16.5	13.3	39 166	17 345	11 147	119 639	13.7	2.40	9.5	29.8
Little Rock-North Little Rock-Conway, AR	11.7	6.9	5.3	51.4	534 943	610 518	14.1	14.6	87 371	51 288	39 826	279 225	15.8	2.45	14.4	27.7
Logan, UT-ID	7.4	4.4	3.8	50.2	79 416	102 720	29.3	22.1	24 339	4 743	438	38 801	25.1	3.14	7.6	16.5
Longview, TX	11.9	7.5	6.6	50.1	180 053	194 042	7.8	10.5	27 884	19 583	5 730	79 199	8.0	2.58	13.7	25.8
Longview, WA	13.8	8.6	6.8	50.6	82 119	92 948	13.2	10.2	11 793	9 000	6 806	40 244	12.3	2.51	11.8	25.8
Los Angeles-Long Beach-Santa Ana, CA	10.4	5.9	5.1	50.7	11 273 720	12 365 627	9.7	3.7	1 814 842	710 713	-532 441	4 233 985	4.1	2.98	14.5	23.4
Los Angeles-Long Beach-Glendale, CA Div	10.3	5.8	5.1	50.7	8 863 052	9 519 338	7.4	3.1	1 402 112	553 030	-474 695	3 241 204	3.4	2.98	15.3	24.2
Santa Ana-Anaheim-Irvine, CA Div	10.7	6.2	5.4	50.5	2 410 668	2 846 289	18.1	5.8	412 730	157 683	-57 746	992 781	6.1	2.99	11.6	20.9
Louisville-Jefferson County, KY-IN	12.4	7.0	5.8	51.2	1 056 156	1 161 975	10.0	10.5	150 523	101 831	51 405	514 214	11.2	2.45	13.9	28.3
Lubbock, TX	9.8	5.9	5.2	50.6	229 940	249 700	8.6	14.1	38 580	19 392	8 026	108 018	13.7	2.53	13.5	27.4
Lynchburg, VA	13.0	8.6	7.1	51.8	206 226	228 616	10.9	10.5	24 963	21 321	16 466	99 602	11.0	2.41	12.6	27.0
Macon, GA	12.5	7.2	5.7	52.1	206 786	222 368	7.5	4.5	30 926	21 000	440	88 999	6.5	2.52	19.4	27.8
Madera-Chowchilla, CA	10.5	6.5	4.9	51.8	88 090	123 109	39.8	22.5	22 075	8 657	12 821	43 317	19.8	3.28	13.3	16.7
Madison, WI	11.8	5.7	5.1	50.4	432 323	501 774	16.1	13.3	63 676	31 113	38 840	236 032	16.5	2.35	8.5	29.9
Manchester-Nashua, NH	12.4	6.4	5.5	50.5	335 838	380 841	13.4	5.2	46 552	26 013	6 914	155 466	7.6	2.53	10.5	25.3
Manhattan, KS	7.8	4.2	4.1	49.0	113 720	108 899	-4.2	16.6	17 319	6 186	-4 082	46 364	17.8	2.52	10.9	25.8
Mankato, North Mankato, MN	10.8	5.8	6.1	49.8	82 120	85 712	4.4	12.9	10 359	5 840	3 497	36 646	15.6	2.44	8.5	27.1
Mansfield, OH	13.3	8.5	7.8	49.4	126 137	128 852	2.2	-3.4	14 669	11 456	-6 829	48 921	-1.2	2.40	12.5	28.8
McAllen-Edinburg-Mission, TX	7.8	5.1	4.2	51.3	383 545	569 463	48.5	36.1	152 574	29 453	52 865	216 471	38.0	3.55	18.8	14.0
Medford, OR	14.9	9.3	8.4	51.3	146 387	181 269	23.8	12.1	20 549	18 127	18 455	83 076	16.1	2.40	11.0	27.7
Memphis, TN-MS-AR	11.4	6.0	4.6	52.0	1 067 263	1 205 204	12.9	9.2	183 816	98 315	11 907	491 198	9.5	2.63	20.3	26.4
Merced, CA	8.9	5.2	4.2	49.7	178 403	210 554	18.0	21.5	40 173	13 493	8 734	75 642	18.5	3.32	15.8	17.4
Miami-Fort Lauderdale-Pompano Beach, FL	11.5	8.0	8.0	51.6	4 056 228	5 007 564	23.5	11.1	649 535	438 106	234 874	2 097 626	10.1	2.62	15.8	27.0
Fort Lauderdale-Pompano Beach-Deerfield Beach, FL Div	11.9	7.2	7.1	51.6	1 255 531	1 623 018	29.3	7.7	209 107	142 933	75 947	686 047	4.8	2.52	15.3	28.8
Miami-Miami Beach-Kendall, FL Div	10.9	7.5	6.6	51.6	1 937 194	2 253 362	16.3	10.8	303 660	170 459	23 116	867 352	11.7	2.83	18.8	23.5
West Palm Beach-Boca Raton-Boynton Beach, FL Div	12.1	9.9	11.7	51.6	863 503	1 131 184	31.0	16.7	136 768	124 714	135 811	544 227	14.8	2.39	11.7	30.1
Michigan City-La Porte, IN	13.3	7.7	6.5	48.3	107 066	110 106	2.8	1.2	12 719	9 750	-1 371	42 331	3.1	2.48	12.8	27.3
Midland, TX	10.8	5.6	5.4	50.9	106 611	116 009	8.8	18.0	18 512	8 634	7 106	50 845	18.9	2.66	12.8	24.8
Milwaukee-Waukesha-West Allis, WI	11.8	6.2	6.3	51.4	1 432 149	1 500 741	4.8	3.7	199 213	119 253	-46 621	622 087	5.9	2.45	13.4	29.9
Minneapolis-St. Paul-Bloomington, MN	11.3	5.7	4.9	50.6	2 538 776	2 968 806	16.9	10.5	424 024	175 755	67 662	1 272 677	12.0	2.53	10.2	27.5
Missoula, MT	12.7	6.4	5.0	49.7	78 687	95 802	21.8	14.1	11 186	6 412	8 520	45 926	19.5	2.30	9.2	30.3
Mobile, AL	12.1	7.3	5.7	52.0	378 643	399 843	5.6	3.3	55 073	36 423	-4 324	158 435	5.5	2.56	18.8	26.5
Modesto, CA	10.1	5.8	4.9	50.5	370 522	446 997	20.6	15.1	75 988	33 683	23 505	165 180	13.8	3.08	14.6	19.3
Monroe, LA	11.4	7.0	5.9	52.0	162 987	170 053	4.3	3.8	24 463	15 212	-4 179	67 835	5.9	2.51	19.4	27.8
Monroe, MI	13.3	7.3	6.1	50.7	133 600	145 945	9.2	4.2	16 183	11 347	2 839	58 230	8.3	2.59	11.1	23.5
Montgomery, AL	11.4	6.8	5.2	52.0	305 175	346 528	13.6	8.1	48 013	29 562	3 380	142 855	10.1	2.52	18.5	27.4
Morgantown, WV	11.4	6.4	5.2	48.4	104 546	111 200	6.4	16.6	11 371	8 858	7 249	52 672	17.1	2.28	8.4	30.0
Morristown, TN	13.2	9.7	6.3	51.0	100 591	123 081	22.4	11.0	15 553	12 446	12 123	53 453	9.9	2.51	11.8	24.3
Mount Vernon-Anacortes, WA	13.9	8.8	7.4	50.4	79 545	102 979	29.5	13.5	13 550	9 372	12 884	45 557	17.3	2.53	10.1	25.6
Muncie, IN	11.4	7.8	6.8	51.9	119 659	118 769	-0.7	-0.9	12 229	10 812	-4 300	46 516	-1.3	2.34	12.2	29.6
Muskegon-Norton Shores, MI	12.6	7.1	6.4	50.4	158 983	170 200	7.1	1.2	21 984	14 743	-2 413	65 616	3.6	2.53	15.4	26.4
Myrtle Beach-North Myrtle Beach-Conway, SC	14.3	10.5	6.6	51.1	144 053	196 629	36.5	37.0	27 141	19 857	60 476	112 225	37.2	2.37	12.5	26.8
Napa, CA	13.1	7.7	7.4	50.1	110 765	124 279	12.2	9.8	15 219	11 522	7 498	48 876	7.7	2.69	10.3	25.3

1. No spouse present.

Area name	Persons in group quarters, 2010	Daytime population, 2010 Number	Employ-ment/residence ratio	Births, average 2006–2008 Total	Rate[1]	Deaths, average 2006–2008 Number	Rate[1]	Persons under 65 with no health insurance 2009 Number	Percent	Medicare, 2011 Enrolled in original Medicare	Enrolled in Medicare Advantage	Enrolled in a Medicare prescription drug plan	Serious crimes known to police,[2] 2010 Total Number	Rate[3]
	32	33	34	35	36	37	38	39	40	41	42	43	44	45
Kokomo, IN	1 487	D	D	D	D	1 009	10.1	11 541	14.3	20 245	1 481	8 551	3 279	3 323
La Crosse, WI-MN	5 452	136 935	1.04	D	D	1 095	8.4	10 582	9.4	22 130	9 094	7 175	3 221	2 463
Lafayette, IN	14 661	209 371	1.07	D	D	1 302	6.8	27 951	16.4	25 160	3 674	12 021	5 285	2 707
Lafayette, LA	5 851	289 214	1.12	3 985	15.5	2 021	7.9	42 062	18.3	36 951	2 497	19 200	12 104	4 557
Lake Charles, LA	3 796	D	D	2 850	14.8	1 911	9.9	29 902	18.0	32 286	3 867	14 197	9 577	4 993
Lake Havasu City-Kingman, AZ	2 629	D	D	2 488	12.8	2 533	13.0	29 500	19.9	50 598	10 444	18 366	6 916	3 455
Lakeland-Winter Haven, FL	12 261	577 051	0.89	8 239	14.4	5 581	9.8	104 683	22.3	119 134	43 641	33 718	23 218	3 880
Lancaster, PA	12 638	504 907	0.94	7 215	14.5	4 451	8.9	58 039	13.9	90 498	27 401	36 814	10 511	2 024
Lansing-East Lansing, MI	20 717	475 702	1.06	D	D	3 242	7.1	50 582	13.0	68 422	15 240	20 916	13 137	2 881
Laredo, TX	3 479	D	D	6 020	25.7	1 085	4.6	77 572	35.8	25 195	1 534	14 652	13 217	5 280
Las Cruces, NM	4 581	205 376	0.94	3 340	16.9	1 308	6.6	46 430	26.3	30 444	6 939	12 732	7 013	3 414
Las Vegas-Paradise, NV	21 992	1 960 580	1.01	30 085	16.5	12 789	7.0	417 112	24.9	248 286	87 967	63 881	71 098	3 644
Lawrence, KS	8 792	107 576	0.94	1 282	11.3	573	5.1	14 668	14.3	12 410	1 111	6 550	5 079	4 583
Lawton, OK	10 343	130 034	1.08	1 999	17.9	932	8.4	18 866	19.5	15 703	444	6 049	6 558	5 285
Lebanon, PA	3 657	D	D	1 656	12.9	1 340	10.5	12 316	11.7	26 305	8 396	8 867	2 369	1 812
Lewiston, ID-WA	1 140	D	D	D	D	636	10.6	7 718	15.9	13 735	2 450	5 545	2 134	3 505
Lewiston-Auburn, ME	2 760	D	D	1 414	13.2	1 015	9.5	11 168	12.7	21 063	3 365	11 415	2 752	2 555
Lexington-Fayette, KY	16 922	497 105	1.10	D	D	3 365	7.5	64 445	15.9	66 642	12 981	31 560	18 875	4 004
Lima, OH	5 934	D	D	1 417	13.4	1 040	9.9	13 019	15.0	19 205	4 049	9 829	4 299	4 063
Lincoln, NE	15 112	308 927	1.04	4 164	14.3	1 915	6.6	31 822	12.3	40 080	2 768	21 844	12 186	4 138
Little Rock-North Little Rock-Conway, AR	14 285	716 905	1.05	9 612	14.5	5 746	8.6	94 416	16.1	114 234	13 254	51 129	38 067	5 974
Logan, UT-ID	3 696	123 244	0.96	D	D	513	4.3	17 628	15.3	12 021	4 859	3 539	1 533	1 222
Longview, TX	10 140	221 407	1.08	D	D	2 128	10.4	42 911	24.8	36 383	4 757	16 908	8 818	4 136
Longview, WA	1 207	D	D	1 350	13.4	1 011	10.1	13 873	16.1	20 639	8 346	6 135	3 923	3 831
Los Angeles-Long Beach-Santa Ana, CA	210 917	13 076 552	1.04	194 124	15.0	75 843	5.9	2 673 041	23.6	1 602 136	637 716	569 801	351 108	2 737
Los Angeles-Long Beach-Glendale, CA Div	171 681	9 999 671	1.04	150 540	15.2	58 738	5.9	2 150 986	24.8	1 209 358	467 871	454 198	283 354	2 886
Santa Ana-Anaheim-Irvine, CA Div	39 236	3 076 881	1.04	43 584	14.5	17 105	5.7	522 055	19.7	392 778	169 845	115 603	67 754	2 251
Louisville-Jefferson County, KY-IN	25 265	1 288 503	1.00	D	D	11 028	8.9	155 526	14.6	213 040	45 392	103 241	48 222	3 885
Lubbock, TX	11 099	290 114	1.01	4 279	16.1	2 174	8.2	56 421	23.7	38 375	5 456	16 780	16 005	5 618
Lynchburg, VA	12 915	246 914	0.96	D	D	2 372	9.8	30 350	15.0	50 309	8 462	26 005	5 767	2 283
Macon, GA	7 802	D	D	D	D	2 285	9.9	36 484	18.7	40 268	9 828	16 322	13 007	5 630
Madera-Chowchilla, CA	8 624	D	D	2 590	17.6	955	6.5	31 570	24.3	20 269	6 245	7 735	3 971	2 632
Madison, WI	14 515	597 055	1.09	6 832	12.3	3 408	6.2	42 274	8.5	76 293	15 344	30 072	16 511	2 905
Manchester-Nashua, NH	7 759	386 497	0.93	4 903	12.2	2 904	7.2	40 995	11.8	61 092	4 042	28 265	9 594	2 541
Manhattan, KS	10 273	132 558	1.07	D	D	658	5.8	14 503	13.3	12 459	771	5 955	2 977	2 343
Mankato, North Mankato, MN	7 249	D	D	D	D	641	7.0	8 428	10.5	13 729	5 606	7 149	2 484	2 568
Mansfield, OH	7 263	D	D	1 598	12.7	1 258	10.0	14 797	14.5	24 467	4 776	13 086	5 325	4 344
McAllen-Edinburg-Mission, TX	6 982	770 300	0.96	17 152	24.1	3 339	4.7	247 348	37.9	80 452	11 604	47 325	38 800	5 008
Medford, OR	3 492	204 414	1.01	2 374	11.9	2 031	10.2	34 768	21.3	43 017	12 623	14 801	6 513	3 205
Memphis, TN-MS-AR	24 145	1 331 193	1.03	19 948	15.6	10 554	8.2	192 638	17.1	179 241	28 979	80 951	73 375	5 704
Merced, CA	4 896	245 741	0.88	4 606	18.7	1 459	5.9	46 305	21.4	29 647	2 324	16 186	9 692	3 789
Miami-Fort Lauderdale-Pompano Beach, FL	76 921	5 600 754	1.01	72 328	13.3	46 174	8.5	1 353 696	29.7	902 150	411 878	281 998	265 573	4 773
Fort Lauderdale-Pompano Beach-Deerfield Beach, FL Div	16 892	1 684 659	0.91	22 867	12.9	14 782	8.4	393 201	26.5	255 947	123 333	66 834	75 974	4 346
Miami-Miami Beach-Kendall, FL Div	40 057	2 575 579	1.07	33 911	14.2	18 085	7.5	709 529	33.9	383 142	204 761	123 383	136 434	5 465
West Palm Beach-Boca Raton-Boynton Beach, FL Div	19 972	1 340 516	1.03	15 550	12.3	13 307	10.5	250 966	25.6	263 061	83 784	91 781	53 165	4 027
Michigan City-La Porte, IN	6 623	D	D	1 395	12.6	1 099	10.0	15 924	17.2	19 330	1 264	10 097	4 358	4 036
Midland, TX	1 678	D	D	2 217	17.5	952	7.5	27 449	23.8	16 955	1 557	8 171	4 699	3 433
Milwaukee-Waukesha-West Allis, WI	33 087	1 604 130	1.06	21 697	14.1	12 654	8.2	146 445	11.1	237 455	69 139	83 264	59 452	3 821
Minneapolis-St. Paul-Bloomington, MN	64 055	3 315 900	1.02	46 699	14.6	19 146	6.0	276 445	9.6	425 105	207 867	133 523	103 649	3 171
Missoula, MT	3 634	112 974	1.06	1 293	12.3	717	6.8	19 384	20.6	15 952	1 534	7 658	3 574	3 270
Mobile, AL	6 808	420 385	1.04	6 202	15.3	4 051	10.0	60 350	17.2	70 467	26 188	18 767	21 665	5 246
Modesto, CA	6 305	502 600	0.93	8 702	17.0	3 672	7.2	90 325	20.2	69 582	26 846	25 644	23 450	4 558
Monroe, LA	5 949	D	D	D	D	1 718	10.0	30 452	20.8	28 429	3 900	12 722	9 210	5 322
Monroe, MI	1 462	D	D	1 713	11.1	1 285	8.4	15 339	11.9	25 662	6 092	8 820	4 014	2 711
Montgomery, AL	15 116	384 877	1.05	5 235	14.4	3 274	9.0	44 368	14.3	60 679	15 502	15 820	15 184	4 054
Morgantown, WV	9 640	138 288	1.13	D	D	945	8.1	15 860	15.4	17 956	3 722	10 465	2 975	2 392
Morristown, TN	2 663	D	D	D	D	1 408	10.5	20 877	18.3	28 961	9 821	10 817	5 625	4 118
Mount Vernon-Anacortes, WA	1 624	D	D	1 564	13.4	1 051	9.0	17 408	17.5	22 715	6 888	7 558	6 063	5 186
Muncie, IN	8 830	D	D	1 277	11.1	1 177	10.2	16 493	17.2	21 394	2 235	9 818	3 309	2 812
Muskegon-Norton Shores, MI	6 345	D	D	2 377	13.6	1 590	9.1	20 786	14.0	32 747	10 153	11 729	7 822	4 543
Myrtle Beach-North Myrtle Beach-Conway, SC	2 952	272 888	1.02	3 357	13.5	2 282	9.2	50 690	24.1	57 712	5 904	23 269	17 287	6 427
Napa, CA	4 918	140 272	1.06	1 697	12.7	1 186	8.9	19 954	17.7	24 143	9 046	6 569	3 475	2 546

1. Per 1,000 estimated resident population.   2. Data for serious crimes have not been adjusted for underreporting; this may affect comparability between geographic areas and over time.   3. Per 100,000 population estimated by the FBI.

Area name	Serious crimes known to police,[1] 2010 (cont.) Rate[2] Violent	Property	Education School enrollment and attainment, 2010 Enrollment[3] Total	Percent private	Attainment[4] (percent) High school graduate or less	Bachelor's degree or more	Local government expenditures,[5] 2008–2009 Total current expenditures (mil dol)	Current expenditures per student (dollars)	Income and Poverty, 2010 Per capita income[6] (dollars)	Median household income (dollars)	Percent of households with income of less than $25,000	Percent of households with income of $100,000 or more	Percent of households with income of $200,000 or more	Percent below poverty level All persons	Children under 18 years	Children under 5
	46	47	48	49	50	51	52	53	54	55	56	57	58	59	60	61
Kokomo, IN	208	3 115	27 023	6.5	50.9	19.0	155.7	9 388	22 587	41 180	29.0	10.8	1.8	14.3	20.9	25.7
La Crosse, WI-MN	168	2 294	39 971	16.1	37.8	29.3	223.5	11 155	24 031	47 696	26.8	14.5	1.7	12.1	6.5	8.4
Lafayette, IN	196	2 511	76 158	7.0	43.9	30.4	227.5	8 809	21 806	40 577	33.3	14.3	2.2	19.1	17.7	32.8
Lafayette, LA	596	3 960	77 521	18.9	50.0	25.2	362.8	9 531	23 909	46 730	29.4	17.4	3.2	19.8	26.5	27.2
Lake Charles, LA	642	4 351	51 265	14.4	51.8	19.5	352.1	10 356	22 960	40 194	30.5	16.1	2.2	18.0	24.7	29.5
Lake Havasu City-Kingman, AZ	192	3 262	44 841	8.7	48.4	12.6	187.9	7 027	20 347	36 456	29.1	7.6	1.7	17.7	32.0	36.5
Lakeland-Winter Haven, FL	400	3 480	144 524	14.9	54.5	17.9	815.2	8 612	20 124	41 174	29.0	10.1	1.6	17.5	28.7	35.6
Lancaster, PA	182	1 841	129 156	26.5	54.4	24.1	847.0	12 313	24 871	51 740	21.9	17.6	2.6	10.5	14.8	16.3
Lansing-East Lansing, MI	407	2 475	158 627	10.6	33.3	30.0	770.2	10 613	23 359	47 731	26.5	15.4	2.0	16.9	19.0	24.1
Laredo, TX	509	4 772	87 137	3.8	56.9	16.8	566.7	8 558	14 000	35 770	35.9	11.7	2.4	31.7	42.1	48.6
Las Cruces, NM	352	3 062	67 321	4.3	44.4	24.5	366.3	9 255	17 938	35 230	36.8	11.7	1.7	26.3	35.5	44.3
Las Vegas-Paradise, NV	777	2 867	480 542	11.0	45.9	21.6	2 539.5	8 120	24 748	51 437	22.1	18.4	3.0	15.1	22.8	26.5
Lawrence, KS	423	4 160	45 236	7.5	25.0	49.9	129.1	9 397	24 030	47 263	28.8	16.3	1.9	16.5	10.1	12.9
Lawton, OK	711	4 574	33 730	4.7	47.2	17.8	169.3	7 750	21 048	43 817	26.9	10.8	2.3	17.6	29.4	33.0
Lebanon, PA	186	1 626	30 816	25.0	60.1	19.1	187.9	9 943	25 880	51 436	19.2	16.7	3.0	10.9	16.9	20.4
Lewiston, ID-WA	169	3 336	14 048	6.3	47.9	18.2	83.9	9 379	23 543	39 959	30.1	9.4	2.1	11.6	19.6	24.3
Lewiston-Auburn, ME	159	2 396	25 011	16.7	51.7	18.6	185.6	11 240	22 734	41 190	29.3	11.1	1.8	14.8	19.5	23.0
Lexington-Fayette, KY	439	3 564	132 964	15.5	40.7	31.2	565.2	8 687	24 983	46 257	27.8	16.6	2.3	18.8	25.6	31.9
Lima, OH	395	3 668	29 556	15.3	55.0	16.4	156.0	9 608	20 657	41 057	32.6	11.2	1.0	19.3	35.0	36.9
Lincoln, NE	438	3 700	92 097	19.6	31.7	33.7	389.1	9 363	25 183	50 091	24.0	16.6	2.7	16.4	19.2	19.2
Little Rock-North Little Rock-Conway, AR	791	5 183	186 637	14.7	43.0	26.2	958.9	8 850	24 602	45 991	26.3	15.8	2.4	15.2	21.1	26.0
Logan, UT-ID	58	1 164	47 591	6.4	32.0	31.7	163.3	6 424	18 746	46 215	25.1	12.5	1.8	15.6	17.1	19.7
Longview, TX	460	3 676	54 550	9.3	51.1	15.7	336.2	8 772	20 885	41 842	29.2	13.4	2.6	17.8	27.5	31.1
Longview, WA	319	3 511	25 325	12.2	42.7	14.4	161.1	9 091	21 317	41 054	32.0	11.9	1.7	22.4	32.7	57.5
Los Angeles-Long Beach-Santa Ana, CA	445	2 292	3 689 635	14.5	42.3	31.0	21 010.6	9 845	27 051	56 691	22.1	26.0	6.2	16.3	22.6	23.5
Los Angeles-Long Beach-Glendale, CA Div	512	2 374	2 816 272	14.7	44.6	29.2	16 525.5	10 139	25 724	52 684	24.1	23.6	5.5	17.5	24.5	25.5
Santa Ana-Anaheim-Irvine, CA Div	229	2 021	873 363	14.0	34.6	36.6	4 485.1	8 897	31 373	70 880	15.8	33.7	8.4	12.2	16.4	16.9
Louisville-Jefferson County, KY-IN	396	3 489	324 015	21.7	44.4	25.8	1 736.2	9 174	24 511	44 678	26.6	15.8	2.9	15.3	22.4	25.8
Lubbock, TX	790	4 828	99 071	8.0	41.5	28.0	394.2	8 399	21 575	42 126	31.3	14.0	2.7	21.4	28.2	35.7
Lynchburg, VA	285	1 998	71 413	34.3	52.4	21.3	334.4	9 468	21 676	41 248	29.5	12.1	1.8	16.2	21.8	35.9
Macon, GA	465	5 165	61 652	20.2	52.0	20.3	340.8	9 075	20 322	37 507	34.5	15.4	2.3	23.2	35.8	39.6
Madera-Chowchilla, CA	434	2 199	40 519	5.0	54.9	15.4	270.5	9 198	18 300	48 268	23.3	18.9	3.0	21.0	31.3	46.3
Madison, WI	244	2 661	161 906	12.6	28.5	43.3	901.5	11 401	30 263	57 594	19.9	22.0	3.9	11.8	12.0	13.6
Manchester-Nashua, NH	230	2 311	102 283	25.9	37.3	35.1	667.1	11 154	33 406	68 312	14.7	30.3	5.4	7.1	10.4	14.6
Manhattan, KS	336	2 007	45 800	5.1	30.3	34.2	176.1	9 833	21 179	46 150	24.7	11.8	2.2	18.0	17.0	18.9
Mankato, North Mankato, MN	153	2 415	32 743	19.3	34.3	31.1	124.5	10 170	23 215	51 127	20.8	13.0	1.2	14.9	11.2	6.5
Mansfield, OH	177	4 167	28 597	19.6	54.3	14.6	200.3	11 543	20 674	41 572	25.1	10.8	1.6	12.9	20.2	24.6
McAllen-Edinburg-Mission, TX	314	4 694	261 381	5.0	62.6	15.8	1 826.4	9 082	13 525	33 732	37.8	9.8	1.9	33.4	45.3	44.3
Medford, OR	271	2 934	45 251	9.5	38.8	23.7	274.4	9 674	22 644	40 177	31.0	13.4	2.3	14.9	20.0	21.8
Memphis, TN-MS-AR	1 027	4 677	371 785	17.0	43.7	25.1	1 894.7	8 268	22 919	45 377	27.3	17.0	2.9	19.1	27.6	32.2
Merced, CA	566	3 223	82 525	5.9	58.1	12.3	547.2	9 744	18 150	42 449	31.4	13.3	3.4	23.0	31.5	35.3
Miami-Fort Lauderdale-Pompano Beach, FL	611	4 162	1 391 800	20.8	45.1	28.1	7 096.7	9 185	24 982	45 352	27.9	18.4	4.2	17.1	22.9	24.9
Fort Lauderdale-Pompano Beach-Deerfield Beach, FL Div	485	3 861	457 470	21.9	41.3	29.3	2 365.1	9 226	26 373	48 063	25.5	19.7	3.9	14.6	19.7	21.2
Miami-Miami Beach-Kendall, FL Div	741	4 724	629 365	20.8	51.0	25.2	3 144.3	9 100	20 970	40 219	32.6	15.6	3.6	20.4	25.4	26.9
West Palm Beach-Boca Raton-Boynton Beach, FL Div	530	3 498	304 965	19.4	39.5	31.8	1 587.3	9 296	30 735	49 879	23.4	21.0	5.4	14.2	22.7	25.9
Michigan City-La Porte, IN	211	3 825	27 039	15.1	52.0	17.6	166.5	9 111	20 982	43 765	30.8	11.8	1.4	16.5	25.3	22.9
Midland, TX	330	3 104	36 958	9.6	43.8	20.3	191.2	8 099	29 255	53 170	20.2	20.2	6.6	14.7	25.3	20.5
Milwaukee-Waukesha-West Allis, WI	466	3 355	433 599	23.5	38.8	31.7	2 736.0	11 726	26 997	49 774	25.1	19.9	3.3	15.5	24.2	29.0
Minneapolis-St. Paul-Bloomington, MN	287	2 884	911 095	19.6	30.5	37.9	5 907.7	11 121	31 471	62 352	17.8	26.4	4.9	10.9	14.8	15.6
Missoula, MT	286	2 984	32 387	9.0	27.9	40.7	125.0	9 536	24 450	45 596	26.9	14.4	1.9	14.2	13.6	13.5
Mobile, AL	582	4 664	109 825	18.4	48.9	21.0	565.2	8 822	21 274	39 998	32.4	13.7	2.3	20.2	28.1	36.9
Modesto, CA	519	4 039	151 711	9.1	52.6	16.0	994.9	9 415	20 719	48 044	27.1	17.7	2.3	19.9	29.1	30.6
Monroe, LA	417	4 906	45 805	9.7	51.7	19.6	311.1	10 016	21 184	37 819	33.9	13.3	2.0	20.9	30.6	34.6
Monroe, MI	265	2 446	40 781	13.6	46.0	18.3	242.8	10 108	23 842	50 034	23.0	16.6	1.7	12.7	20.0	23.3
Montgomery, AL	299	3 755	104 050	21.6	44.9	27.6	475.9	8 494	23 363	45 513	27.5	18.1	2.3	17.8	26.6	33.9
Morgantown, WV	343	2 048	44 003	4.0	48.8	29.6	153.7	10 349	22 784	43 470	33.6	13.9	2.9	20.9	14.2	15.6
Morristown, TN	389	3 729	33 517	14.2	59.8	14.1	147.6	7 092	19 235	37 065	34.5	8.3	1.4	18.9	28.8	41.3
Mount Vernon-Anacortes, WA	211	4 975	26 881	16.3	35.1	22.2	196.6	10 187	25 535	55 458	20.1	18.1	1.7	11.5	17.8	16.2
Muncie, IN	246	2 566	39 066	4.3	47.2	23.8	147.6	9 481	19 789	35 902	34.5	10.1	1.3	24.3	28.3	40.4
Muskegon-Norton Shores, MI	462	4 080	43 032	8.6	49.3	16.1	320.3	10 093	19 347	38 621	33.7	9.6	0.9	21.1	29.4	40.2
Myrtle Beach-North Myrtle Beach-Conway, SC	663	5 765	58 018	8.0	45.1	23.3	373.6	9 845	22 731	41 568	29.1	10.9	2.1	20.1	34.2	35.2
Napa, CA	477	2 069	34 387	15.8	37.1	27.9	213.6	10 595	32 283	64 401	19.7	29.0	7.3	11.7	15.4	20.3

1. Data for serious crimes have not been adjusted for underreporting; this may affect comparability between geographic areas and over time. 2. Per 100,000 population estimated by the FBI. 3. All persons 3 years old and over enrolled in nursery school through college. 4. Persons 25 years old and over. 5. Elementary and secondary education expenditures. 6. Based on resident population estimated as of July 1, 2009.

Table C. Metropolitan Areas — **Personal Income**

Area name	Personal income, 2009 Total (mil dol)	Percent change, 2008–2009	Per capita[1] Dollars	Rank	Wages and salaries[2] (mil dol)	Proprietors' income (mil dol)	Dividends, interest, and rent (mil dol)	Transfer payments Total (mil dol)	Government payments to individuals Total (mil dol)	Social Security (mil dol)	Medical payments (mil dol)	Income maintenance (mil dol)	Unemployment insurance (mil dol)
	62	63	64	65	66	67	68	69	70	71	72	73	74
Kokomo, IN	3 129	-5.0	31 677	287	2 192	182	449	834	816	326	311	68	66
La Crosse, WI-MN	4 773	1.5	35 908	166	3 351	247	860	886	861	302	370	56	51
Lafayette, IN	6 012	-1.1	30 620	314	4 339	555	943	992	956	378	316	86	87
Lafayette, LA	10 966	-1.3	41 670	56	7 827	1 173	1 970	1 624	1 576	486	719	198	36
Lake Charles, LA	7 030	-2.6	36 210	159	4 735	484	1 221	1 397	1 362	454	633	149	30
Lake Havasu City-Kingman, AZ	5 101	-1.7	26 185	359	1 968	298	940	1 626	1 590	710	556	140	54
Lakeland-Winter Haven, FL	18 865	-2.2	32 336	259	9 568	1 160	3 913	4 274	4 168	1 634	1 547	485	180
Lancaster, PA	18 450	-1.2	36 336	154	11 047	1 458	3 402	3 425	3 333	1 330	1 257	223	309
Lansing-East Lansing, MI	15 510	-1.1	34 192	209	11 156	928	2 264	3 051	2 969	1 058	1 115	304	263
Laredo, TX	5 624	1.0	23 294	364	3 424	593	655	1 418	1 374	243	630	339	54
Las Cruces, NM	5 814	3.6	28 165	348	3 284	385	828	1 444	1 406	356	635	215	50
Las Vegas-Paradise, NV	69 855	-5.3	36 711	143	46 708	4 785	14 045	10 488	10 142	3 391	3 734	961	1 288
Lawrence, KS	3 732	1.1	32 070	269	2 176	189	724	516	494	181	184	46	30
Lawton, OK	4 140	2.9	36 564	148	3 227	130	469	760	741	206	258	90	19
Lebanon, PA	4 809	1.4	36 850	138	2 210	227	757	983	959	379	371	58	82
Lewiston, ID-WA	2 072	-0.3	34 166	210	1 160	182	396	518	507	192	209	48	13
Lewiston-Auburn, ME	3 777	0.7	35 455	178	2 237	243	389	990	970	271	484	113	39
Lexington-Fayette, KY	16 816	-1.1	35 715	172	12 718	1 255	2 894	2 781	2 695	928	948	265	160
Lima, OH	3 193	-1.8	30 596	315	2 454	282	485	793	774	269	295	80	45
Lincoln, NE	11 134	-0.5	37 361	133	8 086	739	2 019	1 580	1 526	560	606	129	47
Little Rock-North Little Rock-Conway, AR	27 029	1.2	39 431	81	18 348	1 998	4 789	4 902	4 778	1 587	1 959	472	217
Logan, UT-ID	3 221	-0.8	25 176	362	2 080	162	567	495	472	164	171	50	24
Longview, TX	7 782	-1.7	37 616	126	4 594	1 045	1 393	1 617	1 579	511	773	143	54
Longview, WA	3 147	1.1	30 859	305	1 830	171	558	889	870	307	306	116	65
Los Angeles-Long Beach-Santa Ana, CA	550 832	-3.0	42 784	41	362 742	61 670	106 920	84 146	81 798	19 115	38 890	11 009	5 922
Los Angeles-Long Beach-Glendale, CA Div	402 459	-2.5	40 867	X	268 394	44 759	77 335	67 792	65 996	14 039	32 680	9 559	4 426
Santa Ana-Anaheim-Irvine, CA Div	148 373	-4.3	49 020	X	94 348	16 911	29 585	16 354	15 802	5 076	6 210	1 450	1 496
Louisville-Jefferson County, KY-IN	47 433	-0.8	37 688	122	31 183	3 890	7 493	8 953	8 723	3 038	3 522	866	550
Lubbock, TX	9 428	1.6	34 079	212	5 524	920	1 810	1 878	1 828	516	939	195	51
Lynchburg, VA	8 242	-0.6	33 308	235	4 868	428	1 444	1 856	1 811	701	731	168	54
Macon, GA	7 968	-0.3	34 407	203	4 598	481	1 312	1 810	1 768	531	726	268	78
Madera-Chowchilla, CA	3 982	0.4	26 790	356	2 122	505	634	933	905	267	362	135	69
Madison, WI	24 572	-0.9	43 107	37	18 583	1 520	4 566	3 090	2 987	1 118	1 170	269	217
Manchester-Nashua, NH	17 948	-2.7	44 217	35	12 343	1 364	2 405	2 357	2 283	879	943	169	130
Manhattan, KS	4 913	2.1	39 918	73	4 157	148	654	524	505	166	177	58	25
Mankato, North Mankato, MN	3 287	-1.9	35 258	184	2 220	283	608	567	550	183	216	46	41
Mansfield, OH	3 689	-2.2	29 635	331	2 349	142	564	999	976	346	388	94	62
McAllen-Edinburg-Mission, TX	15 200	3.6	20 509	366	8 394	1 485	1 731	4 617	4 481	757	2 060	1 131	208
Medford, OR	6 907	-0.6	34 314	206	3 534	666	1 649	1 591	1 555	586	542	149	137
Memphis, TN-MS-AR	49 095	-2.2	37 623	125	33 788	5 609	6 358	8 468	8 231	2 485	3 234	1 533	331
Merced, CA	6 750	-1.4	27 517	354	3 241	841	950	1 716	1 671	355	735	288	144
Miami-Fort Lauderdale-Pompano Beach, FL	237 215	-3.1	42 764	42	130 209	15 412	67 254	40 728	39 718	11 440	19 539	4 300	1 882
Fort Lauderdale-Pompano Beach-Deerfield Beach, FL Div	72 752	-4.2	41 185	X	40 559	3 949	17 767	11 433	11 111	3 523	5 101	1 041	590
Miami-Miami Beach-Kendall, FL Div	90 916	-0.8	36 357	X	59 202	7 432	17 340	19 198	18 742	3 941	10 173	2 635	880
West Palm Beach-Boca Raton-Boynton Beach, FL Div	73 547	-4.9	57 461	X	30 449	4 031	32 147	10 098	9 864	3 977	4 265	625	411
Michigan City-La Porte, IN	3 354	-3.1	30 199	318	1 970	179	512	803	783	297	299	75	60
Midland, TX	7 167	-7.0	54 164	7	3 908	1 557	1 403	755	731	243	315	102	28
Milwaukee-Waukesha-West Allis, WI	65 978	-1.0	42 303	47	46 868	3 855	11 570	11 691	11 407	3 574	5 017	1 450	778
Minneapolis-St. Paul-Bloomington, MN	149 795	-3.0	45 811	30	109 187	9 200	26 950	20 139	19 543	6 122	8 653	1 710	1 525
Missoula, MT	3 819	0.6	35 156	187	2 519	413	792	632	612	209	229	54	32
Mobile, AL	12 713	0.2	30 878	304	8 965	742	1 863	3 109	3 034	1 004	1 246	447	91
Modesto, CA	15 949	-0.8	31 248	296	8 498	1 450	2 517	3 508	3 415	898	1 400	475	333
Monroe, LA	5 959	1.8	34 229	207	3 407	628	995	1 373	1 341	374	630	202	31
Monroe, MI	4 881	-4.6	31 961	274	2 037	230	690	1 069	1 041	405	380	83	106
Montgomery, AL	13 147	-0.8	35 882	169	9 003	943	2 065	2 618	2 551	828	968	411	71
Morgantown, WV	4 189	3.6	34 813	194	3 081	336	564	819	797	259	363	63	26
Morristown, TN	3 792	0.1	27 559	353	1 930	259	486	1 114	1 089	396	440	116	56
Mount Vernon-Anacortes, WA	4 569	-0.6	38 225	109	2 346	396	1 099	929	907	320	336	92	71
Muncie, IN	3 389	-0.5	29 418	337	2 079	215	491	902	881	325	348	84	59
Muskegon-Norton Shores, MI	4 834	-1.5	27 792	350	2 726	236	658	1 453	1 422	486	534	195	128
Myrtle Beach-North Myrtle Beach-Conway, SC	7 679	-1.0	29 101	343	4 390	486	1 548	1 998	1 950	803	680	176	106
Napa, CA	6 706	-3.0	49 805	15	4 018	569	1 565	906	882	310	381	48	60

1. Based on the resident population estimated as of July 1 of the year shown.   2. Includes other labor income.

Table C. Metropolitan Areas — Earnings, Social Security, and Housing

Area name	Earnings, 2009 Total (mil dol)	Farm	Goods-related[1] Total	Manu-facturing	Infor-mation, profes-sional, and technical services	Retail trade	Finance, insur-ance, and real estate	Health care and social services	Govern-ment	Social Security beneficiaries, December 2010 Number	Rate[2]	Supple-mental Security Income recipients, December 2009	Housing units, 2010 Total	Percent change, 2000–2010
	75	76	77	78	79	80	81	82	83	84	85	86	87	88
Kokomo, IN	2 374	2.4	D	41.3	3.7	6.2	3.4	D	16.9	23 630	239	2 258	45 677	2.8
La Crosse, WI-MN	3 597	0.5	D	13.5	D	6.9	6.4	22.4	15.2	24 420	183	2 367	57 003	10.4
Lafayette, IN	4 893	2.5	D	21.2	D	5.6	4.6	NA	27.8	28 660	142	2 234	84 505	19.3
Lafayette, LA	9 000	0.2	30.9	6.5	10.1	6.6	6.3	12.2	11.4	41 270	151	7 675	115 597	17.6
Lake Charles, LA	5 219	0.0	32.5	17.8	D	NA	D	10.4	16.2	36 425	182	5 963	85 651	5.3
Lake Havasu City-Kingman, AZ	2 267	0.1	14.1	6.8	5.2	13.4	5.1	19.8	20.5	56 875	284	4 014	110 911	38.5
Lakeland-Winter Haven, FL	10 728	0.8	16.0	9.6	7.8	7.7	6.9	13.8	15.0	133 160	221	17 248	281 214	24.2
Lancaster, PA	12 505	1.1	28.1	18.1	7.7	7.3	5.6	13.9	10.1	98 815	190	9 249	202 952	12.8
Lansing-East Lansing, MI	12 085	0.5	13.9	9.5	D	5.6	9.6	12.2	32.1	78 170	168	8 812	199 026	9.4
Laredo, TX	4 018	0.2	10.1	0.8	4.3	8.3	4.6	10.8	31.2	27 860	111	11 656	73 496	33.1
Las Cruces, NM	3 669	3.2	9.3	4.4	9.6	6.0	3.2	13.9	36.2	33 220	159	7 169	81 492	25.0
Las Vegas-Paradise, NV	51 494	0.0	13.6	2.9	8.6	6.7	7.1	8.2	16.1	271 030	139	30 893	840 343	50.1
Lawrence, KS	2 365	0.2	15.7	10.5	11.0	6.5	4.4	7.5	34.3	13 500	122	1 155	46 731	16.1
Lawton, OK	3 357	-0.2	D	7.7	D	5.0	3.3	5.1	60.5	18 040	145	3 002	50 739	11.7
Lebanon, PA	2 437	1.8	24.2	19.3	4.2	7.7	2.7	13.2	22.2	29 040	217	2 176	55 592	12.7
Lewiston, ID-WA	1 341	1.8	D	13.9	5.0	9.2	7.5	16.4	19.3	15 340	252	1 721	27 310	7.9
Lewiston-Auburn, ME	2 480	0.5	19.5	12.8	7.6	8.2	7.0	21.8	11.9	23 505	218	3 619	49 090	6.8
Lexington-Fayette, KY	13 973	1.5	D	17.3	D	6.5	4.8	NA	20.2	73 530	156	11 334	209 138	19.3
Lima, OH	2 737	1.1	D	24.9	4.2	6.8	3.4	19.5	13.8	21 185	199	2 827	44 999	1.7
Lincoln, NE	8 825	1.2	D	9.8	8.3	6.0	8.7	NA	23.0	42 795	142	4 318	127 750	15.5
Little Rock-North Little Rock-Conway, AR	20 346	0.4	D	6.7	D	5.9	7.1	NA	24.8	129 445	185	22 354	306 882	17.2
Logan, UT-ID	2 241	1.8	28.9	23.7	6.8	7.2	3.4	NA	25.0	13 325	106	917	41 552	26.3
Longview, TX	5 639	0.2	34.6	12.6	D	7.8	4.5	NA	10.2	41 070	192	6 500	87 318	7.6
Longview, WA	2 001	-0.1	32.7	21.4	4.2	7.2	3.5	13.8	16.4	23 515	230	3 271	43 450	12.5
Los Angeles-Long Beach-Santa Ana, CA	424 412	0.1	15.5	10.4	19.2	5.7	9.3	9.3	13.8	1 525 495	119	484 340	4 493 983	6.0
Los Angeles-Long Beach-Glendale, CA Div	313 153	0.1	14.0	9.8	20.6	5.6	8.3	9.5	15.0	1 148 135	117	413 058	3 445 076	5.3
Santa Ana-Anaheim-Irvine, CA Div	111 259	0.1	19.5	11.9	15.2	6.0	12.2	8.5	10.6	377 360	125	71 282	1 048 907	8.2
Louisville-Jefferson County, KY-IN	35 072	0.2	D	NA	D	5.7	9.5	NA	13.9	238 965	186	35 127	559 837	13.7
Lubbock, TX	6 445	0.7	D	NA	D	8.3	D	NA	23.6	42 040	148	6 334	117 966	13.7
Lynchburg, VA	5 296	-0.5	D	19.5	D	6.8	7.6	NA	14.4	56 480	224	6 185	112 515	14.7
Macon, GA	5 079	0.4	D	NA	D	NA	D	NA	15.3	45 225	195	8 964	101 587	8.0
Madera-Chowchilla, CA	2 627	13.3	D	7.2	3.9	6.5	2.1	15.6	25.5	22 500	149	4 740	49 140	21.7
Madison, WI	20 103	0.4	D	9.8	13.1	6.6	10.2	NA	24.2	94 060	148	7 858	252 878	18.9
Manchester-Nashua, NH	13 707	0.0	22.1	16.7	15.8	7.9	9.8	11.8	11.1	68 120	170	6 090	166 053	10.7
Manhattan, KS	4 305	0.4	D	3.6	D	3.8	2.5	D	64.2	14 015	110	1 275	51 355	20.4
Mankato, North Mankato, MN	2 504	5.0	D	14.6	D	6.6	4.3	NA	19.6	14 915	154	1 336	39 075	17.7
Mansfield, OH	2 490	0.5	29.0	24.6	5.1	8.0	3.5	15.3	18.9	27 050	217	3 017	54 599	2.9
McAllen-Edinburg-Mission, TX	9 879	0.6	8.4	2.6	5.1	9.5	4.1	21.5	28.0	89 745	116	40 227	248 287	28.9
Medford, OR	4 200	0.5	15.4	7.0	6.7	11.7	5.3	17.9	16.2	47 270	233	3 912	90 937	20.1
Memphis, TN-MS-AR	39 397	0.4	D	9.7	D	6.4	8.2	NA	15.6	204 485	155	44 144	550 896	14.6
Merced, CA	4 082	13.5	D	11.0	3.8	6.8	2.9	9.8	25.8	32 595	127	10 940	83 698	22.1
Miami-Fort Lauderdale-Pompano Beach, FL	145 622	0.4	9.6	3.9	13.8	7.4	9.6	11.5	16.1	932 095	168	197 664	2 464 417	14.6
Fort Lauderdale-Pompano Beach-Deerfield Beach, FL Div	44 508	0.0	10.5	4.3	13.5	8.5	9.8	10.5	16.3	277 735	159	37 583	810 388	9.4
Miami-Miami Beach-Kendall, FL Div	66 635	0.3	8.7	3.6	14.0	6.8	9.3	11.1	17.3	371 465	149	140 916	989 435	16.1
West Palm Beach-Boca Raton-Boynton Beach, FL Div	34 480	1.1	10.3	4.0	13.7	7.4	9.9	13.8	13.5	282 895	214	19 165	664 594	19.4
Michigan City-La Porte, IN	2 149	1.6	28.8	21.3	3.5	7.5	3.1	13.9	17.9	22 360	201	2 077	48 448	6.2
Midland, TX	5 465	0.0	51.1	3.7	6.7	4.6	4.7	5.1	9.0	18 750	137	2 356	54 351	13.1
Milwaukee-Waukesha-West Allis, WI	50 723	0.1	D	17.0	11.3	5.0	9.2	13.5	11.7	265 765	171	42 592	669 879	8.4
Minneapolis-St. Paul-Bloomington, MN	118 388	0.2	D	12.3	D	5.1	D	NA	13.4	456 325	139	53 443	1 354 973	15.8
Missoula, MT	2 932	-0.1	11.3	4.4	9.5	8.9	6.8	17.3	19.9	17 190	157	1 881	50 106	21.3
Mobile, AL	9 707	0.3	19.9	10.8	9.2	6.9	7.8	11.4	18.6	82 220	199	14 411	178 196	7.9
Modesto, CA	9 948	5.1	19.9	14.1	4.6	7.6	4.5	15.8	18.4	75 480	147	21 044	179 503	19.0
Monroe, LA	4 035	0.7	16.3	9.9	11.7	8.1	6.6	NA	18.8	31 190	177	7 217	75 827	6.8
Monroe, MI	2 267	1.1	D	16.1	8.7	6.8	3.9	10.3	15.4	29 940	197	2 545	62 971	11.5
Montgomery, AL	9 945	0.6	D	10.4	D	6.1	6.5	10.2	31.3	69 670	186	14 510	161 573	11.7
Morgantown, WV	3 417	-0.2	18.0	8.5	6.5	5.6	2.9	18.2	32.2	20 055	155	2 966	58 335	16.3
Morristown, TN	2 189	0.0	D	28.6	D	8.1	D	D	15.2	33 605	246	4 305	61 356	14.2
Mount Vernon-Anacortes, WA	2 742	2.5	25.6	16.8	4.7	10.5	6.1	9.7	22.5	24 655	211	2 258	51 473	20.6
Muncie, IN	2 294	1.0	D	11.0	6.8	7.5	5.8	21.2	23.2	24 605	209	2 758	52 357	2.6
Muskegon-Norton Shores, MI	2 963	0.6	D	23.2	4.6	10.8	4.1	17.6	17.6	38 330	223	6 031	73 561	7.3
Myrtle Beach-North Myrtle Beach-Conway, SC	4 876	0.1	10.9	3.5	6.8	12.3	10.5	10.6	17.9	65 290	242	5 120	185 992	52.3
Napa, CA	4 587	2.5	26.8	19.3	7.1	5.5	5.4	10.7	16.1	24 595	180	2 416	54 759	12.8

1. Includes mining, construction, and manufacturing.   2. Per 1,000 resident population enumerated in the 2010 census.

Table C. Metropolitan Areas — **Housing, Labor Force, and Employment**

Area name	Housing units, 2010								Civilian labor force, 2010				Civilian employment,[5] 2010		
	Occupied units										Unemployment			Percent	
	Owner-occupied					Renter-occupied									
				Median owner cost as a percent of income											
	Total	Percent	Median value[1]	With a mortgage	Without a mortgage	Median rent[2]	Median rent as a percent of income	Sub-stand-ard units[3] (percent)	Total	Percent change, 2009–2010	Total	Rate[4]	Total	Management, business, science, and arts occupations	Construction, production, and maintenance occupations
	89	90	91	92	93	94	95	96	97	98	99	100	101	102	103
Kokomo, IN	40 775	70.3	99 800	19.8	10.0	604	33.5	NA	42 281	-1.0	5 181	12.3	41 764	29.2	28.0
La Crosse, WI-MN	53 627	66.3	151 500	22.1	13.0	660	32.6	2.5	76 845	-0.2	5 004	6.5	70 323	32.7	23.2
Lafayette, IN	76 945	60.3	123 800	21.3	10.9	724	36.2	1.7	96 225	-2.1	8 829	9.2	96 088	36.7	22.3
Lafayette, LA	103 181	66.6	149 300	19.8	10.0	687	28.1	3.0	136 592	0.8	8 138	6.0	129 034	32.1	23.2
Lake Charles, LA	75 197	74.5	119 500	19.7	10.7	726	32.3	2.0	95 266	0.4	6 655	7.0	85 532	29.5	26.0
Lake Havasu City-Kingman, AZ	82 166	70.7	143 100	30.1	12.9	762	31.2	3.8	92 454	0.1	10 388	11.2	72 433	25.2	22.3
Lakeland-Winter Haven, FL	221 073	71.1	119 100	26.9	14.0	828	35.5	3.5	275 449	0.6	34 546	12.5	237 723	29.7	25.5
Lancaster, PA	194 028	69.6	187 400	24.4	12.6	822	30.8	1.9	267 237	-0.6	20 172	7.5	249 828	31.9	28.7
Lansing-East Lansing, MI	178 797	66.7	135 100	23.5	13.5	760	33.6	1.2	241 779	-0.7	23 731	9.8	212 975	37.5	18.9
Laredo, TX	66 716	59.8	109 900	27.7	15.1	677	34.2	18.2	95 694	1.7	8 273	8.6	99 263	23.7	22.1
Las Cruces, NM	73 614	62.9	145 600	23.8	10.0	641	36.2	6.4	93 644	3.6	7 639	8.2	84 796	32.5	22.9
Las Vegas-Paradise, NV	698 955	55.0	170 100	28.6	11.7	986	31.6	5.6	969 098	-0.2	147 501	15.2	872 794	27.4	16.9
Lawrence, KS	43 385	48.2	187 600	22.7	12.8	820	31.9	NA	63 316	0.9	3 922	6.2	59 164	44.6	13.8
Lawton, OK	46 141	56.1	114 200	21.1	10.7	663	27.7	NA	48 413	2.4	3 105	6.4	47 730	31.3	27.5
Lebanon, PA	50 701	71.9	165 300	22.8	12.2	692	28.6	1.9	72 834	0.4	5 254	7.2	62 284	32.3	24.6
Lewiston, ID-WA	25 143	72.0	167 200	22.1	12.4	636	29.9	NA	29 295	1.1	2 311	7.9	27 507	26.6	24.5
Lewiston-Auburn, ME	43 918	66.6	158 400	24.4	16.4	640	31.2	NA	58 283	0.4	4 703	8.1	49 715	33.8	22.5
Lexington-Fayette, KY	190 535	58.3	158 400	21.9	10.0	696	30.2	2.2	241 965	1.1	20 835	8.6	232 855	39.0	20.6
Lima, OH	40 615	68.7	110 200	21.4	13.2	642	33.5	NA	50 932	-1.1	5 415	10.6	44 717	25.2	28.1
Lincoln, NE	120 407	60.5	148 200	21.6	11.4	685	28.8	2.7	166 304	-0.9	7 030	4.2	159 090	39.7	20.0
Little Rock-North Little Rock-Conway, AR	272 455	65.4	132 700	20.9	10.7	731	30.2	2.6	342 309	0.3	24 013	7.0	323 730	35.8	20.8
Logan, UT-ID	40 170	65.3	187 000	23.8	10.0	581	26.9	5.1	68 543	-0.2	3 911	5.7	58 559	33.8	25.8
Longview, TX	76 660	70.1	104 100	21.3	11.0	726	29.6	5.4	111 508	2.4	8 262	7.4	90 932	25.5	30.8
Longview, WA	40 475	62.0	194 200	26.5	12.6	691	38.8	NA	44 695	-0.5	5 704	12.8	38 046	27.1	29.4
Los Angeles-Long Beach-Santa Ana, CA	4 188 650	49.8	455 900	32.1	11.1	1 196	34.8	12.5	6 491 393	0.0	770 306	11.9	5 805 528	36.2	19.7
Los Angeles-Long Beach-Glendale, CA Div	3 202 353	46.9	429 500	32.6	11.4	1 147	35.1	13.2	4 910 534	0.1	619 137	12.6	4 391 268	35.2	20.6
Santa Ana-Anaheim-Irvine, CA Div	986 297	59.2	528 200	30.7	10.3	1 402	33.8	10.1	1 580 859	-0.5	151 169	9.6	1 414 260	39.3	17.1
Louisville-Jefferson County, KY-IN	510 653	68.3	148 100	22.9	11.1	671	29.1	1.9	636 947	0.0	65 764	10.3	590 422	34.0	23.6
Lubbock, TX	107 367	58.0	107 900	22.3	11.6	757	35.7	5.3	146 492	1.4	9 082	6.2	136 655	32.5	19.5
Lynchburg, VA	96 553	70.8	157 700	24.2	10.5	679	32.3	NA	123 650	-0.5	9 631	7.8	111 799	32.2	25.0
Macon, GA	82 543	63.6	130 200	24.0	13.5	684	34.9	1.8	111 661	-1.2	11 542	10.3	87 055	36.4	21.3
Madera-Chowchilla, CA	42 189	60.4	203 900	31.4	13.1	877	29.4	11.1	66 960	0.6	10 420	15.6	54 262	26.4	36.0
Madison, WI	235 533	62.9	224 000	24.9	12.4	824	31.0	2.0	344 324	0.1	20 441	5.9	312 928	45.4	15.6
Manchester-Nashua, NH	152 652	68.1	257 100	25.9	16.7	1 019	29.4	2.1	229 175	-0.3	14 442	6.3	210 628	41.9	19.8
Manhattan, KS	45 851	49.7	148 000	21.8	11.2	811	27.4	NA	64 466	3.4	3 691	5.7	57 886	37.6	18.4
Mankato, North Mankato, MN	36 886	67.8	163 900	24.0	10.4	721	30.0	NA	58 369	0.8	3 584	6.1	53 530	31.5	23.1
Mansfield, OH	47 654	69.6	106 300	22.9	10.8	573	22.2	1.1	60 490	-2.0	7 112	11.8	51 205	29.2	31.1
McAllen-Edinburg-Mission, TX	212 743	68.0	80 400	24.6	12.5	608	33.4	15.7	305 786	3.1	36 133	11.8	278 649	26.2	23.0
Medford, OR	81 508	63.8	236 200	29.1	14.8	818	38.3	2.0	102 524	0.1	12 969	12.6	84 959	31.5	20.4
Memphis, TN-MS-AR	474 304	63.1	138 700	24.5	11.9	793	33.9	3.6	609 410	-1.1	60 863	10.0	575 047	33.8	22.7
Merced, CA	73 885	54.6	146 100	27.5	11.2	807	32.7	9.3	107 381	1.7	20 291	18.9	94 048	19.5	36.8
Miami-Fort Lauderdale-Pompano Beach, FL	1 984 559	64.0	195 700	33.1	17.2	1 063	37.8	4.7	2 835 313	1.4	325 701	11.5	2 479 649	32.9	17.6
Fort Lauderdale-Pompano Beach-Deerfield Beach, FL Div	658 025	66.2	179 600	32.2	18.1	1 126	36.1	4.2	985 251	0.1	99 336	10.1	826 452	34.2	15.9
Miami-Miami Beach-Kendall, FL Div	809 689	57.0	207 100	35.3	17.2	997	39.6	6.0	1 231 368	3.0	153 926	12.5	1 075 625	30.5	20.0
West Palm Beach-Boca Raton-Boynton Beach, FL Div	516 845	72.2	199 500	31.4	16.6	1 103	36.0	3.3	618 694	0.2	72 439	11.7	577 572	35.5	15.8
Michigan City-La Porte, IN	42 552	73.7	125 800	21.5	10.9	667	34.4	3.5	51 018	-2.7	6 106	12.0	46 537	26.6	29.9
Midland, TX	48 730	69.1	151 000	22.0	11.5	848	26.9	3.0	77 066	2.9	4 076	5.3	65 211	30.5	27.6
Milwaukee-Waukesha-West Allis, WI	615 244	62.2	203 600	24.9	15.0	764	31.5	2.3	794 359	-1.1	69 325	8.7	747 245	37.5	19.8
Minneapolis-St. Paul-Bloomington, MN	1 267 805	71.3	225 500	24.4	12.0	845	30.4	2.5	1 844 518	0.0	133 330	7.2	1 695 128	42.0	17.4
Missoula, MT	44 572	63.2	238 800	24.7	11.4	744	33.2	2.5	58 534	0.5	4 246	7.3	56 935	36.3	14.6
Mobile, AL	153 676	67.1	131 800	24.3	13.2	695	35.1	2.6	186 352	-0.6	19 006	10.2	170 552	29.1	24.6
Modesto, CA	165 761	59.5	176 800	29.4	12.6	978	35.5	8.9	237 400	1.1	41 346	17.4	198 972	26.9	31.4
Monroe, LA	65 267	63.2	107 700	19.7	10.0	657	31.4	3.5	81 860	0.8	6 396	7.8	76 916	28.8	24.9
Monroe, MI	58 596	78.8	147 400	24.8	13.1	757	31.2	2.7	71 165	-3.2	8 859	12.4	66 791	26.5	29.8
Montgomery, AL	140 996	66.6	133 100	22.8	10.7	781	32.3	2.3	167 902	-2.3	15 311	9.1	162 467	33.8	22.1
Morgantown, WV	48 447	64.0	128 400	18.8	10.0	683	35.6	NA	63 917	0.0	3 924	6.1	61 273	37.2	21.8
Morristown, TN	52 262	72.2	117 900	23.5	12.9	600	29.5	1.5	63 977	-0.6	7 416	11.6	56 547	26.4	33.8
Mount Vernon-Anacortes, WA	44 856	68.7	278 600	28.5	12.3	897	32.0	4.5	58 833	0.6	6 141	10.4	49 678	29.3	27.9
Muncie, IN	46 933	63.2	94 800	20.2	11.4	638	36.2	2.1	54 114	-1.9	6 074	11.2	50 428	34.7	18.9
Muskegon-Norton Shores, MI	65 892	72.7	103 900	23.2	13.8	649	34.2	1.8	84 273	-3.0	11 292	13.4	67 493	28.3	29.6
Myrtle Beach-North Myrtle Beach-Conway, SC	111 352	70.4	161 300	27.2	13.0	780	33.4	7.7	131 995	0.3	15 764	11.9	118 696	25.7	17.7
Napa, CA	49 754	62.2	424 100	30.5	11.4	1 186	32.5	7.7	74 424	-1.5	7 308	9.8	62 966	36.1	21.1

1. Specified owner-occupied units.　2. Specified renter-occupied units. A value of 10.0 represents 10 percent or less.　3. Overcrowded or lacking complete plumbing facilities.　4. Percent of civilian labor force.　5. Persons 16 years old and over.

Table C. Metropolitan Areas — Nonfarm Employment and Agriculture

Area name	Private nonfarm establishments, employment and payroll, 2009 — Number of establishments	Employment — Total	Employment — Health care and social assistance	Employment — Manufacturing	Employment — Retail trade	Employment — Finance and insurance	Employment — Professional, scientific, and technical services	Annual payroll — Total (mil dol)	Annual payroll — Average per employee (dollars)	Agriculture, 2007 — Farms — Number	Percent with: Fewer than 50 acres	Percent with: 500 acres or more	Farm operators whose principal occupation is farming (percent)
	104	105	106	107	108	109	110	111	112	113	114	115	116
Kokomo, IN	2 155	33 519	6 144	9 000	5 217	812	682	1 526	45 520	1 059	46.6	18.5	51.5
La Crosse, WI-MN	3 436	60 717	12 141	7 283	8 878	2 910	2 099	1 977	32 567	1 886	20.3	9.1	46.8
Lafayette, IN	3 879	65 310	9 069	15 436	9 974	3 085	2 439	2 141	32 780	1 737	43.0	21.1	46.7
Lafayette, LA	8 755	132 226	22 170	9 278	17 509	3 688	8 992	4 874	36 858	1 068	72.3	6.3	38.6
Lake Charles, LA	4 442	70 745	12 263	8 099	11 067	2 002	3 576	2 561	36 199	1 310	48.7	12.5	38.0
Lake Havasu City-Kingman, AZ	3 869	42 107	8 511	3 081	9 590	1 234	1 162	1 170	27 785	334	57.8	21.6	48.8
Lakeland-Winter Haven, FL	10 995	163 343	25 371	15 410	23 993	11 169	7 164	5 570	34 103	2 768	66.2	6.4	42.5
Lancaster, PA	11 981	211 461	34 020	35 813	30 460	7 300	9 924	7 538	35 645	5 462	46.6	1.7	64.1
Lansing-East Lansing, MI	9 673	153 933	25 995	16 561	22 116	12 425	7 981	5 593	36 333	3 409	47.6	9.0	43.8
Laredo, TX	4 695	64 376	12 699	687	12 649	2 618	1 485	1 574	24 451	663	15.7	41.3	34.1
Las Cruces, NM	3 731	50 549	12 096	2 203	8 015	1 766	4 069	1 378	27 263	1 762	80.5	5.6	41.4
Las Vegas-Paradise, NV	39 755	762 726	66 048	20 784	94 865	28 107	38 325	28 432	37 276	193	74.6	5.2	40.4
Lawrence, KS	2 669	37 319	5 388	3 500	6 014	1 063	2 224	1 047	28 047	1 040	38.8	9.2	35.4
Lawton, OK	2 218	32 225	6 223	3 354	5 326	2 178	1 353	962	29 852	1 126	24.5	21.0	42.6
Lebanon, PA	2 636	43 082	7 403	8 950	6 536	902	1 047	1 368	31 750	1 193	52.9	1.4	54.8
Lewiston, ID-WA	1 610	20 884	3 882	3 012	3 597	1 362	718	657	31 456	665	36.8	31.7	51.6
Lewiston-Auburn, ME	2 766	44 030	10 013	6 036	6 147	2 869	1 459	1 507	34 216	378	47.9	5.3	52.4
Lexington-Fayette, KY	11 841	204 641	32 154	27 009	28 086	6 662	11 705	7 683	37 542	4 988	43.2	7.4	45.8
Lima, OH	2 567	46 048	11 455	7 211	6 496	1 248	896	1 542	33 483	946	40.7	13.1	37.8
Lincoln, NE	8 176	132 423	22 001	12 586	17 553	12 350	8 707	4 411	33 311	2 591	39.9	17.8	43.9
Little Rock-North Little Rock-Conway, AR	17 668	274 444	56 350	22 795	36 244	14 752	13 277	10 433	38 017	3 763	44.2	9.0	40.1
Logan, UT-ID	3 336	39 429	5 250	11 294	5 841	1 201	2 230	1 122	28 455	1 934	45.6	11.9	38.3
Longview, TX	5 276	80 869	12 118	11 097	11 639	2 884	3 015	2 761	34 147	3 514	43.7	6.0	36.1
Longview, WA	2 240	30 640	5 466	5 910	4 540	897	921	1 177	38 424	481	67.8	1.9	44.3
Los Angeles-Long Beach-Santa Ana, CA	333 006	5 039 574	616 212	575 669	533 419	254 732	462 318	240 950	47 812	2 059	86.2	2.8	36.6
Los Angeles-Long Beach-Glendale, CA Div	NA	NA	NA	NA	NA	NA	NA	NA	NA	1 734	86.9	2.8	35.8
Santa Ana-Anaheim-Irvine, CA Div	NA	NA	NA	NA	NA	NA	NA	NA	NA	325	82.8	2.8	40.9
Louisville-Jefferson County, KY-IN	29 727	525 101	80 039	64 018	61 079	35 185	27 312	19 744	37 600	10 328	44.8	4.8	40.8
Lubbock, TX	6 925	104 591	21 899	5 724	16 795	5 113	3 497	3 136	29 985	1 576	31.8	29.4	43.8
Lynchburg, VA	6 092	95 732	13 579	17 137	13 874	4 271	5 388	3 275	34 205	2 897	30.5	6.9	60.1
Macon, GA	5 281	81 469	16 563	5 626	11 945	8 346	2 790	2 763	33 911	842	37.2	7.8	47.5
Madera-Chowchilla, CA	1 955	24 031	5 661	3 367	3 733	635	530	862	35 853	1 708	46.4	13.1	54.4
Madison, WI	15 235	275 676	44 908	29 387	38 479	23 824	18 940	10 980	39 829	6 729	38.2	8.0	44.6
Manchester-Nashua, NH	10 841	177 056	27 517	27 815	27 153	7 978	12 151	8 600	48 572	615	57.9	1.8	48.1
Manhattan, KS	2 691	36 771	6 187	3 044	6 927	1 361	1 666	998	27 133	1 604	21.0	26.5	46.4
Mankato, North Mankato, MN	2 567	46 358	9 899	7 699	6 829	1 268	1 388	1 363	29 393	2 074	27.1	20.9	55.5
Mansfield, OH	2 798	43 964	7 917	9 176	6 576	1 124	1 032	1 333	30 313	1 009	43.0	4.5	41.8
McAllen-Edinburg-Mission, TX	10 660	164 066	49 556	5 242	33 562	6 058	5 003	4 108	25 037	2 151	61.6	14.9	44.1
Medford, OR	5 896	65 112	11 441	5 481	11 175	2 783	2 537	2 094	32 167	1 976	69.5	3.5	45.5
Memphis, TN-MS-AR	26 096	519 483	75 224	38 446	59 818	21 860	18 305	20 530	39 520	4 220	37.7	13.9	40.9
Merced, CA	2 921	40 447	6 063	8 678	7 201	1 299	869	1 321	32 671	2 607	55.7	12.6	59.5
Miami-Fort Lauderdale-Pompano Beach, FL	169 725	1 855 542	280 292	68 842	272 259	96 629	138 004	74 989	40 413	4 308	91.5	2.1	51.6
Fort Lauderdale-Pompano Beach-Deerfield Beach, FL Div	NA	NA	NA	NA	NA	NA	NA	NA	NA	547	92.3	0.5	50.3
Miami-Miami Beach-Kendall, FL Div	NA	NA	NA	NA	NA	NA	NA	NA	NA	2 498	93.2	0.9	50.4
West Palm Beach-Boca Raton-Boynton Beach, FL Div	NA	NA	NA	NA	NA	NA	NA	NA	NA	1 263	87.8	5.3	54.4
Michigan City-La Porte, IN	2 487	34 772	5 315	7 296	5 840	821	947	1 089	31 311	869	51.6	18.1	44.3
Midland, TX	4 496	61 008	6 448	2 154	7 822	1 957	3 364	2 711	44 441	601	51.1	16.5	28.6
Milwaukee-Waukesha-West Allis, WI	38 989	755 162	120 706	115 989	81 174	57 005	41 116	32 726	43 337	2 115	50.4	6.0	49.8
Minneapolis-St. Paul-Bloomington, MN	90 472	1 625 406	246 391	178 335	175 389	118 031	116 306	76 599	47 126	11 672	43.8	6.9	42.4
Missoula, MT	4 203	47 442	9 152	1 767	8 376	2 674	2 811	1 481	31 211	699	59.2	8.0	30.3
Mobile, AL	9 016	150 599	23 433	16 065	20 427	6 297	8 198	5 458	36 245	876	60.8	4.8	39.7
Modesto, CA	8 578	127 658	23 533	19 791	21 345	3 711	5 048	4 814	37 707	4 114	69.4	6.1	54.1
Monroe, LA	4 541	67 993	13 488	6 734	10 058	4 096	4 342	2 064	30 361	928	43.1	6.1	42.9
Monroe, MI	2 424	36 045	5 215	6 003	5 130	954	D	1 296	35 952	1 119	52.4	10.0	44.2
Montgomery, AL	7 909	131 641	20 146	17 864	18 869	6 199	7 492	4 467	33 931	2 066	34.9	15.8	40.9
Morgantown, WV	2 741	45 045	12 969	3 809	7 216	1 022	2 573	1 508	33 485	1 505	27.8	3.8	42.9
Morristown, TN	2 265	40 119	5 452	12 288	6 035	917	533	1 181	29 437	2 934	49.6	1.5	40.8
Mount Vernon-Anacortes, WA	3 485	37 356	6 893	5 363	6 967	1 543	1 443	1 325	35 467	1 215	74.7	4.4	39.4
Muncie, IN	2 450	38 335	10 622	4 074	6 116	1 606	1 543	1 107	28 867	659	58.0	11.1	48.1
Muskegon-Norton Shores, MI	3 406	49 479	10 322	11 045	7 581	1 108	1 308	1 616	32 665	525	52.2	5.7	45.3
Myrtle Beach-North Myrtle Beach-Conway, SC	8 418	97 155	9 824	3 216	20 880	3 813	3 328	2 529	26 035	914	37.1	7.5	46.2
Napa, CA	3 996	55 167	10 152	9 896	6 411	1 297	1 960	2 444	44 299	1 638	73.0	5.3	41.4

Table C. Metropolitan Areas — **Agriculture**

Area name	Land in farms					Value of land and buildings (dollars)		Value of machinery and equipment, average per farm (dollars)	Value of products sold				Percent of farms with sales of:		Government payments	
				Acres							Percent from:					
	Acreage (1,000)	Percent change, 2002–2007	Average size of farm	Total irrigated (1,000)	Total cropland (1,000)	Average per farm	Average per acre		Total (mil dol)	Average per farm (dollars)	Crops	Live-stock and poultry products	$10,000 or more	$100,000 or more	Total ($1,000)	Percent of farms
	117	118	119	120	121	122	123	124	125	126	127	128	129	130	131	132
Kokomo, IN	328	6.5	310	0.1	311.0	1 280 954	4 134	137 159	192.9	182 117	74.7	25.3	61.0	29.5	6 409	74.7
La Crosse, WI-MN	410	-4.2	217	1.0	215.2	601 091	2 767	91 513	151.8	80 485	30.1	69.9	45.7	18.9	5 821	73.2
Lafayette, IN	681	1.6	392	9.9	640.5	1 479 765	3 772	156 954	402.6	231 741	77.5	22.5	58.7	32.9	13 820	67.5
Lafayette, LA	146	-6.4	137	11.5	108.2	393 405	2 872	71 694	61.4	57 501	89.8	10.2	23.1	6.3	1 731	15.2
Lake Charles, LA	584	5.8	446	24.0	180.5	794 338	1 782	59 362	27.9	21 276	44.4	55.6	27.3	4.5	4 251	29.3
Lake Havasu City-Kingman, AZ	858	8.2	2 570	17.1	31.2	1 450 681	564	57 373	18.6	55 784	65.2	34.8	28.1	5.1	761	4.5
Lakeland-Winter Haven, FL	549	-12.4	198	98.4	136.3	1 417 168	7 144	57 381	399.0	144 132	91.1	8.9	62.7	22.8	211	1.7
Lancaster, PA	425	3.2	78	5.4	326.6	726 059	9 324	83 136	1 072.2	196 293	13.9	86.1	69.5	44.3	4 547	23.0
Lansing-East Lansing, MI	680	0.1	199	8.1	565.9	695 306	3 486	97 308	320.7	94 101	54.4	45.6	40.1	14.7	8 980	47.3
Laredo, TX	1 856	-9.2	2 799	5.1	58.8	2 090 515	747	57 689	24.7	37 297	1.2	98.8	26.4	5.4	298	5.0
Las Cruces, NM	589	1.4	334	79.0	95.8	636 656	1 903	77 539	388.8	220 651	43.2	56.8	36.8	9.9	2 338	13.1
Las Vegas-Paradise, NV	88	27.5	458	6.5	6.2	1 391 798	3 039	64 840	10.2	53 062	46.1	53.9	21.2	7.3	91	6.7
Lawrence, KS	221	10.0	212	1.8	134.7	408 136	1 924	66 492	41.3	39 675	67.8	32.2	34.3	7.9	1 994	44.2
Lawton, OK	498	17.2	442	1.4	160.7	506 837	1 147	52 948	38.8	34 484	22.7	77.3	36.7	6.0	3 169	40.0
Lebanon, PA	113	-9.6	95	1.3	89.6	791 376	8 319	100 682	257.1	215 505	8.6	91.4	51.6	33.4	1 495	29.2
Lewiston, ID-WA	627	0.5	943	0.9	284.0	1 121 528	1 189	112 883	72.1	108 374	D	D	37.1	19.8	7 352	50.7
Lewiston-Auburn, ME	51	-8.9	135	0.5	23.1	402 339	2 991	112 469	68.4	181 071	11.2	88.8	36.2	16.4	487	15.1
Lexington-Fayette, KY	808	2.3	162	2.6	368.2	802 819	4 958	67 341	1 248.5	250 275	5.7	94.3	42.0	14.1	2 541	18.4
Lima, OH	187	-0.5	198	0.4	170.4	708 676	3 581	86 747	87.6	92 629	73.7	26.3	54.1	20.6	3 921	79.7
Lincoln, NE	754	-7.3	291	143.0	596.0	737 329	2 534	103 101	347.8	134 255	62.4	37.6	46.4	22.4	13 648	70.7
Little Rock-North Little Rock-Conway, AR	808	-6.6	215	248.7	487.0	539 290	2 510	76 088	257.4	68 389	59.6	40.4	30.9	8.5	14 229	18.7
Logan, UT-ID	476	-2.9	246	129.7	275.5	649 863	2 638	94 283	214.9	111 077	18.7	81.3	44.1	14.8	4 993	41.1
Longview, TX	544	5.4	155	2.6	139.1	365 068	2 357	49 264	108.8	30 969	22.0	78.0	22.4	3.1	293	2.0
Longview, WA	31	-22.5	64	3.0	10.9	485 875	7 612	51 689	26.5	55 006	40.2	59.8	18.3	5.6	29	1.9
Los Angeles-Long Beach-Santa Ana, CA	196	9.5	95	38.7	63.8	1 252 511	13 165	82 634	662.3	321 646	96.0	4.0	31.2	13.6	176	1.9
Los Angeles-Long Beach-Glendale, CA Div	108	-2.7	63	29.7	49.2	877 388	14 027	67 008	325.9	187 935	92.7	7.3	27.8	11.2	138	1.6
Santa Ana-Anaheim-Irvine, CA Div	87	27.9	269	9.0	14.6	3 253 936	12 095	166 005	336.4	1 035 046	99.2	0.8	49.5	26.8	38	3.4
Louisville-Jefferson County, KY-IN	1 417	-1.6	137	6.0	809.9	491 673	3 584	60 403	392.9	38 040	D	D	33.3	6.8	12 481	32.2
Lubbock, TX	1 068	2.0	678	269.4	704.8	634 326	936	143 751	301.7	191 466	D	D	40.0	26.0	29 437	64.3
Lynchburg, VA	517	NA	178	1.5	166.8	675 462	3 785	61 428	64.0	22 126	15.2	84.8	30.4	3.4	1 391	19.3
Macon, GA	169	-17.6	200	7.2	51.4	621 040	3 100	65 938	86.0	102 137	22.1	77.9	28.3	8.3	1 119	14.4
Madera-Chowchilla, CA	680	-0.3	398	281.7	290.7	2 699 315	6 783	139 667	990.1	579 696	63.2	36.8	64.8	38.8	4 608	11.3
Madison, WI	1 217	-1.1	181	14.1	861.0	699 298	3 867	100 029	795.2	118 177	31.5	68.5	43.3	19.6	22 912	65.3
Manchester-Nashua, NH	50	25.0	82	0.8	13.1	560 697	6 864	55 096	17.1	27 800	67.6	32.4	24.6	5.4	60	4.6
Manhattan, KS	809	-6.7	504	28.3	328.5	614 890	1 219	86 189	157.4	98 155	41.4	58.6	51.5	17.3	5 323	65.3
Mankato, North Mankato, MN	689	3.9	332	D	625.7	1 156 641	3 480	167 231	564.3	272 058	44.5	55.5	65.1	43.1	14 000	80.3
Mansfield, OH	147	-7.5	145	0.1	110.2	525 268	3 616	77 684	72.8	72 127	52.6	47.4	41.8	18.3	1 934	41.3
McAllen-Edinburg-Mission, TX	723	21.9	336	169.3	404.3	732 730	2 181	88 682	314.2	146 098	91.8	8.2	35.1	11.0	10 723	19.6
Medford, OR	244	-3.2	124	56.4	56.5	721 613	5 843	44 133	79.1	40 042	64.8	35.2	21.3	3.0	458	2.6
Memphis, TN-MS-AR	1 496	-3.9	355	243.3	1 069.9	853 535	2 407	99 029	350.2	82 999	D	D	28.0	10.9	37 241	43.3
Merced, CA	1 041	3.5	399	514.2	537.7	2 879 524	7 210	198 153	2 330.4	893 904	37.7	62.3	72.7	39.6	11 968	19.8
Miami-Fort Lauderdale-Pompano Beach, FL	601	-7.5	140	428.4	509.3	986 213	7 064	67 777	1 643.1	381 412	D	D	45.8	17.4	8 585	7.6
Fort Lauderdale-Pompano Beach-Deerfield Beach, FL Div	9	-62.5	16	1.7	4.9	424 408	26 571	32 949	50.3	91 945	97.0	3.0	29.4	10.2	680	5.5
Miami-Miami Beach-Kendall, FL Div	67	-25.6	27	39.0	53.8	742 119	27 648	45 341	661.1	264 652	D	D	51.5	18.3	5 450	8.9
West Palm Beach-Boca Raton-Boynton Beach, FL Div	526	-1.9	416	387.8	450.7	1 712 306	4 114	127 234	931.7	737 713	99.1	0.9	41.7	18.8	2 455	6.1
Michigan City-La Porte, IN	256	5.3	295	47.8	231.9	1 077 366	3 655	131 009	152.3	175 237	67.4	32.6	49.0	26.6	5 128	59.7
Midland, TX	457	26.2	760	8.3	90.0	660 020	869	59 919	15.4	25 621	77.7	22.3	18.5	5.5	2 750	29.8
Milwaukee-Waukesha-West Allis, WI	293	-5.2	138	2.4	236.0	715 564	5 173	96 063	222.0	104 961	45.5	54.5	44.9	19.6	4 444	48.3
Minneapolis-St. Paul-Bloomington, MN	1 920	D	165	105.9	1 445.8	674 933	4 103	93 603	D	D	D	D	39.7	14.9	D	52.0
Missoula, MT	282	9.3	403	16.6	27.9	895 806	2 221	39 176	7.6	10 840	35.8	64.2	16.9	2.9	102	6.4
Mobile, AL	114	12.9	130	3.5	44.2	414 764	3 197	69 495	83.2	94 946	90.1	9.9	29.3	10.0	2 538	12.9
Modesto, CA	789	-0.1	192	375.0	351.2	1 817 304	9 476	119 526	1 820.6	442 529	40.4	59.6	61.4	28.7	4 379	10.0
Monroe, LA	153	-8.4	165	7.4	69.1	419 611	2 550	67 543	167.4	180 404	8.4	91.6	33.1	14.7	2 197	15.5
Monroe, MI	208	-4.1	186	6.5	189.5	710 533	3 826	102 813	130.1	116 237	93.8	6.2	51.4	18.8	3 127	48.9
Montgomery, AL	623	-1.4	302	6.9	187.7	591 570	1 961	66 400	131.3	63 485	D	D	32.2	7.6	5 709	25.4
Morgantown, WV	212	4.4	141	0.1	63.0	350 475	2 494	43 631	16.7	11 111	19.0	81.0	23.7	1.1	92	6.2
Morristown, TN	263	-2.2	90	D	127.9	370 697	4 138	48 951	76.0	25 928	D	D	22.5	2.6	248	8.0
Mount Vernon-Anacortes, WA	109	-4.4	89	16.3	69.8	602 607	6 746	80 332	256.2	210 904	68.0	32.0	26.5	10.8	630	8.9
Muncie, IN	154	-18.9	234	0.5	143.4	824 551	3 518	95 643	68.6	104 109	88.2	11.8	44.6	18.7	2 670	58.4
Muskegon-Norton Shores, MI	80	8.1	152	9.8	58.1	601 241	3 962	100 785	91.2	173 669	44.2	55.8	34.1	14.5	790	23.0
Myrtle Beach-North Myrtle Beach-Conway, SC	164	-12.8	179	1.3	97.3	619 386	3 460	77 868	65.9	72 046	65.9	34.1	29.3	10.7	2 240	47.4
Napa, CA	223	-6.3	136	51.6	66.2	3 696 510	27 122	76 502	376.9	230 078	98.7	1.3	72.6	31.2	233	1.6

Table C. Metropolitan Areas — Water Use, Wholesale Trade, Retail Trade, and Real Estate

Area name	Water use, 2005		Wholesale trade,[1] 2007				Retail trade, 2007				Real estate and rental and leasing, 2007			
	Total water withdrawn (mil gal/day)	Gallons withdrawn per person	Number of establishments	Number of employees	Sales (mil dol)	Annual payroll (mil dol)	Number of establishments	Number of employees	Sales (mil dol)	Annual payroll (mil dol)	Number of establishments	Number of employees	Receipts (mil dol)	Annual payroll (mil dol)
	133	134	135	136	137	138	139	140	141	142	143	144	145	146
Kokomo, IN	23.1	228	92	767	604.1	35.3	426	5 665	1 330.7	117.4	98	355	49.7	8.0
La Crosse, WI-MN	72.8	565	167	2 890	3 248.0	110.6	526	9 273	1 952.1	178.1	131	614	84.0	15.2
Lafayette, IN	42.7	233	153	1 613	1 510.1	68.4	668	10 651	2 232.6	205.4	213	1 099	190.2	35.7
Lafayette, LA	104.8	423	555	8 890	4 254.2	439.7	1 178	17 005	4 221.9	374.8	480	4 046	1 092.4	214.4
Lake Charles, LA	341.6	1 752	227	2 617	2 260.2	109.9	853	11 942	2 812.8	249.6	215	1 053	231.5	35.6
Lake Havasu City-Kingman, AZ	138.6	741	129	1 060	458.3	36.1	730	10 672	2 837.7	248.0	280	876	133.3	22.7
Lakeland-Winter Haven, FL	219.3	405	696	9 822	16 436.7	407.0	1 876	25 321	6 420.1	586.4	741	3 423	517.8	95.9
Lancaster, PA	102.6	209	690	13 363	12 187.5	500.4	2 000	30 083	6 542.3	644.4	348	2 223	420.1	74.3
Lansing-East Lansing, MI	259.7	570	424	6 358	7 545.2	290.1	1 590	23 293	5 115.0	468.3	456	3 348	399.8	88.9
Laredo, TX	88.8	395	374	2 742	1 593.4	86.1	819	12 864	2 913.6	235.4	205	724	119.6	18.9
Las Cruces, NM	465.2	2 456	127	1 136	507.3	36.0	536	7 881	1 925.6	159.5	229	1 009	143.2	22.2
Las Vegas-Paradise, NV	607.7	355	2 002	27 453	16 605.7	1 380.0	5 744	99 817	26 676.6	2 656.9	3 356	25 654	5 235.4	925.5
Lawrence, KS	22.0	213	95	842	455.7	32.8	407	6 121	1 202.2	110.5	170	711	93.4	17.5
Lawton, OK	22.6	204	63	550	213.4	15.5	435	5 540	1 206.8	108.0	135	484	66.7	10.9
Lebanon, PA	124.5	992	117	3 287	2 859.9	124.1	451	6 611	1 488.6	144.1	68	271	43.5	7.3
Lewiston, ID-WA	34.1	576	62	701	716.5	27.2	273	3 586	911.8	90.5	64	241	29.6	5.9
Lewiston-Auburn, ME	15.8	146	114	1 321	471.9	53.1	489	6 386	1 704.3	145.2	119	509	82.0	13.4
Lexington-Fayette, KY	304.9	709	595	13 415	12 467.8	813.9	1 831	29 937	6 901.1	679.3	647	2 907	484.7	85.2
Lima, OH	27.5	259	151	3 397	2 326.7	119.2	464	6 950	1 577.5	133.6	105	481	67.1	12.2
Lincoln, NE	159.7	567	339	4 425	3 189.9	190.8	1 108	17 746	3 772.5	356.2	376	1 575	252.9	48.4
Little Rock-North Little Rock-Conway, AR	662.0	1 029	1 092	18 488	22 361.1	842.0	2 709	37 562	9 186.1	813.6	904	4 417	768.4	131.5
Logan, UT-ID	484.3	4 177	147	1 033	462.1	36.1	440	5 855	1 208.6	106.1	202	590	65.5	13.5
Longview, TX	2 527.0	12 541	329	4 261	2 354.8	175.2	942	11 426	2 976.2	264.8	217	1 437	302.8	58.5
Longview, WA	147.8	1 518	94	1 379	1 538.5	66.8	360	5 018	1 219.7	117.1	117	442	54.3	9.7
Los Angeles-Long Beach-Santa Ana, CA	4 528.7	350	31 642	415 986	465 512.5	22 339.7	40 170	577 963	164 134.4	15 153.5	19 651	134 213	37 478.6	6 290.8
Los Angeles-Long Beach-Glendale, CA Div	3 811.1	384	23 856	294 204	313 461.3	14 526.0	30 179	418 153	119 111.8	10 849.2	14 085	90 847	26 790.4	4 129.2
Santa Ana-Anaheim-Irvine, CA Div	717.6	240	7 786	121 782	152 051.1	7 813.7	9 991	159 810	45 022.5	4 304.3	5 566	43 366	10 688.2	2 161.6
Louisville-Jefferson County, KY-IN	1 138.4	942	1 750	25 858	26 461.4	1 224.5	4 423	64 772	15 331.4	1 422.8	1 404	8 538	2 222.0	300.4
Lubbock, TX	330.1	1 275	455	5 970	4 832.8	257.8	1 064	16 919	3 948.7	348.5	383	2 264	239.8	51.4
Lynchburg, VA	50.7	214	223	2 763	1 577.0	104.5	1 039	13 775	3 187.2	286.2	288	908	128.4	25.9
Macon, GA	138.2	604	282	3 641	2 805.9	160.5	1 011	12 921	2 769.7	271.2	259	1 310	235.5	36.9
Madera-Chowchilla, CA	834.8	5 846	89	745	397.6	30.5	368	3 663	1 010.2	89.3	100	409	36.7	9.4
Madison, WI	336.8	627	779	13 290	8 758.7	632.4	2 113	39 786	9 471.6	934.2	744	5 106	684.1	156.7
Manchester-Nashua, NH	58.6	146	649	8 676	6 030.9	601.8	1 657	27 793	7 647.3	678.7	443	2 664	554.7	96.4
Manhattan, KS	58.7	551	71	1 128	456.5	33.9	464	6 783	1 307.7	122.8	160	678	75.7	14.1
Mankato, North Mankato, MN	38.7	436	131	1 827	1 568.3	79.4	441	7 099	1 376.3	128.3	105	766	85.0	16.1
Mansfield, OH	16.3	128	149	2 499	1 190.3	90.3	497	7 387	1 489.5	145.8	108	571	59.2	12.3
McAllen-Edinburg-Mission, TX	394.4	581	744	8 485	5 117.1	286.5	2 132	32 803	7 898.8	635.3	491	2 289	366.9	53.2
Medford, OR	352.8	1 806	249	2 459	1 176.6	97.8	991	12 243	3 422.4	290.1	360	1 563	205.4	36.5
Memphis, TN-MS-AR	965.3	766	1 841	38 271	49 114.8	2 074.1	4 479	64 473	15 818.3	1 491.0	1 285	9 229	1 675.3	351.1
Merced, CA	1 624.9	6 723	113	1 674	1 673.3	65.9	578	8 005	2 001.3	179.9	153	641	85.6	15.1
Miami-Fort Lauderdale-Pompano Beach, FL	3 972.7	732	15 850	137 754	139 829.9	6 580.6	23 239	304 024	84 738.4	7 682.8	11 250	55 949	11 006.6	2 137.1
Fort Lauderdale-Pompano Beach-Deerfield Beach, FL Div	1 837.9	1 056	4 706	43 584	49 935.2	2 118.6	7 382	104 336	30 886.3	2 710.6	3 624	18 044	3 555.6	648.1
Miami-Miami Beach-Kendall, FL Div	602.3	249	8 654	72 193	72 464.3	3 269.7	10 293	123 559	34 530.5	3 055.6	4 935	25 546	5 367.9	985.2
West Palm Beach-Boca Raton-Boynton Beach, FL Div	1 532.5	1 211	2 490	21 977	17 430.4	1 192.3	5 564	76 129	19 321.7	1 916.5	2 691	12 359	2 083.2	503.8
Michigan City-La Porte, IN	37.3	338	142	1 718	1 002.8	69.2	495	6 054	1 363.6	114.9	102	438	60.4	11.1
Midland, TX	31.1	256	286	3 717	2 745.6	184.8	551	7 744	2 276.7	183.9	227	1 418	270.7	56.8
Milwaukee-Waukesha-West Allis, WI	1 576.1	1 042	2 654	46 102	40 493.1	2 541.1	5 012	86 028	18 898.8	1 853.3	1 474	9 657	1 673.8	337.7
Minneapolis-St. Paul-Bloomington, MN	1 868.9	595	6 087	104 304	117 099.0	7 100.9	10 933	188 242	46 284.7	4 394.6	5 034	31 686	8 295.0	1 148.4
Missoula, MT	112.7	1 126	195	2 019	1 073.9	76.4	587	8 668	2 179.4	194.6	227	952	126.3	21.6
Mobile, AL	1 130.9	2 817	619	7 671	4 340.3	336.5	1 644	22 271	5 225.5	483.4	448	2 460	417.2	77.8
Modesto, CA	1 457.9	2 884	451	6 078	4 402.7	277.0	1 500	23 394	5 661.9	561.1	500	2 988	472.6	90.3
Monroe, LA	83.0	485	217	3 179	2 033.7	111.2	809	10 259	2 369.7	208.0	198	874	151.1	27.7
Monroe, MI	1 846.7	11 997	107	1 716	1 841.4	77.2	427	5 637	1 465.3	120.3	95	373	48.8	7.5
Montgomery, AL	134.2	376	413	6 975	5 264.2	293.8	1 448	19 572	4 558.3	428.6	389	2 617	329.4	79.0
Morgantown, WV	279.9	2 445	73	573	511.5	22.0	487	7 365	1 510.8	127.9	151	625	82.7	15.5
Morristown, TN	21.3	163	93	1 692	751.0	67.8	505	6 220	1 688.8	133.3	97	387	54.0	8.1
Mount Vernon-Anacortes, WA	44.2	390	140	1 641	926.6	66.9	616	7 788	2 134.8	200.4	181	653	105.5	18.3
Muncie, IN	17.7	152	111	1 231	1 215.5	47.5	484	6 563	1 516.8	130.8	113	575	89.0	17.2
Muskegon-Norton Shores, MI	323.1	1 840	133	1 816	2 250.8	91.1	608	7 878	1 656.7	154.5	112	484	67.0	12.0
Myrtle Beach-North Myrtle Beach-Conway, SC	171.2	754	277	2 299	952.4	84.4	1 810	21 072	4 967.2	459.4	708	5 839	829.9	187.4
Napa, CA	51.8	390	172	2 036	2 858.5	134.0	537	6 463	1 665.0	180.7	206	893	153.0	31.1

1. Merchant wholesalers, except manufacturers' sales branches and offices.

Table C. Metropolitan Areas — Professional Services, Manufacturing, and Accommodation and Food Services

Area name	Professional, scientific, and technical services,[1] 2007				Manufacturing, 2007				Accommodation and food services, 2007			
	Number of establishments	Number of employees	Sales (mil dol)	Annual payroll (mil dol)	Number of establishments	Number of employees	Sales (mil dol)	Annual payroll (mil dol)	Number of establishments	Number of employees	Sales (mil dol)	Annual payroll (mil dol)
	147	148	149	150	151	152	153	154	155	156	157	158
Kokomo, IN	154	D	D	D	100	13 074	3 285.3	914.9	213	4 220	160.3	47.2
La Crosse, WI-MN	253	D	D	D	189	7 756	1 930.6	274.0	355	6 275	222.5	64.8
Lafayette, IN	334	D	D	D	172	16 830	13 018.7	780.3	432	8 989	337.0	98.2
Lafayette, LA	1 213	D	D	D	344	10 151	2 361.6	403.1	590	13 477	629.8	167.0
Lake Charles, LA	455	D	D	D	134	8 358	31 622.3	592.2	332	10 366	879.9	181.9
Lake Havasu City-Kingman, AZ	251	D	D	D	164	3 814	1 350.0	139.6	381	6 380	274.3	77.3
Lakeland-Winter Haven, FL	1 093	6 654	781.8	310.5	438	16 160	7 178.0	697.4	765	16 084	699.6	199.4
Lancaster, PA	939	D	D	D	920	40 077	13 269.9	1 735.9	935	17 060	763.9	221.2
Lansing-East Lansing, MI	1 087	7 810	928.7	375.1	385	20 365	14 472.8	1 187.2	901	17 436	652.2	194.7
Laredo, TX	309	D	D	D	89	914	242.4	30.7	360	7 489	317.3	86.5
Las Cruces, NM	315	D	D	D	141	2 349	931.9	84.2	298	5 955	238.7	64.9
Las Vegas-Paradise, NV	5 282	43 063	6 982.5	2 498.8	1 096	26 478	7 180.7	1 086.3	3 797	266 845	24 857.8	7 431.8
Lawrence, KS	285	D	D	D	88	3 848	976.5	143.0	299	5 937	213.7	60.1
Lawton, OK	175	D	D	D	48	3 549	1 232.4	171.0	204	4 330	154.5	46.4
Lebanon, PA	193	D	D	D	213	9 655	2 393.6	363.3	241	3 075	125.3	35.3
Lewiston, ID-WA	109	D	D	D	62	3 312	964.6	166.3	134	2 278	87.5	27.6
Lewiston-Auburn, ME	182	D	D	D	158	6 945	2 186.2	300.2	226	3 422	149.7	44.0
Lexington-Fayette, KY	1 347	D	D	D	459	30 392	17 925.5	1 502.4	960	22 013	985.7	286.2
Lima, OH	170	D	D	D	136	8 661	10 009.0	475.9	219	4 469	173.2	47.4
Lincoln, NE	804	8 361	1 112.3	386.2	272	14 390	4 541.2	577.4	685	12 466	486.1	136.3
Little Rock-North Little Rock-Conway, AR	2 013	D	D	D	615	24 783	8 828.2	1 033.8	1 238	25 036	1 087.4	307.0
Logan, UT-ID	363	D	D	D	234	10 810	3 685.3	420.5	155	2 921	101.0	31.2
Longview, TX	436	D	D	D	250	12 506	4 642.8	522.3	380	7 316	296.7	86.3
Longview, WA	150	D	D	D	128	7 001	2 914.7	356.7	215	2 782	124.0	38.2
Los Angeles-Long Beach-Santa Ana, CA	44 767	571 476	79 845.9	31 400.9	20 509	628 771	202 475.6	29 161.5	26 330	481 517	28 486.0	7 936.8
Los Angeles-Long Beach-Glendale, CA Div	30 754	D	D	D	15 158	451 656	153 343.7	20 520.1	19 476	339 815	20 238.1	5 570.1
Santa Ana-Anaheim-Irvine, CA Div	14 013	D	D	D	5 351	177 115	49 131.9	8 641.4	6 854	141 702	8 247.8	2 366.7
Louisville-Jefferson County, KY-IN	3 134	D	D	D	1 400	75 811	34 623.8	3 457.3	2 284	52 254	2 548.0	717.8
Lubbock, TX	585	3 410	374.5	128.7	258	D		204.5	587	13 168	541.3	142.7
Lynchburg, VA	518	D	D	D	302	18 731	5 973.9	898.0	431	7 932	297.0	89.0
Macon, GA	486	D	D	D	187	6 403	1 838.2	266.2	470	8 618	346.1	92.6
Madera-Chowchilla, CA	124	D	D	D	116	4 143	1 452.9	170.3	192	2 265	125.1	33.1
Madison, WI	1 715	D	D	D	727	33 367	9 107.7	1 525.6	1 459	28 022	1 106.8	321.9
Manchester-Nashua, NH	1 347	D	D	D	633	31 243	7 707.6	1 944.4	875	15 987	732.3	224.9
Manhattan, KS	235	D	D	D	68	3 040	685.6	109.7	263	5 139	189.2	52.9
Mankato, North Mankato, MN	169	D	D	D	140	8 903	3 601.1	309.0	214	4 840	164.5	48.6
Mansfield, OH	194	1 044	110.4	41.0	192	11 080	3 563.7	555.3	277	4 802	178.9	52.5
McAllen-Edinburg-Mission, TX	793	D	D	D	276	6 007	1 503.2	183.5	896	17 219	758.0	186.5
Medford, OR	491	D	D	D	324	6 115	2 037.5	228.8	590	7 946	372.9	108.9
Memphis, TN-MS-AR	2 273	18 556	2 378.9	973.1	1 017	43 692	22 469.6	1 988.6	2 257	62 998	3 489.6	954.9
Merced, CA	170	D	D	D	122	9 208	3 954.2	348.6	302	5 130	219.4	55.2
Miami-Fort Lauderdale-Pompano Beach, FL	27 747	141 555	22 331.1	8 589.8	5 041	83 698	20 748.5	3 370.1	10 669	218 145	13 303.6	3 719.0
Fort Lauderdale-Pompano Beach-Deerfield Beach, FL Div	9 509	46 243	6 635.1	2 550.4	1 734	29 333	7 160.8	1 185.5	3 693	70 373	4 209.1	1 140.1
Miami-Miami Beach-Kendall, FL Div	11 294	60 310	9 603.2	3 755.1	2 312	40 446	9 347.1	1 556.0	4 358	91 230	6 005.9	1 659.8
West Palm Beach-Boca Raton-Boynton Beach, FL Div	6 944	35 002	6 092.8	2 284.2	995	13 919	4 240.7	628.6	2 618	56 542	3 088.6	919.0
Michigan City-La Porte, IN	169	D	D	D	184	8 808	2 364.0	363.9	259	5 254	389.7	80.1
Midland, TX	436	D	D	D	140	2 366	533.8	95.2	254	5 324	259.2	69.3
Milwaukee-Waukesha-West Allis, WI	3 967	40 641	5 592.7	2 312.5	2 740	130 675	41 284.2	6 590.5	3 194	59 644	2 465.0	701.4
Minneapolis-St. Paul-Bloomington, MN	13 279	119 276	18 443.4	7 620.1	4 997	200 650	63 158.2	10 420.0	6 326	138 810	6 590.5	1 980.6
Missoula, MT	458	D	D	D	112	2 159	674.9	93.8	332	6 209	269.1	70.0
Mobile, AL	901	D	D	D	385	16 776	12 407.2	840.9	652	13 252	562.4	155.0
Modesto, CA	701	D	D	D	443	24 127	9 476.0	1 032.9	842	13 881	615.1	171.7
Monroe, LA	462	D	D	D	146	6 927	D	D	302	6 798	260.5	70.4
Monroe, MI	147	944	84.3	39.6	143	8 555	3 503.0	440.6	274	4 682	171.5	47.8
Montgomery, AL	817	7 278	1 020.9	377.5	318	18 749	D	D	653	13 159	539.5	150.2
Morgantown, WV	231	D	D	D	98	3 918	1 480.9	173.7	266	5 401	205.1	56.4
Morristown, TN	130	D	D	D	194	16 517	4 248.2	566.4	192	3 881	145.6	41.0
Mount Vernon-Anacortes, WA	305	D	D	D	205	6 387	8 918.2	294.5	347	4 734	251.0	74.1
Muncie, IN	169	D	D	D	150	5 268	1 280.6	232.7	216	4 981	160.8	48.3
Muskegon-Norton Shores, MI	239	D	D	D	290	13 271	3 675.8	609.1	344	5 763	221.0	64.6
Myrtle Beach-North Myrtle Beach-Conway, SC	660	D	D	D	168	4 103	894.8	166.8	1 178	25 931	1 483.8	396.2
Napa, CA	419	D	D	D	436	13 165	4 529.3	632.4	363	8 904	620.4	195.4

1. Establishments subject to federal tax.

Table C. Metropolitan Areas — Health Care and Social Assistance, Other Services, and Federal Funds

Area name	Health care and social assistance,[1] 2007				Other services,[1] 2007				Federal funds and grants, 2009–2010 Expenditures (mil dol)			
									Total	Direct payments for individuals		
	Number of establishments	Number of employees	Receipts (mil dol)	Annual payroll (mil dol)	Number of establishments	Number of employees	Receipts (mil dol)	Annual payroll (mil dol)		Social Security and government retirement	Medicare	Food stamps and Supplemental Security Income
	159	160	161	162	163	164	165	166	167	168	169	170
Kokomo, IN	253	6 193	571.4	216.9	160	838	66.4	17.2	797.8	408.1	173.6	36.4
La Crosse, WI-MN	315	11 491	1 137.5	453.6	275	2 041	137.7	43.2	912.4	382.2	154.9	33.9
Lafayette, IN	364	9 594	935.2	353.2	299	1 980	249.4	49.5	1 245.0	438.5	172.5	35.2
Lafayette, LA	1 020	20 357	1 929.3	708.9	494	3 590	324.0	89.9	1 650.0	597.0	321.3	87.5
Lake Charles, LA	520	11 058	1 037.5	352.5	284	1 733	176.7	47.0	1 486.8	554.2	344.6	73.7
Lake Havasu City-Kingman, AZ	456	7 612	911.1	284.4	315	1 895	129.4	38.0	1 474.8	868.4	294.3	80.2
Lakeland-Winter Haven, FL	971	24 347	2 613.7	926.8	727	3 850	323.5	94.6	4 156.6	1 954.4	1 105.1	266.6
Lancaster, PA	1 062	32 573	2 878.0	1 163.1	1 042	6 812	587.2	157.1	2 993.7	1 497.6	683.1	94.5
Lansing-East Lansing, MI	1 182	24 945	2 329.6	970.0	864	6 760	748.4	209.1	7 633.8	1 242.4	575.8	160.3
Laredo, TX	441	12 142	723.4	284.3	257	1 465	124.3	28.6	1 613.9	325.1	210.5	164.0
Las Cruces, NM	474	10 748	798.2	323.2	230	1 237	94.1	27.7	2 062.5	567.9	160.8	130.9
Las Vegas-Paradise, NV	3 978	67 163	8 517.4	3 017.6	2 313	18 791	1 602.5	473.7	11 254.2	4 651.5	1 579.7	494.2
Lawrence, KS	283	5 331	375.5	163.3	190	1 429	277.4	33.7	689.9	246.9	76.3	18.1
Lawton, OK	274	6 219	580.1	223.7	170	879	63.3	15.2	3 180.5	477.1	114.1	56.3
Lebanon, PA	266	7 662	626.6	286.9	233	1 059	93.0	25.2	1 398.6	491.7	205.8	22.5
Lewiston, ID-WA	190	3 784	356.0	121.9	119	607	39.9	11.6	601.9	253.9	98.8	29.9
Lewiston-Auburn, ME	421	9 495	872.4	355.7	203	945	69.8	21.2	874.9	352.8	171.4	57.0
Lexington-Fayette, KY	1 323	31 132	3 415.2	1 316.8	844	6 104	586.4	171.1	4 087.5	1 191.4	707.8	141.8
Lima, OH	330	11 408	999.0	417.5	213	1 448	93.3	27.9	1 079.7	526.6	182.7	48.5
Lincoln, NE	874	22 175	1 978.1	811.0	700	4 372	561.1	121.1	2 912.4	761.2	239.2	56.6
Little Rock-North Little Rock-Conway, AR	2 041	48 896	5 101.1	1 964.0	1 188	7 197	810.6	191.3	8 126.7	2 228.2	843.6	257.0
Logan, UT-ID	326	4 717	376.9	185.6	181	847	65.3	15.8	747.8	208.0	109.7	17.0
Longview, TX	534	11 452	1 080.6	387.2	338	2 189	221.1	60.5	1 537.7	651.5	375.8	82.0
Longview, WA	249	5 122	487.3	198.6	146	894	76.9	22.8	779.0	356.7	134.8	53.8
Los Angeles-Long Beach-Santa Ana, CA	37 695	577 980	69 501.3	25 483.8	21 200	152 375	18 866.4	4 337.0	100 586.1	22 206.6	21 974.1	4 892.8
Los Angeles-Long Beach-Glendale, CA Div	27 728	444 806	53 200.9	19 568.8	16 089	117 748	15 230.4	3 369.6	82 544.3	16 317.2	17 792.2	4 259.6
Santa Ana-Anaheim-Irvine, CA Div	9 967	133 174	16 300.4	5 915.0	5 111	34 627	3 636.0	967.4	18 041.8	5 889.5	4 181.8	633.2
Louisville-Jefferson County, KY-IN	3 257	77 550	7 682.4	2 918.7	2 130	17 244	1 652.4	425.7	12 859.1	3 768.3	2 625.1	312.8
Lubbock, TX	824	D	D	D	481	3 383	298.8	78.1	1 967.8	661.0	480.5	109.8
Lynchburg, VA	532	12 079	1 026.4	439.4	458	2 354	175.5	53.0	2 163.6	932.7	289.5	77.0
Macon, GA	637	16 562	1 755.5	639.9	371	2 086	213.6	57.3	2 105.7	782.1	419.8	165.4
Madera-Chowchilla, CA	221	5 836	554.7	255.8	119	609	48.9	12.9	847.3	327.4	188.3	45.6
Madison, WI	1 357	42 786	4 355.3	1 777.5	1 189	8 991	1 398.4	275.2	6 991.6	1 352.1	517.4	92.8
Manchester-Nashua, NH	1 020	26 771	2 503.8	1 065.3	828	5 317	501.5	155.6	3 353.3	1 143.0	408.1	88.2
Manhattan, KS	269	6 429	444.4	185.2	232	1 950	303.8	56.0	3 855.4	306.1	88.7	23.0
Mankato, North Mankato, MN	270	9 523	694.8	321.8	220	1 326	205.1	28.4	594.8	231.8	106.4	14.4
Mansfield, OH	354	7 670	663.5	263.1	238	1 533	109.3	29.3	950.7	414.3	216.4	47.1
McAllen-Edinburg-Mission, TX	1 655	44 931	2 877.2	1 137.1	573	3 257	238.5	61.9	4 297.2	973.0	654.8	575.5
Medford, OR	627	11 160	1 173.9	434.7	357	2 107	182.0	56.9	1 624.4	769.7	250.3	87.8
Memphis, TN-MS-AR	2 702	71 899	7 409.8	2 946.3	1 730	14 358	1 988.2	402.3	12 902.4	3 385.4	2 450.0	852.8
Merced, CA	443	6 048	592.2	235.3	209	899	73.9	19.3	1 519.8	461.0	273.2	126.0
Miami-Fort Lauderdale-Pompano Beach, FL	18 858	276 188	34 308.5	11 820.3	12 419	68 297	7 169.9	1 706.1	50 255.7	13 113.2	18 594.2	2 809.5
Fort Lauderdale-Pompano Beach-Deerfield Beach, FL Div	5 732	88 155	10 883.5	3 647.7	4 174	22 705	2 171.8	586.7	12 480.1	4 158.7	4 960.3	545.3
Miami-Miami Beach-Kendall, FL Div	8 311	120 152	15 042.3	5 194.3	5 065	27 878	3 185.8	659.3	27 110.5	4 568.7	9 894.6	1 956.9
West Palm Beach-Boca Raton-Boynton Beach, FL Div	4 815	67 881	8 382.6	2 978.3	3 180	17 714	1 812.2	460.1	10 665.1	4 385.8	3 739.3	307.3
Michigan City-La Porte, IN	236	4 900	521.2	188.2	207	1 172	74.6	22.2	756.1	357.8	183.6	38.0
Midland, TX	359	5 999	697.2	241.4	255	2 469	287.0	65.5	638.5	281.9	156.8	40.0
Milwaukee-Waukesha-West Allis, WI	4 879	118 780	11 226.9	4 710.5	2 926	21 389	2 254.9	615.4	12 331.2	4 184.9	2 473.3	805.6
Minneapolis-St. Paul-Bloomington, MN	8 405	227 776	22 299.0	9 658.7	6 589	49 916	5 202.8	1 332.5	24 336.5	7 306.3	3 955.4	737.5
Missoula, MT	451	8 022	754.8	278.6	288	1 618	150.7	37.8	818.8	299.5	93.6	28.0
Mobile, AL	741	23 845	2 160.0	894.7	666	4 681	412.6	116.5	3 934.1	1 327.4	768.5	269.2
Modesto, CA	1 108	21 628	2 662.6	967.7	650	4 205	380.9	119.5	3 048.2	1 091.0	705.9	198.7
Monroe, LA	616	13 311	1 181.0	416.2	245	1 573	138.5	38.1	1 379.0	464.3	339.1	93.8
Monroe, MI	284	4 733	381.3	158.7	195	1 172	93.7	30.3	885.2	468.7	218.6	37.2
Montgomery, AL	917	19 608	1 977.5	741.6	654	4 413	398.6	115.6	5 924.7	1 336.2	530.9	201.9
Morgantown, WV	272	11 546	1 169.3	421.2	186	1 190	177.2	27.3	1 418.0	328.1	153.2	40.1
Morristown, TN	245	5 377	439.6	165.3	148	651	47.5	13.2	1 201.5	523.4	304.0	66.0
Mount Vernon-Anacortes, WA	342	6 346	614.5	241.6	237	1 158	94.1	27.6	846.6	417.2	158.3	40.4
Muncie, IN	316	10 078	836.1	335.6	203	1 206	119.8	26.7	932.8	377.0	182.0	52.1
Muskegon-Norton Shores, MI	398	9 463	864.8	374.1	283	1 440	116.0	27.8	1 299.3	564.9	261.1	96.9
Myrtle Beach-North Myrtle Beach-Conway, SC	611	9 079	976.0	358.7	512	3 110	265.6	65.3	1 722.0	1 023.9	245.0	78.9
Napa, CA	425	10 004	1 150.0	502.2	219	1 172	142.5	38.4	1 011.6	412.9	312.3	21.3

1. Establishments subject to federal tax.

Table C. Metropolitan Areas — Federal Funds, Residential Construction and Local Government Finances

Area name	Salaries and wages	Defense	Other	Medicaid and other health-related	Nutrition and family welfare	Education	Other	New construction ($1,000)	Number of housing units	Total (mil dol)	Inter-govern-mental (mil dol)	Total (mil dol)	Per capita[1] Total	Per capita[1] Property
	171	172	173	174	175	176	177	178	179	180	181	182	183	184
Kokomo, IN	36.6	0.5	6.2	91.5	15.9	1.9	10.3	2 654	18	491.0	132.6	135.5	1 357	1 261
La Crosse, WI-MN	57.8	39.6	32.3	132.2	23.0	8.4	13.6	42 394	327	583.4	280.8	190.1	1 452	1 339
Lafayette, IN	72.0	17.6	20.1	161.1	19.6	10.3	237.1	86 743	531	487.5	185.1	198.8	1 035	907
Lafayette, LA	152.3	32.3	33.5	235.6	44.1	29.8	45.2	116 657	849	756.1	266.3	352.8	1 375	463
Lake Charles, LA	101.2	45.8	72.8	152.0	34.0	17.1	53.6	128 564	975	909.3	276.6	410.3	2 138	820
Lake Havasu City-Kingman, AZ	36.4	6.0	15.3	84.6	25.0	12.8	29.3	48 555	262	613.2	254.1	253.3	1 299	749
Lakeland-Winter Haven, FL	153.2	49.3	24.1	306.9	97.8	47.9	49.1	208 680	1 200	2 004.3	841.8	655.6	1 141	856
Lancaster, PA	177.0	44.0	95.9	238.2	63.5	13.4	51.1	214 508	1 381	1 635.2	540.9	714.1	1 433	1 148
Lansing-East Lansing, MI	337.4	520.7	133.6	654.4	529.6	843.4	2 401.7	101 666	677	1 965.3	944.4	592.5	1 298	1 211
Laredo, TX	205.4	2.8	40.7	421.4	132.8	21.3	39.6	93 949	663	1 057.5	514.3	342.7	1 470	1 182
Las Cruces, NM	218.7	309.3	203.7	273.0	47.7	15.0	64.9	166 683	974	633.2	389.2	159.6	803	331
Las Vegas-Paradise, NV	1 452.3	443.1	893.0	790.9	162.4	87.6	466.0	577 931	5 474	9 530.4	3 523.8	3 157.6	1 720	1 078
Lawrence, KS	52.4	12.5	18.6	110.8	13.8	27.9	77.8	41 580	288	429.5	85.5	157.0	1 384	1 048
Lawton, OK	1 851.8	466.2	26.4	87.4	25.3	20.5	22.5	53 879	326	403.3	143.2	85.4	751	385
Lebanon, PA	423.9	36.7	83.5	61.2	14.6	2.2	45.5	38 916	240	428.2	136.1	157.2	1 229	937
Lewiston, ID-WA	23.1	2.1	17.7	97.9	15.0	10.1	14.8	12 497	75	183.8	92.4	50.3	837	752
Lewiston-Auburn, ME	46.5	1.1	5.4	178.8	17.7	6.3	18.2	28 397	206	330.4	146.7	142.8	1 337	1 325
Lexington-Fayette, KY	282.5	463.2	303.2	452.3	62.5	38.5	144.5	179 930	1 361	1 117.4	312.8	612.1	1 369	563
Lima, OH	41.1	87.4	6.3	108.5	24.3	8.3	9.2	13 505	116	397.7	197.7	129.4	1 230	858
Lincoln, NE	331.7	19.0	91.4	284.1	116.2	160.7	773.3	139 148	1 032	991.2	253.8	510.4	1 747	1 314
Little Rock-North Little Rock-Conway, AR	1 183.4	450.3	248.2	659.1	232.4	306.1	1 519.3	371 990	3 559	1 928.9	964.9	507.6	762	335
Logan, UT-ID	42.2	52.6	24.8	55.4	20.6	24.0	150.7	79 236	655	305.4	137.4	89.2	737	448
Longview, TX	53.5	1.4	12.0	278.3	36.1	6.3	13.1	46 416	491	684.5	247.3	323.1	1 587	1 246
Longview, WA	46.3	17.2	6.0	92.5	19.4	18.2	16.7	28 221	131	372.1	160.5	105.3	1 048	664
Los Angeles-Long Beach-Santa Ana, CA	5 900.3	12 663.2	6 235.7	15 628.9	3 451.2	1 018.7	4 302.2	2 381 242	10 394	76 654.5	35 407.6	22 598.3	1 755	1 172
Los Angeles-Long Beach-Glendale, CA Div	4 489.4	10 637.0	5 805.2	13 950.6	2 840.6	852.6	3 697.1	NA	NA	61 779.9	29 562.5	17 192.0	1 740	1 120
Santa Ana-Anaheim-Irvine, CA Div	1 410.9	2 026.2	430.5	1 678.3	610.6	166.1	605.1	NA	NA	14 874.7	5 845.1	5 406.3	1 804	1 344
Louisville-Jefferson County, KY-IN	879.2	3 130.3	262.0	1 080.2	187.5	115.7	203.5	377 746	2 525	3 732.4	1 234.0	1 393.9	1 130	680
Lubbock, TX	156.8	13.8	17.6	258.3	44.1	10.3	111.7	219 523	1 451	1 022.6	296.9	348.0	1 302	987
Lynchburg, VA	93.9	115.4	313.5	178.1	26.4	16.5	19.3	123 777	700	694.5	336.2	252.0	1 034	693
Macon, GA	193.1	12.5	48.2	292.4	51.5	28.6	39.4	48 757	368	763.2	282.5	328.4	1 429	839
Madera-Chowchilla, CA	44.6	0.9	7.9	144.3	33.6	9.9	14.9	24 379	192	598.1	351.0	131.1	895	715
Madison, WI	475.5	166.8	239.4	1 033.9	300.7	454.4	2 195.6	232 421	1 198	2 389.4	852.4	1 084.8	1 952	1 800
Manchester-Nashua, NH	369.5	700.2	111.2	271.3	39.2	22.6	101.1	94 983	682	1 330.6	420.3	697.9	1 735	1 686
Manhattan, KS	2 861.5	324.0	20.9	68.4	20.4	21.0	79.4	116 345	830	384.0	148.0	142.3	1 252	898
Mankato, North Mankato, MN	62.3	6.1	6.6	78.1	15.4	5.5	15.5	44 804	331	351.9	167.7	79.0	864	782
Mansfield, OH	57.7	7.8	8.2	119.8	24.8	10.7	23.4	7 537	45	490.3	239.1	173.6	1 381	907
McAllen-Edinburg-Mission, TX	296.2	-35.5	207.6	1 025.4	205.3	97.6	84.4	421 852	3 552	2 583.5	1 512.6	687.4	968	774
Medford, OR	132.1	13.7	104.2	176.9	31.5	14.5	25.0	64 241	373	629.4	302.0	211.7	1 062	872
Memphis, TN-MS-AR	1 028.2	1 645.7	609.7	1 896.3	321.0	102.5	281.0	469 037	2 429	4 881.4	1 759.5	2 007.0	1 567	1 117
Merced, CA	54.0	54.7	64.5	260.0	73.7	26.1	48.7	22 930	106	1 419.6	825.1	251.4	1 024	823
Miami-Fort Lauderdale-Pompano Beach, FL	2 948.1	1 045.7	1 068.1	6 789.3	807.8	329.4	1 575.7	1 028 266	5 877	31 511.9	8 246.7	12 682.0	2 343	1 884
Fort Lauderdale-Pompano Beach-Deerfield Beach, FL Div	672.6	202.1	285.6	601.0	203.9	104.8	326.9	NA	NA	10 074.0	2 472.5	3 722.3	2 115	1 746
Miami-Miami Beach-Kendall, FL Div	1 812.5	396.7	472.7	5 786.5	443.0	166.9	1 018.8	NA	NA	14 420.4	4 219.0	5 277.1	2 211	1 651
West Palm Beach-Boca Raton-Boynton Beach, FL Div	463.0	446.9	309.7	401.8	160.8	57.8	230.1	NA	NA	7 017.5	1 555.2	3 682.6	2 908	2 513
Michigan City-La Porte, IN	37.9	4.2	5.8	86.8	17.7	2.6	5.0	27 474	228	386.6	163.7	106.7	972	806
Midland, TX	57.0	0.2	10.5	53.0	9.0	4.2	10.7	54 595	394	587.8	144.8	231.6	1 832	1 400
Milwaukee-Waukesha-West Allis, WI	782.7	292.8	444.9	2 037.7	337.5	127.8	604.5	371 214	1 929	6 708.0	2 770.3	2 679.2	1 735	1 624
Minneapolis-St. Paul-Bloomington, MN	2 228.8	1 360.4	1 118.0	3 320.3	616.7	540.8	2 098.8	1 182 155	5 726	14 119.4	6 409.0	4 167.3	1 299	1 192
Missoula, MT	103.8	5.5	52.8	117.3	17.7	8.6	58.9	35 509	368	266.9	105.7	114.6	1 085	1 048
Mobile, AL	317.4	507.9	65.7	333.9	74.8	37.7	104.8	125 841	1 026	1 348.0	605.0	535.3	1 324	417
Modesto, CA	93.7	18.4	33.7	535.9	145.3	36.1	78.6	40 531	292	2 994.5	1 529.2	678.5	1 327	984
Monroe, LA	77.4	10.1	13.3	228.6	29.8	18.7	42.2	60 939	441	575.8	259.6	242.1	1 405	443
Monroe, MI	23.8	1.1	5.6	72.5	25.0	10.1	4.8	19 896	117	529.2	247.3	182.9	1 191	1 160
Montgomery, AL	832.7	422.8	97.4	439.2	213.3	392.7	1 334.0	100 179	993	918.9	453.6	331.1	905	254
Morgantown, WV	205.4	23.4	352.0	162.4	16.4	10.1	82.0	30 076	301	254.5	106.6	83.9	712	544
Morristown, TN	33.1	25.4	10.4	164.9	24.8	11.4	6.7	34 317	206	256.2	115.8	95.5	710	357
Mount Vernon-Anacortes, WA	29.4	19.2	34.2	69.5	23.5	15.8	19.7	40 141	207	655.4	196.6	178.4	1 533	973
Muncie, IN	56.0	0.4	20.6	156.3	21.6	4.4	25.1	7 887	50	304.8	150.1	87.5	758	697
Muskegon-Norton Shores, MI	41.1	37.2	6.6	195.6	44.5	17.7	13.4	16 995	106	697.5	353.7	177.1	1 016	945
Myrtle Beach-North Myrtle Beach-Conway, SC	64.1	6.7	8.1	151.2	30.3	14.0	29.6	224 299	1 508	984.4	221.7	404.4	1 618	1 288
Napa, CA	22.6	24.8	9.1	102.5	32.0	10.9	35.0	61 077	110	773.9	256.2	327.3	2 469	1 962

1. Based on the resident population estimated as of July 1 of the year shown.

Table C. Metropolitan Areas — Local Government Finances, Government Employment, and Voting

Area name	Local government finances, 2007 (cont.) Direct general expenditure Total (mil dol)	Per capita[1] (dollars)	Education	Health and hospitals	Police protection	Public welfare	Highways	Debt outstanding Total (mil dol)	Per capita[1] (dollars)	Government employment, 2009 Federal civilian	Federal military	State and local	Presidential election[2] 2008 Percent of vote cast: Democratic	Republican	All other
	185	186	187	188	189	190	191	192	193	194	195	196	197	198	199
Kokomo, IN	508.6	5 094	33.5	32.9	4.0	1.8	2.7	278.2	2 786	309	332	7 514	45.5	53.2	1.3
La Crosse, WI-MN	590.4	4 509	48.2	2.7	4.5	14.4	6.4	455.7	3 480	540	403	10 354	60.0	38.4	1.7
Lafayette, IN	532.0	2 768	49.1	1.0	3.0	3.5	6.9	493.7	2 569	674	712	23 486	53.2	45.5	1.3
Lafayette, LA	703.2	2 742	45.6	1.6	7.5	0.0	5.8	1 097.8	4 280	1 122	1 107	16 000	34.7	63.8	1.5
Lake Charles, LA	827.7	4 313	38.3	6.9	6.2	0.2	6.3	1 011.3	5 269	636	896	15 149	35.9	62.3	1.8
Lake Havasu City-Kingman, AZ	607.7	3 117	33.3	2.7	8.5	0.8	7.5	509.9	2 616	527	417	7 746	32.7	65.6	1.7
Lakeland-Winter Haven, FL	1 985.5	3 455	50.8	2.7	6.7	0.9	6.0	2 648.1	4 607	1 378	1 157	28 275	46.5	52.6	0.9
Lancaster, PA	1 704.0	3 419	57.0	3.5	4.3	3.6	3.2	3 018.1	6 055	1 468	1 338	20 375	43.7	55.5	0.9
Lansing-East Lansing, MI	2 008.5	4 400	51.0	8.1	4.5	2.1	4.5	2 287.2	5 011	2 479	1 285	56 045	60.1	38.3	1.6
Laredo, TX	1 026.5	4 402	63.3	1.1	5.2	0.5	0.9	1 283.2	5 504	3 092	569	18 738	71.4	28.0	0.5
Las Cruces, NM	605.1	3 044	58.2	3.1	4.2	0.8	2.8	401.1	2 018	4 050	594	17 629	58.1	40.5	1.3
Las Vegas-Paradise, NV	8 762.7	4 772	34.3	7.6	8.9	2.7	10.3	18 383.2	10 011	11 710	13 283	85 158	58.5	39.5	2.0
Lawrence, KS	378.9	3 339	32.9	31.9	6.2	0.1	3.9	522.0	4 600	511	534	14 906	64.4	33.6	2.0
Lawton, OK	395.6	3 476	46.6	31.8	4.1	0.0	1.7	141.9	1 247	4 028	12 251	9 980	41.2	58.8	0.0
Lebanon, PA	452.1	3 535	52.0	5.2	2.3	12.1	2.9	710.8	5 558	2 475	407	5 519	40.0	58.9	1.2
Lewiston, ID-WA	181.9	3 029	45.9	4.8	6.0	0.4	7.7	50.5	841	236	220	4 996	40.8	57.3	1.9
Lewiston-Auburn, ME	325.1	3 043	50.6	0.2	3.6	0.2	4.5	321.5	3 010	362	357	5 202	56.5	41.3	2.1
Lexington-Fayette, KY	1 059.4	2 369	46.4	2.8	6.9	1.8	1.8	2 323.0	5 195	4 593	1 510	43 166	46.2	52.5	1.3
Lima, OH	390.5	3 711	48.9	3.1	5.8	6.2	4.3	181.4	1 724	404	269	6 343	38.8	59.6	1.6
Lincoln, NE	1 056.5	3 616	48.1	3.2	4.2	2.1	7.6	1 828.3	6 257	3 021	1 305	32 104	50.7	47.4	1.9
Little Rock-North Little Rock-Conway, AR	1 994.7	2 993	50.9	3.1	6.1	0.0	4.5	2 059.1	3 090	9 516	8 346	61 812	44.5	53.7	1.8
Logan, UT-ID	286.8	2 369	50.8	6.8	5.0	0.3	5.1	227.7	1 880	413	565	10 798	23.5	71.9	4.6
Longview, TX	618.6	3 038	64.0	3.9	4.8	0.1	3.1	611.7	3 004	485	490	11 670	28.7	70.7	0.6
Longview, WA	352.0	3 503	42.9	4.2	5.1	0.0	6.6	638.1	6 351	238	316	5 588	54.4	43.2	2.4
Los Angeles-Long Beach-Santa Ana, CA	71 175.2	5 528	39.2	8.4	7.3	7.5	3.1	95 156.9	7 390	62 776	24 271	693 711	63.6	34.3	2.0
Los Angeles-Long Beach-Glendale, CA Div	56 883.7	5 758	38.2	9.7	7.3	8.0	2.9	73 718.0	7 462	51 046	18 559	552 318	69.2	28.8	2.0
Santa Ana-Anaheim-Irvine, CA Div	14 291.5	4 769	43.2	8.0	7.4	5.6	4.0	21 438.8	7 153	11 730	5 712	141 393	47.6	50.2	2.2
Louisville-Jefferson County, KY-IN	3 603.5	2 921	45.4	11.4	4.3	0.9	3.1	6 352.1	5 149	10 495	4 243	68 596	49.2	49.7	1.1
Lubbock, TX	1 082.0	3 975	40.1	29.8	4.8	0.1	3.0	1 365.7	5 111	1 357	678	25 083	31.3	67.9	0.8
Lynchburg, VA	693.9	2 849	52.4	2.8	5.7	6.0	2.4	382.9	1 572	778	852	14 237	37.4	61.4	1.1
Macon, GA	761.9	3 315	48.5	5.7	7.3	0.4	3.7	742.6	3 231	1 380	824	13 537	51.5	47.9	0.6
Madera-Chowchilla, CA	691.1	4 717	49.3	3.3	3.4	8.0	4.8	386.0	2 635	322	243	11 050	42.4	55.7	1.9
Madison, WI	2 415.8	4 348	45.6	2.0	5.6	8.8	6.6	2 676.5	4 817	5 243	1 707	79 527	71.1	27.5	1.4
Manchester-Nashua, NH	1 845.6	3 345	51.1	0.7	5.8	3.9	4.3	1 045.4	2 599	3 940	1 364	18 555	51.2	47.5	1.3
Manhattan, KS	365.2	3 214	48.0	14.2	5.5	0.0	5.4	366.4	3 224	3 800	17 079	15 224	40.5	57.5	2.0
Mankato, North Mankato, MN	363.6	3 975	38.7	4.0	4.4	5.1	15.1	359.8	3 933	392	352	7 995	54.8	42.7	2.5
Mansfield, OH	479.8	3 818	47.7	7.1	5.3	5.5	6.8	143.1	1 139	634	319	7 713	42.1	55.7	2.2
McAllen-Edinburg-Mission, TX	2 724.7	3 835	70.2	1.7	3.5	0.8	2.3	2 783.8	3 918	3 287	1 749	49 704	69.0	30.3	0.7
Medford, OR	598.7	3 004	44.0	6.5	7.5	0.0	7.3	575.5	2 887	1 739	572	9 563	48.6	48.5	2.9
Memphis, TN-MS-AR	5 015.8	3 917	49.4	8.0	7.8	0.8	3.2	7 650.1	5 974	14 962	6 720	77 074	56.5	42.8	0.7
Merced, CA	1 437.0	5 853	49.3	3.6	3.8	9.6	3.0	688.0	2 802	772	401	16 315	53.3	45.0	1.7
Miami-Fort Lauderdale-Pompano Beach, FL	31 624.3	5 842	32.5	12.1	7.3	2.4	2.0	36 405.7	6 725	34 146	13 836	284 725	61.9	37.7	0.4
Fort Lauderdale-Pompano Beach-Deerfield Beach, FL Div	10 081.9	5 730	30.6	21.2	8.5	1.5	1.6	9 068.5	5 154	7 821	3 887	94 091	67.1	32.4	0.5
Miami-Miami Beach-Kendall, FL Div	14 688.6	6 153	33.7	10.0	6.5	3.0	2.0	20 249.0	8 482	19 895	7 341	130 927	57.9	41.8	0.4
West Palm Beach-Boca Raton-Boynton Beach, FL Div	6 853.8	5 412	32.9	3.3	7.3	2.4	2.4	7 088.2	5 597	6 430	2 608	59 707	61.2	38.3	0.5
Michigan City-La Porte, IN	352.4	3 210	57.1	1.3	2.1	2.0	7.3	269.9	2 459	204	391	7 216	60.2	38.2	1.6
Midland, TX	564.0	4 462	39.4	32.9	4.4	0.0	1.9	394.8	3 123	641	311	8 069	21.0	78.2	0.8
Milwaukee-Waukesha-West Allis, WI	6 855.1	4 439	44.2	7.1	7.3	4.7	5.5	7 487.8	4 848	11 409	5 005	80 272	54.0	44.8	1.2
Minneapolis-St. Paul-Bloomington, MN	14 634.1	4 561	42.4	6.5	5.4	6.7	6.7	21 879.2	6 820	22 056	12 889	212 598	56.1	42.0	1.9
Missoula, MT	281.7	2 666	46.3	3.9	5.5	0.7	4.4	200.7	1 900	1 422	550	8 521	61.8	35.1	3.0
Mobile, AL	1 241.0	3 069	48.4	3.3	6.9	0.5	4.8	1 144.8	2 831	2 639	2 998	25 823	45.3	54.0	0.7
Modesto, CA	2 929.4	5 730	52.0	7.3	4.7	8.4	2.9	3 299.0	6 453	884	838	26 189	49.9	48.1	2.0
Monroe, LA	543.3	3 154	49.5	2.9	5.6	0.1	4.8	396.9	2 304	598	730	13 406	35.7	63.2	1.1
Monroe, MI	519.5	3 382	55.8	6.3	3.9	0.7	7.7	565.9	3 684	263	280	5 666	51.3	46.9	1.8
Montgomery, AL	1 000.6	2 734	48.9	1.2	6.9	0.3	5.9	696.7	1 904	6 803	4 939	34 628	48.2	51.2	0.6
Morgantown, WV	261.5	2 220	59.2	2.9	4.9	0.3	1.6	262.4	2 228	1 914	639	16 267	47.1	51.1	1.8
Morristown, TN	258.8	1 923	61.3	2.7	5.2	0.1	3.6	199.2	1 480	370	464	6 877	28.8	69.6	1.6
Mount Vernon-Anacortes, WA	668.9	5 747	25.6	41.8	3.1	0.0	3.7	488.5	4 197	430	369	10 402	53.8	44.2	2.1
Muncie, IN	373.1	3 232	51.4	1.3	3.9	4.7	2.7	233.5	2 023	371	392	10 360	56.9	41.9	1.1
Muskegon-Norton Shores, MI	748.6	4 293	53.1	10.7	3.7	2.9	4.2	815.1	4 674	366	343	8 265	63.9	34.6	1.5
Myrtle Beach-North Myrtle Beach-Conway, SC	982.5	3 931	45.9	11.4	5.3	0.3	2.6	1 240.3	4 963	568	1 154	14 168	37.1	61.7	1.3
Napa, CA	789.2	5 954	41.2	5.1	6.7	3.7	4.4	766.1	5 779	399	220	9 933	65.1	32.7	2.2

1. Based on the resident population estimated as of July 1 of the year shown.   2. © 2009 Election Data Services, Inc. All rights reserved.

Table C. Metropolitan Areas — Land Area and Population

CBSA code[1]	Area name	Land area,[2] 2010 (sq km)	Population and population characteristics, 2010 — Total persons	Rank	Per square kilometer	White	Black	American Indian, Alaska Native	Asian and Pacific Islander	Percent Hispanic or Latino[3]	Under 5 years	5 to 17 years	18 to 24 years	25 to 34 years	35 to 44 years	45 to 54 years
		1	2	3	4	5	6	7	8	9	10	11	12	13	14	15
34940	Naples-Marco Island, FL	5 176	321 520	149	62.1	66.3	6.6	0.4	1.5	25.9	5.2	14.2	6.9	10.1	11.1	12.7
34980	Nashville-Davidson—Murfreesboro—Franklin, TN..............................	14 734	1 589 934	38	107.9	75.4	15.9	0.7	2.8	6.6	6.9	17.5	9.8	14.7	14.4	14.7
35300	New Haven-Milford, CT	1 566	862 477	60	550.8	68.9	12.8	0.6	4.0	15.0	5.6	16.7	9.9	12.5	13.2	15.4
35380	New Orleans-Metairie-Kenner, LA	7 667	1 167 764	46	152.3	54.9	34.3	0.8	3.2	7.9	6.6	16.8	9.9	14.2	12.8	15.1
35620	New York-Northern New Jersey-Long Island, NY-NJ-PA	17 319	18 897 109	1	1 091.1	49.9	16.8	0.5	10.8	22.9	6.2	16.6	9.4	14.2	14.1	14.8
35620	Edison-New Brunswick, NJ Div............................	4 424	2 340 249	X	529.0	68.6	7.4	0.4	11.9	12.8	6.1	17.5	8.4	11.7	13.7	15.8
35620	Nassau-Suffolk, NY Div ...	3 100	2 832 882	X	913.8	69.7	9.2	0.4	6.1	15.6	5.6	18.0	8.6	10.9	13.8	16.4
35620	Newark-Union, NJ-PA Div	5 649	2 147 727	X	380.2	55.4	21.3	0.4	5.9	17.9	6.2	18.1	8.3	12.0	14.6	16.2
35620	New York-White Plains-Wayne, NY-NJ Div	4 146	11 576 251	X	2 792.1	40.3	19.8	0.5	12.6	27.7	6.3	15.9	10.1	16.0	14.1	14.0
35660	Niles-Benton Harbor, MI	1 470	156 813	254	106.7	78.0	16.2	1.2	2.1	4.5	6.1	17.3	8.5	11.0	12.2	15.3
35840	North Port-Bradenton-Sarasota, FL.............................	3 364	702 281	73	208.8	80.7	6.9	0.5	1.9	11.1	4.7	13.3	6.4	9.1	10.7	13.6
35980	Norwich-New London, CT ...	1 722	274 055	167	159.1	80.6	6.8	1.8	5.1	8.5	5.5	16.3	9.8	11.9	13.2	16.3
36100	Ocala, FL	4 104	331 298	147	80.7	75.2	12.6	0.8	1.7	10.9	5.2	14.2	7.2	9.6	10.8	13.4
36140	Ocean City, NJ	651	97 265	347	149.4	88.2	5.2	0.6	1.2	6.2	4.7	14.2	8.0	9.4	10.6	15.8
36220	Odessa, TX	2 325	137 130	283	59.0	41.8	4.4	0.8	1.0	52.7	8.8	20.2	11.2	14.4	12.0	13.3
36260	Ogden-Clearfield, UT	3 844	547 184	94	142.3	84.5	1.6	0.9	3.0	11.8	9.7	22.8	9.9	15.6	12.2	11.8
36420	Oklahoma City, OK.............	14 275	1 252 987	44	87.8	71.2	11.6	6.6	3.6	11.3	7.3	17.7	10.8	14.7	12.6	13.9
36500	Olympia, WA.......................	1 870	252 264	181	134.9	82.8	3.8	2.6	8.2	7.1	6.1	16.9	9.1	13.5	13.1	14.7
36540	Omaha-Council Bluffs, NE-IA	11 266	865 350	59	76.8	80.4	8.8	1.0	2.7	9.0	7.6	18.6	9.5	14.7	13.1	14.2
36740	Orlando-Kissimmee-Sanford, FL.............................	9 009	2 134 411	26	236.9	54.6	15.9	0.6	4.8	25.2	6.2	17.2	11.0	13.9	14.0	14.4
36780	Oshkosh-Neenah, WI	1 125	166 994	238	148.4	91.8	2.2	0.9	2.7	3.5	5.9	15.7	11.9	13.1	12.8	15.3
36980	Owensboro, KY...................	2 327	114 752	323	49.3	92.5	5.1	0.4	0.9	2.4	6.8	17.7	8.4	12.2	12.7	15.0
37100	Oxnard-Thousand Oaks-Ventura, CA	4 774	823 318	63	172.5	50.7	2.1	0.8	8.3	40.3	6.7	19.0	9.9	12.8	13.5	15.0
37340	Palm Bay-Melbourne-Titusville, FL.............................	2 631	543 376	95	206.5	79.3	10.6	0.8	2.9	8.1	4.9	14.9	7.9	10.1	11.4	16.7
37380	Palm Coast, FL...................	1 257	95 696	352	76.1	77.5	11.8	0.7	2.7	8.6	5.0	14.9	6.3	9.4	11.2	13.2
37460	Panama City-Lynn Haven-Panama City Beach, FL..	1 964	168 852	236	86.0	81.6	11.6	1.5	3.1	4.8	6.3	15.7	9.5	13.1	12.8	15.7
37620	Parkersburg-Marietta-Vienna, WV-OH............	3 525	162 056	244	46.0	97.3	1.7	0.8	0.8	0.8	5.5	15.9	8.0	11.1	12.6	15.6
37700	Pascagoula, MS..................	3 112	162 246	243	52.1	73.8	20.1	0.9	2.4	4.2	6.9	18.8	8.8	12.8	13.4	15.0
37860	Pensacola-Ferry Pass-Brent, FL......................	4 320	448 991	110	103.9	74.9	17.8	1.7	3.6	4.6	6.2	16.1	11.4	12.6	12.2	15.2
37900	Peoria, IL	6 399	379 186	135	59.3	85.8	10.1	0.6	2.3	2.8	6.6	17.4	8.9	12.8	12.4	14.3
37980	Philadelphia-Camden-Wilmington, PA-NJ-DE-MD	11 919	5 965 343	5	500.5	66.3	21.2	0.6	5.6	7.8	6.2	17.1	10.1	12.9	13.2	15.3
37980	Camden, NJ Div..............	3 475	1 250 679	X	359.9	70.3	16.6	0.6	4.9	9.2	6.1	17.8	8.8	12.1	13.8	16.1
37980	Philadelphia, PA Div	5 583	4 008 994	X	718.1	64.7	22.7	0.6	6.1	7.4	6.2	16.9	10.4	13.2	13.0	15.0
37980	Wilmington, DE-MD-NJ Div..............................	2 861	705 670	X	246.7	68.3	20.9	0.7	4.1	7.8	6.2	17.3	10.3	12.7	13.6	15.5
38060	Phoenix-Mesa-Glendale, AZ...	37 725	4 192 887	14	111.1	60.3	5.4	2.3	4.3	29.5	7.5	19.0	9.7	14.3	13.7	13.1
38220	Pine Bluff, AR	5 258	100 258	343	19.1	49.4	48.2	0.7	0.8	1.8	6.2	17.0	10.7	12.8	12.5	14.8
38300	Pittsburgh, PA	13 679	2 356 285	22	172.3	88.3	9.2	0.5	2.1	1.3	5.1	15.0	9.1	11.6	12.3	15.8
38340	Pittsfield, MA	2 400	131 219	294	54.7	92.3	3.6	0.6	1.7	3.5	4.7	14.9	9.4	9.8	11.7	16.1
38540	Pocatello, ID	6 517	90 656	355	13.9	86.3	1.1	3.5	2.2	8.7	8.5	19.2	11.9	15.0	11.0	12.0
38860	Portland-South Portland-Biddeford, ME...................	5 386	514 098	101	95.5	94.9	2.0	0.9	2.1	1.6	5.2	15.8	8.4	11.4	13.6	16.7
38900	Portland-Vancouver-Hillsboro, OR-WA................	17 311	2 226 009	23	128.6	79.2	3.6	1.7	7.8	10.9	6.5	17.2	8.7	15.1	14.6	14.3
38940	Port St. Lucie, FL...............	2 889	424 107	118	146.8	68.9	14.7	0.6	1.9	15.1	5.3	15.4	7.3	10.0	11.8	14.5
39100	Poughkeepsie-Newburgh-Middletown, NY	4 163	670 301	78	161.0	72.6	10.2	0.7	3.5	14.7	6.2	18.8	10.3	10.9	13.7	16.2
39140	Prescott, AZ........................	21 040	211 033	200	10.0	83.5	0.9	2.2	1.4	13.6	5.0	14.1	7.1	8.8	9.7	14.1
39300	Providence-New Bedford-Fall River, RI-MA	4 110	1 600 852	37	389.5	81.1	5.4	0.9	3.1	10.2	5.5	16.1	10.8	12.0	13.4	15.5
39340	Provo-Orem, UT	13 975	526 810	98	37.7	86.1	0.8	0.9	3.5	10.7	11.3	24.0	15.6	17.0	10.9	8.4
39380	Pueblo, CO	6 180	159 063	249	25.7	55.3	2.1	1.2	1.1	41.4	6.6	17.8	9.4	11.9	11.9	14.1
39460	Punta Gorda, FL.................	1 762	159 978	248	90.8	87.2	6.0	0.6	1.6	5.8	3.5	10.8	5.4	7.0	8.8	13.3
39540	Racine, WI..........................	861	195 408	217	227.0	76.0	12.0	0.7	1.4	11.5	6.5	18.3	8.1	12.2	13.2	16.3
39580	Raleigh-Cary, NC...............	5 486	1 130 490	48	206.1	64.9	20.7	0.8	5.1	10.1	7.3	18.9	9.3	14.6	16.2	14.6
39660	Rapid City, SD...................	16 181	126 382	303	7.8	86.2	1.8	9.7	1.7	3.8	7.5	17.3	9.7	13.7	11.5	14.7
39740	Reading, PA........................	2 218	411 442	125	185.5	78.0	4.7	0.4	1.6	16.4	6.1	17.7	10.0	11.2	13.1	15.2
39820	Redding, CA	9 778	177 223	228	18.1	85.6	1.4	4.5	3.5	8.4	5.8	16.6	9.0	11.3	11.0	15.0
39900	Reno-Sparks, NV	17 004	425 417	116	25.0	68.4	2.8	2.0	7.1	22.1	6.6	16.9	10.6	13.3	13.1	14.6
40060	Richmond, VA......................	14 724	1 258 251	43	85.5	61.5	30.6	0.9	3.8	5.0	6.2	17.1	9.8	13.1	13.7	15.4
40140	Riverside-San Bernardino-Ontario, CA...................	70 612	4 224 851	13	59.8	38.4	8.0	1.0	7.4	47.3	7.6	21.1	10.9	13.4	13.4	13.5
40220	Roanoke, VA.......................	4 840	308 707	152	63.8	82.1	13.6	0.6	2.0	3.1	5.8	15.7	8.3	11.2	13.0	15.5
40340	Rochester, MN....................	4 184	186 011	223	44.5	87.4	4.4	0.5	5.0	4.1	7.3	18.1	7.6	14.4	12.7	15.4
40380	Rochester, NY.....................	7 584	1 054 323	51	139.0	79.7	12.0	0.7	3.1	6.1	5.7	16.9	10.8	11.6	12.6	15.6
40420	Rockford, IL	2 057	349 431	144	169.9	74.7	11.5	0.6	2.6	12.3	6.7	18.9	8.4	12.2	13.4	14.9
40580	Rocky Mount, NC...............	2 708	152 392	261	56.3	48.8	45.2	0.9	0.7	5.3	6.3	17.9	8.4	11.5	12.9	15.3
40660	Rome, GA............................	1 321	96 317	349	72.9	74.9	14.8	0.6	1.6	9.3	6.8	17.6	10.3	12.1	13.0	13.9

1. CBSA = Core Based Statistical Area. DIV = Metropolitan Division. See Appendix A for explanation. See Appendix B for list of metropolitan areas identified by type. 2. Dry land or land partially or temporarily covered by water. 3. May be of any race.

Table C. Metropolitan Areas — **Population and Households**

Area name	55 to 64 years	65 to 74 years	75 years and over	Percent female	Total persons 1990	Total persons 2000	Percent change 1990–2000	Percent change 2000–2010	Births	Deaths	Net migration	Households Number	Percent change 2000–2010	Persons per household	Female family householder[1]	One person
	16	17	18	19	20	21	22	23	24	25	26	27	28	29	30	31
Naples-Marco Island, FL	13.4	14.4	12.1	50.7	152 099	251 377	65.3	27.9	35 226	23 589	56 618	133 179	29.3	2.38	8.6	26.7
Nashville-Davidson—Murfreesboro—Franklin, TN	11.2	6.1	4.6	51.1	1 048 216	1 311 789	25.1	21.2	195 857	103 319	160 855	615 374	20.6	2.52	12.8	26.8
New Haven-Milford, CT	12.2	7.0	7.3	51.9	804 219	824 008	2.5	4.7	94 809	70 856	5 498	334 502	4.8	2.49	14.5	28.9
New Orleans-Metairie-Kenner, LA	12.5	6.7	5.4	51.3	1 264 383	1 316 510	4.1	-11.3	156 469	105 892	-287 001	455 146	-8.7	2.52	17.4	28.4
New York-Northern New Jersey-Long Island, NY-NJ-PA	11.5	6.8	6.3	51.8	16 863 671	18 323 002	8.7	3.1	2 371 167	1 303 749	-845 904	6 918 950	3.6	2.67	15.3	27.6
Edison-New Brunswick, NJ Div	12.1	7.4	7.4	51.4	1 898 329	2 173 869	14.5	7.7	273 599	183 710	66 904	854 039	6.8	2.69	10.6	24.7
Nassau-Suffolk, NY Div	12.4	7.3	7.1	51.2	2 609 212	2 753 913	5.5	2.9	322 313	206 584	-96 298	948 450	3.5	2.93	11.7	20.4
Newark-Union, NJ-PA Div	11.9	6.6	5.9	51.4	1 959 933	2 098 843	7.1	2.3	263 163	152 613	-71 470	776 210	3.3	2.71	14.6	24.8
New York-White Plains-Wayne, NY-NJ Div	11.1	6.6	5.9	52.2	10 396 197	11 296 377	8.7	2.5	1 512 092	760 842	-745 040	4 340 251	3.1	2.61	17.2	30.2
Niles-Benton Harbor, MI	13.3	8.5	7.8	51.3	161 378	162 453	0.7	-3.5	19 493	14 899	-5 624	63 054	-0.8	2.43	13.6	28.7
North Port-Bradenton-Sarasota, FL	14.7	13.9	13.7	52.0	489 483	589 959	20.5	19.0	61 482	76 047	115 557	311 475	18.7	2.22	9.6	30.5
Norwich-New London, CT	12.8	7.4	6.8	50.1	254 957	259 088	1.6	5.8	28 828	20 422	618	107 057	7.2	2.44	11.8	27.6
Ocala, FL	13.9	14.2	11.5	52.0	194 833	258 916	32.9	28.0	30 627	35 732	75 565	137 726	29.0	2.35	12.0	26.7
Ocean City, NJ	15.7	11.3	10.2	51.4	95 089	102 326	7.6	-4.9	8 935	11 919	-2 581	40 812	-3.2	2.32	11.0	31.2
Odessa, TX	10.0	5.6	4.6	50.6	118 934	121 123	1.8	13.2	21 870	9 969	2 232	48 688	11.0	2.77	15.4	24.5
Ogden-Clearfield, UT	8.9	4.9	4.1	49.8	351 799	442 656	25.8	23.6	91 531	25 029	26 862	175 118	26.0	3.09	10.4	18.0
Oklahoma City, OK	11.3	6.5	5.2	50.7	971 042	1 095 421	12.8	14.4	164 222	91 410	65 768	489 654	13.9	2.49	12.7	27.8
Olympia, WA	13.6	7.2	5.7	51.3	161 238	207 355	28.6	21.7	25 107	16 894	35 240	100 650	23.3	2.46	11.4	25.9
Omaha-Council Bluffs, NE-IA	11.1	5.9	5.2	50.7	685 797	767 041	11.8	12.8	120 459	55 216	22 118	334 379	13.5	2.54	11.7	27.5
Orlando-Kissimmee-Sanford, FL	11.0	6.9	5.5	51.1	1 224 844	1 644 561	34.3	29.8	248 070	129 308	323 492	798 445	27.7	2.62	14.6	24.1
Oshkosh-Neenah, WI	11.8	6.7	6.7	49.7	140 320	156 763	11.7	6.5	17 328	11 856	2 183	67 875	11.0	2.34	9.1	29.9
Owensboro, KY	12.6	7.9	6.9	51.3	104 681	109 875	5.0	4.4	14 627	10 094	-64	45 737	5.8	2.45	12.4	27.6
Oxnard-Thousand Oaks-Ventura, CA	11.4	6.2	5.5	50.8	669 016	753 197	12.6	9.3	110 905	45 038	-11 182	266 920	9.7	3.04	11.8	19.9
Palm Bay-Melbourne-Titusville, FL	13.7	10.6	9.8	51.0	398 978	476 230	19.4	14.1	48 677	51 627	65 900	229 692	15.9	2.33	11.8	28.4
Palm Coast, FL	15.5	14.2	10.3	51.9	28 701	49 832	73.6	92.0	6 403	7 341	42 701	39 186	84.0	2.42	11.0	23.1
Panama City-Lynn Haven-Panama City Beach, FL	12.4	8.1	6.4	50.5	126 994	148 217	16.7	13.9	20 302	13 666	10 716	68 438	14.8	2.41	13.0	27.5
Parkersburg-Marietta-Vienna, WV-OH	14.1	9.5	7.5	51.2	161 907	164 624	1.7	-1.6	16 851	16 604	-2 969	67 410	1.2	2.35	10.8	28.0
Pascagoula, MS	11.9	7.6	4.9	50.5	131 916	150 564	14.1	7.8	20 469	12 808	-1 816	60 187	10.6	2.66	15.7	22.9
Pensacola-Ferry Pass-Brent, FL	12.3	7.9	6.0	50.2	344 406	412 153	19.7	8.9	53 775	36 076	27 431	173 148	11.8	2.46	14.7	26.4
Peoria, IL	12.7	7.6	7.3	51.2	358 552	366 899	2.3	3.3	45 947	33 703	-1 208	151 801	5.7	2.44	11.8	28.2
Philadelphia-Camden-Wilmington, PA-NJ-DE-MD	11.9	6.8	6.5	51.7	5 435 550	5 687 147	4.6	4.9	701 530	493 781	11 165	2 260 312	5.9	2.56	14.8	27.4
Camden, NJ Div	12.1	6.8	6.3	51.4	1 127 972	1 186 999	5.2	5.4	142 061	98 613	23 567	461 569	7.1	2.66	13.9	24.6
Philadelphia, PA Div	11.8	6.8	6.7	51.9	3 728 991	3 849 647	3.2	4.1	474 911	343 515	-35 138	1 533 935	5.1	2.53	15.2	28.6
Wilmington, DE-MD-NJ Div	11.9	6.7	5.7	51.4	578 587	650 501	12.4	8.5	84 558	51 653	22 736	264 808	8.3	2.59	14.4	25.5
Phoenix-Mesa-Glendale, AZ	10.5	6.9	5.4	50.3	2 238 498	3 251 876	45.3	28.9	599 688	243 463	763 865	1 537 173	28.7	2.68	12.4	25.4
Pine Bluff, AR	12.6	7.4	6.0	49.3	106 958	107 341	0.4	-6.6	12 991	10 027	-9 105	36 496	-4.2	2.50	19.9	27.6
Pittsburgh, PA	13.8	8.3	9.0	51.7	2 468 289	2 431 087	-1.5	-3.1	229 854	258 848	-32 236	1 001 627	0.6	2.29	11.4	31.9
Pittsfield, MA	14.9	9.0	9.5	51.9	139 352	134 953	-3.2	-2.8	11 642	14 190	-2 251	56 091	0.2	2.23	11.5	33.0
Pocatello, ID	11.1	6.1	5.1	50.0	73 112	83 103	13.7	9.1	14 614	5 823	-3 868	33 323	12.0	2.67	10.7	24.5
Portland-South Portland-Biddeford, ME	14.0	7.8	7.0	51.4	441 257	487 568	10.5	5.4	50 963	40 390	21 537	213 436	8.5	2.35	9.7	28.3
Portland-Vancouver-Hillsboro, OR-WA	12.3	6.2	5.1	50.6	1 523 741	1 927 881	26.5	15.5	267 329	137 903	195 654	867 794	16.4	2.52	10.5	27.0
Port St. Lucie, FL	13.2	11.5	11.0	50.9	251 071	319 426	27.2	32.8	38 753	38 207	87 710	172 422	30.4	2.42	11.3	26.7
Poughkeepsie-Newburgh-Middletown, NY	11.8	6.5	5.6	50.1	567 033	621 517	9.6	7.8	77 770	43 738	25 118	233 890	9.1	2.73	11.7	23.9
Prescott, AZ	17.2	13.7	10.4	51.0	107 714	167 517	55.5	26.0	19 235	20 658	50 085	90 903	29.5	2.28	9.0	29.1
Providence-New Bedford-Fall River, RI-MA	12.4	7.1	7.3	51.7	1 509 789	1 582 997	4.8	1.1	176 664	136 548	-12 990	626 610	2.1	2.46	13.7	28.9
Provo-Orem, UT	6.2	3.6	2.9	49.9	269 407	376 774	39.9	39.8	106 808	16 970	39 091	143 695	40.3	3.57	8.1	11.7
Pueblo, CO	13.0	7.9	7.4	50.8	123 051	141 472	15.0	12.4	18 954	13 894	11 526	62 972	15.4	2.46	14.1	28.9
Punta Gorda, FL	17.1	18.1	16.0	51.4	110 975	141 627	27.6	13.0	10 231	20 328	25 749	73 370	14.9	2.14	8.5	28.5
Racine, WI	12.3	6.9	6.3	50.5	175 034	188 831	7.9	3.5	24 129	14 364	-1 079	75 651	6.8	2.52	13.0	26.4
Raleigh-Cary, NC	10.2	5.3	3.7	51.2	544 031	797 071	46.5	41.8	139 447	47 820	232 684	430 577	40.5	2.57	11.7	25.6
Rapid City, SD	12.5	7.0	6.2	49.9	103 221	112 818	9.3	12.0	17 446	8 253	3 383	51 154	17.7	2.40	11.2	28.0
Reading, PA	12.1	7.2	7.3	50.9	336 523	373 638	11.0	10.1	46 021	33 196	23 088	154 356	9.0	2.59	12.0	24.5
Redding, CA	14.4	9.3	7.6	50.8	147 036	163 256	11.0	8.6	19 345	17 279	16 619	70 346	10.9	2.48	12.2	25.9
Reno-Sparks, NV	12.7	7.3	4.9	49.5	257 193	342 885	33.3	24.1	52 174	27 114	53 262	165 187	23.7	2.54	11.2	27.2
Richmond, VA	12.4	6.7	5.4	51.6	949 244	1 096 957	15.6	14.7	144 117	90 468	93 598	488 330	14.9	2.50	14.7	26.6
Riverside-San Bernardino-Ontario, CA	9.7	5.8	4.6	50.3	2 588 793	3 254 821	25.7	29.8	577 348	236 537	563 449	1 297 878	25.4	3.20	14.7	18.5
Roanoke, VA	14.2	8.7	7.6	51.8	268 513	288 309	7.4	7.1	31 861	29 593	11 375	128 454	7.6	2.34	12.5	29.6
Rochester, MN	11.4	6.9	6.1	50.9	141 945	163 618	15.3	13.7	24 787	10 446	8 794	73 362	17.4	2.49	8.5	26.5
Rochester, NY	12.7	7.2	6.9	51.4	1 002 410	1 037 831	3.5	1.6	112 443	81 933	-26 858	420 554	5.9	2.41	13.2	29.2
Rockford, IL	12.1	7.2	6.2	51.0	283 719	320 204	12.9	9.1	43 905	26 114	13 929	134 006	9.3	2.57	13.5	26.4
Rocky Mount, NC	13.6	7.9	6.2	52.4	133 369	143 026	7.2	6.5	18 483	14 026	-66	59 462	10.0	2.50	18.9	27.3
Rome, GA	12.0	7.7	6.5	51.6	81 251	90 565	11.5	6.4	12 998	9 128	2 411	35 930	5.6	2.58	14.8	26.0

1. No spouse present.

Area name	Daytime population, 2010			Births, average 2006–2008		Deaths, average 2006–2008		Persons under 65 with no health insurance 2009		Medicare, 2011			Serious crimes known to police,[2] 2010 Total	
	Persons in group quarters, 2010	Number	Employ-ment/ residence ratio	Total	Rate[1]	Number	Rate[1]	Number	Percent	Enrolled in original Medicare	Enrolled in Medicare Advantage	Enrolled in a Medicare prescription drug plan	Number	Rate[3]
	32	33	34	35	36	37	38	39	40	41	42	43	44	45
Naples-Marco Island, FL......	4 546	328 805	1.05	4 043	12.8	2 645	8.4	64 812	28.4	72 238	9 724	31 958	6 760	2 103
Nashville-Davidson—Mur-freesboro—Franklin, TN	38 454	1 614 950	1.03	21 593	14.3	11 533	7.6	210 261	15.3	215 416	70 444	70 361	64 519	4 058
New Haven-Milford, CT	29 198	833 236	0.93	10 253	12.1	7 550	8.9	73 071	10.3	143 487	33 068	52 622	28 060	3 469
New Orleans-Metairie-Ken-ner, LA	19 379	1 202 602	1.06	14 290	13.4	9 694	9.1	221 348	21.8	179 424	82 385	46 739	43 564	3 731
New York-Northern New Jer-sey-Long Island, NY-NJ-PA........................	394 769	19 111 956	1.02	257 005	13.6	135 676	7.2	2 349 410	14.5	2 798 051	652 904	1 070 695	402 092	2 128
Edison-New Brunswick, NJ Div	42 638	2 221 768	0.89	29 900	12.9	19 557	8.4	247 543	12.6	394 342	49 233	162 770	47 348	2 023
Nassau-Suffolk, NY Div.....	51 072	D	D	33 714	12.0	21 708	7.7	267 469	11.0	474 317	89 875	156 587	52 479	1 853
Newark-Union, NJ-PA Div.	46 231	2 158 388	1.01	27 686	13.0	15 927	7.5	263 213	14.4	309 306	40 738	129 448	50 316	2 343
New York-White Plains-Wayne, NY-NJ Div........	254 828	12 065 753	1.09	165 705	14.3	78 484	6.8	1 571 185	15.7	1 620 086	473 058	621 890	251 949	2 177
Niles-Benton Harbor, MI ...	3 527	D	D	2 063	12.9	1 613	10.1	21 079	15.9	31 342	5 782	14 163	4 925	3 185
North Port-Bradenton-Sara-sota, FL..........................	10 439	696 024	0.97	7 210	10.5	8 295	12.1	117 637	23.9	181 881	38 287	68 181	29 354	4 180
Norwich-New London, CT.....	12 782	276 758	1.02	3 041	11.5	2 216	8.4	20 705	9.3	46 284	5 915	18 140	NA	NA
Ocala, FL	8 239	D	D	3 660	11.3	4 030	12.5	58 034	24.0	92 672	27 247	29 052	10 090	3 046
Ocean City, NJ..................	2 628	D	D	930	9.6	1 259	13.0	10 530	14.2	23 924	2 360	11 495	4 793	4 928
Odessa, TX......................	2 175	D	D	2 625	20.2	1 133	8.7	34 540	29.2	17 153	1 892	8 688	5 706	4 161
Ogden-Clearfield, UT..........	5 802	512 545	0.84	10 351	20.1	2 825	5.5	69 157	14.2	59 464	19 592	12 588	17 027	3 112
Oklahoma City, OK.............	31 897	1 266 822	1.02	18 813	15.8	10 101	8.5	213 725	20.3	180 984	32 027	73 021	59 663	4 762
Olympia, WA	4 222	239 130	0.88	2 929	12.2	1 846	7.7	28 758	13.3	41 373	12 732	10 700	8 714	3 454
Omaha-Council Bluffs, NE-IA.......................	17 599	872 131	1.01	D	D	6 060	7.3	88 979	12.1	118 207	20 826	53 081	29 878	3 456
Orlando-Kissimmee-Sanford, FL....................	44 468	2 196 701	1.06	29 070	14.4	14 178	7.0	426 006	24.2	308 465	93 025	96 432	89 647	4 200
Oshkosh-Neenah, WI..........	8 239	176 256	1.11	1 925	11.9	1 312	8.1	14 081	10.2	26 615	12 231	6 429	3 547	2 124
Owensboro, KY	2 753	D	D	D	D	1 101	9.8	13 957	14.8	22 616	2 782	13 225	2 812	2 451
Oxnard-Thousand Oaks-Ven-tura, CA........................	10 600	783 546	0.89	12 244	15.3	4 954	6.2	126 443	18.1	114 077	30 411	41 166	17 773	2 159
Palm Bay-Melbourne-Titus-ville, FL	7 735	535 948	0.97	5 605	10.5	5 668	10.6	83 632	20.1	122 311	37 218	30 498	20 350	3 745
Palm Coast, FL	684	D	D	943	10.8	920	10.5	14 838	22.0	26 245	8 181	7 031	2 478	2 589
Panama City-Lynn Haven-Panama City Beach, FL...	3 817	D	D	2 345	14.3	1 506	9.2	31 271	22.8	30 373	2 500	12 373	8 416	4 984
Parkersburg-Marietta-Vienna, WV-OH	3 450	D	D	1 658	10.3	1 792	11.1	19 565	15.0	35 440	5 345	20 849	2 934	1 906
Pascagoula, MS	1 854	D	D	D	D	1 370	9.0	26 402	20.0	26 671	3 167	12 156	5 672	3 496
Pensacola-Ferry Pass-Brent, FL.................................	22 203	437 292	0.93	6 172	13.8	3 991	8.9	80 528	21.1	80 846	15 373	25 268	17 759	3 955
Peoria, IL	9 190	385 009	1.04	D	D	3 652	9.8	34 980	11.2	65 681	10 947	26 794	10 482	3 059
Philadelphia-Camden-Wil-mington, PA-NJ-DE-MD.	167 826	5 944 667	0.99	78 378	13.4	52 386	9.0	586 988	11.7	946 970	250 884	356 596	193 510	3 248
Camden, NJ Div	24 851	1 157 474	0.84	15 927	12.8	10 473	8.4	134 100	12.5	198 391	33 360	79 611	36 152	2 891
Philadelphia, PA Div.........	123 013	4 080 519	1.04	52 965	13.6	36 225	9.3	386 837	11.5	640 710	211 931	223 642	129 146	3 228
Wilmington, DE-MD-NJ Div	19 962	706 674	1.00	9 486	13.7	5 688	8.2	66 051	11.0	107 869	5 593	53 343	28 212	3 998
Phoenix-Mesa-Glendale, AZ....	79 422	4 199 551	0.99	70 160	16.8	27 027	6.5	763 512	20.1	561 683	232 660	140 829	164 305	3 921
Pine Bluff, AR	9 027	D	D	D	D	1 059	10.4	16 885	20.3	18 074	2 852	9 103	5 331	5 416
Pittsburgh, PA	62 679	2 374 360	1.02	24 597	10.4	27 329	11.6	197 933	10.5	478 689	292 626	75 706	53 652	2 292
Pittsfield, MA	6 159	D	D	1 233	9.5	1 495	11.5	4 759	4.7	29 510	730	17 083	3 637	2 875
Pocatello, ID	1 839	D	D	1 462	16.7	623	7.1	14 130	18.0	12 929	3 642	5 718	2 630	2 901
Portland-South Portland-Bid-deford, ME	12 560	513 708	1.00	5 044	9.8	4 325	8.4	48 649	11.3	96 413	14 468	43 693	13 609	2 647
Portland-Vancouver-Hills-boro, OR-WA	38 319	2 237 440	1.00	29 291	13.5	15 169	7.0	330 356	16.9	308 925	161 169	70 954	75 704	3 419
Port St. Lucie, FL..............	6 986	400 236	0.85	4 835	12.1	4 237	10.6	75 257	24.5	95 585	22 219	33 924	12 397	2 923
Poughkeepsie-Newburgh-Middletown, NY.............	32 195	623 049	0.84	8 481	12.6	4 715	7.0	69 017	11.8	100 376	12 266	35 441	14 686	2 345
Prescott, AZ	3 525	D	D	2 339	11.0	2 395	11.3	31 768	19.7	58 689	12 143	20 783	5 112	2 422
Providence-New Bedford-Fall River, RI-MA	58 531	1 540 688	0.92	17 463	10.9	14 613	9.1	141 551	10.6	288 050	78 254	115 497	46 356	2 896
Provo-Orem, UT................	14 034	507 447	0.89	12 181	24.2	1 940	3.9	71 918	14.1	41 548	17 045	10 534	12 267	2 329
Pueblo, CO	4 321	D	D	2 146	13.9	1 552	10.0	23 471	17.8	30 609	8 389	10 097	7 601	4 779
Punta Gorda, FL	3 012	D	D	1 206	7.9	2 137	14.0	23 024	22.8	50 912	11 900	17 360	4 580	2 863
Racine, WI	4 995	183 973	0.87	2 653	13.5	1 574	8.0	19 191	11.3	32 636	9 041	10 599	5 922	3 031
Raleigh-Cary, NC...............	24 394	1 117 979	0.96	16 428	15.7	5 499	5.3	148 279	14.9	130 704	21 191	50 564	30 539	2 716
Rapid City, SD	3 372	D	D	D	D	884	7.3	16 885	16.1	22 254	3 138	9 535	4 156	3 288
Reading, PA	12 023	384 194	0.85	5 149	12.8	3 508	8.7	41 909	12.4	71 270	23 081	27 235	10 334	2 512
Redding, CA.....................	2 654	D	D	2 202	12.2	2 024	11.3	26 528	17.7	40 679	3 855	20 217	6 239	3 520
Reno-Sparks, NV	5 277	425 665	1.00	6 034	14.8	3 118	7.6	86 920	23.8	63 790	17 022	19 463	13 545	3 184
Richmond, VA	36 912	1 257 419	0.99	D	D	9 826	8.1	143 509	13.7	189 703	31 547	80 366	34 415	2 735
Riverside-San Bernardino-Ontario, CA...................	75 883	4 015 633	0.86	68 263	16.8	26 101	6.4	805 062	22.0	507 204	249 079	130 991	129 858	3 074
Roanoke, VA.....................	7 928	318 922	1.07	D	D	3 245	10.9	34 528	14.2	63 357	10 521	30 538	9 008	2 918
Rochester, MN	3 165	192 361	1.06	D	D	1 159	6.4	12 928	8.2	28 278	8 507	9 460	3 628	1 986
Rochester, NY...................	39 346	1 065 583	1.02	11 625	11.2	8 828	8.5	85 574	9.9	187 988	109 214	37 561	32 067	3 041
Rockford, IL	4 995	347 321	0.99	4 887	13.9	2 853	8.1	44 195	14.7	58 423	10 146	26 185	15 170	4 442
Rocky Mount, NC...............	3 640	D	D	2 027	13.9	1 515	10.4	22 117	18.1	27 894	1 711	16 658	6 164	4 045
Rome, GA	3 733	D	D	1 434	15.0	988	10.3	17 762	22.0	17 533	2 890	9 014	3 853	4 000

1. Per 1,000 estimated resident population.   2. Data for serious crimes have not been adjusted for underreporting; this may affect comparability between geographic areas and over time.   3. Per 100,000 population estimated by the FBI.

Table C. Metropolitan Areas — Crime, Education, Money Income, and Poverty

Area name	Serious crimes known to police,[1] 2010 (cont.) Rate[2] Violent	Property	Education School enrollment and attainment, 2010 Enrollment[3] Total	Percent private	Attainment[4] (percent) High school graduate or less	Bachelor's degree or more	Local government expenditures,[5] 2008–2009 Total current expenditures (mil dol)	Current expenditures per student (dollars)	Income and Poverty, 2010 Per capita income[6] (dollars)	Median household income (dollars)	Percent of households with income of less than $25,000	Percent of households with income of $100,000 or more	Percent of households with income of $200,000 or more	Percent below poverty level All persons	Children under 18 years	Children under 5
	46	47	48	49	50	51	52	53	54	55	56	57	58	59	60	61
Naples-Marco Island, FL	318	1 785	68 039	14.2	41.7	31.1	426.2	10 019	31 952	52 730	20.3	22.0	6.6	16.2	27.3	32.1
Nashville-Davidson—Mur-freesboro—Franklin, TN	639	3 419	420 264	21.7	43.0	29.7	1 928.0	8 091	25 472	47 975	24.9	17.8	3.6	15.4	22.8	27.7
New Haven-Milford, CT	416	3 053	227 940	23.3	43.1	31.8	1 867.1	14 464	31 041	57 056	22.3	26.0	5.0	11.7	16.5	19.2
New Orleans-Metairie-Ken-ner, LA	480	3 251	298 659	31.3	45.8	26.8	1 762.4	12 592	25 625	46 134	28.2	18.7	3.8	17.4	25.8	32.8
New York-Northern New Jer-sey-Long Island, NY-NJ-PA	395	1 733	4 893 113	23.6	42.0	36.0	49 051.3	18 501	33 208	61 927	21.6	30.6	8.3	13.8	19.5	21.3
Edison-New Brunswick, NJ Div	158	1 866	612 716	21.9	38.4	38.1	5 420.8	15 199	35 345	74 819	15.5	35.9	8.3	7.9	11.6	14.5
Nassau-Suffolk, NY Div	165	1 689	741 478	20.1	38.2	36.6	9 418.1	20 324	37 114	85 900	12.1	42.6	11.1	6.0	7.3	9.0
Newark-Union, NJ-PA Div	389	1 954	571 307	18.2	40.5	36.4	5 982.7	17 117	35 187	68 849	18.3	33.9	10.1	11.1	15.5	18.7
New York-White Plains-Wayne, NY-NJ Div	500	1 676	2 967 612	25.9	43.9	35.3	28 229.7	19 052	31 453	53 540	25.5	26.3	7.4	17.4	25.1	25.8
Niles-Benton Harbor, MI	350	2 834	39 715	20.3	45.6	22.1	278.6	10 466	22 337	40 329	31.0	12.9	1.8	16.8	28.5	34.5
North Port-Bradenton-Sara-sota, FL	508	3 671	129 709	16.6	43.6	26.9	817.7	9 776	26 837	45 283	26.2	15.5	3.4	13.6	22.5	25.8
Norwich-New London, CT	NA	NA	64 813	19.3	41.1	30.1	569.7	13 896	32 053	62 349	17.3	27.4	5.8	8.8	10.8	14.9
Ocala, FL	542	2 504	63 932	17.1	53.7	16.3	350.2	8 215	20 100	37 044	31.3	7.8	1.2	19.8	31.3	34.6
Ocean City, NJ	251	4 677	18 376	8.8	47.2	27.4	247.0	18 073	33 905	53 392	21.6	25.1	5.5	10.5	18.7	30.5
Odessa, TX	650	3 511	37 642	7.9	56.4	13.2	212.3	7 584	21 890	42 282	33.5	13.6	2.6	20.0	30.1	36.3
Ogden-Clearfield, UT	149	2 963	175 837	8.9	32.0	30.1	723.3	6 207	23 403	59 171	15.8	22.1	2.9	10.2	13.0	14.0
Oklahoma City, OK	547	4 214	351 526	11.9	40.0	27.6	1 520.0	7 479	24 305	46 238	26.8	16.6	2.7	15.9	23.8	25.8
Olympia, WA	249	3 205	65 608	12.4	31.6	31.1	379.6	9 201	28 265	61 011	19.5	22.4	2.4	10.1	12.3	17.1
Omaha-Council Bluffs, NE-IA	386	3 070	251 737	20.1	34.3	33.0	1 346.7	9 512	26 907	54 060	22.1	20.1	2.8	12.4	17.7	18.7
Orlando-Kissimmee-Sanford, FL	613	3 588	604 934	18.9	41.0	28.1	2 678.2	8 114	23 165	46 478	24.5	16.5	2.8	14.7	20.4	24.6
Oshkosh-Neenah, WI	206	1 918	45 099	9.7	45.2	22.1	240.6	10 382	25 409	48 177	22.0	13.1	1.8	12.3	12.3	18.6
Owensboro, KY	117	2 334	29 714	15.2	55.7	16.5	167.3	8 889	19 925	41 021	31.4	8.7	1.2	16.2	27.9	26.7
Oxnard-Thousand Oaks-Ven-tura, CA	212	1 946	230 361	14.7	36.7	30.8	1 244.1	8 794	31 135	71 864	15.9	34.7	8.6	10.7	14.3	15.1
Palm Bay-Melbourne-Titus-ville, FL	588	3 157	120 890	18.7	42.2	25.1	602.4	8 241	26 022	46 262	25.3	17.2	2.8	13.4	19.5	24.6
Palm Coast, FL	239	2 350	19 435	9.3	39.2	25.7	101.4	7 866	23 556	43 993	26.2	11.1	3.3	18.1	21.1	20.1
Panama City-Lynn Haven-Panama City Beach, FL	513	4 471	40 560	11.3	44.4	20.0	211.3	8 139	22 175	44 881	24.4	13.2	1.7	14.2	16.2	16.2
Parkersburg-Marietta-Vienna, WV-OH	274	1 633	38 839	12.5	51.9	16.5	249.6	9 912	22 187	40 352	30.7	11.9	1.6	16.0	23.3	27.3
Pascagoula, MS	261	3 235	41 574	8.6	49.0	17.2	245.4	8 522	21 163	44 878	27.9	13.7	1.6	16.6	25.9	38.6
Pensacola-Ferry Pass-Brent, FL	583	3 372	112 933	19.6	40.4	24.5	548.1	8 265	22 558	43 974	28.1	14.7	2.2	17.1	24.8	30.3
Peoria, IL	422	2 636	99 822	20.4	42.0	26.2	570.4	9 705	26 282	50 983	22.9	17.7	2.8	12.4	17.5	23.1
Philadelphia-Camden-Wil-mington, PA-NJ-DE-MD	558	2 690	1 623 198	26.7	42.8	33.1	12 011.7	14 138	30 250	58 095	21.9	26.5	5.6	12.7	17.1	19.0
Camden, NJ Div	337	2 553	338 472	18.8	42.4	30.8	3 257.6	15 730	31 527	66 313	16.7	29.4	5.8	8.4	12.0	14.2
Philadelphia, PA Div	613	2 615	1 089 453	30.0	43.0	34.3	7 478.3	13 823	30 013	55 389	23.8	25.6	5.8	14.3	18.9	20.1
Wilmington, DE-MD-NJ Div	642	3 356	195 273	22.0	42.6	30.4	1 275.8	12 567	29 332	59 927	20.1	26.3	4.3	11.4	16.3	21.0
Phoenix-Mesa-Glendale, AZ	371	3 550	1 146 584	11.2	38.8	27.2	5 597.9	7 569	24 809	50 385	23.1	19.7	3.6	16.3	22.7	25.8
Pine Bluff, AR	796	4 619	28 309	4.6	55.0	13.2	146.3	8 921	17 784	33 446	36.9	9.4	0.6	22.4	35.2	42.4
Pittsburgh, PA	322	1 970	565 878	21.6	45.3	29.1	3 941.4	12 257	27 075	46 700	27.0	16.7	3.1	12.2	16.8	19.7
Pittsfield, MA	442	2 433	30 892	24.0	44.1	28.9	278.2	15 337	27 106	44 190	28.5	15.3	3.1	12.1	18.3	20.9
Pocatello, ID	213	2 688	27 348	13.9	36.2	26.7	106.9	6 872	19 710	39 175	27.8	11.0	1.2	13.4	15.6	25.6
Portland-South Portland-Bid-deford, ME	136	2 511	124 404	17.4	36.6	33.7	901.2	12 558	28 992	56 530	20.8	20.2	2.9	10.3	14.2	18.8
Portland-Vancouver-Hills-boro, OR-WA	274	3 145	578 456	16.8	33.0	33.0	3 215.7	9 602	27 451	53 078	21.2	20.7	3.5	13.4	17.6	20.1
Port St. Lucie, FL	364	2 559	99 499	13.8	46.5	21.7	495.7	8 710	25 449	41 346	25.0	15.7	2.9	15.2	23.3	23.8
Poughkeepsie-Newburgh-Middletown, NY	271	2 074	193 033	23.3	41.1	30.9	1 854.0	16 679	29 607	67 269	16.8	29.8	5.2	9.4	13.6	18.4
Prescott, AZ	325	2 098	40 766	8.1	36.7	21.6	188.7	7 191	22 619	40 274	29.6	11.3	1.7	19.2	29.0	37.8
Providence-New Bedford-Fall River, RI-MA	371	2 525	418 207	24.0	45.5	28.5	3 126.5	13 591	27 132	51 935	26.0	21.3	3.4	13.7	18.3	22.5
Provo-Orem, UT	87	2 241	208 762	28.2	24.7	35.2	672.3	5 796	18 964	54 201	20.3	18.3	2.7	14.6	12.6	13.4
Pueblo, CO	577	4 202	42 308	9.2	44.4	19.5	225.8	8 235	20 526	38 326	33.9	10.4	1.3	20.0	26.5	28.8
Punta Gorda, FL	238	2 625	26 838	18.1	45.5	22.3	157.3	9 059	23 930	42 031	29.1	10.8	1.0	13.5	25.5	24.8
Racine, WI	262	2 769	50 618	16.9	46.7	23.5	338.0	11 081	25 555	51 377	26.0	18.1	2.3	14.7	20.1	23.3
Raleigh-Cary, NC	250	2 466	328 994	16.0	28.8	41.0	1 509.9	8 183	28 767	57 840	19.8	24.2	4.9	12.9	17.2	20.8
Rapid City, SD	406	2 883	32 957	15.0	36.1	27.7	158.4	8 038	24 776	47 074	22.7	15.4	2.8	12.7	17.6	18.8
Reading, PA	332	2 180	108 444	16.3	54.3	22.8	841.7	11 997	25 384	51 759	23.2	18.9	2.6	14.1	23.2	24.2
Redding, CA	822	2 698	47 661	16.9	36.9	19.4	286.5	10 107	21 495	41 023	30.3	11.1	1.7	18.5	25.3	29.4
Reno-Sparks, NV	417	2 766	115 601	9.2	38.7	26.0	558.8	8 486	27 626	50 699	23.8	20.6	4.1	15.8	21.7	27.1
Richmond, VA	267	2 468	323 192	15.5	41.1	31.7	1 998.3	9 948	28 883	55 325	19.6	23.4	4.1	11.6	14.6	20.4
Riverside-San Bernardino-Ontario, CA	370	2 704	1 286 227	11.0	47.4	19.5	7 289.3	8 696	21 371	53 548	22.2	21.1	3.1	17.1	24.1	27.3
Roanoke, VA	298	2 620	72 465	19.2	43.6	27.6	456.0	10 099	25 603	45 569	24.5	15.6	2.2	13.7	21.5	24.0
Rochester, MN	185	1 801	46 350	12.8	32.0	35.3	264.3	8 865	30 403	59 702	17.8	23.7	4.0	7.6	9.0	11.8
Rochester, NY	307	2 734	287 343	22.9	38.6	33.0	2 533.7	15 440	26 382	50 211	24.2	18.5	2.8	14.2	20.8	26.7
Rockford, IL	801	3 640	90 318	18.9	49.0	21.0	573.3	9 855	22 254	45 457	28.2	15.0	2.0	17.7	28.5	35.2
Rocky Mount, NC	587	3 458	39 525	11.6	54.1	14.0	225.0	8 311	20 502	38 077	32.0	9.8	1.5	17.5	28.2	39.3
Rome, GA	468	3 532	25 850	20.8	55.9	18.6	173.0	10 682	19 015	36 934	34.3	9.2	2.3	17.9	20.5	19.6

1. Data for serious crimes have not been adjusted for underreporting; this may affect comparability between geographic areas and over time. 2. Per 100,000 population estimated by the FBI. 3. All persons 3 years old and over enrolled in nursery school through college. 4. Persons 25 years old and over. 5. Elementary and secondary education expenditures. 6. Based on resident population estimated as of July 1, 2009.

Table C. Metropolitan Areas — **Personal Income**

Area name	Total (mil dol)	Percent change, 2008–2009	Per capita[1] Dollars	Per capita[1] Rank	Wages and salaries[2] (mil dol)	Proprietors' income (mil dol)	Dividends, interest, and rent (mil dol)	Transfer payments Total (mil dol)	Government payments to individuals Total (mil dol)	Social Security (mil dol)	Medical payments (mil dol)	Income maintenance (mil dol)	Unemployment insurance (mil dol)
	62	63	64	65	66	67	68	69	70	71	72	73	74
Naples-Marco Island, FL.......	19 128	-4.8	60 049	2	6 137	875	10 708	2 270	2 212	1 050	798	135	95
Nashville-Davidson—Mur-freesboro—Franklin, TN	61 164	-2.4	38 656	98	40 793	9 605	8 030	9 223	8 935	3 104	3 655	1 003	472
New Haven-Milford, CT	40 184	-1.3	47 387	20	22 978	3 003	6 699	7 218	7 063	2 104	3 447	588	541
New Orleans-Metairie-Ken-ner, LA	50 818	-2.1	42 705	43	31 137	5 666	10 461	7 871	7 655	2 392	3 628	893	177
New York-Northern New Jer-sey-Long Island, NY-NJ-PA.............................	992 331	-3.9	52 037	10	657 646	91 072	180 619	162 619	159 141	39 819	83 246	16 787	10 286
Edison-New Brunswick, NJ Div	118 195	-3.0	50 610	X	67 638	8 467	21 024	16 670	16 244	6 130	6 515	787	1 692
Nassau-Suffolk, NY Div.....	157 922	-4.1	54 912	X	79 024	10 272	32 832	21 550	21 026	7 625	9 661	1 224	1 083
Newark-Union, NJ-PA Div..	115 495	-3.6	54 318	X	73 192	9 979	19 851	15 454	15 066	4 694	6 528	1 301	1 583
New York-White Plains-Wayne, NY-NJ Div........	600 720	-4.1	51 203	X	437 791	62 354	106 913	108 945	106 805	21 370	60 543	13 473	5 929
Niles-Benton Harbor, MI	5 377	-1.5	33 507	233	3 079	367	875	1 371	1 341	466	563	145	96
North Port-Bradenton-Sara-sota, FL.........................	33 388	-2.6	48 521	17	12 337	1 903	13 183	6 041	5 916	2 615	2 383	320	216
Norwich-New London, CT.....	12 499	-0.8	46 841	21	8 978	704	2 276	1 997	1 950	669	869	130	157
Ocala, FL	10 217	-1.2	31 097	299	4 206	334	2 549	3 009	2 950	1 292	1 083	241	105
Ocean City, NJ....................	4 452	0.2	46 329	25	1 876	287	967	1 037	1 020	364	445	50	106
Odessa, TX........................	4 516	-4.6	33 544	231	3 139	383	599	850	825	235	399	105	39
Ogden-Clearfield, UT...........	17 717	-0.1	32 714	250	10 007	829	3 130	2 256	2 158	723	776	222	138
Oklahoma City, OK..............	47 547	-1.5	38 742	95	30 352	6 484	7 561	7 634	7 412	2 490	2 992	837	261
Olympia, WA	10 240	1.4	40 801	62	5 453	549	1 771	1 726	1 681	589	555	160	113
Omaha-Council Bluffs, NE-IA...................................	36 514	-1.1	42 982	38	25 200	3 093	6 629	5 081	4 927	1 655	2 137	454	142
Orlando-Kissimmee-Sanford, FL....................	73 466	-2.7	35 279	183	51 505	4 593	13 229	13 110	12 731	4 144	5 217	1 434	753
Oshkosh-Neenah, WI..........	6 059	0.0	37 088	136	4 920	216	1 067	1 012	982	397	382	60	78
Owensboro, KY...................	3 729	0.7	32 817	247	2 248	274	607	901	880	319	362	86	45
Oxnard-Thousand Oaks-Ven-tura, CA.........................	36 863	-1.6	45 908	29	19 601	2 564	7 170	4 598	4 452	1 511	1 701	396	408
Palm Bay-Melbourne-Titus-ville, FL..........................	20 089	-0.4	37 454	131	11 416	905	4 483	4 368	4 270	1 731	1 697	281	169
Palm Coast, FL..................	2 993	0.6	32 671	251	774	21	992	768	751	381	236	50	30
Panama City-Lynn Haven-Panama City Beach, FL...	5 984	0.3	36 316	156	3 758	277	1 232	1 266	1 236	398	527	121	47
Parkersburg-Marietta-Vienna, WV-OH	5 128	1.1	31 869	279	3 284	272	729	1 419	1 389	507	581	129	59
Pascagoula, MS..................	5 277	0.8	33 916	218	3 483	187	705	1 088	1 059	391	458	107	30
Pensacola-Ferry Pass-Brent, FL...................................	15 438	0.9	33 921	217	8 955	566	2 778	3 256	3 175	1 067	1 282	335	100
Peoria, IL..........................	14 966	-1.9	39 818	75	10 403	883	2 597	2 603	2 535	987	926	243	219
Philadelphia-Camden-Wil-mington, PA-NJ-DE-MD.	274 986	-0.9	46 075	27	179 219	22 921	44 071	46 929	45 842	14 013	21 229	4 214	3 364
Camden, NJ Div	53 608	-0.1	42 753	X	30 592	3 003	7 241	9 418	9 190	2 990	3 816	694	1 021
Philadelphia, PA Div.........	191 620	-0.9	47 755	X	126 802	17 828	31 851	32 582	31 850	9 390	15 232	3 152	2 051
Wilmington, DE-MD-NJ Div...............................	29 758	-2.2	42 404	X	21 825	2 089	4 979	4 929	4 801	1 633	2 182	368	292
Phoenix-Mesa-Glendale, AZ....	150 352	-3.0	34 452	202	99 293	11 727	25 993	25 831	25 037	8 026	10 624	2 207	997
Pine Bluff, AR	2 975	1.2	29 541	333	1 843	161	401	831	813	233	307	120	42
Pittsburgh, PA	99 611	-0.7	42 298	48	62 529	9 087	15 679	21 102	20 673	7 102	9 332	1 435	1 384
Pittsfield, MA.....................	5 537	-1.3	42 826	40	3 050	409	1 142	1 325	1 302	407	628	120	93
Pocatello, ID......................	2 574	0.0	28 513	346	1 558	188	382	568	552	168	203	56	29
Portland-South Portland-Bid-deford, ME	21 403	-1.2	41 412	58	14 052	1 546	3 654	3 744	3 650	1 281	1 692	286	134
Portland-Vancouver-Hills-boro, OR-WA	87 894	-1.2	39 206	86	59 166	6 346	16 789	13 731	13 323	4 319	4 764	1 353	1 426
Port St. Lucie, FL...............	16 076	-3.1	39 568	78	5 981	629	6 214	3 405	3 331	1 368	1 347	243	149
Poughkeepsie-Newburgh-Middletown, NY..............	26 454	-1.4	39 070	89	14 193	1 150	4 163	4 636	4 514	1 551	1 992	387	258
Prescott, AZ......................	6 284	-2.8	29 134	342	2 479	315	1 900	1 659	1 659	815	518	96	53
Providence-New Bedford-Fall River, RI-MA	65 353	-0.9	40 829	61	37 512	4 044	10 248	13 902	13 611	3 893	6 243	1 342	1 206
Provo-Orem, UT.................	13 026	-1.0	23 448	363	8 266	1 191	2 143	1 879	1 778	578	669	194	106
Pueblo, CO	4 970	2.7	31 613	290	2 696	274	723	1 537	1 509	354	806	156	54
Punta Gorda, FL	5 628	-2.1	35 858	171	1 788	252	2 089	1 550	1 522	729	569	69	50
Racine, WI	7 364	-0.8	36 708	144	3 956	307	1 239	1 380	1 344	502	539	122	117
Raleigh-Cary, NC...............	42 789	-1.2	38 007	113	28 848	2 278	6 738	5 528	5 322	1 821	2 140	515	454
Rapid City, SD	4 657	-0.3	37 330	134	2 909	330	1 056	785	763	292	290	71	13
Reading, PA.......................	14 793	-0.4	36 336	154	8 791	912	2 395	3 034	2 960	1 064	1 158	252	282
Redding, CA.......................	6 170	-0.6	34 068	213	3 016	619	1 174	1 734	1 701	539	710	180	117
Reno-Sparks, NV	17 773	-5.1	42 390	46	10 526	1 294	4 874	2 445	2 368	859	862	170	288
Richmond, VA	50 966	-2.0	41 161	59	36 244	2 949	8 665	7 672	7 447	2 744	3 023	771	363
Riverside-San Bernardino-Ontario, CA....................	122 969	-1.6	29 680	330	64 025	8 810	18 976	24 552	23 799	6 632	9 191	3 330	2 260
Roanoke, VA......................	11 512	-0.7	38 322	106	7 983	667	2 109	2 241	2 186	854	806	193	70
Rochester, MN...................	7 836	0.2	42 216	49	6 072	470	1 313	1 132	1 099	390	482	79	75
Rochester, NY....................	40 424	-0.7	39 036	90	26 410	2 745	6 733	8 603	8 414	2 852	3 665	946	431
Rockford, IL.......................	11 308	-2.5	31 970	273	7 345	538	1 866	2 380	2 315	875	785	261	264
Rocky Mount, NC................	4 682	0.8	31 936	276	2 793	302	687	1 274	1 247	370	535	178	73
Rome, GA	3 065	-0.7	31 840	280	1 859	205	531	712	695	249	271	81	37

1. Based on the resident population estimated as of July 1 of the year shown.   2. Includes other labor income.

Table C. Metropolitan Areas — Earnings, Social Security, and Housing

Area name	Earnings, 2009 Total (mil dol)	Farm	Goods-related[1] Total	Manu-facturing	Information, profes-sional, and technical services	Retail trade	Finance, insur-ance, and real estate	Health care and social services	Govern-ment	Social Security beneficiaries, December 2010 Number	Rate[2]	Supplemental Security Income recipients, December 2009	Housing units, 2010 Total	Percent change, 2000–2010
	75	76	77	78	79	80	81	82	83	84	85	86	87	88
Naples-Marco Island, FL	7 012	2.3	12.8	2.6	8.3	9.1	9.5	14.6	12.4	75 290	234	3 085	197 298	36.5
Nashville-Davidson—Murfreesboro—Franklin, TN	50 398	0.0	D	9.4	D	6.6	D	NA	11.9	242 575	153	27 910	667 655	22.9
New Haven-Milford, CT	25 981	0.1	D	11.3	11.9	6.0	5.8	15.8	16.5	153 535	178	18 060	362 004	6.2
New Orleans-Metairie-Kenner, LA	36 803	0.1	D	8.3	D	NA	5.9	NA	17.1	196 205	168	41 220	538 239	-1.9
New York-Northern New Jersey-Long Island, NY-NJ-PA	748 719	0.0	D	NA	19.2	4.8	17.9	10.9	13.8	2 900 230	153	604 737	7 527 752	6.2
Edison-New Brunswick, NJ Div	76 106	0.1	D	9.2	19.0	6.1	8.3	10.8	15.0	424 890	182	28 352	954 389	9.0
Nassau-Suffolk, NY Div	89 296	0.1	13.0	6.4	13.4	7.0	9.4	15.0	19.0	515 380	182	40 198	1 038 331	5.9
Newark-Union, NJ-PA Div	83 171	0.0	D	10.2	16.9	5.6	9.7	10.2	16.1	330 315	154	44 268	852 179	5.9
New York-White Plains-Wayne, NY-NJ Div	500 146	0.0	D	NA	20.6	4.0	22.3	10.3	12.4	1 629 645	141	491 919	4 682 853	5.7
Niles-Benton Harbor, MI	3 446	1.2	31.8	27.8	4.5	5.9	5.1	11.9	14.4	35 485	226	4 905	76 922	4.7
North Port-Bradenton-Sarasota, FL	14 241	1.3	D	6.1	11.8	9.0	7.5	16.6	12.4	195 240	278	8 929	401 103	25.1
Norwich-New London, CT	9 681	0.4	20.3	16.2	9.3	5.1	2.2	10.2	34.2	50 020	183	3 497	120 994	9.3
Ocala, FL	4 540	-0.3	16.6	8.6	6.8	10.3	7.0	15.4	20.7	102 810	310	7 772	164 050	33.7
Ocean City, NJ	2 163	0.3	D	1.4	6.0	10.2	6.7	11.8	30.2	26 685	274	1 774	98 309	8.0
Odessa, TX	3 522	0.0	34.8	7.4	5.7	6.9	4.8	8.0	14.5	19 285	141	3 845	53 027	7.1
Ogden-Clearfield, UT	10 836	0.1	D	11.9	D	7.1	4.7	NA	31.3	62 290	114	5 392	186 763	27.3
Oklahoma City, OK	36 836	0.0	D	9.1	D	5.9	5.9	NA	23.2	201 285	161	26 239	539 077	14.2
Olympia, WA	6 002	0.3	8.5	3.1	6.2	6.6	5.2	12.5	41.7	46 365	184	4 755	108 182	24.8
Omaha-Council Bluffs, NE-IA	28 293	1.4	D	6.5	D	5.7	9.8	NA	15.9	127 895	148	13 040	362 327	16.3
Orlando-Kissimmee-Sanford, FL	56 098	0.3	D	5.0	13.9	7.0	8.5	10.9	12.8	343 620	161	48 556	942 312	37.9
Oshkosh-Neenah, WI	5 135	0.2	D	33.0	7.2	4.4	3.9	10.8	12.5	30 360	182	2 264	73 329	13.3
Owensboro, KY	2 523	3.8	D	20.7	D	7.2	D	9.4	20.1	26 095	227	4 240	49 450	6.5
Oxnard-Thousand Oaks-Ventura, CA	22 165	3.6	22.0	15.9	10.8	6.6	8.2	8.6	18.0	117 290	142	16 484	281 695	11.9
Palm Bay-Melbourne-Titusville, FL	12 320	0.1	20.9	16.0	11.6	6.5	4.2	12.9	18.4	134 980	248	10 068	269 864	21.5
Palm Coast, FL	795	1.5	D	4.4	D	11.7	4.8	13.9	25.5	29 105	304	1 488	48 595	98.7
Panama City-Lynn Haven-Panama City Beach, FL	4 035	0.0	11.6	5.5	9.6	7.8	6.4	11.0	31.5	33 940	201	4 301	99 650	27.0
Parkersburg-Marietta-Vienna, WV-OH	3 556	-0.1	D	NA	D	8.2	D	15.6	18.4	40 220	248	6 032	75 203	1.6
Pascagoula, MS	3 670	0.0	48.0	38.0	6.5	4.9	2.4	NA	20.2	31 305	193	3 802	69 397	17.2
Pensacola-Ferry Pass-Brent, FL	9 521	0.1	10.0	3.9	8.3	6.9	5.5	14.5	33.4	91 040	203	11 632	201 463	15.9
Peoria, IL	11 286	2.3	30.1	24.5	D	5.1	D	15.5	10.9	73 330	193	6 944	164 283	7.2
Philadelphia-Camden-Wilmington, PA-NJ-DE-MD	202 140	0.2	D	NA	D	5.3	11.1	13.5	13.2	1 024 620	172	171 324	2 433 611	6.7
Camden, NJ Div	33 596	0.3	16.3	10.2	11.3	7.3	7.3	13.6	19.5	219 935	176	24 507	490 354	7.5
Philadelphia, PA Div	144 630	0.1	D	8.5	18.6	4.8	11.2	13.7	11.5	684 525	171	134 381	1 657 226	5.8
Wilmington, DE-MD-NJ Div	23 914	0.3	D	D	D	5.0	15.5	11.9	14.1	120 160	170	12 436	286 031	10.0
Phoenix-Mesa-Glendale, AZ	111 019	0.2	15.5	8.5	11.1	7.7	10.7	11.4	14.5	622 345	148	60 286	1 798 501	35.1
Pine Bluff, AR	2 005	4.1	D	15.2	D	NA	D	D	32.4	20 285	202	5 119	41 930	-2.8
Pittsburgh, PA	71 617	0.0	18.0	10.0	13.2	5.9	7.9	14.0	11.5	532 220	226	68 362	1 102 048	2.2
Pittsfield, MA	3 459	0.0	18.6	11.2	9.7	8.3	6.5	19.3	13.2	32 095	245	4 149	68 508	3.3
Pocatello, ID	1 747	1.6	D	11.1	D	7.4	D	13.2	24.9	13 810	152	1 819	36 135	13.1
Portland-South Portland-Biddeford, ME	15 597	0.2	15.8	10.2	11.1	7.3	9.2	14.9	18.2	103 365	201	9 228	262 718	12.6
Portland-Vancouver-Hillsboro, OR-WA	65 512	0.6	D	13.6	D	5.7	D	NA	14.8	334 440	150	39 164	925 076	17.0
Port St. Lucie, FL	6 609	0.9	D	4.4	8.8	9.6	5.7	16.1	18.1	104 375	246	7 404	215 160	37.3
Poughkeepsie-Newburgh-Middletown, NY	15 343	0.1	17.1	12.2	7.2	7.8	4.0	14.2	27.8	113 535	169	12 341	255 663	11.7
Prescott, AZ	2 794	0.2	16.5	5.0	6.0	10.0	5.0	15.6	23.1	64 235	304	3 297	110 432	35.1
Providence-New Bedford-Fall River, RI-MA	41 555	0.1	D	11.1	10.4	6.7	7.4	15.2	17.8	313 095	196	52 726	693 923	5.7
Provo-Orem, UT	9 457	0.3	17.9	11.1	D	7.7	4.6	NA	14.4	47 040	89	4 126	151 852	41.8
Pueblo, CO	2 969	0.1	D	9.6	4.5	8.0	4.1	19.0	23.8	32 175	202	5 782	69 526	18.0
Punta Gorda, FL	2 041	1.1	8.5	1.4	7.3	12.7	6.2	23.5	18.7	55 725	348	2 301	100 632	26.2
Racine, WI	4 263	0.5	D	34.0	6.1	5.9	4.3	12.7	13.6	37 635	193	4 639	82 164	10.0
Raleigh-Cary, NC	31 126	0.3	D	7.9	18.4	6.4	6.9	NA	17.8	143 940	127	16 194	466 095	41.5
Rapid City, SD	3 239	0.3	D	4.5	D	8.2	6.1	16.7	27.8	24 475	194	2 160	55 949	18.0
Reading, PA	9 703	0.6	25.3	18.7	7.8	7.6	6.0	13.4	14.0	79 760	194	9 684	164 827	9.7
Redding, CA	3 635	0.2	D	3.8	6.8	9.9	4.6	18.5	22.4	44 875	253	9 850	77 313	12.4
Reno-Sparks, NV	11 820	0.0	D	7.1	D	NA	D	NA	17.5	68 840	162	5 871	186 831	28.4
Richmond, VA	39 192	0.1	D	NA	D	5.4	D	NA	20.6	210 840	168	25 782	531 648	17.4
Riverside-San Bernardino-Ontario, CA	72 835	0.7	16.2	7.8	6.4	8.3	4.8	10.7	25.5	549 460	130	125 914	1 500 344	26.5
Roanoke, VA	8 650	0.0	D	NA	D	6.8	7.2	D	15.7	68 150	221	7 322	144 987	11.9
Rochester, MN	6 542	1.1	D	13.5	D	4.7	3.2	NA	9.7	30 580	164	2 438	78 439	20.4
Rochester, NY	29 155	0.5	D	17.1	10.8	5.8	4.9	NA	17.0	212 215	201	30 783	455 397	6.6
Rockford, IL	7 884	0.3	30.0	24.6	5.4	6.3	6.0	16.3	13.0	65 880	189	7 354	145 935	12.4
Rocky Mount, NC	3 095	3.0	D	21.7	6.6	7.6	3.7	D	18.1	32 060	210	6 193	67 124	9.9
Rome, GA	2 064	0.6	D	17.1	6.2	6.1	4.0	24.0	17.4	20 185	210	2 973	40 551	10.7

1. Includes mining, construction, and manufacturing.   2. Per 1,000 resident population enumerated in the 2010 census.

Table C. Metropolitan Areas — Housing, Labor Force, and Employment

Area name	Housing units, 2010 — Occupied units — Owner-occupied — Total	Percent	Median value[1]	Median owner cost as a percent of income — With a mortgage	Without a mortgage	Renter-occupied — Median rent[2]	Median rent as a percent of income	Sub-standard units[3] (percent)	Civilian labor force, 2010 — Total	Percent change, 2009–2010	Unemployment — Total	Rate[4]	Civilian employment,[5] 2010 — Total	Percent — Management, business, science, and arts occupations	Construction, production, and maintenance occupations
	89	90	91	92	93	94	95	96	97	98	99	100	101	102	103
Naples-Marco Island, FL......	118 258	74.7	255 500	32.2	14.1	942	32.9	4.2	144 557	0.5	17 293	12.0	123 674	29.8	16.8
Nashville-Davidson—Murfreesboro—Franklin, TN	599 775	66.4	173 500	24.3	11.3	783	32.1	2.6	815 569	1.2	70 489	8.6	741 473	37.6	20.1
New Haven-Milford, CT	329 595	63.5	269 200	27.7	19.0	1 015	33.4	2.6	454 652	1.0	45 710	10.1	420 431	39.6	17.4
New Orleans-Metairie-Kenner, LA	451 411	64.1	176 900	24.4	12.2	884	33.2	3.6	544 044	1.9	40 092	7.4	534 683	35.0	21.6
New York-Northern New Jersey-Long Island, NY-NJ-PA	6 800 883	52.2	426 500	29.6	18.1	1 150	32.0	6.7	9 469 921	-0.4	841 717	8.9	8 782 161	40.0	16.4
Edison-New Brunswick, NJ Div............................	850 344	74.8	347 900	28.6	18.8	1 222	32.1	2.8	1 200 115	-0.5	105 236	8.8	1 104 286	42.4	16.7
Nassau-Suffolk, NY Div.....	938 995	79.8	427 300	30.4	19.4	1 390	34.4	2.7	1 474 285	-0.5	109 146	7.4	1 361 183	40.6	16.8
Newark-Union, NJ-PA Div.	761 447	63.4	381 000	29.0	18.5	1 067	32.0	5.3	1 086 819	-1.0	101 321	9.3	1 001 946	40.3	18.1
New York-White Plains-Wayne, NY-NJ Div........	4 250 097	39.5	475 800	30.0	17.1	1 139	31.9	8.7	5 708 702	-0.2	526 014	9.2	5 314 746	39.3	15.9
Niles-Benton Harbor, MI	59 915	73.7	130 500	23.1	13.4	586	32.8	NA	76 713	0.1	9 455	12.3	66 786	31.5	21.7
North Port-Bradenton-Sarasota, FL	289 448	74.1	173 000	29.9	14.5	913	34.2	2.4	303 659	-0.4	37 079	12.2	274 268	32.9	17.5
Norwich-New London, CT.....	106 808	68.5	265 000	25.6	16.0	955	29.3	2.3	150 822	0.2	13 139	8.7	133 119	37.3	18.4
Ocala, FL	131 753	78.4	118 100	30.0	14.1	821	35.7	3.3	135 005	-0.4	18 671	13.8	113 661	28.5	20.9
Ocean City, NJ	42 763	76.1	327 300	27.8	19.6	1 007	33.7	NA	58 308	1.2	6 939	11.9	43 681	34.3	18.3
Odessa, TX	48 630	62.4	88 000	22.9	10.1	638	27.6	8.0	72 680	1.8	5 660	7.8	62 517	23.3	33.3
Ogden-Clearfield, UT	177 989	74.0	209 900	23.7	10.0	784	27.8	2.4	264 298	-1.0	20 497	7.8	245 945	36.8	22.5
Oklahoma City, OK	474 558	66.2	127 400	22.6	11.2	713	30.4	2.8	568 903	0.5	37 523	6.6	584 588	35.1	20.7
Olympia, WA	99 869	65.9	250 200	26.2	12.4	934	28.2	1.8	130 969	-0.5	10 793	8.2	110 855	41.4	17.8
Omaha-Council Bluffs, NE-IA..	334 319	67.9	146 100	22.1	12.4	753	29.3	1.9	446 673	-0.6	23 064	5.2	447 432	37.4	18.9
Orlando-Kissimmee-Sanford, FL	748 210	65.0	169 000	29.6	13.9	976	36.2	2.3	1 121 746	1.1	128 374	11.4	982 276	34.8	16.4
Oshkosh-Neenah, WI............	67 793	67.1	141 200	22.9	13.2	620	26.0	1.9	95 331	0.1	6 876	7.2	84 739	28.0	27.1
Owensboro, KY	44 507	70.3	101 400	21.5	10.2	561	27.1	NA	58 082	0.7	5 425	9.3	49 402	27.4	33.8
Oxnard-Thousand Oaks-Ventura, CA.........................	265 904	64.0	458 200	29.5	11.3	1 381	32.9	6.4	430 924	0.2	46 607	10.8	387 454	37.2	19.8
Palm Bay-Melbourne-Titusville, FL	221 945	75.0	149 100	26.4	12.8	873	32.8	2.0	268 149	0.2	30 930	11.5	227 358	39.3	17.6
Palm Coast, FL	35 218	81.5	172 800	30.4	14.2	1 000	38.2	2.7	33 498	2.2	5 186	15.5	31 840	34.9	14.3
Panama City-Lynn Haven-Panama City Beach, FL...	63 654	63.6	163 600	26.4	12.5	919	32.9	2.9	90 215	1.2	9 249	10.3	75 029	31.5	19.7
Parkersburg-Marietta-Vienna, WV-OH	65 240	76.7	100 600	20.7	10.3	570	30.2	1.8	76 265	-3.0	7 350	9.6	66 383	29.9	28.0
Pascagoula, MS	57 593	74.3	116 600	24.0	10.4	812	31.0	4.1	73 937	3.5	7 034	9.5	65 924	28.4	32.8
Pensacola-Ferry Pass-Brent, FL..........................	165 645	69.8	148 300	27.5	11.9	825	32.8	1.9	211 236	1.6	22 214	10.5	177 676	33.5	17.1
Peoria, IL...............................	150 898	73.3	128 900	21.2	12.1	658	30.3	1.4	203 733	1.4	20 812	10.2	171 516	37.3	23.4
Philadelphia-Camden-Wilmington, PA-NJ-DE-MD.	2 220 711	68.6	246 300	25.7	15.5	945	32.8	2.0	2 955 611	-1.0	266 235	9.0	2 781 740	41.4	16.6
Camden, NJ Div..............	458 638	74.3	236 600	27.3	18.1	996	34.3	1.7	665 389	-0.7	65 681	9.9	597 982	40.0	17.2
Philadelphia, PA Div.........	1 501 715	66.7	250 200	25.3	15.2	929	32.5	2.1	1 947 193	-0.9	169 650	8.7	1 846 818	42.0	16.0
Wilmington, DE-MD-NJ Div...................................	260 358	70.0	250 000	24.5	12.8	962	32.0	2.5	343 029	-2.5	30 904	9.0	336 940	40.0	18.8
Phoenix-Mesa-Glendale, AZ....	1 503 107	64.3	172 900	26.5	11.3	883	31.7	4.7	2 126 253	0.6	196 344	9.2	1 806 646	36.3	18.2
Pine Bluff, AR	35 976	63.3	73 200	20.4	12.5	615	30.8	NA	44 006	-1.2	4 263	9.7	38 218	25.3	30.8
Pittsburgh, PA	978 959	70.4	122 200	21.3	13.2	656	28.8	1.0	1 212 590	-0.6	97 397	8.0	1 102 914	37.3	19.8
Pittsfield, MA	56 517	66.2	204 000	25.5	16.1	730	29.7	NA	73 531	0.4	6 039	8.2	61 667	36.8	19.6
Pocatello, ID	31 856	69.5	144 100	23.4	10.0	575	27.2	NA	43 488	2.3	3 730	8.6	39 426	31.4	25.7
Portland-South Portland-Biddeford, ME	209 787	72.1	235 500	24.8	14.1	833	29.5	2.7	288 116	0.3	19 703	6.8	265 337	40.4	18.6
Portland-Vancouver-Hillsboro, OR-WA	857 389	61.8	271 700	27.5	13.2	867	31.2	3.7	1 189 828	0.4	126 187	10.6	1 038 699	39.3	18.8
Port St. Lucie, FL.................	165 072	75.6	144 900	31.8	14.7	908	33.1	1.7	189 632	1.4	25 287	13.3	166 093	30.9	20.3
Poughkeepsie-Newburgh-Middletown, NY............	231 561	69.8	292 200	28.7	17.5	1 053	32.4	3.5	322 495	-0.7	26 105	8.1	308 040	37.4	19.3
Prescott, AZ	90 607	69.0	188 600	29.7	11.9	782	33.3	4.9	98 213	-1.0	10 283	10.5	79 070	31.4	17.6
Providence-New Bedford-Fall River, RI-MA	612 291	61.3	266 700	27.5	15.6	831	31.0	2.3	870 156	1.2	99 806	11.5	746 445	39.1	19.9
Provo-Orem, UT...................	143 324	69.4	223 000	26.1	10.0	797	32.9	4.9	227 110	-0.6	17 649	7.8	218 095	39.5	17.8
Pueblo, CO	62 686	67.5	141 200	25.4	11.8	642	36.0	1.8	74 737	-0.2	7 756	10.4	64 170	29.1	22.2
Punta Gorda, FL	69 176	77.8	147 800	32.3	14.1	931	33.9	1.2	69 969	1.4	8 684	12.4	53 046	35.3	16.2
Racine, WI	74 808	69.2	177 600	25.1	14.7	719	31.4	1.8	98 046	-1.4	9 790	10.0	89 471	34.0	26.7
Raleigh-Cary, NC..................	421 955	68.0	207 800	22.9	11.6	851	29.2	2.7	561 912	-0.2	48 719	8.7	553 176	46.0	15.1
Rapid City, SD	51 016	64.9	151 700	23.6	12.6	739	28.0	2.6	66 766	-0.5	3 364	5.0	61 355	33.9	19.8
Reading, PA..........................	155 329	71.3	175 700	24.6	14.5	785	32.7	2.1	202 918	-0.2	18 689	9.2	193 364	33.0	26.1
Redding, CA..........................	67 909	65.8	225 600	32.7	13.0	885	37.6	3.1	83 887	-0.2	13 422	16.0	64 021	33.1	18.1
Reno-Sparks, NV..................	164 809	57.9	215 900	28.3	13.0	873	32.1	4.0	222 995	-0.4	31 544	14.1	195 413	33.3	18.5
Richmond, VA........................	475 685	68.8	227 400	24.7	11.4	903	31.3	2.5	655 119	-0.3	50 624	7.7	594 613	39.9	18.4
Riverside-San Bernardino-Ontario, CA...................	1 265 050	65.7	225 600	31.1	12.6	1 078	36.4	9.1	1 769 461	-0.3	256 206	14.5	1 646 193	28.1	25.4
Roanoke, VA.........................	129 280	71.0	176 300	25.6	11.8	704	27.8	2.2	157 307	-0.5	11 645	7.4	143 591	36.5	21.2
Rochester, MN	72 998	78.0	169 600	22.6	10.2	715	29.7	1.1	105 512	0.3	6 455	6.1	99 397	43.3	18.6
Rochester, NY.......................	414 096	68.5	127 400	22.4	14.4	735	32.1	1.8	527 430	-0.6	42 717	8.1	494 082	39.6	20.0
Rockford, IL...........................	129 937	70.8	136 100	24.4	14.2	691	31.9	1.8	172 771	1.6	26 379	15.3	151 311	30.1	26.4
Rocky Mount, NC..................	59 832	64.0	99 500	23.0	16.1	706	31.9	3.2	70 652	-1.3	9 483	13.4	64 280	26.2	30.3
Rome, GA..............................	35 634	64.3	112 600	24.8	13.9	703	33.5	3.3	48 307	-2.0	5 154	10.7	37 769	32.3	24.8

1. Specified owner-occupied units. 2. Specified renter-occupied units. A value of 10.0 represents 10 percent or less. 3. Overcrowded or lacking complete plumbing facilities. 4. Percent of civilian labor force. 5. Persons 16 years old and over.

Table C. Metropolitan Areas — **Nonfarm Employment and Agriculture**

Area name	Private nonfarm establishments, employment and payroll, 2009									Agriculture, 2007			
		Employment						Annual payroll		Farms			
												Percent with:	
	Number of establishments	Total	Health care and social assistance	Manufacturing	Retail trade	Finance and insurance	Professional, scientific, and technical services	Total (mil dol)	Average per employee (dollars)	Number	Fewer than 50 acres	500 acres or more	Farm operators whose principal occupation is farming (percent)
	104	105	106	107	108	109	110	111	112	113	114	115	116
Naples-Marco Island, FL.......	9 860	101 535	15 124	2 485	17 988	3 737	5 096	3 657	36 012	322	70.5	9.9	53.1
Nashville-Davidson—Murfreesboro—Franklin, TN	37 883	669 162	101 537	59 675	80 726	38 987	36 330	28 308	42 304	14 063	45.7	3.6	37.0
New Haven-Milford, CT	19 893	327 054	70 574	36 209	42 257	12 260	16 064	14 635	44 749	573	70.5	1.4	50.6
New Orleans-Metairie-Kenner, LA	29 100	455 195	69 845	30 589	59 309	18 754	30 899	18 763	41 220	986	64.7	9.8	47.0
New York-Northern New Jersey-Long Island, NY-NJ-PA....................	531 446	7 390 128	1 296 063	363 414	819 413	580 364	678 832	445 399	60 269	6 110	78.5	2.0	43.9
Edison-New Brunswick, NJ Div	NA	NA	NA	NA	NA	NA	NA	NA	NA	1 868	83.1	2.5	44.5
Nassau-Suffolk, NY Div.....	NA	NA	NA	NA	NA	NA	NA	NA	NA	644	75.5	1.1	62.3
Newark-Union, NJ-PA Div.	NA	NA	NA	NA	NA	NA	NA	NA	NA	3 187	75.6	2.0	39.6
New York-White Plains-Wayne, NY-NJ Div........	NA	NA	NA	NA	NA	NA	NA	NA	NA	411	84.9	1.2	46.2
Niles-Benton Harbor, MI	3 736	51 686	8 985	8 466	7 003	1 280	2 001	1 839	35 584	1 300	57.8	5.5	49.1
North Port-Bradenton-Sarasota, FL......................	19 900	202 921	37 743	12 987	36 720	8 565	11 956	6 795	33 484	1 099	67.8	8.2	43.7
Norwich-New London, CT.....	5 878	104 745	16 307	D	14 072	2 194	5 785	4 323	41 272	793	58.9	1.5	44.6
Ocala, FL	6 890	76 897	14 071	6 235	15 166	4 685	3 757	2 349	30 547	3 496	81.9	1.9	50.6
Ocean City, NJ.....................	3 869	24 315	4 572	459	5 337	1 104	1 074	896	36 864	201	80.6	1.0	50.7
Odessa, TX	3 248	50 980	7 600	3 878	7 167	1 422	2 099	1 945	38 152	301	74.4	13.0	29.2
Ogden-Clearfield, UT	11 484	146 973	19 449	19 572	24 242	7 881	10 545	4 677	31 819	1 813	75.3	4.3	34.5
Oklahoma City, OK	32 898	465 006	73 589	30 603	60 592	25 405	28 743	16 989	36 534	10 772	35.8	11.7	39.6
Olympia, WA........................	5 858	64 807	11 285	2 628	11 841	2 710	5 357	2 222	34 286	1 288	76.9	2.0	40.5
Omaha-Council Bluffs, NE-IA.........................	22 066	395 884	54 190	32 357	51 118	36 875	34 585	15 758	39 805	5 783	33.6	24.5	54.7
Orlando-Kissimmee-Sanford, FL......................	55 166	867 848	101 920	37 595	117 249	37 236	63 905	31 906	36 765	3 415	80.0	4.1	43.0
Oshkosh-Neenah, WI...........	3 628	82 414	13 919	22 501	7 645	2 948	2 304	3 408	41 348	1 001	39.6	8.1	44.5
Owensboro, KY	2 577	44 576	8 072	8 268	6 207	2 127	1 090	1 490	33 437	1 810	37.2	11.6	45.1
Oxnard-Thousand Oaks-Ventura, CA........................	19 677	245 788	31 025	24 862	37 200	16 689	21 219	10 889	44 303	2 437	77.8	4.1	47.7
Palm Bay-Melbourne-Titusville, FL......................	13 005	165 707	26 491	19 994	25 074	5 538	13 099	6 637	40 052	531	79.8	4.9	46.7
Palm Coast, FL	1 781	16 572	2 065	755	3 156	560	443	442	26 682	82	47.6	24.4	53.7
Panama City-Lynn Haven-Panama City Beach, FL....	4 510	54 350	9 161	3 285	10 226	2 658	3 310	1 707	31 406	133	69.2	2.3	38.3
Parkersburg-Marietta-Vienna, WV-OH..............	3 784	58 011	11 707	8 088	9 410	2 658	1 570	1 807	31 144	2 242	28.4	2.4	39.2
Pascagoula, MS	2 678	52 086	5 954	D	6 251	1 187	1 872	2 155	41 370	1 058	58.1	2.6	38.8
Pensacola-Ferry Pass-Brent, FL.........................	9 124	118 922	21 742	4 115	19 765	5 900	7 391	3 852	32 390	1 319	58.3	4.7	36.0
Peoria, IL............................	8 756	164 611	28 492	21 114	19 335	6 876	7 193	7 127	43 298	3 679	33.9	21.6	52.4
Philadelphia-Camden-Wilmington, PA-NJ-DE-MD.	145 714	2 480 290	442 351	189 488	300 008	177 582	205 901	122 084	49 222	6 987	66.2	4.1	48.9
Camden, NJ Div	NA	NA	NA	NA	NA	NA	NA	NA	NA	1 816	76.8	3.4	46.3
Philadelphia, PA Div..........	NA	NA	NA	NA	NA	NA	NA	NA	NA	3 482	64.2	2.9	49.2
Wilmington, DE-MD-NJ Div........................	NA	NA	NA	NA	NA	NA	NA	NA	NA	1 689	58.8	7.5	51.2
Phoenix-Mesa-Glendale, AZ....	89 014	1 497 003	196 412	102 312	212 911	110 673	90 924	62 121	41 497	2 578	71.2	12.5	51.2
Pine Bluff, AR	1 724	26 393	5 271	6 058	3 931	928	1 319	849	32 159	1 114	35.6	19.7	53.9
Pittsburgh, PA	59 426	1 042 405	186 280	93 673	129 223	56 348	74 213	42 541	40 810	7 926	39.8	2.8	39.7
Pittsfield, MA	4 088	55 460	11 857	5 195	8 699	2 091	D	2 009	36 216	522	49.8	4.8	48.7
Pocatello, ID.......................	2 202	29 074	6 045	2 903	4 774	1 590	1 309	776	26 687	1 273	43.4	24.7	39.6
Portland-South Portland-Biddeford, ME	17 292	221 349	42 998	23 502	32 782	15 472	13 806	8 466	38 246	1 521	55.1	2.1	43.9
Portland-Vancouver-Hillsboro, OR-WA	62 363	879 302	119 625	95 345	103 319	45 076	60 706	38 759	44 079	11 457	78.7	2.0	41.0
Port St. Lucie, FL.................	9 862	100 378	17 787	4 852	21 857	3 481	5 016	3 204	31 915	857	67.4	11.2	44.3
Poughkeepsie-Newburgh-Middletown, NY..............	16 734	195 066	37 202	19 771	35 568	6 961	9 248	7 511	38 506	1 298	46.3	5.2	58.3
Prescott, AZ	5 875	53 702	10 815	2 649	10 926	1 382	1 674	1 544	28 759	756	63.0	13.8	46.2
Providence-New Bedford-Fall River, RI-MA	41 431	608 402	119 322	74 263	80 830	33 683	29 162	24 010	39 464	1 996	69.7	0.7	49.5
Provo-Orem, UT..................	10 806	157 453	19 098	15 690	22 976	4 576	13 081	5 209	33 083	2 510	69.4	8.2	33.5
Pueblo, CO	3 193	46 927	11 707	3 736	7 722	1 368	1 427	1 484	31 618	881	41.2	23.7	38.7
Punta Gorda, FL	3 539	40 953	7 990	400	7 998	1 197	1 244	1 076	26 267	242	57.9	13.6	49.2
Racine, WI	4 094	65 755	10 657	13 607	8 560	2 486	2 364	2 463	37 461	652	53.7	7.5	44.6
Raleigh-Cary, NC................	28 660	420 422	56 834	24 047	57 264	20 859	37 454	17 372	41 319	2 665	49.9	6.6	46.6
Rapid City, SD	4 231	49 534	9 789	2 779	8 983	2 791	1 986	1 592	32 130	1 534	18.8	49.1	55.6
Reading, PA	8 413	144 462	23 753	28 407	20 339	6 840	6 217	5 704	39 486	1 980	49.5	4.0	54.5
Redding, CA	4 428	47 789	10 415	2 335	9 236	2 198	2 125	1 582	33 101	1 473	69.5	8.5	46.8
Reno-Sparks, NV	12 106	173 472	21 440	13 726	22 635	6 192	10 037	6 688	38 555	398	67.6	6.0	37.7
Richmond, VA	31 379	505 999	71 762	37 782	67 547	48 779	32 072	21 681	42 849	4 330	42.1	8.7	41.3
Riverside-San Bernardino-Ontario, CA	65 921	999 660	135 704	99 136	162 244	29 166	33 615	34 018	34 030	4 868	85.8	2.8	48.1
Roanoke, VA.......................	8 353	141 793	24 276	17 544	18 134	11 120	6 567	5 061	35 693	2 219	37.4	6.1	42.5
Rochester, MN	4 428	86 945	D	11 180	11 790	2 129	2 314	3 499	40 245	3 083	33.1	13.2	49.5
Rochester, NY.....................	23 465	419 313	70 888	58 030	56 686	15 146	23 312	15 986	38 124	3 728	40.1	10.2	54.8
Rockford, IL	7 610	131 890	20 980	28 832	16 676	4 877	4 728	4 692	35 578	1 400	56.1	13.4	48.9
Rocky Mount, NC.................	3 014	52 808	8 231	11 303	7 238	2 344	1 317	1 740	32 942	787	39.3	17.5	53.0
Rome, GA	1 964	34 138	7 890	6 498	4 360	959	850	1 089	31 906	553	42.0	6.5	40.0

Table C. Metropolitan Areas — **Agriculture**

	Agriculture, 2007 (cont.)														
	Land in farms				Value of land and buildings (dollars)			Value of products sold				Percent of farms with sales of:		Government payments	
			Acres				Value of machinery and equipment, average per farm (dollars)			Percent from:					
Area name	Acreage (1,000)	Percent change, 2002–2007	Average size of farm	Total irrigated (1,000)	Total cropland (1,000)	Average per farm	Average per acre		Total (mil dol)	Average per farm (dollars)	Crops	Live-stock and poultry products	$10,000 or more	$100,000 or more	Total ($1,000)	Percent of farms
	117	118	119	120	121	122	123	124	125	126	127	128	129	130	131	132
Naples-Marco Island, FL	110	-39.2	341	31.4	69.9	2 039 523	5 974	87 700	278.8	865 907	98.5	1.5	40.7	20.5	132	4.3
Nashville-Davidson—Murfreesboro—Franklin, TN	1 701	-12.3	121	6.4	786.1	473 528	3 914	53 869	285.1	20 270	47.4	52.6	24.0	3.2	4 289	14.6
New Haven-Milford, CT	46	76.9	80	1.5	13.8	1 061 198	13 310	64 600	90.2	157 370	90.3	9.7	36.8	12.7	344	6.1
New Orleans-Metairie-Kenner, LA	228	D	231	D	D	D	D	D	D	D	D	57.3	31.2	7.8	1 041	9.5
New York-Northern New Jersey-Long Island, NY-NJ-PA	369	D	60	D	D	D	D	D	594.2	97 267	84.8	15.0	32.4	11.1	D	5.7
Edison-New Brunswick, NJ Div	105	-10.3	56	10.1	65.3	1 217 607	21 579	64 385	177.7	95 125	78.5	21.5	33.5	10.3	708	4.6
Nassau-Suffolk, NY Div.	36	2.9	55	13.8	26.6	1 165 722	21 034	174 458	258.7	401 758	91.5	8.5	69.9	37.0	253	8.5
Newark-Union, NJ-PA Div.	210	D	66	2.9	111.8	1 068 544	16 203	48 059	123.9	38 913	81.5	18.5	23.5	5.6	D	6.3
New York-White Plains-Wayne, NY-NJ Div.	17	D	42	D	D	D	D	D	33.9	82 387	78.1	17.9	38.4	17.0	D	1.7
Niles-Benton Harbor, MI	169	-2.9	130	18.4	138.6	600 093	4 616	102 068	136.3	104 815	90.5	9.5	47.3	17.0	2 241	27.4
North Port-Bradenton-Sarasota, FL	286	-32.4	260	53.1	86.0	1 695 414	6 512	71 523	342.8	311 954	D	D	36.8	14.3	90	0.8
Norwich-New London, CT	63	6.8	80	0.6	25.1	953 549	11 931	52 855	110.1	138 799	46.5	53.5	29.8	8.1	479	9.6
Ocala, FL	267	-1.5	76	9.7	59.9	725 733	9 518	46 830	173.7	49 697	15.7	84.3	22.6	5.9	476	1.3
Ocean City, NJ	8	-20.0	40	2.3	4.3	637 097	16 055	59 369	14.6	72 567	96.2	3.8	35.8	8.0	20	4.0
Odessa, TX	424	-15.9	1 408	1.1	7.0	560 521	398	43 889	3.6	11 824	27.5	72.5	15.3	3.3	109	4.3
Ogden-Clearfield, UT	457	D	252	55.7	67.0	663 693	2 635	60 361	81.8	45 119	54.5	45.5	25.0	6.3	781	8.7
Oklahoma City, OK	2 665	3.1	247	22.0	1 001.8	396 265	1 601	56 498	413.5	38 386	21.5	78.5	31.1	5.4	11 165	23.2
Olympia, WA	81	9.5	63	6.9	26.3	535 414	8 554	56 688	117.9	91 526	36.5	63.5	18.9	4.7	297	2.8
Omaha-Council Bluffs, NE-IA	2 159	-11.4	373	D	1 877.8	1 154 999	3 094	138 136	1 102.6	190 674	67.9	32.1	58.8	33.9	36 293	71.9
Orlando-Kissimmee-Sanford, FL	939	-6.8	275	60.1	104.3	1 209 527	4 397	50 079	570.1	166 958	D	D	42.1	13.6	D	0.8
Oshkosh-Neenah, WI	164	-3.5	164	0.3	133.3	563 264	3 438	93 394	107.8	107 654	28.6	71.4	45.2	19.2	2 690	69.9
Owensboro, KY	464	2.7	256	D	357.1	744 187	2 902	97 802	289.3	159 815	47.8	52.2	43.0	17.6	5 154	55.5
Oxnard-Thousand Oaks-Ventura, CA	259	-22.0	106	91.3	113.9	2 421 700	22 782	95 150	1 316.3	540 137	99.0	1.0	62.2	25.2	554	1.9
Palm Bay-Melbourne-Titusville, FL	167	-11.2	315	20.5	22.1	1 238 223	3 936	56 362	46.7	87 913	85.2	14.8	50.1	9.0	21	1.5
Palm Coast, FL	58	-14.7	712	6.8	8.7	2 833 332	3 979	88 146	35.1	428 537	97.6	2.4	43.9	20.7	27	4.9
Panama City-Lynn Haven-Panama City Beach, FL	12	9.1	94	D	2.7	718 873	7 667	33 325	5.0	37 812	92.3	7.7	19.5	2.3	5	4.5
Parkersburg-Marietta-Vienna, WV-OH	280	-0.7	125	D	95.2	286 437	2 293	42 158	D	D	38.2	D	17.8	2.5	D	10.6
Pascagoula, MS	110	3.8	104	0.9	41.8	330 052	3 186	57 467	25.4	24 009	64.8	35.2	24.2	4.2	2 012	15.0
Pensacola-Ferry Pass-Brent, FL	152	2.7	115	5.1	85.6	602 464	5 223	52 955	52.7	39 967	84.5	15.5	24.6	6.7	6 999	40.0
Peoria, IL	1 251	-1.4	340	37.4	1 137.3	1 382 199	4 064	133 647	676.2	183 812	86.8	13.2	61.9	35.8	23 316	75.7
Philadelphia-Camden-Wilmington, PA-NJ-DE-MD.	679	D	97	D	489.0	1 056 233	10 868	89 344	1 084.2	155 149	D	D	39.9	16.4	D	16.7
Camden, NJ Div	141	-18.0	78	28.2	93.4	1 037 852	13 347	70 900	198.8	109 438	94.1	5.9	36.9	13.1	1 473	8.1
Philadelphia, PA Div.	289	D	83	D	205.5	871 207	10 486	92 411	663.9	190 647	D	D	41.1	18.4	D	16.0
Wilmington, DE-MD-NJ Div	249	1.6	147	21.8	190.1	1 457 443	9 904	102 852	221.5	131 115	D	D	40.6	15.7	4 005	27.4
Phoenix-Mesa-Glendale, AZ	1 533	-14.3	594	414.5	523.3	3 078 081	5 177	154 163	1 613.3	625 796	39.1	60.9	36.4	19.1	34 774	16.6
Pine Bluff, AR	520	1.8	467	D	400.2	1 036 953	2 221	161 530	455.3	408 683	38.4	61.6	47.5	30.0	15 857	44.2
Pittsburgh, PA	876	-3.5	111	2.4	484.0	469 623	4 247	62 321	228.4	28 817	50.5	49.5	26.0	5.6	4 518	18.1
Pittsfield, MA	66	-4.3	127	0.2	22.6	1 113 751	8 762	54 632	20.6	39 466	37.5	62.5	28.4	8.2	205	6.1
Pocatello, ID	773	-1.2	607	153.3	536.0	749 754	1 235	102 779	198.4	155 841	77.3	22.7	28.6	12.1	11 923	42.2
Portland-South Portland-Biddeford, ME	130	-1.5	85	1.7	46.9	398 209	4 671	56 909	43.3	28 439	D	D	27.5	7.3	641	7.6
Portland-Vancouver-Hillsboro, OR-WA	662	-7.4	58	95.1	389.4	631 364	10 932	59 345	D	D	D	D	26.3	8.3	3 387	6.6
Port St. Lucie, FL	283	-33.9	330	117.8	114.6	2 016 864	6 111	74 821	302.8	353 315	88.7	11.3	43.8	18.9	473	4.7
Poughkeepsie-Newburgh-Middletown, NY	183	-16.8	141	5.9	93.2	762 975	5 402	95 761	118.6	91 382	62.9	37.1	49.0	18.3	1 161	18.6
Prescott, AZ	639	-11.3	845	7.9	25.3	1 503 944	1 779	52 064	D	D	D	D	26.2	5.0	282	3.6
Providence-New Bedford-Fall River, RI-MA	107	10.3	54	6.2	39.7	885 545	16 508	61 580	110.1	55 186	83.7	16.3	36.5	9.8	1 298	8.2
Provo-Orem, UT	606	-1.1	241	104.6	183.5	710 678	2 943	66 251	201.5	80 297	38.3	61.7	28.8	6.3	2 550	14.5
Pueblo, CO	911	17.7	1 034	24.6	73.5	692 240	670	68 533	49.3	55 904	32.2	67.8	29.3	8.3	1 667	18.8
Punta Gorda, FL	166	-13.5	686	20.0	28.7	2 224 000	3 241	61 849	65.6	270 921	89.5	10.5	39.7	16.5	306	2.5
Racine, WI	120	-3.2	185	3.5	105.0	883 553	4 782	131 796	101.9	156 324	61.3	38.7	45.1	18.3	2 081	52.8
Raleigh-Cary, NC	392	-5.5	147	14.9	223.3	725 673	4 934	74 020	293.4	110 049	51.6	48.4	32.7	12.0	7 406	34.3
Rapid City, SD	3 394	-1.3	2 212	14.5	800.7	1 254 455	567	104 686	134.4	87 644	28.9	71.1	52.7	22.6	9 241	43.8
Reading, PA	222	2.8	112	1.3	170.8	772 086	6 882	101 016	367.8	185 778	45.0	55.0	52.5	24.8	3 280	33.0
Redding, CA	391	17.1	265	48.7	40.2	837 861	3 158	43 514	44.7	30 329	D	D	22.6	4.1	252	3.8
Reno-Sparks, NV	486	D	1 221	D	19.0	971 262	793	66 029	D	D	D	44.7	21.6	4.5	284	2.0
Richmond, VA	850	NA	196	13.8	412.4	849 890	4 331	78 561	288.8	66 707	D	D	28.8	8.1	8 946	25.0
Riverside-San Bernardino-Ontario, CA	869	-20.0	179	197.0	255.8	1 483 376	8 310	72 148	1 755.7	360 662	49.6	50.4	46.0	15.3	6 980	2.9
Roanoke, VA	325	NA	147	1.0	114.3	614 239	4 189	67 391	77.9	35 114	17.2	82.8	30.1	5.5	1 019	15.6
Rochester, MN	806	-0.9	262	D	635.3	891 032	3 407	130 622	472.1	153 129	48.1	51.9	54.5	28.3	14 620	72.6
Rochester, NY	863	6.7	231	8.8	650.6	497 601	2 151	124 029	649.8	174 326	57.8	42.2	47.8	22.1	10 289	37.2
Rockford, IL	321	-5.0	229	2.2	291.4	1 062 738	4 638	98 406	171.3	122 371	83.9	16.1	43.6	23.6	7 779	55.8
Rocky Mount, NC	293	-9.6	373	13.2	198.2	1 105 896	2 967	131 295	290.8	369 551	48.3	51.7	45.5	29.6	8 386	50.6
Rome, GA	85	-6.6	153	1.1	28.0	565 269	3 695	63 954	49.4	89 351	5.9	94.1	26.6	8.0	769	16.8

Table C. Metropolitan Areas — Water Use, Wholesale Trade, Retail Trade, and Real Estate

Area name	Water use, 2005		Wholesale trade,[1] 2007				Retail trade, 2007				Real estate and rental and leasing, 2007			
	Total water withdrawn (mil gal/day)	Gallons withdrawn per person	Number of establishments	Number of employees	Sales (mil dol)	Annual payroll (mil dol)	Number of establishments	Number of employees	Sales (mil dol)	Annual payroll (mil dol)	Number of establishments	Number of employees	Receipts (mil dol)	Annual payroll (mil dol)
	133	134	135	136	137	138	139	140	141	142	143	144	145	146
Naples-Marco Island, FL.......	193.2	608	385	2 933	1 838.1	145.5	1 500	20 122	5 186.5	535.5	958	2 874	552.3	118.0
Nashville-Davidson—Murfreesboro—Franklin, TN	1 212.4	852	2 155	39 397	37 880.7	1 939.0	5 869	84 667	21 088.0	1 997.6	1 846	12 182	2 703.5	420.2
New Haven-Milford, CT	342.7	405	1 130	16 584	12 043.2	939.9	3 172	46 058	11 785.3	1 112.5	780	5 470	1 611.1	192.9
New Orleans-Metairie-Kenner, LA	5 738.2	4 349	1 773	22 985	23 831.4	1 136.4	4 311	61 162	15 554.7	1 496.4	1 268	9 069	1 700.0	318.0
New York-Northern New Jersey-Long Island, NY-NJ-PA...........................	11 840.4	632	40 354	526 717	643 078.2	33 175.4	75 619	856 298	237 554.8	23 310.4	33 481	186 514	57 284.2	9 294.6
Edison-New Brunswick, NJ Div	2 341.1	1 016	4 153	75 469	98 802.1	5 226.4	8 886	129 943	35 419.5	3 348.5	2 375	14 060	3 870.6	603.2
Nassau-Suffolk, NY Div.....	2 059.5	733	7 000	85 309	78 816.5	4 752.1	13 106	168 238	47 632.6	4 491.6	4 314	18 290	4 787.8	825.4
Newark-Union, NJ-PA Div.	196.8	91	3 902	69 907	78 972.4	5 003.3	8 275	101 421	28 129.1	2 673.6	2 477	18 407	4 667.5	938.9
New York-White Plains-Wayne, NY-NJ Div....	7 243.0	631	25 299	296 032	386 487.3	18 193.6	45 352	456 696	126 373.6	12 796.7	24 315	135 757	43 958.3	6 927.1
Niles-Benton Harbor, MI	2 327.2	14 311	171	2 063	1 789.3	77.3	609	7 360	1 622.8	153.9	189	796	105.6	19.3
North Port-Bradenton-Sarasota, FL.............................	182.4	271	955	7 671	4 500.5	333.2	2 927	39 824	9 474.3	943.1	1 479	5 402	929.9	169.3
Norwich-New London, CT.....	2 259.1	8 473	174	2 286	1 698.6	120.1	1 123	15 660	3 883.0	390.4	232	D	D	D
Ocala, FL..............................	54.4	179	370	4 691	2 421.0	182.3	1 208	16 639	4 218.8	379.2	466	1 598	217.9	39.9
Ocean City, NJ......................	217.6	2 191	71	D	D	D	746	6 103	1 584.9	164.8	258	836	177.1	27.0
Odessa, TX...........................	64.0	511	319	4 654	2 324.3	247.5	476	6 660	2 090.6	167.6	157	1 383	338.4	74.3
Ogden-Clearfield, UT...........	437.4	874	502	6 539	4 660.3	261.8	1 517	24 999	6 070.9	537.6	752	2 215	322.2	50.7
Oklahoma City, OK...............	204.6	177	1 770	25 698	36 154.4	1 182.1	4 391	61 143	15 683.4	1 371.5	1 650	10 607	1 631.5	370.3
Olympia, WA........................	46.2	202	203	2 083	1 227.6	100.1	822	12 136	3 103.0	313.2	323	1 234	238.8	31.6
Omaha-Council Bluffs, NE-IA..	2 087.6	2 567	1 376	20 154	20 914.4	1 059.6	2 857	51 994	13 053.0	1 153.4	1 018	6 713	1 146.9	215.1
Orlando-Kissimmee-Sanford, FL.........................	559.3	286	3 281	42 454	48 564.7	2 007.3	8 295	126 325	32 378.4	2 870.5	4 241	36 652	7 857.9	1 398.3
Oshkosh-Neenah, WI............	76.6	480	184	3 375	1 487.3	137.1	540	8 027	1 796.5	162.1	125	756	97.5	19.6
Owensboro, KY.....................	491.6	4 405	117	1 452	933.7	52.5	488	6 298	1 359.0	129.7	85	537	51.3	11.2
Oxnard-Thousand Oaks-Ventura, CA..............................	1 198.6	1 506	1 170	17 854	34 976.8	1 218.5	2 766	40 773	11 083.6	1 074.8	1 051	5 064	1 006.1	196.0
Palm Bay-Melbourne-Titusville, FL	957.3	1 799	606	4 267	2 639.7	179.3	2 073	28 911	6 594.0	630.4	777	2 795	401.1	74.8
Palm Coast, FL.....................	19.3	245	59	298	92.9	10.9	208	2 899	684.1	66.3	195	508	66.9	13.8
Panama City-Lynn Haven-Panama City Beach, FL...	291.9	1 805	193	1 736	868.3	72.1	816	10 186	2 472.0	227.1	314	1 172	167.7	88.8
Parkersburg-Marietta-Vienna, WV-OH	1 113.5	6 851	181	1 709	1 045.4	54.8	711	9 986	2 425.5	194.1	135	667	117.0	18.1
Pascagoula, MS....................	57.7	367	71	926	318.6	19.5	534	6 244	1 536.6	132.4	114	388	50.5	9.6
Pensacola-Ferry Pass-Brent, FL......................................	358.0	813	415	4 592	2 718.6	182.1	1 596	21 249	5 163.6	471.0	591	2 008	333.3	55.7
Peoria, IL..............................	676.4	1 832	490	8 246	16 183.5	445.1	1 404	20 008	4 598.1	430.9	352	1 589	259.4	42.4
Philadelphia-Camden-Wilmington, PA-NJ-DE-MD.	5 258.7	903	8 743	144 877	160 429.2	9 316.9	20 970	316 013	84 725.2	7 790.6	5 693	43 149	19 440.1	1 911.9
Camden, NJ Div.............	235.2	189	1 802	D	D	D	4 494	69 542	17 217.0	1 694.6	1 046	D	D	D
Philadelphia, PA Div.........	1 814.1	466	6 137	91 849	87 723.7	6 056.8	13 900	207 225	57 105.7	5 162.6	3 686	D	D	D
Wilmington, DE-MD-NJ Div...................................	3 209.4	4 671	804	D	D	D	2 576	39 246	10 402.5	933.5	961	4 251	10 805.6	167.8
Phoenix-Mesa-Glendale, AZ.	3 256.2	842	5 216	83 170	75 372.4	4 476.5	11 992	226 298	60 721.4	5 507.8	6 325	38 676	7 904.0	1 582.1
Pine Bluff, AR	556.6	5 308	79	D	D	D	363	4 353	937.2	84.6	83	259	47.9	6.8
Pittsburgh, PA	2 311.9	969	3 251	46 323	51 610.7	2 308.7	8 858	132 058	32 663.5	2 755.0	2 016	13 928	2 677.3	508.2
Pittsfield, MA	35.6	270	124	1 334	529.3	58.1	766	8 942	1 901.8	208.8	128	770	123.3	22.9
Pocatello, ID.........................	747.1	8 697	95	864	557.6	32.0	373	5 185	1 149.7	101.6	103	350	54.0	7.1
Portland-South Portland-Biddeford, ME	253.2	492	775	9 597	6 901.6	435.9	2 637	34 309	7 984.1	803.3	900	3 763	622.5	126.8
Portland-Vancouver-Hillsboro, OR-WA	787.1	376	4 056	57 847	62 236.2	3 234.9	7 404	113 736	29 223.1	2 847.1	3 702	20 226	3 772.1	729.1
Port St. Lucie, FL.................	1 491.0	3 912	524	3 753	2 145.5	159.2	1 514	24 047	6 168.1	578.3	653	2 609	377.2	72.5
Poughkeepsie-Newburgh-Middletown, NY.............	893.8	1 338	771	11 008	9 421.6	523.3	2 681	36 977	9 328.4	873.6	811	3 435	667.5	108.3
Prescott, AZ	91.5	460	201	1 728	886.6	63.9	920	11 795	2 695.4	266.6	469	1 776	293.9	55.4
Providence-New Bedford-Fall River, RI-MA	1 462.2	901	2 123	34 240	24 749.2	1 829.5	6 499	87 944	20 934.2	2 061.9	1 705	8 944	1 844.9	297.8
Provo-Orem, UT....................	476.2	1 024	476	6 412	3 188.4	292.2	1 391	24 306	5 884.3	523.1	755	2 462	334.4	60.1
Pueblo, CO	301.3	1 991	96	959	472.8	41.6	548	8 064	1 864.6	192.4	165	667	94.9	18.3
Punta Gorda, FL	40.1	260	114	658	279.3	25.1	582	8 761	1 898.1	187.9	289	877	120.7	22.1
Racine, WI	42.3	216	213	3 442	4 657.4	166.2	654	10 082	2 230.0	198.7	140	596	64.5	13.4
Raleigh-Cary, NC..................	164.0	173	1 546	22 231	20 942.0	1 361.4	3 899	58 236	14 941.7	1 340.3	1 502	7 839	1 990.0	337.6
Rapid City, SD	44.7	378	208	2 259	1 289.7	90.5	686	8 604	2 162.1	194.1	187	771	128.2	18.1
Reading, PA	61.0	154	448	7 216	7 091.9	358.9	1 327	20 433	4 953.2	466.8	273	1 384	210.2	39.4
Redding, CA	236.2	1 313	196	1 936	1 166.0	77.5	722	10 287	2 526.4	260.1	225	1 201	128.2	26.1
Reno-Sparks, NV..................	120.6	306	688	11 434	8 716.2	521.2	1 577	25 079	6 674.2	672.1	765	4 008	705.9	129.4
Richmond, VA	4 085.9	3 475	1 756	29 714	27 573.3	1 520.7	4 622	69 570	17 888.3	1 591.0	1 470	9 303	1 929.3	370.1
Riverside-San Bernardino-Ontario, CA	1 843.5	471	4 401	63 310	59 701.7	2 764.3	10 338	173 855	45 863.8	4 276.1	3 960	21 722	4 366.9	731.4
Roanoke, VA.........................	54.3	185	527	7 785	5 305.7	343.0	1 338	18 897	4 121.3	413.8	411	2 288	328.2	61.1
Rochester, MN	55.8	315	176	2 638	1 541.0	140.9	774	11 860	2 484.6	254.6	179	859	120.6	22.2
Rochester, NY.......................	714.5	688	1 305	19 642	11 387.3	1 047.8	3 547	56 071	12 056.1	1 185.1	1 029	7 181	1 158.2	213.5
Rockford, IL..........................	52.0	153	469	5 939	4 056.5	256.1	1 154	17 650	4 306.9	383.0	270	1 653	219.2	47.5
Rocky Mount, NC..................	37.5	258	148	4 535	3 152.0	137.1	636	7 312	1 595.9	144.6	123	533	96.0	13.9
Rome, GA	588.9	6 252	101	1 410	692.1	52.5	431	4 718	1 039.8	94.0	82	353	58.0	10.1

1. Merchant wholesalers, except manufacturers' sales branches and offices.

Table C. Metropolitan Areas — **Professional Services, Manufacturing, and Accommodation and Food Services**

Area name	Professional, scientific, and technical services,[1] 2007				Manufacturing, 2007				Accommodation and food services, 2007			
	Number of establishments	Number of employees	Sales (mil dol)	Annual payroll (mil dol)	Number of establishments	Number of employees	Sales (mil dol)	Annual payroll (mil dol)	Number of establishments	Number of employees	Sales (mil dol)	Annual payroll (mil dol)
	147	148	149	150	151	152	153	154	155	156	157	158
Naples-Marco Island, FL	1 271	D	D	D	228	3 035	606.7	109.5	704	17 421	1 037.2	308.3
Nashville-Davidson—Murfreesboro—Franklin, TN	3 653	D	D	D	1 583	74 547	D	3 135.7	3 096	69 674	3 463.8	987.1
New Haven-Milford, CT	2 015	D	D	D	1 289	40 188	10 493.0	1 976.9	1 920	24 768	1 345.9	371.7
New Orleans-Metairie-Kenner, LA	3 710	28 673	4 672.5	1 655.4	764	35 267	D	1 939.1	2 830	60 410	3 677.0	1 043.7
New York-Northern New Jersey-Long Island, NY-NJ-PA	67 946	672 812	135 779.9	54 004.4	18 482	449 307	144 942.5	21 711.5	41 108	538 990	39 932.8	10 809.3
Edison-New Brunswick, NJ Div	9 804	D	D	D	2 010	D	D	3 789.0	5 055	66 830	3 787.7	1 016.2
Nassau-Suffolk, NY Div	12 596	D	D	D	3 577	D	D	4 056.0	6 466	79 474	4 815.7	1 331.5
Newark-Union, NJ-PA Div	7 888	102 853	16 262.9	7 903.4	2 552	87 290	38 292.3	5 050.9	4 595	58 397	3 637.6	982.3
New York-White Plains-Wayne, NY-NJ Div	37 658	D	D	D	10 343	202 733	58 514.0	8 815.6	24 992	334 289	27 691.8	7 479.3
Niles-Benton Harbor, MI	287	D	D	D	332	10 831	2 298.3	474.7	413	5 519	219.5	64.1
North Port-Bradenton-Sarasota, FL	2 687	D	D	D	630	17 798	4 351.7	763.1	1 335	26 200	1 288.2	381.4
Norwich-New London, CT	555	D	D	D	201	D	D	848.8	690	30 404	3 444.7	856.8
Ocala, FL	698	3 459	361.6	132.0	221	8 904	1 841.5	320.9	443	7 784	353.1	100.0
Ocean City, NJ	250	D	D	D	81	662	D	18.9	832	5 615	517.0	144.9
Odessa, TX	224	D	D	D	240	4 814	2 049.7	222.0	245	5 213	228.6	59.4
Ogden-Clearfield, UT	1 278	D	D	D	529	22 140	9 104.3	909.8	737	14 674	541.1	149.1
Oklahoma City, OK	3 836	D	D	D	1 138	32 649	10 181.0	1 278.9	2 428	52 115	2 111.7	588.3
Olympia, WA	598	D	D	D	189	3 118	870.1	120.7	497	7 612	346.7	102.7
Omaha-Council Bluffs, NE-IA	2 196	D	D	D	748	33 757	14 272.2	1 377.6	1 826	37 671	1 782.4	479.4
Orlando-Kissimmee-Sanford, FL	7 667	D	D	D	1 473	43 017	14 027.0	2 060.2	4 190	126 780	8 735.7	2 143.5
Oshkosh-Neenah, WI	250	D	D	D	319	23 777	9 198.9	1 149.8	377	6 071	212.1	58.4
Owensboro, KY	182	D	D	D	135	9 342	4 765.0	424.3	196	4 171	152.7	45.9
Oxnard-Thousand Oaks-Ventura, CA	2 597	16 457	6 370.8	1 032.7	954	33 602	8 769.0	1 643.4	1 602	29 832	1 478.2	422.9
Palm Bay-Melbourne-Titusville, FL	1 683	19 711	3 364.7	1 589.6	473	22 772	6 767.6	1 172.5	1 019	19 057	855.5	240.1
Palm Coast, FL	197	674	105.6	46.6	52	1 031	235.7	29.9	131	2 401	114.8	31.6
Panama City-Lynn Haven-Panama City Beach, FL	406	D	D	D	116	3 702	1 254.3	153.4	442	9 154	480.4	135.8
Parkersburg-Marietta-Vienna, WV-OH	249	1 975	180.3	69.4	178	9 219	5 203.7	474.0	364	6 463	249.0	72.6
Pascagoula, MS	221	D	D	D	96	14 386	D	672.2	254	4 509	191.5	50.2
Pensacola-Ferry Pass-Brent, FL	1 042	8 005	936.0	379.3	246	5 710	2 191.9	271.1	718	14 399	629.0	173.6
Peoria, IL	679	D	D	D	362	D	D	D	920	15 634	733.7	193.3
Philadelphia-Camden-Wilmington, PA-NJ-DE-MD	18 282	190 964	32 765.7	13 547.2	5 881	224 483	122 509.8	12 018.5	12 138	185 109	9 991.3	2 727.1
Camden, NJ Div	3 525	D	D	D	1 180	48 041	25 901.8	2 543.0	2 398	35 317	1 715.2	470.0
Philadelphia, PA Div	12 688	D	D	D	4 182	150 767	73 597.8	7 873.8	8 407	126 476	7 062.3	1 932.9
Wilmington, DE-MD-NJ Div	2 069	D	D	D	519	25 675	23 010.2	1 601.7	1 333	23 316	1 213.8	324.2
Phoenix-Mesa-Glendale, AZ	11 954	100 017	14 346.2	5 938.7	3 520	124 958	42 332.0	6 195.2	7 078	162 741	8 750.9	2 534.5
Pine Bluff, AR	99	D	D	D	69	5 260	1 477.9	173.9	156	2 324	91.7	23.9
Pittsburgh, PA	5 990	D	D	D	2 755	101 747	38 078.2	4 809.8	5 348	93 669	3 940.7	1 134.7
Pittsfield, MA	366	D	D	D	173	6 204	1 425.5	317.1	516	7 600	401.9	125.6
Pocatello, ID	170	D	D	D	66	3 320	1 206.5	130.5	197	3 126	120.4	32.5
Portland-South Portland-Biddeford, ME	1 868	D	D	D	715	26 666	6 744.0	1 187.9	1 733	23 504	1 285.5	383.2
Portland-Vancouver-Hillsboro, OR-WA	7 698	D	D	D	3 281	110 749	47 590.7	5 358.2	5 340	83 103	4 170.4	1 226.8
Port St. Lucie, FL	1 178	D	D	D	295	6 106	1 772.6	231.8	665	13 151	547.4	161.6
Poughkeepsie-Newburgh-Middletown, NY	1 679	D	D	D	554	23 458	6 176.5	1 584.1	1 493	16 927	879.4	240.4
Prescott, AZ	584	D	D	D	233	3 618	764.0	143.6	578	8 737	456.5	126.2
Providence-New Bedford-Fall River, RI-MA	4 206	D	D	D	2 628	88 819	20 939.6	4 034.3	4 132	65 292	3 033.9	883.7
Provo-Orem, UT	1 442	16 746	1 354.1	509.0	530	18 472	4 867.1	815.1	564	11 935	458.8	130.2
Pueblo, CO	251	D	D	D	106	3 838	1 705.8	180.3	344	5 602	220.9	61.8
Punta Gorda, FL	366	D	D	D	64	430	103.7	14.6	240	4 322	178.0	53.2
Racine, WI	346	D	D	D	345	17 183	7 863.3	890.8	388	6 239	242.7	66.1
Raleigh-Cary, NC	4 380	36 371	5 527.1	2 270.9	810	27 491	17 544.0	1 263.7	2 087	41 492	1 945.2	537.0
Rapid City, SD	326	D	D	D	163	3 201	713.8	112.3	412	6 538	320.0	88.8
Reading, PA	735	6 289	1 449.0	389.4	550	32 597	8 461.8	1 487.9	715	11 030	446.0	124.4
Redding, CA	400	D	D	D	167	2 794	662.9	117.1	403	5 862	281.0	74.9
Reno-Sparks, NV	1 696	10 101	1 444.2	549.1	507	15 502	5 884.3	765.8	1 003	35 540	2 404.2	730.6
Richmond, VA	3 401	30 395	4 176.1	1 861.6	1 035	42 516	22 849.0	2 196.1	2 319	45 274	2 090.9	583.5
Riverside-San Bernardino-Ontario, CA	5 662	35 199	4 326.5	1 583.0	3 668	122 090	32 530.9	4 855.0	6 404	128 663	7 590.0	2 021.0
Roanoke, VA	744	5 864	808.4	288.7	346	17 968	4 915.0	733.0	628	12 451	520.1	156.6
Rochester, MN	334	D	D	D	160	12 447	4 212.7	711.4	395	8 214	355.7	101.7
Rochester, NY	2 433	D	D	D	1 333	66 957	21 530.8	3 036.9	2 170	33 119	1 412.2	409.7
Rockford, IL	727	4 914	534.9	217.9	756	33 901	13 467.0	1 742.1	662	11 409	492.4	135.5
Rocky Mount, NC	222	1 232	133.0	48.1	145	12 735	4 183.1	500.7	266	5 058	200.2	55.2
Rome, GA	174	703	80.1	24.8	109	7 726	3 346.1	312.7	198	3 423	144.3	38.1

1. Establishments subject to federal tax.

Table C. Metropolitan Areas — Health Care and Social Assistance, Other Services, and Federal Funds

Area name	Health care and social assistance,[1] 2007				Other services,[1] 2007				Federal funds and grants, 2009–2010 Expenditures (mil dol)			
									Total	Direct payments for individuals		
	Number of establishments	Number of employees	Receipts (mil dol)	Annual payroll (mil dol)	Number of establishments	Number of employees	Receipts (mil dol)	Annual payroll (mil dol)	Total	Social Security and government retirement	Medicare	Food stamps and Supplemental Security Income
	159	160	161	162	163	164	165	166	167	168	169	170
Naples-Marco Island, FL.......	914	14 861	1 796.1	703.8	828	4 364	393.3	113.0	2 069.4	1 202.8	492.5	54.2
Nashville-Davidson—Murfreesboro—Franklin, TN	3 820	89 796	10 518.5	3 917.0	2 529	20 895	1 944.3	614.7	15 209.1	3 935.9	2 386.8	513.4
New Haven-Milford, CT	2 371	68 663	6 467.8	2 792.6	1 772	10 629	948.2	288.9	11 538.3	2 403.0	5 657.1	291.9
New Orleans-Metairie-Kenner, LA	3 027	61 663	6 835.2	2 484.5	1 935	12 290	1 654.5	360.5	15 844.0	3 119.2	2 819.8	697.8
New York-Northern New Jersey-Long Island, NY-NJ-PA	55 243	1 255 893	130 730.9	54 812.1	44 877	256 021	41 257.8	8 606.9	169 410.6	44 503.5	38 973.7	8 037.3
Edison-New Brunswick, NJ Div	6 848	125 226	13 035.7	5 180.4	4 877	27 864	3 369.7	824.0	19 043.9	7 014.8	4 236.9	289.6
Nassau-Suffolk, NY Div.....	10 014	179 244	19 852.0	8 240.8	7 604	37 690	3 737.3	1 042.6	23 918.0	8 659.2	5 576.1	398.7
Newark-Union, NJ-PA Div.	6 504	131 899	13 247.6	5 867.9	4 926	28 360	3 128.5	837.8	17 359.5	5 300.6	4 068.9	627.9
New York-White Plains-Wayne, NY-NJ Div........	31 877	819 524	84 595.6	35 523.0	27 470	162 107	31 022.2	5 902.6	109 089.3	23 528.9	25 091.9	6 721.1
Niles-Benton Harbor, MI	394	8 821	701.7	282.8	281	1 468	112.2	35.1	1 365.2	568.7	292.2	90.6
North Port-Bradenton-Sarasota, FL.........................	2 244	35 836	3 772.8	1 384.5	1 431	7 361	577.6	160.1	6 387.1	3 283.7	1 962.4	154.7
Norwioh-New London, CT.....	703	16 048	1 467.8	617.5	479	2 549	234.3	59.3	6 569.1	887.6	1 336.7	55.3
Ocala, FL	817	14 493	1 590.4	566.1	467	2 408	201.6	51.4	2 844.7	1 621.9	717.0	121.2
Ocean City, NJ...................	268	D	D	D	288	1 124	91.2	29.5	961.9	429.9	310.1	20.2
Odessa, TX	300	6 988	644.3	248.5	246	2 115	283.6	64.3	749.5	287.9	194.9	70.3
Ogden-Clearfield, UT...........	1 154	18 393	1 597.3	620.7	715	4 457	326.2	97.2	5 122.2	1 524.7	679.8	110.4
Oklahoma City, OK ,.............	3 832	73 078	8 033.8	2 723.7	2 034	12 913	1 348.9	318.7	12 811.2	3 852.5	1 467.4	439.1
Olympia, WA.......................	710	11 596	1 238.4	447.6	464	2 812	273.7	88.2	4 306.4	924.1	232.8	71.1
Omaha-Council Bluffs, NE-IA...............................	2 141	53 429	5 209.5	2 133.1	1 591	10 887	1 256.8	284.8	7 087.1	2 428.1	957.7	217.3
Orlando-Kissimmee-Sanford, FL.....................	4 863	92 989	9 853.3	3 908.8	3 611	24 032	2 345.8	664.8	16 831.3	6 109.2	3 077.5	687.8
Oshkosh-Neenah, WI...........	430	12 589	1 344.9	476.6	290	2 355	199.8	61.9	8 060.3	447.7	214.4	25.8
Owensboro, KY...................	324	8 026	662.0	252.7	178	1 207	78.7	25.0	952.5	379.4	268.7	53.5
Oxnard-Thousand Oaks-Ventura, CA.........................	2 317	29 522	3 140.0	1 200.9	1 196	7 303	839.6	195.9	5 559.1	1 945.1	1 102.6	147.1
Palm Bay-Melbourne-Titusville, FL.........................	1 417	26 415	2 796.8	1 085.6	1 039	4 868	395.3	121.0	8 154.8	2 539.4	1 110.3	165.0
Palm Coast, FL...................	149	1 807	175.1	70.7	126	484	35.2	9.4	631.4	469.7	101.0	17.6
Panama City-Lynn Haven-Panama City Beach, FL...	493	9 501	985.3	354.0	315	1 767	122.2	38.1	2 261.4	730.5	337.2	74.5
Parkersburg-Marietta-Vienna, WV-OH ,............	460	11 253	924.5	346.7	307	1 568	127.0	28.9	1 521.5	632.8	305.8	79.7
Pascagoula, MS...................	318	5 980	622.4	243.8	175	849	71.7	19.9	1 226.4	531.3	216.1	54.2
Pensacola-Ferry Pass-Brent, FL...................................	983	23 199	2 412.9	894.2	649	3 468	283.2	86.2	4 928.0	2 006.9	877.4	198.1
Peoria, IL...........................	845	27 673	2 527.2	1 059.6	669	5 352	467.9	180.5	2 779.0	1 119.8	587.3	116.8
Philadelphia-Camden-Wilmington, PA-NJ-DE-MD.	16 323	415 348	42 566.2	17 480.6	11 395	74 963	9 790.7	2 169.8	62 636.7	17 098.9	14 133.7	2 440.0
Camden, NJ Div	3 328	68 999	7 081.3	2 808.5	2 319	14 328	1 135.9	363.6	11 837.1	3 792.6	2 214.6	306.7
Philadelphia, PA Div.........	11 159	300 011	30 720.5	12 542.3	7 826	52 579	7 889.0	1 584.7	45 563.0	11 294.6	10 871.2	1 925.8
Wilmington, DE-MD-NJ Div	1 836	46 338	4 764.4	2 129.9	1 250	8 056	765.9	221.5	5 236.6	2 011.7	1 047.8	207.4
Phoenix-Mesa-Glendale, AZ....	10 008	180 870	20 217.1	7 822.2	5 750	47 116	4 481.5	1 223.9	33 532.2	10 122.3	4 348.1	1 242.3
Pine Bluff, AR	289	4 791	411.5	150.4	116	763	57.6	22.0	1 329.6	350.7	171.3	83.9
Pittsburgh, PA.....................	7 734	184 576	17 470.8	6 919.7	5 279	31 880	3 755.4	782.5	28 473.6	8 645.4	7 805.0	938.1
Pittsfield, MA.......................	450	10 869	981.1	429.8	309	1 742	142.3	38.5	1 352.8	459.3	357.1	48.0
Pocatello, ID.......................	303	4 956	404.5	152.6	145	712	63.4	15.2	652.9	258.0	77.9	40.3
Portland-South Portland-Biddeford, ME	2 031	40 747	3 487.0	1 505.2	1 188	6 117	543.7	147.9	5 091.1	1 706.7	636.1	159.0
Portland-Vancouver-Hillsboro, OR-WA	6 374	114 594	12 607.5	5 005.4	4 041	24 286	2 985.0	726.9	15 688.0	5 585.8	2 331.1	707.8
Port St. Lucie, FL................	1 087	17 254	1 857.4	671.3	734	3 709	288.0	85.8	3 198.9	1 722.0	978.4	116.3
Poughkeepsie-Newburgh-Middletown, NY.............	1 901	37 055	3 337.4	1 453.5	1 354	6 464	697.6	167.1	5 175.0	1 860.0	890.1	146.7
Prescott, AZ	737	10 268	930.0	370.7	386	1 822	141.9	41.0	1 624.2	996.3	244.7	51.4
Providence-New Bedford-Fall River, RI-MA	4 642	118 319	10 073.1	4 455.6	3 434	20 277	1 914.7	504.6	17 257.8	4 687.4	3 140.9	646.5
Provo-Orem, UT...................	1 035	19 210	1 648.7	644.1	547	3 039	245.4	64.4	2 575.7	749.3	496.5	67.6
Pueblo, CO	410	11 085	872.7	388.5	237	1 160	92.3	25.4	1 440.6	554.1	256.1	92.2
Punta Gorda, FL..................	474	7 731	897.1	308.2	275	1 186	90.0	24.7	1 438.9	829.2	490.9	31.4
Racine, WI..........................	417	11 897	946.4	478.0	343	2 167	162.7	49.1	1 319.4	599.0	262.3	65.9
Raleigh-Cary, NC.................	2 601	52 345	4 949.4	2 062.5	1 869	13 363	1 516.1	408.2	9 618.5	2 418.0	752.5	224.0
Rapid City, SD	365	9 404	977.3	381.2	304	1 674	145.6	37.7	1 394.5	472.0	115.4	40.5
Reading, PA.........................	799	21 887	2 014.4	848.1	781	4 670	398.8	108.0	2 648.7	1 186.8	686.4	108.4
Redding, CA........................	661	10 015	1 124.5	420.3	320	1 697	168.2	43.3	1 678.2	724.9	355.0	93.5
Reno-Sparks, NV.................	1 113	19 938	2 642.3	1 000.5	765	5 594	703.9	148.9	3 495.6	1 167.4	382.4	99.1
Richmond, VA......................	2 937	70 736	7 079.7	2 874.6	2 496	16 629	2 014.7	481.3	13 630.3	3 963.6	1 482.6	386.0
Riverside-San Bernardino-Ontario, CA...................	7 225	129 700	14 971.5	5 514.6	4 810	32 342	2 927.7	850.7	24 553.0	8 445.0	5 113.2	1 239.8
Roanoke, VA........................	763	22 840	2 378.1	928.0	685	3 976	299.1	92.3	2 553.1	1 133.3	428.3	83.7
Rochester, MN.....................	421	19 262	2 036.4	829.5	345	D	D	D	1 037.0	445.4	213.1	30.7
Rochester, NY......................	2 454	69 515	5 675.0	2 437.8	1 693	9 937	967.1	253.1	10 403.0	3 204.2	1 672.7	380.0
Rockford, IL.........................	734	20 112	1 949.3	814.3	617	4 043	332.5	97.7	2 108.5	967.7	385.0	105.5
Rocky Mount, NC.................	343	9 283	711.5	306.7	213	1 198	197.6	29.8	1 296.2	490.9	220.3	98.5
Rome, GA............................	259	7 910	785.1	310.9	108	D	D	D	705.5	304.8	152.1	42.4

1. Establishments subject to federal tax.

Table C. Metropolitan Areas — **Federal Funds, Residential Construction and Local Government Finances**

Area name	Salaries and wages	Defense	Other	Medicaid and other health-related	Nutrition and family welfare	Education	Other	New construction ($1,000)	Number of housing units	Total (mil dol)	Inter-govern-mental (mil dol)	Total (mil dol)	Per capita[1] (dollars) Total	Property
	171	172	173	174	175	176	177	178	179	180	181	182	183	184
Naples-Marco Island, FL........	53.2	61.7	19.9	63.1	62.5	11.5	14.8	371 116	1 259	1 632.7	314.3	935.7	2 963	2 487
Nashville-Davidson—Murfreesboro—Franklin, TN .	1 180.6	181.3	1 164.5	1 846.6	433.2	1 019.0	2 008.7	852 116	5 092	4 745.9	1 342.2	2 214.3	1 455	860
New Haven-Milford, CT..........	480.1	79.2	179.4	1 810.1	129.2	70.3	256.3	186 209	1 019	3 404.4	1 294.9	1 764.1	2 086	2 046
New Orleans-Metairie-Kenner, LA	1 168.6	4 493.1	801.8	1 624.5	252.9	163.4	479.0	339 636	2 171	5 638.9	1 775.8	2 079.9	2 019	830
New York-Northern New Jersey-Long Island, NY-NJ-PA	10 184.2	8 653.9	5 053.8	35 663.7	4 029.2	1 370.2	8 116.6	3 053 583	18 668	137 447.6	42 994.4	72 397.9	3 848	2 306
Edison-New Brunswick, NJ Div....................	1 218.1	3 237.4	533.7	1 434.3	280.3	55.6	382.2	NA	NA	10 162.1	2 541.4	6 010.9	2 591	2 541
Nassau-Suffolk, NY Div.....	1 557.6	2 458.4	1 208.9	2 726.0	529.3	152.2	305.0	NA	NA	18 984.9	4 839.8	11 977.9	4 340	3 390
Newark-Union, NJ-PA Div ..	1 319.5	1 240.5	596.6	2 285.1	371.6	88.1	1 091.1	NA	NA	10 053.9	3 015.0	5 675.5	2 666	2 593
New York-White Plains-Wayne, NY-NJ Div.........	6 089.0	1 717.5	2 714.5	29 218.3	2 848.1	1 074.3	6 338.3	NA	NA	98 246.7	32 598.2	48 733.6	4 198	1 948
Niles-Benton Harbor, MI	31.8	2.9	16.0	249.9	36.3	15.7	32.6	36 640	133	590.1	307.2	173.2	1 085	1 060
North Port-Bradenton-Sarasota, FL	228.4	224.2	38.9	186.0	76.7	35.0	126.0	433 105	1 955	3 477.2	617.2	1 460.5	2 125	1 736
Norwich-New London, CT.....	342.9	3 520.5	55.9	234.1	35.3	19.9	33.0	64 859	344	1 033.0	375.8	540.4	2 021	1 959
Ocala, FL..............................	57.6	15.9	17.1	163.8	42.2	18.5	24.2	88 836	481	968.0	357.1	320.2	986	783
Ocean City, NJ....................	75.3	7.4	17.1	61.7	15.9	4.0	5.8	110 257	434	633.6	155.7	372.3	3 861	3 709
Odessa, TX...........................	28.1	0.0	3.8	92.7	28.4	8.5	16.4	79 162	708	609.9	162.7	189.3	1 461	1 149
Ogden-Clearfield, UT	1 158.6	916.1	181.2	333.0	71.7	13.4	35.9	306 710	1 509	1 432.6	590.7	482.8	931	616
Oklahoma City, OK	2 251.8	987.1	495.3	930.8	376.1	352.9	1 416.5	561 796	3 635	3 651.6	1 168.8	1 381.7	1 158	587
Olympia, WA	122.2	119.1	24.2	287.1	340.4	673.5	1 437.6	232 869	1 156	882.4	347.7	334.2	1 401	841
Omaha-Council Bluffs, NE-IA	1 043.8	735.9	278.9	844.4	134.8	66.5	165.9	441 727	3 223	3 077.0	980.9	1 419.8	1 711	1 290
Orlando-Kissimmee-Sanford, FL.................................	1 044.0	3 485.6	630.6	708.6	240.5	135.8	287.2	1 140 613	5 254	9 424.9	2 900.8	3 544.8	1 744	1 210
Oshkosh-Neenah, WI............	82.1	7 100.1	11.7	112.5	23.6	7.7	10.5	55 905	359	566.0	263.6	202.6	1 249	1 209
Owensboro, KY	39.5	2.2	7.7	85.2	28.5	7.1	29.5	29 512	338	351.9	133.1	96.1	857	499
Oxnard-Thousand Oaks-Ventura, CA	602.1	681.1	175.4	445.3	153.9	52.6	159.5	110 971	590	4 288.6	1 876.2	1 310.9	1 642	1 348
Palm Bay-Melbourne-Titusville, FL............................	617.8	2 092.1	1 237.4	154.1	63.8	28.4	65.6	248 553	1 144	1 940.6	575.9	770.6	1 437	1 095
Palm Coast, FL	13.8	0.4	3.2	7.1	6.8	2.9	4.1	51 882	278	366.4	107.4	156.2	1 767	1 578
Panama City-Lynn Haven-Panama City Beach, FL....	420.0	425.6	56.4	109.4	33.1	14.2	12.5	39 713	309	877.5	228.1	282.9	1 725	1 267
Parkersburg-Marietta-Vienna, WV-OH................	180.8	16.5	40.7	170.0	27.4	15.0	19.8	18 908	159	450.9	202.8	152.6	950	716
Pascagoula, MS	113.9	118.1	48.0	59.2	26.4	8.7	37.9	49 519	329	849.6	289.0	161.9	1 065	997
Pensacola-Ferry Pass-Brent, FL.................................	514.0	532.2	163.6	369.4	82.4	36.1	55.4	270 553	1 754	1 509.6	673.1	457.5	1 009	739
Peoria, IL...............................	231.5	253.7	53.1	204.5	57.5	11.0	57.1	142 662	793	1 316.6	517.7	512.6	1 381	1 173
Philadelphia-Camden-Wilmington, PA-NJ-DE-MD.......	4 899.5	6 849.6	4 627.6	8 409.3	994.8	282.1	1 866.0	1 033 367	7 053	28 819.0	11 352.5	12 391.9	2 126	1 483
Camden, NJ Div	1 268.2	2 149.8	645.7	885.0	186.8	50.0	130.6	NA	NA	5 997.4	2 118.1	2 704.2	2 170	2 136
Philadelphia, PA Div..........	3 218.2	4 616.2	3 811.0	6 800.0	678.8	195.1	1 463.3	NA	NA	20 605.5	8 216.6	8 909.8	2 292	1 384
Wilmington, DE-MD-NJ Div	413.1	83.5	170.8	724.4	129.2	37.0	272.1	NA	NA	2 216.2	1 017.9	777.8	1 121	869
Phoenix-Mesa-Glendale, AZ....	1 920.1	4 444.2	933.6	4 349.4	869.5	777.1	2 408.9	1 664 617	8 300	16 700.4	6 455.8	6 225.7	1 490	852
Pine Bluff, AR......................	97.1	256.5	43.4	217.3	24.2	16.3	19.7	8 358	126	252.5	164.5	54.5	537	233
Pittsburgh, PA	1 614.9	2 023.4	1 588.6	3 906.8	463.7	114.7	752.5	673 102	3 615	10 276.0	4 522.4	3 874.9	1 645	1 213
Pittsfield, MA	54.6	111.3	29.3	202.4	27.1	12.7	31.0	34 941	139	442.7	189.6	203.0	1 564	1 520
Pocatello, ID.........................	60.4	0.4	12.2	107.3	15.0	3.2	19.5	20 429	149	365.2	117.2	69.3	791	749
Portland-South Portland-Biddeford, ME	543.2	1 094.4	91.1	511.4	73.5	18.6	157.1	252 583	1 260	1 706.5	484.1	939.3	1 831	1 800
Portland-Vancouver-Hillsboro, OR-WA..................	1 546.5	563.3	683.2	2 366.8	330.4	152.2	1 053.1	951 296	4 476	8 948.6	3 360.4	3 325.9	1 529	1 096
Port St. Lucie, FL.................	83.6	5.7	21.7	118.8	48.1	20.8	32.8	120 408	492	1 906.0	533.3	861.7	2 154	1 803
Poughkeepsie-Newburgh-Middletown, NY..............	954.9	199.0	95.0	702.7	140.0	41.9	69.4	178 374	1 343	3 554.2	1 219.8	1 833.3	2 737	2 083
Prescott, AZ	70.5	1.1	46.3	147.1	24.0	12.9	5.6	64 052	339	692.9	249.7	293.3	1 380	903
Providence-New Bedford-Fall River, RI-MA	1 149.9	2 362.0	383.6	2 795.2	379.8	314.4	942.4	246 040	1 439	5 688.9	2 261.4	2 713.2	1 695	1 641
Provo-Orem, UT...................	166.8	497.2	27.7	244.7	56.4	13.7	131.0	401 203	1 985	1 329.0	554.5	433.7	879	577
Pueblo, CO...........................	85.8	42.0	20.4	258.3	33.6	16.6	39.7	39 615	234	490.8	226.0	183.4	1 187	747
Punta Gorda, FL	26.1	0.8	5.5	16.6	19.3	4.9	5.5	59 443	425	668.6	125.2	347.4	2 273	1 705
Racine, WI............................	53.3	54.5	10.7	196.2	34.6	13.0	18.6	39 605	240	724.8	359.2	255.6	1 310	1 266
Raleigh-Cary, NC.................	704.4	186.1	205.3	889.8	554.7	1 091.9	2 278.7	909 221	5 213	3 468.0	1 311.5	1 247.8	1 191	886
Rapid City, SD	350.4	134.8	40.6	81.2	21.6	16.4	64.0	81 807	642	380.7	116.8	185.8	1 545	1 097
Reading, PA	146.1	65.2	29.9	225.9	52.4	11.3	78.4	73 420	415	1 848.0	724.3	738.8	1 838	1 472
Redding, CA	96.8	3.9	75.2	199.0	50.8	18.4	30.1	42 773	253	953.9	513.4	222.1	1 238	962
Reno-Sparks, NV..................	274.7	674.8	135.5	292.4	58.6	35.3	315.8	118 007	606	1 810.5	781.1	633.6	1 544	1 089
Richmond, VA	2 084.2	1 096.7	328.0	1 076.9	347.9	606.5	2 004.6	478 253	3 456	4 384.5	1 802.0	1 847.3	1 523	1 110
Riverside-San Bernardino-Ontario, CA	2 362.5	2 713.9	448.8	2 202.6	737.4	265.9	551.6	1 230 710	6 336	23 957.5	11 947.5	6 066.6	1 486	1 093
Roanoke, VA.........................	228.5	129.4	143.0	224.4	37.9	20.0	34.9	84 824	436	1 019.9	454.7	446.5	1 506	975
Rochester, MN......................	107.6	3.4	40.9	103.4	24.0	10.3	20.9	94 627	477	732.5	332.8	194.1	1 072	950
Rochester, NY.......................	460.4	1 939.3	253.2	1 509.4	264.4	160.4	296.8	244 065	1 449	5 326.6	2 262.9	2 255.8	2 189	1 636
Rockford, IL..........................	124.3	153.5	25.4	185.1	38.1	11.8	38.9	35 644	299	1 207.5	495.5	500.1	1 419	1 257
Rocky Mount, NC.................	61.0	16.0	10.3	271.1	38.7	12.9	17.2	30 738	212	469.2	269.9	120.1	825	623
Rome, GA	35.5	0.0	8.9	86.1	19.0	7.5	5.0	6 526	55	530.9	181.6	115.9	1 212	720

1. Based on the resident population estimated as of July 1 of the year shown.

Table C. Metropolitan Areas — Local Government Finances, Government Employment, and Voting

Area name	Total (mil dol)	Per capita[1] (dollars)	Education	Health and hospitals	Police protection	Public welfare	Highways	Total (mil dol)	Per capita[1] (dollars)	Federal civilian	Federal military	State and local	Democratic	Republican	All other
	Local government finances, 2007 (cont.)									Government employment, 2009			Presidential election,[2] 2008		
	Direct general expenditure							Debt outstanding					Percent of vote cast:		
			Percent of total for:												
	185	186	187	188	189	190	191	192	193	194	195	196	197	198	199
Naples-Marco Island, FL......	1 757.0	5 563	38.1	2.3	8.8	0.2	8.2	3 007.6	9 523	673	630	12 293	38.3	60.8	0.8
Nashville-Davidson—Mur-freesboro—Franklin, TN	4 675.5	3 073	40.6	7.5	7.2	0.9	3.9	7 627.7	5 013	12 449	6 071	88 029	44.3	54.4	1.3
New Haven-Milford, CT	3 336.5	3 946	57.5	0.9	4.8	0.5	3.5	2 951.8	3 491	5 764	1 796	45 551	61.0	37.8	1.2
New Orleans-Metairie-Ken-ner, LA	4 944.9	4 799	29.5	19.0	6.8	0.3	3.3	6 274.4	6 089	12 738	7 968	77 208	46.1	52.3	1.6
New York-Northern New Jer-sey-Long Island, NY-NJ-PA....................	129 641.2	6 890	37.4	7.4	5.9	10.1	2.4	165 011.4	8 770	123 169	37 103	1 162 491	64.2	35.0	0.8
Edison-New Brunswick, NJ Div	10 703.2	4 614	55.7	0.9	5.7	2.5	3.1	9 930.7	4 281	15 739	6 100	132 939	50.2	48.6	1.1
Nassau-Suffolk, NY Div....	19 216.3	6 963	50.0	5.5	7.0	5.4	3.3	14 662.0	5 313	18 107	5 328	175 613	53.2	46.0	0.8
Newark-Union, NJ-PA Div.	10 538.2	4 951	51.3	1.7	6.7	2.4	2.3	8 940.1	4 200	18 175	4 496	149 316	59.2	40.0	0.9
New York-White Plains-Wayne, NY-NJ Div........	89 183.5	7 683	30.9	9.3	5.6	12.9	2.2	131 478.5	11 327	71 148	21 179	704 623	72.6	26.7	0.7
Niles-Benton Harbor, MI	592.1	3 710	53.6	7.8	5.6	1.1	4.9	334.7	2 098	368	315	8 789	52.0	46.5	1.5
North Port-Bradenton-Sara-sota, FL.................	3 398.0	4 945	35.1	15.0	5.8	0.8	5.3	3 541.2	5 153	1 975	1 392	25 064	48.1	51.1	0.8
Norwich-New London, CT.....	1 092.9	4 087	63.7	0.4	4.8	0.6	5.1	682.5	2 553	2 734	8 052	35 861	59.9	38.8	1.3
Ocala, FL.................	959.0	2 952	50.3	1.7	10.2	0.7	8.4	760.8	2 342	742	652	16 843	43.7	55.3	1.0
Ocean City, NJ.................	730.0	7 570	37.5	1.2	5.3	3.6	5.2	626.5	6 497	467	1 258	9 147	45.0	53.7	1.3
Odessa, TX.................	554.0	4 275	41.9	34.4	3.8	0.0	2.2	306.9	2 369	178	319	9 479	25.6	73.6	0.8
Ogden-Clearfield, UT...........	1 470.7	2 837	50.9	2.6	5.9	2.0	3.8	1 208.1	2 331	19 185	6 535	26 401	30.2	67.1	2.7
Oklahoma City, OK..............	3 744.3	3 139	43.8	8.9	6.6	0.2	5.7	3 308.0	2 773	26 189	12 635	94 334	37.2	62.8	0.0
Olympia, WA.................	845.2	3 543	48.3	6.0	3.8	0.0	5.0	708.9	2 972	960	801	36 202	59.9	38.2	1.9
Omaha-Council Bluffs, NE-IA.................	2 988.8	3 601	50.4	3.2	5.4	0.6	5.1	5 775.9	6 960	9 013	9 652	53 536	47.9	50.5	1.7
Orlando-Kissimmee-Sanford, FL............	9 060.4	4 458	41.7	3.3	6.3	0.8	5.7	14 883.2	7 323	12 089	4 416	101 371	54.1	45.3	0.7
Oshkosh-Neenah, WI...........	592.7	3 655	40.8	2.6	5.6	11.6	8.2	694.9	4 285	501	478	11 972	54.9	43.3	1.8
Owensboro, KY.................	348.4	3 108	42.4	1.7	3.8	0.1	3.3	1 772.3	15 809	340	376	9 523	44.8	53.7	1.5
Oxnard-Thousand Oaks-Ven-tura, CA.................	4 176.2	5 231	39.4	8.7	7.5	4.3	4.1	2 696.6	3 378	7 398	6 470	36 318	55.2	42.9	1.9
Palm Bay-Melbourne-Titus-ville, FL.................	1 977.4	3 688	44.4	8.3	6.0	0.3	4.8	2 145.2	4 001	6 282	2 955	23 127	44.3	54.7	0.9
Palm Coast, FL.................	414.3	4 686	35.3	1.3	4.2	0.2	7.2	447.0	5 057	157	181	3 580	50.4	48.8	0.7
Panama City-Lynn Haven-Panama City Beach, FL...	846.1	5 159	36.6	29.6	5.2	0.0	3.0	797.3	4 862	3 533	4 327	10 618	29.2	69.9	1.0
Parkersburg-Marietta-Vienna, WV-OH...............	467.5	2 848	58.1	4.3	5.2	2.8	5.2	493.0	3 069	2 483	680	8 415	37.7	60.6	1.7
Pascagoula, MS.................	775.8	5 103	33.0	35.3	2.9	0.1	4.1	501.4	3 298	847	1 362	10 887	30.4	68.7	1.0
Pensacola-Ferry Pass-Brent, FL.................	1 540.3	3 397	46.8	3.8	6.2	0.3	4.3	1 882.3	4 151	6 554	14 606	21 589	35.1	63.9	1.0
Peoria, IL.................	1 281.4	3 452	47.8	1.5	5.7	1.3	6.8	770.8	2 077	2 236	795	19 586	49.8	48.6	1.7
Philadelphia-Camden-Wil-mington, PA-NJ-DE-MD.	28 218.2	4 842	48.3	6.5	5.1	4.8	2.0	42 828.0	7 349	56 629	22 778	297 230	65.2	33.9	0.9
Camden, NJ Div	6 100.4	4 895	57.2	1.9	4.8	2.6	2.1	6 980.2	5 601	9 535	7 289	76 719	61.5	37.4	1.1
Philadelphia, PA Div..........	19 685.3	5 063	44.3	8.6	5.0	6.1	1.9	33 740.4	8 679	41 749	11 992	178 400	66.5	32.7	0.8
Wilmington, DE-MD-NJ Div	2 432.4	3 505	59.0	1.0	7.5	0.7	2.0	2 107.4	3 037	5 345	3 497	42 111	64.3	34.3	1.4
Phoenix-Mesa-Glendale, AZ....	16 103.8	3 853	40.8	4.4	7.5	1.9	5.6	27 140.8	6 494	23 077	14 838	217 621	44.0	54.8	1.2
Pine Bluff, AR.................	272.4	2 684	65.1	0.2	5.8	0.0	3.9	149.3	1 471	2 154	509	9 244	56.1	41.5	2.4
Pittsburgh, PA.................	9 931.6	4 216	47.2	6.4	3.4	7.5	3.5	17 650.1	7 492	18 620	6 704	109 101	50.8	48.1	1.0
Pittsfield, MA.................	500.5	3 856	60.3	0.5	3.4	0.1	5.3	347.1	2 674	452	322	8 109	75.2	22.6	2.2
Pocatello, ID.................	381.5	4 355	26.9	40.5	4.4	0.4	6.1	157.0	1 793	582	354	8 160	41.7	55.6	2.7
Portland-South Portland-Bid-deford, ME	1 662.1	3 239	50.0	0.8	5.0	1.7	5.9	1 279.4	2 493	8 349	5 339	28 892	61.8	36.4	1.7
Portland-Vancouver-Hills-boro, OR-WA	8 842.2	4 065	39.3	4.1	5.2	2.4	6.2	14 538.1	6 684	18 589	7 120	122 660	62.6	34.9	2.5
Port St. Lucie, FL.................	1 904.6	4 760	41.5	2.2	6.8	1.0	8.7	2 616.8	6 540	1 080	881	18 518	50.6	48.6	0.8
Poughkeepsie-Newburgh-Middletown, NY...............	3 631.4	5 421	54.2	3.6	3.5	9.0	3.7	2 540.4	3 792	6 564	7 121	44 086	52.6	46.3	1.1
Prescott, AZ.................	676.3	3 181	35.2	1.6	7.3	4.9	10.7	475.8	2 237	1 439	472	9 822	37.0	61.4	1.6
Providence-New Bedford-Fall River, RI-MA	5 733.3	3 581	56.9	0.4	6.5	0.4	2.6	3 764.5	2 352	11 580	8 596	81 712	62.4	35.9	1.7
Provo-Orem, UT.................	1 237.3	2 508	51.4	3.5	5.9	0.3	4.4	2 038.0	4 131	1 088	2 472	26 328	18.8	77.6	3.5
Pueblo, CO	498.3	3 224	43.3	0.9	6.1	4.6	4.6	446.2	2 887	1 042	420	11 624	56.7	41.8	1.5
Punta Gorda, FL.................	645.6	4 225	30.2	3.1	8.6	1.3	9.5	627.2	4 104	280	312	5 930	45.8	53.1	1.1
Racine, WI.................	733.5	3 760	46.9	4.9	8.3	6.0	7.2	719.6	3 688	377	579	8 991	53.1	45.7	1.3
Raleigh-Cary, NC.................	3 752.7	3 582	43.6	7.3	4.5	4.6	2.5	13 091.7	12 496	5 486	3 624	86 049	53.9	45.2	1.0
Rapid City, SD	368.4	3 063	46.2	2.2	6.3	0.3	7.4	239.5	1 991	2 914	4 090	7 386	37.2	60.7	2.1
Reading, PA.................	1 817.4	4 521	55.4	4.1	3.6	7.3	2.6	3 268.4	8 131	1 171	1 087	23 006	53.9	44.7	1.4
Redding, CA.................	983.2	5 480	41.0	6.6	5.0	9.3	2.5	684.3	3 814	1 271	298	12 348	35.9	61.7	2.4
Reno-Sparks, NV	1 655.6	4 035	33.3	1.4	7.4	3.7	6.5	3 087.6	7 526	3 588	1 013	24 500	55.1	42.7	2.2
Richmond, VA.................	4 321.0	3 562	48.2	3.3	7.3	4.4	3.1	4 536.1	3 740	15 644	11 510	99 427	52.7	46.4	0.9
Riverside-San Bernardino-Ontario, CA.................	23 139.3	5 669	41.5	9.1	5.7	6.7	4.1	23 606.5	5 784	20 310	24 917	223 650	51.1	46.9	2.0
Roanoke, VA.................	1 031.0	3 477	47.6	0.5	6.0	6.5	2.6	1 016.8	3 429	4 054	1 042	17 538	44.2	54.6	1.2
Rochester, MN.................	773.7	4 273	37.9	1.6	4.5	9.3	6.5	1 736.2	9 588	1 041	699	9 292	49.5	48.3	2.2
Rochester, NY.................	5 606.0	5 440	49.1	3.8	3.5	11.4	3.6	3 829.8	3 716	4 596	1 761	72 227	54.8	43.9	1.3
Rockford, IL.................	1 254.9	3 562	47.7	1.3	5.6	2.7	5.4	954.7	2 710	1 121	709	16 395	54.9	43.4	1.7
Rocky Mount, NC.................	475.2	3 264	52.2	5.7	5.3	8.1	1.4	88.0	604	501	369	10 828	55.4	44.0	0.5
Rome, GA.................	541.5	5 663	32.4	42.5	2.6	0.1	2.8	233.9	2 446	243	307	6 829	31.2	67.6	1.1

1. Based on the resident population estimated as of July 1 of the year shown.   2. © 2009 Election Data Services, Inc. All rights reserved.

Table C. Metropolitan Areas — Land Area and Population

CBSA code[1]	Area name	Land area,[2] 2010 (sq km)	Total persons	Rank	Per square kilometer	White	Black	American Indian, Alaska Native	Asian and Pacific Islander	Percent Hispanic or Latino[3]	Under 5 years	5 to 17 years	18 to 24 years	25 to 34 years	35 to 44 years	45 to 54 years
		1	2	3	4	5	6	7	8	9	10	11	12	13	14	15
40900	Sacramento—Arden-Arcade—Roseville, CA.	13 194	2 149 127	24	162.9	58.9	8.3	1.6	14.8	20.2	6.7	18.2	10.3	13.6	13.2	14.5
40980	Saginaw-Saginaw Township North, MI	2 072	200 169	212	96.6	72.0	19.6	0.8	1.3	7.8	5.9	17.5	10.6	11.0	12.0	14.7
41060	St. Cloud, MN	4 536	189 093	221	41.7	92.4	3.5	0.6	2.3	2.6	6.7	16.8	14.6	13.7	11.8	13.9
41100	St. George, UT	6 284	138 115	281	22.0	87.1	0.8	1.6	2.4	9.8	9.0	21.2	9.7	13.0	10.0	9.7
41140	St. Joseph, MO-KS	4 288	127 329	300	29.7	89.5	5.9	1.0	1.1	4.2	6.4	16.5	10.3	13.1	12.5	14.9
41180	St. Louis, MO-IL	22 334	2 812 896	18	125.9	76.5	19.1	0.7	2.7	2.6	6.3	17.5	9.2	13.1	12.9	15.5
41420	Salem, OR	4 981	390 738	131	78.4	73.3	1.4	2.3	3.5	21.9	7.3	18.7	10.2	13.3	12.3	13.0
41500	Salinas, CA	8 497	415 057	122	48.8	34.8	3.3	0.8	7.9	55.4	7.8	18.9	11.1	15.0	13.2	12.8
41540	Salisbury, MD	1 798	125 203	307	69.6	65.3	29.0	0.7	2.6	4.3	5.9	15.3	15.6	12.2	11.7	14.2
41620	Salt Lake City, UT	24 748	1 124 197	50	45.4	76.6	1.8	1.0	5.6	16.6	8.8	20.7	10.4	16.9	13.2	12.1
41660	San Angelo, TX	6 665	111 823	326	16.8	59.3	4.1	0.8	1.5	35.5	7.0	16.6	13.8	13.3	11.0	13.1
41700	San Antonio-New Braunfels, TX	18 940	2 142 508	25	113.1	37.2	6.6	0.6	2.7	54.1	7.3	19.5	10.4	13.9	13.4	13.7
41740	San Diego-Carlsbad-San Marcos, CA	10 895	3 095 313	17	284.1	51.1	5.6	1.0	13.3	32.0	6.6	16.8	11.9	15.2	13.6	13.9
41780	Sandusky, OH	652	77 079	362	118.2	87.1	10.2	0.8	0.8	3.4	5.4	16.8	7.4	10.3	12.0	15.9
41860	San Francisco-Oakland-Fremont, CA	6 399	4 335 391	11	677.5	45.4	9.1	0.9	26.4	21.7	6.0	15.2	8.9	15.0	15.1	15.0
41860	Oakland-Fremont-Hayward, CA Div	3 768	2 559 296	X	679.2	42.8	12.0	1.0	24.7	23.3	6.4	17.1	9.3	14.0	14.7	15.1
41860	San Francisco-San Mateo-Redwood City, CA Div	2 630	1 776 095	X	675.3	49.1	4.8	0.7	29.0	19.3	5.4	12.6	8.3	16.5	15.7	14.9
41940	San Jose-Sunnyvale-Santa Clara, CA	6 938	1 836 911	31	264.8	37.8	2.8	0.6	33.7	27.8	7.0	17.3	8.9	15.1	15.6	14.8
42020	San Luis Obispo-Paso Robles, CA	8 543	269 637	170	31.6	73.3	2.3	1.3	4.4	20.8	4.9	13.9	14.7	11.9	11.0	14.6
42060	Santa Barbara-Santa Maria-Goleta, CA	7 084	423 895	119	59.8	49.8	2.2	1.0	6.1	42.9	6.5	16.7	14.9	13.6	11.9	13.0
42100	Santa Cruz-Watsonville, CA	1 153	262 382	175	227.6	62.1	1.4	1.2	5.8	32.0	5.7	15.4	13.8	12.9	12.6	14.8
42140	Santa Fe, NM	4 945	144 170	271	29.2	44.9	0.9	2.8	1.6	50.6	5.7	15.3	7.4	11.5	12.6	15.5
42220	Santa Rosa-Petaluma, CA	4 081	483 878	104	118.6	68.6	2.1	1.7	5.4	24.9	5.8	16.2	9.5	12.7	12.5	15.2
42340	Savannah, GA	3 471	347 611	145	100.1	58.7	34.4	0.7	2.8	5.0	7.0	17.1	11.9	14.8	12.7	13.7
42540	Scranton—Wilkes-Barre, PA	4 524	563 631	91	124.6	90.1	3.2	0.4	1.5	5.8	5.3	15.1	9.6	11.1	12.7	15.1
42660	Seattle-Tacoma-Bellevue, WA	15 209	3 439 809	15	226.2	71.8	6.8	2.0	14.8	9.0	6.5	16.4	9.3	15.2	14.8	15.2
42660	Seattle-Bellevue-Everett, WA Div	10 885	2 644 584	X	243.0	70.8	6.2	1.8	16.2	8.9	6.3	15.9	9.1	15.6	15.2	15.3
42660	Tacoma, WA Div	4 324	795 225	X	183.9	75.2	8.8	2.7	10.2	9.2	7.0	17.9	9.9	14.1	13.6	15.0
42680	Sebastian-Vero Beach, FL	1 302	138 028	282	106.0	78.4	9.3	0.6	1.6	11.2	4.7	14.1	6.6	9.0	10.3	13.7
43100	Sheboygan, WI	1 324	115 507	320	87.2	88.0	1.9	0.7	5.0	5.5	6.2	17.7	7.7	12.0	13.0	16.1
43300	Sherman-Denison, TX	2 416	120 877	313	50.0	80.5	6.4	2.4	1.2	11.3	6.5	17.6	9.3	11.4	12.2	14.9
43340	Shreveport-Bossier City, LA	6 719	398 604	130	59.3	55.8	39.5	0.9	1.6	3.5	7.1	17.8	9.8	14.0	12.1	14.0
43580	Sioux City, IA-NE-SD	5 371	143 577	273	26.7	78.1	3.1	2.3	2.7	15.6	7.8	19.2	9.7	12.6	12.2	13.7
43620	Sioux Falls, SD	6 671	228 261	193	34.2	90.3	3.7	2.5	1.8	3.4	8.0	18.0	9.1	15.6	13.1	14.2
43780	South Bend-Mishawaka, IN-MI	2 455	319 224	150	130.0	79.6	12.8	1.1	2.2	6.6	6.5	18.0	10.7	12.2	12.3	14.3
43900	Spartanburg, SC	2 093	284 307	163	135.8	71.2	21.2	0.6	2.4	5.9	6.7	17.8	9.8	11.9	13.7	14.4
44060	Spokane, WA	4 568	471 221	107	103.2	89.7	2.7	2.7	3.7	4.5	6.4	16.8	11.4	13.2	12.3	14.4
44100	Springfield, IL	3 063	210 170	201	68.6	85.2	12.3	0.6	1.9	1.7	6.3	17.4	8.3	12.7	12.5	15.5
44140	Springfield, MA	4 775	692 942	76	145.1	75.9	6.6	0.6	3.0	15.4	5.4	16.4	12.8	11.3	12.2	15.1
44180	Springfield, MO	7 788	436 712	112	56.1	93.3	2.7	1.5	1.7	2.7	6.6	16.7	11.8	13.4	12.3	13.9
44220	Springfield, OH	1 029	138 333	280	134.4	87.4	10.2	0.8	1.0	2.8	6.3	17.3	9.0	11.0	12.1	14.4
44300	State College, PA	2 875	153 990	255	53.6	89.2	3.4	0.4	5.9	2.4	4.4	11.5	28.9	12.2	10.4	11.6
44600	Steubenville-Weirton, WV-OH	1 503	124 454	309	82.8	94.5	4.8	0.5	0.6	1.0	5.0	14.9	8.7	10.1	12.1	15.4
44700	Stockton, CA	3 604	685 306	77	190.2	38.4	8.1	1.3	16.5	38.9	7.9	21.4	10.4	13.3	13.2	13.4
44940	Sumter, SC	1 723	107 456	335	62.4	48.2	47.5	0.8	1.7	3.3	7.4	18.1	10.8	13.2	12.1	14.1
45060	Syracuse, NY	6 177	662 577	80	107.3	85.5	8.8	1.3	2.8	3.4	5.8	17.1	11.7	11.5	12.4	15.6
45220	Tallahassee, FL	6 184	367 413	137	59.4	59.1	33.0	0.8	2.9	5.8	5.7	14.6	18.9	14.1	11.7	13.1
45300	Tampa-St. Petersburg-Clearwater, FL	6 510	2 783 243	19	427.5	69.0	12.0	0.7	3.6	16.2	5.6	15.6	8.6	12.1	13.1	14.9
45460	Terre Haute, IN	3 794	172 425	233	45.4	91.7	5.8	0.7	1.5	1.9	5.8	16.2	11.9	12.7	12.7	14.2
45500	Texarkana, TX-Texarkana, AR	3 912	136 027	288	34.8	69.1	25.0	1.3	1.0	5.2	6.7	17.6	8.8	13.4	13.1	14.2
45780	Toledo, OH	4 192	651 429	81	155.4	79.1	14.4	0.7	1.8	5.8	6.4	17.1	11.5	12.1	12.3	14.7
45820	Topeka, KS	8 372	233 870	189	27.9	82.3	7.8	2.5	1.4	8.8	6.8	18.1	8.1	12.3	11.8	14.9
45940	Trenton-Ewing, NJ	582	366 513	138	629.7	55.8	20.3	0.5	9.8	15.1	5.9	16.8	10.9	12.8	14.1	15.2
46060	Tucson, AZ	23 794	980 263	52	41.2	56.8	3.8	3.0	3.5	34.6	6.4	16.6	11.0	12.9	11.8	13.4
46140	Tulsa, OK	16 237	937 478	54	57.7	73.0	9.5	12.6	2.3	8.4	7.1	18.5	9.1	13.4	12.9	14.3
46220	Tuscaloosa, AL	6 767	219 461	196	32.4	62.0	34.2	0.5	1.4	2.8	6.0	15.9	18.4	13.1	11.6	12.6
46340	Tyler, TX	2 387	209 714	202	87.9	63.2	18.4	0.8	1.5	17.2	7.1	18.5	10.8	12.8	12.2	13.1
46540	Utica-Rome, NY	6 796	299 397	157	44.1	88.5	5.7	0.6	2.7	4.0	5.6	16.3	9.8	11.1	12.3	15.4
46660	Valdosta, GA	4 116	139 588	278	33.9	58.7	34.5	0.8	1.9	5.5	7.6	17.3	15.6	14.1	12.2	12.7
46700	Vallejo-Fairfield, CA	2 128	413 344	123	194.2	44.8	16.2	1.5	18.6	24.0	6.5	18.1	9.8	13.3	13.2	15.5
47020	Victoria, TX	5 804	115 384	322	19.9	49.0	5.6	0.5	1.8	43.8	7.3	19.1	8.7	12.2	11.8	14.4
47220	Vineland-Millville-Bridgeton, NJ	1 253	156 898	253	125.2	51.7	20.0	1.5	1.5	27.1	6.9	17.1	9.5	14.4	14.1	14.2

1. CBSA = Core Based Statistical Area. DIV = Metropolitan Division. See Appendix A for explanation. See Appendix B for list of metropolitan areas identified by type. 2. Dry land or land partially or temporarily covered by water. 3. May be of any race.

Table C. Metropolitan Areas — Population and Households

Area name	Population, 2010 (cont.) Age (percent) (cont.) 55 to 64 years	65 to 74 years	75 years and over	Percent female	Population change and components of change, 1990–2010 Total persons 1990	2000	Percent change 1990–2000	2000–2010	Components of change, 2000–2009 Births	Deaths	Net migration	Households, 2010 Number	Percent change, 2000–2010	Persons per household	Percent Female family householder[1]	One person
	16	17	18	19	20	21	22	23	24	25	26	27	28	29	30	31
Sacramento—Arden-Arcade—Roseville, CA..	11.5	6.4	5.6	51.0	1 506 792	1 796 857	19.3	19.6	265 752	133 652	207 891	787 667	18.4	2.68	13.0	24.8
Saginaw-Saginaw Township North, MI	13.0	8.0	7.3	51.7	211 946	210 039	-0.9	-4.7	24 330	19 082	-14 154	79 011	-1.8	2.44	16.0	28.2
St. Cloud, MN	10.6	6.0	6.0	49.6	149 509	167 392	12.0	13.0	22 909	10 270	5 297	71 311	17.5	2.52	8.5	25.4
St. George, UT	10.1	9.3	8.0	50.6	48 560	90 354	86.1	52.9	21 799	7 547	33 149	46 334	54.8	2.94	8.4	18.8
St. Joseph, MO-KS	11.8	7.4	7.0	48.8	115 816	122 336	5.6	4.1	14 507	12 045	-1 479	48 184	3.6	2.46	12.0	28.1
St. Louis, MO-IL	12.1	7.0	6.4	51.6	2 580 720	2 698 687	4.6	4.2	339 347	233 675	-12 683	1 119 020	6.7	2.46	13.7	28.5
Salem, OR	12.0	7.0	6.3	50.4	278 024	347 214	24.9	12.5	51 654	28 396	27 795	141 245	13.3	2.68	12.0	24.6
Salinas, CA	10.4	5.5	5.2	48.6	355 660	401 762	13.0	3.3	68 134	21 904	-35 690	125 946	3.9	3.15	12.7	21.7
Salisbury, MD	11.8	7.1	6.1	51.1	97 779	109 391	11.9	14.5	13 910	10 293	7 836	46 008	13.4	2.50	15.2	26.5
Salt Lake City, UT	9.3	4.8	3.8	49.7	768 075	968 858	26.1	16.0	188 828	52 286	8 343	373 583	17.4	2.97	10.7	21.6
San Angelo, TX	11.4	7.2	6.7	51.0	100 087	105 781	5.7	5.7	15 127	9 271	-844	42 984	6.9	2.48	13.3	28.1
San Antonio-New Braunfels, TX	10.7	6.1	4.9	50.9	1 407 745	1 711 703	21.6	25.2	283 210	123 764	210 708	763 022	26.9	2.74	15.5	24.3
San Diego-Carlsbad-San Marcos, CA	10.6	5.8	5.5	49.8	2 498 016	2 813 833	12.6	10.0	423 374	181 546	-23 412	1 086 865	9.3	2.75	12.1	24.0
Sandusky, OH	14.8	9.1	8.2	51.0	76 781	79 551	3.6	-3.1	8 320	7 682	-2 816	31 860	0.4	2.37	12.9	28.6
San Francisco-Oakland-Fremont, CA	12.2	6.7	5.9	50.7	3 711 756	4 123 740	11.1	5.1	520 322	268 980	-80 856	1 627 360	4.9	2.61	11.2	28.0
Oakland-Fremont-Hayward, CA Div.	11.8	6.3	5.4	51.1	2 108 078	2 392 557	13.5	7.0	321 583	151 615	-16 475	920 502	6.1	2.73	12.7	24.7
San Francisco-San Mateo-Redwood City, CA Div.	12.7	7.2	6.8	50.1	1 603 678	1 731 183	8.0	2.6	198 739	117 365	-64 381	706 858	3.3	2.45	9.3	32.3
San Jose-Sunnyvale-Santa Clara, CA	10.4	6.0	5.1	49.8	1 534 274	1 735 819	13.1	5.8	258 376	83 942	-63 577	621 009	6.7	2.91	10.8	21.6
San Luis Obispo-Paso Robles, CA	13.8	7.9	7.4	48.8	217 162	246 681	13.6	9.3	24 628	19 136	16 300	102 016	10.0	2.48	9.3	26.2
Santa Barbara-Santa Maria-Goleta, CA	10.6	6.3	6.5	49.8	369 608	399 347	8.0	6.1	55 821	26 635	-19 175	142 104	4.0	2.86	10.9	24.8
Santa Cruz-Watsonville, CA	13.7	6.0	5.1	50.1	229 734	255 602	11.3	2.7	32 171	15 045	-15 384	94 355	3.5	2.66	10.5	26.4
Santa Fe, NM	16.8	9.3	5.8	51.3	98 928	129 292	30.7	11.5	15 180	8 099	11 881	61 963	18.1	2.28	11.0	33.7
Santa Rosa-Petaluma, CA	14.2	7.3	6.6	50.8	388 222	458 614	18.1	5.5	53 617	34 996	-2 730	185 825	7.8	2.55	10.6	27.3
Savannah, GA	11.2	6.5	5.1	51.5	257 899	293 000	13.6	18.6	44 820	25 444	32 133	131 868	18.7	2.53	16.5	26.2
Scranton—Wilkes-Barre, PA	13.5	8.5	9.2	51.4	575 322	560 625	-2.6	0.5	52 481	67 636	7 680	230 395	1.2	2.36	12.5	31.2
Seattle-Tacoma-Bellevue, WA	11.8	5.9	4.9	50.2	2 559 136	3 043 878	18.9	13.0	392 652	198 862	172 107	1 357 475	13.4	2.49	10.2	28.4
Seattle-Bellevue-Everett, WA Div	11.8	5.8	4.9	50.1	1 972 933	2 343 058	18.8	12.9	294 984	145 187	118 989	1 057 557	13.0	2.46	9.4	29.3
Tacoma, WA Div	11.5	6.2	4.9	50.6	586 203	700 820	19.6	13.5	97 668	50 675	53 118	299 918	15.0	2.59	13.0	25.1
Sebastian-Vero Beach, FL	14.4	13.1	14.1	51.6	90 208	112 947	25.2	22.2	11 821	15 670	26 537	60 176	22.5	2.26	9.8	29.8
Sheboygan, WI	12.7	7.3	7.3	49.8	103 877	112 646	8.4	2.5	12 630	9 702	-320	46 390	6.5	2.42	8.6	27.9
Sherman-Denison, TX	12.6	8.5	7.0	51.3	95 019	110 595	16.4	9.3	14 731	11 608	6 936	46 905	9.5	2.53	12.2	25.5
Shreveport-Bossier City, LA	11.9	7.1	6.1	51.9	360 009	375 965	4.4	6.0	53 138	34 715	-724	157 916	9.4	2.47	18.8	28.9
Sioux City, IA-NE-SD	11.8	6.6	6.3	50.5	131 350	143 053	8.9	0.4	21 107	11 460	-7 683	54 396	1.5	2.58	11.9	27.0
Sioux Falls, SD	10.8	5.6	5.5	50.2	153 500	187 093	21.9	22.0	30 953	14 057	28 075	89 297	23.2	2.48	9.6	27.4
South Bend-Mishawaka, IN-MI	12.4	6.9	6.9	51.3	296 529	316 663	6.8	0.8	40 305	26 604	-11 102	123 673	2.7	2.49	13.1	28.3
Spartanburg, SC	12.4	7.8	5.7	51.5	226 793	253 791	11.9	12.0	32 846	24 070	25 536	109 246	11.8	2.53	15.1	26.2
Spokane, WA	12.5	6.8	6.1	50.6	361 333	417 939	15.7	12.7	53 083	34 345	34 266	187 167	14.4	2.44	11.2	28.6
Springfield, IL	13.3	7.3	6.6	52.0	189 550	201 437	6.3	4.3	24 975	17 990	-855	88 126	5.4	2.34	13.0	31.4
Springfield, MA	12.9	6.9	7.0	52.2	672 964	680 014	1.0	1.9	71 467	58 633	1 590	269 091	3.2	2.44	15.2	29.5
Springfield, MO	11.5	7.4	6.5	51.1	298 818	368 374	23.3	18.6	50 553	33 582	47 495	174 584	20.2	2.42	10.4	27.4
Springfield, OH	13.6	8.6	7.6	51.6	147 538	144 742	-1.9	-4.4	16 772	15 016	-6 159	55 244	-2.5	2.45	14.1	27.7
State College, PA	9.7	5.9	5.3	48.2	124 812	135 758	8.8	13.4	12 056	8 245	7 492	57 573	16.7	2.38	6.4	28.7
Steubenville-Weirton, WV-OH	15.3	9.4	9.2	51.8	142 523	132 008	-7.4	-5.7	11 874	16 024	-6 209	52 426	-3.8	2.31	12.0	30.0
Stockton, CA	10.0	5.6	4.8	50.2	480 628	563 598	17.3	21.6	100 619	42 408	55 975	215 007	18.4	3.12	15.4	19.7
Sumter, SC	11.3	7.3	5.6	51.9	101 276	104 646	3.3	2.7	15 326	8 854	-5 993	40 398	7.1	2.59	20.2	25.8
Syracuse, NY	12.3	7.0	6.8	51.4	659 924	650 154	-1.5	1.9	71 776	52 169	-19 701	261 840	3.9	2.43	13.0	29.2
Tallahassee, FL	11.5	6.0	4.4	51.4	259 107	320 304	23.6	14.7	39 983	21 820	23 286	144 033	14.7	2.40	15.0	28.9
Tampa-St. Petersburg-Clearwater, FL	12.7	9.0	8.3	51.6	2 067 959	2 395 997	15.9	16.2	292 213	264 578	336 925	1 151 263	14.1	2.37	12.9	29.9
Terre Haute, IN	12.3	7.5	6.7	49.3	166 578	170 943	2.6	0.9	19 327	17 599	-1 803	66 250	0.7	2.42	12.3	28.8
Texarkana, TX-Texarkana, AR	12.1	7.7	6.4	49.9	120 132	129 749	8.0	4.8	16 336	12 117	4 249	51 888	6.6	2.47	16.8	27.6
Toledo, OH	12.6	6.9	6.5	51.4	654 157	659 188	0.8	-1.2	80 448	56 535	-31 978	263 001	1.2	2.41	14.1	29.9
Topeka, KS	13.1	7.7	7.0	51.2	210 257	224 551	6.8	4.2	29 434	20 515	-1 207	94 483	5.4	2.42	11.5	29.2
Trenton-Ewing, NJ	11.7	6.4	6.2	51.2	325 759	350 761	7.7	4.5	42 596	26 783	1 914	133 155	5.8	2.61	14.2	26.9
Tucson, AZ	12.5	8.3	7.1	50.9	666 957	843 746	26.5	16.2	121 594	73 661	100 945	388 660	16.9	2.46	12.8	29.2
Tulsa, OK	11.8	7.1	5.7	50.9	761 019	859 532	12.9	9.1	123 481	76 011	26 942	367 091	8.9	2.51	12.6	27.3
Tuscaloosa, AL	11.1	6.1	5.2	51.6	176 151	192 034	9.0	14.3	24 500	16 732	9 715	86 178	15.1	2.42	15.8	29.4
Tyler, TX	11.3	7.6	6.6	51.6	151 309	174 706	15.5	20.0	26 991	15 869	19 952	79 055	20.3	2.60	13.3	25.3
Utica-Rome, NY	13.0	8.0	8.3	50.4	316 645	299 896	-5.3	-0.2	30 134	29 764	-5 171	119 352	2.7	2.38	12.7	30.7
Valdosta, GA	10.0	6.1	4.4	51.1	99 244	119 560	20.5	16.8	18 449	9 389	7 821	51 141	19.9	2.60	16.7	24.6
Vallejo-Fairfield, CA	12.4	6.3	5.0	50.1	339 469	394 542	16.2	4.8	53 542	24 963	-13 463	141 758	8.7	2.83	14.7	21.9
Victoria, TX	12.4	7.6	6.5	50.8	99 394	111 663	12.3	3.3	16 304	9 014	-2 923	42 821	6.6	2.65	13.7	24.3
Vineland-Millville-Bridgeton, NJ	11.1	6.7	5.9	48.5	138 053	146 438	6.1	7.1	21 247	13 643	4 684	51 931	5.7	2.79	18.6	24.0

1. No spouse present.

Table C. Metropolitan Areas — **Population, Vital Statistics, Medicare, and Crime**

Area name	Daytime population, 2010			Births, average 2006–2008		Deaths, average 2006–2008		Persons under 65 with no health insurance 2009		Medicare, 2011			Serious crimes known to police,[2] 2010 Total	
	Persons in group quarters, 2010	Number	Employment/residence ratio	Total	Rate[1]	Number	Rate[1]	Number	Percent	Enrolled in original Medicare	Enrolled in Medicare Advantage	Enrolled in a Medicare prescription drug plan	Number	Rate[3]
	32	33	34	35	36	37	38	39	40	41	42	43	44	45
Sacramento—Arden-Arcade—Roseville, CA..	35 946	2 152 977	1.00	30 344	14.5	14 701	7.0	274 069	14.9	316 243	131 327	86 231	77 470	3 605
Saginaw-Saginaw Township North, MI	7 116	D	D	2 492	12.3	2 090	10.3	21 747	13.0	39 411	8 353	13 310	7 347	3 670
St. Cloud, MN	9 261	192 968	1.04	D	D	1 112	6.0	16 748	10.3	27 145	12 210	11 637	4 487	2 373
St. George, UT	1 853	D	D	2 744	20.7	889	6.7	21 684	19.6	24 973	7 805	7 432	2 824	2 045
St. Joseph, MO-KS	8 674	D	D	D	D	1 311	10.6	16 504	15.6	21 666	1 147	11 946	4 799	3 769
St. Louis, MO-IL	56 232	2 823 012	1.01	34 689	12.4	25 066	8.9	298 272	12.5	456 610	115 830	177 739	104 035	3 751
Salem, OR	12 314	389 328	0.99	5 914	15.3	3 169	8.2	77 111	22.9	62 616	34 788	15 074	12 568	3 216
Salinas, CA	18 702	414 427	0.99	7 487	18.3	2 273	5.6	86 616	24.0	51 448	1 503	26 045	12 442	2 998
Salisbury, MD	10 054	D	D	D	D	1 149	9.6	17 197	16.9	19 889	472	9 722	5 252	4 195
Salt Lake City, UT	14 477	1 196 012	1.13	20 558	18.8	5 802	5.3	171 513	16.8	117 211	44 482	33 643	53 824	4 789
San Angelo, TX	5 165	D	D	1 667	15.5	1 008	9.4	23 826	25.7	18 746	1 318	7 823	4 933	4 411
San Antonio-New Braunfels, TX	49 032	2 146 386	0.99	31 060	15.6	13 805	6.9	422 916	23.4	295 989	91 401	73 661	120 288	5 617
San Diego-Carlsbad-San Marcos, CA	101 966	3 136 372	1.02	47 074	15.8	19 306	6.5	500 631	18.8	409 903	165 409	113 597	79 489	2 568
Sandusky, OH	1 677	D	D	851	11.0	861	11.1	8 401	13.6	15 802	2 883	7 475	2 240	2 945
San Francisco-Oakland-Fremont, CA	89 917	4 410 074	1.03	56 123	13.3	28 312	6.7	522 457	13.9	626 938	257 682	195 616	157 495	3 633
Oakland-Fremont-Hayward, CA Div	47 756	2 469 489	0.91	34 585	13.9	16 201	6.5	314 659	14.2	347 386	149 398	103 092	95 797	3 743
San Francisco-San Mateo-Redwood City, CA Div	42 161	1 940 585	1.18	21 538	12.5	12 111	7.0	207 798	13.6	279 552	108 284	92 524	61 698	3 474
San Jose-Sunnyvale-Santa Clara, CA	30 639	1 930 444	1.10	27 917	15.5	9 167	5.1	228 322	13.9	227 615	80 982	82 385	46 600	2 537
San Luis Obispo-Paso Robles, CA	17 006	266 621	0.97	2 784	10.6	2 104	8.0	38 869	17.5	47 847	6 467	20 131	6 897	2 558
Santa Barbara-Santa Maria-Goleta, CA	17 782	437 657	1.07	6 260	15.5	2 837	7.0	67 463	19.5	63 161	11 545	28 774	10 544	2 487
Santa Cruz-Watsonville, CA	10 969	254 646	0.93	3 569	14.2	1 584	6.3	40 480	18.1	35 795	4 786	17 558	9 580	3 651
Santa Fe, NM	2 613	146 893	1.03	1 694	11.8	945	6.6	29 922	24.0	25 745	6 298	9 842	6 406	4 443
Santa Rosa-Petaluma, CA	10 043	466 337	0.91	5 800	12.4	3 750	8.0	64 511	16.1	79 827	29 492	24 814	10 704	2 212
Savannah, GA	13 596	360 225	1.07	4 763	14.5	2 790	8.5	58 199	19.8	48 879	11 591	17 464	13 634	3 922
Scranton—Wilkes-Barre, PA	20 456	569 167	1.02	5 555	10.1	7 104	12.9	49 357	11.3	120 858	27 863	56 452	13 462	2 398
Seattle-Tacoma-Bellevue, WA	65 473	3 496 494	1.03	45 649	13.8	21 699	6.6	403 535	13.4	452 977	132 533	154 635	145 232	4 222
Seattle-Bellevue-Everett, WA Div	47 528	2 738 709	1.07	34 287	13.5	16 055	6.3	301 042	13.0	340 599	105 101	118 891	109 313	4 133
Tacoma, WA Div	17 945	757 785	0.89	11 362	14.7	5 644	7.3	102 493	14.7	112 378	27 432	35 744	35 919	4 517
Sebastian-Vero Beach, FL	1 794	D	D	1 403	10.7	1 689	12.9	24 768	25.6	37 816	5 582	14 924	4 696	3 402
Sheboygan, WI	3 023	D	D	1 410	12.3	1 036	9.0	9 479	9.9	19 811	6 627	5 731	2 428	2 102
Sherman-Denison, TX	2 214	D	D	1 583	13.3	1 285	10.8	25 202	25.4	22 967	1 818	9 986	3 944	3 263
Shreveport-Bossier City, LA	8 423	411 395	1.07	6 058	15.6	3 816	9.8	61 380	18.6	64 538	8 242	25 607	16 807	4 293
Sioux City, IA-NE-SD	3 055	145 733	1.03	D	D	1 265	8.8	17 032	13.9	22 556	4 731	11 464	4 127	2 966
Sioux Falls, SD	7 040	231 965	1.02	3 500	15.6	1 566	7.0	25 425	12.4	33 171	4 017	18 247	6 264	2 759
South Bend-Mishawaka, IN-MI	11 746	316 817	0.98	4 421	13.9	2 913	9.2	43 082	16.1	52 427	12 252	20 800	13 425	4 214
Spartanburg, SC	7 986	D	D	3 889	14.1	2 605	9.4	50 204	20.9	52 587	15 532	19 799	11 767	4 146
Spokane, WA	14 692	481 363	1.04	6 045	13.3	3 876	8.5	59 673	14.9	78 258	21 884	27 348	25 447	5 400
Springfield, IL	4 120	220 540	1.10	2 522	12.2	1 905	9.2	17 979	10.3	36 169	1 952	14 527	11 006	5 451
Springfield, MA	37 104	673 921	0.94	D	D	6 272	9.2	27 996	4.8	125 832	24 069	52 787	24 768	3 644
Springfield, MO	14 413	437 615	1.01	D	D	3 701	8.9	61 899	17.1	77 246	28 869	26 070	22 703	5 199
Springfield, OH	2 798	D	D	1 837	13.1	1 581	11.2	15 775	13.8	26 923	11 657	12 846	6 628	4 802
State College, PA	16 989	162 399	1.12	1 303	9.1	900	6.3	13 929	11.2	19 739	8 452	6 511	2 612	1 696
Steubenville-Weirton, WV-OH	3 310	D	D	D	D	1 712	13.9	13 143	13.7	27 778	8 702	13 939	2 103	1 777
Stockton, CA	14 354	662 489	0.90	11 471	17.1	4 685	7.0	114 489	19.2	87 661	24 766	36 511	33 820	4 935
Sumter, SC	2 774	D	D	1 697	16.3	966	9.3	17 373	20.0	17 984	2 209	7 102	4 830	4 495
Syracuse, NY	27 156	672 285	1.03	D	D	5 597	8.7	58 588	10.8	114 794	28 557	36 667	17 453	2 671
Tallahassee, FL	21 922	373 027	1.03	D	D	2 359	6.8	57 769	18.6	46 942	16 748	12 570	15 985	4 358
Tampa-St. Petersburg-Clearwater, FL	49 245	2 781 272	0.99	33 933	12.5	28 187	10.4	494 469	22.2	528 081	216 817	136 499	108 218	3 888
Terre Haute, IN	12 393	D	D	D	D	1 807	10.7	24 052	16.9	30 883	2 407	16 593	NA	NA
Texarkana, TX-Texarkana, AR	7 686	D	D	1 903	14.1	1 335	9.9	26 234	22.9	24 276	2 888	10 565	6 633	4 876
Toledo, OH	17 825	665 782	1.05	D	D	6 093	9.4	80 292	14.1	108 276	34 846	51 916	19 636	3 172
Topeka, KS	5 049	234 293	0.98	D	D	2 245	9.8	26 554	13.8	43 156	2 525	22 047	10 623	4 619
Trenton-Ewing, NJ	18 805	419 593	1.31	4 713	12.9	2 895	7.9	40 818	13.0	57 810	7 153	23 633	9 354	2 552
Tucson, AZ	24 139	981 599	1.00	13 764	14.1	8 041	8.2	154 841	18.2	166 634	73 268	36 708	28 776	2 936
Tulsa, OK	15 486	945 831	1.02	13 003	14.3	8 579	9.5	163 417	20.5	148 486	41 251	57 159	38 428	4 099
Tuscaloosa, AL	10 802	224 420	1.05	D	D	1 838	9.0	26 126	14.5	35 504	2 505	15 168	9 497	4 340
Tyler, TX	4 127	216 007	1.06	3 074	15.5	1 767	8.9	42 660	25.1	36 208	4 098	16 222	8 538	4 107
Utica-Rome, NY	14 831	300 465	1.01	3 271	11.1	3 125	10.6	27 524	11.5	60 805	16 279	21 865	7 557	2 563
Valdosta, GA	6 670	D	D	D	D	1 027	7.9	25 931	22.0	18 795	2 906	8 802	5 083	3 799
Vallejo-Fairfield, CA	12 452	379 242	0.80	5 755	14.1	2 750	6.7	51 536	14.5	57 475	25 427	10 560	14 281	3 455
Victoria, TX	1 850	D	D	D	D	1 026	9.0	24 516	25.2	19 571	1 543	9 515	5 094	4 415
Vineland-Millville-Bridgeton, NJ	12 111	157 004	1.00	2 495	16.0	1 400	9.0	24 955	18.6	25 054	3 112	12 910	6 064	3 865

1. Per 1,000 estimated resident population.   2. Data for serious crimes have not been adjusted for underreporting; this may affect comparability between geographic areas and over time.   3. Per 100,000 population estimated by the FBI.

Table C. Metropolitan Areas — Crime, Education, Money Income, and Poverty

Area name	Serious crimes known to police,[1] 2010 (cont.) Rate[2] Violent	Property	Education — School enrollment and attainment, 2010 Enrollment[3] Total	Percent private	Attainment[4] (percent) High school graduate or less	Bachelor's degree or more	Local government expenditures,[5] 2008-2009 Total current expenditures (mil dol)	Current expenditures per student (dollars)	Income and Poverty, 2010 Per capita income[6] (dollars)	Median household income (dollars)	Percent of households with income of less than $25,000	Percent of households with income of $100,000 or more	Percent of households with income of $200,000 or more	Percent below poverty level All persons	Children under 18 years	Children under 5
	46	47	48	49	50	51	52	53	54	55	56	57	58	59	60	61
Sacramento—Arden-Arcade—Roseville, CA..	481	3 124	640 070	13.0	34.3	29.4	3 231.0	9 029	26 992	56 233	21.0	23.7	3.9	15.1	20.5	21.4
Saginaw-Saginaw Township North, MI	860	2 810	53 680	14.4	48.9	17.8	341.7	10 198	21 025	41 938	29.5	12.4	1.7	16.9	24.1	33.9
St. Cloud, MN	177	2 196	57 071	22.7	39.0	22.1	274.5	9 666	23 507	50 085	21.8	14.3	1.5	12.3	12.4	15.7
St. George, UT	109	1 935	42 086	7.0	36.0	27.2	170.5	6 369	21 226	49 058	23.2	12.7	2.8	14.3	20.8	16.9
St. Joseph, MO-KS	297	3 472	32 667	8.2	54.0	18.9	165.8	9 094	22 006	43 178	30.5	12.5	1.5	14.2	17.8	22.9
St. Louis, MO-IL	519	3 232	760 473	23.7	39.6	29.9	4 452.8	10 567	27 242	50 912	24.0	20.2	3.6	13.3	18.8	23.1
Salem, OR	234	2 983	102 523	14.5	43.0	22.6	660.6	9 962	21 530	45 584	24.9	13.5	1.7	17.9	27.4	31.9
Salinas, CA	491	2 507	118 791	9.8	49.5	22.8	726.3	10 295	24 950	54 534	20.4	23.1	5.8	17.1	26.4	26.9
Salisbury, MD	652	3 543	37 204	11.2	52.2	23.4	227.4	12 993	21 926	47 128	24.5	14.6	2.2	17.0	24.0	37.2
Salt Lake City, UT	355	4 434	344 238	13.0	36.1	29.0	1 345.8	6 348	24 006	57 419	19.5	21.3	3.3	13.1	17.1	19.4
San Angelo, TX	274	4 138	29 233	10.5	50.8	19.3	158.5	8 611	21 099	38 234	35.1	12.3	2.0	20.3	27.9	31.3
San Antonio-New Braunfels, TX	476	5 142	623 575	13.0	43.0	25.4	3 319.2	8 385	23 434	50 225	24.2	18.1	3.2	16.3	23.8	26.4
San Diego-Carlsbad-San Marcos, CA	376	2 192	880 968	14.4	34.0	33.7	4 693.7	9 541	28 498	59 923	19.8	26.6	5.7	14.8	19.2	19.2
Sandusky, OH	289	2 656	16 966	14.0	53.1	19.3	168.0	12 936	24 203	42 246	27.6	14.3	2.4	15.7	29.5	37.8
San Francisco-Oakland-Fremont, CA	529	3 104	1 116 287	19.6	30.5	43.4	5 435.8	9 805	37 693	73 027	17.6	36.7	10.7	10.9	13.3	13.6
Oakland-Fremont-Hayward, CA Div	578	3 165	700 314	15.7	32.7	39.6	3 478.9	9 150	33 456	70 415	17.6	34.5	9.2	11.7	15.3	15.8
San Francisco-San Mateo-Redwood City, CA Div	457	3 016	415 973	26.1	27.5	48.3	1 956.9	11 234	43 808	78 247	17.5	39.6	12.7	9.7	9.4	10.0
San Jose-Sunnyvale-Santa Clara, CA	266	2 271	515 390	19.3	30.0	45.3	2 665.4	9 767	37 177	83 944	14.8	42.8	12.8	10.6	13.5	13.6
San Luis Obispo-Paso Robles, CA	266	2 292	74 264	7.9	33.8	30.8	325.9	9 391	28 231	53 978	21.4	22.4	4.4	14.4	12.6	11.6
Santa Barbara-Santa Maria-Goleta, CA	434	2 053	132 683	11.0	39.0	29.7	626.6	9 505	28 781	56 767	22.5	26.1	6.0	18.0	21.8	23.6
Santa Cruz-Watsonville, CA	500	3 151	82 327	13.1	32.4	33.7	386.6	9 993	29 060	61 071	20.9	27.8	5.5	14.6	17.3	18.5
Santa Fe, NM	375	4 069	32 094	17.2	35.4	37.9	143.6	9 118	29 873	47 080	29.0	19.5	3.6	18.0	26.9	19.6
Santa Rosa-Petaluma, CA	388	1 824	123 170	10.9	33.4	32.1	687.3	9 781	29 510	59 055	20.0	23.8	5.4	13.1	15.0	19.6
Savannah, GA	332	3 590	100 301	17.7	41.8	28.4	495.3	9 451	24 273	46 755	27.0	17.5	2.5	17.3	23.9	29.1
Scranton—Wilkes-Barre, PA	233	2 165	132 363	28.0	52.0	22.2	864.8	10 966	23 462	42 368	28.9	13.9	2.2	14.9	25.0	34.1
Seattle-Tacoma-Bellevue, WA	349	3 874	862 861	17.3	30.3	37.0	4 721.1	9 496	32 401	63 088	17.9	27.7	5.3	11.7	15.6	18.2
Seattle-Bellevue-Everett, WA Div	309	3 824	659 158	17.9	27.8	40.9	3 489.9	9 525	34 275	65 552	17.3	29.8	6.1	11.6	15.1	17.9
Tacoma, WA Div	480	4 037	203 703	15.2	38.9	28.4	1 231.2	9 417	26 148	56 510	19.7	20.4	2.4	12.0	16.8	18.9
Sebastian-Vero Beach, FL	325	3 078	27 174	9.7	43.6	25.9	150.6	8 555	26 925	47 335	25.7	15.9	3.4	14.6	27.2	25.0
Sheboygan, WI	145	1 957	29 631	18.5	49.5	20.0	215.8	10 938	23 609	49 440	22.5	14.2	1.5	9.4	14.9	27.6
Sherman-Denison, TX	280	2 982	29 649	9.4	47.4	19.2	182.1	8 665	22 332	45 577	27.3	13.4	2.2	14.4	18.5	20.2
Shreveport-Bossier City, LA	624	3 669	101 790	12.5	50.2	20.4	688.9	10 259	22 547	40 762	33.8	14.4	2.5	18.0	29.1	30.0
Sioux City, IA-NE-SD	252	2 714	38 471	24.3	47.9	22.4	266.0	10 215	22 640	44 038	27.0	14.6	2.0	13.8	20.9	29.9
Sioux Falls, SD	245	2 514	60 026	20.8	37.2	31.8	277.0	7 570	26 043	52 050	20.8	17.1	2.7	10.3	11.7	14.4
South Bend-Mishawaka, IN-MI	342	3 872	93 689	28.8	46.4	24.4	470.4	9 761	21 941	41 991	28.7	14.1	2.0	15.5	23.8	30.2
Spartanburg, SC	519	3 627	73 572	14.9	48.3	20.6	431.9	9 200	20 964	41 850	29.2	13.6	1.5	17.1	26.0	29.5
Spokane, WA	347	5 053	124 744	17.5	31.9	28.5	721.1	9 542	24 410	47 039	25.7	14.7	2.5	14.3	15.9	19.2
Springfield, IL	876	4 575	54 531	16.6	36.8	31.4	323.0	10 086	27 656	50 423	22.9	19.0	2.9	12.9	19.5	26.6
Springfield, MA	583	3 061	199 728	21.8	43.3	29.1	1 486.4	14 091	25 198	49 209	27.3	19.3	2.5	15.8	22.3	30.5
Springfield, MO	447	4 751	113 783	16.1	42.9	24.9	505.5	7 796	21 256	40 084	31.4	10.6	1.8	17.5	23.8	35.7
Springfield, OH	369	4 432	34 602	17.2	53.2	17.1	216.1	9 456	20 594	39 580	33.2	10.5	1.4	20.6	31.5	44.8
State College, PA	103	1 594	61 903	8.1	39.8	40.9	167.0	12 174	22 589	44 746	27.5	17.0	2.2	20.9	16.8	21.1
Steubenville-Weirton, WV-OH	139	1 637	25 667	19.9	57.6	14.4	183.8	10 267	20 250	35 666	35.7	8.8	0.8	16.7	27.1	39.9
Stockton, CA	806	4 129	202 501	11.0	49.2	17.7	1 213.6	9 005	21 147	50 011	22.2	18.9	2.8	19.2	26.5	29.4
Sumter, SC	881	3 614	31 557	13.9	51.0	15.6	146.2	8 323	16 862	36 457	37.0	8.1	0.4	20.4	31.5	39.3
Syracuse, NY	282	2 388	184 594	19.2	41.9	29.2	1 639.5	15 227	25 579	49 694	25.7	18.7	2.7	14.3	20.3	24.1
Tallahassee, FL	768	3 590	125 371	10.6	38.0	34.2	390.3	8 615	22 722	41 511	32.5	14.3	2.0	25.7	26.7	32.9
Tampa-St. Petersburg-Clearwater, FL	500	3 388	670 524	15.9	43.2	26.2	3 335.1	8 605	24 958	43 547	27.5	15.0	2.9	15.4	21.6	27.5
Terre Haute, IN	NA	NA	46 782	14.4	53.7	17.7	243.9	9 176	21 628	41 200	29.7	12.6	2.5	15.9	22.9	26.8
Texarkana, TX-Texarkana, AR	722	4 154	33 704	8.2	49.7	16.1	212.0	8 746	21 092	40 547	32.3	11.5	1.9	17.8	27.4	31.7
Toledo, OH	508	2 664	189 111	16.2	44.3	24.3	1 174.3	10 958	23 196	41 583	30.2	14.6	2.3	17.4	25.0	28.6
Topeka, KS	388	4 231	60 699	11.8	42.6	27.3	372.4	9 952	23 907	45 360	26.7	14.1	2.3	16.6	26.1	34.4
Trenton-Ewing, NJ	452	2 101	102 053	23.9	39.7	38.5	1 000.0	16 686	34 884	70 956	17.9	35.3	9.6	12.1	17.3	21.1
Tucson, AZ	429	2 506	271 535	11.1	35.8	30.0	1 162.8	7 777	23 747	44 274	27.6	15.4	2.5	17.8	24.7	28.7
Tulsa, OK	607	3 493	244 954	13.7	42.6	24.8	1 226.9	7 679	24 194	44 519	26.7	15.2	2.9	15.5	22.7	26.7
Tuscaloosa, AL	441	3 899	64 826	10.8	45.8	25.1	275.8	8 554	21 395	41 047	30.9	14.1	2.0	18.4	25.1	30.4
Tyler, TX	418	3 689	56 950	12.2	39.7	24.9	271.3	8 301	24 217	43 209	27.0	17.4	3.0	14.4	19.2	23.2
Utica-Rome, NY	253	2 310	72 294	13.3	46.8	21.3	670.6	14 708	22 806	46 625	26.4	15.6	1.0	15.1	24.3	29.5
Valdosta, GA	344	3 455	40 748	8.9	51.0	20.5	206.1	9 316	17 869	36 028	35.2	10.6	1.1	23.0	30.0	28.0
Vallejo-Fairfield, CA	455	3 000	114 116	10.5	38.7	22.8	607.6	8 818	26 842	63 384	16.9	27.5	3.5	12.4	19.4	29.4
Victoria, TX	567	3 848	27 651	14.7	52.7	15.5	175.2	8 478	23 381	45 802	29.2	16.6	2.3	19.5	32.0	42.6
Vineland-Millville-Bridgeton, NJ	504	3 361	36 804	11.4	63.8	13.2	438.0	16 383	21 641	51 619	28.3	20.4	2.6	16.9	26.3	31.3

1. Data for serious crimes have not been adjusted for underreporting; this may affect comparability between geographic areas and over time.　2. Per 100,000 population estimated by the FBI.　3. All persons 3 years old and over enrolled in nursery school through college.　4. Persons 25 years old and over.　5. Elementary and secondary education expenditures.　6. Based on resident population estimated as of July 1, 2009.

Table C. Metropolitan Areas — **Personal Income**

Area name	\[Personal income, 2009\] Total (mil dol)	Per capita[1] Percent change, 2008–2009	Per capita[1] Dollars	Per capita[1] Rank	Wages and salaries[2] (mil dol)	Proprietors' income (mil dol)	Dividends, interest, and rent (mil dol)	Transfer payments Total (mil dol)	Government payments to individuals Total (mil dol)	Government payments to individuals Social Security (mil dol)	Government payments to individuals Medical payments (mil dol)	Government payments to individuals Income maintenance (mil dol)	Government payments to individuals Unemployment insurance (mil dol)
	62	63	64	65	66	67	68	69	70	71	72	73	74
Sacramento—Arden-Arcade—Roseville, CA..	85 746	-1.3	40 306	69	56 321	6 991	14 823	14 667	14 279	4 003	6 009	1 681	1 130
Saginaw-Saginaw Township North, MI	6 029	-0.4	30 137	320	4 002	333	902	1 767	1 730	612	676	238	119
St. Cloud, MN	6 350	-1.7	33 571	229	4 518	473	1 147	1 153	1 119	346	455	86	94
St. George, UT	3 595	-1.7	26 147	360	1 903	206	930	798	773	339	268	60	39
St. Joseph, MO-KS	4 074	1.7	32 168	267	2 618	276	557	914	891	299	405	82	37
St. Louis, MO-IL	115 220	-3.3	40 728	64	77 166	6 780	21 711	19 584	19 069	6 706	8 133	1 787	1 052
Salem, OR	12 802	0.7	32 320	262	7 331	1 028	2 369	2 828	2 756	867	1 119	302	227
Salinas, CA	17 127	-0.7	41 735	55	9 565	2 373	3 832	2 337	2 263	650	896	250	209
Salisbury, MD	3 984	0.9	33 153	239	2 577	191	642	930	908	279	412	101	47
Salt Lake City, UT	42 386	-1.1	37 500	129	34 099	3 514	7 846	4 976	4 770	1 629	1 817	504	288
San Angelo, TX	3 952	0.6	35 892	167	2 171	356	882	773	754	248	346	72	23
San Antonio-New Braunfels, TX	75 186	1.3	36 285	157	45 797	7 683	13 563	13 026	12 654	3 595	5 540	1 514	438
San Diego-Carlsbad-San Marcos, CA	139 577	-1.7	45 706	31	92 789	11 825	27 493	18 538	18 000	5 140	7 511	1 756	1 501
Sandusky, OH	2 789	-1.9	36 236	158	1 587	237	474	649	635	229	255	49	39
San Francisco-Oakland-Fremont, CA	259 043	-2.6	59 993	3	166 738	24 861	57 063	27 565	26 778	7 986	11 465	2 541	2 331
Oakland-Fremont-Hayward, CA Div.	130 640	-2.2	51 580	X	74 789	9 879	24 684	16 374	15 912	4 486	6 951	1 592	1 448
San Francisco-San Mateo-Redwood City, CA Div...	128 403	-3.0	71 930	X	91 949	14 982	32 378	11 191	10 865	3 500	4 514	949	883
San Jose-Sunnyvale-Santa Clara, CA	101 495	-3.9	55 169	6	88 273	6 972	21 329	10 140	9 805	2 881	3 901	895	1 146
San Luis Obispo-Paso Robles, CA	10 706	-1.7	40 103	71	5 300	1 100	3 036	1 600	1 551	642	533	116	102
Santa Barbara-Santa Maria-Goleta, CA	18 955	-2.1	46 565	24	10 740	1 803	5 856	2 351	2 278	837	836	216	141
Santa Cruz-Watsonville, CA .	12 592	-2.9	49 145	16	5 122	1 249	3 086	1 537	1 490	466	570	132	156
Santa Fe, NM	6 292	-2.6	42 645	44	3 334	707	1 624	904	877	342	353	74	37
Santa Rosa-Petaluma, CA....	21 142	-4.2	44 784	33	10 392	1 968	5 250	3 032	2 946	1 080	1 142	200	258
Savannah, GA	13 157	-0.5	38 348	105	8 327	638	2 326	2 200	2 139	687	793	252	107
Scranton—Wilkes-Barre, PA	19 865	0.8	36 154	160	11 533	1 334	3 210	5 135	5 035	1 683	2 145	356	416
Seattle-Tacoma-Bellevue, WA	171 681	-0.9	50 378	13	121 165	14 395	34 540	20 968	20 352	6 275	6 962	2 077	2 206
Seattle-Bellevue-Everett, WA Div	139 348	-1.5	53 369	X	102 711	12 478	29 705	15 569	15 094	4 726	5 133	1 453	1 718
Tacoma, WA Div	32 333	1.5	40 577	X	18 454	1 917	4 835	5 398	5 259	1 549	1 828	623	488
Sebastian-Vero Beach, FL....	7 610	-5.0	56 303	5	2 279	280	4 109	1 242	1 218	549	480	69	49
Sheboygan, WI	4 328	-1.9	37 783	121	2 966	285	763	743	722	299	264	47	76
Sherman-Denison, TX	3 849	1.2	32 066	270	1 978	198	743	931	909	318	414	68	30
Shreveport-Bossier City, LA....	15 018	-0.3	38 358	104	9 078	1 835	2 660	2 923	2 852	845	1 288	399	67
Sioux City, IA-NE-SD	5 012	-1.4	34 719	196	3 306	549	837	904	878	314	373	89	36
Sioux Falls, SD	9 466	0.3	39 753	76	6 418	1 102	1 852	1 146	1 103	458	447	90	23
South Bend-Mishawaka, IN-MI	10 859	-4.4	34 196	208	6 436	1 141	1 672	2 211	2 153	793	820	223	170
Spartanburg, SC	8 674	-1.2	30 242	317	6 144	499	1 306	2 059	2 006	750	763	188	115
Spokane, WA	16 216	0.8	34 599	199	10 730	901	3 080	3 523	3 438	1 044	1 311	420	223
Springfield, IL	8 425	0.8	40 467	66	6 001	702	1 455	1 400	1 362	510	520	149	88
Springfield, MA	26 480	0.1	37 888	118	14 851	1 534	3 837	6 732	6 605	1 608	3 334	826	490
Springfield, MO	13 683	-0.1	31 754	285	8 537	1 139	2 445	2 941	2 863	1 020	1 189	253	119
Springfield, OH	4 557	0.3	32 627	253	2 217	214	599	1 190	1 164	365	508	124	58
State College, PA	4 972	0.9	34 006	214	3 756	324	854	809	783	289	265	38	61
Steubenville-Weirton, WV-OH	3 829	0.1	31 661	289	2 022	192	535	1 197	1 175	421	512	102	57
Stockton, CA	20 969	-0.7	31 071	300	11 198	1 965	3 268	4 851	4 727	1 105	2 157	657	415
Sumter, SC	3 078	-0.1	29 458	336	1 985	140	401	824	805	234	303	123	39
Syracuse, NY	23 797	0.5	36 833	139	16 371	1 200	3 658	5 076	4 958	1 717	2 076	547	272
Tallahassee, FL	12 180	-0.3	33 833	220	8 510	619	2 235	1 975	1 909	635	704	263	65
Tampa-St. Petersburg-Clearwater, FL	103 386	-1.5	37 632	124	63 326	5 747	23 021	21 185	20 686	7 342	8 748	1 855	892
Terre Haute, IN	5 106	0.2	30 067	322	3 142	333	754	1 329	1 298	446	553	121	81
Texarkana, TX-Texarkana, AR	4 553	0.7	33 118	241	2 663	332	853	1 049	1 024	306	481	120	32
Toledo, OH	22 303	-1.2	33 178	238	15 182	1 414	3 248	5 246	5 124	1 500	2 186	572	314
Topeka, KS	8 487	1.0	36 770	141	5 569	410	1 508	1 687	1 645	585	632	151	88
Trenton-Ewing, NJ	19 024	-3.3	51 947	11	16 297	1 687	3 347	2 837	2 771	870	1 245	233	257
Tucson, AZ	34 516	-1.1	33 833	220	19 481	1 801	7 785	7 659	7 474	2 284	3 674	646	228
Tulsa, OK	37 534	-2.7	40 402	68	22 227	5 556	6 662	6 246	6 077	2 192	2 515	572	234
Tuscaloosa, AL	7 066	-0.6	33 515	232	4 606	535	1 121	1 518	1 480	502	611	189	43
Tyler, TX	7 843	-0.6	38 319	107	4 560	1 019	1 709	1 467	1 430	504	631	128	51
Utica-Rome, NY	9 757	1.3	33 269	237	5 987	442	1 507	2 571	2 518	836	1 116	280	110
Valdosta, GA	3 963	0.1	29 184	341	2 611	238	600	872	848	242	341	127	41
Vallejo-Fairfield, CA	15 866	-0.3	38 961	92	8 457	787	2 338	2 511	2 438	726	903	268	229
Victoria, TX	4 201	-2.5	36 408	152	2 413	457	844	851	830	269	393	86	28
Vineland-Millville-Bridgeton, NJ	5 028	1.1	31 877	278	3 286	266	620	1 370	1 341	368	605	148	146

1. Based on the resident population estimated as of July 1 of the year shown.   2. Includes other labor income.

Table C. Metropolitan Areas — **Earnings, Social Security, and Housing**

Area name	Earnings, 2009									Social Security beneficiaries, December 2010			Housing units, 2010	
			Percent by selected industries											
			Goods-related[1]		Service-related and health							Supplemental Security Income recipients, December 2009		Percent change, 2000–2010
	Total (mil dol)	Farm	Total	Manufacturing	Information, professional, and technical services	Retail trade	Finance, insurance, and real estate	Health care and social services	Government	Number	Rate[2]		Total	
	75	76	77	78	79	80	81	82	83	84	85	86	87	88
Sacramento—Arden-Arcade—Roseville, CA..	63 312	0.6	11.7	4.6	11.9	6.0	8.3	10.8	31.7	324 270	151	77 253	871 793	21.9
Saginaw-Saginaw Township North, MI	4 335	0.9	D	19.1	6.4	7.7	5.9	18.2	16.0	45 935	229	8 079	86 844	1.6
St. Cloud, MN	4 992	3.0	23.9	16.2	6.1	7.3	5.2	16.5	17.1	29 755	157	2 495	78 114	22.5
St. George, UT	2 109	-0.2	15.2	5.1	D	11.4	5.3	17.9	17.5	27 245	197	1 083	57 734	58.3
St. Joseph, MO-KS	2 894	3.2	D	NA	D	7.1	5.1	NA	17.4	24 180	190	2 803	53 638	6.1
St. Louis, MO-IL	83 946	0.4	D	NA	D	5.7	D	NA	14.0	508 010	181	58 212	1 236 222	9.1
Salem, OR	8 359	3.5	12.8	6.9	5.3	6.5	4.8	16.7	30.3	70 300	180	8 295	151 250	14.0
Salinas, CA	11 938	11.1	8.0	3.5	6.4	6.0	3.8	7.7	25.7	54 005	130	9 229	139 048	5.6
Salisbury, MD	2 768	1.0	D	8.3	6.9	7.5	4.5	18.5	22.2	22 715	181	2 922	52 322	17.6
Salt Lake City, UT	37 613	0.0	17.8	10.1	D	7.1	10.0	8.3	16.9	127 690	114	12 777	410 031	19.8
San Angelo, TX	2 528	0.1	20.2	8.2	D	6.7	D	NA	27.7	20 825	186	2 883	47 427	5.8
San Antonio-New Braunfels, TX	53 480	0.0	D	5.7	10.1	6.4	10.0	NA	24.7	325 350	152	60 193	837 999	29.2
San Diego-Carlsbad-San Marcos, CA	104 615	0.4	14.5	8.7	17.6	5.4	7.1	8.0	26.5	415 805	134	82 461	1 164 786	12.0
Sandusky, OH	1 825	0.5	D	21.2	3.7	6.9	3.9	14.8	17.2	17 235	224	1 474	37 845	5.4
San Francisco-Oakland-Fremont, CA	191 599	0.1	D	8.5	22.9	5.1	12.0	8.8	13.8	601 700	139	141 161	1 741 999	8.4
Oakland-Fremont-Hayward, CA Div	84 668	0.1	D	10.8	16.8	5.6	7.7	11.4	15.4	340 940	133	78 591	982 812	9.8
San Francisco-San Mateo-Redwood City, CA Div	106 932	0.1	D	6.6	27.7	4.7	15.3	6.7	12.6	260 760	147	62 570	759 187	6.6
San Jose-Sunnyvale-Santa Clara, CA	95 244	0.2	D	24.9	D	4.3	4.3	7.5	8.7	212 395	116	48 827	649 790	9.1
San Luis Obispo-Paso Robles, CA	6 401	1.3	15.3	5.4	9.7	8.3	5.1	11.5	22.1	50 215	186	5 212	117 315	14.7
Santa Barbara-Santa Maria-Goleta, CA	12 543	4.3	15.6	8.4	13.3	6.4	5.5	10.3	21.6	65 395	154	9 634	152 834	6.9
Santa Cruz-Watsonville, CA	6 371	5.6	D	5.8	9.3	8.1	4.9	12.6	19.7	37 520	143	5 845	104 476	5.7
Santa Fe, NM	4 041	0.2	D	1.9	D	9.6	6.5	11.8	29.6	27 605	191	2 676	71 267	23.5
Santa Rosa-Petaluma, CA	12 360	0.9	22.1	13.0	12.0	7.5	6.1	13.3	15.5	82 525	171	9 779	204 572	11.7
Savannah, GA	8 965	0.1	D	13.5	5.6	6.3	4.6	NA	23.3	54 415	157	7 451	151 049	23.2
Scranton—Wilkes-Barre, PA	12 867	0.0	18.3	13.1	8.7	7.6	6.4	NA	15.1	135 820	241	16 987	258 834	2.4
Seattle-Tacoma-Bellevue, WA	135 560	0.1	18.4	12.2	20.2	5.7	7.6	9.1	16.9	470 945	137	64 067	1 463 295	16.5
Seattle-Bellevue-Everett, WA Div	115 188	0.1	19.3	13.8	22.8	5.6	7.9	8.3	13.3	348 170	132	46 294	1 137 920	16.3
Tacoma, WA Div	20 371	0.1	13.6	6.0	5.4	5.7	5.5	13.6	37.4	122 775	154	17 773	325 375	17.4
Sebastian-Vero Beach, FL	2 559	1.5	D	3.9	9.2	9.9	7.1	18.4	14.2	40 895	296	1 922	76 346	31.9
Sheboygan, WI	3 251	0.5	D	39.9	3.5	5.4	5.2	12.9	10.4	22 500	195	1 628	50 766	10.5
Sherman-Denison, TX	2 176	0.3	26.4	18.7	4.5	9.0	6.6	17.7	14.7	25 345	210	2 824	53 727	11.2
Shreveport-Bossier City, LA	10 912	0.1	23.1	6.6	6.4	6.6	4.1	NA	24.4	70 660	177	16 733	173 669	8.7
Sioux City, IA-NE-SD	3 855	5.8	D	NA	D	6.9	D	NA	13.9	25 085	175	2 403	58 083	2.0
Sioux Falls, SD	7 520	4.2	D	8.4	7.7	7.1	D	18.6	10.4	36 360	159	2 743	95 862	26.8
South Bend-Mishawaka, IN-MI	7 577	0.7	24.0	19.3	D	6.0	6.0	14.8	11.9	59 740	187	6 360	140 736	7.5
Spartanburg, SC	6 643	0.1	30.8	25.5	5.2	6.3	5.2	8.9	17.4	60 455	213	6 763	122 628	14.6
Spokane, WA	11 631	0.2	15.2	8.3	7.7	8.0	7.5	17.3	21.1	84 400	179	12 511	201 434	15.1
Springfield, IL	6 704	2.5	D	3.0	8.1	5.2	7.9	NA	32.2	40 660	193	4 992	95 555	5.3
Springfield, MA	16 385	0.1	D	10.8	7.2	6.8	7.6	17.1	21.0	135 260	195	35 016	288 536	4.4
Springfield, MO	9 676	-0.2	D	8.5	D	8.4	6.5	NA	16.2	86 020	197	9 309	192 346	22.9
Springfield, OH	2 431	2.0	19.6	16.2	4.1	6.9	6.5	16.4	16.9	29 160	211	3 692	61 419	0.6
State College, PA	4 081	-0.1	10.1	5.2	10.3	5.5	3.8	9.3	47.6	21 625	140	1 587	63 297	19.1
Steubenville-Weirton, WV-OH	2 215	0.0	D	20.1	D	6.3	3.1	D	13.5	31 670	254	4 005	58 334	-1.4
Stockton, CA	13 163	4.8	15.9	9.0	4.4	7.2	5.5	12.6	20.8	93 195	136	28 573	233 755	23.6
Sumter, SC	2 125	1.0	20.8	14.6	3.7	5.7	3.2	11.1	37.8	20 885	194	4 056	46 011	10.2
Syracuse, NY	17 570	0.3	D	12.2	9.4	6.1	6.7	13.2	19.7	130 715	197	19 126	287 712	3.5
Tallahassee, FL	9 129	0.4	D	2.7	D	6.0	6.0	NA	39.1	51 710	141	8 900	163 078	19.3
Tampa-St. Petersburg-Clearwater, FL	69 072	0.4	D	6.3	13.8	7.4	10.1	13.7	15.4	586 940	211	66 691	1 353 158	18.3
Terre Haute, IN	3 476	1.6	D	19.1	3.9	7.3	4.0	NA	20.1	35 570	206	4 342	74 136	2.2
Texarkana, TX-Texarkana, AR	2 995	0.3	12.7	8.6	D	8.0	6.0	15.2	29.6	26 930	198	5 814	57 774	6.6
Toledo, OH	16 596	0.8	D	17.6	D	6.4	4.8	NA	17.3	117 155	180	18 749	301 322	5.5
Topeka, KS	5 979	0.5	D	7.2	D	5.2	D	NA	26.8	46 330	198	5 340	103 809	7.7
Trenton-Ewing, NJ	17 984	0.0	7.3	4.2	21.6	3.8	10.3	9.4	25.3	62 400	170	8 654	143 169	7.4
Tucson, AZ	21 282	0.1	17.1	11.5	10.9	6.7	4.9	14.8	25.5	182 545	186	18 785	440 909	20.2
Tulsa, OK	27 783	0.1	D	16.2	D	5.9	5.6	NA	11.0	169 010	180	20 362	409 820	11.9
Tuscaloosa, AL	5 141	1.5	D	19.5	D	6.0	4.0	NA	28.3	41 880	191	8 956	97 534	15.7
Tyler, TX	5 579	0.2	21.8	8.3	9.3	7.6	7.4	21.6	12.4	39 520	188	5 105	87 309	21.8
Utica-Rome, NY	6 429	0.4	13.7	10.0	6.7	7.0	7.1	16.2	31.1	68 540	229	10 317	137 561	2.0
Valdosta, GA	2 849	2.0	D	NA	D	8.3	D	NA	36.3	21 780	156	4 383	57 434	19.2
Vallejo-Fairfield, CA	9 243	1.4	21.3	13.4	5.1	6.9	4.5	13.7	27.6	60 430	146	12 167	152 698	13.5
Victoria, TX	2 870	-0.2	D	17.6	D	8.5	D	NA	14.6	22 025	191	3 287	50 537	8.4
Vineland-Millville-Bridgeton, NJ	3 552	2.1	21.9	15.5	4.0	7.5	2.9	13.2	29.9	28 655	183	5 212	55 834	5.6

1. Includes mining, construction, and manufacturing.   2. Per 1,000 resident population enumerated in the 2010 census.

Table C. Metropolitan Areas — Housing, Labor Force, and Employment

Area name	Housing units, 2010								Civilian labor force, 2010				Civilian employment,[5] 2010		
	Occupied units							Sub-stand-ard units[3] (percent)			Unemployment			Percent	
	Owner-occupied					Renter-occupied										
				Median owner cost as a percent of income		Median rent[2]	Median rent as a percent of income							Management, business, science, and arts occupations	Construction, production, and maintenance occupations
	Total	Percent	Median value[1]	With a mortgage	Without a mortgage				Total	Percent change, 2009-2010	Total	Rate[4]	Total		
	89	90	91	92	93	94	95	96	97	98	99	100	101	102	103
Sacramento—Arden-Arcade—Roseville, CA..	781 425	61.0	279 100	29.2	11.3	1 005	34.2	4.6	1 040 838	-1.0	130 751	12.6	912 753	38.8	16.0
Saginaw-Saginaw Township North, MI	75 609	73.8	104 200	23.1	13.5	686	31.2	NA	91 827	-1.4	10 838	11.8	79 870	29.1	22.0
St. Cloud, MN	71 145	72.3	170 700	24.6	11.4	658	27.5	1.7	108 992	1.1	8 013	7.4	98 493	30.3	24.6
St. George, UT	47 413	68.6	217 400	31.6	10.0	851	29.5	4.3	58 965	-2.9	5 962	10.1	51 780	29.7	25.5
St. Joseph, MO-KS	48 133	67.4	111 200	19.4	11.9	579	28.5	1.2	67 946	-2.3	5 916	8.7	57 084	27.2	27.6
St. Louis, MO-IL	1 112 442	70.5	161 400	22.7	12.2	734	30.5	1.9	1 437 267	-0.2	143 729	10.0	1 326 409	37.0	19.2
Salem, OR	143 114	62.6	204 900	27.2	12.3	763	34.2	5.2	199 534	0.4	21 544	10.8	162 478	31.7	25.1
Salinas, CA	125 446	50.9	381 700	32.6	10.1	1 157	33.6	13.2	219 661	2.0	28 032	12.8	175 878	25.6	28.1
Salisbury, MD	43 998	63.9	182 600	24.8	14.5	882	33.2	NA	62 636	-0.4	5 683	9.1	55 994	34.5	22.0
Salt Lake City, UT	369 754	68.5	236 800	24.9	10.0	835	30.2	4.9	607 497	-0.7	45 308	7.5	531 485	34.8	21.2
San Angelo, TX	42 192	67.4	94 100	22.0	12.3	627	33.3	5.5	54 819	2.1	3 493	6.4	46 159	28.5	21.2
San Antonio-New Braunfels, TX	749 906	63.4	131 700	22.7	11.6	788	28.9	5.3	988 725	2.4	72 505	7.3	958 883	34.4	20.4
San Diego-Carlsbad-San Marcos, CA	1 061 210	53.9	407 000	30.8	10.8	1 249	34.5	6.9	1 558 186	0.3	164 320	10.5	1 348 077	39.7	16.3
Sandusky, OH	32 243	69.1	134 100	23.3	13.4	648	29.8	NA	42 747	0.1	4 426	10.4	35 269	30.0	22.7
San Francisco-Oakland-Fremont, CA	1 601 506	54.4	588 300	30.1	10.5	1 314	30.6	6.3	2 239 684	-0.5	231 722	10.3	2 108 199	45.3	14.4
Oakland-Fremont-Hayward, CA Div	905 293	58.5	467 700	29.9	10.4	1 224	32.2	5.6	1 277 903	-0.6	144 206	11.3	1 179 752	43.7	16.3
San Francisco-San Mateo-Redwood City, CA Div	696 213	49.1	749 800	30.7	10.5	1 425	29.1	7.1	961 781	-0.4	87 516	9.1	928 447	47.2	11.9
San Jose-Sunnyvale-Santa Clara, CA	616 837	57.3	631 400	29.7	10.0	1 412	29.1	8.5	900 111	0.0	101 951	11.3	857 511	49.8	14.8
San Luis Obispo-Paso Robles, CA	99 653	60.1	425 200	30.4	12.3	1 137	36.4	3.3	136 162	-0.1	13 827	10.2	116 949	37.1	18.5
Santa Barbara-Santa Maria-Goleta, CA	140 842	53.4	446 800	29.5	10.8	1 267	34.5	8.8	220 463	0.3	20 625	9.4	187 202	34.0	22.7
Santa Cruz-Watsonville, CA	91 264	59.4	558 000	32.8	11.8	1 284	33.2	6.3	147 848	0.1	18 849	12.7	117 481	41.7	21.5
Santa Fe, NM	61 494	68.8	284 800	31.1	10.2	829	31.8	3.6	77 296	0.8	5 452	7.1	66 852	42.4	13.1
Santa Rosa-Petaluma, CA	185 711	59.7	414 000	31.9	11.8	1 204	34.8	5.1	254 195	-0.9	26 630	10.5	227 836	33.5	20.0
Savannah, GA	130 517	61.1	172 900	25.1	11.2	873	34.0	1.9	174 291	-1.0	15 626	9.0	154 766	33.2	22.4
Scranton—Wilkes-Barre, PA	225 165	67.8	129 500	23.6	14.3	632	28.7	1.6	279 519	-0.9	27 063	9.7	253 095	31.4	24.4
Seattle-Tacoma-Bellevue, WA	1 353 765	60.6	333 100	27.5	13.2	1 017	30.1	3.5	1 889 529	-0.3	175 897	9.3	1 678 265	42.7	17.7
Seattle-Bellevue-Everett, WA Div	1 053 889	60.4	360 700	27.2	13.3	1 033	29.7	3.6	1 493 022	-0.4	136 483	9.1	1 333 668	45.4	16.4
Tacoma, WA Div	299 876	61.4	252 000	28.4	13.1	964	32.0	3.3	396 507	-0.1	39 414	9.9	344 597	32.1	22.8
Sebastian-Vero Beach, FL	53 151	75.3	163 900	27.3	14.0	877	36.2	NA	62 464	0.0	8 743	14.0	52 019	30.2	18.8
Sheboygan, WI	46 153	72.1	158 000	24.3	16.1	633	25.1	NA	63 307	-2.5	5 483	8.7	57 675	29.5	33.5
Sherman-Denison, TX	44 885	67.8	104 600	22.7	13.8	766	28.2	2.3	57 431	1.2	4 838	8.4	52 118	30.8	29.7
Shreveport-Bossier City, LA	154 252	63.3	122 900	21.0	10.8	691	31.9	3.3	184 673	0.5	12 939	7.0	177 533	30.2	24.2
Sioux City, IA-NE-SD	54 012	67.7	101 100	19.7	11.4	586	27.0	3.0	78 379	0.3	5 176	6.6	71 964	28.8	32.5
Sioux Falls, SD	89 664	67.1	153 900	22.1	10.0	653	27.3	NA	128 481	-0.4	6 394	5.0	123 874	35.6	21.4
South Bend-Mishawaka, IN-MI	119 517	71.0	123 400	22.0	11.2	670	31.0	1.1	152 237	-0.9	17 326	11.4	139 281	33.9	22.6
Spartanburg, SC	105 598	70.5	128 000	22.8	10.3	639	30.0	2.7	135 287	-1.3	15 488	11.4	122 856	29.0	28.4
Spokane, WA	187 672	63.3	187 000	24.5	10.9	718	31.9	1.9	237 502	-0.9	22 807	9.6	210 995	33.8	18.8
Springfield, IL	88 364	69.5	120 700	20.1	11.8	664	28.2	NA	117 957	3.3	9 433	8.0	104 241	37.1	15.5
Springfield, MA	270 260	63.3	220 700	24.9	14.7	780	32.3	2.4	354 896	0.3	32 424	9.1	317 047	36.4	20.7
Springfield, MO	173 946	65.5	129 800	22.2	11.4	638	31.8	2.6	218 089	-0.2	19 067	8.7	197 596	32.0	21.0
Springfield, OH	55 459	64.6	102 000	22.8	11.2	641	32.1	3.6	69 991	-1.0	7 312	10.4	57 900	27.8	25.5
State College, PA	56 358	58.7	192 100	22.1	11.9	826	38.7	1.9	75 038	-0.1	4 648	6.2	73 162	44.7	16.9
Steubenville-Weirton, WV-OH	52 107	76.9	81 200	19.4	11.0	575	31.9	NA	56 658	-2.4	7 577	13.4	51 628	24.1	29.0
Stockton, CA	215 469	57.7	213 400	29.7	11.3	995	34.7	9.3	298 937	0.2	51 786	17.3	264 858	28.9	27.5
Sumter, SC	38 363	63.1	107 900	21.7	14.1	680	29.0	2.3	45 562	0.6	5 416	11.9	38 806	30.8	25.5
Syracuse, NY	255 612	67.3	122 700	22.1	13.7	704	30.2	1.4	325 595	-1.0	27 661	8.5	305 126	36.8	19.4
Tallahassee, FL	141 996	59.8	167 800	25.4	11.6	894	38.5	3.5	193 186	0.2	16 450	8.5	159 239	44.4	14.0
Tampa-St. Petersburg-Clearwater, FL	1 116 299	67.6	152 200	28.8	14.5	900	34.3	2.2	1 302 921	0.3	157 580	12.1	1 207 195	35.9	17.5
Terre Haute, IN	64 742	68.6	87 200	18.7	10.6	615	28.9	1.8	80 065	-0.6	8 934	11.2	72 912	32.1	26.4
Texarkana, TX-Texarkana, AR	50 248	68.4	89 100	19.7	10.8	670	29.4	2.5	65 112	1.6	4 901	7.5	58 150	29.3	26.3
Toledo, OH	256 437	66.5	123 800	23.6	13.4	645	32.1	0.9	327 781	-1.1	36 953	11.3	289 599	32.4	23.1
Topeka, KS	94 949	66.2	122 300	21.9	12.2	649	27.9	1.9	124 147	1.0	8 776	7.1	110 408	34.8	20.3
Trenton-Ewing, NJ	131 500	67.5	293 600	26.2	17.4	1 082	32.0	3.1	203 947	-0.2	15 934	7.8	175 496	43.1	14.3
Tucson, AZ	382 574	63.6	173 200	25.3	12.5	768	32.0	4.2	491 362	0.2	44 400	9.0	412 292	37.4	15.9
Tulsa, OK	364 083	67.1	128 400	21.9	11.6	688	29.4	3.0	438 459	0.0	34 622	7.9	432 143	33.2	23.1
Tuscaloosa, AL	77 180	66.5	145 500	22.5	13.5	738	33.5	2.1	98 166	-1.4	8 699	8.9	93 320	31.6	30.6
Tyler, TX	79 341	67.1	118 800	22.2	12.4	798	33.5	5.5	101 403	1.0	7 974	7.9	96 804	29.4	19.5
Utica-Rome, NY	115 856	70.5	101 900	20.4	12.9	653	27.9	1.5	140 520	-0.7	11 099	7.9	129 483	35.0	20.6
Valdosta, GA	50 009	58.4	128 200	25.5	10.0	730	33.7	2.1	66 346	-2.4	5 832	8.8	56 113	29.1	22.7
Vallejo-Fairfield, CA	140 202	62.5	262 600	30.0	10.0	1 201	33.0	6.3	214 954	0.2	25 864	12.0	180 913	34.1	22.0
Victoria, TX	41 779	67.7	111 200	22.0	12.6	660	32.6	NA	58 962	1.3	4 482	7.6	51 075	31.7	28.3
Vineland-Millville-Bridgeton, NJ	50 237	66.1	177 600	25.5	14.7	903	39.0	5.3	70 675	0.3	9 430	13.3	62 728	28.3	27.7

1. Specified owner-occupied units. 2. Specified renter-occupied units. A value of 10.0 represents 10 percent or less. 3. Overcrowded or lacking complete plumbing facilities. 4. Percent of civilian labor force. 5. Persons 16 years old and over.

Table C. Metropolitan Areas — Nonfarm Employment and Agriculture

Area name	Number of establishments	Total	Health care and social assistance	Manufacturing	Retail trade	Finance and insurance	Professional, scientific, and technical services	Total (mil dol)	Average per employee (dollars)	Number	Fewer than 50 acres	500 acres or more	Farm operators whose principal occupation is farming (percent)
	104	105	106	107	108	109	110	111	112	113	114	115	116
Sacramento—Arden-Arcade—Roseville, CA..	45 327	644 269	98 636	36 627	90 411	43 659	45 278	26 933	41 803	5 132	71.4	7.0	47.0
Saginaw-Saginaw Township North, MI	4 510	76 018	17 179	9 818	12 348	3 094	2 753	2 553	33 585	1 533	43.4	10.0	48.3
St. Cloud, MN	5 231	88 614	16 728	14 784	12 596	3 864	3 609	2 993	33 770	4 287	25.7	8.2	53.9
St. George, UT	3 974	39 405	6 949	2 150	7 689	1 334	1 852	1 083	27 480	593	60.4	13.2	31.0
St. Joseph, MO-KS	3 176	49 262	8 264	11 775	6 833	2 251	1 366	1 603	32 538	3 420	27.0	14.2	41.2
St. Louis, MO-IL	70 840	1 205 316	174 487	105 606	142 770	64 550	84 173	50 258	41 697	12 686	38.6	13.5	42.6
Salem, OR	9 061	106 821	19 495	11 013	17 750	3 903	4 351	3 370	31 545	3 922	69.1	5.4	45.5
Salinas, CA	8 500	100 735	14 540	6 106	16 416	3 683	7 370	3 973	39 440	1 199	45.0	24.9	64.1
Salisbury, MD	2 928	41 743	9 319	3 966	7 126	1 303	1 639	1 386	33 192	837	46.2	9.3	50.9
Salt Lake City, UT	31 801	537 712	57 875	49 611	65 371	38 893	35 876	21 485	39 957	1 595	66.1	10.6	32.0
San Angelo, TX	2 645	36 328	7 038	2 967	6 193	1 525	1 191	1 058	29 128	1 336	43.3	27.5	38.1
San Antonio-New Braunfels, TX	40 201	722 469	113 854	43 982	96 990	54 227	39 049	25 986	35 968	14 552	44.0	10.1	39.6
San Diego-Carlsbad-San Marcos, CA	76 345	1 119 643	139 226	93 819	138 162	52 930	118 403	50 265	44 894	6 687	91.1	1.3	37.8
Sandusky, OH	1 912	29 155	4 877	5 911	4 496	625	681	973	33 357	403	47.9	11.7	42.7
San Francisco-Oakland-Fremont, CA	118 485	1 809 415	236 284	127 022	192 895	114 494	216 600	112 088	61 947	1 749	63.7	12.9	44.3
Oakland-Fremont-Hayward, CA Div	NA	NA	NA	NA	NA	NA	NA	NA	NA	1 159	67.7	10.4	39.9
San Francisco-San Mateo-Redwood City, CA Div	NA	NA	NA	NA	NA	NA	NA	NA	NA	590	55.8	18.0	53.1
San Jose-Sunnyvale-Santa Clara, CA	45 067	861 722	93 027	91 529	80 491	27 022	116 052	65 305	75 784	1 693	68.5	11.7	50.1
San Luis Obispo-Paso Robles, CA	7 950	82 573	14 948	5 508	13 472	2 819	4 991	2 848	34 489	2 784	56.7	12.5	49.6
Santa Barbara-Santa Maria-Goleta, CA	11 203	136 826	19 451	12 022	18 665	4 892	11 178	5 735	41 918	1 597	64.9	11.1	50.9
Santa Cruz-Watsonville, CA	6 885	71 708	12 150	4 676	11 992	2 075	4 535	2 851	39 766	682	77.7	2.2	61.9
Santa Fe, NM	4 875	45 986	8 530	764	9 289	2 024	2 537	1 609	34 981	489	66.9	13.5	42.7
Santa Rosa-Petaluma, CA	13 383	149 366	22 767	19 124	23 094	6 756	8 164	6 315	42 279	3 429	72.4	5.3	47.3
Savannah, GA	8 359	127 591	20 342	14 683	18 119	3 747	5 466	4 453	34 901	313	46.6	9.3	38.3
Scranton—Wilkes-Barre, PA	13 409	231 067	48 140	30 665	33 260	11 235	9 139	7 313	31 647	1 676	37.6	2.3	34.1
Seattle-Tacoma-Bellevue, WA	97 293	1 481 865	196 278	143 882	165 168	67 702	118 877	77 821	52 515	4 908	85.5	0.9	41.1
Seattle-Bellevue-Everett, WA Div	NA	NA	NA	NA	NA	NA	NA	NA	NA	3 460	85.8	1.0	40.8
Tacoma, WA Div	NA	NA	NA	NA	NA	NA	NA	NA	NA	1 448	84.6	0.4	41.9
Sebastian-Vero Beach, FL	3 874	37 847	8 127	1 805	7 628	1 202	1 706	1 252	33 093	415	68.7	9.6	50.1
Sheboygan, WI	2 699	51 338	6 873	16 816	6 194	2 019	1 549	1 742	33 933	1 059	42.0	9.4	53.7
Sherman-Denison, TX	2 582	38 107	7 555	6 699	6 233	2 501	911	1 200	31 491	2 723	55.3	4.9	35.1
Shreveport-Bossier City, LA	9 088	148 626	32 502	10 637	21 446	5 010	5 309	5 003	33 663	1 737	49.6	10.5	43.9
Sioux City, IA-NE-SD	3 817	67 876	9 951	12 330	8 692	3 550	1 310	2 136	31 476	2 516	23.8	27.0	52.7
Sioux Falls, SD	6 978	123 776	24 655	13 177	16 041	15 305	5 235	4 414	35 661	3 316	28.1	29.0	56.3
South Bend-Mishawaka, IN-MI	6 809	122 153	19 222	16 468	15 634	4 489	5 412	4 318	35 346	1 523	49.2	10.8	42.7
Spartanburg, SC	6 396	112 163	13 973	23 852	13 908	2 433	3 479	4 103	36 577	1 242	53.8	2.4	39.7
Spokane, WA	12 515	177 847	35 391	14 361	25 492	11 083	8 782	6 493	36 507	2 502	54.8	10.6	36.3
Springfield, IL	5 369	83 630	19 078	2 953	12 362	5 579	4 965	2 967	35 473	1 564	45.3	22.8	47.7
Springfield, MA	15 033	245 496	56 511	29 105	34 057	12 839	9 163	8 724	35 537	1 960	55.7	2.1	47.7
Springfield, MO	11 255	169 919	31 847	15 674	24 572	9 161	7 976	5 232	30 790	8 122	38.0	6.2	39.6
Springfield, OH	2 486	41 505	8 608	5 767	6 123	2 563	1 158	1 263	30 431	744	53.5	14.1	42.9
State College, PA	3 180	42 376	6 567	3 997	8 081	1 748	3 414	1 347	31 798	1 146	40.2	4.3	44.2
Steubenville-Weirton, WV-OH	2 385	38 343	7 517	7 103	5 058	1 084	824	1 137	29 655	688	28.8	4.5	49.0
Stockton, CA	11 044	165 952	27 015	20 422	24 982	6 231	4 314	5 972	35 989	3 624	64.1	8.6	55.9
Sumter, SC	1 842	28 652	4 526	6 892	4 324	820	796	832	29 055	554	43.0	12.8	49.6
Syracuse, NY	15 312	254 128	43 372	27 030	34 950	15 038	17 527	9 754	38 382	2 075	31.4	10.4	54.7
Tallahassee, FL	8 765	105 165	19 230	3 696	17 994	5 450	10 602	3 627	34 490	1 498	56.7	6.9	37.3
Tampa-St. Petersburg-Clearwater, FL	69 376	951 382	162 195	53 258	133 905	72 374	75 734	37 092	38 988	4 955	82.2	2.7	44.5
Terre Haute, IN	3 703	59 315	11 015	11 427	8 947	1 604	1 510	1 920	32 377	1 924	48.0	16.2	46.9
Texarkana, TX-Texarkana, AR	2 889	42 956	8 051	4 480	7 804	1 582	1 186	1 293	30 111	2 211	46.9	8.7	38.1
Toledo, OH	14 902	262 624	51 409	36 847	32 919	7 949	12 098	9 490	36 136	2 893	45.8	12.9	42.6
Topeka, KS	5 469	86 872	20 594	7 058	11 357	5 736	4 017	3 024	34 812	4 901	26.6	15.6	38.7
Trenton-Ewing, NJ	9 818	177 461	27 279	7 195	19 399	15 206	22 319	9 792	55 176	311	70.7	2.3	40.8
Tucson, AZ	20 547	309 243	56 070	26 958	47 950	13 169	15 749	11 041	35 702	622	74.0	12.1	41.2
Tulsa, OK	24 267	388 992	56 105	53 465	45 857	18 809	20 949	15 213	39 108	9 916	39.6	10.8	38.1
Tuscaloosa, AL	4 360	74 117	12 136	13 653	10 584	1 797	2 467	2 578	34 787	1 408	30.5	14.9	44.5
Tyler, TX	5 363	85 043	19 379	8 169	11 880	3 082	3 944	3 016	35 464	2 514	53.1	4.5	35.0
Utica-Rome, NY	6 075	101 533	22 718	13 525	14 100	7 597	4 170	3 244	31 954	1 685	24.6	8.7	58.1
Valdosta, GA	3 068	41 849	7 487	3 606	7 558	1 292	1 254	1 108	26 476	1 093	39.2	13.4	37.3
Vallejo-Fairfield, CA	6 839	100 025	19 888	9 514	17 039	3 299	3 750	4 076	40 753	890	62.0	12.1	52.8
Victoria, TX	2 766	41 213	7 179	5 014	6 884	1 417	1 146	1 423	34 527	2 725	33.5	17.9	40.3
Vineland-Millville-Bridgeton, NJ	2 978	46 428	8 533	8 259	7 833	1 546	1 223	1 667	35 897	615	62.0	5.7	52.7

Table C. Metropolitan Areas — **Agriculture**

Area name	Land in farms Acreage (1,000)	Percent change, 2002–2007	Acres Average size of farm	Total irrigated (1,000)	Total cropland (1,000)	Value of land and buildings (dollars) Average per farm	Average per acre	Value of machinery and equipment, average per farm (dollars)	Value of products sold Total (mil dol)	Average per farm (dollars)	Percent from: Crops	Live-stock and poultry products	Percent of farms with sales of: $10,000 or more	$100,000 or more	Government payments Total ($1,000)	Percent of farms
	117	118	119	120	121	122	123	124	125	126	127	128	129	130	131	132
Sacramento—Arden-Arcade—Roseville, CA..	1 048	-5.8	204	399.9	510.5	1 415 346	6 933	79 048	795.2	154 964	76.9	23.1	34.9	12.3	14 924	10.3
Saginaw-Saginaw Township North, MI	324	-0.3	212	1.8	287.2	599 832	2 835	100 851	142.5	92 959	88.8	11.2	49.5	17.6	5 355	70.8
St. Cloud, MN	894	1.9	209	56.1	664.5	599 831	2 875	126 760	633.3	147 727	15.1	84.9	55.7	29.3	15 029	69.0
St. George, UT	174	-19.8	294	13.8	42.8	915 375	3 116	56 838	9.8	16 587	39.0	61.0	26.1	3.4	268	10.3
St. Joseph, MO-KS	944	10.5	276	D	655.8	598 249	2 166	71 963	239.0	69 838	74.4	25.6	45.6	14.8	13 979	68.8
St. Louis, MO-IL	3 076	0.7	242	D	2 338.3	842 983	3 477	97 692	1 084.7	85 517	73.1	26.9	41.7	16.7	40 472	54.5
Salem, OR	474	-7.1	121	113.0	345.2	774 463	6 404	100 949	733.4	186 999	81.5	18.5	34.6	16.5	2 483	11.8
Salinas, CA	1 328	5.3	1 108	233.0	311.1	5 144 255	4 645	305 191	2 178.5	1 816 906	98.2	1.8	59.8	37.9	1 316	7.8
Salisbury, MD	153	5.5	183	7.3	87.1	1 099 106	6 009	99 176	390.4	466 417	14.2	85.8	55.1	38.6	3 031	56.6
Salt Lake City, UT	775	-11.2	486	58.4	83.2	852 923	1 755	55 518	79.5	49 814	34.0	66.0	25.7	6.5	394	4.8
San Angelo, TX	1 548	12.1	1 159	35.0	235.5	1 036 726	895	76 156	139.1	104 093	36.5	63.6	28.7	12.2	6 309	25.4
San Antonio-New Braunfels, TX	3 534	-3.0	243	94.3	810.4	554 483	2 283	44 811	330.7	22 717	49.5	50.5	19.4	2.4	8 675	11.3
San Diego-Carlsbad-San Marcos, CA	304	-25.5	45	62.2	102.5	874 683	19 247	40 032	1 054.2	157 646	91.2	8.8	42.0	10.8	342	0.5
Sandusky, OH	84	-11.6	209	0.2	75.3	833 263	3 994	133 276	40.4	100 166	87.1	12.9	55.8	21.1	1 615	55.3
San Francisco-Oakland-Fremont, CA	542	D	310	42.3	88.8	1 700 623	5 488	70 494	315.3	180 236	73.9	26.1	41.1	14.7	1 185	5.3
Oakland-Fremont-Hayward, CA Div	352	2.3	303	37.1	66.4	1 522 267	5 018	63 521	121.2	104 545	77.4	22.6	36.7	11.2	557	4.2
San Francisco-San Mateo-Redwood City, CA Div...	190	D	323	5.2	22.4	2 050 985	6 357	84 191	194.1	328 924	71.6	28.4	49.7	21.5	628	7.3
San Jose-Sunnyvale-Santa Clara, CA	880	-2.1	520	52.6	88.5	1 967 370	3 786	88 895	458.8	270 991	89.1	10.9	41.2	13.8	528	4.5
San Luis Obispo-Paso Robles, CA	1 370	3.9	492	98.9	299.6	2 236 326	4 546	69 792	560.6	201 367	93.2	6.8	46.3	15.9	4 492	8.2
Santa Barbara-Santa Maria-Goleta, CA	727	-4.0	455	95.1	125.0	3 223 533	7 081	104 111	951.3	595 696	96.0	4.0	57.2	25.9	132	1.0
Santa Cruz-Watsonville, CA .	47	-29.9	70	19.6	23.6	1 561 362	22 423	101 383	447.4	656 037	96.9	3.1	59.4	30.4	40	0.7
Santa Fe, NM	569	-16.8	1 164	50.0	21.5	778 559	669	42 309	12.6	25 796	68.1	31.9	20.2	3.5	49	4.5
Santa Rosa-Petaluma, CA....	531	-15.3	155	78.3	134.4	2 459 725	15 887	68 139	647.6	188 854	65.2	34.8	56.9	20.6	711	2.6
Savannah, GA	65	-17.7	208	D	22.4	599 680	2 887	69 752	12.8	40 965	86.4	13.6	24.6	6.1	D	23.3
Scranton—Wilkes-Barre, PA	184	9.5	110	0.8	101.4	466 597	4 243	56 554	47.9	28 558	60.5	39.5	23.2	7.0	1 714	26.9
Seattle-Tacoma-Bellevue, WA	174	3.6	35	13.3	72.3	491 170	13 870	43 251	336.3	68 519	40.7	59.3	21.6	5.6	1 014	2.8
Seattle-Bellevue-Everett, WA Div	126	14.5	36	8.8	55.0	493 504	13 539	43 681	252.9	73 089	41.4	58.6	23.9	6.0	946	3.4
Tacoma, WA Div	48	-15.8	33	4.5	17.3	485 594	14 748	42 222	83.4	57 598	38.8	61.2	16.1	4.5	68	1.2
Sebastian-Vero Beach, FL...	157	-17.8	379	66.9	81.3	1 986 694	5 245	104 511	136.1	327 911	D	D	61.0	24.1	68	3.6
Sheboygan, WI	192	-1.5	181	0.1	157.6	700 484	3 869	124 039	166.9	157 569	20.3	79.7	54.3	26.3	2 134	59.2
Sherman-Denison, TX	400	-9.3	147	3.1	166.5	446 159	3 034	48 025	52.8	19 405	56.5	43.5	21.0	3.0	1 251	11.1
Shreveport-Bossier City, LA..	422	1.7	243	10.4	151.3	544 328	2 240	67 978	68.2	39 278	50.7	49.3	27.6	6.2	5 373	13.1
Sioux City, IA-NE-SD	1 140	-0.6	453	92.4	973.2	1 112 904	2 457	142 988	579.5	230 334	57.2	42.8	59.9	34.3	21 110	79.3
Sioux Falls, SD	1 489	4.6	449	30.4	1 227.3	1 139 529	2 538	141 650	651.0	196 351	58.4	41.6	66.2	37.8	19 796	73.7
South Bend-Mishawaka, IN-MI	369	4.2	242	64.0	315.4	866 012	3 575	109 273	191.4	125 673	68.3	31.7	43.7	19.0	5 913	57.1
Spartanburg, SC	110	-12.7	89	2.1	41.5	432 985	4 892	41 123	26.3	21 171	57.4	42.6	18.0	2.7	499	10.6
Spokane, WA	626	-2.6	250	13.5	394.9	588 545	2 351	65 660	117.1	46 789	84.2	15.8	23.6	8.3	5 929	24.5
Springfield, IL	687	10.3	439	3.6	636.1	1 702 347	3 877	167 151	374.7	239 628	94.1	5.9	49.8	33.0	12 252	69.8
Springfield, MA	169	3.7	86	3.9	61.2	755 959	8 764	60 526	121.1	61 835	71.1	28.9	35.1	10.9	1 447	10.9
Springfield, MO	1 266	-10.3	156	2.0	509.0	400 097	2 568	44 928	267.6	32 953	8.6	91.4	37.3	6.3	2 242	10.7
Springfield, OH	177	7.3	238	1.5	153.5	911 967	3 826	112 592	137.0	184 200	67.1	32.9	44.9	21.5	3 093	53.4
State College, PA	148	-10.3	130	0.6	86.1	660 008	5 095	60 906	69.7	60 786	25.1	74.9	39.4	17.2	1 266	26.8
Steubenville-Weirton, WV-OH	95	8.0	137	D	39.9	312 292	2 273	51 411	10.7	15 494	36.9	63.1	25.4	3.6	376	20.6
Stockton, CA	738	-9.2	204	454.0	492.0	2 069 142	10 168	127 313	1 564.4	431 665	63.4	36.6	65.5	33.9	4 444	8.5
Sumter, SC	153	12.5	277	9.5	88.8	552 862	1 996	91 687	88.8	160 338	37.3	62.7	25.6	11.0	4 016	54.0
Syracuse, NY	439	2.6	212	3.2	271.2	417 445	1 973	107 941	263.0	126 769	29.9	70.1	47.4	20.7	4 215	29.5
Tallahassee, FL	314	9.8	209	6.1	64.1	908 795	4 341	45 544	124.1	82 911	89.1	10.9	24.5	3.1	1 682	20.7
Tampa-St. Petersburg-Clearwater, FL	427	-18.0	86	42.2	D	803 173	9 310	46 114	637.6	128 671	79.1	20.9	30.5	9.2	D	1.2
Terre Haute, IN	589	4.6	306	D	507.9	947 330	3 096	118 263	250.0	129 906	90.2	9.8	46.3	23.0	9 485	69.2
Texarkana, TX-Texarkana, AR	467	0.2	211	5.0	197.4	392 245	1 859	55 289	97.1	43 934	30.7	69.3	28.3	5.7	2 579	11.0
Toledo, OH	638	-8.2	220	2.3	597.8	757 544	3 438	109 471	353.5	122 226	78.3	21.7	57.2	23.1	12 203	73.6
Topeka, KS	1 682	1.0	343	D	759.0	429 700	1 252	66 304	263.4	53 761	50.3	49.7	41.6	10.9	11 453	51.8
Trenton-Ewing, NJ	22	-12.0	70	1.0	15.4	1 314 520	18 813	64 690	18.6	59 955	80.5	19.5	41.2	11.9	286	13.2
Tucson, AZ	D	D	D	35.7	49.6	1 951 879	D	80 179	67.5	108 521	73.2	26.8	27.2	9.8	3 771	6.6
Tulsa, OK	3 025	6.4	305	11.6	693.3	437 580	1 434	47 276	288.6	29 106	18.3	81.7	27.6	3.6	3 734	13.4
Tuscaloosa, AL	416	6.1	295	1.6	110.1	562 865	1 907	72 824	106.2	75 450	D	D	28.0	9.0	3 429	29.8
Tyler, TX	302	5.2	120	2.7	91.8	377 217	3 136	53 392	68.0	27 049	62.5	37.5	23.3	2.8	68	1.7
Utica-Rome, NY	332	-12.6	197	0.5	186.9	365 662	1 854	91 371	152.2	90 358	21.3	78.7	48.8	21.4	3 069	34.4
Valdosta, GA	324	-9.5	297	35.6	148.1	883 515	2 977	90 995	138.7	126 913	82.4	17.6	34.9	14.5	8 745	42.0
Vallejo-Fairfield, CA	358	2.0	403	146.0	154.9	1 985 813	4 934	99 718	244.3	274 489	83.1	16.9	41.0	19.3	2 289	17.4
Victoria, TX	1 194	-5.8	438	7.3	281.9	696 286	1 589	65 633	92.4	33 907	52.2	47.8	31.8	6.2	5 771	15.6
Vineland-Millville-Bridgeton, NJ	69	-2.8	113	18.4	52.3	1 056 005	9 346	118 184	156.9	255 185	97.4	2.6	48.0	22.9	413	9.3

Table C. Metropolitan Areas — Water Use, Wholesale Trade, Retail Trade, and Real Estate

Area name	Water use, 2005 Total water withdrawn (mil gal/day)	Gallons withdrawn per person	Wholesale trade,[1] 2007 Number of establishments	Number of employees	Sales (mil dol)	Annual payroll (mil dol)	Retail trade, 2007 Number of establishments	Number of employees	Sales (mil dol)	Annual payroll (mil dol)	Real estate and rental and leasing, 2007 Number of establishments	Number of employees	Receipts (mil dol)	Annual payroll (mil dol)
	133	134	135	136	137	138	139	140	141	142	143	144	145	146
Sacramento—Arden-Arcade—Roseville, CA..	1 768.3	866	2 204	35 604	34 925.8	1 714.1	6 166	99 917	25 165.5	2 583.3	2 808	17 197	2 790.3	601.2
Saginaw-Saginaw Township North, MI	20.2	97	204	2 542	1 254.6	101.7	973	12 584	2 534.3	243.3	149	751	101.8	17.4
St. Cloud, MN	73.6	406	240	5 488	2 437.8	233.9	842	13 555	2 918.8	265.7	206	1 126	121.3	27.4
St. George, UT	98.9	778	157	1 320	590.8	50.8	593	8 035	2 087.8	185.9	367	856	122.0	20.0
St. Joseph, MO-KS	106.1	870	143	1 858	1 467.5	73.4	486	7 006	1 671.9	147.9	144	526	63.5	10.9
St. Louis, MO-IL	3 968.1	1 428	4 337	60 274	70 978.7	3 325.4	9 989	148 889	35 738.2	3 661.6	3 266	20 731	3 990.4	720.7
Salem, OR	327.4	872	392	4 456	3 860.8	188.0	1 259	18 547	4 391.6	438.1	556	2 924	359.1	69.7
Salinas, CA	1 129.2	2 740	453	6 994	6 581.3	375.2	1 497	18 392	4 541.1	487.8	487	2 423	500.6	86.6
Salisbury, MD	24.4	210	148	2 475	1 536.2	119.1	506	7 890	1 886.0	175.6	173	745	112.5	23.4
Salt Lake City, UT	651.7	611	2 115	35 199	28 056.2	1 760.8	3 818	65 130	17 922.2	1 612.3	2 390	12 775	2 257.2	427.5
San Angelo, TX	44.9	426	134	1 215	597.9	43.8	452	6 052	1 558.2	132.7	135	631	76.0	15.8
San Antonio-New Braunfels, TX	969.3	513	2 007	31 051	22 838.4	1 418.0	5 913	95 964	27 169.2	2 233.7	2 164	13 556	2 433.7	464.0
San Diego-Carlsbad-San Marcos, CA	4 085.1	1 393	4 569	64 810	49 017.1	4 804.4	9 948	151 425	38 710.6	3 889.2	5 810	33 067	7 190.2	1 345.2
Sandusky, OH	35.2	448	72	1 038	599.0	38.9	351	5 086	1 034.9	101.8	79	360	40.9	8.8
San Francisco-Oakland-Fremont, CA	3 707.1	893	7 079	100 925	111 769.0	6 831.0	14 412	210 050	56 860.9	6 077.9	7 206	45 485	12 223.8	2 307.7
Oakland-Fremont-Hayward, CA Div	1 850.9	750	3 979	63 505	69 710.8	4 032.4	7 325	113 400	29 672.8	3 125.0	3 484	19 990	4 688.8	820.5
San Francisco-San Mateo-Redwood City, CA Div	1 856.2	1 101	3 100	37 420	42 058.2	2 798.7	7 087	96 650	27 188.1	2 952.9	3 722	25 495	7 535.0	1 487.2
San Jose-Sunnyvale-Santa Clara, CA	365.5	208	2 973	87 492	89 981.1	8 953.8	5 421	87 932	26 844.4	2 947.0	2 664	14 946	5 189.2	752.0
San Luis Obispo-Paso Robles, CA	2 774.1	10 858	319	2 511	1 213.5	110.5	1 262	14 652	3 548.4	353.6	475	2 050	293.4	56.7
Santa Barbara-Santa Maria-Goleta, CA	239.6	598	491	6 446	5 371.5	391.5	1 605	20 281	4 983.4	524.4	681	3 452	620.7	119.5
Santa Cruz-Watsonville, CA	73.7	295	315	7 288	6 357.7	497.9	981	12 454	3 725.4	316.0	380	1 793	311.1	58.6
Santa Fe, NM	47.4	336	158	1 377	1 155.0	64.9	887	9 949	2 426.3	261.6	311	1 092	206.0	40.8
Santa Rosa-Petaluma, CA	114.3	245	676	9 568	6 887.4	606.1	1 925	26 177	6 427.2	718.5	718	3 237	604.1	114.2
Savannah, GA	395.2	1 259	410	5 287	4 771.8	262.0	1 491	18 989	4 551.8	422.8	487	2 223	387.6	68.6
Scranton—Wilkes-Barre, PA	156.7	285	650	10 799	6 226.5	431.6	2 383	34 129	8 691.1	694.7	393	2 628	385.5	72.1
Seattle-Tacoma-Bellevue, WA	554.0	173	6 002	87 932	85 085.5	5 055.2	11 549	176 728	55 952.6	4 867.7	6 187	33 954	7 698.4	1 345.0
Seattle-Bellevue-Everett, WA Div	355.5	145	5 191	75 356	76 985.3	4 534.1	9 243	140 913	46 211.0	3 915.4	5 093	28 259	6 727.9	1 183.7
Tacoma, WA Div	198.5	263	811	12 576	8 100.2	521.0	2 306	35 815	9 741.6	952.3	1 094	5 695	970.6	161.2
Sebastian-Vero Beach, FL	285.7	2 197	159	D	D	D	699	9 096	1 851.7	203.3	260	945	146.5	24.1
Sheboygan, WI	402.3	3 510	105	1 605	1 160.4	79.3	427	6 386	1 398.7	131.5	80	372	73.8	12.1
Sherman-Denison, TX	23.6	202	120	1 170	779.0	39.7	497	6 333	1 594.7	140.4	114	456	69.9	11.1
Shreveport-Bossier City, LA	904.0	2 359	477	7 147	7 498.1	319.2	1 557	21 638	5 633.3	483.8	422	2 432	362.4	65.1
Sioux City, IA-NE-SD	1 031.4	7 234	233	3 172	2 454.4	134.4	608	9 140	2 023.5	174.2	132	680	106.0	18.0
Sioux Falls, SD	58.7	282	467	6 144	4 507.6	282.7	1 035	16 679	4 364.2	370.8	245	1 577	238.5	46.2
South Bend-Mishawaka, IN-MI	78.0	245	457	7 008	4 395.1	310.9	1 072	17 506	3 866.8	367.4	267	1 498	225.2	44.4
Spartanburg, SC	100.7	377	488	7 196	6 641.4	322.7	1 089	13 937	3 638.4	309.0	279	1 279	220.8	45.1
Spokane, WA	191.7	435	757	10 996	8 498.9	459.0	1 712	26 853	6 741.2	697.7	662	3 426	630.3	105.1
Springfield, IL	415.3	2 021	238	3 191	2 215.7	132.0	842	12 798	2 931.6	255.8	235	1 069	163.0	25.2
Springfield, MA	238.8	347	654	10 229	9 587.3	476.6	2 560	34 910	7 905.8	789.4	587	2 817	463.1	86.4
Springfield, MO	242.3	609	651	10 134	7 331.5	409.9	1 781	25 165	6 142.0	548.1	589	3 103	379.1	73.9
Springfield, OH	27.9	196	103	1 977	1 944.3	76.1	460	6 625	1 398.7	131.7	101	485	64.0	10.9
State College, PA	101.6	723	98	D	D	D	548	8 014	1 604.3	151.0	129	922	184.7	26.2
Steubenville-Weirton, WV-OH	2 413.4	19 084	85	979	929.8	35.8	443	5 421	1 118.1	105.3	82	351	42.2	7.4
Stockton, CA	1 483.5	2 234	630	11 301	12 465.7	516.6	1 756	27 329	7 109.7	653.0	634	3 363	577.5	104.4
Sumter, SC	24.9	236	83	943	403.4	31.3	417	4 919	1 021.5	91.8	87	308	36.7	6.8
Syracuse, NY	1 409.6	2 163	944	15 728	22 145.7	723.5	2 368	35 712	8 023.1	762.2	763	3 899	714.7	134.0
Tallahassee, FL	84.1	234	321	3 407	1 440.2	137.2	1 298	19 641	4 230.5	396.2	505	2 565	381.4	71.7
Tampa-St. Petersburg-Clearwater, FL	4 714.6	1 788	4 201	52 123	50 581.7	2 349.9	10 024	148 740	40 337.4	3 561.3	4 391	22 538	3 987.4	813.4
Terre Haute, IN	1 678.6	9 988	163	1 732	1 101.7	61.0	705	10 036	2 312.1	199.5	129	720	88.0	19.5
Texarkana, TX-Texarkana, AR	247.3	1 848	163	2 018	2 198.6	78.0	629	7 921	1 943.1	172.0	123	549	77.8	13.0
Toledo, OH	944.2	1 438	892	12 516	9 268.5	548.4	2 419	35 261	8 219.6	751.0	652	3 780	1 120.0	131.0
Topeka, KS	49.5	216	232	2 556	1 239.4	100.8	926	11 716	2 569.8	237.7	269	1 133	167.2	31.8
Trenton-Ewing, NJ	691.6	1 888	414	10 266	9 049.0	851.9	1 412	20 683	5 089.1	505.0	357	D	D	D
Tucson, AZ	306.8	332	855	9 543	4 838.2	398.8	2 982	51 830	11 928.5	1 208.9	1 449	8 133	1 211.7	251.8
Tulsa, OK	190.0	214	1 475	21 606	20 496.6	1 139.0	3 152	45 953	11 623.2	996.3	1 169	8 958	1 468.7	289.3
Tuscaloosa, AL	463.0	2 352	171	1 916	885.9	82.3	858	11 097	2 566.2	233.5	204	1 182	175.5	32.2
Tyler, TX	45.5	239	291	3 019	1 516.0	135.4	855	12 347	3 110.1	287.8	229	1 447	204.5	41.3
Utica-Rome, NY	57.7	194	246	2 877	1 356.0	109.0	1 091	14 414	3 254.1	309.9	250	1 014	172.0	22.4
Valdosta, GA	43.3	346	169	1 987	992.0	67.3	632	7 478	1 938.4	152.4	144	803	84.6	19.3
Vallejo-Fairfield, CA	467.9	1 137	293	5 152	3 639.4	246.4	1 167	19 117	4 828.0	482.7	404	1 913	347.9	58.5
Victoria, TX	77.3	682	139	1 759	948.2	78.5	496	7 072	1 793.8	157.5	142	944	175.3	37.9
Vineland-Millville-Bridgeton, NJ	58.1	379	173	2 807	1 753.1	103.9	564	7 602	1 952.7	185.4	125	540	88.3	16.2

1. Merchant wholesalers, except manufacturers' sales branches and offices.

Table C. Metropolitan Areas —

Professional Services, Manufacturing, and Accommodation and Food Services

Area name	Professional, scientific, and technical services,[1] 2007				Manufacturing, 2007				Accommodation and food services, 2007			
	Number of establishments	Number of employees	Sales (mil dol)	Annual payroll (mil dol)	Number of establishments	Number of employees	Sales (mil dol)	Annual payroll (mil dol)	Number of establishments	Number of employees	Sales (mil dol)	Annual payroll (mil dol)
	147	148	149	150	151	152	153	154	155	156	157	158
Sacramento—Arden-Arcade—Roseville, CA..	5 856	50 677	7 296.2	3 360.2	1 598	44 504	12 821.8	1 859.3	4 304	77 056	4 168.6	1 100.2
Saginaw-Saginaw Township North, MI	355	3 009	429.9	121.3	219	11 437	4 604.8	659.0	383	8 620	337.3	102.2
St. Cloud, MN	351	D	D	D	330	17 503	4 584.6	694.0	452	8 241	293.3	83.6
St. George, UT	432	D	D	D	154	3 225	609.6	117.4	279	5 631	254.5	74.5
St. Joseph, MO-KS	209	D	D	D	126	9 871	4 934.8	413.4	232	4 492	165.7	48.5
St. Louis, MO-IL	7 330	D	D	D	2 976	132 161	67 121.1	6 916.2	5 835	121 229	5 558.7	1 586.9
Salem, OR	826	4 270	445.6	172.5	448	12 783	3 262.0	438.1	773	13 231	768.8	195.6
Salinas, CA	818	D	D	D	301	7 333	2 227.6	268.4	983	18 026	1 197.1	345.4
Salisbury, MD	251	D	D	D	100	D	1 124.3	D	225	4 300	194.7	53.2
Salt Lake City, UT	4 111	34 053	4 964.4	1 944.3	1 560	53 639	19 597.6	2 442.0	2 048	46 050	2 138.6	635.8
San Angelo, TX	188	D	D	D	121	2 932	877.8	114.0	210	4 301	180.1	50.1
San Antonio-New Braunfels, TX	4 284	35 667	5 087.5	1 997.8	1 332	48 294	15 945.7	1 869.9	3 944	86 014	4 291.7	1 200.1
San Diego-Carlsbad-San Marcos, CA	11 972	117 497	18 834.7	7 694.0	3 182	102 168	27 541.1	5 244.6	6 599	144 287	9 551.5	2 567.2
Sandusky, OH	132	D	D	D	110	7 149	2 329.9	344.9	279	5 661	254.7	69.0
San Francisco-Oakland-Fremont, CA	18 729	225 698	44 312.5	17 801.0	4 462	143 318	77 651.2	8 277.1	11 166	184 046	12 142.9	3 499.3
Oakland-Fremont-Hayward, CA Div	8 416	D	D	D	2 703	99 553	57 258.3	5 791.5	5 162	75 932	4 370.0	1 203.1
San Francisco-San Mateo-Redwood City, CA Div...	10 313	D	D	D	1 759	43 765	20 392.9	2 485.6	6 004	108 114	7 772.9	2 296.2
San Jose-Sunnyvale-Santa Clara, CA	7 885	123 833	21 593.3	13 561.5	2 683	145 580	45 719.1	10 397.9	4 190	69 623	4 197.8	1 173.9
San Luis Obispo-Paso Robles, CA	930	5 709	593.8	222.6	377	6 517	2 548.2	260.4	850	14 903	767.9	219.7
Santa Barbara-Santa Maria-Goleta, CA	1 359	D	D	D	505	13 149	3 174.1	676.8	1 029	21 380	1 361.5	360.1
Santa Cruz-Watsonville, CA .	914	D	D	D	329	6 689	1 502.4	301.6	657	9 774	513.8	148.8
Santa Fe, NM	693	D	D	D	153	980	D	34.5	398	9 203	540.4	166.3
Santa Rosa-Petaluma, CA....	1 538	D	D	D	885	24 077	5 841.9	1 201.2	1 173	17 739	1 005.4	283.8
Savannah, GA	816	D	D	D	226	15 650	8 463.5	899.2	921	18 424	933.8	252.9
Scranton—Wilkes-Barre, PA	1 107	9 715	844.2	340.5	649	32 526	11 135.4	1 238.4	1 369	19 758	825.7	225.5
Seattle-Tacoma-Bellevue, WA	11 939	D	D	D	4 024	165 676	64 901.7	8 809.4	8 615	134 167	7 701.2	2 239.4
Seattle-Bellevue-Everett, WA Div	10 553	D	D	D	3 356	145 350	59 943.1	7 915.2	7 037	110 091	6 528.7	1 906.7
Tacoma, WA Div	1 386	D	D	D	668	20 326	4 958.6	894.2	1 578	24 076	1 172.5	332.7
Sebastian-Vero Beach, FL....	473	2 076	235.3	97.2	99	2 179	413.0	87.7	232	4 557	190.5	56.2
Sheboygan, WI	176	1 743	209.1	70.5	246	18 774	6 126.1	816.0	271	4 869	193.0	54.8
Sherman-Denison, TX	220	1 086	92.5	34.5	132	6 148	2 542.8	293.7	226	4 001	167.7	48.6
Shreveport-Bossier City, LA.....	788	5 212	593.9	206.3	303	12 519	8 801.5	615.0	692	22 372	1 397.5	352.7
Sioux City, IA-NE-SD	245	D	D	D	166	D	D	408.9	351	5 692	199.2	57.4
Sioux Falls, SD	556	D	D	D	264	13 300	4 044.2	541.4	510	10 672	423.2	127.4
South Bend-Mishawaka, IN-MI	616	D	D	D	512	20 781	8 722.3	975.8	618	11 918	466.8	134.1
Spartanburg, SC	467	D	D	D	462	26 108	11 731.8	1 204.9	528	10 002	411.5	113.6
Spokane, WA	1 231	8 631	1 157.2	432.4	589	17 412	3 895.4	730.7	993	17 046	780.2	232.2
Springfield, IL	594	4 726	567.6	230.3	123	3 172	683.4	137.1	543	9 450	373.8	112.2
Springfield, MA	1 366	D	D	D	941	32 853	8 264.3	1 501.5	1 502	22 047	967.5	283.7
Springfield, MO	1 033	D	D	D	538	18 405	4 428.8	664.6	881	18 123	691.8	202.4
Springfield, OH	163	D	D	D	182	7 164	2 494.3	299.2	241	4 574	173.1	49.6
State College, PA	376	D	D	D	150	4 341	1 216.5	181.0	301	5 961	240.1	68.8
Steubenville-Weirton, WV-OH	161	D	D	D	83	8 433	5 467.0	428.3	308	3 446	131.6	34.2
Stockton, CA	801	D	D	D	585	23 442	8 272.5	938.6	1 079	15 195	745.8	199.3
Sumter, SC	139	D	D	D	82	7 707	1 922.0	253.3	149	3 173	109.4	29.8
Syracuse, NY	1 462	15 052	2 395.7	845.1	633	29 539	10 634.2	1 467.2	1 527	22 740	989.9	286.6
Tallahassee, FL	1 488	10 506	1 982.0	684.9	152	4 293	1 027.4	177.7	684	14 779	597.7	161.9
Tampa-St. Petersburg-Clearwater, FL	10 175	74 476	10 297.6	4 104.9	2 323	65 945	18 564.6	2 763.0	4 995	99 165	5 143.5	1 423.0
Terre Haute, IN	279	D	D	D	190	11 628	4 552.6	519.3	372	6 181	244.5	67.0
Texarkana, TX-Texarkana, AR	208	D	D	D	94	4 825	2 442.1	233.0	232	4 856	210.2	62.1
Toledo, OH	1 251	D	D	D	927	49 565	28 585.1	2 557.9	1 567	28 162	1 055.8	305.4
Topeka, KS	534	D	D	D	156	6 810	2 418.2	300.1	442	8 874	456.5	110.9
Trenton-Ewing, NJ	1 646	30 900	5 790.4	2 345.3	293	9 352	D	420.1	834	12 103	695.8	197.7
Tucson, AZ	2 692	16 250	1 886.4	777.8	760	30 567	10 365.2	1 877.0	1 758	42 002	2 135.2	601.8
Tulsa, OK	2 815	18 151	2 527.6	937.0	1 448	55 034	21 574.6	2 496.5	1 809	34 896	1 421.1	399.5
Tuscaloosa, AL	370	2 599	225.7	84.7	171	14 378	11 142.2	755.9	395	8 389	331.8	88.6
Tyler, TX	548	D	D	D	224	10 737	5 423.5	474.5	339	7 563	337.3	93.6
Utica-Rome, NY	462	D	D	D	329	13 713	3 798.2	547.0	662	7 136	314.7	89.3
Valdosta, GA	230	D	D	D	128	4 881	2 326.4	180.1	272	5 615	212.7	56.2
Vallejo-Fairfield, CA	598	D	D	D	296	10 357	8 377.3	578.9	731	12 523	573.3	153.4
Victoria, TX	198	D	D	D	99	5 007	11 902.9	346.6	242	3 777	155.8	41.7
Vineland-Millville-Bridgeton, NJ	231	D	D	D	175	9 037	2 591.4	341.6	262	3 263	155.1	40.0

1. Establishments subject to federal tax.

Area name	Health care and social assistance,[1] 2007				Other services,[1] 2007				Federal funds and grants, 2009–2010 Expenditures (mil dol)			
										Direct payments for individuals		
	Number of establishments	Number of employees	Receipts (mil dol)	Annual payroll (mil dol)	Number of establishments	Number of employees	Receipts (mil dol)	Annual payroll (mil dol)	Total	Social Security and government retirement	Medicare	Food stamps and Supplemental Security Income
	159	160	161	162	163	164	165	166	167	168	169	170
Sacramento—Arden-Arcade—Roseville, CA..	5 027	96 068	12 292.4	4 739.2	3 314	28 694	4 276.2	1 121.0	32 388.0	5 596.7	2 668.6	786.4
Saginaw-Saginaw Township North, MI	584	16 811	1 512.5	605.3	369	2 191	178.2	46.5	1 822.0	749.9	366.7	145.4
St. Cloud, MN	487	15 066	1 357.3	637.4	450	2 917	216.5	62.0	1 217.3	513.9	200.2	30.0
St. George, UT	393	6 648	628.5	250.2	198	1 116	95.0	27.4	1 063.0	435.9	120.4	18.5
St. Joseph, MO-KS	352	8 067	744.7	298.8	235	1 391	120.4	40.7	959.9	374.6	220.9	48.9
St. Louis, MO-IL	7 544	170 320	15 882.5	6 161.2	5 193	35 614	3 393.0	1 003.8	34 277.1	8 588.8	4 849.7	1 079.3
Salem, OR	1 047	17 339	1 580.1	655.6	596	2 876	235.9	70.3	4 403.2	1 106.7	448.1	159.9
Salinas, CA	970	13 789	1 876.6	723.7	556	3 651	425.9	104.6	3 298.5	932.2	553.5	91.2
Salisbury, MD	386	8 982	823.2	368.0	207	1 303	112.1	32.0	1 054.9	352.7	339.7	38.8
Salt Lake City, UT	2 844	55 193	5 899.6	2 256.9	2 059	14 359	1 381.6	383.3	9 696.7	2 187.2	1 579.4	230.4
San Angelo, TX	260	6 778	590.2	245.3	214	1 170	107.2	26.8	1 016.3	355.2	152.9	39.9
San Antonio-New Braunfels, TX	4 849	109 941	10 646.6	3 893.2	3 063	21 362	1 732.3	509.8	23 110.7	6 821.9	2 454.8	850.4
San Diego-Carlsbad-San Marcos, CA	7 924	133 893	15 954.7	5 872.9	5 176	37 084	3 732.5	1 015.3	37 302.9	7 771.6	4 652.8	790.1
Sandusky, OH	195	4 986	434.3	162.8	155	815	49.6	14.5	666.7	297.9	153.9	23.6
San Francisco-Oakland-Fremont, CA	13 103	221 320	28 727.4	11 570.0	8 537	59 689	12 556.2	2 072.7	40 303.3	9 748.0	7 459.6	1 269.6
Oakland-Fremont-Hayward, CA Div	6 975	118 515	15 333.8	6 289.8	4 270	28 823	3 413.6	946.9	21 436.0	5 551.9	4 046.2	768.4
San Francisco-San Mateo-Redwood City, CA Div	6 128	102 805	13 393.6	5 280.3	4 267	30 866	9 142.6	1 125.8	18 867.3	4 196.0	3 413.4	491.3
San Jose-Sunnyvale-Santa Clara, CA	5 161	88 995	12 403.9	4 736.6	2 970	19 637	2 838.4	664.1	16 250.0	3 352.8	2 115.6	474.5
San Luis Obispo-Paso Robles, CA	864	14 341	1 341.2	546.4	464	2 808	222.0	60.3	1 783.4	769.8	416.5	44.5
Santa Barbara-Santa Maria-Goleta, CA	1 322	19 124	2 076.4	784.0	767	5 005	816.9	141.4	3 677.4	1 037.4	621.1	91.6
Santa Cruz-Watsonville, CA	863	11 416	1 441.4	505.0	452	2 702	258.2	72.1	1 598.2	550.8	387.8	56.7
Santa Fe, NM	518	8 465	809.4	318.0	341	1 849	231.0	54.1	2 153.9	470.9	117.4	28.7
Santa Rosa-Petaluma, CA	1 516	23 219	2 623.9	1 065.9	873	4 877	508.1	138.8	3 142.9	1 300.7	800.3	86.8
Savannah, GA	767	20 019	2 012.8	825.9	538	3 467	306.5	91.1	7 185.6	1 002.3	481.0	172.6
Scranton—Wilkes-Barre, PA	1 761	43 009	3 621.4	1 482.7	1 034	5 467	429.8	114.6	5 883.8	2 071.6	1 750.2	187.4
Seattle-Tacoma-Bellevue, WA	10 071	189 085	21 143.3	8 376.0	6 953	43 575	6 464.1	1 857.4	33 849.9	8 520.3	3 411.8	1 062.3
Seattle-Bellevue-Everett, WA Div	8 191	147 038	16 748.1	6 594.7	5 652	35 082	5 661.0	1 106.2	21 905.7	6 023.9	2 674.5	748.0
Tacoma, WA Div	1 880	42 047	4 395.2	1 781.3	1 301	8 493	803.1	251.2	11 944.2	2 496.4	737.4	314.3
Sebastian-Vero Beach, FL	446	7 230	836.4	300.9	264	1 169	97.0	26.7	1 224.1	654.7	422.4	26.9
Sheboygan, WI	292	6 709	501.4	242.7	217	1 093	76.8	20.2	765.1	334.6	141.0	18.9
Sherman-Denison, TX	382	8 254	706.2	279.6	165	820	59.1	16.6	868.6	401.2	214.3	37.4
Shreveport-Bossier City, LA	1 033	28 793	2 713.9	1 122.7	606	4 172	316.2	89.5	3 640.2	1 181.0	667.8	210.2
Sioux City, IA-NE-SD	424	9 421	834.8	325.4	270	1 736	142.1	42.6	1 304.1	388.9	224.3	38.0
Sioux Falls, SD	599	22 420	2 079.8	952.0	456	2 690	227.0	62.2	1 894.1	607.9	190.6	38.4
South Bend-Mishawaka, IN-MI	728	18 605	1 990.8	718.8	581	4 088	431.2	102.9	3 311.7	885.6	469.8	117.5
Spartanburg, SC	510	13 349	1 287.4	520.8	433	2 920	283.9	69.8	1 826.7	951.9	320.5	93.8
Spokane, WA	1 424	33 424	3 273.7	1 325.9	863	5 436	479.1	132.2	4 074.6	1 547.5	616.2	199.1
Springfield, IL	477	D	D	D	501	3 555	387.4	109.6	5 593.0	614.6	333.0	70.0
Springfield, MA	1 778	49 008	4 274.5	1 849.1	1 268	7 575	627.2	185.4	5 994.5	1 959.1	1 294.3	411.1
Springfield, MO	981	30 796	2 692.2	1 152.4	851	5 346	465.0	133.8	2 936.9	1 339.5	510.3	127.7
Springfield, OH	319	8 186	619.8	258.2	237	1 402	188.1	38.4	1 247.9	511.9	288.8	64.5
State College, PA	332	6 543	549.7	238.6	228	1 270	100.7	27.6	1 405.5	336.6	165.5	19.1
Steubenville-Weirton, WV-OH	306	7 421	547.3	226.1	207	1 016	61.2	16.7	1 287.0	589.5	370.1	65.6
Stockton, CA	1 351	26 658	3 045.8	1 141.3	879	5 576	462.8	144.6	4 164.3	1 413.7	851.2	287.4
Sumter, SC	180	4 812	469.3	172.7	152	1 141	69.7	21.7	1 422.2	401.7	121.4	78.0
Syracuse, NY	1 658	42 157	4 003.5	1 689.2	1 158	7 158	629.1	177.8	6 233.8	2 021.2	948.9	239.4
Tallahassee, FL	783	19 119	1 879.5	713.5	721	4 825	727.3	168.1	9 141.2	900.3	548.5	153.8
Tampa-St. Petersburg-Clearwater, FL	7 869	147 093	16 779.4	6 161.0	5 037	31 222	2 816.9	781.2	26 756.0	9 642.6	7 343.4	1 026.2
Terre Haute, IN	477	10 700	1 051.3	353.2	284	1 811	133.1	36.3	1 548.2	563.4	340.2	63.4
Texarkana, TX-Texarkana, AR	373	8 177	736.6	290.9	193	1 214	93.7	26.5	1 482.9	504.7	273.1	77.5
Toledo, OH	1 698	48 747	4 266.3	1 830.8	1 176	7 730	687.5	181.6	5 031.9	1 769.6	1 309.4	317.7
Topeka, KS	593	18 560	1 465.1	651.6	489	3 159	303.2	85.6	3 278.0	883.0	318.8	69.5
Trenton-Ewing, NJ	1 147	26 724	2 609.3	1 180.7	860	6 084	828.6	214.7	6 657.9	1 020.4	810.3	91.2
Tucson, AZ	2 672	51 151	5 459.8	2 073.5	1 494	12 045	1 020.6	289.4	14 248.6	3 301.3	1 318.0	381.9
Tulsa, OK	2 622	53 658	5 098.5	2 001.8	1 502	8 672	926.6	228.3	6 426.0	2 693.1	1 268.7	327.7
Tuscaloosa, AL	422	12 490	1 066.5	494.1	257	1 789	137.5	39.0	1 920.5	638.8	332.0	112.0
Tyler, TX	636	19 044	2 002.7	784.8	334	2 556	192.7	71.9	1 498.6	640.5	307.9	66.0
Utica-Rome, NY	727	22 040	1 606.9	754.0	513	3 534	223.8	66.2	2 843.0	1 047.0	559.4	124.5
Valdosta, GA	359	7 813	638.7	260.9	190	867	69.4	22.6	1 241.8	363.7	165.4	77.9
Vallejo-Fairfield, CA	861	18 135	2 136.5	895.9	541	3 240	324.0	92.5	3 454.6	1 261.9	407.1	118.6
Victoria, TX	364	7 029	635.6	252.9	212	1 417	134.2	38.7	846.5	340.3	178.3	49.1
Vineland-Millville-Bridgeton, NJ	399	8 351	820.8	333.3	273	1 439	103.0	31.1	1 295.5	434.9	354.9	63.3

1. Establishments subject to federal tax.

Table C. Metropolitan Areas —

Federal Funds, Residential Construction and Local Government Finances

Area name	Federal funds and grants, 2009–2010 (cont.)							Value of residential construction authorized by building permits, 2010		Local government finances, 2007				
	Expenditures (mil dol) (cont.)									General revenue				
	Procurement contract awards			Grants								Taxes		
													Per capita[1] (dollars)	
	Salaries and wages	Defense	Other	Medicaid and other health-related	Nutrition and family welfare	Education	Other	New construction ($1,000)	Number of housing units	Total (mil dol)	Inter-governmental (mil dol)	Total (mil dol)	Total	Property
	171	172	173	174	175	176	177	178	179	180	181	182	183	184
Sacramento—Arden-Arcade—Roseville, CA ...	1 258.0	4 694.0	488.7	2 822.1	2 812.7	3 074.1	7 628.0	615 552	2 702	12 365.1	5 339.3	3 593.5	1 718	1 250
Saginaw-Saginaw Township North, MI	102.1	16.2	31.3	262.1	58.9	19.0	55.0	25 204	137	749.6	432.9	168.2	831	732
St. Cloud, MN	128.5	1.0	56.7	145.4	29.5	9.5	15.5	57 612	314	700.6	350.7	171.0	921	821
St. George, UT	377.3	0.4	27.3	27.9	11.5	4.2	17.9	168 923	893	442.8	162.8	155.0	1 158	767
St. Joseph, MO-KS	55.1	15.2	11.3	141.7	13.9	7.8	27.9	18 131	131	356.0	132.5	136.5	1 107	738
St. Louis, MO-IL	3 503.0	9 200.0	1 003.6	3 653.4	402.0	188.9	1 190.5	962 831	5 660	9 708.2	3 240.8	4 387.9	1 565	1 087
Salem, OR	264.8	29.4	39.4	500.6	268.0	300.5	1 189.4	130 093	699	1 336.4	696.3	376.1	973	839
Salinas, CA	588.4	385.9	170.6	285.9	114.4	35.1	93.0	67 126	279	2 775.3	1 150.3	709.4	1 740	1 280
Salisbury, MD	45.6	14.1	12.5	144.6	27.2	11.5	26.7	29 789	194	466.8	215.7	157.0	1 313	764
Salt Lake City, UT	1 280.0	944.9	308.1	1 146.3	236.3	230.7	1 350.0	516 281	2 989	3 574.8	1 081.5	1 479.5	1 345	918
San Angelo, TX	205.4	64.0	5.5	112.7	22.8	3.8	16.9	24 682	177	298.8	127.6	122.6	1 135	849
San Antonio-New Braunfels, TX	4 647.3	4 014.7	609.1	2 319.4	360.0	130.9	353.0	1 059 634	6 865	7 279.7	2 504.1	2 880.3	1 447	1 208
San Diego-Carlsbad-San Marcos, CA	4 765.8	11 593.0	1 288.7	3 866.8	677.8	239.4	990.5	772 067	3 494	16 065.9	6 632.0	5 448.0	1 831	1 394
Sandusky, OH	33.6	25.3	35.8	47.4	16.2	5.5	21.0	11 186	47	382.6	124.9	143.7	1 859	1 381
San Francisco-Oakland-Fremont, CA	3 330.8	1 586.8	4 836.0	7 369.9	858.4	412.3	2 633.7	1 154 311	4 621	29 510.4	10 613.2	10 634.5	2 530	1 716
Oakland-Fremont-Hayward, CA Div	1 581.8	604.4	3 307.2	3 306.1	508.0	216.3	1 140.6	NA	NA	17 127.4	6 717.7	5 452.8	2 195	1 558
San Francisco-San Mateo-Redwood City, CA Div	1 749.0	982.4	1 528.9	4 063.7	350.4	196.0	1 493.1	NA	NA	12 383.1	3 895.5	5 181.6	3 012	1 945
San Jose-Sunnyvale-Santa Clara, CA	965.3	4 727.3	1 076.4	2 027.3	346.7	119.6	793.4	755 561	4 179	11 689.2	3 794.5	4 423.8	2 453	1 836
San Luis Obispo-Paso Robles, CA	126.0	56.0	25.0	176.0	70.7	13.3	44.4	114 809	468	1 183.8	434.3	521.1	1 986	1 598
Santa Barbara-Santa Maria-Goleta, CA	416.1	701.1	65.0	332.1	93.3	38.4	201.3	138 930	400	2 499.6	956.2	791.8	1 959	1 459
Santa Cruz-Watsonville, CA ..	53.2	9.7	19.4	275.4	54.0	21.4	116.7	37 720	158	1 409.1	614.7	454.6	1 806	1 403
Santa Fe, NM	136.2	45.2	43.5	254.6	123.5	151.5	743.4	12 802	96	511.3	237.0	184.0	1 287	676
Santa Rosa-Petaluma, CA	203.3	47.1	78.1	359.9	84.6	26.4	103.0	87 521	477	2 520.7	903.4	933.6	2 010	1 589
Savannah, GA	4 120.0	735.9	33.3	290.7	75.2	32.7	48.3	155 856	1 301	1 837.4	356.0	665.4	2 020	1 229
Scranton—Wilkes-Barre, PA..	378.7	374.1	138.6	617.0	104.1	16.3	79.6	124 111	687	1 760.0	694.0	737.4	1 342	984
Seattle-Tacoma-Bellevue, WA	8 503.3	3 712.7	1 080.6	4 499.1	522.2	184.9	1 830.8	1 900 709	10 040	15 920.4	5 052.5	6 142.1	1 856	1 024
Seattle-Bellevue-Everett, WA Div	2 219.0	3 067.7	936.9	3 774.8	388.0	128.0	1 553.8	NA	NA	12 963.1	3 851.1	5 048.3	1 990	1 063
Tacoma, WA Div	6 284.9	644.9	143.8	724.3	134.3	56.9	277.0	NA	NA	2 957.3	1 201.4	1 093.9	1 415	896
Sebastian-Vero Beach, FL.....	33.2	0.1	10.4	38.1	17.6	6.6	5.8	103 644	307	581.3	109.6	324.0	2 458	1 835
Sheboygan, WI	28.1	38.1	90.0	78.4	16.4	5.6	4.7	17 112	69	493.2	225.5	180.9	1 580	1 523
Sherman-Denison, TX	25.3	6.5	10.0	123.9	16.0	2.7	7.8	21 820	327	363.4	126.4	155.6	1 311	1 087
Shreveport-Bossier City, LA......	623.1	159.8	51.1	471.2	81.4	41.1	60.2	211 354	1 300	1 399.9	501.5	690.8	1 782	773
Sioux City, IA-NE-SD	97.2	282.0	20.2	138.8	26.6	8.4	21.4	49 828	275	563.8	234.6	225.0	1 576	1 152
Sioux Falls, SD	219.2	43.2	105.8	136.4	21.0	4.3	133.5	138 512	1 081	621.7	172.8	333.9	1 470	979
South Bend-Mishawaka, IN-MI	153.0	1 124.3	30.7	305.7	42.5	12.3	88.7	66 883	383	1 024.5	447.0	349.8	1 105	1 047
Spartanburg, SC	85.6	4.8	10.7	239.6	37.1	19.4	22.2	70 033	562	1 277.3	308.7	290.4	1 054	930
Spokane, WA	486.6	237.7	134.2	482.5	91.6	32.6	129.8	238 193	1 609	1 575.8	697.5	548.2	1 202	709
Springfield, IL	273.0	25.2	32.9	282.4	396.1	940.2	2 563.2	74 033	399	703.6	275.4	294.0	1 423	1 249
Springfield, MA	504.7	106.5	148.1	987.3	147.3	65.5	212.3	128 006	633	2 455.1	1 318.8	895.3	1 312	1 282
Springfield, MO	266.1	8.9	49.1	380.3	52.2	26.8	70.6	164 437	1 338	1 129.9	390.1	448.9	1 069	592
Springfield, OH	72.3	22.3	5.4	188.8	27.6	11.8	28.5	9 893	57	580.8	303.3	164.6	1 172	789
State College, PA	72.0	236.8	68.0	179.8	22.9	11.9	192.3	78 298	426	400.8	139.2	181.2	1 253	907
Steubenville-Weirton, WV-OH	31.6	5.3	7.4	148.6	24.2	9.6	16.9	4 463	25	431.3	217.5	120.0	979	725
Stockton, CA	285.9	93.9	65.0	739.1	153.5	47.5	89.5	166 494	813	3 836.6	1 957.0	986.4	1 470	1 065
Sumter, SC	294.5	176.0	76.3	180.0	28.4	13.9	15.1	37 678	353	256.0	124.9	98.3	946	684
Syracuse, NY	396.9	1 191.0	214.4	750.9	169.9	60.5	143.1	157 153	1 139	3 396.8	1 536.9	1 316.2	2 040	1 452
Tallahassee, FL	208.5	42.3	40.9	840.5	644.2	2 166.6	3 343.5	88 533	625	1 355.6	555.3	430.0	1 220	891
Tampa-St. Petersburg-Clearwater, FL	2 400.1	2 146.8	1 042.0	1 538.0	387.1	194.4	429.2	1 289 270	6 501	11 250.7	3 906.6	4 592.7	1 686	1 317
Terre Haute, IN	146.0	25.6	58.2	241.3	31.6	6.1	22.0	24 106	189	500.3	219.1	135.5	800	695
Texarkana, TX-Texarkana, AR	172.1	133.4	12.9	216.0	26.5	7.0	21.0	19 043	237	391.7	196.8	122.5	912	648
Toledo, OH	291.9	38.5	53.0	734.3	126.6	59.5	126.1	117 322	775	2 991.3	1 130.6	1 237.8	1 901	1 213
Topeka, KS	316.1	24.9	58.2	270.5	146.0	227.5	898.3	59 067	381	852.0	320.2	344.7	1 507	1 173
Trenton-Ewing, NJ	320.8	177.4	175.7	690.6	349.7	578.2	2 175.8	94 562	655	1 979.0	683.1	990.7	2 711	2 675
Tucson, AZ	1 074.4	5 268.8	388.9	1 668.4	174.1	107.4	341.9	424 149	1 938	3 481.7	1 650.1	1 289.2	1 333	911
Tulsa, OK	462.0	251.7	209.3	628.1	170.8	74.5	181.9	417 682	2 616	2 611.2	945.7	1 080.9	1 193	646
Tuscaloosa, AL	113.4	122.9	152.0	228.7	36.9	21.5	82.9	89 144	623	940.5	286.9	173.6	846	330
Tyler, TX	80.8	56.3	30.8	223.4	25.1	8.5	17.5	37 614	266	557.5	164.4	281.6	1 417	1 075
Utica-Rome, NY	236.6	162.1	24.0	490.4	81.2	27.4	40.5	49 744	314	1 456.9	721.1	524.4	1 778	1 162
Valdosta, GA	286.4	89.1	5.1	135.3	34.1	12.8	12.6	70 430	852	401.3	173.1	166.7	1 281	653
Vallejo-Fairfield, CA	689.1	363.8	49.4	264.2	71.7	24.2	163.2	103 818	467	2 176.4	1 047.1	670.5	1 641	1 187
Victoria, TX	41.5	16.9	6.0	138.5	22.7	4.7	6.3	14 698	103	552.0	112.4	208.7	1 834	1 545
Vineland-Millville-Bridgeton, NJ	61.2	42.0	14.4	232.9	41.0	11.5	17.7	28 038	246	758.8	469.5	192.0	1 234	1 205

1. Based on the resident population estimated as of July 1 of the year shown.

Table C. Metropolitan Areas — Local Government Finances, Government Employment, and Voting

Area name	Local government finances, 2007 (cont.)									Government employment, 2009			Presidential election,[2] 2008		
	Direct general expenditure							Debt outstanding					Percent of vote cast:		
			Percent of total for:												
	Total (mil dol)	Per capita[1] (dollars)	Education	Health and hospitals	Police protection	Public welfare	Highways	Total (mil dol)	Per capita[1] (dollars)	Federal civilian	Federal military	State and local	Democratic	Republican	All other
	185	186	187	188	189	190	191	192	193	194	195	196	197	198	199
Sacramento—Arden-Arcade—Roseville, CA..	12 885.3	6 162	34.6	5.1	5.0	7.6	6.8	20 284.8	9 700	12 812	4 375	243 683	54.8	43.2	2.0
Saginaw-Saginaw Township North, MI	770.9	3 811	48.9	13.1	4.2	0.7	5.5	503.7	2 490	1 197	386	10 344	57.9	40.6	1.5
St. Cloud, MN	688.3	3 709	42.4	7.1	4.7	4.5	12.6	1 258.3	6 781	2 117	715	11 573	45.0	52.5	2.5
St. George, UT	406.0	3 035	48.1	2.7	6.5	0.0	5.3	645.9	4 828	548	608	6 424	21.9	75.3	2.8
St. Joseph, MO-KS	355.6	2 883	51.1	1.7	4.1	0.1	6.0	518.3	4 202	621	536	9 506	45.1	52.9	2.0
St. Louis, MO-IL	9 511.1	3 392	50.8	2.5	6.7	0.5	5.3	11 371.8	4 056	30 443	15 593	146 881	57.5	41.4	1.1
Salem, OR	1 367.8	3 537	53.1	6.6	5.3	0.3	4.7	1 736.6	4 491	1 602	1 133	39 238	49.4	47.8	2.9
Salinas, CA	2 680.5	6 576	35.2	21.3	4.5	4.9	4.8	1 456.7	3 574	5 345	5 524	26 051	68.2	29.9	2.0
Salisbury, MD	455.6	3 809	57.5	0.9	4.8	3.9	4.3	271.1	2 267	401	389	10 418	46.8	51.9	1.3
Salt Lake City, UT	3 281.7	2 983	40.0	1.5	6.6	1.6	4.7	6 352.8	5 775	12 517	5 486	86 057	48.3	48.9	2.7
San Angelo, TX	287.2	2 657	53.7	3.9	6.3	0.3	3.0	218.1	2 017	1 355	3 271	7 671	28.5	70.6	0.9
San Antonio-New Braunfels, TX	7 423.0	3 729	52.6	11.1	5.0	1.0	2.7	16 637.3	8 358	32 308	36 743	125 714	47.1	52.1	0.8
San Diego-Carlsbad-San Marcos, CA	16 037.1	5 391	40.2	9.0	6.0	6.5	2.9	17 352.6	5 833	43 765	112 014	187 442	54.1	43.9	1.9
Sandusky, OH	363.6	4 702	49.0	2.2	5.8	6.0	4.2	235.3	3 043	238	196	5 471	56.1	42.3	1.6
San Francisco-Oakland-Fremont, CA	29 792.9	7 087	26.1	13.6	5.6	6.0	3.5	45 709.5	10 873	34 729	9 121	268 010	76.4	21.7	1.9
Oakland-Fremont-Hayward, CA Div	17 899.6	7 206	28.1	11.5	5.3	5.4	3.7	27 119.1	10 918	15 641	5 453	141 089	74.2	23.9	1.9
San Francisco-San Mateo-Redwood City, CA Div	11 893.4	6 915	23.1	16.8	6.0	7.0	3.3	18 590.5	10 808	19 088	3 668	126 921	79.2	18.8	2.0
San Jose-Sunnyvale-Santa Clara, CA	11 417.7	6 330	33.0	16.3	5.0	5.5	3.1	15 026.0	8 331	10 903	3 372	83 253	69.2	28.8	2.0
San Luis Obispo-Paso Robles, CA	1 122.2	4 276	38.3	5.7	6.4	8.8	5.0	704.1	2 683	638	470	20 482	51.4	46.0	2.6
Santa Barbara-Santa Maria-Goleta, CA	2 477.1	6 129	37.4	14.0	5.5	5.4	4.7	1 475.7	3 651	3 746	3 437	31 418	60.4	37.5	2.1
Santa Cruz-Watsonville, CA	1 495.0	5 939	37.8	6.0	4.3	8.0	3.1	1 194.1	4 743	554	419	17 618	77.5	19.8	2.7
Santa Fe, NM	462.7	3 237	43.5	3.0	6.5	3.1	5.8	626.5	4 382	1 040	396	17 886	76.9	21.9	1.2
Santa Rosa-Petaluma, CA	2 662.5	5 733	35.4	8.3	6.4	4.9	4.3	2 522.0	5 430	1 665	1 550	26 050	73.6	24.0	2.3
Savannah, GA	1 841.7	5 592	26.0	31.0	5.7	0.2	4.1	1 351.0	4 102	2 995	7 672	20 391	49.7	49.6	0.6
Scranton—Wilkes-Barre, PA	1 850.3	3 368	50.1	0.3	3.2	3.8	4.3	2 109.4	3 839	4 796	1 483	27 507	57.0	42.0	1.0
Seattle-Tacoma-Bellevue, WA	15 163.6	4 582	34.2	9.4	4.9	0.7	4.7	26 380.5	7 972	36 232	50 798	230 522	64.7	33.6	1.7
Seattle-Bellevue-Everett, WA Div	12 137.2	4 786	31.4	10.8	4.9	0.7	4.5	22 184.6	8 747	24 484	14 190	183 819	67.3	31.1	1.6
Tacoma, WA Div	3 026.4	3 914	45.2	3.8	5.1	0.4	5.5	4 196.0	5 427	11 748	36 606	46 703	55.2	43.0	1.8
Sebastian-Vero Beach, FL	528.1	4 006	35.5	3.8	7.4	0.6	7.4	540.1	4 097	408	267	5 443	42.1	56.9	1.0
Sheboygan, WI	509.8	4 452	52.0	6.2	5.0	8.7	7.4	481.1	4 202	223	349	5 865	48.9	49.6	1.5
Sherman-Denison, TX	365.4	3 079	62.8	2.5	4.5	0.1	3.3	392.7	3 309	358	284	5 997	30.6	68.5	1.0
Shreveport-Bossier City, LA..	1 329.4	3 430	49.7	1.4	7.7	0.0	3.7	1 303.1	3 362	4 630	6 785	30 138	44.1	55.1	0.9
Sioux City, IA-NE-SD	550.9	3 858	55.5	2.1	5.4	0.9	8.0	440.9	3 088	988	642	8 377	47.3	51.2	1.5
Sioux Falls, SD	633.3	2 788	47.1	1.8	5.3	0.6	7.1	677.5	2 982	2 619	1 526	9 971	47.3	50.9	1.8
South Bend-Mishawaka, IN-MI	1 086.4	3 431	52.1	1.6	4.5	4.0	2.8	1 075.8	3 397	1 239	1 026	15 929	56.9	42.0	1.1
Spartanburg, SC	1 311.4	4 760	35.2	42.2	3.2	0.4	1.5	2 196.7	7 973	517	1 254	18 499	38.4	60.0	1.5
Spokane, WA	1 516.3	3 324	49.0	4.6	5.4	0.1	5.0	957.6	2 099	4 807	4 164	30 962	48.2	49.3	2.5
Springfield, IL	678.9	3 286	54.4	1.2	8.2	1.8	6.0	1 083.5	5 245	1 971	434	26 683	50.8	47.6	1.6
Springfield, MA	2 453.2	3 594	60.9	0.6	4.6	0.5	3.4	2 059.7	3 017	5 889	1 907	50 715	65.5	32.3	2.2
Springfield, MO	1 107.5	2 637	50.6	7.4	8.0	0.8	9.7	1 408.4	3 353	2 669	1 792	25 050	38.3	60.3	1.3
Springfield, OH	533.2	3 795	49.5	6.3	6.0	8.4	3.9	240.3	1 711	717	365	6 651	47.9	50.4	1.8
State College, PA	425.6	2 942	51.8	4.4	3.0	7.7	5.2	425.5	2 942	469	452	44 696	55.4	43.5	1.1
Steubenville-Weirton, WV-OH	401.6	3 276	45.8	8.5	4.4	7.7	4.8	150.3	1 226	338	453	5 793	47.2	50.9	1.9
Stockton, CA	3 766.6	5 613	43.4	8.4	5.5	8.1	2.8	3 448.9	5 140	4 133	1 134	34 303	54.4	43.8	1.8
Sumter, SC	251.4	2 418	60.8	1.6	6.9	0.0	2.4	433.8	4 174	1 310	5 020	5 956	57.3	41.9	0.8
Syracuse, NY	3 517.6	5 451	48.9	3.6	3.3	10.4	4.8	3 224.4	4 997	4 604	1 352	50 577	56.8	41.4	1.8
Tallahassee, FL	1 366.3	3 878	44.0	1.1	6.7	0.1	9.9	3 225.4	9 155	1 985	820	60 023	60.3	38.9	0.8
Tampa-St. Petersburg-Clearwater, FL	10 560.7	3 877	40.6	2.3	7.3	2.3	3.6	12 459.9	4 574	22 766	12 488	126 878	52.0	47.0	1.0
Terre Haute, IN	546.5	3 227	50.2	4.6	2.9	2.0	3.9	387.4	2 287	1 393	600	11 937	53.9	44.7	1.4
Texarkana, TX-Texarkana, AR	375.5	2 798	65.5	0.5	5.8	0.2	3.7	440.7	3 284	5 292	443	8 488	31.2	67.8	1.0
Toledo, OH	3 079.3	4 730	42.4	6.6	5.6	5.8	4.8	2 810.0	4 317	2 456	1 846	47 522	60.3	38.1	1.6
Topeka, KS	836.3	3 657	54.8	1.8	5.7	0.3	4.2	1 208.8	5 286	3 181	1 221	25 524	45.9	52.3	1.9
Trenton-Ewing, NJ	2 085.4	5 706	53.1	1.0	5.4	4.4	1.3	1 899.1	5 197	2 382	791	49 093	67.4	31.4	1.2
Tucson, AZ	3 541.9	3 662	35.0	8.9	8.4	2.7	6.5	4 775.0	4 937	11 799	8 420	66 304	52.4	46.4	1.2
Tulsa, OK	2 623.3	2 896	51.8	2.9	5.4	1.0	3.7	4 063.4	4 486	4 728	4 100	50 596	35.6	64.4	0.0
Tuscaloosa, AL	979.3	4 772	32.5	41.0	4.0	0.0	5.1	616.7	3 005	1 703	1 031	23 385	45.6	53.5	0.8
Tyler, TX	599.0	3 015	63.3	5.0	4.6	0.4	3.7	786.9	3 960	919	485	11 812	29.8	69.4	0.8
Utica-Rome, NY	1 465.7	4 971	51.2	2.6	2.9	11.1	7.1	1 424.5	4 831	2 761	545	30 287	45.8	52.6	1.7
Valdosta, GA	427.8	3 287	53.0	8.2	6.0	0.5	8.9	68.6	527	859	4 943	11 766	43.6	55.7	0.7
Vallejo-Fairfield, CA	2 178.6	5 332	37.7	4.8	8.0	6.8	5.1	2 079.0	5 088	3 918	7 330	21 761	63.4	34.8	1.8
Victoria, TX	516.2	4 536	44.7	26.2	4.7	0.4	3.0	576.5	5 066	324	333	8 292	34.3	64.9	0.7
Vineland-Millville-Bridgeton, NJ	747.9	4 808	62.4	2.2	3.5	3.7	1.8	357.1	2 296	644	324	14 381	60.1	38.5	1.4

1. Based on the resident population estimated as of July 1 of the year shown.　2. © 2009 Election Data Services, Inc. All rights reserved.

Table C. Metropolitan Areas — **Land Area and Population**

CBSA code[1]	Area name	Land area,[2] 2010 (sq km)	Total persons	Rank	Per square kilometer	White	Black	American Indian, Alaska Native	Asian and Pacific Islander	Percent Hispanic or Latino[3]	Under 5 years	5 to 17 years	18 to 24 years	25 to 34 years	35 to 44 years	45 to 54 years
		1	2	3	4	5	6	7	8	9	10	11	12	13	14	15
47260	Virginia Beach-Norfolk-Newport News, VA-NC	6 811	1 671 683	36	245.4	59.5	32.2	1.1	4.7	5.4	6.5	17.0	11.9	14.1	12.8	15.0
47300	Visalia-Porterville, CA	12 495	442 179	111	35.4	33.8	1.5	1.3	3.9	60.6	9.3	23.3	10.7	14.0	12.4	11.8
47380	Waco, TX	2 686	234 906	188	87.5	60.1	15.1	0.7	1.7	23.6	7.1	18.3	14.3	12.9	11.4	12.9
47580	Warner Robins, GA	973	139 900	277	143.8	62.4	29.4	0.9	3.4	6.1	7.3	19.5	9.5	14.3	13.5	15.2
47900	Washington-Arlington-Alexandria, DC-VA-MD-WV.	14 500	5 582 170	7	385.0	50.7	26.5	0.7	10.7	13.8	6.7	17.1	9.2	15.3	15.1	15.3
47900	Bethesda-Rockville-Frederick, MD Div	2 982	1 205 162	X	404.1	56.9	16.2	0.6	13.4	15.1	6.5	17.8	7.7	13.3	14.6	16.0
47900	Washington-Arlington-Alexandria, DC-VA-MD-WV Div	11 517	4 377 008	X	380.0	49.0	29.3	0.8	9.9	13.4	6.8	17.0	9.7	15.9	15.2	15.1
47940	Waterloo-Cedar Falls, IA	3 893	167 819	237	43.1	88.3	8.0	0.5	1.6	3.1	6.4	15.7	14.4	12.6	10.9	13.0
48140	Wausau, WI	4 001	134 063	290	33.5	91.2	1.0	0.8	5.8	2.2	6.5	18.0	7.8	12.2	13.2	15.6
48300	Wenatchee-East Wenatchee, WA	12 276	110 884	328	9.0	71.2	0.5	1.5	1.5	26.8	7.0	18.8	8.5	11.8	11.8	14.3
48540	Wheeling, WV-OH	2 443	147 950	267	60.6	95.4	3.9	0.5	0.7	0.7	5.1	14.6	8.9	11.1	12.0	15.4
48620	Wichita, KS	10 746	623 061	84	58.0	76.3	8.8	2.0	4.1	11.6	7.6	19.4	9.5	13.6	12.3	14.4
48660	Wichita Falls, TX	6 785	151 306	263	22.3	73.1	9.6	1.5	2.4	15.2	6.6	16.5	13.2	13.4	11.5	14.1
48700	Williamsport, PA	3 182	116 111	318	36.5	93.4	5.4	0.6	0.8	1.3	5.6	15.3	11.0	11.0	12.1	15.3
48900	Wilmington, NC	4 942	362 315	141	73.3	78.9	14.8	1.0	1.3	5.4	5.7	14.3	9.9	12.9	12.7	13.8
49020	Winchester, VA-WV	2 753	128 472	299	46.7	86.2	5.7	0.6	1.7	7.4	6.2	17.8	8.7	12.2	13.8	15.4
49180	Winston-Salem, NC	3 771	477 717	105	126.7	67.7	20.8	0.7	1.8	10.3	6.5	17.5	9.2	12.1	13.6	14.9
49340	Worcester, MA	3 913	798 552	67	204.1	82.2	4.3	0.6	4.6	9.4	5.9	17.6	9.6	11.6	14.2	16.4
49420	Yakima, WA	11 125	243 231	187	21.9	49.2	1.1	4.7	1.6	45.0	8.8	21.6	9.9	13.1	12.1	12.5
49620	York-Hanover, PA	2 342	434 972	113	185.7	87.6	6.1	0.5	1.6	5.6	6.1	17.3	8.3	11.6	13.9	15.9
49660	Youngstown-Warren-Boardman, OH-PA	4 409	565 773	90	128.3	85.7	11.6	0.6	0.9	2.7	5.4	16.4	8.4	10.5	12.0	15.3
49700	Yuba City, CA	3 197	166 892	239	52.2	57.3	3.2	3.0	13.0	27.1	8.0	20.2	10.0	13.8	12.5	13.4
49740	Yuma, AZ	14 281	195 751	216	13.7	36.3	2.0	1.4	1.7	59.7	7.7	20.5	10.8	12.4	11.7	11.5

1. CBSA = Core Based Statistical Area. DIV = Metropolitan Division. See Appendix A for explanation. See Appendix B for list of metropolitan areas identified by type.   2. Dry land or land partially or temporarily covered by water.   3. May be of any race.

Table C. Metropolitan Areas — **Population and Households**

Area name	55 to 64 years	65 to 74 years	75 years and over	Percent female	Total persons 1990	Total persons 2000	Percent change 1990–2000	Percent change 2000–2010	Births	Deaths	Net migration	Number	Percent change, 2000–2010	Persons per household	Female family householder[1]	One person
	16	17	18	19	20	21	22	23	24	25	26	27	28	29	30	31
Virginia Beach-Norfolk-Newport News, VA-NC	11.1	6.4	5.1	51.0	1 450 855	1 576 370	8.7	6.0	220 165	113 125	-17 992	628 572	8.3	2.55	15.8	25.0
Visalia-Porterville, CA	9.1	5.2	4.3	49.9	311 932	368 021	18.0	20.2	73 748	25 133	15 609	130 352	18.1	3.36	16.1	16.6
Waco, TX	10.7	6.5	6.0	51.4	189 123	213 517	12.9	10.0	31 310	18 546	8 593	86 892	10.2	2.60	14.7	26.2
Warner Robins, GA	10.3	6.0	4.4	51.3	89 208	110 765	24.2	26.3	17 415	7 941	15 946	53 051	29.7	2.61	16.2	24.0
Washington-Arlington-Alexandria, DC-VA-MD-WV ..	11.2	5.7	4.3	51.3	4 122 259	4 796 183	16.3	16.4	720 960	279 860	213 169	2 074 730	15.2	2.64	12.5	27.0
Bethesda-Rockville-Frederick, MD Div	12.2	6.4	5.7	51.8	913 083	1 068 618	17.0	12.8	152 866	63 458	40 651	441 886	12.0	2.70	11.1	24.4
Washington-Arlington-Alexandria, DC-VA-MD-WV Div	11.0	5.6	3.9	51.2	3 209 176	3 727 565	16.2	17.4	568 094	216 402	172 518	1 632 844	16.2	2.63	12.9	27.7
Waterloo-Cedar Falls, IA	12.3	7.3	7.4	51.3	158 640	163 706	3.2	2.5	19 086	13 630	-3 342	66 986	5.4	2.39	10.4	28.2
Wausau, WI	12.4	7.2	6.9	49.8	115 400	125 834	9.0	6.5	14 783	9 077	886	53 176	11.5	2.49	8.5	25.8
Wenatchee-East Wenatchee, WA	12.9	8.0	7.0	50.1	78 455	99 219	26.5	11.8	13 345	7 812	5 765	41 721	13.5	2.63	10.0	24.4
Wheeling, WV-OH	15.0	8.9	9.0	50.8	159 301	153 172	-3.8	-3.4	14 048	17 360	-4 377	61 462	-1.3	2.29	11.5	31.1
Wichita, KS	11.3	6.1	5.9	50.5	511 111	571 166	11.7	9.1	86 425	46 243	4 837	240 359	9.0	2.55	11.8	27.9
Wichita Falls, TX	11.0	7.1	6.5	48.9	140 375	151 524	7.9	-0.1	19 410	13 539	-9 252	56 873	1.4	2.45	12.8	28.5
Williamsport, PA	13.2	8.1	8.3	51.0	118 710	120 044	1.1	-3.3	12 366	11 485	-3 329	46 700	-0.6	2.37	10.8	28.2
Wilmington, NC	14.3	9.8	6.5	51.1	200 124	274 532	37.2	32.0	34 798	25 469	71 865	152 676	33.1	2.32	11.6	28.0
Winchester, VA-WV	12.3	7.8	5.9	50.2	84 168	102 997	22.4	24.7	14 296	8 638	15 846	49 066	22.5	2.57	10.5	24.5
Winston-Salem, NC	12.3	7.6	6.3	52.2	361 426	421 961	16.7	13.2	57 242	36 852	33 462	192 310	13.3	2.43	13.8	28.8
Worcester, MA	12.0	6.4	6.3	50.8	709 711	750 963	5.8	6.3	91 922	62 070	15 187	303 080	6.7	2.55	12.2	26.2
Yakima, WA	10.4	6.2	5.3	50.0	188 823	222 581	17.9	9.3	39 326	16 143	-5 419	80 592	8.9	2.97	14.7	21.6
York-Hanover, PA	12.8	7.5	6.5	50.7	339 574	381 751	12.4	13.9	45 804	31 498	35 276	168 372	13.6	2.53	10.6	23.7
Youngstown-Warren-Boardman, OH-PA	14.1	8.7	9.2	51.4	613 604	602 964	-1.7	-6.2	59 236	63 485	-32 332	231 165	-3.0	2.37	13.9	30.3
Yuba City, CA	10.6	6.4	5.1	50.1	122 643	139 149	13.5	19.9	24 211	11 354	14 311	55 744	17.2	2.95	13.4	21.1
Yuma, AZ	9.7	8.9	6.8	49.9	106 895	160 026	49.7	22.3	30 013	10 865	18 965	64 767	20.3	2.93	13.8	19.6

1. No spouse present.

Area name	Daytime population, 2010			Births, average 2006–2008		Deaths, average 2006–2008		Persons under 65 with no health insurance 2009		Medicare, 2011			Serious crimes known to police,[2] 2010	
													Total	
	Persons in group quarters, 2010	Number	Employ-ment/ residence ratio	Total	Rate[1]	Number	Rate[1]	Number	Percent	Enrolled in original Medicare	Enrolled in Medicare Advantage	Enrolled in a Medicare prescription drug plan	Number	Rate[3]
	32	33	34	35	36	37	38	39	40	41	42	43	44	45
Virginia Beach-Norfolk-New-port News, VA-NC	69 128	1 688 637	1.02	D	D	12 385	7.5	195 207	13.7	235 440	31 228	77 907	63 987	3 828
Visalia-Porterville, CA	4 772	436 552	0.96	8 443	20.0	2 772	6.6	89 238	23.5	51 446	6 702	27 910	17 832	4 033
Waco, TX	9 085	240 942	1.05	3 499	15.3	2 031	8.9	45 794	23.1	35 661	6 498	14 412	10 887	4 635
Warner Robins, GA..............	1 599	D	D	2 058	15.8	886	6.8	19 690	16.8	18 795	2 175	5 218	5 302	3 790
Washington-Arlington-Alex-andria, DC-VA-MD-WV..	102 275	5 787 426	1.06	80 353	15.1	30 349	5.7	566 229	11.8	629 474	59 412	199 445	163 777	2 934
Bethesda-Rockville-Fred-erick, MD Div	13 082	1 147 643	0.90	16 791	14.4	6 696	5.8	124 095	12.0	156 030	11 904	52 596	27 341	2 269
Washington-Arlington-Alex-andria, DC-VA-MD-WV Div....................	89 193	4 639 783	1.10	63 562	15.3	23 653	5.7	442 134	11.8	473 444	47 508	146 849	136 436	3 117
Waterloo-Cedar Falls, IA	7 839	171 566	1.08	D	D	1 464	9.0	13 779	10.2	29 195	3 731	13 998	4 515	2 690
Wausau, WI	1 655	136 260	1.03	1 692	13.0	1 023	7.8	11 274	10.2	22 183	8 416	6 137	2 518	1 878
Wenatchee-East Wenat-chee, WA	1 118	109 600	0.96	1 587	14.8	873	8.1	18 386	20.0	19 685	2 524	8 975	2 879	2 596
Wheeling, WV-OH................	6 899	D	D	D	D	1 860	12.8	16 589	14.3	31 442	12 957	12 823	2 297	1 673
Wichita, KS	11 281	623 902	1.01	8 969	15.0	5 039	8.4	78 474	14.9	91 534	12 539	48 713	27 226	4 390
Wichita Falls, TX..................	12 143	D	D	D	D	1 456	9.9	29 563	23.8	24 935	959	11 086	6 670	4 408
Williamsport, PA..................	5 437	D	D	1 313	11.2	1 235	10.6	11 658	12.4	23 354	6 197	10 758	2 535	2 183
Wilmington, NC....................	8 631	359 460	0.97	D	D	2 953	8.7	52 951	18.4	71 667	5 860	33 189	14 180	3 969
Winchester, VA-WV	2 451	D	D	D	D	951	7.9	16 497	15.9	21 044	2 150	9 875	3 161	2 467
Winston-Salem, NC	10 976	476 344	0.99	6 017	13.0	4 059	8.8	69 684	17.2	81 217	37 081	22 686	22 719	4 784
Worcester, MA	27 045	755 742	0.88	9 700	12.4	6 654	8.5	31 241	4.6	127 145	43 745	43 146	20 611	2 611
Yakima, WA	3 485	243 941	0.99	4 438	19.0	1 778	7.6	50 892	24.6	35 214	6 402	16 313	11 959	4 917
York-Hanover, PA.................	8 430	398 416	0.82	5 238	12.5	3 496	8.3	36 334	10.2	74 712	22 539	26 030	10 034	2 307
Youngstown-Warren-Board-man, OH-PA	18 460	559 700	0.98	6 260	10.9	6 913	12.0	61 808	13.6	120 440	50 833	44 884	20 226	3 579
Yuba City, CA	2 231	D	D	2 833	17.3	1 218	7.4	29 446	20.4	24 423	1 723	12 763	4 783	2 866
Yuma, AZ.............................	5 921	194 119	0.97	3 332	17.5	1 203	6.3	36 955	23.6	27 095	5 306	10 003	4 866	2 858

1. Per 1,000 estimated resident population.   2. Data for serious crimes have not been adjusted for underreporting; this may affect comparability between geographic areas and over time.   3. Per 100,000 population estimated by the FBI.

Table C. Metropolitan Areas — Crime, Education, Money Income, and Poverty

Area name	Serious crimes known to police,[1] 2010 (cont.) Rate[2] Violent	Property	Education: School enrollment and attainment, 2010 Enrollment[3] Total	Percent private	Attainment[4] (percent) High school graduate or less	Bachelor's degree or more	Local government expenditures,[5] 2008–2009 Total current expenditures (mil dol)	Current expenditures per student (dollars)	Income and Poverty, 2010 Per capita income[6] (dollars)	Median household income (dollars)	Percent of households with income of less than $25,000	Percent of households with income of $100,000 or more	Percent of households with income of $200,000 or more	Percent below poverty level All persons	Children under 18 years	Children under 5
	46	47	48	49	50	51	52	53	54	55	56	57	58	59	60	61
Virginia Beach-Norfolk-Newport News, VA-NC	342	3 485	459 747	15.5	36.7	28.5	2 842.8	10 443	27 497	57 315	18.5	22.2	3.2	10.6	16.0	20.5
Visalia-Porterville, CA	469	3 563	135 849	5.9	56.1	13.4	905.5	9 395	17 365	43 397	29.0	15.6	1.9	24.5	33.3	36.3
Waco, TX	542	4 092	72 730	25.6	47.2	22.5	362.8	8 702	19 427	39 143	32.3	12.2	1.2	21.5	30.1	34.6
Warner Robins, GA	327	3 463	43 010	8.9	41.8	20.3	246.1	9 364	23 812	58 401	21.6	17.6	2.0	14.3	22.8	32.5
Washington-Arlington-Alexandria, DC-VA-MD-WV	380	2 554	1 539 559	22.4	30.1	46.8	11 286.3	13 403	40 528	84 523	12.2	42.4	11.8	8.4	10.7	10.4
Bethesda-Rockville-Frederick, MD Div	210	2 059	331 068	23.9	25.6	53.0	2 640.6	14 723	42 960	87 595	11.7	44.4	13.4	7.2	9.1	8.2
Washington-Arlington-Alexandria, DC-VA-MD-WV Div	426	2 691	1 208 491	22.0	31.4	45.1	8 645.7	13 046	39 859	83 429	12.4	41.8	11.4	8.7	11.1	10.9
Waterloo-Cedar Falls, IA	375	2 316	48 500	13.6	45.4	24.8	258.5	10 269	24 159	45 811	27.3	14.1	2.4	16.7	26.9	29.1
Wausau, WI	127	1 751	33 670	9.1	48.9	20.5	221.9	11 110	23 757	49 356	21.2	15.4	1.2	12.2	21.6	23.0
Wenatchee-East Wenatchee, WA	143	2 453	28 149	11.4	45.3	19.2	194.2	9 842	23 381	47 839	20.8	16.6	2.6	12.7	17.9	18.9
Wheeling, WV-OH	183	1 490	33 247	14.6	53.3	19.5	205.2	10 690	23 319	38 415	31.5	11.8	1.3	15.6	26.3	31.2
Wichita, KS	585	3 805	176 295	14.9	40.1	27.1	1 009.3	9 714	23 693	46 131	25.5	16.0	1.9	13.8	18.1	24.7
Wichita Falls, TX	350	4 058	39 690	8.7	52.1	18.4	216.7	8 580	20 298	39 633	30.2	10.9	1.7	17.0	22.7	17.7
Williamsport, PA	171	2 013	27 814	12.9	57.3	18.2	195.9	11 729	20 146	41 037	31.2	9.0	1.0	18.0	27.6	33.7
Wilmington, NC	357	3 612	88 314	12.0	36.6	32.3	413.6	9 081	25 712	44 825	29.0	15.4	2.7	17.6	23.7	27.9
Winchester, VA-WV	167	2 300	31 048	14.2	55.2	21.5	210.9	10 254	24 857	46 626	27.2	20.1	2.5	12.5	12.6	15.6
Winston-Salem, NC	471	4 312	121 410	17.3	44.8	27.1	650.5	8 653	24 072	42 644	27.3	13.5	2.9	16.3	25.1	28.3
Worcester, MA	465	2 146	219 226	22.2	40.2	32.7	1 667.2	12 614	29 316	61 212	21.8	26.2	4.8	10.8	14.1	15.9
Yakima, WA	340	4 577	66 163	9.6	54.9	15.6	490.9	9 844	20 256	40 648	31.0	14.6	2.1	24.3	37.4	41.2
York-Hanover, PA	209	2 098	103 524	18.2	52.9	21.7	729.6	10 871	26 702	56 368	18.6	20.9	2.4	9.2	13.3	16.6
Youngstown-Warren-Boardman, OH-PA	285	3 294	133 569	14.6	54.1	19.3	946.4	10 870	21 324	39 240	31.9	9.8	1.3	17.1	28.5	34.3
Yuba City, CA	365	2 501	47 675	8.4	47.2	17.4	311.9	9 196	20 146	46 314	24.3	14.8	1.7	19.3	26.5	35.9
Yuma, AZ	377	2 482	55 667	8.7	51.3	13.8	269.0	7 116	17 795	42 240	28.1	11.1	0.8	20.1	29.2	24.1

1. Data for serious crimes have not been adjusted for underreporting; this may affect comparability between geographic areas and over time.　2. Per 100,000 population estimated by the FBI.　3. All persons 3 years old and over enrolled in nursery school through college.　4. Persons 25 years old and over.　5. Elementary and secondary education expenditures.　6. Based on resident population estimated as of July 1, 2009.

Table C. Metropolitan Areas — **Personal Income**

	Personal income, 2009												
			Per capita[1]						Transfer payments				
										Government payments to individuals			
Area name	Total (mil dol)	Percent change, 2008–2009	Dollars	Rank	Wages and salaries[2] (mil dol)	Proprietors' income (mil dol)	Dividends, interest, and rent (mil dol)	Total (mil dol)	Total (mil dol)	Social Security (mil dol)	Medical payments (mil dol)	Income mainte-nance (mil dol)	Unemploy-ment insurance (mil dol)
	62	63	64	65	66	67	68	69	70	71	72	73	74
Virginia Beach-Norfolk-New-port News, VA-NC	66 173	-0.4	39 518	79	48 868	3 280	9 848	9 817	9 528	3 149	3 689	1 096	337
Visalia-Porterville, CA	11 911	-0.9	27 721	351	6 410	1 374	1 737	2 967	2 889	623	1 229	563	221
Waco, TX	7 530	2.2	32 265	264	4 902	473	1 328	1 502	1 460	472	576	175	51
Warner Robins, GA..............	4 494	1.4	33 114	242	3 805	192	656	774	750	219	292	100	37
Washington-Arlington-Alex-andria, DC-VA-MD-WV ..	312 059	0.4	56 984	4	252 800	22 362	51 474	25 821	24 830	7 690	11 133	2 325	1 227
Bethesda-Rockville-Fred-erick, MD Div	74 639	-0.5	62 221	X	44 070	5 221	15 364	5 769	5 551	1 984	2 401	394	305
Washington-Arlington-Alex-andria, DC-VA-MD-WV Div.....................................	237 420	0.7	55 515	X	208 731	17 141	36 111	20 052	19 279	5 706	8 732	1 931	922
Waterloo-Cedar Falls, IA	5 999	0.2	36 376	153	4 197	455	1 021	1 144	1 114	427	440	103	58
Wausau, WI	4 746	-1.4	36 058	162	3 296	280	760	832	808	313	298	60	87
Wenatchee-East Wenat-chee, WA	3 661	0.8	33 299	236	2 123	205	761	811	791	269	312	84	49
Wheeling, WV-OH.................	4 674	-0.2	32 318	263	2 861	210	810	1 304	1 278	455	559	111	48
Wichita, KS	23 855	-1.8	38 935	93	15 753	2 395	3 982	4 034	3 922	1 355	1 529	426	357
Wichita Falls, TX..................	5 632	-1.8	38 202	110	3 077	859	1 050	1 033	1 007	331	452	92	36
Williamsport, PA	3 727	1.5	31 900	277	2 286	231	616	940	919	332	353	73	92
Wilmington, NC	12 041	-0.2	33 964	215	6 636	766	2 714	2 696	2 631	1 024	1 062	205	150
Winchester, VA-WV	4 227	-0.3	34 094	211	2 711	223	744	719	696	288	254	64	39
Winston-Salem, NC	16 970	-2.9	34 996	191	10 973	1 247	3 540	3 339	3 251	1 187	1 355	301	205
Worcester, MA	33 773	-1.2	42 021	51	18 308	2 171	4 493	6 042	5 895	1 727	2 681	583	591
Yakima, WA	7 474	0.6	31 265	295	4 255	619	1 277	1 886	1 842	456	806	333	98
York-Hanover, PA.................	15 427	-0.2	35 966	164	8 981	709	2 547	2 842	2 764	1 105	1 002	187	276
Youngstown-Warren-Board-man, OH-PA	17 851	-1.6	31 709	286	9 731	993	2 930	5 221	5 118	1 751	2 165	485	312
Yuba City, CA	5 178	1.6	31 279	294	2 508	706	785	1 265	1 236	299	542	169	101
Yuma, AZ.............................	4 994	2.6	25 356	361	3 106	349	646	1 281	1 245	330	513	180	104

1. Based on the resident population estimated as of July 1 of the year shown.   2. Includes other labor income.

Table C. Metropolitan Areas — Earnings, Social Security, and Housing

Area name	Earnings, 2009									Social Security beneficiaries, December 2010			Housing units, 2010	
	Total (mil dol)	Percent by selected industries										Supplemental Security Income recipients, December 2009		
		Farm	Goods-related[1]		Service-related and health				Govern-ment	Number	Rate[2]		Total	Percent change, 2000–2010
			Total	Manu-facturing	Infor-mation, profes-sional, and technical services	Retail trade	Finance, insur-ance, and real estate	Health care and social services						
	75	76	77	78	79	80	81	82	83	84	85	86	87	88
Virginia Beach-Norfolk-Newport News, VA-NC	52 147	0.1	D	NA	D	5.0	D	NA	40.0	257 720	154	32 289	686 297	10.2
Visalia-Porterville, CA	7 784	10.5	13.5	8.2	4.1	7.5	3.7	7.8	25.2	57 290	130	18 824	141 696	18.4
Waco, TX	5 375	0.0	26.7	19.6	5.9	6.0	7.6	11.6	17.6	39 755	169	6 930	95 124	12.2
Warner Robins, GA	3 997	0.1	D	7.2	9.1	5.0	2.4	5.2	58.2	20 500	147	3 043	58 325	31.0
Washington-Arlington-Alexandria, DC-VA-MD-WV	275 163	0.0	D	NA	D	D	D	NA	29.9	605 427	108	78 878	2 213 752	17.1
Bethesda-Rockville-Frederick, MD Div	49 291	0.1	9.9	4.1	24.1	4.4	9.2	9.4	23.8	146 705	122	14 842	466 041	14.3
Washington-Arlington-Alexandria, DC-VA-MD-WV Div	225 872	0.0	D	NA	D	D	D	NA	31.2	458 722	105	64 036	1 747 711	17.9
Waterloo-Cedar Falls, IA	4 652	2.9	D	25.6	5.4	6.3	6.5	D	16.2	32 460	193	3 331	71 332	7.4
Wausau, WI	3 576	0.8	29.7	24.2	6.6	7.1	10.1	13.4	11.8	24 925	186	2 030	57 734	14.6
Wenatchee-East Wenatchee, WA	2 327	6.8	D	5.3	D	8.5	4.4	17.2	23.3	21 530	194	1 954	51 469	18.7
Wheeling, WV-OH	3 071	-0.1	D	8.8	D	8.3	5.0	D	16.8	35 110	207	4 628	69 542	0.5
Wichita, KS	18 148	0.6	D	28.1	6.0	5.7	3.8	NA	14.3	102 120	164	11 640	263 043	10.3
Wichita Falls, TX	3 937	0.2	28.4	10.8	D	6.0	4.4	NA	29.6	27 585	182	4 051	64 823	4.3
Williamsport, PA	2 517	0.2	27.6	22.1	5.9	7.4	4.4	15.6	19.4	26 325	227	3 465	52 500	0.1
Wilmington, NC	7 402	0.7	D	9.4	12.0	8.4	6.4	NA	20.1	80 040	221	7 188	205 642	35.4
Winchester, VA-WV	2 934	-0.2	D	15.8	D	9.4	5.3	NA	18.1	23 310	181	2 212	56 906	26.2
Winston-Salem, NC	12 220	0.5	19.8	15.2	D	7.3	8.7	NA	11.0	91 660	192	9 155	214 375	17.1
Worcester, MA	20 479	0.1	19.7	14.2	10.3	6.3	6.9	16.4	15.8	136 615	171	22 061	326 788	9.6
Yakima, WA	4 874	12.8	12.6	8.1	3.4	7.1	3.6	15.8	20.6	38 795	159	7 016	85 474	8.0
York-Hanover, PA	9 690	0.4	30.5	22.7	6.3	6.7	4.3	13.2	15.1	83 805	193	7 811	178 671	14.0
Youngstown-Warren-Boardman, OH-PA	10 725	0.2	23.0	17.0	5.3	8.7	4.9	17.4	16.3	134 890	238	18 266	259 729	1.2
Yuba City, CA	3 215	10.4	10.3	3.9	4.1	7.2	3.6	D	33.0	26 615	159	7 892	61 493	20.7
Yuma, AZ	3 455	5.6	7.3	2.4	4.0	7.2	3.2	10.8	36.8	30 520	156	4 026	87 850	18.5

1. Includes mining, construction, and manufacturing.   2. Per 1,000 resident population enumerated in the 2010 census.

Table C. Metropolitan Areas — Housing, Labor Force, and Employment

Area name	Housing units, 2010								Civilian labor force, 2010		Unemployment		Civilian employment,[5] 2010		
	Occupied units													Percent	
		Owner-occupied				Renter-occupied									
				Median owner cost as a percent of income											
	Total	Percent	Median value[1]	With a mortgage	Without a mortgage	Median rent[2]	Median rent as a percent of income	Sub-stand-ard units[3] (percent)	Total	Percent change, 2009–2010	Total	Rate[4]	Total	Management, business, science, and arts occupations	Construction, production, and maintenance occupations
	89	90	91	92	93	94	95	96	97	98	99	100	101	102	103
Virginia Beach-Norfolk-New-port News, VA-NC	618 426	63.9	246 200	26.7	12.4	1 022	32.1	3.0	825 695	-0.2	60 962	7.4	764 168	37.1	20.3
Visalia-Porterville, CA	129 590	58.6	170 300	28.4	11.1	798	33.4	12.5	207 727	2.1	34 960	16.8	169 217	22.0	36.8
Waco, TX	83 212	59.0	109 000	23.2	12.6	743	34.2	3.7	115 706	1.7	8 507	7.4	105 442	32.7	22.5
Warner Robins, GA..............	50 823	67.1	136 400	20.2	10.0	806	28.8	3.4	71 182	1.0	5 408	7.6	60 696	37.6	20.4
Washington-Arlington-Alex-andria, DC-VA-MD-WV ..	2 042 154	64.2	376 200	24.9	11.4	1 351	29.6	2.9	3 073 918	0.5	192 019	6.2	2 944 846	50.7	12.5
Bethesda-Rockville-Fred-erick, MD Div	443 440	68.0	409 600	24.8	12.0	1 428	31.2	2.6	636 065	-0.5	36 908	5.8	646 035	54.0	11.2
Washington-Arlington-Alex-andria, DC-VA-MD-WV Div	1 598 714	63.2	366 800	25.0	11.2	1 330	29.3	3.0	2 437 853	0.8	155 111	6.4	2 298 811	49.8	12.9
Waterloo-Cedar Falls, IA	64 831	68.2	123 600	19.3	10.1	622	31.8	1.6	95 257	0.6	5 574	5.9	82 203	29.2	27.4
Wausau, WI	51 851	73.9	142 900	23.0	12.6	629	27.2	2.1	73 551	-1.9	6 491	8.8	69 887	30.6	29.9
Wenatchee-East Wenat-chee, WA	40 402	65.9	241 600	23.7	10.1	714	29.0	NA	63 848	-0.5	5 403	8.5	48 191	26.3	29.4
Wheeling, WV-OH................	60 776	75.7	87 500	19.1	10.0	500	27.9	1.0	69 381	-0.1	6 780	9.8	61 861	30.5	23.4
Wichita, KS	235 977	67.9	119 000	21.8	11.6	654	30.1	2.0	314 416	-1.8	27 000	8.6	292 136	33.0	23.7
Wichita Falls, TX	54 996	65.8	85 500	22.6	13.8	667	30.8	4.3	72 977	0.7	5 638	7.7	63 883	28.3	24.6
Williamsport, PA..................	45 611	67.7	127 000	25.0	14.2	602	28.9	1.6	59 931	0.1	5 388	9.0	52 784	26.3	29.8
Wilmington, NC	151 338	67.8	205 400	26.7	13.5	842	34.0	2.3	178 102	-0.9	18 261	10.3	159 635	38.1	21.0
Winchester, VA-WV	49 365	65.5	214 400	24.9	11.3	804	34.3	2.4	65 225	0.3	4 886	7.5	57 179	32.7	24.8
Winston-Salem, NC	187 786	69.4	145 000	22.6	11.7	666	29.6	2.8	237 345	-1.7	23 874	10.1	212 587	36.3	22.4
Worcester, MA	296 295	65.3	268 100	24.8	15.0	867	29.7	1.8	407 924	0.3	38 039	9.3	381 625	39.5	18.5
Yakima, WA	79 875	61.0	160 300	22.9	10.6	718	33.7	7.1	127 027	1.0	12 313	9.7	100 062	25.7	33.9
York-Hanover, PA................	170 055	76.9	185 500	24.7	15.2	796	29.5	1.6	223 818	-1.0	19 731	8.8	215 887	33.3	26.7
Youngstown-Warren-Board-man, OH-PA	228 960	72.5	98 600	23.2	13.5	588	31.9	1.4	273 284	-1.4	31 203	11.4	232 097	28.3	25.7
Yuba City, CA	55 241	59.6	189 500	27.5	11.5	795	29.0	10.2	70 246	-0.1	13 712	19.5	60 425	26.6	28.9
Yuma, AZ...........................	67 750	71.9	131 800	26.4	10.5	781	31.8	6.3	91 707	3.9	23 166	25.3	68 598	28.8	24.6

1. Specified owner-occupied units.   2. Specified renter-occupied units. A value of 10.0 represents 10 percent or less.   3. Overcrowded or lacking complete plumbing facilities.   4. Percent of civilian labor force.   5. Persons 16 years old and over.

Table C. Metropolitan Areas — **Nonfarm Employment and Agriculture**

Area name	Private nonfarm establishments, employment and payroll, 2009									Agriculture, 2007			
		Employment						Annual payroll		Farms			
												Percent with:	
	Number of establish-ments	Total	Health care and social assistance	Manufac-turing	Retail trade	Finance and insurance	Professional, scientific, and technical services	Total (mil dol)	Average per employee (dollars)	Number	Fewer than 50 acres	500 acres or more	Farm operators whose principal occu-pation is farming (percent)
	104	105	106	107	108	109	110	111	112	113	114	115	116
Virginia Beach-Norfolk-New-port News, VA-NC	37 907	603 702	80 205	58 250	88 607	28 570	51 981	21 871	36 228	1 500	60.3	11.5	51.5
Visalia-Porterville, CA	6 276	87 794	14 409	12 574	14 521	3 310	2 558	2 823	32 160	5 240	64.3	8.0	53.2
Waco, TX	4 955	94 548	15 234	14 618	11 752	5 011	2 537	2 936	31 058	2 798	52.9	7.0	34.8
Warner Robins, GA..............	2 304	33 434	5 006	4 047	6 582	1 186	3 873	974	29 121	298	54.0	5.7	51.0
Washington-Arlington-Alex-andria, DC-VA-MD-WV ..	140 672	2 397 777	278 096	55 419	254 930	103 034	478 758	134 510	56 098	8 257	54.6	5.0	45.3
Bethesda-Rockville-Fred-erick, MD Div	NA	NA	NA	NA	NA	NA	NA	NA	NA	2 003	51.5	5.6	48.0
Washington-Arlington-Alex-andria, DC-VA-MD-WV Div	NA	NA	NA	NA	NA	NA	NA	NA	NA	6 254	55.6	4.8	44.4
Waterloo-Cedar Falls, IA	4 073	74 713	14 096	15 665	10 586	3 820	3 075	2 570	34 399	2 737	32.9	18.9	52.8
Wausau, WI	3 425	63 576	9 892	16 802	7 901	4 977	2 220	2 230	35 070	2 545	25.3	6.4	53.8
Wenatchee-East Wenat-chee, WA	3 125	31 801	5 839	2 018	5 733	1 027	1 319	1 107	34 799	1 934	58.3	14.4	55.6
Wheeling, WV-OH................	3 418	54 737	13 369	3 065	8 515	2 296	2 405	1 665	30 410	1 674	25.8	3.5	38.3
Wichita, KS	14 760	262 258	40 734	57 864	31 564	10 002	11 348	9 903	37 762	4 774	29.8	23.1	44.6
Wichita Falls, TX..................	3 548	48 655	10 524	5 894	8 090	1 956	1 350	1 433	29 460	2 102	25.6	26.4	42.7
Williamsport, PA..................	2 805	43 559	7 940	9 175	7 070	1 535	1 533	1 332	30 580	1 211	32.6	3.1	41.4
Wilmington, NC	9 957	114 551	19 675	9 096	19 435	3 835	6 018	3 756	32 790	694	58.9	7.5	48.7
Winchester, VA-WV	3 102	45 172	8 109	6 942	8 058	1 542	1 834	1 640	36 313	1 353	41.1	7.3	39.0
Winston-Salem, NC	10 457	185 797	34 776	25 141	22 731	11 752	7 746	7 280	39 183	3 260	52.3	2.4	44.5
Worcester, MA	17 786	272 872	58 787	33 107	38 141	15 950	14 901	11 286	41 360	1 547	59.4	0.8	44.8
Yakima, WA	4 681	62 674	12 820	7 423	9 961	1 622	1 996	2 178	34 755	3 540	69.8	6.0	51.6
York-Hanover, PA................	8 647	156 561	22 125	35 366	21 819	4 235	6 287	5 795	37 017	2 370	58.9	5.2	45.2
Youngstown-Warren-Board-man, OH-PA	13 028	200 687	40 431	29 584	29 737	6 561	5 728	6 182	30 805	2 768	38.8	4.1	46.8
Yuba City, CA	2 607	29 506	6 336	1 948	5 619	1 104	873	965	32 694	2 091	55.7	11.5	55.7
Yuma, AZ.............................	3 029	42 617	6 580	2 818	8 313	1 378	1 164	1 150	26 983	452	60.6	19.5	57.5

Table C. Metropolitan Areas — **Agriculture**

Area name	Acreage (1,000)	Percent change, 2002–2007	Average size of farm	Total irrigated (1,000)	Total cropland (1,000)	Average per farm	Average per acre	Value of machinery and equipment, average per farm (dollars)	Total (mil dol)	Average per farm (dollars)	Crops	Live-stock and poultry products	$10,000 or more	$100,000 or more	Total ($1,000)	Percent of farms
	117	118	119	120	121	122	123	124	125	126	127	128	129	130	131	132
Virginia Beach-Norfolk-Newport News, VA-NC	326	D	217	3.4	246.5	968 267	4 457	103 337	167.5	111 603	66.5	18.2	37.8	16.7	9 008	33.7
Visalia-Porterville, CA	1 169	-16.1	223	550.3	638.8	1 843 502	8 266	125 007	3 335.0	636 453	36.2	63.8	69.9	32.8	20 335	11.3
Waco, TX	530	-1.5	189	2.9	241.6	390 384	2 062	49 514	104.7	37 431	39.8	60.2	21.9	3.7	2 612	16.0
Warner Robins, GA..............	47	-37.3	157	4.5	20.3	577 908	3 692	64 949	15.6	52 339	44.8	55.2	28.9	6.4	1 095	24.2
Washington-Arlington-Alexandria, DC-VA-MD-WV ..	1 050	D	127	10.1	556.5	924 408	7 271	70 848	343.0	41 536	D	D	28.6	6.6	7 164	17.0
Bethesda-Rockville-Frederick, MD Div	270	-0.4	135	2.3	192.2	1 165 883	8 659	95 938	160.2	79 994	38.2	61.8	37.5	13.1	3 899	30.6
Washington-Arlington-Alexandria, DC-VA-MD-WV Div	780	D	125	7.8	364.3	847 070	6 791	62 812	182.8	29 219	D	D	25.7	4.5	3 265	12.6
Waterloo-Cedar Falls, IA	841	-1.5	307	0.5	787.0	1 206 628	3 926	155 560	573.3	209 491	66.4	33.6	67.1	38.9	21 637	80.3
Wausau, WI	491	-7.5	193	7.1	323.6	526 977	2 734	100 135	307.4	120 800	14.8	85.2	54.9	29.0	4 727	50.3
Wenatchee-East Wenatchee, WA	977	-1.4	505	47.6	583.0	857 223	1 697	81 409	402.2	207 946	97.5	2.5	61.4	31.2	11 939	21.3
Wheeling, WV-OH................	256	0.4	153	0.1	83.6	308 242	2 018	42 010	20.1	11 972	23.5	76.5	17.9	2.2	211	9.4
Wichita, KS	2 346	1.2	491	94.5	1 564.7	570 428	1 161	98 717	498.6	104 442	39.7	60.3	42.9	15.4	21 492	58.7
Wichita Falls, TX.................	1 500	0.5	714	8.7	356.9	803 795	1 126	71 421	145.1	69 035	18.2	81.8	42.4	12.5	4 070	31.7
Williamsport, PA.................	160	-9.6	132	1.7	88.0	458 300	3 459	61 706	53.4	44 080	38.7	61.3	33.8	11.5	1 832	39.9
Wilmington, NC	110	D	159	8.0	66.0	680 116	4 288	85 287	215.9	311 147	34.1	65.9	36.9	17.1	926	23.8
Winchester, VA-WV	227	NA	168	0.3	71.4	880 815	5 239	60 379	60.5	44 720	38.5	61.5	28.2	6.1	593	14.0
Winston-Salem, NC	310	-11.9	95	2.0	150.4	488 299	5 141	52 156	154.7	47 453	32.0	68.0	26.5	7.2	1 124	12.7
Worcester, MA	106	1.9	69	0.9	35.6	810 727	11 792	50 355	80.6	52 069	55.5	44.5	29.2	6.9	1 034	7.6
Yakima, WA	1 649	-1.8	466	267.6	344.5	712 970	1 530	97 908	1 203.8	340 058	65.4	34.6	52.6	21.8	4 705	9.2
York-Hanover, PA	293	2.8	123	1.0	225.4	701 059	5 680	81 789	212.6	89 719	47.1	52.9	38.4	13.9	2 722	22.7
Youngstown-Warren-Boardman, OH-PA	361	-1.6	131	0.9	245.3	443 488	3 387	73 223	147.4	53 427	44.1	55.9	41.7	11.6	3 529	36.9
Yuba City, CA	521	-14.0	249	302.7	345.4	1 585 064	6 365	123 374	430.5	205 890	94.4	5.6	57.5	27.5	21 983	22.9
Yuma, AZ............................	210	-9.1	466	174.2	193.1	3 893 483	8 361	373 336	960.0	2 123 823	D	D	60.0	37.4	4 395	20.8

Area name	Water use, 2005		Wholesale trade,[1] 2007				Retail trade, 2007				Real estate and rental and leasing, 2007			
	Total water withdrawn (mil gal/day)	Gallons withdrawn per person	Number of establish-ments	Number of employees	Sales (mil dol)	Annual payroll (mil dol)	Number of establish-ments	Number of employees	Sales (mil dol)	Annual payroll (mil dol)	Number of establish-ments	Number of employees	Receipts (mil dol)	Annual payroll (mil dol)
	133	134	135	136	137	138	139	140	141	142	143	144	145	146
Virginia Beach-Norfolk-Newport News, VA-NC	3 909.7	2 373	1 552	26 377	15 913.8	1 074.5	6 285	94 923	20 958.7	2 050.9	2 237	16 873	2 359.8	532.6
Visalia-Porterville, CA	2 275.0	5 537	393	4 748	3 850.6	190.4	1 140	16 005	3 900.9	367.4	294	1 260	189.1	32.3
Waco, TX	198.4	883	275	3 629	5 947.1	137.7	872	11 703	2 942.6	248.7	211	1 408	281.7	54.3
Warner Robins, GA..............	29.4	233	54	408	168.7	13.8	452	6 600	1 524.3	143.9	133	510	72.6	12.5
Washington-Arlington-Alexandria, DC-VA-MD-WV ..	6 669.1	1 271	4 397	71 935	67 941.6	4 616.7	16 959	271 527	69 885.5	7 074.5	7 153	57 318	15 438.3	3 048.1
Bethesda-Rockville-Frederick, MD Div	692.6	603	1 111	17 102	12 148.6	1 204.2	3 742	60 739	16 322.1	1 654.7	1 732	16 740	4 566.7	922.2
Washington-Arlington-Alexandria, DC-VA-MD-WV Div.....................	5 976.5	1 458	3 286	54 833	55 793.0	3 412.5	13 217	210 788	53 563.4	5 419.9	5 421	40 578	10 871.6	2 125.9
Waterloo-Cedar Falls, IA	43.1	266	204	3 004	1 836.9	117.2	683	10 226	2 307.2	208.9	177	809	135.5	24.1
Wausau, WI	232.9	1 806	207	3 190	1 295.2	131.0	505	10 000	2 139.1	196.5	99	473	75.4	11.9
Wenatchee-East Wenatchee, WA	130.1	1 242	155	2 596	1 104.7	90.0	505	5 984	1 435.6	145.4	146	628	86.4	15.6
Wheeling, WV-OH................	1 004.1	6 754	137	2 276	3 518.2	80.9	640	8 930	1 811.2	171.2	126	681	70.0	14.6
Wichita, KS	161.0	274	834	10 875	19 098.8	548.8	2 159	30 972	7 547.8	670.3	712	3 670	533.8	98.5
Wichita Falls, TX	115.7	791	196	2 078	1 324.4	86.6	589	7 894	1 832.9	164.9	189	856	102.9	19.6
Williamsport, PA.................	14.5	123	128	2 740	961.1	85.9	519	6 968	1 458.4	130.8	94	444	80.7	11.4
Wilmington, NC	1 617.4	5 132	475	5 031	2 958.2	217.1	1 657	20 685	5 161.5	471.5	703	2 829	460.8	92.0
Winchester, VA-WV	11.0	95	142	2 623	1 507.8	117.7	557	8 428	2 231.6	192.4	143	569	108.2	20.4
Winston-Salem, NC	1 310.4	2 921	592	8 954	6 313.2	381.7	1 810	24 580	6 075.9	548.7	497	2 240	786.5	67.4
Worcester, MA	446.5	570	998	15 838	12 545.8	991.7	2 738	40 506	10 057.2	971.0	673	3 794	692.2	138.6
Yakima, WA	658.3	2 843	282	5 725	3 343.5	221.6	780	9 900	2 425.6	239.5	255	977	161.6	23.7
York-Hanover, PA	2 596.5	6 352	429	7 690	5 321.6	341.6	1 344	21 762	4 942.7	455.6	285	2 158	294.5	75.5
Youngstown-Warren-Boardman, OH-PA	245.0	413	634	9 060	6 195.8	355.6	2 352	31 815	6 785.7	625.9	447	2 936	398.2	78.5
Yuba City, CA	1 185.4	7 598	109	D	D	D	430	6 136	1 489.0	147.0	136	723	80.9	15.5
Yuma, AZ	1 166.1	6 433	139	1 984	1 209.3	77.5	540	8 905	2 004.6	180.2	190	734	119.2	17.5

1. Merchant wholesalers, except manufacturers' sales branches and offices.

Table C. Metropolitan Areas — Professional Services, Manufacturing, and Accommodation and Food Services

Area name	Professional, scientific, and technical services,[1] 2007				Manufacturing, 2007				Accommodation and food services, 2007			
	Number of establishments	Number of employees	Sales (mil dol)	Annual payroll (mil dol)	Number of establishments	Number of employees	Sales (mil dol)	Annual payroll (mil dol)	Number of establishments	Number of employees	Sales (mil dol)	Annual payroll (mil dol)
	147	148	149	150	151	152	153	154	155	156	157	158
Virginia Beach-Norfolk-Newport News, VA-NC	3 957	50 947	6 937.7	2 714.0	1 000	57 622	16 143.4	2 588.4	3 631	74 162	3 403.5	953.9
Visalia-Porterville, CA	446	D	D	D	278	12 443	5 016.0	458.3	558	8 282	379.4	102.8
Waco, TX	352	D	D	D	255	13 971	5 888.9	550.4	468	9 123	375.3	100.9
Warner Robins, GA	281	D	D	D	64	2 511	1 422.9	97.2	248	5 246	206.1	54.8
Washington-Arlington-Alexandria, DC-VA-MD-WV	27 953	447 594	94 021.2	36 863.4	2 453	63 946	17 576.7	3 312.5	11 141	219 832	14 530.1	4 019.5
Bethesda-Rockville-Frederick, MD Div	6 399	78 940	14 969.5	5 972.7	640	17 874	6 267.8	982.7	2 145	37 600	2 229.3	614.1
Washington-Arlington-Alexandria, DC-VA-MD-WV Div	21 554	368 654	79 051.7	30 890.8	1 813	46 072	11 308.9	2 329.7	8 996	182 232	12 300.9	3 405.3
Waterloo-Cedar Falls, IA	295	D	D	D	215	15 137	6 723.9	652.4	355	6 885	215.6	65.2
Wausau, WI	235	D	D	D	250	18 678	D	765.6	321	4 813	173.7	48.8
Wenatchee-East Wenatchee, WA	226	D	D	D	121	2 168	700.7	88.3	327	4 080	201.6	60.4
Wheeling, WV-OH	271	1 967	250.1	77.0	129	3 032	994.2	122.1	316	5 713	215.8	61.3
Wichita, KS	1 288	D	D	D	724	60 130	25 390.9	3 212.5	1 266	24 281	950.5	275.0
Wichita Falls, TX	252	D	D	D	155	6 336	1 548.8	271.7	306	6 775	258.8	81.0
Williamsport, PA	183	1 367	102.9	39.6	183	10 240	3 358.2	408.7	277	3 721	147.9	40.0
Wilmington, NC	1 118	D	D	D	312	9 167	4 808.7	441.9	923	16 719	711.6	204.1
Winchester, VA-WV	274	D	D	D	128	8 970	3 459.9	D	267	4 790	208.6	59.1
Winston-Salem, NC	1 123	D	D	D	480	24 818	18 942.7	1 095.6	890	16 714	738.1	204.7
Worcester, MA	1 888	14 149	2 693.0	917.8	1 099	39 334	10 706.1	1 953.9	1 691	24 156	1 150.7	330.8
Yakima, WA	320	D	D	D	255	8 696	2 686.1	304.4	427	5 287	245.6	70.8
York-Hanover, PA	726	5 437	620.4	240.9	600	38 016	11 957.4	1 669.8	736	13 112	527.9	146.4
Youngstown-Warren-Boardman, OH-PA	937	D	D	D	840	37 611	14 779.7	1 879.9	1 249	20 511	752.6	213.9
Yuba City, CA	199	D	D	D	116	2 470	664.9	94.6	238	3 553	153.1	42.1
Yuma, AZ	208	D	D	D	82	2 856	891.6	88.0	316	5 942	271.9	69.6

1. Establishments subject to federal tax.

Area name	Health care and social assistance,[1] 2007				Other services,[1] 2007				Federal funds and grants, 2009–2010			
									Expenditures (mil dol)			
										Direct payments for individuals		
	Number of establishments	Number of employees	Receipts (mil dol)	Annual payroll (mil dol)	Number of establishments	Number of employees	Receipts (mil dol)	Annual payroll (mil dol)	Total	Social Security and government retirement	Medicare	Food stamps and Supplemental Security Income
	159	160	161	162	163	164	165	166	167	168	169	170
Virginia Beach-Norfolk-Newport News, VA-NC	3 385	79 324	7 792.4	3 220.5	2 998	20 356	2 143.1	526.1	27 891.6	6 512.0	1 823.6	595.0
Visalia-Porterville, CA	806	13 734	1 295.3	493.8	384	2 298	208.1	62.9	2 559.9	749.5	525.0	196.5
Waco, TX	525	15 510	1 219.3	504.2	394	2 615	244.7	64.2	2 019.0	701.0	261.8	104.5
Warner Robins, GA..............	256	4 784	461.8	176.5	166	932	67.1	17.0	2 499.9	601.1	113.9	48.8
Washington-Arlington-Alexandria, DC-VA-MD-WV ..	14 178	259 815	29 523.9	11 613.2	12 486	132 740	30 096.7	6 657.7	169 492.6	18 118.3	6 322.7	1 058.9
Bethesda-Rockville-Frederick, MD Div	3 907	64 067	7 490.2	2 943.8	2 339	19 995	3 645.3	832.2	23 309.8	3 499.7	1 752.6	152.4
Washington-Arlington-Alexandria, DC-VA-MD-WV Div................................	10 271	195 748	22 033.7	8 669.4	10 147	112 745	26 451.4	5 825.5	146 182.8	14 618.6	4 570.1	906.5
Waterloo-Cedar Falls, IA	423	12 317	963.0	414.7	294	1 978	150.9	42.3	1 272.3	498.1	278.7	58.3
Wausau, WI	345	9 438	926.4	379.0	253	1 591	139.1	36.2	828.7	350.2	152.5	30.7
Wenatchee-East Wenatchee, WA	261	5 526	547.9	248.4	204	806	69.8	16.6	800.5	341.5	128.7	34.5
Wheeling, WV-OH................	485	11 961	937.5	371.9	310	1 787	124.8	34.2	1 326.9	532.8	347.6	70.6
Wichita, KS	1 608	39 696	3 939.7	1 452.5	1 046	6 775	604.3	180.6	5 408.5	1 715.4	819.7	181.4
Wichita Falls, TX..................	399	10 734	840.2	336.2	284	1 544	144.7	35.7	1 642.4	545.0	239.6	56.9
Williamsport, PA..................	285	8 065	675.8	272.5	244	1 521	150.1	33.0	969.5	391.6	250.7	45.6
Wilmington, NC	950	22 009	2 105.9	882.9	626	3 672	293.5	81.2	2 725.5	1 375.4	381.9	128.4
Winchester, VA-WV	352	7 680	775.7	341.1	202	1 181	104.3	31.5	805.7	406.7	115.3	25.3
Winston-Salem, NC	971	32 257	3 051.8	1 188.7	749	4 549	435.8	106.7	3 416.7	1 476.9	563.7	150.9
Worcester, MA	1 945	55 586	5 551.2	2 200.6	1 346	7 695	772.5	224.3	6 321.4	2 028.3	1 564.3	283.5
Yakima, WA	537	11 636	1 119.8	441.2	297	1 767	132.9	33.9	1 822.9	574.3	269.3	140.3
York-Hanover, PA................	925	20 265	1 931.3	790.7	746	5 098	582.7	115.6	3 882.1	1 330.7	654.7	77.2
Youngstown-Warren-Boardman, OH-PA	1 768	38 812	3 156.1	1 254.2	1 030	6 263	474.1	130.4	5 279.6	2 133.5	1 498.1	305.0
Yuba City, CA	347	5 793	722.4	228.5	186	991	95.8	26.5	1 364.9	439.3	245.3	74.0
Yuma, AZ............................	329	6 463	654.6	235.7	208	1 217	85.2	26.0	1 761.7	495.9	212.6	96.0

1. Establishments subject to federal tax.

Table C. Metropolitan Areas — Federal Funds, Residential Construction and Local Government Finances

	Federal funds and grants, 2009–2010 (cont.)							Value of residential construction authorized by building permits, 2010		Local government finances, 2007				
	Expenditures (mil dol) (cont.)									General revenue				
	Procurement contract awards			Grants								Taxes		
Area name													Per capita[1] (dollars)	
	Salaries and wages	Defense	Other	Medicaid and other health-related	Nutrition and family welfare	Education	Other	New con-struction ($1,000)	Number of housing units	Total (mil dol)	Inter-govern-mental (mil dol)	Total (mil dol)	Total	Property
	171	172	173	174	175	176	177	178	179	180	181	182	183	184
Virginia Beach-Norfolk-Newport News, VA-NC	6 402.6	9 027.1	1 160.6	956.1	193.2	158.4	377.7	692 087	3 966	7 247.2	2 801.2	2 903.9	1 751	1 205
Visalia-Porterville, CA	77.9	12.8	73.0	569.1	116.0	40.5	68.2	199 680	1 367	2 844.1	1 469.6	387.4	919	613
Waco, TX	190.6	256.7	34.8	300.0	33.5	11.5	35.7	82 962	602	1 359.6	479.5	300.6	1 318	1 012
Warner Robins, GA...............	982.5	572.7	67.4	55.7	25.1	7.4	2.1	109 400	646	597.5	168.8	172.5	1 316	721
Washington-Arlington-Alexandria, DC-VA-MD-WV	42 792.8	37 778.4	43 558.9	4 596.1	818.6	1 006.4	9 991.6	2 104 284	13 065	30 893.9	8 530.0	17 190.3	3 239	1 718
Bethesda-Rockville-Frederick, MD Div....................	5 396.8	3 125.5	7 314.8	959.1	122.4	34.3	758.4	NA	NA	5 574.5	1 195.3	3 543.9	3 067	1 344
Washington-Arlington-Alexandria, DC-VA-MD-WV Div..................................	37 396.1	34 652.9	36 244.1	3 637.0	696.3	972.1	9 233.2	NA	NA	25 319.4	7 334.7	13 646.4	3 287	1 822
Waterloo-Cedar Falls, IA........	89.6	15.3	33.8	155.2	28.1	8.8	45.7	70 532	391	647.1	248.3	232.8	1 426	1 116
Wausau, WI..........................	72.1	2.2	42.5	122.5	19.4	6.0	6.0	45 568	262	538.7	241.1	193.6	1 489	1 374
Wenatchee-East Wenatchee, WA....................................	53.0	15.3	14.1	85.1	22.8	5.7	45.4	61 297	320	453.8	196.7	129.3	1 207	764
Wheeling, WV-OH.................	77.3	9.4	18.9	157.8	30.9	11.4	35.2	5 538	38	506.2	234.9	152.9	1 051	670
Wichita, KS..........................	704.2	1 077.6	157.4	412.3	97.8	29.0	92.2	161 447	1 259	2 115.8	918.4	811.5	1 361	965
Wichita Falls, TX	380.1	181.1	9.6	145.0	28.1	6.0	16.8	32 866	187	421.3	140.7	189.1	1 277	979
Williamsport, PA	64.5	20.3	16.9	107.0	24.2	4.8	20.0	35 096	207	397.9	173.9	143.6	1 229	892
Wilmington, NC	138.8	124.3	45.3	309.2	45.6	20.2	91.2	328 551	1 830	1 715.5	427.5	465.3	1 370	996
Winchester, VA-WV	128.5	9.2	19.0	66.2	9.3	7.3	4.6	64 274	346	384.4	149.2	180.8	1 492	986
Winston-Salem, NC...............	153.7	53.4	79.2	642.9	61.2	44.4	83.4	142 029	1 201	1 392.4	652.4	490.6	1 059	816
Worcester, MA	313.7	165.3	113.1	1 290.4	135.6	62.6	243.3	230 305	1 391	2 659.9	1 294.8	1 073.9	1 374	1 341
Yakima, WA	134.0	62.6	30.9	333.3	103.9	48.1	58.2	90 398	624	808.0	483.0	196.6	844	524
York-Hanover, PA	216.5	1 323.7	41.4	211.8	48.0	7.3	31.6	165 331	1 059	1 629.2	579.2	662.4	1 573	1 241
Youngstown-Warren-Boardman, OH-PA...................	231.8	53.1	43.2	681.6	131.5	47.8	68.1	61 247	325	2 072.6	1 071.0	708.0	1 241	892
Yuba City, CA	244.2	12.9	19.5	201.4	42.0	19.3	13.9	25 659	150	886.8	481.6	202.7	1 235	967
Yuma, AZ	235.1	324.8	45.2	209.7	51.8	19.1	30.8	59 100	455	669.9	368.7	193.9	1 017	548

1. Based on the resident population estimated as of July 1 of the year shown.

Table C. Metropolitan Areas — Local Government Finances, Government Employment, and Voting

Area name	Local government finances, 2007 (cont.)									Government employment, 2009			Presidential election,[2] 2008		
	Direct general expenditure							Debt outstanding					Percent of vote cast:		
			Percent of total for:												
	Total (mil dol)	Per capita[1] (dollars)	Education	Health and hospitals	Police protection	Public welfare	Highways	Total (mil dol)	Per capita[1] (dollars)	Federal civilian	Federal military	State and local	Democratic	Republican	All other
	185	186	187	188	189	190	191	192	193	194	195	196	197	198	199
Virginia Beach-Norfolk-Newport News, VA-NC	6 951.5	4 191	45.4	6.5	4.9	4.1	3.1	7 717.4	4 653	48 450	98 409	111 794	55.2	43.9	0.9
Visalia-Porterville, CA	2 828.2	6 709	40.6	21.2	3.1	8.7	2.8	1 178.2	2 795	1 309	702	30 376	41.5	56.8	1.7
Waco, TX	1 351.0	5 922	29.1	1.9	3.4	0.3	1.4	15 878.1	69 603	3 584	616	14 010	37.7	61.6	0.8
Warner Robins, GA	604.1	4 611	46.0	28.7	3.8	0.2	4.5	126.5	966	14 648	4 249	9 138	39.5	59.7	0.8
Washington-Arlington-Alexandria, DC-VA-MD-WV	29 967.0	5 647	40.6	3.8	5.4	9.5	2.2	35 715.8	6 730	379 223	72 388	309 080	68.3	30.6	1.1
Bethesda-Rockville-Frederick, MD Div	5 432.0	4 701	50.8	2.6	4.7	3.1	3.9	4 556.8	3 943	49 980	8 169	51 152	66.9	31.6	1.5
Washington-Arlington-Alexandria, DC-VA-MD-WV Div	24 534.9	5 911	38.4	4.0	5.6	10.9	1.8	31 159.1	7 506	329 243	64 219	257 928	68.7	30.4	1.0
Waterloo-Cedar Falls, IA	689.5	4 222	51.3	10.0	4.0	0.8	7.3	451.5	2 765	659	698	13 819	57.9	40.7	1.5
Wausau, WI	586.2	4 511	46.6	14.1	4.0	3.7	9.8	477.0	3 670	533	381	7 249	53.5	44.7	1.8
Wenatchee-East Wenatchee, WA	384.6	3 588	47.9	11.0	4.4	0.0	7.6	1 742.9	16 263	889	347	7 974	41.6	56.6	1.8
Wheeling, WV-OH	494.1	3 397	45.1	1.5	5.0	5.1	6.3	442.1	3 040	711	588	9 657	46.8	51.4	1.8
Wichita, KS	1 966.0	3 296	52.1	4.0	6.4	0.5	4.8	3 636.4	6 097	5 910	5 200	36 254	41.0	57.1	1.9
Wichita Falls, TX	393.0	2 653	54.0	5.2	6.5	0.6	4.6	702.9	4 745	2 349	7 910	10 182	28.2	71.0	0.8
Williamsport, PA	377.8	3 234	55.4	0.0	2.6	4.4	4.6	503.7	4 312	477	310	9 265	37.3	61.5	1.2
Wilmington, NC	1 772.3	5 220	26.1	35.9	4.3	4.0	1.1	1 606.9	4 733	1 479	1 112	24 684	45.4	53.6	1.0
Winchester, VA-WV	391.4	3 230	62.3	1.1	4.3	3.2	1.4	407.6	3 364	1 358	470	7 164	40.7	57.8	1.5
Winston-Salem, NC	1 412.8	3 050	48.0	5.7	5.7	5.7	2.1	1 361.0	2 939	1 646	1 224	23 928	48.2	50.8	1.0
Worcester, MA	2 872.2	3 676	59.7	0.6	4.3	0.1	3.5	2 447.7	3 133	2 915	2 008	49 066	55.8	42.1	2.1
Yakima, WA	822.6	3 529	66.3	1.4	4.6	1.2	5.4	518.4	2 224	1 291	843	16 253	43.9	54.4	1.7
York-Hanover, PA	1 595.0	3 788	45.1	4.3	2.9	10.1	2.6	2 349.1	5 579	4 680	1 601	16 935	42.7	56.3	1.1
Youngstown-Warren-Boardman, OH-PA	2 082.9	3 650	54.9	5.2	5.3	5.1	3.9	1 393.7	2 442	2 061	1 467	30 716	58.9	38.9	2.1
Yuba City, CA	897.1	5 466	51.6	4.8	4.7	8.4	2.7	443.3	2 701	1 478	3 600	10 119	41.0	56.9	2.1
Yuma, AZ	749.5	3 933	47.7	1.1	6.0	0.3	6.6	534.1	2 803	3 705	4 240	10 674	42.6	56.3	1.1

1. Based on the resident population estimated as of July 1 of the year shown.   2. © 2009 Election Data Services, Inc. All rights reserved.

Cities of 25,000 or More

(For explanation of symbols, see page viii)

Page

City Highlights and Rankings

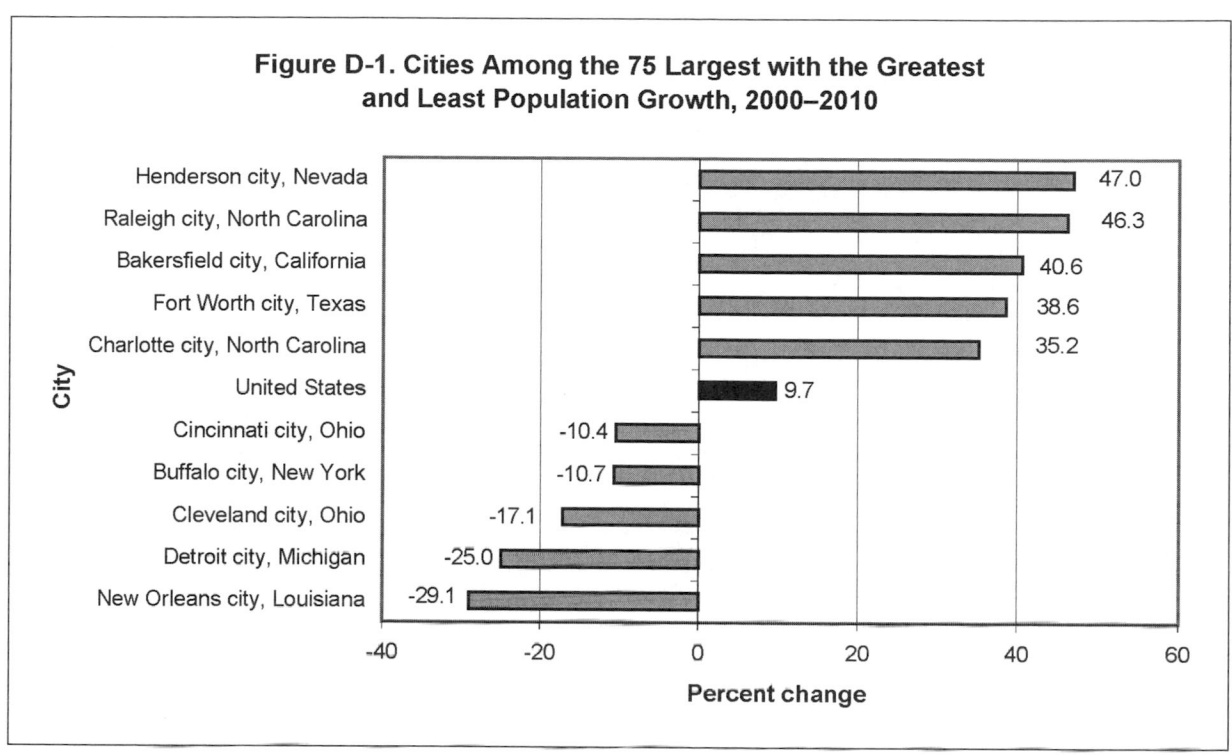

Figure D-1. Cities Among the 75 Largest with the Greatest and Least Population Growth, 2000–2010

City	Percent change
Henderson city, Nevada	47.0
Raleigh city, North Carolina	46.3
Bakersfield city, California	40.6
Fort Worth city, Texas	38.6
Charlotte city, North Carolina	35.2
United States	9.7
Cincinnati city, Ohio	-10.4
Buffalo city, New York	-10.7
Cleveland city, Ohio	-17.1
Detroit city, Michigan	-25.0
New Orleans city, Louisiana	-29.1

In 2010, 9 cities had more than 1 million residents, led by New York City with nearly 8.2 million people, Los Angeles with 3.8 million people, and Chicago with 2.7 million people. California had 13 cities among the nation's 75 most populous, as well as 4 among the top 15 (Los Angeles, San Diego, San Jose, and San Francisco). Texas had 9 cities in the top 75, and also had 4 among the top 15 (Houston, San Antonio, Dallas, and Austin).

Among the largest cities, 10 had growth rates exceeding 20 percent from 2000 to 2010. Three of these cities were in North Carolina (Raleigh, Charlotte, and Greensboro) and two each were in Texas (Fort Worth and Austin) and Nevada (Henderson and Las Vegas); Henderson, (a suburb of Las Vegas) had the highest growth rate, at 47.0 percent. Among the ten highest growth rates was Fort Wayne, IN, unusual among the cities of the Midwest. Fort Wayne's population grew by 23 percent, but its land area increased by 40 percent through annexation. Thirty-three of the largest cities exceeded the U.S. growth rate of 9.7 percent.

Among the 75 largest cities, 16 lost population between 2000 and 2010. Cincinnati, Buffalo, Cleveland, Detroit, and New Orleans all lost more than 10 percent of their populations. Though New Orleans lost 29.1 percent of its population between 2000 and 2010, it actually grew by nearly two-thirds between 2006 and 2010, after losing more than half of its population after Hurricane Katrina in 2005.

Among all cities of 25,000 or more, 555 cities had unemployment rates of 10 percent or more, up from 433 cities in 2009, 67 cities in 2008 and 25 cities in 2007. Nineteen of the twenty-five cities with the highest unemployment rates were located in California and four were located in Michigan. Among the largest cities, Detroit, MI had the highest unemployment rate at 23.1 percent followed by Stockton, CA at 20.7 percent. Among the largest cities, Lincoln and Omaha, NE had the lowest unemployment rates, both under

6 percent. Nine cities had unemployment rates of 4 percent or lower, five of them in North Dakota and three in Iowa.

While the 2010 census provides updated counts of the population and basic demographic characteristics, updated information on social and economic characteristics is now obtained through the ongoing American Community Survey (ACS). This book includes some of the recently released data for cities with populations of 20,000 or more. These 3-year estimates for 2008–2010 include data on education, income, housing characteristics, and more. Between the 2000 census and the late-decade information from the ACS, housing values increased dramatically in many cities, while the median household income increased less markedly. Among the largest cities, the same five cities topped the rankings for median household income in 2000 and 2008–2010: Plano, San Jose, Henderson, Anchorage, and San Francisco. But the housing value rankings have shifted, with California's housing inflation pushing more California cities to the top of the list. San Francisco retains its spot at the top with an estimated median housing value of $773,600 up from $396,400 in 2000. Buffalo and Detroit had the lowest median housing values among the large cities.

In the 2008–2010 time period, there were nine cities where more than 10 percent of the residents had moved there during the previous year. This may result from population growth: Raleigh, NC had one of the highest growth rates during the decade and the highest proportion of people who had moved there in the past year. Other cities have large shifts because of student or military population groups: Pittsburgh, PA lost 8.5 percent of its population during the decade but 11.1 percent of its population were new residents in the 2008–2010 time period, reflecting the 16.9 percent of residents who were between the ages of 18 and 24, well above the 9.9 percent national average.

75 Largest Cities by 2010 Population
Selected Rankings

Population, 2010			Land area, 2010				Population density, 2010			
Population rank	City	Population [col 2]	Population rank	Land area rank	City	Land area (square kilometers) [col 1]	Population rank	Density rank	City	Density (per square kilometer) [col 4]
1	New York city, New York	8 175 133	64	1	Anchorage municipality, Alaska	4 415.1	1	1	New York city, New York	10 430
2	Los Angeles city, California	3 792 621	12	2	Jacksonville city, Florida	1 934.7	13	2	San Francisco city, California	6 633
3	Chicago city, Illinois	2 695 598	31	3	Oklahoma City, Oklahoma	1 570.6	75	3	Jersey City city, New Jersey	6 461
4	Houston city, Texas	2 099 451	4	4	Houston city, Texas	1 552.9	24	4	Boston city, Massachusetts	4 939
5	Philadelphia city, Pennsylvania	1 526 006	6	5	Phoenix city, Arizona	1 338.3	57	5	Santa Ana city, California	4 595
6	Phoenix city, Arizona	1 445 632	22	6	Nashville-Davidson, Tennessee	1 305.4	3	6	Chicago city, Illinois	4 572
7	San Antonio city, Texas	1 327 407	2	7	Los Angeles city, California	1 213.9	68	7	Newark city, New Jersey	4 424
8	San Diego city, California	1 307 402	7	8	San Antonio city, Texas	1 193.8	5	8	Philadelphia city, Pennsylvania	4 394
9	Dallas city, Texas	1 197 816	17	9	Louisville/Jefferson County, Kentucky	985.3	44	9	Miami city, Florida	4 299
10	San Jose city, California	945 942	11	10	Indianapolis city, Indiana	949.1	26	10	Washington city, District of Columbia	3 806
11	Indianapolis city, Indiana	829 718	9	11	Dallas city, Texas	881.9	36	11	Long Beach city, California	3 549
12	Jacksonville city, Florida	821 784	16	12	Fort Worth city, Texas	880.1	2	12	Los Angeles city, California	3 124
13	San Francisco city, California	805 235	8	13	San Diego city, California	842.2	23	13	Baltimore city, Maryland	2 962
14	Austin city, Texas	790 390	21	14	Memphis city, Tennessee	816.0	25	14	Seattle city, Washington	2 800
15	Columbus city, Ohio	787 033	37	15	Kansas City city, Missouri	815.7	48	15	Minneapolis city, Minnesota	2 737
16	Fort Worth city, Texas	741 206	1	16	New York city, New York	783.8	47	16	Oakland city, California	2 704
17	Louisville/Jefferson County, Kentucky	741 096	14	17	Austin city, Texas	771.6	54	17	Anaheim city, California	2 605
18	Charlotte city, North Carolina	731 424	18	18	Charlotte city, North Carolina	771.0	70	18	Buffalo city, New York	2 498
19	Detroit city, Michigan	713 777	63	19	Lexington-Fayette urban cnty, Kentucky	734.7	28	19	Milwaukee city, Wisconsin	2 389
20	El Paso city, Texas	649 121	20	20	El Paso city, Texas	661.1	53	20	Urban Honolulu CDP, Hawaii	2 152
21	Memphis city, Tennessee	646 889	39	21	Virginia Beach city, Virginia	645.0	59	21	Pittsburgh city, Pennsylvania	2 132
22	Nashville-Davidson, Tennessee	626 681	3	22	Chicago city, Illinois	589.6	67	22	St. Paul city, Minnesota	2 118
23	Baltimore city, Maryland	620 961	33	23	Tucson city, Arizona	587.2	10	23	San Jose city, California	2 069
24	Boston city, Massachusetts	617 594	15	24	Columbus city, Ohio	562.5	58	24	St. Louis city, Missouri	1 991
25	Seattle city, Washington	608 660	46	25	Tulsa city, Oklahoma	509.6	19	25	Detroit city, Michigan	1 986
26	Washington city, District of Columbia	601 723	41	26	Colorado Springs city, Colorado	503.9	45	26	Cleveland city, Ohio	1 972
27	Denver city, Colorado	600 158	32	27	Albuquerque city, New Mexico	486.2	35	27	Sacramento city, California	1 840
28	Milwaukee city, Wisconsin	594 833	10	28	San Jose city, California	457.2	65	28	Stockton city, California	1 826
29	Portland city, Oregon	583 776	52	29	New Orleans city, Louisiana	438.8	34	29	Fresno city, California	1 706
30	Las Vegas city, Nevada	583 756	60	30	Corpus Christi city, Texas	416.0	29	30	Portland city, Oregon	1 689
31	Oklahoma City city, Oklahoma	579 999	49	31	Wichita city, Kansas	412.6	30	31	Las Vegas city, Nevada	1 660
32	Albuquerque city, New Mexico	545 852	56	32	Aurora city, Colorado	400.8	8	32	San Diego city, California	1 552
33	Tucson city, Arizona	520 116	27	33	Denver city, Colorado	396.3	27	33	Denver city, Colorado	1 514
34	Fresno city, California	494 665	43	34	Raleigh city, North Carolina	370.1	50	34	Arlington city, Texas	1 472
35	Sacramento city, California	466 488	51	35	Bakersfield city, California	368.2	62	35	Cincinnati city, Ohio	1 471
36	Long Beach city, California	462 257	19	36	Detroit city, Michigan	359.4	61	36	Riverside city, California	1 446
37	Kansas City city, Missouri	459 787	38	37	Mesa city, Arizona	353.4	71	37	Plano city, Texas	1 402
38	Mesa city, Arizona	439 041	30	38	Las Vegas city, Nevada	351.8	15	38	Columbus city, Ohio	1 399
39	Virginia Beach city, Virginia	437 994	5	39	Philadelphia city, Pennsylvania	347.3	66	39	Toledo city, Ohio	1 374
40	Atlanta city, Georgia	420 003	29	40	Portland city, Oregon	345.6	9	40	Dallas city, Texas	1 358
41	Colorado Springs city, Colorado	416 427	40	41	Atlanta city, Georgia	344.9	4	41	Houston city, Texas	1 352
42	Omaha city, Nebraska	408 958	42	42	Omaha city, Nebraska	329.2	42	42	Omaha city, Nebraska	1 242
43	Raleigh city, North Carolina	403 892	69	43	Greensboro city, North Carolina	327.7	38	43	Mesa city, Arizona	1 242
44	Miami city, Florida	399 457	55	44	Tampa city, Florida	293.7	40	44	Atlanta city, Georgia	1 218
45	Cleveland city, Ohio	396 815	34	45	Fresno city, California	290.0	55	45	Tampa city, Florida	1 143
46	Tulsa city, Oklahoma	391 906	74	46	Fort Wayne city, Indiana	286.5	32	46	Albuquerque city, New Mexico	1 123
47	Oakland city, California	390 724	73	47	Henderson city, Nevada	279.0	72	47	Lincoln city, Nebraska	1 120
48	Minneapolis city, Minnesota	382 578	35	48	Sacramento city, California	253.6	7	48	San Antonio city, Texas	1 112
49	Wichita city, Kansas	382 368	28	49	Milwaukee city, Wisconsin	249.0	43	49	Raleigh city, North Carolina	1 091
50	Arlington city, Texas	365 438	50	50	Arlington city, Texas	248.3	6	50	Phoenix city, Arizona	1 080
51	Bakersfield city, California	347 483	72	51	Lincoln city, Nebraska	230.8	14	51	Austin city, Texas	1 024
52	New Orleans city, Louisiana	343 829	25	52	Seattle city, Washington	217.4	20	52	El Paso city, Texas	981.9
53	Urban Honolulu CDP, Hawaii	337 256	61	53	Riverside city, California	210.2	18	53	Charlotte city, North Carolina	948.7
54	Anaheim city, California	336 265	23	54	Baltimore city, Maryland	209.6	51	54	Bakersfield city, California	943.7
55	Tampa city, Florida	335 709	66	55	Toledo city, Ohio	209.0	49	55	Wichita city, Kansas	926.8
56	Aurora city, Colorado	325 078	62	56	Cincinnati city, Ohio	201.9	73	56	Henderson city, Nevada	923.7
57	Santa Ana city, California	324 528	45	57	Cleveland city, Ohio	201.2	33	57	Tucson city, Arizona	885.8
58	St. Louis city, Missouri	319 294	71	58	Plano city, Texas	185.4	74	58	Fort Wayne city, Indiana	885.5
59	Pittsburgh city, Pennsylvania	305 704	58	59	St. Louis city, Missouri	160.3	11	59	Indianapolis city, Indiana	874.2
60	Corpus Christi city, Texas	305 215	65	60	Stockton city, California	159.7	16	60	Fort Worth city, Texas	842.2
61	Riverside city, California	303 871	26	61	Washington city, District of Columbia	158.1	41	61	Colorado Springs city, Colorado	826.5
62	Cincinnati city, Ohio	296 943	53	62	Urban Honolulu CDP, Hawaii	156.8	69	62	Greensboro city, North Carolina	823.0
63	Lexington-Fayette urban cnty, Kentucky	295 803	47	63	Oakland city, California	144.5	56	63	Aurora city, Colorado	811.2
64	Anchorage municipality, Alaska	291 826	59	64	Pittsburgh city, Pennsylvania	143.4	21	64	Memphis city, Tennessee	792.8
65	Stockton city, California	291 707	48	65	Minneapolis city, Minnesota	139.8	52	65	New Orleans city, Louisiana	783.6
66	Toledo city, Ohio	287 208	67	66	St. Paul city, Minnesota	134.6	46	66	Tulsa city, Oklahoma	769.1
67	St. Paul city, Minnesota	285 068	36	67	Long Beach city, California	130.3	17	67	Louisville/Jefferson County, Kentucky	752.2
68	Newark city, New Jersey	277 140	54	68	Anaheim city, California	129.1	60	68	Corpus Christi city, Texas	733.7
69	Greensboro city, North Carolina	269 666	24	69	Boston city, Massachusetts	125.0	39	69	Virginia Beach city, Virginia	679.1
70	Buffalo city, New York	261 310	13	70	San Francisco city, California	121.4	37	70	Kansas City city, Missouri	563.7
71	Plano city, Texas	259 841	70	71	Buffalo city, New York	104.6	22	71	Nashville-Davidson, Tennessee	480.1
72	Lincoln city, Nebraska	258 379	44	72	Miami city, Florida	92.9	12	72	Jacksonville city, Florida	424.8
73	Henderson city, Nevada	257 729	57	73	Santa Ana city, California	70.6	63	73	Lexington-Fayette urban cnty, Kentucky	402.6
74	Fort Wayne city, Indiana	253 691	68	74	Newark city, New Jersey	62.6	31	74	Oklahoma City city, Oklahoma	369.3
75	Jersey City city, New Jersey	247 597	75	75	Jersey City city, New Jersey	38.3	64	75	Anchorage municipality, Alaska	66.1

75 Largest Cities by 2010 Population
Selected Rankings

Population rank	Percent change rank	City	Percent change [col 26]	Population rank	White rank	City	Percent White [col 5]	Population rank	Black rank	City	Percent Black [col 6]
		Percent population change, 2000–2010				**Percent White, alone or in combination, 2010**				**Percent Black, alone or in combination, 2010**	
73	1	Henderson city, Nevada	47.0	72	1	Lincoln city, Nebraska	85.3	19	1	Detroit city, Michigan	83.6
43	2	Raleigh city, North Carolina	46.3	29	2	Portland city, Oregon	75.5	23	2	Baltimore city, Maryland	64.4
51	3	Bakersfield city, California	40.6	63	3	Lexington-Fayette urban cnty, Kentucky	74.9	21	3	Memphis city, Tennessee	63.8
16	4	Fort Worth city, Texas	38.6	41	4	Colorado Springs city, Colorado	73.7	52	4	New Orleans city, Louisiana	60.4
18	5	Charlotte city, North Carolina	35.2	74	5	Fort Wayne city, Indiana	72.8	40	5	Atlanta city, Georgia	54.4
74	6	Fort Wayne city, Indiana	23.3	17	6	Louisville/Jefferson County, Kentucky	72.2	45	6	Cleveland city, Ohio	53.9
30	7	Las Vegas city, Nevada	22.0	73	7	Henderson city, Nevada	71.6	26	7	Washington city, District of Columbia	51.3
32	8	Albuquerque city, New Mexico	21.7	25	8	Seattle city, Washington	70.1	68	8	Newark city, New Jersey	50.6
14	9	Austin city, Texas	20.4	42	9	Omaha city, Nebraska	69.8	58	9	St. Louis city, Missouri	50.3
69	9	Greensboro city, North Carolina	20.4	64	10	Anchorage municipality, Alaska	68.5	62	10	Cincinnati city, Ohio	46.2
65	11	Stockton city, California	19.7	49	11	Wichita city, Kansas	67.3	5	11	Philadelphia city, Pennsylvania	43.4
61	12	Riverside city, California	19.1	39	12	Virginia Beach city, Virginia	67.2	69	12	Greensboro city, North Carolina	41.6
56	13	Aurora city, Colorado	17.6	59	13	Pittsburgh city, Pennsylvania	66.7	28	13	Milwaukee city, Wisconsin	40.9
71	14	Plano city, Texas	17.0	38	14	Mesa city, Arizona	66.0	70	14	Buffalo city, New York	39.0
7	15	San Antonio city, Texas	16.0	66	15	Toledo city, Ohio	64.0	18	15	Charlotte city, North Carolina	35.6
34	16	Fresno city, California	15.7	48	16	Minneapolis city, Minnesota	63.1	3	16	Chicago city, Illinois	33.0
41	17	Colorado Springs city, Colorado	15.4	46	17	Tulsa city, Oklahoma	62.0	12	17	Jacksonville city, Florida	31.2
20	18	El Paso city, Texas	15.2	15	18	Columbus city, Ohio	61.7	37	18	Kansas City city, Missouri	31.0
31	19	Oklahoma City city, Oklahoma	14.6	11	19	Indianapolis city, Indiana	60.7	43	19	Raleigh city, North Carolina	29.8
35	19	Sacramento city, California	14.6	71	20	Plano city, Texas	60.2	15	20	Columbus city, Ohio	29.6
72	21	Lincoln city, Nebraska	14.5	31	21	Oklahoma City city, Oklahoma	60.0	47	21	Oakland city, California	29.2
63	22	Lexington-Fayette urban cnty, Kentucky	13.5	22	22	Nashville-Davidson, Tennessee	59.0	66	22	Toledo city, Ohio	28.9
64	23	Anchorage municipality, Alaska	12.1	67	23	St. Paul city, Minnesota	58.6	11	23	Indianapolis city, Indiana	28.6
12	24	Jacksonville city, Florida	11.7	12	24	Jacksonville city, Florida	56.9	22	24	Nashville-Davidson, Tennessee	28.5
49	25	Wichita city, Kansas	11.1	37	25	Kansas City city, Missouri	56.8	59	25	Pittsburgh city, Pennsylvania	27.3
38	26	Mesa city, Arizona	10.8	43	26	Raleigh city, North Carolina	54.8	55	26	Tampa city, Florida	25.8
15	27	Columbus city, Ohio	10.6	27	27	Denver city, Colorado	53.9	9	27	Dallas city, Texas	26.1
55	27	Tampa city, Florida	10.6	14	28	Austin city, Texas	50.3	75	28	Jersey City city, New Jersey	24.9
29	29	Portland city, Oregon	10.3	30	29	Las Vegas city, Nevada	50.2	24	29	Boston city, Massachusetts	23.8
44	30	Miami city, Florida	10.2	62	30	Cincinnati city, Ohio	50.0	1	30	New York city, New York	23.6
22	31	Nashville-Davidson, Tennessee	10.0	56	31	Aurora city, Colorado	49.9	4	30	Houston city, Texas	23.6
60	31	Corpus Christi city, Texas	10.0	33	32	Tucson city, Arizona	48.9	17	32	Louisville/Jefferson County, Kentucky	21.8
50	33	Arlington city, Texas	9.8	24	33	Boston city, Massachusetts	48.5	39	33	Virginia Beach city, Virginia	20.6
6	34	Phoenix city, Arizona	9.4	6	34	Phoenix city, Arizona	48.0	48	34	Minneapolis city, Minnesota	20.4
27	35	Denver city, Colorado	8.2	55	35	Tampa city, Florida	47.9	50	35	Arlington city, Texas	19.3
25	36	Seattle city, Washington	8.0	8	36	San Diego city, California	47.8	16	36	Fort Worth city, Texas	19.2
4	37	Houston city, Texas	7.5	70	37	Buffalo city, New York	47.7	46	37	Tulsa city, Oklahoma	17.4
8	38	San Diego city, California	6.9	69	38	Greensboro city, North Carolina	47.1	67	38	St. Paul city, Minnesota	17.3
33	38	Tucson city, Arizona	6.9	50	39	Arlington city, Texas	46.5	74	39	Fort Wayne city, Indiana	17.1
17	40	Louisville/Jefferson County, Kentucky	6.8	18	40	Charlotte city, North Carolina	46.4	56	40	Aurora city, Colorado	17.0
10	41	San Jose city, California	5.7	13	41	San Francisco city, California	44.6	44	41	Miami city, Florida	16.7
26	42	Washington city, District of Columbia	5.2	58	42	St. Louis city, Missouri	43.8	31	42	Oklahoma City city, Oklahoma	16.4
42	43	Omaha city, Nebraska	4.9	32	43	Albuquerque city, New Mexico	43.7	35	43	Sacramento city, California	15.9
11	44	Indianapolis city, Indiana	4.8	16	44	Fort Worth city, Texas	43.0	63	44	Lexington-Fayette urban cnty, Kentucky	15.6
24	44	Boston city, Massachusetts	4.8	51	45	Bakersfield city, California	39.6	42	45	Omaha city, Nebraska	14.9
37	46	Kansas City city, Missouri	4.1	28	46	Milwaukee city, Wisconsin	38.8	36	46	Long Beach city, California	14.1
13	47	San Francisco city, California	3.7	5	47	Philadelphia city, Pennsylvania	38.1	49	47	Wichita city, Kansas	12.8
75	48	Jersey City city, New Jersey	3.1	35	48	Sacramento city, California	37.7	65	47	Stockton city, California	12.8
39	49	Virginia Beach city, Virginia	3.0	40	49	Atlanta city, Georgia	37.4	30	49	Las Vegas city, Nevada	11.8
2	50	Los Angeles city, California	2.6	26	50	Washington city, District of Columbia	36.3	27	50	Denver city, Colorado	10.8
54	51	Anaheim city, California	2.5	61	51	Riverside city, California	35.9	2	51	Los Angeles city, California	9.8
1	52	New York city, New York	2.1	45	52	Cleveland city, Ohio	34.9	25	52	Seattle city, Washington	9.1
68	53	Newark city, New Jersey	1.3	1	53	New York city, New York	34.3	51	53	Bakersfield city, California	8.5
9	54	Dallas city, Texas	0.8	60	54	Corpus Christi city, Texas	34.1	34	54	Fresno city, California	8.4
40	54	Atlanta city, Georgia	0.8	3	55	Chicago city, Illinois	32.7	14	55	Austin city, Texas	8.3
5	56	Philadelphia city, Pennsylvania	0.6	34	56	Fresno city, California	31.6	71	56	Plano city, Texas	8.0
36	57	Long Beach city, California	0.2	36	57	Long Beach city, California	31.4	29	57	Portland city, Oregon	7.4
48	58	Minneapolis city, Minnesota	0.0	52	57	New Orleans city, Louisiana	31.4	61	57	Riverside city, California	7.4
53	58	Urban Honolulu CDP, Hawaii	0.0	10	59	San Jose city, California	30.9	8	59	San Diego city, California	7.3
46	60	Tulsa city, Oklahoma	-0.3	2	60	Los Angeles city, California	30.3	41	59	Colorado Springs city, Colorado	7.3
28	61	Milwaukee city, Wisconsin	-0.4	9	61	Dallas city, Texas	29.6	64	61	Anchorage municipality, Alaska	7.1
21	62	Memphis city, Tennessee	-0.5	23	62	Baltimore city, Maryland	29.2	6	62	Phoenix city, Arizona	6.8
67	63	St. Paul city, Minnesota	-0.7	54	63	Anaheim city, California	29.0	7	62	San Antonio city, Texas	6.8
47	64	Oakland city, California	-2.2	47	64	Oakland city, California	28.6	13	64	San Francisco city, California	6.7
57	65	Santa Ana city, California	-4.0	21	65	Memphis city, Tennessee	28.3	73	65	Henderson city, Nevada	5.9
23	66	Baltimore city, Maryland	-4.6	7	66	San Antonio city, Texas	27.6	33	66	Tucson city, Arizona	5.3
3	67	Chicago city, Illinois	-6.9	53	67	Urban Honolulu CDP, Hawaii	26.5	72	67	Lincoln city, Nebraska	5.0
58	68	St. Louis city, Missouri	-8.3	4	68	Houston city, Texas	26.4	60	68	Corpus Christi city, Texas	4.2
66	69	Toledo city, Ohio	-8.4	65	69	Stockton city, California	25.3	38	69	Mesa city, Arizona	4.0
59	70	Pittsburgh city, Pennsylvania	-8.6	75	70	Jersey City city, New Jersey	22.7	10	70	San Jose city, California	3.4
62	71	Cincinnati city, Ohio	-10.4	20	71	El Paso city, Texas	14.9	32	71	Albuquerque city, New Mexico	3.3
70	72	Buffalo city, New York	-10.7	68	72	Newark city, New Jersey	12.5	20	72	El Paso city, Texas	3.1
45	73	Cleveland city, Ohio	-17.1	44	73	Miami city, Florida	12.3	54	73	Anaheim city, California	2.8
19	74	Detroit city, Michigan	-25.0	57	74	Santa Ana city, California	9.8	53	74	Urban Honolulu CDP, Hawaii	2.3
52	75	New Orleans city, Louisiana	-29.1	19	75	Detroit city, Michigan	8.9	57	75	Santa Ana city, California	1.1

75 Largest Cities by 2010 Population
Selected Rankings

Percent American Indian, Alaska Native, 2010				Percent Asian and Pacific Islander, 2010				Percent Hispanic or Latino,[1] 2010			
Population rank	American Indian, Alaska Native rank	City	Percent American Indian, Alaska Native [col 7]	Population rank	Asian and Pacific Islander rank	City	Percent Asian and Pacific Islander [col 8]	Population rank	Hispanic or Latino rank	City	Percent Hispanic or Latino [col 10]
64	1	Anchorage municipality, Alaska	11.5	53	1	Urban Honolulu CDP, Hawaii	65.9	20	1	El Paso city, Texas	80.7
46	2	Tulsa city, Oklahoma	8.5	13	2	San Francisco city, California	35.2	57	2	Santa Ana city, California	78.2
31	3	Oklahoma City city, Oklahoma	5.6	10	3	San Jose city, California	33.7	44	3	Miami city, Florida	70.0
32	4	Albuquerque city, New Mexico	4.5	75	4	Jersey City city, New Jersey	24.8	7	4	San Antonio city, Texas	63.2
48	5	Minneapolis city, Minnesota	2.8	65	5	Stockton city, California	22.6	60	5	Corpus Christi city, Texas	59.7
38	6	Mesa city, Arizona	2.5	35	6	Sacramento city, California	20.2	54	6	Anaheim city, California	52.8
33	7	Tucson city, Arizona	2.3	47	7	Oakland city, California	18.4	61	7	Riverside city, California	49.0
6	8	Phoenix city, Arizona	2.1	71	8	Plano city, Texas	18.1	2	8	Los Angeles city, California	48.5
49	8	Wichita city, Kansas	2.1	8	9	San Diego city, California	17.7	34	9	Fresno city, California	46.9
29	10	Portland city, Oregon	1.9	25	10	Seattle city, Washington	16.3	32	10	Albuquerque city, New Mexico	46.7
67	10	St. Paul city, Minnesota	1.9	54	11	Anaheim city, California	15.8	51	11	Bakersfield city, California	45.5
25	12	Seattle city, Washington	1.7	67	11	St. Paul city, Minnesota	15.8	4	12	Houston city, Texas	43.8
35	12	Sacramento city, California	1.7	36	13	Long Beach city, California	14.0	9	13	Dallas city, Texas	42.4
41	14	Colorado Springs city, Colorado	1.5	1	14	New York city, New York	13.6	33	14	Tucson city, Arizona	41.6
51	15	Bakersfield city, California	1.4	34	15	Fresno city, California	13.3	6	15	Phoenix city, Arizona	40.8
34	16	Fresno city, California	1.3	2	16	Los Angeles city, California	12.3	36	15	Long Beach city, California	40.8
56	16	Aurora city, Colorado	1.3	57	17	Santa Ana city, California	10.8	65	17	Stockton city, California	40.3
65	16	Stockton city, California	1.3	64	18	Anchorage municipality, Alaska	9.9	14	18	Austin city, Texas	35.1
27	19	Denver city, Colorado	1.2	24	19	Boston city, Massachusetts	9.7	16	19	Fort Worth city, Texas	34.1
28	19	Milwaukee city, Wisconsin	1.2	73	20	Henderson city, Nevada	8.9	68	20	Newark city, New Jersey	33.8
37	19	Kansas City city, Missouri	1.2	29	21	Portland city, Oregon	8.7	10	21	San Jose city, California	33.2
42	19	Omaha city, Nebraska	1.2	61	22	Riverside city, California	8.2	27	22	Denver city, Colorado	31.8
47	19	Oakland city, California	1.2	39	23	Virginia Beach city, Virginia	7.5	30	23	Las Vegas city, Nevada	31.5
53	19	Urban Honolulu CDP, Hawaii	1.2	50	24	Arlington city, Texas	7.4	3	24	Chicago city, Illinois	28.9
70	19	Buffalo city, New York	1.2	30	25	Las Vegas city, Nevada	7.3	8	25	San Diego city, California	28.8
72	19	Lincoln city, Nebraska	1.2	14	26	Austin city, Texas	7.1	56	26	Aurora city, Colorado	28.7
69	27	Greensboro city, North Carolina	1.1	5	27	Philadelphia city, Pennsylvania	6.9	1	27	New York city, New York	28.6
73	27	Henderson city, Nevada	1.1	51	28	Bakersfield city, California	6.7	75	28	Jersey City city, New Jersey	27.6
19	29	Detroit city, Michigan	1.0	4	29	Houston city, Texas	6.5	50	29	Arlington city, Texas	27.4
30	29	Las Vegas city, Nevada	1.0	48	29	Minneapolis city, Minnesota	6.5	35	30	Sacramento city, California	26.9
39	29	Virginia Beach city, Virginia	1.0	3	31	Chicago city, Illinois	6.0	38	31	Mesa city, Arizona	26.4
12	32	Jacksonville city, Florida	0.9	56	32	Aurora city, Colorado	5.9	47	32	Oakland city, California	25.4
15	32	Columbus city, Ohio	0.9	18	33	Charlotte city, North Carolina	5.5	55	33	Tampa city, Florida	23.1
23	32	Baltimore city, Maryland	0.9	49	33	Wichita city, Kansas	5.5	24	34	Boston city, Massachusetts	17.5
36	32	Long Beach city, California	0.9	12	35	Jacksonville city, Florida	5.1	28	35	Milwaukee city, Wisconsin	17.3
50	32	Arlington city, Texas	0.9	43	36	Raleigh city, North Carolina	5.0	31	36	Oklahoma City city, Oklahoma	17.2
58	32	St. Louis city, Missouri	0.9	59	36	Pittsburgh city, Pennsylvania	5.0	41	37	Colorado Springs city, Colorado	16.1
61	32	Riverside city, California	0.9	15	38	Columbus city, Ohio	4.7	49	38	Wichita city, Kansas	15.3
66	32	Toledo city, Ohio	0.9	31	39	Oklahoma City city, Oklahoma	4.6	13	39	San Francisco city, California	15.1
74	32	Fort Wayne city, Indiana	0.9	69	40	Greensboro city, North Carolina	4.5	73	40	Henderson city, Nevada	14.9
8	41	San Diego city, California	0.8	72	41	Lincoln city, Nebraska	4.4	71	41	Plano city, Texas	14.7
13	41	San Francisco city, California	0.8	26	42	Washington city, District of Columbia	4.3	46	42	Tulsa city, Oklahoma	14.1
16	41	Fort Worth city, Texas	0.8	41	42	Colorado Springs city, Colorado	4.3	18	43	Charlotte city, North Carolina	13.1
18	41	Charlotte city, North Carolina	0.8	16	44	Fort Worth city, Texas	4.2	42	43	Omaha city, Nebraska	13.1
26	41	Washington city, District of Columbia	0.8	27	45	Denver city, Colorado	4.1	5	45	Philadelphia city, Pennsylvania	12.3
45	41	Cleveland city, Ohio	0.8	55	45	Tampa city, Florida	4.1	43	46	Raleigh city, North Carolina	11.4
62	41	Cincinnati city, Ohio	0.8	28	47	Milwaukee city, Wisconsin	3.9	48	47	Minneapolis city, Minnesota	10.5
71	41	Plano city, Texas	0.8	63	48	Lexington-Fayette urban cnty, Kentucky	3.8	70	47	Buffalo city, New York	10.5
5	49	Philadelphia city, Pennsylvania	0.7	74	48	Fort Wayne city, Indiana	3.8	37	49	Kansas City city, Missouri	10.0
10	49	San Jose city, California	0.7	6	50	Phoenix city, Arizona	3.7	45	49	Cleveland city, Ohio	10.0
11	49	Indianapolis city, Indiana	0.7	40	50	Atlanta city, Georgia	3.7	22	51	Nashville-Davidson, Tennessee	9.8
14	49	Austin city, Texas	0.7	22	52	Nashville-Davidson, Tennessee	3.6	67	52	St. Paul city, Minnesota	9.6
17	49	Louisville/Jefferson County, Kentucky	0.7	70	52	Buffalo city, New York	3.6	11	53	Indianapolis city, Indiana	9.4
22	49	Nashville-Davidson, Tennessee	0.7	33	54	Tucson city, Arizona	3.5	29	53	Portland city, Oregon	9.4
24	49	Boston city, Massachusetts	0.7	58	55	St. Louis city, Missouri	3.4	26	55	Washington city, District of Columbia	9.1
40	49	Atlanta city, Georgia	0.7	9	56	Dallas city, Texas	3.2	74	56	Fort Wayne city, Indiana	8.0
43	49	Raleigh city, North Carolina	0.7	32	56	Albuquerque city, New Mexico	3.2	12	57	Jacksonville city, Florida	7.7
59	49	Pittsburgh city, Pennsylvania	0.7	52	56	New Orleans city, Louisiana	3.2	64	58	Anchorage municipality, Alaska	7.6
75	49	Jersey City city, New Jersey	0.7	37	59	Kansas City city, Missouri	3.0	69	59	Greensboro city, North Carolina	7.5
9	60	Dallas city, Texas	0.6	42	60	Omaha city, Nebraska	2.9	66	60	Toledo city, Ohio	7.4
52	60	New Orleans city, Louisiana	0.6	7	61	San Antonio city, Texas	2.8	63	61	Lexington-Fayette urban cnty, Kentucky	6.9
55	60	Tampa city, Florida	0.6	23	61	Baltimore city, Maryland	2.8	19	62	Detroit city, Michigan	6.8
63	60	Lexington-Fayette urban cnty, Kentucky	0.6	46	61	Tulsa city, Oklahoma	2.8	25	63	Seattle city, Washington	6.6
68	60	Newark city, New Jersey	0.6	17	64	Louisville/Jefferson County, Kentucky	2.6	39	63	Virginia Beach city, Virginia	6.6
1	65	New York city, New York	0.5	11	65	Indianapolis city, Indiana	2.5	21	65	Memphis city, Tennessee	6.5
2	65	Los Angeles city, California	0.5	38	65	Mesa city, Arizona	2.5	72	66	Lincoln city, Nebraska	6.3
3	65	Chicago city, Illinois	0.5	62	67	Cincinnati city, Ohio	2.3	15	67	Columbus city, Ohio	5.6
7	65	San Antonio city, Texas	0.5	45	68	Cleveland city, Ohio	2.1	53	68	Urban Honolulu CDP, Hawaii	5.4
21	65	Memphis city, Tennessee	0.5	60	68	Corpus Christi city, Texas	2.1	40	69	Atlanta city, Georgia	5.2
54	65	Anaheim city, California	0.5	21	70	Memphis city, Tennessee	1.8	52	69	New Orleans city, Louisiana	5.2
60	65	Corpus Christi city, Texas	0.5	68	70	Newark city, New Jersey	1.8	17	71	Louisville/Jefferson County, Kentucky	4.4
4	72	Houston city, Texas	0.4	66	72	Toledo city, Ohio	1.5	23	72	Baltimore city, Maryland	4.2
20	72	El Paso city, Texas	0.4	20	73	El Paso city, Texas	1.4	58	73	St. Louis city, Missouri	3.5
57	74	Santa Ana city, California	0.3	19	74	Detroit city, Michigan	1.3	62	74	Cincinnati city, Ohio	2.8
44	75	Miami city, Florida	0.2	44	75	Miami city, Florida	1.2	59	75	Pittsburgh city, Pennsylvania	2.3

1. Persons of hispanic origin may be of any race.

75 Largest Cities by 2010 Population
Selected Rankings

Percent under 18 years old, 2010

Population rank	Under 18 years old rank	City	Percent under 18 years old [col 12 and 13]
51	1	Bakersfield city, California	31.5
57	2	Santa Ana city, California	30.7
34	3	Fresno city, California	30.1
65	4	Stockton city, California	29.9
16	5	Fort Worth city, Texas	29.3
20	6	El Paso city, Texas	29.2
6	7	Phoenix city, Arizona	28.3
50	8	Arlington city, Texas	27.9
54	9	Anaheim city, California	27.4
56	9	Aurora city, Colorado	27.4
28	11	Milwaukee city, Wisconsin	27.1
61	12	Riverside city, California	26.8
7	13	San Antonio city, Texas	26.8
19	14	Detroit city, Michigan	26.6
9	15	Dallas city, Texas	26.5
49	15	Wichita city, Kansas	26.5
74	17	Fort Wayne city, Indiana	26.4
38	18	Mesa city, Arizona	26.3
71	19	Plano city, Texas	25.9
21	20	Memphis city, Tennessee	25.9
64	20	Anchorage municipality, Alaska	25.9
4	22	Houston city, Texas	25.8
60	22	Corpus Christi city, Texas	25.8
30	24	Las Vegas city, Nevada	25.6
68	25	Newark city, New Jersey	25.5
31	26	Oklahoma City city, Oklahoma	25.4
18	27	Charlotte city, North Carolina	25.3
42	28	Omaha city, Nebraska	25.1
67	28	St. Paul city, Minnesota	25.1
11	30	Indianapolis city, Indiana	25.0
41	30	Colorado Springs city, Colorado	25.0
10	32	San Jose city, California	24.9
35	33	Sacramento city, California	24.9
36	33	Long Beach city, California	24.9
45	35	Cleveland city, Ohio	24.6
46	36	Tulsa city, Oklahoma	24.5
37	37	Kansas City city, Missouri	24.1
66	37	Toledo city, Ohio	24.1
39	39	Virginia Beach city, Virginia	24.1
32	40	Albuquerque city, New Mexico	24.0
12	41	Jacksonville city, Florida	23.9
70	42	Buffalo city, New York	23.6
33	43	Tucson city, Arizona	23.4
17	44	Louisville/Jefferson County, Kentucky	23.2
15	45	Columbus city, Ohio	23.2
3	46	Chicago city, Illinois	23.1
43	46	Raleigh city, North Carolina	23.1
2	48	Los Angeles city, California	23.0
73	49	Henderson city, Nevada	22.7
69	50	Greensboro city, North Carolina	22.7
72	50	Lincoln city, Nebraska	22.7
55	52	Tampa city, Florida	22.6
5	53	Philadelphia city, Pennsylvania	22.5
62	54	Cincinnati city, Ohio	22.2
14	55	Austin city, Texas	22.2
22	56	Nashville-Davidson, Tennessee	21.7
1	57	New York city, New York	21.6
23	58	Baltimore city, Maryland	21.5
27	58	Denver city, Colorado	21.5
8	60	San Diego city, California	21.4
47	61	Oakland city, California	21.3
52	61	New Orleans city, Louisiana	21.3
63	63	Lexington-Fayette urban cnty, Kentucky	21.2
75	63	Jersey City city, New Jersey	21.2
58	65	St. Louis city, Missouri	21.1
48	66	Minneapolis city, Minnesota	20.2
40	67	Atlanta city, Georgia	19.4
29	68	Portland city, Oregon	19.1
44	69	Miami city, Florida	18.4
53	70	Urban Honolulu CDP, Hawaii	17.4
26	71	Washington city, District of Columbia	16.7
24	72	Boston city, Massachusetts	16.7
59	73	Pittsburgh city, Pennsylvania	16.2
25	74	Seattle city, Washington	15.4
13	75	San Francisco city, California	13.4

Percent 65 years old and over, 2010

Population rank	65 years and over rank	City	Percent 65 years old and over [col 19 and 20]
53	1	Urban Honolulu CDP, Hawaii	17.9
44	2	Miami city, Florida	16.0
73	3	Henderson city, Nevada	14.2
38	4	Mesa city, Arizona	14.1
59	5	Pittsburgh city, Pennsylvania	13.7
13	6	San Francisco city, California	13.6
17	7	Louisville/Jefferson County, Kentucky	13.4
46	8	Tulsa city, Oklahoma	12.4
5	9	Philadelphia city, Pennsylvania	12.1
32	9	Albuquerque city, New Mexico	12.1
1	11	New York city, New York	12.1
66	11	Toledo city, Ohio	12.1
30	13	Las Vegas city, Nevada	12.0
45	13	Cleveland city, Ohio	12.0
74	13	Fort Wayne city, Indiana	12.0
33	16	Tucson city, Arizona	11.9
60	16	Corpus Christi city, Texas	11.9
23	18	Baltimore city, Maryland	11.7
19	19	Detroit city, Michigan	11.5
49	19	Wichita city, Kansas	11.5
69	19	Greensboro city, North Carolina	11.5
70	22	Buffalo city, New York	11.4
26	23	Washington city, District of Columbia	11.4
42	23	Omaha city, Nebraska	11.4
31	25	Oklahoma City city, Oklahoma	11.3
20	26	El Paso city, Texas	11.2
47	27	Oakland city, California	11.1
12	28	Jacksonville city, Florida	11.0
37	28	Kansas City city, Missouri	11.0
52	28	New Orleans city, Louisiana	11.0
58	28	St. Louis city, Missouri	11.0
41	32	Colorado Springs city, Colorado	10.9
55	33	Tampa city, Florida	10.9
62	34	Cincinnati city, Ohio	10.8
8	35	San Diego city, California	10.7
25	35	Seattle city, Washington	10.7
72	35	Lincoln city, Nebraska	10.7
39	38	Virginia Beach city, Virginia	10.6
11	39	Indianapolis city, Indiana	10.6
35	39	Sacramento city, California	10.6
22	41	Nashville-Davidson, Tennessee	10.5
63	41	Lexington-Fayette urban cnty, Kentucky	10.5
2	43	Los Angeles city, California	10.4
21	43	Memphis city, Tennessee	10.4
27	43	Denver city, Colorado	10.4
29	43	Portland city, Oregon	10.4
7	47	San Antonio city, Texas	10.4
3	48	Chicago city, Illinois	10.3
10	49	San Jose city, California	10.0
24	49	Boston city, Massachusetts	10.0
65	49	Stockton city, California	10.0
40	52	Atlanta city, Georgia	9.9
34	53	Fresno city, California	9.4
54	54	Anaheim city, California	9.3
36	55	Long Beach city, California	9.2
4	56	Houston city, Texas	9.1
67	57	St. Paul city, Minnesota	9.0
75	57	Jersey City city, New Jersey	9.0
28	59	Milwaukee city, Wisconsin	8.9
9	60	Dallas city, Texas	8.9
56	60	Aurora city, Colorado	8.9
71	62	Plano city, Texas	8.8
15	63	Columbus city, Ohio	8.6
61	63	Riverside city, California	8.6
68	63	Newark city, New Jersey	8.6
6	66	Phoenix city, Arizona	8.5
18	66	Charlotte city, North Carolina	8.5
51	68	Bakersfield city, California	8.4
16	69	Fort Worth city, Texas	8.2
43	69	Raleigh city, North Carolina	8.2
50	69	Arlington city, Texas	8.2
48	72	Minneapolis city, Minnesota	8.0
64	73	Anchorage municipality, Alaska	7.3
14	74	Austin city, Texas	7.0
57	75	Santa Ana city, California	6.8

Percent high school graduate or less, 2008–2010

Population rank	Percent high school graduate or less rank	City	Percent high school graduate or less [col 40]
57	1	Santa Ana city, California	69.0
68	2	Newark city, New Jersey	65.8
44	3	Miami city, Florida	59.9
45	4	Cleveland city, Ohio	57.4
19	5	Detroit city, Michigan	55.8
5	6	Philadelphia city, Pennsylvania	55.5
23	7	Baltimore city, Maryland	51.7
66	8	Toledo city, Ohio	51.0
28	9	Milwaukee city, Wisconsin	50.7
54	9	Anaheim city, California	50.7
65	11	Stockton city, California	50.4
20	12	El Paso city, Texas	49.0
34	13	Fresno city, California	48.6
9	14	Dallas city, Texas	48.5
21	14	Memphis city, Tennessee	48.5
4	16	Houston city, Texas	48.3
70	17	Buffalo city, New York	48.1
30	18	Las Vegas city, Nevada	47.4
51	19	Bakersfield city, California	46.6
60	20	Corpus Christi city, Texas	46.4
61	21	Riverside city, California	46.3
16	22	Fort Worth city, Texas	46.1
1	23	New York city, New York	45.9
7	24	San Antonio city, Texas	45.8
11	25	Indianapolis city, Indiana	45.6
2	26	Los Angeles city, California	45.5
17	27	Louisville/Jefferson County, Kentucky	44.8
6	28	Phoenix city, Arizona	44.5
58	29	St. Louis city, Missouri	43.9
3	30	Chicago city, Illinois	43.1
12	31	Jacksonville city, Florida	42.9
55	32	Tampa city, Florida	42.4
74	32	Fort Wayne city, Indiana	42.4
62	34	Cincinnati city, Ohio	42.2
52	35	New Orleans city, Louisiana	41.7
56	35	Aurora city, Colorado	41.7
31	37	Oklahoma City city, Oklahoma	41.4
59	38	Pittsburgh city, Pennsylvania	40.9
33	39	Tucson city, Arizona	40.8
38	40	Mesa city, Arizona	40.7
36	41	Long Beach city, California	40.6
49	42	Wichita city, Kansas	40.5
22	43	Nashville-Davidson, Tennessee	40.1
46	44	Tulsa city, Oklahoma	40.0
37	45	Kansas City city, Missouri	39.7
75	46	Jersey City city, New Jersey	39.3
15	47	Columbus city, Ohio	39.2
50	47	Arlington city, Texas	39.2
35	49	Sacramento city, California	39.0
47	50	Oakland city, California	38.4
53	51	Urban Honolulu CDP, Hawaii	38.3
24	52	Boston city, Massachusetts	38.2
67	53	St. Paul city, Minnesota	37.8
69	54	Greensboro city, North Carolina	37.2
10	55	San Jose city, California	36.9
32	56	Albuquerque city, New Mexico	36.2
42	56	Omaha city, Nebraska	36.2
27	58	Denver city, Colorado	35.9
40	59	Atlanta city, Georgia	34.4
73	60	Henderson city, Nevada	34.0
63	61	Lexington-Fayette urban cnty, Kentucky	32.9
18	62	Charlotte city, North Carolina	32.8
26	63	Washington city, District of Columbia	32.7
14	64	Austin city, Texas	31.7
39	65	Virginia Beach city, Virginia	31.5
48	66	Minneapolis city, Minnesota	31.0
72	67	Lincoln city, Nebraska	30.8
8	68	San Diego city, California	30.0
64	69	Anchorage municipality, Alaska	29.9
41	70	Colorado Springs city, Colorado	28.8
29	71	Portland city, Oregon	28.7
13	72	San Francisco city, California	28.5
43	73	Raleigh city, North Carolina	25.6
71	74	Plano city, Texas	20.9
25	75	Seattle city, Washington	19.2

75 Largest Cities by 2010 Population
Selected Rankings

Percent college graduates (bachelor's degree or more), 2008–2010

Population rank	Percent college graduate rank	City	Percent college graduates [col 41]
25	1	Seattle city, Washington	55.8
71	2	Plano city, Texas	53.9
13	3	San Francisco city, California	51.2
26	4	Washington city, District of Columbia	49.8
43	5	Raleigh city, North Carolina	47.0
40	6	Atlanta city, Georgia	45.5
14	7	Austin city, Texas	43.9
48	8	Minneapolis city, Minnesota	43.6
24	9	Boston city, Massachusetts	43.1
29	10	Portland city, Oregon	42.4
75	11	Jersey City city, New Jersey	41.2
8	12	San Diego city, California	40.8
27	13	Denver city, Colorado	40.6
18	14	Charlotte city, North Carolina	38.7
63	14	Lexington-Fayette urban cnty, Kentucky	38.7
47	16	Oakland city, California	37.1
67	17	St. Paul city, Minnesota	36.9
10	18	San Jose city, California	36.4
41	19	Colorado Springs city, Colorado	36.1
72	20	Lincoln city, Nebraska	34.8
59	21	Pittsburgh city, Pennsylvania	34.5
69	22	Greensboro city, North Carolina	34.2
1	23	New York city, New York	33.4
22	24	Nashville-Davidson, Tennessee	33.3
53	24	Urban Honolulu CDP, Hawaii	33.3
3	26	Chicago city, Illinois	32.9
64	26	Anchorage municipality, Alaska	32.9
15	28	Columbus city, Ohio	32.3
52	29	New Orleans city, Louisiana	32.2
32	30	Albuquerque city, New Mexico	32.0
42	30	Omaha city, Nebraska	32.0
55	32	Tampa city, Florida	31.7
62	33	Cincinnati city, Ohio	31.5
39	34	Virginia Beach city, Virginia	31.4
73	35	Henderson city, Nevada	30.8
2	36	Los Angeles city, California	30.4
37	37	Kansas City city, Missouri	29.9
46	38	Tulsa city, Oklahoma	29.4
9	39	Dallas city, Texas	28.8
35	39	Sacramento city, California	28.8
50	41	Arlington city, Texas	28.4
4	42	Houston city, Texas	28.2
36	43	Long Beach city, California	27.9
49	44	Wichita city, Kansas	27.8
58	45	St. Louis city, Missouri	27.7
11	46	Indianapolis city, Indiana	27.4
31	47	Oklahoma City city, Oklahoma	26.7
17	48	Louisville/Jefferson County, Kentucky	25.8
56	49	Aurora city, Colorado	25.7
16	50	Fort Worth city, Texas	25.6
6	51	Phoenix city, Arizona	25.3
74	51	Fort Wayne city, Indiana	25.3
23	53	Baltimore city, Maryland	25.2
33	54	Tucson city, Arizona	24.6
12	55	Jacksonville city, Florida	23.8
38	55	Mesa city, Arizona	23.8
7	57	San Antonio city, Texas	23.6
54	58	Anaheim city, California	23.5
44	59	Miami city, Florida	22.6
21	60	Memphis city, Tennessee	22.5
5	61	Philadelphia city, Pennsylvania	22.4
70	62	Buffalo city, New York	22.1
20	63	El Paso city, Texas	21.9
61	64	Riverside city, California	21.8
28	65	Milwaukee city, Wisconsin	21.3
30	66	Las Vegas city, Nevada	20.6
60	66	Corpus Christi city, Texas	20.6
34	68	Fresno city, California	20.3
51	69	Bakersfield city, California	19.6
66	70	Toledo city, Ohio	17.1
65	71	Stockton city, California	17.0
45	72	Cleveland city, Ohio	13.4
68	73	Newark city, New Jersey	12.6
57	74	Santa Ana city, California	11.9
19	75	Detroit city, Michigan	11.8

Percent female-headed family households, 2010

Population rank	Female households rank	City	Percent female households [col 29]
19	1	Detroit city, Michigan	31.4
68	2	Newark city, New Jersey	28.9
21	3	Memphis city, Tennessee	25.3
45	3	Cleveland city, Ohio	25.3
23	5	Baltimore city, Maryland	23.8
28	6	Milwaukee city, Wisconsin	22.6
5	7	Philadelphia city, Pennsylvania	22.5
70	8	Buffalo city, New York	22.0
52	9	New Orleans city, Louisiana	20.9
20	10	El Paso city, Texas	20.7
66	11	Toledo city, Ohio	19.9
58	12	St. Louis city, Missouri	19.4
34	13	Fresno city, California	19.3
62	14	Cincinnati city, Ohio	19.1
65	15	Stockton city, California	18.9
1	16	New York city, New York	18.7
75	17	Jersey City city, New Jersey	18.2
44	18	Miami city, Florida	18.1
3	19	Chicago city, Illinois	17.7
7	20	San Antonio city, Texas	17.6
11	21	Indianapolis city, Indiana	17.2
12	22	Jacksonville city, Florida	17.1
55	23	Tampa city, Florida	16.8
60	24	Corpus Christi city, Texas	16.6
40	25	Atlanta city, Georgia	16.5
69	25	Greensboro city, North Carolina	16.5
26	27	Washington city, District of Columbia	16.4
36	27	Long Beach city, California	16.4
24	29	Boston city, Massachusetts	16.3
4	30	Houston city, Texas	16.2
51	30	Bakersfield city, California	16.2
37	32	Kansas City city, Missouri	16.1
57	32	Santa Ana city, California	16.1
9	34	Dallas city, Texas	16.0
15	35	Columbus city, Ohio	15.9
35	36	Sacramento city, California	15.8
47	37	Oakland city, California	15.7
18	38	Charlotte city, North Carolina	15.6
17	39	Louisville/Jefferson County, Kentucky	15.4
33	39	Tucson city, Arizona	15.4
16	41	Fort Worth city, Texas	15.3
61	42	Riverside city, California	15.1
50	43	Arlington city, Texas	15.0
2	44	Los Angeles city, California	14.9
6	44	Phoenix city, Arizona	14.9
59	44	Pittsburgh city, Pennsylvania	14.9
54	47	Anaheim city, California	14.8
67	47	St. Paul city, Minnesota	14.8
74	47	Fort Wayne city, Indiana	14.8
22	50	Nashville-Davidson, Tennessee	14.7
46	51	Tulsa city, Oklahoma	14.6
32	52	Albuquerque city, New Mexico	14.3
56	53	Aurora city, Colorado	14.2
30	54	Las Vegas city, Nevada	14.1
31	55	Oklahoma City city, Oklahoma	13.9
39	55	Virginia Beach city, Virginia	13.9
42	57	Omaha city, Nebraska	13.7
43	58	Raleigh city, North Carolina	13.5
49	59	Wichita city, Kansas	13.1
10	60	San Jose city, California	12.6
38	60	Mesa city, Arizona	12.6
63	62	Lexington-Fayette urban cnty, Kentucky	12.3
53	63	Urban Honolulu CDP, Hawaii	12.1
48	64	Minneapolis city, Minnesota	11.7
64	64	Anchorage municipality, Alaska	11.7
41	66	Colorado Springs city, Colorado	11.6
8	67	San Diego city, California	11.4
14	68	Austin city, Texas	11.0
73	68	Henderson city, Nevada	11.0
27	70	Denver city, Colorado	10.6
72	71	Lincoln city, Nebraska	10.2
29	72	Portland city, Oregon	10.1
71	73	Plano city, Texas	9.7
13	74	San Francisco city, California	8.3
25	75	Seattle city, Washington	7.3

Percent of households composed of one person, 2010

Population rank	One-person household rank	City	Percent one-person households [col 30]
26	1	Washington city, District of Columbia	44.0
40	1	Atlanta city, Georgia	44.0
62	3	Cincinnati city, Ohio	43.4
58	4	St. Louis city, Missouri	42.6
59	5	Pittsburgh city, Pennsylvania	41.7
25	6	Seattle city, Washington	41.3
27	7	Denver city, Colorado	40.6
48	8	Minneapolis city, Minnesota	40.3
70	9	Buffalo city, New York	39.7
45	10	Cleveland city, Ohio	39.5
13	11	San Francisco city, California	38.6
24	12	Boston city, Massachusetts	37.1
23	13	Baltimore city, Maryland	36.1
52	14	New Orleans city, Louisiana	35.9
67	15	St. Paul city, Minnesota	35.8
15	16	Columbus city, Ohio	35.1
3	17	Chicago city, Illinois	35.0
66	18	Toledo city, Ohio	34.8
37	19	Kansas City city, Missouri	34.7
22	20	Nashville-Davidson, Tennessee	34.5
29	20	Portland city, Oregon	34.5
46	20	Tulsa city, Oklahoma	34.5
5	23	Philadelphia city, Pennsylvania	34.1
14	24	Austin city, Texas	34.0
19	24	Detroit city, Michigan	34.0
9	26	Dallas city, Texas	33.9
47	26	Oakland city, California	33.9
69	28	Greensboro city, North Carolina	33.8
28	29	Milwaukee city, Wisconsin	33.6
55	29	Tampa city, Florida	33.6
44	31	Miami city, Florida	33.3
33	32	Tucson city, Arizona	33.1
53	33	Urban Honolulu CDP, Hawaii	32.9
43	34	Raleigh city, North Carolina	32.8
63	35	Lexington-Fayette urban cnty, Kentucky	32.7
42	36	Omaha city, Nebraska	32.3
21	37	Memphis city, Tennessee	32.2
11	38	Indianapolis city, Indiana	32.1
1	39	New York city, New York	32.0
17	39	Louisville/Jefferson County, Kentucky	32.0
32	41	Albuquerque city, New Mexico	31.9
72	42	Lincoln city, Nebraska	31.3
74	43	Fort Wayne city, Indiana	31.2
49	44	Wichita city, Kansas	31.1
4	45	Houston city, Texas	31.0
31	46	Oklahoma City city, Oklahoma	30.5
35	46	Sacramento city, California	30.5
18	48	Charlotte city, North Carolina	30.3
75	49	Jersey City city, New Jersey	30.2
41	50	Colorado Springs city, Colorado	29.6
36	51	Long Beach city, California	28.5
2	52	Los Angeles city, California	28.3
12	53	Jacksonville city, Florida	28.2
8	54	San Diego city, California	28.0
68	55	Newark city, New Jersey	27.9
56	56	Aurora city, Colorado	27.7
6	57	Phoenix city, Arizona	27.1
7	58	San Antonio city, Texas	26.9
38	59	Mesa city, Arizona	26.6
16	60	Fort Worth city, Texas	26.5
30	61	Las Vegas city, Nevada	26.0
60	62	Corpus Christi city, Texas	25.6
50	63	Arlington city, Texas	24.9
64	63	Anchorage municipality, Alaska	24.9
71	65	Plano city, Texas	24.4
73	66	Henderson city, Nevada	24.2
39	67	Virginia Beach city, Virginia	23.3
34	68	Fresno city, California	22.1
20	69	El Paso city, Texas	21.5
65	69	Stockton city, California	21.5
61	71	Riverside city, California	19.9
10	72	San Jose city, California	19.7
51	73	Bakersfield city, California	19.6
54	74	Anaheim city, California	17.8
57	75	Santa Ana city, California	12.6

75 Largest Cities by 2010 Population
Selected Rankings

Median household income, 2008–2010

Population rank	Median income rank	City	Median income (dollars) [col 43]
71	1	Plano city, Texas	80 210
10	2	San Jose city, California	78 149
64	3	Anchorage municipality, Alaska	74 272
13	4	San Francisco city, California	71 779
73	5	Henderson city, Nevada	65 047
39	6	Virginia Beach city, Virginia	64 065
8	7	San Diego city, California	61 282
25	8	Seattle city, Washington	60 619
26	9	Washington city, District of Columbia	59 822
54	10	Anaheim city, California	56 496
61	11	Riverside city, California	56 261
75	12	Jersey City city, New Jersey	56 119
53	13	Urban Honolulu CDP, Hawaii	55 809
57	14	Santa Ana city, California	53 266
30	15	Las Vegas city, Nevada	52 382
41	16	Colorado Springs city, Colorado	52 179
51	17	Bakersfield city, California	52 145
36	18	Long Beach city, California	51 891
18	19	Charlotte city, North Carolina	51 419
50	20	Arlington city, Texas	51 260
43	21	Raleigh city, North Carolina	51 173
24	22	Boston city, Massachusetts	50 710
14	23	Austin city, Texas	50 147
47	24	Oakland city, California	50 094
1	25	New York city, New York	50 038
29	26	Portland city, Oregon	49 326
16	27	Fort Worth city, Texas	48 970
35	28	Sacramento city, California	48 826
2	29	Los Angeles city, California	48 746
56	30	Aurora city, Colorado	48 519
72	31	Lincoln city, Nebraska	48 203
38	32	Mesa city, Arizona	47 994
12	33	Jacksonville city, Florida	47 356
6	34	Phoenix city, Arizona	47 187
63	35	Lexington-Fayette urban cnty, Kentucky	47 104
32	36	Albuquerque city, New Mexico	46 532
48	37	Minneapolis city, Minnesota	46 232
65	38	Stockton city, California	46 209
3	39	Chicago city, Illinois	46 195
27	40	Denver city, Colorado	45 526
42	41	Omaha city, Nebraska	45 115
40	42	Atlanta city, Georgia	44 771
22	43	Nashville-Davidson, Tennessee	44 630
49	44	Wichita city, Kansas	44 477
67	45	St. Paul city, Minnesota	44 265
60	46	Corpus Christi city, Texas	44 067
31	47	Oklahoma City city, Oklahoma	43 744
37	48	Kansas City city, Missouri	43 587
4	49	Houston city, Texas	43 349
74	50	Fort Wayne city, Indiana	43 069
7	51	San Antonio city, Texas	42 656
15	52	Columbus city, Ohio	42 368
55	53	Tampa city, Florida	42 359
17	54	Louisville/Jefferson County, Kentucky	42 174
34	55	Fresno city, California	41 698
11	56	Indianapolis city, Indiana	41 170
9	57	Dallas city, Texas	41 011
69	58	Greensboro city, North Carolina	40 760
23	59	Baltimore city, Maryland	39 113
46	60	Tulsa city, Oklahoma	39 021
20	61	El Paso city, Texas	37 836
59	62	Pittsburgh city, Pennsylvania	36 723
52	63	New Orleans city, Louisiana	36 208
21	64	Memphis city, Tennessee	36 142
33	65	Tucson city, Arizona	36 065
5	66	Philadelphia city, Pennsylvania	35 952
28	67	Milwaukee city, Wisconsin	34 944
68	68	Newark city, New Jersey	34 816
58	69	St. Louis city, Missouri	33 657
62	70	Cincinnati city, Ohio	33 425
66	71	Toledo city, Ohio	32 251
70	72	Buffalo city, New York	29 714
44	73	Miami city, Florida	28 506
19	74	Detroit city, Michigan	27 050
45	75	Cleveland city, Ohio	26 137

Median value of owner-occupied housing units, 2008–2010

Population rank	Median value rank	City	Median value (dollars) [col 52]
13	1	San Francisco city, California	773 600
10	2	San Jose city, California	598 600
53	3	Urban Honolulu CDP, Hawaii	544 300
1	4	New York city, New York	518 400
2	5	Los Angeles city, California	493 200
47	6	Oakland city, California	475 700
8	7	San Diego city, California	464 400
36	8	Long Beach city, California	464 100
25	9	Seattle city, Washington	456 600
26	10	Washington city, District of Columbia	446 300
54	11	Anaheim city, California	438 200
24	12	Boston city, Massachusetts	378 800
57	13	Santa Ana city, California	356 300
75	14	Jersey City city, New Jersey	354 900
29	15	Portland city, Oregon	297 700
68	16	Newark city, New Jersey	281 600
39	17	Virginia Beach city, Virginia	280 700
61	18	Riverside city, California	277 800
64	19	Anchorage municipality, Alaska	273 200
73	20	Henderson city, Nevada	267 400
35	21	Sacramento city, California	265 500
3	22	Chicago city, Illinois	264 200
44	23	Miami city, Florida	260 400
27	24	Denver city, Colorado	245 500
40	25	Atlanta city, Georgia	236 600
48	26	Minneapolis city, Minnesota	226 500
34	27	Fresno city, California	220 100
71	28	Plano city, Texas	216 700
41	29	Colorado Springs city, Colorado	216 000
30	30	Las Vegas city, Nevada	214 100
14	31	Austin city, Texas	214 000
43	32	Raleigh city, North Carolina	213 800
51	33	Bakersfield city, California	206 600
65	34	Stockton city, California	204 700
67	35	St. Paul city, Minnesota	199 400
6	36	Phoenix city, Arizona	197 000
32	37	Albuquerque city, New Mexico	195 000
55	38	Tampa city, Florida	191 200
52	39	New Orleans city, Louisiana	183 100
56	40	Aurora city, Colorado	182 200
38	41	Mesa city, Arizona	180 000
18	42	Charlotte city, North Carolina	179 100
12	43	Jacksonville city, Florida	168 800
22	43	Nashville-Davidson, Tennessee	168 800
23	45	Baltimore city, Maryland	167 500
33	46	Tucson city, Arizona	164 100
63	47	Lexington-Fayette urban cnty, Kentucky	159 300
69	48	Greensboro city, North Carolina	147 000
5	49	Philadelphia city, Pennsylvania	142 100
72	49	Lincoln city, Nebraska	142 100
17	51	Louisville/Jefferson County, Kentucky	139 800
28	52	Milwaukee city, Wisconsin	139 500
15	53	Columbus city, Ohio	139 200
37	54	Kansas City city, Missouri	137 500
42	55	Omaha city, Nebraska	134 200
50	56	Arlington city, Texas	132 700
62	57	Cincinnati city, Ohio	131 300
9	58	Dallas city, Texas	130 800
31	59	Oklahoma City city, Oklahoma	128 300
4	60	Houston city, Texas	126 700
16	61	Fort Worth city, Texas	123 200
58	62	St. Louis city, Missouri	122 900
46	63	Tulsa city, Oklahoma	122 200
11	64	Indianapolis city, Indiana	121 400
49	65	Wichita city, Kansas	115 600
20	66	El Paso city, Texas	114 800
7	67	San Antonio city, Texas	114 000
60	68	Corpus Christi city, Texas	113 300
74	69	Fort Wayne city, Indiana	101 000
21	70	Memphis city, Tennessee	99 400
66	71	Toledo city, Ohio	93 800
59	72	Pittsburgh city, Pennsylvania	89 000
45	73	Cleveland city, Ohio	84 300
19	74	Detroit city, Michigan	68 900
70	75	Buffalo city, New York	66 600

Median gross rent of renter-occupied housing units, 2008–2010

Population rank	Median rent rank	City	Median rent (dollars) [col 56]
10	1	San Jose city, California	1 364
13	2	San Francisco city, California	1 363
54	3	Anaheim city, California	1 275
8	4	San Diego city, California	1 262
57	5	Santa Ana city, California	1 256
24	6	Boston city, Massachusetts	1 212
73	7	Henderson city, Nevada	1 177
39	8	Virginia Beach city, Virginia	1 176
53	9	Urban Honolulu CDP, Hawaii	1 171
75	10	Jersey City city, New Jersey	1 116
26	11	Washington city, District of Columbia	1 112
2	12	Los Angeles city, California	1 104
61	13	Riverside city, California	1 103
1	14	New York city, New York	1 098
36	15	Long Beach city, California	1 057
64	16	Anchorage municipality, Alaska	1 017
47	17	Oakland city, California	1 016
30	18	Las Vegas city, Nevada	1 005
25	19	Seattle city, Washington	988
71	20	Plano city, Texas	976
35	21	Sacramento city, California	962
65	22	Stockton city, California	925
68	23	Newark city, New Jersey	921
51	24	Bakersfield city, California	908
14	25	Austin city, Texas	900
52	25	New Orleans city, Louisiana	900
3	27	Chicago city, Illinois	894
40	28	Atlanta city, Georgia	887
55	29	Tampa city, Florida	886
12	30	Jacksonville city, Florida	881
44	31	Miami city, Florida	879
23	32	Baltimore city, Maryland	875
56	33	Aurora city, Colorado	865
6	34	Phoenix city, Arizona	851
38	35	Mesa city, Arizona	846
43	36	Raleigh city, North Carolina	840
29	37	Portland city, Oregon	835
34	38	Fresno city, California	831
18	39	Charlotte city, North Carolina	825
5	40	Philadelphia city, Pennsylvania	824
27	41	Denver city, Colorado	816
50	42	Arlington city, Texas	815
60	43	Corpus Christi city, Texas	813
16	44	Fort Worth city, Texas	805
4	45	Houston city, Texas	797
9	46	Dallas city, Texas	790
48	47	Minneapolis city, Minnesota	784
22	48	Nashville-Davidson, Tennessee	778
41	49	Colorado Springs city, Colorado	776
21	50	Memphis city, Tennessee	765
7	51	San Antonio city, Texas	759
15	51	Columbus city, Ohio	759
19	53	Detroit city, Michigan	748
28	54	Milwaukee city, Wisconsin	744
67	55	St. Paul city, Minnesota	742
37	56	Kansas City city, Missouri	727
11	57	Indianapolis city, Indiana	720
32	57	Albuquerque city, New Mexico	720
59	57	Pittsburgh city, Pennsylvania	720
42	60	Omaha city, Nebraska	712
63	61	Lexington-Fayette urban cnty, Kentucky	706
69	62	Greensboro city, North Carolina	705
33	63	Tucson city, Arizona	696
46	64	Tulsa city, Oklahoma	683
31	65	Oklahoma City city, Oklahoma	675
58	66	St. Louis city, Missouri	672
72	67	Lincoln city, Nebraska	669
70	68	Buffalo city, New York	650
17	69	Louisville/Jefferson County, Kentucky	649
20	70	El Paso city, Texas	642
49	71	Wichita city, Kansas	633
45	72	Cleveland city, Ohio	628
74	73	Fort Wayne city, Indiana	619
66	74	Toledo city, Ohio	607
62	75	Cincinnati city, Ohio	605

75 Largest Cities by 2010 Population
Selected Rankings

Percent of population below the poverty level, 2008–2010				Unemployment rate, 2010				Percent change in civilian labor force, 2009–2010			
Population rank	Poverty rate rank	City	Poverty rate [col 46]	Population rank	Unemployment rate rank	City	Unemployment rate [col 64]	Population rank	Percent change rank	City	Percent change [col 62]
19	1	Detroit city, Michigan	31.2	19	1	Detroit city, Michigan	23.1	43	1	Raleigh city, North Carolina	11.7
45	2	Cleveland city, Ohio	28.5	65	2	Stockton city, California	20.7	40	2	Atlanta city, Georgia	11.4
70	3	Buffalo city, New York	26.9	47	3	Oakland city, California	16.9	30	3	Las Vegas city, Nevada	11.1
68	4	Newark city, New Jersey	24.1	34	4	Fresno city, California	15.8	59	3	Pittsburgh city, Pennsylvania	11.1
62	5	Cincinnati city, Ohio	23.1	68	5	Newark city, New Jersey	15.4	48	5	Minneapolis city, Minnesota	11.0
44	6	Miami city, Florida	22.9	57	6	Santa Ana city, California	14.9	35	6	Sacramento city, California	10.6
28	7	Milwaukee city, Wisconsin	22.7	35	7	Sacramento city, California	14.8	27	7	Denver city, Colorado	10.5
34	8	Fresno city, California	21.0	30	8	Las Vegas city, Nevada	14.6	38	7	Mesa city, Arizona	10.5
58	8	St. Louis city, Missouri	21.0	61	8	Riverside city, California	14.6	56	9	Aurora city, Colorado	10.3
21	10	Memphis city, Tennessee	20.8	2	10	Los Angeles city, California	13.9	24	10	Boston city, Massachusetts	9.9
52	11	New Orleans city, Louisiana	20.6	36	11	Long Beach city, California	13.8	41	10	Colorado Springs city, Colorado	9.9
66	11	Toledo city, Ohio	20.6	44	12	Miami city, Florida	13.7	52	12	New Orleans city, Louisiana	9.8
5	13	Philadelphia city, Pennsylvania	20.4	73	13	Henderson city, Nevada	13.1	14	13	Austin city, Texas	9.6
40	14	Atlanta city, Georgia	20.0	58	14	St. Louis city, Missouri	12.8	25	14	Seattle city, Washington	9.5
9	15	Dallas city, Texas	19.6	40	15	Atlanta city, Georgia	12.7	55	15	Tampa city, Florida	9.4
20	16	El Paso city, Texas	19.4	10	16	San Jose city, California	12.2	61	15	Riverside city, California	9.4
65	17	Stockton city, California	18.2	55	16	Tampa city, Florida	12.2	62	15	Cincinnati city, Ohio	9.4
4	18	Houston city, Texas	17.9	54	18	Anaheim city, California	12.1	73	15	Henderson city, Nevada	9.4
23	19	Baltimore city, Maryland	17.8	66	18	Toledo city, Ohio	12.1	58	19	St. Louis city, Missouri	9.2
3	20	Chicago city, Illinois	17.7	23	20	Baltimore city, Maryland	11.9	50	20	Arlington city, Texas	9.1
67	21	St. Paul city, Minnesota	17.4	28	20	Milwaukee city, Wisconsin	11.9	67	20	St. Paul city, Minnesota	9.1
15	22	Columbus city, Ohio	16.9	3	22	Chicago city, Illinois	11.7	39	22	Virginia Beach city, Virginia	8.9
33	22	Tucson city, Arizona	16.9	45	23	Cleveland city, Ohio	11.5	16	23	Fort Worth city, Texas	8.8
57	24	Santa Ana city, California	16.8	75	24	Jersey City city, New Jersey	11.4	33	24	Tucson city, Arizona	8.7
2	25	Los Angeles city, California	16.6	21	25	Memphis city, Tennessee	11.3	63	24	Lexington-Fayette urban cnty, Kentucky	8.7
1	26	New York city, New York	16.4	6	26	Phoenix city, Arizona	11.2	29	26	Portland city, Oregon	8.5
47	27	Oakland city, California	16.1	12	26	Jacksonville city, Florida	11.2	31	26	Oklahoma City city, Oklahoma	8.5
6	28	Phoenix city, Arizona	15.8	51	26	Bakersfield city, California	11.2	72	26	Lincoln city, Nebraska	8.5
48	28	Minneapolis city, Minnesota	15.8	74	29	Fort Wayne city, Indiana	11.1	15	29	Columbus city, Ohio	8.4
55	28	Tampa city, Florida	15.8	5	30	Philadelphia city, Pennsylvania	10.8	36	29	Long Beach city, California	8.4
7	31	San Antonio city, Texas	15.4	56	30	Aurora city, Colorado	10.8	54	29	Anaheim city, California	8.4
36	31	Long Beach city, California	15.4	70	30	Buffalo city, New York	10.8	37	32	Kansas City city, Missouri	8.2
24	33	Boston city, Massachusetts	15.1	8	33	San Diego city, California	10.5	64	32	Anchorage municipality, Alaska	8.2
27	33	Denver city, Colorado	15.1	17	34	Louisville/Jefferson County, Kentucky	10.4	26	34	Washington city, District of Columbia	8.1
59	33	Pittsburgh city, Pennsylvania	15.1	33	34	Tucson city, Arizona	10.4	46	35	Tulsa city, Oklahoma	7.8
11	36	Indianapolis city, Indiana	15.0	62	34	Cincinnati city, Ohio	10.4	8	36	San Diego city, California	7.7
22	37	Nashville-Davidson, Tennessee	14.5	37	37	Kansas City city, Missouri	10.3	71	36	Plano city, Texas	7.7
46	37	Tulsa city, Oklahoma	14.5	69	37	Greensboro city, North Carolina	10.3	6	38	Phoenix city, Arizona	7.5
60	37	Corpus Christi city, Texas	14.5	26	39	Washington city, District of Columbia	10.1	69	38	Greensboro city, North Carolina	7.5
75	40	Jersey City city, New Jersey	14.4	11	40	Indianapolis city, Indiana	10.0	18	40	Charlotte city, North Carolina	7.4
26	41	Washington city, District of Columbia	14.3	27	41	Denver city, Colorado	9.9	22	40	Nashville-Davidson, Tennessee	7.4
16	42	Fort Worth city, Texas	14.1	18	42	Charlotte city, North Carolina	9.7	51	40	Bakersfield city, California	7.4
17	42	Louisville/Jefferson County, Kentucky	14.1	29	42	Portland city, Oregon	9.7	9	43	Dallas city, Texas	7.3
51	42	Bakersfield city, California	14.1	49	42	Wichita city, Kansas	9.7	47	44	Oakland city, California	7.0
35	45	Sacramento city, California	13.9	13	45	San Francisco city, California	9.6	57	45	Santa Ana city, California	6.9
14	46	Austin city, Texas	13.5	1	46	New York city, New York	9.5	42	46	Omaha city, Nebraska	6.8
37	46	Kansas City city, Missouri	13.5	41	46	Colorado Springs city, Colorado	9.5	60	47	Corpus Christi city, Texas	6.7
31	48	Oklahoma City city, Oklahoma	13.4	20	48	El Paso city, Texas	9.0	32	48	Albuquerque city, New Mexico	6.5
56	48	Aurora city, Colorado	13.4	9	49	Dallas city, Texas	8.9	45	48	Cleveland city, Ohio	6.5
69	50	Greensboro city, North Carolina	12.9	22	49	Nashville-Davidson, Tennessee	8.9	44	50	Miami city, Florida	6.4
32	51	Albuquerque city, New Mexico	12.2	38	49	Mesa city, Arizona	8.9	65	50	Stockton city, California	6.4
49	52	Wichita city, Kansas	12.1	52	49	New Orleans city, Louisiana	8.9	53	52	Urban Honolulu CDP, Hawaii	6.3
63	52	Lexington-Fayette urban cnty, Kentucky	12.1	15	53	Columbus city, Ohio	8.6	4	53	Houston city, Texas	6.1
74	52	Fort Wayne city, Indiana	12.1	4	54	Houston city, Texas	8.5	23	53	Baltimore city, Maryland	6.1
54	55	Anaheim city, California	11.9	25	55	Seattle city, Washington	8.4	12	55	Jacksonville city, Florida	6.0
43	56	Raleigh city, North Carolina	11.8	16	56	Fort Worth city, Texas	8.3	70	55	Buffalo city, New York	6.0
29	57	Portland city, Oregon	11.6	59	57	Pittsburgh city, Pennsylvania	8.2	11	57	Indianapolis city, Indiana	5.7
50	58	Arlington city, Texas	11.3	24	58	Boston city, Massachusetts	8.0	66	57	Toledo city, Ohio	5.7
12	59	Jacksonville city, Florida	11.2	50	58	Arlington city, Texas	8.0	13	59	San Francisco city, California	5.6
18	60	Charlotte city, North Carolina	11.1	63	58	Lexington-Fayette urban cnty, Kentucky	8.0	49	59	Wichita city, Kansas	5.6
42	61	Omaha city, Nebraska	11.0	43	61	Raleigh city, North Carolina	7.8	75	59	Jersey City city, New Jersey	5.6
30	62	Las Vegas city, Nevada	10.7	67	62	St. Paul city, Minnesota	7.7	7	62	San Antonio city, Texas	5.4
61	63	Riverside city, California	10.6	32	63	Albuquerque city, New Mexico	7.6	28	63	Milwaukee city, Wisconsin	5.3
8	64	San Diego city, California	10.3	7	64	San Antonio city, Texas	7.3	10	64	San Jose city, California	5.1
41	65	Colorado Springs city, Colorado	9.8	46	64	Tulsa city, Oklahoma	7.3	17	64	Louisville/Jefferson County, Kentucky	5.1
38	66	Mesa city, Arizona	9.6	60	66	Corpus Christi city, Texas	7.2	34	64	Fresno city, California	5.1
72	67	Lincoln city, Nebraska	8.9	71	66	Plano city, Texas	7.2	74	67	Fort Wayne city, Indiana	5.0
10	68	San Jose city, California	8.2	48	68	Minneapolis city, Minnesota	7.0	21	68	Memphis city, Tennessee	4.8
53	69	Urban Honolulu CDP, Hawaii	7.5	64	69	Anchorage municipality, Alaska	6.8	68	69	Newark city, New Jersey	4.7
13	70	San Francisco city, California	7.4	14	70	Austin city, Texas	6.5	20	70	El Paso city, Texas	4.5
25	71	Seattle city, Washington	6.1	31	71	Oklahoma City city, Oklahoma	6.4	2	71	Los Angeles city, California	4.4
71	72	Plano city, Texas	5.8	39	72	Virginia Beach city, Virginia	6.3	3	72	Chicago city, Illinois	3.8
64	73	Anchorage municipality, Alaska	5.4	42	73	Omaha city, Nebraska	5.3	5	73	Philadelphia city, Pennsylvania	3.7
73	74	Henderson city, Nevada	5.3	72	74	Lincoln city, Nebraska	4.1	19	73	Detroit city, Michigan	3.7
39	75	Virginia Beach city, Virginia	4.9	53		Urban Honolulu CDP, Hawaii	NA	1	75	New York city, New York	2.1

75 Largest Cities by 2010 Population
Selected Rankings

	Per capita local government taxes, 2007				Per capita city government debt outstanding, 2007				Violent crime rate, 2010 (violent crimes known to police)		
Population rank	Local taxes rank	City	Local per capita taxes (dollars) [col 121]	Population rank	Debt rank	City	Debt per capita (dollars) [col 138]	Population rank	Violent crime rate rank	City	Violent crimes (per 100,000 population) [col 37]
26	1	Washington city, District of Columbiaa...	8 826	26	1	Washington city, District of Columbia.....	14 497	19	1	Detroit city, Michigan	2 378
1	2	New York city, New York	4 611	40	2	Atlanta city, Georgia	13 604	58	2	St. Louis city, Missouri	1 943
13	3	San Francisco city, California	3 154	12	3	Jacksonville city, Florida	13 560	21	3	Memphis city, Tennessee	1 608
24	4	Boston city, Massachusetts	2 168	13	4	San Francisco city, California	11 380	47	4	Oakland city, California	1 604
5	5	Philadelphia city, Pennsylvania	1 971	1	5	New York city, New York	10 961	23	5	Baltimore city, Maryland	1 500
22	6	Nashville-Davidson, Tennessee	1 966	27	6	Denver city, Colorado	8 576	45	6	Cleveland city, Ohio	1 393
39	7	Virginia Beach city, Virginia	1 941	19	7	Detroit city, Michigan	8 410	65	7	Stockton city, California	1 383
23	8	Baltimore city, Maryland	1 680	52	8	New Orleans city, Louisiana	8 088	70	8	Buffalo city, New York	1 377
64	9	Anchorage municipality, Alaska	1 677	48	9	Minneapolis city, Minnesota	7 883	40	9	Atlanta city, Georgia	1 369
52	10	New Orleans city, Louisiana	1 636	9	10	Dallas city, Texas	7 136	26	10	Washington city, District of Columbia.....	1 241
37	11	Kansas City city, Missouri	1 493	47	11	Oakland city, California	7 000	37	11	Kansas City city, Missouri	1 227
47	12	Oakland city, California	1 466	22	12	Nashville-Davidson, Tennessee	6 531	44	12	Miami city, Florida	1 221
27	13	Denver city, Colorado	1 454	14	13	Austin city, Texas	6 251	62	13	Cincinnati city, Ohio	1 217
25	14	Seattle city, Washington	1 287	45	14	Cleveland city, Ohio	5 976	5	14	Philadelphia city, Pennsylvania	1 215
58	14	St. Louis city, Missouri	1 287	64	15	Anchorage municipality, Alaska	5 936	11	15	Indianapolis city, Indiana	1 160
62	16	Cincinnati city, Ohio	1 275	25	16	Seattle city, Washington	5 869	22	16	Nashville-Davidson, Tennessee	1 124
11	17	Indianapolis city, Indiana	1 170	3	17	Chicago city, Illinois	5 693	46	17	Tulsa city, Oklahoma	1 098
59	18	Pittsburgh city, Pennsylvania	1 064	11	18	Indianapolis city, Indiana	5 681	4	18	Houston city, Texas	1 071
48	19	Minneapolis city, Minnesota	1 009	4	19	Houston city, Texas	5 510	28	19	Milwaukee city, Wisconsin	1 065
2	20	Los Angeles city, California	1 008	37	20	Kansas City city, Missouri	5 478	48	20	Minneapolis city, Minnesota	1 062
8	21	San Diego city, California	981	41	21	Colorado Springs city, Colorado	5 325	3	21	Chicago city, Illinois	1 054
45	22	Cleveland city, Ohio	968	50	22	Arlington city, Texas	5 239	68	22	Newark city, New Jersey	1 041
19	23	Detroit city, Michigan	948	54	23	Anaheim city, California	5 128	66	23	Toledo city, Ohio	994
21	24	Memphis city, Tennessee	930	18	24	Charlotte city, North Carolina	5 110	24	24	Boston city, Massachusetts	942
12	25	Jacksonville city, Florida	925	7	25	San Antonio city, Texas	4 825	31	25	Oklahoma City city, Oklahoma	914
63	26	Lexington-Fayette urban cnty, Kentucky....	911	10	26	San Jose city, California	4 747	59	26	Pittsburgh city, Pennsylvania	913
35	27	Sacramento city, California	887	58	27	St. Louis city, Missouri	4 715	35	27	Sacramento city, California	881
31	28	Oklahoma City city, Oklahoma	876	5	28	Philadelphia city, Pennsylvania	4 683	30	28	Las Vegas city, Nevada	875
68	29	Newark city, New Jersey	866	29	29	Portland city, Oregon	4 674	64	29	Anchorage municipality, Alaska	833
10	30	San Jose city, California	856	6	30	Phoenix city, Arizona	4 563	49	30	Wichita city, Kansas	795
55	31	Tampa city, Florida	851	55	31	Tampa city, Florida	4 553	32	31	Albuquerque city, New Mexico	786
44	32	Miami city, Florida	844	36	32	Long Beach city, California	4 494	9	32	Dallas city, Texas	765
54	33	Anaheim city, California	828	21	33	Memphis city, Tennessee	4 380	52	33	New Orleans city, Louisiana	754
29	34	Portland city, Oregon	820	61	34	Riverside city, California	4 368	67	34	St. Paul city, Minnesota	740
40	35	Atlanta city, Georgia	796	2	35	Los Angeles city, California	4 317	75	35	Jersey City city, New Jersey	739
15	36	Columbus city, Ohio	790	23	36	Baltimore city, Maryland	3 839	13	36	San Francisco city, California	714
71	37	Plano city, Texas	781	35	37	Sacramento city, California	3 747	15	37	Columbus city, Ohio	695
61	38	Riverside city, California	769	46	38	Tulsa city, Oklahoma	3 679	60	38	Corpus Christi city, Texas	678
9	39	Dallas city, Texas	757	72	39	Lincoln city, Nebraska	3 649	12	39	Jacksonville city, Florida	664
4	40	Houston city, Texas	728	59	40	Pittsburgh city, Pennsylvania	3 263	55	40	Tampa city, Florida	646
36	41	Long Beach city, California	720	67	41	St. Paul city, Minnesota	3 154	33	41	Tucson city, Arizona	640
3	42	Chicago city, Illinois	719	39	42	Virginia Beach city, Virginia	3 128	7	42	San Antonio city, Texas	635
16	42	Fort Worth city, Texas	719	60	43	Corpus Christi city, Texas	3 047	18	43	Charlotte city, North Carolina	627
56	44	Aurora city, Colorado	703	75	44	Jersey City city, New Jersey	2 955	34	44	Fresno city, California	613
66	45	Toledo city, Ohio	698	56	45	Aurora city, Colorado	2 852	51	45	Bakersfield city, California	605
65	46	Stockton city, California	691	63	46	Lexington-Fayette urban cnty, Kentucky....	2 739	1	46	New York city, New York	593
6	47	Phoenix city, Arizona	687	43	47	Raleigh city, North Carolina	2 596	36	47	Long Beach city, California	588
75	48	Jersey City city, New Jersey	684	38	48	Mesa city, Arizona	2 522	63	48	Lexington-Fayette urban cnty, Kentucky....	583
46	49	Tulsa city, Oklahoma	681	8	49	San Diego city, California	2 450	16	49	Fort Worth city, Texas	580
32	50	Albuquerque city, New Mexico	680	15	50	Columbus city, Ohio	2 445	25	50	Seattle city, Washington	577
42	51	Omaha city, Nebraska	660	70	51	Buffalo city, New York	2 443	2	51	Los Angeles city, California	566
14	52	Austin city, Texas	634	65	52	Stockton city, California	2 424	17	52	Louisville/Jefferson County, Kentucky..	565
57	53	Santa Ana city, California	624	24	53	Boston city, Massachusetts	2 404	27	53	Denver city, Colorado	564
18	54	Charlotte city, North Carolina	614	49	54	Wichita city, Kansas	2 268	69	54	Greensboro city, North Carolina	561
50	55	Arlington city, Texas	604	62	55	Cincinnati city, Ohio	2 181	42	55	Omaha city, Nebraska	556
69	56	Greensboro city, North Carolina	601	33	56	Tucson city, Arizona	2 162	6	56	Phoenix city, Arizona	553
70	57	Buffalo city, New York	600	28	57	Milwaukee city, Wisconsin	2 101	50	57	Arlington city, Texas	527
73	58	Henderson city, Nevada	593	34	58	Fresno city, California	2 000	29	58	Portland city, Oregon	523
60	59	Corpus Christi city, Texas	569	31	59	Oklahoma City city, Oklahoma	1 980	72	59	Lincoln city, Nebraska	487
72	60	Lincoln city, Nebraska	566	42	60	Omaha city, Nebraska	1 941	14	60	Austin city, Texas	480
41	61	Colorado Springs city, Colorado	558	32	61	Albuquerque city, New Mexico	1 837	61	61	Riverside city, California	477
34	62	Fresno city, California	553	20	62	El Paso city, Texas	1 812	41	62	Colorado Springs city, Colorado	471
51	63	Bakersfield city, California	522	69	63	Greensboro city, North Carolina	1 804	57	63	Santa Ana city, California	465
33	64	Tucson city, Arizona	514	16	64	Fort Worth city, Texas	1 735	56	64	Aurora city, Colorado	446
20	65	El Paso city, Texas	490	68	65	Newark city, New Jersey	1 677	20	65	El Paso city, Texas	441
74	65	Fort Wayne city, Indiana	490	73	66	Henderson city, Nevada	1 622	43	66	Raleigh city, North Carolina	431
43	67	Raleigh city, North Carolina	473	44	67	Miami city, Florida	1 328	8	67	San Diego city, California	430
7	68	San Antonio city, Texas	461	57	68	Santa Ana city, California	1 243	38	68	Mesa city, Arizona	408
67	69	St. Paul city, Minnesota	457	71	69	Plano city, Texas	1 221	54	69	Anaheim city, California	345
49	70	Wichita city, Kansas	451	66	70	Toledo city, Ohio	1 219	10	70	San Jose city, California	340
30	71	Las Vegas city, Nevada	450	74	71	Fort Wayne city, Indiana	1 189	74	71	Fort Wayne city, Indiana	294
28	72	Milwaukee city, Wisconsin	410	30	72	Las Vegas city, Nevada	631	73	72	Henderson city, Nevada	211
38	73	Mesa city, Arizona	391	51	73	Bakersfield city, California	382	39	73	Virginia Beach city, Virginia	190
17	NA	Louisville/Jefferson County, Kentucky..	NA	17	NA	Louisville/Jefferson County, Kentucky..	NA	71	74	Plano city, Texas	186
53	NA	Urban Honolulu CDP, Hawaii	NA	53	NA	Urban Honolulu CDP, Hawaii	NA	53	NA	Urban Honolulu CDP, Hawaii	NA

All Cities
Selected Rankings

Defense procurement contracts for all cities, 2009–2010				Non-defense procurement contracts for all cities, 2009–2010				Federal grants, 2009–2010			
Population rank	Defense contract rank	City	Defense contracts (millions of dollars) [col 108]	Population rank	Non-defense contract rank	City	Non-defense contracts (millions of dollars) [col 109]	Population rank	Grants rank	City	Grants (millions of dollars) [col 110]
16	1	Fort Worth city, Texas	7 742.9	26	1	Washington city, District of Columbia	16 598.9	1	1	New York city, New York	34 534.2
498	2	Oshkosh city, Wisconsin	7 026.8	4	2	Houston city, Texas	4 174.0	26	2	Washington city, District of Columbia	10 872.0
33	3	Tucson city, Arizona	5 200.9	1 224	3	Oak Ridge city, Tennessee	3 380.3	35	3	Sacramento city, California	9 252.3
8	4	San Diego city, California	4 772.4	746	4	Richland city, Washington	3 100.3	14	4	Austin city, Texas	7 296.9
127	5	Huntsville city, Alabama	4 741.0	32	5	Albuquerque city, New Mexico	2 752.9	24	5	Boston city, Massachusetts	6 428.2
26	6	Washington city, District of Columbia	4 651.0	1 214	6	Aiken city, South Carolina	2 319.8	714	6	Harrisburg city, Pennsylvania	4 756.8
174	7	Sunnyvale city, California	3 983.8	1	7	New York city, New York	2 225.2	124	7	Tallahassee city, Florida	4 447.5
36	8	Long Beach city, California	3 814.0	547	8	Rockville city, Maryland	2 072.2	286	8	Albany city, New York	4 416.7
612	9	Marietta city, Georgia	3 485.4	40	9	Atlanta city, Georgia	1 859.6	3	9	Chicago city, Illinois	4 225.5
79	10	Orlando city, Florida	3 058.4	379	10	Livermore city, California	1 571.9	40	10	Atlanta city, Georgia	4 102.9
58	11	St. Louis city, Missouri	3 022.3	328	11	Santa Monica city, California	1 456.1	23	11	Baltimore city, Maryland	4 036.3
126	12	Newport News city, Virginia	3 012.1	606	12	Idaho Falls city, Idaho	1 344.4	15	12	Columbus city, Ohio	3 619.3
513	13	Rancho Cordova city, California	2 999.6	37	13	Kansas City city, Missouri	1 268.1	2	13	Los Angeles city, California	3 310.9
7	14	San Antonio city, Texas	2 791.9	8	14	San Diego city, California	897.1	25	14	Seattle city, Washington	3 027.0
119	15	Amarillo city, Texas	2 394.6	5	15	Philadelphia city, Pennsylvania	882.3	5	15	Philadelphia city, Pennsylvania	2 976.3
52	16	New Orleans city, Louisiana	2 386.5	229	16	Berkeley city, California	795.6	43	16	Raleigh city, North Carolina	2 880.8
131	17	Grand Prairie city, Texas	2 252.0	3	17	Chicago city, Illinois	726.4	225	17	Lansing city, Michigan	2 770.2
188	18	Sterling Heights city, Michigan	2 108.9	175	18	Alexandria city, Virginia	721.1	82	18	Madison city, Wisconsin	2 762.3
78	19	Norfolk city, Virginia	2 099.7	13	19	San Francisco city, California	706.1	13	19	San Francisco city, California	2 739.5
39	20	Virginia Beach city, Virginia	1 962.6	30	20	Las Vegas city, Nevada	696.6	8	20	San Diego city, California	2 736.8
41	21	Colorado Springs city, Colorado	1 892.4	23	21	Baltimore city, Maryland	688.6	85	21	Baton Rouge city, Louisiana	2 574.9
6	22	Phoenix city, Arizona	1 873.8	24	22	Boston city, Massachusetts	614.8	22	22	Nashville-Davidson, Tennessee	2 476.4
62	23	Cincinnati city, Ohio	1 784.8	810	23	Coeur d'Alene city, Idaho	602.7	11	23	Indianapolis city, Indiana	2 170.3
98	24	Rochester city, New York	1 754.9	27	24	Denver city, Colorado	566.3	4	24	Houston city, Texas	2 135.2
839	25	Leesburg town, Virginia	1 640.9	566	25	Gaithersburg city, Maryland	548.3	221	25	Springfield city, Illinois	2 100.1
4	26	Houston city, Texas	1 530.1	119	26	Amarillo city, Texas	537.6	6	26	Phoenix city, Arizona	2 074.8
21	27	Memphis city, Tennessee	1 513.6	208	27	Charleston city, South Carolina	505.0	104	27	Richmond city, Virginia	2 033.0
311	28	Kent city, Washington	1 475.2	21	28	Memphis city, Tennessee	495.9	353	28	Trenton city, New Jersey	1 913.7
626	29	Taunton city, Massachusetts	1 386.7	1 018	29	Leavenworth city, Kansas	487.8	27	29	Denver city, Colorado	1 880.5
322	30	Lynn city, Massachusetts	1 384.5	137	30	Chattanooga city, Tennessee	483.1	58	30	St. Louis city, Missouri	1 828.5
1 398	31	Greenville city, Texas	1 345.3	25	31	Seattle city, Washington	482.7	775	31	Olympia city, Washington	1 715.6
11	32	Indianapolis city, Indiana	1 289.4	52	32	New Orleans city, Louisiana	481.2	59	32	Pittsburgh city, Pennsylvania	1 697.2
753	33	Poway city, California	1 275.1	79	33	Orlando city, Florida	472.0	123	33	Salt Lake City city, Utah	1 688.1
820	34	York city, Pennsylvania	1 207.2	1 376	34	Batavia city, Illinois	440.2	29	34	Portland city, Oregon	1 443.6
38	35	Mesa city, Arizona	1 145.0	22	35	Nashville-Davidson, Tennessee	438.7	256	35	Cambridge city, Massachusetts	1 398.8
855	36	Littleton city, Colorado	1 138.3	290	36	Boulder city, Colorado	436.4	226	36	Ann Arbor city, Michigan	1 384.4
731	37	West Sacramento city, California	1 131.2	256	37	Cambridge city, Massachusetts	435.6	86	37	Durham city, North Carolina	1 372.5
194	38	Cedar Rapids city, Iowa	1 097.7	238	38	Murfreesboro city, Tennessee	429.3	828	38	Jefferson City city, Missouri	1 371.9
25	39	Seattle city, Washington	1 044.2	19	39	Detroit city, Michigan	428.2	31	39	Oklahoma City city, Oklahoma	1 360.0
419	40	Melbourne city, Florida	1 040.8	9	40	Dallas city, Texas	425.0	116	40	Little Rock city, Arkansas	1 319.0
55	41	Tampa city, Florida	998.2	14	41	Austin city, Texas	418.7	105	41	Des Moines city, Iowa	1 314.5
49	42	Wichita city, Kansas	988.4	29	42	Portland city, Oregon	408.9	67	42	St. Paul city, Minnesota	1 309.5
956	43	Hurst city, Texas	976.0	1 121	43	Menlo Park city, California	390.8	149	43	Salem city, Oregon	1 226.4
64	44	Anchorage municipality, Alaska	963.9	127	44	Huntsville city, Alabama	384.8	133	44	Jackson city, Mississippi	1 183.5
1 123	45	Deer Park city, Texas	952.9	6	45	Phoenix city, Arizona	378.1	48	45	Minneapolis city, Minnesota	1 161.7
31	46	Oklahoma City city, Oklahoma	921.8	128	46	Knoxville city, Tennessee	372.9	45	46	Cleveland city, Ohio	1 129.0
270	47	South Bend city, Indiana	876.9	7	47	San Antonio city, Texas	366.0	190	47	Columbia city, South Carolina	1 115.1
12	48	Jacksonville city, Florida	845.0	11	48	Indianapolis city, Indiana	356.9	685	48	Charleston city, West Virginia	1 101.6
175	49	Alexandria city, Virginia	834.3	45	49	Cleveland city, Ohio	355.4	102	49	Montgomery city, Alabama	1 069.9
74	50	Fort Wayne city, Indiana	822.0	2	50	Los Angeles city, California	343.7	1 401	50	Frankfort city, Kentucky	1 068.1
185	51	McKinney city, Texas	815.7	55	51	Tampa city, Florida	342.0	68	51	Newark city, New Jersey	1 054.9
490	52	Redondo Beach city, California	815.6	1 207	52	Morgantown city, West Virginia	321.4	44	52	Miami city, Florida	1 039.2
156	53	Palmdale city, California	804.4	62	53	Cincinnati city, Ohio	302.2	9	53	Dallas city, Texas	991.8
218	54	Independence city, Missouri	793.9	515	54	Palo Alto city, California	300.6	187	54	New Haven city, Connecticut	971.6
945	55	Manassas city, Virginia	746.3	48	55	Minneapolis city, Minnesota	296.3	198	55	Hartford city, Connecticut	932.8
40	56	Atlanta city, Georgia	702.4	86	56	Durham city, North Carolina	279.9	601	56	Chapel Hill town, North Carolina	914.9
2	57	Los Angeles city, California	675.7	64	57	Anchorage municipality, Alaska	278.6	129	57	Providence city, Rhode Island	881.9
256	58	Cambridge city, Massachusetts	660.7	507	58	Frederick city, Maryland	275.4	97	58	Birmingham city, Alabama	842.1
932	59	Annapolis city, Maryland	658.8	18	59	Charlotte city, North Carolina	270.5	28	59	Milwaukee city, Wisconsin	819.7
937	60	Woburn city, Massachusetts	654.8	262	60	Richmond city, California	265.9	98	60	Rochester city, New York	797.7
323	61	Sparks city, Nevada	633.3	15	61	Columbus city, Ohio	262.5	52	61	New Orleans city, Louisiana	772.0
1	62	New York city, New York	611.4	31	62	Oklahoma City city, Oklahoma	257.6	7	62	San Antonio city, Texas	738.5
341	63	Nashua city, New Hampshire	583.6	177	63	Hampton city, Virginia	252.2	290	63	Boulder city, Colorado	717.6
92	64	Scottsdale city, Arizona	568.2	97	64	Birmingham city, Alabama	236.4	62	64	Cincinnati city, Ohio	699.6
3	65	Chicago city, Illinois	543.6	194	65	Cedar Rapids city, Iowa	233.2	72	65	Lincoln city, Nebraska	697.7
854	66	Dublin city, Ohio	538.7	419	66	Melbourne city, Florida	231.8	47	66	Oakland city, California	695.2
15	67	Columbus city, Ohio	535.1	63	67	Lexington-Fayette urban cnty, Kentucky	230.9	192	67	Topeka city, Kansas	673.4
123	68	Salt Lake City city, Utah	529.1	59	68	Pittsburgh city, Pennsylvania	225.0	19	68	Detroit city, Michigan	653.1
1 264	69	Monroeville municipality, Pennsylvania	523.5	16	69	Fort Worth city, Texas	221.8	229	69	Berkeley city, California	638.0
714	70	Harrisburg city, Pennsylvania	522.5	42	70	Omaha city, Nebraska	217.4	932	70	Annapolis city, Maryland	608.0
48	71	Minneapolis city, Minnesota	516.9	44	71	Miami city, Florida	216.9	475	71	Santa Fe city, New Mexico	598.5
13	72	San Francisco city, California	508.7	276	72	Round Rock city, Texas	213.9	21	72	Memphis city, Tennessee	587.3
225	73	Lansing city, Michigan	508.2	12	73	Jacksonville city, Florida	213.6	103	73	Boise City city, Idaho	583.7
1 182	74	Clearfield city, Utah	493.4	20	74	El Paso city, Texas	206.7	33	74	Tucson city, Arizona	579.6
177	75	Hampton city, Virginia	482.7	988	75	Lancaster city, Texas	206.2	64	75	Anchorage municipality, Alaska	576.9

Table D. Cities — **Land Area and Population**

STATE Place code	City	Population, 2010				Race alone or in combination, not of Hispanic origin (percent), 2010					Percent Hispanic or Latino[2], 2010	Percent Foreign born, 2008–2010
		Land area,[1] 2010 (sq km)	Total persons	Rank	Per square kilometer	White	Black	American Indian, Alaska Native	Asian	Hawaiian Pacific Islander		
		1	2	3	4	5	6	7	8	9	10	11

1. Dry land or land partially or temporarily covered by water. 2. May be of any race.

Table D. Cities — **Population**

City	Age of population (percent), 2010											Population			
												Census counts		Percent change	
	Under 5 years	5 to 17 years	18 to 24 years	25 to 34 years	35 to 44 years	45 to 54 years	55 to 64 years	65 to 74 years	75 years and over	Median age	Percent female	1990	2000	1990–2000	2000–2010
	12	13	14	15	16	17	18	19	20	21	22	23	24	25	26

Table D. Cities — **Households, Group Quarters, Crime, and Education**

City	Households, 2010				Persons in group quarters, 2010				Serious crimes known to police,[2] 2010				Educational attainment, 2008–2010		
		Percent				Institutional			Total		Rate[3]			Attainment[4] (percent)	
	Number	Persons per household	Female family householder[1]	One-person	Total	Total	Persons in nursing facilities	Non-institutional	Number	Rate[3]	Violent	Property	Population age 25 and older	High school graduate or less	Bachelor's degree or more
	27	28	29	30	31	32	33	34	35	36	37	38	39	40	41

1. No spouse present. 2. Data for serious crimes have not been adjusted for underreporting. This may affect comparability between geographic areas and over time. 3. Per 100,000 population estimated by the FBI. 4. Persons 25 years old and over.

Table D. Cities — **Income, Poverty, and Housing**

City	Money income, 2008–2010					Housing units, 2010			Occupied Housing units 2008–2010				
		Households								Owner-occupied		Median owner costs as a percent of income	
	Per capita income[1] (dollars)	Median income	Percent with income of $200,000 or more	Percent with income of less than $25,000	Families with income below poverty (percent)	Total	Percent change, 2000–2010	Vacant units for sale or rent[2]	Total	Percent	Median value[3] (dollars)	With a mortgage[4]	Without a mortgage[5]
	42	43	44	45	46	47	48	49	50	51	52	53	54

1. Based on population estimated by the American Community Survey. 2. Includes units rented or sold but not occupied. 3. Specified owner-occupied units; $1,000,000 represents $1,000,000 or more. 4. 50.0 represents 50 percent or more. 5. 10.0 represents 10 percent or less.

Table D. Cities — Housing, Labor Force, and Employment

City	Occupied housing units, 2008–2010 (cont.)				Migration, 2008–2010		Civilian labor force, 2010				Civilian employment[4], 2008–2010			
									Unemployment			Percent		
	Percent renter occupied	Median gross rent[1]	Median rent as a percent of income[2]	Percent with no vehicle available	Percent who lived in the same house one year ago	Percent who lived outside this city one year ago	Total	Percent change, 2009–2010	Total	Rate[3]	Population age 16 and older	In labor force	Full-year full-time worker	Households with no workers (percent)
	55	56	57	58	59	60	61	62	63	64	65	66	67	68

1. $2,000 represents $2,000 or more.   2. 50.0 represents 50 percent or more.   3. Percent of civilian labor force.   4. Persons 16 years old and over.

Table D. Cities — Construction, Wholesale Trade, and Retail Trade

City	Value of residential construction authorized by building permits, 2010			Wholesale trade,[1] 2007				Retail trade,[2] 2007			
	New construction ($1,000)	Number of housing units	Percent single family	Number of establish-ments	Number of employees	Sales (mil dol)	Annual payroll (mil dol)	Number of establish-ments	Number of employees	Sales (mil dol)	Annual payroll (mil dol)
	69	70	71	72	73	74	75	76	77	78	79

1. Merchant wholesalers except manufacturers' sales branches and offices.   2. Establishments with payroll.

Table D. Cities — Real Estate, Professional Services, and Manufacturing

City	Real estate and rental and leasing, 2007				Professional, scientific, and technical services,[1] 2007				Manufacturing, 2007			
	Number of establish-ments	Number of employees	Receipts (mil dol)	Annual payroll (mil dol)	Number of establish-ments	Number of employees	Receipts (mil dol)	Annual payroll (mil dol)	Number of establish-ments	Number of employees	Receipts (mil dol)	Annual payroll (mil dol)
	80	81	82	83	84	85	86	87	88	89	90	91

1. Establishments subject to federal tax.

Table D. Cities — Accommodation and Food Services, Arts, Entertainment, and Recreation, and Health Care and Social Assistance

City	Accommodation and food services, 2007				Arts, entertainment, and recreation,[1] 2007				Health care and social assistance,[1] 2007			
	Number of establish-ments	Number of employees	Sales (mil dol)	Annual payroll (mil dol)	Number of establish-ments	Number of employees	Receipts (mil dol)	Annual payroll (mil dol)	Number of establish-ments	Number of employees	Receipts (mil dol)	Annual payroll (mil dol)
	92	93	94	95	96	97	98	99	100	101	102	103

1. Establishments subject to federal tax.

Table D. Cities — Other Services and Federal Funds

| City | Other services[1], 2007 | | | | Selected federal funds, 2009–2010 (mil dol) | | | | | | | | |
| | | | | | Procurement contracts | | Grants | | | | | | |
	Number of establish-ments	Number of employees	Receipts (mil dol)	Annual payroll (mil dol)	Defense	Other	Total[2]	Medicaid and other health related	Nutrition and family welfare	Energy and envi-ronment	Disasters and emergency prepared-ness	Housing and community develop-ment	Employment and training
	104	105	106	107	108	109	110	111	112	113	114	115	116

1. Establishments subject to federal tax.   2. Includes program categories not shown separately. State totals include additional categories not allocated by city.

Table D. Cities — City Government Finances

City	City government finances, 2007									
	General revenue							General expenditure		
	Intergovernmental			Taxes					Per capita[1] (dollars)	
					Per capita[1] (dollars)					
	Total (mil dol)	Total (mil dol)	Percent from state government	Total (mil dol)	Total	Property	Sales and gross receipts	Total (mil dol)	Total	Capital outlays
	117	118	119	120	121	122	123	124	125	126

1. Based on population estimated as of July 1 of the year shown.

Table D. Cities — City Government Finances

City	City government finances, 2007 (cont.)									
	General expenditure (cont.)									
	Percent of total for:									
	Public welfare	Highways	Parking facilities	Education	Health and hospitals	Police protection	Sewerage and sanitation	Parks and recreation	Housing and community development	Interest on debt
	127	128	129	130	131	132	133	134	135	136

Table D. Cities — City Government Finances, City Government Employment, and Climate

City	City government finances, 2007 (cont.)				Climate[2]							
	Debt outstanding				Average daily temperature (degrees Fahrenheit)							
					Mean		Limits					
	Total (mil dol)	Per capita[1] (dollars)	Debt issued during year	City government employment, 2010	January	July	January[3]	July[4]	Annual precipitation (inches)	Heating degree days	Cooling degree days
	137	138	139	140	141	142	143	144	145	146	147

1. Based on the population estimated as of July 1 of the year shown.   2. Represents normal values based on the 30-year period, 1971–2000.   3. Average daily minimum.   4. Average daily maximum.

Table D. Cities — Land Area and Population

STATE Place code	City		Population, 2010			Race alone or in combination, not of Hispanic origin (percent), 2010						
		Land area,[1] 2010 (sq km)	Total persons	Rank	Per square kilometer	White	Black	American Indian, Alaska Native	Asian	Hawaiian Pacific Islander	Percent Hispanic or Latino[2], 2010	Percent Foreign born, 2008–2010
		1	2	3	4	5	6	7	8	9	10	11
00 00000	United States..............	9 147 592.7	308 745 538	X	33.8	65.4	13.0	1.3	5.4	0.3	16.3	12.8
01 00000	ALABAMA	131 170.8	4 779 736	X	36.4	68.2	26.6	1.1	1.4	0.1	3.9	3.5
01 00820	Alabaster	64.9	30 352	1 342	468.0	76.1	14.0	0.7	1.2	0.1	9.0	7.1
01 03076	Auburn..........................	150.4	53 380	712	354.9	74.7	16.9	0.7	5.9	0.1	2.9	7.3
01 05980	Bessemer	103.2	27 456	1 503	266.0	24.2	71.6	0.6	0.3	0.0	4.1	3.0
01 07000	Birmingham..................	378.3	212 237	98	561.0	21.7	73.7	0.5	1.2	0.1	3.6	3.8
01 20104	Decatur.........................	139.0	55 683	675	400.6	64.4	22.5	1.1	1.1	0.1	12.4	9.3
01 21184	Dothan..........................	231.5	65 496	536	282.9	62.9	33.2	0.8	1.4	0.1	2.9	2.8
01 24184	Enterprise.....................	80.9	26 562	1 560	328.3	67.9	21.4	1.2	2.8	0.3	8.8	6.4
01 26896	Florence	67.3	39 319	1 006	584.0	75.2	20.2	0.9	1.6	0.1	3.6	3.5
01 28696	Gadsden.......................	96.3	36 856	1 077	382.9	57.4	37.2	0.7	0.7	0.1	5.4	3.2
01 35800	Homewood	21.7	25 167	1 653	1 161.9	72.9	17.5	0.4	2.7	0.1	7.3	6.2
01 35896	Hoover..........................	122.2	81 619	390	668.2	73.6	15.2	0.5	5.7	0.1	6.0	11.8
01 37000	Huntsville.....................	541.5	180 105	131	332.6	59.8	31.9	1.3	3.0	0.2	5.8	7.0
01 45784	Madison	76.7	42 938	914	560.2	73.3	15.2	1.1	8.0	0.2	4.3	7.7
01 50000	Mobile..........................	360.3	195 111	118	541.5	44.8	51.1	0.7	2.1	0.1	2.4	3.6
01 51000	Montgomery	413.3	205 764	104	497.9	36.9	57.1	0.5	2.6	0.1	3.9	4.5
01 57048	Opelika	154.3	26 477	1 565	171.6	50.0	44.0	0.5	1.9	0.1	4.4	6.0
01 59472	Phenix City	71.9	32 822	1 242	456.6	48.4	47.2	0.8	1.1	0.3	4.0	1.9
01 62328	Prattville......................	85.1	33 960	1 189	399.1	78.3	17.2	0.9	2.0	0.1	3.1	2.5
01 77256	Tuscaloosa...................	156.0	90 468	335	579.9	53.3	41.9	0.5	2.1	0.1	3.0	4.0
01 78552	Vestavia Hills...............	50.3	34 033	1 187	677.0	89.6	4.0	0.4	4.2	0.0	2.5	6.1
02 00000	ALASKA	1 477 953.2	710 231	X	0.5	69.8	4.3	18.8	6.8	1.5	5.5	7.0
02 03000	Anchorage....................	4 415.1	291 826	64	66.1	68.5	7.1	11.5	9.9	2.6	7.6	9.2
02 24230	Fairbanks.....................	82.1	31 535	1 294	384.2	67.7	10.6	13.4	5.0	1.2	9.0	5.7
02 36400	Juneau..........................	6 998.0	31 275	1 304	4.5	74.7	1.7	18.1	8.8	1.3	5.1	6.0
04 00000	ARIZONA	294 207.3	6 392 017	X	21.7	59.4	4.4	4.6	3.3	0.3	29.6	13.8
04 02830	Apache Junction...........	90.6	35 840	1 112	395.5	82.6	1.6	1.5	1.1	0.2	14.4	7.5
04 04720	Avondale......................	118.1	76 238	435	645.5	35.8	9.8	1.4	4.1	0.6	50.3	16.5
04 07940	Buckeye........................	971.9	50 876	759	52.3	51.6	7.5	1.7	2.3	0.3	38.3	10.5
04 08220	Bullhead City	153.8	39 540	1 001	257.1	72.6	1.6	1.4	1.8	0.3	23.7	9.7
04 10530	Casa Grande................	284.0	48 571	803	171.0	51.2	4.9	4.1	2.1	0.3	39.0	9.8
04 12000	Chandler.......................	166.8	236 123	80	1 415.4	63.7	5.4	1.6	9.2	0.4	21.9	14.0
04 22220	El Mirage	26.0	31 797	1 283	1 224.4	43.3	7.2	1.6	2.2	0.4	47.6	17.3
04 23620	Flagstaff.......................	165.4	65 870	530	398.2	66.5	2.3	12.0	2.7	0.4	18.4	6.9
04 23760	Florence	135.9	25 536	1 627	188.0	47.3	6.7	14.6	1.1	0.1	31.2	23.7
04 27400	Gilbert..........................	176.0	208 453	102	1 184.3	75.0	4.0	1.1	6.9	0.4	14.9	8.6
04 27820	Glendale.......................	155.3	226 721	88	1 459.5	53.3	6.6	1.7	4.5	0.3	35.5	15.3
04 28380	Goodyear......................	495.9	65 275	538	131.6	60.2	7.3	1.4	5.1	0.3	27.8	10.4
04 37620	Kingman........................	90.2	28 068	1 472	311.2	83.1	1.5	2.3	2.1	0.5	12.5	4.8
04 39370	Lake Havasu City..........	115.1	52 527	725	456.4	85.3	0.9	1.4	1.4	0.2	12.1	4.9
04 44270	Marana	314.6	34 961	1 151	111.1	70.6	2.9	1.4	4.5	0.3	22.1	9.2
04 44410	Maricopa......................	123.0	43 482	904	353.7	60.2	10.6	2.1	5.0	0.5	24.4	9.8
04 46000	Mesa............................	353.4	439 041	38	1 242.3	66.0	4.0	2.5	2.5	0.5	26.4	13.0
04 51600	Oro Valley	92.0	41 011	968	445.7	83.4	1.8	0.7	3.9	0.3	11.5	9.3
04 54050	Peoria..........................	451.7	154 065	156	341.1	73.9	3.9	1.2	3.9	0.3	18.6	9.3
04 55000	Phoenix	1 338.3	1 445 632	6	1 080.2	48.0	6.8	2.1	3.7	0.3	40.8	21.0
04 57380	Prescott........................	107.1	39 843	989	372.1	88.3	0.9	1.5	1.7	0.2	8.6	6.6
04 57450	Prescott Valley	100.1	38 822	1 017	387.8	80.3	1.2	1.6	1.5	0.3	16.7	10.7
04 58150	Queen Creek................	72.6	26 361	1 571	363.0	75.9	4.1	0.9	3.6	0.3	17.3	5.0
04 62140	Sahuarita	80.4	25 259	1 645	314.2	62.4	3.4	1.2	2.8	0.4	32.0	6.1
04 63470	San Luis	83.0	25 505	1 630	307.5	1.0	0.1	0.1	0.2	0.0	98.7	44.9
04 65000	Scottsdale....................	476.4	217 385	93	456.4	85.2	2.1	1.0	4.2	0.2	8.8	11.2
04 66820	Sierra Vista	394.4	43 888	896	111.3	66.3	9.9	1.6	5.9	1.0	19.4	9.2
04 71510	Surprise	273.9	117 517	221	429.1	73.2	5.8	1.0	3.4	0.4	18.5	9.1
04 73000	Tempe..........................	103.4	161 719	149	1 563.7	64.4	6.6	3.0	6.6	0.6	21.1	14.6
04 77000	Tucson..........................	587.2	520 116	33	885.8	48.9	5.3	2.3	3.5	0.3	41.6	15.7
04 85540	Yuma............................	311.5	93 064	321	298.7	39.2	3.2	1.5	2.3	0.3	54.8	19.6
05 00000	ARKANSAS...............	134 771.3	2 915 918	X	21.6	76.0	15.9	1.5	1.5	0.2	6.4	4.4
05 04840	Bella Vista	114.6	26 461	1 568	230.8	95.1	0.8	1.7	0.7	0.1	2.6	2.5
05 05290	Benton..........................	57.6	30 681	1 321	532.6	88.0	6.6	1.0	1.1	0.1	4.5	2.4
05 05320	Bentonville...................	81.0	35 301	1 140	435.6	78.9	2.8	2.1	9.0	0.3	8.7	7.3
05 15190	Conway	117.4	58 908	620	501.6	76.6	16.4	1.0	2.4	0.3	5.1	6.3
05 23290	Fayetteville	139.5	73 580	462	527.6	83.2	6.8	2.1	3.7	0.3	6.4	6.2
05 24550	Fort Smith....................	160.5	86 209	361	537.2	67.4	10.1	3.2	5.8	0.1	16.5	12.2
05 33400	Hot Springs	90.7	35 193	1 145	388.1	74.1	18.1	1.4	1.2	0.1	7.5	7.3

1. Dry land or land partially or temporarily covered by water. 2. May be of any race.

Table D. Cities — **Population**

City	Age of population (percent), 2010											Population			
												Census counts		Percent change	
	Under 5 years	5 to 17 years	18 to 24 years	25 to 34 years	35 to 44 years	45 to 54 years	55 to 64 years	65 to 74 years	75 years and over	Median age	Percent female	1990	2000	1990–2000	2000–2010
	12	13	14	15	16	17	18	19	20	21	22	23	24	25	26
United States	6.5	17.5	9.9	13.3	13.3	14.6	11.8	7.0	6.0	37.2	50.8	248 790 925	281 421 906	13.1	9.7
ALABAMA	6.4	17.3	10.0	12.7	13.0	14.5	12.3	7.8	6.0	37.9	51.5	4 040 389	4 447 100	10.1	7.5
Alabaster	7.5	20.7	7.1	13.7	16.9	14.7	10.2	5.3	3.8	35.6	50.7	14 619	22 619	54.7	34.2
Auburn	4.9	12.5	38.0	13.4	9.7	8.2	6.3	3.6	3.2	23.3	49.9	33 830	42 987	27.1	24.2
Bessemer	7.1	17.6	9.2	12.8	11.2	14.0	13.0	7.0	8.0	38.0	53.3	33 581	29 672	-11.6	-7.5
Birmingham	6.9	14.7	12.4	15.6	11.5	14.3	12.3	6.2	6.2	35.4	53.2	265 347	242 820	-8.5	-12.6
Decatur	6.7	17.4	9.0	13.4	12.7	14.2	12.1	8.0	6.5	37.9	51.9	49 917	53 929	8.0	3.3
Dothan	6.9	17.6	8.5	13.3	12.8	14.0	12.3	7.8	6.9	38.0	52.7	54 131	57 737	6.7	13.4
Enterprise	7.5	17.9	9.3	16.1	13.0	12.4	10.9	6.8	6.1	34.4	51.0	20 119	21 178	5.3	25.4
Florence	5.9	14.2	15.4	12.3	10.4	12.7	11.8	8.5	8.8	37.1	53.8	36 426	36 264	-0.4	8.4
Gadsden	6.4	16.0	9.7	12.6	12.5	13.4	12.6	8.2	8.6	39.3	52.5	42 523	38 978	-8.3	-5.4
Homewood	7.3	15.4	17.4	18.2	12.6	11.3	8.6	3.9	5.2	29.8	53.1	23 644	25 043	5.9	0.5
Hoover	6.8	18.2	7.8	14.6	14.1	14.7	11.9	6.3	5.6	37.0	51.9	39 988	62 742	56.9	30.1
Huntsville	6.2	15.3	12.5	14.3	11.9	14.5	11.2	7.6	6.6	36.5	51.4	159 880	158 216	-1.0	13.8
Madison	6.2	22.2	7.5	11.5	14.9	18.9	10.5	5.0	3.2	37.0	50.7	14 792	29 329	98.3	46.4
Mobile	6.7	17.4	11.2	13.8	11.5	13.9	11.7	7.0	6.7	35.7	53.0	199 973	198 915	-0.5	-1.9
Montgomery	7.2	17.7	11.7	14.6	12.7	13.4	10.8	6.2	5.6	34.0	53.0	190 350	201 568	5.9	2.1
Opelika	7.7	17.7	8.9	15.0	13.0	13.7	11.7	6.9	5.3	35.5	52.5	22 122	23 498	6.2	12.7
Phenix City	8.3	18.6	10.4	15.3	12.6	12.7	10.2	6.3	5.5	33.1	53.3	25 311	28 265	11.7	16.1
Prattville	6.5	20.6	8.5	12.4	15.4	14.5	10.1	7.0	4.9	36.3	52.3	19 816	24 303	22.8	39.7
Tuscaloosa	5.0	12.4	31.9	12.9	9.1	9.8	9.1	4.9	4.9	25.4	51.9	77 866	77 906	0.1	16.1
Vestavia Hills	6.4	18.9	6.0	12.2	13.8	14.7	12.7	7.0	8.3	39.7	52.4	19 550	24 476	25.2	39.0
ALASKA	7.6	18.8	10.5	14.5	13.1	15.6	12.1	5.0	2.8	33.8	48.0	550 043	626 932	14.0	13.3
Anchorage	7.5	18.4	11.2	15.6	13.4	15.3	11.3	4.6	2.7	32.9	49.2	226 338	260 283	15.0	12.1
Fairbanks	9.6	16.3	16.7	19.1	11.2	10.9	8.9	4.1	3.2	27.9	46.8	30 843	30 224	-2.0	4.3
Juneau	6.3	17.1	8.9	13.8	13.8	17.4	14.2	5.5	2.9	38.1	49.0	26 751	30 711	14.8	1.8
ARIZONA	7.1	18.4	9.9	13.4	12.9	13.2	11.4	7.8	6.0	35.9	50.3	3 665 339	5 130 632	40.0	24.6
Apache Junction	5.4	14.4	6.6	8.7	10.7	12.9	14.2	14.7	11.4	47.5	51.4	18 092	31 814	75.8	12.7
Avondale	9.3	23.3	11.7	15.9	15.0	11.7	7.7	3.6	1.9	28.6	50.4	17 595	35 883	103.9	112.5
Buckeye	9.1	21.5	8.7	18.8	15.7	10.7	8.9	5.0	1.7	30.7	45.4	NA	6 537	NA	678.3
Bullhead City	5.4	14.2	7.4	8.9	9.8	14.3	16.1	14.7	9.3	48.2	50.6	21 951	33 769	53.8	17.1
Casa Grande	7.9	20.0	8.5	12.3	11.7	11.5	12.2	9.6	6.2	36.0	51.5	19 076	25 224	32.2	92.6
Chandler	7.6	20.0	8.8	15.0	16.6	14.7	9.6	4.7	3.1	34.1	50.9	89 862	176 581	96.5	33.7
El Mirage	10.5	25.0	9.7	17.7	14.2	9.9	6.7	4.2	2.2	28.1	50.4	NA	7 609	NA	317.9
Flagstaff	6.1	14.5	26.2	15.6	11.1	11.2	9.0	3.9	2.5	26.6	50.6	45 857	52 894	15.3	24.5
Florence	1.8	5.1	13.8	26.3	21.2	14.4	8.2	5.7	3.4	36.2	17.9	7 321	17 054	132.9	49.7
Gilbert	8.5	23.6	8.0	14.8	17.1	13.6	8.4	4.1	2.0	31.9	50.8	29 149	109 697	276.3	90.0
Glendale	7.6	20.4	11.4	13.7	13.2	14.1	10.4	5.3	3.9	32.5	50.9	147 070	218 812	48.8	3.6
Goodyear	7.3	19.7	9.1	14.0	15.6	12.7	10.8	7.5	3.4	34.9	53.1	6 258	18 911	202.2	245.2
Kingman	6.4	16.9	8.3	10.9	11.3	13.8	13.4	10.7	8.4	41.7	51.1	13 208	20 069	51.9	39.9
Lake Havasu City	4.5	13.4	6.1	8.9	10.0	14.2	16.1	15.5	11.4	50.3	50.6	24 363	41 938	72.1	25.2
Marana	7.8	17.8	6.2	14.0	14.4	12.4	12.6	10.2	4.7	37.7	50.1	2 565	13 556	428.5	157.9
Maricopa	10.7	21.9	6.3	19.0	16.0	10.8	9.1	4.7	1.6	31.2	50.4	NA	1 040	NA	4 081.0
Mesa	7.7	18.6	10.0	14.2	12.6	12.6	10.3	7.3	6.8	34.6	50.8	289 199	396 375	37.1	10.8
Oro Valley	3.9	15.3	6.1	7.0	10.7	15.3	15.7	13.6	12.5	49.8	52.4	8 627	29 700	244.3	38.1
Peoria	6.4	19.6	8.4	11.6	14.1	14.5	11.1	7.4	6.9	38.1	52.0	51 080	108 364	112.1	42.2
Phoenix	8.3	20.0	10.4	15.5	14.3	13.5	9.6	4.9	3.6	32.2	49.8	988 015	1 321 045	33.7	9.4
Prescott	3.1	10.4	9.8	7.4	7.9	12.6	17.9	15.9	14.9	54.1	50.8	26 592	33 938	27.6	17.4
Prescott Valley	6.9	17.2	8.3	11.6	11.0	12.9	13.0	10.7	8.4	40.6	51.5	8 904	23 535	164.3	65.0
Queen Creek	10.4	27.0	6.7	15.0	17.2	11.1	7.4	3.8	1.4	29.8	49.9	NA	4 316	NA	510.8
Sahuarita	9.5	20.3	5.4	16.0	14.1	9.0	11.0	10.0	4.7	34.4	51.2	NA	3 242	NA	679.1
San Luis	9.2	27.7	12.4	12.5	13.8	12.2	6.4	3.6	2.3	25.5	50.5	4 212	15 322	263.8	66.5
Scottsdale	4.2	13.6	6.8	12.2	12.8	15.5	15.0	10.8	9.2	45.4	51.7	130 099	202 705	55.8	7.2
Sierra Vista	7.5	15.5	12.5	16.9	12.0	11.2	9.7	8.0	6.6	33.1	49.1	32 983	37 775	14.5	16.2
Surprise	7.9	19.5	6.1	13.7	13.8	9.4	10.7	11.9	7.1	36.8	51.7	7 122	30 848	333.1	281.0
Tempe	5.0	11.8	25.8	18.1	10.6	11.1	9.1	4.7	3.7	28.1	47.9	141 993	158 625	11.7	2.0
Tucson	6.9	16.5	14.3	15.0	12.2	12.8	10.6	6.1	5.8	33.0	50.5	415 444	486 699	17.2	6.9
Yuma	7.9	20.3	12.7	13.8	12.2	11.6	8.9	6.8	5.8	31.3	49.2	56 966	77 515	36.1	20.1
ARKANSAS	6.8	17.6	9.7	12.9	12.6	14.0	12.0	8.0	6.4	37.4	50.9	2 350 624	2 673 400	13.7	9.1
Bella Vista	5.5	12.4	3.7	10.8	11.1	11.4	13.7	16.6	15.0	50.8	52.0	9 083	16 582	82.6	59.6
Benton	7.6	19.2	7.9	15.3	14.1	12.8	10.4	6.7	6.0	35.0	51.6	18 177	21 906	20.5	40.1
Bentonville	9.2	21.9	8.1	18.8	16.0	11.9	6.9	3.7	3.4	30.6	51.0	11 257	19 730	75.3	78.9
Conway	7.0	15.6	22.8	15.6	11.6	10.6	7.9	4.5	4.3	27.3	51.7	26 481	43 167	63.0	36.5
Fayetteville	6.0	12.5	26.2	18.6	11.1	9.8	8.0	3.9	3.9	27.2	49.7	42 247	58 047	37.4	26.8
Fort Smith	7.6	17.8	10.7	13.7	12.4	13.9	11.1	6.6	6.1	35.1	51.3	72 798	80 268	10.3	7.4
Hot Springs	6.0	14.5	8.5	11.9	10.7	13.6	13.4	9.6	11.7	43.5	52.7	33 095	35 750	8.0	-1.6

City	Households, 2010				Persons in group quarters, 2010				Serious crimes known to police,[2] 2010				Educational attainment, 2008–2010		
			Percent			Institutional			Total		Rate[3]			Attainment[4] (percent)	
	Number	Persons per house-hold	Female family house-holder[1]	One-person	Total	Total	Persons in nursing facilities	Non-institu-tional	Number	Rate[3]	Violent	Property	Population age 25 and older	High school graduate or less	Bachelor's degree or more
	27	28	29	30	31	32	33	34	35	36	37	38	39	40	41
United States	116 716 292	2.58	13.1	26.7	7 987 323	3 993 659	1 502 264	3 993 664	10 329 135	3 346	404	2 942	202 053 193	43.1	28.0
ALABAMA	1 883 791	2.48	15.3	27.4	115 816	67 004	22 995	48 812	186 148	3 895	378	3 517	3 142 304	49.5	21.9
Alabaster	10 628	2.83	10.1	18.7	300	297	293	3	548	1 805	109	1 697	20 464	33.7	32.9
Auburn	22 111	2.24	8.8	33.8	3 827	130	130	3 697	1 901	3 561	155	3 406	22 347	19.7	60.4
Bessemer	10 711	2.48	29.7	30.9	871	519	472	352	2 478	9 025	1 053	7 973	18 719	57.2	12.8
Birmingham	89 382	2.27	25.0	37.7	9 035	3 300	1 559	5 735	9 980	4 702	633	4 070	142 937	47.0	20.6
Decatur	22 576	2.42	15.6	29.9	966	767	246	199	2 963	5 321	381	4 940	37 700	48.5	21.0
Dothan	26 845	2.39	17.7	28.8	1 369	1 171	484	198	3 547	5 416	628	4 788	43 289	46.1	21.9
Enterprise	10 513	2.50	13.9	25.6	279	245	245	34	1 062	3 998	467	3 531	16 804	40.3	27.5
Florence	17 267	2.18	15.0	35.5	1 701	524	370	1 177	1 770	4 502	226	4 275	24 647	45.6	25.1
Gadsden	15 171	2.31	19.5	34.9	1 752	1 189	380	563	2 938	7 972	863	7 109	25 033	50.7	16.6
Homewood	10 092	2.31	12.2	34.4	1 864	18	0	1 846	1 654	6 572	453	6 119	14 335	19.4	58.2
Hoover	32 478	2.50	10.0	25.8	408	393	361	15	2 248	2 754	92	2 662	52 773	18.8	56.1
Huntsville	77 033	2.25	14.5	34.7	6 786	1 924	874	4 862	10 950	6 080	656	5 424	118 048	32.9	37.6
Madison	16 111	2.65	9.9	23.4	270	270	225	0	1 007	2 345	191	2 154	26 677	19.5	55.6
Mobile	78 959	2.40	21.6	32.2	5 598	2 632	1 196	2 966	15 881	6 324	678	5 647	124 584	44.2	25.8
Montgomery	81 486	2.44	21.8	31.1	6 879	2 967	1 005	3 912	12 057	5 860	387	5 472	129 624	42.0	30.7
Opelika	10 523	2.46	20.1	28.2	572	481	141	91	1 648	6 224	589	5 635	17 822	49.3	23.5
Phenix City	13 243	2.44	23.9	30.1	557	494	203	63	1 785	5 438	478	4 960	19 859	49.4	14.7
Prattville	12 711	2.64	14.0	22.9	398	362	181	36	1 386	4 081	265	3 816	20 488	38.6	30.2
Tuscaloosa	36 185	2.23	16.2	35.4	9 659	942	144	8 717	5 277	5 833	496	5 337	48 028	42.8	31.7
Vestavia Hills	13 987	2.42	7.7	29.3	141	138	138	3	549	1 613	53	1 560	23 278	13.5	68.9
ALASKA	258 058	2.65	10.7	25.6	26 352	6 458	1 626	19 894	24 796	3 491	639	2 852	439 507	35.2	27.4
Anchorage	107 332	2.64	11.7	24.9	8 450	2 828	1 137	5 622	12 646	4 333	833	3 500	180 004	29.9	32.9
Fairbanks	11 534	2.52	12.2	29.9	2 518	427	81	2 091	1 651	5 235	901	4 335	18 422	40.0	19.4
Juneau	12 187	2.49	10.4	26.9	887	408	57	479	1 656	5 295	425	4 870	21 110	26.8	34.8
ARIZONA	2 380 990	2.63	12.4	26.1	139 384	84 788	13 819	54 596	251 978	3 942	408	3 534	4 088 405	39.5	26.1
Apache Junction	15 574	2.28	10.7	31.4	283	120	120	163	1 179	3 290	299	2 991	26 128	48.9	13.1
Avondale	23 386	3.25	17.0	15.5	160	146	132	14	3 931	5 156	261	4 895	41 795	52.1	18.1
Buckeye	14 424	3.17	11.7	15.2	5 094	5 084	0	10	1 288	2 532	85	2 447	27 051	44.4	19.8
Bullhead City	16 761	2.35	12.2	27.8	166	96	93	70	1 599	4 044	149	3 895	29 451	53.0	13.5
Casa Grande	17 651	2.74	14.0	22.3	282	47	3	235	3 097	6 376	515	5 862	28 012	45.2	19.4
Chandler	86 924	2.71	11.8	22.7	546	136	94	410	8 207	3 476	293	3 183	147 300	26.5	38.3
El Mirage	9 416	3.38	17.9	14.8	13	0	0	13	929	2 922	261	2 661	16 439	47.7	12.9
Flagstaff	22 836	2.53	11.8	25.6	8 076	668	114	7 408	3 222	4 891	405	4 486	34 931	25.5	41.9
Florence	3 330	2.35	10.1	26.2	17 700	17 700	0	0	286	1 120	153	967	19 882	59.9	5.6
Gilbert	69 372	3.00	10.6	16.1	304	4	0	300	4 351	2 087	99	1 988	120 155	22.7	37.6
Glendale	79 114	2.82	16.0	24.0	3 257	1 000	836	2 257	14 487	6 390	425	5 965	137 014	43.0	21.3
Goodyear	21 491	2.86	9.9	16.0	3 828	3 670	164	158	2 125	3 255	205	3 050	39 170	32.6	29.1
Kingman	11 217	2.44	11.7	27.9	699	541	132	158	1 657	5 904	296	5 608	18 869	43.0	15.1
Lake Havasu City	23 168	2.26	8.8	26.6	201	151	142	50	1 356	2 582	198	2 384	38 808	41.9	15.8
Marana	13 073	2.63	8.5	18.7	520	499	0	21	1 123	3 212	80	3 132	22 929	26.8	37.0
Maricopa	14 359	3.03	10.9	15.6	0	0	0	0	961	2 210	113	2 097	25 038	27.8	24.7
Mesa	165 374	2.63	12.6	26.6	3 538	1 344	928	2 194	16 666	3 796	408	3 388	284 924	40.7	23.8
Oro Valley	17 804	2.30	6.9	25.1	68	63	42	5	804	1 960	73	1 887	30 051	18.6	47.7
Peoria	57 457	2.66	11.6	23.5	1 227	868	826	359	4 912	3 188	183	3 005	99 214	36.2	24.4
Phoenix	514 806	2.77	14.9	27.1	21 738	13 589	2 696	8 149	69 416	4 802	553	4 248	890 133	44.5	25.3
Prescott	18 611	2.03	7.5	35.1	2 008	675	474	1 333	1 386	3 479	339	3 140	30 792	31.1	33.7
Prescott Valley	15 364	2.51	11.4	23.9	209	158	118	51	779	2 007	281	1 726	25 934	37.6	16.8
Queen Creek	7 720	3.41	8.4	10.4	16	0	0	16	NA	NA	NA	NA	13 583	24.9	28.4
Sahuarita	9 020	2.79	8.5	16.3	63	44	44	19	383	1 516	55	1 461	15 742	24.4	33.8
San Luis	5 953	4.20	19.8	5.7	524	502	0	22	NA	NA	NA	NA	13 517	71.8	8.2
Scottsdale	101 273	2.14	7.6	34.4	1 159	686	622	473	6 916	3 181	162	3 019	163 474	19.2	52.0
Sierra Vista	17 059	2.39	10.7	28.9	3 037	233	217	2 804	1 517	3 457	276	3 181	28 169	28.2	31.1
Surprise	43 272	2.71	9.8	19.0	274	89	80	185	2 084	1 773	90	1 683	73 439	32.7	27.0
Tempe	66 000	2.30	10.7	32.3	10 188	298	280	9 890	9 251	5 720	482	5 239	92 781	26.4	41.0
Tucson	205 390	2.43	15.4	33.1	20 706	9 920	1 798	10 786	11 766	2 262	640	1 622	324 413	40.8	24.6
Yuma	30 714	2.86	15.5	21.8	5 128	3 291	308	1 837	4 620	3 018	414	2 605	53 160	46.3	16.0
ARKANSAS	1 147 084	2.47	13.4	27.1	78 931	47 287	18 532	31 644	118 510	4 064	505	3 559	1 904 101	52.5	19.0
Bella Vista	11 729	2.24	4.8	23.4	133	133	133	0	170	642	68	574	19 679	29.9	33.8
Benton	11 834	2.55	13.5	24.3	493	462	289	31	1 502	4 896	473	4 423	20 035	42.0	25.1
Bentonville	13 253	2.64	11.6	25.1	258	179	160	79	774	2 193	178	2 014	20 488	34.8	35.5
Conway	22 399	2.45	12.8	27.0	4 038	1 118	372	2 920	2 862	4 858	436	4 422	30 569	35.0	34.7
Fayetteville	30 726	2.17	9.6	36.5	6 818	1 124	405	5 694	3 074	4 178	446	3 732	40 621	30.8	43.4
Fort Smith	34 352	2.45	14.3	31.2	1 930	1 083	592	847	5 478	6 354	771	5 583	55 468	50.8	19.6
Hot Springs	15 575	2.15	14.5	38.5	1 692	1 127	578	565	3 533	10 039	1 145	8 894	25 134	52.8	19.9

1. No spouse present.   2. Data for serious crimes have not been adjusted for underreporting. This may affect comparability between geographic areas and over time.   3. Per 100,000 population estimated by the FBI.   4. Persons 25 years old and over.

Table D. Cities — Income, Poverty, and Housing

City	Money income, 2008–2010 — Per capita income[1] (dollars)	Households — Median income	Households — Percent with income of $200,000 or more	Households — Percent with income of less than $25,000	Families with income below poverty (percent)	Housing units, 2010 — Total	Housing units, 2010 — Percent change, 2000–2010	Housing units, 2010 — Vacant units for sale or rent[2]	Occupied Housing units 2008–2010 — Owner-occupied — Total	Occupied Housing units 2008–2010 — Owner-occupied — Percent	Occupied Housing units 2008–2010 — Owner-occupied — Median value[3] (dollars)	Median owner costs as a percent of income — With a mortgage[4]	Median owner costs as a percent of income — Without a mortgage[5]
	42	43	44	45	46	47	48	49	50	51	52	53	54
United States.............	26 942	51 222	4.1	24.0	10.5	131 704 730	13.6	14 988 438	114 596 927	65.9	187 500	25.1	12.6
ALABAMA	22 752	41 788	2.3	30.9	13.2	2 171 853	10.6	288 062	1 823 831	70.5	121 800	22.4	11.8
Alabaster	27 877	65 956	1.6	12.3	3.9	11 295	28.3	667	10 911	86.3	162 200	23.0	10.8
Auburn.....................	24 510	35 500	3.1	39.1	7.1	24 646	22.7	2 535	21 270	48.1	215 100	24.3	13.9
Bessemer	16 394	26 980	0.0	47.9	19.3	12 369	-3.2	1 658	11 348	58.7	82 700	29.6	15.9
Birmingham	19 129	31 532	1.3	40.6	21.4	108 981	-2.9	19 599	88 690	50.4	86 600	26.7	14.8
Decatur.....................	22 483	40 765	1.6	32.3	14.7	24 538	2.2	1 962	22 274	60.6	132 200	20.7	10.0
Dothan......................	23 810	41 640	2.7	30.7	13.7	29 274	12.6	2 429	25 299	61.6	136 700	20.5	10.0
Enterprise	23 997	48 648	1.9	27.2	15.1	11 616	20.2	1 103	9 755	66.4	149 300	21.0	10.0
Florence	20 699	32 839	2.1	40.4	18.1	19 299	9.1	2 032	16 738	58.3	106 000	22.8	10.0
Gadsden...................	19 124	28 543	1.5	43.8	22.0	17 672	-5.9	2 501	15 481	61.0	72 000	22.8	13.8
Homewood................	28 700	54 689	3.5	23.1	7.6	11 385	0.5	1 293	9 582	56.4	289 100	24.5	11.2
Hoover......................	37 071	72 103	8.4	13.2	3.7	35 474	31.2	2 996	30 373	68.3	268 700	22.4	10.0
Huntsville.................	29 582	47 238	3.8	27.7	12.1	84 949	15.4	7 916	74 096	60.7	154 600	19.6	10.0
Madison	40 406	91 011	9.7	9.3	3.4	17 203	43.1	1 092	15 468	74.7	231 900	17.4	10.0
Mobile......................	22 318	36 851	3.0	34.5	17.8	89 127	3.5	10 168	76 953	57.9	127 200	23.7	13.3
Montgomery	23 740	42 304	2.4	30.3	16.3	92 115	6.1	10 629	79 772	60.2	122 100	22.8	10.4
Opelika.....................	22 861	37 768	1.9	36.7	16.9	11 751	14.4	1 228	11 061	66.4	125 800	22.4	13.4
Phenix City................	20 140	34 752	1.2	35.9	18.9	15 198	15.0	1 955	12 490	57.2	115 500	24.7	13.2
Prattville...................	26 611	59 751	1.7	15.2	4.4	13 541	40.7	830	12 011	73.2	149 100	21.9	10.0
Tuscaloosa................	20 753	33 362	3.3	39.9	18.0	40 842	16.8	4 657	31 726	48.6	158 700	24.2	10.3
Vestavia Hills.............	49 059	82 049	12.8	11.7	2.8	14 952	40.8	965	13 632	74.6	324 400	22.2	10.0
ALASKA	31 085	67 016	4.8	14.8	6.2	306 967	17.6	48 909	251 468	65.2	235 300	23.9	11.0
Anchorage................	34 999	74 272	6.6	11.5	5.4	113 032	12.6	5 700	105 079	62.3	273 200	23.9	11.0
Fairbanks..................	26 745	53 694	1.5	18.6	7.1	13 056	5.2	1 522	12 370	41.1	199 900	28.1	10.2
Juneau......................	36 563	74 827	5.3	10.4	5.0	13 055	6.3	868	12 394	62.0	297 400	25.3	12.0
ARIZONA	24 820	49 214	3.2	23.9	11.6	2 844 526	29.9	463 536	2 333 172	66.5	195 400	26.6	11.1
Apache Junction..........	21 677	38 456	1.0	32.2	8.0	22 564	-1.0	6 990	15 145	79.1	99 000	25.9	12.9
Avondale	20 567	60 990	1.5	15.9	13.2	27 001	136.6	3 615	21 451	64.9	163 400	27.1	14.9
Buckeye....................	21 327	61 831	2.7	13.3	9.5	18 207	NA	3 783	14 325	74.7	162 700	27.8	12.1
Bullhead City..............	20 340	37 386	1.0	30.4	14.5	23 464	27.5	6 703	16 628	63.3	128 700	32.0	13.4
Casa Grande..............	20 148	46 129	1.0	25.7	13.7	22 400	104.8	4 749	16 274	68.1	140 300	25.5	13.5
Chandler...................	31 527	67 213	4.7	12.7	6.4	94 404	41.7	7 480	86 036	65.5	248 800	24.2	10.0
El Mirage	16 169	47 299	0.2	19.8	16.9	11 326	NA	1 910	8 834	71.6	121 400	29.6	14.1
Flagstaff....................	22 719	48 178	1.7	26.0	10.7	26 254	22.5	3 418	22 539	47.2	299 200	25.7	10.0
Florence	9 144	42 528	0.7	26.9	7.0	5 224	60.5	1 894	2 745	74.0	120 100	30.8	10.0
Gilbert......................	30 005	75 895	4.9	9.6	5.5	74 907	102.2	5 535	67 169	71.3	259 000	25.9	10.0
Glendale...................	22 088	50 404	2.3	23.6	12.3	90 505	13.6	11 391	78 377	60.7	182 300	25.9	12.6
Goodyear..................	26 495	71 845	2.9	10.7	5.7	25 027	275.6	3 536	19 756	75.2	231 500	26.9	10.0
Kingman....................	21 681	42 045	0.9	28.8	10.1	12 724	48.6	1 607	10 871	66.1	142 500	23.8	10.0
Lake Havasu City.........	24 227	42 979	2.2	23.1	8.6	32 327	40.6	9 159	22 419	71.1	219 200	30.9	11.8
Marana	30 982	70 090	4.1	10.2	2.8	14 726	160.3	1 653	12 022	78.6	236 400	25.3	10.0
Maricopa...................	24 065	63 992	1.4	11.7	3.1	17 240	NA	2 881	13 379	78.0	155 700	28.0	14.0
Mesa........................	23 987	47 994	2.2	22.4	9.6	201 173	14.5	35 799	166 796	64.3	180 000	26.1	10.8
Oro Valley	37 927	65 584	6.1	15.1	3.5	20 340	45.2	2 536	17 289	75.8	306 800	26.2	11.1
Peoria......................	27 983	60 876	3.8	16.0	6.4	64 818	51.9	7 361	54 474	74.1	213 100	27.1	11.9
Phoenix	23 626	47 187	3.4	25.6	15.8	590 149	19.0	75 343	510 695	58.3	197 000	27.4	12.1
Prescott....................	28 075	41 497	2.9	29.5	5.7	22 159	27.1	3 548	18 892	65.0	284 200	29.3	11.7
Prescott Valley	20 837	43 441	1.2	24.8	7.7	17 494	84.5	2 130	15 167	67.4	193 300	28.2	11.6
Queen Creek..............	26 516	86 067	3.7	5.3	2.9	8 557	NA	837	6 834	83.9	250 000	27.5	10.7
Sahuarita	29 316	71 113	1.7	8.8	2.8	10 615	NA	1 595	8 753	81.7	228 400	24.3	10.1
San Luis	8 484	26 821	0.0	46.4	33.6	6 525	95.8	572	6 420	72.5	138 600	32.8	17.4
Scottsdale.................	49 337	71 021	12.1	16.6	4.4	124 001	18.2	22 728	99 699	71.0	428 100	26.3	12.0
Sierra Vista...............	27 827	57 855	3.0	15.8	5.8	18 742	20.0	1 683	16 601	56.5	205 600	20.4	10.0
Surprise	24 451	59 306	1.3	13.1	6.3	52 586	222.5	9 314	40 429	77.5	210 400	27.6	11.1
Tempe......................	25 758	47 868	3.2	26.3	13.1	73 462	9.6	7 462	62 671	46.0	233 100	23.7	10.0
Tucson......................	19 522	36 065	1.0	35.2	16.9	229 762	9.5	24 372	204 676	52.4	164 100	26.2	12.8
Yuma........................	19 570	43 416	1.2	27.5	15.9	38 626	10.2	7 912	33 383	59.3	155 500	25.0	10.1
ARKANSAS...............	20 981	38 851	1.8	32.4	13.8	1 316 299	12.2	169 215	1 120 028	67.2	105 400	21.3	11.0
Bella Vista	30 913	58 401	3.0	13.9	4.1	13 241	49.2	1 512	10 809	87.6	156 800	19.7	10.0
Benton	25 130	48 441	2.3	27.2	9.3	12 902	38.9	1 068	11 465	70.8	131 000	20.9	12.7
Bentonville................	26 876	54 151	4.2	20.8	8.2	14 693	84.9	1 440	12 488	57.7	168 300	21.2	10.0
Conway	22 904	42 640	2.4	31.7	10.7	24 402	41.2	2 003	21 380	51.1	145 500	19.0	10.0
Fayetteville................	23 928	35 365	2.8	37.1	12.9	36 188	42.9	5 462	30 112	42.6	175 800	23.1	10.0
Fort Smith.................	21 339	36 796	2.9	34.2	18.3	37 899	7.2	3 547	33 712	57.0	113 000	20.3	11.3
Hot Springs	19 752	30 666	1.6	40.0	17.4	18 947	1.2	3 372	14 829	55.8	120 000	26.7	13.0

1. Based on population estimated by the American Community Survey. 2. Includes units rented or sold but not occupied. 3. Specified owner-occupied units; $1,000,000 represents $1,000,000 or more. 4. 50.0 represents 50 percent or more. 5. 10.0 represents 10 percent or less.

Table D. Cities — Housing, Labor Force, and Employment

City	Occupied housing units, 2008–2010 (cont.)				Migration, 2008–2010		Civilian labor force, 2010		Unemployment		Civilian employment[4], 2008–2010	Percent		
	Percent renter occupied	Median gross rent[1]	Median rent as a percent of income[2]	Percent with no vehicle available	Percent who lived in the same house one year ago	Percent who lived outside this city one year ago	Total	Percent change, 2009–2010	Total	Rate[3]	Population age 16 and older	In labor force	Full-year full-time worker	Households with no workers (percent)
	55	56	57	58	59	60	61	62	63	64	65	66	67	68
United States	34.1	850	30.9	8.9	84.5	9.7	27 715	22.0	1 940	7.0	45 851	65.7	45.9	19.4
ALABAMA	29.5	658	30.7	6.4	84.6	10.3	12 234	-1.3	1 330	10.9	22 508	56.4	32.3	35.1
Alabaster	13.7	951	22.0	1.3	88.0	7.9	24 106	-1.6	2 192	9.1	43 206	51.8	31.9	40.2
Auburn	51.9	718	37.9	4.1	62.2	19.2	17 296	5.9	1 500	8.7	25 794	65.2	44.7	23.4
Bessemer	41.3	667	33.6	16.9	89.6	4.0	94 940	1.9	8 591	9.0	159 368	63.4	41.7	27.5
Birmingham	49.6	699	35.2	14.4	77.3	8.9	12 067	-2.8	1 163	9.6	21 064	65.1	42.3	27.4
Decatur	39.4	574	28.0	6.9	85.8	6.8	14 059	8.6	1 142	8.1	24 389	64.9	42.2	28.8
Dothan	38.4	603	28.0	7.5	82.8	8.2	16 306	4.9	1 085	6.7	24 745	68.4	48.8	22.9
Enterprise	33.6	663	26.0	9.2	80.7	11.6	41 630	-1.7	3 660	8.8	73 335	54.1	31.1	32.2
Florence	41.7	553	33.1	7.7	78.1	11.9	15 564	11.5	842	5.4	26 668	67.3	46.3	23.9
Gadsden	39.0	583	27.8	8.7	79.8	10.0	363 949	1.5	29 010	8.0	536 112	72.3	42.7	19.5
Homewood	43.6	850	33.8	4.3	75.6	20.1	156 732	1.4	10 644	6.8	221 199	75.2	48.7	15.9
Hoover	31.7	927	28.2	1.6	81.3	12.8	13 232	-11.6	1 049	7.9	24 231	71.3	50.2	21.4
Huntsville	39.3	663	29.7	7.1	80.1	8.6	18 484	0.1	1 068	5.8	24 798	75.3	46.9	15.9
Madison	25.3	786	23.2	2.4	86.1	9.0	132 145	4.7	9 889	7.5	175 647	75.3	51.0	15.7
Mobile	42.1	717	34.3	8.9	85.0	5.9	14 997	20.2	2 160	14.4	20 254	70.4	41.5	14.3
Montgomery	39.8	780	34.1	8.9	77.6	6.8	37 225	-1.4	2 541	6.8	54 034	70.8	35.4	16.7
Opelika	33.6	604	31.8	10.3	82.7	8.8	3 208	NA	373	11.6	23 512	0.0	10.6	51.0
Phenix City	42.8	671	30.6	8.0	74.0	14.2	112 536	-1.0	6 279	5.6	143 612	77.9	52.0	11.8
Prattville	26.8	857	24.9	4.6	84.8	9.4	117 459	-18.6	11 715	10.0	171 004	67.8	42.8	22.4
Tuscaloosa	51.4	713	38.1	9.4	74.5	11.0	3 100 253	-1.8	325 485	10.5	4 897 769	62.1	39.6	28.2
Vestavia Hills	25.4	1 038	30.4	6.4	84.9	12.7	15 283	2.6	1 271	8.3	29 477	49.6	30.0	46.6
ALASKA	34.8	981	27.6	9.6	78.6	11.6	36 276	-5.3	3 391	9.3	52 341	72.2	51.7	13.5
Anchorage	37.7	1 017	28.0	5.9	76.6	8.2	21 612	69.1	2 624	12.1	32 439	65.5	50.2	16.3
Fairbanks	58.9	1 082	30.4	8.5	70.4	18.2	21 397	-1.3	2 438	11.4	32 996	53.5	29.9	45.1
Juneau	38.0	1 132	27.3	9.0	78.9	8.7	21 727	5.7	2 395	11.0	34 217	63.7	36.7	28.2
ARIZONA	33.5	863	31.1	6.6	79.9	11.3	154 253 483	0.3	14 860 461	9.6	241 366 686	65.1	41.3	26.1
Apache Junction	20.9	725	31.0	8.1	87.7	9.1	2 179 163	0.4	206 776	9.5	3 754 375	60.6	39.3	30.8
Avondale	35.1	1 124	28.7	3.4	77.6	15.0	16 363	5.3	1 031	6.3	23 006	74.1	52.8	16.6
Buckeye	25.3	1 097	27.5	2.1	73.2	19.6	24 121	-6.0	1 868	7.7	44 378	59.7	28.0	28.1
Bullhead City	36.7	814	32.3	6.2	76.0	12.1	10 096	-3.5	1 352	13.4	21 912	56.6	36.5	38.6
Casa Grande	31.9	790	34.9	6.8	74.1	11.3	90 937	-5.3	10 716	11.8	172 894	61.3	36.5	32.1
Chandler	34.5	1 001	28.4	3.7	76.5	14.8	26 495	0.4	2 596	9.8	43 903	64.3	40.8	31.1
El Mirage	28.4	1 089	34.5	1.6	81.9	13.7	29 069	-1.8	2 437	8.4	51 041	60.7	40.4	29.0
Flagstaff	52.8	960	35.9	4.3	71.2	15.6	11 126	5.1	780	7.0	20 208	59.0	44.3	29.5
Florence	26.0	657	21.8	6.1	50.4	38.9	17 979	4.9	1 572	8.7	31 369	57.7	32.5	36.7
Gilbert	28.7	1 193	28.0	1.6	75.9	17.0	14 112	2.2	1 587	11.2	29 361	51.2	30.9	44.3
Glendale	39.3	843	32.7	8.0	80.0	13.2	13 787	6.8	830	6.0	20 087	68.6	42.0	21.4
Goodyear	24.8	1 152	24.6	2.5	76.4	18.0	43 161	16.4	2 419	5.6	60 959	69.8	48.1	18.8
Kingman	33.9	786	29.8	8.6	71.8	13.7	90 889	1.1	6 796	7.5	143 997	67.1	42.4	26.7
Lake Havasu City	28.9	845	28.9	4.2	80.6	7.0	24 057	9.6	1 301	5.4	31 923	72.3	51.5	11.8
Marana	21.4	1 109	24.7	3.4	79.1	16.4	89 068	4.8	9 269	10.4	153 672	61.5	39.0	30.9
Maricopa	22.0	1 183	29.1	1.7	76.1	19.3	21 330	5.0	2 774	13.0	27 478	74.5	54.5	12.5
Mesa	35.7	846	31.4	6.4	80.5	10.5	222 234	-13.1	19 719	8.9	341 778	63.6	40.5	29.3
Oro Valley	24.2	1 031	26.1	1.8	82.3	13.7	18 777	15.9	1 246	6.6	33 564	53.8	33.8	40.5
Peoria	25.9	1 129	30.9	4.3	85.2	9.7	75 030	11.2	5 209	6.9	116 198	67.6	45.8	24.0
Phoenix	41.7	851	31.9	9.0	78.4	7.5	741 933	-13.8	83 461	11.2	1 084 657	67.1	45.3	20.7
Prescott	35.0	749	33.6	6.6	77.7	13.4	18 295	-3.6	1 790	9.8	34 781	48.5	26.9	44.9
Prescott Valley	32.6	857	31.0	3.0	78.1	15.1	13 582	-3.4	1 512	11.1	29 615	61.3	34.1	34.4
Queen Creek	16.1	1 410	27.0	0.6	79.1	13.4	0	NA	0	0.0	15 991	0.0	52.7	10.7
Sahuarita	18.3	1 194	27.2	2.0	80.0	14.5	12 490	NA	1 094	8.8	17 430	61.4	42.4	32.8
San Luis	27.5	468	26.4	11.8	NA	NA	8 234	NA	4 084	49.6	17 488	44.6	20.5	34.0
Scottsdale	29.0	1 096	29.7	5.1	83.6	10.6	119 196	-16.1	8 606	7.2	184 615	63.4	42.1	29.1
Sierra Vista	43.5	879	24.2	6.5	71.4	17.8	19 521	-1.1	1 047	5.4	34 431	63.5	46.7	28.3
Surprise	22.5	1 218	32.7	2.1	80.8	12.2	44 443	29.0	5 309	11.9	82 955	59.1	39.0	32.6
Tempe	54.0	884	31.5	8.2	69.0	19.6	97 553	-20.1	8 250	8.5	137 210	71.3	39.1	20.8
Tucson	47.6	696	33.7	11.7	74.8	8.7	257 898	-9.8	26 753	10.4	413 026	62.7	36.8	28.2
Yuma	40.7	810	31.2	6.1	75.5	11.2	47 685	2.5	9 886	20.7	68 636	64.3	41.6	28.5
ARKANSAS	32.8	622	29.4	6.6	82.3	11.3	1 356 625	0.0	107 712	7.9	2 269 018	60.7	39.4	30.7
Bella Vista	12.4	1 109	28.1	1.5	87.6	8.3	8 424	1.2	556	6.6	21 026	50.6	37.0	42.2
Benton	29.2	698	30.8	6.0	80.1	14.2	13 945	4.8	896	6.4	23 732	64.4	43.4	26.7
Bentonville	42.3	649	24.8	6.5	73.2	16.1	14 971	1.3	1 143	7.6	24 396	69.4	54.0	16.7
Conway	48.9	682	31.7	4.9	67.1	15.9	28 385	2.1	1 753	6.2	45 540	68.1	41.1	21.9
Fayetteville	57.4	628	32.1	6.5	65.4	18.0	38 659	-0.3	2 452	6.3	60 705	67.2	37.8	23.6
Fort Smith	43.0	571	28.6	6.9	81.9	7.9	42 328	-0.1	3 498	8.3	66 878	59.6	40.6	28.6
Hot Springs	44.2	654	31.6	14.3	76.4	12.1	17 019	-0.8	1 696	10.0	29 001	52.6	31.5	39.5

1. $2,000 represents $2,000 or more. 2. 50.0 represents 50 percent or more. 3. Percent of civilian labor force. 4. Persons 16 years old and over.

Table D. Cities — Construction, Wholesale Trade, and Retail Trade

City	Value of residential construction authorized by building permits, 2010			Wholesale trade,[1] 2007				Retail trade,[2] 2007			
	New construction ($1,000)	Number of housing units	Percent single family	Number of establishments	Number of employees	Sales (mil dol)	Annual payroll (mil dol)	Number of establishments	Number of employees	Sales (mil dol)	Annual payroll (mil dol)
	69	70	71	72	73	74	75	76	77	78	79
United States..............	138 694	511	100.0	17	D	D	D	109	2 955	631.7	61.4
ALABAMA	6 901	35	100.0	19	240	136.9	9.5	154	3 085	993.6	72.5
Alabaster	14 426	93	87.1	58	361	97.5	10.8	272	3 279	862.8	82.4
Auburn	101 362	511	67.1	21	255	98.8	12.1	98	3 098	748.7	72.1
Bessemer	46 459	620	31.8	263	4 995	3 039.3	211.3	952	13 945	3 132.0	304.9
Birmingham	38 325	342	50.9	30	671	659.2	26.9	207	2 792	675.1	54.1
Decatur........................	70 924	660	39.4	13	205	74.1	8.9	114	1 077	233.2	21.2
Dothan........................	26 030	191	70.7	21	123	39.5	4.2	169	2 312	598.2	58.4
Enterprise	67 023	493	45.0	85	1 051	473.6	45.0	504	7 545	1 693.2	159.4
Florence	17 395	39	100.0	37	686	443.4	46.9	146	1 689	388.4	38.3
Gadsden	204 680	904	83.3	658	8 262	4 563.6	391.6	2 641	34 977	9 303.4	936.8
Homewood	116 574	480	79.4	339	5 498	2 914.0	261.0	923	15 842	4 482.7	441.8
Hoover.........................	0	0	0.0	51	714	355.1	33.4	244	4 031	1 185.6	113.4
Huntsville....................	12 879	53	86.8	33	D	D	D	172	1 933	465.3	52.0
Madison	151 653	509	100.0	220	4 198	4 585.9	291.8	694	15 714	3 608.3	353.3
Mobile.........................	0	0	0.0	5	43	17.9	1.7	25	487	89.1	10.0
Montgomery	16 137	183	29.5	66	856	405.9	29.8	362	5 566	1 174.4	119.0
Opelika	20 024	173	100.0	NA	NA	NA	NA	17	104	30.0	2.8
Phenix City	166 090	1 060	100.0	147	1 450	649.3	59.7	441	8 466	2 079.1	207.2
Prattville.....................	25 408	130	56.9	135	2 079	1 013.5	70.0	714	15 566	3 627.8	332.3
Tuscaloosa..................	2 424 190	12 370	86.9	5 874	84 029	57 573.6	4 116.4	19 384	337 529	86 758.8	8 010.8
Vestavia Hills..............	13 607	104	100.0	17	66	24.7	1.8	96	2 181	447.5	45.4
ALASKA	12 382	59	100.0	14	181	73.4	11.3	126	4 287	1 601.3	126.1
Anchorage...................	76 996	380	100.0	9	D	D	D	48	449	215.2	14.2
Fairbanks....................	7 695	28	100.0	9	70	26.1	2.5	146	2 668	570.7	58.1
Juneau........................	16 192	137	100.0	23	374	139.4	12.8	195	2 981	676.7	64.4
ARIZONA	101 943 061	604 610	74.0	369 387	5 098 545	4 174 286.5	260 532.1	1 128 112	15 515 396	3 917 663.5	362 818.7
Apache Junction...........	1 546 975	11 261	77.3	4 824	70 469	52 252.8	3 032.2	19 722	238 922	57 344.9	5 112.0
Avondale	4 980	29	100.0	38	330	806.5	14.6	98	1 700	388.7	42.6
Buckeye.......................	80 371	420	68.6	22	200	88.3	6.8	207	3 148	672.4	62.5
Bullhead City...............	996	8	100.0	70	1 208	60.9	60.0	211	2 550	633.2	60.2
Casa Grande	54 579	457	24.1	537	11 374	6 667.8	523.1	1 137	15 093	4 690.4	358.1
Chandler......................	9 630	56	100.0	82	1 163	793.0	51.6	355	4 319	1 159.6	97.5
El Mirage.....................	42 285	242	79.3	140	D	D	D	651	7 329	1 790.2	167.1
Flagstaff	21 061	234	52.1	10	58	15.3	1.7	177	2 196	570.2	49.3
Florence	11 258	140	48.6	50	443	143.3	13.0	307	4 425	951.7	87.0
Gilbert.........................	816	16	100.0	38	331	168.7	11.6	276	3 364	722.6	63.6
Glendale	3 001	8	100.0	78	864	670.5	43.7	257	3 891	662.8	82.8
Goodyear.....................	64 806	301	100.0	81	1 092	1 045.4	90.8	418	8 411	2 117.6	197.0
Kingman	45 377	1 073	100.0	238	3 505	2 425.2	166.1	1 016	15 593	3 675.8	351.6
Lake Havasu City.........	103 648	281	100.0	48	634	382.7	33.7	133	2 066	530.8	48.2
Marana	40 787	286	54.2	350	4 591	2 311.0	208.0	1 004	15 513	3 557.8	341.6
Maricopa.....................	32 291	188	100.0	7	D	D	D	30	524	149.6	11.2
Mesa...........................	134 490	487	100.0	301	3 372	2 037.3	174.1	1 507	28 855	6 294.5	653.9
Oro Valley	24 259	57	100.0	11	38	11.8	1.3	79	1 999	395.9	37.0
Peoria	53 153	442	100.0	56	368	251.2	14.8	353	8 143	2 340.4	216.9
Phoenix	302 754	1 695	65.5	1 946	34 585	23 670.5	1 650.7	4 266	77 534	21 859.5	1 913.7
Prescott	20 520	103	51.5	64	509	276.5	22.0	318	5 205	1 227.5	121.5
Prescott Valley	9 686	71	29.6	29	611	393.1	22.4	109	1 274	281.2	28.8
Queen Creek...............	44 269	161	100.0	15	94	42.8	2.6	36	1 033	241.1	21.9
Sahuarita	65 786	306	100.0	3	22	3.5	1.0	19	766	168.0	19.1
San Luis	11 227	85	100.0	5	25	7.0	0.8	34	383	77.2	6.3
Scottsdale...................	120 791	294	54.4	538	5 811	3 445.5	314.3	1 378	22 923	6 645.4	664.9
Sierra Vista.................	27 321	169	100.0	13	120	28.4	3.5	163	3 284	726.4	73.8
Surprise	49 480	215	98.1	23	97	20.4	3.5	147	4 064	888.2	85.7
Tempe.........................	57 215	296	17.2	511	11 117	7 286.1	722.2	847	16 389	6 172.5	447.5
Tucson........................	72 480	388	88.7	473	5 730	2 124.6	224.0	2 080	37 716	8 647.0	887.8
Yuma..........................	29 355	172	100.0	79	1 318	817.9	51.8	391	7 294	1 683.6	153.0
ARKANSAS...............	880 263	7 177	64.8	2 977	38 988	29 659.8	1 536.3	11 906	140 018	32 974.3	2 889.2
Bella Vista	NA	NA	NA	6	18	2.9	0.4	30	415	66.9	8.6
Benton	38 374	229	97.4	17	106	75.4	3.6	146	1 839	488.4	38.7
Bentonville..................	60 363	276	93.5	63	1 624	447.3	52.9	134	2 038	703.3	55.6
Conway	69 977	950	23.6	47	438	229.7	17.6	301	4 595	1 077.3	91.8
Fayetteville.................	72 806	248	100.0	60	798	440.2	30.6	430	7 281	1 646.9	147.5
Fort Smith...................	54 751	365	67.9	172	2 275	1 216.1	90.0	545	7 273	1 667.4	152.7
Hot Springs	4 175	38	100.0	48	325	120.6	10.3	386	4 741	1 184.0	104.4

1. Merchant wholesalers except manufacturers' sales branches and offices.   2. Establishments with payroll.

Table D. Cities — Real Estate, Professional Services, and Manufacturing

City	Real estate and rental and leasing, 2007				Professional, scientific, and technical services,[1] 2007				Manufacturing, 2007			
	Number of establishments	Number of employees	Receipts (mil dol)	Annual payroll (mil dol)	Number of establishments	Number of employees	Receipts (mil dol)	Annual payroll (mil dol)	Number of establishments	Number of employees	Receipts (mil dol)	Annual payroll (mil dol)
	80	81	82	83	84	85	86	87	88	89	90	91
United States.............	61	166	33.7	5.6	67	355	36.6	15.1	20	760	185.5	30.2
ALABAMA	53	181	26.5	5.7	65	D	D	D	NA	NA	NA	NA
Alabaster	108	307	55.8	8.0	100	350	45.3	14.5	78	1 399	238.6	49.8
Auburn.........................	40	107	14.6	3.2	53	205	20.4	7.0	28	783	243.7	39.1
Bessemer	292	2 333	288.1	71.5	633	6 216	876.2	335.8	176	11 155	6 943.7	499.7
Birmingham	38	175	21.3	3.6	69	D	D	D	47	2 801	D	112.5
Decatur........................	38	136	18.5	2.7	42	205	13.8	4.6	29	1 659	D	93.5
Dothan.........................	32	124	19.3	3.4	57	D	D	D	21	1 335	D	D
Enterprise	142	925	142.0	26.0	262	1 978	180.0	66.7	64	5 390	2 115.6	216.1
Florence	67	D	D	D	147	D	D	D	NA	NA	NA	NA
Gadsden......................	852	4 370	840.6	160.2	1 799	12 509	2 006.8	745.4	544	13 298	8 204.0	489.5
Homewood...................	378	2 416	453.5	94.0	1 092	D	D	D	194	2 305	D	D
Hoover........................	91	518	116.9	22.9	140	D	D	D	NA	NA	NA	NA
Huntsville....................	58	241	41.1	5.9	95	D	D	D	NA	NA	NA	NA
Madison......................	301	1 171	228.0	37.7	610	7 138	373.9	490.9	162	8 577	3 956.0	502.4
Mobile........................	7	15	3.2	0.4	6	D	D	D	NA	NA	NA	NA
Montgomery	156	533	105.5	17.1	255	D	D	D	72	3 429	1 314.2	213.1
Opelika.......................	4	11	0.7	0.2	7	D	D	D	NA	NA	NA	NA
Phenix City..................	307	1 003	185.2	34.7	462	D	D	D	115	2 941	415.9	94.5
Prattville.....................	250	1 208	202.9	30.9	302	D	D	D	159	3 904	913.0	193.7
Tuscaloosa..................	9 441	52 627	10 077.6	1 994.3	16 563	128 188	17 617.1	7 239.5	5 074	172 438	57 977.8	8 774.3
Vestavia Hills...............	42	123	23.5	3.8	30	122	9.7	2.7	NA	NA	NA	NA
ALASKA	54	228	32.6	8.6	44	200	20.6	6.2	NA	NA	NA	NA
Anchorage...................	15	58	46.9	2.3	22	149	22.1	7.1	NA	NA	NA	NA
Fairbanks.....................	65	231	33.9	6.0	51	D	D	D	NA	NA	NA	NA
Juneau........................	61	244	40.4	7.3	49	D	D	D	28	1 624	1 040.0	73.6
ARIZONA	384 297	2 188 479	485 058.6	84 764.9	842 607	7 678 304	1 220 434.1	489 965.4	332 536	13 395 670	5 319 456.3	613 768.6
Apache Junction...........	4 554	27 100	4 073.2	823.4	9 437	92 759	13 623.2	4 996.4	4 928	271 986	112 858.8	11 351.6
Avondale	11	53	8.5	1.4	60	600	268.2	31.4	25	1 094	287.6	45.8
Buckeye......................	62	357	44.4	8.8	105	D	D	D	55	3 672	869.0	135.3
Bullhead City...............	35	131	17.5	4.1	75	D	D	D	51	1 780	373.1	70.3
Casa Grande................	339	3 706	526.1	145.8	901	D	D	D	305	15 835	4 724.8	749.4
Chandler......................	74	290	39.9	6.7	159	970	80.9	31.8	90	4 463	2 650.1	204.3
El Mirage	115	D	D	D	222	D	D	D	102	5 180	1 153.6	183.0
Flagstaff......................	49	223	24.7	5.6	57	346	41.8	10.4	18	856	318.4	24.8
Florence	62	255	40.5	7.2	154	D	D	D	64	2 700	987.2	100.3
Gilbert........................	46	226	41.0	5.6	118	626	51.3	19.9	58	4 239	977.8	167.6
Glendale......................	65	438	76.0	16.7	183	1 545	241.3	79.7	27	1 297	594.3	57.6
Goodyear.....................	97	720	247.7	25.5	280	2 269	460.3	136.1	NA	NA	NA	NA
Kingman......................	330	1 720	277.8	54.7	997	28 335	5 091.5	1 988.4	195	21 059	8 209.6	1 028.7
Lake Havasu City..........	59	253	48.2	7.9	130	D	D	D	33	1 205	D	50.1
Marana	324	1 729	282.3	51.3	739	D	D	D	156	7 341	2 338.8	362.5
Maricopa......................	14	33	3.2	0.6	29	83	5.5	3.7	NA	NA	NA	NA
Mesa..........................	594	2 834	524.9	80.1	1 081	7 105	708.1	301.8	257	8 764	3 072.5	585.6
Oro Valley	72	D	D	D	125	481	49.4	24.4	13	D	D	D
Peoria.........................	152	710	114.5	25.1	218	D	D	D	54	1 341	267.8	45.3
Phoenix.......................	2 227	17 353	3 261.0	746.4	5 038	46 488	7 094.6	2 922.4	1 626	57 398	16 926.9	2 733.3
Prescott	188	444	81.9	11.5	237	D	D	D	71	1 536	267.6	61.2
Prescott Valley	54	187	39.0	6.2	50	200	12.2	4.4	42	856	214.5	31.9
Queen Creek................	31	46	4.2	0.8	50	117	11.2	3.2	NA	NA	NA	NA
Sahuarita	5	17	1.4	0.3	11	27	2.3	0.8	NA	NA	NA	NA
San Luis	10	22	3.4	0.4	5	D	D	D	NA	NA	NA	NA
Scottsdale...................	1 102	5 637	1 992.0	335.8	1 970	D	D	D	252	8 620	4 806.6	611.1
Sierra Vista.................	62	337	44.3	9.1	102	D	D	D	NA	NA	NA	NA
Surprise	55	445	48.1	6.8	83	437	27.5	11.1	NA	NA	NA	NA
Tempe........................	451	3 423	768.9	138.5	1 005	10 930	1 321.4	606.0	453	17 621	5 877.6	835.4
Tucson........................	865	5 832	834.2	176.8	1 759	12 057	1 416.0	567.6	459	10 964	3 446.1	489.9
Yuma..........................	143	572	90.3	13.2	169	D	D	D	53	2 662	830.4	82.6
ARKANSAS...............	3 162	14 115	1 968.1	374.9	5 588	D	D	D	3 088	184 568	60 735.6	6 518.4
Bella Vista	36	73	7.9	1.7	35	69	6.5	2.0	NA	NA	NA	NA
Benton........................	33	106	14.5	2.0	62	210	15.8	5.7	29	571	124.3	D
Bentonville..................	66	223	32.1	5.2	186	2 300	191.4	135.6	25	1 074	293.8	57.6
Conway	98	336	48.7	8.8	159	614	62.3	19.0	56	5 036	1 540.8	207.2
Fayetteville.................	160	1 797	126.9	48.4	354	D	D	D	59	5 223	1 309.7	178.0
Fort Smith...................	150	675	128.8	20.2	265	D	D	D	160	18 247	5 080.4	589.3
Hot Springs	97	491	68.5	11.7	150	D	D	D	47	D	D	D

1. Establishments subject to federal tax.

Table D. Cities — Accommodation and Food Services, Arts, Entertainment, and Recreation, and Health Care and Social Assistance

City	Accommodation and food services, 2007				Arts, entertainment, and recreation,[1] 2007				Health care and social assistance,[1] 2007			
	Number of establish-ments	Number of employees	Sales (mil dol)	Annual payroll (mil dol)	Number of establish-ments	Number of employees	Receipts (mil dol)	Annual payroll (mil dol)	Number of establish-ments	Number of employees	Receipts (mil dol)	Annual payroll (mil dol)
	92	93	94	95	96	97	98	99	100	101	102	103
United States	76	2 167	105.1	32.5	10	D	D	D	101	D	D	D
ALABAMA	93	1 716	75.6	21.0	9	D	D	D	104	D	D	D
Alabaster	136	2 574	104.7	30.3	14	255	12.2	3.0	161	D	D	D
Auburn	88	1 903	76.8	20.9	12	D	D	D	38	D	D	D
Bessemer	456	9 565	395.9	110.4	31	D	D	D	572	8 657	931.2	356.1
Birmingham	75	1 893	71.4	21.3	3	D	D	D	83	D	D	D
Decatur	65	1 156	45.9	11.8	5	D	D	D	49	D	D	D
Dothan	87	2 054	83.3	23.7	6	D	D	D	61	D	D	D
Enterprise	276	6 318	260.7	68.7	17	266	11.8	4.4	219	2 808	282.4	122.7
Florence	66	1 218	50.4	13.5	14	257	14.0	5.6	88	D	D	D
Gadsden	1 996	25 638	1 851.3	529.8	392	3 738	291.8	55.1	1 603	15 416	1 820.6	714.2
Homewood	720	14 031	933.3	283.9	109	D	D	D	851	9 685	1 181.7	451.7
Hoover	139	2 569	155.7	43.1	26	765	25.6	5.0	131	D	D	D
Huntsville	97	1 228	86.9	21.6	24	D	D	D	87	648	65.7	26.4
Madison	456	10 153	500.9	153.6	48	2 316	314.3	66.6	557	5 196	540.8	186.1
Mobile	7	47	2.4	0.7	1	D	D	D	4	D	D	D
Montgomery	269	5 546	294.5	77.3	30	630	23.8	9.3	292	2 407	259.8	107.0
Opelika	18	379	28.7	5.5	4	D	D	D	11	D	D	D
Phenix City	248	4 450	191.2	54.5	35	D	D	D	421	D	D	D
Prattville	394	7 516	340.7	97.5	37	1 444	97.7	69.9	514	6 077	747.4	291.7
Tuscaloosa	11 610	250 716	13 268.5	3 766.3	1 510	39 112	3 816.4	1 171.2	13 643	154 061	16 655.7	6 572.3
Vestavia Hills	58	915	36.3	8.5	8	161	6.2	1.5	39	D	D	D
ALASKA	97	2 113	94.6	26.1	11	D	D	D	85	D	D	D
Anchorage	25	271	17.2	4.1	5	D	D	D	9	D	D	D
Fairbanks	80	1 240	54.6	15.3	7	231	5.9	3.8	106	D	D	D
Juneau	80	1 758	75.2	20.4	7	94	4.9	1.5	107	1 424	127.8	52.1
ARIZONA	634 361	11 600 751	613 795.7	170 826.8	100 656	1 496 869	151 958.0	45 916.0	647 120	8 322 326	818 394.6	330 887.7
Apache Junction	8 093	150 791	6 426.3	1 751.4	843	11 475	950.1	188.1	8 502	134 925	12 637.2	5 167.2
Avondale	44	737	38.4	10.0	5	D	D	D	93	D	D	D
Buckeye	168	3 419	123.1	32.7	14	D	D	D	79	D	D	D
Bullhead City	75	1 427	62.3	16.6	11	128	12.8	3.2	87	D	D	D
Casa Grande	549	11 539	587.7	165.0	45	749	61.4	13.4	738	13 898	1 705.5	701.3
Chandler	144	3 009	122.4	33.1	10	D	D	D	219	2 770	259.0	97.8
El Mirage	208	4 333	174.0	47.8	17	D	D	D	255	D	D	D
Flagstaff	74	1 401	47.5	12.4	8	D	D	D	73	D	D	D
Florence	113	3 145	118.7	36.0	14	D	D	D	190	D	D	D
Gilbert	105	2 299	94.6	27.3	7	D	D	D	185	4 572	514.5	182.6
Glendale	121	2 962	142.5	38.8	5	D	D	D	177	D	D	D
Goodyear	176	4 257	224.0	64.5	20	292	18.5	4.3	196	D	D	D
Kingman	480	10 921	471.9	133.4	48	D	D	D	593	D	D	D
Lake Havasu City	89	1 580	72.7	19.3	9	102	3.1	1.0	85	1 270	93.5	36.5
Marana	461	10 113	427.5	122.1	42	485	23.4	6.5	470	10 484	983.1	458.6
Maricopa	30	457	18.3	5.0	2	D	D	D	22	D	D	D
Mesa	788	16 920	753.2	210.0	79	1 677	80.5	22.6	1 096	12 584	1 403.7	543.9
Oro Valley	52	1 630	81.8	23.1	9	221	6.7	3.7	93	1 323	142.7	53.6
Peoria	217	6 006	258.5	78.5	30	623	30.9	11.3	293	3 900	350.9	152.0
Phoenix	2 600	61 385	3 644.4	1 027.3	333	7 211	729.6	285.8	3 232	39 166	4 469.4	1 897.0
Prescott	164	2 528	111.2	32.8	14	109	3.9	1.3	294	2 682	241.5	92.7
Prescott Valley	72	993	40.6	12.0	8	258	10.8	3.0	90	783	53.9	19.6
Queen Creek	34	527	25.6	6.8	7	D	D	D	55	508	31.7	15.5
Sahuarita	14	217	7.8	2.0	3	D	D	D	10	D	D	D
San Luis	14	234	11.0	2.4	1	D	D	D	7	D	D	D
Scottsdale	705	22 206	1 314.3	403.3	160	4 435	306.6	102.6	1 272	10 821	1 295.3	516.9
Sierra Vista	99	1 854	86.8	24.2	5	D	D	D	124	1 347	122.3	52.1
Surprise	112	2 720	115.1	34.8	11	D	D	D	111	D	D	D
Tempe	566	11 197	606.8	163.2	61	1 420	292.7	159.2	495	7 572	960.3	306.7
Tucson	1 210	27 059	1 214.9	347.5	137	1 582	74.6	22.6	1 476	18 451	1 869.0	784.8
Yuma	232	5 084	230.0	60.3	13	D	D	D	259	3 240	305.6	116.7
ARKANSAS	5 112	89 933	3 559.8	994.1	607	6 136	346.2	92.6	5 718	77 215	7 150.8	2 895.5
Bella Vista	19	178	8.6	2.3	2	D	D	D	22	298	18.7	8.7
Benton	55	856	33.3	9.5	9	55	2.8	0.8	79	D	D	D
Bentonville	123	2 275	88.5	26.5	11	182	7.6	2.5	97	1 531	173.6	63.5
Conway	135	3 325	122.3	33.0	15	D	D	D	194	2 488	202.1	81.4
Fayetteville	281	5 943	231.9	66.1	23	284	11.2	4.5	245	3 139	355.4	136.7
Fort Smith	233	4 785	197.0	54.0	16	D	D	D	294	5 620	516.1	248.4
Hot Springs	188	4 262	168.9	52.6	34	D	D	D	186	3 079	342.2	140.0

1. Establishments subject to federal tax.

Table D. Cities — Other Services and Federal Funds

City	Other services[1], 2007				Selected federal funds, 2009–2010 (mil dol)								
	Number of establishments	Number of employees	Receipts (mil dol)	Annual payroll (mil dol)	Procurement contracts		Grants						
					Defense	Other	Total[2]	Medicaid and other health related	Nutrition and family welfare	Energy and environment	Disasters and emergency preparedness	Housing and community development	Employment and training
	104	105	106	107	108	109	110	111	112	113	114	115	116
United States..............	35	181	9.2	3.3	61.9	0.2	0.6	0.0	0.0	0.5	0.0	0.0	0.0
ALABAMA	51	438	32.0	10.0	5.3	2.5	2.3	0.0	0.0	0.0	0.0	1.6	0.0
Alabaster	122	689	47.7	14.3	0.6	4.2	0.4	0.0	0.0	0.0	0.0	0.0	0.0
Auburn	57	D	D	D	1.7	0.5	5.2	2.4	0.0	0.0	0.0	0.0	0.0
Bessemer	311	D	D	D	406.5	68.6	1 069.9	127.5	156.2	85.9	-3.5	71.2	127.3
Birmingham	43	175	14.6	3.9	1.4	1.1	5.1	0.0	0.0	0.0	0.0	5.0	0.0
Decatur	50	D	D	D	0.6	0.3	8.1	0.0	1.9	0.2	0.0	5.2	0.0
Dothan	43	D	D	D	0.0	0.0	1.9	0.0	0.0	0.6	0.0	0.4	0.0
Enterprise	118	1 122	76.9	25.5	120.1	142.6	115.1	24.6	6.7	15.0	0.0	9.4	0.5
Florence	60	422	25.1	9.8	0.0	0.0	0.0	0.0	0.0	0.0	0.0	0.0	0.0
Gadsden	871	4 874	477.0	145.2	1 776.3	687.9	3 465.2	1 065.9	283.0	260.3	15.8	174.4	56.0
Homewood	394	2 642	241.2	78.2	963.9	278.6	576.9	39.1	18.2	26.9	3.3	73.1	9.0
Hoover	88	648	60.5	19.8	77.8	66.1	114.2	25.3	7.0	22.5	0.0	10.8	0.0
Huntsville......................	47	228	18.1	5.1	2.0	41.2	466.9	34.6	45.0	114.2	0.2	19.5	43.7
Madison	237	2 032	136.7	53.4	189.0	9.0	10.1	0.1	0.0	2.3	0.0	6.8	0.0
Mobile	18	79	5.8	1.7	0.0	0.0	2.2	0.0	0.0	0.0	0.7	0.0	0.0
Montgomery	132	890	58.7	18.8	3.8	14.4	80.1	11.3	14.7	11.3	0.8	4.1	0.2
Opelika	4	D	D	D	0.0	37.0	5.9	0.0	0.0	0.0	0.0	0.0	0.0
Phenix City..................	198	1 083	68.4	19.9	48.0	23.4	5.8	0.0	0.0	1.8	3.0	0.8	0.0
Prattville......................	297	1 597	127.0	40.4	29.7	2.3	17.2	0.0	0.0	2.4	0.0	13.0	0.0
Tuscaloosa	7 444	52 045	3 940.2	1 230.9	10 831.4	1 981.7	14 361.0	8 500.6	1 460.7	449.2	12.7	710.9	146.4
Vestavia Hills................	43	143	10.2	3.0	0.0	0.0	0.0	0.0	0.0	0.0	0.0	0.0	0.0
ALASKA	43	322	19.7	6.8	0.0	0.0	0.5	0.0	0.0	0.0	-0.9	0.5	0.0
Anchorage..................	7	D	D	D	0.0	0.1	4.6	0.0	0.0	0.0	4.2	0.0	0.0
Fairbanks......................	40	223	16.9	4.8	0.0	1.5	0.3	0.0	0.0	0.3	0.0	0.0	0.0
Juneau......................	58	426	23.6	7.5	0.0	0.0	9.8	1.9	0.0	2.1	0.0	3.7	0.0
ARIZONA	432 302	2 598 622	219 837.5	66 828.9	329 872.9	184 951.4	675 282.4	357 482.0	74 796.2	26 084.7	6 668.4	35 873.9	9 977.6
Apache Junction..........	5 606	33 791	3 102.5	851.5	8 140.1	2 341.6	9 273.4	4 946.9	949.1	370.3	46.6	382.0	137.5
Avondale......................	37	D	D	D	185.2	0.0	0.0	0.0	0.0	0.0	0.0	0.0	0.0
Buckeye......................	62	367	20.2	6.6	21.3	2.9	68.0	6.3	5.9	4.8	0.0	2.9	0.0
Bullhead City..................	54	492	62.3	15.5	4.8	0.1	66.8	0.0	0.0	0.0	0.0	7.2	0.0
Casa Grande................	409	3 825	367.7	123.2	42.8	236.4	842.1	481.8	17.6	167.6	2.2	87.1	1.2
Chandler......................	96	D	D	D	7.9	0.3	20.0	0.2	12.1	0.0	0.0	7.3	0.0
El Mirage	153	D	D	D	3.9	0.8	17.9	0.5	7.0	0.0	0.0	5.1	3.0
Flagstaff......................	48	D	D	D	41.2	7.9	3.1	0.0	0.0	0.0	0.0	0.8	0.0
Florence	87	D	D	D	0.9	1.1	8.2	0.8	1.2	0.0	0.0	5.4	0.0
Gilbert......................	56	D	D	D	0.1	8.6	21.8	7.1	2.0	0.1	0.0	3.4	0.0
Glendale......................	65	440	38.9	12.7	5.8	14.3	0.0	0.0	0.0	0.0	0.0	0.0	0.0
Goodyear......................	91	570	54.3	17.8	0.2	0.4	0.4	0.0	0.0	0.0	0.0	0.0	0.0
Kingman......................	289	2 629	502.4	71.1	4 741.0	384.8	108.8	15.4	3.4	13.8	0.0	14.6	0.0
Lake Havasu City.........	38	206	12.6	3.9	187.0	12.2	0.2	0.0	0.0	0.0	0.0	0.0	0.0
Marana......................	345	2 892	177.2	65.0	466.9	42.9	109.9	39.3	0.4	3.9	2.0	38.3	0.0
Maricopa......................	12	D	D	D	0.0	0.0	2.0	0.2	0.0	0.4	0.0	0.7	0.0
Mesa......................	596	5 247	320.5	103.4	1 145.0	66.1	41.5	0.7	0.3	0.6	4.0	17.6	0.0
Oro Valley......................	47	D	D	D	1.1	0.7	0.0	0.0	0.0	0.0	0.0	0.0	0.0
Peoria......................	185	1 009	80.0	22.2	1.3	5.3	4.7	0.0	0.0	3.1	0.0	1.5	0.0
Phoenix	1 829	15 911	1 318.6	380.6	1 873.8	378.1	2 074.8	173.1	364.3	121.2	-0.1	374.0	123.1
Prescott......................	115	552	41.8	12.6	0.3	8.4	4.4	0.9	0.0	0.5	0.0	0.3	0.0
Prescott Valley	54	207	15.9	5.2	0.0	0.1	0.6	0.0	0.0	0.0	0.0	0.0	0.0
Queen Creek................	26	114	9.2	3.0	0.0	0.0	0.4	0.0	0.0	0.0	0.0	0.0	0.0
Sahuarita......................	6	D	D	D	0.1	0.0	0.0	0.0	0.0	0.0	0.0	0.0	0.0
San Luis	4	D	D	D	47.0	1.6	1.7	0.0	0.0	0.0	0.0	0.0	0.0
Scottsdale......................	531	3 388	257.0	85.0	568.2	133.2	90.6	21.2	2.7	4.4	0.0	10.2	0.1
Sierra Vista...................	41	252	14.5	4.7	192.8	8.4	2.1	0.0	0.0	0.2	0.0	0.8	0.0
Surprise......................	76	425	48.0	17.1	0.1	0.1	6.5	4.3	0.0	1.1	0.0	0.8	0.0
Tempe	286	2 437	202.4	69.8	362.3	34.6	251.2	36.1	0.0	80.0	0.6	12.0	0.0
Tucson......................	810	5 535	417.7	133.5	5 200.9	160.7	579.6	208.8	28.7	54.1	0.1	99.6	3.9
Yuma......................	125	728	52.3	16.8	19.4	20.7	31.9	0.6	8.5	3.1	0.0	9.6	0.1
ARKANSAS...............	3 325	18 421	1 407.7	426.5	1 137.5	613.5	6 843.0	3 731.0	680.6	109.3	76.9	265.1	100.8
Bella Vista......................	7	D	D	D	NA	NA	NA	NA	NA	NA	NA	NA	NA
Benton......................	50	237	20.4	5.9	-0.1	0.0	6.6	0.0	3.2	0.0	0.0	3.4	0.0
Bentonville......................	54	638	28.3	20.8	0.0	0.2	4.2	0.8	0.0	1.1	0.0	0.2	0.0
Conway......................	79	D	D	D	0.3	0.7	38.0	0.1	6.4	0.0	24.1	2.1	0.0
Fayetteville......................	118	765	43.4	14.6	7.9	55.8	87.3	9.4	4.5	9.6	0.6	3.9	0.0
Fort Smith......................	140	D	D	D	5.6	12.8	17.4	1.6	0.5	0.9	0.0	8.7	0.0
Hot Springs	84	411	25.3	8.5	2.3	1.5	4.9	0.0	0.0	0.0	0.0	4.0	0.0

1. Establishments subject to federal tax.   2. Includes program categories not shown separately. State totals include additional categories not allocated by city.

Table D. Cities — City Government Finances

City	General revenue Total (mil dol)	Intergovernmental Total (mil dol)	Intergovernmental Percent from state government	Taxes Total (mil dol)	Taxes Per capita (dollars) Total	Taxes Per capita (dollars) Property	Taxes Per capita (dollars) Sales and gross receipts	General expenditure Total (mil dol)	General expenditure Per capita (dollars) Total	General expenditure Capital outlays
	117	118	119	120	121	122	123	124	125	126
United States.............	206.2	103.1	100.0	68.3	1 293	234	1 059	152.2	2 880	1 545
ALABAMA	43.1	16.3	100.0	15.3	552	16	537	40.1	1 447	245
Alabaster	88.2	27.4	82.8	33.4	590	116	475	146.4	2 586	1 399
Auburn......................	67.7	16.6	63.8	42.7	1 340	0	1 340	104.6	3 283	1 674
Bessemer	240.4	32.7	45.4	175.6	860	131	729	212.7	1 042	97
Birmingham................	50.8	4.7	12.7	35.6	1 377	260	812	42.4	1 640	293
Decatur......................	32.7	2.0	71.6	20.8	679	130	548	33.6	1 097	287
Dothan........................	28.8	0.4	0.0	20.5	639	56	583	25.1	784	0
Enterprise....................	120.8	29.2	43.6	65.0	732	115	608	108.9	1 227	213
Florence	33.3	2.5	53.3	25.6	825	374	451	30.2	973	81
Gadsden......................	X	X	X	X	X	X	X	X	X	X
Homewood..................	1 143.1	467.0	93.0	469.1	1 677	1 461	217	1 089.1	3 894	733
Hoover.......................	43.2	8.5	84.9	17.3	500	337	163	35.3	1 023	192
Huntsville...................	246.3	57.4	90.9	80.7	2 631	1 223	1 407	235.9	7 686	1 599
Madison......................	313.2	88.1	92.8	143.4	582	109	473	381.3	1 548	543
Mobile.......................	31.2	12.3	100.0	9.1	343	83	260	22.7	860	0
Montgomery	149.2	39.5	78.1	66.6	1 114	291	823	117.9	1 973	271
Opelika	20.4	8.5	95.5	5.6	314	17	297	15.8	887	134
Phenix City.................	287.2	73.0	78.8	163.1	738	89	649	260.9	1 257	603
Prattville.....................	367.8	126.9	82.9	138.6	547	52	496	301.9	1 192	32
Tuscaloosa	X	X	X	X	X	X	X	X	X	X
Vestavia Hills...............	38.5	17.6	100.0	17.0	533	0	533	32.6	1 021	0
ALASKA	110.0	25.2	94.0	61.4	770	55	715	101.8	1 276	380
Anchorage....................	45.8	5.2	95.9	33.7	1 125	195	925	30.6	1 020	9
Fairbanks.....................	58.8	22.2	100.0	19.2	468	4	464	49.0	1 195	12
Juneau........................	76.6	14.7	82.9	37.4	982	65	917	58.2	1 525	269
ARIZONA	X	X	X	X	X	X	X	X	X	X
Apache Junction...........	X	X	X	X	X	X	X	X	X	X
Avondale	41.1	2.6	100.0	17.4	606	85	451	36.0	1 254	331
Buckeye......................	73.2	2.4	60.3	52.3	963	241	578	51.2	943	212
Bullhead City...............	50.1	6.1	58.8	35.8	1 248	222	863	49.7	1 786	270
Casa Grande................	490.6	42.5	38.5	380.5	1 656	239	1 059	398.2	1 733	130
Chandler.....................	87.2	10.5	100.0	41.3	741	44	697	94.8	1 702	214
El Mirage	68.6	3.2	16.0	49.0	748	42	706	74.5	1 138	66
Flagstaff.....................	25.0	2.4	96.3	17.7	726	113	614	25.9	1 059	203
Florence	62.4	12.3	94.6	40.0	1 069	262	807	51.6	1 377	100
Gilbert........................	63.0	3.0	26.1	48.4	1 311	108	849	64.6	1 749	54
Glendale......................	53.7	0.4	100.0	45.3	1 893	612	1 281	27.2	1 137	65
Goodyear.....................	104.5	5.2	57.0	82.9	1 186	126	1 034	94.3	1 349	162
Kingman	305.0	23.1	69.7	200.8	1 172	235	937	212.8	1 242	104
Lake Havasu City.........	32.9	1.9	84.2	22.8	597	138	459	40.8	1 066	313
Marana.......................	357.5	25.8	27.4	247.1	1 291	68	1 051	266.4	1 392	178
Maricopa.....................	54.9	8.3	100.0	29.5	778	58	720	17.4	459	181
Mesa..........................	538.7	190.6	82.6	177.0	391	0	378	618.8	1 366	224
Oro Valley	58.4	31.8	95.2	16.1	400	41	294	58.8	1 463	766
Peoria........................	260.1	64.5	73.9	101.0	688	122	566	290.9	1 983	824
Phoenix......................	3 081.9	1 018.4	63.4	1 066.6	687	137	549	2 912.4	1 876	764
Prescott	107.7	17.9	94.2	37.2	880	67	813	85.1	2 014	752
Prescott Valley	46.0	13.3	100.0	16.4	435	0	435	50.1	1 327	449
Queen Creek................	42.4	4.2	99.3	24.3	1 030	0	1 030	89.9	3 806	2 191
Sahuarita....................	39.3	9.6	93.8	23.3	1 444	0	1 444	76.8	4 755	1 789
San Luis	18.6	8.9	96.3	4.8	203	0	203	63.6	2 671	1 837
Scottsdale....................	575.0	92.5	92.4	268.2	1 138	215	923	402.9	1 710	317
Sierra Vista..................	57.4	19.2	91.6	23.9	554	115	439	51.5	1 195	77
Surprise......................	215.8	57.2	98.5	72.5	799	59	741	221.6	2 442	1 493
Tempe	385.3	136.0	40.9	167.8	964	159	805	312.3	1 794	400
Tucson........................	749.7	284.2	71.1	270.4	514	72	443	643.4	1 224	177
Yuma.........................	125.9	38.6	91.0	53.6	604	83	521	148.8	1 677	593
ARKANSAS...............	X	X	X	X	X	X	X	X	X	X
Bella Vista	NA	NA	NA	NA	NA	NA	NA	NA	NA	NA
Benton........................	18.2	2.7	60.0	11.0	388	51	337	21.8	769	183
Bentonville...................	47.1	7.2	39.6	20.8	615	116	499	46.2	1 369	557
Conway.......................	69.6	4.1	66.1	29.1	511	37	474	55.1	966	136
Fayetteville	104.0	22.1	40.3	43.7	605	43	562	131.8	1 825	869
Fort Smith...................	125.0	28.4	40.6	58.7	696	119	577	106.0	1 257	426
Hot Springs	65.0	8.6	89.3	30.6	782	1	781	54.3	1 389	273

1. Based on population estimated as of July 1 of the year shown.

City	Public welfare	Highways	Parking facilities	Education	Health and hospitals	Police protection	Sewerage and sanitation	Parks and recreation	Housing and community development	Interest on debt
	127	128	129	130	131	132	133	134	135	136
United States.............	0.0	7.8	0.0	0.0	0.0	7.5	12.7	2.3	4.0	3.5
ALABAMA	0.0	22.9	0.0	0.0	0.0	21.3	9.8	9.9	0.0	2.1
Alabaster	0.0	5.4	0.0	0.0	0.0	8.3	55.5	6.5	0.3	3.8
Auburn..........................	0.0	47.7	0.0	0.0	0.0	9.7	0.0	5.7	0.2	2.2
Bessemer	0.0	13.1	0.1	1.1	0.1	18.6	0.9	14.1	2.3	4.0
Birmingham	0.0	14.1	0.0	10.4	0.6	14.9	12.6	6.4	0.4	7.5
Decatur.........................	0.1	9.5	0.0	0.0	0.2	14.1	14.6	16.9	0.0	6.4
Dothan..........................	0.0	3.6	0.0	0.0	0.0	21.9	17.9	7.2	0.0	4.7
Enterprise	0.0	10.5	0.0	0.0	0.2	20.6	18.9	4.0	3.1	2.5
Florence	0.0	3.7	0.0	2.5	0.6	15.1	8.1	9.2	0.1	4.8
Gadsden.......................	X	X	X	X	X	X	X	X	X	X
Homewood	0.0	8.8	0.6	52.0	2.2	7.8	5.8	6.1	0.0	2.9
Hoover..........................	0.0	23.5	0.6	0.0	0.0	19.9	1.0	0.0	0.0	1.8
Huntsville......................	0.0	3.9	0.1	34.6	27.8	5.6	4.2	3.7	1.1	2.4
Madison........................	0.0	22.9	0.0	0.0	0.0	17.2	6.2	0.1	4.8	4.2
Mobile..........................	0.0	6.5	0.0	0.0	0.0	32.4	17.4	3.7	5.5	1.9
Montgomery	0.0	23.6	0.0	0.0	0.0	12.3	15.3	0.0	10.8	2.5
Opelika	0.0	10.7	0.0	0.0	0.0	12.1	23.5	7.0	1.3	1.1
Phenix City	0.0	14.1	0.0	0.0	0.0	11.9	16.5	21.1	0.5	3.7
Prattville.......................	0.2	8.6	0.0	0.0	0.0	18.7	13.0	6.0	2.5	7.8
Tuscaloosa	X	X	X	X	X	X	X	X	X	X
Vestavia Hills...............	0.0	25.6	0.0	0.0	0.0	24.8	0.0	12.3	5.3	0.9
ALASKA	0.5	12.1	0.0	0.0	1.2	15.9	21.0	8.8	4.3	3.7
Anchorage	0.0	6.2	0.0	0.0	0.0	25.2	20.5	2.3	0.0	1.2
Fairbanks......................	0.0	19.9	0.0	0.0	0.0	27.2	7.1	4.4	0.5	3.1
Juneau..........................	0.0	8.6	0.0	0.0	0.0	17.8	16.1	6.5	4.3	2.2
ARIZONA	X	X	X	X	X	X	X	X	X	X
Apache Junction............	X	X	X	X	X	X	X	X	X	X
Avondale	0.0	9.2	0.0	0.0	0.0	13.6	15.9	7.6	0.0	9.0
Buckeye........................	0.1	7.2	0.0	0.0	0.4	14.3	15.8	18.7	0.0	7.3
Bullhead City	2.5	4.3	0.0	2.1	0.0	18.9	7.9	2.2	4.6	1.7
Casa Grande................	0.0	18.6	2.4	0.3	0.4	16.7	5.4	6.4	0.2	6.0
Chandler.......................	0.1	2.8	0.0	0.0	0.7	11.7	15.3	6.7	2.9	13.9
El Mirage	0.1	6.6	0.0	4.0	1.0	19.0	18.4	12.8	0.0	0.0
Flagstaff.......................	0.5	10.7	0.0	17.9	2.2	15.2	17.6	9.0	0.0	3.5
Florence	0.0	9.5	0.1	14.8	0.7	15.0	6.5	8.8	0.9	9.5
Gilbert..........................	0.0	1.2	0.0	0.9	0.0	13.0	11.1	8.9	2.2	5.3
Glendale.......................	0.0	0.0	0.0	0.0	0.2	27.9	7.5	11.1	0.0	9.0
Goodyear......................	0.0	6.3	0.0	7.5	0.3	19.3	6.8	12.1	0.3	5.5
Kingman	0.0	4.1	0.9	0.0	0.6	15.8	10.0	8.5	5.1	11.9
Lake Havasu City..........	0.0	38.1	0.0	0.0	0.0	11.5	0.0	4.8	0.0	12.5
Marana.........................	0.0	5.6	4.2	0.0	0.2	20.4	11.4	10.9	0.0	6.4
Maricopa.......................	0.0	11.9	0.0	0.0	0.0	14.0	0.0	7.4	2.6	0.0
Mesa............................	0.6	9.9	0.0	0.0	0.0	24.4	16.1	8.4	3.1	7.0
Oro Valley	0.0	58.0	0.0	0.0	0.0	19.5	0.0	3.8	0.0	2.1
Peoria	0.0	8.3	0.0	0.2	0.0	9.2	27.4	12.0	0.7	2.8
Phoenix	0.4	8.1	0.2	0.7	0.0	15.4	17.6	13.3	4.4	6.7
Prescott	0.0	25.1	0.1	0.0	0.0	14.2	19.2	6.3	3.9	1.9
Prescott Valley	0.0	23.4	0.0	0.0	0.0	14.1	12.6	5.0	0.5	8.8
Queen Creek................	0.0	24.3	0.0	0.0	0.0	3.0	16.8	4.8	0.0	1.4
Sahuarita......................	0.0	37.5	0.0	0.0	0.0	4.6	9.8	11.2	0.3	1.9
San Luis	0.0	4.4	0.0	0.0	0.0	5.3	17.0	3.8	0.8	4.7
Scottsdale.....................	0.0	14.6	0.0	0.0	0.0	19.4	15.3	10.4	1.8	9.5
Sierra Vista	0.0	23.1	0.0	0.0	0.0	21.9	14.2	11.4	3.1	2.3
Surprise	0.0	9.7	0.0	0.0	0.0	22.2	31.7	7.2	0.3	1.1
Tempe	0.0	6.2	0.0	0.0	0.3	21.5	16.0	15.1	8.5	5.1
Tucson..........................	0.0	8.5	0.0	0.0	0.0	19.3	6.3	7.5	16.3	3.8
Yuma............................	0.0	19.6	0.0	0.0	0.0	18.3	17.3	11.2	1.3	4.0
ARKANSAS...............	X	X	X	X	X	X	X	X	X	X
Bella Vista	NA	NA	NA	NA	NA	NA	NA	NA	NA	NA
Benton	0.0	14.8	0.0	0.0	1.7	18.0	16.1	6.4	2.1	1.4
Bentonville....................	0.0	34.8	0.0	0.0	0.0	9.0	12.5	3.3	0.0	1.2
Conway	0.0	2.9	0.0	0.0	0.0	17.7	23.9	2.6	1.1	12.8
Fayetteville	0.0	8.7	0.5	0.0	0.7	9.5	51.0	2.9	0.8	5.1
Fort Smith.....................	0.0	23.7	0.3	0.0	0.1	12.0	25.3	3.0	1.8	1.6
Hot Springs	0.0	7.7	0.2	0.0	1.0	18.4	31.4	3.7	1.2	2.5

Table D. Cities — City Government Finances, City Government Employment, and Climate

City	City government finances, 2007 (cont.) Debt outstanding Total (mil dol)	Per capita[1] (dollars)	Debt issued during year	City government employment, 2010	Climate[2] Average daily temperature (degrees Fahrenheit) Mean January	July	Limits January[3]	July[4]	Annual precipitation (inches)	Heating degree days	Cooling degree days
	137	138	139	140	141	142	143	144	145	146	147
United States..............	189.5	3 585	42.9	558	NA	NA	NA	NA	NA	NA	NA
ALABAMA	21.8	786	3.7	NA	NA	NA	NA	NA	NA	NA	NA
Alabaster	197.8	3 494	37.0	NA	53.9	95.2	42.9	107.5	6.25	1 230	4 523
Auburn	64.5	2 025	29.0	NA	NA	NA	NA	NA	NA	NA	NA
Bessemer	201.1	985	37.1	2 869	46.6	81.8	35.5	92.7	54.77	2 194	2 252
Birmingham	93.8	3 631	1.9	380	NA	NA	NA	NA	NA	NA	NA
Decatur.......................	123.2	4 017	50.8	382	46.8	82.0	36.6	91.7	48.57	2 154	2 296
Dothan........................	60.6	1 891	33.0	369	NA	NA	NA	NA	NA	NA	NA
Enterprise	193.3	2 179	41.5	1 252	42.9	80.4	32.5	90.8	54.99	2 787	1 893
Florence	32.2	1 037	0.0	266	NA	NA	NA	NA	NA	NA	NA
Gadsden......................	X	X	X	NA	X	X	X	X	X	X	X
Homewood	1 660.0	5 936	127.7	9 941	15.8	58.4	9.3	65.3	16.08	10 470	3
Hoover........................	11.4	331	0.0	186	-9.7	62.4	-19.0	73.0	10.34	13 980	74
Huntsville....................	182.5	5 946	50.1	1 914	25.7	56.8	20.7	64.3	58.33	8 574	0
Madison......................	446.1	1 810	134.9	1 652	54.3	91.3	41.5	105.7	9.23	1 271	3 798
Mobile........................	20.4	771	12.5	182	NA	NA	NA	NA	NA	NA	NA
Montgomery	147.8	2 474	50.1	813	29.7	66.1	16.5	82.2	22.91	6 999	126
Opelika.......................	14.4	807	0.4	NA	NA	NA	NA	NA	NA	NA	NA
Phenix City..................	450.4	2 170	146.2	1 134	54.3	91.3	41.5	105.7	9.23	1 271	3 798
Prattville.....................	864.6	3 415	177.8	1 927	52.5	90.6	39.2	104.2	7.78	1 535	3 488
Tuscaloosa..................	X	X	X	NA	X	X	X	X	X	X	X
Vestavia Hills..............	16.7	524	6.1	NA	52.7	89.5	40.0	104.3	12.29	1 542	3 443
ALASKA	87.2	1 093	21.0	411	54.7	93.5	41.3	107.6	9.03	1 173	4 166
Anchorage...................	29.9	998	15.0	NA	NA	NA	NA	NA	NA	NA	NA
Fairbanks....................	56.4	1 377	0.0	NA	54.4	95.6	43.3	111.7	5.84	1 164	4 508
Juneau........................	25.0	656	0.5	NA	52.4	90.4	37.3	105.1	9.22	1 572	3 554
ARIZONA	X	X	X	NA	X	X	X	X	X	X	X
Apache Junction...........	X	X	X	NA	X	X	X	X	X	X	X
Avondale.....................	72.3	2 520	15.2	230	NA	NA	NA	NA	NA	NA	NA
Buckeye......................	216.2	3 978	15.6	535	44.7	79.9	34.2	89.7	52.63	2 507	1 932
Bullhead City...............	43.0	1 501	1.5	542	42.9	81.0	30.8	93.6	59.38	2 766	1 943
Casa Grande................	930.7	4 050	329.2	4 911	42.6	80.2	32.3	90.0	53.99	2 823	1 881
Chandler......................	226.6	4 066	5.3	695	38.9	79.2	29.1	90.3	55.31	3 469	1 609
El Mirage....................	56.6	805	0.0	986	47.7	81.3	36.2	93.3	56.61	2 058	2 264
Flagstaff......................	20.8	854	1.3	580	NA	NA	NA	NA	NA	NA	NA
Florence	125.0	3 337	1.9	805	39.9	80.2	30.7	90.6	55.80	3 236	1 789
Gilbert........................	86.2	2 335	0.0	698	40.3	79.8	29.9	90.5	56.10	3 220	1 716
Glendale......................	50.1	2 095	0.0	358	42.6	80.2	32.3	90.6	53.99	2 823	1 881
Goodyear.....................	118.3	1 693	0.0	662	42.9	81.0	30.8	93.6	59.38	2 766	1 943
Kingman......................	684.0	3 992	68.1	2 703	39.8	79.5	30.7	89.4	57.51	3 262	1 671
Lake Havasu City.........	103.9	2 714	0.8	374	46.6	81.8	35.5	92.7	54.77	2 194	2 252
Marana	536.0	2 800	66.0	2 991	50.1	81.5	39.5	91.2	66.29	1 681	2 539
Maricopa.....................	0.0	0	0.0	NA	NA	NA	NA	NA	NA	NA	NA
Mesa..........................	1 142.4	2 522	230.4	3 514	54.3	91.3	41.5	105.7	9.23	1 271	3 798
Oro Valley	72.1	1 794	9.6	NA	50.6	86.3	34.6	100.7	12.40	1 831	2 810
Peoria.........................	403.4	2 749	214.4	1 208	54.7	93.5	41.3	107.6	9.03	1 173	4 166
Phoenix	7 082.8	4 563	958.8	14 366	54.2	92.8	43.4	104.2	8.29	1 125	4 189
Prescott......................	54.6	1 292	8.9	570	37.1	73.4	23.3	88.3	19.19	4 849	742
Prescott Valley	69.4	1 836	0.0	212	NA	NA	NA	NA	NA	NA	NA
Queen Creek................	81.2	3 440	81.2	NA	NA	NA	NA	NA	NA	NA	NA
Sahuarita	28.3	1 750	0.0	NA	NA	NA	NA	NA	NA	NA	NA
San Luis	73.3	3 079	5.5	204	NA	NA	NA	NA	NA	NA	NA
Scottsdale....................	968.8	4 111	221.5	2 489	54.2	92.8	43.4	104.2	8.29	1 125	4 189
Sierra Vista	25.5	593	1.6	415	47.7	79.1	33.7	92.6	14.02	2 369	1 739
Surprise	103.0	1 135	52.0	777	54.7	93.5	41.3	107.6	9.03	1 173	4 166
Tempe........................	604.1	3 470	168.5	1 888	54.1	89.9	40.1	103.6	9.36	1 390	3 655
Tucson........................	1 136.0	2 162	303.3	5 300	54.0	88.5	41.9	100.5	12.00	1 333	3 501
Yuma..........................	157.2	1 773	0.0	964	58.1	94.1	46.2	107.3	3.01	782	4 540
ARKANSAS...............	X	X	X	NA	X	X	X	X	X	X	X
Bella Vista	NA	NA	NA	NA	NA	NA	NA	NA	NA	NA	NA
Benton........................	51.0	1 800	26.5	261	NA	NA	NA	NA	NA	NA	NA
Bentonville..................	34.8	1 030	5.0	430	NA	NA	NA	NA	NA	NA	NA
Conway.......................	179.3	3 145	33.1	475	38.3	82.1	28.1	92.4	48.67	3 320	1 961
Fayetteville	172.8	2 393	61.0	718	34.3	78.9	24.2	89.1	46.02	4 166	1 439
Fort Smith...................	239.4	2 837	87.2	875	38.0	82.2	27.8	92.9	43.87	3 437	1 929
Hot Springs	42.3	1 083	4.8	612	40.2	82.2	29.6	94.3	57.69	3 133	1 993

1. Based on the population estimated as of July 1 of the year shown.   2. Represents normal values based on the 30-year period, 1971–2000.   3. Average daily minimum.   4. Average daily maximum.

Table D. Cities — **Land Area and Population**

STATE Place code	City	Land area,[1] 2010 (sq km)	Population, 2010 Total persons	Rank	Per square kilometer	Race alone or in combination, not of Hispanic origin (percent), 2010 White	Black	American Indian, Alaska Native	Asian	Hawaiian Pacific Islander	Percent Hispanic or Latino[2], 2010	Percent Foreign born, 2008–2010
		1	2	3	4	5	6	7	8	9	10	11
	ARKANSAS—Cont'd											
05 34750	Jacksonville.........	72.8	28 364	1 456	389.7	57.7	34.4	1.4	2.9	0.2	6.7	3.6
05 35710	Jonesboro.........	206.9	67 263	510	325.2	74.4	19.3	0.8	1.8	0.1	5.2	4.4
05 41000	Little Rock.........	308.7	193 524	119	626.8	47.7	42.9	0.7	3.0	0.1	6.8	7.9
05 50450	North Little Rock.........	133.4	62 304	570	467.2	53.0	40.6	1.0	1.3	0.1	5.7	3.9
05 53390	Paragould.........	80.8	26 113	1 591	323.1	95.5	1.2	1.0	0.5	0.1	2.8	1.3
05 55310	Pine Bluff.........	115.5	49 083	786	425.1	22.1	76.1	0.5	0.7	0.0	1.5	1.3
05 60410	Rogers.........	98.3	55 964	671	569.5	63.4	1.7	1.5	2.9	0.4	31.5	20.3
05 61670	Russellville.........	73.2	27 920	1 480	381.3	80.7	6.1	1.2	1.9	0.1	11.7	5.9
05 63800	Sherwood.........	53.4	29 523	1 394	553.1	75.2	19.4	1.0	2.1	0.1	4.0	5.1
05 66080	Springdale.........	108.3	69 797	488	644.7	54.2	2.1	1.6	2.3	5.9	35.4	24.2
05 68810	Texarkana.........	107.9	29 919	1 366	277.3	62.8	33.9	1.1	0.8	0.1	2.8	1.9
05 74540	West Memphis.........	73.7	26 245	1 579	356.3	34.3	63.9	0.4	0.5	0.0	1.6	0.5
06 00000	**CALIFORNIA......**	403 466.3	37 253 956	X	92.3	42.3	6.5	1.0	14.3	0.6	37.6	27.2
06 00296	Adelanto.........	145.1	31 765	1 284	219.0	18.8	21.1	1.0	2.2	0.8	58.3	18.3
06 00562	Alameda.........	27.5	73 812	460	2 686.0	50.0	7.6	1.2	34.6	1.0	11.0	28.3
06 00884	Alhambra.........	19.8	83 089	384	4 204.9	11.1	1.6	0.4	53.7	0.3	34.4	50.2
06 00947	Aliso Viejo.........	19.4	47 823	821	2 471.5	65.6	2.5	0.6	17.7	0.6	17.1	24.4
06 02000	Anaheim.........	129.1	336 265	54	2 605.3	29.0	2.8	0.5	15.8	0.7	52.8	38.6
06 02252	Antioch.........	73.4	102 372	277	1 394.3	39.2	18.6	1.5	12.3	1.2	31.7	21.9
06 02364	Apple Valley.........	189.6	69 135	492	364.7	58.0	9.8	1.5	3.6	0.6	29.2	7.4
06 02462	Arcadia.........	28.3	56 364	662	1 991.7	27.1	1.4	0.4	60.5	0.3	12.1	47.7
06 03064	Atascadero.........	66.4	28 310	1 459	426.3	79.1	2.5	1.7	3.2	0.3	15.6	5.9
06 03162	Atwater.........	15.8	28 168	1 465	1 786.2	37.6	4.6	1.1	5.7	0.5	52.6	21.3
06 03386	Azusa.........	25.0	46 361	850	1 853.7	20.5	3.2	0.5	9.3	0.3	67.6	31.5
06 03526	Bakersfield.........	368.2	347 483	51	943.7	39.6	8.5	1.4	6.7	0.2	45.5	18.2
06 03666	Baldwin Park.........	17.2	75 390	445	4 390.8	4.6	1.0	0.2	14.2	0.2	80.1	45.5
06 03820	Banning.........	59.8	29 603	1 387	494.8	45.1	7.7	2.0	6.7	0.2	41.1	19.8
06 04758	Beaumont.........	80.1	36 877	1 076	460.6	44.9	6.6	1.4	8.6	0.4	40.3	17.8
06 04870	Bell.........	6.5	35 477	1 133	5 474.8	5.2	0.7	0.3	0.9	0.0	93.1	46.1
06 04982	Bellflower.........	15.8	76 616	432	4 836.9	21.0	14.4	0.7	12.3	1.1	52.3	30.9
06 04996	Bell Gardens.........	6.4	42 072	936	6 604.7	2.8	0.5	0.3	0.6	0.1	95.7	45.4
06 05108	Belmont.........	12.0	25 835	1 606	2 158.3	65.5	2.2	0.7	23.1	1.4	11.5	29.7
06 05290	Benicia.........	33.5	26 997	1 532	806.1	70.4	6.7	1.5	13.6	1.0	12.0	10.0
06 06000	Berkeley.........	27.1	112 580	236	4 151.2	58.9	11.1	1.0	22.3	0.4	10.8	22.2
06 06308	Beverly Hills.........	14.8	34 109	1 185	2 307.8	82.8	2.6	0.4	12.3	0.3	5.7	38.9
06 08100	Brea.........	31.3	39 282	1 008	1 255.8	54.8	1.7	0.7	19.7	0.5	25.0	24.1
06 08142	Brentwood.........	38.3	51 481	744	1 344.2	57.9	7.4	1.2	10.0	0.9	26.8	14.2
06 08786	Buena Park.........	27.3	80 530	401	2 954.1	29.5	4.0	0.6	27.8	0.8	39.3	37.3
06 08954	Burbank.........	44.9	103 340	273	2 301.0	61.0	3.0	0.6	13.4	0.3	24.5	34.4
06 09066	Burlingame.........	11.4	28 806	1 434	2 524.6	63.6	1.6	0.4	22.8	0.7	13.8	25.9
06 09710	Calexico.........	21.7	38 572	1 025	1 775.1	1.7	0.1	0.1	1.1	0.0	96.8	45.2
06 10046	Camarillo.........	50.6	65 201	541	1 289.1	64.5	2.3	0.8	11.9	0.5	22.9	17.5
06 10345	Campbell.........	15.0	39 349	1 005	2 619.8	61.8	3.6	0.9	18.6	0.7	18.4	22.6
06 11194	Carlsbad.........	97.7	105 328	262	1 078.1	77.7	1.7	0.6	9.1	0.5	13.3	14.8
06 11530	Carson.........	48.5	91 714	328	1 891.0	9.0	24.3	0.6	26.6	3.0	38.6	35.3
06 12048	Cathedral City.........	55.7	51 200	755	919.5	33.5	2.6	0.8	5.3	0.2	58.8	31.2
06 12524	Ceres.........	20.8	45 417	868	2 188.8	33.3	2.7	1.5	7.6	1.0	56.0	27.9
06 12552	Cerritos.........	22.6	49 041	789	2 170.0	18.4	7.2	0.4	63.7	0.7	12.0	45.3
06 13014	Chico.........	85.3	86 187	362	1 010.8	76.9	2.9	2.2	5.5	0.5	15.4	8.1
06 13210	Chino.........	76.8	77 983	417	1 015.8	29.1	6.3	0.7	11.1	0.3	53.8	25.7
06 13214	Chino Hills.........	115.7	74 799	454	646.4	35.6	4.9	0.5	31.8	0.4	29.1	28.2
06 13392	Chula Vista.........	128.5	243 916	77	1 897.6	22.5	4.9	0.6	15.6	0.8	58.2	30.6
06 13588	Citrus Heights.........	36.9	83 301	383	2 260.5	75.9	4.1	1.9	4.6	0.7	16.5	12.1
06 13756	Claremont.........	34.6	34 926	1 154	1 010.3	62.0	5.3	0.8	15.1	0.4	19.8	16.5
06 14218	Clovis.........	60.3	95 631	309	1 586.2	59.9	3.1	1.7	11.8	0.4	25.6	11.4
06 14260	Coachella.........	75.0	40 704	975	542.9	2.5	0.4	0.2	0.5	0.0	96.4	39.3
06 14890	Colton.........	39.7	52 154	731	1 314.0	14.2	9.7	0.6	5.3	0.4	71.0	25.3
06 15044	Compton.........	25.9	96 455	308	3 719.8	1.2	32.9	0.5	0.4	0.8	65.0	29.2
06 16000	Concord.........	79.1	122 067	211	1 543.0	53.7	4.1	1.1	13.2	1.0	30.6	26.1
06 16350	Corona.........	100.6	152 374	162	1 515.3	40.1	6.2	0.7	11.1	0.6	43.6	25.2
06 16532	Costa Mesa.........	40.5	109 960	242	2 712.4	54.1	1.7	0.7	9.2	0.8	35.8	25.4
06 16742	Covina.........	18.2	47 796	825	2 626.2	31.5	4.3	0.7	12.6	0.4	52.4	21.5
06 17568	Culver City.........	13.2	38 883	1 015	2 936.8	51.4	10.7	0.8	17.0	0.5	23.2	26.0
06 17610	Cupertino.........	29.2	58 302	631	2 000.1	31.7	0.8	0.4	65.8	0.3	3.6	49.8
06 17750	Cypress.........	17.0	47 802	824	2 805.3	46.3	3.6	0.8	33.2	0.8	18.4	28.2
06 17918	Daly City.........	19.9	101 123	280	5 094.4	15.8	4.0	0.4	57.2	1.2	23.7	53.2
06 17946	Dana Point.........	16.8	33 351	1 216	1 981.6	78.4	1.1	1.0	4.2	0.3	17.0	12.5
06 17988	Danville.........	46.7	42 039	937	900.4	81.2	1.2	0.5	12.9	0.4	6.8	12.1
06 18100	Davis.........	25.6	65 622	535	2 562.4	62.7	2.8	0.9	24.6	0.4	12.5	18.0

1. Dry land or land partially or temporarily covered by water.   2. May be of any race.

City	Under 5 years	5 to 17 years	18 to 24 years	25 to 34 years	35 to 44 years	45 to 54 years	55 to 64 years	65 to 74 years	75 years and over	Median age	Percent female	1990	2000	1990–2000	2000–2010
					Age of population (percent), 2010							Census counts		Percent change	
	12	13	14	15	16	17	18	19	20	21	22	23	24	25	26
ARKANSAS—Cont'd															
Jacksonville	8.9	18.0	13.1	15.5	11.9	12.3	9.9	5.9	4.4	30.8	50.7	29 101	29 916	2.8	-5.2
Jonesboro	7.6	17.2	15.0	15.3	11.6	11.7	9.8	6.2	5.7	31.3	51.7	46 535	55 515	19.3	21.2
Little Rock	7.0	17.2	9.5	16.3	13.2	13.8	11.8	5.8	5.5	35.1	52.3	175 727	183 133	4.2	5.7
North Little Rock	7.4	16.8	9.5	15.2	12.5	13.8	11.8	6.4	6.6	35.9	52.7	61 829	60 433	-2.3	3.1
Paragould	7.4	18.3	9.4	13.6	12.9	12.9	11.0	7.6	7.0	36.0	52.0	18 540	22 017	18.8	18.6
Pine Bluff	7.3	18.2	13.4	13.0	11.4	13.4	11.0	6.2	6.2	33.4	52.5	57 140	55 085	-3.6	-10.9
Rogers	9.1	21.5	9.1	15.3	14.7	12.6	8.4	4.7	4.6	31.7	51.0	24 692	38 829	57.3	44.1
Russellville	7.2	14.5	22.4	13.2	10.6	10.8	9.1	6.2	6.2	29.1	51.1	21 260	23 682	11.4	17.9
Sherwood	7.0	17.1	8.0	15.1	13.8	13.9	12.5	7.4	5.2	37.0	52.6	18 890	21 511	13.9	37.2
Springdale	10.3	22.3	9.8	16.5	13.5	11.1	7.6	4.7	4.1	29.6	50.3	29 945	45 798	52.9	52.4
Texarkana	7.5	16.3	9.8	14.6	12.5	13.3	12.2	7.3	6.3	36.2	51.2	22 631	26 448	16.9	13.1
West Memphis	8.7	21.1	9.8	12.9	11.8	13.5	10.8	6.4	5.0	32.9	53.8	28 259	27 666	-2.1	-5.1
CALIFORNIA	6.8	18.2	10.5	14.3	13.9	14.1	10.8	6.1	5.3	35.2	50.3	29 785 857	33 871 648	13.7	10.0
Adelanto	10.3	26.8	12.3	15.7	13.5	10.7	6.2	2.8	1.6	25.3	48.6	6 815	18 130	166.0	75.2
Alameda	5.7	15.1	7.4	12.9	15.6	16.1	13.8	6.9	6.6	40.7	52.2	73 979	72 259	-2.3	2.1
Alhambra	5.2	13.7	9.5	15.1	14.9	15.1	12.2	6.9	7.4	39.3	52.7	82 087	85 804	4.5	-3.2
Aliso Viejo	7.7	18.2	7.8	16.0	19.8	16.8	8.3	3.3	2.1	35.1	51.9	7 612	40 166	427.7	19.1
Anaheim	7.7	19.7	10.9	15.5	14.6	13.3	9.2	5.1	4.2	32.4	50.3	266 406	328 014	23.1	2.5
Antioch	7.1	21.0	10.3	13.0	13.8	15.3	10.6	5.1	3.7	33.8	51.3	62 195	90 532	45.6	13.1
Apple Valley	6.9	21.0	9.4	10.7	11.1	13.7	11.7	8.5	6.9	37.0	51.0	46 079	54 239	17.7	27.5
Arcadia	4.3	17.5	7.3	9.9	13.9	17.5	13.3	8.2	8.2	43.1	52.3	48 284	53 054	9.9	6.2
Atascadero	5.9	15.5	8.1	13.4	12.1	16.5	15.4	7.1	5.9	41.0	49.2	23 138	26 411	14.1	7.2
Atwater	8.9	23.1	10.5	14.2	12.4	11.8	8.7	5.9	4.5	30.0	51.1	22 282	23 113	3.7	21.9
Azusa	7.5	19.2	16.7	14.5	13.9	11.9	8.5	4.4	3.3	29.3	51.0	41 203	44 712	8.5	3.7
Bakersfield	9.0	22.5	10.8	14.7	13.2	12.4	8.9	4.7	3.7	30.0	51.0	176 264	247 057	40.2	40.6
Baldwin Park	7.8	22.1	11.7	14.6	14.1	12.5	9.2	4.6	3.4	30.5	50.4	69 330	75 837	9.4	-0.6
Banning	6.2	16.7	9.2	11.1	9.3	10.9	10.7	11.6	14.3	42.3	51.7	20 572	23 562	14.5	25.6
Beaumont	9.1	21.0	7.9	16.1	13.9	11.1	10.4	6.8	3.8	32.5	51.2	9 685	11 384	17.5	223.9
Bell	8.8	23.2	11.6	15.9	14.5	11.5	7.7	3.9	2.9	28.9	49.6	34 365	36 664	6.7	-3.2
Bellflower	7.6	20.8	11.1	14.9	14.3	13.2	9.5	4.9	3.7	31.9	51.4	61 815	72 878	17.9	5.1
Bell Gardens	9.3	24.7	12.4	15.9	14.3	11.2	6.9	3.2	2.0	27.3	50.1	42 315	44 054	4.1	-4.5
Belmont	6.6	14.3	6.5	13.0	16.5	15.9	12.3	7.4	7.5	40.9	51.2	24 165	25 123	4.0	2.8
Benicia	4.8	18.6	7.1	9.7	12.9	18.1	16.4	7.4	5.0	42.9	51.9	24 437	26 865	9.9	0.6
Berkeley	3.7	8.6	26.9	15.7	11.1	10.9	11.3	6.6	5.1	31.0	51.1	102 724	102 743	0.0	9.6
Beverly Hills	3.8	15.7	7.4	12.3	12.7	15.6	13.4	9.0	10.1	43.6	54.3	31 971	33 784	5.7	1.0
Brea	5.5	17.6	9.3	12.5	14.7	16.0	11.9	6.8	5.8	38.7	51.2	32 873	35 410	7.7	10.9
Brentwood	7.0	24.2	7.5	10.8	16.7	14.4	8.4	6.5	4.9	35.6	51.5	7 563	23 302	208.1	120.9
Buena Park	6.5	18.8	10.7	14.0	14.2	15.0	10.3	5.6	5.0	35.1	50.7	68 784	78 282	13.8	2.9
Burbank	5.0	14.9	8.7	15.5	16.0	15.7	11.0	6.8	6.6	38.9	51.6	93 649	100 316	7.1	3.0
Burlingame	6.5	15.2	5.2	13.7	17.1	16.3	12.0	6.7	7.3	40.5	52.5	26 666	28 158	5.6	2.3
Calexico	7.7	23.4	11.0	11.4	12.8	12.6	9.5	6.0	5.5	31.8	52.7	18 633	27 109	45.5	42.3
Camarillo	5.7	17.5	7.9	11.6	12.8	15.1	12.3	8.0	9.2	40.8	51.6	52 297	57 077	9.1	14.2
Campbell	6.6	14.5	7.6	16.2	16.4	16.5	11.1	5.7	5.5	38.3	51.0	36 088	38 138	5.7	3.2
Carlsbad	6.0	18.1	6.4	11.6	15.0	16.3	12.5	6.8	7.3	40.4	51.1	63 292	78 247	23.6	34.6
Carson	5.7	18.2	10.9	12.0	13.2	14.3	11.9	8.1	5.6	37.6	52.1	83 995	89 730	6.8	2.2
Cathedral City	6.9	20.1	9.6	12.1	13.2	13.6	10.1	7.7	6.6	36.0	48.6	30 085	42 647	41.8	20.1
Ceres	8.7	23.5	11.2	14.2	13.4	12.8	8.5	4.5	3.3	29.4	50.5	26 413	34 609	31.0	31.2
Cerritos	3.9	16.5	8.3	10.0	12.7	15.3	15.6	11.3	6.4	44.0	51.9	53 244	51 488	-3.3	-4.8
Chico	5.7	13.8	23.9	15.2	10.7	10.5	9.5	4.9	5.7	28.6	50.4	39 970	59 954	50.0	43.8
Chino	6.7	18.6	10.9	16.6	15.6	14.5	9.8	4.4	2.9	33.2	48.6	59 682	67 168	12.5	16.1
Chino Hills	5.8	21.3	9.6	11.1	15.9	18.0	11.2	4.4	2.7	36.6	50.6	37 868	66 787	76.4	12.0
Chula Vista	7.2	20.8	10.1	13.7	15.2	13.8	9.2	5.3	4.7	33.7	51.6	135 160	173 556	28.4	40.5
Citrus Heights	6.7	16.4	10.2	15.1	12.5	14.2	11.6	6.8	6.5	36.2	51.5	107 439	85 071	-20.8	-2.1
Claremont	3.7	14.8	19.4	8.8	11.1	13.4	12.3	7.7	8.8	38.6	53.1	32 610	33 998	4.3	2.7
Clovis	7.2	20.9	10.0	13.1	13.6	14.0	10.7	5.6	5.0	34.1	51.8	50 323	68 468	36.1	39.7
Coachella	11.0	27.8	12.0	16.4	12.8	10.1	5.4	2.8	1.7	24.5	50.2	16 896	22 724	34.5	79.1
Colton	9.4	22.6	12.2	15.8	12.9	11.9	8.2	3.9	3.1	28.4	51.0	40 213	47 662	18.5	9.4
Compton	9.2	23.9	12.3	14.4	13.1	12.0	7.5	4.2	3.3	28.0	51.3	90 454	93 493	3.4	3.2
Concord	6.8	16.1	9.0	15.3	14.0	15.2	11.7	6.3	5.5	37.0	50.3	111 308	121 780	9.4	0.2
Corona	7.4	22.5	10.2	13.2	15.9	14.8	8.7	4.3	3.0	32.5	50.8	75 943	124 966	64.6	21.9
Costa Mesa	6.5	15.0	11.7	19.2	15.6	13.6	9.2	4.8	4.4	33.6	49.1	96 357	108 724	12.8	1.1
Covina	6.3	18.6	10.6	13.5	14.0	14.9	10.6	5.9	5.7	35.7	51.7	43 332	46 837	8.1	2.0
Culver City	5.3	13.5	7.0	15.2	16.0	15.5	12.6	7.3	7.7	40.5	52.9	38 793	38 816	0.1	0.2
Cupertino	5.4	22.1	5.6	8.6	18.2	17.3	10.2	6.2	6.3	39.9	50.7	39 967	50 546	26.5	15.3
Cypress	5.0	18.8	9.8	10.3	14.2	17.5	11.6	7.3	5.6	39.9	51.5	42 655	46 229	8.4	3.4
Daly City	5.4	13.9	10.4	15.7	13.6	14.6	12.9	7.2	6.3	38.3	50.6	92 088	103 621	12.5	-2.4
Dana Point	4.7	13.2	7.6	12.1	12.7	16.9	15.9	9.0	8.0	44.8	50.5	31 896	35 110	10.1	-5.0
Danville	4.9	21.8	5.0	5.7	13.4	19.8	15.0	8.1	6.3	44.5	51.7	31 306	41 715	33.2	0.8
Davis	3.7	12.7	33.2	13.0	9.6	10.4	9.0	4.5	4.0	25.2	52.5	46 322	60 308	30.2	8.8

Table D. Cities — Households, Group Quarters, Crime, and Education

City	Households, 2010 Number	Persons per household	Female family householder[1]	One-person	Persons in group quarters, 2010 Total	Institutional Total	Persons in nursing facilities	Non-institutional	Serious crimes known to police,[2] 2010 Number	Rate[3]	Violent	Property	Population age 25 and older	High school graduate or less	Bachelor's degree or more
	27	28	29	30	31	32	33	34	35	36	37	38	39	40	41
ARKANSAS—Cont'd															
Jacksonville	10 936	2.52	18.5	27.1	847	100	98	747	1 552	5 472	712	4 760	16 960	51.2	14.9
Jonesboro	26 111	2.45	15.3	28.3	3 412	1 238	800	2 174	3 247	4 827	459	4 368	39 869	46.4	27.3
Little Rock	82 018	2.30	17.5	34.8	4 543	2 781	1 074	1 762	17 778	9 186	1 522	7 665	125 705	33.1	36.6
North Little Rock	26 530	2.32	19.4	34.2	870	638	583	232	5 654	9 075	902	8 173	41 763	44.8	24.3
Paragould	10 288	2.48	14.6	26.3	550	391	226	159	1 840	7 046	329	6 717	16 715	57.4	12.7
Pine Bluff	18 071	2.49	27.7	31.3	3 999	2 512	429	1 487	4 435	9 036	1 400	7 636	29 777	53.0	17.2
Rogers	19 675	2.82	11.8	23.8	624	312	312	138	2 264	4 045	393	3 652	32 960	49.8	25.0
Russellville	10 318	2.39	14.4	30.1	3 251	448	277	2 803	1 345	4 817	351	4 466	15 633	51.2	22.0
Sherwood	12 207	2.41	13.9	27.0	85	85	85	0	1 095	3 709	440	3 269	19 979	40.2	26.4
Springdale	22 805	3.02	13.3	21.5	830	678	577	152	2 454	3 516	466	3 050	38 906	60.8	17.3
Texarkana	12 032	2.36	19.9	29.8	1 468	1 251	300	217	2 233	7 463	996	6 467	19 614	52.4	13.4
West Memphis	9 835	2.61	29.2	28.1	608	505	206	103	2 956	11 263	2 610	8 653	15 335	64.0	8.3
CALIFORNIA	12 577 498	2.90	13.3	23.3	819 816	397 142	111 884	422 674	1 146 072	3 076	441	2 636	23 787 044	40.1	30.0
Adelanto	7 809	3.84	23.8	11.7	1 753	1 723	0	30	968	3 047	762	2 286	14 883	60.8	8.6
Alameda	30 123	2.40	12.0	31.0	1 496	639	639	857	2 137	2 895	234	2 661	51 707	28.0	44.9
Alhambra	29 217	2.82	16.5	22.2	614	482	455	132	2 260	2 720	223	2 497	59 965	41.5	30.1
Aliso Viejo	18 204	2.60	10.8	24.3	469	19	19	450	NA	NA	NA	NA	31 604	17.0	53.9
Anaheim	98 294	3.38	14.8	17.8	3 557	1 537	1 376	2 020	9 634	2 865	345	2 520	206 172	50.7	23.5
Antioch	32 252	3.15	17.7	16.4	664	260	229	404	3 960	3 868	844	3 024	60 981	42.2	19.4
Apple Valley	23 598	2.91	15.0	20.1	461	300	104	161	2 077	3 004	272	2 732	42 720	45.1	17.0
Arcadia	19 592	2.83	12.4	19.7	862	223	220	639	1 825	3 238	156	3 082	39 030	23.5	53.5
Atascadero	10 737	2.51	11.0	23.3	1 324	1 100	91	224	699	2 469	279	2 190	19 707	33.7	28.8
Atwater	8 838	3.18	17.6	18.3	102	71	63	31	1 242	4 409	405	4 005	15 779	50.8	12.1
Azusa	12 716	3.43	17.9	17.6	2 802	111	97	2 691	1 362	2 938	487	2 450	24 848	53.9	18.2
Bakersfield	111 132	3.10	16.2	19.6	3 395	1 301	749	2 094	17 301	4 979	605	4 373	194 953	46.6	19.6
Baldwin Park	17 189	4.36	19.5	8.6	406	318	276	88	2 005	2 660	336	2 324	44 099	69.9	12.1
Banning	10 838	2.61	13.7	28.5	1 365	1 111	177	254	701	2 368	524	1 844	21 344	54.3	17.6
Beaumont	11 801	3.08	12.3	16.2	474	211	137	263	868	2 354	236	2 118	22 659	41.1	26.8
Bell	8 870	3.93	21.2	10.9	579	89	89	490	842	2 373	679	1 694	19 452	80.0	3.9
Bellflower	23 651	3.21	20.3	19.5	739	340	329	399	2 191	2 860	542	2 318	45 688	49.9	17.5
Bell Gardens	9 655	4.31	22.2	7.8	424	299	299	125	1 150	2 733	499	2 234	22 453	82.9	4.9
Belmont	10 575	2.39	7.8	27.5	514	120	120	394	393	1 521	101	1 421	18 508	16.1	57.5
Benicia	10 686	2.52	11.9	24.6	26	0	0	26	521	1 930	185	1 745	19 151	21.3	37.5
Berkeley	46 029	2.17	8.4	36.7	12 849	419	237	12 430	6 476	5 752	473	5 279	67 954	13.9	68.4
Beverly Hills	14 869	2.29	9.1	36.3	121	0	0	121	1 060	3 108	220	2 888	24 887	21.5	55.0
Brea	14 266	2.75	11.3	21.5	69	0	0	69	1 542	3 925	181	3 745	26 458	26.6	41.2
Brentwood	16 494	3.11	11.1	15.9	146	5	5	141	1 229	2 387	218	2 170	29 232	31.2	28.6
Buena Park	23 686	3.37	16.0	14.3	814	261	242	553	2 248	2 792	299	2 492	50 204	41.5	26.9
Burbank	41 940	2.45	11.9	30.6	573	282	268	291	2 908	2 814	214	2 600	74 380	30.2	37.7
Burlingame	12 361	2.29	8.4	34.6	449	294	294	155	761	2 642	205	2 437	20 725	21.3	50.7
Calexico	10 116	3.80	22.9	11.9	100	0	0	100	1 506	3 904	200	3 705	21 295	60.3	14.5
Camarillo	24 504	2.64	9.7	24.4	496	341	227	155	1 026	1 574	83	1 491	44 170	26.9	36.0
Campbell	16 163	2.42	10.8	29.7	201	122	114	79	1 534	3 898	211	3 688	27 793	23.9	43.5
Carlsbad	41 345	2.53	9.2	23.9	915	456	451	459	2 015	1 913	185	1 728	71 896	18.1	50.7
Carson	25 432	3.56	18.8	14.8	1 303	133	49	1 170	2 825	3 080	544	2 536	59 362	43.3	23.1
Cathedral City	17 047	2.99	13.4	25.2	295	32	32	263	1 754	3 426	486	2 939	31 671	54.0	16.3
Ceres	12 692	3.55	17.4	12.5	353	60	38	293	2 114	4 655	370	4 285	26 165	61.0	10.4
Cerritos	15 526	3.15	12.1	11.6	104	18	18	86	1 789	3 648	190	3 458	33 871	23.9	48.0
Chico	34 805	2.38	11.4	29.9	3 178	587	577	2 591	2 592	3 007	284	2 723	49 334	25.2	33.5
Chino	20 772	3.41	14.6	13.7	7 064	6 900	3	164	2 273	2 915	339	2 576	50 608	48.5	19.0
Chino Hills	22 941	3.25	10.4	11.8	155	147	0	8	1 058	1 414	107	1 308	46 876	24.7	43.2
Chula Vista	75 515	3.21	16.6	16.7	1 736	1 080	538	656	5 787	2 373	272	2 101	144 228	38.5	26.8
Citrus Heights	32 686	2.53	14.3	27.1	486	182	131	304	4 316	5 181	462	4 719	56 813	37.2	18.7
Claremont	11 608	2.57	10.5	25.5	5 124	198	192	4 926	926	2 651	140	2 511	20 690	19.3	54.7
Clovis	33 419	2.85	13.6	21.0	388	258	221	130	3 734	3 905	173	3 732	57 546	29.5	31.3
Coachella	8 998	4.52	21.4	5.2	58	0	0	58	1 816	4 461	474	3 987	19 037	78.9	4.3
Colton	14 971	3.46	21.6	16.4	330	245	243	85	1 749	3 354	326	3 028	29 420	58.8	10.9
Compton	23 062	4.15	27.6	12.9	755	112	84	643	4 111	4 262	1 376	2 886	50 400	68.2	6.8
Concord	44 278	2.73	12.7	23.5	1 047	535	469	512	4 350	3 564	451	3 112	83 433	36.6	30.6
Corona	44 950	3.38	13.3	14.4	511	282	268	229	3 735	2 451	131	2 321	89 873	41.9	24.0
Costa Mesa	39 946	2.68	10.9	27.4	2 970	738	581	2 232	3 434	3 123	218	2 905	73 930	31.5	33.6
Covina	15 855	2.99	17.8	19.9	435	367	341	68	1 814	3 795	358	3 438	30 211	38.8	24.4
Culver City	16 779	2.30	11.2	33.7	311	227	227	84	1 787	4 596	383	4 213	29 120	19.2	50.8
Cupertino	20 181	2.87	6.9	17.6	337	276	258	61	1 041	1 786	103	1 683	39 136	10.8	73.4
Cypress	15 654	3.02	14.1	15.3	502	0	0	502	850	1 778	132	1 646	31 939	28.2	36.8
Daly City	31 090	3.23	15.0	18.8	681	408	397	273	2 054	2 031	247	1 784	70 935	35.5	32.8
Dana Point	14 182	2.33	8.7	28.3	241	81	77	160	661	1 982	198	1 784	24 575	21.5	44.6
Danville	15 420	2.71	7.4	18.2	243	187	183	56	563	1 339	76	1 263	27 866	10.9	63.7
Davis	24 873	2.55	7.6	23.9	2 100	277	203	1 823	1 837	2 799	151	2 649	34 030	11.4	69.1

1. No spouse present.　2. Data for serious crimes have not been adjusted for underreporting. This may affect comparability between geographic areas and over time.　3. Per 100,000 population estimated by the FBI.　4. Persons 25 years old and over.

Table D. Cities — Income, Poverty, and Housing

| City | Money income, 2008–2010 | | | | | Housing units, 2010 | | | Occupied Housing units 2008–2010 | | | | |
| | Households | | | | Families with income below poverty (percent) | Total | Percent change, 2000–2010 | Vacant units for sale or rent[2] | Owner-occupied | | | Median owner costs as a percent of income | |
	Per capita income[1] (dollars)	Median income	Percent with income of $200,000 or more	Percent with income of less than $25,000					Total	Percent	Median value[3] (dollars)	With a mortgage[4]	Without a mortgage[5]
	42	43	44	45	46	47	48	49	50	51	52	53	54
ARKANSAS—Cont'd													
Jacksonville	20 253	39 675	0.5	30.3	15.8	12 412	4.8	1 476	11 020	52.5	108 900	22.0	11.8
Jonesboro	22 641	36 184	3.7	36.7	18.8	28 321	16.5	2 210	25 637	53.5	131 000	19.6	10.2
Little Rock	28 505	42 466	4.6	28.6	14.7	91 288	7.5	9 270	80 231	55.7	148 700	22.4	11.4
North Little Rock	23 155	37 711	1.9	34.2	17.0	29 437	6.8	2 907	26 046	49.2	117 600	20.7	11.1
Paragould	18 170	38 033	0.6	34.1	13.4	11 070	12.9	782	10 142	55.2	98 900	19.9	11.0
Pine Bluff	15 694	28 820	1.3	44.9	23.5	20 923	-6.2	2 852	16 869	55.1	69 100	22.3	15.5
Rogers	24 238	46 497	3.8	23.8	10.5	22 022	47.9	2 347	19 845	60.5	154 100	22.9	10.9
Russellville	17 958	36 532	1.2	35.6	19.7	11 124	8.9	806	9 734	52.6	113 100	19.9	10.0
Sherwood	27 038	54 465	2.4	19.1	7.9	12 924	40.5	717	11 865	65.5	141 500	19.7	10.1
Springdale	17 520	40 663	1.5	27.8	18.0	25 614	50.4	2 809	22 505	51.6	143 600	22.5	10.9
Texarkana	20 035	39 800	0.9	35.1	14.8	13 375	13.5	1 343	11 592	61.4	94 600	20.5	10.8
West Memphis	15 322	26 698	0.9	47.4	32.2	10 966	-0.5	1 131	9 750	46.3	90 700	24.8	13.0
CALIFORNIA	28 551	60 016	6.3	20.5	10.8	13 680 081	12.0	1 102 583	12 392 347	56.4	405 800	31.2	11.1
Adelanto	11 878	40 000	0.6	31.7	25.7	9 086	62.6	1 277	7 164	58.3	119 600	34.4	11.0
Alameda	37 721	76 092	8.4	16.7	8.3	32 351	2.2	2 228	28 444	47.9	648 900	30.4	10.0
Alhambra	23 527	50 352	3.0	25.1	12.3	30 915	2.8	1 698	28 738	40.9	493 100	32.5	11.0
Aliso Viejo	42 047	93 208	9.4	7.5	1.7	18 867	13.6	663	18 322	62.9	504 700	30.9	10.0
Anaheim	22 306	56 496	3.7	18.9	11.9	104 237	4.7	5 943	99 664	48.4	438 200	32.2	10.6
Antioch	24 129	60 814	4.0	19.2	11.1	34 849	15.5	2 597	31 515	63.1	277 000	32.6	10.3
Apple Valley	22 802	47 248	3.1	27.9	14.0	26 117	29.5	2 519	22 752	69.7	214 700	30.6	13.5
Arcadia	37 358	75 566	11.8	16.3	7.9	20 686	3.5	1 094	19 334	82.1	772 000	30.4	10.0
Atascadero	30 422	66 705	2.9	16.9	7.4	11 505	16.8	768	10 259	72.4	433 000	32.4	10.0
Atwater	17 217	42 119	1.6	26.0	21.2	9 771	20.8	933	8 105	50.0	146 800	29.8	11.3
Azusa	16 829	48 076	1.3	24.1	13.2	13 386	3.6	670	12 529	51.0	342 200	35.9	14.3
Bakersfield	22 283	52 145	2.9	22.8	14.1	120 725	36.9	9 593	107 557	59.2	206 600	28.6	11.0
Baldwin Park	15 032	48 060	2.5	23.0	15.9	17 736	1.8	547	17 330	60.0	307 000	35.9	10.0
Banning	19 898	36 268	0.9	32.0	16.4	12 144	24.7	1 306	12 507	68.3	194 800	36.5	14.4
Beaumont	25 381	67 948	2.6	16.0	7.0	12 908	203.1	1 107	11 869	76.6	248 600	33.1	11.5
Bell	11 857	34 089	0.1	32.7	25.3	9 217	0.0	347	8 996	27.5	313 900	37.6	11.0
Bellflower	19 963	51 334	1.5	23.1	10.5	24 897	2.9	1 246	23 883	39.0	373 500	32.6	11.5
Bell Gardens	11 470	36 417	0.1	32.3	25.1	9 956	2.0	331	10 186	24.5	301 500	37.6	14.4
Belmont	50 661	101 613	16.3	9.6	1.4	11 028	3.8	453	10 267	60.6	895 100	30.1	10.3
Benicia	41 500	83 476	9.6	10.2	4.8	11 306	7.1	620	10 814	66.7	464 100	28.8	10.6
Berkeley	37 024	60 690	9.7	24.6	6.7	49 454	5.5	3 425	43 536	41.5	721 900	27.1	10.5
Beverly Hills	65 526	77 938	18.0	18.1	6.6	16 394	3.4	1 525	14 890	39.0	1 000 000	44.4	14.2
Brea	35 021	77 524	7.0	14.1	3.8	14 785	11.4	519	14 502	64.4	551 700	28.8	10.0
Brentwood	30 986	86 333	6.8	11.5	7.0	17 523	125.6	1 029	15 336	78.5	384 400	33.2	12.0
Buena Park	22 706	62 139	3.8	15.7	7.6	24 623	3.1	937	22 587	55.5	435 600	31.6	10.0
Burbank	34 095	65 188	6.1	19.1	5.7	44 309	3.4	2 369	41 378	44.8	588 700	32.0	10.0
Burlingame	48 282	74 154	16.2	14.8	6.3	13 027	1.3	666	11 543	51.1	1 000 000	32.0	10.0
Calexico	14 063	34 757	1.8	38.8	25.1	10 651	52.5	535	9 831	56.4	167 300	32.3	13.3
Camarillo	36 790	80 180	8.8	12.9	3.9	25 702	17.2	1 198	23 770	69.5	494 900	28.9	12.2
Campbell	43 002	80 591	10.8	13.7	4.1	16 950	3.7	787	16 202	49.8	685 400	28.6	10.2
Carlsbad	42 012	83 238	11.3	13.0	6.1	44 673	32.5	3 328	40 308	67.8	627 900	30.4	10.9
Carson	23 142	70 754	3.5	14.4	6.2	26 226	3.6	794	24 896	75.0	385 500	31.2	10.0
Cathedral City	21 667	47 418	2.2	24.3	12.7	20 995	17.9	3 948	16 968	65.4	242 500	33.9	15.7
Ceres	17 382	46 883	1.0	26.1	17.2	13 673	26.6	981	13 267	64.1	198 700	35.8	12.0
Cerritos	31 865	84 305	8.7	11.6	7.0	15 859	1.6	333	15 233	79.9	611 500	30.4	10.0
Chico	24 243	42 504	2.3	29.8	12.7	37 050	52.1	2 245	33 775	45.3	298 400	28.5	11.7
Chino	22 409	72 363	4.0	13.8	5.3	21 797	21.0	1 025	19 849	72.4	363 000	32.6	11.2
Chino Hills	34 733	100 326	10.0	6.6	4.1	23 617	15.8	676	21 951	81.5	524 500	28.4	10.2
Chula Vista	24 498	64 488	4.0	17.3	7.9	79 416	33.4	3 901	72 913	59.9	384 000	34.6	10.0
Citrus Heights	25 359	52 466	1.2	17.9	9.2	35 075	0.4	2 389	32 753	57.4	230 700	30.3	12.6
Claremont	35 160	78 379	12.0	14.7	5.9	12 156	5.0	548	11 121	66.7	571 000	28.6	10.0
Clovis	27 003	62 405	3.3	19.2	7.9	35 306	40.4	1 887	32 731	61.7	278 900	27.9	11.7
Coachella	11 499	40 566	1.0	28.2	24.5	9 903	98.8	905	8 639	66.2	161 500	35.1	17.4
Colton	16 089	41 620	0.9	26.2	18.2	16 350	3.6	1 379	14 954	50.7	198 600	29.6	12.6
Compton	13 547	43 765	0.6	27.5	20.1	24 523	3.1	1 461	23 339	53.2	282 400	38.0	12.5
Concord	29 852	64 665	4.3	16.3	6.5	47 125	4.8	2 847	44 417	61.7	404 300	31.8	12.3
Corona	26 010	75 795	5.0	13.7	7.6	47 174	20.2	2 224	42 533	67.4	359 600	31.4	10.6
Costa Mesa	32 525	63 542	5.8	16.4	10.4	42 120	4.3	2 174	39 732	43.2	604 400	32.2	10.0
Covina	25 215	64 046	2.3	14.9	7.3	16 576	0.9	721	15 477	56.7	414 900	29.8	10.4
Culver City	42 049	73 689	10.0	14.7	3.5	17 491	2.1	712	17 065	57.6	631 300	31.2	11.8
Cupertino	49 842	120 636	23.9	9.6	2.4	21 027	12.4	846	20 104	63.9	1 000 000	28.6	10.0
Cypress	31 493	77 783	6.1	10.4	3.8	16 068	0.3	414	15 923	71.7	553 300	28.6	10.1
Daly City	27 284	73 898	4.4	12.8	5.1	32 588	4.3	1 498	31 057	56.0	578 300	31.7	11.0
Dana Point	48 453	78 125	14.7	10.6	4.1	15 938	1.8	1 756	14 140	59.1	782 300	33.1	10.0
Danville	59 297	129 720	25.3	5.3	2.3	15 934	3.9	514	15 110	83.9	857 000	30.9	10.0
Davis	31 820	61 030	7.8	24.3	7.9	25 869	9.6	996	24 130	46.9	548 600	24.9	10.0

1. Based on population estimated by the American Community Survey.   2. Includes units rented or sold but not occupied.   3. Specified owner-occupied units; $1,000,000 represents $1,000,000 or more.   4. 50.0 represents 50 percent or more.   5. 10.0 represents 10 percent or less.

Table D. Cities — Housing, Labor Force, and Employment

City	Occupied housing units, 2008–2010 (cont.)				Migration, 2008–2010		Civilian labor force, 2010				Civilian employment[4], 2008–2010			
									Unemployment			Percent		
	Percent renter occupied	Median gross rent[1]	Median rent as a percent of income[2]	Percent with no vehicle available	Percent who lived in the same house one year ago	Percent who lived outside this city one year ago	Total	Percent change, 2009–2010	Total	Rate[3]	Population age 16 and older	In labor force	Full-year full-time worker	Households with no workers (percent)
	55	56	57	58	59	60	61	62	63	64	65	66	67	68
ARKANSAS—Cont'd														
Jacksonville	47.5	647	27.5	10.9	72.7	17.6	13 255	-1.7	1 159	8.7	21 566	67.4	49.9	23.6
Jonesboro	46.5	606	28.0	10.0	72.6	9.8	32 769	1.5	2 573	7.9	51 584	64.3	39.3	28.8
Little Rock	44.3	744	31.1	7.8	79.5	7.4	96 722	-1.9	7 145	7.4	150 529	68.9	46.4	24.6
North Little Rock	50.8	742	33.4	11.5	75.9	14.4	30 898	-2.0	2 108	6.8	48 212	63.7	44.8	28.5
Paragould	44.8	576	25.1	8.4	80.7	8.5	10 818	NA	1 031	9.5	20 265	61.8	41.3	30.2
Pine Bluff	44.9	615	38.8	12.2	76.6	10.9	21 550	-1.8	2 479	11.5	38 118	57.3	33.7	34.2
Rogers	39.5	756	28.2	5.6	82.0	10.6	27 276	1.2	1 668	6.1	40 311	70.6	49.0	20.1
Russellville	47.4	644	30.9	7.1	76.8	11.3	12 957	-0.4	1 016	7.8	22 125	65.7	33.4	27.5
Sherwood	34.5	744	26.2	3.9	80.7	14.8	12 277	NA	708	5.8	23 112	66.8	49.9	22.3
Springdale	48.4	665	27.4	6.9	74.2	11.3	28 913	-0.1	2 066	7.1	47 372	71.3	48.7	20.0
Texarkana	38.6	664	27.7	8.4	75.3	12.3	13 480	-0.4	869	6.4	23 311	60.9	41.1	31.1
West Memphis	53.7	635	34.8	16.1	69.8	13.3	11 081	-6.0	1 477	13.3	19 442	62.6	36.3	31.9
CALIFORNIA	43.6	1 163	33.1	7.7	83.9	9.0	18 316 411	0.6	2 264 898	12.4	28 800 443	64.9	39.4	23.8
Adelanto	41.7	847	42.7	7.2	73.5	17.5	6 953	0.2	1 491	21.4	19 762	53.4	28.5	29.1
Alameda	52.1	1 288	27.5	9.2	83.9	8.5	39 631	-0.4	3 081	7.8	59 310	69.1	43.2	23.1
Alhambra	59.1	1 145	33.0	8.1	89.1	7.5	45 458	0.1	4 956	10.9	69 530	63.1	40.8	18.2
Aliso Viejo	37.1	1 800	31.0	1.7	81.2	14.0	27 316	-0.4	1 376	5.0	36 213	79.7	57.3	11.3
Anaheim	51.6	1 275	36.0	7.1	83.1	8.4	175 170	0.0	21 187	12.1	251 405	69.3	43.3	18.5
Antioch	36.9	1 229	37.6	5.8	79.9	8.9	49 160	-0.4	6 172	12.6	75 824	65.4	37.4	21.9
Apple Valley	30.3	937	40.0	4.7	82.4	10.7	26 198	-0.3	4 048	15.5	51 956	58.2	30.7	34.6
Arcadia	37.9	1 323	32.0	5.4	89.3	7.3	27 578	-0.2	2 001	7.3	45 475	61.1	42.2	22.2
Atascadero	27.6	1 056	35.4	4.0	84.3	12.1	15 343	0.2	1 247	8.1	23 500	60.9	36.4	22.9
Atwater	50.0	858	28.5	5.3	81.5	8.1	12 843	3.5	2 460	19.2	19 505	61.2	35.0	29.1
Azusa	49.0	1 149	34.9	8.2	86.2	9.4	21 488	0.4	2 936	13.7	35 603	67.2	39.9	15.5
Bakersfield	40.8	908	33.8	7.0	79.1	7.4	155 107	1.2	17 361	11.2	246 073	64.6	39.7	22.7
Baldwin Park	40.0	1 166	36.3	4.7	90.0	6.8	33 831	0.6	5 293	15.6	55 210	63.4	37.8	15.8
Banning	31.7	882	42.0	8.0	88.1	8.2	11 981	2.7	1 979	16.5	23 880	44.2	26.9	50.2
Beaumont	23.4	956	40.1	3.3	84.1	9.9	7 001	2.7	1 152	16.5	25 730	59.1	41.5	25.7
Bell	72.5	941	35.9	12.7	90.8	7.9	16 135	0.7	2 674	16.6	24 889	60.6	39.7	18.9
Bellflower	61.0	1 136	31.5	8.1	84.8	11.6	36 717	0.3	4 694	12.8	56 614	64.8	45.7	20.0
Bell Gardens	75.5	1 005	34.5	11.2	91.5	5.6	17 774	1.0	3 516	19.8	29 163	62.5	40.1	15.9
Belmont	39.4	1 428	22.7	3.0	86.0	10.4	14 406	0.2	1 082	7.5	20 624	70.3	47.0	20.2
Benicia	33.3	1 271	27.6	2.0	88.9	6.7	16 777	-0.3	1 268	7.6	22 442	68.4	43.3	22.5
Berkeley	58.5	1 220	35.5	21.4	70.2	16.5	58 765	-0.2	6 299	10.7	98 780	57.5	29.7	29.0
Beverly Hills	61.0	1 800	31.3	6.9	86.8	9.6	19 066	-0.1	1 683	8.8	28 623	62.6	37.3	27.7
Brea	35.6	1 315	28.8	6.4	87.5	8.6	21 072	-0.4	1 376	6.5	31 206	68.3	43.3	20.0
Brentwood	21.5	1 642	35.7	0.8	85.9	9.7	10 839	-0.6	1 071	9.9	35 119	63.6	39.8	23.3
Buena Park	44.5	1 353	34.8	4.3	85.2	10.3	42 225	-0.1	4 976	11.8	61 770	64.8	40.5	18.8
Burbank	55.2	1 331	30.3	8.0	86.7	7.3	60 091	0.1	6 172	10.3	85 173	68.7	44.7	21.3
Burlingame	48.9	1 341	31.3	8.1	88.1	9.7	15 580	0.1	994	6.4	22 850	65.5	42.0	19.2
Calexico	43.6	727	38.4	13.9	86.3	1.7	15 557	1.5	5 138	33.0	27 583	60.5	27.6	28.2
Camarillo	30.5	1 507	32.2	3.3	82.8	9.6	31 911	0.5	2 470	7.7	50 927	64.3	41.9	26.6
Campbell	50.2	1 384	27.5	6.4	83.9	12.7	22 496	0.3	2 131	9.5	31 484	72.7	48.0	19.6
Carlsbad	32.2	1 523	34.3	3.1	85.0	10.4	47 552	0.7	3 336	7.0	81 413	66.3	42.4	22.6
Carson	25.0	1 281	31.6	4.6	89.8	7.0	46 199	0.3	5 872	12.7	72 540	66.6	42.5	19.0
Cathedral City	34.6	1 069	34.3	5.7	81.4	7.8	26 858	2.6	3 809	14.2	38 896	65.4	37.5	27.0
Ceres	35.9	884	40.1	6.5	80.0	13.0	18 973	1.8	4 045	21.3	32 969	67.6	35.8	24.5
Cerritos	20.1	1 873	37.1	2.3	91.8	5.5	28 597	-0.2	1 982	6.9	40 018	60.9	41.0	22.1
Chico	54.7	881	34.3	8.5	68.4	11.6	33 783	-1.2	4 370	12.9	71 964	65.2	31.1	29.8
Chino	27.6	1 204	33.5	4.0	76.8	17.0	34 603	-0.6	4 389	12.7	61 753	60.3	37.6	16.7
Chino Hills	18.5	1 759	36.7	2.3	89.6	6.5	39 071	-1.0	2 834	7.3	56 882	72.4	46.7	10.0
Chula Vista	40.1	1 217	37.4	5.6	87.2	6.8	92 622	1.1	11 349	12.3	178 607	67.0	42.8	19.7
Citrus Heights	42.6	981	30.4	6.2	78.0	14.6	50 251	-1.3	4 513	9.0	67 342	68.5	40.4	25.1
Claremont	33.3	1 194	33.7	6.8	83.9	11.2	16 272	-0.2	1 085	6.7	28 778	58.2	29.9	26.9
Clovis	38.3	972	30.4	5.6	84.5	10.2	42 392	-0.6	3 888	9.2	71 280	67.6	40.8	20.8
Coachella	33.8	843	40.0	3.5	84.3	6.6	12 747	3.2	2 865	22.5	25 338	69.4	35.2	15.8
Colton	49.3	969	38.9	7.1	87.0	9.4	24 988	-0.3	3 814	15.3	36 910	65.9	41.5	17.9
Compton	46.8	962	37.7	9.2	88.6	6.7	37 454	1.1	7 911	21.1	66 100	63.0	38.3	22.9
Concord	38.3	1 181	32.9	7.2	85.5	7.6	69 959	-0.4	8 398	12.0	97 535	71.1	41.5	21.2
Corona	32.6	1 269	35.5	3.6	82.7	10.3	85 692	2.3	9 214	10.8	111 200	70.6	42.8	13.4
Costa Mesa	56.8	1 430	31.0	4.6	83.2	10.0	65 872	-0.3	5 595	8.5	89 092	74.1	44.5	17.9
Covina	43.3	1 179	29.9	3.8	86.9	9.9	25 703	0.0	2 300	8.9	37 161	66.9	40.9	20.9
Culver City	42.4	1 434	28.6	5.6	86.6	11.3	24 270	-0.1	2 113	8.7	32 042	71.7	47.4	22.4
Cupertino	36.1	1 963	23.5	3.6	84.8	9.3	24 144	0.3	1 729	7.2	43 813	62.8	43.7	20.0
Cypress	28.3	1 390	31.1	4.5	91.6	5.7	27 066	-0.2	2 706	10.0	38 360	65.4	42.2	18.3
Daly City	44.0	1 430	33.0	8.3	86.3	8.7	54 076	0.2	5 848	10.8	84 286	68.5	43.5	18.7
Dana Point	40.9	1 775	35.7	1.9	86.2	10.0	21 955	-0.3	1 513	6.9	28 032	68.2	43.5	23.9
Danville	16.1	2 000	26.7	1.6	91.8	6.9	22 914	-0.9	1 353	5.9	31 425	64.4	42.2	20.3
Davis	53.1	1 217	41.9	6.6	67.9	15.5	38 276	-1.5	3 142	8.2	55 239	63.3	29.9	23.6

1. $2,000 represents $2,000 or more.   2. 50.0 represents 50 percent or more.   3. Percent of civilian labor force.   4. Persons 16 years old and over.

Table D. Cities — Construction, Wholesale Trade, and Retail Trade

City	Value of residential construction authorized by building permits, 2010			Wholesale trade,[1] 2007				Retail trade,[2] 2007			
	New construction ($1,000)	Number of housing units	Percent single family	Number of establishments	Number of employees	Sales (mil dol)	Annual payroll (mil dol)	Number of establishments	Number of employees	Sales (mil dol)	Annual payroll (mil dol)
	69	70	71	72	73	74	75	76	77	78	79
ARKANSAS—Cont'd											
Jacksonville	12 996	153	100.0	15	163	49.7	6.1	101	1 594	347.2	37.9
Jonesboro	55 893	546	67.0	104	1 204	495.5	50.2	440	6 193	1 335.6	119.1
Little Rock	74 161	428	80.4	387	7 632	3 999.3	339.0	1 008	14 560	3 359.2	330.4
North Little Rock	43 473	516	31.8	192	3 792	7 809.5	175.7	422	6 705	1 509.5	132.7
Paragould	12 218	162	68.5	31	269	82.1	7.8	161	1 554	336.8	31.3
Pine Bluff	4 142	83	25.3	52	394	211.9	13.7	280	3 646	798.7	74.2
Rogers	47 914	301	73.8	55	1 124	314.2	42.1	308	4 921	995.1	104.2
Russellville	6 135	68	94.1	50	331	204.6	13.3	251	3 290	852.8	68.1
Sherwood	17 067	101	100.0	30	173	78.8	7.4	92	1 480	579.7	39.2
Springdale	22 164	99	91.9	148	1 706	865.2	73.6	259	3 536	875.2	87.6
Texarkana	6 027	45	82.2	41	D	D	D	133	1 438	397.2	30.2
West Memphis	655	3	100.0	32	383	668.7	17.8	122	1 805	586.5	36.5
CALIFORNIA	9 120 592	43 716	58.8	53 963	745 785	598 456.5	42 334.5	114 438	1 683 023	455 032.3	44 328.9
Adelanto	12 280	54	100.0	5	48	25.2	2.3	13	205	52.2	5.0
Alameda	5 985	16	100.0	62	1 405	2 014.7	146.9	180	2 258	517.3	58.6
Alhambra	8 831	57	22.8	261	1 088	561.3	36.6	249	4 014	1 491.5	113.4
Aliso Viejo	23 397	109	54.1	65	1 903	1 273.0	136.9	69	1 078	662.8	28.8
Anaheim	16 142	87	67.8	797	12 461	7 962.1	580.1	866	14 042	3 679.3	367.0
Antioch	31 572	108	100.0	27	261	162.8	17.6	253	4 315	957.1	104.2
Apple Valley	9 026	79	84.8	15	32	12.6	1.6	106	2 213	493.0	49.0
Arcadia	15 868	93	35.5	293	1 233	619.7	45.8	330	4 965	900.1	98.0
Atascadero	1 831	12	100.0	24	121	32.3	4.8	126	1 556	356.3	36.8
Atwater	539	4	100.0	2	D	D	D	54	632	151.9	15.1
Azusa	11 824	35	100.0	73	890	404.0	41.7	96	1 162	427.0	31.2
Bakersfield	194 985	1 074	76.0	274	4 127	3 299.9	193.0	1 062	19 677	5 104.1	487.2
Baldwin Park	2 070	12	100.0	145	1 044	546.8	41.1	134	2 451	643.9	59.8
Banning	0	0	0.0	13	452	95.9	13.1	63	771	233.2	20.8
Beaumont	54 104	333	100.0	4	6	1.2	0.2	53	1 109	298.1	27.8
Bell	1 078	7	100.0	51	747	639.5	40.5	62	664	212.4	21.0
Bellflower	2 316	11	100.0	39	244	76.3	8.7	189	1 676	438.2	45.2
Bell Gardens	0	0	0.0	37	534	155.8	18.7	72	854	186.6	21.5
Belmont	867	2	100.0	19	D	D	D	58	916	363.8	99.2
Benicia	6 559	19	100.0	79	1 468	859.1	78.8	74	868	175.5	29.9
Berkeley	3 404	18	11.1	118	1 394	620.3	66.8	506	5 975	1 274.6	168.3
Beverly Hills	54 282	29	100.0	137	741	725.7	63.6	443	6 018	2 512.0	269.8
Brea	3 285	24	100.0	262	5 315	4 709.8	258.2	329	6 144	1 079.6	123.2
Brentwood	33 748	167	100.0	18	63	24.4	3.5	128	1 969	463.2	48.6
Buena Park	4 611	22	100.0	175	2 543	1 770.0	120.4	230	4 538	1 649.8	138.1
Burbank	7 410	18	83.3	213	3 581	6 364.4	219.5	426	8 247	2 276.9	195.5
Burlingame	20 440	61	26.2	153	1 040	935.4	61.1	201	2 425	819.4	94.5
Calexico	0	0	0.0	73	414	346.7	9.8	195	2 591	545.2	50.6
Camarillo	2 049	4	100.0	132	1 651	647.2	87.2	299	4 855	1 276.2	134.9
Campbell	2 754	8	100.0	82	906	470.0	57.2	174	3 008	691.4	79.6
Carlsbad	114 528	378	99.5	247	3 622	2 305.2	225.1	513	8 049	2 270.1	236.3
Carson	NA	NA	NA	369	6 927	4 918.7	335.5	237	4 830	1 703.9	180.3
Cathedral City	8 589	64	6.3	22	108	44.2	5.0	160	2 478	962.7	83.7
Ceres	309	2	100.0	19	289	205.6	11.0	88	1 633	402.9	38.0
Cerritos	0	0	0.0	257	4 835	5 247.7	288.1	266	8 177	2 681.5	232.4
Chico	43 974	422	15.9	86	983	434.1	38.3	464	8 018	1 642.3	174.1
Chino	3 499	20	40.0	390	4 599	2 468.8	197.2	236	4 455	952.0	95.7
Chino Hills	7 877	36	100.0	72	159	79.2	5.6	124	2 311	597.7	53.7
Chula Vista	103 529	518	70.8	297	2 045	1 156.6	83.7	651	11 801	2 754.1	271.1
Citrus Heights	4 574	19	89.5	21	31	12.0	1.5	309	5 362	1 151.8	113.7
Claremont	9 203	78	3.8	35	116	84.1	6.1	89	1 021	442.8	37.0
Clovis	86 608	387	100.0	41	175	87.6	7.3	286	5 804	1 569.5	137.9
Coachella	13 621	124	100.0	18	352	178.2	19.4	57	695	197.7	15.2
Colton	2 910	19	100.0	42	647	420.2	29.7	111	2 120	645.5	66.5
Compton	3 713	34	100.0	122	3 251	2 195.2	176.3	158	1 124	267.9	30.0
Concord	0	0	0.0	135	1 302	553.7	69.4	505	8 856	2 578.5	256.5
Corona	15 385	69	44.9	299	5 283	6 720.2	280.7	485	8 950	2 418.9	229.8
Costa Mesa	1 810	9	55.6	336	4 639	4 176.2	303.2	740	14 696	3 875.8	401.4
Covina	0	0	0.0	82	524	250.8	20.3	193	3 013	765.3	81.6
Culver City	914	3	100.0	150	3 233	1 965.9	206.2	334	5 847	1 605.6	163.6
Cupertino	12 828	24	100.0	66	1 194	1 139.3	96.5	157	3 266	3 703.0	77.2
Cypress	1 854	13	0.0	110	3 530	7 669.6	262.6	104	2 011	597.4	51.5
Daly City	2 484	5	100.0	25	D	D	D	217	4 005	943.2	90.9
Dana Point	15 506	14	100.0	44	150	188.7	10.1	123	1 115	351.7	32.0
Danville	15 970	24	83.3	42	156	105.6	7.8	131	1 324	316.8	35.1
Davis	6 154	27	100.0	15	170	171.6	10.3	146	2 061	480.5	50.8

1. Merchant wholesalers except manufacturers' sales branches and offices. 2. Establishments with payroll.

Table D. Cities — **Real Estate, Professional Services, and Manufacturing**

City	Real estate and rental and leasing, 2007				Professional, scientific, and technical services,[1] 2007				Manufacturing, 2007			
	Number of establish-ments	Number of employees	Receipts (mil dol)	Annual payroll (mil dol)	Number of establish-ments	Number of employees	Receipts (mil dol)	Annual payroll (mil dol)	Number of establish-ments	Number of employees	Receipts (mil dol)	Annual payroll (mil dol)
	80	81	82	83	84	85	86	87	88	89	90	91
ARKANSAS—Cont'd												
Jacksonville	43	157	15.5	3.1	33	D	D	D	30	1 192	378.6	48.5
Jonesboro	99	468	73.2	11.7	157	D	D	D	101	6 186	1 703.7	221.2
Little Rock	414	2 643	455.0	87.8	1 173	D	D	D	188	8 669	3 918.1	402.2
North Little Rock	89	434	142.9	11.6	193	1 544	122.6	47.6	80	2 500	767.0	106.4
Paragould	27	D	D	D	51	355	19.7	7.9	36	3 648	D	D
Pine Bluff	60	182	35.5	5.1	73	D	D	D	44	D	1 151.5	119.0
Rogers	98	529	69.3	17.7	179	1 816	220.4	82.8	68	5 922	1 607.5	207.5
Russellville	66	213	42.0	5.4	100	D	D	D	52	4 024	1 318.0	D
Sherwood	29	105	17.7	3.1	55	431	45.9	16.5	NA	NA	NA	NA
Springdale	94	397	56.6	9.9	150	947	89.5	39.7	107	9 022	2 131.7	289.8
Texarkana	21	66	10.5	1.5	37	D	D	D	26	D	D	D
West Memphis	27	136	17.8	4.4	41	D	D	D	31	D	D	38.1
CALIFORNIA	51 597	312 488	76 805.0	13 446.7	111 954	1 231 372	194 406.3	80 738.1	44 296	1 448 485	491 372.1	71 247.3
Adelanto	10	21	2.0	0.3	5	46	4.7	1.6	43	1 829	385.8	71.9
Alameda	113	D	D	D	247	2 254	642.6	202.3	59	2 567	1 219.3	186.1
Alhambra	116	597	66.1	17.8	245	D	D	D	98	1 944	393.7	69.4
Aliso Viejo	69	1 013	135.4	58.0	234	D	D	D	35	1 437	558.2	78.1
Anaheim	377	3 858	677.4	168.9	717	D	D	D	818	30 787	7 648.1	1 479.1
Antioch	64	311	46.4	9.3	106	777	65.6	27.0	NA	NA	NA	NA
Apple Valley	55	268	41.7	7.1	63	267	25.3	9.3	NA	NA	NA	NA
Arcadia	150	540	135.8	17.3	282	1 726	388.6	92.9	67	1 044	192.5	43.4
Atascadero	37	123	21.4	2.8	84	D	D	D	NA	NA	NA	NA
Atwater	16	66	7.6	1.2	12	D	D	D	11	519	158.6	17.5
Azusa	36	189	30.9	6.9	22	127	7.0	2.9	123	4 986	1 444.6	247.7
Bakersfield	358	1 956	309.4	63.4	752	D	D	D	152	2 514	820.8	102.6
Baldwin Park	29	124	20.9	3.5	28	129	9.1	2.8	119	2 207	383.0	79.0
Banning	30	202	18.6	5.0	12	61	4.4	1.8	22	890	176.6	21.9
Beaumont	19	67	11.8	1.8	21	53	5.6	2.1	18	543	131.7	18.7
Bell	19	D	D	D	9	D	D	D	23	1 004	396.6	43.9
Bellflower	82	367	37.4	10.9	74	420	28.1	12.2	NA	NA	NA	NA
Bell Gardens	9	54	3.8	0.9	9	53	4.7	1.4	57	1 020	237.6	38.8
Belmont	52	482	49.1	18.4	95	309	60.9	22.4	NA	NA	NA	NA
Benicia	51	273	58.6	10.9	103	640	93.4	35.6	84	2 520	D	193.3
Berkeley	181	766	185.4	25.5	589	3 864	750.5	256.3	155	4 733	D	262.9
Beverly Hills	498	2 568	851.9	146.9	1 017	D	D	D	NA	NA	NA	NA
Brea	107	520	134.1	30.3	257	2 326	360.5	131.6	172	6 822	1 690.6	299.4
Brentwood	54	223	36.9	6.4	74	356	33.1	14.9	NA	NA	NA	NA
Buena Park	65	239	52.0	7.3	129	1 124	161.8	51.2	106	4 906	1 671.4	226.0
Burbank	239	2 543	810.8	127.0	527	144 144	6 976.0	3 869.3	220	5 429	1 028.5	249.5
Burlingame	149	1 025	219.0	34.9	264	D	D	D	60	1 678	364.3	83.6
Calexico	26	137	11.4	2.7	32	119	8.9	3.3	NA	NA	NA	NA
Camarillo	103	714	125.9	28.1	268	D	D	D	145	6 110	1 530.4	316.3
Campbell	108	592	121.2	23.5	296	D	D	D	111	1 977	371.5	109.9
Carlsbad	342	1 883	328.5	71.5	760	D	D	D	178	11 834	3 775.2	733.4
Carson	68	4 455	1 141.3	210.4	117	1 859	356.6	121.8	263	12 324	12 083.3	621.0
Cathedral City	54	308	53.0	7.8	45	142	13.0	4.6	NA	NA	NA	NA
Ceres	38	144	20.9	3.3	20	171	12.4	4.8	30	613	122.0	21.2
Cerritos	97	411	115.7	12.7	178	3 990	304.0	113.1	155	3 548	852.2	145.3
Chico	147	947	107.5	20.9	297	D	D	D	84	2 009	504.6	70.8
Chino	76	381	71.6	13.0	128	912	103.2	34.0	244	9 023	1 902.9	332.3
Chino Hills	52	125	33.0	3.6	144	371	39.3	13.7	NA	NA	NA	NA
Chula Vista	307	1 156	215.9	31.9	331	D	D	D	160	4 237	1 233.2	274.0
Citrus Heights	88	441	64.2	10.6	135	1 196	102.9	40.1	NA	NA	NA	NA
Claremont	60	D	D	D	147	D	D	D	27	803	118.3	26.8
Clovis	81	292	59.4	7.2	168	1 084	117.6	41.7	51	3 547	719.2	151.1
Coachella	13	56	6.5	0.9	5	D	D	D	15	551	108.3	25.4
Colton	29	187	29.2	5.3	50	505	57.4	21.6	57	4 043	1 157.0	128.9
Compton	19	180	98.4	3.4	21	D	D	D	133	4 940	1 083.7	176.9
Concord	166	1 014	242.2	42.4	323	D	D	D	120	2 705	528.6	122.9
Corona	200	909	184.9	38.2	315	2 105	211.0	115.0	372	16 971	4 279.7	708.0
Costa Mesa	294	2 676	686.1	128.6	764	D	D	D	258	7 604	1 962.7	386.2
Covina	102	542	75.7	20.5	159	682	79.5	27.8	103	1 833	393.7	72.8
Culver City	129	1 305	161.9	53.7	384	2 692	609.6	283.6	82	2 384	566.7	118.5
Cupertino	91	D	D	D	394	D	D	D	46	1 786	669.8	148.0
Cypress	68	255	40.7	8.3	131	1 949	649.1	150.4	44	1 683	431.2	97.9
Daly City	63	290	96.3	10.2	81	262	25.0	8.3	NA	NA	NA	NA
Dana Point	79	233	70.0	10.0	185	699	108.8	43.7	NA	NA	NA	NA
Danville	108	399	110.9	20.8	201	854	159.2	59.5	NA	NA	NA	NA
Davis	112	640	69.0	18.2	197	D	D	D	NA	NA	NA	NA

1. Establishments subject to federal tax.

Table D. Cities — Accommodation and Food Services, Arts, Entertainment, and Recreation, and Health Care and Social Assistance

City	Accommodation and food services, 2007				Arts, entertainment, and recreation,[1] 2007				Health care and social assistance,[1] 2007			
	Number of establishments	Number of employees	Sales (mil dol)	Annual payroll (mil dol)	Number of establishments	Number of employees	Receipts (mil dol)	Annual payroll (mil dol)	Number of establishments	Number of employees	Receipts (mil dol)	Annual payroll (mil dol)
	92	93	94	95	96	97	98	99	100	101	102	103
ARKANSAS—Cont'd												
Jacksonville	49	1 016	39.8	11.0	6	D	D	D	55	D	D	D
Jonesboro	171	3 866	144.0	40.7	12	D	D	D	246	D	D	D
Little Rock	522	11 312	532.7	154.3	60	872	55.2	15.2	846	10 964	1 447.6	595.8
North Little Rock	201	4 206	184.5	51.3	24	D	D	D	222	D	D	D
Paragould	57	967	37.5	10.4	3	D	D	D	66	D	D	D
Pine Bluff	115	1 912	77.6	20.3	5	D	D	D	191	D	D	D
Rogers	120	3 283	142.1	42.5	13	D	D	D	126	D	D	D
Russellville	98	2 144	74.6	19.9	7	D	D	D	110	D	D	D
Sherwood	32	477	19.8	5.4	2	D	D	D	56	D	D	D
Springdale	130	2 893	105.9	30.8	15	123	4.2	1.6	135	D	D	D
Texarkana	58	1 113	42.1	12.2	4	D	D	D	52	D	D	D
West Memphis	64	1 304	51.9	14.6	8	D	D	D	68	790	64.5	25.8
CALIFORNIA	75 989	1 366 926	80 852.8	22 374.8	18 025	243 993	31 778.7	10 364.4	84 335	883 552	102 703.1	38 944.0
Adelanto	16	143	8.9	2.2	4	D	D	D	3	D	D	D
Alameda	191	1 983	107.8	30.4	30	D	D	D	178	1 562	178.8	68.7
Alhambra	204	3 116	143.1	41.0	11	D	D	D	255	2 512	270.4	84.3
Aliso Viejo	83	964	53.5	15.7	12	D	D	D	105	D	D	D
Anaheim	686	22 020	1 405.3	438.7	74	D	D	D	781	9 799	1 159.6	435.0
Antioch	152	2 528	121.3	33.8	15	D	D	D	200	2 204	343.5	102.3
Apple Valley	67	1 035	49.5	13.4	6	D	D	D	172	D	D	D
Arcadia	189	3 531	180.3	48.8	72	1 913	208.8	54.4	371	D	D	D
Atascadero	60	850	36.8	10.6	7	D	D	D	78	D	D	D
Atwater	38	583	27.9	6.7	4	D	D	D	24	D	D	D
Azusa	84	936	44.6	11.6	4	D	D	D	43	D	D	D
Bakersfield	631	12 254	593.1	163.4	61	1 638	57.0	19.3	871	10 618	1 240.1	440.9
Baldwin Park	81	1 198	66.5	15.9	2	D	D	D	67	D	D	D
Banning	50	821	39.2	10.8	2	D	D	D	49	738	76.2	21.9
Beaumont	36	448	25.0	7.8	4	162	6.8	3.0	32	D	D	D
Bell	52	794	41.8	10.7	1	D	D	D	23	D	D	D
Bellflower	109	1 262	61.8	16.9	11	108	5.8	1.8	144	D	D	D
Bell Gardens	61	774	48.5	10.6	2	D	D	D	27	489	35.6	15.2
Belmont	53	722	45.8	13.4	8	D	D	D	49	407	33.4	12.8
Benicia	61	908	35.4	9.7	11	142	3.7	1.0	56	305	41.4	10.5
Berkeley	424	5 666	323.8	96.2	63	970	131.3	28.9	401	2 931	392.5	160.7
Beverly Hills	214	7 899	648.9	196.1	846	5 001	2 182.7	890.5	980	5 865	1 104.5	350.9
Brea	155	4 055	211.1	61.8	14	D	D	D	135	D	D	D
Brentwood	86	1 194	58.6	15.4	9	308	12.3	4.6	70	443	37.9	15.1
Buena Park	189	3 086	173.2	45.5	15	D	D	D	142	1 327	162.9	42.7
Burbank	289	6 989	427.3	113.2	276	D	D	D	411	D	D	D
Burlingame	144	3 984	286.5	85.2	20	246	21.1	4.1	149	D	D	D
Calexico	65	955	44.8	11.8	4	D	D	D	26	106	8.6	3.2
Camarillo	165	3 002	146.2	39.4	26	D	D	D	207	1 806	158.3	59.9
Campbell	126	2 267	130.9	36.7	13	D	D	D	134	D	D	D
Carlsbad	220	6 891	551.8	148.8	56	1 133	88.2	30.8	214	2 106	244.2	81.3
Carson	145	2 422	124.0	32.9	21	D	D	D	131	977	78.4	27.3
Cathedral City	90	1 441	69.5	21.2	12	336	19.1	5.5	58	583	38.4	18.2
Ceres	67	1 061	50.0	13.5	2	D	D	D	44	D	D	D
Cerritos	148	2 850	145.8	42.8	10	158	11.3	2.3	162	1 948	196.8	76.6
Chico	268	5 112	207.8	57.9	24	780	21.7	7.1	371	3 703	333.5	116.6
Chino	131	2 579	115.8	32.4	18	D	D	D	145	1 724	208.7	65.6
Chino Hills	110	1 681	81.2	20.9	16	D	D	D	104	D	D	D
Chula Vista	383	6 389	333.5	93.3	34	799	65.8	13.5	464	3 697	383.6	139.9
Citrus Heights	129	2 660	120.5	33.5	11	D	D	D	154	1 834	144.0	58.7
Claremont	79	1 238	64.4	18.6	13	D	D	D	120	1 035	80.3	32.7
Clovis	182	3 223	132.4	36.9	15	141	8.4	1.9	166	D	D	D
Coachella	42	538	27.8	6.8	2	D	D	D	10	55	2.9	1.3
Colton	94	1 311	60.3	16.9	5	D	D	D	82	D	D	D
Compton	77	1 270	86.5	21.5	4	6	0.4	0.1	61	451	35.6	13.7
Concord	272	4 480	241.0	66.2	26	716	41.5	11.7	345	3 376	349.0	144.8
Corona	300	5 785	247.7	69.3	38	D	D	D	293	2 858	287.7	98.5
Costa Mesa	402	8 460	512.1	142.0	46	544	47.8	11.6	310	3 058	274.3	103.9
Covina	117	1 886	91.8	23.3	10	D	D	D	185	2 824	236.0	104.6
Culver City	173	2 837	189.5	51.2	139	897	185.1	89.6	164	3 302	257.0	105.5
Cupertino	141	2 774	163.1	47.9	14	238	13.5	5.3	170	1 499	145.4	54.4
Cypress	109	2 044	105.4	27.9	22	D	D	D	105	D	D	D
Daly City	137	2 424	142.2	39.1	9	D	D	D	225	D	D	D
Dana Point	107	3 837	290.5	84.6	27	D	D	D	73	D	D	D
Danville	88	1 370	69.8	20.9	16	445	36.2	11.5	116	880	96.5	35.9
Davis	164	D	D	D	17	D	D	D	119	1 072	165.6	42.3

1. Establishments subject to federal tax.

Table D. Cities — Other Services and Federal Funds

City	Other services[1], 2007				Selected federal funds, 2009–2010 (mil dol)								
					Procurement contracts		Grants						
	Number of establish-ments	Number of employees	Receipts (mil dol)	Annual payroll (mil dol)	Defense	Other	Total[2]	Medicaid and other health related	Nutrition and family welfare	Energy and environ-ment	Disasters and emergency prepared-ness	Housing and community develop-ment	Employment and training
	104	105	106	107	108	109	110	111	112	113	114	115	116
ARKANSAS—Cont'd													
Jacksonville	33	D	D	D	32.8	0.0	6.4	0.0	0.0	0.0	0.0	4.1	0.0
Jonesboro	100	D	D	D	5.6	5.3	15.3	0.4	0.1	0.8	0.0	8.7	0.0
Little Rock	322	2 405	179.6	53.0	49.0	77.6	1 319.0	200.9	139.7	56.3	0.3	137.9	89.5
North Little Rock	133	762	57.5	17.0	1.7	113.9	42.2	0.6	0.3	11.8	2.4	16.2	0.0
Paragould	40	D	D	D	0.9	0.1	2.7	0.1	0.0	0.0	0.0	2.2	0.0
Pine Bluff	67	D	D	D	19.0	2.7	32.2	4.9	2.6	0.8	0.0	5.6	0.0
Rogers	84	518	26.4	9.0	4.9	6.6	4.3	0.1	3.0	0.6	0.0	0.5	0.0
Russellville	68	344	22.9	7.6	0.0	1.5	17.1	0.0	7.9	0.1	0.0	3.6	0.0
Sherwood	43	193	16.7	4.8	0.1	0.1	0.5	0.0	0.0	0.0	0.0	0.0	0.0
Springdale	102	824	54.2	21.6	141.5	5.9	7.3	3.2	0.0	0.0	0.0	1.5	0.0
Texarkana	27	D	D	D	1.9	2.8	4.9	0.3	0.1	0.0	0.0	2.2	0.0
West Memphis	46	D	D	D	1.4	0.1	10.6	1.5	0.0	0.0	0.0	3.8	3.4
CALIFORNIA	47 780	308 788	30 937.3	8 721.2	41 323.3	16 213.6	78 868.9	41 931.1	11 743.7	2 723.1	148.7	4 890.8	1 299.6
Adelanto	6	D	D	D	2.6	0.1	0.6	0.0	0.0	0.1	0.0	0.0	0.1
Alameda	98	386	33.9	11.1	56.9	93.2	50.0	1.8	2.2	19.0	0.0	26.3	0.0
Alhambra	105	453	45.7	10.9	0.1	0.6	5.9	0.0	0.0	0.0	0.0	2.4	0.0
Aliso Viejo	43	D	D	D	4.3	-1.9	1.4	1.4	0.0	0.0	0.0	0.0	0.0
Anaheim	376	2 850	270.6	85.3	204.9	9.5	102.7	0.8	0.1	18.7	0.0	79.8	0.0
Antioch	98	716	62.0	18.9	0.8	1.4	7.4	0.0	0.0	3.8	0.0	1.5	0.0
Apple Valley	32	174	10.5	4.5	0.7	3.8	19.9	0.0	0.0	18.0	0.0	1.4	0.0
Arcadia	99	432	36.6	9.9	3.9	32.2	99.1	86.1	0.0	10.1	0.0	0.0	0.0
Atascadero	37	165	13.9	4.2	1.2	0.5	0.0	0.0	0.0	0.0	0.0	0.0	0.0
Atwater	20	D	D	D	28.3	30.9	0.2	0.0	0.0	0.0	0.0	0.0	0.0
Azusa	70	292	27.0	7.9	29.8	5.2	0.9	0.8	0.0	0.1	0.0	0.0	0.0
Bakersfield	351	2 690	231.1	65.2	13.5	44.4	99.8	0.4	22.9	1.7	0.0	38.3	5.0
Baldwin Park	48	D	D	D	2.2	1.5	10.2	0.9	0.0	0.6	0.0	7.3	0.0
Banning	30	148	9.6	3.3	0.1	0.0	4.6	1.9	0.2	0.6	0.0	0.0	0.0
Beaumont	31	D	D	D	0.0	0.0	0.0	0.0	0.0	0.0	0.0	0.0	0.0
Bell	27	D	D	D	0.0	0.0	0.8	0.0	0.0	0.1	0.0	0.0	0.0
Bellflower	135	606	61.7	18.6	2.2	-0.1	2.9	0.0	0.0	0.0	0.0	2.5	0.0
Bell Gardens	35	177	18.1	4.5	0.6	0.1	0.0	0.0	0.0	0.0	0.0	0.0	0.0
Belmont	48	261	23.7	7.1	0.3	0.2	72.7	-0.2	0.0	0.0	0.0	70.1	2.6
Benicia	50	558	86.6	23.1	99.4	5.2	4.4	0.0	0.0	0.0	0.0	4.4	0.0
Berkeley	194	1 512	103.3	57.1	1.4	795.6	638.0	323.8	6.3	33.6	0.5	31.9	0.2
Beverly Hills	266	1 963	218.2	56.2	0.3	1.8	1.3	1.2	0.0	0.0	0.0	0.1	0.0
Brea	109	1 028	93.4	31.6	24.0	5.7	0.1	0.0	0.0	0.1	0.0	0.0	0.0
Brentwood	58	373	35.3	10.4	0.0	0.0	0.0	0.0	0.0	0.0	0.0	0.0	0.0
Buena Park	76	D	D	D	3.4	0.2	1.8	0.0	0.0	0.7	0.0	1.1	0.0
Burbank	250	2 210	195.8	78.5	12.2	3.6	33.1	0.0	0.0	20.0	0.0	11.0	0.0
Burlingame	114	671	54.9	17.9	107.8	0.4	16.2	14.8	0.0	0.0	0.0	1.1	0.0
Calexico	20	D	D	D	0.0	1.2	3.1	0.0	0.0	0.0	0.0	2.2	0.0
Camarillo	104	832	88.8	26.1	55.1	5.2	9.3	0.3	0.4	0.3	0.0	0.5	0.0
Campbell	171	999	91.2	29.2	2.9	9.3	15.4	0.0	0.3	15.0	0.0	0.1	0.0
Carlsbad	133	1 245	109.3	30.4	159.1	11.3	11.3	2.7	0.0	0.0	0.0	7.3	0.0
Carson	110	1 136	138.1	34.1	425.5	1.7	11.1	1.0	0.6	0.1	0.0	1.2	0.0
Cathedral City	89	612	49.5	15.2	0.0	0.0	0.6	0.0	0.0	0.0	0.0	0.0	0.0
Ceres	50	D	D	D	1.0	0.3	0.1	0.0	0.0	0.0	0.0	0.0	0.0
Cerritos	63	630	69.5	18.5	2.8	5.5	0.2	0.0	0.0	0.0	0.0	0.1	0.0
Chico	155	779	68.6	19.2	0.4	27.3	39.1	1.7	0.2	1.7	0.0	14.8	4.3
Chino	118	1 486	114.1	49.7	1.8	61.8	22.7	0.0	0.0	21.8	0.0	0.8	0.0
Chino Hills	62	334	15.5	5.1	0.1	0.5	1.3	0.0	0.0	0.6	0.0	0.5	0.0
Chula Vista	216	1 585	135.5	38.4	24.5	13.6	17.6	0.0	0.2	1.9	0.0	3.6	0.4
Citrus Heights	83	673	80.3	17.9	0.0	3.7	1.5	0.0	0.0	0.4	0.0	1.1	0.0
Claremont	31	139	9.2	3.2	1.6	0.1	21.3	12.4	0.5	0.2	0.0	0.0	0.0
Clovis	120	657	52.3	15.5	0.0	11.6	1.5	0.4	0.0	0.1	0.0	0.7	0.0
Coachella	11	D	D	D	94.9	2.4	1.1	0.0	0.3	0.4	0.0	0.0	0.0
Colton	52	671	55.9	15.1	0.1	0.4	0.7	0.0	0.0	0.5	0.0	0.0	0.0
Compton	62	392	23.2	7.7	5.3	0.7	12.6	-0.2	0.0	0.9	0.0	11.2	0.0
Concord	221	1 246	141.4	42.7	24.8	5.7	10.7	0.0	0.0	3.6	0.0	1.9	0.0
Corona	221	1 312	129.4	36.3	60.1	3.1	4.5	0.3	0.0	0.0	0.0	3.5	0.0
Costa Mesa	332	2 166	222.6	67.8	52.1	19.4	10.8	0.3	0.0	1.1	0.1	3.3	0.0
Covina	117	711	71.0	20.0	1.9	0.0	3.0	0.0	0.0	2.1	0.0	0.0	0.0
Culver City	136	2 856	115.9	49.9	1.8	7.6	18.4	0.2	0.0	0.5	0.0	1.8	0.0
Cupertino	58	398	23.9	8.8	5.1	2.8	2.8	2.3	0.0	0.0	0.0	0.5	0.0
Cypress	77	472	58.4	14.7	3.9	0.1	0.0	0.0	0.0	0.0	0.0	0.0	0.0
Daly City	84	505	40.1	12.4	0.0	-0.7	2.0	0.1	0.0	0.0	0.0	1.9	0.0
Dana Point	50	347	53.3	8.7	0.4	0.1	0.1	0.0	0.0	0.0	0.0	0.0	0.0
Danville	63	297	22.9	6.6	0.3	2.0	0.2	0.0	0.0	0.0	0.0	0.0	0.0
Davis	51	248	22.8	7.3	3.6	6.0	475.8	368.0	0.4	28.4	0.0	1.6	0.0

1. Establishments subject to federal tax. 2. Includes program categories not shown separately. State totals include additional categories not allocated by city.

Table D. Cities — City Government Finances

City	City government finances, 2007									
	General revenue							General expenditure		
	Intergovernmental			Taxes					Per capita[1] (dollars)	
					Per capita[1] (dollars)					
	Total (mil dol)	Total (mil dol)	Percent from state government	Total (mil dol)	Total	Property	Sales and gross receipts	Total (mil dol)	Total	Capital outlays
	117	118	119	120	121	122	123	124	125	126
ARKANSAS—Cont'd										
Jacksonville	78.4	9.6	37.7	9.3	299	30	269	70.2	2 251	89
Jonesboro	62.7	16.0	28.2	20.5	324	51	273	58.6	928	97
Little Rock	304.1	66.2	10.1	103.6	553	189	364	350.4	1 869	482
North Little Rock	91.9	19.1	21.9	50.9	856	131	726	112.7	1 894	705
Paragould	25.9	5.3	39.8	6.4	260	29	230	20.6	841	46
Pine Bluff	41.3	12.5	38.3	15.7	309	66	243	43.1	850	59
Rogers	68.1	17.5	33.6	27.9	507	67	440	53.3	971	339
Russellville	23.9	5.0	35.0	13.3	499	15	484	17.5	656	109
Sherwood	23.4	5.5	30.6	10.4	429	16	413	20.4	846	98
Springdale	70.3	15.9	29.3	34.1	510	74	436	72.0	1 076	483
Texarkana	25.3	5.5	40.0	11.3	382	110	272	22.0	744	17
West Memphis	25.4	5.3	59.2	11.5	419	21	399	26.9	979	37
CALIFORNIA	X	X	X	X	X	X	X	X	X	X
Adelanto	27.8	2.9	100.0	9.0	325	181	138	28.7	1 035	37
Alameda	138.7	16.3	80.0	72.9	1 037	578	398	170.8	2 430	649
Alhambra	95.6	13.2	51.9	49.8	577	311	261	100.8	1 168	309
Aliso Viejo	19.4	3.2	100.0	13.7	332	162	137	20.3	489	179
Anaheim	578.9	100.5	28.9	275.9	828	348	474	663.2	1 990	514
Antioch	77.4	8.2	86.0	44.4	446	285	155	80.5	808	217
Apple Valley	55.6	3.8	94.0	30.7	436	221	144	55.1	784	273
Arcadia	61.6	4.0	65.4	40.9	728	357	363	63.6	1 132	171
Atascadero	37.4	5.7	92.4	22.6	805	428	222	33.9	1 211	532
Atwater	23.7	4.0	45.7	10.1	373	242	93	27.5	1 020	292
Azusa	60.1	3.5	71.9	34.4	739	339	373	78.8	1 690	332
Bakersfield	387.1	37.4	37.1	164.8	522	279	237	303.3	960	192
Baldwin Park	42.5	7.7	58.7	25.9	333	202	128	41.9	538	47
Banning	34.3	6.7	85.9	12.8	440	258	179	38.7	1 331	356
Beaumont	38.0	1.9	100.0	7.0	230	60	147	30.3	1 004	430
Bell	27.3	2.4	68.7	18.2	493	307	184	61.5	1 668	878
Bellflower	36.2	4.8	73.6	25.5	348	161	184	35.5	483	114
Bell Gardens	36.8	3.1	81.7	25.5	568	179	388	31.7	706	59
Belmont	39.0	2.3	92.5	25.3	1 026	741	267	39.7	1 610	114
Benicia	51.1	3.4	95.8	30.8	1 171	572	560	43.7	1 059	314
Berkeley	295.4	25.5	84.7	133.1	1 313	641	485	290.6	2 867	113
Beverly Hills	210.8	5.5	73.5	134.6	3 892	1 119	2 739	163.3	4 720	376
Brea	93.9	6.1	77.4	57.4	1 495	1 000	488	86.6	2 257	497
Brentwood	95.7	2.9	100.0	37.3	770	463	145	110.6	2 282	750
Buena Park	100.0	14.1	34.3	70.0	883	514	364	70.2	886	119
Burbank	299.5	31.2	33.7	145.0	1 404	774	621	301.8	2 922	778
Burlingame	57.4	2.1	100.0	34.4	1 247	408	820	58.8	2 133	582
Calexico	37.3	6.2	39.7	16.6	442	143	268	38.1	1 013	53
Camarillo	73.9	9.7	56.9	37.8	599	315	274	69.9	1 108	312
Campbell	43.1	2.0	91.6	28.7	760	435	308	43.3	1 149	167
Carlsbad	212.4	21.0	43.0	113.3	1 187	559	614	183.9	1 926	613
Carson	115.0	10.1	74.2	78.2	843	477	359	100.4	1 082	190
Cathedral City	72.8	8.8	88.4	46.3	885	645	228	68.6	1 311	239
Ceres	39.9	2.9	91.4	23.4	547	241	242	38.5	902	269
Cerritos	116.3	2.7	100.0	69.9	1 354	831	516	117.7	2 279	185
Chico	112.5	9.2	51.3	73.7	887	487	394	117.9	1 418	597
Chino	127.7	7.6	88.7	54.3	655	426	222	132.1	1 595	219
Chino Hills	88.0	5.8	92.6	22.4	301	137	156	86.5	1 163	499
Chula Vista	238.6	18.9	77.4	130.6	601	286	308	277.7	1 277	212
Citrus Heights	59.8	16.6	82.0	36.1	428	203	222	44.5	527	96
Claremont	40.9	2.7	94.5	23.2	664	296	356	38.6	1 104	152
Clovis	108.6	7.5	69.5	49.2	542	268	268	108.9	1 199	323
Coachella	40.1	8.7	78.7	16.9	435	248	141	47.9	1 236	334
Colton	61.0	4.4	71.1	35.0	689	399	279	58.9	1 159	218
Compton	86.0	15.9	29.5	44.7	474	186	282	91.4	968	33
Concord	141.0	9.5	86.2	81.7	676	366	305	123.4	1 021	205
Corona	234.4	14.5	65.5	128.6	855	490	327	254.2	1 691	263
Costa Mesa	126.6	9.1	69.5	93.4	857	383	468	106.6	978	85
Covina	50.4	4.3	89.1	33.6	712	362	342	47.5	1 005	173
Culver City	163.8	17.2	60.7	100.2	2 578	1 002	1 479	129.8	3 341	463
Cupertino	53.7	2.5	66.7	34.7	651	268	353	54.8	1 028	149
Cypress	51.7	4.1	79.4	36.2	768	422	339	46.7	990	276
Daly City	104.8	13.8	40.4	53.4	529	301	218	102.1	1 012	105
Dana Point	34.1	2.7	100.0	26.6	746	257	472	37.3	1 046	352
Danville	37.4	2.8	100.0	23.7	578	323	194	32.1	783	187
Davis	102.2	17.7	93.2	49.1	783	384	307	99.6	1 587	261

1. Based on population estimated as of July 1 of the year shown.

Table D. Cities — **City Government Finances**

City	City government finances, 2006 (cont.)									
	General expenditure (cont.)									
	Percent of total for:									
	Public welfare	Highways	Parking facilities	Education	Health and hospitals	Police protection	Sewerage and sanitation	Parks and recreation	Housing and community development	Interest on debt
	127	128	129	130	131	132	133	134	135	136
ARKANSAS—Cont'd										
Jacksonville	0.0	3.1	0.0	0.0	63.8	7.2	10.1	3.2	0.5	0.9
Jonesboro....................	0.0	16.8	0.0	0.0	0.6	15.8	14.6	3.8	0.1	18.5
Little Rock	0.0	9.4	0.2	0.0	4.4	14.7	18.5	10.2	1.0	4.3
North Little Rock	0.0	5.6	0.0	0.0	0.4	14.3	12.4	34.7	1.0	1.7
Paragould	0.3	7.9	0.0	0.0	0.7	12.2	17.9	6.0	0.0	5.3
Pine Bluff	0.0	8.2	0.0	0.0	0.8	24.1	19.2	8.9	3.8	1.8
Rogers........................	0.0	4.8	0.0	0.0	0.0	12.4	25.7	5.5	0.0	4.4
Russellville	0.3	22.6	0.0	0.0	0.0	22.2	14.5	3.8	0.0	1.9
Sherwood	0.0	12.3	0.0	0.0	1.6	21.2	21.1	9.0	0.0	1.2
Springdale	0.0	36.7	0.0	0.0	0.4	13.2	8.8	11.0	0.9	2.6
Texarkana	0.0	8.5	0.0	0.0	0.4	29.1	21.8	0.9	3.0	1.9
West Memphis	0.0	9.6	0.0	0.0	0.7	21.8	11.9	4.5	1.3	3.6
CALIFORNIA..............	X	X	X	X	X	X	X	X	X	X
Adelanto	0.0	3.7	0.0	0.0	0.6	16.5	8.4	1.9	5.5	9.5
Alameda	0.0	4.6	0.0	0.0	9.5	14.9	3.0	6.1	16.7	2.8
Alhambra	0.0	7.0	1.6	0.0	2.6	20.9	9.4	7.4	20.0	5.2
Aliso Viejo	0.0	8.3	0.0	0.0	0.4	26.2	0.0	0.3	0.5	0.0
Anaheim	0.0	6.9	0.0	0.0	0.1	15.8	7.1	14.1	18.5	10.5
Antioch	0.0	21.3	0.0	0.0	1.0	32.0	5.0	9.6	10.6	4.9
Apple Valley	0.0	21.0	0.0	0.0	1.8	15.6	13.5	8.4	18.2	1.3
Arcadia	0.0	7.7	0.0	0.0	3.6	22.2	1.5	3.9	3.4	2.3
Atascadero	0.0	14.5	0.0	0.0	0.0	15.3	9.5	19.1	12.2	2.3
Atwater	0.0	6.4	0.0	0.0	0.0	16.0	25.1	3.7	5.5	1.5
Azusa	0.0	4.8	0.0	0.0	0.5	17.8	5.4	4.6	20.5	5.1
Bakersfield...................	0.0	6.2	0.0	0.0	0.0	21.4	15.2	9.8	1.3	2.1
Baldwin Park	0.0	10.6	0.0	0.0	0.0	36.2	0.8	5.4	17.4	4.9
Banning	0.0	2.8	0.0	0.0	0.4	24.3	17.0	13.4	17.5	3.1
Beaumont.....................	0.0	2.5	0.0	0.0	0.4	15.4	10.1	3.5	4.1	16.4
Bell	0.0	2.8	0.0	0.0	0.0	14.4	3.2	4.1	12.1	5.5
Bellflower......................	0.0	17.7	0.0	0.0	0.0	28.6	0.0	12.3	17.6	6.2
Bell Gardens	0.0	10.0	0.0	0.0	0.0	38.0	4.3	20.1	3.6	6.6
Belmont........................	0.0	5.3	0.0	0.0	0.0	20.5	16.1	8.2	12.5	4.8
Benicia.........................	0.0	17.7	0.0	0.0	0.0	20.4	13.0	13.0	0.1	4.3
Berkeley	0.0	5.6	2.3	0.0	10.3	15.9	13.0	6.1	11.9	2.1
Beverly Hills	0.0	6.7	5.1	0.0	3.4	21.0	15.5	9.9	0.1	5.1
Brea	0.0	13.0	0.0	0.0	3.4	26.8	3.5	9.9	13.7	11.5
Brentwood	0.0	26.9	0.0	0.0	0.0	11.4	14.1	9.4	9.3	11.3
Buena Park	0.0	15.2	0.0	0.0	0.3	30.7	4.4	6.8	14.5	2.3
Burbank	0.0	7.2	0.3	0.0	4.0	12.8	7.9	4.8	24.7	4.5
Burlingame	0.0	22.7	1.9	0.0	0.0	14.1	14.0	9.9	0.0	2.5
Calexico.......................	0.0	7.6	0.0	0.0	0.4	17.7	14.5	3.3	7.7	0.5
Camarillo	0.0	27.5	0.0	0.0	0.2	18.0	15.7	0.4	10.0	3.8
Campbell	0.0	11.4	0.0	0.0	0.0	26.3	0.0	14.1	13.9	3.0
Carlsbad	0.0	12.9	0.0	0.0	0.1	13.6	9.7	23.5	3.8	2.9
Carson.........................	0.0	12.4	0.0	0.0	0.4	19.5	0.1	17.6	18.0	5.4
Cathedral City	0.0	6.9	0.0	0.0	3.0	17.8	0.7	0.0	24.8	11.8
Ceres..........................	0.0	12.2	0.0	0.0	0.0	22.8	12.3	9.3	10.6	7.7
Cerritos........................	0.0	8.8	0.0	0.0	0.1	10.4	4.2	14.7	9.2	14.5
Chico	0.0	4.9	0.9	0.0	0.8	17.9	6.6	5.5	31.4	5.9
Chino	0.0	8.3	0.0	0.0	4.4	19.7	13.7	10.8	15.3	6.8
Chino Hills	0.0	28.7	0.0	0.0	0.3	11.7	8.9	21.8	0.0	5.2
Chula Vista...................	0.0	8.7	0.1	0.0	1.4	18.8	8.1	8.8	4.1	8.9
Citrus Heights...............	0.0	26.9	0.0	0.0	1.2	36.6	1.0	0.0	2.5	5.0
Claremont.....................	0.0	9.3	0.0	0.0	1.4	24.5	13.1	9.3	11.6	3.7
Clovis...........................	0.0	8.7	0.0	0.0	1.4	21.4	28.2	5.5	4.1	4.1
Coachella	0.0	30.2	0.0	0.0	0.3	12.4	7.0	0.9	9.6	7.1
Colton..........................	0.0	15.7	0.0	0.0	0.0	24.5	7.7	7.4	6.5	8.4
Compton.......................	0.0	10.2	0.0	0.0	1.0	16.3	9.4	2.3	10.6	2.7
Concord........................	0.0	16.2	0.0	0.0	0.0	31.2	13.9	13.4	7.6	3.1
Corona.........................	0.0	8.5	0.1	0.0	0.9	14.9	10.2	4.8	18.1	9.8
Costa Mesa..................	0.0	6.5	0.0	0.0	0.8	37.1	0.1	4.0	3.9	1.1
Covina	0.0	7.1	0.2	0.0	0.4	26.1	11.8	4.9	12.6	5.0
Culver City...................	0.0	5.0	0.1	0.0	2.7	22.5	10.8	5.0	15.6	8.7
Cupertino......................	0.0	23.9	0.0	0.0	0.4	12.7	3.9	16.4	0.9	4.1
Cypress	0.0	14.3	0.0	0.0	0.2	27.6	1.8	24.2	14.1	3.3
Daly City......................	0.0	6.0	0.0	0.0	0.0	21.9	12.2	16.1	3.1	1.5
Dana Point	0.0	26.0	0.0	0.0	0.6	20.9	0.0	20.5	1.1	0.0
Danville........................	0.0	17.5	0.0	0.0	0.5	19.1	0.0	9.3	2.8	2.6
Davis	0.0	11.9	0.0	0.0	0.0	13.8	16.1	28.4	8.6	2.0

Table D. Cities — City Government Finances, City Government Employment, and Climate

City	City government finances, 2007 (cont.) Debt outstanding				Climate[2]						
					Average daily temperature (degrees Fahrenheit)						
					Mean		Limits				
	Total (mil dol)	Per capita[1] (dollars)	Debt issued during year	City government employment, 2010	January	July	January[3]	July[4]	Annual precipitation (inches)	Heating degree days	Cooling degree days
	137	138	139	140	141	142	143	144	145	146	147
ARKANSAS—Cont'd											
Jacksonville	17.4	558	4.5	347	38.2	79.9	27.4	91.1	50.56	3 470	1 699
Jonesboro	313.8	4 966	5.9	680	35.6	81.6	25.8	92.3	46.18	3 737	1 858
Little Rock	380.2	2 028	23.1	2 512	40.1	82.4	30.8	92.8	50.93	3 084	2 086
North Little Rock	141.8	2 384	12.0	949	40.1	82.4	30.8	92.8	50.93	3 084	2 086
Paragould	46.8	1 910	0.0	256	NA	NA	NA	NA	NA	NA	NA
Pine Bluff	21.0	415	0.0	429	40.8	82.4	31.5	92.4	52.48	2 935	2 099
Rogers	104.7	1 905	15.4	472	32.9	77.5	22.0	88.8	46.92	4 483	1 269
Russellville	7.3	275	0.0	235	NA	NA	NA	NA	NA	NA	NA
Sherwood	6.2	255	0.0	264	NA	NA	NA	NA	NA	NA	NA
Springdale	136.4	2 039	127.6	560	34.3	78.9	24.2	89.1	46.02	4 166	1 439
Texarkana	54.5	1 839	0.7	233	44.3	82.7	35.6	92.7	47.38	2 421	2 280
West Memphis	30.3	1 104	0.0	377	37.5	81.5	28.5	90.9	52.80	3 417	1 903
CALIFORNIA	X	X	X	NA	X	X	X	X	X	X	X
Adelanto	63.7	2 301	8.0	NA	NA	NA	NA	NA	NA	NA	NA
Alameda	137.2	1 953	4.0	NA	50.9	64.9	44.7	72.7	22.94	2 400	377
Alhambra	109.4	1 267	0.0	442	56.3	75.6	42.6	89.0	18.56	1 295	1 575
Aliso Viejo	0.0	0	0.0	NA	56.7	72.4	47.2	82.3	14.03	1 465	1 183
Anaheim	1 708.8	5 128	537.1	2 567	56.9	73.2	45.2	84.0	11.23	1 286	1 294
Antioch	73.0	733	0.0	369	45.7	74.4	37.8	90.7	13.33	2 714	1 179
Apple Valley	21.6	307	9.0	NA	45.5	80.0	31.4	99.1	6.20	2 929	1 735
Arcadia	33.9	603	0.0	NA	56.3	75.6	42.6	89.0	18.56	1 295	1 575
Atascadero	15.1	537	1.0	NA	47.3	71.6	33.1	91.3	14.71	2 932	785
Atwater	13.3	492	10.8	NA	NA	NA	NA	NA	NA	NA	NA
Azusa	208.2	4 467	126.7	NA	54.6	73.8	41.5	88.7	16.96	1 727	1 191
Bakersfield	120.6	382	1.3	1 457	47.8	83.1	39.3	96.9	6.49	2 120	2 286
Baldwin Park	89.4	1 149	12.8	254	56.3	75.6	42.6	89.0	18.56	1 295	1 575
Banning	55.5	1 911	30.0	NA	NA	NA	NA	NA	NA	NA	NA
Beaumont	146.6	4 852	31.1	NA	NA	NA	NA	NA	NA	NA	NA
Bell	83.3	2 260	0.0	NA	58.8	76.6	47.9	88.9	14.44	949	1 837
Bellflower	37.5	511	2.6	NA	57.0	73.8	46.0	82.9	12.94	1 211	1 186
Bell Gardens	72.0	1 606	0.4	NA	58.8	76.6	47.9	88.9	14.44	949	1 837
Belmont	45.3	1 837	0.0	NA	48.1	69.7	36.4	88.2	28.71	2 769	569
Benicia	79.2	3 007	0.0	NA	46.3	71.2	38.8	87.4	19.58	2 757	786
Berkeley	192.0	1 894	0.0	1 533	50.0	62.8	43.6	70.4	25.40	2 857	142
Beverly Hills	273.6	7 908	117.1	1 019	57.9	69.5	49.4	76.9	18.68	1 379	893
Brea	232.9	6 067	0.0	NA	56.9	73.2	45.2	84.0	11.23	1 286	1 294
Brentwood	216.8	4 475	0.0	NA	NA	NA	NA	NA	NA	NA	NA
Buena Park	51.8	653	0.0	348	57.0	73.8	46.0	82.9	12.94	1 211	1 186
Burbank	423.1	4 096	52.9	1 354	54.8	76.5	42.0	88.9	17.49	1 575	1 455
Burlingame	36.3	1 317	33.0	NA	50.0	62.7	42.9	70.5	23.35	2 720	184
Calexico	5.9	158	0.0	NA	55.8	91.4	41.3	107.0	2.96	1 080	3 952
Camarillo	108.7	1 723	27.6	NA	55.7	66.0	45.3	74.0	13.61	1 961	389
Campbell	33.6	891	0.0	NA	48.7	70.3	38.8	85.4	22.64	2 641	613
Carlsbad	108.5	1 137	0.0	804	54.7	67.6	45.4	72.1	11.13	2 009	505
Carson	165.3	1 781	61.0	518	56.3	69.4	46.2	77.6	14.79	1 526	742
Cathedral City	250.3	4 787	115.8	NA	57.3	92.1	44.2	108.2	5.23	951	4 224
Ceres	55.1	1 290	38.1	NA	47.2	77.7	40.1	93.6	13.12	2 358	1 570
Cerritos	267.4	5 177	1.0	NA	57.0	73.8	46.0	82.9	12.94	1 211	1 186
Chico	150.4	1 810	0.0	NA	44.5	76.9	35.2	93.0	26.23	2 945	1 334
Chino	247.0	2 982	89.5	442	54.6	73.8	41.5	88.7	16.96	1 727	1 191
Chino Hills	185.4	2 493	49.7	192	56.9	73.2	45.2	84.0	11.23	1 286	1 294
Chula Vista	850.8	3 912	26.8	1 291	57.3	70.1	46.1	76.1	9.95	1 321	862
Citrus Heights	50.2	595	0.0	202	46.9	77.7	39.2	94.8	24.61	2 532	1 528
Claremont	29.3	837	0.0	NA	54.6	73.8	41.5	88.7	16.96	1 727	1 191
Clovis	281.4	3 098	68.5	505	46.0	81.4	38.4	96.6	11.23	2 447	1 963
Coachella	102.3	2 641	10.1	NA	NA	NA	NA	NA	NA	NA	NA
Colton	90.2	1 776	0.4	NA	54.4	79.6	41.8	96.0	16.43	1 599	1 937
Compton	97.7	1 034	53.1	495	57.0	73.8	46.0	82.9	12.94	1 211	1 186
Concord	117.8	975	0.6	472	46.3	71.2	38.8	87.4	19.58	2 757	786
Corona	621.6	4 135	61.4	793	54.7	75.9	41.5	92.0	12.00	1 599	1 534
Costa Mesa	57.0	523	30.0	605	55.9	67.3	48.2	71.4	11.65	1 719	543
Covina	59.5	1 260	0.3	NA	54.6	73.8	41.5	88.7	16.96	1 727	1 191
Culver City	199.1	5 125	1.6	NA	56.7	70.8	46.1	80.0	13.32	1 344	959
Cupertino	50.1	940	0.0	NA	48.7	70.3	38.8	85.4	22.64	2 641	613
Cypress	51.1	1 084	29.9	NA	57.0	73.8	46.0	82.9	12.94	1 211	1 186
Daly City	56.1	556	0.0	605	50.6	57.3	44.6	61.1	19.77	3 665	17
Dana Point	0.0	0	0.0	NA	55.4	68.7	43.9	77.3	13.56	1 756	666
Danville	14.8	360	0.0	NA	47.5	72.4	39.3	85.2	23.96	3 267	983
Davis	49.0	782	21.1	NA	45.2	74.3	37.1	92.7	19.05	2 853	1 127

1. Based on the population estimated as of July 1 of the year shown. 2. Represents normal values based on the 30-year period, 1971–2000. 3. Average daily minimum. 4. Average daily maximum.

Table D. Cities — Land Area and Population

STATE Place code	City	Land area,[1] 2010 (sq km)	Population, 2010 Total persons	Rank	Per square kilometer	Race alone or in combination, not of Hispanic origin (percent), 2010 White	Black	American Indian, Alaska Native	Asian	Hawaiian Pacific Islander	Percent Hispanic or Latino[2], 2010	Percent Foreign born, 2008–2010
		1	2	3	4	5	6	7	8	9	10	11
	CALIFORNIA—Cont'd											
06 18394	Delano	37.0	53 041	716	1 432.0	8.0	7.7	0.4	12.8	0.2	71.5	36.6
06 18996	Desert Hot Springs	61.2	25 938	1 600	424.1	36.2	8.6	1.2	3.0	0.5	52.6	20.8
06 19192	Diamond Bar	38.5	55 544	677	1 441.2	22.9	4.4	0.4	53.8	0.5	20.1	42.4
06 19766	Downey	32.1	111 772	238	3 477.7	18.5	3.7	0.4	7.2	0.3	70.7	36.7
06 20018	Dublin	38.6	46 036	857	1 192.3	48.0	10.0	0.9	29.7	1.1	14.5	22.8
06 20956	East Palo Alto	6.5	28 155	1 466	4 338.2	7.4	16.8	0.7	4.6	8.2	64.5	41.4
06 21712	El Cajon	37.4	99 478	290	2 661.3	60.8	7.3	1.2	5.9	1.0	28.2	27.5
06 21782	El Centro	28.7	42 598	925	1 484.3	14.0	2.3	0.4	2.1	0.1	81.6	29.4
06 22020	Elk Grove	109.3	153 015	159	1 400.3	42.2	12.7	1.3	29.3	2.0	18.0	23.4
06 22230	El Monte	24.8	113 475	234	4 581.1	5.2	0.5	0.2	25.2	0.1	69.0	53.6
06 22300	El Paso de Robles (Paso Robles)	49.5	29 793	1 375	601.6	60.9	2.4	1.2	2.5	0.3	34.5	16.4
06 22678	Encinitas	48.7	59 518	612	1 221.6	81.1	0.9	0.7	5.5	0.4	13.7	14.1
06 22804	Escondido	95.3	143 911	174	1 509.5	42.1	2.7	0.9	6.9	0.4	48.9	28.7
06 23042	Eureka	24.3	27 191	1 519	1 119.0	78.0	2.7	6.2	5.1	1.0	11.6	8.3
06 23182	Fairfield	96.8	105 321	263	1 087.6	40.0	17.7	1.6	17.9	2.0	27.3	21.1
06 24638	Folsom	56.8	72 203	468	1 270.3	69.3	6.1	1.0	14.4	0.5	11.2	14.3
06 24680	Fontana	109.9	196 069	116	1 784.1	16.6	9.9	0.6	7.1	0.4	66.8	31.4
06 25338	Foster City	9.7	30 567	1 328	3 141.5	45.3	2.2	0.4	48.1	1.0	6.5	41.2
06 25380	Fountain Valley	23.4	55 313	680	2 367.9	51.9	1.2	0.7	35.2	0.7	13.1	29.4
06 26000	Fremont	200.6	214 089	96	1 067.1	29.9	3.8	0.7	53.8	1.0	14.8	43.3
06 27000	Fresno	290.0	494 665	34	1 705.9	31.6	8.4	1.3	13.3	0.3	46.9	21.2
06 28000	Fullerton	57.9	135 161	188	2 334.8	40.1	2.5	0.6	24.0	0.5	34.4	31.0
06 28168	Gardena	15.1	58 829	621	3 896.0	10.8	24.8	0.6	27.2	1.1	37.7	33.7
06 29000	Garden Grove	46.5	170 883	140	3 677.3	23.9	1.3	0.4	38.1	0.9	36.9	44.7
06 29504	Gilroy	41.8	48 821	795	1 167.4	33.2	1.9	0.8	7.9	0.4	57.8	24.4
06 30000	Glendale	78.9	191 719	121	2 430.8	64.6	1.5	0.3	18.8	0.4	17.4	55.3
06 30014	Glendora	50.2	50 073	769	996.9	59.2	2.1	0.6	9.3	0.4	30.7	14.9
06 30378	Goleta	20.5	29 888	1 367	1 460.1	55.9	1.9	0.9	10.5	0.2	32.9	27.1
06 31960	Hanford	43.0	53 967	703	1 255.9	43.2	5.3	1.1	5.1	0.3	47.1	16.5
06 32548	Hawthorne	15.8	84 293	375	5 351.9	11.4	27.7	0.5	7.4	1.4	52.9	34.9
06 33000	Hayward	117.4	144 186	172	1 228.3	21.3	12.4	1.0	24.2	4.2	40.7	36.9
06 33182	Hemet	72.1	78 657	414	1 090.6	54.0	7.0	1.5	3.7	0.6	35.8	13.8
06 33434	Hesperia	189.3	90 173	338	476.3	42.7	6.1	1.0	2.6	0.4	48.9	13.5
06 33588	Highland	48.6	53 104	715	1 093.1	32.7	11.7	1.0	8.3	0.5	48.1	21.9
06 34120	Hollister	18.9	34 928	1 153	1 850.0	30.4	1.0	0.9	3.2	0.2	65.7	22.7
06 36000	Huntington Beach	69.3	189 992	123	2 742.4	70.1	1.3	0.9	13.0	0.7	17.1	16.9
06 36056	Huntington Park	7.8	58 114	634	7 450.5	1.7	0.4	0.1	0.6	0.0	97.1	51.6
06 36294	Imperial Beach	10.8	26 324	1 575	2 441.9	38.9	5.1	1.2	8.3	1.1	49.0	20.6
06 36448	Indio	75.6	76 036	440	1 006.0	27.7	2.3	0.5	2.3	0.1	67.8	26.6
06 36546	Inglewood	23.5	109 673	243	4 668.9	3.7	44.2	0.8	1.7	0.5	50.6	29.0
06 36770	Irvine	171.2	212 375	97	1 240.4	49.2	2.2	0.4	42.7	0.4	9.2	35.0
06 39220	Laguna Hills	17.3	30 344	1 343	1 756.0	64.9	1.7	0.6	15.1	0.4	20.6	23.4
06 39248	Laguna Niguel	38.4	62 979	564	1 639.2	75.7	1.5	0.6	11.1	0.4	13.9	21.4
06 39290	La Habra	19.1	60 239	603	3 155.5	31.6	1.7	0.6	10.0	0.3	57.2	28.1
06 39486	Lake Elsinore	93.8	51 821	740	552.6	40.1	5.8	1.0	6.6	0.6	48.4	20.5
06 39496	Lake Forest	46.1	77 264	422	1 674.6	60.0	2.0	0.7	15.1	0.6	24.6	22.1
06 39892	Lakewood	24.4	80 048	406	3 283.3	43.6	9.3	0.9	17.9	1.4	30.1	21.0
06 40004	La Mesa	23.5	57 065	650	2 427.3	65.1	8.6	1.2	7.3	0.9	20.5	13.3
06 40032	La Mirada	20.3	48 527	804	2 389.3	39.6	2.4	0.6	18.8	0.6	39.7	23.4
06 40130	Lancaster	244.2	156 633	151	641.5	36.5	21.4	1.2	5.1	0.4	38.0	12.5
06 40340	La Puente	9.0	39 816	990	4 419.1	4.9	1.3	0.3	8.5	0.2	85.1	42.8
06 40354	La Quinta	91.0	37 467	1 059	412.0	64.6	2.0	0.6	3.7	0.2	30.3	15.2
06 40830	La Verne	21.8	31 063	1 310	1 423.0	57.4	3.7	0.9	8.7	0.4	31.0	14.2
06 40886	Lawndale	5.1	32 769	1 244	6 412.7	17.8	10.1	0.6	10.7	1.3	61.0	38.1
06 41124	Lemon Grove	10.1	25 320	1 642	2 519.4	37.4	14.6	1.1	7.7	1.5	41.2	18.0
06 41474	Lincoln	52.1	42 819	917	822.3	73.6	1.9	1.3	7.6	0.6	17.7	11.2
06 41992	Livermore	65.2	80 968	397	1 241.8	67.8	2.5	1.0	10.4	0.6	20.9	16.3
06 42202	Lodi	35.3	62 134	576	1 762.7	55.3	0.9	1.2	7.8	0.4	36.4	19.5
06 42524	Lompoc	30.0	42 434	929	1 412.6	38.7	6.4	1.6	4.7	0.6	50.8	24.5
06 43000	Long Beach	130.3	462 257	36	3 548.7	31.4	14.1	0.9	14.0	1.4	40.8	27.1
06 43280	Los Altos	16.8	28 976	1 422	1 724.8	71.5	0.7	0.3	26.9	0.3	3.9	24.2
06 44000	Los Angeles	1 213.9	3 792 621	2	3 124.5	30.3	9.8	0.5	12.3	0.3	48.5	39.6
06 44028	Los Banos	25.9	35 972	1 108	1 390.0	27.9	3.7	0.9	3.5	0.6	64.9	27.3
06 44112	Los Gatos	28.7	29 413	1 397	1 024.8	80.4	1.2	0.7	13.5	0.4	7.2	16.8
06 44574	Lynwood	12.5	69 772	490	5 564.0	2.4	9.9	0.2	0.6	0.3	86.6	41.2
06 45022	Madera	40.9	61 416	581	1 502.0	17.8	3.0	0.9	2.4	0.1	76.7	29.4
06 45400	Manhattan Beach	10.2	35 135	1 148	3 444.6	83.1	1.3	0.5	11.6	0.4	6.9	9.3
06 45484	Manteca	45.9	67 096	512	1 460.8	49.8	4.8	1.4	8.6	0.9	37.7	16.0
06 46114	Martinez	31.4	35 824	1 114	1 140.2	72.6	4.5	1.7	10.3	0.8	14.7	11.7
06 46492	Maywood	3.1	27 395	1 505	8 982.0	1.9	0.2	0.1	0.3	0.1	97.4	49.0
06 46842	Menifee	120.4	77 519	419	644.1	56.4	5.5	1.1	5.9	0.7	33.0	14.9

1. Dry land or land partially or temporarily covered by water.   2. May be of any race.

City	Age of population (percent), 2010											Population			
												Census counts		Percent change	
	Under 5 years	5 to 17 years	18 to 24 years	25 to 34 years	35 to 44 years	45 to 54 years	55 to 64 years	65 to 74 years	75 years and over	Median age	Percent female	1990	2000	1990– 2000	2000– 2010
	12	13	14	15	16	17	18	19	20	21	22	23	24	25	26
CALIFORNIA—Cont'd															
Delano	8.0	20.5	14.7	18.0	14.6	11.5	6.7	3.4	2.7	28.5	40.1	22 762	38 824	70.6	36.6
Desert Hot Springs	9.0	22.1	10.5	13.7	12.9	13.4	8.9	5.6	4.0	31.0	49.9	11 668	16 582	42.1	56.4
Diamond Bar	4.3	17.1	10.1	11.0	13.5	17.8	14.6	7.2	4.4	41.0	51.2	53 672	56 287	4.9	-1.3
Downey	7.0	19.8	10.8	14.7	14.8	12.9	9.5	5.2	5.2	33.3	51.5	91 444	107 323	17.4	4.1
Dublin	7.4	15.0	8.0	18.9	19.3	14.8	9.3	4.7	2.6	35.3	47.9	23 229	29 973	29.0	53.6
East Palo Alto	9.3	22.6	12.4	17.5	14.1	11.1	7.1	3.4	2.5	28.1	49.3	23 451	29 506	25.8	-4.6
El Cajon	7.6	18.1	11.3	14.7	12.9	14.3	10.1	5.6	5.4	33.7	51.1	88 918	94 869	6.7	4.9
El Centro	7.9	21.9	11.3	12.7	12.3	13.2	10.1	5.7	5.0	31.8	51.4	31 405	37 835	20.5	12.6
Elk Grove	7.2	22.9	8.6	12.2	15.7	15.2	9.8	4.8	3.5	34.3	51.6	17 483	59 984	243.1	155.1
El Monte	7.9	20.5	11.3	15.2	14.2	12.4	9.2	5.1	4.3	31.6	49.8	106 162	115 965	9.2	-2.1
El Paso de Robles (Paso Robles)	7.8	18.5	9.5	13.8	12.6	13.5	10.9	6.6	6.8	35.3	51.3	18 583	24 297	30.7	22.6
Encinitas	5.4	15.3	6.3	13.4	14.5	16.9	15.4	6.6	6.3	41.5	50.5	55 406	58 014	4.7	2.6
Escondido	8.1	19.6	10.7	15.0	13.5	13.1	9.6	5.1	5.3	32.5	50.5	108 648	133 559	22.9	7.8
Eureka	6.1	13.9	11.4	16.9	12.6	14.0	13.3	6.3	5.5	36.2	48.6	27 025	26 128	-3.3	4.1
Fairfield	7.4	19.7	10.7	13.9	13.5	14.4	10.1	5.4	4.8	33.7	50.8	78 650	96 178	22.3	9.5
Folsom	6.1	18.2	7.4	14.1	17.8	16.6	10.2	5.1	4.5	37.6	46.7	29 802	51 884	74.1	39.2
Fontana	8.6	24.3	11.7	14.5	14.9	12.7	7.6	3.4	2.2	28.7	50.3	87 535	128 929	47.3	52.1
Foster City	6.8	15.8	5.0	14.6	17.5	14.6	12.3	8.1	5.3	39.3	51.7	28 176	28 803	2.2	6.1
Fountain Valley	4.6	16.4	8.4	10.5	13.5	15.7	13.2	10.4	7.2	42.6	51.3	53 691	54 978	2.4	0.6
Fremont	7.1	17.7	7.3	14.7	16.5	15.8	10.6	5.6	4.5	36.8	50.3	173 339	203 413	17.3	5.2
Fresno	8.9	21.2	12.7	15.3	12.1	11.6	9.0	4.9	4.5	29.3	50.9	354 091	427 652	20.8	15.7
Fullerton	5.9	17.4	13.0	14.0	14.0	14.3	9.7	5.8	5.9	34.8	50.9	114 144	126 003	10.4	7.3
Gardena	6.3	16.5	9.1	13.9	14.4	14.2	11.5	7.2	6.9	37.9	51.9	51 481	57 746	12.2	1.9
Garden Grove	6.7	18.9	10.2	13.2	15.5	14.6	10.1	5.9	4.9	35.6	50.1	142 965	165 196	15.5	3.4
Gilroy	8.5	22.2	9.2	13.8	15.1	13.5	9.2	4.8	3.6	32.4	50.4	31 487	41 464	31.7	17.7
Glendale	4.8	13.9	8.7	14.2	14.2	16.0	12.7	8.0	7.6	41.0	52.3	180 038	194 973	8.3	-1.7
Glendora	6.0	18.5	9.8	10.5	13.1	16.5	12.4	7.4	6.8	40.2	51.6	47 832	49 415	3.3	1.3
Goleta	5.5	15.6	12.7	14.3	12.3	14.8	11.2	6.3	7.3	36.5	49.7	NA	55 204	NA	-45.9
Hanford	9.1	21.9	10.2	14.6	12.7	12.3	9.3	5.2	4.7	30.9	51.0	30 463	41 686	36.8	29.5
Hawthorne	8.0	19.4	11.3	17.1	15.0	13.1	8.7	4.8	3.1	31.5	51.7	71 349	84 112	17.9	0.2
Hayward	7.5	17.1	11.1	16.5	14.0	13.4	10.3	5.3	4.8	33.5	50.7	114 705	140 030	22.1	3.0
Hemet	7.2	18.6	8.7	11.3	10.7	10.8	10.5	9.8	12.4	39.0	52.9	43 366	58 812	35.6	33.7
Hesperia	8.4	23.9	10.5	13.1	12.7	13.0	9.3	5.2	3.9	30.5	50.4	50 418	62 582	24.1	44.1
Highland	8.4	23.5	11.1	12.4	13.6	13.9	9.4	4.8	3.0	30.6	51.3	34 439	44 605	29.5	19.1
Hollister	8.5	23.2	10.1	14.0	14.4	13.9	8.4	3.8	3.6	30.8	50.3	19 318	34 413	78.1	1.8
Huntington Beach	5.1	15.5	8.4	13.8	14.7	15.9	12.6	8.1	6.1	40.2	50.4	181 519	189 594	4.4	0.2
Huntington Park	8.8	23.0	12.0	15.8	15.0	11.2	7.6	4.0	2.7	28.9	50.1	56 129	61 348	9.3	-5.3
Imperial Beach	7.5	17.9	13.8	16.1	12.8	13.4	9.4	4.8	4.2	31.0	49.7	26 512	26 992	1.8	-2.5
Indio	8.5	21.6	9.5	14.2	13.0	11.2	9.6	7.6	4.8	32.2	50.7	36 850	49 116	33.3	54.8
Inglewood	7.3	19.4	10.8	14.7	14.1	14.1	10.2	5.6	3.7	33.4	52.5	109 602	112 580	2.7	-2.6
Irvine	5.7	15.9	14.3	15.8	15.6	14.0	10.1	5.1	3.6	33.9	51.3	110 330	143 072	29.7	48.4
Laguna Hills	5.2	17.1	8.6	11.4	13.7	17.0	14.1	6.9	5.9	40.8	51.2	22 719	31 178	37.2	-2.7
Laguna Niguel	5.1	17.4	7.5	9.8	13.5	19.0	14.7	7.5	5.5	42.8	51.5	44 723	61 891	38.4	1.8
La Habra	7.2	19.4	10.5	14.7	14.1	13.6	9.5	5.4	5.5	33.6	50.8	51 263	58 974	15.0	2.1
Lake Elsinore	9.2	23.6	10.2	15.0	15.4	13.0	7.9	3.6	2.2	29.8	49.9	19 733	28 928	46.6	79.1
Lake Forest	6.3	18.5	8.8	13.4	15.2	17.1	11.6	5.4	3.8	37.2	50.3	56 065	58 707	4.7	31.6
Lakewood	6.1	18.3	9.5	12.6	15.0	15.7	11.5	5.9	5.5	37.5	51.5	73 553	79 345	7.9	0.9
La Mesa	6.3	13.2	11.2	16.3	13.1	14.5	11.2	6.0	8.2	37.1	52.4	52 911	54 749	3.5	4.2
La Mirada	5.1	16.0	14.6	11.0	13.0	14.3	10.9	7.3	7.9	37.9	52.0	40 452	46 783	15.7	3.7
Lancaster	8.0	22.1	11.9	14.1	13.1	14.0	8.7	4.5	3.6	30.4	49.9	97 300	118 718	22.0	31.9
La Puente	7.5	21.2	11.7	14.5	14.3	13.1	8.6	5.1	4.1	31.5	50.1	36 955	41 063	11.1	-3.0
La Quinta	4.8	17.1	6.7	8.6	11.9	14.5	15.5	13.3	7.5	45.6	51.7	11 215	23 694	111.3	58.1
La Verne	4.4	16.9	10.0	10.1	11.4	16.4	13.9	8.7	8.2	42.9	52.7	30 843	31 638	2.6	-1.8
Lawndale	7.5	19.7	11.4	16.3	15.9	13.5	8.7	4.1	2.8	31.9	49.7	27 331	31 711	16.0	3.3
Lemon Grove	7.0	18.5	10.2	14.3	13.0	14.8	11.1	5.4	5.7	35.0	51.2	23 984	24 918	3.9	1.6
Lincoln	7.8	16.5	5.5	12.7	12.6	9.5	11.9	14.2	9.3	40.5	51.9	7 248	11 205	54.6	282.1
Livermore	6.6	18.9	7.6	12.3	15.5	17.7	11.0	5.8	4.5	38.3	50.4	56 741	73 345	29.3	10.4
Lodi	7.9	19.9	9.4	13.7	11.9	13.2	10.4	6.3	7.2	34.3	51.2	51 874	56 999	9.9	9.0
Lompoc	7.6	18.8	10.5	14.5	14.3	14.7	9.6	5.3	4.6	33.9	46.5	37 649	41 103	9.2	3.2
Long Beach	7.0	17.9	11.7	15.9	14.6	13.6	10.0	5.0	4.2	33.2	51.0	429 321	461 522	7.5	0.2
Los Altos	5.4	20.7	3.5	4.7	13.5	18.6	13.7	9.5	10.5	46.2	51.8	26 599	27 693	4.1	4.6
Los Angeles	6.6	16.4	11.5	16.8	15.0	13.3	9.9	5.5	4.9	34.1	50.2	3 485 557	3 694 820	6.0	2.6
Los Banos	9.0	24.6	10.3	13.0	13.7	12.6	8.2	4.7	3.8	29.8	50.2	14 519	25 869	78.2	39.1
Los Gatos	4.7	17.6	4.9	8.5	14.4	18.7	13.3	9.1	8.8	45.0	52.1	27 357	28 592	4.5	2.9
Lynwood	9.1	23.9	12.5	15.7	14.7	11.4	7.3	3.4	2.0	27.8	51.4	61 945	69 845	12.8	-0.1
Madera	10.7	24.0	12.6	15.7	12.5	9.9	7.0	4.0	3.5	26.6	49.0	29 283	43 207	47.5	42.1
Manhattan Beach	5.8	19.1	5.0	11.5	15.7	17.5	12.9	7.2	5.5	40.9	49.9	32 063	33 852	5.6	3.8
Manteca	7.7	21.2	9.8	13.1	13.8	14.6	9.8	5.6	4.3	33.6	50.8	40 773	49 258	20.8	36.2
Martinez	5.0	15.5	7.9	12.1	13.6	18.4	15.4	7.3	4.8	42.2	50.8	31 800	35 866	12.8	-0.1
Maywood	9.4	23.1	12.4	16.5	15.0	10.5	7.0	3.6	2.4	27.9	48.9	27 893	28 083	0.7	-2.4
Menifee	6.9	19.0	8.3	12.0	12.2	12.3	10.4	9.3	9.6	38.1	51.9	NA	NA	NA	NA

Table D. Cities — **Households, Group Quarters, Crime, and Education**

City	Number	Persons per household	Female family householder[1]	One-person	Total	Total	Persons in nursing facilities	Non-institutional	Number	Rate[3]	Violent	Property	Population age 25 and older	High school graduate or less	Bachelor's degree or more
	27	28	29	30	31	32	33	34	35	36	37	38	39	40	41
CALIFORNIA—Cont'd															
Delano	10 260	4.11	20.4	9.6	10 897	10 719	189	178	1 898	3 578	466	3 113	30 523	75.0	6.3
Desert Hot Springs	8 650	2.98	18.5	23.9	118	0	0	118	1 754	6 762	1 442	5 320	14 360	54.4	13.5
Diamond Bar	17 880	3.10	12.1	12.9	129	27	22	102	856	1 541	86	1 455	38 451	24.6	47.5
Downey	33 936	3.27	18.5	16.9	683	561	534	122	4 350	3 892	353	3 539	68 956	52.8	18.8
Dublin	14 913	2.70	9.3	21.5	5 774	5 682	0	92	789	1 714	150	1 564	30 997	28.7	44.6
East Palo Alto	6 940	4.03	21.8	17.2	154	4	0	150	1 117	3 967	963	3 005	15 609	63.1	14.8
El Cajon	34 134	2.84	16.6	23.1	2 482	1 350	1 339	1 132	3 153	3 170	389	2 781	60 799	50.6	15.9
El Centro	13 108	3.19	21.7	18.8	816	520	98	296	2 605	6 115	462	5 653	24 610	51.1	15.4
Elk Grove	47 927	3.18	13.7	15.1	669	209	133	460	3 733	2 440	346	2 094	89 963	27.4	31.8
El Monte	27 814	4.04	19.0	11.3	1 080	763	618	317	3 198	2 818	529	2 289	69 698	71.8	11.2
El Paso de Robles (Paso Robles)	10 833	2.73	12.4	22.9	169	5	0	164	1 101	3 695	319	3 377	18 688	42.8	21.2
Encinitas	24 082	2.45	8.1	26.2	528	405	405	123	1 093	1 836	245	1 591	43 119	18.7	54.5
Escondido	45 484	3.12	13.4	20.9	2 119	786	657	1 333	4 630	3 217	415	2 802	88 952	48.4	22.0
Eureka	11 150	2.27	13.0	35.6	1 883	449	8	1 434	1 760	6 473	677	5 796	18 705	39.4	19.8
Fairfield	34 484	2.98	15.1	19.7	2 489	1 268	332	1 221	3 897	3 700	477	3 223	64 407	38.5	22.7
Folsom	24 951	2.61	8.8	23.2	6 960	6 772	96	188	1 589	2 201	145	2 055	48 797	28.6	40.9
Fontana	49 116	3.98	16.4	9.8	444	228	194	216	4 440	2 265	387	1 877	107 233	53.6	15.0
Foster City	12 016	2.53	8.0	23.4	109	57	57	52	440	1 439	79	1 361	21 821	13.4	63.5
Fountain Valley	18 648	2.94	11.3	18.5	437	180	160	257	1 395	2 522	186	2 336	39 368	28.2	38.3
Fremont	71 004	2.99	10.0	16.3	1 651	682	662	969	4 902	2 290	228	2 062	145 595	29.6	49.0
Fresno	158 349	3.07	19.3	22.1	8 867	4 552	1 825	4 315	27 494	5 558	613	4 945	281 321	48.6	20.3
Fullerton	45 391	2.91	12.1	21.5	3 077	759	629	2 318	4 272	3 161	314	2 846	86 083	32.4	36.8
Gardena	20 558	2.82	19.1	25.0	794	672	631	122	1 793	3 048	590	2 458	40 226	45.4	22.0
Garden Grove	46 037	3.67	14.9	14.1	1 941	707	624	1 234	4 129	2 416	315	2 101	109 603	52.2	19.2
Gilroy	14 175	3.39	15.6	15.1	806	164	128	642	1 760	3 605	420	3 185	28 514	44.8	23.0
Glendale	72 269	2.63	12.3	24.9	1 429	1 206	1 181	223	3 994	2 083	144	1 939	138 127	34.3	39.5
Glendora	17 141	2.88	13.3	19.0	765	573	519	192	1 311	2 618	124	2 494	31 917	33.0	29.7
Goleta	10 903	2.72	9.8	25.1	201	178	170	23	464	1 552	191	1 362	19 647	28.9	45.7
Hanford	17 492	3.03	16.2	19.9	899	616	296	283	1 340	2 483	335	2 148	32 721	47.1	15.6
Hawthorne	28 486	2.94	22.4	25.0	539	331	311	208	2 853	3 385	775	2 610	52 273	51.3	16.5
Hayward	45 365	3.12	16.5	20.6	2 724	770	723	1 954	4 405	3 055	452	2 603	93 013	48.7	22.9
Hemet	30 092	2.59	14.5	30.3	614	459	421	155	3 256	4 139	469	3 670	50 551	52.5	12.6
Hesperia	26 431	3.41	16.0	15.3	28	6	6	22	2 206	2 446	318	2 128	48 878	55.5	10.0
Highland	15 471	3.42	18.6	14.6	172	96	96	76	1 734	3 265	456	2 810	29 447	49.6	18.8
Hollister	9 860	3.53	15.3	13.4	115	106	102	9	1 048	3 000	455	2 545	20 683	53.6	16.2
Huntington Beach	74 285	2.55	10.3	24.9	890	403	391	487	5 122	2 696	236	2 460	134 489	24.3	39.4
Huntington Park	14 597	3.96	22.0	11.3	255	7	0	248	2 654	4 567	962	3 605	32 503	78.7	6.0
Imperial Beach	9 112	2.82	18.7	22.5	619	0	0	619	598	2 272	551	1 721	15 674	48.3	15.0
Indio	23 378	3.21	15.3	16.5	949	584	135	365	3 182	4 185	596	3 589	44 222	51.8	18.9
Inglewood	36 389	2.97	24.7	25.7	1 502	515	405	987	3 515	3 205	769	2 436	67 905	50.2	17.2
Irvine	78 978	2.61	9.6	23.4	6 556	588	55	5 968	2 918	1 374	57	1 317	129 708	12.9	65.7
Laguna Hills	10 469	2.86	9.4	19.5	369	136	136	233	553	1 822	142	1 681	20 542	25.6	45.7
Laguna Niguel	24 232	2.59	9.4	22.2	248	0	0	248	681	1 081	64	1 018	44 173	15.1	52.5
La Habra	18 977	3.16	15.3	19.2	340	171	167	169	1 405	2 332	281	2 052	37 227	48.7	21.4
Lake Elsinore	14 788	3.48	14.0	13.2	432	208	0	224	1 679	3 240	208	3 032	27 888	48.6	16.5
Lake Forest	26 224	2.93	10.3	18.6	515	216	216	299	1 051	1 360	119	1 241	51 759	24.5	42.8
Lakewood	26 543	3.01	15.0	17.8	109	0	0	109	2 172	2 713	370	2 344	52 653	36.9	26.9
La Mesa	24 512	2.30	12.7	32.7	657	533	512	124	2 209	3 871	322	3 549	39 647	29.0	32.2
La Mirada	14 681	3.11	11.8	17.3	2 857	271	271	2 586	800	1 649	152	1 496	30 707	37.7	28.5
Lancaster	46 992	3.16	20.2	19.7	8 259	6 775	486	1 484	4 311	2 752	575	2 178	90 371	48.8	16.7
La Puente	9 451	4.21	19.3	10.5	43	0	0	43	743	1 866	407	1 459	23 134	69.6	10.1
La Quinta	14 820	2.52	9.7	21.3	57	7	7	50	1 425	3 803	366	3 438	25 728	31.2	31.7
La Verne	11 261	2.70	12.8	22.4	676	175	104	501	699	2 250	180	2 070	20 916	32.0	31.4
Lawndale	9 681	3.37	18.7	18.2	175	17	0	158	741	2 261	696	1 566	19 082	55.0	15.2
Lemon Grove	8 434	2.96	16.8	22.9	346	146	129	200	687	2 713	616	2 097	15 861	44.5	17.7
Lincoln	16 479	2.59	7.3	21.3	115	85	85	30	475	1 109	65	1 044	28 384	28.8	31.7
Livermore	29 134	2.76	9.7	20.6	510	121	121	389	2 093	2 585	399	2 186	52 725	27.2	36.6
Lodi	22 097	2.78	13.2	25.1	677	490	470	187	2 245	3 613	391	3 222	39 117	50.1	18.3
Lompoc	13 355	2.90	15.4	24.7	3 656	3 557	163	99	1 243	2 929	733	2 196	25 279	51.4	16.1
Long Beach	163 531	2.78	16.4	28.5	8 277	2 956	2 370	5 321	14 362	3 107	588	2 519	287 559	40.6	27.9
Los Altos	10 745	2.68	5.6	19.4	227	193	193	34	241	832	28	804	20 460	7.4	76.2
Los Angeles	1 318 168	2.81	14.9	28.3	84 601	26 415	13 845	58 186	111 188	2 932	566	2 365	2 470 825	45.5	30.4
Los Banos	10 259	3.49	14.4	15.1	181	78	78	103	1 189	3 305	386	2 919	19 264	62.2	10.4
Los Gatos	12 355	2.35	7.7	29.9	350	258	238	92	610	2 074	116	1 958	21 101	8.9	66.4
Lynwood	14 680	4.57	22.2	7.2	2 652	2 203	370	449	1 943	2 785	881	1 903	39 287	76.8	4.3
Madera	15 938	3.82	18.3	14.9	591	173	173	418	1 676	2 729	581	2 148	31 890	65.5	10.7
Manhattan Beach	14 038	2.50	6.4	25.8	28	0	0	28	887	2 525	137	2 388	24 262	8.3	72.9
Manteca	21 618	3.08	13.9	18.0	495	345	341	150	2 124	3 166	359	2 806	39 522	46.7	15.3
Martinez	14 287	2.42	12.3	27.4	1 296	1 061	268	235	920	2 568	204	2 364	26 131	29.7	32.0
Maywood	6 559	4.16	19.1	9.1	119	119	119	0	634	2 314	551	1 763	14 846	83.0	3.4
Menifee	27 461	2.82	10.0	24.0	188	107	106	81	1 403	1 810	83	1 727	49 960	46.0	16.4

1. No spouse present. 2. Data for serious crimes have not been adjusted for underreporting. This may affect comparability between geographic areas and over time. 3. Per 100,000 population estimated by the FBI. 4. Persons 25 years old and over.

Table D. Cities — Income, Poverty, and Housing

City	Per capita income[1] (dollars)	Median income	Percent with income of $200,000 or more	Percent with income of less than $25,000	Families with income below poverty (percent)	Total	Percent change, 2000–2010	Vacant units for sale or rent[2]	Total	Percent	Median value[3] (dollars)	With a mortgage[4]	Without a mortgage[5]
	42	43	44	45	46	47	48	49	50	51	52	53	54
CALIFORNIA—Cont'd													
Delano	9 920	34 096	1.0	35.8	28.2	10 713	21.0	453	9 888	55.3	161 300	31.2	10.2
Desert Hot Springs	15 644	34 443	0.4	32.1	18.3	10 902	55.2	2 252	8 560	52.8	160 000	35.1	17.9
Diamond Bar	32 464	85 163	8.3	8.8	3.9	18 455	2.8	575	17 453	82.9	541 900	30.2	10.0
Downey	22 430	57 379	2.5	18.0	8.7	35 601	2.4	1 665	33 193	50.0	463 600	33.1	10.0
Dublin	38 944	103 183	13.4	8.5	2.2	15 782	59.6	869	14 239	62.8	602 400	30.8	12.3
East Palo Alto	17 779	49 146	2.8	19.2	13.6	7 819	10.8	879	7 232	41.9	417 500	37.3	10.0
El Cajon	19 797	44 800	2.1	29.9	19.6	35 850	1.9	1 716	31 951	40.5	346 500	29.6	11.4
El Centro	18 430	40 475	2.1	35.7	22.2	14 476	17.8	1 368	13 293	51.4	175 800	29.2	11.6
Elk Grove	27 492	76 282	4.4	10.4	7.7	50 634	167.9	2 707	45 661	74.4	292 500	30.1	11.0
El Monte	14 052	42 385	0.8	26.4	19.2	29 069	4.8	1 255	27 226	39.1	367 400	35.0	10.1
El Paso de Robles (Paso Robles)	25 196	55 760	2.2	18.7	8.4	11 426	30.1	593	10 779	61.2	378 900	30.8	12.7
Encinitas	45 323	86 603	13.7	15.4	7.3	25 740	7.8	1 658	23 107	64.0	716 000	30.8	11.0
Escondido	21 977	49 900	3.4	20.2	11.9	48 044	6.8	2 560	43 562	53.7	351 500	33.2	12.7
Eureka	21 670	32 191	1.3	41.0	12.5	11 891	2.6	741	11 496	44.9	275 000	28.1	10.0
Fairfield	26 590	67 224	3.8	15.6	8.6	37 184	16.7	2 700	33 811	63.2	320 000	31.1	10.0
Folsom	35 230	91 669	9.2	9.9	3.1	26 109	45.5	1 158	23 032	70.1	420 900	27.7	11.4
Fontana	18 519	60 754	2.4	16.9	12.2	51 857	44.5	2 741	46 858	69.3	278 100	34.9	11.0
Foster City	52 528	111 250	18.2	9.4	3.0	12 458	3.7	442	12 023	58.7	873 700	25.7	10.0
Fountain Valley	32 900	78 778	6.8	10.6	4.2	19 164	3.7	516	18 452	71.5	614 200	29.1	10.0
Fremont	37 182	94 864	11.7	10.4	3.5	73 989	6.5	2 985	69 692	64.2	621 700	28.7	10.0
Fresno	19 324	41 698	2.5	31.7	21.0	171 288	15.0	12 939	155 795	48.6	220 100	28.6	11.3
Fullerton	29 906	67 632	6.4	17.4	9.1	47 869	7.0	2 478	44 837	54.2	518 800	30.3	10.0
Gardena	22 105	48 220	2.1	26.8	13.5	21 472	2.1	914	20 822	45.8	371 400	32.0	10.0
Garden Grove	20 285	59 951	2.9	19.0	11.6	47 755	2.0	1 718	45 327	57.2	429 300	31.6	10.0
Gilroy	27 557	73 056	7.3	17.2	7.0	14 854	22.1	679	14 388	60.7	501 000	34.2	12.1
Glendale	29 233	53 980	6.5	26.0	11.4	76 269	3.5	4 000	71 342	39.7	610 500	33.0	12.8
Glendora	32 037	74 912	6.3	12.4	4.7	17 778	3.5	637	16 391	69.3	481 100	31.1	10.0
Goleta	32 201	66 921	5.6	12.9	3.8	11 473	-43.6	570	10 802	52.4	692 600	28.3	10.0
Hanford	21 539	51 973	1.5	21.1	11.6	18 493	25.4	1 001	16 810	59.2	210 100	25.0	10.3
Hawthorne	19 763	44 714	2.0	26.4	15.5	29 869	1.0	1 383	28 712	26.5	438 400	34.7	10.0
Hayward	24 389	61 805	3.8	16.6	8.2	48 296	5.1	2 931	43 717	54.0	359 500	32.8	10.1
Hemet	18 694	34 266	0.8	37.3	15.8	35 305	19.8	5 213	30 082	62.0	141 700	31.3	15.6
Hesperia	17 208	47 423	1.2	25.2	16.7	29 004	36.2	2 573	25 202	69.4	183 400	32.0	11.7
Highland	21 318	55 522	5.1	23.8	17.5	16 578	10.9	1 107	14 547	65.2	283 200	29.0	11.6
Hollister	22 637	60 361	3.2	19.7	13.0	10 401	4.5	541	10 500	61.8	335 600	34.1	11.3
Huntington Beach	40 222	77 971	9.7	13.3	4.6	78 003	2.9	3 718	74 611	60.4	653 900	30.6	11.2
Huntington Park	12 069	36 511	0.7	33.8	25.2	15 151	-1.2	554	14 262	28.4	359 500	36.0	11.8
Imperial Beach	20 683	46 574	2.2	26.9	12.8	9 882	1.5	770	9 044	31.1	377 000	28.0	11.0
Indio	20 501	48 871	2.6	25.6	16.3	28 971	71.4	5 593	23 128	64.4	236 000	33.4	13.4
Inglewood	20 086	44 116	1.5	27.0	16.9	38 429	-0.5	2 040	36 313	36.0	370 300	33.6	11.3
Irvine	41 175	88 571	12.2	14.8	5.6	83 899	56.2	4 921	73 718	52.3	647 100	29.1	10.0
Laguna Hills	43 926	85 975	14.0	9.6	5.1	11 046	-2.5	577	10 615	77.3	570 700	31.1	10.0
Laguna Niguel	49 625	93 427	16.6	10.4	4.1	25 312	5.9	1 080	24 351	74.6	696 200	32.1	10.5
La Habra	23 504	60 927	5.1	18.2	9.5	19 924	2.0	947	18 456	56.0	414 100	32.5	11.7
Lake Elsinore	21 376	64 296	2.7	16.3	10.6	16 253	70.6	1 465	14 018	67.6	234 000	35.0	17.0
Lake Forest	39 951	91 676	11.9	8.1	2.6	27 088	31.6	864	26 956	71.2	543 600	28.3	10.0
Lakewood	29 051	76 454	2.9	11.1	5.3	27 470	0.7	927	26 205	72.2	452 700	29.3	10.0
La Mesa	29 293	53 248	2.0	23.6	10.3	26 167	5.1	1 655	23 781	46.2	392 300	32.0	10.7
La Mirada	27 440	79 954	4.4	13.8	4.1	15 092	1.9	411	14 187	80.1	447 900	29.1	10.0
Lancaster	20 344	51 633	2.5	26.8	17.1	51 835	24.4	4 843	46 902	62.1	199 800	31.0	12.3
La Puente	14 687	50 846	1.3	18.3	10.7	9 761	1.0	310	9 203	59.7	322 400	36.7	10.0
La Quinta	43 450	72 181	11.0	14.5	4.9	23 489	99.7	8 669	13 881	73.8	389 000	32.6	12.6
La Verne	31 385	74 843	5.0	16.3	4.2	11 686	3.5	425	11 051	76.6	470 600	30.6	15.9
Lawndale	18 837	50 271	2.1	22.7	10.5	10 151	2.8	470	9 718	32.5	403 400	37.6	14.8
Lemon Grove	22 106	47 844	2.1	27.1	13.7	8 868	1.2	434	8 636	55.0	317 500	35.5	10.0
Lincoln	31 153	72 554	3.4	12.5	5.5	17 457	322.6	978	15 194	80.1	352 200	34.3	12.6
Livermore	39 783	90 206	11.1	11.6	3.1	30 342	14.3	1 208	28 613	71.3	530 000	29.7	10.0
Lodi	23 599	46 802	4.0	25.2	12.6	23 792	11.2	1 695	21 384	52.3	272 600	27.8	13.1
Lompoc	19 368	47 466	0.5	26.8	16.3	14 416	5.8	1 061	13 061	51.0	279 900	28.3	10.4
Long Beach	26 033	51 891	4.4	23.6	15.4	176 032	2.5	12 501	159 137	41.4	464 100	30.8	10.0
Los Altos	75 674	145 811	35.2	7.6	2.2	11 204	4.4	459	10 945	83.9	1 000 000	31.5	10.6
Los Angeles	27 346	48 746	5.9	27.0	16.6	1 413 995	5.7	95 827	1 312 002	38.2	493 200	35.3	12.5
Los Banos	18 621	53 893	3.3	23.6	15.8	11 375	40.9	1 116	9 872	63.2	171 200	31.3	10.9
Los Gatos	66 752	117 581	27.3	8.2	2.6	13 050	5.2	695	12 340	65.0	1 000 000	28.6	10.0
Lynwood	11 922	40 294	0.3	28.9	19.4	15 277	1.8	597	15 156	46.5	340 800	38.9	10.1
Madera	14 118	40 818	1.3	30.5	22.8	17 049	34.7	1 111	15 904	49.3	184 500	33.2	13.0
Manhattan Beach	79 677	126 103	28.0	7.4	1.5	14 929	-1.1	891	14 066	69.0	1 000 000	27.0	10.0
Manteca	23 361	61 136	1.5	14.8	6.4	23 132	36.9	1 514	21 794	62.8	246 600	31.1	13.0
Martinez	37 519	77 162	6.9	13.2	3.7	14 976	2.3	689	14 248	68.9	445 200	30.4	10.0
Maywood	11 567	35 965	0.1	32.2	21.3	6 766	1.0	207	6 721	23.6	276 100	42.3	10.0
Menifee	23 256	51 328	1.0	23.2	8.4	30 269	NA	2 808	26 788	79.4	216 200	35.1	13.5

1. Based on population estimated by the American Community Survey.   2. Includes units rented or sold but not occupied.   3. Specified owner-occupied units; $1,000,000 represents $1,000,000 or more.   4. 50.0 represents 50 percent or more.   5. 10.0 represents 10 percent or less.

City	Occupied housing units, 2008–2010 (cont.)				Migration, 2008–2010		Civilian labor force, 2010				Civilian employment[4], 2008–2010			
									Unemployment			Percent		
	Percent renter occupied	Median gross rent[1]	Median rent as a percent of income[2]	Percent with no vehicle available	Percent who lived in the same house one year ago	Percent who lived outside this city one year ago	Total	Percent change, 2009–2010	Total	Rate[3]	Population age 16 and older	In labor force	Full-year full-time worker	Households with no workers (percent)
	55	56	57	58	59	60	61	62	63	64	65	66	67	68
CALIFORNIA—Cont'd														
Delano	44.7	722	36.6	9.4	72.3	17.0	20 258	4.3	7 642	37.7	38 378	44.2	23.7	23.9
Desert Hot Springs	47.2	827	33.6	10.3	77.9	11.4	9 804	NA	1 979	20.2	17 918	61.4	36.0	33.7
Diamond Bar	17.1	1 632	36.1	1.6	90.9	5.7	32 176	0.0	2 917	9.1	45 472	63.3	43.8	14.2
Downey	50.0	1 161	32.4	4.7	86.0	9.2	53 633	0.1	5 461	10.2	84 926	66.9	42.6	18.2
Dublin	37.2	1 710	25.7	3.4	74.1	19.7	15 258	-0.4	1 050	6.9	36 236	61.4	44.9	13.1
East Palo Alto	58.1	1 205	39.2	10.1	NA	NA	13 490	0.5	2 719	20.2	20 914	67.2	37.6	16.5
El Cajon	59.5	1 017	36.6	9.7	80.1	9.5	53 610	1.3	7 636	14.2	75 161	63.6	36.8	25.7
El Centro	48.6	704	36.1	12.3	81.5	7.3	22 353	1.2	6 349	28.4	30 455	63.3	34.6	30.0
Elk Grove	25.6	1 401	36.6	2.6	81.5	9.4	35 189	-1.1	3 644	10.4	108 053	70.7	44.4	16.3
El Monte	60.9	1 039	36.3	9.1	89.1	5.6	52 410	0.6	8 117	15.5	87 093	62.2	38.7	15.7
El Paso de Robles (Paso Robles)	38.8	958	30.8	6.0	82.9	7.3	13 129	0.6	1 540	11.7	22 024	65.2	38.9	26.9
Encinitas	36.0	1 645	29.9	3.7	85.0	11.1	38 761	0.7	2 914	7.5	48 205	67.9	39.4	20.8
Escondido	46.3	1 142	36.2	7.2	84.1	7.6	73 393	1.0	8 035	10.9	108 740	63.4	38.0	21.5
Eureka	55.1	754	33.7	9.0	79.5	11.0	11 964	0.5	1 455	12.2	22 464	59.4	33.3	33.2
Fairfield	36.8	1 187	32.9	4.2	79.4	9.8	49 517	0.3	6 505	13.1	78 645	66.8	41.8	21.2
Folsom	29.9	1 271	27.4	2.7	81.1	14.5	26 881	-1.7	1 569	5.8	56 280	59.0	38.9	18.7
Fontana	30.7	1 078	36.9	4.3	83.2	10.5	62 377	-0.4	9 183	14.7	136 383	68.6	40.2	15.0
Foster City	41.3	1 862	24.6	3.5	83.9	11.5	16 284	0.1	1 053	6.5	24 260	68.4	48.1	18.9
Fountain Valley	28.5	1 461	34.3	4.8	90.2	7.2	32 447	-0.3	2 568	7.9	45 712	63.2	40.1	22.1
Fremont	35.8	1 436	26.4	5.1	87.5	6.5	109 005	-0.4	8 901	8.2	165 752	67.2	45.2	17.8
Fresno	51.4	831	36.1	12.1	81.2	5.1	230 773	0.2	36 530	15.8	358 202	63.2	35.2	29.1
Fullerton	45.8	1 321	33.5	4.0	81.2	11.4	70 893	-0.1	7 521	10.6	105 766	68.0	40.4	19.8
Gardena	54.2	1 028	33.3	9.5	89.6	7.8	29 566	0.2	3 497	11.8	46 489	63.5	41.0	25.0
Garden Grove	42.8	1 296	36.4	5.9	87.1	7.6	84 852	-0.1	9 998	11.8	132 120	65.2	39.7	18.7
Gilroy	39.3	1 177	33.2	5.0	83.8	8.9	21 429	0.3	3 489	16.3	34 209	71.7	41.9	18.6
Glendale	60.3	1 246	38.9	10.5	88.0	5.7	104 349	0.1	11 502	11.0	160 237	63.8	38.5	24.7
Glendora	30.7	1 375	30.7	4.4	90.7	6.3	27 672	-0.3	1 833	6.6	39 188	63.2	38.8	22.0
Goleta	47.6	1 547	30.8	6.0	85.0	10.6	17 330	0.0	806	4.7	23 520	71.3	43.3	22.5
Hanford	40.8	842	29.0	8.1	82.1	8.2	24 151	0.1	3 501	14.5	39 900	63.3	41.6	21.5
Hawthorne	73.5	981	31.0	9.7	89.0	7.8	42 813	0.6	6 976	16.3	63 237	67.2	45.1	16.8
Hayward	46.0	1 209	32.2	6.9	81.5	9.4	70 551	-0.1	8 833	12.5	111 666	69.1	40.6	21.5
Hemet	38.0	954	44.1	11.0	73.3	13.4	27 559	2.9	4 991	18.1	59 441	50.0	26.5	47.7
Hesperia	30.6	1 036	37.3	3.6	85.3	8.5	30 807	-0.1	5 561	18.1	63 185	59.5	34.3	29.6
Highland	34.8	949	37.4	7.5	83.8	10.8	23 200	-0.1	4 112	17.7	36 874	64.2	37.2	21.7
Hollister	38.2	1 126	32.8	6.0	84.9	9.0	17 154	4.3	3 290	19.2	25 204	70.2	39.1	19.0
Huntington Beach	39.6	1 470	29.8	3.2	86.3	7.5	120 635	-0.3	9 355	7.8	155 978	69.2	42.9	21.9
Huntington Park	71.6	861	36.4	19.2	90.2	5.3	27 247	0.9	5 068	18.6	41 221	64.6	41.2	14.6
Imperial Beach	68.9	1 083	33.4	12.8	80.8	12.7	14 223	1.5	2 373	16.7	20 361	65.3	38.9	20.8
Indio	35.6	945	37.9	5.3	81.2	9.3	28 103	2.7	4 400	15.7	54 274	64.0	35.5	28.0
Inglewood	64.0	997	35.8	10.0	88.9	7.7	54 723	0.6	8 584	15.7	82 978	67.1	41.4	23.6
Irvine	47.7	1 765	29.5	4.1	77.1	12.8	82 457	-0.3	5 893	7.1	169 238	64.6	42.9	17.7
Laguna Hills	22.7	1 686	40.6	4.9	83.8	12.5	17 676	-0.3	1 422	8.0	24 488	68.8	41.5	17.9
Laguna Niguel	25.4	1 715	32.1	2.6	87.8	9.4	37 100	-0.3	2 752	7.4	50 898	67.4	43.6	20.4
La Habra	44.0	1 229	35.3	5.4	82.8	9.6	31 551	-0.1	3 371	10.7	45 602	69.5	43.8	19.6
Lake Elsinore	32.4	1 235	33.9	5.1	76.1	15.9	17 638	2.6	2 481	14.1	35 209	70.6	41.9	16.5
Lake Forest	28.8	1 644	29.1	2.5	89.0	8.1	36 182	-0.4	2 385	6.6	59 948	73.5	50.2	13.1
Lakewood	27.8	1 441	30.0	3.0	88.8	9.2	44 411	-0.1	3 647	8.2	62 890	68.9	46.7	18.3
La Mesa	53.8	1 156	34.8	6.9	76.3	19.1	34 071	0.8	3 007	8.8	47 001	69.0	40.6	26.2
La Mirada	19.9	1 348	47.2	4.4	87.7	10.0	24 170	-0.2	1 870	7.7	38 525	62.3	38.8	23.8
Lancaster	37.9	1 079	39.2	6.8	85.7	7.4	56 942	0.8	10 005	17.6	111 837	57.9	40.0	25.9
La Puente	40.3	1 066	35.6	7.3	95.1	3.0	19 264	0.5	2 843	14.8	29 943	62.5	40.7	14.9
La Quinta	26.2	1 442	33.8	2.8	85.9	7.9	14 960	2.1	1 152	7.7	29 187	60.3	36.2	30.8
La Verne	23.4	1 175	32.7	7.3	89.5	7.8	18 143	-0.2	1 328	7.3	25 178	63.4	38.7	28.2
Lawndale	67.5	1 318	35.9	8.3	87.5	10.7	16 446	0.3	2 057	12.5	25 061	70.7	40.7	17.6
Lemon Grove	45.0	1 109	38.4	6.6	88.5	9.7	13 980	1.2	1 833	13.1	19 605	62.1	39.2	29.9
Lincoln	19.9	1 579	34.7	2.4	84.5	12.6	7 933	-0.5	1 601	20.2	31 781	54.8	34.0	37.8
Livermore	28.7	1 334	32.6	4.3	86.6	7.4	40 810	-0.4	3 013	7.4	61 760	72.1	46.0	19.3
Lodi	47.7	1 007	36.6	7.6	81.3	6.0	31 816	-0.1	4 201	13.2	47 304	60.0	36.2	29.4
Lompoc	49.0	903	34.0	9.5	83.3	7.2	20 712	1.3	3 377	16.3	31 718	59.9	38.2	27.2
Long Beach	58.6	1 057	32.9	10.8	80.2	8.4	238 584	0.4	33 027	13.8	357 621	68.4	40.1	21.4
Los Altos	16.1	2 000	22.6	3.4	91.1	8.0	12 592	0.4	710	5.6	21 936	59.8	37.8	29.3
Los Angeles	61.8	1 104	35.0	12.8	85.4	4.4	1 926 827	0.4	267 696	13.9	2 997 934	67.0	40.6	22.6
Los Banos	36.8	965	30.6	6.5	79.7	8.7	13 704	3.5	2 704	19.7	24 701	67.8	36.0	24.0
Los Gatos	35.0	1 701	27.4	3.4	85.5	9.9	15 278	0.3	1 112	7.3	23 098	62.6	42.4	27.9
Lynwood	53.5	949	41.5	7.6	89.4	7.9	28 449	1.0	5 592	19.7	50 688	55.9	35.7	14.6
Madera	50.7	863	33.2	8.4	82.1	5.7	24 349	1.2	5 285	21.7	41 046	59.8	31.9	38.6
Manhattan Beach	31.0	1 961	24.1	2.1	88.1	6.9	22 001	-0.5	991	4.5	26 882	67.6	46.4	19.9
Manteca	37.2	1 116	29.9	3.8	80.0	10.8	27 646	0.2	4 177	15.1	48 404	72.3	41.3	22.0
Martinez	31.1	1 259	31.8	3.8	89.2	8.6	21 749	-0.7	1 945	8.9	30 118	65.3	40.6	21.2
Maywood	76.4	958	33.3	15.1	NA	NA	12 468	0.8	2 263	18.2	19 506	66.3	39.2	14.5
Menifee	20.6	1 193	43.5	4.1	82.6	13.2	23 693	NA	3 662	15.5	57 940	57.8	33.5	38.2

1. $2,000 represents $2,000 or more. 2. 50.0 represents 50 percent or more. 3. Percent of civilian labor force. 4. Persons 16 years old and over.

City	Value of residential construction authorized by building permits, 2010			Wholesale trade,[1] 2007				Retail trade,[2] 2007			
	New construction ($1,000)	Number of housing units	Percent single family	Number of establish-ments	Number of employees	Sales (mil dol)	Annual payroll (mil dol)	Number of establish-ments	Number of employees	Sales (mil dol)	Annual payroll (mil dol)
	69	70	71	72	73	74	75	76	77	78	79
CALIFORNIA—Cont'd											
Delano	6 399	87	19.5	16	247	208.8	11.4	81	1 072	258.9	23.8
Desert Hot Springs	436	3	100.0	NA	NA	NA	NA	38	639	120.9	13.9
Diamond Bar	5 097	21	100.0	203	698	463.5	31.6	125	1 576	391.9	34.2
Downey	2 468	6	100.0	96	947	376.1	37.7	320	5 367	1 216.2	132.1
Dublin	129 879	344	66.3	57	503	251.8	25.5	185	3 939	1 249.9	114.8
East Palo Alto	0	0	0.0	5	D	D	D	22	819	220.2	19.4
El Cajon	9 791	42	100.0	129	1 243	459.1	47.3	508	7 503	1 968.4	193.6
El Centro	0	0	0.0	48	363	202.2	13.6	213	3 848	756.0	81.7
Elk Grove	69 472	411	72.0	54	D	D	D	274	6 684	1 950.0	177.9
El Monte	2 131	9	100.0	339	1 976	858.9	66.1	300	4 461	2 140.4	153.6
El Paso de Robles (Paso Robles)	10 708	95	14.7	38	317	166.6	16.0	172	2 401	634.7	59.1
Encinitas	7 331	35	100.0	91	423	155.1	18.1	302	4 309	1 082.8	105.9
Escondido	26 876	139	60.4	160	1 328	642.0	64.8	593	10 151	2 698.3	267.6
Eureka	2 411	21	14.3	48	469	159.3	18.5	274	3 689	968.6	87.4
Fairfield	22 791	139	100.0	62	1 616	681.9	68.9	344	5 687	1 346.3	135.0
Folsom	15 326	74	64.9	33	405	824.8	31.4	288	6 074	1 766.7	157.2
Fontana	40 253	305	33.8	138	3 302	2 405.0	148.0	336	6 599	1 852.5	167.8
Foster City	0	0	0.0	42	D	D	D	37	885	279.6	25.2
Fountain Valley	1 002	3	100.0	124	1 925	6 251.7	138.8	250	3 805	1 283.1	99.9
Fremont	68 818	315	31.7	500	10 709	11 312.2	801.9	456	8 160	2 721.8	254.5
Fresno	216 542	1 199	82.6	533	8 235	4 831.4	362.0	1 658	25 728	6 358.8	611.1
Fullerton	6 609	59	81.4	235	3 219	2 275.7	143.4	401	6 034	1 608.6	152.9
Gardena	4 945	23	100.0	185	1 875	1 049.5	84.3	182	2 702	757.4	78.7
Garden Grove	17 073	94	66.0	246	2 541	1 379.0	113.2	418	4 760	1 410.7	119.5
Gilroy	29 309	84	100.0	53	649	274.0	31.3	330	4 907	1 141.0	112.9
Glendale	16 621	99	7.1	244	2 112	894.2	97.0	734	11 451	3 224.0	298.7
Glendora	4 774	22	4.5	43	471	145.0	25.6	141	2 500	727.6	66.6
Goleta	291	2	100.0	63	1 662	1 166.2	124.9	125	2 346	668.3	62.1
Hanford	20 937	134	61.2	27	376	164.6	16.4	201	3 186	733.0	68.4
Hawthorne	21 528	117	7.7	75	1 423	549.2	57.6	176	3 460	1 039.2	88.4
Hayward	57 537	248	100.0	493	7 787	4 967.5	403.8	443	6 868	1 785.7	188.8
Hemet	56 462	170	76.5	28	149	30.6	4.5	243	4 614	876.4	115.1
Hesperia	6 487	69	2.9	43	324	274.5	12.1	186	1 977	508.7	48.0
Highland	8 804	23	100.0	12	186	38.3	4.7	60	677	160.5	15.6
Hollister	7 847	41	100.0	22	547	128.8	25.4	102	1 393	315.0	37.3
Huntington Beach	6 925	20	20.0	457	6 703	4 698.0	426.4	596	9 070	2 364.8	230.3
Huntington Park	0	0	0.0	60	1 113	463.0	44.3	219	2 514	652.2	63.7
Imperial Beach	540	2	100.0	4	13	2.6	0.3	39	271	68.1	6.0
Indio	56 688	268	100.0	45	567	237.5	26.6	171	2 797	789.3	80.3
Inglewood	13 316	163	3.1	91	1 825	958.0	69.2	263	3 849	1 099.6	88.5
Irvine	292 308	1 754	36.5	902	18 358	33 740.7	1 324.0	636	13 736	4 566.8	438.6
Laguna Hills	2 081	2	100.0	85	548	252.3	30.3	226	3 124	571.1	62.9
Laguna Niguel	18 873	45	100.0	94	374	161.5	19.2	174	3 853	1 304.3	117.1
La Habra	7 668	24	100.0	69	560	235.4	24.7	183	3 446	971.7	85.4
Lake Elsinore	57 534	318	100.0	42	290	69.0	9.7	171	2 938	773.2	71.4
Lake Forest	6 975	26	100.0	218	3 761	2 875.0	244.4	241	3 826	1 225.8	103.0
Lakewood	4 142	18	100.0	36	174	46.5	4.6	241	5 437	1 056.0	109.0
La Mesa	233	1	100.0	25	124	37.6	4.6	264	4 631	1 236.3	117.5
La Mirada	0	0	0.0	123	3 364	5 047.9	187.2	104	1 554	424.5	42.6
Lancaster	58 272	277	100.0	65	905	928.6	40.1	343	6 023	1 754.4	156.5
La Puente	1 527	11	81.8	33	230	97.5	6.4	113	1 205	227.3	27.3
La Quinta	20 793	79	100.0	21	57	20.1	2.1	108	3 127	784.7	72.6
La Verne	807	2	100.0	92	1 036	472.0	48.2	94	1 380	288.3	31.0
Lawndale	784	3	100.0	17	150	43.2	5.1	93	871	253.5	22.5
Lemon Grove	340	4	100.0	15	123	31.9	4.3	76	1 266	402.1	36.0
Lincoln	16 786	90	100.0	17	244	115.7	11.0	52	848	193.5	20.5
Livermore	21 794	95	82.1	159	3 337	2 130.0	206.4	240	4 278	1 315.2	138.0
Lodi	596	5	100.0	49	331	436.0	13.8	236	3 617	853.9	91.7
Lompoc	15	1	100.0	7	47	8.3	1.6	128	1 725	385.3	39.2
Long Beach	18 131	106	41.5	331	4 884	7 337.1	286.7	1 012	13 851	4 320.9	323.2
Los Altos	35 429	83	96.4	24	50	36.8	2.3	113	1 163	265.0	35.1
Los Angeles	868 845	4 109	15.5	8 693	84 842	49 819.9	3 788.8	11 880	140 076	36 672.8	3 602.7
Los Banos	1 072	5	100.0	9	81	62.2	3.2	94	1 487	350.9	33.3
Los Gatos	28 359	32	100.0	44	540	321.5	42.8	187	2 387	721.0	68.4
Lynwood	196	1	100.0	41	709	334.4	32.8	132	1 345	274.1	27.1
Madera	6 844	59	89.8	28	271	169.0	11.8	175	2 363	518.9	52.2
Manhattan Beach	24 913	45	100.0	38	D	D	D	182	3 187	721.9	71.8
Manteca	54 077	355	100.0	27	285	163.7	13.0	174	2 826	679.6	72.1
Martinez	598	2	100.0	23	143	38.1	5.1	72	1 256	312.0	35.6
Maywood	625	3	100.0	23	409	171.1	15.3	50	563	104.2	13.0
Menifee	95 771	399	100.0	NA	NA	NA	NA	NA	NA	NA	NA

1. Merchant wholesalers except manufacturers' sales branches and offices.   2. Establishments with payroll.

City	Real estate and rental and leasing, 2007				Professional, scientific, and technical services,[1] 2007				Manufacturing, 2007			
	Number of establishments	Number of employees	Receipts (mil dol)	Annual payroll (mil dol)	Number of establishments	Number of employees	Receipts (mil dol)	Annual payroll (mil dol)	Number of establishments	Number of employees	Receipts (mil dol)	Annual payroll (mil dol)
	80	81	82	83	84	85	86	87	88	89	90	91
CALIFORNIA—Cont'd												
Delano	21	58	9.0	1.2	20	D	D	D	NA	NA	NA	NA
Desert Hot Springs	14	155	14.7	4.7	11	292	5.9	3.6	NA	NA	NA	NA
Diamond Bar	100	322	53.7	9.1	245	1 342	198.1	64.2	24	968	319.5	43.8
Downey	197	1 217	154.0	31.0	142	D	D	D	95	2 738	1 141.7	109.9
Dublin	52	319	75.6	13.5	150	1 184	190.8	81.2	23	1 430	D	92.8
East Palo Alto	15	44	24.3	1.7	16	D	D	D	NA	NA	NA	NA
El Cajon	175	843	150.8	24.0	208	1 303	125.5	47.8	183	5 660	999.1	233.7
El Centro	58	221	31.6	4.9	84	D	D	D	NA	NA	NA	NA
Elk Grove	103	368	67.1	10.6	177	835	88.8	35.9	39	1 155	281.5	48.0
El Monte	73	499	46.6	13.8	122	D	D	D	182	4 537	806.7	180.9
El Paso de Robles (Paso Robles)	55	164	30.4	5.0	95	392	59.7	16.9	85	2 418	489.5	98.4
Encinitas	217	473	114.6	18.8	474	D	D	D	NA	NA	NA	NA
Escondido	197	948	482.9	42.2	386	D	D	D	197	3 321	572.2	126.4
Eureka	68	297	53.6	9.3	111	D	D	D	34	557	117.4	19.6
Fairfield	97	401	85.5	12.9	162	1 148	111.2	50.0	62	2 642	1 358.5	139.8
Folsom	120	494	100.5	17.6	276	D	D	D	33	502	110.7	24.9
Fontana	88	598	115.6	21.7	78	D	D	D	127	6 095	1 839.3	231.3
Foster City	48	609	161.2	47.4	182	D	D	D	20	D	D	D
Fountain Valley	102	412	77.4	15.6	289	2 186	455.1	136.3	99	2 926	3 201.1	154.1
Fremont	281	1 441	407.7	56.8	948	D	D	D	343	22 496	8 724.6	1 577.6
Fresno	487	3 393	507.9	104.2	1 154	D	D	D	366	13 192	3 965.6	495.9
Fullerton	183	1 097	221.8	37.8	394	D	D	D	226	6 982	2 128.2	287.8
Gardena	50	392	35.0	8.4	68	375	43.2	13.2	276	5 692	1 426.1	220.4
Garden Grove	133	743	109.4	24.5	277	D	D	D	333	8 131	1 705.1	324.1
Gilroy	52	D	D	D	75	D	D	D	59	1 846	566.1	81.6
Glendale	309	2 441	1 049.5	150.9	806	7 801	1 854.0	543.7	240	5 156	606.6	206.8
Glendora	80	252	49.2	7.9	130	1 107	89.7	39.6	35	965	388.8	36.1
Goleta	56	348	44.6	10.3	155	D	D	D	123	5 686	1 658.8	376.2
Hanford	49	215	30.6	4.7	58	337	31.3	10.4	28	962	343.5	38.9
Hawthorne	69	340	42.3	8.5	69	869	149.5	44.9	81	2 976	516.3	116.4
Hayward	167	1 207	241.9	46.1	256	D	D	D	340	12 570	3 295.8	580.8
Hemet	74	399	55.8	9.0	93	525	49.8	16.9	28	970	185.3	33.5
Hesperia	51	220	39.4	6.6	67	543	34.6	11.5	73	718	112.3	28.1
Highland	22	75	12.4	1.5	29	93	9.9	3.3	NA	NA	NA	NA
Hollister	39	91	11.5	2.5	41	151	17.4	4.9	38	1 639	355.5	53.6
Huntington Beach	341	1 692	337.7	57.9	797	D	D	D	380	13 155	4 423.5	849.2
Huntington Park	24	123	17.4	2.8	35	244	21.4	5.6	127	3 412	561.9	106.0
Imperial Beach	26	96	13.7	2.4	16	73	4.8	1.7	NA	NA	NA	NA
Indio	56	365	57.0	9.7	67	D	D	D	41	774	124.5	29.3
Inglewood	77	650	108.3	19.0	58	D	D	D	69	2 184	438.0	102.0
Irvine	622	8 462	1 739.3	462.0	2 428	D	D	D	433	29 937	8 761.5	1 704.0
Laguna Hills	92	843	127.8	37.4	364	1 726	250.2	94.4	72	583	D	26.7
Laguna Niguel	150	571	115.5	20.0	315	1 410	292.8	79.1	NA	NA	NA	NA
La Habra	57	262	44.4	6.8	84	468	39.8	17.3	70	1 250	215.0	46.7
Lake Elsinore	44	162	60.6	4.9	49	307	29.0	9.1	62	892	121.0	31.7
Lake Forest	124	1 203	200.1	52.9	399	3 383	452.7	208.1	111	4 953	1 238.8	238.2
Lakewood	52	296	73.2	7.8	64	236	20.3	8.3	NA	NA	NA	NA
La Mesa	161	985	117.1	29.4	256	1 343	140.5	55.2	NA	NA	NA	NA
La Mirada	40	341	83.0	16.8	62	646	75.8	33.0	58	2 726	859.9	118.6
Lancaster	116	654	114.8	17.8	144	D	D	D	56	1 192	258.6	50.2
La Puente	21	72	11.6	1.9	17	D	D	D	NA	NA	NA	NA
La Quinta	81	204	42.5	7.5	92	419	60.2	20.6	NA	NA	NA	NA
La Verne	30	145	20.8	4.0	68	281	30.9	10.0	54	1 398	294.6	54.6
Lawndale	24	324	62.5	9.6	35	D	D	D	NA	NA	NA	NA
Lemon Grove	22	99	19.5	1.8	25	118	8.1	3.2	NA	NA	NA	NA
Lincoln	27	82	15.9	2.0	46	D	D	D	24	868	214.2	40.7
Livermore	109	593	179.4	27.5	192	D	D	D	150	5 221	1 803.8	299.9
Lodi	91	928	67.0	22.0	114	670	63.6	24.5	92	3 433	687.1	114.1
Lompoc	35	151	22.3	4.7	37	D	D	D	NA	NA	NA	NA
Long Beach	504	3 206	1 099.2	134.4	1 005	D	D	D	273	12 425	6 198.3	856.7
Los Altos	88	371	127.7	19.8	270	D	D	D	NA	NA	NA	NA
Los Angeles	5 912	38 870	13 742.3	1 904.9	14 157	178 164	27 271.5	10 738.3	6 118	129 537	41 805.6	5 391.5
Los Banos	23	57	10.4	1.1	23	130	12.7	4.9	11	604	412.9	25.9
Los Gatos	106	726	822.5	80.5	288	1 360	251.1	102.4	31	620	112.6	32.6
Lynwood	15	63	10.0	2.9	16	D	D	D	57	1 630	374.1	58.6
Madera	37	120	16.0	3.5	33	D	D	D	41	D	394.6	58.2
Manhattan Beach	134	556	81.0	23.8	281	1 119	194.8	92.1	NA	NA	NA	NA
Manteca	65	236	37.9	6.2	49	239	19.4	6.6	32	941	293.7	41.3
Martinez	48	176	29.1	6.0	92	D	D	D	26	949	D	D
Maywood	3	D	D	D	5	D	D	D	NA	NA	NA	NA
Menifee	NA	NA	NA	NA	NA	NA	NA	NA	NA	NA	NA	NA

1. Establishments subject to federal tax.

Table D. Cities — Accommodation and Food Services, Arts, Entertainment, and Recreation, and Health Care and Social Assistance

City	Accommodation and food services, 2007				Arts, entertainment, and recreation,[1] 2007				Health care and social assistance,[1] 2007			
	Number of establishments	Number of employees	Sales (mil dol)	Annual payroll (mil dol)	Number of establishments	Number of employees	Receipts (mil dol)	Annual payroll (mil dol)	Number of establishments	Number of employees	Receipts (mil dol)	Annual payroll (mil dol)
	92	93	94	95	96	97	98	99	100	101	102	103
CALIFORNIA—Cont'd												
Delano	43	495	25.9	5.8	2	D	D	D	69	807	64.8	25.3
Desert Hot Springs	33	353	18.2	4.4	1	D	D	D	13	D	D	D
Diamond Bar	116	1 377	64.7	17.4	10	D	D	D	161	1 223	108.4	36.2
Downey	202	3 424	181.5	50.4	13	197	14.7	3.6	293	4 008	455.3	174.0
Dublin	123	2 287	135.8	36.5	12	D	D	D	79	653	59.1	23.4
East Palo Alto	13	668	41.9	17.8	2	D	D	D	14	133	21.1	11.3
El Cajon	244	3 526	171.3	45.9	17	D	D	D	232	3 318	265.9	109.4
El Centro	107	1 857	81.9	23.3	3	D	D	D	119	741	81.9	32.4
Elk Grove	208	4 110	169.6	47.7	18	D	D	D	225	2 184	294.2	72.5
El Monte	161	1 526	84.0	19.9	5	D	D	D	146	1 865	146.7	55.5
El Paso de Robles (Paso Robles)	113	2 193	98.0	29.4	14	D	D	D	62	521	32.8	11.7
Encinitas	193	3 638	180.1	50.6	44	D	D	D	318	2 422	296.9	101.7
Escondido	276	4 149	211.6	57.8	30	564	28.3	8.1	305	3 511	332.5	140.6
Eureka	133	1 928	91.8	25.5	11	D	D	D	109	1 086	91.9	34.4
Fairfield	193	3 467	162.3	42.3	18	D	D	D	218	2 200	295.1	93.8
Folsom	200	3 442	159.1	48.0	23	505	24.1	6.1	197	D	D	D
Fontana	202	3 325	158.0	42.1	13	245	15.2	4.0	132	D	D	D
Foster City	60	1 236	78.6	22.8	10	D	D	D	63	537	66.6	25.2
Fountain Valley	146	2 093	115.3	30.1	18	D	D	D	357	D	D	D
Fremont	384	5 456	296.6	80.7	37	719	41.9	12.6	552	6 413	787.1	303.6
Fresno	944	17 909	813.6	229.4	92	2 061	116.1	32.3	1 326	15 864	1 749.4	729.6
Fullerton	293	5 125	253.5	69.2	22	384	33.1	7.4	339	D	D	D
Gardena	180	1 842	102.2	24.9	10	D	D	D	153	1 940	225.3	74.4
Garden Grove	359	5 564	344.2	89.8	20	D	D	D	447	4 441	450.7	157.0
Gilroy	120	2 070	103.3	28.0	11	D	D	D	124	1 231	151.3	45.8
Glendale	376	5 760	324.0	86.6	131	658	94.5	30.5	842	6 977	780.0	281.9
Glendora	94	1 298	68.8	18.9	21	D	D	D	189	D	D	D
Goleta	91	1 862	93.0	24.4	9	140	9.4	2.9	109	812	85.8	35.4
Hanford	97	D	D	D	8	D	D	D	120	1 197	106.9	44.7
Hawthorne	129	1 840	103.2	24.1	11	D	D	D	114	1 812	165.8	62.3
Hayward	306	3 593	210.5	51.6	17	D	D	D	234	4 312	575.6	254.5
Hemet	139	2 340	113.2	32.3	14	D	D	D	208	D	D	D
Hesperia	107	1 653	86.2	21.9	8	D	D	D	68	470	39.0	13.9
Highland	35	490	24.3	6.0	3	D	D	D	46	D	D	D
Hollister	63	783	36.4	10.3	11	D	D	D	68	D	D	D
Huntington Beach	416	7 878	445.0	125.1	51	645	43.6	9.2	567	4 484	495.4	191.9
Huntington Park	100	1 634	86.2	21.3	3	D	D	D	113	D	D	D
Imperial Beach	39	380	20.1	4.7	3	D	D	D	19	149	12.1	3.7
Indio	104	D	D	D	12	D	D	D	105	1 484	182.1	70.4
Inglewood	159	2 285	129.6	33.2	39	D	D	D	276	2 691	358.4	113.6
Irvine	534	12 383	755.8	204.4	68	2 360	160.2	39.2	752	7 108	1 063.8	393.9
Laguna Hills	110	2 363	115.5	36.1	7	D	D	D	298	D	D	D
Laguna Niguel	119	1 814	98.1	27.1	21	D	D	D	202	1 077	117.8	39.4
La Habra	131	2 001	99.6	27.2	6	D	D	D	99	D	D	D
Lake Elsinore	104	1 622	73.1	21.0	11	234	12.1	4.7	47	D	D	D
Lake Forest	186	3 615	172.7	49.2	25	D	D	D	158	D	D	D
Lakewood	156	3 150	155.5	41.3	10	263	14.8	3.5	139	1 708	223.7	80.5
La Mesa	146	3 359	155.6	51.9	13	D	D	D	293	D	D	D
La Mirada	92	1 443	77.7	19.3	10	D	D	D	111	1 301	123.1	45.4
Lancaster	222	3 733	178.1	45.9	19	D	D	D	367	5 511	701.4	213.3
La Puente	81	685	36.6	9.2	2	D	D	D	52	D	D	D
La Quinta	74	3 505	219.2	70.3	21	D	D	D	58	269	30.7	10.3
La Verne	78	1 239	58.1	17.0	8	169	10.4	2.6	45	321	32.1	11.3
Lawndale	47	599	34.4	8.8	5	13	2.7	0.7	55	236	22.0	6.1
Lemon Grove	51	D	D	D	4	45	1.3	0.4	38	592	35.2	15.8
Lincoln	55	637	28.7	8.3	8	D	D	D	52	487	93.1	25.7
Livermore	159	2 296	132.0	36.2	16	D	D	D	141	1 241	151.1	50.6
Lodi	148	2 020	90.6	24.3	10	D	D	D	180	D	D	D
Lompoc	85	1 275	59.1	14.9	5	23	0.8	0.2	64	D	D	D
Long Beach	852	17 187	924.8	266.0	77	1 597	106.8	25.8	1 007	12 146	1 257.0	485.9
Los Altos	56	959	67.1	17.2	14	120	6.9	4.4	137	1 012	114.6	46.7
Los Angeles	7 609	130 390	8 271.8	2 279.2	6 627	31 958	8 263.6	3 056.4	9 129	98 549	11 732.8	4 226.3
Los Banos	53	957	42.7	10.8	7	D	D	D	39	245	23.3	9.4
Los Gatos	121	2 281	125.9	41.6	17	D	D	D	289	D	D	D
Lynwood	72	1 036	59.4	13.4	1	D	D	D	105	D	D	D
Madera	74	890	46.9	11.2	8	D	D	D	110	D	D	D
Manhattan Beach	141	3 357	206.9	57.6	57	322	50.5	19.2	158	D	D	D
Manteca	116	1 654	86.5	22.9	11	316	12.0	3.6	100	2 172	333.3	123.2
Martinez	73	777	43.2	10.5	6	51	5.9	0.9	37	D	D	D
Maywood	34	393	21.1	5.2	1	D	D	D	30	D	D	D
Menifee	NA	NA	NA	NA	NA	NA	NA	NA	NA	NA	NA	NA

1. Establishments subject to federal tax.

Table D. Cities — Other Services and Federal Funds

City	Other services[1], 2007				Selected federal funds, 2009–2010 (mil dol)								
					Procurement contracts		Grants						
	Number of establishments	Number of employees	Receipts (mil dol)	Annual payroll (mil dol)	Defense	Other	Total[2]	Medicaid and other health related	Nutrition and family welfare	Energy and environment	Disasters and emergency preparedness	Housing and community development	Employment and training
	104	105	106	107	108	109	110	111	112	113	114	115	116
CALIFORNIA—Cont'd													
Delano	18	103	10.3	4.7	0.0	1.0	2.0	0.0	0.0	1.1	0.0	0.9	0.0
Desert Hot Springs	15	28	6.2	0.6	0.1	0.0	0.2	0.0	0.0	0.0	0.0	0.0	0.0
Diamond Bar	75	247	17.4	5.0	22.9	5.5	74.1	0.0	0.0	74.1	0.0	0.0	0.0
Downey	140	818	73.1	18.9	0.6	1.3	215.7	1.8	210.1	0.0	0.0	3.1	0.0
Dublin	80	511	52.9	16.6	29.0	2.9	1.3	0.0	0.0	0.0	0.0	0.3	0.0
East Palo Alto	8	D	D	D	0.0	0.0	0.2	0.0	0.0	0.0	0.0	0.0	0.0
El Cajon	162	974	90.4	23.7	13.8	2.5	8.8	0.2	0.2	0.9	0.0	1.9	0.0
El Centro	59	D	D	D	0.5	39.7	3.9	0.7	0.0	0.2	0.0	0.2	0.0
Elk Grove	112	610	52.1	15.4	0.1	6.1	4.8	0.0	0.0	2.7	0.0	0.0	0.0
El Monte	134	704	58.4	16.1	8.5	0.3	8.1	0.0	0.0	6.6	0.0	-0.3	0.5
El Paso de Robles (Paso Robles)	43	249	23.4	6.7	0.3	0.0	0.2	0.0	0.0	0.0	0.0	0.2	0.0
Encinitas	127	785	64.2	20.8	7.5	1.6	6.8	4.2	0.0	0.5	0.0	1.7	0.0
Escondido	240	1 349	137.9	39.1	4.7	1.8	10.7	2.3	0.0	0.1	0.0	5.4	0.3
Eureka	85	497	41.9	12.5	1.4	3.7	15.4	1.2	0.5	1.8	0.0	6.4	0.6
Fairfield	123	699	60.2	18.2	103.4	5.9	24.3	1.1	0.2	1.2	0.0	11.9	0.0
Folsom	77	505	41.5	12.8	98.6	116.2	5.1	0.7	0.0	2.9	0.0	0.1	0.0
Fontana	165	1 149	92.5	29.4	0.6	0.4	6.7	0.0	0.0	1.7	0.0	3.1	0.0
Foster City	21	123	7.9	2.7	7.4	16.3	0.0	0.0	0.0	0.0	0.0	0.0	0.0
Fountain Valley	102	610	61.1	18.0	7.8	3.0	2.7	0.0	0.0	0.5	0.0	0.5	1.6
Fremont	265	2 159	168.7	61.8	24.0	31.7	27.9	9.2	10.6	2.3	0.0	4.0	0.0
Fresno	578	4 197	371.4	107.5	23.3	98.8	274.9	4.4	31.9	18.0	0.0	129.9	3.9
Fullerton	183	732	73.0	19.1	245.8	1.3	32.7	4.8	7.4	1.8	0.0	2.6	0.0
Gardena	124	778	65.2	21.1	7.2	0.2	1.4	0.0	0.0	0.0	0.0	1.0	0.0
Garden Grove	243	1 117	89.5	24.3	6.2	0.4	33.0	0.7	0.0	0.5	0.0	30.7	0.0
Gilroy	68	431	41.1	12.9	0.5	0.3	2.7	0.0	0.0	0.0	0.0	1.8	0.0
Glendale	308	2 041	156.6	58.0	129.7	9.8	51.0	0.7	0.0	22.6	0.0	21.0	0.0
Glendora	97	D	D	D	0.4	0.6	8.6	0.0	0.0	0.7	0.0	0.4	0.0
Goleta	62	D	D	D	311.5	21.9	23.7	0.8	10.4	3.0	0.0	0.6	0.0
Hanford	48	D	D	D	0.0	0.0	16.9	0.0	6.5	0.0	0.0	6.4	0.0
Hawthorne	103	405	39.8	9.7	8.4	22.3	6.6	0.0	0.0	0.0	0.0	6.2	0.1
Hayward	209	1 653	158.1	44.1	25.8	7.0	115.3	7.1	0.0	7.0	0.0	85.3	0.0
Hemet	89	446	29.7	7.8	0.7	0.3	1.9	0.0	0.0	0.9	0.0	0.8	0.0
Hesperia	85	449	41.3	11.6	0.6	0.1	8.2	0.0	0.0	0.0	0.0	0.8	0.0
Highland	33	191	11.4	3.8	1.4	0.3	0.7	0.0	0.0	0.2	0.0	0.0	0.0
Hollister	48	D	D	D	1.4	1.5	1.4	0.7	0.0	0.0	0.0	0.0	0.0
Huntington Beach	342	1 994	153.9	46.6	476.1	55.3	12.4	0.0	0.0	8.1	0.0	2.5	0.0
Huntington Park	47	D	D	D	0.0	0.0	4.4	0.0	0.0	0.0	0.0	4.3	0.0
Imperial Beach	18	75	4.7	1.4	5.6	22.0	1.1	0.7	0.0	0.1	0.0	0.0	0.0
Indio	61	366	37.7	9.9	0.1	0.3	11.2	0.0	0.0	1.0	0.0	9.3	0.0
Inglewood	143	993	78.1	22.3	61.8	22.9	25.9	0.3	0.0	1.0	0.0	13.0	0.0
Irvine	278	2 176	188.5	62.3	305.8	62.9	367.0	279.2	0.0	19.7	0.0	4.6	0.0
Laguna Hills	71	470	34.4	10.7	7.7	0.3	0.0	0.0	0.0	0.0	0.0	0.0	0.0
Laguna Niguel	86	538	45.0	14.6	1.9	14.3	0.7	0.0	0.0	0.0	0.0	0.7	0.0
La Habra	123	653	61.8	16.5	0.0	0.0	2.1	0.1	0.0	0.0	0.0	1.7	0.0
Lake Elsinore	51	341	21.9	6.9	18.0	0.3	2.9	0.0	0.0	1.9	0.0	0.0	0.0
Lake Forest	112	768	84.2	22.2	20.9	3.9	14.1	0.0	0.0	0.7	12.2	0.9	0.0
Lakewood	70	D	D	D	0.4	0.5	3.1	0.0	0.0	0.4	0.0	2.3	0.0
La Mesa	118	697	44.3	13.7	0.0	0.5	2.1	0.0	0.0	0.9	0.0	1.1	0.0
La Mirada	33	309	14.2	6.4	26.7	1.4	0.1	0.0	0.0	0.0	0.0	0.0	0.0
Lancaster	150	917	74.2	21.2	9.7	0.8	19.1	1.2	0.0	0.0	0.0	2.0	0.0
La Puente	41	147	8.8	2.4	3.8	0.7	0.0	0.0	0.0	0.0	0.0	0.0	0.0
La Quinta	29	217	9.3	3.6	0.2	0.0	1.7	0.0	0.0	0.0	0.0	0.0	0.0
La Verne	42	D	D	D	88.9	1.8	1.0	0.0	0.0	0.0	0.0	0.0	0.0
Lawndale	64	D	D	D	0.1	0.2	0.5	0.0	0.0	0.0	0.0	0.0	0.0
Lemon Grove	52	223	21.5	5.6	0.4	0.0	0.6	0.0	0.0	0.0	0.0	0.1	0.0
Lincoln	29	D	D	D	2.6	0.2	0.0	0.0	0.0	0.0	0.0	0.0	0.0
Livermore	117	630	63.7	22.8	16.0	1 571.9	23.1	4.7	0.0	1.8	0.0	9.0	0.0
Lodi	112	637	54.5	17.5	0.7	17.9	3.3	0.0	0.0	0.0	0.0	1.6	0.0
Lompoc	44	223	20.9	5.5	11.9	11.5	41.0	0.0	0.0	0.0	0.0	36.7	0.0
Long Beach	538	4 265	470.4	114.9	3 814.0	38.3	569.9	11.7	18.4	368.4	0.0	117.2	1.2
Los Altos	44	189	13.2	4.8	0.6	0.2	8.9	6.7	0.0	0.3	0.0	0.0	0.0
Los Angeles	5 424	36 122	3 211.8	885.5	675.7	343.7	3 310.9	1 453.2	28.8	157.1	0.3	901.5	15.4
Los Banos	22	D	D	D	0.0	8.7	1.9	0.0	0.0	1.9	0.0	0.0	0.0
Los Gatos	97	515	40.0	11.5	0.3	0.8	24.0	1.2	0.0	21.3	0.0	0.0	0.0
Lynwood	46	190	20.6	4.4	1.3	0.3	3.6	0.1	0.0	0.6	0.0	2.4	0.0
Madera	51	278	25.0	6.2	0.0	0.1	14.8	2.3	3.3	0.1	0.0	7.2	0.0
Manhattan Beach	76	474	31.4	9.1	0.1	7.4	0.5	0.4	0.0	0.0	0.0	0.1	0.0
Manteca	80	333	25.5	7.4	0.7	0.7	1.5	0.0	0.0	0.5	0.0	0.0	0.0
Martinez	47	232	23.6	7.7	4.4	42.1	127.6	2.2	20.8	3.6	0.0	98.8	0.0
Maywood	22	D	D	D	0.0	0.0	0.0	0.0	0.0	0.0	0.0	0.0	0.0
Menifee	NA	NA	NA	NA	NA	NA	NA	NA	NA	NA	NA	NA	NA

1. Establishments subject to federal tax. 2. Includes program categories not shown separately. State totals include additional categories not allocated by city.

Table D. Cities — City Government Finances

	City government finances, 2007									
	General revenue							General expenditure		
		Intergovernmental		Taxes					Per capita[1] (dollars)	
					Per capita[1] (dollars)					
City	Total (mil dol)	Total (mil dol)	Percent from state government	Total (mil dol)	Total	Property	Sales and gross receipts	Total (mil dol)	Total	Capital outlays
	117	118	119	120	121	122	123	124	125	126
CALIFORNIA—Cont'd										
Delano	34.3	11.2	86.3	15.0	286	176	90	31.0	592	53
Desert Hot Springs	23.5	2.4	90.3	16.6	682	260	231	30.1	1 238	441
Diamond Bar	29.4	8.4	96.2	14.0	245	89	130	25.1	437	106
Downey	95.8	11.6	67.7	56.6	524	253	267	89.7	829	38
Dublin	69.8	2.7	86.5	49.2	1 120	538	377	64.8	1 473	364
East Palo Alto	32.2	2.2	68.5	22.3	675	492	173	24.9	753	79
El Cajon	101.7	11.2	87.6	59.9	648	358	285	101.8	1 100	155
El Centro	137.1	9.6	52.3	30.3	764	374	352	124.8	3 147	389
Elk Grove	139.6	9.1	66.9	95.0	724	287	431	186.5	1 422	413
El Monte	90.0	13.8	65.4	67.2	550	274	267	93.3	763	103
El Paso de Robles (Paso Robles)	50.0	3.7	81.5	34.3	1 198	579	611	38.3	1 338	271
Encinitas	78.2	5.2	97.0	46.8	780	552	219	83.2	1 388	422
Escondido	192.4	17.0	56.2	91.6	672	422	244	166.4	1 214	245
Eureka	35.2	4.1	75.6	22.0	867	376	488	41.3	1 625	206
Fairfield	166.4	23.9	41.8	103.9	999	568	425	140.4	1 350	342
Folsom	132.2	6.7	89.5	82.8	1 229	448	687	138.9	2 060	730
Fontana	268.3	26.7	77.8	166.9	909	634	269	324.3	1 768	789
Foster City	60.1	1.2	100.0	38.7	1 339	1 079	251	65.8	2 275	343
Fountain Valley	57.9	4.4	84.6	37.7	679	409	266	47.1	849	99
Fremont	237.2	28.4	74.3	161.7	803	485	254	231.2	1 148	348
Fresno	574.0	102.4	51.1	260.3	553	297	252	568.8	1 209	295
Fullerton	146.8	11.7	64.3	77.5	587	379	200	127.7	967	174
Gardena	69.7	9.4	66.8	51.9	883	202	507	69.1	1 177	115
Garden Grove	166.3	44.0	24.4	90.7	548	332	212	155.5	939	117
Gilroy	75.8	6.0	45.2	37.5	764	265	372	88.3	1 758	754
Glendale	328.1	59.2	23.4	146.9	746	383	357	366.2	1 859	648
Glendora	46.3	5.6	91.8	29.7	597	389	202	51.6	1 038	350
Goleta	25.9	5.1	91.5	17.5	692	272	245	24.2	821	102
Hanford	52.9	8.9	85.4	21.8	439	257	140	48.0	968	323
Hawthorne	118.7	48.5	24.9	50.9	603	263	335	144.4	1 710	504
Hayward	172.5	17.7	88.7	98.9	702	398	251	204.5	1 451	567
Hemet	85.1	14.4	78.5	38.3	545	336	202	84.2	1 197	183
Hesperia	62.7	12.2	93.0	38.9	455	190	186	68.1	796	187
Highland	34.2	7.5	81.5	17.2	336	220	61	36.4	709	340
Hollister	39.1	1.6	72.8	21.6	619	497	113	50.1	1 434	616
Huntington Beach	236.2	25.7	89.1	131.0	679	335	338	217.2	1 126	162
Huntington Park	60.9	7.9	60.7	34.6	564	339	223	67.6	1 103	333
Imperial Beach	28.2	1.3	95.1	14.4	545	432	108	34.7	1 313	151
Indio	127.9	4.5	68.5	55.0	655	320	327	110.8	1 320	328
Inglewood	147.0	8.8	73.3	84.9	749	319	375	141.6	1 249	59
Irvine	318.3	23.5	65.3	152.7	759	326	433	281.2	1 398	259
Laguna Hills	27.2	4.4	28.3	17.9	561	304	248	28.5	893	347
Laguna Niguel	43.4	3.9	91.2	32.8	509	297	205	38.7	601	213
La Habra	57.3	9.6	80.8	33.8	571	287	276	51.4	868	105
Lake Elsinore	91.6	1.9	99.6	29.1	596	217	248	93.1	1 906	518
Lake Forest	48.5	3.8	79.8	38.1	503	259	238	37.3	492	79
Lakewood	60.0	5.9	54.1	38.6	488	273	212	60.8	770	125
La Mesa	53.3	4.9	86.3	30.9	573	305	257	54.1	1 002	175
La Mirada	53.7	3.7	52.7	38.1	765	488	272	68.5	1 376	692
Lancaster	189.6	15.7	69.5	134.8	939	629	303	185.6	1 292	309
La Puente	16.8	2.8	69.2	10.1	246	132	100	14.1	345	24
La Quinta	141.9	5.2	99.4	110.1	2 553	2 076	376	136.6	3 165	828
La Verne	44.6	5.9	98.9	25.8	778	478	288	40.5	1 224	208
Lawndale	22.2	3.1	61.8	15.9	505	262	239	18.1	573	107
Lemon Grove	22.2	1.6	77.7	13.8	573	333	236	22.6	938	69
Lincoln	72.8	8.9	94.5	28.9	686	231	416	129.0	3 063	1 929
Livermore	142.8	7.4	73.1	66.0	830	476	342	151.5	1 905	389
Lodi	68.4	7.9	77.4	41.2	668	277	351	55.5	900	127
Lompoc	52.0	6.0	69.9	22.9	565	257	271	58.8	1 454	285
Long Beach	1 535.0	175.9	38.1	335.7	720	403	312	1 327.1	2 845	352
Los Altos	34.4	2.0	92.9	20.6	735	410	300	42.4	1 513	136
Los Angeles	8 472.8	682.8	50.7	3 866.6	1 008	443	494	7 602.3	1 983	365
Los Banos	39.3	3.7	70.4	20.2	580	328	162	45.8	1 314	576
Los Gatos	43.8	2.4	97.2	30.5	1 046	614	406	38.5	1 318	181
Lynwood	51.6	7.6	82.1	31.1	442	264	172	63.1	897	122
Madera	54.9	4.8	54.8	26.9	482	268	150	73.9	1 322	672
Manhattan Beach	65.6	2.3	100.0	39.5	1 082	597	462	81.2	2 222	291
Manteca	124.1	12.1	95.7	41.1	641	481	160	111.0	1 733	680
Martinez	25.5	2.9	97.4	17.0	485	295	185	23.7	674	44
Maywood	18.5	4.7	54.2	9.5	336	237	92	23.7	834	234
Menifee	NA	NA	NA	NA	NA	NA	NA	NA	NA	NA

1. Based on population estimated as of July 1 of the year shown.

City	Public welfare	Highways	Parking facilities	Education	Health and hospitals	Police protection	Sewerage and sanitation	Parks and recreation	Housing and community development	Interest on debt
					City government finances, 2006 (cont.)					
					General expenditure (cont.)					
					Percent of total for:					
	127	128	129	130	131	132	133	134	135	136
CALIFORNIA—Cont'd										
Delano	0.0	4.5	0.0	0.0	1.0	40.8	10.5	6.4	5.9	4.5
Desert Hot Springs	0.0	19.5	0.0	0.0	1.0	19.0	0.0	11.8	16.6	3.6
Diamond Bar	0.0	23.6	0.0	0.0	0.4	0.0	1.5	22.1	2.4	2.0
Downey	0.0	7.4	0.0	0.0	3.0	29.5	2.0	11.5	4.1	3.7
Dublin	0.0	13.0	0.0	0.0	0.7	18.3	2.5	26.0	0.9	0.5
East Palo Alto	0.0	6.0	0.0	0.0	0.0	39.8	7.1	2.4	9.8	11.5
El Cajon	0.0	9.7	0.0	0.0	5.9	34.1	11.1	5.0	9.7	3.1
El Centro	0.0	7.8	0.0	0.0	57.3	6.4	8.7	2.0	4.4	2.0
Elk Grove	0.0	53.2	0.0	0.0	0.3	16.4	4.7	0.8	0.3	2.9
El Monte	0.0	9.1	0.1	0.0	0.1	31.4	0.0	6.1	12.0	6.0
El Paso de Robles (Paso Robles)	0.0	18.6	0.0	0.0	0.0	23.0	7.5	14.5	3.3	5.4
Encinitas	0.0	9.9	0.0	0.0	1.2	12.6	4.6	22.2	1.3	0.5
Escondido	0.0	11.2	0.0	0.0	0.4	27.3	16.8	6.8	3.9	4.0
Eureka	0.0	9.4	0.0	0.0	0.0	19.8	8.9	7.3	15.5	5.2
Fairfield	0.0	27.3	0.0	0.0	0.5	20.1	0.0	8.8	12.7	6.0
Folsom	0.0	25.5	0.0	0.0	0.5	14.4	8.1	12.0	6.8	3.7
Fontana	0.0	20.8	0.0	0.0	0.7	11.8	3.6	1.5	33.4	9.8
Foster City	0.0	2.6	0.0	0.0	0.0	12.9	5.6	8.3	12.0	3.6
Fountain Valley	0.0	14.6	0.0	0.0	4.8	28.8	7.0	6.6	6.3	4.4
Fremont	0.0	13.7	0.0	0.0	4.1	23.4	2.3	8.0	8.8	6.0
Fresno	0.0	9.9	1.0	0.0	1.7	23.6	18.5	8.5	3.9	7.7
Fullerton	0.0	6.5	0.0	0.0	4.9	28.0	8.0	6.0	10.1	8.3
Gardena	0.0	5.0	0.0	0.0	3.6	54.3	0.5	4.4	1.3	2.3
Garden Grove	0.0	9.4	0.0	0.0	3.9	25.8	5.9	4.0	25.0	6.7
Gilroy	0.0	3.5	0.0	0.0	0.4	20.5	3.5	1.2	44.5	1.8
Glendale	0.0	8.0	1.5	0.0	0.3	14.3	12.0	5.1	25.8	1.3
Glendora	0.0	9.7	0.0	0.0	0.3	23.7	0.2	9.0	32.9	5.3
Goleta	0.0	15.2	0.0	0.0	1.6	24.1	0.0	2.8	12.2	0.6
Hanford	0.0	15.0	0.0	0.0	0.3	15.4	18.9	22.5	3.4	4.4
Hawthorne	0.0	13.3	0.0	0.0	0.0	22.6	0.7	2.4	31.6	4.6
Hayward	0.0	8.8	0.0	0.0	0.8	22.6	23.5	0.9	11.0	2.0
Hemet	0.0	20.5	0.0	0.0	0.2	24.4	17.4	1.2	10.6	1.1
Hesperia	0.0	12.9	0.0	0.0	2.4	15.1	0.0	0.9	19.3	4.8
Highland	0.0	11.0	0.0	0.0	3.2	16.3	0.0	4.9	7.2	5.8
Hollister	0.0	36.4	0.0	0.0	0.8	10.7	25.1	2.6	2.0	4.9
Huntington Beach	0.0	14.0	0.9	0.0	2.8	26.3	9.0	9.8	1.9	3.9
Huntington Park	0.0	21.7	0.8	0.0	0.3	21.6	2.8	3.6	11.9	7.2
Imperial Beach	0.0	10.7	0.0	0.0	0.7	32.0	18.5	4.7	16.1	4.6
Indio	0.0	52.9	0.0	0.0	3.7	15.1	0.0	2.3	4.3	1.6
Inglewood	0.0	6.3	0.3	0.0	1.8	25.3	8.7	5.5	17.1	4.3
Irvine	0.0	25.6	0.0	0.0	0.8	18.3	0.0	13.3	4.2	15.4
Laguna Hills	0.0	27.0	0.0	0.0	0.1	20.7	0.0	26.7	0.0	2.9
Laguna Niguel	0.0	31.8	0.0	0.0	0.7	20.0	0.0	20.5	0.2	0.0
La Habra	0.0	14.7	0.0	0.0	3.2	26.5	6.5	15.3	5.0	2.9
Lake Elsinore	0.0	8.1	0.0	0.0	0.2	8.6	0.0	8.3	10.6	23.8
Lake Forest	0.0	25.2	0.0	0.0	0.7	26.7	0.0	10.9	9.2	1.1
Lakewood	0.0	16.4	0.0	0.0	0.3	18.5	7.6	19.4	12.8	4.6
La Mesa	0.0	10.3	0.2	0.0	0.2	23.9	19.9	8.5	0.9	5.6
La Mirada	0.0	13.2	0.0	0.0	0.1	11.4	0.0	45.8	14.0	7.7
Lancaster	0.0	18.0	0.0	0.0	0.2	10.3	0.0	7.3	40.7	9.0
La Puente	0.0	2.7	0.0	0.0	1.2	31.0	1.5	11.0	9.2	2.9
La Quinta	0.0	8.7	0.0	0.0	0.3	6.3	0.0	5.7	47.4	14.2
La Verne	0.0	11.6	0.0	0.0	4.6	27.4	1.7	7.2	14.9	5.3
Lawndale	0.0	15.2	0.0	0.0	0.9	22.9	0.2	15.3	11.2	3.5
Lemon Grove	0.0	9.2	0.0	0.0	0.7	20.0	14.2	7.1	12.4	4.4
Lincoln	0.0	4.3	0.0	0.0	0.0	4.9	11.2	2.2	1.3	7.2
Livermore	0.0	14.8	0.0	0.0	0.5	15.7	13.3	2.8	4.9	4.6
Lodi	0.0	6.0	0.0	0.0	0.5	24.9	15.2	9.2	1.2	0.1
Lompoc	0.0	9.4	0.0	0.0	0.6	28.0	29.2	6.8	3.5	1.6
Long Beach	0.0	5.1	0.0	0.0	4.3	17.3	5.5	8.1	7.5	7.5
Los Altos	0.0	6.7	0.0	0.0	6.1	37.4	12.2	7.5	2.2	0.1
Los Angeles	0.0	7.7	0.3	0.0	2.6	17.3	9.0	5.1	4.8	5.7
Los Banos	0.0	18.2	0.0	0.0	0.5	16.1	22.1	18.5	5.5	2.8
Los Gatos	0.0	8.2	0.0	0.0	0.4	31.3	0.6	7.2	15.4	4.2
Lynwood	0.0	14.4	0.0	0.0	0.8	19.9	0.0	16.7	6.4	3.8
Madera	0.0	12.8	0.0	0.0	1.4	12.0	37.7	5.0	9.4	3.6
Manhattan Beach	0.0	24.1	2.9	0.0	4.5	29.3	6.3	9.9	0.0	0.6
Manteca	0.0	19.6	0.0	0.0	0.2	11.6	24.9	5.2	18.2	6.3
Martinez	0.0	14.2	1.3	0.0	0.0	38.3	0.0	14.7	0.1	0.5
Maywood	0.0	4.1	0.0	0.0	0.2	42.4	0.0	3.7	35.3	1.7
Menifee	NA	NA	NA	NA	NA	NA	NA	NA	NA	NA

Table D. Cities — City Government Finances, City Government Employment, and Climate

City	City government finances, 2007 (cont.) Debt outstanding — Total (mil dol)	Per capita[1] (dollars)	Debt issued during year	City government employment, 2010	Climate[2] — Average daily temperature (degrees Fahrenheit) — Mean — January	July	Limits — January[3]	July[4]	Annual precipitation (inches)	Heating degree days	Cooling degree days
	137	138	139	140	141	142	143	144	145	146	147
CALIFORNIA—Cont'd											
Delano	22.0	420	0.0	NA	46.6	81.1	36.5	99.0	7.34	2 434	1 990
Desert Hot Springs	21.6	889	7.0	NA	NA	NA	NA	NA	NA	NA	NA
Diamond Bar	13.3	231	0.0	NA	54.6	73.8	41.5	88.7	16.96	1 727	1 191
Downey	41.1	380	0.0	541	57.0	73.8	46.0	82.9	12.94	1 211	1 186
Dublin	8.1	183	0.0	NA	47.2	72.0	37.4	89.1	14.82	2 755	858
East Palo Alto	68.7	2 077	1.4	NA	49.0	68.0	40.4	78.8	15.71	2 584	452
El Cajon	80.5	870	15.8	469	54.9	74.7	41.6	87.0	11.96	1 560	1 371
El Centro	70.1	1 767	32.1	1 121	55.8	91.4	41.3	107.0	2.96	1 080	3 852
Elk Grove	105.2	802	0.2	269	46.3	75.4	38.8	92.4	17.93	2 666	1 248
El Monte	125.1	1 023	4.2	320	56.3	75.6	42.6	89.0	18.56	1 295	1 575
El Paso de Robles (Paso Robles)	52.8	1 842	1.2	NA	NA	NA	NA	NA	NA	NA	NA
Encinitas	50.6	844	0.0	NA	55.5	75.1	42.5	88.6	15.10	1 464	1 436
Escondido	280.1	2 056	159.0	946	55.5	75.1	42.5	88.6	15.10	1 464	1 436
Eureka	35.1	1 381	0.0	300	47.9	58.1	40.8	63.3	38.10	4 430	7
Fairfield	202.4	1 946	0.0	567	46.1	72.6	37.5	88.8	23.46	2 649	975
Folsom	174.2	2 584	16.9	500	46.9	77.7	39.2	94.8	24.61	2 532	1 528
Fontana	636.4	3 468	41.0	735	56.6	78.3	45.3	95.0	14.77	1 364	1 901
Foster City	29.0	1 004	0.0	NA	48.4	68.0	39.1	80.8	20.16	2 764	422
Fountain Valley	33.6	605	0.0	NA	58.0	72.9	46.6	87.7	13.84	1 153	1 299
Fremont	421.0	2 091	0.0	879	49.8	68.0	42.0	78.3	14.85	2 367	530
Fresno	940.9	2 000	22.5	3 965	46.0	81.4	38.4	96.6	11.23	2 447	1 963
Fullerton	199.6	1 512	74.6	756	56.9	73.2	45.2	84.0	11.23	1 286	1 294
Gardena	35.7	607	0.0	NA	56.3	69.4	46.2	77.6	14.79	1 526	742
Garden Grove	161.9	978	3.9	688	58.0	72.9	46.6	87.7	13.84	1 153	1 299
Gilroy	31.8	647	0.0	NA	49.7	72.0	39.4	88.3	20.60	2 278	913
Glendale	240.2	1 219	0.0	1 862	54.8	75.5	42.0	88.9	17.49	1 575	1 455
Glendora	55.0	1 106	0.0	NA	54.6	73.8	41.5	88.7	16.96	1 727	1 191
Goleta	1.9	64	0.0	NA	53.1	67.0	40.8	76.7	16.93	2 121	482
Hanford	48.7	983	0.5	272	44.7	79.6	35.7	95.9	8.58	2 749	1 724
Hawthorne	182.0	2 156	31.2	361	57.1	69.3	48.6	75.3	13.15	1 274	679
Hayward	215.2	1 527	54.6	846	49.7	64.6	41.7	75.2	26.30	2 810	261
Hemet	21.7	308	3.9	NA	52.4	79.9	38.4	97.8	12.55	1 914	1 903
Hesperia	94.4	1 103	0.0	203	45.5	80.0	31.4	99.1	6.20	2 929	1 735
Highland	87.8	1 711	43.0	NA	54.4	79.6	41.8	96.0	16.43	1 599	1 937
Hollister	43.8	1 255	0.0	NA	49.5	66.6	37.8	80.9	13.61	2 724	405
Huntington Beach	315.7	1 637	15.0	1 178	55.9	67.3	48.2	71.4	11.65	1 719	543
Huntington Park	278.0	4 533	27.9	NA	58.3	74.2	48.5	83.8	15.14	928	1 506
Imperial Beach	24.9	941	0.0	NA	57.3	70.1	46.1	76.1	9.95	1 321	862
Indio	157.6	1 878	101.1	259	56.8	92.8	42.0	107.1	3.15	903	4 388
Inglewood	195.5	1 724	6.1	835	57.1	69.3	48.6	75.3	13.15	1 274	679
Irvine	1 155.2	5 743	187.3	930	54.5	72.1	41.4	83.8	13.87	1 794	1 102
Laguna Hills	20.5	641	0.0	NA	56.7	72.4	47.2	82.3	14.03	1 465	1 183
Laguna Niguel	0.0	0	0.0	NA	55.4	68.7	43.9	77.3	13.56	1 756	666
La Habra	32.9	555	0.0	NA	56.9	73.2	45.2	84.0	11.23	1 286	1 294
Lake Elsinore	415.9	8 512	58.7	NA	52.2	79.6	38.3	98.1	12.09	1 924	1 874
Lake Forest	10.1	134	0.0	80	56.7	72.4	47.2	82.3	14.03	1 465	1 183
Lakewood	45.8	581	3.1	260	57.0	73.8	46.0	82.9	12.94	1 211	1 186
La Mesa	74.4	1 378	0.2	264	57.1	73.0	45.7	83.6	13.75	1 313	1 261
La Mirada	117.5	2 360	0.0	NA	58.8	76.6	47.9	88.9	14.44	949	1 837
Lancaster	435.9	3 035	40.0	378	43.9	80.8	31.0	95.5	7.40	3 241	1 733
La Puente	13.4	327	4.8	NA	58.8	76.6	47.9	88.9	14.44	949	1 837
La Quinta	357.4	8 285	0.1	NA	NA	NA	NA	NA	NA	NA	NA
La Verne	41.6	1 255	0.4	196	54.6	73.8	41.5	88.7	16.96	1 727	1 191
Lawndale	13.2	419	0.0	NA	57.1	69.3	48.6	75.3	13.15	1 274	679
Lemon Grove	32.4	1 348	14.1	NA	NA	NA	NA	NA	NA	NA	NA
Lincoln	193.6	4 596	118.8	NA	NA	NA	NA	NA	NA	NA	NA
Livermore	177.5	2 232	10.4	452	47.2	72.0	37.4	89.1	14.82	2 755	858
Lodi	1.9	31	0.0	491	46.1	73.8	37.5	91.1	18.22	2 710	1 057
Lompoc	62.3	1 540	24.5	NA	53.7	64.5	41.4	75.4	15.85	2 250	322
Long Beach	2 096.3	4 494	110.5	6 131	57.0	73.8	46.0	82.9	12.94	1 211	1 186
Los Altos	0.4	14	0.0	NA	49.0	68.0	40.4	78.8	15.71	2 584	452
Los Angeles	16 553.5	4 317	2 050.5	51 022	58.3	74.2	48.5	83.8	15.14	928	1 506
Los Banos	30.7	881	17.5	NA	45.9	78.1	36.8	94.6	9.95	2 570	1 547
Los Gatos	12.4	426	0.0	NA	48.7	70.3	38.8	85.4	22.64	2 641	613
Lynwood	46.5	661	0.0	NA	58.3	74.2	48.5	83.8	15.14	928	1 506
Madera	79.2	1 417	2.9	NA	45.7	79.6	37.2	96.5	11.94	2 670	1 706
Manhattan Beach	46.3	1 268	6.8	NA	57.1	69.3	48.6	75.3	13.15	1 274	679
Manteca	218.4	3 411	22.7	NA	46.0	77.3	38.1	93.8	13.84	2 563	1 456
Martinez	11.3	323	0.0	NA	46.3	71.2	38.8	87.4	19.58	2 757	786
Maywood	29.2	1 027	21.7	NA	58.3	74.2	48.5	83.8	15.14	928	1 506
Menifee	NA	NA	NA	NA	NA	NA	NA	NA	NA	NA	NA

1. Based on the population estimated as of July 1 of the year shown.   2. Represents normal values based on the 30-year period, 1971–2000.   3. Average daily minimum.   4. Average daily maximum.

Table D. Cities — Land Area and Population

STATE Place code	City	Land area,[1] 2010 (sq km)	Population, 2010			Race alone or in combination, not of Hispanic origin (percent), 2010					Percent Hispanic or Latino[2], 2010	Percent Foreign born, 2008–2010
			Total persons	Rank	Per square kilometer	White	Black	American Indian, Alaska Native	Asian	Hawaiian Pacific Islander		
		1	2	3	4	5	6	7	8	9	10	11
	CALIFORNIA—Cont'd											
06 46870	Menlo Park	25.4	32 026	1 270	1 263.4	65.0	5.3	0.6	12.4	1.7	18.4	24.7
06 46898	Merced	60.4	78 958	411	1 307.5	31.9	6.6	1.2	12.6	0.3	49.6	19.3
06 47766	Milpitas	35.2	66 790	517	1 897.4	16.8	3.4	0.6	64.3	0.9	16.8	49.6
06 48256	Mission Viejo	45.9	93 305	319	2 031.0	72.0	1.8	0.6	11.4	0.4	17.0	18.9
06 48354	Modesto	95.5	201 165	108	2 106.7	52.0	4.7	1.5	7.9	1.5	35.5	15.4
06 48648	Monrovia	35.2	36 590	1 088	1 038.3	43.2	7.2	0.9	12.2	0.4	38.4	25.0
06 48788	Montclair	14.3	36 664	1 083	2 565.7	15.3	5.1	0.5	9.5	0.3	70.2	39.8
06 48816	Montebello	21.6	62 500	567	2 896.2	9.0	0.7	0.3	11.0	0.2	79.3	37.0
06 48872	Monterey	21.9	27 810	1 485	1 268.1	74.6	3.5	1.2	10.2	0.8	13.7	20.0
06 48914	Monterey Park	19.9	60 269	602	3 033.2	5.8	0.5	0.3	67.5	0.2	26.9	54.3
06 49138	Moorpark	32.6	34 421	1 172	1 056.5	59.7	1.9	0.7	8.6	0.3	31.4	17.1
06 49270	Moreno Valley	132.8	193 365	120	1 456.1	20.9	18.7	0.9	7.0	0.7	54.4	25.5
06 49278	Morgan Hill	33.4	37 882	1 045	1 135.6	53.3	2.4	0.9	11.9	0.7	34.0	19.6
06 49670	Mountain View	31.1	74 066	458	2 383.8	49.1	2.6	0.5	28.5	0.8	21.7	40.1
06 50076	Murrieta	87.0	103 466	272	1 189.8	58.8	6.1	1.0	11.1	0.7	25.9	15.2
06 50258	Napa	46.2	76 915	426	1 664.8	58.9	0.8	1.1	3.0	0.3	37.6	22.8
06 50398	National City	18.9	58 582	625	3 107.8	13.0	5.2	0.6	19.0	1.0	63.0	45.4
06 50916	Newark	35.9	42 573	926	1 184.6	30.6	5.1	0.7	29.9	2.4	35.2	36.7
06 51182	Newport Beach	61.7	85 186	365	1 381.8	84.5	0.9	0.5	8.7	0.3	7.2	13.5
06 51560	Norco	36.2	27 063	1 527	748.4	58.0	7.2	1.2	3.8	0.3	31.1	11.9
06 52526	Norwalk	25.1	105 549	260	4 198.4	13.1	4.2	0.5	12.3	0.5	70.1	36.3
06 52582	Novato	71.1	51 904	736	730.3	68.7	3.4	0.8	8.3	0.4	21.3	20.8
06 53000	Oakland	144.5	390 724	47	2 704.3	28.6	29.2	1.2	18.4	0.8	25.4	28.5
06 53070	Oakley	41.1	35 432	1 135	862.9	50.7	8.0	1.4	7.9	0.7	34.9	19.6
06 53322	Oceanside	106.8	167 086	143	1 564.5	51.2	5.3	0.9	8.3	1.8	35.9	21.5
06 53896	Ontario	129.4	163 924	147	1 267.3	19.2	6.4	0.5	5.5	0.4	69.0	30.4
06 53980	Orange	64.2	136 416	185	2 124.2	48.5	1.8	0.6	12.3	0.4	38.1	27.2
06 54652	Oxnard	69.7	197 899	115	2 840.9	16.1	2.8	0.5	8.0	0.4	73.5	38.6
06 54806	Pacifica	32.8	37 234	1 062	1 135.9	59.8	3.3	1.0	22.3	1.4	16.8	20.0
06 55156	Palmdale	274.4	152 750	161	556.6	26.2	15.3	0.9	4.9	0.3	54.4	24.5
06 55184	Palm Desert	69.4	48 445	807	697.7	71.6	2.0	0.6	4.0	0.2	22.8	18.3
06 55254	Palm Springs	243.8	44 552	884	182.8	65.0	4.7	1.2	5.0	0.3	25.3	19.3
06 55282	Palo Alto	61.9	64 403	547	1 041.1	64.0	2.2	0.4	30.0	0.4	6.2	31.6
06 55520	Paradise	47.4	26 218	1 581	552.9	90.3	0.7	2.5	1.8	0.3	7.0	5.5
06 55618	Paramount	12.3	54 098	701	4 416.2	6.1	11.5	0.4	3.2	0.9	78.6	39.8
06 56000	Pasadena	59.5	137 122	184	2 305.0	41.1	11.1	0.6	15.8	0.3	33.7	30.3
06 56700	Perris	81.3	68 386	497	841.1	12.3	12.4	0.6	4.0	0.6	71.8	29.8
06 56784	Petaluma	37.3	57 941	636	1 555.5	72.0	1.8	1.0	5.8	0.5	21.5	17.6
06 56924	Pico Rivera	21.5	62 942	565	2 928.9	5.5	0.7	0.3	2.5	0.1	91.2	33.3
06 57456	Pittsburg	44.6	63 264	560	1 418.5	22.6	18.7	1.0	17.3	1.5	42.4	33.4
06 57526	Placentia	17.0	50 533	762	2 970.8	46.4	2.0	0.6	16.1	0.3	36.4	24.1
06 57764	Pleasant Hill	18.3	33 152	1 225	1 809.6	71.7	2.7	0.9	16.2	0.5	12.1	18.5
06 57792	Pleasanton	62.5	70 285	484	1 125.5	64.0	2.1	0.7	25.8	0.5	10.3	23.2
06 58072	Pomona	59.4	149 058	164	2 507.7	13.5	7.3	0.5	9.0	0.3	70.5	34.4
06 58240	Porterville	45.6	54 165	699	1 187.8	31.7	1.1	1.5	5.0	0.2	61.9	19.9
06 58520	Poway	101.2	47 811	823	472.4	71.9	2.0	0.9	12.0	0.5	15.7	17.1
06 59444	Rancho Cordova	86.8	64 776	545	746.4	56.2	11.9	1.7	14.1	1.4	19.7	26.9
06 59451	Rancho Cucamonga	103.2	165 269	145	1 601.3	45.0	9.8	0.7	11.6	0.6	34.9	17.6
06 59514	Rancho Palos Verdes	34.9	41 643	943	1 194.2	59.5	2.9	0.4	31.8	0.4	8.5	27.2
06 59587	Rancho Santa Margarita	33.6	47 853	819	1 425.9	70.0	2.4	0.6	11.2	0.5	18.6	16.7
06 59920	Redding	154.5	89 861	339	581.7	84.6	2.0	3.8	4.2	0.4	8.7	5.9
06 59962	Redlands	93.6	68 747	493	734.8	56.3	5.7	0.9	8.8	0.6	30.3	15.4
06 60018	Redondo Beach	16.1	66 748	519	4 158.8	69.0	3.5	0.7	14.8	0.7	15.2	19.9
06 60102	Redwood City	50.3	76 815	427	1 527.1	46.5	2.8	0.6	12.5	1.4	38.8	33.2
06 60466	Rialto	57.9	99 171	293	1 713.1	13.6	16.5	0.6	2.5	0.5	67.6	25.9
06 60620	Richmond	77.9	103 701	270	1 331.5	19.1	27.5	0.9	14.7	0.7	39.5	33.7
06 60704	Ridgecrest	53.8	27 616	1 493	513.5	72.1	4.9	2.0	5.8	0.9	17.9	7.8
06 62000	Riverside	210.2	303 871	61	1 446.0	35.9	7.4	0.9	8.2	0.6	49.0	24.6
06 62364	Rocklin	50.6	56 974	651	1 125.7	78.9	2.0	1.3	9.4	0.6	11.5	10.7
06 62546	Rohnert Park	18.1	40 971	971	2 258.6	69.7	2.7	1.6	6.8	0.9	22.1	14.6
06 62896	Rosemead	13.4	53 764	707	4 021.2	5.2	0.4	0.2	60.9	0.1	33.8	58.0
06 62938	Roseville	93.8	118 788	217	1 266.3	74.1	2.6	1.3	10.2	0.5	14.6	12.7
06 64000	Sacramento	253.6	466 488	35	1 839.5	37.7	15.9	1.7	20.2	2.1	26.9	21.8
06 64224	Salinas	60.0	150 441	163	2 506.1	16.7	2.0	0.6	6.7	0.5	75.0	36.8
06 65000	San Bernardino	153.3	209 924	100	1 369.1	20.5	15.4	0.9	4.5	0.5	60.0	24.0
06 65028	San Bruno	14.2	41 114	963	2 897.4	38.6	2.6	0.7	27.6	4.4	29.2	38.4
06 65042	San Buenaventura (Ventura)	56.1	106 433	255	1 897.5	62.4	2.0	1.4	4.5	0.4	31.8	13.8
06 65070	San Carlos	14.3	28 406	1 451	1 980.9	76.8	1.2	0.6	14.4	0.5	10.1	19.2
06 65084	San Clemente	48.5	63 522	556	1 310.8	78.3	0.9	0.9	5.1	0.3	16.8	11.8
06 66000	San Diego	842.2	1 307 402	8	1 552.3	47.8	7.3	0.8	17.7	0.8	28.8	25.8
06 66070	San Dimas	39.0	33 371	1 213	856.8	54.6	3.6	0.8	11.6	0.3	31.4	22.7

1. Dry land or land partially or temporarily covered by water.   2. May be of any race.

Table D. Cities — Population

City	Age of population (percent), 2010									Median age	Percent female	Population			
	Under 5 years	5 to 17 years	18 to 24 years	25 to 34 years	35 to 44 years	45 to 54 years	55 to 64 years	65 to 74 years	75 years and over			Census counts		Percent change	
												1990	2000	1990–2000	2000–2010
	12	13	14	15	16	17	18	19	20	21	22	23	24	25	26
CALIFORNIA—Cont'd															
Menlo Park	7.7	16.7	5.7	14.1	15.8	14.7	11.1	6.7	7.6	38.7	51.6	28 403	30 785	8.4	4.0
Merced	9.4	22.4	13.3	14.7	11.8	11.1	8.6	4.6	4.2	28.1	50.9	56 155	63 893	13.8	23.6
Milpitas	6.9	16.0	8.8	16.3	16.3	15.2	10.9	5.7	3.8	36.1	48.9	50 690	62 698	23.7	6.5
Mission Viejo	4.9	17.9	8.4	9.7	13.5	17.8	13.2	7.7	6.8	42.2	51.2	79 464	93 102	17.2	0.2
Modesto	7.4	19.5	10.4	13.7	12.7	13.7	11.0	6.1	5.6	34.2	51.3	164 746	188 856	14.6	6.5
Monrovia	6.5	16.8	8.4	14.1	15.2	15.3	12.1	6.2	5.4	37.9	52.2	35 733	36 929	3.3	-0.9
Montclair	8.1	21.3	11.7	15.1	14.0	12.5	8.9	4.9	3.6	30.7	50.2	28 434	33 049	16.2	10.9
Montebello	6.9	18.9	10.3	14.3	13.8	12.3	9.8	6.6	7.0	34.7	51.7	59 564	62 150	4.3	0.6
Monterey	5.1	10.2	13.8	18.1	12.4	12.4	12.5	7.2	8.3	36.9	49.7	31 954	29 674	-7.1	-6.3
Monterey Park	4.5	13.6	8.6	12.1	13.8	15.4	12.7	8.5	10.8	43.1	52.0	60 738	60 051	-1.1	0.4
Moorpark	6.6	20.9	10.5	12.3	13.3	17.7	11.5	4.2	2.9	34.7	50.4	25 494	31 415	23.2	9.6
Moreno Valley	8.4	24.0	12.2	14.5	13.3	13.0	8.5	3.9	2.4	28.6	51.2	118 779	142 381	19.9	35.8
Morgan Hill	7.4	21.2	7.7	11.4	15.0	16.5	11.3	5.7	3.8	36.8	50.5	23 928	33 556	40.2	12.9
Mountain View	7.1	12.6	7.3	21.1	17.5	13.9	9.9	5.6	5.0	35.9	49.1	67 365	70 708	5.0	4.7
Murrieta	7.0	23.4	9.6	11.9	15.3	14.7	8.1	5.2	4.9	33.4	51.2	18 557	44 282	138.6	133.7
Napa	6.6	17.9	8.7	13.6	13.6	14.1	11.8	6.8	6.9	37.4	50.7	61 865	72 585	17.3	6.0
National City	6.9	18.6	16.2	14.7	12.4	12.0	8.6	5.0	5.6	30.2	48.7	54 249	54 260	0.0	8.0
Newark	7.4	18.0	9.0	15.0	14.8	14.7	10.5	6.3	4.3	35.4	50.2	37 861	42 471	12.2	0.2
Newport Beach	3.8	13.5	7.8	13.7	12.5	15.8	13.9	9.8	9.1	44.0	50.7	66 643	70 032	5.1	21.6
Norco	4.5	15.7	10.3	13.2	15.9	19.0	11.7	6.4	3.2	39.5	42.2	23 302	24 157	3.7	12.0
Norwalk	7.0	20.6	11.4	14.4	14.1	13.1	9.5	5.4	4.5	32.5	50.4	94 279	103 298	9.6	2.2
Novato	5.9	16.7	6.5	10.6	13.9	15.9	14.8	8.7	7.0	42.6	51.7	47 585	47 630	0.1	9.0
Oakland	6.7	14.6	9.3	17.4	15.6	13.6	11.7	5.9	5.2	36.2	51.5	372 242	399 484	7.3	-2.2
Oakley	7.5	23.0	10.0	13.6	15.1	15.1	9.1	4.1	2.7	32.0	50.3	18 374	25 619	39.4	38.3
Oceanside	7.0	16.9	11.4	14.5	12.9	14.0	10.5	6.1	6.8	35.2	50.7	128 090	161 029	25.7	3.8
Ontario	8.4	21.8	11.8	15.9	14.3	12.7	8.4	4.0	2.8	29.9	50.2	133 179	158 007	18.6	3.7
Orange	6.4	17.2	12.0	14.7	14.3	14.4	10.3	5.7	5.0	34.8	49.6	110 658	128 821	16.4	5.9
Oxnard	8.9	20.9	12.1	15.8	13.5	12.0	8.5	4.6	3.7	29.9	49.3	142 560	170 358	19.5	16.2
Pacifica	5.4	15.3	7.6	12.2	14.7	17.4	15.2	7.0	5.2	41.5	51.1	37 670	38 390	1.9	-3.0
Palmdale	8.3	24.8	11.2	12.2	14.0	14.3	8.6	3.9	2.7	29.7	51.2	73 314	116 670	59.1	30.9
Palm Desert	4.2	11.4	6.9	9.0	9.1	12.1	14.6	15.8	17.1	53.0	53.0	23 252	41 155	77.0	17.7
Palm Springs	3.9	9.9	5.8	8.9	10.5	17.2	17.5	14.0	12.6	51.6	43.6	40 144	42 807	6.6	4.1
Palo Alto	5.4	18.0	4.9	11.9	14.8	16.1	11.8	7.9	9.2	41.9	51.1	55 900	58 598	4.8	9.9
Paradise	4.4	12.8	7.1	8.8	9.6	15.2	17.1	11.1	13.9	50.2	52.5	25 401	26 408	4.0	-0.7
Paramount	8.7	23.9	11.8	15.5	14.6	11.7	7.6	3.9	2.4	28.6	51.4	47 669	55 266	15.9	-2.1
Pasadena	6.0	13.3	9.2	18.1	15.0	13.7	11.1	6.9	6.7	37.2	51.2	131 586	133 936	1.8	2.4
Perris	10.0	27.0	11.6	14.9	14.5	11.1	6.1	3.0	1.9	26.0	50.4	21 500	36 189	68.3	89.0
Petaluma	6.0	17.2	7.9	11.9	14.1	16.5	13.3	6.9	6.2	40.3	50.9	43 166	54 548	26.4	6.2
Pico Rivera	6.8	19.9	11.1	13.6	13.7	13.1	9.7	6.1	6.1	34.0	51.2	59 177	63 428	7.2	-0.8
Pittsburg	7.9	19.6	10.8	15.3	13.7	13.7	10.5	5.0	3.6	32.5	51.3	47 607	56 769	19.2	11.4
Placentia	6.6	18.0	10.3	13.6	14.0	13.9	11.1	6.9	5.6	36.0	50.8	41 259	46 488	12.7	8.7
Pleasant Hill	5.5	14.3	9.6	12.9	13.9	15.9	14.0	6.7	7.2	40.7	51.5	31 583	32 837	4.0	1.0
Pleasanton	5.6	21.5	6.2	9.0	15.5	19.3	11.9	6.3	4.6	40.5	51.0	50 570	63 654	25.9	10.4
Pomona	8.1	21.4	13.5	14.8	13.6	12.5	8.6	4.2	3.4	29.5	50.0	131 700	149 473	13.5	-0.3
Porterville	9.9	23.7	10.9	14.2	12.1	11.3	8.6	5.0	4.4	28.8	50.5	29 521	39 615	34.2	36.7
Poway	5.1	19.9	8.2	9.7	12.2	18.6	13.9	6.7	5.7	41.3	50.7	43 396	48 044	10.7	-0.5
Rancho Cordova	8.3	18.0	9.9	16.8	13.4	13.5	9.9	5.7	5.4	33.1	51.1	48 731	55 060	13.0	17.6
Rancho Cucamonga	6.2	19.6	10.5	14.4	15.0	15.7	10.8	4.7	3.2	34.5	50.6	101 409	127 743	26.0	29.4
Rancho Palos Verdes	3.7	18.5	5.6	5.2	11.7	18.3	13.7	11.6	11.6	47.8	51.5	41 667	41 145	-1.3	1.2
Rancho Santa Margarita	6.3	22.7	7.9	11.8	16.9	19.5	9.3	3.2	2.5	36.0	51.1	11 390	47 214	314.5	1.4
Redding	6.3	16.6	10.5	13.1	11.1	13.6	12.5	8.1	8.3	38.5	51.6	66 176	80 865	22.2	11.1
Redlands	6.0	17.6	11.9	13.0	12.3	14.0	12.1	6.5	6.5	36.2	52.4	62 667	63 591	1.5	8.1
Redondo Beach	6.3	13.0	6.3	16.4	18.3	17.0	12.3	6.0	4.5	39.3	50.2	60 167	63 261	5.1	5.5
Redwood City	7.5	16.2	7.8	15.7	16.6	14.9	10.8	5.6	5.0	36.7	50.2	66 072	75 402	14.1	1.9
Rialto	8.7	24.2	12.3	13.7	13.3	12.4	8.4	4.1	2.8	28.3	51.4	72 395	91 873	26.9	7.9
Richmond	7.4	17.5	10.0	15.4	14.3	13.8	11.4	5.9	4.3	34.8	51.3	86 019	99 216	15.3	4.5
Ridgecrest	8.2	19.1	9.6	14.6	11.4	13.9	10.9	6.8	5.6	33.8	49.9	28 295	24 927	-11.9	10.8
Riverside	7.2	19.6	15.5	14.3	12.8	12.9	9.0	4.6	4.0	30.0	50.6	226 546	255 166	12.6	19.1
Rocklin	6.3	21.1	9.3	11.2	15.4	15.8	10.0	5.8	5.2	36.7	51.6	18 806	36 330	93.2	56.8
Rohnert Park	5.6	15.3	16.7	14.6	12.3	14.8	11.3	4.9	4.4	33.0	51.2	36 326	42 236	16.3	-3.0
Rosemead	5.4	17.3	9.7	13.2	14.6	15.0	11.8	6.7	6.2	38.1	50.7	51 638	53 505	3.6	0.5
Roseville	6.8	19.5	7.9	13.3	14.8	14.3	10.1	6.4	7.0	36.8	52.1	44 685	79 921	78.9	48.6
Sacramento	7.5	17.4	11.2	16.6	13.2	12.8	10.7	5.5	5.1	33.0	51.3	369 365	407 018	10.2	14.6
Salinas	9.5	21.8	12.0	16.5	13.4	11.5	7.8	3.8	3.7	28.8	49.5	108 777	151 060	38.9	-0.4
San Bernardino	9.3	22.7	12.7	14.1	12.7	12.4	8.2	4.3	3.6	28.5	50.7	170 036	185 401	9.0	13.2
San Bruno	6.0	15.0	8.7	15.0	14.3	15.7	12.7	6.8	5.9	38.8	50.7	38 961	40 165	3.1	2.4
San Buenaventura (Ventura)	5.8	16.7	9.0	13.4	13.7	15.8	12.4	6.5	6.8	39.0	50.6	92 557	100 916	9.0	5.5
San Carlos	6.6	17.0	4.1	9.7	17.3	17.6	13.5	7.4	6.9	42.6	51.7	26 382	27 718	5.1	2.5
San Clemente	6.5	18.0	7.9	11.3	14.7	16.1	12.5	7.0	6.2	39.7	49.8	41 100	49 936	21.5	27.2
San Diego	6.2	15.2	13.1	17.6	14.1	13.2	10.1	5.5	5.2	33.6	49.5	1 110 623	1 223 400	10.2	6.9
San Dimas	4.4	16.6	9.8	10.6	12.0	16.4	14.7	8.7	6.8	42.6	52.5	32 398	34 980	8.0	-4.6

Table D. Cities — Households, Group Quarters, Crime, and Education

City	Households, 2010				Persons in group quarters, 2010				Serious crimes known to police,[2] 2010				Educational attainment, 2008–2010		
			Percent			Institutional			Total		Rate[3]			Attainment[4] (percent)	
	Number	Persons per house-hold	Female family house-holder[1]	One-person	Total	Total	Persons in nursing facilities	Non-institu-tional	Number	Rate[3]	Violent	Property	Population age 25 and older	High school graduate or less	Bachelor's degree or more
	27	28	29	30	31	32	33	34	35	36	37	38	39	40	41
CALIFORNIA—Cont'd															
Menlo Park	12 347	2.53	8.4	29.7	845	246	236	599	686	2 142	128	2 014	22 916	16.9	68.1
Merced	24 899	3.13	19.8	21.5	1 080	588	343	492	3 357	4 252	695	3 556	43 834	50.6	15.7
Milpitas	19 184	3.34	11.9	12.9	2 698	2 594	34	104	2 072	3 102	136	2 966	45 422	35.4	39.6
Mission Viejo	33 208	2.78	8.9	19.0	942	83	66	859	1 205	1 291	75	1 216	63 923	19.9	44.0
Modesto	69 107	2.87	15.6	23.0	2 955	1 766	1 169	1 189	10 781	5 359	695	4 664	124 404	47.7	17.9
Monrovia	13 762	2.65	15.1	26.5	156	95	76	61	1 152	3 148	197	2 952	24 612	35.7	31.3
Montclair	9 523	3.81	18.7	13.0	396	181	181	215	1 925	5 250	472	4 779	22 061	58.9	12.6
Montebello	19 012	3.27	21.2	17.6	400	361	350	39	2 155	3 448	342	3 106	40 725	58.4	15.7
Monterey	12 184	2.08	7.4	39.2	2 503	293	293	2 210	1 337	4 808	554	4 254	19 320	22.0	45.4
Monterey Park	19 963	3.01	16.2	18.2	230	189	186	41	956	1 586	159	1 427	43 291	45.3	28.2
Moorpark	10 484	3.28	10.6	12.8	0	0	0	0	431	1 252	139	1 113	20 973	29.5	37.2
Moreno Valley	51 592	3.74	19.4	11.8	554	83	27	471	5 946	3 075	374	2 701	103 687	51.9	14.1
Morgan Hill	12 326	3.04	11.9	16.2	386	222	144	164	696	1 837	143	1 695	23 199	31.3	37.3
Mountain View	31 957	2.31	7.7	34.3	265	120	107	145	1 626	2 195	227	1 969	54 302	21.3	58.0
Murrieta	32 749	3.15	11.6	15.9	429	138	56	291	1 506	1 456	96	1 360	57 473	30.9	29.3
Napa	28 166	2.69	11.4	26.5	1 237	669	343	568	1 802	2 343	319	2 024	50 987	40.9	27.2
National City	15 502	3.41	22.2	17.4	5 752	411	411	5 341	2 277	3 887	731	3 156	34 567	59.3	14.3
Newark	12 972	3.27	13.2	15.0	145	0	0	145	1 615	3 793	439	3 354	28 613	45.7	29.1
Newport Beach	38 751	2.19	6.7	33.1	402	251	221	151	2 293	2 692	137	2 554	63 049	12.0	63.4
Norco	7 023	3.23	11.1	14.7	4 397	4 322	0	75	710	2 624	151	2 472	18 204	45.2	17.0
Norwalk	27 130	3.83	18.6	12.6	1 615	1 300	474	315	2 521	2 388	425	1 963	65 304	53.7	15.7
Novato	20 279	2.53	11.0	26.4	626	177	175	449	1 134	2 185	191	1 994	36 453	26.2	43.3
Oakland	153 791	2.49	15.7	33.9	8 138	2 463	1 349	5 675	23 592	6 038	1 604	4 434	268 353	38.4	37.1
Oakley	10 727	3.29	13.2	14.2	103	28	6	75	532	1 501	138	1 363	20 099	49.5	13.1
Oceanside	59 238	2.80	11.7	23.8	936	134	91	802	4 559	2 729	389	2 340	107 964	38.6	24.4
Ontario	44 931	3.63	17.6	15.0	758	347	347	411	5 548	3 384	384	3 000	96 019	56.6	13.7
Orange	43 367	3.00	12.1	19.6	6 253	3 666	299	2 587	2 719	1 993	110	1 883	88 793	37.7	32.6
Oxnard	49 797	3.95	15.3	14.2	1 434	502	465	932	4 709	2 379	349	2 030	114 350	58.3	14.4
Pacifica	13 967	2.65	11.4	22.4	182	118	115	64	829	2 226	185	2 041	27 155	25.6	38.8
Palmdale	42 952	3.55	18.2	13.6	199	41	0	158	4 166	2 727	545	2 183	81 808	51.7	14.3
Palm Desert	23 117	2.08	9.4	34.4	308	210	210	98	1 959	4 044	99	3 945	39 208	31.1	32.4
Palm Springs	22 746	1.93	8.7	44.0	539	196	190	343	2 255	5 062	633	4 429	36 579	32.8	33.1
Palo Alto	26 493	2.41	7.0	30.1	583	378	323	205	1 404	2 180	90	2 090	45 125	7.7	79.7
Paradise	11 893	2.17	11.0	34.0	408	269	246	139	650	2 479	397	2 083	20 198	34.9	20.8
Paramount	13 881	3.87	22.4	13.7	310	283	283	27	1 897	3 507	634	2 873	29 622	73.5	8.5
Pasadena	55 270	2.42	11.1	34.1	3 493	1 021	890	2 472	4 628	3 375	404	2 971	98 211	31.4	46.1
Perris	16 365	4.16	19.1	8.8	240	100	71	140	1 895	2 771	234	2 537	34 115	63.3	10.3
Petaluma	21 737	2.63	10.4	24.7	724	363	363	361	975	1 683	340	1 343	39 776	31.4	35.1
Pico Rivera	16 566	3.77	20.1	13.7	454	415	415	39	1 800	2 860	392	2 467	39 330	66.0	10.1
Pittsburg	19 527	3.22	18.3	17.6	291	138	123	153	2 209	3 492	243	3 248	38 223	51.6	15.7
Placentia	16 365	3.07	12.6	17.6	337	84	73	253	929	1 838	168	1 670	32 246	32.6	36.6
Pleasant Hill	13 708	2.38	9.9	28.7	463	312	291	151	1 501	4 528	284	4 244	24 019	19.1	49.6
Pleasanton	25 245	2.77	8.0	19.3	456	136	129	320	1 372	1 952	111	1 841	45 152	19.2	53.9
Pomona	38 477	3.77	18.1	15.1	4 138	1 356	1 166	2 782	5 381	3 610	588	3 022	83 539	60.2	14.9
Porterville	15 644	3.39	18.9	17.1	1 147	940	931	207	2 074	3 829	410	3 419	29 923	53.6	11.8
Poway	16 128	2.93	10.4	15.3	550	266	260	284	615	1 286	188	1 098	31 731	22.9	45.3
Rancho Cordova	23 448	2.75	16.3	24.8	325	155	143	170	2 680	4 137	597	3 540	40 298	39.1	22.8
Rancho Cucamonga	54 383	2.98	13.8	18.3	3 124	2 988	73	136	4 043	2 446	206	2 241	103 041	31.9	28.3
Rancho Palos Verdes	15 561	2.65	7.8	18.9	340	27	27	313	464	1 114	101	1 013	29 850	12.1	66.7
Rancho Santa Margarita	16 665	2.87	10.2	19.2	2	0	0	2	390	815	54	761	29 158	17.4	46.4
Redding	36 130	2.43	13.3	28.6	2 020	882	543	1 138	3 830	4 262	882	3 380	58 533	33.3	23.2
Redlands	24 764	2.68	13.7	24.6	2 368	512	485	1 856	2 779	4 042	353	3 689	43 265	28.6	38.8
Redondo Beach	29 011	2.29	8.7	31.9	431	64	64	367	1 767	2 647	315	2 333	49 421	16.7	57.4
Redwood City	27 957	2.69	11.2	26.5	1 547	1 139	53	408	1 815	2 363	227	2 136	51 210	32.2	40.8
Rialto	25 202	3.92	20.5	12.5	447	193	153	254	3 062	3 088	501	2 586	53 630	62.6	9.5
Richmond	36 093	2.83	19.2	26.4	1 583	913	172	670	5 799	5 592	1 134	4 458	66 749	43.5	27.6
Ridgecrest	10 781	2.54	12.5	27.6	196	87	87	109	741	2 683	471	2 212	17 740	32.4	22.8
Riverside	91 932	3.18	15.1	19.9	11 549	2 624	1 153	8 925	11 411	3 755	477	3 279	176 238	46.3	21.8
Rocklin	20 800	2.71	10.5	21.2	637	181	176	456	1 091	1 915	104	1 811	35 029	21.2	40.5
Rohnert Park	15 808	2.57	11.9	26.4	397	6	6	391	1 000	2 441	400	2 040	25 172	33.5	24.7
Rosemead	14 247	3.74	17.6	12.2	413	278	208	135	1 285	2 390	311	2 079	36 487	62.2	13.3
Roseville	45 059	2.62	10.9	24.5	847	369	361	478	4 136	3 482	281	3 201	75 937	26.2	33.9
Sacramento	174 624	2.62	15.8	30.5	8 314	4 046	1 367	4 268	24 312	5 212	881	4 330	297 093	39.0	28.8
Salinas	40 387	3.66	16.9	17.1	2 465	1 807	531	658	5 810	3 862	772	3 090	83 706	61.7	13.4
San Bernardino	59 283	3.42	22.8	18.9	7 325	4 247	878	3 078	10 591	5 045	774	4 272	117 525	60.5	12.5
San Bruno	14 701	2.77	12.4	24.9	398	82	72	316	990	2 408	197	2 211	28 649	31.6	34.7
San Buenaventura (Ventura)	40 438	2.57	12.2	27.1	2 493	1 738	293	755	3 721	3 496	247	3 249	71 078	30.8	31.1
San Carlos	11 524	2.46	7.2	25.8	91	12	12	79	470	1 655	84	1 570	20 318	15.5	56.8
San Clemente	23 906	2.65	7.9	21.7	273	28	0	245	843	1 327	96	1 231	42 949	18.3	46.6
San Diego	483 092	2.60	11.4	28.0	51 956	7 050	2 902	44 906	36 369	2 782	430	2 352	849 008	30.0	40.8
San Dimas	12 030	2.73	12.2	22.2	540	220	128	320	743	2 226	240	1 987	22 969	29.8	32.4

1. No spouse present. 2. Data for serious crimes have not been adjusted for underreporting. This may affect comparability between geographic areas and over time. 3. Per 100,000 population estimated by the FBI. 4. Persons 25 years old and over.

Table D. Cities — Income, Poverty, and Housing

City	Per capita income[1] (dollars)	Median income	Percent with income of $200,000 or more	Percent with income of less than $25,000	Families with income below poverty (percent)	Total	Percent change, 2000–2010	Vacant units for sale or rent[2]	Total	Percent	Median value[3] (dollars)	With a mortgage[4]	Without a mortgage[5]
	42	43	44	45	46	47	48	49	50	51	52	53	54
CALIFORNIA—Cont'd													
Menlo Park	63 325	105 909	23.1	9.9	3.2	13 085	2.7	738	12 630	54.5	1 000 000	29.3	10.0
Merced	16 710	36 499	1.7	35.4	21.8	27 446	27.4	2 547	23 778	41.3	163 800	26.3	11.8
Milpitas	31 335	96 599	9.9	10.5	4.0	19 806	14.0	622	18 564	67.7	566 600	29.4	10.0
Mission Viejo	40 934	92 555	11.2	9.1	2.2	34 228	4.0	1 020	33 435	77.9	577 000	28.8	10.0
Modesto	22 473	49 116	2.5	25.8	15.2	75 044	11.5	5 937	68 026	56.5	209 000	30.6	11.0
Monrovia	30 641	64 901	5.3	20.3	7.5	14 473	3.9	711	13 630	48.6	532 300	31.6	10.0
Montclair	16 304	49 283	2.9	22.5	19.0	9 911	8.0	388	8 907	60.8	283 400	34.1	10.0
Montebello	19 570	50 850	1.8	24.1	13.6	19 768	1.8	756	18 647	48.1	421 400	34.5	11.8
Monterey	35 557	62 314	5.3	19.0	5.5	13 584	1.2	1 400	12 256	36.8	715 200	27.2	13.2
Monterey Park	24 325	51 488	3.1	24.9	9.1	20 850	3.3	887	19 632	56.2	484 200	29.0	10.0
Moorpark	34 462	96 007	11.0	8.9	3.5	10 738	18.1	254	10 627	79.6	567 300	31.2	10.0
Moreno Valley	17 793	54 513	1.8	19.8	15.4	55 559	34.0	3 967	49 940	63.8	211 800	33.2	11.1
Morgan Hill	38 619	89 236	15.3	13.5	8.4	12 859	15.7	533	12 371	72.4	624 000	31.9	10.9
Mountain View	48 700	91 282	13.5	14.6	3.3	33 881	4.5	1 924	30 769	41.1	766 300	28.5	12.2
Murrieta	27 199	75 866	4.8	11.9	5.7	35 294	136.5	2 545	29 918	72.9	302 800	31.4	13.9
Napa	30 063	61 676	5.0	19.0	9.4	30 149	8.6	1 983	28 414	60.2	466 300	29.8	11.2
National City	15 995	36 143	0.9	32.2	17.9	16 762	8.0	1 260	16 255	35.1	305 100	36.7	13.3
Newark	29 698	80 831	4.8	9.5	3.8	13 414	2.0	442	13 016	69.1	471 600	32.1	10.0
Newport Beach	79 537	105 366	24.6	11.4	4.2	44 193	18.4	5 442	38 161	55.0	1 000 000	31.3	10.0
Norco	24 910	80 358	6.4	14.1	7.0	7 322	17.7	299	6 821	81.0	448 200	31.3	11.4
Norwalk	19 525	60 612	1.7	17.1	9.4	28 083	1.9	953	27 288	64.7	346 600	31.3	10.0
Novato	40 858	77 554	10.0	16.5	4.7	21 158	11.5	879	20 213	69.3	631 400	33.4	10.5
Oakland	30 242	50 094	6.3	28.1	16.1	169 710	7.7	15 919	153 285	41.2	475 700	33.1	12.0
Oakley	26 313	67 827	6.7	16.8	6.2	11 484	44.0	757	10 409	74.8	272 400	30.8	14.5
Oceanside	27 126	60 864	3.5	17.0	7.8	64 435	8.3	5 197	58 596	58.7	377 900	32.5	11.9
Ontario	18 647	53 478	1.8	16.6	11.8	47 449	5.2	2 518	44 308	57.2	286 200	31.7	12.3
Orange	31 163	76 283	8.2	13.1	6.2	45 111	8.0	1 744	42 661	60.0	549 600	30.9	10.0
Oxnard	19 843	58 251	3.4	19.5	12.8	52 772	16.8	2 975	50 673	53.6	365 100	32.4	10.4
Pacifica	40 827	87 767	8.9	9.1	2.1	14 523	1.9	556	14 092	67.6	635 900	31.0	10.0
Palmdale	18 258	52 731	2.5	20.7	14.4	46 544	25.3	3 592	40 785	69.0	206 500	32.5	14.0
Palm Desert	40 273	51 727	6.3	23.2	7.2	37 073	32.1	13 956	24 192	68.9	346 000	34.0	16.7
Palm Springs	38 031	44 731	6.6	26.6	8.4	34 794	12.3	12 048	23 357	58.5	316 000	33.7	18.3
Palo Alto	70 144	117 127	29.0	10.7	3.3	28 216	7.9	1 723	25 504	57.4	1 000 000	24.7	10.0
Paradise	24 797	41 517	1.4	31.8	10.1	12 961	5.4	1 088	11 882	71.9	230 700	28.5	14.8
Paramount	13 289	38 100	0.3	30.9	20.3	14 571	-0.4	690	14 363	42.8	294 900	37.1	10.0
Pasadena	38 367	64 692	9.1	20.2	9.0	59 551	10.0	4 281	52 395	45.7	632 900	29.7	12.9
Perris	13 925	48 687	0.7	23.6	23.1	17 906	70.5	1 541	15 479	65.2	172 100	34.9	10.4
Petaluma	34 766	73 855	7.2	13.9	5.3	22 736	11.8	999	21 610	68.7	474 600	30.7	10.3
Pico Rivera	17 770	55 774	1.1	20.8	11.3	17 109	1.8	543	16 328	68.3	371 100	31.0	10.0
Pittsburg	22 424	56 886	2.4	18.4	10.3	21 126	14.9	1 599	18 740	60.9	269 000	32.9	12.9
Placentia	29 535	73 088	5.7	15.0	7.1	16 872	9.4	507	16 278	68.0	536 500	29.5	10.0
Pleasant Hill	42 513	78 999	11.9	12.4	4.4	14 321	2.0	613	13 757	62.0	573 900	28.4	10.0
Pleasanton	48 682	115 494	19.7	8.2	2.8	26 053	8.6	808	23 643	68.5	739 000	28.0	10.0
Pomona	16 185	48 072	1.3	24.2	15.7	40 685	2.7	2 208	38 792	54.7	302 800	35.7	11.3
Porterville	16 989	43 742	0.8	30.0	20.5	16 734	31.4	1 090	15 806	57.8	170 200	27.5	10.6
Poway	38 239	93 676	10.7	7.5	2.6	16 715	5.6	587	15 513	73.3	544 400	26.5	10.0
Rancho Cordova	23 672	53 899	1.8	19.7	13.4	25 479	18.5	2 031	22 832	56.5	227 300	29.8	10.3
Rancho Cucamonga	32 110	76 383	5.7	9.3	3.5	56 618	34.1	2 235	52 923	66.6	395 800	31.4	10.0
Rancho Palos Verdes	58 084	113 192	24.2	8.7	2.8	16 179	3.3	618	15 131	83.0	993 800	28.3	10.0
Rancho Santa Margarita	38 825	97 813	11.1	7.3	3.6	17 260	3.7	595	16 212	71.4	548 900	29.4	11.4
Redding	22 453	43 142	1.8	29.3	13.6	38 679	14.5	2 549	34 936	56.3	257 900	30.3	13.2
Redlands	32 134	68 851	6.2	17.7	8.1	26 634	7.1	1 870	24 025	61.8	335 200	25.9	10.0
Redondo Beach	50 137	91 701	14.3	13.9	3.6	30 609	3.6	1 598	28 502	51.2	740 800	27.8	11.1
Redwood City	38 300	76 390	11.4	15.6	6.0	29 167	0.8	1 210	27 895	51.9	792 700	32.0	12.9
Rialto	15 435	49 583	1.1	21.9	16.1	27 203	5.4	2 001	24 148	62.7	222 800	32.9	10.0
Richmond	24 760	53 738	3.7	22.5	13.5	39 328	8.8	3 235	35 235	50.9	339 200	32.8	10.2
Ridgecrest	26 710	58 465	2.0	20.4	7.1	11 915	4.8	1 134	10 712	58.7	184 700	19.7	10.0
Riverside	21 861	56 261	3.2	20.1	10.6	98 444	14.4	6 512	89 195	57.6	277 800	30.4	10.0
Rocklin	33 629	77 821	5.6	13.5	4.1	22 010	52.4	1 210	20 767	69.1	359 200	30.3	13.1
Rohnert Park	27 562	56 491	2.5	19.1	4.4	16 551	4.6	743	15 830	56.4	345 500	32.6	13.7
Rosemead	17 164	47 657	1.6	21.7	14.0	14 805	3.4	558	14 069	51.9	459 400	39.6	10.0
Roseville	32 249	72 857	4.9	13.6	5.2	47 757	49.3	2 698	43 988	66.9	346 800	28.8	11.1
Sacramento	24 619	48 826	2.9	25.2	13.9	190 911	16.5	16 287	174 721	49.1	265 500	29.9	10.7
Salinas	17 632	48 849	1.9	24.4	17.8	42 651	7.7	2 264	41 730	43.8	311 800	35.9	10.0
San Bernardino	15 231	38 386	1.3	33.4	24.2	65 401	3.1	6 118	60 272	51.6	191 200	32.6	11.9
San Bruno	34 712	76 066	7.8	12.7	5.7	15 356	2.7	655	15 096	59.0	641 700	30.4	10.0
San Buenaventura (Ventura)	30 476	64 294	4.0	18.4	7.2	42 827	7.5	2 389	39 969	55.4	475 800	29.4	10.0
San Carlos	56 784	110 515	22.2	6.5	2.5	12 018	3.6	494	11 144	70.6	937 300	28.6	10.0
San Clemente	46 286	81 983	13.8	11.4	4.5	25 966	25.7	2 060	24 020	65.7	781 700	33.1	11.8
San Diego	31 981	61 282	6.5	20.1	10.3	516 033	9.9	32 941	477 518	48.8	464 400	30.5	10.0
San Dimas	32 778	73 716	9.9	15.3	4.0	12 506	-0.6	476	11 317	67.9	453 100	25.9	10.2

1. Based on population estimated by the American Community Survey.　2. Includes units rented or sold but not occupied.　3. Specified owner-occupied units; $1,000,000 represents $1,000,000 or more.　4. 50.0 represents 50 percent or more.　5. 10.0 represents 10 percent or less.

Table D. Cities — Housing, Labor Force, and Employment

City	Occupied housing units, 2008–2010 (cont.)				Migration, 2008–2010		Civilian labor force, 2010				Civilian employment[4], 2008–2010			
									Unemployment			Percent		
	Percent renter occupied	Median gross rent[1]	Median rent as a percent of income[2]	Percent with no vehicle available	Percent who lived in the same house one year ago	Percent who lived outside this city one year ago	Total	Percent change, 2009–2010	Total	Rate[3]	Population age 16 and older	In labor force	Full-year full-time worker	Households with no workers (percent)
	55	56	57	58	59	60	61	62	63	64	65	66	67	68
CALIFORNIA—Cont'd														
Menlo Park	45.5	1 705	26.7	5.7	82.7	12.2	15 716	0.1	1 111	7.1	24 915	68.6	44.9	22.2
Merced	58.7	757	34.4	12.4	79.3	8.2	32 353	3.4	6 028	18.6	56 049	58.6	32.2	30.8
Milpitas	32.3	1 585	29.7	2.7	85.3	10.0	31 917	0.3	3 613	11.3	52 879	63.9	44.6	12.5
Mission Viejo	22.1	1 659	35.2	3.6	89.5	7.4	54 222	-0.3	3 738	6.9	74 101	68.6	46.0	19.5
Modesto	43.5	976	34.3	8.1	78.6	8.7	102 580	1.3	15 384	15.0	150 959	62.6	35.7	27.5
Monrovia	51.4	1 254	29.4	6.9	88.1	8.0	20 666	0.2	2 300	11.1	29 393	68.8	43.9	19.8
Montclair	39.2	1 056	35.3	6.8	81.0	13.4	16 157	-0.5	2 194	13.6	27 946	67.4	35.9	16.1
Montebello	51.9	1 054	32.3	12.1	89.8	7.6	29 042	0.4	4 077	14.0	47 690	61.0	40.1	24.2
Monterey	63.2	1 301	29.7	8.5	71.8	21.6	17 664	1.5	1 016	5.8	24 102	68.3	43.9	26.7
Monterey Park	43.8	1 158	38.6	10.7	90.5	4.8	29 289	0.0	2 805	9.6	50 197	57.1	37.4	27.7
Moorpark	20.4	1 681	36.1	1.1	92.3	5.5	18 799	0.7	1 894	10.1	26 166	73.0	49.3	12.1
Moreno Valley	36.2	1 275	39.2	4.8	83.6	7.9	90 327	2.8	15 091	16.7	134 978	66.0	37.6	16.3
Morgan Hill	27.6	1 404	33.7	1.9	87.1	7.7	17 753	0.3	2 501	14.1	27 828	69.9	40.5	20.0
Mountain View	58.9	1 444	22.8	7.3	77.6	14.1	41 882	0.3	3 428	8.2	60 903	73.8	48.4	18.1
Murrieta	27.1	1 361	34.1	2.0	77.6	15.8	27 846	2.2	2 687	9.6	72 498	66.9	39.7	20.3
Napa	39.8	1 184	32.7	6.8	84.5	6.4	45 240	0.2	4 562	10.1	60 241	66.6	39.5	24.4
National City	64.9	903	34.6	15.6	84.5	7.8	25 039	1.8	4 981	19.9	43 433	62.0	40.9	24.1
Newark	30.9	1 434	28.7	3.3	90.9	6.3	22 407	-0.2	2 351	10.5	33 765	70.0	47.9	17.6
Newport Beach	45.0	1 816	27.7	3.3	80.7	12.3	43 856	-0.4	2 614	6.0	71 913	65.6	42.4	24.3
Norco	19.0	1 800	33.8	2.3	84.3	13.3	13 940	2.4	1 654	11.9	21 815	53.9	31.8	22.6
Norwalk	35.3	1 235	32.1	7.0	90.4	5.4	49 360	0.4	6 564	13.3	80 037	64.2	42.3	17.4
Novato	30.7	1 444	34.5	4.2	87.8	6.7	26 289	0.9	2 493	9.5	40 858	66.6	39.5	24.4
Oakland	58.8	1 016	32.8	18.0	83.8	7.0	204 714	0.2	34 532	16.9	314 175	66.0	38.9	27.3
Oakley	25.2	1 353	41.1	3.2	85.4	12.2	13 626	-0.8	1 099	8.1	25 620	66.1	36.2	22.2
Oceanside	41.3	1 291	33.6	4.9	81.3	9.2	86 174	0.9	8 646	10.0	130 879	66.4	42.2	24.8
Ontario	42.8	1 213	33.6	5.7	82.7	9.7	82 140	-0.3	12 336	15.0	121 862	70.0	39.0	16.4
Orange	40.0	1 408	31.1	5.3	84.6	9.8	72 364	-0.2	6 329	8.7	106 084	69.5	43.7	17.2
Oxnard	46.4	1 215	35.0	6.6	85.1	5.1	91 669	1.1	13 339	14.6	145 512	66.7	40.7	19.4
Pacifica	32.4	1 552	29.5	3.0	87.3	9.6	22 465	0.2	2 251	10.0	30 505	71.2	49.0	19.0
Palmdale	31.0	1 125	40.9	5.6	83.8	8.7	56 236	0.6	8 752	15.6	104 667	62.3	37.2	21.8
Palm Desert	31.1	1 191	35.6	8.1	84.2	11.0	25 424	2.1	2 215	8.7	42 514	50.3	26.1	48.0
Palm Springs	41.5	921	29.9	6.6	82.2	9.3	26 825	2.3	3 042	11.3	39 776	56.0	31.8	40.7
Palo Alto	42.6	1 723	25.1	6.4	83.0	9.7	31 197	0.3	1 853	5.9	49 377	65.4	43.5	24.2
Paradise	28.1	790	41.3	7.2	88.0	6.3	11 925	-1.5	1 291	10.8	22 667	48.9	28.2	45.0
Paramount	57.2	1 094	40.4	6.3	90.7	5.6	25 166	0.8	4 582	18.2	38 697	63.2	39.7	17.6
Pasadena	54.3	1 322	31.4	9.2	81.3	12.2	75 846	0.0	7 331	9.7	114 342	65.9	40.6	24.9
Perris	34.8	1 123	39.5	5.0	78.0	12.9	20 449	3.2	4 518	22.1	44 255	66.1	33.0	18.1
Petaluma	31.3	1 417	35.5	5.7	87.9	6.9	31 326	-0.9	2 990	9.5	46 121	70.1	42.7	21.2
Pico Rivera	31.7	1 151	36.6	6.8	91.9	5.6	29 076	0.2	3 422	11.8	48 598	59.8	40.3	20.1
Pittsburg	39.1	1 229	34.4	5.9	82.4	9.6	30 791	0.0	5 354	17.4	47 144	68.1	38.5	20.4
Placentia	32.0	1 420	36.6	4.1	84.3	12.7	27 716	-0.3	2 339	8.4	39 162	66.7	40.0	19.3
Pleasant Hill	38.0	1 369	29.9	5.6	83.1	12.1	20 199	-0.7	1 832	9.1	27 270	68.2	38.6	26.3
Pleasanton	31.5	1 579	26.5	3.1	84.5	10.4	34 977	-0.5	2 008	5.7	52 420	71.2	46.2	18.8
Pomona	45.3	1 025	36.9	6.1	84.3	10.1	67 003	0.4	9 370	14.0	108 860	64.0	38.0	18.3
Porterville	42.2	713	31.1	6.4	83.8	6.1	21 541	1.3	3 345	15.5	36 856	65.3	39.5	25.6
Poway	26.7	1 379	29.1	3.9	86.8	7.8	28 008	0.6	1 762	6.3	36 860	69.5	45.4	18.7
Rancho Cordova	43.5	953	31.7	7.8	74.5	13.8	31 072	-0.6	4 513	14.5	48 612	69.3	40.7	23.2
Rancho Cucamonga	33.4	1 417	31.6	2.7	81.4	11.7	76 281	-0.9	7 116	9.3	126 774	70.1	43.6	15.7
Rancho Palos Verdes	17.0	2 000	36.1	2.7	89.3	7.8	20 999	-0.5	917	4.4	33 237	56.0	36.1	30.2
Rancho Santa Marga- rita	28.6	1 512	31.7	4.1	87.4	7.5	28 592	-0.4	1 743	6.1	35 420	75.0	49.4	11.5
Redding	43.7	866	35.9	9.2	80.0	9.6	42 138	0.0	5 811	13.8	70 923	59.7	31.5	35.7
Redlands	38.2	1 062	29.2	6.6	84.1	9.5	36 574	-0.8	3 814	10.4	53 993	64.9	39.9	23.2
Redondo Beach	48.8	1 589	28.7	3.2	85.7	8.4	44 605	-0.2	3 011	6.8	54 864	74.8	49.2	18.0
Redwood City	48.1	1 317	31.6	5.9	84.5	9.2	41 548	0.2	3 626	8.7	58 223	71.6	45.2	18.5
Rialto	37.3	1 047	39.7	5.4	81.6	11.2	44 229	-0.1	7 947	18.0	69 272	64.6	36.2	18.9
Richmond	49.1	1 136	32.3	9.7	79.1	10.9	53 660	0.0	9 525	17.8	79 862	66.5	38.9	27.3
Ridgecrest	41.3	775	26.9	6.6	77.9	11.1	15 756	1.0	1 448	9.2	21 272	63.5	42.4	27.4
Riverside	42.4	1 103	36.1	5.4	79.6	9.4	164 915	2.6	24 098	14.6	228 126	64.7	37.2	21.5
Rocklin	30.9	1 265	31.1	5.0	82.4	11.3	26 649	-1.5	2 207	8.3	41 977	69.6	43.8	24.0
Rohnert Park	43.6	1 265	36.4	4.9	77.5	12.1	24 939	-0.8	2 555	10.2	33 630	71.1	39.8	22.2
Rosemead	48.1	1 143	36.9	6.4	93.2	2.7	24 882	0.2	2 768	11.1	43 813	58.6	38.2	16.0
Roseville	33.1	1 196	31.9	4.4	81.5	11.5	55 590	-1.2	6 403	11.5	88 478	67.5	43.1	26.1
Sacramento	50.9	962	32.8	9.9	75.4	10.6	217 168	-0.6	32 239	14.8	361 691	64.9	37.4	28.5
Salinas	56.2	980	33.5	7.9	85.1	4.3	77 339	2.4	13 658	17.7	106 134	67.9	37.8	18.8
San Bernardino	48.4	899	39.5	10.4	77.6	10.7	85 419	0.0	16 064	18.8	151 545	58.0	34.3	27.3
San Bruno	41.0	1 454	27.4	5.7	86.7	11.3	21 928	0.2	1 667	7.6	33 099	72.8	48.6	19.8
San Buenaventura (Ven- tura)	44.6	1 325	31.9	5.0	82.8	9.0	61 588	0.7	6 011	9.8	83 690	68.0	40.2	24.8
San Carlos	29.4	1 437	25.6	2.2	88.1	8.0	15 236	0.1	906	5.9	22 247	68.3	44.6	20.7
San Clemente	34.3	1 614	31.6	2.4	85.7	10.0	28 900	-0.3	2 224	7.7	48 412	66.7	43.2	22.5
San Diego	51.2	1 262	32.6	7.1	80.6	7.7	702 007	1.0	73 870	10.5	1 052 301	66.9	42.7	22.5
San Dimas	32.1	1 478	30.1	4.6	84.9	12.2	19 865	-0.2	1 477	7.4	27 503	63.3	44.1	21.4

1. $2,000 represents $2,000 or more. 2. 50.0 represents 50 percent or more. 3. Percent of civilian labor force. 4. Persons 16 years old and over.

Table D. Cities — **Construction, Wholesale Trade, and Retail Trade**

City	Value of residential construction authorized by building permits, 2010			Wholesale trade,[1] 2007				Retail trade,[2] 2007			
	New construction ($1,000)	Number of housing units	Percent single family	Number of establishments	Number of employees	Sales (mil dol)	Annual payroll (mil dol)	Number of establishments	Number of employees	Sales (mil dol)	Annual payroll (mil dol)
	69	70	71	72	73	74	75	76	77	78	79
CALIFORNIA—Cont'd											
Menlo Park	8 638	12	100.0	45	640	411.0	50.2	115	1 483	354.3	48.2
Merced	418	2	100.0	32	818	1 204.2	35.7	270	4 509	1 057.5	103.5
Milpitas	16 645	62	9.7	146	5 498	4 231.2	512.4	312	5 088	993.9	103.3
Mission Viejo	800	1	100.0	117	1 385	598.4	89.7	372	7 291	1 727.6	181.8
Modesto	3 780	16	100.0	108	1 147	1 311.9	52.7	737	12 116	2 599.3	268.2
Monrovia	1 510	8	100.0	82	931	475.8	43.6	135	2 753	907.2	81.3
Montclair	14 578	75	33.3	77	699	257.8	24.1	260	5 046	1 136.0	123.1
Montebello	9 694	59	61.0	106	1 635	759.0	64.7	212	3 782	820.0	80.0
Monterey	657	2	100.0	45	1 701	2 172.2	94.1	227	2 684	512.9	70.4
Monterey Park	6 304	19	100.0	228	1 354	653.7	47.5	222	1 937	477.2	41.1
Moorpark	13 725	40	100.0	54	731	401.8	34.6	60	1 013	192.8	20.3
Moreno Valley	34 476	161	56.5	30	147	62.1	5.5	310	5 564	1 853.2	129.5
Morgan Hill	40 704	157	68.8	63	2 221	1 332.4	144.7	112	1 584	418.3	40.2
Mountain View	34 583	134	49.3	125	3 295	2 750.6	373.0	262	4 609	1 290.1	131.9
Murrieta	15 148	64	62.5	79	409	238.2	19.1	229	4 293	1 073.7	98.0
Napa	14 123	46	100.0	67	557	302.7	28.3	324	4 411	1 129.0	116.3
National City	890	7	100.0	96	940	946.4	43.8	322	5 688	1 483.3	150.3
Newark	0	0	0.0	57	1 734	755.4	79.0	195	3 705	781.8	76.5
Newport Beach	51 726	74	78.4	224	2 091	2 564.4	174.1	467	7 369	2 614.3	250.3
Norco	531	2	100.0	28	244	123.5	8.6	98	1 659	521.0	51.1
Norwalk	0	0	0.0	85	769	385.1	31.9	163	3 410	1 160.4	98.5
Novato	24 541	124	47.6	87	1 259	596.3	90.1	188	2 919	969.4	90.4
Oakland	69 493	624	27.5	424	5 473	3 541.5	277.3	1 099	11 176	2 987.1	314.0
Oakley	46 796	210	79.0	8	D	D	D	49	499	141.3	12.0
Oceanside	36 675	175	46.9	144	1 516	502.5	54.4	400	6 646	1 688.3	159.2
Ontario	5 689	50	60.0	596	12 375	13 263.9	539.7	583	10 441	3 160.6	268.2
Orange	13 494	94	37.2	349	4 806	6 253.9	253.2	608	7 997	2 101.9	211.0
Oxnard	28 516	180	33.9	193	4 187	2 837.6	207.0	458	7 877	2 348.6	212.2
Pacifica	3 131	5	100.0	8	D	D	D	65	663	177.5	15.9
Palmdale	30 296	149	100.0	34	259	51.3	8.1	314	7 319	1 670.4	163.2
Palm Desert	25 651	96	77.1	76	559	195.2	23.0	472	6 874	1 538.1	163.9
Palm Springs	8 349	25	100.0	50	249	106.3	10.8	222	2 753	643.7	71.4
Palo Alto	55 975	181	80.7	70	941	1 584.9	64.0	340	5 719	1 535.7	182.6
Paradise	1 134	5	100.0	6	17	6.1	0.6	88	878	168.5	19.7
Paramount	1 355	5	100.0	239	1 965	1 163.4	79.6	120	1 710	423.9	42.3
Pasadena	14 609	56	92.9	150	D	D	D	652	10 857	2 707.8	280.7
Perris	24 282	207	100.0	15	234	78.2	9.6	79	2 638	537.3	61.0
Petaluma	1 894	7	100.0	100	1 460	795.8	110.7	289	3 803	947.3	104.1
Pico Rivera	1 419	9	100.0	108	2 268	1 218.7	90.6	116	2 611	927.7	55.6
Pittsburg	21 895	178	37.6	33	398	217.9	21.3	123	2 535	650.0	69.6
Placentia	4 371	23	60.9	128	1 105	480.1	55.3	104	1 354	384.5	38.6
Pleasant Hill	468	2	100.0	26	146	113.8	9.1	140	2 472	510.8	54.8
Pleasanton	14 197	42	100.0	138	2 228	3 957.5	172.4	355	6 810	1 605.1	179.6
Pomona	103	1	100.0	302	3 199	1 629.7	139.6	291	4 139	1 102.6	100.4
Porterville	18 859	127	44.9	23	140	44.6	5.5	158	2 448	540.1	56.2
Poway	16 178	91	15.4	106	2 104	1 444.6	146.8	147	3 097	1 002.8	90.6
Rancho Cordova	51 183	205	91.2	102	1 053	453.8	56.8	191	2 828	543.9	68.7
Rancho Cucamonga	34 354	155	100.0	292	3 728	3 078.3	170.4	444	8 301	1 803.6	175.4
Rancho Palos Verdes	16 691	73	6.8	33	119	123.8	6.1	56	481	112.6	11.0
Rancho Santa Margarita	0	0	0.0	68	622	345.4	32.1	86	2 005	608.4	54.1
Redding	24 546	156	47.4	129	1 429	724.2	58.5	500	7 820	1 953.9	199.2
Redlands	2 223	15	26.7	49	650	174.7	25.1	253	5 303	1 581.1	133.4
Redondo Beach	12 838	45	100.0	63	295	102.2	12.6	303	4 570	815.7	101.6
Redwood City	10 002	46	100.0	73	1 243	1 189.7	114.5	245	4 925	1 613.7	175.2
Rialto	16 940	141	46.8	47	698	766.6	38.3	130	2 420	524.4	52.7
Richmond	17 536	129	36.4	94	1 871	1 127.9	94.9	261	4 139	1 024.6	103.5
Ridgecrest	5 360	38	100.0	6	33	12.0	1.6	96	1 442	298.2	32.1
Riverside	51 161	373	28.7	312	5 066	2 854.9	229.3	922	16 855	4 757.5	439.1
Rocklin	40 718	137	88.3	71	1 433	855.4	88.0	142	1 927	545.9	60.0
Rohnert Park	0	0	0.0	31	475	225.3	24.9	114	2 220	610.8	57.4
Rosemead	4 569	19	100.0	113	447	220.5	11.1	172	2 201	453.9	42.0
Roseville	149 594	635	100.0	107	2 175	2 233.8	109.0	549	13 868	3 923.2	372.1
Sacramento	28 969	191	49.7	488	9 008	8 940.1	402.1	1 282	20 067	4 307.5	486.9
Salinas	28 960	139	25.2	159	2 031	1 588.9	111.7	507	7 654	1 933.2	194.9
San Bernardino	9 454	86	7.0	142	2 655	2 265.4	96.8	592	10 661	2 845.1	268.5
San Bruno	0	0	0.0	23	224	340.5	9.9	133	2 403	512.7	53.7
San Buenaventura (Ventura)	19 286	175	10.3	179	1 885	747.8	91.9	568	7 907	1 980.7	201.9
San Carlos	0	0	0.0	101	933	455.6	55.6	148	1 669	494.5	51.8
San Clemente	21 994	47	95.7	162	2 010	914.9	107.7	197	2 185	580.7	56.7
San Diego	201 346	1 076	51.8	1 902	33 209	21 927.7	3 017.4	4 368	65 695	16 525.8	1 687.8
San Dimas	188	1	100.0	81	570	371.3	25.4	116	2 583	542.0	53.3

1. Merchant wholesalers except manufacturers' sales branches and offices.   2. Establishments with payroll.

Table D. Cities — **Real Estate, Professional Services, and Manufacturing**

City	Real estate and rental and leasing, 2007				Professional, scientific, and technical services,[1] 2007				Manufacturing, 2007			
	Number of establish-ments	Number of employees	Receipts (mil dol)	Annual payroll (mil dol)	Number of establish-ments	Number of employees	Receipts (mil dol)	Annual payroll (mil dol)	Number of establish-ments	Number of employees	Receipts (mil dol)	Annual payroll (mil dol)
	80	81	82	83	84	85	86	87	88	89	90	91
CALIFORNIA—Cont'd												
Menlo Park	95	454	126.4	21.7	307	D	D	D	60	3 102	1 095.0	191.9
Merced	69	374	50.3	9.8	103	D	D	D	35	1 979	605.7	81.5
Milpitas	88	520	167.2	13.8	220	D	D	D	179	16 051	4 831.9	1 432.6
Mission Viejo	186	884	233.6	43.4	408	1 545	232.4	84.2	61	1 038	548.0	66.0
Modesto	235	1 251	245.9	39.0	445	D	D	D	97	6 161	2 924.1	326.1
Monrovia	51	522	106.1	36.3	142	1 940	373.2	132.3	112	2 832	501.9	119.4
Montclair	41	191	38.1	6.3	34	214	17.8	6.7	83	999	177.7	36.4
Montebello	74	524	133.6	20.7	70	983	75.6	18.0	102	6 193	955.2	244.4
Monterey	98	592	79.0	17.6	260	D	D	D	49	836	152.3	38.4
Monterey Park	82	747	59.0	16.7	174	D	D	D	47	895	165.8	35.9
Moorpark	23	102	22.5	4.4	94	318	59.1	17.1	58	3 026	661.5	128.9
Moreno Valley	80	334	73.9	9.5	79	590	37.4	15.2	21	1 255	248.5	45.0
Morgan Hill	82	215	59.0	9.7	145	3 503	132.1	56.7	93	3 607	922.0	216.8
Mountain View	137	738	159.6	27.2	541	15 440	3 164.0	1 548.6	148	6 514	1 751.4	430.6
Murrieta	128	373	72.4	13.9	185	700	92.0	34.9	69	914	124.9	32.5
Napa	99	419	69.7	13.8	247	D	D	D	112	3 299	D	177.9
National City	59	339	76.2	11.0	62	546	42.4	16.1	93	2 215	332.1	78.7
Newark	42	D	D	D	111	1 979	496.8	184.0	78	3 754	954.3	196.3
Newport Beach	702	6 702	3 369.6	519.1	1 294	D	D	D	92	3 369	495.2	167.2
Norco	34	154	25.2	5.3	59	1 004	97.8	35.7	34	630	81.0	28.8
Norwalk	62	364	58.3	10.6	68	D	D	D	60	990	188.2	33.9
Novato	113	721	95.0	23.1	266	D	D	D	57	515	99.6	24.4
Oakland	475	2 942	763.2	112.0	1 442	14 607	2 039.2	1 104.7	407	8 970	1 797.7	387.0
Oakley	20	62	14.0	2.8	24	110	10.7	3.3	NA	NA	NA	NA
Oceanside	163	823	142.3	21.8	297	1 217	134.4	44.5	171	3 973	698.2	138.2
Ontario	194	1 535	680.8	72.8	246	D	D	D	443	17 492	4 945.1	655.4
Orange	299	2 198	485.8	100.3	741	D	D	D	294	8 054	1 721.4	334.9
Oxnard	148	672	128.8	24.9	224	D	D	D	185	11 928	3 490.0	567.8
Pacifica	31	80	14.0	2.1	64	218	30.7	10.3	NA	NA	NA	NA
Palmdale	119	591	66.0	10.5	109	1 048	171.5	53.7	44	5 026	1 277.9	342.5
Palm Desert	180	780	159.4	33.1	312	D	D	D	NA	NA	NA	NA
Palm Springs	151	850	167.7	22.9	186	767	125.7	38.9	32	737	D	D
Palo Alto	193	1 215	917.6	104.4	775	12 475	3 061.8	1 523.5	72	6 530	2 767.7	496.3
Paradise	35	224	16.6	4.5	34	118	10.0	2.7	NA	NA	NA	NA
Paramount	31	231	28.4	6.2	37	251	23.7	8.6	228	4 847	1 554.7	226.4
Pasadena	322	1 812	421.8	93.7	1 182	D	D	D	104	1 467	327.1	71.2
Perris	30	189	34.3	5.7	24	97	14.9	4.4	40	2 894	462.4	104.2
Petaluma	93	463	83.4	17.5	214	D	D	D	115	4 248	1 213.7	206.5
Pico Rivera	45	244	40.6	7.3	34	219	23.7	6.4	77	1 631	434.7	62.4
Pittsburg	39	308	43.7	11.9	46	297	29.6	10.7	45	2 112	1 526.5	138.0
Placentia	59	285	58.0	9.7	115	534	63.6	23.0	134	2 644	478.8	103.9
Pleasant Hill	63	265	78.6	14.8	149	723	109.2	41.5	NA	NA	NA	NA
Pleasanton	189	1 017	360.2	45.0	528	5 335	958.7	409.3	89	2 608	590.2	159.2
Pomona	87	640	125.3	21.7	125	D	D	D	244	7 424	1 829.3	264.4
Porterville	37	124	22.6	3.0	50	229	18.5	5.2	24	1 117	243.3	34.7
Poway	93	490	69.6	19.0	253	1 756	253.1	106.7	103	5 111	1 317.6	256.8
Rancho Cordova	86	470	71.5	16.5	207	D	D	D	93	5 233	1 016.2	296.5
Rancho Cucamonga	235	1 170	244.9	43.5	371	D	D	D	266	9 878	3 182.4	409.2
Rancho Palos Verdes	66	D	D	D	140	1 012	98.3	47.0	NA	NA	NA	NA
Rancho Santa Margarita	72	368	52.3	15.4	197	D	D	D	48	1 846	544.8	100.0
Redding	155	795	90.3	18.3	310	D	D	D	84	929	172.1	34.4
Redlands	99	460	87.2	14.0	214	D	D	D	53	1 234	194.3	42.5
Redondo Beach	117	340	66.6	12.0	298	D	D	D	37	D	D	D
Redwood City	121	915	184.8	37.6	412	D	D	D	79	3 813	985.3	214.3
Rialto	47	190	33.9	5.1	36	225	16.4	7.0	75	2 720	596.0	98.3
Richmond	84	431	85.6	13.3	122	D	D	D	121	4 313	D	250.1
Ridgecrest	22	118	14.9	2.9	56	826	96.7	40.9	NA	NA	NA	NA
Riverside	334	1 953	402.7	66.4	636	D	D	D	303	9 480	2 569.9	380.9
Rocklin	77	D	D	D	156	1 485	242.8	86.0	38	710	143.4	27.8
Rohnert Park	52	320	52.9	14.3	66	403	40.0	18.5	44	968	194.9	45.1
Rosemead	32	99	13.5	2.5	68	278	26.2	7.7	59	1 038	191.4	30.1
Roseville	235	2 824	473.3	103.0	467	4 209	671.5	243.5	69	4 969	2 114.7	176.5
Sacramento	591	4 017	687.3	181.3	1 766	D	D	D	388	11 961	3 985.5	442.8
Salinas	132	613	152.1	18.8	221	D	D	D	102	3 523	1 232.1	124.9
San Bernardino	143	704	112.9	20.1	264	D	D	D	131	3 008	837.0	115.1
San Bruno	33	284	35.7	8.3	69	509	93.1	46.5	NA	NA	NA	NA
San Buenaventura (Ventura)	196	1 134	168.1	32.7	493	D	D	D	162	2 579	457.1	108.9
San Carlos	74	271	74.3	14.4	216	D	D	D	121	2 443	846.7	134.7
San Clemente	122	486	449.9	34.6	372	1 843	270.9	112.3	97	1 844	431.5	86.3
San Diego	2 902	20 071	4 600.7	905.2	7 038	90 341	15 331.3	6 345.2	1 213	45 502	12 989.0	2 520.1
San Dimas	67	560	70.5	14.1	144	1 959	343.6	94.5	85	1 805	1 850.9	74.6

1. Establishments subject to federal tax.

Accommodation and Food Services, Arts, Entertainment, and Recreation, and Health Care and Social Assistance

City	Accommodation and food services, 2007				Arts, entertainment, and recreation,[1] 2007				Health care and social assistance,[1] 2007			
	Number of establish-ments	Number of employees	Sales (mil dol)	Annual payroll (mil dol)	Number of establish-ments	Number of employees	Receipts (mil dol)	Annual payroll (mil dol)	Number of establish-ments	Number of employees	Receipts (mil dol)	Annual payroll (mil dol)
	92	93	94	95	96	97	98	99	100	101	102	103
CALIFORNIA—Cont'd												
Menlo Park	96	1 375	92.0	28.9	21	112	10.0	3.4	111	910	94.0	43.0
Merced	139	2 582	104.9	26.4	9	D	D	D	241	2 195	218.1	80.2
Milpitas	259	4 520	278.8	76.6	23	D	D	D	173	1 390	227.8	62.0
Mission Viejo	187	2 980	148.4	42.3	25	D	D	D	397	D	D	D
Modesto	416	7 813	338.5	95.4	30	585	27.3	7.9	616	10 051	1 245.5	477.3
Monrovia	92	1 770	91.1	25.6	19	D	D	D	75	1 045	155.8	77.7
Montclair	89	1 881	84.3	23.9	5	D	D	D	81	1 379	131.1	52.6
Montebello	124	1 796	97.0	25.0	7	D	D	D	172	D	D	D
Monterey	216	5 359	374.3	113.1	23	D	D	D	277	D	D	D
Monterey Park	162	2 162	109.3	30.2	6	D	D	D	250	3 310	428.0	144.2
Moorpark	51	951	47.0	13.8	11	154	8.9	3.4	25	D	D	D
Moreno Valley	200	3 684	176.0	48.0	9	D	D	D	203	1 559	154.2	54.7
Morgan Hill	103	1 292	70.2	20.0	11	D	D	D	78	D	D	D
Mountain View	278	3 796	275.1	71.6	25	278	30.8	6.1	290	D	D	D
Murrieta	142	2 097	96.1	27.1	28	D	D	D	189	D	D	D
Napa	176	3 429	213.4	63.2	19	265	12.2	3.6	241	2 343	295.7	117.4
National City	175	2 429	132.9	32.8	6	96	8.7	1.9	136	1 301	117.5	38.0
Newark	139	1 956	113.3	30.4	4	D	D	D	65	351	40.5	13.4
Newport Beach	354	10 889	695.8	219.1	99	1 175	123.8	38.7	777	D	D	D
Norco	75	1 125	57.5	14.8	6	D	D	D	32	272	26.0	9.8
Norwalk	137	1 805	89.4	22.3	7	327	11.0	3.8	125	D	D	D
Novato	115	1 834	93.0	26.6	21	D	D	D	146	1 267	174.3	65.0
Oakland	826	11 240	749.5	200.1	77	1 953	350.4	203.5	892	11 401	1 454.0	755.9
Oakley	24	295	15.4	3.5	6	D	D	D	18	D	D	D
Oceanside	294	4 866	243.4	66.3	36	862	57.4	16.3	249	2 099	232.3	78.5
Ontario	309	7 496	417.5	112.7	29	547	45.5	11.0	181	2 562	232.1	86.0
Orange	364	7 252	390.7	102.7	47	D	D	D	603	7 938	945.9	402.6
Oxnard	266	4 962	225.8	58.4	28	542	38.4	11.1	391	3 732	404.5	151.1
Pacifica	70	667	37.1	9.5	11	121	4.6	1.4	40	D	D	D
Palmdale	177	3 649	181.9	50.5	14	D	D	D	158	1 293	128.1	45.3
Palm Desert	196	5 865	321.5	98.0	34	1 171	88.1	27.9	193	1 730	186.4	66.9
Palm Springs	252	4 927	298.3	88.8	31	1 398	221.0	36.7	244	4 290	633.4	200.8
Palo Alto	271	5 585	348.6	107.0	24	458	18.4	6.6	333	D	D	D
Paradise	44	546	21.4	6.7	7	D	D	D	99	D	D	D
Paramount	80	706	41.8	9.6	3	29	2.1	0.5	83	D	D	D
Pasadena	449	10 635	623.8	182.1	137	1 009	107.9	40.3	720	9 243	1 140.8	431.9
Perris	62	906	52.7	11.4	5	D	D	D	40	256	35.6	14.1
Petaluma	169	2 351	132.5	36.0	31	D	D	D	174	1 602	195.5	63.8
Pico Rivera	105	1 467	81.5	20.7	3	D	D	D	73	867	68.2	25.9
Pittsburg	82	1 331	69.9	18.6	3	D	D	D	65	576	48.0	22.1
Placentia	106	1 359	74.3	18.0	9	D	D	D	99	1 365	130.9	51.6
Pleasant Hill	80	1 507	89.3	23.0	15	184	11.5	4.3	109	1 173	88.0	34.7
Pleasanton	230	4 001	242.3	67.8	35	827	59.3	22.5	257	2 449	436.5	135.5
Pomona	202	3 080	165.7	43.7	15	D	D	D	261	3 419	318.8	119.2
Porterville	77	1 176	48.8	13.6	6	D	D	D	132	1 451	113.3	41.5
Poway	109	1 692	81.7	21.8	30	D	D	D	139	D	D	D
Rancho Cordova	136	1 756	95.5	23.6	11	164	9.2	2.1	84	D	D	D
Rancho Cucamonga	315	6 865	341.0	94.7	32	D	D	D	285	3 533	296.7	109.6
Rancho Palos Verdes ...	53	D	D	D	12	D	D	D	99	D	D	D
Rancho Santa Marga-rita	90	1 795	86.1	25.3	23	D	D	D	94	D	D	D
Redding	256	4 780	220.6	59.6	24	D	D	D	467	4 993	487.2	188.5
Redlands	173	3 330	160.5	45.8	22	D	D	D	242	2 509	353.7	106.8
Redondo Beach	188	3 470	196.2	57.0	39	D	D	D	184	1 080	187.4	53.8
Redwood City	226	3 120	214.5	58.0	24	550	33.7	10.5	249	2 861	454.6	206.5
Rialto	96	1 424	68.7	18.1	6	D	D	D	100	967	65.3	24.6
Richmond	128	1 199	64.5	16.6	24	D	D	D	137	2 358	292.7	133.4
Ridgecrest	55	897	45.5	12.1	4	D	D	D	51	D	D	D
Riverside	531	9 412	456.5	129.8	51	830	46.3	12.1	693	11 292	1 314.8	526.5
Rocklin	104	1 631	71.4	21.0	15	D	D	D	119	D	D	D
Rohnert Park	97	1 862	94.9	26.5	13	D	D	D	77	708	81.4	23.3
Rosemead	130	1 733	87.6	24.2	5	130	17.5	2.8	109	D	D	D
Roseville	333	7 021	344.2	97.8	31	839	38.5	11.7	377	5 257	807.8	302.2
Sacramento	1 055	19 705	1 021.4	294.9	90	2 939	327.9	106.1	1 025	13 515	1 875.7	756.7
Salinas	268	3 602	190.0	49.7	12	160	16.9	3.2	289	2 817	332.7	125.4
San Bernardino	343	6 514	330.5	87.1	27	D	D	D	356	4 923	421.0	165.9
San Bruno	104	1 427	83.3	23.0	7	D	D	D	66	648	112.5	26.5
San Buenaventura (Ven-tura)	333	5 799	309.8	87.1	50	764	41.5	11.6	442	3 917	406.7	162.4
San Carlos	87	919	57.2	16.5	8	10	1.6	0.4	90	523	46.9	17.7
San Clemente	158	2 374	122.4	31.1	28	D	D	D	185	981	111.1	37.6
San Diego	3 345	77 459	5 154.5	1 402.6	422	9 206	988.9	403.7	3 258	34 412	4 510.9	1 730.2
San Dimas	69	1 208	64.7	15.1	12	261	31.8	6.6	100	D	D	D

1. Establishments subject to federal tax.

Table D. Cities — Other Services and Federal Funds

City	Other services[1], 2007				Selected federal funds, 2009–2010 (mil dol)								
					Procurement contracts		Grants						
	Number of establishments	Number of employees	Receipts (mil dol)	Annual payroll (mil dol)	Defense	Other	Total[2]	Medicaid and other health related	Nutrition and family welfare	Energy and environment	Disasters and emergency preparedness	Housing and community development	Employment and training
	104	105	106	107	108	109	110	111	112	113	114	115	116
CALIFORNIA—Cont'd													
Menlo Park	60	D	D	D	115.3	390.8	90.9	31.9	0.0	30.5	0.0	0.0	0.0
Merced	67	343	28.9	8.7	0.0	2.4	66.1	12.0	8.7	1.6	0.0	22.0	0.0
Milpitas	99	1 017	172.5	35.0	8.7	31.6	4.8	0.0	0.0	4.0	0.0	0.7	0.0
Mission Viejo	156	972	89.8	24.5	1.7	2.9	4.0	0.0	0.2	0.9	0.0	0.5	0.0
Modesto	258	1 621	130.7	38.0	7.8	3.1	117.6	0.0	43.0	3.8	1.8	61.3	0.0
Monrovia	70	465	71.3	11.1	191.1	3.3	4.4	0.2	0.0	0.0	0.0	0.0	0.0
Montclair	76	D	D	D	1.6	1.4	0.1	0.0	0.0	0.0	0.0	0.1	0.0
Montebello	90	694	48.6	16.3	0.6	13.8	7.1	0.0	0.0	0.6	0.0	0.3	0.0
Monterey	60	484	31.3	11.5	253.3	55.1	15.9	0.0	0.3	1.2	0.0	0.8	0.0
Monterey Park	72	D	D	D	5.2	9.3	496.2	1.1	0.0	0.0	0.0	320.2	0.2
Moorpark	16	110	8.9	2.8	25.9	0.1	2.9	0.0	0.0	0.0	0.0	0.0	0.0
Moreno Valley	120	619	43.7	12.6	0.2	1.1	9.3	0.5	0.0	1.7	0.0	4.4	0.0
Morgan Hill	66	341	35.2	10.8	5.0	0.0	0.0	0.0	0.0	0.0	0.0	0.0	0.0
Mountain View	154	944	113.8	32.0	49.8	89.6	26.5	10.3	0.0	2.8	0.0	1.2	0.0
Murrieta	143	862	78.0	21.9	3.6	0.2	1.3	0.0	0.0	0.9	0.0	0.0	0.0
Napa	127	681	64.3	22.7	24.4	3.9	31.9	0.9	9.1	0.5	0.0	12.2	0.0
National City	119	698	60.9	20.3	8.8	0.9	25.3	0.0	13.9	0.0	0.0	11.1	0.0
Newark	61	D	D	D	0.3	73.4	1.2	0.2	0.0	0.0	0.0	0.0	0.0
Newport Beach	197	1 320	115.4	33.3	10.2	6.1	1.2	0.0	0.0	0.0	0.0	0.9	0.0
Norco	54	309	38.1	8.2	67.4	0.7	8.1	0.0	0.0	0.8	0.0	0.0	0.0
Norwalk	67	338	30.9	7.9	5.7	2.1	16.8	0.0	0.0	0.0	0.0	11.6	0.0
Novato	91	671	86.1	28.5	14.3	8.3	29.1	27.5	0.0	0.4	0.0	0.7	0.0
Oakland	600	3 665	318.9	93.0	156.1	110.4	695.2	171.2	16.7	10.3	-0.2	236.4	7.8
Oakley	22	D	D	D	0.0	12.7	0.1	0.0	0.0	0.0	0.0	0.1	0.0
Oceanside	184	1 195	100.1	30.5	11.3	2.0	55.4	0.0	0.0	0.0	0.0	17.7	0.0
Ontario	212	2 110	192.3	62.0	14.3	4.7	9.0	0.3	0.0	1.5	1.4	4.4	0.0
Orange	289	1 813	158.1	43.5	35.0	4.6	54.7	2.5	0.0	4.6	0.0	2.4	0.0
Oxnard	179	947	91.2	24.9	24.0	40.6	66.6	0.0	11.1	22.5	0.0	25.1	0.0
Pacifica	36	127	10.8	3.2	1.1	0.1	4.4	0.0	0.0	4.4	0.0	0.0	0.0
Palmdale	109	615	48.4	12.0	804.4	5.9	9.3	0.0	0.0	1.2	0.0	3.9	0.2
Palm Desert	118	796	54.3	17.7	0.3	0.4	3.5	0.0	0.0	0.2	0.0	0.9	0.0
Palm Springs	76	372	29.7	9.6	5.8	4.0	2.8	0.1	0.1	0.5	0.0	0.5	0.0
Palo Alto	102	974	86.7	30.2	115.2	300.6	153.1	29.2	0.0	16.6	0.0	1.1	0.0
Paradise	37	121	13.5	3.0	0.0	0.0	1.9	0.0	0.0	0.0	0.0	0.2	0.0
Paramount	65	684	80.6	26.6	1.2	0.3	4.0	0.0	0.0	0.3	0.0	3.7	0.0
Pasadena	305	2 180	374.8	77.3	71.5	25.2	357.5	123.7	11.5	39.8	0.0	20.1	10.0
Perris	29	D	D	D	0.4	2.7	11.7	0.0	0.0	11.6	0.0	0.0	0.0
Petaluma	104	543	48.1	15.2	8.8	16.5	11.5	1.3	0.0	3.6	0.0	0.6	0.0
Pico Rivera	69	685	56.6	17.2	1.1	0.0	9.1	0.0	0.0	0.0	0.0	6.6	0.0
Pittsburg	61	347	31.0	9.1	-0.6	0.2	17.9	0.6	0.0	0.0	0.0	16.7	0.0
Placentia	69	419	32.3	9.7	6.0	4.5	58.8	0.0	0.0	0.2	0.0	0.0	0.0
Pleasant Hill	43	281	20.5	5.9	0.0	0.0	0.6	0.0	0.0	0.0	0.0	0.2	0.0
Pleasanton	133	834	91.4	29.9	6.0	7.7	6.3	1.4	0.0	3.6	0.0	0.4	0.0
Pomona	148	923	85.0	25.4	11.8	9.8	28.9	5.2	0.0	1.5	0.0	16.3	0.0
Porterville	38	230	17.0	10.4	3.0	8.3	16.4	6.3	0.0	0.7	0.0	5.0	0.1
Poway	91	562	43.2	13.0	1 275.1	29.7	0.2	0.1	0.0	0.0	0.0	0.0	0.0
Rancho Cordova	79	394	34.9	11.2	2 999.6	15.8	82.7	0.5	9.6	42.5	0.0	0.9	0.0
Rancho Cucamonga	209	1 245	150.7	37.9	83.6	3.1	6.3	0.5	0.0	1.6	0.0	2.1	0.0
Rancho Palos Verdes	31	221	31.6	9.1	1.1	0.0	0.4	0.0	0.0	0.4	0.0	0.0	0.0
Rancho Santa Margarita	47	408	27.7	8.1	4.0	0.6	0.3	0.0	0.0	0.0	0.0	0.3	0.0
Redding	195	1 095	90.5	27.9	3.7	18.2	48.4	5.1	11.7	1.7	0.0	15.3	0.0
Redlands	102	606	42.2	12.8	28.0	12.0	4.4	0.5	0.1	1.3	0.0	1.3	0.0
Redondo Beach	124	846	145.3	28.7	815.6	9.2	7.9	0.0	0.0	0.0	0.0	6.6	0.0
Redwood City	123	1 049	247.6	43.6	20.1	22.4	23.7	-0.9	0.1	10.6	0.0	4.7	0.0
Rialto	73	331	41.5	9.9	0.3	0.1	3.2	0.0	0.0	1.5	0.0	1.4	0.0
Richmond	86	406	45.6	13.2	10.3	265.9	26.3	-0.1	0.0	1.2	0.0	23.5	0.5
Ridgecrest	30	150	11.8	3.3	26.4	1.4	1.7	0.0	0.0	0.2	0.0	0.0	0.0
Riverside	396	2 521	214.2	67.0	4.7	29.7	264.7	34.3	37.8	18.0	0.7	103.8	0.0
Rocklin	72	D	D	D	6.6	1.6	0.8	0.0	0.0	0.0	0.0	0.4	0.0
Rohnert Park	50	299	26.6	7.9	0.4	4.9	5.4	0.0	-0.1	1.4	0.0	0.0	0.0
Rosemead	92	374	30.7	6.8	15.5	4.7	66.4	0.0	0.0	65.1	0.0	1.2	0.0
Roseville	172	D	D	D	3.2	3.8	7.3	0.0	0.0	0.0	0.0	5.2	0.0
Sacramento	627	4 186	392.7	116.6	68.3	89.3	9 252.3	776.5	2 433.3	603.2	19.9	274.6	1 167.3
Salinas	157	1 027	103.9	28.1	41.4	4.0	78.4	3.9	12.6	3.7	0.0	44.8	0.0
San Bernardino	209	1 287	113.9	31.6	61.8	18.4	222.1	15.2	35.4	14.9	0.0	96.1	4.4
San Bruno	56	259	31.4	9.4	38.6	10.4	1.2	0.0	0.0	0.2	0.0	0.0	0.0
San Buenaventura (Ventura)	194	1 086	104.6	29.4	36.2	28.0	22.3	0.0	0.0	1.4	0.0	18.6	0.0
San Carlos	95	778	71.7	26.6	14.8	66.7	45.2	0.2	0.3	0.0	0.0	0.0	0.0
San Clemente	86	454	34.0	9.5	9.8	3.9	2.4	0.1	0.0	0.3	0.0	1.7	0.0
San Diego	1 982	13 678	1 183.4	360.3	4 772.4	897.1	2 736.8	1 750.2	83.0	234.4	0.3	321.2	8.8
San Dimas	55	D	D	D	2.3	6.6	0.0	0.0	0.0	0.0	0.0	0.0	0.0

1. Establishments subject to federal tax.   2. Includes program categories not shown separately. State totals include additional categories not allocated by city.

Table D. Cities — **City Government Finances**

City	City government finances, 2007									
	General revenue							General expenditure		
		Intergovernmental		Taxes					Per capita[1] (dollars)	
					Per capita[1] (dollars)					
	Total (mil dol)	Total (mil dol)	Percent from state government	Total (mil dol)	Total	Property	Sales and gross receipts	Total (mil dol)	Total	Capital outlays
	117	118	119	120	121	122	123	124	125	126
CALIFORNIA—Cont'd										
Menlo Park	62.6	3.5	90.6	36.1	1 206	775	412	47.1	1 571	217
Merced	108.6	10.3	68.7	42.9	558	308	238	115.0	1 495	409
Milpitas	143.3	5.0	55.3	78.4	1 174	744	424	156.7	2 347	667
Mission Viejo	76.4	8.9	57.3	58.0	613	378	230	82.3	870	184
Modesto	234.2	22.6	50.1	128.3	629	211	414	231.2	1 134	232
Monrovia	50.8	7.3	94.2	32.8	872	552	311	54.4	1 447	277
Montclair	52.4	5.7	82.3	36.5	1 004	538	462	62.8	1 728	719
Montebello	99.7	18.4	78.0	59.7	959	482	460	71.4	1 146	260
Monterey	88.5	4.3	88.5	43.4	1 525	513	1 004	89.2	3 131	447
Monterey Park	64.6	9.0	56.3	38.3	622	386	230	61.9	1 007	142
Moorpark	39.5	2.0	79.2	22.9	633	351	143	33.0	913	253
Moreno Valley	162.5	16.2	80.0	83.0	440	207	225	141.5	749	94
Morgan Hill	81.5	5.1	43.2	49.5	1 317	940	219	85.1	2 263	1 247
Mountain View	165.0	5.4	80.7	91.7	1 302	765	408	167.2	2 374	524
Murrieta	85.7	8.6	99.9	49.9	551	299	244	140.2	1 548	983
Napa	110.9	18.5	35.5	57.8	779	385	388	101.0	1 360	239
National City	80.9	18.9	31.7	46.8	796	443	347	77.1	1 312	355
Newark	41.0	2.6	89.1	30.6	733	346	374	43.8	1 050	60
Newport Beach	173.5	10.9	85.9	119.9	1 507	931	576	179.5	2 257	532
Norco	48.6	2.9	99.0	27.9	1 036	758	231	57.3	2 128	766
Norwalk	84.6	23.1	40.0	51.2	493	238	253	78.8	760	93
Novato	52.1	3.5	76.9	34.4	660	444	194	53.7	1 030	268
Oakland	1 265.9	166.6	49.0	588.4	1 466	796	439	1 509.3	3 759	1 206
Oakley	36.9	2.3	70.0	21.2	696	300	146	44.7	1 469	786
Oceanside	237.2	38.5	100.0	102.1	605	386	214	231.7	1 374	188
Ontario	369.2	21.7	80.2	188.9	1 105	553	547	301.1	1 761	313
Orange	157.1	16.7	89.8	104.8	781	430	342	148.7	1 107	283
Oxnard	289.6	27.5	89.2	113.3	613	401	207	350.5	1 897	646
Pacifica	39.2	3.2	97.9	19.6	526	347	170	42.2	1 131	23
Palmdale	174.9	18.7	88.7	125.5	891	473	241	158.1	1 122	131
Palm Desert	210.6	3.5	73.8	133.0	2 621	1 894	713	242.2	4 774	1 985
Palm Springs	157.2	27.1	17.6	80.3	1 677	825	772	153.1	3 195	746
Palo Alto	199.2	6.5	49.6	70.3	1 206	463	642	205.0	3 519	469
Paradise	14.6	3.5	96.6	9.2	348	259	77	17.5	660	172
Paramount	43.9	6.8	77.8	31.3	563	324	236	38.0	683	112
Pasadena	667.4	41.2	70.0	176.7	1 225	558	659	372.0	2 594	619
Perris	79.4	2.4	92.9	48.2	899	395	494	63.2	1 179	350
Petaluma	107.2	9.6	76.3	49.5	900	530	356	154.9	2 842	1 593
Pico Rivera	52.2	12.2	54.3	31.0	489	259	228	52.8	832	48
Pittsburg	129.9	15.0	89.4	67.8	1 085	916	164	170.6	2 729	864
Placentia	36.0	3.6	95.8	24.7	497	291	200	41.8	842	61
Pleasant Hill	30.7	2.2	79.7	24.3	744	372	347	28.0	857	133
Pleasanton	146.5	5.6	81.9	79.8	1 199	771	415	140.9	2 117	362
Pomona	176.5	28.6	37.3	107.9	707	377	316	185.7	1 217	217
Porterville	52.0	7.9	77.1	24.0	466	149	233	46.9	910	206
Poway	106.9	2.7	90.8	67.2	1 379	1 045	298	104.2	2 140	439
Rancho Cordova	76.9	3.5	97.7	62.6	1 027	262	758	59.5	976	300
Rancho Cucamonga	243.3	9.9	82.8	180.5	1 060	797	255	190.1	1 117	196
Rancho Palos Verdes	26.8	2.4	89.8	18.6	449	249	192	24.5	591	92
Rancho Santa Margarita	19.7	2.8	85.7	15.0	302	149	146	17.5	352	91
Redding	184.9	35.8	37.7	71.7	799	400	330	189.2	2 108	861
Redlands	108.3	15.7	70.3	55.0	787	406	374	96.9	1 386	288
Redondo Beach	101.1	6.9	83.1	58.8	878	424	408	99.3	1 482	83
Redwood City	134.3	11.5	89.3	78.5	1 066	608	448	156.8	2 130	603
Rialto	112.6	7.7	73.1	66.6	675	356	315	119.8	1 213	406
Richmond	224.2	39.6	32.3	135.1	1 331	744	516	227.8	2 245	363
Ridgecrest	24.6	1.6	96.5	15.0	590	363	222	17.6	691	159
Riverside	412.5	39.4	67.5	226.5	769	421	335	544.4	1 849	677
Rocklin	73.4	8.9	71.5	38.9	754	351	241	79.6	1 542	310
Rohnert Park	63.6	2.1	100.0	31.5	777	527	246	85.2	2 102	457
Rosemead	30.6	3.1	69.2	17.4	318	156	127	25.2	461	79
Roseville	423.8	25.2	79.0	104.8	964	461	494	382.7	3 519	1 569
Sacramento	901.1	92.5	90.2	408.3	887	416	444	1 046.7	2 274	763
Salinas	131.3	19.9	57.6	91.1	635	260	372	125.5	875	185
San Bernardino	266.7	30.8	58.0	146.4	734	339	386	247.6	1 242	125
San Bruno	49.3	2.6	100.0	23.6	591	276	299	56.1	1 402	77
San Buenaventura (Ventura)	131.0	11.2	80.7	74.4	721	305	411	129.0	1 250	213
San Carlos	41.3	3.4	100.0	23.5	871	543	316	37.8	1 401	187
San Clemente	84.9	8.7	63.3	41.3	675	427	236	79.3	1 295	454
San Diego	2 537.8	375.5	42.5	1 242.6	981	532	399	2 069.4	1 634	236
San Dimas	33.6	2.7	64.2	24.0	681	371	305	39.7	1 125	225

1. Based on population estimated as of July 1 of the year shown.

Table D. Cities — **City Government Finances**

City	Public welfare	Highways	Parking facilities	Education	Health and hospitals	Police protection	Sewerage and sanitation	Parks and recreation	Housing and community development	Interest on debt
	127	128	129	130	131	132	133	134	135	136
CALIFORNIA—Cont'd										
Menlo Park	0.0	10.2	1.1	0.0	0.0	23.7	4.1	18.1	11.7	8.0
Merced	0.0	11.1	0.0	0.0	0.3	18.1	12.2	17.1	12.3	2.2
Milpitas	0.0	5.8	0.0	0.0	7.6	12.8	5.4	4.5	35.7	6.0
Mission Viejo	0.0	23.1	0.0	0.0	1.4	15.5	0.0	24.7	5.7	3.1
Modesto	0.0	11.7	0.5	0.0	0.5	23.6	11.7	12.3	10.7	1.9
Monrovia	0.0	6.8	0.0	0.0	2.6	21.7	2.5	19.8	9.3	6.4
Montclair	0.0	7.4	0.0	0.0	1.0	32.2	5.8	2.3	20.7	4.3
Montebello	0.0	6.3	0.0	0.0	0.0	25.7	4.3	17.2	8.5	6.3
Monterey	0.0	19.0	5.5	0.0	0.0	12.4	2.4	17.0	2.7	3.5
Monterey Park	0.0	5.8	0.0	0.0	0.9	21.6	9.6	6.0	11.4	5.2
Moorpark	0.0	19.7	0.0	0.0	0.9	16.2	0.4	8.3	18.4	4.2
Moreno Valley	0.0	18.7	0.0	0.0	3.0	24.5	0.0	9.2	9.6	2.8
Morgan Hill	0.0	9.5	0.0	0.0	0.1	11.2	10.4	8.5	39.1	1.4
Mountain View	0.0	5.5	5.6	0.0	0.0	11.6	15.2	18.4	0.8	1.9
Murrieta	0.0	21.3	0.0	0.0	0.0	12.8	0.0	9.5	6.5	2.7
Napa	0.0	14.7	0.7	0.0	2.5	17.5	16.0	8.9	16.7	2.6
National City	0.0	3.3	0.0	0.0	0.8	24.3	8.0	3.9	24.0	3.8
Newark	0.0	12.4	0.0	0.0	10.0	31.6	0.5	16.9	0.5	1.5
Newport Beach	0.0	7.9	0.0	0.0	3.0	24.5	2.2	22.4	3.2	6.4
Norco	0.0	5.9	0.0	0.0	4.1	20.3	19.4	11.7	16.9	8.0
Norwalk	0.0	19.5	0.5	0.0	6.2	16.1	0.0	10.2	17.2	9.0
Novato	0.0	25.3	0.0	0.0	0.9	22.0	0.0	13.1	5.6	12.4
Oakland	0.0	4.0	0.7	0.0	3.7	12.4	2.3	2.9	7.9	8.4
Oakley	0.0	31.5	0.0	0.0	0.2	12.8	0.0	10.0	18.4	1.9
Oceanside	0.0	7.3	0.4	0.0	0.1	19.5	19.4	6.3	13.6	4.8
Ontario	0.0	6.6	0.0	0.0	0.2	18.7	11.9	10.9	9.7	4.1
Orange	0.0	13.9	0.0	0.0	3.9	23.3	6.6	6.1	12.1	2.3
Oxnard	0.0	10.3	0.2	0.0	0.0	18.8	30.1	13.8	4.5	5.9
Pacifica	0.0	11.4	0.0	0.0	1.1	22.6	18.9	9.0	0.5	2.8
Palmdale	0.0	14.3	0.0	0.0	0.4	11.1	0.0	9.3	33.8	9.4
Palm Desert	0.0	12.5	0.0	0.0	0.5	5.0	0.0	8.2	50.9	9.1
Palm Springs	0.0	4.5	0.2	0.0	0.9	14.5	3.3	16.2	4.9	6.3
Palo Alto	0.0	7.6	0.1	0.0	0.2	10.9	28.5	10.8	0.1	1.3
Paradise	0.0	31.8	0.0	0.0	0.0	24.6	2.1	0.0	2.5	2.0
Paramount	0.0	18.4	0.0	0.0	0.0	26.2	0.0	12.1	15.9	7.2
Pasadena	0.0	8.4	2.5	0.0	4.6	14.3	3.5	7.3	5.9	11.1
Perris	0.0	18.0	0.0	0.0	0.7	8.4	2.5	7.6	10.8	15.0
Petaluma	0.0	17.2	0.0	0.0	1.9	10.2	40.3	4.3	12.3	3.1
Pico Rivera	0.0	19.4	0.0	0.0	0.0	17.2	0.0	12.1	24.4	7.1
Pittsburg	0.0	12.9	0.0	0.0	0.5	8.3	2.7	2.2	52.8	11.7
Placentia	0.0	11.7	0.0	0.0	0.0	30.0	7.2	8.5	6.5	8.0
Pleasant Hill	0.0	24.8	0.0	0.0	0.4	37.1	0.3	0.0	12.3	3.1
Pleasanton	0.0	9.6	0.0	0.0	1.2	18.3	8.0	17.4	0.8	3.7
Pomona	0.0	10.8	0.0	0.0	0.2	30.3	6.9	3.6	23.0	6.3
Porterville	0.0	7.5	0.1	0.0	0.3	15.7	27.8	9.5	4.6	5.7
Poway	0.0	10.5	0.0	0.0	0.2	8.8	7.1	6.1	18.7	18.1
Rancho Cordova	0.0	2.6	0.0	0.0	0.7	23.4	0.0	0.0	5.2	1.9
Rancho Cucamonga	0.0	19.7	0.0	0.0	1.4	12.5	0.5	4.0	17.0	13.1
Rancho Palos Verdes	0.0	12.0	0.0	0.0	1.3	12.8	1.5	10.3	1.4	5.7
Rancho Santa Margarita	0.0	35.2	0.0	0.0	0.2	33.5	0.0	10.0	0.0	0.0
Redding	0.0	1.3	0.0	0.0	0.3	12.5	18.8	10.1	10.5	3.2
Redlands	0.0	10.2	0.0	0.0	3.6	25.2	18.3	7.7	4.9	2.0
Redondo Beach	0.0	7.6	0.0	0.0	4.0	25.8	5.7	5.3	7.6	2.5
Redwood City	0.0	12.6	1.3	0.0	0.5	17.4	10.6	6.1	6.7	4.5
Rialto	0.0	7.6	0.0	0.0	3.2	19.0	11.2	7.7	26.9	5.1
Richmond	0.0	16.7	0.0	0.0	0.5	19.4	4.8	6.9	21.7	7.8
Ridgecrest	0.0	27.3	0.0	0.0	0.0	34.0	5.4	12.4	7.3	2.5
Riverside	0.0	12.1	0.6	0.0	0.0	15.4	6.9	6.7	9.5	4.2
Rocklin	0.0	8.3	0.0	0.0	0.0	16.1	0.0	19.3	8.8	6.4
Rohnert Park	0.0	4.8	0.0	0.0	1.2	29.1	15.6	7.0	15.0	0.9
Rosemead	0.0	15.3	0.0	0.0	0.1	19.7	0.0	0.3	23.5	6.0
Roseville	0.0	29.4	0.0	0.0	0.0	7.7	17.9	7.0	5.8	7.3
Sacramento	0.0	11.8	1.4	0.0	1.5	12.6	8.3	9.0	5.5	10.7
Salinas	0.0	16.5	1.0	0.0	2.9	30.7	3.4	8.0	3.3	2.5
San Bernardino	0.0	9.0	0.0	0.0	1.2	23.4	17.2	3.4	6.9	6.5
San Bruno	0.0	7.3	0.0	0.0	0.0	18.0	16.2	7.4	1.3	0.8
San Buenaventura (Ventura)	0.0	13.5	0.0	0.0	0.9	24.3	9.9	11.0	2.3	2.7
San Carlos	0.0	6.0	0.0	0.0	0.0	20.3	13.0	13.4	7.7	2.9
San Clemente	0.0	18.3	0.0	0.0	2.4	12.7	18.8	19.8	1.2	2.3
San Diego	0.0	6.7	0.1	0.0	2.4	18.1	15.1	8.9	16.4	6.8
San Dimas	0.0	13.5	0.1	0.0	0.3	25.4	0.1	8.5	16.9	3.2

Table D. Cities — City Government Finances, City Government Employment, and Climate

	City government finances, 2007 (cont.)				Climate[2]						
	Debt outstanding				Average daily temperature (degrees Fahrenheit)						
					Mean		Limits				
City	Total (mil dol)	Per capita[1] (dollars)	Debt issued during year	City government employment, 2010	January	July	January[3]	July[4]	Annual precipitation (inches)	Heating degree days	Cooling degree days
	137	138	139	140	141	142	143	144	145	146	147
CALIFORNIA—Cont'd											
Menlo Park	93.0	3 103	0.0	NA	49.0	68.0	40.4	78.8	15.71	2 584	452
Merced	69.2	901	0.0	504	46.3	78.6	37.5	96.5	12.50	2 602	1 578
Milpitas	309.2	4 631	26.2	424	50.5	70.9	41.7	84.3	15.08	2 171	811
Mission Viejo	58.9	623	0.2	188	56.7	72.4	47.2	82.3	14.03	1 465	1 183
Modesto	247.7	1 214	37.3	1 198	47.2	77.7	40.1	93.6	13.12	2 358	1 570
Monrovia	82.9	2 206	19.5	NA	56.1	75.3	44.3	89.4	21.09	1 398	1 558
Montclair	51.2	1 408	13.4	NA	54.6	73.8	41.5	88.7	16.96	1 727	1 191
Montebello	83.7	1 344	8.9	NA	58.8	76.6	47.9	88.9	14.44	949	1 837
Monterey	71.7	2 519	0.0	NA	51.6	60.2	43.4	68.1	20.35	3 092	74
Monterey Park	75.3	1 224	2.6	NA	56.3	75.6	42.6	89.0	18.56	1 295	1 575
Moorpark	30.1	832	11.7	NA	54.7	68.3	41.2	80.7	18.41	1 911	602
Moreno Valley	67.4	357	0.5	673	54.2	77.4	42.0	93.5	10.67	1 674	1 697
Morgan Hill	39.7	1 056	1.8	NA	43.5	70.7	37.5	78.2	23.73	4 566	747
Mountain View	78.4	1 112	0.0	NA	49.0	68.0	40.4	78.8	15.71	2 584	452
Murrieta	74.0	817	0.0	347	52.2	79.6	38.3	98.1	12.09	1 924	1 874
Napa	85.8	1 156	47.4	NA	47.9	68.6	39.2	82.6	26.46	2 689	529
National City	62.0	1 054	0.0	NA	57.3	70.1	46.1	76.1	9.95	1 321	862
Newark	14.5	347	0.0	NA	49.8	68.0	42.0	78.3	14.85	2 367	530
Newport Beach	301.2	3 786	0.0	856	55.9	67.3	48.2	71.4	11.65	1 719	543
Norco	147.5	5 480	0.0	NA	NA	NA	NA	NA	NA	NA	NA
Norwalk	158.1	1 524	2.5	360	57.0	73.8	46.0	82.9	12.94	1 211	1 186
Novato	216.7	4 160	5.4	224	48.8	67.7	41.3	80.9	34.29	2 621	451
Oakland	2 810.4	7 000	230.1	3 563	50.9	64.9	44.7	72.7	22.94	2 400	377
Oakley	16.5	543	8.5	NA	45.7	74.4	37.8	90.7	13.33	2 714	1 179
Oceanside	313.7	1 861	0.7	999	54.7	67.6	45.4	72.1	11.13	2 009	505
Ontario	292.8	1 713	0.0	1 069	54.6	73.8	41.5	88.7	16.96	1 727	1 191
Orange	122.2	910	0.0	723	58.0	72.9	46.6	82.7	13.84	1 153	1 299
Oxnard	454.3	2 459	44.7	1 550	55.6	65.9	45.5	72.7	15.62	1 936	403
Pacifica	47.4	1 271	0.0	NA	49.4	62.8	42.9	71.1	20.11	2 862	142
Palmdale	252.0	1 789	38.0	300	46.6	81.7	34.3	97.5	7.36	2 704	1 998
Palm Desert	598.6	11 799	334.9	NA	56.8	92.8	42.0	107.1	3.15	903	4 388
Palm Springs	181.4	3 787	2.0	NA	57.3	92.1	44.2	108.2	5.23	951	4 224
Palo Alto	51.5	884	0.0	965	49.0	68.0	40.4	78.8	15.71	2 584	452
Paradise	6.3	240	1.5	NA	45.7	77.8	37.7	91.7	56.20	3 145	1 464
Paramount	61.7	1 109	0.0	NA	57.0	73.8	46.0	82.9	12.94	1 211	1 186
Pasadena	679.0	4 735	21.6	1 939	56.1	75.3	44.3	89.4	21.09	1 398	1 558
Perris	299.6	5 591	68.3	NA	51.2	78.3	36.1	97.8	11.40	2 123	1 710
Petaluma	183.7	3 371	108.8	NA	48.4	67.3	38.9	82.7	25.85	2 741	385
Pico Rivera	154.3	2 433	1.2	NA	58.3	74.2	48.5	83.8	15.14	928	1 506
Pittsburg	598.2	9 570	208.7	NA	45.7	74.4	37.8	90.7	13.33	2 714	1 179
Placentia	54.6	1 099	0.0	NA	58.0	72.9	46.6	82.7	13.84	1 153	1 299
Pleasant Hill	32.0	979	0.0	NA	46.3	71.2	38.8	87.4	19.58	2 757	786
Pleasanton	139.6	2 097	3.1	NA	47.2	72.0	37.4	89.1	14.82	2 755	858
Pomona	290.7	1 905	60.9	770	54.6	73.8	41.5	88.7	16.96	1 727	1 191
Porterville	62.3	1 208	0.0	NA	48.7	82.8	39.4	98.1	11.49	2 053	2 246
Poway	317.8	6 524	25.1	NA	55.3	70.9	43.5	80.8	11.97	1 808	979
Rancho Cordova	27.7	455	0.3	NA	48.2	77.4	41.3	93.8	19.87	2 226	1 597
Rancho Cucamonga	521.2	3 061	58.3	674	56.6	78.3	45.3	95.0	14.77	1 364	1 901
Rancho Palos Verdes	22.4	540	1.2	NA	56.3	69.4	46.2	77.6	14.79	1 526	742
Rancho Santa Margarita	0.0	0	0.0	NA	56.7	72.4	47.2	82.3	14.03	1 465	1 183
Redding	286.3	3 189	39.7	823	45.5	81.3	35.5	98.5	33.52	2 961	1 741
Redlands	74.5	1 065	0.0	NA	52.9	78.0	40.4	94.4	13.62	1 904	1 714
Redondo Beach	69.8	1 041	0.0	528	57.1	69.3	48.6	75.3	13.15	1 274	679
Redwood City	212.4	2 886	15.2	NA	48.4	68.0	39.1	80.8	20.16	2 764	422
Rialto	179.2	1 816	25.0	445	54.4	79.6	41.8	96.0	16.43	1 599	1 937
Richmond	485.0	4 781	0.0	858	50.0	62.7	42.9	70.5	23.35	2 720	184
Ridgecrest	18.6	730	0.0	NA	NA	NA	NA	NA	NA	NA	NA
Riverside	1 286.2	4 368	301.0	2 218	55.3	78.7	42.7	94.1	10.22	1 475	1 863
Rocklin	102.2	1 980	15.9	NA	46.9	77.7	39.2	94.8	24.61	2 532	1 528
Rohnert Park	95.2	2 349	63.1	NA	48.7	67.6	39.5	82.2	31.01	2 694	526
Rosemead	37.5	687	24.2	NA	56.3	75.6	42.6	89.0	18.56	1 295	1 575
Roseville	972.8	8 945	208.9	1 191	46.9	77.7	39.2	94.8	24.61	2 532	1 528
Sacramento	1 724.6	3 747	278.3	4 996	46.3	75.4	38.8	92.4	17.93	2 666	1 248
Salinas	53.1	370	0.0	616	51.2	63.2	41.3	71.3	12.91	2 770	210
San Bernardino	395.7	1 985	8.1	1 553	54.4	79.6	41.8	96.0	16.43	1 599	1 937
San Bruno	8.7	218	0.0	259	49.4	62.8	42.9	71.1	20.11	2 862	142
San Buenaventura (Ventura)	98.8	957	0.4	681	55.6	65.9	45.5	72.7	15.62	1 936	403
San Carlos	29.6	1 097	0.0	NA	48.4	68.0	39.1	80.8	20.16	2 764	422
San Clemente	29.7	485	0.0	NA	55.4	68.7	43.9	77.3	13.56	1 756	666
San Diego	3 103.5	2 450	501.5	10 173	57.8	70.9	49.7	75.8	10.77	1 063	866
San Dimas	41.5	1 177	0.0	NA	54.6	73.8	41.5	88.7	16.96	1 727	1 191

1. Based on the population estimated as of July 1 of the year shown.　2. Represents normal values based on the 30-year period, 1971–2000.　3. Average daily minimum.　4. Average daily maximum.

Table D. Cities — **Land Area and Population**

STATE Place code	City	Land area,[1] 2010 (sq km)	Population, 2010 Total persons	Rank	Per square kilometer	Race alone or in combination, not of Hispanic origin (percent), 2010 White	Black	American Indian, Alaska Native	Asian	Hawaiian Pacific Islander	Percent Hispanic or Latino[2], 2010	Percent Foreign born, 2008–2010
		1	2	3	4	5	6	7	8	9	10	11
	CALIFORNIA—Cont'd											
06 67000	San Francisco	121.4	805 235	13	6 632.9	44.6	6.7	0.8	35.2	0.7	15.1	35.5
06 67042	San Gabriel	10.7	39 718	991	3 701.6	12.4	1.0	0.3	61.5	0.2	25.7	55.6
06 67112	San Jacinto	66.6	44 199	887	663.6	37.1	7.2	1.7	3.7	0.4	52.3	22.5
06 68000	San Jose	457.2	945 942	10	2 069.0	30.9	3.4	0.7	33.7	0.7	33.2	38.5
06 68028	San Juan Capistrano	36.6	34 593	1 165	946.2	57.3	0.6	0.8	3.7	0.3	38.7	23.8
06 68084	San Leandro	34.6	84 950	369	2 458.0	29.5	13.0	0.9	31.2	1.2	27.4	32.2
06 68154	San Luis Obispo	33.1	45 119	873	1 363.5	78.4	1.5	1.0	6.8	0.4	14.7	9.3
06 68196	San Marcos	63.1	83 781	380	1 327.3	51.3	2.8	0.7	10.8	0.7	36.6	23.3
06 68252	San Mateo	31.4	97 207	302	3 093.8	49.5	2.7	0.5	21.2	2.7	26.6	32.0
06 68294	San Pablo	6.8	29 139	1 413	4 272.6	11.4	16.4	0.8	15.9	0.9	56.5	45.3
06 68364	San Rafael	42.7	57 713	639	1 352.9	61.3	2.4	0.7	7.5	0.4	30.0	28.5
06 68378	San Ramon	46.8	72 148	469	1 542.3	52.1	3.4	0.6	38.7	0.6	8.7	29.8
06 69000	Santa Ana	70.6	324 528	57	4 594.8	9.8	1.1	0.3	10.8	0.3	78.2	49.1
06 69070	Santa Barbara	50.4	88 410	348	1 753.5	56.5	1.7	0.9	4.4	0.2	38.0	24.1
06 69084	Santa Clara	47.7	116 468	227	2 443.2	38.9	3.2	0.6	40.1	0.9	19.4	39.8
06 69088	Santa Clarita	136.5	176 320	135	1 291.4	58.4	3.6	0.7	9.9	0.4	29.5	20.8
06 69112	Santa Cruz	33.0	59 946	606	1 816.5	70.3	2.5	1.4	9.7	0.5	19.4	11.7
06 69196	Santa Maria	58.9	99 553	289	1 689.1	22.8	1.5	0.7	5.4	0.3	70.4	35.2
06 70000	Santa Monica	21.8	89 736	342	4 118.2	73.3	4.6	0.7	11.2	0.3	13.1	23.8
06 70042	Santa Paula	11.9	29 321	1 404	2 466.0	19.1	0.4	0.7	0.8	0.1	79.5	31.3
06 70098	Santa Rosa	107.0	167 815	141	1 569.1	62.3	3.1	1.9	6.3	0.7	28.6	20.2
06 70224	Santee	42.1	53 413	711	1 270.2	76.8	2.7	1.3	5.5	1.0	16.3	8.9
06 70280	Saratoga	32.1	29 926	1 365	933.1	54.3	0.6	0.3	43.9	0.3	3.5	35.9
06 70742	Seaside	23.9	33 025	1 236	1 380.6	36.0	9.8	1.2	12.2	2.3	43.4	30.5
06 72016	Simi Valley	107.4	124 237	208	1 156.4	65.4	1.8	1.0	10.9	0.4	23.3	20.0
06 72520	Soledad	11.4	25 738	1 611	2 251.8	13.8	11.2	0.7	3.0	0.4	71.1	31.3
06 73080	South Gate	18.7	94 396	313	5 037.1	3.6	0.7	0.2	0.7	0.1	94.8	45.1
06 73220	South Pasadena	8.8	25 619	1 618	2 904.6	46.9	3.6	0.4	33.6	0.2	18.6	28.4
06 73262	South San Francisco.....	23.7	63 632	553	2 688.3	24.2	2.9	0.6	38.5	2.5	34.0	44.2
06 73962	Stanton	8.2	38 186	1 034	4 679.7	23.1	2.2	0.6	23.9	0.8	50.8	43.8
06 75000	Stockton	159.7	291 707	65	1 826.4	25.3	12.8	1.3	22.6	1.0	40.3	26.5
06 75630	Suisun City	10.6	28 111	1 467	2 644.5	34.3	22.5	1.6	22.4	2.5	24.0	23.9
06 77000	Sunnyvale....................	57.0	140 081	179	2 459.7	37.1	2.3	0.6	43.1	0.7	18.9	43.2
06 78120	Temecula.....................	78.1	100 097	282	1 281.8	60.4	4.8	1.2	11.8	0.7	24.7	15.5
06 78148	Temple City	10.4	35 558	1 130	3 428.9	24.0	0.9	0.3	56.7	0.3	19.3	44.8
06 78582	Thousand Oaks	142.5	126 683	199	888.8	72.6	1.6	0.6	10.4	0.3	16.8	19.3
06 80000	Torrance	53.0	145 438	169	2 742.0	45.7	3.2	0.6	37.2	0.8	16.1	30.3
06 80238	Tracy	57.0	82 922	385	1 455.0	39.8	8.0	1.1	17.1	1.4	36.9	25.5
06 80644	Tulare	54.2	59 278	618	1 093.5	36.4	3.9	1.2	2.5	0.3	57.5	22.3
06 80812	Turlock.......................	43.8	68 549	495	1 563.6	55.3	2.0	1.1	7.0	0.8	36.4	26.1
06 80854	Tustin.........................	28.7	75 540	444	2 632.1	37.0	2.5	0.5	21.9	0.6	39.7	34.6
06 80994	Twentynine Palms.........	153.2	25 048	1 661	163.5	64.6	9.6	2.1	5.7	2.0	20.8	6.5
06 81204	Union City....................	50.4	69 516	491	1 378.7	17.7	6.9	0.6	54.3	2.0	22.9	44.8
06 81344	Upland........................	40.5	73 732	461	1 822.8	45.9	7.5	0.7	9.4	0.4	38.0	18.3
06 81554	Vacaville.....................	73.5	92 428	323	1 257.9	58.9	11.5	1.6	8.3	1.1	22.9	12.6
06 81666	Vallejo........................	79.4	115 942	229	1 459.5	28.3	23.7	1.5	27.1	1.8	22.6	27.7
06 82590	Victorville....................	189.5	115 903	230	611.5	30.6	17.7	1.5	4.8	0.6	47.8	15.6
06 82954	Visalia........................	93.9	124 442	206	1 325.5	45.9	2.2	1.4	5.9	0.2	46.0	14.2
06 82996	Vista	48.4	93 834	317	1 939.5	43.0	3.8	0.9	5.5	1.1	48.4	26.1
06 83332	Walnut........................	23.3	29 172	1 411	1 252.6	13.9	3.0	0.3	65.0	0.5	19.1	48.0
06 83346	Walnut Creek	51.2	64 173	551	1 254.1	76.6	2.1	0.6	14.8	0.4	8.6	21.3
06 83542	Wasco........................	24.4	25 545	1 625	1 046.5	14.8	7.2	0.6	0.8	0.0	76.7	27.0
06 83668	Watsonville..................	17.3	51 199	756	2 956.1	14.6	0.6	0.6	3.5	0.1	81.4	43.2
06 84200	West Covina	41.6	106 098	258	2 553.5	16.5	4.5	0.5	26.4	0.3	53.2	34.1
06 84410	West Hollywood	4.9	34 399	1 174	7 034.6	80.4	3.9	0.7	6.8	0.3	10.5	31.1
06 84550	Westminster	26.0	89 701	343	3 446.1	27.4	1.1	0.6	48.7	0.7	23.6	46.4
06 84816	West Sacramento.........	55.5	48 744	799	878.4	51.1	5.5	1.8	12.6	1.9	31.4	22.7
06 85292	Whittier	37.9	85 331	364	2 249.1	29.2	1.1	0.5	4.1	0.2	65.7	20.9
06 85446	Wildomar	61.4	32 176	1 264	524.5	56.1	3.7	1.4	5.7	0.5	35.3	19.1
06 85922	Windsor	18.8	26 801	1 544	1 424.1	63.0	1.2	1.8	4.2	0.5	31.8	13.7
06 86328	Woodland	39.6	55 468	678	1 399.6	43.9	1.7	1.4	7.1	0.5	47.4	21.1
06 86832	Yorba Linda.................	50.5	64 234	549	1 273.0	68.1	1.6	0.6	17.5	0.3	14.4	17.8
06 86972	Yuba City....................	37.8	64 925	542	1 719.4	50.2	3.0	2.1	18.9	0.6	28.4	25.0
06 87042	Yucaipa......................	72.2	51 367	749	711.2	67.8	2.0	1.3	3.5	0.3	27.1	10.8
08 00000	COLORADO..............	268 431.3	5 029 196	X	18.7	71.8	4.5	1.3	3.5	0.2	20.7	9.9
08 03455	Arvada........................	91.0	106 433	256	1 169.3	82.8	1.2	0.9	2.7	0.1	13.7	5.4
08 04000	Aurora........................	400.8	325 078	56	811.2	49.9	17.0	1.3	5.9	0.5	28.7	21.2
08 07850	Boulder.......................	63.9	97 385	301	1 524.5	85.0	1.3	0.8	6.0	0.2	8.7	11.3
08 08675	Brighton	51.8	33 352	1 215	644.4	56.3	1.5	1.1	1.7	0.1	40.5	11.7
08 09280	Broomfield	85.6	55 889	673	653.2	81.1	1.3	0.9	7.1	0.2	11.1	7.6

1. Dry land or land partially or temporarily covered by water.　　2. May be of any race.

Table D. Cities — **Population**

City	Age of population (percent), 2010											Population			
												Census counts		Percent change	
	Under 5 years	5 to 17 years	18 to 24 years	25 to 34 years	35 to 44 years	45 to 54 years	55 to 64 years	65 to 74 years	75 years and over	Median age	Percent female	1990	2000	1990–2000	2000–2010
	12	13	14	15	16	17	18	19	20	21	22	23	24	25	26
CALIFORNIA—Cont'd															
San Francisco	4.4	9.0	9.6	20.9	16.6	13.9	12.0	6.7	6.9	38.5	49.3	723 959	776 733	7.3	3.7
San Gabriel	5.2	14.6	9.0	13.2	15.4	16.5	12.2	6.7	7.3	40.3	51.8	37 120	39 804	7.2	-0.2
San Jacinto	8.8	23.9	10.0	13.9	13.0	11.6	8.2	5.6	5.0	30.3	51.1	17 614	23 779	35.0	85.9
San Jose	7.3	17.6	9.5	15.4	15.8	14.4	10.1	5.6	4.4	35.2	49.7	782 224	894 943	14.4	5.7
San Juan Capistrano	6.2	18.4	8.9	10.6	12.0	14.9	13.4	8.1	7.5	40.2	50.4	26 183	33 826	29.2	2.3
San Leandro.................	6.2	16.1	8.3	13.4	14.2	15.6	12.4	6.5	7.2	39.3	52.0	68 223	79 452	16.5	6.9
San Luis Obispo...........	3.3	8.9	34.7	13.2	8.1	10.1	9.6	5.3	6.8	26.5	47.8	41 958	44 174	5.3	2.1
San Marcos.................	8.4	19.4	11.0	14.4	15.8	12.2	8.7	5.1	5.0	32.9	51.1	38 974	54 977	41.1	52.4
San Mateo....................	6.8	14.1	7.1	15.5	16.1	14.7	11.4	6.7	7.7	38.9	51.2	85 619	92 482	8.0	5.1
San Pablo....................	8.3	20.0	11.1	15.8	14.1	12.9	9.0	4.5	4.3	31.6	50.3	25 158	30 215	20.1	-3.6
San Rafael	6.2	13.1	8.6	14.6	14.7	14.0	13.0	7.5	8.3	40.2	50.1	48 410	56 063	15.8	2.9
San Ramon	7.9	21.7	4.9	11.7	19.9	16.1	10.0	5.1	2.7	37.1	50.9	35 303	44 722	26.7	61.3
Santa Ana...................	8.9	21.8	12.1	16.6	14.9	11.6	7.3	3.9	2.9	29.1	48.9	293 827	337 977	15.0	-4.0
Santa Barbara..............	5.5	13.2	12.2	16.6	13.1	13.0	12.2	6.6	7.6	36.8	50.4	85 571	92 325	7.9	-4.2
Santa Clara	7.8	13.5	10.7	19.8	16.2	12.9	9.1	5.1	4.9	34.1	49.5	93 613	102 361	9.3	13.8
Santa Clarita	6.3	19.9	10.0	12.3	14.9	16.4	10.8	5.4	4.1	36.2	50.7	120 050	151 088	25.9	16.7
Santa Cruz	3.9	9.7	29.1	13.6	11.5	12.0	11.3	4.8	4.1	29.9	49.9	49 711	54 593	9.8	9.8
Santa Maria.................	9.9	21.5	12.2	16.3	12.3	10.8	7.5	4.5	4.9	28.6	49.5	61 552	77 423	25.8	28.6
Santa Monica	4.1	9.9	7.2	19.4	16.9	15.0	12.6	7.4	7.6	40.4	51.8	86 905	84 084	-3.2	6.7
Santa Paula.................	8.7	21.1	11.2	14.3	13.1	11.8	9.3	5.5	5.0	31.1	49.5	25 062	28 598	14.1	2.5
Santa Rosa	6.8	16.6	9.5	15.0	12.8	13.8	12.0	6.4	7.1	36.7	51.2	113 261	147 595	30.3	13.7
Santee	6.6	17.2	9.5	13.7	14.0	16.3	12.0	6.0	4.8	37.2	51.7	52 902	52 975	0.1	0.8
Saratoga	3.3	20.7	4.6	4.2	11.4	21.0	14.4	10.2	10.1	47.8	51.1	28 061	29 843	6.4	0.3
Seaside	8.9	18.1	13.4	16.7	14.1	11.7	8.5	4.3	4.3	30.6	49.9	38 826	31 696	-18.4	4.2
Simi Valley	6.1	18.9	8.9	12.4	14.9	16.5	11.7	6.1	4.5	37.8	50.9	100 218	111 351	11.1	11.6
Soledad	6.1	15.9	9.5	18.6	20.8	16.3	8.1	2.7	1.9	34.9	29.8	13 426	11 263	-16.1	128.5
South Gate..................	8.4	22.7	12.0	15.4	14.3	11.9	8.3	4.2	2.8	29.4	50.9	86 284	96 375	11.7	-2.1
South Pasadena...........	5.2	18.2	6.2	12.7	16.3	17.1	12.2	6.6	5.5	40.1	52.5	23 936	24 292	1.5	5.5
South San Francisco.....	6.2	15.5	8.9	15.0	14.3	15.1	12.0	6.7	6.4	38.1	50.6	54 312	60 552	11.5	5.1
Stanton	7.9	19.7	10.6	14.6	15.0	13.1	9.0	5.2	4.8	33.0	50.5	30 491	37 403	22.7	2.1
Stockton	8.4	21.5	11.7	13.8	12.5	12.1	9.9	5.4	4.6	30.8	51.0	210 943	243 771	15.6	19.7
Suisun City	7.5	20.0	10.5	14.9	13.0	15.0	11.3	4.7	3.0	33.0	50.8	22 704	26 118	15.0	7.6
Sunnyvale....................	8.0	14.4	6.7	19.6	16.7	13.8	9.6	5.8	5.4	35.6	49.6	117 324	131 760	12.3	6.3
Temecula....................	7.0	23.6	9.3	12.0	15.9	15.7	8.7	4.5	3.3	33.4	51.0	27 177	57 716	112.4	73.4
Temple City	4.5	16.7	8.1	10.9	14.4	16.7	13.7	7.9	7.2	42.0	52.5	31 153	33 377	7.1	6.5
Thousand Oaks............	5.2	18.5	8.1	9.8	13.7	17.0	13.0	7.9	6.8	41.5	51.1	104 381	117 005	12.1	8.3
Torrance	5.2	16.7	7.5	11.5	14.8	17.4	12.0	7.3	7.7	41.3	51.4	133 107	137 946	3.6	5.4
Tracy ,,,,,,,,,,,,,,,,,,	8.0	24.2	9.0	12.5	16.2	14.9	8.3	4.0	2.9	32.3	50.4	33 558	56 929	69.6	46.7
Tulare	9.4	23.9	10.5	14.5	12.9	11.5	8.2	4.9	4.2	29.1	50.9	33 249	43 994	32.3	34.7
Turlock,,,,,,,,,,,,,,,	7.5	19.9	11.8	14.1	12.6	12.8	9.6	5.8	5.8	32.5	51.3	42 224	55 810	32.2	22.8
Tustin..........................	7.6	19.2	9.1	16.8	16.4	13.6	8.9	4.8	3.7	33.4	51.4	50 689	67 504	33.2	11.9
Twentynine Palms........	11.1	14.5	30.0	17.4	8.1	7.3	5.8	3.3	2.6	23.5	43.7	11 821	14 764	24.9	69.7
Union City	6.8	17.4	9.3	14.6	14.7	14.2	11.9	6.3	4.8	36.2	50.6	53 762	66 869	24.4	4.0
Upland........................	6.2	18.3	10.2	13.8	13.2	14.5	11.7	6.5	5.5	36.1	51.8	63 374	68 393	7.9	7.8
Vacaville.....................	6.0	17.3	9.7	14.2	14.3	16.7	11.5	5.5	4.9	37.2	47.1	71 476	88 625	24.0	4.3
Vallejo........................	6.5	16.7	10.1	13.4	12.5	15.1	13.6	6.6	5.4	37.9	51.5	109 199	116 760	6.9	-0.7
Victorville	8.9	23.9	10.5	15.0	13.9	12.0	7.7	4.5	3.6	29.5	49.9	50 103	64 029	27.8	81.0
Visalia........................	8.6	21.4	10.0	14.6	12.6	12.5	9.8	5.5	4.8	31.6	51.2	75 659	91 565	21.0	35.9
Vista	8.0	18.8	12.5	16.2	13.2	13.3	8.7	4.3	4.9	31.1	49.8	71 861	89 857	25.0	4.4
Walnut	3.5	17.4	10.6	9.5	11.4	18.7	16.7	7.7	4.5	43.1	51.0	29 105	30 004	3.1	-2.8
Walnut Creek	4.1	12.6	5.6	11.8	11.8	14.1	13.4	10.5	16.1	47.9	53.7	60 569	64 296	6.2	-0.2
Wasco	8.6	20.1	14.4	19.0	14.7	11.4	6.6	3.0	2.1	28.3	38.4	12 412	21 263	71.3	20.1
Watsonville	9.5	22.0	11.7	15.7	13.3	11.4	8.2	4.1	4.2	29.2	50.2	31 099	44 265	42.3	15.7
West Covina................	6.0	18.6	10.7	13.4	13.8	14.2	11.2	6.4	5.7	36.0	51.8	96 226	105 080	9.2	1.0
West Hollywood	1.9	2.7	7.0	26.8	20.4	15.5	10.8	6.7	8.2	40.4	43.8	36 118	35 716	-1.1	-3.7
Westminster................	5.9	17.4	9.6	11.8	15.0	14.6	11.4	7.8	6.4	38.7	50.6	78 293	88 207	12.7	1.7
West Sacramento.........	8.4	18.3	9.1	16.5	14.5	13.1	10.2	5.3	4.5	33.6	50.6	28 898	31 615	9.4	54.2
Whittier.......................	6.7	18.7	10.8	13.3	14.4	14.0	10.4	5.6	6.1	35.4	51.5	77 671	83 680	7.7	2.0
Wildomar	7.1	20.8	10.1	12.5	13.4	15.4	10.0	5.6	5.0	34.6	50.6	10 411	14 064	35.1	128.8
Windsor	6.8	21.2	8.3	11.2	14.3	16.2	11.1	5.5	5.5	37.0	50.9	12 002	22 744	89.5	17.8
Woodland	7.9	19.6	10.0	14.3	13.2	13.6	10.5	5.6	5.3	33.7	50.8	40 230	49 151	22.2	12.9
Yorba Linda.................	4.8	19.8	8.7	8.8	12.7	18.5	14.8	7.0	4.8	41.7	51.3	52 422	58 918	12.4	9.0
Yuba City....................	8.1	20.1	10.2	14.2	12.8	12.8	10.0	6.3	5.4	33.0	50.5	27 385	36 758	34.2	76.6
Yucaipa......................	6.6	19.6	8.7	11.6	12.8	15.5	11.9	6.9	6.4	37.8	50.8	32 819	41 207	25.6	24.7
COLORADO..............	6.8	17.5	9.7	14.4	13.9	14.8	11.9	6.2	4.8	36.1	49.9	3 294 473	4 301 261	30.6	16.9
Arvada........................	5.9	17.5	7.8	11.8	13.4	16.4	13.4	7.6	6.3	40.5	51.2	89 261	102 153	14.4	4.2
Aurora........................	8.4	19.0	9.3	16.2	14.5	13.4	10.4	5.1	3.8	33.2	50.8	222 103	276 393	24.4	17.6
Boulder.......................	4.1	9.8	29.1	16.0	11.7	10.8	9.6	4.6	4.3	28.7	48.7	85 127	94 673	11.2	2.9
Brighton......................	8.6	21.3	8.9	15.7	15.1	12.6	8.9	4.9	3.9	32.2	49.4	14 203	20 905	47.2	59.5
Broomfield	7.1	19.2	7.7	13.9	16.0	15.5	10.8	5.6	4.3	36.4	50.4	24 638	38 272	55.3	46.0

City	Households, 2010 Number [27]	Persons per household [28]	Percent — Female family householder[1] [29]	Percent — One-person [30]	Persons in group quarters, 2010 — Total [31]	Institutional — Total [32]	Persons in nursing facilities [33]	Non-institutional [34]	Serious crimes known to police,[2] 2010 — Total — Number [35]	Total — Rate[3] [36]	Rate[3] — Violent [37]	Rate[3] — Property [38]	Educational attainment, 2008–2010 — Population age 25 and older [39]	Attainment[4] (percent) — High school graduate or less [40]	Attainment[4] (percent) — Bachelor's degree or more [41]
CALIFORNIA—Cont'd															
San Francisco	345 811	2.26	8.3	38.6	24 264	5 362	2 942	18 902	38 112	4 733	714	4 019	615 745	28.5	51.2
San Gabriel	12 542	3.13	15.6	16.9	452	418	395	34	651	1 639	214	1 425	28 637	46.6	28.1
San Jacinto	13 152	3.34	16.1	18.7	228	59	43	169	1 479	3 346	244	3 102	25 136	53.1	11.7
San Jose	301 366	3.09	12.6	19.7	13 322	3 780	2 190	9 542	25 296	2 674	340	2 334	613 578	36.9	36.4
San Juan Capistrano	11 394	3.03	9.6	20.9	87	0	0	87	544	1 573	119	1 454	21 874	34.4	34.3
San Leandro	30 717	2.74	14.7	26.8	650	368	364	282	3 484	4 101	408	3 693	58 397	45.0	25.1
San Luis Obispo	19 193	2.29	7.0	32.4	1 182	215	206	967	1 812	4 016	279	3 737	22 382	22.7	45.5
San Marcos	27 202	3.05	11.2	19.0	844	108	108	736	1 879	2 243	283	1 960	50 390	37.0	30.1
San Mateo	38 233	2.51	10.0	30.7	1 316	341	306	975	2 197	2 260	300	1 960	68 895	29.0	43.3
San Pablo	8 761	3.28	19.6	21.2	441	373	373	68	1 610	5 525	827	4 698	17 801	63.5	12.0
San Rafael	22 764	2.44	8.8	32.7	2 119	805	497	1 314	1 839	3 186	409	2 778	42 003	28.5	46.3
San Ramon	25 284	2.85	7.9	18.5	75	23	0	52	1 010	1 400	49	1 351	46 392	13.7	59.4
Santa Ana	73 174	4.37	16.1	12.6	4 658	3 243	895	1 415	8 090	2 493	465	2 028	183 206	69.0	11.9
Santa Barbara	35 449	2.45	9.7	33.7	1 627	455	375	1 172	2 869	3 245	386	2 859	61 672	29.3	42.8
Santa Clara	43 021	2.63	9.5	25.4	3 196	336	318	2 860	3 198	2 746	156	2 590	77 907	25.5	49.1
Santa Clarita	59 507	2.94	11.6	19.6	1 410	129	111	1 281	3 045	1 727	213	1 514	110 858	31.9	32.0
Santa Cruz	21 657	2.39	8.5	31.3	8 289	379	2	7 910	3 489	5 820	922	4 898	33 039	20.7	51.7
Santa Maria	26 908	3.66	14.7	18.9	1 007	419	263	588	3 090	3 104	774	2 329	54 751	59.5	12.9
Santa Monica	46 917	1.87	7.5	48.4	2 126	827	783	1 299	3 512	3 914	437	3 477	71 124	16.8	62.1
Santa Paula	8 347	3.50	15.2	15.9	133	89	89	44	618	2 108	344	1 763	17 517	59.6	11.6
Santa Rosa	63 590	2.59	12.1	28.3	3 410	1 713	830	1 697	4 863	2 898	457	2 441	109 645	35.8	29.4
Santee	19 306	2.72	13.5	20.6	966	889	274	77	1 112	2 082	286	1 795	35 308	39.8	18.3
Saratoga	10 734	2.77	5.7	16.2	199	165	161	34	287	959	74	886	21 207	6.5	75.9
Seaside	10 093	3.16	14.2	19.1	1 127	0	0	1 127	721	2 183	391	1 793	19 535	45.2	19.8
Simi Valley	41 237	3.00	11.3	17.2	660	178	123	482	2 338	1 882	104	1 778	81 254	33.1	30.6
Soledad	3 664	4.27	16.0	8.2	10 103	10 103	55	0	406	1 577	291	1 286	17 429	75.1	3.2
South Gate	23 278	4.05	20.2	9.8	88	72	72	16	3 201	3 391	634	2 758	54 793	73.9	7.4
South Pasadena	10 467	2.43	12.1	29.4	163	155	151	8	448	1 749	98	1 651	17 818	9.2	65.4
South San Francisco	20 938	3.01	13.8	20.5	579	51	18	528	1 631	2 563	239	2 324	43 223	38.4	30.3
Stanton	10 825	3.50	16.6	18.1	350	258	240	92	799	2 092	409	1 684	23 391	60.0	16.9
Stockton	90 605	3.16	18.9	21.5	5 734	1 838	1 558	3 896	20 210	6 928	1 383	5 546	169 359	50.4	17.0
Suisun City	8 918	3.15	16.6	16.2	44	17	5	27	746	2 654	288	2 366	17 189	35.4	22.6
Sunnyvale	53 384	2.61	8.7	25.2	849	469	457	380	2 396	1 710	121	1 590	99 149	21.0	56.6
Temecula	31 781	3.15	11.8	13.8	129	8	0	121	2 425	2 423	74	2 349	57 821	29.9	30.0
Temple City	11 606	3.03	14.8	17.0	422	393	388	29	491	1 381	172	1 209	24 680	35.8	36.4
Thousand Oaks	45 836	2.73	9.3	21.2	1 742	352	348	1 390	2 175	1 717	110	1 607	83 474	21.7	48.9
Torrance	56 001	2.58	11.0	25.8	1 146	640	578	506	3 149	2 165	199	1 966	101 865	24.9	45.9
Tracy	24 331	3.40	13.1	13.7	316	247	245	69	2 240	2 701	163	2 539	46 732	43.9	20.6
Tulare	17 720	3.33	18.0	16.2	278	216	216	62	3 003	5 066	658	4 408	33 366	57.2	11.7
Turlock	22 772	2.96	13.9	20.9	1 207	520	445	687	3 347	4 883	680	4 203	42 454	48.2	23.6
Tustin	25 203	2.98	13.9	20.5	520	180	150	340	1 695	2 244	169	2 074	46 578	33.2	37.7
Twentynine Palms	8 095	2.68	12.9	21.1	3 347	0	0	3 347	636	2 539	475	2 064	11 050	41.5	16.5
Union City	20 433	3.38	13.5	13.4	518	96	75	422	2 134	3 070	466	2 604	45 751	38.6	38.0
Upland	25 823	2.83	15.6	20.0	682	377	359	305	2 566	3 480	282	3 198	47 324	34.2	28.7
Vacaville	31 092	2.71	13.1	22.7	8 022	7 989	171	33	2 138	2 313	294	2 019	60 306	39.7	20.5
Vallejo	40 559	2.82	17.8	24.3	1 663	533	483	1 130	5 923	5 109	709	4 400	77 487	38.3	23.8
Victorville	32 558	3.40	19.9	15.6	5 103	4 762	294	341	4 355	3 757	588	3 170	61 510	52.0	11.8
Visalia	41 349	2.98	15.7	20.3	1 326	720	408	606	5 912	4 751	464	4 286	73 229	42.8	19.9
Vista	29 317	3.13	13.7	19.7	2 045	1 384	588	661	2 515	2 680	432	2 249	57 556	47.1	21.9
Walnut	8 533	3.41	11.5	7.3	34	12	10	22	476	1 632	99	1 532	19 422	23.5	48.3
Walnut Creek	30 443	2.08	6.8	39.0	1 002	826	826	176	2 487	3 875	179	3 696	49 187	14.5	60.5
Wasco	5 131	3.86	19.3	11.2	5 720	5 710	0	10	NA	NA	NA	NA	14 125	77.3	4.4
Watsonville	13 528	3.75	17.6	18.2	528	206	201	322	1 866	3 645	639	3 006	28 804	66.7	10.9
West Covina	31 596	3.34	17.1	15.2	674	323	299	351	3 297	3 108	300	2 808	66 905	41.7	26.6
West Hollywood	22 511	1.52	3.8	59.7	109	0	0	109	1 934	5 622	1 131	4 491	30 670	19.5	53.7
Westminster	26 164	3.40	14.1	16.2	670	289	197	381	2 798	3 119	289	2 831	59 837	49.6	19.1
West Sacramento	17 421	2.78	14.8	24.5	338	92	82	246	1 517	3 112	353	2 759	31 284	43.3	23.9
Whittier	28 273	2.96	16.1	21.6	1 635	552	434	1 083	2 776	3 253	402	2 851	53 910	40.6	24.0
Wildomar	9 992	3.22	11.8	16.0	42	4	4	38	762	2 368	183	2 185	19 531	44.9	18.1
Windsor	8 970	2.98	10.1	19.4	51	0	0	51	358	1 336	142	1 194	16 777	36.4	23.9
Woodland	18 721	2.91	14.1	21.9	985	829	323	156	1 674	3 018	290	2 728	34 614	43.6	23.6
Yorba Linda	21 576	2.97	8.5	14.5	190	93	93	97	862	1 342	90	1 252	42 213	17.8	45.6
Yuba City	21 550	2.99	13.8	22.1	580	455	247	125	1 999	3 079	333	2 746	39 542	44.7	20.4
Yucaipa	18 231	2.79	12.2	23.0	554	327	242	227	944	1 838	271	1 567	33 076	37.0	22.8
COLORADO	1 972 868	2.49	10.1	27.9	115 878	61 591	18 079	54 287	151 125	3 005	321	2 684	3 268 020	33.2	36.2
Arvada	42 701	2.48	10.7	26.3	506	343	314	163	2 855	2 682	128	2 555	73 388	31.9	33.4
Aurora	121 901	2.65	14.2	27.7	2 556	1 850	1 145	706	11 505	3 539	446	3 093	202 182	41.7	25.7
Boulder	41 302	2.16	5.5	35.8	8 105	1 080	531	7 025	2 932	3 011	216	2 795	55 354	12.1	69.7
Brighton	10 788	2.95	12.5	20.9	1 546	1 518	197	28	1 262	3 784	207	3 577	20 651	49.9	18.7
Broomfield	21 414	2.60	8.0	23.9	282	279	207	3	1 208	2 161	75	2 086	35 868	24.4	44.0

1. No spouse present. 2. Data for serious crimes have not been adjusted for underreporting. This may affect comparability between geographic areas and over time. 3. Per 100,000 population estimated by the FBI. 4. Persons 25 years old and over.

City	Money income, 2008–2010				Housing units, 2010			Occupied Housing units 2008–2010				
		Households							Owner-occupied		Median owner costs as a percent of income	
	Per capita income[1] (dollars)	Median income	Percent with income of $200,000 or more	Percent with income of less than $25,000	Families with income below poverty (percent)	Total	Percent change, 2000–2010	Vacant units for sale or rent[2]	Total	Percent	Median value[3] (dollars)	With a mortgage[4]	Without a mortgage[5]
	42	43	44	45	46	47	48	49	50	51	52	53	54
CALIFORNIA—Cont'd													
San Francisco	45 078	71 779	12.0	21.3	7.4	376 942	8.8	31 131	336 613	37.0	773 600	30.0	10.0
San Gabriel	24 971	57 463	5.4	23.1	9.8	13 237	3.0	695	12 189	49.4	562 900	29.1	10.6
San Jacinto	17 765	47 837	1.5	26.3	11.9	14 977	58.7	1 825	12 657	70.7	162 100	34.0	14.4
San Jose	32 237	78 149	10.0	15.1	8.2	314 038	11.5	12 672	299 480	58.9	598 600	30.8	10.0
San Juan Capistrano	38 764	75 628	12.7	15.9	8.1	11 940	5.3	546	11 127	76.0	618 900	36.2	13.5
San Leandro	26 658	58 978	2.6	20.1	7.0	32 419	3.6	1 702	29 783	56.6	413 500	33.9	10.9
San Luis Obispo	25 400	42 461	3.3	33.2	7.1	20 553	6.3	1 360	18 931	38.2	562 600	26.8	10.0
San Marcos	24 697	55 264	4.8	18.6	7.5	28 641	51.5	1 439	26 268	61.4	389 700	33.7	14.4
San Mateo	44 128	85 758	12.0	11.8	4.2	40 014	4.7	1 781	37 732	54.2	738 900	31.1	10.7
San Pablo	17 314	43 506	0.2	28.9	17.6	9 571	2.5	810	8 520	48.0	239 800	39.1	10.2
San Rafael	42 276	71 841	11.3	15.5	5.8	24 011	4.6	1 247	23 669	53.1	771 200	30.3	10.0
San Ramon	48 237	117 866	19.2	5.5	2.5	26 222	50.5	938	24 489	71.7	720 500	29.6	10.7
Santa Ana	15 774	53 266	1.9	18.7	16.8	76 896	3.3	3 722	71 944	48.0	356 300	33.3	10.0
Santa Barbara	36 183	61 937	7.1	20.4	9.7	37 820	1.7	2 371	35 015	41.5	923 600	32.7	10.7
Santa Clara	38 691	87 187	10.1	14.4	5.8	45 147	14.0	2 126	42 602	45.2	630 500	28.4	10.0
Santa Clarita	32 502	81 210	6.7	13.2	5.2	62 055	18.3	2 548	58 495	70.5	413 100	30.5	12.6
Santa Cruz	29 430	59 155	7.6	26.0	6.8	23 316	8.6	1 659	21 171	46.1	696 300	29.5	10.1
Santa Maria	18 132	50 216	1.9	22.4	14.8	28 294	24.0	1 386	26 443	51.3	283 200	31.3	12.5
Santa Monica	55 473	67 438	12.1	21.1	5.5	50 912	6.4	3 995	45 987	28.3	984 400	29.2	12.2
Santa Paula	20 130	51 621	4.0	25.2	13.2	8 749	4.5	402	8 428	53.1	358 500	33.2	12.8
Santa Rosa	28 817	57 334	4.6	21.0	8.6	67 396	17.2	3 806	62 560	54.4	405 600	30.4	13.1
Santee	26 330	66 029	1.8	14.4	5.9	20 048	6.6	742	17 795	71.1	341 000	31.9	12.7
Saratoga	66 438	146 942	37.1	7.6	2.4	11 123	4.3	389	10 510	85.1	1 000 000	31.0	10.2
Seaside	22 586	60 047	2.6	16.0	8.6	10 872	-1.2	779	10 105	46.4	483 900	36.0	10.0
Simi Valley	33 802	84 321	8.1	11.1	5.7	42 506	13.9	1 269	40 763	73.0	481 500	31.1	10.5
Soledad	9 810	44 343	1.7	22.3	15.4	3 876	52.4	212	3 837	57.9	242 400	37.3	10.0
South Gate	13 883	40 809	0.8	27.9	20.6	24 160	-0.5	882	24 254	43.1	327 600	37.1	10.0
South Pasadena	44 915	80 892	12.4	13.6	6.0	11 118	2.5	651	10 641	45.6	823 100	29.0	10.0
South San Francisco	30 606	72 674	6.6	12.6	3.9	21 814	8.2	876	21 066	60.3	627 500	32.7	10.0
Stanton	19 201	48 823	2.0	20.4	15.3	11 283	3.1	458	11 256	45.8	291 600	30.4	10.4
Stockton	19 321	46 209	2.0	27.0	18.2	99 637	21.3	9 032	90 957	52.1	204 700	32.0	10.2
Suisun City	25 315	71 435	2.0	10.6	6.8	9 454	16.0	536	8 703	73.0	278 400	30.7	11.2
Sunnyvale	43 937	90 701	12.3	11.6	4.0	55 791	3.8	2 407	53 929	49.0	706 000	28.4	10.0
Temecula	27 706	72 433	4.9	14.4	7.2	34 004	78.8	2 223	30 543	68.6	327 400	33.1	12.0
Temple City	25 170	61 472	4.1	16.0	8.1	12 117	3.5	511	11 162	61.6	569 000	31.4	10.4
Thousand Oaks	44 263	99 980	14.5	10.9	4.1	47 497	10.6	1 661	44 674	73.4	632 600	29.1	11.0
Torrance	35 368	74 131	7.2	15.3	5.8	58 377	4.3	2 376	54 843	57.2	644 000	31.2	10.0
Tracy	26 147	74 712	4.3	14.1	8.2	25 963	48.9	1 632	23 750	67.1	291 900	31.8	11.9
Tulare	17 532	44 583	1.7	24.4	16.1	18 863	32.6	1 143	17 724	58.1	189 600	27.8	12.7
Turlock	22 231	51 296	2.2	27.1	11.8	24 627	29.3	1 855	23 260	55.3	232 800	27.7	13.1
Tustin	31 090	72 661	8.2	14.6	8.2	26 476	3.9	1 273	24 448	61.4	558 300	31.3	11.6
Twentynine Palms	20 049	40 723	0.5	30.5	13.5	9 431	38.9	1 336	7 666	35.0	168 500	25.7	10.0
Union City	29 391	80 649	6.6	14.2	6.1	21 258	12.7	825	20 431	70.3	526 600	30.4	10.5
Upland	28 419	65 127	5.9	17.7	7.5	27 355	7.4	1 532	25 057	58.9	436 700	28.4	10.0
Vacaville	28 076	69 816	5.3	12.9	6.4	32 814	14.4	1 722	29 725	64.4	315 400	28.7	11.6
Vallejo	25 990	60 453	3.5	20.8	10.9	44 433	7.9	3 874	40 212	60.5	277 500	31.8	10.0
Victorville	17 295	52 679	1.4	24.0	18.5	36 655	61.8	4 097	31 612	60.8	169 400	30.7	13.7
Visalia	22 961	53 019	3.1	22.4	12.0	44 205	34.8	2 856	39 821	62.0	212 100	28.4	11.1
Vista	21 207	49 911	1.7	17.0	9.6	30 986	3.5	1 669	29 024	51.8	365 900	34.2	10.7
Walnut	32 036	91 364	12.2	10.9	4.8	8 753	4.3	220	8 452	87.8	641 200	29.3	11.3
Walnut Creek	48 175	78 499	10.0	14.2	2.2	32 681	3.8	2 238	30 312	67.9	587 600	27.9	15.9
Wasco	11 028	41 170	0.7	29.4	24.5	5 477	28.2	346	4 828	57.0	152 000	27.3	10.0
Watsonville	15 821	45 549	0.6	27.7	18.2	14 089	19.7	561	13 656	46.1	366 300	37.4	12.8
West Covina	24 914	67 700	4.2	14.0	6.4	32 705	2.2	1 109	30 670	63.7	410 300	29.6	10.0
West Hollywood	53 092	51 486	5.8	25.7	7.8	24 588	2.0	2 077	22 738	23.3	657 300	34.1	19.5
Westminster	21 570	57 386	2.9	23.0	12.6	27 650	2.7	1 486	26 965	55.5	483 400	31.7	10.0
West Sacramento	24 597	56 442	1.5	24.8	12.9	18 681	54.1	1 260	17 581	60.3	272 300	31.0	10.2
Whittier	26 906	65 289	4.4	16.5	8.3	29 591	1.9	1 318	27 698	56.3	458 100	32.8	10.0
Wildomar	24 073	60 574	3.9	15.7	9.5	10 806	128.0	814	9 741	74.4	251 600	35.4	12.9
Windsor	29 069	71 964	5.2	11.9	3.0	9 549	23.4	579	9 137	75.2	406 700	30.7	17.4
Woodland	24 620	55 902	2.4	20.1	8.1	19 806	15.8	1 085	19 151	55.5	310 300	28.7	10.0
Yorba Linda	47 031	109 948	19.0	7.7	1.4	22 305	14.2	729	21 194	84.3	713 900	30.8	10.0
Yuba City	20 935	48 699	1.5	24.0	11.8	23 174	66.6	1 624	21 783	57.1	215 900	28.6	13.2
Yucaipa	26 136	57 656	3.9	20.8	8.7	19 642	21.9	1 411	17 328	76.3	270 800	28.9	13.7
COLORADO	29 791	55 945	4.5	21.0	8.8	2 212 898	22.4	240 030	1 942 049	66.7	238 800	25.0	10.1
Arvada	31 102	65 029	2.9	16.9	4.5	44 427	12.1	1 726	42 918	73.2	240 700	25.1	11.1
Aurora	23 427	48 519	2.0	24.8	13.4	131 040	20.1	9 139	121 651	61.9	182 200	26.6	11.4
Boulder	36 036	52 276	8.4	26.8	7.5	43 479	6.6	2 177	40 667	48.1	498 100	24.1	10.2
Brighton	24 269	64 476	1.7	14.1	6.7	11 387	63.0	599	10 724	70.9	194 400	25.8	11.8
Broomfield	34 164	73 616	6.0	12.8	2.4	22 646	57.8	1 232	21 163	70.3	261 700	23.5	10.0

1. Based on population estimated by the American Community Survey.   2. Includes units rented or sold but not occupied.   3. Specified owner-occupied units; $1,000,000 represents $1,000,000 or more.   4. 50.0 represents 50 percent or more.   5. 10.0 represents 10 percent or less.

Table D. Cities — Housing, Labor Force, and Employment

City	Occupied housing units, 2008–2010 (cont.) Percent renter occupied	Median gross rent[1]	Median rent as a percent of income[2]	Percent with no vehicle available	Migration, 2008–2010 Percent who lived in the same house one year ago	Percent who lived outside this city one year ago	Civilian labor force, 2010 Total	Percent change, 2009–2010	Unemployment Total	Rate[3]	Civilian employment[4], 2008–2010 Population age 16 and older	Percent In labor force	Full-year full-time worker	Households with no workers (percent)
	55	56	57	58	59	60	61	62	63	64	65	66	67	68
CALIFORNIA—Cont'd														
San Francisco	63.0	1 363	28.1	30.6	84.6	5.6	456 589	-0.7	43 623	9.6	704 518	69.6	44.9	25.1
San Gabriel	50.6	1 212	34.5	7.0	86.0	8.3	20 531	0.1	2 132	10.4	33 104	62.7	41.9	17.5
San Jacinto	29.3	1 219	34.0	5.7	78.0	13.5	12 912	3.1	2 776	21.5	30 862	58.7	31.8	31.8
San Jose	41.1	1 364	31.0	5.4	85.8	5.1	463 473	0.3	56 508	12.2	728 682	68.4	42.5	18.3
San Juan Capistrano	24.0	1 662	40.0	4.0	88.5	6.5	17 495	-0.3	1 468	8.4	25 973	63.5	40.3	25.3
San Leandro	43.4	1 164	30.2	6.3	87.4	9.1	41 674	-0.2	4 633	11.1	67 162	68.0	42.0	24.3
San Luis Obispo	61.8	1 166	48.0	8.3	63.8	15.3	27 912	0.5	3 032	10.9	39 758	62.4	28.2	29.0
San Marcos	38.6	1 264	39.9	5.2	85.4	9.8	31 248	1.0	3 289	10.5	60 348	62.5	39.8	24.2
San Mateo	45.8	1 492	27.1	6.8	86.9	7.9	49 105	0.1	3 421	7.0	77 958	71.6	46.6	22.4
San Pablo	52.0	971	37.9	15.7	81.1	10.9	14 273	0.3	3 100	21.7	22 296	65.2	33.7	26.2
San Rafael	46.9	1 387	32.9	6.2	83.2	11.0	30 473	0.9	2 898	9.5	48 066	66.8	39.8	24.2
San Ramon	28.3	1 565	25.2	2.5	85.9	10.0	27 911	-1.0	1 296	4.6	50 994	73.8	50.2	13.3
Santa Ana	52.0	1 256	34.2	6.2	81.5	6.9	161 553	0.1	24 008	14.9	235 629	68.7	41.3	12.7
Santa Barbara	58.5	1 382	34.1	10.6	76.8	9.8	55 737	0.2	3 688	6.6	74 373	67.5	40.0	28.9
Santa Clara	54.8	1 445	24.9	5.6	79.9	12.5	56 638	0.3	5 712	10.1	91 930	69.4	44.9	19.6
Santa Clarita	29.5	1 486	32.4	5.2	84.8	8.8	88 710	-0.1	6 920	7.8	135 032	71.3	43.6	19.2
Santa Cruz	53.9	1 304	38.4	8.0	71.7	14.8	32 482	-0.2	3 425	10.5	51 789	59.1	26.3	29.8
Santa Maria	48.7	1 076	33.7	7.8	80.0	4.8	40 647	1.1	5 887	14.5	70 185	64.5	37.0	23.9
Santa Monica	71.7	1 401	29.2	9.9	82.4	12.3	57 164	0.1	5 966	10.4	78 602	67.5	40.5	27.7
Santa Paula	46.9	1 096	33.3	7.0	85.8	6.3	15 166	1.4	2 663	17.6	21 590	66.8	40.3	27.1
Santa Rosa	45.6	1 139	32.5	7.1	79.9	8.8	81 318	-0.8	8 477	10.4	130 192	67.9	37.3	27.7
Santee	28.9	1 195	29.6	3.3	89.6	8.1	32 928	0.8	2 914	8.8	42 221	63.5	39.8	22.8
Saratoga	14.9	1 780	28.0	4.5	92.0	5.2	13 231	0.3	741	5.6	23 831	54.4	35.6	31.3
Seaside	53.6	1 427	32.6	6.6	73.0	18.9	16 596	1.6	1 242	7.5	25 180	71.2	40.1	16.4
Simi Valley	27.0	1 625	30.6	3.4	87.9	5.8	69 908	0.6	6 231	8.9	96 314	71.0	46.1	16.9
Soledad	42.1	1 024	30.7	8.4	78.8	18.1	5 978	2.2	958	16.0	20 723	35.9	17.8	15.3
South Gate	56.9	944	35.4	9.5	91.2	5.6	41 876	0.6	6 695	16.0	69 999	64.6	41.3	16.9
South Pasadena	54.4	1 349	24.2	3.3	89.1	9.2	15 103	-0.3	954	6.3	20 050	72.9	48.1	20.0
South San Francisco	39.7	1 393	30.8	8.1	90.2	5.2	31 634	0.2	3 392	10.7	50 357	67.8	46.6	22.6
Stanton	54.2	1 233	37.2	7.2	85.4	10.8	18 674	0.1	2 820	15.1	29 044	67.6	41.4	17.4
Stockton	47.9	925	37.0	9.6	78.4	6.4	127 550	0.9	26 397	20.7	213 371	61.6	33.3	27.7
Suisun City	27.0	1 369	38.2	2.6	79.2	16.3	14 970	0.2	1 855	12.4	21 533	71.4	45.0	17.2
Sunnyvale	51.0	1 452	22.4	4.9	84.0	8.9	75 153	0.3	7 102	9.5	111 006	70.2	47.6	17.9
Temecula	31.4	1 375	32.9	3.0	81.4	12.1	37 346	2.2	3 721	10.0	71 862	70.3	41.8	16.9
Temple City	38.4	1 384	35.9	3.8	89.1	7.4	17 975	-0.1	1 477	8.2	28 899	63.1	41.4	19.7
Thousand Oaks	26.6	1 764	31.5	3.0	87.6	7.1	71 341	0.6	5 984	8.4	98 557	68.7	42.9	22.0
Torrance	42.8	1 373	30.5	5.4	87.3	6.4	78 764	-0.3	4 993	6.3	117 080	67.0	43.7	22.7
Tracy	32.9	1 260	32.2	4.1	77.3	10.2	32 681	-0.4	3 570	10.9	57 333	72.3	42.6	15.7
Tulare	41.9	889	34.0	6.3	88.2	4.2	24 017	1.2	3 476	14.5	40 781	61.5	40.6	25.3
Turlock	44.7	896	33.5	6.5	81.0	8.6	28 935	1.1	3 831	13.2	52 951	63.2	37.1	27.9
Tustin	48.6	1 397	33.4	4.2	81.0	12.8	41 535	-0.2	3 875	9.3	56 321	73.3	47.1	15.1
Twentynine Palms	65.0	879	33.1	7.9	58.8	21.3	6 169	-0.2	1 044	16.9	19 832	72.3	55.0	24.6
Union City	29.7	1 332	32.7	5.0	91.0	5.9	34 312	-0.2	3 629	10.6	53 536	67.6	45.5	18.4
Upland	41.1	1 139	33.3	4.0	84.1	11.4	39 777	-0.8	3 899	9.8	56 684	67.4	38.7	21.7
Vacaville	35.6	1 307	31.5	4.5	82.3	9.3	45 385	-0.1	4 086	9.0	72 457	62.0	39.6	21.8
Vallejo	39.5	1 150	33.6	7.9	82.5	6.8	65 881	0.5	9 699	14.7	92 388	66.0	38.9	25.9
Victorville	39.2	1 055	36.1	6.3	77.7	13.3	30 157	-0.2	5 113	17.0	76 849	59.3	35.0	26.5
Visalia	38.0	924	32.8	7.0	83.9	5.0	55 509	0.8	5 886	10.6	89 235	63.8	41.4	24.1
Vista	48.2	1 212	35.0	4.3	81.8	12.4	49 241	1.1	5 756	11.7	72 268	64.2	41.0	20.0
Walnut	12.2	1 783	39.5	2.2	91.4	4.2	16 317	-0.3	1 010	6.2	24 385	61.6	42.2	16.1
Walnut Creek	32.1	1 384	28.6	8.8	83.8	11.0	33 945	-0.8	2 565	7.6	54 022	59.1	38.1	37.3
Wasco	43.0	606	32.8	6.1	71.1	19.5	8 805	NA	2 497	28.4	18 536	42.6	24.8	23.5
Watsonville	53.9	1 047	33.6	6.2	84.4	5.8	23 923	1.8	6 175	25.8	36 469	66.6	32.8	20.6
West Covina	36.3	1 302	32.9	5.0	86.2	9.1	55 231	0.2	6 153	11.1	83 033	66.2	41.2	18.4
West Hollywood	76.7	1 224	31.2	16.6	79.2	17.1	26 939	0.1	2 880	10.7	33 325	74.6	46.0	26.2
Westminster	44.5	1 222	39.4	5.8	86.9	9.0	45 950	-0.1	4 838	10.5	71 162	61.5	35.8	24.4
West Sacramento	39.7	915	31.6	7.6	77.6	10.3	16 784	0.0	3 246	19.3	36 104	69.0	40.7	25.2
Whittier	43.7	1 121	30.6	6.0	87.1	9.5	43 347	0.0	3 927	9.1	66 676	65.3	42.0	22.3
Wildomar	25.6	1 371	37.6	3.7	79.8	12.6	NA	NA	NA	NA	23 696	67.3	39.9	21.4
Windsor	24.8	1 630	34.8	4.8	90.0	5.0	12 479	-0.9	1 161	9.3	19 803	69.9	45.3	23.4
Woodland	44.5	966	31.0	8.7	78.4	8.0	28 981	-0.6	4 320	14.9	42 207	65.9	40.3	24.6
Yorba Linda	15.7	1 915	37.2	3.0	89.0	7.2	34 807	-0.4	2 201	6.3	50 125	67.6	43.6	17.5
Yuba City	42.9	825	29.9	7.6	80.6	6.1	20 210	2.6	4 350	21.5	47 813	64.6	34.3	29.1
Yucaipa	23.7	964	36.9	4.1	84.6	8.4	21 817	-0.7	2 493	11.4	39 145	64.9	39.1	26.5
COLORADO	33.3	862	30.9	5.8	80.8	11.9	2 725 202	-0.1	243 755	8.9	3 889 293	69.9	44.6	21.6
Arvada	26.8	929	28.6	5.3	84.5	11.0	58 722	0.5	5 790	9.9	84 996	70.7	46.2	23.1
Aurora	38.1	865	33.9	6.7	78.4	10.3	179 891	3.3	19 360	10.8	240 359	72.2	48.1	20.0
Boulder	51.9	1 052	40.6	7.5	64.1	19.3	63 051	0.9	5 072	8.0	85 421	65.6	31.8	20.8
Brighton	29.1	896	27.7	4.3	80.7	13.1	12 782	2.8	1 395	10.9	24 430	67.4	48.2	15.6
Broomfield	29.7	975	28.2	3.7	81.6	12.0	30 887	1.2	2 418	7.8	41 752	74.5	52.3	16.7

1. $2,000 represents $2,000 or more.   2. 50.0 represents 50 percent or more.   3. Percent of civilian labor force.   4. Persons 16 years old and over.

Table D. Cities — Construction, Wholesale Trade, and Retail Trade

City	Value of residential construction authorized by building permits, 2010			Wholesale trade,[1] 2007				Retail trade,[2] 2007			
	New construction ($1,000)	Number of housing units	Percent single family	Number of establishments	Number of employees	Sales (mil dol)	Annual payroll (mil dol)	Number of establishments	Number of employees	Sales (mil dol)	Annual payroll (mil dol)
	69	70	71	72	73	74	75	76	77	78	79
CALIFORNIA—Cont'd											
San Francisco	194 472	779	2.8	1 195	11 786	10 562.2	668.1	3 710	45 079	12 400.0	1 395.9
San Gabriel	3 667	11	100.0	146	726	220.1	21.5	221	1 651	440.4	35.5
San Jacinto	5 078	38	100.0	13	167	60.0	5.9	54	744	195.6	19.5
San Jose	335 540	2 422	3.1	1 098	21 549	30 166.7	1 922.0	2 397	41 343	11 482.4	1 666.4
San Juan Capistrano	6 839	26	100.0	62	414	318.7	21.9	150	1 883	535.9	53.9
San Leandro	2 758	7	100.0	263	5 151	2 428.6	271.5	320	5 597	1 557.9	151.9
San Luis Obispo	9 974	65	13.8	74	855	312.9	38.2	382	5 357	1 283.3	125.4
San Marcos	32 678	120	60.8	155	1 757	800.0	72.7	263	4 611	1 224.6	129.9
San Mateo	766	2	100.0	101	887	438.3	69.3	408	7 320	1 652.2	203.4
San Pablo	976	6	33.3	8	D	D	D	82	956	222.8	23.1
San Rafael	449	1	100.0	138	1 523	1 049.6	82.9	373	5 583	1 657.5	178.3
San Ramon	0	0	0.0	90	956	2 534.8	75.7	136	2 546	679.1	70.4
Santa Ana	1 948	8	100.0	560	7 262	2 881.5	372.9	920	13 893	3 346.1	372.8
Santa Barbara	11 150	39	46.2	111	1 330	558.9	51.8	617	7 579	1 729.6	205.3
Santa Clara	6 221	33	54.5	399	12 368	7 464.8	1 298.6	403	5 602	1 806.7	192.1
Santa Clarita	43 844	118	83.1	194	3 053	6 452.9	169.3	531	10 207	2 903.2	251.6
Santa Cruz	12 953	41	43.9	48	927	622.4	62.2	287	3 601	830.5	95.0
Santa Maria	19 581	153	9.8	108	1 218	673.7	52.3	349	5 531	1 448.8	139.3
Santa Monica	56 167	302	7.3	171	3 840	3 259.4	191.9	750	10 025	4 944.7	340.1
Santa Paula	9 472	94	4.3	14	D	D	D	64	724	168.6	17.7
Santa Rosa	32 027	224	38.4	157	2 514	1 522.5	155.8	729	11 971	2 977.2	334.8
Santee	31 495	164	70.7	51	447	152.8	16.8	131	2 835	672.9	64.2
Saratoga	10 318	14	100.0	24	145	75.9	7.5	51	542	108.8	13.1
Seaside	777	4	100.0	13	62	33.6	2.0	96	1 871	563.3	53.1
Simi Valley	3 573	18	100.0	140	2 137	852.5	100.5	468	6 857	1 689.6	159.3
Soledad	0	0	0.0	5	D	D	D	31	290	72.7	6.3
South Gate	1 158	12	100.0	64	915	717.4	41.2	185	2 518	787.0	61.8
South Pasadena	445	1	100.0	27	122	163.5	8.6	66	837	192.3	21.8
South San Francisco	4 259	10	100.0	332	5 350	3 150.1	339.0	193	2 676	791.9	83.3
Stanton	3 699	20	100.0	34	331	100.0	13.4	117	1 293	347.5	34.1
Stockton	27 196	123	100.0	248	4 783	3 701.8	199.4	759	13 076	3 340.1	301.2
Suisun City	6 107	28	100.0	4	D	D	D	33	520	172.5	13.9
Sunnyvale	99 103	856	13.1	228	12 043	10 557.8	1 587.1	316	5 524	1 863.1	159.2
Temecula	65 583	348	100.0	166	2 804	2 112.1	104.6	480	8 447	2 371.3	206.5
Temple City	13 536	38	100.0	90	327	112.2	7.6	110	964	180.6	18.5
Thousand Oaks	12 862	35	57.1	184	2 365	1 462.0	170.5	594	9 292	2 863.8	273.1
Torrance	9 918	47	87.2	586	6 226	13 175.4	321.5	762	14 145	4 877.8	371.1
Tracy	3 631	14	100.0	59	981	1 101.0	57.9	269	4 306	1 106.0	101.3
Tulare	14 565	133	85.0	41	541	182.3	21.7	185	2 838	662.4	65.4
Turlock	7 596	54	100.0	53	667	265.9	27.9	238	4 092	987.2	96.9
Tustin	5 378	36	91.7	195	2 709	1 343.4	160.8	286	4 961	1 849.9	147.2
Twentynine Palms	5 242	47	100.0	4	15	4.1	0.4	31	326	93.8	7.4
Union City	16 712	102	2.0	140	3 814	2 905.4	235.0	120	2 716	665.3	84.4
Upland	2 943	13	100.0	103	665	188.4	25.7	280	4 124	918.8	94.8
Vacaville	53 147	214	100.0	35	D	D	D	348	6 010	1 430.5	135.5
Vallejo	8 414	38	100.0	29	599	398.7	30.0	269	4 432	1 192.8	123.9
Victorville	48 389	283	100.0	39	217	169.9	11.0	372	7 457	1 939.5	173.1
Visalia	66 144	331	100.0	134	1 334	1 566.1	60.2	468	7 658	1 943.0	177.9
Vista	13 710	54	100.0	196	3 485	1 694.8	169.6	294	4 914	1 246.6	135.0
Walnut	23 896	49	100.0	265	988	611.5	36.0	106	1 082	209.7	21.2
Walnut Creek	944	2	100.0	74	484	583.0	31.0	356	7 089	1 918.4	231.7
Wasco	0	0	0.0	3	28	12.7	1.0	39	432	82.4	8.3
Watsonville	3 873	41	61.0	71	1 494	1 081.9	78.0	166	2 627	1 540.4	69.6
West Covina	5 460	65	0.0	72	182	100.2	5.0	284	6 118	1 563.9	144.7
West Hollywood	4 528	11	54.5	121	771	369.9	44.2	348	4 397	1 285.7	130.6
Westminster	11 097	48	25.0	103	487	229.8	16.1	442	6 101	1 625.6	147.8
West Sacramento	17 063	83	100.0	143	4 622	5 685.7	203.3	127	2 296	523.6	57.7
Whittier	591	3	100.0	74	414	157.1	15.2	228	3 661	815.0	80.5
Wildomar	16 618	60	100.0	5	D	D	D	31	367	126.7	10.3
Windsor	0	0	0.0	23	322	80.1	17.0	52	1 120	278.9	29.6
Woodland	5 898	52	17.3	74	1 020	528.8	43.6	178	2 748	586.0	60.6
Yorba Linda	86 750	255	96.9	112	1 614	1 021.1	120.1	119	1 878	578.0	49.5
Yuba City	4 716	20	100.0	45	527	199.3	21.4	262	4 323	983.7	100.0
Yucaipa	5 066	38	100.0	19	96	33.7	3.4	86	973	229.5	23.4
COLORADO	2 608 302	11 591	75.8	5 850	81 144	53 599.0	4 191.0	19 428	261 962	65 896.8	6 537.5
Arvada	46 389	190	98.9	83	661	532.6	33.6	279	4 037	958.8	97.7
Aurora	160 181	764	75.0	237	6 062	5 839.6	295.2	909	16 098	3 664.5	366.7
Boulder	72 313	453	25.4	194	2 414	1 131.8	212.2	614	8 421	1 919.5	224.0
Brighton	9 577	50	100.0	28	465	378.0	19.6	87	1 757	476.5	45.7
Broomfield	55 983	232	100.0	68	D	D	D	279	5 355	1 139.8	111.3

1. Merchant wholesalers except manufacturers' sales branches and offices.   2. Establishments with payroll.

Table D. Cities — **Real Estate, Professional Services, and Manufacturing**

City	Real estate and rental and leasing, 2007				Professional, scientific, and technical services,[1] 2007				Manufacturing, 2007			
	Number of establishments	Number of employees	Receipts (mil dol)	Annual payroll (mil dol)	Number of establishments	Number of employees	Receipts (mil dol)	Annual payroll (mil dol)	Number of establishments	Number of employees	Receipts (mil dol)	Annual payroll (mil dol)
	80	81	82	83	84	85	86	87	88	89	90	91
CALIFORNIA—Cont'd												
San Francisco	1 843	14 332	4 309.7	984.3	5 600	D	D	D	788	11 339	2 077.5	422.5
San Gabriel	92	510	75.2	10.6	119	349	40.1	12.1	NA	NA	NA	NA
San Jacinto	23	104	15.6	2.5	23	180	16.0	6.1	34	640	83.7	20.0
San Jose	1 124	6 677	1 637.4	278.1	2 771	44 768	5 497.4	5 265.1	960	43 662	17 377.9	2 967.7
San Juan Capistrano	88	399	78.5	21.9	211	897	145.9	46.3	30	1 086	229.5	49.9
San Leandro	130	2 372	426.1	89.7	127	1 010	141.5	58.7	211	6 620	2 061.6	285.8
San Luis Obispo	137	802	106.9	23.6	330	D	D	D	64	979	166.6	39.3
San Marcos	106	500	100.0	19.2	221	D	D	D	188	4 916	1 141.6	220.2
San Mateo	205	1 065	462.8	76.1	526	D	D	D	57	579	D	27.1
San Pablo	25	78	16.0	2.2	11	D	D	D	NA	NA	NA	NA
San Rafael	167	1 019	535.4	46.9	518	D	D	D	88	832	154.4	32.8
San Ramon	125	897	192.4	41.4	439	5 264	996.0	429.9	NA	NA	NA	NA
Santa Ana	347	2 868	443.7	125.3	1 012	10 987	1 650.8	664.6	875	23 728	5 339.9	954.4
Santa Barbara	269	1 408	293.0	53.3	684	4 647	897.8	307.6	117	1 326	233.3	58.4
Santa Clara	193	1 411	364.6	77.7	850	D	D	D	542	18 177	5 296.3	1 306.0
Santa Clarita	225	1 012	186.3	31.6	501	D	D	D	246	9 292	1 860.4	463.1
Santa Cruz	89	415	87.5	11.7	306	D	D	D	100	1 600	310.9	69.0
Santa Maria	93	523	84.5	17.7	159	1 195	133.3	59.3	100	3 020	666.8	110.3
Santa Monica	438	3 095	1 205.9	194.7	1 192	D	D	D	100	1 201	256.0	46.2
Santa Paula	26	138	26.8	5.2	25	146	17.2	6.4	23	563	123.8	23.4
Santa Rosa	274	1 267	267.8	44.1	606	D	D	D	182	7 583	1 124.2	481.8
Santee	73	252	41.4	7.7	88	D	D	D	88	1 401	232.1	54.0
Saratoga	82	226	90.5	10.9	169	504	77.1	29.6	NA	NA	NA	NA
Seaside	15	97	12.4	2.7	18	D	D	D	NA	NA	NA	NA
Simi Valley	127	501	75.8	14.1	360	2 001	422.4	124.7	158	4 012	831.6	181.1
Soledad	7	25	2.5	0.4	4	28	1.5	0.6	NA	NA	NA	NA
South Gate	52	251	172.4	8.3	36	310	34.2	12.1	146	6 065	2 260.3	245.7
South Pasadena	46	163	26.9	5.3	158	D	D	D	NA	NA	NA	NA
South San Francisco	94	979	164.4	36.3	178	D	D	D	130	13 709	D	975.8
Stanton	27	157	27.3	3.2	30	176	12.9	5.0	76	978	131.3	37.8
Stockton	280	1 569	250.5	54.3	403	D	D	D	204	7 622	2 506.6	303.1
Suisun City	15	50	8.8	1.1	20	168	46.6	8.6	NA	NA	NA	NA
Sunnyvale	147	1 184	298.2	56.2	741	17 893	3 543.1	1 623.4	276	40 837	10 241.2	3 029.2
Temecula	196	747	132.9	32.2	377	D	D	D	129	7 716	1 929.2	377.3
Temple City	52	170	24.6	5.3	69	232	20.2	6.6	NA	NA	NA	NA
Thousand Oaks	290	1 294	359.1	67.4	787	5 177	4 358.1	359.6	132	3 373	1 113.9	234.1
Torrance	352	2 184	420.2	72.2	897	D	D	D	280	14 673	5 621.3	816.0
Tracy	77	235	139.0	7.7	112	514	45.8	16.2	53	2 512	1 063.0	111.1
Tulare	45	166	37.8	4.5	48	258	38.9	16.0	32	1 786	1 165.2	76.4
Turlock	62	334	37.0	8.1	71	515	46.9	16.5	77	3 762	1 605.0	137.5
Tustin	206	1 196	179.1	42.3	560	D	D	D	131	4 401	1 654.1	215.4
Twentynine Palms	16	113	9.5	1.5	11	92	11.3	2.5	NA	NA	NA	NA
Union City	48	395	116.3	19.7	106	433	70.0	23.9	90	4 149	1 088.0	218.8
Upland	106	965	366.5	57.1	220	1 498	182.5	73.1	116	1 078	210.7	44.4
Vacaville	90	565	95.9	17.0	121	639	77.3	25.9	54	3 414	1 054.7	172.3
Vallejo	92	413	59.8	10.2	123	D	D	D	NA	NA	NA	NA
Victorville	93	711	92.8	19.9	104	D	D	D	31	1 272	501.8	60.3
Visalia	131	695	104.6	20.8	259	D	D	D	81	2 657	617.4	99.6
Vista	142	599	105.7	20.1	252	D	D	D	197	8 746	2 730.7	347.4
Walnut	41	118	30.7	6.3	108	337	47.9	12.8	NA	NA	NA	NA
Walnut Creek	243	1 439	313.9	73.7	747	6 760	1 399.6	566.2	39	1 144	531.9	57.3
Wasco	10	41	4.8	0.9	5	22	2.1	0.4	NA	NA	NA	NA
Watsonville	59	253	46.3	9.1	79	D	D	D	74	1 982	459.4	80.2
West Covina	84	703	78.6	16.4	149	1 355	101.9	42.6	NA	NA	NA	NA
West Hollywood	137	982	434.5	42.1	372	D	D	D	NA	NA	NA	NA
Westminster	91	425	83.1	12.3	161	667	111.9	21.7	105	1 104	195.3	34.8
West Sacramento	69	565	120.6	24.9	88	D	D	D	59	1 962	588.0	84.2
Whittier	101	372	49.3	10.1	178	1 074	102.4	41.9	61	1 287	214.3	48.3
Wildomar	12	112	7.9	2.6	23	68	4.4	1.6	NA	NA	NA	NA
Windsor	27	214	42.1	7.3	54	290	36.4	8.2	26	814	136.5	33.2
Woodland	60	273	47.9	8.3	77	D	D	D	68	2 896	841.2	108.0
Yorba Linda	130	449	119.5	18.0	219	1 135	143.0	46.8	64	1 638	713.1	113.6
Yuba City	89	589	58.4	12.7	112	D	D	D	55	1 245	421.8	D
Yucaipa	47	196	27.9	5.4	66	270	35.6	8.9	NA	NA	NA	NA
COLORADO	10 011	47 568	8 460.9	1 793.0	22 522	156 859	28 932.6	10 515.7	5 288	137 880	46 332.0	6 789.7
Arvada	131	415	47.3	10.8	371	1 675	191.6	79.8	105	2 239	508.7	106.5
Aurora	335	1 555	325.3	58.5	620	D	D	D	132	3 144	767.2	137.4
Boulder	321	1 336	270.6	50.7	1 196	D	D	D	216	7 933	2 193.3	442.8
Brighton	34	127	14.7	3.2	52	D	D	D	NA	NA	NA	NA
Broomfield	91	525	105.3	15.3	271	D	D	D	85	3 939	2 255.5	192.9

1. Establishments subject to federal tax.

Table D. Cities — Accommodation and Food Services, Arts, Entertainment, and Recreation, and Health Care and Social Assistance

City	Accommodation and food services, 2007				Arts, entertainment, and recreation,[1] 2007				Health care and social assistance,[1] 2007			
	Number of establish-ments	Number of employees	Sales (mil dol)	Annual payroll (mil dol)	Number of establish-ments	Number of employees	Receipts (mil dol)	Annual payroll (mil dol)	Number of establish-ments	Number of employees	Receipts (mil dol)	Annual payroll (mil dol)
	92	93	94	95	96	97	98	99	100	101	102	103
CALIFORNIA—Cont'd												
San Francisco	3 525	66 365	5 039.2	1 496.8	325	6 697	871.5	300.1	2 252	15 376	2 123.6	823.6
San Gabriel	167	1 318	71.6	18.5	5	D	D	D	178	D	D	D
San Jacinto	34	396	21.0	5.5	1	D	D	D	18	147	11.1	3.5
San Jose	1 793	30 188	1 714.6	474.1	134	4 474	403.1	160.8	2 010	22 791	2 620.3	1 078.0
San Juan Capistrano	71	1 287	68.5	20.5	18	D	D	D	117	2 632	275.7	125.0
San Leandro	173	2 162	118.5	32.1	15	D	D	D	225	2 637	291.7	110.7
San Luis Obispo	196	4 507	223.9	63.6	18	182	7.8	2.6	276	3 411	416.4	160.2
San Marcos	158	2 632	122.5	36.1	15	D	D	D	113	1 113	109.6	43.8
San Mateo	277	4 506	306.4	87.0	37	726	85.5	18.6	382	2 552	303.3	110.0
San Pablo	53	516	29.8	7.4	3	D	D	D	31	752	61.7	29.4
San Rafael	197	2 335	136.4	38.8	62	466	66.6	14.5	220	2 573	303.2	162.2
San Ramon	127	2 434	161.8	44.6	15	405	30.1	7.8	248	2 948	377.5	136.7
Santa Ana	518	7 690	447.4	119.2	29	333	28.7	6.2	745	8 689	960.6	384.0
Santa Barbara	400	7 984	447.1	124.4	59	843	43.6	17.8	457	3 945	519.1	194.7
Santa Clara	369	6 250	455.3	121.2	33	1 811	296.7	168.3	200	D	D	D
Santa Clarita	328	6 417	301.5	84.6	108	893	67.2	21.2	391	3 664	445.3	132.8
Santa Cruz	230	3 745	193.0	55.4	23	962	55.8	19.7	166	1 544	191.5	72.0
Santa Maria	168	2 993	150.5	41.7	14	249	9.0	2.7	262	2 144	212.7	78.0
Santa Monica	401	10 715	791.3	221.9	719	2 419	684.4	272.9	821	6 413	941.3	308.2
Santa Paula	45	522	22.0	5.6	3	D	D	D	39	298	29.4	10.3
Santa Rosa	394	5 911	300.2	84.4	50	756	35.2	12.0	609	7 234	941.9	398.9
Santee	89	1 522	68.4	20.8	10	186	9.7	3.1	57	486	38.7	14.8
Saratoga	51	561	38.5	11.4	6	84	5.4	2.4	86	561	50.2	19.5
Seaside	62	950	56.6	16.4	4	D	D	D	15	110	7.8	2.6
Simi Valley	252	4 191	204.9	59.3	53	D	D	D	270	2 059	216.9	79.9
Soledad	21	222	12.8	2.8	1	D	D	D	7	D	D	D
South Gate	113	1 137	62.2	15.0	5	D	D	D	74	744	74.1	24.9
South Pasadena	48	787	39.7	11.5	30	D	D	D	90	D	D	D
South San Francisco	203	3 466	289.6	73.7	16	131	11.4	2.9	160	2 413	272.2	141.7
Stanton	85	918	51.9	12.5	7	D	D	D	27	D	D	D
Stockton	471	6 765	343.5	89.5	37	687	40.0	14.5	602	8 582	972.7	367.3
Suisun City	29	411	17.5	4.5	4	D	D	D	26	85	6.1	2.2
Sunnyvale	327	4 318	270.7	75.2	25	D	D	D	302	3 741	375.3	188.1
Temecula	287	6 255	304.0	87.2	30	D	D	D	270	1 763	187.3	62.1
Temple City	65	845	40.0	11.2	11	20	1.0	0.8	93	968	69.1	23.5
Thousand Oaks	308	6 796	347.9	102.6	99	832	57.7	18.8	549	5 540	680.5	250.1
Torrance	432	8 920	503.2	140.5	59	D	D	D	936	8 131	1 136.1	353.8
Tracy	152	2 127	101.5	28.6	17	D	D	D	144	D	D	D
Tulare	95	1 184	59.7	16.0	8	D	D	D	88	D	D	D
Turlock	141	2 382	105.5	28.9	11	D	D	D	155	D	D	D
Tustin	201	3 407	176.4	55.2	20	D	D	D	343	2 771	292.5	109.9
Twentynine Palms	33	402	23.8	5.5	5	D	D	D	7	D	D	D
Union City	115	1 770	90.6	25.6	6	D	D	D	115	936	72.0	32.8
Upland	158	2 259	107.2	30.3	26	D	D	D	315	D	D	D
Vacaville	160	3 544	154.3	42.4	15	D	D	D	149	1 864	237.0	80.2
Vallejo	201	2 874	145.6	38.1	22	D	D	D	231	4 519	435.2	283.4
Victorville	199	3 777	182.0	49.9	13	D	D	D	171	3 260	325.6	113.8
Visalia	221	4 420	187.1	53.2	15	D	D	D	322	3 294	336.7	132.3
Vista	182	2 368	103.0	28.2	20	D	D	D	215	2 532	241.3	97.0
Walnut	67	641	32.8	8.2	4	D	D	D	70	722	43.8	19.6
Walnut Creek	202	4 666	258.8	76.6	35	524	30.4	9.6	412	D	D	D
Wasco	21	D	D	D	1	D	D	D	12	D	D	D
Watsonville	99	1 238	69.4	18.1	6	D	D	D	119	1 349	180.9	74.5
West Covina	200	3 635	177.5	49.0	15	D	D	D	281	D	D	D
West Hollywood	205	6 211	423.7	124.8	473	D	D	D	214	1 009	128.8	44.6
Westminster	232	2 780	139.3	39.2	17	D	D	D	275	2 164	229.7	75.3
West Sacramento	91	D	D	D	9	D	D	D	47	D	D	D
Whittier	168	2 970	144.0	41.9	11	D	D	D	309	D	D	D
Wildomar	20	245	13.0	3.3	8	155	4.9	1.3	45	D	D	D
Windsor	46	632	32.4	9.2	4	90	4.9	1.7	40	213	18.4	6.5
Woodland	109	D	D	D	10	D	D	D	90	1 126	108.6	54.9
Yorba Linda	87	1 706	78.6	24.6	22	D	D	D	153	1 228	139.0	44.4
Yuba City	126	2 274	90.7	25.6	13	D	D	D	202	D	D	D
Yucaipa	57	820	35.0	9.6	10	D	D	D	82	1 165	77.1	31.2
COLORADO	12 075	231 721	11 440.4	3 408.2	1 957	41 153	3 253.2	1 051.0	11 557	127 029	12 599.1	5 234.2
Arvada	169	2 963	128.1	35.4	19	D	D	D	187	1 382	121.1	46.1
Aurora	529	9 480	444.8	128.3	40	568	31.4	9.1	545	8 884	875.7	339.9
Boulder	402	8 121	390.5	120.6	90	944	59.9	15.1	510	3 719	352.1	158.3
Brighton	69	1 279	52.9	15.5	7	D	D	D	53	D	D	D
Broomfield	137	3 370	163.4	53.3	25	D	D	D	101	866	71.7	30.1

1. Establishments subject to federal tax.

Table D. Cities — Other Services and Federal Funds

City	Other services[1], 2007 Number of establish-ments	Number of employees	Receipts (mil dol)	Annual payroll (mil dol)	Selected federal funds, 2009–2010 (mil dol) Procurement contracts Defense	Other	Grants Total[2]	Medicaid and other health related	Nutrition and family welfare	Energy and environment	Disasters and emergency preparedness	Housing and community development	Employment and training
	104	105	106	107	108	109	110	111	112	113	114	115	116
CALIFORNIA—Cont'd													
San Francisco	1 489	9 487	843.1	247.3	508.7	706.1	2 739.5	1 362.4	24.6	66.6	0.7	216.3	16.2
San Gabriel	79	448	40.7	13.3	2.9	0.1	0.0	0.0	0.0	0.0	0.0	0.0	0.0
San Jacinto	27	80	7.9	1.9	0.2	0.0	1.9	0.0	0.2	0.4	0.0	0.0	0.0
San Jose	1 100	7 036	896.0	232.2	170.9	80.3	541.1	19.9	22.7	47.6	1.2	311.8	19.2
San Juan Capistrano	46	295	21.0	6.7	2.6	0.9	0.0	0.0	0.0	0.0	0.0	0.0	0.0
San Leandro.................	158	1 201	182.8	46.2	12.3	8.3	20.6	13.5	0.5	1.9	0.0	0.8	0.4
San Luis Obispo...........	112	648	55.4	14.9	20.1	1.3	70.7	1.4	27.7	2.7	0.0	21.1	0.1
San Marcos	132	776	72.6	22.9	8.7	0.5	18.7	9.8	0.0	0.7	0.0	0.8	0.0
San Mateo....................	213	1 052	104.9	30.2	23.9	2.0	14.2	8.2	0.0	0.4	0.0	1.6	0.0
San Pablo....................	35	D	D	D	0.0	0.0	3.1	1.1	0.0	0.0	0.0	0.0	0.0
San Rafael	192	1 222	154.4	52.2	1.5	3.2	55.1	3.7	4.1	4.5	0.0	36.3	0.0
San Ramon	107	706	67.5	22.2	25.0	1.7	1.5	0.0	0.0	0.0	0.0	0.0	0.0
Santa Ana	415	2 658	254.6	69.5	60.7	18.0	259.8	8.2	34.3	4.5	0.0	196.4	0.7
Santa Barbara	201	1 315	101.0	29.0	20.0	5.6	182.2	38.7	0.2	18.0	0.0	35.8	0.2
Santa Clara	227	1 477	162.3	48.2	290.7	4.9	34.6	3.2	0.9	21.9	0.0	2.9	0.0
Santa Clarita	244	1 784	171.0	45.8	61.2	6.9	21.2	1.0	0.0	2.1	0.0	2.7	0.0
Santa Cruz	103	618	56.7	17.0	1.1	6.1	168.3	52.7	4.9	8.3	0.0	51.4	0.0
Santa Maria	122	776	76.5	20.6	96.6	3.5	9.9	0.9	0.0	0.0	4.4	0.1	0.0
Santa Monica	328	2 365	196.0	53.0	7.5	1 456.1	184.0	70.6	0.0	3.6	0.0	21.8	5.0
Santa Paula	26	D	D	D	0.1	0.1	6.2	0.0	0.0	0.1	0.0	5.6	0.0
Santa Rosa	264	1 588	154.1	47.2	6.5	2.2	91.5	5.1	5.8	13.8	0.0	48.0	4.2
Santee	91	562	68.3	18.5	2.6	0.7	2.2	0.0	0.0	1.2	0.0	0.5	0.0
Saratoga	32	D	D	D	4.0	0.0	4.9	0.0	0.0	3.8	0.0	0.0	0.0
Seaside	49	202	23.9	6.4	31.3	93.5	9.2	0.0	0.0	0.1	0.0	0.4	0.0
Simi Valley	179	D	D	D	34.6	42.0	3.9	0.0	0.0	0.0	0.0	0.8	0.0
Soledad	4	D	D	D	0.0	0.0	1.2	0.0	0.0	0.0	0.0	0.0	0.0
South Gate	74	316	28.4	8.4	3.0	0.0	8.5	0.0	0.0	0.0	0.0	8.4	0.0
South Pasadena...........	32	D	D	D	0.1	1.0	1.4	1.1	0.0	0.0	0.0	0.0	0.0
South San Francisco.....	117	1 419	136.2	46.5	92.1	45.5	12.3	4.3	6.7	0.0	0.2	0.8	0.0
Stanton	58	266	27.1	7.1	1.4	0.0	0.0	0.0	0.0	0.0	0.0	0.0	0.0
Stockton	322	2 500	194.9	65.0	35.8	8.2	108.9	1.1	24.8	7.3	0.0	51.0	0.5
Suisun City	20	D	D	D	0.3	0.0	3.1	0.0	0.2	0.0	0.0	2.9	0.0
Sunnyvale....................	154	874	120.6	33.0	3 983.8	31.8	29.9	6.9	0.0	17.0	0.0	2.1	0.3
Temecula.....................	185	997	80.7	22.7	5.2	18.4	9.7	0.2	0.3	7.6	0.0	0.0	0.0
Temple City	53	239	15.7	3.5	0.0	0.0	0.0	0.0	0.0	0.0	0.0	0.0	0.0
Thousand Oaks............	217	1 172	105.8	29.1	97.1	18.1	50.1	0.1	0.0	15.0	0.0	31.5	0.0
Torrance......................	257	1 669	166.5	55.5	132.8	34.4	73.2	37.7	0.3	10.8	0.0	6.8	0.0
Tracy	96	434	37.9	10.0	24.7	3.5	1.9	0.0	0.0	0.6	0.0	1.0	0.0
Tulare	58	338	35.7	9.3	0.0	0.4	4.9	1.9	0.0	1.2	0.0	1.0	0.0
Turlock........................	84	716	50.8	16.7	3.2	8.2	8.3	0.0	0.0	0.6	0.0	2.5	0.0
Tustin..........................	113	893	95.6	28.2	40.3	12.9	3.0	0.7	0.0	0.6	0.0	0.9	0.0
Twentynine Palms........	13	D	D	D	400.8	0.1	1.4	0.0	0.0	0.1	0.0	0.0	0.0
Union City....................	61	542	88.2	19.1	7.7	1.0	5.6	2.5	0.0	0.0	0.0	0.7	0.0
Upland.........................	152	769	63.9	18.5	0.4	2.1	8.3	1.5	0.0	0.0	0.0	6.6	0.0
Vacaville	94	515	41.7	11.8	3.5	1.3	16.0	0.0	0.0	0.1	0.0	10.7	0.0
Vallejo.........................	119	615	50.8	15.9	19.9	22.6	121.9	3.8	0.2	1.0	0.0	27.1	0.0
Victorville	108	753	95.8	19.1	19.0	10.3	11.6	0.2	0.0	1.0	0.0	1.3	0.0
Visalia.........................	159	1 096	94.8	26.2	0.1	1.8	64.4	0.1	18.0	1.4	0.0	25.3	9.3
Vista	127	759	75.1	22.4	34.3	2.6	8.0	3.0	0.0	0.8	0.0	0.0	0.0
Walnut	69	D	D	D	3.8	0.2	5.0	0.0	0.0	0.0	0.0	0.0	2.2
Walnut Creek	161	1 121	101.5	31.4	4.3	5.7	3.2	0.8	0.0	1.8	0.0	0.4	0.0
Wasco	11	33	3.5	0.7	0.0	0.0	3.6	0.0	0.0	3.6	0.0	0.0	0.0
Watsonville..................	68	234	23.8	6.0	0.0	3.4	4.2	1.5	0.0	0.0	0.0	1.8	0.0
West Covina.................	98	518	35.9	9.7	5.2	2.7	28.7	3.0	7.1	2.4	0.0	1.3	0.0
West Hollywood	165	1 107	82.2	21.3	0.0	0.1	1.2	0.3	0.0	0.0	0.0	0.0	0.0
Westminster	139	614	61.5	15.8	0.5	0.5	1.3	0.0	0.0	0.8	0.0	0.0	0.0
West Sacramento..........	78	576	68.6	20.1	1 131.2	5.6	4.0	0.0	0.0	0.0	0.0	3.0	0.1
Whittier	125	D	D	D	3.9	1.2	8.5	0.0	0.0	0.9	0.0	1.5	0.0
Wildomar	13	D	D	D	NA	NA	NA	NA	NA	NA	NA	NA	NA
Windsor	29	142	12.8	4.1	0.1	0.8	0.2	0.0	0.0	0.0	0.0	0.0	0.0
Woodland	86	535	41.5	11.9	4.3	0.3	23.7	0.0	3.9	0.9	0.0	12.5	0.0
Yorba Linda.................	83	484	48.7	13.4	7.3	8.7	2.4	0.0	0.0	1.7	0.0	0.0	0.0
Yuba City....................	94	D	D	D	0.2	7.7	11.4	3.7	0.0	0.0	0.0	5.6	0.0
Yucaipa	43	192	15.0	3.7	12.2	0.3	4.9	0.0	0.0	4.7	0.0	0.0	0.0
COLORADO..............	7 904	45 358	3 811.5	1 178.5	5 631.6	4 735.5	8 792.9	3 665.3	967.6	568.8	7.7	399.6	130.0
Arvada........................	167	856	56.6	17.6	10.3	51.8	4.9	0.0	0.0	0.5	0.0	4.3	0.0
Aurora.........................	379	2 366	197.5	58.5	33.2	66.2	393.2	357.7	1.2	3.1	0.0	19.1	0.0
Boulder.......................	220	1 480	127.3	44.8	161.0	436.4	717.6	104.6	1.2	151.8	0.0	17.1	0.0
Brighton	56	292	28.0	8.3	0.1	0.0	6.3	0.0	3.1	1.4	0.0	1.6	0.0
Broomfield	76	577	92.6	37.8	24.7	7.1	15.3	0.3	0.0	0.0	0.0	0.2	0.0

1. Establishments subject to federal tax.   2. Includes program categories not shown separately. State totals include additional categories not allocated by city.

Table D. Cities — City Government Finances

City	General revenue Total (mil dol)	Intergovernmental Total (mil dol)	Intergovernmental Percent from state government	Taxes Total (mil dol)	Taxes Per capita¹ Total	Taxes Per capita¹ Property	Taxes Per capita¹ Sales and gross receipts	General expenditure Total (mil dol)	General expenditure Per capita¹ Total	General expenditure Per capita¹ Capital outlays
	117	118	119	120	121	122	123	124	125	126
CALIFORNIA—Cont'd										
San Francisco	5 978.3	2 003.3	73.3	2 412.5	3 154	1 542	905	5 225.2	6 831	577
San Gabriel	31.6	2.4	86.6	22.9	564	313	232	29.2	719	44
San Jacinto	38.4	2.3	89.6	22.1	593	300	134	30.4	816	83
San Jose	1 620.0	150.8	48.7	804.1	856	450	334	1 727.5	1 838	476
San Juan Capistrano	46.3	3.6	77.3	28.0	809	507	282	37.9	1 094	155
San Leandro	127.6	10.4	87.4	83.9	1 079	506	514	118.5	1 525	181
San Luis Obispo	76.6	7.1	77.8	43.3	994	344	619	62.8	1 444	230
San Marcos	165.0	5.2	88.7	102.4	1 307	980	252	168.8	2 156	765
San Mateo	141.3	10.9	66.2	86.5	943	522	290	165.7	1 805	586
San Pablo	46.3	2.6	65.6	34.9	1 136	590	543	41.4	1 348	570
San Rafael	84.8	6.2	69.8	54.2	974	494	454	85.0	1 528	139
San Ramon	68.4	4.6	84.4	39.1	798	498	283	88.9	1 817	738
Santa Ana	382.2	79.8	42.1	211.9	624	337	283	414.2	1 220	259
Santa Barbara	234.8	33.5	34.9	95.6	1 109	497	605	209.5	2 430	473
Santa Clara	259.0	24.7	93.1	110.9	1 010	554	444	231.4	2 109	463
Santa Clarita	165.5	13.6	64.3	113.0	665	203	456	105.6	621	186
Santa Cruz	123.4	11.2	72.7	55.7	1 007	479	508	122.7	2 218	403
Santa Maria	122.6	14.5	62.8	61.8	722	233	375	127.3	1 486	437
Santa Monica	531.7	51.2	58.0	276.6	3 172	1 126	1 972	387.2	4 439	830
Santa Paula	26.5	3.6	84.0	12.4	432	299	99	29.6	1 033	208
Santa Rosa	262.3	16.8	62.0	119.7	776	311	441	250.5	1 624	303
Santee	65.6	9.7	35.2	37.3	702	423	180	65.9	1 240	542
Saratoga	18.5	1.3	78.3	12.7	419	273	126	21.3	704	88
Seaside	35.6	2.8	56.9	27.1	808	477	329	39.0	1 161	391
Simi Valley	120.6	15.4	33.4	76.0	631	386	238	116.6	968	254
Soledad	19.3	1.2	71.3	6.4	228	169	57	13.4	478	62
South Gate	82.0	16.8	29.1	35.6	367	213	152	82.5	850	210
South Pasadena	27.2	6.0	40.1	15.2	620	388	203	24.2	986	189
South San Francisco	137.8	5.3	86.5	72.0	1 179	784	367	110.7	1 789	310
Stanton	35.7	2.6	70.9	24.3	646	450	178	39.6	1 053	444
Stockton	397.4	57.6	63.5	198.6	691	326	361	346.6	1 207	155
Suisun City	42.2	5.0	34.2	24.6	911	741	163	39.1	1 446	504
Sunnyvale	229.7	19.6	39.6	100.1	763	371	369	226.7	1 729	100
Temecula	131.9	20.5	65.8	78.1	824	381	374	117.7	1 242	398
Temple City	17.4	2.1	79.0	11.1	293	131	131	13.0	341	6
Thousand Oaks	154.5	9.1	74.8	91.9	745	381	356	168.6	1 286	170
Torrance	248.9	24.5	64.3	161.4	1 141	376	760	221.8	1 568	210
Tracy	136.1	8.6	72.4	63.0	791	421	363	148.2	1 860	758
Tulare	83.4	4.1	78.2	44.0	796	257	343	68.4	1 236	137
Turlock	87.2	10.7	69.8	43.9	645	319	213	85.8	1 259	538
Tustin	89.4	6.8	46.7	63.1	891	473	407	101.5	1 432	488
Twentynine Palms	11.8	1.2	86.6	9.5	305	176	115	9.8	315	72
Union City	83.9	5.7	74.9	58.2	830	518	254	94.9	1 354	390
Upland	93.0	5.9	87.8	39.4	543	373	158	91.3	1 260	180
Vacaville	177.5	34.2	33.1	89.5	971	615	352	170.3	1 850	670
Vallejo	223.0	48.6	28.5	85.4	739	320	386	243.5	2 107	255
Victorville	172.4	27.2	21.9	81.1	756	297	317	198.2	1 849	347
Visalia	156.9	24.5	34.7	77.6	654	253	395	152.4	1 285	472
Vista	112.8	10.6	81.9	57.2	629	393	230	103.1	1 135	233
Walnut	38.2	2.2	87.3	29.8	963	865	94	36.5	1 180	34
Walnut Creek	80.2	3.2	78.2	49.9	789	377	382	78.1	1 235	160
Wasco	31.8	3.8	36.0	6.1	252	156	95	15.4	635	88
Watsonville	81.7	15.2	75.1	37.4	752	458	270	102.9	2 067	679
West Covina	102.2	8.0	84.9	63.6	598	367	227	117.5	1 105	396
West Hollywood	94.5	2.7	96.4	50.0	1 386	562	811	69.1	1 915	216
Westminster	95.8	9.0	59.1	71.0	801	532	266	85.2	961	166
West Sacramento	139.8	4.8	56.7	78.4	1 687	948	731	143.7	3 091	1 428
Whittier	82.1	6.5	78.8	44.3	535	254	274	79.6	961	54
Wildomar	NA	NA	NA	NA	NA	NA	NA	NA	NA	NA
Windsor	29.8	2.0	100.0	17.8	703	404	240	24.4	965	241
Woodland	80.7	4.5	82.5	55.1	1 027	320	696	101.0	1 881	864
Yorba Linda	77.8	3.0	74.3	50.2	767	572	185	78.3	1 197	225
Yuba City	62.3	3.9	80.5	38.0	622	293	210	76.7	1 253	351
Yucaipa	36.5	2.0	83.8	23.7	474	222	100	31.8	636	167
COLORADO	X	X	X	X	X	X	X	X	X	X
Arvada	133.9	15.0	27.4	65.8	619	98	521	119.4	1 123	279
Aurora	361.9	35.8	46.6	219.3	703	104	599	379.3	1 216	138
Boulder	194.7	19.2	100.0	125.9	1 346	227	1 119	194.8	2 083	303
Brighton	43.4	3.3	43.6	20.2	658	76	577	36.1	1 176	435
Broomfield	155.8	10.6	38.8	90.4	1 684	559	1 125	101.8	1 897	105

1. Based on population estimated as of July 1 of the year shown.

City	Public welfare	Highways	Parking facilities	Education	Health and hospitals	Police protection	Sewerage and sanitation	Parks and recreation	Housing and community development	Interest on debt
	City government finances, 2006 (cont.)									
	General expenditure (cont.)									
	Percent of total for:									
	127	128	129	130	131	132	133	134	135	136
CALIFORNIA—Cont'd										
San Francisco	11.3	3.8	1.9	2.1	26.8	6.6	3.3	4.2	3.2	7.2
San Gabriel	0.0	7.5	0.0	0.0	0.0	33.1	0.2	9.9	0.4	0.7
San Jacinto	0.0	9.5	0.0	0.0	0.0	23.2	8.1	5.6	15.0	7.0
San Jose	0.0	6.6	0.6	0.0	0.6	13.8	13.1	8.9	7.0	11.9
San Juan Capistrano	0.0	14.1	0.0	0.0	0.0	14.2	8.4	16.9	11.8	5.5
San Leandro	0.0	8.8	0.3	0.0	1.2	22.2	6.9	7.8	9.6	2.0
San Luis Obispo	0.0	7.5	5.5	0.0	0.0	19.3	12.9	11.7	2.0	3.5
San Marcos	0.0	16.8	0.0	0.0	1.8	12.2	0.0	8.5	27.2	14.1
San Mateo	0.0	7.0	0.9	0.0	0.3	17.4	16.6	7.8	12.9	5.6
San Pablo	0.0	22.9	0.0	0.0	0.0	26.2	0.0	5.4	20.9	10.7
San Rafael	0.0	10.5	2.9	0.0	5.2	22.3	0.0	11.1	2.8	2.1
San Ramon	0.0	8.9	0.0	0.0	0.0	13.9	0.1	15.1	16.9	3.8
Santa Ana	0.0	14.3	1.0	0.0	0.9	24.8	4.1	5.7	14.1	7.4
Santa Barbara	0.0	15.3	2.7	0.0	7.8	15.0	1.5	9.8	8.0	2.1
Santa Clara	0.0	8.5	0.6	0.0	1.4	16.7	12.0	7.9	13.6	4.6
Santa Clarita	0.0	38.1	0.0	0.0	0.0	13.5	1.0	9.4	3.4	1.2
Santa Cruz	0.0	9.8	1.5	0.0	1.7	14.8	19.7	14.7	8.6	2.9
Santa Maria	0.0	32.2	0.0	0.0	0.0	15.3	19.7	7.1	1.4	1.7
Santa Monica	0.0	8.6	0.1	0.0	6.3	17.1	8.7	10.7	13.4	2.5
Santa Paula	0.0	11.4	0.0	0.0	0.5	17.8	19.0	6.8	16.0	0.8
Santa Rosa	0.0	10.5	1.8	0.0	0.8	17.5	17.1	11.2	4.7	7.8
Santee	0.0	32.2	0.0	0.0	3.3	16.5	0.0	2.6	14.8	1.7
Saratoga	0.0	22.7	0.0	0.0	2.7	15.9	0.0	12.6	0.3	3.5
Seaside	0.0	10.8	0.0	0.0	0.3	23.1	0.0	4.0	13.3	5.1
Simi Valley	0.0	14.5	0.0	0.0	0.9	24.4	12.7	0.5	15.6	5.3
Soledad	0.0	17.3	0.0	0.0	2.0	18.5	19.8	2.7	4.4	3.0
South Gate	0.0	19.4	0.0	0.0	0.5	25.6	4.6	5.4	6.1	11.4
South Pasadena	0.0	21.6	0.0	0.0	2.3	26.0	3.0	5.0	2.9	0.5
South San Francisco	0.0	15.8	0.4	0.0	5.8	16.3	12.6	7.1	9.9	6.7
Stanton	0.0	10.3	0.0	0.0	0.2	18.9	1.7	3.8	45.7	5.1
Stockton	0.0	5.2	1.1	0.0	1.1	28.3	12.8	7.2	8.7	3.5
Suisun City	0.0	9.9	0.0	0.0	0.0	11.3	0.0	6.3	54.3	8.2
Sunnyvale	0.0	6.7	0.7	0.0	0.2	12.6	27.5	8.2	2.6	1.8
Temecula	0.0	30.8	0.0	0.0	0.1	14.1	0.0	16.8	12.4	2.2
Temple City	0.0	13.8	0.9	0.0	1.7	26.3	0.1	14.4	5.8	3.9
Thousand Oaks	0.0	14.6	0.0	0.0	0.5	14.4	10.5	5.6	16.5	4.1
Torrance	0.0	8.3	0.0	0.0	3.8	25.2	5.8	8.3	3.4	2.7
Tracy	0.0	8.2	0.0	0.0	3.7	12.0	26.8	8.1	8.2	7.3
Tulare	0.0	12.6	0.0	0.0	1.4	14.3	22.3	6.1	18.1	4.9
Turlock	0.0	15.8	0.0	0.0	0.4	15.5	21.7	4.4	14.2	2.7
Tustin	0.0	27.2	0.0	0.0	0.1	21.0	0.0	6.0	20.9	5.8
Twentynine Palms	0.0	29.9	0.0	0.0	3.3	25.1	0.0	15.7	5.0	0.8
Union City	0.0	6.2	0.0	0.0	0.4	19.4	1.7	15.5	19.3	7.7
Upland	0.0	15.7	0.0	0.0	1.5	17.3	14.0	2.4	19.1	3.5
Vacaville	0.0	13.0	0.0	0.0	4.4	15.4	9.1	5.6	29.2	6.6
Vallejo	0.0	8.3	0.0	0.0	0.1	16.5	7.2	23.4	10.6	2.9
Victorville	0.0	10.8	0.0	0.0	0.4	8.3	10.6	6.1	4.8	8.4
Visalia	0.0	21.3	0.0	0.0	0.0	15.7	12.1	5.3	3.3	1.7
Vista	0.0	8.3	0.0	0.0	3.9	15.0	21.6	10.0	8.0	3.0
Walnut	0.0	10.2	0.0	0.0	0.7	8.3	0.0	9.4	51.6	10.2
Walnut Creek	0.0	11.3	2.5	0.0	0.0	24.6	0.0	25.9	3.1	0.6
Wasco	0.0	18.0	0.0	0.0	1.5	17.8	23.9	0.2	5.6	2.2
Watsonville	0.0	15.0	0.0	0.0	0.5	14.0	16.4	5.1	15.8	1.8
West Covina	0.0	10.4	0.4	0.0	3.3	22.9	0.0	25.9	10.0	4.1
West Hollywood	0.0	13.2	9.2	0.0	8.6	14.7	2.3	5.2	13.0	1.4
Westminster	0.0	11.7	0.0	0.0	1.0	29.6	0.0	4.9	19.6	2.2
West Sacramento	0.0	16.0	0.0	0.0	0.3	10.4	12.2	8.2	12.0	10.1
Whittier	0.0	9.8	0.0	0.0	0.0	35.7	12.0	15.2	4.9	3.3
Wildomar	NA	NA	NA	NA	NA	NA	NA	NA	NA	NA
Windsor	0.0	25.4	0.0	0.0	0.8	19.6	0.0	3.7	6.5	3.9
Woodland	0.0	25.0	0.0	0.0	0.0	14.3	9.8	17.7	1.6	3.7
Yorba Linda	0.0	28.5	0.0	0.0	0.4	12.3	5.3	15.5	14.6	6.1
Yuba City	0.0	4.5	0.0	0.0	0.4	25.2	8.9	5.1	7.7	2.8
Yucaipa	0.0	39.5	0.0	0.0	2.6	16.3	0.0	9.2	1.2	5.7
COLORADO	X	X	X	X	X	X	X	X	X	X
Arvada	0.0	10.8	0.0	0.0	0.0	18.0	9.8	22.8	3.8	2.5
Aurora	0.0	13.4	0.0	0.0	0.0	18.7	9.3	9.5	2.7	2.4
Boulder	0.0	13.2	1.3	0.0	0.0	12.5	14.8	12.4	8.8	4.4
Brighton	0.0	25.0	0.0	0.0	0.4	14.1	12.0	15.7	1.3	2.8
Broomfield	9.2	10.0	0.0	0.0	1.7	12.1	4.8	11.2	0.1	18.1

Table D. Cities — City Government Finances, City Government Employment, and Climate

City	City government finances, 2007 (cont.) Debt outstanding Total (mil dol)	Per capita[1] (dollars)	Debt issued during year	City government employment, 2010	Climate[2] Average daily temperature (degrees Fahrenheit) Mean January	July	Limits January[3]	July[4]	Annual precipitation (inches)	Heating degree days	Cooling degree days
	137	138	139	140	141	142	143	144	145	146	147
CALIFORNIA—Cont'd											
San Francisco	8 705.7	11 380	960.8	27 329	52.3	61.3	46.4	68.2	22.28	2 597	163
San Gabriel	2.3	56	0.3	NA	56.3	75.6	42.6	89.0	18.56	1 295	1 575
San Jacinto	41.3	1 109	0.0	NA	NA	NA	NA	NA	NA	NA	NA
San Jose	4 461.3	4 747	909.0	6 731	50.5	70.9	41.7	84.3	15.08	2 171	811
San Juan Capistrano	40.1	1 159	0.0	NA	55.4	68.7	43.9	77.3	13.56	1 756	666
San Leandro.................	68.4	880	23.4	402	50.0	62.8	43.6	70.4	25.40	2 857	142
San Luis Obispo...........	85.9	1 975	16.9	NA	53.3	66.5	41.9	80.3	24.36	2 138	476
San Marcos	517.2	6 607	14.1	271	56.4	71.6	45.1	82.2	13.69	1 514	1 047
San Mateo....................	190.7	2 078	46.1	598	48.4	68.0	39.1	80.8	20.16	2 764	422
San Pablo....................	91.9	2 995	36.2	NA	48.8	67.7	41.3	80.9	34.29	2 621	451
San Rafael	55.6	999	6.2	NA	48.8	67.7	41.3	80.9	34.29	2 621	451
San Ramon	105.3	2 152	55.2	NA	47.2	72.0	37.4	89.1	14.82	2 755	858
Santa Ana	422.2	1 243	0.0	1 477	58.0	72.9	46.6	87.7	13.84	1 153	1 299
Santa Barbara.............	138.7	1 609	0.0	1 156	53.1	67.0	40.8	76.7	16.93	2 121	482
Santa Clara	470.3	4 285	0.0	1 045	50.5	70.9	41.7	84.3	15.08	2 171	811
Santa Clarita	52.7	310	13.8	445	50.3	74.1	36.1	94.2	13.96	2 502	1 139
Santa Cruz...................	154.6	2 794	4.1	737	50.6	63.7	40.2	74.8	30.67	2 836	162
Santa Maria	94.6	1 104	0.0	534	51.6	63.5	39.3	73.5	14.01	2 783	121
Santa Monica	236.6	2 713	1.1	2 139	57.0	65.5	50.2	68.8	13.27	1 810	429
Santa Paula.................	35.4	1 235	0.0	NA	54.7	68.3	41.2	80.7	18.41	1 911	602
Santa Rosa	509.5	3 303	68.3	1 284	48.7	67.6	39.5	82.2	31.01	2 694	526
Santee	25.1	472	0.0	NA	57.1	73.0	45.7	83.6	13.75	1 313	1 261
Saratoga......................	13.9	458	0.0	NA	50.5	70.9	41.7	84.3	15.08	2 171	811
Beaside	45.5	1 355	7.2	NA	51.6	60.2	43.4	68.1	20.35	3 092	74
Simi Valley	240.4	1 995	0.0	620	53.7	76.0	39.5	95.0	17.79	1 822	1 485
Soledad	10.1	359	0.0	NA	NA	NA	NA	NA	NA	NA	NA
South Gate..................	212.3	2 186	0.0	350	58.3	74.2	48.5	83.8	15.14	928	1 506
South Pasadena...........	10.6	432	0.1	NA	NA	NA	NA	NA	NA	NA	NA
South San Francisco.....	160.4	2 593	0.0	NA	49.4	62.8	42.9	71.1	20.11	2 862	142
Stanton.......................	46.3	1 233	0.0	NA	58.0	72.9	46.6	87.7	13.84	1 163	1 299
Stockton......................	696.3	2 424	191.5	1 573	46.0	77.3	38.1	93.8	13.84	2 563	1 456
Suisun City	87.4	3 239	0.0	NA	46.1	72.6	37.5	88.8	23.46	2 649	975
Sunnyvale....................	98.7	752	2.2	919	50.5	70.9	41.7	84.3	15.08	2 171	811
Temecula.....................	76.5	808	21.1	202	51.2	78.3	36.1	97.8	11.40	2 123	1 710
Temple City..................	12.2	320	0.0	NA	56.3	75.6	42.6	89.0	18.56	1 295	1 575
Thousand Oaks.............	173.8	1 409	0.0	491	53.7	76.0	39.5	95.0	17.79	1 822	1 485
Torrance......................	120.3	851	0.0	1 454	56.3	69.4	46.2	77.6	14.79	1 526	742
Tracy	285.3	3 579	0.0	440	47.1	76.4	38.5	92.5	12.61	2 421	1 470
Tulare.........................	128.5	2 323	6.3	NA	45.8	79.3	37.4	93.8	11.03	2 588	1 685
Turlock........................	68.4	1 004	0.0	NA	46.4	77.6	39.0	93.3	12.43	2 519	1 506
Tustin.........................	122.9	1 734	25.0	307	54.5	72.1	41.4	83.8	13.87	1 794	1 102
Twentynine Palms........	1.2	38	0.4	NA	50.0	88.4	36.1	105.8	4.57	1 910	3 064
Union City....................	138.8	1 981	0.0	NA	49.8	68.0	42.0	78.3	14.85	2 367	530
Upland........................	61.0	842	15.0	NA	54.6	73.8	41.5	88.7	16.96	1 727	1 191
Vacaville.....................	188.4	2 046	19.3	618	47.2	77.3	38.8	95.8	24.55	2 410	1 498
Vallejo........................	353.6	3 060	46.5	555	46.3	71.2	38.8	87.4	19.58	2 757	786
Victorville....................	411.0	3 833	244.1	507	45.5	80.0	31.4	99.1	6.20	2 929	1 735
Visalia........................	55.3	467	6.2	597	45.8	79.3	37.4	93.8	11.03	2 588	1 685
Vista..........................	103.1	1 135	0.0	340	56.4	71.6	45.1	82.2	13.69	1 514	1 047
Walnut........................	78.3	2 533	0.0	NA	54.6	73.8	41.5	88.7	16.96	1 727	1 191
Walnut Creek	10.7	169	0.0	NA	47.5	72.4	39.3	85.2	23.96	3 267	983
Wasco.........................	7.4	306	0.3	NA	NA	NA	NA	NA	NA	NA	NA
Watsonville..................	44.9	902	0.0	NA	49.7	62.4	38.7	72.0	23.25	3 080	123
West Covina................	132.0	1 240	23.9	473	56.3	75.6	42.6	89.0	18.56	1 295	1 575
West Hollywood	32.8	908	0.0	NA	58.3	74.2	48.5	83.8	15.14	928	1 506
Westminster	37.4	422	0.1	313	58.0	72.9	46.6	82.7	13.84	1 153	1 299
West Sacramento.........	400.4	8 612	8.6	NA	46.3	75.4	38.8	92.4	17.93	2 666	1 248
Whittier.......................	102.2	1 233	37.3	497	56.3	75.6	42.6	89.0	18.56	1 295	1 575
Wildomar.....................	NA	NA	NA	NA	NA	NA	NA	NA	NA	NA	NA
Windsor.......................	39.1	1 543	0.0	NA	NA	NA	NA	NA	NA	NA	NA
Woodland.....................	116.9	2 178	6.9	NA	45.7	76.4	37.6	94.0	20.78	2 683	1 417
Yorba Linda.................	104.2	1 592	1.8	NA	56.9	73.2	45.2	84.0	11.23	1 286	1 294
Yuba City.....................	68.1	1 113	25.2	NA	46.3	78.9	37.8	96.3	22.07	2 488	1 687
Yucaipa	45.3	906	0.4	NA	52.9	78.0	40.4	94.4	13.62	1 904	1 714
COLORADO.............	X	X	X	NA	X	X	X	X	X	X	X
Arvada........................	70.4	662	0.0	677	31.2	71.5	15.6	88.3	18.17	5 988	496
Aurora........................	889.2	2 852	189.0	2 590	29.2	73.4	15.2	88.0	15.81	6 128	696
Boulder.......................	224.2	2 396	20.5	1 219	32.5	71.6	19.2	87.2	19.93	5 687	552
Brighton......................	28.1	914	0.0	266	NA	NA	NA	NA	NA	NA	NA
Broomfield	352.8	6 571	0.0	769	32.5	71.6	19.2	87.2	19.93	5 687	552

1. Based on the population estimated as of July 1 of the year shown.   2. Represents normal values based on the 30-year period, 1971–2000.   3. Average daily minimum.   4. Average daily maximum.

Table D. Cities — **Land Area and Population**

STATE Place code	City	Land area,[1] 2010 (sq km)	Total persons	Rank	Per square kilometer	White	Black	American Indian, Alaska Native	Asian	Hawaiian Pacific Islander	Percent Hispanic or Latino[2], 2010	Percent Foreign born, 2008–2010
		1	2	3	4	5	6	7	8	9	10	11
	COLORADO—Cont'd											
08 12415	Castle Rock............	87.5	48 231	811	551.1	86.6	1.6	0.9	2.6	0.2	10.0	5.5
08 12815	Centennial	74.4	100 377	281	1 349.3	84.4	4.0	0.8	5.3	0.3	7.4	7.7
08 16000	Colorado Springs	503.9	416 427	41	826.5	73.7	7.3	1.5	4.3	0.5	16.1	7.9
08 16495	Commerce City	88.8	45 913	860	517.0	47.4	3.4	1.1	2.8	0.2	46.8	16.5
08 20000	Denver........................	396.3	600 158	27	1 514.5	53.9	10.8	1.2	4.1	0.2	31.8	16.4
08 24785	Englewood...................	17.0	30 255	1 348	1 781.8	77.0	2.7	1.6	2.5	0.3	18.1	9.9
08 27425	Fort Collins	140.6	143 986	173	1 024.2	85.1	1.6	1.1	3.9	0.2	10.1	6.1
08 27865	Fountain	62.1	25 846	1 605	416.1	66.4	12.1	2.0	3.9	1.1	19.4	4.9
08 31660	Grand Junction.............	99.0	58 566	626	591.7	83.5	1.1	1.2	1.6	0.2	13.9	4.1
08 32155	Greeley........................	120.6	92 889	322	770.5	60.6	1.7	0.9	1.7	0.2	36.0	10.9
08 43000	Lakewood.....................	111.1	142 980	175	1 287.4	72.5	1.8	1.3	3.7	0.2	22.0	9.7
08 45255	Littleton.......................	33.6	41 737	941	1 241.4	83.4	1.8	1.1	2.8	0.1	12.4	7.3
08 45970	Longmont.....................	67.8	86 270	359	1 272.0	70.8	1.2	1.0	3.9	0.1	24.6	13.9
08 46465	Loveland......................	87.0	66 859	515	768.4	86.2	0.9	1.0	1.4	0.1	11.7	4.6
08 54330	Northglenn...................	19.2	35 789	1 118	1 865.0	62.7	2.6	1.3	4.2	0.2	30.6	9.3
08 57630	Parker.........................	53.0	45 297	869	854.2	86.5	2.0	0.8	4.3	0.2	8.2	4.0
08 62000	Pueblo.........................	138.9	106 595	252	767.3	46.3	2.5	1.2	1.0	0.1	49.8	4.4
08 77290	Thornton	90.2	118 772	218	1 316.2	61.6	2.2	1.0	5.1	0.2	31.7	11.2
08 83835	Westminster	81.7	106 114	257	1 298.5	71.9	1.8	1.0	6.1	0.2	20.7	10.6
08 84440	Wheat Ridge	24.1	30 166	1 351	1 252.2	75.6	1.4	1.4	2.0	0.2	20.9	6.6
09 00000	CONNECTICUT	12 541.6	3 574 097	X	285.0	72.6	10.2	0.6	4.3	0.1	13.4	13.5
09 08000	Bridgeport...................	41.4	144 229	171	3 486.3	23.9	33.5	0.6	3.7	0.2	38.2	26.3
09 08420	Bristol	68.4	60 477	598	884.2	84.7	4.5	0.6	2.3	0.1	9.6	9.1
09 18430	Danbury.......................	108.5	80 893	398	745.6	59.3	7.2	0.5	7.2	0.1	25.0	31.4
09 37000	Hartford......................	45.0	124 775	205	2 771.5	16.8	36.6	0.7	3.1	0.2	43.4	22.1
09 46450	Meriden.......................	61.6	60 868	588	987.8	60.3	9.4	0.7	2.4	0.1	28.9	10.4
09 47290	Middletown	106.2	47 648	831	448.5	74.0	13.9	0.8	5.6	0.1	8.3	9.9
09 47500	Milford........................	57.4	52 759	722	918.7	86.6	2.8	0.4	5.9	0.1	5.2	9.9
09 49880	Naugatuck	42.2	31 862	1 280	754.3	82.3	5.4	0.5	3.3	0.1	9.2	10.4
09 50370	New Britain..................	34.7	73 206	464	2 110.3	49.4	12.1	0.5	2.8	0.1	36.8	21.0
09 52000	New Haven...................	48.4	129 779	193	2 682.5	33.4	34.9	0.9	5.2	0.1	27.4	16.5
09 52280	New London..................	14.5	27 620	1 492	1 899.6	51.9	18.0	1.9	3.4	0.4	28.3	15.7
09 55990	Norwalk	59.2	85 603	363	1 445.8	56.9	14.2	0.4	5.2	0.1	24.3	23.3
09 56200	Norwich	72.7	40 493	981	557.1	67.5	12.1	2.3	8.3	0.3	12.6	16.7
09 68100	Shelton	79.3	39 559	999	498.7	87.6	2.6	0.4	4.1	0.0	5.9	11.1
09 73000	Stamford......................	97.5	122 643	209	1 258.1	54.4	13.8	0.3	8.5	0.1	23.8	39.2
09 76500	Torrington	103.0	36 383	1 095	353.4	86.5	3.2	0.7	2.4	0.1	8.8	8.5
09 80000	Waterbury....................	73.9	110 366	241	1 494.3	47.2	19.6	0.8	2.1	0.2	31.2	14.7
09 82800	West Haven..................	27.8	55 564	676	1 996.6	58.7	19.8	0.6	4.3	0.2	18.3	13.0
10 00000	DELAWARE	5 046.7	897 934	X	177.9	67.0	22.1	0.9	3.7	0.1	8.2	8.4
10 21200	Dover..........................	60.0	36 047	1 105	601.3	48.1	43.6	1.4	3.5	0.2	6.6	4.8
10 50670	Newark	23.8	31 454	1 298	1 322.2	81.1	7.3	0.5	8.1	0.1	4.8	9.7
10 77580	Wilmington...................	28.2	70 851	480	2 508.9	29.0	58.1	0.8	1.2	0.1	12.4	6.2
11 00000	DISTRICT OF COLUMBIA..............	158.1	601 723	X	3 805.7	36.3	51.3	0.8	4.3	0.1	9.1	13.1
11 50000	Washington	158.1	601 723	26	3 805.7	36.3	51.3	0.8	4.3	0.1	9.1	13.1
12 00000	FLORIDA...................	138 887.5	18 801 310	X	135.4	59.1	15.9	0.6	2.9	0.2	22.5	19.2
12 00950	Altamonte Springs.........	23.3	41 496	952	1 777.9	58.8	13.9	0.7	3.9	0.2	24.3	15.3
12 01700	Apopka	80.9	41 542	948	513.4	50.9	20.6	0.5	3.8	0.2	25.4	15.5
12 02681	Aventura	6.9	35 762	1 119	5 205.5	58.6	3.7	0.1	2.1	0.1	35.8	43.2
12 07300	Boca Raton	76.0	84 392	374	1 110.9	80.1	5.4	0.3	2.9	0.1	11.9	19.1
12 07525	Bonita Springs	100.0	43 914	895	439.3	75.6	0.8	0.3	1.2	0.1	22.5	19.3
12 07875	Boynton Beach..............	41.9	68 217	499	1 628.5	54.6	30.6	0.4	2.6	0.2	12.8	25.4
12 07950	Bradenton....................	36.7	49 546	778	1 349.3	65.8	16.5	0.6	1.3	0.1	17.0	12.9
12 10275	Cape Coral...................	273.7	154 305	155	563.8	74.8	4.4	0.5	1.9	0.1	19.5	15.7
12 11050	Casselberry	18.1	26 241	1 580	1 449.0	66.5	8.0	0.8	3.6	0.2	22.6	11.8
12 12875	Clearwater...................	66.2	107 685	249	1 626.7	72.5	11.4	0.6	2.6	0.2	14.2	15.1
12 12925	Clermont......................	35.3	28 742	1 437	814.0	62.0	14.5	0.8	5.4	0.3	17.8	15.8
12 13275	Coconut Creek	30.7	52 909	719	1 724.0	61.1	14.0	0.3	4.5	0.2	20.4	27.8
12 14125	Cooper City	20.8	28 547	1 441	1 371.1	66.2	5.2	0.4	6.4	0.1	22.8	22.5
12 14250	Coral Gables	33.5	46 780	845	1 398.1	40.9	2.8	0.1	3.2	0.0	53.6	37.4
12 14400	Coral Springs	61.6	121 096	213	1 965.2	53.0	18.3	0.4	5.9	0.2	23.5	25.6
12 15968	Cutler Bay	25.5	40 286	984	1 581.7	29.5	13.8	0.3	3.0	0.2	54.5	33.0
12 16335	Dania Beach.................	21.0	29 639	1 384	1 414.1	53.7	21.8	0.5	2.5	0.1	22.4	25.8
12 16475	Davie	90.4	91 992	327	1 018.1	58.0	8.1	0.5	5.3	0.2	29.1	24.0
12 16525	Daytona Beach..............	151.3	61 005	586	403.3	55.9	36.0	0.8	2.6	0.1	6.2	9.6

1. Dry land or land partially or temporarily covered by water.   2. May be of any race.

Table D. Cities — **Population**

City	Age of population (percent), 2010											Population			
												Census counts		Percent change	
	Under 5 years	5 to 17 years	18 to 24 years	25 to 34 years	35 to 44 years	45 to 54 years	55 to 64 years	65 to 74 years	75 years and over	Median age	Percent female	1990	2000	1990–2000	2000–2010
	12	13	14	15	16	17	18	19	20	21	22	23	24	25	26
COLORADO—Cont'd															
Castle Rock	9.2	23.2	5.7	14.0	19.0	14.1	8.6	4.0	2.2	33.8	50.4	8 710	20 224	132.2	138.5
Centennial	5.3	19.8	6.7	10.2	13.6	17.8	14.7	6.8	5.0	41.1	50.8	NA	NA	NA	NA
Colorado Springs	7.1	17.9	10.5	14.6	13.0	14.9	11.1	5.9	5.0	34.9	51.0	280 430	360 890	28.7	15.4
Commerce City	10.9	22.2	7.7	18.7	15.6	11.1	8.1	3.5	2.3	30.4	49.6	16 466	20 991	27.5	118.7
Denver	7.3	14.2	10.4	20.5	15.0	12.1	10.3	5.4	5.0	33.7	50.0	467 610	554 636	18.6	8.2
Englewood	6.4	11.9	9.7	18.8	13.8	15.6	11.3	5.5	6.9	37.1	50.0	29 396	31 727	7.9	-4.6
Fort Collins	5.7	14.2	21.4	16.9	12.1	11.7	9.3	4.5	4.3	29.6	50.1	87 491	118 652	35.6	21.4
Fountain	10.2	23.5	9.5	17.8	15.5	11.8	6.5	3.5	1.8	28.7	50.8	10 754	15 197	41.3	70.1
Grand Junction	6.5	14.7	12.5	14.3	11.2	13.1	12.1	7.3	8.3	36.7	50.6	32 893	41 986	27.6	39.5
Greeley	7.8	18.0	16.9	13.9	11.5	11.3	9.8	5.4	5.3	29.8	50.9	60 454	76 930	27.3	20.7
Lakewood	6.0	14.8	9.7	14.3	12.8	15.3	12.6	7.6	6.9	39.2	51.1	126 475	144 126	14.0	-0.8
Littleton	5.7	15.9	7.8	12.7	12.9	16.2	13.0	7.5	8.2	41.3	51.7	33 711	40 340	19.7	3.5
Longmont	7.2	19.0	7.9	13.5	14.7	15.3	11.2	6.0	5.2	36.6	50.7	51 976	71 093	36.8	21.3
Loveland	6.8	17.2	7.9	13.4	12.9	14.6	12.4	7.8	7.1	38.7	51.7	37 357	50 608	35.5	32.1
Northglenn	7.5	18.0	10.7	16.6	13.2	13.4	9.2	6.2	5.1	33.1	50.2	27 195	31 575	16.1	13.3
Parker	8.7	24.2	5.7	13.7	20.3	14.5	8.0	3.3	1.5	33.6	50.6	5 450	23 558	332.3	92.3
Pueblo	6.9	17.1	10.5	12.7	11.5	13.3	12.2	7.8	8.4	37.5	51.2	98 640	102 121	3.5	4.4
Thornton	8.6	20.9	9.0	16.6	16.1	13.1	9.2	4.0	2.5	32.0	50.5	55 031	82 384	49.7	44.2
Westminster	7.0	17.0	9.5	16.2	14.2	15.3	11.5	5.2	3.9	35.1	50.4	74 619	100 940	35.3	5.1
Wheat Ridge	5.4	13.3	7.1	13.6	12.2	16.1	13.6	8.1	10.5	43.7	51.4	29 419	32 913	11.9	-8.3
CONNECTICUT	5.7	17.2	9.1	11.8	13.6	16.1	12.4	7.1	7.0	40.0	51.3	3 287 116	3 405 565	3.6	4.9
Bridgeport	7.4	17.6	12.4	16.1	13.8	13.3	9.3	5.3	4.8	32.6	51.5	141 686	139 529	-1.5	3.4
Bristol	5.6	15.8	7.9	13.5	13.9	16.0	12.2	7.1	7.8	40.3	51.8	60 640	60 062	-1.0	0.7
Danbury	6.7	14.4	10.6	16.4	15.4	14.6	10.8	5.7	5.4	36.2	50.9	65 585	74 848	14.1	8.1
Hartford	7.6	18.2	15.4	15.5	12.6	12.6	9.2	5.0	3.8	30.2	51.7	139 739	121 578	-13.0	2.6
Meriden	6.7	17.2	8.5	14.1	13.6	15.1	11.9	6.3	6.6	37.7	51.6	59 479	58 244	-2.1	4.5
Middletown	5.4	13.7	13.1	15.3	13.4	14.6	11.3	6.5	6.7	37.0	51.4	42 762	43 167	0.9	10.4
Milford	4.7	15.3	6.7	11.5	14.3	17.2	14.1	8.3	8.0	43.5	51.8	48 139	52 305	8.7	0.9
Naugatuck	5.9	17.2	8.6	14.1	14.3	16.3	11.6	6.8	5.7	38.2	51.0	30 625	30 989	1.2	2.8
New Britain	6.9	16.4	14.3	15.6	11.9	12.7	10.2	5.2	6.7	32.6	51.5	75 491	71 538	-5.2	2.3
New Haven	7.1	15.7	16.8	19.0	12.6	11.2	8.4	5.0	4.3	29.9	51.8	130 474	123 626	-5.2	5.0
New London	6.0	14.4	21.3	14.6	11.6	12.3	10.0	5.0	5.0	30.3	50.6	28 540	25 671	-10.1	7.6
Norwalk	6.9	15.2	7.3	15.7	15.5	15.2	11.4	6.7	6.1	38.2	51.0	78 331	82 951	5.9	3.2
Norwich	6.3	16.1	9.3	14.4	13.3	15.2	12.2	6.4	6.7	38.0	51.6	37 391	36 117	-3.4	12.1
Shelton	4.7	16.4	6.7	9.7	13.6	17.6	13.9	8.8	8.6	44.4	51.5	35 418	38 101	7.6	3.8
Stamford	6.8	14.8	7.8	17.4	15.1	14.2	10.8	6.4	6.8	37.1	50.7	108 056	117 083	8.4	4.7
Torrington	5.7	15.3	7.7	11.9	13.4	16.9	12.9	7.2	8.9	42.4	51.0	33 687	35 202	4.5	3.4
Waterbury	7.2	18.4	10.1	14.1	13.3	13.9	10.4	6.1	6.5	35.2	52.4	108 961	107 271	-1.6	2.9
West Haven	5.9	14.9	13.1	14.1	13.1	14.7	11.7	6.2	6.3	38.6	51.8	54 021	52 360	-3.1	6.1
DELAWARE	6.2	16.7	10.1	12.4	12.9	14.9	12.4	8.1	6.3	38.8	51.6	666 168	783 600	17.6	14.6
Dover	6.6	15.0	18.8	13.7	10.3	11.6	9.5	6.9	7.5	31.3	53.6	27 630	32 135	16.3	12.2
Newark	2.8	7.9	48.0	9.4	6.9	8.0	7.6	4.8	4.6	22.2	53.3	26 463	28 547	7.9	10.2
Wilmington	7.3	17.0	10.0	16.6	13.3	13.9	10.3	6.0	5.6	34.3	52.5	71 529	72 664	1.6	-2.5
DISTRICT OF COLUMBIA	5.4	11.3	14.5	20.7	13.4	12.6	10.6	6.1	5.3	33.8	52.8	606 900	572 059	-5.7	5.2
Washington	5.4	11.3	14.5	20.7	13.4	12.6	10.6	6.1	5.3	33.8	52.8	606 900	572 059	-5.7	5.2
FLORIDA	5.7	15.6	9.3	12.2	12.9	14.6	12.4	9.2	8.1	40.7	51.1	12 938 071	15 982 378	23.5	17.6
Altamonte Springs	5.9	14.0	10.3	19.1	14.1	13.3	10.7	6.5	6.0	35.5	53.0	35 167	41 200	17.2	0.7
Apopka	8.1	19.3	7.9	14.1	16.0	14.1	10.5	5.8	4.2	35.4	51.5	13 611	26 642	95.7	55.9
Aventura	5.4	10.1	5.5	13.5	14.3	11.8	13.0	11.7	14.9	46.1	54.2	14 914	25 267	69.4	41.5
Boca Raton	3.9	13.3	11.2	9.5	11.5	15.7	14.0	10.2	10.8	45.4	51.1	61 486	74 764	21.6	12.9
Bonita Springs	4.4	9.4	5.6	10.2	9.0	11.2	16.5	20.1	13.7	55.2	49.6	13 600	32 797	141.2	33.9
Boynton Beach	5.8	13.5	8.0	13.6	13.2	13.5	11.0	9.2	12.2	41.9	52.8	46 284	60 389	30.5	13.0
Bradenton	6.5	15.0	8.4	11.7	10.9	12.5	12.0	9.1	14.0	42.8	53.4	43 769	49 504	13.1	0.1
Cape Coral	5.4	17.1	7.1	10.7	13.4	15.4	14.0	10.0	7.0	42.4	51.2	74 991	102 286	36.4	50.9
Casselberry	5.4	14.2	11.6	15.5	13.2	14.0	12.0	7.6	6.5	37.5	51.6	20 736	22 629	9.1	16.0
Clearwater	5.3	13.4	8.3	12.4	12.2	14.9	13.7	9.5	10.3	43.8	51.7	98 669	108 787	10.3	-1.0
Clermont	5.7	17.8	7.6	10.8	13.8	12.4	11.9	11.7	8.4	40.9	52.7	NA	9 333	NA	208.0
Coconut Creek	5.7	15.8	7.3	13.5	14.8	14.2	10.2	6.9	11.6	40.3	53.4	27 269	43 566	59.8	21.4
Cooper City	4.7	21.1	8.7	8.4	13.5	20.6	14.2	5.2	3.6	41.0	51.6	21 335	27 939	31.0	2.2
Coral Gables	4.7	13.2	16.6	10.6	13.2	14.0	12.0	8.1	7.5	38.8	52.7	40 091	42 249	5.4	10.7
Coral Springs	5.8	20.8	9.4	12.0	14.8	17.3	12.0	4.6	3.3	36.5	51.9	78 864	117 549	49.1	3.0
Cutler Bay	6.8	18.9	9.0	13.3	16.2	15.4	9.8	5.9	4.7	36.3	51.7	NA	NA	NA	NA
Dania Beach	5.9	12.8	8.2	14.4	13.8	16.3	13.7	8.3	6.5	41.0	50.7	13 183	20 061	52.2	47.7
Davie	5.7	17.7	10.4	13.2	13.9	17.0	11.5	5.9	4.7	37.5	51.6	47 143	75 720	60.6	21.5
Daytona Beach	5.2	10.5	17.9	11.8	9.8	13.5	12.7	9.0	9.6	39.8	50.0	61 991	64 112	3.4	-4.8

City	Households, 2010 Number	Persons per house-hold	Female family house-holder[1] Percent	One-person	Persons in group quarters, 2010 Total	Institutional Total	Persons in nursing facilities	Non-institu-tional	Serious crimes known to police,[2] 2010 Number	Rate[3]	Violent	Property	Educational attainment, 2008-2010 Population age 25 and older	Attainment[4] (percent) High school graduate or less	Bachelor's degree or more
	27	28	29	30	31	32	33	34	35	36	37	38	39	40	41
COLORADO—Cont'd															
Castle Rock	16 688	2.86	8.5	17.7	460	390	108	70	506	1 049	54	995	29 212	20.3	44.5
Centennial....................	37 449	2.63	9.0	20.5	1 701	1 559	307	142	1 616	1 610	159	1 451	67 832	17.5	54.9
Colorado Springs............	167 788	2.44	11.6	29.6	7 629	3 467	1 657	4 162	18 754	4 504	471	4 033	263 919	28.8	36.1
Commerce City.............	14 479	3.15	13.1	17.4	351	191	191	160	1 475	3 213	264	2 949	25 732	51.0	20.9
Denver	263 107	2.22	10.6	40.6	15 981	6 518	2 333	9 463	24 073	4 011	564	3 447	401 651	35.9	40.6
Englewood...................	14 375	2.08	11.1	40.1	291	238	238	53	2 113	6 984	479	6 505	21 229	41.5	29.1
Fort Collins..................	57 829	2.37	8.1	28.4	7 085	1 437	514	5 648	4 992	3 467	305	3 162	82 103	19.9	50.8
Fountain	8 724	2.96	15.6	16.8	0	0	0	0	NA	NA	NA	NA	14 220	32.8	22.8
Grand Junction	24 311	2.29	9.7	32.6	2 884	1 077	395	1 807	2 374	4 054	352	3 702	38 744	35.7	31.0
Greeley	33 427	2.63	11.9	26.9	4 853	1 627	627	3 226	3 398	3 658	460	3 198	53 077	42.6	26.7
Lakewood....................	61 986	2.27	11.9	33.5	2 171	1 552	1 064	619	6 593	4 611	432	4 179	99 084	33.8	35.9
Littleton.....................	18 312	2.25	9.5	34.7	491	448	313	43	1 238	2 966	127	2 839	28 831	24.5	42.5
Longmont....................	33 252	2.58	10.7	26.8	639	498	482	141	2 483	2 878	320	2 558	55 437	30.6	38.1
Loveland.....................	27 153	2.44	10.6	26.7	510	416	414	94	1 720	2 573	191	2 381	44 212	33.4	33.2
Northglenn...................	13 492	2.64	14.6	26.2	129	129	129	0	1 157	3 233	277	2 956	22 298	51.8	17.2
Parker.......................	15 917	2.84	8.8	18.9	28	0	0	28	546	1 205	75	1 130	26 887	16.4	48.9
Pueblo.......................	43 290	2.37	16.4	33.1	4 045	3 050	1 444	995	5 884	5 520	831	4 689	69 581	46.7	17.8
Thornton.....................	41 359	2.86	12.2	20.1	462	430	430	32	4 681	3 941	889	3 052	72 404	41.0	25.5
Westminster.................	42 041	2.51	10.9	26.4	467	448	348	19	3 505	3 303	220	3 083	68 002	34.1	33.0
Wheat Ridge	13 976	2.12	11.6	38.4	554	434	381	120	1 486	4 926	573	4 353	22 568	39.9	29.4
CONNECTICUT...........	1 371 087	2.52	12.9	27.3	118 152	49 370	26 371	68 782	88 443	2 475	281	2 193	2 416 034	39.5	35.6
Bridgeport	51 266	2.72	24.2	29.0	4 838	1 960	759	2 878	6 095	4 226	979	3 247	88 170	60.1	16.1
Bristol........................	25 320	2.35	12.8	30.4	849	637	611	212	1 535	2 538	331	2 207	42 857	49.8	23.6
Danbury	28 907	2.66	11.8	26.4	3 953	1 904	538	2 049	1 631	2 016	143	1 873	54 507	48.5	30.2
Hartford......................	45 124	2.57	30.0	33.1	8 951	2 194	777	6 757	7 119	5 705	1 302	4 404	72 328	61.9	14.0
Meriden......................	23 977	2.50	17.0	29.4	955	688	660	267	1 981	3 255	237	3 018	40 371	50.8	21.1
Middletown...................	19 863	2.21	13.0	35.7	3 731	998	552	2 733	1 202	2 523	124	2 399	33 677	43.0	34.3
Milford.......................	21 708	2.41	9.9	29.3	472	355	344	117	1 683	3 190	104	3 086	36 333	34.1	39.7
Naugatuck....................	12 339	2.56	13.5	25.4	267	236	236	31	665	2 087	97	1 990	22 475	48.6	22.3
New Britain	28 158	2.49	20.7	31.0	3 194	790	557	2 404	3 360	4 590	421	4 169	46 640	58.3	18.5
New Haven	48 877	2.43	22.4	35.4	11 220	1 774	768	9 446	9 244	7 123	1 536	5 586	76 794	47.2	32.7
New London..................	10 373	2.30	18.4	38.0	3 713	225	225	3 488	1 197	4 334	1 032	3 302	16 034	50.0	22.4
Norwalk......................	33 217	2.55	13.0	28.6	797	461	405	336	2 225	2 599	401	2 199	63 050	36.1	41.3
Norwich......................	16 599	2.41	17.2	31.3	514	219	205	295	1 115	2 754	356	2 398	26 747	45.6	21.8
Shelton.......................	15 325	2.55	9.0	24.2	502	446	442	56	518	1 309	71	1 239	28 546	42.8	33.4
Stamford.....................	47 357	2.56	12.2	28.9	1 280	662	653	618	2 330	1 900	286	1 614	85 507	38.5	41.3
Torrington....................	15 243	2.33	12.1	31.9	838	611	559	227	919	2 526	140	2 386	25 278	52.2	18.3
Waterbury	42 761	2.54	22.3	30.7	1 938	1 149	886	789	5 012	4 541	332	4 210	70 222	57.5	17.4
West Haven	21 112	2.50	16.7	29.9	2 857	458	362	2 399	1 828	3 290	770	2 520	38 913	51.8	20.3
DELAWARE...............	342 297	2.55	14.2	25.6	24 413	11 673	4 591	12 740	36 538	4 069	621	3 448	596 009	44.4	28.0
Dover	13 771	2.35	19.0	33.6	3 745	569	340	3 176	2 362	6 553	655	5 898	20 851	39.0	26.6
Newark.......................	9 834	2.47	6.5	26.8	7 128	0	0	7 128	1 087	3 456	445	3 011	13 733	25.6	51.0
Wilmington	28 615	2.36	24.8	38.1	3 226	2 324	531	902	5 573	7 866	1 986	5 880	47 028	50.9	24.7
DISTRICT OF COLUMBIA.............................	266 707	2.11	16.4	44.0	40 021	7 339	3 064	32 682	36 760	6 109	1 330	4 779	405 733	32.7	49.8
Washington...................	266 707	2.11	16.4	44.0	40 021	7 339	3 064	32 682	34 606	5 751	1 241	4 510	405 733	32.7	49.8
FLORIDA	7 420 802	2.48	13.5	27.2	421 709	254 506	73 372	167 203	771 004	4 101	542	3 558	12 931 148	44.5	25.7
Altamonte Springs	19 126	2.15	15.3	37.6	448	444	444	4	1 529	3 685	398	3 287	30 286	31.3	31.9
Apopka.......................	14 360	2.88	13.9	17.9	178	118	118	60	1 655	3 984	587	3 397	26 911	34.4	29.5
Aventura......................	17 892	1.99	9.0	39.3	96	96	96	0	2 271	6 350	154	6 197	27 195	29.0	46.7
Boca Raton	36 778	2.20	8.3	32.2	3 444	430	415	3 014	2 683	3 179	209	2 971	61 668	23.5	49.5
Bonita Springs	20 017	2.19	5.3	27.0	157	12	0	145	NA	NA	NA	NA	35 130	40.9	29.0
Boynton Beach	29 104	2.31	13.1	34.3	1 000	649	630	351	3 780	5 541	858	4 684	50 349	44.4	24.2
Bradenton	21 405	2.23	14.6	36.5	1 757	1 074	966	683	2 447	4 939	773	4 166	34 613	49.4	21.8
Cape Coral...................	60 767	2.53	12.0	21.4	445	350	307	95	4 063	2 633	179	2 454	105 920	46.6	20.6
Casselberry..................	11 430	2.29	14.8	32.5	51	12	5	39	1 082	4 123	812	3 312	18 232	43.0	19.8
Clearwater....................	47 638	2.19	12.5	36.5	3 584	1 011	1 000	2 573	5 113	4 748	720	4 028	80 207	42.2	26.8
Clermont.....................	11 216	2.54	11.6	23.5	199	177	177	22	1 025	3 566	324	3 243	19 400	37.6	28.5
Coconut Creek...............	22 754	2.32	12.3	32.8	146	138	65	8	1 522	2 877	168	2 708	36 630	37.3	30.6
Cooper City	9 628	2.96	13.5	12.2	40	0	0	40	674	2 361	175	2 186	17 928	29.8	39.1
Coral Gables	17 946	2.35	9.8	29.2	4 540	1	0	4 539	2 046	4 374	199	4 175	28 775	15.4	67.2
Coral Springs	41 814	2.89	16.7	17.3	359	227	222	132	3 145	2 597	216	2 382	76 811	32.1	35.4
Cutler Bay....................	13 338	3.00	16.3	17.7	338	245	199	93	2 069	5 136	514	4 622	24 803	36.5	31.7
Dania Beach	12 877	2.28	15.3	33.0	329	294	87	35	1 704	5 749	766	4 983	21 587	46.5	25.0
Davie........................	34 315	2.64	14.6	23.0	1 355	86	50	1 269	4 010	4 359	399	3 960	60 294	36.5	28.8
Daytona Beach	27 314	2.05	15.1	41.1	5 048	1 094	1 059	3 954	5 446	8 927	1 329	7 598	39 261	47.7	21.0

1. No spouse present.   2. Data for serious crimes have not been adjusted for underreporting. This may affect comparability between geographic areas and over time.   3. Per 100,000 population estimated by the FBI.   4. Persons 25 years old and over.

Table D. Cities — Income, Poverty, and Housing

City	Money income, 2008–2010 Households — Per capita income[1] (dollars)	Median income	Percent with income of $200,000 or more	Percent with income of less than $25,000	Families with income below poverty (percent)	Housing units, 2010 — Total	Percent change, 2000–2010	Vacant units for sale or rent[2]	Occupied Housing units 2008–2010 Owner-occupied — Total	Percent	Median value[3] (dollars)	Median owner costs as a percent of income — With a mortgage[4]	Without a mortgage[5]
	42	43	44	45	46	47	48	49	50	51	52	53	54
COLORADO—Cont'd													
Castle Rock	32 943	84 080	6.4	8.6	3.3	17 626	135.5	938	16 087	76.9	279 700	24.8	10.1
Centennial	40 520	86 832	9.7	8.1	3.4	38 779	NA	1 330	37 353	85.1	287 200	22.4	10.0
Colorado Springs	27 753	52 179	3.3	22.9	9.8	179 607	20.7	11 819	163 393	60.5	216 000	24.3	10.0
Commerce City	21 856	56 912	1.1	20.0	13.4	15 452	123.7	973	13 996	68.3	201 700	27.5	14.9
Denver	30 806	45 526	4.9	28.5	15.1	285 797	13.7	22 690	256 810	51.3	245 500	25.1	10.8
Englewood	25 811	43 138	1.7	26.1	9.9	15 478	4.0	1 103	13 885	51.1	216 000	26.1	13.1
Fort Collins	27 491	49 512	3.5	26.0	7.8	60 503	26.7	2 674	56 412	55.3	245 500	24.1	10.0
Fountain	21 253	53 015	0.0	20.8	12.0	9 371	80.1	647	8 683	69.5	184 200	26.4	10.0
Grand Junction	27 084	48 172	2.7	26.1	8.5	26 170	38.7	1 859	24 198	63.4	234 100	24.8	10.0
Greeley	20 907	42 303	2.3	31.9	15.6	36 323	25.9	2 896	33 505	58.5	169 600	24.7	11.6
Lakewood	29 790	52 263	3.1	20.8	9.4	65 758	5.3	3 772	61 220	58.2	237 900	25.2	10.0
Littleton	33 024	55 330	4.9	22.6	6.5	19 434	7.1	1 122	18 037	63.3	270 300	23.8	10.1
Longmont	28 378	54 577	3.8	19.7	9.5	35 008	27.6	1 756	33 409	62.8	242 300	25.4	10.0
Loveland	26 824	53 991	2.3	19.8	7.9	28 557	40.5	1 404	26 828	68.5	211 200	24.6	10.0
Northglenn	22 182	53 483	1.1	20.3	11.3	14 274	17.5	782	12 313	57.2	194 900	25.2	12.0
Parker	33 978	90 502	4.9	8.5	3.2	16 533	97.8	616	15 801	76.3	290 300	24.9	10.0
Pueblo	19 554	34 142	1.3	38.2	17.6	47 593	10.4	4 303	42 581	61.2	120 200	25.8	11.5
Thornton	25 699	64 154	2.0	13.8	7.6	43 230	46.6	1 871	39 780	71.0	210 100	25.0	11.3
Westminster	29 571	61 872	2.8	16.4	8.3	43 968	11.4	1 927	40 587	66.6	225 100	24.8	10.2
Wheat Ridge	28 999	45 857	1.4	28.1	9.8	14 868	-0.7	892	14 349	59.7	238 300	24.6	12.1
CONNECTICUT	36 412	67 067	8.0	18.3	6.9	1 487 891	7.4	116 804	1 361 186	68.6	294 300	26.7	17.1
Bridgeport	19 066	39 637	1.3	33.8	18.9	57 012	4.9	5 757	51 383	44.0	233 500	36.6	22.4
Bristol	29 186	57 294	2.6	18.4	7.2	27 011	3.4	1 691	25 214	65.1	217 900	26.1	17.7
Danbury	28 942	62 541	4.5	17.3	7.2	31 154	9.2	2 247	29 229	63.1	329 700	29.2	15.2
Hartford	15 851	28 069	1.1	45.9	29.1	51 822	2.3	6 698	46 121	25.9	189 900	33.3	18.3
Meriden	25 862	52 674	1.9	23.8	11.7	25 892	5.1	1 915	23 567	63.0	209 200	29.2	18.0
Middletown	30 835	55 570	2.6	25.5	7.2	21 223	7.7	1 360	20 765	57.3	241 400	27.7	16.9
Milford	38 351	77 449	7.3	12.5	3.3	23 074	5.1	1 366	20 426	76.1	332 800	27.4	20.7
Naugatuck	28 422	60 186	2.4	18.9	9.1	13 061	5.8	722	12 745	70.1	227 400	27.7	18.2
New Britain	20 350	39 423	0.6	34.1	17.6	31 226	0.2	3 068	29 224	43.9	173 700	30.7	19.8
New Haven	21 900	38 585	2.7	36.3	20.7	54 967	3.8	6 090	48 679	30.3	233 500	30.2	17.4
New London	20 430	44 510	1.2	26.4	14.7	11 840	2.4	1 467	10 141	36.7	197 800	29.5	17.9
Norwalk	43 522	74 229	10.4	16.2	7.3	35 415	4.9	2 198	36 386	66.0	465 000	32.3	19.0
Norwich	25 998	52 075	2.0	22.3	11.5	18 659	12.4	2 060	16 245	54.4	208 700	28.4	16.5
Shelton	39 187	77 998	8.3	13.1	3.0	16 146	9.8	821	15 132	82.5	372 200	28.4	17.2
Stamford	41 227	73 965	12.6	18.0	8.6	50 573	6.9	3 216	45 039	54.2	563 000	28.1	19.0
Torrington	25 269	47 958	1.6	24.0	7.8	16 761	3.8	1 518	15 225	67.3	189 900	28.2	18.0
Waterbury	21 145	38 636	0.9	33.9	18.0	47 991	2.5	5 230	43 165	47.6	166 300	29.5	22.6
West Haven	26 619	51 220	2.8	21.7	7.6	22 446	0.5	1 334	22 048	56.4	233 500	31.4	20.4
DELAWARE	28 708	57 613	3.8	19.5	7.5	405 885	18.3	63 588	331 643	73.2	248 200	24.9	11.5
Dover	22 800	48 896	2.0	24.2	13.1	15 024	12.5	1 253	12 971	56.4	194 400	26.4	11.0
Newark	23 744	49 575	3.8	34.4	4.7	10 475	12.5	641	9 820	54.2	292 500	19.5	10.0
Wilmington	24 084	36 736	3.0	36.2	19.4	32 820	2.1	4 205	28 726	48.8	185 600	24.9	16.1
DISTRICT OF COLUMBIA	42 066	59 822	10.1	23.8	14.3	296 719	8.0	30 012	256 081	42.7	446 300	24.7	10.7
Washington	42 066	59 822	10.1	23.8	14.3	296 719	8.0	30 012	256 081	42.7	446 300	24.7	10.7
FLORIDA	25 482	46 077	3.4	25.9	10.8	8 989 580	23.1	1 568 778	7 087 691	68.8	187 400	29.7	14.0
Altamonte Springs	26 887	48 251	1.3	19.1	6.1	22 088	9.5	2 962	17 456	53.7	184 400	28.9	15.1
Apopka	25 952	57 079	2.8	16.4	9.9	15 707	55.9	1 347	14 756	80.7	206 500	28.7	12.1
Aventura	45 301	52 115	9.1	24.0	7.6	26 120	30.5	8 228	16 837	69.4	301 100	35.9	25.0
Boca Raton	47 531	69 266	12.8	17.7	6.0	44 539	18.3	7 761	35 535	73.8	390 500	31.3	15.5
Bonita Springs	38 657	51 605	8.0	18.5	7.7	31 716	35.2	11 699	18 487	81.9	268 200	33.4	13.3
Boynton Beach	25 463	42 816	1.6	27.2	9.8	36 289	18.6	7 185	28 376	66.7	167 800	32.8	17.8
Bradenton	22 892	41 105	1.1	29.7	11.2	26 767	7.3	5 362	20 726	58.7	163 400	28.2	14.6
Cape Coral	23 541	49 111	1.8	20.8	9.1	78 948	72.7	18 181	55 085	74.9	173 200	31.5	16.1
Casselberry	23 260	42 801	1.2	29.1	13.5	12 708	22.5	1 278	9 993	66.1	163 900	30.2	14.8
Clearwater	26 350	40 542	3.0	29.6	11.7	59 156	4.3	11 518	45 752	62.4	178 800	31.3	18.0
Clermont	26 095	52 526	1.6	17.8	5.4	12 730	NA	1 514	10 787	74.7	217 200	30.6	13.1
Coconut Creek	26 730	50 347	0.9	21.2	5.9	25 926	17.1	3 172	21 864	69.7	170 300	31.6	25.4
Cooper City	34 002	86 943	7.8	9.2	3.4	9 912	7.4	284	9 243	86.7	331 800	27.0	13.5
Coral Gables	52 503	85 684	20.6	17.7	5.0	20 266	13.9	2 320	16 429	68.1	648 100	32.4	15.8
Coral Springs	30 403	67 310	6.4	15.3	6.5	45 433	10.0	3 619	40 612	68.7	305 600	30.4	13.8
Cutler Bay	25 832	62 044	4.6	20.2	10.7	14 620	NA	1 282	12 804	72.5	244 500	30.0	12.9
Dania Beach	24 862	42 362	1.3	29.4	10.9	15 671	44.1	2 794	12 909	58.1	182 100	30.2	21.5
Davie	29 265	58 378	4.7	20.3	9.0	37 306	19.6	2 991	32 758	74.3	240 700	29.0	16.2
Daytona Beach	18 162	29 727	1.6	43.9	19.4	33 920	1.6	6 606	24 694	51.1	156 400	32.4	14.8

1. Based on population estimated by the American Community Survey.   2. Includes units rented or sold but not occupied.   3. Specified owner-occupied units; $1,000,000 represents $1,000,000 or more.   4. 50.0 represents 50 percent or more.   5. 10.0 represents 10 percent or less.

Table D. Cities — Housing, Labor Force, and Employment

City	Occupied housing units, 2008–2010 (cont.)				Migration, 2008–2010		Civilian labor force, 2010				Civilian employment[4], 2008–2010			
			Median rent as a percent of income[2]	Percent with no vehicle available	Percent who lived in the same house one year ago	Percent who lived outside this city one year ago		Percent change, 2009–2010	Unemployment		Population age 16 and older	Percent		Households with no workers (percent)
	Percent renter occupied	Median gross rent[1]					Total		Total	Rate[3]		In labor force	Full-year full-time worker	
	55	56	57	58	59	60	61	62	63	64	65	66	67	68
COLORADO—Cont'd														
Castle Rock	23.1	1 072	29.8	2.8	79.8	10.1	19 177	1.3	1 911	10.0	32 904	77.9	53.7	12.6
Centennial	14.9	1 184	27.7	2.7	88.8	9.5	65 710	2.8	4 292	6.5	79 220	72.4	47.2	16.1
Colorado Springs	39.5	776	29.2	7.0	76.6	9.9	216 789	1.4	20 621	9.5	316 698	70.0	44.4	22.3
Commerce City	31.7	873	33.2	7.2	80.7	13.3	11 969	3.4	1 823	15.2	30 245	75.9	48.7	17.1
Denver	48.7	816	30.9	12.8	76.8	10.5	323 088	0.5	32 085	9.9	474 928	71.2	44.9	24.2
Englewood	48.9	745	31.0	10.0	78.6	16.5	21 361	3.3	2 162	10.1	24 605	74.8	46.9	22.6
Fort Collins	44.7	874	35.0	5.1	69.6	15.3	85 381	1.7	7 253	8.5	117 247	71.3	38.8	19.4
Fountain	30.5	944	36.7	2.6	79.1	16.6	8 550	NA	1 170	13.7	18 081	69.0	48.4	17.7
Grand Junction	36.6	823	29.5	7.6	77.0	13.6	28 629	-2.0	3 078	10.8	46 856	62.7	39.5	29.2
Greeley	41.5	695	33.1	6.9	75.2	12.1	50 822	1.8	6 067	11.9	70 729	65.8	39.4	25.9
Lakewood	41.8	888	29.7	7.2	76.7	14.8	83 680	0.3	7 729	9.2	117 499	68.6	43.1	24.0
Littleton	36.7	840	29.8	5.9	80.7	13.8	26 176	3.0	2 032	7.8	33 324	68.0	43.4	26.1
Longmont	37.2	900	31.5	4.6	80.7	9.0	44 156	0.8	3 203	7.3	64 774	71.6	42.5	19.2
Loveland	31.5	852	32.0	4.4	83.2	9.5	34 159	1.5	2 204	6.5	51 484	68.5	42.7	25.2
Northglenn	42.8	872	27.8	3.5	82.4	13.6	22 191	2.7	2 306	10.4	27 591	71.3	47.8	18.8
Parker	23.7	1 135	28.3	2.4	85.1	11.3	21 307	0.9	1 092	5.1	31 199	79.6	54.7	9.9
Pueblo	38.8	635	35.2	10.2	78.6	7.9	52 971	2.7	6 181	11.7	83 182	56.7	33.7	37.5
Thornton	29.0	982	31.6	3.9	83.2	12.4	57 767	2.4	4 784	8.3	85 613	74.8	52.2	12.6
Westminster	33.4	933	28.8	3.7	82.5	14.6	68 851	1.5	5 686	8.3	81 535	74.7	48.8	16.8
Wheat Ridge	40.3	766	33.2	7.9	80.2	16.2	17 736	0.4	1 818	10.3	25 887	66.3	42.7	29.8
CONNECTICUT	31.4	994	31.5	8.7	87.8	7.9	1 916 596	1.6	178 138	9.3	2 841 460	68.3	42.5	24.1
Bridgeport	56.0	1 012	36.6	22.1	86.4	4.8	67 731	5.9	9 202	13.6	109 483	65.8	38.2	29.0
Bristol	34.9	868	27.9	7.3	87.7	6.4	34 586	-1.4	3 511	10.2	49 041	70.4	44.8	25.2
Danbury	36.9	1 203	31.2	9.1	85.5	7.5	45 959	2.5	3 593	7.8	64 267	72.2	45.1	20.1
Hartford	74.1	824	37.0	35.2	77.1	9.0	51 571	1.5	8 553	16.6	95 579	60.7	31.1	37.0
Meriden	37.0	898	33.5	11.0	84.9	6.3	33 115	2.2	3 739	11.3	47 759	69.9	42.7	24.5
Middletown	42.7	908	29.6	8.4	81.5	9.6	27 022	-1.2	2 406	8.9	39 191	68.3	42.9	23.3
Milford	23.9	1 356	30.1	4.2	88.2	6.4	31 133	-5.3	2 878	9.2	41 065	71.3	47.0	20.9
Naugatuck	29.9	928	31.7	4.6	92.3	5.1	17 161	-0.1	1 977	11.5	25 922	73.2	43.7	24.4
New Britain	56.1	856	32.9	16.9	82.2	7.2	36 944	3.2	4 827	13.1	58 163	68.2	37.7	28.0
New Haven	69.7	1 043	34.2	27.1	77.1	9.6	59 622	5.2	7 795	13.1	103 598	65.5	34.0	29.2
New London	63.3	882	28.1	18.4	66.1	18.0	14 680	4.8	1 631	11.1	22 676	66.9	39.6	30.4
Norwalk	34.0	1 227	31.4	8.7	89.3	4.3	49 835	1.8	3 912	7.8	69 275	72.2	48.6	21.5
Norwich	45.6	923	29.7	12.8	79.4	8.0	23 133	8.5	2 294	9.9	31 541	71.6	42.8	24.7
Shelton	17.5	994	27.8	5.5	94.1	4.3	22 957	-1.4	1 914	8.3	31 702	68.1	42.7	23.3
Stamford	45.8	1 465	33.0	11.0	85.6	5.5	68 826	1.7	5 314	7.7	98 320	72.3	43.3	18.8
Torrington	32.7	776	31.1	8.8	87.8	5.1	20 271	1.6	2 249	11.1	29 263	66.5	39.8	30.2
Waterbury	52.4	845	36.7	18.2	86.1	4.0	51 978	2.8	7 651	14.7	84 700	64.5	37.8	32.1
West Haven	43.6	1 005	33.2	11.6	86.3	9.2	31 703	5.8	3 336	10.5	45 465	71.9	42.6	24.8
DELAWARE	26.8	952	31.7	7.0	85.3	11.6	436 822	0.4	35 116	8.0	710 308	65.0	42.8	25.9
Dover	43.6	940	30.4	10.7	74.9	14.5	16 275	-1.6	1 540	9.5	28 604	63.4	43.0	27.7
Newark	45.8	939	48.3	13.4	57.8	24.9	15 567	3.3	1 011	6.5	28 104	50.4	24.9	31.5
Wilmington	51.2	827	33.9	25.8	76.8	10.8	30 934	-4.6	3 660	11.8	56 023	63.1	39.0	31.5
DISTRICT OF COLUMBIA	57.3	1 112	29.8	35.5	80.4	8.1	343 379	3.4	34 690	10.1	502 268	67.5	45.9	25.2
Washington	57.3	1 112	29.8	35.5	80.4	8.1	343 379	3.4	34 690	10.1	502 268	67.5	45.9	25.2
FLORIDA	31.2	957	34.9	6.6	83.4	11.6	9 132 470	-0.1	1 030 146	11.3	15 153 656	61.2	38.5	31.1
Altamonte Springs	46.3	935	29.2	7.4	81.1	12.2	26 073	-0.9	2 591	9.9	34 740	74.1	47.8	17.7
Apopka	19.3	946	38.6	4.0	90.8	6.4	21 874	4.7	2 254	10.3	31 287	70.9	50.7	17.3
Aventura	30.6	1 613	36.8	8.1	78.5	16.2	17 126	14.2	1 604	9.4	29 839	54.1	37.2	39.9
Boca Raton	26.2	1 289	38.2	3.7	86.0	9.1	41 630	-6.1	3 722	8.9	72 023	60.9	38.0	29.4
Bonita Springs	18.1	947	34.4	2.5	89.6	5.0	18 830	-2.1	2 020	10.7	38 068	48.1	28.2	48.6
Boynton Beach	33.3	1 207	36.0	6.4	80.3	13.1	32 448	-4.6	3 602	11.1	57 719	63.4	37.2	36.7
Bradenton	41.3	891	38.2	7.2	79.9	10.8	21 512	-12.4	2 694	12.5	40 755	60.3	36.1	38.0
Cape Coral	25.1	1 005	35.5	2.8	82.0	8.5	76 117	-5.7	9 491	12.5	122 043	63.4	38.0	29.6
Casselberry	33.9	942	35.6	3.7	85.7	11.6	14 950	1.3	1 549	10.4	21 661	68.5	42.3	22.9
Clearwater	37.6	931	34.7	8.9	83.5	11.1	52 039	-1.7	5 433	10.4	91 171	58.4	38.3	35.3
Clermont	25.3	970	34.8	2.5	81.9	12.6	13 517	NA	1 292	9.6	22 408	62.3	35.2	32.7
Coconut Creek	30.3	1 341	32.6	5.1	81.2	12.5	29 196	3.7	2 588	8.9	41 517	65.0	44.6	28.1
Cooper City	13.3	1 672	33.3	1.2	90.8	6.9	17 406	-3.1	1 363	7.8	22 417	71.2	46.3	14.5
Coral Gables	31.9	1 194	29.9	5.6	80.8	12.4	26 336	3.0	2 138	8.1	38 349	56.9	37.0	22.8
Coral Springs	31.3	1 250	36.0	4.5	85.0	8.9	72 573	-4.2	6 439	8.9	93 842	73.7	46.9	14.3
Cutler Bay	27.5	1 351	34.0	9.5	NA	NA	22 412	29.2	2 477	11.1	29 428	68.7	49.4	22.0
Dania Beach	41.9	1 118	35.3	7.6	83.5	13.3	17 277	4.5	1 413	8.2	24 265	70.8	44.4	25.9
Davie	25.7	1 136	32.7	4.9	84.3	10.2	54 682	1.3	4 340	7.9	72 358	70.1	45.9	19.6
Daytona Beach	48.9	745	38.0	13.7	74.7	18.1	31 314	-4.7	3 751	12.0	54 541	49.1	25.3	41.7

1. $2,000 represents $2,000 or more. 2. 50.0 represents 50 percent or more. 3. Percent of civilian labor force. 4. Persons 16 years old and over.

City	Value of residential construction authorized by building permits, 2010			Wholesale trade,[1] 2007				Retail trade,[2] 2007			
	New construction ($1,000)	Number of housing units	Percent single family	Number of establish-ments	Number of employees	Sales (mil dol)	Annual payroll (mil dol)	Number of establish-ments	Number of employees	Sales (mil dol)	Annual payroll (mil dol)
	69	70	71	72	73	74	75	76	77	78	79
COLORADO—Cont'd											
Castle Rock	77 317	376	90.4	26	163	48.3	7.6	210	2 869	636.9	69.8
Centennial	4 542	34	100.0	190	2 740	1 970.0	181.8	264	3 983	1 942.9	128.6
Colorado Springs	NA	NA	NA	358	4 471	2 482.4	225.2	1 741	27 411	7 027.3	678.4
Commerce City	37 543	240	92.1	129	2 820	2 015.9	154.2	101	1 496	458.6	40.5
Denver	183 136	1 232	51.3	1 174	21 245	14 920.9	1 064.5	2 271	27 979	6 835.4	752.6
Englewood	1 231	7	100.0	106	1 845	667.0	97.4	226	2 968	1 598.1	80.7
Fort Collins	45 084	246	73.2	101	933	371.7	50.1	595	9 642	2 152.3	222.3
Fountain	NA	NA	NA	3	D	D	D	42	1 070	242.8	24.6
Grand Junction	NA	NA	NA	160	1 856	921.5	79.3	535	7 495	2 002.3	191.5
Greeley	12 131	85	100.0	92	1 115	606.1	53.0	341	5 563	1 222.6	122.4
Lakewood	45 053	200	58.5	129	877	475.8	46.9	695	10 817	2 671.8	271.3
Littleton	36 333	281	0.4	67	961	288.2	43.2	255	4 575	1 688.6	150.0
Longmont	21 443	110	64.5	66	736	669.5	57.5	309	4 761	1 054.5	106.4
Loveland	83 965	720	15.3	62	900	387.1	39.3	350	5 218	1 211.7	117.8
Northglenn	0	0	0.0	17	280	65.2	8.9	91	1 559	366.2	41.0
Parker	32 511	112	100.0	33	396	127.9	9.8	135	2 460	629.4	57.2
Pueblo	NA	NA	NA	57	525	244.0	23.3	441	6 907	1 563.9	163.8
Thornton	52 562	260	71.2	28	207	118.2	16.7	194	5 057	1 267.0	131.7
Westminster	14 284	48	83.3	64	1 011	452.4	71.0	358	6 595	1 421.5	140.0
Wheat Ridge	324	2	100.0	61	570	178.5	29.3	186	2 402	637.7	69.8
CONNECTICUT	861 356	3 932	66.9	3 848	58 291	107 917.0	3 587.9	13 807	196 133	52 165.5	5 160.4
Bridgeport	4 264	101	10.9	125	1 732	794.3	94.8	313	3 555	1 122.2	112.3
Bristol	4 095	37	100.0	37	600	253.4	27.9	178	3 046	803.3	74.9
Danbury	21 604	128	93.0	99	1 041	1 037.3	65.0	473	8 219	2 176.7	217.6
Hartford	6 896	64	6.3	130	2 759	1 413.4	128.1	381	3 620	1 299.1	110.2
Meriden	1 164	17	100.0	36	451	169.2	22.6	257	3 907	828.6	78.9
Middletown	3 900	28	92.9	40	761	262.0	34.4	139	1 868	526.7	52.8
Milford	NA	NA	NA	113	1 763	840.5	94.4	332	5 958	1 546.1	138.4
Naugatuck	1 302	8	100.0	27	429	240.6	25.8	71	1 066	275.4	24.0
New Britain	3 034	14	71.4	43	613	407.4	26.7	164	2 079	589.8	55.9
New Haven	99 333	478	4.8	78	1 042	1 077.9	51.7	345	3 366	907.2	88.0
New London	5 865	35	100.0	13	264	266.3	12.4	124	1 542	505.4	50.1
Norwalk	8 098	40	42.5	139	2 437	2 929.7	143.4	689	6 949	2 164.2	230.5
Norwich	3 081	43	62.8	18	450	248.3	27.0	151	2 134	517.6	51.4
Shelton	4 069	31	80.6	57	1 235	977.3	91.3	109	1 984	648.6	64.0
Stamford	32 129	152	10.5	222	4 587	64 886.5	568.9	492	6 157	1 596.1	186.7
Torrington	1 120	8	100.0	37	294	197.4	15.2	176	2 621	725.5	65.8
Waterbury	2 528	32	93.8	95	1 000	622.9	52.7	442	6 706	1 526.4	152.7
West Haven	455	4	100.0	62	1 148	486.8	58.0	129	1 487	443.1	40.9
DELAWARE	354 135	3 072	87.0	819	9 065	5 727.4	416.9	3 907	55 432	14 202.1	1 322.8
Dover	13 385	130	73.1	38	730	216.4	27.0	300	4 944	1 291.4	103.9
Newark	1 040	9	100.0	37	355	349.5	22.5	161	2 956	894.9	79.9
Wilmington	1 691	58	31.0	100	1 016	700.0	46.7	331	4 128	1 105.7	109.5
DISTRICT OF COLUMBIA	105 471	739	24.0	316	3 680	2 118.0	216.4	1 827	19 117	3 843.7	485.9
Washington	105 471	739	24.0	316	3 680	2 118.0	216.4	1 827	19 117	3 843.7	485.9
FLORIDA	7 823 543	38 679	77.7	27 442	279 300	221 641.5	12 566.1	73 794	1 016 290	262 341.1	24 049.7
Altamonte Springs	1 755	18	0.0	83	1 081	328.1	37.1	372	6 966	1 503.8	152.0
Apopka	82 954	289	100.0	55	464	128.6	14.4	144	2 082	567.7	48.8
Aventura	0	0	0.0	106	429	929.8	22.1	327	6 995	1 390.1	145.2
Boca Raton	27 322	65	92.3	421	4 906	5 249.8	314.8	746	10 183	2 348.5	272.7
Bonita Springs	45 746	249	100.0	38	410	188.3	15.0	228	2 762	663.1	73.7
Boynton Beach	1 082	11	81.8	119	963	457.4	42.8	356	6 019	1 191.8	118.8
Bradenton	8 357	48	58.3	42	574	322.4	27.0	216	2 930	718.4	71.5
Cape Coral	26 048	216	100.0	98	422	115.5	13.4	391	5 407	1 228.0	122.7
Casselberry	5 376	28	100.0	35	118	36.1	4.1	153	2 618	578.9	56.6
Clearwater	6 620	30	86.7	184	1 773	902.4	90.8	675	11 269	2 938.8	260.9
Clermont	NA	NA	NA	18	120	34.7	4.4	131	2 935	703.2	63.6
Coconut Creek	15 741	77	100.0	80	394	327.5	20.1	131	3 121	1 437.4	110.3
Cooper City	21 995	310	100.0	50	169	81.3	7.2	86	1 556	278.8	29.7
Coral Gables	32 383	61	27.9	169	1 124	7 011.7	93.3	316	4 545	1 436.4	151.2
Coral Springs	0	0	0.0	208	2 019	1 009.5	63.4	508	8 734	1 900.2	184.9
Cutler Bay	5 193	130	70.0	NA	NA	NA	NA	NA	NA	NA	NA
Dania Beach	926	4	100.0	134	1 054	581.3	52.2	193	2 053	564.1	55.5
Davie	22 646	182	86.3	253	1 589	633.3	76.0	412	6 288	2 010.5	170.0
Daytona Beach	30 798	130	100.0	96	1 054	447.8	40.5	500	7 644	1 810.6	168.7

1. Merchant wholesalers except manufacturers' sales branches and offices.   2. Establishments with payroll.

Table D. Cities — Real Estate, Professional Services, and Manufacturing

City	Real estate and rental and leasing, 2007				Professional, scientific, and technical services,[1] 2007				Manufacturing, 2007			
	Number of establish-ments	Number of employees	Receipts (mil dol)	Annual payroll (mil dol)	Number of establish-ments	Number of employees	Receipts (mil dol)	Annual payroll (mil dol)	Number of establish-ments	Number of employees	Receipts (mil dol)	Annual payroll (mil dol)
	80	81	82	83	84	85	86	87	88	89	90	91
COLORADO—Cont'd												
Castle Rock	93	237	36.3	6.4	158	422	54.4	19.6	NA	NA	NA	NA
Centennial	246	1 688	336.3	67.2	719	4 300	772.7	283.7	76	1 451	436.5	75.6
Colorado Springs	942	3 364	521.5	99.7	1 871	D	D	D	379	11 518	3 819.9	577.9
Commerce City	48	380	111.1	18.6	35	189	20.8	7.2	78	2 424	4 019.7	125.9
Denver	1 451	11 600	2 536.4	623.7	3 856	D	D	D	840	19 480	5 189.9	826.0
Englewood	79	414	57.5	15.6	172	D	D	D	147	4 032	988.4	183.5
Fort Collins	289	1 274	185.2	34.0	768	D	D	D	126	5 852	2 179.3	367.0
Fountain	15	61	6.4	1.0	18	62	4.5	1.0	11	563	296.2	16.6
Grand Junction	232	830	203.1	32.2	373	D	D	D	106	2 082	D	83.0
Greeley	133	586	80.7	17.2	198	D	D	D	69	3 814	1 821.0	135.7
Lakewood	264	1 089	177.1	36.2	816	D	D	D	111	2 598	744.5	118.9
Littleton	113	466	58.7	12.6	351	D	D	D	34	D	D	D
Longmont	137	479	84.2	13.6	350	2 353	410.7	168.9	119	3 102	587.8	125.0
Loveland	112	462	60.1	13.4	210	1 108	125.1	41.4	92	2 885	563.6	181.6
Northglenn	44	257	19.8	5.4	51	179	14.9	6.0	36	804	128.4	29.5
Parker	66	176	26.2	4.1	186	580	80.1	28.7	NA	NA	NA	NA
Pueblo	121	581	85.1	16.5	202	D	D	D	59	2 046	D	104.6
Thornton	77	276	49.7	7.0	160	983	152.9	53.3	NA	NA	NA	NA
Westminster	158	584	87.6	17.1	335	D	D	D	52	813	271.7	41.2
Wheat Ridge	52	175	24.0	4.0	180	913	127.0	56.4	49	1 101	248.3	56.1
CONNECTICUT	3 609	22 455	5 686.6	994.0	9 828	101 384	15 771.7	7 988.8	4 924	190 790	58 404.9	10 345.1
Bridgeport	96	507	156.6	17.3	200	D	D	D	199	4 736	946.8	211.8
Bristol	40	138	30.1	4.1	74	416	38.5	17.2	148	3 675	719.2	160.1
Danbury	84	1 956	287.6	107.9	238	3 976	398.7	219.9	100	5 096	1 736.9	311.6
Hartford	174	1 562	257.6	77.4	404	7 844	1 666.5	639.6	80	1 314	242.9	51.5
Meriden	49	404	63.4	10.7	78	781	82.0	37.4	73	2 974	652.6	160.9
Middletown	49	404	140.7	21.6	113	D	D	D	64	3 390	1 668.0	199.8
Milford	60	910	863.6	43.0	187	2 126	224.6	95.9	167	3 477	1 102.4	190.5
Naugatuck	15	48	9.2	1.1	39	151	15.3	6.4	52	1 488	355.7	72.1
New Britain	45	153	30.0	4.7	94	D	D	D	103	3 382	713.2	157.6
New Haven	137	956	159.9	34.4	390	D	D	D	79	2 999	584.0	125.1
New London	27	166	21.2	6.3	106	D	D	D	NA	NA	NA	NA
Norwalk	100	386	92.2	18.1	374	D	D	D	131	3 220	991.2	207.6
Norwich	41	159	22.0	3.9	64	453	40.9	16.6	34	981	176.7	46.1
Shelton	44	263	93.5	19.3	152	D	D	D	74	4 316	1 195.7	301.0
Stamford	232	1 856	569.9	126.1	701	D	D	D	125	4 371	2 200.5	224.2
Torrington	28	123	15.9	4.1	65	254	30.4	8.9	63	1 998	415.4	90.4
Waterbury	89	352	87.1	12.0	159	D	D	D	177	4 187	1 009.4	186.5
West Haven	44	179	36.3	5.5	64	D	D	D	50	1 549	377.9	72.7
DELAWARE	1 248	5 807	11 057.2	222.4	2 383	D	D	D	673	34 866	25 679.9	1 759.7
Dover	60	388	60.5	15.5	143	D	D	D	26	D	1 413.5	D
Newark	66	D	D	D	117	D	D	D	36	4 372	3 070.0	311.7
Wilmington	244	861	2 285.7	39.0	567	D	D	D	77	1 578	397.2	76.2
DISTRICT OF COLUMBIA	1 140	9 663	2 747.8	624.8	4 373	82 107	24 177.7	8 660.6	137	2 015	332.8	80.8
Washington	1 140	9 663	2 747.8	624.8	4 373	82 107	24 177.7	8 660.6	137	2 015	332.8	80.8
FLORIDA	33 653	170 859	32 235.4	6 094.2	69 083	427 536	61 599.8	24 264.5	14 324	355 386	104 832.9	15 227.2
Altamonte Springs	142	783	137.5	28.1	332	2 172	264.2	98.0	NA	NA	NA	NA
Apopka	44	162	23.2	3.9	103	360	36.8	12.0	35	878	173.2	38.2
Aventura	174	828	217.1	32.1	261	864	145.1	55.0	NA	NA	NA	NA
Boca Raton	516	3 740	555.0	179.9	1 544	D	D	D	150	1 997	385.2	95.3
Bonita Springs	124	475	112.6	22.1	199	976	168.4	52.0	NA	NA	NA	NA
Boynton Beach	115	462	96.6	13.6	271	906	101.8	35.7	73	777	108.1	27.8
Bradenton	97	355	55.7	10.4	248	D	D	D	26	618	100.0	19.1
Cape Coral	295	637	82.1	15.5	347	1 318	136.9	48.8	85	745	101.2	27.9
Casselberry	59	295	49.1	9.0	108	411	50.5	15.3	NA	NA	NA	NA
Clearwater	286	1 151	198.5	39.5	772	D	D	D	112	1 301	219.6	49.6
Clermont	80	235	33.8	5.9	103	408	37.0	14.6	NA	NA	NA	NA
Coconut Creek	42	D	D	D	145	368	38.8	12.7	NA	NA	NA	NA
Cooper City	44	99	23.2	3.0	136	376	43.9	13.3	NA	NA	NA	NA
Coral Gables	385	2 418	403.9	89.7	1 424	D	D	D	45	512	D	27.7
Coral Springs	241	905	209.2	38.2	801	2 940	341.6	111.9	84	903	166.0	36.4
Cutler Bay	NA	NA	NA	NA	NA	NA	NA	NA	NA	NA	NA	NA
Dania Beach	69	204	52.4	7.2	154	638	85.1	29.9	59	792	131.8	29.5
Davie	219	875	213.1	35.0	503	D	D	D	99	2 449	331.4	113.3
Daytona Beach	158	1 515	209.2	41.9	333	D	D	D	62	1 382	316.3	58.7

1. Establishments subject to federal tax.

Table D. Cities — **Accommodation and Food Services, Arts, Entertainment, and Recreation, and Health Care and Social Assistance**

City	Accommodation and food services, 2007				Arts, entertainment, and recreation,[1] 2007				Health care and social assistance,[1] 2007			
	Number of establishments	Number of employees	Sales (mil dol)	Annual payroll (mil dol)	Number of establishments	Number of employees	Receipts (mil dol)	Annual payroll (mil dol)	Number of establishments	Number of employees	Receipts (mil dol)	Annual payroll (mil dol)
	92	93	94	95	96	97	98	99	100	101	102	103
COLORADO—Cont'd												
Castle Rock	93	1 680	67.3	21.3	14	D	D	D	92	818	55.7	25.0
Centennial	168	2 680	125.4	36.1	33	D	D	D	305	2 419	230.1	98.7
Colorado Springs	1 008	20 874	1 011.9	309.4	146	1 492	81.9	22.5	1 354	14 224	1 406.1	583.1
Commerce City	52	814	37.1	11.3	4	D	D	D	14	262	17.1	7.7
Denver	1 778	38 701	2 279.0	656.3	204	4 981	626.2	320.9	1 595	22 442	2 562.4	1 047.8
Englewood	104	1 469	65.7	19.6	13	D	D	D	218	4 579	651.1	259.0
Fort Collins	392	8 324	328.0	99.9	52	813	35.1	9.8	486	5 257	531.3	223.6
Fountain	37	528	25.4	6.7	3	53	2.1	0.8	11	121	12.0	4.3
Grand Junction	210	4 746	211.3	61.0	34	733	18.4	6.8	313	D	D	D
Greeley	187	3 828	134.5	40.7	20	197	7.0	1.8	228	3 326	273.9	116.4
Lakewood	350	7 742	347.4	108.1	44	727	30.9	10.1	440	5 841	504.5	226.8
Littleton	127	2 229	94.6	29.3	19	160	7.5	2.6	203	2 238	244.2	114.8
Longmont	183	3 285	144.5	45.6	27	226	6.4	1.9	226	2 350	201.4	91.1
Loveland	181	3 274	128.6	37.4	26	D	D	D	180	1 842	177.5	68.7
Northglenn	56	1 516	69.3	20.6	8	D	D	D	42	495	38.7	16.4
Parker	98	2 117	87.9	26.0	12	D	D	D	107	D	D	D
Pueblo	282	4 840	194.1	55.0	24	D	D	D	318	D	D	D
Thornton	143	3 048	135.5	38.8	17	D	D	D	162	2 845	316.5	120.2
Westminster	234	5 207	259.6	82.5	26	D	D	D	206	2 579	232.4	108.6
Wheat Ridge	99	1 553	67.1	18.8	16	100	5.0	1.3	167	1 666	189.4	91.7
CONNECTICUT	7 941	132 001	9 138.4	2 483.1	1 206	14 325	1 834.8	457.0	7 687	122 425	11 534.8	5 062.3
Bridgeport	193	D	D	D	17	315	30.7	6.9	214	3 925	364.7	161.7
Bristol	101	1 251	62.1	16.9	12	169	30.8	7.7	108	D	D	D
Danbury	208	3 248	200.3	54.3	16	D	D	D	195	D	D	D
Hartford	350	5 163	294.9	84.8	15	746	123.7	57.6	248	4 850	714.9	346.3
Meriden	120	1 402	72.5	19.9	9	D	D	D	95	1 616	145.8	62.3
Middletown	117	1 238	83.4	21.3	8	84	3.8	0.8	118	2 491	245.4	114.5
Milford	184	2 470	129.0	35.9	20	229	19.1	6.2	134	2 416	231.6	101.7
Naugatuck	51	398	20.1	5.1	4	D	D	D	39	1 081	50.8	23.7
New Britain	81	1 091	49.1	14.8	8	D	D	D	104	1 366	193.4	84.7
New Haven	331	3 739	266.0	66.2	17	340	80.9	7.8	277	4 295	431.1	209.7
New London	94	D	D	D	13	113	11.6	4.8	85	D	D	D
Norwalk	238	2 777	207.0	54.0	53	720	101.8	30.9	196	2 901	283.3	124.4
Norwich	89	D	D	D	9	D	D	D	120	1 890	195.3	74.7
Shelton	95	1 683	99.2	30.4	10	D	D	D	92	1 923	223.7	72.7
Stamford	349	4 437	353.1	106.8	57	D	D	D	340	3 368	424.1	169.5
Torrington	90	1 114	56.6	15.6	7	D	D	D	102	1 834	170.1	70.4
Waterbury	215	2 848	138.7	40.8	16	161	8.6	2.1	242	6 276	552.2	252.4
West Haven	118	1 358	74.5	20.9	6	D	D	D	61	D	D	D
DELAWARE	1 850	32 194	1 910.8	468.8	291	3 722	349.3	82.6	1 877	25 319	2 620.7	1 155.8
Dover	123	3 732	378.6	57.0	16	D	D	D	165	2 272	205.7	90.6
Newark	124	2 513	138.6	32.2	12	135	7.1	2.4	161	2 563	334.4	151.5
Wilmington	212	3 315	198.1	56.4	27	380	31.7	10.0	253	3 791	521.9	218.2
DISTRICT OF COLUMBIA	2 148	52 998	4 278.2	1 238.4	198	4 721	612.3	240.4	1 419	19 710	2 098.8	944.4
Washington	2 148	52 998	4 278.2	1 238.4	198	4 721	612.3	240.4	1 419	19 710	2 098.8	944.4
FLORIDA	35 012	746 214	41 922.1	11 470.0	6 629	133 359	13 402.7	3 497.8	46 687	538 050	61 636.7	22 586.4
Altamonte Springs	161	4 366	219.1	65.5	19	D	D	D	220	D	D	D
Apopka	67	1 112	51.9	14.0	11	D	D	D	71	537	59.9	29.4
Aventura	86	3 455	237.0	69.0	24	120	12.7	2.7	219	2 603	439.8	131.2
Boca Raton	398	10 638	682.8	202.2	92	661	78.8	14.1	700	7 297	935.2	341.9
Bonita Springs	107	1 978	104.5	29.3	36	1 146	72.5	27.6	112	813	114.8	32.5
Boynton Beach	150	3 081	138.0	43.5	24	D	D	D	283	D	D	D
Bradenton	123	2 196	103.9	27.6	24	220	10.9	4.0	262	5 984	765.1	241.2
Cape Coral	178	2 822	125.9	36.0	40	246	18.9	3.9	232	2 145	263.6	85.2
Casselberry	76	1 251	49.8	14.8	13	225	10.4	2.5	56	612	45.1	20.2
Clearwater	358	6 966	361.3	102.3	57	771	43.8	12.5	474	5 699	634.8	264.1
Clermont	85	1 862	80.7	23.8	15	D	D	D	101	D	D	D
Coconut Creek	51	537	27.9	7.8	20	D	D	D	82	D	D	D
Cooper City	49	875	33.0	10.0	32	174	15.5	5.6	97	D	D	D
Coral Gables	210	4 645	292.2	93.0	42	237	25.3	10.0	454	D	D	D
Coral Springs	275	4 595	246.9	64.7	67	623	35.6	10.3	497	D	D	D
Cutler Bay	NA	NA	NA	NA	NA	NA	NA	NA	NA	NA	NA	NA
Dania Beach	80	1 646	106.4	26.9	25	D	D	D	37	D	D	D
Davie	217	3 335	175.4	46.0	62	D	D	D	190	1 187	140.7	36.3
Daytona Beach	267	6 442	337.1	85.5	34	D	D	D	229	3 544	356.4	160.1

1. Establishments subject to federal tax.

Table D. Cities — Other Services and Federal Funds

City	Other services[1], 2007				Selected federal funds, 2009–2010 (mil dol)								
					Procurement contracts		Grants						
	Number of establishments	Number of employees	Receipts (mil dol)	Annual payroll (mil dol)	Defense	Other	Total[2]	Medicaid and other health related	Nutrition and family welfare	Energy and environment	Disasters and emergency preparedness	Housing and community development	Employment and training
	104	105	106	107	108	109	110	111	112	113	114	115	116
COLORADO—Cont'd													
Castle Rock	79	405	29.4	9.8	0.1	4.2	4.3	0.0	0.0	3.0	0.0	0.9	0.0
Centennial	167	872	94.6	27.4	127.9	54.3	0.8	0.0	0.0	0.0	0.1	0.0	0.0
Colorado Springs	690	4 198	324.7	101.7	1 892.4	69.8	97.7	8.0	9.4	2.6	0.1	25.3	0.1
Commerce City	81	684	79.1	20.8	0.1	0.5	28.5	0.0	0.0	0.0	0.0	14.7	0.0
Denver	1 131	8 938	732.5	229.9	166.6	566.3	1 880.5	293.6	329.1	135.1	3.5	206.0	109.6
Englewood	142	874	89.8	29.5	185.1	92.0	54.6	6.4	4.9	-0.2	0.0	3.9	0.0
Fort Collins	221	1 252	84.2	28.3	8.5	129.5	235.6	70.8	3.2	42.3	0.6	10.0	0.4
Fountain	13	D	D	D	4.1	0.0	14.5	0.0	0.0	0.0	0.0	1.8	0.0
Grand Junction	198	1 227	116.9	31.8	35.0	90.9	17.2	0.4	0.0	5.7	0.0	6.3	0.0
Greeley	123	633	48.7	14.5	0.4	7.4	18.6	1.6	0.0	0.2	0.0	7.0	0.0
Lakewood	271	1 301	99.1	33.3	5.7	150.2	61.8	0.4	1.0	39.3	0.0	12.2	3.6
Littleton	101	497	42.2	12.9	1 138.3	2.3	31.8	1.7	0.0	25.3	0.0	4.4	0.0
Longmont	149	794	53.8	17.9	0.2	5.0	113.9	1.9	1.4	0.9	0.0	4.6	0.0
Loveland	127	733	53.6	18.1	8.9	21.1	9.2	0.0	0.9	0.8	0.0	4.6	0.0
Northglenn	54	D	D	D	0.0	0.1	0.7	0.0	0.0	0.0	0.0	0.0	0.0
Parker	100	489	35.6	11.4	3.8	0.6	0.0	0.0	0.0	0.0	0.0	0.0	0.0
Pueblo	141	724	56.4	15.6	31.4	15.0	51.8	6.5	0.0	8.0	2.7	17.3	0.0
Thornton	83	699	48.3	19.7	0.8	1.3	1.0	0.0	0.0	0.0	0.0	0.6	0.0
Westminster	123	783	46.8	15.8	4.9	0.4	2.0	0.4	0.0	0.0	0.0	0.7	0.0
Wheat Ridge	108	512	48.1	14.7	6.9	9.5	23.0	2.7	0.2	7.2	0.0	11.8	0.0
CONNECTICUT	5 911	36 724	3 068.8	980.2	11 113.6	843.0	8 298.9	4 768.8	847.6	189.2	20.4	522.2	140.6
Bridgeport	159	760	72.3	19.3	107.8	2.9	79.4	7.4	8.9	2.7	0.0	41.9	8.1
Bristol	97	427	33.7	9.7	0.4	0.3	7.8	0.0	0.0	0.0	0.0	7.7	0.0
Danbury	160	1 023	90.8	28.0	85.0	14.6	23.2	0.2	1.8	11.0	0.0	9.2	0.0
Hartford	208	2 359	139.9	47.3	27.7	25.5	932.8	134.3	178.1	40.2	8.6	195.4	2.1
Meriden	78	385	28.6	10.0	11.4	1.2	10.8	0.2	0.1	0.0	0.0	9.3	0.0
Middletown	77	380	51.2	11.6	60.8	1.0	29.0	9.7	0.0	0.2	0.0	9.4	0.0
Milford	133	782	61.5	19.8	0.0	0.0	5.7	0.6	0.0	2.1	0.0	3.0	0.0
Naugatuck	38	192	14.1	4.4	3.4	0.2	2.7	0.0	0.0	0.0	0.0	2.4	0.0
New Britain	81	335	29.7	9.5	1.5	3.2	26.4	1.0	3.0	1.5	0.0	11.6	0.1
New Haven	174	967	76.8	24.4	7.1	38.5	971.6	803.8	6.8	16.1	0.0	68.5	0.0
New London	48	314	23.1	7.7	4.7	38.1	5.9	0.0	0.0	0.0	0.0	4.2	0.0
Norwalk	186	1 017	99.2	29.4	170.1	3.6	28.6	0.0	1.7	2.3	0.0	16.9	0.0
Norwich	72	515	32.3	10.9	0.4	1.1	18.4	0.4	0.1	10.6	0.0	6.5	0.0
Shelton	59	351	22.4	7.3	2.3	2.8	0.7	0.0	0.0	0.2	0.0	0.4	0.0
Stamford	221	1 431	125.4	39.5	38.4	19.8	40.5	0.2	2.7	5.5	0.0	28.1	0.0
Torrington	73	542	30.5	21.9	2.4	0.0	3.5	0.2	0.0	0.3	0.0	2.0	0.0
Waterbury	152	1 092	72.9	25.4	4.3	0.7	39.2	1.8	4.1	6.5	0.0	24.1	0.0
West Haven	81	368	37.3	11.0	7.9	58.9	15.2	0.0	1.3	0.5	0.0	12.0	0.0
DELAWARE	1 256	7 893	569.1	195.3	218.1	144.5	2 055.2	983.3	207.3	105.0	8.3	78.2	27.7
Dover	65	626	34.4	12.0	120.2	2.2	332.0	4.2	0.8	30.1	2.4	27.1	0.0
Newark	64	430	20.4	7.9	20.6	7.1	157.8	51.6	6.6	16.4	0.0	1.0	0.0
Wilmington	148	1 043	76.4	27.8	21.9	74.2	183.3	28.1	12.4	45.7	0.0	49.8	25.1
DISTRICT OF COLUMBIA	969	7 011	566.2	170.4	4 651.0	16 598.9	10 872.0	2 282.6	377.8	865.6	16.8	342.6	226.0
Washington	969	7 011	566.2	170.4	4 651.0	16 598.9	10 872.0	2 282.6	377.8	865.6	16.8	342.6	226.0
FLORIDA	28 522	149 369	11 718.0	3 529.5	12 814.2	5 166.5	28 066.3	14 386.2	3 377.4	807.6	110.2	1 635.9	393.6
Altamonte Springs	109	640	41.0	13.5	0.3	0.5	0.4	0.0	0.0	0.1	0.0	0.0	0.0
Apopka	59	293	20.8	6.2	170.0	1.5	0.0	0.0	0.0	0.0	0.0	0.0	0.0
Aventura	65	411	23.1	7.5	0.0	0.0	0.0	0.0	0.0	0.0	0.0	0.0	0.0
Boca Raton	347	1 954	142.7	47.5	75.3	12.6	29.9	7.7	0.0	4.0	0.0	6.4	0.0
Bonita Springs	68	318	18.8	6.6	0.7	0.1	49.6	0.0	0.0	24.3	0.0	0.0	0.0
Boynton Beach	133	772	52.7	15.5	0.9	4.6	1.6	0.1	0.0	0.0	0.0	1.3	0.0
Bradenton	95	393	28.6	8.9	11.3	1.2	34.0	0.4	5.3	2.5	0.0	14.3	0.0
Cape Coral	203	831	65.3	18.4	0.9	1.0	2.1	0.0	0.0	1.4	0.0	0.7	0.0
Casselberry	63	299	22.9	6.8	0.2	0.0	0.9	0.4	0.0	0.4	0.0	0.0	0.0
Clearwater	240	1 253	100.1	30.8	357.4	11.5	31.9	2.8	-0.1	5.0	0.0	19.5	0.5
Clermont	45	211	13.6	4.1	3.0	5.8	0.0	0.0	0.0	0.0	0.0	0.0	0.0
Coconut Creek	65	276	37.0	8.5	0.0	0.0	0.4	0.0	0.0	0.0	0.0	0.3	0.0
Cooper City	43	D	D	D	0.0	0.0	0.0	0.0	0.0	0.0	0.0	0.0	0.0
Coral Gables	132	653	48.9	15.4	0.4	0.7	285.1	244.8	0.0	0.7	0.0	0.1	0.0
Coral Springs	242	1 001	76.5	20.8	8.2	21.1	0.9	0.0	0.0	0.0	0.0	0.9	0.0
Cutler Bay	NA	NA	NA	NA	NA	NA	NA	NA	NA	NA	NA	NA	NA
Dania Beach	102	583	57.8	16.3	10.5	4.3	0.0	0.0	0.0	0.0	0.0	0.0	0.0
Davie	216	1 096	105.3	29.2	4.1	1.4	4.5	0.0	0.0	1.3	0.0	0.7	0.0
Daytona Beach	132	853	51.7	15.1	71.3	27.3	38.4	1.2	0.1	1.3	0.0	11.4	0.0

1. Establishments subject to federal tax. 2. Includes program categories not shown separately. State totals include additional categories not allocated by city.

Table D. Cities — City Government Finances

City	General revenue Total (mil dol) 117	Intergovernmental Total (mil dol) 118	Intergovernmental Percent from state government 119	Taxes Total (mil dol) 120	Taxes Per capita[1] (dollars) Total 121	Property 122	Sales and gross receipts 123	General expenditure Total (mil dol) 124	General expenditure Per capita[1] (dollars) Total 125	Capital outlays 126
COLORADO—Cont'd										
Castle Rock	89.5	3.3	100.0	63.0	1 484	84	1 400	66.1	1 557	405
Centennial	44.8	8.1	59.9	30.4	306	81	225	44.8	452	39
Colorado Springs	936.7	58.8	43.7	209.9	558	57	501	881.4	2 341	517
Commerce City	54.6	4.0	28.2	44.5	1 087	102	985	34.5	843	0
Denver	1 963.0	226.0	17.5	855.5	1 454	369	974	2 147.9	3 651	545
Englewood	53.2	3.0	47.6	29.9	920	119	801	68.7	2 111	566
Fort Collins	250.4	39.9	8.3	108.0	806	119	688	243.1	1 815	545
Fountain	22.8	1.0	90.1	8.6	438	131	307	11.2	575	16
Grand Junction	109.5	15.2	47.6	53.8	1 112	146	966	135.5	2 799	1 084
Greeley	107.2	13.4	10.6	53.5	593	92	501	116.1	1 285	391
Lakewood	137.4	16.8	49.3	84.0	598	61	485	118.6	845	107
Littleton	64.5	15.4	15.6	30.5	751	88	663	67.5	1 661	103
Longmont	105.8	7.7	68.4	61.5	723	164	559	114.7	1 349	347
Loveland	103.0	7.2	95.8	63.6	988	115	872	77.6	1 205	303
Northglenn	34.7	3.6	28.9	19.7	588	148	441	31.3	933	253
Parker	50.4	5.9	26.1	31.3	732	30	700	52.3	1 223	584
Pueblo	116.6	15.3	37.4	59.9	577	89	489	113.3	1 092	299
Thornton	157.0	13.1	56.1	86.6	781	157	624	110.2	994	196
Westminster	161.3	14.1	33.5	83.7	788	54	734	238.3	2 244	806
Wheat Ridge	27.9	3.6	100.0	18.2	591	127	455	33.4	1 082	119
CONNECTICUT	X	X	X	X	X	X	X	X	X	X
Bridgeport	650.6	357.6	94.1	238.7	1 747	1 714	25	568.2	4 157	382
Bristol	200.0	69.9	98.1	107.0	1 756	1 704	28	228.4	3 750	553
Danbury	224.3	60.4	98.7	138.9	1 753	1 691	62	211.8	2 674	521
Hartford	748.2	489.7	98.2	238.2	1 912	1 851	40	731.7	5 874	704
Meriden	207.5	84.0	98.7	104.4	1 763	1 752	12	204.1	3 446	209
Middletown	172.8	75.1	99.7	84.4	1 766	1 750	9	189.2	3 959	1 373
Milford	176.4	24.4	98.2	132.2	2 462	2 395	33	176.4	3 286	215
Naugatuck	99.8	34.7	98.2	57.1	1 789	1 755	34	103.7	3 249	4
New Britain	265.1	137.8	97.2	100.3	1 420	1 369	51	231.3	3 273	452
New Haven	712.4	444.0	97.5	186.1	1 502	1 458	19	641.2	5 174	736
New London	109.1	57.0	96.8	38.0	1 467	1 418	25	135.7	5 236	1 427
Norwalk	308.6	44.9	97.4	225.6	2 704	2 584	119	266.1	3 189	127
Norwich	123.8	52.9	99.8	53.3	1 462	1 436	0	129.5	3 555	195
Shelton	111.3	16.7	98.5	85.6	2 140	2 068	72	130.4	3 259	829
Stamford	479.5	79.4	93.8	348.9	2 945	2 811	89	516.6	4 360	796
Torrington	114.0	36.1	99.9	64.7	1 826	1 826	0	110.1	3 107	162
Waterbury	415.7	183.4	96.5	200.6	1 872	1 816	25	449.0	4 190	162
West Haven	159.9	64.8	100.0	86.3	1 639	1 628	11	154.2	2 928	41
DELAWARE	X	X	X	X	X	X	X	X	X	X
Dover	38.4	5.2	69.8	16.4	458	362	75	46.7	1 304	172
Newark	19.5	2.5	74.2	7.4	246	127	58	26.1	870	57
Wilmington	169.4	47.0	11.1	86.8	1 191	415	91	197.9	2 716	361
DISTRICT OF COLUMBIA	X	X	X	X	X	X	X	X	X	X
Washington	9 507.7	2 775.7	0.0	5 192.2	8 826	2 577	2 464	8 740.9	14 858	2 403
FLORIDA	X	X	X	X	X	X	X	X	X	X
Altamonte Springs	53.5	5.2	97.1	26.9	668	233	435	49.9	1 238	462
Apopka	49.7	17.1	49.4	20.5	548	182	366	46.3	1 238	444
Aventura	42.8	10.7	69.7	26.9	912	478	434	36.5	1 239	347
Boca Raton	221.0	52.2	22.5	121.0	1 416	768	648	205.9	2 410	353
Bonita Springs	35.1	7.2	100.0	13.3	314	170	144	40.4	955	654
Boynton Beach	133.5	23.1	46.6	56.2	827	491	336	122.5	1 804	371
Bradenton	65.5	15.7	42.9	21.9	410	236	171	63.4	1 186	182
Cape Coral	270.8	35.9	68.3	103.1	657	485	172	230.4	1 468	524
Casselberry	30.5	5.1	68.4	13.0	523	251	272	29.3	1 181	70
Clearwater	213.4	49.2	75.8	75.6	709	451	258	200.8	1 883	336
Clermont	34.5	3.1	88.9	11.8	911	437	474	31.7	2 446	865
Coconut Creek	56.1	14.6	38.4	26.2	521	289	232	41.7	829	81
Cooper City	37.9	10.2	28.9	18.5	633	355	277	38.0	1 295	73
Coral Gables	135.3	8.0	74.7	91.4	2 171	1 469	702	130.4	3 097	212
Coral Springs	129.1	34.6	43.7	58.7	462	256	198	145.3	1 145	109
Cutler Bay	10.1	2.4	100.0	7.6	260	123	137	8.2	281	5
Dania Beach	39.2	3.2	99.1	23.8	840	556	205	42.5	1 503	146
Davie	95.6	26.0	99.0	50.9	563	275	289	105.5	1 168	132
Daytona Beach	125.0	24.5	55.9	51.1	794	456	338	103.7	1 611	169

1. Based on population estimated as of July 1 of the year shown.

Table D. Cities — **City Government Finances**

City					Percent of total for:					
	Public welfare	Highways	Parking facilities	Education	Health and hospitals	Police protection	Sewerage and sanitation	Parks and recreation	Housing and community development	Interest on debt
	127	128	129	130	131	132	133	134	135	136
COLORADO—Cont'd										
Castle Rock	0.0	22.0	0.0	0.0	0.0	8.9	17.5	20.2	0.0	1.9
Centennial	0.0	20.8	0.0	0.0	0.0	37.4	0.0	0.0	0.0	0.1
Colorado Springs	0.0	8.5	0.3	0.0	45.9	9.1	9.4	2.7	0.8	2.5
Commerce City	0.0	14.0	0.0	0.0	0.0	30.5	0.0	13.9	6.4	0.0
Denver	5.2	2.8	0.0	0.0	6.6	7.6	6.2	5.7	3.0	2.5
Englewood	0.0	5.1	0.0	0.0	0.0	12.9	39.4	10.7	2.0	4.9
Fort Collins	0.0	29.8	0.0	0.0	0.0	16.0	5.8	16.1	0.2	2.7
Fountain	0.0	12.7	0.0	0.0	7.0	36.0	0.0	7.5	0.1	0.0
Grand Junction	0.0	40.7	1.6	0.0	0.0	13.3	8.8	10.4	1.7	2.2
Greeley	0.0	11.7	0.7	0.0	0.4	17.2	5.4	21.4	0.8	3.2
Lakewood	0.0	14.3	0.0	0.0	0.4	27.7	3.4	14.7	0.5	2.3
Littleton	0.5	8.3	0.3	0.0	0.4	14.2	10.3	3.7	0.1	3.5
Longmont	0.0	18.1	0.0	0.0	0.0	15.4	14.1	15.9	2.3	1.6
Loveland	0.0	9.7	0.0	0.0	0.0	16.1	20.5	13.1	0.4	1.1
Northglenn	0.0	19.6	0.0	0.0	0.0	23.4	18.2	7.7	4.0	0.3
Parker	0.0	29.1	0.0	0.0	0.0	14.6	1.7	27.9	0.0	1.5
Pueblo	0.0	8.8	0.2	0.0	0.0	20.3	8.0	5.1	3.5	2.1
Thornton	0.0	9.9	0.0	0.0	1.9	17.2	11.8	13.4	0.0	4.8
Westminster	0.0	3.2	0.0	0.0	0.0	8.0	12.5	8.0	19.2	4.0
Wheat Ridge	0.0	19.9	0.0	0.0	0.0	24.3	0.0	19.0	3.9	0.8
CONNECTICUT	X	X	X	X	X	X	X	X	X	X
Bridgeport	0.3	2.0	0.3	53.7	1.7	7.4	4.5	1.1	2.4	7.4
Bristol	0.0	4.4	0.0	56.1	3.7	5.3	4.7	1.9	0.0	0.8
Danbury	0.0	2.8	0.8	59.0	1.7	9.9	2.6	0.6	0.3	2.2
Hartford	1.8	1.9	0.5	61.4	1.1	4.7	2.1	0.1	5.5	1.2
Meriden	2.1	1.6	0.0	56.7	1.5	5.0	3.5	1.4	0.5	2.1
Middletown	0.0	8.5	0.1	54.1	1.0	5.0	10.3	1.2	0.2	1.1
Milford	0.5	2.1	0.0	55.8	1.4	5.4	6.6	0.6	0.6	1.4
Naugatuck	0.0	1.5	0.0	56.9	6.8	4.7	1.3	1.5	0.1	3.6
New Britain	0.5	2.0	0.0	60.5	0.6	5.8	4.2	3.9	1.4	0.0
New Haven	0.6	1.6	0.3	62.8	0.6	5.4	1.0	0.0	3.2	2.9
New London	0.0	1.0	0.3	60.6	0.1	6.9	7.1	1.3	2.1	0.9
Norwalk	0.1	0.1	1.1	62.0	0.2	7.1	2.3	5.3	0.4	3.4
Norwich	1.4	11.3	0.0	54.7	0.0	8.4	6.1	1.9	1.7	1.1
Shelton	0.0	2.0	0.0	50.8	0.3	4.5	4.1	1.1	0.0	1.2
Stamford	0.0	1.0	1.1	59.0	1.0	8.8	6.6	1.4	0.0	3.4
Torrington	0.3	4.0	0.0	58.2	3.0	6.3	3.6	1.3	0.4	1.5
Waterbury	0.0	6.1	0.0	51.8	0.7	5.5	4.7	0.8	1.0	1.6
West Haven	0.1	6.5	0.0	55.2	0.6	8.0	5.0	0.5	0.8	3.9
DELAWARE	X	X	X	X	X	X	X	X	X	X
Dover	0.0	6.7	0.2	0.0	0.4	26.0	14.2	3.1	1.0	0.2
Newark	0.0	9.3	1.8	0.0	0.0	28.9	22.7	8.2	2.5	0.5
Wilmington	0.0	3.9	2.3	0.0	0.0	24.1	7.4	5.3	3.9	2.9
DISTRICT OF COLUMBIA	X	X	X	X	X	X	X	X	X	X
Washington	24.7	1.2	0.0	17.7	6.1	5.7	6.0	4.2	5.1	4.3
FLORIDA	X	X	X	X	X	X	X	X	X	X
Altamonte Springs	0.0	34.4	0.0	0.0	0.0	18.0	4.5	11.0	0.0	0.9
Apopka	0.0	9.9	0.0	0.0	0.0	13.6	17.2	3.7	0.0	0.4
Aventura	0.0	15.7	0.0	13.3	0.0	31.3	1.4	6.0	0.0	4.8
Boca Raton	0.0	7.6	0.0	0.0	0.0	16.9	9.3	16.9	1.1	2.5
Bonita Springs	0.0	54.2	0.0	0.0	0.9	2.1	0.0	20.7	7.0	4.1
Boynton Beach	0.0	1.2	0.0	0.0	0.0	17.1	22.4	9.1	1.4	0.6
Bradenton	4.4	3.7	11.5	0.0	0.0	16.5	16.6	3.8	13.9	0.1
Cape Coral	0.0	16.0	0.0	1.7	0.0	14.2	7.6	23.7	0.5	1.7
Casselberry	0.0	7.7	0.0	0.0	0.3	17.9	26.4	6.6	0.0	1.5
Clearwater	0.2	5.2	1.8	0.0	0.0	17.0	20.6	15.0	0.9	2.6
Clermont	0.0	2.6	0.0	0.0	0.2	12.9	19.0	32.0	0.5	4.2
Coconut Creek	0.0	4.4	0.0	0.0	0.0	29.1	2.4	14.2	0.1	3.3
Cooper City	0.0	3.6	0.1	0.0	0.0	19.8	12.4	33.7	0.0	0.7
Coral Gables	0.0	2.5	2.6	0.0	0.0	27.7	15.8	5.4	0.5	1.8
Coral Springs	0.0	4.3	0.0	0.0	5.5	24.5	6.1	11.2	0.0	1.8
Cutler Bay	0.0	0.0	0.0	0.0	0.0	65.2	0.0	7.9	0.0	0.0
Dania Beach	0.0	4.7	0.0	0.0	0.0	18.8	18.7	10.3	0.0	1.5
Davie	0.0	21.0	0.0	0.0	0.0	26.8	0.0	4.8	4.7	2.0
Daytona Beach	0.0	11.8	0.3	0.0	0.2	27.1	18.5	8.9	2.4	3.8

City	Total (mil dol) [137]	Per capita[1] (dollars) [138]	Debt issued during year [139]	City government employment, 2010 [140]	January [141]	July [142]	January[3] [143]	July[4] [144]	Annual precipitation (inches) [145]	Heating degree days [146]	Cooling degree days [147]
COLORADO—Cont'd											
Castle Rock	48.6	1 145	9.7	NA	NA	NA	NA	NA	NA	NA	NA
Centennial	3.1	31	0.0	58	NA	NA	NA	NA	NA	NA	NA
Colorado Springs	2 004.3	5 325	144.5	7 640	28.1	69.6	14.5	84.4	17.40	6 480	404
Commerce City	154.5	3 774	122.8	NA	NA	NA	NA	NA	NA	NA	NA
Denver	5 045.8	8 576	931.0	12 287	31.2	71.5	15.6	88.3	18.17	5 988	496
Englewood	94.0	2 889	0.1	507	28.2	70.2	12.7	85.8	17.06	6 773	435
Fort Collins	240.9	1 799	1.7	1 422	28.2	71.5	14.5	86.2	13.98	6 256	524
Fountain	11.8	605	0.0	199	NA	NA	NA	NA	NA	NA	NA
Grand Junction	77.9	1 609	15.3	717	27.4	77.5	16.8	91.9	9.06	5 489	1 098
Greeley	166.2	1 840	25.0	854	27.8	74.0	15.6	88.7	14.22	5 980	759
Lakewood	96.2	685	52.1	1 038	28.2	70.2	12.7	85.8	17.06	6 773	435
Littleton	70.9	1 745	0.0	NA	28.2	70.2	12.7	85.8	17.06	6 773	435
Longmont	72.0	847	21.0	862	27.1	72.2	12.0	88.9	14.15	6 415	587
Loveland	22.3	347	0.0	615	28.2	71.5	14.5	86.2	13.98	6 256	524
Northglenn	22.3	666	0.0	NA	30.0	72.0	16.2	87.9	13.25	6 074	590
Parker	20.4	476	17.0	312	NA	NA	NA	NA	NA	NA	NA
Pueblo	112.1	1 080	19.2	946	30.8	77.0	14.7	93.8	12.60	5 346	997
Thornton	211.8	1 910	0.0	844	30.0	72.0	16.2	87.9	13.25	6 074	590
Westminster	275.2	2 591	52.0	998	29.2	73.4	15.2	88.0	15.81	6 128	696
Wheat Ridge	12.5	404	0.1	267	31.2	71.5	15.6	88.3	18.17	5 988	496
CONNECTICUT	X	X	X	NA	X	X	X	X	X	X	X
Bridgeport	696.7	5 097	0.0	4 281	29.9	74.0	22.9	81.9	44.15	5 466	789
Bristol	59.8	981	21.6	1 692	23.4	70.5	12.6	83.3	51.03	6 825	395
Danbury	124.0	1 565	31.8	1 803	26.5	72.5	17.6	83.9	51.77	6 159	597
Hartford	235.5	1 890	0.0	5 421	25.9	73.6	16.3	83.8	44.29	6 121	654
Meriden	110.9	1 872	20.2	1 679	28.3	73.4	20.3	84.2	52.35	5 791	669
Middletown	41.4	866	7.9	1 624	29.9	74.0	22.9	81.9	44.15	5 466	789
Milford	59.2	1 103	0.0	2 026	29.9	74.0	22.9	81.9	44.15	5 466	789
Naugatuck	90.7	2 840	0.0	921	29.9	74.0	22.9	81.9	44.15	5 466	789
New Britain	244.4	3 459	13.6	2 259	28.3	73.4	20.3	84.2	52.35	5 791	669
New Haven	584.4	4 716	109.1	5 127	25.9	72.5	16.9	82.8	52.73	6 271	558
New London	41.8	1 611	12.2	875	28.9	71.8	20.0	80.7	48.72	5 799	511
Norwalk	236.7	2 837	25.0	2 641	27.8	73.4	18.8	84.2	48.38	5 854	662
Norwich	36.3	996	0.0	1 096	27.6	73.2	17.3	83.8	52.78	5 916	627
Shelton	60.8	1 518	27.4	1 012	29.9	74.0	22.9	81.9	44.15	5 466	789
Stamford	493.1	4 162	0.0	3 987	28.7	73.5	19.2	85.4	52.79	5 582	692
Torrington	44.9	1 266	26.3	973	23.6	69.5	13.9	80.7	54.59	6 839	323
Waterbury	177.0	1 651	27.8	3 762	25.9	72.5	16.9	82.8	52.73	6 271	558
West Haven	142.9	2 713	0.0	1 428	25.9	72.5	16.9	82.8	52.73	6 271	558
DELAWARE	X	X	X	NA	X	X	X	X	X	X	X
Dover	27.4	765	0.0	377	35.3	77.8	26.9	87.4	46.28	4 212	1 262
Newark	19.2	639	0.0	256	32.5	76.4	23.5	87.6	45.35	4 746	1 047
Wilmington	147.8	2 028	0.0	1 327	31.5	76.6	23.7	86.0	42.81	4 888	1 125
DISTRICT OF COLUMBIA	X	X	X	NA	X	X	X	X	X	X	X
Washington	8 528.4	14 497	1 853.9	33 990	34.9	79.2	27.3	88.3	39.35	4 055	1 531
FLORIDA	X	X	X	NA	X	X	X	X	X	X	X
Altamonte Springs	6.6	163	0.0	NA	58.7	81.5	47.0	91.9	51.31	799	3 017
Apopka	29.0	775	1.5	NA	58.7	81.5	47.0	91.9	51.31	799	3 017
Aventura	35.3	1 196	0.0	NA	67.9	82.7	62.6	87.0	46.60	141	4 090
Boca Raton	169.8	1 989	0.0	1 386	67.2	83.3	57.8	91.8	57.27	219	4 241
Bonita Springs	32.2	762	0.0	NA	64.3	82.0	53.4	91.2	51.90	316	3 646
Boynton Beach	99.6	1 466	11.3	861	66.2	82.5	57.3	90.1	61.39	246	3 999
Bradenton	34.4	643	3.6	523	61.6	81.9	50.9	91.3	54.12	538	3 327
Cape Coral	366.9	2 337	60.4	1 376	62.7	81.3	50.3	91.3	50.07	427	3 287
Casselberry	27.7	1 118	0.0	NA	NA	NA	NA	NA	NA	NA	NA
Clearwater	258.6	2 425	28.8	1 752	61.3	82.5	52.4	89.7	44.77	591	3 482
Clermont	28.9	2 224	5.3	275	NA	NA	NA	NA	NA	NA	NA
Coconut Creek	37.5	746	0.0	341	67.2	83.3	57.8	91.8	57.27	219	4 241
Cooper City	20.7	705	1.3	NA	67.5	82.6	59.2	89.8	64.19	167	4 120
Coral Gables	60.6	1 438	6.0	801	67.9	82.7	62.6	87.0	46.60	141	4 090
Coral Springs	110.4	871	0.0	830	67.2	83.3	57.8	91.8	57.27	219	4 241
Cutler Bay	2.7	92	0.0	NA	NA	NA	NA	NA	NA	NA	NA
Dania Beach	14.5	512	1.5	172	NA	NA	NA	NA	NA	NA	NA
Davie	110.3	1 221	41.5	617	66.2	82.5	57.3	90.1	61.39	246	3 999
Daytona Beach	181.6	2 822	0.0	949	57.1	81.2	44.5	91.2	57.03	954	2 819

1. Based on the population estimated as of July 1 of the year shown.   2. Represents normal values based on the 30-year period, 1971–2000.   3. Average daily minimum.   4. Average daily maximum.

Table D. Cities — Land Area and Population

STATE Place code	City	Land area,[1] 2010 (sq km)	Population, 2010			Race alone or in combination, not of Hispanic origin (percent), 2010					Percent Hispanic or Latino[2], 2010	Percent Foreign born, 2008–2010
			Total persons	Rank	Per square kilometer	White	Black	American Indian, Alaska Native	Asian	Hawaiian Pacific Islander		
		1	2	3	4	5	6	7	8	9	10	11
	FLORIDA—Cont'd											
12 16725	Deerfield Beach	39.1	75 018	451	1 919.6	57.4	25.8	0.4	1.9	0.2	14.2	33.9
12 16875	DeLand	45.6	27 031	1 528	593.0	68.4	17.5	0.8	2.1	0.1	12.7	9.7
12 17100	Delray Beach	40.9	60 522	596	1 478.3	60.0	28.4	0.4	2.2	0.3	9.5	21.3
12 17200	Deltona	97.2	85 182	366	876.4	58.4	10.4	0.8	1.6	0.1	30.2	8.1
12 17935	Doral	35.9	45 704	864	1 271.7	15.0	1.8	0.1	3.7	0.0	79.5	61.6
12 18575	Dunedin	26.8	35 321	1 139	1 317.0	88.6	3.7	0.6	2.0	0.2	5.9	10.0
12 24000	Fort Lauderdale	90.0	165 521	144	1 838.3	53.4	31.2	0.5	1.9	0.2	13.7	21.0
12 24125	Fort Myers	103.5	62 298	571	602.0	45.8	32.3	0.5	1.9	0.2	20.0	18.1
12 24300	Fort Pierce	53.3	41 590	944	780.7	36.2	41.4	0.7	1.1	0.2	21.6	19.5
12 25175	Gainesville	158.8	124 354	207	783.2	59.8	23.6	0.7	7.8	0.2	10.0	11.9
12 27322	Greenacres	15.0	37 573	1 053	2 504.9	41.8	16.9	0.3	3.4	0.2	38.3	36.1
12 28452	Hallandale Beach	10.9	37 113	1 065	3 398.6	48.4	18.2	0.3	1.8	0.1	31.8	41.9
12 30000	Hialeah	55.6	224 669	90	4 044.4	4.3	0.6	0.1	0.4	0.0	94.7	74.8
12 32000	Hollywood	70.9	140 768	178	1 986.0	48.5	16.2	0.4	2.9	0.2	32.6	34.4
12 32275	Homestead	39.2	60 512	597	1 543.3	16.7	19.1	0.3	1.5	0.3	62.9	34.6
12 35000	Jacksonville	1 934.7	821 784	12	424.8	56.9	31.2	0.9	5.1	0.2	7.7	9.4
12 35875	Jupiter	55.6	55 156	687	992.0	83.6	1.7	0.4	2.5	0.1	12.7	12.6
12 36950	Kissimmee	54.9	59 682	611	1 087.3	27.2	10.3	0.4	3.7	0.2	58.9	23.7
12 38250	Lakeland	169.1	97 422	300	576.3	64.5	21.4	0.7	2.1	0.2	12.6	10.2
12 39075	Lake Worth	15.2	34 910	1 155	2 295.2	39.0	19.8	1.2	1.2	0.2	39.6	44.6
12 39425	Largo	45.6	77 648	418	1 701.7	82.3	6.1	0.7	3.1	0.3	9.0	12.1
12 39525	Lauderdale Lakes	9.5	32 593	1 251	3 416.5	12.0	81.3	0.5	1.7	0.6	5.4	45.3
12 39550	Lauderhill	22.1	66 887	514	3 027.9	14.5	76.4	0.4	2.2	0.4	7.4	36.1
12 43125	Margate	22.9	53 284	713	2 323.8	47.2	26.1	0.4	4.7	0.3	22.2	29.9
12 43975	Melbourne	87.7	76 068	439	867.4	77.3	11.0	0.9	4.0	0.2	8.9	9.5
12 45000	Miami	92.9	399 457	44	4 299.4	12.3	16.7	0.2	1.2	0.1	70.0	58.2
12 45025	Miami Beach	19.8	87 779	352	4 444.5	41.4	3.5	0.3	2.2	0.1	53.0	50.9
12 45060	Miami Gardens	47.2	107 167	250	2 269.5	3.0	74.4	0.3	0.8	0.3	22.0	27.7
12 45100	Miami Lakes	14.6	29 361	1 401	2 012.4	14.8	2.6	0.1	1.6	0.0	81.1	51.0
12 45975	Miramar	76.5	122 041	212	1 596.1	12.6	45.0	0.3	6.0	0.3	36.9	41.3
12 49425	North Lauderdale	11.9	41 023	967	3 450.2	17.2	53.8	0.4	3.7	0.4	25.8	41.5
12 49450	North Miami	21.8	58 786	622	2 699.1	12.9	58.0	0.5	2.1	0.5	27.1	50.0
12 49475	North Miami Beach	12.5	41 523	949	3 321.8	19.1	40.6	0.4	3.9	0.6	36.6	51.4
12 49675	North Port	257.9	57 357	644	222.4	82.9	7.6	0.6	1.4	0.1	8.7	9.4
12 50575	Oakland Park	19.3	41 363	954	2 140.9	46.3	26.1	0.5	2.5	0.3	25.6	30.6
12 50750	Ocala	116.1	56 315	663	485.0	64.6	21.3	0.7	3.0	0.1	11.7	8.5
12 51075	Ocoee	38.1	35 579	1 128	933.8	54.9	17.8	0.6	6.5	0.3	20.8	16.3
12 53000	Orlando	265.2	238 300	79	898.6	42.8	27.8	0.6	4.4	0.2	25.4	18.3
12 53150	Ormond Beach	82.7	38 137	1 036	461.2	90.0	3.6	0.6	2.7	0.1	4.1	8.5
12 53575	Oviedo	39.4	33 342	1 217	846.5	71.1	8.7	0.5	4.7	0.1	16.3	9.3
12 54000	Palm Bay	170.2	103 190	274	606.4	66.0	18.5	0.8	2.5	0.2	14.1	15.1
12 54075	Palm Beach Gardens	142.7	48 452	806	339.6	83.2	4.8	0.3	3.6	0.1	8.9	16.1
12 54200	Palm Coast	232.8	75 180	447	323.0	74.3	13.2	0.6	3.0	0.2	10.0	13.9
12 54700	Panama City	75.8	36 484	1 090	481.1	70.6	22.9	1.2	2.3	0.2	5.1	4.7
12 55775	Pembroke Pines	85.8	154 750	153	1 803.8	34.0	19.5	0.3	5.7	0.2	41.4	36.7
12 55925	Pensacola	58.4	51 923	734	889.4	65.9	28.6	1.2	2.6	0.2	3.3	5.5
12 56975	Pinellas Park	40.2	49 079	787	1 222.1	76.9	5.1	0.8	7.9	0.2	10.7	16.1
12 57425	Plantation	56.3	84 955	368	1 508.7	55.0	20.6	0.4	4.8	0.2	20.4	27.1
12 57550	Plant City	70.4	34 721	1 160	493.1	54.6	15.2	0.7	1.8	0.1	28.8	14.4
12 58050	Pompano Beach	62.2	99 845	286	1 606.0	51.7	29.0	0.4	1.6	0.2	17.5	24.0
12 58575	Port Orange	69.1	56 048	670	811.7	89.5	3.7	0.7	2.8	0.1	4.5	7.6
12 58715	Port St. Lucie	295.1	164 603	146	557.7	63.0	16.7	0.6	2.5	0.2	18.4	17.1
12 60975	Riviera Beach	22.1	32 488	1 254	1 470.7	23.8	66.3	0.6	2.7	0.3	7.4	16.2
12 62100	Royal Palm Beach	29.0	34 140	1 183	1 177.2	52.5	22.9	0.4	5.0	0.2	20.4	21.7
12 62625	St. Cloud	46.0	35 183	1 146	765.0	62.5	5.4	0.6	2.3	0.2	29.2	11.5
12 63000	St. Petersburg	159.9	244 769	76	1 530.7	65.9	24.5	0.7	3.8	0.1	6.6	9.9
12 63650	Sanford	59.5	53 570	710	900.9	46.5	30.5	0.9	3.3	0.2	20.2	11.5
12 64175	Sarasota	38.0	51 917	735	1 367.3	66.9	15.4	0.6	1.7	0.1	16.6	15.1
12 69700	Sunrise	46.9	84 439	373	1 801.6	37.9	32.1	0.4	4.8	0.3	25.6	36.8
12 70600	Tallahassee	259.6	181 376	128	698.6	54.9	35.5	0.7	4.2	0.1	6.3	7.4
12 70675	Tamarac	30.1	60 427	599	2 008.2	49.9	23.2	0.3	3.1	0.2	24.3	30.8
12 71000	Tampa	293.7	335 709	55	1 142.9	47.9	25.8	0.6	4.1	0.2	23.1	15.0
12 71900	Titusville	76.1	43 761	899	575.3	78.2	14.1	1.1	1.8	0.2	6.5	6.7
12 75812	Wellington	116.3	56 508	660	486.0	66.1	10.8	0.3	4.6	0.2	19.4	21.2
12 76582	Weston	65.2	65 333	537	1 002.5	45.9	4.5	0.3	5.2	0.1	44.9	39.1
12 76600	West Palm Beach	143.2	99 919	284	697.7	42.6	32.5	0.5	2.7	0.3	22.6	27.8
12 78250	Winter Garden	39.9	34 568	1 167	866.1	55.6	16.4	0.5	6.1	0.3	22.0	14.5
12 78275	Winter Haven	81.1	33 874	1 192	417.9	59.2	27.9	0.5	2.3	0.2	11.0	12.1
12 78300	Winter Park	22.5	27 852	1 483	1 239.0	83.0	7.9	0.5	2.9	0.1	7.0	7.4
12 78325	Winter Springs	38.0	33 282	1 219	876.1	76.9	5.8	0.6	3.0	0.1	15.0	11.7

1. Dry land or land partially or temporarily covered by water. 2. May be of any race.

Table D. Cities — **Population**

City	Under 5 years	5 to 17 years	18 to 24 years	25 to 34 years	35 to 44 years	45 to 54 years	55 to 64 years	65 to 74 years	75 years and over	Median age	Percent female	Census counts 1990	Census counts 2000	Percent change 1990–2000	Percent change 2000–2010
	12	13	14	15	16	17	18	19	20	21	22	23	24	25	26
FLORIDA—Cont'd															
Deerfield Beach	5.6	12.4	7.6	13.8	12.9	14.2	12.1	9.9	11.6	43.3	51.7	46 997	64 583	37.4	16.2
DeLand	6.2	14.8	13.5	10.7	11.3	12.0	11.1	8.7	11.7	39.1	54.6	16 622	20 904	25.8	29.3
Delray Beach	4.7	11.4	8.0	12.4	12.1	14.4	13.3	10.2	13.5	46.0	51.9	47 184	60 020	27.2	0.8
Deltona	6.2	19.0	8.6	12.4	13.9	15.3	11.5	7.1	5.9	37.8	51.3	49 429	69 543	40.7	22.5
Doral	7.7	20.6	8.4	15.4	20.6	14.1	7.3	4.0	2.1	34.0	51.9	3 126	20 438	553.8	123.6
Dunedin	3.7	11.1	5.7	9.0	10.8	15.6	16.1	12.9	15.0	51.3	53.6	34 427	35 691	3.7	-1.0
Fort Lauderdale	5.2	12.4	8.1	14.4	14.0	16.6	14.0	8.4	6.9	42.2	47.2	149 238	152 397	2.1	8.6
Fort Myers	7.3	15.4	10.8	15.4	12.9	12.6	11.2	7.8	6.6	35.8	49.9	44 947	48 208	7.3	29.2
Fort Pierce	8.2	17.7	10.5	12.8	11.5	13.2	10.9	7.8	7.5	35.7	50.7	36 830	37 516	1.9	10.9
Gainesville	4.4	8.9	36.8	16.9	8.1	8.5	8.0	4.1	4.2	24.9	51.6	91 482	95 447	4.3	30.3
Greenacres	7.3	17.5	8.8	14.5	14.3	11.9	9.3	7.6	8.9	36.3	52.5	18 683	27 569	47.6	36.3
Hallandale Beach	5.2	10.2	6.5	12.7	13.2	13.5	13.7	12.0	13.1	46.7	52.5	30 997	34 282	10.6	8.3
Hialeah	5.0	14.2	9.1	11.2	15.1	15.0	11.2	9.9	9.2	42.2	51.7	188 008	226 419	20.4	-0.8
Hollywood	5.9	14.4	7.9	13.1	14.7	16.3	12.7	7.7	7.4	41.1	51.0	121 720	139 357	14.5	1.0
Homestead	10.5	20.7	10.8	19.0	15.1	10.6	6.8	3.7	2.8	29.1	49.6	26 694	31 909	19.5	89.6
Jacksonville	7.0	16.9	10.5	14.9	13.6	14.8	11.4	6.1	4.9	35.5	51.5	635 042	735 617	15.8	11.7
Jupiter	4.5	14.9	6.6	11.2	13.2	16.1	13.6	10.4	9.6	44.7	50.3	26 753	39 328	47.0	40.2
Kissimmee	7.4	18.3	11.2	15.2	14.6	14.0	9.8	5.8	3.6	33.5	51.4	30 337	47 814	57.6	24.8
Lakeland	6.2	14.8	11.4	12.3	10.9	12.0	11.7	9.8	10.9	39.8	53.1	70 576	78 452	11.2	24.2
Lake Worth	7.4	14.8	11.0	16.8	14.3	14.3	10.2	5.9	5.4	35.0	46.0	28 564	35 133	23.0	-0.6
Largo	4.5	11.1	7.1	11.4	11.2	14.5	14.1	12.3	13.7	48.2	52.8	65 910	69 371	5.3	11.9
Lauderdale Lakes	7.0	17.7	9.9	12.4	11.8	13.4	12.1	8.6	7.0	37.6	54.1	27 341	31 705	16.0	2.8
Lauderhill	7.7	17.9	10.0	13.8	13.2	13.8	10.7	6.5	6.4	35.5	54.2	49 015	57 585	17.5	16.2
Margate	5.7	14.7	7.9	12.2	13.2	14.4	12.8	9.6	9.5	42.3	53.2	42 985	53 909	25.4	-1.2
Melbourne	5.1	13.1	10.3	12.3	11.1	15.5	12.5	9.4	10.5	43.3	51.5	60 034	71 382	18.9	6.6
Miami	6.0	12.4	9.4	16.5	14.9	14.0	10.8	8.0	8.0	38.8	50.2	358 648	362 470	1.1	10.2
Miami Beach	4.2	8.5	7.4	19.8	18.1	14.7	11.0	7.8	8.4	40.3	47.6	92 639	87 933	-5.1	-0.2
Miami Gardens	6.9	20.0	11.9	13.0	12.9	13.2	10.9	6.9	4.3	33.5	53.2	NA	NA	NA	NA
Miami Lakes	5.1	18.0	9.1	11.8	16.1	16.6	10.3	7.3	5.9	38.9	52.8	12 750	22 676	77.9	29.5
Miramar	7.4	21.6	9.5	13.6	17.1	15.1	8.7	4.3	2.6	33.6	52.8	40 663	72 739	78.9	67.8
North Lauderdale	8.2	20.7	10.9	17.0	14.7	13.5	8.5	4.0	2.5	30.9	52.2	26 473	32 264	21.9	27.1
North Miami	6.9	16.9	12.8	14.3	13.8	14.4	11.2	5.8	4.3	34.4	51.9	50 001	59 880	19.8	-1.8
North Miami Beach	6.4	17.1	10.6	14.2	13.4	16.5	11.8	6.2	5.0	36.4	52.1	35 361	40 786	15.3	1.8
North Port	6.2	18.0	6.6	11.2	13.5	13.7	13.0	10.7	7.1	40.9	51.2	11 973	22 797	90.4	151.6
Oakland Park	6.3	13.9	8.4	15.4	16.2	18.2	11.9	5.7	4.0	38.8	46.5	26 326	30 966	17.6	33.6
Ocala	7.0	16.4	10.5	13.3	12.3	13.5	10.7	7.8	9.4	38.2	52.4	42 045	45 943	9.3	22.6
Ocoee	7.1	20.6	8.5	13.1	16.4	15.6	10.0	4.9	3.7	35.4	51.2	12 778	24 391	90.9	45.9
Orlando	7.1	14.9	11.2	20.6	15.1	12.8	9.0	4.9	4.5	32.8	51.4	164 674	185 951	12.9	28.2
Ormond Beach	3.7	13.5	6.0	7.4	10.7	15.6	15.8	12.9	14.3	50.7	52.8	29 721	36 301	22.1	5.1
Oviedo	5.6	22.6	10.8	10.6	15.9	17.6	9.5	4.3	3.1	35.3	50.8	11 114	26 316	136.8	26.7
Palm Bay	6.2	17.7	8.6	11.8	12.3	15.8	12.2	8.4	6.9	39.8	51.7	62 543	79 413	27.0	29.9
Palm Beach Gardens	4.4	12.0	5.4	11.6	12.1	14.1	15.2	13.3	12.0	48.3	53.1	24 139	35 058	45.2	38.2
Palm Coast	5.4	16.1	6.4	10.1	11.9	12.8	14.4	13.3	9.7	45.1	52.2	14 287	32 732	129.1	129.7
Panama City	6.2	14.5	10.2	13.7	12.2	14.8	12.1	7.5	8.8	39.7	50.9	34 396	36 417	5.9	0.2
Pembroke Pines	5.7	18.1	8.4	11.7	14.7	15.9	10.7	6.8	8.0	39.5	53.8	65 566	137 427	109.6	12.6
Pensacola	5.5	14.1	9.3	12.7	11.2	15.3	14.3	8.6	9.1	42.6	52.6	59 198	56 255	-5.0	-7.7
Pinellas Park	5.3	14.2	7.6	12.7	13.2	15.4	13.0	9.8	8.8	42.7	51.4	43 571	45 658	4.8	7.5
Plantation	5.8	15.6	7.9	14.0	14.4	15.7	13.0	7.2	6.2	39.7	52.6	66 814	82 934	24.1	2.4
Plant City	8.1	20.2	9.7	14.1	13.2	13.0	10.3	6.4	5.0	33.3	51.6	22 754	29 915	31.5	16.1
Pompano Beach	5.7	12.6	8.4	13.3	13.3	15.5	12.3	8.6	10.3	42.7	49.0	72 411	78 191	8.0	27.7
Port Orange	4.2	13.9	8.1	10.1	11.2	14.8	15.2	11.8	10.7	46.9	51.8	35 399	45 823	29.4	22.3
Port St. Lucie	6.2	18.3	7.5	11.4	14.1	14.8	11.9	8.8	7.0	39.8	51.4	55 761	88 769	59.2	85.4
Riviera Beach	7.2	17.8	9.9	12.1	12.8	14.0	11.4	8.3	6.6	37.5	52.2	27 646	29 884	8.1	8.7
Royal Palm Beach	6.4	20.7	8.6	10.8	15.2	16.7	10.8	5.6	5.2	37.7	52.2	15 532	21 523	38.6	58.6
St. Cloud	6.8	19.4	8.6	12.9	14.4	14.3	10.3	7.1	6.2	36.8	52.1	12 684	20 074	58.3	75.3
St. Petersburg	5.4	14.1	8.7	12.9	13.5	16.3	13.4	7.9	7.8	41.6	51.9	240 318	248 232	3.3	-1.4
Sanford	8.0	18.1	11.2	16.9	13.7	13.3	9.6	5.0	4.3	32.4	52.0	32 387	38 291	18.2	39.9
Sarasota	5.2	11.7	10.7	11.7	11.3	13.7	13.3	10.4	12.1	44.5	51.4	50 897	52 715	3.6	-1.5
Sunrise	6.0	16.4	8.6	13.3	14.4	14.9	11.3	6.9	8.2	39.1	53.5	65 683	85 779	30.6	-1.6
Tallahassee	5.5	11.7	30.0	16.3	10.0	9.7	8.6	4.3	3.8	26.1	52.9	124 773	150 624	20.7	20.4
Tamarac	5.0	11.6	6.0	12.2	12.3	12.5	12.9	10.9	16.5	47.1	55.4	44 822	55 588	24.0	8.7
Tampa	6.4	16.2	12.5	15.4	14.0	14.2	10.4	5.8	5.1	34.6	51.1	280 015	303 447	8.4	10.6
Titusville	5.7	14.9	8.0	11.1	11.2	15.6	12.9	10.3	10.2	44.3	51.9	39 394	40 670	3.2	7.6
Wellington	5.1	21.9	7.8	8.8	15.1	18.1	12.6	6.3	4.2	39.9	51.8	20 670	38 216	84.9	47.9
Weston	5.4	25.3	7.6	7.8	18.0	18.7	9.2	4.6	3.4	37.9	51.5	9 829	49 286	401.4	32.6
West Palm Beach	6.4	13.5	10.2	15.9	13.0	13.3	11.8	8.4	7.6	38.1	51.4	67 764	82 103	21.2	21.7
Winter Garden	7.8	20.3	7.9	14.4	16.9	13.9	9.2	5.1	4.5	34.7	51.6	9 863	14 351	45.5	140.9
Winter Haven	6.5	15.8	7.9	11.8	10.9	12.2	12.6	10.8	11.5	42.3	53.7	24 725	26 487	7.1	27.9
Winter Park	4.3	14.0	11.3	9.8	11.4	15.4	13.8	8.7	11.2	44.3	53.2	24 260	24 090	-0.7	15.6
Winter Springs	4.4	18.1	8.3	10.7	13.2	17.7	14.2	7.5	5.9	41.8	52.1	22 151	31 666	43.0	5.1

City	Households, 2010				Persons in group quarters, 2010				Serious crimes known to police,[2] 2010				Educational attainment, 2008–2010		
			Percent			Institutional			Total		Rate[3]			Attainment[4] (percent)	
	Number	Persons per house-hold	Female family house-holder[1]	One-person	Total	Total	Persons in nursing facilities	Non-institu-tional	Number	Rate[3]	Violent	Property	Population age 25 and older	High school graduate or less	Bachelor's degree or more
	27	28	29	30	31	32	33	34	35	36	37	38	39	40	41
FLORIDA—Cont'd															
Deerfield Beach	33 370	2.22	12.7	37.0	1 046	863	229	183	2 938	3 916	572	3 345	56 115	52.9	21.1
DeLand	10 746	2.29	14.9	35.1	2 377	595	587	1 782	1 519	5 619	566	5 053	17 367	43.0	25.9
Delray Beach	27 193	2.18	10.6	38.3	1 114	584	539	530	3 930	6 494	975	5 519	44 913	35.6	34.4
Deltona	30 223	2.81	15.3	18.1	166	127	127	39	NA	NA	NA	NA	56 535	48.0	14.4
Doral	15 244	3.00	15.5	14.9	6	0	0	6	2 825	6 181	193	5 989	27 549	21.9	54.8
Dunedin	17 618	1.98	9.5	39.9	385	344	338	41	1 268	3 590	306	3 284	28 220	39.1	27.1
Fort Lauderdale	74 786	2.17	12.3	39.4	3 418	1 861	324	1 557	11 270	6 809	819	5 990	120 562	39.7	32.0
Fort Myers	24 968	2.37	17.9	33.1	3 236	2 520	598	716	3 397	5 453	1 120	4 332	41 087	52.9	20.3
Fort Pierce	15 850	2.59	20.6	30.6	577	455	314	122	2 878	6 920	1 159	5 761	26 721	63.2	12.9
Gainesville	51 029	2.19	12.4	34.5	12 493	1 796	748	10 697	6 310	5 074	729	4 346	59 763	29.9	44.3
Greenacres	14 384	2.61	16.5	27.9	51	5	5	46	1 236	3 290	476	2 813	25 748	51.8	19.8
Hallandale Beach	18 301	2.02	12.4	40.9	101	0	0	101	2 132	5 745	932	4 812	28 439	47.6	24.7
Hialeah	71 205	3.13	20.1	16.4	1 493	727	700	766	8 809	3 921	423	3 498	164 283	65.9	12.8
Hollywood	58 438	2.39	14.3	32.3	1 203	608	476	595	7 861	5 584	423	5 161	100 792	45.2	26.8
Homestead	18 996	3.16	22.6	18.1	450	227	223	223	3 869	6 394	1 416	4 978	32 011	57.5	17.8
Jacksonville	323 106	2.48	17.1	28.2	19 747	8 158	3 155	11 589	42 893	5 210	664	4 546	533 855	42.9	23.8
Jupiter	23 920	2.29	9.4	29.6	393	131	131	262	1 190	2 158	221	1 936	39 095	30.3	42.5
Kissimmee	20 726	2.85	21.1	20.0	595	317	54	278	3 817	6 396	1 004	5 392	37 398	52.7	14.1
Lakeland	40 758	2.29	15.2	32.8	4 126	1 140	1 094	2 986	5 558	5 705	471	5 234	66 548	46.9	24.4
Lake Worth	12 958	2.65	13.1	33.1	618	518	409	100	2 126	6 090	1 286	4 804	23 264	62.5	19.7
Largo	38 022	2.02	11.2	39.6	1 026	941	836	85	3 853	4 962	652	4 310	60 396	49.7	19.4
Lauderdale Lakes	11 891	2.71	26.1	27.5	392	387	363	5	1 931	5 925	1 009	4 915	22 286	55.2	17.5
Lauderhill	24 826	2.67	25.9	28.2	592	225	225	367	3 120	4 665	804	3 860	42 747	51.4	19.3
Margate	21 483	2.47	14.2	30.8	169	6	6	163	1 292	2 425	283	2 141	37 723	50.5	23.5
Melbourne	34 040	2.17	13.4	35.7	2 125	746	713	1 379	4 357	5 728	901	4 827	55 587	42.0	24.5
Miami	158 317	2.47	18.1	33.3	8 161	5 133	1 526	3 028	26 097	6 533	1 221	5 312	284 297	59.9	22.6
Miami Beach	47 168	1.84	8.4	49.0	1 026	534	473	492	9 607	10 945	984	9 960	67 698	33.6	43.1
Miami Gardens	32 219	3.28	32.3	17.6	1 367	64	11	1 303	6 471	6 038	990	5 048	64 392	58.2	15.3
Miami Lakes	10 253	2.86	14.6	19.3	28	0	0	28	727	2 476	187	2 289	19 648	31.6	32.4
Miramar	37 420	3.26	22.2	13.5	87	24	11	63	4 191	3 434	442	2 992	71 710	34.8	33.1
North Lauderdale	12 977	3.16	25.0	18.8	31	0	0	31	1 295	3 157	483	2 674	24 712	58.2	15.1
North Miami	19 275	2.96	21.8	25.2	1 640	539	539	1 101	3 987	6 782	1 048	5 734	36 792	54.4	18.6
North Miami Beach	14 412	2.86	21.0	25.1	236	151	148	85	2 455	5 912	833	5 079	27 145	50.4	23.0
North Port	22 431	2.55	11.2	21.6	119	100	100	19	1 580	2 755	338	2 416	38 072	47.6	16.7
Oakland Park	17 499	2.35	15.0	34.0	205	19	0	186	2 421	5 853	725	5 128	30 693	43.5	24.3
Ocala	23 103	2.30	17.0	34.2	3 281	2 856	922	425	3 632	6 449	819	5 631	36 672	47.8	22.6
Ocoee	11 792	2.99	14.6	16.3	287	225	225	62	1 414	3 974	447	3 527	22 077	39.8	26.5
Orlando	102 521	2.29	16.9	34.6	3 294	1 227	1 009	2 067	18 139	7 612	1 080	6 532	156 252	39.5	31.1
Ormond Beach	17 062	2.21	9.8	30.3	458	434	434	24	1 636	4 290	658	3 632	29 720	33.1	30.9
Oviedo	11 125	2.99	12.1	12.7	103	94	94	9	642	1 925	234	1 692	18 863	27.1	39.0
Palm Bay	39 482	2.60	15.3	23.0	430	331	320	99	2 981	2 889	505	2 384	67 948	47.8	16.7
Palm Beach Gardens	22 804	2.11	8.8	31.4	235	205	154	30	1 686	3 480	149	3 331	36 510	26.5	46.0
Palm Coast	29 805	2.51	11.7	21.3	319	282	144	37	NA	NA	NA	NA	52 564	42.1	22.1
Panama City	14 792	2.28	16.8	34.1	2 782	2 453	553	329	2 700	7 401	759	6 641	24 698	48.0	17.9
Pembroke Pines	56 873	2.70	15.0	24.0	1 397	1 187	125	210	5 302	3 426	178	3 248	105 632	36.3	31.7
Pensacola	23 592	2.17	15.7	36.3	727	284	224	443	2 965	5 710	809	4 901	37 227	36.9	33.0
Pinellas Park	20 623	2.32	13.3	31.1	1 165	510	337	655	3 083	6 282	536	5 746	35 246	50.0	18.6
Plantation	34 190	2.47	13.6	26.3	363	307	304	56	4 046	4 763	343	4 420	60 544	29.0	41.8
Plant City	12 239	2.82	17.5	22.2	185	118	118	67	1 807	5 204	530	4 674	21 303	57.6	15.8
Pompano Beach	42 182	2.27	13.3	36.7	4 267	3 680	415	587	5 989	5 998	994	5 005	74 085	51.0	23.6
Port Orange	24 841	2.25	10.8	29.2	167	118	102	49	1 513	2 699	182	2 517	41 795	44.2	22.9
Port St. Lucie	60 902	2.69	12.9	19.5	711	330	322	381	3 598	2 186	235	1 951	108 582	49.3	17.7
Riviera Beach	12 380	2.60	24.3	28.2	323	134	134	189	2 435	7 495	1 798	5 697	20 330	50.0	21.4
Royal Palm Beach	11 556	2.93	15.8	16.9	236	229	119	7	1 173	3 436	325	3 111	21 021	34.9	28.4
St. Cloud	12 565	2.76	15.6	20.9	448	375	349	73	1 082	3 075	378	2 697	22 595	48.1	17.7
St. Petersburg	108 815	2.19	15.1	36.2	6 607	2 719	2 364	3 888	16 573	6 771	1 127	5 644	174 733	42.6	27.6
Sanford	20 118	2.59	21.1	27.5	1 531	996	180	535	3 723	6 950	665	6 285	33 626	45.9	19.6
Sarasota	23 142	2.09	12.6	40.2	3 582	1 632	738	1 950	3 698	7 123	982	6 141	38 240	45.0	26.6
Sunrise	32 493	2.58	17.0	27.3	578	506	496	72	4 310	5 104	400	4 704	58 185	42.3	25.6
Tallahassee	74 815	2.23	14.4	34.1	14 623	3 231	718	11 392	10 381	5 723	994	4 730	94 512	26.4	45.7
Tamarac	28 415	2.12	14.1	37.3	261	234	234	27	1 455	2 408	308	2 100	46 853	45.3	23.0
Tampa	135 955	2.38	16.8	33.6	12 282	2 138	876	10 144	13 623	4 058	646	3 412	218 578	42.4	31.7
Titusville	19 017	2.28	14.5	31.7	473	344	344	129	1 836	4 196	800	3 396	31 727	45.4	17.0
Wellington	19 659	2.87	12.2	15.9	2	0	0	2	1 715	3 035	221	2 814	35 338	29.7	39.9
Weston	21 220	3.08	12.1	13.0	0	0	0	0	794	1 215	58	1 157	38 743	18.2	56.6
West Palm Beach	42 912	2.26	14.8	36.5	2 943	1 196	1 093	1 747	5 841	5 846	790	5 056	70 378	42.9	28.8
Winter Garden	11 875	2.87	14.7	19.0	497	483	483	14	1 234	3 570	463	3 107	21 087	37.6	34.0
Winter Haven	14 323	2.32	15.8	32.5	598	491	490	107	2 159	6 374	720	5 653	22 152	55.4	17.6
Winter Park	12 228	2.15	9.0	36.5	1 609	338	338	1 271	948	3 404	248	3 156	19 830	26.8	47.6
Winter Springs	13 101	2.54	12.5	22.1	31	31	0	0	468	1 406	168	1 238	22 501	32.2	36.0

1. No spouse present.   2. Data for serious crimes have not been adjusted for underreporting. This may affect comparability between geographic areas and over time.   3. Per 100,000 population estimated by the FBI.   4. Persons 25 years old and over.

Table D. Cities — Income, Poverty, and Housing

City	Money income, 2008–2010 Households — Per capita income[1] (dollars)	Median income	Percent with income of $200,000 or more	Percent with income of less than $25,000	Families with income below poverty (percent)	Housing units, 2010 — Total	Percent change, 2000–2010	Vacant units for sale or rent[2]	Occupied Housing units 2008–2010 Owner-occupied — Total	Percent	Median value[3] (dollars)	Median owner costs as a percent of income — With a mortgage[4]	Without a mortgage[5]
	42	43	44	45	46	47	48	49	50	51	52	53	54
FLORIDA—Cont'd													
Deerfield Beach	22 869	37 014	1.4	34.0	14.1	42 671	14.3	9 301	32 138	66.8	151 800	35.2	19.3
DeLand	19 528	35 139	1.3	39.2	16.1	12 610	35.6	1 864	10 171	60.0	166 500	27.9	17.9
Delray Beach	35 579	49 218	5.9	22.4	9.7	34 156	7.9	6 963	26 224	65.0	235 000	33.7	17.7
Deltona	20 844	51 034	1.6	21.2	10.1	34 089	28.4	3 866	28 878	83.4	163 900	29.3	12.8
Doral	28 364	67 867	6.6	12.7	6.7	17 785	89.4	2 541	14 079	57.6	329 200	40.0	16.1
Dunedin	28 680	45 776	2.1	27.3	6.6	21 113	5.0	3 495	16 523	68.3	181 800	26.9	17.2
Fort Lauderdale	33 692	46 966	6.4	26.1	13.7	93 159	15.3	18 373	70 974	56.9	279 300	35.0	17.4
Fort Myers	20 548	35 978	2.9	35.9	17.7	35 138	60.9	10 170	22 726	45.1	159 500	29.3	11.9
Fort Pierce	15 395	28 363	0.8	45.3	24.7	21 357	24.1	5 507	14 856	49.9	113 900	32.1	19.9
Gainesville	18 754	31 208	2.3	42.9	16.3	57 576	43.5	6 547	46 745	39.8	169 200	26.4	11.6
Greenacres	21 589	41 902	1.3	29.9	11.0	17 249	21.0	2 865	13 916	68.8	154 900	33.2	17.1
Hallandale Beach	23 730	34 682	1.0	36.2	12.4	27 057	7.8	8 756	17 650	60.6	165 300	41.0	21.5
Hialeah	14 638	30 766	0.5	41.0	18.0	74 067	2.6	2 862	72 439	52.1	202 900	38.6	17.5
Hollywood	25 267	44 293	3.0	27.5	9.7	71 070	3.9	12 632	55 764	62.6	218 200	33.8	18.5
Homestead	15 342	36 308	1.0	34.9	27.2	23 419	111.0	4 423	17 452	37.6	178 400	34.7	13.9
Jacksonville	24 478	47 356	2.3	24.9	11.2	366 273	18.6	43 167	307 831	62.4	168 800	26.7	12.2
Jupiter	42 524	65 707	9.9	16.7	5.4	29 825	41.7	5 905	22 359	74.1	281 300	31.7	13.5
Kissimmee	16 965	36 984	0.6	29.7	12.9	26 275	33.6	5 549	21 616	44.0	153 400	30.3	11.6
Lakeland	23 884	40 205	2.4	31.2	12.5	48 218	23.3	7 460	40 107	56.1	137 700	25.7	13.6
Lake Worth	17 548	38 259	0.9	33.4	27.7	16 473	3.6	3 515	11 571	51.4	166 800	31.1	14.8
Largo	25 337	39 263	1.5	28.5	6.9	46 859	16.4	8 837	36 465	61.3	113 700	27.4	14.7
Lauderdale Lakes	17 483	35 925	0.6	34.7	17.7	15 000	4.5	3 109	12 180	63.7	109 500	39.4	16.6
Lauderhill	18 119	36 339	0.6	33.8	19.8	29 519	15.0	4 693	23 599	63.2	151 000	34.1	19.9
Margate	23 668	43 972	2.1	26.9	7.7	24 863	0.5	3 380	21 013	77.8	153 100	32.6	17.0
Melbourne	23 940	40 851	1.8	29.9	9.5	38 955	15.7	4 915	33 055	61.9	152 400	27.3	11.7
Miami	19 723	28 506	3.0	45.3	22.9	183 994	23.9	25 677	149 708	34.9	260 400	40.7	19.7
Miami Beach	39 878	42 330	8.2	31.3	9.7	67 499	13.0	20 331	42 997	41.0	324 100	36.6	23.4
Miami Gardens	15 743	42 430	0.5	28.4	17.3	34 284	NA	2 065	30 789	68.4	186 500	36.1	13.0
Miami Lakes	29 039	62 034	5.3	16.0	5.8	10 698	18.8	445	9 883	65.2	335 500	32.3	15.1
Miramar	23 785	60 485	4.5	14.7	8.1	40 294	55.6	2 874	35 282	73.8	250 000	36.2	16.7
North Lauderdale	16 149	40 187	0.2	24.9	18.9	14 709	28.1	1 732	12 308	57.5	151 100	35.5	18.5
North Miami	16 963	35 867	1.1	34.9	20.5	22 110	-0.7	2 835	18 382	55.2	208 500	42.6	18.2
North Miami Beach	18 577	42 526	0.9	27.3	14.9	16 402	7.1	1 990	13 379	58.8	207 000	36.9	15.5
North Port	21 942	46 795	1.5	20.0	7.6	27 986	170.2	5 555	20 479	78.0	152 000	31.3	13.4
Oakland Park	23 682	41 765	0.5	26.0	11.0	20 076	38.1	2 577	17 829	60.7	165 400	34.5	12.2
Ocala	23 003	36 812	3.3	35.2	17.7	26 764	29.8	3 661	21 922	53.5	140 400	26.0	15.0
Ocoee	25 463	62 770	2.0	13.9	7.0	12 802	53.8	1 010	11 278	77.5	214 000	28.8	11.4
Orlando	24 643	40 669	3.1	28.3	12.9	121 254	35.8	18 733	96 846	40.3	205 500	30.7	13.2
Ormond Beach	30 848	48 353	5.4	24.6	5.3	19 576	12.8	2 514	16 116	81.3	205 000	28.8	16.5
Oviedo	26 705	77 188	3.7	13.4	5.7	11 720	28.9	595	9 730	83.0	258 800	27.8	10.0
Palm Bay	20 297	43 737	1.1	25.5	10.2	45 220	37.3	5 738	36 954	74.8	138 300	28.3	11.5
Palm Beach Gardens	51 382	69 020	12.6	12.8	1.3	27 663	52.6	4 859	20 853	75.4	314 700	29.3	13.0
Palm Coast	22 101	48 207	1.8	21.9	9.5	35 058	132.0	5 253	26 875	79.3	194 500	30.6	13.2
Panama City	20 221	38 066	1.2	33.2	17.0	17 438	5.5	2 646	14 883	54.3	150 000	27.7	13.9
Pembroke Pines	26 976	59 968	3.4	19.2	5.5	61 703	11.6	4 830	53 813	75.8	241 400	32.3	20.7
Pensacola	28 577	40 438	4.1	31.8	13.5	26 848	-0.3	3 256	23 256	61.0	166 200	27.4	13.0
Pinellas Park	22 180	43 245	0.6	26.3	8.3	23 458	7.5	2 835	20 477	71.1	135 500	27.4	15.7
Plantation	34 151	61 713	6.1	15.7	5.9	37 587	7.1	3 397	34 301	70.9	279 100	31.1	13.9
Plant City	21 656	46 831	1.5	25.3	13.5	13 732	16.5	1 493	11 754	60.6	163 700	29.6	15.4
Pompano Beach	24 458	38 259	2.6	33.5	13.4	55 885	25.9	13 703	41 339	61.7	191 100	35.4	17.9
Port Orange	27 331	47 371	2.5	24.9	6.1	27 972	34.2	3 131	23 240	77.3	176 600	27.0	14.8
Port St. Lucie	21 499	47 276	1.4	20.3	9.9	70 877	92.0	9 975	56 548	78.4	163 800	34.6	16.9
Riviera Beach	21 848	36 225	2.3	38.3	23.7	17 124	19.4	4 744	12 357	56.0	174 300	36.1	16.9
Royal Palm Beach	25 811	64 196	2.0	12.3	6.8	12 854	58.1	1 298	10 901	85.4	228 700	33.8	13.9
St. Cloud	19 995	47 571	1.3	23.4	10.9	14 544	68.6	1 979	12 554	72.2	164 300	31.5	14.0
St. Petersburg	26 828	43 915	2.5	27.3	10.2	129 401	3.9	20 586	105 789	63.3	166 800	30.3	15.6
Sanford	19 221	41 661	1.5	31.1	18.0	23 061	49.0	2 943	18 562	57.9	147 800	28.8	10.8
Sarasota	28 598	38 755	4.5	33.1	14.0	29 151	8.2	6 009	21 853	59.5	198 000	35.6	18.3
Sunrise	23 126	47 819	0.7	21.8	8.0	37 609	5.5	5 116	31 493	73.9	175 300	34.5	22.1
Tallahassee	23 227	36 925	2.8	35.6	15.5	84 248	23.2	9 433	73 598	43.5	191 500	25.1	12.7
Tamarac	24 440	40 389	0.7	30.9	7.6	32 794	10.3	4 379	27 517	80.9	150 700	35.7	23.6
Tampa	27 186	42 359	4.9	30.4	15.8	157 130	15.8	21 175	132 667	53.0	191 200	29.5	14.0
Titusville	22 870	42 871	1.3	27.0	9.3	22 729	18.2	3 712	17 732	68.3	136 400	27.7	11.0
Wellington	34 765	75 268	10.2	12.1	6.3	22 685	54.2	3 026	18 158	79.7	309 800	31.0	13.8
Weston	39 947	89 646	16.2	9.9	4.2	24 394	28.9	3 174	20 567	73.8	403 100	29.0	17.6
West Palm Beach	28 891	42 411	4.1	28.9	15.4	54 179	34.1	11 267	41 516	52.3	207 400	32.2	17.0
Winter Garden	25 861	61 630	3.6	15.9	4.3	13 260	128.8	1 385	10 976	72.5	230 600	29.1	16.1
Winter Haven	19 248	36 108	1.0	35.6	16.4	17 037	22.3	2 714	13 409	56.6	133 900	28.1	14.4
Winter Park	44 337	52 261	11.1	21.7	7.5	13 626	18.2	1 398	11 664	62.0	362 200	27.2	13.3
Winter Springs	32 021	67 138	6.9	12.8	5.0	14 052	14.3	951	11 824	77.8	227 600	25.1	10.0

1. Based on population estimated by the American Community Survey.   2. Includes units rented or sold but not occupied.   3. Specified owner-occupied units; $1,000,000 represents $1,000,000 or more.   4. 50.0 represents 50 percent or more.   5. 10.0 represents 10 percent or less.

Table D. Cities — Housing, Labor Force, and Employment

City	Occupied housing units, 2008–2010 (cont.)				Migration, 2008–2010		Civilian labor force, 2010		Unemployment		Civilian employment[4], 2008–2010			
												Percent		
	Percent renter occupied	Median gross rent[1]	Median rent as a percent of income[2]	Percent with no vehicle available	Percent who lived in the same house one year ago	Percent who lived outside this city one year ago	Total	Percent change, 2009–2010	Total	Rate[3]	Population age 16 and older	In labor force	Full-year full-time worker	Households with no workers (percent)
	55	56	57	58	59	60	61	62	63	64	65	66	67	68
FLORIDA—Cont'd														
Deerfield Beach	33.2	1 111	39.3	10.8	81.9	12.6	39 016	-0.1	3 666	9.4	64 337	62.9	37.4	35.2
DeLand	40.0	833	40.2	15.3	80.0	16.0	11 905	-1.6	1 385	11.6	20 972	54.6	33.8	43.9
Delray Beach	35.0	1 232	34.2	7.1	82.0	10.4	27 999	-9.8	3 214	11.5	51 869	62.9	39.1	36.8
Deltona	16.6	1 112	29.7	3.4	88.0	9.6	46 010	0.0	5 509	12.0	66 320	64.1	42.7	23.6
Doral	42.4	1 631	32.8	3.0	78.9	11.8	25 151	74.5	1 976	7.9	32 034	70.6	53.2	9.2
Dunedin	31.7	903	32.9	6.6	84.0	12.3	16 281	-5.0	1 844	11.3	30 467	58.2	35.6	39.9
Fort Lauderdale	43.1	1 040	34.1	9.0	80.5	9.7	93 472	-10.0	8 481	9.1	137 787	66.0	40.3	27.9
Fort Myers	54.9	845	36.5	11.7	74.3	13.7	27 730	-8.2	3 198	11.5	49 646	59.8	33.4	31.9
Fort Pierce	50.1	806	43.7	13.8	80.3	10.3	17 621	-2.4	2 829	16.1	32 365	56.5	28.9	36.2
Gainesville	60.2	831	41.3	10.6	62.1	18.8	63 318	6.2	4 954	7.8	110 127	56.0	29.5	28.0
Greenacres	31.2	1 101	42.9	7.0	84.2	13.4	17 043	10.6	1 680	9.9	29 428	68.5	41.0	31.3
Hallandale Beach	39.4	1 004	37.7	14.4	78.4	12.9	17 537	-4.5	1 950	11.1	31 604	56.2	35.7	40.4
Hialeah	47.9	938	43.2	13.4	92.8	1.9	102 123	0.5	16 177	15.8	190 273	58.6	40.2	28.1
Hollywood	37.4	978	36.2	8.5	82.3	9.1	79 097	-1.3	7 819	9.9	116 311	66.1	39.8	26.2
Homestead	62.4	984	40.5	12.3	78.3	11.1	27 915	-0.4	2 892	10.4	38 908	68.5	46.5	19.4
Jacksonville	37.6	881	32.1	7.8	80.3	6.0	416 171	-0.8	46 809	11.2	642 767	67.9	44.3	23.9
Jupiter	25.9	1 361	30.4	3.7	84.8	8.3	28 159	7.4	2 442	8.7	43 756	62.7	42.3	30.6
Kissimmee	56.0	958	39.7	9.4	79.6	13.9	31 876	-7.4	3 812	12.0	45 944	72.5	44.1	19.5
Lakeland	43.9	844	32.1	9.7	79.1	13.4	43 638	1.0	4 951	11.3	79 739	58.3	36.0	36.0
Lake Worth	48.6	905	37.1	17.5	76.4	9.4	17 384	-5.9	1 885	10.8	28 187	71.7	40.7	28.5
Largo	38.7	889	31.9	9.7	83.6	11.2	34 975	2.5	3 804	10.9	67 243	56.0	37.8	39.0
Lauderdale Lakes	36.3	988	35.7	13.0	87.0	9.7	15 344	3.7	1 774	11.6	26 201	68.4	39.8	27.6
Lauderhill	36.8	989	43.9	11.2	84.3	11.0	34 661	-0.6	3 430	9.9	50 715	69.1	42.0	25.0
Margate	22.2	1 243	39.2	8.0	88.3	9.2	29 330	-2.4	2 997	10.2	43 386	66.6	42.0	27.5
Melbourne	38.1	843	34.3	7.3	82.3	11.2	38 690	-3.7	3 984	10.3	64 675	58.8	34.6	36.2
Miami	65.1	879	39.8	20.4	81.9	6.4	174 777	-7.7	23 932	13.7	330 629	59.8	37.6	31.0
Miami Beach	59.0	1 029	34.2	25.5	76.0	10.6	47 583	-2.0	4 752	10.0	75 519	68.1	46.3	27.0
Miami Gardens	31.6	994	45.8	8.5	89.9	6.5	52 840	-5.9	8 461	16.0	80 329	63.3	41.7	23.1
Miami Lakes	34.8	1 356	32.6	3.7	92.8	6.4	NA	NA	NA	NA	23 244	67.4	50.4	18.4
Miramar	26.2	1 413	37.6	2.9	84.5	10.2	67 268	11.2	6 131	9.1	87 116	74.8	49.4	11.6
North Lauderdale	42.5	1 167	42.6	7.0	86.5	11.6	23 399	-2.2	2 102	9.0	30 499	72.7	46.4	13.9
North Miami	44.8	951	44.4	9.7	85.4	8.9	28 035	-0.4	3 679	13.1	45 146	68.0	42.7	20.5
North Miami Beach	41.2	959	35.3	8.8	86.2	9.9	19 807	3.4	2 602	13.1	33 172	68.7	46.0	18.1
North Port	22.0	1 039	33.9	2.9	83.8	10.6	24 942	-1.3	3 074	12.3	43 226	61.0	35.1	32.2
Oakland Park	39.3	1 003	38.5	6.3	78.0	17.2	26 362	-3.0	2 068	7.8	34 176	78.0	48.5	21.1
Ocala	46.5	855	34.6	8.9	73.3	14.5	24 398	0.6	3 034	12.4	44 334	60.0	36.2	31.9
Ocoee	22.5	1 205	31.5	2.7	86.2	10.6	19 821	4.5	1 860	9.4	26 890	75.3	50.9	13.3
Orlando	59.7	944	34.1	8.6	70.1	14.2	133 069	-1.2	14 625	11.0	191 123	74.7	46.0	20.4
Ormond Beach	18.7	977	38.7	5.9	91.8	5.4	19 142	0.0	1 806	9.4	32 953	52.0	30.9	40.5
Oviedo	17.0	1 127	39.7	3.4	89.3	8.6	18 727	-2.1	1 610	8.6	24 009	71.0	44.9	14.6
Palm Bay	25.2	921	36.1	4.1	83.9	8.7	52 604	-0.2	5 866	11.2	81 177	64.7	38.6	27.9
Palm Beach Gardens	24.6	1 264	33.4	4.4	85.2	10.4	24 190	-6.3	1 848	7.6	40 624	61.7	40.6	33.1
Palm Coast	20.7	1 047	36.1	3.7	88.4	6.8	26 373	1.5	3 842	14.6	59 677	52.1	30.5	40.3
Panama City	45.7	822	33.4	10.1	73.4	16.7	17 931	-3.1	1 907	10.6	29 723	59.6	35.2	30.5
Pembroke Pines	24.2	1 343	35.4	7.5	85.8	9.2	86 883	5.4	7 530	8.7	122 318	66.2	43.8	24.8
Pensacola	39.0	783	34.9	12.4	80.7	12.5	25 287	-2.6	2 214	8.8	43 205	64.9	39.6	33.4
Pinellas Park	28.9	949	32.2	8.2	87.0	8.3	23 444	-1.1	2 613	11.1	40 322	61.4	40.6	33.6
Plantation	29.1	1 289	33.1	4.2	83.2	12.7	52 578	0.5	4 171	7.9	69 263	71.8	47.5	19.3
Plant City	39.4	839	33.1	6.5	84.2	8.3	15 421	1.2	1 893	12.3	25 571	65.3	42.2	25.8
Pompano Beach	38.3	1 026	43.4	10.5	79.8	13.0	50 229	-3.1	4 570	9.1	83 818	60.3	35.5	35.2
Port Orange	22.7	910	28.7	3.5	87.0	8.9	29 565	2.5	2 753	9.3	47 043	58.8	36.9	36.4
Port St. Lucie	21.6	1 153	34.5	3.1	80.7	9.4	78 066	2.1	9 732	12.5	125 283	64.8	38.0	28.9
Riviera Beach	44.0	963	45.5	9.2	87.9	6.4	13 961	-13.9	1 821	13.0	24 532	64.1	39.8	32.2
Royal Palm Beach	14.6	1 344	39.0	4.1	90.3	6.8	18 406	6.5	1 667	9.1	25 981	72.6	45.8	16.3
St. Cloud	27.8	1 002	36.3	4.7	82.8	10.0	16 397	16.0	1 779	10.8	26 287	66.2	41.4	25.9
St. Petersburg	36.7	898	32.7	10.1	83.8	6.5	119 702	-3.5	13 761	11.5	201 987	65.5	43.1	28.7
Sanford	42.1	893	32.0	8.7	81.5	12.8	25 767	0.8	3 044	11.8	39 626	66.9	45.3	25.8
Sarasota	40.5	876	36.7	11.9	79.4	11.0	23 328	-6.2	2 730	11.7	44 392	56.4	32.7	39.7
Sunrise	26.1	1 289	35.8	6.9	87.8	8.8	47 305	-5.3	4 694	9.9	66 963	72.8	48.3	23.2
Tallahassee	56.5	876	39.4	8.3	64.9	14.5	96 491	1.7	7 683	8.0	152 205	65.1	36.2	24.2
Tamarac	19.1	1 184	38.0	8.4	87.0	9.9	29 868	0.6	3 309	11.1	51 189	60.5	38.3	39.0
Tampa	47.0	886	32.8	10.5	78.1	9.4	156 193	-4.5	19 013	12.2	265 054	67.4	43.2	25.4
Titusville	31.7	843	33.8	6.6	76.7	12.0	20 883	-3.0	2 483	11.9	36 195	55.3	35.3	36.2
Wellington	20.3	1 482	34.5	2.6	86.8	10.9	28 916	-1.1	2 588	9.0	41 239	69.0	46.7	19.0
Weston	26.2	1 739	31.4	2.4	84.5	6.1	35 194	2.3	2 687	7.6	47 443	69.9	45.0	13.2
West Palm Beach	47.7	1 011	35.0	10.0	80.0	11.7	49 538	-3.9	5 479	11.1	82 286	63.6	40.1	31.0
Winter Garden	27.5	956	29.3	4.5	82.8	14.4	17 438	11.7	1 619	9.3	24 652	73.3	49.1	15.8
Winter Haven	43.4	772	36.1	12.2	80.1	13.5	13 679	-1.6	1 571	11.5	26 801	54.1	32.8	38.6
Winter Park	38.0	1 014	29.6	8.5	82.7	13.1	13 324	-4.4	1 213	9.1	23 705	56.5	34.6	31.3
Winter Springs	22.2	1 080	30.0	3.5	88.2	9.5	18 120	-2.8	1 788	9.9	27 001	68.7	44.2	20.5

1. $2,000 represents $2,000 or more.   2. 50.0 represents 50 percent or more.   3. Percent of civilian labor force.   4. Persons 16 years old and over.

City	Value of residential construction authorized by building permits, 2010			Wholesale trade,[1] 2007				Retail trade,[2] 2007			
	New construction ($1,000)	Number of housing units	Percent single family	Number of establishments	Number of employees	Sales (mil dol)	Annual payroll (mil dol)	Number of establishments	Number of employees	Sales (mil dol)	Annual payroll (mil dol)
	69	70	71	72	73	74	75	76	77	78	79
FLORIDA—Cont'd											
Deerfield Beach............	889	7	100.0	204	3 698	10 610.9	210.4	327	4 122	1 145.9	110.3
DeLand........................	35 966	127	100.0	34	258	99.5	10.8	177	2 821	674.8	66.9
Delray Beach...............	18 958	165	12.7	118	994	477.9	44.3	395	4 993	1 568.8	143.5
Deltona.......................	6 474	28	100.0	14	47	7.6	1.2	95	1 461	294.3	27.0
Doral..........................	18 780	178	62.9	1 277	13 811	17 259.1	597.7	571	8 569	2 282.9	212.7
Dunedin......................	0	0	0.0	29	197	81.4	9.3	126	1 218	225.0	24.9
Fort Lauderdale.............	23 801	42	100.0	612	6 433	3 213.9	288.4	1 216	13 480	4 715.7	406.5
Fort Myers...................	70 306	308	69.8	156	2 381	1 049.5	100.8	624	9 748	2 577.7	245.9
Fort Pierce..................	5 116	34	35.3	52	263	130.1	11.3	239	3 260	966.7	78.8
Gainesville...................	12 404	168	26.8	131	1 691	1 089.2	63.6	639	9 918	2 168.4	211.8
Greenacres...................	2 256	12	100.0	15	70	23.0	3.1	101	1 584	473.2	44.2
Hallandale Beach	2 075	10	80.0	78	348	208.4	15.1	132	1 537	360.9	36.2
Hialeah.......................	448	5	60.0	512	3 463	1 438.1	116.2	1 055	11 206	2 449.7	244.0
Hollywood...................	655	3	100.0	309	1 940	1 278.6	98.4	594	6 753	1 781.7	162.8
Homestead..................	21 208	158	80.4	46	321	155.4	9.8	143	2 043	512.7	45.7
Jacksonville.................	251 182	1 465	95.4	1 116	19 604	17 104.0	953.9	3 169	49 068	12 749.7	1 165.2
Jupiter........................	56 829	178	98.9	89	769	401.6	42.4	291	3 544	828.5	85.0
Kissimmee...................	7 266	47	85.1	46	D	D	D	297	4 262	1 003.2	96.7
Lakeland.....................	31 336	159	95.0	150	2 848	10 346.8	138.5	598	9 096	2 250.1	209.6
Lake Worth..................	4 673	38	13.2	61	698	364.4	37.2	172	1 290	312.1	33.4
Largo.........................	3 548	14	100.0	83	D	D	D	354	5 197	1 308.0	128.2
Lauderdale Lakes.........	500	10	0.0	25	176	52.0	4.8	81	1 090	243.7	23.7
Lauderhill...................	0	0	0.0	32	161	104.6	4.8	200	1 800	355.9	39.9
Margate	0	0	0.0	59	345	163.9	12.5	194	3 041	1 071.4	88.3
Melbourne	33 764	199	51.8	125	1 276	675.7	61.0	479	7 029	1 695.4	162.2
Miami.........................	96 316	712	3.8	1 438	9 237	11 188.2	420.8	2 362	20 112	5 622.5	498.8
Miami Beach................	22 695	12	58.3	136	487	409.6	27.9	528	5 232	1 102.3	119.7
Miami Gardens.............	3 214	35	77.1	187	3 917	1 820.1	207.2	277	4 364	1 592.6	124.8
Miami Lakes.................	2 160	10	100.0	111	1 656	974.4	74.0	94	1 186	376.7	33.7
Miramar......................	24 386	161	29.2	154	2 920	2 158.9	169.3	184	4 052	1 881.9	123.9
North Lauderdale	0	0	0.0	21	65	10.2	1.3	71	1 012	226.1	22.1
North Miami.................	1 427	5	100.0	94	522	292.2	22.1	204	1 833	434.1	44.9
North Miami Beach	4 085	29	100.0	83	287	148.9	10.5	234	2 483	731.1	64.1
North Port...................	15 326	63	100.0	21	161	32.3	4.1	61	1 256	257.9	26.2
Oakland Park	838	12	100.0	158	890	430.4	43.7	270	2 444	594.3	59.9
Ocala.........................	13 513	81	100.0	170	2 228	1 071.6	86.4	597	9 774	2 529.6	233.5
Ocoee........................	70 048	230	100.0	27	837	551.6	44.4	191	3 505	573.7	61.4
Orlando......................	72 746	560	40.0	589	9 294	5 439.6	450.3	1 552	23 831	7 481.2	580.2
Ormond Beach.............	20 156	82	100.0	49	931	393.7	32.2	188	2 433	525.7	50.7
Oviedo	72 890	264	64.4	40	180	107.6	10.8	147	1 979	310.3	34.4
Palm Bay.....................	31 499	147	100.0	41	241	122.1	11.4	189	2 945	719.1	63.6
Palm Beach Gardens....	48 271	98	100.0	52	230	185.8	11.8	342	6 687	1 380.2	151.5
Palm Coast..................	36 364	223	52.5	34	96	37.1	4.1	121	2 154	532.5	50.2
Panama City................	NA	NA	NA	67	539	275.1	25.0	381	5 211	1 327.8	116.7
Pembroke Pines...........	11 853	68	100.0	163	563	320.5	24.5	597	11 008	3 020.6	265.1
Pensacola...................	6 924	34	100.0	73	957	472.3	39.0	437	5 921	1 160.4	115.9
Pinellas Park	19 520	181	30.4	180	2 550	1 030.5	93.9	304	6 201	2 770.0	185.3
Plantation	2 206	5	100.0	127	567	332.8	21.6	364	6 326	1 343.9	130.7
Plant City....................	4 133	27	88.9	89	1 508	860.6	52.9	155	2 615	711.7	68.4
Pompano Beach...........	3 199	11	100.0	515	7 335	4 374.9	332.9	654	9 001	3 788.0	274.4
Port Orange................	21 806	117	100.0	41	346	383.8	15.6	166	2 603	519.0	51.3
Port St. Lucie...............	15 955	198	97.0	99	309	108.9	12.2	302	8 458	2 177.3	210.4
Riviera Beach..............	60	1	100.0	112	2 816	1 383.4	140.1	129	1 328	474.8	41.6
Royal Palm Beach	7 863	26	100.0	23	54	15.4	1.7	123	2 632	592.6	59.9
St. Cloud....................	40 474	224	100.0	14	D	D	D	103	1 727	411.6	37.9
St. Petersburg..............	31 195	338	20.7	205	1 976	806.3	83.4	970	13 597	3 261.7	298.0
Sanford......................	21 804	131	95.4	88	1 581	570.5	61.5	364	5 966	1 462.3	126.2
Sarasota.....................	27 335	97	29.9	87	629	308.4	27.4	491	5 483	1 117.6	127.8
Sunrise.......................	27 090	106	86.8	250	2 908	1 828.5	156.3	500	8 288	2 125.2	186.2
Tallahassee.................	38 105	289	85.5	162	1 641	533.7	65.3	890	14 333	2 927.8	286.2
Tamarac	208	1	100.0	71	1 015	955.1	45.2	149	2 977	546.6	88.7
Tampa........................	172 907	1 098	41.4	634	8 805	6 460.5	423.1	1 726	24 672	6 572.1	620.1
Titusville.....................	8 109	37	100.0	25	320	108.6	11.3	164	2 698	613.1	59.9
Wellington...................	38 692	92	100.0	90	285	195.5	13.5	250	3 310	558.6	66.6
Weston.......................	354	2	100.0	224	1 914	1 577.3	107.4	154	1 952	404.9	48.7
West Palm Beach	2 285	8	100.0	167	1 712	1 068.0	79.0	578	9 352	3 028.8	260.9
Winter Garden.............	37 815	196	100.0	37	434	303.3	17.1	119	1 005	298.0	28.5
Winter Haven	22 893	194	58.8	41	464	205.7	16.4	213	3 007	667.5	66.4
Winter Park	14 409	26	100.0	54	382	230.9	20.8	253	2 997	785.4	73.4
Winter Springs.............	1 041	6	100.0	23	105	30.8	3.7	51	323	84.2	7.6

1. Merchant wholesalers except manufacturers' sales branches and offices. 2. Establishments with payroll.

Table D. Cities — Real Estate, Professional Services, and Manufacturing

City	Real estate and rental and leasing, 2007				Professional, scientific, and technical services,[1] 2007				Manufacturing, 2007			
	Number of establishments	Number of employees	Receipts (mil dol)	Annual payroll (mil dol)	Number of establishments	Number of employees	Receipts (mil dol)	Annual payroll (mil dol)	Number of establishments	Number of employees	Receipts (mil dol)	Annual payroll (mil dol)
	80	81	82	83	84	85	86	87	88	89	90	91
FLORIDA—Cont'd												
Deerfield Beach............	147	905	142.8	35.2	384	2 273	312.7	101.5	119	2 642	496.9	104.6
DeLand......................	77	342	36.3	7.3	132	726	69.6	27.0	52	2 269	403.1	90.8
Delray Beach...............	156	555	111.3	21.0	434	1 938	238.3	94.1	64	652	152.3	22.5
Deltona....................	44	98	11.0	2.6	78	237	19.4	6.4	NA	NA	NA	NA
Doral......................	206	686	249.7	30.1	503	D	D	D	131	3 187	632.3	130.3
Dunedin....................	49	140	26.2	3.0	176	3 115	98.2	49.1	NA	NA	NA	NA
Fort Lauderdale............	729	3 653	742.5	147.6	2 323	D	D	D	324	4 977	1 068.8	208.2
Fort Myers.................	226	1 469	277.1	45.1	469	D	D	D	93	2 002	367.8	73.9
Fort Pierce.................	72	252	47.0	7.4	142	D	D	D	35	681	145.8	24.6
Gainesville.................	255	1 350	235.1	40.0	495	D	D	D	88	2 132	589.2	96.6
Greenacres.................	28	120	27.4	4.5	68	335	29.8	13.1	NA	NA	NA	NA
Hallandale Beach..........	94	188	36.5	5.9	146	429	63.1	19.8	NA	NA	NA	NA
Hialeah	271	768	188.7	20.3	364	1 289	127.6	37.1	468	6 542	917.0	205.4
Hollywood..................	334	1 128	201.7	35.7	885	D	D	D	121	2 181	401.3	76.8
Homestead.................	43	138	21.2	3.8	98	395	32.9	13.7	NA	NA	NA	NA
Jacksonville...............	1 257	7 869	1 955.8	347.0	2 820	D	D	D	624	25 890	11 145.3	1 233.1
Jupiter.....................	159	697	90.0	25.0	390	D	D	D	57	1 127	515.7	62.5
Kissimmee..................	176	797	134.3	30.0	171	687	70.5	28.6	NA	NA	NA	NA
Lakeland...................	204	1 197	189.0	33.7	385	D	D	D	84	3 540	1 001.5	138.5
Lake Worth.................	59	143	26.0	3.8	149	D	D	D	58	547	146.2	20.9
Largo......................	139	1 562	236.0	80.6	252	D	D	D	92	3 512	640.9	144.3
Lauderdale Lakes..........	19	211	20.0	5.6	38	107	8.8	3.8	NA	NA	NA	NA
Lauderhill.................	57	493	76.8	15.7	99	375	35.8	11.9	NA	NA	NA	NA
Margate	84	392	66.4	11.3	147	656	68.9	23.4	NA	NA	NA	NA
Melbourne	183	929	146.7	26.4	396	3 372	590.4	196.8	114	6 354	2 784.6	339.8
Miami......................	1 115	4 189	1 317.6	197.2	3 235	23 525	4 436.8	1 906.4	396	4 176	1 079.4	139.1
Miami Beach	458	2 249	602.3	162.0	559	D	D	D	NA	NA	NA	NA
Miami Gardens.............	66	279	85.3	9.7	98	476	44.7	18.3	73	2 716	547.6	98.4
Miami Lakes................	116	700	156.2	32.8	266	1 306	215.2	59.3	27	3 455	D	216.5
Miramar	83	224	69.6	7.8	229	1 191	175.7	69.4	41	1 157	203.9	64.3
North Lauderdale	24	111	19.0	2.6	56	D	D	D	NA	NA	NA	NA
North Miami	108	265	45.2	8.3	163	847	83.7	39.7	33	613	114.9	20.5
North Miami Beach	91	534	74.4	11.4	216	D	D	D	NA	NA	NA	NA
North Port.................	33	79	10.5	2.0	48	191	13.9	6.6	NA	NA	NA	NA
Oakland Park	119	555	73.3	17.3	263	D	D	D	131	1 338	246.7	49.6
Ocala......................	222	990	139.3	25.5	389	2 171	240.8	94.0	112	6 586	1 297.9	236.9
Ocoee......................	32	1 133	37.4	29.6	93	449	36.8	14.7	NA	NA	NA	NA
Orlando....................	779	8 239	2 231.9	363.2	1 835	D	D	D	281	12 806	5 742.1	707.5
Ormond Beach.............	97	453	62.4	11.6	176	989	98.3	34.8	48	951	152.8	35.3
Oviedo	75	171	48.8	5.4	154	D	D	D	NA	NA	NA	NA
Palm Bay...................	79	219	33.2	5.1	120	D	D	D	52	10 509	2 894.8	D
Palm Beach Gardens....	131	591	117.9	30.4	458	D	D	D	20	605	135.5	39.8
Palm Coast.................	133	316	40.5	8.7	133	429	79.3	37.4	23	768	D	D
Panama City................	107	426	66.9	12.2	206	D	D	D	45	1 622	862.4	72.1
Pembroke Pines...........	213	698	180.7	19.6	564	1 763	193.4	68.5	NA	NA	NA	NA
Pensacola..................	136	543	122.3	15.3	444	4 210	477.8	215.6	48	934	300.5	41.8
Pinellas Park	71	305	54.2	8.9	164	D	D	D	256	10 171	2 230.7	419.3
Plantation	229	1 417	210.3	56.8	676	D	D	D	39	1 023	D	61.8
Plant City..................	53	235	39.4	5.5	80	D	D	D	63	3 846	1 215.6	140.0
Pompano Beach...........	260	1 585	285.9	57.7	505	2 028	354.2	93.2	307	7 410	1 562.8	273.5
Port Orange................	95	394	52.7	10.5	123	483	49.9	18.3	NA	NA	NA	NA
Port St. Lucie	169	500	80.6	13.7	260	1 248	115.6	45.3	44	854	408.4	40.9
Riviera Beach..............	47	219	60.6	8.6	68	369	47.7	16.7	90	1 499	1 199.7	61.2
Royal Palm Beach	32	94	12.1	2.2	85	314	37.9	11.2	NA	NA	NA	NA
St. Cloud	56	123	16.2	2.6	54	221	19.9	9.3	NA	NA	NA	NA
St. Petersburg	388	1 905	304.1	66.7	1 132	D	D	D	157	4 557	1 601.2	213.3
Sanford....................	89	557	148.5	16.6	134	D	D	D	72	2 405	701.6	86.5
Sarasota	271	932	206.0	31.7	656	D	D	D	60	672	93.6	31.4
Sunrise	120	532	249.6	19.7	367	2 420	297.8	115.6	65	787	211.0	35.3
Tallahassee................	373	2 141	330.0	61.1	1 183	9 322	1 822.7	629.6	83	1 976	574.2	84.9
Tamarac	80	379	52.8	11.4	150	744	68.3	23.7	28	634	86.8	21.6
Tampa......................	845	5 600	1 167.2	254.0	2 497	23 091	3 950.6	1 662.3	371	9 239	2 836.5	380.4
Titusville	48	231	26.7	4.7	89	561	59.7	26.3	NA	NA	NA	NA
Wellington.................	128	549	76.1	25.2	277	823	109.9	40.6	NA	NA	NA	NA
Weston.....................	187	346	84.2	11.1	461	1 342	196.5	94.3	20	534	55.6	18.5
West Palm Beach	288	1 547	284.8	64.8	1 013	7 964	1 374.6	608.4	114	2 482	473.6	123.1
Winter Garden..............	63	179	28.8	7.0	81	313	30.5	12.4	25	527	212.4	18.1
Winter Haven	81	383	62.3	12.2	130	584	58.4	25.4	27	567	279.2	25.5
Winter Park	181	586	82.5	23.5	482	3 471	560.2	239.7	NA	NA	NA	NA
Winter Springs.............	39	48	8.6	1.3	102	238	21.0	8.6	NA	NA	NA	NA

1. Establishments subject to federal tax.

988 FL(Deerfield Beach)—FL(Winter Springs)   Items 80—91

Table D. Cities — Accommodation and Food Services, Arts, Entertainment, and Recreation, and Health Care and Social Assistance

City	Accommodation and food services, 2007				Arts, entertainment, and recreation,[1] 2007				Health care and social assistance,[1] 2007			
	Number of establish-ments	Number of employees	Sales (mil dol)	Annual payroll (mil dol)	Number of establish-ments	Number of employees	Receipts (mil dol)	Annual payroll (mil dol)	Number of establish-ments	Number of employees	Receipts (mil dol)	Annual payroll (mil dol)
	92	93	94	95	96	97	98	99	100	101	102	103
FLORIDA—Cont'd												
Deerfield Beach	162	3 235	184.3	48.3	28	299	50.5	6.6	186	D	D	D
DeLand	84	1 539	57.7	17.0	11	D	D	D	109	1 643	204.0	60.4
Delray Beach	204	3 683	218.4	59.5	45	308	23.5	7.2	335	3 854	570.6	185.0
Deltona	46	694	27.2	6.6	12	D	D	D	68	550	46.6	18.0
Doral	186	4 503	308.8	80.3	37	D	D	D	151	2 539	315.9	114.9
Dunedin	88	1 151	48.7	13.1	15	D	D	D	109	D	D	D
Fort Lauderdale	679	18 389	1 356.2	363.0	153	1 105	131.9	32.0	773	11 439	1 196.1	481.1
Fort Myers	257	4 685	260.1	66.8	33	988	52.3	19.6	340	4 660	591.5	230.9
Fort Pierce	118	2 217	97.7	28.0	9	152	14.4	3.0	178	2 792	353.2	115.8
Gainesville	359	7 338	315.0	84.8	36	751	32.4	10.2	397	6 146	697.1	259.7
Greenacres	58	987	41.6	11.5	7	19	0.8	0.2	70	662	56.6	20.1
Hallandale Beach	77	2 145	98.2	35.4	22	D	D	D	140	D	D	D
Hialeah	312	4 015	232.2	55.9	38	D	D	D	811	8 639	1 067.7	323.6
Hollywood	332	5 433	395.1	119.8	92	425	49.0	7.3	509	D	D	D
Homestead	74	1 428	65.6	17.6	11	139	37.6	3.6	132	989	101.9	33.9
Jacksonville	1 655	31 715	1 568.2	441.2	213	3 762	396.7	143.1	1 804	25 425	2 813.3	1 141.4
Jupiter	138	2 925	132.0	39.0	41	1 019	63.0	25.5	260	D	D	D
Kissimmee	124	3 419	291.5	77.6	26	D	D	D	232	3 496	499.7	169.4
Lakeland	234	6 154	261.1	76.1	33	512	24.9	8.2	308	5 434	665.2	208.7
Lake Worth	88	1 056	47.1	14.7	18	D	D	D	80	1 035	74.8	32.9
Largo	175	2 843	127.7	38.8	22	D	D	D	310	6 535	626.9	242.5
Lauderdale Lakes	36	411	22.9	5.8	2	D	D	D	99	D	D	D
Lauderhill	86	1 010	48.7	12.3	17	D	D	D	117	1 317	97.2	29.8
Margate	101	1 403	73.3	18.9	17	D	D	D	177	D	D	D
Melbourne	202	3 872	165.8	50.0	36	483	20.2	6.2	354	5 573	705.7	288.4
Miami	994	19 303	1 337.8	355.2	191	2 853	385.2	158.4	1 797	13 565	1 659.3	539.6
Miami Beach	549	16 909	1 345.6	386.9	112	1 411	140.1	39.2	370	2 520	297.6	113.2
Miami Gardens	90	1 372	76.5	18.6	18	D	D	D	119	1 121	86.6	29.2
Miami Lakes	60	1 556	84.7	25.4	17	D	D	D	145	D	D	D
Miramar	95	1 470	69.4	18.9	26	D	D	D	165	D	D	D
North Lauderdale	34	508	26.9	6.4	4	D	D	D	35	D	D	D
North Miami	94	1 550	78.8	20.1	17	D	D	D	126	1 110	95.8	32.0
North Miami Beach	104	1 592	90.3	22.7	18	264	13.6	2.8	232	2 466	274.8	89.3
North Port	29	524	20.2	6.1	4	54	2.0	1.0	47	581	39.0	15.7
Oakland Park	109	1 648	82.7	21.7	20	D	D	D	135	1 853	207.7	70.4
Ocala	242	5 391	245.6	70.9	28	D	D	D	497	7 844	969.9	337.6
Ocoee	74	1 081	54.9	14.7	21	D	D	D	99	1 135	130.9	50.6
Orlando	851	22 678	1 514.5	373.8	133	15 577	1 613.8	418.3	793	8 550	1 133.7	503.3
Ormond Beach	117	2 473	105.8	32.0	23	D	D	D	223	D	D	D
Oviedo	64	1 126	41.1	11.3	14	224	8.0	2.0	116	D	D	D
Palm Bay	99	1 701	70.4	19.4	9	D	D	D	126	1 605	123.6	56.4
Palm Beach Gardens	150	5 178	277.7	86.8	37	D	D	D	329	3 630	513.3	163.3
Palm Coast	76	1 776	88.4	24.8	15	213	12.2	4.2	104	D	D	D
Panama City	166	2 987	133.7	38.5	16	D	D	D	300	4 517	570.2	198.4
Pembroke Pines	284	5 793	271.3	76.0	54	D	D	D	501	D	D	D
Pensacola	187	4 497	208.6	59.4	22	D	D	D	338	6 369	827.5	329.5
Pinellas Park	119	1 878	128.8	34.9	14	144	6.9	2.3	126	1 592	140.5	56.1
Plantation	186	3 569	194.4	51.9	39	D	D	D	534	5 622	787.1	245.9
Plant City	80	1 597	77.5	19.1	5	D	D	D	98	D	D	D
Pompano Beach	266	3 739	197.7	50.2	62	D	D	D	269	2 650	282.6	93.3
Port Orange	88	1 785	70.6	20.1	20	D	D	D	117	D	D	D
Port St. Lucie	158	3 292	127.5	35.9	30	D	D	D	284	4 051	486.2	153.0
Riviera Beach	39	950	44.9	10.4	14	685	53.1	19.4	36	190	14.5	5.7
Royal Palm Beach	83	1 436	61.1	17.8	13	106	6.4	1.8	116	1 857	248.6	75.8
St. Cloud	63	1 340	57.3	16.0	8	D	D	D	43	D	D	D
St. Petersburg	465	8 782	451.1	126.6	56	1 412	200.1	90.3	774	9 186	1 214.4	427.9
Sanford	129	2 932	123.8	36.1	14	D	D	D	103	1 765	226.8	73.8
Sarasota	258	5 897	350.1	103.6	37	684	39.9	11.1	464	5 185	676.8	241.0
Sunrise	186	3 596	181.7	48.8	36	D	D	D	244	3 991	497.3	225.0
Tallahassee	538	12 939	514.5	142.2	52	998	112.0	15.7	504	8 075	801.3	353.6
Tamarac	86	1 310	64.5	15.1	15	D	D	D	203	2 744	305.0	106.8
Tampa	956	23 982	1 376.2	377.7	126	6 136	659.7	287.3	1 197	14 681	2 066.7	719.4
Titusville	97	1 986	89.2	23.1	11	113	5.6	1.6	137	D	D	D
Wellington	101	2 125	92.5	27.5	54	260	18.2	3.8	176	D	D	D
Weston	98	2 203	120.6	31.9	30	D	D	D	195	D	D	D
West Palm Beach	295	6 038	326.6	91.0	60	608	88.5	26.0	509	7 574	1 095.9	366.0
Winter Garden	48	547	25.7	6.7	8	D	D	D	43	515	41.7	18.2
Winter Haven	106	1 625	70.0	18.9	5	D	D	D	168	D	D	D
Winter Park	128	3 271	152.0	46.2	31	D	D	D	272	3 373	441.9	165.4
Winter Springs	26	257	9.6	2.5	14	D	D	D	29	D	D	D

1. Establishments subject to federal tax.

Table D. Cities — **Other Services and Federal Funds**

City	Other services[1], 2007				Selected federal funds, 2009–2010 (mil dol)								
					Procurement contracts		Grants						
	Number of establish-ments	Number of employees	Receipts (mil dol)	Annual payroll (mil dol)	Defense	Other	Total[2]	Medicaid and other health related	Nutrition and family welfare	Energy and envi-ronment	Disasters and emergency prepared-ness	Housing and community develop-ment	Employment and training
	104	105	106	107	108	109	110	111	112	113	114	115	116
FLORIDA—Cont'd													
Deerfield Beach	161	879	64.9	21.3	5.7	5.4	5.3	0.0	0.0	0.0	0.0	5.3	0.0
DeLand	71	371	24.4	8.4	0.1	0.3	16.6	0.0	0.0	2.4	0.0	12.5	0.0
Delray Beach	181	743	63.7	15.9	23.4	0.5	13.9	0.0	0.0	0.1	0.0	13.3	0.0
Deltona	44	165	7.4	2.4	0.0	0.0	1.2	0.0	0.0	0.7	0.0	0.5	0.0
Doral	130	1 131	134.6	30.2	3.2	8.1	0.8	0.0	0.0	0.0	0.0	0.0	0.0
Dunedin	79	260	29.3	5.7	0.2	0.1	2.1	0.0	0.0	0.2	0.0	0.0	0.0
Fort Lauderdale	559	3 246	314.4	91.4	44.8	43.1	145.6	27.4	0.2	3.0	0.6	47.4	4.3
Fort Myers	238	1 417	131.8	36.0	1.0	7.0	57.1	7.3	5.5	5.1	0.1	21.1	0.0
Fort Pierce	91	372	28.7	9.5	0.1	3.0	20.8	0.5	0.1	3.7	0.0	9.3	0.0
Gainesville	207	1 182	84.0	26.0	10.0	125.8	407.9	224.6	4.8	17.0	0.0	21.7	0.4
Greenacres	48	125	7.7	2.5	0.0	0.1	0.0	0.0	0.0	0.0	0.0	0.0	0.0
Hallandale Beach	88	471	34.9	11.6	NA	NA	NA	NA	NA	NA	NA	NA	NA
Hialeah	478	1 814	146.7	38.5	42.2	2.7	42.6	0.4	0.0	2.4	0.0	38.7	0.0
Hollywood	264	1 888	138.5	45.5	2.2	1.4	15.3	0.9	0.0	0.7	0.0	9.1	0.0
Homestead	58	216	15.6	4.1	51.9	2.2	20.5	0.3	0.0	0.5	0.0	18.5	0.0
Jacksonville	1 368	D	D	D	845.0	213.6	346.7	38.6	32.1	117.8	0.0	78.3	5.9
Jupiter	143	665	46.7	15.8	10.9	1.3	11.4	0.4	0.0	1.4	0.0	0.0	0.0
Kissimmee	111	407	32.7	9.3	4.9	0.5	11.4	1.0	0.0	0.0	0.0	2.1	0.0
Lakeland	156	875	61.7	20.2	2.0	1.5	34.6	0.4	0.0	15.8	0.0	13.0	0.3
Lake Worth	98	347	24.7	7.8	3.4	0.0	27.1	0.0	0.0	0.3	0.0	23.7	0.3
Largo	160	676	50.2	16.1	29.9	3.9	19.2	0.4	0.0	0.0	0.0	1.6	0.0
Lauderdale Lakes	31	83	7.5	2.2	0.0	0.1	74.6	0.3	0.0	0.0	0.0	74.2	0.0
Lauderhill	83	341	24.1	6.7	0.0	0.0	2.6	0.0	0.0	0.6	0.0	2.0	0.0
Margate	107	399	35.5	8.0	0.2	0.6	0.9	0.0	0.0	0.5	0.0	0.4	0.0
Melbourne	167	802	54.4	18.7	1 040.8	231.8	20.5	0.9	0.0	1.0	0.2	12.5	0.0
Miami	879	4 795	360.0	97.3	200.6	216.9	1 039.2	92.5	54.1	217.8	70.6	337.3	0.2
Miami Beach	176	1 483	112.6	24.6	0.5	7.8	41.1	10.9	0.0	0.8	0.0	28.6	0.0
Miami Gardens	51	1 605	44.1	20.0	0.0	0.0	2.3	0.1	0.0	0.0	0.0	1.4	0.0
Miami Lakes	30	92	7.0	2.1	0.3	0.5	0.0	0.0	0.0	0.0	0.0	0.0	0.0
Miramar	92	395	33.4	10.4	10.2	10.4	4.0	2.4	0.0	0.8	0.0	0.8	0.0
North Lauderdale	45	221	23.8	7.1	0.0	0.0	0.5	0.0	0.5	0.0	0.0	0.0	0.0
North Miami	99	392	26.3	6.0	1.1	0.6	2.4	0.0	0.0	0.5	0.0	1.8	0.0
North Miami Beach	103	394	28.3	8.0	0.0	0.0	0.1	0.0	0.0	0.0	0.0	0.0	0.0
North Port	38	118	8.7	2.8	0.0	0.0	0.0	0.0	0.0	0.0	0.0	0.0	0.0
Oakland Park	185	584	51.7	14.1	0.0	0.0	0.3	0.0	0.0	0.0	0.0	0.0	0.0
Ocala	181	1 059	79.9	23.2	15.3	5.4	26.0	0.0	0.1	4.0	0.0	11.4	4.4
Ocoee	53	D	D	D	3.2	0.1	0.8	0.0	0.0	0.0	0.0	0.0	0.0
Orlando	501	4 728	334.7	100.1	3 058.4	472.0	290.7	36.2	16.3	70.1	0.3	62.7	1.1
Ormond Beach	74	308	18.3	5.6	1.3	0.4	1.7	0.0	0.0	0.0	-0.1	1.5	0.0
Oviedo	58	300	19.0	5.7	13.6	0.8	2.8	0.0	0.0	0.3	0.0	2.5	0.0
Palm Bay	96	326	27.5	8.5	393.8	48.2	15.5	1.3	0.0	3.4	0.0	0.6	0.0
Palm Beach Gardens	95	498	38.8	13.8	15.9	146.4	0.1	0.0	0.0	0.1	0.0	0.0	0.0
Palm Coast	58	213	11.7	3.6	0.4	0.0	1.3	0.0	0.8	0.0	0.0	0.0	0.0
Panama City	92	624	40.1	12.3	274.6	46.4	13.7	1.3	5.1	0.2	0.0	3.5	0.0
Pembroke Pines	196	1 128	78.6	21.7	1.5	1.3	4.1	0.0	0.0	1.5	0.0	0.9	0.0
Pensacola	111	820	58.4	17.0	340.2	129.7	62.3	1.9	6.9	4.4	0.0	20.7	0.3
Pinellas Park	147	869	84.5	25.5	20.5	0.7	5.7	3.3	1.4	0.0	0.0	0.1	0.0
Plantation	154	858	52.5	24.3	8.6	5.1	1.4	0.0	0.0	0.8	0.0	0.5	0.0
Plant City	51	269	20.8	6.6	7.8	0.4	1.8	0.0	0.0	0.2	0.0	1.5	0.0
Pompano Beach	297	1 607	157.0	40.4	31.9	44.3	103.6	1.9	0.0	0.0	0.0	10.9	0.0
Port Orange	82	413	21.6	6.5	0.1	0.6	0.8	0.0	0.5	0.0	0.0	0.3	0.0
Port St. Lucie	125	424	31.4	9.4	1.4	1.5	3.6	1.5	0.0	1.3	0.0	0.7	0.0
Riviera Beach	67	355	48.2	12.4	0.0	22.0	0.3	0.0	0.0	0.0	0.0	0.2	0.0
Royal Palm Beach	57	275	19.2	5.6	0.0	0.3	0.0	0.0	0.0	0.0	0.0	0.0	0.0
St. Cloud	41	D	D	D	0.3	0.0	0.1	0.0	0.0	0.0	0.0	0.0	0.0
St. Petersburg	418	1 877	120.7	40.4	424.5	190.7	82.1	3.4	13.4	16.2	0.0	33.6	2.6
Sanford	113	647	54.1	18.0	22.2	1.6	28.9	4.0	0.0	3.2	0.0	9.8	0.3
Sarasota	164	1 171	72.1	23.3	1.7	1.5	62.4	4.7	3.2	1.4	0.0	39.0	0.0
Sunrise	127	521	41.1	11.9	64.8	7.6	17.9	0.6	13.5	1.4	0.0	2.3	0.0
Tallahassee	312	1 966	132.7	45.5	27.1	21.6	4 447.5	527.5	582.2	176.8	32.3	155.3	356.7
Tamarac	63	278	15.6	4.7	0.3	4.5	2.2	0.0	0.0	1.3	0.0	0.4	0.0
Tampa	769	7 266	431.8	130.5	998.2	342.0	496.2	200.1	24.7	10.2	1.4	197.1	1.8
Titusville	73	528	45.1	20.9	27.0	13.8	4.5	0.0	0.0	0.0	0.0	3.8	0.0
Wellington	94	527	38.8	13.1	137.8	1.9	0.5	0.0	0.0	0.5	0.0	0.0	0.0
Weston	84	496	30.4	11.1	0.8	4.9	1.1	1.0	0.0	0.1	0.0	0.0	0.0
West Palm Beach	203	1 198	85.8	28.0	55.5	11.5	189.6	19.6	15.0	1.9	0.4	122.2	0.0
Winter Garden	41	193	15.4	4.1	0.0	0.7	0.2	0.0	0.0	0.2	0.0	0.0	0.0
Winter Haven	60	228	18.9	5.7	0.4	1.0	11.8	0.0	5.6	0.0	0.0	1.3	2.9
Winter Park	107	506	35.4	11.8	21.5	0.6	7.7	0.9	1.3	0.0	0.0	0.3	0.0
Winter Springs	28	65	5.5	1.4	6.1	0.0	2.4	0.0	0.0	0.0	0.0	0.0	0.0

1. Establishments subject to federal tax.   2. Includes program categories not shown separately. State totals include additional categories not allocated by city.

Table D. Cities — **City Government Finances**

City	City government finances, 2007									
	General revenue							General expenditure		
	Intergovernmental			Taxes					Per capita[1] (dollars)	
					Per capita[1] (dollars)					
	Total (mil dol)	Total (mil dol)	Percent from state government	Total (mil dol)	Total	Property	Sales and gross receipts	Total (mil dol)	Total	Capital outlays
	117	118	119	120	121	122	123	124	125	126
FLORIDA—Cont'd										
Deerfield Beach	116.2	23.8	94.7	51.4	690	478	212	110.0	1 475	128
DeLand	35.6	3.6	70.8	18.6	691	281	410	37.0	1 377	431
Delray Beach	142.5	18.1	48.4	80.8	1 261	952	232	158.4	2 471	719
Deltona	57.0	10.8	84.6	27.5	324	116	208	42.3	498	70
Doral	52.8	3.5	82.8	34.6	1 510	750	760	45.8	1 996	1 140
Dunedin	47.3	4.5	90.1	21.7	598	244	354	54.8	1 511	391
Fort Lauderdale	447.7	128.1	18.3	193.6	1 054	685	370	394.6	2 149	188
Fort Myers	171.9	24.9	39.9	74.6	1 161	459	702	141.1	2 196	183
Fort Pierce	105.4	50.4	21.4	23.3	580	302	278	81.1	2 018	432
Gainesville	176.1	15.9	60.1	48.5	424	193	232	195.2	1 707	339
Greenacres	27.4	6.0	100.0	15.6	482	258	224	22.3	690	140
Hallandale Beach	63.7	8.5	55.0	31.7	820	512	307	66.1	1 712	212
Hialeah	215.3	53.2	54.0	109.5	516	256	260	223.8	1 054	139
Hollywood	277.5	57.3	48.3	122.4	859	559	300	272.8	1 915	234
Homestead	80.0	14.7	91.9	34.1	603	189	414	76.6	1 354	183
Jacksonville	1 810.6	262.0	73.8	745.0	925	511	413	1 627.8	2 021	369
Jupiter	66.7	9.8	63.1	36.6	750	410	340	61.0	1 250	269
Kissimmee	79.9	28.3	40.5	30.7	497	234	262	78.1	1 264	249
Lakeland	161.4	29.3	61.1	54.1	583	226	358	173.7	1 872	201
Lake Worth	74.4	28.5	23.1	24.2	681	398	283	67.8	1 906	249
Largo	105.8	12.6	81.8	41.3	564	204	360	99.5	1 358	180
Lauderdale Lakes	39.7	9.9	64.8	16.3	522	219	304	34.8	1 112	252
Lauderhill	61.3	16.4	46.6	29.7	440	208	232	64.4	953	0
Margate	72.4	18.1	90.5	30.3	554	376	178	69.4	1 271	28
Melbourne	116.9	18.6	59.5	45.9	591	224	367	102.9	1 324	135
Miami	683.7	168.6	36.4	346.6	844	609	234	734.5	1 793	273
Miami Beach	409.0	74.8	14.9	208.3	2 450	1 407	1 043	335.2	3 942	364
Miami Gardens	52.0	19.4	63.9	30.4	312	120	192	54.0	555	43
Miami Lakes	25.4	9.5	38.5	14.4	661	324	337	24.5	1 126	100
Miramar	162.6	34.1	37.1	74.9	692	400	292	134.3	1 241	149
North Lauderdale	37.7	11.2	45.0	15.3	365	176	178	37.8	904	26
North Miami	76.3	17.2	41.8	33.6	598	336	261	75.0	1 336	27
North Miami Beach	75.6	17.0	33.1	27.6	723	414	309	66.8	1 748	217
North Port	107.7	19.2	24.2	52.7	971	259	708	66.3	1 221	232
Oakland Park	61.3	8.1	22.8	28.7	681	350	331	86.5	2 053	131
Ocala	92.4	12.3	76.5	33.5	627	333	294	93.4	1 747	173
Ocoee	40.4	11.0	72.6	15.0	472	240	231	35.8	1 122	325
Orlando	542.4	124.2	42.4	205.3	901	413	488	504.5	2 214	129
Ormond Beach	51.9	8.4	44.4	25.1	653	309	344	48.3	1 257	168
Oviedo	33.0	7.5	73.9	16.6	538	302	236	37.8	1 226	338
Palm Bay	92.6	16.6	78.0	50.2	502	233	269	80.4	803	83
Palm Beach Gardens	76.1	9.6	100.0	50.7	1 036	837	199	69.6	1 423	152
Palm Coast	52.7	7.0	98.8	25.0	350	206	143	63.8	893	346
Panama City	58.3	8.7	88.6	28.8	783	272	511	50.8	1 380	146
Pembroke Pines	204.7	48.3	34.2	88.0	600	290	310	242.2	1 650	110
Pensacola	132.4	49.6	27.4	45.0	830	280	550	129.7	2 390	687
Pinellas Park	74.5	11.7	69.4	32.9	693	298	396	75.6	1 593	43
Plantation	129.0	38.2	34.9	58.3	691	365	326	130.5	1 547	139
Plant City	59.2	15.2	81.5	21.8	675	252	422	45.6	1 410	112
Pompano Beach	166.6	25.8	38.0	89.8	874	479	395	145.4	1 415	120
Port Orange	69.5	8.7	75.6	23.8	433	224	210	52.9	964	135
Port St. Lucie	258.4	20.1	61.8	88.6	585	250	335	239.7	1 583	632
Riviera Beach	75.1	3.8	78.2	39.8	1 087	747	340	70.0	1 914	140
Royal Palm Beach	30.7	4.6	70.7	15.3	504	175	329	22.8	750	94
St. Cloud	80.4	17.0	30.2	27.5	1 004	157	847	72.4	2 644	198
St. Petersburg	400.9	83.6	39.9	158.5	643	374	269	341.7	1 387	194
Sanford	87.4	24.8	24.2	31.5	624	263	361	69.8	1 384	334
Sarasota	135.3	28.0	56.5	51.6	982	425	558	114.0	2 173	160
Sunrise	179.1	22.2	55.2	67.7	754	375	379	137.7	1 534	138
Tallahassee	283.5	54.0	67.8	97.3	576	188	388	314.3	1 860	74
Tamarac	87.6	18.7	9.3	32.5	545	332	212	72.3	1 212	170
Tampa	659.9	123.2	58.6	286.7	851	419	433	566.8	1 683	229
Titusville	40.4	7.3	92.6	19.9	452	228	225	41.7	950	110
Wellington	76.0	14.7	47.8	33.4	614	268	346	62.2	1 141	250
Weston	73.3	14.2	100.0	25.5	398	151	247	63.5	989	106
West Palm Beach	245.0	44.6	27.3	119.3	1 200	773	427	220.5	2 219	305
Winter Garden	54.5	5.9	91.9	10.7	373	202	172	39.5	1 377	523
Winter Haven	53.4	5.9	72.7	22.2	680	308	372	49.6	1 522	369
Winter Park	62.1	9.1	87.8	29.0	1 038	645	393	60.9	2 180	271
Winter Springs	35.2	4.4	95.8	19.2	582	231	351	28.0	849	140

1. Based on population estimated as of July 1 of the year shown.

Table D. Cities — **City Government Finances**

City	City government finances, 2006 (cont.)									
	General expenditure (cont.)									
	Percent of total for:									
	Public welfare	Highways	Parking facilities	Education	Health and hospitals	Police protection	Sewerage and sanitation	Parks and recreation	Housing and community development	Interest on debt
	127	128	129	130	131	132	133	134	135	136
FLORIDA—Cont'd										
Deerfield Beach............	13.5	1.9	0.1	0.0	0.0	13.3	20.3	6.7	1.0	1.7
DeLand........................	0.0	3.7	0.0	0.0	0.0	17.0	13.3	9.3	2.4	1.9
Delray Beach................	0.0	1.6	12.2	0.0	0.0	16.5	5.7	14.8	9.1	1.6
Deltona.......................	0.0	12.2	0.0	0.0	0.0	17.0	20.1	6.9	5.4	0.0
Doral..........................	0.0	2.1	0.0	0.0	0.0	24.4	0.0	58.4	0.0	1.0
Dunedin......................	0.0	4.0	0.0	0.0	0.0	8.4	22.1	27.6	0.0	0.8
Fort Lauderdale............	0.0	2.4	2.2	0.0	0.0	22.4	4.4	12.4	9.5	1.1
Fort Myers...................	0.0	6.9	0.5	0.0	0.0	16.5	23.7	12.5	6.1	3.8
Fort Pierce..................	0.0	4.8	0.0	0.0	0.0	17.2	18.1	10.2	11.9	1.7
Gainesville..................	0.5	5.4	0.2	0.0	0.0	18.1	24.6	5.6	2.6	6.9
Greenacres..................	0.0	11.9	0.0	0.0	0.0	28.0	3.9	7.6	0.0	1.1
Hallandale Beach.........	2.0	1.5	0.0	0.0	0.0	22.0	18.4	3.4	9.8	0.5
Hialeah	0.0	10.7	0.0	0.0	0.1	17.7	17.0	6.2	3.1	2.4
Hollywood....................	0.0	3.1	1.6	0.0	0.0	24.1	15.7	7.9	1.7	3.3
Homestead..................	0.0	5.3	0.0	0.0	0.0	32.2	17.1	8.8	9.1	1.2
Jacksonville.................	5.1	4.9	0.1	0.0	1.3	10.7	11.8	4.5	1.5	20.7
Jupiter.........................	0.0	10.1	0.0	0.0	0.0	26.7	6.5	6.8	0.0	2.9
Kissimmee...................	0.0	17.9	0.0	0.0	0.0	21.3	7.9	9.2	0.0	4.1
Lakeland......................	0.0	7.8	0.5	0.0	0.0	16.7	15.2	16.4	1.8	2.0
Lake Worth...................	0.0	5.2	0.1	0.0	0.0	20.1	28.0	8.6	0.0	1.0
Largo	0.0	1.4	0.0	0.0	0.0	16.6	26.4	9.2	10.1	1.5
Lauderdale Lakes.........	1.5	9.4	0.0	0.0	0.0	19.1	6.5	19.7	1.2	3.8
Lauderhill....................	0.0	14.5	0.0	0.0	7.0	19.7	2.3	9.1	1.1	4.4
Margate	0.0	2.3	0.0	0.0	0.0	26.0	7.4	5.7	2.7	0.2
Melbourne	0.0	15.0	0.0	0.0	0.0	16.1	14.3	9.7	2.4	2.4
Miami..........................	0.0	7.0	3.6	0.0	0.0	17.2	4.1	8.2	7.1	2.9
Miami Beach	0.0	3.2	6.3	0.0	3.9	20.7	12.9	19.9	0.9	4.5
Miami Gardens.............	0.0	16.4	0.0	0.0	0.0	50.7	0.0	7.3	0.0	0.6
Miami Lakes	0.0	30.8	0.0	0.0	0.0	25.2	0.0	13.0	0.0	0.0
Miramar	0.0	2.2	0.0	0.0	0.0	21.2	5.5	10.8	0.9	3.8
North Lauderdale	0.0	3.2	0.0	8.5	0.0	19.3	12.7	10.7	1.1	1.8
North Miami.................	0.0	4.6	0.0	0.0	0.0	18.4	28.1	7.0	4.8	2.0
North Miami Beach	0.0	1.6	0.0	0.0	0.0	30.7	19.2	5.4	0.4	3.1
North Port....................	0.0	22.4	0.0	0.0	0.0	13.7	21.0	4.6	0.0	0.4
Oakland Park	0.0	2.3	0.0	0.0	0.0	11.7	24.7	6.2	0.0	0.6
Ocala..........................	0.2	14.6	0.1	0.0	1.1	21.9	22.5	5.5	1.0	2.0
Ocoee.........................	0.0	20.0	0.0	0.0	0.0	20.1	8.9	8.8	0.0	4.4
Orlando.......................	0.0	7.0	2.4	0.0	0.0	21.1	14.8	11.1	2.4	3.5
Ormond Beach..............	0.0	9.1	0.0	0.0	0.0	15.2	22.1	10.6	0.0	0.9
Oviedo.........................	0.0	25.0	0.0	0.0	0.0	14.2	5.7	19.8	0.0	2.8
Palm Bay.....................	0.0	17.0	0.0	0.0	0.0	23.8	13.2	6.4	5.2	1.6
Palm Beach Gardens....	0.0	1.0	0.0	0.0	0.0	29.6	0.0	21.5	0.0	2.1
Palm Coast..................	0.0	13.2	0.0	0.0	0.0	2.8	36.7	7.7	0.0	3.8
Panama City.................	0.1	12.8	0.0	0.0	0.4	17.0	9.6	12.7	0.8	1.1
Pembroke Pines...........	1.1	3.1	0.0	0.0	0.0	10.3	14.8	6.5	2.6	8.3
Pensacola....................	0.0	4.2	0.0	0.0	0.0	13.1	4.8	4.6	6.6	3.5
Pinellas Park	0.0	5.6	0.0	0.0	2.5	16.4	23.9	5.1	0.5	0.9
Plantation	0.0	4.8	0.0	0.0	4.3	24.8	7.9	10.4	2.0	1.9
Plant City....................	0.0	5.8	0.0	0.0	0.5	15.4	34.7	10.5	6.1	2.0
Pompano Beach...........	0.0	3.0	0.0	0.0	7.5	26.8	11.0	11.5	2.2	0.4
Port Orange.................	0.0	9.0	0.0	0.0	0.0	19.4	24.6	13.5	1.6	2.8
Port St. Lucie	0.0	45.9	0.0	0.0	0.6	12.8	4.6	5.0	0.8	5.6
Riviera Beach...............	0.1	0.9	0.0	0.0	0.0	19.3	11.9	7.5	3.6	0.4
Royal Palm Beach	0.0	14.5	0.0	0.0	0.0	24.9	10.8	18.1	0.0	0.7
St. Cloud	0.0	10.1	0.0	0.0	1.7	10.2	17.2	13.5	0.0	2.7
St. Petersburg	0.0	5.2	1.1	0.0	2.8	24.0	13.1	20.5	2.3	2.4
Sanford.......................	0.0	10.1	0.0	0.0	0.6	15.9	29.6	7.4	0.6	0.2
Sarasota	0.0	8.5	0.4	0.0	0.0	23.4	18.1	16.2	11.7	1.0
Sunrise.......................	0.0	3.4	0.0	0.0	0.0	18.0	29.0	8.2	0.8	1.8
Tallahassee	0.0	24.6	0.1	0.0	0.0	13.3	15.9	8.7	1.9	2.6
Tamarac	0.0	6.7	0.0	0.0	0.0	13.0	11.6	9.1	2.9	3.5
Tampa.........................	0.0	10.3	2.6	0.0	0.0	21.0	25.5	12.0	4.8	5.7
Titusville	0.0	4.4	0.0	0.0	0.0	21.8	16.7	9.5	10.1	0.6
Wellington	0.0	7.3	0.0	0.0	0.0	8.4	16.8	14.1	0.0	1.7
Weston	0.0	0.0	0.0	0.0	0.0	11.9	4.8	9.0	2.4	0.4
West Palm Beach	0.0	6.6	1.5	0.0	1.5	19.8	11.9	6.4	6.5	2.8
Winter Garden..............	0.1	18.5	0.0	0.0	0.0	12.6	24.1	5.9	1.9	2.1
Winter Haven...............	0.0	4.7	0.0	0.0	0.0	16.9	26.0	11.8	0.0	2.1
Winter Park	0.0	4.1	0.0	0.0	0.0	16.9	18.6	10.5	0.8	1.8
Winter Springs..............	0.0	11.2	0.0	0.0	0.0	20.3	14.1	7.6	0.1	4.3

Table D. Cities — City Government Finances, City Government Employment, and Climate

City	City government finances, 2007 (cont.)				Climate[2]						
	Debt outstanding				Average daily temperature (degrees Fahrenheit)						
					Mean		Limits				
	Total (mil dol)	Per capita[1] (dollars)	Debt issued during year	City government employment, 2010	January	July	January[3]	July[4]	Annual precipitation (inches)	Heating degree days	Cooling degree days
	137	138	139	140	141	142	143	144	145	146	147
FLORIDA—Cont'd											
Deerfield Beach..............	63.4	850	6.2	617	67.2	83.3	57.8	91.8	57.27	219	4 241
DeLand........................	38.7	1 440	13.3	NA	NA	NA	NA	NA	NA	NA	NA
Delray Beach................	93.6	1 459	7.9	777	66.2	82.5	57.3	90.1	61.39	246	3 999
Deltona......................	99.1	1 166	18.6	317	57.1	81.2	44.5	91.2	57.03	954	2 819
Doral.........................	21.3	927	21.3	NA	NA	NA	NA	NA	NA	NA	NA
Dunedin......................	36.3	1 002	3.2	381	60.9	82.5	50.2	91.3	52.42	623	3 414
Fort Lauderdale............	218.8	1 192	16.9	2 478	67.5	82.6	59.2	89.8	64.19	167	4 120
Fort Myers...................	247.9	3 858	40.7	916	64.9	83.0	54.5	91.7	54.19	302	3 957
Fort Pierce..................	153.7	3 823	20.2	644	62.6	81.7	50.7	91.5	53.50	477	3 430
Gainesville..................	783.8	6 853	394.0	2 112	54.4	81.1	41.8	92.4	49.56	1 249	2 608
Greenacres..................	6.1	189	0.0	NA	66.2	82.5	57.3	90.1	61.39	246	3 999
Hallandale Beach.........	14.2	368	0.0	472	68.1	83.7	59.6	90.9	58.53	149	4 361
Hialeah	145.1	684	10.1	1 668	67.9	82.7	62.6	87.0	46.60	141	4 090
Hollywood...................	347.2	2 437	31.2	1 450	67.5	82.6	59.2	89.8	64.19	167	4 120
Homestead..................	29.5	521	1.2	362	67.0	81.8	56.2	90.6	55.55	238	3 923
Jacksonville................	10 924.0	13 560	1 203.5	9 402	54.5	82.5	42.6	92.7	51.88	1 222	2 810
Jupiter.......................	85.6	1 755	0.0	389	66.2	82.5	57.3	90.1	61.39	246	3 999
Kissimmee...................	408.5	6 613	10.6	899	59.7	81.8	47.7	91.6	48.01	694	3 111
Lakeland.....................	940.7	10 137	189.0	2 190	62.5	84.0	51.1	94.6	49.13	487	3 886
Lake Worth..................	94.7	2 663	12.9	342	66.1	81.1	52.5	91.3	58.44	273	3 438
Largo.........................	30.1	410	0.0	878	61.3	82.5	52.4	89.7	44.77	591	3 482
Lauderdale Lakes..........	16.1	514	1.5	NA	67.2	83.3	57.8	91.8	57.27	219	4 241
Lauderhill...................	82.3	1 218	0.0	449	67.5	82.6	59.2	89.8	64.19	167	4 120
Margate......................	24.7	453	0.0	539	67.2	83.3	57.8	91.8	57.27	219	4 241
Melbourne	120.2	1 548	7.3	889	60.9	81.2	50.0	90.5	48.29	595	3 186
Miami.........................	544.0	1 328	43.0	4 055	68.1	83.7	59.6	90.9	58.53	149	4 361
Miami Beach	471.4	5 544	62.6	1 926	68.1	83.7	59.6	90.9	58.53	149	4 361
Miami Gardens............	11.0	113	0.0	561	NA	NA	NA	NA	NA	NA	NA
Miami Lakes................	0.0	0	0.0	NA	NA	NA	NA	NA	NA	NA	NA
Miramar......................	132.6	1 225	6.7	901	68.1	83.7	59.6	90.9	58.53	149	4 361
North Lauderdale..........	14.2	339	0.0	NA	67.5	82.6	59.2	89.8	64.19	167	4 120
North Miami.................	22.2	395	1.2	521	68.1	83.7	59.6	90.9	58.53	149	4 361
North Miami Beach	108.7	2 845	0.0	558	68.1	83.7	59.6	90.9	58.53	149	4 361
North Port...................	44.1	812	6.2	523	NA	NA	NA	NA	NA	NA	NA
Oakland Park	23.0	545	0.0	NA	67.5	82.6	59.2	89.8	64.19	167	4 120
Ocala.........................	186.6	3 488	7.6	985	58.1	81.7	45.7	92.2	49.68	902	2 971
Ocoee........................	60.1	1 885	5.6	NA	NA	NA	NA	NA	NA	NA	NA
Orlando......................	480.8	2 110	85.1	2 985	60.9	82.4	49.9	92.2	48.35	580	3 428
Ormond Beach.............	34.0	884	8.3	340	60.9	82.4	49.9	92.2	48.35	580	3 428
Oviedo	40.2	1 304	0.1	291	58.7	81.5	47.0	91.9	51.31	799	3 017
Palm Bay....................	140.7	1 405	47.4	771	60.9	81.2	50.0	90.5	48.29	595	3 186
Palm Beach Gardens....	36.2	739	6.1	490	66.2	82.5	57.3	90.1	61.39	246	3 999
Palm Coast..................	114.1	1 598	10.9	NA	57.4	82.8	46.4	92.0	49.79	909	3 193
Panama City................	42.5	1 155	0.0	548	50.3	80.0	38.7	89.0	64.76	1 810	2 174
Pembroke Pines...........	308.0	2 098	0.0	935	67.5	82.6	59.2	89.8	64.19	167	4 120
Pensacola...................	91.3	1 681	0.0	895	52.0	82.6	42.7	90.7	64.28	1 498	2 650
Pinellas Park	42.8	903	0.0	522	61.7	83.4	54.0	90.2	49.58	548	3 718
Plantation...................	67.1	795	0.0	853	67.5	82.6	59.2	89.8	64.19	167	4 120
Plant City...................	35.5	1 098	2.2	NA	61.1	81.5	49.8	90.8	51.17	625	3 261
Pompano Beach...........	62.6	609	49.4	733	67.2	83.3	57.8	91.8	57.27	219	4 241
Port Orange................	159.2	2 899	38.8	NA	57.1	81.2	44.5	91.2	57.03	954	2 819
Port St. Lucie	774.4	5 115	174.8	1 102	64.5	81.8	54.7	89.5	59.53	315	3 600
Riviera Beach..............	49.1	1 343	7.4	495	66.2	82.5	57.3	90.1	61.39	246	3 999
Royal Palm Beach	4.6	152	0.0	NA	NA	NA	NA	NA	NA	NA	NA
St. Cloud....................	48.1	1 757	9.5	NA	NA	NA	NA	NA	NA	NA	NA
St. Petersburg	573.0	2 325	66.4	2 983	61.7	83.4	54.0	90.2	49.58	548	3 718
Sanford......................	50.0	991	11.5	619	58.7	81.5	47.0	91.9	51.31	799	3 017
Sarasota.....................	86.1	1 640	0.8	669	61.7	83.4	54.0	90.2	49.58	548	3 718
Sunrise......................	300.0	3 341	3.6	933	67.5	82.6	59.2	89.8	64.19	167	4 120
Tallahassee.................	675.5	3 998	146.0	2 939	51.8	82.4	39.7	92.0	63.21	1 604	2 551
Tamarac.....................	53.4	895	20.6	NA	67.2	83.3	57.8	91.8	57.27	219	4 241
Tampa........................	1 533.7	4 553	36.3	4 368	61.3	82.5	52.4	89.7	44.77	591	3 482
Titusville	64.9	1 478	0.0	488	59.9	82.4	49.5	91.4	52.79	677	3 300
Wellington...................	40.9	750	0.0	NA	66.2	82.5	57.3	90.1	61.39	246	3 999
Weston.......................	6.8	106	0.0	NA	67.5	82.6	59.2	89.8	64.19	167	4 120
West Palm Beach	272.5	2 742	42.9	1 522	66.2	82.5	57.3	90.1	61.39	246	3 999
Winter Garden.............	30.6	1 066	12.0	NA	NA	NA	NA	NA	NA	NA	NA
Winter Haven..............	85.4	2 622	0.0	464	62.3	82.3	51.0	92.5	50.22	538	3 551
Winter Park	147.2	5 268	9.1	NA	NA	NA	NA	NA	NA	NA	NA
Winter Springs..............	43.3	1 314	0.4	NA	60.9	82.4	49.9	92.2	48.35	580	3 428

1. Based on the population estimated as of July 1 of the year shown.   2. Represents normal values based on the 30-year period, 1971–2000.   3. Average daily minimum.   4. Average daily maximum.

Table D. Cities — Land Area and Population

STATE Place code	City	Land area,[1] 2010 (sq km)	Population, 2010 Total persons	Rank	Per square kilometer	Race alone or in combination, not of Hispanic origin (percent), 2010 White	Black	American Indian, Alaska Native	Asian	Hawaiian Pacific Islander	Percent Hispanic or Latino[2], 2010	Percent Foreign born, 2008–2010
		1	2	3	4	5	6	7	8	9	10	11
13 00000	GEORGIA................	148 959.2	9 687 653	X	65.0	57.1	30.9	0.7	3.7	0.1	8.8	9.8
13 01052	Albany......................	142.8	77 434	420	542.4	25.2	72.0	0.5	1.0	0.1	2.1	2.2
13 01696	Alpharetta................	69.7	57 551	641	825.7	66.5	11.4	0.5	14.5	0.2	8.5	21.8
13 03436	Athens-Clarke County ...	308.7	116 714	226	378.0	58.5	27.1	0.5	4.8	0.1	10.4	11.4
13 04000	Atlanta....................	344.9	420 003	40	1 217.9	37.4	54.4	0.7	3.7	0.1	5.2	7.8
13 04200	Augusta-Richmond County ...	840.0	200 549	110	238.7	39.7	54.9	0.8	2.2	0.3	4.1	3.7
13 19000	Columbus..................	560.4	189 885	124	338.8	45.4	46.3	0.8	2.8	0.3	6.4	5.0
13 21380	Dalton.....................	53.2	33 128	1 228	622.7	43.4	6.6	0.3	2.5	0.1	48.0	28.3
13 23900	Douglasville.............	58.2	30 961	1 312	532.2	35.0	56.5	0.7	2.1	0.2	7.2	8.9
13 24600	Duluth.....................	25.9	26 600	1 556	1 027.4	43.1	20.7	0.7	23.3	0.1	14.0	31.3
13 24768	Dunwoody.................	33.5	46 267	854	1 379.9	65.3	13.0	0.6	12.1	0.1	10.3	22.6
13 25720	East Point................	38.0	33 712	1 201	887.2	12.7	75.2	0.8	1.1	0.1	11.5	8.8
13 31908	Gainesville..............	82.7	33 804	1 195	408.8	40.1	15.4	0.5	3.5	0.1	41.6	31.3
13 38964	Hinesville...............	52.8	33 437	1 211	633.8	38.1	48.4	1.1	3.6	1.1	11.5	9.7
13 42425	Johns Creek.............	79.6	76 728	430	964.0	61.6	9.8	0.4	24.6	0.1	5.2	25.3
13 43192	Kennesaw................	24.5	29 783	1 376	1 218.1	60.8	23.1	0.7	6.1	0.1	10.8	14.7
13 44340	LaGrange	102.3	29 588	1 390	289.2	44.4	48.8	0.5	2.7	0.1	4.7	5.4
13 45488	Lawrenceville............	34.7	28 546	1 442	822.9	39.8	32.4	0.6	6.3	0.1	22.3	27.4
13 49000	Macon.....................	144.3	91 351	331	633.0	28.5	68.5	0.5	1.0	0.1	2.5	2.8
13 49756	Marietta	59.8	56 579	659	946.5	44.4	32.0	0.6	3.4	0.2	20.6	23.7
13 51670	Milton	99.8	32 661	1 250	327.4	73.9	9.5	0.5	11.3	0.1	6.0	17.0
13 55020	Newnan	47.4	33 039	1 232	696.4	56.0	30.9	0.7	3.2	0.2	11.0	9.0
13 59724	Peachtree City............	63.6	34 364	1 175	540.7	79.6	8.1	0.6	6.2	0.2	7.1	10.4
13 66668	Rome......................	80.1	36 303	1 100	453.4	53.7	28.6	0.6	2.2	0.1	16.2	11.2
13 67284	Roswell...................	105.5	88 346	349	837.6	67.1	12.2	0.5	4.8	0.1	16.6	20.3
13 68516	Sandy Springs.............	97.5	93 853	315	962.7	60.2	20.3	0.6	5.7	0.1	14.2	21.9
13 69000	Savannah..................	267.2	136 286	186	510.1	37.6	56.0	0.7	2.5	0.2	4.7	6.0
13 71492	Smyrna....................	39.8	51 271	752	1 289.5	48.3	32.2	0.8	5.6	0.1	14.9	17.3
13 73256	Statesboro	35.0	28 422	1 450	813.0	54.5	40.7	0.5	2.4	0.2	3.0	4.3
13 73704	Stockbridge	34.5	25 636	1 617	743.7	26.9	56.5	0.9	8.3	0.2	9.5	14.7
13 78800	Valdosta	92.8	54 518	692	587.5	42.7	51.6	0.6	2.1	0.2	4.0	3.9
13 80508	Warner Robins	90.8	66 588	521	733.1	52.2	38.1	0.9	3.6	0.2	7.6	5.0
15 00000	HAWAII....................	16 634.5	1 360 301	X	81.8	36.5	2.5	1.7	53.4	22.9	8.9	18.1
15 06290	East Honolulu CDP	59.6	49 914	772	837.5	40.6	1.1	1.2	63.8	12.2	4.1	15.2
15 14650	Hilo CDP	138.3	43 263	907	312.9	34.5	1.2	2.1	55.1	33.0	10.4	9.0
15 22700	Kahului CDP...............	37.4	26 337	1 574	703.8	19.1	1.0	1.2	66.5	25.4	9.4	26.9
15 23150	Kailua CDP (Honolulu County)	20.1	38 635	1 023	1 921.2	62.1	1.5	1.9	38.5	22.8	6.5	8.4
15 28250	Kaneohe CDP..............	16.9	34 597	1 164	2 045.9	39.1	1.2	1.9	58.9	29.0	8.4	8.6
15 51050	Mililani Town CDP.........	10.4	27 629	1 491	2 661.8	33.1	3.2	1.6	65.4	19.0	9.3	13.3
15 62600	Pearl City CDP............	23.6	47 698	830	2 021.1	26.5	3.7	1.2	67.2	16.4	8.2	12.4
15 71550	Urban Honolulu CDP	156.8	337 256	53	2 151.6	26.5	2.3	1.2	65.9	16.7	5.4	28.3
15 79700	Waipahu CDP	7.2	38 216	1 033	5 278.5	9.5	1.5	0.6	75.5	21.5	5.8	39.9
16 00000	IDAHO.....................	214 044.7	1 567 582	X	7.3	85.6	0.9	1.9	1.8	0.3	11.2	5.9
16 08830	Boise City................	205.6	205 671	105	1 000.6	87.3	1.9	1.2	4.2	0.4	7.1	7.9
16 12250	Caldwell..................	57.1	46 237	855	809.2	62.4	0.8	1.3	1.5	0.3	35.4	12.1
16 16750	Coeur d'Alene	40.3	44 137	888	1 094.4	93.2	0.8	2.2	1.4	0.3	4.3	2.8
16 39700	Idaho Falls...............	57.9	56 813	653	981.6	84.5	1.0	1.3	1.5	0.2	12.9	5.5
16 46540	Lewiston	44.6	31 894	1 278	714.6	94.2	0.6	2.8	1.3	0.2	2.8	2.3
16 52120	Meridian..................	69.4	75 092	450	1 082.2	90.1	1.2	0.9	2.7	0.3	6.8	4.7
16 56260	Nampa....................	80.8	81 557	392	1 009.5	74.5	1.0	1.5	1.4	0.5	22.9	8.6
16 64090	Pocatello.................	83.5	54 255	697	650.1	88.6	1.4	2.1	2.2	0.4	7.2	2.4
16 64810	Post Falls	36.5	27 574	1 496	756.5	93.2	0.7	1.9	1.4	0.2	4.6	2.1
16 67420	Rexburg	25.3	25 484	1 633	1 008.1	92.0	0.8	0.5	1.9	0.4	5.6	2.2
16 82810	Twin Falls................	46.9	44 125	889	941.0	83.7	0.8	1.2	2.4	0.2	13.1	9.1
17 00000	ILLINOIS..................	143 793.4	12 830 632	X	89.2	64.9	15.0	0.5	5.1	0.1	15.8	13.8
17 00243	Addison...................	25.3	36 942	1 074	1 460.2	48.3	4.0	0.3	8.0	0.1	40.1	35.8
17 00685	Algonquin	31.7	30 046	1 357	948.7	83.8	2.0	0.4	8.1	0.1	6.8	14.0
17 01114	Alton	40.1	27 865	1 481	695.4	70.5	29.1	1.0	0.8	0.1	1.9	1.8
17 02154	Arlington Heights..........	43.0	75 101	449	1 745.7	85.6	1.4	0.2	7.9	0.1	5.7	18.3
17 03012	Aurora....................	116.4	197 899	114	1 700.5	41.2	11.1	0.4	7.3	0.1	41.3	25.0
17 04013	Bartlett	40.5	41 208	958	1 018.2	74.3	2.6	0.4	15.2	0.1	8.6	16.6
17 04078	Batavia	25.0	26 045	1 597	1 043.5	88.7	2.8	0.3	2.3	0.0	6.8	4.1
17 04845	Belleville	58.9	44 478	885	755.1	70.5	26.8	0.8	1.6	0.2	2.6	1.8
17 05092	Belvidere	31.3	25 585	1 620	817.9	65.8	3.0	0.5	1.3	0.1	30.6	16.3
17 05573	Berwyn	10.1	56 657	657	5 604.1	31.8	6.3	0.4	2.8	0.1	59.4	25.3
17 06613	Bloomington	70.5	76 610	433	1 086.8	76.8	11.5	0.6	7.6	0.1	5.6	7.7
17 07133	Bolingbrook	62.3	73 366	463	1 177.8	43.4	21.2	0.5	12.2	0.1	24.5	24.3
17 09447	Buffalo Grove	24.6	41 496	951	1 686.1	77.6	1.2	0.2	16.9	0.1	4.9	26.1

1. Dry land or land partially or temporarily covered by water.   2. May be of any race.

City	Age of population (percent), 2010									Median age	Percent female	Population Census counts 1990	2000	Population Percent change 1990–2000	2000–2010
	Under 5 years	5 to 17 years	18 to 24 years	25 to 34 years	35 to 44 years	45 to 54 years	55 to 64 years	65 to 74 years	75 years and over						
	12	13	14	15	16	17	18	19	20	21	22	23	24	25	26
GEORGIA	7.1	18.6	10.0	13.8	14.4	14.4	11.0	6.3	4.4	35.3	51.2	6 478 149	8 186 453	26.4	18.3
Albany	7.9	18.4	14.2	14.0	11.4	12.2	10.6	5.9	5.4	31.4	53.9	78 804	76 939	-2.4	0.6
Alpharetta	6.5	22.3	6.0	12.6	17.7	18.0	9.5	4.0	3.4	36.8	51.3	13 002	34 854	168.1	65.1
Athens-Clarke County	6.0	11.5	30.4	16.8	10.1	8.9	7.9	4.6	3.9	25.9	52.5	86 522	101 489	17.3	15.0
Atlanta	6.4	13.0	14.3	19.8	14.8	12.3	9.6	5.5	4.4	32.9	50.2	393 929	416 474	5.7	0.8
Augusta-Richmond County	7.4	17.2	12.5	15.1	11.6	13.7	11.2	6.3	5.0	33.2	51.6	NA	199 775	NA	0.4
Columbus	7.4	18.1	11.4	14.9	12.3	13.5	10.6	6.0	5.6	33.5	52.1	178 685	186 291	4.3	1.9
Dalton	9.1	20.4	10.8	14.8	14.0	11.4	8.7	5.6	5.1	31.3	50.7	22 218	27 912	25.6	18.7
Douglasville	8.2	20.1	9.5	15.9	17.3	13.2	8.9	4.3	2.5	32.7	53.2	11 635	20 065	72.5	54.3
Duluth	7.3	17.1	8.2	17.0	16.8	15.7	10.6	4.4	2.8	35.2	52.2	9 029	22 122	145.0	20.2
Dunwoody	7.3	16.1	6.6	18.7	16.8	12.6	9.6	6.9	5.5	35.7	51.9	26 302	32 808	24.7	41.0
East Point	7.9	18.0	10.8	16.3	13.8	13.4	11.1	5.4	3.3	33.1	52.6	34 595	39 595	14.5	-14.9
Gainesville	10.1	20.3	13.1	16.7	12.5	9.1	7.6	4.8	5.8	28.5	52.2	17 885	25 578	43.0	32.2
Hinesville	10.3	20.4	12.9	17.2	12.2	13.3	8.5	3.7	1.7	28.2	52.7	21 596	30 392	40.7	10.0
Johns Creek	6.0	24.8	5.7	8.5	17.9	19.8	10.6	4.0	2.7	38.4	51.4	NA	NA	NA	NA
Kennesaw	7.4	19.5	10.6	16.4	16.8	13.6	8.2	4.0	3.3	32.3	52.7	8 936	21 675	142.6	37.4
LaGrange	8.3	19.2	11.6	13.1	12.4	12.5	10.1	6.0	6.8	33.0	53.8	25 574	25 998	1.7	13.8
Lawrenceville	8.8	21.0	9.1	15.1	14.9	12.7	9.1	4.4	4.8	32.4	52.2	17 250	22 397	29.8	27.5
Macon	8.1	18.5	12.1	13.2	11.3	13.2	11.1	6.3	6.0	33.3	53.9	107 365	97 255	-9.4	-6.1
Marietta	8.2	15.2	11.6	18.8	14.5	12.2	9.3	4.9	5.1	32.6	51.1	44 129	58 748	33.1	-3.7
Milton	6.3	24.6	5.7	11.1	17.9	18.9	9.3	3.9	2.3	36.7	51.1	NA	NA	NA	NA
Newnan	9.5	19.0	8.7	17.4	15.7	11.6	8.9	5.2	4.0	32.3	52.5	12 497	16 242	30.0	103.4
Peachtree City	4.7	22.8	6.0	7.8	14.0	19.0	13.7	6.8	5.2	41.7	51.7	19 027	31 580	66.0	8.8
Rome	8.2	17.5	10.0	14.2	12.3	12.7	11.0	6.8	7.4	35.1	52.4	30 425	34 980	15.0	3.8
Roswell	7.4	18.2	6.7	13.7	15.7	15.5	12.4	5.9	4.5	37.6	50.7	47 986	79 334	65.3	11.4
Sandy Springs	6.8	14.4	8.6	20.3	15.0	13.1	10.9	5.5	5.2	34.9	51.8	67 842	85 781	26.4	9.4
Savannah	7.1	15.2	16.1	16.2	11.1	12.2	10.3	5.9	5.7	31.3	52.1	137 812	131 510	-4.6	3.6
Smyrna	9.1	13.5	8.1	22.1	18.4	12.6	8.5	4.1	3.7	33.7	52.0	32 453	40 999	26.3	25.1
Statesboro	4.9	8.8	50.7	11.8	5.8	6.2	5.1	3.3	3.5	22.0	50.7	20 770	22 698	9.3	25.2
Stockbridge	7.8	22.7	8.8	14.9	18.3	13.3	7.9	3.8	2.4	32.4	53.6	NA	9 853	NA	160.2
Valdosta	7.7	15.1	23.3	15.1	9.8	10.2	8.7	5.3	4.8	26.9	53.1	40 038	43 724	9.2	24.7
Warner Robins	8.4	19.6	10.4	16.9	13.4	13.2	8.7	5.1	4.3	31.2	52.2	43 861	48 804	11.3	36.4
HAWAII	6.4	15.9	9.6	13.6	13.0	14.2	12.9	7.4	7.0	38.6	49.9	1 108 229	1 211 537	9.3	12.3
East Honolulu CDP	4.6	14.7	5.5	8.8	12.7	16.3	16.2	10.8	10.2	47.2	51.1	NA	NA	NA	NA
Hilo CDP	6.0	15.3	11.3	11.5	10.6	13.4	13.8	8.5	9.5	40.5	51.2	37 808	40 759	7.8	6.1
Kahului CDP	7.0	17.9	8.9	13.3	13.8	13.8	9.9	7.3	8.5	37.2	50.7	16 889	20 146	19.3	30.7
Kailua CDP (Honolulu County)	5.4	15.1	7.8	12.0	12.7	16.6	15.0	8.3	8.1	42.8	50.7	36 818	36 513	-0.8	5.8
Kaneohe CDP	5.8	15.0	8.8	12.5	11.8	15.5	12.9	8.2	9.6	41.9	51.4	35 448	34 970	-1.3	-1.1
Mililani Town CDP	5.7	16.0	9.2	12.6	11.9	14.4	16.7	8.5	5.0	40.3	50.2	29 359	28 608	-2.6	-3.4
Pearl City CDP	5.8	13.5	11.1	13.6	12.2	12.1	12.3	10.2	9.2	39.9	47.4	30 993	30 976	-0.1	54.0
Urban Honolulu CDP	4.9	12.5	9.7	14.5	13.2	14.2	13.2	8.1	9.8	41.3	50.6	NA	NA	NA	NA
Waipahu CDP	7.1	17.7	10.0	12.8	12.5	12.8	11.2	8.0	7.9	37.0	50.5	31 435	33 108	5.3	15.4
IDAHO	7.8	19.6	9.9	13.3	12.2	13.3	11.5	7.0	5.4	34.6	49.9	1 006 734	1 293 953	28.5	21.1
Boise City	6.4	16.3	11.2	15.6	13.2	14.4	11.8	5.9	5.2	35.3	50.6	126 685	185 787	46.7	10.7
Caldwell	10.7	22.4	11.5	16.4	12.0	10.3	7.8	5.0	3.9	28.2	50.6	18 586	25 967	39.7	78.1
Coeur d'Alene	6.7	16.1	11.8	14.8	11.9	12.7	11.3	7.0	7.6	35.4	51.4	24 561	34 514	40.5	27.9
Idaho Falls	9.2	20.1	9.2	15.1	11.2	12.8	10.5	5.9	5.8	32.2	50.5	43 973	50 730	15.4	12.0
Lewiston	5.7	15.8	10.8	12.2	11.6	13.6	12.0	8.3	9.9	39.9	50.8	28 082	30 904	10.0	3.2
Meridian	9.3	24.1	6.5	14.1	16.4	12.1	8.6	5.0	3.9	32.5	51.0	9 596	34 919	263.9	115.0
Nampa	9.8	22.5	9.9	15.5	13.1	10.6	8.3	5.4	4.9	30.1	51.0	28 365	51 867	82.9	57.2
Pocatello	8.3	17.5	14.4	16.6	10.8	11.4	10.4	5.6	5.1	30.2	50.1	46 117	51 466	11.6	5.4
Post Falls	8.6	20.5	8.7	15.0	13.6	12.5	10.0	6.8	4.5	33.0	51.2	7 349	17 247	134.7	59.9
Rexburg	9.6	10.8	49.2	15.6	4.3	3.9	2.9	1.8	1.9	22.3	52.7	14 298	17 257	20.7	47.7
Twin Falls	8.8	18.1	11.8	15.4	11.1	11.5	9.8	6.7	6.7	31.9	51.3	27 634	34 469	24.7	28.0
ILLINOIS	6.5	17.9	9.7	13.8	13.5	14.6	11.5	6.6	5.9	36.6	51.0	11 430 602	12 419 293	8.6	3.3
Addison	7.7	18.6	9.8	15.9	13.3	13.5	10.7	6.3	4.1	33.7	49.8	32 053	35 914	12.0	2.9
Algonquin	6.6	22.4	6.5	10.0	17.3	18.4	10.8	4.9	3.2	38.3	50.7	11 764	23 276	97.9	29.1
Alton	7.3	16.8	9.8	14.9	11.8	14.3	11.3	6.8	7.1	36.0	52.2	33 000	30 496	-7.8	-8.6
Arlington Heights	5.5	16.6	6.3	11.3	13.6	16.4	13.1	8.0	9.2	42.7	52.0	75 463	76 031	0.8	-1.2
Aurora	9.1	22.4	9.1	16.8	16.1	12.3	7.8	3.7	2.8	30.7	50.4	99 672	142 990	43.5	38.4
Bartlett	6.8	20.5	6.9	11.6	16.7	17.5	11.7	4.8	3.6	38.0	51.0	19 395	36 706	89.3	12.3
Batavia	5.7	21.8	7.2	8.7	14.0	18.6	12.7	5.1	6.2	40.4	51.3	17 076	23 866	39.8	9.1
Belleville	6.7	16.6	9.3	15.5	13.0	15.0	10.9	5.9	7.1	36.5	52.5	42 806	41 410	-3.3	7.4
Belvidere	7.8	22.3	9.0	12.8	14.7	12.8	8.7	6.3	5.6	33.6	50.6	16 059	20 820	29.6	22.9
Berwyn	8.0	19.8	9.9	15.5	15.0	12.8	9.5	4.9	4.5	32.9	50.5	45 426	54 016	18.9	4.9
Bloomington	7.0	17.5	10.3	16.4	13.8	14.3	10.6	5.1	5.0	34.1	51.3	51 869	64 808	24.9	18.2
Bolingbrook	8.0	22.7	8.7	13.5	17.0	14.2	9.6	4.2	2.1	33.1	50.4	40 843	56 321	37.9	30.3
Buffalo Grove	4.8	18.8	6.4	10.1	14.6	19.3	14.1	6.2	5.7	41.9	51.6	36 417	42 909	17.8	-3.3

Table D. Cities — Households, Group Quarters, Crime, and Education

City	Households, 2010 Number	Persons per household	Female family householder[1]	One-person	Persons in group quarters, 2010 Total	Institutional Total	Persons in nursing facilities	Non-institutional	Serious crimes known to police[2] 2010 Number	Rate[3]	Violent	Property	Population age 25 and older	High school graduate or less	Bachelor's degree or more
	27	28	29	30	31	32	33	34	35	36	37	38	39	40	41
GEORGIA	3 585 584	2.63	15.8	25.4	253 199	144 545	34 738	108 654	391 751	4 044	403	3 640	6 154 545	45.2	27.4
Albany	29 781	2.46	27.7	31.8	4 288	1 421	400	2 867	5 759	7 437	932	6 505	45 360	48.9	18.7
Alpharetta	21 742	2.64	9.3	25.6	69	57	19	12	1 516	2 634	85	2 549	36 358	17.5	61.6
Athens-Clarke County	45 414	2.37	13.4	30.6	9 183	779	348	8 404	5 304	4 589	321	4 268	59 169	38.3	40.5
Atlanta	185 142	2.11	16.5	44.0	29 484	6 756	1 626	22 728	36 549	8 702	1 369	7 333	275 755	34.4	45.5
Augusta-Richmond County	76 924	2.47	22.6	30.4	10 508	3 907	1 137	6 601	15 387	7 857	554	7 303	122 042	48.1	20.0
Columbus	74 081	2.47	21.3	29.9	7 017	3 486	898	3 531	14 447	7 608	529	7 079	116 936	44.6	21.0
Dalton	11 337	2.84	15.2	27.3	904	754	340	150	1 258	3 797	229	3 568	19 544	63.0	19.3
Douglasville	11 627	2.58	21.7	28.3	937	826	0	111	2 382	7 694	675	7 019	18 974	37.3	28.3
Duluth	10 555	2.52	14.1	28.4	34	0	0	34	685	2 575	158	2 417	17 732	28.0	43.3
Dunwoody	19 944	2.31	8.1	33.7	154	0	0	154	1 794	3 877	223	3 655	31 527	14.3	66.5
East Point	13 333	2.50	26.1	33.5	420	44	27	376	4 003	11 874	1 065	10 809	21 412	46.3	26.0
Gainesville	11 273	2.85	18.2	28.9	1 713	649	434	1 064	1 742	5 153	352	4 801	19 220	57.9	20.4
Hinesville	12 324	2.69	22.7	21.7	310	263	0	47	1 828	5 467	449	5 018	18 602	43.8	17.8
Johns Creek	26 266	2.92	9.0	16.2	0	0	0	0	694	904	65	839	47 202	14.1	63.4
Kennesaw	11 413	2.59	15.2	26.8	244	244	99	0	546	1 833	67	1 766	17 587	30.7	39.1
LaGrange	11 243	2.52	26.1	30.2	1 242	627	381	615	1 838	6 212	446	5 766	17 565	56.6	21.9
Lawrenceville	9 973	2.84	19.3	25.6	268	238	238	30	1 349	4 726	343	4 382	17 099	50.5	21.2
Macon	35 603	2.45	27.8	33.8	4 292	2 026	680	2 266	8 027	8 787	770	8 017	55 697	55.7	17.6
Marietta	23 065	2.38	15.6	34.1	1 769	758	730	1 011	3 319	5 866	817	5 050	37 277	39.3	36.1
Milton	11 659	2.80	8.6	20.2	4	0	0	4	327	1 001	40	961	19 923	14.6	66.2
Newnan	12 439	2.61	18.7	27.1	518	518	135	0	1 347	4 077	397	3 680	20 127	42.8	31.3
Peachtree City	12 726	2.69	9.5	19.9	118	118	118	0	487	1 417	35	1 382	22 301	17.7	51.9
Rome	13 885	2.50	19.2	32.1	1 606	1 409	447	197	2 223	6 123	642	5 482	22 658	56.7	23.6
Roswell	33 945	2.59	10.5	24.8	516	356	305	160	1 993	2 266	148	2 108	58 797	23.9	52.0
Sandy Springs	42 334	2.21	9.5	37.1	327	205	205	122	2 855	3 042	201	2 841	66 166	19.7	58.3
Savannah	52 545	2.40	22.4	32.7	10 014	4 499	584	5 515	10 045	4 495	377	4 118	82 941	48.5	23.5
Smyrna	23 002	2.22	12.4	38.3	279	269	112	10	1 627	3 173	322	2 852	35 457	25.6	50.9
Statesboro	10 207	2.36	15.0	31.0	4 290	266	266	4 024	1 708	6 009	883	5 126	10 571	44.6	26.9
Stockbridge	9 499	2.70	22.0	26.6	8	0	0	8	NA	NA	NA	NA	15 469	36.3	30.9
Valdosta	20 471	2.46	20.4	28.9	4 122	1 147	444	2 975	2 903	5 325	495	4 830	28 293	48.6	23.3
Warner Robins	26 136	2.53	19.6	28.2	338	223	208	115	3 916	5 881	512	5 369	39 369	42.9	20.7
HAWAII	455 338	2.89	12.6	23.3	42 880	11 306	5 198	31 574	48 657	3 577	263	3 314	916 380	38.7	29.2
East Honolulu CDP	17 684	2.81	9.4	16.0	235	160	160	75	NA	NA	NA	NA	37 442	19.2	53.3
Hilo CDP	15 483	2.69	14.7	25.8	1 648	605	575	1 043	NA	NA	NA	NA	29 967	35.4	30.8
Kahului CDP	7 111	3.46	16.6	19.5	1 740	1 296	564	444	NA	NA	NA	NA	16 666	56.7	16.3
Kailua CDP (Honolulu County)	12 921	2.98	11.5	17.1	119	30	8	89	NA	NA	NA	NA	27 267	27.5	45.4
Kaneohe CDP	11 138	3.05	14.4	18.0	643	411	411	232	NA	NA	NA	NA	23 867	33.8	34.3
Mililani Town CDP	9 038	3.06	11.4	13.2	0	0	0	0	NA	NA	NA	NA	21 026	31.4	34.1
Pearl City CDP	14 268	3.08	13.1	16.5	3 694	165	156	3 529	NA	NA	NA	NA	32 757	39.8	28.0
Urban Honolulu CDP	129 408	2.51	12.1	32.9	13 052	4 247	1 823	8 805	NA	NA	NA	NA	244 927	38.3	33.3
Waipahu CDP	8 383	4.45	19.3	12.9	910	390	369	520	NA	NA	NA	NA	25 715	61.0	13.8
IDAHO	579 408	2.66	9.6	23.8	28 951	17 076	4 820	11 875	34 751	2 217	221	1 996	972 106	40.2	24.2
Boise City	85 704	2.36	10.3	30.6	3 717	1 762	548	1 955	6 284	3 055	265	2 791	135 804	28.9	36.8
Caldwell	14 895	3.00	15.5	21.7	1 532	913	149	619	1 318	2 851	327	2 524	25 498	58.4	11.5
Coeur d'Alene	18 395	2.33	11.6	31.4	1 215	813	428	402	1 833	4 153	575	3 577	28 788	37.6	25.2
Idaho Falls	21 203	2.63	11.3	26.5	1 011	477	72	534	1 765	3 107	320	2 786	35 212	36.2	26.1
Lewiston	13 324	2.32	10.3	30.2	966	594	385	372	1 394	4 371	166	4 205	21 599	45.7	19.2
Meridian	25 302	2.96	10.4	16.6	307	126	103	181	1 299	1 730	145	1 585	44 036	29.3	31.9
Nampa	27 729	2.88	13.5	22.0	1 751	540	360	1 211	2 586	3 171	338	2 832	45 612	47.9	15.8
Pocatello	20 832	2.53	11.3	27.5	1 519	630	307	889	1 877	3 460	245	3 214	32 124	35.0	28.7
Post Falls	10 263	2.68	12.7	21.9	84	42	42	42	682	2 473	141	2 332	16 289	37.5	17.8
Rexburg	7 179	3.41	4.4	9.2	1 027	127	44	900	253	993	39	954	7 627	15.8	37.9
Twin Falls	16 744	2.58	12.2	26.6	897	592	314	305	1 526	3 458	331	3 127	26 666	45.3	15.7
ILLINOIS	4 836 972	2.59	12.9	27.8	301 773	159 989	81 516	141 784	399 824	3 116	435	2 681	8 407 186	40.8	30.6
Addison	11 940	3.08	12.8	17.7	112	46	0	66	894	2 420	181	2 239	24 212	52.1	23.3
Algonquin	10 247	2.93	7.4	16.4	0	0	0	0	608	2 024	263	1 761	19 299	25.6	47.1
Alton	11 734	2.33	19.2	34.4	518	356	202	162	1 470	5 275	528	4 748	17 893	44.5	19.1
Arlington Heights	30 919	2.41	7.1	30.1	723	545	538	178	1 192	1 587	53	1 534	53 528	26.4	49.4
Aurora	62 564	3.12	13.7	20.0	2 477	751	577	1 726	4 401	2 224	320	1 903	114 913	44.6	31.0
Bartlett	14 073	2.92	7.5	17.5	58	58	58	0	394	956	51	905	25 674	26.4	43.0
Batavia	9 554	2.71	8.8	23.1	157	148	148	9	549	2 108	154	1 954	16 564	23.1	48.9
Belleville	18 795	2.30	16.4	34.4	1 246	1 167	740	79	2 256	5 072	569	4 503	29 472	38.0	22.4
Belvidere	8 803	2.88	13.7	24.4	230	221	150	9	582	2 275	262	2 013	14 453	64.4	13.4
Berwyn	18 910	2.99	16.5	24.6	52	17	14	35	1 462	2 580	362	2 219	35 018	54.2	19.4
Bloomington	31 663	2.35	10.7	32.6	2 234	566	280	1 668	2 345	3 061	503	2 558	47 872	30.5	45.3
Bolingbrook	22 212	3.29	12.5	14.2	279	279	279	0	1 388	1 892	180	1 712	44 514	38.9	31.9
Buffalo Grove	16 206	2.55	7.5	24.7	118	112	112	6	400	964	19	945	29 277	19.7	60.3

1. No spouse present.   2. Data for serious crimes have not been adjusted for underreporting. This may affect comparability between geographic areas and over time.   3. Per 100,000 population estimated by the FBI.   4. Persons 25 years old and over.

Table D. Cities — Income, Poverty, and Housing

City	Money income, 2008–2010					Housing units, 2010			Occupied Housing units 2008–2010				
		Households			Families with income below poverty (percent)				Owner-occupied			Median owner costs as a percent of income	
	Per capita income[1] (dollars)	Median income	Percent with income of $200,000 or more	Percent with income of less than $25,000		Total	Percent change, 2000–2010	Vacant units for sale or rent[2]	Total	Percent	Median value[3] (dollars)	With a mortgage[4]	Without a mortgage[5]
	42	43	44	45	46	47	48	49	50	51	52	53	54
GEORGIA	24 561	48 448	3.6	25.9	12.6	4 088 801	24.6	503 217	3 488 349	66.7	162 400	24.5	11.5
Albany	17 434	29 508	1.9	43.8	26.4	33 436	3.9	3 655	28 752	42.6	99 800	23.6	12.3
Alpharetta	43 017	89 589	13.7	8.7	2.8	23 029	57.2	1 287	20 844	65.7	333 000	21.4	10.8
Athens-Clarke County	19 023	33 750	2.6	41.2	17.3	51 068	21.2	5 654	40 006	45.6	163 800	24.2	10.8
Atlanta	34 475	44 771	8.1	32.0	20.0	224 573	20.1	39 431	178 239	46.6	236 600	26.4	15.1
Augusta-Richmond County	20 012	37 798	1.6	34.1	20.0	86 331	4.9	9 407	72 005	56.5	99 700	24.6	12.3
Columbus	21 697	38 940	2.3	32.8	16.9	82 690	8.5	8 609	72 515	55.0	134 200	23.5	11.6
Dalton	19 003	37 026	2.6	36.6	27.8	13 378	29.8	2 041	11 134	48.4	134 200	23.5	10.0
Douglasville	25 230	49 324	2.5	23.8	13.8	13 163	66.4	1 536	11 421	56.1	168 500	26.9	11.2
Duluth	27 972	58 186	2.0	18.0	9.1	11 313	23.6	758	10 521	60.8	198 200	27.6	13.5
Dunwoody	44 066	74 297	11.4	13.3	6.1	21 671	48.4	1 727	19 035	57.0	376 600	22.0	12.4
East Point	20 691	41 226	1.9	28.6	17.2	17 225	11.1	3 892	12 642	47.0	145 100	26.0	13.4
Gainesville	19 753	37 488	3.5	34.6	26.6	12 967	45.5	1 694	11 984	35.6	182 300	26.3	15.0
Hinesville	19 829	42 157	1.5	25.2	14.7	14 653	24.4	2 329	12 540	52.8	123 300	25.2	10.0
Johns Creek	44 192	103 951	15.4	8.5	4.1	27 744	NA	1 478	24 889	81.4	344 100	23.2	11.6
Kennesaw	27 278	60 779	2.5	14.4	7.9	12 328	40.7	915	10 935	70.0	173 800	24.0	11.7
LaGrange	18 641	31 102	3.0	40.3	26.4	12 846	16.7	1 603	11 076	44.2	132 300	24.1	11.7
Lawrenceville	18 421	45 007	1.7	27.9	20.4	11 187	45.8	1 214	9 337	55.2	149 300	24.2	12.6
Macon	16 353	26 876	1.5	47.8	25.2	42 794	-3.8	7 191	34 229	47.1	96 900	25.5	12.3
Marietta	26 323	44 958	3.9	25.9	17.8	26 918	6.0	3 853	23 015	44.2	221 200	24.8	11.6
Milton	52 339	110 652	21.4	8.8	7.3	12 328	NA	669	10 857	74.9	466 800	22.4	10.0
Newnan	24 006	49 623	1.8	24.2	11.4	13 860	108.6	1 421	12 427	52.5	185 900	25.3	13.6
Peachtree City	40 241	93 044	9.2	9.8	3.4	13 538	17.8	812	12 364	76.1	283 000	22.7	10.0
Rome	20 431	32 303	4.1	39.5	18.3	15 797	9.3	1 912	13 439	51.7	125 600	24.8	14.7
Roswell	39 192	76 195	10.6	13.6	5.6	36 344	15.8	2 399	32 752	68.2	309 300	22.6	12.7
Sandy Springs	49 304	66 386	14.1	16.1	5.6	46 955	9.9	4 621	40 761	51.1	437 000	23.4	11.7
Savannah	19 464	32 699	1.3	38.8	18.6	61 883	7.6	9 338	51 540	46.8	151 900	26.3	13.3
Smyrna	36 061	55 313	6.0	16.9	9.3	25 745	30.6	2 743	22 741	57.2	224 500	23.1	10.0
Statesboro	12 620	21 063	0.2	55.7	21.5	11 602	25.3	1 395	9 751	27.4	120 900	20.0	12.7
Stockbridge	25 232	54 612	1.3	16.2	9.3	10 312	NA	813	9 751	61.1	167 000	30.1	10.1
Valdosta	18 147	31 645	1.7	40.8	19.7	22 709	19.5	2 238	20 015	44.7	128 800	24.7	11.3
Warner Robins	21 455	45 262	0.6	24.7	14.1	29 084	33.2	2 948	25 117	57.2	111 900	20.6	10.0
HAWAII	28 417	66 201	5.3	17.2	6.9	519 508	12.8	64 170	443 806	58.9	534 900	29.8	10.0
East Honolulu CDP	48 051	108 910	16.7	7.1	2.2	18 774	NA	1 090	17 510	82.1	783 800	28.1	10.3
Hilo CDP	24 316	50 151	3.6	29.6	11.8	16 905	5.5	1 422	15 594	62.7	321 600	23.5	10.0
Kahului CDP	21 480	56 156	2.5	21.6	8.7	7 773	28.6	662	6 816	55.9	575 200	31.8	10.0
Kailua CDP (Honolulu County)	37 864	88 178	12.4	9.9	5.6	13 650	6.9	729	12 963	71.5	779 900	31.4	11.4
Kaneohe CDP	32 643	79 510	6.0	12.5	5.3	11 553	0.7	415	11 418	68.3	622 400	26.5	10.0
Mililani Town CDP	32 795	89 063	5.8	6.1	0.0	9 272	0.0	234	9 886	77.2	551 700	27.8	10.0
Pearl City CDP	30 711	82 304	7.0	10.1	3.6	14 622	60.5	354	14 296	69.9	581 300	24.9	10.0
Urban Honolulu CDP	29 609	55 809	4.7	21.1	7.5	143 173	NA	13 765	127 387	45.0	544 300	28.4	11.3
Waipahu CDP	19 700	65 993	6.9	18.6	8.9	8 850	10.2	467	8 178	56.1	519 500	26.7	10.0
IDAHO	21 864	45 824	2.0	25.3	10.3	667 796	26.5	88 388	574 773	70.6	173 200	24.7	10.5
Boise City	27 221	48 506	2.9	23.5	9.2	92 700	18.9	6 996	85 573	60.8	200 800	23.7	10.7
Caldwell	15 566	36 740	1.4	32.1	16.4	16 323	68.4	1 428	15 121	61.2	122 600	27.5	10.7
Coeur d'Alene	23 746	39 963	1.8	29.2	12.1	20 219	36.8	1 824	19 172	55.2	196 000	27.1	12.1
Idaho Falls	23 157	45 994	2.2	24.6	10.8	22 977	15.9	1 774	20 725	67.0	152 800	21.6	10.3
Lewiston	22 890	44 656	0.9	29.6	8.0	14 057	5.0	733	13 164	65.2	167 600	21.2	12.6
Meridian	25 748	63 036	2.7	14.7	4.8	26 674	117.1	1 372	25 133	77.7	206 900	24.0	10.3
Nampa	16 283	41 329	0.6	30.3	15.2	30 507	56.2	2 778	26 230	67.4	137 900	27.0	12.2
Pocatello	20 916	41 837	1.8	31.1	10.2	22 404	8.3	1 572	20 361	67.5	132 100	22.5	10.9
Post Falls	21 530	45 832	1.7	23.3	13.3	11 150	66.7	887	10 181	67.2	190 100	24.3	12.9
Rexburg	12 192	25 409	2.1	49.4	30.6	7 617	69.2	438	6 750	34.6	174 000	24.7	10.0
Twin Falls	18 901	41 612	0.9	27.4	12.6	18 033	27.4	1 289	16 160	61.0	146 100	24.3	10.0
ILLINOIS	28 424	55 010	4.7	22.3	9.6	5 296 715	8.4	459 743	4 768 404	68.5	202 000	25.7	13.6
Addison	25 038	57 945	3.4	19.7	8.8	12 581	7.3	641	12 118	71.8	278 800	28.7	19.9
Algonquin	37 481	99 555	9.3	5.7	1.9	10 727	33.4	480	10 240	87.8	285 100	25.5	12.7
Alton	18 945	37 447	0.9	37.2	18.6	13 266	-4.5	1 532	11 213	61.3	86 000	22.2	12.7
Arlington Heights	38 617	71 776	9.8	13.3	2.3	32 795	3.4	1 876	30 019	76.5	364 500	26.4	14.8
Aurora	24 872	58 747	4.1	17.1	10.2	67 273	37.5	4 709	62 869	68.7	205 000	28.4	16.0
Bartlett	33 828	89 709	6.1	9.9	4.0	14 509	17.4	436	13 454	87.9	321 900	28.4	14.3
Batavia	36 864	84 360	9.8	19.5	9.5	10 042	13.9	488	9 600	78.3	291 500	26.2	14.0
Belleville	24 809	46 872	1.4	27.5	11.0	21 099	9.4	2 304	18 170	61.7	111 000	21.9	13.9
Belvidere	19 850	48 073	1.8	22.8	10.7	9 565	20.5	762	8 399	73.1	135 900	26.4	13.4
Berwyn	20 236	47 456	1.4	21.9	11.3	20 719	0.1	1 809	18 825	59.3	237 500	31.4	15.6
Bloomington	31 183	56 099	4.8	19.5	4.8	34 339	20.4	2 676	30 148	65.3	158 400	21.3	13.4
Bolingbrook	26 935	80 387	4.9	10.4	6.5	23 141	29.2	929	21 829	84.6	239 100	27.6	13.9
Buffalo Grove	43 806	88 272	11.2	10.1	3.0	17 034	6.9	828	16 159	82.9	335 100	27.3	16.8

1. Based on population estimated by the American Community Survey.   2. Includes units rented or sold but not occupied.   3. Specified owner-occupied units; $1,000,000 represents $1,000,000 or more.   4. 50.0 represents 50 percent or more.   5. 10.0 represents 10 percent or less.

Table D. Cities — **Housing, Labor Force, and Employment**

City	Occupied housing units, 2008–2010 (cont.)				Migration, 2008–2010		Civilian labor force, 2010				Civilian employment[4], 2008–2010			
									Unemployment			Percent		
	Percent renter occupied	Median gross rent[1]	Median rent as a percent of income[2]	Percent with no vehicle available	Percent who lived in the same house one year ago	Percent who lived outside this city one year ago	Total	Percent change, 2009–2010	Total	Rate[3]	Population age 16 and older	In labor force	Full-year full-time worker	Households with no workers (percent)
	55	56	57	58	59	60	61	62	63	64	65	66	67	68
GEORGIA	33.3	812	31.3	6.7	83.1	13.1	4 694 930	-1.5	481 055	10.2	7 409 259	65.3	42.7	24.1
Albany	57.4	643	34.2	12.1	74.5	11.4	34 267	5.7	4 101	12.0	58 546	58.4	35.7	33.1
Alpharetta	34.3	1 022	23.7	2.6	82.5	11.0	30 208	13.2	2 311	7.7	41 641	73.4	54.9	14.0
Athens-Clarke County	54.4	740	36.5	7.5	75.8	11.9	65 611	2.5	5 015	7.6	96 792	57.1	30.9	27.6
Atlanta	53.4	887	31.4	18.2	75.2	11.4	187 414	-21.2	23 873	12.7	344 099	65.3	41.7	26.2
Augusta-Richmond County	43.5	677	31.1	NA	78.0	9.9	87 505	-4.4	9 469	10.8	151 792	63.3	39.9	28.7
Columbus	45.0	727	31.9	10.4	73.1	13.7	83 687	-2.1	8 151	9.7	145 525	63.8	41.0	27.4
Dalton	51.6	639	31.0	8.9	73.7	13.0	13 568	-8.3	1 858	13.7	23 540	63.8	38.3	24.2
Douglasville	43.9	870	30.6	5.6	73.3	20.0	14 924	0.1	1 777	11.9	22 739	70.2	47.4	19.8
Duluth	39.2	952	29.6	1.6	84.3	12.6	16 078	2.0	1 493	9.3	20 050	74.3	52.1	17.3
Dunwoody	43.0	1 116	25.6	5.3	81.4	13.7	NA	NA	NA	NA	35 455	69.9	49.7	21.3
East Point	53.0	814	33.3	15.1	78.4	16.7	15 422	-20.8	2 364	15.3	27 044	70.8	41.3	24.0
Gainesville	64.4	779	30.0	15.7	77.3	11.0	15 043	-4.3	1 491	9.9	23 912	68.3	46.8	25.3
Hinesville	47.2	764	28.4	6.7	76.4	15.7	15 070	-0.1	1 279	8.5	24 852	69.3	47.3	14.5
Johns Creek	18.6	1 155	26.1	1.0	88.4	8.8	35 541	26.2	2 964	8.3	54 349	72.3	52.2	12.2
Kennesaw	30.0	994	30.6	3.0	83.6	14.1	16 637	-4.8	2 023	12.2	21 822	78.3	51.8	15.6
LaGrange	55.8	631	31.3	15.7	74.3	12.4	13 519	3.6	1 688	12.5	22 377	59.3	38.7	32.1
Lawrenceville	44.8	851	34.9	6.5	75.4	16.5	14 291	-3.0	1 967	13.8	20 158	71.9	42.1	20.5
Macon	52.9	631	37.6	16.4	79.0	8.2	39 601	-3.6	5 031	12.7	69 902	55.2	31.5	35.6
Marietta	55.8	852	30.0	10.5	73.9	17.6	30 836	-15.0	3 173	10.3	45 426	74.1	44.4	17.7
Milton	25.1	1 085	25.3	0.8	83.5	12.8	NA	NA	NA	NA	22 748	71.0	50.4	10.6
Newnan	47.5	879	29.3	7.7	76.5	14.5	14 569	7.7	1 522	10.4	24 029	65.7	46.6	25.1
Peachtree City	23.9	1 180	27.5	2.3	85.5	9.3	16 320	-1.4	1 192	7.3	26 052	66.9	43.7	18.9
Rome	48.3	688	32.9	16.8	80.4	10.2	17 227	-1.9	2 183	12.7	28 356	58.0	33.0	36.6
Roswell	31.8	982	30.8	3.9	84.5	10.5	47 746	-0.8	3 706	7.8	66 795	73.6	53.6	16.1
Sandy Springs	48.9	970	26.3	6.5	75.9	16.0	54 631	11.4	4 269	7.8	76 056	72.6	50.6	17.7
Savannah	53.2	832	35.3	13.0	87.0	6.5	63 196	-2.0	6 645	10.5	108 578	58.0	39.2	29.9
Smyrna	42.8	928	29.8	3.2	76.0	19.2	29 304	2.7	3 067	10.5	40 988	79.0	52.5	15.3
Statesboro	72.6	586	42.5	9.4	65.2	21.4	12 292	-1.6	1 480	12.0	24 632	49.8	24.1	28.8
Stockbridge	38.9	982	29.2	2.5	85.6	11.2	12 862	NA	1 601	12.4	17 820	76.6	54.1	17.0
Valdosta	55.3	737	34.9	8.5	73.2	14.0	26 458	3.4	2 486	9.4	42 278	64.2	35.0	28.2
Warner Robins	42.8	772	28.9	5.7	76.5	11.7	32 853	3.4	2 776	8.4	48 824	68.6	43.2	21.3
HAWAII	41.1	1 286	33.0	8.7	84.5	10.0	649 158	2.8	44 636	6.9	1 080 889	67.4	45.4	21.5
East Honolulu CDP	17.9	2 000	34.5	3.5	90.9	5.8	NA	NA	NA	NA	40 896	66.0	48.0	21.0
Hilo CDP	37.3	862	39.5	9.6	79.2	12.0	NA	NA	NA	NA	37 935	59.2	35.6	30.8
Kahului CDP	44.1	1 020	31.4	8.6	79.6	6.9	NA	NA	NA	NA	19 745	62.4	41.9	28.1
Kailua CDP (Honolulu County)	28.5	1 918	32.3	4.9	86.6	7.9	NA	NA	NA	NA	31 041	70.3	48.1	15.5
Kaneohe CDP	31.7	1 673	29.7	5.8	86.1	9.4	NA	NA	NA	NA	27 639	65.8	47.7	22.4
Mililani Town CDP	22.8	1 863	36.2	1.9	88.4	9.2	NA	NA	NA	NA	24 324	68.1	50.0	15.0
Pearl City CDP	30.1	1 626	32.9	4.5	87.5	10.9	NA	NA	NA	NA	37 359	64.7	46.8	19.2
Urban Honolulu CDP	55.0	1 171	32.3	17.5	84.6	6.3	NA	NA	NA	NA	285 669	65.2	44.4	23.5
Waipahu CDP	43.9	1 088	30.0	11.2	87.8	7.1	NA	NA	NA	NA	31 428	63.0	42.6	18.8
IDAHO	29.4	697	29.2	4.2	82.1	11.4	763 498	1.7	66 983	8.8	1 174 540	65.2	39.1	25.6
Boise City	39.2	753	29.8	6.2	77.5	9.8	107 430	-0.5	9 115	8.5	165 107	70.3	43.2	22.1
Caldwell	38.8	713	30.5	6.7	77.8	11.5	20 309	8.1	2 260	11.1	32 362	66.8	36.0	24.4
Coeur d'Alene	44.8	721	31.8	5.7	77.3	14.8	23 112	1.7	2 302	10.0	35 053	65.0	38.0	28.7
Idaho Falls	33.0	667	30.2	5.9	80.6	10.0	27 774	1.0	1 986	7.2	41 923	66.3	41.6	25.3
Lewiston	34.8	615	27.2	7.5	82.6	7.3	15 761	2.4	1 057	6.7	25 940	63.9	38.5	33.1
Meridian	22.3	996	29.0	2.2	83.6	12.3	36 598	10.6	2 940	8.0	50 761	72.2	47.5	19.1
Nampa	32.6	740	31.1	4.1	76.3	13.5	36 658	0.4	3 915	10.7	56 383	64.4	35.0	26.9
Pocatello	32.5	581	29.4	6.7	77.2	11.3	27 458	-2.3	2 123	7.7	41 380	68.1	38.9	27.0
Post Falls	32.8	799	28.4	1.2	82.4	8.9	13 898	4.0	1 474	10.6	19 355	72.9	40.8	25.8
Rexburg	65.4	594	40.5	2.5	43.7	28.2	10 775	-7.6	585	5.4	20 359	60.7	19.5	18.4
Twin Falls	39.0	667	28.1	6.2	82.8	6.8	21 783	0.1	1 840	8.4	33 242	65.3	44.0	23.3
ILLINOIS	31.5	839	30.6	10.5	86.8	7.3	6 602 654	0.2	691 911	10.5	10 030 465	66.9	41.9	25.0
Addison	28.2	897	33.8	3.2	86.6	7.7	19 913	0.2	2 131	10.7	28 120	72.2	45.2	16.7
Algonquin	12.2	1 486	26.2	2.5	92.9	5.6	16 691	0.0	1 503	9.0	22 669	76.0	49.8	11.2
Alton	38.7	692	33.8	9.8	85.0	9.2	13 200	-5.2	1 675	12.7	21 230	60.4	36.4	32.4
Arlington Heights	23.5	1 095	27.4	6.0	90.7	6.3	41 749	2.6	3 134	7.5	60 380	67.2	43.3	25.0
Aurora	31.3	969	32.7	6.3	86.6	6.6	106 263	17.4	10 769	10.1	138 467	74.8	47.4	16.2
Bartlett	12.1	1 051	38.5	4.0	92.5	4.3	23 668	-1.4	2 138	9.0	30 791	74.8	48.6	12.1
Batavia	21.7	969	32.9	4.7	88.4	10.2	14 336	-3.9	1 288	9.0	19 443	73.5	43.1	22.6
Belleville	38.3	692	30.8	7.4	83.5	10.9	22 953	7.0	2 560	11.2	35 040	70.7	46.0	25.4
Belvidere	26.9	685	31.0	8.4	89.0	4.2	12 578	-1.9	2 240	17.8	17 730	64.5	38.8	28.1
Berwyn	40.7	831	31.5	10.7	87.1	6.9	28 697	13.3	3 196	11.1	42 380	69.8	41.7	21.7
Bloomington	34.7	696	24.2	7.2	81.5	8.4	43 005	4.5	3 422	8.0	59 628	71.5	45.8	22.2
Bolingbrook	15.4	929	32.0	3.4	90.7	5.6	41 383	4.0	4 062	9.8	54 701	77.9	51.8	12.0
Buffalo Grove	17.1	1 208	23.7	4.2	91.3	7.3	23 241	-2.7	1 946	8.4	32 730	72.4	50.0	17.7

1. $2,000 represents $2,000 or more.   2. 50.0 represents 50 percent or more.   3. Percent of civilian labor force.   4. Persons 16 years old and over.

Table D. Cities — Construction, Wholesale Trade, and Retail Trade

City	Value of residential construction authorized by building permits, 2010			Wholesale trade,[1] 2007				Retail trade,[2] 2007			
	New construction ($1,000)	Number of housing units	Percent single family	Number of establishments	Number of employees	Sales (mil dol)	Annual payroll (mil dol)	Number of establishments	Number of employees	Sales (mil dol)	Annual payroll (mil dol)
	69	70	71	72	73	74	75	76	77	78	79
GEORGIA	2 659 234	17 265	85.6	11 545	166 619	141 962.4	8 246.5	36 218	475 344	117 516.9	10 760.2
Albany	4 790	54	53.7	137	1 857	1 108.6	73.6	495	6 561	1 428.5	129.1
Alpharetta	19 319	57	100.0	167	4 459	18 722.2	338.4	404	8 233	1 941.3	185.8
Athens-Clarke County ...	15 081	94	100.0	106	1 994	1 782.5	84.1	553	7 752	1 669.1	161.5
Atlanta	40 749	279	29.7	706	9 721	7 523.6	501.2	1 943	26 962	5 594.1	643.9
Augusta-Richmond County	62 793	373	98.1	196	2 249	916.4	94.3	895	11 084	2 505.1	233.6
Columbus	31 807	339	66.1	173	1 906	1 173.6	81.2	845	12 642	2 889.2	260.7
Dalton	1 255	16	31.3	132	2 689	977.8	103.3	312	3 304	828.4	73.2
Douglasville	3 613	14	100.0	25	175	57.5	8.4	270	5 181	1 034.5	100.4
Duluth	25 724	79	100.0	129	2 692	2 034.2	226.5	263	4 656	1 766.7	166.3
Dunwoody	624	1	100.0	57	D	D	D	286	6 132	1 016.3	126.8
East Point	2 486	23	100.0	32	591	437.9	29.6	103	1 325	271.2	26.4
Gainesville	300	1	100.0	107	1 554	3 411.9	65.1	341	4 748	1 138.6	115.1
Hinesville	13 248	59	100.0	2	D	D	D	137	1 585	379.8	33.6
Johns Creek	24 784	134	100.0	70	316	327.8	20.3	161	2 240	409.2	47.3
Kennesaw	4 399	23	100.0	97	1 790	971.6	91.6	169	2 587	665.6	64.7
LaGrange	6 888	81	25.9	30	577	365.5	23.9	212	2 831	670.2	60.6
Lawrenceville	500	5	100.0	116	1 348	1 083.1	63.6	381	4 681	1 074.3	112.8
Macon	9 178	110	83.6	142	2 113	1 085.4	91.3	677	9 114	1 838.5	186.0
Marietta	18 158	153	39.9	300	4 304	2 585.3	213.1	463	7 449	2 465.7	223.1
Milton	12 699	68	100.0	17	81	76.8	11.2	30	351	61.4	7.7
Newnan	28 225	124	100.0	28	562	345.8	23.7	201	3 320	736.0	71.5
Peachtree City	3 634	15	100.0	91	985	620.1	50.1	159	2 667	533.2	53.9
Rome	NA	NA	NA	72	1 028	510.7	37.4	315	4 049	897.2	81.9
Roswell	16 111	60	100.0	191	1 892	1 568.3	135.3	386	5 589	1 761.7	162.0
Sandy Springs	21 122	172	29.1	150	3 211	6 167.9	285.4	270	3 899	1 176.9	121.0
Savannah	43 909	520	46.3	183	2 113	1 633.9	106.6	941	11 511	2 521.2	250.3
Smyrna	11 392	77	100.0	87	2 677	2 088.3	139.8	213	2 981	1 069.6	83.1
Statesboro	6 550	85	24.7	22	119	60.3	3.9	227	3 163	636.9	62.6
Stockbridge	NA	NA	NA	9	D	D	D	95	1 827	391.9	41.2
Valdosta	25 002	378	19.3	90	828	565.8	33.9	693	5 343	1 220.8	109.1
Warner Robins	42 777	319	100.0	23	222	59.9	8.3	295	4 669	1 080.6	104.3
HAWAII	773 013	3 442	55.8	1 629	17 707	8 894.7	699.1	5 012	70 661	17 611.9	1 766.4
East Honolulu CDP	NA	NA	NA	NA	NA	NA	NA	NA	NA	NA	NA
Hilo CDP	NA	NA	NA	77	950	428.4	30.2	258	4 178	1 156.3	108.9
Kahului CDP	NA	NA	NA	52	652	356.3	32.8	213	4 591	1 329.0	133.1
Kailua CDP (Honolulu County)	NA	NA	NA	23	74	21.8	3.5	103	1 578	350.9	38.2
Kaneohe CDP	NA	NA	NA	19	39	15.1	1.6	129	2 113	555.3	51.6
Mililani Town CDP	NA	NA	NA	7	10	2.2	0.3	36	1 106	248.1	26.0
Pearl City CDP	NA	NA	NA	32	378	228.8	15.2	50	1 666	474.2	39.1
Urban Honolulu CDP	NA	NA	NA	NA	NA	NA	NA	NA	NA	NA	NA
Waipahu CDP	NA	NA	NA	51	904	302.9	34.2	104	2 560	858.3	80.1
IDAHO	732 442	4 153	85.9	1 846	21 844	14 286.7	900.0	6 300	80 447	20 526.6	1 833.6
Boise City	62 554	352	100.0	354	5 159	4 925.8	259.2	1 002	16 168	3 893.1	366.1
Caldwell	18 972	179	73.2	35	240	83.4	9.5	132	2 148	611.8	54.1
Coeur d'Alene	27 431	239	56.5	46	713	379.1	28.0	333	4 317	1 234.6	110.5
Idaho Falls	10 021	155	48.4	96	1 192	1 151.1	47.5	389	5 750	1 453.1	121.4
Lewiston	4 601	24	83.3	41	490	434.9	19.6	202	2 700	680.5	67.0
Meridian	120 904	509	100.0	85	1 463	683.9	76.2	204	3 967	1 329.0	112.5
Nampa	14 268	104	97.1	94	1 148	709.7	54.2	311	5 342	1 483.9	134.9
Pocatello	7 716	74	100.0	65	579	383.1	20.8	250	3 246	762.6	67.8
Post Falls	22 632	168	70.2	21	318	181.8	16.8	108	1 598	519.9	41.4
Rexburg	32 046	241	11.6	27	342	139.5	8.5	102	1 586	386.3	35.3
Twin Falls	18 240	133	98.5	75	897	330.6	29.4	354	4 897	1 150.3	108.6
ILLINOIS	2 412 386	12 318	61.9	16 704	259 758	231 082.8	14 319.6	43 055	639 147	165 450.5	14 895.5
Addison	354	1	100.0	205	3 703	1 899.4	203.5	112	2 793	1 090.5	95.3
Algonquin	1 244	2	100.0	24	79	38.7	4.6	155	3 105	635.4	55.6
Alton	334	4	100.0	26	268	189.2	10.9	181	2 774	601.0	62.0
Arlington Heights	3 352	13	100.0	202	1 856	1 395.4	119.5	256	4 269	978.0	98.5
Aurora	9 657	71	100.0	138	2 866	7 694.2	151.8	597	10 131	2 148.1	204.5
Bartlett	250	1	100.0	51	548	318.2	26.1	49	744	150.8	16.2
Batavia	2 480	5	100.0	81	1 533	2 074.0	81.6	89	2 032	470.8	42.2
Belleville	6 508	48	100.0	38	424	207.0	18.4	203	2 498	616.4	66.2
Belvidere	1 104	8	100.0	11	119	78.2	5.8	79	1 366	365.2	30.9
Berwyn	0	0	0.0	10	54	7.0	1.2	127	1 378	328.8	36.9
Bloomington	32 263	187	98.4	75	1 344	3 984.1	73.8	382	5 581	1 298.3	118.7
Bolingbrook	11 473	100	37.0	86	5 309	4 024.5	250.8	204	4 916	1 046.4	102.9
Buffalo Grove	11 293	54	100.0	119	2 491	2 170.3	157.3	128	1 703	491.8	46.7

1. Merchant wholesalers except manufacturers' sales branches and offices. 2. Establishments with payroll.

Table D. Cities — **Real Estate, Professional Services, and Manufacturing**

City	Real estate and rental and leasing, 2007				Professional, scientific, and technical services,[1] 2007				Manufacturing, 2007			
	Number of establish-ments	Number of employees	Receipts (mil dol)	Annual payroll (mil dol)	Number of establish-ments	Number of employees	Receipts (mil dol)	Annual payroll (mil dol)	Number of establish-ments	Number of employees	Receipts (mil dol)	Annual payroll (mil dol)
	80	81	82	83	84	85	86	87	88	89	90	91
GEORGIA..................	12 620	65 875	14 021.9	2 903.2	27 668	213 419	34 966.0	12 689.5	8 699	411 158	144 280.8	16 128.1
Albany	129	564	78.6	14.9	192	D	D	D	70	4 975	3 263.0	246.5
Alpharetta.....................	219	1 135	305.0	62.5	870	D	D	D	NA	NA	NA	NA
Athens-Clarke County ...	224	839	128.3	24.3	283	D	D	D	91	6 632	1 971.2	255.2
Atlanta..........................	1 231	12 285	2 727.8	752.2	3 250	42 668	9 456.3	3 651.7	346	12 257	5 304.3	504.2
Augusta-Richmond County	233	1 449	220.1	38.5	437	3 181	397.2	144.3	129	9 055	5 256.3	452.0
Columbus	259	1 549	292.8	54.0	348	D	D	D	141	7 055	2 111.4	266.7
Dalton..........................	66	281	41.4	7.7	117	D	D	D	191	16 869	6 207.2	531.4
Douglasville..................	60	225	33.0	6.7	130	587	51.9	21.6	NA	NA	NA	NA
Duluth	138	711	179.8	29.7	302	2 440	300.7	129.8	49	1 176	389.7	69.5
Dunwoody	147	1 016	551.9	122.8	505	5 866	921.7	381.2	16	D	D	D
East Point.....................	36	620	92.7	14.1	71	D	D	D	31	854	295.9	36.5
Gainesville...................	97	300	76.0	10.5	201	D	D	D	111	8 629	2 533.2	308.6
Hinesville	42	182	26.8	4.6	34	194	16.1	4.6	NA	NA	NA	NA
Johns Creek	107	475	67.5	17.1	446	1 699	257.3	95.1	11	D	D	D
Kennesaw.....................	65	268	46.7	8.1	166	645	73.7	27.6	58	1 380	326.3	58.5
LaGrange	50	406	34.8	8.0	62	325	29.8	13.6	47	4 325	1 613.2	184.0
Lawrenceville................	89	438	73.4	16.0	251	D	D	D	74	2 976	933.7	133.5
Macon..........................	147	838	163.1	23.3	311	D	D	D	91	2 482	644.5	113.5
Marietta........................	193	1 326	228.6	48.6	635	D	D	D	148	11 727	3 782.9	695.1
Milton	37	103	13.0	2.9	122	D	D	D	NA	NA	NA	NA
Newnan........................	66	233	40.8	7.4	87	420	54.3	19.5	34	1 378	344.6	47.7
Peachtree City..............	84	182	30.6	6.2	156	D	D	D	43	3 037	1 622.7	150.5
Rome...........................	66	303	51.7	8.9	135	617	71.1	21.9	71	5 141	2 006.6	188.0
Roswell........................	214	839	193.5	37.1	792	7 311	811.2	307.9	57	694	107.3	27.5
Sandy Springs..............	368	D	D	D	976	10 482	2 097.8	754.7	NA	NA	NA	NA
Savannah.....................	253	1 422	231.4	43.1	506	D	D	D	107	4 136	2 160.5	183.4
Smyrna.........................	115	674	144.6	37.0	281	3 256	1 102.5	227.9	43	781	144.6	31.0
Statesboro	64	278	38.2	5.8	82	555	55.3	18.2	31	1 649	472.5	55.3
Stockbridge	36	100	18.4	2.8	77	487	60.2	20.4	NA	NA	NA	NA
Valdosta.......................	94	675	64.1	16.7	168	D	D	D	71	3 570	1 918.8	124.4
Warner Robins	83	377	51.5	9.3	168	D	D	D	31	668	181.9	29.9
HAWAII......................	2 084	16 759	3 974.0	653.8	3 254	21 772	3 068.3	1 193.5	984	14 127	8 799.3	511.5
East Honolulu CDP	NA	NA	NA	NA	NA	NA	NA	NA	NA	NA	NA	NA
Hilo CDP	88	442	76.5	10.0	116	D	D	D	55	544	110.6	19.3
Kahului CDP..................	51	718	180.7	23.1	43	243	24.0	8.2	NA	NA	NA	NA
Kailua CDP (Honolulu County)......................	44	186	33.8	6.7	102	490	90.0	27.7	NA	NA	NA	NA
Kaneohe CDP	24	96	16.6	3.0	51	D	D	D	NA	NA	NA	NA
Mililani Town CDP........	13	48	5.4	1.2	21	79	6.0	1.7	NA	NA	NA	NA
Pearl City CDP	12	53	6.1	1.3	16	90	8.5	4.0	NA	NA	NA	NA
Urban Honolulu CDP	NA	NA	NA	NA	NA	NA	NA	NA	NA	NA	NA	NA
Waipahu CDP	30	156	20.9	4.6	14	156	9.8	3.9	NA	NA	NA	NA
IDAHO	2 530	8 371	1 241.7	233.5	4 189	D	D	D	1 942	64 778	18 011.0	2 829.4
Boise City.....................	545	2 533	396.3	88.0	1 173	D	D	D	223	18 120	4 442.3	1 138.1
Caldwell........................	51	220	20.1	4.4	50	D	D	D	69	2 147	D	66.6
Coeur d'Alene	122	580	117.6	20.1	250	D	D	D	67	1 211	388.1	45.5
Idaho Falls...................	119	451	74.6	10.4	308	D	D	D	76	1 302	376.8	48.0
Lewiston.......................	37	D	D	D	74	D	D	D	29	D	D	45.2
Meridian.......................	155	530	69.0	18.7	171	860	131.3	38.1	51	1 342	225.3	47.3
Nampa.........................	121	323	39.7	6.5	137	762	68.0	27.7	97	4 996	1 412.6	184.2
Pocatello......................	81	263	43.4	5.8	136	D	D	D	45	D	634.8	D
Post Falls	44	123	15.0	2.9	52	668	61.3	25.8	47	1 266	217.0	45.4
Rexburg.......................	47	145	19.6	2.6	52	873	34.0	9.7	18	D	D	D
Twin Falls	90	307	45.5	7.5	174	D	D	D	62	1 803	614.1	59.1
ILLINOIS..................	13 899	87 468	21 725.0	3 985.2	38 797	363 231	61 896.1	24 197.9	15 704	663 586	257 760.7	31 715.9
Addison	44	278	76.3	16.3	97	501	91.7	27.9	346	7 508	1 286.6	317.5
Algonquin	34	D	D	D	105	336	32.3	12.1	35	715	111.9	29.7
Alton	35	142	21.3	3.8	61	D	D	D	26	848	D	36.5
Arlington Heights..........	128	802	144.5	31.5	529	D	D	D	93	2 322	768.7	122.6
Aurora..........................	132	818	127.6	20.2	413	2 269	297.6	115.6	157	9 917	4 331.0	506.8
Bartlett.........................	27	75	13.4	2.6	125	285	48.5	14.8	26	1 102	274.2	49.6
Batavia.........................	27	132	18.3	3.7	129	D	D	D	96	3 688	1 066.4	162.8
Belleville	64	239	32.7	6.3	171	1 118	132.1	64.3	49	1 856	435.7	73.7
Belvidere	18	57	6.9	1.1	41	D	D	D	35	5 701	5 359.5	348.1
Berwyn.........................	45	127	18.0	2.6	77	312	27.7	11.1	14	503	D	D
Bloomington	103	565	90.9	14.4	224	D	D	D	60	2 753	821.0	129.9
Bolingbrook	45	172	31.3	4.5	149	932	99.8	37.7	52	3 218	1 362.4	131.7
Buffalo Grove	57	432	57.6	20.3	316	3 424	477.2	199.6	64	4 219	1 160.8	188.6

1. Establishments subject to federal tax.

Accommodation and Food Services, Arts, Entertainment, and Recreation, and Health Care and Social Assistance

City	Accommodation and food services, 2007				Arts, entertainment, and recreation,[1] 2007				Health care and social assistance,[1] 2007			
	Number of establishments	Number of employees	Sales (mil dol)	Annual payroll (mil dol)	Number of establishments	Number of employees	Receipts (mil dol)	Annual payroll (mil dol)	Number of establishments	Number of employees	Receipts (mil dol)	Annual payroll (mil dol)
	92	93	94	95	96	97	98	99	100	101	102	103
GEORGIA	18 640	355 423	16 976.2	4 704.4	2 319	31 121	2 527.7	836.4	18 379	229 101	23 274.0	9 144.8
Albany	208	4 015	165.6	41.3	18	D	D	D	237	D	D	D
Alpharetta	318	7 164	377.1	108.6	33	D	D	D	298	3 491	395.5	162.1
Athens-Clarke County	331	7 062	293.4	80.3	36	408	28.6	6.3	355	D	D	D
Atlanta	1 528	41 275	2 743.7	770.6	224	2 961	589.0	243.9	1 203	14 437	1 982.7	753.8
Augusta-Richmond County	431	9 726	395.4	108.6	32	D	D	D	548	7 955	964.8	347.7
Columbus	418	9 898	428.2	120.7	37	D	D	D	484	6 110	635.8	246.8
Dalton	143	2 775	117.2	31.6	8	D	D	D	132	D	D	D
Douglasville	137	3 446	145.2	40.0	9	210	10.0	2.4	108	D	D	D
Duluth	158	1 969	81.9	26.2	24	298	39.6	5.8	155	D	D	D
Dunwoody	119	3 326	198.3	59.0	13	D	D	D	180	2 292	259.8	98.3
East Point	74	1 889	119.7	34.9	13	31	11.6	2.8	82	D	D	D
Gainesville	156	2 562	116.4	30.6	16	D	D	D	245	D	D	D
Hinesville	70	1 294	50.2	12.0	1	D	D	D	42	461	28.2	11.9
Johns Creek	112	2 087	85.3	26.6	21	210	26.1	12.2	121	D	D	D
Kennesaw	100	1 760	76.1	21.7	19	D	D	D	74	D	D	D
LaGrange	92	1 878	71.7	19.3	6	D	D	D	86	D	D	D
Lawrenceville	137	2 044	106.7	27.6	20	D	D	D	231	D	D	D
Macon	261	4 791	184.4	49.9	14	D	D	D	393	D	D	D
Marietta	271	4 116	207.5	55.5	27	D	D	D	339	D	D	D
Milton	25	191	13.7	3.3	10	212	14.6	4.6	16	D	D	D
Newnan	104	2 566	104.0	30.4	7	D	D	D	72	D	D	D
Peachtree City	87	2 101	83.4	25.0	20	D	D	D	95	D	D	D
Rome	156	2 981	125.6	33.0	9	D	D	D	203	4 802	537.4	196.3
Roswell	239	3 862	181.7	52.9	44	441	30.7	9.2	340	5 303	459.1	183.0
Sandy Springs	264	4 087	250.2	65.2	44	574	38.7	12.4	598	7 763	1 218.0	497.0
Savannah	521	12 365	663.2	180.9	51	543	36.8	8.9	457	7 158	895.1	364.6
Smyrna	163	2 993	147.2	40.2	27	D	D	D	186	D	D	D
Statesboro	124	D	D	D	7	D	D	D	136	D	D	D
Stockbridge	68	957	39.7	9.4	11	D	D	D	131	D	D	D
Valdosta	171	4 114	159.6	41.9	9	76	4.3	1.1	244	D	D	D
Warner Robins	143	3 217	121.4	32.9	8	D	D	D	153	D	D	D
HAWAII	3 528	98 353	8 042.2	2 209.8	397	7 676	563.7	163.1	2 778	29 023	2 978.6	1 244.1
East Honolulu CDP	NA	NA	NA	NA	NA	NA	NA	NA	NA	NA	NA	NA
Hilo CDP	149	2 616	132.0	36.3	6	79	4.2	1.0	178	2 407	194.8	82.5
Kahului CDP	94	D	D	D	10	D	D	D	76	669	85.9	36.0
Kailua CDP (Honolulu County)	95	1 510	69.9	19.3	10	76	5.3	2.0	110	863	74.7	35.2
Kaneohe CDP	78	1 135	59.6	14.5	14	D	D	D	78	744	74.2	29.0
Mililani Town CDP	39	1 055	47.2	12.2	4	118	7.9	2.0	25	D	D	D
Pearl City CDP	43	716	36.8	9.7	1	D	D	D	32	409	45.1	19.3
Urban Honolulu CDP	NA	NA	NA	NA	NA	NA	NA	NA	NA	NA	NA	NA
Waipahu CDP	69	1 033	56.4	14.5	1	D	D	D	70	581	57.8	19.9
IDAHO	3 482	56 662	2 416.0	662.7	590	7 065	310.3	97.3	3 974	44 499	3 510.2	1 422.7
Boise City	606	13 055	593.2	163.9	67	1 514	56.5	16.7	832	9 567	901.7	402.3
Caldwell	63	971	36.8	10.3	6	D	D	D	90	1 327	118.2	44.3
Coeur d'Alene	192	3 801	180.7	50.1	29	D	D	D	246	D	D	D
Idaho Falls	166	3 070	124.0	33.5	21	D	D	D	382	4 361	379.9	147.3
Lewiston	91	1 664	63.9	20.0	10	D	D	D	125	D	D	D
Meridian	149	2 876	117.5	34.1	13	D	D	D	192	2 448	187.7	71.5
Nampa	145	2 698	97.0	25.9	15	426	7.3	2.5	175	D	D	D
Pocatello	130	2 350	92.7	25.1	14	D	D	D	225	D	D	D
Post Falls	62	1 034	39.1	12.1	8	D	D	D	80	D	D	D
Rexburg	46	1 028	29.5	8.3	7	111	4.2	1.0	74	D	D	D
Twin Falls	143	2 606	104.5	27.2	17	D	D	D	234	D	D	D
ILLINOIS	26 774	468 827	25 469.0	6 894.3	3 666	51 012	5 306.0	1 579.8	25 651	325 085	32 056.1	13 445.1
Addison	77	1 491	83.8	22.5	10	76	4.5	1.5	59	882	63.1	34.2
Algonquin	81	1 665	67.6	22.3	13	D	D	D	74	D	D	D
Alton	96	1 697	73.6	20.6	10	D	D	D	113	1 376	127.4	55.8
Arlington Heights	181	3 120	177.7	48.5	23	121	6.7	1.8	363	D	D	D
Aurora	267	4 486	211.9	57.6	31	1 781	475.8	43.6	277	4 139	491.5	190.6
Bartlett	50	615	33.3	7.7	8	139	4.0	1.5	54	D	D	D
Batavia	70	1 043	47.8	14.5	8	D	D	D	53	D	D	D
Belleville	145	1 964	87.4	23.0	14	D	D	D	203	3 418	332.9	166.7
Belvidere	51	754	35.3	9.3	6	49	2.3	0.5	39	D	D	D
Berwyn	94	1 184	61.5	15.4	9	76	5.3	1.7	138	3 191	343.6	156.5
Bloomington	233	5 530	221.2	65.5	24	355	11.8	3.7	184	2 680	306.2	138.0
Bolingbrook	139	2 787	143.5	41.2	14	257	10.1	4.7	100	907	72.3	33.0
Buffalo Grove	97	1 742	85.7	23.2	18	D	D	D	143	1 049	124.7	48.4

1. Establishments subject to federal tax.

City	Other services[1], 2007				Selected federal funds, 2009–2010 (mil dol)								
					Procurement contracts		Grants						
	Number of establishments	Number of employees	Receipts (mil dol)	Annual payroll (mil dol)	Defense	Other	Total[2]	Medicaid and other health related	Nutrition and family welfare	Energy and environment	Disasters and emergency preparedness	Housing and community development	Employment and training
	104	105	106	107	108	109	110	111	112	113	114	115	116
GEORGIA	12 420	81 240	6 485.3	2 183.1	8 377.5	4 083.2	16 750.6	8 036.6	2 202.4	368.4	99.5	936.8	217.3
Albany	136	D	D	D	78.2	29.9	29.4	4.9	0.5	0.8	0.0	4.5	0.0
Alpharetta	150	D	D	D	60.4	14.9	34.8	0.2	0.0	34.5	0.0	0.0	0.0
Athens-Clarke County	160	D	D	D	0.0	0.0	4.4	0.0	0.0	0.8	0.0	0.2	0.0
Atlanta	904	8 419	671.6	204.2	702.4	1 859.6	4 102.9	1 051.6	413.0	229.3	33.7	251.1	206.9
Augusta-Richmond County	226	1 628	125.0	41.6	NA	NA	NA	NA	NA	NA	NA	NA	NA
Columbus	277	1 862	122.7	42.3	24.6	2.5	43.6	3.3	6.2	1.9	0.0	22.8	0.0
Dalton	79	404	37.7	11.6	1.6	1.5	1.3	0.6	0.0	0.0	0.0	0.5	0.0
Douglasville	91	D	D	D	0.5	0.6	1.0	0.0	0.0	0.0	0.0	0.3	0.0
Duluth	163	1 111	93.4	41.0	8.5	2.2	0.7	0.7	0.0	0.0	0.0	0.0	0.0
Dunwoody	73	436	26.3	9.1	NA	NA	NA	NA	NA	NA	NA	NA	NA
East Point	43	D	D	D	1.2	2.9	4.8	0.4	0.0	0.0	0.0	4.1	0.0
Gainesville	110	D	D	D	263.9	34.8	24.0	0.1	20.6	0.6	0.0	1.5	0.0
Hinesville	44	D	D	D	33.9	0.0	11.5	0.0	0.0	0.0	0.0	0.5	0.0
Johns Creek	91	D	D	D	NA	NA	NA	NA	NA	NA	NA	NA	NA
Kennesaw	105	D	D	D	3.5	20.8	6.6	0.7	0.0	0.0	0.0	0.0	0.0
LaGrange	55	D	D	D	1.0	0.5	3.4	0.7	0.0	0.0	0.0	0.8	0.0
Lawrenceville	138	990	96.7	33.0	28.4	6.1	15.9	0.9	0.0	0.0	0.0	6.6	0.0
Macon	176	943	81.6	24.8	11.7	29.2	45.8	6.3	5.4	0.9	0.0	24.6	0.0
Marietta	232	1 399	153.9	46.5	3 485.4	183.6	68.7	4.5	3.1	18.1	0.0	28.0	0.1
Milton	19	D	D	D	NA	NA	NA	NA	NA	NA	NA	NA	NA
Newnan	69	235	21.7	5.5	1.0	2.3	1.6	0.0	0.0	0.0	0.0	1.5	0.0
Peachtree City	79	D	D	D	11.6	1.2	0.1	0.0	0.0	0.0	0.0	0.0	0.0
Rome	67	D	D	D	0.0	6.1	5.6	0.7	0.0	0.0	0.0	3.8	0.0
Roswell	205	D	D	D	1.7	1.1	1.3	0.0	0.0	1.1	0.0	0.2	0.0
Sandy Springs	155	D	D	D	4.6	10.0	1.5	0.0	0.0	0.0	0.0	1.5	0.0
Savannah	227	1 505	124.1	38.6	255.1	8.8	71.6	6.1	6.7	4.3	-1.7	32.9	0.3
Smyrna	99	434	41.8	12.0	2.9	5.1	2.9	1.3	0.0	0.0	1.4	0.0	0.0
Statesboro	60	298	21.9	5.6	1.3	0.3	6.3	1.0	0.0	0.3	0.0	0.5	0.0
Stockbridge	44	D	D	D	0.4	0.4	0.0	0.0	0.0	0.0	0.0	0.0	0.0
Valdosta	96	432	28.0	8.4	29.0	0.4	18.8	0.8	6.6	0.0	0.0	2.2	3.4
Warner Robins	84	D	D	D	318.1	3.3	9.3	0.0	7.3	0.0	0.0	1.3	0.0
HAWAII	1 615	11 669	908.6	279.4	2 350.8	394.0	3 025.6	1 232.7	331.2	141.4	6.0	170.3	50.2
East Honolulu CDP	NA	NA	NA	NA	NA	NA	NA	NA	NA	NA	NA	NA	NA
Hilo CDP	72	470	39.1	10.8	NA	NA	NA	NA	NA	NA	NA	NA	NA
Kahului CDP	60	577	46.3	13.9	NA	NA	NA	NA	NA	NA	NA	NA	NA
Kailua CDP (Honolulu County)	39	193	14.4	4.9	NA	NA	NA	NA	NA	NA	NA	NA	NA
Kaneohe CDP	43	363	22.0	7.9	NA	NA	NA	NA	NA	NA	NA	NA	NA
Mililani Town CDP	10	58	4.1	1.1	NA	NA	NA	NA	NA	NA	NA	NA	NA
Pearl City CDP	30	177	16.6	5.1	NA	NA	NA	NA	NA	NA	NA	NA	NA
Urban Honolulu CDP	NA	NA	NA	NA	NA	NA	NA	NA	NA	NA	NA	NA	NA
Waipahu CDP	52	258	22.0	6.5	NA	NA	NA	NA	NA	NA	NA	NA	NA
IDAHO	2 114	11 031	837.1	249.3	264.9	2 368.4	2 979.5	1 473.1	282.9	199.2	8.6	71.0	68.1
Boise City	368	2 413	175.6	62.7	28.0	112.7	583.7	44.4	44.6	142.0	4.9	53.5	66.7
Caldwell	46	307	24.9	7.8	0.4	1.1	12.3	0.7	7.5	0.0	0.0	0.0	1.1
Coeur d'Alene	91	579	37.6	11.4	0.1	602.7	3.7	1.1	0.0	0.5	0.0	0.6	0.0
Idaho Falls	92	D	D	D	64.8	1 344.4	16.5	10.8	1.9	1.0	0.0	0.7	0.0
Lewiston	68	D	D	D	0.4	13.8	7.8	0.1	3.4	0.4	0.0	0.5	0.0
Meridian	89	508	29.0	8.9	1.3	0.6	18.9	0.1	0.0	0.8	0.0	0.2	0.0
Nampa	105	598	42.2	12.1	-0.3	7.0	12.8	4.9	0.0	0.1	0.0	6.7	0.0
Pocatello	81	D	D	D	0.4	4.8	20.4	4.1	1.5	2.0	0.0	3.5	0.2
Post Falls	47	294	19.0	5.5	0.0	0.3	0.2	0.0	0.0	0.0	0.0	0.0	0.0
Rexburg	21	D	D	D	0.3	0.0	3.0	2.3	0.0	0.1	0.0	0.0	0.0
Twin Falls	94	722	48.0	15.2	0.1	3.2	9.9	2.4	4.6	0.7	0.0	0.3	0.0
ILLINOIS	18 732	122 938	10 459.8	3 264.5	7 118.7	4 481.8	24 060.1	12 147.7	2 913.9	769.9	259.9	1 735.3	405.0
Addison	115	615	72.1	23.3	9.0	2.4	0.1	0.0	0.0	0.0	0.0	0.1	0.0
Algonquin	49	275	15.4	5.1	0.0	0.0	0.0	0.0	0.0	0.0	0.0	0.0	0.0
Alton	50	250	18.3	6.1	1.5	0.6	9.9	0.4	7.0	0.0	0.0	0.9	0.0
Arlington Heights	157	1 033	91.8	29.1	0.3	3.7	36.1	0.0	0.0	0.8	0.0	0.5	0.0
Aurora	184	1 136	102.6	25.8	20.1	0.7	16.0	1.9	0.0	1.6	0.0	11.4	0.4
Bartlett	46	D	D	D	0.0	0.0	0.0	0.0	0.0	0.0	0.0	0.0	0.0
Batavia	52	479	51.5	18.1	0.3	440.2	11.8	0.0	0.0	7.6	3.4	0.0	0.0
Belleville	112	661	47.6	17.4	26.9	0.2	24.1	0.0	1.6	2.1	0.4	16.8	0.0
Belvidere	33	D	D	D	0.2	0.0	1.0	0.0	0.0	0.0	0.0	1.0	0.0
Berwyn	61	195	19.3	4.7	0.0	0.1	2.2	0.0	0.0	0.4	0.0	1.4	0.0
Bloomington	120	956	66.5	22.1	0.3	8.5	24.4	6.7	3.3	0.7	0.0	7.7	0.1
Bolingbrook	80	444	44.2	13.7	5.8	1.7	2.8	0.0	0.0	2.5	0.0	0.3	0.0
Buffalo Grove	71	572	34.7	13.4	9.2	30.3	0.0	0.0	0.0	0.0	0.0	0.0	0.0

1. Establishments subject to federal tax.   2. Includes program categories not shown separately. State totals include additional categories not allocated by city.

Table D. Cities — City Government Finances

City	City government finances, 2007									
	General revenue							General expenditure		
		Intergovernmental		Taxes					Per capita[1] (dollars)	
					Per capita[1] (dollars)					
	Total (mil dol)	Total (mil dol)	Percent from state government	Total (mil dol)	Total	Property	Sales and gross receipts	Total (mil dol)	Total	Capital outlays
	117	118	119	120	121	122	123	124	125	126
GEORGIA..................	X	X	X	X	X	X	X	X	X	X
Albany	108.5	43.4	8.5	25.4	335	196	140	95.5	1 260	223
Alpharetta	64.2	10.4	2.1	38.6	778	465	313	58.9	1 185	290
Athens-Clarke County ...	190.0	63.2	22.3	61.6	540	355	183	172.6	1 513	347
Atlanta	1 600.8	206.1	30.5	413.5	796	403	392	1 851.5	3 566	1 521
Augusta-Richmond County	306.1	99.9	22.1	87.9	457	258	197	269.7	1 403	252
Columbus	328.9	123.5	38.9	120.0	641	453	186	265.7	1 420	199
Dalton	76.8	9.4	4.2	16.9	507	366	141	93.7	2 804	1 064
Douglasville	29.1	10.9	10.3	12.1	401	140	261	30.3	1 007	370
Duluth	27.0	10.0	10.3	10.7	414	219	195	23.8	915	422
Dunwoody	NA	NA	NA	NA	NA	NA	NA	NA	NA	NA
East Point	40.3	11.2	1.0	14.2	330	200	130	46.5	1 084	91
Gainesville..................	103.0	20.5	11.1	18.8	540	268	272	106.2	3 050	1 159
Hinesville	23.2	5.9	13.9	9.5	310	182	128	23.3	764	100
Johns Creek................	51.0	13.0	13.9	20.8	349	205	144	51.2	860	113
Kennesaw	12.5	1.0	13.5	5.4	170	47	123	17.7	561	48
LaGrange	31.8	5.2	11.8	4.5	181	2	159	47.5	1 697	488
Lawrenceville,.............	20.1	5.5	2.8	6.2	214	78	130	24.9	859	226
Macon	96.1	40.6	3.3	36.5	392	203	190	92.0	988	52
Marietta	87.5	22.0	1.6	30.8	459	184	268	85.4	1 274	168
Milton	24.8	10.4	5.4	7.5	494	243	251	23.8	1 578	372
Newnan	22.6	8.3	8.7	9.7	337	138	200	19.7	682	190
Peachtree City..............	38.1	12.4	4.9	15.9	461	260	201	35.0	1 013	173
Rome	60.4	18.0	7.3	18.6	510	251	212	52.4	1 437	337
Roswell......................	88.7	23.1	0.4	40.1	459	288	171	73.6	843	73
Sandy Springs..............	77.4	23.1	1.5	50.3	604	316	287	59.3	713	46
Savannah	353.0	108.1	6.8	92.1	707	381	309	341.5	2 620	596
Smyrna	47.2	8.3	11.0	22.3	449	348	100	51.0	1 030	188
Statesboro	27.6	4.8	4.3	7.8	293	130	163	33.0	1 242	274
Stockbridge ,,,,,,,,,,,,,,	13.8	6.3	7.1	3.1	217	7	210	12.6	892	341
Valdosta	56.5	23.7	5.4	17.0	357	176	181	54.2	1 139	269
Warner Robins	44.5	3.5	6.3	22.5	373	210	162	50.8	840	117
HAWAII.....................	X	X	X	X	X	X	X	X	X	X
East Honolulu CDP .,,,,	NA	NA	NA	NA	NA	NA	NA	NA	NA	NA
Hilo ODP	NA	NA	NA	NA	NA	NA	NA	NA	NA	NA
Kahului CDP................	NA	NA	NA	NA	NA	NA	NA	NA	NA	NA
Kailua CDP (Honolulu County)	NA	NA	NA	NA	NA	NA	NA	NA	NA	NA
Kaneohe CDP	NA	NA	NA	NA	NA	NA	NA	NA	NA	NA
Mililani Town CDP........	NA	NA	NA	NA	NA	NA	NA	NA	NA	NA
Pearl City CDP.............	NA	NA	NA	NA	NA	NA	NA	NA	NA	NA
Urban Honolulu CDP	NA	NA	NA	NA	NA	NA	NA	NA	NA	NA
Waipahu CDP	NA	NA	NA	NA	NA	NA	NA	NA	NA	NA
IDAHO	X	X	X	X	X	X	X	X	X	X
Boise City	243.6	36.4	43.9	99.1	489	412	76	202.6	999	120
Caldwell......................	37.4	5.7	66.5	15.8	395	314	82	37.6	942	294
Coeur d'Alene	42.8	6.9	61.9	19.4	459	308	151	45.9	1 085	342
Idaho Falls..................	70.7	17.3	48.9	22.0	412	386	27	69.1	1 297	409
Lewiston	39.5	10.1	80.1	14.2	448	415	33	33.6	1 057	107
Meridian.....................	38.5	4.3	73.0	13.5	209	168	41	34.0	526	176
Nampa.......................	74.3	10.3	84.0	29.3	370	282	89	89.2	1 126	437
Pocatello.....................	61.1	15.7	45.3	21.0	385	342	42	56.1	1 028	316
Post Falls	27.4	2.9	100.0	14.2	558	251	307	35.4	1 395	865
Rexburg	16.7	5.4	77.3	4.3	157	99	59	16.6	602	213
Twin Falls	33.7	6.4	80.9	13.2	318	288	30	30.9	743	172
ILLINOIS..................	X	X	X	X	X	X	X	X	X	X
Addison	40.3	12.8	99.4	18.7	507	252	237	41.9	1 135	230
Algonquin	26.9	10.3	100.0	10.5	348	156	192	26.8	884	290
Alton	40.2	19.7	100.0	9.9	337	174	163	46.6	1 584	254
Arlington Heights...........	97.1	21.4	97.1	62.3	845	576	269	104.9	1 423	436
Aurora	211.2	67.8	89.5	118.9	696	431	235	215.7	1 263	185
Bartlett	31.0	7.4	97.5	14.1	342	232	88	31.2	755	139
Batavia	33.3	10.7	83.8	11.2	409	218	190	28.9	1 057	128
Belleville	49.0	14.0	99.2	20.4	497	339	158	46.1	1 122	256
Belvidere	22.1	7.4	96.1	5.2	200	170	30	20.3	775	171
Berwyn	59.4	13.8	87.8	33.8	671	436	178	56.4	1 121	67
Bloomington	98.3	28.7	95.4	41.9	578	235	344	109.8	1 516	331
Bolingbrook	92.4	21.8	90.2	41.9	594	193	402	83.1	1 179	92
Buffalo Grove	42.3	11.0	98.6	18.2	422	245	177	39.5	916	0

1. Based on population estimated as of July 1 of the year shown.

City	City government finances, 2006 (cont.)									
	General expenditure (cont.)									
	Percent of total for:									
	Public welfare	Highways	Parking facilities	Education	Health and hospitals	Police protection	Sewerage and sanitation	Parks and recreation	Housing and community development	Interest on debt
	127	128	129	130	131	132	133	134	135	136
GEORGIA................	X	X	X	X	X	X	X	X	X	X
Albany	0.0	6.6	0.0	0.0	0.0	13.4	23.6	8.2	6.8	0.4
Alpharetta...................	0.0	28.6	0.0	0.2	0.0	14.0	4.3	13.0	0.1	4.8
Athens-Clarke County ...	0.3	7.0	0.5	0.0	6.1	13.0	14.7	6.0	3.4	0.2
Atlanta......................	0.0	3.2	0.0	0.0	0.0	11.3	19.7	6.6	1.1	7.4
Augusta-Richmond County	0.3	6.5	0.1	0.0	7.8	11.9	22.3	5.8	6.8	0.6
Columbus	0.1	8.8	0.0	0.0	6.1	12.6	14.0	5.7	2.6	4.0
Dalton	0.0	8.1	0.0	0.0	0.0	7.8	32.4	5.0	0.0	1.4
Douglasville.................	0.1	35.0	0.0	0.0	0.0	23.6	12.9	5.7	2.6	1.9
Duluth	0.0	14.5	0.0	0.0	0.0	23.3	0.3	7.5	4.5	0.0
Dunwoody	NA	NA	NA	NA	NA	NA	NA	NA	NA	NA
East Point..................	0.0	3.5	0.0	0.0	0.0	22.7	11.8	2.3	0.8	6.4
Gainesville..................	2.9	2.9	0.0	0.0	0.0	7.2	38.8	3.3	1.0	16.7
Hinesville...................	0.0	14.3	0.0	0.0	0.0	23.5	24.7	1.9	4.5	0.0
Johns Creek................	0.0	14.3	0.0	0.0	0.0	23.5	24.7	1.9	4.5	0.0
Kennesaw...................	0.0	12.1	0.0	0.0	0.0	21.0	11.5	10.3	1.6	5.6
LaGrange	0.0	8.2	0.0	0.0	0.4	15.4	31.7	1.8	2.8	3.6
Lawrenceville...............	0.0	16.3	0.0	0.0	0.0	26.1	13.9	4.3	0.8	0.4
Macon.......................	0.0	4.2	0.1	0.0	0.3	17.5	9.0	5.4	2.9	1.6
Marietta	6.6	8.6	0.0	0.0	0.0	15.2	15.8	2.0	5.1	5.2
Milton.......................	0.0	13.8	0.0	0.0	0.0	19.8	21.0	8.8	0.9	0.3
Newnan	0.0	17.5	0.0	0.0	0.3	26.3	0.0	11.8	1.7	0.0
Peachtree City..............	0.4	18.4	0.0	0.0	0.6	15.6	1.5	12.1	0.0	2.0
Rome........................	0.0	8.8	0.1	0.0	0.0	14.9	31.4	1.8	2.3	1.1
Roswell......................	0.0	11.1	0.0	0.0	0.0	21.3	12.5	14.2	5.3	3.0
Sandy Springs..............	0.0	16.3	0.0	0.0	0.0	19.4	0.0	1.5	8.5	0.6
Savannah	0.3	3.7	1.3	0.0	0.0	15.5	29.4	6.6	6.0	1.6
Smyrna	0.0	15.6	0.0	0.0	0.0	18.3	19.2	12.2	0.0	4.1
Statesboro	0.0	9.3	0.0	0.0	0.2	26.1	27.1	3.5	1.2	0.3
Stockbridge	0.0	22.0	0.0	0.0	0.0	1.0	18.6	1.5	19.4	2.7
Valdosta	0.0	13.8	0.0	0.0	0.0	19.8	21.0	8.8	0.9	0.3
Warner Robins	0.1	18.2	0.0	0.0	0.7	20.9	22.5	5.0	5.1	0.0
HAWAII......................	X	X	X	X	X	X	X	X	X	X
East Honolulu CDP	NA	NA	NA	NA	NA	NA	NA	NA	NA	NA
Hilo CDP	NA	NA	NA	NA	NA	NA	NA	NA	NA	NA
Kahului CDP................	NA	NA	NA	NA	NA	NA	NA	NA	NA	NA
Kailua CDP (Honolulu County)...................	NA	NA	NA	NA	NA	NA	NA	NA	NA	NA
Kaneohe CDP	NA	NA	NA	NA	NA	NA	NA	NA	NA	NA
Mililani Town CDP.........	NA	NA	NA	NA	NA	NA	NA	NA	NA	NA
Pearl City CDP.............	NA	NA	NA	NA	NA	NA	NA	NA	NA	NA
Urban Honolulu CDP	NA	NA	NA	NA	NA	NA	NA	NA	NA	NA
Waipahu CDP	NA	NA	NA	NA	NA	NA	NA	NA	NA	NA
IDAHO	X	X	X	X	X	X	X	X	X	X
Boise City	0.0	1.2	0.3	0.0	0.0	15.6	24.4	8.3	0.9	2.8
Caldwell.....................	0.0	12.0	0.0	0.0	0.0	15.3	24.8	5.4	5.9	2.4
Coeur d'Alene	0.0	10.2	0.1	0.0	0.0	16.1	35.7	6.2	0.0	1.0
Idaho Falls..................	0.0	10.1	0.0	0.0	3.7	12.8	22.9	9.5	0.0	0.5
Lewiston	0.0	11.0	0.0	0.0	0.0	17.4	22.0	8.9	3.1	0.0
Meridian	0.0	0.0	0.0	0.0	0.0	19.6	28.9	10.4	0.0	0.3
Nampa.......................	0.0	7.5	0.0	0.0	0.0	13.3	17.4	12.9	1.9	2.9
Pocatello....................	0.0	26.0	0.0	0.0	4.3	15.6	17.5	5.1	1.9	1.4
Post Falls	0.0	13.1	0.0	0.0	0.2	9.2	50.2	3.4	0.0	1.5
Rexburg	0.0	18.1	0.0	0.0	6.0	9.5	19.3	14.0	0.0	1.3
Twin Falls	0.0	10.6	0.1	0.0	0.6	19.2	17.1	5.9	0.0	1.4
ILLINOIS...................	X	X	X	X	X	X	X	X	X	X
Addison	0.0	16.2	0.0	0.0	0.0	27.3	5.0	0.0	6.2	6.7
Algonquin	0.0	14.1	0.0	0.0	0.0	23.6	32.5	10.6	0.0	3.3
Alton........................	0.0	14.5	0.0	0.0	0.4	18.3	9.7	12.5	0.0	2.1
Arlington Heights...........	0.3	10.2	1.1	0.0	1.3	17.5	1.5	0.3	0.5	2.4
Aurora.......................	0.0	15.7	1.4	0.0	0.4	27.2	1.0	5.1	2.2	5.9
Bartlett......................	0.0	25.6	0.3	0.0	0.0	29.7	7.9	7.1	0.0	5.7
Batavia	0.0	20.9	0.0	0.0	0.0	22.4	8.8	0.0	0.0	0.8
Belleville	0.0	21.8	0.2	0.0	0.0	16.5	14.9	3.3	0.0	2.7
Belvidere	0.0	12.4	0.0	0.0	0.1	17.3	13.1	0.0	0.0	1.6
Berwyn	0.0	6.9	0.0	0.0	0.0	33.4	7.6	2.1	2.0	5.5
Bloomington	0.0	6.1	0.7	0.0	0.0	15.0	15.5	25.3	3.9	3.5
Bolingbrook	0.0	16.1	0.0	0.0	0.0	19.1	8.1	12.9	0.4	10.4
Buffalo Grove	0.0	11.5	0.4	0.0	0.0	25.6	10.6	8.0	0.0	1.3

Table D. Cities — City Government Finances, City Government Employment, and Climate

City	City government finances, 2007 (cont.) Debt outstanding Total (mil dol)	Per capita[1] (dollars)	Debt issued during year	City government employment, 2010	Climate[2] Average daily temperature (degrees Fahrenheit) Mean January	Mean July	Limits January[3]	Limits July[4]	Annual precipitation (inches)	Heating degree days	Cooling degree days
	137	138	139	140	141	142	143	144	145	146	147
GEORGIA	X	X	X	NA	X	X	X	X	X	X	X
Albany	88.4	1 166	6.6	1 204	47.5	81.4	35.1	92.5	53.40	2 106	2 264
Alpharetta	89.3	1 797	21.8	449	39.5	77.2	29.1	87.5	51.82	3 490	1 327
Athens-Clarke County	35.0	307	0.0	1 721	42.2	79.8	32.9	90.2	47.83	2 861	1 785
Atlanta	7 062.5	13 604	271.3	8 142	41.7	79.5	31.3	90.6	49.10	3 004	1 679
Augusta-Richmond County	651.3	3 390	63.6	2 555	44.8	80.8	33.1	92.0	44.58	2 525	1 986
Columbus	353.5	1 890	50.4	3 208	46.8	82.0	36.6	91.7	48.57	2 154	2 296
Dalton	128.6	3 849	14.5	784	39.4	78.0	28.8	89.8	53.64	3 534	1 393
Douglasville	11.3	376	0.0	201	NA	NA	NA	NA	NA	NA	NA
Duluth	0.0	0	0.0	NA	NA	NA	NA	NA	NA	NA	NA
Dunwoody	NA	NA	NA	NA	NA	NA	NA	NA	NA	NA	NA
East Point	134.7	3 137	19.6	633	42.7	80.0	33.5	89.4	50.20	2 827	1 810
Gainesville	653.7	18 776	133.9	686	36.0	72.9	24.7	84.0	58.19	4 421	752
Hinesville	8.9	293	0.0	207	51.6	82.6	40.7	93.3	48.32	1 551	2 539
Johns Creek	19.7	330	0.0	NA	NA	NA	NA	NA	NA	NA	NA
Kennesaw	23.6	746	0.0	225	NA	NA	NA	NA	NA	NA	NA
LaGrange	82.4	2 946	7.7	415	42.2	78.7	31.3	89.3	53.38	3 078	1 551
Lawrenceville	5.2	181	0.0	252	NA	NA	NA	NA	NA	NA	NA
Macon	35.6	382	0.1	1 183	45.5	81.1	34.5	91.8	45.00	2 364	2 115
Marietta	156.4	2 333	0.0	731	39.4	77.9	28.5	89.3	54.43	3 505	1 403
Milton	4.8	316	0.0	NA	NA	NA	NA	NA	NA	NA	NA
Newnan	0.0	0	0.0	316	NA	NA	NA	NA	NA	NA	NA
Peachtree City	16.0	464	1.1	267	42.6	79.4	31.8	90.5	50.10	2 958	1 679
Rome	82.7	2 269	0.0	572	39.4	77.5	29.1	87.7	56.16	3 510	1 360
Roswell	45.0	516	0.0	782	39.5	77.2	29.1	87.5	51.82	3 490	1 327
Sandy Springs	0.0	0	0.0	250	NA	NA	NA	NA	NA	NA	NA
Savannah	203.1	1 559	0.0	2 664	49.2	82.1	38.0	92.3	49.58	1 799	2 454
Smyrna	44.0	888	0.0	396	42.7	80.0	33.5	89.4	50.20	2 827	1 810
Statesboro	10.2	384	0.0	276	NA	NA	NA	NA	NA	NA	NA
Stockbridge	23.2	1 641	9.8	NA	NA	NA	NA	NA	NA	NA	NA
Valdosta	10.9	228	0.2	763	50.0	80.9	38.0	92.0	53.06	1 782	2 319
Warner Robins	18.7	309	0.0	516	45.5	81.1	34.5	91.8	45.00	2 364	2 115
HAWAII	X	X	X	NA	X	X	X	X	X	X	X
East Honolulu CDP	NA	NA	NA	NA	NA	NA	NA	NA	NA	NA	NA
Hilo CDP	NA	NA	NA	NA	NA	NA	NA	NA	NA	NA	NA
Kahului CDP	NA	NA	NA	NA	NA	NA	NA	NA	NA	NA	NA
Kailua CDP (Honolulu County)	NA	NA	NA	NA	NA	NA	NA	NA	NA	NA	NA
Kaneohe CDP	NA	NA	NA	NA	NA	NA	NA	NA	NA	NA	NA
Mililani Town CDP	NA	NA	NA	NA	NA	NA	NA	NA	NA	NA	NA
Pearl City CDP	NA	NA	NA	NA	NA	NA	NA	NA	NA	NA	NA
Urban Honolulu CDP	NA	NA	NA	NA	NA	NA	NA	NA	NA	NA	NA
Waipahu CDP	NA	NA	NA	NA	NA	NA	NA	NA	NA	NA	NA
IDAHO	X	X	X	NA	X	X	X	X	X	X	X
Boise City	201.6	994	0.8	1 626	30.2	74.7	23.6	89.2	12.19	5 727	807
Caldwell	24.3	609	0.2	239	29.3	68.8	19.6	85.7	10.90	6 749	410
Coeur d'Alene	26.6	629	17.8	351	28.4	68.7	22.1	82.6	26.07	6 540	426
Idaho Falls	52.3	982	7.7	649	19.3	68.4	11.1	85.9	11.02	7 917	322
Lewiston	0.0	0	0.0	287	33.7	73.5	28.0	87.6	12.74	5 220	792
Meridian	2.2	34	0.0	316	29.4	71.8	22.1	89.2	9.94	5 752	579
Nampa	43.1	544	0.0	584	28.9	73.3	20.8	90.5	11.37	5 873	692
Pocatello	37.1	681	0.6	566	24.4	69.2	16.3	87.5	12.58	7 109	387
Post Falls	15.4	607	0.0	178	NA	NA	NA	NA	NA	NA	NA
Rexburg	2.3	82	0.0	118	NA	NA	NA	NA	NA	NA	NA
Twin Falls	42.5	1 023	34.7	291	28.2	72.2	19.7	87.9	9.42	6 300	587
ILLINOIS	X	X	X	NA	X	X	X	X	X	X	X
Addison	77.8	2 105	18.5	260	22.0	73.3	14.3	83.5	36.27	6 498	830
Algonquin	20.5	676	0.1	NA	NA	NA	NA	NA	NA	NA	NA
Alton	27.2	924	2.2	228	27.7	78.4	19.4	88.1	38.54	5 149	1 354
Arlington Heights	78.3	1 062	36.5	587	22.0	73.3	14.3	83.5	36.27	6 498	830
Aurora	362.5	2 122	69.4	1 434	20.0	72.4	10.5	84.2	38.39	6 859	661
Bartlett	31.9	772	0.0	179	19.3	72.6	10.9	83.0	37.22	6 975	679
Batavia	69.5	2 545	41.9	NA	NA	NA	NA	NA	NA	NA	NA
Belleville	30.8	751	1.4	349	30.9	78.1	22.1	89.6	39.37	4 612	1 339
Belvidere	8.1	309	0.0	NA	NA	NA	NA	NA	NA	NA	NA
Berwyn	65.5	1 301	8.9	369	25.8	75.3	17.3	86.2	40.96	5 555	1 027
Bloomington	82.9	1 145	0.3	708	22.4	75.2	13.7	85.6	37.45	6 190	998
Bolingbrook	272.1	3 861	63.5	395	23.1	74.8	14.2	86.8	37.94	6 053	942
Buffalo Grove	10.4	241	0.0	253	18.4	72.1	9.6	82.3	36.56	7 149	624

1. Based on the population estimated as of July 1 of the year shown.   2. Represents normal values based on the 30-year period, 1971–2000.   3. Average daily minimum.   4. Average daily maximum.

Table D. Cities — Land Area and Population

STATE Place code	City	Land area,[1] 2010 (sq km)	Population, 2010 Total persons	Rank	Per square kilometer	Race alone or in combination, not of Hispanic origin (percent), 2010 White	Black	American Indian, Alaska Native	Asian	Hawaiian Pacific Islander	Percent Hispanic or Latino[2], 2010	Percent Foreign born, 2008–2010
		1	2	3	4	5	6	7	8	9	10	11
	ILLINOIS—Cont'd											
17 09642	Burbank	10.8	28 925	1 425	2 675.8	69.0	1.8	0.3	3.1	0.1	26.6	30.8
17 10487	Calumet City	18.6	37 042	1 070	1 990.4	14.0	71.0	0.6	0.5	0.1	15.0	8.5
17 11163	Carbondale	44.3	25 902	1 601	585.4	62.5	26.8	1.1	6.7	0.2	5.4	8.1
17 11332	Carol Stream	23.6	39 711	992	1 686.2	64.5	6.3	0.3	15.8	0.1	14.2	21.6
17 11358	Carpentersville	20.5	37 691	1 050	1 841.3	37.7	6.9	0.4	5.9	0.0	50.1	27.4
17 12385	Champaign	58.1	81 055	395	1 395.1	67.0	16.7	0.6	11.6	0.2	6.3	12.5
17 14000	Chicago	589.6	2 695 598	3	4 572.1	32.7	33.0	0.5	6.0	0.1	28.9	21.0
17 14026	Chicago Heights	26.1	30 276	1 347	1 160.4	24.3	42.0	0.5	0.5	0.1	33.9	13.1
17 14351	Cicero	15.2	83 891	379	5 522.8	9.4	3.3	0.1	0.7	0.0	86.6	43.4
17 15599	Collinsville	38.0	25 579	1 621	672.8	84.5	11.0	0.7	1.1	0.1	4.3	1.6
17 17887	Crystal Lake	47.5	40 743	974	857.2	84.6	1.4	0.5	3.1	0.0	11.7	9.7
17 18563	Danville	46.3	33 027	1 235	712.9	62.0	31.9	0.8	1.5	0.1	6.5	3.8
17 18823	Decatur	109.4	76 122	437	696.1	73.2	25.3	0.7	1.1	0.1	2.2	1.6
17 19161	DeKalb	38.0	43 862	897	1 155.8	70.4	13.4	0.5	4.7	0.1	12.5	9.5
17 19642	Des Plaines	37.0	58 364	630	1 577.8	69.1	2.0	0.3	12.2	0.1	17.2	28.2
17 20591	Downers Grove	37.1	47 833	820	1 291.0	86.1	3.3	0.3	6.3	0.1	5.2	8.4
17 22255	East St. Louis	36.2	27 006	1 530	745.2	1.2	98.4	0.5	0.2	0.1	0.5	NA
17 23074	Elgin	96.3	108 188	248	1 124.0	43.8	7.7	0.4	5.8	0.1	43.6	26.0
17 23256	Elk Grove Village	29.4	33 127	1 229	1 127.5	78.5	1.7	0.3	11.0	0.1	9.5	20.8
17 23620	Elmhurst	26.6	44 121	890	1 661.2	86.2	2.2	0.2	5.9	0.0	6.6	9.7
17 24582	Evanston	20.2	74 486	455	3 696.6	63.8	19.2	0.7	10.0	0.1	9.0	16.3
17 27884	Freeport	30.5	25 638	1 616	840.6	78.5	18.6	0.7	1.1	0.1	4.1	3.3
17 28326	Galesburg	46.0	32 195	1 262	700.3	80.5	13.2	0.7	1.1	0.1	6.9	4.1
17 29730	Glendale Heights	13.9	34 208	1 179	2 459.2	40.5	6.2	0.5	23.2	0.1	30.7	30.0
17 29756	Glen Ellyn	17.1	27 450	1 504	1 603.4	83.8	3.1	0.3	7.3	0.1	6.6	10.6
17 29938	Glenview	36.1	44 692	883	1 237.0	80.5	1.2	0.2	13.4	0.1	5.8	21.8
17 30926	Granite City	50.0	29 849	1 372	597.5	88.6	6.3	0.8	0.8	0.1	5.0	2.9
17 32018	Gurnee	35.0	31 295	1 303	895.2	68.5	8.3	0.6	12.7	0.2	11.7	13.9
17 32746	Hanover Park	16.4	37 973	1 042	2 316.8	39.2	7.3	0.5	16.0	0.1	38.3	38.5
17 33383	Harvey	16.3	25 282	1 643	1 549.1	4.3	76.3	0.5	0.9	0.1	19.0	9.4
17 34722	Highland Park	31.6	29 763	1 377	942.2	87.9	2.0	0.2	3.5	0.1	7.3	12.8
17 35411	Hoffman Estates	53.9	51 895	737	963.5	57.8	5.1	0.4	24.0	0.1	14.1	31.9
17 38570	Joliet	160.9	147 433	166	916.5	54.3	16.5	0.4	2.3	0.0	27.8	14.4
17 38934	Kankakee	36.6	27 537	1 499	752.2	39.9	42.2	0.6	0.8	0.0	18.5	6.7
17 41183	Lake in the Hills	26.9	28 965	1 424	1 077.6	81.0	2.3	0.4	6.0	0.1	11.6	13.9
17 42028	Lansing	17.6	28 331	1 458	1 611.5	52.9	32.1	0.5	1.1	0.0	14.5	6.4
17 44407	Lombard	26.6	43 165	909	1 625.8	77.2	5.0	0.3	10.6	0.1	8.1	14.1
17 45694	McHenry	38.2	26 992	1 534	707.0	84.8	0.9	0.4	1.8	0.1	12.8	9.1
17 48242	Melrose Park	11.0	25 411	1 635	2 314.3	23.1	5.5	0.2	1.9	0.0	69.6	39.7
17 49867	Moline	42.6	43 483	903	1 021.9	76.7	6.1	0.5	2.7	0.1	15.6	10.6
17 51089	Mount Prospect	26.8	54 167	698	2 022.7	70.0	2.6	0.3	12.5	0.1	15.5	32.3
17 51349	Mundelein	24.8	31 064	1 309	1 254.1	59.4	1.6	0.3	9.5	0.1	30.1	29.7
17 51622	Naperville	100.4	141 853	176	1 412.7	74.6	5.1	0.4	16.1	0.1	5.3	15.9
17 53000	Niles	15.1	29 803	1 373	1 968.5	72.7	1.6	0.2	17.9	0.1	8.7	46.1
17 53234	Normal	47.5	52 497	726	1 104.7	84.3	9.1	0.4	3.8	0.1	4.1	4.6
17 53481	Northbrook	34.2	33 170	1 224	971.0	85.0	0.8	0.1	12.5	0.0	2.5	19.3
17 53559	North Chicago	20.5	32 574	1 253	1 592.1	38.5	30.5	1.0	4.9	0.6	27.2	21.1
17 54638	Oak Forest	15.4	27 962	1 479	1 814.5	77.8	4.9	0.4	4.5	0.1	13.4	10.1
17 54820	Oak Lawn	22.3	56 690	656	2 546.7	78.1	5.4	0.3	2.7	0.1	14.3	15.3
17 54885	Oak Park	12.2	51 878	739	4 262.8	66.3	22.9	0.6	6.1	0.1	6.8	10.5
17 55249	O'Fallon	37.2	28 281	1 460	760.7	77.6	16.8	0.8	3.9	0.2	3.5	4.3
17 56640	Orland Park	56.7	56 767	654	1 001.9	87.0	1.8	0.2	5.6	0.1	6.2	13.4
17 56887	Oswego	40.2	30 355	1 341	754.7	79.6	5.5	0.3	4.2	0.1	11.7	7.3
17 57225	Palatine	35.3	68 557	494	1 943.8	68.6	3.0	0.3	11.1	0.1	18.0	22.9
17 57875	Park Ridge	18.4	37 480	1 057	2 041.4	91.0	0.6	0.2	4.3	0.0	4.7	15.6
17 58447	Pekin	37.7	34 094	1 186	904.1	94.4	2.5	0.8	0.9	0.1	2.4	1.1
17 59000	Peoria	124.3	115 007	231	924.9	63.2	29.0	0.7	5.1	0.1	4.9	5.5
17 60287	Plainfield	60.2	39 581	998	658.0	75.7	6.0	0.3	8.5	0.1	10.7	11.8
17 62367	Quincy	41.2	40 633	978	986.2	91.9	6.8	0.6	1.1	0.1	1.4	2.1
17 65000	Rockford	158.2	152 871	160	966.3	60.7	21.8	0.7	3.3	0.1	15.8	10.4
17 65078	Rock Island	43.6	39 018	1 014	894.3	70.3	19.9	0.8	2.2	0.1	9.4	6.0
17 65442	Romeoville	47.8	39 680	994	831.0	51.7	12.2	0.6	7.0	0.1	29.9	23.0
17 66040	Round Lake Beach	13.1	28 175	1 464	2 149.1	44.7	4.5	0.5	3.5	0.1	48.0	29.5
17 66703	St. Charles	37.8	32 974	1 239	871.6	84.0	2.7	0.3	3.6	0.1	10.2	12.1
17 68003	Schaumburg	49.8	74 227	457	1 491.1	66.5	4.5	0.4	21.0	0.1	8.8	24.5
17 70122	Skokie	26.1	64 784	544	2 486.0	57.6	7.8	0.4	27.4	0.2	8.8	41.2
17 72000	Springfield	154.1	116 250	228	754.6	76.9	20.1	0.7	2.6	0.1	2.0	3.8
17 73157	Streamwood	20.2	39 858	988	1 969.3	52.1	4.6	0.4	16.0	0.1	28.2	29.8
17 75484	Tinley Park	41.5	56 703	655	1 366.7	85.3	3.8	0.3	4.5	0.1	6.9	9.0
17 77005	Urbana	30.2	41 250	957	1 366.8	60.0	17.2	0.5	19.0	0.2	5.2	18.7
17 77694	Vernon Hills	20.0	25 113	1 655	1 258.2	66.8	2.4	0.2	20.4	0.1	11.4	26.6

1. Dry land or land partially or temporarily covered by water. 2. May be of any race.

Table D. Cities — Population

City	Under 5 years	5 to 17 years	18 to 24 years	25 to 34 years	35 to 44 years	45 to 54 years	55 to 64 years	65 to 74 years	75 years and over	Median age	Percent female	Census counts 1990	Census counts 2000	Percent change 1990–2000	Percent change 2000–2010
	12	13	14	15	16	17	18	19	20	21	22	23	24	25	26
ILLINOIS—Cont'd															
Burbank	6.2	18.3	10.5	12.8	12.5	15.0	11.4	7.0	6.3	36.8	50.5	27 600	27 902	1.1	3.7
Calumet City	7.0	21.2	9.7	11.9	13.8	14.0	10.6	6.1	5.7	35.1	54.0	37 840	39 071	3.3	-5.2
Carbondale	4.0	8.3	44.4	16.1	7.2	6.4	6.0	3.3	4.2	23.5	46.9	27 033	20 681	-23.5	25.2
Carol Stream	6.5	18.8	10.0	14.1	13.5	17.5	11.0	4.3	4.3	35.5	51.1	31 759	40 438	27.3	-1.8
Carpentersville	10.1	23.8	9.1	17.1	16.2	11.5	6.8	3.2	2.0	29.4	49.6	23 049	30 586	32.7	23.2
Champaign	5.4	11.9	31.2	16.0	9.8	9.8	8.2	3.9	3.7	25.7	49.1	63 502	67 518	6.3	20.0
Chicago	6.9	16.2	11.2	19.1	14.0	12.6	9.8	5.6	4.7	32.9	51.5	2 783 726	2 896 016	4.0	-6.9
Chicago Heights	8.7	22.0	10.6	13.9	12.4	12.4	9.4	5.4	5.2	31.2	51.1	32 966	32 776	-0.6	-7.6
Cicero	9.8	24.0	11.6	16.4	14.5	10.7	7.0	3.3	2.7	27.8	49.1	67 436	85 616	27.0	-2.0
Collinsville	6.9	15.1	9.6	16.5	12.5	14.6	11.8	6.6	6.5	36.4	51.1	22 424	24 707	10.2	3.5
Crystal Lake	6.1	22.0	8.0	11.5	14.7	17.5	10.2	5.2	4.8	37.0	50.6	24 692	38 000	53.9	7.2
Danville	7.7	18.0	9.1	14.0	11.4	13.3	11.6	7.2	7.7	36.1	50.0	33 828	33 904	0.2	-2.6
Decatur	6.7	15.4	10.8	12.7	10.7	13.9	12.9	7.9	9.0	39.1	53.2	83 900	81 860	-2.4	-7.0
DeKalb	6.0	11.6	37.3	14.4	8.2	8.3	6.7	3.5	4.0	23.6	49.7	35 076	39 018	11.2	12.4
Des Plaines	5.4	14.8	7.7	13.0	12.9	15.8	13.4	8.0	9.2	42.2	51.3	53 414	58 720	9.9	-0.6
Downers Grove	5.5	17.2	7.2	10.6	12.8	17.0	14.5	7.6	7.7	42.6	51.8	47 464	48 724	2.7	-1.8
East St. Louis	8.4	20.9	10.4	11.8	11.3	12.6	11.3	7.3	6.0	33.6	54.6	40 944	31 542	-23.0	-14.4
Elgin	8.8	19.7	9.6	16.0	14.8	12.9	9.6	4.8	3.9	32.5	50.2	77 014	94 487	22.7	14.5
Elk Grove Village	4.9	15.7	8.0	12.3	12.8	17.7	13.8	7.6	7.2	42.4	51.8	33 429	34 727	3.9	-4.6
Elmhurst	6.1	20.4	9.2	7.9	14.0	16.6	11.4	6.7	7.7	40.1	51.8	42 029	42 762	1.7	3.2
Evanston	5.8	13.5	16.7	14.8	13.0	12.8	11.2	6.1	6.1	34.3	52.4	73 233	74 239	1.4	0.3
Freeport	8.7	16.5	8.4	11.5	11.2	14.4	12.2	8.3	10.8	41.3	53.2	25 840	26 443	2.3	-3.0
Galesburg	5.5	14.2	12.4	12.7	11.3	13.3	12.5	8.2	9.9	39.7	49.5	33 530	33 706	0.5	-4.5
Glendale Heights	7.7	18.6	10.6	18.1	14.6	13.1	10.1	4.9	2.4	32.0	49.1	27 915	31 765	13.8	7.7
Glen Ellyn	6.4	21.4	6.3	9.3	13.8	17.1	12.7	6.3	6.8	40.3	51.6	24 919	26 999	8.3	1.7
Glenview	5.2	19.4	5.4	6.6	12.7	16.4	14.6	9.2	10.6	45.5	52.6	38 436	41 847	8.9	6.8
Granite City	6.4	16.5	9.3	13.7	12.5	15.0	11.6	7.0	7.9	38.2	51.5	32 766	31 301	-4.5	+4.6
Gurnee	6.3	21.9	6.9	11.0	15.8	18.1	11.2	4.9	3.9	37.9	52.2	13 715	28 834	110.2	8.5
Hanover Park	7.9	21.5	10.5	15.6	14.8	13.9	9.7	4.1	2.0	31.5	49.5	32 918	38 278	16.3	-0.8
Harvey	8.3	23.2	11.0	13.0	12.4	11.9	9.7	6.4	4.1	30.8	51.3	29 771	30 000	0.8	-15.7
Highland Park	5.3	20.6	4.5	6.1	12.7	16.2	15.3	9.9	9.5	45.4	51.6	30 575	31 365	2.6	-5.1
Hoffman Estates	6.6	18.4	8.2	14.0	14.8	16.2	12.5	6.5	3.9	37.0	50.7	46 363	49 495	6.8	4.8
Joliet	8.9	22.0	9.1	15.5	16.1	12.2	7.9	4.2	4.1	31.7	50.6	77 217	106 221	37.6	38.8
Kankakee	8.8	19.5	10.2	15.1	12.1	12.6	9.8	5.4	6.4	32.2	51.1	27 541	27 491	-0.2	0.2
Lake In the Hills	8.1	23.4	6.7	13.4	19.9	15.2	8.0	3.5	1.7	33.9	50.3	5 900	23 152	292.4	25.1
Lansing	5.9	19.0	8.3	12.6	12.9	15.7	12.0	6.6	6.9	38.3	52.8	28 131	28 332	0.7	0.0
Lombard	6.0	15.5	8.4	14.9	13.6	15.8	11.5	6.5	7.7	39.1	51.8	39 408	42 322	7.4	2.0
McHenry	6.7	19.2	7.9	13.2	15.0	15.7	10.8	5.9	5.6	37.2	51.5	16 343	21 501	31.6	25.5
Melrose Park	9.5	20.5	10.1	16.3	14.3	11.3	8.2	4.9	4.8	30.9	49.9	20 859	23 171	11.1	9.7
Moline	6.5	16.3	8.5	13.7	12.1	13.9	12.9	7.9	8.3	39.2	51.7	43 080	43 768	1.6	-0.7
Mount Prospect	6.3	16.6	7.2	13.3	14.0	15.1	11.6	7.8	8.1	39.7	50.7	53 168	56 265	5.8	-3.7
Mundelein	7.5	19.5	8.4	14.5	14.6	16.2	10.9	5.0	3.5	35.1	49.3	21 224	30 935	45.8	0.4
Naperville	5.8	22.9	7.4	10.4	15.3	18.2	11.4	4.8	3.9	37.9	51.4	85 806	128 358	49.6	10.5
Niles	4.1	12.6	7.2	10.3	11.3	14.7	14.1	10.1	15.6	48.2	52.8	28 375	30 068	6.0	-0.9
Normal	5.2	12.6	35.7	12.4	9.3	9.4	7.2	3.9	4.4	23.5	52.9	40 023	45 386	13.4	15.7
Northbrook	4.5	19.1	4.9	5.4	11.6	16.5	15.7	10.6	11.8	48.0	52.2	32 565	33 435	2.7	-0.8
North Chicago	6.7	13.4	38.4	18.1	7.9	6.5	4.7	2.4	1.9	22.8	39.5	34 978	35 918	2.7	-9.3
Oak Forest	6.1	18.2	9.0	13.3	13.6	16.1	12.4	6.7	4.5	37.7	50.6	26 202	28 051	7.1	-0.3
Oak Lawn	5.6	16.2	8.5	12.5	11.8	15.0	12.3	8.0	10.0	41.2	52.4	56 182	55 245	-1.7	2.6
Oak Park	6.5	17.7	6.2	13.8	15.8	15.6	13.7	6.1	4.6	38.9	53.6	53 648	52 524	-2.1	-1.2
O'Fallon	6.3	21.1	8.1	12.5	15.4	16.5	11.0	5.3	3.8	36.4	51.5	16 064	21 910	36.4	29.1
Orland Park	4.5	17.1	7.5	9.3	11.0	16.5	15.0	9.3	9.8	45.4	52.4	35 720	51 077	43.0	11.1
Oswego	8.4	24.2	6.3	12.9	19.4	13.8	8.2	4.2	2.6	33.9	50.9	3 949	13 326	237.5	127.8
Palatine	6.6	17.3	7.6	15.8	14.9	15.8	11.5	5.9	4.6	36.8	50.6	41 554	65 479	57.6	4.7
Park Ridge	5.0	19.4	6.5	7.1	12.3	17.7	13.7	8.3	10.0	44.8	52.1	37 075	37 775	1.9	-0.8
Pekin	6.4	15.5	8.4	14.5	13.1	14.4	11.8	7.4	8.5	38.9	50.9	32 254	33 857	5.0	0.7
Peoria	7.5	17.1	12.0	14.7	11.9	12.5	11.3	6.3	6.8	34.0	52.4	113 508	112 936	-0.5	1.8
Plainfield	8.8	26.4	6.0	10.7	21.1	14.1	7.6	3.2	2.0	33.8	50.4	4 557	13 038	186.1	203.6
Quincy	6.6	15.7	10.2	12.7	11.2	13.6	11.7	7.9	10.4	39.4	52.1	39 682	40 366	1.7	0.7
Rockford	7.6	18.2	9.3	13.8	12.7	13.4	11.1	6.5	7.4	35.8	51.7	142 815	150 115	5.1	1.8
Rock Island	6.7	15.7	12.7	12.7	11.0	13.5	12.3	7.2	8.2	37.0	52.0	40 630	39 684	-2.3	-1.7
Romeoville	8.1	22.4	10.8	14.7	17.5	12.0	7.1	4.7	2.5	31.3	50.6	14 101	21 153	50.0	87.6
Round Lake Beach	8.8	24.1	9.5	15.3	16.2	12.9	7.6	3.5	2.0	30.2	49.6	16 406	25 859	57.6	9.0
St. Charles	5.5	19.4	7.6	11.9	13.9	16.0	13.2	6.4	6.0	39.4	49.8	22 636	27 896	23.2	18.2
Schaumburg	6.1	14.3	7.7	17.7	14.5	14.9	12.6	6.7	5.6	37.8	51.7	68 586	75 386	9.9	-1.5
Skokie	5.3	16.5	7.9	11.3	12.1	15.0	14.5	8.2	9.2	42.6	52.6	59 432	63 348	6.6	2.3
Springfield	6.5	16.4	9.5	14.0	11.9	14.4	13.0	7.1	7.1	38.2	52.8	105 412	111 454	5.7	4.3
Streamwood	7.9	18.4	8.1	16.0	15.9	14.7	10.9	5.1	2.9	34.7	50.4	31 197	36 407	16.7	9.5
Tinley Park	5.8	17.6	8.0	12.6	12.6	16.9	13.3	7.0	6.3	40.0	52.0	37 115	48 401	30.4	17.2
Urbana	4.5	8.2	38.0	18.1	7.7	7.8	7.1	3.8	4.9	24.8	49.9	36 383	36 395	0.0	13.3
Vernon Hills	6.6	20.3	6.2	11.4	17.0	17.7	11.6	4.5	4.8	38.5	52.0	15 319	20 120	31.3	24.8

Table D. Cities — Households, Group Quarters, Crime, and Education

City	Households, 2010 Number	Persons per house-hold	Percent Female family house-holder[1]	Percent One-person	Persons in group quarters, 2010 Total	Institutional Total	Persons in nursing facilities	Non-institutional	Serious crimes known to police,[2] 2010 Total Number	Rate[3]	Violent	Property	Population age 25 and older	High school graduate or less	Bachelor's degree or more
	27	28	29	30	31	32	33	34	35	36	37	38	39	40	41
ILLINOIS—Cont'd															
Burbank	9 287	3.09	12.8	18.6	242	186	186	56	678	2 344	232	2 112	18 450	62.8	13.4
Calumet City	13 978	2.65	27.3	31.4	24	4	0	20	2 941	7 940	667	7 273	23 333	47.9	15.6
Carbondale	11 035	2.02	9.2	42.7	3 600	359	193	3 241	1 399	5 401	942	4 459	10 745	22.5	53.8
Carol Stream	14 264	2.78	11.6	23.1	44	44	44	0	626	1 576	111	1 466	25 850	32.5	35.5
Carpentersville	10 852	3.47	14.4	15.5	5	0	0	5	622	1 650	114	1 536	22 101	56.2	20.0
Champaign	32 207	2.25	10.0	35.9	8 514	392	341	8 122	3 189	3 934	930	3 004	40 288	25.6	47.1
Chicago	1 045 560	2.52	17.7	35.0	60 246	27 250	14 382	32 996	148 447	5 507	1 054	4 453	1 770 967	43.1	32.9
Chicago Heights	9 587	3.09	26.0	22.1	644	507	502	137	1 514	5 001	922	4 079	16 934	52.9	13.0
Cicero	22 101	3.79	17.6	15.5	196	173	173	23	2 465	2 938	476	2 463	45 962	71.5	8.0
Collinsville	10 927	2.33	13.2	30.4	65	59	59	6	785	3 069	215	2 854	17 542	41.9	24.3
Crystal Lake	14 421	2.81	10.1	22.1	267	163	163	104	881	2 162	133	2 030	25 873	28.3	39.8
Danville	12 843	2.38	19.7	34.5	2 422	2 243	159	179	2 526	7 648	1 054	6 595	21 176	56.5	15.3
Decatur	32 344	2.23	16.9	35.2	3 918	1 908	1 005	2 010	3 589	4 715	615	4 100	50 091	48.8	18.8
DeKalb	15 386	2.44	11.2	29.7	6 292	363	363	5 929	1 408	3 210	369	2 841	18 937	32.0	34.7
Des Plaines	22 700	2.53	8.8	29.8	888	822	702	66	786	1 347	98	1 249	41 951	41.7	29.5
Downers Grove	19 187	2.46	8.0	29.1	548	176	153	372	988	2 066	88	1 978	32 930	20.4	51.4
East St. Louis	10 119	2.63	40.0	33.4	433	109	90	324	4 327	16 022	6 506	9 516	16 427	55.3	10.9
Elgin	35 094	3.03	13.3	22.4	1 953	1 041	699	912	2 541	2 349	328	2 021	66 327	48.6	24.3
Elk Grove Village	13 307	2.48	9.6	28.4	132	96	96	36	790	2 385	115	2 270	23 187	34.6	32.3
Elmhurst	15 765	2.72	8.1	24.0	1 298	373	373	925	677	1 534	50	1 485	27 978	23.3	54.1
Evanston	30 047	2.25	9.7	37.5	7 024	1 297	1 150	5 727	2 314	3 107	286	2 821	47 557	18.0	64.7
Freeport	11 032	2.26	14.8	36.4	754	613	468	141	929	3 624	191	3 432	18 577	45.4	16.7
Galesburg	13 008	2.19	14.0	37.9	3 771	2 468	485	1 303	1 456	4 522	531	3 991	21 634	55.8	14.0
Glendale Heights	11 257	3.04	12.3	20.4	1	0	0	1	621	1 815	114	1 701	20 337	42.6	26.3
Glen Ellyn	10 424	2.63	8.0	26.0	5	0	0	5	399	1 454	36	1 417	18 008	17.4	61.9
Glenview	16 783	2.62	7.0	24.3	642	606	606	36	752	1 683	145	1 537	31 059	17.8	62.7
Granite City	12 214	2.42	15.4	30.4	256	158	158	98	935	3 132	529	2 603	20 886	59.9	9.7
Gurnee	11 536	2.71	10.5	24.4	89	61	61	28	1 393	4 451	89	4 362	20 070	23.7	46.4
Hanover Park	10 921	3.48	13.7	13.2	0	0	0	0	585	1 541	129	1 412	22 024	45.8	25.6
Harvey	7 947	3.15	32.2	24.1	252	192	192	60	2 167	8 571	1 586	6 985	13 613	60.2	10.8
Highland Park	11 410	2.59	6.9	22.3	255	183	173	72	381	1 280	57	1 223	21 140	11.9	66.0
Hoffman Estates	18 132	2.84	10.1	19.6	435	172	172	263	807	1 555	112	1 443	34 679	30.9	44.4
Joliet	48 019	3.01	14.0	22.1	2 945	2 185	1 189	760	4 733	3 210	368	2 842	86 841	45.8	21.9
Kankakee	9 646	2.67	23.7	31.5	1 810	921	305	889	1 377	5 001	890	4 111	16 625	61.3	9.7
Lake in the Hills	9 544	3.03	8.6	16.0	0	0	0	0	270	932	110	822	17 506	31.0	32.2
Lansing	10 957	2.58	17.9	27.7	91	83	83	8	1 485	5 242	180	5 062	19 085	41.7	21.9
Lombard	17 405	2.45	9.5	30.7	502	288	288	214	1 240	2 873	123	2 750	29 823	29.9	42.7
McHenry	10 075	2.66	10.4	25.3	194	186	186	8	579	2 145	137	2 008	17 890	41.1	25.1
Melrose Park	7 958	3.19	15.4	23.5	52	0	0	52	730	2 873	256	2 617	14 694	67.6	8.9
Moline	18 573	2.32	12.1	33.2	322	280	280	42	1 703	3 916	497	3 420	29 391	42.4	25.8
Mount Prospect	20 564	2.63	8.6	24.9	121	0	0	121	701	1 294	65	1 230	37 950	35.9	38.5
Mundelein	10 507	2.94	9.2	19.6	203	0	0	203	433	1 394	39	1 355	20 264	37.6	39.3
Naperville	50 009	2.79	7.9	20.5	2 489	1 188	1 108	1 301	2 191	1 545	89	1 456	90 001	14.1	65.5
Niles	11 906	2.41	9.4	32.4	1 118	1 100	1 100	18	788	2 644	87	2 557	22 748	50.4	28.1
Normal	17 993	2.45	9.7	27.0	8 332	391	377	7 941	1 643	3 130	278	2 852	25 716	27.5	45.7
Northbrook	12 642	2.57	6.1	22.5	678	611	611	67	458	1 381	24	1 357	23 239	14.6	65.7
North Chicago	6 620	3.00	20.3	27.8	12 741	196	0	12 545	NA	NA	NA	NA	15 003	52.3	16.0
Oak Forest	10 208	2.74	11.5	23.3	43	5	5	38	498	1 781	139	1 642	17 990	44.7	20.1
Oak Lawn	22 361	2.51	11.8	31.4	493	479	479	14	1 206	2 127	157	1 970	38 831	45.7	26.0
Oak Park	22 670	2.27	12.2	36.2	383	255	224	128	1 917	3 695	370	3 325	35 575	10.9	68.6
O'Fallon	10 747	2.63	12.5	22.9	0	0	0	0	737	2 606	117	2 489	17 284	22.0	45.9
Orland Park	21 639	2.60	8.6	24.7	464	451	451	13	1 182	2 082	41	2 042	39 347	35.4	37.2
Oswego	9 935	3.05	8.5	15.3	52	47	47	5	505	1 664	105	1 558	17 811	22.3	44.3
Palatine	26 876	2.54	9.0	27.8	168	134	134	34	927	1 352	44	1 308	45 539	29.5	46.6
Park Ridge	14 118	2.62	8.7	24.8	492	434	399	58	586	1 564	40	1 523	25 455	24.3	51.1
Pekin	13 820	2.32	13.8	31.6	2 042	1 933	281	109	959	2 813	340	2 473	23 613	50.9	16.5
Peoria	47 152	2.36	16.5	34.4	3 832	1 313	1 109	2 519	6 042	5 254	764	4 489	72 590	37.8	32.5
Plainfield	11 920	3.31	7.9	11.5	109	109	109	0	535	1 352	53	1 299	22 237	26.3	44.5
Quincy	17 151	2.25	12.6	35.6	2 087	1 378	1 015	709	1 525	3 333	458	3 295	26 877	51.4	20.2
Rockford	59 973	2.48	17.7	31.9	4 179	2 881	1 728	1 298	10 118	6 619	1 493	5 125	101 097	52.2	20.6
Rock Island	15 930	2.30	15.3	35.1	2 441	685	452	1 756	1 613	4 134	787	3 347	24 962	45.6	22.7
Romeoville	11 987	3.21	12.8	16.1	1 188	0	0	1 188	808	2 036	81	1 956	23 615	45.1	24.9
Round Lake Beach	8 055	3.48	12.2	16.8	139	139	139	0	714	2 534	227	2 307	15 489	59.3	15.8
St. Charles	12 424	2.56	8.8	25.5	1 211	1 121	161	90	730	2 214	88	2 126	22 244	28.8	45.1
Schaumburg	31 539	2.34	9.3	32.4	414	374	374	40	2 376	3 201	115	3 086	51 682	28.9	43.7
Skokie	23 531	2.72	12.0	23.9	706	494	475	212	1 957	3 021	242	2 778	45 440	28.9	46.8
Springfield	50 714	2.23	14.8	36.7	3 396	1 489	831	1 907	9 019	7 758	1 249	6 509	77 904	36.3	31.8
Streamwood	13 034	3.04	10.6	18.7	288	268	160	20	733	1 839	88	1 751	25 953	43.5	28.4
Tinley Park	21 666	2.62	9.5	26.1	45	0	0	45	1 024	1 806	86	1 719	39 409	36.1	31.1
Urbana	16 961	2.02	8.2	42.5	7 050	781	339	6 269	1 437	3 484	419	3 064	19 712	22.2	53.9
Vernon Hills	9 517	2.63	8.4	25.9	43	43	43	0	679	2 704	24	2 680	15 987	22.4	55.7

1. No spouse present.   2. Data for serious crimes have not been adjusted for underreporting. This may affect comparability between geographic areas and over time.   3. Per 100,000 population estimated by the FBI.   4. Persons 25 years old and over.

Table D. Cities — Income, Poverty, and Housing

City	Money income, 2008–2010 Per capita income[1] (dollars)	Households Median income	Households Percent with income of $200,000 or more	Households Percent with income of less than $25,000	Families with income below poverty (percent)	Housing units, 2010 Total	Percent change, 2000–2010	Vacant units for sale or rent[2]	Occupied Housing units 2008–2010 Total	Owner-occupied Percent	Median value[3] (dollars)	Median owner costs as a percent of income With a mortgage[4]	Without a mortgage[5]
	42	43	44	45	46	47	48	49	50	51	52	53	54
ILLINOIS—Cont'd													
Burbank	20 606	54 279	1.8	18.8	7.5	9 721	2.0	434	8 559	80.4	231 300	29.1	13.9
Calumet City	21 161	41 961	0.8	27.1	15.7	15 646	-1.8	1 668	14 556	58.6	147 200	29.5	15.2
Carbondale	15 030	19 214	1.6	56.2	26.1	12 419	12.7	1 384	9 171	32.5	114 000	20.0	11.1
Carol Stream	28 700	70 774	3.1	17.0	8.2	15 050	6.2	786	14 725	68.3	259 400	26.3	14.1
Carpentersville	20 087	57 134	2.5	16.1	11.2	11 583	29.6	731	10 938	80.3	177 500	32.9	14.2
Champaign	23 244	39 873	3.2	35.0	11.3	34 434	20.4	2 227	30 907	46.8	151 700	22.1	11.3
Chicago	26 967	46 195	4.7	29.6	17.7	1 194 337	3.6	148 777	1 029 203	46.6	264 200	29.8	15.2
Chicago Heights	15 589	41 469	0.4	31.0	22.9	11 060	-3.7	1 473	9 289	61.4	137 000	27.6	13.4
Cicero	14 674	45 466	0.4	25.0	17.4	24 329	-1.3	2 228	21 715	52.3	201 300	35.5	15.6
Collinsville	26 803	46 444	1.4	26.9	12.6	11 891	7.1	964	11 407	61.8	122 900	21.1	13.5
Crystal Lake	30 058	74 663	4.5	11.7	3.0	15 176	13.6	755	14 411	78.6	232 200	26.5	15.5
Danville	18 233	33 777	0.8	41.0	24.6	14 719	-1.0	1 876	13 404	56.1	65 800	20.4	12.3
Decatur	22 296	36 437	2.2	33.2	14.5	36 134	-3.0	3 790	31 107	63.3	80 300	20.8	11.7
DeKalb	18 488	36 829	2.3	38.0	13.7	16 436	21.4	1 050	15 184	43.6	181 400	28.0	14.2
Des Plaines	29 251	61 792	2.8	16.6	4.6	24 075	4.9	1 375	22 319	80.2	276 900	28.9	16.8
Downers Grove	41 486	77 660	10.4	12.0	2.9	20 478	4.9	1 291	18 480	83.2	351 600	23.9	14.5
East St. Louis	11 323	19 130	0.0	61.7	41.5	12 055	-6.6	1 936	11 075	47.5	60 200	40.3	17.8
Elgin	23 437	56 983	2.1	16.1	10.3	37 848	15.7	2 754	35 769	72.7	208 000	29.8	15.8
Elk Grove Village	32 527	66 083	4.9	13.1	3.4	13 905	3.3	598	13 046	76.2	290 200	26.5	13.7
Elmhurst	40 185	88 373	13.6	12.7	2.4	16 590	2.1	825	15 135	80.4	380 200	25.9	13.1
Evanston	41 307	66 271	13.1	19.4	6.2	33 181	7.7	3 134	28 933	57.6	376 600	26.0	13.7
Freeport	22 537	35 589	1.1	36.6	14.2	12 396	-0.7	1 364	11 471	62.8	82 500	19.7	14.5
Galesburg	17 811	33 765	0.6	38.7	11.6	14 280	1.2	1 272	13 022	56.9	74 800	23.0	12.8
Glendale Heights	24 646	63 515	2.3	14.9	9.3	11 864	7.3	607	10 966	73.7	214 800	28.8	14.0
Glen Ellyn	49 363	90 036	19.2	14.3	2.8	11 051	4.3	627	10 389	78.9	420 700	25.6	14.5
Glenview	52 596	101 937	18.7	12.0	2.4	17 746	12.2	963	16 567	84.8	534 700	27.8	15.2
Granite City	18 730	38 038	0.6	33.7	17.7	13 578	-3.9	1 364	12 436	72.4	85 200	23.4	13.6
Gurnee	35 639	81 018	10.1	10.8	2.3	12 031	11.2	495	11 322	74.9	288 400	24.8	17.2
Hanover Park	21 684	67 018	3.1	11.9	8.0	11 483	0.7	562	10 681	80.0	215 700	32.4	12.2
Harvey	13 145	31 013	0.4	40.2	26.1	9 805	-3.6	1 858	7 197	54.1	105 600	36.1	16.2
Highland Park	61 287	106 231	22.3	10.1	4.5	12 256	2.8	846	11 856	84.1	558 200	29.0	16.3
Hoffman Estates	31 906	76 772	6.2	9.7	4.2	18 970	8.5	838	17 490	77.5	292 100	26.0	13.3
Joliet	21 866	59 236	0.9	18.8	10.8	51 285	34.3	3 266	46 992	73.6	191 500	28.0	14.1
Kankakee	14 816	30 975	0.8	40.8	24.0	10 935	-0.1	1 289	9 503	49.8	99 200	28.1	14.7
Lake in the Hills	30 298	82 304	3.8	8.4	4.1	9 885	25.8	341	9 687	90.1	240 100	29.3	12.7
Lansing	24 056	50 593	0.6	21.7	7.5	11 741	0.1	784	11 145	73.3	152 600	27.5	13.4
Lombard	32 800	69 082	3.8	15.1	1.8	18 454	8.9	1 049	17 366	70.6	270 700	27.2	13.8
McHenry	29 524	65 103	3.6	19.7	6.6	10 741	32.1	666	10 116	77.9	221 800	27.3	14.8
Melrose Park	16 346	44 915	0.0	25.4	14.1	8 525	7.2	567	7 480	54.4	256 000	34.6	16.6
Moline	26 808	45 883	3.5	23.6	6.2	19 856	1.9	1 283	18 047	68.9	112 200	21.2	11.8
Mount Prospect	32 576	67 823	5.2	12.4	3.3	21 836	-1.1	1 272	20 428	73.2	332 000	27.8	15.1
Mundelein	33 533	80 433	9.2	8.0	4.0	10 992	8.3	485	10 343	81.7	257 300	27.1	15.8
Naperville	44 331	99 488	14.4	7.9	3.0	52 270	14.7	2 261	49 001	76.3	394 400	24.8	11.6
Niles	26 481	47 666	2.2	23.1	6.3	12 572	1.9	666	11 289	76.0	313 100	31.8	16.4
Normal	22 981	52 265	1.1	29.9	7.7	18 816	20.3	823	18 207	57.8	160 800	21.8	11.2
Northbrook	52 770	102 267	20.4	11.5	4.1	13 434	7.6	792	12 341	89.3	523 400	26.8	14.2
North Chicago	18 263	46 051	2.2	26.4	19.0	7 745	-7.3	1 125	6 891	37.6	142 200	36.7	18.8
Oak Forest	26 346	72 004	1.9	15.6	5.9	10 672	6.8	464	9 361	81.5	226 400	26.6	13.4
Oak Lawn	28 567	57 983	2.7	19.3	6.1	23 517	2.6	1 156	21 737	83.3	228 400	26.6	16.6
Oak Park	45 681	73 625	12.3	15.7	4.7	24 519	3.4	1 849	21 721	64.8	391 100	26.5	13.9
O'Fallon	31 154	72 405	5.5	14.8	7.3	11 414	32.7	667	9 966	65.8	200 500	23.5	11.3
Orland Park	34 589	77 795	6.2	12.1	2.5	22 443	17.6	804	20 988	89.3	300 500	27.1	15.2
Oswego	33 527	95 967	5.7	5.0	1.9	10 388	125.0	453	9 457	87.6	264 300	25.2	12.7
Palatine	34 222	72 045	6.8	13.7	6.5	28 621	9.2	1 745	25 511	71.1	303 300	26.8	14.8
Park Ridge	41 261	82 901	12.6	10.4	2.2	15 030	2.8	912	13 807	85.4	441 100	29.1	14.5
Pekin	24 177	43 761	1.7	25.6	10.1	14 714	5.1	894	14 046	75.5	100 600	21.0	12.4
Peoria	28 857	45 872	4.8	30.1	15.7	52 621	7.3	5 469	46 846	59.9	123 400	20.2	11.7
Plainfield	31 620	103 820	6.4	6.8	3.5	12 532	174.2	612	10 746	89.3	316 900	27.7	14.5
Quincy	22 799	39 266	2.2	32.5	13.2	18 655	3.7	1 504	16 648	65.2	94 600	20.9	11.3
Rockford	20 958	37 537	2.1	33.7	19.5	66 700	4.9	6 727	59 781	58.5	113 300	24.3	14.5
Rock Island	23 216	43 553	2.3	29.8	8.4	17 422	-0.5	1 492	15 185	70.5	101 100	21.1	12.7
Romeoville	22 829	66 314	1.7	9.2	5.2	12 623	71.3	636	11 637	88.7	204 000	30.8	15.8
Round Lake Beach	19 136	57 276	1.3	17.5	13.7	8 587	13.5	532	8 063	81.3	171 600	29.9	10.0
St. Charles	39 222	74 375	10.2	12.2	3.0	13 157	18.9	733	12 158	70.5	301 100	27.6	15.8
Schaumburg	35 183	65 988	4.3	14.6	5.8	33 610	1.6	2 071	30 841	67.7	252 900	26.8	13.4
Skokie	32 256	66 175	6.8	17.2	6.1	25 066	5.8	1 535	22 839	73.1	339 600	30.6	14.2
Springfield	27 987	48 414	3.3	26.0	12.4	55 729	3.4	5 015	49 833	65.7	114 500	20.6	12.0
Streamwood	27 531	68 138	3.4	11.0	3.6	13 629	10.0	595	13 384	85.6	225 300	28.8	13.5
Tinley Park	31 876	77 412	3.6	12.0	3.4	22 491	24.7	825	21 225	85.4	250 500	26.2	14.8
Urbana	18 900	32 773	1.9	40.4	14.5	19 090	25.2	2 129	16 025	36.5	146 500	21.4	10.0
Vernon Hills	38 409	82 003	11.5	8.2	2.2	9 956	25.2	439	9 121	76.7	333 300	27.4	18.7

1. Based on population estimated by the American Community Survey.   2. Includes units rented or sold but not occupied.   3. Specified owner-occupied units; $1,000,000 represents $1,000,000 or more.   4. 50.0 represents 50 percent or more.   5. 10.0 represents 10 percent or less.

Table D. Cities — Housing, Labor Force, and Employment

City	Occupied housing units, 2008–2010 (cont.)				Migration, 2008–2010		Civilian labor force, 2010				Civilian employment[4], 2008–2010			
									Unemployment			Percent		
	Percent renter occupied	Median gross rent[1]	Median rent as a percent of income[2]	Percent with no vehicle available	Percent who lived in the same house one year ago	Percent who lived outside this city one year ago	Total	Percent change, 2009–2010	Total	Rate[3]	Population age 16 and older	In labor force	Full-year full-time worker	Households with no workers (percent)
	55	56	57	58	59	60	61	62	63	64	65	66	67	68
ILLINOIS—Cont'd														
Burbank	19.6	899	31.3	5.8	90.6	7.3	15 130	5.5	1 582	10.5	22 227	65.2	40.2	22.0
Calumet City	41.4	844	32.9	13.2	86.8	11.4	18 432	1.9	2 637	14.3	28 946	64.5	40.4	30.7
Carbondale	67.5	605	46.5	14.8	58.1	27.0	14 204	-0.7	1 123	7.9	22 687	55.6	20.7	34.0
Carol Stream	31.7	932	33.0	6.6	88.7	7.0	22 941	-0.2	2 120	9.2	31 126	76.4	46.8	18.5
Carpentersville	19.7	958	28.7	3.7	91.2	6.3	18 968	1.3	2 543	13.4	26 549	72.5	46.2	11.7
Champaign	53.2	766	38.1	12.7	66.4	17.6	41 977	-2.1	3 674	8.8	67 779	62.5	33.1	21.2
Chicago	53.4	894	32.2	26.5	83.5	3.8	1 261 515	-4.3	147 340	11.7	2 140 548	66.2	41.2	25.9
Chicago Heights	38.6	849	43.3	13.7	86.5	10.0	13 463	-0.8	2 207	16.4	21 507	62.2	37.2	29.3
Cicero	47.7	776	30.4	11.1	85.3	6.2	33 807	4.5	4 444	13.1	56 931	69.9	43.1	17.5
Collinsville	38.2	725	30.4	6.3	87.0	8.6	13 989	-2.5	1 349	9.6	20 410	67.1	42.4	27.7
Crystal Lake	21.4	1 102	28.9	3.9	92.1	4.8	21 974	-1.5	2 186	9.9	30 958	72.6	45.8	17.1
Danville	43.9	575	32.0	17.9	79.2	7.8	13 488	3.1	1 812	13.4	25 994	56.4	34.5	38.7
Decatur	36.7	597	29.1	12.0	81.1	7.1	36 276	-2.4	4 835	13.3	60 240	58.5	36.0	35.2
DeKalb	56.4	732	43.5	9.3	64.9	19.0	23 611	-2.8	2 071	8.8	37 116	66.5	27.2	25.6
Des Plaines	19.8	948	30.5	7.6	91.8	5.2	31 147	3.0	3 220	10.3	47 566	66.7	43.3	26.3
Downers Grove	16.8	928	27.4	4.7	91.8	5.9	26 521	-1.9	2 099	7.9	38 316	70.2	44.0	20.7
East St. Louis	52.5	520	35.8	24.5	83.5	9.3	9 354	-6.1	1 707	18.2	20 189	48.1	25.6	49.2
Elgin	27.3	889	32.3	4.5	86.3	6.1	59 556	2.1	7 482	12.6	79 892	72.3	46.9	17.1
Elk Grove Village	23.8	956	29.0	6.7	92.5	6.0	19 960	0.0	1 755	8.8	27 060	72.2	46.8	22.2
Elmhurst	19.6	1 072	31.1	5.8	90.3	7.2	23 856	-3.2	1 805	7.6	33 576	66.6	40.2	23.8
Evanston	42.4	1 088	32.9	14.9	79.9	10.1	40 861	-3.1	3 238	7.9	60 705	65.4	39.3	24.3
Freeport	37.2	582	35.6	13.0	84.2	7.4	12 662	-1.4	1 623	12.8	20 840	63.1	35.2	37.6
Galesburg	43.1	571	29.4	12.8	85.7	7.7	15 116	5.0	1 493	9.9	26 433	51.5	29.3	39.3
Glendale Heights	26.3	1 003	31.9	4.0	87.7	8.9	20 263	7.2	1 956	9.7	24 229	80.4	52.2	12.9
Glen Ellyn	23.1	838	28.0	3.8	91.2	6.4	14 584	1.6	1 038	7.1	20 514	64.9	43.3	23.7
Glenview	15.2	1 365	30.5	4.3	92.0	5.6	23 124	-2.7	1 635	7.1	35 007	61.3	40.6	26.9
Granite City	27.6	642	33.2	7.1	86.8	6.1	14 638	-5.8	1 708	11.7	23 829	62.0	36.9	36.4
Gurnee	25.1	1 041	30.6	2.9	87.9	9.3	17 157	2.9	1 583	9.2	23 180	75.3	50.5	16.0
Hanover Park	20.0	957	27.8	2.3	93.1	5.2	21 628	3.9	2 459	11.4	27 670	78.2	49.3	9.2
Harvey	45.9	886	33.1	16.5	82.9	10.8	10 259	-7.0	1 821	17.8	16 794	59.2	29.3	39.9
Highland Park	15.9	1 340	30.5	3.3	90.3	6.6	15 180	-4.6	1 054	6.9	23 455	65.8	39.4	23.8
Hoffman Estates	22.5	1 073	27.0	3.9	88.8	7.9	30 052	-2.6	2 557	8.5	40 485	72.8	49.1	13.7
Joliet	26.4	808	33.5	6.3	86.9	7.8	73 559	1.8	9 616	13.1	105 210	70.7	43.2	20.1
Kankakee	50.2	650	39.3	16.1	78.7	6.8	12 077	3.0	2 007	16.6	20 538	62.4	32.5	34.9
Lake in the Hills	9.9	1 192	27.7	0.2	93.8	6.1	16 756	-1.5	1 552	9.3	20 577	78.5	52.5	9.9
Lansing	26.7	856	32.7	5.2	91.5	6.8	15 181	6.3	1 728	11.4	22 045	67.8	45.0	26.9
Lombard	29.4	1 138	27.7	5.6	86.3	9.3	24 579	1.2	2 183	8.9	35 341	72.8	46.5	22.4
McHenry	22.1	942	41.2	5.4	90.0	7.7	15 315	1.2	1 561	10.2	20 722	73.2	41.0	22.9
Melrose Park	45.6	829	32.3	10.1	92.1	5.8	12 447	NA	1 430	11.5	17 877	69.8	42.5	20.2
Moline	31.1	639	26.7	6.7	86.5	6.6	23 569	0.9	2 146	9.1	35 014	68.8	41.8	26.1
Mount Prospect	26.8	939	27.0	7.0	90.4	6.6	30 361	1.9	2 386	7.9	43 335	67.7	46.0	24.6
Mundelein	18.3	999	23.5	1.7	91.7	4.9	16 616	-6.3	1 829	11.0	24 247	78.6	50.4	13.4
Naperville	23.7	1 163	25.7	2.8	87.6	8.3	75 776	-0.3	5 986	7.9	105 519	70.6	46.1	14.1
Niles	24.0	929	37.6	12.1	91.4	6.0	14 611	4.0	1 257	8.6	25 146	54.2	35.2	36.5
Normal	42.2	680	39.7	6.4	67.0	21.4	27 790	0.8	2 089	7.5	42 976	68.0	34.6	21.3
Northbrook	10.7	1 619	40.0	3.4	93.2	4.7	16 678	-1.4	1 165	7.0	26 604	61.3	39.8	25.0
North Chicago	62.4	988	29.0	7.9	50.5	43.0	8 658	-6.9	1 519	17.5	26 662	77.1	49.1	24.9
Oak Forest	18.5	922	23.2	3.6	93.3	5.1	15 987	1.4	1 627	10.2	21 645	71.2	40.8	20.1
Oak Lawn	16.7	875	27.7	7.4	91.5	6.2	28 219	7.0	3 005	10.6	45 448	65.3	40.0	28.4
Oak Park	35.2	949	29.0	12.7	85.9	9.1	31 412	5.1	2 357	7.5	39 747	74.2	51.3	19.1
O'Fallon	34.2	961	27.5	5.2	86.4	10.6	14 187	1.9	1 191	8.4	20 400	71.7	46.3	18.5
Orland Park	10.7	946	32.0	3.8	93.2	5.0	29 605	3.1	2 630	8.9	45 223	63.7	39.0	27.7
Oswego	12.4	1 286	29.9	2.7	90.5	7.0	16 900	-3.2	1 497	8.9	20 500	76.6	51.9	12.3
Palatine	28.9	998	28.8	2.8	86.8	8.3	41 462	2.8	3 545	8.5	52 654	75.5	50.6	16.5
Park Ridge	14.6	1 128	26.7	4.4	94.5	2.6	19 342	1.9	1 454	7.5	29 535	65.9	42.0	24.5
Pekin	24.5	583	28.3	5.9	85.2	8.5	17 839	1.3	2 219	12.4	27 408	60.6	39.9	29.6
Peoria	40.1	676	31.4	12.7	79.5	8.2	57 076	-1.4	6 440	11.3	89 574	63.8	38.6	28.9
Plainfield	10.7	1 414	24.8	0.8	87.7	9.8	21 244	6.3	1 924	9.1	25 666	73.4	50.4	9.7
Quincy	34.8	586	28.3	9.6	82.2	6.3	22 344	0.7	1 808	8.1	32 671	63.8	41.6	31.2
Rockford	41.5	659	33.8	10.6	85.2	5.5	70 836	-1.2	11 997	16.9	119 925	61.0	34.8	33.0
Rock Island	29.5	584	29.4	14.3	82.2	9.7	19 993	1.8	2 013	10.1	30 585	62.2	38.5	32.3
Romeoville	11.3	1 317	30.0	2.2	90.7	6.1	23 323	5.0	2 461	10.6	28 203	72.0	48.1	14.6
Round Lake Beach	18.7	873	43.8	3.6	88.2	7.9	15 051	1.3	2 185	14.5	19 112	77.5	48.5	10.6
St. Charles	29.5	1 007	29.6	3.7	85.1	9.7	19 214	1.6	1 610	8.4	25 629	72.4	47.3	19.3
Schaumburg	32.3	1 159	28.5	5.5	85.4	10.4	46 188	3.6	3 693	8.0	59 704	75.0	50.2	18.8
Skokie	26.9	1 010	31.2	9.4	89.1	5.4	32 981	-2.0	2 804	8.5	52 958	64.8	40.7	24.7
Springfield	34.3	671	31.1	9.4	81.1	8.4	63 728	-0.4	5 360	8.4	91 382	67.9	44.7	27.2
Streamwood	14.4	1 440	33.4	1.2	92.2	6.5	23 696	7.1	2 427	10.2	31 174	77.5	53.7	11.5
Tinley Park	14.6	933	27.4	3.4	93.5	4.8	31 478	-3.7	3 010	9.6	45 626	70.2	45.6	21.9
Urbana	63.5	728	37.0	18.8	58.4	20.4	20 547	0.2	1 938	9.4	36 672	58.1	26.1	31.5
Vernon Hills	23.3	1 318	32.9	8.3	90.6	8.0	14 662	NA	1 163	7.9	18 570	73.3	50.0	16.6

1. $2,000 represents $2,000 or more.   2. 50.0 represents 50 percent or more.   3. Percent of civilian labor force.   4. Persons 16 years old and over.

City	Value of residential construction authorized by building permits, 2010			Wholesale trade,[1] 2007				Retail trade,[2] 2007			
	New construction ($1,000)	Number of housing units	Percent single family	Number of establishments	Number of employees	Sales (mil dol)	Annual payroll (mil dol)	Number of establishments	Number of employees	Sales (mil dol)	Annual payroll (mil dol)
	69	70	71	72	73	74	75	76	77	78	79
ILLINOIS—Cont'd											
Burbank	1 005	8	100.0	5	17	6.6	0.5	96	1 592	367.9	30.0
Calumet City	0	0	0.0	10	96	35.0	6.0	186	3 191	529.7	64.5
Carbondale	4 236	60	16.7	9	134	29.9	4.5	175	3 185	557.1	55.4
Carol Stream	786	11	100.0	117	3 082	6 930.4	180.9	93	1 557	385.2	35.6
Carpentersville	5 769	35	100.0	12	95	29.3	5.2	57	876	239.0	19.4
Champaign	35 759	329	19.1	61	1 644	922.4	61.0	405	7 172	1 354.4	126.8
Chicago	451 267	1 877	8.7	2 449	34 677	28 519.3	1 827.9	7 544	89 349	19 842.7	2 114.8
Chicago Heights	0	0	0.0	33	311	353.2	16.2	79	845	167.2	18.7
Cicero	0	0	0.0	46	635	479.6	29.8	135	1 996	536.7	43.1
Collinsville	547	3	100.0	33	334	208.9	16.5	103	1 581	473.0	39.8
Crystal Lake	2 194	12	100.0	82	712	485.2	37.7	223	4 188	1 077.4	101.0
Danville	560	5	100.0	44	D	D	D	168	2 405	512.3	48.6
Decatur	3 908	20	100.0	83	992	491.9	46.1	316	4 449	1 120.4	101.9
DeKalb	660	3	100.0	18	178	44.9	6.8	152	3 008	618.0	56.4
Des Plaines	6 576	37	100.0	138	3 148	2 063.7	200.8	197	2 520	740.9	65.1
Downers Grove	9 415	24	100.0	131	2 098	3 132.4	151.2	264	5 066	1 526.6	126.1
East St. Louis	8 716	38	21.1	17	239	351.1	8.5	65	516	80.8	10.4
Elgin	22 290	182	100.0	196	3 454	3 304.3	212.6	223	3 337	1 099.2	97.6
Elk Grove Village	340	1	100.0	499	7 758	4 987.2	429.0	124	2 844	815.0	88.0
Elmhurst	64 383	229	20.1	139	3 424	1 709.5	264.4	155	2 185	812.3	66.6
Evanston	13 251	156	6.4	53	552	395.3	26.9	250	4 311	1 010.6	108.0
Freeport	0	0	0.0	26	165	62.8	4.9	114	1 715	377.6	35.6
Galesburg	0	0	0.0	23	230	109.7	6.9	171	3 358	618.3	62.8
Glendale Heights	0	0	0.0	67	1 673	1 111.6	100.4	59	1 403	392.6	35.5
Glen Ellyn	6 008	13	100.0	34	280	276.9	14.7	111	1 443	359.8	33.6
Glenview	8 815	14	100.0	110	1 645	1 127.2	105.9	215	4 002	1 456.7	162.6
Granite City	7 838	58	25.9	29	360	363.2	19.0	86	1 270	297.8	29.6
Gurnee	341	1	100.0	73	1 072	777.1	68.7	273	5 456	1 116.7	102.0
Hanover Park	2 072	20	100.0	39	1 395	1 052.6	69.9	72	995	186.4	19.5
Harvey	0	0	0.0	26	297	108.6	14.2	67	531	175.7	15.2
Highland Park	10 572	44	31.8	67	198	591.3	18.2	204	3 007	1 003.3	86.1
Hoffman Estates	1 958	10	100.0	69	725	798.8	62.9	133	2 411	930.6	76.5
Joliet	13 832	84	92.9	98	1 099	511.8	51.9	420	8 659	1 985.3	185.5
Kankakee	244	2	0.0	22	207	134.8	10.4	89	1 057	246.3	23.5
Lake in the Hills	672	3	100.0	21	194	207.2	8.5	49	733	195.1	18.2
Lansing	0	0	0.0	25	301	109.2	18.7	122	2 282	479.0	48.4
Lombard	1 340	5	100.0	122	1 332	1 141.5	68.8	249	4 758	920.4	94.4
McHenry	1 315	8	100.0	46	2 056	789.1	118.8	148	2 636	607.7	57.3
Melrose Park	255	3	100.0	63	2 330	942.2	80.1	94	2 167	537.3	45.6
Moline	0	0	0.0	38	439	224.9	19.1	284	4 919	994.8	100.1
Mount Prospect	799	3	100.0	91	1 951	1 887.6	125.3	168	3 688	3 841.8	100.5
Mundelein	6 071	49	100.0	68	1 130	791.1	87.4	107	1 519	305.3	33.8
Naperville	35 446	94	100.0	217	4 725	3 000.6	391.0	495	9 752	3 362.0	262.2
Niles	1 919	3	100.0	89	1 459	610.0	80.3	276	6 189	1 618.3	147.0
Normal	14 864	177	45.2	23	711	372.6	39.8	134	2 868	636.4	56.4
Northbrook	16 359	24	100.0	212	2 524	2 692.6	169.5	257	4 273	1 038.9	117.9
North Chicago	0	0	0.0	16	451	333.7	29.7	34	207	71.4	5.1
Oak Forest	738	4	100.0	21	124	72.8	5.8	54	780	241.7	18.6
Oak Lawn	901	5	100.0	25	96	36.3	3.3	184	3 814	1 106.2	101.1
Oak Park	835	2	100.0	20	35	13.3	2.0	187	1 743	315.3	36.1
O'Fallon	53 782	372	37.6	17	74	23.5	3.2	109	2 493	812.5	64.8
Orland Park	9 330	38	100.0	50	345	100.6	13.0	398	8 924	1 900.6	187.3
Oswego	17 534	116	100.0	20	110	34.4	4.8	91	1 908	403.2	39.9
Palatine	6 055	16	100.0	89	486	450.0	26.7	191	3 270	831.7	74.4
Park Ridge	3 454	8	100.0	49	236	237.4	14.5	100	1 180	389.5	35.1
Pekin	5 572	30	100.0	16	210	128.5	6.9	151	2 363	561.9	53.1
Peoria	47 373	349	41.8	173	2 397	1 188.0	113.9	585	9 177	1 895.2	190.9
Plainfield	15 997	59	100.0	34	303	230.6	23.0	115	2 166	471.5	43.5
Quincy	20 314	138	36.2	68	1 276	563.7	45.8	281	4 382	838.5	81.4
Rockford	2 705	26	92.3	204	3 253	1 871.7	134.9	544	9 578	2 276.6	216.3
Rock Island	9 912	79	11.4	63	1 634	828.0	74.6	97	1 055	213.7	22.4
Romeoville	1 876	9	100.0	55	1 127	890.7	56.9	65	841	224.4	20.3
Round Lake Beach	0	0	0.0	5	9	2.9	0.5	65	1 537	313.6	29.8
St. Charles	2 589	8	100.0	113	1 209	1 240.5	64.2	210	4 171	996.5	97.4
Schaumburg	0	0	0.0	277	4 190	3 955.1	299.1	551	13 348	3 290.2	320.6
Skokie	1 100	2	100.0	147	D	D	D	367	6 024	1 224.5	134.4
Springfield	41 210	205	51.7	120	2 176	1 396.8	84.6	608	10 676	2 366.9	215.1
Streamwood	728	6	100.0	24	175	59.0	8.6	69	1 632	300.9	32.8
Tinley Park	1 745	8	100.0	59	702	429.5	37.3	167	3 799	1 134.9	94.2
Urbana	5 086	30	93.3	25	692	773.0	26.1	89	1 616	446.7	40.0
Vernon Hills	24 276	235	1.7	67	2 832	1 637.7	156.1	227	6 239	2 720.0	182.3

1. Merchant wholesalers except manufacturers' sales branches and offices.   2. Establishments with payroll.

Table D. Cities — Real Estate, Professional Services, and Manufacturing

City	Real estate and rental and leasing, 2007				Professional, scientific, and technical services,[1] 2007				Manufacturing, 2007			
	Number of establish-ments	Number of employees	Receipts (mil dol)	Annual payroll (mil dol)	Number of establish-ments	Number of employees	Receipts (mil dol)	Annual payroll (mil dol)	Number of establish-ments	Number of employees	Receipts (mil dol)	Annual payroll (mil dol)
	80	81	82	83	84	85	86	87	88	89	90	91
ILLINOIS—Cont'd												
Burbank	14	63	11.4	2.0	28	92	7.0	2.2	NA	NA	NA	NA
Calumet City	19	79	32.1	1.6	29	D	D	D	NA	NA	NA	NA
Carbondale	48	282	31.6	5.0	64	D	D	D	NA	NA	NA	NA
Carol Stream	49	284	44.9	9.8	97	D	D	D	101	5 322	1 527.9	259.4
Carpentersville	20	100	19.0	3.2	36	126	18.0	6.7	28	1 968	535.8	86.1
Champaign	116	1 040	242.6	32.3	263	D	D	D	56	1 898	897.7	74.7
Chicago	3 479	28 882	8 128.6	1 706.8	9 751	139 501	30 057.1	11 723.3	2 185	73 447	22 115.6	3 113.1
Chicago Heights	20	153	13.2	2.8	34	340	18.6	8.9	60	3 317	1 757.4	163.6
Cicero	24	101	17.0	2.9	38	293	13.3	4.3	93	3 371	1 051.5	157.2
Collinsville	27	170	26.6	5.7	68	471	54.5	19.7	NA	NA	NA	NA
Crystal Lake	59	373	61.6	13.6	214	863	160.2	40.1	90	3 406	751.9	164.9
Danville	41	183	25.1	3.8	62	307	37.5	10.5	52	4 183	1 805.3	185.3
Decatur	80	416	59.1	11.2	139	1 019	106.4	43.9	85	7 555	D	353.6
DeKalb	40	457	41.3	9.3	56	D	D	D	43	1 502	375.6	68.3
Des Plaines	94	1 405	1 224.9	68.6	259	D	D	D	125	9 476	2 294.5	446.1
Downers Grove	109	488	102.1	21.8	376	D	D	D	81	3 524	736.9	185.8
East St. Louis	15	65	7.9	1.7	14	D	D	D	NA	NA	NA	NA
Elgin	96	545	94.4	18.7	249	1 647	245.6	89.1	201	8 938	2 142.4	424.1
Elk Grove Village	66	531	134.4	28.0	172	2 318	373.0	107.1	477	18 094	4 638.5	821.2
Elmhurst	82	532	118.8	29.3	248	1 220	166.6	67.0	82	2 125	401.8	97.0
Evanston	109	629	86.4	19.5	438	D	D	D	61	1 347	315.9	69.6
Freeport	24	76	9.1	1.8	58	364	30.9	12.7	35	2 342	439.9	D
Galesburg	27	129	16.6	2.4	54	D	D	D	33	D	364.0	29.0
Glendale Heights	20	99	59.4	3.6	58	291	30.8	12.0	53	3 209	711.1	140.6
Glen Ellyn	44	165	33.5	7.8	196	821	122.8	48.9	NA	NA	NA	NA
Glenview	100	566	411.8	30.7	280	1 510	146.9	121.5	51	809	200.3	38.2
Granite City	29	213	24.2	5.2	51	D	D	D	33	4 851	2 388.4	276.4
Gurnee	49	276	61.7	12.6	133	367	70.8	19.9	76	2 157	664.5	101.1
Hanover Park	12	23	3.6	0.6	49	148	21.7	6.6	12	536	D	26.7
Harvey	10	75	27.3	3.6	7	46	2.7	1.2	32	1 939	697.4	88.0
Highland Park	68	203	87.2	11.0	245	547	109.4	39.6	28	898	234.8	30.5
Hoffman Estates	47	243	45.1	10.0	231	2 663	413.1	210.1	24	822	266.2	76.8
Joliet	101	478	77.1	14.7	233	D	D	D	84	3 672	1 596.7	201.9
Kankakee	27	93	14.2	2.5	58	D	D	D	31	1 912	969.7	106.2
Lake in the Hills	20	86	8.4	1.9	64	131	36.9	5.1	NA	NA	NA	NA
Lansing	33	121	28.6	3.8	75	281	26.4	11.0	33	1 565	289.0	65.4
Lombard	72	2 245	503.1	91.0	237	2 437	802.7	167.5	80	1 747	505.5	80.3
McHenry	37	249	24.2	6.3	81	505	60.1	28.9	66	1 940	336.9	76.2
Melrose Park	21	126	23.9	4.5	22	208	12.4	12.4	116	6 001	2 323.9	312.3
Moline	56	302	52.0	6.6	127	1 116	169.2	37.4	47	2 367	781.5	115.6
Mount Prospect	63	267	79.9	11.0	188	1 449	346.5	112.0	48	1 622	438.1	84.0
Mundelein	22	64	8.6	1.3	105	500	78.2	21.9	68	2 418	569.5	116.2
Naperville	227	842	253.1	34.5	1 002	D	D	D	99	2 472	579.3	119.8
Niles	54	410	81.4	14.6	94	467	69.3	20.6	81	3 541	1 048.1	171.4
Normal	37	337	44.2	9.5	71	D	D	D	28	2 342	D	125.3
Northbrook	137	614	143.1	38.0	610	19 892	1 308.5	715.2	89	3 140	696.9	151.4
North Chicago	10	68	12.5	6.3	11	D	D	D	19	1 365	355.9	D
Oak Forest	22	109	10.8	4.4	58	185	23.3	7.5	NA	NA	NA	NA
Oak Lawn	68	313	41.8	8.0	111	D	D	D	NA	NA	NA	NA
Oak Park	97	401	57.4	12.1	314	1 178	135.0	58.7	NA	NA	NA	NA
O'Fallon	48	D	D	D	81	D	D	D	NA	NA	NA	NA
Orland Park	92	311	80.9	7.6	241	1 078	124.8	48.0	41	1 477	496.7	90.9
Oswego	26	75	11.3	1.9	65	D	D	D	24	500	D	22.2
Palatine	90	308	52.1	9.9	330	1 481	206.3	75.6	41	1 786	670.0	81.0
Park Ridge	85	486	75.9	14.8	247	1 774	205.6	84.7	NA	NA	NA	NA
Pekin	25	89	11.8	2.5	50	294	22.2	9.5	30	1 224	D	55.7
Peoria	175	926	147.4	26.1	350	D	D	D	95	4 217	D	174.5
Plainfield	36	108	15.1	2.8	114	209	31.4	9.9	19	1 002	178.5	37.5
Quincy	53	249	28.4	6.0	121	749	61.6	22.3	55	D	D	D
Rockford	164	1 313	170.9	39.1	454	D	D	D	390	17 157	5 349.8	884.6
Rock Island	33	151	18.4	3.9	102	D	D	D	50	2 170	397.6	72.5
Romeoville	18	143	36.4	6.9	31	226	26.2	8.2	56	1 884	439.1	83.0
Round Lake Beach	12	46	7.3	1.0	22	D	D	D	NA	NA	NA	NA
St. Charles	92	339	99.9	15.4	265	1 700	249.5	111.1	105	5 588	1 559.1	259.1
Schaumburg	168	1 303	294.3	62.2	589	D	D	D	160	5 593	3 074.4	254.4
Skokie	115	1 199	188.0	42.7	398	2 529	552.1	197.9	154	6 021	1 355.1	289.8
Springfield	167	819	136.9	21.3	452	4 033	513.6	205.7	71	2 373	545.5	107.6
Streamwood	17	50	7.6	1.4	75	261	22.8	7.9	37	922	216.7	40.4
Tinley Park	52	175	27.0	4.3	148	1 273	156.8	45.6	43	1 421	358.8	65.8
Urbana	42	204	61.4	10.0	79	D	D	D	25	D	D	D
Vernon Hills	24	260	58.3	7.4	149	1 465	248.1	101.7	29	1 982	519.3	123.5

1. Establishments subject to federal tax.

— **Accommodation and Food Services, Arts, Entertainment, and Recreation, and Health Care and Social Assistance**

City	Accommodation and food services, 2007				Arts, entertainment, and recreation,[1] 2007				Health care and social assistance,[1] 2007			
	Number of establish-ments	Number of employees	Sales (mil dol)	Annual payroll (mil dol)	Number of establish-ments	Number of employees	Receipts (mil dol)	Annual payroll (mil dol)	Number of establish-ments	Number of employees	Receipts (mil dol)	Annual payroll (mil dol)
	92	93	94	95	96	97	98	99	100	101	102	103
ILLINOIS—Cont'd												
Burbank	62	751	38.7	9.3	3	D	D	D	38	D	D	D
Calumet City	88	1 285	54.7	14.7	8	85	4.9	1.3	65	1 957	69.0	37.1
Carbondale	106	2 217	80.2	22.4	3	D	D	D	86	1 562	131.8	51.0
Carol Stream	66	992	55.2	12.6	9	206	4.4	1.3	59	563	49.5	22.5
Carpentersville	40	961	33.7	10.1	3	D	D	D	18	65	5.7	2.3
Champaign	288	6 348	241.5	68.8	21	283	9.2	3.5	151	2 550	293.0	111.9
Chicago	5 572	105 396	7 663.3	2 049.8	676	D	D	D	4 725	57 699	5 867.6	2 193.0
Chicago Heights	45	641	27.0	6.9	5	17	1.5	0.3	56	1 194	120.9	57.1
Cicero	84	978	57.6	13.8	12	D	D	D	52	677	49.2	19.3
Collinsville	80	1 597	64.9	18.7	10	D	D	D	50	374	25.9	10.3
Crystal Lake	107	2 373	99.0	29.9	21	216	7.1	1.7	182	1 890	185.2	85.4
Danville	99	1 764	64.0	19.4	9	D	D	D	82	D	D	D
Decatur	178	3 751	138.2	41.2	16	D	D	D	208	2 696	313.4	133.2
DeKalb	98	1 808	69.8	17.7	3	D	D	D	38	726	63.1	28.9
Des Plaines	166	2 446	134.6	34.1	13	D	D	D	185	2 611	264.7	96.0
Downers Grove	147	3 069	165.4	46.7	15	D	D	D	194	D	D	D
East St. Louis	37	D	D	D	1	D	D	D	31	471	25.0	12.5
Elgin	159	2 270	106.3	29.3	19	D	D	D	215	2 893	279.3	132.2
Elk Grove Village	85	1 384	85.5	21.7	16	D	D	D	118	D	D	D
Elmhurst	119	1 986	99.4	27.0	15	24	1.9	0.3	203	D	D	D
Evanston	212	3 654	210.3	56.0	44	322	29.1	9.3	269	3 216	501.8	268.6
Freeport	71	1 050	39.7	12.4	8	D	D	D	61	D	D	D
Galesburg	102	1 547	60.2	16.9	9	D	D	D	81	D	D	D
Glendale Heights	49	741	37.0	9.6	9	99	5.8	1.6	32	D	D	D
Glen Ellyn	60	866	42.6	11.3	8	211	6.7	2.5	80	972	99.4	42.1
Glenview	202	5 145	266.4	79.1	40	272	23.6	8.3	212	2 977	291.6	116.0
Granite City	63	1 176	42.9	12.9	10	D	D	D	61	1 567	156.0	60.6
Gurnee	121	2 985	141.0	40.8	13	D	D	D	146	1 163	152.7	60.8
Hanover Park	47	585	27.3	6.8	3	D	D	D	26	D	D	D
Harvey	43	411	22.2	5.1	1	D	D	D	48	D	D	D
Highland Park	73	1 294	68.1	20.9	25	228	10.6	4.4	164	D	D	D
Hoffman Estates	110	2 236	129.8	39.5	21	D	D	D	196	D	D	D
Joliet	229	6 100	564.3	107.9	24	520	72.5	11.0	285	3 936	475.4	210.1
Kankakee	62	756	28.4	6.9	6	D	D	D	72	D	D	D
Lake in the Hills	26	490	20.9	5.8	8	86	6.7	2.3	39	281	30.2	10.1
Lansing	60	1 220	53.4	15.5	8	D	D	D	48	364	24.4	9.6
Lombard	128	2 936	161.3	48.0	15	D	D	D	119	1 558	193.9	73.9
McHenry	78	1 301	59.4	15.6	9	69	5.8	1.4	86	D	D	D
Melrose Park	69	1 042	55.9	13.7	9	D	D	D	104	D	D	D
Moline	157	3 155	122.2	35.4	11	D	D	D	157	D	D	D
Mount Prospect	105	1 408	70.4	18.4	11	D	D	D	97	739	62.7	31.9
Mundelein	68	934	48.1	13.3	15	128	9.5	3.1	47	326	26.6	10.7
Naperville	311	6 770	335.2	100.8	48	600	28.6	9.5	508	D	D	D
Niles	128	1 851	102.2	26.5	3	D	D	D	140	2 499	189.7	72.5
Normal	93	2 468	91.4	27.4	5	D	D	D	61	D	D	D
Northbrook	103	2 029	158.2	50.3	30	D	D	D	254	2 408	242.9	103.9
North Chicago	39	595	27.5	7.1	1	D	D	D	9	D	D	D
Oak Forest	34	542	24.2	6.3	8	D	D	D	53	D	D	D
Oak Lawn	103	2 349	116.4	31.5	13	D	D	D	252	D	D	D
Oak Park	96	1 486	71.5	21.4	21	122	14.9	3.9	249	2 503	205.8	91.2
O'Fallon	69	1 460	54.1	15.9	11	D	D	D	49	809	65.3	21.7
Orland Park	156	4 138	176.5	53.1	31	D	D	D	262	D	D	D
Oswego	59	952	46.9	12.8	11	D	D	D	48	D	D	D
Palatine	126	1 841	85.9	23.4	21	D	D	D	123	985	78.8	34.1
Park Ridge	63	725	35.2	9.5	11	D	D	D	188	D	D	D
Pekin	89	1 342	53.1	15.0	9	D	D	D	75	902	64.4	30.7
Peoria	332	6 428	272.5	78.9	32	D	D	D	343	6 072	707.3	349.4
Plainfield	65	1 543	58.8	16.6	15	D	D	D	91	D	D	D
Quincy	122	2 280	79.4	22.7	15	D	D	D	103	1 682	244.7	80.3
Rockford	356	7 378	320.1	88.4	30	362	20.7	5.9	371	5 860	647.8	305.7
Rock Island	78	1 253	44.2	13.7	10	D	D	D	72	822	58.5	25.2
Romeoville	59	1 105	52.1	13.9	8	494	22.4	6.2	28	D	D	D
Round Lake Beach	39	706	43.1	8.5	5	D	D	D	26	D	D	D
St. Charles	139	3 102	156.4	48.6	15	212	14.9	4.2	148	1 483	165.1	72.4
Schaumburg	273	8 038	458.0	133.8	23	D	D	D	228	2 276	205.1	79.2
Skokie	150	3 055	172.3	47.6	24	362	26.8	7.1	332	3 530	339.9	141.3
Springfield	379	7 782	311.8	95.5	34	505	68.3	6.4	295	D	D	D
Streamwood	57	786	42.0	11.0	5	D	D	D	42	D	D	D
Tinley Park	111	2 632	124.2	32.4	19	D	D	D	145	1 754	157.1	51.8
Urbana	97	1 949	78.5	20.9	9	68	2.9	1.3	43	2 715	322.6	172.9
Vernon Hills	85	1 804	97.0	30.0	15	D	D	D	92	899	105.0	41.0

1. Establishments subject to federal tax.

Table D. Cities — **Other Services and Federal Funds**

City	Other services[1], 2007				Selected federal funds, 2009–2010 (mil dol)								
					Procurement contracts		Grants						
	Number of establishments	Number of employees	Receipts (mil dol)	Annual payroll (mil dol)	Defense	Other	Total[2]	Medicaid and other health related	Nutrition and family welfare	Energy and environment	Disasters and emergency preparedness	Housing and community development	Employment and training
	104	105	106	107	108	109	110	111	112	113	114	115	116
ILLINOIS—Cont'd													
Burbank	30	D	D	D	0.0	0.0	0.2	0.0	0.0	0.0	0.0	0.2	0.0
Calumet City	41	179	14.4	4.5	0.0	0.0	0.1	0.0	0.0	0.1	0.0	0.0	0.0
Carbondale	44	D	D	D	0.8	3.2	44.9	20.8	3.2	0.9	0.0	0.0	0.0
Carol Stream	63	407	40.1	12.2	9.0	0.3	0.2	0.0	0.0	0.2	0.0	0.0	0.0
Carpentersville	24	107	5.5	1.6	0.5	0.0	0.0	0.0	0.0	0.0	0.0	0.0	0.0
Champaign	106	727	45.2	15.0	14.5	5.8	445.2	159.8	0.3	45.4	-0.3	14.7	0.0
Chicago	3 320	23 822	2 101.5	609.9	543.6	726.4	4 225.5	1 110.6	389.1	95.3	6.5	1 297.2	377.7
Chicago Heights	44	313	19.6	6.4	13.7	4.1	13.2	11.0	0.2	0.0	0.0	0.0	0.0
Cicero	66	242	22.6	6.3	0.1	0.2	3.4	0.0	0.0	0.5	0.0	2.7	0.0
Collinsville	44	263	20.9	5.6	0.1	0.2	8.1	0.0	0.0	0.0	0.0	8.0	0.0
Crystal Lake	96	690	50.8	15.9	2.2	0.1	0.0	0.0	0.0	0.0	0.0	0.0	0.0
Danville	55	443	25.0	7.3	14.7	65.5	13.3	0.2	3.8	0.4	0.0	4.3	0.0
Decatur	114	D	D	D	1.9	12.1	188.4	5.9	2.7	165.9	0.0	10.6	0.0
DeKalb	47	275	17.3	5.1	0.0	0.2	62.6	0.0	0.0	1.9	0.0	6.0	0.0
Des Plaines	148	806	100.3	28.7	11.8	21.5	39.9	3.7	0.0	33.2	0.0	1.4	0.0
Downers Grove	115	1 075	154.0	49.0	13.6	3.8	0.7	0.4	0.0	0.2	0.0	0.0	0.0
East St. Louis	17	122	6.9	2.3	0.0	0.1	26.4	11.2	0.0	0.0	0.0	12.5	0.4
Elgin	145	1 449	136.5	47.6	10.4	5.3	16.8	2.6	0.0	1.0	0.0	11.0	0.0
Elk Grove Village	99	1 163	124.9	40.6	22.1	1.2	6.1	5.3	0.0	0.5	0.0	0.0	0.0
Elmhurst	98	810	72.7	27.1	0.9	6.7	0.2	0.0	0.0	0.0	0.0	0.0	0.0
Evanston	114	820	49.7	18.8	17.9	15.9	527.2	411.0	1.0	20.5	0.0	21.1	0.0
Freeport	51	D	D	D	0.6	0.3	3.6	0.0	1.2	0.0	0.0	1.2	0.0
Galesburg	49	D	D	D	0.0	0.3	5.4	0.5	0.0	0.0	0.0	2.1	0.0
Glendale Heights	34	D	D	D	0.1	0.2	0.0	0.0	0.0	0.0	0.0	0.0	0.0
Glen Ellyn	51	298	16.5	7.1	0.0	0.0	0.9	0.7	0.0	0.0	0.0	0.0	0.0
Glenview	109	699	54.4	19.6	43.2	0.3	0.0	0.0	0.0	0.0	0.0	0.0	0.0
Granite City	47	349	39.4	10.0	31.8	0.6	10.8	0.1	1.8	0.0	0.0	1.5	0.0
Gurnee	54	479	39.0	10.5	0.6	0.7	0.6	0.0	0.0	0.0	0.0	0.6	0.0
Hanover Park	36	D	D	D	1.0	1.0	0.0	0.0	0.0	0.0	0.0	0.0	0.0
Harvey	16	D	D	D	1.1	0.3	2.4	0.7	0.0	0.0	0.0	0.0	0.0
Highland Park	80	531	41.3	14.9	0.3	0.0	0.7	0.0	0.0	0.5	0.0	0.0	0.0
Hoffman Estates	50	371	21.2	11.6	0.1	0.1	0.4	0.0	0.0	0.1	0.0	0.3	0.0
Joliet	164	1 266	96.0	28.0	13.2	11.4	35.0	1.7	6.0	2.8	1.2	21.3	0.0
Kankakee	56	370	30.3	9.3	0.0	0.0	13.1	0.0	2.7	0.0	0.0	7.8	0.0
Lake in the Hills	30	D	D	D	0.0	0.0	0.0	0.0	0.0	0.0	0.0	0.0	0.0
Lansing	48	411	27.9	9.2	0.1	0.0	0.0	0.0	0.0	0.0	0.0	0.0	0.0
Lombard	106	826	63.6	22.8	1.8	3.1	0.4	0.4	0.0	0.0	0.0	0.0	0.0
McHenry	56	D	D	D	0.1	0.2	0.2	0.0	0.0	0.0	0.0	0.2	0.0
Melrose Park	43	D	D	D	15.4	0.1	0.3	0.0	0.0	0.0	0.0	0.0	0.0
Moline	84	600	43.9	13.8	71.6	6.9	8.2	0.0	0.0	0.0	0.0	3.5	0.0
Mount Prospect	83	515	40.6	12.0	0.1	1.2	0.6	0.0	0.0	0.2	0.0	0.4	0.0
Mundelein	56	D	D	D	2.2	9.3	0.4	0.0	0.0	0.0	0.0	0.0	0.0
Naperville	236	1 832	126.3	42.6	18.2	19.4	25.6	0.0	0.4	14.5	0.0	0.7	0.0
Niles	71	306	25.2	6.9	3.8	0.5	2.2	0.0	0.0	2.2	0.0	0.0	0.0
Normal	50	475	26.6	10.0	0.0	0.1	11.7	1.7	0.0	1.3	0.0	0.4	0.0
Northbrook	74	535	39.7	13.3	8.8	1.4	1.7	0.1	0.0	0.0	0.0	0.0	0.0
North Chicago	18	148	17.7	4.9	38.1	50.6	28.2	13.8	0.0	0.0	0.0	4.9	0.5
Oak Forest	38	164	18.2	4.8	0.0	0.0	0.0	0.0	0.0	0.0	0.0	0.0	0.0
Oak Lawn	99	734	52.7	17.0	0.0	0.1	0.4	0.0	0.0	0.0	0.0	0.3	0.0
Oak Park	87	536	33.3	11.4	0.0	2.4	10.0	3.5	0.0	0.3	0.0	6.1	0.0
O'Fallon	49	298	18.2	5.8	1.1	0.1	0.5	0.0	0.0	0.0	0.0	0.0	0.0
Orland Park	113	961	80.3	25.3	0.0	2.2	0.1	0.0	0.0	0.0	0.0	0.0	0.0
Oswego	51	362	24.7	7.8	0.6	0.8	0.0	0.0	0.0	0.0	0.0	0.0	0.0
Palatine	134	922	64.7	20.4	4.8	5.9	1.5	0.0	0.0	0.6	0.0	0.9	0.0
Park Ridge	59	303	20.0	7.1	33.3	2.0	0.4	0.0	0.0	0.4	0.0	0.0	0.0
Pekin	53	281	18.2	4.9	3.2	3.9	0.9	0.0	0.0	0.0	0.0	0.7	0.0
Peoria	178	2 909	254.2	120.5	10.3	21.3	59.4	2.8	5.4	8.4	0.0	16.1	0.5
Plainfield	54	D	D	D	1.1	0.1	0.0	0.0	0.0	0.0	0.0	0.0	0.0
Quincy	95	549	45.5	12.9	5.3	0.8	11.4	0.7	1.7	0.5	0.0	1.9	0.0
Rockford	247	2 058	164.3	51.5	117.7	6.5	43.5	5.0	0.1	1.5	0.0	27.7	0.5
Rock Island	50	402	34.7	11.2	7.8	0.7	30.2	0.0	4.8	0.5	0.0	22.6	0.0
Romeoville	38	480	60.2	16.5	0.3	0.0	1.2	0.1	0.0	0.1	0.0	0.0	0.0
Round Lake Beach	27	D	D	D	0.0	0.0	0.0	0.0	0.0	0.0	0.0	0.0	0.0
St. Charles	80	535	42.1	14.0	4.4	0.1	0.2	0.0	0.0	0.0	0.0	0.0	0.0
Schaumburg	204	1 621	135.5	45.7	7.7	19.5	52.6	1.5	0.0	0.0	0.0	0.5	0.0
Skokie	154	1 085	95.8	30.8	1.1	4.5	1.7	0.0	0.0	0.4	0.0	0.6	0.0
Springfield	190	1 536	104.6	35.6	25.0	15.8	2 100.1	121.1	367.8	256.9	227.3	15.6	15.9
Streamwood	47	307	19.0	6.6	0.1	0.0	0.0	0.0	0.0	0.4	0.0	1.1	0.0
Tinley Park	64	560	34.1	12.6	4.2	0.0	1.5	0.0	0.0	0.4	0.0	1.1	0.0
Urbana	44	D	D	D	8.2	7.1	110.4	1.8	4.1	12.9	0.0	2.5	0.0
Vernon Hills	34	406	25.6	9.1	141.3	134.5	0.3	0.0	0.0	0.0	0.0	0.0	0.0

1. Establishments subject to federal tax. 2. Includes program categories not shown separately. State totals include additional categories not allocated by city.

Table D. Cities — **City Government Finances**

City	General revenue Total (mil dol)	Intergovernmental Total (mil dol)	Percent from state government	Taxes Total (mil dol)	Taxes Per capita (dollars) Total	Property	Sales and gross receipts	General expenditure Total (mil dol)	Per capita (dollars) Total	Capital outlays
	117	118	119	120	121	122	123	124	125	126
ILLINOIS—Cont'd										
Burbank	21.3	6.9	100.0	12.9	465	252	214	20.6	746	104
Calumet City	44.2	12.8	98.9	27.0	729	454	270	45.0	1 214	97
Carbondale	28.6	12.5	80.5	8.9	339	28	311	27.8	1 055	96
Carol Stream	30.0	11.0	100.0	9.5	239	13	203	25.9	651	49
Carpentersville	28.9	11.2	98.8	10.1	269	181	88	29.1	775	56
Champaign	83.7	26.1	98.0	43.6	578	241	337	77.3	1 023	252
Chicago	5 612.0	1 465.4	57.9	2 038.7	719	128	497	6 914.2	2 437	526
Chicago Heights	34.4	9.7	84.5	18.4	596	414	182	30.3	983	33
Cicero	100.1	16.1	96.6	61.2	756	508	248	86.8	1 072	208
Collinsville	25.1	11.1	98.1	6.1	237	137	100	23.1	893	158
Crystal Lake	44.6	16.7	98.8	15.8	380	298	82	41.7	1 001	178
Danville	37.4	14.9	88.5	14.4	442	198	244	30.8	949	0
Decatur	69.7	30.9	81.4	31.6	412	155	256	72.4	944	103
DeKalb	43.1	15.1	72.1	22.5	514	226	288	44.8	1 025	285
Des Plaines	81.1	18.4	97.3	46.5	815	487	307	82.3	1 444	225
Downers Grove	58.7	21.3	98.1	29.5	601	309	292	51.2	1 045	145
East St. Louis	36.5	20.2	88.0	14.7	507	334	173	39.8	1 373	209
Elgin	140.1	51.3	97.1	51.6	495	390	105	123.3	1 183	266
Elk Grove Village	58.1	15.8	81.2	33.3	994	476	472	62.7	1 570	139
Elmhurst	58.6	16.9	99.9	26.7	588	314	259	59.3	1 307	78
Evanston	148.6	31.8	91.3	74.8	986	542	384	142.6	1 879	375
Freeport	23.5	9.8	85.8	7.2	291	146	145	22.5	909	43
Galesburg	29.7	12.0	87.0	11.5	368	222	146	26.1	838	18
Glendale Heights	32.0	10.3	96.7	13.2	412	234	155	26.8	839	33
Glen Ellyn	34.2	6.9	96.0	12.4	457	296	130	29.7	1 091	223
Glenview	103.2	24.0	76.0	49.4	1 066	785	280	85.0	1 834	324
Granite City	38.0	16.9	93.3	11.9	389	241	148	35.8	1 166	158
Gurnee	35.1	23.2	89.4	7.0	230	15	215	31.2	1 021	53
Hanover Park	31.0	7.1	97.7	16.2	438	279	154	28.7	778	89
Harvey	23.3	7.3	94.0	12.4	439	295	144	24.7	876	39
Highland Park	56.9	12.5	96.6	31.0	984	411	484	53.3	1 694	259
Hoffman Estates	103.1	13.3	96.4	55.8	1 050	790	239	103.9	1 955	1 011
Joliet	192.4	80.0	95.7	64.7	448	209	213	168.5	1 168	95
Kankakee	41.1	14.3	86.3	16.0	563	416	147	39.2	1 472	117
Lake in the Hills	16.9	5.9	99.5	8.5	286	180	107	22.3	752	253
Lansing	36.1	9.1	100.0	19.9	740	591	148	25.2	940	41
Lombard	53.8	18.7	89.5	20.8	486	166	320	113.5	2 648	1 678
McHenry	23.2	10.0	99.4	5.1	194	167	27	24.3	919	192
Melrose Park	35.2	9.9	100.0	19.2	871	637	234	39.9	1 811	13
Moline	62.5	19.6	89.7	27.9	647	366	282	68.2	1 586	332
Mount Prospect	62.8	16.7	97.0	37.9	707	448	239	58.7	1 092	63
Mundelein	38.0	9.0	100.0	17.9	547	279	268	32.2	983	179
Naperville	153.3	49.4	93.7	71.2	500	290	168	155.4	1 091	173
Niles	47.1	17.5	97.8	22.8	791	211	558	41.5	1 439	81
Normal	54.0	15.4	90.0	23.6	456	144	312	61.9	1 196	152
Northbrook	51.2	14.3	100.0	26.0	764	416	348	52.2	1 532	211
North Chicago	22.5	9.8	87.3	9.5	288	156	121	27.5	837	261
Oak Forest	21.3	6.2	100.0	11.7	420	336	83	23.9	856	181
Oak Lawn	58.0	20.1	97.4	26.1	488	335	153	53.8	1 008	28
Oak Park	79.2	14.6	81.3	45.7	917	637	184	96.4	1 933	563
O'Fallon	28.1	12.9	97.6	7.9	294	171	123	31.6	1 168	464
Orland Park	91.4	36.4	82.1	35.2	633	377	256	80.4	1 445	329
Oswego	16.2	5.4	98.2	4.7	163	35	128	20.8	718	230
Palatine	71.2	18.1	92.9	41.6	618	430	188	63.6	945	180
Park Ridge	40.6	8.9	98.9	27.3	741	409	312	46.5	1 261	162
Pekin	35.0	12.9	97.5	10.9	325	167	158	32.2	964	133
Peoria	160.6	60.0	92.7	67.9	598	232	366	179.7	1 583	488
Plainfield	30.2	7.9	99.6	10.8	306	121	184	46.5	1 315	665
Quincy	41.2	19.5	93.0	12.2	304	83	221	36.3	906	185
Rockford	174.1	85.1	83.0	66.8	427	322	105	169.8	1 084	110
Rock Island	52.7	16.1	86.5	19.8	518	329	188	48.9	1 279	74
Romeoville	54.2	8.8	98.3	22.4	604	316	266	53.0	1 428	499
Round Lake Beach	18.5	7.5	99.8	8.7	312	178	134	21.3	763	383
St. Charles	52.3	14.9	96.5	23.8	726	350	376	62.3	1 902	557
Schaumburg	123.4	42.6	95.9	48.8	676	33	643	167.4	2 320	935
Skokie	82.8	25.9	92.6	46.7	700	410	277	74.5	1 117	118
Springfield	139.7	62.8	65.0	54.4	465	194	270	119.2	1 018	2
Streamwood	30.4	9.0	94.8	13.7	368	189	154	31.8	851	281
Tinley Park	54.4	20.2	95.3	24.7	418	347	72	45.8	775	151
Urbana	36.0	12.2	85.1	15.2	386	163	223	35.5	898	151
Vernon Hills	23.9	13.3	95.9	5.6	232	0	232	25.8	1 071	315

1. Based on population estimated as of July 1 of the year shown.

City	Public welfare	Highways	Parking facilities	Education	Health and hospitals	Police protection	Sewerage and sanitation	Parks and recreation	Housing and community development	Interest on debt
	City government finances, 2006 (cont.)									
	General expenditure (cont.)									
	Percent of total for:									
	127	128	129	130	131	132	133	134	135	136
ILLINOIS—Cont'd										
Burbank	0.0	33.1	0.0	0.0	0.0	34.1	0.0	0.0	0.0	2.4
Calumet City	0.0	16.1	0.0	0.0	0.5	21.5	5.2	0.0	0.0	4.0
Carbondale	0.0	22.2	0.5	0.0	0.0	25.0	9.1	0.6	2.3	3.3
Carol Stream	0.0	25.9	0.0	0.0	0.0	41.4	8.9	0.0	0.0	4.2
Carpentersville	0.0	22.3	0.0	0.0	0.0	28.7	7.9	0.2	0.0	3.3
Champaign	2.5	10.3	1.4	0.0	0.0	20.6	2.9	0.0	1.7	2.5
Chicago	3.7	7.2	0.1	0.0	2.9	18.0	4.5	0.7	1.7	10.5
Chicago Heights	0.0	6.7	0.0	0.0	0.0	27.0	10.7	0.5	0.2	6.7
Cicero	0.3	17.6	0.0	0.0	0.7	22.1	5.8	0.2	2.0	7.2
Collinsville	0.5	9.7	0.0	0.0	0.6	20.7	20.7	0.0	0.0	3.4
Crystal Lake	0.0	12.1	0.0	0.0	0.3	20.3	5.9	0.0	0.0	2.7
Danville	0.0	14.0	0.6	0.0	0.0	25.3	12.6	7.3	2.8	1.5
Decatur	0.0	24.0	0.7	0.0	0.0	23.8	1.7	0.1	2.7	4.1
DeKalb	0.0	14.6	0.0	0.0	0.0	18.9	3.7	0.0	4.0	2.9
Des Plaines	0.6	18.3	0.3	0.0	0.0	20.7	4.7	0.0	0.3	6.0
Downers Grove	0.0	13.3	1.8	0.0	0.0	24.7	0.0	0.0	0.0	3.9
East St. Louis	0.0	21.5	0.0	0.0	0.0	16.6	0.9	0.0	5.3	2.3
Elgin	0.0	7.0	0.0	0.0	0.0	23.4	10.5	11.7	0.6	3.0
Elk Grove Village	0.0	22.1	0.0	0.0	1.2	28.1	3.7	0.4	0.0	2.0
Elmhurst	0.2	16.0	0.8	0.0	0.7	20.7	10.7	2.4	0.0	5.5
Evanston	1.4	10.4	2.9	0.0	2.7	13.7	11.3	9.6	5.4	8.1
Freeport	0.0	4.9	0.0	0.0	0.2	16.7	21.1	1.2	0.4	5.4
Galesburg	0.0	11.5	0.0	0.0	0.0	19.9	5.3	7.9	0.0	2.1
Glendale Heights	0.0	25.2	0.0	0.0	0.0	24.1	10.1	15.7	0.0	1.9
Glen Ellyn	0.0	15.2	0.7	0.0	0.0	18.7	15.5	9.8	0.0	2.7
Glenview	0.0	14.0	0.5	0.0	0.0	16.5	4.8	0.0	0.0	7.3
Granite City	0.0	25.4	0.0	0.0	0.0	19.4	15.0	0.0	1.1	0.0
Gurnee	0.0	15.5	0.0	0.0	0.0	31.4	3.3	0.0	0.0	1.5
Hanover Park	0.0	10.1	1.0	0.0	0.0	32.2	8.7	0.0	0.0	3.2
Harvey	0.0	12.9	1.1	0.0	0.0	20.9	6.8	0.0	0.3	2.0
Highland Park	0.0	18.4	1.8	0.0	0.0	25.8	0.0	5.3	0.0	3.6
Hoffman Estates	0.0	8.3	0.0	0.0	0.6	13.3	2.4	0.2	0.0	5.9
Joliet	0.0	14.8	0.6	0.0	0.1	20.6	8.4	5.0	1.8	1.9
Kankakee	0.0	15.1	0.0	0.0	0.0	18.8	18.3	0.2	3.1	6.0
Lake in the Hills	0.0	25.4	2.8	0.0	0.0	26.5	0.0	9.6	0.0	0.5
Lansing	0.0	6.7	0.0	0.0	0.0	31.8	8.8	0.1	0.0	3.9
Lombard	0.0	3.4	0.1	0.0	0.0	9.5	3.9	0.0	0.0	4.7
McHenry	0.0	22.2	0.0	0.0	0.0	29.4	7.4	14.9	0.0	3.1
Melrose Park	0.0	5.9	0.0	0.0	3.4	26.1	1.4	9.3	0.0	12.6
Moline	0.0	14.1	0.2	0.0	0.0	15.8	8.0	5.3	1.0	7.0
Mount Prospect	1.8	15.3	0.7	0.0	0.2	22.2	11.0	0.6	0.5	2.2
Mundelein	0.0	20.0	0.1	0.0	0.0	25.8	11.8	0.0	0.0	2.9
Naperville	0.1	23.4	0.5	0.0	0.0	21.9	8.5	5.4	0.0	1.9
Niles	0.0	18.4	0.0	0.0	0.0	26.7	3.8	4.0	0.0	4.4
Normal	0.0	8.4	0.0	0.0	0.0	14.0	6.8	12.4	0.0	3.8
Northbrook	0.0	23.0	0.4	0.0	0.0	22.8	2.1	0.0	2.3	3.3
North Chicago	0.0	5.9	0.0	0.0	0.0	25.3	7.3	0.0	1.0	2.3
Oak Forest	0.0	16.0	0.9	0.0	0.0	26.5	3.4	0.0	0.0	3.1
Oak Lawn	0.0	10.3	0.2	0.0	0.6	19.6	8.6	0.5	0.5	4.0
Oak Park	0.0	16.4	11.7	0.0	1.8	15.7	6.0	0.0	1.1	2.4
O'Fallon	0.5	9.2	0.0	0.0	3.6	13.4	7.8	3.8	0.0	3.9
Orland Park	0.0	11.1	0.2	0.0	0.0	27.3	4.8	13.2	0.0	3.9
Oswego	0.0	27.7	0.0	0.0	0.0	28.8	9.8	0.0	0.0	4.1
Palatine	0.0	7.3	1.0	0.0	0.0	24.4	8.4	0.0	0.5	5.5
Park Ridge	0.0	7.5	0.7	0.0	0.4	17.6	7.9	1.6	0.0	4.0
Pekin	0.0	12.0	0.0	0.0	0.0	21.6	10.7	0.2	0.1	6.4
Peoria	0.0	13.3	1.6	0.0	0.0	17.4	3.0	1.5	1.5	4.5
Plainfield	0.0	27.2	0.0	0.0	0.0	31.0	12.1	0.0	0.0	4.0
Quincy	0.0	22.2	0.0	0.0	0.0	20.4	9.2	0.2	4.0	2.2
Rockford	9.7	14.6	0.8	0.0	0.1	24.0	4.6	0.1	7.6	3.6
Rock Island	0.0	12.1	0.5	0.0	0.0	19.7	11.3	10.6	1.1	0.9
Romeoville	0.0	19.0	0.0	0.0	0.0	18.4	9.1	6.8	0.0	4.3
Round Lake Beach	0.0	10.8	0.0	0.0	0.0	24.9	0.0	0.2	0.0	4.4
St. Charles	0.0	29.7	0.0	0.0	1.1	15.5	8.1	0.0	0.0	6.8
Schaumburg	0.0	12.2	0.3	0.0	0.3	15.5	1.0	1.4	0.2	5.5
Skokie	0.0	11.4	0.0	0.0	2.3	17.5	5.5	2.7	0.7	3.5
Springfield	0.0	14.4	0.6	0.0	0.0	24.4	2.9	2.4	2.7	10.5
Streamwood	0.0	6.7	0.0	0.0	0.0	23.4	6.3	1.0	0.5	2.2
Tinley Park	0.0	12.1	1.3	0.0	0.0	29.1	9.9	0.0	0.0	3.2
Urbana	0.5	23.9	1.0	0.0	0.0	16.7	4.7	0.0	8.6	2.2
Vernon Hills	0.0	13.2	0.0	0.0	0.0	27.4	0.0	3.3	0.0	1.7

Table D. Cities — City Government Finances, City Government Employment, and Climate

City	City government finances, 2007 (cont.) Debt outstanding Total (mil dol)	Per capita[1] (dollars)	Debt issued during year	City government employment, 2010	Climate[2] Average daily temperature (degrees Fahrenheit) Mean January	July	Limits January[3]	July[4]	Annual precipitation (inches)	Heating degree days	Cooling degree days
	137	138	139	140	141	142	143	144	145	146	147
ILLINOIS—Cont'd											
Burbank	10.2	369	0.4	151	23.5	75.5	16.2	84.7	38.35	6 083	1 001
Calumet City	52.5	1 415	4.8	314	22.0	74.2	14.8	83.7	38.65	6 355	866
Carbondale	38.3	1 454	6.7	249	NA	NA	NA	NA	NA	NA	NA
Carol Stream	28.1	707	0.0	192	23.1	74.8	14.2	86.8	37.94	6 053	942
Carpentersville	29.1	776	10.0	227	19.3	72.6	10.9	83.0	37.22	6 975	679
Champaign	44.6	591	0.0	593	33.7	79.0	25.0	89.5	47.93	4 183	1 501
Chicago	16 150.0	5 693	933.7	34 094	25.3	75.4	18.3	84.4	38.01	5 787	994
Chicago Heights	57.8	1 875	0.0	313	22.0	74.2	14.8	83.7	38.65	6 355	866
Cicero	148.7	1 836	3.6	645	22.0	73.3	14.3	83.5	36.27	6 498	830
Collinsville	22.2	857	20.0	NA	NA	NA	NA	NA	NA	NA	NA
Crystal Lake	34.9	839	8.4	316	28.6	76.3	19.0	87.2	46.96	5 168	1 112
Danville	17.2	530	4.0	298	25.8	75.3	17.3	86.2	40.96	5 555	1 027
Decatur	62.3	813	5.0	567	25.8	76.2	17.1	87.8	39.74	5 458	1 142
DeKalb	31.8	727	0.0	232	18.5	73.1	10.3	83.6	37.38	6 979	736
Des Plaines	122.9	2 156	0.0	458	22.0	73.3	14.3	83.5	36.27	6 498	830
Downers Grove	124.2	2 535	44.7	399	23.1	74.8	14.2	86.8	37.94	6 053	942
East St. Louis	21.1	728	0.2	207	29.1	78.6	20.0	88.7	40.33	4 826	1 378
Elgin	133.4	1 279	13.8	727	19.3	72.6	10.9	83.0	37.22	6 975	679
Elk Grove Village	19.1	568	0.8	325	22.0	73.3	14.3	83.5	36.27	6 498	830
Elmhurst	68.2	1 504	17.9	600	23.1	74.8	14.2	86.8	37.94	6 053	942
Evanston	293.5	3 867	29.2	872	22.0	72.9	13.7	83.2	36.80	6 630	702
Freeport	28.9	1 166	10.0	206	17.2	71.9	9.0	82.0	34.79	7 317	611
Galesburg	19.9	448	0.0	288	21.3	74.9	13.5	84.5	37.22	6 347	941
Glendale Heights	14.7	461	3.0	229	22.0	73.3	14.3	83.5	36.27	6 498	830
Glen Ellyn	26.2	966	1.0	NA	21.7	74.4	12.2	85.7	38.58	6 359	888
Glenview	156.3	3 374	37.9	363	22.0	73.3	14.3	83.5	36.27	6 498	830
Granite City	0.0	0	0.0	236	27.7	78.4	19.4	88.1	38.54	5 149	1 354
Gurnee	11.4	372	0.0	204	19.9	72.2	12.1	82.2	36.50	6 955	634
Hanover Park	20.7	559	0.0	219	18.4	72.1	9.6	82.3	36.56	7 149	624
Harvey	16.5	585	0.0	207	22.0	74.2	14.8	83.7	38.65	6 355	866
Highland Park	50.9	1 619	0.0	292	22.0	72.9	13.7	83.2	36.80	6 630	702
Hoffman Estates	150.3	2 827	2.0	367	18.4	72.1	9.6	82.3	36.56	7 149	624
Joliet	80.4	557	6.3	953	21.7	73.7	13.5	84.6	36.96	6 464	809
Kankakee	59.5	2 237	9.6	297	21.7	74.4	12.2	85.7	38.58	6 359	888
Lake in the Hills	6.5	219	5.6	NA	NA	NA	NA	NA	NA	NA	NA
Lansing	19.9	742	0.0	224	21.7	74.4	12.2	85.7	38.58	6 359	888
Lombard	212.7	4 964	5.3	308	23.1	74.8	14.2	86.8	37.94	6 053	942
McHenry	18.5	700	3.0	NA	NA	NA	NA	NA	NA	NA	NA
Melrose Park	103.9	4 717	14.9	288	NA	NA	NA	NA	NA	NA	NA
Moline	86.0	1 999	0.0	400	21.8	76.4	13.3	85.1	35.10	6 179	1 100
Mount Prospect	42.8	797	10.0	446	22.0	73.3	14.3	83.5	36.27	6 498	830
Mundelein	19.9	607	0.0	NA	18.4	72.1	9.6	82.3	36.56	7 149	624
Naperville	126.0	885	0.0	1 182	23.1	74.8	14.2	86.8	37.94	6 053	942
Niles	41.2	1 428	0.0	308	22.0	73.3	14.3	83.5	36.27	6 498	830
Normal	72.6	1 404	34.7	398	25.8	76.2	17.1	87.8	39.74	5 458	1 142
Northbrook	63.0	1 852	13.1	290	22.0	72.9	13.7	83.2	36.80	6 630	702
North Chicago	16.2	492	0.0	183	20.3	71.5	12.0	81.7	34.09	7 031	613
Oak Forest	16.6	596	0.0	NA	22.0	74.2	14.8	83.7	38.65	6 355	866
Oak Lawn	62.0	1 161	7.5	448	23.5	75.5	16.2	84.7	38.35	6 083	1 001
Oak Park	117.8	2 362	40.2	448	22.0	73.3	14.3	83.5	36.27	6 498	830
O'Fallon	42.7	1 577	24.0	NA	NA	NA	NA	NA	NA	NA	NA
Orland Park	80.8	1 452	12.0	437	23.5	75.5	16.2	84.7	38.35	6 083	1 001
Oswego	25.2	868	11.6	NA	NA	NA	NA	NA	NA	NA	NA
Palatine	93.0	1 382	4.3	362	18.4	72.1	9.6	82.3	36.56	7 149	624
Park Ridge	48.5	1 317	20.6	286	22.0	73.3	14.3	83.5	36.27	6 498	830
Pekin	50.2	1 501	0.0	256	24.4	75.8	15.7	87.4	35.71	5 695	1 088
Peoria	183.9	1 620	9.8	856	22.5	75.1	14.3	85.7	36.03	6 097	998
Plainfield	42.6	1 205	0.0	134	NA	NA	NA	NA	NA	NA	NA
Quincy	20.1	500	1.3	413	24.9	76.8	16.0	88.0	35.63	5 707	1 117
Rockford	129.8	829	17.5	1 166	19.0	72.9	10.8	83.1	36.63	6 933	768
Rock Island	19.9	520	4.9	359	21.8	76.4	13.3	85.1	35.10	6 179	1 100
Romeoville	46.1	1 242	0.0	317	NA	NA	NA	NA	NA	NA	NA
Round Lake Beach	28.9	1 032	3.9	NA	19.9	72.2	12.1	82.2	35.50	6 955	634
St. Charles	97.7	2 981	16.5	287	19.3	72.6	10.9	83.0	37.22	6 975	679
Schaumburg	318.4	4 413	4.7	516	18.4	72.1	9.6	82.3	36.56	7 149	624
Skokie	56.9	853	0.0	614	22.0	73.3	14.3	83.5	36.27	6 498	830
Springfield	513.9	4 389	0.0	1 648	25.1	76.3	17.1	86.5	35.56	5 596	1 165
Streamwood	15.7	422	0.0	196	19.3	72.6	10.9	83.0	37.22	6 975	679
Tinley Park	34.7	587	0.0	349	21.8	76.4	13.3	85.1	35.10	6 179	1 100
Urbana	18.4	467	0.0	306	20.7	73.2	12.4	83.7	34.47	6 606	774
Vernon Hills	15.5	642	5.1	109	NA	NA	NA	NA	NA	NA	NA

1. Based on the population estimated as of July 1 of the year shown.   2. Represents normal values based on the 30-year period, 1971–2000.   3. Average daily minimum.   4. Average daily maximum.

Table D. Cities — Land Area and Population

STATE Place code	City	Land area,[1] 2010 (sq km)	Population, 2010 Total persons	Rank	Per square kilometer	Race alone or in combination, not of Hispanic origin (percent), 2010 White	Black	American Indian, Alaska Native	Asian	Hawaiian Pacific Islander	Percent Hispanic or Latino,[2] 2010	Percent Foreign born, 2008–2010
		1	2	3	4	5	6	7	8	9	10	11
	ILLINOIS—Cont'd											
17 79293	Waukegan	61.3	89 078	345	1 452.9	22.9	19.2	0.5	4.6	0.1	53.4	32.6
17 80060	West Chicago	38.3	27 086	1 525	706.7	40.6	2.4	0.3	6.4	0.1	51.1	36.9
17 81048	Wheaton	29.1	52 894	720	1 815.2	85.2	4.8	0.4	6.2	0.1	4.9	11.0
17 81087	Wheeling	22.5	37 648	1 051	1 670.3	53.3	2.4	0.4	13.5	0.0	31.2	42.5
17 82075	Wilmette	14.0	27 087	1 524	1 936.2	84.7	1.0	0.2	12.3	0.1	3.3	14.8
17 83245	Woodridge	24.4	32 971	1 240	1 351.3	64.8	9.4	0.4	13.3	0.1	13.4	20.9
18 00000	INDIANA	92 789.2	6 483 802	X	69.9	82.9	9.8	0.6	1.9	0.1	6.0	4.5
18 01468	Anderson	107.2	56 129	669	523.8	79.0	16.7	0.8	0.7	0.1	4.8	2.8
18 05860	Bloomington	60.0	80 405	403	1 340.5	83.5	5.5	0.7	9.1	0.1	3.5	10.7
18 10342	Carmel	122.9	79 191	409	644.2	85.2	3.4	0.4	9.8	0.1	2.5	9.5
18 14734	Columbus	71.2	44 061	892	618.7	85.5	3.5	0.5	5.9	0.2	5.8	8.1
18 16138	Crown Point	45.9	27 317	1 510	595.4	83.7	6.6	0.3	2.1	0.0	8.1	6.3
18 19486	East Chicago	36.5	29 698	1 379	813.9	7.7	41.5	0.4	0.1	0.1	50.9	14.5
18 20728	Elkhart	60.7	50 949	758	838.8	60.8	17.4	0.9	1.2	0.1	22.5	13.0
18 22000	Evansville	114.4	117 429	222	1 026.8	83.3	14.4	0.7	1.3	0.1	2.6	2.5
18 23278	Fishers	87.0	76 794	428	882.8	85.0	6.3	0.3	6.4	0.1	3.4	7.3
18 25000	Fort Wayne	286.5	253 691	74	885.5	72.8	17.1	0.9	3.8	0.1	8.0	6.9
18 27000	Gary	129.2	80 294	405	621.7	9.9	85.2	0.8	0.4	0.0	5.1	1.8
18 28386	Goshen	42.0	31 719	1 288	754.7	68.0	3.1	0.6	1.5	0.1	28.1	12.8
18 29898	Greenwood	55.0	49 791	774	905.5	89.0	2.4	0.6	4.3	0.1	5.0	4.8
18 31000	Hammond	59.0	80 830	400	1 370.2	42.7	22.7	0.6	1.2	0.1	34.1	10.5
18 34114	Hobart	68.2	29 059	1 418	426.1	78.0	7.3	0.7	1.3	0.0	13.9	3.9
18 36000	Indianapolis	949.1	829 718	11	874.2	60.7	28.6	0.7	2.5	0.1	9.4	8.5
18 38358	Jeffersonville	88.2	44 953	878	509.5	81.0	15.0	0.8	1.5	0.2	4.1	3.2
18 40392	Kokomo	47.9	45 468	867	949.0	84.5	12.5	1.0	1.3	0.1	3.3	1.7
18 40788	Lafayette	71.9	67 140	511	934.4	80.1	7.1	0.8	1.7	0.1	12.1	7.6
18 42426	Lawrence	52.1	46 001	858	882.3	61.0	27.5	0.8	2.1	0.2	11.2	7.2
18 46908	Marion	40.7	29 948	1 363	736.0	78.6	16.7	0.8	1.1	0.1	5.5	1.8
18 48528	Merrillville	86.0	35 246	1 143	409.7	41.6	45.1	0.5	1.6	0.1	12.9	4.4
18 48798	Michigan City	50.7	31 479	1 296	620.5	65.0	30.1	0.9	1.0	0.1	5.9	3.5
18 49932	Mishawaka	44.0	48 252	810	1 096.1	86.1	8.2	1.0	2.3	0.2	4.5	5.8
18 51876	Muncie	70.4	70 085	487	995.0	85.0	12.4	0.8	1.6	0.2	2.3	2.4
18 52326	New Albany	38.7	36 372	1 096	940.1	86.5	10.4	0.8	1.0	0.1	3.7	2.1
18 54180	Noblesville	81.3	51 969	733	639.5	90.0	4.2	0.5	2.2	0.1	4.3	4.5
18 60246	Plainfield	57.7	27 631	1 490	479.0	84.4	8.6	0.5	3.8	0.1	4.0	4.9
18 61092	Portage	66.4	36 828	1 079	554.8	75.3	7.6	0.8	1.2	0.1	16.4	3.0
18 64260	Richmond	61.9	36 812	1 080	594.3	85.5	11.1	1.1	1.5	0.3	4.1	3.4
18 68220	Schererville	38.1	29 243	1 408	767.5	80.9	5.7	0.3	3.2	0.1	10.6	10.3
18 71000	South Bend	107.4	101 168	279	942.1	58.6	28.6	1.0	1.7	0.2	13.0	7.1
18 75428	Terre Haute	89.5	60 785	591	679.5	83.8	12.7	1.0	1.8	0.1	3.1	3.3
18 78326	Valparaiso	40.2	31 730	1 287	788.9	87.1	3.8	0.6	2.7	0.1	7.1	6.5
18 82700	Westfield	69.5	30 068	1 355	432.6	89.1	2.6	0.4	3.0	0.0	5.8	5.4
18 82862	West Lafayette	19.7	29 596	1 388	1 500.8	75.9	3.2	0.4	18.5	0.2	3.6	19.6
19 00000	IOWA	144 669.3	3 046 355	X	21.1	89.9	3.6	0.7	2.1	0.1	5.0	4.3
19 01855	Ames	62.7	58 965	619	940.3	84.0	4.0	0.5	9.6	0.1	3.4	11.4
19 02305	Ankeny	76.0	45 582	866	600.1	94.3	1.6	0.4	2.4	0.1	2.3	3.0
19 06355	Bettendorf	55.0	33 217	1 222	604.5	90.6	2.9	0.5	3.6	0.1	3.6	3.9
19 09550	Burlington	37.5	25 663	1 615	684.2	88.7	8.8	0.8	1.1	0.1	3.1	2.3
19 11755	Cedar Falls	74.5	39 260	1 010	527.3	93.6	2.7	0.4	2.8	0.1	2.0	3.6
19 12000	Cedar Rapids	183.4	126 326	201	688.9	88.4	7.1	0.8	2.7	0.2	3.3	3.5
19 14430	Clinton	91.1	26 885	1 541	295.3	91.3	5.6	0.9	1.0	0.0	3.3	2.0
19 16860	Council Bluffs	106.1	62 230	573	586.4	88.4	2.6	1.0	1.0	0.1	8.5	5.0
19 19000	Davenport	163.0	99 685	287	611.5	79.4	12.7	1.0	2.6	0.1	7.3	4.3
19 21000	Des Moines	209.5	203 433	107	971.3	72.7	11.7	0.8	5.0	0.1	12.0	10.5
19 22395	Dubuque	77.6	57 637	640	742.6	91.7	4.8	0.6	1.5	0.5	2.4	1.7
19 28515	Fort Dodge	41.6	25 206	1 648	606.4	88.3	6.6	0.6	1.1	0.1	5.0	4.1
19 38595	Iowa City	64.8	67 862	502	1 047.6	81.6	6.5	0.6	7.7	0.1	5.3	10.3
19 49485	Marion	41.6	34 768	1 157	836.4	94.1	2.9	0.6	1.9	0.1	2.0	3.0
19 49755	Marshalltown	49.9	27 552	1 497	551.7	71.5	2.8	0.6	2.1	0.2	24.1	15.4
19 50160	Mason City	72.0	28 079	1 470	389.9	92.1	2.6	0.6	1.1	0.1	5.1	3.1
19 60465	Ottumwa	41.1	25 023	1 664	609.3	85.5	2.4	0.7	1.1	0.2	11.3	7.7
19 73335	Sioux City	148.5	82 684	388	556.6	75.6	4.1	2.9	3.2	0.2	16.4	9.5
19 79950	Urbandale	56.8	39 463	1 003	695.1	90.3	3.4	0.3	4.1	0.1	3.1	8.2
19 82425	Waterloo	159.0	68 406	496	430.2	77.3	17.2	0.7	1.4	0.3	5.6	6.6
19 83910	West Des Moines	99.9	56 609	658	566.4	86.4	4.0	0.4	5.4	0.1	5.2	9.4

1. Dry land or land partially or temporarily covered by water.   2. May be of any race.

Table D. Cities — Population

City	Age of population (percent), 2010											Population			
												Census counts		Percent change	
	Under 5 years	5 to 17 years	18 to 24 years	25 to 34 years	35 to 44 years	45 to 54 years	55 to 64 years	65 to 74 years	75 years and over	Median age	Percent female	1990	2000	1990–2000	2000–2010
	12	13	14	15	16	17	18	19	20	21	22	23	24	25	26
ILLINOIS—Cont'd															
Waukegan	9.2	21.3	10.5	16.0	14.1	12.8	8.6	4.1	3.3	30.5	49.6	69 481	87 901	26.5	1.3
West Chicago	9.3	23.1	9.8	14.8	15.2	13.2	8.3	3.9	2.3	30.1	48.6	14 808	23 469	58.5	15.4
Wheaton	5.5	18.3	11.5	11.0	12.3	16.2	12.9	6.2	6.0	38.4	51.2	51 441	55 416	7.7	-4.6
Wheeling	7.0	15.0	8.2	18.1	13.9	13.9	11.7	6.2	6.0	36.1	50.8	29 911	34 496	15.3	9.1
Wilmette	5.4	24.0	4.7	4.1	12.2	18.1	14.8	8.3	8.5	44.8	52.0	26 694	27 651	3.6	-2.0
Woodridge	6.8	17.2	8.6	15.9	14.7	16.2	12.4	5.6	2.7	36.1	50.8	26 359	30 934	17.4	6.6
INDIANA	6.7	18.1	10.0	12.8	13.0	14.6	11.9	7.0	6.0	37.0	50.8	5 544 156	6 080 485	9.7	6.6
Anderson	6.7	15.7	11.6	12.7	12.1	13.3	11.6	7.9	8.4	37.8	52.1	59 518	59 734	0.4	-6.0
Bloomington	3.9	7.5	44.4	15.6	7.4	6.9	6.3	3.6	4.3	23.3	49.7	62 735	69 291	10.5	16.0
Carmel	6.5	22.9	5.3	9.4	15.9	17.7	11.9	5.9	4.4	39.2	51.3	25 380	37 733	48.7	109.9
Columbus	7.1	18.1	8.2	13.7	13.6	13.4	11.4	7.3	7.1	37.1	51.6	33 948	39 059	15.1	12.8
Crown Point	5.7	15.5	8.0	14.5	13.2	14.2	12.8	7.9	8.2	39.6	50.0	17 728	19 806	11.7	37.9
East Chicago	9.6	21.8	9.7	14.0	11.4	12.4	9.8	5.7	5.6	30.9	53.2	33 892	32 414	-4.4	-8.4
Elkhart	9.5	19.6	9.4	14.5	13.0	12.7	9.8	5.8	5.8	32.7	51.8	44 661	51 874	16.2	-1.8
Evansville	6.8	15.3	11.6	14.6	11.5	14.2	11.6	6.8	7.5	36.5	51.9	126 272	121 582	-3.7	-3.4
Fishers	8.9	24.1	4.9	15.2	19.3	14.4	7.7	3.4	2.1	33.2	51.4	7 189	37 835	426.3	103.0
Fort Wayne	7.6	18.8	10.2	14.1	12.5	13.6	11.3	6.0	6.0	34.5	51.6	195 680	205 727	5.1	23.3
Gary	7.8	20.3	8.7	11.4	10.3	14.0	13.0	7.8	6.7	36.7	54.0	116 646	102 746	-11.9	-21.9
Goshen	8.9	18.5	11.4	14.3	11.8	11.2	8.9	6.4	8.6	32.4	51.1	23 794	29 383	23.5	8.0
Greenwood	7.9	18.7	9.0	15.9	13.9	12.9	10.1	6.1	5.5	34.0	51.6	26 507	36 037	36.0	38.2
Hammond	7.7	19.9	10.2	14.5	12.8	13.8	10.4	5.4	5.3	33.3	51.0	84 236	83 048	-1.4	-2.7
Hobart	6.3	16.7	8.0	14.7	13.3	14.6	12.0	7.4	7.0	38.0	51.5	24 440	25 363	3.8	14.6
Indianapolis	7.6	17.4	10.6	16.1	13.1	14.0	10.6	5.6	5.0	33.7	51.7	731 728	791 926	8.2	4.8
Jeffersonville	7.0	16.3	8.0	15.6	13.7	14.8	12.8	6.7	5.2	37.3	51.2	24 016	27 362	13.9	64.3
Kokomo	7.4	16.6	8.8	13.4	11.9	14.1	12.1	8.0	7.8	38.2	53.2	44 996	46 113	2.5	-1.4
Lafayette	8.0	15.9	13.0	17.7	12.0	12.1	10.1	5.8	5.5	31.9	51.3	45 933	56 397	22.8	19.0
Lawrence	7.7	20.4	8.1	14.9	14.4	14.9	10.0	4.9	4.6	34.2	52.5	26 849	38 915	44.9	18.2
Marion	6.4	14.6	16.3	11.3	10.7	13.2	11.4	7.7	8.3	36.2	53.0	32 607	31 320	-3.9	-4.4
Merrillville	6.4	19.2	8.6	13.6	13.2	13.8	11.6	6.3	7.3	36.7	53.0	27 257	30 560	12.1	15.3
Michigan City	6.9	16.6	9.0	15.0	12.8	14.7	11.5	6.8	6.8	37.1	48.6	33 822	32 900	-2.7	-4.3
Mishawaka	6.8	16.2	11.5	15.8	12.5	12.9	10.7	6.2	7.4	34.7	52.9	42 635	46 557	9.2	3.6
Muncie	5.5	12.2	27.6	11.9	9.5	10.7	9.6	6.5	6.5	28.1	52.5	71 170	67 430	-5.3	3.9
New Albany	7.0	16.9	10.0	14.6	12.3	14.2	12.0	6.9	7.0	37.1	52.5	36 322	37 603	3.5	-3.3
Noblesville	9.3	20.9	6.6	16.6	16.3	12.6	9.0	5.0	3.8	33.0	51.6	17 655	28 590	61.9	81.8
Plainfield	6.6	18.0	8.9	15.7	15.1	14.1	10.3	5.9	5.4	35.5	47.2	14 953	18 396	23.0	50.2
Portage	6.6	19.1	8.6	13.7	13.7	14.5	11.7	6.6	5.5	36.4	51.6	29 062	33 496	15.3	9.9
Richmond	7.0	15.2	11.4	12.8	11.6	13.8	11.8	7.9	8.5	38.4	52.1	38 705	39 124	1.1	-5.9
Schererville	5.5	16.6	7.8	12.3	13.7	15.9	14.3	7.8	6.2	40.9	51.5	20 155	24 851	23.3	17.7
South Bend	8.2	19.1	10.0	15.0	12.0	12.6	10.5	5.5	7.0	33.3	51.6	105 511	107 789	2.2	-6.1
Terre Haute	6.0	14.0	18.2	14.6	11.8	12.4	10.3	6.0	6.6	32.7	48.4	57 475	59 614	3.7	2.0
Valparaiso	5.9	15.4	15.9	14.9	12.0	12.2	10.6	5.7	7.4	33.4	51.4	24 414	27 428	12.3	15.7
Westfield	8.8	23.0	6.0	14.2	17.4	14.8	8.9	4.1	2.8	33.7	51.1	NA	9 293	NA	223.6
West Lafayette	3.5	8.3	49.5	11.8	6.6	6.4	5.2	3.2	5.5	22.8	45.8	26 144	28 778	10.1	2.8
IOWA	6.6	17.3	10.0	12.6	12.0	14.4	12.2	7.4	7.5	38.1	50.5	2 776 831	2 926 324	5.4	4.1
Ames	4.5	8.9	40.6	15.4	7.5	7.6	7.4	4.1	4.0	23.8	47.0	47 198	50 731	7.5	16.2
Ankeny	9.2	18.5	9.1	18.4	15.3	11.8	9.3	4.9	3.5	31.9	51.0	18 482	27 117	46.7	68.1
Bettendorf	6.0	19.5	5.8	11.4	13.2	15.6	13.7	7.6	7.1	40.7	51.4	28 139	31 275	11.1	6.2
Burlington	6.9	16.8	7.8	13.0	11.6	13.9	12.5	8.1	9.3	39.7	51.9	27 208	26 839	-1.4	-4.4
Cedar Falls	5.0	12.3	29.8	11.9	8.6	10.0	10.1	5.6	6.8	26.8	51.9	34 298	36 145	5.4	8.6
Cedar Rapids	6.7	16.8	11.2	14.9	12.5	13.7	11.1	6.4	6.8	35.3	50.9	108 772	120 758	11.0	4.6
Clinton	6.6	16.5	9.3	11.7	11.1	15.3	12.4	8.2	8.9	40.4	51.5	29 201	27 772	-4.9	-3.2
Council Bluffs	7.3	16.8	10.8	14.0	12.0	14.1	11.5	6.8	6.7	35.9	51.3	54 315	58 268	7.3	6.8
Davenport	7.3	16.7	10.8	14.9	12.3	13.8	11.6	6.3	6.2	35.3	51.3	95 333	98 359	3.2	1.3
Des Moines	7.9	16.9	10.9	16.3	13.0	13.4	10.6	5.6	5.4	33.5	51.1	193 189	198 682	2.8	2.4
Dubuque	6.2	15.3	13.0	12.8	10.5	13.8	12.0	7.4	9.1	38.0	51.6	57 538	57 686	0.3	-0.1
Fort Dodge	6.1	15.6	13.3	13.1	10.3	13.3	12.1	7.2	9.0	36.8	48.7	26 057	25 136	-3.5	0.3
Iowa City	4.7	10.2	33.5	16.5	9.3	9.1	8.7	4.1	4.0	25.6	50.3	59 735	62 220	4.2	9.1
Marion	7.5	19.0	7.0	14.9	14.4	13.6	10.6	7.0	6.1	36.1	51.7	20 422	26 294	28.8	32.2
Marshalltown	7.8	18.3	9.3	12.3	10.8	12.8	12.1	7.5	9.2	37.3	50.2	25 178	26 009	3.3	5.9
Mason City	6.2	15.7	9.7	11.9	11.2	14.9	13.2	7.7	9.4	40.9	51.8	29 040	29 172	0.5	-3.7
Ottumwa	7.2	16.1	10.8	13.1	11.7	13.4	11.6	7.1	8.9	37.4	51.6	24 488	24 998	2.1	0.1
Sioux City	8.1	18.5	11.5	13.5	12.0	12.9	11.1	6.2	6.2	33.7	50.8	80 505	85 013	5.6	-2.7
Urbandale	7.0	19.0	6.3	13.5	15.4	15.0	11.9	6.2	5.6	37.8	51.6	23 775	29 072	22.3	35.7
Waterloo	7.5	16.2	10.3	14.9	11.5	13.2	12.3	6.9	7.1	35.9	51.6	66 467	68 747	3.4	-0.5
West Des Moines	7.1	17.0	9.2	18.7	13.9	13.3	10.1	5.7	5.0	33.5	51.7	31 702	46 403	46.4	22.0

Table D. Cities — Households, Group Quarters, Crime, and Education

City	Households, 2010 Number (27)	Persons per house-hold (28)	Female family house-holder[1] (29)	One-person (30)	Persons in group quarters, 2010 Total (31)	Institutional Total (32)	Persons in nursing facilities (33)	Non-institu-tional (34)	Serious crimes known to police[2] 2010 Number (35)	Rate[3] (36)	Violent (37)	Property (38)	Population age 25 and older (39)	High school graduate or less (40)	Bachelor's degree or more (41)
ILLINOIS—Cont'd															
Waukegan	28 079	3.10	18.0	23.4	2 077	1 586	842	491	2 978	3 343	384	2 959	52 148	58.6	17.5
West Chicago	7 330	3.65	10.4	12.4	333	325	325	8	390	1 440	107	1 333	14 686	50.2	26.1
Wheaton	19 191	2.58	8.2	25.7	3 379	1 395	578	1 984	810	1 531	45	1 486	34 014	15.9	60.5
Wheeling	14 461	2.57	9.7	29.2	465	461	461	4	698	1 854	165	1 690	25 292	39.3	37.1
Wilmette	9 742	2.77	7.1	20.8	126	69	69	57	NA	NA	NA	NA	18 047	9.0	76.6
Woodridge	12 646	2.60	11.3	25.2	88	86	0	2	477	1 447	146	1 301	22 276	25.9	45.7
INDIANA	2 502 154	2.52	12.4	26.9	186 923	95 336	41 158	91 587	217 649	3 357	314	3 042	4 200 431	48.9	22.7
Anderson	23 560	2.28	17.1	34.5	2 401	910	527	1 491	3 271	5 828	355	5 473	37 383	58.5	15.6
Bloomington	31 425	2.09	7.5	38.2	14 669	543	282	14 126	3 449	4 290	381	3 909	35 697	21.6	57.1
Carmel	28 997	2.71	6.3	20.8	600	579	470	21	939	1 186	53	1 133	49 758	12.2	66.9
Columbus	17 787	2.43	11.7	29.7	870	704	450	166	2 347	5 327	177	5 150	29 081	39.0	31.5
Crown Point	10 394	2.45	10.0	27.5	1 863	1 839	338	24	541	1 980	70	1 911	18 566	41.1	30.8
East Chicago	10 724	2.75	31.4	29.0	178	98	92	80	2 168	7 300	704	6 596	16 352	63.8	7.8
Elkhart	19 261	2.60	18.5	30.8	915	611	611	304	2 486	4 879	306	4 573	31 276	61.5	13.6
Evansville	50 588	2.23	15.6	36.5	4 727	2 103	1 194	2 624	6 037	5 141	420	4 721	78 355	51.2	18.4
Fishers	27 218	2.82	7.9	19.8	27	27	27	0	748	974	23	951	47 457	14.5	60.1
Fort Wayne	101 585	2.44	14.8	31.2	5 356	2 680	1 643	2 676	9 606	3 786	294	3 492	160 353	42.4	25.3
Gary	31 380	2.54	30.9	32.8	708	261	237	447	6 107	7 606	928	6 678	53 015	55.3	12.1
Goshen	11 344	2.67	13.1	27.4	1 467	808	411	659	1 073	3 383	104	3 279	19 876	54.9	19.5
Greenwood	19 615	2.51	11.6	27.8	481	456	405	25	1 951	3 918	360	3 559	31 876	43.3	25.4
Hammond	29 949	2.67	19.7	30.3	975	82	71	893	4 544	5 622	820	4 801	51 145	60.4	11.9
Hobart	11 650	2.48	12.1	28.2	144	1	0	143	1 545	5 317	268	5 048	19 689	51.6	16.5
Indianapolis	336 186	2.42	17.2	32.1	16 040	8 750	4 382	7 290	55 590	6 686	1 160	5 526	526 191	45.6	27.4
Jeffersonville	18 580	2.37	13.9	30.5	878	535	109	343	1 677	3 731	719	3 012	30 336	46.0	20.2
Kokomo	19 848	2.25	16.6	35.4	722	532	426	190	2 532	5 569	334	5 234	29 625	52.8	16.9
Lafayette	28 545	2.30	13.7	34.9	1 433	1 058	477	375	2 968	4 421	393	4 027	42 430	45.0	27.5
Lawrence	17 864	2.56	17.5	27.6	333	289	223	44	NA	NA	NA	NA	28 223	40.8	30.1
Marion	11 828	2.25	17.0	36.7	3 364	797	481	2 567	1 525	5 092	301	4 792	18 933	64.3	14.0
Merrillville	13 696	2.54	17.9	29.7	455	366	362	89	1 368	3 881	270	3 612	22 721	45.7	19.3
Michigan City	12 136	2.37	19.0	34.3	2 670	2 506	234	164	2 163	6 871	467	6 404	21 583	55.5	15.6
Mishawaka	21 343	2.21	14.4	37.4	1 013	212	83	801	3 207	6 646	294	6 352	32 231	48.7	24.6
Muncie	27 722	2.22	14.1	35.2	8 508	1 267	744	7 241	2 328	3 322	348	2 974	38 078	53.4	20.6
New Albany	15 575	2.27	18.2	33.7	1 008	724	429	284	2 347	6 453	300	6 153	24 414	55.3	17.6
Noblesville	19 080	2.69	10.8	21.6	661	632	316	29	903	1 738	60	1 678	31 804	25.1	48.5
Plainfield	9 747	2.57	12.3	25.7	2 615	2 595	145	20	720	2 606	130	2 475	17 465	44.4	26.9
Portage	13 992	2.61	14.6	24.3	255	233	233	22	1 320	3 584	266	3 318	24 273	51.8	15.8
Richmond	15 098	2.29	16.3	34.2	2 292	1 198	561	1 094	1 790	4 863	462	4 401	24 846	58.5	17.3
Schererville	11 883	2.45	9.7	27.7	120	63	0	57	781	2 671	51	2 619	20 421	37.4	31.9
South Bend	39 760	2.48	18.9	33.3	2 692	1 697	773	995	6 675	6 598	737	5 861	64 175	49.5	20.8
Terre Haute	22 645	2.29	15.7	34.9	8 875	4 173	589	4 702	4 348	7 153	240	6 913	37 290	49.6	18.9
Valparaiso	12 610	2.28	10.9	34.5	2 936	1 070	546	1 866	857	2 701	145	2 556	19 278	35.5	34.0
Westfield	10 490	2.85	9.3	18.0	139	99	99	40	448	1 490	57	1 433	17 819	20.1	53.5
West Lafayette	11 945	2.22	4.4	34.2	3 069	155	155	2 914	534	1 804	162	1 642	11 626	13.2	72.2
IOWA	1 221 576	2.41	9.3	28.4	98 112	43 282	26 871	54 830	76 648	2 516	274	2 243	2 000 692	43.2	24.8
Ames	22 759	2.25	5.4	30.5	7 767	294	181	7 473	1 733	2 939	300	2 639	26 582	15.8	60.1
Ankeny	17 433	2.58	7.2	22.6	663	174	146	489	754	1 654	103	1 551	27 722	20.2	45.7
Bettendorf	13 681	2.42	8.4	28.2	176	172	158	4	504	1 517	75	1 442	22 361	24.3	44.7
Burlington	10 938	2.30	14.2	32.5	495	367	235	128	1 168	4 551	647	3 904	17 308	45.6	18.0
Cedar Falls	14 608	2.37	7.2	28.0	4 574	354	354	4 220	761	1 938	183	1 755	21 138	29.0	42.0
Cedar Rapids	53 236	2.31	11.0	32.5	3 518	1 561	769	1 957	5 371	4 252	306	3 946	82 648	34.1	30.4
Clinton	11 246	2.33	12.7	32.1	713	379	347	334	1 315	4 891	550	4 341	18 186	51.5	14.4
Council Bluffs	24 793	2.43	15.0	30.0	1 908	964	440	944	4 301	6 911	1 024	5 888	40 218	51.0	14.8
Davenport	40 620	2.38	14.3	31.5	3 111	1 247	751	1 864	5 781	5 799	871	4 929	64 386	40.0	26.2
Des Moines	81 360	2.43	14.2	32.5	6 104	1 641	1 005	4 463	10 897	5 357	533	4 824	130 573	45.5	23.9
Dubuque	23 506	2.28	11.1	33.7	4 027	1 133	806	2 894	1 940	3 366	291	3 074	37 492	46.2	26.6
Fort Dodge	10 275	2.21	13.0	36.8	2 509	1 651	345	858	1 372	5 443	294	5 150	16 080	47.0	21.4
Iowa City	27 657	2.22	7.2	34.3	6 585	296	168	6 289	1 729	2 548	277	2 271	34 167	17.2	59.3
Marion	14 108	2.44	9.8	28.4	292	214	210	78	641	1 844	158	1 685	22 500	31.3	32.1
Marshalltown	10 335	2.55	11.9	29.8	1 190	1 040	985	150	1 168	4 239	388	3 851	17 879	51.7	19.6
Mason City	12 366	2.20	10.8	35.0	856	448	344	408	1 105	3 935	167	3 768	19 322	38.4	19.9
Ottumwa	10 251	2.36	12.9	32.9	826	371	248	455	1 015	4 056	404	3 653	16 635	55.6	15.0
Sioux City	31 571	2.54	13.8	29.4	2 565	743	437	1 822	3 425	4 143	353	3 789	50 715	48.9	20.5
Urbandale	15 596	2.52	7.2	25.0	234	230	222	4	780	1 977	147	1 830	26 339	22.4	46.4
Waterloo	28 607	2.35	14.9	31.6	1 165	687	515	478	3 006	4 394	639	3 756	44 355	48.8	18.8
West Des Moines	24 311	2.32	8.6	31.2	273	262	262	11	1 853	3 273	194	3 079	37 387	22.9	48.1

1. No spouse present.   2. Data for serious crimes have not been adjusted for underreporting. This may affect comparability between geographic areas and over time.   3. Per 100,000 population estimated by the FBI.   4. Persons 25 years old and over.

Table D. Cities — Income, Poverty, and Housing

City	Money income, 2008–2010					Housing units, 2010			Occupied Housing units 2008–2010				
	Households				Families with income below poverty (percent)				Owner-occupied			Median owner costs as a percent of income	
	Per capita income[1] (dollars)	Median income	Percent with income of $200,000 or more	Percent with income of less than $25,000		Total	Percent change, 2000–2010	Vacant units for sale or rent[2]	Total	Percent	Median value[3] (dollars)	With a mortgage[4]	Without a mortgage[5]
	42	43	44	45	46	47	48	49	50	51	52	53	54
ILLINOIS—Cont'd													
Waukegan	19 859	47 366	1.8	24.0	14.2	30 746	5.1	2 667	28 667	56.9	162 800	28.6	17.6
West Chicago	24 284	60 397	4.6	15.2	8.4	7 763	15.2	433	7 450	61.9	253 200	29.3	14.5
Wheaton	40 145	83 492	11.3	13.0	3.3	20 112	1.1	921	18 803	72.7	355 600	25.1	11.6
Wheeling	26 555	57 069	2.3	19.4	7.4	15 397	12.5	936	14 248	65.4	236 400	31.6	16.5
Wilmette	67 047	127 608	30.0	8.9	1.6	10 290	-0.4	548	9 542	84.9	667 500	24.1	13.8
Woodridge	32 536	71 081	4.4	13.0	3.9	13 392	14.6	746	12 570	67.7	270 900	28.5	13.7
INDIANA	23 605	46 529	2.2	25.3	10.2	2 795 541	10.4	293 387	2 471 619	71.1	124 100	21.9	11.6
Anderson	18 252	34 154	0.5	35.5	18.7	27 953	1.3	4 393	22 965	61.4	75 700	23.6	13.3
Bloomington	18 187	26 564	2.6	47.3	18.2	33 239	17.2	1 814	30 538	34.5	170 500	21.5	10.9
Carmel	48 384	100 003	15.7	8.8	2.4	30 738	117.0	1 741	28 153	78.7	293 900	20.1	10.0
Columbus	27 551	48 506	3.1	23.9	8.4	19 700	14.9	1 913	18 084	64.8	142 600	19.3	11.2
Crown Point	32 273	67 361	5.9	13.2	4.0	10 976	36.0	582	9 663	80.1	182 000	21.8	11.7
East Chicago	12 598	26 773	0.2	46.2	36.0	12 958	-2.3	2 234	9 375	44.4	89 000	28.4	17.1
Elkhart	17 337	33 217	0.8	38.1	24.0	22 699	4.9	3 438	18 835	54.0	90 800	22.9	15.3
Evansville	20 593	34 785	1.1	35.3	15.3	57 799	1.2	7 211	50 937	55.4	91 000	21.7	13.0
Fishers	37 849	87 460	7.7	6.1	2.5	28 511	82.0	1 293	27 120	81.4	214 300	20.8	10.1
Fort Wayne	22 821	43 069	1.8	26.8	12.1	113 541	24.9	11 956	100 753	64.5	101 000	20.4	10.1
Gary	14 889	27 230	0.3	47.0	28.7	39 531	-9.4	8 151	30 815	54.2	67 300	27.5	16.9
Goshen	20 010	39 266	1.5	29.2	12.3	12 631	12.2	1 287	11 931	65.9	102 800	22.5	13.9
Greenwood	26 712	53 482	2.3	19.7	9.3	21 309	33.6	1 724	19 325	63.1	132 800	20.9	11.7
Hammond	17 765	37 300	0.6	33.5	16.0	32 945	-3.5	2 996	30 017	62.0	97 900	25.4	14.0
Hobart	23 782	51 962	0.0	21.9	5.5	12 399	20.6	749	11 211	73.3	137 200	22.2	19.6
Indianapolis	23 449	41 170	2.1	29.4	15.0	384 414	7.6	48 228	323 352	57.2	121 400	22.7	12.3
Jeffersonville	24 238	48 543	1.4	25.2	7.1	19 991	60.9	1 411	17 928	65.7	124 700	20.5	12.0
Kokomo	19 826	35 581	0.8	35.7	17.2	23 010	3.0	3 162	19 108	61.2	85 900	21.0	11.6
Lafayette	21 577	37 162	1.3	33.7	14.2	31 260	22.4	2 715	28 770	51.4	103 400	21.8	10.0
Lawrence	24 493	52 164	2.4	21.1	7.4	19 515	19.9	1 651	16 651	73.1	134 400	23.8	13.8
Marion	16 226	27 864	0.5	44.5	18.8	13 715	-0.6	1 887	11 952	54.3	66 500	21.9	13.4
Merrillville	22 993	49 469	1.1	25.0	8.9	14 842	19.8	1 146	13 461	69.1	133 900	25.5	13.4
Michigan City	18 883	35 497	1.3	35.2	15.6	14 435	1.5	2 299	12 088	61.4	95 500	23.9	12.3
Mishawaka	21 303	36 195	1.3	35.2	14.3	24 088	11.4	2 745	21 193	55.2	94 600	23.7	13.1
Muncie	16 013	29 202	0.8	41.8	18.8	31 958	5.8	4 236	27 569	52.8	75 200	22.8	12.9
New Albany	20 226	36 916	0.6	33.5	14.5	17 315	1.6	1 740	15 916	56.6	110 000	23.7	12.4
Noblesville	29 877	65 551	3.2	14.5	6.0	21 121	86.3	2 041	19 078	74.8	169 300	22.6	10.2
Plainfield	24 425	53 760	2.2	16.1	8.1	10 086	38.3	639	9 243	71.9	149 700	22.4	12.0
Portage	22 861	46 814	0.6	26.0	10.1	14 807	11.1	815	14 232	70.9	141 500	21.6	16.1
Richmond	20 445	33 184	1.6	38.3	22.5	17 649	-0.4	2 551	15 281	55.8	88 000	21.1	10.9
Schererville	31 983	66 160	4.3	16.3	4.3	12 393	24.0	810	11 503	76.7	199 600	23.4	10.0
South Bend	17 955	32 917	1.0	35.5	20.9	46 324	0.2	6 564	38 938	60.5	87 800	23.3	12.6
Terre Haute	17 393	31 153	1.0	39.8	21.1	25 518	-0.3	2 873	22 423	57.4	77 300	21.4	12.6
Valparaiso	24 176	48 248	2.5	26.1	9.2	13 506	15.8	896	12 186	60.3	170 100	22.9	14.2
Westfield	33 767	86 438	7.1	9.6	5.1	11 209	NA	719	10 317	84.7	208 300	21.9	11.2
West Lafayette	22 728	30 307	3.1	46.8	9.0	12 591	16.5	646	12 042	35.3	171 800	19.1	10.0
IOWA	25 357	48 827	2.3	23.8	7.6	1 336 417	8.4	114 841	1 219 737	72.7	122 000	21.1	11.6
Ames	23 363	40 073	2.2	33.1	6.8	23 876	27.6	1 117	22 804	42.2	167 600	20.1	10.0
Ankeny	30 790	69 405	2.5	11.8	4.0	18 339	69.8	906	16 790	79.9	176 500	22.0	11.4
Bettendorf	34 932	65 176	6.8	16.2	4.5	14 437	10.6	756	13 251	77.1	165 800	19.4	10.0
Burlington	23 179	38 336	0.8	33.8	9.7	11 899	-1.0	961	10 936	67.6	83 800	21.7	12.4
Cedar Falls	23 385	47 037	1.7	27.4	9.1	15 477	16.4	869	14 246	65.7	158 600	19.4	10.3
Cedar Rapids	27 714	50 870	2.7	22.3	7.6	57 217	9.7	3 981	52 900	69.9	130 000	20.8	11.9
Clinton	21 908	41 911	1.4	30.0	8.8	12 202	-1.8	956	10 952	68.5	96 300	21.0	12.5
Council Bluffs	20 577	41 129	0.5	28.5	12.2	26 594	9.1	1 801	24 548	62.5	111 200	22.5	12.5
Davenport	23 902	42 475	1.8	29.3	13.2	44 087	6.6	3 467	41 302	63.4	119 000	22.0	12.1
Des Moines	23 533	43 455	1.6	28.6	12.1	88 729	4.3	7 360	83 242	62.5	119 800	23.4	13.2
Dubuque	23 482	42 447	2.1	24.3	8.1	25 029	5.1	1 523	23 477	66.8	124 100	20.8	11.9
Fort Dodge	21 478	36 403	0.6	34.2	12.6	11 215	0.1	940	10 697	63.9	80 100	19.5	12.1
Iowa City	24 285	40 320	3.1	37.5	8.6	29 270	12.4	1 613	26 563	47.9	182 000	22.2	11.0
Marion	28 573	54 200	2.0	15.5	3.8	15 064	37.2	956	13 924	74.1	142 900	20.1	12.2
Marshalltown	20 468	40 874	0.8	27.7	10.5	11 171	2.9	836	10 612	70.0	91 500	21.6	11.7
Mason City	24 224	40 673	1.7	31.0	9.4	13 352	2.3	986	13 135	65.8	95 700	19.9	11.4
Ottumwa	21 068	35 653	1.4	34.1	14.4	11 257	2.6	1 006	10 380	71.9	68 600	20.1	13.5
Sioux City	20 838	41 330	1.4	29.1	13.3	33 425	-1.1	1 854	31 347	63.1	94 400	21.0	11.6
Urbandale	39 131	82 147	7.5	10.3	2.6	16 319	37.7	723	15 746	78.3	194 600	20.3	10.0
Waterloo	21 601	40 280	1.3	30.2	14.6	30 723	4.2	2 116	28 776	65.1	103 000	20.3	12.0
West Des Moines	37 271	64 134	6.2	12.4	3.5	26 219	26.2	1 908	23 584	63.9	184 100	21.3	10.0

1. Based on population estimated by the American Community Survey. 2. Includes units rented or sold but not occupied. 3. Specified owner-occupied units; $1,000,000 represents $1,000,000 or more. 4. 50.0 represents 50 percent or more. 5. 10.0 represents 10 percent or less.

Table D. Cities — Housing, Labor Force, and Employment

City	Occupied housing units, 2008–2010 (cont.)				Migration, 2008–2010		Civilian labor force, 2010		Unemployment		Civilian employment[4], 2008–2010			
												Percent		
	Percent renter occupied	Median gross rent[1]	Median rent as a percent of income[2]	Percent with no vehicle available	Percent who lived in the same house one year ago	Percent who lived outside this city one year ago	Total	Percent change, 2009–2010	Total	Rate[3]	Population age 16 and older	In labor force	Full-year full-time worker	Households with no workers (percent)
	55	56	57	58	59	60	61	62	63	64	65	66	67	68
ILLINOIS—Cont'd														
Waukegan	43.1	827	30.6	12.5	84.5	6.1	43 195	-0.6	6 150	14.2	64 207	69.7	43.3	21.2
West Chicago	38.1	879	29.1	3.4	83.4	9.7	14 865	3.0	1 609	10.8	18 917	76.9	46.6	13.4
Wheaton	27.3	1 083	28.9	5.1	85.1	8.9	28 507	-2.1	2 162	7.6	42 375	67.8	42.7	20.4
Wheeling	34.6	955	28.3	6.1	88.5	6.7	22 591	4.7	1 897	8.4	29 676	75.4	49.7	17.8
Wilmette	15.1	1 362	26.9	4.4	89.6	6.3	12 907	3.3	854	6.6	20 448	61.9	40.5	23.8
Woodridge	32.3	987	25.3	4.1	86.5	10.1	19 607	-1.9	1 783	9.1	26 458	74.1	45.0	17.0
INDIANA	28.9	686	29.8	6.4	84.3	9.4	3 176 657	-0.2	320 240	10.1	5 036 761	65.4	40.1	26.8
Anderson	38.6	653	32.9	12.0	79.1	6.1	25 952	-1.8	3 239	12.5	45 398	59.0	33.2	40.1
Bloomington	65.5	715	44.2	13.0	53.1	25.4	40 018	6.4	2 776	6.9	71 686	53.5	21.9	31.1
Carmel	21.3	957	25.5	1.8	86.7	9.3	38 360	15.0	2 326	6.1	56 721	70.2	47.4	16.4
Columbus	35.2	747	28.4	6.3	78.8	8.5	21 272	7.8	2 002	9.4	33 669	68.3	43.3	26.6
Crown Point	19.9	936	27.4	3.8	83.9	13.2	13 079	NA	1 237	9.5	21 140	64.0	43.1	21.8
East Chicago	55.6	666	34.5	22.1	77.8	15.4	9 936	-3.4	1 465	14.7	20 368	52.7	29.4	39.0
Elkhart	46.0	654	30.2	11.9	79.1	9.7	22 535	-2.2	3 531	15.7	37 368	65.9	34.7	28.4
Evansville	44.6	646	31.8	12.2	80.9	6.9	58 694	0.7	5 606	9.6	94 309	64.0	41.5	30.3
Fishers	18.6	988	22.9	0.9	86.7	10.1	42 956	8.2	2 615	6.1	54 016	76.7	55.4	9.5
Fort Wayne	35.5	619	26.5	8.2	84.6	5.0	124 830	-0.5	13 854	11.1	193 058	66.1	41.6	27.2
Gary	45.8	672	41.3	16.2	83.4	7.0	28 819	-17.5	3 926	13.6	63 250	51.0	26.4	43.6
Goshen	34.1	705	33.2	9.6	78.2	10.7	14 184	-1.1	1 904	13.4	24 002	67.7	35.9	28.2
Greenwood	36.9	760	26.7	4.8	82.4	12.2	26 713	2.1	2 326	8.7	37 609	70.0	46.6	23.5
Hammond	38.0	734	31.5	11.7	88.2	8.7	34 097	2.4	4 220	12.4	61 950	62.0	36.9	31.0
Hobart	26.7	778	28.5	5.5	87.1	9.2	14 083	0.1	1 592	11.3	22 940	66.9	38.8	27.8
Indianapolis	42.8	720	31.9	8.7	80.2	5.7	421 784	0.9	42 125	10.0	634 543	68.9	41.6	25.3
Jeffersonville	34.3	712	28.6	6.7	87.2	8.6	22 114	41.4	1 748	7.9	35 327	71.7	47.4	23.1
Kokomo	38.8	615	33.2	10.3	79.9	8.1	19 374	0.2	2 660	13.7	34 450	57.6	32.0	41.1
Lafayette	48.6	680	31.3	7.7	74.1	12.0	34 368	-0.9	3 525	10.3	52 675	72.6	42.8	24.2
Lawrence	26.9	752	29.2	2.9	89.1	8.7	24 359	4.2	2 188	9.0	33 720	73.4	46.6	21.8
Marion	45.7	569	29.3	10.9	81.6	8.7	13 039	-0.6	1 724	13.2	23 572	54.5	28.5	44.9
Merrillville	30.9	901	37.2	8.2	85.3	11.6	17 369	3.1	1 721	9.9	26 533	65.9	41.5	28.0
Michigan City	38.6	659	30.4	9.0	79.1	10.1	13 680	-5.2	1 753	12.8	25 816	60.1	33.3	27.9
Mishawaka	44.8	649	27.2	8.8	80.7	12.6	24 991	-4.7	2 943	11.8	37 834	69.6	39.6	26.5
Muncie	47.2	621	36.2	10.6	61.6	14.8	31 361	4.9	3 533	11.3	58 776	60.1	25.8	37.4
New Albany	43.4	657	29.9	9.5	78.9	9.8	17 397	-5.4	1 842	10.6	28 949	66.4	42.4	29.0
Noblesville	25.2	837	28.2	4.0	82.8	10.4	26 604	18.7	2 115	7.9	37 008	75.4	50.4	14.6
Plainfield	28.1	835	24.4	2.9	81.8	15.1	13 673	-2.6	1 152	8.4	20 222	61.8	42.8	22.8
Portage	29.1	755	32.0	2.2	86.7	9.7	17 870	-3.3	1 839	10.3	28 168	65.9	40.9	26.0
Richmond	44.2	556	32.2	15.9	75.1	8.3	15 900	-5.9	2 057	12.9	29 735	57.2	32.7	37.3
Schererville	23.3	813	29.3	2.6	90.8	7.3	15 454	-1.5	1 302	8.4	23 253	72.8	47.3	21.0
South Bend	39.5	701	32.8	10.9	77.0	9.9	44 675	-2.8	5 845	13.1	76 868	65.4	35.2	31.6
Terre Haute	42.6	592	31.2	11.2	81.7	11.2	27 463	1.2	3 186	11.6	49 773	52.7	30.1	38.8
Valparaiso	39.7	805	29.5	5.7	79.4	12.4	15 828	1.8	1 291	8.2	24 726	63.5	37.4	29.3
Westfield	15.3	795	23.0	0.5	88.1	8.6	14 601	NA	912	6.2	20 369	77.3	55.6	12.1
West Lafayette	64.7	791	50.0	12.3	63.3	19.3	13 057	-8.7	773	5.9	26 209	55.7	23.4	34.2
IOWA	27.3	623	27.4	5.9	84.2	9.1	1 669 841	0.3	104 823	6.3	2 391 813	69.2	44.9	24.7
Ames	57.8	709	35.7	6.9	60.5	18.2	32 659	0.9	1 373	4.2	51 124	69.1	29.9	19.7
Ankeny	20.1	718	24.4	3.5	84.5	10.1	26 812	4.9	1 080	4.0	32 851	79.1	55.3	13.1
Bettendorf	22.9	684	25.8	4.9	86.6	9.0	18 060	1.1	989	5.5	25 281	67.6	47.6	22.1
Burlington	32.4	569	27.7	9.7	82.0	9.6	12 830	1.0	1 042	8.1	20 361	64.2	38.3	32.8
Cedar Falls	34.3	690	42.0	4.6	73.0	15.6	24 314	0.9	983	4.0	33 259	66.2	34.9	24.4
Cedar Rapids	30.1	657	27.3	7.2	79.2	8.7	72 665	-1.8	4 504	6.2	99 642	71.6	47.6	22.9
Clinton	31.5	542	29.5	12.1	84.1	7.6	14 452	0.8	1 130	7.8	21 398	64.3	40.2	32.2
Council Bluffs	37.5	676	31.6	8.1	79.2	9.6	31 671	1.3	1 653	5.2	48 298	69.0	46.1	25.2
Davenport	36.6	620	28.8	6.7	82.7	7.5	52 223	-1.5	3 918	7.5	77 867	66.8	42.8	25.4
Des Moines	37.5	682	31.0	10.4	77.0	8.3	107 990	1.0	7 985	7.4	157 223	71.8	47.2	23.8
Dubuque	33.2	597	27.9	10.0	83.3	7.1	32 089	2.4	1 929	6.0	47 001	69.1	39.8	24.2
Fort Dodge	36.1	510	25.3	10.9	85.7	7.2	12 744	-2.9	917	7.2	20 143	67.0	37.0	27.8
Iowa City	52.1	760	46.2	8.8	63.4	17.2	42 033	-1.7	1 644	3.9	58 372	69.9	31.9	22.2
Marion	25.9	603	27.2	5.5	84.1	10.4	21 064	5.1	992	4.7	25 877	72.1	50.7	20.5
Marshalltown	30.0	528	29.0	10.8	85.2	5.5	13 184	2.7	948	7.2	21 289	62.7	40.9	30.8
Mason City	34.2	557	27.5	7.6	82.4	7.6	15 599	0.8	1 111	7.1	22 534	71.1	45.9	27.3
Ottumwa	28.1	559	28.1	9.4	81.3	5.1	12 441	2.5	1 034	8.3	19 878	65.0	38.0	31.3
Sioux City	36.9	605	30.4	8.6	80.9	7.6	44 715	0.4	3 076	6.9	63 079	69.2	45.4	22.5
Urbandale	21.7	789	24.5	2.5	85.6	10.6	23 247	1.6	1 060	4.6	29 412	79.3	59.3	14.3
Waterloo	34.9	602	30.5	10.0	80.4	8.4	36 511	0.8	2 705	7.4	53 515	66.5	41.6	28.4
West Des Moines	36.1	784	23.4	2.7	80.3	13.4	33 684	-0.8	1 517	4.5	44 161	76.7	55.9	16.6

1. $2,000 represents $2,000 or more. 2. 50.0 represents 50 percent or more. 3. Percent of civilian labor force. 4. Persons 16 years old and over.

City	Value of residential construction authorized by building permits, 2010			Wholesale trade,[1] 2007				Retail trade,[2] 2007			
	New construction ($1,000)	Number of housing units	Percent single family	Number of establish-ments	Number of employees	Sales (mil dol)	Annual payroll (mil dol)	Number of establish-ments	Number of employees	Sales (mil dol)	Annual payroll (mil dol)
	69	70	71	72	73	74	75	76	77	78	79
ILLINOIS—Cont'd											
Waukegan	4 108	27	63.0	67	1 398	1 285.6	76.0	236	4 515	1 112.9	139.7
West Chicago	500	6	100.0	80	1 592	946.9	84.1	93	1 241	372.0	35.8
Wheaton	10 432	18	100.0	58	253	168.7	17.4	191	3 068	603.8	61.6
Wheeling	1 652	9	100.0	137	2 218	1 125.9	127.3	108	1 271	334.2	35.6
Wilmette	17 775	24	100.0	28	75	102.3	4.2	129	1 398	297.8	38.1
Woodridge	936	5	100.0	55	1 904	1 509.1	115.2	92	1 702	428.3	40.9
INDIANA	1 960 774	13 083	74.7	6 756	97 219	67 634.9	4 295.6	23 692	333 172	78 745.6	7 123.1
Anderson	6 086	27	85.2	38	707	212.3	26.2	269	4 063	863.0	79.4
Bloomington	NA	NA	NA	49	628	450.6	27.5	394	6 324	1 267.8	122.0
Carmel	89 631	539	55.8	100	985	1 276.5	67.1	249	3 602	786.3	82.5
Columbus	NA	NA	NA	55	885	677.7	47.0	236	3 787	822.0	81.1
Crown Point	27 511	132	100.0	25	259	244.0	11.7	88	1 239	257.1	25.0
East Chicago	4 925	15	66.7	33	507	380.8	20.0	53	450	130.2	11.4
Elkhart	464	5	100.0	143	2 152	1 330.5	91.1	283	4 492	1 121.6	100.3
Evansville	6 320	78	50.0	194	4 327	2 395.3	230.9	728	11 399	2 450.3	245.5
Fishers	107 055	770	62.5	86	1 493	761.3	90.6	171	3 367	910.0	83.7
Fort Wayne	1 134	8	100.0	422	6 310	4 927.4	242.8	1 157	19 477	4 392.0	402.2
Gary	0	0	0.0	55	1 323	802.3	75.6	198	1 522	548.1	29.8
Goshen	7 376	79	24.1	26	461	220.4	17.9	172	3 175	737.3	72.5
Greenwood	39 590	373	56.0	41	742	456.0	32.5	310	5 811	1 216.2	122.9
Hammond	376	2	100.0	64	1 067	512.8	53.8	236	3 116	1 031.8	70.3
Hobart	2 728	13	100.0	26	223	316.1	10.5	267	5 547	1 073.4	99.4
Indianapolis	145 588	1 342	46.1	1 264	24 462	15 103.1	1 201.6	3 036	49 297	12 140.2	1 192.8
Jeffersonville	12 138	99	90.9	41	761	629.0	33.3	106	1 435	330.7	32.8
Kokomo	204	2	100.0	46	388	237.2	18.0	328	4 829	1 078.4	97.3
Lafayette	18 420	152	60.5	74	859	285.3	37.8	431	7 594	1 596.7	150.1
Lawrence	9 411	62	100.0	37	281	205.1	12.9	123	2 004	408.3	43.3
Marion	NA	NA	NA	27	249	95.0	9.7	203	2 684	607.0	55.3
Merrillville	13 138	223	9.0	30	323	195.8	15.2	199	3 869	1 071.2	90.4
Michigan City	2 026	31	100.0	38	559	332.9	22.3	262	3 721	730.1	68.0
Mishawaka	3 338	22	100.0	65	890	991.9	52.7	385	7 739	1 766.8	152.1
Muncie	941	12	83.3	63	801	320.7	25.3	379	5 143	1 044.6	99.6
New Albany	3 344	23	100.0	57	802	1 390.8	30.4	154	2 463	615.3	53.0
Noblesville	59 083	419	79.0	69	442	147.5	20.9	165	3 199	727.9	73.5
Plainfield	12 560	71	100.0	28	2 020	2 337.3	84.5	137	2 849	715.6	60.8
Portage	1 887	12	100.0	29	637	472.4	31.3	103	1 886	454.0	41.3
Richmond	8 508	131	55.7	43	427	248.2	16.5	220	3 612	902.5	76.6
Schererville	8 766	46	47.8	26	173	68.0	8.0	131	2 499	625.9	60.1
South Bend	NA	NA	NA	168	3 485	1 880.0	142.8	336	6 510	1 425.2	148.7
Terre Haute	5 586	72	61.1	83	1 001	432.7	36.2	362	5 627	1 174.3	112.5
Valparaiso	10 833	49	87.8	37	308	206.5	25.8	204	3 626	852.1	79.1
Westfield	50 802	223	95.5	29	433	180.9	20.2	100	2 268	492.6	47.0
West Lafayette	13 449	70	94.3	10	107	22.9	3.2	85	1 504	268.7	26.9
IOWA	1 222 078	7 607	78.2	4 361	55 874	41 068.3	2 276.7	13 203	177 156	39 234.6	3 561.1
Ames	26 634	132	43.9	42	270	150.6	12.0	224	3 950	836.1	80.0
Ankeny	102 510	519	100.0	56	1 262	1 118.3	54.9	122	2 988	755.5	65.2
Bettendorf	28 362	135	88.1	40	462	503.9	22.2	108	1 586	306.9	34.2
Burlington	3 800	25	100.0	24	308	331.5	10.2	121	1 633	261.0	29.8
Cedar Falls	40 233	212	100.0	42	776	416.1	29.4	161	2 767	611.0	57.3
Cedar Rapids	36 244	441	77.6	211	3 637	1 974.4	173.6	562	11 148	2 774.6	236.6
Clinton	3 335	23	100.0	25	177	66.2	5.7	142	2 145	470.9	42.5
Council Bluffs	16 242	116	98.3	59	1 115	1 984.8	50.9	253	5 378	1 294.8	106.1
Davenport	16 286	184	42.9	184	2 949	2 268.3	128.2	523	9 471	2 168.1	200.0
Des Moines	60 232	404	35.4	278	4 779	2 667.7	221.4	718	10 528	2 240.8	229.1
Dubuque	24 478	315	35.9	85	1 156	1 079.9	46.0	355	5 778	1 156.7	110.8
Fort Dodge	1 114	9	100.0	43	429	189.7	19.6	164	2 555	531.7	49.4
Iowa City	43 175	212	72.2	32	507	208.4	18.9	276	4 064	889.5	88.7
Marion	20 638	194	74.7	29	346	242.1	15.1	116	1 714	384.2	38.0
Marshalltown	860	6	66.7	23	289	186.7	13.5	145	1 984	373.0	39.1
Mason City	4 619	22	90.9	49	497	323.8	19.6	192	3 470	719.0	67.3
Ottumwa	1 332	11	100.0	21	223	123.4	7.8	140	2 323	458.8	43.3
Sioux City	10 454	55	67.3	137	2 298	1 492.6	97.6	418	7 017	1 425.6	136.0
Urbandale	40 058	177	83.1	103	1 440	817.5	72.1	164	2 938	961.1	93.5
Waterloo	7 588	63	71.4	82	1 411	641.8	51.6	320	5 346	1 134.5	108.0
West Des Moines	68 360	421	60.6	47	589	275.1	28.5	408	8 702	1 228.5	144.6

1. Merchant wholesalers except manufacturers' sales branches and offices. 2. Establishments with payroll.

Table D. Cities — **Real Estate, Professional Services, and Manufacturing**

City	Real estate and rental and leasing, 2007				Professional, scientific, and technical services,[1] 2007				Manufacturing, 2007			
	Number of establish- ments	Number of employees	Receipts (mil dol)	Annual payroll (mil dol)	Number of establish- ments	Number of employees	Receipts (mil dol)	Annual payroll (mil dol)	Number of establish- ments	Number of employees	Receipts (mil dol)	Annual payroll (mil dol)
	80	81	82	83	84	85	86	87	88	89	90	91
ILLINOIS—Cont'd												
Waukegan..................	55	304	53.8	8.6	158	D	D	D	86	5 521	1 601.4	287.8
West Chicago..............	32	226	52.2	10.4	82	D	D	D	107	5 323	2 130.7	224.2
Wheaton......................	67	306	46.2	11.3	401	D	D	D	NA	NA	NA	NA
Wheeling....................	34	119	60.0	4.7	126	966	125.9	58.8	166	9 448	2 714.0	421.2
Wilmette	64	297	72.9	11.8	182	415	74.5	27.4	NA	NA	NA	NA
Woodridge..................	33	273	36.6	9.1	89	875	211.6	68.0	32	1 682	365.4	71.9
INDIANA..................	6 389	34 272	5 448.1	1 061.6	12 959	95 701	12 128.9	4 785.9	9 015	536 907	221 877.8	24 474.7
Anderson......................	64	276	41.4	6.4	123	D	D	D	56	1 984	D	77.5
Bloomington	145	854	113.8	20.9	222	D	D	D	52	D	D	85.7
Carmel........................	141	2 014	385.4	102.8	442	3 251	501.2	197.6	51	783	459.4	31.5
Columbus....................	63	244	36.2	7.6	133	D	D	D	103	10 953	4 714.6	475.1
Crown Point................	32	101	17.6	2.7	84	D	D	D	35	948	221.2	35.4
East Chicago..............	13	106	27.2	5.5	18	116	9.7	3.2	51	9 604	6 191.5	568.5
Elkhart	76	391	68.9	11.5	135	D	D	D	323	18 896	4 281.5	696.3
Evansville	171	1 105	153.9	28.0	358	D	D	D	184	10 577	5 534.5	454.6
Fishers........................	82	343	94.4	11.3	242	1 457	206.9	65.9	24	659	138.2	30.4
Fort Wayne..................	340	1 736	288.4	48.7	751	6 416	676.9	320.1	413	19 604	D	927.7
Gary............................	51	326	40.2	7.1	55	D	D	D	37	5 998	D	336.6
Goshen........................	42	166	20.4	4.3	74	D	D	D	116	13 960	3 666.5	587.1
Greenwood..................	84	370	69.6	9.6	129	791	66.6	23.8	45	D	D	D
Hammond....................	56	376	42.9	11.8	105	D	D	D	76	3 563	1 779.6	193.8
Hobart........................	28	131	24.8	3.6	48	D	D	D	22	546	87.3	17.8
Indianapolis	1 236	10 076	1 891.2	381.8	2 671	D	D	D	928	48 817	21 317.5	2 715.6
Jeffersonville..............	47	345	53.6	9.4	95	450	51.4	17.1	89	5 104	1 364.8	213.1
Kokomo	73	296	44.6	7.0	109	D	D	D	63	11 686	D	865.5
Lafayette....................	125	730	138.0	25.7	181	D	D	D	83	8 459	5 253.9	390.9
Lawrence....................	30	182	23.3	5.2	83	D	D	D	NA	NA	NA	NA
Marion	37	146	18.2	3.3	62	D	D	D	46	3 349	1 171.8	213.1
Merrillville	73	560	73.8	15.7	185	1 476	137.0	58.5	33	660	122.0	27.3
Michigan City..............	39	185	32.8	3.8	63	380	38.0	13.5	60	3 439	1 107.2	143.5
Mishawaka	67	465	79.9	13.7	106	873	73.7	29.3	106	3 665	1 542.7	156.5
Muncie........................	87	383	63.5	9.9	118	D	D	D	84	3 684	950.3	171.8
New Albany	52	254	27.3	5.3	115	D	D	D	89	D	D	227.0
Noblesville	59	190	28.4	4.7	151	D	D	D	55	2 173	568.1	85.0
Plainfield....................	27	105	14.8	2.2	42	648	60.3	25.3	24	580	125.1	D
Portage........................	37	221	31.4	5.8	47	331	43.2	13.0	23	1 874	D	113.2
Richmond....................	47	241	26.5	6.1	64	333	27.9	10.7	93	5 978	2 178.1	233.2
Schererville..................	40	167	35.4	4.0	85	D	D	D	20	729	201.3	37.2
South Bend	104	740	99.5	22.4	305	D	D	D	186	7 811	2 210.1	353.3
Terre Haute................	78	498	60.1	14.5	171	1 067	99.1	33.5	85	6 902	D	309.9
Valparaiso	67	348	39.8	7.8	129	898	96.1	34.6	55	2 053	1 004.8	108.9
Westfield....................	26	81	12.7	2.1	67	D	D	D	28	1 547	267.5	59.6
West Lafayette	45	284	35.8	7.1	64	D	D	D	NA	NA	NA	NA
IOWA........................	2 969	14 667	2 556.0	473.0	6 181	42 118	5 015.6	1 883.8	3 802	223 049	97 592.1	9 525.7
Ames	71	290	29.5	7.5	127	744	65.5	31.6	40	2 586	1 418.7	140.2
Ankeny........................	60	174	36.4	5.3	81	472	46.2	21.1	28	2 392	1 178.1	135.0
Bettendorf....................	45	175	46.0	4.9	94	D	D	D	29	3 255	1 350.6	180.6
Burlington	28	593	94.2	22.8	41	266	23.9	11.2	36	D	920.8	D
Cedar Falls..................	48	199	51.5	6.5	93	1 446	107.7	90.3	41	1 254	D	47.5
Cedar Rapids	179	1 488	330.4	86.6	374	3 720	474.6	203.5	144	15 137	6 894.3	1 004.4
Clinton........................	34	104	16.2	3.0	50	318	26.9	11.9	28	3 097	3 532.8	149.0
Council Bluffs	79	384	62.7	9.7	114	D	D	D	46	4 342	D	156.9
Davenport....................	123	1 577	212.1	40.0	266	D	D	D	107	7 431	4 016.5	345.2
Des Moines..................	213	1 670	281.7	57.9	523	D	D	D	189	6 405	3 552.9	274.8
Dubuque......................	80	416	70.1	16.0	131	D	D	D	89	4 912	1 059.9	186.5
Fort Dodge	38	114	17.7	2.8	66	D	D	D	37	1 572	D	77.2
Iowa City	86	443	75.3	13.0	140	D	D	D	46	3 319	D	137.5
Marion	33	138	13.6	2.9	55	433	51.1	23.2	42	719	121.7	27.2
Marshalltown	35	344	43.2	10.1	46	329	48.9	11.8	39	D	D	D
Mason City	44	134	19.9	3.4	63	D	D	D	37	3 214	1 210.3	133.4
Ottumwa......................	25	78	12.8	2.0	43	D	D	D	21	D	D	D
Sioux City....................	90	554	83.7	14.1	165	D	D	D	82	4 396	2 288.0	177.8
Urbandale....................	52	197	32.7	5.6	176	1 444	182.6	80.2	31	1 411	556.9	60.1
Waterloo......................	92	481	61.4	12.2	124	D	D	D	92	8 328	4 506.4	396.9
West Des Moines.........	114	807	225.7	38.4	321	2 946	448.4	153.8	32	1 117	257.3	56.0

1. Establishments subject to federal tax.

Accommodation and Food Services, Arts, Entertainment, and Recreation, and Health Care and Social Assistance

City	Accommodation and food services, 2007				Arts, entertainment, and recreation,[1] 2007				Health care and social assistance,[1] 2007			
	Number of establishments	Number of employees	Sales (mil dol)	Annual payroll (mil dol)	Number of establishments	Number of employees	Receipts (mil dol)	Annual payroll (mil dol)	Number of establishments	Number of employees	Receipts (mil dol)	Annual payroll (mil dol)
	92	93	94	95	96	97	98	99	100	101	102	103
ILLINOIS—Cont'd												
Waukegan	148	2 162	110.9	28.4	10	126	8.3	1.9	105	2 413	282.4	103.8
West Chicago	58	736	31.5	8.7	6	73	5.5	1.8	21	361	23.6	10.1
Wheaton	106	1 973	89.0	26.4	17	336	14.6	5.3	168	1 721	152.2	74.7
Wheeling	68	1 920	110.9	36.2	7	D	D	D	62	D	D	D
Wilmette	45	D	D	D	21	D	D	D	102	675	57.9	25.7
Woodridge	39	800	37.4	10.7	6	D	D	D	79	461	44.9	16.4
INDIANA	12 932	254 293	11 669.8	3 175.2	1 687	25 762	2 558.3	769.6	11 919	181 493	17 014.6	6 813.4
Anderson	156	3 285	117.0	33.2	21	D	D	D	151	D	D	D
Bloomington	298	6 769	268.0	73.3	19	183	10.3	2.3	214	3 369	311.6	140.4
Carmel	140	2 845	134.9	40.3	36	368	17.0	6.3	276	5 761	657.7	235.8
Columbus	126	2 581	105.4	30.7	11	D	D	D	161	2 037	177.3	76.4
Crown Point	58	924	33.9	9.0	12	D	D	D	63	883	77.6	37.7
East Chicago	41	D	D	D	1	D	D	D	32	305	25.3	9.5
Elkhart	192	3 695	133.4	37.9	16	D	D	D	121	1 892	268.9	92.1
Evansville	366	9 033	426.8	118.6	35	D	D	D	388	D	D	D
Fishers	138	2 961	125.8	34.9	20	D	D	D	160	D	D	D
Fort Wayne	614	14 155	506.1	156.1	78	D	D	D	750	17 070	1 801.5	707.4
Gary	105	1 744	168.4	31.1	9	D	D	D	94	1 519	92.6	39.9
Goshen	91	2 019	71.4	19.4	6	D	D	D	71	935	84.5	35.7
Greenwood	148	3 414	134.2	41.0	19	317	11.7	4.0	111	D	D	D
Hammond	156	D	D	D	6	D	D	D	67	D	D	D
Hobart	92	D	D	D	8	135	3.7	1.2	53	D	D	D
Indianapolis	1 957	43 393	2 138.2	632.9	248	D	D	D	1 865	31 197	3 338.9	1 377.5
Jeffersonville	75	1 643	66.1	20.2	7	D	D	D	108	1 544	167.7	70.5
Kokomo	165	3 728	143.5	42.3	13	D	D	D	168	D	D	D
Lafayette	223	5 259	194.9	60.2	17	228	7.4	2.3	187	3 658	441.0	178.9
Lawrence	85	1 332	57.3	15.9	19	D	D	D	40	D	D	D
Marion	98	1 924	68.6	18.9	10	D	D	D	116	D	D	D
Merrillville	127	3 190	141.2	35.9	10	275	9.9	2.8	240	D	D	D
Michigan City	104	3 383	313.9	60.6	4	D	D	D	78	D	D	D
Mishawaka	181	4 692	179.5	53.3	20	D	D	D	130	D	D	D
Muncie	170	4 336	139.9	42.0	22	D	D	D	204	4 250	391.1	174.2
New Albany	78	1 358	57.0	15.9	10	D	D	D	140	2 025	161.4	66.7
Noblesville	96	1 830	75.5	21.6	20	D	D	D	120	D	D	D
Plainfield	77	1 933	82.7	23.3	6	D	D	D	40	D	D	D
Portage	72	1 310	53.5	14.6	7	D	D	D	55	915	76.5	29.2
Richmond	100	2 445	85.2	25.1	10	73	2.2	0.6	91	D	D	D
Schererville	88	D	D	D	6	114	3.3	1.1	76	D	D	D
South Bend	252	4 667	188.2	52.4	16	163	31.2	3.6	246	4 390	638.2	228.0
Terre Haute	206	4 053	171.6	47.9	15	151	26.1	3.0	229	D	D	D
Valparaiso	113	2 433	93.8	26.5	7	104	4.6	1.3	159	1 955	208.2	85.5
Westfield	58	1 441	58.4	17.6	13	D	D	D	40	D	D	D
West Lafayette	125	2 508	97.1	26.5	6	D	D	D	41	D	D	D
IOWA	7 014	116 838	4 737.7	1 276.0	978	13 748	1 216.6	259.1	5 399	70 263	5 853.9	2 731.9
Ames	182	3 872	136.2	39.4	13	189	6.6	2.3	88	1 719	174.9	79.5
Ankeny	95	1 926	70.2	20.8	18	D	D	D	71	761	54.4	22.8
Bettendorf	64	2 150	153.6	33.1	11	D	D	D	86	D	D	D
Burlington	83	1 811	63.4	19.0	9	D	D	D	64	563	35.0	13.4
Cedar Falls	99	2 785	81.2	25.1	7	25	1.1	0.3	58	D	D	D
Cedar Rapids	382	7 800	299.1	86.9	30	829	29.0	9.6	291	4 089	463.7	201.1
Clinton	79	1 173	45.5	12.3	7	D	D	D	79	1 069	84.5	33.0
Council Bluffs	153	5 312	431.9	92.4	14	D	D	D	132	1 692	148.2	68.6
Davenport	296	6 211	239.8	70.9	30	754	94.3	14.0	252	2 797	309.9	142.8
Des Moines	497	8 479	378.1	110.5	50	544	34.0	9.7	364	6 110	788.0	383.9
Dubuque	193	3 815	125.2	37.6	25	D	D	D	134	2 711	272.8	141.7
Fort Dodge	70	1 321	58.7	14.9	9	D	D	D	75	D	D	D
Iowa City	177	3 671	125.1	36.0	11	314	6.6	2.0	140	1 606	147.3	60.3
Marion	44	815	28.9	9.1	5	D	D	D	50	641	38.1	15.1
Marshalltown	75	1 143	39.3	10.9	8	D	D	D	41	D	D	D
Mason City	96	1 575	55.4	15.9	10	D	D	D	64	D	D	D
Ottumwa	69	1 085	40.9	11.2	6	D	D	D	70	D	D	D
Sioux City	225	4 384	149.4	44.6	21	715	66.5	13.4	198	2 175	246.1	102.2
Urbandale	81	1 752	71.9	20.1	15	D	D	D	63	727	50.5	20.9
Waterloo	159	3 077	101.8	31.8	22	D	D	D	140	1 818	188.6	95.2
West Des Moines	185	4 429	186.5	58.1	24	D	D	D	212	2 859	337.4	160.9

1. Establishments subject to federal tax.

Table D. Cities — Other Services and Federal Funds

	Other services[1], 2007				Selected federal funds, 2009–2010 (mil dol)								
					Procurement contracts		Grants						
City	Number of establish-ments	Number of employees	Receipts (mil dol)	Annual payroll (mil dol)	Defense	Other	Total[2]	Medicaid and other health related	Nutrition and family welfare	Energy and envi-ronment	Disasters and emergency prepared-ness	Housing and community develop-ment	Employment and training
	104	105	106	107	108	109	110	111	112	113	114	115	116
ILLINOIS—Cont'd													
Waukegan	100	500	43.9	13.0	235.0	35.0	28.2	3.1	5.7	0.8	0.0	15.4	0.1
West Chicago	46	231	23.1	6.3	4.4	0.9	1.7	0.0	0.0	0.1	0.0	0.0	0.0
Wheaton	95	682	35.9	13.6	0.0	0.0	45.5	2.1	0.0	6.2	0.0	34.9	0.0
Wheeling	62	735	75.3	20.5	4.5	3.9	1.0	0.2	0.0	0.8	0.0	0.0	0.0
Wilmette	56	381	31.6	10.3	0.0	0.4	0.4	0.2	0.0	0.0	0.0	0.2	0.0
Woodridge	34	339	13.9	10.5	2.6	0.1	0.0	0.0	0.0	0.0	0.0	0.0	0.0
INDIANA	8 961	56 731	4 531.3	1 397.9	4 369.9	1 128.5	11 964.8	6 228.9	1 304.6	611.2	24.8	633.7	226.3
Anderson	94	664	44.1	14.7	4.5	0.4	35.4	1.3	2.6	0.0	0.0	9.4	0.0
Bloomington	109	D	D	D	4.6	7.3	419.2	319.5	2.6	8.4	0.0	10.9	0.0
Carmel	107	650	44.6	15.5	0.4	24.5	26.1	3.4	0.0	22.3	0.0	0.0	0.0
Columbus	80	652	48.4	15.6	19.4	0.6	54.0	1.4	2.6	43.6	0.0	4.3	0.0
Crown Point	65	514	45.0	11.4	0.7	0.1	9.4	0.8	0.0	3.0	0.0	4.2	0.0
East Chicago	25	155	15.5	3.9	5.8	0.0	40.3	1.1	0.0	31.6	0.0	7.6	0.0
Elkhart	129	931	77.9	26.3	7.2	-2.4	9.7	0.7	0.0	0.6	0.0	7.0	0.0
Evansville	214	1 736	131.6	43.8	128.3	2.4	42.4	2.7	5.0	3.1	0.0	16.2	0.4
Fishers	83	666	29.6	12.4	2.1	0.1	0.7	0.0	0.0	0.6	0.0	0.0	0.0
Fort Wayne	469	3 671	264.3	93.8	822.0	54.2	56.6	1.9	5.2	10.4	0.0	21.8	0.4
Gary	71	500	41.4	12.8	1.3	1.0	30.4	0.7	0.2	0.6	0.0	21.3	0.0
Goshen	60	434	33.3	11.8	7.5	0.1	4.8	0.0	0.1	1.8	0.0	2.4	0.0
Greenwood	93	831	64.3	21.3	1.0	0.2	0.3	0.0	0.0	0.0	0.0	0.0	0.0
Hammond	120	880	88.1	27.6	9.5	0.3	11.4	0.3	0.0	1.0	0.0	10.0	0.0
Hobart	48	296	16.3	5.9	0.1	0.0	0.4	0.0	0.0	0.0	0.0	0.0	0.0
Indianapolis	1 133	9 402	830.9	258.2	1 289.4	356.9	2 170.3	163.9	298.5	360.4	7.4	415.4	219.2
Jeffersonville	61	542	40.9	13.8	2.3	30.7	6.3	0.5	2.4	0.4	0.0	2.7	0.0
Kokomo	89	D	D	D	0.5	0.5	12.9	0.0	2.7	0.9	0.0	5.4	0.0
Lafayette	145	D	D	D	1.4	4.6	32.1	1.3	3.5	1.5	0.0	8.4	0.0
Lawrence	64	307	24.7	7.0	0.0	0.0	0.0	0.0	0.0	0.0	0.0	0.0	0.0
Marion	46	237	12.9	4.1	0.1	30.2	6.4	0.1	2.0	0.0	0.0	2.5	0.0
Merrillville	69	458	37.2	12.1	1.4	2.5	16.2	0.6	9.9	0.0	0.0	0.0	4.7
Michigan City	53	265	17.7	5.7	0.0	0.0	5.9	0.0	2.0	0.2	0.0	3.1	0.0
Mishawaka	106	672	46.1	15.9	240.9	2.3	3.6	0.4	0.2	0.0	0.0	2.6	0.0
Muncie	123	804	57.3	17.8	0.0	14.1	29.9	2.2	1.5	5.7	0.0	10.5	0.0
New Albany	70	388	23.3	7.8	3.4	1.4	7.2	0.0	1.8	0.2	0.0	5.2	0.0
Noblesville	80	421	27.4	8.4	0.6	0.3	4.3	0.0	0.3	0.0	0.0	2.0	0.0
Plainfield	42	226	19.7	5.9	0.9	40.5	0.0	0.0	0.0	0.0	0.0	0.0	0.1
Portage	56	368	30.8	9.7	1.4	0.0	8.4	2.0	0.0	0.2	0.0	0.0	0.0
Richmond	58	250	20.6	6.4	2.2	1.2	7.6	0.4	1.8	0.0	0.0	1.8	0.0
Schererville	65	539	45.3	12.9	0.0	0.0	0.0	0.0	0.0	0.0	0.0	0.0	0.0
South Bend	197	1 845	164.8	49.8	876.9	9.2	42.3	1.5	5.9	1.3	0.0	22.1	0.3
Terre Haute	103	945	55.7	18.7	4.3	48.6	23.3	1.2	2.3	1.6	0.0	8.0	0.0
Valparaiso	89	681	48.7	17.7	3.7	5.0	4.3	1.8	0.0	0.2	0.5	0.2	0.0
Westfield	36	D	D	D	0.3	0.1	0.0	0.0	0.0	0.0	0.0	0.0	0.0
West Lafayette	29	D	D	D	8.4	1.1	292.8	77.1	0.0	31.5	2.4	0.5	0.0
IOWA	4 878	24 331	1 856.5	544.9	1 556.7	815.9	6 394.4	2 962.1	661.9	100.1	245.4	698.1	92.1
Ames	67	D	D	D	15.0	59.4	189.0	38.9	0.4	21.2	0.4	2.5	0.0
Ankeny	68	481	38.7	10.5	1.3	0.1	7.6	0.1	0.0	5.1	0.0	0.5	0.9
Bettendorf	59	D	D	D	1.1	0.2	3.2	0.0	0.0	0.0	0.0	2.6	0.0
Burlington	52	241	19.8	4.9	0.7	0.1	7.0	0.0	3.3	0.0	0.0	2.6	0.0
Cedar Falls	41	306	27.2	8.0	0.0	0.1	12.8	0.0	0.2	1.3	0.0	1.5	0.0
Cedar Rapids	230	1 605	108.0	36.4	1 097.7	233.2	39.0	1.8	0.3	1.4	0.0	7.7	0.0
Clinton	54	281	13.1	8.5	0.2	0.0	7.5	0.3	0.0	0.0	0.0	1.8	0.0
Council Bluffs	101	505	37.5	11.0	0.6	0.8	15.4	1.4	0.1	0.6	0.0	5.7	0.0
Davenport	180	1 258	87.2	29.3	49.2	2.4	40.2	9.7	4.1	1.4	0.0	6.5	0.0
Des Moines	297	2 100	146.3	48.2	19.6	44.4	1 314.5	89.2	133.7	52.4	54.2	588.6	83.9
Dubuque	126	1 038	63.9	19.6	3.4	1.1	31.6	0.8	1.7	0.7	0.0	10.9	2.1
Fort Dodge	48	D	D	D	3.0	0.2	10.3	1.2	1.8	0.8	0.0	4.6	0.0
Iowa City	102	646	42.5	14.6	11.7	59.9	421.8	370.2	1.9	4.4	0.0	8.8	0.2
Marion	45	198	15.9	5.1	0.2	-0.2	0.3	0.0	0.0	0.0	0.0	0.0	0.0
Marshalltown	50	D	D	D	0.0	1.9	26.2	0.1	3.5	0.0	0.0	2.6	0.0
Mason City	64	348	23.5	7.7	0.0	0.1	9.1	0.5	2.4	0.0	0.0	3.3	0.0
Ottumwa	41	176	11.8	3.7	0.2	1.1	8.1	1.7	2.0	0.7	0.0	1.3	0.0
Sioux City	133	D	D	D	4.3	4.7	28.1	2.6	3.1	1.3	0.0	10.3	4.5
Urbandale	64	407	33.5	11.0	0.1	0.9	0.1	0.0	0.0	0.0	0.0	0.0	0.0
Waterloo	101	786	54.9	18.3	-0.1	21.1	39.3	4.1	5.0	1.4	0.0	10.4	0.2
West Des Moines	82	487	28.2	12.1	18.4	40.2	2.2	0.5	0.5	0.6	0.0	0.3	0.0

1. Establishments subject to federal tax.   2. Includes program categories not shown separately. State totals include additional categories not allocated by city.

Table D. Cities — City Government Finances

City	General revenue Total (mil dol)	Intergovernmental Total (mil dol)	Intergovernmental Percent from state government	Taxes Total (mil dol)	Taxes Per capita[1] (dollars) Total	Taxes Per capita[1] (dollars) Property	Taxes Per capita[1] (dollars) Sales and gross receipts	General expenditure Total (mil dol)	General expenditure Per capita[1] (dollars) Total	General expenditure Per capita[1] (dollars) Capital outlays
	117	118	119	120	121	122	123	124	125	126
ILLINOIS—Cont'd										
Waukegan	84.8	30.6	90.3	38.0	417	243	150	91.3	1 002	186
West Chicago	26.2	7.0	95.8	8.1	305	142	163	24.4	920	153
Wheaton	49.5	14.0	97.5	25.6	469	319	132	56.2	1 031	169
Wheeling	44.3	12.2	98.4	23.3	644	377	267	43.1	1 192	266
Wilmette	34.8	7.1	96.8	19.9	748	408	288	32.6	1 228	179
Woodridge	28.0	9.0	93.0	12.7	371	181	166	21.1	618	7
INDIANA	X	X	X	X	X	X	X	X	X	X
Anderson	68.6	24.7	38.1	16.2	283	267	15	85.5	1 492	276
Bloomington	76.3	28.9	65.2	22.6	313	303	10	62.8	869	93
Carmel	79.6	32.1	35.7	28.1	437	381	55	145.4	2 258	236
Columbus	50.9	19.7	61.6	15.2	383	375	8	57.1	1 435	151
Crown Point	14.2	4.9	75.2	6.6	278	237	41	14.5	606	43
East Chicago	79.5	18.1	85.4	44.2	1 465	1 459	6	145.7	4 833	391
Elkhart	76.4	34.8	72.0	25.9	492	407	26	63.0	1 196	64
Evansville	196.3	52.7	55.9	45.5	391	308	22	227.2	1 954	107
Fishers	45.6	18.3	33.5	15.0	227	153	75	77.9	1 178	128
Fort Wayne	292.7	44.0	71.1	123.1	490	285	18	265.0	1 055	101
Gary	156.0	36.3	97.8	76.1	789	774	14	157.8	1 637	101
Goshen	35.2	12.7	70.4	11.3	354	276	25	104.2	3 266	282
Greenwood	45.1	11.3	53.1	10.8	233	227	6	41.4	892	168
Hammond	128.2	66.4	86.6	48.1	623	522	23	144.7	1 875	138
Hobart	34.3	5.2	87.5	14.1	508	473	31	20.0	719	114
Indianapolis	2 229.6	490.8	83.8	931.1	1 170	902	119	2 369.9	2 979	832
Jeffersonville	42.5	12.2	52.8	11.6	388	275	53	40.9	1 380	95
Kokomo	61.0	18.6	58.3	22.3	486	456	5	59.8	1 303	38
Lafayette	65.2	19.6	54.5	23.8	373	289	8	87.0	1 366	388
Lawrence	24.1	9.4	52.4	11.0	257	227	29	26.5	619	43
Marion	28.3	10.6	60.7	11.1	366	359	8	32.1	1 057	58
Merrillville	17.8	6.8	67.5	7.8	242	215	15	24.6	763	52
Michigan City	49.3	22.2	87.9	16.7	524	356	24	14.7	462	144
Mishawaka	64.6	21.7	80.5	29.0	587	529	29	69.6	1 408	266
Muncie	55.3	19.7	63.4	21.3	326	298	3	65.9	1 008	38
New Albany	30.5	11.8	53.8	11.7	316	179	12	30.8	832	41
Noblesville	62.7	16.4	36.8	20.1	484	361	36	97.4	2 344	509
Plainfield	28.0	5.6	95.1	11.3	439	328	54	30.5	1 186	182
Portage	34.2	13.2	39.3	10.4	284	261	23	31.9	873	327
Richmond	40.4	14.6	69.2	12.5	338	304	13	45.4	1 227	191
Schererville	41.0	4.7	82.5	9.6	334	297	29	44.6	1 550	164
South Bend	150.1	28.3	100.0	57.3	551	523	28	135.7	1 304	142
Terre Haute	77.8	16.7	67.1	29.4	498	401	17	89.8	1 523	289
Valparaiso	51.0	10.9	78.4	10.8	360	322	23	57.5	1 919	95
Westfield	18.2	5.6	24.8	3.7	179	130	30	30.6	1 494	158
West Lafayette	35.5	8.7	72.8	9.1	292	236	3	36.7	1 181	185
IOWA	X	X	X	X	X	X	X	X	X	X
Ames	219.5	18.5	82.4	24.0	438	351	87	187.0	3 416	410
Ankeny	36.8	3.8	83.2	21.1	520	463	57	57.8	1 424	778
Bettendorf	42.0	8.2	65.3	24.3	748	543	205	40.7	1 255	298
Burlington	28.5	6.7	78.2	12.7	501	378	123	32.3	1 273	358
Cedar Falls	58.3	7.1	57.0	24.6	654	503	151	52.8	1 406	533
Cedar Rapids	221.3	37.9	34.7	86.3	683	607	76	184.8	1 462	253
Clinton	35.7	8.7	64.2	16.6	625	449	176	31.2	1 171	340
Council Bluffs	87.9	17.8	65.8	46.9	783	530	254	80.9	1 351	369
Davenport	130.1	28.2	67.0	66.1	668	560	107	137.4	1 388	315
Des Moines	353.8	53.5	38.4	139.6	708	578	130	360.7	1 831	449
Dubuque	92.0	19.2	39.9	34.3	598	364	235	85.1	1 485	391
Fort Dodge	27.5	6.2	45.0	13.0	514	399	114	27.7	1 099	241
Iowa City	103.5	20.3	36.3	44.3	660	617	43	91.7	1 368	264
Marion	23.5	3.0	92.1	13.9	431	399	32	25.0	778	142
Marshalltown	27.8	6.5	47.1	14.0	543	360	183	22.8	882	126
Mason City	34.6	8.6	39.6	16.3	591	405	186	36.1	1 314	426
Ottumwa	39.1	11.9	37.8	14.8	603	439	164	40.3	1 641	701
Sioux City	126.6	30.1	47.6	61.8	747	530	217	125.5	1 518	419
Urbandale	32.5	4.7	87.5	22.6	594	522	73	29.9	785	185
Waterloo	100.6	22.3	31.8	49.8	750	552	198	104.2	1 570	455
West Des Moines	83.7	9.5	61.3	53.2	971	899	72	66.3	1 212	232

1. Based on population estimated as of July 1 of the year shown.

City	City government finances, 2006 (cont.)									
	General expenditure (cont.)									
	Percent of total for:									
	Public welfare	Highways	Parking facilities	Education	Health and hospitals	Police protection	Sewerage and sanitation	Parks and recreation	Housing and community development	Interest on debt
	127	128	129	130	131	132	133	134	135	136
ILLINOIS—Cont'd										
Waukegan	0.0	11.3	0.4	0.0	0.0	28.6	7.2	6.9	1.5	5.6
West Chicago	0.0	9.9	0.5	0.0	0.0	30.8	14.4	2.1	0.0	9.6
Wheaton	0.2	13.2	0.9	0.0	0.0	21.2	4.1	1.5	0.0	4.0
Wheeling	0.0	9.7	0.1	0.0	0.0	24.7	4.9	0.0	0.0	6.0
Wilmette	0.0	22.3	0.8	0.0	0.6	24.3	13.9	0.3	0.2	4.6
Woodridge	0.0	13.4	0.0	0.0	0.0	40.2	2.7	0.0	0.0	2.9
INDIANA	X	X	X	X	X	X	X	X	X	X
Anderson	0.2	5.6	0.1	0.0	0.7	12.1	28.9	4.7	2.4	3.2
Bloomington	0.0	7.8	3.0	0.0	1.6	13.7	19.4	11.0	6.8	7.0
Carmel	0.0	11.3	0.0	0.0	0.6	8.0	4.7	1.1	0.0	5.7
Columbus	0.0	5.6	0.0	0.0	0.6	11.8	11.8	12.2	1.3	0.1
Crown Point	0.0	11.3	0.0	0.0	0.0	23.6	0.4	5.4	0.0	1.8
East Chicago	0.0	1.9	0.0	0.0	3.3	7.2	22.7	5.2	0.6	0.5
Elkhart	0.0	5.2	2.1	0.0	0.0	12.9	11.8	8.2	1.1	0.8
Evansville	0.1	3.1	0.4	0.0	2.1	12.8	12.4	5.9	1.4	2.6
Fishers	0.0	5.7	0.0	0.0	0.0	10.3	8.4	2.4	0.1	3.5
Fort Wayne	0.0	7.2	0.6	0.0	0.8	15.5	21.1	5.2	3.4	2.6
Gary	0.8	2.9	0.0	0.0	2.3	14.2	17.9	12.8	2.9	1.6
Goshen	0.0	2.9	0.0	0.0	0.0	3.4	4.1	1.4	1.8	8.2
Greenwood	0.0	3.5	0.0	0.0	0.0	12.5	33.8	5.1	0.0	2.0
Hammond	0.0	2.6	0.0	0.0	0.6	46.3	3.3	4.0	2.0	1.3
Hobart	0.0	8.2	0.0	0.0	0.2	18.8	8.6	11.9	0.0	3.5
Indianapolis	4.4	1.7	0.1	0.0	26.5	7.1	5.8	11.6	3.8	8.6
Jeffersonville	0.0	3.3	0.0	0.0	0.3	7.6	24.6	3.4	1.2	2.6
Kokomo	0.4	10.4	0.0	0.0	0.0	21.1	16.3	4.7	1.5	2.6
Lafayette	0.0	14.8	0.3	0.0	0.0	0.7	7.4	6.7	1.0	7.5
Lawrence	0.0	11.4	0.0	0.0	3.3	19.5	5.5	3.9	0.0	3.9
Marion	0.0	9.8	0.0	0.0	0.0	18.0	11.6	5.0	0.5	2.4
Merrillville	0.0	11.1	0.0	0.0	3.8	19.0	0.0	1.2	12.7	12.0
Michigan City	0.0	9.4	0.0	0.0	0.0	0.2	0.0	15.2	0.0	11.4
Mishawaka	0.0	4.6	0.0	0.0	1.6	9.5	25.0	4.3	0.9	2.3
Muncie	0.0	4.9	0.0	0.0	0.5	16.1	34.4	2.2	2.6	1.2
New Albany	0.0	5.8	0.2	0.0	3.3	19.8	9.7	5.1	0.1	11.2
Noblesville	0.0	18.5	0.0	0.0	0.0	6.8	8.8	4.4	0.5	5.0
Plainfield	0.0	3.8	0.0	0.0	0.0	13.9	12.7	9.5	0.0	0.0
Portage	0.0	11.3	0.0	0.0	0.3	0.2	4.0	10.2	0.0	0.0
Richmond	0.0	6.5	0.2	0.0	1.1	15.3	23.1	7.8	0.0	2.0
Schererville	0.0	13.6	0.0	0.0	0.2	11.1	37.9	3.5	0.9	1.8
South Bend	0.0	1.5	0.4	0.0	1.2	19.5	15.9	3.0	0.1	2.2
Terre Haute	0.0	5.2	0.1	0.0	1.6	8.3	17.5	3.4	4.2	4.6
Valparaiso	0.0	3.3	0.0	0.0	0.0	5.3	12.9	5.6	0.0	2.5
Westfield	0.0	6.0	0.0	0.0	0.3	10.7	28.6	5.7	1.3	5.5
West Lafayette	0.0	12.2	0.0	0.0	0.0	11.6	34.5	3.1	5.4	4.6
IOWA	X	X	X	X	X	X	X	X	X	X
Ames	0.5	1.9	0.4	0.0	75.1	3.4	4.2	1.5	0.9	1.5
Ankeny	0.1	18.9	0.0	0.0	2.5	8.4	9.9	10.7	1.7	3.5
Bettendorf	0.0	21.7	0.0	0.0	0.0	14.1	12.3	13.7	1.1	6.5
Burlington	0.0	13.7	0.3	0.0	1.7	13.6	14.0	12.8	0.0	5.3
Cedar Falls	0.0	15.8	0.4	0.0	1.6	7.2	15.4	8.1	3.1	2.2
Cedar Rapids	0.0	13.1	1.4	0.0	0.4	12.8	19.9	4.2	4.4	7.0
Clinton	0.0	11.8	0.3	0.0	3.0	18.0	21.7	17.0	1.4	3.8
Council Bluffs	0.0	5.7	0.1	0.0	1.0	15.8	9.9	5.9	1.0	3.4
Davenport	0.0	8.6	0.8	0.0	0.0	15.9	10.3	6.3	4.5	9.4
Des Moines	0.3	13.4	2.7	0.0	0.0	13.5	15.5	6.6	5.8	6.1
Dubuque	0.6	14.3	2.6	0.0	1.9	12.3	11.9	10.6	6.3	2.3
Fort Dodge	3.1	7.8	0.3	0.0	0.2	10.9	10.4	7.4	3.5	4.6
Iowa City	0.0	7.0	3.4	0.0	0.6	10.0	12.0	6.1	9.9	9.6
Marion	0.0	10.6	0.0	0.0	0.1	17.6	11.4	5.4	2.0	2.2
Marshalltown	0.2	9.2	0.2	0.0	6.0	20.5	13.7	7.4	6.5	5.0
Mason City	1.8	11.3	0.2	0.0	3.7	14.4	14.8	7.4	0.5	2.5
Ottumwa	0.2	11.1	0.0	0.0	1.1	8.0	31.4	21.1	0.0	3.1
Sioux City	0.0	19.0	1.2	0.0	0.2	13.7	19.9	9.4	5.0	4.1
Urbandale	0.0	12.6	0.0	0.0	3.0	17.4	5.0	10.9	1.6	6.1
Waterloo	0.3	20.3	0.3	0.0	1.5	12.2	12.6	7.1	6.6	9.4
West Des Moines	1.5	9.0	0.0	0.0	3.6	11.7	11.6	5.8	0.9	8.9

Table D. Cities — City Government Finances, City Government Employment, and Climate

City	City government finances, 2007 (cont.) Debt outstanding — Total (mil dol)	Per capita[1] (dollars)	Debt issued during year	City government employment, 2010	Climate[2] Avg daily temp — Mean January	Mean July	Limits January[3]	Limits July[4]	Annual precipitation (inches)	Heating degree days	Cooling degree days
	137	138	139	140	141	142	143	144	145	146	147
ILLINOIS—Cont'd											
Waukegan	116.1	1 274	10.4	522	20.3	71.5	12.0	81.7	34.09	7 031	613
West Chicago	55.4	2 087	0.0	NA	NA	NA	NA	NA	NA	NA	NA
Wheaton	50.1	919	0.0	448	23.1	74.8	14.2	86.8	37.94	6 053	942
Wheeling	59.4	1 645	0.0	230	18.4	72.1	9.6	82.3	36.56	7 149	624
Wilmette	57.9	2 181	0.0	212	22.0	73.3	14.3	83.5	36.27	6 498	830
Woodridge	13.0	381	0.0	174	23.1	74.8	14.2	86.8	37.94	6 053	942
INDIANA	X	X	X	NA	X	X	X	X	X	X	X
Anderson	70.6	1 233	0.0	678	25.7	74.0	18.4	83.8	39.82	5 807	872
Bloomington	116.6	1 614	16.6	782	27.9	75.4	19.3	86.0	44.91	5 348	1 017
Carmel	338.8	5 261	157.2	713	25.3	74.2	17.0	84.5	42.85	5 901	873
Columbus	4.5	112	1.0	421	27.9	75.9	19.1	86.4	41.94	5 367	1 059
Crown Point	17.5	734	4.7	195	NA	NA	NA	NA	NA	NA	NA
East Chicago	61.5	2 041	33.2	745	23.7	74.0	15.3	84.8	38.13	6 055	887
Elkhart	20.5	390	6.1	622	22.8	72.1	14.3	83.3	38.56	6 487	663
Evansville	191.4	1 646	6.3	1 241	33.2	79.6	24.8	90.5	45.76	4 140	1 616
Fishers	65.0	984	13.2	360	25.3	74.2	17.0	84.5	42.85	5 901	873
Fort Wayne	298.6	1 189	69.7	2 043	23.6	73.4	16.1	84.3	36.55	6 205	830
Gary	84.4	876	9.6	1 947	22.2	73.5	13.9	83.9	38.02	6 497	776
Goshen	268.9	8 432	3.4	232	24.3	73.7	17.0	84.5	36.59	6 075	826
Greenwood	22.7	488	1.5	280	25.7	74.7	18.0	84.0	40.24	5 783	942
Hammond	50.6	655	14.2	876	22.2	73.5	13.9	83.9	38.02	6 497	776
Hobart	11.9	428	12.0	222	22.2	73.5	13.9	83.9	38.02	6 497	776
Indianapolis	4 518.8	5 681	652.8	13 667	26.5	75.4	18.5	85.6	40.95	5 521	1 042
Jeffersonville	27.8	939	1.6	316	31.3	75.8	21.4	88.5	45.47	4 829	1 079
Kokomo	42.2	919	0.3	487	22.8	73.0	15.0	84.1	41.54	6 368	771
Lafayette	186.4	2 927	56.9	730	23.0	73.5	14.3	84.5	36.90	6 206	842
Lawrence	21.9	511	9.6	290	25.7	74.7	18.0	84.0	40.24	5 783	942
Marion	20.3	667	0.0	242	24.2	73.8	16.3	84.5	39.01	6 143	819
Merrillville	70.1	2 180	0.0	143	21.1	72.7	12.1	83.6	40.04	6 642	734
Michigan City	34.2	1 073	0.0	366	23.4	73.0	15.7	83.1	39.70	6 294	812
Mishawaka	97.2	1 967	10.0	576	24.3	73.7	17.0	84.5	36.59	6 075	826
Muncie	25.4	388	6.2	523	24.4	72.5	15.9	83.9	41.23	6 215	717
New Albany	74.6	2 014	12.1	266	31.3	75.8	21.4	88.5	45.47	4 829	1 079
Noblesville	162.4	3 909	80.8	379	25.3	74.2	17.0	84.5	42.85	5 901	873
Plainfield	0.0	0	0.0	278	NA	NA	NA	NA	NA	NA	NA
Portage	0.0	0	0.0	259	22.9	73.0	15.5	83.1	40.06	6 270	745
Richmond	25.1	679	4.0	531	25.7	73.1	17.2	84.6	39.55	5 942	769
Schererville	21.7	752	0.0	177	NA	NA	NA	NA	NA	NA	NA
South Bend	174.3	1 675	22.2	1 282	23.4	73.0	15.7	83.1	39.70	6 294	812
Terre Haute	74.2	1 259	0.0	619	26.5	76.2	17.7	87.3	42.47	5 433	1 107
Valparaiso	44.7	1 494	16.3	311	22.9	73.0	15.5	83.1	40.06	6 270	745
Westfield	45.3	2 213	7.2	183	NA	NA	NA	NA	NA	NA	NA
West Lafayette	45.2	1 453	0.8	202	25.2	75.5	17.2	86.3	36.32	5 732	1 024
IOWA	X	X	X	NA	X	X	X	X	X	X	X
Ames	61.4	1 121	5.3	612	18.5	73.8	9.6	84.3	34.07	6 791	830
Ankeny	110.9	2 732	17.4	251	18.2	74.8	8.7	85.8	33.38	6 961	881
Bettendorf	60.7	1 870	14.6	261	21.1	76.2	13.2	85.4	34.11	6 246	1 072
Burlington	44.3	1 744	11.0	245	22.8	76.3	15.1	85.4	37.94	5 948	1 095
Cedar Falls	67.7	1 802	0.0	451	16.1	73.6	6.3	85.0	33.15	7 348	758
Cedar Rapids	337.6	2 671	87.9	1 290	19.9	74.8	11.5	85.3	36.62	6 488	910
Clinton	23.8	895	2.3	220	20.4	74.7	12.5	85.0	35.68	6 416	915
Council Bluffs	95.4	1 592	14.1	470	21.1	76.2	10.4	87.7	33.25	6 323	1 057
Davenport	248.6	2 512	25.7	924	21.1	76.2	13.2	85.4	34.11	6 246	1 072
Des Moines	613.7	3 115	226.5	2 102	20.4	76.1	11.7	86.0	34.72	6 436	1 052
Dubuque	39.9	696	0.7	636	17.8	75.1	8.7	85.4	33.96	6 891	908
Fort Dodge	39.8	1 576	3.2	189	15.4	73.1	5.8	84.3	34.39	7 513	746
Iowa City	215.9	3 219	12.2	815	21.7	76.9	13.4	87.5	37.27	6 052	1 134
Marion	11.5	357	0.3	182	16.8	73.9	7.1	84.4	36.40	7 191	787
Marshalltown	26.4	1 022	0.0	195	16.8	73.9	7.1	84.4	36.40	7 191	787
Mason City	35.4	1 287	6.3	302	13.9	72.4	5.1	83.3	34.48	7 765	655
Ottumwa	30.9	1 261	7.5	278	NA	NA	NA	NA	NA	NA	NA
Sioux City	136.7	1 653	20.1	792	18.6	74.6	8.5	86.2	25.99	6 900	914
Urbandale	46.6	1 224	6.4	202	20.4	76.1	11.7	86.0	34.72	6 436	1 052
Waterloo	127.0	1 913	27.7	611	16.1	73.6	6.3	85.0	33.15	7 348	758
West Des Moines	160.5	2 934	4.1	449	20.4	76.1	11.7	86.0	34.72	6 436	1 052

1. Based on the population estimated as of July 1 of the year shown.   2. Represents normal values based on the 30-year period, 1971–2000.   3. Average daily minimum.   4. Average daily maximum.

Table D. Cities — **Land Area and Population**

STATE Place code	City	Population, 2010				Race alone or in combination, not of Hispanic origin (percent), 2010					Percent Hispanic or Latino[2], 2010	Percent Foreign born, 2008–2010
		Land area,[1] 2010 (sq km)	Total persons	Rank	Per square kilometer	White	Black	American Indian, Alaska Native	Asian	Hawaiian Pacific Islander		
		1	2	3	4	5	6	7	8	9	10	11
20 00000	KANSAS..................	211 754.1	2 853 118	X	13.5	80.3	6.7	1.7	2.9	0.1	10.5	6.4
20 18250	Dodge City	37.4	27 340	1 509	731.0	38.2	2.6	0.7	1.8	0.2	57.5	28.4
20 25325	Garden City	22.8	26 658	1 554	1 167.2	44.0	2.9	0.7	4.5	0.1	48.6	20.4
20 33625	Hutchinson	58.8	42 080	935	716.0	84.0	5.4	1.3	0.8	0.0	10.6	2.9
20 36000	Kansas City	323.3	145 786	168	451.0	42.1	27.9	1.4	2.9	0.2	27.8	14.7
20 38900	Lawrence	86.9	87 643	353	1 008.2	82.0	6.0	4.1	5.5	0.2	5.7	7.4
20 39000	Leavenworth	62.3	35 251	1 142	566.1	73.8	16.8	1.7	2.8	0.5	8.1	3.9
20 39075	Leawood	39.0	31 867	1 279	816.9	91.8	2.2	0.4	4.5	0.1	2.2	5.4
20 39350	Lenexa	88.3	48 190	813	545.6	82.4	6.6	0.9	4.5	0.2	7.3	9.9
20 44250	Manhattan	48.6	52 281	729	1 076.0	82.8	6.6	1.1	6.2	0.3	5.8	7.5
20 52575	Olathe....................	154.5	125 872	202	814.6	79.8	6.3	0.9	4.8	0.1	10.2	9.6
20 53775	Overland Park	193.8	173 372	139	894.4	82.5	5.0	0.8	7.0	0.1	6.3	9.5
20 62700	Salina	65.0	47 707	829	733.5	82.7	5.1	1.1	2.9	0.1	10.7	6.2
20 64500	Shawnee	108.4	62 209	574	573.9	83.6	6.1	0.9	3.8	0.2	7.5	7.9
20 71000	Topeka....................	155.8	127 473	198	818.0	72.9	13.0	2.4	1.8	0.1	13.4	5.2
20 79000	Wichita...................	412.6	382 368	49	926.8	67.3	12.8	2.1	5.5	0.2	15.3	9.3
21 00000	KENTUCKY...............	102 269.1	4 339 367	X	42.4	87.7	8.5	0.6	1.4	0.1	3.1	3.2
21 08902	Bowling Green.............	97.9	58 067	635	593.4	74.9	15.1	0.6	4.6	0.2	6.5	11.8
21 17848	Covington	34.2	40 640	977	1 189.0	83.4	13.8	0.9	0.7	0.2	3.6	2.4
21 24274	Elizabethtown	65.7	28 531	1 443	434.4	80.8	13.2	0.9	3.5	0.4	4.3	4.6
21 27982	Florence	26.7	29 951	1 362	1 122.2	86.4	5.5	0.6	3.5	0.2	5.5	6.1
21 28900	Frankfort	37.1	25 527	1 628	688.4	78.0	18.3	0.8	1.6	0.1	3.8	4.2
21 30700	Georgetown...............	41.0	29 098	1 415	709.0	87.1	8.1	0.5	1.5	0.1	4.3	3.6
21 35866	Henderson................	39.6	28 757	1 436	725.6	85.2	13.0	0.5	0.7	0.1	2.3	1.1
21 37918	Hopkinsville	79.4	31 577	1 292	397.6	62.9	33.2	0.8	1.4	0.3	3.5	3.2
21 40222	Jeffersontown	25.7	26 595	1 657	1 034.4	81.7	12.3	0.6	2.2	0.2	5.0	12.4
21 46027	Lexington-Fayette.........	734.7	295 803	63	402.6	74.9	15.6	0.6	3.8	0.1	6.9	8.6
21 48003	Louisville/Jefferson County	985.3	741 096	17	752.2	72.2	21.8	0.7	2.6	0.1	4.4	6.2
21 56136	Nicholasville	33.7	28 015	1 475	831.3	91.3	5.4	0.8	0.9	0.1	3.5	2.9
21 58620	Owensboro	49.5	57 265	645	1 158.0	88.2	9.0	0.4	1.1	0.1	3.2	2.5
21 58836	Paducah	51.5	25 024	1 663	485.5	72.3	25.7	0.9	1.2	0.1	2.7	3.0
21 65226	Richmond	59.1	31 364	1 301	531.0	87.6	9.3	0.9	1.6	0.1	2.7	3.4
22 00000	LOUISIANA	111 897.6	4 533 372	X	40.5	61.4	32.5	1.1	1.8	0.1	4.2	3.6
22 00975	Alexandria	73.6	47 723	827	648.6	38.5	58.0	0.9	2.2	0.0	1.8	1.5
22 05000	Baton Rouge	199.3	229 493	85	1 151.6	38.6	54.9	0.5	3.6	0.1	3.3	4.9
22 08920	Bossier City	109.7	61 315	583	559.1	63.5	26.5	0.9	2.8	0.3	8.1	4.8
22 13960	Central...................	161.2	26 864	1 542	166.7	89.1	8.6	0.8	0.7	0.0	1.6	1.1
22 36255	Houma....................	37.3	33 727	1 199	903.2	65.5	25.1	4.8	1.1	0.1	4.8	3.8
22 39475	Kenner	38.5	66 702	520	1 732.1	49.8	24.0	0.5	4.1	0.1	22.4	17.5
22 40735	Lafayette..................	127.5	120 623	214	946.0	62.9	31.6	0.7	2.1	0.1	3.8	5.0
22 41155	Lake Charles...............	108.9	71 993	471	660.9	46.8	48.6	0.9	1.9	0.1	2.9	3.3
22 51410	Monroe	75.7	48 815	796	645.2	33.6	64.3	0.5	1.3	0.1	1.1	2.0
22 54035	New Iberia	28.9	30 617	1 324	1 061.2	52.3	42.1	0.5	3.0	0.1	3.1	4.9
22 55000	New Orleans	438.8	343 829	52	783.6	31.4	60.4	0.6	3.2	0.1	5.2	5.7
22 70000	Shreveport................	272.9	199 311	111	730.3	40.9	55.2	0.8	1.6	0.1	2.5	2.7
22 70805	Slidell....................	38.4	27 068	1 526	704.2	74.2	17.8	0.9	2.0	0.1	6.3	5.0
23 00000	MAINE	79 882.8	1 328 361	X	16.6	95.8	1.6	1.3	1.4	0.1	1.3	3.3
23 02795	Bangor....................	88.7	33 039	1 233	372.4	93.9	2.2	2.1	2.0	0.1	1.5	3.3
23 38740	Lewiston	88.4	36 592	1 087	413.7	87.6	9.8	1.1	1.5	0.1	2.0	4.7
23 60545	Portland..................	55.2	66 194	523	1 199.4	85.7	7.9	1.0	4.3	0.1	3.0	10.9
23 71990	South Portland	31.0	25 002	1 666	805.5	91.7	2.6	0.7	4.4	0.1	2.2	7.2
24 00000	MARYLAND	25 141.6	5 773 552	X	229.6	56.4	30.2	0.8	6.3	0.1	8.2	13.5
24 01600	Annapolis.................	18.6	38 394	1 031	2 063.1	54.9	26.7	0.6	2.5	0.1	16.8	16.7
24 04000	Baltimore	209.6	620 961	23	2 962.0	29.2	64.4	0.9	2.8	0.1	4.2	7.2
24 08775	Bowie.....................	47.7	54 727	689	1 146.8	41.1	50.0	1.1	5.1	0.1	5.6	12.3
24 18750	College Park..............	14.6	30 413	1 338	2 083.1	60.5	14.9	0.6	14.2	0.1	11.9	17.9
24 30325	Frederick	57.0	65 239	539	1 145.5	60.6	19.9	0.8	6.8	0.2	14.4	16.6
24 31175	Gaithersburg	26.4	59 933	607	2 268.5	42.2	16.7	0.7	18.4	0.2	24.2	40.7
24 36075	Hagerstown	30.5	39 662	995	1 299.1	77.4	18.3	0.8	1.7	0.2	5.6	6.4
24 45900	Laurel	11.1	25 115	1 654	2 254.5	26.1	49.7	0.9	9.9	0.1	15.5	27.5
24 67675	Rockville..................	35.0	61 209	585	1 749.8	55.0	10.0	0.5	22.2	0.2	14.3	35.6
24 69925	Salisbury..................	34.7	30 343	1 344	874.7	55.0	35.7	0.7	3.8	0.1	7.0	10.5
25 00000	MASSACHUSETTS ...	20 202.1	6 547 629	X	324.1	77.6	6.8	0.5	5.9	0.1	9.6	14.8
25 00840	Agawam Town	60.4	28 438	1 448	471.1	93.3	1.7	0.4	2.1	0.1	3.3	7.7
25 02690	Attleboro	69.4	43 593	901	627.8	85.4	3.6	0.6	5.1	0.1	6.3	10.3
25 03690	Barnstable Town	154.9	45 193	871	291.8	89.7	4.1	1.3	1.6	0.1	3.1	9.0

1. Dry land or land partially or temporarily covered by water.   2. May be of any race.

Table D. Cities — **Population**

City	Age of population (percent), 2010											Population			
												Census counts		Percent change	
	Under 5 years	5 to 17 years	18 to 24 years	25 to 34 years	35 to 44 years	45 to 54 years	55 to 64 years	65 to 74 years	75 years and over	Median age	Percent female	1990	2000	1990–2000	2000–2010
	12	13	14	15	16	17	18	19	20	21	22	23	24	25	26
KANSAS	7.2	18.3	10.1	13.2	12.2	14.2	11.6	6.7	6.5	36.0	50.4	2 477 588	2 688 418	8.5	6.1
Dodge City	10.3	21.5	11.8	15.5	12.5	11.5	8.1	4.3	4.6	28.9	48.6	21 129	25 176	19.2	8.6
Garden City	9.6	21.6	11.6	13.7	12.2	13.1	9.2	4.7	4.3	29.9	50.2	24 097	28 451	18.1	-6.3
Hutchinson	6.8	16.2	10.6	13.3	11.1	13.7	11.6	7.7	8.9	37.8	49.7	39 308	40 787	3.8	3.2
Kansas City	8.8	19.6	9.7	15.2	12.5	13.4	10.3	5.6	4.9	32.5	50.6	151 521	146 866	-3.1	-0.7
Lawrence	5.5	12.0	28.6	17.1	10.4	9.9	8.5	4.0	4.0	26.7	49.8	65 608	80 098	22.1	9.4
Leavenworth	8.1	17.9	8.5	15.9	15.8	13.7	10.2	5.4	4.6	34.8	46.1	38 495	35 420	-8.0	-0.5
Leawood	5.5	22.6	4.2	5.3	12.9	18.1	16.3	8.2	7.1	44.7	51.5	19 693	27 656	40.4	15.2
Lenexa	7.1	17.6	8.2	14.9	13.3	15.2	13.3	5.3	5.0	36.6	51.3	34 110	40 238	18.0	19.8
Manhattan	5.6	9.8	39.0	16.5	7.5	7.5	6.7	3.5	4.0	23.8	49.1	43 081	44 831	4.1	16.6
Olathe	8.9	21.1	7.5	15.9	16.2	13.8	9.4	4.0	3.2	32.9	50.5	63 402	92 962	46.6	35.4
Overland Park	6.4	18.4	7.3	14.4	13.7	15.5	12.0	6.2	6.2	37.8	51.7	111 790	149 080	33.4	16.3
Salina	7.6	17.5	10.0	13.4	11.9	13.8	11.5	7.0	7.3	36.4	50.6	42 299	45 679	8.0	4.4
Shawnee	7.5	20.2	6.9	13.4	15.4	15.3	11.3	5.7	4.4	36.4	51.1	37 962	47 996	26.4	29.6
Topeka	7.5	16.9	9.8	14.6	11.5	13.4	12.0	6.9	7.4	36.0	52.2	119 883	122 377	2.1	4.2
Wichita	8.0	18.5	10.2	14.7	12.3	13.8	11.0	5.8	5.7	33.9	50.7	304 017	344 284	13.2	11.1
KENTUCKY	6.5	17.1	9.5	13.0	13.3	14.8	12.4	7.5	5.8	38.1	50.8	3 686 892	4 041 769	9.6	7.4
Bowling Green	6.1	14.0	24.9	15.2	10.4	10.5	8.2	5.3	5.4	27.6	51.7	41 688	49 296	18.2	17.8
Covington	7.9	15.4	9.7	17.5	13.5	14.8	10.7	5.3	5.2	34.6	49.9	43 646	43 370	-0.6	-6.3
Elizabethtown	7.6	17.5	9.8	14.6	12.9	13.9	10.5	6.5	6.8	35.4	52.1	18 167	22 542	24.1	26.6
Florence	8.2	16.4	9.5	15.7	13.6	12.7	10.8	6.9	6.2	35.2	52.0	18 586	23 551	26.7	27.2
Frankfort	6.4	14.4	13.1	14.0	12.6	13.6	11.9	7.1	7.0	36.7	51.9	26 535	27 741	4.5	-8.0
Georgetown	8.6	19.3	11.3	16.5	15.5	12.0	8.5	4.7	3.6	31.7	51.8	11 414	18 080	58.4	60.9
Henderson	7.3	16.0	8.7	13.9	12.6	14.2	12.6	7.3	7.4	38.3	53.0	25 945	27 373	5.5	5.1
Hopkinsville	7.7	17.3	9.8	13.7	12.1	13.4	11.4	7.1	7.5	36.1	52.9	29 809	30 089	0.9	4.9
Jeffersontown	6.1	16.6	8.2	14.6	13.2	14.5	13.0	7.5	6.2	38.4	52.0	23 223	26 633	14.7	-0.1
Lexington-Fayette	6.5	14.7	14.1	16.6	13.3	13.5	10.8	5.7	4.8	33.7	50.8	225 366	260 512	15.6	13.5
Louisville/Jefferson County	6.6	16.6	9.2	14.1	12.9	14.9	12.3	6.9	6.5	37.9	51.7	NA	693 604	NA	6.8
Nicholasville	8.8	19.2	8.8	16.1	14.6	13.3	9.5	5.4	4.3	33.1	52.3	13 603	19 680	44.7	42.4
Owensboro	7.4	16.3	9.5	13.4	11.7	13.7	11.8	7.9	8.3	38.1	52.9	53 577	54 067	0.9	5.9
Paducah	6.3	15.4	8.0	13.0	11.4	14.5	13.2	8.5	9.7	41.4	54.0	27 256	26 307	-3.5	-4.9
Richmond	6.0	11.8	28.8	16.3	10.7	9.7	7.3	4.6	4.7	26.6	52.1	21 183	27 152	28.2	15.5
LOUISIANA	6.9	17.7	10.5	13.9	12.5	14.4	11.8	6.9	5.4	35.8	51.0	4 221 826	4 468 976	5.9	1.4
Alexandria	7.2	19.4	8.9	13.4	11.6	14.1	11.4	7.0	7.0	36.0	53.1	49 049	46 342	-5.5	3.0
Baton Rouge	6.5	15.9	17.4	15.6	10.7	12.2	10.4	5.8	5.4	30.7	51.9	219 531	227 818	3.8	0.7
Bossier City	8.1	18.0	11.0	16.1	12.2	12.7	9.6	6.3	5.9	32.6	51.1	52 721	56 461	7.1	8.6
Central	6.0	17.1	8.6	12.1	12.0	16.3	14.0	8.5	5.3	40.6	51.0	NA	NA	NA	NA
Houma	7.3	18.4	9.2	13.7	12.5	14.8	11.6	6.6	6.0	36.2	50.9	30 495	32 393	6.2	4.1
Kenner	6.7	16.3	9.6	14.4	12.2	14.8	13.4	7.1	5.4	37.4	51.2	72 033	70 517	-2.1	-5.4
Lafayette	6.1	15.7	15.4	14.9	11.2	13.7	11.2	6.1	5.6	33.2	51.4	101 865	110 257	8.2	9.4
Lake Charles	7.0	16.5	12.2	14.3	10.8	13.6	11.7	7.0	7.0	35.0	51.7	70 580	71 757	1.7	0.3
Monroe	7.8	19.3	14.1	13.0	10.5	12.1	10.6	5.9	6.7	31.4	54.1	54 909	53 107	-3.3	-8.1
New Iberia	7.9	19.3	9.3	13.0	11.1	14.1	11.5	7.1	6.6	35.4	52.3	31 828	32 623	2.5	-6.1
New Orleans	6.4	14.9	12.8	16.4	12.4	14.2	12.0	6.1	4.9	34.6	51.6	496 938	484 674	-2.5	-29.1
Shreveport	7.3	17.7	10.8	14.6	11.5	13.2	11.6	6.5	6.6	34.6	53.2	198 518	200 145	0.8	-0.4
Slidell	7.1	18.4	8.5	13.2	12.7	14.2	11.9	7.2	6.8	37.3	51.5	24 124	25 695	6.5	5.3
MAINE	5.2	15.4	8.7	10.9	12.9	16.5	14.5	8.5	7.4	42.7	51.1	1 227 928	1 274 923	3.8	4.2
Bangor	5.5	12.3	16.1	14.4	11.6	13.7	12.1	6.6	7.8	36.7	51.8	33 181	31 473	-5.1	5.0
Lewiston	7.2	14.9	12.9	12.4	11.8	13.7	11.6	7.4	8.1	37.4	51.9	39 757	35 690	-10.2	2.5
Portland	5.4	11.7	11.4	19.2	13.9	14.3	11.5	5.9	6.7	36.7	51.2	64 157	64 249	0.1	3.0
South Portland	5.9	14.5	9.7	13.9	14.5	15.1	12.8	7.0	6.7	39.4	52.3	23 163	23 324	0.7	7.2
MARYLAND	6.3	17.1	9.7	13.2	13.8	15.6	12.1	6.7	5.6	38.0	51.6	4 780 753	5 296 486	10.8	9.0
Annapolis	7.5	13.4	9.9	17.8	13.2	12.9	12.5	7.1	5.9	36.0	52.2	33 195	35 838	8.0	7.1
Baltimore	6.6	14.9	12.6	16.7	12.3	14.1	11.1	6.2	5.5	34.4	52.9	736 014	651 154	-11.5	-4.6
Bowie	5.9	18.6	7.5	10.8	15.4	18.3	11.9	6.4	5.1	40.1	53.1	37 642	50 269	33.5	8.9
College Park	2.4	5.3	60.6	10.0	5.6	6.2	4.8	2.8	2.4	21.3	46.9	23 714	24 657	4.0	23.3
Frederick	7.7	16.0	9.8	17.0	14.9	13.8	9.9	5.0	5.8	34.6	51.8	40 186	52 767	31.3	23.6
Gaithersburg	8.3	15.9	7.9	17.8	16.0	14.3	10.3	4.8	4.7	35.1	51.4	39 676	52 613	32.6	13.9
Hagerstown	8.7	17.2	9.3	15.4	13.1	13.5	10.4	6.1	6.3	34.5	52.7	35 306	36 687	3.9	8.1
Laurel	8.0	14.7	9.4	20.4	16.8	14.4	9.4	4.2	2.8	33.7	52.3	19 086	19 960	4.6	25.8
Rockville	6.5	14.9	7.2	15.4	15.6	14.7	11.6	6.8	7.1	38.7	52.1	44 830	47 388	5.7	29.2
Salisbury	7.3	14.4	22.8	14.8	10.7	10.6	8.3	5.1	6.0	28.1	53.7	20 592	23 743	15.3	27.8
MASSACHUSETTS	5.6	16.1	10.4	12.9	13.5	15.5	12.3	7.0	6.8	39.1	51.6	6 016 425	6 349 097	5.5	3.1
Agawam Town	4.7	15.6	7.3	10.3	13.1	16.7	14.3	8.2	9.9	44.4	52.2	27 323	28 144	3.0	1.0
Attleboro	6.4	16.3	7.9	12.9	15.6	16.5	11.5	6.5	6.4	39.5	51.2	38 383	42 068	9.6	3.6
Barnstable Town	4.6	13.7	6.9	9.7	11.3	17.0	15.7	10.5	10.5	47.3	51.8	40 949	47 821	16.8	-5.5

Table D. Cities — Households, Group Quarters, Crime, and Education

City	Households, 2010				Persons in group quarters, 2010				Serious crimes known to police,[2] 2010				Educational attainment, 2008–2010		
		Percent				Institutional			Total		Rate[3]			Attainment[4] (percent)	
	Number	Persons per household	Female family householder[1]	One-person	Total	Total	Persons in nursing facilities	Non-institutional	Number	Rate[3]	Violent	Property	Population age 25 and older	High school graduate or less	Bachelor's degree or more
	27	28	29	30	31	32	33	34	35	36	37	38	39	40	41
KANSAS	1 112 096	2.49	10.4	27.8	79 074	41 393	20 672	37 681	99 546	3 489	369	3 120	1 824 029	38.6	29.6
Dodge City	8 777	3.05	13.0	22.7	596	363	207	233	1 021	3 734	486	3 248	15 369	58.4	15.9
Garden City	9 071	2.88	13.9	24.0	548	231	96	317	1 145	4 295	469	3 826	15 116	59.5	15.1
Hutchinson	16 981	2.31	12.3	33.2	2 850	2 402	447	448	3 140	7 462	585	6 877	28 008	40.7	19.6
Kansas City	53 925	2.68	18.9	28.8	1 109	815	421	294	8 558	5 870	565	5 306	89 389	58.8	14.6
Lawrence	34 970	2.28	8.8	32.0	7 984	430	270	7 554	4 292	4 897	478	4 419	44 316	21.5	53.3
Leavenworth	12 256	2.55	13.2	28.7	4 031	3 352	72	679	1 492	4 233	735	3 498	23 019	38.7	31.1
Leawood	11 781	2.70	4.8	18.1	11	0	0	11	496	1 556	41	1 516	21 111	8.7	74.8
Lenexa	19 288	2.48	9.0	25.2	348	327	325	21	1 065	2 210	137	2 073	32 028	20.8	51.7
Manhattan	20 008	2.30	8.2	30.3	6 227	401	306	5 826	NA	NA	NA	NA	23 290	20.3	52.8
Olathe	44 507	2.80	9.6	20.0	1 418	789	661	629	2 523	2 004	172	1 833	77 520	24.4	45.2
Overland Park	71 443	2.41	8.4	29.8	1 343	1 215	1 040	128	4 474	2 581	167	2 414	118 060	17.0	57.0
Salina	19 391	2.39	11.8	31.6	1 435	545	377	890	2 479	5 196	398	4 798	30 517	44.6	24.1
Shawnee	23 651	2.61	9.8	23.1	406	384	384	22	1 340	2 154	190	1 964	39 919	27.3	42.4
Topeka	53 943	2.29	14.2	35.9	4 083	2 648	1 246	1 435	8 201	6 434	545	5 888	83 060	42.1	27.1
Wichita	151 818	2.48	13.1	31.1	6 420	3 555	1 666	2 865	21 338	5 580	795	4 786	240 142	40.5	27.8
KENTUCKY	1 719 965	2.45	12.7	27.5	125 870	70 779	26 044	55 091	121 237	2 794	243	2 551	2 879 829	52.6	20.5
Bowling Green	22 735	2.28	14.1	35.4	6 147	1 173	492	4 974	2 826	4 867	260	4 607	31 474	46.6	29.5
Covington	17 033	2.30	17.2	37.3	1 406	946	420	460	2 664	6 555	792	5 763	27 365	54.4	17.0
Elizabethtown	11 711	2.34	15.1	32.1	1 075	995	284	80	1 007	3 529	175	3 354	18 481	43.1	25.2
Florence	12 493	2.38	13.8	32.5	268	265	265	3	1 661	5 546	214	5 332	19 811	50.4	19.2
Frankfort	11 140	2.14	16.7	38.3	1 644	648	188	996	1 027	4 023	298	3 725	17 096	51.4	25.0
Georgetown	10 733	2.59	14.9	24.9	1 284	211	136	1 073	1 134	3 897	433	3 464	17 409	46.0	23.4
Henderson	12 091	2.28	16.2	33.7	1 162	806	262	356	1 068	3 714	80	3 634	19 979	56.8	15.2
Hopkinsville	12 854	2.35	19.8	32.4	1 425	1 204	348	221	1 384	4 383	415	3 968	20 463	53.4	15.8
Jeffersontown	11 065	2.37	12.3	29.4	351	351	351	0	622	2 339	184	2 155	18 993	38.6	31.2
Lexington-Fayette	123 043	2.30	12.3	32.7	12 804	3 996	1 092	8 808	12 748	4 310	583	3 727	188 892	32.9	38.7
Louisville/Jefferson County	309 175	2.35	15.4	32.0	14 153	8 529	4 831	5 624	33 285	5 039	565	4 473	396 450	44.8	25.8
Nicholasville	10 492	2.64	16.7	22.3	312	269	80	43	1 244	4 440	186	4 255	17 161	50.1	17.6
Owensboro	24 215	2.29	15.5	34.0	1 817	1 025	806	792	2 372	4 142	206	3 936	37 698	53.7	16.6
Paducah	11 462	2.09	16.4	41.5	1 090	1 024	510	66	1 327	5 303	372	4 931	17 892	44.7	19.4
Richmond	12 435	2.17	13.8	35.6	4 344	480	207	3 864	2 057	6 558	402	6 157	16 335	46.4	25.7
LOUISIANA	1 728 360	2.55	17.2	26.9	127 427	88 104	24 524	39 323	190 243	4 197	549	3 648	2 900 712	52.8	21.1
Alexandria	18 272	2.48	24.5	31.2	2 356	1 611	531	745	4 379	9 176	1 240	7 935	29 682	49.8	22.2
Baton Rouge	91 474	2.40	20.6	32.7	9 554	3 531	1 129	6 023	14 999	6 536	1 104	5 432	134 575	40.5	32.2
Bossier City	23 866	2.50	16.9	28.4	1 614	811	671	803	3 073	5 012	651	4 361	37 766	46.1	21.9
Central	10 179	2.63	11.9	18.8	59	0	0	59	NA	NA	NA	NA	18 246	49.4	22.0
Houma	12 751	2.63	17.4	26.1	212	134	114	78	1 830	5 426	753	4 673	21 873	57.9	20.7
Kenner	24 844	2.67	17.2	25.6	422	319	303	103	2 561	3 839	313	3 526	45 591	49.2	20.3
Lafayette	49 444	2.35	15.5	31.9	4 509	1 775	613	2 734	7 929	6 573	779	5 794	74 609	40.1	32.4
Lake Charles	28 940	2.38	19.4	32.4	3 149	2 018	596	1 131	3 535	4 910	678	4 232	45 840	48.0	24.1
Monroe	18 445	2.47	27.6	33.5	3 273	1 229	663	2 044	4 985	10 212	836	9 376	29 064	51.3	24.9
New Iberia	11 706	2.58	21.9	28.8	433	367	367	66	NA	NA	NA	NA	18 730	62.0	14.7
New Orleans	142 158	2.33	20.9	35.9	13 165	5 509	1 509	7 656	15 238	4 432	754	3 678	213 791	41.7	32.2
Shreveport	80 651	2.40	23.0	32.6	5 574	3 588	1 975	1 986	10 992	5 515	769	4 746	126 444	47.3	22.9
Slidell	10 050	2.66	16.2	23.4	315	286	286	29	1 655	6 114	392	5 723	17 562	43.6	24.1
MAINE	557 219	2.32	10.0	28.6	35 545	12 409	7 878	23 136	34 555	2 601	122	2 479	934 836	44.4	26.5
Bangor	14 475	2.10	12.6	37.9	2 690	854	561	1 836	1 782	5 394	157	5 236	22 051	38.7	27.6
Lewiston	15 267	2.26	13.7	34.4	2 117	365	344	1 752	1 150	3 143	254	2 889	23 722	53.7	15.6
Portland	30 725	2.07	10.1	40.5	2 613	1 065	592	1 548	3 163	4 778	366	4 413	46 895	29.0	44.3
South Portland	10 877	2.24	12.0	31.9	636	195	73	441	950	3 800	196	3 604	17 667	33.4	36.8
MARYLAND	2 156 411	2.61	14.6	26.1	138 375	66 838	28 001	71 537	204 671	3 545	548	2 997	3 826 074	38.4	35.6
Annapolis	16 136	2.34	14.9	35.0	603	143	143	460	1 327	3 456	589	2 868	27 294	35.6	43.3
Baltimore	249 903	2.38	23.8	36.1	25 199	9 951	3 793	15 248	37 596	6 054	1 500	4 554	407 252	51.7	25.2
Bowie	19 950	2.73	14.0	23.4	255	148	145	107	1 150	2 101	194	1 908	35 787	26.0	45.5
College Park	6 757	2.79	7.9	24.8	11 535	0	0	11 535	NA	NA	NA	NA	9 616	29.8	49.0
Frederick	25 352	2.50	12.8	30.7	1 785	803	803	982	2 166	3 320	696	2 624	42 935	34.8	34.8
Gaithersburg	22 000	2.70	12.7	26.7	547	372	366	175	NA	NA	NA	NA	41 218	26.3	52.5
Hagerstown	16 449	2.36	18.4	34.5	806	546	508	260	1 613	4 067	446	3 621	26 282	56.3	15.2
Laurel	10 498	2.37	15.7	37.6	183	0	0	183	1 232	4 905	589	4 316	16 808	34.9	35.7
Rockville	23 686	2.54	9.9	27.0	1 103	833	665	270	NA	NA	NA	NA	43 191	21.8	59.9
Salisbury	11 983	2.42	19.1	32.5	1 391	155	135	1 236	2 687	8 855	1 480	7 376	17 169	45.9	25.3
MASSACHUSETTS	2 547 075	2.48	12.5	28.7	238 882	74 667	43 833	164 215	184 458	2 817	467	2 351	4 418 255	37.2	38.5
Agawam Town	11 664	2.38	10.3	30.0	677	669	669	8	307	1 080	165	914	20 674	40.6	25.0
Attleboro	16 884	2.55	11.3	26.4	564	451	429	113	994	2 280	358	1 922	29 486	44.3	27.8
Barnstable Town	19 225	2.33	10.6	29.0	363	106	79	257	1 683	3 724	788	2 936	33 967	30.0	37.3

1. No spouse present. 2. Data for serious crimes have not been adjusted for underreporting. This may affect comparability between geographic areas and over time. 3. Per 100,000 population estimated by the FBI. 4. Persons 25 years old and over.

Table D. Cities — Income, Poverty, and Housing

City	Money income, 2008–2010					Housing units, 2010			Occupied Housing units 2008–2010				
		Households			Families with income below poverty (percent)				Owner-occupied			Median owner costs as a percent of income	
	Per capita income[1] (dollars)	Median income	Percent with income of $200,000 or more	Percent with income of less than $25,000		Total	Percent change, 2000–2010	Vacant units for sale or rent[2]	Total	Percent	Median value[3] (dollars)	With a mortgage[4]	Without a mortgage[5]
	42	43	44	45	46	47	48	49	50	51	52	53	54
KANSAS	25 815	49 444	3.0	23.8	8.6	1 233 215	9.0	121 119	1 106 198	68.6	126 600	21.5	11.7
Dodge City	19 240	46 734	1.5	24.2	14.5	9 378	4.3	601	8 886	64.6	83 300	22.3	13.9
Garden City	19 063	41 693	2.2	21.9	11.0	9 656	-1.7	585	8 749	67.2	96 600	23.9	12.4
Hutchinson	21 601	40 298	1.2	30.4	13.2	18 580	5.1	1 599	17 259	64.6	89 900	22.0	13.4
Kansas City	18 208	36 110	0.7	34.5	19.3	61 969	0.8	8 044	52 233	61.3	95 900	25.6	15.5
Lawrence	23 195	41 953	2.8	32.5	10.8	37 502	14.4	2 532	34 153	44.2	178 300	23.0	11.8
Leavenworth	23 467	49 545	2.0	25.5	7.0	13 670	5.9	1 414	12 272	51.5	126 400	21.9	14.1
Leawood	64 118	132 976	27.7	9.4	1.7	12 384	22.2	603	11 864	92.6	399 300	21.1	10.0
Lenexa	35 987	74 935	6.3	13.2	4.4	20 832	27.4	1 544	18 931	64.2	215 800	20.6	10.0
Manhattan	20 358	36 917	2.2	36.4	10.6	21 619	22.1	1 611	19 118	40.6	167 800	22.2	11.3
Olathe	30 311	74 320	4.2	12.0	4.1	46 851	40.6	2 344	43 449	73.4	195 600	21.7	10.9
Overland Park	39 170	70 775	7.6	13.3	3.9	76 280	21.7	4 837	72 388	64.8	227 600	21.3	10.8
Salina	23 375	41 822	1.8	26.0	10.5	20 803	6.1	1 412	18 738	65.7	113 600	21.3	11.1
Shawnee	32 762	72 342	4.1	12.5	4.3	24 954	30.6	1 303	23 304	73.3	203 800	21.9	11.9
Topeka	22 959	39 169	1.6	31.2	15.9	59 582	5.5	5 639	55 231	57.2	96 000	21.2	12.2
Wichita	24 517	44 477	2.6	27.1	12.1	167 310	10.0	15 492	151 767	61.8	115 600	20.9	11.0
KENTUCKY	22 200	40 990	2.1	31.5	13.9	1 927 164	10.1	207 199	1 684 824	69.0	119 400	21.9	11.0
Bowling Green	18 738	32 152	1.1	36.8	18.9	24 712	16.6	1 977	22 099	43.1	128 500	22.8	10.4
Covington	20 005	36 087	1.3	36.7	20.4	20 053	-1.9	3 020	17 304	49.7	110 200	23.1	12.2
Elizabethtown	23 627	40 720	1.3	31.6	14.7	12 664	26.3	953	11 383	53.8	160 900	21.3	10.0
Florence	22 714	46 225	1.1	26.8	11.4	13 447	31.2	954	11 973	53.1	140 300	23.5	10.0
Frankfort	22 027	39 376	0.6	32.6	19.8	12 938	-3.4	1 798	11 447	49.7	126 200	23.7	10.0
Georgetown	23 197	50 971	1.2	24.3	13.2	11 957	66.8	1 224	10 990	59.5	148 300	19.6	10.0
Henderson	20 003	32 840	0.3	39.1	16.6	13 171	4.0	1 080	12 541	60.5	96 000	23.2	10.5
Hopkinsville	18 498	35 154	1.1	36.4	19.1	14 318	7.8	1 464	12 765	54.8	100 800	22.7	11.5
Jeffersontown	26 212	51 626	1.5	18.7	7.1	11 800	5.5	735	10 621	65.7	160 300	22.6	10.7
Lexington-Fayette	27 881	47 104	3.9	27.5	12.1	135 160	16.3	12 117	121 966	56.2	159 300	21.6	10.0
Louisville/Jefferson County	24 238	42 174	2.6	29.9	14.1	337 616	NA	28 441	240 446	62.1	139 800	22.8	11.3
Nicholasville	18 807	43 086	0.3	25.0	12.9	11 405	47.0	913	10 208	56.6	142 700	23.2	10.0
Owensboro	19 811	35 004	1.4	37.2	14.4	26 072	7.0	1 857	23 340	56.9	97 600	22.3	11.9
Paducah	20 430	31 220	1.4	40.2	18.1	12 851	-2.5	1 399	11 055	50.1	97 800	20.7	11.0
Richmond	17 606	30 716	1.1	42.5	19.7	13 788	16.5	1 353	11 939	39.5	143 000	22.0	10.0
LOUISIANA	23 293	43 362	2.7	30.2	13.6	1 964 981	6.4	236 621	1 678 868	67.9	135 600	21.5	10.0
Alexandria	21 205	35 013	2.4	37.7	21.3	20 366	2.4	2 094	17 112	53.2	121 800	22.0	11.3
Baton Rouge	23 616	36 816	3.5	36.1	16.9	100 801	3.6	9 327	88 151	50.5	158 400	21.9	10.7
Bossier City	22 960	44 587	2.1	26.2	13.9	25 579	11.7	1 713	23 151	57.6	128 000	21.3	10.0
Central	29 068	64 223	3.7	15.4	4.5	10 574	NA	395	10 110	86.6	167 700	20.0	10.0
Houma	24 605	44 223	2.6	28.1	13.2	13 924	12.1	1 173	12 422	68.3	150 100	22.4	10.0
Kenner	25 347	49 286	3.7	23.6	11.5	28 076	2.5	3 232	24 174	60.8	189 000	23.7	10.6
Lafayette	26 849	44 520	4.6	31.2	13.5	53 356	13.9	3 912	47 085	57.6	167 500	21.7	11.1
Lake Charles	23 370	35 979	2.6	34.0	16.6	32 469	3.7	3 529	28 699	58.4	117 600	21.0	10.0
Monroe	19 350	28 581	2.4	45.4	32.8	20 570	-3.5	2 125	18 011	45.1	117 700	24.4	11.4
New Iberia	18 390	32 242	1.6	38.7	21.2	13 059	1.1	1 353	11 810	60.8	104 400	23.2	12.4
New Orleans	24 721	36 208	3.8	37.2	20.6	189 896	-11.7	47 738	139 939	48.2	183 100	28.5	14.2
Shreveport	22 455	35 404	2.8	36.0	15.6	88 253	1.5	7 602	77 043	55.8	120 500	22.0	10.9
Slidell	21 999	48 122	1.7	24.3	12.3	11 155	10.4	1 105	9 995	71.4	160 600	26.2	12.2
MAINE	25 186	46 405	2.1	26.1	8.6	721 830	10.7	164 611	550 376	72.4	178 600	24.6	14.1
Bangor	23 274	37 724	1.8	32.4	14.8	15 674	7.5	1 199	14 265	48.6	153 500	22.8	16.7
Lewiston	20 203	35 624	1.2	35.9	17.3	16 731	1.6	1 464	14 775	50.6	157 900	25.5	19.7
Portland	27 708	43 063	1.9	29.0	12.5	33 836	6.2	3 111	30 984	45.6	249 100	27.2	13.5
South Portland	28 227	51 296	2.0	19.7	9.1	11 484	11.0	607	11 005	64.2	225 200	28.1	15.3
MARYLAND	34 469	70 017	7.2	15.6	6.1	2 378 814	10.9	222 403	2 122 769	68.2	321 400	25.8	12.7
Annapolis	39 909	67 394	8.9	17.8	8.7	17 845	10.2	1 709	16 165	52.7	413 300	24.2	11.8
Baltimore	22 975	39 113	2.5	33.9	17.8	296 685	-1.3	46 782	237 886	48.7	167 500	26.3	16.2
Bowie	40 691	101 082	9.1	6.6	1.8	20 687	11.1	737	19 704	86.9	348 100	27.5	10.7
College Park	18 119	61 222	7.7	31.5	3.2	8 212	31.4	1 455	6 465	52.1	344 000	27.7	10.8
Frederick	31 932	65 130	3.7	14.1	5.4	27 559	25.0	2 207	25 428	58.2	280 300	26.5	16.0
Gaithersburg	38 457	79 795	7.7	12.6	6.4	23 337	13.5	1 337	22 894	57.0	372 100	24.8	10.8
Hagerstown	20 078	34 863	1.0	36.7	19.0	18 682	9.5	2 233	16 642	41.8	174 100	27.6	13.9
Laurel	31 535	64 498	2.4	12.0	1.7	11 397	19.4	899	9 673	51.7	285 100	31.7	13.0
Rockville	47 266	91 664	13.7	8.9	2.5	25 199	41.6	1 513	23 428	58.6	488 900	23.9	11.0
Salisbury	19 545	37 361	1.0	32.3	10.9	13 401	37.2	1 418	11 911	40.3	172 600	31.7	13.1
MASSACHUSETTS	33 969	63 961	6.8	20.6	7.5	2 808 254	7.1	261 179	2 521 984	63.3	342 000	26.5	15.5
Agawam Town	28 838	62 384	1.6	17.9	6.5	12 139	4.1	475	11 647	76.8	232 100	24.8	14.6
Attleboro	28 872	62 049	3.1	16.8	5.1	18 022	8.9	1 138	16 221	67.8	290 900	28.6	15.4
Barnstable Town	35 795	61 545	5.7	17.3	5.9	26 343	5.3	7 118	19 983	77.0	370 500	30.6	17.6

1. Based on population estimated by the American Community Survey.   2. Includes units rented or sold but not occupied.   3. Specified owner-occupied units; $1,000,000 represents $1,000,000 or more.   4. 50.0 represents 50 percent or more.   5. 10.0 represents 10 percent or less.

Table D. Cities — Housing, Labor Force, and Employment

City	Occupied housing units, 2008–2010 (cont.)				Migration, 2008–2010		Civilian labor force, 2010		Unemployment		Civilian employment[4], 2008–2010			
	Percent renter occupied	Median gross rent[1]	Median rent as a percent of income[2]	Percent with no vehicle available	Percent who lived in the same house one year ago	Percent who lived outside this city one year ago	Total	Percent change, 2009–2010	Total	Rate[3]	Population age 16 and older	In labor force	Full-year full-time worker	Households with no workers (percent)
	55	56	57	58	59	60	61	62	63	64	65	66	67	68
KANSAS	31.4	678	27.6	5.3	82.6	9.8	1 504 883	-0.2	107 675	7.2	2 194 029	68.8	45.5	23.3
Dodge City	35.4	571	21.3	9.8	81.7	11.4	14 742	1.4	666	4.5	19 385	70.9	49.2	22.2
Garden City	32.8	621	23.2	4.7	83.3	9.9	13 970	1.5	703	5.0	18 863	0.0	52.3	15.1
Hutchinson	35.4	587	26.8	6.5	79.9	9.2	21 120	-0.6	1 611	7.6	33 583	61.1	41.8	27.7
Kansas City	38.7	704	33.3	10.9	78.8	8.6	66 083	-1.0	7 068	10.7	108 211	67.2	39.3	29.4
Lawrence	55.8	791	34.5	5.4	67.5	13.5	50 692	-0.1	3 323	6.6	73 044	69.7	35.8	18.3
Leavenworth	48.5	790	27.6	8.1	67.0	22.3	15 114	0.2	1 630	10.8	26 988	58.2	40.9	24.6
Leawood	7.4	1 410	31.9	3.7	89.5	8.3	15 848	-1.1	734	4.6	23 750	67.6	43.1	21.3
Lenexa	35.8	861	26.6	4.2	80.4	15.8	28 494	-1.1	2 061	7.2	37 578	77.7	52.2	14.2
Manhattan	59.4	745	36.6	6.2	72.0	15.1	28 937	-1.4	1 455	5.0	45 381	67.8	33.5	21.0
Olathe	26.6	824	26.7	2.7	85.1	8.7	62 534	-1.1	4 156	6.6	90 859	78.7	52.7	13.4
Overland Park	35.2	893	25.7	4.0	82.3	11.1	98 307	-1.1	6 496	6.6	135 067	73.1	50.4	19.3
Salina	34.3	643	28.5	6.5	79.7	7.6	26 156	-2.4	1 722	6.6	36 209	70.3	44.1	23.8
Shawnee	26.7	770	26.1	2.7	84.4	10.3	32 692	-1.1	1 781	5.4	46 189	76.1	50.8	15.0
Topeka	42.8	642	28.9	9.4	78.8	7.8	66 588	0.9	5 567	8.4	99 500	66.9	43.7	28.5
Wichita	38.2	633	28.9	7.0	80.8	5.6	191 007	-2.5	18 502	9.7	289 344	69.7	45.6	23.9
KENTUCKY	31.0	608	28.9	7.9	84.5	10.3	2 060 180	-0.9	210 776	10.2	3 410 542	60.6	38.5	31.7
Bowling Green	56.9	603	30.9	9.3	69.7	17.3	28 999	-1.3	2 618	9.0	47 090	64.3	32.3	29.1
Covington	50.3	640	34.0	18.1	78.3	11.1	19 567	-6.7	2 225	11.4	32 322	65.1	42.2	29.4
Elizabethtown	46.2	608	28.7	5.3	81.1	11.5	13 784	NA	1 136	8.2	21 758	59.3	39.3	28.9
Florence	46.9	743	29.9	11.2	81.4	13.5	16 311	6.1	1 384	8.5	23 242	67.0	41.8	25.7
Frankfort	50.3	613	31.4	7.8	77.9	9.8	12 060	-8.6	1 126	9.3	20 788	64.3	41.1	31.4
Georgetown	40.5	708	26.4	6.8	70.0	19.7	14 192	NA	1 194	8.4	21 608	69.9	45.6	23.8
Henderson	39.5	555	31.7	8.7	81.3	5.8	14 131	0.7	1 411	10.0	22 971	60.9	38.6	35.5
Hopkinsville	45.2	556	26.2	10.3	80.9	9.0	13 549	-7.3	1 513	11.2	24 007	57.1	36.6	36.7
Jeffersontown	34.3	777	26.5	2.4	83.6	10.8	14 202	-2.3	1 266	8.9	21 251	70.5	46.1	21.2
Lexington-Fayette	43.8	706	29.4	7.9	73.4	8.7	152 490	0.5	12 131	8.0	236 987	70.3	43.8	22.2
Louisville/Jefferson County	37.9	649	29.6	11.7	85.6	5.1	362 777	-0.4	37 865	10.4	467 381	66.2	41.0	28.8
Nicholasville	43.4	721	29.7	5.3	72.5	10.7	13 319	1.0	1 166	8.8	20 995	70.6	44.1	20.2
Owensboro	43.1	553	26.1	11.0	80.4	7.2	27 799	0.9	2 490	9.0	44 820	56.0	37.9	36.9
Paducah	49.9	516	27.7	11.5	74.8	13.8	10 528	-3.1	990	9.4	20 417	55.7	36.0	35.7
Richmond	60.5	536	31.1	9.0	63.2	20.8	16 506	-2.9	1 344	8.1	26 112	64.3	28.3	28.6
LOUISIANA	32.1	730	31.4	8.6	85.2	10.0	2 070 068	0.5	154 724	7.5	3 506 906	62.1	41.4	27.4
Alexandria	46.8	748	39.9	13.5	82.9	7.2	19 921	-2.9	1 488	7.5	35 058	58.6	40.2	29.1
Baton Rouge	49.5	733	35.0	11.4	77.6	9.2	107 494	-0.9	8 552	8.0	183 392	65.0	38.5	26.3
Bossier City	42.4	733	29.1	7.7	77.3	13.8	27 740	-4.1	1 621	5.8	46 636	68.1	46.7	23.8
Central	13.4	689	29.8	2.8	89.0	7.0	15 381	NA	731	4.8	21 473	68.6	49.2	21.7
Houma	31.7	664	31.5	11.4	85.4	7.6	16 216	0.5	965	6.0	26 335	60.3	40.2	26.6
Kenner	39.2	900	30.3	6.8	86.9	8.4	33 132	-1.5	2 139	6.5	53 500	68.8	45.7	22.3
Lafayette	42.4	720	29.1	8.8	83.3	8.8	61 703	1.3	3 608	5.8	96 611	65.0	40.4	24.6
Lake Charles	41.6	691	30.5	10.2	76.8	10.3	33 217	-2.7	2 452	7.4	56 490	62.0	37.6	28.1
Monroe	54.9	574	33.6	14.0	82.3	7.7	20 226	-5.6	1 890	9.3	37 172	56.8	35.1	33.7
New Iberia	39.2	630	30.0	13.2	83.7	7.8	13 133	-10.6	1 111	8.5	22 823	59.1	36.0	32.1
New Orleans	51.8	900	38.9	19.0	78.8	9.8	146 021	8.6	12 970	8.9	263 647	63.7	39.8	29.8
Shreveport	44.2	688	31.9	11.6	83.6	5.5	91 381	-1.6	6 817	7.5	154 470	63.2	42.2	29.0
Slidell	28.6	990	33.5	2.4	81.2	11.2	12 487	-2.1	824	6.6	20 983	63.8	41.2	28.2
MAINE	27.6	718	30.4	7.0	86.4	10.6	700 568	0.3	57 324	8.2	1 087 668	65.1	39.9	29.7
Bangor	51.4	706	31.5	11.6	74.6	14.5	17 145	-2.2	1 364	8.0	27 572	68.0	35.6	28.4
Lewiston	49.4	631	31.7	15.4	80.1	10.5	18 473	2.7	1 598	8.7	29 121	61.2	36.1	35.4
Portland	54.4	844	32.3	16.1	75.1	13.5	39 006	3.6	2 476	6.3	56 248	70.0	42.7	27.0
South Portland	35.8	919	29.3	6.2	86.6	8.7	14 618	2.7	914	6.3	19 785	73.1	48.2	23.0
MARYLAND	31.8	1 117	30.7	9.3	86.1	10.0	3 057 271	1.9	239 441	7.8	4 545 628	70.0	47.4	20.8
Annapolis	47.3	1 237	31.3	12.0	83.4	11.1	22 193	5.8	1 552	7.0	31 392	69.4	45.8	21.6
Baltimore	51.3	875	33.7	29.8	82.0	6.1	275 904	-1.1	32 696	11.9	501 802	62.3	39.1	31.7
Bowie	13.1	1 712	33.6	2.6	91.6	7.5	31 306	2.3	1 955	6.2	41 899	76.2	56.2	15.6
College Park	47.9	1 311	42.5	10.8	58.8	30.1	15 731	11.0	1 256	8.0	27 887	53.2	20.6	24.2
Frederick	41.8	1 098	27.8	7.3	79.6	10.5	35 616	10.2	2 635	7.4	50 494	75.1	49.8	18.1
Gaithersburg	43.0	1 357	29.3	7.5	82.9	12.4	33 444	2.0	2 029	6.1	47 247	77.7	54.1	14.3
Hagerstown	58.2	753	33.7	16.0	76.1	11.7	19 294	2.8	2 407	12.5	30 921	65.6	37.8	33.6
Laurel	48.3	1 214	28.4	5.6	79.8	14.9	NA	NA	NA	NA	20 114	80.2	55.8	13.4
Rockville	41.4	1 639	28.1	9.1	82.8	10.8	31 836	0.6	1 783	5.6	48 261	72.4	50.6	17.7
Salisbury	59.7	899	35.9	13.8	71.7	16.3	15 797	6.9	1 622	10.3	24 487	63.2	38.0	30.2
MASSACHUSETTS	36.7	1 008	30.0	12.4	86.2	8.3	3 469 270	-0.2	288 590	8.3	5 268 400	68.1	41.7	25.5
Agawam Town	23.2	845	28.8	5.8	92.3	3.8	15 801	-0.2	1 287	8.1	23 330	68.8	42.8	24.6
Attleboro	32.2	899	26.7	5.8	86.7	7.1	24 863	0.2	2 524	10.2	34 842	73.7	45.8	21.1
Barnstable Town	23.0	1 059	30.5	6.6	90.7	5.4	26 296	-1.4	2 134	8.1	37 820	64.0	39.0	30.1

1. $2,000 represents $2,000 or more.   2. 50.0 represents 50 percent or more.   3. Percent of civilian labor force.   4. Persons 16 years old and over.

Table D. Cities — Construction, Wholesale Trade, and Retail Trade

City	Value of residential construction authorized by building permits, 2010			Wholesale trade,[1] 2007				Retail trade,[2] 2007			
	New construction ($1,000)	Number of housing units	Percent single family	Number of establishments	Number of employees	Sales (mil dol)	Annual payroll (mil dol)	Number of establishments	Number of employees	Sales (mil dol)	Annual payroll (mil dol)
	69	70	71	72	73	74	75	76	77	78	79
KANSAS	811 584	5 140	77.3	3 747	47 285	45 863.9	2 150.4	11 463	149 672	34 538.3	3 133.7
Dodge City	3 800	31	80.6	40	433	333.3	17.6	124	1 571	380.1	33.2
Garden City	2 388	18	44.4	14	132	132.4	5.3	152	2 248	461.2	43.5
Hutchinson	5 253	30	100.0	36	473	464.1	17.1	241	3 264	720.4	68.9
Kansas City	18 456	201	65.7	214	5 328	3 855.9	265.1	422	6 267	1 556.3	158.6
Lawrence	35 940	261	62.5	63	641	354.9	24.8	363	5 823	1 130.5	105.7
Leavenworth	9 836	50	100.0	7	19	5.4	0.7	121	1 529	353.2	32.0
Leawood	6 812	20	100.0	38	355	203.3	23.7	136	2 403	334.1	40.0
Lenexa	19 452	67	88.1	285	5 111	2 182.2	256.3	185	3 734	1 849.1	107.4
Manhattan	67 393	486	45.3	34	567	126.0	18.4	260	4 688	837.1	80.8
Olathe	100 062	364	100.0	136	2 873	1 426.9	140.5	408	7 408	2 090.1	176.5
Overland Park	64 905	222	95.0	272	2 390	9 823.7	196.8	772	15 086	2 809.9	324.8
Salina	10 798	85	97.6	66	909	505.5	35.8	267	4 131	1 047.1	84.6
Shawnee	19 055	66	97.0	49	829	632.8	42.7	194	3 595	726.3	78.9
Topeka	21 977	176	84.1	124	1 454	571.4	60.7	674	9 716	2 136.6	201.2
Wichita	66 126	677	78.4	519	7 491	11 827.5	349.6	1 518	23 854	5 765.6	519.7
KENTUCKY	1 086 665	7 986	74.9	3 794	59 854	74 680.8	2 869.5	16 404	214 782	50 405.9	4 502.2
Bowling Green	21 751	223	58.3	120	1 638	2 071.9	68.7	482	7 172	1 609.8	144.8
Covington	1 898	29	3.4	26	744	158.1	19.1	139	2 025	417.8	42.4
Elizabethtown	31 310	396	39.1	34	365	220.2	12.7	280	4 192	973.0	93.9
Florence	NA	NA	NA	40	697	814.2	37.1	325	6 780	1 579.0	140.1
Frankfort	3 543	28	64.3	14	215	205.3	9.2	140	1 998	402.8	40.0
Georgetown	NA	NA	NA	14	D	D	D	109	1 581	440.7	31.9
Henderson	2 791	34	38.2	26	351	419.3	16.8	168	2 315	581.3	48.7
Hopkinsville	8 590	111	37.8	50	856	776.5	31.8	197	2 427	584.7	54.4
Jeffersontown	4 292	28	71.4	155	2 419	1 186.1	122.6	150	3 074	866.8	74.2
Lexington-Fayette	92 725	822	76.4	375	8 540	4 442.4	568.5	1 249	22 335	4 778.5	510.4
Louisville/Jefferson County	154 632	975	64.9	1 026	16 413	13 000.6	763.2	2 775	43 687	10 002.4	978.5
Nicholasville	6 854	68	82.4	27	D	D	D	118	1 759	621.0	47.0
Owensboro	28 464	332	81.3	69	861	568.8	34.9	361	4 763	1 071.4	100.4
Paducah	12 395	67	62.2	72	1 503	3 423.6	61.2	373	5 842	1 408.6	121.2
Richmond	8 254	112	70.5	25	208	131.8	7.7	206	3 012	662.9	58.8
LOUISIANA	1 765 181	11 343	90.0	4 839	63 911	51 415.6	2 808.8	17 135	231 365	56 543.2	5 096.1
Alexandria	22 527	189	52.4	80	981	442.6	40.4	398	5 762	1 415.2	125.7
Baton Rouge	35 486	208	100.0	346	4 642	5 407.5	204.8	1 173	16 258	3 830.3	374.8
Bossier City	59 133	569	69.1	60	1 307	926.2	60.8	389	5 610	1 559.3	127.3
Central	38 295	137	100.0	NA	NA	NA	NA	NA	NA	NA	NA
Houma	NA	NA	NA	60	684	374.2	31.1	186	2 432	505.2	52.2
Kenner	1 261	9	100.0	124	1 009	518.1	42.9	369	6 512	1 875.1	164.1
Lafayette	NA	NA	NA	257	3 482	1 389.2	147.8	829	13 436	3 273.0	293.3
Lake Charles	51 584	462	77.5	75	937	411.1	34.1	505	6 847	1 507.5	142.2
Monroe	11 798	128	57.8	80	1 184	1 184.4	46.2	395	6 299	1 352.3	125.7
New Iberia	7 271	48	56.3	40	773	256.6	37.2	210	2 982	736.6	65.2
New Orleans	153 978	1 080	75.9	253	3 030	1 938.4	145.6	1 155	11 877	2 718.0	305.5
Shreveport	83 209	344	99.4	274	D	D	D	909	13 397	3 240.4	304.8
Slidell	2 951	28	100.0	36	328	253.1	12.3	288	5 190	1 143.6	109.3
MAINE	525 280	3 034	92.7	1 439	16 939	8 823.7	686.4	6 911	83 279	20 444.0	1 893.7
Bangor	6 583	31	100.0	71	1 272	854.1	50.6	332	6 123	1 824.0	136.5
Lewiston	6 091	60	43.3	46	689	252.8	28.5	169	2 029	561.0	45.2
Portland	5 683	38	94.7	172	2 475	1 124.5	105.2	416	5 116	1 321.8	131.0
South Portland	4 057	32	100.0	57	1 269	1 108.4	50.3	252	5 393	1 069.6	116.5
MARYLAND	1 951 870	11 931	71.2	5 020	79 868	51 276.8	4 158.4	19 601	294 806	75 664.2	7 290.8
Annapolis	3 486	19	100.0	58	495	812.5	30.2	311	3 368	973.6	95.9
Baltimore	45 497	369	32.0	534	9 046	4 843.4	468.9	1 950	16 682	4 348.8	401.5
Bowie	NA	NA	NA	12	47	16.6	2.1	167	4 136	854.4	85.5
College Park	NA	NA	NA	16	56	15.3	3.1	87	2 001	543.6	54.0
Frederick	27 265	164	80.5	78	1 101	487.0	59.8	356	5 491	1 398.0	141.1
Gaithersburg	25 996	160	56.3	73	858	499.1	55.4	371	7 650	2 068.4	202.1
Hagerstown	13 909	114	47.4	53	466	141.5	16.4	225	4 104	1 059.1	95.8
Laurel	3 117	27	81.5	12	139	33.9	7.0	154	2 280	460.1	47.8
Rockville	0	0	0.0	89	1 959	3 282.8	151.2	316	4 343	1 245.3	125.7
Salisbury	2 777	17	76.5	69	813	416.1	31.5	298	5 181	1 104.6	106.3
MASSACHUSETTS	1 816 993	9 075	64.3	7 284	123 267	95 275.7	7 644.3	25 469	360 218	88 083.0	8 916.5
Agawam Town	6 799	41	70.7	NA	NA	NA	NA	NA	NA	NA	NA
Attleboro	5 281	46	95.7	38	619	260.1	31.5	158	2 716	664.8	58.7
Barnstable Town	8 654	32	100.0	41	425	148.9	19.6	434	5 635	1 395.5	143.3

1. Merchant wholesalers except manufacturers' sales branches and offices.   2. Establishments with payroll.

City	Real estate and rental and leasing, 2007				Professional, scientific, and technical services,[1] 2007				Manufacturing, 2007			
	Number of establish-ments	Number of employees	Receipts (mil dol)	Annual payroll (mil dol)	Number of establish-ments	Number of employees	Receipts (mil dol)	Annual payroll (mil dol)	Number of establish-ments	Number of employees	Receipts (mil dol)	Annual payroll (mil dol)
	80	81	82	83	84	85	86	87	88	89	90	91
KANSAS	3 314	15 160	2 428.8	439.7	7 042	55 922	7 781.4	2 736.5	3 170	177 659	76 751.8	7 983.4
Dodge City	26	D	D	D	45	D	D	D	21	D	D	D
Garden City	29	100	13.8	2.4	53	D	D	D	NA	NA	NA	NA
Hutchinson	54	D	D	D	92	D	D	D	45	1 413	315.2	55.8
Kansas City	127	730	126.2	21.2	140	D	D	D	204	10 394	7 369.7	604.1
Lawrence	151	685	90.1	16.9	247	D	D	D	66	3 447	820.1	123.8
Leavenworth	32	175	20.7	4.4	68	D	D	D	14	535	D	19.0
Leawood	109	300	86.3	12.9	211	1 435	240.4	98.2	NA	NA	NA	NA
Lenexa	118	771	139.0	27.9	307	D	D	D	150	7 287	2 087.7	320.3
Manhattan	101	496	53.0	10.5	138	D	D	D	29	1 162	184.0	36.3
Olathe	148	577	108.3	18.5	358	D	D	D	110	5 447	3 245.9	279.9
Overland Park	397	2 043	438.2	80.8	1 155	D	D	D	97	1 358	238.1	57.3
Salina	69	277	44.9	6.3	115	D	D	D	58	3 765	1 026.9	145.9
Shawnee	74	313	58.8	6.9	191	1 372	144.1	47.0	48	1 759	758.1	106.0
Topeka	207	931	144.0	28.1	408	D	D	D	94	3 965	1 658.1	145.1
Wichita	520	3 170	467.8	87.1	983	D	D	D	478	33 140	14 213.2	1 655.3
KENTUCKY	3 898	20 146	3 894.3	593.4	8 075	61 428	7 872.2	2 831.6	4 165	247 096	119 105.4	10 773.2
Bowling Green	114	1 046	107.5	27.1	175	D	D	D	98	9 133	4 473.8	404.8
Covington	39	287	73.1	9.6	135	D	D	D	31	1 052	278.7	41.9
Elizabethtown	58	235	38.8	5.5	90	D	D	D	57	4 359	D	185.6
Florence	71	288	79.3	8.6	111	586	66.6	22.2	41	D	D	D
Frankfort	37	123	17.9	2.9	96	616	78.2	27.5	13	870	D	36.6
Georgetown	42	140	24.2	3.4	47	382	30.1	12.9	22	9 060	D	D
Henderson	35	203	15.8	4.4	73	385	32.4	10.6	59	4 336	D	152.0
Hopkinsville	51	179	22.0	3.2	61	346	30.1	11.4	54	D	D	197.5
Jeffersontown	75	713	194.4	22.9	156	D	D	D	101	4 718	865.7	173.1
Lexington-Fayette	476	2 268	391.2	68.2	1 053	D	D	D	255	9 602	3 061.2	401.7
Louisville/Jefferson County	991	6 888	1 995.1	263.3	2 266	D	D	D	797	45 142	25 695.4	2 233.8
Nicholasville	34	145	25.1	4.5	37	152	12.5	4.3	55	2 584	D	D
Owensboro	63	432	37.9	9.4	140	D	D	D	82	4 930	2 092.4	194.4
Paducah	69	336	53.6	8.8	139	D	D	D	32	1 274	345.2	D
Richmond	53	198	33.3	4.5	72	D	D	D	32	2 192	D	83.8
LOUISIANA	4 625	30 922	6 014.9	1 194.9	11 128	84 666	11 856.6	4 234.6	3 442	148 080	205 054.7	7 564.5
Alexandria	107	590	69.0	14.7	195	1 268	134.5	49.9	34	1 165	D	29.7
Baton Rouge	353	1 827	316.6	58.1	1 148	13 858	2 088.3	722.9	197	4 423	2 443.5	198.7
Bossier City	86	457	81.2	12.3	96	610	54.2	18.2	52	1 671	D	59.2
Central	NA	NA	NA	NA	NA	NA	NA	NA	NA	NA	NA	NA
Houma	79	602	110.2	25.4	168	D	D	D	37	812	138.2	36.3
Kenner	80	1 057	199.7	31.4	165	920	117.8	48.5	55	1 062	150.7	40.7
Lafayette	306	2 156	571.5	107.1	928	D	D	D	128	5 125	1 055.5	187.8
Lake Charles	121	440	77.4	12.8	304	D	D	D	40	2 358	D	184.8
Monroe	122	582	103.8	19.6	308	D	D	D	45	1 546	413.6	63.2
New Iberia	58	654	147.6	33.1	120	549	65.7	17.8	57	2 978	D	117.5
New Orleans	362	1 764	354.4	61.8	1 290	D	D	D	141	7 607	3 088.9	402.0
Shreveport	290	1 839	258.8	49.0	568	4 053	474.9	170.2	162	6 383	D	256.0
Slidell	40	171	31.4	4.1	138	D	D	D	NA	NA	NA	NA
MAINE	1 771	6 942	1 054.0	209.4	3 444	20 504	2 686.1	1 004.9	1 825	58 938	16 363.2	2 524.5
Bangor	96	482	92.3	15.1	163	D	D	D	45	1 022	225.3	41.7
Lewiston	46	285	34.0	6.5	71	D	D	D	70	2 240	537.5	90.2
Portland	248	1 376	261.2	48.8	570	D	D	D	105	3 198	886.7	124.6
South Portland	54	414	83.5	16.7	98	838	99.4	41.8	31	1 595	298.0	95.4
MARYLAND	6 768	49 766	12 391.9	2 262.6	19 345	D	D	D	3 680	127 780	41 456.1	6 453.7
Annapolis	104	618	106.3	25.6	387	D	D	D	47	618	127.6	26.6
Baltimore	647	4 677	837.5	214.9	1 506	D	D	D	479	16 253	5 730.9	726.5
Bowie	54	195	32.8	6.7	164	D	D	D	NA	NA	NA	NA
College Park	20	73	7.9	2.1	61	D	D	D	6	D	D	D
Frederick	105	765	120.1	27.2	368	D	D	D	55	2 317	1 614.3	121.4
Gaithersburg	117	756	207.7	44.4	425	D	D	D	40	1 996	559.5	137.1
Hagerstown	58	250	35.4	6.7	113	1 251	74.4	30.0	64	3 878	1 434.9	214.8
Laurel	36	593	62.3	19.7	91	D	D	D	NA	NA	NA	NA
Rockville	139	2 575	592.3	128.4	871	16 740	2 715.0	1 166.8	65	1 301	199.9	58.1
Salisbury	93	578	81.6	18.5	162	D	D	D	47	3 260	811.6	109.6
MASSACHUSETTS	7 053	48 576	14 029.8	2 287.6	21 773	243 374	49 085.7	20 652.0	7 737	289 256	86 429.0	15 712.0
Agawam Town	NA	NA	NA	NA	NA	NA	NA	NA	NA	NA	NA	NA
Attleboro	34	121	16.7	5.1	76	352	40.9	16.0	109	5 721	1 711.3	289.0
Barnstable Town	76	262	66.1	8.6	201	D	D	D	41	562	D	27.5

1. Establishments subject to federal tax.

Accommodation and Food Services, Arts, Entertainment, and Recreation, and Health Care and Social Assistance

City	Accommodation and food services, 2007				Arts, entertainment, and recreation,[1] 2007				Health care and social assistance,[1] 2007			
	Number of establish-ments	Number of employees	Sales (mil dol)	Annual payroll (mil dol)	Number of establish-ments	Number of employees	Receipts (mil dol)	Annual payroll (mil dol)	Number of establish-ments	Number of employees	Receipts (mil dol)	Annual payroll (mil dol)
	92	93	94	95	96	97	98	99	100	101	102	103
KANSAS..................	5 866	104 795	4 192.3	1 173.7	769	10 017	546.6	146.7	5 778	83 531	7 948.2	3 175.8
Dodge City	66	938	39.6	9.9	6	D	D	D	52	D	D	D
Garden City	65	1 107	48.4	12.3	4	D	D	D	64	D	D	D
Hutchinson	100	1 984	75.3	20.3	5	D	D	D	121	1 942	224.1	97.6
Kansas City	216	4 494	220.7	61.7	24	D	D	D	216	3 372	280.0	129.9
Lawrence.................	262	5 634	203.0	57.6	27	D	D	D	196	1 940	159.3	74.5
Leavenworth	56	933	35.0	9.7	4	D	D	D	57	519	39.3	18.5
Leawood	52	D	D	D	13	95	5.8	3.1	141	D	D	D
Lenexa.................	105	1 778	80.7	24.1	19	275	13.1	4.1	118	3 962	342.7	141.6
Manhattan	152	3 466	125.8	33.4	15	188	8.9	2.3	116	D	D	D
Olathe.................	225	5 329	203.2	61.8	27	603	21.6	6.9	225	2 689	272.7	110.4
Overland Park	438	10 877	525.9	158.3	75	1 669	79.3	25.0	561	10 621	1 331.7	510.3
Salina	120	2 509	94.0	26.2	13	D	D	D	136	1 767	189.1	73.0
Shawnee	108	1 966	82.2	23.1	15	D	D	D	105	D	D	D
Topeka	342	D	D	D	29	D	D	D	359	D	D	D
Wichita.................	937	18 895	758.6	222.1	86	1 813	81.0	23.8	905	17 563	2 125.6	749.3
KENTUCKY.................	7 309	151 551	6 300.9	1 787.4	1 021	12 434	893.9	260.1	8 686	115 673	10 089.6	4 218.4
Bowling Green..............	200	5 185	223.1	61.7	16	D	D	D	246	D	D	D
Covington	135	2 603	124.9	35.3	8	D	D	D	40	D	D	D
Elizabethtown	111	2 954	109.0	31.5	10	D	D	D	184	D	D	D
Florence	159	4 275	185.1	53.7	22	433	24.5	7.7	121	1 718	136.0	59.4
Frankfort.................	83	1 910	70.2	22.1	5	D	D	D	106	1 833	178.4	62.8
Georgetown	67	1 572	65.2	18.0	3	D	D	D	62	D	D	D
Henderson	81	1 298	52.9	14.6	8	D	D	D	108	D	D	D
Hopkinsville	79	1 568	56.8	15.1	7	D	D	D	140	1 482	125.5	43.4
Jeffersontown	108	2 904	131.1	40.9	15	D	D	D	89	2 394	201.8	69.6
Lexington-Fayette..........	704	17 027	785.7	230.3	102	1 609	114.8	40.9	821	11 213	1 149.2	526.2
Louisville/Jefferson County	1 561	35 897	1 629.2	480.6	243	3 741	291.3	95.9	1 909	27 997	2 708.5	1 159.0
Nicholasville	47	1 025	39.8	11.1	6	D	D	D	43	436	27.5	13.2
Owensboro	134	3 322	120.2	37.5	13	D	D	D	221	2 935	245.9	104.8
Paducah	169	4 156	158.9	46.4	9	D	D	D	184	D	D	D
Richmond.................	95	2 528	90.7	25.5	8	87	2.5	0.7	108	D	D	D
LOUISIANA	8 189	180 289	9 729.9	2 679.0	1 082	20 064	2 468.3	578.3	9 725	145 174	13 178.8	4 934.9
Alexandria	158	3 256	129.3	33.1	12	D	D	D	270	5 309	582.5	210.6
Baton Rouge	599	15 567	716.7	197.5	56	2 070	262.5	37.2	725	11 500	1 084.6	417.0
Bossier City	198	9 254	694.5	170.3	28	1 560	155.4	24.8	138	D	D	D
Central........................	NA	NA	NA	NA	NA	NA	NA	NA	NA	NA	NA	NA
Houma.................	105	1 662	90.6	26.2	15	122	6.4	2.2	147	D	D	D
Kenner.................	190	3 710	193.4	52.5	24	1 288	452.3	176.8	149	2 094	217.3	76.8
Lafayette.................	421	11 003	516.5	138.8	34	D	D	D	715	12 024	1 274.8	467.0
Lake Charles	189	6 553	563.8	116.2	29	D	D	D	317	4 658	482.8	168.7
Monroe	170	3 817	142.9	37.7	19	D	D	D	320	3 918	385.7	139.4
New Iberia	76	1 636	62.9	15.6	7	108	6.3	1.1	160	D	D	D
New Orleans	1 058	28 356	2 148.2	602.4	109	2 551	284.1	109.0	594	6 413	847.2	277.8
Shreveport.................	409	11 967	661.4	171.8	58	D	D	D	653	D	D	D
Slidell.................	172	3 029	133.0	36.1	13	D	D	D	197	2 356	283.8	108.1
MAINE	3 938	49 363	2 515.8	747.7	635	5 204	361.3	85.0	3 203	39 757	3 015.8	1 397.3
Bangor.................	140	2 886	136.1	40.7	12	D	D	D	220	3 696	310.0	151.0
Lewiston	83	1 250	52.0	14.8	14	114	5.7	2.0	127	1 589	132.3	58.4
Portland.................	287	5 067	246.0	78.4	40	354	29.1	6.1	312	4 231	397.4	186.2
South Portland	127	3 046	137.6	45.7	9	D	D	D	101	1 261	124.4	60.2
MARYLAND	10 802	192 619	10 758.4	2 915.9	1 735	26 548	2 140.5	743.0	12 542	143 677	15 363.7	6 218.0
Annapolis.................	170	4 132	230.4	70.9	32	560	40.1	11.3	136	D	D	D
Baltimore	1 481	21 456	1 434.7	372.1	104	2 595	312.5	164.3	1 065	13 768	1 480.1	622.9
Bowie	75	D	D	D	13	D	D	D	172	1 381	130.2	48.7
College Park.................	105	1 820	103.4	25.6	5	56	3.0	1.1	33	D	D	D
Frederick	197	3 508	168.4	50.9	23	238	11.9	3.3	300	3 880	422.6	181.0
Gaithersburg.................	238	4 085	265.9	69.0	21	D	D	D	160	1 968	174.0	73.2
Hagerstown	129	2 543	113.9	32.7	12	107	3.8	0.9	124	1 347	156.6	63.8
Laurel	83	1 956	106.8	32.0	19	D	D	D	95	1 256	133.1	57.9
Rockville.................	237	3 440	242.4	63.6	32	331	16.1	4.0	263	3 503	492.4	202.8
Salisbury.................	149	3 313	151.4	40.6	11	D	D	D	169	D	D	D
MASSACHUSETTS ...	16 039	257 302	14 917.2	4 339.7	2 261	34 183	3 137.0	1 122.2	12 828	202 678	21 341.6	9 279.6
Agawam Town	NA	NA	NA	NA	NA	NA	NA	NA	NA	NA	NA	NA
Attleboro	89	2 009	83.9	27.5	10	D	D	D	92	1 579	148.1	58.4
Barnstable Town	193	3 066	185.2	57.0	28	197	17.2	5.0	152	2 027	223.5	104.8

1. Establishments subject to federal tax.

Table D. Cities — Other Services and Federal Funds

City	Other services[1], 2007				Selected federal funds, 2009–2010 (mil dol)								
					Procurement contracts		Grants						
	Number of establishments	Number of employees	Receipts (mil dol)	Annual payroll (mil dol)	Defense	Other	Total[2]	Medicaid and other health related	Nutrition and family welfare	Energy and environment	Disasters and emergency preparedness	Housing and community development	Employment and training
	104	105	106	107	108	109	110	111	112	113	114	115	116
KANSAS.................	4 281	24 265	1 825.9	572.9	1 940.8	1 118.9	4 736.3	2 241.5	600.2	156.7	123.0	133.5	62.6
Dodge City...................	39	D	D	D	0.5	0.6	7.1	0.0	1.7	0.0	0.0	2.3	0.0
Garden City.................	39	D	D	D	0.0	0.5	4.8	1.0	0.0	0.0	0.0	0.1	0.0
Hutchinson..................	73	D	D	D	0.0	0.0	5.6	0.7	2.2	0.0	0.0	0.6	0.1
Kansas City.................	177	D	D	D	18.1	38.9	149.5	111.1	7.5	5.4	0.2	18.8	0.0
Lawrence....................	118	731	45.0	14.3	12.5	15.3	181.6	75.9	2.6	17.5	0.0	6.6	0.1
Leavenworth................	43	269	17.3	5.2	88.8	487.8	2.6	0.0	0.0	0.0	0.0	1.9	0.0
Leawood.....................	42	588	49.8	11.7	8.8	11.3	1.0	0.2	0.0	0.0	0.0	0.5	0.0
Lenexa.......................	84	660	65.7	21.6	7.0	12.7	0.5	0.0	0.0	0.0	0.0	0.0	0.0
Manhattan	81	D	D	D	9.2	16.7	104.8	19.8	1.6	12.0	2.0	3.2	0.0
Olathe.......................	165	1 018	89.9	27.3	13.5	0.9	14.2	0.5	1.4	0.6	0.5	2.8	0.0
Overland Park	289	1 737	118.7	39.0	6.7	18.6	4.3	0.9	1.3	0.8	0.0	0.7	0.0
Salina.......................	91	D	D	D	3.5	1.7	7.7	0.8	3.8	0.1	0.0	1.5	0.0
Shawnee	90	1 682	64.7	32.0	0.9	0.5	0.9	0.0	0.0	0.5	0.0	0.4	0.0
Topeka	217	1 409	102.5	31.7	20.5	12.7	673.4	78.5	110.0	70.3	6.7	39.2	57.4
Wichita......................	605	4 760	301.7	127.2	988.4	68.1	78.2	6.9	12.1	6.9	0.0	25.6	3.2
KENTUCKY..............	5 037	33 941	2 777.7	801.2	5 180.5	2 305.6	9 502.2	5 482.6	1 065.1	161.0	78.3	357.8	137.3
Bowling Green..............	114	911	64.5	18.8	0.1	5.1	71.5	1.0	6.0	5.5	0.0	4.9	1.2
Covington	68	481	32.8	10.9	0.4	9.3	38.8	2.0	4.6	0.0	0.0	29.0	0.0
Elizabethtown..............	69	542	38.4	12.1	4.8	0.8	2.3	0.1	0.0	0.1	0.0	0.3	0.0
Florence.....................	76	592	33.2	11.3	90.0	6.5	0.5	0.0	0.0	0.2	0.0	0.0	0.3
Frankfort....................	51	226	14.7	4.5	0.8	1.5	1 068.1	98.9	210.0	74.0	38.0	87.2	99.1
Georgetown.................	36	D	D	D	0.6	0.0	3.0	0.1	0.0	0.0	0.0	2.7	0.0
Henderson..................	45	D	D	D	0.9	0.2	5.2	0.5	0.0	0.0	0.0	3.8	0.0
Hopkinsville	55	D	D	D	4.3	1.9	5.6	0.5	0.0	0.0	0.0	3.0	0.0
Jeffersontown..............	78	845	118.0	28.8	6.1	1.1	1.2	0.2	0.0	0.0	0.0	0.0	0.0
Lexington-Fayette.........	429	3 634	248.1	92.9	442.7	230.9	350.0	196.7	14.3	18.1	0.1	23.4	0.0
Louisville/Jefferson County	1 108	10 083	928.2	244.7	NA	NA	NA	NA	NA	NA	NA	NA	NA
Nicholasville	50	D	D	D	0.6	5.9	-2.2	0.0	0.0	-3.0	0.0	0.1	0.0
Owensboro	101	755	50.5	17.2	2.2	3.0	39.6	0.1	12.1	1.0	0.0	4.1	0.2
Paducah	80	632	69.9	14.4	0.5	66.2	10.5	0.7	1.8	0.0	-0.2	4.3	0.0
Richmond	48	241	14.1	4.2	312.8	1.0	12.9	2.7	5.4	0.0	-0.5	4.2	0.0
LOUISIANA	5 446	35 039	3 464.7	965.6	5 841.7	1 448.9	15 087.6	6 250.9	1 238.6	213.4	2 909.7	1 731.7	117.0
Alexandria	100	662	52.2	14.4	1.4	43.5	29.1	1.8	6.4	0.0	0.0	8.1	0.3
Baton Rouge	423	3 042	248.2	81.5	172.6	-20.0	2 574.9	115.6	214.2	110.0	55.5	1 264.8	104.6
Bossier City	99	765	47.4	13.8	34.4	0.2	15.1	0.0	3.0	0.7	0.0	5.7	0.0
Central......................	NA	NA	NA	NA	NA	NA	NA	NA	NA	NA	NA	NA	NA
Houma.......................	58	598	104.1	34.7	2.9	0.0	0.0	0.0	0.0	0.0	0.0	0.0	0.0
Kenner	129	851	97.4	24.9	105.3	0.5	9.5	0.0	0.0	0.0	0.0	9.4	0.0
Lafayette....................	261	1 993	151.3	47.3	3.5	15.3	55.8	5.5	9.5	1.6	0.0	14.5	4.9
Lake Charles................	117	759	65.4	19.8	28.2	64.0	30.9	0.0	3.8	8.9	0.0	10.1	0.0
Monroe	74	628	47.6	14.8	4.7	1.6	51.9	3.5	5.1	0.6	0.0	16.9	0.0
New Iberia	72	D	D	D	-0.1	0.0	5.0	1.8	0.1	0.7	0.0	2.1	0.0
New Orleans	408	2 514	196.4	55.7	2 386.5	481.2	772.0	300.3	24.1	17.6	1.0	259.5	0.8
Shreveport..................	308	D	D	D	4.9	35.0	100.1	32.7	11.2	1.7	0.0	20.8	4.3
Slidell.......................	94	487	33.9	10.5	30.3	0.5	4.1	0.0	0.0	0.0	0.0	3.9	0.0
MAINE	2 124	9 136	812.9	218.9	1 336.2	399.5	3 787.4	2 186.8	340.3	250.6	6.3	151.8	58.3
Bangor.......................	75	504	57.3	12.4	50.2	55.8	22.6	2.8	5.4	0.1	0.1	4.4	2.6
Lewiston	58	305	18.8	6.7	0.0	0.0	16.1	0.1	2.8	0.1	0.0	9.9	0.3
Portland	182	1 100	93.9	26.4	243.3	44.1	122.7	22.4	6.7	6.5	0.0	32.8	0.4
South Portland	69	526	31.2	9.6	6.0	2.5	8.9	2.3	0.0	0.0	0.0	4.8	0.0
MARYLAND	8 270	57 508	4 832.5	1 602.5	12 017.6	14 504.9	14 441.4	7 701.5	1 138.0	631.3	53.1	710.2	256.3
Annapolis....................	153	1 034	92.1	32.2	658.8	40.0	608.0	0.5	6.7	22.3	0.1	7.5	0.0
Baltimore	728	6 191	559.3	160.9	383.4	688.6	4 036.3	1 903.0	257.1	314.4	0.4	221.5	147.5
Bowie........................	53	377	25.4	7.6	6.3	28.9	7.6	0.0	0.2	0.7	0.0	0.2	0.0
College Park................	43	D	D	D	4.6	153.7	336.4	76.5	0.1	15.8	2.6	0.7	0.0
Frederick	144	1 016	70.8	24.9	291.4	275.4	24.7	10.0	2.2	0.4	0.0	8.3	1.8
Gaithersburg...............	129	1 057	81.0	33.3	298.1	548.3	45.8	29.2	0.9	0.7	0.0	6.1	0.0
Hagerstown.................	79	445	37.1	10.0	15.5	15.3	28.6	1.4	3.5	2.8	0.0	12.6	1.8
Laurel	47	467	29.6	8.8	7.1	73.5	1.6	0.0	0.0	0.6	0.0	0.6	0.0
Rockville	182	1 047	106.8	33.2	306.1	2 072.2	444.3	283.2	6.2	13.7	-1.3	23.6	24.9
Salisbury....................	89	790	60.0	20.7	9.8	0.8	20.6	0.1	7.8	0.0	0.0	2.4	0.0
MASSACHUSETTS ...	10 744	66 722	6 164.8	1 906.5	12 673.5	3 313.8	22 351.8	14 088.0	1 526.5	867.2	87.3	1 328.9	215.3
Agawam Town	NA	NA	NA	NA	NA	NA	NA	NA	NA	NA	NA	NA	NA
Attleboro....................	60	267	21.3	5.8	2.0	122.0	1.5	0.0	0.0	0.2	0.0	1.3	0.0
Barnstable Town	127	747	60.4	21.5	NA	NA	NA	NA	NA	NA	NA	NA	NA

1. Establishments subject to federal tax.   2. Includes program categories not shown separately. State totals include additional categories not allocated by city.

Table D. Cities — City Government Finances

City	General revenue Total (mil dol)	Intergovernmental Total (mil dol)	Intergovernmental Percent from state government	Taxes Total (mil dol)	Taxes Per capita (dollars) Total	Taxes Per capita (dollars) Property	Taxes Per capita (dollars) Sales and gross receipts	General expenditure Total (mil dol)	General expenditure Per capita (dollars) Total	General expenditure Capital outlays
	117	118	119	120	121	122	123	124	125	126
KANSAS...................	X	X	X	X	X	X	X	X	X	X
Dodge City	37.7	11.9	30.3	12.6	488	247	241	34.2	1 328	402
Garden City	25.0	5.2	20.6	10.9	409	190	219	29.1	1 094	227
Hutchinson	39.7	6.6	21.9	21.3	524	267	257	27.1	666	86
Kansas City	362.8	38.8	89.1	170.4	1 197	659	538	387.2	2 721	469
Lawrence	223.6	14.7	33.5	41.4	460	249	211	193.8	2 157	154
Leavenworth	35.8	6.9	16.4	18.3	527	306	222	33.8	972	207
Leawood	45.7	7.9	20.7	29.0	935	546	389	32.1	1 035	380
Lenexa	81.8	19.2	72.4	51.2	1 121	597	524	104.2	2 280	1 154
Manhattan	52.5	7.9	35.5	29.7	575	321	254	40.6	784	30
Olathe	168.9	16.5	31.7	69.7	590	278	312	170.0	1 440	392
Overland Park	170.2	47.9	60.5	98.3	580	150	430	170.0	1 004	417
Salina	53.9	10.7	33.6	22.0	474	214	260	55.0	1 185	311
Shawnee	50.5	8.2	30.1	34.8	580	261	319	54.9	916	157
Topeka	159.8	20.2	23.1	83.7	682	285	398	167.6	1 367	11
Wichita	377.7	108.8	25.3	163.1	451	330	122	329.4	911	73
KENTUCKY	X	X	X	X	X	X	X	X	X	X
Bowling Green	78.2	12.1	61.3	52.3	963	178	96	73.4	1 354	190
Covington	65.8	11.2	20.8	38.2	886	141	174	46.9	1 089	76
Elizabethtown	31.7	2.1	92.8	17.2	722	117	202	20.5	864	46
Florence	23.5	1.2	96.0	16.3	596	221	91	25.4	930	246
Frankfort	58.2	3.4	59.8	23.5	865	112	139	58.8	2 169	719
Georgetown	63.4	11.6	19.1	17.9	849	61	130	40.8	1 935	656
Henderson	36.0	9.2	18.5	15.0	541	176	179	31.3	1 127	123
Hopkinsville	30.4	5.9	30.4	15.3	483	114	27	32.9	1 040	105
Jeffersontown	15.0	0.2	91.8	14.7	563	138	42	12.6	482	46
Lexington-Fayette	380.1	44.8	16.6	254.3	911	145	144	345.5	1 238	27
Louisville/Jefferson County	NA	NA	NA	NA	NA	NA	NA	NA	NA	NA
Nicholasville	18.7	1.6	95.8	11.4	440	116	126	14.6	564	138
Owensboro	88.7	24.3	10.2	28.4	512	150	79	87.0	1 571	504
Paducah	51.0	9.9	40.1	27.2	1 066	209	193	35.6	1 395	226
Richmond	29.8	3.0	69.8	17.8	550	62	159	30.2	935	251
LOUISIANA	X	X	X	X	X	X	X	X	X	X
Alexandria	80.5	20.1	44.4	42.9	935	135	800	70.8	1 545	238
Baton Rouge	881.2	154.4	54.3	428.2	1 886	551	1 334	753.6	3 319	379
Bossier City	107.8	10.3	74.2	66.1	1 070	154	915	85.8	1 389	286
Central	NA	NA	NA	NA	NA	NA	NA	NA	NA	NA
Houma	347.4	64.8	79.2	97.2	2 980	1 074	1 906	312.1	9 568	1 120
Kenner	87.7	45.8	14.0	21.1	324	115	208	77.1	1 183	226
Lafayette	322.8	59.3	66.3	161.9	1 426	582	843	301.2	2 653	587
Lake Charles	123.1	30.0	10.6	65.7	935	85	850	112.1	1 595	511
Monroe	122.0	24.7	8.5	71.9	1 404	211	1 193	103.1	2 014	539
New Iberia	33.1	4.4	28.9	21.4	650	108	542	28.0	851	162
New Orleans	1 157.0	361.6	22.8	391.1	1 636	784	832	992.2	4 149	537
Shreveport	321.6	54.4	43.4	191.3	959	271	688	301.1	1 509	404
Slidell	48.0	9.5	1.9	31.2	1 148	171	977	39.5	1 453	135
MAINE	X	X	X	X	X	X	X	X	X	X
Bangor	109.9	35.5	84.9	46.2	1 452	1 395	57	113.2	3 555	560
Lewiston	101.9	44.0	100.0	42.7	1 211	1 199	12	112.3	3 186	538
Portland	265.4	55.6	76.6	128.1	2 039	1 976	63	271.4	4 320	366
South Portland	79.3	12.5	95.2	55.7	2 346	2 295	51	72.9	3 068	177
MARYLAND	X	X	X	X	X	X	X	X	X	X
Annapolis	63.8	15.7	39.8	29.5	807	698	107	66.2	1 808	194
Baltimore	3 088.2	1 530.1	83.0	1 071.2	1 680	940	183	2 814.1	4 415	517
Bowie	43.6	10.6	34.9	19.4	364	328	36	32.5	610	76
College Park	10.8	2.3	47.8	6.4	240	181	59	13.1	491	120
Frederick	75.6	14.6	33.1	38.5	651	592	53	71.7	1 210	31
Gaithersburg	42.8	15.3	20.6	19.9	345	287	58	37.8	655	38
Hagerstown	67.0	9.7	44.8	22.6	570	459	94	56.4	1 423	5
Laurel	21.8	4.4	38.5	15.7	726	630	96	21.0	972	204
Rockville	98.4	28.0	28.1	35.0	597	531	59	106.3	1 811	471
Salisbury	46.1	15.2	75.9	17.8	641	576	65	38.8	1 393	171
MASSACHUSETTS ...	X	X	X	X	X	X	X	X	X	X
Agawam Town	NA	NA	NA	NA	NA	NA	NA	NA	NA	NA
Attleboro	119.4	51.5	98.2	52.0	1 207	1 170	37	111.1	2 578	247
Barnstable Town	151.3	29.3	95.9	93.2	1 995	1 924	71	147.0	3 146	197

1. Based on population estimated as of July 1 of the year shown.

Table D. Cities — **City Government Finances**

City	Public welfare	Highways	Parking facilities	Education	Health and hospitals	Police protection	Sewerage and sanitation	Parks and recreation	Housing and community development	Interest on debt
	127	128	129	130	131	132	133	134	135	136
KANSAS..................	X	X	X	X	X	X	X	X	X	X
Dodge City	0.1	16.5	0.0	0.0	0.9	12.2	11.1	13.0	0.0	4.6
Garden City	0.0	4.4	0.0	0.0	0.0	14.3	11.8	10.2	0.9	6.3
Hutchinson	0.5	9.1	0.1	0.0	0.0	20.9	25.3	9.1	0.0	4.4
Kansas City	0.0	7.7	0.0	0.0	4.4	12.6	5.9	1.9	1.9	27.2
Lawrence.....................	0.2	3.5	0.4	0.0	58.7	6.7	9.4	4.2	0.8	3.6
Leavenworth................	0.0	2.1	0.0	0.0	0.6	16.8	16.4	7.7	7.0	4.7
Leawood......................	0.0	8.7	0.0	0.0	0.0	40.1	0.0	9.6	0.0	6.1
Lenexa........................	0.0	41.4	0.0	0.0	0.0	12.1	11.9	4.7	0.0	5.0
Manhattan	0.0	6.7	0.0	0.0	1.4	21.0	9.9	12.6	1.3	7.0
Olathe........................	0.0	5.1	0.0	0.0	0.0	11.6	11.0	0.9	0.0	20.6
Overland Park	0.0	7.0	0.0	0.0	0.0	16.8	1.6	5.8	0.0	1.8
Salina.........................	0.0	5.3	0.0	0.0	1.9	10.4	10.3	10.2	3.3	2.1
Shawnee	0.0	16.5	0.0	0.0	0.0	15.9	6.2	13.3	0.0	16.1
Topeka........................	1.4	5.3	1.1	0.0	0.0	16.3	8.5	7.0	1.5	8.7
Wichita........................	0.4	7.6	0.0	0.0	1.0	18.6	12.3	6.9	7.1	7.5
KENTUCKY	X	X	X	X	X	X	X	X	X	X
Bowling Green.............	0.0	11.6	0.0	0.0	0.0	16.2	6.6	25.1	7.2	5.4
Covington	0.0	12.5	1.7	0.0	0.0	21.3	0.3	4.0	19.0	15.4
Elizabethtown..............	0.0	14.8	0.1	0.0	0.0	15.2	13.7	5.2	3.5	9.5
Florence	0.0	22.6	0.0	0.0	0.0	20.1	0.0	7.0	0.0	14.7
Frankfort.....................	0.0	7.7	0.0	0.0	4.9	7.3	17.5	5.1	0.0	3.1
Georgetown.................	19.0	3.6	0.0	1.2	0.0	9.4	22.0	0.6	0.7	23.5
Henderson...................	0.0	7.3	0.0	0.0	0.0	12.5	22.2	2.9	17.9	0.9
Hopkinsville	0.0	4.6	0.0	0.0	0.0	15.0	16.5	0.0	23.5	14.3
Jeffersontown	0.0	0.6	0.0	0.0	0.0	45.8	10.2	1.0	0.0	33.0
Lexington-Fayette.........	3.1	1.1	0.1	0.0	6.6	14.5	10.9	5.1	0.0	7.7
Louisville/Jefferson County	NA	NA	NA	NA	NA	NA	NA	NA	NA	NA
Nicholasville	0.0	12.6	0.0	0.0	0.0	24.0	26.2	0.0	0.1	1.0
Owensboro	0.0	6.6	0.1	0.0	0.0	11.9	28.9	6.2	8.5	0.6
Paducah	0.0	18.8	0.0	0.0	0.0	15.6	13.9	3.0	17.3	3.5
Richmond....................	0.0	4.1	0.0	0.0	2.1	14.1	21.5	20.1	3.4	4.5
LOUISIANA	X	X	X	X	X	X	X	X	X	X
Alexandria	0.0	13.6	0.0	0.0	0.0	21.5	16.9	8.2	8.4	1.0
Baton Rouge	0.4	8.2	0.1	1.7	9.9	12.4	17.7	2.9	5.4	4.6
Bossier City	0.0	13.6	0.0	0.0	4.8	19.6	9.0	9.0	7.8	4.1
Central........................	NA	NA	NA	NA	NA	NA	NA	NA	NA	NA
Houma........................	0.5	1.8	0.0	0.0	49.0	5.8	6.0	2.5	3.0	2.1
Kenner........................	0.3	12.4	0.0	0.0	0.3	22.4	17.9	8.6	4.8	3.3
Lafayette.....................	0.0	10.7	0.1	0.0	1.1	12.6	9.1	7.2	4.7	8.0
Lake Charles	0.0	16.1	0.0	0.0	0.5	12.5	19.7	8.3	9.4	1.1
Monroe	0.0	9.7	0.0	0.0	0.0	11.0	14.2	9.6	15.7	6.5
New Iberia	0.0	9.4	0.0	0.0	0.0	16.3	33.3	6.3	11.2	4.0
New Orleans	0.0	2.1	0.0	0.0	1.5	13.9	14.0	4.5	9.8	11.1
Shreveport...................	0.0	6.6	0.3	0.0	0.0	16.6	11.5	7.6	10.4	1.4
Slidell.........................	0.0	8.1	0.0	0.0	1.0	16.1	16.5	3.3	2.3	1.9
MAINE	X	X	X	X	X	X	X	X	X	X
Bangor........................	1.2	0.0	0.6	35.1	1.2	5.8	0.0	4.2	2.0	3.0
Lewiston	0.5	3.0	0.4	44.8	0.0	4.4	6.5	1.9	0.7	6.9
Portland	8.1	4.2	0.6	32.5	3.0	5.0	9.1	3.0	1.1	4.7
South Portland	0.4	3.4	0.0	49.8	0.1	5.5	7.0	4.1	0.0	2.0
MARYLAND	X	X	X	X	X	X	X	X	X	X
Annapolis....................	0.0	9.4	3.2	0.0	0.0	25.0	12.9	4.9	1.0	2.5
Baltimore	0.1	6.5	0.7	42.2	4.5	12.6	7.8	3.5	3.5	1.7
Bowie..........................	0.0	13.7	0.0	0.0	0.5	6.8	25.1	17.1	0.8	0.3
College Park................	0.0	21.6	13.8	0.0	0.7	2.9	19.5	8.1	0.7	0.2
Frederick	0.0	7.8	4.0	0.0	0.0	27.9	13.6	12.2	1.2	5.5
Gaithersburg	0.0	10.4	0.0	0.0	0.9	16.5	6.0	23.7	5.0	0.0
Hagerstown	0.0	7.2	0.8	0.0	0.0	19.3	21.2	5.3	3.5	2.5
Laurel	0.0	17.7	0.0	0.0	0.0	33.2	5.7	6.1	0.0	2.2
Rockville.....................	0.0	9.9	0.3	0.0	0.3	6.7	8.9	19.1	1.9	3.1
Salisbury.....................	0.0	11.1	1.4	0.0	0.5	22.0	19.7	7.0	2.4	2.3
MASSACHUSETTS ...	X	X	X	X	X	X	X	X	X	X
Agawam Town	NA	NA	NA	NA	NA	NA	NA	NA	NA	NA
Attleboro.....................	0.5	3.1	0.0	59.8	0.3	5.3	13.1	1.5	0.7	3.8
Barnstable Town	0.2	3.4	0.0	53.3	0.6	7.4	3.2	2.3	0.4	3.6

Items 127—136

Table D. Cities — City Government Finances, City Government Employment, and Climate

City	City government finances, 2007 (cont.) Debt outstanding — Total (mil dol)	Per capita[1] (dollars)	Debt issued during year	City government employment, 2010	Climate[2] — Average daily temperature (degrees Fahrenheit) Mean — January	July	Limits — January[3]	July[4]	Annual precipitation (inches)	Heating degree days	Cooling degree days
	137	138	139	140	141	142	143	144	145	146	147
KANSAS	X	X	X	NA	X	X	X	X	X	X	X
Dodge City	40.0	1 554	1.1	259	30.1	79.8	18.7	92.8	22.35	5 037	1 481
Garden City	51.3	1 926	8.9	300	28.6	77.8	14.7	92.1	18.77	5 423	1 191
Hutchinson	35.9	884	2.6	402	28.5	79.9	17.0	92.7	30.32	5 146	1 454
Kansas City	2 963.9	20 826	68.5	2 635	29.1	79.0	19.9	89.4	40.17	4 847	1 406
Lawrence	259.5	2 888	69.2	1 953	29.9	80.2	20.5	90.6	39.78	4 685	1 582
Leavenworth	34.3	987	1.3	266	26.6	79.1	16.4	89.8	40.94	5 331	1 356
Leawood	52.7	1 698	13.1	265	29.1	79.0	19.9	89.4	40.17	4 847	1 406
Lenexa......................	277.3	6 070	16.4	408	29.1	79.0	19.9	89.4	40.17	4 847	1 406
Manhattan	86.4	1 670	59.1	342	27.8	79.9	16.1	92.5	34.80	5 120	1 465
Olathe	621.3	5 263	53.2	839	29.1	79.0	19.9	89.4	40.17	4 847	1 406
Overland Park	144.6	853	79.6	938	29.1	79.0	19.9	89.4	40.17	4 847	1 406
Salina	47.4	1 020	2.2	554	29.0	81.3	18.8	93.3	32.19	4 952	1 600
Shawnee	197.1	3 287	7.6	286	29.1	79.0	19.9	89.4	40.17	4 847	1 406
Topeka	520.6	4 245	135.9	1 352	27.2	78.4	17.2	89.1	35.64	5 225	1 357
Wichita	819.6	2 268	88.7	3 108	30.2	81.0	20.3	92.9	30.38	4 765	1 658
KENTUCKY	X	X	X	NA	X	X	X	X	X	X	X
Bowling Green.............	265.4	4 892	14.9	696	34.2	78.5	25.4	89.2	51.63	4 243	1 413
Covington	168.6	3 914	9.1	430	32.0	76.1	24.1	85.9	45.91	4 713	1 154
Elizabethtown..............	46.4	1 953	0.0	272	NA	NA	NA	NA	NA	NA	NA
Florence	84.2	3 086	0.0	205	NA	NA	NA	NA	NA	NA	NA
Frankfort....................	55.7	2 055	11.8	570	30.3	75.2	20.8	86.9	43.56	5 129	994
Georgetown................	585.6	27 788	7.2	170	NA	NA	NA	NA	NA	NA	NA
Henderson..................	33.4	1 204	10.0	465	32.6	77.6	23.6	88.4	44.77	4 374	1 344
Hopkinsville	158.0	4 993	9.5	414	33.2	78.2	24.4	88.5	50.92	4 298	1 433
Jeffersontown.............	171.0	6 538	0.0	112	33.0	78.4	24.9	87.0	44.54	4 352	1 443
Lexington-Fayette.........	764.3	2 739	139.6	3 761	31.6	75.9	22.5	86.3	46.39	4 769	1 094
Louisville/Jefferson County	NA	NA	NA	NA	NA	NA	NA	NA	NA	NA	NA
Nicholasville ,,,,,,,,,,,,,,	20.3	903	6.6	219	NA	NA	NA	NA	NA	NA	NA
Owensboro	385.8	6 963	0.0	784	33.5	79.2	24.4	90.7	46.53	4 159	1 565
Paducah	36.4	1 424	6.0	533	35.2	79.9	27.2	90.8	46.04	3 893	1 635
Richmond	134.8	4 169	6.5	313	34.7	75.8	25.6	87.0	47.33	4 231	1 150
LOUISIANA	X	X	X	NA	X	X	X	X	X	X	X
Alexandria	82.2	1 792	0.0	919	48.1	83.3	38.0	92.8	61.44	1 908	2 602
Baton Rouge	1 018.7	4 486	329.5	8 161	50.1	81.7	40.2	90.7	63.08	1 689	2 628
Bossier City	110.9	1 795	37.4	790	48.3	81.0	37.4	91.0	61.06	1 981	2 220
Central......................	NA	NA	NA	NA	NA	NA	NA	NA	NA	NA	NA
Houma......................	166.0	5 088	4.5	2 553	53.1	82.5	43.4	90.7	63.67	1 346	2 804
Kenner......................	59.7	916	0.0	688	52.6	82.7	43.4	91.1	64.16	1 417	2 773
Lafayette...................	745.2	8 563	26.9	3 094	51.3	82.2	41.6	91.2	60.54	1 531	2 671
Lake Charles...............	37.6	536	0.7	1 027	50.9	82.6	41.2	91.0	57.19	1 546	2 705
Monroe	147.1	2 873	6.1	1 127	44.6	83.0	33.5	94.1	58.04	2 399	2 311
New Iberia	25.0	760	3.0	NA	51.3	82.3	41.4	91.1	60.89	1 544	2 680
New Orleans	1 934.1	8 088	281.2	6 844	52.7	82.2	43.3	90.9	65.15	1 416	2 686
Shreveport.................	632.9	3 171	2.2	2 947	46.4	83.4	36.5	93.3	51.30	2 251	2 405
Slidell.......................	27.9	1 027	0.3	NA	50.7	82.1	40.2	91.1	62.66	1 652	2 548
MAINE	X	X	X	NA	X	X	X	X	X	X	X
Bangor......................	81.6	2 561	3.6	1 189	18.0	69.2	8.3	79.6	39.57	7 676	313
Lewiston	120.7	3 425	16.6	1 285	20.5	71.4	11.5	81.5	45.79	7 107	465
Portland	310.8	4 948	26.1	2 865	21.7	68.7	12.5	78.8	45.83	7 318	347
South Portland	29.8	1 254	2.1	913	NA	NA	NA	NA	NA	NA	NA
MARYLAND	X	X	X	NA	X	X	X	X	X	X	X
Annapolis...................	44.8	1 223	0.0	675	32.8	77.5	23.8	87.7	44.78	4 695	1 162
Baltimore	2 446.9	3 839	358.6	26 701	36.8	81.7	29.4	90.6	43.59	4 720	1 147
Bowie.......................	2.9	55	0.0	NA	31.8	75.2	21.2	87.1	44.66	4 970	917
College Park...............	0.3	13	0.0	NA	NA	NA	NA	NA	NA	NA	NA
Frederick	134.9	2 278	0.0	509	33.3	77.9	25.1	88.9	40.64	4 430	1 272
Gaithersburg...............	44.0	763	0.0	326	31.8	75.3	23.8	85.4	43.08	4 990	983
Hagerstown	39.3	991	11.2	491	29.3	75.2	20.8	86.1	39.45	5 249	902
Laurel	12.7	587	3.6	194	NA	NA	NA	NA	NA	NA	NA
Rockville	98.8	1 684	0.3	680	31.8	75.3	23.8	85.4	43.08	4 990	983
Salisbury...................	54.5	1 959	27.4	388	NA	NA	NA	NA	NA	NA	NA
MASSACHUSETTS ...	X	X	X	NA	X	X	X	X	X	X	X
Agawam Town	NA	NA	NA	NA	NA	NA	NA	NA	NA	NA	NA
Attleboro...................	116.4	2 699	5.0	1 166	27.4	72.2	17.8	83.0	48.34	6 012	558
Barnstable Town	143.5	3 069	74.0	NA	29.2	70.5	21.2	77.8	43.03	6 026	413

1. Based on the population estimated as of July 1 of the year shown. 2. Represents normal values based on the 30-year period, 1971–2000. 3. Average daily minimum. 4. Average daily maximum.

Table D. Cities — **Land Area and Population**

STATE Place code	City	Land area,[1] 2010 (sq km)	Population, 2010 — Total persons	Rank	Per square kilometer	Race alone or in combination, not of Hispanic origin (percent), 2010 — White	Black	American Indian, Alaska Native	Asian	Hawaiian Pacific Islander	Percent Hispanic or Latino,[2] 2010	Percent Foreign born, 2008–2010
		1	2	3	4	5	6	7	8	9	10	11
	MASSACHUSETTS— Cont'd											
25 05595	Beverly	39.1	39 502	1 002	1 010.5	92.6	2.1	0.5	2.1	0.1	3.5	5.6
25 07000	Boston	125.0	617 594	24	4 939.2	48.5	23.8	0.7	9.7	0.2	17.5	26.7
25 07740	Braintree Town	35.6	35 744	1 121	1 003.8	86.3	3.2	0.4	8.0	0.1	2.5	10.9
25 09000	Brockton	55.2	93 810	318	1 698.2	45.1	34.5	0.9	2.7	0.5	10.0	25.0
25 11000	Cambridge	16.5	105 162	264	6 358.0	65.1	12.4	0.7	17.1	0.2	7.6	27.4
25 13205	Chelsea	5.7	35 177	1 147	6 139.1	26.5	7.5	0.4	3.5	0.1	62.1	46.1
25 13660	Chicopee	59.1	55 298	681	935.2	80.6	3.4	0.5	1.6	0.1	14.8	9.3
25 21990	Everett	8.9	41 667	942	4 697.5	55.5	14.6	0.5	5.1	0.2	21.1	38.2
25 23000	Fall River	85.8	88 857	346	1 035.5	85.3	4.6	0.7	2.9	0.1	7.4	18.4
25 23875	Fitchburg	72.1	40 318	983	559.4	70.2	5.3	0.6	4.1	0.1	21.6	12.2
25 25172	Franklin Town	69.0	31 635	1 289	458.7	92.6	1.7	0.3	4.5	0.1	2.0	9.4
25 26150	Gloucester	67.9	28 789	1 435	424.3	95.1	1.1	0.4	1.2	0.1	2.7	8.0
25 29405	Haverhill	85.4	60 879	587	713.0	80.9	3.2	0.5	2.0	0.1	14.5	9.9
25 30840	Holyoke	55.1	39 880	987	723.5	47.8	3.0	0.5	1.3	0.0	48.4	6.7
25 34550	Lawrence	17.9	76 377	434	4 257.4	21.0	2.6	0.3	2.5	0.0	73.8	37.0
25 35075	Leominster	74.6	40 759	973	546.1	77.1	5.4	0.5	3.3	0.1	14.5	15.8
25 37000	Lowell	35.2	106 519	253	3 027.8	54.6	6.7	0.4	21.1	0.2	17.3	25.3
25 37490	Lynn	27.8	90 329	336	3 246.9	49.4	11.9	0.6	7.4	0.1	32.1	28.5
25 37875	Malden	13.1	59 450	615	4 552.1	54.6	15.4	0.5	20.8	0.2	8.4	40.0
25 38715	Marlborough	54.0	38 499	1 029	712.4	77.6	3.4	0.5	5.6	0.1	10.8	16.7
25 39835	Medford	21.0	56 173	666	2 677.5	78.1	9.5	0.5	7.6	0.1	4.4	22.0
25 40115	Melrose	12.1	26 983	1 535	2 226.3	90.9	2.8	0.3	4.5	0.0	2.5	11.6
25 40710	Methuen Town	57.6	47 255	839	820.1	75.8	2.3	0.3	4.2	0.1	18.1	15.0
25 45000	New Bedford	51.8	95 072	312	1 835.7	70.5	7.9	1.2	1.2	0.3	16.7	18.4
25 45560	Newton	46.2	85 146	367	1 843.0	81.5	2.9	0.3	12.8	0.1	4.1	20.3
25 46330	Northampton	88.7	28 549	1 440	321.9	86.0	3.2	0.7	5.0	0.1	6.8	9.9
25 52490	Peabody	42.0	51 251	754	1 220.6	88.7	2.4	0.3	2.1	0.1	6.3	14.6
25 53960	Pittsfield	104.8	44 737	881	426.8	88.3	6.8	0.6	1.6	0.1	5.0	4.8
25 55745	Quincy	42.9	92 271	325	2 149.8	66.9	5.1	0.5	24.8	0.1	3.3	27.9
25 56585	Revere	14.7	51 755	741	3 511.2	63.9	5.2	0.4	5.9	0.1	24.4	32.3
25 59105	Salem	21.4	41 340	955	1 928.2	77.5	4.4	0.5	3.1	0.1	15.6	17.8
25 62535	Somerville	10.7	75 754	442	7 106.4	71.5	7.4	0.5	9.8	0.2	10.6	26.1
25 67000	Springfield	82.5	153 060	158	1 854.6	38.4	21.1	0.8	2.7	0.2	38.8	10.5
25 69170	Taunton	121.0	55 874	674	461.9	86.5	6.1	0.7	1.3	0.2	5.5	12.0
25 72600	Waltham	33.0	60 632	594	1 839.0	70.1	6.3	0.3	10.5	0.1	13.7	27.3
25 73440	Watertown Town	10.3	31 915	1 277	3 086.6	83.7	3.5	0.3	8.3	0.1	5.3	25.2
25 76030	Westfield	120.0	41 094	964	342.5	89.6	1.8	0.6	1.6	0.1	7.5	6.9
25 77890	West Springfield Town	43.3	28 391	1 453	655.8	83.5	3.5	0.5	5.0	0.1	8.7	18.1
25 78972	Weymouth Town	43.5	53 743	708	1 235.8	89.5	3.5	0.5	3.6	0.1	2.6	8.7
25 81035	Woburn	32.7	38 120	1 038	1 165.0	82.9	4.5	0.3	7.8	0.0	4.5	15.0
25 82000	Worcester	96.8	181 045	129	1 870.5	61.5	11.5	0.8	6.6	0.1	20.9	20.7
26 00000	MICHIGAN	146 435.1	9 883 640	X	67.5	78.3	14.9	1.2	2.9	0.1	4.4	6.0
26 01380	Allen Park	18.1	28 210	1 461	1 555.1	88.5	2.5	0.9	1.1	0.1	8.1	5.1
26 03000	Ann Arbor	72.1	113 934	233	1 580.7	73.2	8.8	0.8	16.0	0.1	4.1	17.4
26 05920	Battle Creek	110.4	52 347	728	474.4	72.0	20.5	1.5	2.8	0.1	6.7	6.5
26 06020	Bay City	26.3	34 932	1 152	1 326.7	87.2	4.9	1.4	0.7	0.0	8.5	0.9
26 12060	Burton	60.5	29 999	1 360	495.9	88.3	8.3	1.5	1.0	0.1	3.1	1.9
26 21000	Dearborn	62.7	98 153	296	1 564.4	90.4	4.4	0.5	4.6	0.2	3.4	26.0
26 21020	Dearborn Heights	30.4	57 774	637	1 899.8	85.2	8.5	0.8	2.9	0.1	4.7	13.5
26 22000	Detroit	359.4	713 777	19	1 986.2	8.9	83.6	1.0	1.3	0.1	6.8	5.0
26 24120	East Lansing	35.2	48 579	802	1 379.7	78.6	7.7	0.7	11.8	0.1	3.4	14.6
26 24290	Eastpointe	13.3	32 442	1 256	2 435.6	66.7	30.8	1.4	1.5	0.1	2.1	3.6
26 27440	Farmington Hills	86.2	79 740	407	925.2	69.9	18.1	0.6	11.1	0.1	1.9	17.0
26 29000	Flint	86.6	102 434	276	1 183.5	38.4	58.7	1.7	0.7	0.1	3.9	1.7
26 31420	Garden City	15.2	27 692	1 488	1 821.8	91.9	4.1	1.1	1.2	0.1	3.3	3.5
26 34000	Grand Rapids	115.0	188 040	126	1 635.4	61.5	22.2	1.2	2.3	0.1	15.6	10.2
26 38640	Holland	43.0	33 051	1 231	769.2	70.6	4.1	0.7	3.4	0.2	22.7	9.3
26 40680	Inkster	16.2	25 369	1 638	1 566.0	21.9	75.3	1.4	2.0	0.1	2.6	5.8
26 41420	Jackson	28.1	33 534	1 205	1 191.7	73.1	24.0	1.4	0.9	0.1	5.3	1.7
26 42160	Kalamazoo	63.9	74 262	456	1 161.6	69.2	24.6	1.5	2.3	0.1	6.4	5.8
26 42820	Kentwood	54.1	48 707	800	899.6	69.0	17.0	1.1	7.3	0.1	8.5	11.2
26 46000	Lansing	93.4	114 297	232	1 224.1	59.6	26.3	1.8	4.3	0.1	12.5	8.2
26 47800	Lincoln Park	15.3	38 144	1 035	2 501.2	78.2	6.8	1.3	0.7	0.1	14.9	5.1
26 49000	Livonia	92.5	96 942	304	1 048.6	91.3	3.7	0.6	3.1	0.1	2.5	7.5
26 50560	Madison Heights	18.4	29 694	1 380	1 618.2	84.6	7.3	1.0	6.8	0.2	2.5	19.2
26 53780	Midland	87.3	41 863	939	479.7	91.7	2.6	0.7	3.7	0.1	2.4	5.5
26 56020	Mount Pleasant	20.1	26 016	1 598	1 297.6	87.7	4.9	2.7	3.6	0.1	3.3	5.1
26 56320	Muskegon	36.8	38 401	1 030	1 043.2	56.1	36.6	2.0	0.6	0.0	8.2	2.3
26 59440	Novi	78.4	55 224	684	704.6	72.6	8.7	0.5	16.9	0.1	3.0	18.3

1. Dry land or land partially or temporarily covered by water.   2. May be of any race.

Table D. Cities — **Population**

City	Age of population (percent), 2010											Population			
												Census counts		Percent change	
	Under 5 years	5 to 17 years	18 to 24 years	25 to 34 years	35 to 44 years	45 to 54 years	55 to 64 years	65 to 74 years	75 years and over	Median age	Percent female	1990	2000	1990–2000	2000–2010
	12	13	14	15	16	17	18	19	20	21	22	23	24	25	26
MASSACHUSETTS— Cont'd															
Beverly	5.3	14.1	12.2	12.2	12.7	15.7	13.2	6.9	7.7	40.1	52.6	38 195	39 862	4.4	-0.9
Boston	5.2	11.5	19.4	20.7	12.5	11.4	9.1	5.3	4.7	30.8	52.1	574 283	589 141	2.6	4.8
Braintree Town	5.8	17.0	6.5	11.7	14.1	15.8	12.0	7.9	9.0	41.6	52.8	33 836	33 698	-0.4	6.1
Brockton	7.3	18.4	9.8	13.3	13.6	14.5	11.1	6.4	5.5	35.9	51.9	92 788	94 304	1.6	-0.5
Cambridge	4.3	7.1	20.8	28.7	11.9	8.9	8.8	5.2	4.3	30.2	51.4	95 802	101 355	5.8	3.8
Chelsea	8.7	16.6	11.2	19.4	15.4	11.9	8.0	4.4	4.4	31.8	49.1	28 710	35 080	22.2	0.3
Chicopee	5.6	15.1	9.9	13.4	12.2	14.8	12.9	7.7	8.3	40.1	52.2	56 632	54 653	-3.5	1.2
Everett	6.9	15.9	9.8	16.9	15.5	13.9	9.7	5.6	5.8	35.3	50.9	35 701	38 037	6.5	9.5
Fall River	6.5	15.0	9.7	14.9	13.6	13.9	11.3	7.1	8.0	38.0	52.5	92 703	91 938	-0.8	-3.4
Fitchburg	6.7	16.1	14.1	13.3	12.6	14.1	10.5	6.0	6.4	34.7	51.4	41 194	39 102	-5.1	3.1
Franklin Town	6.1	22.4	8.1	8.7	16.0	18.7	10.6	5.0	4.4	38.7	51.0	22 095	29 560	33.8	7.0
Gloucester	4.5	14.1	7.1	9.8	12.2	17.6	17.0	9.2	8.5	46.4	51.9	28 716	30 273	5.4	-4.9
Haverhill	7.0	16.1	8.6	13.7	14.6	16.1	11.9	6.0	6.1	38.5	52.0	51 418	58 969	14.7	3.2
Holyoke	7.7	18.6	10.2	13.4	12.1	13.1	10.7	6.3	7.8	35.0	53.1	43 704	39 838	-8.8	0.1
Lawrence	8.4	20.7	12.2	15.0	13.6	12.6	8.9	4.6	4.0	30.5	51.9	70 207	72 043	2.6	6.0
Leominster	5.9	16.8	8.2	12.4	13.8	16.4	12.2	6.9	7.3	40.0	51.5	38 145	41 303	8.3	-1.3
Lowell	7.3	16.4	13.5	16.1	13.3	13.6	9.7	5.2	4.9	32.6	50.4	103 439	105 167	1.7	1.3
Lynn	7.4	17.5	10.8	14.8	13.6	14.0	10.5	5.9	5.5	34.7	51.0	81 245	89 050	9.6	1.4
Malden	6.3	13.3	9.5	18.9	15.2	14.4	10.7	6.0	5.7	36.2	51.6	53 884	66 340	4.6	5.5
Marlborough	6.6	15.0	7.8	15.4	15.3	16.2	11.1	6.2	6.4	38.5	50.5	31 813	36 255	14.0	6.2
Medford	5.2	11.4	11.6	18.0	13.7	13.7	11.2	6.8	8.4	37.7	52.2	57 407	55 765	-2.9	0.7
Melrose	5.9	16.1	5.5	12.1	15.4	15.9	13.3	7.7	8.1	41.9	53.0	28 150	27 134	-3.6	-0.6
Methuen Town	6.1	17.8	8.3	12.0	14.1	15.8	12.0	6.6	7.2	39.3	52.4	39 990	43 789	9.5	7.9
New Bedford	6.9	16.3	10.1	14.6	12.8	13.7	11.0	6.7	7.9	36.6	52.0	99 922	93 768	-6.2	1.4
Newton	5.3	16.3	12.1	9.7	12.6	14.8	13.8	7.3	8.0	40.5	53.2	82 585	83 829	1.5	1.6
Northampton	3.8	12.4	14.4	13.7	11.9	15.4	14.9	6.7	6.9	40.0	56.9	29 289	28 978	-1.1	-1.6
Peabody	4.9	14.2	7.3	11.3	12.8	15.9	13.0	8.6	11.9	44.6	52.5	47 264	48 129	1.8	6.5
Pittsfield	5.7	15.5	8.0	11.9	12.3	16.9	13.2	8.0	9.5	42.5	52.0	48 622	45 793	-5.8	-2.3
Quincy	5.4	11.2	8.7	18.6	14.2	14.8	12.0	7.2	7.9	39.2	52.1	84 985	88 025	3.6	4.8
Revere	6.2	14.1	9.3	16.1	14.7	14.2	10.8	7.0	7.5	37.9	51.0	42 786	47 283	10.5	9.5
Salem	5.6	13.1	12.8	15.0	13.5	14.7	12.3	6.5	6.5	37.6	53.5	38 091	40 407	6.1	2.3
Somerville	4.6	7.4	15.0	31.4	14.2	10.3	8.0	4.7	4.5	31.4	50.9	76 210	77 478	1.7	-2.2
Springfield	7.3	19.7	13.1	13.4	12.4	12.9	10.3	5.6	5.4	32.2	52.6	156 983	152 082	-3.1	0.6
Taunton	6.3	16.3	8.3	13.4	14.4	16.3	11.6	6.9	6.7	39.3	52.1	49 832	55 976	12.6	-0.2
Waltham	5.3	9.3	18.4	18.8	12.8	12.5	10.7	6.1	6.2	33.9	50.2	57 878	59 226	2.3	2.4
Watertown Town	5.7	9.8	7.0	21.7	15.2	13.8	11.9	7.0	7.9	38.3	53.1	33 284	32 986	-0.9	-3.2
Westfield	5.3	16.1	14.7	10.4	12.3	14.9	12.6	6.9	6.7	38.3	51.1	38 372	40 072	4.4	2.6
West Springfield Town	5.9	15.2	9.1	13.3	12.6	15.6	13.2	7.3	7.8	40.4	51.2	27 537	27 899	1.3	1.8
Weymouth Town	5.9	14.8	7.3	12.9	14.2	16.6	13.2	7.7	7.5	41.7	52.6	54 063	53 988	-0.1	-0.5
Woburn	5.9	13.8	7.4	15.2	14.2	15.7	11.8	7.2	8.7	40.5	51.6	35 943	37 258	3.7	2.3
Worcester	6.6	15.5	15.3	14.7	13.0	13.3	10.0	5.5	6.2	33.4	51.3	169 759	172 648	1.7	4.9
MICHIGAN	6.0	17.7	9.9	11.8	12.9	15.3	12.7	7.3	6.4	38.9	50.9	9 295 287	9 938 444	6.9	-0.6
Allen Park	5.0	16.6	7.9	11.8	13.0	15.9	12.6	6.9	10.3	41.7	51.9	31 092	29 376	-5.5	-4.0
Ann Arbor	4.3	10.1	29.4	17.8	10.0	9.9	9.2	4.8	4.5	27.8	50.7	109 608	114 024	4.0	-0.1
Battle Creek	7.7	18.4	9.1	13.2	12.6	14.0	11.6	6.5	6.9	36.3	52.1	53 516	53 364	-0.3	-1.9
Bay City	7.3	17.5	9.8	14.4	12.8	14.3	11.5	6.3	5.9	35.8	51.3	38 936	36 817	-5.4	-5.1
Burton	6.1	17.9	8.8	12.4	13.6	15.8	12.1	7.0	6.2	38.6	51.2	27 437	30 308	10.5	-1.0
Dearborn	8.0	21.7	10.0	12.8	12.7	12.8	10.1	5.5	6.5	33.0	50.6	89 286	97 775	9.5	0.4
Dearborn Heights	6.6	18.4	8.6	12.4	12.9	14.4	10.8	7.2	8.8	38.3	51.6	60 838	58 264	-4.2	-0.8
Detroit	7.0	19.6	11.5	12.1	13.0	13.7	11.6	6.1	5.4	34.8	52.7	1 027 974	951 270	-7.5	-25.0
East Lansing	2.4	5.2	62.3	10.1	4.5	4.3	4.9	2.8	3.5	21.6	51.5	50 677	46 525	-8.2	4.4
Eastpointe	6.6	19.2	8.8	13.6	14.9	14.8	10.9	4.8	6.5	36.3	51.6	35 283	34 077	-3.4	-4.8
Farmington Hills	5.1	16.5	7.1	12.1	13.1	16.4	13.8	7.6	8.3	42.1	52.9	74 614	82 111	10.0	-2.9
Flint	8.0	19.3	11.3	13.1	12.5	14.3	10.9	5.7	5.0	33.6	52.0	140 925	124 943	-11.3	-18.0
Garden City	5.3	17.0	8.6	12.4	14.1	16.7	11.8	6.8	7.2	39.9	50.9	31 846	30 047	-5.6	-7.8
Grand Rapids	8.0	16.7	14.4	17.1	11.6	11.8	9.4	4.8	6.3	30.8	51.3	189 126	197 800	4.6	-4.9
Holland	7.4	16.5	16.7	13.3	11.3	11.7	9.3	5.3	8.4	31.7	52.5	30 745	35 048	14.0	-5.7
Inkster	7.3	20.6	10.6	12.5	12.9	13.5	11.2	6.4	4.9	34.2	53.2	30 772	30 115	-2.1	-15.8
Jackson	9.0	19.6	10.5	14.7	13.0	12.9	10.1	5.1	5.1	32.2	52.3	37 425	36 316	-3.0	-7.7
Kalamazoo	6.4	14.0	27.0	15.0	9.9	10.0	8.2	4.3	5.1	26.2	50.7	80 277	77 145	-3.9	-3.7
Kentwood	7.3	18.0	9.9	15.6	13.3	13.8	10.5	5.4	6.1	34.3	52.0	37 826	45 255	19.6	7.6
Lansing	7.7	16.6	12.2	17.8	12.4	13.0	10.8	5.1	4.5	32.2	51.6	127 321	119 128	-6.4	-4.1
Lincoln Park	6.7	18.2	8.6	14.2	14.5	14.8	11.5	5.6	5.9	36.7	51.0	41 832	40 008	-4.4	-4.7
Livonia	4.5	16.3	7.8	10.0	12.2	17.6	13.9	7.8	9.9	44.5	51.7	100 850	100 545	-0.3	-3.6
Madison Heights	6.1	14.3	8.8	16.3	14.0	15.3	11.3	6.8	7.1	38.3	50.9	32 196	31 101	-3.4	-4.5
Midland	6.0	17.4	11.0	11.9	11.8	14.8	11.4	6.9	8.7	38.3	51.9	38 053	41 685	9.5	0.4
Mount Pleasant	3.6	7.4	53.1	11.0	5.8	6.4	5.5	3.1	4.1	22.0	52.6	23 299	25 946	11.4	0.3
Muskegon	7.1	16.2	12.2	15.7	13.1	13.6	10.5	5.3	6.3	34.1	47.9	39 809	40 105	0.7	-4.2
Novi	5.8	19.7	6.6	12.2	15.8	17.3	11.3	5.2	6.1	39.1	51.6	32 998	47 386	43.6	16.5

Table D. Cities — **Households, Group Quarters, Crime, and Education**

City	Households, 2010				Persons in group quarters, 2010				Serious crimes known to police,[2] 2010				Educational attainment, 2008–2010		
			Percent			Institutional			Total		Rate[3]			Attainment[4] (percent)	
	Number	Persons per household	Female family householder[1]	One-person	Total	Total	Persons in nursing facilities	Non-institutional	Number	Rate[3]	Violent	Property	Population age 25 and older	High school graduate or less	Bachelor's degree or more
	27	28	29	30	31	32	33	34	35	36	37	38	39	40	41
MASSACHUSETTS— Cont'd															
Beverly	15 850	2.33	10.5	31.3	2 514	533	369	1 981	772	1 954	291	1 663	27 924	29.7	42.7
Boston	252 699	2.26	16.3	37.1	46 214	6 697	3 280	39 517	26 447	4 282	942	3 340	390 175	38.2	43.1
Braintree Town	13 736	2.56	12.0	27.4	545	524	514	21	997	2 789	171	2 619	25 037	35.5	33.8
Brockton	33 303	2.76	22.3	26.9	1 768	1 088	790	680	3 963	4 224	1 161	3 064	59 994	53.1	17.5
Cambridge	44 032	2.00	8.4	40.7	17 102	324	277	16 778	3 708	3 526	453	3 073	72 794	16.2	73.1
Chelsea	11 831	2.92	21.8	29.3	682	570	570	112	1 998	5 680	1 774	3 906	21 637	70.4	11.6
Chicopee	23 739	2.28	15.6	34.3	1 155	341	231	814	1 964	3 552	495	3 056	37 308	54.6	16.9
Everett	15 543	2.67	17.8	27.7	191	150	150	41	1 432	3 437	547	2 890	28 449	62.3	15.2
Fall River	38 457	2.27	18.0	34.9	1 735	1 071	994	664	4 389	4 939	1 224	3 715	61 810	62.1	14.0
Fitchburg	15 165	2.49	16.2	29.8	2 538	669	356	1 869	1 434	3 557	779	2 778	24 801	51.2	21.1
Franklin Town	10 995	2.80	8.5	20.8	875	79	72	796	139	439	38	401	19 422	26.1	47.3
Gloucester	12 486	2.27	10.7	32.8	450	230	216	220	679	2 359	111	2 247	21 894	40.1	34.2
Haverhill	24 150	2.47	14.4	29.6	1 300	671	618	629	1 975	3 244	575	2 669	41 355	39.3	29.9
Holyoke	15 361	2.51	24.9	32.0	1 385	1 086	934	299	3 180	7 974	1 196	6 778	26 553	54.5	19.4
Lawrence	25 181	3.00	30.0	24.5	902	542	310	360	3 018	3 951	826	3 125	44 643	64.4	11.2
Leominster	16 767	2.41	13.5	30.0	327	251	224	76	1 608	3 945	697	3 248	27 925	45.1	24.1
Lowell	38 470	2.66	18.9	29.4	4 346	1 112	1 101	3 234	4 780	4 487	1 128	3 359	68 000	53.9	22.7
Lynn	33 310	2.69	19.3	30.6	835	284	263	551	3 261	3 610	847	2 763	57 909	57.0	17.6
Malden	23 673	2.50	13.9	30.0	373	116	116	257	1 781	2 996	484	2 511	40 534	43.1	32.7
Marlborough	15 395	2.46	10.3	28.7	661	286	253	375	907	2 356	421	1 935	27 700	41.7	37.0
Medford	22 810	2.38	11.4	29.6	1 959	479	465	1 480	718	1 278	107	1 171	40 506	37.3	40.7
Melrose	11 213	2.38	9.1	31.3	267	229	223	38	326	1 208	130	1 078	19 323	26.7	50.1
Methuen Town	17 529	2.67	14.4	24.9	420	277	232	143	1 097	2 321	222	2 099	31 635	43.0	27.9
New Bedford	38 761	2.40	20.0	32.4	1 966	1 415	1 196	551	4 778	5 026	1 223	3 802	62 576	64.2	14.1
Newton	31 168	2.50	8.4	25.6	7 103	483	474	6 620	1 299	1 526	102	1 423	54 147	15.1	73.9
Northampton	12 000	2.12	11.3	37.2	3 156	846	527	2 310	945	3 310	368	2 942	18 604	27.5	53.6
Peabody	21 313	2.38	10.7	31.4	520	397	389	123	1 329	2 593	217	2 377	36 467	41.1	30.7
Pittsfield	19 653	2.22	14.4	35.3	1 184	894	501	290	1 464	3 272	628	2 644	32 055	44.4	25.8
Quincy	40 658	2.24	10.6	37.7	1 400	729	698	671	2 196	2 380	449	1 931	68 148	38.2	38.5
Revere	20 454	2.52	14.9	32.0	280	228	228	52	1 907	3 685	595	3 090	35 489	61.7	15.6
Salem	17 842	2.22	14.4	35.3	1 770	167	156	1 603	1 203	2 910	455	2 455	27 854	36.7	38.3
Somerville	32 105	2.29	8.9	32.0	2 269	37	22	2 232	2 253	2 974	325	2 649	52 702	31.9	52.1
Springfield	56 752	2.60	27.2	30.0	5 677	954	553	4 723	9 649	6 304	1 367	4 937	90 347	57.1	16.5
Taunton	22 332	2.47	15.2	28.9	784	574	406	210	1 246	2 230	548	1 682	38 794	52.9	19.5
Waltham	23 690	2.28	9.1	34.9	6 686	308	287	6 378	1 183	1 951	249	1 702	39 081	35.8	46.0
Watertown Town	14 709	2.15	8.3	35.8	234	104	0	130	599	1 877	201	1 676	24 774	28.5	54.1
Westfield	15 335	2.49	11.4	27.5	2 976	359	294	2 617	905	2 202	231	1 971	26 520	43.8	26.3
West Springfield Town	12 124	2.33	12.2	34.3	170	120	120	50	1 491	5 252	542	4 709	20 104	46.6	25.7
Weymouth Town	22 435	2.37	12.0	32.3	460	373	373	87	1 212	2 255	335	1 920	38 353	38.1	33.4
Woburn	15 524	2.43	11.3	29.9	323	238	238	85	838	2 198	226	1 973	27 295	41.0	32.9
Worcester	68 613	2.46	17.6	31.8	12 152	2 093	1 845	10 059	7 955	4 394	973	3 421	113 659	45.4	29.5
MICHIGAN	3 872 508	2.49	13.2	27.9	229 068	109 867	42 473	119 201	316 661	3 204	490	2 714	6 560 571	42.6	25.0
Allen Park	11 580	2.42	11.6	30.1	171	138	132	33	652	2 311	167	2 145	19 600	42.8	22.5
Ann Arbor	47 060	2.17	7.1	37.4	11 840	78	61	11 762	3 230	3 230	251	2 584	60 811	11.5	70.8
Battle Creek	21 118	2.41	18.5	32.6	1 399	862	228	537	3 835	6 215	1 138	5 077	34 209	47.0	18.3
Bay City	14 436	2.38	16.6	33.7	515	180	0	335	1 318	3 773	733	3 040	22 969	48.7	19.4
Burton	11 964	2.50	16.3	27.0	111	0	0	111	913	3 043	257	2 787	21 085	48.2	12.7
Dearborn	34 342	2.85	11.9	29.6	226	195	180	31	4 097	4 174	379	3 795	60 608	41.9	29.5
Dearborn Heights	22 266	2.57	13.9	30.1	602	504	344	98	1 656	2 866	331	2 536	38 402	49.1	19.0
Detroit	269 445	2.59	31.4	34.0	14 759	6 541	3 365	8 218	64 782	9 076	2 378	6 698	452 844	55.8	11.8
East Lansing	14 774	2.23	5.6	33.3	15 701	193	193	15 508	1 254	2 581	338	2 244	13 900	13.0	68.5
Eastpointe	12 557	2.58	19.5	28.7	21	0	0	21	1 275	3 930	734	3 196	21 421	52.3	12.2
Farmington Hills	33 559	2.36	9.9	31.5	693	319	251	374	1 503	1 885	148	1 737	56 477	23.1	49.8
Flint	40 472	2.45	29.0	33.9	3 193	988	85	2 205	8 647	8 442	2 355	6 087	64 952	56.4	11.3
Garden City	10 894	2.54	13.6	26.8	54	0	0	54	814	2 939	307	2 633	18 529	50.8	13.3
Grand Rapids	72 126	2.49	16.4	32.3	8 260	3 298	2 011	4 962	9 405	5 002	875	4 127	114 887	43.0	28.1
Holland	12 021	2.52	11.9	29.8	2 723	283	273	2 440	1 181	3 573	442	3 132	20 355	41.9	32.6
Inkster	9 821	2.56	30.0	31.6	230	18	3	212	1 406	5 542	1 786	3 757	15 939	55.2	10.2
Jackson	13 294	2.46	22.4	33.9	773	468	263	305	1 905	5 681	948	4 733	21 465	46.9	13.4
Kalamazoo	29 141	2.29	15.6	36.8	7 462	1 126	489	6 336	4 252	5 726	964	4 762	38 305	35.0	31.3
Kentwood	19 741	2.45	13.1	30.9	395	246	114	149	1 768	3 630	427	3 203	31 446	35.1	32.6
Lansing	48 450	2.33	17.9	35.0	1 181	273	120	908	5 454	4 772	1 085	3 687	72 497	39.0	24.0
Lincoln Park	14 924	2.55	16.9	29.0	64	13	0	51	1 754	4 598	383	4 216	25 361	62.2	8.0
Livonia	38 714	2.47	9.7	26.7	1 366	791	764	575	2 200	2 269	158	2 112	68 397	34.6	33.2
Madison Heights	12 712	2.32	12.9	34.1	156	149	149	7	1 027	3 459	263	3 196	21 697	47.1	21.7
Midland	17 506	2.33	9.8	31.8	1 159	489	352	670	785	1 875	124	1 751	26 897	27.0	42.4
Mount Pleasant	8 376	2.35	9.3	31.6	6 365	442	286	5 923	582	2 237	242	1 995	9 735	33.8	38.7
Muskegon	13 967	2.38	22.9	36.0	5 199	4 459	426	740	2 618	6 818	974	5 844	25 095	58.4	10.8
Novi	22 258	2.46	8.6	29.5	360	316	316	44	1 028	1 862	60	1 802	37 377	19.4	54.5

1. No spouse present. 2. Data for serious crimes have not been adjusted for underreporting. This may affect comparability between geographic areas and over time. 3. Per 100,000 population estimated by the FBI. 4. Persons 25 years old and over.

Table D. Cities — Income, Poverty, and Housing

City	Money income, 2008–2010					Housing units, 2010			Occupied Housing units 2008–2010				
	Households				Families with income below poverty (percent)					Owner-occupied		Median owner costs as a percent of income	
	Per capita income[1] (dollars)	Median income	Percent with income of $200,000 or more	Percent with income of less than $25,000		Total	Percent change, 2000–2010	Vacant units for sale or rent[2]	Total	Percent	Median value[3] (dollars)	With a mortgage[4]	Without a mortgage[5]
	42	43	44	45	46	47	48	49	50	51	52	53	54
MASSACHUSETTS— Cont'd													
Beverly	38 063	66 274	7.8	19.4	8.2	16 641	2.2	791	15 726	61.8	371 200	25.8	15.8
Boston	32 261	50 710	6.2	29.4	15.1	272 481	8.2	19 782	248 498	33.4	378 800	27.2	14.6
Braintree Town	36 250	78 627	6.4	13.0	3.5	14 302	10.7	566	13 480	73.8	369 800	26.2	17.2
Brockton	21 459	48 823	1.4	25.2	12.8	35 552	2.1	2 249	33 509	57.5	247 000	31.5	17.3
Cambridge	45 176	67 271	10.4	23.2	9.5	47 291	5.7	3 259	46 108	33.8	556 600	24.9	11.3
Chelsea	17 251	41 840	0.9	32.4	24.0	12 621	2.3	790	10 975	30.8	281 500	31.8	22.5
Chicopee	22 775	44 448	0.9	29.9	11.2	25 140	2.9	1 401	22 532	59.7	184 900	25.1	15.9
Everett	23 066	48 062	1.8	26.9	11.2	16 715	5.1	1 172	14 805	39.9	337 000	38.4	14.9
Fall River	20 021	32 913	1.0	40.1	18.6	42 750	2.1	4 293	37 848	38.1	252 100	30.2	19.8
Fitchburg	21 442	45 481	1.4	30.2	15.0	17 117	7.0	1 952	14 578	56.8	217 800	27.4	17.2
Franklin Town	38 117	89 868	9.5	10.0	2.6	11 394	10.3	399	10 922	79.2	399 100	24.9	17.4
Gloucester	34 337	61 407	6.7	21.0	5.6	14 557	4.3	2 071	12 006	67.0	381 600	30.0	17.5
Haverhill	28 856	59 051	2.4	20.4	8.4	25 657	8.1	1 507	24 176	62.6	274 700	28.0	14.0
Holyoke	18 846	30 770	0.8	45.1	26.2	16 384	1.1	1 023	16 885	39.5	192 500	26.7	15.3
Lawrence	16 557	30 888	1.5	41.2	24.6	27 137	6.0	1 956	26 751	32.3	242 000	38.9	18.3
Leominster	28 250	55 779	2.7	21.7	5.0	17 873	5.3	1 106	16 127	61.2	244 800	27.9	15.4
Lowell	22 940	49 698	1.5	27.1	14.5	41 431	5.0	2 961	39 174	49.0	238 500	27.4	14.4
Lynn	21 764	41 969	1.5	31.5	15.6	35 776	3.1	2 466	33 873	45.8	270 900	32.3	18.0
Malden	26 680	56 055	2.3	25.7	10.0	25 161	6.5	1 488	23 410	44.0	344 200	31.4	14.4
Marlborough	37 130	69 078	7.2	15.9	3.9	16 416	10.2	1 021	16 190	61.7	323 100	25.6	15.3
Medford	31 810	68 022	3.2	18.1	6.1	24 046	6.0	1 236	22 342	59.7	388 500	28.2	19.8
Melrose	38 885	83 410	6.8	15.0	2.2	11 751	4.5	538	10 902	66.5	424 000	24.4	14.2
Methuen Town	28 858	58 389	3.5	20.1	5.4	18 340	8.6	811	17 650	71.0	291 700	27.4	16.3
New Bedford	20 172	34 893	0.8	40.1	19.8	42 933	3.4	4 172	38 714	42.9	239 000	30.1	19.8
Newton	57 284	104 887	23.8	13.1	4.6	32 648	1.7	1 480	30 443	69.6	688 700	24.5	14.4
Northampton	30 939	54 022	4.9	21.3	8.2	12 728	2.6	728	11 241	59.1	284 000	26.0	11.3
Peabody	31 926	64 679	3.8	18.1	3.3	22 220	17.6	907	20 514	66.3	350 000	27.0	13.6
Pittsfield	25 764	41 297	2.1	32.8	11.7	21 487	0.6	1 834	20 047	60.1	176 100	26.0	15.3
Quincy	32 471	59 256	3.6	20.2	6.4	42 838	6.8	2 180	40 287	49.2	353 200	29.9	16.5
Revere	23 346	47 862	1.4	27.7	15.5	22 100	9.5	1 646	18 590	47.8	323 200	34.8	22.5
Salem	30 692	53 285	3.1	25.1	10.2	19 130	5.3	1 288	17 907	50.5	319 300	28.1	17.5
Somerville	31 645	61 613	4.1	19.1	8.5	33 720	3.8	1 615	31 190	31.3	441 800	27.4	20.4
Springfield	17 746	36 114	0.8	37.6	22.0	61 706	0.9	4 954	54 994	51.4	156 400	28.2	17.6
Taunton	25 651	53 035	1.3	22.7	10.1	23 896	4.3	1 564	21 844	63.6	275 500	27.2	15.3
Waltham	32 048	67 956	6.8	19.7	7.7	24 926	4.4	1 236	22 066	48.1	408 800	25.9	15.7
Watertown Town	41 242	74 606	5.7	16.2	3.8	15 584	3.6	875	14 507	52.5	426 900	29.3	22.2
Westfield	26 053	51 053	3.6	26.0	5.0	16 075	4.1	740	15 605	65.2	224 600	23.9	15.3
West Springfield Town	28 239	53 164	2.9	25.6	9.6	12 697	3.6	573	12 011	59.2	215 500	22.2	16.6
Weymouth Town	34 049	65 375	3.9	17.3	5.7	23 480	4.0	1 045	22 174	68.1	331 900	26.9	17.3
Woburn	33 239	68 978	3.0	14.3	5.4	16 309	6.0	785	15 684	61.6	365 500	27.9	16.5
Worcester	23 490	44 580	1.8	30.0	14.3	74 645	5.5	6 032	70 352	45.6	233 700	27.7	17.4
MICHIGAN	24 435	46 861	2.6	26.2	11.3	4 532 233	7.0	659 725	3 815 248	73.4	136 600	24.7	13.8
Allen Park	27 071	56 983	1.3	20.7	6.7	12 206	-0.4	626	11 164	87.6	129 500	21.5	14.4
Ann Arbor	29 404	51 783	5.6	25.3	6.6	49 789	5.5	2 729	43 816	45.2	233 200	23.8	12.7
Battle Creek	20 996	37 632	1.5	32.4	16.2	24 277	3.1	3 159	21 015	62.1	90 700	23.9	13.7
Bay City	18 004	36 555	0.4	34.9	15.1	15 923	-2.1	1 487	14 192	71.9	79 500	23.8	14.7
Burton	20 641	44 798	0.4	23.9	8.1	13 075	5.9	1 111	11 572	78.0	89 600	24.5	13.2
Dearborn	21 727	45 552	2.4	29.9	19.3	37 871	-2.8	3 529	33 698	70.6	127 200	27.7	14.8
Dearborn Heights	21 613	44 944	1.4	25.2	8.7	24 068	0.6	1 802	21 638	79.4	108 400	26.7	14.3
Detroit	14 520	27 050	0.6	46.8	31.2	349 170	-6.9	79 725	261 565	53.2	68 900	31.7	17.9
East Lansing	15 913	31 490	4.0	44.5	8.3	15 787	3.1	1 013	12 532	38.3	184 800	23.4	12.2
Eastpointe	19 642	43 360	0.3	26.2	13.3	13 796	-1.2	1 239	12 635	79.9	89 200	27.5	15.1
Farmington Hills	37 129	65 683	7.0	17.0	5.3	36 178	3.8	2 619	33 507	64.1	219 200	24.2	14.4
Flint	14 372	25 803	0.1	48.9	33.8	51 321	-7.5	10 849	41 511	55.2	57 700	26.1	15.6
Garden City	23 070	55 393	0.3	17.6	5.4	11 616	-0.9	722	10 192	83.4	106 700	24.4	14.0
Grand Rapids	19 100	37 698	1.0	34.0	20.1	80 619	3.4	8 493	71 746	57.5	118 900	24.4	13.9
Holland	21 024	42 000	1.7	25.9	14.3	13 212	5.2	1 191	12 666	67.2	130 400	24.6	14.3
Inkster	15 044	27 340	0.1	46.6	29.5	11 647	-3.0	1 826	10 535	51.8	72 100	28.3	16.3
Jackson	15 846	28 825	0.4	44.3	25.1	15 457	1.4	2 163	13 475	58.8	82 100	24.9	14.8
Kalamazoo	17 899	29 886	1.6	42.9	25.6	32 433	2.0	3 292	28 745	47.2	103 600	25.1	15.1
Kentwood	23 872	45 390	0.9	26.8	10.5	21 584	10.7	1 843	19 823	63.4	138 700	23.1	14.8
Lansing	19 488	37 395	0.6	33.3	18.5	54 181	1.8	5 731	48 085	57.5	96 200	24.6	14.1
Lincoln Park	18 012	39 547	0.1	30.1	14.6	16 530	-1.7	1 606	14 152	74.3	84 900	25.6	15.6
Livonia	30 416	66 654	2.8	15.6	4.0	40 401	4.5	1 687	36 650	86.7	168 300	23.3	13.0
Madison Heights	21 828	40 240	0.7	30.1	14.2	13 685	0.5	973	12 704	63.6	111 400	25.0	16.4
Midland	30 510	48 647	5.9	24.6	6.9	18 578	4.7	1 072	17 661	66.6	136 800	21.5	11.4
Mount Pleasant	15 286	25 910	2.0	48.6	18.2	8 981	0.8	605	8 330	35.6	134 300	22.9	11.2
Muskegon	13 550	23 918	0.5	52.0	31.1	16 105	0.5	2 138	14 640	48.8	77 100	24.1	14.3
Novi	42 207	76 390	10.4	13.1	4.6	24 226	23.2	1 968	22 577	66.8	253 300	23.9	13.9

1. Based on population estimated by the American Community Survey.   2. Includes units rented or sold but not occupied.   3. Specified owner-occupied units; $1,000,000 represents $1,000,000 or more.   4. 50.0 represents 50 percent or more.   5. 10.0 represents 10 percent or less.

Table D. Cities — Housing, Labor Force, and Employment

City	Occupied housing units, 2008-2010 (cont.)				Migration, 2008-2010		Civilian labor force, 2010				Civilian employment[4], 2008-2010			
									Unemployment			Percent		
	Percent renter occupied	Median gross rent[1]	Median rent as a percent of income[2]	Percent with no vehicle available	Percent who lived in the same house one year ago	Percent who lived outside this city one year ago	Total	Percent change, 2009-2010	Total	Rate[3]	Population age 16 and older	In labor force	Full-year full-time worker	Households with no workers (percent)
	55	56	57	58	59	60	61	62	63	64	65	66	67	68
MASSACHUSETTS— Cont'd														
Beverly	38.2	1 023	29.0	9.4	85.4	9.7	21 424	-0.2	1 596	7.4	32 890	68.6	43.9	25.5
Boston	66.6	1 212	31.2	36.0	76.4	9.9	316 133	1.0	25 197	8.0	520 662	69.6	41.1	26.6
Braintree Town	26.2	1 113	28.8	8.1	89.6	7.1	19 130	0.9	1 499	7.8	28 480	69.7	43.5	22.5
Brockton	42.5	976	34.6	13.6	84.1	5.1	45 769	0.6	5 185	11.3	72 956	70.1	40.3	27.5
Cambridge	66.2	1 484	29.5	32.8	70.4	18.1	59 864	-1.0	3 211	5.4	92 513	67.7	42.2	25.3
Chelsea	69.2	1 065	36.2	31.3	81.1	9.0	14 365	-14.5	1 541	10.7	26 412	67.9	40.0	27.4
Chicopee	40.3	725	28.9	12.8	85.4	8.4	28 004	-0.9	2 784	9.9	44 879	61.7	36.7	35.3
Everett	60.1	1 135	34.1	19.6	83.1	10.6	21 151	10.6	1 762	8.3	32 963	72.2	43.9	24.0
Fall River	61.9	657	28.9	18.4	84.8	5.4	43 857	-3.1	6 392	14.6	72 472	60.9	34.6	39.0
Fitchburg	43.2	858	34.4	14.2	82.6	9.8	18 809	-0.4	2 208	11.7	32 469	65.9	36.4	28.1
Franklin Town	20.8	1 087	26.4	2.2	88.7	7.9	16 836	-2.1	1 242	7.4	23 156	75.1	49.2	15.0
Gloucester	33.0	947	30.6	8.5	91.5	4.3	15 720	-5.0	1 581	10.1	24 210	64.8	37.4	28.6
Haverhill	37.4	946	32.1	9.7	86.7	6.7	31 779	0.4	2 896	9.1	47 596	70.9	44.0	25.2
Holyoke	60.5	663	33.8	25.1	85.0	5.5	16 199	-1.8	1 841	11.4	31 444	55.1	31.4	43.1
Lawrence	67.7	918	35.9	24.8	79.3	5.2	31 705	4.3	5 106	16.1	56 550	59.7	35.6	30.0
Leominster	38.8	850	30.7	10.0	85.4	5.7	20 523	-1.2	2 201	10.7	32 372	69.4	43.9	27.3
Lowell	51.0	909	29.1	15.7	82.8	6.8	52 527	2.7	5 433	10.3	83 907	66.2	41.8	28.3
Lynn	54.2	909	33.8	22.4	84.1	5.2	43 270	2.7	4 024	9.3	71 443	66.0	40.1	30.5
Malden	56.0	1 115	28.9	19.4	82.4	12.2	33 236	6.1	2 601	7.8	48 177	73.3	43.0	22.8
Marlborough	38.3	1 043	27.5	10.4	86.2	6.8	22 675	-1.3	1 527	6.7	31 203	75.8	50.3	19.5
Medford	40.3	1 319	28.4	10.7	82.6	11.1	30 652	0.3	2 268	7.4	48 686	70.0	42.7	25.4
Melrose	33.5	1 149	24.9	10.6	88.9	7.0	15 183	0.0	991	6.5	21 652	70.0	43.9	24.3
Methuen Town	29.0	900	29.9	7.5	87.9	6.8	24 301	2.3	2 438	10.0	36 652	67.2	43.0	26.9
New Bedford	57.1	734	30.7	18.2	83.9	5.6	43 696	2.3	6 148	14.1	74 595	62.7	35.8	35.2
Newton	30.4	1 568	27.7	6.0	82.6	12.8	46 995	3.1	2 602	5.5	68 201	63.1	41.3	21.8
Northampton	40.9	859	31.1	11.2	80.7	12.1	16 463	-1.1	960	5.8	24 160	67.3	35.2	25.6
Peabody	33.7	1 127	32.3	10.9	90.7	5.1	27 744	-0.9	2 189	7.9	41 904	66.6	42.3	30.5
Pittsfield	39.9	727	31.5	15.0	87.2	5.1	23 455	1.3	2 018	8.6	36 432	64.5	35.8	33.7
Quincy	50.8	1 124	27.8	16.9	80.9	9.5	53 070	-0.5	4 311	8.1	78 801	71.3	45.2	26.5
Revere	52.2	1 157	37.2	21.0	81.8	10.6	24 808	-13.6	2 295	9.3	41 184	66.8	39.8	29.8
Salem	49.5	1 026	30.3	14.6	79.6	10.8	23 810	-0.6	1 938	8.1	34 088	73.6	45.0	25.5
Somerville	68.7	1 301	27.3	22.3	73.9	16.1	46 504	-0.4	2 869	6.2	66 503	77.5	47.9	18.6
Springfield	48.6	753	33.8	20.4	82.8	7.0	67 360	1.0	8 398	12.5	116 530	58.7	32.8	35.9
Taunton	36.4	836	31.7	8.1	88.5	5.5	31 108	-0.8	2 962	9.5	45 245	71.6	43.2	23.4
Waltham	51.9	1 270	29.0	7.5	75.2	14.7	35 385	0.0	2 297	6.5	53 676	65.7	39.8	19.5
Watertown Town	47.5	1 351	23.1	12.0	87.1	10.6	13 027	0.1	995	7.6	27 836	75.6	52.1	20.3
Westfield	34.8	774	34.9	9.8	88.5	6.2	15 680	1.2	898	5.7	33 176	60.6	37.9	29.7
West Springfield Town..	40.8	707	28.8	9.7	87.9	8.7	14 796	2.0	1 364	9.2	23 132	67.4	42.5	27.2
Weymouth Town	31.9	1 062	30.7	6.9	90.6	6.9	30 073	0.8	2 624	8.7	42 938	71.9	45.1	22.9
Woburn	38.4	1 223	27.8	6.8	87.6	6.8	21 803	2.3	1 651	7.6	31 003	71.1	43.4	23.3
Worcester	54.4	864	29.8	16.8	81.7	7.2	85 077	1.3	8 323	9.8	146 636	63.6	38.1	29.1
MICHIGAN	26.6	724	32.8	7.5	85.2	10.4	4 747 128	-2.3	600 566	12.7	7 831 187	62.8	35.2	31.5
Allen Park	12.4	845	34.6	5.7	93.2	5.1	12 254	-1.9	800	6.5	22 995	63.1	37.2	33.7
Ann Arbor	54.8	923	32.2	11.2	63.3	18.4	62 229	-1.9	5 343	8.6	99 929	60.1	30.8	25.9
Battle Creek	37.9	654	34.1	10.9	78.7	8.9	24 937	-4.1	3 199	12.8	40 742	62.6	33.3	33.7
Bay City	28.1	506	34.0	12.8	81.6	8.5	17 259	-3.1	2 169	12.6	26 936	62.4	34.0	33.7
Burton	22.0	707	31.7	5.2	89.3	6.5	13 041	-4.4	1 423	10.9	24 353	61.3	34.3	35.3
Dearborn	29.4	940	35.6	8.6	86.9	4.4	36 317	-2.2	3 463	9.5	72 412	56.8	30.9	35.9
Dearborn Heights	20.6	960	39.3	6.6	87.1	8.9	24 134	-2.1	2 124	8.8	44 532	57.7	33.0	34.0
Detroit	46.8	748	44.0	22.4	82.7	3.7	363 169	-3.6	83 795	23.1	560 075	54.4	25.6	44.4
East Lansing	61.7	775	49.2	8.8	45.3	27.3	19 701	-4.1	2 364	12.0	44 710	49.5	14.9	29.4
Eastpointe	20.1	1 045	41.7	5.8	80.7	17.5	17 413	-1.3	2 493	14.3	25 055	68.4	36.7	30.6
Farmington Hills	35.9	908	27.4	5.2	86.5	9.4	40 084	-1.0	4 209	10.5	64 337	66.6	41.8	26.4
Flint	44.8	620	47.4	17.9	79.6	6.4	50 467	-5.5	11 807	23.4	78 984	50.3	22.2	50.3
Garden City	16.6	893	30.8	4.7	87.8	10.6	13 563	-2.1	1 176	8.7	22 081	68.9	39.5	26.5
Grand Rapids	42.5	725	34.7	12.8	77.4	10.5	99 461	-3.5	13 987	14.1	146 728	66.5	35.2	29.5
Holland	32.8	667	32.7	9.1	74.4	14.0	17 426	-3.4	2 517	14.4	26 331	65.9	35.7	29.0
Inkster	48.2	683	43.6	15.8	87.1	8.3	12 056	-3.0	2 009	16.7	19 797	52.3	26.7	48.6
Jackson	41.2	563	35.9	21.4	81.1	9.1	16 821	-5.4	3 032	18.0	25 707	56.6	31.2	40.4
Kalamazoo	52.8	666	39.0	14.5	65.2	18.4	39 288	-3.5	5 420	13.8	60 536	65.7	29.7	33.5
Kentwood	36.6	678	28.2	9.2	84.2	11.9	25 563	-3.2	2 372	9.3	38 152	71.8	43.8	23.0
Lansing	42.5	677	34.5	11.8	79.2	9.4	64 053	-4.3	9 086	14.2	89 521	67.9	37.2	29.9
Lincoln Park	25.7	724	37.3	9.2	85.2	9.6	17 721	-2.4	1 977	11.2	29 484	60.2	32.7	34.6
Livonia	13.3	862	28.4	4.8	91.7	5.3	44 634	-1.8	2 581	5.8	79 199	64.6	37.8	30.3
Madison Heights	36.4	706	28.9	9.2	83.7	10.1	15 498	-1.1	2 138	13.8	24 874	63.8	36.8	32.9
Midland	33.4	631	30.7	8.1	81.7	9.2	20 489	-3.2	1 483	7.2	33 204	62.3	38.2	30.8
Mount Pleasant	64.4	658	41.3	14.5	47.8	30.1	13 797	-4.1	1 324	9.6	23 420	59.7	18.5	29.9
Muskegon	51.2	574	41.3	17.6	71.7	16.4	17 123	-5.8	2 949	17.2	30 396	53.8	22.4	41.9
Novi	33.2	907	26.1	4.4	84.9	10.4	24 068	-0.8	1 937	8.0	42 767	70.4	46.8	20.2

1. $2,000 represents $2,000 or more. 2. 50.0 represents 50 percent or more. 3. Percent of civilian labor force. 4. Persons 16 years old and over.

Table D. Cities — Construction, Wholesale Trade, and Retail Trade

City	Value of residential construction authorized by building permits, 2010			Wholesale trade,[1] 2007				Retail trade,[2] 2007			
	New construction ($1,000)	Number of housing units	Percent single family	Number of establishments	Number of employees	Sales (mil dol)	Annual payroll (mil dol)	Number of establishments	Number of employees	Sales (mil dol)	Annual payroll (mil dol)
	69	70	71	72	73	74	75	76	77	78	79
MASSACHUSETTS— Cont'd											
Beverly	3 592	11	100.0	51	368	184.1	21.6	155	2 608	852.3	70.1
Boston	41 017	351	6.6	565	10 156	6 225.7	583.8	2 157	27 909	6 808.8	725.3
Braintree Town	7 368	49	26.5	NA	NA	NA	NA	NA	NA	NA	NA
Brockton	3 587	27	92.6	65	1 062	757.7	54.6	329	5 208	1 263.5	138.6
Cambridge	15 953	38	21.1	90	1 693	2 066.4	189.9	474	6 627	1 287.7	150.6
Chelsea	6 600	112	0.0	90	1 606	2 447.5	94.2	78	1 334	348.2	36.1
Chicopee	3 027	23	73.9	36	922	725.5	42.4	167	2 582	721.3	62.9
Everett	5 112	56	37.5	61	1 566	1 050.6	84.6	120	1 811	496.7	45.7
Fall River	5 546	54	88.9	76	1 642	727.8	63.9	298	3 488	931.2	91.4
Fitchburg	4 594	21	100.0	32	249	105.8	11.8	144	1 876	489.5	42.8
Franklin Town	10 154	45	53.3	NA	NA	NA	NA	NA	NA	NA	NA
Gloucester	8 134	23	91.3	56	417	491.5	21.3	117	1 146	253.7	29.2
Haverhill	9 665	62	71.0	51	722	266.2	39.3	143	2 230	648.0	60.2
Holyoke	1 173	10	40.0	29	421	125.3	16.3	261	4 373	712.6	77.6
Lawrence	1 930	20	30.0	66	1 204	538.2	58.1	173	1 579	429.6	45.9
Leominster	4 367	25	76.0	48	730	429.0	37.3	221	3 896	766.0	76.7
Lowell	4 102	41	95.1	65	964	523.4	51.0	224	2 331	573.9	54.1
Lynn	2 281	18	100.0	41	526	430.8	26.7	215	2 278	623.8	57.1
Malden	0	0	0.0	32	515	229.9	26.2	131	1 397	456.9	35.0
Marlborough	3 134	22	100.0	80	1 973	1 051.3	184.0	225	3 543	758.0	69.4
Medford	140	2	0.0	47	809	413.0	40.0	160	2 312	596.3	59.9
Melrose	4 493	22	54.5	11	73	24.6	4.2	61	768	173.1	19.1
Methuen Town	13 039	51	100.0	33	735	1 721.2	46.0	107	2 157	486.0	49.9
New Bedford	2 296	16	100.0	100	1 746	919.5	79.4	305	3 061	727.0	71.9
Newton	35 131	96	85.4	116	2 246	4 040.0	126.8	378	5 680	1 153.6	156.1
Northampton	6 488	37	56.8	28	217	65.1	7.6	185	2 140	468.9	50.7
Peabody	5 024	29	82.8	76	2 037	4 327.3	141.1	273	5 071	1 219.5	132.5
Pittsfield	3 074	26	46.2	43	561	217.9	22.5	209	3 205	747.8	77.3
Quincy	8 880	74	16.2	58	739	530.4	36.6	245	4 032	1 142.2	105.0
Revere	1 979	17	23.5	26	D	D	D	115	1 665	360.4	34.3
Salem	1 424	7	100.0	39	314	166.3	17.0	173	2 680	544.2	64.4
Somerville	167	1	100.0	46	560	291.2	33.4	172	2 962	761.5	69.1
Springfield	7 365	62	87.1	123	1 892	1 097.0	94.4	485	6 592	1 521.3	150.5
Taunton	8 195	59	98.2	57	1 932	1 393.0	105.4	242	4 868	1 085.1	107.3
Waltham	12 117	64	31.3	115	2 961	8 050.6	283.0	224	2 932	811.3	85.6
Watertown Town	1 550	9	0.0	39	506	193.4	26.5	171	3 392	889.4	97.8
Westfield	4 932	26	76.9	38	1 109	1 826.1	45.0	144	2 198	530.8	61.0
West Springfield Town	2 830	19	89.5	NA	NA	NA	NA	NA	NA	NA	NA
Weymouth Town	12 962	81	55.6	NA	NA	NA	NA	NA	NA	NA	NA
Woburn	7 281	23	100.0	224	3 716	2 178.4	215.0	192	3 601	1 010.7	111.9
Worcester	11 162	114	86.8	209	2 968	1 321.9	139.0	593	8 591	1 923.3	205.4
MICHIGAN	1 553 300	9 075	85.5	9 892	137 315	107 109.3	7 016.1	37 619	470 794	109 102.6	10 001.5
Allen Park	0	0	0.0	17	209	132.8	11.5	111	1 680	297.0	31.2
Ann Arbor	13 879	141	68.1	73	641	364.1	39.4	518	7 836	1 467.2	165.7
Battle Creek	418	4	100.0	39	490	344.6	21.9	261	3 920	757.6	72.7
Bay City	0	0	0.0	46	571	217.1	26.9	156	1 338	274.8	29.1
Burton	104	2	100.0	25	244	68.9	10.5	180	2 799	538.9	55.0
Dearborn	2 101	5	100.0	134	1 549	1 733.8	78.5	556	6 001	1 181.6	110.7
Dearborn Heights	0	0	0.0	42	152	69.4	6.3	193	1 781	377.8	35.0
Detroit	48 589	383	35.0	450	7 278	7 112.1	381.1	2 157	12 933	3 271.8	265.3
East Lansing	601	5	100.0	15	68	55.6	3.9	76	1 488	278.3	24.2
Eastpointe	0	0	0.0	19	56	13.3	2.0	137	1 404	342.7	37.7
Farmington Hills	8 005	28	100.0	212	2 920	2 236.2	188.5	267	4 095	1 151.2	103.6
Flint	655	5	100.0	71	1 557	757.6	95.5	432	4 597	876.5	89.6
Garden City	75	1	100.0	12	50	10.5	1.1	115	1 126	404.4	32.9
Grand Rapids	2 196	18	83.3	222	5 471	3 319.6	280.7	613	6 933	1 500.4	154.5
Holland	1 275	4	100.0	47	767	440.8	43.1	177	2 248	509.1	46.5
Inkster	0	0	0.0	9	152	76.7	11.9	51	278	72.3	5.5
Jackson	375	2	100.0	61	972	733.7	48.6	191	1 868	398.1	40.7
Kalamazoo	180	2	100.0	102	1 503	611.6	61.9	301	3 160	637.3	68.7
Kentwood	4 555	58	96.6	127	2 549	1 395.8	122.3	303	4 914	898.6	95.4
Lansing	1 326	7	100.0	125	1 949	1 657.6	88.9	451	6 709	1 552.2	149.7
Lincoln Park	123	1	100.0	14	165	75.4	7.1	140	1 637	347.3	32.9
Livonia	7 511	26	100.0	279	4 608	4 355.0	224.4	506	7 560	2 683.7	169.0
Madison Heights	186	3	100.0	111	1 943	965.8	102.6	175	3 589	891.5	84.4
Midland	9 271	67	85.1	32	D	D	D	244	3 910	746.7	71.1
Mount Pleasant	982	14	42.9	27	526	197.5	12.6	132	2 661	496.1	47.7
Muskegon	1 406	12	50.0	37	961	394.7	48.8	145	2 121	407.5	43.5
Novi	28 441	185	100.0	151	2 259	3 321.6	139.4	359	6 845	1 361.1	143.7

1. Merchant wholesalers except manufacturers' sales branches and offices. 2. Establishments with payroll.

Items 69—79

City	Real estate and rental and leasing, 2007				Professional, scientific, and technical services,[1] 2007				Manufacturing, 2007			
	Number of establish-ments	Number of employees	Receipts (mil dol)	Annual payroll (mil dol)	Number of establish-ments	Number of employees	Receipts (mil dol)	Annual payroll (mil dol)	Number of establish-ments	Number of employees	Receipts (mil dol)	Annual payroll (mil dol)
	80	81	82	83	84	85	86	87	88	89	90	91
MASSACHUSETTS— Cont'd												
Beverly	43	193	31.8	6.8	164	D	D	D	57	3 090	722.2	208.3
Boston	1 022	11 955	5 544.2	846.9	2 971	52 195	13 235.0	5 456.7	319	9 922	3 193.3	580.7
Braintree Town	NA	NA	NA	NA	NA	NA	NA	NA	NA	NA	NA	NA
Brockton	56	317	49.2	10.0	150	D	D	D	91	2 702	443.3	104.2
Cambridge	160	937	332.5	44.6	824	D	D	D	75	2 906	800.2	184.4
Chelsea	25	137	15.4	4.3	37	385	45.1	20.2	43	2 102	367.8	73.0
Chicopee	44	161	31.2	4.9	48	220	21.0	8.4	85	4 401	1 118.3	192.7
Everett	18	92	17.0	4.2	36	145	12.1	4.2	49	811	145.8	37.5
Fall River	87	339	61.8	9.8	169	D	D	D	164	6 067	1 060.1	215.2
Fitchburg	35	142	18.3	3.5	63	314	28.3	10.6	74	2 271	464.4	102.7
Franklin Town	NA	NA	NA	NA	NA	NA	NA	NA	NA	NA	NA	NA
Gloucester	28	92	11.1	2.4	99	D	D	D	53	2 941	1 218.7	211.9
Haverhill	49	238	40.7	8.9	114	739	80.6	33.3	97	2 658	601.2	109.7
Holyoke	48	422	74.9	11.2	59	D	D	D	82	2 233	451.8	98.6
Lawrence	42	242	38.5	7.6	84	D	D	D	100	4 491	851.2	174.4
Leominster	44	295	46.7	12.8	99	D	D	D	97	3 225	1 024.3	142.3
Lowell	81	543	77.0	13.5	143	D	D	D	77	3 905	762.9	209.9
Lynn	54	275	53.5	8.1	86	D	D	D	43	4 887	D	D
Malden	62	318	111.3	13.5	77	528	37.2	14.7	48	1 694	372.3	71.0
Marlborough	51	242	70.3	8.9	176	D	D	D	73	6 934	2 661.5	638.8
Medford	37	189	43.3	7.0	115	D	D	D	39	506	79.9	23.5
Melrose	22	63	16.1	2.1	78	261	32.3	12.4	NA	NA	NA	NA
Methuen Town	39	136	22.5	4.5	85	369	47.4	19.4	42	1 641	543.5	90.4
New Bedford	81	400	53.6	12.4	181	D	D	D	129	7 611	1 995.0	292.4
Newton	166	1 677	1 370.8	83.8	599	D	D	D	48	787	284.9	43.4
Northampton	39	122	21.0	3.1	123	D	D	D	38	1 381	466.0	73.0
Peabody	46	318	76.0	10.4	112	854	113.1	43.4	74	2 784	708.4	165.4
Pittsfield	44	283	32.0	7.4	134	D	D	D	52	2 787	552.3	152.9
Quincy	96	706	106.2	27.8	294	D	D	D	47	613	246.1	35.3
Revere	23	332	31.2	7.5	44	237	17.8	7.4	16	D	D	D
Salem	39	205	40.2	7.4	171	D	D	D	49	789	157.9	39.4
Somerville	67	263	61.1	10.4	173	D	D	D	67	1 523	269.2	78.3
Springfield	117	772	119.9	27.9	354	D	D	D	123	4 822	1 158.3	226.4
Taunton	39	135	38.4	3.8	107	2 335	576.0	152.1	71	5 292	1 388.5	386.6
Waltham	97	906	196.2	40.6	404	D	D	D	117	4 172	1 017.4	231.3
Watertown Town	39	526	122.6	38.3	120	D	D	D	50	1 692	392.7	108.3
Westfield	37	162	25.0	4.1	62	499	75.0	28.1	97	3 323	783.4	153.3
West Springfield Town	NA	NA	NA	NA	NA	NA	NA	NA	NA	NA	NA	NA
Weymouth Town	NA	NA	NA	NA	NA	NA	NA	NA	NA	NA	NA	NA
Woburn	72	806	139.7	43.8	298	D	D	D	153	4 869	1 596.7	312.3
Worcester	169	1 526	295.0	51.7	451	D	D	D	212	8 673	2 116.0	454.6
MICHIGAN	8 862	54 874	12 858.6	1 685.7	22 552	249 864	29 536.8	15 304.5	13 675	581 739	234 455.8	29 910.3
Allen Park	27	D	D	D	57	1 813	113.7	80.5	NA	NA	NA	NA
Ann Arbor	175	1 685	405.9	58.0	602	7 037	799.1	455.3	64	1 400	D	62.0
Battle Creek	52	337	48.1	9.2	101	D	D	D	78	8 084	3 825.1	392.8
Bay City	31	136	13.1	2.5	97	754	56.3	33.0	52	2 103	613.3	127.0
Burton	19	107	16.2	4.7	40	220	20.8	6.1	NA	NA	NA	NA
Dearborn	102	D	D	D	284	D	D	D	96	10 493	D	759.2
Dearborn Heights	40	D	D	D	70	361	32.7	15.2	NA	NA	NA	NA
Detroit	321	D	D	D	685	13 636	2 451.1	929.0	472	22 962	20 216.1	1 486.3
East Lansing	58	687	61.7	20.5	126	D	D	D	NA	NA	NA	NA
Eastpointe	16	75	9.1	2.1	40	221	14.5	6.7	NA	NA	NA	NA
Farmington Hills	200	4 754	548.4	179.2	743	10 597	1 570.9	759.6	104	2 250	645.3	115.9
Flint	81	519	67.7	12.5	171	D	D	D	76	9 791	D	D
Garden City	13	D	D	D	17	75	7.4	3.1	NA	NA	NA	NA
Grand Rapids	188	1 136	145.9	27.9	615	D	D	D	315	19 627	5 497.9	1 068.9
Holland	39	204	35.3	5.9	98	D	D	D	99	8 901	2 669.1	367.1
Inkster	23	D	D	D	9	25	1.7	0.7	NA	NA	NA	NA
Jackson	45	201	26.3	4.0	102	D	D	D	101	2 578	660.6	107.7
Kalamazoo	98	807	83.3	18.3	236	D	D	D	116	4 462	1 347.5	210.5
Kentwood	56	417	82.1	10.5	132	1 418	173.3	68.9	130	8 624	1 838.1	357.2
Lansing	101	924	119.8	23.2	247	D	D	D	95	5 096	D	327.4
Lincoln Park	18	D	D	D	29	D	D	D	NA	NA	NA	NA
Livonia	139	1 077	150.9	28.1	394	D	D	D	280	11 265	3 195.9	604.9
Madison Heights	43	396	82.4	24.9	122	1 523	173.7	76.0	163	4 288	872.8	200.8
Midland	67	D	D	D	124	D	D	D	36	4 487	D	344.4
Mount Pleasant	33	D	D	D	81	1 141	48.8	26.7	26	D	D	D
Muskegon	19	100	12.4	2.6	86	D	D	D	79	3 806	991.6	173.4
Novi	78	497	94.0	19.0	274	4 007	589.0	259.7	80	2 211	D	109.7

1. Establishments subject to federal tax.

City	Accommodation and food services, 2007				Arts, entertainment, and recreation,[1] 2007				Health care and social assistance,[1] 2007			
	Number of establishments	Number of employees	Sales (mil dol)	Annual payroll (mil dol)	Number of establishments	Number of employees	Receipts (mil dol)	Annual payroll (mil dol)	Number of establishments	Number of employees	Receipts (mil dol)	Annual payroll (mil dol)
	92	93	94	95	96	97	98	99	100	101	102	103
MASSACHUSETTS— Cont'd												
Beverly	117	1 354	72.7	21.3	19	D	D	D	119	D	D	D
Boston	2 073	46 895	3 661.7	1 057.5	182	D	D	D	899	18 698	3 110.4	1 379.7
Braintree Town	NA	NA	NA	NA	NA	NA	NA	NA	NA	NA	NA	NA
Brockton	155	2 812	122.8	40.9	14	248	11.7	3.5	198	3 585	364.3	180.0
Cambridge	398	8 044	594.9	172.8	50	651	133.4	20.7	214	3 195	510.3	195.3
Chelsea	56	556	33.4	8.6	NA	NA	NA	NA	30	635	47.6	20.4
Chicopee	118	1 575	68.7	19.7	3	D	D	D	48	942	62.7	27.5
Everett	77	D	D	D	5	D	D	D	43	D	D	D
Fall River	181	2 574	105.5	29.9	13	D	D	D	200	3 976	351.5	167.6
Fitchburg	89	1 145	53.6	15.4	6	D	D	D	80	1 299	106.6	45.4
Franklin Town	NA	NA	NA	NA	NA	NA	NA	NA	NA	NA	NA	NA
Gloucester	119	1 031	61.1	17.9	15	111	11.5	3.8	55	488	49.8	22.7
Haverhill	124	1 695	84.0	23.3	24	D	D	D	98	2 404	254.5	98.1
Holyoke	96	D	D	D	9	81	5.5	1.5	82	1 262	107.0	52.4
Lawrence	91	858	42.1	11.1	5	39	2.3	0.4	67	1 017	136.9	56.1
Leominster	97	1 874	79.6	25.2	16	D	D	D	97	1 554	132.5	61.1
Lowell	183	2 207	107.9	28.8	17	388	14.1	5.0	145	2 819	252.6	125.8
Lynn	140	1 169	63.4	16.4	9	129	9.1	2.2	103	1 489	119.2	55.0
Malden	96	1 033	52.4	15.4	10	69	5.1	1.6	75	917	96.9	31.1
Marlborough	140	2 462	127.8	38.2	14	278	14.6	3.8	70	1 054	91.4	38.3
Medford	92	1 300	82.6	19.2	10	D	D	D	91	D	D	D
Melrose	36	377	20.4	5.9	2	D	D	D	67	D	D	D
Methuen Town	97	1 485	76.3	22.5	10	310	12.7	3.4	90	864	82.9	40.1
New Bedford	211	2 496	101.3	27.1	19	D	D	D	137	2 700	234.0	105.8
Newton	177	D	D	D	44	359	87.3	22.7	388	6 190	587.1	271.2
Northampton	101	1 874	81.7	25.5	18	113	7.6	2.0	108	1 603	153.7	78.0
Peabody	125	2 468	137.5	40.2	7	D	D	D	112	2 291	281.7	119.9
Pittsfield	131	2 142	92.6	28.1	18	214	10.9	3.2	146	1 679	182.7	86.8
Quincy	234	3 264	188.7	52.0	20	D	D	D	196	3 878	383.1	155.8
Revere	101	1 340	90.1	22.2	5	D	D	D	49	D	D	D
Salem	122	1 710	98.5	29.0	20	234	12.5	3.9	115	D	D	D
Somerville	181	D	D	D	16	D	D	D	59	1 026	117.1	44.7
Springfield	294	4 867	222.5	65.5	18	119	7.8	2.2	291	5 910	618.5	305.1
Taunton	111	2 130	90.8	27.4	6	D	D	D	86	1 045	125.8	50.7
Waltham	272	3 647	252.9	70.5	33	477	29.6	8.0	137	2 360	249.4	102.4
Watertown Town	90	1 117	64.0	17.4	10	303	16.7	5.0	88	1 340	170.9	62.4
Westfield	76	1 039	43.7	12.8	10	D	D	D	79	722	64.5	29.7
West Springfield Town	NA	NA	NA	NA	NA	NA	NA	NA	NA	NA	NA	NA
Weymouth Town	NA	NA	NA	NA	NA	NA	NA	NA	NA	NA	NA	NA
Woburn	100	1 855	115.7	31.1	15	D	D	D	107	1 936	279.3	96.5
Worcester	430	5 843	302.0	85.9	28	1 087	26.5	7.8	401	9 043	1 084.4	439.7
MICHIGAN	19 678	339 181	14 536.6	4 207.3	2 975	41 065	3 940.6	1 170.2	21 150	228 681	21 054.9	9 168.6
Allen Park	77	1 537	61.6	18.7	11	D	D	D	83	1 087	87.5	38.4
Ann Arbor	338	7 686	372.7	108.3	38	230	13.0	3.9	316	D	D	D
Battle Creek	145	2 830	110.2	33.6	14	252	8.4	3.7	159	2 051	192.8	77.3
Bay City	104	1 601	48.4	15.1	12	D	D	D	111	D	D	D
Burton	65	1 158	44.9	12.6	9	104	1.7	0.5	81	D	D	D
Dearborn	281	5 031	255.0	76.8	20	D	D	D	358	D	D	D
Dearborn Heights	99	1 718	64.6	18.5	9	D	D	D	91	926	80.7	34.3
Detroit	958	16 550	1 253.9	333.3	65	8 209	1 388.0	389.9	719	9 945	822.9	356.1
East Lansing	109	2 602	104.8	28.7	6	D	D	D	110	1 757	178.2	95.8
Eastpointe	51	749	28.0	8.5	5	D	D	D	94	D	D	D
Farmington Hills	172	2 758	131.9	37.5	32	D	D	D	417	4 287	432.5	191.1
Flint	183	2 152	87.2	22.5	5	D	D	D	182	1 638	224.9	77.5
Garden City	46	725	28.2	7.1	8	D	D	D	70	D	D	D
Grand Rapids	396	8 765	331.7	105.3	46	647	33.0	10.0	379	5 548	597.9	242.7
Holland	91	1 965	68.3	24.3	6	81	2.4	1.0	95	1 585	132.5	62.2
Inkster	23	187	10.5	2.6	1	D	D	D	17	118	6.3	2.3
Jackson	107	1 749	66.4	18.5	9	115	5.0	1.4	146	1 779	202.9	98.0
Kalamazoo	199	4 543	167.0	54.1	25	411	16.3	5.3	168	3 061	257.0	134.3
Kentwood	105	2 278	94.9	28.2	10	D	D	D	100	1 537	163.1	69.1
Lansing	227	3 774	152.7	44.4	19	398	63.1	8.9	233	D	D	D
Lincoln Park	66	944	39.7	9.5	5	D	D	D	64	638	57.1	26.0
Livonia	243	5 634	246.2	71.4	26	D	D	D	420	4 576	394.7	173.4
Madison Heights	104	1 861	79.7	22.3	10	116	8.8	2.4	99	D	D	D
Midland	102	2 267	97.1	27.8	10	D	D	D	155	D	D	D
Mount Pleasant	89	2 564	87.1	24.4	6	D	D	D	116	1 075	76.7	35.4
Muskegon	80	1 357	53.8	15.1	9	D	D	D	124	1 904	225.4	121.9
Novi	151	3 825	178.7	53.1	16	D	D	D	200	D	D	D

1. Establishments subject to federal tax.

Table D. Cities — Other Services and Federal Funds

City	Other services[1], 2007				Procurement contracts		Grants						
	Number of establishments	Number of employees	Receipts (mil dol)	Annual payroll (mil dol)	Defense	Other	Total[2]	Medicaid and other health related	Nutrition and family welfare	Energy and environment	Disasters and emergency preparedness	Housing and community development	Employment and training
	104	105	106	107	108	109	110	111	112	113	114	115	116
MASSACHUSETTS— Cont'd													
Beverly	66	650	32.8	13.5	12.4	1.5	21.0	10.8	2.2	1.5	1.5	3.6	0.0
Boston	1 041	8 143	704.5	200.9	186.5	614.8	6 428.2	3 771.0	282.9	183.6	58.7	703.2	198.5
Braintree Town	NA	NA	NA	NA	NA	NA	NA	NA	NA	NA	NA	NA	NA
Brockton	136	928	68.9	23.1	12.2	38.5	29.4	3.6	0.0	1.1	0.0	18.6	0.9
Cambridge	147	1 114	104.0	29.4	660.7	435.6	1 398.8	693.7	0.3	113.8	0.0	49.4	0.0
Chelsea	33	D	D	D	10.0	2.7	20.3	0.3	2.2	0.2	1.5	6.6	2.5
Chicopee	86	414	31.4	9.5	40.2	21.0	4.5	0.0	0.0	0.0	0.0	3.3	0.0
Everett	66	468	38.4	14.0	0.0	0.5	4.4	0.0	0.0	0.0	0.0	4.3	0.0
Fall River	148	745	52.9	15.5	23.9	0.5	36.9	2.8	4.0	2.2	-0.4	25.2	0.0
Fitchburg	55	227	21.3	7.0	0.0	0.2	20.6	4.2	5.0	0.0	0.0	3.9	0.0
Franklin Town	NA	NA	NA	NA	NA	NA	NA	NA	NA	NA	NA	NA	NA
Gloucester	56	239	17.5	5.6	8.5	7.0	12.7	0.0	1.3	2.1	0.0	8.9	0.0
Haverhill	80	D	D	D	1.0	1.9	22.0	0.0	1.7	0.5	0.0	5.1	0.0
Holyoke	50	238	16.9	4.9	0.2	1.7	46.1	4.6	11.1	8.5	0.0	13.4	0.0
Lawrence	82	519	43.1	14.7	14.7	5.3	28.0	4.8	4.9	1.0	0.0	15.9	0.0
Leominster	59	239	21.7	5.7	0.0	0.1	2.8	0.0	0.0	0.0	0.0	2.7	0.0
Lowell	142	695	56.9	18.6	31.2	24.3	81.9	12.1	5.8	15.7	-0.1	21.4	0.1
Lynn	105	547	49.3	14.1	1 384.5	0.6	36.1	2.7	2.9	0.0	0.0	30.3	0.0
Malden	98	472	45.2	13.8	2.0	0.4	250.3	2.7	1.6	1.7	0.0	18.1	0.0
Marlborough	64	439	71.0	12.5	392.6	121.4	13.7	5.1	0.0	3.5	0.0	1.7	0.0
Medford	102	592	53.8	17.1	0.8	0.2	42.5	1.2	0.0	8.0	0.0	13.0	0.0
Melrose	34	177	19.0	5.8	0.2	0.0	2.9	0.1	0.0	0.0	0.0	2.8	0.0
Methuen Town	62	D	D	D	0.6	2.8	6.7	0.0	0.0	0.2	0.0	5.3	0.0
New Bedford	150	855	87.6	24.4	145.1	6.9	45.7	1.9	2.7	4.0	0.0	24.7	0.0
Newton	177	1 125	97.4	34.2	13.3	17.8	171.4	43.9	0.0	8.1	0.0	12.4	0.0
Northampton	69	335	22.6	7.7	26.1	32.7	12.9	3.4	0.0	0.1	-0.1	6.2	0.0
Peabody	100	562	55.0	13.9	3.8	12.0	7.2	0.2	0.0	0.7	0.0	6.2	0.0
Pittsfield	83	483	34.3	12.3	110.1	18.9	17.1	0.1	2.5	1.0	0.0	7.1	0.0
Quincy	179	869	86.4	26.2	45.7	1.2	83.7	1.0	3.2	55.4	0.0	18.7	0.0
Revere	74	316	33.4	9.0	0.2	0.0	10.4	0.0	0.0	0.0	0.0	10.2	0.0
Salem	87	366	35.9	10.4	0.7	0.5	18.1	0.9	0.0	0.6	0.0	12.5	0.2
Somerville	99	1 295	99.2	35.3	2.5	7.7	173.4	124.6	4.8	2.1	0.0	16.6	10.5
Springfield	197	1 636	119.8	40.5	4.0	5.3	69.1	11.3	1.1	4.7	0.0	30.9	0.8
Taunton	78	352	26.6	8.2	1 386.7	6.8	25.1	0.8	2.5	0.2	0.0	13.2	0.0
Waltham	128	826	127.5	32.9	171.3	4.6	64.7	37.6	0.0	4.3	0.0	7.5	0.0
Watertown Town	65	842	90.1	43.2	2.8	29.9	393.3	90.3	0.0	257.8	0.0	1.9	0.0
Westfield	62	346	30.7	10.9	8.9	1.7	7.5	0.0	1.4	0.0	0.0	2.3	0.0
West Springfield Town	NA	NA	NA	NA	NA	NA	NA	NA	NA	NA	NA	NA	NA
Weymouth Town	NA	NA	NA	NA	NA	NA	NA	NA	NA	NA	NA	NA	NA
Woburn	95	D	D	D	654.8	70.3	25.7	9.8	0.0	7.1	0.0	3.8	0.0
Worcester	259	1 801	166.9	50.2	49.8	14.2	452.3	358.5	8.9	5.8	0.0	44.2	0.7
MICHIGAN	13 953	79 193	6 221.1	1 956.5	4 080.3	2 386.4	20 577.3	11 165.6	2 752.7	1 031.9	7.1	937.6	542.1
Allen Park	41	250	16.4	5.8	0.0	0.0	0.1	0.0	0.0	0.0	0.0	0.1	0.0
Ann Arbor	147	953	62.6	22.3	74.4	179.7	1 384.4	1 004.1	5.0	43.8	0.3	17.5	0.0
Battle Creek	87	D	D	D	115.8	8.5	20.8	4.3	6.9	0.5	0.0	6.0	0.3
Bay City	63	441	33.4	10.3	1.5	9.7	7.5	0.4	0.1	1.1	0.0	3.1	0.0
Burton	66	298	25.0	7.8	0.0	0.0	0.5	0.0	0.0	0.0	0.0	0.0	0.0
Dearborn	189	875	70.7	21.6	0.8	198.6	12.5	0.0	0.3	6.3	0.0	4.1	0.0
Dearborn Heights	93	434	32.5	10.0	0.0	0.0	3.9	0.0	0.0	0.0	0.0	3.7	0.0
Detroit	698	4 200	321.6	107.5	29.2	428.2	653.1	182.6	54.8	116.4	0.4	130.8	13.4
East Lansing	26	229	9.6	2.7	2.7	5.6	333.0	98.3	0.6	35.6	0.0	0.8	0.4
Eastpointe	57	230	21.3	6.6	0.0	0.0	1.4	0.0	0.0	0.0	0.0	1.4	0.0
Farmington Hills	149	943	82.9	25.9	5.3	17.3	1.5	0.0	0.0	0.0	0.0	1.5	0.0
Flint	129	923	54.4	30.7	1.0	13.9	69.1	5.0	17.4	3.2	0.0	19.0	4.5
Garden City	46	197	13.7	4.2	0.0	0.0	0.1	0.0	0.0	0.0	0.0	0.0	0.0
Grand Rapids	237	1 707	123.8	42.5	8.6	40.3	125.5	22.8	11.8	6.5	0.0	41.5	4.0
Holland	58	515	32.9	13.6	22.9	20.7	10.1	0.1	3.3	0.0	0.1	0.8	0.0
Inkster	19	D	D	D	0.0	0.3	6.7	0.0	0.7	0.0	0.0	5.6	0.0
Jackson	63	524	47.0	15.3	17.2	0.7	20.6	3.1	7.0	0.0	0.0	7.1	0.3
Kalamazoo	132	1 188	97.4	31.5	11.7	4.8	46.2	13.7	4.9	1.8	0.0	5.0	0.4
Kentwood	72	596	41.1	13.0	4.1	0.1	0.0	0.0	0.0	0.0	0.0	0.0	0.0
Lansing	150	1 314	86.5	28.7	508.2	96.8	2 770.2	223.3	454.2	144.8	-2.3	483.5	469.5
Lincoln Park	68	336	25.6	8.0	0.0	0.0	3.1	0.0	0.0	0.0	0.0	3.1	0.0
Livonia	224	1 544	173.2	46.0	23.6	1.8	9.1	0.6	0.0	0.7	0.0	6.9	0.0
Madison Heights	76	761	79.8	25.4	8.1	0.4	2.3	0.1	0.0	0.0	0.0	2.2	0.0
Midland	76	616	47.5	13.4	0.2	1.3	11.5	0.1	0.0	8.6	0.0	1.5	0.0
Mount Pleasant	51	314	16.4	5.0	0.0	1.9	6.2	0.3	0.3	2.8	0.0	1.6	0.0
Muskegon	49	314	21.0	6.8	32.8	0.8	18.7	0.3	6.4	2.2	0.0	2.7	0.0
Novi	90	832	57.3	24.2	4.7	0.6	4.2	1.1	0.0	0.9	0.0	0.0	0.0

1. Establishments subject to federal tax.   2. Includes program categories not shown separately. State totals include additional categories not allocated by city.

Table D. Cities — **City Government Finances**

City	City government finances, 2007									
	General revenue							General expenditure		
		Intergovernmental		Taxes					Per capita[1] (dollars)	
					Per capita[1] (dollars)					
	Total (mil dol)	Total (mil dol)	Percent from state government	Total (mil dol)	Total	Property	Sales and gross receipts	Total (mil dol)	Total	Capital outlays
	117	118	119	120	121	122	123	124	125	126
MASSACHUSETTS— Cont'd										
Beverly	111.6	23.9	94.6	69.9	1 784	1 753	31	105.6	2 695	106
Boston	3 016.3	1 196.8	92.2	1 299.2	2 168	2 022	145	2 815.5	4 698	424
Braintree Town	NA	NA	NA	NA	NA	NA	NA	NA	NA	NA
Brockton	334.1	204.7	98.2	98.3	1 056	1 028	28	325.8	3 500	438
Cambridge	1 129.4	311.5	74.7	258.5	2 550	2 459	91	1 105.8	10 907	759
Chelsea	128.6	79.6	93.4	33.9	887	829	58	133.0	3 480	154
Chicopee	219.4	144.8	97.8	59.5	1 105	1 080	24	169.2	3 141	587
Everett	145.5	69.5	98.9	69.4	1 863	1 843	20	161.8	4 341	1 125
Fall River	260.5	167.7	92.8	66.8	735	711	23	307.8	3 386	592
Fitchburg	120.0	68.2	97.7	37.5	942	904	38	125.9	3 160	159
Franklin Town	NA	NA	NA	NA	NA	NA	NA	NA	NA	NA
Gloucester	88.6	18.8	92.2	52.8	1 743	1 695	48	98.6	3 252	456
Haverhill	174.9	79.6	95.8	75.8	1 266	1 215	51	176.1	2 940	265
Holyoke	168.7	106.8	98.0	43.4	1 092	1 070	22	182.6	4 596	532
Lawrence	289.1	216.1	91.9	44.4	634	610	23	270.2	3 857	277
Leominster	107.0	52.2	98.3	47.3	1 150	1 126	24	110.9	2 695	318
Lowell	364.4	240.8	94.7	94.0	908	881	27	343.5	3 318	309
Lynn	263.5	163.9	97.9	88.4	1 014	990	24	262.3	3 010	150
Malden	161.9	72.9	95.5	61.0	1 094	1 053	41	180.3	3 237	48
Marlborough	119.1	24.2	98.6	85.2	2 238	2 174	64	107.8	2 833	27
Medford	134.6	38.7	92.7	79.1	1 423	1 379	44	136.3	2 453	66
Melrose	93.2	40.2	98.6	43.4	1 621	1 619	2	94.6	3 532	1 014
Methuen Town	118.9	48.9	99.6	58.9	1 339	1 300	39	117.1	2 663	77
New Bedford	348.5	216.0	93.6	92.7	1 009	941	68	294.9	3 211	238
Newton	316.1	55.5	87.3	225.5	2 707	2 629	78	297.4	3 571	194
Northampton	78.8	22.3	88.9	37.7	1 329	1 280	48	77.9	2 741	244
Peabody	155.7	54.1	92.9	79.9	1 552	1 487	65	148.9	2 895	52
Pittsfield	135.4	64.4	90.3	58.4	1 360	1 332	28	131.4	3 061	182
Quincy	267.1	64.2	88.2	152.6	1 666	1 626	40	282.7	3 086	247
Revere	132.3	64.9	97.4	59.9	1 082	1 047	35	125.5	2 267	158
Salem	158.5	77.5	94.2	65.3	1 595	1 575	20	155.6	3 804	866
Somerville	215.6	93.8	95.2	88.4	1 189	1 149	40	224.5	3 017	347
Springfield	573.3	398.4	91.9	147.9	986	958	29	563.8	3 760	152
Taunton	159.0	76.6	97.6	63.5	1 139	1 096	43	166.6	3 381	796
Waltham	207.7	59.5	98.5	127.3	2 130	2 019	111	200.9	3 362	187
Watertown Town	99.3	19.8	99.7	65.2	2 005	1 997	8	99.4	3 057	172
Westfield	131.8	65.1	92.0	52.2	1 299	1 276	24	122.4	3 047	185
West Springfield Town	NA	NA	NA	NA	NA	NA	NA	NA	NA	NA
Weymouth Town	NA	NA	NA	NA	NA	NA	NA	NA	NA	NA
Woburn	171.4	75.5	99.9	79.5	2 145	2 089	56	134.8	3 638	438
Worcester	610.5	353.7	91.9	197.3	1 134	1 097	37	661.2	3 801	318
MICHIGAN	X	X	X	X	X	X	X	X	X	X
Allen Park	38.1	7.6	81.3	16.8	628	579	49	31.0	1 154	56
Ann Arbor	181.4	35.6	54.0	72.5	630	619	11	199.0	1 729	376
Battle Creek	106.5	28.6	58.4	46.7	895	602	21	100.1	1 917	100
Bay City	59.7	16.2	62.1	14.4	422	406	16	57.0	1 674	170
Burton	18.8	5.6	92.3	5.0	165	153	13	17.2	569	115
Dearborn	166.3	25.2	80.1	81.2	910	883	26	188.7	2 115	552
Dearborn Heights	60.9	14.6	65.1	29.5	551	531	20	52.1	972	18
Detroit	2 511.7	773.0	76.8	869.2	948	350	292	2 338.6	2 550	301
East Lansing	59.6	13.2	77.5	19.6	424	396	28	61.3	1 325	171
Eastpointe	40.9	7.5	76.9	20.7	636	614	21	33.3	1 020	69
Farmington Hills	88.7	14.5	86.8	45.0	570	559	11	87.1	1 103	47
Flint	492.5	109.3	81.1	46.8	408	226	19	509.3	4 442	213
Garden City	27.6	6.1	93.7	13.5	490	474	16	25.5	924	38
Grand Rapids	291.9	71.8	53.1	108.3	559	236	21	330.6	1 707	335
Holland	53.0	13.0	60.9	17.9	528	511	16	50.2	1 475	223
Inkster	38.1	15.6	47.0	11.8	430	416	14	39.2	1 428	255
Jackson	50.6	17.6	47.0	20.3	597	361	7	52.0	1 528	176
Kalamazoo	130.3	33.9	72.0	42.7	588	562	27	117.6	1 619	237
Kentwood	37.1	7.5	83.7	17.9	377	345	32	38.0	804	105
Lansing	232.9	46.3	66.0	73.5	639	384	10	235.5	2 049	408
Lincoln Park	37.2	11.6	66.3	16.2	445	429	16	36.7	1 007	45
Livonia	122.2	24.6	64.1	58.3	621	594	26	112.6	1 198	33
Madison Heights	42.2	7.8	72.4	22.6	763	737	26	41.0	1 382	220
Midland	70.2	9.6	89.9	34.7	845	831	15	58.7	1 429	240
Mount Pleasant	19.7	5.5	86.4	7.2	270	256	15	17.9	675	29
Muskegon	45.9	17.3	62.4	16.5	419	205	26	47.3	1 201	190
Novi	73.1	6.8	97.2	37.3	689	646	43	55.6	1 028	48

1. Based on population estimated as of July 1 of the year shown.

City	City government finances, 2006 (cont.)									
	General expenditure (cont.)									
	Percent of total for:									
	Public welfare	Highways	Parking facilities	Education	Health and hospitals	Police protection	Sewerage and sanitation	Parks and recreation	Housing and community development	Interest on debt
	127	128	129	130	131	132	133	134	135	136
MASSACHUSETTS— Cont'd										
Beverly	0.2	3.7	0.0	50.7	0.4	5.5	9.3	1.8	0.5	2.9
Boston	3.2	1.7	0.1	34.7	6.0	10.8	8.7	1.4	3.1	1.9
Braintree Town	NA	NA	NA	NA	NA	NA	NA	NA	NA	NA
Brockton	0.1	2.3	0.1	62.7	0.3	5.3	12.1	0.4	0.6	3.3
Cambridge	0.0	1.0	0.1	13.9	63.3	2.9	1.1	1.2	0.3	0.8
Chelsea	0.2	1.5	0.0	53.2	0.1	5.4	2.3	0.1	3.1	2.8
Chicopee	0.5	2.2	0.0	67.4	0.2	4.9	4.9	1.2	0.8	0.8
Everett	0.2	3.3	0.0	62.5	0.9	5.2	1.8	0.1	0.2	1.4
Fall River	0.5	3.0	0.1	62.9	0.9	6.5	3.4	0.4	2.0	2.3
Fitchburg	0.0	3.0	0.1	55.4	0.5	6.0	8.6	0.5	1.4	2.3
Franklin Town	NA	NA	NA	NA	NA	NA	NA	NA	NA	NA
Gloucester	0.1	2.5	0.0	45.0	0.4	5.3	17.5	0.0	0.0	2.9
Haverhill	0.2	2.5	0.0	59.2	0.7	4.8	7.8	0.2	0.9	2.8
Holyoke	3.8	2.3	0.1	55.8	0.3	6.2	14.0	0.6	1.3	0.9
Lawrence	0.2	1.2	0.3	67.1	0.1	5.4	4.0	0.3	0.8	2.1
Leominster	0.3	4.0	0.0	62.5	0.4	5.5	5.5	1.9	0.7	1.2
Lowell	0.2	1.8	0.7	54.9	0.6	6.4	8.1	1.3	2.5	2.4
Lynn	0.1	2.3	0.3	65.9	0.3	7.0	1.6	0.4	1.1	2.1
Malden	1.5	1.8	0.0	47.0	0.4	4.8	1.9	0.3	4.2	2.8
Marlborough	0.1	4.6	0.0	61.1	0.3	5.8	5.7	0.3	0.1	2.0
Medford	0.2	2.9	0.0	51.5	0.3	8.5	5.1	0.6	1.7	2.0
Melrose	0.1	1.3	0.0	56.6	0.5	3.5	2.9	2.0	0.1	2.2
Methuen Town	0.4	5.5	0.0	62.8	0.7	6.6	6.2	0.1	0.8	2.3
New Bedford	0.4	1.5	0.1	58.8	1.0	7.5	6.8	0.4	2.4	2.8
Newton	0.1	2.8	0.0	59.4	0.7	4.7	3.4	1.5	1.3	0.9
Northampton	0.4	4.0	0.8	44.5	0.6	5.5	5.3	0.3	3.1	3.0
Peabody	0.1	2.4	0.0	53.1	0.7	5.9	2.9	2.0	2.7	1.4
Pittsfield	0.1	3.8	0.0	58.8	0.5	5.1	5.4	1.0	1.8	1.7
Quincy	0.3	3.0	0.0	45.0	0.7	7.0	4.1	1.0	1.7	1.3
Revere	0.5	4.7	0.1	55.6	0.2	5.8	0.5	0.2	0.9	1.7
Salem	0.1	2.0	0.4	61.7	0.3	4.5	3.0	0.7	1.0	1.9
Somerville	0.1	2.5	0.0	46.7	0.5	4.8	3.2	0.3	1.7	1.5
Springfield	0.1	2.2	0.0	64.2	0.2	6.3	1.9	1.5	1.0	2.7
Taunton	3.6	3.1	0.0	65.0	0.4	5.6	3.0	0.6	1.1	1.3
Waltham	0.2	3.6	0.1	44.0	0.3	6.1	4.4	0.6	0.5	1.6
Watertown Town	0.1	2.5	0.2	43.5	0.4	6.6	3.6	0.5	0.3	2.3
Westfield	0.4	4.4	0.0	62.1	1.7	4.9	4.9	0.6	0.6	2.8
West Springfield Town	NA	NA	NA	NA	NA	NA	NA	NA	NA	NA
Weymouth Town	NA	NA	NA	NA	NA	NA	NA	NA	NA	NA
Woburn	0.1	1.4	0.0	56.5	0.4	5.8	2.3	0.6	0.0	1.7
Worcester	0.0	2.5	0.1	52.8	0.5	5.9	5.2	0.6	1.3	4.5
MICHIGAN	X	X	X	X	X	X	X	X	X	X
Allen Park	0.0	10.4	0.0	0.0	0.0	20.3	18.7	4.9	0.8	2.1
Ann Arbor	0.0	7.6	8.0	0.0	0.0	13.4	15.1	5.4	8.3	2.6
Battle Creek	0.0	11.9	0.8	0.0	0.0	14.9	12.7	6.5	4.8	3.5
Bay City	0.0	11.7	0.0	0.0	0.0	13.1	17.4	1.8	11.0	3.0
Burton	0.0	26.5	0.0	0.0	0.0	25.2	24.7	0.5	0.0	3.0
Dearborn	0.0	10.9	0.7	0.0	0.5	14.6	34.5	7.6	3.2	1.0
Dearborn Heights	0.0	12.3	0.0	0.0	0.0	23.3	21.2	1.9	1.9	3.2
Detroit	1.4	4.7	0.3	2.6	2.8	15.2	25.3	3.0	3.4	13.2
East Lansing	0.0	11.9	4.4	0.0	0.2	13.0	14.1	10.3	0.7	4.0
Eastpointe	0.0	8.7	0.0	0.0	0.0	24.8	19.2	4.9	4.3	0.5
Farmington Hills	0.0	11.8	0.0	0.0	0.0	22.5	17.5	10.4	0.5	1.7
Flint	0.0	3.2	0.0	0.0	68.6	6.1	7.2	1.4	2.9	1.0
Garden City	0.0	11.8	0.0	0.0	0.0	17.5	20.3	3.0	0.7	3.3
Grand Rapids	0.0	7.9	3.8	0.0	0.0	13.7	20.4	2.5	14.8	5.7
Holland	0.3	28.0	0.3	0.0	0.8	14.9	15.2	11.2	1.6	3.0
Inkster	0.0	20.1	0.0	0.0	0.0	15.0	10.5	2.7	12.1	1.3
Jackson	0.0	17.7	0.3	0.0	0.3	17.3	9.3	6.6	14.2	4.0
Kalamazoo	0.0	8.6	1.7	0.0	0.0	25.4	19.9	3.6	2.1	13.6
Kentwood	0.0	27.2	0.0	0.0	0.0	25.9	5.7	3.1	0.0	2.1
Lansing	0.0	7.6	1.9	0.0	0.0	13.3	18.7	5.8	7.2	4.7
Lincoln Park	0.0	8.7	0.0	0.0	0.0	21.0	15.2	4.7	11.3	1.3
Livonia	0.0	13.6	0.0	0.0	0.0	19.2	20.6	9.9	8.2	1.6
Madison Heights	0.0	16.7	0.0	0.0	0.0	14.6	14.5	3.5	3.9	0.4
Midland	0.0	18.7	0.2	0.0	0.0	9.9	17.0	10.5	6.1	1.7
Mount Pleasant	0.0	12.7	0.0	0.0	0.0	22.6	14.7	8.2	3.2	2.2
Muskegon	0.0	18.1	0.0	0.0	0.0	18.3	13.6	5.9	8.0	0.5
Novi	0.0	14.4	0.0	0.0	0.0	20.0	12.8	8.5	1.3	6.6

Table D. Cities — **City Government Finances, City Government Employment, and Climate**

City	City government finances, 2007 (cont.) Debt outstanding Total (mil dol)	Per capita[1] (dollars)	Debt issued during year	City government employment, 2010	Climate[2] Average daily temperature (degrees Fahrenheit) Mean January	July	Limits January[3]	July[4]	Annual precipitation (inches)	Heating degree days	Cooling degree days
	137	138	139	140	141	142	143	144	145	146	147
MASSACHUSETTS— Cont'd											
Beverly	70.3	1 794	0.0	NA	28.8	72.6	20.4	82.1	45.51	5 704	582
Boston	1 440.6	2 404	187.6	19 344	29.3	73.9	22.1	82.2	42.53	5 630	777
Braintree Town	NA	NA	NA	NA	NA	NA	NA	NA	NA	NA	NA
Brockton	248.6	2 671	37.0	3 178	27.9	72.1	17.8	83.2	48.25	6 008	529
Cambridge	280.1	2 763	67.9	5 848	29.3	73.9	22.1	82.2	42.53	5 630	777
Chelsea	72.7	1 902	3.2	NA	29.3	73.9	22.1	82.2	42.53	5 630	777
Chicopee	36.2	673	0.0	1 800	21.5	68.9	10.4	81.7	48.07	7 312	287
Everett	82.1	2 204	20.4	1 107	29.3	73.9	22.1	82.2	42.53	5 630	777
Fall River	253.4	2 788	38.0	2 468	28.5	74.2	20.0	83.1	50.77	5 734	740
Fitchburg	87.1	2 187	7.6	NA	24.2	71.9	15.2	81.0	49.13	6 576	548
Franklin Town	NA	NA	NA	NA	NA	NA	NA	NA	NA	NA	NA
Gloucester	122.5	4 040	34.9	NA	28.8	72.6	20.4	82.1	45.51	5 704	582
Haverhill	120.4	2 011	8.2	1 794	25.3	72.2	15.6	83.5	46.88	6 435	550
Holyoke	66.0	1 660	13.4	2 018	21.5	68.9	10.4	81.7	48.07	7 312	287
Lawrence	154.7	2 208	56.4	2 633	24.5	71.8	14.5	82.9	44.09	6 539	510
Leominster	36.9	897	0.0	NA	24.2	71.9	15.2	81.0	49.13	6 576	548
Lowell	219.0	2 115	47.1	2 550	23.6	72.4	14.1	84.5	43.14	6 575	532
Lynn	96.4	1 106	6.7	2 933	29.3	73.9	22.1	82.2	42.63	5 630	777
Malden	116.2	2 085	12.5	1 380	29.3	73.9	22.1	82.2	42.53	5 630	777
Marlborough	57.4	1 507	0.5	1 160	25.9	73.4	16.2	84.0	45.87	6 060	651
Medford	64.5	1 160	4.2	1 152	29.3	73.9	22.1	82.2	42.53	5 630	777
Melrose	50.4	1 883	4.6	NA	29.3	73.9	22.1	82.2	42.53	5 630	777
Methuen Town	74.5	1 693	1.1	1 106	24.5	71.8	14.5	82.9	44.09	6 539	510
New Bedford	259.8	2 828	16.9	2 911	28.5	74.2	20.0	83.1	50.77	5 734	740
Newton	76.9	923	17.2	2 962	25.9	73.4	16.2	84.0	45.87	6 060	651
Northampton	53.8	1 893	9.4	1 235	22.3	71.2	11.2	83.2	45.57	6 856	452
Peabody	56.2	1 093	9.0	1 458	28.8	72.6	20.4	82.1	45.51	5 704	582
Pittsfield	70.8	1 650	0.0	NA	19.9	67.6	11.2	77.5	48.71	7 689	222
Quincy	122.5	1 338	90.1	2 149	26.0	71.6	18.1	81.2	51.19	6 371	558
Revere	33.1	597	12.0	1 152	29.3	73.9	22.1	82.2	42.53	5 630	777
Salem	69.4	1 696	2.3	1 245	28.8	72.6	20.4	82.1	45.51	5 704	582
Somerville	83.3	1 120	37.1	1 701	29.3	73.9	22.1	82.2	42.53	5 630	777
Springfield	347.9	2 320	55.6	6 320	25.7	73.7	17.2	84.9	46.16	6 104	769
Taunton	79.5	1 425	8.8	1 597	27.4	72.2	17.8	83.0	48.34	6 012	558
Waltham	77.4	1 294	26.1	1 529	25.4	71.5	15.7	82.7	46.95	6 370	485
Watertown Town	40.3	1 240	3.5	NA	29.3	73.9	22.1	82.2	42.53	5 630	777
Westfield	83.6	2 083	0.1	1 534	21.5	68.9	10.4	81.7	48.07	7 312	287
West Springfield Town	NA	NA	NA	NA	NA	NA	NA	NA	NA	NA	NA
Weymouth Town	NA	NA	NA	NA	NA	NA	NA	NA	NA	NA	NA
Woburn	58.0	1 565	1.1	NA	25.5	71.5	15.7	82.5	48.31	6 401	472
Worcester	658.1	3 783	51.5	5 632	23.6	70.1	15.8	79.3	49.05	6 831	371
MICHIGAN	X	X	X	NA	X	X	X	X	X	X	X
Allen Park	40.2	1 499	0.0	158	24.5	73.5	17.8	83.4	32.89	6 422	736
Ann Arbor	158.4	1 377	7.5	865	23.4	72.6	16.6	83.0	35.35	6 503	691
Battle Creek	110.6	2 118	0.0	577	23.1	71.0	15.3	82.5	35.15	6 742	559
Bay City	105.9	3 113	2.6	349	21.0	71.5	13.8	81.5	31.25	7 106	545
Burton	13.8	454	0.0	107	21.3	70.6	13.3	82.0	31.61	7 005	555
Dearborn	206.0	2 308	43.7	1 389	24.7	73.7	16.1	85.7	33.58	6 224	788
Dearborn Heights	69.7	1 301	20.6	331	24.7	73.7	16.1	85.7	33.58	6 224	788
Detroit	7 711.2	8 410	1 553.8	12 916	24.7	73.7	16.1	85.7	33.58	6 224	788
East Lansing	81.6	1 764	13.6	407	21.6	70.3	13.9	82.1	31.53	7 098	558
Eastpointe	14.2	434	0.0	188	25.3	73.6	18.8	83.3	33.97	6 160	757
Farmington Hills	34.4	436	6.6	433	24.7	73.7	16.1	85.7	33.58	6 224	788
Flint	135.6	1 182	0.0	3 304	21.3	70.6	13.3	82.0	31.61	7 005	555
Garden City	68.2	2 474	0.0	148	24.7	73.7	16.1	85.7	33.58	6 224	788
Grand Rapids	541.6	2 797	33.5	1 760	22.4	71.4	15.6	82.3	37.13	6 896	613
Holland	55.7	1 638	0.0	476	24.4	71.4	17.6	82.5	36.25	6 589	611
Inkster	34.8	1 269	12.4	223	24.5	73.5	17.8	83.4	32.89	6 422	736
Jackson	51.9	1 526	0.0	337	22.2	71.3	14.7	82.7	30.67	6 873	570
Kalamazoo	395.6	5 446	11.8	777	24.3	73.2	17.0	84.2	37.41	6 235	773
Kentwood	19.7	417	0.0	214	22.4	71.4	15.6	82.3	37.13	6 896	613
Lansing	446.0	3 880	36.7	1 763	21.6	70.3	13.9	82.1	31.53	7 098	558
Lincoln Park	12.3	339	0.0	176	24.5	73.5	17.8	83.4	32.89	6 422	736
Livonia	67.2	715	13.5	726	24.7	73.7	16.1	85.7	33.58	6 224	788
Madison Heights	16.2	546	1.5	197	24.7	73.7	16.1	85.7	33.58	6 224	788
Midland	24.8	603	0.0	419	22.9	72.7	16.2	83.8	30.69	6 645	679
Mount Pleasant	15.8	595	0.0	149	20.7	70.6	13.5	82.2	31.57	7 329	492
Muskegon	46.5	1 180	9.4	273	23.5	69.9	17.1	80.0	32.88	6 943	487
Novi	76.7	1 417	0.0	316	22.1	71.0	14.3	81.7	29.28	6 989	550

1. Based on the population estimated as of July 1 of the year shown.   2. Represents normal values based on the 30-year period, 1971–2000.   3. Average daily minimum.   4. Average daily maximum.

Table D. Cities — **Land Area and Population**

STATE Place code	City	Land area,[1] 2010 (sq km)	Population, 2010			Race alone or in combination, not of Hispanic origin (percent), 2010					Percent Hispanic or Latino[2], 2010	Percent Foreign born, 2008–2010
			Total persons	Rank	Per square kilometer	White	Black	American Indian, Alaska Native	Asian	Hawaiian Pacific Islander		
		1	2	3	4	5	6	7	8	9	10	11
	MICHIGAN—Cont'd											
26 59920	Oak Park	13.4	29 319	1 406	2 191.3	39.0	59.1	1.0	2.2	0.1	1.4	9.1
26 65440	Pontiac	51.7	59 515	613	1 150.5	29.1	53.6	1.3	2.6	0.1	16.5	8.3
26 65560	Portage	83.5	46 292	853	554.7	87.6	6.1	1.0	4.7	0.1	3.1	5.1
26 65820	Port Huron	20.9	30 184	1 350	1 442.1	84.4	11.2	1.7	0.8	0.1	5.4	2.6
26 69035	Rochester Hills	85.0	70 995	479	835.2	81.5	5.0	0.5	11.4	0.0	3.1	16.4
26 69800	Roseville	25.5	47 299	838	1 858.5	84.0	13.0	1.3	2.0	0.1	2.0	4.9
26 70040	Royal Oak	30.5	57 236	646	1 875.4	90.6	4.9	0.7	3.0	0.1	2.3	7.2
26 70520	Saginaw	44.9	51 508	743	1 147.2	39.7	47.0	1.0	0.5	0.1	14.3	1.8
26 70760	St. Clair Shores	30.1	59 715	610	1 984.5	92.9	4.5	0.9	1.5	0.1	1.7	4.4
26 74900	Southfield	68.1	71 739	474	1 054.2	25.9	71.7	0.9	2.2	0.1	1.3	8.6
26 74960	Southgate	17.7	30 047	1 356	1 694.7	85.8	6.1	0.9	2.0	0.1	6.5	7.2
26 76460	Sterling Heights	94.6	129 699	194	1 371.8	85.7	5.6	0.6	7.9	0.2	1.9	24.0
26 79000	Taylor	61.1	63 131	562	1 032.9	76.7	16.9	1.3	2.0	0.1	5.1	4.3
26 80700	Troy	86.7	80 980	396	934.0	74.2	4.4	0.5	20.2	0.1	2.1	23.6
26 84000	Warren	89.1	134 056	189	1 505.4	79.2	14.5	1.1	5.4	0.1	2.1	9.7
26 86000	Westland	52.9	84 094	378	1 589.7	75.3	18.2	1.1	3.5	0.1	3.8	6.6
26 88900	Wyandotte	13.7	25 883	1 603	1 894.8	92.4	1.8	1.3	0.7	0.1	5.1	1.8
26 88940	Wyoming	63.8	72 125	470	1 130.3	70.5	8.1	1.1	3.2	0.1	19.4	9.7
27 00000	**MINNESOTA**	206 232.3	5 303 925	X	25.7	84.8	6.0	1.7	4.6	0.1	4.7	7.1
27 01486	Andover	87.7	30 598	1 325	348.7	93.6	2.2	0.8	2.9	0.1	2.0	5.2
27 01900	Apple Valley	43.7	49 084	785	1 124.0	83.6	6.7	0.7	6.2	0.2	4.9	9.2
27 06382	Blaine	87.7	57 186	648	652.4	84.5	4.5	1.2	8.7	0.1	3.2	8.7
27 06616	Bloomington	89.8	82 893	386	922.8	79.5	8.5	1.0	6.6	0.1	6.8	10.8
27 07948	Brooklyn Center	20.6	30 104	1 354	1 461.4	49.1	28.3	1.4	15.1	0.1	9.6	23.0
27 07966	Brooklyn Park	67.5	75 781	441	1 122.2	52.7	26.3	1.1	16.4	0.2	6.4	20.9
27 08794	Burnsville	64.5	60 306	601	935.0	76.4	11.4	1.0	5.9	0.2	7.9	12.1
27 13114	Coon Rapids	58.6	61 476	580	1 049.8	86.9	6.7	1.5	4.2	0.1	3.2	7.5
27 13456	Cottage Grove	87.1	34 589	1 166	397.2	85.4	4.7	1.0	5.9	0.1	4.8	5.1
27 17000	Duluth	175.6	86 265	360	491.3	92.1	3.4	3.8	2.0	0.1	1.5	3.0
27 17288	Eagan	80.6	64 206	550	796.7	81.4	6.6	0.8	8.8	0.1	4.5	11.1
27 18116	Eden Prairie	84.0	60 797	590	723.4	81.7	6.3	0.5	10.1	0.1	3.0	15.2
27 18188	Edina	40.0	47 941	818	1 197.9	88.1	3.5	0.5	7.0	0.1	2.3	10.1
27 22814	Fridley	26.3	27 208	1 516	1 033.3	75.3	13.1	2.1	5.7	0.1	7.3	11.6
27 31076	Inver Grove Heights	71.9	33 880	1 191	471.1	83.4	4.8	0.9	4.0	0.2	8.9	6.3
27 35180	Lakeville	93.4	55 954	672	599.2	89.2	3.4	0.7	4.9	0.1	3.5	5.6
27 39878	Mankato	46.4	39 309	1 007	847.5	89.7	4.9	0.7	3.4	0.1	2.9	5.9
27 40166	Maple Grove	84.5	61 567	579	728.4	86.6	5.0	0.6	7.0	0.1	2.5	9.7
27 40382	Maplewood	44.0	38 018	1 041	864.6	74.7	9.3	1.0	11.1	0.1	6.2	10.1
27 43000	Minneapolis	139.8	382 578	48	2 736.8	63.1	20.4	2.8	6.5	0.2	10.5	15.0
27 43252	Minnetonka	69.7	49 734	775	713.1	90.3	4.5	0.6	4.0	0.1	2.4	7.2
27 43864	Moorhead	51.3	38 065	1 040	742.2	90.2	2.7	2.3	2.6	0.1	4.1	4.2
27 47680	Oakdale	28.4	27 378	1 506	965.7	81.0	7.1	0.9	8.8	0.1	4.3	9.0
27 49300	Owatonna	37.6	25 599	1 619	680.1	87.7	4.4	0.4	1.2	0.0	7.3	4.7
27 51730	Plymouth	84.7	70 576	482	833.7	84.3	6.1	0.7	7.7	0.1	3.0	10.1
27 54214	Richfield	17.8	35 228	1 144	1 981.3	65.2	10.4	1.3	6.8	0.1	18.3	18.9
27 54880	Rochester	141.4	106 769	251	755.2	81.1	7.2	0.6	7.7	0.1	5.2	12.0
27 55852	Roseville	33.7	33 660	1 203	999.4	81.3	7.1	1.0	8.1	0.1	4.6	11.4
27 56896	St. Cloud	103.7	65 842	532	634.9	85.3	8.9	1.2	4.2	0.1	2.4	5.7
27 57220	St. Louis Park	27.6	45 250	870	1 642.5	83.5	8.7	1.0	4.7	0.2	4.3	10.0
27 58000	St. Paul	134.6	285 068	67	2 117.6	58.6	17.3	1.9	15.8	0.2	9.6	17.0
27 58738	Savage	40.5	26 911	1 537	664.6	82.8	5.2	0.9	9.2	0.4	3.4	11.7
27 59350	Shakopee	72.5	37 076	1 067	511.1	76.2	5.1	1.6	11.2	0.1	7.8	16.5
27 59998	Shoreview	27.9	25 043	1 662	897.3	87.9	2.9	0.7	8.1	0.1	2.2	7.4
27 71032	Winona	48.8	27 592	1 494	565.4	93.1	2.4	0.5	3.2	0.1	1.7	3.6
27 71428	Woodbury	90.0	61 961	577	688.8	81.1	6.4	0.6	10.1	0.1	3.8	9.7
28 00000	**MISSISSIPPI**	121 530.7	2 967 297	X	24.4	58.8	37.4	0.8	1.1	0.1	2.7	2.2
28 06220	Biloxi	99.0	44 054	893	445.1	66.6	20.4	1.0	5.3	0.4	8.7	7.4
28 14420	Clinton	108.3	25 216	1 647	232.8	60.1	34.4	0.5	4.3	0.1	1.5	5.2
28 29180	Greenville	69.7	34 400	1 173	493.8	20.3	78.1	0.3	0.8	0.0	0.9	2.1
28 29700	Gulfport	144.0	67 793	504	470.9	56.5	37.0	0.9	2.3	0.2	5.2	5.7
28 31020	Hattiesburg	138.3	45 989	859	332.6	41.3	53.6	0.5	1.1	0.1	4.3	3.2
28 33700	Horn Lake	41.5	26 066	1 595	628.4	57.7	33.7	0.7	1.3	0.1	8.0	5.2
28 36000	Jackson	287.6	173 514	138	603.3	18.5	79.7	0.4	0.5	0.1	1.6	1.7
28 46640	Meridian	139.2	41 148	962	295.6	35.5	61.8	0.4	1.1	0.1	1.7	2.4
28 54040	Olive Branch	95.1	33 484	1 210	352.3	71.1	23.6	0.4	1.6	0.1	4.2	3.5
28 55760	Pearl	61.1	25 092	1 657	410.5	69.3	23.6	0.6	1.1	0.3	6.4	3.8
28 69280	Southaven	106.8	48 982	791	458.5	70.6	22.8	0.6	2.1	0.1	5.0	3.5
28 74840	Tupelo	132.5	34 546	1 168	260.8	58.7	37.4	0.3	1.2	0.0	3.5	2.7

1. Dry land or land partially or temporarily covered by water.   2. May be of any race.

Table D. Cities — **Population**

City	Under 5 years (12)	5 to 17 years (13)	18 to 24 years (14)	25 to 34 years (15)	35 to 44 years (16)	45 to 54 years (17)	55 to 64 years (18)	65 to 74 years (19)	75 years and over (20)	Median age (21)	Percent female (22)	1990 (23)	2000 (24)	1990–2000 (25)	2000–2010 (26)
MICHIGAN—Cont'd															
Oak Park	6.3	18.5	9.7	12.2	13.5	14.0	12.8	6.4	6.5	37.5	54.9	30 468	29 793	-2.2	-1.6
Pontiac	8.5	18.8	11.2	13.8	14.4	13.6	10.5	5.2	4.1	33.4	50.9	71 136	66 337	-6.7	-10.3
Portage	6.7	18.1	7.9	13.4	13.4	14.6	12.3	7.0	6.6	38.1	52.1	41 042	44 897	9.4	3.1
Port Huron	7.9	17.7	9.8	13.7	12.6	13.8	11.4	6.2	6.9	35.8	52.2	33 694	32 338	-4.0	-6.7
Rochester Hills	5.7	18.0	7.6	10.8	13.8	16.4	14.0	7.2	6.5	40.9	51.6	61 766	68 825	11.4	3.2
Roseville	6.3	16.7	9.0	13.9	14.3	15.6	11.1	6.0	7.1	37.9	51.6	51 412	48 129	-6.4	-1.7
Royal Oak	5.8	10.9	7.5	21.4	14.5	14.6	12.2	5.9	7.1	37.8	51.0	65 410	60 062	-8.2	-4.7
Saginaw	8.2	20.2	10.5	13.0	12.0	13.8	11.3	5.3	5.6	33.5	52.9	69 512	61 799	-11.1	-16.7
St. Clair Shores	5.0	14.1	7.0	12.3	12.7	16.4	13.4	8.1	11.1	44.2	52.2	68 107	63 096	-7.4	-5.4
Southfield	4.8	15.7	8.6	11.7	13.1	14.4	14.8	8.1	8.8	42.0	55.3	75 727	78 296	3.4	-8.4
Southgate	4.9	15.4	9.1	12.9	13.3	15.2	12.9	7.8	8.5	40.8	52.2	30 771	30 136	-2.1	-0.3
Sterling Heights	5.5	16.2	8.7	12.5	13.4	15.3	13.2	8.3	6.9	40.4	51.5	117 810	124 471	5.7	4.2
Taylor	7.1	17.7	10.0	13.0	13.4	14.8	11.3	6.9	5.9	36.9	52.1	70 811	65 868	-7.0	-4.2
Troy	5.2	18.7	6.7	10.5	13.5	17.2	14.5	7.8	6.0	41.8	50.7	72 884	80 959	11.1	0.0
Warren	6.1	16.6	9.0	12.6	13.6	15.1	10.9	7.3	8.8	39.4	51.6	144 864	138 247	-4.6	-3.0
Westland	6.3	15.8	9.5	13.9	13.8	15.3	11.4	6.7	7.3	38.3	52.5	84 724	86 602	2.2	-2.9
Wyandotte	5.4	16.0	8.5	12.6	13.8	16.9	13.0	6.4	7.4	40.4	51.1	30 938	28 006	-9.5	-7.6
Wyoming	8.3	18.8	10.6	16.4	13.3	13.8	9.7	4.7	4.4	32.1	50.7	63 891	69 368	8.6	4.0
MINNESOTA	6.7	17.5	9.5	13.5	12.8	15.2	11.9	6.7	6.2	37.4	50.4	4 375 665	4 919 479	12.4	7.8
Andover	5.7	24.7	7.5	9.4	16.1	19.4	10.4	4.6	2.1	37.3	49.3	15 216	26 588	74.7	15.1
Apple Valley	6.5	18.9	7.4	13.4	14.1	17.0	13.1	6.0	3.6	37.9	51.5	34 598	45 527	31.6	7.8
Blaine	7.9	18.6	7.4	15.1	15.5	15.5	11.5	5.6	2.9	35.6	50.9	38 975	44 942	15.3	27.2
Bloomington	5.4	14.3	7.8	13.6	11.5	15.4	13.5	9.1	9.3	42.7	51.6	86 335	85 172	-1.3	-2.7
Brooklyn Center	8.9	18.7	10.2	15.8	12.2	12.7	9.4	5.5	6.7	32.6	51.3	28 887	29 172	1.0	3.2
Brooklyn Park	8.7	20.3	9.6	15.0	14.0	14.1	10.5	4.7	3.2	32.5	51.1	56 381	67 388	19.5	12.5
Burnsville	7.4	16.7	9.0	15.7	13.0	14.9	11.6	6.7	5.0	35.9	51.3	51 288	60 220	17.4	0.1
Coon Rapids	6.9	17.6	8.9	14.3	13.2	16.0	11.8	6.5	4.8	36.9	51.6	52 978	61 607	16.3	-0.2
Cottage Grove	7.3	21.6	7.8	13.3	15.7	15.4	10.6	5.1	3.2	35.0	50.1	22 935	30 582	33.3	13.1
Duluth	5.6	12.9	19.6	13.4	10.1	12.9	11.9	6.3	7.4	33.6	51.0	85 493	86 918	1.7	-0.8
Eagan	6.4	19.1	8.0	14.2	13.9	19.0	11.8	4.6	3.0	36.8	50.9	47 409	63 557	34.1	1.0
Eden Prairie	6.6	19.9	6.5	13.8	13.9	18.2	12.6	4.9	3.7	37.6	51.5	39 311	54 901	39.7	10.7
Edina	5.4	18.8	4.6	8.9	12.1	15.8	13.8	8.6	12.0	45.2	53.4	46 075	47 425	2.9	1.1
Fridley	7.2	16.3	8.7	15.1	12.8	14.3	11.4	7.9	6.3	37.1	50.5	28 335	27 449	-3.1	-0.9
Inver Grove Heights	6.4	18.1	8.4	13.0	13.3	16.9	12.1	5.9	5.9	38.4	52.0	22 477	29 751	32.4	13.9
Lakeville	7.4	24.4	6.7	11.7	17.0	17.9	9.1	4.0	1.8	34.8	49.9	24 854	43 128	73.5	29.7
Mankato	5.6	10.7	32.7	16.1	8.7	8.6	8.0	4.6	6.0	25.4	50.0	31 469	32 427	3.1	21.2
Maple Grove	7.1	19.8	6.4	13.1	15.6	17.9	12.7	4.8	2.5	37.6	51.2	38 736	50 365	30.0	22.2
Maplewood	6.4	16.5	9.0	13.3	11.8	15.6	12.1	6.9	8.3	39.3	52.0	30 954	34 947	12.9	8.8
Minneapolis	6.9	13.3	15.2	21.0	13.7	12.2	9.7	4.3	3.7	31.4	49.7	368 383	382 618	3.9	0.0
Minnetonka	4.9	15.9	5.9	11.9	11.3	17.0	16.4	8.2	8.5	45.0	52.5	48 370	51 301	6.1	-3.1
Moorhead	6.5	14.4	23.7	13.9	9.6	11.3	9.2	5.1	6.4	28.3	51.6	32 295	32 177	-0.4	18.3
Oakdale	6.2	17.9	9.5	13.2	12.8	17.3	11.9	6.1	5.1	37.9	52.1	18 377	26 653	45.0	2.7
Owatonna	7.8	19.1	7.4	13.1	13.2	14.3	11.3	6.5	7.3	37.2	51.2	19 386	22 434	15.7	14.1
Plymouth	6.0	18.0	6.9	13.6	13.5	16.9	13.2	7.0	5.1	39.5	51.6	50 889	65 894	29.5	7.1
Richfield	7.5	13.8	8.5	18.6	12.8	13.6	11.1	6.0	8.2	36.2	50.8	35 710	34 439	-3.6	2.3
Rochester	7.9	16.9	8.3	16.9	12.6	14.1	10.5	6.3	6.4	35.0	51.6	70 729	85 806	21.3	24.4
Roseville	5.2	13.4	10.8	13.3	10.5	14.1	12.6	8.8	11.3	42.1	52.9	33 485	33 690	0.6	-0.1
St. Cloud	5.9	12.9	23.9	15.5	9.9	11.8	9.6	5.0	5.3	28.8	48.5	48 812	59 107	21.1	11.4
St. Louis Park	6.5	12.0	8.0	22.9	13.6	13.0	11.0	5.7	7.3	35.4	52.2	43 787	44 126	0.8	2.5
St. Paul	7.8	17.3	13.8	17.0	12.5	12.5	10.0	4.6	4.4	30.9	51.1	272 235	287 151	5.5	-0.7
Savage	7.7	23.8	6.1	13.0	17.8	17.6	8.4	3.8	1.7	34.6	49.9	9 906	21 115	113.2	27.4
Shakopee	10.0	20.2	6.6	18.8	18.4	12.2	7.0	3.8	3.0	32.2	51.2	11 739	20 568	75.2	80.3
Shoreview	5.0	16.6	7.1	10.3	11.5	18.5	16.6	8.1	6.3	44.6	52.1	24 587	25 924	5.4	-3.4
Winona	3.9	10.6	33.2	10.5	8.0	10.5	10.0	6.1	7.3	26.7	52.7	25 435	27 069	6.4	1.9
Woodbury	7.5	22.1	6.2	13.4	16.1	16.1	10.3	4.8	3.5	35.6	51.8	20 075	46 463	131.4	33.4
MISSISSIPPI	7.1	18.4	10.3	13.1	12.6	14.1	11.7	7.2	5.6	36.0	51.4	2 575 475	2 844 658	10.5	4.3
Biloxi	7.1	14.8	14.9	15.0	11.7	13.7	10.6	6.4	5.7	33.5	48.6	46 319	50 644	9.3	-13.0
Clinton	6.4	18.2	9.9	13.4	12.8	14.1	11.6	7.0	6.7	36.7	53.8	21 847	23 347	6.9	8.0
Greenville	7.8	21.1	9.4	12.3	11.3	13.6	12.3	6.7	5.6	34.5	54.3	45 226	41 633	-7.9	-17.4
Gulfport	8.0	17.0	10.7	15.3	12.6	13.9	11.0	6.5	5.1	34.3	51.0	64 045	71 127	11.1	-4.7
Hattiesburg	7.4	13.7	22.3	17.6	10.0	10.0	8.2	5.1	5.6	27.8	52.6	45 325	44 779	-1.2	2.7
Horn Lake	8.4	22.5	9.9	16.6	15.2	12.6	8.4	4.1	2.3	30.7	51.5	9 069	14 099	55.5	84.9
Jackson	7.8	19.6	12.8	14.8	11.7	13.1	10.3	5.4	4.6	31.2	53.5	202 062	184 256	-8.8	-5.8
Meridian	8.0	18.6	10.2	13.2	11.9	13.0	11.2	6.6	7.2	34.9	53.8	41 036	39 968	-2.6	3.0
Olive Branch	6.7	21.6	7.4	12.6	16.1	14.5	10.5	6.1	4.5	36.0	51.7	3 567	21 054	490.2	59.0
Pearl	7.9	18.4	9.5	15.8	12.8	13.4	10.3	7.1	4.8	33.9	52.5	19 588	21 961	12.1	14.3
Southaven	7.7	20.5	8.6	15.2	15.0	13.0	9.6	6.2	4.2	33.7	51.9	18 705	28 977	54.9	69.0
Tupelo	7.5	19.6	8.1	13.9	12.7	13.2	10.7	7.1	7.1	35.7	53.1	30 685	34 211	11.5	1.0

Table D. Cities — Households, Group Quarters, Crime, and Education

City	Households, 2010				Persons in group quarters, 2010				Serious crimes known to police,[2] 2010				Educational attainment, 2008–2010		
			Percent			Institutional			Total		Rate[3]			Attainment[4] (percent)	
	Number	Persons per household	Female family householder[1]	One-person	Total	Total	Persons in nursing facilities	Non-institutional	Number	Rate[3]	Violent	Property	Population age 25 and older	High school graduate or less	Bachelor's degree or more
	27	28	29	30	31	32	33	34	35	36	37	38	39	40	41
MICHIGAN—Cont'd															
Oak Park	11 719	2.50	23.9	30.9	58	0	0	58	1 145	3 905	614	3 291	18 979	32.6	26.8
Pontiac	22 220	2.56	27.0	33.1	2 563	1 586	102	977	3 199	5 375	1 897	3 478	36 771	55.9	13.2
Portage	19 199	2.40	10.9	29.1	156	111	111	45	1 917	4 141	220	3 921	30 761	26.2	39.6
Port Huron	12 177	2.42	19.9	33.0	761	235	228	526	1 386	4 592	656	3 936	19 898	54.4	12.8
Rochester Hills	27 578	2.53	8.1	25.7	1 181	507	507	674	NA	NA	NA	NA	49 340	22.4	49.3
Roseville	19 553	2.41	17.4	31.7	245	148	148	97	2 134	4 512	442	4 070	32 794	53.7	10.5
Royal Oak	28 063	2.03	8.1	41.4	404	249	225	155	973	1 700	154	1 546	44 254	25.0	48.5
Saginaw	19 799	2.52	28.7	32.1	1 693	876	346	817	3 421	6 642	2 355	4 287	32 750	58.1	10.5
St. Clair Shores	26 585	2.24	11.9	35.1	277	248	248	29	1 239	2 075	255	1 820	44 284	40.5	23.9
Southfield	31 778	2.22	19.4	37.9	1 189	453	451	736	3 170	4 419	555	3 864	51 258	26.8	37.9
Southgate	13 062	2.29	12.3	33.9	117	88	88	29	1 202	4 000	223	3 777	20 913	50.2	16.7
Sterling Heights	49 451	2.61	10.5	26.5	772	566	554	206	2 616	2 017	153	1 864	90 084	43.6	26.1
Taylor	24 370	2.56	20.4	25.5	673	540	512	133	2 851	4 516	553	3 963	41 253	59.1	9.1
Troy	30 703	2.63	7.3	23.4	310	117	117	193	1 790	2 210	74	2 136	54 873	21.1	57.2
Warren	53 442	2.49	15.9	30.4	1 248	945	945	303	4 472	3 336	574	2 762	91 732	53.0	14.9
Westland	35 886	2.31	16.4	34.3	1 034	779	548	255	2 719	3 233	435	2 798	57 705	51.1	17.3
Wyandotte	10 991	2.35	13.2	33.0	88	0	0	88	710	2 743	182	2 562	18 132	52.9	13.9
Wyoming	26 970	2.66	14.4	25.6	358	149	149	209	1 817	2 519	320	2 199	44 669	48.4	18.5
MINNESOTA	2 087 227	2.48	9.5	28.0	135 395	56 308	32 989	79 087	148 946	2 808	236	2 572	3 492 345	36.1	31.6
Andover	9 811	3.11	7.1	10.6	39	0	0	39	NA	NA	NA	NA	18 744	31.3	29.4
Apple Valley	18 875	2.58	10.2	23.6	316	198	189	118	1 562	3 182	104	3 078	32 300	24.8	45.7
Blaine	21 077	2.71	10.8	20.7	147	71	31	76	2 004	3 504	89	3 415	36 630	31.9	31.1
Bloomington	35 905	2.28	9.7	32.2	991	489	481	502	3 293	3 973	142	3 830	58 758	30.7	38.0
Brooklyn Center	10 756	2.78	18.1	27.7	182	93	86	89	1 510	5 016	488	4 528	18 335	48.9	18.7
Brooklyn Park	26 229	2.88	15.0	22.3	209	17	8	192	3 127	4 126	354	3 773	45 211	36.0	29.9
Burnsville	24 283	2.47	11.5	27.6	443	294	287	149	1 446	2 398	98	2 300	40 498	28.8	35.2
Coon Rapids	23 532	2.60	13.0	23.8	359	205	201	154	2 844	4 626	220	4 407	40 917	38.3	23.5
Cottage Grove	11 719	2.95	9.3	14.9	64	13	7	51	587	1 697	61	1 636	21 138	30.6	32.1
Duluth	35 705	2.23	11.2	35.1	6 640	1 416	924	5 224	4 331	5 021	349	4 672	51 877	34.2	32.1
Eagan	25 249	2.54	9.0	25.9	197	61	61	136	1 661	2 587	56	2 531	42 046	20.8	49.2
Eden Prairie	23 930	2.53	8.0	25.1	208	127	112	81	1 056	1 737	59	1 678	38 866	14.2	61.3
Edina	20 672	2.31	6.4	33.1	190	112	100	78	921	1 921	46	1 875	33 728	14.7	63.9
Fridley	11 110	2.44	14.1	28.8	131	48	48	83	1 420	5 219	334	4 885	18 343	39.7	26.9
Inver Grove Heights	13 476	2.50	11.4	26.2	193	154	140	39	661	1 951	83	1 868	22 321	33.0	31.4
Lakeville	18 683	2.99	9.2	14.0	46	14	6	32	850	1 519	36	1 483	34 353	24.3	43.6
Mankato	14 851	2.35	9.0	30.9	4 347	324	239	4 023	1 615	4 108	224	3 885	20 263	29.3	34.2
Maple Grove	22 867	2.69	8.3	19.3	50	4	4	46	1 284	2 086	70	2 016	39 874	19.2	49.0
Maplewood	14 882	2.48	12.1	29.1	1 131	800	362	331	2 396	6 302	208	6 094	25 214	38.0	31.2
Minneapolis	163 540	2.23	11.7	40.3	18 066	3 896	2 814	14 170	22 363	5 845	1 062	4 783	250 470	31.0	43.6
Minnetonka	21 901	2.25	7.3	31.1	380	292	209	88	1 010	2 031	54	1 977	36 221	18.8	53.7
Moorhead	14 304	2.41	10.6	29.2	3 650	344	263	3 306	1 003	2 635	171	2 464	21 294	36.6	33.3
Oakdale	10 948	2.48	12.7	28.4	177	7	2	170	1 181	4 314	219	4 095	17 995	35.2	26.4
Owatonna	10 068	2.49	10.0	27.9	531	321	203	210	518	2 024	141	1 883	16 772	40.4	27.1
Plymouth	28 663	2.42	8.5	26.4	1 128	730	229	398	1 283	1 818	81	1 737	48 026	17.7	55.0
Richfield	14 818	2.35	10.8	34.3	347	112	110	235	960	2 725	247	2 478	24 413	35.3	33.2
Rochester	43 025	2.42	9.5	30.1	2 615	1 760	646	855	2 664	2 495	220	2 275	70 394	26.6	42.7
Roseville	14 623	2.20	8.4	35.3	1 426	342	292	1 084	1 527	4 537	134	4 403	23 849	28.1	44.5
St. Cloud	25 439	2.37	10.4	30.8	5 615	1 690	448	3 925	2 780	4 222	361	3 861	38 115	36.9	27.5
St. Louis Park	21 743	2.05	9.1	40.1	755	633	630	122	1 529	3 379	124	3 255	32 702	19.4	53.2
St. Paul	111 001	2.47	14.8	35.8	11 438	2 351	1 608	9 087	13 868	4 858	740	4 118	173 740	37.8	36.9
Savage	9 116	2.95	8.2	14.8	6	4	0	2	727	2 701	152	2 549	16 614	23.8	43.7
Shakopee	12 772	2.83	10.5	20.4	884	843	167	41	1 119	3 018	245	2 773	22 849	34.8	34.5
Shoreview	10 402	2.39	7.9	27.3	204	9	0	195	311	1 242	48	1 194	17 404	20.1	52.4
Winona	10 449	2.24	8.5	35.6	4 223	376	324	3 847	520	1 885	112	1 772	15 227	40.0	28.5
Woodbury	22 594	2.73	8.7	20.4	286	161	161	125	1 344	2 169	60	2 109	38 692	17.3	56.3
MISSISSIPPI	1 115 768	2.58	18.5	26.3	91 964	55 135	16 496	36 829	96 577	3 255	270	2 985	1 890 674	50.0	19.6
Biloxi	17 104	2.40	16.2	31.2	3 065	209	158	2 856	2 727	6 190	479	5 711	28 350	37.8	23.7
Clinton	9 766	2.54	15.7	25.4	397	265	265	132	609	2 415	127	2 288	15 581	25.6	45.3
Greenville	12 678	2.68	30.9	27.1	432	370	254	62	2 248	6 535	250	6 285	21 135	52.6	18.3
Gulfport	26 307	2.50	21.0	28.3	1 984	1 222	278	762	3 891	5 740	237	5 502	42 895	46.3	19.1
Hattiesburg	18 501	2.30	21.0	35.7	3 529	832	468	2 697	2 432	5 288	250	5 038	25 605	39.7	30.5
Horn Lake	9 052	2.87	21.3	20.9	56	56	56	0	680	2 609	96	2 513	15 293	51.3	13.1
Jackson	64 523	2.60	29.1	30.2	6 035	1 419	998	4 616	14 968	8 626	990	7 636	103 615	43.7	26.7
Meridian	16 509	2.39	25.6	34.2	1 678	1 161	268	517	2 600	6 319	491	5 828	26 309	46.3	20.9
Olive Branch	12 078	2.77	14.4	19.1	0	0	0	0	1 097	3 276	224	3 052	21 901	39.4	27.1
Pearl	9 792	2.56	18.9	26.5	70	57	57	13	669	2 666	271	2 395	16 822	49.8	16.1
Southaven	17 969	2.71	16.6	21.9	264	264	264	0	2 006	4 095	267	3 828	30 505	42.7	20.1
Tupelo	13 602	2.47	19.2	30.1	895	834	471	61	1 810	5 239	234	5 005	22 298	38.4	28.2

1. No spouse present.   2. Data for serious crimes have not been adjusted for underreporting. This may affect comparability between geographic areas and over time.   3. Per 100,000 population estimated by the FBI.   4. Persons 25 years old and over.

Table D. Cities — Income, Poverty, and Housing

City	Money income, 2008–2010					Housing units, 2010			Occupied Housing units 2008–2010				
	Households				Families with income below poverty (percent)				Owner-occupied			Median owner costs as a percent of income	
	Per capita income[1] (dollars)	Median income	Percent with income of $200,000 or more	Percent with income of less than $25,000		Total	Percent change, 2000–2010	Vacant units for sale or rent[2]	Total	Percent	Median value[3] (dollars)	With a mortgage[4]	Without a mortgage[5]
	42	43	44	45	46	47	48	49	50	51	52	53	54
MICHIGAN—Cont'd													
Oak Park	20 850	42 134	0.5	29.3	17.6	12 782	12.4	1 063	11 412	59.0	113 500	27.9	16.9
Pontiac	15 843	29 068	0.1	44.4	29.5	27 084	2.8	4 864	23 222	51.9	82 100	28.0	18.7
Portage	30 299	57 246	4.2	19.6	6.8	20 559	8.9	1 360	18 803	69.9	156 300	21.9	12.4
Port Huron	17 974	32 896	1.0	40.6	23.4	13 871	-0.9	1 694	12 549	57.3	94 900	26.8	15.0
Rochester Hills	36 980	73 967	8.0	16.0	4.6	29 494	8.1	1 916	27 744	76.2	221 600	23.6	12.4
Roseville	20 744	39 957	0.7	29.7	10.2	21 260	3.6	1 707	20 061	72.9	93 100	27.6	16.2
Royal Oak	35 719	59 854	3.3	17.5	4.0	30 207	0.9	2 144	27 615	67.4	164 700	22.8	13.4
Saginaw	14 242	26 771	0.6	47.1	31.6	23 574	-8.1	3 775	19 581	61.8	61 100	27.5	14.7
St. Clair Shores	28 513	51 243	1.8	22.6	6.5	28 467	0.9	1 882	26 929	82.7	122 000	23.8	14.8
Southfield	27 739	50 664	2.2	22.2	9.2	35 986	0.8	4 208	31 383	52.9	146 200	26.7	17.8
Southgate	23 375	43 958	0.9	26.7	5.8	13 933	4.3	871	12 809	66.9	115 000	26.3	17.1
Sterling Heights	25 603	54 569	1.5	19.8	9.1	52 190	9.8	2 739	49 021	77.7	162 200	24.8	13.6
Taylor	19 252	41 010	0.8	28.7	17.2	26 422	2.0	2 052	23 187	65.2	99 500	24.5	14.2
Troy	40 029	82 635	9.8	14.7	4.3	32 907	6.6	2 204	30 519	75.7	233 400	22.5	12.2
Warren	20 885	43 580	0.6	27.4	12.9	57 938	1.2	4 496	53 574	75.3	112 700	25.5	15.2
Westland	22 642	43 293	0.6	27.1	12.6	39 201	3.0	3 315	33 957	63.0	115 300	25.3	14.1
Wyandotte	24 798	46 933	2.3	23.3	9.0	12 081	-1.8	1 090	10 801	74.4	103 300	24.2	15.8
Wyoming	19 720	41 711	0.8	28.0	15.3	28 983	5.4	2 013	27 169	67.8	113 900	25.0	12.6
MINNESOTA	29 280	56 456	3.9	20.4	7.0	2 347 201	13.6	259 974	2 093 087	73.6	202 700	24.4	12.0
Andover	31 932	84 429	4.9	6.9	2.6	10 091	23.0	280	9 686	92.5	250 800	25.3	10.0
Apple Valley	35 450	78 028	5.7	12.7	4.0	19 600	18.5	725	18 960	82.8	236 300	23.3	10.9
Blaine	30 147	71 276	3.7	11.7	3.3	21 921	35.6	844	20 327	88.9	212 200	25.2	13.7
Bloomington	34 216	57 823	4.7	15.9	4.7	37 641	1.5	1 736	35 801	70.6	236 500	25.2	11.0
Brooklyn Center	21 412	48 325	0.9	21.3	15.5	11 640	0.4	884	10 478	64.6	165 500	27.3	13.1
Brooklyn Park	24 512	57 388	2.4	17.3	9.3	27 841	12.1	1 612	25 637	72.4	214 900	26.3	12.2
Burnsville	31 614	64 423	3.2	14.7	4.7	25 759	6.2	1 476	24 604	67.4	232 900	23.7	11.4
Coon Rapids	28 077	60 876	2.2	17.0	6.1	24 462	7.3	930	23 492	77.2	194 000	25.6	12.0
Cottage Grove	30 132	80 538	3.4	10.0	4.3	12 102	20.8	383	11 460	89.5	227 400	24.2	10.4
Duluth	23 021	38 457	1.7	32.5	11.7	38 208	3.3	2 503	36 367	58.4	149 900	22.3	12.3
Eagan	37 621	75 599	7.6	10.1	3.2	26 414	8.3	1 165	25 224	73.7	254 600	22.9	10.0
Eden Prairie	47 578	86 590	14.7	9.4	5.0	25 075	19.3	1 145	23 189	72.8	321 100	22.5	10.0
Edina	55 009	81 417	16.1	14.3	1.8	22 560	4.2	1 888	20 376	72.1	399 300	23.1	12.7
Fridley	26 040	51 259	1.3	18.3	6.8	11 760	2.2	650	11 504	65.6	203 400	24.9	12.3
Inver Grove Heights	34 063	65 253	4.7	11.5	2.0	14 062	22.8	586	13 438	73.2	233 200	26.0	10.8
Lakeville	35 734	90 142	8.5	7.6	2.8	19 458	41.0	773	18 544	89.7	266 900	23.3	11.8
Mankato	19 960	38 740	1.0	33.9	10.2	15 784	24.0	933	14 702	53.5	158 300	24.1	12.1
Maple Grove	40 444	91 139	8.8	6.1	1.7	23 626	33.2	759	22 437	89.1	256 500	22.1	10.0
Maplewood	27 440	51 557	2.1	19.8	8.5	15 561	11.1	679	14 561	71.8	217 600	26.1	13.8
Minneapolis	29 233	46 232	3.9	29.3	15.8	178 287	5.7	14 747	166 451	50.0	226 500	26.3	14.0
Minnetonka	47 439	79 082	11.5	11.4	2.3	23 294	4.8	1 393	21 644	74.8	308 900	22.6	11.5
Moorhead	21 736	44 683	1.0	29.3	7.8	15 274	25.5	970	14 237	61.3	153 500	22.7	12.0
Oakdale	30 042	66 269	3.4	14.3	4.5	11 388	9.5	440	10 613	79.6	209 700	25.0	10.0
Owatonna	25 293	53 237	2.0	21.0	6.3	10 724	20.0	656	9 998	73.3	157 800	23.7	11.3
Plymouth	47 195	85 083	13.2	11.6	3.2	29 982	18.7	1 319	28 253	73.7	313 100	21.9	10.0
Richfield	26 668	48 736	1.3	24.2	7.8	15 735	2.5	917	14 957	63.9	215 100	25.6	14.0
Rochester	31 798	61 018	5.1	18.1	5.5	45 683	29.7	2 658	42 330	72.5	168 000	22.1	10.0
Roseville	33 074	56 858	3.7	17.8	3.4	15 490	3.8	867	14 629	65.6	233 900	24.0	12.0
St. Cloud	21 550	37 630	2.0	32.5	13.8	27 338	17.8	1 899	26 056	52.8	158 200	24.9	11.3
St. Louis Park	37 945	60 795	4.9	16.2	5.5	23 285	10.2	1 542	21 556	60.2	239 900	24.5	13.8
St. Paul	25 047	44 265	3.3	28.7	17.4	120 795	4.4	9 794	110 906	53.0	199 400	24.7	12.0
Savage	33 528	86 728	6.9	4.5	1.6	9 429	34.5	313	8 865	87.0	272 800	25.2	10.0
Shakopee	29 949	75 509	2.9	11.7	3.6	13 339	71.2	567	12 649	79.0	238 400	24.4	11.0
Shoreview	42 438	80 481	8.7	9.7	0.5	10 826	5.2	424	10 452	82.1	265 000	22.2	11.4
Winona	18 608	34 342	0.7	40.8	11.6	10 989	3.1	540	10 752	62.6	146 000	24.4	10.8
Woodbury	40 169	89 334	9.9	7.9	2.7	23 568	34.4	974	22 051	83.7	281 700	23.3	10.5
MISSISSIPPI	19 760	37 696	1.8	34.8	17.2	1 274 719	9.7	158 951	1 085 467	70.2	99 800	23.1	12.1
Biloxi	25 818	46 550	2.9	26.8	12.1	21 278	-3.9	4 174	17 425	55.1	160 400	22.3	10.0
Clinton	25 656	58 423	2.9	19.9	4.4	10 359	16.2	593	9 049	75.1	155 000	21.5	10.0
Greenville	15 197	25 547	1.1	49.3	31.1	14 561	-10.5	1 883	12 611	51.9	77 300	24.4	13.2
Gulfport	20 752	39 035	1.8	30.4	16.6	31 602	6.8	5 295	25 376	57.3	131 600	25.9	13.0
Hattiesburg	18 270	26 516	1.8	46.5	27.5	21 381	11.5	2 880	18 502	37.6	124 400	27.3	11.7
Horn Lake	17 695	45 500	0.3	24.5	13.3	9 705	90.4	653	8 794	68.9	100 800	23.1	10.7
Jackson	18 454	33 465	2.5	38.5	22.2	74 537	-1.5	10 014	62 202	52.6	93 000	23.8	12.3
Meridian	20 100	31 107	2.2	42.3	25.1	18 591	3.6	2 082	16 476	53.3	82 900	23.7	12.6
Olive Branch	27 762	68 319	2.9	13.0	4.1	12 942	60.6	864	12 292	81.7	168 000	23.4	10.2
Pearl	20 104	40 239	0.3	29.8	11.9	10 396	14.6	604	10 162	63.2	106 600	21.6	10.0
Southaven	23 031	53 502	0.9	19.0	8.8	19 101	66.3	1 132	18 012	67.3	138 400	23.0	10.5
Tupelo	23 458	37 679	3.9	33.8	20.0	15 371	5.0	1 769	13 458	63.0	120 700	24.8	11.9

1. Based on population estimated by the American Community Survey.   2. Includes units rented or sold but not occupied.   3. Specified owner-occupied units; $1,000,000 represents $1,000,000 or more.   4. 50.0 represents 50 percent or more.   5. 10.0 represents 10 percent or less.

City	Occupied housing units, 2008–2010 (cont.)				Migration, 2008–2010		Civilian labor force, 2010				Civilian employment[4], 2008–2010			
									Unemployment			Percent		
	Percent renter occupied	Median gross rent[1]	Median rent as a percent of income[2]	Percent with no vehicle available	Percent who lived in the same house one year ago	Percent who lived outside this city one year ago	Total	Percent change, 2009–2010	Total	Rate[3]	Population age 16 and older	In labor force	Full-year full-time worker	Households with no workers (percent)
	55	56	57	58	59	60	61	62	63	64	65	66	67	68
MICHIGAN—Cont'd														
Oak Park	41.0	950	34.0	9.8	82.7	15.1	14 081	-1.3	2 572	18.3	22 899	63.4	34.8	30.4
Pontiac	48.1	726	40.9	16.1	74.9	8.9	32 010	-1.9	9 453	29.5	45 437	62.0	29.9	39.2
Portage	30.1	686	28.9	4.2	83.3	10.5	24 924	-3.5	1 955	7.8	35 984	70.3	42.6	24.4
Port Huron	42.7	640	34.5	14.4	78.3	8.6	15 485	-6.9	3 323	21.5	23 529	62.9	32.9	37.8
Rochester Hills	23.8	990	29.0	4.2	86.9	9.5	33 008	-0.8	2 439	7.4	56 393	68.2	41.6	24.6
Roseville	27.1	763	35.6	8.9	88.6	7.4	25 903	-2.0	4 985	19.2	38 414	65.6	34.8	34.1
Royal Oak	32.6	804	24.1	5.2	84.4	10.6	32 808	-0.8	2 572	7.8	49 248	72.7	47.9	22.4
Saginaw	38.2	626	45.1	16.6	79.9	9.2	24 811	-3.6	4 923	19.8	39 642	54.2	25.2	43.1
St. Clair Shores	17.3	812	31.2	5.4	92.2	5.0	31 600	-1.4	4 665	14.8	49 787	65.4	38.5	31.6
Southfield	47.1	932	32.6	8.7	78.3	14.0	39 947	-1.2	6 247	15.6	59 011	63.0	38.2	31.9
Southgate	33.1	747	29.0	8.3	84.3	11.9	13 579	-2.1	1 209	8.9	24 534	63.6	38.5	32.8
Sterling Heights	22.3	808	29.1	5.7	89.9	5.5	65 105	-0.8	7 086	10.9	104 702	64.6	37.9	27.6
Taylor	34.8	742	33.0	6.9	81.9	12.8	28 261	-2.4	3 250	11.5	49 371	61.4	30.5	33.3
Troy	24.3	1 003	24.5	4.8	87.9	7.9	40 217	-1.0	4 376	10.9	63 177	67.3	42.1	23.5
Warren	24.7	772	31.6	7.7	87.0	7.6	69 037	-1.6	11 181	16.2	107 155	62.4	34.8	33.9
Westland	37.0	730	32.6	9.3	81.4	12.3	40 425	-2.1	3 332	8.2	68 856	64.1	36.8	32.1
Wyandotte	25.6	656	26.4	8.2	88.6	9.7	12 971	-2.3	1 372	10.6	21 190	63.5	40.1	33.3
Wyoming	32.2	691	31.5	7.3	80.2	12.5	38 900	-3.3	4 176	10.7	54 817	72.6	39.1	23.1
MINNESOTA	26.4	762	30.0	7.0	85.6	9.4	2 958 686	0.3	217 099	7.3	4 148 979	71.0	44.0	23.3
Andover	7.5	1 231	37.1	2.9	94.0	5.5	17 073	-2.1	1 243	7.3	22 384	77.5	48.0	14.2
Apple Valley	17.2	1 040	32.4	3.4	88.8	7.9	29 242	-4.1	2 014	6.9	37 678	76.9	49.8	15.7
Blaine	11.1	1 026	32.6	3.1	86.5	10.3	33 752	0.4	2 458	7.3	42 801	76.7	50.1	16.5
Bloomington	29.4	887	30.4	6.9	87.1	9.3	47 492	-1.0	3 365	7.1	67 478	69.3	43.7	26.2
Brooklyn Center	35.4	857	36.5	10.5	83.6	13.4	16 046	5.9	1 402	8.7	22 343	71.3	44.5	22.9
Brooklyn Park	27.6	781	36.0	8.3	83.1	12.3	43 977	2.9	3 400	7.7	54 086	76.7	49.1	15.3
Burnsville	32.6	906	29.0	5.7	81.9	10.4	36 591	-0.9	2 533	6.9	48 187	76.4	47.8	19.1
Coon Rapids	22.8	890	32.0	5.4	85.1	10.3	35 591	-3.6	2 773	7.8	49 071	75.7	46.8	19.7
Cottage Grove	10.5	1 095	34.4	1.4	91.6	5.1	19 391	-0.3	1 326	6.8	25 359	78.5	49.4	13.8
Duluth	41.6	661	34.2	11.9	73.7	10.1	46 408	0.8	3 549	7.6	72 319	64.9	34.2	28.9
Eagan	26.3	920	26.6	4.4	84.3	10.8	38 383	-2.0	2 455	6.4	49 188	79.6	55.1	14.8
Eden Prairie	27.2	1 017	25.4	4.4	85.4	10.3	34 557	-3.3	2 097	6.1	45 921	74.9	48.8	13.5
Edina	27.9	1 096	24.7	5.2	87.2	9.6	23 303	2.0	1 342	5.8	37 605	65.2	42.4	30.1
Fridley	34.4	824	27.9	4.6	81.4	13.0	15 847	1.7	1 224	7.7	21 427	71.4	45.7	24.6
Inver Grove Heights	26.8	975	27.0	3.1	84.7	10.8	20 100	-0.9	1 471	7.3	26 778	73.4	49.3	20.0
Lakeville	10.3	1 157	32.7	1.1	91.1	7.4	30 877	0.2	2 067	6.7	39 632	79.6	54.0	12.2
Mankato	46.5	683	36.5	8.3	70.4	13.9	24 180	3.3	1 641	6.8	33 345	72.5	33.9	24.0
Maple Grove	10.9	1 192	25.0	1.6	90.9	6.6	37 091	-2.6	2 269	6.1	45 520	79.3	56.0	11.0
Maplewood	28.2	823	33.8	9.9	88.3	10.0	20 507	2.3	1 552	7.6	29 913	63.2	39.5	28.2
Minneapolis	50.0	784	31.3	18.8	74.0	11.0	212 007	-2.7	14 919	7.0	313 858	73.4	42.2	23.2
Minnetonka	25.2	984	27.2	4.3	87.4	10.9	28 805	-3.2	1 788	6.2	40 620	71.5	46.1	21.3
Moorhead	38.7	662	33.3	7.3	76.5	13.2	21 612	-1.0	908	4.2	30 593	71.7	39.0	23.3
Oakdale	20.4	849	30.3	4.3	87.7	10.0	15 496	-1.3	1 180	7.6	21 906	74.5	47.5	21.8
Owatonna	26.7	633	28.2	8.6	83.6	8.3	14 887	NA	1 201	8.1	19 637	72.9	47.6	25.5
Plymouth	26.3	1 045	28.1	2.5	85.9	11.6	40 393	-4.0	2 490	6.2	55 515	73.2	49.8	17.3
Richfield	36.1	747	31.2	10.1	82.4	11.4	20 208	4.2	1 345	6.7	28 588	73.4	43.4	26.6
Rochester	27.5	748	28.8	6.2	84.5	6.9	59 063	2.7	3 542	6.0	81 929	71.5	48.2	20.4
Roseville	34.4	834	27.7	9.7	85.5	11.4	18 337	-0.2	1 193	6.5	28 477	63.7	40.2	30.2
St. Cloud	47.2	663	32.7	9.6	69.5	16.5	38 236	-4.0	2 890	7.6	55 808	67.3	33.2	25.5
St. Louis Park	39.8	896	26.6	7.1	78.4	16.8	27 609	-3.5	1 688	6.1	37 430	75.7	51.1	18.3
St. Paul	47.0	742	32.4	15.4	79.0	9.1	144 710	-0.7	11 202	7.7	221 303	69.9	40.2	24.9
Savage	13.0	1 189	28.3	2.5	91.3	8.0	15 289	-5.1	1 063	7.0	19 369	82.6	52.6	9.2
Shakopee	21.0	918	28.1	4.4	88.1	7.5	21 592	6.8	1 450	6.7	26 237	80.5	57.5	12.0
Shoreview	17.9	880	31.5	3.8	88.6	9.3	14 625	-2.6	914	6.2	20 212	73.0	45.7	24.1
Winona	37.4	603	37.9	9.5	76.5	13.7	15 713	1.6	1 182	7.5	24 331	65.7	30.7	27.2
Woodbury	16.3	1 209	26.3	1.9	90.6	6.8	34 466	7.0	2 005	5.8	44 352	76.6	53.4	14.9
MISSISSIPPI	29.8	657	32.0	7.1	85.1	10.4	1 317 216	1.7	138 445	10.5	2 288 593	59.6	39.1	30.4
Biloxi	44.9	829	29.5	5.7	79.3	14.1	19 343	-7.3	2 063	10.7	35 277	69.0	47.9	24.6
Clinton	24.9	823	31.8	4.0	85.3	8.7	13 672	-2.8	888	6.5	19 800	68.1	47.2	23.5
Greenville	48.1	569	41.2	15.9	80.2	8.2	14 816	4.4	2 272	15.3	25 449	58.6	33.1	36.8
Gulfport	42.7	845	34.4	6.6	73.6	14.7	31 336	-7.3	3 323	10.6	52 712	65.5	42.4	24.7
Hattiesburg	62.4	641	36.6	10.6	71.7	15.6	22 403	-9.3	2 687	12.0	37 538	63.6	36.6	27.5
Horn Lake	31.1	864	31.1	3.9	83.4	11.6	12 556	NA	914	7.3	18 905	72.7	47.9	17.3
Jackson	47.4	737	36.1	10.2	79.8	5.9	80 646	2.0	8 253	10.2	130 495	62.5	41.9	28.3
Meridian	46.7	585	29.2	12.3	78.3	11.5	16 534	7.6	2 432	14.7	31 686	58.2	35.3	30.1
Olive Branch	18.3	971	25.5	1.5	87.5	8.9	16 630	3.3	1 337	8.0	25 375	73.4	50.8	17.3
Pearl	36.8	798	35.6	4.9	75.9	16.2	13 408	NA	947	7.1	19 733	64.1	48.0	24.4
Southaven	32.7	895	28.8	2.1	82.1	12.2	24 416	8.6	1 673	6.9	35 379	71.8	50.8	18.0
Tupelo	37.0	601	31.6	7.4	83.2	6.8	16 331	-1.3	1 926	11.8	26 318	62.3	42.8	24.4

1. $2,000 represents $2,000 or more.   2. 50.0 represents 50 percent or more.   3. Percent of civilian labor force.   4. Persons 16 years old and over.

City	Value of residential construction authorized by building permits, 2010			Wholesale trade,[1] 2007				Retail trade,[2] 2007			
	New construction ($1,000)	Number of housing units	Percent single family	Number of establish-ments	Number of employees	Sales (mil dol)	Annual payroll (mil dol)	Number of establish-ments	Number of employees	Sales (mil dol)	Annual payroll (mil dol)
	69	70	71	72	73	74	75	76	77	78	79
MICHIGAN—Cont'd											
Oak Park	336	3	100.0	62	634	281.9	34.0	131	1 030	221.3	26.1
Pontiac	3 578	37	100.0	54	1 202	788.0	83.6	196	1 566	377.1	35.4
Portage	8 980	43	76.7	49	560	215.6	33.5	318	6 241	1 136.8	109.3
Port Huron	0	0	0.0	18	189	140.1	8.9	130	1 457	237.5	26.3
Rochester Hills	31 729	85	100.0	79	946	450.6	56.5	255	5 071	1 183.2	123.0
Roseville	145	2	100.0	64	747	380.2	36.0	264	5 045	1 178.8	106.9
Royal Oak	23 332	338	23.7	52	549	794.4	34.6	239	2 884	632.5	69.1
Saginaw	75	1	100.0	41	765	241.9	26.1	164	1 340	233.3	25.9
St. Clair Shores	2 357	8	100.0	48	214	95.2	8.2	189	2 125	518.0	52.0
Southfield	2 438	11	100.0	193	3 194	3 250.9	198.4	434	6 216	2 165.7	167.2
Southgate	275	1	100.0	10	47	8.9	1.4	136	2 547	791.5	58.1
Sterling Heights	16 351	103	100.0	149	1 781	774.7	88.5	494	8 239	1 628.0	170.5
Taylor	137	1	100.0	91	1 198	1 205.7	59.4	319	5 453	1 189.1	110.7
Troy	10 261	57	100.0	317	4 196	2 727.4	237.4	601	12 596	2 615.6	298.1
Warren	1 700	20	100.0	191	3 524	1 900.1	170.6	489	6 337	1 517.6	150.6
Westland	1 219	14	100.0	55	547	171.7	22.3	349	5 681	1 119.9	108.0
Wyandotte	1 062	8	50.0	13	50	18.5	1.3	83	532	141.1	12.8
Wyoming	8 243	57	100.0	173	6 179	3 358.9	346.0	278	4 402	978.3	101.0
MINNESOTA	1 810 528	9 840	71.7	6 913	110 487	82 878.1	6 417.8	20 777	307 034	71 384.1	6 685.6
Andover	14 701	71	100.0	11	D	D	D	41	704	145.8	13.0
Apple Valley	17 886	94	52.1	33	170	106.5	8.0	136	3 726	839.3	77.4
Blaine	72 839	331	75.2	68	934	563.0	48.2	261	4 357	766.7	85.3
Bloomington	930	4	100.0	243	5 523	4 442.9	409.7	547	13 463	2 847.6	375.0
Brooklyn Center	474	1	100.0	26	303	99.2	10.0	94	2 331	672.9	60.7
Brooklyn Park	10 609	55	96.4	94	1 505	1 101.7	84.7	161	3 018	851.6	77.4
Burnsville	2 271	10	60.0	155	2 140	775.6	109.0	354	6 030	1 357.5	138.6
Coon Rapids	4 111	18	55.6	29	295	152.1	19.0	207	5 303	1 133.2	117.9
Cottage Grove	15 703	89	50.6	11	D	D	D	59	1 168	226.3	22.7
Duluth	9 689	74	41.9	82	947	590.9	40.3	476	7 090	1 294.7	136.6
Eagan	9 481	33	93.9	155	3 978	1 729.2	234.8	176	3 625	906.9	82.0
Eden Prairie	13 013	67	100.0	207	3 428	7 152.9	218.9	232	6 651	2 684.2	203.7
Edina	16 635	34	100.0	123	1 032	707.8	67.9	317	5 655	984.1	121.5
Fridley	684	3	100.0	74	D	D	D	91	2 346	598.6	60.4
Inver Grove Heights	4 262	12	100.0	20	D	D	D	68	1 467	413.7	35.3
Lakeville	39 217	145	100.0	52	594	255.1	26.4	110	2 048	536.9	45.1
Mankato	17 809	112	83.9	49	837	970.1	38.5	281	5 875	1 128.1	103.4
Maple Grove	80 995	304	94.4	94	1 501	1 119.7	121.0	238	5 145	886.6	94.5
Maplewood	3 483	21	100.0	34	314	175.2	15.2	247	5 272	1 130.3	111.5
Minneapolis	107 704	878	4.7	518	7 683	5 518.6	391.2	1 164	14 740	3 867.0	386.8
Minnetonka	30 952	171	12.9	152	2 435	2 873.4	167.9	324	7 218	1 581.0	153.1
Moorhead	24 713	163	100.0	30	349	261.5	17.0	127	2 153	478.1	42.0
Oakdale	9 995	70	44.3	36	310	159.2	17.1	79	1 513	358.8	37.1
Owatonna	3 728	18	100.0	18	288	176.3	15.1	123	2 340	437.7	43.9
Plymouth	41 554	133	100.0	222	5 164	3 515.5	309.1	210	4 234	1 903.3	133.8
Richfield	209	1	100.0	17	307	78.9	17.5	126	2 400	1 768.0	70.7
Rochester	63 097	342	58.5	78	853	607.7	39.7	503	9 700	1 932.1	204.6
Roseville	1 609	7	100.0	83	1 436	823.4	68.4	314	7 056	1 335.0	137.9
St. Cloud	6 171	42	100.0	77	2 835	1 125.7	133.3	370	7 350	1 481.0	144.5
St. Louis Park	1 354	6	100.0	134	2 016	1 337.4	115.0	178	3 976	1 086.9	106.5
St. Paul	4 199	22	81.8	296	5 321	3 129.2	290.8	752	10 077	1 794.1	209.9
Savage	15 871	85	100.0	36	802	732.9	47.7	74	1 082	274.1	24.6
Shakopee	40 688	167	100.0	36	519	421.2	30.7	121	2 226	544.4	49.3
Shoreview	1 768	9	100.0	29	2 287	912.6	140.0	52	1 073	193.6	19.3
Winona	6 171	62	6.5	39	341	231.0	13.7	140	2 560	461.2	48.2
Woodbury	98 048	519	53.4	40	270	119.9	12.1	224	4 677	922.4	85.0
MISSISSIPPI	715 297	5 259	84.2	2 556	32 382	23 003.6	1 276.0	12 452	141 426	33 751.4	2 910.9
Biloxi	14 478	63	100.0	38	408	160.6	12.7	227	2 532	573.4	52.8
Clinton	6 970	56	100.0	15	97	27.1	4.7	93	906	194.5	17.1
Greenville	246	3	100.0	39	363	555.9	20.9	217	2 295	418.6	42.1
Gulfport	53 102	461	56.2	86	961	604.2	48.8	409	6 087	1 641.2	144.9
Hattiesburg	4 114	28	100.0	72	824	419.9	29.6	496	7 567	2 701.3	159.4
Horn Lake	1 559	17	100.0	11	57	17.8	1.9	69	1 164	288.2	24.7
Jackson	19 356	130	32.3	257	3 995	1 931.9	179.3	788	10 919	2 660.1	255.5
Meridian	783	7	100.0	61	1 261	889.7	50.9	381	4 875	1 100.4	103.8
Olive Branch	10 777	97	100.0	47	846	615.7	37.8	115	1 885	565.8	46.6
Pearl	5 064	39	100.0	61	1 173	743.3	62.1	118	1 818	423.1	39.4
Southaven	11 999	118	100.0	28	1 100	986.0	36.3	208	4 015	1 005.8	88.9
Tupelo	7 991	48	100.0	118	1 446	690.0	52.0	410	5 709	1 212.0	117.6

1. Merchant wholesalers except manufacturers' sales branches and offices.   2. Establishments with payroll.

City	Real estate and rental and leasing, 2007				Professional, scientific, and technical services,[1] 2007				Manufacturing, 2007			
	Number of establishments	Number of employees	Receipts (mil dol)	Annual payroll (mil dol)	Number of establishments	Number of employees	Receipts (mil dol)	Annual payroll (mil dol)	Number of establishments	Number of employees	Receipts (mil dol)	Annual payroll (mil dol)
	80	81	82	83	84	85	86	87	88	89	90	91
MICHIGAN—Cont'd												
Oak Park	36	485	26.9	14.7	40	203	25.5	9.6	61	1 099	189.1	45.8
Pontiac	36	137	21.0	4.1	57	D	D	D	52	4 423	D	416.6
Portage	52	1 232	79.8	35.8	133	D	D	D	64	7 052	4 511.5	439.1
Port Huron	31	134	16.1	3.3	75	D	D	D	62	4 210	1 619.5	184.4
Rochester Hills	47	217	33.4	5.6	253	3 209	553.3	188.2	104	3 147	868.3	167.7
Roseville	54	264	58.8	6.8	52	424	26.7	15.2	145	4 445	748.9	195.9
Royal Oak	69	440	48.5	14.0	255	1 957	184.9	123.2	73	1 982	394.6	59.3
Saginaw	28	100	13.3	2.3	95	1 114	92.1	43.0	62	3 783	1 543.3	232.1
St. Clair Shores	53	231	26.8	7.6	156	602	76.1	27.9	44	1 341	D	53.5
Southfield	252	3 264	661.7	129.5	818	D	D	D	89	3 013	1 041.3	161.4
Southgate	23	D	D	D	44	330	22.0	10.7	NA	NA	NA	NA
Sterling Heights	100	466	115.7	14.7	284	D	D	D	272	14 955	7 662.4	1 018.5
Taylor	48	D	D	D	86	D	D	D	91	4 058	1 251.1	171.4
Troy	147	1 390	263.6	51.5	925	16 536	2 697.5	1 115.9	270	8 351	1 590.5	356.0
Warren	93	655	127.0	21.3	203	D	D	D	381	16 381	7 570.1	873.5
Westland	63	D	D	D	66	432	35.5	12.1	71	1 546	335.1	70.0
Wyandotte	19	D	D	D	43	D	D	D	34	1 390	599.2	101.6
Wyoming	74	696	107.8	23.3	101	D	D	D	174	8 535	2 542.0	443.5
MINNESOTA	6 889	39 430	9 208.0	1 317.4	16 595	140 786	20 473.1	8 425.3	7 951	340 514	107 563.1	15 999.2
Andover	40	182	15.3	3.4	78	331	20.8	9.3	NA	NA	NA	NA
Apple Valley	65	278	43.5	6.0	155	D	D	D	16	551	D	27.6
Blaine	68	251	63.0	6.7	110	D	D	D	152	3 511	477.2	155.4
Bloomington	208	3 531	636.9	184.3	618	D	D	D	145	8 561	1 444.5	478.0
Brooklyn Center	30	D	D	D	67	412	51.1	22.0	33	2 076	346.3	98.7
Brooklyn Park	57	298	43.3	10.2	144	813	155.4	45.3	117	5 704	1 325.6	320.7
Burnsville	119	564	87.3	21.8	301	D	D	D	109	3 522	824.3	162.6
Coon Rapids	78	227	31.9	5.5	131	780	94.4	37.5	67	3 318	866.4	178.9
Cottage Grove	28	69	10.5	1.2	44	99	9.7	3.3	14	1 580	719.9	93.3
Duluth	125	692	102.7	15.2	249	D	D	D	91	3 111	1 081.1	139.8
Eagan	113	535	108.3	19.1	340	D	D	D	93	3 607	1 196.9	176.5
Eden Prairie	147	1 478	485.3	57.4	450	11 071	1 396.2	500.1	109	9 043	1 956.4	516.0
Edina	229	1 990	338.3	73.1	518	D	D	D	73	1 847	578.8	91.8
Fridley	34	274	83.6	5.5	82	446	58.3	27.2	130	7 953	2 612.6	447.6
Inver Grove Heights	30	77	14.5	2.5	108	678	46.3	50.6	29	856	284.9	44.9
Lakeville	87	228	33.3	6.5	162	396	54.2	21.6	74	3 057	714.3	132.5
Mankato	71	620	72.7	13.1	109	D	D	D	51	2 838	2 349.3	116.0
Maple Grove	93	269	41.3	9.9	291	1 120	141.5	74.2	105	7 124	2 443.1	436.8
Maplewood	60	235	43.6	4.3	90	580	123.3	28.5	26	562	165.0	23.7
Minneapolis	651	4 429	3 014.6	159.5	2 305	D	D	D	499	15 783	4 107.5	778.0
Minnetonka	157	1 087	344.2	73.9	485	4 586	698.7	323.6	86	4 543	1 393.9	263.1
Moorhead	31	167	16.0	3.0	44	D	D	D	29	D	D	D
Oakdale	24	90	16.5	2.8	87	596	82.4	28.7	40	997	275.7	46.8
Owatonna	24	241	12.4	4.2	45	142	14.2	4.7	43	5 287	1 309.6	244.8
Plymouth	168	758	827.3	38.2	468	5 079	1 119.4	310.9	194	11 757	3 583.4	662.4
Richfield	26	D	D	D	96	373	42.5	17.8	NA	NA	NA	NA
Rochester	136	735	108.7	19.6	231	D	D	D	62	8 002	2 798.6	535.3
Roseville	74	702	137.2	28.4	210	D	D	D	66	2 435	568.5	111.6
St. Cloud	106	802	91.9	20.3	172	D	D	D	71	7 544	1 926.4	302.6
St. Louis Park	135	1 867	191.1	54.0	359	D	D	D	78	3 302	720.0	158.0
St. Paul	362	3 273	474.6	126.4	968	D	D	D	263	9 382	3 509.0	527.8
Savage	45	105	22.2	3.2	109	254	39.0	11.2	39	1 270	486.9	60.9
Shakopee	44	124	17.6	3.1	90	D	D	D	41	3 413	1 194.9	227.1
Shoreview	36	120	19.2	3.0	124	429	52.6	22.0	30	1 157	295.2	62.1
Winona	39	108	14.4	2.0	60	D	D	D	68	3 313	D	133.5
Woodbury	99	288	63.3	7.8	248	901	141.8	44.0	20	918	202.6	44.5
MISSISSIPPI	2 517	10 169	1 734.6	283.7	4 751	30 855	3 971.9	1 350.3	2 598	159 235	59 869.5	5 756.6
Biloxi	82	326	58.5	9.3	147	D	D	D	NA	NA	NA	NA
Clinton	27	74	10.4	1.4	52	206	20.4	7.3	14	D	D	46.8
Greenville	49	245	27.8	7.5	72	D	D	D	32	1 435	652.9	55.6
Gulfport	118	448	85.5	15.5	189	D	D	D	56	1 809	346.6	65.4
Hattiesburg	111	442	65.4	12.5	201	D	D	D	60	3 846	788.4	117.6
Horn Lake	16	57	13.2	1.3	14	56	3.8	1.1	15	640	187.7	32.5
Jackson	241	1 605	402.4	58.9	613	D	D	D	122	3 732	893.3	157.6
Meridian	65	262	35.7	5.5	105	D	D	D	48	1 662	330.1	50.6
Olive Branch	35	164	26.2	4.9	34	127	10.8	3.4	71	2 903	1 139.9	129.4
Pearl	33	180	30.2	5.4	24	135	26.7	5.4	28	582	407.0	25.7
Southaven	37	144	42.1	4.2	75	509	37.3	14.0	NA	NA	NA	NA
Tupelo	80	365	69.8	10.3	163	D	D	D	89	5 055	1 348.5	188.8

1. Establishments subject to federal tax.

Table D. Cities — Accommodation and Food Services, Arts, Entertainment, and Recreation, and Health Care and Social Assistance

City	Accommodation and food services, 2007				Arts, entertainment, and recreation,[1] 2007				Health care and social assistance,[1] 2007			
	Number of establishments	Number of employees	Sales (mil dol)	Annual payroll (mil dol)	Number of establishments	Number of employees	Receipts (mil dol)	Annual payroll (mil dol)	Number of establishments	Number of employees	Receipts (mil dol)	Annual payroll (mil dol)
	92	93	94	95	96	97	98	99	100	101	102	103
MICHIGAN—Cont'd												
Oak Park	39	454	19.6	5.5	3	3	0.1	0.0	69	604	39.3	14.9
Pontiac	116	1 491	82.8	21.7	14	D	D	D	112	1 117	138.3	61.8
Portage	133	3 641	121.4	37.7	13	D	D	D	161	1 836	152.3	69.7
Port Huron	69	1 059	43.2	12.5	15	D	D	D	133	1 244	156.8	78.8
Rochester Hills	121	D	D	D	15	D	D	D	264	3 063	268.1	123.7
Roseville	107	2 900	116.2	36.1	9	106	5.0	1.2	101	1 071	81.4	37.8
Royal Oak	142	2 966	135.0	39.6	20	D	D	D	165	D	D	D
Saginaw	92	1 172	42.2	11.5	3	D	D	D	118	1 715	167.8	73.4
St. Clair Shores	116	1 995	80.8	23.1	26	D	D	D	193	1 934	200.9	94.2
Southfield	254	4 114	213.8	59.4	27	486	24.2	8.8	682	9 139	988.0	396.1
Southgate	86	2 234	98.5	28.7	2	D	D	D	98	718	90.9	31.6
Sterling Heights	232	5 096	207.6	66.9	30	345	28.5	7.9	292	3 412	282.9	122.9
Taylor	138	2 486	97.9	28.2	11	D	D	D	111	1 632	138.1	54.5
Troy	277	6 365	325.4	96.9	33	D	D	D	432	D	D	D
Warren	309	4 992	216.1	60.1	21	309	14.8	4.1	334	D	D	D
Westland	143	2 825	114.1	32.2	14	D	D	D	139	1 694	129.0	57.2
Wyandotte	58	668	27.7	7.4	5	D	D	D	45	D	D	D
Wyoming	124	2 182	87.9	23.8	16	D	D	D	86	1 035	88.2	38.1
MINNESOTA	11 340	221 081	10 423.7	2 978.4	1 990	28 038	2 185.6	796.1	10 263	157 035	13 229.6	6 021.1
Andover	23	424	15.7	4.5	6	D	D	D	27	D	D	D
Apple Valley	69	1 736	77.6	23.4	12	116	9.5	1.4	105	993	104.0	36.4
Blaine	97	2 430	93.3	29.3	12	D	D	D	69	D	D	D
Bloomington	258	7 752	459.7	137.3	35	684	31.0	9.2	181	3 061	249.3	111.4
Brooklyn Center	50	976	50.5	14.2	5	65	2.5	0.9	79	1 174	91.5	36.6
Brooklyn Park	79	1 745	75.5	23.0	12	D	D	D	103	1 411	81.8	34.2
Burnsville	128	3 128	126.2	39.4	25	760	16.8	4.7	188	D	D	D
Coon Rapids	106	2 918	110.1	33.8	19	D	D	D	130	D	D	D
Cottage Grove	38	693	25.9	7.2	6	84	3.3	1.0	37	453	44.9	15.0
Duluth	230	5 249	211.0	61.8	31	193	9.6	2.4	264	4 379	380.4	174.5
Eagan	128	3 250	166.2	45.4	13	D	D	D	138	2 553	211.5	85.6
Eden Prairie	139	3 182	154.2	51.5	34	D	D	D	119	1 914	229.2	94.8
Edina	100	2 950	161.0	48.2	23	98	7.1	2.2	340	D	D	D
Fridley	47	680	34.8	9.8	7	D	D	D	66	D	D	D
Inver Grove Heights	50	944	41.1	11.9	11	D	D	D	56	526	43.4	19.8
Lakeville	59	1 682	54.4	18.0	19	224	15.0	4.9	77	795	60.7	23.1
Mankato	144	3 813	132.8	39.4	14	110	10.2	1.8	112	D	D	D
Maple Grove	103	3 326	147.6	45.5	18	D	D	D	118	2 183	192.1	80.1
Maplewood	92	2 367	97.5	29.1	16	D	D	D	132	1 808	301.0	98.4
Minneapolis	1 095	24 428	1 333.5	421.5	167	2 758	502.7	235.6	746	13 034	1 258.1	627.4
Minnetonka	108	2 708	142.2	43.9	24	356	22.3	8.0	124	1 749	211.0	84.2
Moorhead	63	1 354	50.0	14.6	7	D	D	D	65	639	39.1	17.2
Oakdale	39	992	66.0	15.6	9	D	D	D	40	248	24.5	7.3
Owatonna	72	1 373	62.7	15.6	7	D	D	D	69	D	D	D
Plymouth	128	2 771	122.3	37.5	25	346	25.0	5.9	190	1 995	262.5	131.3
Richfield	64	1 254	68.6	18.2	6	D	D	D	72	1 414	101.2	42.8
Rochester	278	6 882	312.8	89.6	23	D	D	D	197	D	D	D
Roseville	124	3 672	151.0	51.6	18	D	D	D	129	3 307	285.6	119.5
St. Cloud	160	4 467	164.2	47.3	24	242	19.9	4.1	178	3 917	360.2	212.9
St. Louis Park	93	2 341	106.0	34.6	19	D	D	D	178	D	D	D
St. Paul	598	10 672	499.5	148.0	82	2 225	153.2	70.7	643	12 304	992.8	472.5
Savage	38	D	D	D	9	236	10.0	2.8	38	D	D	D
Shakopee	72	1 520	69.0	21.3	18	D	D	D	67	611	56.2	25.0
Shoreview	29	569	26.2	7.3	4	D	D	D	55	556	48.7	21.0
Winona	78	1 654	58.7	14.8	16	D	D	D	53	D	D	D
Woodbury	97	2 512	96.2	30.0	14	D	D	D	141	D	D	D
MISSISSIPPI	4 817	119 626	7 045.1	1 812.3	506	5 960	425.4	112.4	4 858	72 601	7 228.8	2 752.9
Biloxi	104	11 235	1 247.1	331.2	15	D	D	D	126	2 213	256.7	86.9
Clinton	54	1 168	45.1	11.2	5	D	D	D	46	782	47.3	17.5
Greenville	75	1 462	91.0	19.7	9	D	D	D	113	951	71.5	28.4
Gulfport	162	5 009	304.1	84.3	16	161	10.7	3.8	208	D	D	D
Hattiesburg	213	5 429	217.0	60.2	16	D	D	D	180	D	D	D
Horn Lake	46	1 176	50.9	13.1	5	42	1.4	0.4	11	D	D	D
Jackson	363	7 472	335.7	90.3	24	524	47.3	10.2	505	8 491	1 066.8	406.5
Meridian	140	3 511	131.8	36.9	10	D	D	D	155	D	D	D
Olive Branch	66	1 609	64.5	17.6	9	D	D	D	44	D	D	D
Pearl	62	1 455	61.2	16.6	6	D	D	D	26	250	29.4	9.9
Southaven	118	2 967	124.6	31.9	13	D	D	D	106	D	D	D
Tupelo	164	3 657	131.9	37.0	8	D	D	D	166	D	D	D

1. Establishments subject to federal tax.

Table D. Cities — Other Services and Federal Funds

City	Other services[1], 2007				Procurement contracts		Selected federal funds, 2009–2010 (mil dol) Grants						
	Number of establishments	Number of employees	Receipts (mil dol)	Annual payroll (mil dol)	Defense	Other	Total[2]	Medicaid and other health related	Nutrition and family welfare	Energy and environment	Disasters and emergency preparedness	Housing and community development	Employment and training
	104	105	106	107	108	109	110	111	112	113	114	115	116
MICHIGAN—Cont'd													
Oak Park	34	139	12.3	4.4	0.1	3.2	7.9	0.0	0.0	0.0	0.0	7.7	0.0
Pontiac	65	476	43.0	13.7	3.9	6.2	142.1	2.4	0.0	122.0	0.0	13.2	0.7
Portage	91	D	D	D	0.8	3.0	10.4	0.0	0.0	0.0	0.0	0.2	0.0
Port Huron	40	228	14.0	4.7	26.6	2.8	17.2	0.2	2.9	3.4	0.0	5.7	0.0
Rochester Hills	95	606	40.1	13.4	1.5	0.1	1.4	0.0	0.0	0.0	0.0	0.0	0.0
Roseville	86	464	34.9	10.8	7.2	0.3	2.9	0.0	0.0	0.0	0.0	2.8	0.0
Royal Oak	110	687	48.8	16.2	0.5	0.4	7.5	3.5	0.0	0.5	0.0	2.8	0.0
Saginaw	57	243	16.9	4.8	15.9	17.5	29.2	4.5	7.2	1.4	0.0	12.0	0.0
St. Clair Shores	97	497	28.1	8.9	0.2	0.7	2.6	0.0	0.0	0.5	0.0	1.9	0.0
Southfield	142	808	65.8	21.5	81.5	22.9	30.1	4.5	2.6	15.0	0.0	5.3	0.0
Southgate	54	506	79.9	19.3	0.1	0.0	3.0	0.0	0.0	1.2	0.0	0.1	0.0
Sterling Heights	158	809	62.6	20.5	2 108.9	35.8	7.1	0.5	0.0	1.2	0.0	1.4	0.0
Taylor	112	1 122	99.2	39.2	0.7	0.2	13.8	0.0	0.0	0.0	0.0	12.3	0.0
Troy	198	1 515	117.1	40.1	41.2	138.0	267.8	0.7	9.5	251.9	0.0	2.4	0.4
Warren	222	1 615	168.9	56.0	157.2	17.9	56.2	0.3	0.0	44.3	0.0	1.8	5.0
Westland	118	741	67.2	20.8	1.0	0.2	34.8	0.7	24.1	0.7	0.0	8.8	0.0
Wyandotte	55	237	20.5	5.3	0.2	1.8	3.8	0.0	0.0	3.8	0.0	0.0	0.0
Wyoming	124	790	67.5	23.6	0.5	0.3	10.6	0.0	0.0	0.0	0.0	9.4	0.0
MINNESOTA	8 519	52 215	4 106.5	1 281.6	1 520.3	1 430.1	10 527.8	6 006.5	1 249.2	223.7	26.4	437.2	187.0
Andover	36	D	D	D	0.0	0.0	0.0	0.0	0.0	0.0	0.0	0.0	0.0
Apple Valley	61	422	31.8	11.4	0.1	0.2	0.5	0.0	0.0	0.5	0.0	0.0	0.0
Blaine	113	D	D	D	0.1	0.0	4.2	0.0	4.2	0.0	0.0	0.0	0.0
Bloomington	166	1 575	101.7	41.3	11.7	21.6	8.2	1.6	0.0	0.0	0.0	6.3	0.0
Brooklyn Center	23	146	6.8	2.5	0.1	0.5	0.1	0.0	0.0	0.1	0.0	0.0	0.0
Brooklyn Park	86	613	46.2	16.4	2.5	3.6	2.7	0.0	0.0	0.0	0.0	0.0	2.6
Burnsville	106	819	58.8	20.6	29.7	3.2	2.0	0.0	0.0	0.4	0.0	0.0	0.0
Coon Rapids	77	D	D	D	0.0	0.5	0.5	0.0	0.0	0.4	0.0	0.0	0.0
Cottage Grove	28	D	D	D	0.3	0.1	0.1	0.0	0.0	0.0	0.0	0.0	0.0
Duluth	137	942	54.3	19.5	22.5	22.0	49.7	4.4	3.7	2.8	0.0	15.1	0.0
Eagan	112	1 216	117.9	37.0	160.5	7.1	23.6	0.0	0.0	1.5	0.0	21.9	0.0
Eden Prairie	114	947	70.7	24.8	15.2	70.7	6.6	5.4	0.0	0.6	0.0	0.3	0.0
Edina	81	997	75.1	26.5	2.4	26.3	0.7	0.7	0.0	0.0	0.0	0.0	0.0
Fridley	54	D	D	D	0.4	3.8	0.0	0.0	0.0	0.0	0.0	0.0	0.0
Inver Grove Heights	50	291	19.4	6.9	0.2	9.8	-0.1	0.0	0.0	0.0	0.0	0.0	0.0
Lakeville	79	506	45.2	15.6	0.1	0.0	0.0	0.0	0.0	0.0	0.0	6.8	0.0
Mankato	87	D	D	D	0.0	0.5	12.5	0.1	2.9	0.7	0.0	0.0	0.0
Maple Grove	87	841	59.3	20.9	4.1	1.9	9.2	8.8	0.0	0.0	0.0	0.0	0.0
Maplewood	82	D	D	D	0.0	0.0	3.0	0.0	0.0	0.6	0.0	0.0	0.0
Minneapolis	685	5 055	426.7	130.5	516.9	296.3	1 161.7	601.3	22.0	27.5	3.8	104.4	15.2
Minnetonka	85	703	38.2	14.8	2.1	0.8	0.9	0.7	0.0	0.0	0.0	0.2	0.0
Moorhead	62	D	D	D	50.7	0.0	6.3	2.3	1.8	0.0	0.0	1.1	0.0
Oakdale	34	114	10.3	3.3	1.7	1.9	0.6	0.1	0.0	0.4	0.0	0.1	0.0
Owatonna	49	D	D	D	1.6	0.1	1.1	0.1	0.0	0.0	0.0	0.6	0.0
Plymouth	89	593	42.6	14.7	1.2	6.4	7.6	0.0	0.0	3.9	0.0	3.3	0.0
Richfield	56	337	24.7	9.2	0.1	0.5	1.6	0.1	0.0	0.0	0.0	1.6	0.0
Rochester	147	D	D	D	3.2	5.0	22.1	0.8	2.1	0.0	0.0	4.2	0.0
Roseville	83	940	73.5	25.1	0.0	0.0	3.3	0.0	0.0	0.0	0.0	0.0	0.0
St. Cloud	119	916	76.5	24.6	0.2	36.5	15.5	0.2	3.2	0.0	0.0	6.5	0.0
St. Louis Park	97	501	36.4	11.3	0.1	1.2	8.8	5.9	0.0	0.0	0.0	2.9	0.0
St. Paul	398	2 848	216.0	71.5	80.6	78.2	1 309.5	137.2	183.7	155.6	0.4	168.7	148.5
Savage	50	D	D	D	0.4	0.0	0.0	0.0	0.0	0.0	0.0	0.0	0.0
Shakopee	56	D	D	D	0.0	0.4	5.4	0.0	2.2	0.0	0.0	3.1	0.0
Shoreview	25	D	D	D	0.0	0.0	0.0	0.0	0.0	0.0	0.0	0.0	0.0
Winona	46	D	D	D	2.9	0.3	5.1	0.1	0.0	1.5	0.0	1.3	0.1
Woodbury	73	663	38.4	14.7	0.1	0.0	0.2	0.0	0.0	0.0	0.0	0.2	0.0
MISSISSIPPI	3 076	16 201	1 295.3	373.2	1 634.0	1 031.9	7 871.1	4 459.9	856.9	259.2	185.7	233.4	95.6
Biloxi	48	331	28.7	8.7	168.6	34.9	42.5	5.5	0.5	25.6	0.0	5.7	0.1
Clinton	24	142	10.8	3.9	0.0	0.1	0.3	0.0	0.0	0.0	0.0	0.0	0.0
Greenville	55	D	D	D	1.0	2.6	12.7	0.3	7.3	0.2	0.0	0.0	0.3
Gulfport	119	720	74.6	20.5	90.0	34.7	68.7	0.9	9.3	-1.6	0.0	50.8	0.0
Hattiesburg	89	644	37.1	12.0	31.5	5.3	99.8	16.8	5.9	35.1	0.0	2.5	0.4
Horn Lake	24	D	D	D	0.0	0.3	0.0	0.0	0.0	0.0	0.0	0.0	0.0
Jackson	239	1 797	108.9	36.2	31.0	102.6	1 183.5	171.9	175.3	68.4	101.1	99.2	86.3
Meridian	95	D	D	D	12.9	1.3	15.4	2.8	0.0	0.0	0.0	3.7	4.5
Olive Branch	38	D	D	D	0.1	1.5	0.0	0.0	0.0	0.0	0.0	0.0	0.0
Pearl	50	233	20.9	6.1	0.2	0.4	5.5	4.5	0.0	0.0	0.0	0.0	0.0
Southaven	57	385	29.8	9.9	0.6	0.1	0.2	0.0	0.0	0.2	0.0	0.0	0.0
Tupelo	87	D	D	D	0.6	21.0	2.2	0.0	0.0	0.0	0.0	0.7	0.0

1. Establishments subject to federal tax.   2. Includes program categories not shown separately. State totals include additional categories not allocated by city.

Table D. Cities — City Government Finances

City	City government finances, 2007									
	General revenue							General expenditure		
		Intergovernmental		Taxes					Per capita[1] (dollars)	
					Per capita[1] (dollars)					
	Total (mil dol)	Total (mil dol)	Percent from state government	Total (mil dol)	Total	Property	Sales and gross receipts	Total (mil dol)	Total	Capital outlays
	117	118	119	120	121	122	123	124	125	126
MICHIGAN—Cont'd										
Oak Park	34.3	4.6	95.9	17.4	567	554	13	39.5	1 285	232
Pontiac	107.6	31.6	60.3	47.0	707	465	38	114.0	1 714	136
Portage	40.5	8.0	94.0	22.4	487	462	25	41.5	900	143
Port Huron	58.3	13.3	63.7	23.9	770	540	24	59.3	1 907	335
Rochester Hills	74.4	16.4	59.3	33.0	475	445	30	63.4	914	68
Roseville	58.8	12.0	68.9	29.7	632	623	9	52.8	1 124	67
Royal Oak	75.7	15.6	64.0	31.7	552	505	47	72.2	1 257	136
Saginaw	88.7	28.1	55.7	27.0	480	208	31	82.2	1 461	116
St. Clair Shores	75.9	17.9	61.0	37.5	619	598	21	65.3	1 076	136
Southfield	102.6	21.1	55.6	62.2	826	794	31	110.2	1 461	102
Southgate	34.5	5.2	96.9	18.9	662	643	19	33.5	1 176	29
Sterling Heights	115.7	23.3	85.5	57.4	451	437	14	114.8	901	117
Taylor	128.7	31.4	39.3	53.9	864	821	42	107.6	1 726	8
Troy	102.8	14.0	84.5	56.8	705	687	19	96.0	1 191	171
Warren	157.1	27.9	90.4	87.3	650	633	17	175.4	1 306	224
Westland	90.0	28.4	58.0	33.7	414	399	15	82.0	1 009	27
Wyandotte	45.2	8.0	64.2	18.4	717	696	21	55.2	2 154	330
Wyoming	85.3	21.7	50.3	26.7	379	344	35	101.7	1 443	488
MINNESOTA	X	X	X	X	X	X	X	X	X	X
Andover	20.8	2.7	95.4	10.2	337	317	20	19.1	632	236
Apple Valley	38.0	1.1	97.5	21.7	433	399	34	41.9	838	175
Blaine	41.3	3.0	76.9	21.0	379	326	52	47.4	856	348
Bloomington	100.6	12.6	79.6	62.9	650	459	191	101.1	1 242	280
Brooklyn Center	38.4	2.4	89.8	16.3	593	516	53	38.9	1 415	304
Brooklyn Park	67.9	10.2	84.9	32.2	451	406	45	53.6	750	191
Burnsville	53.5	6.3	54.0	30.1	509	450	59	52.2	883	237
Coon Rapids	43.4	4.3	100.0	21.6	350	276	74	46.3	749	228
Cottage Grove	38.9	4.1	84.3	12.8	386	340	45	32.7	988	409
Duluth	183.4	75.5	60.8	37.5	445	210	234	180.3	2 137	707
Eagan	49.5	2.4	96.5	22.7	357	327	30	47.9	752	175
Eden Prairie	67.4	4.3	85.7	34.4	558	501	57	60.1	974	205
Edina	57.3	2.9	89.3	31.6	689	602	87	53.0	1 154	196
Fridley	25.0	2.6	94.8	9.1	351	317	34	30.7	1 183	120
Inver Grove Heights	25.6	1.7	86.0	13.0	388	354	0	29.4	877	178
Lakeville	39.3	2.4	95.2	20.6	380	331	49	35.2	651	200
Mankato	69.0	15.8	74.8	18.0	445	284	161	69.5	1 937	703
Maple Grove	81.3	5.0	100.0	27.9	462	385	66	80.6	1 303	729
Maplewood	38.4	1.8	96.2	15.7	434	391	43	39.0	1 080	306
Minneapolis	956.7	230.0	75.6	380.8	1 009	713	296	844.3	2 237	235
Minnetonka	48.9	2.5	88.3	30.3	603	525	78	44.5	883	211
Moorhead	63.9	20.2	79.4	5.0	141	89	52	76.6	2 169	1 097
Oakdale	21.7	2.3	74.9	10.2	376	314	35	20.3	752	164
Owatonna	25.7	8.1	76.7	7.6	307	261	35	24.8	1 002	260
Plymouth	52.6	8.0	94.5	26.4	372	328	44	51.7	727	162
Richfield	41.9	11.0	97.3	17.4	520	445	32	38.6	1 157	137
Rochester	169.1	22.6	96.6	50.8	513	342	170	201.5	2 033	941
Roseville	29.6	2.5	100.0	16.4	506	408	98	25.6	788	158
St. Cloud	82.3	21.4	83.5	29.3	441	247	194	90.0	1 353	546
St. Louis Park	58.7	13.4	85.3	27.9	634	563	71	58.7	1 333	113
St. Paul	482.0	165.9	55.7	126.8	457	275	182	461.3	1 664	201
Savage	33.0	3.0	99.2	14.9	540	486	55	34.9	1 263	660
Shakopee	31.5	3.8	66.2	13.5	403	317	80	31.2	933	350
Shoreview	21.4	1.0	76.1	9.4	349	330	19	22.3	825	131
Winona	30.8	16.7	98.2	6.4	239	177	62	35.4	1 326	545
Woodbury	66.6	3.3	89.0	24.3	438	366	71	48.1	868	326
MISSISSIPPI	X	X	X	X	X	X	X	X	X	X
Biloxi	140.4	74.9	44.9	21.3	480	380	100	122.0	2 754	292
Clinton	21.5	9.7	96.4	7.4	280	237	43	24.9	942	401
Greenville	29.1	8.2	83.6	13.4	371	288	83	25.5	706	90
Gulfport	429.2	111.2	31.6	28.5	430	334	96	404.8	6 108	641
Hattiesburg	65.2	36.7	67.9	19.6	390	245	144	52.6	1 047	250
Horn Lake	13.0	4.2	95.6	6.2	257	232	25	12.6	520	35
Jackson	232.6	78.9	62.9	72.0	410	343	67	243.0	1 383	496
Meridian	42.4	16.6	100.0	13.8	360	290	70	31.6	826	37
Olive Branch	28.0	8.8	100.0	9.6	315	277	38	26.4	860	158
Pearl	17.8	8.6	81.0	4.0	165	157	7	18.2	754	97
Southaven	39.1	12.0	100.0	18.0	422	348	74	46.5	1 093	382
Tupelo	61.0	32.1	86.8	11.6	321	298	23	55.4	1 535	485

1. Based on population estimated as of July 1 of the year shown.

City	City government finances, 2006 (cont.)									
	General expenditure (cont.)									
	Percent of total for:									
	Public welfare	Highways	Parking facilities	Education	Health and hospitals	Police protection	Sewerage and sanitation	Parks and recreation	Housing and community development	Interest on debt
	127	128	129	130	131	132	133	134	135	136
MICHIGAN—Cont'd										
Oak Park	0.0	22.9	0.0	0.0	0.0	26.4	18.4	2.9	0.4	4.2
Pontiac	0.0	8.3	1.4	0.0	0.0	13.7	12.7	5.0	10.2	4.6
Portage	0.3	16.9	0.0	0.0	0.0	16.7	15.6	5.4	1.0	7.3
Port Huron	0.0	12.8	0.3	0.0	0.0	13.5	26.5	10.3	9.1	3.8
Rochester Hills	0.0	22.2	0.0	0.0	0.3	11.9	14.8	17.5	0.2	3.7
Roseville	0.0	8.8	0.0	0.0	0.0	20.5	17.8	3.3	6.9	1.7
Royal Oak	0.0	13.1	1.8	0.0	0.6	15.6	19.9	4.3	5.5	1.6
Saginaw	0.0	8.0	0.4	0.0	0.0	16.0	22.4	0.2	16.8	4.1
St. Clair Shores	0.0	10.3	0.0	0.0	0.0	18.7	22.7	7.2	2.9	4.1
Southfield	0.0	18.1	0.0	0.0	0.0	19.1	2.7	7.8	1.9	2.2
Southgate	0.0	10.7	0.0	0.0	0.0	18.2	12.2	5.5	0.5	4.1
Sterling Heights	0.0	16.4	0.0	0.0	0.0	25.1	15.2	3.5	1.8	2.0
Taylor	0.0	11.5	0.0	0.0	0.0	12.8	5.0	6.4	15.3	5.0
Troy	0.0	17.6	0.0	0.0	0.0	24.6	15.7	14.3	0.1	3.7
Warren	0.0	8.6	0.0	0.0	0.0	21.9	15.7	4.4	2.2	3.5
Westland	0.0	10.0	0.0	0.0	0.0	19.0	17.1	5.7	10.6	0.6
Wyandotte	0.0	17.8	0.0	0.0	0.0	10.1	19.8	7.6	0.0	1.3
Wyoming	0.0	10.3	0.0	0.0	0.3	12.0	37.7	3.9	8.4	4.0
MINNESOTA	X	X	X	X	X	X	X	X	X	X
Andover	0.0	30.8	0.0	0.0	0.1	9.7	12.0	14.9	3.8	10.1
Apple Valley	0.0	23.0	0.0	0.0	0.0	16.0	8.9	15.1	0.0	4.8
Blaine	0.0	4.7	0.0	0.0	0.0	27.2	14.1	5.7	7.6	2.7
Bloomington	0.0	22.7	0.0	0.0	6.1	18.0	12.9	11.8	0.8	2.0
Brooklyn Center	0.0	13.4	0.0	0.0	0.0	15.7	12.5	7.0	11.0	3.2
Brooklyn Park	0.0	17.8	0.0	0.0	0.0	19.9	11.1	13.3	9.9	5.9
Burnsville	0.0	23.9	0.0	0.0	0.0	19.7	8.5	11.7	0.0	2.8
Coon Rapids	0.0	8.3	0.0	0.0	0.5	12.9	14.9	9.1	2.7	2.0
Cottage Grove	0.0	12.2	0.0	0.0	3.4	13.4	9.7	11.8	2.4	5.3
Duluth	0.0	7.3	0.0	0.0	5.6	9.4	11.8	10.4	0.2	3.1
Eagan	0.0	11.3	0.0	0.0	0.0	19.2	11.0	14.1	3.7	9.8
Eden Prairie	1.1	13.8	0.0	0.0	0.2	14.3	10.7	11.2	5.0	14.5
Edina	0.0	16.4	0.0	0.0	0.8	15.1	13.4	30.1	2.6	4.3
Fridley	0.0	10.6	0.0	0.0	0.0	15.2	14.0	14.6	14.5	6.4
Inver Grove Heights	0.0	21.1	0.0	0.0	0.0	13.8	7.5	24.9	0.0	4.7
Lakeville	0.0	14.1	0.0	0.0	0.1	20.7	14.3	19.9	0.0	8.4
Mankato	0.0	26.7	0.7	0.0	0.0	9.6	11.5	5.2	20.8	4.9
Maple Grove	0.6	11.0	0.0	0.0	0.0	8.3	5.5	9.1	1.1	1.7
Maplewood	0.0	5.7	0.0	0.0	4.4	17.0	11.9	12.1	3.4	5.5
Minneapolis	0.0	9.4	4.8	0.0	1.7	15.3	10.9	10.1	14.9	10.4
Minnetonka	0.0	19.5	0.0	0.0	0.6	17.0	18.4	15.2	3.3	0.8
Moorhead	0.0	6.2	0.0	0.0	1.1	7.4	10.5	5.0	3.5	6.6
Oakdale	0.0	6.2	0.0	0.0	0.0	17.4	11.5	11.5	0.0	1.6
Owatonna	0.0	27.2	0.0	0.0	0.0	13.5	4.7	15.9	7.5	3.9
Plymouth	6.9	24.2	0.0	0.0	0.0	18.6	11.1	15.4	0.7	2.5
Richfield	0.0	4.1	0.0	0.0	0.2	15.0	8.7	10.2	28.0	2.8
Rochester	0.0	2.8	1.6	0.0	0.1	7.6	21.2	5.6	0.2	15.7
Roseville	0.0	12.6	0.0	0.0	0.0	16.6	13.9	14.0	4.2	2.1
St. Cloud	0.0	28.9	1.6	0.0	0.7	14.0	13.8	7.3	1.2	3.4
St. Louis Park	0.0	12.4	0.0	0.0	0.3	10.6	11.9	10.4	20.6	14.3
St. Paul	0.0	6.0	2.5	0.0	0.8	17.0	6.9	9.6	14.8	8.1
Savage	0.0	33.9	0.0	0.0	0.0	28.1	5.9	6.8	2.9	10.0
Shakopee	0.0	28.8	0.0	0.0	0.0	15.6	11.1	21.2	1.4	2.8
Shoreview	0.0	16.5	0.0	0.0	0.2	11.6	20.0	26.5	0.0	8.9
Winona	0.0	40.2	0.0	0.0	0.2	11.3	8.5	10.8	1.0	1.3
Woodbury	0.0	14.1	0.0	0.0	2.5	14.0	9.6	14.8	2.4	6.0
MISSISSIPPI	X	X	X	X	X	X	X	X	X	X
Biloxi	0.4	13.4	0.0	0.0	0.1	11.3	42.9	3.8	0.5	2.4
Clinton	0.0	27.2	0.0	0.0	0.0	14.5	21.0	13.8	0.0	2.7
Greenville	1.0	14.3	0.0	0.0	0.1	22.2	13.3	3.2	0.0	1.4
Gulfport	0.0	2.9	0.0	0.0	63.5	4.8	4.8	1.1	0.4	2.4
Hattiesburg	0.0	18.7	0.4	0.0	1.4	18.4	12.7	8.5	1.3	2.6
Horn Lake	0.0	13.4	0.0	0.0	5.5	30.0	11.7	2.9	0.0	8.0
Jackson	1.1	12.2	0.0	0.0	0.4	13.8	24.0	3.4	2.5	2.7
Meridian	0.0	13.3	0.5	0.0	0.0	20.8	18.3	6.3	3.5	4.3
Olive Branch	0.0	8.9	0.0	0.0	3.2	17.3	17.1	4.6	0.0	9.0
Pearl	0.0	12.3	0.0	0.0	1.7	13.3	17.6	6.9	2.3	4.6
Southaven	0.0	4.4	0.0	0.0	0.4	14.0	6.8	13.0	0.0	5.1
Tupelo	0.0	22.2	0.0	0.0	0.0	16.3	20.7	7.7	0.0	3.2

Table D. Cities — City Government Finances, City Government Employment, and Climate

City	City government finances, 2007 (cont.) — Debt outstanding — Total (mil dol)	Per capita[1] (dollars)	Debt issued during year	City government employment, 2010	Climate[2] — Average daily temperature (degrees Fahrenheit) — Mean — January	July	Limits — January[3]	July[4]	Annual precipitation (inches)	Heating degree days	Cooling degree days
	137	138	139	140	141	142	143	144	145	146	147
MICHIGAN—Cont'd											
Oak Park	43.6	1 418	0.1	197	24.7	73.7	16.1	85.7	33.58	6 224	788
Pontiac	146.0	2 195	0.0	462	22.9	71.9	15.9	82.3	30.03	6 680	626
Portage	95.7	2 078	0.8	221	24.3	73.2	17.0	84.2	37.41	6 235	773
Port Huron	103.7	3 337	18.8	270	22.8	72.2	15.1	81.9	31.39	6 845	626
Rochester Hills	52.2	753	0.0	268	22.0	70.6	13.7	82.7	35.74	7 046	523
Roseville	18.2	387	4.9	336	25.3	73.6	18.8	83.3	33.97	6 160	757
Royal Oak	134.6	2 345	1.1	360	24.7	73.7	16.1	85.7	33.58	6 224	788
Saginaw	110.5	1 963	1.5	446	21.4	71.2	14.9	81.9	31.61	7 099	548
St. Clair Shores	59.5	982	3.8	302	25.3	73.6	18.8	83.3	33.97	6 160	757
Southfield	86.6	1 148	0.0	766	24.7	73.7	16.1	85.7	33.58	6 224	788
Southgate	25.8	903	0.0	180	24.5	73.5	17.8	83.4	32.89	6 422	736
Sterling Heights	49.5	389	7.9	634	24.4	71.9	18.0	81.8	32.24	6 620	597
Taylor	189.9	3 045	0.3	397	24.5	73.5	17.8	83.4	32.89	6 422	736
Troy	79.4	986	4.3	534	22.9	71.9	15.9	82.3	30.03	6 680	626
Warren	177.7	1 324	11.8	439	24.7	73.7	16.1	85.7	33.58	6 224	788
Westland	18.1	223	0.0	411	24.6	73.9	17.6	84.7	32.80	6 167	828
Wyandotte	78.1	3 048	10.6	269	24.5	73.5	17.8	83.4	32.89	6 422	736
Wyoming	141.6	2 010	32.0	404	22.4	71.4	15.6	82.3	37.13	6 896	613
MINNESOTA	X	X	X	NA	X	X	X	X	X	X	X
Andover	59.7	1 972	12.9	63	10.9	70.4	1.8	80.5	31.36	8 367	500
Apple Valley	42.4	847	6.6	215	9.2	69.4	-1.1	80.5	29.19	8 805	416
Blaine	47.5	857	5.2	199	10.9	70.4	1.8	80.5	31.36	8 367	500
Bloomington	117.9	1 448	31.4	587	13.1	73.2	4.3	83.3	29.41	7 876	699
Brooklyn Center	59.2	2 153	1.5	191	13.0	71.4	2.8	82.8	30.50	7 983	587
Brooklyn Park	83.1	1 164	1.3	432	13.0	71.4	2.8	82.8	30.50	7 983	587
Burnsville	55.5	939	12.8	286	13.8	74.0	3.4	85.8	30.44	7 549	803
Coon Rapids	59.2	959	0.0	256	13.0	71.4	2.8	82.8	30.50	7 983	587
Cottage Grove	58.0	1 752	29.2	128	12.0	72.1	2.5	82.6	29.95	8 032	617
Duluth	437.1	5 179	28.5	1 013	8.4	65.5	-1.2	76.3	31.00	9 724	189
Eagan	91.8	1 437	0.0	287	13.1	73.2	4.3	83.3	29.41	7 876	699
Eden Prairie	263.2	4 268	13.5	313	10.2	71.4	-0.3	82.2	28.82	8 429	567
Edina	79.2	1 724	0.0	255	13.8	74.0	3.4	85.8	30.44	7 549	803
Fridley	8.4	322	2.5	150	10.9	70.4	1.8	80.5	31.36	8 367	500
Inver Grove Heights	44.7	1 334	10.1	155	10.1	71.0	0.0	81.3	34.60	8 345	533
Lakeville	85.1	1 573	10.8	208	13.1	72.2	3.8	83.6	31.43	7 773	658
Mankato	113.4	3 159	14.1	263	12.5	72.1	2.4	83.4	33.42	8 029	650
Maple Grove	216.2	3 494	45.5	305	13.0	71.4	2.8	82.8	30.50	7 983	587
Maplewood	154.9	4 285	6.4	168	14.5	73.0	6.2	83.2	32.59	7 606	715
Minneapolis	2 975.0	7 883	64.7	5 105	13.1	73.2	4.3	83.3	29.41	7 876	699
Minnetonka	19.0	378	0.0	269	13.1	73.2	4.3	83.3	29.41	7 876	699
Moorhead	202.5	5 731	45.4	323	3.8	69.8	-7.1	81.5	21.56	9 628	478
Oakdale	23.2	859	5.0	117	14.5	73.0	6.2	83.2	32.59	7 606	715
Owatonna	26.1	1 054	2.8	230	NA	NA	NA	NA	NA	NA	NA
Plymouth	161.1	2 267	0.0	289	13.0	71.4	2.8	82.8	30.50	7 983	587
Richfield	68.8	2 061	8.6	151	13.1	73.2	4.3	83.3	29.41	7 876	699
Rochester	1 284.8	12 962	40.6	902	9.8	70.0	0.0	80.9	29.10	8 703	474
Roseville	21.7	667	9.6	189	14.5	73.0	6.2	83.2	32.59	7 606	715
St. Cloud	364.2	5 476	50.5	488	8.8	69.8	-1.2	81.7	27.13	8 815	443
St. Louis Park	177.3	4 028	0.0	269	13.0	71.4	2.8	82.8	30.50	7 983	587
St. Paul	874.5	3 154	35.6	2 972	14.5	73.0	6.2	83.2	32.59	7 606	715
Savage	96.5	3 492	20.6	120	NA	NA	NA	NA	NA	NA	NA
Shakopee	116.1	3 470	14.0	197	NA	NA	NA	NA	NA	NA	NA
Shoreview	43.0	1 588	3.5	97	14.5	73.0	6.2	83.2	32.59	7 606	715
Winona	20.5	768	2.3	187	17.6	75.8	9.2	85.3	34.20	6 839	990
Woodbury	120.0	2 164	24.3	208	11.5	72.1	1.9	81.9	29.92	8 104	621
MISSISSIPPI	X	X	X	NA	X	X	X	X	X	X	X
Biloxi	71.3	1 609	8.0	680	50.7	81.7	43.5	88.5	64.84	1 645	2 517
Clinton	33.3	1 262	6.5	198	NA	NA	NA	NA	NA	NA	NA
Greenville	18.4	510	0.0	426	42.3	82.6	33.0	92.6	54.20	2 715	2 216
Gulfport	235.1	3 547	33.6	3 249	51.6	82.6	42.6	91.3	65.20	1 514	2 679
Hattiesburg	94.3	1 877	32.2	733	47.9	81.7	36.0	92.1	62.47	2 024	2 327
Horn Lake	24.4	1 011	1.2	223	NA	NA	NA	NA	NA	NA	NA
Jackson	360.8	2 053	4.5	2 024	45.0	81.4	35.0	91.4	55.95	2 401	2 264
Meridian	63.4	1 656	11.2	537	46.1	81.7	34.7	92.9	58.65	2 352	2 173
Olive Branch	57.4	1 875	4.3	364	NA	NA	NA	NA	NA	NA	NA
Pearl	18.9	786	2.8	223	NA	NA	NA	NA	NA	NA	NA
Southaven	83.1	1 952	28.6	362	37.9	80.4	27.8	90.3	55.06	3 442	1 749
Tupelo	81.7	2 264	14.3	508	40.4	80.6	30.5	91.4	55.86	3 086	1 884

1. Based on the population estimated as of July 1 of the year shown. 2. Represents normal values based on the 30-year period, 1971–2000. 3. Average daily minimum. 4. Average daily maximum.

Table D. Cities — Land Area and Population

STATE Place code	City	Land area,[1] 2010 (sq km)	Population, 2010			Race alone or in combination, not of Hispanic origin (percent), 2010					Percent Hispanic or Latino[2], 2010	Percent Foreign born, 2008–2010
			Total persons	Rank	Per square kilometer	White	Black	American Indian, Alaska Native	Asian	Hawaiian Pacific Islander		
		1	2	3	4	5	6	7	8	9	10	11
29 00000	MISSOURI...............	178 039.7	5 988 927	X	33.6	82.6	12.3	1.1	2.0	0.2	3.5	3.8
29 03160	Ballwin......................	23.3	30 404	1 339	1 305.5	89.1	3.0	0.5	6.3	0.0	2.4	9.7
29 06652	Blue Springs.................	57.7	52 575	723	911.3	86.9	7.4	1.1	1.8	0.3	5.0	2.3
29 11242	Cape Girardeau.............	73.6	37 941	1 043	515.3	82.2	14.1	0.7	2.2	0.1	2.8	3.3
29 13600	Chesterfield	82.3	47 484	834	577.0	85.6	2.9	0.4	9.3	0.1	2.8	9.6
29 15670	Columbia	163.4	108 500	246	664.1	79.5	12.6	0.9	6.0	0.1	3.4	8.5
29 24778	Florissant....................	32.5	52 158	730	1 603.4	70.0	28.0	0.7	1.2	0.1	2.0	1.8
29 27190	Gladstone....................	20.9	25 410	1 636	1 218.1	84.5	6.3	1.4	2.4	0.7	7.3	5.4
29 31276	Hazelwood..................	41.5	25 703	1 613	619.5	64.5	31.8	0.8	1.8	0.1	3.0	3.7
29 35000	Independence...............	200.9	116 830	225	581.5	84.6	6.6	1.4	1.3	0.9	7.7	4.4
29 37000	Jefferson City	93.1	43 079	910	462.7	78.4	17.9	0.8	2.2	0.1	2.6	4.2
29 37592	Joplin..........................	92.1	50 150	766	544.5	88.5	4.6	3.2	2.0	0.4	4.5	2.3
29 38000	Kansas City	815.7	459 787	37	563.7	56.8	31.0	1.2	3.0	0.3	10.0	8.0
29 39044	Kirkwood.....................	23.7	27 540	1 498	1 161.0	89.4	7.6	0.5	1.9	0.1	1.8	3.8
29 41348	Lee's Summit	164.1	91 364	330	556.9	85.6	9.2	0.8	2.3	0.2	3.9	3.1
29 42032	Liberty........................	75.2	29 149	1 412	387.7	90.7	4.5	1.2	1.5	0.2	4.1	2.1
29 46586	Maryland Heights	56.5	27 472	1 500	485.9	73.1	12.8	0.6	10.7	0.1	4.5	17.3
29 54074	O'Fallon	75.6	79 329	408	1 049.3	89.7	4.6	0.6	3.7	0.1	2.7	4.3
29 60788	Raytown	25.7	29 526	1 391	1 148.0	67.9	26.8	1.4	1.5	0.4	5.1	2.6
29 64082	St. Charles	61.3	65 794	534	1 074.2	86.9	6.8	0.7	3.0	0.1	4.2	3.7
29 64550	St. Joseph	113.9	76 780	429	673.9	86.8	7.2	1.0	1.2	0.3	5.7	3.0
29 65000	St. Louis	160.3	319 294	58	1 991.4	43.8	50.3	0.9	3.4	0.1	3.5	6.8
29 65126	St. Peters	57.9	52 575	724	907.6	91.6	4.3	0.6	2.4	0.1	2.5	3.3
29 70000	Springfield	211.7	159 498	150	753.6	89.4	5.3	1.8	2.4	0.3	3.7	3.1
29 75220	University City	15.3	35 371	1 137	2 313.3	51.2	42.4	0.9	5.0	0.1	2.8	8.5
29 78442	Wentzville	51.7	29 010	1 417	562.2	89.7	7.0	0.5	1.5	0.1	2.7	1.2
29 79820	Wildwood....................	172.0	35 517	1 132	206.5	91.7	2.0	0.5	4.8	0.1	2.3	5.1
30 00000	MONTANA	376 961.9	989 415	X	2.6	89.9	0.7	7.5	1.0	0.2	2.9	2.0
30 06550	Billings........................	112.4	104 170	267	926.4	89.0	1.3	5.3	1.2	0.2	5.2	1.8
30 08950	Bozeman	49.5	37 280	1 061	752.8	93.4	0.8	1.8	2.6	0.2	2.9	3.9
30 11390	Butte-Silver Bow..........	1 860.9	34 200	1 180	18.4	93.7	0.5	2.8	0.7	0.1	3.7	2.5
30 32800	Great Falls..................	56.4	58 505	627	1 036.6	89.7	1.7	6.8	1.5	0.2	3.4	2.6
30 35600	Helena........................	42.3	28 190	1 463	665.8	93.8	0.7	3.6	1.1	0.1	2.8	1.5
30 50200	Missoula......................	71.3	66 788	518	937.2	92.6	1.0	3.8	1.9	0.2	2.9	2.7
31 00000	NEBRASKA...............	198 973.7	1 826 341	X	9.2	83.5	5.2	1.3	2.2	0.1	9.2	6.1
31 03950	Bellevue......................	41.1	50 137	767	1 221.1	78.7	7.4	1.2	3.3	0.3	11.9	9.3
31 17670	Fremont......................	22.8	26 397	1 569	1 157.8	86.2	1.0	0.7	0.8	0.2	11.9	7.1
31 19595	Grand Island................	73.6	48 520	805	659.4	69.5	2.3	0.8	1.5	0.1	26.7	13.9
31 25055	Kearney.......................	33.1	30 787	1 316	930.7	89.6	1.4	0.5	2.0	0.0	7.3	3.5
31 28000	Lincoln........................	230.8	258 379	72	1 119.5	85.3	5.0	1.2	4.4	0.1	6.3	7.5
31 37000	Omaha........................	329.2	408 958	42	1 242.4	69.8	14.9	1.2	2.9	0.2	13.1	9.4
32 00000	NEVADA....................	284 331.9	2 700 551	X	9.5	56.6	8.7	1.5	8.5	1.1	26.5	19.3
32 09700	Carson City	374.7	55 274	682	147.5	72.4	2.2	2.8	2.7	0.4	21.3	11.3
32 31900	Henderson...................	279.0	257 729	73	923.7	71.6	5.9	1.1	8.9	1.1	14.9	11.4
32 40000	Las Vegas	351.8	583 756	30	1 659.5	50.2	11.8	1.0	7.3	1.0	31.5	22.2
32 51800	North Las Vegas	262.5	216 961	94	826.6	33.8	20.8	1.0	7.8	1.4	38.8	23.4
32 60600	Reno...........................	266.8	225 221	89	844.2	64.8	3.4	1.6	7.5	1.0	24.3	17.3
32 68400	Sparks	92.6	90 264	337	974.7	63.6	3.2	1.6	7.0	1.0	26.3	16.5
33 00000	NEW HAMPSHIRE.....	23 187.3	1 316 470	X	56.8	93.6	1.5	0.7	2.6	0.1	2.8	5.2
33 14200	Concord......................	166.4	42 695	920	256.6	91.9	2.7	0.9	3.9	0.1	2.1	4.9
33 18820	Dover.........................	69.2	29 987	1 361	433.3	91.2	2.4	0.7	5.3	0.2	2.2	6.0
33 45140	Manchester..................	85.7	109 565	244	1 278.0	83.9	4.6	0.7	4.2	0.1	8.1	11.9
33 50260	Nashua.......................	79.9	86 494	357	1 082.5	80.5	2.9	0.6	7.1	0.1	9.8	12.3
33 65140	Rochester....................	117.6	29 752	1 378	253.0	95.7	1.4	0.8	1.6	0.1	1.8	2.3
34 00000	NEW JERSEY............	19 047.3	8 791 894	X	461.6	60.5	13.5	0.5	8.9	0.1	17.7	20.6
34 02080	Atlantic City	27.8	39 558	1 000	1 421.4	17.1	36.8	0.9	16.4	0.1	30.4	28.1
34 03580	Bayonne......................	15.0	63 024	563	4 193.2	58.2	8.4	0.4	8.2	0.2	25.8	26.6
34 05170	Bergenfield..................	7.5	26 764	1 546	3 592.5	40.5	7.1	0.4	26.6	0.1	26.5	34.4
34 07600	Bridgeton.....................	16.0	25 349	1 639	1 584.3	20.4	35.4	1.5	0.7	0.0	43.6	22.0
34 10000	Camden.......................	23.1	77 344	421	3 346.8	5.6	45.4	0.7	2.3	0.1	47.0	14.5
34 13690	Clifton.........................	29.2	84 136	377	2 885.3	54.6	4.2	0.3	9.8	0.1	31.9	35.9
34 19390	East Orange................	10.2	64 270	548	6 325.8	2.8	88.2	0.9	0.9	0.2	7.9	23.2
34 21000	Elizabeth.....................	31.9	124 969	203	3 916.3	18.9	19.1	0.3	2.3	0.1	59.5	45.4
34 21480	Englewood...................	12.7	27 147	1 520	2 132.5	32.2	32.1	0.8	8.6	0.1	27.5	29.9
34 22470	Fair Lawn	13.3	32 457	1 255	2 438.5	78.3	1.7	0.2	10.3	0.0	10.2	25.4
34 24420	Fort Lee......................	6.6	35 345	1 138	5 371.6	47.8	2.6	0.2	39.3	0.1	11.0	49.8

1. Dry land or land partially or temporarily covered by water.   2. May be of any race.

Table D. Cities — **Population**

City	Under 5 years	5 to 17 years	18 to 24 years	25 to 34 years	35 to 44 years	45 to 54 years	55 to 64 years	65 to 74 years	75 years and over	Median age	Percent female	1990	2000	1990–2000	2000–2010
	12	13	14	15	16	17	18	19	20	21	22	23	24	25	26
MISSOURI	6.5	17.3	9.8	12.9	12.5	14.8	12.1	7.5	6.5	37.9	51.0	5 116 901	5 595 211	9.3	7.0
Ballwin	5.9	19.0	6.8	10.3	13.5	16.5	12.9	8.0	7.1	41.2	51.8	27 054	31 283	15.6	-2.8
Blue Springs	7.2	20.7	8.5	14.0	13.8	14.6	11.8	5.7	3.6	34.7	51.5	40 103	48 080	19.9	9.3
Cape Girardeau	6.1	13.2	20.2	13.6	9.9	11.7	10.6	6.4	8.3	32.1	52.6	34 475	35 349	2.5	7.3
Chesterfield	4.3	17.9	5.7	8.2	11.2	16.8	15.7	10.1	10.0	46.6	52.2	42 325	46 802	10.6	1.5
Columbia	6.0	12.9	27.2	16.3	10.5	10.4	8.4	4.2	4.3	26.8	51.7	69 133	84 531	22.3	28.4
Florissant	6.4	17.5	8.6	14.1	12.1	14.7	11.2	6.7	8.8	38.0	53.2	51 038	50 497	-1.1	3.3
Gladstone	6.4	14.9	7.8	12.7	11.8	14.8	13.9	8.9	8.7	41.7	52.1	26 243	26 365	0.5	-3.6
Hazelwood	6.2	17.0	10.0	14.6	12.5	16.0	11.3	6.6	5.8	36.8	53.0	15 512	26 206	68.9	-1.9
Independence	6.8	16.2	8.7	13.2	11.7	15.0	12.3	8.0	8.1	39.4	52.0	112 301	113 288	0.9	3.1
Jefferson City	6.5	14.4	10.4	15.5	13.0	14.5	12.3	6.3	7.1	37.5	48.8	35 517	39 636	11.6	8.7
Joplin	7.3	15.3	12.8	14.5	11.7	12.7	10.9	7.2	7.6	35.0	52.1	41 175	45 504	10.5	10.2
Kansas City	7.5	16.6	10.0	16.4	13.3	14.1	11.0	5.8	5.2	34.6	51.5	434 829	441 545	1.5	4.1
Kirkwood	5.9	17.3	6.1	11.3	12.4	15.6	14.3	8.0	9.1	42.6	54.0	28 318	27 324	-3.5	0.8
Lee's Summit	6.9	21.2	7.0	12.0	14.8	15.7	10.9	6.0	5.5	37.2	52.1	46 418	70 700	52.3	29.2
Liberty	6.7	19.9	9.7	11.9	14.1	15.3	11.3	5.9	5.2	36.4	51.3	20 459	26 232	28.2	11.1
Maryland Heights	6.0	14.2	10.8	19.0	12.9	14.4	10.4	6.6	5.6	35.0	51.3	25 440	25 756	1.2	6.7
O'Fallon	8.0	22.0	7.1	14.0	16.9	14.8	8.4	5.0	4.0	34.3	51.2	17 427	46 169	164.9	71.8
Raytown	6.1	17.0	8.0	12.4	12.5	15.7	12.1	7.1	9.1	40.3	52.7	30 601	30 388	-0.7	-2.8
St. Charles	5.9	13.8	13.8	14.7	11.3	14.9	11.7	7.1	6.9	36.6	51.0	50 634	60 321	19.1	9.1
St. Joseph	7.1	16.6	11.6	14.0	12.0	13.9	11.0	6.7	7.1	35.6	50.2	71 852	73 990	3.0	3.8
St. Louis	6.6	14.5	12.3	18.1	12.6	14.0	10.8	5.5	5.5	33.9	51.7	396 685	348 189	-12.2	-8.3
St. Peters	5.7	17.5	8.4	13.7	13.2	17.3	12.8	5.9	5.5	38.8	51.8	40 660	51 381	26.4	2.3
Springfield	6.0	12.3	18.4	15.3	10.7	12.3	10.5	6.8	7.7	33.2	51.5	140 494	151 580	7.9	5.2
University City	6.0	13.5	11.3	16.3	12.2	12.3	12.3	8.1	7.9	37.4	53.4	40 087	37 428	-6.6	-5.5
Wentzville	10.6	23.2	6.1	17.4	16.3	11.4	7.7	4.7	2.8	31.2	51.5	NA	6 896	NA	321.5
Wildwood	5.0	25.3	5.8	5.6	14.7	20.6	14.0	5.6	3.3	41.5	50.6	16 527	32 884	99.0	8.0
MONTANA	6.3	16.3	9.6	12.4	11.4	15.1	14.0	8.2	6.7	39.8	49.8	799 065	902 195	12.9	9.7
Billings	7.0	15.6	9.8	14.7	11.5	14.2	12.1	7.2	7.8	37.5	51.7	81 125	89 847	10.8	15.9
Bozeman	5.5	10.2	28.2	20.7	10.7	9.0	7.7	3.5	4.6	27.2	47.4	22 660	27 509	21.4	35.5
Butte-Silver Bow	5.8	15.2	10.8	11.3	11.3	15.5	13.7	8.7	7.7	41.3	49.5	33 252	34 606	4.1	-1.2
Great Falls	6.7	15.8	9.9	13.4	11.2	14.4	12.0	8.2	8.4	39.0	51.1	55 125	56 690	2.8	3.2
Helena	5.9	14.2	11.6	12.9	10.5	14.5	14.9	7.5	8.1	40.3	52.0	24 609	25 780	4.8	9.3
Missoula	5.7	12.2	19.8	18.7	10.9	11.5	10.6	6.2	5.4	30.9	50.1	42 918	57 053	32.9	17.1
NEBRASKA	7.2	17.9	10.0	13.4	12.1	14.2	11.7	6.7	6.8	36.2	50.4	1 578 417	1 711 263	8.4	6.7
Bellevue	7.3	19.1	9.8	14.0	12.6	14.8	10.8	6.8	4.7	34.8	50.8	39 240	44 382	13.1	13.0
Fremont	7.3	17.0	9.7	12.8	11.2	13.6	11.2	7.6	9.6	38.0	51.5	23 680	25 174	6.3	4.9
Grand Island	8.4	19.2	8.7	14.1	12.6	13.3	10.7	6.0	6.9	34.7	50.2	39 487	42 940	8.7	13.0
Kearney	7.5	14.7	20.4	15.4	10.2	11.0	9.6	5.3	5.8	29.0	51.1	24 396	27 431	12.4	12.2
Lincoln	7.2	15.5	15.6	16.0	11.9	12.4	10.5	5.4	5.3	31.8	50.0	191 972	225 581	17.5	14.5
Omaha	7.5	17.6	11.3	15.5	12.3	13.5	10.9	5.8	5.6	33.5	50.8	344 463	390 007	13.2	4.9
NEVADA	6.9	17.7	9.2	14.3	14.2	13.9	11.7	7.3	4.7	36.3	49.5	1 201 675	1 998 257	66.3	35.1
Carson City	5.8	15.5	8.5	12.0	12.6	15.2	13.8	8.7	7.8	41.7	48.1	40 443	52 457	29.7	5.4
Henderson	5.9	16.8	7.8	13.0	14.5	14.3	13.5	9.0	5.2	39.6	50.8	64 948	175 381	170.0	47.0
Las Vegas	7.2	18.4	8.9	14.2	14.7	13.8	10.8	7.0	5.0	35.9	49.6	258 877	478 434	84.8	22.0
North Las Vegas	9.0	22.5	9.7	15.9	15.3	12.0	8.4	4.7	2.4	30.6	50.2	47 849	115 488	141.4	87.9
Reno	7.0	15.8	12.5	15.2	13.0	13.4	11.4	6.6	5.0	34.6	49.2	134 230	180 480	34.5	24.8
Sparks	7.2	18.6	9.7	13.7	13.9	14.2	11.4	6.5	4.8	35.5	50.6	53 367	66 346	24.3	36.1
NEW HAMPSHIRE	5.3	16.5	9.4	11.0	13.6	17.2	13.5	7.4	6.2	41.1	50.7	1 109 252	1 235 786	11.4	6.5
Concord	5.5	15.2	9.3	14.2	13.9	15.9	12.3	6.1	7.7	39.4	50.4	36 006	40 687	13.0	4.9
Dover	6.0	14.2	11.1	16.4	14.1	14.5	10.5	6.0	7.0	36.7	51.0	25 042	26 884	7.4	11.5
Manchester	6.7	14.9	10.2	16.8	13.6	14.8	11.2	5.7	6.1	36.0	50.4	99 332	107 006	7.7	2.4
Nashua	6.3	15.8	9.3	13.8	14.3	15.9	11.9	6.5	6.2	38.5	50.7	79 662	86 605	8.7	-0.1
Rochester	6.0	16.0	7.7	12.7	13.5	16.3	12.9	7.8	6.9	40.7	51.7	26 630	28 461	6.9	4.5
NEW JERSEY	6.2	17.3	8.7	12.6	14.1	15.7	11.9	7.0	6.5	39.0	51.3	7 747 750	8 414 350	8.6	4.5
Atlantic City	7.8	16.8	10.2	13.6	13.2	14.5	11.2	6.9	5.8	36.3	51.0	37 986	40 517	6.7	-2.4
Bayonne	6.1	16.4	8.9	14.2	13.9	15.1	12.3	6.6	6.6	38.4	52.2	61 464	61 842	0.6	1.9
Bergenfield	6.5	17.4	8.6	12.3	13.8	15.7	12.6	6.9	6.2	39.0	52.2	24 458	26 247	7.3	2.0
Bridgeton	9.9	18.0	12.2	20.0	14.6	11.7	6.5	3.8	3.4	29.7	42.5	18 942	22 771	20.2	11.3
Camden	9.2	21.8	13.1	15.6	12.4	12.0	8.2	4.6	3.0	28.5	51.4	87 492	79 904	-8.7	-3.2
Clifton	6.1	15.9	8.8	14.5	13.8	14.8	12.2	6.6	7.3	38.4	51.8	71 984	78 672	9.3	6.9
East Orange	7.2	18.4	10.2	14.2	13.6	14.1	10.5	6.6	5.2	35.0	55.2	73 552	69 824	-5.1	-8.0
Elizabeth	8.0	17.7	10.6	16.5	14.8	13.8	9.5	5.2	4.0	33.2	50.4	110 002	120 568	9.6	3.7
Englewood	6.6	15.6	7.7	14.4	14.5	14.5	12.5	7.8	6.4	38.9	52.6	24 850	26 203	5.4	3.6
Fair Lawn	5.2	16.8	6.8	10.3	13.7	16.4	14.4	7.4	8.9	43.1	52.0	30 548	31 637	3.6	2.6
Fort Lee	5.1	11.8	5.3	12.7	15.5	14.3	13.5	10.6	11.2	44.7	53.5	31 997	35 461	10.8	-0.3

Table D. Cities — Households, Group Quarters, Crime, and Education

City	Households, 2010				Persons in group quarters, 2010				Serious crimes known to police,[2] 2010				Educational attainment, 2008–2010		
			Percent			Institutional			Total		Rate[3]			Attainment[4] (percent)	
	Number	Persons per household	Female family householder[1]	One-person	Total	Total	Persons in nursing facilities	Non-institutional	Number	Rate[3]	Violent	Property	Population age 25 and older	High school graduate or less	Bachelor's degree or more
	27	28	29	30	31	32	33	34	35	36	37	38	39	40	41
MISSOURI	2 375 611	2.45	12.3	28.3	174 142	93 274	44 866	80 868	227 666	3 801	455	3 346	3 943 725	45.2	25.3
Ballwin	11 874	2.56	8.8	23.1	2	0	0	2	337	1 108	53	1 056	20 984	18.0	53.0
Blue Springs	19 522	2.68	13.7	20.4	218	182	182	36	1 800	3 424	188	3 235	34 042	33.9	29.0
Cape Girardeau	15 205	2.27	12.8	33.6	3 466	789	712	2 677	2 701	7 119	627	6 492	23 333	42.9	29.6
Chesterfield	19 224	2.42	5.9	26.1	934	925	925	9	1 042	2 194	97	2 098	33 817	14.0	64.4
Columbia	43 065	2.32	10.6	32.0	8 804	1 146	624	7 658	4 346	4 006	488	3 517	57 638	26.0	52.2
Florissant	21 247	2.42	17.5	29.9	788	668	542	120	1 446	2 772	184	2 588	35 574	43.5	19.6
Gladstone	11 182	2.27	12.3	32.4	42	36	36	6	653	2 570	213	2 357	17 281	39.2	27.7
Hazelwood	10 933	2.34	17.3	33.7	140	0	0	140	1 030	4 007	381	3 626	17 440	38.9	23.3
Independence	48 742	2.37	13.9	31.7	1 225	1 048	982	177	7 707	6 597	414	6 182	77 501	52.9	16.6
Jefferson City	17 278	2.21	12.4	36.2	4 964	3 990	456	974	1 865	4 329	457	3 872	26 829	38.2	34.0
Joplin	20 860	2.31	13.5	33.3	1 988	743	653	1 245	3 749	7 476	584	6 891	32 205	46.4	21.5
Kansas City	192 406	2.34	16.1	34.7	8 812	4 192	2 499	4 620	32 841	7 143	1 227	5 915	303 930	39.7	29.9
Kirkwood	11 894	2.29	9.9	33.6	257	223	218	34	883	3 206	105	3 101	18 706	15.2	61.4
Lee's Summit	34 429	2.63	10.9	22.8	714	626	573	88	2 226	2 436	106	2 330	58 080	25.4	43.5
Liberty	10 582	2.63	11.0	23.4	1 358	585	277	773	608	2 086	141	1 945	18 281	32.5	37.0
Maryland Heights	12 180	2.21	11.4	35.2	559	522	473	37	720	2 621	149	2 472	19 632	34.4	36.0
O'Fallon	28 234	2.80	10.0	19.3	294	254	247	40	1 345	1 695	91	1 605	47 285	29.9	39.2
Raytown	12 104	2.39	16.9	30.7	559	401	395	158	1 205	4 081	396	3 685	19 673	41.9	21.9
St. Charles	26 715	2.29	10.8	31.9	4 623	917	508	3 706	2 017	3 066	192	2 874	44 562	41.8	29.9
St. Joseph	29 727	2.43	14.5	30.7	4 493	3 104	673	1 389	3 910	5 092	397	4 695	49 851	52.9	20.3
St. Louis	142 057	2.16	19.4	42.6	11 978	4 822	2 060	7 156	33 529	10 501	1 943	8 558	211 075	43.9	27.7
St. Peters	20 861	2.51	10.0	26.3	203	184	184	19	1 665	3 167	215	2 952	35 797	32.5	32.4
Springfield	69 754	2.13	11.8	37.3	10 739	3 302	1 443	7 437	16 544	10 373	833	9 540	101 134	42.9	24.8
University City	16 154	2.18	15.0	36.5	232	200	169	32	1 623	4 589	659	3 930	24 639	24.8	51.8
Wentzville	9 767	2.96	11.1	15.6	137	133	133	4	556	1 913	138	1 775	16 679	29.4	31.5
Wildwood	12 112	2.93	6.0	13.6	66	62	40	4	NA	NA	NA	NA	22 473	14.1	61.5
MONTANA	409 607	2.35	9.0	29.7	28 849	11 929	5 200	16 920	27 862	2 816	272	2 544	664 198	39.1	28.2
Billings	43 945	2.29	11.3	32.6	3 351	1 750	753	1 601	5 306	5 094	272	4 822	69 784	37.4	31.0
Bozeman	15 775	2.17	7.0	33.5	3 030	199	145	2 831	1 435	3 849	252	3 597	20 671	17.1	50.1
Butte-Silver Bow	14 932	2.22	10.6	35.1	998	610	276	388	1 574	4 602	275	4 327	22 698	46.7	22.1
Great Falls	25 301	2.26	11.5	33.5	1 263	798	482	465	2 900	4 957	212	4 745	39 286	37.7	24.2
Helena	12 780	2.07	10.6	39.8	1 682	432	191	1 250	1 103	3 913	429	3 484	19 166	24.6	45.0
Missoula	29 081	2.18	9.6	35.0	3 519	766	374	2 753	2 712	4 061	346	3 715	41 000	28.1	41.9
NEBRASKA	721 130	2.46	9.8	28.7	51 165	23 633	13 519	27 532	53 925	2 953	279	2 673	1 174 907	38.6	27.8
Bellevue	19 142	2.62	13.0	24.3	74	31	15	43	1 419	2 830	140	2 691	32 196	36.7	26.8
Fremont	10 725	2.38	11.2	30.2	832	468	386	364	858	3 250	189	3 061	17 436	52.3	16.6
Grand Island	18 326	2.59	12.0	29.1	1 058	781	546	277	2 465	5 080	346	4 734	30 039	50.0	16.2
Kearney	12 201	2.36	9.9	30.4	2 002	390	284	1 612	942	3 060	201	2 858	17 571	34.0	37.8
Lincoln	103 546	2.36	10.2	31.3	13 579	4 236	1 001	9 343	11 476	4 442	487	3 955	157 297	30.8	34.8
Omaha	162 627	2.45	13.7	32.3	11 183	4 676	2 002	6 507	19 608	4 795	556	4 239	259 253	36.2	32.0
NEVADA	1 006 250	2.65	12.7	25.7	36 154	25 835	5 005	10 319	92 773	3 435	661	2 775	1 768 726	44.8	21.9
Carson City	21 427	2.41	12.0	30.4	3 625	3 560	313	65	1 295	2 343	293	2 050	38 563	42.7	22.3
Henderson	101 314	2.53	11.0	24.2	1 104	787	585	317	5 739	2 227	211	2 016	179 315	34.0	30.8
Las Vegas	211 689	2.71	14.1	26.0	9 482	6 514	1 628	2 968	55 867	3 863	875	2 988	380 769	47.4	20.6
North Las Vegas	66 499	3.23	16.8	16.7	2 441	2 167	683	274	7 337	3 382	847	2 535	124 171	51.9	15.7
Reno	90 924	2.43	11.8	32.1	4 583	1 679	323	2 904	8 636	3 834	519	3 316	142 715	38.5	27.3
Sparks	33 502	2.68	13.0	24.3	321	256	256	65	3 118	3 454	396	3 059	58 250	42.5	20.4
NEW HAMPSHIRE	518 973	2.46	9.7	25.6	40 104	13 113	7 767	26 991	30 980	2 353	167	2 186	901 717	38.2	32.8
Concord	17 592	2.26	11.6	33.6	2 903	2 282	454	621	1 318	3 087	223	2 865	30 433	35.3	35.0
Dover	12 827	2.27	10.3	31.8	896	789	358	107	525	1 751	110	1 641	19 711	34.0	38.7
Manchester	45 766	2.34	13.1	32.4	2 578	1 547	662	1 031	4 298	3 923	497	3 426	74 777	46.2	26.1
Nashua	35 044	2.42	11.6	29.4	1 685	546	505	1 139	2 391	2 764	201	2 563	58 359	37.8	34.5
Rochester	12 378	2.38	12.2	27.8	240	192	181	48	1 084	3 643	346	3 297	20 823	48.3	18.6
NEW JERSEY	3 214 360	2.68	13.3	25.2	186 876	100 621	45 512	86 255	210 097	2 390	308	2 082	5 925 769	41.7	34.9
Atlantic City	15 504	2.50	22.2	37.5	802	186	186	616	3 752	9 485	1 979	7 505	26 047	61.7	16.5
Bayonne	25 237	2.49	16.8	31.6	276	0	0	276	1 047	1 661	257	1 404	44 248	50.2	29.7
Bergenfield	8 852	3.02	13.7	19.4	38	0	0	38	137	512	112	400	18 138	37.4	40.8
Bridgeton	6 265	3.36	27.7	25.8	4 276	4 257	0	19	1 367	5 393	1 262	4 130	15 445	75.7	8.1
Camden	24 475	3.02	37.9	24.8	3 321	2 229	290	1 092	5 341	6 906	2 380	4 525	43 749	72.7	7.5
Clifton	30 661	2.74	13.0	26.0	254	192	182	62	1 512	1 797	210	1 587	59 568	46.3	32.0
East Orange	24 945	2.53	29.0	35.8	1 235	780	716	455	1 854	2 885	758	2 127	41 775	52.9	16.3
Elizabeth	41 596	2.94	22.0	23.5	2 545	1 833	398	712	6 126	4 902	1 114	3 788	77 149	67.3	12.1
Englewood	10 057	2.68	17.1	27.3	164	136	136	28	575	2 118	236	1 882	19 009	38.5	43.3
Fair Lawn	11 930	2.70	9.1	21.3	187	152	152	35	387	1 192	83	1 109	22 581	30.6	48.7
Fort Lee	16 371	2.16	8.5	38.4	7	0	0	7	354	1 002	96	905	26 944	25.1	55.1

1. No spouse present.   2. Data for serious crimes have not been adjusted for underreporting. This may affect comparability between geographic areas and over time.   3. Per 100,000 population estimated by the FBI.   4. Persons 25 years old and over.

Table D. Cities — Income, Poverty, and Housing

City	Money income, 2008–2010					Housing units, 2010			Occupied Housing units 2008–2010				
		Households			Families with income below poverty (percent)				Owner-occupied			Median owner costs as a percent of income	
	Per capita income[1] (dollars)	Median income	Percent with income of $200,000 or more	Percent with income of less than $25,000		Total	Percent change, 2000–2010	Vacant units for sale or rent[2]	Total	Percent	Median value[3] (dollars)	With a mortgage[4]	Without a mortgage[5]
	42	43	44	45	46	47	48	49	50	51	52	53	54
MISSOURI..................	24 496	45 829	2.5	26.6	10.2	2 712 729	11.1	337 118	2 355 253	69.3	139 700	22.4	11.5
Ballwin..........................	37 061	79 651	5.8	9.7	2.3	12 435	3.2	561	11 860	80.5	235 900	20.6	10.1
Blue Springs................	27 623	63 860	2.6	14.4	6.1	20 643	16.0	1 121	19 243	72.9	147 800	22.3	11.0
Cape Girardeau............	21 415	38 526	2.6	32.0	13.7	16 760	6.0	1 555	14 906	54.6	133 000	20.7	10.9
Chesterfield.................	51 210	98 309	15.8	11.1	1.4	20 393	8.5	1 169	18 924	80.2	332 700	19.9	11.1
Columbia	23 833	40 816	2.6	31.7	11.0	46 758	30.0	3 693	42 576	48.6	164 900	21.5	10.0
Florissant.....................	24 097	50 124	0.6	19.3	4.9	22 632	8.0	1 385	21 753	76.7	117 600	23.9	12.4
Gladstone.....................	26 254	49 952	2.1	21.4	7.4	12 148	1.8	966	11 084	64.5	137 500	22.5	13.0
Hazelwood...................	23 515	45 797	0.5	22.4	7.3	11 730	2.9	797	11 059	60.1	124 000	23.5	11.1
Independence..............	22 015	43 215	0.8	29.0	11.9	53 834	7.3	5 092	46 547	64.8	108 900	22.4	13.3
Jefferson City..............	24 169	48 026	2.2	24.7	8.6	18 852	10.9	1 574	16 466	60.5	135 700	18.6	10.0
Joplin...........................	23 443	37 438	2.3	32.9	14.7	23 322	9.2	2 462	20 127	54.8	97 700	22.0	11.6
Kansas City.................	25 666	43 587	2.7	28.4	13.5	221 860	9.7	29 454	192 626	57.6	137 500	23.4	12.9
Kirkwood......................	44 250	70 991	9.6	18.3	3.7	12 895	4.6	1 001	11 666	78.0	235 300	21.0	12.2
Lee's Summit	32 912	72 062	4.5	12.5	4.6	36 679	33.9	2 250	33 602	75.4	185 900	21.7	11.5
Liberty.........................	28 010	64 201	3.2	13.8	5.1	11 284	14.5	702	10 592	78.3	161 000	22.8	11.1
Maryland Heights	28 106	52 221	1.3	19.1	7.1	13 092	10.7	912	12 306	53.6	164 700	22.9	11.4
O'Fallon.......................	29 036	75 412	3.2	10.1	2.9	29 376	84.8	1 142	26 800	84.8	209 200	22.5	12.2
Raytown.......................	22 791	48 215	0.9	22.7	5.2	13 276	-0.2	1 172	11 658	72.3	104 700	22.8	13.0
St. Charles	28 113	53 559	2.7	20.8	8.2	28 590	13.4	1 875	26 612	65.9	182 800	22.1	11.9
St. Joseph	21 256	40 861	1.3	29.7	10.7	33 189	4.7	3 462	29 342	63.1	101 200	20.5	11.2
St. Louis	21 605	33 657	1.5	38.6	21.0	176 002	-0.2	33 945	140 844	45.9	122 900	24.0	13.4
St. Peters	30 263	70 679	1.7	10.3	1.6	21 717	15.5	856	20 866	80.6	173 200	21.9	10.0
Springfield...................	20 078	32 279	1.2	38.7	17.8	77 620	11.1	7 866	69 784	49.9	106 900	21.2	10.2
University City	35 314	51 912	8.7	25.1	8.8	18 021	3.0	1 867	15 911	56.2	197 900	21.9	12.2
Wentzville.....................	26 262	69 339	2.5	8.8	2.0	10 305	NA	538	9 281	85.8	201 700	25.7	11.9
Wildwood......................	49 130	115 181	22.1	6.3	1.5	12 604	11.5	492	11 908	91.1	356 000	20.8	10.8
MONTANA	23 844	43 335	1.9	27.8	10.0	482 825	17.0	73 218	404 616	68.9	180 800	24.0	11.6
Billings.........................	26 556	46 065	2.6	24.7	8.8	46 317	18.3	2 372	43 934	64.3	176 100	22.5	11.5
Bozeman	25 611	41 705	2.7	28.8	10.4	17 464	50.0	1 689	15 566	47.5	268 700	23.9	11.4
Butte-Silver Bow..........	21 780	38 660	0.7	32.8	10.7	16 717	3.3	1 785	14 638	66.1	128 500	20.8	12.2
Great Falls...................	22 491	40 768	1.0	28.4	12.0	26 854	6.3	1 553	24 952	64.5	152 000	23.5	11.5
Helena.........................	28 011	47 969	2.6	24.2	6.2	13 457	11.0	677	12 816	58.2	193 300	22.5	10.0
Missoula	22 468	36 872	1.5	35.1	10.0	30 682	22.3	1 601	28 736	49.4	244 300	26.6	11.2
NEBRASKA...............	25 207	49 075	2.5	23.7	7.8	796 793	10.3	75 663	715 188	68.4	126 300	21.9	12.5
Bellevue.......................	24 963	55 607	1.1	17.6	6.4	20 591	18.0	1 449	19 263	67.3	139 200	22.1	11.8
Fremont........................	20 970	44 643	0.8	28.4	9.8	11 427	8.0	702	10 762	62.2	113 400	21.3	13.8
Grand Island................	21 094	44 638	1.0	26.6	8.9	19 426	11.7	1 100	18 181	63.8	106 700	21.3	13.8
Kearney........................	23 033	44 665	1.6	27.8	13.0	12 738	15.7	537	11 613	58.9	134 400	21.6	10.0
Lincoln.........................	24 981	49 203	2.3	25.3	8.9	110 546	16.1	7 000	102 727	59.1	142 100	22.7	11.0
Omaha.........................	25 872	45 115	3.2	26.5	11.0	177 518	7.1	14 891	163 166	59.6	134 200	22.7	13.2
NEVADA..................	26 520	54 065	3.2	20.4	9.5	1 173 814	41.9	167 564	984 519	58.7	220 000	28.9	11.9
Carson City	27 196	54 492	1.8	22.7	9.6	23 534	10.6	2 107	20 986	61.6	250 200	25.9	12.2
Henderson....................	34 075	65 047	5.8	14.7	5.3	113 586	59.0	12 272	100 281	66.2	267 400	28.6	10.9
Las Vegas....................	25 549	52 382	3.3	22.2	10.7	243 701	27.7	32 012	210 805	55.5	214 100	29.2	12.1
North Las Vegas	21 259	57 040	1.9	15.8	10.7	76 073	107.9	9 574	63 798	61.7	189 400	30.6	10.0
Reno............................	26 661	47 355	3.2	26.4	13.1	102 582	28.9	11 658	88 415	47.7	251 800	28.7	11.8
Sparks.........................	24 725	54 385	1.9	20.8	9.5	36 455	39.8	2 953	33 171	59.6	231 100	28.8	13.8
NEW HAMPSHIRE.....	31 256	61 989	4.5	17.4	5.3	614 754	12.4	95 781	515 185	72.0	251 000	26.8	16.5
Concord.......................	28 907	50 827	2.9	21.4	6.3	18 852	11.7	1 260	18 407	51.7	230 200	25.8	19.1
Dover...........................	31 271	53 641	4.3	19.7	7.0	13 685	14.8	858	12 436	52.8	247 700	26.6	17.0
Manchester..................	26 980	51 643	2.2	22.2	10.0	49 288	7.4	3 522	45 022	51.0	233 200	28.4	17.6
Nashua.........................	33 459	63 929	4.2	20.0	6.2	37 168	5.0	2 124	34 609	58.6	254 700	25.4	17.2
Rochester....................	27 404	50 341	1.3	17.8	10.0	13 372	13.0	994	12 748	69.6	192 600	26.3	18.7
NEW JERSEY...........	34 622	69 400	8.3	17.4	7.0	3 553 562	7.3	339 202	3 176 234	66.5	350 300	28.7	18.9
Atlantic City	18 673	29 119	1.9	43.1	26.3	20 013	-1.0	4 509	16 335	37.1	222 800	35.3	22.8
Bayonne.......................	29 398	55 458	4.3	22.7	10.1	27 799	3.6	2 562	25 234	42.1	347 700	33.1	18.4
Bergenfield	35 591	83 191	9.0	15.3	5.3	9 200	0.6	348	9 099	72.7	374 600	30.6	19.0
Bridgeton	12 312	32 470	1.8	41.3	28.7	6 782	-0.2	517	5 920	42.4	127 200	25.8	21.9
Camden........................	12 777	27 024	0.3	45.5	33.5	28 358	-4.7	3 883	24 982	41.2	95 800	33.3	18.5
Clifton..........................	30 552	63 407	4.2	17.8	6.8	31 946	2.9	1 285	29 621	61.6	360 400	32.5	22.5
East Orange.................	20 874	40 312	1.2	32.8	16.0	28 803	1.1	3 858	24 100	26.4	256 900	35.1	28.1
Elizabeth......................	18 559	43 394	1.6	28.6	16.0	45 516	6.3	3 920	39 225	28.6	332 600	39.3	26.8
Englewood...................	38 690	60 073	9.4	22.0	8.9	10 695	11.2	638	10 296	56.6	409 800	36.6	32.3
Fair Lawn.....................	40 908	91 852	10.4	11.7	2.8	12 266	2.2	336	11 792	77.7	430 200	28.3	20.5
Fort Lee.......................	45 355	68 170	8.8	19.5	7.1	17 818	2.1	1 447	16 653	62.3	363 000	28.1	17.7

1. Based on population estimated by the American Community Survey.   2. Includes units rented or sold but not occupied.   3. Specified owner-occupied units; $1,000,000 represents $1,000,000 or more.   4. 50.0 represents 50 percent or more.   5. 10.0 represents 10 percent or less.

Table D. Cities — Housing, Labor Force, and Employment

City	Occupied housing units, 2008–2010 (cont.)				Migration, 2008–2010		Civilian labor force, 2010		Unemployment		Civilian employment[4], 2008–2010			
											Population age 16 and older	Percent		
	Percent renter occupied	Median gross rent[1]	Median rent as a percent of income[2]	Percent with no vehicle available	Percent who lived in the same house one year ago	Percent who lived outside this city one year ago	Total	Percent change, 2009–2010	Total	Rate[3]	Population age 16 and older	In labor force	Full-year full-time worker	Households with no workers (percent)
	55	56	57	58	59	60	61	62	63	64	65	66	67	68
MISSOURI	30.7	677	29.0	7.1	83.4	11.1	3 052 847	0.1	285 541	9.4	4 703 113	65.2	41.8	27.3
Ballwin	19.5	875	26.4	1.2	87.5	9.4	16 329	1.9	1 109	6.8	24 278	72.0	48.2	18.2
Blue Springs	27.1	848	26.1	2.0	85.5	9.8	28 964	-5.6	2 417	8.3	40 999	73.0	50.4	18.1
Cape Girardeau	45.4	595	27.3	7.5	73.0	12.8	19 290	0.0	1 425	7.4	31 154	64.9	38.1	27.7
Chesterfield	19.8	936	26.0	2.8	89.4	8.0	24 605	4.3	1 563	6.4	38 622	63.5	42.1	24.4
Columbia	51.4	747	32.3	7.6	66.4	15.8	59 768	5.2	3 454	5.8	89 303	68.4	37.7	22.3
Florissant	23.3	769	27.0	4.8	89.0	8.7	27 346	3.9	2 634	9.6	42 057	68.7	45.2	27.1
Gladstone	35.5	714	26.5	6.1	79.4	16.3	13 914	-10.2	1 223	8.8	20 443	68.3	45.7	26.5
Hazelwood	39.9	744	27.9	7.0	86.5	12.0	14 955	2.7	1 467	9.8	20 069	71.0	49.3	24.3
Independence	35.2	704	29.6	7.2	85.9	7.2	58 617	5.1	5 850	10.0	91 395	64.5	40.6	30.4
Jefferson City	39.5	534	23.5	8.4	76.7	15.6	21 725	3.6	1 453	6.7	34 685	58.5	42.4	25.6
Joplin	45.2	649	28.7	9.2	76.4	12.2	24 786	2.0	2 066	8.3	40 478	65.4	40.6	28.2
Kansas City	42.4	727	30.1	11.4	80.4	8.2	231 366	2.1	23 832	10.3	357 602	69.4	46.0	25.2
Kirkwood	22.0	904	28.4	5.2	88.2	8.5	14 748	3.8	969	6.6	21 728	69.1	44.3	24.8
Lee's Summit	24.6	917	28.2	4.5	86.6	8.7	47 993	7.6	3 447	7.2	66 766	73.8	50.4	19.3
Liberty	21.7	681	27.1	3.6	80.6	14.7	15 111	-5.3	1 140	7.5	22 161	67.5	45.6	22.2
Maryland Heights	46.4	764	23.2	4.0	77.2	16.7	16 730	6.8	1 231	7.4	23 064	68.2	47.2	19.6
O'Fallon	15.2	864	25.6	2.3	87.0	10.0	42 690	4.7	3 075	7.2	55 894	77.0	52.3	14.5
Raytown	27.7	812	26.3	7.0	83.4	12.5	14 965	4.2	1 613	10.8	23 043	67.9	48.5	26.7
St. Charles	34.1	737	28.1	6.5	82.5	12.3	36 883	3.8	3 048	8.3	54 287	65.3	42.1	27.5
St. Joseph	36.9	625	27.8	9.5	76.2	9.4	42 646	3.3	3 515	8.2	60 226	62.4	40.2	28.5
St. Louis	54.1	672	32.0	21.3	76.8	9.2	145 651	-7.9	18 671	12.8	257 866	66.7	40.4	30.2
St. Peters	19.4	833	22.7	1.8	91.5	7.0	30 640	-3.6	2 455	8.0	42 687	74.8	52.9	15.8
Springfield	50.1	612	31.0	9.1	71.8	13.3	81 777	1.8	6 885	8.4	133 837	63.5	36.0	30.2
University City	43.8	799	28.8	12.8	79.8	14.4	19 144	-1.1	1 636	8.5	28 962	66.0	42.3	27.7
Wentzville	14.2	861	33.5	2.8	89.7	8.7	14 384	NA	1 067	7.4	18 983	77.7	53.9	14.0
Wildwood	8.9	902	28.0	2.3	92.1	6.5	18 431	4.8	1 172	6.4	25 630	70.3	47.3	14.6
MONTANA	31.1	639	28.0	5.3	83.6	10.7	500 078	0.7	34 463	6.9	787 443	65.2	40.1	27.3
Billings	35.7	688	27.2	6.2	81.8	7.9	57 563	-3.8	3 028	5.3	81 809	69.1	44.3	22.6
Bozeman	52.5	746	30.7	6.1	60.6	21.0	20 763	-4.8	1 230	5.9	31 979	70.6	36.2	22.0
Butte-Silver Bow	33.9	528	29.0	10.2	83.6	6.9	17 658	3.2	1 052	6.0	26 882	60.5	38.4	32.1
Great Falls	35.5	551	25.8	8.6	78.9	9.3	29 849	0.7	1 709	5.7	46 723	65.3	41.6	28.0
Helena	41.8	652	28.5	9.7	75.4	15.7	15 280	-6.3	823	5.4	23 440	66.7	41.7	27.6
Missoula	50.6	691	36.1	8.1	72.6	16.9	36 232	-2.5	2 241	6.2	55 880	67.9	36.1	24.7
NEBRASKA	31.6	651	26.9	5.6	82.8	8.8	988 509	0.8	46 434	4.7	1 408 450	71.3	47.6	22.3
Bellevue	32.7	753	27.9	3.1	82.7	10.9	25 928	-1.9	1 304	5.0	38 448	74.1	51.1	18.5
Fremont	37.8	611	25.6	6.1	80.6	7.9	14 068	0.9	690	4.9	20 557	69.9	45.1	27.1
Grand Island	36.2	608	27.0	6.6	80.4	8.9	26 233	3.4	1 155	4.4	35 749	75.8	51.1	20.7
Kearney	41.1	624	27.7	3.5	75.4	12.4	19 124	0.8	600	3.1	24 612	72.6	44.1	16.5
Lincoln	40.9	669	27.9	6.6	76.2	8.5	144 949	0.8	5 950	4.1	203 916	72.8	45.2	21.1
Omaha	40.4	712	29.6	9.7	79.5	6.8	211 784	-9.9	11 314	5.3	316 638	71.9	46.0	23.2
NEVADA	41.3	991	31.0	7.2	77.9	13.4	1 385 729	2.3	190 420	13.7	2 091 705	67.8	43.4	23.7
Carson City	38.4	911	29.5	5.1	81.8	7.7	46 199	0.3	5 872	12.7	44 813	65.5	37.7	33.1
Henderson	33.8	1 177	29.7	3.4	82.6	9.4	142 759	0.4	18 744	13.1	204 700	68.0	45.7	22.9
Las Vegas	44.5	1 005	32.1	9.6	76.4	11.1	289 559	1.2	42 176	14.6	452 986	67.0	42.7	24.7
North Las Vegas	38.3	1 116	33.2	5.1	75.6	13.9	97 249	-2.4	15 952	16.4	151 027	69.7	46.7	15.8
Reno	52.3	866	31.9	10.8	72.3	10.8	119 486	2.2	15 516	13.0	176 978	69.1	40.8	26.1
Sparks	40.4	940	32.2	6.5	75.4	14.2	49 026	-0.2	6 332	12.9	68 048	70.8	44.4	21.2
NEW HAMPSHIRE	28.0	938	29.5	5.1	86.5	9.7	739 349	-0.8	45 364	6.1	1 063 227	70.3	44.3	22.6
Concord	48.3	930	31.1	9.9	80.0	11.3	22 473	0.6	1 213	5.4	35 516	66.4	43.8	24.2
Dover	47.2	907	30.9	8.3	77.4	16.1	17 989	3.9	934	5.2	24 707	71.8	44.4	21.7
Manchester	49.0	938	29.9	9.2	79.4	7.4	62 168	-0.2	4 341	7.0	88 064	71.2	47.0	24.1
Nashua	41.4	1 056	29.5	7.1	83.3	7.2	49 721	1.0	3 322	6.7	69 608	71.6	46.2	24.5
Rochester	30.4	949	35.7	5.5	81.5	9.2	16 481	-4.0	1 118	6.8	24 865	69.4	45.7	22.3
NEW JERSEY	33.5	1 108	31.4	11.7	89.8	7.2	4 554 076	0.6	437 436	9.6	6 936 153	67.2	43.9	23.7
Atlantic City	62.9	774	34.1	41.4	86.9	7.2	16 920	0.0	2 755	16.3	30 364	62.5	35.6	39.3
Bayonne	57.9	1 000	27.8	23.4	94.8	2.5	30 855	6.6	3 546	11.5	51 112	64.9	46.0	26.1
Bergenfield	27.3	1 154	30.4	9.9	93.4	3.5	14 378	2.4	1 153	8.0	21 228	72.1	51.7	17.6
Bridgeton	57.6	910	46.1	20.6	81.8	11.2	8 750	NA	1 389	15.9	19 103	44.5	21.8	38.0
Camden	58.8	807	41.4	34.0	80.9	6.2	27 723	-2.0	5 302	19.1	56 036	58.7	32.4	37.6
Clifton	38.4	1 172	32.7	11.3	91.3	4.5	43 338	5.0	4 409	10.2	67 946	68.6	48.6	22.6
East Orange	73.6	910	29.5	33.3	79.8	11.4	29 024	-2.5	4 021	13.9	50 534	69.4	40.2	31.0
Elizabeth	71.4	974	31.7	24.4	83.8	5.3	56 201	-1.2	7 224	12.8	93 104	69.8	46.7	23.1
Englewood	43.4	1 178	31.4	14.0	88.3	8.1	13 934	-8.2	1 255	9.0	21 466	68.7	44.5	20.2
Fair Lawn	22.3	1 281	27.5	6.9	93.8	5.0	17 256	4.0	1 452	8.4	25 944	68.4	46.6	21.2
Fort Lee	37.7	1 400	30.2	11.2	90.1	4.0	17 991	-4.2	1 194	6.6	30 091	62.3	43.8	27.0

1. $2,000 represents $2,000 or more.   2. 50.0 represents 50 percent or more.   3. Percent of civilian labor force.   4. Persons 16 years old and over.

Table D. Cities — **Construction, Wholesale Trade, and Retail Trade**

City	Value of residential construction authorized by building permits, 2010			Wholesale trade,[1] 2007				Retail trade,[2] 2007			
	New construction ($1,000)	Number of housing units	Percent single family	Number of establishments	Number of employees	Sales (mil dol)	Annual payroll (mil dol)	Number of establishments	Number of employees	Sales (mil dol)	Annual payroll (mil dol)
	69	70	71	72	73	74	75	76	77	78	79
MISSOURI	1 430 225	9 699	71.2	6 903	96 451	81 032.9	4 533.6	23 360	317 318	76 575.2	7 155.3
Ballwin	4 523	12	100.0	17	55	44.9	2.7	101	1 905	523.1	45.9
Blue Springs	5 229	45	100.0	43	278	236.6	13.5	182	2 854	788.5	67.0
Cape Girardeau	5 821	44	59.1	84	1 611	1 625.5	63.3	313	4 809	1 018.2	93.6
Chesterfield	NA	NA	NA	144	1 712	1 194.1	122.5	340	5 576	1 047.6	112.3
Columbia	72 955	451	88.9	96	1 170	508.3	46.3	542	10 194	2 672.8	214.8
Florissant	13 400	95	1.1	24	126	29.7	3.6	190	3 586	737.2	83.9
Gladstone	686	4	100.0	17	59	19.5	2.2	84	1 873	436.2	43.4
Hazelwood	311	2	100.0	61	1 472	870.0	75.6	149	2 975	978.0	83.2
Independence	6 878	60	100.0	81	578	176.3	20.9	490	9 020	1 878.5	186.1
Jefferson City	12 072	88	69.3	53	2 277	620.8	67.1	306	5 229	1 134.4	110.0
Joplin	11 827	99	58.6	88	1 199	487.1	46.8	426	6 272	1 543.5	126.5
Kansas City	27 473	280	24.3	627	12 675	15 540.1	691.5	1 558	25 485	6 713.0	592.7
Kirkwood	5 175	17	100.0	38	237	94.2	13.3	134	2 394	649.0	63.3
Lee's Summit	45 022	170	100.0	94	1 304	589.6	60.6	253	4 732	1 092.0	105.7
Liberty	3 021	14	100.0	20	282	279.6	15.0	97	1 847	411.9	40.9
Maryland Heights	0	0	0.0	232	5 738	3 732.8	322.9	131	3 697	987.0	312.5
O'Fallon	51 737	529	59.5	73	724	705.6	37.5	202	3 285	776.7	75.2
Raytown	317	3	100.0	31	233	78.3	10.2	99	1 519	367.1	36.7
St. Charles	37 600	190	100.0	80	1 449	3 807.1	74.0	295	4 714	1 093.7	104.8
St. Joseph	12 212	93	62.4	92	1 358	1 001.8	54.0	358	5 847	1 419.1	126.9
St. Louis	32 630	259	39.4	522	9 422	5 042.1	462.3	1 028	11 368	2 496.7	263.6
St. Peters	33 601	314	92.4	76	D	D	D	334	5 810	1 545.1	138.2
Springfield	33 931	481	21.8	373	6 953	4 816.0	293.0	1 064	17 200	4 176.4	379.3
University City	1 770	4	100.0	29	284	147.9	20.5	94	987	183.4	22.8
Wentzville	71 118	427	60.7	33	D	D	D	89	1 678	468.7	46.7
Wildwood	NA	NA	NA	41	131	51.9	6.0	37	474	93.6	11.5
MONTANA	303 528	2 022	65.4	1 254	12 849	8 202.8	503.4	5 258	58 883	14 686.9	1 617.8
Billings	69 692	488	71.1	235	3 630	2 226.0	157.6	645	8 951	2 406.3	219.8
Bozeman	40 270	208	78.8	57	722	253.2	27.1	371	5 400	1 210.2	128.6
Butte-Silver Bow	10 376	122	43.4	31	D	D	D	189	2 183	504.7	44.3
Great Falls	16 952	96	83.3	94	942	597.0	37.8	346	5 153	1 226.0	114.3
Helena	25 466	167	46.7	32	335	167.3	12.9	251	3 597	775.5	79.5
Missoula	19 616	293	40.6	118	1 371	688.1	54.3	485	7 019	1 718.6	158.6
NEBRASKA	744 968	5 401	70.0	2 668	32 329	24 019.9	1 323.5	7 888	108 209	26 486.6	2 230.5
Bellevue	29 148	137	100.0	13	39	9.0	1.3	99	2 080	573.1	49.1
Fremont	3 890	26	92.3	33	396	363.0	15.2	142	2 060	580.6	47.3
Grand Island	15 321	103	82.5	81	899	553.4	39.0	306	4 795	962.9	94.1
Kearney	16 034	103	70.9	32	558	473.3	25.7	209	3 197	593.4	59.5
Lincoln	108 226	833	60.1	239	3 562	2 557.8	157.1	996	16 660	3 526.9	333.6
Omaha	186 447	1 579	75.4	675	9 809	5 606.0	460.7	1 707	34 372	7 495.1	759.5
NEVADA	759 740	6 443	83.2	2 614	36 052	19 255.9	1 698.5	8 492	139 829	37 434.0	3 691.7
Carson City	9 963	71	15.5	92	D	D	D	262	3 698	991.5	99.5
Henderson	89 460	768	91.1	183	1 292	566.3	57.1	704	15 060	4 803.0	404.1
Las Vegas	124 979	1 288	71.9	410	3 578	1 566.6	157.5	1 791	32 904	9 178.9	892.6
North Las Vegas	84 757	668	97.0	179	5 661	2 698.7	269.5	276	5 885	1 443.4	137.6
Reno	87 896	485	72.4	294	5 486	3 017.5	234.7	1 087	18 504	5 014.9	503.1
Sparks	18 774	88	100.0	247	4 534	2 998.8	208.4	323	5 092	1 166.4	128.6
NEW HAMPSHIRE	461 754	2 670	70.8	1 561	21 457	14 564.5	1 196.3	6 603	98 333	25 353.9	2 380.5
Concord	2 900	19	89.5	49	1 232	778.0	63.9	318	6 020	1 412.6	133.9
Dover	11 225	75	90.7	37	480	216.3	30.8	113	1 482	381.5	41.8
Manchester	21 595	200	22.5	171	2 531	1 350.6	126.6	489	8 057	2 132.5	196.9
Nashua	18 790	195	27.2	112	1 566	1 250.1	121.2	492	10 041	2 925.2	244.1
Rochester	7 596	78	47.4	13	D	D	D	144	2 419	651.6	65.8
NEW JERSEY	2 036 521	13 535	54.5	14 033	221 729	233 413.0	13 266.6	34 482	460 843	124 813.6	12 050.0
Atlantic City	3 875	42	100.0	13	355	70.9	8.7	316	2 692	554.0	59.5
Bayonne	5 377	46	34.8	46	1 380	622.0	76.0	216	1 605	369.8	36.5
Bergenfield	98	1	100.0	39	239	150.0	10.9	102	955	206.9	23.1
Bridgeton	1 531	20	100.0	14	D	D	D	112	908	241.8	22.4
Camden	8 041	128	11.7	64	1 222	849.4	58.5	192	1 256	270.5	28.0
Clifton	4 307	54	24.1	175	2 801	1 178.8	132.3	306	4 611	1 263.4	119.5
East Orange	233	4	0.0	15	148	143.5	6.8	137	896	237.2	21.9
Elizabeth	11 538	135	3.0	113	3 926	3 548.4	231.2	556	5 925	1 304.0	112.8
Englewood	11 791	48	25.0	113	1 476	933.8	84.4	165	2 048	1 004.5	92.0
Fair Lawn	5 922	29	41.4	57	739	801.1	32.1	112	1 374	440.5	55.4
Fort Lee	15 182	40	55.0	167	2 065	3 797.2	181.2	148	1 126	311.8	28.0

1. Merchant wholesalers except manufacturers' sales branches and offices. 2. Establishments with payroll.

City	Real estate and rental and leasing, 2007				Professional, scientific, and technical services,[1] 2007				Manufacturing, 2007			
	Number of establishments	Number of employees	Receipts (mil dol)	Annual payroll (mil dol)	Number of establishments	Number of employees	Receipts (mil dol)	Annual payroll (mil dol)	Number of establishments	Number of employees	Receipts (mil dol)	Annual payroll (mil dol)
	80	81	82	83	84	85	86	87	88	89	90	91
MISSOURI................	7 003	39 625	7 186.3	1 248.8	13 524	130 786	19 749.8	7 454.7	6 886	295 313	110 907.6	12 996.5
Ballwin.......................	29	94	11.5	1.8	85	187	23.6	8.5	NA	NA	NA	NA
Blue Springs.................	78	250	43.1	6.1	132	D	D	D	34	1 037	D	48.0
Cape Girardeau.............	88	312	51.9	6.9	106	D	D	D	39	2 650	2 605.4	134.8
Chesterfield.................	146	895	186.9	37.2	370	9 133	1 567.9	614.1	48	1 858	479.1	92.4
Columbia.....................	202	903	136.4	23.4	325	D	D	D	63	3 354	1 259.9	129.9
Florissant....................	43	223	29.7	6.2	67	466	22.5	10.1	NA	NA	NA	NA
Gladstone	44	206	30.1	8.0	75	D	D	D	NA	NA	NA	NA
Hazelwood..................	38	384	60.1	15.5	40	1 940	526.5	152.4	39	3 413	1 112.2	202.9
Independence..............	121	569	137.7	13.8	237	D	D	D	97	4 394	1 039.4	201.1
Jefferson City	59	207	36.3	5.0	200	1 312	161.2	59.8	43	3 117	D	134.9
Joplin	92	489	53.9	13.2	148	D	D	D	91	5 843	1 902.5	218.0
Kansas City	622	5 816	1 381.0	213.3	1 543	D	D	D	434	19 070	7 789.3	897.7
Kirkwood.....................	51	180	26.5	5.2	136	675	85.1	31.4	32	591	123.0	27.5
Lee's Summit	136	499	73.0	14.0	291	1 539	256.9	83.6	76	2 143	421.7	89.5
Liberty	41	185	28.1	4.9	102	D	D	D	20	1 311	D	62.4
Maryland Heights	67	345	97.0	16.4	179	2 947	620.4	234.6	111	3 673	1 082.3	173.5
O'Fallon	73	310	46.3	7.7	116	737	74.0	27.7	62	5 519	1 132.9	224.8
Raytown	22	124	13.5	2.8	76	499	37.9	17.2	NA	NA	NA	NA
St. Charles	120	666	256.7	24.7	265	4 800	287.1	121.1	77	2 392	D	121.9
St. Joseph	99	449	48.8	9.4	169	D	D	D	93	D	D	D
St. Louis	418	2 633	606.6	94.7	1 005	D	D	D	543	21 432	10 920.6	998.2
St. Peters	68	302	57.6	8.0	132	768	80.4	25.7	53	1 825	695.2	D
Springfield	375	2 593	322.7	63.7	675	D	D	D	273	13 588	3 554.2	520.0
University City	50	589	67.5	14.0	91	352	39.2	13.7	NA	NA	NA	NA
Wentzville	15	63	9.5	1.5	46	205	18.2	6.4	23	3 095	D	D
Wildwood....................	34	58	13.2	2.5	97	226	38.2	14.6	NA	NA	NA	NA
MONTANA	1 892	6 410	848.3	153.3	3 403	16 547	1 770.9	670.6	1 324	19 525	10 638.1	808.2
Billings.......................	226	805	121.9	23.7	489	D	D	D	126	2 484	D	128.1
Bozeman.....................	169	518	86.8	13.7	394	1 859	229.8	86.8	71	985	228.0	35.9
Butte-Silver Bow...........	45	144	14.9	3.0	107	D	D	D	NA	NA	NA	NA
Great Falls..................	119	349	53.9	7.8	177	D	D	D	53	938	640.2	39.5
Helena	80	603	75.0	13.0	206	1 625	198.6	81.4	NA	NA	NA	NA
Missoula	174	843	105.3	18.9	378	D	D	D	67	D	D	21.0
NEBRASKA...............	2 032	9 974	1 645.5	292.0	4 205	40 692	4 836.4	2 011.0	1 984	99 547	40 158.0	3 788.6
Bellevue......................	46	193	26.8	3.2	75	1 757	324.3	119.9	13	608	123.7	23.3
Fremont......................	43	D	D	D	43	189	15.4	5.5	33	929	395.7	36.8
Grand Island................	64	256	44.4	7.2	91	D	D	D	63	6 524	D	240.2
Kearney......................	48	161	26.9	4.1	66	442	36.3	16.2	23	538	D	D
Lincoln.......................	343	1 536	247.5	42.6	727	7 989	1 082.1	373.8	223	11 908	3 932.9	486.9
Omaha........................	599	5 226	775.7	168.3	1 385	D	D	D	448	20 354	8 853.9	817.4
NEVADA...................	4 613	31 603	6 187.3	1 106.5	7 895	57 357	8 881.4	3 241.1	2 035	51 958	15 735.8	2 290.8
Carson City	147	569	73.4	16.0	381	D	D	D	143	3 528	621.6	141.7
Henderson...................	431	1 532	361.9	58.5	678	D	D	D	128	5 086	1 634.7	197.1
Las Vegas	1 099	5 391	1 048.7	209.8	2 220	14 869	2 496.1	865.1	233	3 744	872.9	137.2
North Las Vegas	139	3 182	318.0	97.1	136	D	D	D	137	5 728	1 311.6	213.5
Reno..........................	505	2 847	509.0	91.0	1 236	D	D	D	249	9 355	3 875.0	496.6
Sparks	126	795	134.7	25.8	157	D	D	D	196	4 760	1 522.3	210.7
NEW HAMPSHIRE.....	1 534	7 266	1 371.8	248.2	3 961	29 160	3 730.8	1 570.2	2 104	81 592	18 592.4	4 196.2
Concord.......................	78	447	83.9	14.2	241	1 820	254.3	113.7	66	2 606	567.4	112.2
Dover..........................	42	189	31.5	4.9	91	D	D	D	45	1 215	167.1	48.9
Manchester..................	141	1 161	234.3	38.9	398	D	D	D	153	6 970	1 493.4	309.1
Nashua.......................	121	520	118.5	21.6	336	D	D	D	134	9 964	2 693.5	924.0
Rochester....................	30	113	15.3	2.4	45	302	25.5	10.7	42	1 531	281.0	60.3
NEW JERSEY..........	9 618	64 021	16 347.6	2 939.1	31 040	330 133	52 442.8	23 639.9	9 250	310 606	116 608.1	16 399.3
Atlantic City	63	739	139.4	20.7	69	D	D	D	NA	NA	NA	NA
Bayonne......................	52	243	48.6	9.0	79	290	27.7	10.0	39	1 208	470.9	58.1
Bergenfield..................	19	44	6.4	1.1	59	146	26.1	6.4	NA	NA	NA	NA
Bridgeton	10	90	10.5	2.0	40	D	D	D	15	659	254.8	29.0
Camden......................	35	196	32.8	5.4	54	D	D	D	56	2 851	641.1	192.0
Clifton........................	99	733	107.0	29.5	263	3 746	472.3	198.9	176	5 671	1 429.0	295.7
East Orange................	70	385	66.9	10.4	56	D	D	D	NA	NA	NA	NA
Elizabeth.....................	110	358	140.0	12.1	114	D	D	D	81	3 314	808.7	154.7
Englewood...................	74	250	59.0	11.4	125	791	154.8	50.3	61	1 582	468.2	67.2
Fair Lawn	34	100	36.4	2.9	218	1 037	257.2	71.3	40	2 031	634.7	97.5
Fort Lee......................	120	574	142.7	22.7	257	1 127	255.0	73.6	NA	NA	NA	NA

1. Establishments subject to federal tax.

City	Accommodation and food services, 2007				Arts, entertainment, and recreation,[1] 2007				Health care and social assistance,[1] 2007			
	Number of establishments	Number of employees	Sales (mil dol)	Annual payroll (mil dol)	Number of establishments	Number of employees	Receipts (mil dol)	Annual payroll (mil dol)	Number of establishments	Number of employees	Receipts (mil dol)	Annual payroll (mil dol)
	92	93	94	95	96	97	98	99	100	101	102	103
MISSOURI..............	12 261	241 438	11 070.6	3 109.1	1 696	25 744	2 735.9	1 026.2	12 881	159 529	14 101.7	5 911.6
Ballwin......................	37	787	27.1	8.4	10	D	D	D	38	D	D	D
Blue Springs................	107	2 203	83.7	22.7	18	D	D	D	113	D	D	D
Cape Girardeau............	126	3 284	119.7	35.1	14	136	7.9	2.6	194	D	D	D
Chesterfield................	161	4 566	191.9	61.2	32	286	17.2	4.4	223	3 750	389.8	176.4
Columbia	362	7 659	286.3	83.7	33	546	17.9	6.8	387	4 126	423.1	177.8
Florissant....................	123	2 577	96.4	28.7	9	D	D	D	146	1 867	146.9	64.1
Gladstone	37	824	33.3	10.1	5	D	D	D	82	806	65.6	27.2
Hazelwood..................	66	1 148	59.2	17.4	6	D	D	D	47	378	41.0	14.2
Independence..............	217	5 267	216.8	67.9	17	D	D	D	224	3 795	432.7	165.1
Jefferson City	140	2 963	118.9	35.2	16	D	D	D	163	D	D	D
Joplin........................	190	4 200	168.3	48.5	9	D	D	D	263	2 508	233.5	113.7
Kansas City	1 110	26 835	1 668.7	426.6	104	2 464	503.4	281.6	886	13 090	1 483.9	645.2
Kirkwood....................	59	1 585	58.5	17.8	12	116	7.3	2.2	111	832	114.5	40.6
Lee's Summit	153	3 172	119.9	37.5	36	74	D	D	195	3 005	334.7	127.1
Liberty	55	1 020	42.7	13.0	5	74	2.6	0.8	85	D	D	D
Maryland Heights	93	4 251	438.0	98.4	9	D	D	D	64	2 747	329.8	103.7
O'Fallon......................	143	3 286	113.2	35.3	25	322	18.1	6.7	133	D	D	D
Raytown	43	693	28.7	8.4	8	D	D	D	50	D	D	D
St. Charles	196	4 467	178.1	52.2	23	D	D	D	158	1 753	181.9	69.3
St. Joseph	189	4 084	151.7	44.8	14	D	D	D	229	D	D	D
St. Louis	934	20 372	1 059.3	311.4	62	2 672	450.0	226.8	722	11 401	1 052.1	365.9
St. Peters	190	3 702	135.2	41.2	24	D	D	D	191	1 766	179.9	74.3
Springfield..................	598	13 951	540.5	160.7	54	470	28.7	7.4	506	D	D	D
University City	77	1 250	52.6	16.3	9	81	2.8	0.8	74	1 240	59.2	23.5
Wentzville..................	62	1 374	45.7	14.4	6	D	D	D	59	551	52.2	18.1
Wildwood..................	24	D	D	D	11	125	5.6	1.4	40	395	24.7	11.8
MONTANA	3 360	46 137	2 079.4	554.2	881	8 207	589.4	110.3	2 438	21 763	1 944.6	801.7
Billings......................	312	7 102	335.8	91.1	82	792	68.6	10.2	368	D	D	D
Bozeman....................	153	3 297	141.0	38.0	44	318	31.9	5.2	206	1 608	150.6	60.2
Butte-Silver Bow............	133	1 946	78.3	22.7	34	278	33.0	3.9	113	1 458	85.9	36.9
Great Falls..................	209	3 588	157.7	44.4	54	D	D	D	197	D	D	D
Helena	145	2 729	106.9	30.3	25	337	14.4	3.0	172	1 531	134.3	56.3
Missoula	260	5 473	233.1	60.8	61	695	53.0	8.9	319	D	D	D
NEBRASKA................	4 241	69 142	2 685.6	749.1	573	6 394	396.8	92.8	3 830	49 338	4 447.4	1 888.7
Bellevue....................	91	1 808	70.8	20.3	9	D	D	D	61	977	59.7	25.7
Fremont......................	77	1 233	47.5	12.4	4	D	D	D	79	D	D	D
Grand Island................	122	2 330	86.2	25.1	13	230	9.3	2.6	129	D	D	D
Kearney......................	118	2 480	98.4	27.2	15	D	D	D	91	1 133	132.1	63.8
Lincoln......................	619	11 603	457.9	128.2	80	1 447	54.4	16.8	677	D	D	D
Omaha......................	1 123	23 858	1 041.5	298.0	129	1 976	119.2	29.4	1 156	17 234	1 853.5	787.1
NEVADA....................	5 570	325 544	28 815.5	8 594.6	1 153	28 815	3 275.5	752.7	5 269	72 716	9 225.8	3 345.0
Carson City	167	2 664	127.7	37.8	48	1 762	138.4	39.5	192	2 048	278.5	101.3
Henderson..................	463	15 786	1 145.5	333.9	128	D	D	D	612	D	D	D
Las Vegas	1 128	42 712	3 134.0	924.7	226	4 369	521.9	120.4	1 593	28 718	4 019.0	1 373.4
North Las Vegas	199	6 458	476.1	127.8	33	1 554	107.8	28.5	141	D	D	D
Reno........................	702	27 677	1 918.0	580.7	103	1 816	161.5	39.0	757	9 418	1 226.5	542.7
Sparks......................	202	5 809	340.3	105.4	24	D	D	D	167	2 083	168.3	68.1
NEW HAMPSHIRE.....	3 508	55 268	2 631.0	799.8	548	9 606	659.1	205.7	2 655	32 711	3 095.7	1 386.1
Concord......................	135	2 769	132.4	41.1	13	217	6.9	2.2	158	2 267	248.0	124.6
Dover........................	79	1 364	58.7	18.8	8	D	D	D	116	1 286	129.6	64.0
Manchester..................	294	5 777	265.3	82.3	30	858	73.4	34.4	236	3 281	322.1	157.8
Nashua......................	228	4 574	231.7	70.4	25	428	28.1	8.0	248	3 236	353.7	151.0
Rochester..................	66	1 048	43.1	12.0	3	D	D	D	66	662	68.3	31.6
NEW JERSEY............	19 526	291 327	19 993.6	5 232.4	2 939	35 241	2 958.6	921.7	22 056	253 078	26 415.5	10 529.7
Atlantic City	238	47 392	5 602.5	1 369.0	16	131	15.8	4.0	48	490	39.5	16.7
Bayonne......................	112	983	49.5	12.4	8	D	D	D	152	1 042	119.0	44.3
Bergenfield	44	342	22.3	5.3	4	D	D	D	52	302	37.3	11.1
Bridgeton....................	35	441	21.2	5.2	1	D	D	D	31	D	D	D
Camden......................	93	600	42.2	9.7	7	84	27.9	3.8	76	1 342	126.6	66.0
Clifton........................	157	D	D	D	17	D	D	D	330	2 687	294.0	110.7
East Orange................	47	703	33.6	8.3	2	D	D	D	130	2 371	139.0	61.0
Elizabeth....................	253	2 627	192.0	49.1	6	D	D	D	188	1 860	175.7	68.7
Englewood..................	54	744	43.8	10.2	14	D	D	D	216	D	D	D
Fair Lawn	69	751	44.2	11.2	12	D	D	D	198	1 872	216.1	88.4
Fort Lee......................	107	1 209	80.6	18.6	25	D	D	D	190	D	D	D

1. Establishments subject to federal tax.

Table D. Cities — Other Services and Federal Funds

City	Other services[1], 2007				Selected federal funds, 2009–2010 (mil dol)								
					Procurement contracts		Grants						
	Number of establish-ments	Number of employees	Receipts (mil dol)	Annual payroll (mil dol)	Defense	Other	Total[2]	Medicaid and other health related	Nutrition and family welfare	Energy and environment	Disasters and emergency prepared-ness	Housing and community develop-ment	Employment and training
	104	105	106	107	108	109	110	111	112	113	114	115	116
MISSOURI.................	9 114	53 749	4 220.1	1 361.4	10 334.5	2 667.9	14 002.5	7 868.9	1 212.9	968.8	87.3	519.6	199.3
Ballwin........................	41	233	14.6	5.6	1.0	0.0	0.0	0.0	0.0	0.0	0.0	0.0	0.0
Blue Springs.................	86	418	30.4	9.7	0.2	0.2	1.0	0.0	0.0	0.5	0.0	0.5	0.0
Cape Girardeau............	87	433	29.7	9.8	5.7	1.8	30.8	1.6	0.0	0.3	0.1	0.2	0.0
Chesterfield	85	876	48.8	16.0	22.9	9.9	73.6	1.0	0.0	71.8	0.0	0.0	0.0
Columbia......................	203	1 451	108.9	31.6	4.8	38.6	263.1	98.6	5.7	10.9	-2.1	11.1	0.4
Florissant.....................	94	597	46.2	14.8	0.1	0.0	2.2	0.0	0.0	0.5	0.0	0.2	0.0
Gladstone.....................	46	275	20.1	6.3	0.0	0.2	0.1	0.0	0.0	0.1	0.0	0.0	0.0
Hazelwood....................	38	271	22.1	7.1	3.4	2.0	3.4	0.0	0.0	0.0	0.0	0.0	3.2
Independence...............	174	833	64.7	19.5	793.9	2.7	12.7	0.0	0.0	0.4	0.0	11.7	0.0
Jefferson City	98	D	D	D	1.9	3.6	1 371.9	139.7	236.9	93.4	12.0	150.1	165.7
Joplin...........................	133	716	44.3	13.5	15.6	10.8	21.4	0.1	6.3	7.2	0.0	5.4	0.0
Kansas City	734	5 132	416.6	131.9	101.9	1 268.1	306.4	87.8	21.9	64.5	2.0	77.7	0.5
Kirkwood......................	52	403	26.7	9.8	0.1	0.5	0.2	0.0	0.0	0.0	0.0	0.1	0.0
Lee's Summit	112	668	46.0	14.7	2.4	5.0	10.8	0.1	0.0	0.8	0.0	5.1	0.0
Liberty.........................	44	259	17.6	6.3	3.3	2.1	3.3	0.0	0.0	0.4	0.0	2.2	0.0
Maryland Heights	59	549	52.7	19.9	230.9	95.0	0.0	0.0	0.0	0.0	0.0	0.0	0.0
O'Fallon.......................	122	862	54.5	18.8	56.2	0.3	1.0	0.0	0.0	0.7	0.0	0.3	0.0
Raytown.......................	65	470	26.5	13.5	0.1	2.0	0.2	0.0	0.0	0.0	0.0	0.1	0.0
St. Charles	127	884	67.0	21.9	273.8	0.2	7.7	0.0	0.0	0.7	0.0	6.8	0.0
St. Joseph...................	150	D	D	D	14.6	4.9	9.4	0.0	0.0	0.0	0.0	6.9	0.0
St. Louis	517	3 996	306.0	106.8	3 022.3	201.9	1 828.5	850.7	36.6	643.1	1.1	101.5	14.1
St. Peters	144	1 123	74.1	26.2	28.0	0.5	0.3	0.0	0.0	0.0	0.0	0.3	0.0
Springfield	449	D	D	D	8.0	23.0	57.1	6.5	11.4	1.5	0.0	9.5	0.0
University City	56	408	34.1	11.7	0.1	0.9	2.9	0.0	0.0	0.1	2.6	0.2	0.0
Wentzville....................	46	D	D	D	1.0	0.0	0.8	0.4	0.0	0.0	0.0	0.0	0.0
Wildwood......................	17	97	5.1	1.5	7.0	0.0	0.0	0.0	0.0	0.0	0.0	0.0	0.0
MONTANA	1 619	7 260	647.7	164.8	312.7	506.7	2 939.4	1 080.2	271.7	254.3	6.6	95.5	54.0
Billings........................	241	1 418	117.5	34.1	2.1	75.9	37.5	16.8	4.7	1.1	0.0	6.4	0.3
Bozeman	80	396	28.2	9.1	17.2	14.5	90.9	33.6	1.2	12.8	-0.1	0.0	0.0
Butte-Silver Bow...........	51	240	19.7	4.8	0.0	0.0	16.1	3.7	1.4	3.3	0.0	0.8	0.0
Great Falls...................	102	D	D	D	17.4	4.6	22.6	6.9	2.6	1.1	-1.7	4.4	0.0
Helena.........................	70	427	32.7	9.4	5.8	18.0	458.1	44.9	47.2	104.2	4.9	39.5	49.1
Missoula	161	955	71.4	21.2	4.1	36.2	86.0	22.3	3.1	8.9	0.0	10.0	0.0
NEBRASKA...............	3 226	17 286	1 299.7	406.5	793.2	513.6	3 507.0	1 703.0	411.7	131.7	37.6	119.9	51.0
Bellevue.......................	60	403	31.3	10.5	32.2	2.3	13.1	0.0	0.0	0.2	0.0	1.4	0.0
Fremont	49	D	D	D	0.5	0.2	6.8	0.0	0.7	0.0	0.0	1.2	0.0
Grand Island................	115	567	45.6	11.3	0.0	3.9	9.0	0.3	0.0	0.0	0.0	2.2	0.0
Kearney	59	281	20.2	5.6	0.0	0.4	7.7	0.0	4.5	0.0	0.0	1.1	0.1
Lincoln.........................	425	2 627	154.9	57.2	13.7	63.3	697.7	91.9	83.4	70.0	14.6	40.1	46.3
Omaha.........................	782	6 236	425.1	161.9	226.6	217.4	310.3	152.2	8.9	27.3	0.1	50.2	2.4
NEVADA....................	2 989	22 756	1 750.6	564.6	1 315.0	1 092.1	3 701.8	1 312.3	423.8	446.2	4.3	225.1	92.0
Carson City	117	820	57.8	20.1	13.0	7.9	550.5	32.1	100.6	57.0	0.9	21.3	86.6
Henderson....................	271	1 908	155.8	49.7	2.4	5.9	6.5	1.4	0.0	1.6	0.0	1.8	0.0
Las Vegas	665	4 876	370.4	119.6	77.9	696.6	470.5	18.9	5.7	196.0	0.2	134.1	4.6
North Las Vegas	131	2 797	198.0	70.6	0.8	21.6	20.7	0.0	0.0	13.8	0.0	0.4	0.5
Reno............................	365	2 887	183.0	67.5	28.8	54.0	351.7	38.4	13.6	115.6	0.3	47.7	0.0
Sparks.........................	178	1 227	126.6	36.1	633.3	3.3	6.7	2.0	0.0	2.4	0.0	0.7	0.3
NEW HAMPSHIRE.....	2 281	12 269	1 117.9	346.5	1 091.9	343.5	2 311.1	1 132.7	209.8	102.2	14.3	120.8	43.3
Concord........................	105	549	48.0	16.0	11.1	18.3	368.3	39.2	48.4	43.6	4.3	20.6	40.2
Dover...........................	50	300	22.4	6.9	3.3	1.0	8.2	1.1	0.0	0.1	0.0	4.0	0.0
Manchester...................	227	1 570	130.1	43.3	15.0	19.6	78.4	3.1	4.2	2.6	0.3	56.1	0.0
Nashua	151	1 172	109.7	36.7	583.6	8.8	25.5	1.5	0.0	2.2	0.0	12.1	0.2
Rochester.....................	51	327	26.2	8.3	2.3	0.7	2.8	0.1	0.0	0.0	0.0	2.4	0.0
NEW JERSEY...........	16 350	85 202	7 212.2	2 257.6	7 857.5	2 378.8	15 456.8	8 131.6	1 857.8	572.3	130.5	1 041.9	272.7
Atlantic City	55	665	45.1	14.8	0.7	4.7	20.0	0.2	6.8	0.0	0.0	12.0	0.0
Bayonne.......................	110	410	30.8	8.3	27.7	2.6	16.1	0.0	1.5	0.5	3.6	7.0	0.0
Bergenfield	62	178	15.9	3.9	0.5	0.0	0.3	0.0	0.0	0.0	0.0	0.0	0.0
Bridgeton......................	26	117	9.6	2.5	0.1	0.1	15.7	3.2	8.9	0.0	0.0	2.5	0.0
Camden........................	56	323	28.2	8.4	131.1	9.9	88.4	4.7	3.1	6.4	0.0	51.5	0.4
Clifton..........................	184	747	64.8	20.7	269.2	1.3	5.0	0.0	0.0	0.7	0.0	4.1	0.0
East Orange	49	D	D	D	0.0	44.7	23.1	3.1	4.3	0.6	0.0	14.9	0.0
Elizabeth......................	191	917	90.6	23.5	24.6	7.0	35.1	2.2	0.2	2.4	0.0	29.1	0.0
Englewood....................	85	381	31.1	9.7	3.2	3.9	52.5	1.9	0.0	0.5	0.0	48.4	0.0
Fair Lawn	76	342	32.6	10.3	1.5	0.1	0.0	0.0	0.0	0.0	0.0	0.0	0.0
Fort Lee.......................	103	381	33.3	10.2	41.3	6.1	7.4	1.6	0.0	0.0	0.0	5.8	0.0

1. Establishments subject to federal tax. 2. Includes program categories not shown separately. State totals include additional categories not allocated by city.

City	General revenue Total (mil dol)	Intergovernmental Total (mil dol)	Intergovernmental Percent from state government	Taxes Total (mil dol)	Taxes Per capita[1] (dollars) Total	Taxes Per capita[1] (dollars) Property	Taxes Per capita[1] (dollars) Sales and gross receipts	General expenditure Total (mil dol)	General expenditure Per capita[1] (dollars) Total	General expenditure Per capita[1] (dollars) Capital outlays
	117	118	119	120	121	122	123	124	125	126
MISSOURI	X	X	X	X	X	X	X	X	X	X
Ballwin	19.5	1.6	57.3	12.8	426	0	416	15.9	529	66
Blue Springs	35.7	7.4	18.5	19.1	348	90	257	30.2	548	23
Cape Girardeau	44.9	3.7	100.0	28.6	770	48	723	39.3	1 059	241
Chesterfield	54.7	26.8	15.1	22.3	482	331	151	39.0	842	206
Columbia	132.1	20.1	23.6	57.6	581	97	484	138.3	1 395	191
Florissant	24.2	12.8	18.6	7.8	152	0	102	30.0	589	60
Gladstone	21.3	2.2	55.9	13.3	477	116	361	31.7	1 135	528
Hazelwood	39.8	12.5	13.4	23.5	924	398	208	38.8	1 521	365
Independence	126.0	15.8	32.4	79.4	717	102	615	158.5	1 431	664
Jefferson City	52.0	3.0	100.0	32.1	792	105	687	46.5	1 146	245
Joplin	62.5	9.0	35.0	36.0	734	37	697	60.1	1 223	439
Kansas City	1 317.7	136.2	15.0	672.4	1 493	320	813	1 359.8	3 019	579
Kirkwood	29.4	7.8	24.2	15.6	581	304	253	19.4	722	10
Lee's Summit	135.2	18.7	12.4	65.2	788	300	488	123.8	1 494	556
Liberty	40.2	1.6	57.2	16.1	535	149	387	50.4	1 680	502
Maryland Heights	42.2	15.8	19.5	19.1	730	69	661	31.5	1 207	275
O'Fallon	63.4	4.8	51.0	34.2	458	149	306	45.7	609	59
Raytown	19.1	2.2	100.0	9.3	327	59	268	16.7	588	0
St. Charles	80.1	10.2	84.5	53.9	847	159	688	83.2	1 307	434
St. Joseph	105.3	12.8	96.1	45.5	615	263	351	102.5	1 387	331
St. Louis	877.5	208.9	59.3	451.5	1 287	215	581	840.8	2 397	152
St. Peters	90.4	6.5	95.9	37.5	681	201	480	62.4	1 132	161
Springfield	282.6	43.9	19.5	120.7	780	145	635	239.9	1 550	319
University City	34.1	11.8	13.7	10.8	295	89	206	28.7	786	0
Wentzville	27.7	5.0	25.1	15.9	709	231	479	38.0	1 693	824
Wildwood	13.8	7.7	17.9	3.5	101	26	75	11.2	327	41
MONTANA	X	X	X	X	X	X	X	X	X	X
Billings	144.1	27.9	66.0	29.3	287	229	36	130.6	1 282	294
Bozeman	51.0	11.3	92.1	17.7	466	315	151	57.3	1 509	486
Butte-Silver Bow	48.3	12.9	73.5	20.0	611	586	25	48.0	1 469	119
Great Falls	51.3	11.3	78.1	14.8	252	220	32	44.7	760	24
Helena	34.0	6.9	71.7	7.4	256	236	20	31.5	1 095	172
Missoula	55.8	13.0	90.3	24.3	362	317	45	56.7	845	174
NEBRASKA	X	X	X	X	X	X	X	X	X	X
Bellevue	35.2	4.6	71.0	22.3	460	246	170	36.2	749	144
Fremont	22.5	5.1	57.9	9.1	360	148	212	19.9	787	151
Grand Island	55.5	8.7	100.0	20.7	463	124	339	55.4	1 236	172
Kearney	32.4	5.9	100.0	10.6	352	63	289	32.6	1 083	239
Lincoln	279.7	68.7	64.1	140.8	566	190	376	309.0	1 242	404
Omaha	427.2	33.3	95.6	280.0	660	224	436	448.5	1 057	142
NEVADA	X	X	X	X	X	X	X	X	X	X
Carson City	112.3	36.1	89.8	34.0	619	301	318	118.9	2 164	466
Henderson	389.2	114.6	91.3	147.9	593	340	254	252.9	1 014	50
Las Vegas	1 041.9	394.0	69.5	251.5	450	246	204	834.0	1 492	260
North Las Vegas	352.5	106.0	51.9	108.9	514	337	177	334.0	1 574	295
Reno	294.7	90.7	65.2	123.1	573	277	296	290.2	1 351	216
Sparks	128.1	35.0	82.6	55.5	637	293	344	96.8	1 111	27
NEW HAMPSHIRE	X	X	X	X	X	X	X	X	X	X
Concord	62.7	6.1	60.6	35.9	846	815	31	74.9	1 767	573
Dover	93.8	29.4	63.9	50.9	1 768	1 741	27	102.8	3 572	706
Manchester	406.7	142.7	78.6	154.5	1 420	1 290	130	401.0	3 684	581
Nashua	246.4	81.4	90.5	135.4	1 559	1 534	25	225.8	2 601	268
Rochester	77.0	36.0	91.0	34.1	1 116	1 000	117	90.1	2 952	524
NEW JERSEY	X	X	X	X	X	X	X	X	X	X
Atlantic City	213.7	34.6	37.5	159.4	4 017	3 846	171	188.5	4 749	178
Bayonne	196.5	68.6	98.3	107.3	1 853	1 836	18	316.4	5 467	1 727
Bergenfield	73.5	3.3	99.6	68.0	2 631	2 605	27	61.8	2 392	199
Bridgeton	31.4	13.9	63.9	8.8	358	327	31	29.7	1 207	231
Camden	188.1	143.2	79.4	27.8	353	294	59	185.8	2 361	229
Clifton	85.5	19.6	77.6	59.9	763	734	29	84.4	1 074	126
East Orange	379.3	278.0	95.7	81.1	1 230	1 211	19	384.1	5 824	739
Elizabeth	219.6	59.0	70.5	111.6	894	813	81	218.0	1 746	188
Englewood	118.5	31.8	79.9	82.5	2 944	2 910	34	116.9	4 172	505
Fair Lawn	41.1	6.0	97.7	33.3	1 081	1 042	39	36.0	1 171	125
Fort Lee	63.0	9.3	32.9	50.7	1 388	1 336	52	59.1	1 619	116

1. Based on population estimated as of July 1 of the year shown.

Table D. Cities — City Government Finances

City	City government finances, 2006 (cont.)									
	General expenditure (cont.)									
	Percent of total for:									
	Public welfare	Highways	Parking facilities	Education	Health and hospitals	Police protection	Sewerage and sanitation	Parks and recreation	Housing and community development	Interest on debt
	127	128	129	130	131	132	133	134	135	136
MISSOURI...............	X	X	X	X	X	X	X	X	X	X
Ballwin......................	0.0	16.0	0.0	0.0	0.0	31.1	3.8	24.2	0.0	10.4
Blue Springs................	0.0	5.9	2.6	0.0	0.0	27.4	16.2	16.6	0.0	8.5
Cape Girardeau............	0.0	21.3	0.0	0.0	0.7	15.0	15.5	10.2	0.5	2.1
Chesterfield.................	0.0	31.3	0.0	0.0	0.0	18.6	0.0	18.1	0.4	13.6
Columbia	0.7	4.5	0.9	0.0	3.5	10.1	15.5	10.5	1.0	1.7
Florissant....................	0.0	0.0	0.0	0.0	2.3	28.0	2.3	20.4	0.8	1.6
Gladstone	0.0	7.2	0.0	0.0	0.0	13.8	9.1	43.6	0.0	2.6
Hazelwood...................	0.0	19.9	0.0	0.0	0.0	16.9	0.3	6.2	0.0	3.3
Independence..............	0.0	7.6	0.0	0.0	1.9	21.4	19.5	8.1	0.4	5.1
Jefferson City	0.0	9.6	1.6	0.0	1.1	16.9	16.5	12.2	0.7	5.8
Joplin.........................	0.4	14.3	0.1	0.0	4.2	14.4	16.8	5.6	1.2	1.6
Kansas City	0.5	4.9	0.3	0.0	4.8	13.0	7.3	3.9	0.7	4.9
Kirkwood.....................	0.0	5.6	0.0	0.0	0.0	23.3	10.6	13.0	0.0	8.1
Lee's Summit	0.0	24.1	0.0	0.0	0.0	12.6	9.7	9.1	1.1	2.9
Liberty........................	0.0	13.2	0.0	0.0	0.0	8.6	36.3	10.4	3.6	3.3
Maryland Heights	0.9	26.6	0.0	0.0	0.0	27.2	6.8	11.1	4.0	5.1
O'Fallon......................	0.0	12.9	0.0	0.0	0.0	21.7	15.8	12.6	0.6	12.8
Raytown	0.0	11.4	0.0	0.0	11.5	31.6	19.6	7.8	2.6	3.3
St. Charles	0.0	21.6	0.4	0.0	0.0	19.5	18.2	7.4	0.4	5.6
St. Joseph	0.0	9.1	0.3	0.0	2.9	11.1	11.0	5.0	2.8	21.7
St. Louis	0.0	1.9	1.2	0.0	5.2	19.7	1.8	3.0	9.5	8.5
St. Peters	0.0	20.6	0.0	0.0	1.1	15.4	19.5	16.6	3.5	3.3
Springfield	0.0	25.2	0.0	0.0	3.5	21.8	7.0	13.9	3.7	3.7
University City	0.0	12.5	0.8	0.0	0.0	25.9	8.4	12.3	0.0	3.5
Wentzville....................	0.0	28.1	0.0	0.0	0.0	12.6	34.8	4.9	0.0	5.0
Wildwood.....................	0.0	28.2	0.0	0.0	0.0	22.0	0.0	3.9	0.0	0.9
MONTANA	X	X	X	X	X	X	X	X	X	X
Billings........................	0.0	15.4	5.4	0.0	0.4	12.8	14.2	4.1	2.3	2.1
Bozeman.....................	6.8	4.9	0.3	0.0	0.0	11.2	11.5	0.0	2.8	0.9
Butte-Silver Bow...........	0.3	6.1	0.4	0.0	8.6	11.3	11.1	4.8	7.7	5.1
Great Falls...................	0.0	8.7	1.7	0.0	0.6	20.8	20.2	9.4	3.1	3.6
Helena........................	0.0	11.6	3.0	0.0	0.4	17.5	25.6	10.9	0.3	2.7
Missoula	0.2	13.9	0.0	0.0	2.2	16.7	10.7	6.5	5.6	1.2
NEBRASKA...............	X	X	X	X	X	X	X	X	X	X
Bellevue......................	1.1	17.8	0.0	0.0	0.0	17.4	6.1	9.4	0.6	4.6
Fremont.......................	0.0	20.9	0.0	0.0	0.0	16.2	26.5	15.2	2.3	1.3
Grand Island	0.0	15.4	0.1	0.0	0.0	13.6	20.2	7.7	0.4	1.5
Kearney......................	0.0	18.8	0.2	0.0	0.0	16.5	20.9	11.0	4.0	2.0
Lincoln........................	0.0	21.0	1.5	0.0	8.0	11.0	18.0	6.4	6.4	2.1
Omaha........................	0.0	12.1	0.5	0.0	0.0	19.3	11.7	5.2	1.5	6.8
NEVADA..................	X	X	X	X	X	X	X	X	X	X
Carson City	1.7	9.6	0.0	0.0	5.4	19.4	5.3	7.6	1.5	3.9
Henderson...................	0.0	4.2	0.0	0.0	0.0	24.7	9.4	15.4	5.1	3.8
Las Vegas	0.1	9.2	0.5	0.0	0.3	16.1	6.0	15.0	3.0	2.3
North Las Vegas	0.0	19.0	0.0	0.0	0.3	18.2	5.2	7.7	2.2	2.7
Reno..........................	0.0	5.0	0.0	0.0	0.0	20.4	21.6	7.4	1.9	6.1
Sparks........................	0.0	8.8	0.0	0.0	0.0	22.2	12.3	8.7	2.7	3.6
NEW HAMPSHIRE.....	X	X	X	X	X	X	X	X	X	X
Concord......................	1.5	9.1	1.0	0.0	0.4	10.5	12.0	4.7	0.0	1.8
Dover..........................	0.6	6.1	0.0	44.8	0.0	6.6	5.4	2.9	0.9	3.2
Manchester..................	0.3	5.1	0.5	38.4	1.1	6.3	5.8	3.3	0.9	5.1
Nashua.......................	0.6	3.2	0.0	51.7	0.7	7.3	10.3	1.3	0.8	5.1
Rochester....................	0.8	7.5	0.0	58.7	0.1	5.3	3.8	1.2	0.2	3.3
NEW JERSEY............	X	X	X	X	X	X	X	X	X	X
Atlantic City	2.3	0.7	0.0	0.0	2.4	21.5	1.7	2.6	13.4	3.0
Bayonne......................	0.0	3.2	0.3	41.4	0.6	7.3	3.3	1.3	7.4	2.7
Bergenfield	0.0	0.0	0.0	64.5	0.6	9.7	7.9	1.1	0.0	1.4
Bridgeton.....................	0.0	5.4	0.0	0.0	0.0	18.0	19.5	1.9	18.4	0.5
Camden.......................	0.0	3.2	0.0	0.0	0.6	21.1	6.6	2.0	17.4	1.8
Clifton	0.1	4.5	0.0	0.0	1.2	20.1	8.4	1.9	2.8	3.0
East Orange.................	0.0	0.6	0.1	65.3	1.9	6.8	2.9	1.1	4.0	0.8
Elizabeth......................	0.0	2.8	0.9	0.0	2.6	18.7	9.6	5.0	14.3	1.6
Englewood...................	0.2	5.1	0.7	54.6	0.9	8.9	2.5	0.9	4.2	0.9
Fair Lawn	0.4	4.9	0.0	0.0	1.5	19.1	14.5	6.0	0.0	4.8
Fort Lee......................	0.2	3.2	0.0	0.0	1.8	24.9	10.9	2.6	8.8	4.2

Table D. Cities — City Government Finances, City Government Employment, and Climate

City	City government finances, 2007 (cont.) Debt outstanding Total (mil dol)	Per capita[1] (dollars)	Debt issued during year	City government employment, 2010	Climate[2] Average daily temperature (degrees Fahrenheit) Mean January	July	Limits January[3]	July[4]	Annual precipitation (inches)	Heating degree days	Cooling degree days
	137	138	139	140	141	142	143	144	145	146	147
MISSOURI..................	X	X	X	NA	X	X	X	X	X	X	X
Ballwin.........................	30.2	1 004	0.0	161	27.5	78.1	17.3	89.2	38.00	5 199	1 293
Blue Springs.................	91.0	1 653	11.4	269	24.6	76.6	14.9	87.2	41.18	5 623	1 137
Cape Girardeau.............	68.2	1 836	0.0	414	32.4	79.5	24.0	90.1	46.54	4 344	1 515
Chesterfield..................	114.5	2 475	0.3	225	27.5	78.1	17.3	89.2	38.00	5 199	1 293
Columbia......................	143.2	1 444	60.6	1 440	27.8	77.4	18.2	88.6	40.28	5 177	1 246
Florissant.....................	14.2	278	3.6	359	29.6	80.2	21.2	89.8	38.75	4 758	1 561
Gladstone.....................	44.9	1 605	28.3	175	29.3	81.3	20.7	90.5	35.51	4 734	1 676
Hazelwood....................	30.7	1 206	6.3	193	29.6	80.2	21.2	89.8	38.75	4 758	1 561
Independence................	203.7	1 840	64.1	1 173	26.6	77.1	17.1	87.5	43.14	5 373	1 176
Jefferson City...............	50.6	1 247	10.1	445	28.2	77.9	17.7	89.4	39.59	5 158	1 261
Joplin..........................	18.4	375	0.0	511	33.1	79.9	23.7	90.4	46.07	4 253	1 555
Kansas City..................	2 467.0	5 478	374.6	6 339	29.3	81.3	20.7	90.5	35.51	4 734	1 676
Kirkwood......................	33.7	1 258	0.3	248	29.6	80.2	21.2	89.8	38.75	4 758	1 561
Lee's Summit	112.4	1 357	17.1	665	24.6	76.6	14.9	87.2	41.18	5 623	1 137
Liberty.........................	49.9	1 665	0.0	211	26.6	77.1	17.1	87.5	43.14	5 373	1 176
Maryland Heights	29.9	1 144	0.6	224	29.5	80.7	21.2	90.5	38.84	4 650	1 633
O'Fallon.......................	343.2	4 577	15.8	411	28.3	79.0	19.0	90.2	38.28	5 020	1 399
Raytown.......................	13.2	464	7.6	164	24.6	76.6	14.9	87.2	41.18	5 623	1 137
St. Charles	154.8	2 432	11.1	448	27.5	78.1	17.3	89.2	38.00	5 199	1 293
St. Joseph....................	375.0	5 073	0.0	669	26.4	78.7	15.9	89.9	35.24	5 345	1 339
St. Louis......................	1 653.9	4 715	492.2	6 783	29.5	80.7	21.2	90.5	38.84	4 650	1 633
St. Peters.....................	61.1	1 108	0.1	494	28.3	79.0	19.0	90.2	38.28	5 020	1 399
Springfield....................	484.9	3 133	137.4	2 647	31.7	78.5	21.8	89.9	44.97	4 602	1 366
University City	23.2	636	0.0	301	29.5	80.7	21.2	90.5	38.84	4 650	1 633
Wentzville.....................	47.5	2 113	4.2	193	NA	NA	NA	NA	NA	NA	NA
Wildwood......................	2.6	75	0.0	NA	27.5	78.1	17.3	89.2	38.00	5 199	1 293
MONTANA	X	X	X	NA	X	X	X	X	X	X	X
Billings........................	101.4	996	27.6	859	24.0	72.0	15.1	85.8	14.77	7 006	583
Bozeman......................	15.2	400	2.2	330	22.6	65.3	12.0	81.8	16.45	7 984	216
Butte-Silver Bow...........	48.1	1 474	0.0	439	17.6	62.7	5.4	79.8	12.78	9 399	127
Great Falls...................	54.0	918	3.6	484	21.7	66.2	11.3	82.0	14.89	7 828	288
Helena.........................	41.9	1 460	0.8	306	20.2	67.8	9.9	83.4	11.32	7 975	277
Missoula.......................	65.8	1 025	21.2	481	23.5	66.9	16.2	83.6	13.82	7 622	256
NEBRASKA................	X	X	X	NA	X	X	X	X	X	X	X
Bellevue.......................	39.2	810	0.0	254	21.7	76.7	11.6	87.4	30.22	6 311	1 095
Fremont........................	46.7	1 843	9.9	289	21.1	76.2	10.4	87.7	29.80	6 444	1 004
Grand Island.................	85.0	1 897	15.0	578	22.4	75.8	12.2	87.1	25.89	6 385	1 027
Kearney.......................	38.5	1 279	5.6	254	22.4	74.7	11.0	85.7	25.20	6 652	852
Lincoln.........................	907.8	3 649	139.0	2 593	22.4	77.8	11.5	89.6	28.37	6 242	1 154
Omaha.........................	823.8	1 941	97.7	2 850	21.7	76.7	11.6	87.4	30.22	6 311	1 095
NEVADA....................	X	X	X	NA	X	X	X	X	X	X	X
Carson City	141.2	2 571	12.4	632	33.7	70.0	21.7	89.2	10.36	5 661	419
Henderson....................	404.6	1 622	2.1	2 243	47.0	91.2	36.8	104.1	4.49	2 239	3 214
Las Vegas....................	352.8	631	34.2	2 869	47.0	91.2	36.8	104.1	4.49	2 239	3 214
North Las Vegas	378.6	1 785	154.9	1 937	47.0	91.2	36.8	104.1	4.49	2 239	3 214
Reno............................	751.0	3 495	45.0	1 514	33.6	71.3	21.8	91.2	7.48	5 600	493
Sparks.........................	108.6	1 247	32.0	841	33.6	71.3	21.8	91.2	7.48	5 600	493
NEW HAMPSHIRE.....	X	X	X	NA	X	X	X	X	X	X	X
Concord.......................	68.5	1 615	13.3	518	20.1	70.0	9.7	82.9	37.60	7 478	442
Dover...........................	108.4	3 768	20.6	932	23.3	70.7	13.1	83.2	42.80	6 748	427
Manchester...................	555.2	5 099	0.0	3 547	18.8	68.4	5.2	82.1	39.82	7 742	263
Nashua........................	165.6	1 907	12.9	2 751	22.8	70.8	12.1	82.5	45.43	6 834	445
Rochester.....................	66.3	2 173	0.0	997	23.3	70.7	13.1	83.2	42.80	6 748	427
NEW JERSEY...........	X	X	X	NA	X	X	X	X	X	X	X
Atlantic City	169.9	4 281	2.5	1 669	35.2	75.2	29.0	80.6	38.37	4 480	951
Bayonne.......................	393.2	6 793	17.4	2 184	31.3	77.2	24.4	85.2	46.25	4 843	1 220
Bergenfield...................	20.7	802	5.0	NA	28.6	75.0	19.5	85.5	51.50	5 522	824
Bridgeton......................	5.7	232	0.0	246	NA	NA	NA	NA	NA	NA	NA
Camden........................	124.7	1 585	3.9	1 367	32.3	76.3	23.2	87.8	48.25	4 801	1 054
Clifton..........................	69.4	883	15.8	611	28.6	75.0	19.5	85.5	51.50	5 522	824
East Orange.................	109.2	1 655	23.0	3 191	31.3	77.2	24.4	85.2	46.25	4 843	1 220
Elizabeth......................	137.6	1 102	22.1	1 383	29.6	74.5	19.8	85.7	50.94	5 450	787
Englewood....................	35.7	1 274	0.0	932	29.6	75.3	22.7	82.5	46.33	5 367	882
Fair Lawn.....................	29.9	971	0.0	267	28.6	75.0	19.5	85.5	51.50	5 522	824
Fort Lee.......................	69.6	1 907	0.0	356	29.6	75.3	22.7	82.5	46.33	5 367	882

1. Based on the population estimated as of July 1 of the year shown.   2. Represents normal values based on the 30-year period, 1971–2000.   3. Average daily minimum.   4. Average daily maximum.

Table D. Cities — Land Area and Population

STATE Place code	City	Land area,[1] 2010 (sq km)	Population, 2010			Race alone or in combination, not of Hispanic origin (percent), 2010					Percent Hispanic or Latino[2], 2010	Percent Foreign born, 2008–2010
			Total persons	Rank	Per square kilometer	White	Black	American Indian, Alaska Native	Asian	Hawaiian Pacific Islander		
		1	2	3	4	5	6	7	8	9	10	11
	NEW JERSEY— Cont'd											
34 25770	Garfield....................	5.4	30 487	1 332	5 604.2	59.8	5.7	0.2	2.6	0.1	32.2	42.0
34 28680	Hackensack.............	10.8	43 010	913	3 971.4	30.8	23.3	0.5	10.9	0.1	35.3	38.3
34 32250	Hoboken..................	3.3	50 005	770	15 153.0	74.7	3.0	0.2	8.2	0.1	15.2	14.5
34 36000	Jersey City	38.3	247 597	75	6 461.3	22.7	24.9	0.7	24.8	0.2	27.6	38.4
34 36510	Kearny....................	22.7	40 684	976	1 789.9	49.8	4.6	0.2	4.7	0.2	39.9	39.4
34 40350	Linden....................	27.7	40 499	980	1 464.7	45.7	26.6	0.6	3.0	0.1	24.9	34.1
34 41310	Long Branch............	13.7	30 719	1 319	2 248.8	54.0	14.1	0.5	2.5	0.1	28.1	29.6
34 46680	Millville..................	108.8	28 400	1 452	261.1	64.2	20.1	1.6	1.5	0.1	14.9	4.8
34 51000	Newark	62.6	277 140	68	4 424.3	12.5	50.6	0.6	1.8	0.1	33.8	25.5
34 51210	New Brunswick..........	13.5	55 181	686	4 075.4	27.7	14.7	0.4	8.0	0.1	49.9	38.2
34 55950	Paramus	27.1	26 342	1 572	971.3	68.1	1.5	0.2	23.9	0.5	7.3	28.4
34 56550	Passaic..................	8.2	69 781	489	8 562.1	16.5	7.8	0.2	4.6	0.0	71.0	45.9
34 57000	Paterson.................	21.8	146 199	167	6 697.2	10.0	29.0	0.4	3.7	0.1	57.6	25.0
34 58200	Perth Amboy............	12.2	50 814	760	4 171.9	12.4	7.7	0.2	1.7	0.0	78.1	36.2
34 59190	Plainfield................	15.6	49 808	773	3 192.8	9.1	49.6	0.7	1.2	0.1	40.4	36.5
34 61530	Rahway..................	10.1	27 346	1 508	2 710.2	41.5	30.9	0.8	4.7	0.1	23.5	21.0
34 65790	Sayreville...............	41.0	42 704	919	1 040.8	60.4	10.6	0.3	16.9	0.1	12.3	23.6
34 74000	Trenton	19.8	84 913	370	4 286.4	14.4	51.1	0.7	1.3	0.1	33.7	24.3
34 74630	Union City...............	3.3	66 455	522	20 016.6	11.0	1.8	0.1	2.4	0.0	84.7	58.3
34 76070	Vineland.................	177.2	60 724	592	342.6	47.4	13.2	0.8	2.0	0.1	38.0	12.6
34 79040	Westfield................	17.4	30 316	1 345	1 742.3	86.0	3.5	0.2	6.7	0.1	4.9	12.4
34 79610	West New York	2.6	49 708	776	19 045.2	13.8	2.0	0.2	6.3	0.0	78.1	60.6
35 00000	**NEW MEXICO**..........	314 160.8	2 059 179	X	6.6	41.7	2.2	9.2	1.7	0.1	46.3	9.8
35 01780	Alamogordo	55.5	30 403	1 340	547.7	61.2	6.1	1.8	2.6	0.5	30.5	7.8
35 02000	Albuquerque............	486.2	545 852	32	1 122.6	43.7	3.3	4.5	3.2	0.2	46.7	11.2
35 12150	Carlsbad.................	74.9	26 138	1 588	348.8	54.1	1.9	1.2	1.2	0.1	42.5	2.1
35 16420	Clovis....................	58.8	37 775	1 048	642.1	49.6	7.2	1.2	1.9	0.1	41.8	9.5
35 25800	Farmington	81.6	45 877	861	562.1	54.4	1.3	23.0	0.9	0.1	22.4	5.3
35 32520	Hobbs....................	62.0	34 122	1 184	550.0	39.1	6.1	1.2	0.7	0.1	53.7	11.2
35 39380	Las Cruces..............	198.1	97 618	298	492.7	38.6	2.4	1.3	1.9	0.2	56.8	12.5
35 63460	Rio Rancho..............	267.7	87 521	354	326.9	55.8	3.3	3.4	2.4	0.3	36.7	5.7
35 64930	Roswell..................	77.3	48 366	808	625.4	42.9	2.3	1.1	0.9	0.1	53.4	10.8
35 70500	Santa Fe.................	119.1	67 947	501	570.6	47.4	1.1	1.9	1.8	0.1	48.7	12.4
36 00000	**NEW YORK**..............	122 056.8	19 378 102	X	158.8	59.5	15.2	0.7	8.0	0.1	17.6	21.9
36 01000	Albany	55.4	97 856	297	1 766.4	56.3	31.0	0.9	5.6	0.2	8.6	11.6
36 03078	Auburn...................	21.6	27 687	1 489	1 282.4	87.1	10.1	0.9	0.8	0.1	3.6	2.9
36 06607	Binghamton.............	27.2	47 376	837	1 743.7	78.2	12.9	1.0	4.8	0.2	6.4	9.8
36 11000	Buffalo...................	104.6	261 310	70	2 498.4	47.7	39.0	1.2	3.6	0.1	10.5	7.6
36 24229	Elmira....................	18.8	29 200	1 410	1 555.7	80.6	17.4	1.2	0.9	0.1	4.3	2.2
36 27485	Freeport..................	12.0	42 860	915	3 574.6	24.6	32.2	0.7	2.0	0.1	41.7	36.6
36 29113	Glen Cove	17.2	26 964	1 536	1 564.0	60.4	7.1	0.4	5.1	0.2	27.9	30.7
36 32402	Harrison..................	43.4	27 472	1 501	632.7	78.3	2.6	0.3	8.3	0.1	11.7	23.2
36 33139	Hempstead..............	9.5	53 891	704	5 649.0	7.2	47.1	0.7	1.6	0.1	44.2	40.3
36 38077	Ithaca....................	14.0	30 014	1 359	2 150.0	69.8	7.5	1.0	17.9	0.2	6.9	17.6
36 38264	Jamestown..............	23.1	31 146	1 305	1 346.0	86.6	5.9	1.3	0.6	0.1	8.8	1.9
36 42554	Lindenhurst.............	9.7	27 253	1 513	2 798.0	86.7	1.6	0.3	2.4	0.0	9.7	10.2
36 43335	Long Beach..............	5.7	33 275	1 220	5 797.0	76.4	6.5	0.3	3.2	0.1	14.1	15.3
36 47042	Middletown..............	13.2	28 086	1 469	2 135.8	39.3	20.2	1.1	2.2	0.1	39.7	22.2
36 49121	Mount Vernon..............	11.4	67 292	509	5 923.6	19.8	63.0	0.9	2.4	0.2	14.3	33.3
36 50034	Newburgh................	9.9	28 866	1 431	2 930.6	22.2	30.0	1.0	1.1	0.1	47.9	23.4
36 50617	New Rochelle............	26.8	77 062	424	2 874.4	49.0	19.0	0.4	4.7	0.1	27.8	26.9
36 51000	New York.................	783.8	8 175 133	1	10 429.6	34.3	23.6	0.5	13.6	0.2	28.6	36.8
36 51055	Niagara Falls	36.5	50 193	764	1 375.9	72.2	23.7	3.0	1.5	0.1	3.0	5.4
36 53682	North Tonawanda........	26.2	31 568	1 293	1 206.7	96.4	1.2	0.8	1.0	0.1	1.7	3.2
36 55530	Ossining	8.2	25 060	1 658	3 071.1	38.0	16.2	0.2	4.7	0.1	41.4	38.3
36 59223	Port Chester.............	6.0	28 967	1 423	4 795.9	32.3	5.7	0.3	2.2	0.0	59.4	46.5
36 59641	Poughkeepsie............	13.3	32 736	1 245	2 457.7	46.0	34.3	0.8	2.0	0.1	19.5	20.1
36 63000	Rochester................	92.7	210 565	99	2 272.2	39.9	41.8	1.1	3.5	0.1	16.4	8.7
36 63418	Rome.....................	193.7	33 725	1 200	174.1	86.5	8.1	0.7	1.4	0.1	5.3	4.6
36 65255	Saratoga Springs	72.7	26 586	1 558	365.7	92.1	3.4	0.6	2.6	0.1	3.2	3.8
36 65508	Schenectady.............	27.9	66 135	525	2 368.7	61.4	22.0	1.7	5.1	0.4	10.5	11.0
36 70420	Spring Valley	5.2	31 347	1 302	6 005.2	28.9	36.6	0.6	4.2	0.3	30.6	48.0
36 73000	Syracuse.................	64.9	145 170	170	2 238.2	56.3	31.1	2.1	6.1	0.2	8.3	10.8
36 75484	Troy	26.8	50 129	768	1 869.1	72.7	17.5	0.8	4.0	0.1	7.9	8.3
36 76540	Utica	43.4	62 235	572	1 433.7	67.1	16.3	0.7	7.9	0.2	10.5	16.1
36 76705	Valley Stream............	9.0	37 511	1 054	4 158.6	46.9	18.4	0.3	12.3	0.2	22.2	31.7
36 78608	Watertown	23.4	27 023	1 529	1 156.8	85.9	7.6	1.2	2.5	0.4	5.6	4.6
36 81677	White Plains	25.3	56 853	652	2 247.2	50.0	13.9	0.3	7.0	0.1	29.6	31.3

1. Dry land or land partially or temporarily covered by water.   2. May be of any race.

Table D. Cities — **Population**

City	Age of population (percent), 2010											Population			
												Census counts		Percent change	
	Under 5 years	5 to 17 years	18 to 24 years	25 to 34 years	35 to 44 years	45 to 54 years	55 to 64 years	65 to 74 years	75 years and over	Median age	Percent female	1990	2000	1990–2000	2000–2010
	12	13	14	15	16	17	18	19	20	21	22	23	24	25	26
NEW JERSEY— Cont'd															
Garfield	6.9	16.5	9.2	16.7	14.2	14.1	11.3	5.5	5.8	35.5	52.3	26 727	29 786	11.4	2.4
Hackensack	6.4	12.2	8.3	19.0	15.6	14.4	11.6	6.5	5.9	37.5	50.5	37 049	42 677	15.2	0.8
Hoboken	6.8	5.4	12.1	38.3	17.5	8.0	5.5	3.3	3.0	31.2	49.5	33 397	38 577	15.5	29.6
Jersey City	7.1	14.1	10.0	22.4	15.2	12.5	9.6	5.3	3.7	33.2	50.6	228 517	240 055	5.0	3.1
Kearny	5.5	15.2	11.0	16.2	15.0	15.3	11.1	5.9	4.8	36.4	48.5	34 874	40 513	16.2	0.4
Linden	5.5	16.3	9.2	13.9	14.1	15.4	12.2	6.6	6.8	38.8	52.3	36 701	39 394	7.3	2.8
Long Branch	7.2	14.5	12.2	17.8	13.3	13.1	10.7	5.7	5.6	33.8	49.9	28 658	31 340	9.4	-2.0
Millville	7.0	18.9	9.9	12.3	12.8	14.0	11.9	7.3	6.0	36.6	52.6	25 992	26 847	3.3	5.8
Newark	7.5	18.0	11.9	16.8	15.0	13.2	8.9	5.1	3.5	32.3	50.5	275 221	273 546	-0.6	1.3
New Brunswick	7.2	13.9	33.2	17.7	10.7	7.3	4.9	2.7	2.5	23.3	48.8	41 711	48 573	16.5	13.6
Paramus	4.0	17.5	7.1	7.4	11.8	17.0	13.3	9.1	12.8	46.3	51.3	25 004	25 737	2.9	2.4
Passaic	9.9	21.6	11.4	16.4	13.3	11.4	8.2	4.4	3.4	29.2	49.8	58 041	67 861	16.9	2.8
Paterson	8.0	19.9	11.4	14.8	14.1	13.3	9.5	5.4	3.5	32.1	51.7	140 891	149 222	5.9	-2.0
Perth Amboy	7.9	19.4	11.0	15.7	14.4	13.2	9.1	5.0	4.3	32.4	50.7	41 967	47 303	12.7	7.4
Plainfield	8.3	17.5	10.5	16.1	14.6	14.0	9.5	5.5	4.0	33.3	49.7	46 577	47 829	2.7	4.1
Rahway	5.9	15.9	8.5	14.4	14.3	15.6	11.9	6.6	6.9	38.8	52.3	25 325	26 500	4.6	3.2
Sayreville	6.6	16.0	8.0	14.3	14.7	16.2	12.1	6.4	5.7	38.6	51.2	34 998	40 377	15.4	5.8
Trenton	7.9	17.1	11.0	17.7	14.9	13.2	9.3	4.8	4.0	32.6	48.4	88 675	85 403	-3.7	-0.6
Union City	7.3	16.4	10.6	17.4	15.0	13.6	9.1	5.7	4.8	33.9	49.9	58 012	67 088	15.6	-0.9
Vineland	7.0	17.5	9.4	12.8	13.4	14.2	11.8	7.2	6.8	37.7	52.0	54 780	56 271	2.7	7.9
Westfield	6.6	23.4	4.7	6.8	15.8	17.7	12.0	6.3	6.8	41.0	51.9	28 870	29 644	2.7	2.3
West New York	7.4	13.6	9.7	19.6	15.8	12.7	9.2	6.1	5.8	34.8	50.4	38 125	45 768	20.0	8.6
NEW MEXICO	7.0	18.1	9.9	13.0	12.1	14.2	12.5	7.5	5.8	36.7	50.6	1 515 069	1 819 046	20.1	13.2
Alamogordo	7.5	16.1	9.6	14.2	11.1	13.5	11.3	8.8	8.0	37.4	50.9	27 596	35 582	28.9	-14.6
Albuquerque	7.0	17.0	10.7	15.2	12.8	13.8	11.5	6.4	5.7	35.1	51.4	384 915	448 607	16.5	21.7
Carlsbad	7.3	18.3	9.0	12.6	11.1	13.6	12.5	7.6	8.0	37.6	50.9	24 952	25 625	2.7	2.0
Clovis	8.8	19.8	10.4	15.1	12.0	12.5	9.6	6.1	5.6	31.8	50.4	30 954	32 667	5.5	15.6
Farmington	8.6	19.3	10.0	15.1	11.7	13.3	10.9	5.5	5.6	32.7	50.7	33 997	37 844	11.3	21.2
Hobbs	9.6	20.2	10.7	15.6	12.0	12.6	9.1	5.3	4.7	30.8	48.6	29 121	28 657	-1.6	19.1
Las Cruces	7.1	17.2	13.7	15.1	11.0	11.9	10.3	7.3	6.4	32.4	51.3	62 360	74 267	19.1	31.4
Rio Rancho	7.2	20.9	7.8	12.9	14.3	14.9	11.2	6.0	4.8	35.9	51.3	32 512	51 765	59.2	69.1
Roswell	8.4	19.8	10.7	12.5	10.8	12.4	10.8	7.0	7.6	33.5	51.3	44 260	45 293	2.3	6.8
Santa Fe	5.5	13.3	7.5	12.3	12.6	14.6	16.6	9.8	7.7	44.0	52.6	56 537	62 203	10.0	9.2
NEW YORK	6.0	16.4	10.2	13.7	13.5	14.9	11.9	7.0	6.5	38.0	51.6	17 990 778	18 976 457	5.5	2.1
Albany	5.5	12.4	21.5	17.0	10.9	11.6	10.0	5.3	5.9	30.3	51.6	100 031	95 658	-4.4	2.3
Auburn	6.2	14.7	9.3	14.9	12.7	14.4	11.5	6.6	9.7	39.1	49.3	31 258	28 574	-8.6	-3.1
Binghamton	6.2	13.8	15.0	14.2	10.5	13.4	11.6	6.9	8.5	35.8	51.0	53 008	47 380	-10.6	0.0
Buffalo	6.7	16.9	13.9	14.6	11.7	14.0	10.9	5.9	5.5	33.2	52.1	328 175	292 648	-10.8	-10.7
Elmira	7.2	16.5	13.1	14.5	11.9	14.3	10.7	5.4	6.4	33.9	49.4	33 724	30 940	-8.3	-5.6
Freeport	6.4	17.0	10.1	13.6	14.2	15.0	11.8	6.5	5.5	37.2	51.3	39 894	43 783	9.7	-2.1
Glen Cove	5.8	14.8	8.7	13.5	13.5	14.7	12.4	7.6	9.0	40.6	51.3	24 149	26 622	10.2	1.3
Harrison	4.8	17.9	19.2	8.6	12.5	14.2	10.0	6.2	6.6	34.6	53.1	23 308	24 154	3.6	13.7
Hempstead	8.5	17.2	11.2	17.1	14.6	12.8	9.2	5.5	4.0	32.5	50.7	45 982	56 554	23.0	-4.7
Ithaca	2.3	5.9	52.5	15.2	6.3	6.1	5.8	2.7	3.2	22.4	49.6	29 541	29 287	-0.9	2.5
Jamestown	7.3	17.3	10.1	13.2	11.7	14.0	11.7	6.6	8.0	36.9	51.4	34 681	31 730	-8.5	-1.8
Lindenhurst	5.0	17.5	9.1	11.3	14.8	18.4	11.8	6.3	5.8	40.3	51.4	26 879	27 819	3.5	-2.0
Long Beach	4.6	11.7	7.1	16.2	14.1	16.1	14.2	7.5	8.5	42.5	51.7	33 510	35 462	5.8	-6.2
Middletown	8.1	19.1	9.8	14.9	14.1	13.5	9.8	5.5	5.1	33.7	51.1	24 160	25 388	5.1	10.6
Mount Vernon	6.6	16.3	9.2	13.3	14.2	15.1	11.4	7.3	6.6	38.4	54.6	67 153	68 381	1.8	-1.6
Newburgh	9.4	21.3	14.0	15.8	13.0	11.0	7.8	4.5	3.3	28.2	51.4	26 454	28 259	6.8	2.1
New Rochelle	6.1	16.6	10.5	12.6	13.1	14.2	11.7	7.1	8.0	38.4	52.0	67 265	72 182	7.3	6.8
New York	6.3	15.3	10.6	17.0	14.1	13.5	10.9	6.5	5.6	35.5	52.5	7 322 564	8 008 278	9.4	2.1
Niagara Falls	6.1	15.9	10.1	12.6	11.6	15.7	12.5	6.9	8.6	39.8	52.3	61 840	55 593	-10.1	-9.7
North Tonawanda	5.1	14.3	9.3	12.7	12.2	16.4	14.3	7.3	8.4	42.4	51.2	34 989	33 262	-4.9	-5.1
Ossining	6.4	14.9	8.2	17.7	16.8	15.0	10.5	5.4	5.1	36.6	46.9	22 582	24 010	6.3	4.4
Port Chester	6.9	15.7	10.0	18.4	15.7	13.2	9.5	5.0	5.6	34.4	47.6	24 728	27 867	12.7	3.9
Poughkeepsie	7.2	15.0	15.8	15.4	11.5	12.1	10.0	6.1	6.9	32.4	52.0	28 844	29 871	3.6	9.6
Rochester	7.5	17.3	14.2	16.8	12.5	12.8	9.9	5.0	4.0	30.8	51.7	230 356	219 773	-4.6	-4.2
Rome	6.1	14.7	9.1	13.8	12.4	14.8	12.6	7.7	8.7	40.2	48.6	44 350	34 950	-21.2	-3.5
Saratoga Springs	4.1	12.9	15.5	12.2	12.1	13.8	13.7	7.8	7.9	39.8	51.7	25 001	26 186	4.7	1.5
Schenectady	7.5	16.9	12.9	14.8	12.4	14.0	10.1	5.3	6.1	33.4	51.6	65 566	61 821	-5.7	7.0
Spring Valley	10.9	20.4	11.3	18.3	13.1	10.8	8.1	4.3	2.8	28.8	49.2	21 802	25 464	16.8	23.1
Syracuse	7.0	16.0	19.1	14.8	10.7	12.1	9.7	4.9	5.6	29.6	52.3	163 860	147 306	-10.1	-1.5
Troy	6.4	13.8	20.8	15.5	10.7	12.0	9.9	5.4	5.5	30.2	49.5	54 269	49 170	-9.4	2.0
Utica	7.5	17.2	12.4	13.1	11.5	12.7	10.7	6.5	8.3	34.8	51.9	68 637	60 651	-11.6	2.6
Valley Stream	5.6	17.5	9.2	11.7	13.8	16.6	12.4	6.0	7.3	39.7	51.9	33 946	36 368	7.1	3.1
Watertown	9.0	15.5	12.1	17.2	11.7	12.0	9.3	5.7	7.5	32.1	52.2	29 429	26 705	-9.3	1.2
White Plains	5.9	14.2	7.6	15.9	14.7	14.1	12.2	7.7	7.6	39.2	51.9	48 718	53 077	8.9	7.1

Table D. Cities — Households, Group Quarters, Crime, and Education

City	Households, 2010 Number	Persons per house-hold	Percent Female family house-holder[1]	Percent One-person	Persons in group quarters, 2010 Total	Institutional Total	Persons in nursing facilities	Non-institu-tional	Serious crimes known to police,[2] 2010 Total Number	Total Rate[3]	Rate[3] Violent	Rate[3] Property	Educational attainment, 2008–2010 Population age 25 and older	Attainment[4] (percent) High school graduate or less	Bachelor's degree or more
	27	28	29	30	31	32	33	34	35	36	37	38	39	40	41
NEW JERSEY—Cont'd															
Garfield	11 073	2.75	17.8	24.7	32	0	0	32	493	1 617	161	1 456	20 910	57.9	18.6
Hackensack	18 142	2.30	13.9	39.3	1 301	985	172	316	1 180	2 744	249	2 495	31 487	42.6	32.7
Hoboken	25 041	1.93	6.9	39.7	1 574	0	0	1 574	1 058	2 116	262	1 854	36 643	19.3	71.7
Jersey City	96 859	2.53	18.2	30.2	2 843	984	914	1 859	7 822	3 159	739	2 420	167 478	39.3	41.2
Kearny	13 462	2.83	15.6	21.0	2 570	2 501	167	69	981	2 411	211	2 200	27 246	59.3	18.5
Linden	14 909	2.70	17.6	26.2	245	242	214	3	1 497	3 696	289	3 407	27 894	57.3	16.6
Long Branch	11 753	2.60	15.6	31.0	184	75	70	109	932	3 034	365	2 669	20 947	55.0	21.1
Millville	10 648	2.65	20.0	26.6	212	117	117	95	1 385	4 877	595	4 282	18 300	62.2	14.2
Newark	94 542	2.76	28.9	27.9	16 367	8 545	1 015	7 822	12 094	4 364	1 041	3 323	171 711	65.8	12.6
New Brunswick	14 119	3.36	17.5	25.8	7 745	182	147	7 563	1 733	3 141	654	2 486	25 887	65.7	22.5
Paramus	8 630	2.92	9.1	17.8	1 165	1 110	521	55	1 849	7 019	349	6 670	18 901	34.5	47.1
Passaic	19 411	3.57	23.7	19.5	458	232	224	226	2 265	3 246	910	2 336	38 346	69.9	15.9
Paterson	44 329	3.24	29.5	21.0	2 628	1 353	212	1 275	6 086	4 163	1 070	3 092	89 284	69.9	10.8
Perth Amboy	15 419	3.25	24.6	20.3	667	445	445	222	1 336	2 629	394	2 236	31 896	67.2	13.3
Plainfield	15 180	3.23	24.1	21.3	732	342	327	390	1 935	3 885	982	2 903	33 232	59.0	18.5
Rahway	10 533	2.58	16.8	29.5	124	109	109	15	570	2 084	355	1 730	18 880	50.2	21.5
Sayreville	15 636	2.72	12.4	22.4	200	193	193	7	677	1 585	98	1 487	29 316	46.5	31.8
Trenton	28 578	2.79	28.1	30.8	5 123	4 250	1 166	873	3 714	4 374	1 411	2 963	53 644	65.3	11.2
Union City	22 814	2.88	21.8	23.8	649	342	341	307	1 571	2 364	393	1 971	43 865	62.2	17.3
Vineland	21 450	2.76	18.2	23.3	1 491	897	593	594	2 350	3 870	367	3 503	39 292	57.8	16.5
Westfield	10 566	2.85	7.5	19.2	220	204	204	16	254	838	56	782	19 806	18.2	65.3
West New York	18 852	2.64	16.8	29.5	14	0	0	14	907	1 825	344	1 481	32 991	58.4	25.2
NEW MEXICO	791 395	2.55	14.0	28.0	42 629	25 266	5 567	17 363	82 868	4 024	589	3 435	1 316 053	43.4	25.2
Alamogordo	12 763	2.33	12.6	30.9	611	515	278	96	1 133	3 727	319	3 408	20 393	41.3	17.5
Albuquerque	224 330	2.40	14.3	31.9	7 659	2 897	1 712	4 762	30 663	5 617	786	4 831	353 890	36.2	32.0
Carlsbad	10 257	2.50	14.0	28.1	533	470	217	63	1 573	6 018	754	5 264	17 462	49.4	14.1
Clovis	14 288	2.60	15.5	27.8	597	503	188	94	2 118	5 607	598	5 009	22 384	44.5	18.9
Farmington	16 446	2.70	13.6	23.7	1 465	979	164	486	2 155	4 697	1 040	3 658	27 938	42.6	19.9
Hobbs	11 629	2.81	15.5	24.1	1 494	1 316	146	178	1 934	5 668	730	4 938	20 017	56.4	14.2
Las Cruces	39 433	2.43	15.7	29.6	1 610	1 186	251	424	4 734	4 850	418	4 432	58 825	36.5	31.3
Rio Rancho	31 892	2.74	12.0	21.5	197	141	141	56	1 636	1 869	183	1 686	54 238	32.2	27.3
Roswell	17 654	2.66	16.4	26.8	1 489	452	216	1 037	2 676	5 533	726	4 807	29 290	48.2	16.2
Santa Fe	31 895	2.10	11.7	40.6	1 119	270	247	849	4 716	6 941	540	6 401	49 135	30.5	42.6
NEW YORK	7 317 755	2.57	14.9	29.1	585 678	231 163	116 558	354 515	452 138	2 333	392	1 941	12 993 461	43.0	32.3
Albany	41 157	2.13	16.0	41.3	10 248	1 452	941	8 796	5 624	5 747	1 002	4 745	58 021	38.6	38.1
Auburn	11 691	2.17	15.9	39.4	2 328	2 139	370	189	1 072	3 872	347	3 525	19 669	49.0	17.4
Binghamton	21 150	2.18	15.6	40.5	1 262	846	458	416	2 351	4 962	561	4 401	30 608	48.4	23.4
Buffalo	112 536	2.24	22.0	39.7	9 371	2 530	1 201	6 841	18 352	7 023	1 377	5 646	163 907	48.1	22.1
Elmira	10 991	2.34	19.5	36.1	3 458	2 380	296	1 078	1 165	3 990	370	3 620	17 883	56.2	12.1
Freeport	13 279	3.18	20.3	22.2	574	354	346	220	1 239	2 891	497	2 394	29 084	51.9	22.7
Glen Cove	9 764	2.69	14.1	26.4	723	404	396	319	250	927	85	842	18 512	43.0	38.2
Harrison	8 375	2.77	9.7	21.2	4 285	0	0	4 285	274	997	73	925	16 761	30.6	49.6
Hempstead	15 234	3.45	27.8	22.1	1 306	686	678	620	1 503	2 789	839	1 950	33 307	61.8	14.7
Ithaca	10 408	2.14	7.0	43.0	7 701	179	172	7 522	1 203	4 008	200	3 808	12 360	22.3	63.7
Jamestown	13 122	2.29	16.8	35.7	1 134	399	353	735	1 461	4 691	578	4 113	20 329	50.7	15.3
Lindenhurst	9 316	2.92	12.2	19.3	29	0	0	29	NA	NA	NA	NA	18 452	48.9	21.2
Long Beach	14 809	2.17	10.5	38.8	1 094	920	822	174	301	905	120	784	25 835	33.3	44.1
Middletown	9 976	2.77	19.0	28.7	489	190	181	299	1 321	4 703	534	4 169	17 980	60.0	15.6
Mount Vernon	26 260	2.53	24.4	32.8	833	429	418	404	2 262	3 361	1 008	2 354	45 632	48.6	24.7
Newburgh	9 030	3.09	26.6	25.9	945	24	0	921	1 654	5 730	1 808	3 922	16 041	66.6	13.9
New Rochelle	27 953	2.64	12.9	29.9	3 277	1 256	999	2 021	1 432	1 858	282	1 577	49 787	41.9	39.0
New York	3 109 784	2.57	18.7	32.0	185 530	70 041	45 516	115 489	188 104	2 301	593	1 708	5 499 923	45.9	33.4
Niagara Falls	22 603	2.20	19.7	38.1	376	159	157	217	3 534	7 041	1 215	5 826	34 053	53.8	13.8
North Tonawanda	14 004	2.24	11.3	34.1	142	74	70	68	637	2 018	171	1 847	22 642	47.2	20.5
Ossining	8 344	2.78	14.0	26.7	1 858	1 830	102	28	287	1 145	156	990	17 866	46.3	36.5
Port Chester	9 240	3.08	14.3	24.2	465	154	154	311	729	2 517	176	2 341	19 023	60.7	21.2
Poughkeepsie	12 400	2.41	20.0	36.1	2 904	921	540	1 983	1 453	4 439	1 216	3 223	21 542	50.0	21.1
Rochester	87 027	2.30	24.1	38.5	10 200	3 657	1 960	6 543	14 049	6 672	1 059	5 613	128 859	48.6	25.0
Rome	13 526	2.28	15.2	34.9	2 882	2 581	462	301	688	2 040	119	1 921	24 347	52.5	17.9
Saratoga Springs	11 312	2.13	7.9	36.7	2 510	445	352	2 065	630	2 370	117	2 253	19 265	24.2	51.5
Schenectady	26 633	2.35	19.7	35.9	3 470	677	296	2 793	4 066	6 148	1 027	5 121	41 380	52.8	17.6
Spring Valley	8 755	3.56	19.9	20.8	216	0	0	216	762	2 431	443	1 987	18 405	53.7	21.3
Syracuse	57 355	2.31	20.8	38.4	12 782	2 332	1 523	10 450	6 999	4 821	889	3 932	83 399	46.7	26.2
Troy	20 505	2.22	18.0	37.1	4 508	493	202	4 015	2 775	5 536	844	4 692	30 082	48.6	21.8
Utica	24 905	2.38	19.0	36.5	3 076	1 171	983	1 905	3 133	5 034	668	4 366	38 020	51.9	15.0
Valley Stream	12 189	3.07	14.4	18.4	41	0	0	41	NA	NA	NA	NA	25 336	43.6	32.2
Watertown	11 409	2.29	15.9	35.4	905	667	473	238	1 284	4 752	437	4 315	16 898	43.1	22.1
White Plains	22 910	2.40	10.7	35.3	1 755	704	460	1 051	1 204	2 118	193	1 924	41 297	35.8	44.2

1. No spouse present.   2. Data for serious crimes have not been adjusted for underreporting. This may affect comparability between geographic areas and over time.   3. Per 100,000 population estimated by the FBI.   4. Persons 25 years old and over.

Table D. Cities — Income, Poverty, and Housing

City	Money income, 2008–2010					Housing units, 2010			Occupied Housing units 2008–2010				
		Households							Owner-occupied			Median owner costs as a percent of income	
	Per capita income[1] (dollars)	Median income	Percent with income of $200,000 or more	Percent with income of less than $25,000	Families with income below poverty (percent)	Total	Percent change, 2000–2010	Vacant units for sale or rent[2]	Total	Percent	Median value[3] (dollars)	With a mortgage[4]	Without a mortgage[5]
	42	43	44	45	46	47	48	49	50	51	52	53	54
NEW JERSEY—Cont'd													
Garfield	24 735	52 279	2.2	21.9	10.1	11 788	0.8	715	11 261	40.4	367 600	38.4	21.1
Hackensack	31 390	54 943	3.5	22.4	9.6	19 375	2.3	1 233	18 744	36.2	346 200	33.6	22.5
Hoboken	68 946	102 458	20.1	14.3	11.0	26 855	34.3	1 814	23 267	32.6	578 400	23.8	21.7
Jersey City	31 066	56 119	6.7	25.0	14.4	108 720	16.1	11 861	94 335	31.2	354 900	31.2	17.9
Kearny	25 194	60 704	2.4	16.9	7.7	14 180	2.2	718	13 679	46.3	368 700	30.5	20.3
Linden	26 494	54 612	2.0	21.2	7.7	15 872	2.0	963	15 051	57.6	332 400	34.4	24.7
Long Branch	29 292	50 968	5.0	20.8	10.8	14 170	1.3	2 417	11 819	42.8	366 100	34.7	17.8
Millville	22 396	46 261	2.1	29.8	13.3	11 435	7.4	787	10 353	62.4	189 700	30.5	14.1
Newark	17 147	34 816	1.2	37.2	24.1	109 520	9.4	14 978	92 139	24.2	281 600	37.5	23.0
New Brunswick	16 517	44 158	2.6	29.1	15.8	15 053	8.3	934	15 033	24.8	278 500	30.5	20.2
Paramus	39 202	101 953	14.8	9.1	1.9	8 915	8.6	285	8 199	90.1	593 800	28.7	14.8
Passaic	13 634	30 317	1.4	40.5	26.6	20 432	1.2	1 021	19 924	26.5	351 500	46.1	22.5
Paterson	15 033	32 933	0.8	38.5	24.7	47 946	1.6	3 617	44 029	31.3	321 500	48.9	22.0
Perth Amboy	18 650	42 992	0.7	30.6	17.1	16 556	8.7	1 137	16 555	36.6	284 400	35.9	23.7
Plainfield	22 751	53 184	3.7	23.0	12.8	16 621	2.7	1 441	15 263	52.3	292 500	33.9	21.7
Rahway	28 920	57 842	3.1	20.5	5.9	11 300	8.9	767	10 317	59.5	326 500	32.2	22.7
Sayreville	32 419	71 719	4.5	11.5	3.3	16 393	7.6	767	15 232	68.6	344 100	26.6	20.6
Trenton	17 066	36 369	1.4	38.2	24.6	33 035	-2.6	4 457	27 504	40.4	129 700	25.8	18.3
Union City	18 618	40 016	1.6	31.7	16.8	24 931	5.0	2 117	22 592	19.9	356 700	39.4	26.9
Vineland	24 368	52 642	2.9	24.6	10.1	22 661	8.1	1 211	20 892	67.9	186 700	25.6	16.6
Westfield	62 890	121 273	29.0	9.1	1.1	10 950	1.2	384	10 315	81.5	641 700	25.3	21.1
West New York	23 782	44 031	3.7	28.9	16.5	20 018	15.3	1 166	17 702	22.0	374 600	39.8	22.3
NEW MEXICO	22 789	43 569	2.4	28.9	14.0	901 388	15.5	109 993	759 896	69.0	163 300	23.7	10.0
Alamogordo	21 205	40 961	1.2	27.0	9.7	14 052	-11.2	1 289	12 407	61.8	111 200	19.9	10.0
Albuquerque	25 612	46 532	2.5	26.1	12.2	239 166	20.4	14 836	219 858	60.7	195 000	24.3	10.0
Carlsbad	24 851	45 833	1.3	26.3	7.4	11 243	-2.4	986	9 578	70.6	91 000	17.6	10.0
Clovis	20 200	36 976	0.9	31.6	15.8	15 573	8.9	1 285	13 869	63.4	112 200	21.2	10.7
Farmington	25 242	53 391	4.0	21.0	13.3	17 648	16.6	1 102	15 709	68.1	186 900	22.2	10.0
Hobbs	19 772	44 489	2.4	29.3	14.8	12 900	7.5	1 271	11 204	67.8	93 900	18.8	10.0
Las Cruces	20 213	37 390	0.9	34.6	16.2	42 370	33.9	2 937	37 401	57.9	158 300	24.1	10.0
Rio Rancho	27 029	59 846	3.1	16.6	6.5	33 964	68.3	2 072	31 123	78.9	182 400	25.3	10.1
Roswell	17 095	34 035	0.9	37.1	16.7	19 743	2.4	2 089	17 413	64.0	86 500	22.5	10.0
Santa Fe	32 872	49 837	4.3	27.0	11.6	37 200	22.0	5 305	31 545	60.4	312 100	29.9	10.0
NEW YORK	30 791	55 217	6.1	23.7	11.0	8 108 103	5.6	790 348	7 221 564	54.7	304 100	26.3	15.5
Albany	23 257	37 733	2.0	34.9	16.6	46 362	2.4	5 205	40 388	40.4	181 100	24.4	13.6
Auburn	20 950	37 983	0.3	36.1	12.3	12 639	0.0	948	12 007	49.2	94 400	20.7	17.4
Binghamton	19 688	29 821	1.6	43.4	21.3	23 842	-0.5	2 692	20 393	46.6	84 700	24.6	15.4
Buffalo	19 296	29 714	1.4	44.2	26.9	133 444	-8.3	20 908	112 163	41.8	66 600	22.1	13.9
Elmira	16 927	29 997	1.4	42.3	23.3	12 313	-4.5	1 322	10 881	48.6	65 100	19.2	14.6
Freeport	28 500	66 933	4.8	18.2	9.6	13 865	0.3	586	14 139	67.1	368 800	34.1	19.4
Glen Cove	36 408	75 876	11.4	16.4	10.3	10 352	6.3	588	9 471	59.4	547 800	30.0	22.8
Harrison	62 780	103 303	25.5	14.0	5.1	8 956	3.5	581	8 915	64.4	824 900	29.8	17.9
Hempstead	19 687	51 261	2.4	27.5	17.2	16 034	3.0	800	16 117	42.4	356 900	38.0	19.3
Ithaca	17 992	31 893	2.5	39.9	9.5	10 950	2.2	542	10 702	30.8	171 100	26.6	13.8
Jamestown	17 831	29 964	0.4	42.5	22.1	14 738	-1.9	1 616	13 810	46.6	62 900	20.2	13.8
Lindenhurst	32 401	83 964	5.8	9.1	0.9	9 665	4.1	349	8 835	85.2	374 200	29.5	20.7
Long Beach	42 640	76 451	7.8	17.5	7.1	16 450	2.0	1 641	14 539	58.9	510 100	30.7	18.4
Middletown	22 853	53 352	1.8	22.1	15.5	10 866	7.1	890	9 682	47.1	224 000	31.5	16.1
Mount Vernon	26 567	49 613	4.4	24.5	10.2	28 990	7.2	2 730	26 107	38.4	430 900	31.8	20.5
Newburgh	16 052	35 350	1.0	33.3	22.3	10 505	0.2	1 475	9 295	34.2	221 500	31.8	19.2
New Rochelle	39 382	63 251	12.2	20.9	9.0	29 586	9.6	1 633	27 836	48.6	592 800	29.0	18.6
New York	30 394	50 038	6.4	27.9	16.4	3 371 062	5.3	261 278	3 056 088	32.5	518 400	30.4	14.6
Niagara Falls	19 821	31 654	0.9	40.7	17.7	26 220	-5.8	3 617	21 971	54.8	68 500	20.8	15.9
North Tonawanda	24 824	44 345	0.9	29.9	6.7	14 757	2.3	753	14 091	66.7	101 200	22.3	14.2
Ossining	29 497	70 196	8.0	18.1	14.7	8 862	4.1	518	8 352	53.5	430 200	31.3	19.4
Port Chester	25 574	52 347	4.5	21.9	13.5	10 046	2.8	806	9 740	47.5	461 200	33.7	21.6
Poughkeepsie	23 364	38 739	2.2	36.8	24.0	13 984	6.3	1 584	13 729	38.6	245 200	30.1	19.2
Rochester	17 913	29 456	1.1	43.4	26.6	97 158	-2.7	10 131	85 710	41.7	75 800	23.9	15.2
Rome	22 787	43 780	1.1	26.7	8.3	14 893	-8.6	1 367	13 943	60.1	89 400	20.4	14.8
Saratoga Springs	35 519	55 905	4.5	22.9	3.0	12 936	11.7	1 624	12 215	58.1	295 100	24.2	13.4
Schenectady	19 241	36 496	1.1	35.3	17.2	30 095	-0.8	3 462	24 766	50.1	117 100	27.9	17.4
Spring Valley	16 987	46 194	3.3	27.3	16.7	9 374	20.2	619	8 953	24.1	323 600	31.4	24.4
Syracuse	18 154	30 588	1.3	42.5	26.4	64 356	-5.6	7 001	56 499	40.1	84 600	22.4	13.7
Troy	20 542	37 157	1.1	32.7	21.7	23 474	1.6	2 969	20 304	39.5	146 100	24.2	14.6
Utica	17 073	32 140	0.7	41.1	23.1	28 166	-3.4	3 261	24 017	49.3	86 900	21.5	15.6
Valley Stream	29 955	80 635	5.5	10.3	4.3	12 625	-0.6	436	11 414	81.6	415 300	32.2	22.2
Watertown	21 476	37 652	1.6	34.3	14.3	12 562	0.9	1 153	11 521	44.2	120 700	21.5	12.1
White Plains	42 979	69 818	13.3	17.8	4.8	24 382	13.0	1 472	23 046	54.9	506 200	27.7	19.7

1. Based on population estimated by the American Community Survey. 2. Includes units rented or sold but not occupied. 3. Specified owner-occupied units; $1,000,000 represents $1,000,000 or more. 4. 50.0 represents 50 percent or more. 5. 10.0 represents 10 percent or less.

Table D. Cities — Housing, Labor Force, and Employment

City	Occupied housing units, 2008–2010 (cont.)				Migration, 2008–2010		Civilian labor force, 2010		Unemployment		Civilian employment[4], 2008–2010	Percent		
	Percent renter occupied	Median gross rent[1]	Median rent as a percent of income[2]	Percent with no vehicle available	Percent who lived in the same house one year ago	Percent who lived outside this city one year ago	Total	Percent change, 2009–2010	Total	Rate[3]	Population age 16 and older	In labor force	Full-year full-time worker	Households with no workers (percent)
	55	56	57	58	59	60	61	62	63	64	65	66	67	68
NEW JERSEY— Cont'd														
Garfield	59.6	1 126	30.5	15.9	96.3	2.4	16 588	2.5	2 140	12.9	24 969	69.5	51.1	18.8
Hackensack	63.8	1 196	29.5	17.7	89.9	5.7	24 105	-1.6	2 435	10.1	35 858	69.7	53.4	21.8
Hoboken	67.4	1 681	23.3	34.0	75.3	12.3	34 104	19.0	1 768	5.2	42 120	81.0	65.1	14.2
Jersey City	68.8	1 116	28.4	38.2	83.0	5.6	117 105	0.3	13 380	11.4	200 006	69.9	48.4	20.7
Kearny	53.7	1 109	29.1	16.4	86.7	9.0	19 698	7.5	2 378	12.1	32 596	69.1	48.6	20.1
Linden	42.4	1 044	30.0	11.9	93.8	4.1	21 495	2.1	2 355	11.0	32 834	68.7	47.9	25.4
Long Branch	57.2	1 160	31.7	16.1	78.9	11.2	15 455	-5.6	1 541	10.0	25 279	73.0	42.0	22.7
Millville	37.6	763	38.8	13.9	88.9	6.0	14 142	-1.6	2 002	14.2	21 716	65.0	38.6	32.0
Newark	75.8	921	33.0	38.4	87.0	4.7	107 796	-1.5	16 575	15.4	212 859	61.4	38.3	30.9
New Brunswick	75.2	1 281	36.1	28.1	71.5	13.4	29 320	7.2	2 282	7.8	45 083	65.6	34.9	22.0
Paramus	9.9	1 477	34.7	3.2	94.1	3.9	12 857	-1.0	1 034	8.0	21 345	60.4	38.1	22.2
Passaic	73.5	990	42.8	43.1	95.9	2.0	29 442	1.5	3 726	12.7	49 121	60.7	33.2	22.7
Paterson	68.7	1 024	40.6	28.4	89.9	2.6	60 385	-1.4	10 168	16.8	110 296	57.0	42.1	29.9
Perth Amboy	63.4	1 082	34.6	23.4	89.8	5.0	23 769	3.8	3 710	15.6	38 374	62.5	46.0	22.6
Plainfield	47.7	1 101	35.6	16.5	86.7	4.8	26 884	5.6	3 133	11.7	39 255	76.2	46.4	22.2
Rahway	40.5	1 104	32.3	9.7	91.1	4.0	14 450	-5.4	1 551	10.7	22 140	65.8	44.3	26.0
Sayreville	31.4	1 067	23.8	6.1	93.7	3.9	23 146	1.0	2 103	9.1	33 717	68.6	46.4	19.8
Trenton	59.6	932	35.8	33.4	82.5	7.1	40 369	3.7	5 162	12.8	65 582	64.8	40.0	32.3
Union City	80.1	975	32.5	43.1	88.2	3.6	28 877	3.3	3 961	13.7	52 107	69.8	46.3	20.6
Vineland	32.1	925	33.0	12.3	86.4	4.2	29 837	3.2	3 964	13.3	47 696	67.0	40.2	27.5
Westfield	18.5	1 322	30.5	4.0	93.0	4.3	15 680	1.2	898	5.7	22 136	66.6	42.4	22.2
West New York	78.0	1 034	31.2	39.5	85.2	9.5	21 934	3.3	2 552	11.6	39 422	72.4	43.0	20.7
NEW MEXICO	31.0	691	29.0	5.6	84.3	8.7	934 380	-0.8	74 176	7.9	1 580 737	61.7	40.1	27.7
Alamogordo	38.2	590	26.2	4.1	77.4	11.3	12 251	-17.5	858	7.0	24 154	59.5	41.4	30.3
Albuquerque	39.3	720	29.4	6.2	82.1	6.5	256 950	-2.6	19 548	7.6	424 897	67.0	44.0	24.4
Carlsbad	29.4	641	23.6	4.8	84.1	7.2	13 620	-3.7	807	5.9	20 188	64.7	42.3	28.4
Clovis	36.6	557	27.3	7.2	77.9	9.0	17 173	3.4	878	5.1	27 376	64.0	39.8	25.3
Farmington	31.9	746	24.1	4.2	80.8	10.3	21 651	-2.7	1 424	6.6	33 679	64.2	44.2	19.8
Hobbs	32.2	698	22.7	4.3	80.3	12.3	14 161	-0.9	1 083	7.6	25 039	59.0	38.6	23.3
Las Cruces	42.1	670	33.9	5.6	75.4	9.7	46 344	2.9	2 926	6.3	74 924	61.8	36.5	29.0
Rio Rancho	21.1	1 017	30.1	2.8	84.1	9.8	39 759	1.7	3 097	7.8	63 435	68.9	48.1	19.1
Roswell	36.0	565	29.7	7.0	76.2	9.1	19 442	-3.9	1 503	7.7	35 658	60.7	36.5	29.0
Santa Fe	39.6	864	32.9	7.2	79.8	10.0	36 977	-7.4	2 238	6.1	56 044	65.7	40.5	31.6
NEW YORK	45.3	996	31.2	28.8	88.5	5.6	9 586 931	-0.9	824 668	8.6	15 503 530	64.0	41.6	26.6
Albany	59.6	809	32.7	25.2	75.6	11.0	47 391	0.1	3 939	8.3	83 027	62.4	36.3	30.9
Auburn	50.8	621	26.3	15.7	77.5	11.6	13 253	-0.4	1 229	9.3	22 877	61.8	38.4	32.8
Binghamton	53.4	580	36.9	23.1	87.0	6.4	21 106	0.5	2 005	9.5	38 863	56.1	29.5	37.1
Buffalo	58.2	650	36.6	30.2	81.2	6.0	116 324	-5.5	12 530	10.8	207 064	60.7	32.6	37.6
Elmira	51.4	558	32.8	26.1	76.8	13.0	11 874	-1.9	1 237	10.4	23 177	53.1	29.9	39.8
Freeport	32.9	1 178	37.4	12.9	89.2	5.5	22 245	-2.5	1 950	8.8	34 235	72.5	44.1	20.5
Glen Cove	40.6	1 547	34.1	10.9	92.1	4.1	13 353	-0.1	997	7.5	21 659	62.9	43.4	21.0
Harrison	35.6	1 666	32.0	7.8	90.5	4.5	13 399	1.3	973	7.3	20 782	62.3	39.1	23.3
Hempstead	57.6	1 209	36.4	27.0	87.5	8.0	26 057	-0.8	2 415	9.3	40 340	70.4	42.9	21.5
Ithaca	69.2	844	38.7	28.9	57.0	23.1	15 657	0.6	980	6.3	27 793	57.8	20.4	30.0
Jamestown	53.4	559	31.8	23.7	78.2	10.5	14 700	1.3	1 411	9.6	24 384	62.6	33.8	40.2
Lindenhurst	14.8	1 580	31.7	5.7	95.5	3.8	14 541	-4.5	1 264	8.7	21 959	69.1	41.4	22.5
Long Beach	41.1	1 585	29.4	11.0	87.9	6.3	18 387	-6.8	1 377	7.5	28 871	64.3	48.6	23.1
Middletown	52.9	1 045	33.2	18.6	81.4	11.3	12 899	6.8	1 188	9.2	21 742	67.8	41.4	25.2
Mount Vernon	61.6	1 076	34.3	26.1	88.6	3.7	33 389	-3.9	3 185	9.5	53 435	68.4	46.3	24.8
Newburgh	65.8	964	36.6	29.1	80.1	3.1	11 768	1.0	1 258	10.7	20 633	61.4	40.8	29.8
New Rochelle	51.4	1 215	34.2	17.4	87.5	5.9	38 864	1.4	3 159	8.1	61 551	63.9	41.8	23.3
New York	67.5	1 098	31.1	55.1	88.7	2.1	3 964 893	-1.0	378 453	9.5	6 569 389	63.4	42.4	26.4
Niagara Falls	45.2	604	34.1	18.3	89.3	3.2	23 279	-4.2	2 768	11.9	41 262	58.3	34.4	38.1
North Tonawanda	33.3	593	31.1	8.0	90.9	4.7	17 503	-2.0	1 433	8.2	26 350	65.7	41.1	34.2
Ossining	46.5	1 272	35.0	11.5	86.7	5.7	18 736	-0.2	1 281	6.8	20 433	70.1	43.0	19.6
Port Chester	52.5	1 361	37.5	21.5	84.2	4.5	14 774	0.0	921	6.2	23 170	73.1	41.4	17.4
Poughkeepsie	61.4	922	41.9	26.8	77.7	7.0	14 651	9.1	1 339	9.1	25 314	65.5	41.2	32.8
Rochester	58.3	702	37.5	26.0	76.3	7.4	94 092	-1.3	10 098	10.7	164 659	60.8	34.4	34.0
Rome	39.9	614	24.4	13.4	82.6	9.4	14 450	-3.3	1 193	8.3	28 195	55.7	36.9	32.0
Saratoga Springs	41.9	871	32.1	11.6	88.6	8.5	14 370	-11.6	946	6.6	22 184	67.7	41.0	28.5
Schenectady	49.9	781	29.7	19.0	87.8	5.9	31 102	3.4	2 892	9.3	52 059	63.7	39.3	31.4
Spring Valley	75.9	1 109	33.0	20.7	88.5	5.1	14 606	15.5	995	6.8	22 762	73.6	39.7	20.6
Syracuse	59.9	671	34.7	26.3	70.8	10.6	63 909	-0.1	6 288	9.8	115 865	58.0	32.0	35.9
Troy	60.5	747	30.7	23.5	77.9	11.0	23 955	1.1	2 246	9.4	40 168	64.3	35.8	29.2
Utica	50.7	604	33.0	23.0	79.4	7.5	26 930	3.4	2 402	8.9	47 572	60.0	33.6	38.8
Valley Stream	18.4	1 324	28.8	5.7	92.4	6.8	19 702	3.5	1 450	7.4	30 011	68.0	43.1	19.9
Watertown	55.8	678	31.2	18.9	73.2	15.7	11 871	0.4	1 084	9.1	21 290	67.3	43.9	28.4
White Plains	45.1	1 278	31.9	17.6	87.7	6.1	30 018	-3.3	2 006	6.7	46 053	69.5	47.2	23.2

1. $2,000 represents $2,000 or more. 2. 50.0 represents 50 percent or more. 3. Percent of civilian labor force. 4. Persons 16 years old and over.

Table D. Cities — Construction, Wholesale Trade, and Retail Trade

City	Value of residential construction authorized by building permits, 2010			Wholesale trade,[1] 2007				Retail trade,[2] 2007			
	New construction ($1,000)	Number of housing units	Percent single family	Number of establishments	Number of employees	Sales (mil dol)	Annual payroll (mil dol)	Number of establishments	Number of employees	Sales (mil dol)	Annual payroll (mil dol)
	69	70	71	72	73	74	75	76	77	78	79
NEW JERSEY— Cont'd											
Garfield	1 956	21	81.0	51	755	236.7	23.4	76	531	152.0	15.6
Hackensack	546	7	28.6	223	2 147	1 699.4	131.2	278	4 052	1 144.3	108.5
Hoboken	53 327	254	2.8	36	245	575.9	16.6	153	1 351	312.4	31.4
Jersey City	26 888	170	1.2	210	4 366	3 264.5	227.9	818	8 754	2 210.1	201.6
Kearny	0	0	0.0	85	1 623	1 154.2	86.6	129	1 789	443.4	46.2
Linden	2 722	24	75.0	119	1 629	1 957.5	84.0	192	2 864	725.3	67.6
Long Branch	7 008	53	35.8	27	D	D	D	93	1 066	248.4	32.3
Millville	6 644	65	100.0	28	D	D	D	98	2 075	484.9	51.5
Newark	17 641	224	0.9	324	4 954	3 119.2	245.3	935	6 467	1 637.2	147.8
New Brunswick	11 959	95	32.6	65	843	623.7	45.7	135	958	201.5	20.3
Paramus	6 739	15	100.0	112	932	1 641.0	67.7	611	15 080	3 621.1	359.8
Passaic	2 057	31	19.4	93	814	422.7	32.9	274	1 874	415.4	42.2
Paterson	12 315	107	18.7	190	2 064	852.2	99.2	492	2 700	642.1	61.6
Perth Amboy	8 675	177	1.1	50	582	361.4	27.1	189	1 336	340.7	32.1
Plainfield	466	2	100.0	26	155	41.4	4.8	125	685	169.3	17.3
Rahway	3 564	52	11.5	61	767	961.2	45.1	87	798	265.7	26.1
Sayreville	8 136	183	88.5	53	420	547.5	23.3	98	1 221	328.7	30.1
Trenton	92	25	0.0	60	854	663.7	45.3	234	1 470	402.3	36.4
Union City	1 450	19	0.0	59	289	110.8	10.2	297	1 367	341.7	28.9
Vineland	8 875	77	97.4	86	1 357	980.4	55.3	281	3 885	1 052.0	94.5
Westfield	9 500	36	100.0	19	99	27.1	3.3	138	1 546	323.5	33.9
West New York	1 780	30	0.0	43	163	48.6	4.1	241	1 284	270.2	27.0
NEW MEXICO	779 509	4 533	88.4	1 763	19 891	10 589.3	805.8	7 208	97 385	24 470.0	2 250.8
Alamogordo	NA	NA	NA	15	62	27.2	2.0	146	2 128	491.4	42.4
Albuquerque	161 458	1 016	80.1	735	10 490	5 165.8	433.3	2 030	34 923	8 951.7	859.0
Carlsbad	8 010	53	100.0	26	182	66.2	6.6	125	1 512	361.4	34.7
Clovis	33 976	161	96.3	40	196	144.6	6.5	186	2 425	562.4	50.1
Farmington	28 900	196	63.3	107	1 111	606.3	54.9	346	5 296	1 368.3	123.4
Hobbs	11 356	77	22.1	67	631	285.1	29.6	142	2 189	628.5	53.4
Las Cruces	112 946	751	76.7	83	812	272.0	25.7	425	7 046	1 723.8	144.4
Rio Rancho	97 426	544	98.3	22	111	57.5	6.4	108	2 501	905.3	64.1
Roswell	882	5	100.0	38	350	237.6	10.8	283	3 102	788.3	66.3
Santa Fe	12 802	96	100.0	98	1 010	512.6	51.2	763	8 769	2 183.9	236.2
NEW YORK	3 165 282	19 568	50.9	30 863	357 459	313 461.9	19 609.0	76 637	892 863	230 718.1	22 336.7
Albany	5 433	39	87.2	130	1 777	1 362.9	95.4	381	5 687	1 362.3	134.1
Auburn	320	4	100.0	26	396	188.9	17.7	161	2 699	583.4	57.0
Binghamton	326	1	100.0	51	622	191.9	22.0	191	2 280	471.7	46.2
Buffalo	17 831	126	37.3	281	4 538	2 037.3	182.5	795	8 315	1 449.6	159.4
Elmira	0	0	0.0	33	404	151.7	16.5	101	1 367	308.3	30.2
Freeport	1 000	28	0.0	87	793	310.0	32.0	185	1 734	665.9	57.4
Glen Cove	1 251	3	100.0	49	192	130.8	8.8	131	1 337	581.8	45.0
Harrison	10 583	21	100.0	71	2 150	5 874.5	176.7	70	310	92.9	10.4
Hempstead	150	1	100.0	46	461	177.8	22.4	197	2 166	839.8	63.5
Ithaca	2 741	23	13.0	21	158	40.6	5.1	187	2 879	610.4	63.3
Jamestown	200	1	100.0	37	D	D	D	127	1 511	359.2	34.1
Lindenhurst	261	1	100.0	39	D	D	D	88	720	243.0	23.4
Long Beach	2 800	14	100.0	25	34	17.9	1.5	87	624	178.3	18.1
Middletown	1 433	19	100.0	33	361	128.5	12.4	131	1 394	457.1	37.5
Mount Vernon	506	5	60.0	100	1 185	541.4	51.8	222	2 491	583.8	64.6
Newburgh	470	5	100.0	57	768	1 365.4	34.9	117	1 397	359.9	31.6
New Rochelle	5 013	13	100.0	88	1 020	865.4	79.4	267	2 886	1 031.5	88.5
New York	123 742	1 064	0.6	16 230	164 336	147 228.0	9 512.3	31 459	287 574	78 206.5	8 041.7
Niagara Falls	2 440	22	9.1	35	362	160.6	14.7	182	2 429	513.0	46.5
North Tonawanda	3 866	20	100.0	36	1 071	220.0	51.6	74	741	137.2	15.7
Ossining	350	2	100.0	22	92	33.5	4.0	73	546	171.3	13.7
Port Chester	395	3	33.3	47	477	174.2	25.9	152	2 037	613.2	56.8
Poughkeepsie	150	1	100.0	34	340	160.1	16.3	153	1 599	405.5	39.3
Rochester	3 575	33	100.0	301	4 041	1 647.9	177.9	695	6 232	1 181.7	128.0
Rome	991	5	100.0	16	81	57.0	4.1	137	2 150	461.0	49.0
Saratoga Springs	11 066	61	59.0	22	121	113.6	6.3	169	2 419	614.0	53.8
Schenectady	893	10	100.0	47	588	340.6	21.9	183	1 712	441.7	42.4
Spring Valley	9 721	75	2.7	42	264	233.3	12.8	114	1 310	460.2	34.1
Syracuse	2 149	30	50.0	161	3 049	1 109.2	139.7	601	7 597	1 654.5	162.4
Troy	4 564	9	100.0	41	457	908.6	16.8	130	1 544	380.1	40.1
Utica	2 531	15	86.7	59	989	524.7	38.6	179	2 604	580.1	55.7
Valley Stream	200	2	100.0	72	418	317.2	22.3	209	2 558	697.9	58.7
Watertown	1 067	6	100.0	32	583	182.9	19.1	222	3 738	905.9	79.7
White Plains	1 025	7	42.9	111	1 426	3 327.6	109.3	471	8 610	2 004.6	221.0

1. Merchant wholesalers except manufacturers' sales branches and offices. 2. Establishments with payroll.

Table D. Cities — **Real Estate, Professional Services, and Manufacturing**

City	Real estate and rental and leasing, 2007				Professional, scientific, and technical services,[1] 2007				Manufacturing, 2007			
	Number of establish-ments	Number of employees	Receipts (mil dol)	Annual payroll (mil dol)	Number of establish-ments	Number of employees	Receipts (mil dol)	Annual payroll (mil dol)	Number of establish-ments	Number of employees	Receipts (mil dol)	Annual payroll (mil dol)
	80	81	82	83	84	85	86	87	88	89	90	91
NEW JERSEY— Cont'd												
Garfield	13	63	9.2	1.5	29	194	11.7	4.1	71	1 136	205.2	46.8
Hackensack	143	727	203.5	35.2	475	2 896	528.2	210.3	105	1 503	269.3	64.0
Hoboken	106	673	136.9	26.9	210	1 310	307.2	96.0	NA	NA	NA	NA
Jersey City	241	1 328	543.9	48.4	534	D	D	D	105	2 649	745.3	97.2
Kearny	43	368	103.6	19.2	58	213	27.7	8.1	62	1 850	552.9	82.0
Linden	41	295	46.0	8.7	57	914	88.3	58.2	112	3 886	D	236.8
Long Branch	30	79	21.1	2.2	49	D	D	D	NA	NA	NA	NA
Millville	18	78	10.9	2.0	49	264	29.4	8.7	48	3 201	829.8	122.5
Newark	222	2 181	533.1	76.1	413	8 444	1 706.2	660.1	309	9 590	3 209.2	413.2
New Brunswick	41	201	61.2	8.9	153	D	D	D	59	1 726	518.5	81.0
Paramus	65	609	355.3	36.9	227	D	D	D	NA	NA	NA	NA
Passaic	61	217	42.8	5.6	55	212	25.0	8.5	119	1 886	313.7	61.3
Paterson	73	353	63.4	11.0	101	517	53.2	18.0	278	5 473	1 153.7	226.4
Perth Amboy	29	109	34.2	4.4	45	D	D	D	49	2 139	938.5	87.4
Plainfield	30	95	24.9	2.4	44	220	22.0	10.7	23	600	82.0	20.7
Rahway	21	174	22.9	9.4	28	299	27.6	13.8	37	4 650	D	D
Sayreville	21	111	25.8	3.7	103	640	82.1	40.7	44	1 867	1 093.5	106.9
Trenton	50	352	51.9	10.9	117	D	D	D	67	1 609	333.8	68.7
Union City	67	178	27.3	4.1	87	270	28.8	8.9	55	505	77.2	14.1
Vineland	79	332	60.9	11.1	125	705	68.3	27.7	90	4 456	1 149.4	156.4
Westfield	33	117	50.8	4.7	170	1 160	215.4	82.2	NA	NA	NA	NA
West New York	69	690	171.2	25.4	67	174	26.1	8.2	NA	NA	NA	NA
NEW MEXICO	2 525	11 678	1 954.7	355.6	4 789	43 001	5 975.8	2 516.7	1 574	35 409	17 122.7	1 560.5
Alamogordo	50	224	23.5	3.7	55	264	16.4	6.6	NA	NA	NA	NA
Albuquerque	886	4 949	848.5	144.4	2 023	D	D	D	559	14 761	3 779.2	653.3
Carlsbad	24	149	15.6	4.2	44	D	D	D	NA	NA	NA	NA
Clovis	48	D	D	D	65	320	22.4	8.6	NA	NA	NA	NA
Farmington	88	686	168.5	37.2	173	D	D	D	50	660	74.6	22.1
Hobbs	44	397	100.5	23.3	50	418	46.8	21.2	NA	NA	NA	NA
Las Cruces	175	789	116.6	17.8	239	D	D	D	69	747	262.4	23.1
Rio Rancho	49	183	27.7	4.4	95	503	47.0	19.1	29	5 323	D	307.4
Roswell	78	240	35.7	6.2	97	745	102.6	33.4	30	520	15.3	15.3
Santa Fe	241	934	183.5	36.3	547	D	D	D	117	736	106.4	26.6
NEW YORK	32 588	171 601	49 867.2	7 941.7	58 087	539 635	112 045.6	41 604.5	18 629	533 835	162 720.2	24 268.0
Albany	164	1 181	249.5	32.7	434	D	D	D	71	1 791	544.3	76.7
Auburn	44	148	23.8	3.3	64	446	32.8	14.7	56	2 151	789.1	100.0
Binghamton	59	378	34.9	8.3	141	D	D	D	63	2 080	589.3	64.3
Buffalo	253	1 884	281.4	48.4	655	D	D	D	360	12 848	4 499.8	614.4
Elmira	38	212	39.1	5.6	55	D	D	D	27	2 156	403.0	86.0
Freeport	46	164	25.7	5.7	114	344	49.7	16.3	90	2 505	569.2	109.9
Glen Cove	29	101	19.9	3.7	88	367	56.3	17.4	NA	NA	NA	NA
Harrison	98	642	117.5	33.6	184	D	D	D	NA	NA	NA	NA
Hempstead	68	341	50.3	10.8	94	D	D	D	NA	NA	NA	NA
Ithaca	51	339	60.0	8.1	121	D	D	D	38	1 462	D	62.1
Jamestown	27	109	14.0	2.3	73	D	D	D	61	1 872	262.4	71.1
Lindenhurst	15	31	3.6	0.9	62	D	D	D	51	530	93.2	21.5
Long Beach	54	163	43.9	5.4	93	200	25.1	8.1	NA	NA	NA	NA
Middletown	31	100	22.4	2.4	64	342	31.8	13.4	36	1 005	198.2	38.2
Mount Vernon	172	511	102.3	17.3	99	319	53.7	12.2	112	2 784	548.7	115.6
Newburgh	47	176	17.3	4.6	62	D	D	D	43	753	122.4	25.3
New Rochelle	165	556	123.2	22.4	252	1 843	112.0	42.0	57	896	182.4	38.5
New York	18 972	106 396	36 219.1	5 588.3	24 909	300 564	76 850.6	27 940.7	6 626	101 310	20 411.6	3 818.4
Niagara Falls	37	248	27.3	6.9	93	D	D	D	51	1 877	1 073.3	114.9
North Tonawanda	11	30	2.6	0.6	41	283	15.5	6.9	58	1 468	416.2	60.5
Ossining	29	129	23.5	3.0	62	574	54.1	29.4	NA	NA	NA	NA
Port Chester	39	D	D	D	69	204	29.6	8.5	34	1 085	148.8	41.9
Poughkeepsie	83	412	71.9	11.3	143	D	D	D	39	6 649	D	D
Rochester	257	1 792	249.3	55.8	679	D	D	D	463	29 362	9 084.3	1 317.6
Rome	44	183	31.8	4.4	71	D	D	D	40	1 377	754.7	63.3
Saratoga Springs	42	244	50.1	7.0	156	D	D	D	24	1 696	540.3	75.4
Schenectady	57	281	35.1	8.3	142	1 173	140.5	65.5	60	2 171	1 096.5	112.7
Spring Valley	50	135	27.5	3.6	45	119	12.6	3.9	NA	NA	NA	NA
Syracuse	260	1 523	294.1	62.3	487	D	D	D	131	5 249	1 558.7	270.4
Troy	39	220	30.5	4.7	116	D	D	D	38	729	103.6	26.8
Utica	71	268	38.7	5.1	137	D	D	D	83	2 200	543.0	83.5
Valley Stream	59	202	45.2	7.6	151	962	99.5	39.4	NA	NA	NA	NA
Watertown	54	268	50.3	6.3	56	468	45.4	18.5	24	1 218	393.0	56.7
White Plains	198	1 206	425.2	71.3	676	D	D	D	NA	NA	NA	NA

1. Establishments subject to federal tax.

City	Accommodation and food services, 2007				Arts, entertainment, and recreation,[1] 2007				Health care and social assistance,[1] 2007			
	Number of establishments	Number of employees	Sales (mil dol)	Annual payroll (mil dol)	Number of establishments	Number of employees	Receipts (mil dol)	Annual payroll (mil dol)	Number of establishments	Number of employees	Receipts (mil dol)	Annual payroll (mil dol)
	92	93	94	95	96	97	98	99	100	101	102	103
NEW JERSEY— Cont'd												
Garfield	51	345	22.9	5.7	4	D	D	D	29	D	D	D
Hackensack	120	2 033	134.7	38.3	13	229	13.5	4.7	317	D	D	D
Hoboken	200	1 894	121.9	31.2	21	D	D	D	98	D	D	D
Jersey City	433	4 265	324.8	75.4	38	D	D	D	404	4 546	371.8	145.0
Kearny	67	538	34.8	9.1	3	D	D	D	71	523	52.7	17.7
Linden	98	793	45.6	11.5	6	62	3.6	1.0	65	956	66.8	28.2
Long Branch	96	D	D	D	6	D	D	D	93	D	D	D
Millville	59	691	32.0	8.7	2	D	D	D	55	761	53.5	24.0
Newark	542	6 939	552.6	135.8	25	344	118.4	85.5	289	3 577	376.9	138.4
New Brunswick	152	1 992	114.7	36.1	6	D	D	D	77	787	93.7	40.6
Paramus	122	2 686	151.5	41.4	16	D	D	D	199	2 216	253.3	89.2
Passaic	88	D	D	D	8	D	D	D	91	D	D	D
Paterson	198	D	D	D	5	D	D	D	147	1 298	137.4	58.6
Perth Amboy	97	512	32.5	7.3	4	14	1.0	0.3	68	D	D	D
Plainfield	70	595	29.6	8.0	4	D	D	D	68	790	70.3	29.5
Rahway	66	592	32.6	8.2	3	72	4.0	1.1	42	D	D	D
Sayreville	86	811	40.0	11.0	13	283	18.3	4.4	65	531	47.3	18.0
Trenton	157	1 107	66.2	16.7	3	D	D	D	104	1 367	150.2	69.1
Union City	130	910	47.7	11.1	4	27	2.9	0.6	152	1 766	102.4	45.1
Vineland	124	1 769	88.9	22.2	11	76	7.8	2.0	156	2 111	245.5	94.8
Westfield	64	719	42.1	11.5	12	205	7.4	2.8	154	1 599	174.2	74.3
West New York	84	D	D	D	7	22	1.8	0.7	96	D	D	D
NEW MEXICO	4 090	80 415	3 734.3	1 054.8	516	12 527	1 335.5	258.5	3 713	57 423	4 854.5	1 958.2
Alamogordo	79	1 293	48.5	13.6	6	D	D	D	75	D	D	D
Albuquerque	1 222	28 156	1 321.6	386.8	148	2 889	468.1	49.9	1 296	21 688	2 043.3	846.3
Carlsbad	73	1 081	51.3	13.1	4	D	D	D	60	1 145	137.7	47.7
Clovis	82	1 925	68.0	17.7	7	D	D	D	79	D	D	D
Farmington	126	3 003	127.8	33.9	9	D	D	D	192	D	D	D
Hobbs	80	1 493	69.1	16.8	9	D	D	D	72	D	D	D
Las Cruces	247	5 276	211.6	57.6	13	D	D	D	361	7 504	637.2	249.4
Rio Rancho	75	1 582	62.9	18.4	14	326	9.9	3.8	93	D	D	D
Roswell	108	2 235	88.9	24.3	2	D	D	D	138	D	D	D
Santa Fé	333	7 985	480.8	144.0	60	282	26.3	8.6	367	3 684	374.4	152.8
NEW YORK	43 791	591 653	39 813.5	10 956.3	9 289	101 381	15 566.1	4 656.2	41 201	459 964	46 577.9	18 427.7
Albany	413	5 321	309.7	76.8	26	811	14.3	5.3	241	3 540	468.7	175.5
Auburn	93	1 392	53.0	13.0	12	D	D	D	115	1 259	101.5	43.0
Binghamton	146	2 387	104.7	27.9	12	122	9.5	2.3	108	1 295	152.1	59.2
Buffalo	600	9 962	414.7	121.0	42	578	114.2	63.3	403	6 236	565.7	263.0
Elmira	66	955	33.3	9.5	4	104	2.2	0.8	82	849	103.7	41.3
Freeport	80	591	38.9	10.1	19	111	18.1	3.4	98	D	D	D
Glen Cove	72	660	36.5	12.1	16	D	D	D	110	D	D	D
Harrison	72	977	88.1	23.4	20	D	D	D	52	D	D	D
Hempstead	94	802	53.3	14.3	4	D	D	D	118	1 756	177.3	63.6
Ithaca	194	2 448	118.8	35.7	13	76	4.9	1.2	63	650	50.6	19.1
Jamestown	74	854	31.4	9.2	9	D	D	D	81	D	D	D
Lindenhurst	64	721	37.2	9.5	7	48	2.2	0.5	35	D	D	D
Long Beach	82	733	39.1	9.5	16	153	10.1	3.5	111	1 050	128.4	43.2
Middletown	88	1 654	77.3	22.0	5	D	D	D	83	974	116.1	63.5
Mount Vernon	97	649	40.8	10.4	14	D	D	D	115	1 524	85.8	36.7
Newburgh	90	1 042	54.0	15.3	9	D	D	D	86	738	77.4	30.4
New Rochelle	156	1 997	132.3	36.1	41	D	D	D	252	1 940	236.0	83.9
New York	17 494	249 519	22 095.1	6 009.6	4 574	49 339	10 570.7	3 162.4	16 239	185 098	18 567.4	7 309.4
Niagara Falls	154	5 174	520.9	110.8	12	D	D	D	82	980	62.7	27.5
North Tonawanda	56	624	24.6	6.6	9	22	2.9	0.5	52	398	27.2	11.4
Ossining	42	427	21.7	8.1	6	D	D	D	44	309	25.3	10.2
Port Chester	86	757	55.0	14.2	8	D	D	D	41	397	46.3	17.6
Poughkeepsie	104	1 518	81.7	22.6	9	174	8.3	2.3	118	1 886	233.4	105.3
Rochester	529	6 870	324.0	90.5	61	1 005	49.0	16.4	281	4 375	402.6	170.2
Rome	81	942	39.5	11.5	10	58	2.4	1.0	88	1 219	84.1	34.8
Saratoga Springs	163	2 358	131.5	40.5	28	D	D	D	102	1 081	113.0	41.7
Schenectady	156	1 452	72.5	18.9	11	D	D	D	155	1 652	163.2	72.0
Spring Valley	41	186	15.3	3.4	1	D	D	D	38	381	32.1	10.3
Syracuse	392	5 488	251.0	75.8	22	143	11.3	3.0	328	4 611	592.5	230.9
Troy	120	1 535	66.8	18.6	9	69	5.4	1.4	124	1 487	158.9	67.7
Utica	140	1 875	85.9	24.8	9	48	2.9	0.6	160	1 647	193.7	73.3
Valley Stream	76	923	48.7	12.7	20	D	D	D	121	D	D	D
Watertown	111	2 076	97.3	27.0	11	48	2.9	0.8	102	1 263	123.2	59.3
White Plains	194	2 668	177.9	50.8	23	465	26.9	9.1	362	5 152	566.8	266.4

1. Establishments subject to federal tax.

Table D. Cities — Other Services and Federal Funds

City	Other services[1], 2007				Selected federal funds, 2009–2010 (mil dol)								
					Procurement contracts		Grants						
	Number of establishments	Number of employees	Receipts (mil dol)	Annual payroll (mil dol)	Defense	Other	Total[2]	Medicaid and other health related	Nutrition and family welfare	Energy and environment	Disasters and emergency preparedness	Housing and community development	Employment and training
	104	105	106	107	108	109	110	111	112	113	114	115	116
NEW JERSEY— Cont'd													
Garfield	63	D	D	D	0.4	0.0	1.0	0.0	0.0	0.0	0.0	0.7	0.0
Hackensack	129	749	63.5	20.2	4.9	1.0	23.6	4.6	3.8	8.3	0.0	3.1	0.0
Hoboken	105	D	D	D	3.4	2.1	24.0	1.3	4.2	0.3	0.0	4.3	0.0
Jersey City	341	1 286	119.1	30.3	78.7	5.7	101.5	3.6	8.4	4.1	0.9	75.1	0.0
Kearny	69	D	D	D	0.0	0.1	0.2	0.0	0.0	0.2	0.0	0.0	0.0
Linden	105	529	50.3	17.0	0.2	0.3	5.4	0.0	0.0	0.0	0.0	4.2	0.0
Long Branch	60	238	19.0	5.6	0.1	0.2	13.0	0.5	0.0	0.0	0.0	10.6	0.0
Millville	35	163	12.3	3.8	4.9	0.0	3.5	0.0	0.0	0.0	0.0	2.7	0.0
Newark	476	3 232	346.3	112.8	15.9	203.8	1 054.9	105.2	30.4	15.2	0.0	138.9	2.5
New Brunswick	72	305	25.7	8.5	6.4	7.6	328.7	192.4	0.0	7.3	2.5	19.5	1.2
Paramus	66	525	45.6	15.8	16.3	2.7	7.4	0.5	0.0	0.0	0.0	19.4	0.0
Passaic	94	346	26.4	8.5	1.9	0.3	23.7	0.9	2.1	0.0	0.0	19.4	0.0
Paterson	193	1 211	100.1	30.8	11.9	2.0	64.7	10.8	7.8	1.5	0.0	37.1	4.9
Perth Amboy	85	D	D	D	0.0	0.0	14.1	0.9	0.0	0.0	0.0	12.9	0.0
Plainfield	75	269	22.3	6.8	35.5	0.0	11.6	2.6	0.0	0.0	0.0	8.7	0.0
Rahway	45	232	22.0	7.0	1.7	0.0	2.3	0.0	0.0	0.0	0.0	2.3	0.0
Sayreville	82	D	D	D	0.9	0.2	2.2	0.0	0.0	0.0	0.0	2.2	0.0
Trenton	92	286	26.5	7.5	45.5	15.1	1 913.7	214.7	291.8	159.0	28.3	272.2	262.3
Union City	94	253	18.0	4.6	0.0	0.0	9.4	1.4	0.0	0.5	0.0	6.7	0.0
Vineland	137	636	47.0	14.3	33.1	3.8	12.5	0.4	0.0	0.3	0.0	4.9	0.7
Westfield	76	427	39.0	12.4	0.0	0.2	0.0	0.0	0.0	0.0	0.0	0.0	0.0
West New York	80	D	D	D	0.0	0.0	12.1	2.2	4.0	0.0	0.0	5.7	0.0
NEW MEXICO	2 202	13 461	1 108.3	324.9	1 519.7	5 979.2	6 720.2	3 712.9	585.8	251.0	3.9	159.9	60.1
Alamogordo	42	D	D	D	14.5	2.4	1.4	0.0	0.0	0.1	0.0	0.0	0.0
Albuquerque	739	5 676	410.1	138.9	398.5	2 752.9	522.2	212.9	19.2	28.1	0.0	61.2	57.7
Carlsbad	39	212	17.3	4.7	0.6	177.7	21.1	0.1	5.3	12.9	0.0	3.2	0.0
Clovis	58	D	D	D	2.1	0.5	40.3	0.0	0.0	0.8	0.0	3.2	0.0
Farmington	101	838	115.1	22.8	0.0	0.3	9.2	0.6	0.3	1.1	0.0	1.6	0.0
Hobbs	61	D	D	D	0.0	0.2	4.0	0.0	2.3	0.0	0.0	0.0	0.0
Las Cruces	127	767	45.9	14.6	47.2	40.6	84.2	23.1	5.5	10.3	0.0	11.7	0.0
Rio Rancho	56	350	30.6	8.3	0.2	0.3	3.4	0.5	0.0	0.4	0.0	0.4	0.0
Roswell	52	D	D	D	3.2	15.9	13.7	0.0	0.0	2.4	0.0	6.8	0.0
Santa Fe	175	891	67.8	21.5	15.8	28.2	598.5	78.8	104.5	104.2	0.0	32.8	1.3
NEW YORK	32 231	155 249	13 318.0	3 874.0	8 809.8	5 073.4	63 103.6	39 959.0	6 704.4	1 201.8	144.2	3 570.2	553.2
Albany	132	778	60.6	18.7	12.5	132.0	4 416.7	255.0	83.2	409.7	1.1	541.9	463.3
Auburn	56	255	19.8	5.2	2.1	2.7	6.9	0.1	2.5	0.9	0.0	2.3	0.0
Binghamton	78	469	33.8	11.3	3.3	7.4	77.8	10.1	5.2	29.9	0.0	8.0	0.0
Buffalo	307	1 649	144.2	43.6	98.2	146.0	316.7	96.7	22.1	10.6	0.2	95.4	0.7
Elmira	32	211	14.8	4.3	1.2	0.2	19.7	0.0	3.0	0.0	0.0	3.1	0.0
Freeport	107	349	34.3	8.7	9.3	6.5	4.0	0.0	0.0	0.0	0.0	3.6	0.0
Glen Cove	74	204	16.5	4.2	0.1	0.0	9.2	0.1	1.4	0.0	0.0	5.1	0.0
Harrison	43	D	D	D	14.2	1.0	0.0	0.0	0.0	0.0	0.0	0.0	0.0
Hempstead	92	751	59.3	18.9	0.0	0.3	24.3	1.1	7.4	0.0	0.0	14.0	0.0
Ithaca	42	279	19.7	6.0	17.9	12.0	412.4	147.5	3.1	32.3	1.2	8.3	1.6
Jamestown	38	192	15.5	4.6	63.1	0.3	6.0	0.2	0.0	0.0	0.1	5.2	0.0
Lindenhurst	76	276	26.1	6.6	7.0	0.1	2.0	0.0	0.0	0.0	0.0	0.0	0.0
Long Beach	54	169	8.9	2.5	0.0	0.0	5.7	0.2	0.0	0.0	0.0	5.5	0.0
Middletown	75	613	118.5	18.5	0.5	1.8	3.8	0.8	1.9	0.0	0.0	0.9	0.0
Mount Vernon	125	697	82.7	22.5	11.5	0.2	9.9	6.6	0.0	0.6	0.0	2.1	0.0
Newburgh	57	232	19.7	5.4	20.3	8.8	9.0	1.4	2.2	0.0	0.0	4.9	0.0
New Rochelle	146	651	56.6	15.0	-0.5	0.7	25.1	0.6	0.0	1.7	0.0	17.2	0.0
New York	13 086	60 996	5 070.5	1 503.3	611.4	2 225.2	34 534.2	25 615.8	2 238.1	249.6	5.4	2 298.3	42.8
Niagara Falls	66	285	21.8	6.9	37.1	4.9	15.2	0.0	3.7	0.6	0.0	8.4	0.0
North Tonawanda	60	194	13.1	4.1	6.4	0.5	2.8	0.0	0.0	0.0	0.0	1.8	0.0
Ossining	37	110	9.4	2.8	0.0	0.0	7.6	4.3	0.0	0.0	0.0	3.0	0.0
Port Chester	72	260	33.4	8.6	0.0	0.0	4.2	0.6	2.1	0.0	0.0	1.2	0.0
Poughkeepsie	88	373	28.2	8.2	0.4	4.2	27.5	0.0	0.3	-0.2	0.0	12.0	0.3
Rochester	307	1 973	180.9	55.1	1 754.9	50.9	797.7	428.2	16.7	80.1	0.2	78.1	16.6
Rome	48	189	19.1	4.9	129.0	2.4	14.1	0.2	7.6	0.0	0.0	5.2	0.0
Saratoga Springs	41	267	17.5	5.5	2.9	1.3	3.8	0.9	0.0	0.0	0.0	1.9	0.0
Schenectady	96	815	69.2	17.9	278.1	0.4	98.0	12.6	4.4	39.8	0.0	26.5	6.4
Spring Valley	35	89	10.7	2.1	0.2	0.5	9.6	1.0	0.0	0.0	0.0	8.4	0.0
Syracuse	206	1 374	110.7	34.9	66.1	134.4	198.7	50.2	10.5	10.5	0.6	52.2	4.5
Troy	58	284	27.1	7.8	5.7	3.5	176.5	18.1	5.2	98.7	0.4	12.0	3.8
Utica	87	513	33.4	9.7	20.6	2.7	31.3	0.0	0.1	0.8	0.0	11.3	5.9
Valley Stream	123	D	D	D	0.0	0.0	0.0	0.0	0.0	0.0	0.0	0.0	0.0
Watertown	56	330	27.4	7.7	26.0	0.7	12.6	0.0	2.2	0.5	0.0	2.4	0.0
White Plains	141	969	77.4	22.9	14.0	12.2	53.6	9.9	0.5	6.0	0.0	18.2	0.0

1. Establishments subject to federal tax.   2. Includes program categories not shown separately. State totals include additional categories not allocated by city.

Table D. Cities — City Government Finances

City	City government finances, 2007									
	General revenue							General expenditure		
		Intergovernmental		Taxes					Per capita[1] (dollars)	
					Per capita[1] (dollars)					
	Total (mil dol)	Total (mil dol)	Percent from state government	Total (mil dol)	Total	Property	Sales and gross receipts	Total (mil dol)	Total	Capital outlays
	117	118	119	120	121	122	123	124	125	126
NEW JERSEY— Cont'd										
Garfield	29.0	6.8	72.0	18.4	632	613	19	29.2	1 000	78
Hackensack	68.9	8.5	64.4	54.6	1 268	1 246	22	57.8	1 342	120
Hoboken	92.7	29.8	56.2	32.5	801	711	90	88.2	2 174	55
Jersey City	548.0	192.3	63.9	165.9	684	614	70	541.6	2 234	145
Kearny	65.1	32.7	99.5	30.2	810	781	29	69.0	1 851	210
Linden	79.1	28.2	88.7	38.5	977	891	87	74.5	1 892	220
Long Branch	60.6	21.6	30.7	28.3	876	826	49	66.4	1 743	115
Millville	42.9	14.7	89.4	18.5	649	600	50	37.2	1 306	75
Newark	843.1	494.2	37.5	242.7	866	636	111	758.4	2 707	171
New Brunswick	236.3	145.4	90.6	53.6	1 061	1 007	54	245.8	4 864	112
Paramus	49.5	6.3	98.6	37.1	1 413	1 295	118	52.7	2 007	135
Passaic	104.1	44.1	59.2	46.0	686	668	18	99.0	1 475	15
Paterson	237.4	97.2	73.1	93.7	639	624	15	222.9	1 521	114
Perth Amboy	88.0	25.6	50.1	42.3	865	850	15	119.0	2 434	776
Plainfield	95.0	27.2	59.7	44.5	957	939	18	88.2	1 897	108
Rahway	46.5	9.5	60.4	32.1	1 140	1 022	118	48.4	1 718	192
Sayreville	47.9	19.8	67.2	21.2	500	476	24	45.6	1 077	155
Trenton	491.6	384.4	97.0	73.4	886	858	28	525.0	6 340	590
Union City	241.4	187.5	96.2	44.3	707	694	13	258.5	4 121	159
Vineland	52.5	11.6	85.9	24.8	424	403	21	76.5	1 308	59
Westfield	33.3	5.1	89.2	23.8	807	752	54	32.7	1 105	85
West New York	172.4	112.3	92.7	39.2	845	819	26	185.9	4 004	159
NEW MEXICO	X	X	X	X	X	X	X	X	X	X
Alamogordo	42.8	16.3	91.3	15.5	436	80	356	36.5	1 024	235
Albuquerque	939.6	298.1	84.2	352.4	680	210	469	769.8	1 485	420
Carlsbad	40.2	9.7	34.4	21.1	844	66	778	37.2	1 486	418
Clovis	43.6	5.9	60.1	23.5	707	37	671	38.3	1 154	281
Farmington	85.3	35.1	96.5	27.2	640	29	611	95.5	2 252	243
Hobbs	65.0	25.2	100.0	25.1	846	45	802	52.8	1 783	574
Las Cruces	174.6	43.4	88.9	78.0	870	104	734	157.2	1 752	328
Rio Rancho	116.2	12.9	49.5	52.3	688	128	523	134.3	1 766	1 029
Roswell	51.8	32.0	90.8	6.6	145	80	65	56.0	1 226	360
Santa Fe	175.1	72.5	81.3	51.9	708	26	682	157.3	2 148	352
NEW YORK	X	X	X	X	X	X	X	X	X	X
Albany	217.9	75.8	27.8	57.0	605	518	88	208.7	2 216	183
Auburn	42.3	16.0	45.1	11.7	427	376	51	38.6	1 414	137
Binghamton	70.6	30.9	36.1	27.9	619	581	38	85.0	1 888	526
Buffalo	1 339.3	1 028.6	82.2	163.5	600	524	76	1 301.4	4 773	716
Elmira	31.2	14.9	34.9	10.0	341	303	38	31.3	1 062	120
Freeport	60.7	8.4	36.9	36.9	870	811	56	66.1	1 557	226
Glen Cove	45.1	18.1	63.8	21.2	813	697	116	55.0	2 112	509
Harrison	14.4	5.9	100.0	7.6	285	202	81	14.4	544	269
Hempstead	63.0	4.3	22.2	49.0	946	898	48	57.8	1 116	38
Ithaca	55.1	14.0	59.6	26.9	898	509	389	55.4	1 849	370
Jamestown	62.0	24.9	74.1	13.3	449	419	29	71.3	2 411	220
Lindenhurst	10.5	1.4	66.0	5.9	215	151	64	11.1	402	79
Long Beach	108.6	9.1	58.4	40.4	1 168	974	194	102.4	2 961	1 288
Middletown	36.2	11.6	26.9	14.8	574	477	97	33.9	1 311	88
Mount Vernon	94.5	15.7	62.1	66.2	975	602	373	91.2	1 344	96
Newburgh	48.0	16.3	41.2	16.9	598	474	124	50.7	1 796	185
New Rochelle	124.3	25.1	45.5	74.8	1 021	568	453	124.4	1 699	247
New York	76 228.4	27 704.3	83.8	38 153.1	4 611	1 595	795	68 299.1	8 254	1 110
Niagara Falls	105.2	55.8	57.7	38.6	747	551	196	89.3	1 728	116
North Tonawanda	42.2	18.6	32.9	16.1	512	450	62	40.2	1 281	91
Ossining	28.6	7.1	8.0	15.1	631	569	62	30.4	1 269	218
Port Chester	41.6	9.8	6.8	22.5	797	733	63	39.0	1 382	231
Poughkeepsie	53.3	26.1	22.6	17.7	597	521	76	62.9	2 122	417
Rochester	1 011.7	723.4	78.7	194.3	940	858	81	997.5	4 824	362
Rome	43.7	13.5	82.0	23.1	681	397	284	48.9	1 444	224
Saratoga Springs	43.0	4.6	55.8	29.2	1 015	588	426	45.6	1 583	140
Schenectady	90.5	29.5	41.4	35.3	574	508	65	85.9	1 396	174
Spring Valley	32.0	12.2	10.0	18.1	688	648	39	31.8	1 211	66
Syracuse	659.1	477.0	77.1	87.8	631	576	56	634.1	4 559	188
Troy	81.1	33.4	42.2	21.3	447	383	64	75.5	1 582	111
Utica	74.3	27.8	66.9	32.1	550	305	243	77.9	1 332	177
Valley Stream	30.9	2.1	55.1	24.3	698	619	80	30.6	878	105
Watertown	44.4	27.0	26.8	9.7	352	306	46	51.4	1 872	416
White Plains	153.4	12.9	55.1	96.1	1 674	689	985	169.2	2 948	208

1. Based on population estimated as of July 1 of the year shown.

City	Public welfare	Highways	Parking facilities	Education	Health and hospitals	Police protection	Sewerage and sanitation	Parks and recreation	Housing and community development	Interest on debt
	127	128	129	130	131	132	133	134	135	136
NEW JERSEY— Cont'd										
Garfield	0.0	11.0	0.0	0.0	1.3	25.3	12.8	3.0	12.0	2.1
Hackensack	0.4	5.4	1.1	0.0	1.3	22.1	8.7	3.3	9.7	1.6
Hoboken	0.0	1.7	9.2	0.0	0.7	15.8	5.3	2.2	16.4	3.1
Jersey City	0.0	2.0	1.3	0.0	1.8	16.7	12.3	2.2	14.8	5.1
Kearny	0.0	7.8	0.0	0.0	1.0	22.0	14.5	1.6	0.0	2.5
Linden	0.5	3.5	0.1	0.0	1.4	17.2	9.9	4.1	1.8	2.1
Long Branch	0.0	2.7	0.0	0.0	1.2	16.7	11.7	3.0	25.7	4.1
Millville	0.0	4.6	0.0	0.0	0.3	15.8	12.3	1.9	7.5	1.7
Newark	0.7	0.9	0.1	0.0	4.7	19.6	10.4	2.0	20.0	1.8
New Brunswick	0.0	0.8	2.5	58.4	0.3	5.9	3.1	0.8	8.7	3.9
Paramus	0.1	3.3	0.0	0.0	1.8	22.0	8.9	4.9	0.0	3.0
Passaic	0.0	2.6	0.2	0.0	2.2	16.8	10.0	1.2	21.2	1.1
Paterson	0.0	2.1	5.9	0.0	3.5	17.7	10.4	2.0	10.5	1.8
Perth Amboy	0.0	12.9	0.4	0.0	1.4	11.3	6.1	1.7	11.1	3.1
Plainfield	0.7	4.0	0.0	0.0	1.7	15.7	21.2	1.3	12.0	2.7
Rahway	0.0	11.4	0.0	0.0	1.7	17.5	11.0	2.9	9.2	3.0
Sayreville	0.0	6.0	0.0	0.0	0.7	22.6	14.8	3.5	10.0	2.1
Trenton	0.1	0.7	0.3	61.0	0.8	7.1	3.6	0.8	3.7	1.8
Union City	0.0	1.4	0.8	62.5	0.7	7.2	2.7	1.3	4.6	1.3
Vineland	0.0	4.0	0.0	0.0	5.6	14.9	10.6	0.8	6.9	2.3
Westfield	0.3	16.7	0.7	0.0	2.6	19.1	6.2	3.4	0.0	1.4
West New York	0.0	1.8	1.3	59.3	0.4	5.9	1.9	1.8	6.4	0.8
NEW MEXICO	X	X	X	X	X	X	X	X	X	X
Alamogordo	6.0	11.1	0.0	0.0	0.0	17.6	13.8	15.8	1.5	2.2
Albuquerque	3.0	12.3	0.4	0.0	1.8	19.8	10.4	12.1	5.1	4.3
Carlsbad	0.0	13.6	0.0	0.0	0.6	16.3	14.7	13.0	0.2	0.5
Clovis	0.0	17.3	0.0	0.0	0.2	18.1	17.8	6.2	0.0	1.1
Farmington	0.0	11.9	0.0	0.0	1.0	14.4	7.7	13.8	0.0	11.5
Hobbs	0.0	16.3	0.0	0.0	0.0	18.6	19.9	8.2	0.2	0.0
Las Cruces	2.6	7.4	0.0	0.0	5.7	14.3	17.0	7.7	2.1	2.6
Rio Rancho	0.9	19.7	0.0	0.0	0.0	10.8	8.5	9.2	0.5	2.5
Roswell	0.0	8.4	0.0	0.0	0.8	13.7	23.6	10.3	0.6	1.8
Santa Fe	3.4	10.3	2.6	0.0	0.0	14.7	9.7	12.0	5.5	9.5
NEW YORK	X	X	X	X	X	X	X	X	X	X
Albany	0.0	4.3	0.0	0.0	0.2	20.8	5.5	3.2	16.4	13.7
Auburn	0.0	8.6	0.7	0.0	0.1	13.7	17.6	3.7	3.9	6.0
Binghamton	0.0	9.8	0.7	0.0	0.2	12.1	24.1	3.7	7.5	4.0
Buffalo	0.0	3.4	0.1	60.6	0.1	5.4	4.3	0.2	4.1	2.4
Elmira	0.0	10.1	1.0	0.0	0.5	20.0	3.6	3.4	3.5	3.8
Freeport	0.0	15.7	0.1	0.0	0.0	19.3	8.1	6.0	1.6	3.8
Glen Cove	0.0	19.5	0.0	0.0	0.3	20.5	13.1	6.5	8.1	6.2
Harrison	0.0	6.4	0.0	0.0	0.0	3.1	25.9	12.0	0.0	11.8
Hempstead	0.0	5.1	0.5	0.0	0.0	31.2	4.8	3.7	3.7	4.0
Ithaca	0.0	20.7	2.7	0.0	0.1	12.4	13.2	7.8	3.7	4.3
Jamestown	0.0	5.6	0.1	50.0	0.1	7.1	7.7	2.3	0.0	1.1
Lindenhurst	0.0	28.4	0.3	0.0	0.0	0.0	5.8	8.6	1.9	1.9
Long Beach	0.0	2.0	0.0	0.0	0.1	10.7	8.8	5.6	0.0	1.5
Middletown	0.0	7.1	0.0	0.0	0.0	19.3	14.2	4.6	6.0	5.2
Mount Vernon	0.0	3.4	0.0	0.0	0.4	19.2	6.7	3.8	6.4	3.0
Newburgh	0.0	5.1	0.2	0.0	0.2	25.5	10.3	4.4	1.1	7.2
New Rochelle	0.0	7.1	1.1	0.0	0.5	22.0	6.0	2.6	12.2	5.6
New York	15.7	1.4	0.0	27.5	10.1	5.7	5.1	1.3	5.4	4.9
Niagara Falls	0.0	6.2	0.6	0.0	0.1	17.7	3.6	2.3	9.6	1.4
North Tonawanda	0.0	10.6	0.0	0.0	0.1	11.4	12.9	4.6	0.9	1.4
Ossining	0.0	7.1	0.1	0.0	0.3	22.6	6.5	18.1	6.8	3.5
Port Chester	0.0	4.2	0.0	0.0	0.6	17.0	6.0	5.9	8.0	5.7
Poughkeepsie	0.0	5.2	0.9	0.0	0.3	18.2	12.2	1.4	7.2	4.8
Rochester	0.0	2.0	0.2	58.9	0.1	6.9	2.3	1.9	1.3	1.8
Rome	0.0	20.3	0.7	0.0	0.2	14.0	8.0	2.8	2.2	3.1
Saratoga Springs	0.0	9.1	0.3	0.0	0.0	14.0	8.6	20.8	0.6	1.9
Schenectady	0.0	5.6	0.7	0.0	0.1	18.1	14.6	2.2	4.4	7.0
Spring Valley	0.0	3.7	0.1	0.0	0.2	23.0	0.2	1.8	28.4	2.4
Syracuse	0.0	3.3	0.0	56.8	0.1	6.8	1.6	1.2	1.1	4.5
Troy	0.0	5.0	0.0	0.0	0.2	18.3	6.6	3.4	4.1	21.2
Utica	0.0	8.1	0.6	0.0	0.1	16.6	4.2	5.0	10.3	8.9
Valley Stream	0.0	18.3	0.7	0.0	0.6	0.7	13.7	10.5	0.0	3.8
Watertown	0.0	24.2	0.1	0.0	0.2	12.7	8.3	3.1	2.1	4.2
White Plains	0.0	9.3	9.8	0.0	0.0	17.1	5.2	4.9	4.0	2.1

City	City government finances, 2007 (cont.)				Climate[2]						
	Debt outstanding				Average daily temperature (degrees Fahrenheit)						
					Mean		Limits				
	Total (mil dol)	Per capita[1] (dollars)	Debt issued during year	City government employment, 2010	January	July	January[3]	July[4]	Annual precipitation (inches)	Heating degree days	Cooling degree days
	137	138	139	140	141	142	143	144	145	146	147
NEW JERSEY—Cont'd											
Garfield	20.8	712	1.0	187	28.6	75.0	19.5	85.5	51.50	5 522	824
Hackensack	23.6	548	0.0	451	28.6	75.0	19.5	85.5	51.50	5 522	824
Hoboken	93.3	2 301	0.0	789	29.6	75.3	22.7	82.5	46.33	5 367	882
Jersey City	716.2	2 955	105.5	3 381	29.6	75.3	22.7	82.5	46.33	5 367	882
Kearny	59.5	1 595	12.6	NA	31.3	77.2	24.4	85.2	46.25	4 843	1 220
Linden	28.3	718	9.5	649	28.5	74.0	18.2	85.8	51.61	5 595	757
Long Branch	66.0	2 041	24.3	NA	31.7	74.1	22.8	82.6	48.63	5 168	750
Millville	29.8	1 047	0.0	306	32.7	76.3	24.1	85.9	43.20	4 835	1 009
Newark	469.8	1 677	0.7	4 500	31.3	77.2	24.4	85.2	46.25	4 843	1 220
New Brunswick	236.9	4 688	24.2	1 945	29.7	74.8	21.1	85.4	48.78	5 346	816
Paramus	44.8	1 706	0.0	NA	28.6	75.0	19.5	85.5	51.50	5 522	824
Passaic	26.3	391	0.0	612	28.6	75.0	19.5	85.5	51.50	5 522	824
Paterson	97.6	666	0.0	1 821	28.6	75.0	19.5	85.5	51.50	5 522	824
Perth Amboy	134.8	2 758	49.9	402	29.7	74.8	21.1	85.4	48.78	5 346	816
Plainfield	40.9	879	0.4	612	30.0	74.9	21.5	86.6	49.63	5 266	854
Rahway	48.6	1 726	8.8	303	29.6	74.5	19.8	85.7	50.94	5 450	787
Sayreville	29.8	703	5.0	267	29.7	74.8	21.1	85.4	48.78	5 346	816
Trenton	365.0	4 408	52.6	3 128	30.4	75.2	21.3	86.9	48.83	5 262	903
Union City	77.1	1 230	33.6	2 239	29.6	75.3	22.7	82.5	46.33	5 367	882
Vineland	86.3	1 475	23.4	799	26.7	70.4	16.8	81.7	53.28	6 281	438
Westfield	16.9	571	0.0	NA	30.0	74.9	21.5	86.6	49.63	5 266	854
West New York	54.8	1 170	31.1	1 416	29.6	75.3	22.7	82.5	46.33	5 367	882
NEW MEXICO	X	X	X	NA	X	X	X	X	X	X	X
Alamogordo	29.7	834	1.5	369	42.2	79.7	28.9	93.0	13.20	31	1 715
Albuquerque	952.1	1 837	162.5	6 528	35.7	78.5	23.8	92.3	9.47	4 281	1 290
Carlsbad	21.7	865	0.0	391	42.7	81.7	27.5	95.8	14.15	2 823	2 029
Clovis	17.4	524	0.0	389	37.9	77.5	25.0	91.0	18.50	3 955	1 305
Farmington	688.8	16 295	0.0	884	29.8	74.9	17.9	90.7	8.39	5 508	805
Hobbs	15.9	536	0.1	434	42.9	80.1	29.1	93.5	18.15	2 849	1 842
Las Cruces	166.1	1 851	30.5	1 316	39.0	78.7	21.1	94.9	11.44	3 818	1 364
Rio Rancho	211.4	2 783	35.6	638	33.8	73.9	19.7	90.0	9.28	4 981	773
Roswell	60.5	1 327	0.4	567	40.0	80.8	24.4	94.8	13.34	3 332	1 814
Santa Fe	294.9	4 029	88.8	1 506	29.3	69.8	15.5	85.6	14.22	6 073	414
NEW YORK	X	X	X	NA	X	X	X	X	X	X	X
Albany	470.7	4 999	31.6	1 515	22.2	71.1	13.3	82.2	38.60	6 860	544
Auburn	65.3	2 390	0.0	318	23.7	71.2	16.0	81.5	36.98	6 694	528
Binghamton	114.4	2 541	0.0	580	21.7	68.7	15.0	78.1	38.65	7 237	396
Buffalo	666.0	2 443	70.6	10 009	24.5	70.8	17.8	79.6	40.54	6 692	548
Elmira	48.3	1 641	5.2	294	23.9	70.3	15.0	82.3	34.95	6 806	446
Freeport	146.6	3 457	1.0	426	30.7	73.8	24.2	81.0	42.97	5 504	779
Glen Cove	81.1	3 112	0.0	NA	31.9	74.2	25.4	82.8	46.36	5 231	839
Harrison	53.4	2 016	8.9	NA	NA	NA	NA	NA	NA	NA	NA
Hempstead	45.3	875	13.9	439	31.9	74.2	25.4	82.8	46.36	5 231	839
Ithaca	64.7	2 158	0.0	457	22.6	68.7	13.9	80.1	36.71	7 182	312
Jamestown	42.8	1 449	24.7	624	22.3	69.2	14.1	80.1	45.68	7 048	389
Lindenhurst	6.6	239	1.9	NA	30.7	73.8	24.2	81.0	42.97	5 504	779
Long Beach	41.8	1 207	5.6	466	31.8	74.8	24.7	82.9	42.46	4 947	949
Middletown	48.3	1 869	3.7	NA	26.5	73.0	17.5	84.0	44.00	5 820	674
Mount Vernon	49.5	729	0.0	955	29.7	74.2	20.1	86.0	46.46	5 400	770
Newburgh	76.2	2 702	0.0	NA	26.6	74.3	17.1	84.9	45.79	5 813	790
New Rochelle	157.0	2 143	19.0	681	29.7	74.2	20.1	86.0	46.46	5 400	770
New York	90 693.9	10 961	12 027.4	413 032	32.1	76.5	26.2	84.2	49.69	4 754	1 151
Niagara Falls	33.4	647	9.4	668	24.2	71.4	16.8	81.8	33.93	6 752	508
North Tonawanda	16.7	533	5.3	NA	24.2	71.4	16.8	81.8	33.93	6 752	508
Ossining	26.9	1 124	0.0	NA	NA	NA	NA	NA	NA	NA	NA
Port Chester	45.4	1 611	3.1	NA	28.4	73.8	21.0	82.5	50.45	5 660	716
Poughkeepsie	77.1	2 600	4.8	451	24.5	71.9	14.7	83.6	44.12	6 438	550
Rochester	355.2	1 718	0.0	10 289	23.9	70.7	16.6	81.4	33.98	6 728	576
Rome	50.6	1 495	7.5	388	20.8	70.2	11.9	81.3	46.27	7 146	416
Saratoga Springs	25.0	869	8.5	NA	20.9	71.2	11.6	83.0	43.31	6 904	477
Schenectady	143.5	2 332	31.7	673	22.2	71.1	13.3	82.2	38.60	6 860	544
Spring Valley	16.0	607	0.9	NA	27.3	73.1	18.2	83.8	51.01	5 809	642
Syracuse	654.6	4 707	20.8	6 652	22.7	70.9	14.0	81.7	40.05	6 803	551
Troy	290.0	6 074	0.0	627	22.2	71.1	13.3	82.2	38.60	6 860	544
Utica	133.1	2 277	22.4	635	22.2	70.5	12.6	83.2	41.90	6 855	441
Valley Stream	29.7	851	0.0	NA	22.2	70.5	12.6	83.2	41.90	6 855	441
Watertown	36.2	1 319	0.0	NA	18.6	70.2	9.1	79.4	42.57	7 517	421
White Plains	77.4	1 348	24.0	1 075	29.7	74.2	20.1	86.0	46.46	5 400	770

1. Based on the population estimated as of July 1 of the year shown.   2. Represents normal values based on the 30-year period, 1971–2000.   3. Average daily minimum.   4. Average daily maximum.

Table D. Cities — **Land Area and Population**

STATE Place code	City	Population, 2010				Race alone or in combination, not of Hispanic origin (percent), 2010					Percent Hispanic or Latino,[2] 2010	Percent Foreign born, 2008–2010
		Land area,[1] 2010 (sq km)	Total persons	Rank	Per square kilometer	White	Black	American Indian, Alaska Native	Asian	Hawaiian Pacific Islander		
		1	2	3	4	5	6	7	8	9	10	11
37 00000	NORTH CAROLINA ...	125 919.8	9 535 483	X	75.7	66.6	22.1	1.7	2.6	0.1	8.4	7.5
37 01520	Apex	39.8	37 476	1 058	941.4	77.7	8.2	0.7	8.1	0.1	7.1	12.7
37 02080	Asheboro	48.0	25 012	1 665	521.1	59.5	12.7	0.8	1.5	0.1	26.9	17.6
37 02140	Asheville	116.4	83 393	382	716.6	78.1	14.4	1.0	1.8	0.2	6.5	6.8
37 09060	Burlington	65.2	49 963	771	766.4	53.5	28.8	0.8	2.3	0.1	16.0	9.5
37 10740	Cary	140.8	135 234	187	960.8	70.7	8.5	0.7	14.2	0.1	7.7	18.3
37 11800	Chapel Hill	54.7	57 233	647	1 046.3	71.5	10.3	0.7	13.1	0.1	6.4	16.9
37 12000	Charlotte	771.0	731 424	18	948.7	46.4	35.6	0.8	5.5	0.1	13.1	15.0
37 14100	Concord	156.1	79 066	410	506.5	67.0	18.4	0.7	3.0	0.1	12.3	11.0
37 19000	Durham	278.1	228 330	86	821.1	39.2	41.6	0.8	5.6	0.1	14.2	14.6
37 22920	Fayetteville	377.7	200 564	109	531.0	44.1	43.1	2.1	3.7	0.7	10.1	6.1
37 25480	Garner	38.2	25 745	1 610	674.1	55.0	33.5	0.9	2.2	0.1	9.9	6.7
37 25580	Gastonia	130.8	71 741	473	548.4	60.9	28.6	0.8	1.6	0.1	9.6	8.4
37 26880	Goldsboro	72.9	36 437	1 093	499.9	39.1	55.2	0.8	2.6	0.2	4.3	3.2
37 28000	Greensboro	327.7	269 666	69	823.0	47.1	41.6	1.1	4.5	0.1	7.5	10.5
37 28080	Greenville	89.6	84 554	372	943.4	56.3	37.8	0.8	3.0	0.1	3.8	4.3
37 31060	Hickory	76.9	40 010	985	520.0	70.9	15.3	0.5	3.5	0.1	11.4	9.1
37 31400	High Point	139.4	104 371	266	749.0	51.8	33.7	0.9	6.5	0.1	8.5	12.0
37 33120	Huntersville	102.6	46 773	846	455.9	80.2	10.0	0.7	3.3	0.1	7.4	7.9
37 33560	Indian Trail	56.2	33 518	1 206	596.6	76.7	10.5	0.9	2.2	0.1	10.9	11.6
37 34200	Jacksonville	120.5	70 145	486	582.3	63.9	21.2	1.3	3.6	0.5	13.0	5.4
37 35200	Kannapolis	82.7	42 625	922	515.3	66.2	21.1	0.8	1.4	0.0	12.1	7.3
37 41960	Matthews	44.3	27 198	1 517	613.7	79.8	10.2	0.6	4.8	0.1	5.8	9.0
37 43920	Monroe	77.1	32 797	1 243	425.5	44.2	25.8	0.6	1.1	0.0	29.4	17.8
37 44220	Mooresville	54.2	32 711	1 248	603.4	78.4	11.8	0.9	3.8	0.1	6.9	6.8
37 46340	New Bern	73.1	29 524	1 393	403.8	57.1	33.8	0.8	4.2	0.2	5.8	4.0
37 55000	Raleigh	370.1	403 892	43	1 091.2	54.8	29.8	0.7	5.0	0.1	11.4	14.7
37 57500	Rocky Mount	113.4	57 477	642	506.8	33.3	61.9	1.1	1.2	0.1	3.7	3.6
37 58860	Salisbury	57.4	33 662	1 202	587.0	49.8	38.3	0.8	1.8	0.1	10.6	7.4
37 59280	Sanford	69.4	28 094	1 468	404.9	45.3	28.0	0.8	1.4	0.1	25.6	16.5
37 67420	Thomasville	43.4	26 757	1 547	616.1	64.4	20.2	1.0	1.3	0.0	14.4	9.5
37 70540	Wake Forest	39.1	30 117	1 352	770.3	75.7	16.0	0.9	3.6	0.1	5.6	9.0
37 74440	Wilmington	133.4	106 476	254	798.4	72.3	20.5	1.0	1.7	0.1	6.1	5.7
37 74540	Wilson	74.5	49 167	783	660.4	41.3	48.4	0.5	1.4	0.1	9.4	8.0
37 75000	Winston-Salem	343.0	229 617	83	669.4	48.4	35.1	0.8	2.4	0.1	14.7	11.2
38 00000	NORTH DAKOTA......	178 711.2	672 591	X	3.8	90.3	1.6	6.2	1.3	0.1	2.0	2.4
38 07200	Bismarck	79.9	61 272	584	767.0	92.9	1.0	5.2	0.8	0.1	1.3	1.2
38 25700	Fargo	126.5	105 549	261	834.7	90.6	3.3	2.0	3.5	0.1	2.2	5.6
38 32060	Grand Forks	51.6	52 838	721	1 025.0	90.1	2.6	3.8	2.8	0.1	2.8	4.3
38 53380	Minot	45.1	40 888	972	905.8	90.9	3.0	4.2	1.4	0.2	2.7	3.1
38 84780	West Fargo	37.4	25 830	1 607	690.6	93.7	2.4	1.6	1.8	0.1	1.8	5.3
39 00000	OHIO	105 828.7	11 536 504	X	109.0	82.7	13.1	0.7	2.0	0.1	3.1	3.9
39 01000	Akron	160.7	199 110	112	1 239.3	63.7	33.3	1.0	2.5	0.1	2.1	4.7
39 03828	Barberton	23.4	26 550	1 561	1 134.1	92.1	7.2	0.9	0.5	0.1	1.4	2.2
39 04720	Beavercreek	68.4	45 193	872	661.0	88.5	3.0	0.7	6.9	0.1	2.6	7.2
39 07972	Bowling Green	32.5	30 028	1 358	923.4	86.4	7.1	0.7	2.6	0.1	4.8	3.9
39 09680	Brunswick	33.5	34 255	1 178	1 024.1	95.0	1.6	0.5	1.5	0.1	2.3	3.3
39 12000	Canton	66.0	73 007	465	1 107.0	72.0	27.5	1.5	0.6	0.1	2.6	1.7
39 15000	Cincinnati	201.9	296 943	62	1 471.0	50.0	46.2	0.8	2.3	0.1	2.8	4.6
39 16000	Cleveland	201.2	396 815	45	1 971.9	34.9	53.9	0.8	2.1	0.1	10.0	4.5
39 16014	Cleveland Heights	21.0	46 121	856	2 196.2	50.9	43.9	0.8	4.8	0.1	2.0	9.0
39 18000	Columbus	562.5	787 033	15	1 399.2	61.7	29.6	0.9	4.7	0.1	5.6	10.6
39 19778	Cuyahoga Falls	66.4	49 652	777	747.4	93.9	4.0	1.0	1.6	0.0	1.4	3.3
39 21000	Dayton	144.1	141 527	177	981.9	52.7	44.5	1.0	1.3	0.1	3.0	2.7
39 21434	Delaware	49.1	34 753	1 158	707.9	91.2	5.8	0.7	1.7	0.1	2.5	2.9
39 22694	Dublin	63.3	41 751	940	659.7	80.7	2.1	0.3	16.4	0.1	1.8	13.3
39 25256	Elyria	53.3	54 533	691	1 023.5	78.8	17.6	1.0	1.1	0.1	4.9	1.6
39 25704	Euclid	27.5	48 920	793	1 777.0	44.8	53.9	0.7	1.1	0.0	1.6	3.5
39 25914	Fairborn	34.1	32 352	1 260	949.3	86.0	9.1	1.0	4.0	0.2	2.4	3.7
39 25970	Fairfield	54.2	42 510	928	783.9	78.8	13.8	0.6	2.9	0.1	5.5	8.1
39 27048	Findlay	49.6	41 202	959	831.4	89.4	2.9	0.6	2.8	0.1	5.7	4.2
39 29106	Gahanna	32.2	33 248	1 221	1 032.9	82.6	12.2	0.8	3.7	0.1	2.6	5.0
39 29428	Garfield Heights	18.7	28 849	1 433	1 540.3	60.4	36.7	0.6	1.7	0.1	2.3	3.1
39 31860	Green	83.0	25 699	1 614	309.6	95.2	2.2	0.5	1.9	0.0	1.2	3.8
39 32592	Grove City	42.0	35 575	1 129	848.0	93.0	3.7	0.8	1.8	0.1	2.6	2.4
39 33012	Hamilton	55.9	62 477	569	1 117.1	84.2	10.0	0.7	0.9	0.1	6.4	5.4
39 35476	Hilliard	34.1	28 435	1 449	833.9	88.8	3.7	0.4	6.3	0.1	2.3	5.9
39 36610	Huber Heights	57.7	38 101	1 039	660.6	80.7	14.9	0.8	3.4	0.2	3.1	7.5
39 39872	Kent	23.8	28 904	1 429	1 216.5	84.0	11.2	0.8	4.3	0.1	2.2	5.1

1. Dry land or land partially or temporarily covered by water. 2. May be of any race.

Table D. Cities — **Population**

City	Age of population (percent), 2010											Population			
												Census counts		Percent change	
	Under 5 years	5 to 17 years	18 to 24 years	25 to 34 years	35 to 44 years	45 to 54 years	55 to 64 years	65 to 74 years	75 years and over	Median age	Percent female	1990	2000	1990–2000	2000–2010
	12	13	14	15	16	17	18	19	20	21	22	23	24	25	26
NORTH CAROLINA...	6.6	17.3	9.8	13.1	13.9	14.4	11.9	7.3	5.6	37.4	51.3	6 632 448	8 049 313	21.4	18.5
Apex	8.5	24.5	5.2	12.9	20.9	15.5	6.9	3.3	2.3	34.3	51.4	4 789	20 212	322.1	85.4
Asheboro	8.6	18.5	9.6	14.7	13.7	11.7	9.4	6.8	7.1	34.0	52.4	16 362	21 672	32.5	15.4
Asheville	5.7	12.8	10.6	16.5	13.1	12.7	12.2	7.5	8.9	38.2	52.8	63 379	68 889	8.7	21.1
Burlington	7.1	17.1	8.9	12.9	13.1	13.7	11.5	7.2	8.5	38.3	53.2	39 498	44 917	13.7	11.2
Cary	7.0	20.8	6.3	13.4	17.1	16.7	10.1	5.1	3.5	36.6	51.3	44 394	94 536	112.9	43.1
Chapel Hill	4.2	13.2	31.5	13.1	10.5	10.4	8.0	4.6	4.6	25.6	53.4	38 711	48 715	25.8	17.5
Charlotte	7.6	17.7	10.1	17.6	15.7	13.4	9.5	4.7	3.8	33.2	51.7	419 558	540 828	28.9	35.2
Concord	8.0	20.4	7.6	14.1	16.2	13.5	9.4	5.8	4.8	34.9	51.8	29 591	55 977	89.2	41.2
Durham	7.7	15.0	13.0	19.4	14.2	12.1	9.6	4.6	4.2	32.1	52.5	138 894	187 035	34.7	22.1
Fayetteville	8.5	17.2	14.5	16.9	11.6	12.2	9.3	5.5	4.2	29.9	51.6	75 850	121 015	59.5	65.7
Garner	7.1	17.3	7.7	14.8	15.6	14.5	11.1	6.4	5.3	37.1	52.5	14 716	17 757	20.7	45.0
Gastonia	7.0	17.7	8.9	12.5	14.1	14.4	11.8	7.1	6.6	38.0	52.7	54 725	66 277	21.1	8.2
Goldsboro	7.3	15.7	11.9	13.9	10.9	13.7	11.5	7.6	7.3	36.1	51.5	40 736	39 043	-4.2	-6.7
Greensboro	6.5	16.2	14.5	14.9	13.2	12.8	10.5	5.9	5.6	33.4	53.0	185 125	223 891	20.9	20.4
Greenville	6.1	12.6	28.8	16.2	10.4	9.6	7.9	4.1	4.2	26.0	54.2	46 274	60 476	30.7	39.8
Hickory	6.8	16.8	10.1	12.7	13.7	13.9	11.7	7.3	7.1	37.7	52.3	28 474	37 222	30.7	7.5
High Point	7.1	18.2	10.3	13.3	14.2	14.1	10.9	6.1	5.8	35.8	53.1	69 428	85 839	23.6	21.6
Huntersville	8.4	20.5	5.8	15.0	19.2	15.1	9.3	4.3	2.6	35.2	51.0	3 455	24 960	622.4	87.4
Indian Trail	8.6	24.1	6.3	13.3	19.3	13.5	8.0	4.7	2.3	33.7	50.9	1 942	11 905	513.0	181.5
Jacksonville	9.7	13.6	35.8	15.9	8.0	6.8	4.7	2.7	2.7	22.9	41.2	78 031	66 715	-14.5	5.1
Kannapolis	8.1	18.6	8.3	14.1	13.9	13.4	10.4	6.9	6.2	35.6	52.1	31 592	36 910	16.8	15.5
Matthews	5.4	19.5	7.2	10.5	14.5	17.2	12.4	6.6	6.8	40.3	51.9	13 756	22 127	60.9	22.9
Monroe	9.2	20.4	9.4	14.8	14.5	11.7	9.0	6.0	5.1	32.5	50.8	18 623	26 228	40.8	25.0
Mooresville	6.9	21.5	9.0	13.8	16.5	14.0	8.5	5.1	4.7	34.2	51.5	9 317	18 823	102.0	73.8
New Bern	7.5	15.3	9.5	13.6	10.7	12.9	12.5	9.0	9.0	38.8	53.3	20 728	23 128	11.6	27.7
Raleigh	7.2	15.9	13.9	18.4	15.2	12.4	8.8	4.4	3.8	31.9	51.7	218 859	276 093	26.2	46.3
Rocky Mount	6.7	17.9	9.3	11.9	12.2	14.8	13.1	7.6	6.0	38.7	54.2	53 078	55 893	5.3	2.8
Salisbury	7.0	15.7	12.1	13.9	11.6	12.6	11.2	7.3	8.6	36.2	50.5	23 626	26 462	12.0	27.2
Sanford	8.5	19.5	9.4	15.0	13.5	12.6	9.8	5.8	5.9	33.3	51.5	18 881	23 220	23.0	21.0
Thomasville	7.6	18.9	8.5	13.4	14.2	13.3	10.2	6.9	7.0	36.2	52.3	15 915	19 788	24.3	35.2
Wake Forest	9.2	23.3	6.0	13.0	19.1	13.3	8.1	4.8	3.4	34.2	51.9	5 832	12 588	115.8	139.3
Wilmington	5.6	12.9	16.9	15.1	11.8	12.3	11.5	7.1	6.8	34.7	52.2	55 530	75 838	36.6	40.4
Wilson	7.2	18.1	9.4	12.7	12.7	13.5	12.3	7.3	6.8	37.2	53.4	38 400	44 405	15.6	10.7
Winston-Salem	7.3	17.2	11.9	14.0	13.0	13.3	10.8	6.3	6.2	34.6	53.0	162 292	185 776	14.5	23.6
NORTH DAKOTA	6.6	15.7	12.0	13.5	11.2	14.4	12.2	7.0	7.5	37.0	49.5	638 800	642 200	0.5	4.7
Bismarck	6.4	14.4	11.0	14.9	11.2	14.5	12.3	7.2	8.1	38.0	51.4	49 272	55 532	12.7	10.3
Fargo	6.4	12.9	19.8	17.9	11.1	11.8	9.9	4.7	5.5	30.2	49.6	74 084	90 599	22.3	16.5
Grand Forks	6.1	12.3	24.7	15.4	9.7	11.8	9.9	5.0	5.1	28.4	48.8	49 417	49 321	-0.2	7.1
Minot	7.1	14.0	14.1	16.2	10.5	12.4	10.8	6.7	8.3	33.8	50.7	34 544	36 567	5.9	11.8
West Fargo	8.7	18.2	9.3	18.0	14.9	12.9	10.1	4.5	3.3	32.6	50.4	12 287	14 940	21.6	72.9
OHIO	6.2	17.4	9.5	12.2	12.8	15.1	12.6	7.4	6.7	38.8	51.2	10 847 115	11 353 140	4.7	1.6
Akron	6.7	16.1	12.5	13.8	12.3	14.0	11.9	6.2	6.4	35.7	51.7	223 019	217 074	-2.7	-8.3
Barberton	6.6	16.9	8.2	12.5	12.2	14.2	12.8	7.5	9.0	39.8	52.1	27 623	27 899	1.0	-4.8
Beavercreek	5.3	17.4	8.6	12.4	12.4	15.7	13.9	8.1	6.2	40.4	50.1	33 626	37 984	13.0	19.0
Bowling Green	4.1	8.7	43.2	12.2	7.2	8.0	7.7	4.2	4.7	23.2	52.0	28 303	29 636	4.7	1.3
Brunswick	5.9	19.4	7.5	11.6	15.4	15.8	12.5	7.3	4.6	39.1	50.9	28 218	33 388	18.3	2.6
Canton	7.9	17.2	10.8	13.4	12.2	14.1	11.7	6.3	6.5	35.6	52.6	84 161	80 806	-4.0	-9.7
Cincinnati	7.4	14.8	14.6	16.6	11.9	13.4	10.7	5.4	5.4	32.5	52.0	364 114	331 285	-9.0	-10.4
Cleveland	7.1	17.5	11.0	13.6	12.5	15.1	11.3	6.2	5.8	35.7	52.0	505 616	478 403	-5.4	-17.1
Cleveland Heights	6.1	16.2	10.5	16.0	11.8	12.6	13.2	7.4	6.1	35.8	53.4	54 052	49 958	-7.6	-7.7
Columbus	7.6	15.6	14.1	18.9	13.4	12.5	9.3	4.7	3.9	31.2	51.2	632 945	711 470	12.4	10.6
Cuyahoga Falls	5.8	15.1	8.5	15.1	12.8	14.8	12.7	7.1	8.2	39.4	52.7	48 950	49 374	0.9	0.6
Dayton	6.9	16.0	14.2	13.5	11.8	14.2	11.5	6.2	5.6	34.4	51.3	182 011	166 179	-8.7	-14.8
Delaware	8.2	17.3	11.9	15.5	15.0	11.8	9.2	5.6	5.4	33.2	52.0	19 966	25 243	26.4	37.7
Dublin	6.8	23.5	4.9	9.7	17.5	17.9	11.7	4.5	3.3	38.3	50.6	16 366	31 392	91.8	33.0
Elyria	6.9	17.3	9.0	13.0	12.7	14.4	12.3	7.1	7.2	38.1	52.2	56 746	55 953	-1.4	-2.5
Euclid	5.8	17.1	7.8	11.6	12.7	15.9	13.1	7.4	8.6	41.0	55.2	54 875	52 717	-3.9	-7.2
Fairborn	7.0	13.5	16.7	15.8	10.5	12.7	10.7	6.9	6.3	32.4	51.1	31 300	32 052	2.4	0.9
Fairfield	6.4	16.7	8.7	14.0	13.2	15.2	12.7	7.0	6.0	38.3	51.8	39 709	42 097	6.0	1.0
Findlay	6.7	15.5	12.9	13.8	11.6	13.4	11.5	7.2	7.3	35.9	52.4	35 703	38 967	9.1	5.7
Gahanna	5.6	19.8	7.1	12.0	13.4	17.2	13.2	6.6	5.2	39.4	52.1	23 898	32 636	36.6	1.9
Garfield Heights	6.2	18.8	8.5	12.1	13.0	14.5	11.5	6.6	8.9	38.5	54.0	31 739	30 734	-3.2	-6.1
Green	5.4	18.7	7.5	9.7	13.4	16.8	13.9	7.7	6.9	41.8	51.3	NA	22 817	NA	12.6
Grove City	6.2	19.2	8.4	12.4	15.0	14.9	11.8	6.4	5.8	37.8	51.7	19 661	27 075	37.7	31.4
Hamilton	8.1	16.7	9.5	15.3	12.3	13.7	11.2	6.3	6.9	35.3	51.2	61 438	60 690	-1.2	2.9
Hilliard	7.0	23.1	6.3	12.2	16.5	17.0	9.3	4.5	4.1	35.9	51.2	11 794	24 230	105.4	17.4
Huber Heights	6.8	18.6	8.3	13.3	13.0	14.4	12.7	7.7	5.2	37.4	51.7	38 696	38 212	-1.3	-0.3
Kent	4.2	9.9	44.0	11.6	7.6	7.9	7.4	3.5	3.9	22.7	53.7	28 835	27 906	-3.2	3.6

Table D. Cities — Households, Group Quarters, Crime, and Education

City	Households, 2010 Number	Persons per household	Percent Female family householder[1]	One-person	Persons in group quarters, 2010 Total	Institutional Total	Persons in nursing facilities	Non-institutional	Serious crimes known to police,[2] 2010 Total Number	Rate[3]	Rate[3] Violent	Property	Population age 25 and older	Attainment[4] (percent) High school graduate or less	Bachelor's degree or more
	27	28	29	30	31	32	33	34	35	36	37	38	39	40	41
NORTH CAROLINA	3 745 155	2.48	13.7	27.0	257 246	113 296	46 638	143 950	363 372	3 811	363	3 447	6 239 345	43.4	26.3
Apex	13 225	2.82	9.7	20.0	121	98	97	23	415	1 107	91	1 017	21 651	12.8	60.4
Asheboro	9 880	2.46	16.0	33.0	665	565	357	100	1 714	6 853	208	6 645	16 211	56.0	18.1
Asheville	37 380	2.12	12.2	38.0	4 249	2 292	1 047	1 957	4 103	4 920	518	4 402	58 428	32.3	38.5
Burlington	20 632	2.38	17.5	33.0	906	464	445	442	3 914	7 834	791	7 043	33 096	45.2	25.2
Cary	51 791	2.61	7.9	23.9	260	211	193	49	2 299	1 700	89	1 611	86 097	15.1	62.3
Chapel Hill	20 564	2.35	8.2	30.6	9 003	258	227	8 745	1 754	3 065	154	2 911	27 601	14.6	72.1
Charlotte	289 860	2.48	15.6	30.3	13 369	5 104	2 595	8 265	39 592	5 079	627	4 451	467 286	32.8	38.7
Concord	29 137	2.68	13.5	23.5	893	797	431	96	2 981	3 770	176	3 594	49 724	41.4	25.0
Durham	93 441	2.34	15.5	33.7	9 936	1 962	1 136	7 974	12 971	5 681	707	4 974	144 745	30.7	46.5
Fayetteville	78 274	2.45	19.5	28.7	8 841	1 253	689	7 588	13 667	6 814	549	6 265	117 725	35.4	23.9
Garner	10 207	2.49	14.7	27.0	284	243	232	41	1 025	3 981	186	3 795	17 255	30.0	37.2
Gastonia	27 770	2.52	19.0	27.1	1 745	1 149	691	596	4 542	6 331	696	5 636	46 802	47.4	21.5
Goldsboro	14 965	2.27	21.7	35.5	2 422	1 606	394	816	2 911	7 989	1 059	6 930	24 123	45.4	17.5
Greensboro	111 731	2.31	16.5	33.8	11 389	2 110	1 407	9 279	15 288	5 669	561	5 109	169 237	37.2	34.2
Greenville	36 071	2.18	15.5	36.6	5 858	760	734	5 098	NA	NA	NA	NA	43 485	32.4	35.3
Hickory	16 614	2.33	14.4	33.7	1 351	312	312	1 039	2 790	6 973	542	6 431	26 675	39.5	29.6
High Point	40 912	2.46	17.6	29.8	3 577	940	599	2 637	5 487	5 257	583	4 675	65 534	42.8	28.5
Huntersville	17 423	2.67	8.6	21.6	268	260	260	8	1 086	2 322	96	2 226	29 780	19.2	51.1
Indian Trail	11 121	3.01	10.9	14.8	0	0	0	0	NA	NA	NA	NA	19 137	33.4	33.5
Jacksonville	19 985	2.69	14.3	20.2	16 413	825	379	15 588	1 750	2 495	214	2 281	29 828	31.6	21.8
Kannapolis	16 375	2.58	17.0	26.3	330	303	278	27	1 189	2 789	242	2 548	27 734	53.4	14.8
Matthews	10 526	2.56	9.5	23.5	269	259	254	10	788	2 897	180	2 717	17 922	21.4	43.3
Monroe	11 120	2.92	17.4	23.7	379	273	248	106	NA	NA	NA	NA	20 240	52.8	15.6
Mooresville	12 374	2.61	13.6	25.2	372	252	252	120	1 535	4 693	257	4 436	20 128	34.6	25.7
New Bern	12 770	2.25	16.0	34.4	753	618	433	135	1 947	6 595	478	6 117	19 273	42.1	23.4
Raleigh	162 999	2.36	13.5	32.8	19 526	5 387	1 443	14 139	14 735	3 648	431	3 217	248 677	25.6	47.0
Rocky Mount	23 097	2.42	22.9	31.4	1 597	906	377	691	4 254	7 401	1 197	6 204	38 230	52.5	17.4
Salisbury	12 567	2.38	19.7	32.6	3 775	2 057	622	1 718	1 878	5 579	627	4 952	20 782	49.9	23.5
Sanford	10 458	2.60	19.3	28.7	858	684	289	174	727	2 588	224	2 363	16 708	48.7	22.0
Thomasville	10 537	2.50	18.3	28.3	390	315	275	75	1 338	5 001	497	4 503	16 873	58.9	12.8
Wake Forest	10 521	2.83	10.4	18.9	303	138	138	165	350	1 162	86	1 076	17 611	20.9	49.1
Wilmington	46 948	2.16	13.4	36.0	5 118	430	382	4 688	6 430	6 039	680	5 359	68 531	34.2	37.1
Wilson	19 585	2.43	20.8	30.8	1 534	1 003	756	531	2 433	4 948	574	4 375	31 336	51.1	23.0
Winston-Salem	92 337	2.38	17.3	33.1	9 431	2 480	1 268	6 951	14 866	6 474	661	5 814	144 373	40.8	31.6
NORTH DAKOTA	281 192	2.30	8.2	31.5	25 056	9 675	6 433	15 381	13 408	1 993	225	1 769	436 232	37.2	26.5
Bismarck	27 263	2.18	9.6	34.8	1 815	1 371	534	444	1 712	2 794	320	2 474	41 392	30.4	33.4
Fargo	46 791	2.15	8.6	36.6	4 924	1 011	678	3 913	3 066	2 905	286	2 619	62 716	26.7	38.6
Grand Forks	22 260	2.21	9.7	34.8	3 754	478	285	3 276	1 549	2 932	225	2 706	29 226	30.2	35.2
Minot	17 863	2.20	9.6	34.9	1 524	527	421	997	809	1 979	262	1 717	25 498	34.0	28.2
West Fargo	10 348	2.49	9.1	26.4	51	0	0	51	500	1 936	178	1 758	16 202	29.6	33.0
OHIO	4 603 435	2.44	13.1	28.9	306 266	166 042	83 019	140 224	410 747	3 560	315	3 245	7 687 669	47.4	24.4
Akron	83 712	2.31	19.5	34.8	6 133	1 981	878	4 152	12 622	6 339	841	5 498	128 917	50.2	20.5
Barberton	11 054	2.37	16.3	32.2	371	259	259	112	1 234	4 648	192	4 456	18 762	60.5	12.2
Beavercreek	18 195	2.47	6.8	24.9	278	257	257	21	1 134	2 509	64	2 445	30 816	24.0	49.2
Bowling Green	11 288	2.16	7.5	35.8	5 632	503	278	5 129	853	2 841	133	2 707	12 184	28.0	46.5
Brunswick	12 967	2.63	10.6	21.9	200	147	147	53	76	222	55	166	22 705	45.7	22.6
Canton	29 705	2.35	21.1	35.4	3 102	1 256	701	1 846	4 781	6 549	893	5 656	47 953	60.2	12.3
Cincinnati	133 420	2.12	19.1	43.4	14 443	4 531	2 199	9 912	24 215	8 155	1 217	6 937	187 678	42.2	31.5
Cleveland	167 490	2.29	25.3	39.5	13 742	6 258	3 062	7 484	29 041	7 319	1 393	5 925	261 705	57.4	13.4
Cleveland Heights	19 957	2.27	15.2	36.1	738	118	118	620	743	1 611	158	1 453	30 908	24.2	51.0
Columbus	331 602	2.31	15.9	35.1	21 099	6 086	3 236	15 013	55 795	7 089	695	6 394	491 807	39.2	32.3
Cuyahoga Falls	22 250	2.21	11.4	35.6	530	345	345	185	1 285	2 588	137	2 451	34 621	40.5	30.4
Dayton	58 404	2.26	21.4	38.8	9 365	2 099	773	7 266	10 456	7 388	1 068	6 320	89 626	50.2	14.8
Delaware	13 253	2.47	11.7	28.4	2 041	572	377	1 469	970	2 791	158	2 633	21 421	38.4	30.1
Dublin	14 984	2.78	5.9	18.4	127	127	127	0	770	1 844	29	1 816	26 410	9.3	70.6
Elyria	22 400	2.39	17.8	30.5	1 040	881	430	159	2 360	4 328	405	3 922	36 705	55.8	12.7
Euclid	22 685	2.13	20.9	41.4	675	489	391	186	1 284	2 625	276	2 349	32 666	45.1	20.7
Fairborn	14 306	2.24	14.4	32.7	275	229	229	46	1 056	3 264	179	3 085	18 719	43.1	26.0
Fairfield	17 415	2.41	13.1	28.7	506	404	384	102	1 433	3 371	294	3 077	28 644	42.3	25.5
Findlay	17 354	2.29	11.8	32.6	1 506	504	383	1 002	1 456	3 534	182	3 352	27 649	44.7	25.9
Gahanna	13 037	2.54	11.5	24.4	171	166	158	5	791	2 379	63	2 316	21 659	26.9	45.7
Garfield Heights	11 691	2.43	21.3	31.8	391	308	265	83	639	2 215	260	1 955	19 671	57.1	13.1
Green	10 070	2.54	10.0	23.9	141	133	130	8	NA	NA	NA	NA	17 731	37.5	34.4
Grove City	13 946	2.53	11.8	25.6	282	248	165	34	1 321	3 713	143	3 570	22 785	40.9	27.0
Hamilton	24 658	2.47	17.3	30.6	1 663	1 354	436	309	4 280	6 851	663	6 188	41 391	63.7	12.9
Hilliard	10 198	2.77	9.2	21.2	155	155	155	0	849	2 986	74	2 912	17 678	26.8	46.0
Huber Heights	14 720	2.58	14.9	22.8	184	64	64	120	324	850	42	808	25 262	41.5	20.6
Kent	10 288	2.22	12.5	33.4	6 067	81	81	5 986	670	2 318	135	2 183	12 760	30.8	39.9

1. No spouse present.   2. Data for serious crimes have not been adjusted for underreporting. This may affect comparability between geographic areas and over time.   3. Per 100,000 population estimated by the FBI.   4. Persons 25 years old and over.

Table D. Cities — Income, Poverty, and Housing

	Money income, 2008–2010				Housing units, 2010			Occupied Housing units 2008–2010				
		Households							Owner-occupied		Median owner costs as a percent of income	
City	Per capita income[1] (dollars)	Median income	Percent with income of $200,000 or more	Percent with income of less than $25,000	Families with income below poverty (percent)	Total	Percent change, 2000–2010	Vacant units for sale or rent[2]	Total	Percent	Median value[3] (dollars)	With a mortgage[4]	Without a mortgage[5]
	42	43	44	45	46	47	48	49	50	51	52	53	54
NORTH CAROLINA...	24 344	44 958	2.9	27.3	12.0	4 327 528	22.8	582 373	3 666 022	67.6	154 500	23.5	11.9
Apex	31 735	84 000	4.7	7.3	1.9	13 922	72.9	697	12 328	74.8	250 900	21.5	10.0
Asheboro	17 409	29 837	1.4	41.7	24.3	11 158	16.7	1 278	10 355	50.4	119 100	25.6	12.6
Asheville	25 980	40 494	2.8	30.5	12.9	41 626	23.9	4 246	37 693	52.2	197 600	24.7	14.1
Burlington	22 325	40 146	2.0	31.2	17.9	23 414	19.9	2 782	20 913	57.0	127 500	23.5	11.5
Cary	41 322	88 629	11.8	9.9	3.6	55 303	50.1	3 512	49 082	72.2	303 500	20.1	10.0
Chapel Hill	31 657	53 743	11.2	27.8	10.0	22 254	16.6	1 690	19 791	48.1	355 900	22.6	10.0
Charlotte	30 453	51 419	5.3	22.1	11.1	319 918	38.8	30 058	286 752	58.5	179 100	24.0	12.0
Concord	25 332	50 863	3.1	21.5	9.4	32 130	43.1	2 993	28 299	68.1	175 300	23.4	11.3
Durham	26 282	46 556	3.2	26.4	12.7	103 221	27.6	9 780	92 466	51.3	180 200	23.3	11.1
Fayetteville	22 611	42 695	1.7	25.9	14.2	87 005	62.7	8 731	75 234	51.8	120 300	23.9	12.4
Garner	28 214	60 497	2.1	13.7	3.8	10 993	51.9	786	9 957	70.0	168 900	22.1	10.0
Gastonia	21 711	38 829	2.5	31.6	17.0	31 238	12.2	3 468	27 532	60.0	131 200	24.5	13.8
Goldsboro	20 268	33 893	1.5	37.2	18.5	16 824	2.3	1 859	15 051	41.5	124 000	24.9	12.5
Greensboro	24 897	40 760	3.2	29.8	12.9	124 074	25.2	12 343	107 988	54.8	147 000	24.6	11.5
Greenville	22 033	33 339	3.3	39.8	19.4	40 564	43.5	4 493	34 237	39.4	148 200	24.3	14.9
Hickory	24 817	35 353	3.1	33.6	13.4	18 719	12.0	2 105	16 597	53.9	151 300	21.4	13.5
High Point	21 447	42 587	1.6	30.5	16.3	46 677	29.9	5 765	38 299	60.4	146 600	25.7	14.4
Huntersville	35 888	78 844	7.5	11.5	5.0	18 477	87.2	1 054	17 310	76.4	251 100	21.0	13.3
Indian Trail	26 374	69 450	3.3	13.0	5.8	11 700	166.4	579	10 579	88.1	187 200	24.0	12.5
Jacksonville	21 225	42 321	1.5	22.6	10.1	21 136	15.2	1 150	19 823	38.0	144 500	24.5	10.0
Kannapolis	21 365	39 377	2.2	32.4	14.4	18 645	17.4	2 270	16 505	64.3	137 600	25.2	14.5
Matthews	32 924	62 750	6.9	15.1	5.8	11 021	33.2	495	10 396	74.0	229 500	21.1	10.0
Monroe	19 209	44 371	0.5	25.4	17.7	12 375	27.4	1 255	11 347	58.1	153 900	24.8	12.9
Mooresville	24 501	52 865	1.2	21.5	7.5	13 655	74.1	1 281	11 713	67.9	193 600	25.7	10.2
New Bern	23 359	32 248	2.6	39.9	20.7	14 471	31.0	1 701	13 093	51.3	160 700	28.1	17.1
Raleigh	29 216	51 173	4.6	22.2	11.8	176 124	45.9	13 125	157 698	64.0	213 800	23.5	10.5
Rocky Mount	21 535	36 335	2.4	35.7	13.8	26 963	11.1	3 856	23 704	55.9	105 500	24.4	14.6
Salisbury	19 827	33 334	2.8	38.7	24.4	14 626	28.5	2 059	12 581	52.8	123 500	24.5	15.0
Sanford	19 824	40 547	1.4	31.8	19.0	11 411	23.1	953	9 783	57.6	129 800	22.1	12.5
Thomasville	16 467	33 701	0.0	40.3	25.9	11 870	39.2	1 333	10 192	60.9	105 700	24.5	13.2
Wake Forest	31 250	69 643	6.5	14.7	5.9	11 370	123.8	849	9 998	72.7	248 900	22.4	10.0
Wilmington	26 767	40 276	8.5	31.9	13.7	53 400	38.3	6 452	45 740	49.5	240 800	26.2	13.4
Wilson	20 034	35 409	1.4	35.8	20.1	21 870	17.1	2 285	19 529	48.8	133 800	26.0	15.5
Winston-Salem	23 542	40 584	3.0	30.3	15.9	103 974	25.8	11 637	89 508	58.2	142 200	23.4	10.9
NORTH DAKOTA	26 499	47 815	2.4	25.1	7.3	317 498	9.6	36 306	278 577	66.9	117 200	19.9	10.6
Bismarck	28 324	48 565	1.9	24.0	8.0	28 648	18.6	1 385	26 756	66.0	154 000	21.0	11.8
Fargo	26 651	42 144	3.0	27.8	6.2	49 956	21.0	3 165	46 623	45.2	149 400	21.9	11.9
Grand Forks	25 336	41 499	2.5	33.0	8.3	23 449	12.6	1 189	21 742	49.9	148 800	22.0	11.7
Minot	25 987	44 154	2.1	25.2	11.6	18 744	13.7	881	17 515	61.9	124 300	20.5	11.5
West Fargo	28 211	59 385	1.6	16.6	5.2	10 760	83.8	412	10 191	69.4	148 200	22.0	12.3
OHIO	24 738	46 563	2.5	26.4	10.8	5 127 508	7.2	524 073	4 544 687	68.5	136 700	23.3	13.1
Akron	19 337	33 144	1.2	39.5	19.4	96 288	-1.0	12 576	84 627	55.2	89 900	24.4	15.1
Barberton	18 938	35 335	0.1	36.2	14.6	12 191	0.2	1 137	11 346	64.0	95 400	25.8	13.6
Beavercreek	36 338	70 482	4.4	9.7	2.3	19 449	31.1	1 254	17 554	76.5	177 400	22.3	11.8
Bowling Green	18 129	31 793	1.8	41.0	15.0	12 301	15.9	1 013	10 139	39.2	178 300	19.0	10.8
Brunswick	25 899	58 913	1.3	14.5	5.3	13 600	10.9	633	13 080	76.4	162 700	22.5	12.2
Canton	16 772	29 427	1.1	42.5	22.3	34 571	-2.6	4 866	30 375	55.3	80 400	24.1	13.4
Cincinnati	23 699	33 425	2.6	40.2	23.1	161 095	-2.9	27 675	130 262	40.4	131 300	24.5	14.6
Cleveland	15 936	26 137	0.4	48.1	28.5	207 536	-3.8	40 046	167 626	46.2	84 300	27.9	16.3
Cleveland Heights	27 460	44 899	3.4	29.4	14.1	22 465	2.9	2 508	19 706	58.2	140 100	26.7	15.9
Columbus	22 884	42 368	1.6	29.7	16.9	370 965	13.3	39 363	317 760	48.4	139 200	24.0	13.3
Cuyahoga Falls	24 870	45 658	1.4	23.4	8.0	23 859	4.9	1 609	22 252	63.7	125 000	23.2	13.1
Dayton	16 020	28 420	0.4	45.1	25.9	74 065	-4.2	15 661	58 941	49.4	75 800	24.3	15.6
Delaware	23 984	56 219	1.3	19.5	9.1	14 192	37.9	939	13 040	62.7	163 700	22.2	13.9
Dublin	50 934	111 626	18.3	5.2	1.5	15 779	31.1	795	14 666	78.6	330 400	21.5	11.8
Elyria	19 872	40 075	0.5	28.8	13.6	25 085	5.2	2 685	22 223	62.5	110 300	24.4	13.0
Euclid	21 510	37 887	1.0	32.8	13.4	26 037	-0.3	3 352	21 388	53.5	106 000	24.5	16.6
Fairborn	21 378	38 501	0.5	38.0	17.5	15 893	10.3	1 587	13 605	50.3	111 100	21.9	10.5
Fairfield	27 425	53 091	1.4	17.4	7.9	18 803	5.7	1 388	17 187	66.6	150 800	21.4	10.9
Findlay	24 876	42 060	2.4	27.0	10.8	19 318	12.5	1 964	18 070	59.1	125 300	22.3	11.7
Gahanna	35 973	70 249	6.6	10.9	1.5	13 577	9.9	540	12 884	76.8	193 200	22.5	13.3
Garfield Heights	20 215	42 469	0.0	27.5	8.7	13 125	1.6	1 434	11 433	73.2	96 400	24.1	17.1
Green	31 927	64 298	4.7	17.5	3.6	10 858	18.3	788	9 802	80.8	178 100	22.8	13.5
Grove City	28 577	63 449	1.9	13.6	5.0	14 720	38.2	774	12 718	71.4	165 800	23.0	13.8
Hamilton	19 130	37 703	0.8	34.1	17.5	27 878	7.5	3 220	24 927	54.8	108 800	24.5	13.8
Hilliard	33 275	79 500	6.2	11.6	3.3	10 637	19.6	439	9 806	77.0	206 900	22.3	12.8
Huber Heights	24 097	54 726	0.9	18.4	6.4	15 875	6.2	1 155	14 428	70.2	115 800	23.0	12.1
Kent	18 339	28 958	0.5	44.6	10.4	11 174	6.8	886	10 752	41.9	141 100	23.9	12.0

1. Based on population estimated by the American Community Survey.   2. Includes units rented or sold but not occupied.   3. Specified owner-occupied units; $1,000,000 represents $1,000,000 or more.   4. 50.0 represents 50 percent or more.   5. 10.0 represents 10 percent or less.

Table D. Cities — Housing, Labor Force, and Employment

City	Occupied housing units, 2008–2010 (cont.)				Migration, 2008–2010		Civilian labor force, 2010		Unemployment		Civilian employment[4], 2008–2010	Percent		Households with no workers (percent)
	Percent renter occupied	Median gross rent[1]	Median rent as a percent of income[2]	Percent with no vehicle available	Percent who lived in the same house one year ago	Percent who lived outside this city one year ago	Total	Percent change, 2009–2010	Total	Rate[3]	Population age 16 and older	In labor force	Full-year full-time worker	
	55	56	57	58	59	60	61	62	63	64	65	66	67	68
NORTH CAROLINA...	32.4	723	29.9	6.5	84.0	10.7	4 616 767	1.4	504 883	10.9	7 424 705	64.8	40.9	27.3
Apex	25.2	947	23.3	1.8	85.5	10.4	18 889	13.1	1 227	6.5	25 077	76.5	53.3	12.5
Asheboro	49.6	584	33.2	7.6	78.7	12.6	11 832	NA	1 150	9.7	18 929	61.3	33.4	34.8
Asheville	47.8	778	28.6	10.1	76.6	13.8	41 778	12.9	3 155	7.6	68 868	65.7	37.7	30.5
Burlington	43.0	703	32.4	8.6	81.2	12.8	22 638	-1.2	2 600	11.5	38 515	66.4	41.0	30.1
Cary	27.8	879	26.0	2.2	85.3	10.1	68 743	5.1	4 519	6.6	99 162	73.3	51.3	14.1
Chapel Hill	51.9	839	36.4	9.8	63.7	21.1	28 413	6.6	1 512	5.3	47 608	60.4	30.3	23.0
Charlotte	41.5	825	28.6	7.6	77.7	7.4	369 744	7.5	35 746	9.7	559 335	73.2	47.1	19.3
Concord	31.9	768	30.3	4.4	86.2	7.9	37 220	20.1	2 896	7.8	58 504	69.6	42.6	23.3
Durham	48.7	786	30.4	9.0	74.6	10.3	116 941	0.4	9 201	7.9	179 249	69.1	43.0	22.4
Fayetteville	48.2	807	28.3	6.8	69.2	15.3	87 395	15.2	6 383	7.3	152 787	68.2	45.8	24.3
Garner	30.0	877	27.5	2.6	85.5	12.4	13 110	-4.0	1 177	9.0	19 933	75.5	51.1	18.1
Gastonia	40.0	716	30.3	8.8	83.6	7.0	31 846	-1.4	3 634	11.4	56 597	61.9	37.7	29.3
Goldsboro	58.5	632	28.9	15.2	73.3	14.3	12 760	-8.5	1 427	11.2	29 183	56.8	36.3	35.7
Greensboro	45.2	705	30.3	9.0	81.9	7.5	137 674	8.7	14 196	10.3	213 851	66.9	40.1	25.3
Greenville	60.6	677	36.2	9.4	65.9	16.8	43 108	3.9	3 829	8.9	68 500	67.9	35.4	25.8
Hickory	46.1	616	30.0	9.5	80.2	12.0	18 462	-1.0	2 250	12.2	32 137	64.7	40.0	29.3
High Point	39.6	712	31.7	9.0	83.8	7.6	51 977	3.7	5 950	11.4	77 657	66.4	40.0	26.2
Huntersville	23.6	822	26.0	2.5	85.5	11.2	23 779	7.3	1 850	7.8	33 298	79.3	54.0	13.7
Indian Trail	11.9	1 100	28.1	1.0	87.5	8.5	16 970	NA	1 164	6.9	22 520	73.6	49.0	15.8
Jacksonville	62.0	931	29.6	4.8	59.1	26.2	19 020	-11.7	1 896	10.0	54 593	77.8	59.2	17.5
Kannapolis	35.7	721	31.3	8.6	85.5	9.0	20 356	0.5	2 468	12.1	32 513	63.8	40.8	30.9
Matthews	26.0	886	33.5	4.2	89.0	8.8	13 717	2.9	1 144	8.3	20 346	70.2	45.1	20.9
Monroe	41.9	729	32.6	7.7	84.4	9.8	14 621	0.8	1 418	9.7	24 086	68.7	43.0	21.6
Mooresville	32.1	852	32.0	3.8	80.5	12.2	15 679	NA	1 692	10.8	24 281	71.4	46.2	21.6
New Bern	48.7	733	33.3	16.4	82.7	8.1	12 675	-6.9	1 217	9.6	23 365	59.6	33.4	37.9
Raleigh	46.0	840	30.3	6.9	75.6	11.7	210 715	3.3	16 374	7.8	314 003	71.9	46.2	18.2
Rocky Mount	44.1	703	32.5	12.8	83.3	7.5	25 905	0.5	3 505	13.5	45 442	61.0	38.0	34.8
Salisbury	47.2	685	30.0	10.1	81.4	12.5	14 382	11.2	1 634	11.4	25 460	54.7	33.3	37.1
Sanford	42.4	631	28.7	15.4	83.6	6.3	12 274	-3.9	1 501	12.2	20 515	68.3	40.6	30.0
Thomasville	39.1	600	28.8	6.0	84.1	9.3	11 876	-4.1	1 497	12.6	19 840	65.1	38.2	30.7
Wake Forest	27.3	902	27.6	4.6	82.0	13.4	NA	NA	NA	NA	20 165	73.1	45.8	17.0
Wilmington	50.5	809	33.8	9.6	75.7	13.4	53 377	5.1	4 854	9.1	88 085	65.2	35.7	28.3
Wilson	51.2	735	32.7	12.8	80.2	8.6	23 212	-5.3	2 873	12.4	37 546	60.7	39.1	34.1
Winston-Salem	41.8	654	31.4	9.3	83.6	6.2	110 561	6.5	10 420	9.4	177 549	62.7	38.4	28.3
NORTH DAKOTA	33.1	567	25.2	5.1	83.1	9.6	375 728	1.9	14 383	3.8	535 314	70.5	46.6	22.9
Bismarck	34.0	582	26.5	5.2	83.2	7.4	35 900	-0.8	1 226	3.4	49 781	70.4	48.9	23.1
Fargo	54.8	606	27.1	7.0	71.7	12.6	62 851	6.1	2 357	3.8	85 621	76.1	46.9	17.6
Grand Forks	50.1	632	30.6	7.6	73.9	11.9	31 430	2.3	1 079	3.4	44 278	73.6	39.7	21.6
Minot	38.1	613	25.7	7.2	77.7	12.3	21 425	7.2	742	3.5	32 501	71.3	46.6	22.8
West Fargo	30.6	655	24.7	2.3	85.5	11.2	14 959	NA	558	3.7	19 321	80.7	58.9	15.5
OHIO	31.5	680	30.0	8.1	85.3	9.2	5 864 025	-1.2	585 515	10.0	9 109 058	64.8	39.9	28.6
Akron	44.8	656	35.2	14.7	84.2	5.9	100 673	-6.5	11 031	11.0	159 076	65.9	37.3	33.4
Barberton	36.0	639	27.9	11.9	92.4	3.9	13 222	-4.0	1 529	11.6	21 418	61.8	35.9	34.8
Beavercreek	23.5	993	22.5	2.2	89.0	8.5	22 770	10.4	1 837	8.1	35 337	65.4	45.1	23.2
Bowling Green	60.8	598	36.0	7.6	49.7	25.9	15 844	-0.4	1 261	8.0	27 247	65.5	22.1	25.1
Brunswick	23.6	771	29.6	2.8	88.3	8.2	19 638	-0.8	1 569	8.0	26 858	73.9	45.1	21.1
Canton	44.7	547	30.6	15.9	78.7	9.8	33 166	-7.5	4 261	12.8	56 810	61.2	33.8	37.1
Cincinnati	59.6	605	31.3	21.7	74.7	9.4	145 065	-11.3	15 086	10.4	237 665	63.9	38.4	31.7
Cleveland	53.8	628	35.9	24.4	79.7	6.5	168 152	-8.0	19 307	11.5	315 845	59.9	32.2	39.1
Cleveland Heights	41.8	780	32.9	11.2	82.3	11.8	26 190	0.9	1 769	6.8	37 476	67.7	41.6	26.5
Columbus	51.6	759	29.9	10.1	76.5	8.4	422 925	-0.4	36 441	8.6	615 850	70.7	44.3	23.7
Cuyahoga Falls	36.3	694	26.5	7.7	92.0	4.6	27 896	-5.4	2 636	9.4	39 912	67.2	44.2	26.4
Dayton	50.6	615	38.2	18.8	75.6	9.2	61 867	-10.6	7 962	12.9	114 362	61.3	30.4	38.0
Delaware	37.3	748	27.9	3.3	76.8	14.9	17 486	-2.8	1 439	8.2	26 151	70.9	46.9	21.0
Dublin	21.4	1 090	23.1	2.1	90.4	7.7	19 942	-1.2	1 342	6.7	29 711	73.5	53.3	11.5
Elyria	37.5	670	29.2	8.0	84.3	7.9	28 982	-1.3	2 707	9.3	43 910	65.1	38.2	28.2
Euclid	46.5	706	33.0	14.1	81.2	11.0	25 372	2.7	2 339	9.2	38 774	65.0	40.0	30.4
Fairborn	49.7	723	39.1	7.6	80.3	13.0	16 101	-2.6	1 707	10.6	26 516	64.7	35.6	29.6
Fairfield	33.4	838	30.2	3.4	82.6	11.4	24 527	-1.2	2 175	8.9	33 823	74.2	47.4	18.2
Findlay	40.9	659	24.9	7.8	77.6	10.0	22 434	10.1	1 922	8.6	33 410	64.2	41.7	30.1
Gahanna	23.2	889	25.0	4.4	88.1	9.3	17 859	-6.3	1 374	7.7	25 635	72.3	50.8	17.5
Garfield Heights	26.8	741	32.8	11.1	87.5	10.0	14 825	3.3	1 443	9.7	22 958	66.7	42.4	28.7
Green	19.2	833	26.8	1.8	91.9	6.4	14 263	NA	1 283	9.0	20 345	69.7	45.7	22.5
Grove City	28.6	791	26.5	3.4	83.3	11.0	18 720	0.5	1 550	8.3	26 609	72.9	47.7	21.1
Hamilton	45.2	664	32.5	11.7	81.4	9.8	30 011	-1.8	3 244	10.8	48 425	62.9	37.5	33.5
Hilliard	23.0	939	28.8	4.8	88.1	10.0	15 334	-2.4	1 119	7.3	20 247	76.5	53.7	19.0
Huber Heights	29.8	805	27.8	3.7	86.8	10.0	19 370	-1.2	2 017	10.4	29 659	67.7	43.6	22.2
Kent	58.1	679	40.4	8.3	59.4	26.2	17 295	0.6	1 345	7.8	25 152	68.1	28.6	26.8

1. $2,000 represents $2,000 or more.   2. 50.0 represents 50 percent or more.   3. Percent of civilian labor force.   4. Persons 16 years old and over.

Table D. Cities — **Construction, Wholesale Trade, and Retail Trade**

City	Value of residential construction authorized by building permits, 2010			Wholesale trade,[1] 2007				Retail trade,[2] 2007			
	New construction ($1,000)	Number of housing units	Percent single family	Number of establish- ments	Number of employees	Sales (mil dol)	Annual payroll (mil dol)	Number of establish- ments	Number of employees	Sales (mil dol)	Annual payroll (mil dol)
	69	70	71	72	73	74	75	76	77	78	79
NORTH CAROLINA...	5 107 163	33 889	76.9	10 049	142 342	88 795.9	6 969.2	36 592	466 577	114 578.2	10 342.7
Apex	38 612	179	92.7	43	469	320.3	26.9	108	1 908	439.9	41.9
Asheboro	4 468	106	39.6	35	339	154.0	14.9	215	2 503	570.9	52.9
Asheville	71 359	703	33.9	134	1 508	785.3	67.0	804	11 457	2 616.9	254.2
Burlington	10 760	83	100.0	67	934	318.7	35.2	415	5 832	1 216.9	117.0
Cary	210 284	1 359	79.7	127	1 999	2 236.7	152.1	524	9 274	2 293.0	209.5
Chapel Hill	14 402	81	67.9	23	398	403.0	35.9	196	2 888	569.5	62.7
Charlotte	NA	NA	NA	1 552	24 881	15 551.6	1 369.3	2 544	38 969	10 101.4	970.9
Concord	NA	NA	NA	100	2 237	1 145.9	103.8	478	7 685	1 995.1	167.7
Durham	171 194	1 187	75.1	183	2 669	2 648.8	169.1	868	13 805	2 978.1	297.3
Fayetteville	139 545	1 506	25.7	111	1 243	552.7	54.6	843	13 255	3 298.5	291.0
Garner	8 773	54	100.0	58	1 009	801.5	50.7	124	2 120	541.1	48.3
Gastonia	27 655	121	86.8	81	692	559.5	28.2	397	6 645	1 391.5	132.2
Goldsboro	7 519	83	32.5	57	1 365	862.8	53.7	347	4 309	1 027.1	85.8
Greensboro	87 202	941	45.7	567	8 524	7 790.2	412.6	1 293	21 155	5 080.7	502.1
Greenville	50 102	537	40.6	67	905	463.2	40.1	457	6 652	1 503.2	140.0
Hickory	NA	NA	NA	140	4 304	2 975.0	181.3	511	7 297	1 807.2	162.9
High Point	34 916	251	64.9	320	4 722	2 663.4	222.5	467	5 734	1 343.0	131.2
Huntersville	NA	NA	NA	51	517	224.5	28.5	156	2 832	823.7	66.5
Indian Trall	NA	NA	NA	86	826	321.2	36.0	97	1 552	462.8	42.0
Jacksonville	42 622	561	63.6	16	103	36.3	5.4	332	5 647	1 473.9	121.2
Kannapolis	NA	NA	NA	19	158	71.2	6.3	191	2 419	596.5	52.5
Matthews	NA	NA	NA	54	605	264.1	39.6	188	3 373	853.6	77.0
Monroe	11 021	47	100.0	73	1 298	653.5	51.5	246	3 583	884.0	76.2
Mooresville	NA	NA	NA	67	694	313.6	33.8	242	3 659	1 054.3	87.3
New Bern	26 652	255	70.2	35	473	698.7	18.3	249	3 150	728.8	67.8
Raleigh	219 911	1 250	81.9	589	8 369	4 243.2	447.4	1 761	28 116	7 066.4	672.2
Rocky Mount	2 406	36	100.0	66	1 408	975.5	55.7	392	4 811	1 045.6	96.1
Salisbury	NA	NA	NA	48	887	442.7	35.0	223	3 161	782.6	68.1
Sanford	11 191	72	100.0	35	673	572.9	26.2	201	2 340	583.0	50.6
Thomasville	4 966	36	100.0	36	577	230.7	22.6	139	1 716	419.6	37.6
Wake Forest	58 120	344	100.0	16	101	42.3	5.1	80	1 593	454.6	38.7
Wilmington	NA	NA	NA	150	1 293	744.6	53.7	845	12 145	3 076.1	284.9
Wilson	20 840	125	52.0	74	842	654.7	42.1	309	3 695	953.7	81.3
Winston-Salem	59 840	588	77.6	268	5 166	2 841.7	217.1	1 081	16 204	3 888.0	357.7
NORTH DAKOTA	481 143	3 833	54.4	1 332	14 866	13 099.3	627.1	3 361	44 054	10 527.3	891.4
Bismarck	63 250	402	85.3	118	1 531	845.9	68.8	375	6 653	1 377.0	133.6
Fargo	80 071	831	40.2	249	4 419	3 067.3	208.5	545	10 379	2 552.5	224.8
Grand Forks	21 125	130	64.6	61	841	528.9	36.9	297	5 634	1 181.5	110.5
Minot	62 088	649	27.9	56	825	943.8	35.9	252	4 392	1 005.7	89.4
West Fargo	31 248	238	76.5	38	464	165.1	20.0	80	1 405	269.1	27.9
OHIO	2 297 494	13 710	77.3	12 591	192 403	135 575.3	8 914.0	40 075	591 237	138 816.0	12 729.5
Akron	8 516	127	51.2	236	3 404	1 540.3	158.8	676	8 221	1 720.2	174.3
Barberton	540	4	100.0	30	1 501	177.8	37.0	68	781	170.5	16.3
Beavercreek	NA	NA	NA	23	D	D	D	232	5 106	887.4	84.4
Bowling Green	NA	NA	NA	15	130	34.0	3.5	111	1 839	394.7	33.9
Brunswick	11 773	72	100.0	56	654	268.9	30.2	115	1 553	594.4	41.6
Canton	9 190	63	36.5	100	1 407	612.4	62.0	232	3 215	725.7	71.0
Cincinnati	18 180	181	45.3	390	6 264	5 749.5	324.4	1 016	13 048	3 310.5	320.4
Cleveland	12 017	127	71.7	606	9 806	4 912.5	506.4	1 314	10 259	2 298.1	232.5
Cleveland Heights	180	1	100.0	6	D	D	D	123	1 748	378.8	40.2
Columbus	183 534	2 107	34.0	825	16 326	11 029.4	769.7	2 641	48 684	12 077.0	1 132.2
Cuyahoga Falls	3 119	27	70.4	46	527	184.1	22.2	184	3 674	986.5	81.3
Dayton	3 824	27	100.0	187	3 202	1 370.4	145.3	422	4 514	961.3	107.4
Delaware	20 006	108	100.0	24	174	63.5	7.5	115	1 606	419.7	37.1
Dublin	28 260	94	87.2	83	3 809	2 043.4	203.1	130	4 095	1 435.3	133.8
Elyria	776	9	100.0	57	527	401.3	24.0	257	4 814	930.8	90.6
Euclid	0	0	0.0	36	511	336.0	27.3	104	1 178	337.1	31.7
Fairborn	10 565	48	100.0	9	308	316.1	18.3	82	1 114	269.0	25.4
Fairfield	4 386	19	100.0	77	1 495	825.4	67.5	172	4 303	1 518.4	127.1
Findlay	4 772	29	89.7	42	D	D	D	245	3 701	819.3	74.4
Gahanna	2 052	10	100.0	43	520	406.0	21.6	90	1 861	587.2	50.1
Garfield Heights	0	0	0.0	28	347	137.2	12.8	83	1 359	256.1	24.0
Green	NA	NA	NA	34	744	501.9	44.7	64	1 416	639.9	43.2
Grove City	25 519	139	82.7	33	980	1 745.0	35.8	115	2 554	557.0	58.7
Hamilton	2 527	20	100.0	39	585	496.6	32.5	217	3 416	694.0	66.1
Hilliard	38 485	421	84.8	46	782	331.4	37.8	84	1 376	360.5	35.6
Huber Heights	NA	NA	NA	23	516	233.1	25.1	99	1 893	377.3	35.6
Kent	948	4	100.0	17	209	130.3	11.5	81	916	318.7	27.1

1. Merchant wholesalers except manufacturers' sales branches and offices.   2. Establishments with payroll.

City	Real estate and rental and leasing, 2007				Professional, scientific, and technical services,[1] 2007				Manufacturing, 2007			
	Number of establish-ments	Number of employees	Receipts (mil dol)	Annual payroll (mil dol)	Number of establish-ments	Number of employees	Receipts (mil dol)	Annual payroll (mil dol)	Number of establish-ments	Number of employees	Receipts (mil dol)	Annual payroll (mil dol)
	80	81	82	83	84	85	86	87	88	89	90	91
NORTH CAROLINA...	11 258	53 563	11 175.1	1 881.4	22 385	182 224	26 003.8	10 698.3	10 150	506 013	205 867.3	19 589.8
Apex	34	88	14.9	2.6	167	419	52.1	19.8	33	1 181	D	61.1
Asheboro	37	173	31.6	4.3	73	376	33.6	11.0	80	8 766	2 758.2	283.2
Asheville	245	900	186.6	33.3	556	D	D	D	115	3 100	D	112.6
Burlington	79	307	51.0	8.1	114	D	D	D	100	5 331	1 001.0	182.3
Cary	213	880	207.0	38.7	806	D	D	D	75	1 808	606.9	86.4
Chapel Hill	88	D	D	D	286	3 208	317.4	126.3	NA	NA	NA	NA
Charlotte	1 460	10 841	2 676.3	513.2	3 009	D	D	D	716	24 523	8 996.3	1 103.9
Concord	127	459	69.4	13.7	208	D	D	D	84	5 967	D	319.3
Durham	289	1 832	351.7	71.0	838	D	D	D	147	8 554	D	514.2
Fayetteville	261	1 238	191.1	33.5	375	D	D	D	62	D	D	D
Garner	34	94	21.3	2.9	76	413	40.3	14.8	22	1 263	606.5	60.5
Gastonia	99	877	143.1	24.6	166	D	D	D	129	6 225	1 805.4	226.1
Goldsboro	57	244	29.8	5.6	109	736	59.4	21.0	46	2 489	399.9	86.3
Greensboro	465	3 336	1 225.1	108.5	992	D	D	D	350	18 969	19 687.6	925.5
Greenville	147	644	90.5	17.0	221	1 223	139.8	53.6	39	2 412	D	118.5
Hickory	111	404	96.4	12.1	210	1 360	146.1	51.9	188	10 207	1 770.4	351.5
High Point	119	790	168.5	26.4	306	2 445	343.1	131.1	284	15 048	3 380.2	540.7
Huntersville	69	139	33.1	4.9	152	660	92.4	37.0	29	1 065	228.7	48.1
Indian Trail	29	104	21.8	4.1	45	207	20.2	8.2	61	1 354	D	49.0
Jacksonville	99	468	79.9	11.6	127	D	D	D	NA	NA	NA	NA
Kannapolis	44	173	21.7	4.6	54	392	40.9	11.4	31	596	D	16.9
Matthews	52	189	24.6	6.2	138	642	98.3	37.4	40	990	277.7	38.6
Monroe	57	241	55.0	8.2	100	538	51.2	19.6	91	7 591	2 721.0	319.0
Mooresville	88	273	60.6	10.8	149	1 900	188.9	75.3	62	1 999	655.5	80.9
New Bern	60	220	33.8	6.5	127	D	D	D	35	3 110	911.8	133.7
Raleigh	787	4 794	1 356.2	235.6	2 132	D	D	D	294	6 235	2 285.7	280.8
Rocky Mount	81	413	75.4	11.4	141	883	95.5	35.8	56	5 697	1 481.0	223.9
Salisbury	57	190	37.1	6.0	109	907	70.1	28.9	68	2 995	D	D
Sanford	49	175	29.1	5.4	68	D	D	D	49	4 633	1 089.8	150.6
Thomasville	26	78	9.7	1.5	51	191	20.3	5.2	82	3 166	D	114.9
Wake Forest	35	68	14.4	2.6	95	326	35.6	13.7	NA	NA	NA	NA
Wilmington	289	1 318	239.5	43.4	647	D	D	D	102	4 009	1 725.8	224.2
Wilson	63	173	28.2	4.1	105	D	D	D	65	6 950	8 024.2	281.4
Winston-Salem	341	D	D	D	711	D	D	D	232	11 806	9 391.1	529.9
NORTH DAKOTA	770	3 748	668.8	96.0	1 432	9 707	1 110.7	416.9	767	26 361	11 349.8	991.4
Bismarck	105	358	53.3	8.2	249	D	D	D	65	1 991	D	81.7
Fargo	223	1 526	215.9	43.8	349	D	D	D	136	6 055	1 805.1	226.1
Grand Forks	53	386	54.7	8.8	107	912	88.7	45.4	43	2 512	D	78.5
Minot	64	433	142.3	10.2	85	D	D	D	NA	NA	NA	NA
West Fargo	25	73	6.3	1.4	33	D	D	D	47	1 842	D	71.8
OHIO	10 973	67 048	15 011.3	2 339.2	24 963	224 265	32 285.4	12 304.2	16 237	760 267	295 890.9	35 485.5
Akron	168	1 083	154.9	33.3	536	D	D	D	306	8 736	2 379.8	404.7
Barberton	7	50	5.0	0.7	43	D	D	D	65	2 292	679.3	88.3
Beavercreek	44	203	49.6	4.8	173	D	D	D	NA	NA	NA	NA
Bowling Green	40	193	20.0	4.4	56	D	D	D	39	2 637	910.1	112.4
Brunswick	27	105	12.9	1.8	71	371	32.6	13.2	48	938	178.3	40.1
Canton	75	282	48.0	7.3	175	861	101.5	32.0	146	9 975	3 526.9	467.2
Cincinnati	450	2 423	505.9	102.3	1 157	20 569	3 124.8	1 408.7	428	18 795	6 446.6	877.5
Cleveland	361	5 548	1 866.6	287.2	1 260	D	D	D	922	26 961	7 497.0	1 271.1
Cleveland Heights	51	183	24.8	3.7	113	229	30.8	10.6	NA	NA	NA	NA
Columbus	993	8 129	1 767.2	325.0	2 122	D	D	D	600	24 027	11 317.9	1 102.5
Cuyahoga Falls	53	282	33.6	8.3	116	699	71.0	29.9	81	4 091	1 170.2	165.4
Dayton	138	918	129.3	26.4	358	D	D	D	303	12 820	3 197.1	571.1
Delaware	44	131	18.6	3.6	53	233	25.7	9.8	34	2 728	1 584.5	142.1
Dublin	82	540	134.9	24.7	341	3 427	499.9	200.8	29	1 978	437.2	86.6
Elyria	54	334	41.9	8.6	77	D	D	D	108	5 650	1 538.0	260.8
Euclid	51	319	37.0	8.7	49	D	D	D	80	5 429	1 671.5	290.5
Fairborn	30	141	14.0	3.3	77	D	D	D	12	572	D	23.5
Fairfield	49	319	132.9	10.9	84	512	50.0	21.2	90	4 636	1 155.8	173.9
Findlay	55	436	46.2	11.5	106	861	74.3	31.0	63	6 513	1 769.5	300.0
Gahanna	41	154	39.4	5.7	146	892	107.1	42.9	34	1 107	238.8	42.3
Garfield Heights	18	73	17.6	2.7	52	376	39.6	19.0	38	1 223	233.3	51.9
Green	26	224	39.0	4.8	63	968	75.5	50.9	44	1 529	403.3	57.6
Grove City	36	145	19.6	4.2	54	321	28.2	10.2	30	1 714	379.7	74.1
Hamilton	47	248	36.8	6.6	112	D	D	D	79	2 827	1 034.2	125.6
Hilliard	49	154	20.0	4.2	76	404	48.6	23.0	31	1 514	355.4	65.5
Huber Heights	24	126	20.4	5.8	34	330	26.9	10.0	34	1 348	432.8	73.7
Kent	24	89	12.5	2.3	50	321	36.4	13.5	63	1 855	D	74.3

1. Establishments subject to federal tax.

Table D. Cities — Accommodation and Food Services, Arts, Entertainment, and Recreation, and Health Care and Social Assistance

City	Accommodation and food services, 2007				Arts, entertainment, and recreation,[1] 2007				Health care and social assistance,[1] 2007			
	Number of establishments	Number of employees	Sales (mil dol)	Annual payroll (mil dol)	Number of establishments	Number of employees	Receipts (mil dol)	Annual payroll (mil dol)	Number of establishments	Number of employees	Receipts (mil dol)	Annual payroll (mil dol)
	92	93	94	95	96	97	98	99	100	101	102	103
NORTH CAROLINA...	18 268	343 235	16 126.9	4 395.1	2 676	37 489	3 588.0	1 148.8	17 964	286 998	22 794.8	10 132.8
Apex	75	1 237	57.1	15.8	10	D	D	D	87	762	51.7	23.1
Asheboro	88	1 649	67.5	18.5	6	D	D	D	122	1 552	125.2	58.2
Asheville	478	11 166	560.1	167.5	51	480	23.7	7.9	464	6 999	776.0	339.8
Burlington	183	3 616	151.8	44.4	17	D	D	D	174	2 696	214.0	103.9
Cary	322	6 654	317.5	88.6	46	821	48.1	15.5	395	4 388	438.8	180.7
Chapel Hill	222	4 683	219.7	64.8	21	229	7.1	3.2	191	D	D	D
Charlotte	1 803	37 995	2 107.7	578.3	211	5 136	559.0	265.3	1 542	24 083	2 463.3	1 129.8
Concord	206	4 796	239.3	67.8	36	1 593	497.4	129.2	196	3 580	288.6	142.9
Durham	550	11 809	652.1	179.5	56	D	D	D	560	D	D	D
Fayetteville	453	10 088	408.1	108.3	36	D	D	D	571	D	D	D
Garner	71	1 637	69.7	18.9	7	D	D	D	69	1 222	78.6	34.7
Gastonia	179	4 008	182.2	49.8	24	186	10.5	2.4	265	D	D	D
Goldsboro	150	2 791	110.0	29.7	15	D	D	D	190	3 116	244.8	102.6
Greensboro	759	16 581	769.6	218.6	80	D	D	D	700	11 476	1 044.9	496.8
Greenville	252	6 365	265.1	71.8	25	305	13.7	4.1	267	D	D	D
Hickory	232	4 776	196.6	56.6	15	173	15.6	3.6	226	5 072	585.7	231.6
High Point	249	4 994	206.3	59.1	24	D	D	D	229	4 335	486.7	194.2
Huntersville	86	2 164	103.9	27.7	30	706	129.9	44.3	113	1 380	141.3	55.3
Indian Trail	51	568	29.0	7.1	9	87	6.3	1.2	21	D	D	D
Jacksonville	174	4 352	183.7	47.4	17	456	18.0	5.3	170	D	D	D
Kannapolis	81	1 275	55.2	15.3	8	D	D	D	58	838	57.8	25.5
Matthews	90	1 940	89.1	23.5	18	D	D	D	109	D	D	D
Monroe	105	2 151	99.7	23.1	5	D	D	D	106	1 726	142.5	64.0
Mooresville	160	2 908	126.7	35.1	51	D	D	D	132	D	D	D
New Bern	103	2 352	91.2	23.8	11	D	D	D	163	D	D	D
Raleigh	980	20 611	999.7	280.6	131	3 172	275.0	90.1	1 111	16 932	1 652.4	771.8
Rocky Mount	155	3 695	150.3	41.0	19	D	D	D	201	3 504	268.0	117.1
Salisbury	128	2 500	103.7	29.1	18	D	D	D	131	2 223	177.0	82.5
Sanford	85	1 643	61.2	15.9	7	D	D	D	127	2 277	168.7	68.6
Thomasville	60	995	36.8	10.6	4	D	D	D	37	687	43.7	20.7
Wake Forest	52	771	34.5	10.0	18	D	D	D	68	D	D	D
Wilmington	418	8 924	373.2	107.0	55	701	33.7	9.7	506	D	D	D
Wilson	117	2 394	105.2	27.0	13	D	D	D	138	D	D	D
Winston-Salem	527	10 856	508.1	142.4	63	557	26.6	7.3	541	D	D	D
NORTH DAKOTA	1 840	30 307	1 214.2	337.8	267	2 539	131.1	35.4	1 176	14 135	1 426.8	570.7
Bismarck	162	4 332	166.9	49.6	20	D	D	D	178	D	D	D
Fargo	296	7 976	314.2	93.5	45	608	44.4	8.2	285	5 745	785.3	304.6
Grand Forks	162	3 980	135.4	39.7	20	170	7.9	2.2	93	D	D	D
Minot	124	2 687	100.2	28.3	17	D	D	D	101	D	D	D
West Fargo	32	528	19.8	5.7	1	D	D	D	36	D	D	D
OHIO	23 959	436 598	17 779.9	5 078.5	3 122	40 269	4 067.9	1 360.1	22 693	346 386	28 636.8	12 631.1
Akron	443	6 065	247.8	67.8	40	570	49.7	13.2	367	6 681	617.6	304.4
Barberton	46	703	23.2	6.3	4	D	D	D	80	1 893	204.9	82.4
Beavercreek	100	D	D	D	4	48	3.3	0.8	108	D	D	D
Bowling Green	96	2 026	62.4	18.8	13	D	D	D	72	870	72.4	32.4
Brunswick	73	1 093	41.0	10.8	8	D	D	D	53	666	40.9	17.9
Canton	160	2 224	79.9	21.8	11	208	5.9	2.1	159	3 037	316.4	150.4
Cincinnati	730	13 938	712.8	207.1	83	1 379	389.9	257.8	698	15 502	1 549.1	811.2
Cleveland	995	16 038	868.1	235.2	97	3 115	589.0	298.8	447	7 487	492.6	220.4
Cleveland Heights	86	1 162	50.8	14.6	12	61	3.4	0.9	96	1 245	80.4	35.3
Columbus	1 852	41 282	1 944.8	553.4	145	3 364	254.2	101.1	1 457	24 611	2 450.4	1 105.0
Cuyahoga Falls	117	2 514	106.8	31.5	6	D	D	D	134	D	D	D
Dayton	294	4 483	190.9	54.7	20	270	21.4	5.5	332	5 790	632.4	315.1
Delaware	85	1 401	55.0	14.2	9	48	4.7	1.2	75	930	68.0	28.9
Dublin	114	3 032	147.4	45.6	26	D	D	D	167	D	D	D
Elyria	139	2 501	89.3	25.9	10	D	D	D	116	1 509	137.7	57.4
Euclid	78	683	26.1	6.8	7	D	D	D	90	D	D	D
Fairborn	84	1 573	64.7	18.2	4	64	1.5	0.4	35	388	25.3	10.1
Fairfield	95	2 099	94.6	25.2	12	D	D	D	152	D	D	D
Findlay	135	2 981	108.5	31.8	8	D	D	D	127	D	D	D
Gahanna	95	1 907	78.2	21.0	10	D	D	D	114	1 989	137.6	67.9
Garfield Heights	55	712	27.5	7.3	3	9	0.5	0.2	66	1 086	153.8	45.0
Green	58	1 195	46.5	13.1	12	140	10.5	3.0	66	D	D	D
Grove City	113	2 551	104.6	32.2	14	D	D	D	85	D	D	D
Hamilton	119	2 341	88.6	26.2	7	D	D	D	113	1 409	143.4	55.7
Hilliard	57	1 514	58.1	17.7	18	257	26.4	9.2	77	783	62.6	23.0
Huber Heights	69	1 389	55.6	16.0	8	D	D	D	68	D	D	D
Kent	74	1 308	54.4	13.4	5	D	D	D	40	520	36.6	16.1

1. Establishments subject to federal tax.

Table D. Cities — Other Services and Federal Funds

| City | Other services[1], 2007 | | | | Selected federal funds, 2009–2010 (mil dol) | | | | | | | | |
| | | | | | Procurement contracts | | Grants | | | | | | |
	Number of establishments	Number of employees	Receipts (mil dol)	Annual payroll (mil dol)	Defense	Other	Total[2]	Medicaid and other health related	Nutrition and family welfare	Energy and environment	Disasters and emergency preparedness	Housing and community development	Employment and training
	104	105	106	107	108	109	110	111	112	113	114	115	116
NORTH CAROLINA...	11 846	67 498	5 307.6	1 628.9	3 626.5	2 464.0	20 098.9	11 594.5	2 009.1	976.2	25.2	644.5	302.8
Apex	51	D	D	D	0.9	26.9	0.1	0.0	0.0	0.0	0.0	0.0	0.0
Asheboro	45	D	D	D	15.6	3.3	11.3	0.6	3.1	0.3	0.3	5.3	0.0
Asheville	200	1 206	80.4	27.3	19.4	71.6	34.6	2.3	7.0	1.6	0.0	14.4	0.5
Burlington	90	528	31.1	10.5	5.0	2.6	6.3	2.7	0.4	0.2	0.0	1.5	0.0
Cary	194	1 823	134.4	48.3	15.1	16.7	15.5	4.5	0.0	7.9	0.0	0.5	0.0
Chapel Hill	61	558	34.0	12.6	3.1	64.3	914.9	749.9	7.9	8.4	0.2	2.2	3.8
Charlotte	1 090	8 624	685.8	231.6	85.9	270.5	462.1	16.6	7.5	288.3	-0.4	87.4	0.1
Concord	116	700	46.1	14.0	1.0	3.0	10.0	0.7	1.2	0.0	1.3	6.7	0.0
Durham	309	2 641	282.8	77.1	70.5	279.9	1 372.5	821.2	3.4	205.8	0.0	40.7	0.0
Fayetteville	252	1 824	116.4	39.3	57.2	30.0	62.8	0.6	6.2	2.2	0.0	18.3	0.1
Garner	52	314	26.0	8.1	0.7	0.3	0.0	0.0	0.0	0.0	0.0	0.0	0.0
Gastonia	122	759	45.7	14.7	0.3	1.1	22.9	2.5	4.2	0.0	0.0	11.6	0.0
Goldsboro	83	D	D	D	14.1	0.5	18.7	0.0	5.0	0.4	0.0	5.6	0.0
Greensboro	425	2 632	213.4	68.6	48.3	30.9	150.9	16.5	8.6	7.6	0.3	24.5	0.1
Greenville	109	707	49.7	13.3	9.9	3.1	36.2	21.6	0.1	0.1	0.0	7.1	0.0
Hickory	114	D	D	D	0.7	3.3	9.6	0.4	0.0	0.0	0.0	8.7	0.3
High Point	171	1 165	91.8	28.1	21.2	79.3	14.3	-1.1	0.0	0.8	0.0	12.4	0.0
Huntersville	65	387	23.4	7.7	0.3	0.3	0.1	0.0	0.0	0.0	0.0	0.1	0.0
Indian Trail	56	D	D	D	0.3	0.1	0.0	0.0	0.0	0.0	0.0	0.0	0.0
Jacksonville	117	758	42.2	14.2	33.8	0.2	27.3	0.2	1.8	0.6	0.0	4.5	0.0
Kannapolis	58	D	D	D	0.0	0.0	2.5	0.0	1.3	0.2	0.0	0.4	0.0
Matthews	66	292	22.1	6.8	0.1	0.3	0.2	0.0	0.0	0.0	0.0	0.0	0.0
Monroe	94	518	43.4	13.5	12.7	6.1	9.0	0.0	4.1	0.7	0.0	3.0	0.0
Mooresville	89	436	34.1	10.2	6.5	0.1	0.3	0.0	0.0	0.0	0.0	0.2	0.0
New Bern	64	309	19.4	5.4	1.3	4.9	8.8	0.0	0.0	0.1	0.0	5.9	0.0
Raleigh	693	5 015	345.4	118.8	64.9	66.0	2 880.8	252.1	450.7	362.4	0.7	118.3	296.1
Rocky Mount	102	D	D	D	11.6	0.6	14.6	0.0	4.6	0.6	0.0	8.0	0.0
Salisbury	49	286	20.0	6.7	0.5	50.7	20.8	0.0	7.1	0.0	0.0	6.2	0.0
Sanford	57	326	21.0	7.1	0.3	0.6	3.2	0.0	0.0	0.0	0.0	3.1	0.0
Thomasville	56	D	D	D	3.4	1.3	1.0	0.0	0.0	0.0	0.0	1.0	0.0
Wake Forest	43	246	24.3	7.6	0.8	0.0	0.0	0.0	0.0	0.0	0.0	0.0	0.0
Wilmington	272	1 638	120.7	36.7	25.5	27.2	99.4	32.1	2.1	29.8	0.0	18.5	0.3
Wilson	74	D	D	D	13.4	1.3	9.8	4.1	0.0	0.2	0.0	4.3	0.0
Winston-Salem	330	2 049	137.4	52.4	20.5	10.5	333.3	241.6	4.3	2.7	2.0	42.5	0.0
NORTH DAKOTA	1 241	6 059	487.1	140.7	288.2	397.1	2 237.3	630.3	202.8	279.8	141.1	75.4	23.8
Bismarck	140	D	D	D	3.8	29.5	290.6	28.5	36.4	42.5	10.3	18.0	22.0
Fargo	225	1 703	112.8	44.1	20.6	179.9	117.0	19.3	4.0	15.6	0.0	9.0	0.0
Grand Forks	103	672	46.2	13.9	10.3	15.6	110.1	20.4	2.3	44.5	0.0	7.7	0.0
Minot	86	505	36.8	10.7	18.9	16.8	29.2	2.1	3.9	0.2	0.0	4.4	0.0
West Fargo	38	239	23.1	7.2	1.1	0.9	3.9	0.0	0.0	0.1	0.0	2.5	0.0
OHIO	16 338	106 072	8 483.2	2 613.6	6 064.3	2 765.1	24 399.0	13 659.6	3 021.0	847.8	15.8	1 215.5	404.6
Akron	313	2 040	166.1	49.7	307.0	8.5	173.0	13.3	11.0	64.3	0.0	59.3	7.2
Barberton	46	250	19.2	6.3	0.5	0.0	2.2	0.0	0.0	0.9	0.0	0.8	0.0
Beavercreek	48	D	D	D	7.9	3.8	0.7	0.4	0.0	0.2	0.0	0.0	0.0
Bowling Green	47	222	14.5	4.4	0.1	0.1	12.5	1.9	0.0	1.6	0.0	0.8	0.0
Brunswick	55	368	29.0	8.1	1.3	0.6	0.0	0.0	0.0	0.0	0.0	0.0	0.0
Canton	132	670	43.7	13.4	5.4	2.0	43.2	1.7	6.0	8.4	0.0	20.1	0.4
Cincinnati	418	2 971	238.8	78.3	1 784.8	302.2	699.6	400.1	29.2	29.3	0.0	152.3	11.6
Cleveland	624	3 972	355.6	93.2	65.4	355.4	1 129.0	570.0	35.5	14.5	0.2	245.2	0.8
Cleveland Heights	53	321	27.3	8.5	0.0	0.7	4.3	0.0	0.0	0.0	0.0	3.7	0.0
Columbus	1 150	9 379	673.5	215.0	535.1	262.5	3 619.3	645.9	651.1	532.3	7.4	252.5	339.4
Cuyahoga Falls	95	550	39.6	13.2	3.7	0.1	3.2	0.0	0.0	0.4	0.0	2.4	0.0
Dayton	195	1 702	150.5	52.6	343.3	118.3	202.9	15.1	20.1	12.2	0.0	85.7	1.0
Delaware	34	169	13.9	4.7	0.3	0.5	4.5	0.1	0.0	0.0	0.0	2.6	0.0
Dublin	40	524	42.5	15.1	538.7	3.7	1.6	0.8	0.0	0.1	0.0	0.0	0.0
Elyria	76	583	67.9	17.2	5.9	1.0	5.4	0.0	0.0	0.9	0.0	1.3	0.0
Euclid	63	289	20.6	10.8	3.0	0.2	4.7	0.0	0.0	2.7	0.0	1.2	0.0
Fairborn	40	187	11.3	3.7	67.0	1.1	0.6	0.0	0.0	0.0	0.0	0.3	0.0
Fairfield	96	594	48.3	15.6	74.2	12.6	4.6	0.1	4.4	0.0	0.0	0.0	0.0
Findlay	85	542	45.8	14.8	0.2	0.4	6.7	0.0	2.6	1.0	0.0	2.9	0.0
Gahanna	56	663	46.2	15.6	0.3	0.8	0.3	0.0	0.0	0.0	0.0	0.1	0.0
Garfield Heights	42	230	11.6	3.7	0.0	0.0	0.0	0.0	0.0	0.0	0.0	0.0	0.0
Green	37	D	D	D	0.0	0.4	0.0	0.0	0.0	0.0	0.0	0.0	0.0
Grove City	63	522	38.7	18.1	14.2	0.1	0.3	0.0	0.0	0.0	0.0	0.0	0.0
Hamilton	78	380	35.4	10.7	0.1	0.2	17.1	0.2	0.0	0.7	0.0	14.0	0.0
Hilliard	43	269	26.1	7.3	1.8	0.0	0.2	0.0	0.0	0.0	0.0	0.1	0.0
Huber Heights	52	226	15.1	6.1	0.0	0.0	0.2	0.0	0.0	0.2	0.0	0.0	0.0
Kent	45	237	11.7	4.6	0.9	0.2	26.8	8.7	0.0	1.4	0.0	0.6	0.0

1. Establishments subject to federal tax. 2. Includes program categories not shown separately. State totals include additional categories not allocated by city.

Table D. Cities — City Government Finances

City	General revenue Total (mil dol)	Intergovernmental Total (mil dol)	Intergovernmental Percent from state government	Taxes Total (mil dol)	Taxes Per capita Total	Taxes Per capita Property	Sales and gross receipts	General expenditure Total (mil dol)	Per capita Total	Capital outlays
	117	118	119	120	121	122	123	124	125	126
NORTH CAROLINA...	X	X	X	X	X	X	X	X	X	X
Apex	37.5	8.1	27.5	13.0	412	366	46	32.6	1 030	310
Asheboro	27.0	7.2	37.7	10.8	447	419	28	24.0	991	62
Asheville	122.1	36.8	26.8	49.4	669	560	110	100.1	1 356	157
Burlington	63.0	16.7	38.2	24.8	499	444	55	54.6	1 101	176
Cary	197.2	35.2	28.8	64.6	530	446	84	159.7	1 312	483
Chapel Hill	79.9	38.3	25.3	32.0	621	557	64	64.3	1 247	320
Charlotte	1 458.3	406.3	25.3	412.2	614	467	147	1 187.2	1 768	491
Concord	105.4	27.6	27.0	36.8	569	529	40	87.9	1 360	200
Durham	293.7	82.8	24.4	117.6	540	465	75	259.4	1 191	157
Fayetteville	196.5	57.5	29.3	64.7	377	341	36	168.7	982	188
Garner	23.1	7.2	27.8	14.4	570	482	88	20.3	801	101
Gastonia	78.8	22.8	29.3	28.2	397	343	54	70.5	992	82
Goldsboro	40.8	12.7	32.0	14.1	374	332	43	37.4	994	132
Greensboro	361.7	90.9	29.4	148.4	601	642	59	370.3	1 498	229
Greenville	94.1	25.4	33.4	27.8	366	306	60	90.2	1 186	151
Hickory	63.2	18.8	28.7	24.4	596	537	58	51.7	1 261	98
High Point	156.3	37.0	46.3	59.7	595	520	75	143.7	1 431	314
Huntersville	25.9	8.0	48.9	13.3	312	280	32	24.6	579	133
Indian Trail	5.2	2.0	68.2	2.6	144	123	21	5.2	288	45
Jacksonville	52.5	20.1	29.6	15.5	207	180	27	52.9	709	168
Kannapolis	38.4	9.2	36.7	13.0	313	292	21	35.2	847	177
Matthews	21.8	5.2	48.0	10.0	375	318	57	16.6	621	89
Monroe	53.3	10.3	31.1	16.0	506	432	73	39.8	1 258	133
Mooresville	44.8	9.7	24.8	20.0	923	895	28	47.7	2 198	890
New Bern	37.9	9.7	43.2	11.2	396	355	41	41.6	1 475	157
Raleigh	485.3	128.8	28.8	177.6	473	383	89	564.0	1 501	512
Rocky Mount	66.7	20.8	29.3	19.5	344	308	35	65.4	1 151	156
Salisbury	43.7	9.3	37.6	15.7	545	520	25	39.0	1 358	166
Sanford	33.0	7.9	36.0	11.6	404	376	29	26.5	925	77
Thomasville	23.9	7.4	28.3	9.7	369	343	26	30.4	1 158	400
Wake Forest	24.3	6.6	26.5	13.2	520	431	89	22.2	878	224
Wilmington	149.4	50.2	21.8	48.4	486	424	62	159.8	1 604	588
Wilson	56.6	13.5	46.0	17.6	368	337	31	54.5	1 141	132
Winston-Salem	274.5	66.4	36.3	98.9	459	398	62	289.9	1 346	318
NORTH DAKOTA	X	X	X	X	X	X	X	X	X	X
Bismarck	82.3	15.0	53.0	29.1	488	232	256	89.4	1 502	564
Fargo	148.4	23.6	53.4	49.1	530	163	347	140.8	1 520	672
Grand Forks	82.7	13.6	53.5	30.3	586	191	395	53.5	1 034	81
Minot	38.8	5.0	78.0	22.4	635	265	370	25.1	711	107
West Fargo	12.1	1.2	92.3	6.8	296	178	118	13.6	591	43
OHIO	X	X	X	X	X	X	X	X	X	X
Akron	323.9	74.6	57.7	145.4	699	157	4	407.5	1 960	320
Barberton	32.7	5.4	76.4	13.4	500	62	8	32.7	1 222	227
Beavercreek	20.7	5.0	93.4	11.9	299	269	29	20.4	513	35
Bowling Green	38.0	4.6	100.0	21.4	717	133	3	30.9	1 035	41
Brunswick	21.9	4.2	98.8	12.6	361	61	33	26.0	747	127
Canton	102.9	23.4	75.1	48.1	614	46	16	103.6	1 323	170
Cincinnati	841.2	286.2	15.9	423.8	1 275	210	88	815.7	2 454	690
Cleveland	970.0	239.7	62.6	424.1	968	152	110	967.7	2 209	367
Cleveland Heights	63.3	14.0	88.3	35.0	755	243	27	57.1	1 232	44
Columbus	1 140.2	197.5	52.8	591.1	790	63	42	1 097.7	1 468	298
Cuyahoga Falls	65.8	8.3	91.3	29.4	576	213	14	64.0	1 254	203
Dayton	311.3	46.2	54.3	139.7	899	156	11	276.2	1 777	109
Delaware	40.4	9.5	95.4	14.2	431	43	28	65.2	1 976	1 121
Dublin	98.1	6.6	39.4	76.3	2 009	210	103	81.6	2 151	668
Elyria	57.0	8.9	89.6	28.3	514	71	32	58.7	1 065	147
Euclid	62.5	11.6	91.0	30.9	646	144	3	59.8	1 248	135
Fairborn	34.9	5.3	100.0	14.2	440	141	13	42.8	1 322	425
Fairfield	51.9	7.3	95.5	28.9	683	128	14	57.6	1 363	490
Findlay	47.0	8.7	97.8	21.4	572	69	9	45.0	1 200	325
Gahanna	41.1	8.1	95.7	18.4	545	59	23	58.9	1 749	847
Garfield Heights	30.2	3.5	95.5	19.9	709	337	10	29.5	1 053	32
Green	24.9	5.2	34.3	18.2	775	66	19	31.7	1 352	501
Grove City	30.9	4.5	74.6	21.3	644	72	41	34.3	1 036	466
Hamilton	66.4	8.7	84.9	29.8	478	45	61	68.9	1 106	90
Hilliard	26.8	4.4	65.5	18.3	667	50	63	33.6	1 222	131
Huber Heights	30.7	2.9	63.7	18.8	502	92	27	28.9	773	160
Kent	28.9	4.9	73.8	14.1	498	103	18	26.5	937	104

1. Based on population estimated as of July 1 of the year shown.

Table D. Cities — City Government Finances

City	City government finances, 2006 (cont.)									
	General expenditure (cont.)									
	Percent of total for:									
	Public welfare	Highways	Parking facilities	Education	Health and hospitals	Police protection	Sewerage and sanitation	Parks and recreation	Housing and community development	Interest on debt
	127	128	129	130	131	132	133	134	135	136
NORTH CAROLINA...	X	X	X	X	X	X	X	X	X	X
Apex	0.0	12.3	0.0	0.0	0.2	17.0	24.8	10.5	0.0	1.6
Asheboro	0.0	7.6	0.0	0.0	0.0	22.0	24.4	11.5	0.0	1.7
Asheville	0.0	8.6	1.0	0.0	0.2	17.0	16.3	13.5	3.6	3.0
Burlington	0.0	16.3	0.0	0.0	1.1	18.0	22.9	10.4	1.1	3.0
Cary	0.0	15.9	0.0	0.0	0.0	9.4	25.8	9.9	0.5	4.7
Chapel Hill	0.0	6.8	1.8	0.0	0.0	16.9	6.2	8.6	3.8	3.0
Charlotte	0.0	8.1	0.1	0.0	0.4	13.7	27.8	3.1	4.2	10.3
Concord	0.0	7.4	0.0	0.0	0.0	15.0	23.8	4.8	1.1	4.2
Durham	0.0	10.4	0.9	0.0	0.0	17.1	17.2	9.8	4.2	3.5
Fayetteville	0.0	7.9	0.1	0.0	0.0	21.5	24.9	10.1	2.0	3.5
Garner	0.0	10.0	0.0	0.0	0.9	27.5	6.5	16.3	0.0	1.9
Gastonia	0.0	5.8	0.0	0.0	0.0	19.1	30.1	6.4	5.0	3.5
Goldsboro	0.0	7.7	0.0	0.0	0.2	17.7	24.8	8.3	3.4	2.3
Greensboro	0.0	7.5	0.3	0.0	0.1	17.7	30.0	10.1	3.2	3.4
Greenville	0.0	5.3	0.0	0.0	0.0	18.6	23.8	7.7	3.3	4.1
Hickory	0.0	9.5	0.0	0.0	0.2	16.5	20.1	6.7	1.3	2.1
High Point	0.0	15.3	0.6	0.0	1.0	15.0	23.2	7.2	1.7	4.6
Huntersville	0.0	17.2	0.0	0.0	0.9	25.3	0.0	31.0	0.0	2.9
Indian Trail	0.0	17.5	0.0	0.0	0.0	8.6	32.7	0.9	0.0	0.0
Jacksonville	0.0	4.9	0.0	0.0	0.0	18.4	32.0	12.9	1.0	1.6
Kannapolis	0.0	21.4	0.0	0.0	0.0	19.1	20.8	5.2	2.6	4.0
Matthews	0.0	12.8	0.0	0.0	2.6	32.8	9.2	11.2	0.0	3.7
Monroe	0.0	6.3	0.0	0.0	0.1	18.2	18.6	16.1	2.9	1.9
Mooresville	0.0	6.4	0.0	0.0	0.0	9.5	31.7	4.3	0.4	2.9
New Bern	0.0	6.4	0.0	0.0	0.3	18.2	28.7	5.7	0.9	2.3
Raleigh	0.1	8.1	5.3	0.0	0.0	12.5	21.5	23.4	2.7	5.3
Rocky Mount	0.0	5.5	0.0	0.0	0.0	16.3	33.6	11.7	3.2	1.3
Salisbury	0.0	11.3	0.0	0.0	0.1	18.2	22.4	6.6	2.1	2.9
Sanford	0.0	9.6	0.0	0.0	0.1	26.4	26.5	2.3	2.9	1.6
Thomasville	0.0	5.8	0.0	0.0	0.0	13.7	47.2	4.7	1.1	1.8
Wake Forest	0.0	9.3	0.0	0.0	0.0	19.2	8.4	15.9	0.0	2.0
Wilmington	0.0	7.8	0.6	0.0	0.0	16.6	38.7	7.2	1.4	3.7
Wilson	0.0	6.1	0.3	0.0	0.0	18.0	26.8	8.5	2.8	3.1
Winston-Salem	0.0	7.1	0.5	0.0	0.0	16.9	31.4	7.4	3.8	6.5
NORTH DAKOTA......	X	X	X	X	X	X	X	X	X	X
Bismarck	0.0	16.3	1.2	0.0	2.1	9.5	17.6	3.9	0.5	1.5
Fargo	0.2	27.7	0.9	0.0	4.7	8.0	21.3	7.3	3.8	7.9
Grand Forks	0.0	7.3	0.6	0.0	2.4	12.5	18.8	2.8	11.3	18.7
Minot	0.0	16.9	0.4	0.0	0.0	19.5	12.5	4.3	0.0	3.2
West Fargo	0.3	5.8	0.0	0.0	0.0	21.4	22.7	0.0	0.0	30.4
OHIO	X	X	X	X	X	X	X	X	X	X
Akron	0.0	13.9	1.0	0.0	7.2	13.4	8.0	5.9	1.5	4.6
Barberton	10.7	6.4	0.0	0.0	7.2	17.3	18.9	4.5	4.8	1.8
Beavercreek	0.0	24.5	0.0	0.0	1.3	31.8	0.0	15.5	2.6	5.9
Bowling Green	0.0	14.3	0.0	0.0	0.7	15.8	19.0	5.3	0.0	4.1
Brunswick	0.6	16.7	0.0	0.5	0.7	23.6	10.9	9.4	0.4	2.2
Canton	0.0	10.8	0.3	0.0	5.4	18.1	14.9	3.0	10.9	1.3
Cincinnati	0.0	2.7	0.8	0.6	4.6	13.8	24.3	5.1	5.2	2.3
Cleveland	0.4	3.4	0.4	0.0	4.7	17.9	6.3	6.0	10.4	9.3
Cleveland Heights	0.0	10.2	1.5	0.0	1.8	16.5	7.5	7.2	11.9	3.2
Columbus	0.0	8.7	0.3	0.0	3.2	20.5	23.2	6.2	0.7	10.1
Cuyahoga Falls	0.0	6.2	0.0	0.0	0.0	17.1	14.0	12.2	2.2	3.1
Dayton	0.0	13.1	0.0	0.0	0.0	18.2	8.8	4.5	4.9	2.9
Delaware	0.0	7.2	0.1	0.0	0.0	7.0	48.1	6.4	0.3	2.4
Dublin	0.0	24.3	0.0	0.0	0.2	11.3	4.7	16.8	0.0	4.0
Elyria	0.0	10.8	0.0	0.0	3.6	18.3	18.7	5.1	1.5	3.8
Euclid	0.0	3.5	0.0	0.0	0.5	17.6	22.4	5.2	1.8	4.1
Fairborn	0.0	7.9	0.0	0.0	0.0	33.8	14.8	0.7	2.5	2.7
Fairfield	0.0	22.1	0.0	0.0	0.1	13.5	9.1	6.5	2.1	3.4
Findlay	0.0	14.5	0.3	0.0	3.4	17.2	10.3	8.6	0.0	4.3
Gahanna	0.0	10.0	0.0	0.0	0.3	12.2	11.8	3.6	7.6	5.6
Garfield Heights	0.0	8.7	0.0	0.0	0.3	21.3	7.2	3.5	0.1	5.8
Green	0.0	11.2	0.0	0.0	0.7	4.5	0.0	10.2	0.0	2.6
Grove City	0.1	14.2	0.8	0.0	0.6	24.1	2.4	8.6	3.3	5.0
Hamilton	0.0	7.4	0.9	0.0	2.3	19.7	19.6	3.9	2.9	2.9
Hilliard	0.0	22.3	0.0	0.0	0.8	21.3	2.4	10.8	0.0	4.9
Huber Heights	0.0	15.8	0.0	0.0	0.0	18.8	10.4	0.9	0.0	7.1
Kent	0.0	6.6	0.0	0.0	1.7	24.8	14.8	6.0	10.4	8.1

Table D. Cities — City Government Finances, City Government Employment, and Climate

City	City government finances, 2007 (cont.) Debt outstanding — Total (mil dol)	Per capita[1] (dollars)	Debt issued during year	City government employment, 2010	Climate[2] Average daily temperature (degrees Fahrenheit) Mean — January	July	Limits January[3]	July[4]	Annual precipitation (inches)	Heating degree days	Cooling degree days
	137	138	139	140	141	142	143	144	145	146	147
NORTH CAROLINA...	X	X	X	NA	X	X	X	X	X	X	X
Apex	13.2	418	0.0	311	NA	NA	NA	NA	NA	NA	NA
Asheboro	12.9	532	0.0	341	NA	NA	NA	NA	NA	NA	NA
Asheville	74.2	1 004	0.0	1 436	36.4	73.9	26.6	84.3	37.32	4 237	877
Burlington	36.5	736	9.3	708	38.7	79.3	27.6	90.6	45.08	3 588	1 489
Cary	263.2	2 161	86.9	1 170	39.5	78.7	30.1	87.9	46.49	3 431	1 456
Chapel Hill	56.2	1 091	8.1	823	38.5	79.4	27.8	88.6	48.04	3 650	1 491
Charlotte	3 431.9	5 110	839.8	6 893	41.7	80.3	32.1	90.1	43.51	3 162	1 681
Concord	151.1	2 337	0.0	939	39.4	79.2	27.9	90.3	47.30	3 463	1 540
Durham	392.9	1 804	102.9	2 399	39.7	78.8	29.6	89.1	43.05	3 465	1 521
Fayetteville	282.7	1 645	4.5	1 987	41.7	80.4	31.1	90.4	46.78	3 097	1 721
Garner	7.9	313	0.0	NA	NA	NA	NA	NA	NA	NA	NA
Gastonia	83.9	1 180	0.0	956	42.0	79.9	31.7	89.9	49.19	3 009	1 701
Goldsboro	49.6	1 319	5.6	483	43.4	81.2	33.0	91.4	49.84	2 771	1 922
Greensboro	445.9	1 804	104.8	3 121	39.7	78.6	29.0	88.9	42.89	3 443	1 438
Greenville	144.6	1 901	24.6	1 247	42.0	78.8	31.9	88.4	49.30	3 113	1 516
Hickory	38.9	948	0.0	674	39.0	77.7	29.2	87.8	48.98	3 608	1 333
High Point	199.2	1 984	0.1	1 447	39.7	78.2	29.6	89.0	46.19	3 399	1 424
Huntersville	15.3	359	0.0	168	NA	NA	NA	NA	NA	NA	NA
Indian Trail	0.0	0	0.0	NA	NA	NA	NA	NA	NA	NA	NA
Jacksonville	38.5	515	10.9	512	44.7	80.2	33.9	89.5	54.07	2 656	1 832
Kannapolis	44.3	1 067	5.1	285	39.4	79.2	27.9	90.3	47.30	3 463	1 540
Matthews	12.5	469	0.0	NA	NA	NA	NA	NA	NA	NA	NA
Monroe	24.9	786	0.0	523	41.5	79.0	31.0	89.7	48.73	3 125	1 538
Mooresville	84.1	3 874	7.8	442	NA	NA	NA	NA	NA	NA	NA
New Bern	42.5	1 507	0.9	498	NA	NA	NA	NA	NA	NA	NA
Raleigh	975.6	2 596	307.4	4 246	39.1	79.4	28.1	89.9	45.70	3 514	1 550
Rocky Mount	23.4	412	0.0	902	41.1	79.2	30.8	89.7	46.51	3 215	1 518
Salisbury	53.6	1 865	6.0	476	40.2	78.7	29.5	89.5	42.86	3 356	1 466
Sanford	25.7	897	3.0	352	NA	NA	NA	NA	NA	NA	NA
Thomasville	27.5	1 047	0.0	NA	NA	NA	NA	NA	NA	NA	NA
Wake Forest	20.3	803	11.5	NA	NA	NA	NA	NA	NA	NA	NA
Wilmington	194.3	1 950	0.0	979	44.8	80.1	33.3	90.0	58.44	2 606	1 791
Wilson	99.2	2 076	55.3	787	40.4	79.2	29.5	90.2	47.19	3 328	1 575
Winston-Salem	553.0	2 568	128.3	2 481	39.7	78.2	29.6	89.0	46.19	3 399	1 424
NORTH DAKOTA...	X	X	X	NA	X	X	X	X	X	X	X
Bismarck	62.7	1 054	20.7	678	10.2	70.4	-0.6	84.5	16.84	8 802	471
Fargo	463.8	5 005	33.7	826	6.8	70.6	-2.3	82.2	21.19	9 092	533
Grand Forks	238.1	4 601	22.6	435	5.3	69.4	-4.3	81.9	19.60	9 489	420
Minot	28.7	812	6.8	365	7.5	68.4	-1.8	80.4	18.65	9 479	422
West Fargo	103.5	4 484	10.0	104	NA	NA	NA	NA	NA	NA	NA
OHIO	X	X	X	NA	X	X	X	X	X	X	X
Akron	700.6	3 370	59.2	2 251	27.2	74.1	20.1	83.9	36.07	5 752	856
Barberton	14.7	550	0.0	261	29.1	73.6	20.3	85.0	39.16	5 348	813
Beavercreek	19.8	499	0.3	147	27.6	73.1	19.5	83.5	40.06	5 531	768
Bowling Green	38.1	1 274	0.5	303	23.1	72.9	15.2	84.2	33.18	6 492	690
Brunswick	12.2	351	0.5	166	25.7	71.9	18.8	81.4	38.71	6 121	702
Canton	50.2	641	23.2	940	25.2	71.8	17.4	82.3	38.47	6 154	678
Cincinnati	725.2	2 181	76.5	5 645	30.6	76.8	22.7	86.8	39.57	4 841	1 210
Cleveland	2 617.6	5 976	453.2	7 926	25.7	71.9	18.8	81.4	38.71	6 121	702
Cleveland Heights	20.5	442	0.0	467	25.7	71.9	18.8	81.4	38.71	6 121	702
Columbus	1 828.4	2 445	416.9	7 877	28.3	74.7	20.2	85.6	40.03	5 349	935
Cuyahoga Falls	63.1	1 238	0.0	523	29.1	73.6	20.3	85.0	39.16	5 348	813
Dayton	235.4	1 514	6.7	2 158	26.3	74.3	19.0	84.2	39.58	5 690	935
Delaware	47.2	1 431	8.7	215	25.1	73.0	16.6	84.6	37.58	6 178	739
Dublin	66.5	1 753	0.0	422	28.3	74.7	20.2	85.6	40.03	5 349	935
Elyria	65.3	1 186	15.2	544	27.1	73.8	19.3	85.0	38.02	5 731	818
Euclid	49.6	1 034	6.8	478	23.0	68.8	14.3	80.0	47.33	6 956	372
Fairborn	21.3	658	0.5	252	27.9	77.0	20.6	87.2	39.41	5 343	1 214
Fairfield	42.5	1 004	7.5	350	28.7	76.6	19.9	88.1	43.36	5 261	1 135
Findlay	28.9	771	0.0	349	24.5	73.6	17.4	83.5	36.91	6 194	809
Gahanna	52.5	1 557	37.4	196	28.3	75.1	20.3	85.3	38.52	5 492	951
Garfield Heights	33.9	1 209	8.0	226	25.7	71.9	18.8	81.4	38.71	6 121	702
Green	36.0	1 535	0.0	NA	NA	NA	NA	NA	NA	NA	NA
Grove City	29.1	880	25.0	164	28.3	74.7	20.2	85.6	40.03	5 349	935
Hamilton	296.8	4 765	48.2	679	28.7	76.6	19.9	88.1	43.36	5 261	1 135
Hilliard	47.3	1 718	1.9	151	NA	NA	NA	NA	NA	NA	NA
Huber Heights	60.3	1 612	9.8	166	27.9	77.0	20.6	87.2	39.41	5 343	1 214
Kent	18.8	666	0.0	215	27.2	74.1	20.1	83.9	36.07	5 752	856

1. Based on the population estimated as of July 1 of the year shown.   2. Represents normal values based on the 30-year period, 1971–2000.   3. Average daily minimum.   4. Average daily maximum.

Table D. Cities — Land Area and Population

STATE Place code	City	Land area,[1] 2010 (sq km)	Total persons	Rank	Per square kilometer	White	Black	American Indian, Alaska Native	Asian	Hawaiian Pacific Islander	Percent Hispanic or Latino,[2] 2010	Percent Foreign born, 2008–2010
		1	2	3	4	5	6	7	8	9	10	11
	OHIO—Cont'd											
39 40040	Kettering	48.4	56 163	667	1 161.1	92.9	4.1	0.7	1.9	0.1	2.1	2.2
39 41664	Lakewood	14.3	52 131	732	3 637.9	87.1	7.4	0.8	2.5	0.1	4.1	7.8
39 41720	Lancaster	48.8	38 780	1 018	794.7	96.5	1.8	0.8	0.7	0.1	1.6	1.8
39 43554	Lima	35.1	38 771	1 019	1 103.6	68.8	29.4	0.9	0.7	0.1	3.7	1.3
39 44856	Lorain	61.3	64 097	552	1 045.5	57.8	18.4	1.0	0.5	0.0	25.2	3.6
39 47138	Mansfield	80.0	47 821	822	598.1	74.8	23.9	0.9	1.0	0.1	1.9	1.8
39 47754	Marion	30.4	36 837	1 078	1 211.7	86.8	10.7	0.7	0.5	0.1	3.0	0.8
39 48188	Mason	48.3	30 712	1 320	636.5	84.0	3.6	0.3	9.9	0.2	3.2	8.7
39 48244	Massillon	48.1	32 149	1 265	668.1	88.4	10.5	0.7	0.5	0.1	2.0	0.9
39 48790	Medina	30.0	26 678	1 552	890.2	94.1	4.2	0.5	1.3	0.0	1.8	2.8
39 49056	Mentor	69.0	47 159	840	683.4	96.2	1.3	0.2	1.7	0.1	1.3	4.7
39 49840	Middletown	67.8	48 694	801	718.0	83.8	13.3	0.7	0.7	0.1	3.8	2.4
39 54040	Newark	54.1	47 573	832	879.5	94.4	4.9	0.9	0.8	0.1	1.2	1.0
39 56882	North Olmsted	30.2	32 718	1 247	1 081.9	91.6	2.4	0.4	3.2	0.1	3.5	9.0
39 56966	North Ridgeville	60.7	29 465	1 396	485.4	93.8	1.9	0.6	1.6	0.0	3.3	6.2
39 57008	North Royalton	55.2	30 444	1 335	551.6	94.4	1.4	0.3	3.2	0.0	1.6	8.1
39 61000	Parma	51.9	81 601	391	1 573.5	92.0	2.7	0.5	2.3	0.1	3.6	10.6
39 66390	Reynoldsburg	28.9	35 893	1 111	1 242.0	70.9	25.3	1.0	2.3	0.1	3.4	6.4
39 67468	Riverside	25.2	25 201	1 649	1 001.2	87.7	7.7	0.9	2.6	0.1	3.3	1.9
39 70380	Sandusky	25.2	25 793	1 609	1 023.9	72.0	25.7	1.0	0.7	0.0	4.9	1.5
39 71682	Shaker Heights	16.3	28 448	1 447	1 748.5	55.7	38.2	0.7	5.5	0.1	2.2	7.6
39 74118	Springfield	65.5	60 608	595	925.2	77.4	20.8	1.1	1.0	0.1	3.0	2.5
39 74944	Stow	44.3	34 837	1 156	787.1	93.3	3.2	0.4	2.9	0.1	1.5	5.2
39 75098	Strongsville	63.8	44 750	880	701.6	91.8	2.1	0.4	4.8	0.1	2.0	9.0
39 77000	Toledo	209.0	287 208	66	1 374.3	64.0	28.9	0.9	1.5	0.1	7.4	3.5
39 77588	Troy	30.4	25 058	1 659	825.4	91.2	5.6	0.6	2.8	0.0	1.8	3.3
39 79002	Upper Arlington	25.5	33 771	1 197	1 325.4	92.3	1.1	0.4	5.7	0.0	1.6	7.5
39 80892	Warren	41.8	41 557	946	994.9	69.5	29.9	1.0	0.6	0.0	1.9	1.7
39 83342	Westerville	32.3	36 120	1 104	1 118.3	89.1	7.2	0.6	2.9	0.0	1.9	6.2
39 83622	Westlake	41.3	32 729	1 246	793.4	90.8	1.9	0.2	5.8	0.1	2.5	12.0
39 86548	Wooster	42.2	26 119	1 589	618.3	92.0	4.9	0.7	2.2	0.1	2.2	3.8
39 86772	Xenia	34.4	25 719	1 612	747.6	83.8	15.4	1.1	0.8	0.2	1.7	1.2
39 88000	Youngstown	87.9	66 982	513	761.7	45.4	46.2	1.1	0.7	0.1	9.3	3.8
39 88084	Zanesville	30.5	25 487	1 632	836.2	87.9	13.3	1.6	0.6	0.1	1.2	1.4
40 00000	**OKLAHOMA**	177 660.0	3 751 351	X	21.1	73.3	8.4	12.2	2.2	0.2	8.9	5.4
40 04450	Bartlesville	58.9	35 750	1 120	606.9	80.7	4.2	12.4	1.8	0.1	5.9	4.2
40 09050	Broken Arrow	159.5	98 850	294	619.9	80.3	5.2	8.4	4.3	0.1	6.5	5.3
40 23200	Edmond	219.4	81 405	393	371.1	83.3	6.3	4.8	3.9	0.2	5.1	5.6
40 23950	Enid	190.8	49 379	781	258.8	80.6	4.5	3.9	1.5	2.3	10.3	6.7
40 41850	Lawton	209.9	96 867	306	461.5	58.6	23.3	6.2	3.9	0.9	12.6	6.7
40 48350	Midwest City	63.2	54 371	695	860.3	66.6	24.0	6.9	2.5	0.3	5.6	3.4
40 49200	Moore	56.5	55 081	688	974.7	79.8	5.9	7.7	3.1	0.2	8.9	4.1
40 50050	Muskogee	109.8	39 223	1 011	357.2	59.9	18.4	21.2	1.0	0.1	7.1	5.7
40 52500	Norman	463.0	110 925	240	239.6	80.6	5.5	7.6	4.7	0.2	6.4	6.5
40 55000	Oklahoma City	1 570.6	579 999	31	369.3	60.0	16.4	5.6	4.6	0.2	17.2	11.7
40 56650	Owasso	42.2	28 915	1 427	685.5	81.7	3.4	10.9	2.4	0.3	6.7	3.7
40 59850	Ponca City	47.6	25 387	1 637	533.6	80.5	4.0	12.0	1.0	0.1	7.2	3.5
40 66800	Shawnee	114.3	29 857	1 371	261.2	75.9	5.5	18.0	1.2	0.1	5.1	1.6
40 70300	Stillwater	76.5	45 688	865	597.2	81.3	5.8	6.7	6.3	0.1	4.3	7.7
40 75000	Tulsa	509.6	391 906	46	769.1	62.0	17.4	8.5	2.8	0.1	14.1	9.5
41 00000	**OREGON**	248 607.8	3 831 074	X	15.4	81.1	2.3	2.3	4.7	0.6	11.7	9.8
41 01000	Albany	45.4	50 158	765	1 104.3	85.4	1.0	2.2	2.2	0.4	11.4	7.8
41 05350	Beaverton	48.5	89 803	340	1 851.2	69.4	3.4	1.3	12.3	0.8	16.3	21.6
41 05800	Bend	85.5	76 639	431	896.5	89.3	0.8	1.4	2.0	0.3	8.2	4.8
41 15800	Corvallis	36.6	54 462	693	1 488.0	83.0	1.7	1.5	9.1	0.7	7.4	10.1
41 23850	Eugene	113.2	156 185	152	1 379.2	85.5	2.2	2.3	5.5	0.6	7.8	7.9
41 30550	Grants Pass	28.2	34 533	1 169	1 226.7	88.7	0.8	2.6	1.7	0.5	8.5	3.5
41 31250	Gresham	60.1	105 594	259	1 757.3	71.6	4.5	1.8	5.4	1.0	18.9	17.9
41 34100	Hillsboro	61.9	91 611	329	1 480.0	65.6	2.5	1.4	10.3	0.9	22.6	20.1
41 38500	Keizer	18.4	36 478	1 091	1 986.8	77.5	1.2	2.1	2.5	1.0	18.3	8.7
41 40550	Lake Oswego	27.7	36 619	1 085	1 323.9	89.3	1.1	0.9	7.2	0.4	3.7	10.6
41 45000	McMinnville	27.4	32 187	1 263	1 175.1	75.8	0.9	2.2	2.3	0.4	20.6	11.4
41 47000	Medford	66.7	74 907	453	1 123.9	82.4	1.4	2.3	2.2	0.7	13.8	6.1
41 55200	Oregon City	23.5	31 859	1 281	1 358.6	89.3	1.1	1.7	2.6	0.5	7.3	5.7
41 59000	Portland	345.6	583 776	29	1 689.3	75.5	7.4	1.9	8.7	0.8	9.4	13.5
41 61200	Redmond	43.5	26 215	1 583	602.8	85.0	0.8	2.2	1.2	0.5	12.5	5.8
41 64900	Salem	124.1	154 637	154	1 246.6	73.3	2.0	2.3	3.7	1.3	20.3	12.0
41 69600	Springfield	40.8	59 403	616	1 457.4	83.9	1.9	3.1	2.1	0.5	12.1	4.8

1. Dry land or land partially or temporarily covered by water.   2. May be of any race.

City	Age of population (percent), 2010											Population			
												Census counts		Percent change	
	Under 5 years	5 to 17 years	18 to 24 years	25 to 34 years	35 to 44 years	45 to 54 years	55 to 64 years	65 to 74 years	75 years and over	Median age	Percent female	1990	2000	1990– 2000	2000– 2010
	12	13	14	15	16	17	18	19	20	21	22	23	24	25	26
OHIO—Cont'd															
Kettering	5.8	15.2	8.4	13.7	11.9	14.6	12.5	8.3	9.7	40.9	52.3	60 569	57 502	-5.1	-2.3
Lakewood	5.8	13.8	9.5	20.1	14.1	14.3	11.4	5.5	5.5	35.4	50.9	59 718	56 646	-5.1	-8.0
Lancaster	7.5	16.6	8.6	14.3	12.7	13.2	11.4	7.7	8.0	37.5	52.0	34 507	35 335	2.4	9.7
Lima	7.5	17.3	13.3	14.6	12.3	13.1	10.5	5.8	5.6	32.9	47.2	45 553	40 081	-12.0	-3.3
Lorain	7.3	19.4	8.8	12.4	12.3	14.0	12.0	6.8	7.1	36.8	52.5	71 245	68 652	-3.6	-6.6
Mansfield	6.2	14.0	10.1	15.0	12.9	14.1	11.9	7.3	8.4	38.5	47.0	50 627	49 346	-2.5	-3.1
Marion	6.6	15.6	9.9	14.9	13.8	15.0	11.5	6.3	6.3	37.3	45.1	34 075	35 318	3.6	4.3
Mason	5.7	25.1	5.7	8.6	17.5	18.1	9.3	5.2	4.8	38.4	51.5	11 450	22 016	92.3	39.5
Massillon	6.4	16.6	8.2	12.7	12.2	14.6	12.5	8.2	8.6	40.1	51.5	30 969	31 325	1.1	2.6
Medina	7.3	21.0	7.4	12.3	15.2	14.9	10.4	5.5	6.1	36.4	51.9	19 231	25 139	30.7	6.1
Mentor	4.6	16.6	6.8	9.6	12.7	17.7	15.5	8.9	7.6	44.8	51.6	47 491	50 278	5.9	-6.2
Middletown	7.5	16.7	9.0	13.0	11.7	14.8	12.3	7.4	7.5	38.3	52.5	46 758	51 605	10.4	-5.6
Newark	7.4	16.6	9.8	13.6	12.1	14.3	11.7	7.3	7.1	37.3	52.2	44 396	46 279	4.2	2.8
North Olmsted	5.0	15.6	7.7	11.6	12.0	15.9	14.4	9.2	8.7	43.5	51.7	34 204	34 113	-0.3	-4.1
North Ridgeville	6.7	16.4	5.9	12.2	14.9	14.7	14.2	9.1	6.0	40.7	50.9	21 564	22 338	3.6	31.9
North Royalton	4.2	15.9	7.6	12.5	11.8	18.0	14.7	7.7	7.4	43.5	51.2	23 197	28 648	23.5	6.3
Parma	5.5	14.9	8.5	13.0	12.7	15.2	12.5	7.8	9.8	41.5	51.9	87 876	85 655	-2.5	-4.7
Reynoldsburg	6.7	19.6	8.0	12.8	14.0	15.3	12.1	6.4	5.2	37.3	52.6	25 748	32 069	24.5	11.9
Riverside	7.5	17.2	10.9	14.6	12.1	13.1	10.7	7.1	6.7	34.8	51.5	1 471	23 545	1 500.6	7.0
Sandusky	7.3	16.6	9.2	13.1	11.1	14.9	12.8	7.2	7.8	38.5	52.4	29 764	27 844	-6.5	-7.4
Shaker Heights	6.1	20.6	5.8	9.9	13.2	15.2	13.7	7.5	8.0	40.9	54.8	30 955	29 405	-5.0	-3.3
Springfield	7.6	16.8	11.5	12.9	11.3	12.8	11.8	7.2	8.1	36.0	52.4	70 487	65 358	-7.3	-7.3
Stow	5.5	17.2	8.1	13.3	13.5	15.8	12.8	6.8	7.0	39.7	51.8	27 998	32 139	14.8	8.4
Strongsville	4.7	18.6	6.5	9.0	12.6	17.5	15.1	8.5	7.5	44.2	51.4	35 308	43 858	24.2	2.0
Toledo	7.4	16.7	12.8	14.2	12.1	13.6	11.2	6.1	6.0	34.2	51.6	332 943	313 619	-5.8	-8.4
Troy	7.3	17.9	7.9	14.4	13.7	13.9	11.9	6.8	6.3	36.9	51.3	19 478	21 999	12.9	13.9
Upper Arlington	5.8	19.3	5.1	9.4	13.5	16.3	13.9	7.7	9.0	42.8	52.2	34 128	33 686	-1.3	0.3
Warren	7.0	16.8	9.2	13.2	11.9	14.2	11.7	7.6	8.4	38.3	51.9	50 793	46 832	-7.8	-11.3
Westerville	5.2	17.2	10.1	10.0	12.2	15.8	15.3	7.5	6.7	41.2	53.0	30 269	35 318	16.7	2.3
Westlake	4.5	17.0	5.7	10.3	12.4	16.2	14.9	8.4	10.6	45.0	52.6	27 018	31 719	17.4	3.2
Wooster	6.1	14.2	14.8	12.3	10.8	12.8	12.4	7.9	8.8	37.3	52.4	22 427	24 811	10.6	5.3
Xenia	7.0	17.8	9.2	13.6	11.9	13.5	11.4	7.6	8.1	37.1	52.8	24 836	24 164	-2.7	6.4
Youngstown	6.4	16.4	10.9	12.7	11.7	13.8	12.3	6.9	8.9	38.0	50.8	95 732	82 026	-14.3	-18.3
Zanesville	7.7	17.4	9.7	13.5	12.1	12.9	11.5	7.0	8.2	36.3	53.4	26 778	25 586	-4.5	-0.4
OKLAHOMA	7.0	17.7	10.2	13.5	12.3	14.0	11.7	7.5	6.0	36.2	50.8	3 145 576	3 450 654	9.7	8.7
Bartlesville	6.7	16.9	8.7	12.0	11.3	14.3	12.5	8.4	9.3	39.9	52.2	34 256	34 748	1.4	2.9
Broken Arrow	7.2	20.2	7.9	13.8	14.2	14.7	11.7	6.1	4.4	35.7	51.4	58 082	74 859	28.9	32.0
Edmond	6.3	18.5	12.9	12.5	12.0	14.7	11.9	6.4	4.7	34.8	51.6	52 310	68 315	30.6	19.2
Enid	8.0	16.8	9.6	14.4	11.1	13.6	11.2	7.3	7.8	36.0	51.0	45 309	47 045	3.8	5.0
Lawton	8.0	16.9	15.3	18.1	12.0	11.9	8.4	5.0	4.4	29.7	48.1	80 561	92 757	15.1	4.4
Midwest City	7.8	17.6	9.9	14.6	11.7	13.8	11.5	6.8	6.5	36.2	52.6	52 267	54 088	3.5	0.5
Moore	8.6	19.3	9.2	18.5	13.5	12.7	9.6	5.4	3.2	31.5	51.2	40 318	41 138	2.0	33.9
Muskogee	7.7	17.7	10.2	13.4	11.0	13.4	11.8	7.3	7.7	36.0	52.3	37 708	38 310	1.6	2.4
Norman	5.8	14.0	21.8	15.6	10.9	11.8	10.0	5.5	4.5	29.6	50.3	80 071	95 694	19.5	15.9
Oklahoma City	7.9	17.5	10.1	15.8	12.8	13.6	10.9	6.1	5.2	34.0	50.8	444 724	506 132	13.8	14.6
Owasso	8.0	21.6	8.9	15.0	14.9	13.7	8.5	4.8	4.5	32.7	51.7	11 151	18 502	65.9	56.3
Ponca City	7.7	17.7	8.3	13.1	10.5	13.2	12.6	8.0	8.9	38.1	51.1	26 359	25 919	-1.7	-2.1
Shawnee	7.6	16.8	13.7	13.0	10.9	12.8	10.6	7.5	7.0	33.9	52.7	26 017	28 692	10.3	4.1
Stillwater	5.0	9.8	39.0	15.7	7.8	7.9	6.7	4.1	4.1	23.9	49.4	36 676	39 065	6.5	17.0
Tulsa	7.5	17.0	10.8	15.1	12.3	13.4	11.4	6.3	6.1	34.7	51.3	367 302	393 049	7.0	-0.3
OREGON	6.2	16.4	9.4	13.7	13.0	14.1	13.3	7.6	6.4	38.4	50.5	2 842 337	3 421 399	20.4	12.0
Albany	7.1	17.8	9.7	14.4	13.0	12.8	11.9	7.0	6.2	35.6	51.2	33 523	40 852	21.9	22.8
Beaverton	6.8	16.1	9.2	18.3	14.7	13.7	10.8	5.3	5.2	34.7	51.4	53 307	76 129	42.8	18.0
Bend	6.9	16.8	8.7	15.4	14.7	13.3	11.8	6.6	5.9	36.6	51.0	23 740	52 029	119.2	47.3
Corvallis	4.3	10.6	32.4	13.8	9.0	10.0	9.3	4.8	5.7	26.4	49.7	44 757	49 322	10.2	10.4
Eugene	4.9	13.3	18.7	14.6	11.5	12.0	12.4	6.2	6.4	33.8	51.1	112 733	137 893	22.3	13.3
Grants Pass	6.8	17.5	8.5	12.4	11.3	12.9	12.1	8.2	10.4	39.3	52.7	17 503	23 003	31.4	50.1
Gresham	7.8	18.7	10.2	15.3	12.9	13.5	11.0	5.7	5.0	33.6	51.0	68 285	90 205	32.1	17.1
Hillsboro	8.4	18.4	9.3	19.5	15.7	12.0	8.8	4.3	3.5	32.0	49.8	37 598	70 186	86.7	30.5
Keizer	7.1	20.2	8.1	13.6	12.9	13.2	11.5	6.8	6.6	35.7	52.0	21 884	32 203	47.2	13.3
Lake Oswego	4.1	18.0	5.7	8.7	12.4	17.9	17.2	8.6	7.5	45.8	52.7	30 576	35 278	15.4	3.8
McMinnville	7.4	18.4	12.7	12.7	12.0	11.5	10.7	6.9	7.7	34.0	51.8	17 894	26 499	48.1	21.5
Medford	7.2	16.9	9.1	13.5	12.0	13.3	12.0	7.2	9.0	37.9	51.6	47 021	63 154	34.3	18.6
Oregon City	6.7	18.8	8.9	13.8	14.9	13.9	11.8	5.9	5.3	36.3	50.7	14 698	25 754	75.2	23.7
Portland	6.0	13.1	9.7	19.6	15.9	13.3	11.9	5.4	5.0	35.8	50.5	485 975	529 121	8.9	10.3
Redmond	8.1	19.8	8.7	15.0	13.8	11.9	9.9	6.5	6.2	33.9	51.7	7 165	13 481	88.2	94.5
Salem	7.4	17.8	10.7	14.7	13.0	13.0	11.4	6.0	5.9	34.5	50.1	107 793	136 924	27.0	12.9
Springfield	7.3	16.9	10.2	16.2	12.8	13.6	11.4	6.1	5.4	34.5	51.0	44 664	52 864	18.4	12.4

Table D. Cities — Households, Group Quarters, Crime, and Education

City	Households, 2010 Number	Persons per house-hold	Percent Female family house-holder[1]	One-person	Persons in group quarters, 2010 Total	Institutional Total	Persons in nursing facilities	Non-institu-tional	Serious crimes Total Number	Rate[3]	Rate[3] Violent	Property	Population age 25 and older	Attainment[4] (percent) High school graduate or less	Bachelor's degree or more
	27	28	29	30	31	32	33	34	35	36	37	38	39	40	41
OHIO—Cont'd															
Kettering	25 427	2.19	11.3	34.9	427	304	304	123	1 361	2 423	109	2 315	39 888	32.3	32.2
Lakewood	25 274	2.05	10.8	44.8	370	304	303	66	983	1 886	146	1 740	36 703	32.8	39.4
Lancaster	16 048	2.36	14.2	31.7	871	692	383	179	2 301	5 933	266	5 668	26 289	54.7	16.5
Lima	14 221	2.42	22.1	33.5	4 300	3 401	279	899	2 558	6 598	867	5 731	23 565	60.0	8.7
Lorain	25 529	2.48	21.0	30.8	662	444	423	218	3 514	5 482	535	4 947	40 804	57.8	12.1
Mansfield	18 696	2.21	16.6	37.1	6 594	5 881	519	713	3 105	6 493	330	6 163	33 702	58.2	12.5
Marion	12 868	2.45	17.1	30.4	5 267	5 112	363	155	2 039	5 535	247	5 288	25 066	64.4	8.8
Mason	11 016	2.77	8.4	22.4	186	76	76	110	471	1 534	23	1 511	18 867	23.8	53.9
Massillon	13 140	2.37	14.9	31.1	951	683	348	268	876	2 725	124	2 600	22 488	60.5	13.2
Medina	10 382	2.53	12.0	27.8	361	345	186	16	NA	NA	NA	NA	17 364	39.9	35.2
Mentor	19 166	2.44	9.4	25.7	403	381	381	22	1 240	2 629	85	2 545	33 751	39.7	26.5
Middletown	20 238	2.38	18.1	31.5	573	472	399	101	4 343	8 919	706	8 213	32 454	61.0	14.4
Newark	19 840	2.35	14.8	31.9	1 011	750	486	261	2 322	4 881	217	4 664	32 643	56.2	16.3
North Olmsted	13 645	2.37	9.6	30.1	323	264	264	59	422	1 290	70	1 220	23 643	33.0	30.9
North Ridgeville	11 500	2.54	8.6	21.9	225	213	213	12	252	855	88	767	21 264	42.1	22.7
North Royalton	12 944	2.33	7.9	31.0	247	226	226	21	NA	NA	NA	NA	21 949	35.2	34.3
Parma	34 489	2.34	12.4	31.8	1 063	897	792	166	517	634	92	542	58 572	49.0	19.8
Reynoldsburg	14 387	2.49	15.9	28.0	25	0	0	25	1 250	3 483	256	3 226	23 165	38.4	29.7
Riverside	10 284	2.45	15.0	28.9	0	0	0	0	771	3 059	214	2 845	17 009	52.1	14.9
Sandusky	11 082	2.28	19.7	35.1	579	305	240	274	1 423	5 517	582	4 935	17 309	60.0	11.4
Shaker Heights	11 840	2.39	15.3	31.1	156	119	44	37	630	2 215	123	2 092	19 359	14.7	64.6
Springfield	24 459	2.38	18.6	34.1	2 497	1 128	854	1 369	4 974	8 207	792	7 415	39 028	57.8	13.3
Stow	14 226	2.42	9.0	27.2	454	405	405	49	647	1 857	72	1 785	23 213	30.9	40.6
Strongsville	17 659	2.52	7.4	24.9	304	277	264	27	773	1 727	20	1 707	30 708	31.9	41.0
Toledo	119 730	2.33	19.9	34.8	8 475	2 987	1 239	5 488	11 338	3 948	994	2 954	182 616	51.0	17.1
Troy	10 353	2.38	12.9	30.5	420	263	163	157	NA	NA	NA	NA	16 720	50.6	21.8
Upper Arlington	13 754	2.44	7.3	26.9	254	254	254	0	542	1 605	65	1 540	23 414	12.5	71.0
Warren	17 003	2.30	21.3	35.6	2 517	2 302	525	215	2 586	6 223	633	5 590	26 954	63.2	11.7
Westerville	13 859	2.48	9.1	24.4	1 685	454	454	1 231	927	2 566	53	2 514	24 226	23.4	50.1
Westlake	13 870	2.30	6.9	34.2	871	830	830	41	7	21	0	21	23 861	28.2	49.1
Wooster	10 733	2.21	11.3	35.4	2 381	387	230	1 994	929	3 557	172	3 385	16 870	47.7	25.8
Xenia	10 390	2.39	16.3	31.0	925	700	312	225	1 178	4 580	171	4 409	16 693	51.1	15.8
Youngstown	26 839	2.28	24.8	37.8	5 831	3 929	644	1 902	5 124	7 650	1 036	6 614	45 772	64.1	10.3
Zanesville	10 864	2.29	19.1	36.2	582	514	290	68	1 762	6 913	330	6 584	16 952	61.2	11.8
OKLAHOMA	1 460 450	2.49	12.3	27.5	112 017	64 411	21 678	47 606	146 113	3 895	479	3 415	2 411 893	46.2	22.6
Bartlesville	14 977	2.34	11.8	30.7	658	256	145	402	1 372	3 838	408	3 429	23 829	43.6	29.7
Broken Arrow	36 141	2.72	10.3	19.2	468	466	466	2	2 180	2 205	145	2 061	61 994	29.9	31.3
Edmond	31 475	2.54	9.6	23.2	1 586	313	268	1 273	1 765	2 168	91	2 077	48 649	21.4	50.8
Enid	19 726	2.41	11.9	30.5	1 824	1 005	593	819	2 399	4 858	458	4 401	31 564	50.4	21.9
Lawton	34 901	2.48	15.8	29.4	10 143	3 772	523	6 371	6 085	6 282	858	5 424	56 477	47.1	18.9
Midwest City	22 726	2.38	17.5	31.3	285	260	235	25	3 002	5 521	487	5 034	35 939	41.5	20.0
Moore	20 446	2.68	14.1	21.1	309	179	179	130	2 203	4 000	105	3 894	34 420	42.8	22.2
Muskogee	15 704	2.41	17.3	32.7	1 353	834	430	519	2 070	5 278	956	4 321	25 364	47.2	17.5
Norman	44 661	2.33	10.1	30.7	6 757	1 124	566	5 633	3 689	3 326	124	3 201	63 285	27.3	42.8
Oklahoma City	230 233	2.47	13.9	30.5	12 144	6 609	2 521	5 535	38 567	6 649	914	5 735	369 572	41.4	26.7
Owasso	10 689	2.68	11.6	22.5	242	214	173	28	868	3 002	145	2 857	17 268	31.3	29.3
Ponca City	10 395	2.37	12.3	31.8	700	433	245	267	1 349	5 314	445	4 869	17 116	46.5	21.7
Shawnee	11 619	2.43	16.0	30.7	1 670	468	249	1 202	2 030	6 799	914	5 885	18 939	50.5	20.2
Stillwater	17 941	2.16	8.3	35.0	6 945	367	180	6 578	1 648	3 607	219	3 388	20 671	23.3	46.1
Tulsa	163 975	2.34	14.6	34.5	8 386	4 284	2 033	4 102	25 659	6 547	1 098	5 449	253 569	40.0	29.4
OREGON	1 518 938	2.47	10.5	27.4	86 642	36 612	11 491	50 030	125 083	3 265	252	3 013	2 580 193	36.0	28.8
Albany	19 705	2.50	12.4	26.7	824	560	256	264	1 373	2 737	171	2 566	32 431	40.8	22.0
Beaverton	37 213	2.39	10.6	30.9	945	460	393	485	2 012	2 240	266	1 974	60 115	24.3	42.0
Bend	31 790	2.39	9.9	27.1	578	183	157	395	2 657	3 467	322	3 145	52 360	23.8	36.3
Corvallis	22 283	2.22	7.0	33.2	4 899	116	74	4 783	1 435	2 635	105	2 530	28 159	19.3	51.7
Eugene	66 419	2.24	10.0	33.2	7 249	1 131	585	6 118	7 444	4 766	266	4 500	98 153	26.1	40.0
Grants Pass	14 313	2.34	14.5	32.8	1 051	627	355	424	1 717	4 972	211	4 761	22 989	46.1	12.8
Gresham	38 704	2.69	14.3	25.2	1 514	553	491	961	4 525	4 285	445	3 840	66 432	46.3	18.0
Hillsboro	33 289	2.71	11.0	24.0	1 528	989	220	539	2 298	2 508	188	2 321	56 320	31.8	34.1
Keizer	13 703	2.64	13.3	24.2	364	190	190	174	952	2 610	175	2 434	22 920	36.9	24.7
Lake Oswego	15 893	2.29	7.4	30.1	222	187	148	35	525	1 434	82	1 352	26 106	12.0	65.2
McMinnville	11 674	2.61	13.0	26.4	1 716	396	183	1 320	1 116	3 467	186	3 281	19 615	44.5	22.0
Medford	30 079	2.44	13.1	28.9	1 553	691	450	862	3 690	4 926	419	4 507	50 266	38.9	22.9
Oregon City	11 973	2.61	12.4	23.5	650	555	157	95	967	3 035	119	2 916	20 339	37.0	21.9
Portland	248 546	2.28	10.1	34.5	17 754	4 821	2 160	12 933	31 442	5 386	523	4 863	408 630	28.7	42.4
Redmond	9 947	2.61	13.9	24.0	300	181	181	119	1 454	5 546	340	5 207	16 060	42.1	15.5
Salem	57 290	2.55	13.0	28.8	8 635	5 610	639	3 025	6 605	4 271	321	3 950	100 151	40.9	24.4
Springfield	23 665	2.49	15.2	27.9	587	181	140	406	2 780	4 680	244	4 436	38 270	46.4	14.7

1. No spouse present. 2. Data for serious crimes have not been adjusted for underreporting. This may affect comparability between geographic areas and over time. 3. Per 100,000 population estimated by the FBI. 4. Persons 25 years old and over.

Table D. Cities — Income, Poverty, and Housing

City	Money income, 2008–2010					Housing units, 2010			Occupied Housing units 2008–2010				
	Households				Families with income below poverty (percent)				Owner-occupied			Median owner costs as a percent of income	
	Per capita income[1] (dollars)	Median income	Percent with income of $200,000 or more	Percent with income of less than $25,000		Total	Percent change, 2000–2010	Vacant units for sale or rent[2]	Total	Percent	Median value[3] (dollars)	With a mortgage[4]	Without a mortgage[5]
	42	43	44	45	46	47	48	49	50	51	52	53	54
OHIO—Cont'd													
Kettering	29 466	48 802	2.8	24.2	7.0	27 602	2.5	2 175	25 544	64.3	135 500	22.6	12.7
Lakewood	27 222	41 976	2.3	29.5	12.2	28 498	0.3	3 224	24 889	42.0	134 600	24.4	14.3
Lancaster	21 719	40 978	1.5	29.4	12.0	17 685	11.6	1 637	16 131	59.3	123 800	23.1	10.8
Lima	13 902	26 943	0.1	47.1	27.5	16 784	-5.0	2 563	14 292	51.9	73 700	24.1	14.7
Lorain	17 353	32 787	0.7	40.2	28.3	29 144	3.3	3 615	25 786	55.6	104 100	25.4	12.8
Mansfield	17 054	31 986	1.1	38.1	18.1	22 022	-1.4	3 326	18 398	55.3	83 400	23.1	14.3
Marion	15 318	31 201	0.2	41.2	23.6	15 066	2.3	2 198	13 104	60.7	79 100	22.8	14.6
Mason	35 725	78 180	11.2	12.6	4.6	11 471	41.1	455	10 928	83.8	215 900	22.9	16.4
Massillon	19 026	36 666	0.4	34.9	12.5	14 497	7.1	1 357	13 267	65.2	100 500	24.5	13.4
Medina	27 433	57 652	4.0	22.6	8.1	11 152	13.9	770	10 527	67.0	171 300	23.1	11.8
Mentor	30 141	61 754	3.1	13.8	5.3	20 218	4.8	1 052	18 555	86.9	171 300	23.2	13.9
Middletown	19 354	36 074	0.7	32.6	16.4	23 296	0.5	3 058	19 930	61.3	107 500	24.9	15.1
Newark	21 273	36 178	1.0	34.3	14.1	21 976	6.3	2 136	20 441	56.4	116 700	21.5	10.0
North Olmsted	28 378	54 389	2.8	19.1	4.1	14 500	3.1	855	13 551	80.7	157 400	26.3	15.5
North Ridgeville	29 145	64 822	0.9	12.7	2.2	12 109	41.0	609	11 634	88.9	163 300	23.6	13.2
North Royalton	31 901	61 298	4.6	14.6	3.6	13 710	16.6	766	12 423	72.8	199 200	24.0	15.8
Parma	24 512	48 774	0.6	21.7	5.4	36 608	0.5	2 119	33 516	75.6	127 600	23.4	14.8
Reynoldsburg	27 939	53 225	2.1	21.0	9.4	15 611	15.9	1 224	14 267	65.9	150 300	23.2	12.6
Riverside	20 416	39 400	0.0	27.4	14.4	11 304	8.8	1 020	10 316	56.9	98 600	23.2	14.5
Sandusky	18 053	32 135	1.1	39.7	20.4	13 386	0.4	2 304	11 033	52.5	85 900	23.6	13.9
Shaker Heights	48 569	74 471	16.7	18.7	6.1	13 318	2.5	1 478	11 375	62.3	238 100	22.4	15.9
Springfield	18 454	35 086	0.9	37.7	19.3	28 437	-2.9	3 978	24 470	54.9	84 300	22.2	12.7
Stow	30 052	61 872	2.9	13.9	5.8	15 141	17.8	915	13 551	69.0	165 800	21.6	12.9
Strongsville	32 947	70 976	4.5	16.2	4.2	18 476	9.6	817	17 031	79.8	202 300	23.5	15.0
Toledo	18 045	32 251	0.7	39.3	20.6	138 039	-1.3	18 309	119 282	57.0	93 800	24.3	14.6
Troy	22 821	49 606	0.6	25.1	8.8	11 166	17.1	813	10 168	62.0	129 400	20.7	12.1
Upper Arlington	51 080	92 528	15.5	9.5	2.2	14 544	0.8	790	13 347	81.8	310 700	22.0	14.0
Warren	16 089	28 764	0.6	44.2	27.2	20 384	-4.5	3 381	16 361	55.4	72 300	23.9	15.5
Westerville	36 740	80 932	7.7	12.0	3.5	14 467	10.1	608	13 420	77.0	211 800	20.1	10.8
Westlake	41 289	69 286	8.3	12.2	3.1	14 843	8.4	973	13 432	73.5	231 200	23.9	12.2
Wooster	24 999	38 628	2.4	30.5	14.1	11 822	10.0	1 089	10 982	63.6	126 500	23.4	13.1
Xenia	19 196	38 032	0.0	31.4	18.2	11 424	15.4	1 034	10 469	62.9	98 900	22.5	12.0
Youngstown	14 659	24 354	0.3	50.9	27.7	33 123	-10.9	6 284	28 395	61.0	50 200	24.9	16.1
Zanesville	17 317	27 913	0.9	45.8	22.5	12 385	5.4	1 521	10 784	45.4	82 000	24.7	13.9
OKLAHOMA	22 898	42 829	2.2	28.5	12.0	1 664 378	9.9	203 928	1 429 873	67.7	108 500	21.3	10.8
Bartlesville	25 904	44 647	2.7	27.8	12.1	16 768	4.1	1 791	15 419	66.8	107 500	20.3	11.6
Broken Arrow	29 127	64 460	3.7	12.3	3.7	38 013	40.2	1 872	35 088	81.6	147 300	21.5	10.0
Edmond	36 008	67 376	8.6	17.7	4.7	33 178	25.8	1 703	29 745	69.3	190 900	21.1	10.0
Enid	22 209	36 894	1.9	30.2	14.8	21 936	3.2	2 210	19 510	62.5	87 000	20.7	11.2
Lawton	19 938	42 112	1.4	28.7	14.6	39 409	8.2	4 508	34 089	50.1	104 200	20.9	10.0
Midwest City	22 825	42 217	1.0	27.4	12.0	24 723	3.9	1 997	22 407	62.2	96 700	21.7	10.0
Moore	23 888	54 481	1.2	17.4	7.9	21 444	34.8	998	19 642	73.7	114 500	22.1	11.3
Muskogee	18 463	32 890	1.0	35.1	21.6	18 055	2.8	2 351	15 810	58.3	81 700	22.7	11.1
Norman	26 485	44 634	3.1	28.2	9.6	47 965	15.5	3 304	42 147	57.2	148 400	20.8	10.3
Oklahoma City	24 625	43 744	2.6	27.4	13.4	256 930	12.6	26 697	225 639	60.8	128 300	22.4	11.2
Owasso	27 004	65 131	2.5	12.7	5.4	11 346	64.9	657	9 989	73.8	151 400	21.6	10.0
Ponca City	21 888	38 345	2.0	33.4	11.4	11 950	0.5	1 555	10 244	68.1	82 000	18.8	11.9
Shawnee	19 047	35 711	0.9	36.4	15.9	13 205	4.0	1 586	11 285	60.5	88 100	20.3	11.2
Stillwater	18 789	29 734	1.6	45.1	11.6	19 753	17.5	1 812	18 107	36.7	151 100	22.1	11.0
Tulsa	25 608	39 021	3.5	31.1	14.5	185 127	3.1	21 152	164 906	54.0	122 200	22.6	11.9
OREGON	25 679	48 446	2.9	24.8	10.1	1 675 562	15.3	156 624	1 506 878	63.0	257 700	27.1	12.8
Albany	21 991	44 902	0.9	24.9	13.0	20 979	20.6	1 274	19 822	59.1	183 700	26.4	12.3
Beaverton	29 680	54 026	3.5	19.0	8.3	39 500	21.5	2 287	36 689	49.0	301 700	24.8	13.4
Bend	28 557	50 855	3.5	21.6	8.6	36 110	60.5	4 320	31 880	59.3	298 700	28.7	12.6
Corvallis	22 277	35 437	3.4	38.0	11.3	23 423	12.1	1 140	21 297	43.5	256 900	24.8	11.1
Eugene	24 645	40 713	2.7	33.2	10.5	69 951	14.1	3 532	65 436	50.7	251 000	26.3	13.5
Grants Pass	19 755	33 290	0.9	36.1	15.8	15 561	57.8	1 248	14 675	52.6	217 600	29.1	13.0
Gresham	20 941	46 487	1.1	25.5	13.2	41 015	16.2	2 311	37 989	52.9	245 400	27.3	13.9
Hillsboro	26 636	63 147	2.3	14.3	6.3	35 487	30.5	2 198	31 582	57.0	265 200	25.9	11.9
Keizer	24 645	53 042	2.5	19.0	12.1	14 445	13.1	742	13 550	60.3	225 300	26.3	10.7
Lake Oswego	47 849	77 858	12.7	11.6	4.9	16 995	8.5	1 102	15 647	69.6	533 900	26.7	11.5
McMinnville	21 145	40 774	1.7	28.6	11.3	12 389	26.0	715	11 327	59.5	220 400	25.9	14.8
Medford	23 117	40 419	1.9	30.2	14.8	32 430	23.3	2 351	31 015	51.6	241 200	29.5	13.7
Oregon City	24 322	51 499	1.0	23.2	12.2	12 900	26.9	927	12 286	63.2	289 200	28.2	14.1
Portland	29 634	49 326	4.2	25.8	11.6	265 439	11.9	16 893	245 567	54.5	297 700	27.3	14.5
Redmond	19 233	40 846	0.9	29.3	13.3	10 965	92.8	1 018	9 863	57.7	213 600	32.6	13.9
Salem	22 542	43 534	1.9	26.9	12.7	61 276	14.0	3 986	57 198	57.6	202 800	26.4	13.7
Springfield	18 867	35 104	0.9	33.3	15.0	24 809	15.0	1 144	23 616	52.3	181 000	27.6	13.9

1. Based on population estimated by the American Community Survey.   2. Includes units rented or sold but not occupied.   3. Specified owner-occupied units; $1,000,000 represents $1,000,000 or more.   4. 50.0 represents 50 percent or more.   5. 10.0 represents 10 percent or less.

Table D. Cities — Housing, Labor Force, and Employment

City	Occupied housing units, 2008–2010 (cont.)				Migration, 2008–2010		Civilian labor force, 2010				Civilian employment[4], 2008–2010			
									Unemployment			Percent		
	Percent renter occupied	Median gross rent[1]	Median rent as a percent of income[2]	Percent with no vehicle available	Percent who lived in the same house one year ago	Percent who lived outside this city one year ago	Total	Percent change, 2009–2010	Total	Rate[3]	Population age 16 and older	In labor force	Full-year full-time worker	Households with no workers (percent)
	55	56	57	58	59	60	61	62	63	64	65	66	67	68
OHIO—Cont'd														
Kettering	35.7	706	28.6	5.4	84.4	10.6	28 862	1.2	2 843	9.9	45 747	66.9	42.5	28.1
Lakewood	58.0	679	28.4	13.5	78.7	13.6	31 675	2.5	2 372	7.5	43 446	75.8	47.2	24.7
Lancaster	40.7	686	29.9	7.8	78.8	10.4	18 884	-0.5	1 813	9.6	30 529	62.9	39.1	31.0
Lima	48.1	586	37.3	16.9	79.2	8.9	16 824	-1.2	2 051	12.2	29 862	56.5	27.8	38.7
Lorain	44.4	593	36.4	13.6	79.6	7.3	30 487	-8.7	3 434	11.3	48 382	60.1	33.0	37.1
Mansfield	44.7	575	29.3	13.4	79.6	10.6	21 596	-6.6	2 574	11.9	39 126	53.3	30.9	34.7
Marion	39.3	626	35.9	9.8	77.5	12.0	16 523	-2.1	1 797	10.9	29 790	53.1	31.8	34.6
Mason	16.2	1 011	31.9	2.0	90.0	6.0	16 089	2.3	1 209	7.5	22 041	74.6	48.8	15.4
Massillon	34.8	584	30.5	8.3	82.7	9.3	15 701	-3.3	1 783	11.4	26 168	59.6	33.7	35.6
Medina	33.0	730	30.3	8.7	84.4	10.8	14 397	3.1	1 085	7.5	19 867	69.4	46.1	22.4
Mentor	13.1	876	32.6	4.0	91.4	6.2	27 942	-8.0	2 086	7.5	38 527	68.9	44.6	22.8
Middletown	38.7	677	33.3	12.0	81.7	8.0	24 266	-7.0	2 613	10.8	38 354	59.9	36.7	36.5
Newark	43.6	614	29.8	13.1	81.6	9.4	22 897	-4.4	2 321	10.1	37 651	62.0	38.5	35.5
North Olmsted	19.3	722	30.9	4.1	92.7	5.2	18 540	4.5	1 434	7.7	26 975	67.9	40.2	27.8
North Ridgeville	11.1	705	33.3	2.4	92.6	5.9	17 632	4.6	1 306	7.4	23 506	68.8	46.6	21.6
North Royalton	27.2	756	21.5	5.4	92.7	5.7	18 006	3.4	1 328	7.4	25 038	67.6	44.9	23.8
Parma	24.4	712	28.6	5.5	88.4	7.7	43 142	4.2	3 878	9.0	67 519	66.7	39.8	28.3
Reynoldsburg	34.1	774	30.9	5.4	80.1	13.4	19 222	0.4	1 639	8.5	26 967	70.0	48.1	26.3
Riverside	43.1	691	24.8	7.9	84.5	11.2	11 855	-3.9	1 322	11.2	19 707	64.4	37.5	33.0
Sandusky	47.5	581	31.8	13.7	82.6	5.5	13 994	-2.1	1 547	11.1	20 353	60.9	30.9	35.5
Shaker Heights	37.7	892	30.3	8.2	86.2	10.5	15 257	7.7	1 006	6.6	22 254	65.5	43.1	24.5
Springfield	45.1	617	31.7	13.7	79.4	7.8	28 095	-4.2	3 044	10.8	48 275	59.7	35.1	35.1
Stow	31.0	818	25.5	3.2	89.8	7.2	19 708	-0.5	1 651	8.4	27 666	70.5	46.8	21.5
Strongsville	20.2	731	28.4	4.3	92.2	6.5	25 400	4.8	1 750	6.9	35 026	68.0	43.7	24.1
Toledo	43.0	607	33.7	13.7	80.9	5.7	134 625	-4.7	16 335	12.1	226 425	64.3	33.7	35.0
Troy	38.0	663	25.4	8.0	83.8	8.2	13 091	NA	1 353	10.3	19 018	67.4	44.4	25.6
Upper Arlington	18.2	944	28.1	4.8	91.6	5.3	16 670	0.9	1 097	6.6	26 440	64.5	43.4	24.2
Warren	44.6	592	31.7	12.0	84.2	6.8	18 139	-8.0	2 286	12.6	31 799	50.6	28.4	41.2
Westerville	23.0	838	28.2	3.6	88.5	7.4	19 231	-4.9	1 471	7.6	28 232	70.2	47.4	19.8
Westlake	26.5	959	24.6	5.6	89.9	7.2	17 378	7.5	1 241	7.1	26 709	62.6	41.3	25.1
Wooster	36.4	603	27.4	9.0	78.2	9.9	13 374	-2.3	1 178	8.8	21 195	63.1	39.8	29.2
Xenia	37.1	626	38.4	9.5	84.8	8.1	12 147	-7.6	1 454	12.0	19 939	62.1	40.5	30.3
Youngstown	39.0	539	37.8	18.0	83.4	8.0	26 332	-9.8	3 569	13.6	55 020	52.4	24.3	45.5
Zanesville	54.6	554	29.9	17.8	79.9	8.4	10 221	-1.6	1 357	13.3	19 825	57.2	33.0	40.5
OKLAHOMA	32.3	640	28.3	5.7	81.5	10.7	1 771 234	1.1	122 412	6.9	2 897 306	63.1	42.5	27.2
Bartlesville	33.2	590	26.0	7.0	81.1	7.0	19 481	-1.9	1 044	5.4	28 237	62.6	44.8	30.4
Broken Arrow	18.4	870	27.0	2.1	85.2	9.9	49 572	3.0	2 785	5.6	73 583	73.9	52.2	14.5
Edmond	30.7	849	29.8	2.9	79.1	12.4	39 588	-1.3	1 813	4.6	62 601	68.2	46.1	19.5
Enid	37.5	596	25.3	5.4	81.7	6.4	26 141	2.9	1 268	4.9	38 061	65.3	45.0	27.3
Lawton	49.9	670	27.7	6.7	66.4	16.7	35 936	-1.2	2 315	6.4	73 421	66.5	43.2	22.5
Midwest City	37.8	679	29.1	4.2	79.8	13.2	23 597	-6.5	1 770	7.5	41 575	65.7	46.4	26.5
Moore	26.3	818	26.6	2.0	81.2	11.6	25 981	0.6	1 526	5.9	40 443	73.0	50.8	18.4
Muskogee	41.7	582	31.1	11.1	86.7	7.0	17 100	-0.7	1 270	7.4	30 234	57.9	38.1	31.9
Norman	42.8	707	31.5	5.1	72.6	12.9	54 725	0.0	2 805	5.1	90 133	66.1	40.1	21.1
Oklahoma City	39.2	675	29.6	6.7	79.0	8.5	262 217	1.6	16 668	6.4	442 612	68.4	45.6	23.8
Owasso	26.2	776	22.9	3.1	80.3	13.0	12 449	-6.0	750	6.0	20 420	0.0	53.7	14.2
Ponca City	31.9	592	28.9	6.5	80.8	8.0	12 474	-1.8	1 038	8.3	20 008	62.3	42.0	31.6
Shawnee	39.5	600	27.7	8.6	81.0	11.1	14 513	-2.1	905	6.2	23 332	61.2	38.0	29.3
Stillwater	63.3	609	36.3	6.6	59.9	18.2	22 010	-2.6	1 101	5.0	39 386	63.4	28.2	25.9
Tulsa	46.0	683	29.7	8.6	78.7	7.8	187 728	-1.3	13 794	7.3	306 505	65.8	43.3	26.4
OREGON	37.0	811	31.3	7.7	82.1	11.3	1 983 572	0.2	211 356	10.7	3 040 756	64.5	37.2	28.8
Albany	40.9	748	29.2	7.2	83.2	10.2	25 345	4.2	2 998	11.8	38 913	62.1	39.1	29.7
Beaverton	51.0	884	29.5	9.4	78.7	14.2	50 394	-1.7	4 334	8.6	70 846	72.0	44.5	22.2
Bend	40.7	877	29.3	5.4	83.7	7.4	40 739	-0.9	5 293	13.0	59 728	68.3	40.7	27.6
Corvallis	56.5	727	42.5	11.7	69.3	17.1	27 627	4.2	1 939	7.0	46 426	59.5	27.2	30.1
Eugene	49.3	786	36.2	11.4	72.8	11.9	82 951	2.9	7 857	9.5	129 597	62.1	31.3	31.0
Grants Pass	47.4	713	34.8	10.0	84.7	6.9	14 714	1.6	1 860	12.6	27 100	59.4	32.8	39.9
Gresham	47.1	816	33.5	9.9	80.9	12.0	54 917	4.7	5 731	10.4	80 874	67.3	38.4	26.7
Hillsboro	43.0	971	27.7	5.3	79.4	12.0	49 702	-1.5	4 334	8.7	68 360	73.4	45.7	16.5
Keizer	39.7	809	28.0	6.5	81.9	11.4	19 682	3.2	2 014	10.2	27 581	67.3	40.2	25.0
Lake Oswego	30.4	1 111	27.4	4.8	86.1	9.1	19 603	0.2	1 447	7.4	29 225	66.4	42.1	24.0
McMinnville	40.5	773	32.5	8.4	76.9	10.7	14 854	3.4	1 585	10.7	24 385	63.4	34.1	31.6
Medford	48.4	796	35.7	9.7	78.4	11.1	37 473	1.9	4 468	11.9	59 045	61.1	34.8	35.7
Oregon City	36.8	907	38.2	9.5	78.2	13.5	16 997	2.2	1 855	10.9	24 799	67.3	39.2	25.5
Portland	45.5	835	31.6	14.9	79.6	8.5	321 787	4.7	31 057	9.7	477 021	70.3	40.7	24.8
Redmond	42.3	808	34.0	5.2	80.8	11.5	12 897	NA	1 507	11.7	19 803	67.6	39.4	33.4
Salem	42.4	714	32.5	9.6	80.1	9.8	77 568	2.0	8 162	10.5	120 352	61.9	37.0	27.2
Springfield	47.7	733	32.8	9.7	75.3	14.2	30 601	1.3	3 802	12.4	47 045	66.0	34.9	28.1

1. $2,000 represents $2,000 or more.   2. 50.0 represents 50 percent or more.   3. Percent of civilian labor force.   4. Persons 16 years old and over.

Table D. Cities — Construction, Wholesale Trade, and Retail Trade

City	Value of residential construction authorized by building permits, 2010			Wholesale trade,[1] 2007				Retail trade,[2] 2007			
	New construction ($1,000)	Number of housing units	Percent single family	Number of establishments	Number of employees	Sales (mil dol)	Annual payroll (mil dol)	Number of establishments	Number of employees	Sales (mil dol)	Annual payroll (mil dol)
	69	70	71	72	73	74	75	76	77	78	79
OHIO—Cont'd											
Kettering	4 058	26	100.0	32	255	116.5	11.7	170	3 629	1 550.1	81.4
Lakewood	0	0	0.0	32	D	D	D	124	1 273	238.5	25.4
Lancaster	4 178	28	71.4	32	231	81.9	7.5	238	3 172	576.4	59.3
Lima	741	8	50.0	48	725	401.2	29.5	129	1 423	289.0	29.6
Lorain	3 905	42	100.0	35	488	233.7	21.3	123	1 662	319.1	30.5
Mansfield	451	3	100.0	74	1 215	630.1	48.7	196	2 510	531.3	56.9
Marion	1 749	9	55.6	24	401	277.3	14.9	86	893	206.5	20.0
Mason	13 265	46	100.0	45	1 409	634.4	80.6	84	1 168	226.1	23.7
Massillon	8 346	89	39.3	33	474	318.4	20.7	124	2 536	574.1	54.8
Medina	0	0	0.0	46	550	349.8	23.3	115	1 894	334.8	32.4
Mentor	9 099	43	100.0	116	1 431	631.3	65.7	325	6 577	1 478.8	139.4
Middletown	1 162	10	100.0	40	838	482.0	40.0	173	3 252	852.3	70.6
Newark	41 123	289	100.0	42	569	495.1	22.6	162	2 071	496.3	43.0
North Olmsted	144	2	100.0	22	129	144.8	8.6	283	5 132	1 130.5	102.4
North Ridgeville	29 786	245	99.2	33	182	79.2	7.8	64	885	195.1	20.3
North Royalton	10 216	44	100.0	58	408	247.5	18.2	69	715	147.9	14.9
Parma	699	5	100.0	61	735	199.2	34.6	301	4 662	963.1	86.1
Reynoldsburg	462	2	100.0	17	67	43.8	2.8	113	1 938	416.2	41.2
Riverside	NA	NA	NA	12	115	49.5	3.7	57	506	130.4	10.9
Sandusky	1 139	4	100.0	28	272	105.5	11.6	121	1 424	283.4	27.8
Shaker Heights	0	0	0.0	9	17	6.7	1.0	62	698	134.7	13.9
Springfield	1 234	13	69.2	51	1 482	1 706.1	55.5	242	4 072	914.8	84.6
Stow	2 074	11	100.0	40	801	625.0	47.5	106	2 302	481.4	43.7
Strongsville	14 748	54	100.0	72	1 741	950.5	88.4	246	4 691	831.5	87.7
Toledo	8 597	81	48.1	302	4 740	2 924.2	206.8	1 065	14 799	2 831.8	292.7
Troy	NA	NA	NA	17	D	D	D	104	1 786	413.7	38.1
Upper Arlington	3 802	6	100.0	18	47	13.6	1.9	90	1 040	159.9	19.0
Warren	124	2	100.0	41	551	1 168.1	21.1	168	2 240	589.2	50.1
Westerville	16 295	69	100.0	49	860	379.7	40.6	134	2 286	442.6	49.7
Westlake	4 936	13	100.0	105	1 567	915.2	87.2	159	2 544	481.6	48.9
Wooster	3 354	18	77.8	35	530	579.1	20.0	182	2 890	608.7	59.4
Xenia	NA	NA	NA	13	D	D	D	83	1 398	307.1	32.4
Youngstown	50	1	100.0	104	2 226	872.0	81.8	230	2 075	365.4	41.3
Zanesville	70	1	100.0	27	D	D	D	232	3 437	726.1	62.4
OKLAHOMA	1 225 761	8 140	84.3	3 917	52 262	48 074.7	2 312.2	13 554	170 984	43 095.4	3 610.4
Bartlesville	10 659	58	100.0	22	D	D	D	172	2 369	588.9	50.8
Broken Arrow	64 464	366	100.0	126	1 625	713.9	82.7	237	4 185	1 164.6	96.9
Edmond	79 801	296	99.3	88	D	D	D	341	4 480	999.1	91.8
Enid	15 756	70	100.0	62	637	763.9	28.7	242	3 211	716.7	66.5
Lawton	35 844	213	91.5	46	366	117.2	9.5	375	5 143	1 152.2	103.1
Midwest City	24 182	157	100.0	16	413	94.7	10.9	174	3 585	1 011.5	87.5
Moore	52 459	345	88.4	40	524	159.8	18.4	122	2 117	440.7	43.1
Muskogee	8 436	56	100.0	53	864	498.9	46.3	232	3 029	763.8	63.2
Norman	78 338	782	43.0	58	957	442.9	39.5	437	6 907	1 768.0	147.1
Oklahoma City	201 989	1 408	93.2	1 008	D	D	D	2 223	32 456	8 430.8	751.0
Owasso	35 119	452	49.6	15	111	28.8	3.7	102	2 258	490.6	43.7
Ponca City	300	3	100.0	26	127	45.7	4.7	141	1 812	391.5	35.6
Shawnee	10 298	83	92.8	23	205	70.8	6.8	199	2 598	631.8	52.3
Stillwater	18 553	106	96.2	22	291	387.0	14.0	213	3 137	632.9	59.8
Tulsa	89 121	446	75.1	806	13 655	8 307.1	712.7	1 800	28 095	7 081.7	626.9
OREGON	1 377 070	6 868	76.6	4 806	67 040	51 910.8	3 215.5	14 991	204 793	50 370.9	4 916.3
Albany	18 578	104	90.4	40	377	225.6	13.2	188	2 997	770.9	70.3
Beaverton	25 402	175	46.9	215	2 525	2 952.0	172.3	425	7 793	2 594.3	215.3
Bend	43 910	210	97.1	145	1 590	1 001.4	73.7	572	7 977	2 087.9	201.0
Corvallis	11 061	55	67.3	26	416	323.4	16.2	224	3 185	633.6	67.1
Eugene	44 011	238	70.6	278	3 362	1 569.6	154.5	780	12 435	2 582.5	279.3
Grants Pass	8 378	50	76.0	31	328	270.9	9.7	264	3 713	862.5	93.2
Gresham	20 904	125	60.8	60	1 182	1 428.5	55.3	290	4 468	1 256.9	111.0
Hillsboro	42 376	232	60.8	102	2 073	1 072.3	130.8	330	6 609	1 902.9	152.0
Keizer	8 110	48	70.8	15	63	34.3	1.5	75	1 053	198.4	21.7
Lake Oswego	16 744	49	91.8	84	1 115	764.0	66.5	161	1 540	322.4	35.5
McMinnville	8 124	44	84.1	24	305	160.7	14.0	125	1 928	518.7	46.9
Medford	28 001	182	56.0	122	1 478	711.7	58.3	547	7 889	2 045.7	189.1
Oregon City	21 066	114	95.6	17	296	109.5	12.3	117	1 799	395.8	39.3
Portland	182 321	1 100	39.5	1 176	21 291	20 566.4	1 053.0	2 562	33 811	8 174.1	888.5
Redmond	9 959	58	89.7	43	268	131.7	10.4	143	1 587	438.0	45.0
Salem	46 875	232	90.9	165	1 753	2 260.8	75.0	642	10 742	2 617.1	262.9
Springfield	21 958	124	87.1	52	1 101	499.1	47.0	227	3 650	755.6	75.1

1. Merchant wholesalers except manufacturers' sales branches and offices. 2. Establishments with payroll.

City	Real estate and rental and leasing, 2007				Professional, scientific, and technical services,[1] 2007				Manufacturing, 2007			
	Number of establish-ments	Number of employees	Receipts (mil dol)	Annual payroll (mil dol)	Number of establish-ments	Number of employees	Receipts (mil dol)	Annual payroll (mil dol)	Number of establish-ments	Number of employees	Receipts (mil dol)	Annual payroll (mil dol)
	80	81	82	83	84	85	86	87	88	89	90	91
OHIO—Cont'd												
Kettering	57	339	62.2	9.9	132	D	D	D	47	2 164	530.9	100.9
Lakewood	56	189	32.5	4.6	116	424	45.8	18.8	35	535	106.1	24.5
Lancaster	58	206	23.4	4.2	77	D	D	D	58	2 919	669.0	131.1
Lima	41	244	23.0	6.6	83	D	D	D	38	2 845	7 330.7	D
Lorain	48	166	19.2	4.1	76	D	D	D	52	2 517	1 744.2	165.6
Mansfield	59	306	24.0	6.3	123	704	65.6	27.0	118	6 538	2 130.7	281.7
Marion	37	132	18.5	3.7	45	D	D	D	35	2 030	1 159.2	86.5
Mason	32	132	18.2	3.8	110	1 112	106.8	107.4	40	4 128	1 148.1	182.7
Massillon	28	126	15.1	2.7	52	301	20.7	10.7	65	3 810	1 199.6	155.3
Medina	34	107	18.7	2.7	110	504	55.5	20.6	60	3 216	1 031.3	138.9
Mentor	68	576	95.1	15.5	173	868	103.9	33.8	232	7 497	1 944.1	326.7
Middletown	60	233	36.5	6.6	74	538	54.6	23.8	58	3 834	4 793.1	239.5
Newark	42	239	22.2	5.4	86	D	D	D	45	3 198	927.0	128.5
North Olmsted	36	160	42.3	5.1	83	366	30.6	11.6	NA	NA	NA	NA
North Ridgeville	16	52	6.9	0.8	44	224	24.5	12.0	41	1 325	253.5	49.2
North Royalton	23	D	D	D	86	287	27.3	11.0	77	862	131.5	36.4
Parma	67	364	50.1	9.7	116	D	D	D	51	2 492	890.4	184.3
Reynoldsburg	39	131	14.7	2.4	80	444	42.0	14.3	NA	NA	NA	NA
Riverside	26	101	22.7	2.7	42	D	D	D	NA	NA	NA	NA
Sandusky	33	132	19.6	3.9	54	D	D	D	47	1 805	473.5	86.6
Shaker Heights	38	122	20.0	3.8	101	438	83.2	30.3	NA	NA	NA	NA
Springfield	62	313	38.1	7.2	103	D	D	D	94	3 997	967.5	164.5
Stow	35	165	23.0	3.7	95	593	60.0	25.1	52	1 695	320.0	87.2
Strongsville	50	231	51.8	5.1	127	495	62.6	19.7	75	2 988	659.1	132.5
Toledo	276	2 022	745.1	76.3	510	D	D	D	365	15 647	10 634.8	908.7
Troy	33	157	29.4	4.1	60	326	33.7	14.5	64	4 033	1 431.6	187.6
Upper Arlington	53	196	37.4	6.4	136	D	D	D	NA	NA	NA	NA
Warren	33	150	18.5	3.4	107	449	38.1	13.2	55	7 339	1 882.4	445.7
Westerville	66	362	39.1	10.7	216	D	D	D	38	1 384	297.4	48.7
Westlake	67	925	124.1	26.7	221	1 618	154.4	102.5	52	1 764	426.8	73.0
Wooster	43	131	15.6	3.4	75	461	49.1	16.0	35	3 887	1 245.0	177.8
Xenia	27	95	9.6	1.7	38	175	12.8	3.5	34	699	133.5	D
Youngstown	60	283	30.7	6.5	106	D	D	D	115	3 210	1 147.8	143.6
Zanesville	41	205	29.1	5.1	67	D	D	D	39	1 582	537.6	76.1
OKLAHOMA	4 003	24 887	3 852.3	806.2	9 128	D	D	D	3 964	142 351	60 681.4	5 971.2
Bartlesville	45	213	28.3	5.1	80	D	D	D	37	978	293.6	42.8
Broken Arrow	95	D	D	D	237	1 159	132.2	52.9	132	4 754	1 504.2	223.6
Edmond	158	2 132	237.5	58.2	378	D	D	D	NA	NA	NA	NA
Enid	68	324	39.0	8.1	119	544	56.0	19.6	56	2 120	D	64.3
Lawton	128	D	D	D	146	D	D	D	42	3 395	D	D
Midwest City	72	290	47.8	6.3	87	D	D	D	NA	NA	NA	NA
Moore	35	136	29.8	4.5	49	346	26.5	12.4	NA	NA	NA	NA
Muskogee	56	533	43.5	10.1	88	D	D	D	50	2 857	972.6	129.2
Norman	197	884	162.6	27.7	426	D	D	D	80	2 255	931.0	95.5
Oklahoma City	879	5 974	996.7	238.7	2 253	D	D	D	702	23 758	7 711.8	954.0
Owasso	39	109	22.8	2.9	61	214	21.1	7.6	23	786	191.9	29.0
Ponca City	31	D	D	D	68	381	35.8	13.9	37	2 093	D	66.8
Shawnee	36	168	19.1	3.6	83	D	D	D	41	2 624	864.3	113.1
Stillwater	56	193	27.5	4.0	114	D	D	D	36	1 900	984.6	71.3
Tulsa	744	5 083	871.9	170.6	1 958	14 698	2 170.9	811.8	725	24 382	8 815.2	1 108.2
OREGON	6 391	30 978	5 077.2	950.3	11 363	83 190	9 750.4	4 869.5	5 717	183 953	66 880.7	8 138.9
Albany	65	254	32.3	5.7	101	D	D	D	69	2 289	714.5	100.4
Beaverton	249	1 173	221.0	40.5	446	D	D	D	123	6 822	1 855.8	406.1
Bend	284	872	138.6	25.9	445	D	D	D	171	3 198	529.7	122.9
Corvallis	98	495	53.6	10.0	210	D	D	D	54	3 506	408.6	178.5
Eugene	323	1 547	257.1	39.1	714	D	D	D	305	9 542	2 276.1	400.3
Grants Pass	78	355	39.3	8.3	95	D	D	D	79	2 170	340.1	70.3
Gresham	136	476	62.7	11.2	128	425	33.7	13.8	71	6 000	1 939.5	319.4
Hillsboro	103	656	172.4	21.4	214	D	D	D	164	8 924	9 152.2	500.0
Keizer	46	147	19.1	2.9	55	188	20.2	5.9	NA	NA	NA	NA
Lake Oswego	151	612	210.2	40.1	314	D	D	D	43	993	D	52.4
McMinnville	39	122	17.4	3.1	85	D	D	D	54	2 304	868.8	93.6
Medford	183	947	135.6	24.9	255	D	D	D	101	1 756	375.9	63.7
Oregon City	46	129	27.0	3.4	104	D	D	D	44	923	243.5	41.2
Portland	1 307	9 115	1 676.4	350.8	3 116	D	D	D	1 035	30 694	8 434.6	1 315.5
Redmond	59	267	34.2	7.0	39	201	18.5	6.2	63	1 228	217.6	44.3
Salem	303	1 658	240.3	48.2	520	D	D	D	188	5 541	1 294.1	191.4
Springfield	79	342	57.6	8.2	86	510	39.6	15.6	86	2 164	1 029.2	94.6

1. Establishments subject to federal tax.

City	Accommodation and food services, 2007				Arts, entertainment, and recreation,[1] 2007				Health care and social assistance,[1] 2007			
	Number of establishments	Number of employees	Sales (mil dol)	Annual payroll (mil dol)	Number of establishments	Number of employees	Receipts (mil dol)	Annual payroll (mil dol)	Number of establishments	Number of employees	Receipts (mil dol)	Annual payroll (mil dol)
	92	93	94	95	96	97	98	99	100	101	102	103
OHIO—Cont'd												
Kettering	109	2 389	88.9	26.9	12	D	D	D	181	D	D	D
Lakewood	114	1 420	61.1	16.6	13	85	5.0	1.3	117	1 145	87.1	38.2
Lancaster	110	2 550	90.9	26.2	8	D	D	D	148	D	D	D
Lima	78	1 161	47.1	12.4	5	D	D	D	170	D	D	D
Lorain	84	1 044	40.4	10.2	14	122	7.5	1.8	105	1 493	149.1	68.4
Mansfield	132	2 036	73.8	21.6	11	D	D	D	211	D	D	D
Marion	50	830	30.6	8.8	5	D	D	D	107	D	D	D
Mason	66	2 038	87.6	25.3	18	330	24.9	7.8	90	1 251	97.1	42.4
Massillon	84	1 330	51.7	13.7	3	9	0.2	0.1	55	1 636	81.3	34.5
Medina	66	1 245	43.8	12.4	6	D	D	D	103	1 396	106.7	48.5
Mentor	168	3 812	157.8	43.4	13	D	D	D	138	D	D	D
Middletown	107	2 584	97.0	29.0	8	103	2.8	1.0	116	D	D	D
Newark	107	2 198	84.2	23.1	12	D	D	D	115	2 879	189.7	102.0
North Olmsted	124	2 467	103.5	28.7	8	84	2.8	0.9	74	1 055	73.8	28.6
North Ridgeville	40	548	20.6	5.1	8	74	3.2	1.0	31	D	D	D
North Royalton	41	475	18.3	4.8	1	D	D	D	57	D	D	D
Parma	190	2 915	103.2	29.3	14	D	D	D	194	2 895	266.8	119.2
Reynoldsburg	71	1 175	51.2	14.8	7	44	1.8	0.5	85	1 158	58.0	27.2
Riverside	52	847	33.6	9.4	4	D	D	D	35	D	D	D
Sandusky	82	1 116	70.9	14.2	16	D	D	D	62	D	D	D
Shaker Heights	37	540	19.1	5.4	6	140	6.4	2.6	61	742	44.0	21.0
Springfield	162	3 379	129.4	36.8	10	94	4.2	1.4	202	2 889	237.9	104.5
Stow	76	1 795	62.3	18.3	10	D	D	D	69	D	D	D
Strongsville	114	2 769	104.4	28.1	12	151	4.1	1.2	93	971	102.9	39.0
Toledo	624	11 505	428.7	120.7	64	893	39.2	10.6	592	9 105	801.1	411.8
Troy	69	1 555	62.0	17.9	6	D	D	D	72	D	D	D
Upper Arlington	60	D	D	D	6	D	D	D	79	1 010	94.8	51.1
Warren	97	1 207	45.1	12.6	11	83	2.3	0.8	161	2 126	144.1	65.0
Westerville	96	2 085	86.8	22.5	13	D	D	D	203	D	D	D
Westlake	101	2 665	124.4	35.2	7	D	D	D	228	3 251	287.4	129.5
Wooster	71	1 798	61.1	19.0	5	D	D	D	77	1 327	118.1	53.4
Xenia	50	894	35.6	10.1	5	D	D	D	61	486	51.1	16.7
Youngstown	111	1 191	47.2	12.5	10	D	D	D	141	2 528	198.3	90.5
Zanesville	109	2 213	83.7	23.7	5	D	D	D	126	D	D	D
OKLAHOMA	6 900	129 159	5 106.6	1 401.3	862	22 167	2 330.9	412.6	8 577	121 175	10 860.0	4 171.7
Bartlesville	100	1 740	67.7	16.8	11	D	D	D	124	D	D	D
Broken Arrow	151	3 392	125.5	35.9	28	D	D	D	170	D	D	D
Edmond	189	4 635	155.0	46.0	28	424	23.1	8.2	346	3 152	320.9	117.6
Enid	108	D	D	D	10	49	3.7	0.7	180	D	D	D
Lawton	179	3 665	131.4	34.6	15	D	D	D	216	2 748	230.5	78.0
Midwest City	114	2 485	99.3	26.6	12	D	D	D	174	3 258	409.5	128.7
Moore	83	1 963	74.3	20.3	9	D	D	D	66	D	D	D
Muskogee	109	2 203	80.6	21.0	12	71	2.0	0.5	156	D	D	D
Norman	285	7 112	281.6	79.0	40	1 059	92.4	19.3	358	D	D	D
Oklahoma City	1 239	27 218	1 163.9	325.0	136	2 409	190.8	49.5	1 883	31 441	3 405.0	1 278.7
Owasso	79	1 748	67.0	17.9	6	44	1.7	0.5	68	D	D	D
Ponca City	67	1 217	43.6	10.9	4	D	D	D	92	D	D	D
Shawnee	105	2 393	90.7	24.1	5	D	D	D	89	1 283	95.5	39.1
Stillwater	120	2 746	98.2	26.3	9	D	D	D	104	D	D	D
Tulsa	1 051	21 344	929.0	264.5	110	2 142	232.5	42.9	1 415	21 613	2 657.9	1 049.8
OREGON	10 241	150 538	7 555.8	2 152.9	1 211	17 801	1 105.7	408.0	9 011	91 816	9 444.8	3 751.5
Albany	116	1 783	86.3	22.6	15	D	D	D	96	1 060	86.6	34.3
Beaverton	275	4 565	226.6	69.2	41	605	63.5	9.5	277	3 488	322.9	119.8
Bend	302	4 742	231.3	67.7	49	1 493	60.4	19.4	341	D	D	D
Corvallis	179	2 966	120.3	34.3	19	D	D	D	148	D	D	D
Eugene	508	8 243	369.8	107.5	43	656	22.9	7.5	503	6 188	737.8	256.7
Grants Pass	149	2 034	92.1	27.7	15	D	D	D	189	2 364	205.8	71.5
Gresham	223	3 640	166.2	50.3	22	D	D	D	266	2 517	229.1	89.8
Hillsboro	230	3 770	194.3	54.5	18	235	13.0	3.3	217	2 137	212.0	81.9
Keizer	47	1 014	42.0	11.3	12	159	7.2	3.1	52	583	45.4	16.5
Lake Oswego	102	1 742	85.7	26.7	16	79	5.2	1.4	161	D	D	D
McMinnville	82	1 212	52.5	15.3	6	D	D	D	107	1 735	167.1	66.6
Medford	263	4 248	202.0	58.7	28	437	21.8	6.6	294	D	D	D
Oregon City	71	1 085	57.3	16.0	8	100	5.1	1.6	102	D	D	D
Portland	2 205	34 188	1 842.4	539.5	227	2 730	311.5	166.5	1 725	16 888	2 022.3	822.3
Redmond	89	1 355	57.3	15.8	6	D	D	D	73	D	D	D
Salem	393	6 630	309.5	86.5	34	605	37.8	13.4	509	6 251	587.2	248.5
Springfield	157	2 502	120.7	33.2	20	D	D	D	126	2 539	312.7	126.3

1. Establishments subject to federal tax.

Table D. Cities — Other Services and Federal Funds

City	Other services[1], 2007				Selected federal funds, 2009–2010 (mil dol)								
					Procurement contracts		Grants						
	Number of establish-ments	Number of employees	Receipts (mil dol)	Annual payroll (mil dol)	Defense	Other	Total[2]	Medicaid and other health related	Nutrition and family welfare	Energy and envi-ronment	Disasters and emergency prepared-ness	Housing and community develop-ment	Employment and training
	104	105	106	107	108	109	110	111	112	113	114	115	116
OHIO—Cont'd													
Kettering	87	560	30.7	10.6	0.0	0.0	1.1	0.3	0.0	0.0	0.0	0.8	0.0
Lakewood	50	295	18.5	6.2	0.0	0.8	2.9	0.0	0.0	0.0	0.0	2.9	0.0
Lancaster	68	D	D	D	0.2	1.4	10.1	0.0	1.7	0.0	0.0	7.1	0.0
Lima	58	376	28.9	7.6	87.2	2.4	10.0	1.3	0.0	0.0	0.0	7.6	0.0
Lorain	70	515	30.7	9.9	0.9	0.3	38.1	2.8	6.8	1.0	0.0	24.1	0.0
Mansfield	91	829	52.0	15.6	6.8	0.3	26.2	1.5	0.5	0.0	0.0	19.4	0.0
Marion	39	228	15.1	4.9	0.1	0.2	8.8	1.2	5.8	0.0	0.0	0.1	0.0
Mason	39	287	13.2	5.5	12.8	4.2	0.0	0.0	0.0	0.0	0.0	0.0	0.0
Massillon	56	389	40.0	12.9	0.3	0.0	1.0	0.0	0.0	0.1	0.0	0.9	0.0
Medina	60	457	30.7	10.4	3.3	0.6	3.4	0.0	0.0	0.0	0.0	3.4	0.0
Mentor	135	1 109	90.6	29.1	24.5	3.3	1.5	0.4	0.7	0.0	0.0	0.3	0.0
Middletown	58	288	21.8	6.7	0.1	0.1	16.6	1.4	0.0	0.9	0.0	11.8	0.0
Newark	63	469	32.6	11.6	14.6	0.8	15.4	0.3	3.3	0.0	0.0	10.4	0.0
North Olmsted	93	557	33.8	12.1	0.1	1.2	0.0	0.0	0.0	0.0	0.0	0.0	0.0
North Ridgeville	44	168	11.3	3.4	0.5	0.1	0.0	0.0	0.0	0.0	0.0	0.0	0.0
North Royalton	59	279	26.5	8.3	13.1	0.9	0.0	0.0	0.0	0.0	0.0	0.0	0.0
Parma	136	1 003	90.2	30.1	0.1	0.2	7.2	0.0	0.0	1.0	0.0	6.2	0.0
Reynoldsburg	47	253	19.4	6.2	1.8	1.4	5.0	1.4	0.0	3.1	0.3	0.0	0.0
Riverside	17	78	6.2	2.2	0.0	0.0	0.0	0.0	0.0	0.0	0.0	0.0	0.0
Sandusky	35	190	11.9	3.4	24.9	32.5	22.8	0.0	2.0	0.0	0.0	8.2	0.0
Shaker Heights	23	131	6.8	2.2	0.1	0.2	1.0	0.4	0.4	0.0	0.0	0.2	0.0
Springfield	101	694	115.6	19.7	19.6	0.7	30.0	0.5	0.0	0.6	0.0	20.1	0.0
Stow	51	448	26.4	8.7	5.9	0.0	0.0	0.0	0.0	0.0	0.0	0.0	0.0
Strongsville	62	716	54.5	19.2	1.8	0.5	0.0	0.0	0.0	0.0	0.0	0.0	0.0
Toledo	415	2 866	240.0	67.9	5.3	11.4	167.5	38.4	14.0	23.1	3.0	55.7	0.2
Troy	44	358	17.0	5.9	52.0	0.3	6.6	0.4	0.0	0.0	0.0	5.5	0.0
Upper Arlington	31	266	13.9	4.8	2.7	0.2	5.2	0.8	0.0	0.0	0.0	4.4	0.0
Warren	65	329	22.5	6.2	2.0	0.3	20.3	0.0	4.7	0.0	0.0	10.5	0.3
Westerville	64	D	D	D	17.9	-3.8	3.1	0.0	0.0	0.4	0.0	0.1	0.0
Westlake	65	592	29.5	11.6	6.4	2.7	0.5	0.5	0.0	0.0	0.0	0.0	0.0
Wooster	46	328	19.8	7.1	2.6	0.3	18.7	0.2	4.6	0.1	0.0	5.2	0.0
Xenia	35	182	12.6	4.2	7.7	0.5	12.3	1.0	0.1	0.0	0.0	8.9	0.0
Youngstown	83	D	D	D	7.3	3.4	49.4	2.6	7.3	6.3	0.0	21.9	0.6
Zanesville	78	702	44.4	14.2	0.4	6.0	11.8	0.0	1.9	0.4	0.0	5.8	3.0
OKLAHOMA	4 462	25 063	1 975.4	564.4	2 409.9	964.9	7 854.8	3 961.4	1 023.5	301.8	117.8	352.7	90.7
Bartlesville	51	D	D	D	0.1	2.2	1.7	0.0	0.0	0.2	0.0	0.0	0.0
Broken Arrow	125	922	70.7	25.1	39.1	0.2	0.5	0.0	0.0	0.0	0.0	0.0	0.0
Edmond	140	844	52.4	17.4	3.0	3.0	8.4	1.8	2.7	0.8	0.0	0.5	0.0
Enid	94	487	39.9	10.4	78.2	0.3	2.5	0.2	0.1	0.2	0.0	0.7	0.3
Lawton	122	628	37.5	11.2	76.8	19.3	33.2	2.2	0.6	1.0	0.0	7.3	0.4
Midwest City	60	439	26.7	8.3	1.2	0.4	1.3	0.1	0.0	0.5	0.0	0.6	0.0
Moore	52	D	D	D	0.0	1.0	0.4	0.0	0.0	0.4	0.0	0.0	0.0
Muskogee	58	422	26.4	8.0	6.8	32.1	8.8	0.0	2.8	0.6	0.0	3.9	0.0
Norman	117	D	D	D	4.0	31.2	80.4	1.9	7.3	10.1	0.0	8.8	0.6
Oklahoma City	838	6 390	516.6	151.1	921.8	257.6	1 360.0	252.9	184.7	229.1	0.2	143.7	85.3
Owasso	34	D	D	D	0.2	0.0	0.3	0.0	0.0	0.0	0.0	0.0	0.0
Ponca City	41	198	16.2	4.3	185.5	0.9	4.4	0.4	0.5	0.2	0.0	1.7	0.1
Shawnee	43	D	D	D	4.2	0.2	27.9	1.7	3.7	0.5	0.0	12.6	0.1
Stillwater	59	360	20.0	5.6	20.3	12.7	80.2	10.0	0.1	2.1	0.0	3.9	0.0
Tulsa	717	4 694	374.5	115.4	46.6	108.4	136.6	13.2	11.4	9.8	0.2	43.6	0.4
OREGON	5 333	29 509	2 595.4	799.5	891.5	1 155.6	8 694.5	4 360.1	926.3	456.7	49.4	345.9	206.8
Albany	66	D	D	D	1.3	5.1	17.8	0.1	0.0	0.1	0.0	15.3	0.0
Beaverton	160	1 240	105.3	33.0	14.7	6.7	14.1	0.3	0.0	2.2	0.0	0.7	5.0
Bend	157	895	73.5	23.1	4.6	17.0	20.2	1.2	0.3	11.0	0.0	0.4	0.4
Corvallis	63	384	21.2	8.2	47.7	40.4	169.5	41.6	0.9	18.3	-0.3	1.2	0.4
Eugene	284	1 930	158.6	51.6	7.0	14.1	252.1	130.4	1.4	9.2	0.0	22.0	0.2
Grants Pass	76	328	24.6	7.0	2.3	4.5	11.2	2.8	0.0	0.9	0.0	4.0	0.0
Gresham	117	569	45.9	13.1	0.2	0.3	8.0	0.1	5.2	1.2	0.0	1.0	0.0
Hillsboro	135	926	110.5	42.3	4.0	10.2	41.0	0.5	4.4	3.6	0.0	27.3	0.0
Keizer	36	174	10.4	3.4	0.0	0.0	0.4	0.1	0.0	0.2	0.0	0.0	0.0
Lake Oswego	71	292	25.7	7.7	20.9	3.0	1.2	1.2	0.0	0.0	0.0	0.0	0.0
McMinnville	36	170	12.5	4.2	0.7	0.5	14.8	0.1	1.8	0.1	0.0	9.8	0.0
Medford	151	1 154	96.6	35.5	1.0	12.7	24.3	3.9	0.3	1.3	0.0	12.0	0.4
Oregon City	47	222	19.3	6.3	1.0	0.7	30.8	1.5	2.1	0.1	0.0	17.1	0.9
Portland	1 164	7 975	784.9	231.9	309.9	408.9	1 443.6	519.5	16.3	171.3	0.2	104.4	12.6
Redmond	35	D	D	D	0.0	0.1	14.6	0.0	1.4	0.3	0.0	7.8	0.0
Salem	233	1 204	93.1	29.9	13.3	9.6	1 226.4	51.9	216.6	40.1	7.9	64.0	186.4
Springfield	83	437	34.9	11.0	2.5	5.1	8.4	0.0	5.4	0.4	0.0	0.7	0.0

1. Establishments subject to federal tax.   2. Includes program categories not shown separately. State totals include additional categories not allocated by city.

City	General revenue							General expenditure		
		Intergovernmental		Taxes					Per capita[1] (dollars)	
					Per capita[1] (dollars)					
	Total (mil dol)	Total (mil dol)	Percent from state government	Total (mil dol)	Total	Property	Sales and gross receipts	Total (mil dol)	Total	Capital outlays
	117	118	119	120	121	122	123	124	125	126
OHIO—Cont'd										
Kettering	66.6	11.2	86.0	41.2	761	174	10	61.5	1 137	160
Lakewood	65.9	13.7	79.6	34.9	681	271	43	77.2	1 505	304
Lancaster	48.6	7.3	86.7	18.0	487	114	1	49.6	1 342	235
Lima	45.7	9.1	83.4	18.4	484	35	27	46.1	1 214	68
Lorain	66.2	18.3	100.0	26.4	376	64	24	67.4	961	138
Mansfield	66.3	11.8	88.1	38.0	765	166	163	70.6	1 422	145
Marion	39.2	8.2	88.3	16.7	467	54	13	38.4	1 076	95
Mason	56.5	7.6	100.0	30.9	1 046	992	54	68.9	2 331	866
Massillon	37.3	7.0	85.1	15.4	476	58	12	38.5	1 188	159
Medina	32.6	5.7	100.0	17.9	685	120	10	25.5	972	149
Mentor	57.3	10.5	95.6	36.8	711	112	32	63.2	1 222	208
Middletown	76.2	22.2	92.7	24.4	476	115	12	67.7	1 320	107
Newark	46.8	9.8	92.6	25.1	532	70	33	44.6	945	84
North Olmsted	44.2	6.8	95.7	25.0	792	330	40	44.3	1 402	259
North Ridgeville	30.4	3.5	94.3	13.8	501	188	42	30.0	1 087	295
North Royalton	25.9	4.0	100.0	13.6	462	154	13	25.0	850	60
Parma	65.2	13.2	86.3	43.0	546	89	18	61.9	785	105
Reynoldsburg	28.1	4.9	100.0	11.9	354	106	16	32.4	965	326
Riverside	11.9	2.4	100.0	7.0	275	92	2	11.6	456	100
Sandusky	32.8	5.1	58.7	15.9	614	91	218	32.3	1 249	207
Shaker Heights	62.2	20.4	100.0	28.8	1 076	287	34	52.8	1 972	256
Springfield	85.6	21.2	94.7	32.6	523	39	34	79.6	1 276	364
Stow	33.8	6.9	96.6	20.9	612	231	27	44.0	1 294	526
Strongsville	62.1	5.8	100.0	37.8	882	210	0	57.3	1 337	167
Toledo	387.2	64.3	46.0	205.8	698	59	65	474.2	1 607	432
Troy	32.9	4.1	100.0	15.3	694	90	4	32.4	1 470	295
Upper Arlington	38.8	5.2	100.0	23.9	752	220	23	69.9	2 203	237
Warren	62.4	10.0	62.2	24.3	548	31	64	61.4	1 387	143
Westerville	61.8	10.9	98.6	33.9	948	314	32	61.1	1 710	344
Westlake	51.9	7.6	99.6	32.1	1 045	393	30	53.7	1 749	607
Wooster	124.7	15.9	97.7	12.9	494	108	28	124.6	4 789	1 156
Xenia	27.0	6.1	97.3	11.6	491	75	54	24.7	1 043	166
Youngstown	94.9	18.3	77.1	50.9	689	28	16	102.5	1 389	260
Zanesville	32.6	7.8	100.0	16.1	639	50	22	29.4	1 170	41
OKLAHOMA	X	X	X	X	X	X	X	X	X	X
Bartlesville	35.6	2.1	15.6	20.7	584	79	484	34.0	961	208
Broken Arrow	71.0	2.5	76.5	43.2	476	89	367	81.2	895	347
Edmond	87.5	12.4	36.9	45.4	580	1	544	89.5	1 144	248
Enid	49.4	6.2	35.0	30.1	640	12	601	36.6	778	170
Lawton	73.4	5.2	24.5	43.7	477	40	420	73.2	800	159
Midwest City	51.0	2.0	17.9	29.2	522	43	466	50.3	898	33
Moore	37.7	2.6	17.9	21.5	421	40	365	36.7	719	78
Muskogee	132.5	3.7	63.1	30.6	764	9	697	138.2	3 454	231
Norman	331.2	7.5	29.8	57.4	538	21	500	387.3	3 630	1 015
Oklahoma City	1 013.0	85.6	45.1	479.2	876	102	711	986.9	1 803	637
Owasso	26.1	0.5	62.6	17.7	672	0	642	23.5	893	213
Ponca City	30.4	1.1	21.2	14.5	590	15	547	39.6	1 612	349
Shawnee	28.6	2.0	60.9	17.9	591	4	567	25.8	854	62
Stillwater	41.8	0.8	100.0	25.9	552	28	498	47.3	1 007	51
Tulsa	601.7	74.1	18.0	261.6	681	69	613	462.3	1 204	149
OREGON	X	X	X	X	X	X	X	X	X	X
Albany	58.5	7.7	58.2	33.4	708	454	254	80.3	1 701	779
Beaverton	72.8	12.7	67.7	41.4	457	296	160	59.3	654	83
Bend	82.8	13.7	51.0	44.7	599	276	324	83.6	1 121	306
Corvallis	64.6	9.3	53.1	26.4	517	372	145	55.8	1 092	105
Eugene	267.9	47.4	23.8	107.2	720	593	126	229.9	1 543	209
Grants Pass	35.1	4.3	54.4	20.9	630	374	256	34.4	1 038	196
Gresham	102.1	32.1	71.8	39.1	392	217	175	102.4	1 026	175
Hillsboro	99.7	9.6	99.2	55.1	602	384	218	87.7	959	126
Keizer	19.4	3.1	99.6	9.0	256	175	81	20.8	589	193
Lake Oswego	59.6	3.7	71.5	35.6	971	759	212	75.3	2 053	816
McMinnville	42.6	3.7	78.8	14.8	480	315	165	27.2	881	115
Medford	82.9	9.2	61.6	49.8	690	344	346	71.0	984	227
Oregon City	41.4	5.8	98.2	22.5	723	368	355	37.4	1 202	380
Portland	1 048.5	193.7	39.6	451.5	820	493	327	1 208.8	2 196	599
Redmond	53.0	13.7	66.9	19.5	818	360	458	47.0	1 977	739
Salem	206.8	40.9	53.9	87.9	578	390	189	206.7	1 361	197
Springfield	99.9	10.8	99.3	27.7	489	341	148	81.7	1 442	262

1. Based on population estimated as of July 1 of the year shown.

City	Public welfare	Highways	Parking facilities	Education	Health and hospitals	Police protection	Sewerage and sanitation	Parks and recreation	Housing and community development	Interest on debt
				City government finances, 2006 (cont.)						
				General expenditure (cont.)						
				Percent of total for:						
	127	128	129	130	131	132	133	134	135	136
OHIO—Cont'd										
Kettering	0.0	21.4	0.0	0.0	0.3	21.0	0.0	17.5	2.9	1.9
Lakewood	0.7	2.8	1.5	0.0	5.3	14.1	25.1	1.3	6.1	6.6
Lancaster	0.0	7.2	0.0	0.0	0.6	14.6	29.9	3.9	2.1	2.9
Lima	0.0	6.4	0.0	0.0	0.0	18.2	28.9	2.4	6.5	3.8
Lorain	6.3	3.9	2.3	0.0	2.6	16.5	18.7	1.5	13.7	2.1
Mansfield	0.0	14.9	0.0	0.0	0.2	18.9	18.9	1.3	6.3	0.5
Marion	0.0	10.2	0.0	0.0	2.7	16.1	29.3	3.5	1.9	7.6
Mason	0.0	10.2	0.0	0.0	0.0	4.0	12.8	15.0	0.0	8.8
Massillon	0.0	9.2	0.0	0.0	1.7	11.2	23.0	8.1	0.5	3.7
Medina	0.0	14.5	0.0	0.0	0.5	25.8	11.3	12.1	3.7	7.6
Mentor	0.0	29.7	0.0	0.0	0.0	17.7	1.1	12.8	2.2	3.5
Middletown	0.0	10.4	0.2	0.0	2.8	13.7	11.7	3.7	16.0	12.4
Newark	0.0	7.3	0.0	0.0	4.1	20.7	11.2	1.6	3.9	4.1
North Olmsted	1.2	17.9	0.0	0.0	0.1	16.2	15.5	7.3	0.0	7.5
North Ridgeville	0.0	9.4	0.0	0.0	3.8	15.8	34.2	1.2	4.0	2.2
North Royalton	1.2	7.0	0.0	0.0	0.3	25.4	18.2	1.6	3.7	4.9
Parma	0.0	12.3	0.0	0.0	0.5	18.3	8.2	5.4	4.0	2.4
Reynoldsburg	0.0	3.9	0.0	0.0	0.5	20.5	21.1	3.0	0.0	3.9
Riverside	0.0	14.8	0.0	0.0	0.0	31.4	0.0	0.5	0.0	1.4
Sandusky	0.0	10.8	0.1	0.0	0.0	17.4	19.4	7.2	12.7	4.0
Shaker Heights	0.0	6.7	0.0	0.0	1.1	24.0	8.8	9.9	8.9	2.1
Springfield	1.1	4.2	0.0	0.0	11.9	16.1	9.6	3.8	3.6	2.0
Stow	0.0	7.2	0.0	0.0	1.2	8.1	3.0	31.0	3.4	1.5
Strongsville	0.6	13.8	0.0	0.0	0.6	10.4	15.8	7.8	0.0	3.8
Toledo	0.0	12.6	0.1	0.0	0.4	16.7	30.8	2.7	2.7	3.5
Troy	0.0	6.5	0.1	0.0	0.0	13.6	11.7	9.7	19.6	2.9
Upper Arlington	0.0	8.1	0.0	0.0	0.2	9.2	4.5	51.2	0.0	1.7
Warren	0.0	7.4	0.2	0.0	1.5	13.0	23.5	2.9	7.7	1.9
Westerville	0.0	6.5	0.0	0.0	0.0	17.0	12.9	14.4	0.0	2.2
Westlake	0.0	2.9	0.0	0.0	1.3	12.5	5.2	8.0	0.1	6.2
Wooster	0.0	3.9	0.0	0.0	67.0	3.8	14.3	1.5	0.6	1.0
Xenia	0.0	6.8	0.3	0.0	0.3	20.2	17.0	1.5	0.9	1.2
Youngstown	0.0	6.6	0.0	0.0	2.3	19.5	15.5	3.2	5.1	2.0
Zanesville	0.0	4.2	0.0	0.0	0.5	34.2	21.9	3.9	0.0	0.5
OKLAHOMA	X	X	X	X	X	X	X	X	X	X
Bartlesville	0.0	12.6	0.0	0.0	0.0	12.4	19.1	8.5	2.4	1.7
Broken Arrow	0.0	11.3	0.0	0.0	0.4	17.3	23.8	10.1	0.7	3.9
Edmond	1.4	18.1	0.0	0.0	0.0	17.8	10.2	11.1	0.9	4.7
Enid	0.5	19.5	0.0	0.0	0.0	19.5	11.4	5.8	0.7	0.0
Lawton	0.0	9.3	0.0	0.0	0.0	19.8	13.0	9.9	2.7	1.2
Midwest City	0.0	5.7	0.0	0.0	1.5	19.9	16.9	6.1	4.0	4.5
Moore	0.0	9.6	0.0	0.0	0.0	18.6	6.1	4.3	1.5	2.0
Muskogee	0.1	2.2	0.0	0.0	66.7	5.4	5.4	3.8	0.4	1.5
Norman	0.0	5.2	0.0	0.0	65.2	4.8	12.7	1.5	1.3	1.6
Oklahoma City	0.0	9.1	0.0	0.0	0.0	13.9	18.2	9.3	1.0	3.0
Owasso	0.0	4.2	0.0	0.0	3.4	19.6	10.9	9.1	2.0	5.9
Ponca City	0.0	10.2	0.0	0.0	1.8	14.3	14.0	9.6	3.1	1.5
Shawnee	0.0	6.8	0.0	0.0	0.0	22.6	12.2	2.0	3.3	4.4
Stillwater	0.6	11.1	0.0	0.0	0.8	18.7	11.5	8.0	0.0	2.9
Tulsa	5.3	6.0	0.8	0.0	8.2	16.4	21.9	5.2	1.7	5.7
OREGON	X	X	X	X	X	X	X	X	X	X
Albany	0.0	6.8	0.0	0.0	2.6	13.2	49.5	6.1	0.0	1.6
Beaverton	0.0	6.8	0.0	0.0	0.0	31.0	12.5	0.2	0.8	1.2
Bend	0.0	14.6	0.5	0.0	0.0	16.2	9.5	0.0	1.9	4.2
Corvallis	0.0	7.2	0.3	0.0	0.0	18.3	15.0	11.2	7.2	6.3
Eugene	0.0	1.8	1.4	0.0	0.0	18.2	11.3	10.3	4.7	1.2
Grants Pass	0.0	5.4	0.0	0.0	0.0	19.3	19.2	8.1	3.5	1.6
Gresham	0.0	15.5	0.0	0.0	0.0	19.3	20.6	1.6	3.1	3.7
Hillsboro	0.0	9.4	0.0	0.0	0.0	23.1	21.0	17.7	0.0	0.0
Keizer	0.0	13.6	0.0	0.0	0.0	24.6	20.0	1.5	6.5	4.7
Lake Oswego	0.0	5.6	0.0	0.0	0.0	11.1	11.9	8.3	1.8	3.5
McMinnville	0.0	6.0	0.0	0.0	10.6	20.4	12.1	10.3	0.2	5.0
Medford	0.0	17.5	0.5	0.0	0.0	23.7	12.5	9.6	0.9	3.7
Oregon City	0.0	12.8	0.7	0.0	0.0	12.9	26.5	7.6	8.4	3.9
Portland	0.0	14.8	0.4	0.0	0.0	11.8	19.8	8.7	3.8	9.8
Redmond	0.0	23.4	0.0	0.0	0.0	11.6	15.4	9.3	3.5	3.3
Salem	0.0	9.1	0.6	0.0	1.0	13.9	24.5	5.2	10.7	6.5
Springfield	0.0	9.6	0.0	0.0	6.0	18.8	26.7	0.0	5.4	0.7

Table D. Cities — City Government Finances, City Government Employment, and Climate

	City government finances, 2007 (cont.)				Climate[2]						
	Debt outstanding				Average daily temperature (degrees Fahrenheit)						
					Mean		Limits				
City	Total (mil dol)	Per capita[1] (dollars)	Debt issued during year	City government employment, 2010	January	July	January[3]	July[4]	Annual precipitation (inches)	Heating degree days	Cooling degree days
	137	138	139	140	141	142	143	144	145	146	147
OHIO—Cont'd											
Kettering	11.1	205	0.0	499	27.9	77.0	20.6	87.2	39.41	5 343	1 214
Lakewood	120.9	2 357	24.6	480	25.7	71.9	18.8	81.4	38.71	6 121	702
Lancaster	34.6	937	0.0	432	26.5	73.1	17.8	84.4	36.55	5 887	764
Lima	28.6	753	4.5	388	25.5	73.6	18.1	84.0	37.20	5 932	835
Lorain	43.0	613	0.0	448	27.1	73.8	19.3	85.0	38.02	5 731	818
Mansfield	9.0	182	0.0	490	24.3	71.0	16.2	81.8	43.24	6 364	653
Marion	40.7	1 141	24.5	289	24.5	72.7	16.0	83.7	38.35	6 300	703
Mason	111.3	3 766	0.0	247	NA	NA	NA	NA	NA	NA	NA
Massillon	31.9	985	0.0	281	25.2	71.8	17.4	82.3	38.47	6 154	678
Medina	42.8	1 633	0.0	206	23.7	71.3	16.2	82.0	38.34	6 525	558
Mentor	35.1	679	0.0	445	23.0	68.8	14.3	80.0	47.33	6 956	372
Middletown	131.4	2 561	80.2	417	27.5	74.2	18.3	86.3	39.54	5 609	879
Newark	27.3	579	4.8	405	25.8	72.7	17.3	83.8	41.62	6 084	687
North Olmsted	60.9	1 925	38.7	258	25.7	71.9	18.8	81.4	38.71	6 121	702
North Ridgeville	24.9	901	13.8	208	NA	NA	NA	NA	NA	NA	NA
North Royalton	7.7	263	0.0	193	25.7	71.9	18.8	81.4	38.71	6 121	702
Parma	82.4	1 045	10.8	474	25.7	71.9	18.8	81.4	38.71	6 121	702
Reynoldsburg	31.3	932	9.7	133	28.3	75.1	20.3	85.3	38.52	5 492	951
Riverside	3.8	148	0.0	NA	NA	NA	NA	NA	NA	NA	NA
Sandusky	31.3	1 209	0.1	231	25.6	73.8	18.9	81.8	34.46	6 065	785
Shaker Heights	27.5	1 026	2.8	392	25.7	71.9	18.8	81.4	38.71	6 121	702
Springfield	41.6	666	3.8	607	26.1	73.5	18.2	83.8	37.70	5 921	796
Stow	24.8	728	0.0	286	27.2	74.1	20.1	83.9	36.07	5 752	856
Strongsville	43.8	1 023	11.7	326	25.7	71.9	18.8	81.4	38.71	6 121	702
Toledo	359.7	1 219	74.8	2 583	27.5	77.6	21.7	87.1	33.52	5 464	1 257
Troy	29.0	1 316	0.0	203	NA	NA	NA	NA	NA	NA	NA
Upper Arlington	25.8	814	4.0	256	28.3	75.1	20.3	85.3	38.52	5 492	951
Warren	26.7	604	1.7	400	24.0	70.2	15.3	82.4	37.80	6 678	458
Westerville	35.4	991	0.0	523	27.7	74.4	19.7	85.4	39.35	5 434	924
Westlake	48.4	1 575	0.0	256	27.1	73.8	19.3	85.0	38.02	5 731	818
Wooster	122.7	4 719	0.0	887	NA	NA	NA	NA	NA	NA	NA
Xenia	9.7	409	2.1	215	NA	NA	NA	NA	NA	NA	NA
Youngstown	43.4	588	8.4	771	24.9	69.9	17.4	81.0	38.02	6 451	552
Zanesville	7.5	298	0.0	313	24.3	68.4	16.3	78.7	36.91	6 639	573
OKLAHOMA	X	X	X	NA	X	X	X	X	X	X	X
Bartlesville	58.8	1 660	8.1	348	35.4	82.2	23.7	94.5	38.99	3 743	1 894
Broken Arrow	121.0	1 334	20.5	608	34.8	81.3	23.5	92.9	40.46	3 917	1 746
Edmond	170.2	2 175	3.8	699	36.7	82.0	26.2	93.1	35.85	3 663	1 907
Enid	44.6	948	0.3	479	33.1	82.6	21.9	94.4	34.25	4 269	1 852
Lawton	63.4	693	0.0	879	38.2	84.2	26.4	95.7	31.64	3 326	2 199
Midwest City	46.3	828	0.0	494	36.7	82.0	26.2	93.1	35.85	3 663	1 907
Moore	16.3	319	0.4	278	36.7	82.0	26.2	93.1	35.85	3 663	1 907
Muskogee	68.4	1 711	24.3	501	36.1	82.1	25.2	93.1	43.77	3 667	1 858
Norman	298.5	2 798	127.8	3 255	35.8	82.1	23.2	93.9	41.65	3 713	1 906
Oklahoma City	1 083.8	1 980	178.5	4 409	36.7	82.0	26.2	93.1	35.85	3 663	1 907
Owasso	35.7	1 353	8.5	203	NA	NA	NA	NA	NA	NA	NA
Ponca City	27.0	1 099	16.0	409	33.8	82.9	23.8	94.1	36.41	4 053	1 964
Shawnee	37.9	1 253	13.7	255	37.3	83.0	25.5	94.5	40.87	3 460	2 024
Stillwater	42.2	899	0.2	1 264	34.5	82.3	21.9	93.6	36.71	3 899	1 881
Tulsa	1 412.5	3 678	174.9	3 867	37.4	81.9	27.1	92.2	45.10	3 413	1 905
OREGON	X	X	X	NA	X	X	X	X	X	X	X
Albany	93.2	1 973	37.6	411	40.3	66.5	33.6	81.2	43.66	4 715	247
Beaverton	41.6	459	1.0	487	40.0	66.8	33.8	79.2	39.95	4 723	287
Bend	82.5	1 107	5.8	439	31.2	63.5	22.6	80.7	11.73	7 042	147
Corvallis	78.4	1 533	0.0	453	38.1	63.8	31.6	77.4	67.76	5 501	139
Eugene	351.5	2 359	12.9	1 908	39.8	66.2	33.0	81.5	50.90	4 786	242
Grants Pass	24.6	740	9.8	210	NA	NA	NA	NA	NA	NA	NA
Gresham	79.7	800	3.8	545	40.0	68.3	33.5	81.5	45.70	4 491	450
Hillsboro	51.8	566	0.0	765	40.5	67.6	35.1	80.4	38.19	4 532	323
Keizer	27.8	787	4.2	95	40.3	66.8	33.5	81.5	40.00	4 784	257
Lake Oswego	76.7	2 090	26.7	348	41.8	69.3	35.7	82.6	46.05	4 132	475
McMinnville	40.6	1 313	13.1	263	39.6	66.6	33.0	81.9	41.66	4 815	288
Medford	84.9	1 176	19.0	469	39.1	72.7	30.9	90.2	18.37	4 539	711
Oregon City	30.6	983	3.1	165	41.8	69.3	35.7	82.6	46.05	4 132	475
Portland	2 572.7	4 674	411.3	5 816	41.8	69.3	35.7	82.6	46.05	4 132	475
Redmond	52.1	2 192	1.9	194	NA	NA	NA	NA	NA	NA	NA
Salem	520.8	3 429	72.8	1 255	40.3	66.8	33.5	81.5	40.00	4 784	257
Springfield	52.4	925	31.8	586	39.8	66.2	33.0	81.5	50.90	4 786	242

1. Based on the population estimated as of July 1 of the year shown. 2. Represents normal values based on the 30-year period, 1971–2000. 3. Average daily minimum. 4. Average daily maximum.

Table D. Cities — **Land Area and Population**

STATE Place code	City	Land area,[1] 2010 (sq km)	Total persons	Rank	Per square kilometer	White	Black	American Indian, Alaska Native	Asian	Hawaiian Pacific Islander	Percent Hispanic or Latino[2], 2010	Percent Foreign born, 2008–2010
			Population, 2010			Race alone or in combination, not of Hispanic origin (percent), 2010						
		1	2	3	4	5	6	7	8	9	10	11
	OREGON—Cont'd											
41 73650	Tigard	30.6	48 035	817	1 570.3	76.7	2.3	1.4	8.8	1.3	12.7	14.0
41 74950	Tualatin	21.3	26 054	1 596	1 224.3	76.4	1.7	1.2	5.2	1.3	17.3	14.1
41 80150	West Linn	19.1	25 109	1 656	1 311.9	90.6	1.1	1.0	5.5	0.4	4.0	7.5
42 00000	**PENNSYLVANIA**	115 883.1	12 702 379	X	109.6	80.7	11.3	0.5	3.1	0.1	5.7	5.7
42 02000	Allentown	45.4	118 032	220	2 597.5	45.0	11.0	0.5	2.5	0.1	42.8	14.5
42 02184	Altoona	25.7	46 320	852	1 805.1	94.8	4.5	0.4	0.6	0.1	1.3	1.4
42 06064	Bethel Park	30.2	32 313	1 261	1 068.9	96.2	1.6	0.2	1.8	0.1	1.0	2.7
42 06088	Bethlehem	49.5	74 982	452	1 515.7	66.9	6.4	0.4	3.2	0.1	24.4	7.0
42 13208	Chester	12.5	33 972	1 188	2 711.3	16.4	74.8	1.0	0.9	0.1	9.0	2.6
42 21648	Easton	10.6	26 800	1 545	2 540.3	61.6	17.8	0.9	2.8	0.1	19.9	9.9
42 24000	Erie	49.4	101 786	278	2 059.6	74.7	18.7	0.7	1.9	0.1	6.9	6.3
42 32800	Harrisburg	21.1	49 528	779	2 351.8	27.5	52.8	1.0	3.8	0.1	18.0	7.1
42 33408	Hazleton	15.6	25 340	1 640	1 627.5	59.7	2.3	0.3	0.9	0.0	37.3	21.0
42 41216	Lancaster	18.7	59 322	617	3 170.6	43.7	15.5	0.8	3.3	0.1	39.3	9.3
42 42168	Lebanon	10.8	25 477	1 634	2 361.2	62.7	4.6	0.5	1.2	0.1	32.1	6.6
42 50528	Monroeville	51.1	28 386	1 454	555.3	80.4	12.9	0.5	6.5	0.1	1.5	8.0
42 54656	Norristown	9.1	34 324	1 176	3 763.6	34.0	37.2	0.8	2.4	0.1	28.3	21.3
42 60000	Philadelphia	347.3	1 526 006	5	4 393.7	38.1	43.4	0.7	6.9	0.1	12.3	11.4
42 61000	Pittsburgh	143.4	305 704	59	2 131.8	66.7	27.3	0.7	5.0	0.1	2.3	6.8
42 61536	Plum	74.0	27 126	1 521	366.4	94.1	4.1	0.3	1.4	0.1	0.9	1.5
42 63624	Reading	25.6	88 082	351	3 440.7	30.2	11.4	0.5	1.2	0.1	58.2	17.1
42 69000	Scranton	65.6	76 089	438	1 160.8	81.8	5.9	0.5	3.4	0.1	9.9	7.5
42 73808	State College	11.8	42 034	938	3 562.2	82.3	4.2	0.4	10.8	0.1	3.9	10.2
42 85152	Wilkes-Barre	18.1	41 498	950	2 295.2	76.8	11.8	0.5	1.6	0.0	11.3	4.4
42 85312	Williamsport	22.6	29 381	1 398	1 299.5	83.0	16.1	0.9	1.0	0.0	2.6	1.3
42 87048	York	13.7	43 718	900	3 188.8	44.5	28.5	1.0	1.5	0.0	28.5	7.9
44 00000	**RHODE ISLAND**	2 677.6	1 052 567	X	393.1	78.0	6.2	1.0	3.4	0.1	12.4	12.7
44 19180	Cranston	73.4	80 387	404	1 095.2	78.6	5.5	0.7	5.6	0.1	10.8	11.9
44 22960	East Providence	34.3	47 037	842	1 371.7	84.6	7.8	1.4	1.9	0.2	4.1	16.3
44 54640	Pawtucket	22.5	71 148	476	3 163.5	59.0	15.4	0.9	1.9	0.4	19.7	24.2
44 59000	Providence	47.7	178 042	134	3 735.7	39.6	15.2	1.7	7.0	0.2	38.1	28.9
44 74300	Warwick	90.8	82 672	389	910.8	92.1	2.2	0.8	2.7	0.1	3.4	6.1
44 80780	Woonsocket	20.0	41 186	960	2 055.2	74.1	7.2	1.1	6.2	0.1	14.2	9.1
45 00000	**SOUTH CAROLINA**	77 856.8	4 625 364	X	59.4	65.2	28.5	0.8	1.6	0.1	5.1	4.8
45 00550	Aiken	53.6	29 524	1 392	550.8	66.5	29.0	0.7	2.3	0.1	2.6	5.5
45 01360	Anderson	37.8	26 686	1 551	706.0	61.2	34.6	0.7	1.1	0.1	4.1	6.3
45 13330	Charleston	282.3	120 083	215	425.4	69.7	25.8	0.6	2.1	0.2	2.9	4.6
45 16000	Columbia	342.4	129 272	196	377.5	50.8	42.7	0.7	2.8	0.2	4.3	4.6
45 25810	Florence	54.1	37 056	1 069	685.0	50.2	46.6	0.6	2.1	0.1	1.5	1.9
45 29815	Goose Creek	103.8	35 938	1 110	346.2	70.8	19.2	1.1	5.0	0.3	6.1	4.7
45 30850	Greenville	74.3	58 409	628	786.7	62.4	30.6	0.6	1.7	0.1	5.9	5.8
45 30985	Greer	53.5	25 515	1 629	477.4	65.7	18.0	0.5	2.5	0.1	14.5	14.2
45 34045	Hilton Head Island	107.1	37 099	1 066	346.3	75.8	7.6	0.3	1.1	0.0	15.8	14.8
45 48535	Mount Pleasant	116.8	67 843	503	581.0	90.2	5.4	0.4	2.0	0.1	2.7	3.7
45 49075	Myrtle Beach	60.4	27 109	1 523	448.8	69.8	14.7	1.0	2.3	0.3	13.7	20.4
45 50875	North Charleston	189.6	97 471	299	514.2	39.5	47.9	0.8	2.5	0.2	10.9	10.7
45 61405	Rock Hill	92.5	66 154	524	715.0	53.7	39.2	0.9	2.0	0.1	5.7	5.3
45 68290	Spartanburg	51.2	37 013	1 072	722.9	45.1	50.1	0.6	2.1	0.1	3.4	4.1
45 70270	Summerville	46.7	43 392	906	928.4	71.5	22.4	1.0	2.2	0.2	5.0	3.7
45 70405	Sumter	83.1	40 524	979	487.7	45.2	49.7	0.7	2.2	0.2	3.6	4.7
46 00000	**SOUTH DAKOTA**	196 349.6	814 180	X	4.1	86.4	1.7	9.7	1.2	0.1	2.7	2.4
46 00100	Aberdeen	40.2	26 091	1 593	649.7	92.7	1.1	4.5	1.5	0.2	1.6	1.1
46 52980	Rapid City	143.5	67 956	500	473.6	81.6	1.9	13.9	1.8	0.2	4.1	1.9
46 59020	Sioux Falls	189.0	153 888	157	814.3	86.8	5.2	3.3	2.2	0.1	4.4	6.9
47 00000	**TENNESSEE**	106 797.9	6 346 105	X	59.4	76.9	17.2	0.8	1.7	0.1	4.6	4.5
47 03440	Bartlett	69.0	54 613	690	791.1	78.3	16.5	0.5	3.1	0.1	2.7	3.9
47 08280	Brentwood	106.7	37 060	1 068	347.4	89.6	3.2	0.5	5.9	0.1	2.1	7.6
47 08540	Bristol	83.7	26 702	1 549	319.2	93.6	3.9	0.8	1.0	0.1	1.9	1.9
47 14000	Chattanooga	355.2	167 674	142	472.0	57.2	35.7	0.7	2.2	0.1	5.5	6.0
47 15160	Clarksville	252.8	132 929	190	525.8	64.4	24.7	1.4	3.5	0.7	9.3	5.5
47 15400	Cleveland	69.7	41 285	956	592.7	83.2	8.3	0.9	1.7	0.1	7.5	6.5
47 16420	Collierville	75.9	43 965	894	579.6	79.0	11.1	0.5	7.7	0.1	2.6	6.3
47 16540	Columbia	81.7	34 681	1 163	424.6	71.1	22.0	0.7	1.0	0.0	7.0	3.5
47 16920	Cookeville	84.6	30 435	1 336	359.6	87.1	4.1	0.9	2.4	0.1	7.0	4.6

1. Dry land or land partially or temporarily covered by water.   2. May be of any race.

City	Age of population (percent), 2010											Population			
												Census counts		Percent change	
	Under 5 years	5 to 17 years	18 to 24 years	25 to 34 years	35 to 44 years	45 to 54 years	55 to 64 years	65 to 74 years	75 years and over	Median age	Percent female	1990	2000	1990–2000	2000–2010
	12	13	14	15	16	17	18	19	20	21	22	23	24	25	26
OREGON—Cont'd															
Tigard	6.8	17.4	8.0	14.6	14.6	15.2	12.2	5.9	5.4	37.4	51.0	29 435	41 223	40.0	16.5
Tualatin	7.3	19.6	8.4	15.3	15.7	15.2	11.5	4.1	2.9	34.6	50.9	14 664	22 791	55.4	14.3
West Linn	5.7	20.6	6.0	8.8	14.5	17.9	15.5	6.8	4.3	41.5	51.3	16 389	22 261	35.8	12.8
PENNSYLVANIA	5.7	16.2	9.9	11.9	12.7	15.3	12.8	7.7	7.7	40.1	51.3	11 882 842	12 281 054	3.4	3.4
Allentown	7.9	18.3	12.3	14.5	12.4	13.0	9.7	5.5	6.4	32.7	51.8	105 301	106 632	1.3	10.7
Altoona	6.4	16.2	10.4	12.4	12.2	14.0	12.6	7.8	7.8	38.9	52.0	51 881	49 523	-4.5	-6.5
Bethel Park	4.6	16.1	5.8	9.7	12.1	16.9	14.6	9.5	10.7	46.1	52.3	33 823	33 556	-0.8	-3.7
Bethlehem	5.6	14.3	15.6	13.7	11.1	12.4	11.0	6.8	9.4	35.7	51.9	71 427	71 329	-0.1	5.1
Chester	8.1	19.1	16.0	12.8	11.0	12.5	10.1	5.3	5.1	29.9	52.8	41 856	36 854	-12.0	-7.8
Easton	6.8	15.7	17.6	14.1	12.7	13.3	9.5	5.1	5.1	31.9	49.6	26 276	26 263	0.0	2.0
Erie	7.5	16.4	14.1	14.1	11.4	12.9	10.6	5.9	7.0	33.2	51.7	108 718	103 717	-4.6	-1.9
Harrisburg	8.9	17.9	11.0	15.7	12.6	13.7	11.1	5.1	3.9	32.2	51.9	52 376	48 950	-6.5	1.2
Hazleton	7.1	18.2	10.3	11.6	12.6	13.4	10.8	7.6	8.5	37.6	51.7	24 730	23 329	-5.7	8.6
Lancaster	8.0	17.6	14.5	16.6	12.9	12.6	9.2	4.9	3.7	30.5	50.3	55 551	56 348	1.4	5.3
Lebanon	8.0	18.0	9.3	14.1	12.5	13.3	11.1	6.7	7.0	35.6	51.8	24 800	24 461	-1.4	4.2
Monroeville	4.9	13.7	7.1	12.0	11.1	15.2	14.6	9.2	12.2	45.9	52.8	29 169	29 349	0.6	-3.3
Norristown	8.9	17.3	11.3	18.6	13.5	12.3	8.9	4.8	4.3	31.2	50.2	30 754	31 282	1.7	9.7
Philadelphia	6.6	15.9	13.3	16.1	12.3	13.0	10.5	6.2	5.9	33.5	52.8	1 585 577	1 517 550	-4.3	0.6
Pittsburgh	4.9	11.3	18.9	16.9	10.5	12.4	11.2	6.4	7.3	33.2	51.6	369 879	334 563	-9.5	-8.6
Plum	5.3	16.9	7.1	11.1	13.2	16.5	13.1	8.9	7.9	42.6	51.2	25 609	26 940	5.2	0.7
Reading	9.5	21.5	13.1	14.0	12.4	11.7	8.5	4.7	4.6	28.9	51.5	78 380	81 207	3.6	8.5
Scranton	6.1	14.4	13.9	12.7	11.3	13.3	12.0	7.2	9.2	37.9	51.8	81 805	76 415	-6.6	-0.4
State College	1.8	3.2	70.6	9.4	8.7	3.3	3.2	2.0	2.7	21.5	46.0	38 981	38 420	-1.4	9.4
Wilkes-Barre	5.7	14.5	15.7	12.5	11.4	13.1	10.8	6.9	9.3	36.5	51.1	47 523	43 123	-9.3	-3.8
Williamsport	6.5	14.2	22.4	12.9	10.2	12.3	10.1	5.4	6.0	29.7	48.9	31 933	30 706	-3.8	-4.3
York	9.2	19.5	13.2	14.7	12.4	12.5	9.5	5.0	4.0	30.1	51.8	42 192	40 862	-3.2	7.0
RHODE ISLAND	5.5	15.8	11.4	12.1	13.0	15.4	12.4	7.0	7.4	39.4	51.7	1 003 464	1 048 319	4.5	0.4
Cranston	5.0	15.4	9.1	12.7	13.9	16.0	12.5	6.8	8.5	40.8	50.6	76 060	79 269	4.2	1.4
East Providence	5.4	14.1	7.9	13.1	12.8	15.5	12.9	8.1	10.2	42.6	53.2	50 380	48 688	-3.4	-3.4
Pawtucket	7.0	16.3	9.9	14.5	14.0	14.9	10.7	6.2	6.4	36.7	52.1	72 644	72 958	0.4	-2.5
Providence	6.9	16.4	20.3	16.2	12.2	11.0	8.3	4.3	4.4	28.5	51.8	160 728	173 618	8.0	2.5
Warwick	4.7	14.4	7.6	11.8	13.4	16.8	14.1	8.0	9.1	43.7	52.2	85 427	85 808	0.4	-3.7
Woonsocket	7.6	16.4	9.3	14.5	13.1	14.5	11.4	6.1	7.1	36.8	51.6	43 877	43 224	-1.5	-4.7
SOUTH CAROLINA	6.5	16.8	10.3	12.8	13.0	14.3	12.6	8.0	5.7	37.9	51.4	3 486 310	4 012 012	15.1	15.3
Aiken	5.2	14.5	10.3	10.3	9.9	13.0	14.8	11.7	10.2	44.8	54.0	20 386	25 337	24.3	16.5
Anderson	7.7	15.7	12.1	12.3	11.5	12.0	10.7	7.5	10.4	36.8	55.5	26 385	25 514	-3.3	4.6
Charleston	6.3	11.7	17.3	18.1	11.6	11.7	11.0	6.4	5.8	32.5	52.7	88 256	96 650	9.5	24.2
Columbia	5.4	11.5	26.1	17.5	10.9	11.0	8.9	4.4	4.3	28.1	48.5	110 734	116 278	5.0	11.2
Florence	7.3	17.2	8.8	13.5	13.4	13.4	12.4	7.5	6.5	37.4	54.5	29 913	30 248	1.1	22.5
Goose Creek	7.4	17.5	16.5	15.0	13.0	13.6	9.6	5.0	2.4	30.2	48.4	24 692	29 208	18.3	23.0
Greenville	6.5	12.9	14.0	17.3	13.1	12.7	10.8	6.2	6.6	34.6	51.9	58 256	56 002	-3.9	4.3
Greer	8.5	18.1	8.6	16.3	15.0	13.0	9.5	5.9	5.1	33.9	52.5	10 322	16 843	63.2	51.5
Hilton Head Island	4.6	12.0	5.9	10.0	10.3	12.3	16.0	15.5	13.4	50.9	50.9	23 694	33 862	42.9	9.6
Mount Pleasant	6.0	18.2	6.2	13.5	16.0	15.4	12.6	6.7	5.6	39.1	51.9	30 108	47 609	58.1	42.5
Myrtle Beach	5.8	12.8	9.8	16.1	13.4	14.5	12.5	8.5	6.7	39.2	49.2	24 848	22 759	-8.4	19.1
North Charleston	8.8	16.7	13.2	18.1	12.7	12.9	9.2	4.8	3.7	30.6	50.4	70 304	79 641	13.3	22.4
Rock Hill	7.4	17.0	14.7	15.1	13.4	12.3	9.7	5.4	5.0	31.9	54.0	42 112	49 765	18.2	32.9
Spartanburg	7.6	16.0	13.9	12.0	11.3	13.0	11.6	7.2	7.4	35.5	55.9	43 479	39 673	-8.8	-6.7
Summerville	7.4	19.6	8.8	14.6	14.4	13.8	10.9	5.7	4.8	34.7	52.8	22 519	27 752	23.2	56.4
Sumter	8.3	17.6	13.1	13.8	11.1	11.9	10.1	6.9	7.0	32.5	52.9	40 977	39 643	-3.3	2.2
SOUTH DAKOTA	7.3	17.6	10.0	12.9	11.4	14.4	12.0	7.1	7.2	36.9	50.0	696 004	754 844	8.5	7.9
Aberdeen	7.0	15.2	12.8	13.5	10.6	13.2	11.2	6.8	9.6	36.4	52.4	24 995	24 658	-1.3	5.8
Rapid City	7.5	16.4	10.7	14.7	11.1	13.5	11.6	7.1	7.4	35.6	50.5	54 523	59 607	9.3	14.0
Sioux Falls	8.0	16.6	10.6	16.8	12.9	13.6	10.5	5.4	5.5	33.6	50.4	100 836	123 975	22.9	24.1
TENNESSEE	6.4	17.1	9.6	13.0	13.5	14.6	12.4	7.7	5.8	38.0	51.3	4 877 203	5 689 283	16.7	11.5
Bartlett	5.3	20.0	7.5	10.0	14.2	16.7	13.8	7.1	5.4	40.4	51.7	27 038	40 543	49.9	34.7
Brentwood	5.3	25.7	4.8	4.8	14.8	19.8	13.9	6.7	4.3	41.9	50.9	16 392	23 445	43.0	58.1
Bristol	5.4	15.2	8.7	11.3	13.1	14.7	13.5	9.0	9.1	42.3	52.4	23 421	24 821	6.0	7.6
Chattanooga	6.4	14.5	12.0	14.4	12.0	13.7	12.4	7.3	7.3	37.3	52.4	152 393	155 554	2.1	7.8
Clarksville	9.6	18.9	13.7	18.8	13.0	11.3	7.5	4.2	3.0	28.6	51.3	75 542	103 455	37.0	28.5
Cleveland	6.5	15.4	15.2	13.2	12.0	12.4	10.6	7.6	7.2	34.8	52.4	32 236	37 192	15.4	11.0
Collierville	5.7	23.2	6.5	8.9	15.8	18.8	12.1	5.4	3.6	39.2	51.2	14 501	31 872	119.8	37.9
Columbia	7.6	17.1	9.7	14.3	11.7	13.7	11.6	6.8	7.5	36.0	53.2	28 583	33 055	15.6	4.9
Cookeville	5.8	12.8	23.9	13.5	10.1	10.5	9.8	6.8	6.8	29.7	50.1	21 744	23 923	10.0	27.2

Table D. Cities — Households, Group Quarters, Crime, and Education

City	Households, 2010				Persons in group quarters, 2010				Serious crimes known to police,[2] 2010				Educational attainment, 2008–2010		
			Percent			Institutional			Total		Rate[3]			Attainment[4] (percent)	
	Number	Persons per house-hold	Female family house-holder[1]	One-person	Total	Total	Persons in nursing facilities	Non-institu-tional	Number	Rate[3]	Violent	Property	Population age 25 and older	High school graduate or less	Bachelor's degree or more
	27	28	29	30	31	32	33	34	35	36	37	38	39	40	41
OREGON—Cont'd															
Tigard	19 157	2.49	10.0	26.9	347	111	78	236	2 044	4 255	185	4 070	32 565	27.2	38.8
Tualatin	10 000	2.60	11.4	24.6	87	45	45	42	761	2 921	96	2 825	16 524	27.0	42.5
West Linn	9 523	2.62	9.0	20.6	127	63	60	64	304	1 211	36	1 175	17 476	11.4	54.2
PENNSYLVANIA	5 018 904	2.45	12.2	28.6	426 113	197 112	87 775	229 001	322 537	2 539	366	2 173	8 604 107	49.5	26.7
Allentown	42 804	2.64	20.6	29.9	5 070	2 089	885	2 981	5 821	4 932	620	4 312	71 624	60.0	16.3
Altoona	19 301	2.34	15.2	32.8	1 189	452	443	737	1 114	2 405	361	2 044	30 877	57.5	16.2
Bethel Park	13 659	2.35	7.6	29.0	217	184	184	33	329	1 018	105	913	23 421	32.8	42.7
Bethlehem	29 365	2.34	15.3	33.0	6 265	955	882	5 310	2 303	3 071	312	2 759	46 662	47.0	27.0
Chester	11 662	2.64	35.6	31.2	3 151	1 328	143	1 823	2 163	6 367	2 682	3 685	19 829	67.8	8.4
Easton	9 307	2.55	18.8	30.9	3 087	1 093	311	1 994	920	3 433	474	2 959	16 557	59.2	16.8
Erie	40 913	2.36	18.5	34.9	5 244	1 578	715	3 666	3 980	3 910	481	3 429	62 552	56.6	19.9
Harrisburg	20 605	2.36	25.6	39.4	987	265	89	722	3 015	6 087	1 575	4 513	30 750	59.9	18.0
Hazleton	9 798	2.54	19.8	31.9	410	384	218	26	599	2 364	355	2 009	16 746	68.0	11.4
Lancaster	21 793	2.58	21.4	31.6	3 189	1 214	121	1 975	3 368	5 677	861	4 816	34 918	63.5	16.6
Lebanon	10 358	2.42	17.9	34.8	364	106	102	258	776	3 046	385	2 661	15 950	71.1	8.8
Monroeville	12 612	2.21	10.5	33.8	520	457	457	63	475	1 673	303	1 370	21 096	33.4	38.7
Norristown	11 963	2.79	23.0	29.5	947	224	224	723	1 442	4 201	1 148	3 053	21 547	61.2	16.9
Philadelphia	599 736	2.45	22.5	34.1	57 383	19 376	7 887	38 007	76 323	5 001	1 215	3 787	971 738	55.5	22.4
Pittsburgh	136 217	2.07	14.9	41.7	24 329	6 967	2 242	17 362	14 094	4 581	913	3 668	199 540	40.9	34.5
Plum	10 886	2.48	9.4	24.5	132	132	122	0	195	719	144	575	18 877	39.5	34.3
Reading	29 979	2.85	26.3	28.6	2 545	485	265	2 060	4 428	5 027	870	4 157	49 672	70.9	9.1
Scranton	30 069	2.35	15.2	35.3	5 472	2 380	1 444	3 092	2 656	3 491	308	3 183	48 787	57.1	19.8
State College	12 610	2.30	3.8	33.6	13 071	194	155	12 877	966	1 712	131	1 581	9 876	20.4	61.0
Wilkes-Barre	16 874	2.28	16.5	38.3	3 065	1 115	420	1 950	2 010	4 844	472	4 371	25 949	58.5	14.4
Williamsport	11 646	2.27	16.4	35.8	2 896	408	143	2 488	1 322	4 500	347	4 152	17 639	52.7	18.8
York	16 253	2.62	25.3	32.5	1 121	113	0	1 008	2 492	5 700	963	4 737	24 683	71.5	9.4
RHODE ISLAND	413 600	2.44	13.5	29.6	42 663	12 932	8 420	29 731	29 611	2 813	257	2 557	708 650	43.7	30.4
Cranston	31 012	2.45	13.6	29.6	4 523	4 004	224	519	2 018	2 510	144	2 366	56 882	43.6	29.4
East Providence	20 201	2.29	13.6	33.2	800	759	680	41	796	1 692	136	1 556	34 593	52.1	22.5
Pawtucket	29 022	2.43	18.9	31.7	524	357	335	167	2 573	3 616	410	3 206	49 144	56.8	17.9
Providence	62 718	2.60	20.8	31.7	15 086	1 200	1 152	13 886	9 472	5 320	683	4 637	99 945	51.2	28.3
Warwick	35 234	2.33	10.9	31.8	660	502	494	158	2 211	2 674	105	2 569	61 114	43.2	27.8
Woonsocket	17 062	2.37	17.8	33.4	802	568	568	234	1 358	3 297	430	2 867	26 151	59.6	12.5
SOUTH CAROLINA	1 801 181	2.49	15.6	26.5	139 154	63 765	19 020	75 389	208 055	4 498	598	3 900	3 035 053	46.8	24.2
Aiken	12 773	2.20	13.2	32.7	1 382	469	427	913	1 307	4 427	373	4 054	20 522	25.7	45.0
Anderson	11 080	2.25	20.8	36.3	1 751	716	577	1 035	2 149	8 053	764	7 288	17 013	53.1	19.2
Charleston	52 341	2.18	13.1	34.6	5 770	300	291	5 470	4 373	3 642	356	3 286	77 283	26.9	46.8
Columbia	45 666	2.18	17.1	38.0	29 919	7 777	920	22 142	9 228	7 138	1 007	6 131	74 829	35.3	38.5
Florence	14 979	2.43	21.2	29.6	654	389	384	265	3 237	8 735	953	7 783	23 664	42.2	30.0
Goose Creek	12 356	2.72	14.0	18.5	2 322	0	0	2 322	1 049	2 919	501	2 418	20 474	37.0	26.5
Greenville	25 599	2.08	14.7	41.7	5 129	1 393	208	3 736	3 757	6 432	824	5 609	37 825	37.7	41.0
Greer	10 012	2.52	16.3	27.9	272	130	130	142	976	3 825	541	3 284	16 791	47.8	23.9
Hilton Head Island	16 535	2.23	6.8	28.3	202	202	202	0	NA	NA	NA	NA	28 613	25.5	49.9
Mount Pleasant	27 742	2.43	8.1	26.5	568	544	544	24	1 440	2 123	230	1 893	46 115	15.7	62.0
Myrtle Beach	12 113	2.22	12.8	35.8	217	22	22	195	4 651	17 157	1 800	15 357	18 481	45.9	26.3
North Charleston	36 915	2.54	21.7	28.8	3 859	2 139	283	1 720	6 849	7 027	895	6 132	58 000	51.0	16.8
Rock Hill	25 966	2.43	18.8	30.3	3 005	612	442	2 393	3 060	4 626	818	3 808	40 093	42.4	26.8
Spartanburg	15 184	2.27	24.3	35.9	2 489	302	175	2 187	3 686	9 959	1 656	8 302	23 095	42.2	28.4
Summerville	16 866	2.55	15.4	25.3	318	251	160	67	1 756	4 047	346	3 701	27 015	34.8	27.9
Sumter	15 633	2.48	21.1	30.9	1 790	364	330	1 426	3 235	7 983	1 167	6 816	24 675	43.5	25.3
SOUTH DAKOTA	322 282	2.42	9.7	29.4	34 050	14 797	7 005	19 253	17 268	2 121	268	1 852	525 495	42.3	25.5
Aberdeen	11 418	2.18	9.5	36.9	1 191	433	351	758	597	2 288	249	2 039	17 128	44.7	23.2
Rapid City	28 586	2.29	13.1	32.9	2 471	1 331	491	1 140	3 272	4 815	583	4 232	44 230	35.6	29.1
Sioux Falls	61 707	2.40	10.9	30.6	6 085	3 336	982	2 749	5 365	3 486	316	3 170	98 333	36.8	31.7
TENNESSEE	2 493 552	2.48	13.9	26.9	153 472	84 371	33 041	69 101	271 053	4 271	613	3 658	4 208 374	49.8	22.9
Bartlett	19 456	2.77	10.8	17.3	703	688	244	15	946	1 732	192	1 540	35 538	30.1	33.7
Brentwood	12 170	3.02	5.4	11.0	349	312	275	37	469	1 266	78	1 187	22 946	12.2	68.2
Bristol	11 456	2.26	12.9	32.8	833	226	218	607	1 143	4 281	532	3 749	18 901	49.1	18.9
Chattanooga	70 749	2.26	17.3	35.3	7 562	3 067	1 212	4 495	12 543	7 481	934	6 547	110 961	45.8	25.8
Clarksville	49 439	2.63	16.3	23.7	2 921	904	419	2 017	4 928	3 707	603	3 104	74 597	40.0	21.7
Cleveland	16 107	2.40	14.3	30.0	2 703	786	430	1 917	2 343	5 675	853	4 823	25 534	45.3	23.8
Collierville	15 179	2.89	9.1	14.8	62	62	62	0	809	1 840	152	1 688	27 741	22.6	48.6
Columbia	14 012	2.41	18.8	30.0	863	795	462	68	1 679	4 841	813	4 028	22 216	55.2	15.2
Cookeville	12 471	2.25	12.0	33.9	2 410	431	201	1 979	1 867	6 134	325	5 809	17 119	48.4	25.5

1. No spouse present.   2. Data for serious crimes have not been adjusted for underreporting. This may affect comparability between geographic areas and over time.   3. Per 100,000 population estimated by the FBI.   4. Persons 25 years old and over.

Table D. Cities — Income, Poverty, and Housing

City	Money income, 2008–2010					Housing units, 2010			Occupied Housing units 2008–2010				
	Households				Families with income below poverty (percent)				Owner-occupied			Median owner costs as a percent of income	
	Per capita income[1] (dollars)	Median income	Percent with income of $200,000 or more	Percent with income of less than $25,000		Total	Percent change, 2000–2010	Vacant units for sale or rent[2]	Total	Percent	Median value[3] (dollars)	With a mortgage[4]	Without a mortgage[5]
	42	43	44	45	46	47	48	49	50	51	52	53	54
OREGON—Cont'd													
Tigard	32 009	59 245	5.8	16.9	5.1	20 068	15.4	911	18 963	61.0	321 100	26.4	13.2
Tualatin	29 245	57 177	3.5	15.5	10.8	10 528	14.2	528	9 983	54.8	332 700	26.8	10.4
West Linn	39 247	80 391	7.2	9.3	4.0	10 035	14.8	512	10 104	80.0	398 800	27.5	14.0
PENNSYLVANIA	27 004	50 289	3.6	24.6	8.8	5 567 315	6.0	548 411	4 952 621	70.5	165 200	23.7	13.8
Allentown	17 018	34 688	0.8	37.6	22.8	46 921	2.1	4 117	43 519	49.4	147 100	26.6	15.3
Altoona	19 167	34 009	1.2	36.5	15.4	21 179	-2.3	1 878	18 810	67.3	83 700	20.3	13.1
Bethel Park	31 323	63 011	2.8	13.2	1.5	14 311	3.2	652	13 062	80.0	152 100	21.3	12.3
Bethlehem	23 205	44 321	2.1	28.6	13.7	31 221	5.4	1 856	29 443	54.1	178 500	25.2	14.3
Chester	15 615	27 688	1.1	44.4	26.4	13 745	-8.2	2 083	12 134	39.5	74 100	24.8	14.1
Easton	18 520	37 074	1.1	36.7	25.3	10 356	-1.8	1 049	9 226	49.7	140 600	30.1	18.2
Erie	18 047	31 995	1.2	40.5	19.8	44 790	-0.4	3 877	40 209	54.2	83 000	23.6	14.1
Harrisburg	17 789	30 774	0.5	43.4	30.5	24 269	-0.3	3 664	20 742	38.5	86 100	24.0	15.9
Hazleton	18 350	32 950	0.6	34.9	14.2	11 409	-1.0	1 611	10 085	55.1	92 000	25.6	16.0
Lancaster	15 650	32 952	0.6	39.3	23.4	23 377	1.5	1 584	21 775	43.9	100 900	25.6	13.2
Lebanon	17 496	34 134	0.6	37.9	24.1	11 278	0.5	920	10 766	45.1	88 600	20.7	13.8
Monroeville	30 151	56 535	2.7	19.6	4.7	13 496	2.6	884	12 408	68.5	124 400	22.1	11.6
Norristown	20 409	43 156	0.7	25.7	13.4	13 420	-0.8	1 457	12 661	43.0	153 800	28.0	15.4
Philadelphia	21 061	35 952	1.9	37.6	20.4	670 171	1.2	70 435	578 990	54.1	142 100	25.8	15.7
Pittsburgh	25 233	36 723	3.4	37.0	15.1	156 165	-4.4	19 948	132 854	49.5	89 000	21.3	14.5
Plum	28 912	64 450	2.7	13.2	3.6	11 494	8.2	608	10 528	81.6	139 200	22.6	11.9
Reading	13 130	27 212	0.2	46.6	33.4	34 208	-0.3	4 229	31 241	42.5	68 800	26.2	14.6
Scranton	19 160	35 763	1.1	34.7	14.7	33 853	-4.2	3 784	29 533	54.2	109 700	24.8	17.0
State College	12 935	23 903	1.8	51.5	13.9	13 007	4.2	397	11 535	19.6	245 700	20.9	11.4
Wilkes-Barre	16 361	28 904	0.5	44.0	18.1	19 595	-3.4	2 721	16 524	49.6	79 600	22.5	17.3
Williamsport	17 250	27 464	1.0	46.0	23.2	12 864	-4.9	1 218	11 870	41.8	96 100	24.0	13.1
York	13 705	28 845	0.5	43.0	30.2	18 496	-0.2	2 243	16 166	41.7	85 000	26.5	14.8
RHODE ISLAND	28 615	53 887	3.9	24.2	8.8	463 388	5.4	49 788	408 457	61.9	271 000	27.5	18.0
Cranston	27 988	57 361	3.5	22.3	7.0	33 117	3.3	2 105	30 575	66.8	248 400	28.0	18.4
East Providence	26 470	47 570	1.8	28.2	6.8	21 440	0.6	1 239	20 068	57.0	238 300	28.0	15.4
Pawtucket	21 527	38 945	1.0	31.7	15.6	32 055	0.7	3 033	29 181	46.0	219 800	29.8	17.3
Providence	20 513	36 831	3.4	36.9	22.8	71 530	5.3	8 812	60 963	36.7	233 600	31.9	15.7
Warwick	29 971	57 370	2.3	20.6	5.0	37 730	1.7	2 496	35 383	74.5	227 900	27.7	17.0
Woonsocket	19 145	36 359	0.9	37.1	20.1	19 214	2.4	2 152	15 878	40.3	214 600	30.4	16.9
SOUTH CAROLINA	23 003	43 208	2.3	29.3	12.8	2 137 683	21.9	336 502	1 753 036	69.6	138 800	23.2	11.3
Aiken	31 847	53 560	3.4	24.1	12.3	14 162	25.3	1 389	12 818	66.3	185 000	19.3	10.0
Anderson	18 605	30 292	1.5	43.7	24.7	12 938	7.3	1 858	10 327	50.6	132 100	23.6	11.6
Charleston	30 487	48 773	5.1	26.7	12.9	59 522	34.8	7 181	49 911	53.7	265 400	26.4	12.4
Columbia	23 958	36 546	3.6	34.8	16.1	52 471	13.9	6 805	47 486	46.4	166 300	22.3	12.0
Florence	26 521	41 701	2.6	30.4	14.4	16 666	27.5	1 686	14 759	61.3	148 700	19.5	10.0
Goose Creek	23 903	61 795	1.1	15.3	8.2	13 484	42.4	1 128	11 126	70.5	170 900	23.4	10.0
Greenville	30 370	40 536	5.6	33.1	14.4	29 418	7.5	3 819	24 678	48.7	200 100	22.3	11.1
Greer	22 093	40 714	0.8	33.3	13.8	11 127	48.5	1 115	10 243	65.4	142 300	25.2	13.7
Hilton Head Island	46 424	67 995	11.2	15.9	4.8	33 306	35.0	16 771	16 826	74.3	487 000	32.8	12.5
Mount Pleasant	39 148	74 439	9.1	12.8	4.3	30 674	52.4	2 932	26 350	74.9	355 900	27.2	11.0
Myrtle Beach	25 858	36 707	5.1	33.7	16.6	23 262	59.2	11 149	11 474	52.4	174 100	28.2	12.2
North Charleston	18 702	39 415	0.9	32.9	17.9	42 219	25.5	5 304	34 431	47.7	151 800	25.4	14.2
Rock Hill	21 013	39 854	1.4	31.4	14.4	29 159	42.4	3 193	25 185	54.9	138 900	24.1	13.4
Spartanburg	20 090	33 086	2.3	39.9	17.0	17 516	-1.1	2 332	14 560	53.0	115 600	22.8	12.4
Summerville	26 404	52 535	3.4	21.2	10.7	18 557	64.9	1 691	15 692	65.5	187 400	23.0	10.7
Sumter	20 443	37 547	1.8	35.5	18.9	18 150	12.6	2 517	14 789	55.7	126 600	22.6	13.3
SOUTH DAKOTA	24 286	46 520	2.3	25.6	8.6	363 438	12.4	41 156	317 182	68.5	127 600	22.2	11.0
Aberdeen	23 080	40 567	1.7	30.5	7.3	12 158	8.1	740	11 002	64.3	124 600	22.1	13.6
Rapid City	25 349	42 894	2.8	27.0	11.3	30 254	20.4	1 668	28 027	56.9	153 600	24.0	11.8
Sioux Falls	27 561	50 415	3.2	21.5	7.5	66 283	28.1	4 576	60 581	61.8	150 600	21.7	10.0
TENNESSEE	23 264	42 612	2.7	29.3	12.7	2 812 133	15.3	318 581	2 454 343	69.1	138 600	23.6	11.0
Bartlett	29 581	73 194	3.0	9.1	3.7	20 143	43.9	687	18 766	85.8	177 600	23.0	11.2
Brentwood	53 130	132 310	27.0	3.8	1.7	12 577	58.5	407	11 772	94.0	493 800	20.6	10.0
Bristol	21 192	32 893	2.7	39.4	14.6	12 773	10.9	1 317	11 674	67.7	101 400	26.5	12.6
Chattanooga	22 304	35 664	2.2	35.6	18.6	79 607	10.4	8 858	69 802	55.1	134 200	24.1	12.2
Clarksville	20 151	45 676	0.9	25.2	13.0	54 815	36.9	5 376	47 045	58.6	130 400	23.3	10.2
Cleveland	21 042	36 078	3.2	36.4	14.7	17 841	8.4	1 734	15 990	49.4	147 700	23.3	12.6
Collierville	38 745	97 302	11.3	9.4	3.6	15 781	46.7	602	14 435	83.7	281 700	23.4	10.0
Columbia	19 600	37 591	1.8	35.7	14.8	15 906	10.7	1 894	14 160	59.9	116 500	22.9	13.1
Cookeville	18 121	29 469	1.9	43.6	13.3	13 706	26.9	1 235	11 530	45.8	146 700	22.9	11.7

1. Based on population estimated by the American Community Survey.   2. Includes units rented or sold but not occupied.   3. Specified owner-occupied units; $1,000,000 represents $1,000,000 or more.   4. 50.0 represents 50 percent or more.   5. 10.0 represents 10 percent or less.

Table D. Cities — Housing, Labor Force, and Employment

City	Occupied housing units, 2008–2010 (cont.)				Migration, 2008–2010		Civilian labor force, 2010				Civilian employment[4], 2008–2010			
									Unemployment			Percent		
	Percent renter occupied	Median gross rent[1]	Median rent as a percent of income[2]	Percent with no vehicle available	Percent who lived in the same house one year ago	Percent who lived outside this city one year ago	Total	Percent change, 2009–2010	Total	Rate[3]	Population age 16 and older	In labor force	Full-year full-time worker	Households with no workers (percent)
	55	56	57	58	59	60	61	62	63	64	65	66	67	68
OREGON—Cont'd														
Tigard	39.0	864	27.8	5.7	84.3	12.9	26 628	-0.7	2 286	8.6	37 977	71.6	44.7	20.5
Tualatin	45.2	897	31.0	5.7	83.4	11.0	14 879	-1.3	1 196	8.0	20 147	73.5	47.0	17.7
West Linn	20.0	969	29.9	2.6	88.2	7.0	13 400	0.1	1 042	7.8	19 856	71.4	42.5	20.0
PENNSYLVANIA	29.5	751	29.6	11.5	87.6	8.8	6 389 595	0.1	540 922	8.5	10 210 077	63.4	40.3	28.7
Allentown	50.6	785	36.9	21.4	76.7	8.0	55 927	7.4	6 545	11.7	88 425	61.5	36.4	32.6
Altoona	32.7	505	30.2	13.0	85.6	7.5	22 856	-1.9	1 942	8.5	36 959	58.7	36.5	36.0
Bethel Park	20.0	783	24.9	4.5	91.3	6.2	17 563	1.4	1 070	6.1	26 499	66.7	44.0	26.5
Bethlehem	45.9	850	30.4	14.5	76.2	10.8	35 746	2.1	3 663	10.2	61 970	59.0	35.1	31.1
Chester	60.5	766	33.1	37.9	80.5	10.5	13 734	-8.7	1 840	13.4	25 759	54.1	31.6	35.7
Easton	50.3	805	31.0	21.1	68.0	19.0	12 712	0.9	1 265	10.0	22 062	54.0	30.4	31.4
Erie	45.8	594	31.9	18.0	80.0	7.0	47 814	-2.7	4 830	10.1	79 469	62.0	34.5	31.3
Harrisburg	61.5	724	34.7	27.4	76.2	12.0	23 227	1.5	2 630	11.3	37 404	62.6	39.4	32.9
Hazleton	44.9	603	28.9	17.8	83.0	5.0	12 065	11.2	1 564	13.0	19 581	59.4	39.4	35.3
Lancaster	56.1	687	34.6	22.2	78.9	10.2	27 793	4.7	2 939	10.6	45 615	63.2	35.1	30.7
Lebanon	54.9	589	30.5	23.5	79.5	8.7	13 020	3.5	1 282	9.8	19 529	65.8	39.5	35.6
Monroeville	31.5	849	27.0	7.3	90.0	7.5	15 549	1.8	1 061	6.8	23 668	64.9	42.1	27.9
Norristown	57.0	930	32.0	21.4	86.1	5.7	17 488	4.0	1 552	8.9	26 171	73.8	47.7	20.1
Philadelphia	45.9	824	34.1	34.1	86.1	3.7	643 996	2.2	69 846	10.8	1 212 028	59.1	35.8	34.9
Pittsburgh	50.5	720	31.2	25.9	77.7	11.1	151 242	-1.5	12 413	8.2	260 845	61.8	36.8	31.4
Plum	18.4	820	22.9	3.9	91.2	7.1	15 104	2.5	1 025	6.8	21 732	70.3	44.9	22.2
Reading	57.5	664	35.5	26.6	73.8	8.8	36 103	6.9	4 440	12.3	64 827	60.3	32.0	36.4
Scranton	45.8	624	28.5	15.6	84.2	8.4	36 226	1.6	3 468	9.6	62 110	59.1	35.5	31.8
State College	80.4	822	50.0	21.1	38.9	41.1	18 654	1.3	1 169	6.3	40 639	40.2	14.0	32.5
Wilkes-Barre	50.4	593	31.8	23.1	78.6	13.2	19 228	-1.9	2 024	10.5	34 532	56.1	31.7	36.1
Williamsport	58.2	556	33.2	20.3	80.3	9.4	14 438	0.7	1 391	9.6	24 058	61.0	30.1	34.2
York	58.3	637	35.0	25.6	72.7	11.7	20 180	4.8	2 692	13.3	32 359	61.6	30.6	35.9
RHODE ISLAND	38.1	876	30.6	9.7	86.4	8.5	570 301	0.7	66 725	11.7	855 861	66.1	39.7	28.2
Cranston	33.2	941	33.0	5.8	89.2	7.4	42 779	1.3	5 093	11.9	65 812	63.5	39.6	28.1
East Providence	43.0	790	27.8	9.4	89.6	3.9	25 600	-2.0	3 258	12.7	38 994	66.3	40.3	32.7
Pawtucket	54.0	789	31.1	15.5	86.3	6.7	37 184	-1.2	4 803	12.9	57 184	68.0	40.6	30.5
Providence	63.3	892	32.9	20.5	74.7	10.3	82 532	4.1	11 162	13.5	141 854	62.7	33.7	31.8
Warwick	25.5	965	29.9	6.4	91.1	4.4	47 874	-1.0	5 410	11.3	69 379	67.4	41.4	27.5
Woonsocket	59.7	723	29.1	16.0	84.1	5.9	21 306	-4.3	2 895	13.6	31 502	60.5	36.4	35.2
SOUTH CAROLINA	30.4	710	30.6	7.1	84.9	12.3	2 150 576	-1.1	241 162	11.2	3 631 888	62.7	39.8	29.4
Aiken	33.7	779	28.7	8.7	86.2	8.6	13 521	-13.1	1 060	7.8	24 164	54.1	35.9	35.8
Anderson	49.4	632	34.7	13.4	70.2	15.5	10 371	-19.3	1 370	13.2	21 918	55.9	29.7	38.6
Charleston	46.3	892	34.4	10.1	77.6	14.3	59 913	2.1	4 924	8.2	98 719	68.3	44.1	23.6
Columbia	53.6	749	34.8	13.2	65.1	24.0	53 771	-10.6	5 556	10.3	110 187	63.9	36.2	26.4
Florence	38.7	647	29.6	11.3	80.5	11.4	16 570	-1.2	1 668	10.1	28 830	64.1	42.7	27.1
Goose Creek	29.5	989	31.9	3.5	75.8	20.1	14 581	-12.4	1 301	8.9	27 189	75.4	54.0	12.6
Greenville	51.3	680	28.1	9.7	76.0	15.3	29 386	-11.4	2 600	8.8	48 163	67.1	41.2	28.8
Greer	34.6	641	31.2	7.8	84.9	8.2	11 641	NA	1 019	8.8	19 404	66.0	39.6	30.5
Hilton Head Island	25.7	1 074	31.6	6.5	87.9	7.0	16 154	-2.4	1 075	6.7	31 755	50.6	32.6	40.3
Mount Pleasant	25.1	1 221	29.3	3.7	83.5	9.2	36 183	0.1	2 123	5.9	51 547	70.2	49.3	19.9
Myrtle Beach	47.6	811	33.2	11.9	83.7	10.9	14 353	-26.3	1 547	10.8	21 689	68.4	40.1	30.9
North Charleston	52.3	807	32.8	11.9	78.4	14.3	43 612	1.0	4 784	11.0	73 545	67.8	43.1	22.9
Rock Hill	45.1	733	32.2	8.9	75.8	11.4	32 805	-9.5	5 721	17.4	50 871	71.1	42.5	24.3
Spartanburg	47.0	613	32.1	12.5	77.6	12.8	15 494	-21.6	2 114	13.6	29 930	59.2	31.8	36.3
Summerville	34.5	859	31.0	5.0	82.3	14.9	21 468	-15.1	1 594	7.4	31 911	68.3	46.1	22.8
Sumter	44.3	654	26.1	13.2	87.1	9.0	15 274	1.7	1 674	11.0	31 115	62.0	42.0	31.2
SOUTH DAKOTA	31.5	577	26.2	5.6	84.0	9.3	443 444	-0.1	22 378	5.0	630 017	69.3	47.2	24.3
Aberdeen	35.7	466	21.6	10.0	85.7	7.2	15 380	3.0	632	4.1	20 857	70.5	47.5	28.5
Rapid City	43.1	663	29.0	7.4	74.5	11.7	36 380	-0.5	2 171	6.0	53 236	68.4	41.9	27.6
Sioux Falls	38.2	661	26.6	6.6	81.2	6.7	87 970	0.4	4 682	5.3	118 986	74.4	53.6	19.4
TENNESSEE	30.9	687	30.3	6.1	84.1	9.9	3 084 127	1.1	301 100	9.8	4 981 320	62.8	40.0	28.8
Bartlett	14.2	1 143	30.1	1.2	91.6	7.1	28 773	11.8	2 208	7.7	41 489	71.3	51.4	16.3
Brentwood	6.0	1 469	26.8	0.9	92.2	6.3	17 631	3.1	1 081	6.1	26 196	63.8	41.6	16.1
Bristol	32.3	595	32.9	6.7	82.2	9.2	13 071	3.5	1 072	8.2	21 778	54.7	36.2	36.4
Chattanooga	44.9	672	30.7	11.7	79.5	8.8	77 634	-1.1	7 437	9.6	134 303	65.2	38.8	31.0
Clarksville	41.4	759	28.9	4.4	73.7	14.1	56 070	10.9	5 166	9.2	95 855	68.3	44.2	21.3
Cleveland	50.6	650	31.1	6.9	74.3	11.0	19 267	2.7	1 878	9.7	32 935	61.0	33.9	30.9
Collierville	16.3	975	30.0	0.8	90.6	7.0	21 667	8.7	1 469	6.8	31 908	70.4	47.0	14.0
Columbia	40.1	652	31.8	7.3	77.5	13.3	15 262	1.8	2 358	15.5	26 733	62.4	38.6	30.8
Cookeville	54.2	574	32.2	4.4	72.4	17.8	15 619	6.1	1 406	9.0	25 383	52.2	29.7	34.4

1. $2,000 represents $2,000 or more. 2. 50.0 represents 50 percent or more. 3. Percent of civilian labor force. 4. Persons 16 years old and over.

Table D. Cities — Construction, Wholesale Trade, and Retail Trade

City	Value of residential construction authorized by building permits, 2010			Wholesale trade,[1] 2007				Retail trade,[2] 2007			
	New construction ($1,000)	Number of housing units	Percent single family	Number of establish-ments	Number of employees	Sales (mil dol)	Annual payroll (mil dol)	Number of establish-ments	Number of employees	Sales (mil dol)	Annual payroll (mil dol)
	69	70	71	72	73	74	75	76	77	78	79
OREGON—Cont'd											
Tigard	27 806	148	66.2	177	2 928	2 572.7	187.6	345	7 479	1 807.4	188.2
Tualatin	6 441	22	100.0	110	2 197	971.4	109.5	124	2 241	483.3	55.0
West Linn	12 967	40	100.0	24	78	106.6	4.1	50	550	113.6	11.9
PENNSYLVANIA	3 293 099	19 740	85.5	13 161	200 151	142 859.2	10 100.7	46 532	672 042	166 842.8	14 862.3
Allentown	9 786	59	100.0	150	2 980	1 576.9	218.5	368	5 329	1 299.7	126.0
Altoona	1 118	17	35.3	46	682	272.0	22.6	217	4 426	917.1	84.1
Bethel Park	3 058	10	100.0	37	357	123.7	13.4	168	3 786	684.6	69.9
Bethlehem	5 199	34	82.4	64	D	D	D	215	3 236	696.9	71.6
Chester	937	14	100.0	22	232	114.3	10.5	55	345	94.5	9.4
Easton	5 523	59	11.9	22	478	238.9	24.5	94	1 098	268.4	26.6
Erie	2 184	20	100.0	108	1 541	646.0	65.3	336	4 931	945.9	100.3
Harrisburg	212	1	100.0	52	2 143	2 551.3	93.5	214	2 871	560.9	57.1
Hazleton	250	1	100.0	32	477	199.0	21.0	145	1 748	540.3	38.5
Lancaster	1 535	13	100.0	64	868	412.4	31.5	339	5 062	950.9	101.1
Lebanon	636	3	100.0	19	232	95.0	7.2	120	1 263	232.6	26.2
Monroeville	940	6	100.0	50	542	242.5	24.4	314	6 621	1 497.4	127.2
Norristown	320	6	100.0	50	755	399.5	42.6	80	601	168.5	18.8
Philadelphia	138 790	984	45.4	1 067	18 338	11 566.1	956.3	4 420	50 225	11 167.8	1 158.1
Pittsburgh	21 800	147	100.0	396	6 948	7 097.2	353.4	1 161	16 455	3 413.0	367.6
Plum	8 017	54	100.0	32	350	178.0	14.2	52	558	121.2	14.1
Reading	10 302	59	0.0	60	1 233	569.3	60.1	225	2 954	733.6	69.0
Scranton	8 754	48	100.0	100	1 973	844.5	73.2	341	4 370	957.6	94.5
State College	11 041	58	1.7	9	17	10.8	1.0	164	2 560	363.1	39.7
Wilkes-Barre	410	2	100.0	51	581	230.2	24.4	249	5 134	1 878.7	113.6
Williamsport	1 237	7	100.0	40	795	363.6	26.3	114	1 524	270.6	29.4
York	2 913	19	0.0	70	911	786.0	45.1	134	1 624	328.9	38.0
RHODE ISLAND	155 073	934	77.8	1 277	18 128	9 182.8	914.9	4 080	50 865	12 286.5	1 215.4
Cranston	6 551	53	84.9	142	2 191	1 223.1	110.7	314	4 726	1 050.9	109.2
East Providence	1 229	11	81.8	87	1 474	885.4	75.7	147	2 058	554.2	53.7
Pawtucket	893	5	60.0	70	753	291.6	31.2	194	1 765	468.1	45.2
Providence	1 824	21	38.1	195	1 785	1 001.7	89.1	660	7 461	1 474.0	156.0
Warwick	6 292	67	31.3	161	1 720	774.5	94.1	484	8 503	2 153.7	211.9
Woonsocket	490	6	100.0	42	480	192.8	23.4	148	1 885	441.9	43.0
SOUTH CAROLINA	2 489 139	14 021	90.5	4 323	58 524	40 498.0	2 599.4	18 886	231 685	54 298.4	4 878.1
Aiken	9 521	85	100.0	23	D	D	D	229	2 711	529.5	49.6
Anderson	8 857	63	100.0	44	478	178.0	14.9	315	4 231	761.9	78.4
Charleston	71 714	564	70.9	106	1 362	856.2	67.2	796	10 386	2 183.7	228.3
Columbia	30 621	299	67.9	173	2 737	1 449.0	124.0	723	12 683	2 720.2	265.8
Florence	NA	NA	NA	49	946	366.4	40.1	364	5 512	1 173.1	106.2
Goose Creek	32 822	285	100.0	12	447	201.4	22.4	84	1 439	336.5	30.3
Greenville	21 000	106	88.7	178	3 685	4 957.4	197.9	713	10 133	2 356.7	221.1
Greer	9 251	104	100.0	42	335	145.1	16.3	152	2 450	737.4	59.3
Hilton Head Island	20 921	41	100.0	57	227	95.9	12.3	326	3 375	736.0	82.4
Mount Pleasant	73 559	226	100.0	66	260	121.2	13.0	366	5 072	1 016.2	106.7
Myrtle Beach	19 894	119	100.0	81	591	234.9	22.3	606	7 762	1 773.1	171.9
North Charleston	35 970	388	96.4	215	4 229	2 186.1	198.8	599	9 752	2 321.2	222.8
Rock Hill	39 168	210	90.0	58	718	425.8	33.8	320	4 361	1 059.8	89.4
Spartanburg	8 704	60	100.0	67	749	640.5	28.2	372	5 963	1 251.1	117.5
Summerville	27 393	124	100.0	43	358	133.4	15.5	206	3 142	751.9	63.4
Sumter	NA	NA	NA	33	347	120.8	13.9	313	4 079	826.3	74.9
SOUTH DAKOTA	403 140	2 946	74.2	1 248	13 402	11 400.5	550.8	4 172	50 842	12 266.2	1 045.3
Aberdeen	7 024	140	45.0	42	600	1 121.6	25.4	176	2 761	622.7	59.9
Rapid City	33 542	190	94.7	137	1 725	889.4	67.1	496	7 339	1 855.7	167.8
Sioux Falls	89 539	758	72.0	282	4 460	2 681.5	207.3	775	14 756	3 875.9	334.2
TENNESSEE	2 344 869	16 475	70.6	6 282	99 238	80 116.5	4 593.4	24 234	320 739	77 547.3	7 244.6
Bartlett	13 995	81	100.0	60	1 035	472.6	57.6	151	3 196	986.7	88.2
Brentwood	50 467	137	100.0	61	848	505.7	49.3	172	2 949	931.0	84.3
Bristol	7 324	53	100.0	48	741	455.7	45.9	140	2 079	610.6	51.7
Chattanooga	34 627	273	75.5	416	5 506	2 799.8	251.2	1 188	17 322	4 054.0	395.5
Clarksville	98 214	1 435	47.0	62	562	320.1	24.2	478	7 524	1 753.2	170.7
Cleveland	22 064	299	16.1	35	D	D	D	320	3 756	977.7	90.1
Collierville	21 844	54	100.0	53	734	510.9	40.3	186	3 698	800.2	88.5
Columbia	5 646	44	100.0	39	515	194.3	24.1	246	3 073	743.0	67.0
Cookeville	19 059	155	53.5	55	472	300.4	16.7	295	3 940	979.2	89.8

1. Merchant wholesalers except manufacturers' sales branches and offices. 2. Establishments with payroll.

City	Real estate and rental and leasing, 2007				Professional, scientific, and technical services,[1] 2007				Manufacturing, 2007			
	Number of establishments	Number of employees	Receipts (mil dol)	Annual payroll (mil dol)	Number of establishments	Number of employees	Receipts (mil dol)	Annual payroll (mil dol)	Number of establishments	Number of employees	Receipts (mil dol)	Annual payroll (mil dol)
	80	81	82	83	84	85	86	87	88	89	90	91
OREGON—Cont'd												
Tigard	144	799	287.7	34.9	365	4 087	445.4	216.6	108	2 596	D	129.7
Tualatin	41	773	123.1	26.7	92	D	D	D	128	7 068	2 007.1	331.1
West Linn	46	103	20.9	3.1	125	365	38.1	15.2	NA	NA	NA	NA
PENNSYLVANIA	9 904	68 954	13 602.6	2 611.8	29 534	292 791	45 888.3	18 184.2	15 406	650 804	234 840.4	29 433.0
Allentown	98	603	95.1	17.0	223	D	D	D	184	3 350	779.3	135.5
Altoona	37	213	40.8	5.3	101	924	78.2	32.7	51	1 060	227.6	35.1
Bethel Park	31	153	55.5	3.6	96	374	48.6	17.1	41	522	79.6	16.7
Bethlehem	55	286	50.0	7.5	187	1 196	185.2	71.1	65	5 383	1 509.9	286.6
Chester	11	54	8.4	1.2	19	D	D	D	29	1 625	D	108.5
Easton	19	71	14.1	1.6	79	329	34.4	12.1	26	1 076	299.7	50.5
Erie	64	406	45.2	12.1	194	D	D	D	158	6 486	1 595.3	284.4
Harrisburg	36	238	210.7	13.4	282	3 327	641.9	216.3	43	1 269	348.0	48.5
Hazleton	27	340	64.7	6.7	54	257	21.4	8.8	53	2 977	1 063.3	113.2
Lancaster	52	278	77.5	9.2	230	D	D	D	95	5 270	1 517.8	234.6
Lebanon	29	169	25.3	4.7	52	D	D	D	50	1 749	381.8	55.9
Monroeville	47	309	55.0	10.3	114	3 036	662.6	199.5	18	622	119.1	31.4
Norristown	26	125	23.2	4.0	94	D	D	D	31	827	185.5	28.2
Philadelphia	1 088	9 813	1 956.1	433.9	2 703	44 302	9 243.3	3 533.1	946	32 672	18 069.4	1 396.7
Pittsburgh	433	3 813	681.0	170.9	1 539	D	D	D	341	8 408	2 535.0	362.8
Plum	16	76	5.5	2.3	39	329	49.5	24.1	33	546	137.0	20.4
Reading	53	360	46.7	10.5	137	D	D	D	116	8 043	2 783.0	424.7
Scranton	49	347	32.4	9.1	210	D	D	D	89	3 023	662.4	110.9
State College	58	486	78.4	13.3	112	714	86.6	35.9	NA	NA	NA	NA
Wilkes-Barre	28	214	47.7	7.5	132	D	D	D	35	1 440	315.1	58.4
Williamsport	26	81	10.3	1.8	81	769	54.6	22.8	55	4 329	1 418.0	178.5
York	33	257	32.9	8.3	164	D	D	D	89	5 749	2 800.8	284.6
RHODE ISLAND	1 233	6 493	1 462.8	227.2	3 096	22 732	2 777.8	1 173.9	1 831	53 718	12 061.5	2 374.8
Cranston	96	616	90.1	17.8	238	1 598	181.8	68.1	192	4 815	1 606.7	214.0
East Providence	68	383	462.5	17.7	148	1 408	163.5	61.0	101	3 128	740.2	126.8
Pawtucket	55	263	33.7	8.8	114	D	D	D	163	4 805	912.4	204.9
Providence	218	1 458	244.9	53.6	799	7 799	1 057.1	512.3	303	5 828	1 050.5	214.2
Warwick	128	1 219	213.8	44.9	346	1 958	252.8	92.5	174	4 581	1 414.1	185.5
Woonsocket	39	161	20.4	4.0	48	260	40.3	11.9	59	1 306	192.6	45.2
SOUTH CAROLINA	5 473	30 417	5 194.1	989.8	9 459	74 372	9 343.3	3 622.6	4 335	242 153	93 977.5	10 061.5
Aiken	67	266	37.3	6.5	117	D	D	D	23	D	D	D
Anderson	60	240	44.5	7.3	143	D	D	D	59	3 230	860.3	126.8
Charleston	297	1 593	263.2	57.6	608	4 331	688.8	265.4	61	1 024	409.9	43.7
Columbia	262	2 385	616.0	92.9	865	D	D	D	93	3 888	D	203.4
Florence	76	439	61.8	10.2	127	D	D	D	21	D	D	D
Goose Creek	32	434	51.2	9.3	62	699	107.1	26.8	14	1 025	666.6	62.4
Greenville	245	1 822	429.6	73.8	728	6 866	1 376.5	450.7	107	4 053	978.4	162.0
Greer	37	191	27.9	4.4	70	273	24.2	9.6	37	5 333	D	D
Hilton Head Island	250	2 482	306.3	98.3	263	1 287	193.2	91.3	NA	NA	NA	NA
Mount Pleasant	187	507	136.1	18.7	354	D	D	D	NA	NA	NA	NA
Myrtle Beach	256	2 495	441.3	81.8	227	1 281	162.3	62.9	47	1 561	D	71.1
North Charleston	152	1 278	221.9	37.0	292	D	D	D	138	7 832	3 944.9	369.0
Rock Hill	87	459	66.8	12.4	168	D	D	D	57	3 000	1 145.1	139.1
Spartanburg	103	532	79.8	22.3	217	D	D	D	42	D	D	D
Summerville	78	214	40.2	5.8	106	503	41.3	15.7	27	D	D	D
Sumter	62	240	28.5	5.5	110	520	43.2	12.7	35	1 661	345.6	60.3
SOUTH DAKOTA	888	3 844	523.9	90.3	1 735	10 073	1 093.4	385.9	1 052	40 961	13 051.1	1 539.3
Aberdeen	53	D	D	D	70	364	34.4	13.5	32	D	D	D
Rapid City	134	637	106.0	15.5	258	D	D	D	100	2 575	623.6	90.9
Sioux Falls	202	1 288	214.6	38.7	460	D	D	D	160	10 329	3 113.0	428.1
TENNESSEE	6 087	37 737	6 950.4	1 243.0	11 278	D	D	D	6 752	369 165	140 447.8	15 165.6
Bartlett	44	242	96.6	5.5	110	741	104.5	37.4	33	937	299.3	39.4
Brentwood	115	739	121.1	25.6	344	3 706	627.9	274.2	NA	NA	NA	NA
Bristol	38	151	27.7	4.1	66	491	44.0	21.1	51	D	1 445.1	110.2
Chattanooga	314	2 049	326.2	93.6	620	D	D	D	370	18 580	6 159.7	798.8
Clarksville	139	559	109.1	14.9	150	D	D	D	53	3 604	1 827.2	145.7
Cleveland	68	378	82.1	10.7	131	D	D	D	92	D	4 222.7	285.7
Collierville	49	211	36.0	5.1	100	385	42.0	16.0	32	3 466	1 582.4	130.3
Columbia	67	241	38.9	5.9	80	D	D	D	39	D	D	D
Cookeville	60	204	36.9	4.8	121	D	D	D	91	4 100	D	153.4

1. Establishments subject to federal tax.

Table D. Cities — Accommodation and Food Services, Arts, Entertainment, and Recreation, and Health Care and Social Assistance

City	Accommodation and food services, 2007				Arts, entertainment, and recreation,[1] 2007				Health care and social assistance,[1] 2007			
	Number of establishments	Number of employees	Sales (mil dol)	Annual payroll (mil dol)	Number of establishments	Number of employees	Receipts (mil dol)	Annual payroll (mil dol)	Number of establishments	Number of employees	Receipts (mil dol)	Annual payroll (mil dol)
	92	93	94	95	96	97	98	99	100	101	102	103
OREGON—Cont'd												
Tigard	165	2 940	147.0	43.0	13	D	D	D	175	1 904	183.6	72.0
Tualatin	82	1 487	75.4	23.4	11	D	D	D	126	D	D	D
West Linn	43	707	29.9	8.8	12	D	D	D	81	546	44.8	18.9
PENNSYLVANIA	26 910	420 209	19 625.4	5 454.0	3 420	53 939	4 743.5	1 682.1	27 138	368 531	35 089.4	15 093.0
Allentown	258	3 250	150.3	42.5	25	425	17.4	5.8	296	3 821	400.4	169.8
Altoona	113	1 750	64.1	17.1	10	D	D	D	151	D	D	D
Bethel Park	73	1 621	61.4	17.2	13	D	D	D	98	1 201	109.0	49.0
Bethlehem	213	2 815	141.4	39.5	10	157	5.0	1.3	195	2 197	223.0	105.6
Chester	39	295	16.2	4.0	NA	NA	NA	NA	45	1 401	197.0	90.8
Easton	87	1 117	50.1	12.3	1	D	D	D	44	1 657	226.4	67.7
Erie	220	3 227	122.7	32.5	26	D	D	D	351	5 218	481.3	257.4
Harrisburg	183	2 657	137.7	39.1	18	158	8.8	2.2	103	1 513	157.7	71.1
Hazleton	84	944	38.2	10.8	4	D	D	D	107	955	108.4	36.3
Lancaster	145	2 614	127.4	38.8	14	61	4.9	1.6	149	3 072	349.5	151.9
Lebanon	64	547	26.2	5.9	4	D	D	D	77	850	71.9	36.8
Monroeville	121	3 138	144.2	39.6	11	221	6.1	2.2	171	2 784	241.5	107.6
Norristown	55	410	21.7	4.8	3	D	D	D	72	1 391	148.1	74.6
Philadelphia	3 396	48 552	3 051.4	837.9	214	7 245	1 000.8	595.0	2 382	38 459	4 274.2	1 818.6
Pittsburgh	1 144	20 474	1 042.9	310.8	102	2 542	563.1	278.1	885	18 910	2 173.7	1 068.3
Plum	34	602	17.1	4.8	12	76	3.5	1.0	22	133	7.3	3.2
Reading	137	D	D	D	13	332	20.5	6.1	100	1 522	110.2	44.3
Scranton	195	3 044	128.2	34.7	15	D	D	D	212	2 712	286.2	138.6
State College	125	2 827	100.0	28.9	8	44	4.8	1.2	85	1 179	118.2	55.1
Wilkes-Barre	122	2 044	91.1	23.9	7	D	D	D	115	1 147	116.7	48.6
Williamsport	81	1 105	47.2	12.3	3	D	D	D	96	1 712	145.6	78.5
York	92	1 492	65.3	17.5	4	49	1.3	0.4	56	848	75.9	37.8
RHODE ISLAND	2 926	44 426	2 148.7	622.1	395	6 863	526.8	143.4	2 502	34 762	3 015.1	1 309.5
Cranston	188	3 227	144.4	40.7	20	D	D	D	231	3 318	230.5	109.8
East Providence	113	1 600	68.6	17.9	16	D	D	D	129	2 288	231.3	113.0
Pawtucket	144	1 668	65.2	18.1	10	74	14.8	6.3	135	2 060	153.7	72.5
Providence	517	9 156	472.0	138.1	87	1 596	44.6	14.0	447	5 447	639.0	294.3
Warwick	249	5 817	264.4	77.6	39	D	D	D	307	4 301	369.8	156.2
Woonsocket	95	1 249	53.9	14.5	6	D	D	D	82	1 394	105.0	49.9
SOUTH CAROLINA	9 291	182 899	8 383.5	2 311.0	1 271	19 444	1 105.6	316.1	7 883	115 669	11 213.4	4 523.3
Aiken	108	2 160	80.4	21.7	24	423	25.2	7.2	140	3 129	300.1	103.3
Anderson	155	3 447	126.8	35.1	12	140	5.8	2.3	195	D	D	D
Charleston	435	10 992	641.3	173.6	61	1 169	89.2	29.5	419	4 511	626.3	260.7
Columbia	491	10 913	496.0	140.7	41	D	D	D	472	7 864	863.7	373.3
Florence	140	3 211	135.7	37.1	12	D	D	D	217	D	D	D
Goose Creek	63	1 014	43.7	11.2	3	D	D	D	42	D	D	D
Greenville	367	8 250	385.6	112.2	41	851	36.1	12.6	298	4 660	537.5	241.2
Greer	82	1 307	53.0	13.7	8	D	D	D	71	D	D	D
Hilton Head Island	218	5 313	321.6	120.9	53	D	D	D	148	D	D	D
Mount Pleasant	196	3 810	181.1	54.1	43	D	D	D	269	D	D	D
Myrtle Beach	532	13 682	797.8	218.5	69	1 893	128.3	29.2	210	D	D	D
North Charleston	275	6 474	306.8	78.2	17	681	22.6	7.3	253	5 838	741.3	228.4
Rock Hill	170	3 829	157.9	43.5	15	D	D	D	183	4 639	563.8	202.6
Spartanburg	202	4 322	176.3	51.1	16	92	5.7	1.7	178	D	D	D
Summerville	114	3 049	116.1	32.4	8	D	D	D	125	D	D	D
Sumter	118	2 837	96.4	26.6	10	48	1.9	0.4	139	2 065	178.6	74.4
SOUTH DAKOTA	2 426	36 710	1 622.8	436.2	535	4 868	399.3	75.8	1 535	17 404	1 697.4	666.9
Aberdeen	97	1 858	70.5	18.9	21	D	D	D	116	D	D	D
Rapid City	229	5 384	231.9	67.8	60	467	36.1	6.7	259	D	D	D
Sioux Falls	391	9 548	387.3	118.4	96	1 475	118.7	19.6	343	4 728	612.1	266.5
TENNESSEE	11 592	239 379	10 626.8	3 009.2	2 006	21 937	2 873.8	885.3	11 720	185 582	19 249.5	7 599.6
Bartlett	87	1 956	75.8	21.0	8	153	4.8	1.6	98	D	D	D
Brentwood	83	2 193	107.9	30.2	64	D	D	D	273	D	D	D
Bristol	85	1 725	61.2	16.0	10	D	D	D	118	D	D	D
Chattanooga	586	12 921	554.8	164.9	65	1 169	49.9	14.6	699	11 422	1 395.6	547.2
Clarksville	279	5 871	235.5	61.4	19	D	D	D	222	D	D	D
Cleveland	143	D	D	D	14	D	D	D	159	D	D	D
Collierville	81	1 605	66.1	19.4	13	D	D	D	61	D	D	D
Columbia	105	2 321	81.8	23.6	8	51	1.7	0.7	134	D	D	D
Cookeville	132	3 106	128.5	36.2	10	D	D	D	162	1 720	164.3	59.8

1. Establishments subject to federal tax.

Table D. Cities — **Other Services and Federal Funds**

City	Other services[1], 2007				Selected federal funds, 2009–2010 (mil dol)								
					Procurement contracts		Grants						
	Number of establishments	Number of employees	Receipts (mil dol)	Annual payroll (mil dol)	Defense	Other	Total[2]	Medicaid and other health related	Nutrition and family welfare	Energy and environment	Disasters and emergency preparedness	Housing and community development	Employment and training
	104	105	106	107	108	109	110	111	112	113	114	115	116
OREGON—Cont'd													
Tigard	119	780	68.6	22.1	5.5	1.1	6.1	3.5	0.0	0.0	0.0	0.0	0.0
Tualatin	65	490	49.8	15.3	2.4	1.7	1.4	1.2	0.0	0.1	0.0	0.0	0.0
West Linn	31	139	7.8	2.9	2.3	0.2	0.0	0.0	0.0	0.0	0.0	0.0	0.0
PENNSYLVANIA	20 165	113 790	9 502.5	2 798.3	11 900.9	7 451.5	29 411.2	16 147.3	2 976.8	1 336.9	32.0	1 242.1	427.4
Allentown	200	1 202	95.1	28.6	44.6	6.5	495.3	2.2	8.9	436.0	0.0	18.9	0.0
Altoona	112	582	38.8	11.9	1.3	55.0	18.4	0.4	3.1	0.0	0.0	8.3	0.0
Bethel Park	80	552	31.8	11.4	0.0	0.0	0.3	0.3	0.0	0.0	0.0	0.0	0.0
Bethlehem	102	788	80.6	27.9	10.8	1.1	233.2	4.1	0.0	5.7	0.0	9.4	197.0
Chester	32	275	17.8	5.7	5.1	1.2	22.6	2.8	0.0	0.0	0.0	18.5	0.0
Easton	44	246	19.1	6.8	1.8	10.4	13.8	0.3	0.0	2.5	0.0	10.2	0.0
Erie	165	744	53.6	16.4	39.7	29.0	45.7	2.5	6.3	2.2	0.0	19.8	0.0
Harrisburg	71	355	33.8	10.5	522.5	21.6	4 756.8	231.4	590.5	338.6	0.8	107.5	163.0
Hazleton	55	209	14.1	4.3	0.4	0.2	4.4	0.0	0.0	0.0	0.0	3.0	0.0
Lancaster	99	566	37.6	12.8	20.4	3.1	55.4	0.8	6.7	5.4	0.0	22.4	0.0
Lebanon	51	215	14.7	4.6	3.8	74.7	7.5	0.0	0.0	0.0	0.0	4.8	0.0
Monroeville	89	594	31.3	10.9	523.5	0.7	-0.2	0.0	0.0	0.0	-0.2	0.0	0.0
Norristown	41	237	18.0	4.4	2.2	0.8	76.8	2.6	3.4	35.9	0.0	32.5	0.4
Philadelphia	1 903	10 803	836.4	252.6	421.6	882.3	2 976.3	1 657.1	52.6	247.2	0.0	431.0	46.7
Pittsburgh	574	3 536	265.6	81.6	224.3	225.0	1 697.2	1 039.3	32.1	84.6	0.3	170.9	2.5
Plum	34	178	16.7	3.6	0.1	0.2	0.0	0.0	0.0	0.0	0.0	0.0	0.0
Reading	97	823	63.8	24.0	54.8	8.0	48.2	1.1	4.6	3.8	0.0	23.9	0.4
Scranton	138	794	62.7	17.7	119.8	11.2	32.0	4.5	5.6	0.9	0.0	13.1	0.0
State College	41	257	15.3	5.0	23.7	1.9	309.3	120.4	0.3	29.6	0.0	1.7	0.0
Wilkes-Barre	74	329	22.2	5.7	2.4	3.8	38.0	2.6	6.8	2.6	0.0	18.5	0.0
Williamsport	51	364	37.1	9.5	17.7	8.5	23.4	0.1	3.6	0.9	0.0	5.7	0.4
York	46	338	34.5	9.9	1 207.2	14.2	38.0	3.1	3.3	5.6	0.1	16.6	0.4
RHODE ISLAND	1 929	10 073	820.0	264.1	776.9	224.5	3 152.0	1 752.5	292.4	57.9	53.3	144.4	55.0
Cranston	180	1 110	79.0	28.9	13.5	0.8	80.8	9.7	24.4	1.6	0.0	4.1	34.2
East Providence	97	482	50.8	15.2	1.4	1.1	12.4	5.8	0.0	0.0	2.4	3.7	0.0
Pawtucket	120	706	67.6	19.1	0.1	5.8	18.7	6.5	0.0	0.2	0.0	10.1	0.0
Providence	269	2 010	151.1	51.7	14.1	49.5	881.9	317.5	40.8	45.9	35.2	68.8	17.9
Warwick	184	983	83.6	25.8	5.8	15.0	37.4	1.2	4.1	2.8	0.1	5.1	2.8
Woonsocket	65	312	29.5	8.6	13.3	1.2	21.5	3.8	1.9	0.0	0.0	15.1	0.0
SOUTH CAROLINA	5 842	35 233	2 710.9	846.7	4 496.7	3 674.6	8 210.5	4 833.3	853.8	157.2	7.8	250.2	144.0
Aiken	61	526	24.0	8.0	6.1	2 319.8	11.7	0.0	2.6	0.7	0.0	5.8	0.0
Anderson	77	D	D	D	12.1	0.9	16.6	0.9	0.0	0.4	0.0	4.8	0.0
Charleston	182	1 296	73.1	25.9	175.3	505.0	297.9	208.8	0.1	3.8	0.0	29.2	0.0
Columbia	234	1 828	120.5	42.0	475.4	113.9	1 115.1	208.2	151.0	48.9	0.3	83.6	128.2
Florence	57	576	36.0	10.8	4.7	6.5	29.0	2.3	5.9	0.0	0.0	6.4	4.3
Goose Creek	40	165	10.5	3.0	54.6	1.3	0.0	0.0	0.0	0.0	0.0	0.0	0.0
Greenville	186	1 133	69.3	24.3	252.0	4.6	62.7	6.6	12.9	3.0	0.0	24.5	0.0
Greer	58	D	D	D	49.6	1.0	1.7	0.0	0.0	0.0	0.0	1.7	0.0
Hilton Head Island	95	399	32.7	10.3	4.6	0.0	0.0	0.0	0.0	0.0	0.0	0.0	0.0
Mount Pleasant	142	963	64.6	23.8	18.1	1.4	0.6	0.0	0.0	0.5	0.0	0.0	0.0
Myrtle Beach	125	653	47.7	12.9	5.1	1.0	14.7	0.0	0.0	0.0	0.0	4.6	0.0
North Charleston	192	1 863	193.6	62.9	235.3	176.6	21.9	0.0	0.0	0.0	0.0	15.1	0.0
Rock Hill	103	858	60.5	19.8	2.2	1.6	25.3	3.8	6.9	0.7	0.0	5.8	0.2
Spartanburg	101	784	57.5	14.8	0.6	1.8	34.3	6.5	4.9	0.1	0.0	17.8	0.4
Summerville	89	449	34.5	10.7	16.9	0.2	1.2	0.4	0.0	0.0	0.0	0.2	0.0
Sumter	84	564	38.1	11.6	30.9	4.8	27.8	1.2	7.2	3.1	0.0	6.5	0.5
SOUTH DAKOTA	1 359	6 196	465.7	129.1	560.7	352.2	2 250.2	761.9	216.0	233.4	56.2	89.0	34.2
Aberdeen	52	D	D	D	57.4	8.1	6.9	0.2	2.7	0.1	0.0	1.9	0.0
Rapid City	166	988	71.6	22.2	76.7	13.7	81.3	13.9	8.1	11.1	0.0	9.5	0.1
Sioux Falls	262	1 905	128.4	40.0	36.3	40.5	145.9	18.2	4.7	75.4	0.0	14.9	0.0
TENNESSEE	7 153	50 425	3 847.7	1 234.7	3 100.9	7 039.8	14 094.4	8 035.9	1 360.7	285.7	199.5	545.3	149.9
Bartlett	78	582	45.0	14.4	5.0	5.1	0.0	0.0	0.0	0.0	0.0	0.0	0.0
Brentwood	67	623	46.9	15.6	3.3	28.9	0.0	0.0	0.0	0.0	0.0	0.0	0.0
Bristol	57	761	71.3	20.9	0.1	3.5	3.4	0.0	0.0	0.0	0.0	3.0	0.0
Chattanooga	369	3 439	222.7	82.0	31.7	483.1	183.0	6.2	7.6	114.9	0.0	28.2	0.0
Clarksville	165	946	62.8	18.6	20.4	1.3	13.8	0.0	1.5	1.0	0.0	2.4	0.0
Cleveland	76	D	D	D	0.1	2.3	17.0	0.1	11.8	0.0	0.0	2.0	0.0
Collierville	50	D	D	D	4.3	0.0	0.2	0.0	0.0	0.2	0.0	0.0	0.0
Columbia	57	D	D	D	0.5	3.3	1.2	0.0	0.0	0.0	0.0	0.5	0.0
Cookeville	81	D	D	D	1.8	56.7	19.9	0.3	9.3	0.9	0.0	1.2	0.0

1. Establishments subject to federal tax.   2. Includes program categories not shown separately. State totals include additional categories not allocated by city.

Table D. Cities — City Government Finances

City	General revenue Total (mil dol)	Intergovernmental Total (mil dol)	Intergovernmental Percent from state government	Taxes Total (mil dol)	Taxes Per capita (dollars) Total	Taxes Per capita (dollars) Property	Taxes Per capita (dollars) Sales and gross receipts	General expenditure Total (mil dol)	Per capita (dollars) Total	Per capita (dollars) Capital outlays
	117	118	119	120	121	122	123	124	125	126
OREGON—Cont'd										
Tigard	33.5	5.1	60.9	21.1	425	233	192	32.1	646	112
Tualatin	30.3	2.7	66.0	16.5	626	419	206	31.2	1 186	329
West Linn	61.4	4.1	98.3	40.4	1 618	832	786	62.3	2 496	959
PENNSYLVANIA	X	X	X	X	X	X	X	X	X	X
Allentown	116.2	14.3	41.4	50.3	469	278	100	115.1	1 075	79
Altoona	25.7	7.1	35.6	14.5	312	180	75	28.5	613	37
Bethel Park	21.4	2.7	54.2	11.9	375	117	31	21.8	688	47
Bethlehem	69.1	15.3	82.9	31.8	438	260	74	70.4	970	0
Chester	35.9	4.7	71.5	19.2	524	199	109	33.7	919	13
Easton	36.8	5.9	61.7	10.6	406	254	65	39.4	1 511	33
Erie	103.0	25.7	29.8	39.4	380	263	52	89.6	865	32
Harrisburg	86.8	8.8	55.3	25.4	538	273	174	85.0	1 801	88
Hazleton	19.3	8.2	38.3	6.7	307	80	70	15.9	729	110
Lancaster	56.4	11.1	59.7	23.6	432	283	73	60.3	1 102	74
Lebanon	14.2	1.1	98.3	9.5	396	115	8	12.9	536	41
Monroeville	25.1	1.7	95.5	20.5	741	153	325	27.8	1 003	107
Norristown	25.8	3.1	42.7	19.2	618	315	93	26.9	866	98
Philadelphia	6 421.1	2 606.1	73.2	2 857.5	1 971	273	185	5 767.3	3 978	275
Pittsburgh	619.0	219.1	77.3	331.1	1 064	418	297	476.3	1 530	91
Plum	10.2	1.2	86.4	7.5	287	146	29	9.9	378	0
Reading	94.3	14.6	99.0	39.8	492	186	114	96.2	1 191	36
Scranton	74.0	16.3	49.3	41.2	568	167	81	73.5	1 014	1
State College	27.1	3.3	33.6	10.1	252	106	38	33.4	837	167
Wilkes-Barre	55.5	24.4	73.0	21.4	522	155	87	58.1	1 415	245
Williamsport	28.4	11.8	48.7	14.1	478	294	117	20.7	700	116
York	57.6	9.0	37.7	20.5	509	323	130	53.2	1 323	34
RHODE ISLAND	X	X	X	X	X	X	X	X	X	X
Cranston	263.1	76.1	97.9	147.2	1 830	1 830	0	281.0	3 492	158
East Providence	132.9	42.6	98.5	74.2	1 521	1 491	30	129.5	2 654	48
Pawtucket	198.7	110.2	84.0	75.8	1 048	1 037	11	193.0	2 668	95
Providence	750.5	343.4	95.6	290.6	1 685	1 632	53	731.4	4 241	385
Warwick	293.3	61.9	97.4	196.4	2 308	2 246	62	298.2	3 504	112
Woonsocket	144.0	82.8	99.2	43.9	1 007	949	58	143.9	3 300	58
SOUTH CAROLINA	X	X	X	X	X	X	X	X	X	X
Aiken	37.3	2.6	57.0	20.0	684	279	405	34.3	1 175	172
Anderson	33.1	3.5	63.4	17.9	677	391	285	35.3	1 336	110
Charleston	174.8	23.0	32.3	70.3	639	409	230	188.0	1 709	64
Columbia	129.2	9.6	35.9	71.7	574	324	250	128.1	1 027	90
Florence	36.9	2.8	51.6	19.6	622	253	369	29.8	948	59
Goose Creek	16.7	3.2	31.0	9.9	272	96	176	13.8	377	0
Greenville	86.1	8.0	100.0	59.8	1 017	422	596	81.4	1 385	0
Greer	23.8	1.5	62.6	15.1	644	308	315	29.0	1 239	145
Hilton Head Island	59.7	6.8	98.6	41.7	1 227	450	777	51.9	1 526	442
Mount Pleasant	65.3	5.8	95.6	41.0	634	311	323	68.4	1 057	170
Myrtle Beach	123.6	14.4	92.0	56.5	1 884	692	1 192	119.0	3 970	658
North Charleston	103.1	16.6	31.1	63.5	695	376	289	93.8	1 026	209
Rock Hill	79.9	7.5	28.9	35.8	552	353	199	74.7	1 151	210
Spartanburg	40.3	5.9	1.9	28.2	726	393	333	35.5	915	0
Summerville	25.3	2.1	69.0	19.2	436	157	279	19.1	434	52
Sumter	41.7	8.0	29.1	21.1	545	179	366	39.2	1 012	213
SOUTH DAKOTA	X	X	X	X	X	X	X	X	X	X
Aberdeen	32.7	5.0	18.0	18.9	773	219	554	44.4	1 819	798
Rapid City	99.9	14.1	9.9	54.4	851	188	663	93.8	1 465	415
Sioux Falls	179.8	9.6	29.0	128.4	847	231	616	203.0	1 340	541
TENNESSEE	X	X	X	X	X	X	X	X	X	X
Bartlett	52.9	6.0	94.9	31.6	665	299	366	47.5	999	136
Brentwood	44.7	6.4	100.0	25.3	721	265	455	33.0	941	218
Bristol	73.6	33.2	57.2	22.9	901	746	132	69.6	2 730	254
Chattanooga	337.9	105.9	35.5	110.3	649	529	121	308.0	1 813	189
Clarksville	93.2	36.2	39.0	30.6	256	187	69	100.8	845	205
Cleveland	84.1	37.5	65.8	27.1	692	398	295	83.7	2 135	229
Collierville	54.2	15.2	42.2	21.2	540	412	129	48.2	1 230	283
Columbia	33.5	4.3	100.0	13.3	392	201	186	37.5	1 104	285
Cookeville	184.4	3.6	90.0	7.0	241	175	66	181.5	6 280	1 237

1. Based on population estimated as of July 1 of the year shown.

City	City government finances, 2006 (cont.)									
	General expenditure (cont.)									
	Percent of total for:									
	Public welfare	Highways	Parking facilities	Education	Health and hospitals	Police protection	Sewerage and sanitation	Parks and recreation	Housing and community development	Interest on debt
	127	128	129	130	131	132	133	134	135	136
OREGON—Cont'd										
Tigard	0.5	12.1	0.0	0.0	0.0	28.7	9.1	4.5	0.0	1.8
Tualatin	0.0	6.6	0.0	0.0	0.0	12.1	20.6	7.0	9.0	1.5
West Linn	0.0	10.2	0.0	0.0	0.0	12.5	27.8	7.4	5.5	3.9
PENNSYLVANIA	X	X	X	X	X	X	X	X	X	X
Allentown	0.0	9.9	0.0	0.0	5.9	19.1	17.9	2.7	4.6	3.4
Altoona	0.0	19.0	0.0	0.0	0.2	14.9	0.0	1.0	8.9	3.2
Bethel Park	0.0	32.5	0.0	0.0	0.0	23.0	23.6	4.8	0.5	0.8
Bethlehem	0.0	9.1	0.0	0.0	4.8	14.2	13.8	4.8	6.1	10.4
Chester	0.0	6.2	0.0	0.0	1.3	32.2	3.6	2.0	4.7	3.0
Easton	0.0	4.0	0.8	0.0	0.3	18.8	19.7	6.3	2.4	6.5
Erie	0.0	8.6	0.0	0.0	0.0	14.1	15.2	4.5	8.1	5.6
Harrisburg	0.0	6.8	0.0	0.0	0.2	21.2	31.1	3.4	8.9	3.5
Hazleton	0.0	17.3	0.0	0.0	0.7	19.1	10.9	1.9	9.8	2.5
Lancaster	0.0	4.5	0.0	0.0	0.7	24.5	16.4	2.5	4.8	5.0
Lebanon	0.0	20.9	0.0	0.0	0.0	20.0	4.4	18.7	0.0	7.0
Monroeville	0.0	19.7	0.0	0.0	0.3	30.8	4.6	13.2	1.6	2.8
Norristown	0.0	16.3	0.0	0.0	1.5	23.6	5.4	2.0	0.0	5.5
Philadelphia	8.7	1.5	0.0	0.4	23.0	9.2	5.4	1.5	3.7	2.6
Pittsburgh	0.0	2.7	0.0	0.0	2.8	13.1	5.1	2.3	12.5	8.7
Plum	0.0	33.6	0.0	0.0	0.0	31.5	11.7	0.4	0.0	1.6
Reading	0.0	6.9	0.0	0.0	3.1	26.2	18.0	2.1	13.7	3.1
Scranton	0.0	4.8	0.0	0.0	0.6	19.0	4.7	2.0	9.0	4.5
State College	0.0	13.1	15.8	0.0	0.8	20.8	21.7	2.9	4.3	3.9
Wilkes-Barre	0.0	32.1	0.5	0.0	3.1	14.0	3.5	1.3	15.1	2.3
Williamsport	0.0	19.9	0.0	0.0	0.0	27.8	0.2	7.5	4.7	0.8
York	0.0	5.3	1.0	0.0	3.2	14.6	20.1	4.2	8.8	7.0
RHODE ISLAND	X	X	X	X	X	X	X	X	X	X
Cranston	0.0	5.3	0.0	54.0	1.1	10.8	5.5	1.4	0.9	1.4
East Providence	0.0	2.6	0.0	56.9	0.3	8.4	6.0	2.3	0.8	1.5
Pawtucket	0.0	1.3	0.0	59.7	0.0	8.4	1.8	1.4	2.4	1.4
Providence	0.0	0.7	0.0	51.8	0.0	7.3	1.2	2.5	0.0	2.4
Warwick	0.7	2.0	0.0	56.1	0.5	8.5	2.8	0.9	0.5	2.8
Woonsocket	0.2	1.3	0.0	55.6	0.0	5.5	9.6	0.9	2.2	5.3
SOUTH CAROLINA	X	X	X	X	X	X	X	X	X	X
Aiken	0.0	8.6	0.0	0.0	0.0	23.5	16.9	14.4	5.2	0.3
Anderson	0.0	0.0	0.0	0.0	0.0	15.8	22.7	10.3	4.8	2.7
Charleston	0.4	5.3	3.9	0.0	0.0	16.5	15.2	11.4	2.3	19.0
Columbia	0.0	3.0	1.6	0.0	0.8	18.5	8.3	6.8	2.8	3.6
Florence	0.0	6.7	0.0	0.0	0.1	24.4	20.2	10.8	3.3	0.6
Goose Creek	0.0	4.1	1.6	0.0	4.7	34.1	8.2	10.1	0.0	4.1
Greenville	0.0	11.2	2.9	0.0	0.0	19.2	5.8	20.0	4.3	5.5
Greer	0.0	11.2	0.0	0.0	0.0	14.1	25.9	5.1	0.0	13.5
Hilton Head Island	0.0	0.0	3.9	0.0	0.0	4.9	1.6	7.2	0.0	8.9
Mount Pleasant	0.0	6.8	0.0	0.0	0.0	12.2	23.1	5.7	0.0	1.9
Myrtle Beach	0.1	5.2	0.6	0.0	0.0	14.9	13.6	19.3	3.7	7.3
North Charleston	0.0	0.0	9.6	0.0	0.0	25.1	11.0	5.2	4.2	4.7
Rock Hill	0.0	10.3	0.0	0.0	0.0	15.2	20.0	9.6	5.1	2.7
Spartanburg	0.0	9.9	0.2	0.0	0.0	18.6	11.3	4.9	2.4	5.5
Summerville	0.0	1.6	0.0	0.0	0.0	29.9	16.6	11.6	0.0	0.1
Sumter	0.0	0.9	0.0	0.0	0.2	22.4	20.2	7.7	4.5	1.0
SOUTH DAKOTA	X	X	X	X	X	X	X	X	X	X
Aberdeen	0.0	13.6	0.0	0.0	1.6	6.4	19.5	24.7	0.0	0.3
Rapid City	0.1	12.2	0.4	0.0	3.2	14.4	12.6	11.9	3.3	4.5
Sioux Falls	0.0	10.4	1.0	0.0	4.7	11.6	32.8	13.9	5.9	1.7
TENNESSEE	X	X	X	X	X	X	X	X	X	X
Bartlett	0.0	10.9	0.0	0.0	0.0	23.6	13.9	12.0	0.0	1.6
Brentwood	0.0	11.6	0.0	0.7	0.2	15.8	6.3	4.5	0.0	3.3
Bristol	0.2	6.5	0.0	50.8	0.0	9.5	10.8	6.1	1.7	0.9
Chattanooga	4.5	7.4	0.2	0.0	0.5	14.2	17.0	6.2	3.4	6.9
Clarksville	0.0	8.7	0.1	0.0	0.0	18.8	37.1	4.4	2.0	6.9
Cleveland	0.0	7.5	0.0	44.5	0.6	12.3	11.4	2.5	0.7	3.5
Collierville	0.0	12.9	0.0	0.0	0.9	18.3	25.8	9.0	0.0	3.9
Columbia	0.0	7.8	0.0	0.0	0.0	15.7	34.2	3.7	0.0	2.0
Cookeville	0.0	0.5	0.0	0.0	87.5	3.7	1.3	1.0	0.0	2.1

City	City government finances, 2007 (cont.)			Climate[2]							
	Debt outstanding				Average daily temperature (degrees Fahrenheit)						
					Mean		Limits				
	Total (mil dol)	Per capita[1] (dollars)	Debt issued during year	City government employment, 2010	January	July	January[3]	July[4]	Annual precipitation (inches)	Heating degree days	Cooling degree days
	137	138	139	140	141	142	143	144	145	146	147
OREGON—Cont'd											
Tigard	13.7	275	0.0	288	40.0	66.8	33.8	79.2	39.95	4 723	287
Tualatin	22.0	835	4.2	NA	NA	NA	NA	NA	NA	NA	NA
West Linn	60.7	2 433	0.0	NA	NA	NA	NA	NA	NA	NA	NA
PENNSYLVANIA	X	X	X	NA	X	X	X	X	X	X	X
Allentown	130.6	1 219	15.3	869	27.1	73.3	19.1	83.9	45.17	5 830	787
Altoona	30.8	663	0.0	266	26.5	71.1	18.2	81.9	42.69	6 055	546
Bethel Park	3.0	94	0.0	NA	28.6	73.1	19.8	84.5	37.78	5 727	709
Bethlehem	192.2	2 650	0.0	731	27.1	73.3	19.1	83.9	45.17	5 830	787
Chester	21.7	590	12.5	315	33.7	78.7	27.9	87.5	40.66	4 469	1 333
Easton	35.7	1 367	0.8	238	27.1	73.3	19.1	83.9	45.17	5 830	787
Erie	198.7	1 917	6.1	679	26.9	72.1	20.3	80.4	42.77	6 243	620
Harrisburg	161.2	3 415	17.9	554	30.3	75.9	23.1	85.7	41.45	5 201	955
Hazleton	8.4	384	0.0	NA	NA	NA	NA	NA	NA	NA	NA
Lancaster	77.3	1 415	16.3	543	29.1	74.4	20.7	84.7	43.47	5 448	809
Lebanon	22.5	934	0.0	155	NA	NA	NA	NA	NA	NA	NA
Monroeville	22.9	826	0.0	154	28.6	73.1	19.8	84.5	37.78	5 727	709
Norristown	42.2	1 355	0.0	173	30.2	76.1	20.4	86.6	43.87	5 174	884
Philadelphia	6 788.3	4 683	687.0	29 878	32.3	77.6	25.5	85.5	42.05	4 759	1 235
Pittsburgh	1 015.6	3 263	241.8	3 303	27.5	72.6	19.9	82.7	37.85	5 829	726
Plum	2.8	109	0.0	NA	28.6	73.1	19.8	84.5	37.78	5 727	709
Reading	172.4	2 135	75.5	691	27.1	73.6	19.1	83.8	45.28	5 876	723
Scranton	73.5	1 014	0.0	566	26.3	72.1	18.5	82.6	37.56	6 234	611
State College	33.7	845	0.0	170	25.4	71.2	18.3	80.7	39.76	6 345	538
Wilkes-Barre	60.1	1 465	9.1	288	21.5	67.7	13.2	77.4	47.89	7 466	234
Williamsport	0.0	2	0.0	205	25.5	72.4	17.9	83.2	41.59	6 063	709
York	89.9	2 235	0.0	370	30.0	74.6	20.9	86.5	43.00	5 233	862
RHODE ISLAND	X	X	X	NA	X	X	X	X	X	X	X
Cranston	90.0	1 119	0.0	2 250	28.7	73.3	20.3	82.6	46.45	5 754	714
East Providence	34.8	713	0.0	1 284	28.7	73.3	20.3	82.6	46.45	5 754	714
Pawtucket	154.9	2 141	0.0	1 862	28.7	73.3	20.3	82.6	46.45	5 754	714
Providence	478.9	2 777	89.9	5 234	28.7	73.3	20.3	82.6	46.45	5 754	714
Warwick	214.9	2 526	9.5	2 613	28.7	73.6	20.3	82.6	46.45	5 754	714
Woonsocket	137.7	3 158	1.2	1 306	25.4	72.9	13.3	84.3	48.75	6 302	534
SOUTH CAROLINA	X	X	X	NA	X	X	X	X	X	X	X
Aiken	6.5	222	0.0	357	45.6	81.7	33.4	93.7	52.43	2 413	2 081
Anderson	89.8	3 401	6.9	406	41.7	79.7	31.3	90.5	46.67	3 087	1 700
Charleston	1 031.5	9 376	170.3	2 038	49.8	82.8	42.4	88.5	46.39	1 755	2 473
Columbia	177.8	1 424	0.0	2 158	47.3	83.6	36.5	95.2	47.14	2 044	2 475
Florence	37.1	1 180	0.0	476	45.0	81.2	35.2	90.7	44.76	2 523	2 029
Goose Creek	8.2	226	0.0	272	47.9	81.7	36.9	90.9	51.53	2 005	2 306
Greenville	114.1	1 943	8.1	1 137	40.8	78.8	31.4	88.8	50.24	3 272	1 526
Greer	89.1	3 810	10.5	NA	NA	NA	NA	NA	NA	NA	NA
Hilton Head Island	108.0	3 176	0.0	247	47.9	80.5	37.3	88.2	52.52	2 128	2 012
Mount Pleasant	101.8	1 573	0.0	583	47.1	81.1	37.5	88.5	49.38	2 260	2 124
Myrtle Beach	192.6	6 427	35.3	885	NA	NA	NA	NA	NA	NA	NA
North Charleston	122.3	1 337	11.6	1 009	47.9	81.7	36.9	90.9	51.53	2 005	2 306
Rock Hill	151.9	2 342	14.1	813	42.2	80.1	32.5	90.1	48.32	2 934	1 721
Spartanburg	138.8	3 573	0.0	649	42.1	79.3	30.1	91.1	49.95	3 080	1 591
Summerville	5.8	131	5.7	368	49.1	81.8	38.0	91.8	48.24	1 907	2 251
Sumter	52.4	1 350	32.7	549	44.9	80.7	33.6	91.8	48.65	2 577	1 913
SOUTH DAKOTA	X	X	X	NA	X	X	X	X	X	X	X
Aberdeen	37.8	1 547	9.7	295	NA	NA	NA	NA	NA	NA	NA
Rapid City	89.1	1 393	2.1	1 074	22.3	70.2	10.3	82.7	18.45	7 623	480
Sioux Falls	178.6	1 179	48.4	1 152	14.0	73.0	2.9	85.6	24.69	7 812	747
TENNESSEE	X	X	X	NA	X	X	X	X	X	X	X
Bartlett	40.7	856	5.0	511	37.3	79.6	27.3	89.9	55.09	3 665	1 635
Brentwood	33.3	949	0.0	NA	NA	NA	NA	NA	NA	NA	NA
Bristol	17.3	678	0.0	885	NA	NA	NA	NA	NA	NA	NA
Chattanooga	675.3	3 975	176.7	2 958	39.4	79.6	29.9	89.8	54.52	3 427	1 608
Clarksville	828.5	6 946	119.1	1 052	35.2	79.0	25.0	90.4	51.78	4 058	1 512
Cleveland	124.1	3 166	24.5	1 007	38.0	77.5	27.7	88.5	55.42	3 782	1 333
Collierville	69.8	1 782	1.6	471	37.9	81.1	28.2	91.1	53.63	3 491	1 838
Columbia	49.0	1 442	8.5	524	35.6	77.2	25.0	88.5	56.13	4 183	1 267
Cookeville	124.2	4 297	7.0	2 187	NA	NA	NA	NA	NA	NA	NA

1. Based on the population estimated as of July 1 of the year shown.   2. Represents normal values based on the 30-year period, 1971–2000.   3. Average daily minimum.   4. Average daily maximum.

Table D. Cities — **Land Area and Population**

STATE Place code	City	Land area,[1] 2010 (sq km)	Total persons	Rank	Per square kilometer	White	Black	American Indian, Alaska Native	Asian	Hawaiian Pacific Islander	Percent Hispanic or Latino[2], 2010	Percent Foreign born, 2008–2010
		1	2	3	4	5	6	7	8	9	10	11
	TENNESSEE— Cont'd											
47 27740	Franklin	106.8	62 487	568	585.1	81.5	7.2	0.6	4.3	0.1	7.6	8.2
47 28540	Gallatin	80.8	30 278	1 346	374.7	75.9	15.6	0.7	1.0	0.1	8.0	4.6
47 28960	Germantown	51.7	38 844	1 016	750.9	88.9	3.8	0.4	5.7	0.1	1.9	8.7
47 33280	Hendersonville	81.3	51 372	748	632.3	88.0	6.9	0.8	2.0	0.1	3.6	5.1
47 37640	Jackson	139.2	65 211	540	468.6	48.9	46.4	0.4	1.4	0.1	4.0	4.0
47 38320	Johnson City	111.2	63 152	561	567.8	86.8	7.6	0.8	2.3	0.1	4.2	5.1
47 39560	Kingsport	129.0	48 205	812	373.7	92.4	4.9	0.8	1.2	0.1	2.1	1.7
47 40000	Knoxville	255.2	178 874	132	701.0	76.1	18.3	0.9	2.0	0.2	4.6	4.1
47 41200	La Vergne	64.6	32 588	1 252	504.6	60.4	24.2	0.6	3.8	0.2	13.0	11.5
47 41520	Lebanon	100.1	26 190	1 587	261.7	80.0	13.1	0.8	1.5	0.1	6.2	6.5
47 46380	Maryville	43.5	27 465	1 502	631.1	91.6	3.9	0.8	1.9	0.1	3.2	3.4
47 48000	Memphis	816.0	646 889	21	792.8	28.3	63.8	0.5	1.8	0.1	6.5	6.1
47 50280	Morristown	72.3	29 137	1 414	403.2	72.6	7.7	0.7	1.0	0.2	19.7	12.9
47 51560	Murfreesboro	143.4	108 755	245	758.7	75.0	16.3	0.8	4.0	0.1	5.9	7.4
47 52004	Nashville-Davidson	1 305.4	626 681	22	480.1	59.0	28.5	0.7	3.6	0.1	9.8	12.3
47 55120	Oak Ridge	220.8	29 330	1 403	132.8	84.3	9.5	1.2	3.0	0.1	4.6	7.0
47 69420	Smyrna	76.7	39 974	986	521.4	73.3	12.3	0.8	4.8	0.1	10.7	5.9
47 70580	Spring Hill	70.1	29 036	1 420	414.2	86.9	6.1	0.6	2.1	0.3	5.6	4.0
48 00000	**TEXAS**	676 587.0	25 145 561	X	37.2	46.4	12.0	0.7	4.2	0.1	37.6	16.3
48 01000	Abilene	276.6	117 063	223	423.2	64.1	10.0	0.9	2.1	0.2	24.5	5.8
48 01924	Allen	68.1	84 246	376	1 237.1	66.8	8.8	1.0	14.0	0.1	11.2	14.9
48 03000	Amarillo	257.6	190 695	122	740.2	61.1	7.0	1.0	3.4	0.1	28.8	10.1
48 04000	Arlington	248.3	365 438	50	1 471.6	46.5	19.3	0.9	7.4	0.2	27.4	19.9
48 05000	Austin	771.6	790 390	14	1 024.4	50.3	8.3	0.7	7.1	0.1	35.1	19.7
48 06128	Baytown	91.8	71 802	472	782.2	39.5	15.6	0.5	1.6	0.1	43.4	16.3
48 07000	Beaumont	214.5	118 296	219	551.6	35.7	47.7	0.7	3.5	0.1	13.4	9.0
48 07132	Bedford	25.9	46 979	843	1 811.8	75.1	7.5	1.1	5.1	0.5	12.5	10.5
48 08236	Big Spring	49.5	27 282	1 512	551.5	47.6	7.9	0.9	1.1	0.1	43.1	19.2
48 10768	Brownsville	342.7	175 023	137	510.7	5.9	0.2	0.1	0.7	0.0	93.2	29.3
48 10912	Bryan	115.0	76 201	436	662.4	44.0	18.2	0.6	2.0	0.1	36.2	11.7
48 11428	Burleson	67.4	36 690	1 082	544.7	84.6	2.7	1.0	1.4	0.1	11.5	2.8
48 13024	Carrollton	94.0	119 097	216	1 266.9	47.6	8.7	0.7	14.3	0.1	30.0	24.3
48 13492	Cedar Hill	92.8	45 028	875	485.4	27.1	52.5	0.9	2.4	0.1	18.7	8.1
48 13552	Cedar Park	59.2	48 937	792	827.1	71.3	4.8	0.9	6.0	0.2	19.0	8.3
48 15364	Cleburne	76.6	29 337	1 402	382.9	67.2	4.8	0.7	0.7	0.4	27.1	10.0
48 15976	College Station	128.1	93 857	314	733.0	69.7	7.0	0.6	10.0	0.2	14.0	14.6
48 16432	Conroe	136.5	56 207	664	411.7	49.3	10.4	0.7	2.0	0.1	38.5	24.5
48 16612	Coppell	37.3	38 659	1 022	1 037.0	67.7	4.8	0.8	17.0	0.2	11.3	17.6
48 16624	Copperas Cove	46.7	32 032	1 269	686.1	62.5	20.0	1.7	4.4	1.5	15.0	5.9
48 17000	Corpus Christi	416.0	305 215	60	733.7	34.1	4.2	0.5	2.1	0.1	59.7	7.6
48 19000	Dallas	881.9	1 197 816	9	1 358.2	29.6	25.1	0.6	3.2	0.1	42.4	24.7
48 19624	Deer Park	27.1	32 010	1 272	1 182.1	70.4	1.6	0.7	1.7	0.2	26.3	5.1
48 19792	Del Rio	52.2	35 591	1 127	682.1	14.0	1.2	0.3	0.5	0.1	84.1	22.4
48 19972	Denton	227.8	113 383	235	497.8	63.7	10.9	1.2	4.8	0.2	21.2	13.2
48 20092	DeSoto	56.0	49 047	788	876.0	18.3	69.0	0.6	1.1	0.1	12.1	6.1
48 21628	Duncanville	29.1	38 524	1 027	1 323.8	33.3	30.1	0.7	1.9	0.0	35.0	15.3
48 21892	Eagle Pass	24.8	26 248	1 578	1 058.0	3.7	0.2	0.2	0.5	0.0	95.5	35.9
48 22660	Edinburg	97.5	77 100	423	791.0	8.2	1.4	0.1	2.2	0.0	88.2	19.6
48 24000	El Paso	661.1	649 121	20	981.9	14.9	3.1	0.4	1.4	0.2	80.7	25.4
48 24768	Euless	42.0	51 277	751	1 221.2	57.2	11.4	1.1	11.1	2.3	19.0	18.0
48 25452	Farmers Branch	30.6	28 616	1 438	936.7	45.2	4.9	0.7	4.8	0.0	45.4	23.9
48 26232	Flower Mound	107.2	64 669	546	603.3	79.1	3.5	0.9	9.4	0.2	8.4	9.4
48 27000	Fort Worth	880.1	741 206	16	842.2	43.0	19.2	0.8	4.2	0.2	34.1	17.8
48 27648	Friendswood	53.7	35 805	1 115	666.6	78.8	3.7	0.7	5.4	0.1	12.5	8.2
48 27684	Frisco	160.1	116 989	224	730.9	69.2	8.6	0.9	11.2	0.1	12.1	15.8
48 28068	Galveston	106.8	47 743	826	447.2	46.3	19.2	1.0	3.5	0.1	31.3	13.7
48 29000	Garland	147.9	226 876	87	1 534.5	37.8	14.8	0.8	9.9	0.1	37.8	27.4
48 29336	Georgetown	124.0	47 400	836	382.4	73.3	3.9	0.7	1.4	0.1	21.8	10.0
48 30464	Grand Prairie	186.8	175 396	136	939.2	30.3	20.5	0.8	6.9	0.1	42.7	21.3
48 30644	Grapevine	82.7	46 334	851	560.2	73.5	3.6	0.9	5.1	0.3	18.0	11.5
48 30920	Greenville	84.5	25 557	1 624	302.4	59.0	17.2	1.2	1.2	0.3	22.4	10.3
48 31928	Haltom City	32.0	42 409	931	1 326.5	48.3	4.4	0.9	8.4	0.3	38.9	23.0
48 32312	Harker Heights	39.3	26 700	1 550	679.2	56.5	21.3	1.4	5.5	1.3	18.4	9.2
48 32372	Harlingen	103.1	64 849	543	629.0	18.3	0.7	0.2	1.4	0.1	79.5	18.4
48 35000	Houston	1 552.9	2 099 451	4	1 351.9	26.4	23.6	0.4	6.5	0.1	43.8	28.9
48 35528	Huntsville	92.9	38 548	1 026	415.1	54.3	25.8	0.6	1.6	0.1	18.7	7.2
48 35576	Hurst	25.7	37 337	1 060	1 453.9	71.0	6.1	1.2	2.8	0.5	20.1	13.2
48 37000	Irving	173.6	216 290	95	1 246.1	32.0	12.5	0.8	14.7	0.2	41.1	33.0
48 38632	Keller	47.8	39 627	996	829.2	85.8	2.6	0.9	4.6	0.2	7.4	7.1

1. Dry land or land partially or temporarily covered by water. 2. May be of any race.

Table D. Cities — Population

City	Age of population (percent), 2010									Median age	Percent female	Population			
												Census counts		Percent change	
	Under 5 years	5 to 17 years	18 to 24 years	25 to 34 years	35 to 44 years	45 to 54 years	55 to 64 years	65 to 74 years	75 years and over			1990	2000	1990–2000	2000–2010
	12	13	14	15	16	17	18	19	20	21	22	23	24	25	26
TENNESSEE— Cont'd															
Franklin	7.4	20.0	6.6	13.3	16.8	15.5	10.4	5.3	4.8	36.8	52.2	20 098	41 842	108.2	49.3
Gallatin	7.5	16.7	9.0	14.7	13.2	13.8	11.5	7.5	6.1	36.6	52.0	18 794	23 230	23.6	30.3
Germantown	4.9	19.2	5.6	7.2	12.1	17.5	17.5	9.5	6.6	45.7	51.6	33 159	37 348	12.6	4.0
Hendersonville	6.4	19.4	7.3	11.9	15.3	15.1	11.8	7.5	5.3	38.5	51.7	32 188	40 620	26.2	26.5
Jackson	7.4	17.3	13.4	13.4	12.0	13.1	10.6	6.4	6.3	33.8	53.8	49 145	59 643	21.4	9.3
Johnson City	5.3	13.8	15.7	13.1	11.8	13.2	11.8	7.7	7.6	36.9	51.9	50 354	55 469	10.2	13.9
Kingsport	5.8	15.3	7.3	10.5	12.4	14.4	13.5	10.3	10.5	44.0	53.6	40 457	44 905	11.0	7.3
Knoxville	6.2	12.9	17.7	16.0	11.8	12.3	10.5	6.0	6.6	32.7	52.0	169 761	173 890	2.4	2.9
La Vergne	8.7	23.1	7.8	17.4	17.0	13.0	7.7	3.6	1.6	31.2	50.9	7 499	18 687	149.2	74.4
Lebanon	7.5	16.9	10.3	13.5	13.1	13.3	10.9	7.7	6.7	36.3	52.3	15 208	20 235	33.1	29.4
Maryville	5.3	19.0	10.1	10.4	13.8	13.8	10.6	7.6	9.5	39.1	53.4	19 208	23 120	20.4	18.8
Memphis	7.6	18.3	11.4	15.2	12.6	13.5	11.0	5.5	4.9	33.0	52.5	618 652	650 100	5.1	-0.5
Morristown	8.1	16.7	9.5	14.1	12.5	12.1	11.0	7.8	8.2	36.2	52.1	22 513	24 965	10.9	16.7
Murfreesboro	7.1	16.4	18.7	17.0	13.1	11.4	8.2	4.5	3.7	29.0	50.9	44 922	68 816	53.2	58.0
Nashville-Davidson	7.1	14.6	11.7	18.1	13.7	13.6	10.7	5.6	4.9	33.9	51.6	488 188	569 891	16.7	10.0
Oak Ridge	5.5	16.5	7.1	11.0	11.7	15.0	13.9	8.4	10.9	43.5	52.8	27 310	27 387	0.3	7.1
Smyrna	8.6	19.3	9.0	16.3	15.3	13.8	9.1	5.2	3.4	33.0	51.3	14 720	25 569	73.7	56.3
Spring Hill	10.6	23.3	5.3	17.1	19.0	12.5	7.3	3.3	1.7	31.9	51.5	NA	7 715	NA	276.4
TEXAS	7.7	19.6	10.2	14.4	13.8	13.7	10.3	5.9	4.5	33.6	50.4	16 986 335	20 851 820	22.8	20.6
Abilene	7.5	15.9	15.5	15.1	11.2	12.5	9.6	6.2	6.3	31.7	49.5	106 707	115 930	8.6	1.0
Allen	8.2	24.3	6.1	11.9	19.6	16.2	8.2	3.6	2.0	34.7	50.9	19 315	43 554	125.5	93.4
Amarillo	8.3	19.1	9.8	14.7	12.2	13.2	10.7	6.2	5.8	33.4	51.5	157 571	173 627	10.2	9.8
Arlington	7.8	20.1	11.1	15.2	14.4	13.7	9.5	4.8	3.4	32.1	50.9	261 717	332 969	27.2	9.8
Austin	7.3	14.9	14.5	20.7	14.8	12.1	8.7	3.9	3.1	31.0	49.4	472 020	656 562	39.1	20.4
Baytown	8.6	20.6	10.5	14.3	13.0	12.4	10.4	5.4	4.7	32.1	51.2	63 843	66 430	4.1	8.1
Beaumont	7.3	17.5	12.0	14.0	11.8	14.0	11.3	6.1	6.1	34.4	51.3	114 323	113 866	-0.4	3.9
Bedford	5.3	14.6	8.7	14.8	13.2	15.7	14.0	7.7	6.1	40.3	52.5	43 762	47 152	7.7	-0.4
Big Spring	6.7	15.6	11.5	14.6	11.9	17.6	10.9	6.0	5.9	36.5	42.0	23 093	25 233	9.3	8.1
Brownsville	9.0	25.1	10.0	13.4	13.2	10.8	8.7	5.4	4.5	29.5	52.8	107 027	139 722	30.5	25.3
Bryan	8.3	17.3	17.4	17.1	11.7	11.2	8.0	4.6	4.5	28.5	49.8	55 002	65 660	19.4	16.1
Burleson	8.4	21.8	7.8	15.1	14.9	13.0	9.4	5.8	4.0	32.9	51.3	16 113	20 976	30.2	74.9
Carrollton	6.7	19.3	8.5	14.6	15.2	16.5	11.2	5.1	2.9	35.6	51.1	82 169	109 576	33.4	8.7
Cedar Hill	7.3	22.8	8.4	12.8	15.9	15.4	10.3	4.2	2.9	34.1	53.3	19 988	32 093	60.6	40.3
Cedar Park	8.6	21.9	7.3	15.2	18.5	13.9	7.9	3.8	2.9	33.4	51.4	5 161	26 049	404.7	67.9
Cleburne	8.4	19.5	9.6	13.8	13.2	12.0	10.5	6.8	6.3	33.9	51.0	22 205	26 005	17.1	12.8
College Station	4.8	9.9	47.3	14.8	7.6	6.2	4.7	2.7	2.0	22.3	49.2	52 443	67 890	29.5	38.2
Conroe	8.9	17.7	11.4	17.5	13.1	11.2	9.3	5.8	5.1	31.5	49.5	27 675	36 811	33.0	52.7
Coppell	6.0	24.4	6.1	10.0	16.4	21.7	10.2	3.2	2.1	37.7	50.9	16 881	35 958	113.0	7.5
Copperas Cove	9.7	19.6	12.4	17.7	12.7	11.9	8.2	5.2	2.6	29.0	51.5	24 079	29 592	22.9	8.2
Corpus Christi	7.1	18.7	10.4	13.9	12.2	14.2	11.6	6.3	5.6	34.8	51.0	257 454	277 454	7.8	10.0
Dallas	8.6	17.9	10.5	18.4	14.2	12.5	9.1	4.8	4.1	31.8	50.0	1 007 618	1 188 580	18.0	0.8
Deer Park	6.9	20.3	8.9	13.5	13.6	14.6	11.9	6.1	4.2	35.3	50.7	27 424	28 520	4.0	12.2
Del Rio	8.2	21.2	9.6	13.1	13.1	11.8	9.9	7.2	6.0	33.4	50.3	30 705	33 867	10.3	5.1
Denton	6.1	14.3	25.0	16.2	11.4	10.1	7.9	5.1	3.8	27.1	51.2	66 270	80 537	21.5	40.8
DeSoto	6.5	20.4	7.9	11.2	14.8	15.4	13.1	6.4	4.4	37.8	54.2	30 544	37 646	23.3	30.3
Duncanville	7.4	20.5	9.0	12.6	13.0	13.7	12.0	6.9	4.9	35.4	52.5	35 008	36 081	3.1	6.8
Eagle Pass	8.2	23.6	8.8	11.7	12.9	11.2	10.3	7.1	6.2	33.1	52.4	20 651	22 413	8.5	17.1
Edinburg	8.9	22.0	13.9	16.4	13.9	10.3	7.2	4.1	3.2	28.0	50.3	31 091	48 465	55.9	59.1
El Paso	7.9	21.3	10.8	13.2	13.0	12.9	9.7	5.9	5.3	32.5	52.0	515 342	563 662	9.4	15.2
Euless	7.1	16.9	9.2	17.8	16.0	15.3	10.1	5.0	2.7	34.4	51.0	38 149	46 005	20.6	11.5
Farmers Branch	6.6	17.3	9.5	15.7	13.4	13.9	10.3	7.2	6.1	35.6	50.8	24 250	27 508	13.4	4.0
Flower Mound	6.0	26.7	5.6	7.3	18.8	20.5	9.6	3.7	1.9	38.1	50.4	15 527	50 702	226.5	27.5
Fort Worth	9.0	20.3	10.2	16.4	14.6	12.5	8.8	4.5	3.7	31.2	50.9	447 619	534 694	19.5	38.6
Friendswood	5.2	22.3	7.2	8.9	13.8	18.2	12.7	6.7	5.0	40.2	51.5	22 814	29 037	27.3	23.3
Frisco	9.6	23.7	4.9	13.9	22.5	13.0	7.0	3.7	1.7	33.9	51.1	6 138	33 714	449.3	247.0
Galveston	5.9	13.5	13.1	13.6	11.1	15.8	13.5	7.6	6.0	38.8	48.9	59 067	57 247	-3.1	-16.6
Garland	7.6	20.9	9.6	13.7	14.4	14.2	10.5	5.5	3.7	33.7	51.0	180 635	215 768	19.4	5.1
Georgetown	5.7	15.4	8.8	10.3	10.8	10.8	12.5	14.7	11.0	44.0	51.8	14 840	28 339	91.0	67.3
Grand Prairie	8.5	22.4	9.7	15.2	15.5	13.4	8.8	4.1	2.5	31.3	51.1	99 606	127 427	27.9	37.6
Grapevine	5.7	19.4	8.0	13.3	15.2	18.7	11.8	4.6	3.2	37.5	50.5	29 407	42 059	43.0	10.2
Greenville	8.5	17.9	10.1	14.7	11.9	12.8	9.7	7.2	7.2	34.0	51.3	23 071	23 960	3.9	6.7
Haltom City	8.8	19.1	11.0	15.9	13.6	12.9	9.1	5.3	4.3	31.7	49.7	32 856	39 018	18.8	8.7
Harker Heights	8.0	22.5	9.4	14.7	16.2	13.6	8.3	4.3	2.9	31.6	50.6	12 932	17 308	33.8	54.3
Harlingen	8.6	21.8	9.4	12.9	12.2	11.5	10.0	6.6	7.0	32.8	52.2	48 746	57 564	18.1	12.7
Houston	8.1	17.7	11.0	17.8	13.9	12.8	9.7	5.1	4.0	32.1	49.8	1 654 348	1 953 631	18.1	7.5
Huntsville	4.7	9.3	29.3	15.4	12.2	12.4	8.3	4.5	4.0	28.6	40.9	30 628	35 078	14.5	9.9
Hurst	6.9	17.2	7.9	13.1	13.2	15.0	11.8	8.0	6.9	38.8	51.7	33 574	36 273	8.0	2.9
Irving	8.6	17.9	10.5	20.1	15.7	12.4	7.9	4.1	2.9	31.3	50.0	155 037	191 615	23.6	12.9
Keller	5.5	24.9	5.8	7.0	16.6	20.3	11.3	4.8	3.8	39.9	51.2	13 683	27 345	99.8	44.9

Table D. Cities — **Households, Group Quarters, Crime, and Education**

City	Households, 2010				Persons in group quarters, 2010				Serious crimes known to police,[2] 2010				Educational attainment, 2008–2010		
		Percent				Institutional			Total		Rate[3]			Attainment[4] (percent)	
	Number	Persons per house-hold	Female family house-holder[1]	One-person	Total	Total	Persons in nursing facilities	Non-institu-tional	Number	Rate[3]	Violent	Property	Population age 25 and older	High school graduate or less	Bachelor's degree or more
	27	28	29	30	31	32	33	34	35	36	37	38	39	40	41
TENNESSEE—Cont'd															
Franklin	24 040	2.57	10.0	25.5	795	792	491	3	1 173	1 877	166	1 711	40 519	21.4	54.2
Gallatin	11 871	2.48	15.7	27.9	890	870	308	20	653	2 157	386	1 770	20 052	48.8	17.5
Germantown	14 910	2.60	6.4	19.7	43	43	43	0	496	1 277	100	1 177	27 415	11.0	63.2
Hendersonville	20 111	2.55	11.2	24.4	139	128	128	11	1 402	2 729	280	2 449	33 147	32.7	34.0
Jackson	25 191	2.42	21.4	30.8	4 297	1 456	557	2 841	4 603	7 059	833	6 226	40 687	46.0	26.8
Johnson City	27 017	2.19	11.8	35.4	3 936	750	626	3 186	3 298	5 222	442	4 781	40 941	36.1	35.2
Kingsport	21 289	2.22	13.5	33.9	887	744	660	143	3 248	6 738	782	5 956	34 282	48.4	24.2
Knoxville	78 048	2.16	14.6	38.3	10 048	1 723	1 287	8 325	14 167	7 920	988	6 932	113 424	41.3	30.2
La Vergne	10 916	2.98	16.9	17.2	5	0	0	5	1 092	3 351	393	2 958	18 479	47.1	16.4
Lebanon	10 130	2.48	16.2	28.0	1 101	609	375	492	1 456	5 559	821	4 738	16 263	53.7	20.7
Maryville	10 712	2.41	12.8	30.4	1 644	886	529	758	981	3 572	222	3 350	18 375	41.8	30.1
Memphis	250 344	2.52	25.3	32.2	16 536	10 165	2 710	6 371	52 579	8 128	1 608	6 520	406 168	48.5	22.5
Morristown	11 412	2.47	16.0	31.0	903	763	487	140	2 343	8 041	831	7 211	19 159	58.3	15.7
Murfreesboro	41 940	2.49	13.1	27.3	4 434	1 348	458	3 086	5 222	4 802	555	4 246	62 606	35.0	34.7
Nashville-Davidson	259 499	2.32	14.7	34.5	25 870	9 226	2 169	16 644	37 038	6 122	1 124	4 998	395 727	40.1	33.3
Oak Ridge	12 772	2.26	12.9	33.3	483	226	218	257	1 370	4 671	453	4 218	20 181	33.1	40.9
Smyrna	14 807	2.68	15.0	23.0	365	353	215	12	919	2 299	220	2 079	24 505	41.7	23.1
Spring Hill	9 861	2.94	9.9	16.5	47	30	0	17	447	1 539	134	1 405	17 385	27.4	36.4
TEXAS	8 922 933	2.75	14.1	24.2	581 139	375 392	94 278	205 747	1 064 477	4 233	450	3 783	15 448 794	45.2	25.8
Abilene	43 612	2.46	13.7	28.7	9 592	5 306	816	4 286	5 475	4 677	494	4 183	71 812	45.7	22.5
Allen	27 870	3.02	9.9	14.8	171	171	164	0	1 684	1 999	77	1 922	50 825	19.4	49.2
Amarillo	73 918	2.55	14.1	27.9	1 881	1 419	1 019	462	12 291	6 445	629	5 816	119 464	43.0	22.3
Arlington	133 072	2.72	15.0	24.9	3 132	1 061	1 053	2 071	21 275	5 822	527	5 295	219 828	39.2	28.4
Austin	324 892	2.37	11.0	34.0	20 261	4 199	1 869	16 062	49 616	6 277	480	5 798	493 297	31.7	43.9
Baytown	24 955	2.85	16.3	24.1	601	507	507	94	4 150	5 780	419	5 361	42 592	50.5	14.9
Beaumont	45 648	2.48	19.2	30.7	5 133	2 634	513	2 499	6 841	5 783	761	5 022	73 376	48.3	22.5
Bedford	21 016	2.22	10.8	34.0	331	325	287	6	1 976	4 206	447	3 759	33 264	24.7	33.8
Big Spring	8 267	2.56	16.7	28.8	6 080	5 768	280	312	1 579	5 788	652	5 135	18 700	57.4	10.0
Brownsville	49 871	3.48	22.9	15.2	1 637	963	671	674	9 879	5 644	322	5 323	93 578	61.1	15.1
Bryan	27 725	2.64	15.4	28.1	3 097	2 822	361	275	4 057	5 324	538	4 786	40 916	51.2	24.7
Burleson	12 888	2.84	12.7	18.3	108	108	108	0	1 032	2 813	188	2 625	22 111	38.5	23.5
Carrollton	43 299	2.74	12.4	22.5	376	350	350	26	3 694	3 102	154	2 947	78 674	34.1	36.7
Cedar Hill	15 506	2.89	19.3	20.3	293	171	171	122	1 846	4 100	231	3 869	27 033	29.1	31.6
Cedar Park	17 817	2.74	11.7	21.4	137	107	107	30	854	1 745	119	1 627	29 873	22.6	42.3
Cleburne	10 439	2.73	14.1	25.0	876	794	316	82	1 512	5 154	593	4 561	18 758	60.1	13.8
College Station	35 037	2.38	7.7	27.5	10 347	201	201	10 146	2 875	3 063	234	2 829	35 566	20.5	57.2
Conroe	20 017	2.69	14.5	27.9	2 263	2 088	291	175	3 030	5 391	441	4 950	33 462	52.7	18.2
Coppell	13 806	2.80	9.3	18.7	3	0	0	3	692	1 790	171	1 619	24 647	13.1	63.9
Copperas Cove	11 858	2.68	15.8	21.9	284	174	174	110	1 224	3 821	465	3 356	19 449	39.5	16.1
Corpus Christi	112 795	2.66	16.6	25.6	5 640	3 199	1 344	2 441	17 169	5 625	678	4 948	191 568	46.4	20.6
Dallas	458 057	2.57	16.0	33.9	18 725	12 739	3 693	5 986	73 286	6 118	765	5 353	749 847	48.5	28.8
Deer Park	11 133	2.87	12.3	17.9	109	87	87	22	1 043	3 258	87	3 171	19 940	42.4	18.4
Del Rio	11 599	2.95	17.8	22.0	1 373	1 347	203	26	804	2 259	205	2 054	21 409	59.1	17.0
Denton	42 635	2.45	10.2	29.5	8 976	1 646	391	7 330	3 595	3 171	275	2 895	61 718	33.2	35.5
DeSoto	18 210	2.68	19.6	25.7	304	275	275	29	1 794	3 658	275	3 382	31 778	32.5	26.0
Duncanville	13 280	2.89	19.2	20.4	176	165	165	11	1 797	4 665	350	4 314	23 584	46.0	25.9
Eagle Pass	8 272	3.13	20.1	19.6	342	311	59	31	1 144	4 358	221	4 137	15 469	56.9	20.9
Edinburg	23 099	3.16	20.4	17.3	4 072	3 008	169	1 064	4 831	6 266	301	5 965	41 703	51.6	20.3
El Paso	216 894	2.95	20.7	21.5	9 414	5 777	1 482	3 637	20 265	3 122	441	2 681	382 555	49.0	21.9
Euless	21 531	2.38	13.5	32.4	109	99	99	10	2 149	4 191	275	3 916	33 658	36.4	28.3
Farmers Branch	10 797	2.64	11.5	28.6	103	0	0	103	1 211	4 232	178	4 054	18 796	44.7	30.1
Flower Mound	21 011	3.07	7.8	11.4	159	155	110	4	635	982	66	915	38 862	13.5	57.7
Fort Worth	262 652	2.77	15.3	26.5	13 977	8 117	2 410	5 860	39 437	5 321	580	4 740	439 544	46.1	25.6
Friendswood	12 726	2.80	9.5	18.7	207	201	201	6	415	1 159	70	1 089	23 017	21.5	45.5
Frisco	39 901	2.93	8.1	17.5	225	225	225	0	2 792	2 387	110	2 276	69 040	14.5	56.8
Galveston	19 943	2.27	14.7	36.7	2 477	1 261	86	1 216	3 554	7 444	781	6 663	32 010	45.6	26.7
Garland	75 696	2.99	16.1	20.8	567	478	463	89	9 118	4 019	217	3 802	139 718	47.7	22.2
Georgetown	18 830	2.38	9.4	25.0	2 499	1 436	389	1 063	914	1 928	114	1 814	31 007	31.2	36.4
Grand Prairie	58 171	3.01	16.3	21.0	257	188	188	69	8 082	4 608	342	4 266	101 298	50.2	20.4
Grapevine	18 502	2.49	10.5	27.1	242	226	226	16	1 717	3 706	162	3 544	30 082	25.4	45.0
Greenville	9 716	2.56	15.8	29.1	678	604	316	74	1 493	5 842	822	5 020	15 468	53.7	18.0
Haltom City	15 269	2.77	14.5	26.8	96	96	96	0	2 022	4 768	408	4 360	25 951	63.1	13.6
Harker Heights	9 488	2.80	14.7	19.3	166	166	166	0	925	3 464	169	3 296	14 735	35.3	27.4
Harlingen	21 645	2.95	19.7	21.2	1 070	457	415	613	4 804	7 408	615	6 793	40 429	54.4	20.0
Houston	782 643	2.64	16.2	31.0	37 071	18 243	4 778	18 828	137 814	6 564	1 071	5 493	1 318 591	48.3	28.2
Huntsville	11 791	2.32	12.8	31.9	11 239	8 489	190	2 750	1 333	3 458	412	3 046	21 247	49.9	21.2
Hurst	14 652	2.53	12.7	25.3	245	239	224	6	2 292	6 139	447	5 691	25 766	38.4	27.3
Irving	82 538	2.61	13.6	30.1	873	393	393	480	8 273	3 825	245	3 580	133 571	42.9	32.5
Keller	13 514	2.91	7.3	14.6	251	251	251	0	524	1 322	45	1 277	24 515	19.2	50.1

1. No spouse present.   2. Data for serious crimes have not been adjusted for underreporting. This may affect comparability between geographic areas and over time.   3. Per 100,000 population estimated by the FBI.   4. Persons 25 years old and over.

Table D. Cities — Income, Poverty, and Housing

City	Money income, 2008–2010 Per capita income[1] (dollars)	Households Median income	Households Percent with income of $200,000 or more	Households Percent with income of less than $25,000	Families with income below poverty (percent)	Housing units, 2010 Total	Housing units, 2010 Percent change, 2000–2010	Housing units, 2010 Vacant units for sale or rent[2]	Occupied Housing units 2008–2010 Owner-occupied Total	Owner-occupied Percent	Owner-occupied Median value[3] (dollars)	Median owner costs as a percent of income With a mortgage[4]	Median owner costs as a percent of income Without a mortgage[5]
	42	43	44	45	46	47	48	49	50	51	52	53	54
TENNESSEE— Cont'd													
Franklin	35 410	74 803	6.6	14.7	6.0	25 586	48.6	1 546	23 690	69.1	313 700	23.1	10.0
Gallatin	22 994	42 351	1.9	26.1	11.0	13 093	35.8	1 222	12 276	56.2	156 900	24.2	11.7
Germantown	53 043	110 532	17.4	6.3	1.4	15 536	13.4	626	14 729	88.6	289 800	20.8	11.7
Hendersonville	29 073	61 598	4.7	18.1	8.1	21 543	30.6	1 432	18 926	70.5	204 300	23.7	10.0
Jackson	21 959	36 149	3.2	36.2	16.4	28 052	9.8	2 861	24 258	59.1	112 600	23.9	13.5
Johnson City	25 485	37 240	5.0	34.8	15.2	30 583	19.5	3 566	26 199	56.0	156 400	22.5	10.6
Kingsport	23 945	39 255	2.3	33.9	14.2	23 784	9.0	2 495	20 631	67.3	119 200	21.5	10.0
Knoxville	21 786	31 994	1.8	38.7	16.5	88 009	3.7	9 961	83 133	52.2	116 400	23.9	12.8
La Vergne	21 030	56 019	1.1	18.4	12.0	11 612	66.3	696	10 420	75.8	141 600	24.7	10.0
Lebanon	23 481	44 285	2.6	28.6	10.9	11 030	26.1	900	9 817	62.9	178 300	23.6	11.9
Maryville	26 051	46 394	3.0	25.8	9.0	11 629	19.1	917	10 971	65.8	178 400	23.1	11.9
Memphis	20 471	36 142	2.5	35.1	20.8	291 883	7.4	41 539	241 869	53.0	99 400	26.2	14.3
Morristown	17 567	33 357	0.3	38.5	17.0	12 705	15.2	1 293	11 449	61.5	106 700	24.9	15.1
Murfreesboro	24 152	47 662	2.2	25.4	11.6	45 500	57.2	3 560	40 297	54.6	175 500	23.2	10.0
Nashville-Davidson	26 153	44 630	3.6	27.2	14.5	283 978	12.3	24 479	243 190	55.9	168 800	25.2	11.3
Oak Ridge	30 379	51 131	2.9	24.5	9.5	14 494	8.0	1 722	12 498	63.6	149 000	18.8	10.0
Smyrna	24 400	49 481	1.2	17.5	10.4	15 787	57.9	980	15 270	68.3	156 100	23.4	10.0
Spring Hill	26 561	73 324	3.5	7.6	2.6	10 569	NA	708	9 350	84.4	197 700	23.7	10.0
TEXAS	24 671	49 585	4.0	25.0	13.2	9 977 436	22.3	1 054 503	8 666 137	64.2	127 400	23.1	12.3
Abilene	20 968	39 694	1.7	29.8	13.5	47 783	4.8	4 171	42 261	58.5	94 300	21.4	12.7
Allen	35 805	92 717	9.4	9.4	3.8	28 877	89.4	1 007	27 204	80.4	196 200	22.0	10.0
Amarillo	23 179	43 550	2.4	27.8	12.2	80 298	11.0	6 380	71 088	62.3	109 800	21.2	11.2
Arlington	24 678	51 260	3.0	21.3	11.3	144 805	10.7	11 733	132 104	57.9	132 700	23.1	11.8
Austin	29 655	50 147	5.0	23.9	13.5	354 241	28.1	29 349	320 425	45.6	214 000	24.0	12.7
Baytown	21 009	48 387	2.0	24.5	15.8	28 998	10.2	4 043	23 749	62.1	99 500	21.7	12.8
Beaumont	22 471	40 522	3.0	32.2	18.4	50 689	3.8	5 041	44 154	66.3	96 700	20.7	12.5
Bedford	34 374	60 985	3.7	14.7	5.5	22 301	5.6	1 285	20 662	55.1	152 100	20.6	11.6
Big Spring	15 808	36 738	1.5	28.5	11.3	9 640	-2.4	1 373	7 809	59.9	58 200	20.7	11.2
Brownsville	12 416	30 568	1.0	43.6	32.1	53 936	28.8	4 065	46 207	60.8	78 900	26.4	14.1
Bryan	18 748	34 810	2.0	35.4	21.2	30 582	18.6	2 857	27 134	48.4	111 100	22.5	13.1
Burleson	28 330	65 490	3.2	8.8	2.6	18 591	74.5	703	12 441	79.8	119 900	21.9	10.6
Carrollton	30 923	67 030	4.7	13.6	7.6	45 508	12.3	2 209	43 124	65.2	167 800	23.1	11.5
Cedar Hill	27 099	63 725	4.1	12.5	5.0	16 338	47.0	832	14 931	73.5	132 400	24.9	10.9
Cedar Park	31 322	74 002	2.7	10.7	4.2	18 726	108.8	909	16 965	73.3	187 600	23.9	12.9
Cleburne	20 437	45 898	1.2	25.0	10.8	11 418	14.5	979	10 557	58.0	97 200	22.0	13.9
College Station	20 158	32 297	3.3	43.8	16.7	37 226	43.1	2 189	32 301	35.6	174 700	21.8	11.6
Conroe	20 567	44 053	2.2	26.1	16.8	22 215	54.5	2 198	18 847	51.4	126 900	24.5	12.3
Coppell	45 434	101 510	15.7	5.4	1.9	14 343	14.2	537	13 879	70.8	268 900	20.6	10.1
Copperas Cove	20 961	49 706	1.3	20.7	13.3	13 094	16.7	1 236	9 835	63.7	103 400	21.8	10.0
Corpus Christi	23 055	44 067	2.4	29.0	14.5	125 469	16.3	12 674	109 523	59.7	113 300	24.3	13.5
Dallas	26 032	41 011	5.2	29.9	19.6	516 639	6.7	58 582	450 646	45.0	130 800	25.5	13.6
Deer Park	28 993	72 834	4.0	11.6	6.2	11 742	18.6	609	10 408	79.6	126 700	20.4	10.9
Del Rio	15 956	34 362	0.8	38.2	19.2	12 958	9.5	1 359	11 290	62.7	87 400	22.6	13.7
Denton	22 258	45 177	2.3	29.2	8.7	46 211	41.1	3 576	39 312	46.2	147 300	22.5	12.4
DeSoto	25 999	56 332	1.9	21.1	7.6	19 488	38.1	1 278	17 849	68.6	140 300	28.0	14.1
Duncanville	23 849	55 089	2.2	17.6	11.1	14 011	5.6	731	13 150	68.5	114 100	24.8	10.7
Eagle Pass	14 643	29 765	1.7	44.1	28.5	9 019	17.6	747	7 883	58.6	100 800	27.4	13.2
Edinburg	15 849	37 603	1.8	35.4	24.8	25 167	57.8	2 068	22 373	58.4	94 500	23.8	14.4
El Paso	18 119	37 836	1.8	34.0	19.4	227 605	17.5	10 711	209 086	60.5	114 800	24.0	11.4
Euless	29 479	56 014	2.0	16.9	7.2	23 447	16.8	1 916	21 248	45.4	143 300	21.7	12.3
Farmers Branch	28 715	54 725	3.9	17.7	7.7	11 549	13.0	752	10 778	60.4	144 900	25.8	11.8
Flower Mound	43 786	112 334	14.5	5.5	2.5	21 570	27.1	559	20 553	92.4	253 700	22.2	10.5
Fort Worth	23 482	48 970	3.0	25.5	14.1	291 086	37.8	28 434	258 224	59.4	123 200	23.8	13.7
Friendswood	40 139	99 199	13.4	8.3	3.6	13 254	28.3	528	12 081	82.7	208 100	21.4	11.9
Frisco	41 601	103 373	12.8	6.8	3.7	42 306	209.0	2 405	38 110	78.4	253 700	22.5	12.5
Galveston	24 560	37 197	3.5	34.6	15.6	32 368	8.0	12 425	20 551	49.6	129 100	24.0	12.9
Garland	21 413	51 810	2.0	19.0	9.9	80 834	7.4	5 138	72 624	64.9	118 800	24.7	12.8
Georgetown	29 961	60 917	4.0	15.1	5.1	20 037	81.6	1 207	17 799	68.3	183 600	23.7	12.3
Grand Prairie	21 476	50 213	1.8	22.3	12.5	62 424	34.9	4 253	57 163	61.6	124 500	24.5	12.1
Grapevine	36 116	71 219	7.6	13.3	6.3	19 685	19.2	1 183	18 131	57.3	225 900	21.8	14.7
Greenville	19 380	34 866	2.3	37.1	25.9	10 838	9.3	1 122	8 692	53.3	81 900	23.9	12.2
Haltom City	18 256	40 242	0.7	24.7	15.5	16 626	5.0	1 357	15 140	55.2	87 300	25.0	13.5
Harker Heights	23 584	57 574	2.0	19.5	10.9	10 347	51.2	859	8 562	56.9	171 100	25.9	12.6
Harlingen	16 628	35 155	1.1	39.2	24.5	25 585	10.1	3 940	21 177	60.7	77 600	21.5	13.9
Houston	25 700	43 349	4.8	28.9	17.9	892 646	14.1	110 003	767 352	46.4	126 700	24.2	12.8
Huntsville	12 193	27 627	1.0	46.3	17.9	12 853	12.7	1 062	10 953	35.7	127 800	20.1	15.0
Hurst	28 436	54 795	3.6	20.8	7.9	15 761	6.8	1 109	14 429	69.1	139 300	21.7	13.9
Irving	25 768	46 354	4.1	22.9	14.4	91 128	13.5	8 590	81 509	39.3	137 000	26.4	11.9
Keller	43 938	114 207	16.0	7.8	2.9	14 051	52.9	537	12 904	86.8	269 300	22.0	12.7

1. Based on population estimated by the American Community Survey. 2. Includes units rented or sold but not occupied. 3. Specified owner-occupied units; $1,000,000 represents $1,000,000 or more. 4. 50.0 represents 50 percent or more. 5. 10.0 represents 10 percent or less.

Table D. Cities — Housing, Labor Force, and Employment

City	Occupied housing units, 2008–2010 (cont.)				Migration, 2008–2010		Civilian labor force, 2010				Civilian employment[4], 2008–2010			
									Unemployment			Percent		
	Percent renter occupied	Median gross rent[1]	Median rent as a percent of income[2]	Percent with no vehicle available	Percent who lived in the same house one year ago	Percent who lived outside this city one year ago	Total	Percent change, 2009–2010	Total	Rate[3]	Population age 16 and older	In labor force	Full-year full-time worker	Households with no workers (percent)
	55	56	57	58	59	60	61	62	63	64	65	66	67	68
TENNESSEE— Cont'd														
Franklin	30.9	1 026	27.9	3.0	80.7	12.2	33 192	7.4	2 323	7.0	46 481	73.1	48.4	16.9
Gallatin	43.8	737	27.6	6.5	74.3	14.7	13 828	2.2	1 349	9.8	23 606	65.8	40.1	24.6
Germantown	11.4	1 174	23.4	1.4	89.4	7.7	19 486	1.3	1 245	6.4	30 759	67.3	44.3	21.1
Hendersonville	29.5	845	29.5	4.7	82.6	11.9	27 439	8.3	2 162	7.9	37 943	69.5	48.1	21.2
Jackson	40.9	714	36.4	7.9	81.5	8.1	30 871	3.3	3 365	10.9	50 261	64.4	38.3	32.6
Johnson City	44.0	606	30.0	7.5	77.6	13.8	32 738	2.5	2 770	8.5	51 146	59.6	36.9	32.4
Kingsport	32.7	512	28.0	10.2	81.9	9.4	20 677	8.7	1 902	9.2	38 937	55.1	34.7	38.2
Knoxville	47.8	662	32.1	9.4	81.3	8.3	91 338	-2.2	8 097	8.9	148 838	60.9	36.9	31.9
La Vergne	24.2	971	26.6	4.0	81.8	13.0	18 595	8.6	1 729	9.3	22 336	75.3	52.6	15.5
Lebanon	37.1	703	31.3	7.1	75.2	13.2	12 931	NA	1 235	9.6	19 768	60.0	38.3	29.5
Maryville	34.2	651	30.3	6.3	80.3	14.5	13 244	1.6	1 122	8.5	21 836	62.3	36.0	31.4
Memphis	47.0	765	34.7	12.3	78.8	4.8	290 900	-5.5	32 974	11.3	498 997	64.5	40.0	27.5
Morristown	38.5	586	28.1	10.2	78.8	10.6	13 134	3.7	1 526	11.6	22 618	58.5	35.0	41.1
Murfreesboro	45.4	795	31.9	4.6	72.1	15.0	57 693	7.2	5 169	9.0	84 249	71.4	42.3	20.4
Nashville-Davidson	44.1	778	30.7	7.6	78.7	7.4	325 381	1.5	28 918	8.9	478 654	68.7	43.6	23.1
Oak Ridge	36.4	656	24.8	8.8	79.9	13.5	14 299	7.3	1 142	8.0	23 094	60.4	38.9	32.9
Smyrna	31.7	769	26.1	4.0	79.3	15.3	21 982	5.8	2 087	9.5	29 788	72.7	50.7	19.7
Spring Hill	15.6	1 032	24.5	1.3	83.6	14.0	14 995	12.8	1 288	8.6	19 212	76.6	52.3	11.5
TEXAS	35.8	795	29.7	6.0	82.0	10.1	12 269 727	3.1	1 004 979	8.2	18 756 735	65.8	44.7	21.4
Abilene	41.5	740	32.2	6.5	74.8	11.5	58 425	-0.6	3 867	6.6	93 356	63.1	41.5	23.6
Allen	19.6	1 120	32.1	1.9	83.6	12.0	45 050	6.1	3 136	7.0	57 354	77.4	54.9	9.7
Amarillo	37.7	673	29.7	6.7	79.3	6.0	102 000	1.3	5 568	5.5	143 037	69.2	48.0	21.6
Arlington	42.1	815	31.0	4.0	78.9	9.1	198 702	-2.9	15 894	8.0	271 582	73.8	48.7	16.5
Austin	54.4	900	30.8	7.3	72.7	9.6	439 454	4.8	28 680	6.5	623 884	73.3	48.4	17.1
Baytown	37.9	785	30.7	5.6	81.4	9.1	33 364	1.5	3 994	12.0	52 200	62.4	43.7	23.1
Beaumont	43.7	718	29.7	9.3	79.1	7.4	58 520	6.5	5 633	9.6	91 264	62.5	39.7	28.4
Bedford	44.9	877	26.7	3.8	78.0	17.0	30 382	-2.9	2 320	7.6	38 163	75.4	53.3	17.0
Big Spring	40.1	632	30.9	11.1	73.0	13.8	10 465	5.5	845	8.1	21 248	42.7	29.6	32.6
Brownsville	39.2	588	33.3	10.7	86.7	4.3	67 414	2.3	8 092	12.0	117 378	58.7	35.7	24.5
Bryan	51.6	706	34.8	9.8	72.9	16.6	39 043	-1.0	2 562	6.6	57 535	66.5	39.9	23.5
Burleson	20.2	968	28.2	2.3	88.2	7.5	19 016	4.4	1 333	7.0	25 214	74.1	54.7	17.6
Carrollton	34.8	926	27.0	3.5	82.4	10.8	68 559	-2.4	5 217	7.6	92 063	76.8	53.2	12.8
Cedar Hill	26.5	1 118	33.8	4.7	88.6	8.3	24 239	3.3	2 191	9.0	32 272	75.0	55.6	16.1
Cedar Park	26.7	955	28.5	2.3	82.3	13.0	25 910	-21.6	1 713	6.6	34 666	75.4	55.4	12.5
Cleburne	42.0	843	30.1	4.5	81.6	8.8	13 251	-3.1	1 140	8.6	22 672	63.5	42.1	24.3
College Station	64.4	807	50.0	6.0	56.5	23.3	48 204	4.8	3 036	6.3	79 440	59.5	27.8	24.2
Conroe	48.6	784	31.4	6.5	75.0	13.6	26 848	-0.5	1 761	6.6	41 609	67.6	43.4	20.0
Coppell	29.2	1 077	24.6	1.7	85.1	10.0	20 432	1.1	1 504	7.4	28 224	76.1	55.9	9.8
Copperas Cove	36.3	815	28.5	4.3	79.3	15.8	13 342	1.7	962	7.2	23 911	65.1	45.9	22.8
Corpus Christi	40.3	813	32.5	8.3	78.8	6.7	157 291	5.8	11 383	7.2	232 770	64.9	42.0	24.7
Dallas	55.0	790	29.9	9.8	79.8	7.3	569 611	-3.8	50 734	8.9	906 134	67.5	46.3	21.2
Deer Park	20.4	962	28.9	3.1	86.6	8.6	17 327	2.2	1 498	8.6	24 005	68.3	48.7	16.7
Del Rio	37.3	545	29.6	7.7	83.0	6.5	16 186	-3.3	1 406	8.7	25 903	61.2	39.5	29.1
Denton	53.8	778	37.1	5.4	67.7	18.2	61 771	-2.0	4 006	6.5	92 964	66.3	36.2	20.1
DeSoto	31.4	878	33.0	6.0	86.2	10.4	26 367	5.2	2 421	9.2	37 443	66.4	48.4	19.4
Duncanville	31.5	981	32.1	3.8	88.8	8.8	19 767	8.7	1 788	9.0	28 820	68.2	48.4	19.4
Eagle Pass	41.4	516	29.3	10.5	84.9	5.7	13 056	-1.5	2 061	15.8	18 216	59.2	34.7	28.4
Edinburg	41.6	624	34.0	6.8	77.6	12.8	33 960	5.8	2 855	8.4	54 377	62.6	37.1	22.2
El Paso	39.5	642	30.3	8.9	84.0	4.5	270 282	3.5	24 347	9.0	473 919	61.1	40.5	23.4
Euless	54.6	893	24.6	3.4	79.1	14.1	30 382	-2.9	2 320	7.6	40 062	78.3	54.2	13.0
Farmers Branch	39.6	972	25.1	3.0	80.0	12.6	15 177	10.1	1 200	7.9	22 531	71.0	43.5	20.5
Flower Mound	7.6	1 419	28.8	0.6	89.5	6.6	34 489	-3.9	2 354	6.8	44 847	74.9	53.6	10.5
Fort Worth	40.6	805	30.8	6.7	81.2	8.8	344 668	4.7	28 616	8.3	533 318	68.8	47.2	19.7
Friendswood	17.3	1 091	30.3	1.9	85.7	11.1	18 580	3.9	1 329	7.2	26 824	68.2	48.7	17.1
Frisco	21.6	1 131	26.8	2.0	81.0	12.1	61 959	19.5	4 119	6.6	77 383	79.2	57.6	9.7
Galveston	50.4	769	36.6	13.5	72.9	14.2	21 654	-17.6	1 993	9.2	40 222	63.3	38.9	28.8
Garland	35.1	881	29.2	4.0	82.7	9.2	113 923	5.5	9 540	8.4	168 678	72.3	48.2	15.5
Georgetown	31.7	931	27.5	4.5	78.8	14.0	21 621	-4.7	1 543	7.1	36 323	56.9	39.0	37.4
Grand Prairie	38.4	848	31.1	4.2	80.5	11.9	87 796	12.5	7 353	8.4	123 102	73.7	51.8	15.4
Grapevine	42.7	997	25.5	3.2	81.8	12.7	26 613	-8.5	1 817	6.8	35 672	76.7	51.5	13.5
Greenville	46.7	699	36.5	8.9	74.0	13.9	11 419	1.8	938	8.2	18 512	55.2	36.3	29.4
Haltom City	44.8	743	27.6	4.5	78.9	13.9	21 851	4.7	1 818	8.3	31 777	68.6	45.7	21.5
Harker Heights	43.1	804	26.9	3.5	68.4	22.8	12 042	3.7	831	6.9	18 524	67.3	46.6	17.5
Harlingen	39.3	643	28.7	10.4	90.6	5.3	26 359	1.5	2 365	9.0	47 913	51.4	37.0	34.8
Houston	53.6	797	29.6	9.9	80.1	6.1	995 685	-7.3	85 059	8.5	1 601 311	68.3	45.9	19.5
Huntsville	64.3	650	38.1	5.0	68.3	25.6	15 692	-3.8	1 166	7.4	34 242	37.5	20.2	26.5
Hurst	30.9	763	31.1	2.0	82.3	13.1	20 050	-3.4	1 642	8.2	30 050	68.1	47.6	21.5
Irving	60.7	853	27.5	5.1	75.6	11.8	119 262	9.4	9 004	7.5	160 671	74.5	49.9	14.4
Keller	13.2	1 103	28.9	1.3	91.3	7.1	20 412	0.8	1 359	6.7	29 010	71.5	51.1	13.8

1. $2,000 represents $2,000 or more.　　2. 50.0 represents 50 percent or more.　　3. Percent of civilian labor force.　　4. Persons 16 years old and over.

Table D. Cities — Construction, Wholesale Trade, and Retail Trade

City	Value of residential construction authorized by building permits, 2010			Wholesale trade,[1] 2007				Retail trade,[2] 2007			
	New construction ($1,000)	Number of housing units	Percent single family	Number of establish-ments	Number of employees	Sales (mil dol)	Annual payroll (mil dol)	Number of establish-ments	Number of employees	Sales (mil dol)	Annual payroll (mil dol)
	69	70	71	72	73	74	75	76	77	78	79
TENNESSEE—Cont'd											
Franklin	88 973	286	100.0	115	1 321	2 156.7	94.0	483	8 846	2 024.0	198.1
Gallatin	14 327	102	98.0	46	669	470.3	25.4	146	1 904	477.8	45.9
Germantown	NA	NA	NA	42	467	265.5	20.0	176	2 293	365.0	44.0
Hendersonville	20 689	166	100.0	49	D	D	D	168	2 571	621.0	58.0
Jackson	26 630	165	100.0	125	1 774	988.5	72.9	459	6 786	1 553.8	146.2
Johnson City	48 238	450	27.8	106	1 737	1 025.2	60.6	442	7 266	1 674.9	150.2
Kingsport	13 681	81	85.2	80	966	379.4	35.6	373	5 355	1 260.8	117.2
Knoxville	70 664	842	22.8	452	6 580	3 106.5	318.3	1 452	27 067	6 470.5	648.3
La Vergne	14 469	102	100.0	71	3 466	5 145.4	166.3	50	550	159.8	14.2
Lebanon	33 068	430	30.7	39	1 056	862.5	52.8	231	2 778	767.8	63.6
Maryville	6 862	51	100.0	26	205	527.4	9.1	184	2 788	543.8	53.6
Memphis	NA	NA	NA	1 048	22 822	25 485.6	1 173.2	2 571	36 773	8 975.2	880.5
Morristown	3 943	41	100.0	49	D	D	D	277	4 011	1 018.2	87.9
Murfreesboro	63 886	530	65.3	102	898	526.1	42.9	538	8 282	2 008.1	184.7
Nashville-Davidson	253 094	1 568	63.8	1 009	20 028	11 942.6	983.6	2 795	42 241	10 581.8	1 046.2
Oak Ridge	4 167	35	68.6	18	118	94.0	6.1	129	2 055	477.1	44.3
Smyrna	15 723	169	58.6	34	996	526.0	43.0	107	1 949	467.8	41.9
Spring Hill	21 392	218	100.0	7	77	45.3	3.8	46	734	159.2	14.4
TEXAS	13 739 563	88 461	75.7	27 066	386 370	424 238.2	20 260.6	78 795	1 138 440	311 334.8	26 395.2
Abilene	43 078	387	69.5	125	1 372	988.0	50.3	547	8 023	1 897.2	176.4
Allen	132 732	444	100.0	43	543	213.7	37.7	217	3 179	647.1	61.0
Amarillo	176 825	855	59.6	227	3 368	2 351.2	142.7	859	12 913	3 720.1	288.8
Arlington	54 606	352	81.3	357	5 707	4 470.0	280.8	1 091	18 017	4 890.4	421.7
Austin	388 351	2 774	60.0	918	17 256	12 730.5	1 254.5	3 094	51 460	13 493.5	1 300.7
Baytown	10 600	123	46.3	42	385	186.5	14.8	270	4 221	1 242.1	94.0
Beaumont	41 891	479	73.3	180	3 112	2 269.7	148.2	660	9 983	2 474.6	228.6
Bedford	3 087	23	100.0	35	233	470.6	14.2	127	1 957	618.8	56.0
Big Spring	385	2	100.0	16	98	48.3	4.1	103	1 202	320.4	26.4
Brownsville	57 282	600	96.3	193	1 618	783.0	41.2	617	9 329	2 024.3	177.7
Bryan	33 557	273	98.5	74	1 102	520.1	39.3	294	3 600	991.3	87.5
Burleson	48 467	590	33.4	18	109	42.5	3.8	146	2 738	674.7	61.2
Carrollton	73 501	623	21.0	378	7 000	4 226.5	346.5	361	5 154	1 808.8	183.4
Cedar Hill	18 776	85	100.0	13	164	97.9	7.3	105	2 466	478.1	46.8
Cedar Park	107 081	643	92.8	34	283	95.6	11.6	135	1 927	484.0	44.0
Cleburne	2 907	27	92.6	35	411	242.8	17.6	155	2 364	639.5	58.4
College Station	82 511	705	69.6	20	212	173.7	8.5	323	5 380	1 092.6	99.4
Conroe	59 487	431	55.0	114	1 420	4 002.7	61.2	367	6 146	1 921.9	154.1
Coppell	37 400	83	100.0	67	2 208	1 881.7	125.1	57	1 079	413.1	35.7
Copperas Cove	72 847	293	62.1	5	5	1.3	0.1	74	1 012	249.2	21.4
Corpus Christi	98 508	912	68.9	358	4 002	2 682.6	184.2	1 081	16 200	4 133.8	350.2
Dallas	479 731	2 609	33.2	2 101	31 471	19 169.4	1 546.6	4 209	60 028	16 256.5	1 563.1
Deer Park	14 435	84	100.0	35	713	406.9	45.3	60	1 067	258.1	24.2
Del Rio	4 270	38	78.9	23	127	39.3	3.7	163	2 136	512.8	40.8
Denton	157 396	858	44.4	83	1 685	1 266.8	59.5	408	6 516	1 695.3	140.9
DeSoto	23 162	114	100.0	34	535	256.8	26.9	82	1 363	345.8	32.1
Duncanville	2 523	8	100.0	23	237	67.0	11.7	133	1 482	462.3	37.7
Eagle Pass	9 711	205	76.1	29	161	94.7	7.1	171	2 263	493.5	40.6
Edinburg	48 515	581	92.1	68	1 320	524.1	40.1	199	3 256	890.2	64.5
El Paso	569 327	4 062	61.0	846	8 016	4 793.1	290.2	2 131	32 240	7 892.9	653.3
Euless	22 985	76	100.0	45	401	279.7	25.2	96	1 167	366.1	27.8
Farmers Branch	3 723	8	100.0	227	6 362	3 631.9	385.4	167	2 217	619.9	66.2
Flower Mound	38 476	100	100.0	54	515	251.2	25.6	144	2 799	547.5	49.4
Fort Worth	454 256	3 577	77.1	689	14 729	11 371.3	782.4	1 956	30 304	9 586.1	816.1
Friendswood	44 765	148	100.0	22	82	34.4	3.0	86	1 084	330.9	23.9
Frisco	322 022	1 284	100.0	83	1 047	2 266.8	75.5	421	7 750	1 918.3	175.4
Galveston	23 903	105	100.0	31	502	1 084.7	17.4	238	2 786	558.4	57.3
Garland	31 882	147	100.0	183	2 941	1 470.5	140.6	626	9 531	2 320.0	225.2
Georgetown	132 174	542	100.0	41	336	188.6	17.7	195	3 307	1 084.1	89.3
Grand Prairie	67 693	387	100.0	258	5 486	3 794.6	249.8	299	4 954	1 470.6	129.9
Grapevine	3 828	17	100.0	87	1 813	3 263.3	93.2	365	5 623	1 611.4	133.0
Greenville	4 280	29	100.0	21	198	101.5	5.1	138	2 265	600.8	60.2
Haltom City	859	9	100.0	87	1 034	381.5	44.8	164	1 611	496.6	43.6
Harker Heights	34 446	180	97.8	2	D	D	D	55	1 064	279.4	25.0
Harlingen	14 422	106	100.0	75	866	374.3	25.3	329	5 074	1 149.5	102.4
Houston	563 624	4 591	53.4	4 409	78 172	189 998.4	4 899.1	8 646	130 578	36 570.2	3 266.0
Huntsville	54 805	629	32.0	27	233	152.6	8.7	130	2 171	589.1	45.2
Hurst	1 699	13	84.6	29	187	151.9	8.0	292	5 835	1 227.8	117.2
Irving	103 935	338	100.0	380	9 717	13 529.5	643.1	645	14 897	4 784.6	376.6
Keller	66 759	228	100.0	26	185	43.9	4.8	91	1 417	355.5	30.1

1. Merchant wholesalers except manufacturers' sales branches and offices.   2. Establishments with payroll.

Table D. Cities — **Real Estate, Professional Services, and Manufacturing**

City	Real estate and rental and leasing, 2007				Professional, scientific, and technical services,[1] 2007				Manufacturing, 2007			
	Number of establish-ments	Number of employees	Receipts (mil dol)	Annual payroll (mil dol)	Number of establish-ments	Number of employees	Receipts (mil dol)	Annual payroll (mil dol)	Number of establish-ments	Number of employees	Receipts (mil dol)	Annual payroll (mil dol)
	80	81	82	83	84	85	86	87	88	89	90	91
TENNESSEE— Cont'd												
Franklin	125	1 838	273.5	56.7	324	D	D	D	81	2 501	848.9	93.6
Gallatin	45	400	121.9	19.3	54	D	D	D	74	3 000	860.8	111.7
Germantown	64	D	D	D	107	478	71.6	23.6	NA	NA	NA	NA
Hendersonville	73	297	49.5	8.8	117	601	72.1	36.3	62	852	139.3	32.6
Jackson	98	728	97.0	17.4	178	D	D	D	89	8 828	4 012.9	389.3
Johnson City	112	911	107.7	16.9	192	D	D	D	101	5 611	1 433.3	194.7
Kingsport	70	305	54.4	8.1	133	877	135.2	35.6	45	11 452	D	D
Knoxville	385	2 497	477.4	79.9	831	D	D	D	270	D	D	D
La Vergne	16	144	41.9	4.9	12	D	D	D	52	4 422	1 401.8	221.1
Lebanon	61	271	57.4	8.1	89	D	D	D	54	5 236	D	233.9
Maryville	33	138	25.1	3.6	99	D	D	D	35	3 628	D	176.8
Memphis	818	7 093	1 240.3	274.1	1 467	14 364	1 936.2	802.6	569	23 906	14 709.6	1 174.0
Morristown	54	265	41.0	6.3	70	D	D	D	88	12 463	3 142.6	438.5
Murfreesboro	150	800	297.6	20.2	234	D	D	D	93	5 328	2 273.3	223.4
Nashville-Davidson	934	6 617	1 588.0	252.2	1 912	23 798	2 943.3	1 285.4	633	23 715	7 347.2	999.0
Oak Ridge	47	246	36.0	6.0	159	D	D	D	52	5 916	1 006.6	395.2
Smyrna	39	145	35.5	3.9	51	353	38.9	16.8	33	7 897	D	428.2
Spring Hill	20	110	18.0	3.9	21	D	D	D	5	D	D	D
TEXAS	26 593	173 745	36 399.2	7 067.2	57 373	534 386	90 668.7	35 376.4	21 115	893 842	593 541.5	42 835.7
Abilene	156	628	132.2	19.1	260	D	D	D	88	2 282	D	D
Allen	61	285	54.2	9.4	218	1 252	174.5	69.1	20	1 545	440.6	D
Amarillo	256	1 199	203.0	35.0	429	D	D	D	164	6 376	D	235.2
Arlington	380	1 742	326.4	56.7	774	D	D	D	261	12 392	12 265.1	616.6
Austin	1 537	11 708	2 286.4	471.0	4 095	45 252	6 926.2	3 401.9	590	31 091	27 028.0	1 615.5
Baytown	84	483	102.5	13.7	117	1 482	85.4	114.3	48	4 833	D	464.1
Beaumont	194	988	175.9	34.5	386	D	D	D	116	6 480	D	396.9
Bedford	71	302	66.9	12.5	155	981	172.9	55.1	NA	NA	NA	NA
Big Spring	35	178	36.0	3.4	42	183	13.9	4.9	16	572	D	25.2
Brownsville	141	604	60.9	12.4	252	D	D	D	102	2 889	928.6	108.0
Bryan	95	487	80.8	14.6	164	D	D	D	73	3 948	788.6	129.6
Burleson	31	130	25.9	5.1	68	310	25.5	8.6	38	1 078	192.0	38.4
Carrollton	140	985	211.8	50.3	411	D	D	D	199	11 698	3 090.8	554.4
Cedar Hill	16	31	7.7	0.8	44	118	13.4	4.2	26	1 318	160.5	38.4
Cedar Park	58	318	35.3	14.0	110	460	60.5	22.5	25	981	419.8	50.0
Cleburne	39	119	26.7	3.6	72	356	42.1	13.3	37	1 725	698.9	83.7
College Station	115	566	83.2	14.3	177	D	D	D	21	613	D	24.5
Conroe	78	357	89.7	12.8	185	1 087	102.6	38.3	97	3 278	D	148.3
Coppell	56	504	52.8	14.3	155	921	145.7	53.2	22	1 203	297.2	38.3
Copperas Cove	43	136	15.9	2.6	29	247	34.5	17.6	NA	NA	NA	NA
Corpus Christi	394	2 413	384.7	73.2	757	D	D	D	191	5 961	D	310.6
Dallas	2 179	23 891	5 259.0	1 361.5	5 402	D	D	D	1 318	71 657	21 239.9	3 722.1
Deer Park	30	295	135.6	18.0	54	982	89.1	55.4	37	3 892	14 234.2	327.2
Del Rio	26	92	11.3	2.1	39	D	D	D	NA	NA	NA	NA
Denton	143	661	113.3	19.9	233	D	D	D	85	4 346	2 411.0	211.0
DeSoto	33	129	17.9	3.5	64	194	18.1	6.3	29	1 314	459.1	64.3
Duncanville	32	181	26.6	4.6	54	199	21.1	6.7	26	1 154	186.1	37.4
Eagle Pass	34	84	15.1	1.9	39	D	D	D	NA	NA	NA	NA
Edinburg	63	225	36.8	6.5	154	D	D	D	39	970	276.0	32.2
El Paso	635	3 439	612.6	104.3	1 109	D	D	D	513	14 792	14 103.1	577.0
Euless	47	308	68.0	8.8	84	316	41.4	14.4	39	983	148.6	40.5
Farmers Branch	98	1 008	222.4	45.6	283	3 421	518.7	208.5	110	5 769	1 417.5	267.6
Flower Mound	72	314	51.5	10.6	247	D	D	D	17	547	125.0	D
Fort Worth	656	3 915	1 555.2	175.9	1 534	15 959	2 246.6	1 113.6	731	65 224	24 367.5	3 606.7
Friendswood	33	126	16.0	3.1	115	336	41.7	15.9	NA	NA	NA	NA
Frisco	104	492	153.6	22.4	323	D	D	D	28	551	253.6	D
Galveston	75	388	57.6	10.1	113	480	83.4	30.7	NA	NA	NA	NA
Garland	183	1 137	197.3	31.7	301	3 291	757.9	278.3	297	10 604	4 338.5	445.1
Georgetown	65	246	77.1	10.7	144	513	59.2	22.3	45	943	227.6	42.5
Grand Prairie	116	2 146	333.5	90.0	183	1 128	124.6	44.4	210	14 061	3 733.7	736.5
Grapevine	72	580	184.1	25.5	190	1 141	135.7	43.5	47	1 533	427.7	56.9
Greenville	46	206	28.9	5.1	61	D	D	D	43	13 016	2 784.1	D
Haltom City	45	251	57.0	8.1	55	275	24.7	9.0	113	2 884	614.7	96.0
Harker Heights	37	149	17.9	3.8	26	D	D	D	NA	NA	NA	NA
Harlingen	107	559	71.7	10.2	144	D	D	D	62	1 246	229.8	35.1
Houston	3 576	31 940	7 873.4	1 462.7	8 915	D	D	D	2 582	97 035	49 122.0	4 774.3
Huntsville	44	D	D	D	68	354	23.8	6.9	22	585	D	25.1
Hurst	63	279	79.1	9.0	167	749	97.7	37.5	NA	NA	NA	NA
Irving	351	4 341	1 571.2	242.7	844	D	D	D	187	9 661	3 441.1	465.2
Keller	34	189	44.8	6.4	148	476	69.8	20.1	NA	NA	NA	NA

1. Establishments subject to federal tax.

Table D. Cities — Accommodation and Food Services, Arts, Entertainment, and Recreation, and Health Care and Social Assistance

City	Accommodation and food services, 2007				Arts, entertainment, and recreation,[1] 2007				Health care and social assistance,[1] 2007			
	Number of establishments	Number of employees	Sales (mil dol)	Annual payroll (mil dol)	Number of establishments	Number of employees	Receipts (mil dol)	Annual payroll (mil dol)	Number of establishments	Number of employees	Receipts (mil dol)	Annual payroll (mil dol)
	92	93	94	95	96	97	98	99	100	101	102	103
TENNESSEE— Cont'd												
Franklin	220	4 926	229.4	65.9	80	567	70.9	15.2	220	3 880	434.2	221.3
Gallatin	75	1 073	45.6	11.5	7	D	D	D	76	D	D	D
Germantown	73	1 638	70.7	20.4	13	D	D	D	149	D	D	D
Hendersonville	97	2 018	78.0	23.8	26	D	D	D	131	D	D	D
Jackson	206	5 457	203.7	54.9	19	D	D	D	240	D	D	D
Johnson City	212	5 577	220.3	66.6	19	207	11.4	2.8	245	D	D	D
Kingsport	186	4 302	172.0	47.6	20	D	D	D	223	D	D	D
Knoxville	696	18 112	780.3	233.8	58	998	45.6	13.2	746	10 784	1 375.2	604.9
La Vergne	30	399	18.0	4.5	3	D	D	D	16	D	D	D
Lebanon	105	2 138	90.8	26.8	10	D	D	D	132	2 661	236.9	91.6
Maryville	90	1 877	73.1	22.3	8	D	D	D	134	D	D	D
Memphis	1 345	31 224	1 463.1	407.8	96	2 244	231.5	123.8	1 424	22 942	2 471.7	997.2
Morristown	100	D	D	D	11	38	2.0	0.7	134	D	D	D
Murfreesboro	266	6 483	257.7	73.3	18	159	9.5	2.0	277	D	D	D
Nashville-Davidson	1 605	38 979	2 203.0	626.4	622	5 305	1 557.7	484.8	1 504	29 785	3 704.3	1 365.8
Oak Ridge	72	1 756	79.4	22.4	4	D	D	D	101	1 385	152.5	72.4
Smyrna	92	1 884	76.0	22.0	5	D	D	D	88	D	D	D
Spring Hill	36	578	19.1	5.8	6	56	2.0	0.6	23	D	D	D
TEXAS	43 509	866 189	42 054.6	11 502.3	5 002	79 475	6 731.7	2 220.8	48 875	780 459	71 221.3	27 771.8
Abilene	268	D	D	D	39	272	16.9	3.4	301	D	D	D
Allen	109	2 152	99.5	26.7	13	D	D	D	194	D	D	D
Amarillo	462	9 616	428.3	113.5	43	521	28.6	6.5	569	8 906	1 017.5	349.2
Arlington	625	13 989	647.1	176.3	76	2 190	419.7	247.2	806	11 518	1 402.2	495.8
Austin	2 121	49 569	2 655.7	745.4	255	4 457	388.8	115.8	2 005	31 869	3 705.7	1 457.1
Baytown	139	2 846	133.0	34.4	12	D	D	D	190	D	D	D
Beaumont	261	6 190	258.4	75.4	37	D	D	D	503	6 944	570.7	228.2
Bedford	89	2 232	102.3	27.1	17	D	D	D	219	D	D	D
Big Spring	68	D	D	D	2	D	D	D	66	D	D	D
Brownsville	280	4 870	200.9	51.3	24	288	11.1	3.5	388	10 497	575.3	236.2
Bryan	130	2 153	89.6	23.3	16	385	17.9	7.9	217	2 468	279.7	104.9
Burleson	93	2 061	83.9	24.2	8	28	1.1	0.3	63	1 591	79.3	37.3
Carrollton	197	2 857	147.9	38.4	33	D	D	D	297	3 531	324.6	125.3
Cedar Hill	72	D	D	D	10	89	4.9	1.7	58	706	41.1	18.9
Cedar Park	82	1 424	65.6	16.8	15	D	D	D	103	D	D	D
Cleburne	70	1 338	54.1	14.2	8	61	2.5	0.6	87	D	D	D
College Station	230	6 283	248.7	67.8	16	D	D	D	114	2 192	268.9	87.7
Conroe	145	3 242	148.2	40.3	19	190	9.8	2.5	169	3 820	597.1	167.9
Coppell	66	D	D	D	10	D	D	D	80	D	D	D
Copperas Cove	48	921	32.1	8.4	5	37	1.2	0.3	28	311	14.9	5.9
Corpus Christi	717	14 005	607.1	170.7	59	1 304	68.2	19.4	890	D	D	D
Dallas	2 647	57 958	3 378.6	954.1	301	5 043	547.3	200.0	3 180	45 235	6 245.5	2 727.9
Deer Park	42	736	32.9	8.0	3	7	0.3	0.1	50	D	D	D
Del Rio	80	1 415	57.8	15.2	8	D	D	D	71	2 335	75.1	34.0
Denton	229	4 995	207.5	56.8	22	231	11.7	3.0	339	5 726	722.4	243.6
DeSoto	60	1 235	46.0	14.9	6	106	7.9	2.2	144	D	D	D
Duncanville	57	1 491	66.3	17.5	6	D	D	D	103	1 137	79.1	30.3
Eagle Pass	60	D	D	D	6	D	D	D	72	D	D	D
Edinburg	108	2 037	80.3	21.5	12	D	D	D	256	8 284	476.9	224.0
El Paso	1 194	23 499	990.6	258.0	82	1 288	134.0	22.5	1 137	D	D	D
Euless	83	2 182	131.5	39.2	8	140	7.6	2.1	69	747	75.4	26.8
Farmers Branch	93	1 321	76.8	21.8	13	370	19.2	7.6	136	D	D	D
Flower Mound	100	2 056	79.9	24.4	24	D	D	D	140	D	D	D
Fort Worth	1 103	23 998	1 246.1	339.1	128	2 245	243.5	50.1	1 325	19 388	2 197.9	856.8
Friendswood	74	D	D	D	11	159	9.7	3.2	94	D	D	D
Frisco	178	4 689	257.7	74.7	29	D	D	D	225	D	D	D
Galveston	203	5 316	275.9	76.6	19	D	D	D	84	D	D	D
Garland	299	5 150	227.9	62.9	31	681	41.9	10.4	378	D	D	D
Georgetown	96	1 727	77.5	21.3	12	D	D	D	126	2 146	170.6	75.7
Grand Prairie	190	3 784	191.2	49.2	26	D	D	D	185	2 236	138.7	58.4
Grapevine	221	9 432	697.9	195.5	19	449	19.1	5.8	184	D	D	D
Greenville	64	1 319	55.0	16.2	6	66	1.7	0.5	100	1 165	107.6	45.2
Haltom City	67	889	33.8	8.8	6	106	4.5	1.5	33	D	D	D
Harker Heights	48	583	24.5	5.6	10	60	5.0	0.6	28	D	D	D
Harlingen	155	3 136	129.6	33.6	15	268	9.1	2.7	311	D	D	D
Houston	5 177	111 291	6 263.9	1 660.1	464	8 787	1 445.8	509.2	5 956	85 100	8 718.9	3 273.8
Huntsville	84	1 740	63.8	16.7	4	D	D	D	83	D	D	D
Hurst	97	2 035	100.4	25.7	12	D	D	D	104	1 196	109.7	42.4
Irving	489	12 088	722.7	199.5	49	D	D	D	450	D	D	D
Keller	69	1 042	48.9	13.5	9	188	8.4	2.0	105	939	86.9	32.9

1. Establishments subject to federal tax.

Table D. Cities — Other Services and Federal Funds

City	Other services¹, 2007				Selected federal funds, 2009–2010 (mil dol)								
					Procurement contracts		Grants						
	Number of establishments	Number of employees	Receipts (mil dol)	Annual payroll (mil dol)	Defense	Other	Total²	Medicaid and other health related	Nutrition and family welfare	Energy and environment	Disasters and emergency preparedness	Housing and community development	Employment and training
	104	105	106	107	108	109	110	111	112	113	114	115	116
TENNESSEE— Cont'd													
Franklin	130	998	77.1	23.4	24.8	1.6	3.5	1.8	0.1	0.1	0.0	1.1	0.0
Gallatin	50	324	17.6	5.4	0.0	0.2	2.6	0.0	0.0	0.4	0.0	0.7	0.0
Germantown	51	512	23.3	10.1	0.0	3.8	0.3	0.0	0.0	0.0	0.0	0.3	0.0
Hendersonville	84	522	38.9	11.2	1.8	0.1	0.1	0.0	0.0	0.0	0.0	0.0	0.0
Jackson	106	772	57.4	20.9	0.1	3.7	18.1	0.0	0.0	0.0	0.0	12.2	0.0
Johnson City	128	756	51.2	16.2	10.4	1.7	27.1	11.1	0.3	0.0	0.0	5.1	0.0
Kingsport	94	730	47.4	14.6	204.8	2.8	19.2	0.0	7.8	1.9	0.0	8.6	0.0
Knoxville	429	3 172	228.3	77.7	71.5	372.9	210.1	28.8	8.2	30.2	0.0	39.4	0.0
La Vergne	27	674	88.8	26.4	1.0	0.0	0.0	0.0	0.0	0.0	0.0	0.0	0.0
Lebanon	52	305	26.1	7.0	1.4	7.8	9.1	0.1	6.9	0.4	0.0	0.6	0.0
Maryville	65	D	D	D	5.8	0.6	5.6	1.0	0.3	0.0	0.0	2.4	0.0
Memphis	857	7 640	632.5	192.5	1 513.6	495.9	587.3	225.3	90.7	7.0	-1.3	110.0	3.1
Morristown	52	263	17.8	5.3	24.6	0.5	14.0	0.0	7.3	0.0	0.0	3.7	0.3
Murfreesboro	162	927	70.6	23.5	3.5	429.3	17.0	0.8	0.0	1.6	0.0	5.5	0.0
Nashville-Davidson	981	10 214	724.8	273.9	16.0	438.7	2 476.4	907.1	275.9	113.3	160.3	277.1	142.4
Oak Ridge	46	D	D	D	65.4	3 380.3	53.0	38.2	0.0	7.9	0.0	2.0	0.0
Smyrna	41	D	D	D	1.7	7.0	1.0	0.0	0.0	0.0	0.0	0.0	0.9
Spring Hill	21	D	D	D	0.0	0.0	0.0	0.0	0.0	0.0	0.0	0.0	0.0
TEXAS	28 404	209 702	17 917.8	5 592.5	30 331.5	10 263.0	44 624.1	23 603.8	5 505.0	1 098.2	533.5	3 383.1	492.2
Abilene	176	1 144	82.2	23.3	19.1	0.9	21.0	0.0	3.0	0.4	0.0	8.1	0.0
Allen	67	499	28.6	11.1	27.8	2.1	2.8	0.0	0.0	0.7	1.8	0.3	0.0
Amarillo	302	2 230	169.5	46.6	2 394.6	537.6	65.5	0.0	10.1	17.3	0.0	20.4	0.0
Arlington	406	3 093	225.6	71.3	415.0	2.1	97.3	8.5	1.8	23.2	0.4	30.0	3.0
Austin	1 246	11 182	899.4	315.4	446.7	418.7	7 296.9	674.6	990.0	484.9	42.3	1 957.2	407.2
Baytown	105	D	D	D	124.7	0.0	8.6	0.0	0.0	0.0	0.0	7.1	0.0
Beaumont	191	1 680	141.1	43.6	12.7	15.5	27.6	0.9	3.0	0.0	0.0	15.0	0.0
Bedford	51	329	21.0	7.6	8.4	0.7	0.4	0.0	0.0	0.0	0.0	0.0	0.0
Big Spring	38	D	D	D	0.6	12.6	4.1	0.0	0.0	0.0	0.0	1.5	0.0
Brownsville	126	570	33.7	8.6	14.4	27.0	54.2	9.3	0.0	0.6	0.0	22.5	0.0
Bryan	119	D	D	D	11.6	2.3	33.9	2.1	4.3	0.5	0.0	12.6	0.0
Burleson	50	D	D	D	0.0	0.0	0.7	0.4	0.0	0.0	0.3	0.0	0.0
Carrollton	166	1 685	192.9	64.0	3.2	18.4	1.7	0.0	0.0	0.0	0.0	1.7	0.0
Cedar Hill	39	D	D	D	0.0	0.0	0.3	0.0	0.0	0.0	0.0	0.0	0.0
Cedar Park	72	D	D	D	1.7	0.6	0.0	0.0	0.0	0.0	0.0	0.0	0.0
Cleburne	56	375	29.4	8.6	0.0	11.7	2.4	0.0	0.0	0.0	0.0	1.8	0.0
College Station	67	458	23.2	7.5	34.5	18.9	305.9	95.9	1.8	29.7	1.3	1.9	0.2
Conroe	111	758	73.6	19.7	0.3	0.0	10.7	0.7	0.4	3.8	0.0	5.5	0.0
Coppell	46	D	D	D	0.0	2.1	0.9	0.0	0.0	0.9	0.0	0.0	0.0
Copperas Cove	43	336	39.8	10.7	0.0	0.3	14.7	0.0	0.0	0.0	0.0	0.1	0.0
Corpus Christi	408	3 133	308.9	98.3	271.1	53.7	59.5	4.0	9.3	9.1	0.0	18.6	0.4
Dallas	1 567	12 760	1 252.6	351.6	195.3	425.0	991.8	410.0	36.6	15.9	1.3	260.5	0.9
Deer Park	67	D	D	D	952.9	0.0	0.0	0.0	0.0	0.0	0.0	0.0	0.0
Del Rio	30	D	D	D	18.7	11.5	6.0	0.0	2.1	0.0	0.0	3.4	0.0
Denton	139	766	57.5	17.6	7.3	19.9	38.7	2.4	1.3	2.6	0.0	13.8	0.0
DeSoto	37	156	16.2	4.1	2.5	0.4	0.0	0.0	0.0	0.0	0.0	0.0	0.0
Duncanville	70	376	31.2	9.4	0.0	0.4	0.0	0.0	0.0	0.0	0.0	0.0	0.0
Eagle Pass	26	D	D	D	0.6	0.2	10.8	4.1	0.7	0.1	0.0	3.1	0.0
Edinburg	77	253	18.6	4.9	0.1	1.5	64.1	2.3	24.2	4.5	0.0	5.8	0.0
El Paso	705	4 510	278.2	84.6	446.8	206.7	245.5	32.6	29.4	12.0	1.8	55.8	1.3
Euless	52	D	D	D	16.1	0.8	0.8	0.4	0.0	0.5	0.0	0.0	0.0
Farmers Branch	74	1 254	71.1	31.3	1.8	4.4	0.0	0.0	0.0	0.0	0.0	0.0	0.0
Flower Mound	79	696	29.9	14.5	0.1	1.1	0.9	0.0	0.0	0.6	0.0	0.2	0.0
Fort Worth	699	6 713	548.7	177.5	7 742.9	221.8	199.1	40.3	22.5	0.5	0.0	81.8	0.0
Friendswood	54	D	D	D	0.0	0.1	0.0	0.0	0.0	0.0	0.0	0.0	0.0
Frisco	115	935	58.5	20.2	0.4	1.5	0.2	0.0	0.0	0.0	0.2	0.0	0.0
Galveston	73	422	27.9	8.5	171.0	42.5	245.1	181.8	7.0	1.1	0.0	17.2	4.7
Garland	256	1 263	107.1	33.9	196.3	5.4	17.2	0.0	0.0	2.0	0.0	15.2	0.0
Georgetown	71	475	30.2	9.5	0.4	0.2	11.0	0.7	5.4	1.5	0.0	2.2	0.0
Grand Prairie	122	1 761	110.1	43.4	2 252.0	106.7	28.3	0.0	0.0	0.5	0.0	22.9	0.0
Grapevine	78	866	76.3	20.1	0.3	2.2	1.4	0.0	0.0	0.5	0.0	0.6	0.0
Greenville	45	202	15.7	4.6	1 345.3	0.3	8.5	2.9	1.1	0.4	0.0	3.7	0.0
Haltom City	67	728	72.3	16.5	0.2	0.0	0.2	0.0	0.0	0.0	0.0	0.2	0.0
Harker Heights	22	83	6.6	1.6	0.3	0.6	0.8	0.0	0.0	0.0	0.0	0.8	0.0
Harlingen	91	570	36.2	10.2	0.8	13.9	25.8	9.0	0.0	1.0	0.0	6.5	0.0
Houston	3 343	32 243	2 860.5	952.6	1 530.1	4 174.0	2 135.2	1 103.7	50.7	330.0	0.9	248.1	6.1
Huntsville	47	298	19.2	5.1	10.2	0.0	8.2	0.7	0.0	0.0	0.1	1.5	0.0
Hurst	73	D	D	D	976.0	15.9	3.9	0.0	0.0	0.0	0.0	0.0	0.0
Irving	248	2 866	292.5	89.9	44.2	12.8	48.0	0.0	0.0	2.2	0.0	3.5	36.6
Keller	46	D	D	D	0.9	0.0	0.0	0.0	0.0	0.0	0.0	0.0	0.0

1. Establishments subject to federal tax.　2. Includes program categories not shown separately. State totals include additional categories not allocated by city.

Table D. Cities — City Government Finances

City	City government finances, 2007									
	General revenue							General expenditure		
		Intergovernmental		Taxes					Per capita[1] (dollars)	
					Per capita[1] (dollars)					
	Total (mil dol)	Total (mil dol)	Percent from state government	Total (mil dol)	Total	Property	Sales and gross receipts	Total (mil dol)	Total	Capital outlays
	117	118	119	120	121	122	123	124	125	126
TENNESSEE—Cont'd										
Franklin	83.3	10.3	82.6	50.5	880	171	709	81.9	1 428	479
Gallatin	32.0	8.7	42.3	10.0	348	269	79	27.5	956	188
Germantown	54.0	14.3	61.2	22.6	606	537	70	45.3	1 214	133
Hendersonville	28.4	14.0	38.6	10.3	218	149	69	27.9	593	51
Jackson	85.3	10.6	77.9	56.5	895	445	430	81.3	1 287	81
Johnson City	134.5	38.5	97.6	54.1	886	479	406	129.7	2 125	24
Kingsport	146.1	69.4	47.5	50.3	1 133	963	170	116.9	2 631	141
Knoxville	327.2	77.2	50.2	154.5	842	520	322	291.1	1 586	474
La Vergne	17.0	2.8	26.1	8.7	298	111	188	14.0	482	59
Lebanon	25.1	2.5	91.1	14.3	595	109	486	30.2	1 251	120
Maryville	90.2	43.5	100.0	34.5	1 290	1 277	14	74.7	2 790	95
Memphis	2 055.1	1 097.3	60.5	626.5	930	703	225	1 902.6	2 823	173
Morristown	18.5	1.1	76.9	6.2	226	0	225	21.2	773	219
Murfreesboro	161.7	84.7	46.7	42.7	434	303	131	178.5	1 814	435
Nashville-Davidson	2 125.7	470.0	98.1	1 161.6	1 966	1 290	674	2 104.6	3 562	494
Oak Ridge	118.7	73.6	30.6	31.6	1 150	684	446	115.8	4 209	49
Smyrna	44.0	6.8	58.2	16.1	439	175	264	45.5	1 243	328
Spring Hill	14.2	3.9	17.4	1.7	73	0	73	15.9	668	194
TEXAS	X	X	X	X	X	X	X	X	X	X
Abilene	117.7	18.3	39.2	65.3	562	208	354	119.0	1 024	235
Allen	83.7	2.0	100.0	56.2	724	378	346	78.0	1 005	188
Amarillo	195.3	20.5	29.3	95.7	514	133	381	218.2	1 173	252
Arlington	514.4	55.8	9.1	224.1	604	283	321	473.0	1 275	421
Austin	1 198.0	154.8	13.7	471.1	634	316	318	1 165.8	1 569	299
Baytown	86.6	9.5	77.1	35.3	503	227	276	75.1	1 071	173
Beaumont	142.5	16.2	43.8	79.1	722	299	423	125.8	1 148	132
Bedford	36.0	1.1	12.6	25.6	522	255	267	32.5	663	5
Big Spring	79.4	58.5	4.0	11.7	487	129	359	77.5	3 221	25
Brownsville	144.5	10.7	25.8	65.2	377	164	214	158.1	915	144
Bryan	76.4	3.2	19.8	37.6	522	239	283	75.7	1 051	235
Burleson	37.4	0.5	79.2	21.5	645	261	384	43.1	1 291	453
Carrollton	128.9	6.5	87.5	83.4	674	413	260	88.8	717	6
Cedar Hill	48.1	2.6	60.7	32.3	727	385	342	46.7	1 052	294
Cedar Park	50.7	0.5	100.0	35.2	605	221	384	39.0	672	195
Cleburne	33.8	0.0	100.0	19.1	645	327	318	30.0	1 015	0
College Station	72.3	3.5	28.0	39.1	487	207	280	86.2	1 074	211
Conroe	57.8	3.1	78.7	43.1	821	187	634	55.9	1 065	257
Coppell	60.6	0.5	11.2	42.5	1 085	670	415	52.9	1 350	291
Copperas Cove	20.6	0.2	6.0	9.8	327	200	126	17.6	587	42
Corpus Christi	313.1	24.0	29.4	162.5	569	249	320	343.0	1 202	304
Dallas	2 386.1	171.5	24.6	938.7	757	428	329	2 523.6	2 034	603
Deer Park	34.4	1.4	0.0	14.9	485	295	191	26.3	860	0
Del Rio	31.6	5.3	32.7	12.0	327	125	202	26.8	733	103
Denton	138.3	5.2	67.2	75.0	649	260	389	117.7	1 019	125
DeSoto	49.9	1.7	77.3	29.7	633	391	243	50.8	1 085	240
Duncanville	36.0	1.4	100.0	23.0	636	337	299	33.7	930	46
Eagle Pass	39.6	15.4	100.0	7.9	299	99	200	38.2	1 455	513
Edinburg	52.6	3.6	65.0	27.1	395	212	183	46.1	671	46
El Paso	611.5	101.6	38.3	297.1	490	247	243	531.6	876	231
Euless	64.3	0.9	28.5	41.0	783	215	568	63.0	1 203	191
Farmers Branch	56.3	3.5	53.6	36.9	1 395	629	766	59.8	2 260	372
Flower Mound	48.8	0.9	9.7	37.3	546	355	191	53.7	786	210
Fort Worth	818.1	56.4	100.0	490.1	719	386	333	829.7	1 217	335
Friendswood	25.0	0.5	18.4	16.7	500	337	162	24.7	738	153
Frisco	176.8	30.0	60.9	103.0	1 163	453	710	211.8	2 393	1 195
Galveston	114.0	10.0	17.4	50.7	890	283	607	86.7	1 522	159
Garland	212.8	17.6	13.8	100.1	458	305	153	268.8	1 228	361
Georgetown	46.0	0.5	5.8	23.9	509	190	319	38.7	825	0
Grand Prairie	257.7	31.3	24.1	115.9	731	344	388	217.2	1 371	349
Grapevine	95.4	1.0	100.0	63.0	1 257	525	732	80.2	1 600	136
Greenville	48.0	2.2	52.2	16.1	627	301	325	44.9	1 749	616
Haltom City	22.7	0.5	0.0	13.8	345	135	210	30.0	748	196
Harker Heights	13.9	0.6	15.6	8.9	364	193	172	15.0	610	26
Harlingen	73.0	8.5	5.7	35.8	558	200	357	64.0	997	21
Houston	3 112.6	299.0	22.0	1 607.1	728	380	347	3 338.9	1 512	300
Huntsville	28.1	1.3	100.0	12.3	326	105	221	28.2	747	138
Hurst	46.9	2.0	67.5	31.9	830	276	554	44.2	1 150	23
Irving	236.3	11.1	34.4	160.4	804	383	421	230.0	1 153	130
Keller	47.8	1.0	100.0	28.2	739	390	350	37.3	980	129

1. Based on population estimated as of July 1 of the year shown.

Table D. Cities — **City Government Finances**

City	City government finances, 2006 (cont.)									
	General expenditure (cont.)									
	Percent of total for:									
	Public welfare	Highways	Parking facilities	Education	Health and hospitals	Police protection	Sewerage and sanitation	Parks and recreation	Housing and community development	Interest on debt
	127	128	129	130	131	132	133	134	135	136
TENNESSEE— Cont'd										
Franklin	0.7	17.8	0.0	0.0	0.0	17.0	19.2	5.6	0.0	4.6
Gallatin	0.0	10.3	0.0	0.0	0.2	19.7	21.1	13.0	0.0	0.0
Germantown	0.0	10.4	0.0	0.0	0.5	18.6	12.6	15.9	3.4	2.5
Hendersonville	0.5	6.1	0.0	0.1	0.0	20.7	9.5	5.9	0.0	1.8
Jackson	0.0	4.4	0.0	11.6	5.0	17.6	10.8	8.3	0.1	3.9
Johnson City	1.1	5.0	0.0	45.6	0.0	8.1	9.5	2.7	0.1	10.7
Kingsport	0.0	3.7	0.0	49.4	0.0	8.3	7.1	3.9	0.4	2.5
Knoxville	0.0	3.1	0.2	0.0	0.0	14.6	37.7	2.1	2.3	6.3
La Vergne	0.0	3.5	0.0	0.0	0.6	29.2	16.9	4.9	0.0	3.2
Lebanon	0.0	11.6	0.0	0.0	0.0	24.1	21.8	7.2	0.0	3.1
Maryville	0.0	4.1	3.4	59.6	0.4	6.6	4.8	2.3	0.3	2.2
Memphis	0.0	3.3	0.0	56.7	0.6	8.9	4.2	2.8	2.6	3.6
Morristown	0.0	3.1	0.0	0.0	0.0	15.5	36.8	3.1	0.0	2.2
Murfreesboro	0.1	16.8	0.1	31.5	0.0	10.1	10.9	6.4	0.2	3.5
Nashville-Davidson	1.4	2.4	0.0	32.6	8.6	8.2	6.6	4.3	0.0	7.2
Oak Ridge	0.0	1.3	0.0	41.0	0.0	4.8	1.6	3.3	0.5	2.5
Smyrna	0.6	14.1	0.0	0.0	0.0	17.4	4.6	15.2	0.6	3.4
Spring Hill	0.0	3.2	0.0	0.0	0.0	15.9	37.7	3.1	0.0	0.0
TEXAS	X	X	X	X	X	X	X	X	X	X
Abilene	0.0	6.5	0.0	0.0	5.7	15.8	14.1	5.0	2.1	1.9
Allen	0.0	5.7	0.0	0.0	0.0	14.4	13.5	16.0	3.2	7.2
Amarillo	0.1	8.7	0.0	0.0	8.6	13.4	14.7	5.9	4.7	0.2
Arlington	0.1	9.6	0.0	0.0	0.4	14.2	9.6	30.3	0.9	15.6
Austin	0.0	5.4	0.0	0.0	10.8	16.2	15.4	7.8	2.9	6.4
Baytown	0.0	9.2	0.0	0.0	4.2	20.0	16.6	6.2	1.4	6.9
Beaumont	0.0	11.6	0.0	0.0	5.8	20.9	11.3	4.6	2.8	4.1
Bedford	0.0	7.9	0.0	0.0	1.1	25.8	13.2	7.2	0.0	7.4
Big Spring	0.0	2.4	0.0	0.0	2.0	5.1	5.2	1.6	0.0	0.1
Brownsville	0.0	5.1	0.3	0.0	1.0	16.2	13.6	4.5	1.4	15.9
Bryan	0.0	8.2	0.0	0.0	0.0	15.9	16.8	5.8	3.3	7.7
Burleson	0.0	30.5	0.0	0.0	1.1	11.9	16.9	7.1	0.0	4.6
Carrollton	0.0	5.9	0.0	0.0	2.4	20.7	13.5	9.4	0.6	7.1
Cedar Hill	0.0	25.1	0.0	0.0	0.0	13.8	10.5	5.1	0.3	5.2
Cedar Park	0.0	21.7	0.0	0.0	0.3	12.8	19.6	4.9	1.6	8.2
Cleburne	0.0	6.4	0.0	0.0	1.4	17.9	22.7	9.2	0.0	5.9
College Station	0.0	11.0	0.6	0.0	0.0	11.7	17.3	14.3	2.1	6.6
Conroe	0.0	12.3	0.0	0.0	0.0	17.2	17.7	7.1	1.2	5.5
Coppell	0.0	18.1	0.0	0.0	0.4	15.7	3.1	12.9	0.0	6.2
Copperas Cove	0.0	9.2	0.0	0.0	0.0	21.8	18.7	10.3	0.0	4.4
Corpus Christi	0.0	6.2	0.1	0.0	3.8	17.3	23.4	11.2	1.2	5.7
Dallas	0.4	12.7	0.1	0.0	1.2	13.0	9.8	5.3	2.4	15.8
Deer Park	0.0	2.5	0.0	0.0	0.6	17.0	18.3	6.5	0.0	5.2
Del Rio	1.7	16.2	0.0	0.0	1.7	18.1	16.6	4.6	0.0	5.8
Denton	0.0	4.2	0.0	0.0	0.2	16.0	25.1	8.4	1.7	6.8
DeSoto	0.0	9.0	0.0	0.0	0.6	12.2	19.6	8.1	0.0	9.9
Duncanville	0.0	11.4	0.0	0.0	2.5	18.5	18.3	4.8	0.0	4.6
Eagle Pass	0.0	5.2	0.0	0.0	0.1	11.8	31.9	17.1	0.9	5.4
Edinburg	0.0	7.2	0.0	0.0	2.9	18.8	23.2	13.8	1.7	3.0
El Paso	0.0	9.2	0.0	0.0	4.6	17.4	12.5	11.1	5.4	6.2
Euless	0.0	10.9	0.0	0.0	0.5	13.2	3.3	11.8	0.0	4.8
Farmers Branch	0.0	17.3	0.0	0.0	0.0	27.2	13.4	11.8	0.0	1.4
Flower Mound	0.0	21.9	0.0	0.0	1.8	16.8	8.5	12.9	0.0	5.9
Fort Worth	0.0	11.7	0.0	0.0	1.7	20.6	16.2	6.9	1.2	2.7
Friendswood	0.0	6.0	0.0	0.0	0.7	21.7	8.9	7.5	1.1	3.0
Frisco	0.0	15.2	0.0	4.4	0.1	6.3	6.7	3.0	0.0	10.1
Galveston	0.0	7.6	0.5	0.0	0.5	16.0	10.7	17.8	5.3	9.7
Garland	1.4	8.1	0.0	0.0	1.1	14.4	17.6	4.1	6.4	5.8
Georgetown	0.7	4.5	0.0	0.0	0.0	17.0	22.1	8.3	0.0	6.5
Grand Prairie	0.0	14.7	0.0	0.0	0.8	12.6	13.8	11.2	11.3	8.2
Grapevine	0.0	8.8	0.0	0.0	0.0	12.7	7.7	12.1	0.1	8.5
Greenville	0.0	4.0	0.0	0.0	0.3	15.5	18.2	3.3	1.7	4.7
Haltom City	0.0	11.9	0.0	0.0	0.8	21.6	17.6	3.2	0.2	3.6
Harker Heights	0.0	4.8	0.0	0.0	0.0	20.9	13.9	6.5	0.0	4.3
Harlingen	0.0	5.7	0.0	0.0	5.6	15.4	17.3	8.6	1.8	1.8
Houston	0.0	7.4	0.1	0.0	3.0	15.1	10.4	5.2	2.3	13.3
Huntsville	0.0	5.7	0.0	0.0	0.7	13.8	43.4	3.6	0.0	3.8
Hurst	0.0	8.1	0.0	0.0	2.2	28.0	14.6	14.5	0.0	0.7
Irving	0.0	9.9	0.0	0.0	0.7	17.7	15.7	8.9	2.3	3.4
Keller	0.0	7.0	0.0	0.0	0.3	14.5	8.5	15.0	3.3	16.8

City	City government finances, 2007 (cont.) Debt outstanding Total (mil dol)	Debt outstanding Per capita[1] (dollars)	Debt issued during year	City government employment, 2010	Climate[2] Average daily temperature (degrees Fahrenheit) Mean January	Mean July	Limits January[3]	Limits July[4]	Annual precipitation (inches)	Heating degree days	Cooling degree days
	137	138	139	140	141	142	143	144	145	146	147
TENNESSEE—Cont'd											
Franklin	103.3	1 800	20.3	675	35.1	77.4	25.2	88.9	54.33	4 199	1 294
Gallatin	18.0	628	7.5	404	NA	NA	NA	NA	NA	NA	NA
Germantown	28.5	763	9.8	381	37.9	81.1	28.2	91.1	53.63	3 491	1 838
Hendersonville	14.3	305	7.7	NA	36.8	79.1	27.9	88.7	48.11	3 677	1 652
Jackson	121.8	1 927	0.0	732	37.1	79.6	28.2	89.4	54.86	3 649	1 648
Johnson City	496.3	8 133	62.6	2 028	34.2	74.2	24.3	84.8	41.33	4 445	956
Kingsport	129.1	2 995	37.1	1 966	35.6	76.2	26.2	86.9	44.44	4 178	1 139
Knoxville	652.5	3 555	0.0	2 542	38.5	78.7	30.3	88.2	48.22	3 531	1 527
La Vergne	31.0	1 069	0.0	NA	NA	NA	NA	NA	NA	NA	NA
Lebanon	31.2	1 292	2.7	366	NA	NA	NA	NA	NA	NA	NA
Maryville	82.8	3 095	31.0	974	NA	NA	NA	NA	NA	NA	NA
Memphis	2 952.3	4 380	292.0	23 505	39.9	82.5	31.3	92.1	54.65	3 041	2 187
Morristown	12.9	470	1.1	436	NA	NA	NA	NA	NA	NA	NA
Murfreesboro	288.3	2 930	69.8	1 959	35.4	78.1	25.3	89.1	54.98	4 107	1 388
Nashville-Davidson	3 858.6	6 531	254.9	21 689	36.8	79.1	27.9	88.7	48.11	3 677	1 652
Oak Ridge	154.8	5 628	26.0	935	36.6	77.3	27.2	88.1	55.05	3 993	1 301
Smyrna	41.9	1 146	10.8	435	36.8	79.1	27.9	88.7	48.11	3 677	1 652
Spring Hill	8.5	357	0.0	NA	NA	NA	NA	NA	NA	NA	NA
TEXAS	X	X	X	NA	X	X	X	X	X	X	X
Abilene	122.7	1 055	25.7	1 145	43.5	83.5	31.8	94.8	23.78	2 659	2 386
Allen	109.6	1 412	7.1	NA	41.8	82.4	31.1	92.7	41.01	2 843	2 060
Amarillo	161.4	867	20.9	2 005	35.8	78.2	22.6	91.0	19.71	4 318	1 344
Arlington	1 943.9	5 239	479.6	2 578	44.1	85.0	34.0	95.4	34.73	2 370	2 568
Austin	4 644.7	6 251	635.7	12 312	50.2	84.2	40.0	95.0	33.65	1 648	2 974
Baytown	158.9	2 266	38.0	723	51.6	83.6	41.9	91.6	53.75	1 471	2 841
Beaumont	225.6	2 059	28.8	1 228	51.1	83.1	41.1	92.7	57.38	1 548	2 734
Bedford	61.5	1 256	0.0	NA	44.1	85.0	34.0	95.4	34.73	2 370	2 568
Big Spring	10.0	414	5.6	286	42.7	82.7	29.6	94.3	20.12	2 724	2 243
Brownsville	506.6	2 932	20.7	1 645	59.6	83.9	50.5	92.4	27.55	644	3 874
Bryan	174.3	2 420	54.4	920	50.2	84.6	39.8	95.6	39.67	1 616	2 939
Burleson	72.0	2 158	9.0	NA	NA	NA	NA	NA	NA	NA	NA
Carrollton	176.0	1 422	24.8	774	44.1	85.0	34.0	95.4	34.73	2 370	2 568
Cedar Hill	85.0	1 914	19.6	NA	43.7	84.3	33.2	94.9	34.54	2 437	2 508
Cedar Park	126.9	2 184	2.8	348	47.2	83.8	35.1	95.7	36.42	1 998	2 584
Cleburne	99.3	3 359	12.9	NA	45.9	84.5	34.0	97.0	36.25	2 158	2 604
College Station	188.8	2 350	32.7	881	50.2	84.6	39.8	95.6	39.67	1 616	2 938
Conroe	76.6	1 458	15.0	516	50.3	83.7	40.0	94.3	49.32	1 647	2 793
Coppell	72.6	1 851	8.2	NA	44.1	85.0	34.0	95.4	34.73	2 370	2 568
Copperas Cove	44.2	1 471	9.3	NA	46.0	83.5	34.0	95.3	32.88	2 190	2 477
Corpus Christi	869.9	3 047	89.8	2 765	56.1	83.8	46.2	93.2	32.26	950	3 497
Dallas	8 852.4	7 136	852.6	15 111	45.9	86.5	36.4	96.1	37.05	2 219	2 878
Deer Park	44.3	1 445	0.0	307	54.3	84.5	45.2	93.6	53.96	1 174	3 179
Del Rio	71.3	1 950	0.7	477	51.3	85.3	39.7	96.2	18.80	1 417	3 226
Denton	401.6	3 477	24.9	1 239	42.7	83.6	32.0	94.1	37.79	2 650	2 269
DeSoto	105.4	2 248	8.9	NA	46.0	84.6	35.0	96.0	38.81	2 130	2 608
Duncanville	34.4	951	4.7	NA	45.9	86.5	36.4	96.1	37.05	2 219	2 878
Eagle Pass	58.6	2 229	11.7	NA	NA	NA	NA	NA	NA	NA	NA
Edinburg	56.2	818	27.4	NA	58.7	85.1	48.2	95.5	22.61	719	3 898
El Paso	1 100.0	1 812	173.6	5 622	45.1	83.3	32.9	94.5	9.43	2 543	2 254
Euless	76.3	1 457	9.7	NA	44.1	85.0	34.0	95.4	34.73	2 370	2 568
Farmers Branch	19.2	723	0.0	NA	45.9	86.5	36.4	96.1	37.05	2 219	2 878
Flower Mound	119.0	1 741	15.6	NA	44.1	85.0	34.0	95.4	34.73	2 370	2 568
Fort Worth	1 183.0	1 735	46.1	6 234	43.3	84.5	31.4	96.6	34.01	2 509	2 466
Friendswood	51.0	1 522	24.3	212	54.3	84.5	45.2	93.6	53.96	1 174	3 179
Frisco	641.0	7 240	95.3	594	41.8	82.4	31.1	92.7	41.01	2 843	2 060
Galveston	309.5	5 436	47.8	825	55.8	84.3	49.7	88.7	43.84	1 008	3 268
Garland	659.8	3 015	88.2	2 062	45.9	86.5	36.4	96.1	37.05	2 219	2 878
Georgetown	107.1	2 284	33.1	NA	47.2	83.8	35.1	95.7	36.42	1 998	2 584
Grand Prairie	358.8	2 265	18.2	1 171	44.1	85.0	34.0	95.4	34.73	2 370	2 568
Grapevine	230.2	4 594	11.4	585	42.4	84.0	30.8	95.5	34.66	2 649	2 340
Greenville	69.7	2 713	4.9	NA	NA	NA	NA	NA	NA	NA	NA
Haltom City	51.9	1 294	3.4	298	43.0	84.1	31.4	95.7	34.12	2 608	2 358
Harker Heights	36.3	1 477	17.3	NA	NA	NA	NA	NA	NA	NA	NA
Harlingen	48.6	756	8.6	NA	58.6	84.4	48.4	94.5	28.13	737	3 736
Houston	12 167.5	5 510	1 370.0	22 615	54.3	84.5	45.2	93.6	53.96	1 174	3 179
Huntsville	49.2	1 303	1.1	NA	48.5	83.2	39.0	93.8	48.51	1 835	2 600
Hurst	46.2	1 202	8.1	NA	44.1	85.0	34.0	95.4	34.73	2 370	2 568
Irving	368.1	1 845	91.2	1 906	45.9	86.5	36.4	96.1	37.05	2 219	2 878
Keller	152.0	3 991	5.4	NA	43.0	84.1	31.4	95.7	34.12	2 608	2 358

1. Based on the population estimated as of July 1 of the year shown.   2. Represents normal values based on the 30-year period, 1971–2000.   3. Average daily minimum.   4. Average daily maximum.

Table D. Cities — Land Area and Population

STATE Place code	City	Land area,[1] 2010 (sq km)	Population, 2010 Total persons	Rank	Per square kilometer	Race alone or in combination, not of Hispanic origin (percent), 2010 White	Black	American Indian, Alaska Native	Asian	Hawaiian Pacific Islander	Percent Hispanic or Latino[2], 2010	Percent Foreign born, 2008–2010
		1	2	3	4	5	6	7	8	9	10	11
	TEXAS—Cont'd											
48 39148	Killeen	138.8	127 921	197	921.8	38.0	35.1	1.3	5.4	1.7	22.9	10.4
48 39352	Kingsville	35.8	26 213	1 584	731.8	21.6	4.2	0.3	2.8	0.1	71.4	6.4
48 39952	Kyle	49.4	28 016	1 474	566.8	46.8	5.8	0.7	1.5	0.2	46.3	6.1
48 40588	Lake Jackson	50.4	26 849	1 543	533.2	70.9	5.4	0.8	3.4	0.1	20.5	9.4
48 41212	Lancaster	78.4	36 361	1 097	463.6	13.8	69.4	0.6	0.5	0.1	17.0	5.9
48 41440	La Porte	48.3	33 800	1 196	700.4	62.8	6.5	0.9	1.5	0.1	29.4	7.9
48 41464	Laredo	230.3	236 091	81	1 025.3	3.5	0.2	0.1	0.6	0.0	95.6	29.1
48 41980	League City	132.8	83 560	381	629.0	69.8	7.5	0.7	6.2	0.1	17.3	10.4
48 42016	Leander	59.2	26 521	1 562	448.1	68.0	5.2	1.1	3.1	0.2	24.5	8.1
48 42508	Lewisville	94.3	95 290	311	1 010.8	51.3	11.8	0.9	8.4	0.1	29.2	22.0
48 43012	Little Elm	37.7	25 898	1 602	686.2	57.4	15.2	1.2	4.2	0.2	24.0	14.3
48 43888	Longview	144.2	80 455	402	557.8	57.4	23.4	0.8	1.6	0.1	18.0	10.1
48 45000	Lubbock	317.0	229 573	84	724.1	56.7	8.6	0.7	2.7	0.1	32.1	5.6
48 45072	Lufkin	86.4	35 067	1 149	405.7	46.7	27.7	0.5	1.8	0.0	24.1	11.4
48 45384	McAllen	125.2	129 877	192	1 037.3	12.0	0.7	0.2	2.7	0.0	84.6	29.1
48 45744	McKinney	161.1	131 117	191	813.8	66.2	11.1	1.0	4.8	0.1	18.6	12.7
48 46452	Mansfield	94.2	56 368	661	598.2	66.1	14.8	0.9	4.5	0.2	15.4	9.7
48 47892	Mesquite	119.2	139 824	181	1 173.1	43.0	22.3	0.8	3.6	0.1	31.6	15.0
48 48072	Midland	186.7	111 147	239	595.5	52.8	8.0	0.8	1.5	0.1	37.6	8.1
48 48768	Mission	88.0	77 058	425	875.3	12.5	0.5	0.2	1.6	0.0	85.4	25.3
48 48804	Missouri City	73.6	67 358	507	915.2	26.2	42.2	0.7	17.1	0.1	15.3	24.6
48 50256	Nacogdoches	70.1	32 996	1 238	471.0	52.4	29.3	0.7	2.1	0.1	16.8	9.6
48 50820	New Braunfels	113.6	57 740	638	508.1	61.8	2.0	0.6	1.3	0.1	35.0	7.0
48 52356	North Richland Hills	47.1	63 343	558	1 345.7	76.2	5.1	1.1	3.3	0.2	15.6	8.6
48 53388	Odessa	108.7	99 940	283	919.7	42.3	5.7	0.8	1.2	0.1	50.6	11.3
48 55080	Paris	94.5	25 171	1 652	266.2	66.2	24.4	2.8	1.1	0.1	8.2	2.5
48 56000	Pasadena	110.8	149 043	165	1 345.8	33.3	2.2	0.4	2.3	0.1	62.2	26.1
48 56348	Pearland	121.8	91 252	332	749.4	50.2	16.9	0.7	13.2	0.1	20.5	15.0
48 57176	Pflugerville	57.8	46 936	844	811.9	49.3	16.0	0.7	8.1	0.2	27.7	13.5
48 57200	Pharr	60.7	70 400	483	1 160.8	6.1	0.2	0.1	0.5	0.0	93.0	31.2
48 58016	Plano	185.4	259 841	71	1 401.6	60.2	8.0	0.8	18.1	0.2	14.7	24.1
48 58820	Port Arthur	199.2	53 818	705	270.2	23.5	41.0	0.6	6.1	0.1	29.6	16.8
48 61796	Richardson	74.0	99 223	291	1 341.2	59.8	8.9	0.8	16.2	0.1	16.0	21.7
48 62828	Rockwall	71.7	37 490	1 056	523.0	74.0	6.2	0.9	3.5	0.1	16.6	12.0
48 63284	Rosenberg	58.2	30 618	1 323	525.8	25.6	13.2	0.3	1.1	0.1	60.3	17.9
48 63500	Round Rock	88.4	99 887	285	1 130.6	55.8	10.2	0.8	6.0	0.2	29.0	12.5
48 63572	Rowlett	51.5	56 199	665	1 091.0	63.0	13.8	1.0	7.2	0.1	16.5	10.5
48 64472	San Angelo	147.3	93 200	320	632.8	55.6	4.7	0.8	1.5	0.2	38.5	8.1
48 65000	San Antonio	1 193.8	1 327 407	7	1 111.9	27.6	6.8	0.5	2.8	0.2	63.2	13.8
48 65516	San Juan	29.7	33 856	1 193	1 141.1	3.0	0.1	0.0	0.1	0.0	96.7	32.0
48 65600	San Marcos	78.3	44 894	879	573.6	55.1	5.6	0.8	2.0	0.2	37.8	5.5
48 66128	Schertz	73.6	31 465	1 297	427.6	62.7	9.3	1.0	3.5	0.3	25.7	5.2
48 66644	Seguin	89.3	25 175	1 651	282.1	36.1	7.7	0.4	0.9	0.0	55.4	7.6
48 67496	Sherman	107.2	38 521	1 028	359.4	65.5	11.9	2.3	2.0	0.1	20.5	10.7
48 68636	Socorro	57.1	32 013	1 271	560.9	2.2	0.2	0.9	0.1	0.0	96.7	33.7
48 69032	Southlake	56.7	26 575	1 559	469.0	85.7	2.4	0.7	7.2	0.1	5.5	8.9
48 70808	Sugar Land	83.9	78 817	413	939.9	46.0	7.6	0.5	36.8	0.1	10.6	33.0
48 72176	Temple	178.7	66 102	526	369.9	57.1	17.4	0.8	2.5	0.2	23.7	7.0
48 72368	Texarkana	75.2	36 411	1 094	484.1	54.6	37.9	1.1	1.6	0.1	6.4	3.7
48 72392	Texas City	165.3	45 099	874	272.9	42.1	29.9	0.8	1.2	0.1	27.0	6.8
48 72530	The Colony	36.3	36 328	1 099	1 000.8	64.1	8.8	1.3	6.6	0.1	21.2	16.3
48 74144	Tyler	139.5	96 900	305	694.7	51.9	25.2	0.7	2.2	0.1	21.2	11.8
48 75428	Victoria	91.9	62 592	566	681.2	42.7	7.8	0.5	1.5	0.0	48.3	6.5
48 76000	Waco	230.4	124 805	204	541.6	47.1	21.8	0.6	2.1	0.1	29.6	10.0
48 76816	Waxahachie	123.4	29 621	1 386	240.0	63.1	13.0	1.0	0.7	0.2	23.2	7.2
48 76864	Weatherford	64.4	25 250	1 646	392.2	82.5	2.8	1.3	1.1	0.1	13.6	7.7
48 77272	Weslaco	38.1	35 670	1 125	935.7	13.5	0.3	0.2	1.2	0.0	85.0	21.0
48 79000	Wichita Falls	186.8	104 553	265	559.6	65.4	13.2	1.4	2.9	0.2	18.9	8.2
48 80356	Wylie	54.5	41 427	953	760.3	63.5	13.0	1.0	6.3	0.2	17.9	13.4
49 00000	UTAH	212 818.3	2 763 885	X	13.0	82.0	1.3	1.4	2.7	1.3	13.0	8.2
49 01310	American Fork	23.8	26 263	1 577	1 101.6	90.4	0.6	0.8	1.5	1.1	7.4	4.3
49 07690	Bountiful	34.8	42 552	927	1 221.4	91.9	0.8	0.5	2.0	1.2	4.9	4.4
49 11320	Cedar City	95.4	28 857	1 432	302.5	87.7	1.0	3.0	1.5	0.7	7.9	4.3
49 13850	Clearfield	19.7	30 112	1 353	1 525.4	76.7	3.9	1.3	3.8	1.1	16.1	9.7
49 16270	Cottonwood Heights	22.9	33 433	1 212	1 461.9	90.0	1.3	0.6	4.2	0.7	5.1	6.6
49 20120	Draper	77.9	42 274	933	542.5	88.0	1.6	0.8	3.7	1.0	7.0	8.0
49 36070	Holladay	20.5	26 472	1 566	1 290.7	90.8	1.2	0.6	3.5	0.6	4.7	6.2
49 40360	Kaysville	27.1	27 300	1 511	1 008.1	93.7	0.7	0.4	1.4	0.4	4.5	3.4
49 43660	Layton	57.0	67 311	508	1 181.3	84.0	2.2	0.8	3.1	0.8	11.2	4.1

1. Dry land or land partially or temporarily covered by water. 2. May be of any race.

Table D. Cities — **Population**

City	Age of population (percent), 2010											Population			
												Census counts		Percent change	
	Under 5 years	5 to 17 years	18 to 24 years	25 to 34 years	35 to 44 years	45 to 54 years	55 to 64 years	65 to 74 years	75 years and over	Median age	Percent female	1990	2000	1990–2000	2000–2010
	12	13	14	15	16	17	18	19	20	21	22	23	24	25	26
TEXAS—Cont'd															
Killeen	10.6	19.9	14.1	20.7	12.8	10.5	6.4	3.2	2.0	27.1	51.0	63 535	86 911	36.8	47.2
Kingsville	8.0	16.8	20.1	14.3	10.4	10.2	9.1	6.1	5.0	27.6	49.2	25 276	25 575	1.2	2.5
Kyle	10.3	23.5	7.3	19.2	17.9	11.1	6.5	2.9	1.3	30.2	50.2	NA	5 314	NA	427.2
Lake Jackson	6.6	19.8	8.5	12.5	12.9	16.0	11.8	6.1	5.8	37.1	51.0	22 771	26 386	15.9	1.8
Lancaster	8.2	23.0	8.9	13.8	15.6	13.9	9.4	4.3	3.0	32.3	54.2	22 117	25 894	17.1	40.4
La Porte	7.3	20.1	9.4	13.9	14.1	15.0	11.6	5.3	3.3	34.5	50.4	27 923	31 880	14.2	6.0
Laredo	9.7	25.3	10.9	14.1	13.8	10.8	7.4	4.4	3.5	27.9	51.6	122 893	176 576	43.7	33.7
League City	7.8	20.7	7.3	15.1	16.5	15.4	9.9	4.6	2.7	34.5	50.9	30 159	45 444	50.7	83.9
Leander	9.5	24.6	6.5	16.1	18.6	12.2	7.6	3.2	1.7	31.4	50.7	NA	7 596	NA	249.1
Lewisville	8.3	17.4	11.2	20.5	15.3	12.9	7.9	3.8	2.7	30.9	50.6	46 521	77 737	67.1	22.6
Little Elm	11.1	23.8	5.9	18.9	20.4	10.1	5.8	2.7	1.3	30.8	50.9	NA	3 646	NA	610.3
Longview	7.7	17.7	10.9	14.4	12.1	13.3	10.5	6.5	6.9	34.4	51.2	70 311	73 344	4.3	9.7
Lubbock	7.3	16.2	19.0	15.3	10.6	11.6	9.3	5.5	5.2	29.2	50.9	186 206	199 564	7.2	15.0
Lufkin	8.3	18.6	10.6	13.7	11.6	12.5	10.3	6.9	7.5	34.0	52.9	30 210	32 709	8.3	7.2
McAllen	8.1	21.9	9.6	14.3	13.8	11.8	9.5	5.8	5.1	32.2	52.2	84 021	106 414	26.7	22.0
McKinney	8.9	23.0	7.0	15.0	18.5	12.7	7.8	4.2	2.8	32.7	50.9	21 283	54 369	155.5	141.2
Mansfield	7.2	24.6	7.6	12.1	17.9	15.3	8.8	4.1	2.4	34.0	50.9	15 615	28 031	79.5	101.1
Mesquite	7.8	22.0	10.1	13.8	14.1	14.6	9.1	4.7	3.8	32.3	52.3	101 484	124 523	22.7	12.3
Midland	8.2	19.1	10.4	14.8	11.6	14.0	10.6	5.5	5.8	33.0	51.3	89 343	94 996	6.3	17.0
Mission	8.9	24.7	9.5	13.2	13.9	10.7	7.9	6.0	5.4	30.4	51.9	28 653	45 408	58.5	69.7
Missouri City	5.9	20.3	8.3	10.9	14.3	17.2	14.2	5.8	3.2	38.5	52.3	36 143	52 913	46.4	27.3
Nacogdoches	6.5	13.7	31.0	12.7	8.6	9.2	8.2	4.8	5.3	24.6	54.3	30 872	29 914	-3.1	10.3
New Braunfels	7.5	19.7	7.8	14.1	14.0	12.7	10.5	6.8	6.9	35.6	52.0	27 334	36 494	33.5	58.2
North Richland Hills	6.5	17.7	8.7	13.0	13.6	15.7	12.4	6.5	5.9	38.3	51.5	45 895	55 635	21.2	13.9
Odessa	8.6	19.6	11.5	14.7	11.9	13.0	9.9	5.6	5.1	31.6	51.0	89 699	90 943	1.4	9.9
Paris	7.3	17.7	10.5	12.1	12.1	12.9	10.9	8.3	8.3	37.1	53.4	24 799	25 898	4.4	-2.8
Pasadena	8.7	22.0	10.9	14.5	13.4	13.2	9.0	4.6	3.7	30.7	50.3	119 604	141 674	18.5	5.2
Pearland	9.1	20.5	6.8	15.3	17.3	14.0	9.4	4.6	3.1	34.1	51.4	18 927	37 640	98.9	142.4
Pflugerville	7.8	22.8	6.9	14.5	17.9	15.6	8.6	3.6	2.4	33.8	51.6	4 444	16 335	267.6	187.3
Pharr	10.1	25.3	10.2	14.7	12.9	9.3	7.5	5.4	4.6	28.0	52.0	32 921	46 660	41.7	50.9
Plano	6.3	19.6	7.5	13.5	15.8	16.9	11.6	5.5	3.3	37.2	51.1	127 885	222 030	73.6	17.0
Port Arthur	8.0	19.0	9.8	13.0	11.8	14.1	11.1	6.4	6.9	35.3	50.8	58 551	57 755	-1.4	-6.8
Richardson	6.3	16.9	10.2	14.2	13.9	14.6	11.4	6.8	5.8	36.8	50.8	74 840	91 802	22.7	8.1
Rockwall	7.2	22.1	6.5	12.1	16.1	14.7	10.6	6.3	4.3	36.4	51.1	10 486	17 976	71.4	108.6
Rosenberg	8.8	21.8	10.4	15.3	13.5	11.9	8.8	5.4	4.1	30.7	51.5	20 183	24 043	19.1	27.3
Round Rock	8.8	22.3	8.0	16.4	17.6	13.4	8.1	3.3	2.1	32.0	50.8	30 923	61 136	97.7	63.4
Rowlett	6.3	22.7	7.4	11.1	16.5	17.7	10.7	4.5	3.1	36.7	51.0	23 260	44 503	91.3	26.3
San Angelo	7.3	16.1	15.0	14.1	10.7	12.4	10.7	6.9	6.9	32.8	51.3	84 462	88 439	4.7	5.4
San Antonio	7.6	19.2	11.4	14.9	13.2	13.2	10.1	5.6	4.8	32.7	51.2	976 514	1 144 646	17.2	16.0
San Juan	9.9	25.3	10.8	14.9	13.1	10.2	8.1	4.4	3.4	27.7	51.6	12 561	26 229	108.8	29.1
San Marcos	4.4	9.8	44.8	16.2	7.3	8.3	5.5	3.2	3.5	23.1	50.3	28 738	34 733	20.9	29.3
Schertz	6.3	20.8	7.5	11.7	15.3	16.2	10.6	6.9	4.6	37.8	51.7	10 597	18 694	76.4	68.3
Seguin	7.4	18.0	12.4	11.9	11.1	12.0	11.2	7.5	8.5	35.3	51.7	18 692	22 011	17.8	14.4
Sherman	7.9	17.3	13.1	13.9	11.9	12.6	10.1	6.4	6.8	33.2	52.2	31 584	35 082	11.1	9.8
Socorro	8.3	24.2	11.4	12.9	12.5	12.3	9.7	5.3	3.4	29.5	51.8	22 995	27 152	18.1	17.9
Southlake	5.2	29.0	4.8	3.6	15.2	23.9	12.4	3.8	2.0	40.9	49.9	7 082	21 519	203.9	23.5
Sugar Land	5.3	19.3	7.5	9.9	13.5	18.6	15.4	6.1	4.3	41.2	50.4	33 712	63 328	87.9	24.5
Temple	8.4	18.0	9.2	14.9	11.7	13.2	10.8	6.4	7.4	34.6	52.2	46 150	54 514	18.1	21.3
Texarkana	7.1	18.7	9.6	13.3	12.5	13.4	10.9	6.7	7.8	36.0	52.5	32 294	34 782	7.7	4.7
Texas City	7.5	18.8	8.9	13.7	12.2	13.9	12.2	6.4	6.4	35.9	52.1	40 822	41 521	1.7	8.6
The Colony	7.3	19.7	8.9	17.2	16.7	15.9	9.2	3.4	1.6	33.1	50.1	22 113	26 531	20.0	36.9
Tyler	7.2	17.1	14.3	13.9	11.3	11.7	10.0	6.7	7.7	32.8	52.8	75 450	83 650	10.9	15.8
Victoria	7.9	19.1	9.5	13.6	11.5	13.5	11.4	6.9	6.6	34.9	52.0	55 076	60 603	10.0	3.3
Waco	7.7	17.0	19.8	14.3	10.4	10.9	8.7	5.2	6.0	28.2	52.1	103 590	113 726	9.8	9.7
Waxahachie	9.0	19.2	11.2	15.2	12.4	11.7	10.0	6.0	5.4	31.7	51.8	17 934	21 426	19.1	38.2
Weatherford	7.5	17.4	10.6	13.7	12.1	12.7	10.8	7.5	7.7	35.7	51.9	14 804	19 000	28.3	32.9
Weslaco	9.0	22.4	9.2	12.8	12.2	10.0	8.9	7.3	8.2	32.5	52.6	22 739	26 935	18.5	32.4
Wichita Falls	7.0	15.7	15.8	14.7	11.3	12.9	10.1	6.1	6.2	32.4	48.2	96 259	104 197	8.2	0.3
Wylie	9.7	24.0	6.9	16.1	19.2	12.4	6.8	3.2	1.9	31.7	51.3	8 716	15 132	73.6	173.8
UTAH	9.5	22.0	11.5	16.1	12.0	11.1	8.7	5.0	4.0	29.2	49.8	1 722 850	2 233 169	29.6	23.8
American Fork	10.6	27.1	8.7	14.9	12.3	10.4	7.3	4.6	4.1	27.6	49.9	15 722	21 941	39.6	19.7
Bountiful	8.3	20.4	8.9	13.3	10.5	12.4	10.0	7.7	8.6	34.2	51.2	37 544	41 301	10.0	3.0
Cedar City	9.5	18.7	22.4	15.8	9.2	8.8	7.0	4.9	3.7	24.8	50.9	13 443	20 527	52.7	40.6
Clearfield	12.0	22.7	13.6	19.7	11.7	8.9	5.9	3.0	2.5	25.8	49.3	21 435	25 974	21.2	15.9
Cottonwood Heights	6.1	16.9	9.7	14.9	12.0	14.0	13.1	8.3	5.0	36.9	50.2	28 766	27 569	-4.2	21.3
Draper	8.6	24.4	8.5	15.7	17.1	12.9	7.4	3.4	2.0	30.7	46.4	7 143	25 220	253.1	67.6
Holladay	6.8	18.3	8.1	12.9	11.3	13.0	12.3	8.3	9.1	38.5	51.6	NA	14 561	NA	81.8
Kaysville	10.4	28.9	8.0	12.4	13.0	12.4	7.6	3.9	3.3	27.6	49.9	13 961	20 351	45.8	34.1
Layton	9.9	23.6	9.9	15.6	12.8	12.2	9.0	4.2	2.9	29.4	49.9	41 784	58 474	39.9	15.1

Table D. Cities — Households, Group Quarters, Crime, and Education

City	Households, 2010 Number	Persons per household	Percent Female family householder[1]	Percent One-person	Persons in group quarters, 2010 Total	Institutional Total	Persons in nursing facilities	Non-institutional	Serious crimes known to police,[2] 2010 Total Number	Total Rate[3]	Rate[3] Violent	Rate[3] Property	Educational attainment 2008–2010 Population age 25 and older	Attainment[4] High school graduate or less	Attainment[4] Bachelor's degree or more
	27	28	29	30	31	32	33	34	35	36	37	38	39	40	41
TEXAS—Cont'd															
Killeen	48 052	2.66	17.2	24.4	179	97	60	82	6 830	5 339	776	4 563	68 992	38.3	15.6
Kingsville	9 095	2.69	17.5	24.7	1 791	293	173	1 498	1 498	5 715	1 015	4 700	14 495	46.3	23.3
Kyle	8 759	3.15	13.7	14.5	391	388	0	3	477	1 703	182	1 521	15 375	32.7	26.2
Lake Jackson	10 319	2.60	10.1	23.9	57	56	56	1	734	2 734	183	2 551	17 600	28.5	31.6
Lancaster	12 520	2.88	27.1	22.3	360	359	359	1	52	143	3	140	21 701	48.5	19.2
La Porte	11 890	2.84	13.1	20.3	64	46	46	18	753	2 228	139	2 089	20 889	48.6	16.5
Laredo	63 545	3.66	21.1	13.5	3 479	2 014	367	1 465	12 606	5 339	484	4 856	125 089	54.9	18.0
League City	30 192	2.75	10.2	20.3	471	471	368	0	2 090	2 501	83	2 419	52 496	24.8	40.9
Leander	8 557	3.10	12.6	14.0	0	0	0	0	320	1 207	109	1 097	15 292	28.8	31.0
Lewisville	37 496	2.53	12.5	30.1	399	286	264	113	3 776	3 963	252	3 711	59 670	36.2	29.2
Little Elm	8 160	3.17	11.5	14.3	0	0	0	0	320	1 236	42	1 193	14 390	30.2	28.9
Longview	30 562	2.51	15.4	29.1	3 690	1 913	767	1 777	4 890	6 078	723	5 355	50 984	47.4	20.2
Lubbock	88 506	2.48	14.0	28.8	9 933	2 400	1 214	7 533	14 392	6 269	872	5 397	130 261	39.9	29.6
Lufkin	12 928	2.62	18.6	27.8	1 239	823	536	416	2 455	7 001	522	6 479	22 466	49.7	18.2
McAllen	41 573	3.10	19.0	19.1	1 110	899	890	211	7 697	5 926	230	5 696	76 501	48.1	28.3
McKinney	44 353	2.91	10.9	18.7	2 192	1 454	439	738	3 346	2 552	171	2 381	75 515	24.2	44.8
Mansfield	18 305	3.06	11.4	14.4	363	355	159	8	1 070	1 898	140	1 758	31 421	27.5	40.2
Mesquite	48 390	2.88	18.9	22.4	663	644	644	19	6 998	5 005	345	4 660	83 744	47.7	18.1
Midland	41 887	2.62	13.5	26.0	1 567	684	362	883	4 006	3 604	366	3 238	67 412	40.6	23.8
Mission	23 117	3.33	17.1	14.9	179	162	162	17	3 335	4 328	119	4 209	41 671	54.3	21.7
Missouri City	22 376	3.00	15.2	15.8	180	138	138	42	1 374	2 040	276	1 764	42 890	24.1	39.3
Nacogdoches	12 142	2.30	15.7	35.2	5 025	632	428	4 393	1 735	5 258	997	4 261	15 330	41.8	29.9
New Braunfels	21 259	2.67	12.5	23.7	940	666	411	274	2 087	3 614	210	3 405	37 170	39.8	28.3
North Richland Hills	24 854	2.54	11.9	24.8	294	267	267	27	2 337	3 689	357	3 333	42 337	34.6	28.9
Odessa	36 608	2.67	16.1	26.3	2 143	1 285	437	858	4 249	4 252	726	3 525	59 458	53.1	15.0
Paris	10 306	2.38	19.6	32.8	614	406	258	208	1 753	6 964	580	6 384	16 337	53.8	17.1
Pasadena	48 471	3.06	15.1	21.4	884	737	547	147	6 162	4 134	410	3 724	85 542	60.5	13.5
Pearland	31 222	2.91	11.2	17.1	318	312	299	6	1 879	2 059	140	1 919	53 447	25.3	44.6
Pflugerville	15 789	2.96	13.4	17.0	183	131	131	52	966	2 058	145	1 913	27 672	26.4	35.2
Pharr	19 699	3.57	20.8	13.7	19	15	0	4	3 943	5 601	357	5 244	37 691	69.4	13.0
Plano	99 131	2.61	9.7	24.4	859	791	733	68	7 221	2 779	186	2 593	171 328	20.9	53.9
Port Arthur	20 183	2.63	19.8	30.1	687	515	501	172	3 171	5 892	779	5 114	34 639	58.8	9.1
Richardson	38 714	2.54	10.1	26.8	931	517	501	414	3 200	3 225	196	3 030	65 734	24.4	50.2
Rockwall	13 212	2.81	10.0	20.0	325	325	158	0	1 002	2 673	69	2 603	23 203	28.8	38.5
Rosenberg	10 163	3.00	19.8	21.1	134	129	129	5	746	2 436	297	2 139	18 000	62.5	12.5
Round Rock	35 050	2.84	12.5	20.8	454	398	251	56	3 132	3 136	116	3 019	59 858	30.4	34.0
Rowlett	18 371	3.04	11.4	12.6	335	335	334	0	1 008	1 794	135	1 658	34 273	31.9	33.6
San Angelo	36 117	2.45	14.2	29.8	4 858	788	365	4 070	4 517	4 847	299	4 547	57 116	48.7	21.2
San Antonio	479 642	2.71	17.6	26.9	27 800	11 979	5 617	15 821	96 787	7 291	635	6 656	808 015	45.8	23.6
San Juan	8 882	3.80	19.2	9.9	121	112	112	9	1 903	5 621	659	4 962	17 213	74.0	9.8
San Marcos	17 031	2.27	10.2	33.1	6 202	729	300	5 473	1 878	4 183	339	3 845	18 545	40.1	31.8
Schertz	11 379	2.75	11.8	18.6	188	188	188	0	679	2 158	226	1 932	19 013	29.4	31.8
Seguin	8 794	2.68	17.9	27.3	1 644	881	396	763	1 329	5 279	437	4 842	16 042	58.6	16.8
Sherman	14 805	2.51	14.7	29.8	1 368	509	285	859	1 636	4 247	467	3 780	24 363	49.2	18.8
Socorro	8 792	3.64	19.1	10.9	25	0	0	25	695	2 171	284	1 887	17 696	69.4	8.4
Southlake	8 193	3.24	3.9	7.5	0	0	0	0	557	2 096	60	2 036	15 883	11.1	68.1
Sugar Land	26 709	2.90	8.6	15.6	1 413	1 245	313	168	2 021	2 564	180	2 384	51 491	20.3	53.9
Temple	26 113	2.47	14.9	31.0	1 613	989	908	624	2 321	3 511	319	3 192	43 705	43.2	24.9
Texarkana	14 422	2.41	20.4	32.4	1 641	1 469	554	172	2 877	7 901	1 447	6 454	23 513	44.4	22.2
Texas City	16 628	2.66	20.3	26.2	937	916	470	21	1 947	4 317	432	3 885	29 936	50.0	12.3
The Colony	13 168	2.76	11.5	21.5	0	0	0	0	670	1 844	146	1 698	22 927	28.9	33.7
Tyler	37 896	2.46	15.2	31.2	3 647	1 709	893	1 938	5 809	5 995	677	5 318	60 177	38.4	28.7
Victoria	23 421	2.62	16.6	26.3	1 324	1 053	478	271	3 708	5 924	620	5 304	39 460	49.9	17.6
Waco	46 402	2.52	17.4	31.0	8 019	3 026	1 488	4 993	7 277	5 831	671	5 159	68 100	47.9	22.1
Waxahachie	10 457	2.72	15.7	23.3	1 209	715	232	494	1 044	3 525	277	3 248	17 658	45.4	25.9
Weatherford	9 770	2.47	12.7	28.3	1 077	845	450	232	753	2 982	246	2 737	15 524	42.6	21.5
Weslaco	11 212	3.12	19.4	18.6	637	590	488	47	2 921	8 189	549	7 639	20 898	57.5	17.6
Wichita Falls	38 454	2.41	14.3	31.0	11 889	5 334	1 072	6 555	5 777	5 525	443	5 083	64 128	50.6	19.6
Wylie	13 237	3.12	12.1	14.0	155	155	155	0	738	1 781	84	1 697	23 405	32.3	32.3
UTAH	877 692	3.10	9.7	18.7	46 152	22 161	5 854	23 991	93 759	3 392	213	3 180	1 546 535	33.8	29.2
American Fork	7 274	3.57	9.5	13.6	283	72	62	211	1 049	2 909	114	2 795	13 752	26.4	33.0
Bountiful	14 504	2.91	8.8	20.4	330	318	318	12	975	2 291	143	2 148	26 043	22.5	41.0
Cedar City	9 469	2.94	10.0	18.5	986	259	83	727	862	2 987	159	2 828	13 856	30.9	33.2
Clearfield	9 361	3.08	15.0	18.9	1 263	144	96	1 119	888	2 949	136	2 813	16 035	39.1	20.5
Cottonwood Heights	12 459	2.68	9.4	21.2	14	0	0	14	1 052	3 147	159	2 988	21 892	18.4	46.6
Draper	11 544	3.32	7.7	13.4	3 960	3 960	71	0	851	2 013	147	1 866	23 739	23.8	37.4
Holladay	9 927	2.65	9.7	24.3	166	160	160	6	NA	NA	NA	NA	17 785	19.7	49.1
Kaysville	7 524	3.63	7.5	11.7	24	0	0	24	581	2 128	51	2 077	14 391	19.2	45.1
Layton	21 375	3.15	11.1	16.5	44	26	0	18	2 453	3 644	162	3 482	37 209	29.2	32.4

1. No spouse present.   2. Data for serious crimes have not been adjusted for underreporting. This may affect comparability between geographic areas and over time.   3. Per 100,000 population estimated by the FBI.   4. Persons 25 years old and over.

Table D. Cities — Income, Poverty, and Housing

City	Money income, 2008–2010 Per capita income[1] (dollars) 42	Households Median income 43	Percent with income of $200,000 or more 44	Percent with income of less than $25,000 45	Families with income below poverty (percent) 46	Housing units, 2010 Total 47	Percent change, 2000–2010 48	Vacant units for sale or rent[2] 49	Occupied Housing units 2008–2010 Owner-occupied Total 50	Percent 51	Median value[3] (dollars) 52	Median owner costs as a percent of income With a mortgage[4] 53	Without a mortgage[5] 54
TEXAS—Cont'd													
Killeen	19 662	44 029	0.6	23.2	13.2	53 913	52.8	5 861	43 832	49.8	107 500	24.3	11.6
Kingsville	17 908	33 971	3.0	37.4	16.5	10 354	-0.6	1 259	8 849	55.9	70 900	25.6	10.0
Kyle	22 254	67 588	2.3	11.1	8.0	9 226	NA	467	7 925	82.2	143 300	24.5	13.5
Lake Jackson	27 934	72 044	3.8	15.9	7.0	11 149	6.3	830	9 309	73.0	143 700	19.9	10.9
Lancaster	20 365	53 750	0.1	23.1	10.8	13 622	41.7	1 102	12 214	68.4	111 800	27.7	17.6
La Porte	25 102	64 247	0.5	16.0	7.7	12 875	10.2	985	11 537	78.5	119 800	21.3	12.6
Laredo	14 653	37 945	1.8	33.5	24.7	68 610	36.2	5 065	62 586	62.5	113 100	27.8	15.1
League City	37 003	86 268	7.1	9.6	3.1	32 119	86.3	1 927	29 407	77.4	182 100	22.4	13.1
Leander	26 362	69 301	3.6	8.1	2.4	8 949	NA	392	8 128	82.6	156 300	23.4	13.5
Lewisville	27 773	56 075	1.9	15.3	6.3	39 967	26.0	2 471	36 436	46.5	152 300	22.9	12.3
Little Elm	24 428	77 839	1.1	7.7	7.8	8 581	NA	421	7 400	82.0	146 300	23.6	12.4
Longview	22 808	41 874	2.4	29.4	12.8	32 751	6.8	2 189	29 648	56.3	124 900	21.6	11.7
Lubbock	22 915	41 937	2.7	31.0	13.2	95 926	14.2	7 420	87 686	56.9	109 100	22.5	11.7
Lufkin	20 255	33 821	1.7	36.4	14.8	14 183	5.9	1 255	13 332	59.8	88 900	23.1	13.4
McAllen	19 866	38 288	3.3	34.2	24.0	45 862	21.0	4 289	40 965	61.2	106 200	23.7	13.8
McKinney	31 154	77 826	6.5	13.7	6.6	47 915	146.7	3 562	41 498	73.9	186 100	24.0	13.1
Mansfield	32 960	90 417	6.2	9.1	4.6	19 106	103.0	801	17 082	81.4	180 300	23.2	12.0
Mesquite	21 615	49 873	1.3	20.9	10.7	51 952	11.9	3 562	47 346	62.8	113 500	24.3	11.1
Midland	31 005	55 661	7.1	19.3	9.7	44 708	12.3	2 821	40 407	66.3	142 900	20.0	11.2
Mission	17 050	39 337	3.7	33.9	23.2	27 291	54.0	4 174	21 542	72.2	94 900	24.6	12.2
Missouri City	30 088	78 171	7.4	10.8	6.4	23 374	34.0	998	21 302	85.3	158 800	24.3	12.4
Nacogdoches	15 298	25 114	1.1	49.8	27.1	13 635	10.3	1 493	11 427	41.3	112 200	21.5	13.9
New Braunfels	25 729	56 399	3.5	18.9	7.7	23 381	55.7	2 122	20 425	65.9	155 600	20.9	12.5
North Richland Hills	30 849	61 490	3.4	16.8	6.2	26 395	22.8	1 541	24 220	65.2	151 700	22.3	12.8
Odessa	24 599	47 223	2.8	26.7	13.1	39 806	4.8	3 198	36 521	60.8	94 800	19.4	10.9
Paris	18 067	30 406	0.7	39.4	20.5	11 883	1.0	1 577	10 130	54.4	75 300	19.6	14.3
Pasadena	19 477	42 664	2.5	28.3	17.9	53 899	6.9	5 428	47 857	56.6	104 100	23.4	11.6
Pearland	33 946	85 090	6.4	8.4	3.8	33 169	138.7	1 947	29 838	80.9	180 800	23.3	12.3
Pflugerville	28 238	72 004	3.4	9.4	6.5	16 418	209.9	629	14 926	75.2	164 400	22.6	12.8
Pharr	12 166	29 864	0.6	43.4	32.8	22 796	37.4	3 097	19 079	63.2	69 500	30.2	12.9
Plano	39 482	80 210	10.7	12.9	5.8	103 672	20.4	4 541	97 146	66.4	218 700	22.1	10.1
Port Arthur	17 761	31 449	0.9	41.8	23.2	23 577	-4.6	3 394	21 586	60.6	65 300	23.3	12.4
Richardson	33 987	66 899	6.3	15.9	5.6	40 630	11.7	1 916	38 034	62.9	179 900	23.1	12.5
Rockwall	29 748	73 135	3.0	12.1	6.5	13 957	96.1	745	12 657	75.2	202 500	23.9	16.5
Rosenberg	19 458	42 197	1.6	25.4	12.6	11 162	32.2	999	10 253	53.9	103 000	26.1	13.5
Round Rock	27 502	62 664	3.5	12.5	5.8	37 223	71.9	2 173	34 216	56.7	164 600	26.4	11.6
Rowlett	31 013	80 551	5.0	7.1	3.4	18 969	30.1	558	18 040	88.8	165 000	23.9	13.0
San Angelo	21 753	40 186	1.7	31.0	12.7	39 548	4.8	3 431	35 654	62.2	90 500	21.0	11.9
San Antonio	21 613	42 656	2.5	29.5	15.4	524 246	21.0	44 604	464 189	57.4	114 000	23.3	12.1
San Juan	11 175	30 946	0.8	39.2	26.1	9 740	25.8	858	8 515	72.2	83 800	27.5	13.3
San Marcos	15 179	26 304	0.3	48.3	18.5	18 179	36.8	1 148	16 437	30.0	120 300	24.0	15.1
Schertz	28 862	71 625	4.7	12.2	5.5	12 047	74.5	668	10 148	78.6	163 900	21.3	10.2
Seguin	19 952	40 037	1.3	33.0	17.7	9 714	18.7	920	9 287	55.9	102 200	20.2	12.6
Sherman	21 147	40 617	2.1	29.1	14.7	16 404	10.0	1 599	15 014	54.5	93 900	24.5	11.7
Socorro	12 182	32 778	0.6	39.0	22.7	9 313	28.0	521	8 621	84.0	79 900	28.6	12.4
Southlake	65 330	178 364	43.3	5.7	3.1	8 494	28.7	301	7 821	96.1	497 900	22.6	12.0
Sugar Land	41 683	101 912	16.4	8.3	3.4	27 727	31.0	1 018	25 604	79.4	247 200	22.6	10.0
Temple	26 785	50 061	3.2	24.7	10.6	28 442	21.2	2 309	23 433	59.5	108 900	20.6	10.0
Texarkana	21 377	35 090	1.8	36.5	14.7	16 115	6.5	1 693	13 924	53.1	93 700	22.6	12.4
Texas City	22 797	46 268	1.2	30.8	11.6	18 773	12.6	2 145	16 961	59.4	96 100	22.3	12.5
The Colony	31 944	74 211	3.5	7.0	1.8	14 052	59.0	884	13 268	70.7	142 800	21.1	11.5
Tyler	27 052	42 000	5.0	30.5	13.5	41 742	17.4	3 846	37 975	56.3	122 700	21.6	11.1
Victoria	22 145	45 034	1.5	29.0	14.3	25 660	6.1	2 239	23 308	60.4	101 100	21.4	13.0
Waco	17 237	31 521	1.4	41.1	22.0	51 452	12.2	5 050	45 068	46.4	91 800	24.2	13.2
Waxahachie	22 844	51 361	2.7	24.1	12.3	11 554	47.0	1 097	10 564	60.8	130 500	22.5	14.1
Weatherford	23 253	45 023	2.4	29.0	11.4	10 853	31.3	1 083	9 715	61.5	132 700	24.3	14.6
Weslaco	15 538	36 810	2.3	37.0	25.7	14 394	41.0	3 182	10 810	65.4	67 600	22.8	12.3
Wichita Falls	21 498	41 261	2.4	29.1	12.6	43 632	4.3	5 178	37 460	59.6	90 300	22.1	12.7
Wylie	26 593	70 838	2.0	9.6	2.6	13 840	162.5	603	13 209	84.9	157 700	24.8	13.6
UTAH	22 828	55 764	3.0	18.3	8.2	979 709	27.5	102 017	873 647	70.5	225 400	24.8	10.0
American Fork	20 444	68 174	1.8	15.6	6.8	7 598	24.2	324	7 216	78.1	227 800	25.3	10.0
Bountiful	28 905	63 717	5.4	15.3	4.7	15 193	10.1	689	14 257	74.9	253 100	22.6	10.0
Cedar City	15 976	38 001	0.6	32.8	16.7	10 860	52.2	1 391	10 012	51.9	201 300	28.5	11.2
Clearfield	17 813	47 490	0.5	20.3	12.5	10 062	19.7	701	9 804	51.4	159 300	25.2	10.0
Cottonwood Heights	34 526	71 667	9.0	11.6	2.8	13 194	33.2	735	12 058	73.5	315 600	22.6	10.0
Draper	30 529	88 412	9.0	7.2	3.8	12 125	84.3	581	11 068	80.0	386 200	26.4	10.0
Holladay	35 479	61 258	7.5	16.9	3.9	10 537	99.0	610	9 903	76.2	356 100	25.3	10.2
Kaysville	25 552	85 469	4.3	9.8	4.8	7 700	35.3	176	7 290	90.3	279 000	23.9	10.0
Layton	22 985	59 968	2.9	13.7	7.7	22 356	16.8	981	21 470	74.2	216 000	23.7	10.4

1. Based on population estimated by the American Community Survey.   2. Includes units rented or sold but not occupied.   3. Specified owner-occupied units; $1,000,000 represents $1,000,000 or more.   4. 50.0 represents 50 percent or more.   5. 10.0 represents 10 percent or less.

City	Occupied housing units, 2008–2010 (cont.)				Migration, 2008–2010		Civilian labor force, 2010				Civilian employment[4], 2008–2010			
									Unemployment			Percent		
	Percent renter occupied	Median gross rent[1]	Median rent as a percent of income[2]	Percent with no vehicle available	Percent who lived in the same house one year ago	Percent who lived outside this city one year ago	Total	Percent change, 2009–2010	Total	Rate[3]	Population age 16 and older	In labor force	Full-year full-time worker	Households with no workers (percent)
	55	56	57	58	59	60	61	62	63	64	65	66	67	68
TEXAS—Cont'd														
Killeen	50.2	818	28.0	4.6	68.1	15.5	51 038	7.9	4 222	8.3	89 407	72.4	51.4	16.5
Kingsville	44.1	642	30.4	7.9	75.6	12.7	14 012	2.2	953	6.8	19 882	58.3	33.9	31.2
Kyle	17.8	1 203	25.3	1.1	80.7	16.3	13 090	7.7	723	5.5	17 708	75.2	55.3	9.5
Lake Jackson	27.0	804	27.6	2.1	79.1	12.9	13 165	-3.5	1 124	8.5	20 574	64.0	46.1	21.0
Lancaster	31.6	868	30.4	4.6	88.7	7.3	17 475	4.3	1 855	10.6	25 491	72.8	53.7	18.8
La Porte	21.5	993	24.3	3.3	85.2	10.2	18 240	-2.1	1 812	9.9	25 510	72.0	50.6	15.7
Laredo	37.5	700	33.1	8.8	82.8	2.6	92 635	3.6	7 673	8.3	158 527	63.8	41.7	17.0
League City	22.6	1 005	27.3	2.2	84.9	9.2	44 821	14.7	3 139	7.0	60 540	76.1	56.6	11.3
Leander	17.4	1 280	32.9	1.8	81.5	13.5	13 222	-0.8	747	5.6	17 096	0.0	58.1	10.1
Lewisville	53.5	903	26.7	3.5	70.5	16.5	56 764	-3.7	3 958	7.0	71 924	81.4	58.1	11.2
Little Elm	18.0	1 320	27.4	1.7	80.2	15.7	13 688	NA	689	5.0	16 248	81.5	56.6	7.4
Longview	43.8	691	28.2	8.7	77.8	10.3	43 065	3.0	3 275	7.6	61 288	64.4	40.6	26.7
Lubbock	43.1	737	33.6	6.0	73.3	10.7	118 255	-0.6	7 362	6.2	179 158	66.8	40.8	22.4
Lufkin	40.2	689	32.5	10.2	81.0	8.5	16 331	-1.2	1 332	8.2	27 257	60.5	38.1	29.1
McAllen	38.8	690	32.4	7.2	84.1	6.1	60 026	-2.1	4 948	8.2	95 155	61.9	41.0	22.0
McKinney	26.1	961	29.3	3.0	82.9	11.9	65 599	10.9	4 823	7.4	89 852	71.4	51.5	13.4
Mansfield	18.6	1 100	29.4	2.7	85.7	10.3	29 553	18.4	1 974	6.7	37 606	73.1	53.3	12.0
Mesquite	37.2	903	32.2	4.0	85.7	8.9	73 923	8.5	6 281	8.5	102 186	71.8	54.3	15.1
Midland	33.7	839	28.3	4.2	81.1	6.4	64 019	4.0	3 386	5.3	82 682	69.0	50.2	18.6
Mission	27.8	644	36.2	5.8	86.0	8.2	31 028	11.7	3 031	9.8	51 137	58.9	37.4	24.6
Missouri City	14.7	1 383	34.6	1.5	88.6	8.8	37 102	-10.1	3 083	8.3	50 545	70.1	52.0	11.5
Nacogdoches	58.7	641	40.1	9.7	67.9	16.4	16 948	1.9	1 172	6.9	26 055	60.4	32.6	27.5
New Braunfels	34.1	914	28.7	4.8	78.6	12.7	28 571	5.4	1 694	5.9	42 478	66.1	45.5	21.4
North Richland Hills	34.8	864	30.8	4.1	82.9	13.3	35 073	-2.7	2 538	7.2	48 820	72.9	50.6	18.1
Odessa	39.2	687	25.1	5.5	81.1	8.1	53 702	0.9	4 087	7.6	74 178	68.7	46.8	20.5
Paris	45.6	577	29.7	11.9	79.8	9.1	11 549	-2.1	1 142	9.9	19 710	59.0	37.7	36.0
Pasadena	43.4	736	31.7	6.1	81.0	7.8	67 629	0.8	6 956	10.3	106 486	64.4	43.2	22.3
Pearland	19.1	1 077	25.6	2.0	88.4	8.4	48 405	7.6	3 134	6.5	63 053	75.2	56.5	12.4
Pflugerville	24.8	1 151	32.7	3.5	83.2	11.9	25 872	17.4	1 479	5.7	31 865	77.1	56.0	11.3
Pharr	36.8	633	31.1	8.3	85.5	8.0	27 127	5.9	2 805	10.3	46 855	56.2	33.4	29.9
Plano	34.6	976	27.5	3.3	86.2	7.7	144 525	-0.4	10 435	7.2	198 645	72.6	52.8	13.4
Port Arthur	39.4	592	28.1	13.2	86.0	6.2	23 242	-3.3	3 569	15.4	41 255	55.3	36.0	38.4
Richardson	37.1	1 026	28.4	3.5	82.7	11.1	54 472	0.2	3 977	7.3	78 781	70.2	48.6	17.4
Rockwall	24.8	1 150	28.7	2.1	81.1	11.9	19 754	8.3	1 286	6.5	26 665	70.3	48.6	19.3
Rosenberg	46.1	812	28.2	5.1	78.3	12.9	14 562	-9.0	1 256	8.6	22 414	65.2	50.6	22.6
Round Rock	43.3	977	28.0	4.3	75.0	18.2	52 596	-4.6	3 505	6.7	70 141	77.3	53.5	11.6
Rowlett	11.2	1 350	29.8	0.9	92.5	5.1	29 711	3.7	2 438	8.2	42 119	72.0	54.2	12.0
San Angelo	37.8	638	30.0	7.1	73.3	13.4	45 697	2.9	2 974	6.5	73 031	66.3	44.6	26.1
San Antonio	42.6	759	30.2	9.7	80.2	5.4	613 580	-3.1	44 731	7.3	1 000 025	65.0	43.4	23.8
San Juan	27.8	524	37.8	7.6	NA	NA	13 190	-1.9	1 668	12.6	22 225	61.0	34.7	24.0
San Marcos	70.0	789	47.1	5.5	58.0	25.7	24 587	-12.6	1 488	6.1	38 396	58.4	28.6	22.8
Schertz	21.4	946	25.4	1.6	86.9	11.5	15 583	0.3	982	6.3	22 333	67.1	45.7	20.7
Seguin	44.1	755	30.6	9.4	81.3	7.3	11 067	-7.1	789	7.1	19 435	62.2	39.6	25.4
Sherman	45.5	720	26.0	6.3	70.1	11.8	17 777	1.2	1 479	8.3	29 464	63.4	40.7	28.6
Socorro	16.0	526	32.6	5.1	NA	NA	11 591	-2.2	1 283	11.1	23 161	62.4	37.3	18.8
Southlake	3.9	1 902	32.6	0.7	92.2	5.6	12 287	-0.3	873	7.1	18 492	67.4	47.4	12.5
Sugar Land	20.6	1 350	27.2	2.1	90.2	6.8	40 808	-3.0	2 659	6.5	60 758	67.9	50.4	11.9
Temple	40.5	762	29.4	7.4	82.1	9.6	32 994	8.4	2 119	6.4	50 820	61.8	45.1	27.9
Texarkana	46.9	655	29.6	11.5	82.8	11.1	17 392	2.4	1 438	8.3	28 555	61.1	36.2	34.8
Texas City	40.6	799	31.5	7.6	79.7	12.4	20 568	-0.2	2 381	11.6	34 994	62.0	41.9	27.5
The Colony	29.3	1 129	23.2	1.0	83.2	12.8	20 454	-10.6	1 659	8.1	27 553	82.1	59.8	9.8
Tyler	43.7	761	32.3	8.7	77.1	11.8	47 716	-2.3	3 785	7.9	75 344	64.9	42.0	27.8
Victoria	39.6	694	31.0	7.2	77.4	8.9	33 192	1.6	2 394	7.2	47 103	65.8	44.3	25.4
Waco	53.6	717	35.1	9.2	74.1	11.7	56 729	0.3	4 370	7.7	95 541	61.4	35.9	27.9
Waxahachie	39.2	842	29.3	5.2	78.0	10.7	14 028	5.8	1 094	7.8	22 063	69.7	46.4	19.1
Weatherford	38.5	819	28.1	11.4	77.7	15.3	11 738	-6.8	854	7.3	19 281	59.0	40.2	31.5
Weslaco	34.6	586	29.7	9.0	88.4	5.5	14 428	5.4	1 689	11.7	25 197	54.3	33.2	35.6
Wichita Falls	40.4	691	30.2	6.4	74.6	12.8	47 907	2.4	3 885	8.1	82 971	62.6	39.3	25.9
Wylie	15.1	1 032	31.8	1.5	87.9	9.0	21 838	11.8	1 514	6.9	26 859	79.4	60.4	9.3
UTAH	29.5	797	28.7	4.3	82.3	12.1	1 361 756	-1.6	109 041	8.0	1 950 837	69.2	42.4	19.0
American Fork	21.9	843	38.1	2.1	86.6	10.2	10 666	-14.0	982	9.2	17 015	64.7	39.4	15.1
Bountiful	25.1	745	25.8	4.8	86.5	9.8	20 575	-18.7	1 434	7.0	31 496	62.6	38.8	24.7
Cedar City	48.1	625	29.5	3.7	73.9	10.7	13 494	0.1	1 254	9.3	21 378	67.5	33.2	22.7
Clearfield	48.6	892	28.4	2.7	74.8	19.3	13 146	-5.8	1 292	9.8	19 506	74.3	50.2	15.0
Cottonwood Heights	26.5	930	24.1	3.3	86.2	12.1	19 828	-14.6	1 374	6.9	25 946	69.0	44.3	19.7
Draper	20.0	1 104	27.9	1.7	86.4	10.1	18 890	44.9	1 266	6.7	28 432	63.1	43.6	9.8
Holladay	23.8	871	26.9	2.7	88.7	8.7	13 965	61.0	914	6.5	20 938	61.9	38.8	28.4
Kaysville	9.7	682	27.5	2.0	89.2	7.7	11 770	4.0	756	6.4	17 127	70.1	42.1	14.0
Layton	25.8	806	29.5	2.7	83.2	12.2	33 356	-10.0	2 549	7.6	46 487	70.6	44.8	16.1

1. $2,000 represents $2,000 or more.   2. 50.0 represents 50 percent or more.   3. Percent of civilian labor force.   4. Persons 16 years old and over.

City	Value of residential construction authorized by building permits, 2010			Wholesale trade,[1] 2007				Retail trade,[2] 2007			
	New construction ($1,000)	Number of housing units	Percent single family	Number of establishments	Number of employees	Sales (mil dol)	Annual payroll (mil dol)	Number of establishments	Number of employees	Sales (mil dol)	Annual payroll (mil dol)
	69	70	71	72	73	74	75	76	77	78	79
TEXAS—Cont'd											
Killeen	145 765	1 110	94.1	21	153	72.5	9.5	384	5 886	1 525.1	129.7
Kingsville	2 154	19	100.0	3	D	D	D	102	1 868	624.2	46.3
Kyle	32 441	299	100.0	7	111	51.8	3.7	27	273	112.7	12.0
Lake Jackson	8 648	115	16.5	11	48	16.1	2.1	120	2 683	582.4	52.6
Lancaster	9 903	54	100.0	14	264	97.6	11.2	60	1 004	227.1	23.6
La Porte	2 823	21	100.0	33	407	211.3	26.9	72	752	259.6	19.1
Laredo	93 949	663	95.9	348	2 501	1 468.1	78.8	811	12 789	2 900.5	234.5
League City	160 669	976	78.9	38	339	100.9	12.9	154	2 159	728.9	62.0
Leander	57 905	242	100.0	8	47	44.7	1.7	30	698	112.1	12.1
Lewisville	23 204	199	39.7	105	2 012	1 233.9	106.7	446	8 523	2 488.5	209.8
Little Elm	97 179	389	100.0	3	D	D	D	22	280	65.0	5.6
Longview	35 293	331	50.5	162	2 394	1 051.7	99.3	551	7 414	1 855.9	176.3
Lubbock	211 751	1 399	60.3	321	4 431	3 536.4	197.3	946	16 033	3 715.9	329.8
Lufkin	9 415	106	24.5	50	595	276.0	22.3	293	4 327	1 018.7	93.4
McAllen	97 199	650	72.6	255	2 504	1 828.8	86.8	893	15 462	3 599.1	303.1
McKinney	328 611	1 051	100.0	92	910	730.6	46.6	300	6 504	2 002.3	165.3
Mansfield	45 624	236	100.0	62	1 129	408.0	48.5	115	2 134	574.7	46.3
Mesquite	5 183	42	100.0	66	968	782.6	48.8	455	7 872	1 871.5	165.7
Midland	54 595	394	100.0	147	1 525	1 562.3	73.8	501	7 285	2 137.6	169.5
Mission	50 581	386	89.6	54	312	140.0	8.8	205	3 440	845.8	69.6
Missouri City	26 363	138	100.0	48	167	108.5	7.1	132	2 544	696.9	51.9
Nacogdoches	22 268	250	15.2	33	449	265.6	15.1	212	2 652	640.7	57.1
New Braunfels	49 227	356	100.0	46	451	712.2	20.3	285	4 089	1 284.6	105.3
North Richland Hills	16 551	80	100.0	35	325	91.6	15.1	190	4 220	1 376.9	116.7
Odessa	79 163	708	37.9	180	2 138	1 052.8	106.4	417	6 188	1 903.7	157.6
Paris	1 508	16	100.0	37	290	115.2	10.9	205	2 467	596.4	52.4
Pasadena	21 059	206	22.8	110	1 134	549.5	56.2	410	6 236	1 479.8	134.9
Pearland	146 392	848	85.1	47	646	334.8	32.1	181	3 195	779.6	71.3
Pflugerville	18 474	164	100.0	13	146	62.8	6.8	61	807	218.6	20.5
Pharr	17 760	282	100.0	105	1 221	622.4	44.1	183	2 416	613.2	51.4
Plano	89 784	614	50.7	372	5 651	4 512.4	422.8	1 086	22 006	7 210.4	585.7
Port Arthur	32 016	414	100.0	26	297	165.1	12.5	197	3 366	1 078.3	73.9
Richardson	18 399	196	28.6	270	9 924	12 498.2	900.6	353	5 001	1 910.8	165.3
Rockwall	47 079	324	61.7	41	173	63.9	7.8	168	2 790	787.0	64.8
Rosenberg	19 438	135	100.0	18	372	187.9	14.5	159	2 827	814.8	75.4
Round Rock	40 617	253	100.0	108	1 450	817.4	86.1	366	8 635	6 550.1	226.0
Rowlett	4 704	24	100.0	33	186	80.2	8.5	91	1 407	364.5	31.7
San Angelo	24 682	177	100.0	105	791	280.3	29.8	426	5 873	1 511.3	128.3
San Antonio	491 040	3 574	65.4	1 284	20 806	11 116.9	946.1	4 104	71 703	20 252.1	1 669.4
San Juan	11 030	123	100.0	10	93	53.9	3.3	57	666	156.6	12.6
San Marcos	97 688	1 294	14.7	31	353	208.8	14.2	379	6 463	1 331.8	112.8
Schertz	80 071	446	100.0	31	1 199	706.3	61.8	54	1 254	392.5	28.9
Seguin	15 454	249	24.9	32	414	143.8	11.4	144	1 744	433.7	39.5
Sherman	15 910	287	12.2	44	471	444.4	14.9	244	4 147	1 014.8	90.3
Socorro	13 461	76	100.0	15	67	24.5	1.4	61	334	69.0	5.6
Southlake	34 825	54	100.0	61	639	656.5	35.9	207	4 324	1 219.6	112.9
Sugar Land	126 406	437	100.0	152	2 248	3 573.1	110.8	410	7 114	1 719.9	154.9
Temple	60 084	426	95.8	62	2 387	3 972.4	103.4	302	4 084	1 133.8	98.0
Texarkana	10 589	149	25.5	75	874	1 459.9	31.9	368	5 330	1 241.0	118.0
Texas City	5 404	66	53.0	30	222	149.9	11.9	155	1 978	499.7	43.2
The Colony	12 505	37	100.0	11	146	121.5	10.3	53	808	204.6	18.2
Tyler	23 176	179	63.7	150	1 455	608.4	65.8	650	10 390	2 653.4	246.5
Victoria	7 305	47	100.0	79	1 046	461.9	45.0	371	5 694	1 346.2	123.6
Waco	56 831	438	70.3	137	2 251	4 248.8	90.8	601	8 393	1 970.7	176.8
Waxahachie	20 498	150	100.0	31	267	116.9	11.4	145	2 102	537.2	48.6
Weatherford	16 660	91	96.7	25	339	317.3	12.0	166	2 770	1 032.0	74.5
Weslaco	21 092	266	44.7	33	481	215.9	13.3	160	2 502	671.3	48.5
Wichita Falls	27 073	147	81.0	120	1 197	429.1	44.9	468	7 054	1 597.3	148.0
Wylie	48 629	271	98.5	21	434	80.9	7.3	43	999	221.5	24.5
UTAH	1 672 395	9 171	75.1	3 043	43 900	25 417.4	2 012.0	8 984	142 266	36 574.2	3 240.7
American Fork	12 234	72	91.7	29	322	160.0	15.2	132	2 605	724.2	57.9
Bountiful	8 741	22	100.0	25	137	19.7	2.8	138	2 165	594.5	52.5
Cedar City	12 416	83	57.8	28	338	250.6	12.7	163	2 016	558.5	43.0
Clearfield	4 210	32	100.0	26	492	349.9	22.4	57	629	123.9	9.7
Cottonwood Heights	5 770	17	76.5	32	349	357.4	25.4	69	1 641	1 048.5	65.4
Draper	19 647	179	63.1	49	481	165.4	26.6	157	2 957	820.7	78.6
Holladay	14 188	20	100.0	24	148	42.7	5.7	105	1 010	142.6	17.9
Kaysville	33 834	136	100.0	22	289	112.1	11.7	51	676	149.9	15.8
Layton	32 685	162	91.4	47	414	188.9	14.7	300	5 530	1 225.3	108.9

1. Merchant wholesalers except manufacturers' sales branches and offices. 2. Establishments with payroll.

Table D. Cities — Real Estate, Professional Services, and Manufacturing

City	Real estate and rental and leasing, 2007				Professional, scientific, and technical services,[1] 2007				Manufacturing, 2007			
	Number of establishments	Number of employees	Receipts (mil dol)	Annual payroll (mil dol)	Number of establishments	Number of employees	Receipts (mil dol)	Annual payroll (mil dol)	Number of establishments	Number of employees	Receipts (mil dol)	Annual payroll (mil dol)
	80	81	82	83	84	85	86	87	88	89	90	91
TEXAS—Cont'd												
Killeen	147	754	100.0	17.1	112	1 247	119.2	47.4	NA	NA	NA	NA
Kingsville	30	D	D	D	33	151	10.4	3.2	NA	NA	NA	NA
Kyle	5	17	1.2	0.4	17	46	12.6	2.2	NA	NA	NA	NA
Lake Jackson	35	326	59.6	11.0	46	D	D	D	NA	NA	NA	NA
Lancaster	20	87	12.4	2.2	18	107	7.6	3.3	30	1 351	259.8	48.3
La Porte	34	378	81.1	18.7	50	2 420	238.0	123.0	28	1 463	D	108.1
Laredo	201	D	D	D	309	D	D	D	89	914	242.4	30.7
League City	47	215	33.5	5.9	135	627	95.8	37.8	NA	NA	NA	NA
Leander	13	30	7.1	1.2	27	131	9.5	3.5	NA	NA	NA	NA
Lewisville	108	496	126.8	16.1	215	D	D	D	99	2 834	597.6	103.7
Little Elm	9	16	2.5	0.3	14	52	4.4	2.0	NA	NA	NA	NA
Longview	137	653	131.0	22.7	289	D	D	D	131	8 125	3 834.7	339.5
Lubbock	352	2 182	227.8	49.3	545	3 289	357.0	122.4	200	4 544	1 256.7	164.5
Lufkin	67	318	39.4	8.3	139	634	77.1	27.4	42	4 309	760.8	148.0
McAllen	234	959	202.2	26.8	427	D	D	D	95	2 197	605.0	70.0
McKinney	113	430	77.9	14.4	302	D	D	D	65	6 134	3 171.6	320.2
Mansfield	35	121	15.5	2.8	92	508	45.0	18.4	80	3 452	964.6	141.2
Mesquite	92	426	103.8	11.9	126	965	87.7	31.4	83	2 849	987.5	135.6
Midland	194	920	176.6	33.5	407	D	D	D	83	1 271	D	42.6
Mission	50	181	25.4	4.2	48	190	19.1	7.0	30	543	117.8	14.6
Missouri City	36	114	19.9	4.0	123	309	32.5	12.2	NA	NA	NA	NA
Nacogdoches	39	130	18.2	2.7	83	D	D	D	46	3 801	1 374.7	119.7
New Braunfels	95	380	63.0	10.1	131	458	44.8	15.6	64	2 516	655.8	89.8
North Richland Hills	61	403	43.6	10.1	111	D	D	D	22	832	385.5	35.9
Odessa	130	673	149.8	22.8	184	D	D	D	116	1 542	366.8	69.7
Paris	42	D	D	D	55	D	D	D	39	3 734	2 232.2	164.5
Pasadena	130	764	133.8	23.1	160	D	D	D	112	5 184	10 066.1	304.5
Pearland	66	430	123.7	15.2	137	512	53.7	22.4	65	2 462	450.0	101.3
Pflugerville	19	77	12.2	1.9	35	211	17.1	7.8	NA	NA	NA	NA
Pharr	40	321	36.0	6.3	54	584	30.6	10.4	NA	NA	NA	NA
Plano	394	3 094	533.4	133.4	1 281	D	D	D	164	4 870	1 072.4	282.7
Port Arthur	40	212	49.1	6.3	54	300	31.9	12.3	35	5 297	26 687.7	362.3
Richardson	166	799	134.4	31.8	667	D	D	D	146	6 824	1 883.9	429.3
Rockwall	36	D	D	D	138	D	D	D	50	D	247.8	D
Rosenberg	37	132	21.8	3.5	34	176	12.3	4.5	35	1 171	D	42.3
Round Rock	127	585	123.1	17.6	239	1 521	212.7	92.9	71	3 203	1 038.1	185.6
Rowlett	28	65	11.0	1.7	80	195	27.3	8.4	47	585	67.6	D
San Angelo	132	620	74.4	15.6	170	D	D	D	104	2 500	791.6	98.0
San Antonio	1 555	10 279	1 917.9	364.3	3 143	D	D	D	865	33 695	11 971.4	1 298.5
San Juan	6	40	2.3	0.4	11	D	D	D	NA	NA	NA	NA
San Marcos	78	306	56.3	7.6	76	1 226	58.4	24.6	38	2 060	532.4	84.8
Schertz	20	125	18.6	3.8	24	77	8.3	3.0	NA	NA	NA	NA
Seguin	35	215	24.7	5.5	48	184	13.3	5.4	49	4 371	1 145.3	176.0
Sherman	57	274	43.7	6.7	124	500	49.4	18.1	53	3 429	1 669.4	193.2
Socorro	7	29	2.3	0.4	4	30	1.2	0.4	NA	NA	NA	NA
Southlake	84	360	52.7	15.5	188	D	D	D	NA	NA	NA	NA
Sugar Land	154	652	175.5	27.8	408	2 930	486.4	182.1	63	4 819	1 577.9	227.7
Temple	82	400	64.5	11.1	100	D	D	D	62	5 283	1 604.2	191.9
Texarkana	79	376	49.5	9.8	133	D	D	D	37	D	D	D
Texas City	45	244	77.4	9.2	47	401	49.0	19.3	29	4 412	23 145.7	449.7
The Colony	17	109	29.6	3.7	35	135	7.5	2.7	NA	NA	NA	NA
Tyler	170	1 055	145.5	30.7	435	D	D	D	120	7 320	4 644.6	351.6
Victoria	107	697	112.6	26.9	138	D	D	D	56	D	D	D
Waco	146	1 150	246.9	47.4	268	D	D	D	153	11 568	5 303.2	463.8
Waxahachie	48	142	27.0	4.4	69	D	D	D	57	3 951	1 276.4	161.1
Weatherford	48	199	29.0	5.7	82	D	D	D	43	1 008	211.4	36.2
Weslaco	37	216	19.5	3.4	47	D	D	D	NA	NA	NA	NA
Wichita Falls	163	798	95.2	18.6	207	D	D	D	104	3 904	932.1	170.8
Wylie	20	84	10.9	1.7	39	D	D	D	38	1 963	608.9	85.1
UTAH	4 886	20 413	3 390.8	617.4	8 203	67 426	8 197.7	3 157.3	3 368	123 249	42 431.7	5 508.5
American Fork	65	193	16.8	6.7	106	2 245	133.1	64.1	24	687	202.2	38.3
Bountiful	78	200	22.7	5.1	180	D	D	D	NA	NA	NA	NA
Cedar City	75	160	26.9	3.5	95	D	D	D	63	D	729.3	57.8
Clearfield	33	117	38.1	3.6	49	1 225	285.8	97.7	45	5 091	1 388.6	209.8
Cottonwood Heights	176	785	146.4	33.9	208	1 630	289.3	121.4	27	834	120.1	36.0
Draper	105	277	55.7	9.1	200	1 172	170.2	58.1	45	1 259	299.9	50.3
Holladay	107	290	57.9	11.2	159	D	D	D	NA	NA	NA	NA
Kaysville	33	D	D	D	88	591	52.4	20.9	NA	NA	NA	NA
Layton	118	293	38.4	6.9	179	D	D	D	40	985	332.0	34.8

1. Establishments subject to federal tax.

Table D. Cities — Accommodation and Food Services, Arts, Entertainment, and Recreation, and Health Care and Social Assistance

City	Accommodation and food services, 2007				Arts, entertainment, and recreation,[1] 2007				Health care and social assistance,[1] 2007			
	Number of establishments	Number of employees	Sales (mil dol)	Annual payroll (mil dol)	Number of establishments	Number of employees	Receipts (mil dol)	Annual payroll (mil dol)	Number of establishments	Number of employees	Receipts (mil dol)	Annual payroll (mil dol)
	92	93	94	95	96	97	98	99	100	101	102	103
TEXAS—Cont'd												
Killeen	215	4 508	191.3	49.9	22	D	D	D	156	1 651	125.0	50.8
Kingsville	62	1 087	39.5	11.1	6	D	D	D	50	D	D	D
Kyle	19	227	11.4	2.3	3	D	D	D	12	D	D	D
Lake Jackson	53	1 227	56.3	14.7	6	146	4.8	1.8	126	D	D	D
Lancaster	34	497	22.3	5.6	6	26	1.7	0.5	40	D	D	D
La Porte	48	934	42.4	11.5	3	D	D	D	46	D	D	D
Laredo	358	D	D	D	29	D	D	D	399	11 210	654.6	258.7
League City	85	1 565	74.8	19.9	21	D	D	D	114	D	D	D
Leander	12	142	5.3	1.5	3	D	D	D	22	D	D	D
Lewisville	217	4 751	240.8	65.3	23	418	19.6	5.4	235	3 693	401.0	150.7
Little Elm	28	361	12.7	3.2	3	D	D	D	8	64	5.5	1.9
Longview	219	4 860	199.7	58.8	19	D	D	D	335	D	D	D
Lubbock	544	12 781	522.9	139.0	53	D	D	D	664	D	D	D
Lufkin	116	2 561	105.6	29.8	13	90	4.2	0.9	203	4 695	309.7	131.4
McAllen	335	7 776	357.5	91.1	22	348	20.7	4.4	627	13 300	1 031.1	402.2
McKinney	180	3 937	178.3	49.7	25	607	28.3	10.3	240	3 278	410.5	142.9
Mansfield	81	1 828	75.9	20.7	19	197	12.0	3.5	117	D	D	D
Mesquite	206	5 128	219.7	63.4	23	D	D	D	294	5 276	379.9	157.3
Midland	242	5 162	246.7	66.0	30	D	D	D	294	D	D	D
Mission	123	1 885	80.8	18.7	12	D	D	D	212	D	D	D
Missouri City	74	1 253	53.2	14.6	13	D	D	D	128	D	D	D
Nacogdoches	101	2 220	86.9	23.0	6	D	D	D	166	D	D	D
New Braunfels	173	3 494	151.3	41.0	24	520	34.4	12.6	196	1 913	185.9	69.9
North Richland Hills	110	2 639	106.3	31.2	14	D	D	D	128	D	D	D
Odessa	214	4 986	219.5	57.3	22	377	11.3	2.9	265	D	D	D
Paris	77	1 326	56.5	15.7	6	D	D	D	156	D	D	D
Pasadena	194	4 157	176.7	45.3	10	124	8.9	2.3	298	4 418	580.8	191.3
Pearland	115	2 679	99.3	29.0	16	D	D	D	144	1 206	96.7	39.5
Pflugerville	49	923	36.6	10.1	6	46	2.9	0.5	29	D	D	D
Pharr	83	1 588	76.1	16.1	9	114	4.2	1.3	116	4 821	106.5	53.6
Plano	596	13 066	655.3	188.1	64	1 364	80.9	21.8	1 099	D	D	D
Port Arthur	82	1 651	73.6	20.7	9	102	4.7	1.6	123	2 001	231.3	74.5
Richardson	263	4 515	254.4	68.3	30	D	D	D	438	D	D	D
Rockwall	89	1 918	81.4	24.3	17	231	9.8	3.2	117	D	D	D
Rosenberg	80	1 511	66.6	19.6	2	D	D	D	41	576	37.5	13.6
Round Rock	229	5 138	271.2	70.8	33	D	D	D	229	3 061	396.4	151.2
Rowlett	65	977	44.8	11.7	11	D	D	D	76	D	D	D
San Angelo	202	4 150	174.1	47.7	21	228	11.9	3.7	215	D	D	D
San Antonio	2 872	68 118	3 545.9	985.1	272	7 854	618.7	208.5	3 221	64 987	6 306.5	2 305.7
San Juan	23	D	D	D	3	D	D	D	36	D	D	D
San Marcos	178	3 896	158.7	43.7	12	D	D	D	125	D	D	D
Schertz	47	980	42.7	11.6	2	D	D	D	23	D	D	D
Seguin	77	1 306	56.1	15.6	10	D	D	D	94	D	D	D
Sherman	101	2 304	102.2	28.8	10	D	D	D	202	D	D	D
Socorro	14	183	8.5	1.9	3	D	D	D	5	D	D	D
Southlake	83	2 199	108.6	31.0	21	389	21.3	6.1	115	D	D	D
Sugar Land	239	5 017	244.4	67.7	23	D	D	D	398	D	D	D
Temple	150	2 943	133.0	34.8	15	241	8.7	2.5	155	D	D	D
Texarkana	118	2 975	139.3	42.4	16	176	7.0	2.3	228	D	D	D
Texas City	75	1 495	60.3	16.2	7	D	D	D	98	D	D	D
The Colony	40	733	33.3	8.7	9	144	8.3	2.2	28	222	15.4	6.5
Tyler	260	6 187	273.9	74.6	31	D	D	D	454	8 564	858.2	390.5
Victoria	160	3 119	128.4	34.8	22	255	12.0	3.2	283	4 405	425.6	167.1
Waco	320	7 206	287.0	80.4	34	D	D	D	337	6 716	458.5	211.6
Waxahachie	75	1 351	58.7	16.8	10	D	D	D	67	1 039	70.2	28.0
Weatherford	90	1 426	63.9	17.1	7	D	D	D	107	D	D	D
Weslaco	83	1 745	70.1	18.3	8	D	D	D	150	D	D	D
Wichita Falls	248	6 052	231.0	72.1	25	310	14.4	3.7	282	4 632	391.5	145.4
Wylie	34	573	27.1	7.5	5	46	2.7	0.6	36	D	D	D
UTAH	4 541	91 808	3 980.6	1 148.6	727	16 419	807.9	282.7	5 731	67 064	6 411.4	2 364.8
American Fork	53	1 253	48.1	13.4	5	D	D	D	117	D	D	D
Bountiful	69	D	D	D	11	D	D	D	173	2 362	208.4	77.9
Cedar City	92	1 517	56.6	15.9	7	D	D	D	91	D	D	D
Clearfield	34	711	23.6	6.1	6	78	1.5	0.4	40	D	D	D
Cottonwood Heights	41	605	31.7	9.4	12	D	D	D	108	D	D	D
Draper	69	1 049	49.9	13.2	8	D	D	D	91	D	D	D
Holladay	52	784	35.5	9.9	9	D	D	D	101	D	D	D
Kaysville	23	D	D	D	10	38	1.0	0.3	40	D	D	D
Layton	126	2 945	112.9	33.2	15	D	D	D	139	2 196	241.7	83.3

1. Establishments subject to federal tax.

Table D. Cities — Other Services and Federal Funds

City	Other services[1], 2007				Selected federal funds, 2009–2010 (mil dol)								
					Procurement contracts		Grants						
	Number of establishments	Number of employees	Receipts (mil dol)	Annual payroll (mil dol)	Defense	Other	Total[2]	Medicaid and other health related	Nutrition and family welfare	Energy and environment	Disasters and emergency preparedness	Housing and community development	Employment and training
	104	105	106	107	108	109	110	111	112	113	114	115	116
TEXAS—Cont'd													
Killeen	140	949	64.7	20.7	42.8	0.1	65.3	0.0	0.0	1.5	0.0	2.5	0.0
Kingsville	36	D	D	D	0.0	0.0	11.7	1.5	0.0	0.8	0.0	2.9	0.0
Kyle	12	D	D	D	2.0	0.0	0.3	0.0	0.0	0.0	0.0	0.1	0.0
Lake Jackson	28	148	8.5	2.6	0.1	0.0	1.3	0.0	0.0	0.2	0.0	0.0	0.0
Lancaster	24	230	33.8	8.9	0.8	206.2	9.1	0.0	0.0	0.0	0.0	8.3	0.0
La Porte	45	1 632	251.4	84.2	0.0	0.0	0.0	0.0	0.0	0.0	0.0	0.0	0.0
Laredo	223	D	D	D	2.7	35.6	132.1	9.4	76.7	2.1	0.0	14.9	0.0
League City	80	686	50.7	17.7	0.0	0.8	1.3	0.1	0.0	0.6	0.0	0.3	0.0
Leander	14	53	5.2	1.4	0.6	0.0	0.0	0.0	0.0	0.0	0.0	0.0	0.0
Lewisville	145	948	82.0	25.4	13.8	16.2	8.8	0.6	0.0	0.0	0.0	0.6	0.0
Little Elm	10	30	2.3	0.6	0.0	0.0	0.2	0.0	0.0	0.0	0.0	0.0	0.0
Longview	168	1 301	133.7	37.6	0.2	1.4	16.0	4.6	0.1	0.0	0.0	5.5	0.0
Lubbock	347	2 670	204.5	61.5	13.8	5.9	146.0	28.0	3.9	8.4	0.0	9.4	0.0
Lufkin	80	D	D	D	10.8	2.6	0.8	0.6	0.0	0.1	0.0	0.1	0.0
McAllen	155	1 103	83.2	24.8	-35.7	20.9	20.3	0.0	0.0	1.3	0.0	8.3	0.0
McKinney	103	665	48.0	15.7	815.7	27.1	5.0	0.0	0.0	1.4	0.0	3.1	0.0
Mansfield	54	338	22.7	7.3	30.5	15.5	0.2	0.0	0.0	0.0	0.0	0.0	0.0
Mesquite	141	1 005	92.0	26.2	0.2	0.5	16.1	0.0	0.0	1.2	0.0	12.9	0.0
Midland	161	D	D	D	0.0	4.4	14.8	0.7	2.1	1.0	0.0	5.2	0.0
Mission	63	338	21.3	5.7	0.0	0.0	11.1	0.0	0.0	0.9	0.0	4.3	0.0
Missouri City	66	D	D	D	2.5	0.4	1.0	0.0	0.0	0.6	0.0	0.3	0.0
Nacogdoches	58	323	22.6	6.3	0.0	0.4	18.4	2.1	5.3	0.0	0.0	7.4	0.0
New Braunfels	90	D	D	D	253.4	1.1	5.4	0.2	0.3	0.5	0.0	2.2	0.0
North Richland Hills	76	D	D	D	0.6	0.1	0.6	0.0	0.0	0.6	0.0	0.0	0.0
Odessa	153	D	D	D	0.1	0.4	27.3	0.4	6.2	0.3	0.0	8.0	0.0
Paris	58	D	D	D	0.8	0.8	4.8	0.0	1.4	0.0	0.0	1.9	0.0
Pasadena	144	1 312	148.3	53.1	2.2	1.9	27.2	0.7	0.0	1.3	0.0	10.0	9.5
Pearland	103	687	74.1	24.6	1.1	0.0	4.1	3.1	0.0	0.7	0.0	0.3	0.0
Pflugerville	41	201	16.9	4.3	0.0	0.0	0.0	0.0	0.0	0.0	0.0	0.0	0.0
Pharr	41	241	23.5	4.7	0.0	0.2	28.1	7.6	0.0	0.6	0.0	17.9	0.0
Plano	354	2 884	226.2	72.2	102.8	125.3	14.1	2.0	1.2	1.1	0.0	8.2	0.0
Port Arthur	40	177	12.0	3.6	35.2	6.7	27.4	1.8	2.3	0.6	-0.7	20.7	0.0
Richardson	151	1 623	151.0	56.8	204.3	51.9	43.9	16.0	7.6	3.0	0.0	0.0	0.0
Rockwall	49	377	20.9	7.4	54.0	0.4	0.3	0.0	0.0	0.0	0.0	0.2	0.0
Rosenberg	55	D	D	D	0.0	0.4	3.1	0.0	0.0	0.0	0.0	3.1	0.0
Round Rock	135	1 676	113.9	45.7	429.1	213.9	16.8	0.0	0.0	1.4	0.0	1.4	0.0
Rowlett	73	D	D	D	0.0	0.0	0.7	0.0	0.0	0.5	0.0	0.2	0.0
San Angelo	166	D	D	D	13.4	2.4	25.3	2.3	5.6	1.0	0.0	5.9	0.0
San Antonio	1 765	13 495	918.4	304.5	2 791.9	366.0	738.5	288.4	66.5	49.2	7.6	158.8	5.1
San Juan	21	55	3.7	0.7	0.0	0.0	1.7	0.0	0.0	0.0	0.5	0.9	0.0
San Marcos	69	487	32.2	11.2	4.0	54.5	25.7	7.5	4.6	0.4	0.0	2.7	0.0
Schertz	34	332	24.4	8.4	0.8	0.0	1.9	0.0	0.0	0.0	0.0	1.1	0.0
Seguin	51	304	19.1	6.3	0.0	0.1	4.1	0.0	2.2	0.0	0.0	1.8	0.0
Sherman	54	380	26.1	7.7	0.1	4.4	5.9	0.0	0.3	0.0	0.0	4.9	0.0
Socorro	23	D	D	D	0.0	0.0	0.0	0.0	0.0	0.0	0.0	0.0	0.0
Southlake	55	498	27.8	10.0	0.0	0.3	0.0	0.0	0.0	0.0	0.0	0.0	0.0
Sugar Land	120	813	58.7	20.8	42.9	36.2	6.2	0.0	0.3	5.3	0.0	0.3	0.0
Temple	115	584	43.1	13.2	59.2	72.9	16.0	3.5	0.8	4.8	0.0	1.2	0.0
Texarkana	95	714	57.3	16.4	87.1	1.2	15.9	0.0	0.5	0.7	0.0	10.6	0.0
Texas City	40	364	36.4	12.6	255.6	0.2	4.4	0.0	0.0	0.0	0.0	3.0	0.0
The Colony	28	D	D	D	2.0	0.7	0.0	0.0	0.0	0.0	0.0	0.0	0.0
Tyler	165	1 330	81.3	29.6	56.2	15.8	33.5	10.4	3.0	0.0	0.0	7.9	0.0
Victoria	124	D	D	D	0.2	1.2	10.9	0.0	4.4	1.1	0.0	2.6	0.0
Waco	184	1 288	90.7	28.8	231.1	18.2	49.3	3.2	6.5	1.6	0.0	19.1	0.0
Waxahachie	40	212	16.1	4.4	1.1	1.6	0.3	0.0	0.0	0.0	0.0	0.1	0.0
Weatherford	56	380	24.1	7.2	0.0	2.4	12.1	0.4	7.6	0.1	0.0	2.8	0.0
Weslaco	36	175	14.3	3.2	0.0	0.4	7.1	0.0	0.0	0.7	0.0	6.3	0.0
Wichita Falls	164	1 024	79.3	24.1	181.0	3.0	22.7	1.0	4.4	0.4	0.0	6.8	0.0
Wylie	29	142	10.9	3.5	2.7	0.0	0.1	0.0	0.0	0.0	0.0	0.0	0.0
UTAH	3 537	21 934	1 751.2	520.6	2 521.6	1 236.8	4 986.7	2 083.8	491.2	653.6	11.1	122.5	75.6
American Fork	46	D	D	D	1.2	0.0	0.1	0.0	0.0	0.0	0.0	0.0	0.0
Bountiful	57	282	21.1	5.5	3.6	0.5	0.1	0.0	0.0	0.0	0.0	0.1	0.0
Cedar City	45	D	D	D	3.1	12.6	10.5	0.8	3.0	1.5	1.0	2.4	0.0
Clearfield	37	188	10.0	3.2	493.4	0.1	10.0	0.0	0.0	0.3	0.0	0.6	0.0
Cottonwood Heights	24	132	5.9	2.1	0.0	0.1	0.1	0.0	0.0	0.0	0.0	0.0	0.0
Draper	65	459	31.7	8.9	4.3	1.3	23.4	0.0	0.0	1.1	0.0	0.0	0.0
Holladay	38	D	D	D	0.0	0.1	0.0	0.0	0.0	0.0	0.0	0.0	0.0
Kaysville	27	D	D	D	0.0	0.0	0.1	0.0	0.0	0.0	0.0	0.1	0.0
Layton	84	579	39.7	10.8	12.1	2.6	1.6	0.0	0.0	1.2	0.0	0.4	0.0

1. Establishments subject to federal tax.   2. Includes program categories not shown separately. State totals include additional categories not allocated by city.

Table D. Cities — **City Government Finances**

City	City government finances, 2007									
	General revenue							General expenditure		
		Intergovernmental		Taxes					Per capita[1] (dollars)	
					Per capita[1] (dollars)					
	Total (mil dol)	Total (mil dol)	Percent from state government	Total (mil dol)	Total	Property	Sales and gross receipts	Total (mil dol)	Total	Capital outlays
	117	118	119	120	121	122	123	124	125	126
TEXAS—Cont'd										
Killeen....................	99.2	12.5	2.8	47.3	420	184	237	109.2	971	356
Kingsville	18.1	0.2	100.0	9.4	385	169	216	14.9	610	70
Kyle....................	12.5	0.0	100.0	7.9	329	94	235	10.9	456	19
Lake Jackson	24.2	0.8	74.7	11.3	410	177	233	22.7	825	156
Lancaster....................	36.1	8.4	0.2	17.7	503	262	241	33.4	950	1
La Porte....................	39.1	1.1	100.0	18.8	550	355	195	37.1	1 083	178
Laredo....................	278.1	42.5	30.3	101.1	465	227	238	247.8	1 139	239
League City	50.7	0.7	100.0	35.3	518	339	178	46.1	676	58
Leander....................	15.9	0.5	16.2	8.0	342	201	141	17.7	752	271
Lewisville	95.7	5.1	79.4	57.1	582	261	322	97.8	997	281
Little Elm	19.8	0.6	100.0	8.4	353	165	188	19.2	802	303
Longview....................	86.8	8.5	45.8	53.4	695	260	435	78.7	1 025	114
Lubbock....................	213.8	32.9	4.9	108.4	499	197	302	216.9	998	214
Lufkin....................	41.8	0.9	12.0	23.1	679	261	419	35.5	1 043	36
McAllen....................	182.0	5.8	26.4	89.1	700	192	508	181.1	1 423	471
McKinney....................	123.4	2.7	6.3	87.6	758	374	384	134.8	1 166	379
Mansfield....................	61.5	0.1	100.0	42.0	953	499	455	69.1	1 568	568
Mesquite....................	130.4	13.2	1.3	81.2	616	269	348	123.4	937	122
Midland....................	109.9	9.4	18.0	64.7	623	248	376	106.1	1 022	169
Mission....................	42.2	4.6	11.9	24.0	368	192	176	41.0	628	113
Missouri City................	39.8	1.2	16.5	32.8	443	272	171	45.7	617	181
Nacogdoches....................	34.8	4.5	32.8	14.3	447	206	241	31.7	992	185
New Braunfels..............	62.4	1.3	51.2	33.8	653	203	449	56.4	1 089	276
North Richland Hills	72.8	1.9	100.0	42.7	663	306	356	59.3	921	109
Odessa....................	74.5	4.2	15.5	39.4	407	170	236	76.9	794	85
Paris....................	30.7	1.9	94.0	17.6	675	291	384	28.3	1 083	176
Pasadena	131.7	14.1	10.3	65.4	446	186	261	123.1	840	148
Pearland....................	81.2	1.4	51.1	49.7	638	353	285	108.9	1 399	636
Pflugerville....................	27.5	0.3	4.0	16.4	477	262	214	44.3	1 286	715
Pharr....................	49.4	8.1	59.1	25.5	401	164	237	47.6	748	134
Plano....................	318.2	9.6	93.4	203.6	781	403	377	329.1	1 262	225
Port Arthur....................	81.1	16.8	46.5	27.1	490	220	269	72.0	1 301	37
Richardson	137.4	2.0	74.6	89.5	898	467	431	135.2	1 357	176
Rockwall....................	29.6	1.1	32.6	21.3	630	265	365	55.2	1 032	881
Rosenberg....................	24.6	1.9	24.4	15.2	462	152	310	21.6	653	32
Round Rock	139.1	1.1	64.0	104.0	1 072	222	850	126.3	1 302	467
Rowlett....................	58.8	0.5	16.5	34.1	614	404	210	61.6	1 108	244
San Angelo....................	81.5	11.2	7.4	46.7	516	251	264	79.7	880	176
San Antonio................	1 515.8	191.1	62.8	612.3	461	220	239	1 503.3	1 131	220
San Juan....................	12.5	0.2	100.0	6.6	200	114	86	11.1	334	23
San Marcos................	61.3	3.1	100.0	35.5	705	177	528	56.7	1 126	359
Schertz....................	22.0	0.0	100.0	9.3	317	147	170	19.2	653	5
Seguin....................	20.4	1.2	10.3	9.0	344	155	189	28.6	1 099	402
Sherman....................	41.3	0.7	41.3	21.6	573	189	384	40.1	1 064	207
Socorro....................	5.1	0.3	100.0	3.7	117	86	32	4.7	149	18
Southlake	55.2	0.0	***********	42.0	1 603	816	787	35.6	1 359	144
Sugar Land................	108.2	10.9	5.1	64.6	810	272	539	114.6	1 438	576
Temple....................	74.5	4.3	92.9	38.2	654	294	360	70.8	1 215	203
Texarkana	42.6	1.8	75.2	25.4	704	274	430	35.5	983	53
Texas City....................	61.8	5.0	15.2	39.9	898	447	451	59.4	1 338	388
The Colony....................	31.8	0.3	28.5	21.6	521	312	209	27.2	656	105
Tyler....................	103.3	12.0	21.8	56.7	587	127	460	95.4	989	165
Victoria	51.9	2.4	28.5	29.5	474	175	300	51.8	832	60
Waco....................	701.4	216.2	3.7	79.3	649	298	351	702.5	5 748	174
Waxahachie....................	34.4	1.5	100.0	23.8	873	395	478	32.8	1 203	288
Weatherford....................	28.3	0.4	54.6	16.3	634	168	466	21.7	842	93
Weslaco....................	30.1	1.4	33.2	17.5	538	214	324	32.8	1 010	194
Wichita Falls................	105.1	10.9	21.1	59.2	583	235	348	90.3	889	86
Wylie....................	34.6	5.6	100.0	17.7	507	352	155	30.9	885	216
UTAH....................	X	X	X	X	X	X	X	X	X	X
American Fork..............	26.7	1.3	66.7	12.3	464	159	305	23.9	904	153
Bountiful	28.3	3.7	97.7	13.5	309	74	235	28.4	648	237
Cedar City	31.9	4.7	21.4	13.2	474	169	305	24.9	895	96
Clearfield....................	21.9	1.7	47.7	11.3	412	166	246	21.7	792	72
Cottonwood Heights......	15.6	1.3	98.2	13.3	377	196	181	13.1	371	53
Draper....................	32.9	1.6	99.8	18.7	484	167	317	28.8	747	248
Holladay	12.9	2.2	78.7	9.5	371	165	206	14.0	547	53
Kaysville	16.0	1.1	88.7	6.7	266	54	212	17.3	692	303
Layton....................	42.9	3.9	65.0	24.4	379	98	282	48.7	757	245

1. Based on population estimated as of July 1 of the year shown.

Table D. Cities — **City Government Finances**

City	City government finances, 2006 (cont.)									
	General expenditure (cont.)									
	Percent of total for:									
	Public welfare	Highways	Parking facilities	Education	Health and hospitals	Police protection	Sewerage and sanitation	Parks and recreation	Housing and community development	Interest on debt
	127	128	129	130	131	132	133	134	135	136
TEXAS—Cont'd										
Killeen	0.3	7.3	0.0	0.0	0.3	15.0	30.9	4.8	0.9	2.9
Kingsville	0.0	10.4	0.0	0.0	0.0	31.1	27.0	2.7	0.0	2.5
Kyle	0.0	0.6	0.0	0.0	0.6	15.0	24.5	11.6	0.0	10.1
Lake Jackson	0.0	21.3	0.0	0.0	3.0	16.5	17.6	20.3	0.9	5.4
Lancaster	0.0	3.1	0.0	0.0	0.0	15.5	12.8	5.8	22.9	2.0
La Porte	0.1	6.4	0.0	0.0	4.3	31.2	12.0	11.7	0.0	3.2
Laredo	0.2	1.6	0.5	0.0	4.2	17.3	10.7	3.0	5.7	4.9
League City	0.0	10.6	0.0	0.0	3.1	20.2	12.4	4.3	0.2	12.0
Leander	0.0	10.2	0.0	0.0	0.4	11.9	8.7	9.1	0.0	8.0
Lewisville	0.0	10.9	0.0	0.0	1.8	14.7	6.6	6.8	0.8	7.1
Little Elm	0.0	12.3	0.0	0.0	0.0	12.7	7.5	2.6	0.0	3.6
Longview	0.0	4.4	0.0	0.0	1.2	20.2	13.8	6.9	6.0	2.8
Lubbock	0.0	12.3	0.0	0.0	2.1	18.0	14.5	8.3	2.7	4.5
Lufkin	0.0	11.0	0.0	0.0	0.0	19.3	24.1	10.5	0.3	5.1
McAllen	1.4	8.0	0.5	0.0	0.5	14.8	10.3	25.7	1.2	2.9
McKinney	0.0	16.7	0.0	0.0	0.9	15.3	15.8	10.6	0.6	4.6
Mansfield	0.0	18.7	0.0	0.0	0.5	9.9	15.3	4.6	0.0	7.3
Mesquite	0.0	10.9	0.0	0.0	1.4	21.8	10.9	10.6	8.2	4.0
Midland	0.0	7.6	0.0	0.0	3.1	15.5	11.9	11.0	2.7	2.6
Mission	0.0	10.9	0.0	0.0	1.1	22.4	22.9	10.0	2.3	2.4
Missouri City	0.0	16.4	0.1	0.0	0.8	17.2	3.4	10.6	0.5	4.2
Nacogdoches	0.0	4.5	0.0	0.0	0.9	16.4	26.6	3.8	1.7	2.0
New Braunfels	0.0	15.1	0.0	0.0	0.6	15.0	20.9	7.1	0.9	5.4
North Richland Hills	0.0	8.3	0.0	0.0	1.3	24.0	12.4	20.1	0.0	4.5
Odessa	0.0	11.9	0.0	0.0	0.8	20.3	14.3	7.8	2.0	1.6
Paris	0.0	13.4	0.0	0.0	9.9	31.3	14.0	3.8	2.6	2.2
Pasadena	0.0	15.6	0.0	0.0	1.8	30.8	13.9	9.3	7.6	3.2
Pearland	0.0	36.7	0.0	0.0	2.3	8.5	19.8	3.0	0.0	7.4
Pflugerville	0.0	19.6	0.0	0.0	0.1	12.3	47.6	4.1	0.0	7.4
Pharr	0.0	5.3	0.0	0.0	0.4	19.6	14.3	7.9	2.7	3.6
Plano	0.0	7.0	0.0	0.0	0.6	14.5	14.6	11.4	0.0	4.0
Port Arthur	1.9	8.2	0.0	0.0	2.6	16.7	13.0	2.2	1.8	6.3
Richardson	0.0	9.6	0.0	0.0	1.3	15.6	17.1	9.9	0.0	6.1
Rockwall	0.0	24.4	0.0	0.0	1.4	11.5	6.8	32.8	0.0	3.5
Rosenberg	0.0	8.7	0.0	0.0	0.4	25.8	16.0	4.7	1.0	5.0
Round Rock	0.0	22.7	0.0	0.0	0.0	14.8	12.6	12.9	0.3	6.4
Rowlett	0.0	9.8	0.0	0.0	1.4	13.0	15.0	7.0	0.0	7.6
San Angelo	0.0	7.9	0.0	0.0	5.3	17.4	7.9	10.4	6.0	3.8
San Antonio	2.8	8.5	0.4	3.0	2.8	16.1	16.7	10.5	2.3	5.4
San Juan	0.0	13.3	0.0	0.0	0.0	20.4	24.6	10.0	0.0	5.1
San Marcos	0.0	3.5	0.0	0.0	2.1	15.6	24.4	3.9	1.0	3.6
Schertz	0.1	1.5	0.0	0.0	10.8	15.8	18.4	2.5	0.0	4.2
Seguin	0.0	20.8	0.0	0.0	0.5	21.1	15.3	5.1	0.0	3.4
Sherman	0.7	5.5	0.0	0.0	0.0	17.7	32.2	8.0	0.3	0.5
Socorro	0.0	14.7	0.0	0.0	5.2	25.9	0.0	0.0	0.0	3.6
Southlake	0.0	15.1	0.0	0.0	0.0	14.7	5.6	9.1	0.0	13.5
Sugar Land	0.0	4.7	0.0	0.0	0.5	10.4	12.3	2.2	0.3	6.7
Temple	0.0	4.4	0.0	0.0	3.5	16.2	21.5	9.3	1.3	3.3
Texarkana	0.0	10.2	0.0	0.0	5.0	21.4	26.7	4.3	1.4	5.8
Texas City	0.0	21.7	0.0	0.0	2.8	14.6	17.0	8.9	1.5	5.9
The Colony	0.0	16.3	0.0	0.0	0.0	17.8	5.3	9.5	0.0	4.0
Tyler	0.0	12.5	0.0	0.0	0.0	19.4	20.3	5.2	7.6	6.4
Victoria	0.0	10.6	0.0	0.0	1.0	18.7	17.9	5.2	2.2	5.2
Waco	0.0	1.1	0.0	0.0	0.9	4.0	3.9	2.1	0.4	81.6
Waxahachie	0.0	9.3	0.0	0.0	2.2	14.7	23.4	8.4	0.0	8.4
Weatherford	0.0	17.1	0.0	0.0	1.9	24.9	19.0	8.6	2.8	2.1
Weslaco	0.0	13.0	0.0	0.0	1.6	16.3	17.6	5.0	1.2	5.9
Wichita Falls	0.0	10.6	0.0	0.0	4.8	19.5	16.0	5.2	7.1	0.8
Wylie	0.0	12.1	0.0	0.0	2.2	14.9	26.2	4.9	0.0	4.2
UTAH	X	X	X	X	X	X	X	X	X	X
American Fork	0.0	6.9	0.0	0.0	0.0	15.5	12.1	21.2	0.5	5.9
Bountiful	0.0	18.5	0.0	0.0	0.0	19.1	20.1	12.9	11.1	1.5
Cedar City	0.0	17.0	0.0	0.0	0.0	14.9	11.3	15.9	0.1	4.0
Clearfield	0.0	10.7	0.0	0.0	0.0	15.2	11.2	11.7	0.0	8.8
Cottonwood Heights	0.0	23.9	0.0	0.0	0.0	30.3	5.6	2.3	0.0	0.0
Draper	0.0	20.4	0.0	0.0	1.4	11.7	10.2	11.5	6.6	4.0
Holladay	0.0	16.1	0.0	0.0	0.0	21.2	0.0	2.0	14.2	2.3
Kaysville	0.0	37.2	0.0	0.0	0.0	11.7	15.6	14.9	0.0	0.5
Layton	0.0	19.0	0.0	0.0	0.0	18.1	19.7	18.0	1.0	0.0

Table D. Cities — City Government Finances, City Government Employment, and Climate

City	City government finances, 2007 (cont.) Debt outstanding Total (mil dol)	Per capita[1] (dollars)	Debt issued during year	City government employment, 2010	Climate[2] Average daily temperature (degrees Fahrenheit) Mean January	July	Limits January[3]	July[4]	Annual precipitation (inches)	Heating degree days	Cooling degree days
	137	138	139	140	141	142	143	144	145	146	147
TEXAS—Cont'd											
Killeen	146.0	1 299	54.8	1 157	46.0	83.5	34.0	95.3	32.88	2 190	2 477
Kingsville	22.2	909	0.5	249	55.9	84.3	43.4	95.5	29.03	1 001	3 404
Kyle	24.8	1 039	0.6	NA	NA	NA	NA	NA	NA	NA	NA
Lake Jackson	40.9	1 488	0.0	NA	54.0	83.7	45.4	90.2	50.66	1 234	3 003
Lancaster	17.1	486	0.0	306	44.4	84.0	33.3	95.7	38.69	2 380	2 452
La Porte	40.6	1 184	7.0	NA	51.6	83.6	41.9	91.6	53.75	1 471	2 841
Laredo	328.5	1 510	48.7	2 371	55.6	88.5	43.7	101.6	21.53	931	4 213
League City	120.9	1 774	4.7	487	52.7	82.7	43.1	91.2	51.73	1 365	2 815
Leander	55.6	2 363	7.2	NA	NA	NA	NA	NA	NA	NA	NA
Lewisville	191.9	1 956	10.8	701	42.7	83.6	32.0	94.1	37.79	2 650	2 269
Little Elm	38.1	1 594	12.2	NA	NA	NA	NA	NA	NA	NA	NA
Longview	129.0	1 680	0.0	815	45.4	83.4	33.7	94.5	49.06	2 319	2 355
Lubbock	576.9	2 654	188.8	2 022	38.1	79.8	24.4	91.9	18.69	3 508	1 769
Lufkin	50.1	1 472	1.1	NA	48.6	82.6	37.9	93.5	46.62	1 900	2 480
McAllen	138.7	1 090	0.0	1 719	58.7	85.1	48.2	95.5	22.61	719	3 898
McKinney	215.7	1 865	94.7	835	41.8	82.4	31.1	92.7	41.01	2 843	2 060
Mansfield	144.4	3 277	12.3	463	43.7	84.3	33.2	94.9	34.54	2 437	2 508
Mesquite	224.5	1 704	63.1	1 092	45.9	86.5	36.4	96.1	37.05	2 219	2 878
Midland	94.5	910	42.1	922	44.5	81.8	29.5	95.6	14.84	2 479	2 241
Mission	59.1	905	22.4	NA	58.8	86.3	47.5	97.7	22.13	740	4 128
Missouri City	55.2	746	16.5	NA	51.8	84.1	41.6	93.7	49.34	1 475	2 950
Nacogdoches	61.2	1 912	1.8	NA	46.5	83.9	36.4	93.5	48.36	2 150	2 555
New Braunfels	62.1	1 199	0.0	NA	48.6	82.7	35.5	94.7	35.74	1 840	2 545
North Richland Hills	74.8	1 161	23.6	NA	44.1	85.0	34.0	95.4	34.73	2 370	2 568
Odessa	76.0	785	5.4	876	43.2	81.7	29.6	94.3	14.80	2 716	2 139
Paris	43.7	1 676	0.0	NA	40.6	83.1	29.9	94.3	47.82	2 972	2 197
Pasadena	148.9	1 016	0.0	1 025	54.3	84.5	45.2	93.6	53.96	1 174	3 179
Pearland	271.4	3 486	84.0	NA	54.3	84.5	45.2	93.6	53.96	1 174	3 179
Pflugerville	120.9	3 511	15.9	244	NA	NA	NA	NA	NA	NA	NA
Pharr	50.1	787	1.5	NA	60.1	85.9	50.3	96.1	22.96	624	4 181
Plano	318.5	1 221	46.4	2 168	44.1	85.0	34.0	95.4	34.73	2 370	2 568
Port Arthur	97.1	1 756	0.0	704	52.2	82.7	42.9	91.6	59.89	1 447	2 823
Richardson	262.3	2 632	87.6	1 031	45.9	86.5	36.4	96.1	37.05	2 219	2 878
Rockwall	94.1	2 783	41.0	242	NA	NA	NA	NA	NA	NA	NA
Rosenberg	28.7	871	0.0	217	NA	NA	NA	NA	NA	NA	NA
Round Rock	158.1	1 630	6.2	812	47.2	83.8	35.1	95.7	36.42	1 998	2 584
Rowlett	164.0	2 953	38.1	NA	42.1	82.8	30.8	94.2	40.06	2 710	2 212
San Angelo	81.4	900	19.8	925	44.9	82.4	31.8	94.4	20.91	2 396	2 383
San Antonio	6 412.2	4 825	607.2	15 421	50.3	84.3	38.6	94.6	32.92	1 573	3 038
San Juan	17.5	527	2.2	NA	60.1	85.9	50.3	96.1	22.96	624	4 181
San Marcos	136.0	2 700	20.8	NA	49.9	84.4	38.6	95.1	37.19	1 629	2 913
Schertz	78.2	2 666	0.0	NA	NA	NA	NA	NA	NA	NA	NA
Seguin	33.6	1 291	14.3	884	NA	NA	NA	NA	NA	NA	NA
Sherman	4.9	129	1.6	401	41.5	82.8	32.2	92.7	42.04	2 850	2 137
Socorro	3.6	114	0.0	81	44.9	83.6	29.2	98.7	9.71	2 557	2 372
Southlake	152.2	5 802	11.5	274	NA	NA	NA	NA	NA	NA	NA
Sugar Land	194.7	2 444	71.5	631	51.8	84.1	41.6	93.7	49.34	1 475	2 950
Temple	91.6	1 571	3.8	724	46.1	83.7	34.9	95.0	35.81	2 191	2 551
Texarkana	66.0	1 827	5.3	NA	41.6	82.6	30.7	93.1	51.24	2 893	2 138
Texas City	84.9	1 912	0.0	NA	55.8	84.3	49.7	88.7	43.84	1 008	3 268
The Colony	85.5	2 063	27.1	NA	42.7	83.6	32.0	94.1	37.79	2 650	2 269
Tyler	200.0	2 074	0.0	825	47.5	83.4	37.7	93.6	45.27	1 958	2 521
Victoria	143.5	2 306	9.9	606	53.2	84.2	43.6	93.4	40.10	1 248	3 203
Waco	10 174.6	83 247	2 578.0	1 517	46.1	85.4	35.1	96.7	33.34	2 164	2 840
Waxahachie	88.2	3 229	0.2	NA	NA	NA	NA	NA	NA	NA	NA
Weatherford	63.9	2 483	24.0	338	NA	NA	NA	NA	NA	NA	NA
Weslaco	60.9	1 874	1.3	NA	58.6	84.5	47.7	95.4	25.37	755	3 791
Wichita Falls	170.3	1 676	0.0	1 227	40.5	84.8	28.9	97.2	28.83	3 024	2 396
Wylie	70.9	2 029	38.0	NA	NA	NA	NA	NA	NA	NA	NA
UTAH	X	X	X	NA	X	X	X	X	X	X	X
American Fork	32.5	1 229	0.0	185	NA	NA	NA	NA	NA	NA	NA
Bountiful	7.3	168	0.0	192	29.1	75.8	21.6	88.4	22.40	5 937	861
Cedar City	25.0	898	0.0	NA	NA	NA	NA	NA	NA	NA	NA
Clearfield	31.5	1 147	13.0	166	27.6	74.2	18.6	89.9	20.75	6 142	746
Cottonwood Heights	0.0	0	0.0	NA	NA	NA	NA	NA	NA	NA	NA
Draper	19.2	499	0.0	148	31.6	78.0	22.0	95.3	15.76	5 251	1 172
Holladay	12.9	507	6.0	NA	NA	NA	NA	NA	NA	NA	NA
Kaysville	0.8	31	0.0	NA	NA	NA	NA	NA	NA	NA	NA
Layton	10.0	155	5.2	354	27.6	74.2	18.6	89.9	20.75	6 142	746

1. Based on the population estimated as of July 1 of the year shown. 2. Represents normal values based on the 30-year period, 1971–2000. 3. Average daily minimum. 4. Average daily maximum.

Table D. Cities — Land Area and Population

STATE Place code	City	Land area,[1] 2010 (sq km)	Population, 2010 Total persons	Rank	Per square kilometer	White	Black	American Indian, Alaska Native	Asian	Hawaiian Pacific Islander	Percent Hispanic or Latino[2], 2010	Percent Foreign born, 2008–2010
		1	2	3	4	5	6	7	8	9	10	11
	UTAH—Cont'd											
49 44320	Lehi	68.2	47 407	835	695.0	90.6	0.7	0.7	2.2	1.3	6.4	4.9
49 45860	Logan	46.5	48 174	814	1 036.9	80.5	1.2	1.1	4.0	0.7	13.9	9.0
49 49710	Midvale	15.4	27 964	1 478	1 819.4	69.9	1.8	1.3	3.0	1.1	24.3	14.1
49 53230	Murray	31.8	46 746	847	1 468.2	85.7	2.1	1.0	3.3	0.7	9.1	7.9
49 55980	Ogden	70.2	82 825	387	1 180.3	65.3	2.5	1.5	1.9	0.6	30.1	12.9
49 57300	Orem	47.4	88 328	350	1 864.2	79.5	0.9	1.0	2.8	1.8	16.1	9.9
49 60930	Pleasant Grove	23.7	33 509	1 208	1 411.5	89.9	0.8	0.8	1.6	1.0	7.7	3.6
49 62470	Provo	107.9	112 488	237	1 042.2	79.6	0.9	1.1	3.6	1.9	15.2	11.2
49 64340	Riverton	32.7	38 753	1 020	1 184.7	91.6	0.7	0.6	1.7	1.0	5.7	3.8
49 65110	Roy	20.5	36 884	1 075	1 799.2	82.8	1.7	1.0	2.8	0.4	13.5	5.5
49 65330	St. George	182.3	72 897	466	399.8	83.5	1.0	1.7	1.4	1.5	12.8	7.9
49 67000	Salt Lake City	287.8	186 440	127	647.9	67.4	3.0	1.4	5.3	2.4	22.3	17.5
49 67440	Sandy	59.2	87 461	355	1 476.6	87.7	1.1	0.7	3.8	1.0	7.4	7.4
49 70850	South Jordan	57.1	50 418	763	882.7	89.7	1.0	0.3	3.4	1.3	6.0	4.7
49 71290	Spanish Fork	39.9	34 691	1 162	870.3	87.2	0.6	0.9	1.1	1.2	10.6	6.9
49 72280	Springville	37.3	29 466	1 395	791.0	86.0	0.7	0.9	1.2	1.1	11.8	5.7
49 75360	Taylorsville	28.1	58 652	624	2 087.3	72.5	2.3	1.0	4.5	2.6	18.6	13.1
49 76680	Tooele	55.6	31 605	1 290	568.9	84.3	1.2	1.5	1.0	0.7	12.9	2.6
49 82950	West Jordan	84.1	103 712	269	1 233.8	76.5	1.3	0.9	3.5	2.1	17.7	10.6
49 83470	West Valley City	92.1	129 480	195	1 406.0	55.3	2.3	1.3	5.5	4.2	33.1	19.6
50 00000	VERMONT	23 871.0	625 741	X	26.2	95.8	1.4	1.1	1.6	0.1	1.5	4.1
50 10675	Burlington	26.7	42 417	930	1 589.2	89.4	4.5	1.0	4.4	0.1	2.7	9.9
51 00000	VIRGINIA	102 278.9	8 001 024	X	78.2	66.8	20.1	0.8	6.4	0.2	7.9	11.0
51 01000	Alexandria	38.9	139 966	180	3 596.2	55.5	22.3	0.7	7.3	0.2	16.1	24.9
51 07784	Blacksburg	51.5	42 620	923	827.3	81.2	4.8	0.6	12.2	0.2	3.5	15.7
51 14968	Charlottesville	26.5	43 475	905	1 639.3	68.7	20.4	0.7	7.6	0.1	5.1	11.0
51 16000	Chesapeake	882.7	222 209	92	251.7	62.6	30.6	1.0	3.9	0.2	4.4	4.4
51 21344	Danville	111.2	43 055	911	387.2	47.6	48.9	0.5	1.1	0.1	2.9	2.8
51 35000	Hampton	133.2	137 436	183	1 032.1	43.1	50.8	1.4	3.1	0.2	4.5	5.3
51 35624	Harrisonburg	45.1	48 914	794	1 084.3	74.3	6.9	0.4	4.4	0.2	15.7	13.7
51 44984	Leesburg	32.1	42 616	924	1 328.0	65.6	10.5	0.7	8.5	0.1	17.4	18.1
51 47672	Lynchburg	127.2	75 568	443	593.9	64.6	30.5	0.8	2.8	0.1	3.0	4.8
51 48952	Manassas	25.6	37 821	1 047	1 478.0	49.7	14.5	0.7	5.7	0.2	31.4	23.8
51 56000	Newport News	178.0	180 719	130	1 015.4	48.6	41.9	1.3	3.8	0.3	7.5	6.8
51 57000	Norfolk	140.2	242 803	78	1 732.2	46.6	43.9	1.2	4.3	0.3	6.6	6.7
51 61832	Petersburg	59.4	32 420	1 259	545.9	16.2	79.7	0.8	1.0	0.1	3.8	3.7
51 64000	Portsmouth	87.2	95 535	310	1 096.1	42.1	54.2	1.2	1.6	0.2	3.1	3.1
51 67000	Richmond	154.9	204 214	106	1 318.4	40.4	51.2	0.8	2.9	0.1	6.3	7.9
51 68000	Roanoke	110.2	97 032	303	880.3	63.9	29.8	0.7	2.1	0.1	5.5	6.7
51 76432	Suffolk	1 036.4	84 585	371	81.6	52.4	43.5	0.8	2.2	0.1	2.9	2.8
51 82000	Virginia Beach	645.0	437 994	39	679.1	67.2	20.6	1.0	7.5	0.3	6.6	8.9
51 86720	Winchester	23.9	26 203	1 585	1 095.9	71.1	12.2	0.5	2.8	0.1	15.4	17.4
53 00000	WASHINGTON	172 119.0	6 724 540	X	39.1	75.8	4.5	2.5	8.7	1.0	11.2	12.8
53 03180	Auburn	76.7	70 180	485	914.8	69.1	6.3	3.3	10.7	2.2	12.9	17.6
53 05210	Bellevue	82.8	122 363	210	1 477.8	62.2	2.8	0.8	30.0	0.4	7.0	33.0
53 05280	Bellingham	70.1	80 885	399	1 153.2	84.7	2.1	2.3	6.8	0.5	7.0	10.0
53 07380	Bothell	31.4	33 505	1 209	1 067.7	78.6	2.3	1.3	12.2	0.5	8.7	13.6
53 07695	Bremerton	73.6	37 729	1 049	512.8	75.0	8.7	3.5	7.8	2.0	9.6	7.5
53 08850	Burien	19.2	33 313	1 218	1 733.2	60.4	6.9	2.2	11.7	2.3	20.7	23.4
53 17635	Des Moines	16.8	29 673	1 382	1 762.1	61.6	10.3	2.0	12.4	2.9	15.2	21.1
53 20750	Edmonds	23.1	39 709	993	1 722.0	83.6	3.4	1.6	8.9	0.7	5.3	13.1
53 22640	Everett	86.6	103 019	275	1 189.2	71.9	5.2	2.3	9.4	1.1	14.2	16.9
53 23515	Federal Way	57.7	89 306	344	1 549.1	55.9	11.6	2.0	16.4	3.4	16.2	23.9
53 33805	Issaquah	29.5	30 434	1 337	1 032.7	74.5	1.9	1.0	19.8	0.4	5.8	23.3
53 35275	Kennewick	69.8	73 917	459	1 059.6	70.9	2.2	1.4	3.1	0.3	24.2	11.3
53 35415	Kent	74.1	92 411	324	1 246.4	53.6	13.0	1.8	17.3	2.6	16.6	27.5
53 35940	Kirkland	27.9	48 787	797	1 746.1	79.4	2.5	1.0	13.7	0.6	6.3	19.6
53 36745	Lacey	41.6	42 393	932	1 019.3	74.3	7.1	2.1	10.6	2.5	9.2	10.3
53 37900	Lake Stevens	23.0	28 069	1 471	1 220.9	84.7	2.6	2.0	5.2	1.0	8.6	6.5
53 38038	Lakewood	44.5	58 163	632	1 307.9	59.8	14.5	2.7	11.9	3.4	15.3	14.7
53 40245	Longview	37.5	36 648	1 084	976.8	85.3	1.5	3.2	2.8	0.6	9.7	5.3
53 40840	Lynnwood	20.3	35 836	1 113	1 765.3	62.1	6.5	1.8	19.4	1.0	13.3	27.4
53 43955	Marysville	53.6	60 020	605	1 120.6	79.5	2.8	3.1	7.6	1.1	10.3	9.1
53 47560	Mount Vernon	31.9	31 743	1 285	996.3	61.6	1.3	1.8	3.3	0.4	33.7	19.0
53 51300	Olympia	46.2	46 478	848	1 006.9	84.2	3.2	2.3	7.6	0.8	6.3	6.5
53 53545	Pasco	79.0	59 781	608	756.9	40.1	2.2	0.8	2.4	0.2	55.7	28.0

1. Dry land or land partially or temporarily covered by water.   2. May be of any race.

Table D. Cities — **Population**

City	Age of population (percent), 2010											Population			
												Census counts		Percent change	
	Under 5 years	5 to 17 years	18 to 24 years	25 to 34 years	35 to 44 years	45 to 54 years	55 to 64 years	65 to 74 years	75 years and over	Median age	Percent female	1990	2000	1990– 2000	2000– 2010
	12	13	14	15	16	17	18	19	20	21	22	23	24	25	26
UTAH—Cont'd															
Lehi	15.8	27.5	6.8	20.6	13.1	6.9	4.7	2.7	1.8	24.9	49.8	8 475	19 028	124.5	149.1
Logan	10.2	14.4	28.6	20.7	7.8	6.7	5.2	2.9	3.5	24.2	50.7	32 771	42 670	30.2	12.9
Midvale	9.2	15.9	11.6	21.6	12.4	11.0	8.2	5.7	4.3	30.6	50.5	11 886	27 029	127.4	3.5
Murray	7.3	16.4	10.3	16.5	11.2	13.0	11.3	7.1	6.8	34.6	51.7	31 274	34 024	8.8	37.4
Ogden	9.7	18.5	12.8	17.5	11.6	11.5	8.8	4.7	4.7	29.6	49.2	63 943	77 226	20.8	7.3
Orem	10.2	20.7	16.2	18.0	9.5	9.3	7.7	4.3	4.0	26.2	50.1	67 561	84 324	24.8	4.7
Pleasant Grove	12.3	26.1	10.0	17.8	12.0	9.0	6.3	3.7	2.9	26.0	50.1	13 476	23 468	74.1	42.8
Provo	8.5	13.9	36.5	18.0	6.8	5.9	4.6	2.9	2.9	23.3	50.5	86 835	105 166	21.1	7.0
Riverton	10.6	27.3	8.6	15.0	14.7	11.7	7.0	3.2	1.9	27.9	49.8	11 261	25 011	122.1	54.9
Roy	9.5	22.0	9.7	17.0	12.4	11.6	8.5	4.8	4.4	30.0	50.3	24 560	32 885	33.9	12.2
St. George	8.7	19.4	11.3	13.5	9.6	9.1	9.4	9.4	9.5	32.5	51.1	28 572	49 663	73.8	46.8
Salt Lake City	7.8	14.8	14.0	20.9	12.9	11.2	9.2	4.7	4.7	30.9	48.7	159 928	181 743	13.6	2.6
Sandy	7.3	21.2	9.5	13.5	12.4	14.4	12.5	5.8	3.5	33.8	50.2	75 240	88 418	17.5	-1.1
South Jordan	9.2	25.6	8.9	13.8	13.7	12.6	9.2	4.2	2.9	29.9	49.9	12 215	29 437	141.0	71.3
Spanish Fork	13.0	27.9	9.1	18.1	12.9	8.1	5.3	3.1	2.4	25.0	49.3	11 272	20 246	79.6	71.3
Springville	12.5	25.4	9.3	17.0	12.1	9.2	6.8	4.2	3.4	26.7	50.2	13 950	20 424	46.4	44.3
Taylorsville	8.6	18.8	11.3	16.9	11.8	12.5	11.1	5.4	3.6	31.4	50.5	51 426	57 439	11.7	2.1
Tooele	10.5	25.2	8.1	15.9	14.0	10.5	7.6	4.5	3.6	29.2	49.9	13 887	22 502	62.0	40.5
West Jordan	10.2	25.0	9.8	17.3	14.1	11.3	7.6	3.0	1.6	28.2	50.3	42 915	68 336	59.2	51.8
West Valley City	10.2	22.8	10.6	17.0	13.4	10.9	8.1	4.4	2.5	28.8	49.6	86 969	108 896	25.2	18.9
VERMONT	5.1	15.5	10.4	11.1	12.5	16.4	14.4	7.9	6.6	41.5	50.7	562 758	608 827	8.2	2.8
Burlington	4.1	9.4	33.2	15.7	9.7	10.0	8.5	4.6	4.8	26.5	51.4	39 127	38 889	-0.6	9.1
VIRGINIA	6.4	16.8	10.0	13.6	13.9	15.2	11.9	6.9	5.3	37.5	50.9	6 189 197	7 078 515	14.4	13.0
Alexandria	7.1	10.0	7.2	24.4	17.7	13.4	11.0	5.2	3.9	35.6	51.9	111 182	128 283	15.4	9.1
Blacksburg	2.5	5.7	59.1	12.7	5.6	5.0	4.3	2.6	2.4	21.9	45.0	34 590	39 573	14.4	7.7
Charlottesville	5.3	9.6	28.1	18.7	10.2	10.0	8.8	4.9	4.4	27.8	52.3	40 475	45 049	11.3	-3.5
Chesapeake	6.5	19.4	9.1	12.6	13.9	16.8	11.3	6.0	4.4	37.0	51.4	151 982	199 184	31.1	11.6
Danville	6.3	15.2	9.5	10.8	10.9	14.2	13.9	8.9	10.1	42.6	54.4	53 056	48 411	-8.8	-11.1
Hampton	6.5	16.3	12.8	13.9	11.7	15.2	11.4	6.8	5.4	35.5	52.2	133 811	146 437	9.4	-6.1
Harrisonburg	5.0	10.1	41.8	12.7	8.2	7.8	6.2	3.7	4.5	22.7	53.4	30 707	40 468	31.8	20.9
Leesburg	9.1	21.8	7.1	15.2	17.7	15.3	8.1	3.4	2.6	33.3	51.1	16 202	28 311	74.7	50.5
Lynchburg	6.1	13.5	22.9	12.5	9.8	11.3	10.0	6.5	7.5	30.3	53.1	66 049	65 269	-1.2	15.8
Manassas	8.4	20.0	9.6	16.5	14.5	14.4	9.6	4.1	2.8	32.1	49.9	27 957	35 135	25.7	7.6
Newport News	7.4	16.9	13.4	15.6	12.2	14.0	9.9	6.7	4.9	32.3	51.7	171 439	180 150	5.1	0.3
Norfolk	6.8	14.1	19.8	17.1	11.4	12.3	9.1	4.7	4.7	29.7	48.2	261 250	234 403	-10.3	3.6
Petersburg	6.5	14.2	11.6	12.9	11.6	15.4	12.8	7.9	7.0	39.8	53.3	37 027	33 740	-8.9	-3.9
Portsmouth	7.4	16.3	10.4	15.0	12.0	14.1	11.6	6.7	6.6	35.7	51.9	103 910	100 565	-3.2	-5.0
Richmond	6.3	12.3	18.1	17.2	11.5	12.6	10.9	5.6	5.5	32.0	52.3	202 798	197 790	-2.5	3.2
Roanoke	7.2	14.6	8.9	14.9	13.1	14.4	12.7	6.8	7.4	38.5	52.2	96 509	94 911	-1.7	2.2
Suffolk	7.0	19.1	7.9	12.0	14.9	16.2	11.4	6.7	4.8	37.9	52.0	52 143	63 677	22.1	32.8
Virginia Beach	6.7	17.4	10.7	15.4	13.6	14.8	10.8	5.9	4.7	34.9	51.0	393 089	425 257	8.2	3.0
Winchester	6.8	15.4	12.9	14.8	11.8	13.4	10.9	6.7	7.3	35.1	50.8	21 947	23 585	7.5	11.1
WASHINGTON	6.5	17.0	9.7	13.9	13.5	14.7	12.4	6.8	5.5	37.3	50.2	4 866 669	5 894 121	21.1	14.1
Auburn	7.4	18.5	10.6	14.3	13.6	14.9	10.6	5.5	4.6	34.4	50.6	33 650	40 314	19.8	74.1
Bellevue	5.6	15.6	7.6	16.5	14.3	15.1	11.4	7.2	6.8	38.5	49.9	95 213	109 569	15.1	11.7
Bellingham	4.6	10.9	23.6	15.3	10.7	10.8	11.2	6.1	6.7	31.3	51.2	52 179	67 171	28.7	20.4
Bothell	6.3	16.1	8.1	14.8	14.5	15.7	12.4	6.0	6.1	38.3	51.2	12 575	30 150	139.8	11.1
Bremerton	7.0	12.5	17.0	17.8	11.3	12.4	10.1	5.7	6.2	31.9	46.9	38 142	37 259	-2.3	1.3
Burien	6.8	15.6	8.4	14.1	14.0	15.4	12.9	6.9	5.9	38.5	49.7	27 507	31 881	15.9	4.5
Des Moines	6.5	15.7	8.6	13.5	13.4	15.2	12.3	6.6	8.2	39.4	51.3	20 830	29 267	40.5	1.4
Edmonds	4.4	14.2	7.0	10.4	12.1	16.7	16.2	9.7	9.5	46.3	52.7	30 743	39 515	28.5	0.5
Everett	7.2	15.5	11.3	16.9	13.8	14.5	10.6	5.3	5.0	34.4	49.1	70 937	91 488	29.0	12.6
Federal Way	7.1	18.5	10.2	14.3	13.4	15.0	11.2	5.8	4.5	34.9	51.0	67 535	83 259	23.3	7.3
Issaquah	8.4	15.3	5.4	17.3	18.2	13.2	9.5	5.2	7.5	36.8	52.3	7 786	11 212	44.0	171.4
Kennewick	8.5	19.7	10.3	14.6	12.1	13.0	10.9	5.8	5.1	32.6	50.1	42 148	54 693	29.8	35.1
Kent	8.0	18.2	10.1	16.6	14.0	14.4	9.9	5.0	3.8	33.0	50.1	37 960	79 524	109.5	16.2
Kirkland	6.0	12.7	8.2	19.0	16.1	15.1	11.9	5.8	5.1	37.5	51.3	40 059	45 054	12.5	8.3
Lacey	7.9	16.7	10.1	16.8	12.7	11.3	10.5	6.8	7.3	34.0	52.6	19 279	31 226	62.0	35.8
Lake Stevens	8.3	21.6	8.5	15.8	16.3	14.6	8.5	4.1	2.4	32.5	50.1	NA	6 361	NA	341.3
Lakewood	7.4	15.4	10.8	14.6	11.7	14.4	12.1	6.9	6.7	36.6	51.0	55 937	58 211	4.1	-0.1
Longview	7.0	16.2	9.3	12.4	11.2	13.4	12.9	8.1	9.4	39.6	51.9	31 499	34 660	10.0	5.7
Lynnwood	6.3	15.4	10.6	14.8	13.3	14.5	11.7	6.6	6.8	37.3	51.0	28 637	33 847	18.2	5.9
Marysville	7.8	19.7	9.0	14.6	14.3	14.4	10.3	5.2	4.7	34.2	50.6	12 248	25 315	106.7	137.1
Mount Vernon	8.8	19.4	10.1	15.4	12.1	11.6	9.8	6.2	6.5	32.3	51.0	17 647	26 232	48.6	21.0
Olympia	5.4	14.1	11.2	15.4	13.2	13.6	13.2	6.6	7.3	38.0	52.7	33 729	42 514	26.0	9.3
Pasco	11.5	24.0	10.6	17.0	12.8	9.8	7.4	3.9	2.9	27.3	49.3	20 337	32 066	57.7	86.4

Table D. Cities — Households, Group Quarters, Crime, and Education

City	Households, 2010 Number	Persons per household	Female family householder[1]	One-person	Persons in group quarters, 2010 Total	Institutional Total	Persons in nursing facilities	Non-institutional	Serious crimes Total Number	Rate[3]	Violent	Property	Population age 25 and older	High school graduate or less	Bachelor's degree or more
	27	28	29	30	31	32	33	34	35	36	37	38	39	40	41
UTAH—Cont'd															
Lehi	12 402	3.81	7.1	9.0	107	16	16	91	752	1 586	36	1 550	22 341	24.6	35.6
Logan	15 828	2.82	9.1	20.8	3 529	502	160	3 027	670	1 391	46	1 345	21 470	28.5	36.8
Midvale	10 913	2.55	13.9	29.0	85	10	0	75	1 851	6 619	501	6 119	17 652	47.2	21.5
Murray	18 226	2.56	12.6	26.6	175	124	97	51	3 342	7 149	462	6 687	31 843	32.3	30.7
Ogden	29 631	2.73	14.4	27.9	2 061	1 421	260	640	5 004	6 042	398	5 643	48 925	50.2	17.3
Orem	25 816	3.35	9.7	14.3	1 790	461	301	1 329	2 621	2 967	77	2 890	47 014	23.7	34.4
Pleasant Grove	9 381	3.57	9.2	12.6	51	42	42	9	550	1 641	72	1 570	17 133	22.6	34.9
Provo	31 524	3.24	8.2	12.8	10 353	1 037	223	9 316	2 948	2 621	174	2 446	43 401	23.4	39.9
Riverton	10 460	3.70	7.6	8.8	45	14	14	31	NA	NA	NA	NA	19 449	25.8	30.3
Roy	12 174	3.02	12.1	18.0	124	115	93	9	1 055	2 860	106	2 755	21 144	40.5	16.2
St. George	25 520	2.82	9.2	21.0	1 053	648	303	405	1 710	2 346	93	2 252	44 475	35.3	25.8
Salt Lake City	74 513	2.44	9.7	34.6	4 795	822	539	3 973	15 150	8 126	694	7 432	117 287	32.9	38.9
Sandy	28 296	3.08	9.5	15.8	365	287	287	78	3 013	3 445	183	3 262	53 457	27.6	36.2
South Jordan	14 333	3.52	6.6	11.0	7	7	7	0	1 082	2 146	56	2 091	26 400	22.6	35.6
Spanish Fork	9 069	3.73	8.4	11.3	832	813	27	19	639	1 842	35	1 807	16 981	27.9	26.7
Springville	8 531	3.44	9.5	13.9	119	119	55	0	927	3 146	132	3 014	15 791	28.0	33.7
Taylorsville	19 761	2.96	12.6	20.6	112	82	82	30	2 747	4 684	380	4 303	35 134	45.2	18.0
Tooele	9 959	3.15	11.9	18.3	243	237	103	6	1 345	4 256	244	4 012	17 394	41.0	15.2
West Jordan	29 849	3.46	12.0	12.7	502	394	162	108	3 375	3 254	251	3 004	55 856	38.2	23.2
West Valley City	37 139	3.48	14.1	15.1	193	158	77	35	6 391	4 936	468	4 468	73 987	54.2	13.0
VERMONT	256 442	2.34	9.6	28.2	25 329	5 571	3 588	19 758	15 096	2 412	130	2 282	429 010	41.1	33.2
Burlington	16 119	2.19	9.1	35.5	7 060	539	476	6 521	1 614	3 805	288	3 517	24 054	32.6	41.1
VIRGINIA	3 056 058	2.54	12.4	26.0	239 834	101 333	30 324	138 501	203 283	2 541	214	2 327	5 281 767	39.1	33.9
Alexandria	68 082	2.03	8.6	43.4	1 827	974	506	853	3 535	2 526	194	2 331	103 918	23.2	58.5
Blacksburg	14 455	2.35	4.6	26.8	8 718	150	134	8 568	733	1 720	89	1 631	13 337	14.1	65.8
Charlottesville	17 778	2.31	11.3	34.1	2 438	228	167	2 210	1 894	4 357	449	3 908	24 458	34.7	46.0
Chesapeake	79 574	2.75	15.6	19.8	3 721	3 258	650	463	8 447	3 801	395	3 407	142 929	36.5	28.4
Danville	18 831	2.21	21.4	36.5	1 483	987	558	496	2 362	5 486	399	5 087	29 812	51.4	17.0
Hampton	55 031	2.42	18.1	29.2	4 454	902	516	3 552	5 753	4 186	287	3 899	88 778	39.6	22.2
Harrisonburg	15 988	2.59	10.1	27.3	7 583	681	378	6 902	1 167	2 386	186	2 200	20 839	46.5	33.0
Leesburg	14 441	2.93	10.5	21.1	256	247	247	9	810	1 901	131	1 769	25 272	29.1	46.4
Lynchburg	28 476	2.30	16.3	33.3	10 198	1 534	863	8 664	2 931	3 879	427	3 451	43 321	44.3	28.3
Manassas	12 527	3.02	13.8	22.1	46	0	0	46	1 142	3 019	362	2 657	22 381	43.0	28.4
Newport News	70 664	2.45	18.9	29.1	7 499	1 555	633	5 944	7 621	4 217	544	3 673	112 147	38.9	24.3
Norfolk	86 485	2.43	19.3	31.1	32 780	2 746	924	30 034	14 651	6 034	597	5 437	143 166	43.7	24.0
Petersburg	13 634	2.30	25.9	36.0	1 058	587	273	471	1 694	5 225	583	4 642	21 616	63.8	14.1
Portsmouth	37 324	2.47	21.7	29.4	3 416	2 541	454	875	6 120	6 406	639	5 768	62 476	47.9	18.1
Richmond	87 151	2.20	18.9	37.9	12 725	2 884	1 312	9 841	10 109	4 950	741	4 209	128 394	43.0	33.3
Roanoke	42 712	2.22	17.3	37.1	2 126	1 083	517	1 043	5 424	5 590	697	4 893	66 991	48.9	22.9
Suffolk	30 868	2.70	16.2	20.9	1 128	1 029	267	99	2 334	2 759	316	2 444	55 067	44.1	25.1
Virginia Beach	165 089	2.60	13.9	23.3	9 253	2 961	1 520	6 292	14 156	3 232	190	3 042	282 976	31.5	31.4
Winchester	10 607	2.38	13.0	34.3	976	157	125	819	1 183	4 515	214	4 301	17 483	48.8	30.0
WASHINGTON	2 620 076	2.51	10.5	27.2	139 375	57 844	22 156	81 531	270 354	4 020	314	3 707	4 436 983	34.1	31.0
Auburn	26 058	2.67	13.0	25.6	668	289	228	379	4 063	5 789	335	5 455	44 886	41.2	20.4
Bellevue	50 355	2.41	7.6	28.1	1 110	154	154	956	3 907	3 193	113	3 080	85 491	15.6	61.2
Bellingham	34 671	2.18	8.9	35.3	5 172	1 065	570	4 107	3 939	4 870	350	4 520	48 369	26.7	38.5
Bothell	13 497	2.46	9.1	27.2	321	188	188	133	920	2 746	96	2 650	23 334	23.6	43.7
Bremerton	14 932	2.24	12.9	37.3	4 255	428	350	3 827	2 049	5 431	697	4 734	23 303	37.1	19.5
Burien	13 253	2.49	11.7	31.0	300	209	119	91	2 336	7 012	687	6 325	23 985	40.3	25.2
Des Moines	11 664	2.49	12.8	30.1	596	382	382	214	1 062	3 579	280	3 299	21 035	40.4	20.3
Edmonds	17 381	2.26	9.1	31.3	476	220	220	256	915	2 304	171	2 133	29 738	19.9	45.2
Everett	41 312	2.39	12.5	34.1	4 145	1 706	404	2 439	8 207	7 966	519	7 447	67 144	42.1	19.8
Federal Way	33 188	2.67	14.0	26.3	831	445	421	386	5 035	5 638	364	5 274	56 782	36.8	25.7
Issaquah	12 841	2.34	7.9	30.1	443	242	242	201	765	2 514	92	2 422	20 738	13.0	61.8
Kennewick	27 266	2.67	13.0	25.7	1 081	930	200	151	2 756	3 729	323	3 405	44 150	43.5	21.6
Kent	34 044	2.67	14.3	28.1	1 390	888	86	502	4 965	5 373	542	4 831	56 931	42.7	24.1
Kirkland	22 445	2.15	7.6	36.0	630	175	150	455	1 423	2 917	127	2 790	35 077	15.7	56.3
Lacey	16 949	2.44	12.9	28.3	998	207	204	791	1 641	3 871	191	3 680	28 818	31.8	28.5
Lake Stevens	9 810	2.86	11.9	19.1	29	5	5	24	684	2 437	167	2 269	17 037	35.5	24.4
Lakewood	24 069	2.36	15.1	32.3	1 268	992	152	276	3 248	5 584	860	4 725	39 440	42.5	20.8
Longview	15 281	2.34	13.4	33.6	962	769	389	193	2 094	5 714	371	5 343	24 750	42.4	16.9
Lynnwood	14 107	2.50	12.2	30.8	618	237	195	381	2 201	6 142	232	5 910	24 153	36.8	26.0
Marysville	21 219	2.80	12.5	20.9	600	225	191	375	1 927	3 211	217	2 994	37 403	41.6	16.8
Mount Vernon	11 342	2.74	12.2	26.8	639	399	173	240	2 198	6 924	280	6 644	19 182	43.6	16.8
Olympia	20 761	2.18	11.3	36.3	1 283	942	415	341	2 712	5 835	323	5 512	30 634	23.1	45.1
Pasco	17 983	3.30	14.9	17.0	385	276	98	109	1 631	2 728	306	2 422	31 249	59.8	13.5

1. No spouse present. 2. Data for serious crimes have not been adjusted for underreporting. This may affect comparability between geographic areas and over time. 3. Per 100,000 population estimated by the FBI. 4. Persons 25 years old and over.

Table D. Cities — Income, Poverty, and Housing

City	Money income, 2008–2010					Housing units, 2010			Occupied Housing units 2008–2010				
	Per capita income[1] (dollars)	Households Median income	Percent with income of $200,000 or more	Percent with income of less than $25,000	Families with income below poverty (percent)	Total	Percent change, 2000–2010	Vacant units for sale or rent[2]	Owner-occupied Total	Percent	Median value[3] (dollars)	Median owner costs as a percent of income With a mortgage[4]	Without a mortgage[5]
	42	43	44	45	46	47	48	49	50	51	52	53	54
UTAH—Cont'd													
Lehi	21 524	69 501	2.5	12.3	6.3	13 064	146.5	662	11 999	82.3	249 500	27.0	10.0
Logan	17 301	36 488	1.5	33.4	17.3	16 790	14.0	962	16 276	39.7	169 500	24.8	10.0
Midvale	21 768	44 116	1.7	20.1	9.1	11 764	9.6	851	10 840	45.1	209 100	25.3	10.0
Murray	28 762	56 163	3.7	18.6	5.4	19 181	44.1	955	18 524	68.0	240 600	23.8	10.6
Ogden	19 364	40 944	1.4	28.9	16.8	32 482	9.1	2 851	30 195	54.4	141 800	25.0	10.0
Orem	20 267	50 007	2.6	21.3	11.0	26 970	11.6	1 154	26 862	62.4	219 200	24.4	10.0
Pleasant Grove	21 862	62 538	4.1	16.8	7.6	9 841	55.1	460	9 420	74.4	244 000	24.3	10.0
Provo	16 130	38 807	2.3	31.1	15.9	33 212	9.2	1 688	30 278	44.0	218 800	26.2	10.0
Riverton	22 670	80 000	1.9	5.8	3.5	10 810	63.9	350	9 838	86.2	287 400	26.6	10.0
Roy	21 876	55 643	0.9	13.1	4.7	12 599	14.3	425	12 331	82.7	163 500	23.3	10.0
St. George	20 851	47 787	1.9	24.0	10.3	32 089	52.2	6 569	25 756	65.0	243 800	29.7	10.0
Salt Lake City	25 617	43 410	3.5	28.5	11.8	80 724	4.8	6 211	74 699	48.1	247 300	24.4	10.1
Sandy	28 858	75 284	5.3	12.1	6.0	29 501	10.8	1 205	27 685	80.0	292 400	23.9	10.0
South Jordan	27 472	90 743	6.0	6.3	2.0	14 943	92.5	610	12 878	84.6	350 800	26.2	10.0
Spanish Fork	18 332	57 092	1.6	10.9	4.6	9 440	62.3	371	9 160	75.5	215 400	26.1	10.0
Springville	21 388	56 067	2.6	14.6	5.8	8 927	42.7	396	8 860	79.1	211 700	26.9	10.0
Taylorsville	21 210	54 881	1.7	19.3	9.7	20 671	7.8	910	19 121	72.7	201 600	24.2	10.0
Tooele	20 500	57 556	0.8	16.4	7.2	10 646	33.6	687	10 187	70.2	175 900	22.4	10.8
West Jordan	21 447	66 138	1.3	11.9	5.9	31 366	60.2	1 517	29 346	78.8	233 100	24.6	10.0
West Valley City	18 301	52 520	0.8	19.3	12.7	38 978	16.4	1 839	38 555	70.0	186 400	25.2	10.9
VERMONT	27 359	51 605	2.7	23.1	7.6	322 539	9.6	66 097	256 003	70.8	215 400	25.9	16.4
Burlington	23 874	38 997	2.4	33.8	13.7	16 897	3.1	778	16 921	39.6	261 600	29.0	15.5
VIRGINIA	31 893	61 090	6.4	19.1	7.5	3 364 939	15.9	308 881	2 986 092	68.1	256 600	24.7	11.0
Alexandria	52 547	80 173	11.2	12.1	6.6	72 376	12.6	4 294	64 000	44.1	473 500	23.6	12.0
Blacksburg	16 799	29 964	2.8	45.6	11.2	15 342	12.5	887	13 341	33.2	253 100	21.7	10.0
Charlottesville	24 146	43 356	2.8	30.5	9.5	19 189	9.1	1 411	17 550	40.5	284 400	24.5	13.5
Chesapeake	29 503	68 058	4.1	14.8	5.5	83 196	14.5	3 622	79 262	73.6	278 500	27.4	13.2
Danville	18 390	30 115	1.0	43.9	20.1	22 438	-2.9	3 607	19 504	63.7	89 400	25.1	13.6
Hampton	24 003	49 793	1.2	22.9	10.1	59 566	3.9	4 535	52 619	58.5	201 800	26.2	13.8
Harrisonburg	15 447	36 935	1.0	36.1	13.1	17 444	27.4	1 456	15 079	37.1	219 800	22.4	10.3
Leesburg	35 445	95 124	10.5	8.9	5.3	15 119	41.7	678	13 566	70.5	400 400	26.2	10.0
Lynchburg	21 190	35 955	2.7	35.9	15.6	31 992	15.7	3 516	28 285	54.9	147 000	23.4	12.4
Manassas	27 349	70 211	5.0	14.4	10.9	13 123	8.3	596	11 713	67.1	259 100	24.1	14.0
Newport News	24 755	50 456	2.1	22.8	10.0	76 198	2.8	5 584	69 986	51.2	211 600	25.1	12.9
Norfolk	23 766	42 180	2.4	28.4	13.5	95 018	0.6	8 533	84 350	46.0	216 200	28.1	14.1
Petersburg	18 593	34 148	1.0	36.5	16.4	16 326	2.3	2 692	12 309	49.6	121 000	26.2	12.1
Portsmouth	22 150	45 277	1.2	24.8	14.0	40 806	-1.9	3 482	36 677	59.9	188 200	28.3	14.6
Richmond	25 814	37 236	3.6	35.8	21.0	98 349	6.6	11 198	83 110	43.7	208 800	27.0	15.3
Roanoke	22 395	35 857	1.4	34.0	16.9	47 453	4.9	4 741	43 031	55.7	136 000	26.7	13.2
Suffolk	28 046	63 830	3.0	19.6	8.8	33 035	33.7	2 167	30 251	75.9	256 200	27.7	13.3
Virginia Beach	30 763	64 065	4.1	12.7	4.9	177 879	9.6	12 790	163 831	64.8	280 700	27.6	13.0
Winchester	26 532	43 654	3.7	30.4	15.8	11 872	12.1	1 265	10 310	50.4	256 700	26.4	13.1
WASHINGTON	29 420	56 911	4.1	20.0	8.4	2 885 677	17.7	265 601	2 601 305	64.0	287 300	26.8	12.0
Auburn	25 529	52 164	2.2	20.9	10.7	27 834	66.3	1 776	27 050	58.2	274 700	27.9	14.7
Bellevue	45 470	81 113	11.0	12.6	3.8	55 551	15.0	5 196	50 632	57.9	554 600	25.6	12.8
Bellingham	23 308	38 063	1.7	32.8	9.1	36 760	24.9	2 089	33 874	45.9	303 700	28.4	12.5
Bothell	36 443	68 936	6.8	11.7	3.3	14 255	15.3	758	13 682	62.7	379 400	25.7	15.5
Bremerton	20 973	38 222	1.0	31.3	14.4	17 273	3.9	2 341	14 984	39.5	228 300	27.4	12.0
Burien	30 231	51 440	4.3	21.5	10.5	14 322	2.1	1 069	13 928	52.5	333 000	27.5	13.4
Des Moines	28 330	61 613	2.2	15.8	10.2	12 588	6.2	924	11 552	66.5	292 400	27.9	14.1
Edmonds	42 807	70 427	6.3	13.7	3.6	18 378	4.9	997	17 673	73.4	415 400	27.8	13.5
Everett	23 624	46 222	1.4	24.3	11.9	44 609	15.6	3 297	41 019	45.7	277 500	29.3	14.8
Federal Way	25 778	56 259	2.5	20.5	9.4	35 444	8.8	2 256	33 980	58.3	283 200	28.5	13.6
Issaquah	43 648	83 948	8.9	12.4	1.4	13 914	173.6	1 073	12 339	63.4	468 300	26.6	14.5
Kennewick	22 887	49 043	1.6	24.7	12.8	28 507	29.3	1 241	26 457	64.0	162 500	21.6	10.4
Kent	25 134	52 704	2.2	22.8	15.1	36 424	12.0	2 380	34 846	50.5	300 300	27.8	12.5
Kirkland	49 417	86 086	9.2	10.9	4.0	24 345	11.0	1 900	21 962	59.2	494 000	27.2	14.7
Lacey	27 686	56 913	1.1	19.2	7.8	18 493	41.4	1 544	17 256	59.4	237 800	26.1	11.6
Lake Stevens	27 555	65 385	1.3	16.2	8.0	10 414	NA	604	9 631	76.0	287 200	29.6	19.4
Lakewood	25 032	38 709	2.9	30.9	12.4	26 548	4.7	2 479	25 226	40.7	254 900	26.6	11.9
Longview	23 396	39 409	1.9	32.3	15.7	16 380	7.7	1 099	15 555	55.7	191 200	25.0	12.0
Lynnwood	25 363	48 702	2.0	22.3	12.8	14 939	8.5	832	14 393	52.6	330 300	29.6	14.2
Marysville	24 885	62 542	1.3	16.0	7.7	22 363	130.6	1 144	21 143	70.2	269 400	30.5	13.3
Mount Vernon	21 496	47 478	1.1	21.5	9.6	12 058	24.0	716	11 412	59.2	238 900	30.6	11.5
Olympia	29 466	49 404	2.5	28.4	10.4	22 086	12.1	1 325	21 055	50.3	269 300	25.3	10.6
Pasco	16 364	47 092	0.7	25.4	18.1	18 782	81.7	799	16 811	63.9	147 700	24.2	10.0

1. Based on population estimated by the American Community Survey.   2. Includes units rented or sold but not occupied.   3. Specified owner-occupied units; $1,000,000 represents $1,000,000 or more.   4. 50.0 represents 50 percent or more.   5. 10.0 represents 10 percent or less.

Table D. Cities — **Housing, Labor Force, and Employment**

City	Occupied housing units, 2008–2010 (cont.)				Migration, 2008–2010		Civilian labor force, 2010				Civilian employment[4], 2008–2010			
									Unemployment			Percent		
	Percent renter occupied	Median gross rent[1]	Median rent as a percent of income[2]	Percent with no vehicle available	Percent who lived in the same house one year ago	Percent who lived outside this city one year ago	Total	Percent change, 2009–2010	Total	Rate[3]	Population age 16 and older	In labor force	Full-year full-time worker	Households with no workers (percent)
	55	56	57	58	59	60	61	62	63	64	65	66	67	68
UTAH—Cont'd														
Lehi	17.7	1 105	27.7	1.6	85.2	11.2	19 897	81.6	1 517	7.6	26 330	72.0	47.7	12.3
Logan	60.3	650	28.6	4.4	63.0	20.9	28 403	-7.3	1 607	5.7	36 876	71.4	33.0	14.0
Midvale	54.9	828	28.9	7.2	74.3	20.4	16 440	-8.7	1 426	8.7	21 568	74.3	49.0	17.7
Murray	32.0	839	29.5	5.9	85.6	10.4	26 664	20.0	2 166	8.1	37 489	71.0	45.5	22.7
Ogden	45.6	683	28.2	9.1	77.4	12.1	38 936	-11.0	4 000	10.3	61 077	67.2	39.3	24.9
Orem	37.6	808	30.3	3.8	80.6	11.8	38 769	-25.0	3 186	8.2	63 713	69.8	39.1	17.2
Pleasant Grove	25.6	879	27.4	2.9	79.8	15.2	13 982	4.1	1 157	8.3	21 424	70.3	41.6	15.6
Provo	56.0	693	32.6	5.8	55.8	24.0	53 258	-22.2	3 731	7.0	90 752	64.4	24.2	15.7
Riverton	13.8	1 060	28.4	1.3	88.1	10.5	19 157	39.2	1 397	7.3	24 409	75.8	48.1	10.7
Roy	17.3	827	25.0	2.5	88.8	8.1	18 700	-5.0	1 645	8.8	25 670	70.1	48.6	18.8
St. George	35.0	851	29.8	4.5	80.2	10.3	31 611	-6.8	3 099	9.8	54 394	57.9	31.8	34.4
Salt Lake City	51.9	732	29.4	11.9	74.0	13.5	102 937	-10.0	7 811	7.6	147 277	72.1	43.1	21.1
Sandy	20.0	978	29.3	3.2	87.7	9.3	48 095	-12.0	3 554	7.4	64 641	71.8	44.8	17.3
South Jordan	15.4	1 441	24.9	3.4	82.9	14.3	25 361	51.6	1 700	6.7	33 085	69.4	45.1	12.8
Spanish Fork	24.5	866	26.1	2.0	84.8	9.3	14 745	24.1	1 220	8.3	21 245	68.5	43.1	14.7
Springville	20.9	743	26.4	2.6	84.9	12.0	12 927	5.4	1 108	8.6	18 816	70.1	45.0	15.6
Taylorsville	27.3	843	33.8	4.4	86.0	11.4	34 245	-10.3	2 823	8.2	43 770	72.5	47.3	16.6
Tooele	29.8	749	28.7	3.7	81.2	12.7	15 733	-1.4	1 345	8.5	20 883	70.1	48.2	16.0
West Jordan	21.2	975	30.0	2.2	85.9	10.8	56 763	33.0	4 413	7.8	69 711	78.4	51.8	11.0
West Valley City	30.0	836	32.4	4.2	85.0	9.7	68 131	2.9	6 051	8.9	91 008	74.4	48.5	15.0
VERMONT	29.2	824	31.1	6.4	86.3	10.7	359 844	-0.1	23 059	6.4	511 717	68.9	41.8	25.3
Burlington	60.4	926	36.6	16.0	66.5	17.4	24 863	8.6	1 299	5.2	37 342	66.9	33.9	27.3
VIRGINIA	31.9	998	29.7	6.3	84.2	11.3	4 255 162	1.8	294 746	6.9	6 295 135	67.5	46.4	22.4
Alexandria	55.9	1 353	27.1	10.4	78.4	13.4	90 013	-5.0	4 612	5.1	115 962	78.7	60.3	13.4
Blacksburg	66.8	782	48.8	6.5	53.8	25.0	18 998	0.7	1 287	6.8	39 330	51.5	20.8	27.1
Charlottesville	59.5	933	32.0	11.5	66.0	20.2	22 603	3.0	1 544	6.8	37 396	60.4	35.4	28.3
Chesapeake	26.4	1 033	31.2	4.6	86.1	8.6	118 778	1.6	8 124	6.8	170 165	70.6	49.8	18.2
Danville	46.3	588	35.4	16.0	79.4	9.6	19 656	-4.4	2 692	13.7	35 375	57.8	31.1	37.8
Hampton	41.5	943	32.2	7.3	85.2	7.7	66 184	-5.2	5 707	8.6	110 117	66.5	46.3	23.2
Harrisonburg	62.9	801	33.3	7.8	66.1	23.7	25 214	8.9	1 981	7.9	41 842	51.6	29.2	24.0
Leesburg	29.5	1 311	33.3	2.2	83.4	7.9	25 132	5.4	1 114	4.4	29 702	77.2	53.6	9.5
Lynchburg	45.1	668	31.1	13.7	76.4	14.1	35 923	2.6	3 141	8.7	62 616	59.9	35.2	31.9
Manassas	32.9	1 238	37.6	7.3	82.4	13.7	21 683	5.0	1 624	7.5	27 372	73.9	51.2	12.4
Newport News	48.8	908	30.2	11.5	74.8	14.0	91 283	1.3	7 468	8.2	142 258	70.9	47.8	22.2
Norfolk	54.0	864	33.1	11.3	76.7	11.9	106 876	4.9	9 567	9.0	195 684	69.9	47.1	23.3
Petersburg	50.4	771	32.7	17.6	91.7	3.1	14 366	-2.9	1 906	13.3	26 547	57.0	36.0	39.5
Portsmouth	40.1	906	32.3	10.6	80.0	9.9	44 942	-4.4	4 133	9.2	75 341	65.8	43.7	24.0
Richmond	56.3	824	35.0	18.4	74.9	12.3	103 191	0.6	10 782	10.4	168 641	64.9	38.3	28.4
Roanoke	44.3	634	30.9	14.2	80.0	8.4	48 848	2.6	4 336	8.9	77 608	62.5	41.9	30.0
Suffolk	24.1	939	34.9	4.6	87.7	6.8	42 639	4.0	3 229	7.6	63 827	67.5	47.4	22.5
Virginia Beach	35.2	1 176	30.2	4.0	80.6	8.9	229 456	1.5	14 447	6.3	342 284	72.5	52.3	18.0
Winchester	49.6	845	34.1	8.7	70.0	15.4	0	NA	0	0.0	21 297	71.5	39.7	26.8
WASHINGTON	36.0	904	29.9	6.5	82.3	11.7	3 516 463	-0.5	349 065	9.9	5 270 897	66.1	41.0	25.3
Auburn	41.8	905	31.7	7.9	80.7	12.4	35 440	21.8	3 287	9.3	53 508	69.3	40.9	23.4
Bellevue	42.1	1 280	25.4	7.0	79.1	10.5	67 511	-4.6	5 140	7.6	98 579	67.9	44.8	20.5
Bellingham	54.1	799	35.6	11.5	75.2	11.7	44 075	-0.8	3 707	8.4	69 343	64.9	30.6	29.6
Bothell	37.3	1 200	29.0	5.2	83.5	12.7	19 395	0.2	1 706	8.8	26 349	71.4	48.2	21.2
Bremerton	60.5	791	33.9	14.1	69.6	18.3	16 276	-0.4	1 660	10.2	30 438	66.9	41.4	31.7
Burien	47.5	897	30.1	8.8	78.6	15.6	17 935	3.0	1 777	9.9	27 055	68.3	42.2	25.4
Des Moines	33.5	918	30.0	6.7	82.6	13.6	15 629	0.2	1 713	11.0	23 489	64.9	42.8	26.9
Edmonds	26.6	964	29.2	3.8	87.9	8.0	21 707	-3.5	1 981	9.1	33 309	68.3	42.0	25.2
Everett	54.3	912	30.7	9.9	75.4	13.9	52 550	2.0	6 040	11.5	80 544	67.2	41.8	23.9
Federal Way	41.7	972	31.6	6.8	80.6	10.8	49 100	2.9	5 076	10.3	68 959	69.0	42.7	22.6
Issaquah	36.6	1 331	27.6	4.2	81.4	12.4	17 852	NA	1 014	5.7	22 670	67.7	47.5	26.0
Kennewick	36.0	713	29.4	5.0	77.9	13.6	41 121	12.4	2 829	6.9	53 443	68.2	43.7	22.6
Kent	49.5	959	33.6	8.1	80.4	10.6	50 807	6.4	5 229	10.3	69 802	71.2	44.8	21.4
Kirkland	40.8	1 339	24.7	4.3	78.9	14.5	31 508	-0.5	2 590	8.2	40 300	74.3	52.2	17.9
Lacey	40.6	1 039	30.9	5.8	78.9	13.1	20 213	0.6	1 679	8.3	32 677	61.6	42.1	31.1
Lake Stevens	24.0	1 252	32.1	1.6	86.0	12.3	14 276	NA	847	5.9	20 558	73.1	45.7	18.7
Lakewood	59.3	765	34.6	10.6	76.3	16.5	25 345	0.4	2 620	10.3	47 821	60.0	37.6	33.3
Longview	44.3	652	36.6	12.4	81.0	8.4	15 582	0.6	1 967	12.6	28 725	60.0	31.5	37.2
Lynnwood	47.4	967	33.0	8.6	79.7	13.0	19 598	3.1	1 975	10.1	29 010	70.5	42.2	23.4
Marysville	29.8	1 061	31.3	4.9	84.8	9.8	29 836	64.9	2 468	8.3	44 726	69.5	44.9	21.9
Mount Vernon	40.8	840	32.4	7.3	79.9	10.4	15 682	1.2	1 611	10.3	22 793	60.6	37.1	33.0
Olympia	49.7	849	32.5	9.8	78.2	12.9	25 196	-1.3	1 916	7.6	37 915	68.8	42.1	27.6
Pasco	36.1	706	30.3	8.5	80.0	9.6	27 538	4.6	2 344	8.5	38 606	67.1	38.3	24.3

1. $2,000 represents $2,000 or more. 2. 50.0 represents 50 percent or more. 3. Percent of civilian labor force. 4. Persons 16 years old and over.

Table D. Cities — Construction, Wholesale Trade, and Retail Trade

City	Value of residential construction authorized by building permits, 2010			Wholesale trade,[1] 2007				Retail trade,[2] 2007			
	New construction ($1,000)	Number of housing units	Percent single family	Number of establishments	Number of employees	Sales (mil dol)	Annual payroll (mil dol)	Number of establishments	Number of employees	Sales (mil dol)	Annual payroll (mil dol)
	69	70	71	72	73	74	75	76	77	78	79
UTAH—Cont'd											
Lehi	88 931	349	100.0	19	148	57.3	6.3	72	2 005	596.4	61.9
Logan	22 527	292	26.4	69	591	315.1	24.1	247	3 611	709.3	63.1
Midvale	9 080	62	74.2	56	664	287.1	29.3	146	2 108	629.0	47.3
Murray	8 151	43	100.0	114	1 184	449.2	53.5	351	6 832	2 046.1	187.2
Ogden	5 985	52	96.2	126	1 276	696.7	51.0	356	4 207	1 018.2	96.1
Orem	23 326	105	96.2	134	1 447	569.2	59.8	464	8 311	1 734.3	165.6
Pleasant Grove	10 555	54	44.4	21	71	32.9	2.8	50	855	215.6	16.9
Provo	51 675	314	24.2	66	1 478	619.5	87.6	316	5 033	1 202.5	103.6
Riverton	17 438	93	79.6	19	70	31.8	2.8	53	725	167.7	15.8
Roy	6 034	65	58.5	6	D	D	D	67	963	217.1	19.3
St. George	40 449	274	98.5	98	848	342.3	31.5	446	6 242	1 672.5	151.1
Salt Lake City	22 173	180	16.7	567	9 776	7 486.3	475.7	972	15 888	4 213.6	398.1
Sandy	20 453	80	100.0	138	1 487	428.8	54.9	380	6 843	2 042.0	169.2
South Jordan	108 837	501	96.0	39	707	577.2	53.8	85	2 045	543.5	46.7
Spanish Fork	30 379	139	98.6	19	692	232.4	17.2	76	998	202.7	16.3
Springville	19 244	118	67.8	27	684	213.2	30.7	71	1 213	303.6	25.4
Taylorsville	25 372	216	10.6	18	D	D	D	107	1 934	457.1	41.0
Tooele	12 394	126	32.5	8	D	D	D	75	1 391	366.6	31.6
West Jordan	64 424	499	37.1	61	1 351	824.0	63.4	203	4 672	931.6	83.8
West Valley City	15 101	145	91.7	154	3 351	2 250.8	191.7	299	5 823	1 563.7	145.7
VERMONT	227 617	1 319	74.3	762	9 852	5 121.7	424.8	3 852	40 416	9 310.1	938.7
Burlington	612	4	100.0	47	561	418.2	29.0	252	3 435	575.2	71.5
VIRGINIA	3 246 376	20 992	76.9	6 502	98 304	60 513.4	4 787.4	29 633	431 634	105 663.3	9 991.9
Alexandria	48 784	468	13.9	91	1 282	525.7	65.2	528	8 052	2 353.8	232.5
Blacksburg	6 632	21	100.0	12	71	20.7	4.2	109	1 271	212.4	19.8
Charlottesville	15 546	93	50.5	55	473	203.4	20.4	349	3 880	699.4	78.1
Chesapeake	200 957	1 086	67.8	239	3 428	2 123.3	156.1	869	16 523	3 977.8	345.5
Danville	7 894	70	100.0	55	462	204.1	18.8	330	4 395	892.2	81.8
Hampton	29 944	134	97.0	60	800	288.9	33.5	436	7 295	1 805.7	162.3
Harrisonburg	17 804	201	65.2	55	1 033	378.5	42.7	375	6 265	1 465.3	158.1
Leesburg	NA	NA	NA	21	128	55.4	8.4	266	4 750	1 238.4	112.5
Lynchburg	23 149	144	83.3	82	1 125	541.5	43.2	419	7 266	1 665.1	151.2
Manassas	5 601	52	100.0	44	D	D	D	187	2 635	921.2	85.3
Newport News	11 230	188	68.6	116	1 470	902.0	68.5	727	10 894	2 431.3	233.8
Norfolk	46 320	304	56.3	250	8 577	3 280.4	247.2	975	13 764	2 724.1	293.5
Petersburg	13 548	177	10.7	29	647	356.1	19.0	155	1 569	324.2	37.5
Portsmouth	10 576	66	100.0	48	611	173.6	27.4	296	3 428	682.1	75.7
Richmond	42 637	607	20.8	289	4 408	2 843.3	231.1	883	9 029	1 922.8	211.6
Roanoke	14 155	77	61.0	198	3 098	2 233.6	130.4	588	9 765	2 039.8	215.4
Suffolk	52 143	297	99.3	50	1 105	715.8	55.7	228	3 174	820.3	70.4
Virginia Beach	106 513	629	84.1	374	5 069	2 835.1	207.4	1 625	25 639	5 579.9	568.5
Winchester	11 405	37	100.0	30	D	D	D	307	4 695	998.7	101.1
WASHINGTON	3 891 040	20 691	71.1	8 181	111 294	76 791.0	5 557.6	23 075	328 053	92 968.5	8 585.3
Auburn	42 172	203	90.6	175	4 037	3 732.6	196.9	294	5 123	1 417.2	141.6
Bellevue	42 255	204	36.8	345	3 999	3 754.5	279.3	729	13 684	4 141.0	407.3
Bellingham	15 972	72	88.9	145	1 746	776.8	79.3	552	8 450	1 944.6	200.3
Bothell	42 821	124	100.0	76	1 391	1 148.6	115.3	107	1 602	505.5	43.1
Bremerton	20 481	190	19.5	25	281	177.4	10.9	153	2 230	696.4	67.9
Burien	5 352	17	100.0	20	88	15.5	3.6	154	2 070	586.8	57.8
Des Moines	2 137	5	100.0	12	131	113.0	21.8	52	730	177.5	19.1
Edmonds	9 615	39	46.2	38	140	197.7	7.7	143	1 636	484.2	53.9
Everett	11 099	62	90.3	139	2 039	1 436.1	114.8	481	7 619	2 079.9	215.7
Federal Way	14 148	51	92.2	59	562	421.7	37.2	285	4 774	1 261.5	118.2
Issaquah	70 085	491	17.1	51	361	299.7	21.7	167	3 547	2 352.3	106.2
Kennewick	71 836	302	99.3	60	594	344.3	26.5	364	5 973	1 404.0	136.7
Kent	48 195	210	98.1	419	9 140	7 016.4	463.9	362	5 401	1 504.4	155.7
Kirkland	37 421	149	49.7	126	1 106	645.8	70.1	241	5 069	1 591.5	151.5
Lacey	41 219	267	100.0	26	242	107.2	11.7	150	3 528	853.7	89.5
Lake Stevens	25 640	124	93.5	8	52	20.2	1.6	39	929	198.9	21.7
Lakewood	8 142	34	88.2	61	871	1 130.6	39.0	274	3 213	743.7	80.6
Longview	4 822	23	47.8	38	560	339.8	26.7	188	3 334	827.7	81.2
Lynnwood	3 514	19	47.4	87	921	332.5	41.0	445	8 594	2 053.2	212.8
Marysville	73 944	370	99.5	37	339	146.3	12.9	171	2 719	706.0	72.1
Mount Vernon	10 866	74	100.0	35	506	151.3	21.5	155	2 186	596.9	60.0
Olympia	41 521	235	57.0	46	351	209.5	17.3	387	5 524	1 335.0	138.6
Pasco	125 422	657	80.7	66	876	550.1	36.7	155	2 388	706.2	66.1

1. Merchant wholesalers except manufacturers' sales branches and offices. 2. Establishments with payroll.

Table D. Cities — **Real Estate, Professional Services, and Manufacturing**

City	Real estate and rental and leasing, 2007				Professional, scientific, and technical services,[1] 2007				Manufacturing, 2007			
	Number of establish-ments	Number of employees	Receipts (mil dol)	Annual payroll (mil dol)	Number of establish-ments	Number of employees	Receipts (mil dol)	Annual payroll (mil dol)	Number of establish-ments	Number of employees	Receipts (mil dol)	Annual payroll (mil dol)
	80	81	82	83	84	85	86	87	88	89	90	91
UTAH—Cont'd												
Lehi	50	53	10.7	2.0	110	1 606	99.6	56.9	35	1 720	D	102.1
Logan	107	415	48.3	10.9	171	D	D	D	109	6 969	2 130.6	284.5
Midvale	71	1 243	133.8	43.1	108	688	100.5	43.4	38	604	96.0	29.7
Murray	159	1 994	215.4	58.7	308	2 658	318.4	135.0	129	2 400	402.2	97.5
Ogden	133	499	59.2	9.6	258	D	D	D	146	9 325	2 752.7	374.6
Orem	210	555	103.3	14.2	385	D	D	D	113	3 629	780.6	153.3
Pleasant Grove	46	98	16.7	2.8	73	386	30.4	10.4	NA	NA	NA	NA
Provo	130	996	109.8	18.8	353	D	D	D	104	2 796	416.6	115.5
Riverton	62	148	10.2	2.7	77	243	13.9	5.3	NA	NA	NA	NA
Roy	17	65	5.8	1.0	38	390	57.7	20.8	NA	NA	NA	NA
St. George	271	675	99.0	15.3	315	D	D	D	93	2 305	465.9	83.5
Salt Lake City	536	3 371	920.2	123.1	1 336	14 855	2 364.4	1 010.1	480	24 868	9 175.7	1 203.5
Sandy	223	772	124.2	23.9	368	1 793	276.2	93.2	97	2 551	608.5	115.9
South Jordan	103	276	38.8	8.4	158	1 469	244.4	71.6	19	D	D	D
Spanish Fork	29	80	14.4	3.2	45	193	19.7	5.8	40	2 040	356.3	80.5
Springville	34	69	7.2	1.1	55	157	18.0	5.8	55	3 659	905.5	192.9
Taylorsville	50	190	20.9	4.5	80	D	D	D	19	699	114.5	31.7
Tooele	22	75	11.0	1.5	29	D	D	D	20	817	D	30.2
West Jordan	113	250	38.0	5.7	122	D	D	D	124	3 679	906.2	153.7
West Valley City	73	339	74.5	11.8	136	D	D	D	190	5 785	1 443.1	256.2
VERMONT	797	3 395	497.3	95.9	2 100	16 346	1 615.6	649.5	1 108	35 571	10 751.5	1 650.1
Burlington	72	464	75.5	13.4	249	D	D	D	33	1 264	224.3	65.4
VIRGINIA	9 475	60 502	12 636.8	2 408.7	27 078	376 172	66 543.7	26 936.8	5 777	277 456	92 417.8	12 169.6
Alexandria	229	2 484	811.8	127.1	1 166	D	D	D	88	1 483	284.5	56.3
Blacksburg	54	353	56.6	10.2	147	D	D	D	27	1 454	D	76.1
Charlottesville	98	557	86.5	19.7	290	D	D	D	51	1 589	677.1	79.1
Chesapeake	273	1 355	274.7	49.0	485	D	D	D	139	4 487	1 437.1	200.1
Danville	66	332	41.4	8.8	76	D	D	D	43	4 485	1 275.9	212.7
Hampton	115	873	113.9	24.2	280	D	D	D	77	2 790	522.4	122.0
Harrisonburg	80	346	68.3	8.8	150	D	D	D	47	2 824	746.3	103.1
Leesburg	54	240	66.9	9.5	262	D	D	D	NA	NA	NA	NA
Lynchburg	107	466	72.4	15.3	203	D	D	D	96	9 486	2 801.6	500.1
Manassas	59	230	41.7	8.3	218	D	D	D	41	4 038	1 408.7	340.5
Newport News	273	2 884	374.2	84.2	345	D	D	D	107	24 155	4 702.7	1 216.0
Norfolk	324	2 898	385.8	98.3	653	D	D	D	166	7 448	1 280.8	300.0
Petersburg	36	192	21.4	4.6	35	D	D	D	42	2 114	595.9	102.1
Portsmouth	93	383	48.6	8.5	144	D	D	D	63	2 360	652.9	105.2
Richmond	302	2 361	636.4	126.2	826	10 582	1 682.7	785.0	224	9 341	10 192.1	545.8
Roanoke	161	1 274	188.6	33.5	321	D	D	D	115	4 544	1 582.4	182.7
Suffolk	74	287	44.5	10.6	122	D	D	D	48	2 362	1 307.8	109.7
Virginia Beach	717	6 190	830.7	197.8	1 310	D	D	D	243	6 544	1 806.5	236.9
Winchester	76	329	63.3	12.0	147	D	D	D	30	D	D	D
WASHINGTON	10 480	51 196	10 467.3	1 818.7	19 242	150 367	23 394.7	9 778.0	7 650	269 851	112 053.3	13 274.5
Auburn	82	280	75.9	9.4	124	646	105.3	25.3	186	8 019	1 767.4	397.5
Bellevue	589	3 913	1 240.4	197.4	1 185	13 914	2 535.2	1 051.0	130	2 358	813.6	102.5
Bellingham	219	907	189.8	25.2	416	2 307	260.1	102.3	136	3 297	614.5	114.1
Bothell	89	326	91.0	10.7	187	D	D	D	37	2 063	D	127.7
Bremerton	70	250	34.0	6.5	74	D	D	D	NA	NA	NA	NA
Burien	72	329	119.3	10.7	90	553	41.6	15.9	NA	NA	NA	NA
Des Moines	29	86	17.0	2.6	29	91	7.7	2.6	NA	NA	NA	NA
Edmonds	98	311	65.3	12.2	176	721	103.5	39.9	NA	NA	NA	NA
Everett	191	926	134.1	30.1	291	3 107	403.0	164.3	136	29 991	18 143.4	1 933.6
Federal Way	125	636	238.7	22.8	185	1 829	147.1	87.5	NA	NA	NA	NA
Issaquah	77	361	92.7	16.4	169	3 278	1 038.9	251.3	24	1 277	510.4	D
Kennewick	119	734	158.3	22.9	176	D	D	D	42	612	D	26.6
Kent	149	890	180.4	28.8	203	D	D	D	264	19 431	6 922.6	1 279.1
Kirkland	191	1 074	337.0	42.6	403	D	D	D	63	877	D	40.3
Lacey	55	262	33.7	5.6	80	2 591	335.6	137.5	NA	NA	NA	NA
Lake Stevens	34	82	13.4	2.5	16	59	4.0	1.3	NA	NA	NA	NA
Lakewood	123	688	86.2	18.8	109	867	64.7	33.7	44	608	125.4	21.6
Longview	62	296	37.7	7.0	83	D	D	D	41	1 657	751.5	88.7
Lynnwood	106	448	138.6	17.8	142	D	D	D	62	686	91.1	23.5
Marysville	59	228	52.9	7.7	63	396	53.3	12.2	74	2 586	300.4	81.8
Mount Vernon	63	209	39.1	5.7	126	498	51.5	17.0	36	860	164.2	27.2
Olympia	117	477	127.3	12.4	297	D	D	D	35	672	237.5	29.0
Pasco	49	240	44.3	6.3	68	D	D	D	39	D	D	D

1. Establishments subject to federal tax.

Table D. Cities — Accommodation and Food Services, Arts, Entertainment, and Recreation, and Health Care and Social Assistance

City	Accommodation and food services, 2007				Arts, entertainment, and recreation,[1] 2007				Health care and social assistance,[1] 2007			
	Number of establishments	Number of employees	Sales (mil dol)	Annual payroll (mil dol)	Number of establishments	Number of employees	Receipts (mil dol)	Annual payroll (mil dol)	Number of establishments	Number of employees	Receipts (mil dol)	Annual payroll (mil dol)
	92	93	94	95	96	97	98	99	100	101	102	103
UTAH—Cont'd												
Lehi	33	551	24.9	6.3	8	18	1.1	0.2	47	D	D	D
Logan	94	2 018	71.6	22.0	14	D	D	D	163	D	D	D
Midvale	72	1 459	60.4	17.2	8	115	3.9	1.0	47	D	D	D
Murray	97	2 203	92.4	27.6	12	D	D	D	259	D	D	D
Ogden	195	3 097	120.8	33.2	14	D	D	D	270	3 051	308.1	118.7
Orem	127	3 081	123.7	36.6	33	D	D	D	214	3 522	265.7	102.4
Pleasant Grove	25	381	12.2	3.1	8	25	3.6	0.6	51	D	D	D
Provo	182	3 840	150.9	43.6	33	D	D	D	265	D	D	D
Riverton	26	565	20.7	6.1	6	6	0.4	0.2	52	D	D	D
Roy	40	672	28.0	6.9	3	D	D	D	50	D	D	D
St. George	193	4 211	187.2	55.5	26	D	D	D	302	D	D	D
Salt Lake City	669	16 676	880.8	264.5	76	2 059	203.9	96.3	594	6 808	820.0	267.9
Sandy	168	3 812	148.3	45.2	37	525	21.2	5.6	237	D	D	D
South Jordan	44	785	34.2	10.5	8	D	D	D	77	627	67.1	21.0
Spanish Fork	35	D	D	D	4	D	D	D	48	D	D	D
Springville	30	534	22.3	5.7	3	D	D	D	53	D	D	D
Taylorsville	93	1 691	71.3	18.6	7	D	D	D	80	833	65.9	23.9
Tooele	41	760	27.5	6.9	4	D	D	D	62	D	D	D
West Jordan	95	D	D	D	9	D	D	D	144	2 053	259.0	74.7
West Valley City	160	2 746	125.5	33.0	18	D	D	D	104	D	D	D
VERMONT	1 942	31 176	1 367.6	427.9	323	6 554	280.4	79.3	1 469	15 381	1 147.3	531.8
Burlington	138	2 343	108.6	34.3	12	94	4.1	1.4	106	D	D	D
VIRGINIA	15 765	302 446	15 340.5	4 273.0	2 011	32 788	2 621.1	713.5	14 942	203 981	19 704.5	8 418.1
Alexandria	355	6 961	471.7	135.1	32	574	41.5	15.6	335	2 688	318.7	134.3
Blacksburg	93	1 679	57.5	17.8	4	D	D	D	77	D	D	D
Charlottesville	261	5 617	303.6	85.8	23	D	D	D	142	D	D	D
Chesapeake	431	8 991	369.8	105.5	43	D	D	D	431	D	D	D
Danville	140	2 741	110.3	30.0	11	D	D	D	182	D	D	D
Hampton	233	5 888	233.6	69.2	27	D	D	D	206	2 877	206.4	95.9
Harrisonburg	175	4 284	168.6	46.7	10	D	D	D	128	D	D	D
Leesburg	106	2 300	124.6	43.0	13	D	D	D	119	1 231	107.0	45.1
Lynchburg	234	5 226	190.0	58.3	21	161	6.8	1.9	202	D	D	D
Manassas	101	1 307	75.6	19.0	8	42	4.5	2.6	160	D	D	D
Newport News	384	7 660	329.1	89.9	36	351	17.5	4.3	328	5 716	497.9	269.1
Norfolk	551	11 667	505.0	140.2	58	600	45.0	13.0	427	7 517	792.0	367.7
Petersburg	70	864	36.6	9.7	4	56	1.8	0.4	99	D	D	D
Portsmouth	169	2 513	106.2	28.8	15	D	D	D	174	3 116	238.8	108.2
Richmond	547	10 136	476.8	143.5	51	490	41.0	7.6	462	11 317	1 110.4	453.7
Roanoke	294	6 162	267.2	83.3	19	144	6.1	2.0	232	3 993	443.2	173.6
Suffolk	121	1 981	72.8	20.2	14	106	5.5	1.9	124	D	D	D
Virginia Beach	1 134	21 694	1 074.2	294.9	146	1 585	111.9	27.4	855	10 228	985.2	424.2
Winchester	123	2 343	104.6	29.5	12	D	D	D	200	D	D	D
WASHINGTON	15 893	233 235	12 389.4	3 618.1	2 021	45 093	4 116.5	1 255.9	15 513	172 010	16 738.9	6 870.8
Auburn	153	2 150	103.8	29.9	24	D	D	D	146	2 235	241.9	89.2
Bellevue	387	7 861	505.9	147.2	61	1 714	128.5	33.5	753	7 473	793.2	322.3
Bellingham	336	5 623	226.6	71.1	37	638	22.2	6.9	408	D	D	D
Bothell	110	1 457	82.7	21.4	5	D	D	D	126	1 156	93.4	39.1
Bremerton	121	1 498	64.9	19.6	10	305	9.7	3.8	115	1 864	182.4	70.8
Burien	90	1 165	57.0	17.3	8	D	D	D	157	1 217	142.8	53.0
Des Moines	43	788	38.8	12.6	3	D	D	D	50	852	58.3	25.2
Edmonds	121	1 482	75.4	23.8	8	264	16.0	4.2	186	D	D	D
Everett	332	4 661	249.5	71.7	27	422	19.5	6.4	344	4 847	537.8	247.3
Federal Way	235	3 505	172.1	47.6	22	519	35.5	10.1	310	D	D	D
Issaquah	113	1 793	91.1	26.5	9	136	4.2	1.4	143	1 635	184.1	62.0
Kennewick	174	2 835	127.8	35.7	21	D	D	D	217	2 526	223.3	78.0
Kent	259	3 331	170.9	47.9	23	240	33.0	6.2	215	2 101	153.7	57.4
Kirkland	187	3 354	176.9	58.0	22	D	D	D	286	D	D	D
Lacey	106	1 796	83.8	23.6	8	175	7.3	2.6	98	1 189	101.3	35.7
Lake Stevens	37	489	28.2	6.3	2	D	D	D	31	D	D	D
Lakewood	189	2 632	125.5	37.5	12	D	D	D	167	1 790	150.0	57.5
Longview	104	1 489	66.5	18.5	8	D	D	D	136	2 377	225.3	90.9
Lynnwood	199	3 384	200.3	52.1	11	D	D	D	177	D	D	D
Marysville	90	1 256	62.4	18.1	6	D	D	D	93	1 060	89.6	36.8
Mount Vernon	92	1 246	53.8	16.2	7	D	D	D	124	1 944	224.5	87.0
Olympia	212	3 628	165.4	52.3	15	195	13.1	3.5	350	3 914	444.9	166.7
Pasco	83	934	46.3	12.9	8	D	D	D	86	632	54.3	18.8

1. Establishments subject to federal tax.

City	Other services[1], 2007				Selected federal funds, 2009–2010 (mil dol)								
					Procurement contracts		Grants						
	Number of establishments	Number of employees	Receipts (mil dol)	Annual payroll (mil dol)	Defense	Other	Total[2]	Medicaid and other health related	Nutrition and family welfare	Energy and environment	Disasters and emergency preparedness	Housing and community development	Employment and training
	104	105	106	107	108	109	110	111	112	113	114	115	116
UTAH—Cont'd													
Lehi	25	D	D	D	0.0	0.3	0.2	0.0	0.0	0.0	0.0	0.0	0.0
Logan	75	469	37.0	9.1	3.6	6.9	103.4	8.2	5.0	9.7	0.0	3.1	0.0
Midvale	65	456	41.5	11.3	1.0	0.8	0.5	0.0	0.0	0.2	0.0	0.0	0.0
Murray	134	933	66.6	19.7	0.5	0.9	1.3	1.2	0.0	0.0	0.0	0.0	0.0
Ogden	140	1 010	77.6	24.7	58.2	26.8	30.5	3.7	5.7	1.0	0.0	10.1	0.3
Orem	142	851	60.2	18.6	0.6	1.6	92.1	0.3	0.6	83.3	0.0	0.2	0.0
Pleasant Grove	32	119	11.5	2.6	479.2	0.1	1.1	0.0	0.0	1.0	0.0	0.1	0.0
Provo	114	598	42.9	11.7	3.6	4.4	51.3	8.7	6.0	9.1	0.0	14.2	0.0
Riverton	35	148	11.1	2.9	0.0	0.0	0.0	0.0	0.0	0.0	0.0	0.0	0.0
Roy	37	213	14.3	4.0	3.6	0.1	0.0	0.0	0.0	0.0	0.0	0.0	0.0
St. George	132	702	63.5	17.5	0.2	1.2	20.7	1.0	0.6	1.1	0.0	1.9	0.0
Salt Lake City	465	3 690	278.8	85.8	529.1	104.3	1 688.1	391.1	103.5	483.1	10.2	46.2	71.8
Sandy	141	1 460	89.7	45.6	2.8	1.1	2.8	0.0	0.0	0.8	0.0	0.4	0.0
South Jordan	36	193	14.3	4.3	0.6	0.3	0.6	0.0	0.0	0.6	0.0	0.0	0.0
Spanish Fork	35	D	D	D	0.4	0.0	0.6	0.0	0.0	0.0	0.0	0.0	0.0
Springville	24	D	D	D	5.1	0.1	1.0	0.0	0.0	1.0	0.0	0.0	0.0
Taylorsville	42	178	13.5	4.2	0.0	0.3	3.8	0.0	0.0	0.5	0.0	0.4	2.8
Tooele	37	D	D	D	24.6	0.9	3.0	0.0	0.0	0.0	0.0	1.3	0.0
West Jordan	96	720	57.2	19.0	0.1	0.5	0.6	0.0	0.0	0.0	0.0	0.5	0.0
West Valley City	134	750	76.1	20.8	4.5	3.1	5.8	-0.1	0.0	0.0	0.0	5.2	0.3
VERMONT	1 107	4 439	389.2	104.8	711.3	220.4	2 379.9	1 088.4	192.4	161.1	0.4	72.4	34.9
Burlington	64	323	20.9	7.6	433.8	10.0	196.5	127.4	3.6	3.1	0.0	17.9	0.8
VIRGINIA	11 978	76 121	6 677.6	2 125.9	40 377.7	17 960.0	12 227.5	5 483.9	1 142.6	427.2	277.1	592.7	273.7
Alexandria	254	2 071	181.2	63.9	834.3	721.1	348.5	17.6	2.8	22.7	200.3	27.8	5.0
Blacksburg	48	D	D	D	45.3	26.0	175.0	44.1	0.0	17.6	0.0	1.8	0.0
Charlottesville	113	929	66.5	23.2	46.9	25.3	338.4	236.9	0.2	13.5	-0.5	8.0	0.0
Chesapeake	375	2 791	314.0	86.9	299.0	54.2	20.9	0.0	0.0	2.1	0.0	14.8	0.0
Danville	108	D	D	D	0.5	4.1	15.2	1.7	1.5	0.7	0.0	7.4	0.0
Hampton	165	1 046	76.5	25.7	482.7	252.2	132.1	1.6	0.2	1.1	0.0	25.1	-0.1
Harrisonburg	107	590	49.3	15.6	21.3	2.4	16.9	0.6	0.1	1.6	0.0	5.4	5.0
Leesburg	81	483	37.6	11.8	1 640.9	28.7	23.2	0.9	0.0	2.1	0.0	10.1	0.0
Lynchburg	135	852	55.1	19.2	22.1	18.8	20.7	0.9	3.1	0.7	0.0	6.5	0.0
Manassas	114	698	58.5	18.1	746.3	46.6	37.3	22.2	2.2	7.2	0.0	0.0	0.0
Newport News	276	1 885	133.5	46.0	3 012.1	193.2	54.0	5.9	4.2	2.1	2.6	25.7	0.0
Norfolk	351	2 706	258.2	86.8	2 099.7	51.2	125.3	18.2	13.4	4.4	0.2	42.2	0.0
Petersburg	69	520	35.2	12.3	0.9	3.5	27.1	0.1	0.0	0.3	0.0	6.1	0.5
Portsmouth	154	1 437	105.2	39.0	168.1	90.2	29.0	1.5	0.0	0.0	0.0	22.4	0.0
Richmond	408	2 897	233.4	79.8	42.7	89.6	2 033.0	321.0	132.8	135.9	3.7	154.8	134.2
Roanoke	218	1 429	110.6	37.1	29.9	65.3	45.7	1.9	9.0	4.2	0.0	17.7	0.0
Suffolk	84	D	D	D	252.4	14.8	9.4	0.0	0.0	0.0	0.0	7.1	0.0
Virginia Beach	783	4 883	310.0	104.4	1 962.6	138.1	71.9	0.0	0.7	4.4	32.6	21.8	0.0
Winchester	73	491	35.0	12.3	2.0	14.2	5.8	0.8	0.0	0.0	0.0	2.3	0.1
WASHINGTON	9 809	54 544	4 643.2	1 461.8	5 150.5	4 890.3	14 725.4	7 161.4	1 608.2	1 129.9	45.7	656.3	259.1
Auburn	141	852	98.4	29.8	5.6	14.3	46.6	3.8	1.4	0.6	0.0	1.8	0.0
Bellevue	300	2 031	193.1	65.6	13.9	14.0	44.1	2.1	0.4	32.3	0.0	0.9	0.0
Bellingham	189	1 065	81.2	25.1	13.8	27.9	82.0	6.7	4.9	1.4	-2.4	24.3	0.5
Bothell	52	330	38.0	10.3	7.0	3.1	2.3	2.3	0.0	0.0	0.0	0.0	0.0
Bremerton	56	294	24.6	7.6	70.5	0.5	26.5	0.9	5.5	2.6	0.0	13.5	0.0
Burien	81	494	36.8	12.2	0.1	0.1	0.5	0.1	0.0	0.0	0.0	0.4	0.0
Des Moines	29	104	9.7	3.2	0.0	1.9	0.7	0.0	0.0	0.0	0.0	0.0	0.0
Edmonds	56	261	19.0	7.1	0.3	3.4	0.0	0.0	0.0	0.0	0.0	0.0	0.0
Everett	197	1 496	126.6	48.7	34.8	6.4	128.9	2.2	0.6	27.9	0.0	64.6	5.1
Federal Way	128	661	47.7	15.3	0.9	1.3	60.9	0.0	0.0	1.2	0.0	0.0	0.0
Issaquah	72	364	30.3	9.5	2.6	2.5	3.0	0.0	0.0	0.5	0.0	0.0	0.0
Kennewick	118	652	47.6	14.7	0.1	0.4	14.1	0.0	0.0	6.0	0.2	7.5	0.0
Kent	193	1 418	126.4	37.5	1 475.2	10.0	2.1	0.1	0.0	0.8	0.0	0.9	0.0
Kirkland	176	884	70.9	22.5	3.4	4.3	1.7	0.5	0.0	0.0	0.0	0.0	0.0
Lacey	64	410	26.5	9.0	47.8	1.4	11.5	0.1	0.3	1.2	0.0	0.0	0.0
Lake Stevens	25	D	D	D	0.0	0.0	0.0	0.0	0.0	0.0	0.0	0.0	0.0
Lakewood	128	701	62.9	20.3	1.2	1.8	23.8	4.8	0.0	0.5	0.0	0.7	0.0
Longview	71	508	39.3	14.6	0.1	0.1	16.6	1.4	2.3	1.0	0.0	8.5	0.0
Lynnwood	122	956	87.5	26.8	1.0	1.9	23.4	0.0	5.7	0.0	0.0	0.0	0.0
Marysville	86	D	D	D	-0.1	0.2	1.7	0.0	0.0	0.0	0.0	0.0	0.0
Mount Vernon	60	318	21.5	6.8	12.9	0.3	9.2	0.8	0.1	1.8	0.0	4.0	0.0
Olympia	122	598	50.7	16.2	2.0	9.3	1 715.6	151.2	303.6	184.3	7.8	44.3	226.8
Pasco	67	D	D	D	1.0	5.9	15.4	2.3	3.9	0.6	0.0	3.0	0.0

1. Establishments subject to federal tax. 2. Includes program categories not shown separately. State totals include additional categories not allocated by city.

Table D. Cities — City Government Finances

City	General revenue Total (mil dol)	Intergovernmental Total (mil dol)	Percent from state government	Taxes Total (mil dol)	Taxes Per capita (dollars) Total	Property	Sales and gross receipts	General expenditure Total (mil dol)	Per capita (dollars) Total	Capital outlays
	117	118	119	120	121	122	123	124	125	126
UTAH—Cont'd										
Lehi	41.0	1.5	100.0	19.8	538	176	362	33.2	899	77
Logan	54.2	4.7	36.2	21.8	454	115	339	47.5	989	139
Midvale	19.2	1.9	61.0	12.3	443	118	325	19.6	704	42
Murray	50.4	2.2	78.6	28.8	629	195	434	63.5	1 390	90
Ogden	95.8	10.0	28.8	43.9	531	231	300	100.4	1 214	274
Orem	75.8	4.1	67.1	38.5	414	116	298	83.4	896	267
Pleasant Grove	24.1	7.0	14.4	8.7	277	82	195	39.9	1 266	776
Provo	89.8	10.7	41.7	39.5	336	109	227	88.5	752	192
Riverton	25.6	1.9	61.3	8.8	229	37	192	16.2	422	124
Roy	20.6	1.3	93.1	10.7	305	99	206	14.4	412	44
St. George	88.4	7.2	38.2	36.9	519	139	381	68.8	967	210
Salt Lake City	502.7	20.1	35.2	190.0	1 052	556	495	433.1	2 398	733
Sandy	69.5	5.6	68.3	42.1	438	138	300	58.8	613	78
South Jordan	45.1	3.6	98.8	22.1	459	187	272	35.2	733	175
Spanish Fork	26.0	2.5	36.5	9.0	316	66	250	17.5	611	32
Springville	29.1	1.2	97.0	9.5	354	85	239	19.5	726	159
Taylorsville	21.8	3.0	69.2	15.5	265	83	182	20.0	342	49
Tooele	24.8	2.0	79.9	10.7	365	124	226	19.9	676	103
West Jordan	63.5	4.2	81.6	33.4	326	116	210	61.8	603	89
West Valley City	98.6	6.4	58.8	60.1	491	220	271	103.3	844	82
VERMONT	X	X	X	X	X	X	X	X	X	X
Burlington	92.2	14.9	20.5	35.9	931	672	259	94.9	2 462	839
VIRGINIA	X	X	X	X	X	X	X	X	X	X
Alexandria	590.7	98.0	60.9	429.0	3 064	2 220	807	593.3	4 237	287
Blacksburg	32.3	8.9	53.8	13.6	329	105	216	33.8	819	262
Charlottesville	198.3	84.3	76.2	86.3	2 094	1 254	827	181.0	4 390	202
Chesapeake	905.2	384.0	94.6	418.2	1 908	1 343	565	804.0	3 669	295
Danville	163.2	83.7	91.6	47.9	1 066	577	481	153.6	3 417	124
Hampton	551.9	238.3	85.8	218.3	1 491	1 014	461	511.7	3 495	344
Harrisonburg	122.6	41.4	91.7	56.9	1 293	539	741	149.6	3 398	846
Leesburg	54.0	6.6	71.6	29.8	775	352	423	55.6	1 445	34
Lynchburg	265.4	106.2	94.0	103.9	1 457	803	654	246.1	3 452	446
Manassas	163.7	50.8	90.7	80.4	2 271	1 676	553	162.4	4 586	575
Newport News	800.5	364.4	88.0	301.9	1 685	1 162	523	724.8	4 046	330
Norfolk	1 108.7	503.7	73.4	396.5	1 682	1 005	677	1 147.4	4 867	704
Petersburg	121.9	73.7	86.0	40.3	1 227	806	410	120.5	3 663	255
Portsmouth	432.0	217.2	89.5	143.6	1 408	977	415	394.7	3 871	203
Richmond	985.7	408.8	78.4	395.9	1 978	1 311	667	977.7	4 885	281
Roanoke	415.2	193.1	88.2	166.5	1 798	1 008	790	406.2	4 387	635
Suffolk	310.6	138.5	85.4	141.0	1 733	1 324	383	298.4	3 669	416
Virginia Beach	1 696.9	649.4	83.9	844.0	1 941	1 349	568	1 578.8	3 632	489
Winchester	109.8	35.4	88.6	60.7	2 360	1 154	1 205	132.6	5 153	1 044
WASHINGTON	X	X	X	X	X	X	X	X	X	X
Auburn	88.9	6.8	58.4	44.7	898	293	536	75.6	1 518	226
Bellevue	258.2	26.9	35.4	153.2	1 263	228	921	243.3	2 005	571
Bellingham	102.9	11.9	44.5	53.9	695	169	477	114.4	1 476	389
Bothell	53.3	7.4	78.6	33.3	1 032	251	682	42.2	1 310	305
Bremerton	66.7	10.6	84.4	26.5	777	220	505	55.4	1 625	365
Burien	26.0	6.5	66.3	16.1	512	162	303	29.6	941	480
Des Moines	26.7	6.1	64.9	13.0	446	143	288	23.7	814	139
Edmonds	42.6	6.4	59.2	26.4	657	286	299	44.6	1 110	283
Everett	169.2	16.3	66.4	105.3	1 071	249	766	148.1	1 507	278
Federal Way	65.0	9.2	82.8	43.9	517	105	348	61.5	725	326
Issaquah	51.2	4.6	49.1	30.5	1 304	232	889	39.5	1 689	293
Kennewick	55.5	5.1	84.4	34.3	552	136	385	56.7	912	241
Kent	134.9	15.5	62.5	75.6	895	308	521	131.3	1 555	407
Kirkland	88.8	6.5	29.0	52.1	1 101	275	677	76.5	1 617	154
Lacey	78.0	6.2	66.0	30.7	806	194	535	43.2	1 133	220
Lake Stevens	6.2	0.5	91.4	3.4	252	81	142	6.2	458	48
Lakewood	43.6	6.5	75.4	27.4	479	96	348	38.3	669	111
Longview	47.1	5.5	48.5	22.7	618	197	401	43.1	1 176	132
Lynnwood	52.9	3.8	78.0	33.5	997	254	688	43.3	1 289	100
Marysville	49.6	4.7	69.6	18.3	543	197	286	46.0	1 369	385
Mount Vernon	37.8	3.2	77.8	19.0	620	193	375	32.0	1 043	216
Olympia	88.3	6.0	49.5	47.6	1 059	206	793	78.2	1 741	285
Pasco	52.7	10.8	33.2	25.2	478	101	359	46.8	888	363

1. Based on population estimated as of July 1 of the year shown.

City	City government finances, 2006 (cont.)									
	General expenditure (cont.)									
	Percent of total for:									
	Public welfare	Highways	Parking facilities	Education	Health and hospitals	Police protection	Sewerage and sanitation	Parks and recreation	Housing and community development	Interest on debt
	127	128	129	130	131	132	133	134	135	136
UTAH—Cont'd										
Lehi	0.0	13.3	0.0	0.0	0.0	13.6	17.0	14.9	0.0	10.3
Logan	0.0	12.9	0.0	0.0	0.0	15.3	24.8	10.7	2.1	2.8
Midvale	0.0	11.4	0.0	0.0	2.7	25.6	10.9	2.4	3.5	1.0
Murray	0.0	6.6	0.0	0.0	0.0	14.8	6.2	10.2	0.3	1.1
Ogden	0.0	4.5	0.0	0.0	0.0	14.8	9.5	6.7	28.7	2.7
Orem	0.0	16.2	0.0	0.0	0.0	13.9	19.9	5.5	1.8	3.0
Pleasant Grove	0.0	6.1	0.0	0.0	0.0	9.0	18.8	5.6	45.9	1.6
Provo	0.0	6.5	0.0	0.0	0.0	14.7	9.6	8.3	9.8	2.3
Riverton	0.0	22.6	0.0	0.0	0.0	14.4	12.6	21.5	0.7	2.3
Roy	0.0	14.7	0.0	0.0	0.0	25.6	2.9	15.8	1.6	0.3
St. George	0.0	13.7	0.0	0.0	0.0	16.6	20.3	22.4	6.0	3.1
Salt Lake City	0.0	8.3	0.0	0.0	0.2	12.2	7.1	4.9	5.5	2.8
Sandy	0.0	8.7	0.0	0.0	0.0	18.4	14.3	12.3	1.4	3.6
South Jordan	0.0	30.4	0.0	0.0	0.0	11.9	5.7	5.6	2.4	6.4
Spanish Fork	0.0	18.0	0.0	0.0	0.0	17.5	15.0	22.5	0.0	0.1
Springville	0.0	7.7	0.0	0.0	1.0	17.2	21.5	18.0	0.0	4.1
Taylorsville	0.0	19.6	0.0	0.0	0.0	29.5	2.0	4.5	0.0	1.1
Tooele	0.0	9.6	0.0	0.0	0.0	15.7	17.1	12.9	11.1	5.4
West Jordan	0.0	19.5	0.0	0.0	0.0	20.3	16.8	4.4	5.5	3.3
West Valley City	0.0	8.0	0.0	0.0	0.0	18.4	7.3	12.0	9.7	5.1
VERMONT	X	X	X	X	X	X	X	X	X	X
Burlington	0.0	4.7	3.8	0.0	0.0	7.3	5.4	4.6	5.3	6.2
VIRGINIA	X	X	X	X	X	X	X	X	X	X
Alexandria	8.0	3.5	0.4	33.9	6.3	8.9	2.6	5.5	3.8	2.2
Blacksburg	0.0	25.6	0.0	0.0	1.3	16.5	11.9	5.5	2.3	1.9
Charlottesville	10.5	3.0	0.1	35.6	6.2	6.7	4.1	2.4	2.1	1.1
Chesapeake	2.8	5.5	0.0	55.9	3.1	5.1	2.7	1.8	0.3	2.9
Danville	5.4	4.8	0.0	45.9	0.5	5.9	6.1	4.1	5.6	1.5
Hampton	5.6	0.9	0.4	45.7	0.7	5.4	4.6	7.3	5.1	3.1
Harrisonburg	1.7	6.8	0.5	51.9	0.7	4.6	7.5	3.6	1.1	3.6
Leesburg	0.0	5.7	0.2	0.0	0.0	15.9	16.0	10.6	1.1	3.6
Lynchburg	3.2	4.7	0.0	38.6	6.1	7.4	8.5	3.6	2.3	1.0
Manassas	0.2	8.0	0.0	58.5	3.5	8.2	7.0	0.8	0.8	2.1
Newport News	6.7	4.2	0.0	45.3	10.6	5.9	2.8	4.2	4.0	0.6
Norfolk	7.0	4.1	1.2	33.1	2.8	5.5	5.2	5.9	10.2	3.1
Petersburg	6.7	3.6	0.0	47.1	0.9	12.5	1.2	1.7	1.4	1.1
Portsmouth	7.0	1.5	0.2	43.6	2.8	7.0	3.7	2.8	6.4	2.9
Richmond	7.7	4.0	0.0	32.7	4.3	11.5	6.3	1.9	7.1	1.1
Roanoke	9.3	3.4	0.8	40.8	0.5	5.0	4.3	2.0	6.4	2.8
Suffolk	3.5	4.9	0.0	48.6	0.4	4.5	4.7	3.1	0.8	6.3
Virginia Beach	2.6	3.8	0.0	52.8	3.8	5.4	5.1	7.0	1.8	0.3
Winchester	5.6	3.6	0.0	49.7	0.4	4.9	5.4	1.8	3.4	3.6
WASHINGTON	X	X	X	X	X	X	X	X	X	X
Auburn	0.0	11.9	0.0	0.0	0.7	15.7	29.5	7.5	0.6	0.6
Bellevue	0.0	15.2	0.0	0.0	5.1	9.5	14.8	11.0	4.2	3.3
Bellingham	0.0	9.1	0.7	0.0	4.3	10.9	17.4	18.8	4.4	2.1
Bothell	0.0	24.2	0.0	0.0	0.0	19.6	11.4	2.5	2.1	0.9
Bremerton	0.0	9.5	0.7	0.1	3.5	23.1	13.0	21.6	3.3	4.4
Burien	0.0	33.4	0.0	0.0	0.8	36.1	1.8	7.1	2.0	0.9
Des Moines	0.0	18.0	0.0	0.0	0.3	28.3	3.2	17.7	0.9	4.5
Edmonds	0.0	12.1	0.0	0.0	2.9	15.7	11.1	9.1	0.0	3.1
Everett	0.2	8.8	0.2	0.0	4.8	14.3	10.0	8.8	1.2	4.0
Federal Way	0.3	22.9	0.0	0.0	0.9	21.3	3.2	32.5	2.0	2.3
Issaquah	0.0	16.2	0.0	0.0	0.0	11.1	11.9	16.4	3.8	3.7
Kennewick	0.0	12.5	0.0	0.0	4.9	18.3	5.0	16.9	0.8	3.4
Kent	0.2	14.8	0.0	0.0	2.1	12.3	15.8	14.4	2.3	3.3
Kirkland	0.7	9.5	0.1	0.0	0.0	13.2	17.9	9.0	0.0	1.7
Lacey	0.0	20.5	0.0	0.0	0.0	14.5	20.8	11.6	0.1	1.0
Lake Stevens	0.2	12.2	0.0	0.0	0.0	29.4	27.0	2.6	2.0	2.8
Lakewood	1.0	20.5	0.0	0.0	0.6	41.7	4.4	4.5	3.4	0.2
Longview	0.3	8.5	0.0	0.0	0.0	16.8	26.5	8.5	4.7	1.4
Lynnwood	0.0	8.1	0.2	0.0	4.9	20.7	8.2	10.4	1.4	3.1
Marysville	0.0	24.2	0.0	0.0	3.0	12.1	14.7	5.8	0.0	8.3
Mount Vernon	0.0	9.7	0.0	0.0	0.2	15.3	32.5	5.8	1.2	1.5
Olympia	0.0	9.5	0.1	0.0	2.3	12.0	23.4	13.5	1.4	0.5
Pasco	0.0	21.3	0.0	0.0	3.9	12.5	15.9	10.1	0.3	4.6

Table D. Cities — City Government Finances, City Government Employment, and Climate

City	City government finances, 2007 (cont.) Debt outstanding Total (mil dol)	Per capita[1] (dollars)	Debt issued during year	City government employment, 2010	Climate[2] Average daily temperature (degrees Fahrenheit) Mean January	July	Limits January[3]	July[4]	Annual precipitation (inches)	Heating degree days	Cooling degree days
	137	138	139	140	141	142	143	144	145	146	147
UTAH—Cont'd											
Lehi	101.3	2 745	15.8	290	NA	NA	NA	NA	NA	NA	NA
Logan	45.6	951	10.9	463	21.8	71.6	12.7	88.3	17.86	7 174	522
Midvale	5.8	207	1.6	182	30.4	78.5	22.1	90.9	26.19	5 441	1 197
Murray	46.9	1 026	19.7	611	29.2	77.0	21.3	90.6	16.50	5 631	1 066
Ogden	92.5	1 119	9.3	659	28.1	76.6	20.1	90.0	23.67	5 868	980
Orem	68.7	738	5.0	515	28.6	76.5	20.3	92.3	12.84	5 564	1 016
Pleasant Grove	43.9	1 392	32.0	NA	NA	NA	NA	NA	NA	NA	NA
Provo	117.6	1 000	10.8	713	30.9	76.9	22.5	93.4	20.13	5 264	1 028
Riverton	43.3	1 126	15.4	NA	31.6	78.0	22.0	95.3	15.76	5 251	1 172
Roy	0.3	9	0.0	185	27.6	74.2	18.6	89.9	20.75	6 142	746
St. George	118.9	1 671	0.0	680	41.8	86.3	28.9	102.8	8.77	3 103	2 471
Salt Lake City	289.0	1 600	5.5	2 959	32.0	78.1	25.4	89.0	17.75	5 095	1 190
Sandy	69.0	719	0.5	527	30.4	78.5	22.1	90.9	26.19	5 441	1 197
South Jordan	66.1	1 376	30.5	392	31.6	78.0	22.0	95.3	15.76	5 251	1 172
Spanish Fork	37.3	1 300	22.0	187	NA	NA	NA	NA	NA	NA	NA
Springville	20.1	749	3.6	212	NA	NA	NA	NA	NA	NA	NA
Taylorsville	13.3	226	10.0	116	29.2	77.0	21.3	90.6	16.50	5 631	1 066
Tooele	38.3	1 301	0.0	NA	NA	NA	NA	NA	NA	NA	NA
West Jordan	42.9	419	7.5	535	30.4	78.5	22.1	90.9	26.19	6 441	1 197
West Valley City	115.3	942	104.2	713	29.2	77.0	21.3	90.6	16.50	5 631	1 066
VERMONT	X	X	X	NA	X	X	X	X	X	X	X
Burlington	179.2	4 651	5.1	745	18.0	70.6	9.3	81.4	36.05	7 665	489
VIRGINIA	X	X	X	NA	X	X	X	X	X	X	X
Alexandria	412.7	2 947	22.8	4 877	34.9	79.2	27.3	88.3	39.35	4 055	1 531
Blacksburg	26.4	640	4.9	NA	30.9	71.1	20.6	82.6	42.63	5 559	533
Charlottesville	75.2	1 825	16.0	1 978	35.5	76.9	26.2	88.0	48.87	4 103	1 212
Chesapeake	683.1	3 117	29.4	9 548	40.1	79.1	32.3	86.8	45.74	3 368	1 612
Danville	144.2	3 207	5.0	2 358	36.6	78.8	25.8	90.0	44.98	3 970	1 418
Hampton	332.9	2 273	0.0	5 332	39.4	78.5	32.0	85.2	47.90	3 535	1 432
Harrisonburg	354.6	8 051	50.0	1 478	30.5	73.5	20.4	85.3	36.12	5 333	758
Leesburg	91.4	2 377	20.2	NA	31.5	78.2	20.8	87.1	43.21	5 031	911
Lynchburg	60.6	850	7.0	2 872	34.5	75.1	24.5	86.4	43.31	4 354	1 075
Manassas	152.5	4 307	0.0	1 446	31.7	75.7	21.9	87.4	41.80	4 925	1 075
Newport News	872.0	4 867	136.9	8 724	41.2	80.3	33.8	87.9	43.53	3 179	1 682
Norfolk	1 484.8	6 298	163.1	13 394	40.1	79.1	32.3	86.8	45.74	3 368	1 612
Petersburg	45.7	1 388	12.8	1 555	39.7	79.6	29.2	91.0	45.26	3 334	1 619
Portsmouth	343.3	3 367	83.3	4 253	40.1	79.1	32.3	86.8	45.74	3 368	1 612
Richmond	1 196.4	5 978	373.2	10 056	36.4	77.9	27.6	87.5	43.91	3 919	1 435
Roanoke	377.1	4 073	13.0	3 901	35.8	76.2	26.6	87.5	42.49	4 284	1 134
Suffolk	388.0	4 770	137.5	3 578	39.6	78.5	30.3	88.1	48.71	3 467	1 427
Virginia Beach	1 359.9	3 128	181.9	17 694	40.7	78.8	32.2	86.9	44.50	3 336	1 482
Winchester	183.3	7 124	23.7	1 388	NA	NA	NA	NA	NA	NA	NA
WASHINGTON	X	X	X	NA	X	X	X	X	X	X	X
Auburn	27.0	542	6.9	427	40.8	66.4	34.6	77.4	39.59	4 624	219
Bellevue	186.8	1 540	14.0	1 355	41.5	65.5	36.0	74.5	38.25	4 615	192
Bellingham	68.7	887	12.0	809	40.5	63.3	34.8	72.5	34.84	4 980	68
Bothell	7.9	244	0.0	287	40.8	65.2	35.2	75.0	35.96	4 756	174
Bremerton	69.9	2 051	1.4	373	40.1	64.6	34.7	75.2	53.96	4 994	158
Burien	15.3	488	9.8	NA	40.9	65.3	35.9	75.3	37.07	4 797	173
Des Moines	27.7	951	2.2	NA	40.9	65.3	35.9	75.3	37.07	4 797	173
Edmonds	34.2	853	0.8	NA	40.8	65.2	35.2	75.0	35.96	4 756	174
Everett	194.8	1 982	7.3	1 169	39.7	63.6	33.6	73.0	37.54	5 199	121
Federal Way	31.5	372	4.1	363	41.0	65.6	35.1	76.1	38.95	4 650	167
Issaquah	53.9	2 308	9.7	242	NA	NA	NA	NA	NA	NA	NA
Kennewick	61.2	985	13.8	362	34.2	75.2	28.0	89.3	8.01	4 731	909
Kent	138.6	1 641	19.8	845	40.8	66.4	34.6	77.4	39.59	4 624	219
Kirkland	31.4	664	0.3	510	40.8	65.2	35.2	75.0	35.96	4 756	174
Lacey	23.7	623	8.5	NA	38.1	62.8	31.8	76.1	50.79	5 531	97
Lake Stevens	6.6	491	1.4	NA	NA	NA	NA	NA	NA	NA	NA
Lakewood	5.5	96	3.8	NA	41.0	65.6	35.1	76.1	38.95	4 650	167
Longview	19.4	529	0.0	319	39.9	64.5	33.8	76.5	48.02	4 900	148
Lynnwood	21.6	642	0.0	NA	40.8	65.2	35.2	75.0	35.96	4 756	174
Marysville	99.3	2 956	2.6	266	39.7	63.6	33.6	73.0	37.54	5 199	121
Mount Vernon	14.9	486	1.6	222	39.9	62.3	34.1	73.0	32.70	5 197	47
Olympia	23.6	524	9.4	NA	38.1	62.8	31.8	76.1	50.79	5 531	97
Pasco	52.9	1 005	0.1	NA	34.2	75.2	28.0	89.3	8.01	4 731	909

1. Based on the population estimated as of July 1 of the year shown.   2. Represents normal values based on the 30-year period, 1971–2000.   3. Average daily minimum.   4. Average daily maximum.

Table D. Cities — **Land Area and Population**

STATE Place code	City	Land area,[1] 2010 (sq km)	Population, 2010			Race alone or in combination, not of Hispanic origin (percent), 2010					Percent Hispanic or Latino[2], 2010	Percent Foreign born, 2008–2010
			Total persons	Rank	Per square kilometer	White	Black	American Indian, Alaska Native	Asian	Hawaiian Pacific Islander		
		1	2	3	4	5	6	7	8	9	10	11
	WASHINGTON—Cont'd											
53 56625	Pullman	25.6	29 799	1 374	1 164.5	79.9	3.0	1.5	13.4	0.7	5.4	12.9
53 56695	Puyallup	36.1	37 022	1 071	1 026.4	85.0	3.3	2.5	5.8	1.2	6.9	6.1
53 57535	Redmond	42.2	54 144	700	1 283.9	64.0	2.2	0.8	27.6	0.3	7.8	28.6
53 57745	Renton	59.9	90 927	334	1 518.5	53.2	12.3	1.5	23.4	1.2	13.1	28.8
53 58235	Richland	92.5	48 058	816	519.5	85.1	1.9	1.5	5.6	0.2	7.8	7.6
53 61115	Sammamish	47.2	45 780	862	969.9	75.0	1.5	0.7	21.8	0.4	3.9	24.7
53 62288	SeaTac	26.0	26 909	1 538	1 035.8	42.9	18.2	2.4	16.5	4.1	20.3	35.9
53 63000	Seattle	217.4	608 660	25	2 799.6	70.1	9.1	1.7	16.3	0.7	6.6	16.8
53 63960	Shoreline	30.2	53 007	717	1 752.9	71.8	6.0	1.9	17.5	0.8	6.6	19.1
53 67000	Spokane	153.5	208 916	101	1 361.5	87.5	3.6	3.3	3.7	0.8	5.0	6.7
53 67167	Spokane Valley	97.8	89 755	341	917.6	91.0	2.0	2.2	2.5	0.4	4.6	4.2
53 70000	Tacoma	128.8	198 397	113	1 540.6	66.1	14.1	3.2	10.6	1.8	11.3	13.6
53 73465	University Place	21.8	31 144	1 306	1 428.0	73.8	11.2	2.1	12.2	1.5	6.7	12.7
53 74060	Vancouver	120.3	161 791	148	1 344.7	79.6	4.1	2.0	6.4	1.4	10.4	12.0
53 75775	Walla Walla	33.2	31 731	1 286	956.9	72.6	3.1	1.9	2.2	0.7	22.0	11.5
53 77105	Wenatchee	20.1	31 925	1 276	1 586.7	68.0	0.7	1.6	1.5	0.3	29.4	10.1
53 80010	Yakima	70.4	91 067	333	1 293.7	54.1	2.0	2.4	2.0	0.2	41.3	16.2
54 00000	WEST VIRGINIA	62 258.7	1 852 994	X	29.8	94.4	4.1	0.7	0.9	0.1	1.2	1.3
54 14600	Charleston	81.6	51 400	746	629.6	80.4	17.4	0.9	2.8	0.1	1.4	2.8
54 39460	Huntington	42.0	49 138	784	1 169.7	88.5	10.2	1.0	1.4	0.1	1.4	1.8
54 55756	Morgantown	26.3	29 660	1 383	1 126.0	89.6	4.9	0.5	4.0	0.1	2.6	5.2
54 62140	Parkersburg	30.6	31 492	1 295	1 028.8	96.0	3.0	0.9	0.7	0.1	1.2	1.0
54 86452	Wheeling	35.7	28 486	1 445	797.5	92.7	6.7	0.7	1.2	0.1	0.9	1.5
55 00000	WISCONSIN	140 268.1	5 686 986	X	40.5	84.6	6.8	1.3	2.6	0.1	5.9	4.6
55 02375	Appleton	63.0	72 623	467	1 152.7	86.7	2.4	1.0	6.4	0.1	5.0	5.6
55 06500	Beloit	45.0	36 966	1 073	821.6	66.4	16.9	1.0	1.6	0.1	17.1	8.5
55 10025	Brookfield	70.2	37 920	1 044	540.5	89.5	1.5	0.3	7.4	0.1	2.2	6.2
55 22300	Eau Claire	83.0	65 883	529	793.9	91.7	1.7	1.0	5.0	0.1	1.9	4.0
55 25950	Fitchburg	90.6	25 260	1 644	278.9	67.3	11.6	0.7	5.5	0.1	17.2	14.2
55 26275	Fond du Lac	48.8	43 021	912	882.5	88.8	3.2	1.0	2.0	0.1	6.4	4.4
55 27300	Franklin	89.6	35 451	1 134	395.8	84.8	5.2	0.6	6.0	0.1	4.5	7.9
55 31000	Green Bay	117.8	104 057	268	883.6	75.3	4.4	4.6	4.4	0.1	13.4	8.1
55 31175	Greenfield	29.8	36 720	1 081	1 231.8	84.7	2.8	1.1	4.4	0.1	8.4	6.6
55 37825	Janesville	87.7	63 575	555	725.0	90.4	3.4	0.6	1.7	0.1	5.4	2.9
55 39225	Kenosha	69.8	99 218	292	1 422.5	71.7	11.2	0.9	2.2	0.1	16.3	8.1
55 40775	La Crosse	53.1	51 320	750	965.8	90.3	3.1	1.0	5.4	0.1	2.0	4.6
55 48000	Madison	198.9	233 209	82	1 172.6	78.0	8.4	0.8	8.3	0.1	6.8	10.0
55 48500	Manitowoc	45.7	33 736	1 198	738.9	88.8	1.4	1.0	5.0	0.1	5.0	4.1
55 51000	Menomonee Falls	85.3	35 626	1 126	417.9	91.3	3.4	0.4	3.9	0.0	2.0	4.8
55 53000	Milwaukee	249.0	594 833	28	2 389.3	38.8	40.9	1.2	3.9	0.1	17.3	9.9
55 54875	Mount Pleasant	87.4	26 197	1 586	299.9	82.7	7.3	0.6	2.5	0.0	8.3	4.3
55 55750	Neenah	23.9	25 501	1 631	1 067.4	92.9	1.8	1.1	1.7	0.1	3.8	3.7
55 56375	New Berlin	94.4	39 584	997	419.4	92.5	1.0	0.5	4.2	0.1	2.6	5.5
55 58800	Oak Creek	73.7	34 451	1 170	467.6	84.5	3.3	1.1	5.2	0.1	7.5	8.5
55 60500	Oshkosh	66.3	66 083	527	997.0	90.2	3.6	1.1	3.6	0.1	2.7	3.7
55 66000	Racine	40.1	78 860	412	1 966.6	55.9	24.0	0.8	1.0	0.1	20.7	7.6
55 72975	Sheboygan	36.2	49 288	782	1 361.9	78.8	2.5	0.9	9.4	0.1	9.9	8.0
55 77200	Stevens Point	41.3	26 717	1 548	646.3	91.3	1.4	0.8	5.1	0.1	2.6	3.8
55 78600	Sun Prairie	31.7	29 364	1 399	927.2	85.3	7.6	0.7	4.4	0.1	4.3	5.0
55 78650	Superior	95.7	27 244	1 514	284.6	93.4	2.4	4.2	1.5	0.1	1.4	1.7
55 84250	Waukesha	64.3	70 718	481	1 100.7	81.8	3.0	0.6	4.0	0.1	12.1	5.4
55 84475	Wausau	48.6	39 106	1 013	804.2	83.6	2.1	1.3	11.8	0.1	2.9	7.6
55 84675	Wauwatosa	34.3	46 396	849	1 352.3	89.2	5.4	0.6	3.4	0.1	3.1	4.7
55 85300	West Allis	29.5	60 411	600	2 048.5	83.8	4.5	1.5	2.4	0.1	9.6	5.0
55 85350	West Bend	37.7	31 078	1 308	823.9	94.0	1.5	0.8	1.0	0.0	3.9	2.1
56 00000	WYOMING	251 470.1	563 626	X	2.2	87.3	1.1	2.8	1.1	0.2	8.9	2.9
56 13150	Casper	69.7	55 316	679	793.9	90.0	1.6	1.4	1.1	0.2	7.4	2.5
56 13900	Cheyenne	63.5	59 466	614	936.3	80.7	3.5	1.3	1.7	0.3	14.5	2.5
56 31855	Gillette	49.1	29 087	1 416	592.0	88.4	0.7	1.7	1.0	0.1	9.5	4.9
56 45050	Laramie	45.9	30 816	1 315	670.9	85.6	1.7	1.1	4.0	0.2	9.2	6.1

1. Dry land or land partially or temporarily covered by water.   2. May be of any race.

City	Age of population (percent), 2010											Population			
												Census counts		Percent change	
	Under 5 years	5 to 17 years	18 to 24 years	25 to 34 years	35 to 44 years	45 to 54 years	55 to 64 years	65 to 74 years	75 years and over	Median age	Percent female	1990	2000	1990–2000	2000–2010
	12	13	14	15	16	17	18	19	20	21	22	23	24	25	26
WASHINGTON— Cont'd															
Pullman	3.9	7.4	51.8	15.1	6.6	5.8	4.7	2.2	2.5	22.3	48.7	23 478	24 675	5.1	20.8
Puyallup	6.5	17.1	10.2	14.1	12.8	15.4	11.4	6.1	6.4	36.8	52.0	23 878	33 011	38.2	12.2
Redmond	8.1	14.7	7.4	21.7	17.1	12.4	9.2	4.7	4.8	34.1	49.1	35 800	45 256	26.4	19.6
Renton	7.8	15.4	8.7	17.6	15.9	14.0	10.4	5.5	4.6	35.2	50.5	41 688	50 052	20.1	81.7
Richland	6.3	17.9	8.1	12.8	11.9	14.9	13.5	7.8	6.8	39.4	51.0	32 315	38 708	19.8	24.2
Sammamish	7.0	25.3	4.8	8.4	19.5	18.5	10.8	3.8	1.9	37.7	49.9	NA	34 104	NA	34.2
SeaTac	7.6	15.5	10.2	17.4	14.4	14.6	10.6	5.5	4.2	34.5	47.6	22 760	25 496	12.0	5.5
Seattle	5.3	10.1	11.8	20.8	16.4	13.2	11.6	5.4	5.3	36.1	50.0	516 259	563 374	9.1	8.0
Shoreline	4.9	14.2	8.1	12.9	13.8	16.3	14.6	7.1	8.0	42.1	51.3	49 229	53 025	7.7	0.0
Spokane	6.9	15.5	12.2	15.5	12.1	13.4	11.6	6.2	6.6	35.0	51.2	177 165	195 629	10.4	6.8
Spokane Valley	6.9	17.2	9.5	13.7	12.3	14.3	12.0	7.1	7.0	37.3	51.1	NA	NA	NA	NA
Tacoma	7.0	16.0	10.8	16.1	13.5	14.2	11.1	5.7	5.6	35.1	50.6	176 664	193 556	9.6	2.5
University Place	5.9	17.8	9.1	12.1	12.1	15.6	13.3	7.5	6.5	39.4	53.0	26 724	29 933	12.0	4.0
Vancouver	7.1	16.9	9.3	15.4	13.5	13.5	11.8	6.6	5.8	35.9	51.2	62 065	143 560	131.3	12.7
Walla Walla	6.2	15.8	14.5	14.2	12.0	12.4	10.7	6.6	8.0	34.4	48.1	26 482	29 686	12.1	6.9
Wenatchee	7.8	18.3	10.0	13.6	11.6	12.6	10.7	6.7	8.4	35.2	51.1	21 746	27 856	28.1	14.6
Yakima	8.6	19.7	10.4	14.3	11.9	11.8	10.1	6.3	6.8	32.7	50.7	58 427	71 845	23.0	26.8
WEST VIRGINIA	5.6	15.3	9.1	11.9	12.8	14.9	14.3	8.8	7.2	41.3	50.7	1 793 477	1 808 344	0.8	2.5
Charleston	5.8	14.3	9.0	12.9	12.0	15.2	14.6	8.0	8.2	41.7	52.4	57 287	53 421	-6.7	-3.8
Huntington	5.5	12.5	16.7	14.8	11.0	12.1	12.1	7.5	7.8	35.4	51.4	54 844	51 475	-6.1	-4.5
Morgantown	2.7	5.5	52.1	12.4	6.0	6.4	6.9	3.8	4.3	22.6	46.5	25 879	26 809	3.6	10.6
Parkersburg	6.4	14.9	8.2	12.8	12.2	14.7	12.8	8.9	9.1	41.2	52.5	33 862	33 099	-2.3	-4.9
Wheeling	5.1	13.4	9.4	11.2	10.6	14.8	14.8	9.1	11.5	45.2	53.1	34 882	31 419	-9.9	-9.3
WISCONSIN	6.3	17.3	9.7	12.7	12.8	15.4	12.3	7.0	6.6	38.5	50.4	4 891 769	5 363 675	9.6	6.0
Appleton	6.9	18.1	10.0	14.6	13.0	15.2	10.9	5.6	5.8	35.3	50.5	65 695	70 087	6.7	3.6
Beloit	7.7	19.4	12.0	13.3	12.4	12.9	10.2	5.8	6.1	33.1	52.1	35 571	35 775	0.6	3.3
Brookfield	4.5	19.0	5.3	7.2	11.2	18.2	14.8	9.3	10.6	46.7	51.5	35 184	38 649	9.8	-1.9
Eau Claire	5.9	13.4	22.3	14.9	10.2	11.2	10.4	5.4	6.2	29.8	51.5	56 806	61 704	8.6	6.8
Fitchburg	8.0	16.5	9.5	19.5	13.5	13.7	11.6	4.6	3.0	32.9	48.4	15 648	20 501	31.0	23.2
Fond du Lac	6.7	15.9	10.1	15.1	12.3	13.6	11.6	6.4	8.3	36.9	52.3	37 755	42 203	11.8	1.9
Franklin	5.3	16.3	7.7	12.2	13.8	17.1	14.3	7.0	6.3	41.5	48.9	21 855	29 494	35.0	20.2
Green Bay	7.7	16.9	11.7	15.3	12.5	13.9	10.6	5.6	5.8	33.7	50.6	96 466	102 313	6.1	1.7
Greenfield	5.0	12.6	8.0	14.0	11.1	14.9	13.8	8.7	11.9	44.4	52.4	33 403	35 476	6.2	3.5
Janesville	6.7	18.1	8.4	14.0	13.8	14.2	10.9	7.2	6.7	37.1	51.1	52 210	59 498	14.0	6.9
Kenosha	7.6	19.2	10.9	14.4	13.8	13.8	9.4	5.3	5.6	33.5	50.9	80 426	90 352	12.3	9.8
La Crosse	5.0	11.2	26.5	14.1	9.0	11.4	9.0	5.5	7.6	29.2	52.1	51 140	51 818	1.3	-1.0
Madison	5.8	11.7	19.5	19.6	11.9	11.5	10.4	4.9	4.7	30.9	50.8	190 766	208 054	9.1	12.1
Manitowoc	6.2	16.1	8.0	12.2	11.5	15.0	12.3	8.1	10.7	41.7	51.8	32 521	34 053	4.7	-0.9
Menomonee Falls	5.7	17.3	6.0	10.5	13.0	17.5	12.1	8.1	9.8	43.3	51.8	26 840	32 647	21.6	9.1
Milwaukee	8.2	18.9	13.7	16.2	12.5	12.2	9.4	4.5	4.4	30.3	51.8	628 088	596 974	-5.0	-0.4
Mount Pleasant	5.4	15.2	6.4	10.0	12.1	16.0	15.2	9.4	10.4	45.8	52.1	NA	NA	NA	NA
Neenah	7.1	17.9	7.8	14.5	13.1	15.7	11.3	5.9	6.8	37.1	51.1	23 219	24 507	5.5	4.1
New Berlin	4.6	16.7	6.2	10.3	12.3	18.2	14.8	8.3	8.6	44.9	51.4	33 592	38 220	13.8	3.6
Oak Creek	6.5	17.1	8.2	14.9	15.0	15.9	11.4	6.0	5.0	37.4	50.9	19 513	28 456	45.8	21.1
Oshkosh	5.5	13.1	18.7	14.4	12.3	13.0	10.0	5.7	7.2	33.5	48.8	55 006	62 916	14.4	5.0
Racine	8.3	19.6	10.0	14.9	12.5	13.8	10.0	5.6	5.3	33.0	51.2	84 298	81 855	-2.9	-3.7
Sheboygan	7.5	17.8	8.8	14.5	12.7	14.0	10.7	6.4	7.5	36.2	50.5	49 587	50 792	2.4	-3.0
Stevens Point	5.0	11.0	31.2	13.5	8.8	10.2	8.3	5.0	7.0	26.5	51.2	23 002	24 551	6.7	8.8
Sun Prairie	8.5	19.3	7.4	17.5	15.4	13.3	9.7	4.6	4.3	33.3	51.5	15 352	20 369	32.7	44.2
Superior	6.5	14.8	13.4	14.9	11.2	14.0	11.9	6.5	6.9	35.4	51.0	27 134	27 368	0.9	-0.5
Waukesha	7.1	16.6	10.8	16.6	13.6	13.8	10.9	5.4	5.2	34.2	51.0	56 894	64 825	13.9	9.1
Wausau	7.3	16.2	10.0	14.5	11.5	13.5	11.3	6.6	9.2	36.8	50.9	37 060	38 426	3.7	1.8
Wauwatosa	6.3	15.6	5.9	15.8	13.0	14.6	12.2	6.0	10.6	39.8	53.4	49 366	47 271	-4.2	-1.9
West Allis	6.5	14.0	8.3	17.6	12.5	15.2	11.3	6.0	8.6	37.7	51.0	63 221	61 254	-3.1	-1.4
West Bend	7.3	17.4	7.5	15.1	13.7	13.5	10.9	6.6	8.0	37.0	51.7	24 470	28 152	15.0	10.4
WYOMING	7.1	16.9	10.0	13.8	11.9	14.8	13.0	7.0	5.4	36.8	49.0	453 589	493 782	8.9	14.1
Casper	7.2	16.7	10.1	14.7	12.0	14.5	12.0	6.1	6.8	36.0	50.3	46 765	49 644	6.2	11.4
Cheyenne	7.4	16.6	9.4	14.6	12.3	14.0	12.2	7.0	6.5	36.5	50.7	50 008	53 011	6.0	12.2
Gillette	9.2	18.8	11.0	18.1	12.5	14.9	9.7	3.4	2.4	30.6	47.7	17 545	19 646	12.0	48.1
Laramie	5.8	10.1	32.7	17.7	8.8	8.9	8.4	3.9	3.6	25.4	48.0	26 687	27 204	1.9	13.3

Table D. Cities — Households, Group Quarters, Crime, and Education

City	Households, 2010 Number	Persons per house-hold	Percent Female family house-holder[1]	One-person	Persons in group quarters, 2010 Total	Institutional Total	Persons in nursing facilities	Non-institu-tional	Serious crimes known to police,[2] 2010 Total Number	Rate[3]	Violent	Property	Educational attainment, 2008–2010 Population age 25 and older	High school graduate or less	Bachelor's degree or more
	27	28	29	30	31	32	33	34	35	36	37	38	39	40	41
WASHINGTON—Cont'd															
Pullman	11 029	2.18	4.7	34.5	5 788	18	18	5 770	655	2 198	141	2 057	10 747	14.0	63.7
Puyallup	14 950	2.43	12.8	28.5	710	443	403	267	2 642	7 136	316	6 820	23 734	40.7	22.8
Redmond	22 550	2.39	6.9	29.6	274	171	171	103	1 624	2 999	116	2 883	37 603	15.6	59.8
Renton	36 009	2.51	11.9	30.3	685	263	191	422	4 394	4 832	308	4 525	60 228	37.5	29.9
Richland	19 707	2.42	10.0	28.2	285	163	163	122	1 022	2 127	137	1 989	30 860	23.2	40.4
Sammamish	15 154	3.01	5.6	11.4	99	0	0	99	398	869	37	832	27 625	7.6	69.7
SeaTac	9 533	2.72	14.0	28.8	1 014	905	74	109	1 435	5 333	439	4 894	17 607	55.6	15.7
Seattle	283 510	2.06	7.3	41.3	24 925	4 904	2 588	20 021	36 701	6 030	577	5 452	439 334	19.2	55.8
Shoreline	21 561	2.39	10.3	29.7	1 415	581	578	834	1 513	2 854	204	2 651	37 595	26.1	43.5
Spokane	87 271	2.31	12.9	34.2	6 949	1 972	1 236	4 977	16 312	7 808	608	7 200	135 621	33.7	28.2
Spokane Valley	36 558	2.43	12.2	29.0	802	439	418	363	4 391	4 892	184	4 708	59 340	38.6	19.9
Tacoma	78 541	2.44	14.8	32.3	6 693	4 084	1 392	2 609	14 421	7 269	859	6 410	130 587	40.3	24.4
University Place	12 819	2.41	14.0	27.7	206	118	118	88	1 028	3 301	363	2 938	21 350	27.3	34.3
Vancouver	65 691	2.43	13.2	30.0	2 056	1 192	429	864	7 215	4 459	415	4 045	107 910	38.7	22.4
Walla Walla	11 537	2.43	12.0	33.4	3 651	2 600	190	1 051	1 408	4 437	369	4 069	20 690	37.3	21.9
Wenatchee	12 379	2.53	11.9	31.2	582	402	88	180	1 261	3 950	251	3 699	20 972	46.5	22.9
Yakima	33 074	2.68	15.7	28.7	2 448	1 841	650	607	6 045	6 638	538	6 100	56 384	51.9	18.2
WEST VIRGINIA	763 831	2.36	11.2	28.4	49 382	28 323	9 748	21 059	47 330	2 554	315	2 240	1 290 151	58.4	17.3
Charleston	23 453	2.11	14.1	39.4	1 940	675	220	1 265	2 547	4 955	718	4 237	37 247	39.1	37.0
Huntington	21 774	2.12	13.7	39.2	3 012	676	412	2 336	2 526	5 141	466	4 675	32 187	45.7	24.3
Morgantown	11 701	2.05	6.5	36.6	5 636	86	19	5 550	877	2 957	367	2 589	11 697	29.5	49.3
Parkersburg	13 807	2.24	14.3	35.0	547	341	326	206	1 152	3 658	673	2 985	22 652	52.4	14.9
Wheeling	12 816	2.11	12.7	40.4	1 436	523	413	913	650	2 282	355	1 927	20 873	45.8	25.6
WISCONSIN	2 279 768	2.43	10.3	28.2	150 214	74 295	33 808	75 919	156 754	2 756	249	2 508	3 773 536	43.9	25.9
Appleton	28 874	2.43	10.5	29.5	2 429	864	487	1 565	1 923	2 648	282	2 366	46 722	39.5	30.0
Beloit	13 781	2.57	18.3	29.4	1 553	242	242	1 311	1 549	4 190	408	3 782	22 170	60.0	13.5
Brookfield	14 576	2.57	5.4	21.4	513	460	460	53	1 204	3 175	79	3 096	26 910	24.0	52.1
Eau Claire	26 803	2.29	9.5	31.7	4 536	613	256	3 923	2 045	3 104	211	2 893	37 553	34.4	32.8
Fitchburg	9 955	2.45	10.5	27.3	822	815	0	7	936	3 705	337	3 369	16 414	33.2	43.5
Fond du Lac	17 942	2.28	11.1	34.4	2 087	1 481	480	606	1 261	2 931	305	2 627	28 638	48.6	17.4
Franklin	13 642	2.45	6.8	26.4	1 982	1 908	42	74	566	1 597	34	1 563	23 697	35.3	33.7
Green Bay	42 244	2.39	12.5	32.4	3 206	1 362	617	1 844	2 965	2 849	356	2 494	66 218	49.1	20.6
Greenfield	16 860	2.13	9.2	37.5	821	728	728	93	1 386	3 775	142	3 633	27 395	41.7	25.7
Janesville	25 828	2.43	12.7	28.2	930	756	309	174	2 581	4 060	267	3 792	42 154	45.8	22.7
Kenosha	37 376	2.56	15.9	28.8	3 488	1 620	736	1 868	3 238	3 264	272	2 991	61 804	46.3	21.9
La Crosse	21 428	2.18	9.7	37.7	4 681	827	540	3 854	1 887	3 677	304	3 373	29 565	39.1	26.2
Madison	102 516	2.17	8.4	36.2	10 740	2 171	1 173	8 569	8 981	3 851	403	3 448	144 177	22.4	52.0
Manitowoc	14 623	2.24	10.0	35.4	956	532	524	424	706	2 093	130	1 962	23 839	49.1	20.8
Menomonee Falls	14 567	2.43	6.9	26.8	217	202	202	15	432	1 213	36	1 176	25 169	33.5	38.0
Milwaukee	230 221	2.50	22.6	33.6	18 401	5 302	2 512	13 099	38 101	6 405	1 065	5 340	351 801	50.7	21.3
Mount Pleasant	11 136	2.33	8.5	29.2	290	268	265	22	695	2 653	141	2 512	18 895	40.6	27.4
Neenah	10 694	2.36	10.5	30.7	277	233	211	44	441	1 729	141	1 588	17 021	40.0	30.4
New Berlin	16 292	2.42	5.8	25.2	161	125	125	36	333	841	33	808	28 476	28.6	41.2
Oak Creek	14 064	2.44	8.2	28.6	125	0	0	125	1 164	3 379	116	3 263	23 063	38.2	28.8
Oshkosh	26 138	2.24	10.0	34.4	7 520	4 056	974	3 464	1 921	2 907	312	2 595	40 399	49.8	21.9
Racine	30 530	2.53	20.1	30.5	1 548	1 276	152	272	3 793	4 810	491	4 319	48 917	54.2	16.9
Sheboygan	20 308	2.38	11.7	33.4	953	766	472	187	1 469	2 980	211	2 769	32 441	52.6	17.4
Stevens Point	10 598	2.21	8.5	34.9	3 330	178	94	3 152	731	2 736	138	2 598	13 783	37.0	31.6
Sun Prairie	11 636	2.51	11.5	26.1	102	82	82	20	761	2 592	123	2 469	18 719	30.8	37.5
Superior	11 670	2.23	13.5	34.6	1 191	393	234	798	1 742	6 394	272	6 122	17 925	40.0	23.1
Waukesha	28 295	2.40	10.7	30.3	2 911	892	228	2 019	1 168	1 652	132	1 520	45 282	36.0	33.5
Wausau	16 487	2.31	11.5	35.4	1 100	820	526	280	1 289	3 296	261	3 035	26 092	46.0	23.5
Wauwatosa	20 435	2.23	8.2	34.3	871	732	615	139	1 916	4 130	164	3 966	33 166	21.3	51.3
West Allis	27 454	2.17	11.9	38.6	829	591	583	238	3 165	5 239	315	4 925	42 361	48.8	19.7
West Bend	12 769	2.39	10.0	29.2	530	429	215	101	853	2 745	119	2 626	21 526	42.4	23.1
WYOMING	226 879	2.42	8.9	28.0	13 712	6 701	2 450	7 011	14 978	2 657	196	2 462	363 880	38.6	23.7
Casper	22 794	2.38	11.2	30.3	1 125	548	483	577	2 513	4 543	195	4 348	36 249	37.5	23.2
Cheyenne	25 557	2.29	12.0	33.5	865	636	330	229	2 400	4 036	220	3 816	38 020	33.3	22.8
Gillette	10 975	2.61	10.3	24.3	422	260	123	162	922	3 170	100	3 070	17 115	41.1	19.8
Laramie	13 394	2.14	6.9	36.9	2 176	78	70	2 098	709	2 301	136	2 164	15 530	20.3	47.7

1. No spouse present.   2. Data for serious crimes have not been adjusted for underreporting. This may affect comparability between geographic areas and over time.   3. Per 100,000 population estimated by the FBI.   4. Persons 25 years old and over.

Table D. Cities — Income, Poverty, and Housing

City	Money income, 2008–2010					Housing units, 2010			Occupied Housing units 2008–2010				
	Households				Families with income below poverty (percent)				Owner-occupied			Median owner costs as a percent of income	
	Per capita income[1] (dollars)	Median income	Percent with income of $200,000 or more	Percent with income of less than $25,000		Total	Percent change, 2000–2010	Vacant units for sale or rent[2]	Total	Percent	Median value[3] (dollars)	With a mortgage[4]	Without a mortgage[5]
	42	43	44	45	46	47	48	49	50	51	52	53	54
WASHINGTON— Cont'd													
Pullman........................	17 087	25 774	2.6	49.4	14.2	11 966	27.4	937	9 490	32.1	234 200	20.4	10.0
Puyallup......................	29 234	57 550	2.3	18.0	6.5	16 171	20.8	1 221	14 814	52.7	285 400	26.0	11.4
Redmond......................	45 245	92 164	10.0	10.3	3.3	24 177	19.1	1 627	22 750	52.3	469 500	25.2	10.0
Renton	30 002	62 949	2.0	14.9	6.9	38 930	71.5	2 921	35 918	56.4	321 100	29.1	12.7
Richland	32 920	65 619	4.6	17.8	7.6	20 876	26.9	1 169	18 800	66.9	191 300	19.6	10.0
Sammamish	53 559	139 065	26.8	4.1	2.1	15 736	34.7	582	14 545	89.6	612 900	24.3	10.0
SeaTac	21 926	46 595	0.7	26.0	11.9	10 360	3.3	827	10 074	54.1	262 300	27.7	12.6
Seattle	40 894	60 619	7.5	20.5	6.1	308 516	14.0	25 006	283 013	48.3	456 600	26.5	13.2
Shoreline	32 630	66 476	4.6	17.1	4.5	22 787	6.8	1 226	21 362	68.4	372 200	29.1	13.4
Spokane	22 976	40 603	2.0	30.4	13.0	94 291	7.0	7 020	88 150	56.5	167 600	25.4	11.9
Spokane Valley	22 840	45 484	1.3	25.1	9.1	38 851	NA	2 293	37 039	62.9	186 900	25.6	11.3
Tacoma	24 850	48 367	1.9	25.7	12.6	85 786	5.9	7 245	79 254	53.1	243 900	28.9	13.5
University Place	31 724	59 892	3.8	17.3	4.8	13 573	6.8	754	12 897	56.3	316 300	25.5	13.5
Vancouver	25 058	48 075	1.6	23.4	12.0	70 005	16.6	4 314	65 086	49.5	232 200	27.3	11.2
Walla Walla	21 601	39 221	1.1	29.3	14.6	12 514	9.3	977	12 167	57.6	192 700	25.0	13.9
Wenatchee	23 792	44 380	2.0	23.4	8.6	13 175	14.6	796	12 038	58.9	215 900	25.7	10.0
Yakima	20 224	39 090	1.7	32.6	16.9	34 829	21.2	1 755	33 172	53.3	161 200	24.6	11.6
WEST VIRGINIA	21 226	38 338	1.6	33.6	12.9	881 917	4.4	118 086	742 157	74.3	95 400	19.9	10.0
Charleston	33 552	44 513	6.5	30.2	11.6	26 205	-3.2	2 752	23 626	61.6	138 500	18.9	10.0
Huntington	19 362	27 675	1.9	46.8	24.7	25 146	-3.0	3 372	21 934	52.6	81 900	22.1	11.3
Morgantown.................	18 084	25 720	2.8	49.6	8.1	12 664	7.2	963	9 500	38.7	176 700	16.7	10.0
Parkersburg.................	19 793	32 554	0.6	40.0	17.4	15 562	-3.2	1 755	13 700	62.8	88 000	19.8	11.3
Wheeling......................	21 999	34 576	1.1	35.7	14.0	14 661	-6.2	1 845	12 827	63.7	90 100	18.5	10.4
WISCONSIN..............	26 279	50 814	2.6	22.9	8.1	2 624 358	13.1	344 590	2 282 507	69.0	171 000	24.5	13.9
Appleton	25 897	50 621	2.6	21.9	8.3	30 348	9.7	1 474	29 115	69.8	138 900	23.4	13.7
Beloit	17 180	37 430	0.5	33.1	18.0	15 177	6.5	1 396	13 583	66.4	90 500	25.1	15.5
Brookfield	44 295	87 449	12.3	10.0	3.8	15 317	7.5	741	14 502	87.3	289 600	22.0	13.3
Eau Claire	22 819	41 333	1.4	33.0	9.6	28 134	13.7	1 331	26 410	56.6	139 100	22.9	13.0
Fitchburg.....................	32 836	59 849	5.5	19.7	10.9	10 668	23.2	713	9 515	51.3	271 500	24.5	10.0
Fond du Lac.................	24 087	42 065	1.7	28.0	10.4	19 181	9.2	1 239	18 031	58.2	122 300	23.0	13.2
Franklin.......................	32 531	75 740	4.9	13.9	3.4	14 356	31.0	714	12 079	78.2	243 400	22.8	14.3
Green Bay....................	22 864	41 443	1.6	27.8	10.6	45 241	4.8	2 997	42 968	59.1	131 100	23.9	13.0
Greenfield....................	27 618	48 410	1.5	22.6	3.0	17 790	9.9	930	16 441	59.9	187 400	25.3	13.3
Janesville....................	23 300	48 257	1.6	24.2	10.4	27 996	11.7	2 168	25 259	70.8	135 400	23.4	13.1
Kenosha	22 383	45 669	1.9	26.9	13.6	40 643	12.4	3 267	37 301	59.0	164 300	27.7	14.8
La Crosse	20 408	36 728	1.1	35.9	14.4	22 628	1.9	1 200	21 346	51.3	127 600	23.0	14.5
Madison	29 929	51 822	3.6	24.8	8.6	108 843	17.9	6 327	101 493	51.1	222 200	25.0	12.3
Manitowoc	25 920	42 543	2.1	27.4	8.4	15 955	6.4	1 332	15 391	67.2	110 800	22.5	13.6
Menomonee Falls.........	32 644	65 463	4.1	15.9	1.7	15 142	15.1	575	14 803	73.6	239 800	23.7	14.5
Milwaukee	18 424	34 944	0.9	36.3	22.7	255 569	2.5	25 348	228 660	45.4	139 500	28.1	17.8
Mount Pleasant	30 550	60 288	2.1	18.5	4.8	11 827	NA	691	11 164	77.0	195 800	23.5	14.6
Neenah........................	28 610	45 708	3.8	22.0	5.0	11 313	11.2	619	10 541	68.0	133 000	23.6	13.3
New Berlin...................	36 654	73 688	4.7	9.9	1.8	16 829	12.7	537	16 019	78.0	249 100	23.6	12.9
Oak Creek	30 574	68 985	2.2	14.2	3.1	14 754	24.0	690	13 377	61.9	224 400	22.7	13.3
Oshkosh	21 079	40 866	1.3	28.6	9.5	28 179	11.1	2 041	25 170	57.8	120 700	23.2	13.5
Racine.........................	19 191	37 217	1.4	33.4	16.9	33 887	1.3	3 357	30 635	57.3	129 800	25.7	16.0
Sheboygan	21 088	41 752	0.3	27.0	9.9	22 339	2.4	2 031	20 711	64.9	118 900	23.3	15.4
Stevens Point..............	20 635	36 235	1.6	36.4	8.2	11 220	15.0	622	11 026	50.5	115 300	22.0	13.5
Sun Prairie	29 497	62 425	1.9	14.0	6.1	12 413	53.0	777	11 174	63.0	216 300	25.5	15.4
Superior.......................	23 026	39 761	1.2	29.8	12.6	12 328	1.0	658	12 280	55.0	119 900	22.5	13.2
Waukesha	27 690	55 149	2.0	19.2	8.2	29 843	11.1	1 548	28 512	59.6	211 800	25.2	13.3
Wausau	22 180	40 389	1.4	27.2	10.7	18 154	8.8	1 667	16 545	59.7	114 200	22.5	13.6
Wauwatosa..................	35 584	63 521	4.6	16.1	2.0	21 520	2.9	1 085	20 137	65.4	231 400	23.0	14.0
West Allis	24 184	43 292	0.8	26.7	10.6	29 353	2.2	1 899	27 173	57.4	159 500	26.5	16.4
West Bend...................	26 632	49 458	1.8	23.7	6.3	13 546	13.7	777	13 383	63.9	183 200	25.3	16.4
WYOMING	27 760	54 297	2.6	20.3	6.7	261 868	17.0	34 989	219 945	70.6	184 700	22.1	10.0
Casper.........................	29 264	51 695	3.7	18.1	3.9	24 536	11.6	1 742	22 383	68.4	184 100	20.2	10.0
Cheyenne.....................	26 607	49 065	1.8	22.7	9.7	27 283	14.6	1 726	24 329	63.4	169 400	23.5	10.0
Gillette.........................	31 172	72 589	1.8	11.5	8.5	12 153	52.3	1 178	10 376	71.3	193 500	21.0	10.0
Laramie	21 882	36 722	1.4	36.6	7.6	14 307	19.2	913	12 749	46.1	188 600	23.3	10.7

1. Based on population estimated by the American Community Survey.   2. Includes units rented or sold but not occupied.   3. Specified owner-occupied units; $1,000,000 represents $1,000,000 or more.   4. 50.0 represents 50 percent or more.   5. 10.0 represents 10 percent or less.

Table D. Cities — Housing, Labor Force, and Employment

City	Occupied housing units, 2008–2010 (cont.)				Migration, 2008–2010		Civilian labor force, 2010				Civilian employment[4], 2008–2010			
									Unemployment			Percent		
	Percent renter occupied	Median gross rent[1]	Median rent as a percent of income[2]	Percent with no vehicle available	Percent who lived in the same house one year ago	Percent who lived outside this city one year ago	Total	Percent change, 2009–2010	Total	Rate[3]	Population age 16 and older	In labor force	Full-year full-time worker	Households with no workers (percent)
	55	56	57	58	59	60	61	62	63	64	65	66	67	68
WASHINGTON— Cont'd														
Pullman	67.9	619	47.6	8.7	60.4	21.7	14 588	3.6	962	6.6	26 519	55.9	20.6	24.5
Puyallup	47.3	984	28.5	8.0	80.3	13.3	19 436	-0.2	1 840	9.5	29 669	68.6	42.7	25.6
Redmond	47.7	1 341	22.0	6.7	75.3	13.2	32 749	5.0	2 361	7.2	42 502	72.5	51.0	15.5
Renton	43.6	1 027	28.6	5.1	78.3	14.2	52 820	38.7	4 133	7.8	70 741	74.1	50.2	19.3
Richland	33.1	813	27.8	5.3	82.8	10.9	26 716	0.3	1 689	6.3	36 397	65.7	42.6	24.9
Sammamish	10.4	1 482	26.0	0.8	90.3	5.4	24 403	9.5	1 633	6.7	31 869	70.5	49.5	9.1
SeaTac	45.9	890	33.3	8.5	82.4	13.6	14 703	1.2	1 657	11.3	21 674	66.1	43.4	23.8
Seattle	51.7	988	29.0	15.3	76.8	9.5	368 977	-1.8	31 080	8.4	520 587	72.9	45.2	20.8
Shoreline	31.6	982	29.4	6.1	86.8	9.8	28 702	-0.9	2 644	9.2	43 446	67.6	42.1	25.7
Spokane	43.5	689	32.5	9.8	78.9	8.7	104 307	-0.1	10 464	10.0	165 605	64.4	36.9	31.1
Spokane Valley	37.1	726	29.5	6.8	82.8	11.5	47 711	4.8	4 800	10.1	70 811	67.4	40.4	27.5
Tacoma	46.9	845	31.8	10.1	78.7	11.3	98 422	-1.4	10 489	10.7	158 206	64.3	40.4	27.6
University Place	43.7	876	30.1	3.7	81.6	14.2	16 873	0.2	1 297	7.7	24 956	71.2	48.9	23.5
Vancouver	50.5	837	30.0	7.4	79.1	10.5	82 673	4.2	11 874	14.4	126 473	65.6	38.4	27.1
Walla Walla	42.4	653	30.3	9.5	83.0	10.4	15 587	3.8	1 269	8.1	25 785	55.8	31.9	33.6
Wenatchee	41.1	716	27.7	8.6	84.7	9.1	17 455	1.8	1 545	8.9	25 046	62.9	40.8	32.5
Yakima	46.7	672	31.9	9.0	79.1	9.4	44 424	3.7	4 047	9.1	67 391	63.2	38.1	29.2
WEST VIRGINIA	25.7	556	29.4	8.7	87.9	9.7	801 895	0.7	68 126	8.5	1 505 886	55.1	36.3	36.1
Charleston	38.4	561	27.0	15.5	82.7	9.3	24 756	0.1	1 683	6.8	42 922	59.6	39.8	33.2
Huntington	47.4	569	36.4	17.0	78.7	10.4	21 512	-3.9	1 626	7.6	41 134	56.4	31.9	37.7
Morgantown	61.3	601	45.0	7.7	61.3	25.0	15 360	-7.7	834	5.4	27 373	52.4	22.8	33.0
Parkersburg	37.2	560	34.5	13.3	83.7	7.6	13 715	-3.2	1 386	10.1	26 030	56.2	33.7	40.6
Wheeling	36.3	518	29.7	15.2	87.1	7.2	12 673	-2.8	1 154	9.1	23 992	59.5	38.8	35.7
WISCONSIN	31.0	715	29.1	6.8	85.7	8.5	3 082 676	-0.6	260 873	8.5	4 488 361	69.1	42.9	25.1
Appleton	30.2	619	26.2	7.8	88.4	6.2	40 645	1.0	4 147	10.2	56 232	70.1	44.7	24.0
Beloit	33.6	666	36.4	9.0	82.3	8.8	17 494	1.3	2 859	16.3	28 100	65.4	32.2	34.6
Brookfield	12.7	1 282	29.7	2.8	91.4	6.2	18 694	-3.1	1 300	7.0	30 724	63.3	40.9	26.9
Eau Claire	43.4	652	33.0	6.1	73.2	11.8	38 746	1.4	2 921	7.5	53 726	72.8	38.5	23.2
Fitchburg	48.7	786	25.5	4.7	73.1	20.4	15 636	NA	1 058	6.8	19 456	72.2	47.0	16.3
Fond du Lac	41.8	634	28.5	9.9	83.9	7.9	23 103	-0.8	2 319	10.0	34 018	71.3	39.6	26.6
Franklin	21.8	883	27.4	3.5	83.6	15.5	19 233	-0.7	1 372	7.1	27 702	66.1	43.5	19.4
Green Bay	40.9	607	29.4	8.3	82.6	7.7	59 842	3.2	6 642	11.1	81 299	69.4	42.7	24.7
Greenfield	40.1	783	26.0	5.4	87.0	10.8	20 180	0.7	1 587	7.9	30 730	64.8	43.2	32.2
Janesville	29.2	731	34.0	6.1	84.1	5.9	32 858	-0.5	3 776	11.5	49 010	67.6	38.3	28.3
Kenosha	41.0	751	31.9	7.9	81.4	7.7	50 908	2.9	5 847	11.5	75 530	66.7	40.1	26.7
La Crosse	48.7	630	33.3	11.6	73.0	11.9	29 087	0.9	2 232	7.7	44 189	67.7	35.7	30.2
Madison	48.9	842	32.9	12.2	72.2	11.2	145 208	1.2	7 918	5.5	195 146	73.8	42.6	21.1
Manitowoc	32.8	549	26.4	7.0	88.4	5.3	17 916	-3.3	2 051	11.4	27 642	65.9	39.7	32.2
Menomonee Falls	26.4	862	30.6	5.3	90.6	6.6	19 217	1.9	1 365	7.1	28 406	68.5	45.5	28.0
Milwaukee	54.6	744	34.7	17.2	77.9	5.3	272 851	-1.4	32 481	11.9	449 283	66.6	38.3	27.2
Mount Pleasant	23.0	751	26.2	5.5	93.1	5.9	13 855	1.1	1 552	11.2	21 520	64.0	43.0	32.1
Neenah	32.0	610	27.0	7.2	87.3	7.2	14 833	0.7	1 535	10.3	19 619	71.4	46.9	24.2
New Berlin	22.0	1 007	25.9	3.7	89.9	7.8	22 172	2.1	1 631	7.4	31 916	68.2	44.6	24.3
Oak Creek	38.1	864	23.9	5.7	84.8	12.1	20 208	1.9	1 495	7.4	27 023	73.9	49.8	19.0
Oshkosh	42.2	594	28.5	7.7	79.5	10.2	37 246	2.9	3 054	8.2	54 315	63.3	36.7	24.9
Racine	42.7	688	34.6	12.5	84.7	5.0	38 381	-2.3	5 855	15.3	59 051	65.8	40.0	30.3
Sheboygan	35.1	606	27.1	10.1	85.4	4.8	26 780	0.0	2 977	11.1	38 500	70.7	42.8	26.4
Stevens Point	49.5	604	33.1	7.7	66.9	19.5	16 017	3.2	1 422	8.9	22 610	66.5	31.0	27.4
Sun Prairie	37.0	841	25.3	3.1	84.4	10.9	17 463	3.8	1 221	7.0	21 797	78.6	54.1	16.1
Superior	45.0	623	29.1	10.1	80.0	9.5	14 500	3.4	1 147	7.9	22 100	70.2	41.8	26.0
Waukesha	40.4	770	27.4	7.3	83.3	9.2	40 723	2.8	3 904	9.6	55 454	74.0	47.8	20.1
Wausau	40.3	602	27.7	10.2	80.6	7.2	20 313	1.6	2 498	12.3	31 754	68.4	40.8	25.4
Wauwatosa	34.6	876	27.1	7.4	86.4	8.4	24 344	2.4	1 620	6.7	37 325	68.9	47.4	25.5
West Allis	42.6	704	28.9	10.8	86.1	9.4	32 565	1.0	2 988	9.2	49 163	70.9	44.4	26.0
West Bend	36.1	754	28.7	8.7	86.4	6.9	17 293	1.8	1 949	11.3	24 333	69.5	41.0	28.2
WYOMING	29.4	692	25.5	3.6	82.1	11.3	303 215	2.1	21 220	7.0	436 097	69.8	47.1	21.5
Casper	31.6	735	28.4	4.4	81.1	8.8	30 875	3.4	1 991	6.4	43 347	70.3	47.4	21.5
Cheyenne	36.6	660	26.7	5.0	77.3	10.9	29 269	3.3	2 035	7.0	45 231	70.5	49.6	21.5
Gillette	28.7	845	22.2	3.4	80.4	10.7	17 819	-1.4	844	4.7	20 481	80.5	59.3	10.2
Laramie	53.9	681	35.3	4.9	69.6	16.9	16 848	3.3	773	4.6	28 462	66.8	36.6	22.9

1. $2,000 represents $2,000 or more.   2. 50.0 represents 50 percent or more.   3. Percent of civilian labor force.   4. Persons 16 years old and over.

City	Value of residential construction authorized by building permits, 2010			Wholesale trade,[1] 2007				Retail trade,[2] 2007			
	New construction ($1,000)	Number of housing units	Percent single family	Number of establish-ments	Number of employees	Sales (mil dol)	Annual payroll (mil dol)	Number of establish-ments	Number of employees	Sales (mil dol)	Annual payroll (mil dol)
	69	70	71	72	73	74	75	76	77	78	79
WASHINGTON—Cont'd											
Pullman	11 813	65	56.9	11	85	55.7	3.8	49	878	187.8	15.7
Puyallup	18 642	117	41.9	54	683	356.3	30.5	254	5 473	1 436.9	142.3
Redmond	36 416	155	63.2	192	3 567	6 602.3	236.5	260	4 178	916.8	108.1
Renton	70 797	335	71.0	108	4 360	2 572.5	235.1	216	4 945	1 584.9	157.7
Richland	121 405	664	51.8	22	307	365.3	11.0	154	2 145	550.7	54.8
Sammamish	56 336	153	100.0	33	52	28.2	2.3	43	512	122.8	12.9
SeaTac	4 769	35	20.0	23	204	146.8	8.9	40	351	125.1	9.2
Seattle	245 532	2 697	8.9	1 188	17 272	11 531.4	1 072.6	2 674	34 791	15 968.8	989.9
Shoreline	2 239	6	100.0	39	151	68.9	6.4	147	2 769	851.9	79.5
Spokane	41 698	215	90.7	296	3 929	1 944.3	169.6	914	14 446	3 115.8	362.5
Spokane Valley	51 987	441	25.6	230	2 936	1 774.4	129.1	475	7 990	2 121.9	210.1
Tacoma	32 994	165	86.7	204	3 168	2 055.2	159.3	779	12 385	3 064.9	331.0
University Place	7 670	29	100.0	22	219	96.6	10.1	58	860	185.0	20.1
Vancouver	17 443	192	71.4	197	2 247	2 952.5	130.4	563	10 489	2 630.6	250.1
Walla Walla	1 619	11	100.0	35	340	158.2	12.0	170	1 917	400.3	45.8
Wenatchee	8 463	47	100.0	62	976	536.6	36.5	193	2 737	655.6	67.9
Yakima	40 891	389	28.8	114	2 201	998.8	79.9	395	5 553	1 387.3	139.6
WEST VIRGINIA	345 589	2 395	75.0	1 372	16 790	11 036.5	656.0	7 047	92 227	20 538.8	1 776.5
Charleston	5 705	23	100.0	112	1 705	782.8	74.3	353	5 292	1 006.1	95.8
Huntington	4 435	38	31.6	83	1 327	477.6	55.0	236	2 896	548.1	57.2
Morgantown	28 646	291	5.5	22	201	53.3	6.1	212	3 569	743.3	63.5
Parkersburg	2 550	52	21.2	47	407	178.0	13.4	237	3 588	820.9	74.2
Wheeling	3 399	20	75.0	63	D	D	D	167	1 846	402.1	39.2
WISCONSIN	1 793 681	10 864	70.8	6 215	99 773	59 996.2	4 639.0	21 205	320 140	72 283.3	6 778.3
Appleton	17 038	78	82.1	94	1 428	486.0	60.8	290	4 596	1 008.6	97.4
Beloit	0	0	0.0	15	323	297.9	19.4	113	1 826	467.1	38.8
Brookfield	9 365	17	100.0	112	1 767	736.3	107.4	327	6 851	1 216.2	132.1
Eau Claire	14 569	125	57.6	80	1 557	818.4	59.2	363	7 046	1 334.9	130.3
Fitchburg	5 969	49	44.9	33	991	597.4	44.1	64	821	221.0	25.2
Fond du Lac	8 916	74	51.4	45	824	511.0	42.0	251	4 291	903.2	81.9
Franklin	17 557	168	14.3	40	331	212.9	19.8	75	1 831	460.1	43.1
Green Bay	27 345	225	17.3	119	2 134	1 327.7	98.1	395	6 406	1 474.6	132.6
Greenfield	2 859	17	64.7	20	75	22.4	2.9	159	3 492	858.3	83.2
Janesville	9 616	49	100.0	55	1 883	1 642.3	97.0	323	6 243	1 630.6	150.1
Kenosha	16 924	154	42.2	58	922	465.7	47.3	327	5 059	1 276.4	115.5
La Crosse	3 501	33	69.7	75	1 774	2 645.1	73.0	269	5 174	1 015.3	97.1
Madison	71 312	526	35.4	272	5 005	2 321.3	243.4	1 024	19 133	4 103.6	397.4
Manitowoc	4 885	31	67.7	23	242	170.8	10.3	169	2 578	529.4	51.2
Menomonee Falls	11 410	40	100.0	108	1 864	884.2	114.4	133	2 916	573.5	67.7
Milwaukee	87 900	693	12.0	490	9 788	5 599.5	486.5	1 447	18 937	4 001.7	410.5
Mount Pleasant	7 743	38	100.0	19	295	113.4	11.2	76	1 472	393.1	35.3
Neenah	7 864	46	100.0	26	430	199.4	21.5	93	1 603	408.8	34.1
New Berlin	11 287	27	92.6	131	2 743	1 404.6	147.4	104	2 274	515.3	56.0
Oak Creek	8 759	43	100.0	34	1 003	794.4	47.1	83	2 316	588.6	53.3
Oshkosh	9 823	122	18.0	62	1 467	600.7	54.3	277	4 853	1 021.0	96.2
Racine	4 835	76	5.3	62	637	278.0	30.1	314	4 240	710.5	70.0
Sheboygan	1 429	7	100.0	45	632	273.4	24.4	201	3 217	714.8	68.1
Stevens Point	5 647	35	68.6	31	717	380.6	18.6	147	2 708	530.4	51.1
Sun Prairie	9 016	49	87.8	29	652	271.2	28.4	68	1 376	293.3	37.8
Superior	1 848	11	100.0	40	D	D	D	123	1 959	468.0	45.4
Waukesha	7 654	38	100.0	127	2 032	1 261.0	110.1	222	4 498	1 248.1	111.8
Wausau	5 818	39	84.6	49	968	434.4	42.7	209	4 752	969.1	94.1
Wauwatosa	0	0	0.0	81	2 306	1 481.9	93.9	295	5 552	1 018.7	104.8
West Allis	439	3	100.0	107	2 026	1 003.8	104.5	276	4 827	1 386.5	116.9
West Bend	14 600	150	46.7	27	353	102.6	12.1	141	3 173	633.8	59.8
WYOMING	435 190	2 298	67.3	705	6 347	6 352.9	306.6	2 951	32 033	8 957.6	758.1
Casper	58 298	664	18.2	87	787	2 387.1	38.3	351	4 679	1 200.0	115.0
Cheyenne	39 460	238	100.0	77	691	354.6	31.0	313	5 108	1 382.7	122.5
Gillette	93 936	309	84.5	54	902	665.8	51.8	164	2 178	693.4	55.7
Laramie	15 909	122	73.8	16	118	107.5	4.3	157	1 871	444.6	36.8

1. Merchant wholesalers except manufacturers' sales branches and offices.   2. Establishments with payroll.

Table D. Cities — Real Estate, Professional Services, and Manufacturing

City	Real estate and rental and leasing, 2007				Professional, scientific, and technical services,[1] 2007				Manufacturing, 2007			
	Number of establishments	Number of employees	Receipts (mil dol)	Annual payroll (mil dol)	Number of establishments	Number of employees	Receipts (mil dol)	Annual payroll (mil dol)	Number of establishments	Number of employees	Receipts (mil dol)	Annual payroll (mil dol)
	80	81	82	83	84	85	86	87	88	89	90	91
WASHINGTON— Cont'd												
Pullman	35	185	18.2	3.2	36	144	14.7	5.5	12	D	D	D
Puyallup	113	595	87.0	15.4	117	D	D	D	41	678	148.9	28.7
Redmond	127	1 324	283.2	60.3	352	D	D	D	147	9 662	4 379.9	603.2
Renton	102	1 284	239.2	47.4	180	1 848	177.4	75.6	62	11 491	D	719.1
Richland	69	231	32.3	6.4	163	4 779	796.8	361.3	35	1 361	511.7	83.9
Sammamish	61	113	34.6	3.4	158	322	53.0	16.5	NA	NA	NA	NA
SeaTac	35	374	132.9	13.1	19	186	25.0	9.5	NA	NA	NA	NA
Seattle	1 622	10 440	2 279.7	472.8	4 328	47 828	8 836.0	3 877.4	970	28 376	7 076.2	1 226.4
Shoreline	95	340	92.2	12.9	96	311	31.2	12.0	NA	NA	NA	NA
Spokane	321	1 767	333.4	54.6	733	5 625	728.8	297.1	230	4 866	965.5	192.7
Spokane Valley	135	774	170.9	24.6	205	1 197	169.6	54.8	209	7 472	1 886.9	313.1
Tacoma	343	2 193	334.9	58.3	499	D	D	D	240	8 785	2 257.3	407.5
University Place	51	D	D	D	71	220	23.3	10.7	NA	NA	NA	NA
Vancouver	282	1 895	281.9	70.5	540	D	D	D	197	7 993	2 689.2	357.5
Walla Walla	52	155	22.1	4.4	83	D	D	D	75	884	D	41.9
Wenatchee	61	276	41.8	7.2	118	D	D	D	31	586	D	D
Yakima	153	660	110.8	17.1	217	D	D	D	111	3 122	680.1	119.1
WEST VIRGINIA	1 586	7 055	1 171.0	175.3	2 906	20 766	2 341.1	857.5	1 413	59 981	25 080.6	2 645.8
Charleston	160	806	188.2	24.0	397	3 541	515.4	164.4	39	694	D	25.5
Huntington	89	325	58.8	8.7	141	D	D	D	57	3 839	1 725.1	174.5
Morgantown	82	323	44.7	7.7	127	D	D	D	NA	NA	NA	NA
Parkersburg	54	331	52.3	8.3	93	D	D	D	33	D	D	D
Wheeling	57	D	D	D	129	D	D	D	51	908	D	30.5
WISCONSIN	5 119	27 226	4 043.5	788.9	11 255	97 445	12 797.3	4 999.0	9 659	487 573	163 563.2	21 850.3
Appleton	69	326	37.3	8.6	193	3 091	276.4	120.9	108	7 032	2 651.0	318.5
Beloit	22	98	47.0	2.8	37	148	12.7	5.6	57	3 310	1 522.9	137.7
Brookfield	110	1 064	102.3	32.5	309	3 601	579.3	225.9	72	2 033	429.7	99.4
Eau Claire	98	677	80.7	14.9	148	1 008	104.1	47.5	89	4 706	1 141.0	196.0
Fitchburg	38	240	36.6	7.8	86	815	266.7	63.8	33	3 596	1 207.8	194.1
Fond du Lac	50	215	27.1	4.2	90	1 019	73.5	56.5	76	4 365	1 535.4	205.4
Franklin	18	83	13.2	1.8	56	429	85.1	18.1	55	3 081	1 014.7	160.6
Green Bay	111	724	98.5	24.1	221	D	D	D	144	11 058	5 193.4	484.8
Greenfield	47	231	50.7	6.3	76	518	43.6	19.1	NA	NA	NA	NA
Janesville	67	269	37.9	6.0	108	D	D	D	97	8 225	10 171.3	497.5
Kenosha	97	440	57.3	8.8	119	617	60.3	25.8	123	3 838	1 584.3	190.3
La Crosse	75	452	59.4	11.3	151	D	D	D	94	4 355	1 438.6	165.8
Madison	393	3 012	436.9	100.6	934	D	D	D	207	9 145	2 418.3	450.2
Manitowoc	22	138	13.1	2.3	52	411	45.2	14.1	86	7 191	1 995.2	289.8
Menomonee Falls	34	319	44.1	17.0	111	907	100.3	42.9	187	9 018	2 070.6	420.6
Milwaukee	437	3 183	572.7	136.3	1 131	17 521	2 458.6	1 110.0	652	28 510	9 058.9	1 406.3
Mount Pleasant	29	105	13.0	2.9	54	305	32.1	15.8	33	2 626	4 040.6	180.0
Neenah	17	193	41.5	7.2	58	420	37.6	29.6	62	6 070	2 197.2	271.6
New Berlin	32	237	44.1	6.4	111	D	D	D	139	5 303	1 312.8	262.9
Oak Creek	35	429	92.4	14.6	36	258	20.9	8.0	64	6 439	2 478.6	312.6
Oshkosh	66	432	35.4	8.0	100	D	D	D	125	8 592	3 869.1	425.8
Racine	58	214	28.0	4.8	140	D	D	D	170	7 717	2 174.1	399.0
Sheboygan	39	260	61.3	10.0	85	632	146.3	34.8	97	7 776	2 059.1	323.1
Stevens Point	21	104	10.7	1.7	54	400	39.6	15.1	36	1 939	539.8	80.0
Sun Prairie	21	66	22.2	2.9	45	318	31.2	14.0	35	1 393	281.7	56.9
Superior	30	D	D	D	54	285	24.7	10.6	41	D	D	D
Waukesha	70	348	79.3	12.1	184	1 658	222.3	90.1	152	10 719	7 548.7	707.2
Wausau	46	188	24.4	4.3	131	D	D	D	73	6 401	1 579.0	238.1
Wauwatosa	49	225	86.1	8.7	267	D	D	D	46	4 017	1 286.4	322.7
West Allis	55	405	89.5	14.9	115	1 324	110.9	52.3	101	3 692	753.1	169.0
West Bend	27	127	16.1	2.3	61	320	30.4	12.0	55	2 299	522.8	93.7
WYOMING	1 121	4 651	991.6	159.7	1 890	8 711	1 079.3	387.5	596	11 904	8 834.8	573.7
Casper	135	610	158.4	23.6	231	D	D	D	43	603	135.0	25.8
Cheyenne	108	438	86.4	12.2	274	1 251	165.1	58.0	47	1 576	2 390.9	76.4
Gillette	62	341	72.1	9.7	89	498	50.8	19.5	NA	NA	NA	NA
Laramie	51	D	D	D	107	D	D	D	NA	NA	NA	NA

1. Establishments subject to federal tax.

Accommodation and Food Services, Arts, Entertainment, and Recreation, and Health Care and Social Assistance

City	Accommodation and food services, 2007				Arts, entertainment, and recreation,[1] 2007				Health care and social assistance,[1] 2007			
	Number of establishments	Number of employees	Sales (mil dol)	Annual payroll (mil dol)	Number of establishments	Number of employees	Receipts (mil dol)	Annual payroll (mil dol)	Number of establishments	Number of employees	Receipts (mil dol)	Annual payroll (mil dol)
	92	93	94	95	96	97	98	99	100	101	102	103
WASHINGTON—Cont'd												
Pullman	88	1 165	42.4	11.6	2	D	D	D	46	D	D	D
Puyallup	159	2 945	125.4	38.5	13	D	D	D	182	D	D	D
Redmond	257	4 434	306.7	88.5	22	D	D	D	169	1 580	161.4	60.4
Renton	219	3 446	229.0	60.7	17	D	D	D	211	2 103	270.6	97.3
Richland	111	1 806	83.1	25.0	10	D	D	D	199	D	D	D
Sammamish	31	532	23.9	7.8	10	177	10.6	3.1	63	413	36.5	15.3
SeaTac	80	2 817	236.4	60.4	6	D	D	D	26	915	19.0	10.7
Seattle	2 569	42 686	2 730.8	822.4	307	4 686	615.7	313.3	1 859	21 038	2 746.2	1 193.7
Shoreline	92	1 017	44.9	13.3	18	D	D	D	156	1 658	127.3	53.5
Spokane	552	10 324	477.3	145.5	56	875	50.4	13.9	703	11 330	1 154.8	510.2
Spokane Valley	215	3 525	164.7	48.1	26	506	22.7	7.4	291	4 759	313.9	139.4
Tacoma	534	7 979	380.7	114.7	44	1 890	248.9	52.0	613	8 885	938.0	427.7
University Place	34	399	17.8	5.4	4	D	D	D	73	D	D	D
Vancouver	404	7 159	326.2	97.3	40	605	29.0	8.6	444	6 682	651.1	283.8
Walla Walla	99	1 556	70.4	21.4	12	47	3.4	0.8	100	D	D	D
Wenatchee	108	1 588	77.4	22.8	9	83	2.4	0.9	121	D	D	D
Yakima	221	3 320	150.8	45.5	23	D	D	D	273	4 411	490.0	188.5
WEST VIRGINIA	3 650	61 711	2 553.3	712.8	563	8 488	1 257.9	149.7	3 741	51 790	4 338.6	1 708.4
Charleston	215	4 144	190.8	54.8	24	D	D	D	344	4 939	591.0	231.6
Huntington	171	3 145	122.0	33.6	13	215	5.2	1.7	205	D	D	D
Morgantown	160	3 183	118.2	30.1	28	205	9.6	2.8	79	D	D	D
Parkersburg	139	2 266	87.1	24.5	15	D	D	D	176	3 218	326.6	119.5
Wheeling	105	1 699	76.5	20.5	17	703	127.4	13.5	167	D	D	D
WISCONSIN	14 439	227 475	9 247.3	2 535.2	2 075	27 979	2 362.6	748.6	11 149	165 008	15 006.0	6 808.4
Appleton	203	3 949	139.1	39.9	23	298	7.2	2.9	198	3 521	423.6	197.4
Beloit	95	1 387	53.6	14.8	5	D	D	D	43	D	D	D
Brookfield	125	3 025	124.0	37.3	21	390	16.0	5.4	257	D	D	D
Eau Claire	208	4 579	157.0	46.2	24	401	21.4	4.1	186	4 609	494.7	274.0
Fitchburg	40	814	34.8	9.7	9	166	5.6	1.8	30	D	D	D
Fond du Lac	125	2 531	87.5	25.5	14	D	D	D	124	D	D	D
Franklin	51	853	33.9	9.3	4	D	D	D	70	1 009	83.6	33.3
Green Bay	274	5 245	203.7	56.7	33	D	D	D	219	6 217	839.7	317.3
Greenfield	85	D	D	D	16	D	D	D	143	D	D	D
Janesville	178	3 239	121.1	34.3	18	372	11.0	3.1	107	2 259	245.3	98.6
Kenosha	236	3 787	147.8	41.1	30	435	29.1	6.9	279	3 483	301.3	135.3
La Crosse	214	3 882	142.9	42.4	22	D	D	D	101	D	D	D
Madison	698	14 968	595.3	177.7	65	1 067	89.2	16.3	414	8 994	1 242.7	529.7
Manitowoc	94	1 783	57.4	16.5	11	89	5.2	1.5	104	D	D	D
Menomonee Falls	61	1 122	39.5	10.6	9	D	D	D	67	D	D	D
Milwaukee	1 134	20 453	949.1	265.9	75	3 629	661.7	251.0	1 313	16 744	1 439.5	768.1
Mount Pleasant	55	1 411	56.9	16.1	4	D	D	D	67	534	48.6	18.6
Neenah	79	1 219	47.3	12.3	8	48	2.9	1.0	83	1 029	136.3	69.8
New Berlin	61	1 363	48.6	13.3	17	D	D	D	76	1 031	111.5	56.2
Oak Creek	59	1 302	50.3	13.2	8	76	4.8	1.3	47	D	D	D
Oshkosh	186	3 694	125.2	35.7	18	D	D	D	146	2 253	206.8	102.0
Racine	167	D	D	D	26	221	16.8	3.7	144	2 238	214.4	119.6
Sheboygan	138	2 133	85.6	23.4	9	D	D	D	155	3 189	239.3	135.3
Stevens Point	102	1 858	61.0	16.9	10	D	D	D	71	D	D	D
Sun Prairie	52	863	27.8	8.2	5	D	D	D	48	784	75.5	27.9
Superior	112	1 840	64.9	18.3	14	D	D	D	48	940	51.5	23.0
Waukesha	149	2 686	100.2	28.1	21	260	11.5	3.1	183	2 386	236.5	116.6
Wausau	133	2 132	82.1	22.7	14	139	6.4	2.3	160	D	D	D
Wauwatosa	130	3 189	133.3	38.7	10	299	9.7	2.7	393	6 044	515.1	252.9
West Allis	168	D	D	D	20	299	21.3	4.4	189	4 352	308.9	148.8
West Bend	80	1 364	50.2	13.6	12	101	5.0	1.2	90	1 052	62.7	27.9
WYOMING	1 768	26 992	1 469.0	411.9	325	3 211	173.3	54.2	1 297	11 680	1 139.3	469.9
Casper	142	3 298	142.7	43.4	18	D	D	D	220	D	D	D
Cheyenne	154	3 278	144.0	44.2	12	D	D	D	209	2 494	213.7	94.1
Gillette	68	1 632	82.6	22.1	3	D	D	D	66	D	D	D
Laramie	94	1 500	58.7	16.8	9	62	2.2	0.6	84	D	D	D

1. Establishments subject to federal tax.

Table D. Cities — **Other Services and Federal Funds**

City	Other services[1], 2007				Selected federal funds, 2009–2010 (mil dol)								
					Procurement contracts		Grants						
	Number of establishments	Number of employees	Receipts (mil dol)	Annual payroll (mil dol)	Defense	Other	Total[2]	Medicaid and other health related	Nutrition and family welfare	Energy and environment	Disasters and emergency preparedness	Housing and community development	Employment and training
	104	105	106	107	108	109	110	111	112	113	114	115	116
WASHINGTON— Cont'd													
Pullman	26	D	D	D	2.5	1.4	120.3	35.2	0.7	10.5	0.0	0.0	0.0
Puyallup	74	715	67.5	22.6	0.2	0.7	0.6	0.0	0.0	0.0	0.0	0.0	0.0
Redmond	125	950	83.7	28.6	57.6	26.6	12.2	1.5	2.7	0.6	0.0	0.1	0.0
Renton	127	832	78.5	26.9	8.7	9.7	8.5	3.3	0.1	0.3	0.0	4.4	0.0
Richland	59	424	32.9	11.4	6.3	3 100.3	133.4	32.3	0.0	93.0	0.0	0.6	0.0
Sammamish	29	134	11.4	3.1	1.3	0.1	0.0	0.0	0.0	0.0	0.0	0.0	0.0
SeaTac	47	697	62.5	16.7	0.7	3.7	0.3	0.0	0.0	0.0	0.0	0.0	0.0
Seattle	1 382	8 585	751.4	239.8	1 044.2	482.7	3 027.0	1 803.9	47.9	151.9	0.3	164.7	20.0
Shoreline	70	386	31.4	10.0	0.2	0.1	1.8	0.0	0.0	0.5	0.0	0.0	0.0
Spokane	385	2 352	182.5	56.9	11.8	82.8	136.1	7.1	9.7	22.9	0.0	47.7	1.0
Spokane Valley	170	1 438	154.2	34.4	0.0	0.0	11.3	0.0	0.0	11.3	0.0	0.0	0.0
Tacoma	333	2 491	202.0	72.2	72.0	80.7	261.3	8.0	6.8	16.1	7.8	54.7	1.2
University Place	39	299	19.5	6.6	0.0	0.1	0.0	0.0	0.0	0.0	0.0	0.0	0.0
Vancouver	277	1 299	99.7	31.4	19.7	47.9	53.7	1.1	6.7	7.2	0.0	23.0	0.0
Walla Walla	37	D	D	D	10.0	33.9	9.0	0.4	1.0	0.0	0.0	4.8	0.0
Wenatchee	69	271	20.1	5.9	0.0	0.9	44.5	3.3	2.7	1.6	0.0	2.8	0.0
Yakima	140	900	61.7	18.6	2.8	9.3	44.0	4.1	11.5	1.4	0.0	8.7	3.7
WEST VIRGINIA	2 211	12 382	1 024.3	298.5	344.6	1 437.9	4 970.2	2 463.2	510.8	422.2	32.0	131.6	53.4
Charleston	124	1 051	53.1	17.2	11.5	28.9	1 101.6	28.7	111.2	358.6	11.1	54.9	52.2
Huntington	89	579	44.7	13.3	2.6	26.9	71.6	17.2	6.2	5.1	0.0	13.0	0.3
Morgantown	63	D	D	D	17.2	321.4	132.6	46.9	1.9	18.9	0.0	1.1	0.5
Parkersburg	76	426	28.3	8.5	8.6	22.5	11.9	0.0	0.0	0.3	0.0	8.6	0.0
Wheeling	74	673	52.9	15.3	7.4	8.0	25.0	0.9	5.2	0.1	0.0	6.2	0.0
WISCONSIN	8 822	51 066	3 865.8	1 235.7	8 469.0	1 336.1	11 992.0	6 592.2	1 312.1	655.1	56.3	460.5	210.1
Appleton	141	1 081	66.9	22.0	16.4	13.9	20.8	0.1	0.0	1.0	0.0	4.1	0.0
Beloit	45	193	11.1	3.7	11.2	4.6	7.6	0.9	0.0	0.0	0.0	4.4	0.0
Brookfield	103	1 042	104.2	28.3	1.6	1.0	2.0	2.0	0.0	0.0	0.0	0.0	0.0
Eau Claire	135	1 009	69.6	24.3	16.1	2.5	11.0	0.3	0.0	0.7	0.0	3.8	0.0
Fitchburg	29	309	15.6	5.6	0.4	0.8	0.4	0.0	0.0	0.0	0.0	0.0	0.0
Fond du Lac	94	695	48.8	14.8	3.1	0.2	8.5	0.6	1.9	0.0	0.0	3.2	0.0
Franklin	48	D	D	D	0.5	0.2	0.0	0.0	0.0	0.0	0.0	0.0	0.0
Green Bay	146	1 055	72.0	21.3	47.8	45.4	39.8	3.8	5.2	6.9	0.0	16.7	0.2
Greenfield	67	532	36.1	12.9	0.1	0.3	0.2	0.1	0.0	0.0	0.0	0.0	0.0
Janesville	105	584	39.1	12.6	193.2	5.9	13.6	0.2	3.6	0.6	0.0	4.5	1.2
Kenosha	152	1 024	60.3	20.3	62.1	1.5	25.1	1.5	2.9	0.3	0.0	15.6	0.0
La Crosse	99	672	44.9	17.9	35.1	19.9	22.9	5.7	2.7	1.6	0.0	3.3	1.5
Madison	337	2 878	242.6	78.8	151.2	128.3	2 762.3	665.3	235.3	194.2	43.3	187.9	198.6
Manitowoc	57	331	21.4	6.4	0.1	5.9	1.3	0.1	0.0	0.5	0.0	0.1	0.0
Menomonee Falls	69	482	41.0	10.9	2.8	0.3	0.0	0.0	0.0	0.0	0.0	0.0	0.0
Milwaukee	711	4 559	381.3	122.9	121.5	166.2	819.7	251.5	32.1	322.3	0.2	122.2	5.5
Mount Pleasant	35	243	17.4	5.4	0.0	0.0	0.0	0.0	0.0	0.0	0.0	0.0	0.0
Neenah	53	415	29.5	9.8	73.0	0.8	2.6	0.5	0.0	0.0	1.2	0.2	0.0
New Berlin	64	D	D	D	15.0	1.9	0.3	0.3	0.0	0.0	0.0	0.0	0.0
Oak Creek	40	D	D	D	1.3	5.8	0.0	0.0	0.0	0.0	0.0	0.0	0.0
Oshkosh	97	723	42.9	14.1	7 026.8	1.7	12.7	0.6	4.1	1.5	0.0	3.4	0.2
Racine	114	831	56.6	19.4	46.2	1.4	21.4	0.1	4.3	2.5	0.0	10.0	0.4
Sheboygan	85	526	32.5	9.6	0.6	4.3	5.5	0.0	1.1	0.0	0.0	2.2	0.0
Stevens Point	49	319	22.2	6.6	0.1	0.5	11.4	0.4	2.8	0.0	0.0	1.6	0.3
Sun Prairie	42	207	12.7	4.0	0.6	0.2	-0.1	0.0	0.0	0.0	0.0	0.0	0.0
Superior	55	D	D	D	0.5	1.4	14.2	0.0	3.7	1.7	0.0	3.6	0.0
Waukesha	130	865	82.4	23.9	88.9	26.4	41.4	0.2	2.4	26.4	0.0	9.8	0.0
Wausau	64	304	22.5	5.9	1.9	0.5	7.2	0.7	1.4	0.4	0.0	2.2	0.0
Wauwatosa	78	713	48.2	18.9	0.5	0.2	9.1	1.9	0.0	0.0	0.0	1.3	0.0
West Allis	135	745	62.0	19.1	0.4	0.3	5.7	1.8	0.0	0.5	0.0	2.8	0.0
West Bend	72	500	33.7	10.2	0.0	0.1	3.7	0.1	1.1	0.5	0.0	1.3	0.0
WYOMING	996	4 850	520.2	141.5	155.4	414.0	2 254.1	441.9	114.6	242.1	0.5	27.7	25.3
Casper	108	D	D	D	0.4	10.8	37.4	2.0	0.0	0.8	0.0	11.4	15.2
Cheyenne	87	521	39.9	13.3	32.2	49.6	372.3	29.9	21.8	180.4	0.1	10.8	9.4
Gillette	71	D	D	D	0.0	13.9	3.8	0.1	0.5	0.2	0.0	0.1	0.0
Laramie	54	D	D	D	2.5	0.1	76.9	16.9	1.6	21.9	0.0	0.1	0.0

1. Establishments subject to federal tax.   2. Includes program categories not shown separately. State totals include additional categories not allocated by city.

Table D. Cities — **City Government Finances**

City	City government finances, 2007									
	General revenue							General expenditure		
		Intergovernmental		Taxes					Per capita[1] (dollars)	
					Per capita[1] (dollars)					
	Total (mil dol)	Total (mil dol)	Percent from state government	Total (mil dol)	Total	Property	Sales and gross receipts	Total (mil dol)	Total	Capital outlays
	117	118	119	120	121	122	123	124	125	126
WASHINGTON—Cont'd										
Pullman	21.6	3.1	65.0	12.1	457	158	298	16.6	627	134
Puyallup	65.2	3.4	87.4	37.1	1 018	319	640	63.7	1 745	401
Redmond	112.1	15.1	27.5	63.3	1 281	255	877	94.2	1 906	538
Renton	116.1	10.0	78.0	65.8	1 091	393	609	108.8	1 804	346
Richland	64.3	7.2	83.8	27.5	614	238	332	55.8	1 246	272
Sammamish	38.9	1.8	92.7	30.3	859	521	209	44.7	1 268	748
SeaTac	57.8	18.1	10.3	32.7	1 272	396	838	40.5	1 574	563
Seattle	1 492.2	179.4	74.2	765.0	1 287	504	780	1 402.7	2 361	364
Shoreline	54.0	22.4	81.6	24.9	473	134	290	61.7	1 171	677
Spokane	307.2	26.2	72.4	127.3	633	261	340	264.0	1 314	317
Spokane Valley	45.9	5.3	91.7	35.5	417	112	275	33.0	389	80
Tacoma	400.5	42.9	70.6	161.9	824	271	505	395.4	2 012	564
University Place	17.8	1.6	83.0	12.0	393	114	237	23.5	773	344
Vancouver	199.1	30.0	67.7	110.8	686	216	424	160.3	993	266
Walla Walla	38.1	5.1	64.9	14.3	465	127	323	35.5	1 151	167
Wenatchee	36.9	6.9	81.3	19.2	644	163	446	32.0	1 074	240
Yakima	95.0	19.9	62.0	47.8	576	161	393	91.0	1 096	289
WEST VIRGINIA	X	X	X	X	X	X	X	X	X	X
Charleston	97.5	5.0	5.3	62.2	1 233	207	1 021	94.7	1 875	146
Huntington	60.5	5.2	31.5	24.6	501	92	410	59.6	1 217	12
Morgantown	52.1	11.4	78.0	18.7	636	118	519	48.7	1 660	241
Parkersburg	40.1	2.2	6.8	16.9	534	141	393	42.5	1 344	682
Wheeling	58.8	4.7	31.5	17.6	603	145	448	56.5	1 941	0
WISCONSIN	X	X	X	X	X	X	X	X	X	X
Appleton	98.1	31.4	70.8	36.7	524	487	30	88.5	1 264	203
Beloit	54.9	25.6	87.1	12.9	352	313	28	61.7	1 684	357
Brookfield	53.1	8.5	77.7	33.0	841	742	92	54.3	1 384	147
Eau Claire	73.7	23.6	73.2	28.5	439	388	45	75.6	1 163	217
Fitchburg	20.3	3.0	89.7	12.2	527	495	31	19.0	817	174
Fond du Lac	53.5	18.4	79.4	20.0	476	432	40	48.2	1 145	196
Franklin	37.6	5.3	84.1	24.2	691	539	151	38.5	1 100	259
Green Bay	119.0	40.5	79.3	44.2	439	410	23	120.5	1 196	194
Greenfield	31.8	5.6	88.5	17.5	485	453	32	39.3	1 088	322
Janesville	75.2	18.0	69.2	27.3	433	397	34	73.8	1 171	382
Kenosha	111.0	35.6	75.8	50.8	528	495	32	106.8	1 109	131
La Crosse	81.5	27.6	81.0	31.7	624	571	44	82.9	1 634	335
Madison	412.0	132.8	61.4	157.3	687	606	76	397.5	1 737	199
Manitowoc	47.7	14.3	85.3	12.6	381	340	36	56.6	1 713	243
Menomonee Falls	47.8	6.6	99.8	24.0	699	633	66	41.8	1 217	69
Milwaukee	871.6	390.8	80.3	246.8	410	387	23	942.6	1 565	245
Mount Pleasant	26.4	3.2	96.7	13.0	505	458	46	27.1	1 050	182
Neenah	29.8	7.7	81.3	14.5	581	549	30	35.0	1 404	291
New Berlin	42.5	4.6	97.2	20.9	536	493	42	37.9	972	61
Oak Creek	36.1	6.3	96.4	18.8	567	509	54	34.8	1 047	211
Oshkosh	88.1	26.4	81.1	29.6	458	411	42	89.0	1 378	351
Racine	130.9	55.1	81.4	44.3	549	522	26	128.3	1 628	163
Sheboygan	69.9	24.0	79.9	26.7	554	496	53	64.2	1 334	206
Stevens Point	30.3	11.4	81.4	11.5	461	410	48	27.3	1 097	196
Sun Prairie	32.2	5.2	88.2	17.8	642	580	53	44.9	1 616	661
Superior	41.6	18.5	89.5	12.1	455	368	80	39.4	1 481	283
Waukesha	83.2	18.9	77.4	43.2	646	603	40	79.8	1 195	208
Wausau	53.5	19.7	79.7	21.6	568	525	39	52.4	1 377	273
Wauwatosa	62.3	12.9	64.0	35.6	782	726	44	61.8	1 357	123
West Allis	82.9	25.4	68.8	36.2	606	568	25	77.3	1 294	208
West Bend	34.9	8.1	76.5	18.1	608	568	39	40.5	1 360	475
WYOMING	X	X	X	X	X	X	X	X	X	X
Casper	84.3	47.8	61.7	7.7	146	70	65	80.9	1 526	373
Cheyenne	88.6	39.9	59.6	11.8	211	84	118	84.5	1 518	413
Gillette	65.6	48.5	62.8	2.4	95	65	30	64.1	2 563	860
Laramie	41.0	23.4	72.3	3.9	144	64	80	36.6	1 343	219

1. Based on population estimated as of July 1 of the year shown.

City	Public welfare	Highways	Parking facilities	Education	Health and hospitals	Police protection	Sewerage and sanitation	Parks and recreation	Housing and community development	Interest on debt
				City government finances, 2006 (cont.)						
				General expenditure (cont.)						
				Percent of total for:						
	127	128	129	130	131	132	133	134	135	136
WASHINGTON—Cont'd										
Pullman	0.0	11.1	0.0	0.0	5.9	19.8	22.2	11.0	0.0	0.3
Puyallup	0.0	18.1	0.0	0.0	3.0	15.7	8.1	8.2	1.0	3.3
Redmond	0.0	16.6	0.0	0.0	6.9	8.9	13.4	9.6	1.0	2.1
Renton	0.0	19.8	0.0	0.0	0.2	11.8	20.0	11.0	1.8	2.1
Richland	0.0	17.8	0.0	0.0	3.7	11.9	12.5	9.7	6.1	4.6
Sammamish	0.0	19.8	0.0	0.0	0.0	8.2	2.1	25.8	1.7	0.4
SeaTac	0.0	33.3	0.0	0.0	0.0	16.8	2.7	7.6	3.1	2.7
Seattle	5.3	6.4	0.3	0.1	1.1	13.0	25.8	12.4	1.9	3.8
Shoreline	0.0	37.8	0.0	0.0	0.0	12.9	1.6	23.2	2.2	0.3
Spokane	0.8	12.5	0.1	0.0	0.0	12.3	33.9	5.3	1.3	3.6
Spokane Valley	0.0	15.7	0.0	0.0	0.2	42.0	3.3	8.3	3.1	1.0
Tacoma	0.8	10.0	0.3	0.0	2.4	14.3	28.0	2.2	0.9	5.5
University Place	0.0	38.9	0.9	0.0	0.6	16.1	3.9	5.0	4.0	4.1
Vancouver	0.0	20.9	0.7	0.0	0.1	14.5	10.2	15.5	2.5	3.8
Walla Walla	0.0	8.4	0.0	0.0	9.2	14.3	21.9	6.9	0.0	2.4
Wenatchee	0.0	21.5	0.0	0.0	0.5	15.8	12.3	10.3	2.6	2.9
Yakima	0.0	14.7	0.0	0.0	0.5	17.1	18.4	5.7	2.8	2.3
WEST VIRGINIA	X	X	X	X	X	X	X	X	X	X
Charleston	0.0	14.2	3.3	0.0	0.0	17.4	18.6	10.1	4.8	2.1
Huntington	1.3	1.7	1.2	0.0	0.2	17.9	19.3	6.2	6.0	4.2
Morgantown	0.0	6.0	3.2	0.0	0.0	12.0	12.9	12.0	17.2	1.0
Parkersburg	0.3	10.4	0.5	0.0	4.5	13.7	30.4	1.8	0.4	3.5
Wheeling	0.1	10.0	0.8	0.0	0.0	12.3	9.3	42.3	1.2	1.6
WISCONSIN	X	X	X	X	X	X	X	X	X	X
Appleton	1.0	21.4	2.1	0.0	1.7	17.2	15.5	5.6	2.1	7.1
Beloit	0.0	16.7	3.4	0.0	2.2	17.4	15.4	5.6	0.9	6.6
Brookfield	0.0	16.8	0.0	0.0	5.0	14.7	27.3	4.7	0.0	6.4
Eau Claire	0.0	19.6	1.1	0.0	7.1	17.5	9.2	11.6	1.5	4.7
Fitchburg	0.1	17.6	0.0	0.0	2.4	25.8	12.1	6.9	0.0	3.1
Fond du Lac	0.0	13.7	0.9	0.0	7.6	16.5	14.8	6.3	4.1	9.2
Franklin	0.0	15.5	0.0	0.0	4.7	20.0	12.8	2.6	2.4	7.5
Green Bay	0.0	16.2	1.8	0.0	0.2	18.9	17.2	8.7	0.8	8.1
Greenfield	0.0	23.7	0.0	0.0	5.5	31.6	11.9	3.2	0.3	1.4
Janesville	0.2	20.2	0.1	0.0	3.5	15.8	15.5	5.0	4.5	3.8
Kenosha	0.0	7.2	0.0	0.0	8.4	20.8	13.3	10.5	6.9	6.4
La Crosse	0.3	15.9	3.7	0.1	0.3	14.0	9.4	9.9	3.1	5.0
Madison	0.0	9.4	1.9	0.0	3.0	13.2	9.0	27.6	4.8	3.1
Manitowoc	0.1	16.7	0.0	0.0	0.7	12.5	14.7	4.9	0.2	14.7
Menomonee Falls	0.0	19.1	0.0	0.0	0.4	19.5	22.3	2.4	0.1	10.6
Milwaukee	0.0	11.4	2.2	0.0	3.8	24.3	12.9	0.5	3.6	4.5
Mount Pleasant	0.0	19.9	0.0	0.0	15.2	16.4	28.6	0.7	0.0	5.7
Neenah	0.0	16.2	1.9	0.0	1.8	14.7	11.8	7.1	0.6	9.6
New Berlin	0.0	13.0	0.0	0.0	1.8	25.4	21.8	6.7	0.0	5.5
Oak Creek	0.0	20.6	0.0	0.0	13.2	24.2	10.4	3.9	0.0	1.7
Oshkosh	0.1	19.6	0.2	0.0	2.3	13.0	10.7	15.8	0.8	10.0
Racine	0.0	14.3	0.9	0.0	5.6	23.0	13.9	7.2	2.5	7.9
Sheboygan	0.0	16.0	0.6	0.0	0.2	17.5	13.9	6.3	8.4	4.5
Stevens Point	0.0	20.5	0.0	0.0	4.4	19.1	12.3	9.5	0.0	1.9
Sun Prairie	0.0	21.7	0.0	0.0	7.8	21.7	7.8	6.4	0.0	7.4
Superior	0.0	18.7	0.0	0.0	0.2	15.9	17.8	5.1	7.7	3.8
Waukesha	0.0	15.7	1.2	0.0	0.0	18.6	14.5	6.5	0.4	6.2
Wausau	0.0	22.2	4.8	0.0	3.7	13.9	10.9	4.7	10.4	5.1
Wauwatosa	0.0	12.3	0.1	0.0	8.8	23.2	10.8	2.1	2.6	5.8
West Allis	0.0	16.6	0.0	0.0	4.6	22.7	10.4	0.6	14.0	4.0
West Bend	0.0	21.1	0.2	0.0	1.2	16.3	13.2	6.6	0.8	10.3
WYOMING	X	X	X	X	X	X	X	X	X	X
Casper	1.3	10.4	0.1	0.0	2.4	11.9	25.6	16.2	0.9	0.2
Cheyenne	1.3	20.3	0.6	0.0	2.3	13.0	18.3	12.7	1.0	3.2
Gillette	0.0	33.3	0.0	0.0	0.5	11.0	18.9	3.1	1.3	1.1
Laramie	0.0	11.8	0.0	0.0	4.7	18.3	14.6	10.1	1.2	1.9

Table D. Cities — City Government Finances, City Government Employment, and Climate

City	Total (mil dol) 137	Per capita[1] (dollars) 138	Debt issued during year 139	City government employment, 2010 140	Mean January 141	Mean July 142	Limits January[3] 143	Limits July[4] 144	Annual precipitation (inches) 145	Heating degree days 146	Cooling degree days 147
WASHINGTON—Cont'd											
Pullman	2.8	105	0.4	NA	NA	NA	NA	NA	NA	NA	NA
Puyallup	56.3	1 543	0.0	NA	39.9	64.9	32.9	77.8	40.51	4 991	153
Redmond	42.2	854	0.3	673	25.1	55.0	20.0	65.0	82.86	9 630	12
Renton	90.1	1 494	18.0	739	40.9	65.3	35.9	75.3	37.07	4 797	173
Richland	131.3	2 935	6.3	NA	33.0	73.2	26.0	87.9	7.55	5 133	739
Sammamish	11.3	320	0.0	NA	40.8	65.2	35.2	75.0	35.96	4 756	174
SeaTac	13.4	520	0.0	NA	40.9	65.3	35.9	75.3	37.07	4 797	173
Seattle	3 487.3	5 869	341.6	12 533	41.5	65.5	36.0	74.5	38.25	4 615	192
Shoreline	23.7	450	18.8	NA	40.8	65.2	35.2	75.0	35.96	4 756	174
Spokane	195.4	972	2.6	2 221	27.3	68.6	21.7	82.5	16.67	6 820	394
Spokane Valley	8.8	103	0.0	97	NA	NA	NA	NA	NA	NA	NA
Tacoma	1 281.7	6 522	174.8	3 712	41.0	65.6	35.1	76.1	38.95	4 650	167
University Place	26.4	868	6.4	NA	41.0	65.6	35.1	76.1	38.95	4 650	167
Vancouver	223.7	1 386	17.5	1 172	39.0	65.4	32.4	77.3	41.92	4 990	197
Walla Walla	56.2	1 826	0.9	289	34.7	75.3	28.8	89.9	20.88	4 882	957
Wenatchee	26.2	878	0.0	188	29.2	74.4	23.2	87.8	9.12	5 533	832
Yakima	56.5	680	0.8	703	29.1	69.1	20.5	87.2	8.26	6 104	431
WEST VIRGINIA	X	X	X	NA	X	X	X	X	X	X	X
Charleston	81.6	1 616	0.0	884	33.4	73.9	24.2	84.9	44.05	4 644	978
Huntington	53.8	1 098	3.9	379	32.1	76.3	23.5	87.1	41.74	4 737	1 128
Morgantown	29.0	987	0.0	422	30.8	73.5	22.3	83.4	43.30	5 174	815
Parkersburg	69.6	2 203	6.2	359	30.7	75.4	22.3	85.8	40.69	5 091	1 038
Wheeling	44.4	1 525	15.6	815	29.6	74.8	21.4	85.2	40.34	5 313	926
WISCONSIN	X	X	X	NA	X	X	X	X	X	X	X
Appleton	143.8	2 053	16.4	705	16.0	71.6	7.8	81.4	30.16	7 721	572
Beloit	76.3	2 083	9.5	379	19.1	72.4	11.6	82.5	35.25	6 969	664
Brookfield	100.1	2 554	6.4	316	20.0	74.3	11.5	85.1	32.09	6 886	791
Eau Claire	74.4	1 146	5.1	565	11.9	71.4	2.5	82.6	32.12	8 196	554
Fitchburg	13.5	581	0.0	165	NA	NA	NA	NA	NA	NA	NA
Fond du Lac	97.6	2 321	8.7	341	16.6	71.8	9.1	81.1	30.15	7 534	586
Franklin	46.8	1 337	10.0	217	20.7	72.0	13.4	81.1	34.81	7 087	616
Green Bay	254.8	2 528	37.9	873	15.6	69.9	7.1	81.2	29.19	7 963	463
Greenfield	15.3	422	10.0	219	19.9	73.8	12.7	81.9	33.86	6 847	764
Janesville	86.1	1 366	21.2	497	17.7	72.1	8.6	83.8	32.78	7 238	629
Kenosha	190.4	1 977	5.5	824	20.8	71.3	13.2	78.7	34.74	6 999	549
La Crosse	90.6	1 786	9.4	579	15.9	74.0	6.3	86.2	32.36	7 340	775
Madison	311.0	1 359	51.6	3 069	17.3	71.6	9.3	82.1	32.95	7 493	582
Manitowoc	167.8	5 081	10.0	441	18.7	69.9	10.8	79.6	30.49	7 563	425
Menomonee Falls	89.3	2 597	4.5	255	16.5	69.3	8.1	80.2	33.45	7 832	407
Milwaukee	1 265.3	2 101	224.5	6 693	20.0	74.3	11.5	85.1	32.09	6 886	791
Mount Pleasant	18.2	705	9.0	209	NA	NA	NA	NA	NA	NA	NA
Neenah	80.7	3 233	22.1	274	NA	NA	NA	NA	NA	NA	NA
New Berlin	46.5	1 192	6.2	257	19.9	73.8	12.7	81.9	33.86	6 847	764
Oak Creek	95.7	2 882	1.3	274	20.7	72.0	13.4	81.1	34.81	7 087	616
Oshkosh	189.3	2 931	38.4	579	16.1	72.0	7.8	81.8	31.57	7 639	591
Racine	243.1	3 085	15.4	881	20.7	71.3	13.3	78.6	35.35	7 032	567
Sheboygan	107.2	2 227	30.9	470	20.9	71.4	13.2	81.4	31.90	7 056	559
Stevens Point	14.7	591	2.5	197	NA	NA	NA	NA	NA	NA	NA
Sun Prairie	70.1	2 526	12.7	194	NA	NA	NA	NA	NA	NA	NA
Superior	57.6	2 164	1.5	275	12.1	66.6	3.4	76.2	30.78	9 006	241
Waukesha	109.4	1 638	28.6	578	19.5	73.8	11.4	84.2	34.64	6 893	784
Wausau	58.6	1 541	5.8	303	13.0	70.1	3.6	80.8	33.36	8 237	464
Wauwatosa	89.0	1 956	4.0	439	20.0	74.3	11.5	85.1	32.09	6 886	791
West Allis	77.4	1 295	13.8	571	19.9	73.8	12.7	81.9	33.86	6 847	764
West Bend	88.5	2 971	14.5	268	18.4	70.6	10.7	81.3	32.85	7 371	502
WYOMING	X	X	X	NA	X	X	X	X	X	X	X
Casper	14.8	280	5.8	583	22.3	70.0	12.2	86.8	13.03	7 571	428
Cheyenne	106.2	1 909	4.3	671	25.9	67.7	14.8	81.9	15.45	7 388	273
Gillette	18.2	727	6.3	263	NA	NA	NA	NA	NA	NA	NA
Laramie	26.3	967	0.1	311	20.3	62.9	7.8	79.4	11.19	9 233	75

1. Based on the population estimated as of July 1 of the year shown. 2. Represents normal values based on the 30-year period, 1971–2000. 3. Average daily minimum. 4. Average daily maximum.

Congressional Districts of the 112th Congress

(For explanation of symbols, see page viii)

Page

Congressional District Highlights and Rankings

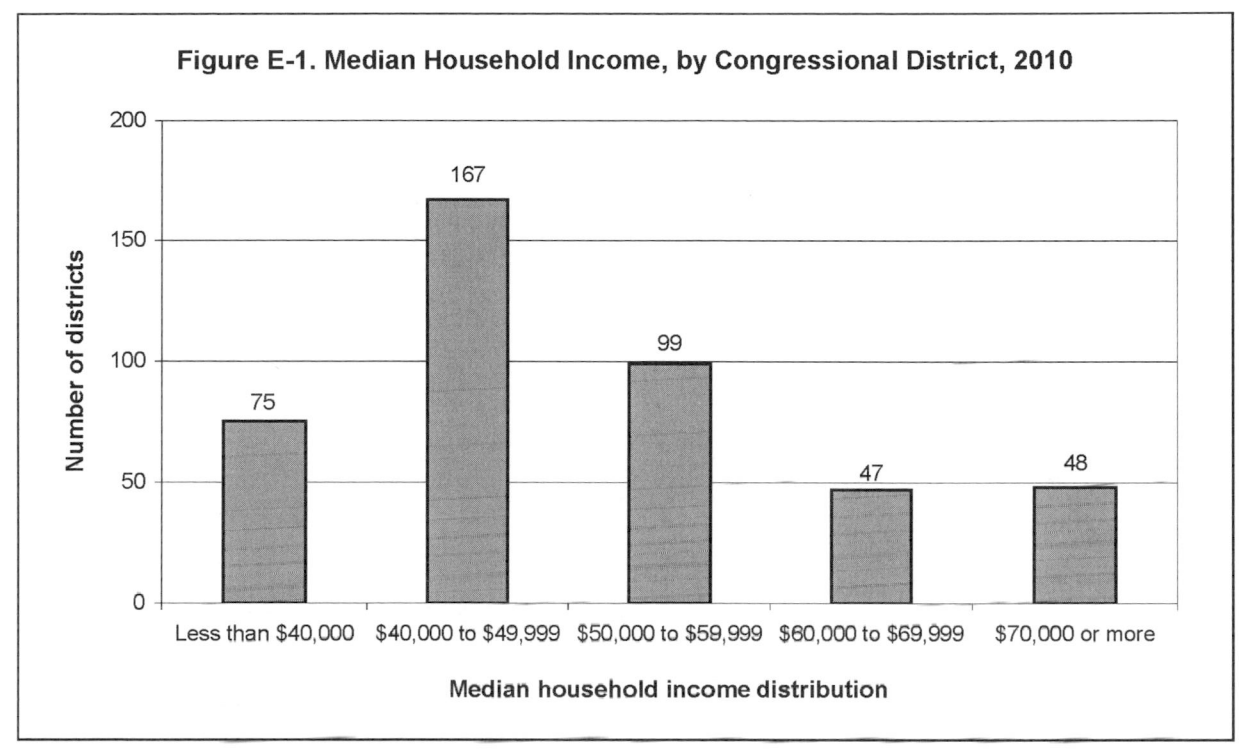

Figure E-1. Median Household Income, by Congressional District, 2010

Every 10 years, the Census Bureau conducts a count to reapportion the seats in the U.S. House of Representatives. The House's 435 seats are divided among the 50 states. (The District of Columbia has no representative in Congress, although it has a nonvoting delegate.) The seats are reapportioned according to the population measured on April 1 of the census year in order to account for population changes among the states over the previous decade. The number of districts within a state may change after each decennial census, and the districts' boundaries may change more than once during a decade. The 108th Congress was the first to reflect the new boundaries based on the 2000 census. The data in Table E are for the boundaries of the 112th Congress.

As the state with the largest population, California had the most representatives with 53. Texas (32) and New York (29) were second and third largest, respectively. There were 6 states with just 1 representative. These states' representatives were considered 'At Large,' as they represented an entire state instead of a specific congressional district within the state.

Because the number of representatives is limited to 435, states with larger population growth add seats, while states with little or no growth lose seats. After the 2000 census, 8 states gained seats. Arizona, Florida, Georgia, and Texas gained 2 seats each. Another 10 states lost 1 or more seats, with New York and Pennsylvania each losing 2 seats. These reapportioned seats reflected the population changes occurring in the United States. The population growth in states in the South and West resulted in a net gain of 5 seats, while the Northeast and the Midwest regions both lost 5 seats.

When the 113th Congress convenes in January 2013, eight states will have more representatives in congress and 10 states will have fewer. Based on the 2010 census, Texas will gain 4 seats, Florida will gain 2, while Washington, Nevada, Utah, Arizona, Georgia, and South Carolina will each gain one seat. New York and Ohio will each lose two seats, while Massachusets, New Jersey, Pennsylvania,

Michigan, Illinois, Iowa, Missouri, and Louisiana will each lose a seat.

As each decade progresses, population shifts alter the size of districts, leading up to the reapportionment of the next census. After the 2000 census, the population of each congressional district was about 645,000. Based on the 2010 census, the new congressional districts will average about 710,000 people. Nevada's 3rd district continues to be the largest congressional district in the United States with over one million people in 2010. Although the population of Louisiana's 2nd district has grown by nearly 25 percent from 2007 to 2010, it remains the least populous congressional district in the nation due to outmigration after Hurricane Katrina.

While most of the congressional districts had about the same population size, they varied widely in other characteristics. In Colorado's 6th district, 96.5 percent of the residents were high school graduates, compared with just 54.9 percent in California's 34th district and 55.7 percent in Texas's 29th district. Texas's 29th district had the lowest proportion of college graduates, with 7.1 percent of its residents holding a bachelor's degree; in New York's 14th district, 64.1 percent of residents were college graduates.

The highest unemployment rates were found in Michigan's 13th and 14th districts while Michigan's 5th district also ranked among the top five. Two districts from Illinois along with one district from California, Florida, Georgia, New York, and New Jersey also ranked among the 10 highest. Eighty congressional districts had 20 percent or more of their populations living in poverty. New York's 16th district had the highest poverty rate in the nation at 38.9 percent and the lowest median household income at $23,773 in 2010. In Virginia's 11th district, the median household income was $105,560, the highest in the nation. Twenty-nine congressional districts had median household incomes exceeding $75,000 per year, while 75 districts had median household incomes below $40,000. The U.S. median household income in 2010 was $50,046.

Congressional Districts of the 112th Congress of the United States
Selected Rankings

Population, 2010			Land area, 2010			Population density, 2010		
Popu-lation rank	State congressional district Representative	Population [col 2]	Land area rank	State congressional district Representative	Land area (square kilometers) [col 1]	Density rank	State congressional district Representative	Population density (per square kilometer) [col 3]
1	NV 3rd: Joseph J. Heck (R)	1 043 855	1	AK At-Large: Don Young (R)	1 477 953	1	NY 15th: Charles B. Rangel (D)	24 078.1
2	MT At-Large Denny Rehberg (R)	989 415	2	MT At-Large Denny Rehberg (R)	376 962	2	NY 16th: José E. Serrano (D)	22 684.1
3	TX 10th Michael T. McCaul (R)	981 367	3	NV 2nd: Mark E. Amodei (R)	271 997	3	NY 11th: Yvette D. Clarke (D)	20 301.2
4	AZ 2nd: Trent Franks (R)	972 839	4	WYAt-Large Cynthia M. Lummis (R)	251 470	4	NY 14th: Carolyn B. Maloney (D)	20 168.0
5	AZ 6th: Jeff Flake (R)	971 733	5	SD At-Large Kristi Noem (R)	196 350	5	NY 8th: Jerrold Nadler (D)	18 523.4
6	UT 3rd: Jason Chaffetz (R)	966 232	6	OR 2nd: Greg Walden (R)	179 979	6	NY 10th: Edolphus Towns (D)	14 560.8
7	FL 5th: Richard B. Nugent (R)	929 533	7	NM 2nd: Steve Pearce (R)	179 859	7	NY 12th: Nydia M. Velázquez (D)	13 960.6
8	TX 26th Michael C. Burgess (R)	915 137	8	ND-At Large Rick Berg (R)	178 711	8	NY 7th: Joseph Crowley (D)	9 792.8
9	CA 45th: Mary Bono Mack (R)	914 209	9	NE 3rd: Adrian Smith (R)	167 043	9	CA 8th: Nancy Pelosi (D)	7 234.6
10	TX 22nd Pete Olson (R)	910 877	10	AZ 1st: Paul R. Gosar (R)	151 704	10	NY 9th: Robert L. Turner (R)	6 883.7
11	UT 1st: Rob Bishop (R)	906 660	11	KS 1st: Tim Huelskamp (R)	148 582	11	NY 6th: Gregory W. Meeks (D)	6 400.6
12	GA 7th: Robert Woodall (R)	903 191	12	CO 3rd: Scott Tipton (R)	139 752	12	MA 8th: Michael E. Capuano (D)	6 264.1
13	Tx 31st John R. Carter (R)	902 101	13	TX 23rd Francisco "Quico" Canseco (R)	125 376	13	CA 31st: Xavier Becerra (D)	6 005.0
14	DE At-Large: John Carney (D)	897 934	14	NM 3rd: Ben Ray Luján (R)	122 094	14	IL 4th: Luis V. Gutierrez (D)	5 918.2
15	UT 2nd: Jim Matheson (D)	890 993	15	UT 2nd: Jim Matheson (D)	118 168	15	CA 33rd: Karen Bass (D)	5 113.5
16	VA 10th: Frank R. Wolf (R)	869 431	16	ID 2nd: Michael K. Simpson (R)	111 837	16	NJ 13th: Albio Sires (D)	4 693.6
17	FL 14th: Connie Mack (R)	858 956	17	TX 13th Mac Thornberry (R)	103 860	17	CA 35th: Maxine Waters (D)	4 632.0
18	SC 1st: Tim Scott (R)	856 956	18	ID 1st: Raul Labrador (R)	102 208	18	CA 47th: Loretta Sanchez (D)	4 437.6
19	TX 21st Lamar Smith (R)	856 954	19	TX 11th K. Michael Conaway (R)	90 614	19	IL 5th: Michael Quigley (D)	4 389.5
20	AZ 7th: Raúl M. Grijalva (D)	855 769	20	OK 3rd: Frank D. Lucas (R)	88 239	20	IL 7th: Danny K. Davis (D)	4 378.4
21	NC 9th: Sue Wilkins Myrick (R)	852 377	21	MN 7th: Collin C. Peterson (D)	82 410	21	CA 34th: Lucille Roybal-Allard (D)	4 334.3
22	TX 28th Henry Cuellar (D)	851 824	22	CO 4th: Cory Gardner (R)	79 930	22	PA 1st: Robert A. Brady (D)	4 324.9
23	TX 23rd Francisco "Quico" Canseco (R)	847 651	23	MN 8th: Chip Cravaack (R)	71 547	23	PA 2nd: Chaka Fattah (D)	4 161.0
24	TX 4th Ralph M. Hall (R)	846 142	24	ME 2nd: Michael H. Michaud (D)	70 730	24	NY 13th: Michael Grimm (R)	4 102.8
25	CA 44th: Ken Calvert (R)	844 756	25	TX 19th Randy Neugebauer (R)	65 378	25	NY 5th: Gary L. Ackerman (D)	3 921.1
26	CA 25th: Howard P. "Buck" McKeon (R)	844 320	26	MI 1st: Dan Benishek (R)	64 304	26	CA 39th: Linda T. Sánchez (D)	3 836.7
27	TX 3rd Sam Johnson (R)	842 449	27	AZ 7th: Raúl M. Grijalva (D)	59 237	27	DC At-Large Eleanor Holmes Norton (D)	3 805.6
28	FL 12th: Dennis Ross (R)	842 199	28	WA 5th: Cathy McMorris Rodgers (R)	59 212	28	NJ 10th: Vacant	3 687.9
29	ID 1st: Raul Labrador (R)	841 930	29	CA 2nd: Wally Herger (R)	56 300	29	CA 36th: Janice Hahn (D)	3 409.1
30	IL 14th: Randy Hultgren (R)	840 956	30	CA 25th: Howard P. "Buck" McKeon (R)	55 603	30	CA 37th: Laura Richardson (D)	3 374.2
31	NV 2nd: Mark E. Amodei (R)	836 562	31	UT 1st: Rob Bishop (R)	53 879	31	CA 28th: Howard L. Berman (D)	3 320.1
32	Tx 8th Kevin Brady (R)	833 770	32	OK 2nd: Dan Boren (D)	53 169	32	IL 9th: Janice D. Schakowsky (D)	3 223.3
33	TX 12th Kay Granger (R)	831 100	33	AR 4th: Mike Ross (D)	53 079	33	NY 4th: Carolyn McCarthy (D)	2 852.5
34	NC 4th: David E. Price (D)	826 878	34	AZ 2nd: Trent Franks (R)	52 376	34	NJ 8th: Steven R. Rothman (D)	2 761.9
35	SC 2nd: Joe Wilson (R)	825 324	35	WA 4th: Doc Hastings (R)	49 321	35	CA 32nd: Judy Chu (D)	2 717.0
36	GA 9th: Tom Graves (R)	823 583	36	WI 7th: Sean P. Duffy (R)	48 567	36	CA 53rd: Susan A. Davis (D)	2 697.8
37	AR 3rd: Steve Womack (R)	822 564	37	MO 8th: Jo Ann Emerson (R)	48 306	37	FL 17th: Frederica Wilson (D)	2 645.4
38	NV 1st: Shelley Berkley (D)	820 134	38	IA 5th: Steve King (R)	47 494	38	CA 40th: Edward R. Royce (R)	2 561.8
39	GA 3rd: Lynn A. Westmoreland (R)	817 247	39	OR 4th: Peter A. DeFazio (D)	44 478	39	CA 29th: Adam B. Schiff (D)	2 454.5
40	TX 25th Lloyd Doggett (D)	814 381	40	AR 1st: Eric A. "Rick" Crawford (R)	44 458	40	NJ 7th: Bill Pascrell Jr. (D)	2 392.5
41	SD At-Large Kristi Noem (R)	814 180	41	CA 4th: Tom McClintock (R)	42 502	41	CA 38th: Grace F. Napolitano (D)	2 375.5
42	FL 15th: Bill Posey (R)	813 570	42	IA 4th: Tom Latham (R)	40 818	42	IL 1st: Bobby L. Rush (D)	2 325.0
43	FL 6th: Cliff Stearns (R)	812 727	43	UT 3rd: Jason Chaffetz (R)	40 771	43	WI 4th: Gwen Moore (D)	2 307.9
44	FL 7th: John L. Mica (R)	812 442	44	MO 4th: Vicky Hartzler (R)	37 553	44	VA 8th: James P. Moran (D)	2 209.5
45	WA 8th: David G. Reichert (R)	810 754	45	KS 2nd: Lynn Jenkins (R)	36 500	45	CA 12th: Jackie Speier (D)	2 161.2
46	IN 5th: Dan Burton (R)	809 107	46	MO 9th: Blaine Luetkemeyer (R)	35 999	46	NY 17th: Eliot L. Engel (D)	2 066.5
47	TX 6th Joe Barton (R)	809 095	47	LA 5th: Rodney Alexander (R)	35 678	47	IL 3rd: Daniel Lipinski (D)	2 057.3
48	FL 25th: David Rivera (R)	807 176	48	MS 2nd: Bennie G. Thompson (D)	35 329	48	FL 21st: Mario Diaz-Balart (R)	2 020.0
49	FL 8th: Daniel Webster (R)	805 608	49	TX 28th Henry Cuellar (D)	35 258	49	WA 7th: Jim McDermott (D)	1 925.6
50	OR 1st: Suzanne Bonamici (D)	802 570	50	WI 3rd: Ron Kind (D)	35 047	50	MN 5th: Keith Ellison (D)	1 925.2
51	FL 24th: Sandy Adams (R)	799 233	51	CA 41st: Jerry Lewis (R)	34 496	51	CA 9th: Barbara Lee (D)	1 893.7
52	CO 6th: Mike Coffman (R)	797 813	52	MN 1st: Timothy J. Walz (D)	34 462	52	TX 9th Al Green (D)	1 856.3
53	FL 16th: Thomas J. Rooney (R)	797 711	53	NY 23rd: William L. Owens (D)	34 219	53	MI 13th: Hansen Clarke (D)	1 853.1
54	CA 49th: Darrell E. Issa (R)	797 428	54	MS 3rd: Gregg Harper (R)	34 127	54	CA 5th: Doris O. Matsui (D)	1 843.4
55	CA 41st: Jerry Lewis (R)	797 133	55	MO 6th: Sam Graves (R)	33 674	55	NV 1st: Shelley Berkley (D)	1 789.4
56	CA 22nd: Kevin McCarthy (R)	797 084	56	NE 1st: Jeff Fortenberry (R)	30 874	56	CA 27th: Brad Sherman (D)	1 754.4
57	CA 11th: Jerry McNerney (D)	796 753	57	KY 1st: Ed Whitfield (R)	30 034	57	MI 14th: John Conyers Jr. (D)	1 742.6
58	GA 11th: Phil Gingrey (R)	794 969	58	IL 19th: John Shimkus (R)	29 794	58	FL 20th: Debbie Wasserman Schultz (D)	1 652.2
59	TN 7th Marsha Blackburn (R)	792 605	59	MS 1st: Alan Nunnelee (R)	29 573	59	TX 32nd Pete Sessions (R)	1 560.4
60	TX 24th Kenny Marchant (R)	792 319	60	GA 1st: Jack Kingston (R)	29 068	60	OH 11th: Marcia L. Fudge (D)	1 551.5
61	VA 11th: Gerald E. Connolly (D)	792 095	61	PA 5th: Glenn Thompson (R)	28 554	61	MI 12th: Sander M. Levin (D)	1 534.8
62	IN 4th: Todd Rokita (R)	789 835	62	CA 1st: Mike Thompson (D)	28 464	62	TX 7th John Abney Culberson (R)	1 534.3
63	TN 6th Diane Black (R)	788 754	63	GA 2nd: Sanford D. Bishop Jr. (D)	28 006	63	TX 20th Charles A. Gonzalez (D)	1 497.9
64	MS 1st: Alan Nunnelee (R)	788 095	64	LA 4th: John Fleming (R)	27 842	64	CO 1st: Diana DeGette (D)	1 495.4
65	TX 15th Rubén Hinojosa (D)	787 124	65	TX 15th Rubén Hinojosa (D)	27 763	65	CA 43rd: Joe Baca (D)	1 487.6
66	VA 1st: Robert J. Wittman (R)	786 237	66	KY 5th: Harold Rogers (R)	27 547	66	MA 7th: Edward J. Markey (D)	1 479.5
67	OK 4th:Tom Cole (R)	785 424	67	AL 2nd: Martha Roby (R)	27 153	67	FL 10th: C. W. Bill Young (R)	1 436.4
68	GA 13th: David Scott (D)	784 445	68	CA 22nd: Kevin McCarthy (R)	26 945	68	PA 14th: Michael F. Doyle (D)	1 395.1
69	CA 21st: Devin Nunes (R)	784 176	69	OK 4th:Tom Cole (R)	26 409	69	NY 3rd: Peter T. King (R)	1 374.7
70	CA 3rd: Daniel E. Lungren (R)	783 317	70	IL 15th: Timothy V. Johnson (R)	26 084	70	AZ 4th: Ed Pastor (D)	1 354.9
71	TX 2nd Ted Poe (R)	782 375	71	TN 4th Scott DesJarlais (R)	25 998	71	HI 1st: Colleen Hanabusa (D)	1 328.9
72	TX 7th John Abney Culberson (R)	780 611	72	WI 8th: Reid Ribble (R)	25 146	72	CA 48th: John Campbell (R)	1 328.1
73	TX 14th Ron Paul (R)	779 704	73	KS 4th: Mike Pompeo (R)	24 670	73	NJ 1st: Frank Pallone Jr. (D)	1 319.4
74	WA 3rd: Jaime Herrera Beutler (R)	779 348	74	TX 4th Ralph M. Hall (R)	24 474	74	IL 2nd: Jesse L. Jackson Jr. (D)	1 258.4
75	WA 4th: Doc Hastings (R)	774 409	75	FL 2nd: Steve Southerland II (R)	24 404	75	TX 18th Sheila Jackson-Lee (D)	1 233.2

Congressional Districts of the 112th Congress of the United States
Selected Rankings

Percent Non-Hispanic White alone, 2010			Percent Black alone, 2010			Percent American Indian, Alaska Native alone, 2010		
Non-Hispanic White alone rank	State congressional district Representative	Percent white [col 11]	Black rank	State congressional district Representative	Percent black [col 5]	American indian Alaska Native rank	State congressional district Representative	Percent American Indian Alaska Native [col 6]
1	KY 5th: Harold Rogers (R)	96.3	1	IL 2nd: Jesse L. Jackson Jr. (D)	69.3	1	AZ 1st: Paul R. Gosar (R)	19.9
2	OH 18th: Bob Gibbs (R)	94.9	2	MS 2nd: Bennie G. Thompson (D)	66.5	2	OK 2nd: Dan Boren (D)	18.8
3	ME 2nd: Michael H. Michaud (D)	94.7	3	TN 9th Steve Cohen (D)	63.5	3	NM 3rd: Ben Ray Luján (D)	18.3
4	WV 1st : David McKinley (R)	94.5	4	AL 7th: Terri A. Sewell (D)	62.8	4	AK At-Large: Don Young (R)	14.8
5	PA 9th: Bill Shuster (R)	94.4	5	IL 1st: Bobby L. Rush (D)	62.6	5	SD At-Large Kristi Noem (R)	8.8
6	VT At-large Peter Welch (D)	94.3	6	NY 10th: Edolphus Towns (D)	62.1	6	NC 7th: Mike McIntyre (D)	8.0
7	ME 1st: Chellie Pingree (D)	94.1	7	OH 11th: Marcia L. Fudge (D)	59.8	7	OK 1st: John Sullivan (R)	6.9
7	OH 6th: Bill Johnson (R)	94.1	8	MI 14th: John Conyers Jr. (D)	59.2	8	OK 3rd: Frank D. Lucas (R)	6.6
9	PA 5th: Glenn Thompson (R)	94.0	9	MI 13th: Hansen Clarke (D)	59.0	9	MT At-Large Denny Rehberg (R)	6.3
10	WI 3rd: Ron Kind (D)	93.8	10	L:A 2nd: Cedric Richmond (D)	58.8	10	OK 4th:Tom Cole (R)	6.2
11	WV 3rd: Nick J. Rahall II (D)	93.4	11	FL 17th: Frederica Wilson (D)	58.5	11	AZ 7th: Raúl M. Grijalva (D)	5.6
12	PA 12th: Mark Critz (D)	93.1	12	NJ 10th: Vacant	57.5	11	NM 2nd: Steve Pearce (R)	5.6
13	MN 8th: Chip Cravaack (R)	92.9	13	PA 2nd: Chaka Fattah (D)	57.3	13	ND-At Large Rick Berg (R)	5.4
13	PA 10th: Tom Marino (R)	92.9	14	GA 13th: David Scott (D)	56.8	14	OK 5th: James Lankford (R)	4.8
13	WI 7th: Sean P. Duffy (R)	92.9	15	MD 4th: Donna F. Edwards (D)	56.6	15	NM 1st: Martin Heinrich (D)	4.2
16	PA 18th: Tim Murphy (R)	92.8	16	MD 7th: Elijah E. Cummings (D)	56.2	16	AZ 4th: Ed Pastor (D)	3.2
17	MI 1st: Dan Benishek (R)	92.5	17	GA 4th: Henry C. "Hank" Johnson Jr. (D)	56.1	17	WI 8th: Reid Ribble (R)	3.1
18	KY 4th: Geoff Davis (R)	92.4	17	NY 11th: Yvette D. Clarke (D)	56.1	18	AZ 5th: David Schweikert (R)	2.9
18	TN 1st David P. Roe (R)	92.4	19	FL 23rd: Alcee L. Hastings (D)	55.9	18	CA 1st: Mike Thompson (D)	2.9
20	IL 19th: John Shimkus (R)	92.3	20	MO 1st: William Lacy Clay (D)	55.6	20	MI 1st: Dan Benishek (R)	2.8
20	NH 1st: Frank Guinta (R)	92.3	21	VA 3rd: Robert C. "Bobby" Scott (D)	55.3	20	MN 7th: Collin C. Peterson (D)	2.8
20	NH 2nd: Charles Bass (R)	92.3	22	SC 6th: James E. Clyburn (D)	54.2	22	MN 8th: Chip Cravaack (R)	2.7
20	PA 4th: Jason Altmire (D)	92.3	23	FL 3rd: Corrine Brown (D)	52.2	23	WA 5th: Cathy McMorris Rodgers (R)	2.4
24	VA 9th: Morgan Griffith (R)	92.0	24	NY 6th: Gregory W. Meeks (D)	51.8	23	WA 6th: Norman D. Dicks (D)	2.4
25	NY 23rd: William L. Owens (D)	91.7	25	IL 7th: Danny K. Davis (D)	51.1	23	WYAt-Large Cynthia M. Lummis (R)	2.4
26	OH 5th: Robert E. Latta (R)	91.6	26	DC At-Large Eleanor Holmes Norton (D)	50.7	26	CA 2nd: Wally Herger (R)	2.2
26	PA 3rd: Mike Kelly (R)	91.6	27	GA 5th: John Lewis (D)	50.3	26	NV 2nd: Mark E. Amodei (R)	2.2
26	WV 2nd: Shelley Moore Capito (R)	91.6	28	NC 1st: G. K. Butterfield (D)	49.6	26	OR 2nd: Greg Walden (R)	2.2
29	IA 4th: Tom Latham (R)	91.5	29	GA 2nd: Sanford D. Bishop Jr. (D)	48.4	29	CO 3rd: Scott Tipton (R)	2.1
29	NY 20th: Christopher P. Gibson (R)	91.5	30	PA 1st: Robert A. Brady (D)	48.1	29	UT 2nd: Jim Matheson (D)	2.1
31	IN 8th: Larry Bucshon (R)	91.3	31	NC 12th: Melvin L. Watt (D)	43.9	29	WA 2nd: Rick Larsen (D)	2.1
32	IN 6th: Mike Pence (R)	91.2	32	GA 12th: John Barrow (D)	43.3	29	WA 4th: Doc Hastings (R)	2.1
33	IN 9th: Todd Young (R)	91.1	33	TX 30th Eddie Bernice Johnson (D)	41.5	33	AZ 2nd: Trent Franks (R)	2.0
33	TN 4th Scott DesJarlais (R)	91.1	34	MD 5th: Steny H. Hoyer (D)	37.3	34	LA 3rd: Jeff Landry (R)	1.9
33	WI 6th: Thomas E. Petri (R)	91.1	35	TX 18th Sheila Jackson-Lee (D)	36.8	34	NC 8th: Larry Kissell (D)	1.9
36	MI 4th: Dave Camp (R)	91.0	36	NY 16th: José E. Serrano (D)	35.9	36	CA 20th: Jim Costa (D)	1.7
37	MO 8th: Jo Ann Emerson (R)	90.9	36	WI 4th: Gwen Moore (D)	35.9	36	NY 16th: José E. Serrano (D)	1.7
38	OH 14th: Steven C. LaTourette (R)	90.8	38	TX 9th Al Green (D)	35.8	38	AZ 3rd: Ben Quayle (R)	1.6
38	OH 16th: Jim Renacci (R)	90.8	39	LA 6th: Bill Cassidy (R)	35.0	38	CA 19th: Jeff Denham (R)	1.6
40	MI 10th: Candice S. Miller (R)	90.7	40	GA 8th: Austin Scott (R)	34.9	38	CA 21st: Devin Nunes (R)	1.6
40	MO 9th: Blaine Luetkemeyer (R)	90.7	41	LA 5th: Rodney Alexander (R)	34.8	38	NC 11th: Heath Shuler (D)	1.6
42	MN 7th: Collin C. Peterson (D)	90.5	41	MS 3rd: Gregg Harper (R)	34.8	38	WI 7th: Sean P. Duffy (R)	1.6
43	MN 6th: Michele Bachmann (R)	90.3	43	LA 4th: John Fleming (R)	33.9	43	MN 5th: Keith Ellison (D)	1.5
43	OH 4th: Jim Jordan (R)	90.3	44	VA 4th: J. Randy Forbes (R)	33.7	44	AR 3rd: Steve Womack (R)	1.4
45	MO 4th: Vicky Hartzler (R)	90.2	45	MD 2nd: C. A. Dutch Ruppersberger (D)	33.6	44	CA 4th: Tom McClintock (R)	1.4
46	NY 29th: Tom Reed (R)	89.9	46	NY 17th: Eliot L. Engel (D)	32.7	44	CA 22nd: Kevin McCarthy (R)	1.4
46	WI 5th: F. James Sensenbrenner Jr. (R)	89.9	47	IN 7th: André Carson (D)	32.6	44	CA 41st: Jerry Lewis (R)	1.4
48	OH 2nd: Jean Schmidt (R)	89.7	48	AL 3rd: Mike Rogers (R)	31.8	44	CO 1st: Diana DeGette (D)	1.4
49	MO 7th: Bill Long (R)	89.6	48	NY 15th: Charles B. Rangel (D)	31.8	44	ID 2nd: Michael K. Simpson (R)	1.4
50	IA 5th: Steve King (R)	89.5	50	AL 2nd: Martha Roby (R)	30.9	44	OR 4th: Peter A. DeFazio (D)	1.4
50	NY 24th: Richard Hanna (R)	89.5	51	SC 5th: Mick Mulvaney (R)	30.6	44	OR 5th: Kurt Schrader (D)	1.4
52	NY 26h: Kathleen C. Hochul (D)	89.3	52	OH 1st: Steve Chabot (R)	30.5	52	AZ 6th: Jeff Flake (R)	1.3
53	MO 2nd: W. Todd Akin (R)	89.2	53	NY 28th: Louise McIntosh Slaughter (D)	30.2	52	CA 18th: Dennis A. Cardoza (D)	1.3
54	IA 1st: Bruce L. Braley (D)	89.1	54	CA 35th: Maxine Waters (D)	29.2	52	CA 23rd: Lois Capps (D)	1.3
55	MN 1st: Timothy J. Walz (D)	89.0	55	NC 13th: Brad Miller (D)	28.5	52	CA 49th: Darrell E. Issa (R)	1.3
56	ND-At Large Rick Berg (R)	88.9	56	NC 2nd: Renee Ellmers (R)	28.4	52	ID 1st: Raul Labrador (R)	1.3
57	WI 8th: Reid Ribble (R)	88.5	56	NC 8th: Larry Kissell (D)	28.4	52	KS 2nd: Lynn Jenkins (R)	1.3
58	KY 1st: Ed Whitfield (R)	88.3	58	FL 11th: Kathy Castor (D)	28.3	52	KS 4th: Mike Pompeo (R)	1.3
58	MA 10th: William Keating (D)	88.3	59	AL 1st: Jo Bonner (R)	27.7	52	NE 1st: Jeff Fortenberry (R)	1.3
60	IN 4th: Todd Rokita (R)	88.2	60	LA 3rd: Jeff Landry (R)	27.4	52	WA 9th: Adam Smith (D)	1.3
61	IN 5th: Dan Burton (R)	88.1	60	MS 1st: Alan Nunnelee (R)	27.4	61	AL 1st: Jo Bonner (R)	1.2
62	IA 2nd: David Loebsack (D)	88.0	62	SC 2nd: Joe Wilson (R)	27.2	61	AZ 8th: Vacant	1.2
63	KY 2nd: Brett Guthrie (R)	87.9	63	LA 7th: Charles W. Boustany Jr. (R)	25.5	61	CA 5th: Doris O. Matsui (D)	1.2
63	MO 6th: Sam Graves (R)	87.9	63	CA 33rd: Karen Bass (D)	25.3	61	CA 17th: Sam Farr (D)	1.2
65	MT At-Large Denny Rehberg (R)	87.8	64	GA 1st: Jack Kingston (R)	25.3	61	CA 25th: Howard P. "Buck" McKeon (R)	1.2
66	PA 19th: Todd Russell Platts (R)	87.3	64	MO 5th: Emanuel Cleaver (D)	25.3	61	CO 7th: Ed Perlmutter (D)	1.2
67	NE 3rd: Adrian Smith (R)	87.2	67	TN 5th Jim Cooper (D)	24.8	67	CA 31st: Xavier Becerra (D)	1.1
68	TN 2nd John J. Duncan Jr. (R)	87.1	68	GA 3rd: Lynn A. Westmoreland (R)	24.5	67	CA 34th: Lucille Roybal-Allard (D)	1.1
69	OH 8th: John A. Boehner (R)	86.9	68	PA 14th: Michael F. Doyle (D)	24.5	67	CA 38th: Grace F. Napolitano (D)	1.1
70	IL 18th: Aaron Schock (R)	86.5	70	AR 4th: Mike Ross (D)	24.3	67	CA 43rd: Joe Baca (D)	1.1
70	NC 11th: Heath Shuler (D)	86.5	71	TN 8th Stephen Fincher (R)	23.3	67	MS 3rd: Gregg Harper (R)	1.1
70	PA 8th: Michael G. Fitzpatrick (R)	86.5	72	MS 4th: Steven Palazzo (R)	23.2	67	NY 23rd: William L. Owens (D)	1.1
73	AL 4th: Robert B. Aderholt (R)	86.4	73	GA 7th: Robert Woodall (R)	22.4	67	OR 3rd: Earl Blumenauer (D)	1.1
74	MI 7th: Tim Walberg (R)	86.3	74	FL 2nd: Steve Southerland II (R)	22.2	67	TX 20th Charles A. Gonzalez (D)	1.1
75	NE 1st: Jeff Fortenberry (R)	86.2	75	VA 2nd: Scott Rigell (R)	22.1	67	WA 3rd: Jaime Herrera Beutler (R)	1.1

Congressional Districts of the 112th Congress of the United States
Selected Rankings

Percent Asian or Pacific Islander alone, 2010			Percent Hispanic or Latino,[1] 2010			Percent foreign born, 2010		
Asian or Pacific Islander rank	State congressional district Representative	Percent Asian or Pacific Islander [col 7]	Hispanic rank	State congressional district Representative	Percent Hispanic [col 10]	Foreign-born rank	State congressional district Representative	Percent foreign born [col 13]
1	HI 1st: Colleen Hanabusa (D)	60.0	1	TX 15th Rubén Hinojosa (D)	82.5	1	FL 21st: Mario Diaz-Balart (R)	58.1
2	HI 2nd: Mazie Hirono (D)	37.9	2	TX 16th Silvestre Reyes (D)	81.5	2	FL 18th: Ileana Ros-Lehtinen (R)	53.2
3	CA 13th: Fortney Pete Stark (D)	37.6	3	TX 28th Henry Cuellar (D)	78.9	3	CA 31st: Xavier Becerra (D)	51.5
4	CA 15th: Michael M. Honda (D)	37.1	4	CA 34th: Lucille Roybal-Allard (D)	78.7	4	NY 5th: Gary L. Ackerman (D)	48.1
5	CA 12th: Jackie Speier (D)	34.8	5	TX 29th Gene Green (D)	76.0	5	CA 47th: Loretta Sanchez (D)	46.9
6	NY 5th: Gary L. Ackerman (D)	32.7	6	FL 21st: Mario Diaz-Balart (R)	75.6	6	FL 25th: David Rivera (R)	46.8
7	CA 8th: Nancy Pelosi (D)	31.9	7	CA 38th: Grace F. Napolitano (D)	75.4	7	CA 29th: Adam B. Schiff (D)	46.3
8	CA 16th: Zoe Lofgren (D)	29.0	8	IL 4th: Luis V. Gutierrez (D)	73.5	8	CA 34th: Lucille Roybal-Allard (D)	44.3
9	CA 29th: Adam B. Schiff (D)	28.1	9	TX 27th Blake Farenthold (R)	73.2	8	NY 6th: Gregory W. Meeks (D)	44.3
10	CA 14th: Anna G. Eshoo (D)	22.5	10	FL 25th: David Rivera (R)	71.6	10	NY 9th: Robert L. Turner (R)	42.1
10	CA 32nd: Judy Chu (D)	22.5	11	TX 20th Charles A. Gonzalez (D)	71.5	11	CA 32nd: Judy Chu (D)	41.7
12	CA 40th: Edward R. Royce (R)	21.1	12	CA 20th: Jim Costa (D)	70.4	12	NY 7th: Joseph Crowley (D)	41.6
13	CA 42nd: Gary G. Miller (R)	20.7	13	CA 43rd: Joe Baca (D)	69.4	13	NJ 13th: Albio Sires (D)	41.5
14	CA 26th: David Dreier (R)	19.4	14	CA 31st: Xavier Becerra (D)	68.2	14	CA 28th: Howard L. Berman (D)	41.2
15	CA 46th: Dana Rohrabacher (R)	19.3	15	CA 47th: Loretta Sanchez (D)	67.6	15	NY 12th: Nydia M. Velázquez (D)	40.0
16	CA 48th: John Campbell (R)	19.2	16	FL 18th: Ileana Ros-Lehtinen (R)	66.9	16	NY 11th: Yvette D. Clarke (D)	39.2
17	CA 9th: Barbara Lee (D)	18.7	17	CA 39th: Linda T. Sánchez (D)	66.5	17	CA 27th: Brad Sherman (D)	38.9
17	NY 9th: Robert L. Turner (R)	18.7	17	NY 16th: José E. Serrano (D)	66.5	18	CA 15th: Michael M. Honda (D)	37.8
19	NY 12th: Nydia M. Velázquez (D)	18.4	19	TX 23rd Francisco "Quico" Canseco (R)	66.4	19	CA 38th: Grace F. Napolitano (D)	37.6
20	CA 5th: Doris O. Matsui (D)	18.1	20	CA 32nd: Judy Chu (D)	64.2	20	CA 16th: Zoe Lofgren (D)	37.4
21	CA 47th: Loretta Sanchez (D)	17.5	21	AZ 4th: Ed Pastor (D)	63.9	21	FL 17th: Frederica Wilson (D)	37.3
22	CA 36th: Janice Hahn (D)	16.9	22	CA 51st: Bob Filner (D)	62.4	22	CA 13th: Fortney Pete Stark (D)	37.1
23	NY 7th: Joseph Crowley (D)	16.4	23	CA 28th: Howard L. Berman (D)	57.5	23	TX 9th Al Green (D)	36.7
24	CA 7th: George Miller (D)	15.9	24	AZ 7th: Raúl M. Grijalva (D)	56.0	24	CA 12th: Jackie Speier (D)	36.3
25	CA 31st: Xavier Becerra (D)	15.3	25	CA 35th: Maxine Waters (D)	54.5	24	NJ 8th: Steven R. Rothman (D)	36.3
26	CA 11th: Jerry McNerney (D)	15.1	26	CA 18th: Dennis A. Cardoza (D)	52.7	26	CA 8th: Nancy Pelosi (D)	35.8
26	NY 8th: Jerrold Nadler (D)	15.1	27	NM 2nd: Steve Pearce (R)	51.8	27	CA 33rd: Karen Bass (D)	35.5
28	NJ 12th: Rush D. Holt (D)	15.0	28	CA 21st: Devin Nunes (R)	51.2	27	NY 16th: José E. Serrano (D)	35.5
28	VA 11th: Gerald E. Connolly (D)	15.0	29	NJ 13th: Albio Sires (D)	50.6	29	MD 8th: Chris Van Hollen (D)	35.2
30	WA 7th: Jim McDermott (D)	14.8	30	CA 17th: Sam Farr (D)	50.4	30	IL 4th: Luis V. Gutierrez (D)	34.9
31	NJ 8th: Steven R. Rothman (D)	14.5	31	CA 23rd: Lois Capps (D)	49.5	31	CA 39th: Linda T. Sánchez (D)	34.4
32	IL 9th: Janice D. Schakowsky (D)	14.4	32	CA 37th: Laura Richardson (D)	49.4	32	FL 20th: Debbie Wasserman Schultz (D)	34.0
33	CA 10th: John Garamendi (D)	14.1	33	NM 1st: Martin Heinrich (D)	48.4	33	NY 8th: Jerrold Nadler (D)	33.9
33	CA 50th: Brian P. Bilbray (R)	14.1	34	NY 15th: Charles B. Rangel (D)	46.1	34	CA 51st: Bob Filner (D)	33.7
35	WA 8th: David G. Reichert (R)	14.0	35	CA 45th: Mary Bono Mack (R)	45.2	35	CA 35th: Maxine Waters (D)	33.5
36	NY 14th: Carolyn B. Maloney (D)	13.6	36	NY 12th: Nydia M. Velázquez (D)	44.6	36	TX 29th Gene Green (D)	33.4
37	CA 33rd: Karen Bass (D)	13.5	37	NY 7th: Joseph Crowley (D)	44.4	37	NY 15th: Charles B. Rangel (D)	33.0
38	CA 37th: Laura Richardson (D)	13.4	38	CA 44th: Ken Calvert (R)	43.5	38	IL 9th: Janice D. Schakowsky (D)	32.8
38	MD 8th: Chris Van Hollen (D)	13.4	38	TX 18th Sheila Jackson-Lee (D)	43.5	39	CA 14th: Anna G. Eshoo (D)	32.1
40	CA 51st: Bob Filner (D)	13.3	40	TX 9th Al Green (D)	42.4	40	FL 23rd: Alcee L. Hastings (D)	31.8
40	NY 6th: Gregory W. Meeks (D)	13.3	40	TX 32nd Pete Sessions (R)	42.4	41	NY 17th: Eliot L. Engel (D)	31.5
42	NY 13th: Michael Grimm (R)	13.2	42	CA 27th: Brad Sherman (D)	42.3	42	CA 40th: Edward R. Royce (R)	30.8
43	TX 22nd Pete Olson (R)	12.8	43	CA 16th: Zoe Lofgren (D)	39.9	43	CA 20th: Jim Costa (D)	30.4
44	CA 27th: Brad Sherman (D)	12.6	44	TX 30th Eddie Bernice Johnson (D)	39.7	44	NY 10th: Edolphus Towns (D)	30.2
44	NJ 7th: Leonard Lance (R)	12.6	45	CA 25th: Howard P. "Buck" McKeon (R)	39.2	45	CA 37th: Laura Richardson (D)	29.6
46	VA 10th: Frank R. Wolf (R)	12.5	46	NM 3rd: Ben Ray Luján (D)	39.0	46	MA 8th: Michael E. Capuano (D)	29.5
47	WA 1st: Vacant	12.4	47	TX 25th Lloyd Doggett (D)	38.8	47	NJ 7th: Bill Pascrell Jr. (D)	29.1
48	TX 3rd Sam Johnson (R)	12.3	48	CA 49th: Darrell E. Issa (R)	38.5	48	CA 43rd: Joe Baca (D)	28.9
49	NJ 6th: Frank Pallone Jr. (D)	11.9	49	CA 33rd: Karen Bass (D)	37.4	49	NY 14th: Carolyn B. Maloney (D)	28.8
50	CA 3rd: Daniel E. Lungren (R)	11.6	50	CA 19th: Jeff Denham (R)	37.3	50	TX 32nd Pete Sessions (R)	28.6
51	CA 38th: Grace F. Napolitano (D)	11.5	51	NV 1st: Shelley Berkley (D)	37.2	51	NY 13th: Michael Grimm (R)	27.5
52	NV 3rd: Joseph J. Heck (R)	11.4	52	TX 11th K. Michael Conaway (R)	36.3	52	VA 8th: James P. Moran (D)	27.4
53	WA 9th: Adam Smith (D)	11.2	53	CA 40th: Edward R. Royce (R)	35.2	53	AZ 4th: Ed Pastor (D)	27.3
54	CA 30th: Henry A. Waxman (D)	11.1	54	CA 41st: Jerry Lewis (R)	34.9	53	CA 17th: Sam Farr (D)	27.3
54	CA 39th: Linda T. Sánchez (D)	11.1	55	IL 3rd: Daniel Lipinski (D)	34.0	53	CA 36th: Janice Hahn (D)	27.3
56	TX 9th Al Green (D)	11.0	56	TX 19th Randy Neugebauer (R)	33.8	56	NJ 10th: Vacant	27.0
57	VA 8th: James P. Moran (D)	10.8	56	WA 4th: Doc Hastings (R)	33.8	57	IL 5th: Michael Quigley (D)	26.9
58	CA 53rd: Susan A. Davis (D)	10.5	58	NJ 7th: Bill Pascrell Jr. (D)	33.2	58	CA 42nd: Gary G. Miller (R)	26.7
59	MN 4th: Betty McCollum (D)	10.3	59	CA 22nd: Kevin McCarthy (R)	32.0	59	CA 9th: Barbara Lee (D)	26.5
60	TX 7th John Abney Culberson (R)	10.2	59	CA 36th: Janice Hahn (D)	32.0	59	VA 11th: Gerald E. Connolly (D)	26.5
61	IL 6th: Peter J. Roskam (R)	10.1	61	CA 53rd: Susan A. Davis (D)	31.9	61	FL 19th: Ted Deutch (D)	26.4
62	MA 8th: Michael E. Capuano (D)	9.9	62	FL 20th: Debbie Wasserman Schultz (D)	31.3	62	CA 48th: John Campbell (R)	26.2
63	CA 18th: Dennis A. Cardoza (D)	9.7	63	CA 26th: David Dreier (R)	30.7	63	CA 23rd: Lois Capps (D)	25.9
63	TX 24th Kenny Marchant (R)	9.7	63	CO 1st: Diana DeGette (D)	30.7	64	TX 16th Silvestre Reyes (D)	25.8
65	IL 13th: Judy Biggert (R)	9.4	65	CA 7th: George Miller (D)	29.7	65	CA 26th: David Dreier (R)	25.6
66	NJ 11th: Rodney P. Frelinghuysen (R)	9.3	66	CA 42nd: Gary G. Miller (R)	29.3	66	CA 7th: George Miller (D)	25.5
67	NJ 5th: Scott Garrett (R)	9.1	67	TX 14th Ron Paul (R)	29.0	66	CA 18th: Dennis A. Cardoza (D)	25.5
68	NJ 13th: Albio Sires (D)	8.9	68	CA 24th: Elton Gallegly (R)	28.8	68	NY 4th: Carolyn McCarthy (D)	25.4
69	GA 7th: Rob Woodall (R)	8.8	68	IL 5th: Michael Quigley (D)	28.8	69	NY 18th: Nita M. Lowey (D)	24.9
70	MA 7th: Edward J. Markey (D)	8.7	68	TX 10th Michael T. McCaul (R)	28.8	70	CA 30th: Henry A. Waxman (D)	24.8
71	IL 10th: Robert Dold (R)	8.5	68	TX 12th Kay Granger (R)	28.8	71	CA 46th: Dana Rohrabacher (R)	24.6
72	CA 44th: Ken Calvert (R)	8.3	72	CO 7th: Ed Perlmutter (D)	28.4	72	TX 18th Sheila Jackson-Lee (D)	24.5
73	IL 8th: Joe Walsh (R)	8.2	73	FL 17th: Frederica Wilson (D)	28.2	72	TX 28th Henry Cuellar (D)	24.5
74	CA 52nd: Duncan Hunter (R)	7.9	74	TX 21st Lamar Smith (R)	28.1	74	NV 1st: Shelley Berkley (D)	24.4
75	GA 6th: Tom Price (R)	7.8	75	FL 11th: Kathy Castor (D)	27.5	75	NJ 6th: Frank Pallone Jr. (D)	24.3

1. May be of any race.

Congressional Districts of the 112th Congress of the United States
Selected Rankings

Percent under 18 years old, 2010			Percent 65 years old and over, 2010			Percent college graduates (bachelor's degree or more), 2010		
Under 18 years old rank	State congressional district Representative	Percent under 18 years old [col 15 and 16]	65 years old and over rank	State congressional district Representative	Percent 65 years old and over [col 22 and 23]	College graduates rank	State congressional district Representative	Percent college graduates [col 28]
1	UT 3rd: Jason Chaffetz (R)	33.8	1	FL 13th: Vern Buchanan (R)	27.6	1	NY 14th: Carolyn B. Maloney (D)	64.1
2	AZ 4th: Ed Pastor (D)	32.8	2	FL 14th: Connie Mack (R)	26.4	2	CA 30th: Henry A. Waxman (D)	60.7
3	CA 20th: Jim Costa (D)	32.7	3	FL 19th: Ted Deutch (D)	25.7	3	VA 8th: James P. Moran (D)	59.1
3	TX 28th Henry Cuellar (D)	32.7	4	FL 5th: Richard B. Nugent (R)	25.0	4	CA 14th: Anna G. Eshoo (D)	57.0
5	CA 43rd: Joe Baca (D)	32.6	5	FL 16th: Thomas J. Rooney (R)	23.9	5	MD 8th: Chris Van Hollen (D)	55.1
5	TX 29th Gene Green (D)	32.6	6	FL 10th: C. W. Bill Young (R)	21.7	6	NY 8th: Jerrold Nadler (D)	54.7
7	UT 1st: Rob Bishop (R)	31.8	7	FL 22nd: Allen West (R)	20.4	7	CA 48th: John Campbell (R)	53.9
8	TX 15th Rubén Hinojosa (D)	31.7	8	MI 1st: Dan Benishek (R)	19.4	8	GA 6th: Tom Price (R)	52.8
9	CA 18th: Dennis A. Cardoza (D)	30.9	9	FL 15th: Bill Posey (R)	19.2	9	IL 10th: Robert Dold (R)	52.5
9	CA 21st: Devin Nunes (R)	30.9	10	NC 11th: Heath Shuler (D)	19.1	10	WA 7th: Jim McDermott (D)	52.1
11	CA 47th: Loretta Sanchez (D)	29.8	11	AZ 2nd: Trent Franks (R)	18.9	11	NC 4th: David E. Price (D)	51.6
11	NY 16th: José E. Serrano (D)	29.8	11	AZ 8th: Vacant	18.9	12	CA 8th: Nancy Pelosi (D)	50.6
13	TX 16th Silvestre Reyes (D)	29.7	13	PA 12th: Mark Critz (D)	18.5	13	DC At-Large Eleanor Holmes Norton (D)	50.1
14	CA 25th: Howard P. "Buck" McKeon (R)	29.5	14	MA 10th: William Keating (D)	18.2	14	VA 11th: Gerald E. Connolly (D)	49.9
15	TX 27th Blake Farenthold (R)	29.3	15	PA 18th: Tim Murphy (R)	18.0	15	TX 7th John Abney Culberson (R)	49.6
16	TX 23rd Francisco "Quico" Canseco (R)	29.0	16	NJ 3rd: Jon Runyan (R)	17.8	16	NJ 11th: Rodney P. Frelinghuysen (R)	48.9
17	GA 7th: Robert Woodall (R)	28.9	17	FL 7th: John L. Mica (R)	17.7	16	NJ 12th: Rush D. Holt (D)	48.9
18	UT 2nd: Jim Matheson (D)	28.8	18	PA 4th: Jason Altmire (D)	17.6	18	NY 18th: Nita M. Lowey (D)	48.6
19	AZ 7th: Raúl M. Grijalva (D)	28.7	19	FL 9th: Gus M. Bilirakis (R)	17.5	18	VA 10th: Frank R. Wolf (R)	48.6
19	WA 4th: Doc Hastings (R)	28.7	20	NE 3rd: Adrian Smith (R)	17.3	20	CO 6th: Mike Coffman (R)	48.5
21	IL 4th: Luis V. Gutierrez (D)	28.6	20	PA 10th: Tom Marino (R)	17.3	21	NJ 7th: Leonard Lance (R)	47.7
21	TX 26th Michael C. Burgess (R)	28.6	22	FL 6th: Cliff Stearns (R)	17.2	22	MA 8th: Michael E. Capuano (D)	47.6
23	CA 35th: Maxine Waters (D)	28.5	22	MN 7th: Collin C. Peterson (D)	17.2	23	CA 15th: Michael M. Honda (D)	47.2
23	TX 9th Al Green (D)	28.5	24	OR 4th: Peter A. DeFazio (D)	17.0	24	MI 9th: Gary C. Peters (D)	46.8
25	CA 34th: Lucille Roybal-Allard (D)	28.3	25	IA 5th: Steve King (R)	16.9	25	CT 4th: James A. Himes (D)	46.7
25	CA 44th: Ken Calvert (R)	28.3	25	TN 1st David P. Roe (R)	16.9	26	IL 13th: Judy Biggert (R)	45.6
27	CA 39th: Linda T. Sánchez (D)	28.2	27	MN 8th: Chip Cravaack (R)	16.8	27	MA 7th: Edward J. Markey (D)	44.8
28	AZ 6th: Jeff Flake (R)	28.1	27	OR 2nd: Greg Walden (R)	16.8	28	IL 9th: Janice D. Schakowsky (D)	44.6
28	CA 37th: Laura Richardson (D)	28.1	27	PA 9th: Bill Shuster (R)	16.8	29	CA 12th: Jackie Speier (D)	44.3
28	TX 3rd Sam Johnson (R)	28.1	30	OH 6th: Bill Johnson (R)	16.7	29	MN 3rd: Erik Paulsen (R)	44.3
28	TX 30th Eddie Bernice Johnson (D)	28.1	30	TN 4th Scott DesJarlais (R)	16.7	31	CA 50th: Brian P. Bilbray (R)	44.1
32	CA 51st: Bob Filner (D)	28.0	32	FL 18th: Ileana Ros-Lehtinen (R)	16.6	32	KS 3rd: Kevin Yoder (R)	44.0
32	GA 13th: David Scott (D)	28.0	33	IL 17th: Bobby Schilling (R)	16.5	32	NJ 5th: Scott Garrett (R)	44.0
32	IL 14th; Randy Hultgren (R)	28.0	33	VA 5th: Robert Hurt (R)	16.5	34	GA 5th: John Lewis (D)	43.9
32	TX 6th Joe Barton (R)	28.0	33	WV 3rd: Nick J. Rahall II (D)	16.5	35	CA 36th: Janice Hahn (D)	43.8
32	Tx 31st John R. Carter (R)	28.0	36	PA 11th; Lou Barletta (R)	16.4	36	CA 9th: Barbara Lee (D)	43.2
37	TX 10th Michael T. McCaul (R)	27.9	36	VA 9th: Morgan Griffith (R)	16.4	36	MD 3rd: John P. Sarbanes (D)	43.2
37	TX 22nd Pete Olson (R)	27.9	36	WI 7th: Sean P. Duffy (R)	16.4	38	TX 3rd Sam Johnson (R)	42.9
39	ID 2nd: Michael K. Simpson (R)	27.8	39	AR 4th: Mike Ross (D)	16.3	39	MO 2nd: W. Todd Akin (R)	42.7
40	CA 11th: Jerry McNerney (D)	27.7	39	MO 8th: Jo Ann Emerson (R)	16.3	40	AZ 5th: David Schweikert (R)	42.4
41	VA 10th: Frank R. Wolf (R)	27.6	41	KS 1st: Tim Huelskamp (R)	16.2	40	CO 2nd: Jared Polis (D)	42.4
42	CA 45th: Mary Bono Mack (R)	27.5	41	ME 2nd: Michael H. Michaud (D)	16.2	42	PA 7th: Patrick Meehan (R)	42.3
42	MN 2nd: John Kline (R)	27.5	41	PA 5th: Glenn Thompson (R)	16.2	43	IL 7th: Danny K. Davis (D)	41.2
44	CA 38th: Grace F. Napolitano (D)	27.4	41	WV 1st : David McKinley (R)	16.2	43	MA 4th: Barney Frank (D)	41.2
44	TX 12th Kay Granger (R)	27.4	45	OK 2nd: Dan Boren (D)	16.1	43	WA 1st: Vacant	41.2
44	TX 18th Sheila Jackson-Lee (D)	27.4	46	AZ 1st: Paul R. Gosar (R)	16.0	46	MA 9th: Stephen F. Lynch (D)	41.1
44	TX 20th Charles A. Gonzalez (D)	27.4	46	AR 1st: Eric A. "Rick" Crawford (R)	16.0	47	MA 6th: John F. Tierney (D)	41.0
48	CO 6th: Mike Coffman (R)	27.3	46	FL 12th: Dennis Ross (R)	16.0	48	WA 8th: David G. Reichert (R)	40.9
49	CA 49th: Darrell E. Issa (R)	27.1	46	HI 1st: Colleen Hanabusa (D)	16.0	49	PA 6th:Jim Gerlach (R)	40.8
49	ID 1st: Raul Labrador (R)	27.1	46	IA 4th: Tom Latham (R)	16.0	50	CA 6th: Lynn C. Woolsey (D)	40.7
49	IL 2nd: Jesse L. Jackson Jr. (D)	27.1	46	PA 3rd: Mike Kelly (R)	16.0	51	MN 5th: Keith Ellison (D)	40.6
49	IN 3rd: Marlin Stutzman (R)	27.1	52	IL 19th: John Shimkus (R)	15.9	52	CA 10th: John Garamendi (D)	40.5
49	NV 1st: Shelley Berkley (D)	27.1	52	NJ 4th: Christopher H. Smith (R)	15.9	52	CO 1st: Diana DeGette (D)	40.5
54	TX 14th Ron Paul (R)	27.0	54	AL 4th: Robert B. Aderholt (R)	15.7	52	WI 5th: F. James Sensenbrenner Jr. (R)	40.5
55	MN 6th: Michele Bachmann (R)	26.9	54	CA 4th: Tom McClintock (R)	15.7	55	CA 46th: Dana Rohrabacher (R)	40.4
56	CA 41st: Jerry Lewis (R)	26.8	54	KY 1st: Ed Whitfield (R)	15.7	55	MA 10th: William Keating (D)	40.4
56	IL 13th: Judy Biggert (R)	26.8	54	MI 4th: Dave Camp (R)	15.7	55	TX 21st Lamar Smith (R)	40.4
56	TX 4th Ralph M. Hall (R)	26.8	54	NY 20th: Christopher P. Gibson (R)	15.7	58	IL 5th: Michael Quigley (D)	40.3
59	CA 22nd: Kevin McCarthy (R)	26.7	54	NY 24th: Richard Hanna (R)	15.7	59	CA 53rd: Susan A. Davis (D)	39.9
59	MS 2nd: Bennie G. Thompson (D)	26.7	54	NY 27th: Brian Higgins (D)	15.7	60	CA 42nd: Gary G. Miller (R)	39.4
59	TX 24th Kenny Marchant (R)	26.7	54	PA 14th: Michael F. Doyle (D)	15.7	61	NC 9th: Sue Wilkins Myrick (R)	39.3
62	CA 19th: Jeff Denham (R)	26.6	62	CA 46th: Dana Rohrabacher (R)	15.6	62	MA 5th: Niki Tsongas (D)	39.2
62	CA 32nd: Judy Chu (D)	26.6	62	IL 18th: Aaron Schock (R)	15.6	63	CA 29th: Adam B. Schiff (D)	39.0
62	GA 11th: Phil Gingrey (R)	26.6	62	NY 9th: Robert L. Turner (R)	15.6	64	IL 6th: Peter J. Roskam (R)	38.3
62	KS 4th: Mike Pompeo (R)	26.6	62	NY 29th: Tom Reed (R)	15.6	65	WI 2nd: Tammy Baldwin (D)	38.1
66	TX 2nd Ted Poe (R)	26.5	62	PA 13th: Allyson Y. Schwartz (D)	15.6	66	FL 22nd: Allen West (R)	37.8
66	WI 4th: Gwen Moore (D)	26.5	62	PA 17th: Tim Holden (D)	15.6	67	NY 9th: Robert L. Turner (R)	37.6
68	AK At-Large: Don Young (R)	26.4	62	VA 6th: Bob Goodlatte (R)	15.6	67	TX 32nd Pete Sessions (R)	37.6
68	MI 13th: Hansen Clarke (D)	26.4	69	ME 1st: Chellie Pingree (D)	15.5	69	OH 12th: Patrick J. Tiberi (R)	37.5
68	NE 2nd: Lee Terry (R)	26.4	69	OH 10th: Dennis J. Kucinich (D)	15.5	69	VA 7th: Eric Cantor (R)	37.5
71	GA 3rd: Lynn A. Westmoreland (R)	26.3	69	OH 14th: Steven C. LaTourette (R)	15.5	71	NY 15th: Charles B. Rangel (D)	37.4
71	NY 10th: Edolphus Towns (D)	26.3	69	OH 16th: Jim Renacci (R)	15.5	72	NY 3rd: Peter T. King (R)	37.2
71	NC 9th: Sue Wilkins Myrick (R)	26.3	69	OH 17th: Tim Ryan (D)	15.5	72	NY 5th: Gary L. Ackerman (D)	37.2
71	OH 12th: Patrick J. Tiberi (R)	26.3	69	SC 3rd: Jeff Duncan (R)	15.5	72	NY 19th: Nan Hayworth (R)	37.2
71	TN 7th Marsha Blackburn (R)	26.3	69	WV 2nd: Shelley Moore Capito (R)	15.5	72	OR 1st: Suzanne Bonamici (D)	37.2

Congressional Districts of the 112th Congress of the United States
Selected Rankings

	Median value of owner-occupied housing units, 2010			Percent female-headed family households, 2010			Percent of households with one person, 2010	
Median value rank	State congressional district Representative	Median value (dollars) [col 44]	Female house-holder rank	State congressional district Representative	Percent with female householder [col 33]	One-person house-hold rank	State congressional district Representative	Percent one-person house-holds [col 34]
1	CA 14th: Anna G. Eshoo (D)	859 800	1	NY 16th: José E. Serrano (D)	37.6	1	NY 14th: Carolyn B. Maloney (D)	47.8
2	CA 30th: Henry A. Waxman (D)	825 400	2	NY 10th: Edolphus Towns (D)	28.3	2	NY 8th: Jerrold Nadler (D)	44.3
3	NY 14th: Carolyn B. Maloney (D)	765 600	3	IL 2nd: Jesse L. Jackson Jr. (D)	27.1	3	DC At-Large Eleanor Holmes Norton (D)	44.0
4	NY 8th: Jerrold Nadler (D)	752 800	4	PA 1st: Robert A. Brady (D)	26.9	4	GA 5th: John Lewis (D)	41.4
5	CA 8th: Nancy Pelosi (D)	742 500	5	IL 1st: Bobby L. Rush (D)	26.4	5	IL 7th: Danny K. Davis (D)	40.9
6	CA 12th: Jackie Speier (D)	725 900	6	MS 2nd: Bennie G. Thompson (D)	26.3	6	CA 8th: Nancy Pelosi (D)	40.8
7	CA 15th: Michael M. Honda (D)	639 700	7	FL 17th: Frederica Wilson (D)	26.1	7	CO 1st: Diana DeGette (D)	40.3
8	CA 36th: Janice Hahn (D)	634 000	8	MI 13th: Hansen Clarke (D)	25.9	8	PA 14th: Michael F. Doyle (D)	39.9
9	CA 48th: John Campbell (R)	626 100	9	MI 14th: John Conyers Jr. (D)	25.6	9	WA 7th: Jim McDermott (D)	39.4
10	CA 46th: Dana Rohrabacher (R)	620 000	10	NJ 10th: Vacant	25.2	10	OH 11th: Marcia L. Fudge (D)	39.0
11	NY 5th: Gary L. Ackerman (D)	594 200	11	NY 6th: Gregory W. Meeks (D)	24.7	11	MN 5th: Keith Ellison (D)	38.2
12	NY 12th: Nydia M. Velázquez (D)	593 400	12	TN 9th Steve Cohen (D)	24.6	11	PA 2nd: Chaka Fattah (D)	38.2
13	NY 15th: Charles B. Rangel (D)	587 700	13	FL 3rd: Corrine Brown (D)	24.0	13	CA 30th: Henry A. Waxman (D)	37.8
14	NY 11th: Yvette D. Clarke (D)	581 300	14	AL 7th: Terri A. Sewell (D)	23.9	14	MA 8th: Michael E. Capuano (D)	37.0
15	CA 29th: Adam B. Schiff (D)	575 000	15	NY 15th: Charles B. Rangel (D)	23.8	15	VA 8th: James P. Moran (D)	36.8
16	NY 18th: Nita M. Lowey (D)	565 600	16	CA 35th: Maxine Waters (D)	23.7	16	NY 15th: Charles B. Rangel (D)	36.5
17	HI 1st: Colleen Hanabusa (D)	555 500	16	NY 11th: Yvette D. Clarke (D)	23.7	17	IL 9th: Janice D. Schakowsky (D)	36.3
18	CA 50th: Brian P. Bilbray (R)	537 700	18	L:A 2nd: Cedric Richmond (D)	22.7	18	FL 10th: C. W. Bill Young (R)	36.2
19	CA 6th: Lynn C. Woolsey (D)	533 100	19	FL 23rd: Alcee L. Hastings (D)	22.6	19	NY 28th: Louise McIntosh Slaughter (D)	36.1
20	CA 42nd: Gary G. Miller (R)	514 400	20	MO 1st: William Lacy Clay (D)	22.5	20	CA 53rd: Susan A. Davis (D)	35.7
21	NY 9th: Robert L. Turner (R)	512 800	21	OH 11th: Marcia L. Fudge (D)	22.3	21	CA 33rd: Karen Bass (D)	34.5
22	CT 4th: James A. Himes (D)	511 400	22	SC 6th: James E. Clyburn (D)	21.8	21	IL 5th: Michael Quigley (D)	34.5
23	CA 16th: Zoe Lofgren (D)	508 900	23	PA 2nd: Chaka Fattah (D)	21.7	21	OH 10th: Dennis J. Kucinich (D)	34.5
24	CA 9th: Barbara Lee (D)	508 500	24	GA 2nd: Sanford D. Bishop Jr. (D)	21.5	24	MI 13th: Hansen Clarke (D)	34.4
25	NY 10th: Edolphus Towns (D)	495 100	24	VA 3rd: Robert C. "Bobby" Scott (D)	21.5	25	MO 1st: William Lacy Clay (D)	34.2
26	HI 2nd: Mazie Hirono (D)	492 300	26	CA 37th: Laura Richardson (D)	21.3	26	WI 4th: Gwen Moore (D)	34.0
27	CA 33rd: Karen Bass (D)	488 000	26	GA 13th: David Scott (D)	21.3	27	TX 7th John Abney Culberson (R)	33.6
28	NY 13th: Michael Grimm (R)	481 200	26	MD 7th: Elijah E. Cummings (D)	21.3	28	FL 22nd: Allen West (R)	33.2
29	CA 40th: Edward R. Royce (R)	472 600	26	WI 4th: Gwen Moore (D)	21.3	28	IN 7th: André Carson (D)	33.2
30	CA 24th: Elton Gallegly (R)	471 800	30	TX 30th Eddie Bernice Johnson (D)	21.0	28	OH 1st: Steve Chabot (R)	33.2
31	CA 13th: Fortney Pete Stark (D)	467 000	31	GA 4th: Henry C. "Hank" Johnson Jr. (D)	20.7	31	MI 12th: Sander M. Levin (D)	33.1
32	CA 26th: David Dreier (R)	466 000	31	TX 18th Sheila Jackson-Lee (D)	20.7	32	MO 5th: Emanuel Cleaver (D)	32.7
33	VA 8th: James P. Moran (D)	462 700	33	NY 7th: Joseph Crowley (D)	20.6	33	CA 9th: Barbara Lee (D)	32.5
34	MD 8th: Chris Van Hollen (D)	459 300	34	TX 16th Silvestre Reyes (D)	20.5	33	TN 5th Jim Cooper (D)	32.5
35	NJ 11th: Rodney P. Frelinghuysen (R)	444 200	35	CA 20th: Jim Costa (D)	20.3	35	MN 4th: Betty McCollum (D)	32.4
36	NY 3rd: Peter T. King (R)	440 800	35	NY 17th: Eliot L. Engel (D)	20.3	36	NY 20th: Paul Tonko (D)	32.3
37	NY 4th: Carolyn McCarthy (D)	433 500	35	TX 9th Al Green (D)	20.3	37	KY 3rd: John A. Yarmuth (D)	32.2
38	CA 10th: John Garamendi (D)	426 900	38	PA 14th: Michael F. Doyle (D)	20.2	37	NY 27th: Brian Higgins (D)	32.2
38	DC At-Large Eleanor Holmes Norton (D)	426 900	38	NC 1st: G. K. Butterfield (D)	20.2	37	TN 9th Steve Cohen (D)	32.2
40	NY 17th: Eliot L. Engel (D)	426 500	40	GA 12th: John Barrow (D)	19.9	40	FL 18th: Ileana Ros-Lehtinen (R)	32.1
41	NJ 5th: Scott Garrett (R)	425 900	40	NC 12th: Melvin L. Watt (D)	19.9	41	TX 32nd Pete Sessions (R)	32.0
42	NY 6th: Gregory W. Meeks (D)	421 400	42	TX 20th Charles A. Gonzalez (D)	19.8	42	FL 11th: Kathy Castor (D)	31.8
43	WA 7th: Jim McDermott (D)	419 600	43	CA 43rd: Joe Baca (D)	19.6	42	MO 3rd: Russ Carnahan (D)	31.8
44	NY 7th: Joseph Crowley (D)	418 400	44	IN 7th: André Carson (D)	19.5	44	AL 7th: Terri A. Sewell (D)	31.7
45	NY 2nd: Steve Israel (D)	416 400	45	AZ 4th: Ed Pastor (D)	19.3	44	IL 1st: Bobby L. Rush (D)	31.7
46	CA 53rd: Susan A. Davis (D)	414 800	45	CA 51st: Bob Filner (D)	19.3	46	ND-At Large Rick Berg (R)	31.5
47	VA 11th: Gerald E. Connolly (D)	413 300	47	NY 28th: Louise McIntosh Slaughter (D)	19.2	47	AZ 5th: David Schweikert (R)	31.3
48	CA 17th: Sam Farr (D)	412 300	48	CA 34th: Lucille Roybal-Allard (D)	18.7	47	FL 19th: Ted Deutch (D)	31.3
48	MA 7th: Edward J. Markey (D)	412 300	48	CA 38th: Grace F. Napolitano (D)	18.7	47	L:A 2nd: Cedric Richmond (D)	31.3
50	CA 27th: Brad Sherman (D)	411 800	50	IL 7th: Danny K. Davis (D)	18.6	47	PA 1st: Robert A. Brady (D)	31.3
51	CA 23rd: Lois Capps (D)	410 900	51	FL 11th: Kathy Castor (D)	18.5	47	RI 1st: David Cicilline (D)	31.3
52	NJ 7th: Leonard Lance (R)	408 900	51	LA 5th: Rodney Alexander (R)	18.5	52	MI 14th: John Conyers Jr. (D)	31.2
53	CA 31st: Xavier Becerra (D)	404 700	53	CA 32nd: Judy Chu (D)	18.4	53	FL 20th: Debbie Wasserman Schultz (D)	31.1
54	CA 52nd: Duncan Hunter (R)	400 400	54	NY 12th: Nydia M. Velázquez (D)	18.3	53	OH 15th: Steve Stivers (R)	31.1
55	MA 8th: Michael E. Capuano (D)	394 700	54	TX 29th Gene Green (D)	18.3	55	MD 7th: Elijah E. Cummings (D)	31.0
56	CA 28th: Howard L. Berman (D)	394 000	56	FL 25th: David Rivera (R)	18.2	55	VA 3rd: Robert C. "Bobby" Scott (D)	31.0
57	VA 10th: Frank R. Wolf (R)	390 400	57	CA 39th: Linda T. Sánchez (D)	18.1	57	IL 17th: Bobby Schilling (R)	30.9
58	NJ 8th: Steven R. Rothman (D)	389 100	57	FL 21st: Mario Diaz-Balart (R)	18.1	58	PA 12th: Mark Critz (D)	30.7
59	MA 6th: John F. Tierney (D)	384 800	59	GA 8th: Austin Scott (R)	17.9	59	OK 5th: James Lankford (R)	30.4
60	NJ 12th: Rush D. Holt (D)	384 700	59	MD 2nd: C. A. Dutch Ruppersberger (D)	17.9	60	NY 22nd: Maurice D. Hinchey (D)	30.3
61	NY 1st: Timothy H. Bishop (D)	381 400	59	TX 15th Rubén Hinojosa (D)	17.9	61	FL 13th: Vern Buchanan (R)	30.2
62	NJ 7th: Bill Pascrell Jr. (D)	379 900	59	TX 27th Blake Farenthold (R)	17.9	61	NY 11th: Yvette D. Clarke (D)	30.2
63	MA 10th: William Keating (D)	376 000	63	NJ 13th: Albio Sires (D)	17.6	61	OH 17th: Tim Ryan (D)	30.2
64	IL 10th: Robert Dold (R)	371 700	64	CA 18th: Dennis A. Cardoza (D)	17.5	61	TX 30th Eddie Bernice Johnson (D)	30.2
65	CA 39th: Linda T. Sánchez (D)	370 900	64	CA 31st: Xavier Becerra (D)	17.5	65	NM 1st: Martin Heinrich (D)	30.1
66	WA 8th: David G. Reichert (R)	367 800	66	LA 4th: John Fleming (R)	17.4	65	OH 9th: Marcy Kaptur (D)	30.1
67	NY 16th: José E. Serrano (D)	362 100	66	OH 1st: Steve Chabot (R)	17.4	67	CA 36th: Janice Hahn (D)	30.0
68	WA 1st: Vacant	360 100	68	SC 5th: Mick Mulvaney (R)	17.3	67	MA 7th: Edward J. Markey (D)	30.0
69	CA 11th: Jerry McNerney (D)	359 400	69	TX 28th Henry Cuellar (D)	17.2	67	OH 3rd: Michael R. Turner (R)	30.0
70	MA 9th: Stephen F. Lynch (D)	357 400	70	CA 5th: Doris O. Matsui (D)	16.9	70	MD 3rd: John P. Sarbanes (D)	29.9
71	NY 19th: Nan Hayworth (R)	354 900	70	LA 3rd: Jeff Landry (R)	16.9	71	AZ 8th: Vacant	29.8
72	CA 32nd: Judy Chu (D)	354 700	72	LA 6th: Bill Cassidy (R)	16.8	71	IL 15th: Timothy V. Johnson (R)	29.8
73	CA 34th: Lucille Roybal-Allard (D)	351 700	72	MI 5th: Dale E. Kildee (D)	16.8	71	NC 12th: Melvin L. Watt (D)	29.8
74	MA 4th: Barney Frank (D)	349 300	74	NC 8th: Larry Kissell (D)	16.7	74	MA 10th: William Keating (D)	29.7
75	CA 35th: Maxine Waters (D)	344 700	75	CA 33rd: Karen Bass (D)	16.6	74	MT At-Large Denny Rehberg (R)	29.7

Congressional Districts of the 112th Congress of the United States
Selected Rankings

	Median household income, 2010			Percent of persons below 65 years with no health insurance, 2010			Percent of persons below the poverty level, 2010	
Median income rank	State congressional district Representative	Median income (dollars) [col 52]	No health insurance rank	State congressional district Representative	Percent with no health insurance [col 64]	Poverty rate rank	State congressional district Representative	Poverty rate [col 54]
1	VA 11th: Gerald E. Connolly (D)	105 560	1	TX 29th: Gene Green (D)	43.9	1	NY 16th: José E. Serrano (D)	38.9
2	VA 10th: Frank R. Wolf (R)	98 789	2	CA 31st: Xavier Becerra (D)	39.9	2	AZ 4th: Ed Pastor (D)	34.4
3	NJ 7th: Leonard Lance (R)	94 843	3	TX 9th Al Green (D)	38.9	3	CA 20th: Jim Costa (D)	33.7
4	CA 14th: Anna G. Eshoo (D)	94 740	4	CA 34th: Lucille Roybal-Allard (D)	37.5	4	MI 13th: Hansen Clarke (D)	32.8
5	NJ 11th: Rodney P. Frelinghuysen (R)	93 514	5	FL 23rd: Alcee L. Hastings (D)	37.2	5	PA 1st: Robert A. Brady (D)	31.6
6	NY 3rd: Peter T. King (R)	92 064	6	FL 17th: Frederica Wilson (D)	37.1	6	MI 14th: John Conyers Jr. (D)	31.1
7	NJ 5th: Scott Garrett (R)	90 587	7	FL 18th: Ileana Ros-Lehtinen (R)	35.9	7	MS 2nd: Bennie G. Thompson (D)	29.8
8	VA 8th: James P. Moran (D)	88 668	8	TX 28th Henry Cuellar (D)	35.8	8	TX 15th Rubén Hinojosa (D)	29.5
9	NJ 12th: Rush D. Holt (D)	86 685	9	FL 21st: Mario Diaz-Balart (R)	35.7	9	CA 31st: Xavier Becerra (D)	28.8
10	MD 8th: Chris Van Hollen (D)	85 926	10	FL 25th: David Rivera (R)	35.3	10	AL 7th: Terri A. Sewell (D)	28.0
11	CA 15th: Michael M. Honda (D)	85 700	11	TX 30th Eddie Bernice Johnson (D)	35.1	10	TX 27th Blake Farenthold (R)	28.0
12	NY 2nd: Steve Israel (D)	84 909	12	TX 15th Rubén Hinojosa (D)	34.5	10	TX 29th Gene Green (D)	28.0
13	NY 18th: Nita M. Lowey (D)	84 607	13	TX 18th Sheila Jackson-Lee (D)	33.5	13	WI 4th: Gwen Moore (D)	27.9
14	CA 42nd: Gary G. Miller (R)	83 029	14	CA 47th: Loretta Sanchez (D)	33.2	14	FL 3rd: Corrine Brown (D)	27.8
15	MD 5th: Steny H. Hoyer (D)	83 020	15	TX 16th Silvestre Reyes (D)	32.5	15	FL 23rd: Alcee L. Hastings (D)	27.7
16	CA 12th: Jackie Speier (D)	82 337	16	TX 32nd Pete Sessions (R)	32.4	16	TX 18th Sheila Jackson-Lee (D)	27.5
17	NY 4th: Carolyn McCarthy (D)	82 102	17	CA 33rd: Karen Bass (D)	31.8	17	GA 2nd: Sanford D. Bishop Jr. (D)	27.3
18	CO 6th: Mike Coffman (R)	82 062	18	CA 35th: Maxine Waters (D)	31.4	17	TX 28th Henry Cuellar (D)	27.3
19	CA 48th: John Campbell (R)	82 047	19	AZ 4th: Ed Pastor (D)	31.1	19	CA 34th: Lucille Roybal-Allard (D)	27.2
20	NY 1st: Timothy H. Bishop (D)	80 674	19	IL 4th: Luis V. Gutierrez (D)	31.1	19	L:A 2nd: Cedric Richmond (D)	27.2
21	IL 13th: Judy Biggert (R)	80 124	21	GA 4th: Henry C. "Hank" Johnson Jr. (D)	30.8	21	KY 5th: Harold Rogers (R)	26.9
22	WA 8th: David G. Reichert (R)	79 260	22	CA 28th: Howard L. Berman (D)	30.5	22	NY 10th: Edolphus Towns (D)	26.3
23	NY 19th: Nan Hayworth (R)	77 920	23	TX 27th Blake Farenthold (R)	30.1	22	PA 2nd: Chaka Fattah (D)	26.3
24	CT 4th: James A. Himes (D)	77 074	24	NV 1st: Shelley Berkley (D)	29.9	22	TX 30th Eddie Bernice Johnson (D)	26.3
25	IL 10th: Robert Dold (R)	77 055	25	CA 38th: Grace F. Napolitano (D)	29.3	25	CA 18th: Dennis A. Cardoza (D)	26.2
26	CA 30th: Henry A. Waxman (D)	76 700	26	CA 20th: Jim Costa (D)	29.0	26	GA 12th: John Barrow (D)	26.1
27	CA 10th: John Garamendi (D)	75 457	26	CA 43rd: Joe Baca (D)	29.0	27	SC 6th: James E. Clyburn (D)	26.0
28	NY 14th: Carolyn B. Maloney (D)	75 348	28	NJ 13th: Albio Sires (D)	28.4	28	NC 1st: G. K. Butterfield (D)	25.6
29	CA 26th: David Dreier (R)	75 086	29	CA 32nd: Judy Chu (D)	28.2	29	FL 17th: Frederica Wilson (D)	25.5
30	CA 24th: Elton Gallegly (R)	74 103	30	TX 11th K. Michael Conaway (R)	28.0	29	TN 9th Steve Cohen (D)	25.5
31	CA 16th: Zoe Lofgren (D)	73 973	31	FL 14th: Connie Mack (R)	27.6	31	OH 11th: Marcia L. Fudge (D)	25.0
32	CA 13th: Fortney Pete Stark (D)	73 539	31	FL 19th: Ted Deutch (D)	27.5	32	IL 1st: Bobby L. Rush (D)	24.8
33	GA 6th: Tom Price (R)	73 528	33	TX 1st Louie Gohmert (R)	27.3	33	CA 35th: Maxine Waters (D)	24.7
34	MA 9th: Stephen F. Lynch (D)	72 927	34	CA 39th: Linda T. Sánchez (D)	27.1	34	IN 7th: André Carson (D)	24.6
35	WA 1st: Vacant	72 438	34	TX 20th Charles A. Gonzalez (D)	27.1	35	MA 8th: Michael E. Capuano (D)	24.5
36	CA 11th: Jerry McNerney (D)	72 075	36	LA 5th: Rodney Alexander (R)	26.6	35	NC 12th: Melvin L. Watt (D)	24.5
37	MD 4th: Donna F. Edwards (D)	71 863	37	CA 37th: Laura Richardson (D)	25.7	37	NY 12th: Nydia M. Velázquez (D)	24.4
38	MN 2nd: John Kline (R)	71 862	38	Tx 5th Jeb Hensarling (R)	25.6	38	GA 5th: John Lewis (D)	24.3
39	MA 7th: Edward J. Markey (D)	71 400	38	TX 13th Mac Thornberry (R)	25.6	39	IL 7th: Danny K. Davis (D)	24.1
40	CA 46th: Dana Rohrabacher (R)	71 332	40	FL 8th: Daniel Webster (R)	25.4	40	AL 3rd: Mike Rogers (R)	24.0
41	NJ 3rd: Jon Runyan (R)	70 743	40	FL 11th: Kathy Castor (D)	25.4	40	NY 15th: Charles B. Rangel (D)	24.0
42	MN 3rd: Erik Paulsen (R)	70 552	40	FL 13th: Vern Buchanan (R)	25.4	42	CA 43rd: Joe Baca (D)	23.9
43	CA 50th: Brian P. Bilbray (R)	70 362	40	TX 23rd Francisco "Quico" Canseco (R)	25.4	43	CA 53rd: Susan A. Davis (D)	23.8
44	MA 6th: John F. Tierney (D)	70 330	44	FL 3rd: Corrine Brown (D)	25.3	44	TX 16th Silvestre Reyes (D)	23.7
45	TX 7th John Abney Culberson (R)	70 229	45	OK 2nd: Dan Boren (D)	25.2	45	NY 28th: Louise McIntosh Slaughter (D)	23.6
46	MO 2nd: W. Todd Akin (R)	70 146	46	GA 13th: David Scott (D)	25.1	45	TX 9th Al Green (D)	23.6
47	MD 3rd: John P. Sarbanes (D)	70 113	47	TX 12th Kay Granger (R)	25.0	47	IL 4th: Luis V. Gutierrez (D)	23.2
48	PA 8th: Michael G. Fitzpatrick (R)	70 008	48	TX 2nd Ted Poe (R)	24.9	48	NM 2nd: Steve Pearce (R)	22.7
49	CA 8th: Nancy Pelosi (D)	69 926	49	FL 16th: Thomas J. Rooney (R)	24.7	49	AZ 7th: Raúl M. Grijalva (D)	22.6
50	MD 6th: Roscoe G. Bartlett (R)	69 501	50	TX 19th Randy Neugebauer (R)	24.6	49	CA 5th: Doris O. Matsui (D)	22.6
51	NJ 6th: Frank Pallone Jr. (D)	69 417	51	CA 23rd: Lois Capps (D)	24.4	51	AZ 1st: Paul R. Gosar (R)	22.3
52	PA 6th:Jim Gerlach (R)	69 222	51	GA 1st: Jack Kingston (R)	24.4	51	FL 11th: Kathy Castor (D)	22.3
53	PA 7th: Patrick Meehan (R)	69 135	53	AZ 7th: Raúl M. Grijalva (D)	24.3	53	CA 21st: Devin Nunes (R)	22.2
54	CT 2nd: Joe Courtney (D)	68 952	54	CA 45th: Mary Bono Mack (R)	24.2	53	CA 33rd: Karen Bass (D)	22.2
55	VA 1st: Robert J. Wittman (R)	68 777	54	GA 2nd: Sanford D. Bishop Jr. (D)	24.2	55	AR 1st: Eric A. "Rick" Crawford (R)	22.1
56	MA 5th: Niki Tsongas (D)	68 241	54	NV 2nd: Mark E. Amodei (R)	24.2	55	LA 5th: Rodney Alexander (R)	22.1
57	IL 8th: Joe Walsh (R)	67 740	54	TX 25th Lloyd Doggett (D)	24.2	57	OH 1st: Steve Chabot (R)	21.9
58	CA 52nd: Duncan Hunter (R)	67 671	58	CA 18th: Dennis A. Cardoza (D)	24.0	58	NY 11th: Yvette D. Clarke (D)	21.6
59	CA 44th: Ken Calvert (R)	67 381	58	WA 4th: Doc Hastings (R)	24.0	59	TX 17th Bill Flores (R)	21.4
60	TX 22nd Pete Olson (R)	67 196	60	FL 12th: Dennis Ross (R)	23.9	59	TX 20th Charles A. Gonzalez (D)	21.4
61	MN 6th: Michele Bachmann (R)	67 049	61	FL 15th: Bill Posey (R)	23.8	61	AR 4th: Mike Ross (D)	21.3
62	MD 1st: Andrew Harris (R)	66 890	61	FL 20th: Debbie Wasserman Schultz (D)	23.8	61	MI 5th: Dale E. Kildee (D)	21.3
63	HI 1st: Colleen Hanabusa (D)	66 111	61	NM 3rd: Ben Ray Luján (D)	23.8	61	MO 1st: William Lacy Clay (D)	21.3
64	TX 3rd Sam Johnson (R)	66 068	64	NM 2nd: Steve Pearce (R)	23.7	64	TX 23rd Francisco "Quico" Canseco (R)	21.2
65	IL 6th: Peter J. Roskam (R)	66 033	65	MS 2nd: Bennie G. Thompson (D)	23.6	65	WV 3rd: Nick J. Rahall II (D)	21.1
66	CA 36th: Janice Hahn (D)	65 717	65	TX 6th Joe Barton (R)	23.6	66	GA 4th: Henry C. "Hank" Johnson Jr. (D)	21.0
67	CA 40th: Edward R. Royce (R)	65 243	67	CA 29th: Adam B. Schiff (D)	23.5	66	TN 1st David P. Roe (R)	21.0
68	MA 10th: William Keating (D)	65 094	67	CA 49th: Darrell E. Issa (R)	23.5	68	CA 47th: Loretta Sanchez (D)	20.9
69	MA 4th: Barney Frank (D)	64 958	69	L:A 2nd: Cedric Richmond (D)	23.4	68	CO 1st: Diana DeGette (D)	20.9
70	WI 5th: F. James Sensenbrenner Jr. (R)	64 869	70	CA 53rd: Susan A. Davis (D)	23.3	68	GA 10th: Paul C. Broun (R)	20.9
71	AK At-Large: Don Young (R)	64 576	70	GA 5th: John Lewis (D)	23.3	71	IL 2nd: Jesse L. Jackson Jr. (D)	20.8
72	CA 6th: Lynn C. Woolsey (D)	64 391	70	OR 2nd: Greg Walden (R)	23.3	71	MS 4th: Steven Palazzo (R)	20.8
73	NJ 4th: Christopher H. Smith (R)	64 265	73	CA 27th: Brad Sherman (D)	23.2	71	NM 3rd: Ben Ray Luján (D)	20.8
74	NC 4th: David E. Price (D)	63 543	73	CA 51st: Bob Filner (D)	23.2	71	NC 7th: Mike McIntyre (D)	20.8
75	IL 14th: Randy Hultgren (R)	63 402	73	GA 12th: John Barrow (D)	23.2	75	FL 2nd: Steve Southerland II (R)	20.5

Table E. Congressional Districts 112th Congress — **Land Area and Population Characteristics**

STATE District	Representative, 112th Congress	Population and population characteristics, 2010												
				Percent									
					Race alone								
		Land area,[1] 2010 (sq km)	Total persons	Per square kilometer	White	Black	American Indian, Alaska Native	Asian and Pacific Islander	Some other race	Two or more races	Hispanic or Latino[2]	Non-Hispanic White alone	Percent female	Percent foreign born	Percent born in state of residence
		1	2	3	4	5	6	7	8	9	10	11	12	13	14

1. Dry land or land partially or temporarily covered by water.   2. May be of any race.

Table E. Congressional Districts 112th Congress — **Age and Education**

STATE District	Population and population characteristics, 2010 (cont.)										Education, 2010			
	Age (percent)										Enrollment[1]		Attainment[2] (percent)	
	Under 5 years	5 to 17 years	18 to 24 years	25 to 34 years	35 to 44 years	45 to 54 years	55 to 64 years	65 to 74 years	75 years and over	Median age	Total	Percent private	High school graduate or more	Bachelor's degree or more
	15	16	17	18	19	20	21	22	23	24	25	26	27	28

1. All persons 3 years old and over enrolled in nursery school through college and graduate or professional school.   2. Persons 25 years old and over.

Table E. Congressional Districts 112th Congress — **Households and Group Quarters**

STATE District	Households, 2010						Group quarters, 2010					
	Number	Persons per household	Family households (percent)	Husband-wife family (percent)	Female family householder[1]	One person households (percent)	Total in group quarters	Percent 65 years and over	Persons in correctional institutions	Persons in nursing homes	Persons in college dormitories	Persons in military quarters
	29	30	31	32	33	34	35	36	37	38	39	40

1. No spouse present.

Table E. Congressional Districts 112th Congress — **Housing and Money Income**

STATE District	Housing units, 2010										Money income, 2010		
		Occupied units										Households	
			Owner-occupied					Renter-occupied					
						Median owner cost as a percent of income							
	Total	Percent occupied	Percent	Median value[1] (dollars)	Percent valued at $500,000 or more	With a mortgage	Without a mortgage[2]	Median rent[3]	Median rent as a percent of income	Sub-standard units[4] (percent)	Per capita income (dollars)	Median income (dollars)	Percent with income of $100,000 or more
	41	42	43	44	45	46	47	48	49	50	51	52	53

1. Specified owner-occupied units.   2. Median monthly owner costs is often in the minimum category—10.0 percent or less, which is indicated as 10.0 percent.   3. Specified renter-occupied units.   4. Overcrowded or lacking complete plumbing facilities.

Table E. Congressional Districts 112th Congress — **Poverty, Labor Force, Employment, and Social Security**

STATE District	Poverty, 2010 (percent)			Civilian labor force, 2010			Civilian employment,[2] 2010					Social Security beneficiaries, December 2010		Supplemental Security Income recipients, December 2010
					Unemployment			Percent						
	Persons below poverty level	Families below poverty level	Households receiving food stamps in past 12 months	Total	Total	Rate[1]	Total	Management, business, science, and arts occupations	Service, sales, and office	Construction and production	Persons under age 65 with no health insurance, 2010 (percent)	Number	Rate[3]	
	54	55	56	57	58	59	60	61	62	63	64	65	66	67

1. Percent of civilian labor force.　　2. Persons 16 years old and over.　　3. Per 1,000 resident population enumerated in the 2010 census.

Table E. Congressional Districts 112th Congress — **Agriculture**

STATE District	Agriculture, 2007												
	Farms		Land in farms		Farm Operators			Value of products sold				Government payments	
						Percent of farm operators				Percent of sales from			
	Number	Operated by family or individual (percent)	Acreage	Average size of farm (acres)	Total	Whose primary occupation is farming	Who live on the farm operated	Total ($1,000)	Average per farm	Crops	Livestock	Total ($1,000)	Percent of farms
	68	69	70	71	72	73	74	75	76	77	78	79	80

STATE District	Representative, 112th Congress	Land area,[1] 2010 (sq km)	Total persons	Per square kilometer	White	Black	American Indian, Alaska Native	Asian and Pacific Islander	Some other race	Two or more races	Hispanic or Latino[2]	Non-Hispanic White alone	Percent female	Percent foreign born	Percent born in state of residence
		1	2	3	4	5	6	7	8	9	10	11	12	13	14
UNITED STATES.............		9 147 593	308 745 538	33.8	72.4	12.6	0.9	5.0	6.2	2.9	16.3	63.7	50.8	12.9	58.8
ALABAMA		131 171	4 779 736	36.4	68.5	26.2	0.6	1.2	2.0	1.5	3.9	67.0	51.5	3.5	70.0
District 1	Jo Bonner (R)	16 328	687 841	42.1	67.1	27.7	1.2	1.3	1.2	1.4	2.8	65.8	51.5	3.2	66.9
District 2	Martha Roby (R)	27 153	673 877	24.8	64.4	30.9	0.5	1.0	1.6	1.6	3.4	63.1	51.4	2.4	70.4
District 3	Mike Rogers (R)	20 250	681 298	33.6	63.7	31.8	0.3	1.4	1.3	1.4	2.8	62.6	51.6	3.3	65.6
District 4	Robert B. Aderholt (R)	21 646	660 162	30.5	88.4	5.0	0.6	0.5	3.9	1.5	6.4	86.4	50.8	4.0	74.9
District 5	Mo Brooks (R)	11 568	718 724	62.1	75.1	17.7	1.0	1.6	2.4	2.3	4.6	73.4	51.0	4.3	62.4
District 6	Spencer Bachus (R)	11 786	754 482	64.0	82.1	12.7	0.3	1.6	2.1	1.2	4.2	80.2	51.2	4.9	69.9
District 7	Terri A. Sewell (D)	22 440	603 352	26.9	33.6	62.8	0.2	0.7	1.7	0.9	3.0	32.7	52.9	2.2	81.6
ALASKA		1 477 953	710 231	0.5	66.7	3.3	14.8	6.4	1.6	7.3	5.5	64.1	48.0	6.9	39.0
At Large	Don Young (R)	1 477 953	710 231	0.5	66.7	3.3	14.8	6.4	1.6	7.3	5.5	64.1	48.0	6.9	39.0
ARIZONA		294 207	6 392 017	21.7	73.0	4.1	4.6	3.0	11.9	3.4	29.6	57.8	50.3	13.4	37.7
District 1	Paul R. Gosar (R)	151 704	774 310	5.1	67.2	1.7	19.9	1.1	7.2	2.9	19.5	57.1	48.8	6.7	48.2
District 2	Trent Franks (R)	52 376	972 839	18.6	79.5	3.7	2.0	2.8	8.7	3.2	20.8	69.3	51.5	9.1	32.9
District 3	Ben Quayle (R)	1 549	707 919	457.0	80.6	3.3	1.6	3.6	7.8	3.0	19.3	70.7	50.5	13.0	33.9
District 4	Ed Pastor (D)	515	698 314	1 354.9	50.5	9.3	3.2	2.5	30.3	4.1	63.9	21.5	49.1	27.3	47.5
District 5	David Schweikert (R)	3 637	656 833	180.6	78.8	4.0	2.9	4.8	6.2	3.2	16.5	70.3	50.3	12.1	29.6
District 6	Jeff Flake (R)	1 873	971 733	518.7	80.1	3.3	1.3	3.9	8.0	3.3	20.7	69.3	51.0	11.1	34.2
Dlstrict 7	Raúl M. Grijalva (D)	59 237	855 769	14.4	62.6	4.1	5.6	2.1	21.6	3.9	56.0	32.6	50.1	19.7	44.2
District 8	Ron Barber (D)	23 317	754 300	32.4	81.8	3.6	1.2	3.0	6.8	3.6	22.7	68.2	50.8	9.8	31.6
ARKANSAS.......................		134 771	2 915 918	21.6	77.0	15.4	0.8	1.4	3.4	2.0	6.4	74.5	50.9	4.5	61.3
District 1	Eric A. "Rick" Crawford (R)	44 458	687 694	15.5	79.7	16.6	0.4	0.5	1.2	1.5	2.7	78.6	50.9	1.8	64.3
District 2	Timothy Griffin (R)	15 302	751 377	49.1	72.7	20.8	0.5	1.5	2.6	1.9	5.2	70.5	51.3	4.7	65.2
District 3	Steve Womack (R)	21 932	822 564	37.5	83.9	2.4	1.4	2.8	6.7	2.7	11.9	79.5	50.5	8.1	50.7
District 4	Mike Ross (D)	53 079	654 283	12.3	70.3	24.3	0.6	0.6	2.6	1.6	4.6	68.7	50.9	2.6	67.3
CALIFORNIA....................		403 466	37 253 956	92.3	57.6	6.2	1.0	13.4	17.0	4.9	37.6	40.1	50.3	27.2	53.8
District 1	Mike Thompson (D)	28 464	704 012	24.7	73.3	1.8	2.9	6.3	10.9	4.9	23.6	63.1	50.1	15.3	63.2
District 2	Wally Herger (R)	56 300	708 596	12.6	78.4	1.4	2.2	4.6	8.5	4.8	19.0	70.2	50.3	10.6	65.3
District 3	Daniel E. Lungren (R)	8 735	783 317	89.7	69.9	6.1	1.0	11.6	5.7	5.8	15.6	62.4	50.5	16.1	61.3
District 4	Tom McClintock (R)	42 502	774 261	18.2	84.6	1.4	1.4	4.5	4.0	4.1	12.1	78.0	50.0	9.1	64.8
District 5	Doris O. Matsui (D)	380	700 443	1 843.4	46.3	14.4	1.2	18.1	12.8	7.2	27.4	35.8	51.2	21.7	58.5
District 6	Lynn C. Woolsey (D)	4 209	664 468	157.9	77.8	2.1	1.0	4.9	9.7	4.5	21.1	68.5	50.9	17.6	56.4
District 7	George Miller (D)	898	655 708	730.4	47.4	15.3	0.7	15.9	14.2	6.6	29.7	35.3	50.6	25.5	55.5
District 8	Nancy Pelosi (D)	92	666 827	7 234.6	48.7	6.8	0.5	31.9	7.4	4.7	16.6	41.7	48.8	35.8	36.8
District 9	Barbara Lee (D)	343	648 766	1 893.7	42.7	20.9	0.7	18.7	11.1	5.9	22.0	34.6	51.4	26.5	50.4
District 10	John Garamendi (D)	2 605	714 750	274.4	62.7	7.5	0.6	14.1	8.7	6.4	21.3	52.8	51.1	21.3	56.1
District 11	Jerry McNerney (D)	5 883	796 753	135.4	62.0	4.9	0.8	15.1	11.2	5.9	26.3	50.3	50.7	19.5	61.7
District 12	Jackie Speier (D)	301	651 322	2 161.2	49.5	2.3	0.4	34.8	7.6	5.3	18.5	40.9	51.2	36.3	47.2
District 13	Fortney Pete Stark (D)	575	665 318	1 157.6	36.3	7.2	0.7	37.6	11.8	6.4	24.9	26.3	50.9	37.1	49.1
District 14	Anna G. Eshoo (D)	2 139	653 935	305.7	60.1	2.5	0.5	22.5	9.8	4.6	20.8	50.9	49.9	32.1	44.1
District 15	Michael M. Honda (D)	742	677 605	913.8	45.9	2.5	0.6	37.1	9.0	4.9	20.7	36.6	50.2	37.8	46.1
District 16	Zoe Lofgren (D)	593	676 880	1 140.5	42.4	3.2	1.0	29.0	19.3	5.0	39.9	25.6	49.4	37.4	49.6
District 17	Sam Farr (D)	12 375	664 240	53.7	59.8	2.3	1.2	5.8	25.8	5.0	50.4	39.2	49.2	27.3	54.3
District 18	Dennis A. Cardoza (D)	7 918	723 607	91.4	51.7	6.1	1.3	9.7	25.6	5.6	52.7	29.5	49.6	25.5	62.2
District 19	Jeff Denham (R)	17 293	757 337	43.8	66.8	4.1	1.6	6.0	16.7	4.8	37.3	49.8	51.0	16.5	66.2
District 20	Jim Costa (D)	12 879	744 350	57.8	46.3	6.5	1.7	5.4	35.8	4.2	70.4	16.6	46.3	30.4	59.1
District 21	Devin Nunes (R)	20 795	784 176	37.7	60.7	2.4	1.6	7.1	23.9	4.3	51.2	37.3	50.3	21.0	65.7
District 22	Kevin McCarthy (R)	26 945	797 084	29.6	68.7	6.5	1.4	4.3	14.5	4.6	32.0	54.3	49.1	12.6	66.5
District 23	Lois Capps (D)	2 694	695 404	258.1	64.8	1.9	1.3	5.7	21.9	4.5	49.5	41.1	49.8	25.9	54.7
District 24	Elton Gallegly (R)	10 048	681 622	67.8	75.9	1.7	0.9	6.5	10.6	4.4	28.8	60.3	50.5	17.7	57.8
District 25	Howard P. "Buck" McKeon (R)	55 603	844 320	15.2	59.5	10.3	1.2	6.1	17.7	5.2	39.2	41.7	49.9	19.0	60.7
District 26	David Dreier (R)	1 947	691 452	355.1	60.0	4.9	0.6	19.4	10.6	4.5	30.7	42.8	51.4	25.6	56.1
District 27	Brad Sherman (D)	390	684 496	1 754.4	58.6	4.7	0.6	12.6	18.6	4.9	42.3	38.0	50.7	38.9	46.1
District 28	Howard L. Berman (D)	199	660 194	3 320.1	56.7	3.8	0.7	6.8	27.7	4.3	57.5	30.5	49.9	41.2	43.3
District 29	Adam B. Schiff (D)	262	642 138	2 454.5	52.8	4.9	0.5	28.1	9.5	4.3	25.0	39.5	52.0	46.3	38.8
District 30	Henry A. Waxman (D)	740	662 319	895.5	78.0	3.0	0.3	11.1	3.3	4.3	10.1	72.1	51.2	24.8	42.6
District 31	Xavier Becerra (D)	102	611 336	6 005.0	39.9	4.3	1.1	15.3	34.6	4.8	68.2	11.3	49.1	51.5	39.3
District 32	Judy Chu (D)	236	642 236	2 717.0	43.4	2.3	1.0	22.5	27.0	3.8	64.2	10.5	50.8	41.7	50.6
District 33	Karen Bass (D)	125	637 122	5 113.5	36.0	25.3	0.7	13.5	19.9	4.6	37.4	21.6	51.4	35.5	42.1
District 34	Lucille Roybal-Allard (D)	151	654 303	4 334.3	47.3	5.2	1.1	6.8	35.6	4.0	78.7	8.8	49.0	44.3	48.8
District 35	Maxine Waters (D)	143	662 413	4 632.0	30.7	29.2	0.7	6.2	28.9	4.4	54.5	9.0	51.6	33.5	52.9
District 36	Janice Hahn (D)	193	659 385	3 409.1	59.0	4.2	0.6	16.9	13.9	5.4	32.0	43.7	50.4	27.3	49.1
District 37	Laura Richardson (D)	192	648 847	3 374.2	32.8	22.0	0.7	13.4	26.4	4.8	49.4	13.7	51.4	29.6	54.5
District 38	Grace F. Napolitano (D)	270	641 410	2 375.5	49.9	3.2	1.1	11.5	30.4	3.9	75.4	9.5	50.6	37.6	56.0

1. Dry land or land partially or temporarily covered by water.   2. May be of any race.

STATE District	Under 5 years	5 to 17 years	18 to 24 years	25 to 34 years	35 to 44 years	45 to 54 years	55 to 64 years	65 to 74 years	75 years and over	Median age	Total	Percent private	High school graduate or more	Bachelor's degree or more
	15	16	17	18	19	20	21	22	23	24	25	26	27	28
UNITED STATES...............	6.5	17.5	9.9	13.3	13.3	14.6	11.8	7.0	6.0	37.2	82 724 222	16.4	85.6	28.2
ALABAMA	6.4	17.3	10.0	12.7	13.0	14.5	12.3	7.8	6.0	37.9	1 238 462	14.4	82.1	21.9
District 1.............................	6.5	17.9	9.1	12.4	12.7	14.6	12.5	8.1	6.1	38.4	175 653	16.0	83.1	21.5
District 2.............................	6.5	17.4	9.8	13.0	12.9	14.3	12.1	7.8	6.1	37.6	170 261	16.1	82.0	20.1
District 3.............................	6.2	17.0	12.0	12.4	12.7	14.1	12.3	7.7	5.7	37.0	194 574	14.4	79.5	19.9
District 4.............................	6.2	17.4	8.3	11.7	13.2	14.5	13.0	9.1	6.6	39.9	148 945	8.7	76.7	12.1
District 5.............................	6.1	17.2	9.6	12.6	13.3	15.5	12.0	7.8	5.9	38.7	192 346	13.8	84.0	26.9
District 6.............................	6.5	17.5	8.3	13.9	14.1	14.7	12.2	7.1	5.8	37.8	188 954	19.3	87.9	33.5
District 7.............................	6.6	16.8	13.8	13.1	11.5	13.8	12.0	6.6	5.8	34.8	167 729	11.2	80.7	16.8
ALASKA	7.6	18.8	10.5	14.5	13.1	15.6	12.1	5.0	2.8	33.8	193 373	13.0	91.0	27.9
At Large	7.6	18.8	10.5	14.5	13.1	15.6	12.1	5.0	2.8	33.8	193 373	13.0	91.0	27.9
ARIZONA	7.1	18.4	9.9	13.4	12.9	13.2	11.4	7.8	6.0	35.9	1 729 192	10.6	85.6	25.9
District 1.............................	6.6	17.4	10.3	11.7	11.3	13.5	13.3	9.5	6.5	38.6	196 673	7.8	83.4	19.1
District 2.............................	6.5	17.8	7.9	11.7	12.3	12.8	12.2	10.3	8.6	40.0	248 890	10.5	88.5	21.4
District 3.............................	6.7	17.4	8.6	13.9	14.5	15.3	12.1	6.6	4.9	37.6	173 567	18.2	91.2	34.0
District 4.............................	10.1	22.7	12.0	16.3	13.8	11.4	7.5	3.7	2.5	28.2	208 268	5.9	66.1	13.1
District 5.............................	5.3	14.7	12.9	14.7	12.6	14.7	12.1	7.3	5.7	37.0	184 739	13.5	92.7	42.4
District 6.............................	7.9	20.2	8.0	13.6	14.3	12.6	10.1	7.3	5.9	35.2	273 035	10.6	90.0	27.9
District 7.............................	8.1	20.6	12.2	14.0	12.6	11.9	9.7	6.5	4.4	31.3	258 461	7.4	75.6	15.0
District 8.............................	5.7	15.3	8.7	12.1	11.5	13.9	13.9	10.3	8.6	42.1	185 559	13.4	92.5	34.7
ARKANSAS.....................	6.8	17.6	9.7	12.9	12.6	14.0	12.0	8.0	6.4	37.4	760 063	10.0	82.9	19.5
District 1.............................	6.5	17.7	8.7	12.1	12.3	14.1	12.5	9.0	7.0	39.1	170 861	8.5	80.3	14.4
District 2.............................	6.8	17.3	10.2	14.0	12.9	14.0	11.8	7.2	5.7	36.2	201 479	15.5	86.5	25.5
District 3.............................	7.2	18.3	10.6	13.6	12.9	13.4	11.1	7.3	5.6	35.2	224 587	8.0	82.8	22.0
District 4.............................	6.4	17.0	9.3	11.5	12.0	14.4	13.0	9.0	7.3	39.9	163 136	7.4	81.9	15.0
CALIFORNIA.....................	6.8	18.2	10.5	14.3	13.9	14.1	10.8	6.1	5.3	35.2	10 648 332	13.6	80.7	30.1
District 1.............................	6.0	16.1	12.1	13.0	12.0	14.0	13.3	7.3	6.2	37.4	201 377	11.6	85.8	28.1
District 2.............................	6.4	17.3	10.7	12.1	11.3	14.0	13.1	8.1	6.8	38.3	197 436	10.7	84.7	20.4
District 3.............................	6.3	18.5	8.6	12.4	13.6	15.4	12.3	7.0	6.0	38.4	221 024	16.1	89.1	25.2
District 4.............................	5.5	17.3	7.7	10.9	12.5	16.0	14.4	8.7	7.0	42.0	202 732	12.1	91.9	29.5
District 5.............................	7.7	17.9	11.4	16.3	12.9	12.9	10.4	5.5	5.0	32.6	204 366	11.0	80.9	24.5
District 6.............................	5.7	15.7	8.3	11.8	13.2	15.7	14.8	7.9	6.8	41.6	165 038	16.5	88.3	40.7
District 7.............................	6.6	17.4	9.6	14.0	13.6	15.4	12.4	6.2	4.8	36.9	176 222	14.7	84.3	24.4
District 8.............................	4.4	8.7	9.4	22.2	17.0	13.7	11.6	6.5	6.6	38.0	138 717	26.3	85.7	50.6
District 9.............................	6.1	14.2	12.0	16.3	14.6	13.6	11.8	6.1	5.3	35.9	183 815	14.6	83.9	43.2
District 10...........................	6.4	18.5	8.4	12.2	14.1	15.6	11.9	6.7	6.2	38.4	198 545	16.0	90.5	40.5
District 11...........................	6.9	20.8	8.5	11.9	14.4	15.4	11.1	6.2	4.8	36.5	231 273	14.3	86.6	32.9
District 12...........................	5.7	14.2	8.2	13.9	15.0	15.5	13.1	7.4	7.1	40.3	164 883	25.1	88.9	44.3
District 13...........................	6.9	17.1	8.7	14.6	15.1	15.0	11.3	6.0	5.3	36.7	176 132	15.2	85.8	36.0
District 14...........................	6.6	16.2	7.9	14.4	14.8	15.3	11.8	6.8	6.2	38.4	175 665	27.5	91.2	57.0
District 15...........................	6.9	17.0	8.2	14.9	16.2	15.4	10.5	5.9	5.1	36.9	193 203	18.6	89.7	47.2
District 16...........................	7.4	17.8	10.2	15.5	15.4	13.9	10.0	5.5	4.2	34.4	188 905	14.8	78.4	33.1
District 17...........................	7.3	18.1	12.4	14.4	13.1	13.2	11.0	5.5	5.1	33.4	198 187	10.1	74.4	24.8
District 18...........................	8.7	22.2	11.5	14.2	12.7	12.4	9.0	5.0	4.2	30.1	224 036	6.1	67.4	10.9
District 19...........................	7.2	19.4	10.3	13.4	12.4	13.5	11.3	6.8	5.7	34.7	214 676	9.2	79.9	21.3
District 20...........................	9.8	22.9	12.5	15.7	13.1	11.5	7.4	3.9	3.1	27.8	220 577	4.8	56.0	7.9
District 21...........................	8.7	22.2	11.0	13.8	12.3	12.3	9.6	5.5	4.7	30.7	248 706	6.8	73.2	18.0
District 22...........................	7.3	19.4	10.7	13.5	12.7	14.4	11.0	6.2	4.8	34.3	234 083	11.7	82.4	20.6
District 23...........................	6.9	16.8	15.2	14.5	12.0	12.3	10.5	6.0	5.9	32.3	206 086	8.1	74.9	27.4
District 24...........................	6.0	18.5	9.0	11.5	13.4	16.2	12.3	6.9	6.2	39.1	195 529	17.4	88.7	34.2
District 25...........................	7.5	22.0	10.6	12.9	14.1	14.8	9.7	5.0	3.5	32.7	271 536	11.0	80.8	20.9
District 26...........................	5.4	18.3	9.9	11.8	13.5	16.0	12.5	6.7	5.7	38.7	209 792	20.2	89.5	36.6
District 27...........................	6.1	16.5	10.6	14.9	14.9	14.5	10.9	6.0	5.5	36.2	189 314	14.6	81.4	30.2
District 28...........................	7.2	17.8	10.6	16.9	15.4	13.3	9.5	5.0	4.3	33.4	185 927	14.1	71.2	28.0
District 29...........................	5.2	14.3	8.8	14.7	14.7	15.5	12.2	7.4	7.2	39.8	167 136	20.1	82.4	39.0
District 30...........................	4.3	12.1	10.6	15.7	14.6	14.7	12.6	7.6	7.8	40.1	161 789	33.0	95.4	60.7
District 31...........................	7.1	17.5	11.7	17.8	15.6	12.6	9.0	4.8	3.8	32.5	168 168	11.6	59.8	19.9
District 32...........................	7.0	19.6	11.4	14.1	14.0	13.2	10.0	5.7	5.1	33.5	189 164	12.5	66.5	16.7
District 33...........................	5.8	14.6	11.8	17.7	15.3	13.7	10.2	5.9	5.1	35.1	174 294	23.3	78.0	33.5
District 34...........................	7.8	20.5	12.0	16.5	14.7	11.9	8.2	4.5	3.9	30.7	191 761	7.4	54.9	12.0
District 35...........................	8.1	20.4	11.7	15.3	14.1	13.0	8.8	4.9	3.7	31.3	191 995	11.8	67.8	18.3
District 36...........................	6.1	15.4	8.4	16.2	16.0	15.0	11.1	6.2	5.5	37.4	170 144	16.7	85.6	43.8
District 37...........................	7.8	20.3	11.9	15.2	14.0	13.0	9.1	4.9	3.8	31.3	203 741	9.2	71.7	19.3
District 38...........................	7.1	20.3	11.8	14.1	13.8	12.9	9.5	5.6	4.8	32.5	202 259	7.3	65.9	15.2

1. All persons 3 years old and over enrolled in nursery school through college and graduate or professional school.   2. Persons 25 years old and over.

Table E. Congressional Districts 112th Congress — Households and Group Quarters

STATE District	Households, 2010						Group quarters, 2010					
	Number	Persons per household	Family households (percent)	Husband-wife family (percent)	Female family householder[1]	One person households (percent)	Total in group quarters	Percent 65 years and over	Persons in correctional institutions	Persons in nursing homes	Persons in college dormitories	Persons in military quarters
	29	30	31	32	33	34	35	36	37	38	39	40
UNITED STATES	116 716 292	2.58	66.4	48.4	13.1	26.7	7 987 323	18.3	2 263 602	1 502 264	2 521 090	338 191
ALABAMA	1 883 791	2.48	67.8	47.9	15.3	27.4	115 816	18.7	41 177	22 995	36 341	2 152
District 1	267 165	2.53	69.0	48.0	16.4	26.2	15 889	19.5	5 651	2 748	2 579	0
District 2	263 982	2.47	67.9	46.7	16.5	27.4	21 055	15.7	13 115	3 638	2 551	1 329
District 3	270 181	2.45	66.2	45.0	16.4	28.0	24 838	15.5	5 460	3 214	8 946	0
District 4	259 673	2.51	70.9	54.2	11.8	25.7	7 624	41.6	2 866	3 915	716	0
District 5	289 131	2.43	67.8	50.7	12.7	27.8	18 363	17.0	5 272	2 892	5 422	823
District 6	294 665	2.52	69.8	55.4	10.7	25.7	9 917	23.8	6 309	3 299	2 830	0
District 7	238 994	2.43	61.9	33.1	23.9	31.7	18 130	13.3	2 504	3 289	13 297	0
ALASKA	258 058	2.65	66.2	49.4	10.7	25.6	26 352	5.9	4 206	1 626	1 872	5 055
At Large	258 058	2.65	66.2	49.4	10.7	25.6	26 352	5.9	4 206	1 626	1 872	5 055
ARIZONA	2 380 990	2.63	66.2	48.1	12.4	26.1	139 384	12.2	67 767	13 819	27 987	5 172
District 1	278 490	2.62	67.2	49.0	12.7	25.8	52 081	4.5	32 114	1 560	8 571	0
District 2	371 984	2.58	69.5	53.5	10.9	24.4	11 027	29.4	5 493	3 258	1 017	656
District 3	284 003	2.47	62.5	45.3	11.6	29.0	5 187	35.4	1 135	1 610	222	0
District 4	214 331	3.18	67.2	38.9	19.3	24.4	16 055	6.2	8 915	1 152	1 162	0
District 5	279 959	2.30	57.0	41.9	10.2	31.3	10 562	12.4	10	1 161	9 513	0
District 6	352 256	2.75	71.2	55.3	10.8	22.3	3 163	47.0	20	1 171	355	0
District 7	283 728	2.93	70.3	47.1	16.5	22.2	23 941	5.5	11 074	951	7 029	1 164
District 8	316 239	2.33	63.0	48.4	10.3	29.8	17 368	19.1	9 006	2 956	118	3 352
ARKANSAS	1 147 084	2.47	67.6	49.5	13.4	27.1	78 931	21.7	25 844	18 532	24 144	619
District 1	271 779	2.46	68.5	49.5	14.2	27.0	18 179	24.8	10 186	5 458	2 669	0
District 2	300 454	2.44	66.0	47.5	14.0	28.0	21 000	21.0	3 474	3 788	6 184	616
District 3	315 393	2.55	68.2	52.7	10.7	25.6	19 091	22.2	1 656	4 129	9 886	0
District 4	259 458	2.43	67.9	48.2	15.0	27.9	20 661	19.2	10 528	5 157	5 405	3
CALIFORNIA	12 577 498	2.90	68.7	49.4	13.3	23.3	819 816	15.4	256 807	111 884	172 843	57 628
District 1	266 894	2.55	61.9	45.5	11.0	27.3	32 529	14.0	5 716	3 046	7 679	3
District 2	269 650	2.59	66.3	48.8	11.8	25.4	12 866	22.8	2 028	2 329	2 607	413
District 3	284 266	2.69	70.5	52.9	12.3	23.1	23 317	16.7	12 558	1 978	22	0
District 4	298 307	2.53	69.2	55.0	9.5	23.9	21 623	14.9	11 492	2 149	630	5
District 5	256 398	2.69	61.2	37.8	16.9	29.2	11 390	19.1	2 254	1 772	1 493	0
District 6	261 659	2.47	61.7	46.8	10.1	28.8	17 021	17.6	6 097	2 983	2 967	390
District 7	227 228	2.82	69.8	47.6	15.9	23.3	16 253	14.7	9 202	1 818	439	0
District 8	292 776	2.21	40.9	29.1	8.2	40.8	7 358	16.6	1 573	1 914	5 594	0
District 9	253 984	2.46	54.6	35.7	13.8	32.5	16 857	12.2	1 044	2 384	11 927	0
District 10	257 421	2.74	70.9	54.6	11.3	22.5	6 781	31.4	1 018	2 412	1 568	908
District 11	267 700	2.92	75.4	58.4	11.4	19.4	18 336	22.1	5 669	2 641	2 187	0
District 12	239 332	2.68	66.3	51.2	10.5	24.8	4 077	37.0	3	2 742	2 557	0
District 13	222 182	2.96	73.3	54.7	13.0	20.3	3 433	39.5	0	2 605	1 076	661
District 14	245 204	2.61	65.9	53.5	8.4	25.8	15 702	15.7	1 090	1 649	7 028	5
District 15	235 711	2.83	71.1	55.2	10.8	21.4	9 295	24.9	2 565	2 397	2 605	0
District 16	205 906	3.23	73.4	53.9	13.0	19.1	7 933	12.2	1 448	894	3 356	0
District 17	210 829	3.01	68.4	50.3	12.3	23.1	35 880	8.6	11 516	1 949	8 411	2 504
District 18	213 822	3.31	75.8	49.9	17.5	18.7	17 504	13.6	8 153	2 297	1 150	0
District 19	256 154	2.89	72.6	52.8	13.5	21.3	16 154	11.5	11 755	1 643	902	0
District 20	187 727	3.68	80.0	50.5	20.3	15.1	45 430	4.9	45 411	1 745	234	2 038
District 21	240 805	3.22	77.1	54.6	15.2	17.8	8 541	31.3	1 521	3 449	1 624	0
District 22	268 076	2.83	71.8	52.1	13.5	22.2	31 670	5.9	25 512	1 513	6 854	426
District 23	226 135	3.00	64.5	47.3	11.6	24.0	19 341	11.8	1 115	1 697	9 419	826
District 24	236 977	2.82	73.0	57.1	10.8	21.0	13 379	14.8	4 895	1 523	2 317	901
District 25	260 665	3.16	76.9	55.4	14.8	17.7	20 629	5.9	13 667	850	1 811	1 401
District 26	233 870	2.90	75.1	56.7	13.0	19.6	14 864	16.8	3 019	1 974	5 401	0
District 27	230 801	2.92	68.4	47.9	13.8	23.2	11 706	36.9	57	3 760	3 080	0
District 28	213 310	3.08	65.1	43.5	14.3	24.9	3 006	37.7	266	1 929	31	0
District 29	238 782	2.66	66.5	47.9	13.1	26.2	13 319	44.9	30	3 939	1 024	0
District 30	297 572	2.15	49.1	38.5	7.4	37.8	17 475	15.7	102	2 769	13 798	0
District 31	194 829	3.09	65.2	38.8	17.5	24.2	8 613	23.4	257	2 333	1 775	0
District 32	173 433	3.66	81.0	53.9	18.4	14.2	19 183	24.9	70	2 375	3 382	0
District 33	247 280	2.51	54.2	31.7	16.6	34.5	18 793	14.9	69	2 693	7 931	0
District 34	186 773	3.39	71.9	44.1	18.7	21.8	19 490	11.1	8 717	2 544	124	0
District 35	202 874	3.22	71.5	39.4	23.7	22.5	7 016	18.2	140	1 526	3 293	0
District 36	259 933	2.51	59.6	43.4	11.1	30.0	5 633	34.7	5	2 046	502	20
District 37	196 736	3.26	69.2	40.2	21.3	22.5	8 702	27.2	84	2 459	794	0
District 38	167 704	3.77	81.9	54.5	18.7	13.7	7 601	20.8	202	2 675	3 310	0

1. No spouse present.

Table E. Congressional Districts 112th Congress — **Housing and Money Income**

STATE District	Housing units, 2010 — Total	Occupied units — Percent occupied	Owner-occupied — Percent	Median value¹ (dollars)	Percent valued at $500,000 or more	Median owner cost as a percent of income — With a mortgage	Without a mortgage²	Renter-occupied — Median rent³	Median rent as a percent of income	Sub-standard units⁴ (percent)	Money income, 2010 — Per capita income (dollars)	Households — Median income (dollars)	Percent with income of $100,000 or more
	41	42	43	44	45	46	47	48	49	50	51	52	53
UNITED STATES..............	131 791 065	86.9	65.4	179 900	10.5	25.1	12.8	855	31.6	3.9	26 059	50 046	20.0
ALABAMA	2 174 428	83.5	70.1	123 900	3.4	23.0	12.3	667	32.2	2.4	21 993	40 474	14.1
District 1..............................	324 851	78.3	69.7	136 000	3.8	24.4	12.8	709	34.8	2.6	21 773	41 172	13.8
District 2..............................	301 606	84.7	67.9	111 200	1.8	22.4	11.9	659	29.8	2.0	21 076	40 567	12.9
District 3..............................	318 023	82.9	66.8	110 100	3.4	24.4	12.6	640	34.1	2.9	19 469	35 452	11.8
District 4..............................	298 854	83.3	75.3	93 400	2.0	22.8	12.3	573	30.0	3.1	19 196	36 715	9.8
District 5..............................	319 162	87.8	72.3	135 600	3.5	20.2	10.7	628	30.1	1.8	25 059	45 856	18.1
District 6..............................	323 767	87.6	77.1	175 300	6.9	23.4	11.6	834	29.4	1.6	28 854	55 559	22.7
District 7..............................	288 165	79.3	60.0	93 900	0.8	24.6	14.8	667	35.7	2.7	17 113	31 047	8.0
ALASKA	307 065	82.9	63.9	241 400	7.1	23.3	10.8	981	29.0	10.2	30 598	64 576	29.5
At Large	307 065	82.9	63.9	241 400	7.1	23.3	10.8	981	29.0	10.2	30 598	64 576	29.5
ARIZONA	2 846 738	82.0	65.2	168 800	6.7	26.5	11.3	844	31.6	5.1	23 618	46 789	17.3
District 1..............................	372 282	71.7	69.7	152 500	6.0	28.0	10.2	757	31.8	8.9	18 429	40 854	10.7
District 2..............................	444 722	82.4	71.7	157 500	2.8	27.1	11.6	952	32.4	3.2	22 763	47 963	14.9
District 3..............................	321 483	84.7	63.0	216 400	13.1	26.0	12.0	855	30.6	3.5	30 948	62 327	24.4
District 4..............................	265 041	83.3	45.5	100 000	0.9	29.8	14.1	747	35.9	13.1	14 246	31 498	8.0
District 5..............................	328 635	83.4	60.7	260 200	20.8	24.9	11.0	883	30.5	2.3	34 476	55 876	26.3
District 6..............................	410 449	83.0	72.3	177 300	3.6	26.0	10.5	943	29.4	3.4	25 684	56 691	22.5
District 7..............................	342 805	82.0	64.4	121 700	1.4	26.9	12.0	765	34.4	7.8	16 736	39 777	10.3
District 8..............................	361 321	86.2	66.9	196 900	7.0	24.9	11.5	801	29.3	1.8	27 961	49 825	18.4
ARKANSAS.....................	1 317 818	84.6	67.4	106 300	2.1	21.5	10.9	638	29.9	3.2	20 725	38 307	11.8
District 1	317 451	84.0	67.6	88 900	1.0	21.2	11.6	579	32.1	3.0	18 682	33 862	9.4
District 2	333 980	87.7	64.8	127 600	3.2	21.0	10.9	720	29.8	3.2	23 889	43 685	14.7
District 3	358 428	86.0	67.4	127 600	2.8	22.1	10.0	640	28.4	3.9	21 181	40 674	12.7
District 4	307 959	80.1	70.2	80 800	1.3	21.7	11.0	596	30.0	2.7	18 651	35 312	9.4
CALIFORNIA...................	13 682 976	90.7	55.6	370 900	33.7	30.6	11.4	1 163	33.8	9.1	27 363	57 708	26.4
District 1..............................	300 223	87.2	58.9	337 600	25.6	30.2	12.3	1 002	35.0	5.1	25 434	48 003	19.3
District 2..............................	303 627	87.5	62.7	221 500	8.4	29.8	13.0	853	32.8	6.0	21 649	42 249	12.7
District 3..............................	311 622	90.9	66.5	264 700	11.9	29.2	10.6	1 047	33.0	3.5	28 100	61 853	26.4
District 4..............................	359 479	81.1	71.8	336 600	20.0	30.8	13.7	1 042	33.8	3.4	29 821	60 629	26.7
District 5..............................	282 678	91.1	48.6	205 000	6.6	28.7	10.8	940	35.5	6.9	21 948	43 953	14.9
District 6..............................	285 761	91.2	60.9	533 100	52.9	31.7	11.7	1 293	35.1	4.8	37 497	64 391	31.3
District 7..............................	244 859	90.7	60.3	288 200	13.7	30.0	10.0	1 189	33.7	7.0	26 413	61 315	26.6
District 8..............................	322 801	88.7	32.3	742 500	81.0	31.0	10.8	1 356	28.0	8.2	44 867	69 926	36.0
District 9..............................	278 229	90.0	44.0	508 500	50.9	30.7	11.8	1 097	33.7	6.9	31 893	53 286	26.2
District 10...........................	277 736	92.0	66.7	426 900	42.4	29.4	11.3	1 311	33.0	3.9	35 580	75 457	37.5
District 11...........................	280 391	94.3	65.8	359 400	36.5	29.4	10.7	1 213	32.3	4.9	32 850	72 075	35.4
District 12...........................	249 253	95.0	60.7	725 900	81.5	30.4	10.0	1 498	29.3	6.2	40 037	82 337	41.6
District 13...........................	231 133	94.3	59.9	467 000	44.5	30.3	10.0	1 272	30.6	6.8	30 293	73 539	35.3
District 14...........................	260 967	93.4	57.7	859 800	79.5	30.0	10.0	1 410	25.4	6.5	49 460	94 740	47.9
District 15...........................	248 074	94.8	55.9	639 700	71.3	29.1	10.0	1 447	28.5	7.1	36 665	85 700	43.7
District 16...........................	212 750	95.4	59.1	508 900	51.0	30.4	11.1	1 333	33.5	12.2	29 205	73 973	36.6
District 17...........................	232 224	89.5	52.1	412 300	41.4	32.6	11.2	1 193	33.7	11.4	24 790	55 026	23.3
District 18...........................	237 826	88.8	52.3	143 800	5.2	29.3	11.4	889	35.4	13.0	16 341	39 297	11.8
District 19...........................	287 267	88.4	62.6	221 200	8.8	29.0	13.1	936	32.2	6.9	22 840	51 553	20.0
District 20...........................	204 783	92.3	45.4	143 900	2.9	29.3	11.4	743	35.0	15.8	12 112	33 089	8.5
District 21...........................	263 717	89.9	60.2	202 800	6.3	27.2	10.1	824	34.2	11.8	19 558	48 113	18.8
District 22...........................	305 806	87.1	62.8	201 400	10.6	27.1	11.0	905	32.8	5.3	24 501	53 626	22.8
District 23...........................	247 572	90.4	51.1	410 900	41.2	29.5	11.2	1 234	36.3	9.9	25 416	54 049	23.6
District 24...........................	249 709	94.5	67.1	471 800	45.0	29.5	11.4	1 431	31.8	3.8	34 425	74 103	36.2
District 25...........................	289 370	87.3	67.0	223 100	12.7	29.9	13.4	1 140	38.5	6.8	22 703	57 862	24.0
District 26...........................	243 006	94.2	65.7	466 000	44.1	29.7	10.0	1 271	31.4	5.5	32 284	75 086	35.4
District 27...........................	250 448	93.2	52.6	411 800	32.7	33.7	14.4	1 192	36.5	9.8	25 820	56 836	25.1
District 28...........................	226 718	92.7	42.6	394 000	38.5	35.7	12.5	1 183	36.5	13.9	25 981	50 607	20.8
District 29...........................	241 100	93.9	43.6	575 000	61.1	31.3	11.3	1 261	34.8	8.3	28 409	57 700	26.3
District 30...........................	323 007	91.3	46.9	825 400	77.7	32.9	13.5	1 523	31.3	2.4	57 321	75 700	38.4
District 31...........................	213 193	92.0	22.8	404 700	33.2	33.7	12.7	937	36.2	26.8	16 429	35 194	10.7
District 32...........................	178 694	94.8	54.8	354 700	15.6	32.8	10.0	1 113	35.4	16.5	17 819	49 529	18.1
District 33...........................	267 525	92.5	29.2	488 000	48.7	35.9	13.8	1 107	36.8	12.6	24 690	41 538	16.6
District 34...........................	200 550	92.7	28.6	351 700	16.7	35.5	10.0	957	37.1	28.5	14 918	36 270	10.1
District 35...........................	215 389	93.2	39.4	344 700	23.1	35.6	11.6	1 021	36.1	18.5	18 780	41 271	15.3
District 36...........................	275 989	92.0	46.0	634 000	67.5	31.5	10.6	1 355	31.1	8.0	36 016	65 717	33.3
District 37...........................	212 318	92.1	42.0	325 900	16.8	32.5	10.2	1 016	34.5	16.9	19 293	46 950	16.9
District 38...........................	177 694	94.6	58.6	324 700	12.6	34.0	10.4	1 103	35.7	19.9	16 783	51 381	16.4

1. Specified owner-occupied units.   2. Median monthly owner costs is often in the minimum category—10.0 percent or less, which is indicated as 10.0 percent.   3. Specified renter-occupied units.   4. Overcrowded or lacking complete plumbing facilities.

Table E. Congressional Districts 112th Congress — Poverty, Labor Force, Employment, and Social Security

STATE District	Poverty, 2010 (percent)			Civilian labor force, 2010			Civilian employment,[2] 2010				Persons under age 65 with no health insurance, 2010 (percent)	Social Security beneficiaries, December 2010		Supplemental Security Income recipients, December 2010
					Unemployment			Percent						
	Persons below poverty level	Families below poverty level	Households receiving food stamps in past 12 months	Total	Total	Rate[1]	Total	Management, business, science, and arts occupations	Service, sales, and office	Construction and production		Number	Rate[3]	
	54	55	56	57	58	59	60	61	62	63	64	65	66	67
UNITED STATES	15.3	11.3	11.9	155 917 013	16 883 085	10.8	139 033 928	35.9	43.0	21.0	17.7	52 641 311	170.5	7 911 333
ALABAMA	19.0	14.7	14.3	2 244 208	265 383	11.8	1 978 825	31.9	42.0	26.2	16.8	1 012 056	211.7	172 223
District 1	19.1	15.4	15.7	318 353	40 650	12.8	277 703	29.7	44.7	25.7	20.1	149 290	217.0	22 441
District 2	18.6	15.2	15.3	311 533	28 858	9.3	282 675	28.4	44.7	26.9	15.0	144 977	215.1	27 285
District 3	24.0	17.7	17.2	310 896	43 339	13.9	267 557	31.4	41.3	27.3	17.1	147 806	216.9	27 671
District 4	19.8	14.8	14.6	290 396	38 483	13.3	251 913	25.2	39.1	35.7	19.2	164 062	248.5	24 430
District 5	15.3	11.8	10.6	355 781	39 859	11.2	315 922	37.1	39.1	23.8	15.1	142 250	197.9	18 643
District 6	10.6	8.0	7.3	379 861	33 017	8.7	346 844	40.9	40.5	18.6	12.3	134 369	178.1	13 083
District 7	28.0	22.6	21.5	277 388	41 177	14.8	236 211	25.9	45.5	28.7	20.1	129 302	214.3	38 670
ALASKA	9.9	7.2	10.6	373 703	36 020	9.6	337 683	35.1	41.0	23.9	21.3	78 208	110.1	12 269
At Large	9.9	7.2	10.6	373 703	36 020	9.6	337 683	35.1	41.0	23.9	21.3	78 208	110.1	12 269
ARIZONA	17.4	12.5	13.2	3 011 568	356 011	11.8	2 655 557	35.6	46.2	18.3	19.4	1 067 717	167.0	110 011
District 1	22.3	15.2	16.1	312 508	42 901	13.7	269 607	30.8	48.3	20.9	21.4	155 201	200.4	20 144
District 2	12.9	9.3	10.1	442 819	55 479	12.5	387 340	32.9	47.4	19.7	17.5	212 890	218.8	12 995
District 3	13.6	9.3	11.3	369 827	34 431	9.3	335 396	42.5	44.2	13.2	16.6	104 135	147.1	9 402
District 4	34.4	29.8	26.5	301 306	43 944	14.6	257 362	23.9	48.4	27.7	31.1	71 780	102.8	22 373
District 5	14.1	8.9	6.8	366 417	35 927	9.8	330 490	44.7	43.2	12.1	14.8	98 598	150.1	5 198
District 6	10.3	7.6	9.2	477 253	52 309	11.0	424 944	37.1	45.9	17.0	15.3	144 599	148.8	8 508
District 7	22.6	17.4	20.4	388 149	57 229	14.7	330 920	26.9	49.2	23.9	24.3	115 472	134.9	20 564
District 8	12.7	8.6	10.3	353 289	33 791	9.6	319 498	42.3	43.7	14.1	13.9	165 042	218.8	10 827
ARKANSAS	18.8	14.1	13.7	1 377 434	132 106	9.6	1 245 328	30.9	41.8	27.4	20.3	635 041	217.8	106 526
District 1	22.1	16.6	16.1	310 046	35 540	11.5	274 506	28.4	40.7	31.0	20.8	168 840	245.5	33 666
District 2	16.3	12.1	11.4	369 851	29 864	8.1	339 987	34.4	43.8	21.8	18.6	146 818	195.4	24 921
District 3	16.5	12.4	11.4	402 115	30 904	7.7	371 211	31.1	42.1	26.8	20.8	160 066	194.6	19 601
District 4	21.3	15.8	16.7	295 422	35 798	12.1	259 624	28.6	39.7	31.7	21.0	159 317	243.5	28 338
CALIFORNIA	15.8	11.8	7.4	18 625 515	2 382 343	12.8	16 243 172	36.5	43.3	20.2	20.7	4 979 141	133.7	1 267 711
District 1	16.7	10.6	6.9	344 909	42 216	12.2	302 693	36.1	43.3	20.6	17.4	126 748	180.0	25 464
District 2	19.0	12.8	10.0	319 897	51 940	16.2	267 957	31.4	45.9	22.7	19.8	147 508	208.2	33 198
District 3	11.1	7.6	7.1	393 215	51 995	13.2	341 220	39.3	44.7	16.0	13.3	124 599	159.1	21 565
District 4	11.2	7.8	5.1	369 132	44 461	12.0	324 671	38.8	44.1	17.1	13.3	157 845	203.9	18 786
District 5	22.6	18.0	12.5	335 654	56 599	16.9	279 055	33.8	49.7	16.6	18.7	93 575	133.6	42 418
District 6	12.2	7.1	4.4	354 895	42 537	12.0	312 358	40.5	43.4	16.1	14.6	114 598	172.5	12 524
District 7	13.3	10.6	7.5	345 679	47 290	13.7	298 389	33.0	45.2	21.7	17.8	91 547	139.6	22 017
District 8	13.1	8.1	4.8	416 474	37 791	9.1	378 683	48.0	41.4	10.6	14.5	89 330	134.0	41 303
District 9	19.3	13.7	7.8	334 916	41 029	12.3	293 887	47.2	37.1	15.7	17.9	81 221	125.2	30 098
District 10	8.0	5.7	3.9	370 246	41 716	11.3	328 530	43.5	40.8	15.7	11.5	106 817	149.4	14 604
District 11	11.1	8.2	5.6	388 667	51 424	13.2	337 243	42.3	40.4	17.4	12.5	108 608	136.3	17 302
District 12	7.0	4.6	1.7	363 693	32 419	8.9	331 274	45.5	41.3	13.1	11.9	98 936	151.9	14 393
District 13	10.5	7.4	5.6	355 352	45 630	12.8	309 722	41.3	40.2	18.5	13.2	82 826	124.5	20 769
District 14	7.1	4.0	2.5	347 824	31 256	9.0	316 568	57.1	31.9	11.0	11.4	81 496	124.6	9 274
District 15	9.5	5.8	4.2	362 715	36 836	10.2	325 879	52.4	34.0	13.6	11.7	80 726	119.1	17 378
District 16	13.1	9.7	7.0	348 929	47 326	13.6	301 603	39.3	41.7	19.0	17.7	71 315	105.4	24 307
District 17	16.8	12.6	6.7	320 712	36 281	11.3	284 431	29.9	43.2	27.0	22.1	90 860	136.8	15 312
District 18	26.2	23.2	16.2	320 521	62 814	19.6	257 707	19.4	43.8	36.8	24.0	96 066	132.8	38 728
District 19	17.9	14.4	12.3	359 002	50 020	13.9	308 982	30.4	44.9	24.6	18.2	119 900	158.3	25 086
District 20	33.7	29.6	22.6	294 099	50 880	17.3	243 219	16.2	38.9	44.9	29.0	71 802	96.5	35 915
District 21	22.2	18.1	18.2	366 602	58 248	15.9	308 354	27.3	41.9	30.8	21.0	102 132	130.2	30 897
District 22	15.7	12.0	8.8	368 029	45 737	12.4	322 292	34.1	43.5	22.3	18.8	123 447	154.9	28 562
District 23	18.5	11.3	7.8	352 754	39 571	11.2	313 183	30.5	44.8	24.8	24.4	102 245	147.0	18 003
District 24	9.0	6.0	4.4	355 473	35 990	10.1	319 483	41.7	42.6	15.7	13.5	107 439	157.6	11 226
District 25	15.7	12.0	8.9	383 621	56 792	14.8	326 829	33.8	45.0	21.2	19.5	92 256	109.3	25 759
District 26	8.9	6.0	3.6	361 739	38 732	10.7	323 007	43.5	42.4	14.0	16.3	96 062	138.9	16 798
District 27	15.3	11.2	4.2	372 078	45 071	12.1	327 007	36.6	45.4	17.9	23.2	82 038	119.9	25 776
District 28	17.7	14.6	7.9	357 933	49 168	13.7	308 765	32.4	45.4	22.3	30.5	66 006	100.0	26 451
District 29	13.1	9.6	5.2	342 455	37 240	10.9	305 215	43.2	43.0	13.8	23.5	81 610	127.1	41 286
District 30	10.6	5.3	1.5	367 783	39 971	10.9	327 812	62.7	31.5	5.7	12.1	100 193	151.3	19 079
District 31	28.8	26.5	10.9	328 573	45 460	13.8	283 113	23.8	48.7	27.5	39.9	51 189	83.7	32 431
District 32	16.1	12.8	8.9	304 036	40 171	13.2	263 865	23.8	47.7	28.5	28.2	74 950	116.7	31 305
District 33	22.2	17.5	7.4	351 567	47 894	13.6	303 673	36.4	48.8	14.9	31.8	72 664	114.1	35 501
District 34	27.2	24.3	12.4	301 300	42 877	14.2	258 423	20.1	46.4	33.5	37.5	61 694	94.3	34 294
District 35	24.7	21.5	13.8	307 714	38 642	12.6	269 072	25.1	48.7	26.2	31.4	68 057	102.7	31 979
District 36	13.2	10.3	4.3	369 323	37 601	10.2	331 722	45.4	40.0	14.6	18.1	84 953	128.8	14 887
District 37	20.3	16.5	13.4	327 817	51 261	15.6	276 556	27.4	47.2	25.4	25.7	70 297	108.3	35 318
District 38	17.3	14.0	10.1	303 844	37 385	12.3	266 459	23.2	47.7	29.0	29.3	77 575	120.9	26 251

1. Percent of civilian labor force.　　2. Persons 16 years old and over.　　3. Per 1,000 resident population enumerated in the 2010 census.

STATE District	Farms		Land in farms		Farm Operators			Value of products sold				Government payments	
						Percent of farm operators				Percent of sales from			
	Number	Operated by family or individual (percent)	Acreage	Average size of farm (acres)	Total	Whose primary occupation is farming	Who live on the farm operated	Total ($1,000)	Average per farm	Crops	Livestock	Total ($1,000)	Percent of farms
	68	69	70	71	72	73	74	75	76	77	78	79	80
UNITED STATES..............	2 204 792	86.5	922 095 840	418	3 337 450	41.9	74.7	297 220 491	134 807	48.3	51.7	7 983 922	38.0
ALABAMA	48 753	92.3	9 033 537	185	70 959	37.5	76.2	4 415 550	90 570	15.3	84.7	124 692	29.6
District 1	3 665	90.5	670 144	183	5 349	38.9	75.8	258 576	70 553	72.6	27.4	16 337	26.9
District 2	9 848	90.1	2 450 645	249	13 975	37.6	69.1	1 138 269	115 584	14.9	85.1	46 030	48.4
District 3	5 714	91.9	1 176 658	206	8 427	36.5	78.0	420 261	73 549	20.8	79.2	9 667	22.3
District 4	14 619	94.7	1 643 321	112	21 567	38.3	83.1	1 817 145	124 300	3.2	96.8	8 653	19.1
District 5	8 272	93.2	1 277 323	154	12 039	35.0	76.7	453 695	54 847	26.2	73.8	29 005	35.5
District 6	2 575	92.5	341 696	133	3 780	37.5	79.8	100 520	39 037	25.0	75.0	1 852	10.4
District 7	4 060	89.6	1 473 750	363	5 822	40.0	62.5	227 082	55 932	13.0	87.0	13 147	34.8
ALASKA	686	80.2	881 585	1 285	1 146	49.6	77.2	57 019	83 118	43.4	56.6	1 645	11.4
At Large	686	80.2	881 585	1 285	1 146	49.6	77.2	57 019	83 118	43.4	56.6	1 645	11.4
ARIZONA	15 637	87.7	26 117 899	1 670	26 183	57.6	75.5	3 234 552	206 852	59.1	40.9	55 947	7.3
District 1	10 208	93.1	18 671 303	1 829	17 353	62.4	77.1	690 126	67 606	50.6	49.4	16 596	5.4
District 2	1 402	87.7	2 385 221	1 701	2 255	52.7	74.5	295 513	210 780	64.6	35.4	7 444	6.8
District 3	273	77.3	12 819	47	466	47.9	76.8	75 358	276 037	97.9	2.1	2 496	6.6
District 4	140	65.0	35 348	252	269	47.2	68.4	60 439	431 707	61.9	38.1	2 438	40.7
District 5	190	73.2	149 812	788	288	51.4	74.7	12 964	68 232	78.2	21.8	19 251	121.1
District 6	567	79.4	60 561	107	947	41.1	79.6	190 905	336 693	40.7	59.3	8 810	31.6
District 7	1 262	71.7	1 219 095	966	2 010	50.2	59.6	1 735 910	1 375 523	61.3	38.7	(D)	0.4
District 8	1 595	75.0	3 583 740	2 247	2 595	44.5	76.8	173 337	108 675	63.5	36.5	(D)	0.3
ARKANSAS......................	49 346	86.1	13 872 862	281	75 308	41.4	76.0	7 508 806	152 166	38.6	61.4	269 448	23.2
District 1	14 657	79.9	7 116 929	486	22 228	46.3	66.9	2 657 732	181 329	82.4	17.6	203 162	43.0
District 2	7 401	88.7	1 290 369	174	11 307	37.0	77.3	516 618	69 804	16.6	83.4	10 446	16.1
District 3	14 312	90.3	2 205 372	154	22 063	38.2	83.7	1 968 401	137 535	2.5	97.5	4 658	11.3
District 4	12 976	86.8	3 260 192	251	19 710	41.9	76.9	2 366 055	182 341	24.4	75.6	51 182	18.1
CALIFORNIA......................	81 033	79.0	25 364 695	313	130 756	46.5	69.7	33 885 064	418 164	67.6	32.4	240 242	9.2
District 1	5 872	77.0	2 013 763	343	9 660	44.1	69.0	1 115 999	190 054	87.9	12.1	6 624	6.4
District 2	10 643	80.8	3 684 702	346	17 581	47.3	71.3	2 035 973	191 297	88.0	12.0	79 675	20.1
District 3	2 687	84.2	796 239	296	4 459	42.3	79.1	417 433	155 353	61.3	38.7	3 046	7.1
District 4	4 880	88.2	1 544 444	316	8 154	41.6	85.7	231 183	47 374	66.1	33.9	5 309	5.1
District 5	82	81.7	11 692	143	127	51.2	44.9	16 567	202 037	41.9	58.1	283	12.2
District 6	2 856	79.3	491 878	172	4 614	43.4	71.5	553 542	193 817	50.3	49.7	1 270	4.1
District 7	347	86.2	65 621	189	563	37.7	73.4	90 888	261 925	91.3	8.7	300	4.9
District 8	6	83.3	7	1	6	33.3	0.0	644	107 333	100.0	0.0		0.0
District 9	76	72.4	70 974	934	117	38.5	82.1	2 785	36 645	33.1	66.9	16	7.9
District 10	831	78.7	341 808	411	1 377	43.1	63.3	151 181	181 927	80.3	19.7	2 804	16.2
District 11	4 108	77.6	937 423	228	6 479	49.3	69.6	1 545 545	376 228	63.7	36.3	4 125	7.4
District 12	50	80.0	6 271	125	97	24.7	40.2	7 085	141 700	97.2	2.8	17	8.0
District 13	111	76.6	32 616	294	192	32.8	49.5	18 073	162 820	53.0	47.0	92	6.3
District 14	625	75.5	76 236	122	993	43.6	65.3	181 984	291 174	96.6	3.4	30	1.9
District 15	446	76.7	68 249	153	704	42.9	69.0	125 508	281 408	96.9	3.1	89	2.9
District 16	235	84.3	47 545	202	375	45.6	82.1	18 644	79 336	80.5	19.5	13	2.1
District 17	2 276	70.3	1 938 674	852	3 813	56.4	56.8	2 799 155	1 229 857	96.9	3.1	1 739	6.2
District 18	4 053	75.1	1 448 595	357	6 478	54.4	66.8	3 269 944	806 796	44.2	55.8	15 234	17.4
District 19	6 089	81.2	1 642 906	270	9 640	49.4	72.3	2 553 350	419 338	51.6	48.4	9 638	9.1
District 20	3 687	72.8	1 885 527	511	6 037	57.5	58.1	4 355 329	1 181 266	66.5	33.5	52 644	21.9
District 21	8 343	77.1	1 848 423	222	12 984	49.2	64.9	4 743 098	568 512	43.3	56.7	26 177	9.2
District 22	4 349	76.1	3 194 994	735	7 280	46.2	68.4	2 507 652	576 604	79.9	20.1	17 394	10.0
District 23	1 190	70.4	318 897	268	1 967	50.9	55.5	1 146 790	963 689	99.1	0.9	727	3.7
District 24	3 185	72.8	782 973	246	5 029	45.8	64.6	1 242 922	390 242	96.3	3.7	600	1.8
District 25	1 123	81.7	397 414	354	1 919	37.8	79.4	220 293	196 165	44.9	55.1	613	2.1
District 26	306	80.1	10 499	34	512	33.8	71.3	35 508	116 039	72.0	28.0	32	1.0
District 27	63	82.5	1 813	29	85	29.4	71.8	23 502	373 048	98.0	2.0	(D)	1.6
District 28	17	70.6	182	11	56	19.6	17.9	4 024	236 706	97.3	2.7		0.0
District 29	42	64.3	2 837	68	62	51.6	30.6	724	17 238	(D)	(D)	2	11.9
District 30	156	78.2	15 825	101	237	44.7	68.4	8 333	53 417	80.6	19.4	(D)	1.3
District 31	2	100.0	(D)	X	3	100.0	66.7	(D)	(D)	(D)	(D)		0.0
District 32	58	62.1	10 299	178	120	39.2	55.0	95 890	1 653 276	99.9	0.1	(D)	1.7
District 33	5	40.0	(D)	X	5	40.0	40.0	(D)	(D)	(D)	(D)	(D)	0.0
District 34	14	85.7	871	62	22	63.6	40.9	1 157	82 643	(D)	(D)	(D)	0.0
District 35	23	39.1	1 331	58	44	54.5	25.0	9 053	393 609	71.2	28.8	(D)	0.0
District 36	21	81.0	899	43	47	53.2	38.3	6 287	299 381	100.0	0.0	(D)	0.0
District 37	27	55.6	(D)	X	42	35.7	11.9	22 462	831 926	99.9	0.1	(D)	0.0
District 38	25	56.0	1 006	40	34	58.8	17.6	6 493	259 720	100.0	0.0	(D)	0.0

1. Specified owner-occupied units.   2. Median monthly owner costs is often in the minimum category—10.0 percent or less, which is indicated as 10.0 percent.   3. Specified renter-occupied units.   4. Overcrowded or lacking complete plumbing facilities.

Table E. Congressional Districts 112th Congress — Land Area and Population Characteristics

STATE District	Representative, 112th Congress	Land area,[1] 2010 (sq km)	Total persons	Per square kilometer	White	Black	American Indian, Alaska Native	Asian and Pacific Islander	Some other race	Two or more races	Hispanic or Latino[2]	Non-Hispanic White alone	Percent female	Percent foreign born	Percent born in state of residence
		1	2	3	4	5	6	7	8	9	10	11	12	13	14
CALIFORNIA—Cont'd															
District 39	Linda T. Sánchez (D)	168	643 115	3 836.7	48.4	5.8	0.9	11.1	29.7	4.1	66.5	15.8	51.1	34.4	56.3
District 40	Edward R. Royce (R)	260	665 653	2 561.8	56.2	2.4	0.7	21.1	15.1	4.4	35.2	39.1	50.6	30.8	53.5
District 41	Jerry Lewis (R)	34 496	797 133	23.1	66.9	6.4	1.4	5.1	15.1	5.0	34.9	50.7	50.6	14.5	61.5
District 42	Gary G. Miller (R)	817	667 638	817.1	61.6	2.6	0.5	20.7	10.2	4.3	29.3	45.1	50.7	26.7	55.9
District 43	Joe Baca (D)	494	735 581	1 487.6	46.7	10.6	1.1	4.5	32.3	4.8	69.4	14.6	50.4	28.9	60.3
District 44	Ken Calvert (R)	1 349	844 756	626.2	61.0	5.6	0.9	8.3	19.5	4.8	43.5	40.5	50.1	23.1	58.7
District 45	Mary Bono Mack (R)	15 490	914 209	59.0	62.5	6.8	1.0	4.9	20.4	4.4	45.2	41.1	50.1	22.7	54.2
District 46	Dana Rohrabacher (R)	680	648 663	953.6	66.2	1.7	0.5	19.3	7.9	4.4	20.2	55.8	50.6	24.6	51.3
District 47	Loretta Sanchez (D)	142	631 422	4 437.6	44.0	1.8	0.9	17.5	32.1	3.7	67.6	12.4	49.3	46.9	45.9
District 48	John Campbell (R)	548	727 833	1 328.1	67.7	1.5	0.4	19.2	6.8	4.5	17.9	58.0	51.3	26.2	48.5
District 49	Darrell E. Issa (R)	4 388	797 428	181.7	65.8	4.7	1.3	5.8	17.1	5.3	38.5	47.9	49.5	19.3	52.5
District 50	Brian P. Bilbray (R)	780	753 135	965.9	68.9	2.0	0.6	14.1	10.0	4.6	22.2	58.5	50.4	22.8	45.6
District 51	Bob Filner (D)	11 871	757 891	63.8	48.7	7.5	1.0	13.3	24.3	5.2	62.4	15.2	50.3	33.7	52.0
District 52	Duncan Hunter (R)	5 478	673 893	123.0	73.8	4.5	0.9	7.9	7.2	5.5	19.4	64.1	50.8	17.0	52.9
District 53	Susan A. Davis (D)	246	662 854	2 697.8	62.0	6.9	0.7	10.5	14.8	5.0	31.9	47.7	48.1	23.3	45.6
COLORADO		268 431	5 029 196	18.7	81.3	4.0	1.1	2.9	7.2	3.4	20.7	70.0	49.9	9.8	42.5
District 1	Diana DeGette (D)	443	662 039	1 495.4	69.7	9.9	1.4	3.5	11.5	4.1	30.7	53.6	50.0	15.7	43.0
District 2	Jared Polis (D)	14 516	733 805	50.6	83.7	1.2	0.8	4.0	7.3	3.0	20.3	72.4	49.4	10.8	41.6
District 3	Scott Tipton (R)	139 752	706 186	5.1	85.1	0.9	2.1	0.8	8.2	2.9	24.2	71.6	49.7	5.6	49.7
District 4	Cory Gardner (R)	79 930	725 041	9.1	86.4	1.2	0.9	1.7	7.2	2.6	20.2	75.0	49.6	8.0	47.3
District 5	Doug Lamborn (R)	19 948	725 902	36.4	81.4	5.6	1.0	2.7	4.5	4.7	14.6	73.6	49.5	6.7	32.6
District 6	Mike Coffman (R)	10 612	797 813	75.2	87.4	2.9	0.5	4.1	2.2	2.9	8.7	81.9	50.7	7.5	38.7
District 7	Ed Perlmutter (D)	3 232	678 410	209.9	73.4	7.2	1.2	3.4	10.9	4.0	28.4	58.7	50.2	15.6	45.4
CONNECTICUT		12 542	3 574 097	285.0	77.6	10.1	0.3	3.8	5.6	2.6	13.4	71.2	51.3	13.6	55.1
District 1	John B. Larson (D)	1 691	710 951	420.4	70.7	14.9	0.3	4.5	6.9	2.7	14.7	64.8	52.1	14.5	58.3
District 2	Joe Courtney (D)	5 251	729 771	139.0	87.5	3.9	0.5	2.9	2.6	2.5	6.7	84.3	49.9	7.5	55.6
District 3	Rosa L. DeLauro (D)	1 186	712 339	600.5	75.1	13.3	0.2	3.9	4.9	2.5	12.7	68.8	52.0	12.0	63.1
District 4	James A. Himes (D)	1 182	706 740	598.1	73.6	12.0	0.3	4.8	6.9	2.5	17.5	64.6	51.4	20.5	42.7
District 5	Christopher S. Murphy (D)	3 232	714 296	221.0	80.7	6.7	0.3	3.1	6.5	2.7	15.6	73.2	51.3	13.8	55.6
DELAWARE		5 047	897 934	177.9	68.9	21.4	0.5	3.2	3.4	2.7	8.2	65.3	51.6	8.0	45.3
At Large	John Carney (D)	5 047	897 934	177.9	68.9	21.4	0.5	3.2	3.4	2.7	8.2	65.3	51.6	8.0	45.3
DISTRICT OF COLUMBIA		158	601 723	3 805.6	38.5	50.7	0.3	3.6	4.1	2.9	9.1	34.8	52.8	13.5	37.3
Delegate District (At Large)	Eleanor Holmes Norton (D)	158	601 723	3 805.6	38.5	50.7	0.3	3.6	4.1	2.9	9.1	34.8	52.8	13.5	37.3
FLORIDA		138 887	18 801 310	135.4	75.0	16.0	0.4	2.5	3.6	2.5	22.5	57.9	51.1	19.4	35.2
District 1	Jeff Miller (R)	11 934	694 158	58.2	77.5	14.5	0.8	2.6	1.4	3.2	5.1	74.6	49.7	5.4	41.7
District 2	Steve Southerland II (R)	24 404	737 519	30.2	71.7	22.2	0.5	1.8	1.6	2.2	5.5	68.5	49.5	5.1	53.6
District 3	Corrine Brown (D)	4 657	659 055	141.5	38.8	52.2	0.5	2.1	3.8	2.7	11.3	32.9	51.4	11.0	56.2
District 4	Ander Crenshaw (R)	10 652	744 418	69.9	76.2	15.0	0.4	3.9	1.9	2.6	7.1	71.8	50.0	8.2	46.7
District 5	Richard B. Nugent (R)	10 443	929 533	89.0	86.9	6.4	0.4	1.8	2.5	2.1	10.8	79.5	51.0	7.2	32.4
District 6	Cliff Stearns (R)	7 557	812 727	107.6	76.7	14.8	0.4	3.4	2.3	2.5	8.9	71.0	51.5	7.9	44.6
District 7	John L. Mica (R)	4 637	812 442	175.2	82.3	10.1	0.3	2.4	2.6	2.3	11.3	74.7	51.5	9.2	35.1
District 8	Daniel Webster (R)	2 543	805 608	316.8	74.6	10.7	0.4	4.8	6.2	3.2	26.0	57.0	51.1	16.2	31.5
District 9	Gus M. Bilirakis (R)	1 609	753 549	468.3	85.0	5.7	0.3	3.4	3.1	2.4	13.6	75.6	51.7	11.9	33.7
District 10	C. W. Bill Young (R)	441	633 889	1 436.4	86.5	5.7	0.3	3.4	1.9	2.2	7.6	81.5	51.7	11.9	28.9
District 11	Kathy Castor (D)	609	673 799	1 106.1	60.3	28.3	0.4	2.8	5.1	3.2	27.5	40.8	51.4	17.3	43.0
District 12	Dennis Ross (R)	4 853	842 199	173.5	72.4	16.1	0.4	2.1	6.2	2.8	21.2	59.4	51.1	12.1	40.7
District 13	Vern Buchanan (R)	6 695	757 805	113.2	86.9	5.5	0.3	1.4	4.1	1.7	12.0	79.9	51.5	12.5	26.6
District 14	Connie Mack (R)	2 660	858 956	322.9	85.2	7.0	0.3	1.4	4.2	1.9	16.7	73.9	51.2	15.8	23.9
District 15	Bill Posey (R)	6 591	813 570	123.4	79.7	9.8	0.4	2.4	4.8	2.9	20.2	66.3	51.2	13.2	28.4
District 16	Thomas J. Rooney (R)	11 749	797 711	67.9	81.4	9.4	0.5	1.6	4.9	2.2	16.5	71.2	50.6	12.3	31.2
District 17	Frederica Wilson (D)	248	655 160	2 645.4	32.6	58.5	0.3	1.7	3.8	3.1	28.2	12.3	52.3	37.3	44.8
District 18	Ileana Ros-Lehtinen (R)	877	712 790	812.9	84.8	7.9	0.2	1.4	3.3	2.3	66.9	24.8	50.2	53.2	26.4
District 19	Ted Deutch (D)	599	736 419	1 230.2	77.1	13.0	0.3	3.0	4.0	2.5	20.6	61.9	53.1	26.4	23.6
District 20	Debbie Wasserman Schultz (D)	419	691 727	1 652.2	77.8	12.3	0.3	3.4	3.4	2.7	31.3	51.8	51.5	34.0	28.9
District 21	Mario Diaz-Balart (R)	343	693 501	2 020.0	83.2	9.0	0.1	2.5	3.0	2.2	75.6	13.8	52.1	58.1	28.4
District 22	Allen West (R)	694	694 259	999.8	84.7	7.4	0.3	2.5	2.9	2.1	16.3	72.3	50.8	20.3	27.3
District 23	Alcee L. Hastings (D)	8 696	684 107	78.7	34.1	55.9	0.7	1.8	4.8	2.8	18.4	22.6	50.4	31.8	42.2
District 24	Sandy Adams (R)	4 086	799 233	195.6	81.2	8.8	0.3	3.4	3.6	2.7	16.3	70.1	50.5	10.9	33.6
District 25	David Rivera (R)	10 890	807 176	74.1	80.8	10.2	0.2	1.6	4.7	2.4	71.6	16.8	51.0	46.8	33.6
GEORGIA		148 959	9 687 653	65.0	59.7	30.5	0.3	3.3	4.0	2.1	8.8	55.9	51.2	9.7	55.2
District 1	Jack Kingston (R)	29 068	722 068	24.8	67.9	25.3	0.4	1.4	2.9	2.1	6.4	65.2	50.5	4.8	59.4
District 2	Sanford D. Bishop Jr. (D)	28 006	631 973	22.6	46.5	48.4	0.3	0.9	2.3	1.6	4.6	44.9	51.0	3.5	71.6

1. Dry land or land partially or temporarily covered by water. 2. May be of any race.

Table E. Congressional Districts 112th Congress — **Age and Education**

	Population and population characteristics, 2010 (cont.)										Education, 2010			
STATE District	Age (percent)									Median age	Enrollment[1]		Attainment[2] (percent)	
	Under 5 years	5 to 17 years	18 to 24 years	25 to 34 years	35 to 44 years	45 to 54 years	55 to 64 years	65 to 74 years	75 years and over		Total	Percent private	High school graduate or more	Bachelor's degree or more
	15	16	17	18	19	20	21	22	23	24	25	26	27	28
CALIFORNIA—Cont'd														
District 39	7.4	20.8	11.4	14.1	14.2	13.1	9.5	5.3	4.2	32.3	193 460	9.7	69.9	17.1
District 40	6.2	18.0	11.0	13.4	14.1	14.8	10.4	6.3	5.7	36.0	195 715	13.3	82.3	30.6
District 41	7.2	19.6	10.6	12.7	12.0	13.8	11.3	7.0	5.9	34.9	218 415	12.7	83.1	20.7
District 42	5.6	18.8	9.4	11.8	14.3	16.9	12.2	6.2	4.8	38.5	207 994	16.2	90.0	39.4
District 43	8.9	23.7	12.1	14.6	13.8	12.4	7.8	3.8	2.7	28.4	236 314	7.3	66.5	11.4
District 44	7.4	20.9	11.7	13.2	14.5	14.1	9.6	5.0	3.7	32.6	272 447	14.2	80.7	26.0
District 45	7.2	20.3	9.3	12.3	12.7	13.0	10.4	7.9	6.9	35.7	261 685	10.4	78.4	20.2
District 46	5.1	15.4	8.8	13.0	14.3	15.4	12.4	8.2	7.4	40.5	168 353	15.7	88.4	40.4
District 47	8.5	21.3	11.8	16.0	15.0	12.2	7.8	4.1	3.3	30.0	191 643	6.7	60.2	15.6
District 48	5.6	16.2	9.8	13.6	14.5	15.4	11.8	6.8	6.3	38.6	210 261	16.6	93.2	53.9
District 49	7.6	19.5	12.4	13.4	12.9	13.5	9.7	5.8	5.4	32.7	226 259	11.1	81.1	22.8
District 50	6.6	17.8	8.5	13.2	14.6	15.2	11.7	6.4	6.1	37.9	204 405	15.1	88.9	44.1
District 51	7.3	20.7	11.3	13.8	13.7	13.3	9.6	5.5	4.8	32.6	239 809	9.0	73.2	18.8
District 52	6.5	17.2	9.6	13.5	13.2	15.7	12.1	6.3	5.8	37.5	190 688	15.8	88.9	31.3
District 53	5.6	12.4	16.7	21.3	13.8	11.7	9.0	4.8	4.7	31.6	192 651	18.5	86.1	39.9
COLORADO	6.8	17.5	9.7	14.4	13.9	14.8	11.9	6.2	4.8	36.1	1 358 511	14.1	89.7	36.4
District 1	7.2	14.2	10.4	20.3	14.8	12.3	10.4	5.4	5.0	33.7	165 468	22.0	84.3	40.5
District 2	6.8	17.2	11.0	15.3	15.0	14.8	11.3	5.2	3.4	34.7	206 379	12.7	90.0	42.4
District 3	6.4	16.9	9.0	12.4	12.1	14.8	13.9	8.0	6.4	39.4	180 336	10.0	89.0	26.9
District 4	6.6	17.5	11.7	13.6	12.8	14.3	11.7	6.5	5.4	35.5	210 241	9.2	89.4	33.6
District 5	6.9	18.2	10.3	13.7	13.1	15.3	11.7	6.3	4.6	35.7	199 623	15.3	91.7	32.9
District 6	6.6	20.7	6.3	11.6	15.7	17.2	12.8	5.7	3.7	38.5	228 047	15.9	96.5	48.5
District 7	7.4	17.5	9.5	15.1	13.7	14.3	11.3	6.2	5.1	35.4	168 417	14.5	85.5	28.1
CONNECTICUT	5.7	17.2	9.1	11.8	13.6	16.1	12.4	7.1	7.0	40.0	948 526	20.6	88.6	35.5
District 1	5.7	16.8	8.7	12.4	13.3	15.7	12.6	7.3	7.5	40.1	190 809	20.2	87.9	32.9
District 2	5.1	16.6	10.4	10.8	13.3	16.9	13.0	7.4	6.5	40.8	191 890	16.5	90.8	32.6
District 3	5.5	15.9	10.5	12.9	13.2	15.3	12.2	7.1	7.5	39.3	183 865	26.4	89.0	31.8
District 4	6.4	19.0	7.7	11.4	14.3	16.2	11.6	6.8	6.7	39.3	196 869	24.7	88.1	46.7
District 5	5.7	17.8	8.3	11.3	13.7	16.5	12.7	7.1	7.0	40.5	185 093	15.0	87.3	34.0
DELAWARE	6.2	16.7	10.1	12.4	12.9	14.9	12.4	8.1	6.3	38.8	236 270	21.1	87.7	27.8
At Large	6.2	16.7	10.1	12.4	12.9	14.9	12.4	8.1	6.3	38.8	236 270	21.1	87.7	27.8
DISTRICT OF COLUMBIA	5.4	11.3	14.5	20.7	13.4	12.6	10.6	6.1	5.3	33.8	158 455	45.8	87.4	50.1
Delegate District (At Large)	5.4	11.3	14.5	20.7	13.4	12.6	10.6	6.1	5.3	33.8	158 455	45.8	87.4	50.1
FLORIDA	5.7	15.6	9.3	12.2	12.9	14.6	12.4	9.2	8.1	40.7	4 614 324	17.6	85.5	25.8
District 1	6.3	16.0	10.9	13.0	12.3	15.3	12.2	8.0	6.0	38.4	169 827	17.4	86.9	22.8
District 2	5.8	14.8	13.8	13.5	12.3	14.3	12.3	7.6	5.6	36.8	209 312	10.8	85.2	25.9
District 3	7.5	17.9	11.5	14.2	12.6	14.1	11.0	6.4	4.8	34.1	183 869	18.7	78.9	14.4
District 4	6.1	15.6	10.2	14.6	13.6	15.0	12.5	7.0	5.4	37.8	188 350	18.8	89.3	26.5
District 5	5.0	14.6	6.5	9.3	11.8	13.4	14.5	14.4	10.6	47.1	197 678	15.9	87.4	20.6
District 6	5.7	15.5	11.9	12.0	11.9	13.6	12.2	9.6	7.6	39.3	221 871	14.9	87.1	24.3
District 7	5.4	16.0	8.5	10.7	12.6	15.3	13.8	9.6	8.1	42.6	203 171	21.2	88.7	29.5
District 8	5.9	16.4	10.4	14.5	14.2	14.7	11.2	6.9	5.9	37.1	217 613	21.2	87.7	28.7
District 9	5.4	16.6	7.7	10.8	13.3	15.6	13.0	8.9	8.6	42.3	187 421	17.5	88.3	29.0
District 10	4.4	12.3	7.1	11.0	12.2	16.2	15.0	10.7	11.0	46.9	124 364	16.8	88.4	27.7
District 11	6.6	16.1	12.1	14.9	13.5	14.1	10.8	6.3	5.4	35.2	183 253	12.8	82.6	25.2
District 12	6.8	17.7	9.0	12.9	12.8	13.3	11.5	8.8	7.2	37.9	213 219	14.9	82.5	19.7
District 13	4.7	13.2	6.5	9.2	10.6	13.5	14.7	14.0	13.6	49.5	139 094	16.3	88.4	26.4
District 14	4.9	13.4	7.0	9.9	10.9	13.1	14.5	14.4	12.0	48.1	168 293	14.1	87.7	26.9
District 15	5.4	15.9	8.0	11.0	12.2	15.3	13.0	10.0	9.2	43.0	189 594	16.5	88.1	23.9
District 16	5.0	15.1	7.1	9.6	11.4	14.4	13.5	12.4	11.5	46.2	177 412	15.5	85.9	23.1
District 17	7.0	18.2	11.1	13.9	13.2	14.3	10.9	6.4	5.0	34.8	180 542	16.7	76.9	16.7
District 18	5.4	12.6	9.2	15.1	15.2	14.5	11.5	8.5	8.1	40.1	154 519	29.6	76.7	30.3
District 19	5.1	14.4	7.1	10.3	12.3	13.2	11.9	10.8	14.9	45.5	168 272	18.3	88.8	30.2
District 20	5.5	15.0	7.6	13.0	15.1	16.2	12.5	7.6	7.5	41.0	172 332	27.1	90.8	35.8
District 21	5.5	16.2	9.5	12.2	15.4	15.5	11.0	7.9	6.9	39.5	172 405	19.4	78.6	26.0
District 22	4.6	13.5	7.1	11.0	13.0	16.3	14.0	10.0	10.4	45.5	150 022	26.1	91.9	37.8
District 23	7.4	17.9	10.6	14.8	13.5	14.1	10.1	6.1	5.4	34.4	188 507	13.1	75.0	16.3
District 24	5.2	15.7	12.1	12.3	12.9	15.2	12.0	7.9	6.6	38.9	221 701	16.1	90.7	29.4
District 25	6.6	18.6	10.0	13.0	15.6	15.0	10.2	6.4	4.6	36.2	231 683	16.4	77.5	23.3
GEORGIA	7.1	18.6	10.0	13.8	14.4	14.4	11.0	6.3	4.4	35.3	2 734 492	15.1	84.3	27.3
District 1	7.4	17.9	11.0	13.5	12.9	13.9	11.4	7.1	4.9	35.2	195 761	8.9	82.6	19.8
District 2	7.1	18.0	10.8	12.8	12.4	14.1	12.0	7.2	5.6	36.1	173 000	8.5	76.9	13.8

1. All persons 3 years old and over enrolled in nursery school through college and graduate or professional school.   2. Persons 25 years old and over.

Table E. Congressional Districts 112th Congress — Households and Group Quarters

STATE District	Households, 2010						Group quarters, 2010					
	Number	Persons per household	Family households (percent)	Husband-wife family (percent)	Female family householder[1]	One person households (percent)	Total in group quarters	Percent 65 years and over	Persons in correctional institutions	Persons in nursing homes	Persons in college dormitories	Persons in military quarters
	29	30	31	32	33	34	35	36	37	38	39	40
CALIFORNIA—Cont'd												
District 39	175 160	3.62	81.7	55.6	18.1	14.0	10 585	20.2	1 919	2 190	2 483	0
District 40	210 735	3.09	74.9	55.4	13.4	18.2	15 431	24.6	2 701	2 499	2 950	0
District 41	272 594	2.87	71.6	51.1	14.1	22.3	20 808	19.5	1 254	2 305	2 814	3 347
District 42	217 235	3.02	78.9	62.6	11.2	16.3	10 701	14.3	6 859	558	822	0
District 43	190 884	3.81	81.6	53.0	19.6	13.7	3 987	15.8	2 577	1 479	53	0
District 44	251 812	3.28	76.9	58.0	12.6	16.6	13 525	10.5	5 489	2 002	7 397	0
District 45	304 220	2.96	71.1	52.4	13.0	22.1	11 305	15.8	9 270	1 249	70	0
District 46	244 925	2.61	64.4	49.6	10.0	26.3	8 661	22.9	1 102	1 642	2 743	16
District 47	151 580	4.11	80.7	55.6	16.3	13.4	8 593	22.8	2 274	1 831	260	0
District 48	279 312	2.57	64.9	51.5	9.4	25.7	10 659	20.6	536	1 119	6 151	0
District 49	253 046	3.06	75.0	57.4	11.8	18.8	23 188	6.2	1 229	885	143	16 563
District 50	269 341	2.76	70.2	55.7	9.9	21.5	16 890	29.9	242	2 081	617	2 926
District 51	216 630	3.39	80.2	54.1	19.3	15.6	19 562	7.7	14 809	1 461	0	5 308
District 52	245 336	2.71	70.5	53.1	12.0	21.9	11 297	26.9	3 489	2 907	185	8
District 53	264 983	2.32	46.8	31.5	10.6	35.7	45 924	5.4	2 737	2 275	15 253	18 959
COLORADO	1 972 868	2.49	63.9	49.2	10.1	27.9	115 878	14.3	40 568	18 079	29 952	10 945
District 1	291 124	2.22	47.9	32.8	10.7	40.3	16 063	12.6	3 960	2 682	4 940	0
District 2	282 514	2.56	63.9	50.2	9.0	25.2	13 825	14.7	811	1 802	6 538	0
District 3	284 848	2.42	64.9	49.7	10.2	28.0	20 021	20.4	4 427	3 696	5 352	0
District 4	275 502	2.53	65.8	52.0	9.2	25.6	21 306	11.9	13 125	3 170	8 916	0
District 5	276 811	2.52	67.7	52.5	10.8	26.3	31 782	7.0	12 105	2 263	2 649	10 678
District 6	298 713	2.66	73.9	61.9	8.2	21.0	2 961	41.0	1 585	1 473	0	0
District 7	263 356	2.53	63.5	45.1	12.7	28.9	9 920	23.0	4 555	2 993	1 557	267
CONNECTICUT	1 371 087	2.52	66.3	49.0	12.9	27.3	118 152	20.9	20 059	26 371	48 537	3 977
District 1	283 063	2.45	64.4	45.1	14.9	29.2	20 279	33.1	1 335	6 778	5 649	0
District 2	276 884	2.49	67.4	52.6	10.4	25.6	44 127	10.7	12 975	4 306	16 779	3 977
District 3	278 954	2.46	63.4	45.0	14.0	29.6	20 516	18.6	902	5 490	16 566	0
District 4	258 141	2.68	69.4	52.8	12.6	24.9	14 359	30.5	1 159	4 486	5 030	0
District 5	274 045	2.54	67.1	50.0	12.6	26.8	18 871	28.1	3 688	5 311	4 513	0
DELAWARE	342 297	2.55	67.4	48.3	14.2	25.6	24 413	16.8	6 457	4 591	10 184	283
At Large	342 297	2.55	67.4	48.3	14.2	25.6	24 413	16.8	6 457	4 591	10 184	283
DISTRICT OF COLUMBIA	266 707	2.11	42.3	22.0	16.4	44.0	40 021	7.8	3 598	3 064	24 087	1 504
Delegate District (At Large)	266 707	2.11	42.3	22.0	16.4	44.0	40 021	7.8	3 598	3 064	24 087	1 504
FLORIDA	7 420 802	2.48	65.2	46.6	13.5	27.2	421 709	17.5	167 453	73 372	85 243	14 612
District 1	268 660	2.46	66.9	48.1	13.9	26.4	34 493	8.0	14 970	2 719	4 832	8 580
District 2	286 377	2.41	62.3	43.6	13.7	28.1	46 360	7.7	30 745	3 539	10 370	513
District 3	246 220	2.59	63.1	32.8	24.0	28.6	29 085	11.0	10 488	2 534	1 551	0
District 4	292 633	2.44	64.9	47.7	12.5	27.3	25 812	11.9	16 769	3 640	2 776	4 662
District 5	379 106	2.40	70.2	56.1	10.0	24.1	16 023	17.6	13 520	3 052	1 130	0
District 6	318 748	2.47	66.5	49.6	12.3	25.1	27 567	13.2	10 390	3 697	9 235	0
District 7	328 948	2.43	66.3	49.8	12.0	26.5	17 982	26.5	1 526	3 987	5 780	0
District 8	313 558	2.53	64.5	46.0	13.4	26.2	9 484	18.8	1 219	3 070	1 480	0
District 9	307 731	2.42	65.2	49.5	11.3	27.8	11 496	39.3	89	3 270	442	0
District 10	293 493	2.12	55.1	40.3	10.7	36.2	9 655	36.1	3 504	4 854	1 677	78
District 11	268 517	2.44	58.1	33.9	18.5	31.8	15 305	17.6	2 195	3 574	8 183	246
District 12	313 963	2.63	69.7	49.9	14.3	24.0	15 884	15.8	8 088	2 803	3 319	0
District 13	333 347	2.23	63.0	49.9	9.3	30.2	15 743	25.2	5 311	3 616	1 569	0
District 14	372 010	2.28	65.3	51.8	9.4	27.7	7 619	27.6	2 727	3 147	2 730	9
District 15	328 153	2.45	66.8	49.6	12.4	26.3	9 765	33.1	1 921	3 006	1 437	182
District 16	325 366	2.41	67.5	52.7	10.3	26.2	8 601	27.7	6 370	3 240	126	0
District 17	219 778	2.94	69.1	35.2	26.1	24.5	12 254	31.2	370	2 761	2 956	0
District 18	287 604	2.43	58.0	37.9	14.0	32.1	12 978	15.5	3 123	2 110	4 895	336
District 19	314 604	2.32	62.5	47.3	11.1	31.3	4 399	33.5	619	1 946	2 444	0
District 20	289 573	2.37	60.4	43.3	12.4	31.1	3 949	24.1	938	1 350	1 328	0
District 21	227 882	3.01	77.2	52.1	18.1	17.2	9 046	24.9	2 296	1 404	2 583	0
District 22	308 490	2.23	58.0	44.7	9.2	33.2	5 696	43.7	12	2 865	1 714	2
District 23	238 582	2.77	64.8	34.9	22.6	27.1	24 489	14.0	15 156	3 527	15	0
District 24	309 979	2.50	66.1	49.6	11.7	24.7	11 121	10.1	8 136	2 604	12 117	4
District 25	247 480	3.21	81.0	55.7	18.2	13.9	36 903	15.0	6 971	1 057	554	0
GEORGIA	3 585 584	2.63	68.5	47.8	15.8	25.4	253 199	12.5	104 012	34 738	72 288	16 072
District 1	268 300	2.58	70.1	49.7	15.7	24.4	27 604	10.3	15 540	3 410	3 962	4 327
District 2	234 984	2.55	68.0	41.3	21.5	27.5	41 119	9.3	16 847	3 594	4 961	5 167

1. No spouse present.

Table E. Congressional Districts 112th Congress — **Housing and Money Income**

STATE District	Housing units, 2010										Money income, 2010		
		Occupied units										Households	
		Owner-occupied						Renter-occupied					
						Median owner cost as a percent of income							
	Total	Percent occupied	Percent	Median value[1] (dollars)	Percent valued at $500,000 or more	With a mortgage	Without a mortgage[2]	Median rent[3]	Median rent as a percent of income	Sub-standard units[4] (percent)	Per capita income (dollars)	Median income (dollars)	Percent with income of $100,000 or more
	41	42	43	44	45	46	47	48	49	50	51	52	53
CALIFORNIA—Cont'd													
District 39	183 503	95.5	59.4	370 900	20.1	31.9	10.0	1 105	38.0	19.0	19 208	53 439	21.6
District 40	217 459	95.2	58.5	472 600	44.1	29.9	10.0	1 323	34.0	10.8	26 800	65 243	30.1
District 41	344 695	77.7	66.7	183 000	5.7	28.8	13.0	979	34.0	6.7	22 299	49 506	18.7
District 42	224 518	95.3	75.4	514 400	52.1	30.2	10.2	1 448	35.8	6.7	32 605	83 029	40.3
District 43	205 348	91.7	57.4	194 300	2.3	32.7	10.6	1 003	39.4	17.9	15 151	46 728	13.3
District 44	267 202	91.7	66.1	321 600	22.7	31.6	10.3	1 215	36.1	9.2	26 164	67 381	30.0
District 45	379 950	76.8	68.3	216 300	11.6	32.5	15.1	1 090	37.1	6.8	22 623	49 508	20.2
District 46	260 167	93.2	60.9	620 000	66.5	29.8	10.2	1 404	32.9	5.5	36 657	71 332	34.7
District 47	162 049	93.9	45.7	343 200	12.1	29.7	10.0	1 216	36.0	28.4	15 999	51 647	18.4
District 48	298 871	92.5	60.5	626 100	64.7	30.7	11.4	1 654	31.7	4.3	43 611	82 047	41.6
District 49	273 783	90.5	64.7	289 400	15.7	32.3	12.1	1 300	36.8	6.4	23 799	57 399	23.2
District 50	283 762	93.1	63.2	537 700	54.3	30.6	11.9	1 446	35.0	3.7	34 819	70 362	35.6
District 51	243 779	89.7	56.7	277 700	10.1	31.9	10.3	1 033	35.7	13.1	19 153	50 316	19.1
District 52	254 972	92.3	61.7	400 400	30.5	29.1	10.6	1 249	32.8	5.2	29 688	67 671	31.0
District 53	289 430	88.3	33.0	414 800	39.1	31.9	10.5	1 177	33.8	8.0	29 280	48 679	19.0
COLORADO	2 214 262	88.5	65.9	236 600	11.4	25.2	10.7	863	31.2	3.2	28 723	54 046	22.7
District 1	316 993	91.8	50.0	245 800	12.7	24.9	11.0	810	30.5	4.1	30 717	44 859	19.4
District 2	339 261	81.9	0.0	276 100	20.2	24.9	10.9	996	31.7	3.3	31 209	62 146	27.0
District 3	350 158	80.2	69.8	202 900	12.1	27.4	11.3	772	32.3	3.2	24 065	44 906	14.3
District 4	305 276	89.8	66.8	211 400	6.8	25.2	10.0	803	31.3	3.4	25 261	50 167	18.7
District 5	306 292	89.9	65.8	210 500	6.4	25.3	10.0	797	30.5	2.7	25 697	50 925	20.7
District 6	318 711	94.7	80.2	294 300	15.3	24.4	10.0	1 117	29.1	1.4	37 824	82 062	38.9
District 7	277 571	93.6	61.9	210 900	4.1	25.8	11.7	862	33.1	4.2	25 088	60 360	18.0
CONNECTICUT	1 488 215	91.3	68.0	288 800	17.6	26.8	17.6	992	32.1	2.4	35 078	64 032	29.9
District 1	303 687	93.1	65.5	245 400	5.7	25.2	17.1	909	30.5	2.1	30 979	59 321	25.7
District 2	305 202	89.8	74.5	269 900	10.7	25.5	15.9	942	29.5	2.2	33 140	68 952	30.6
District 3	301 729	91.5	63.0	274 600	9.3	28.5	18.5	1 061	34.0	2.8	31 320	57 676	25.7
District 4	276 945	91.5	67.2	511 400	51.0	28.9	18.5	1 259	34.1	2.9	47 340	77 074	39.7
District 5	300 652	90.6	69.7	281 700	14.4	27.1	18.6	916	32.8	2.0	32 729	60 460	29.1
DELAWARE	406 489	80.9	73.0	243 600	7.4	24.8	11.8	952	32.3	2.9	27 729	55 847	22.8
At Large	406 489	80.9	73.0	243 600	7.4	24.8	11.8	952	32.3	2.9	27 729	55 847	22.8
DISTRICT OF COLUMBIA	296 836	85.0	42.5	426 900	40.3	24.8	11.0	1 198	30.4	3.5	41 240	60 903	30.5
Delegate District (At Large)	296 836	85.0	42.5	426 900	40.3	24.8	11.0	1 198	30.4	3.5	41 240	60 903	30.5
FLORIDA	8 994 091	78.2	68.1	164 200	6.7	29.5	14.4	947	35.5	3.1	24 272	44 409	15.8
District 1	319 016	80.7	70.0	151 700	4.6	27.0	11.6	849	32.8	2.3	22 981	45 140	14.7
District 2	384 934	72.2	64.6	156 500	5.2	25.4	12.0	879	35.4	3.3	21 959	41 929	13.6
District 3	298 925	76.5	54.9	109 500	2.3	30.6	13.9	807	40.6	3.4	16 037	31 968	6.7
District 4	327 150	85.8	66.9	173 800	6.4	26.5	11.9	930	29.8	2.0	26 638	50 337	17.9
District 5	460 757	80.8	81.7	145 200	3.0	28.4	13.1	891	35.8	2.3	22 010	42 473	12.0
District 6	361 384	84.3	71.1	151 800	3.3	26.3	13.4	892	35.3	2.0	22 382	43 971	14.2
District 7	384 441	78.3	75.0	178 100	8.3	28.7	13.7	940	32.8	2.0	26 375	48 341	18.6
District 8	370 255	81.4	63.3	168 100	6.7	30.2	14.0	986	36.4	2.9	24 212	45 221	16.1
District 9	351 161	84.2	72.1	167 500	5.1	28.6	14.3	915	34.8	2.3	27 065	46 928	19.4
District 10	359 085	78.7	68.4	152 800	6.9	29.0	16.4	927	34.3	1.7	27 921	44 062	14.3
District 11	314 804	83.4	51.9	146 700	6.1	29.8	15.0	858	34.7	2.6	22 107	37 724	11.9
District 12	370 517	81.4	69.5	129 500	1.8	27.4	13.7	864	34.3	3.2	20 560	42 150	11.3
District 13	433 595	71.3	75.1	171 200	7.8	29.8	14.3	903	33.3	2.5	26 339	45 514	15.0
District 14	543 211	61.5	72.8	177 900	13.5	30.0	14.6	890	33.9	2.6	28 412	46 905	18.0
District 15	417 553	74.9	71.5	151 500	4.3	28.0	13.6	910	34.7	2.2	24 070	45 613	15.1
District 16	412 667	75.5	78.2	151 200	7.1	30.3	14.4	935	33.3	1.9	26 254	43 420	15.8
District 17	246 275	81.8	53.5	147 000	3.2	36.5	16.1	914	39.5	7.3	15 691	35 017	7.7
District 18	363 405	73.9	45.6	271 000	23.6	35.5	18.4	990	38.6	6.6	26 619	37 823	17.8
District 19	373 653	79.6	76.6	161 700	5.4	32.2	17.4	1 129	36.6	3.4	27 552	46 919	17.3
District 20	357 388	76.5	68.0	200 600	11.6	31.8	20.4	1 203	34.5	3.3	30 822	50 905	23.4
District 21	237 501	90.8	65.2	220 100	6.8	33.1	16.2	1 051	39.6	5.0	21 230	45 943	18.1
District 22	395 652	75.0	69.8	256 200	17.6	31.1	17.3	1 212	34.7	1.7	38 530	58 319	26.7
District 23	277 103	81.2	54.1	123 500	1.7	35.4	15.7	957	39.1	7.1	16 383	34 942	9.3
District 24	361 124	79.8	73.9	170 500	3.6	27.7	13.4	970	32.9	1.2	24 935	51 960	18.9
District 25	272 535	86.2	69.7	204 100	4.2	34.3	14.6	1 114	39.8	6.2	18 901	49 326	17.8
GEORGIA	4 091 482	85.1	66.2	156 200	5.3	25.2	12.3	819	32.4	3.2	23 383	46 430	17.7
District 1	317 136	84.1	65.6	127 300	4.9	24.8	10.9	735	32.5	3.0	20 685	40 999	13.9
District 2	272 098	84.6	60.1	90 200	1.5	25.1	13.4	631	34.5	3.9	17 166	31 368	9.1

1. Specified owner-occupied units.   2. Median monthly owner costs is often in the minimum category—10.0 percent or less, which is indicated as 10.0 percent.   3. Specified renter-occupied units.   4. Overcrowded or lacking complete plumbing facilities.

STATE District	Poverty, 2010 (percent)			Civilian labor force, 2010			Civilian employment,[2] 2010				Social Security beneficiaries, December 2010			
					Unemployment			Percent						
	Persons below poverty level	Families below poverty level	Households receiving food stamps in past 12 months	Total	Total	Rate[1]	Total	Management, business, science, and arts occupations	Service, sales, and office	Construction and production	Persons under age 65 with no health insurance, 2010 (percent)	Number	Rate[3]	Supplemental Security Income recipients, December 2010
	54	55	56	57	58	59	60	61	62	63	64	65	66	67
CALIFORNIA—Cont'd														
District 39	16.4	14.7	8.8	306 634	42 003	13.7	264 631	28.2	43.4	28.5	27.1	71 741	111.6	21 308
District 40	11.9	8.9	5.5	343 668	38 179	11.1	305 489	35.7	45.1	19.2	22.0	84 847	127.5	16 409
District 41	15.9	10.7	10.1	353 688	52 839	14.9	300 849	31.2	46.0	22.9	20.9	131 010	164.4	27 931
District 42	6.3	4.6	2.3	351 240	34 064	9.7	317 176	43.0	43.4	13.6	14.3	82 783	124.0	11 933
District 43	23.9	19.9	16.4	339 154	61 123	18.0	278 031	18.8	45.5	35.7	29.0	69 273	94.2	28 666
District 44	13.3	9.1	6.6	420 402	62 851	15.0	357 551	33.1	43.1	23.8	21.1	90 791	107.5	19 072
District 45	17.3	13.8	8.4	404 489	68 371	16.9	336 118	26.4	50.5	23.1	24.2	149 788	163.8	24 270
District 46	10.5	6.7	3.1	349 010	35 113	10.1	313 897	45.1	40.6	14.2	16.2	106 873	164.8	16 523
District 47	20.9	17.7	10.8	321 762	46 497	14.5	275 265	19.9	50.3	29.8	33.2	51 980	82.3	24 852
District 48	9.5	5.7	1.9	393 560	35 051	8.9	358 509	52.7	37.8	9.4	13.8	99 840	137.2	9 509
District 49	14.5	10.8	5.1	364 898	50 398	13.8	314 500	30.6	47.0	22.5	23.5	108 810	136.5	14 818
District 50	11.7	9.0	2.0	377 532	37 486	9.9	340 046	47.6	38.0	14.3	16.5	103 068	136.9	12 120
District 51	16.9	14.6	9.1	343 699	51 763	15.1	291 936	27.5	51.1	21.4	23.2	103 087	136.0	34 874
District 52	11.7	8.3	5.7	341 917	38 093	11.1	303 824	41.1	42.9	15.9	14.5	98 660	146.4	16 935
District 53	23.8	17.3	5.3	344 690	38 241	11.1	306 449	42.1	44.5	13.3	23.3	75 460	113.8	22 247
COLORADO	13.4	9.4	7.8	2 714 224	267 550	9.9	2 446 674	39.7	41.9	18.5	17.8	693 341	137.9	65 720
District 1	20.9	15.9	11.1	378 437	44 150	11.7	334 287	41.9	42.4	15.7	20.4	84 518	127.7	14 853
District 2	11.6	6.8	4.7	418 611	38 178	9.1	380 433	42.2	41.8	16.0	16.4	79 263	108.0	5 430
District 3	15.6	11.0	10.3	360 376	38 226	10.6	322 150	32.5	44.4	23.1	23.1	137 286	194.4	14 702
District 4	15.0	10.4	8.6	387 183	36 562	9.4	350 621	38.1	40.2	21.7	17.2	107 355	148.1	8 342
District 5	13.2	10.0	8.6	353 010	36 648	10.4	316 362	39.0	42.4	18.7	16.7	97 284	134.0	8 262
District 6	4.4	2.9	2.5	454 004	31 605	7.0	422 399	49.0	38.5	12.6	9.6	92 808	116.3	3 920
District 7	14.8	11.8	9.3	362 603	42 181	11.6	320 422	31.7	44.8	23.6	23.0	94 827	139.8	10 211
CONNECTICUT	10.1	7.2	10.2	1 939 959	203 513	10.5	1 736 446	40.6	42.4	17.0	10.4	622 167	174.1	58 257
District 1	11.1	8.4	13.3	390 960	43 408	11.1	347 552	40.1	43.4	16.4	10.1	132 576	186.5	15 931
District 2	7.5	4.8	7.0	394 675	35 493	9.0	359 182	39.9	41.2	18.9	8.0	129 267	177.1	7 382
District 3	11.5	8.0	11.4	397 738	45 116	11.3	352 622	39.6	42.9	17.5	10.7	126 371	177.4	12 695
District 4	9.8	7.1	8.4	366 003	38 434	10.5	327 569	43.6	42.4	14.0	12.6	108 366	153.3	9 544
District 5	10.6	7.5	10.5	390 583	41 062	10.5	349 521	40.1	42.4	17.6	10.6	125 587	175.8	12 705
DELAWARE	11.8	8.1	11.3	453 206	42 086	9.3	411 120	37.7	42.7	19.7	11.3	172 441	192.0	15 865
At Large	11.8	8.1	11.3	453 206	42 086	9.3	411 120	37.7	42.7	19.7	11.3	172 441	192.0	15 865
DISTRICT OF COLUMBIA	19.2	14.1	11.4	341 495	42 368	12.4	299 127	59.2	32.9	8.0	8.4	74 417	123.7	24 371
Delegate District (At Large)	19.2	14.1	11.4	341 495	42 368	12.4	299 127	59.2	32.9	8.0	8.4	74 417	123.7	24 371
FLORIDA	16.5	12.0	12.4	9 203 585	1 228 640	13.3	7 974 945	33.5	48.3	18.2	25.4	3 784 225	201.3	485 172
District 1	16.4	12.5	13.0	330 720	48 501	14.7	282 219	32.7	48.8	18.5	20.0	140 044	201.7	17 144
District 2	20.5	12.9	12.7	348 522	41 562	11.9	306 960	37.3	44.3	18.4	18.7	132 564	179.7	19 337
District 3	27.8	22.0	23.7	297 474	51 025	17.2	246 449	24.4	53.6	22.0	25.3	112 951	171.4	30 888
District 4	12.7	8.3	9.2	377 775	38 616	10.2	339 159	36.7	45.0	18.2	18.2	121 565	163.3	13 366
District 5	14.1	10.5	12.3	398 017	56 982	14.3	341 035	32.4	48.0	19.6	21.4	282 803	304.2	16 922
District 6	17.9	12.0	11.5	382 705	52 618	13.7	330 087	34.4	47.5	18.1	19.7	177 654	218.6	15 818
District 7	15.7	11.0	10.4	388 571	46 809	12.0	341 762	36.2	46.7	16.9	22.5	180 337	222.0	14 235
District 8	14.9	11.5	10.7	444 568	55 243	12.4	389 325	35.4	48.3	16.3	25.4	129 871	161.2	16 787
District 9	13.8	9.8	10.5	367 103	42 364	11.5	324 739	38.8	45.0	16.2	19.8	160 228	212.6	12 373
District 10	12.8	8.4	9.9	326 226	38 602	11.8	287 624	36.7	45.3	17.9	22.7	154 432	243.6	11 382
District 11	22.3	17.5	19.3	353 618	57 631	16.3	295 987	34.1	49.1	16.8	25.4	108 896	161.6	30 090
District 12	16.7	13.2	13.3	390 040	53 143	13.6	336 897	29.9	46.4	23.7	23.9	169 170	200.9	22 798
District 13	14.5	9.5	9.0	345 712	47 380	13.7	298 332	31.8	48.0	20.2	25.4	210 828	278.2	9 704
District 14	15.6	9.8	8.8	377 685	58 127	15.4	319 558	30.1	54.5	15.4	27.5	219 644	255.7	11 604
District 15	14.4	10.8	11.0	397 644	53 245	13.4	344 399	32.9	48.6	18.5	23.8	189 165	232.5	16 475
District 16	14.3	10.3	9.7	365 262	53 549	14.7	311 713	32.3	47.7	20.1	24.7	200 391	251.2	12 078
District 17	25.5	21.2	22.2	312 965	56 616	18.1	256 349	24.6	55.1	20.4	37.1	93 554	142.8	34 608
District 18	20.5	15.0	20.2	376 407	42 638	11.3	333 769	32.5	47.9	19.7	35.9	114 090	160.1	43 114
District 19	11.7	8.7	6.9	360 357	50 416	14.0	309 941	34.3	50.3	15.4	27.5	183 985	249.8	8 838
District 20	12.3	9.4	6.8	380 581	44 608	11.7	335 973	40.4	45.6	14.1	23.8	113 310	163.8	12 765
District 21	15.9	13.0	19.9	352 913	43 512	12.3	309 401	30.8	48.9	20.1	35.7	106 001	152.8	37 252
District 22	10.4	6.6	4.9	385 033	41 739	10.8	343 294	39.5	46.3	14.2	21.2	139 159	200.4	7 286
District 23	27.7	23.3	19.2	336 957	61 710	18.3	275 247	23.1	55.5	21.4	37.2	100 538	147.0	25 346
District 24	12.2	8.1	8.7	403 035	44 002	10.9	359 033	39.1	46.1	14.7	18.9	145 696	182.3	11 759
District 25	18.0	15.3	18.4	403 695	48 002	11.9	355 693	29.6	49.8	20.7	35.3	97 349	120.6	33 203
GEORGIA	17.9	13.7	13.5	4 765 482	600 029	12.6	4 165 453	35.4	42.1	22.5	21.9	1 468 209	151.6	228 510
District 1	20.4	16.7	16.2	323 399	34 828	10.8	288 571	28.2	44.7	27.1	24.4	120 885	167.4	19 242
District 2	27.3	22.0	23.1	267 118	38 807	14.5	228 311	28.5	43.3	28.2	24.2	120 204	190.2	29 081

1. Percent of civilian labor force.   2. Persons 16 years old and over.   3. Per 1,000 resident population enumerated in the 2010 census.

Table E. Congressional Districts 112th Congress — **Agriculture**

	Farms		Land in farms		Farm Operators			Value of products sold				Government payments	
						Percent of farm operators				Percent of sales from			
STATE District	Number	Operated by family or individual (percent)	Acreage	Average size of farm (acres)	Total	Whose primary occupation is farming	Who live on the farm operated	Total ($1,000)	Average per farm	Crops	Livestock	Total ($1,000)	Percent of farms
	68	69	70	71	72	73	74	75	76	77	78	79	80
CALIFORNIA—Cont'd													
District 39	21	76.2	728	35	36	52.8	47.2	1 933	92 048	(D)	(D)		0.0
District 40	58	70.7	1 195	21	85	31.8	60.0	17 258	297 552	99.5	0.5	7	6.9
District 41	1 229	83.0	514 593	419	1 950	43.0	74.3	530 475	431 631	25.3	74.7	523	3.2
District 42	221	76.9	10 112	46	346	44.2	65.0	137 961	624 258	34.7	65.3	258	4.1
District 43	138	76.1	5 262	38	230	57.8	62.6	157 365	1 140 326	26.9	73.1	120	8.7
District 44	786	84.7	31 907	41	1 211	40.2	79.6	151 373	192 587	70.2	29.8	106	1.5
District 45	1 707	76.7	229 097	134	2 767	46.5	63.8	656 220	384 429	82.6	17.4	5 425	3.5
District 46	55	72.7	1 536	28	82	32.9	36.6	42 668	775 782	99.9	0.1	(D)	3.6
District 47	13	92.3	173	13	29	20.7	13.8	1 761	135 462	98.9	1.1		0.0
District 48	72	58.3	79 766	1 108	132	54.5	34.8	220 529	3 062 903	99.8	0.2	24	4.2
District 49	4 331	87.4	177 376	41	6 565	37.9	81.6	632 514	146 043	88.2	11.8	234	0.5
District 50	876	79.0	41 706	48	1 304	36.2	62.9	170 221	194 316	91.4	8.6	(D)	0.3
District 51	702	67.7	438 270	624	1 148	56.4	45.0	1 332 407	1 898 016	55.3	44.7	4 888	19.1
District 52	1 834	84.1	123 379	67	2 941	34.0	74.4	244 609	133 375	91.9	8.1	108	0.5
District 53	81	80.2	15 287	189	116	40.5	60.3	22 432	276 938	99.6	0.4	(D)	2.5
COLORADO	37 054	81.4	31 604 911	853	60 684	39.1	74.2	6 061 134	163 576	32.7	67.3	155 980	31.2
District 1	33	57.6	924	28	73	28.8	26.0	(D)	(D)	(D)	(D)	10	15.2
District 2	1 286	74.4	557 291	433	2 170	34.5	76.0	(D)	(D)	(D)	(D)	841	10.6
District 3	13 779	82.4	11 033 099	801	22 456	39.2	78.6	897 667	65 147	51.5	48.5	17 821	18.1
District 4	14 440	79.9	16 257 498	1 126	23 456	42.2	66.9	4 774 894	330 671	26.5	73.5	125 563	54.6
District 5	3 074	85.5	1 389 041	452	5 149	34.6	80.4	73 644	23 925	38.1	61.9	1 039	7.4
District 6	3 431	83.8	1 649 566	481	5 693	32.1	81.5	75 678	22 057	(D)	(D)	4 489	14.0
District 7	1 011	78.8	717 492	710	1 687	36.6	73.0	156 078	154 380	(D)	(D)	6 218	33.5
CONNECTICUT	4 916	80.7	405 616	83	7 913	43.1	78.2	551 553	112 195	72.8	27.2	4 122	7.2
District 1	659	78.1	42 222	64	1 048	41.3	73.6	112 272	170 367	95.0	5.0	(D)	2.3
District 2	2 393	83.3	191 099	80	3 858	42.4	83.2	259 019	108 240	58.3	41.7	2 029	7.9
District 3	438	75.1	42 178	96	741	47.4	70.0	39 440	90 046	80.3	19.7	294	6.6
District 4	232	72.4	34 087	147	380	40.5	67.6	30 931	133 323	76.6	23.4	(D)	0.9
District 5	1 194	80.5	96 030	80	1 886	44.5	76.0	109 891	92 036	80.4	19.6	1 585	9.8
DELAWARE	2 546	78.8	510 253	200	3 928	56.6	77.0	1 083 035	425 387	19.4	80.6	8 896	37.3
At Large	2 546	78.8	510 253	200	3 928	56.6	77.0	1 083 035	425 387	19.4	80.6	8 896	37.3
DISTRICT OF COLUMBIA	X	X	X	X	X	X	X	X	X	X	X	X	X
Delegate District (At Large)	X	X	X	X	X	X	X	X	X	X	X	X	X
FLORIDA	47 463	83.8	9 231 570	195	73 146	41.0	73.0	7 785 228	164 027	80.4	19.6	45 343	9.8
District 1	4 102	92.7	564 096	138	5 979	33.9	77.3	(D)	(D)	(D)	(D)	14 345	44.6
District 2	4 712	90.3	959 342	204	7 071	39.8	76.7	561 641	119 194	42.5	57.5	10 607	24.9
District 3	1 205	87.1	105 803	88	1 877	43.0	76.2	156 394	129 788	91.7	8.3	703	2.7
District 4	3 491	90.1	495 800	142	5 296	37.9	82.3	210 304	60 242	24.2	75.8	2 131	15.6
District 5	5 664	86.8	702 927	124	9 034	40.0	79.3	378 620	66 847	62.2	37.8	3 648	3.1
District 6	5 443	87.8	502 185	92	8 524	41.9	84.9	318 160	58 453	31.5	68.5	1 377	3.9
District 7	1 134	82.4	165 649	146	1 717	41.5	74.1	176 857	155 959	95.9	4.1	96	1.7
District 8	1 477	81.0	90 742	61	2 268	41.8	74.3	185 997	125 929	87.7	12.3	50	0.8
District 9	1 760	85.5	151 064	86	2 689	41.4	78.2	172 539	98 034	78.2	21.8	24	0.7
District 10	76	59.2	961	13	113	27.4	50.4	(D)	(D)	(D)	(D)	(D)	2.6
District 11	238	72.3	16 905	71	372	34.9	59.7	88 331	371 139	98.2	1.8	(D)	1.3
District 12	3 392	78.7	567 969	167	5 059	40.8	61.6	607 632	179 137	92.8	7.2	257	1.7
District 13	3 206	80.3	826 166	258	4 926	39.0	63.6	794 625	247 856	(D)	(D)	431	1.4
District 14	1 040	83.1	103 624	100	1 598	36.5	73.0	220 580	212 096	98.3	1.7	249	1.8
District 15	1 166	76.9	945 251	811	1 883	43.5	58.4	267 661	229 555	82.4	17.6	307	2.6
District 16	3 321	75.5	2 125 486	640	5 314	44.7	62.8	1 608 651	484 388	82.8	17.2	2 767	4.9
District 17	43	72.1	800	19	64	28.1	54.7	2 265	52 674	99.6	0.4		0.0
District 18	299	68.9	7 156	24	481	41.8	43.2	93 632	313 151	97.3	2.7	296	3.7
District 19	222	56.8	41 654	188	334	53.3	49.1	270 400	1 218 018	99.8	0.2	1 392	11.3
District 20	202	60.4	2 914	14	346	48.0	52.0	14 655	72 550	95.8	4.2	368	7.9
District 21	216	74.1	7 275	34	334	38.0	47.9	14 385	66 597	92.7	7.3	86	2.8
District 22	215	71.6	15 273	71	357	49.0	66.1	30 572	142 195	98.5	1.5	212	3.3
District 23	1 120	69.6	477 653	426	1 798	45.4	59.7	578 130	516 188	96.6	3.4	867	4.1
District 24	1 473	82.1	208 426	141	2 318	44.5	73.3	181 950	123 523	94.9	5.1	22	0.7
District 25	2 246	74.9	146 449	65	3 394	50.1	65.5	731 213	325 562	98.5	1.5	5 097	9.5
GEORGIA	47 846	87.2	10 150 539	212	69 060	39.8	77.1	7 112 866	148 662	30.1	69.9	224 523	30.4
District 1	5 358	87.7	1 225 397	229	7 625	40.5	76.9	705 017	131 582	47.7	52.3	30 676	40.3
District 2	7 230	83.4	3 055 668	423	10 113	42.6	70.1	1 495 868	206 897	56.8	43.2	98 562	53.9

1. Specified owner-occupied units.   2. Median monthly owner costs is often in the minimum category—10.0 percent or less, which is indicated as 10.0 percent.   3. Specified renter-occupied units.   4. Overcrowded or lacking complete plumbing facilities.

Table E. Congressional Districts 112th Congress — Land Area and Population Characteristics

STATE District	Representative, 112th Congress	Land area,[1] 2010 (sq km)	Total persons	Per square kilometer	White	Black	American Indian, Alaska Native	Asian and Pacific Islander	Some other race	Two or more races	Hispanic or Latino[2]	Non-Hispanic White alone	Percent female	Percent foreign born	Percent born in state of residence
		1	2	3	4	5	6	7	8	9	10	11	12	13	14
GEORGIA—Cont'd															
District 3	Lynn A. Westmoreland (R)	10 615	817 247	77.0	69.1	24.5	0.3	2.1	2.0	2.0	4.9	66.8	51.6	5.0	60.0
District 4	Henry C. "Hank" Johnson Jr. (D)	851	665 541	782.3	27.6	56.1	0.5	5.5	7.7	2.7	16.1	21.2	51.5	21.0	43.5
District 5	John Lewis (D)	635	630 462	993.3	40.0	50.3	0.3	3.5	3.8	2.1	8.0	36.9	50.7	10.9	49.9
District 6	Tom Price (R)	1 754	767 798	437.8	75.9	10.3	0.3	7.8	3.5	2.3	9.3	70.7	51.1	15.3	36.1
District 7	Robert Woodall (R)	2 494	903 191	362.2	60.3	22.4	0.4	8.8	5.4	2.7	13.2	53.9	51.2	18.6	40.5
District 8	Austin Scott (R)	18 471	715 599	38.7	59.4	34.9	0.3	1.3	2.4	1.7	4.9	57.5	51.5	4.1	72.0
District 9	Tom Graves (R)	11 212	823 583	73.5	86.0	3.3	0.4	1.8	6.7	1.8	13.5	80.0	50.5	9.7	51.5
District 10	Paul C. Broun (R)	15 154	738 248	48.7	73.4	19.4	0.3	2.3	2.7	2.0	6.0	70.7	51.3	5.1	63.1
District 11	Phil Gingrey (R)	6 963	794 969	114.2	75.8	15.6	0.3	2.0	4.0	2.3	8.6	72.1	51.1	8.6	57.7
District 12	John Barrow (D)	22 261	692 529	31.1	51.3	43.3	0.3	1.3	2.2	1.7	4.6	49.6	50.9	4.1	70.7
District 13	David Scott (D)	1 477	784 445	531.2	30.8	56.8	0.4	3.3	6.1	2.7	12.7	25.8	52.4	13.3	48.0
HAWAII		16 635	1 360 301	81.8	24.7	1.6	0.3	48.6	1.2	23.6	8.9	22.7	49.9	18.2	55.0
District 1	Colleen Hanabusa (D)	496	658 672	1 328.9	18.1	1.9	0.2	60.0	0.9	18.9	6.8	16.6	50.1	24.1	53.0
District 2	Mazie Hirono (D)	16 139	701 629	43.5	31.0	1.3	0.4	37.9	1.5	27.9	10.9	28.5	49.7	12.7	56.8
IDAHO		214 045	1 567 582	7.3	89.1	0.6	1.4	1.3	5.1	2.5	11.2	84.0	49.9	5.5	46.9
District 1	Raul Labrador (R)	102 208	841 930	8.2	90.1	0.5	1.3	1.4	4.1	2.6	9.9	85.3	50.0	4.6	42.8
District 2	Michael K. Simpson (R)	111 837	725 652	6.5	87.9	0.7	1.4	1.4	6.2	2.3	12.8	82.5	49.8	6.6	51.7
ILLINOIS		143 793	12 830 632	89.2	71.5	14.5	0.3	4.6	6.7	2.3	15.8	63.7	51.0	13.7	67.1
District 1	Bobby L. Rush (D)	253	587 596	2 325.0	29.6	62.6	0.2	1.8	3.9	1.8	8.8	25.8	54.0	7.0	75.5
District 2	Jesse L. Jackson Jr. (D)	479	602 758	1 258.4	21.7	69.3	0.3	0.6	6.0	2.0	13.0	16.1	53.8	6.7	72.9
District 3	Daniel Lipinski (D)	322	663 381	2 057.3	71.8	7.1	0.4	3.6	14.6	2.4	34.0	54.5	51.0	22.8	67.8
District 4	Luis V. Gutierrez (D)	102	601 156	5 918.2	51.7	5.1	0.9	2.5	36.1	3.7	73.5	18.9	48.8	34.9	50.1
District 5	Michael Quigley (D)	148	648 610	4 389.5	74.5	3.1	0.5	6.7	12.0	3.2	28.8	60.0	50.8	26.9	53.3
District 6	Peter J. Roskam (R)	544	657 131	1 207.1	76.3	3.8	0.4	10.1	7.0	2.3	18.2	66.5	50.7	23.6	62.3
District 7	Danny K. Davis (D)	146	638 105	4 378.4	36.4	51.1	0.2	6.6	3.6	2.0	9.0	32.1	52.4	10.5	63.8
District 8	Joe Walsh (R)	1 592	738 840	464.2	77.9	4.3	0.4	8.2	6.8	2.4	16.9	69.0	50.5	17.8	64.0
District 9	Janice D. Schakowsky (D)	195	628 859	3 223.3	66.6	10.3	0.3	14.4	5.2	3.1	12.7	60.2	51.1	32.8	49.5
District 10	Robert Dold (R)	644	650 425	1 009.8	77.4	5.0	0.4	8.5	6.6	2.1	15.6	69.5	50.7	21.7	58.1
District 11	Adam Kinzinger (R)	10 980	759 445	69.2	83.8	8.5	0.2	1.2	4.2	2.0	11.4	77.5	50.6	5.3	80.0
District 12	Jerry F. Costello (D)	11 379	666 459	58.6	77.9	17.6	0.3	1.1	1.1	2.0	3.0	76.4	50.8	2.0	67.7
District 13	Judy Biggert (R)	914	773 095	845.8	77.5	7.0	0.2	9.4	3.6	2.2	10.7	71.2	51.0	15.9	65.6
District 14	Randy Hultgren (R)	7 376	840 956	114.0	78.4	5.4	0.5	3.3	10.0	2.4	24.5	65.6	50.0	15.1	67.0
District 15	Timothy V. Johnson (R)	26 084	681 580	26.1	85.9	6.8	0.2	3.8	1.4	1.9	3.7	84.0	50.6	5.3	73.2
District 16	Donald A. Manzullo (R)	10 609	718 791	67.8	84.9	6.2	0.3	2.0	4.3	2.2	10.4	79.8	50.5	7.7	69.3
District 17	Bobby Schilling (R)	21 025	634 792	30.2	86.2	8.5	0.2	0.8	2.0	2.2	5.4	83.5	50.7	3.3	74.7
District 18	Aaron Schock (R)	21 207	665 723	31.4	87.9	7.5	0.2	1.5	1.1	1.8	2.8	86.5	50.9	2.9	80.4
District 19	John Shimkus (R)	29 794	672 930	22.6	93.3	3.8	0.2	0.7	0.6	1.3	1.8	92.3	50.0	1.6	76.0
INDIANA		92 789	6 483 802	69.9	84.3	9.1	0.3	1.6	2.7	2.0	6.0	81.5	50.8	4.6	68.3
District 1	Peter J. Visclosky (D)	5 726	705 600	123.2	72.7	18.9	0.3	1.2	4.8	2.2	14.0	64.8	51.4	6.3	59.1
District 2	Joe Donnelly (D)	9 526	679 254	71.3	83.3	8.8	0.4	1.1	3.9	2.5	8.0	80.0	50.6	4.8	68.8
District 3	Marlin Stutzman (R)	8 375	723 633	86.4	86.7	6.0	0.3	1.6	3.2	2.1	6.8	83.7	50.6	4.4	70.7
District 4	Todd Rokita (R)	10 394	789 835	76.0	90.4	3.2	0.3	2.5	2.0	1.7	4.6	88.2	50.3	5.0	71.0
District 5	Dan Burton (R)	8 442	809 107	95.8	89.9	4.0	0.3	2.7	1.3	1.8	3.4	88.1	51.1	4.3	68.2
District 6	Mike Pence (R)	14 351	676 548	47.1	92.4	4.0	0.2	0.8	1.1	1.5	2.5	91.2	50.7	1.7	74.4
District 7	André Carson (D)	677	676 351	999.0	56.0	32.6	0.4	1.8	6.2	3.0	10.6	52.5	51.8	9.6	67.0
District 8	Larry Bucshon (R)	18 229	694 398	38.1	92.3	4.3	0.2	0.9	0.7	1.6	1.8	91.3	50.3	1.9	74.8
District 9	Todd Young (R)	17 070	729 076	42.7	92.6	2.6	0.2	1.5	1.4	1.6	3.1	91.1	50.4	3.6	61.1
IOWA		144 669	3 046 355	21.1	91.3	2.9	0.4	1.8	1.8	1.8	5.0	88.7	50.5	4.6	71.7
District 1	Bruce L. Braley (D)	18 680	596 443	31.9	90.9	4.7	0.2	1.2	1.0	1.9	3.2	89.1	50.8	2.7	74.3
District 2	David Loebsack (D)	19 589	620 856	31.7	90.6	3.2	0.3	2.3	1.6	2.0	4.6	88.0	50.4	5.1	70.2
District 3	Leonard L. Boswell (D)	18 087	642 116	35.5	88.5	4.3	0.5	2.6	2.2	2.0	5.7	85.5	50.7	6.4	72.6
District 4	Tom Latham (R)	40 818	609 487	14.9	94.0	1.3	0.2	1.6	1.5	1.3	4.5	91.5	50.1	3.9	74.3
District 5	Steve King (R)	47 494	577 453	12.2	92.7	1.0	0.6	1.1	3.0	1.5	6.9	89.5	50.5	4.6	66.9
KANSAS		211 754	2 853 118	13.5	83.8	5.9	1.0	2.5	3.9	3.0	10.5	78.2	50.4	6.5	58.2
District 1	Tim Huelskamp (R)	148 582	655 310	4.4	88.5	2.4	0.6	1.2	5.0	2.3	14.8	79.8	49.9	7.3	65.5
District 2	Lynn Jenkins (R)	36 500	710 047	19.5	87.5	4.9	1.3	1.4	1.7	3.2	5.8	84.4	50.1	3.0	62.5
District 3	Kevin Yoder (R)	2 003	767 569	383.3	79.3	8.6	0.7	3.9	4.6	2.9	11.0	73.8	50.9	9.2	42.9
District 4	Mike Pompeo (R)	24 670	720 192	29.2	80.7	7.1	1.3	3.2	4.1	3.6	10.8	75.2	50.5	6.5	64.0

1. Dry land or land partially or temporarily covered by water.   2. May be of any race.

1198   GA(District 3)—KS(District 4)   Items 1—14

Table E. Congressional Districts 112th Congress — **Age and Education**

	Population and population characteristics, 2010 (cont.)										Education, 2010			
	Age (percent)										Enrollment[1]		Attainment[2] (percent)	
STATE District	Under 5 years	5 to 17 years	18 to 24 years	25 to 34 years	35 to 44 years	45 to 54 years	55 to 64 years	65 to 74 years	75 years and over	Median age	Total	Percent private	High school graduate or more	Bachelor's degree or more
	15	16	17	18	19	20	21	22	23	24	25	26	27	28
GEORGIA—Cont'd														
District 3	6.4	19.9	8.8	11.6	14.5	15.2	11.9	6.9	4.7	37.5	236 159	14.5	86.4	25.9
District 4	7.9	18.3	10.0	16.5	15.2	14.0	10.2	4.8	3.2	33.3	194 175	19.4	83.9	27.8
District 5	6.7	13.6	13.4	19.3	14.8	12.5	9.9	5.4	4.4	33.1	172 421	25.7	87.3	43.9
District 6	6.6	19.5	7.0	13.2	16.2	16.2	11.6	5.7	3.8	37.4	209 462	21.8	94.3	52.8
District 7	7.3	21.6	8.1	13.1	16.4	15.5	10.1	4.9	3.1	35.0	272 632	15.0	88.8	33.0
District 8	7.1	18.7	9.6	12.8	13.3	14.4	11.7	7.1	5.4	36.5	196 608	11.7	81.8	16.9
District 9	7.0	19.0	8.4	12.1	14.5	14.3	11.8	7.7	5.1	37.6	210 596	11.7	80.5	22.4
District 10	6.3	16.8	12.5	13.0	12.7	13.6	11.9	7.7	5.5	36.2	207 979	13.6	81.9	25.7
District 11	7.0	19.6	9.7	13.2	15.1	14.7	10.5	6.0	4.1	35.3	228 973	14.3	82.3	25.5
District 12	7.1	17.4	13.2	13.7	12.2	13.7	11.2	6.6	4.9	33.8	202 391	13.5	81.4	17.3
District 13	8.2	19.8	9.4	16.0	16.2	13.7	9.3	4.4	2.9	32.9	234 335	17.5	85.1	26.2
HAWAII	6.4	15.9	9.6	13.6	13.0	14.2	12.9	7.4	7.0	38.6	339 578	24.6	89.9	29.5
District 1	5.8	14.7	9.4	13.9	13.5	14.2	12.6	7.8	8.2	39.7	157 067	25.9	89.6	33.7
District 2	7.0	17.1	9.8	13.3	12.5	14.3	13.2	7.0	5.8	37.4	182 511	23.4	90.2	25.4
IDAHO	7.8	19.6	9.9	13.3	12.2	13.3	11.5	7.0	5.4	34.6	444 069	14.4	88.3	24.4
District 1	7.3	19.8	8.7	12.5	12.8	13.7	12.1	7.5	5.6	36.3	235 233	12.2	88.9	23.6
District 2	8.4	19.4	11.1	14.3	11.5	12.8	10.8	6.4	5.3	32.5	208 836	16.9	87.6	25.3
ILLINOIS	6.5	17.9	9.7	13.8	13.5	14.6	11.5	6.6	5.9	36.6	3 519 499	18.7	86.9	30.8
District 1	6.4	18.7	10.6	12.9	12.1	14.4	11.5	7.1	6.4	36.3	175 889	21.8	84.6	23.2
District 2	6.5	20.6	9.4	11.7	12.8	14.3	11.6	7.2	5.8	36.5	180 553	17.4	85.1	20.6
District 3	6.9	18.6	9.2	13.8	13.5	14.3	11.2	6.1	6.4	36.1	182 062	22.0	82.4	24.7
District 4	8.9	19.7	11.4	21.2	15.0	10.6	7.2	3.5	2.5	29.5	156 165	13.4	66.8	23.2
District 5	6.5	13.3	10.6	21.3	14.8	12.8	10.0	5.5	5.0	33.9	155 919	33.0	84.9	40.3
District 6	6.5	17.9	8.8	13.6	13.9	15.7	11.8	6.2	5.5	37.4	177 193	20.4	88.2	38.3
District 7	6.1	14.8	11.7	20.0	13.6	12.9	10.7	6.0	4.4	33.5	168 121	26.2	84.6	41.2
District 8	6.7	19.5	7.8	13.2	14.9	16.3	11.5	5.9	4.3	37.0	204 846	16.7	90.2	36.2
District 9	5.6	13.8	9.9	15.5	13.8	14.4	12.2	7.1	7.8	38.8	162 133	33.5	87.2	44.6
District 10	5.9	19.4	8.4	10.2	13.0	16.1	12.7	7.1	7.1	40.1	182 881	19.5	90.8	52.5
District 11	6.6	19.0	10.4	12.4	13.6	14.8	11.2	6.4	5.6	36.2	213 554	15.6	89.5	22.7
District 12	6.3	17.0	10.4	12.9	12.5	14.9	11.9	7.3	6.8	37.8	179 752	10.9	86.4	20.9
District 13	6.4	20.4	7.7	12.0	15.0	16.2	11.0	5.9	4.7	37.6	230 097	20.8	93.7	45.6
District 14	7.6	20.4	9.7	13.5	14.5	14.2	10.4	5.5	4.3	34.2	250 854	16.4	86.0	30.6
District 15	6.0	16.0	13.8	12.9	11.6	13.9	11.7	7.2	6.9	36.2	210 826	8.8	89.2	27.3
District 16	6.4	19.3	7.9	11.3	13.7	15.7	12.2	7.4	6.1	39.0	191 454	17.1	87.9	23.8
District 17	6.1	16.3	10.2	11.9	11.6	14.4	12.8	8.3	8.2	39.8	159 114	15.5	86.8	17.9
District 18	6.2	16.9	8.6	12.4	12.4	14.8	13.1	8.0	7.6	39.9	169 307	18.8	90.5	25.0
District 19	5.9	16.6	8.9	11.9	12.5	15.4	12.8	8.3	7.6	40.4	168 779	13.4	89.7	21.0
INDIANA	6.7	18.1	10.0	12.8	13.0	14.6	11.9	7.0	6.0	37.0	1 752 227	16.3	87.0	22.7
District 1	6.5	18.8	8.8	12.5	12.8	15.0	12.3	7.0	6.2	37.7	193 930	15.9	88.3	21.3
District 2	6.7	18.2	9.4	12.4	12.6	14.5	12.3	7.2	6.7	37.8	184 854	20.5	85.7	19.1
District 3	7.4	19.7	9.1	12.5	12.8	14.2	11.7	6.7	5.8	36.0	193 016	19.1	85.8	21.6
District 4	6.7	18.3	11.3	12.8	13.3	14.4	11.3	6.6	5.3	35.7	227 060	12.8	90.7	27.4
District 5	6.7	19.2	7.9	12.7	14.3	15.2	11.7	6.7	5.5	37.6	223 725	18.9	91.9	35.4
District 6	6.2	17.5	10.1	11.3	12.6	14.5	12.5	8.1	7.1	39.0	175 561	12.2	86.7	17.8
District 7	7.8	17.5	11.1	16.1	13.1	13.9	10.1	5.4	4.9	33.1	179 829	18.5	80.7	21.5
District 8	6.2	16.8	10.5	12.0	12.3	15.0	12.6	7.8	6.8	38.8	175 319	15.9	86.1	17.6
District 9	6.0	16.7	12.0	12.5	12.7	14.6	12.2	7.4	5.9	37.3	198 933	13.2	85.9	19.6
IOWA	6.6	17.3	10.0	12.6	12.0	14.4	12.2	7.4	7.5	38.1	810 644	16.8	90.6	24.9
District 1	6.5	17.0	10.3	12.2	11.7	14.6	12.6	7.7	7.5	38.7	159 822	19.3	90.5	24.4
District 2	6.4	16.7	11.4	13.4	12.1	14.0	12.1	7.0	6.7	36.7	174 372	13.9	90.9	29.1
District 3	7.2	17.9	8.9	14.1	13.2	14.4	11.5	6.6	6.3	36.6	167 004	20.5	91.1	27.1
District 4	6.3	16.9	11.1	11.7	11.3	14.3	12.3	7.7	8.3	38.7	167 761	12.7	91.6	25.2
District 5	6.8	17.7	8.4	11.2	11.4	14.9	12.8	8.0	8.9	40.3	141 685	18.0	88.7	18.5
KANSAS	7.2	18.3	10.1	13.2	12.2	14.2	11.6	6.7	6.5	36.0	794 404	12.8	89.2	29.8
District 1	7.1	17.9	9.5	11.9	11.0	14.4	12.0	7.7	8.5	38.4	165 474	7.6	85.9	20.0
District 2	6.8	17.5	12.0	12.7	11.6	14.0	11.8	7.1	6.6	36.0	200 318	11.5	90.8	27.6
District 3	7.4	18.6	9.6	14.9	13.6	14.3	11.1	5.6	5.0	34.7	228 930	16.4	92.1	44.0
District 4	7.5	19.1	9.4	13.2	12.1	14.4	11.5	6.5	6.3	35.7	199 682	14.5	87.4	25.7

1. All persons 3 years old and over enrolled in nursery school through college and graduate or professional school. 2. Persons 25 years old and over.

Table E. Congressional Districts 112th Congress — **Households and Group Quarters**

STATE District	Households, 2010						Group quarters, 2010					
	Number	Persons per household	Family households (percent)	Husband-wife family (percent)	Female family householder[1]	One person households (percent)	Total in group quarters	Percent 65 years and over	Persons in correctional institutions	Persons in nursing homes	Persons in college dormitories	Persons in military quarters
	29	30	31	32	33	34	35	36	37	38	39	40
GEORGIA—Cont'd												
District 3	296 852	2.71	74.3	55.2	14.5	21.4	12 123	16.8	4 777	2 305	4 659	64
District 4	243 166	2.71	64.9	37.8	20.7	27.6	8 823	18.3	3 717	1 561	980	0
District 5	271 779	2.18	46.5	26.1	16.1	41.4	35 407	5.6	6 731	2 418	21 800	78
District 6	292 798	2.61	70.1	57.1	9.5	24.1	1 526	41.5	646	954	396	0
District 7	305 575	2.93	76.9	58.2	13.8	18.5	5 243	18.6	4 919	1 452	653	0
District 8	266 306	2.60	70.2	47.3	17.9	25.3	22 405	15.9	12 280	4 375	4 361	401
District 9	297 797	2.73	74.2	58.2	11.1	21.2	14 901	21.7	3 930	2 684	3 158	44
District 10	281 833	2.53	67.4	49.7	13.3	25.5	35 672	11.5	5 814	2 870	10 100	5 213
District 11	285 749	2.73	72.4	54.1	13.3	22.0	10 837	18.3	4 254	2 781	5 491	36
District 12	254 196	2.57	66.0	41.1	19.9	26.6	29 506	10.0	18 777	4 564	11 292	742
District 13	286 249	2.71	67.2	40.0	21.3	26.7	8 033	17.3	5 780	1 770	475	0
HAWAII	455 338	2.89	68.9	50.5	12.6	23.3	42 880	12.2	5 673	5 198	7 540	12 551
District 1	227 263	2.80	66.7	49.3	12.1	25.7	20 642	13.3	3 581	2 555	4 641	5 332
District 2	228 075	2.98	71.1	51.8	13.0	21.0	22 238	11.0	2 092	2 643	2 899	7 219
IDAHO	579 408	2.66	69.6	55.3	9.6	23.8	28 951	16.9	11 275	4 820	7 223	466
District 1	310 779	2.65	71.1	56.5	9.8	22.7	15 437	16.0	7 979	2 576	4 359	0
District 2	268 629	2.66	67.8	53.9	9.4	25.1	13 514	18.2	3 296	2 244	2 864	466
ILLINOIS	4 836 972	2.59	65.8	48.2	12.9	27.8	301 773	22.6	70 828	81 516	92 960	12 483
District 1	220 656	2.61	63.2	30.9	26.4	31.7	9 441	18.0	0	3 310	5 666	0
District 2	217 427	2.74	68.1	34.6	27.1	28.0	5 230	38.4	5	3 842	362	0
District 3	233 505	2.82	69.0	49.3	13.8	26.3	5 530	54.2	0	3 843	729	0
District 4	191 160	3.13	65.4	41.2	15.8	23.2	2 419	23.2	0	804	39	0
District 5	264 037	2.43	53.6	39.2	9.8	34.5	8 372	27.7	0	3 022	3 837	0
District 6	237 057	2.74	70.9	56.7	9.8	23.9	9 121	31.5	786	3 091	3 269	0
District 7	270 387	2.26	49.9	27.1	18.6	40.9	21 895	6.1	11 613	3 055	8 238	16
District 8	267 454	2.75	72.0	57.7	10.0	22.8	4 282	56.4	537	2 719	188	0
District 9	260 200	2.33	55.2	41.9	9.5	36.3	22 241	28.0	31	9 229	8 776	0
District 10	234 117	2.69	72.3	60.0	8.9	24.0	13 802	18.5	704	4 944	1 927	12 155
District 11	275 024	2.68	70.1	53.9	11.4	24.0	16 690	20.0	3 217	5 064	11 516	0
District 12	266 220	2.43	64.8	45.3	14.6	29.1	22 693	24.3	7 837	4 848	3 332	307
District 13	274 647	2.78	73.7	61.0	9.2	21.8	9 116	30.1	3 246	3 122	3 172	0
District 14	284 463	2.89	73.6	58.5	10.4	20.6	18 182	18.3	3 469	3 577	7 196	0
District 15	273 812	2.37	62.0	48.1	10.0	29.8	42 511	14.6	6 691	4 860	17 613	0
District 16	272 353	2.61	70.4	54.5	11.2	24.5	9 558	45.5	1 376	4 083	325	0
District 17	258 978	2.35	63.1	46.0	12.5	30.9	29 362	22.5	8 308	6 586	9 551	0
District 18	268 231	2.40	65.7	50.4	11.1	28.9	27 093	24.6	9 778	6 212	4 195	5
District 19	267 244	2.43	67.8	53.6	9.8	27.0	24 235	21.3	13 230	5 305	3 029	0
INDIANA	2 502 154	2.52	66.9	49.6	12.4	26.9	186 923	20.5	48 694	41 158	75 434	228
District 1	267 147	2.60	68.8	48.0	15.3	26.2	10 628	27.7	2 086	3 169	3 782	0
District 2	260 626	2.52	66.7	48.6	12.9	27.5	29 744	17.9	7 330	3 887	7 437	0
District 3	271 378	2.62	69.3	53.2	11.3	25.4	8 973	28.8	3 163	4 459	3 611	0
District 4	297 727	2.57	69.0	54.3	10.1	24.1	27 912	19.7	4 370	5 415	12 847	0
District 5	311 360	2.55	70.0	56.2	9.7	24.7	15 523	25.7	4 434	4 760	6 133	0
District 6	262 685	2.48	67.8	51.5	11.5	26.5	21 013	20.3	7 731	5 178	8 928	178
District 7	274 120	2.41	58.0	32.5	19.5	33.2	13 015	21.6	3 147	3 806	5 233	0
District 8	271 642	2.43	66.5	50.7	11.1	27.9	32 455	16.3	11 831	5 643	12 735	50
District 9	285 469	2.46	65.8	50.2	10.7	26.7	27 660	17.4	4 602	4 841	14 728	0
IOWA	1 221 576	2.41	64.7	51.2	9.3	28.4	98 112	26.1	13 309	26 871	44 574	3
District 1	239 704	2.41	65.0	50.7	10.0	28.3	22 566	25.8	2 012	4 986	9 545	3
District 2	251 124	2.39	62.3	48.7	9.5	29.1	20 893	19.7	3 965	4 353	10 541	0
District 3	254 623	2.46	65.2	51.0	10.0	27.9	17 418	23.9	3 186	4 119	6 130	0
District 4	245 640	2.38	64.4	52.6	7.9	28.6	21 700	27.3	1 968	7 195	12 674	0
District 5	230 485	2.43	66.6	53.1	9.1	28.4	15 535	35.2	2 178	6 218	5 684	0
KANSAS	1 112 096	2.49	66.0	51.1	10.4	27.8	79 074	24.4	18 009	20 672	27 754	3 943
District 1	259 834	2.44	66.1	52.9	8.9	28.9	19 961	33.8	5 222	7 189	5 739	0
District 2	276 133	2.46	65.3	50.6	10.4	27.5	28 746	16.6	7 271	5 394	10 312	3 617
District 3	296 578	2.54	66.1	51.1	10.7	26.8	17 566	22.9	1 496	3 582	7 722	0
District 4	279 551	2.52	66.6	50.0	11.5	28.2	12 801	28.9	4 020	4 507	3 981	326

1. No spouse present.

Table E. Congressional Districts 112th Congress — **Housing and Money Income**

STATE District	Housing units, 2010										Money income, 2010		
	Total	Occupied units									Households		
			Owner-occupied					Renter-occupied					
						Median owner cost as a percent of income							
	Total	Percent occupied	Percent	Median value[1] (dollars)	Percent valued at $500,000 or more	With a mortgage	Without a mortgage[2]	Median rent[3]	Median rent as a percent of income	Sub-standard units[4] (percent)	Per capita income (dollars)	Median income (dollars)	Percent with income of $100,000 or more
	41	42	43	44	45	46	47	48	49	50	51	52	53
GEORGIA—Cont'd													
District 3	324 016	89.8	73.8	163 900	3.9	24.4	12.3	845	31.3	2.3	24 813	52 970	20.3
District 4	276 767	84.6	56.5	151 600	2.6	27.9	12.3	863	35.4	4.1	21 163	43 435	14.1
District 5	321 800	77.8	45.5	234 700	18.4	26.0	14.9	905	31.9	4.1	30 345	43 902	20.6
District 6	317 339	91	71.2	274 000	14.8	23.2	11.1	1 009	28.7	2.1	37 447	73 528	37.1
District 7	332 040	91.5	74.8	179 100	4.3	26.1	11.9	960	30.4	2.9	25 403	60 594	23.9
District 8	302 936	83.9	67.6	117 800	1.4	23.6	12.4	686	32.0	2.7	19 645	40 806	13.6
District 9	350 970	83.2	73.9	163 100	5.8	25.7	11.6	744	31.8	4.2	21 882	45 925	16.5
District 10	332 939	80.9	68.6	151 200	6.4	24.5	12.2	720	32.0	2.1	22 291	41 520	14.8
District 11	315 991	88	71.5	149 300	3.2	24.9	12.3	803	31.5	3.8	22 553	49 434	16.6
District 12	298 258	82.1	61.3	110 600	2.2	25.3	13.8	723	34.6	2.8	17 736	35 475	10.4
District 13	329 192	84.9	63.0	137 900	1.9	28.5	12.0	899	33.2	4.2	21 480	44 704	14.8
HAWAII	519 992	85.7	58.0	525 400	53.0	30.1	10.1	1 291	33.5	9.1	27 537	63 030	27.8
District 1	244 993	91.9	55.3	555 500	57.5	28.3	10.7	1 280	32.2	7.7	29 934	66 111	30.1
District 2	274 999	80.2	60.7	492 300	48.9	32.2	10.0	1 308	35.1	10.6	25 329	60 437	25.3
IDAHO	668 634	86.3	69.6	165 100	5.0	24.7	10.6	683	30.5	3.6	20 991	43 490	12.2
District 1	360 679	85.8	71.8	170 600	5.3	25.8	11.2	736	32.0	3.3	21 401	44 949	12.6
District 2	307 955	86.7	67.1	158 200	4.7	23.6	10.0	635	29.0	3.9	20 519	42 042	11.7
ILLINOIS	5 297 077	89.7	67.7	191 800	8.0	25.9	13.8	848	31.5	3.1	27 325	52 972	21.9
District 1	263 159	84.2	53.4	180 100	2.2	28.5	15.6	847	39.3	3.6	20 437	38 299	14.1
District 2	255 011	85.1	62.5	145 400	1.4	28.4	15.0	876	35.8	3.9	20 322	43 515	12.7
District 3	245 638	91	73.9	226 600	6.1	29.4	15.1	864	29.4	4.3	25 184	55 322	20.7
District 4	213 989	85.7	41.6	245 100	9.9	35.5	16.5	856	30.6	8.8	18 883	42 646	14.7
District 5	281 686	89.9	53.8	294 900	17.4	29.3	16.3	960	28.4	3.0	31 638	57 026	24.9
District 6	248 717	93.3	75.1	268 100	9.9	27.8	15.1	966	30.4	4.0	30 504	66 033	29.6
District 7	316 870	83.4	44.1	288 600	20.4	29.0	16.9	996	32.8	4.7	34 665	48 698	24.3
District 8	279 136	92.6	76.4	235 800	9.8	27.3	14.8	978	32.4	3.6	30 351	67 740	30.3
District 9	281 897	90.5	57.4	294 000	14.2	28.5	17.1	914	32.8	5.3	30 408	52 691	23.8
District 10	253 605	93	76.3	371 700	31.9	28.4	15.8	1 045	31.0	2.3	42 341	77 055	38.3
District 11	292 823	91.2	74.5	174 600	3.2	25.1	13.7	775	29.7	1.9	24 757	55 276	20.5
District 12	298 609	87.1	69.2	99 600	1.2	21.9	12.6	679	31.3	1.6	22 397	42 718	14.4
District 13	289 294	94.3	79.6	296 200	16.0	27.1	13.6	1 074	31.2	2.0	35 792	80 124	38.1
District 14	303 536	93.5	75.7	218 000	6.5	27.4	15.1	892	33.4	3.6	27 661	63 402	27.9
District 15	303 065	88.6	67.9	115 400	1.4	21.3	12.2	680	30.0	1.6	24 315	46 373	16.1
District 16	298 802	90.2	75.6	160 200	2.2	25.2	14.1	723	29.8	1.6	24 916	52 903	19.4
District 17	288 460	89.3	68.8	90 500	1.5	21.7	12.5	593	29.5	2.1	21 181	39 021	10.1
District 18	292 964	91.2	73.5	118 100	1.5	20.9	11.8	638	28.4	1.4	25 738	50 322	16.6
District 19	289 816	90.4	77.3	109 800	1.5	20.9	12.1	622	26.8	1.8	24 767	48 513	16.5
INDIANA	2 797 172	88.3	70.3	123 300	2.2	21.6	11.0	683	30.8	2.2	22 806	44 613	14.3
District 1	293 036	89	71.5	147 400	1.8	22.6	11.4	758	32.6	3.0	22 600	47 613	15.4
District 2	296 837	86.9	70.7	113 000	1.4	22.1	11.3	647	30.8	2.3	20 643	40 356	11.1
District 3	312 079	86.6	73.5	121 600	2.2	21.1	10.0	631	26.6	2.1	22 605	47 197	13.3
District 4	324 175	91.2	72.8	137 400	3.0	21.2	11.2	743	32.6	2.1	25 095	51 085	17.8
District 5	334 256	92.4	74.7	155 500	4.4	20.7	10.1	751	27.6	1.2	29 147	56 440	23.3
District 6	293 024	89.2	71.7	101 800	1.4	21.1	11.6	629	29.5	2.3	20 975	41 110	11.3
District 7	323 000	82.6	53.5	104 500	1.6	23.5	12.0	702	35.6	2.6	19 275	34 139	9.2
District 8	303 433	88.1	72.4	104 400	1.4	20.6	11.3	622	29.5	2.1	22 028	42 843	12.7
District 9	317 332	88.8	70.7	124 400	1.7	22.5	11.0	667	30.6	2.5	21 395	42 314	11.9
IOWA	1 337 563	91.5	72.4	123 400	2.1	21.3	11.5	629	28.1	1.7	24 883	47 961	15.2
District 1	258 734	92.1	72.3	127 400	2.4	21.0	11.1	612	28.9	1.8	24 708	46 704	14.4
District 2	272 502	92.1	70.8	128 600	1.9	21.5	12.2	678	29.3	1.5	25 486	48 387	15.6
District 3	276 531	92.4	71.9	140 300	2.2	22.1	12.1	688	27.7	1.7	25 882	51 542	18.1
District 4	272 171	90.8	73.4	115 200	2.0	20.9	11.5	597	27.1	1.8	25 114	47 317	15.1
District 5	257 625	89.8	73.5	102 400	2.0	20.5	10.9	559	27.0	1.9	23 061	46 031	12.4
KANSAS	1 234 037	89.3	68.1	127 300	2.5	21.8	11.8	682	28.1	2.2	24 911	48 257	16.6
District 1	296 716	87.1	71.2	88 400	0.9	20.9	11.2	573	25.7	2.6	22 443	43 367	11.6
District 2	306 074	90.1	66.1	121 100	1.9	21.9	12.3	691	28.5	2.5	23 035	45 992	14.2
District 3	321 007	90.8	66.9	188 600	5.0	22.3	12.4	801	28.5	1.8	30 373	60 507	25.0
District 4	310 240	88.9	68.3	111 000	1.9	21.7	11.6	636	29.8	2.0	23 144	45 291	14.9

1. Specified owner-occupied units. 2. Median monthly owner costs is often in the minimum category—10.0 percent or less, which is indicated as 10.0 percent. 3. Specified renter-occupied units. 4. Overcrowded or lacking complete plumbing facilities.

STATE District	Poverty, 2010 (percent)			Civilian labor force, 2010			Civilian employment,[2] 2010				Persons under age 65 with no health insurance, 2010 (percent)	Social Security beneficiaries, December 2010		Supplemental Security Income recipients, December 2010
					Unemployment			Percent						
	Persons below poverty level	Families below poverty level	Households receiving food stamps in past 12 months	Total	Total	Rate[1]	Total	Management, business, science, and arts occupations	Service, sales, and office	Construction and production		Number	Rate[3]	
	54	55	56	57	58	59	60	61	62	63	64	65	66	67
GEORGIA—Cont'd														
District 3	13.4	11.0	11.9	399 129	47 568	11.9	351 561	34.1	42.3	23.6	17.2	139 442	170.6	15 548
District 4	21.0	16.7	15.2	362 032	65 512	18.1	296 520	33.6	43.7	22.7	30.8	78 860	118.5	15 513
District 5	24.3	19.4	15.9	342 128	49 572	14.5	292 556	47.3	37.3	15.4	23.3	80 842	128.2	20 575
District 6	7.2	5.4	4.6	417 807	37 085	8.9	380 722	49.9	39.8	10.4	14.7	86 689	112.9	4 960
District 7	11.9	9.2	9.4	480 379	56 765	11.8	423 614	37.6	43.3	19.1	22.3	100 397	111.2	11 086
District 8	19.2	15.8	16.3	315 650	39 086	12.4	276 564	32.4	41.1	26.5	19.9	131 691	184.0	23 987
District 9	15.9	11.4	11.5	397 226	46 168	11.6	351 058	31.2	41.1	27.7	21.2	141 347	171.6	13 794
District 10	20.9	14.0	12.9	333 749	33 772	10.1	299 977	34.2	41.6	24.2	20.8	135 834	184.0	17 161
District 11	14.3	11.7	10.7	395 202	48 956	12.4	346 246	35.4	41.0	23.6	19.4	123 320	155.1	15 442
District 12	26.1	18.5	16.3	305 932	34 787	11.4	271 145	28.9	44.2	27.0	23.2	121 714	175.8	25 869
District 13	17.6	13.8	14.9	425 731	67 123	15.8	358 608	33.0	44.5	22.4	25.1	86 984	110.9	16 252
HAWAII	10.7	7.4	9.1	694 445	56 254	8.1	638 191	33.0	48.7	18.3	9.0	227 914	167.5	24 945
District 1	7.7	4.3	6.3	343 174	16 923	4.9	326 251	35.5	48.1	16.5	7.7	115 383	175.2	12 067
District 2	13.5	10.3	12.0	351 271	39 331	11.2	311 940	30.4	49.5	20.1	10.1	112 531	160.4	12 878
IDAHO	15.7	11.6	12.5	757 590	75 683	10.0	681 907	33.6	42.3	24.1	20.2	269 293	171.8	27 294
District 1	14.9	10.8	12.2	397 666	44 259	11.1	353 407	33.8	43.0	23.3	19.9	155 432	184.6	15 044
District 2	16.6	12.5	12.8	359 924	31 424	8.7	328 500	33.4	41.6	25.0	20.6	113 861	156.9	12 250
ILLINOIS	13.8	10.1	11.0	6 674 563	763 068	11.4	5 911 495	36.1	42.8	21.1	15.5	2 033 345	158.5	273 310
District 1	24.8	19.8	21.3	285 571	59 796	20.9	225 775	33.0	48.4	18.5	19.4	99 906	170.0	31 166
District 2	20.8	16.8	20.3	288 378	52 879	18.3	235 499	31.3	47.8	21.0	21.3	104 879	174.0	25 906
District 3	11.8	9.1	9.3	339 142	41 432	12.2	297 710	28.7	45.7	25.6	18.8	99 936	150.6	10 691
District 4	23.2	20.6	17.7	309 665	42 971	13.9	266 694	26.8	42.9	30.3	31.1	49 953	83.1	18 257
District 5	13.1	9.0	7.6	386 358	41 904	10.8	344 454	39.8	41.5	18.6	19.5	80 932	124.8	12 876
District 6	8.5	5.9	6.0	368 051	37 881	10.3	330 170	37.6	43.4	18.9	13.8	90 642	137.9	6 161
District 7	24.1	19.1	19.5	323 116	46 246	14.3	276 870	47.4	41.0	11.6	17.5	85 088	133.3	32 056
District 8	8.1	6.0	6.4	412 179	48 737	11.8	363 442	37.8	42.1	20.1	13.6	97 113	131.4	6 535
District 9	13.3	8.5	8.9	342 129	33 192	9.7	308 937	44.8	41.5	13.7	19.9	98 452	156.6	19 101
District 10	7.2	5.4	5.7	335 792	30 155	9.0	305 637	47.2	38.1	14.7	11.5	103 515	159.1	7 047
District 11	11.6	8.2	10.1	387 219	46 466	12.0	340 753	30.6	45.0	24.3	12.9	123 383	162.5	9 808
District 12	16.9	13.2	15.5	322 235	30 982	9.6	291 253	30.9	45.8	23.3	13.6	127 725	191.6	19 752
District 13	5.6	3.9	4.3	424 831	38 459	9.1	386 372	43.7	40.4	16.0	10.0	101 468	131.2	5 690
District 14	10.4	7.2	8.1	445 609	46 214	10.4	399 395	35.0	42.4	22.7	13.2	106 383	126.5	7 062
District 15	15.5	9.1	9.6	350 735	30 735	8.8	320 000	36.5	41.5	21.9	12.6	120 691	177.1	11 240
District 16	13.3	9.6	10.1	379 284	46 208	12.2	333 076	33.3	41.8	25.0	12.6	130 746	181.9	10 592
District 17	16.5	12.3	13.8	306 680	30 140	9.8	276 540	28.1	45.1	26.8	14.4	135 786	213.9	15 337
District 18	11.9	8.9	10.0	333 314	29 760	8.9	303 554	35.4	41.4	23.2	11.4	134 805	202.5	11 781
District 19	12.3	8.4	9.3	334 275	28 911	8.6	305 364	32.6	41.9	25.5	11.6	141 942	210.9	12 252
INDIANA	15.3	11.0	11.6	3 250 476	351 715	10.8	2 898 761	32.3	41.5	26.1	16.9	1 191 768	183.8	118 065
District 1	15.3	10.5	13.3	340 507	39 906	11.7	300 601	31.0	41.0	28.0	15.8	130 112	184.4	14 976
District 2	16.8	13.4	14.6	331 679	44 402	13.4	287 277	30.0	41.7	28.4	16.9	131 167	193.1	13 544
District 3	13.5	9.6	10.2	366 396	39 321	10.7	327 075	30.5	39.5	30.1	20.1	126 411	174.7	10 709
District 4	12.6	8.2	8.4	403 678	35 898	8.9	367 780	35.9	40.4	23.7	14.6	125 560	159.0	8 030
District 5	9.5	7.0	6.3	426 709	34 593	8.1	392 116	41.9	39.6	18.5	13.3	125 688	155.3	8 146
District 6	17.5	11.9	12.8	326 844	37 422	11.4	289 422	30.5	41.5	28.0	18.2	147 487	218.0	13 287
District 7	24.6	20.3	17.6	350 535	53 882	15.4	296 653	29.2	49.0	21.9	22.1	120 467	178.1	21 756
District 8	14.1	10.0	11.5	337 231	28 240	8.4	308 991	28.3	41.7	30.0	16.4	142 596	205.4	14 429
District 9	15.5	10.7	11.0	366 897	38 051	10.4	328 846	30.4	40.5	29.0	15.6	142 280	195.2	13 188
IOWA	12.6	8.2	10.8	1 651 501	111 463	6.7	1 540 038	33.5	40.7	25.8	10.8	584 113	191.7	47 687
District 1	13.7	9.5	11.1	316 137	22 820	7.2	293 317	31.6	40.6	27.8	9.8	118 511	198.7	11 442
District 2	13.2	7.9	11.6	338 221	23 903	7.1	314 318	35.5	40.3	24.2	10.7	111 804	180.1	10 249
District 3	11.3	7.8	11.5	358 049	24 447	6.8	333 602	34.7	43.3	22.0	10.8	109 875	171.1	9 619
District 4	12.3	7.2	9.4	328 678	21 083	6.4	307 595	35.9	38.9	25.3	10.2	121 332	199.1	7 068
District 5	12.4	8.8	10.4	310 416	19 210	6.2	291 206	29.5	40.6	30.0	12.7	122 591	212.3	9 309
KANSAS	13.6	9.5	8.7	1 491 225	118 195	7.9	1 373 030	35.6	41.9	22.4	15.9	488 765	171.3	45 793
District 1	13.9	9.8	8.2	336 199	19 915	5.9	316 284	31.2	38.8	30.0	16.8	129 545	197.7	9 573
District 2	14.9	10.6	9.3	357 857	29 468	8.2	328 389	35.4	43.3	21.3	14.4	128 491	181.0	13 117
District 3	11.3	7.2	6.1	424 957	30 952	7.3	394 005	42.4	42.1	15.5	15.1	105 517	137.5	9 078
District 4	14.4	10.4	11.5	372 212	37 860	10.2	334 352	32.0	43.3	24.7	17.4	125 212	173.9	14 025

1. Percent of civilian labor force. 2. Persons 16 years old and over. 3. Per 1,000 resident population enumerated in the 2010 census.

Table E. Congressional Districts 112th Congress — Agriculture

	Farms		Land in farms		Farm Operators			Value of products sold				Government payments	
						Percent of farm operators				Percent of sales from			
STATE District	Number	Operated by family or individual (percent)	Acreage	Average size of farm (acres)	Total	Whose primary occupation is farming	Who live on the farm operated	Total ($1,000)	Average per farm	Crops	Livestock	Total ($1,000)	Percent of farms
	68	69	70	71	72	73	74	75	76	77	78	79	80
GEORGIA—Cont'd													
District 3	4 260	88.6	544 276	128	6 377	36.8	81.7	257 940	60 549	11.6	88.4	1 533	10.9
District 4	109	90.8	4 625	42	194	35.6	77.3	805	7 385	86.8	13.3	(D)	5.5
District 5	18	83.3	4 914	273	23	30.4	56.5	75	4 167	14.7	85.3	(D)	11.1
District 6	532	82.9	27 421	52	809	46.6	86.2	41 752	78 481	11.2	88.8	58	7.0
District 7	1 259	86.2	105 263	84	1 867	38.1	78.6	103 229	81 993	25.5	74.5	325	14.0
District 8	5 953	85.6	1 624 260	273	8 431	42.3	73.4	716 808	120 411	60.1	39.9	51 883	46.9
District 9	5 443	89.2	489 581	90	8 071	38.5	82.7	1 090 839	200 411	2.3	97.7	1 404	10.1
District 10	8 128	88.8	988 371	122	12 089	40.4	81.1	1 717 655	211 326	5.1	94.9	4 314	16.7
District 11	3 112	90.2	366 663	118	4 594	37.9	81.3	397 701	127 796	6.6	93.4	2 447	14.6
District 12	6 158	86.9	1 701 104	276	8 422	36.6	71.0	581 332	94 403	55.2	44.8	33 282	42.9
District 13	286	82.9	12 996	45	445	42.9	79.3	3 844	13 441	78.3	21.7	23	4.5
HAWAII	7 521	84.6	1 121 329	149	11 412	48.2	68.6	513 626	68 292	83.7	16.3	2 378	2.9
District 1	264	82.2	9 508	36	373	62.5	40.8	24 024	91 000	76.8	23.2	247	2.7
District 2	7 257	84.7	1 111 821	153	11 039	47.7	69.6	489 603	67 466	84.0	16.0	2 131	2.9
IDAHO	25 349	84.1	11 497 383	454	40 427	41.5	79.9	5 688 765	224 418	40.9	59.1	99 494	36.3
District 1	11 826	86.9	4 054 031	343	18 866	39.5	83.8	1 289 138	109 009	45.7	54.3	32 048	29.8
District 2	13 523	81.6	7 443 352	550	21 561	43.3	76.6	4 399 628	325 344	39.5	60.5	67 446	42.1
ILLINOIS	76 860	85.5	26 775 100	348	111 089	46.1	68.4	13 329 107	173 421	81.6	18.4	487 293	73.9
District 1	X	X	X	X	X	X	X	X	X	X	X	X	X
District 2	118	57.6	6 894	58	229	41.0	41.5	13 149	111 432	97.1	2.9	90	18.6
District 3	25	36.0	184	7	56	76.8	26.0	1 111	44 440	97.3	2.7	X	0.0
District 4	X	X	X	X	X	X	X	X	X	X	X	X	X
District 5	2	100.0	(D)	(D)	2	(D)	(D)	(D)	(D)	(D)	(D)	(D)	(D)
District 6	35	45.7	1 592	46	62	48.4	50.0	3 965	113 286	99.4	0.6	(D)	20.0
District 7	2	50.0	(D)	(D)	4	50.0	75.0	(D)	(D)	(D)	(D)	(D)	(D)
District 8	713	78.0	89 397	125	1 149	48.9	74.1	62 984	88 337	78.2	21.8	1 578	21.6
District 9	7	28.6	(D)	(D)	47	10.6	14.9	(D)	(D)	(D)	(D)	(D)	14.3
District 10	65	60.0	7 285	112	91	39.6	47.3	9 394	144 523	(D)	(D)	96	10.8
District 11	5 521	85.4	2 212 326	401	8 013	49.6	68.2	1 248 694	226 172	91.7	8.3	39 377	75.7
District 12	6 225	86.1	1 737 799	279	8 823	41.0	71.8	508 210	81 640	84.8	15.2	26 938	66.6
District 13	100	74.0	16 249	162	162	38.9	48.1	16 840	168 400	99.0	1.0	245	32.0
District 14	3 952	83.2	1 443 419	365	5 885	50.3	70.2	975 957	246 953	81.6	18.4	31 104	68.4
District 15	12 708	86.3	5 427 672	427	18 118	50.5	64.7	2 841 227	223 578	88.5	11.5	100 370	80.3
District 16	7 283	86.2	2 089 985	287	10 917	46.8	75.7	1 430 225	196 379	63.0	37.0	48 346	67.1
District 17	10 528	84.7	3 840 010	365	15 364	47.7	67.2	1 871 728	177 786	79.0	21.0	67 895	75.0
District 18	10 600	84.6	4 040 489	381	15 227	46.8	64.0	1 994 100	188 123	85.2	14.8	72 008	76.9
District 19	18 976	86.9	5 861 607	309	26 940	41.0	70.1	2 351 113	123 899	77.3	22.7	99 200	76.0
INDIANA	60 938	86.2	14 773 184	242	91 590	39.7	77.1	8 271 291	135 733	64.3	35.7	260 809	58.9
District 1	2 411	82.6	1 026 137	426	3 626	46.1	68.0	732 729	303 911	62.0	38.0	19 226	71.5
District 2	6 122	85.7	1 703 052	278	8 995	42.6	75.6	995 533	162 616	68.7	31.3	33 802	67.6
District 3	9 482	88.3	1 310 689	138	14 370	32.8	80.5	922 069	97 244	44.6	55.4	25 442	52.2
District 4	6 155	85.3	1 855 650	301	9 359	41.9	76.3	996 627	161 922	76.3	23.7	32 180	55.2
District 5	5 813	84.1	1 580 829	272	8 804	41.0	76.9	930 577	160 085	72.1	27.9	28 551	65.2
District 6	10 771	85.8	2 580 726	240	16 100	41.9	78.0	1 427 873	132 566	63.1	36.9	49 626	63.7
District 7	177	85.3	10 747	61	279	36.6	65.2	8 864	50 079	96.0	4.0	150	19.2
District 8	9 217	85.5	2 785 128	302	14 000	42.5	74.8	1 344 760	145 900	76.4	23.6	44 428	59.5
District 9	10 790	88.4	1 920 226	178	16 057	36.1	78.5	912 259	84 547	44.1	55.9	27 404	50.8
IOWA	92 856	83.4	30 747 550	331	136 068	48.5	68.5	20 418 096	219 890	50.7	49.3	706 286	80.7
District 1	14 837	85.2	3 996 927	269	22 139	48.8	72.8	2 681 638	180 740	48.7	51.3	106 885	81.7
District 2	13 727	84.1	3 664 861	267	20 129	43.0	70.7	1 701 763	123 972	58.4	41.6	89 832	77.5
District 3	11 751	83.3	3 714 923	316	17 203	45.6	68.8	1 991 751	169 496	62.9	37.1	87 529	80.2
District 4	25 891	82.8	9 144 470	353	37 710	50.4	67.0	6 434 725	248 531	54.8	45.2	217 684	82.5
District 5	26 650	82.7	10 226 369	384	38 887	50.8	66.3	7 608 220	285 487	42.9	57.1	204 355	80.3
KANSAS	65 531	85.0	46 345 827	707	97 150	43.2	66.0	14 413 182	219 944	33.9	66.1	427 144	67.8
District 1	34 214	81.8	33 354 280	975	49 922	47.3	57.4	12 054 130	352 316	31.3	68.7	326 837	80.7
District 2	20 950	89.0	7 489 422	357	31 526	38.3	75.7	1 437 825	68 631	53.8	46.2	59 118	53.5
District 3	1 091	86.1	188 469	173	1 670	31.7	70.2	60 581	55 528	73.4	26.6	1 432	25.0
District 4	9 276	87.8	5 313 656	573	14 032	41.4	74.3	860 646	92 782	34.2	65.8	39 756	57.8

1. Specified owner-occupied units. 2. Median monthly owner costs is often in the minimum category—10.0 percent or less, which is indicated as 10.0 percent. 3. Specified renter-occupied units. 4. Overcrowded or lacking complete plumbing facilities.

Table E. Congressional Districts 112th Congress — **Land Area and Population Characteristics**

STATE District	Representative, 112th Congress	Land area,[1] 2010 (sq km)	Total persons	Per square kilometer	White	Black	American Indian, Alaska Native	Asian and Pacific Islander	Some other race	Two or more races	Hispanic or Latino[2]	Non-Hispanic White alone	Percent female	Percent foreign born	Percent born in state of residence
		1	2	3	4	5	6	7	8	9	10	11	12	13	14
KENTUCKY		102 269	4 339 367	42.4	87.8	7.8	0.2	1.2	1.3	1.7	3.1	86.3	50.8	3.2	70.3
District 1	Ed Whitfield (R)	30 034	686 989	22.9	89.6	6.9	0.3	0.6	1.0	1.7	2.6	88.3	50.8	1.6	68.3
District 2	Brett Guthrie (R)	19 431	760 032	39.1	89.6	5.8	0.3	1.1	1.3	2.0	3.3	87.9	50.7	3.0	72.3
District 3	John A. Yarmuth (D)	938	721 626	769.2	72.4	21.1	0.2	2.3	1.7	2.2	4.3	70.3	51.8	6.5	69.1
District 4	Geoff Davis (R)	14 654	741 464	50.6	93.6	2.7	0.2	1.0	1.0	1.5	2.4	92.4	50.2	2.3	63.9
District 5	Harold Rogers (R)	27 547	670 051	24.3	96.9	1.3	0.2	0.3	0.3	0.9	1.1	96.3	50.3	0.6	79.8
District 6	Ben Chandler (D)	9 664	759 205	78.6	85.3	8.5	0.2	1.7	2.2	2.0	4.5	83.4	51.1	5.2	69.0
LOUISIANA		111 898	4 533 372	40.5	62.6	32.0	0.7	1.5	1.5	1.6	4.2	60.3	51.0	3.8	78.8
District 1	Steve Scalise (R)	6 197	686 961	110.8	77.6	15.9	0.4	1.9	2.4	1.8	7.6	73.0	51.2	6.5	73.5
District 2	Cedric Richmond (D)	656	493 352	752.2	32.5	58.8	0.4	3.5	2.8	1.9	7.3	29.1	51.8	7.2	76.2
District 3	Jeff Landry (R)	17 441	637 371	36.5	66.0	27.4	1.9	1.2	1.7	1.8	4.1	64.1	50.7	3.1	86.9
District 4	John Fleming (R)	27 842	667 109	24.0	61.1	33.9	0.9	1.1	1.1	1.9	3.4	59.4	50.9	2.5	72.3
District 5	Rodney Alexander (R)	35 678	644 296	18.1	62.0	34.8	0.5	0.7	0.7	1.2	1.9	61.1	50.8	1.8	80.0
District 6	Bill Cassidy (R)	7 962	727 498	91.4	60.2	35.0	0.3	1.9	1.3	1.2	3.4	58.4	50.8	3.6	78.0
District 7	Charles W. Boustany Jr. (R)	16 122	676 785	42.0	70.4	25.5	0.4	1.1	1.0	1.6	2.8	69.0	51.3	2.7	84.5
MAINE		79 883	1 328 361	16.6	95.2	1.2	0.6	1.0	0.3	1.6	1.3	94.4	51.1	3.4	64.0
District 1	Chellie Pingree (D)	9 153	668 515	73.0	95.0	1.3	0.3	1.4	0.4	1.6	1.4	94.1	51.3	4.0	58.6
District 2	Michael H. Michaud (D)	70 730	659 846	9.3	95.5	1.0	1.0	0.7	0.3	1.5	1.1	94.7	50.8	2.8	69.5
MARYLAND		25 142	5 773 552	229.6	58.2	29.4	0.4	5.6	3.6	2.9	8.2	54.7	51.6	13.9	47.6
District 1	Andrew Harris (R)	9 360	744 275	79.5	82.9	11.6	0.2	2.1	1.2	1.9	3.5	81.0	51.2	4.9	59.8
District 2	C. A. Dutch Ruppersberger (D)	917	700 893	764.6	57.4	33.6	0.4	3.8	1.9	2.9	5.0	55.2	52.5	9.6	65.5
District 3	John P. Sarbanes (D)	757	719 856	950.7	68.3	20.3	0.3	5.4	2.9	2.8	6.8	65.2	51.5	12.1	52.6
District 4	Donna F. Edwards (D)	815	714 316	876.7	25.6	56.6	0.4	7.0	7.1	3.3	14.2	20.6	52.5	22.1	24.7
District 5	Steny H. Hoyer (D)	3 862	767 369	198.7	51.0	37.3	0.4	4.3	3.7	3.2	7.9	48.0	51.2	11.5	36.8
District 6	Roscoe G. Bartlett (R)	7 910	738 943	93.4	87.4	6.6	0.2	2.2	1.5	2.1	4.2	85.0	50.2	5.5	61.2
District 7	Elijah E. Cummings (D)	758	659 776	870.4	33.1	56.2	0.3	6.7	1.2	2.4	3.5	31.6	52.5	10.4	61.1
District 8	Chris Van Hollen (D)	761	728 124	956.9	56.3	16.9	0.5	13.4	9.0	4.0	20.0	47.5	51.8	35.2	20.9
MASSACHUSETTS		20 202	6 547 629	324.1	80.4	6.6	0.3	5.3	4.7	2.6	9.6	76.1	51.6	15.0	63.1
District 1	John W. Olver (D)	8 004	644 956	80.6	89.4	2.5	0.3	2.1	3.4	2.3	8.6	85.2	51.2	7.1	69.5
District 2	Richard E. Neal (D)	2 383	661 045	277.4	83.0	6.5	0.3	2.1	5.7	2.4	13.2	77.1	52.0	8.5	66.6
District 3	James P. McGovern (D)	1 499	664 919	443.4	83.8	4.6	0.2	5.2	3.8	2.4	8.9	79.3	51.2	13.4	62.7
District 4	Barney Frank (D)	1 884	656 083	348.3	86.4	3.2	0.3	4.6	2.8	2.6	5.2	83.7	52.0	13.6	65.6
District 5	Niki Tsongas (D)	1 456	662 269	454.9	78.3	3.5	0.3	7.6	7.6	2.7	15.6	72.3	50.8	16.4	62.3
District 6	John F. Tierney (D)	1 223	650 161	531.6	87.5	3.1	0.2	3.5	3.6	2.0	7.7	84.5	51.9	12.0	71.0
District 7	Edward J. Markey (D)	438	648 162	1 479.5	77.6	5.7	0.2	8.7	4.8	2.8	8.8	73.1	51.9	24.0	57.3
District 8	Michael E. Capuano (D)	105	660 414	6 264.1	54.5	21.6	0.4	9.9	9.3	4.3	18.8	46.9	51.6	29.5	39.1
District 9	Stephen F. Lynch (D)	805	650 381	808.0	74.2	13.4	0.2	5.1	4.1	2.9	6.6	71.3	51.9	15.7	67.1
District 10	William Keating (D)	2 405	649 239	270.0	89.7	2.2	0.4	4.5	1.4	1.8	2.2	88.3	51.9	9.6	69.6
MICHIGAN		146 435	9 883 640	67.5	78.9	14.2	0.6	2.4	1.5	2.3	4.4	76.6	50.9	6.0	76.6
District 1	Dan Benishek (R)	64 304	650 222	10.1	93.3	1.2	2.8	0.5	0.2	1.9	1.2	92.5	49.3	1.8	81.2
District 2	Bill Huizenga (R)	13 702	698 831	51.0	88.7	4.7	0.7	1.3	2.5	2.2	6.6	85.3	50.5	4.1	80.3
District 3	Justin Amash (R)	4 768	694 695	145.7	82.0	8.8	0.5	2.1	3.9	2.7	8.6	78.4	50.5	5.7	78.5
District 4	Dave Camp (R)	19 227	686 378	35.7	92.9	2.7	1.0	0.9	0.7	1.7	3.1	91.0	50.2	1.9	84.7
District 5	Dale E. Kildee (D)	4 500	635 129	141.1	76.1	18.8	0.5	0.8	1.2	2.6	4.3	73.7	51.7	2.0	83.5
District 6	Fred Upton (R)	8 593	671 883	78.2	84.1	8.9	0.6	1.3	2.3	2.7	5.2	81.9	50.8	3.9	68.7
District 7	Tim Walberg (R)	11 088	676 899	61.0	88.8	5.9	0.4	1.2	1.2	2.4	4.2	86.3	50.1	3.4	77.9
District 8	Mike Rogers (R)	5 784	707 572	122.3	87.7	5.3	0.5	2.7	1.3	2.5	4.6	85.1	50.7	5.3	77.3
District 9	Gary C. Peters (D)	802	657 590	820.1	77.0	11.6	0.3	7.6	1.2	2.3	4.1	74.6	51.5	13.4	68.6
District 10	Candice S. Miller (R)	9 148	719 712	78.7	92.5	2.9	0.3	1.8	0.8	1.7	2.8	90.7	50.5	7.7	82.0
District 11	Thaddeus G. McCotter (R)	1 030	695 888	675.3	82.4	9.3	0.3	5.2	0.7	2.0	3.0	80.4	51.4	8.3	74.8
District 12	Sander M. Levin (D)	415	636 601	1 534.8	72.7	21.2	0.3	2.8	0.5	2.5	2.0	71.5	52.3	9.4	76.2
District 13	Hansen Clarke (D)	280	519 570	1 853.1	32.3	59.0	0.5	1.2	4.5	2.6	10.5	27.6	51.7	6.3	74.4
District 14	John Conyers Jr. (D)	316	550 465	1 742.6	35.5	59.2	0.3	1.8	0.8	2.3	2.7	34.1	52.7	8.5	72.0
District 15	John D. Dingell (D)	2 478	682 205	275.3	77.3	13.8	0.4	4.5	1.1	2.9	4.1	74.8	51.0	7.9	66.8
MINNESOTA		206 232	5 303 925	25.7	85.3	5.2	1.1	4.0	1.9	2.4	4.7	83.1	50.4	7.1	68.8
District 1	Timothy J. Walz (D)	34 462	644 787	18.7	91.8	2.2	0.3	2.2	2.0	1.5	5.2	89.0	50.5	4.9	69.7
District 2	John Kline (R)	7 827	732 515	93.6	87.9	3.3	0.5	4.1	1.9	2.3	4.8	85.5	50.3	7.0	68.5
District 3	Erik Paulsen (R)	1 204	650 185	540.2	80.7	7.8	0.4	6.8	1.8	2.6	4.0	78.8	51.4	11.2	61.7
District 4	Betty McCollum (D)	511	614 624	1 203.7	72.5	9.9	0.8	10.3	3.1	3.4	7.6	69.1	51.5	12.4	63.6
District 5	Keith Ellison (D)	320	616 482	1 925.2	68.7	15.4	1.5	5.3	4.9	4.1	9.5	65.3	50.4	14.1	57.2
District 6	Michele Bachmann (R)	7 952	759 478	95.5	91.7	2.4	0.4	2.9	0.8	1.8	2.4	90.3	49.6	4.1	76.7
District 7	Collin C. Peterson (D)	82 410	625 512	7.6	92.7	0.8	2.8	0.9	1.2	1.6	3.8	90.5	50.0	2.8	73.0
District 8	Chip Cravaack (R)	71 547	660 342	9.2	93.6	0.9	2.7	0.6	0.3	1.9	1.3	92.9	49.4	1.5	78.2

1. Dry land or land partially or temporarily covered by water.   2. May be of any race.

Table E. Congressional Districts 112th Congress — Age and Education

STATE District	Population and population characteristics, 2010 (cont.)										Education, 2010			
	Age (percent)										Enrollment[1]		Attainment[2] (percent)	
	Under 5 years	5 to 17 years	18 to 24 years	25 to 34 years	35 to 44 years	45 to 54 years	55 to 64 years	65 to 74 years	75 years and over	Median age	Total	Percent private	High school graduate or more	Bachelor's degree or more
	15	16	17	18	19	20	21	22	23	24	25	26	27	28
KENTUCKY	6.5	17.1	9.5	13.0	13.3	14.8	12.4	7.5	5.8	38.1	1 093 037	14.5	81.9	20.5
District 1	6.6	16.8	9.3	12.1	12.4	14.3	12.9	8.8	6.9	39.4	159 450	9.0	81.2	13.6
District 2	6.7	17.9	9.7	12.8	13.2	14.9	12.0	7.3	5.4	37.3	200 865	12.4	83.6	16.6
District 3	6.5	16.6	9.1	14.0	12.9	15.0	12.4	6.9	6.6	38.0	180 658	26.1	87.5	30.8
District 4	6.7	18.4	8.2	12.8	14.0	15.4	12.2	7.1	5.3	38.1	190 245	16.0	84.1	22.4
District 5	6.0	16.6	9.0	12.4	13.6	15.0	13.4	8.4	5.7	39.6	153 339	7.9	69.6	11.5
District 6	6.5	16.2	11.6	14.1	13.6	14.3	11.8	6.7	5.3	36.2	208 480	13.9	84.7	27.3
LOUISIANA	6.9	17.7	10.5	13.9	12.5	14.4	11.8	6.9	5.4	35.8	1 179 298	19.4	81.9	21.4
District 1	6.4	16.8	8.9	13.4	12.7	15.1	13.1	7.4	6.3	38.8	171 271	29.9	86.4	29.6
District 2	6.8	16.4	12.0	15.3	12.4	14.5	11.9	6.2	4.5	34.6	131 595	31.0	79.6	22.9
District 3	7.2	18.8	9.6	13.2	12.9	15.2	11.4	6.7	4.9	36.0	161 546	17.7	76.7	14.1
District 4	7.1	17.7	10.1	13.8	12.2	13.8	11.8	7.4	6.0	36.1	169 289	11.1	83.2	18.1
District 5	6.9	18.0	10.6	13.1	12.0	13.9	11.9	7.5	6.1	36.2	166 152	12.4	79.3	16.4
District 6	6.8	17.7	11.9	14.8	12.8	14.0	11.4	6.1	4.5	34.0	201 666	19.5	86.2	27.8
District 7	7.3	18.5	10.5	13.7	12.2	14.5	11.3	6.7	5.5	35.2	177 779	16.3	80.5	19.8
MAINE	5.2	15.4	8.7	10.9	12.9	16.5	14.5	8.5	7.4	42.7	311 096	15.7	90.3	26.8
District 1	5.2	15.7	8.0	11.1	13.4	16.7	14.4	8.2	7.3	42.7	154 937	16.7	92.1	31.9
District 2	5.3	15.2	9.5	10.6	12.4	16.2	14.5	8.7	7.6	42.8	156 159	14.6	88.5	21.6
MARYLAND	6.3	17.1	9.7	13.2	13.8	15.6	12.1	6.7	5.6	38.0	1 579 378	20.3	88.1	36.1
District 1	5.6	17.2	8.9	10.2	12.8	16.3	13.6	8.5	6.8	41.6	197 029	20.2	89.5	32.0
District 2	6.9	16.8	10.2	14.5	13.2	14.9	11.4	6.2	5.9	36.3	188 136	16.6	85.8	23.7
District 3	6.4	14.8	10.4	16.2	13.8	14.2	11.7	6.5	6.0	36.6	189 013	26.4	88.6	43.2
District 4	7.0	18.2	9.3	14.3	14.6	15.3	11.7	5.8	3.8	35.9	203 199	18.4	88.6	36.1
District 5	6.3	18.0	11.0	12.2	14.4	16.4	11.6	6.1	4.1	37.1	229 583	17.4	89.8	32.0
District 6	5.7	18.0	8.6	10.9	14.1	16.8	12.6	7.2	6.2	40.3	193 594	18.5	89.4	31.0
District 7	6.1	17.1	11.3	13.3	12.8	15.7	11.8	6.5	5.5	37.0	188 921	19.3	83.8	34.2
District 8	6.6	16.7	7.6	14.4	14.5	15.2	12.0	6.6	6.3	38.3	189 903	26.0	88.2	55.1
MASSACHUSETTS	5.6	16.1	10.4	12.9	13.5	15.5	12.3	7.0	6.8	39.1	1 758 536	28.2	89.1	39.0
District 1	5.2	15.9	12.0	10.6	12.4	16.0	13.6	7.2	7.1	40.5	173 389	16.8	88.6	28.5
District 2	5.7	17.6	9.6	11.3	13.6	15.9	12.5	6.8	6.8	39.5	183 360	21.8	86.5	29.1
District 3	6.1	17.7	9.4	11.9	14.4	16.2	11.7	6.3	6.4	38.8	178 478	27.4	88.0	37.0
District 4	5.5	16.9	10.0	11.3	13.6	15.7	12.8	7.3	7.0	40.0	182 310	29.6	80.6	41.2
District 5	6.2	18.8	8.6	11.5	14.1	16.8	11.9	6.4	5.0	38.9	178 294	17.9	87.8	39.2
District 6	5.5	16.9	8.0	10.6	13.5	16.9	13.5	7.5	7.6	42.0	166 086	23.1	92.5	41.0
District 7	6.0	14.6	8.7	14.7	14.5	15.1	11.9	7.0	7.6	39.3	155 467	30.1	90.2	44.8
District 8	5.1	10.4	21.1	23.2	12.4	10.3	8.3	4.9	4.2	29.8	223 761	55.8	85.0	47.6
District 9	5.8	16.5	9.1	13.2	13.9	15.4	12.1	6.9	7.1	39.2	172 998	27.6	91.1	41.1
District 10	5.1	15.4	6.9	10.5	13.0	16.4	14.6	9.3	8.9	44.4	145 393	24.1	94.1	40.4
MICHIGAN	6.0	17.7	9.9	11.8	12.9	15.3	12.7	7.3	6.4	38.9	2 711 955	13.1	88.7	25.2
District 1	4.9	15.1	8.5	9.8	11.2	15.7	15.2	10.6	8.8	45.3	142 691	9.5	89.1	19.6
District 2	6.5	18.4	9.9	11.4	12.3	15.0	12.4	7.6	6.3	38.3	183 386	15.0	88.3	21.5
District 3	7.1	18.8	10.2	13.6	12.9	14.7	11.2	5.9	5.5	35.2	194 803	19.4	89.0	28.0
District 4	5.4	16.2	12.0	10.8	11.7	14.9	13.2	8.6	7.1	40.0	186 994	11.9	88.8	20.2
District 5	6.4	18.4	8.9	11.7	12.7	15.2	12.6	7.5	6.7	38.8	174 225	13.0	87.6	18.4
District 6	6.3	17.6	10.6	11.9	12.2	14.7	12.6	7.5	6.5	38.2	187 738	11.6	89.1	24.1
District 7	5.9	17.8	8.9	11.1	12.9	15.7	13.4	7.7	6.6	40.2	176 239	14.4	90.0	22.2
District 8	5.6	18.1	12.5	11.5	13.0	15.7	12.4	6.5	4.8	37.1	225 041	10.4	92.6	30.9
District 9	5.7	17.3	7.6	12.1	13.7	16.1	13.4	7.3	6.9	40.6	177 279	18.7	92.6	46.8
District 10	5.6	18.4	7.9	10.6	14.0	16.5	13.2	7.8	6.0	40.7	186 711	11.0	89.1	21.5
District 11	5.8	18.1	7.8	11.7	14.5	16.7	12.5	6.6	6.3	39.8	187 143	14.4	92.8	34.2
District 12	5.8	15.9	8.6	13.3	13.7	15.2	12.3	7.3	8.1	39.8	163 828	14.1	87.9	23.0
District 13	7.0	19.4	10.8	12.5	13.0	14.4	11.6	5.7	5.6	35.2	144 877	10.6	77.4	16.5
District 14	6.6	19.5	10.4	11.5	12.9	13.8	11.8	6.8	6.5	36.6	159 596	9.7	81.7	16.5
District 15	6.0	16.9	13.2	13.3	13.2	14.3	11.7	6.2	5.2	35.5	221 404	11.4	89.7	29.7
MINNESOTA	6.7	17.5	9.5	13.5	12.8	15.2	11.9	6.7	6.2	37.4	1 421 768	18.3	91.8	31.8
District 1	6.6	16.8	10.5	12.5	11.5	14.6	12.0	7.4	8.0	38.3	167 569	15.4	90.8	25.3
District 2	7.2	20.3	7.8	13.0	14.9	16.4	10.8	5.5	4.1	36.3	209 200	19.9	94.1	36.9
District 3	6.4	18.4	7.3	12.8	13.2	16.7	12.8	6.6	5.8	39.2	178 107	19.5	94.6	44.3
District 4	6.8	16.6	11.4	14.8	12.0	14.3	11.7	6.1	6.2	35.3	174 606	28.4	90.4	36.6
District 5	6.9	13.6	12.4	19.7	13.5	12.9	10.4	5.2	5.4	33.3	163 448	19.9	89.8	40.6
District 6	7.0	19.9	9.1	13.1	14.5	15.9	10.9	5.6	4.0	35.7	217 010	16.6	94.0	30.5
District 7	6.6	17.2	9.2	11.3	11.0	14.8	12.7	8.4	8.8	40.5	153 877	12.5	88.8	20.0
District 8	6.0	16.2	8.8	11.2	11.6	15.6	13.8	9.0	7.8	41.9	157 951	12.8	91.2	20.7

1. All persons 3 years old and over enrolled in nursery school through college and graduate or professional school.   2. Persons 25 years old and over.

Table E. Congressional Districts 112th Congress — Households and Group Quarters

STATE District	Households, 2010						Group quarters, 2010					
	Number	Persons per household	Family households (percent)	Husband-wife family (percent)	Female family householder[1]	One person households (percent)	Total in group quarters	Percent 65 years and over	Persons in correctional institutions	Persons in nursing homes	Persons in college dormitories	Persons in military quarters
	29	30	31	32	33	34	35	36	37	38	39	40
KENTUCKY	1 719 965	2.45	66.9	49.3	12.7	27.5	125 870	19.2	41 122	26 044	36 340	5 856
District 1	274 585	2.42	68.0	51.7	11.9	27.6	27 546	21.0	6 704	5 248	3 406	3 843
District 2	292 223	2.53	69.9	53.0	12.1	24.9	27 418	20.2	6 001	4 220	6 041	2 013
District 3	301 724	2.34	60.9	40.8	15.3	32.2	13 614	31.1	2 662	4 831	3 307	0
District 4	282 396	2.56	69.7	53.0	11.7	25.0	18 121	22.2	9 364	3 773	2 125	0
District 5	264 956	2.44	69.4	51.3	12.9	26.8	18 259	15.4	11 202	4 395	4 682	0
District 6	304 081	2.40	64.0	47.0	12.4	28.4	20 912	12.3	5 189	3 577	16 779	0
LOUISIANA	1 728 360	2.55	67.1	44.4	17.2	26.9	127 427	16.7	60 804	24 524	24 891	2 861
District 1	271 369	2.50	66.5	47.6	13.6	27.2	9 699	27.0	2 975	2 823	2 228	0
District 2	191 780	2.50	60.3	31.4	22.7	31.3	11 891	11.8	3 749	1 718	5 241	86
District 3	231 069	2.72	72.8	49.5	16.9	22.3	10 764	26.8	4 128	2 611	776	57
District 4	259 133	2.48	67.0	44.4	17.4	28.2	23 086	17.8	12 264	4 949	2 390	2 524
District 5	242 423	2.52	68.1	44.6	18.5	27.4	36 330	12.1	20 330	4 893	6 333	142
District 6	272 562	2.58	66.7	44.4	16.8	25.9	21 055	11.0	13 647	3 248	4 498	52
District 7	260 024	2.55	67.5	46.2	16.0	26.4	14 602	28.7	3 711	4 282	2 935	0
MAINE	557 219	2.32	62.9	48.5	10.0	28.6	35 545	22.5	3 679	7 878	17 251	131
District 1	279 768	2.33	62.8	49.0	9.7	28.5	14 363	26.0	2 708	3 842	5 738	119
District 2	277 451	2.31	63.0	48.0	10.2	28.8	21 182	19.6	971	4 036	11 513	12
MARYLAND	2 156 411	2.61	67.1	47.6	14.6	26.1	138 375	19.4	35 832	28 001	48 141	7 534
District 1	281 707	2.58	71.1	55.8	11.0	23.1	18 080	21.9	5 648	3 877	5 803	59
District 2	272 343	2.54	64.9	41.3	17.9	27.9	10 615	31.9	1 633	3 692	1 099	2 129
District 3	285 062	2.43	61.0	44.3	12.5	29.9	28 172	13.4	6 351	3 484	9 782	4 447
District 4	254 748	2.78	69.1	43.1	20.2	25.0	2 433	30.4	1 892	1 421	242	115
District 5	268 666	2.78	71.3	51.9	14.3	22.3	25 265	13.7	1 111	3 103	14 734	387
District 6	272 022	2.62	71.4	57.1	10.0	23.2	22 953	18.4	12 574	4 481	5 095	183
District 7	250 689	2.53	61.6	35.1	21.3	31.0	22 671	11.9	6 315	3 638	10 895	0
District 8	271 174	2.66	66.3	51.0	11.2	26.6	8 186	54.8	308	4 305	491	214
MASSACHUSETTS	2 547 075	2.48	63.0	46.3	12.5	28.7	238 882	17.7	24 683	43 833	135 773	498
District 1	254 109	2.41	63.1	46.3	12.2	28.9	32 785	13.2	1 830	4 662	22 523	0
District 2	255 653	2.51	66.1	46.7	14.6	27.4	23 843	22.5	1 793	4 706	9 740	0
District 3	252 573	2.56	66.8	50.0	12.4	26.4	19 265	23.9	1 430	4 585	9 747	0
District 4	250 205	2.51	66.0	50.2	11.8	26.8	26 812	17.8	3 559	5 121	16 538	0
District 5	239 936	2.69	70.0	51.9	13.5	24.3	16 626	20.7	6 326	3 853	3 981	0
District 6	253 914	2.51	66.1	51.1	11.1	27.9	13 233	30.8	1 216	4 325	5 120	113
District 7	259 166	2.44	61.7	47.0	10.8	30.0	21 056	24.5	765	4 020	9 303	25
District 8	265 472	2.25	44.1	25.1	15.0	37.0	53 567	3.8	1 901	2 316	50 626	127
District 9	248 413	2.54	63.7	45.9	13.6	28.4	23 358	27.9	3 879	5 840	6 671	207
District 10	267 634	2.39	63.3	49.6	10.0	29.7	8 337	43.1	1 984	4 405	1 524	26
MICHIGAN	3 872 508	2.49	66.0	48.0	13.2	27.9	229 068	19.8	62 083	42 473	78 033	214
District 1	273 298	2.29	64.7	51.4	8.8	29.5	22 767	22.7	10 505	5 123	5 523	124
District 2	263 239	2.58	70.3	55.0	10.8	24.1	22 492	16.3	6 244	2 790	6 380	8
District 3	260 240	2.60	67.8	51.3	12.0	25.5	20 039	18.9	6 388	3 471	3 811	0
District 4	269 770	2.43	66.0	51.5	10.0	26.5	28 711	12.2	10 237	3 184	13 715	0
District 5	253 204	2.47	65.8	43.6	16.8	28.7	11 155	31.6	1 730	2 855	1 303	0
District 6	264 608	2.48	65.6	48.8	12.1	27.1	14 076	22.1	1 476	3 083	6 864	0
District 7	261 363	2.49	68.2	51.5	11.8	26.4	17 855	14.9	13 558	2 914	5 968	82
District 8	269 901	2.54	67.0	52.3	10.3	24.9	27 691	10.6	1 164	1 902	15 387	0
District 9	266 619	2.43	65.0	51.1	10.3	29.4	8 132	29.1	1 665	2 458	2 171	0
District 10	273 911	2.60	71.7	57.3	10.0	23.9	7 669	38.3	2 893	2 370	0	0
District 11	276 392	2.50	67.4	51.7	11.4	27.5	3 308	58.2	2	2 452	139	0
District 12	267 014	2.36	61.0	40.3	15.7	33.1	5 148	45.3	1 142	3 068	502	0
District 13	198 359	2.56	59.8	27.1	25.9	34.4	8 472	14.3	2 760	2 036	1 619	0
District 14	208 162	2.61	64.3	31.9	25.6	31.2	3 679	36.8	461	2 753	778	0
District 15	266 428	2.48	62.9	45.2	13.0	28.6	27 874	10.2	1 858	2 014	13 873	0
MINNESOTA	2 087 227	2.48	64.6	50.8	9.5	28.0	135 395	24.9	20 397	32 989	50 444	0
District 1	256 361	2.43	65.1	52.8	8.3	28.1	19 918	26.3	2 760	5 206	9 723	0
District 2	268 291	2.68	72.5	59.3	8.9	21.8	12 435	21.2	3 201	2 806	4 904	0
District 3	256 307	2.52	67.5	54.1	9.6	26.3	4 546	43.9	461	1 945	226	0
District 4	245 586	2.42	59.2	42.2	12.5	32.4	17 870	18.7	1 045	3 563	9 958	0
District 5	265 321	2.24	48.7	32.9	11.5	38.2	22 276	20.7	876	5 339	8 740	0
District 6	273 605	2.71	72.7	59.7	8.6	20.5	19 489	18.4	5 569	2 687	5 885	0
District 7	252 778	2.41	65.8	53.4	8.1	28.5	19 797	38.5	1 001	6 498	6 518	0
District 8	268 978	2.38	65.0	51.4	8.8	28.5	19 064	25.9	5 484	4 945	4 490	0

1. No spouse present.

1206 KY(District 1)—MN(District 8)

Items 29—40

Table E. Congressional Districts 112th Congress — **Housing and Money Income**

STATE District	Housing units, 2010										Money income, 2010		
		Occupied units									Households		
			Owner-occupied					Renter-occupied					
						Median owner cost as a percent of income							Percent with income of $100,000 or more
	Total	Percent occupied	Percent	Median value[1] (dollars)	Percent valued at $500,000 or more	With a mortgage	Without a mortgage[2]	Median rent[3]	Median rent as a percent of income	Sub-standard units[4] (percent)	Per capita income (dollars)	Median income (dollars)	
	41	42	43	44	45	46	47	48	49	50	51	52	53
KENTUCKY	1 928 617	87.3	68.6	121 600	2.5	22.2	11.3	613	29.8	2.5	21 706	40 062	12.7
District 1	314 025	83.8	73.1	90 000	1.1	21.6	11.1	547	29.2	2.8	19 882	36 752	9.9
District 2	327 340	87.6	70.9	122 500	1.9	22.3	10.3	601	28.8	2.2	20 554	41 459	11.2
District 3	329 801	90.7	62.7	151 600	3.8	22.5	11.6	666	29.8	1.6	25 873	42 397	16.1
District 4	313 685	87.8	73.3	138 000	3.0	22.1	12.2	652	29.5	2.2	23 620	46 707	15.7
District 5	306 374	84	72.6	72 800	1.4	22.9	11.6	501	32.0	3.7	16 588	28 411	7.6
District 6	337 392	89.7	61.0	148 200	3.9	22.1	10.9	652	30.2	2.8	23 214	42 936	14.5
LOUISIANA	1 967 947	85.9	67.6	137 500	3.0	21.6	10.5	736	31.7	3.7	22 862	42 505	15.8
District 1	297 964	88.3	69.1	195 600	5.3	23.7	11.4	869	31.0	2.4	27 865	49 866	21.1
District 2	246 365	78.2	53.9	154 700	4.1	25.8	13.2	867	35.9	5.6	21 298	37 162	12.5
District 3	260 183	87.7	76.5	123 600	2.0	21.4	10.0	684	30.0	4.8	21 740	46 048	16.6
District 4	297 277	85.7	65.5	104 200	2.1	20.3	10.5	682	31.3	3.6	21 207	38 966	13.0
District 5	277 727	83.7	67.0	91 400	2.2	19.7	10.5	603	32.6	4.2	19 746	36 401	11.0
District 6	299 803	88.1	68.3	161 700	3.6	20.9	10.0	757	30.8	2.6	25 172	49 016	19.5
District 7	288 628	88.2	70.1	116 900	1.9	19.9	10.1	651	29.9	3.1	22 187	41 542	15.2
MAINE	722 217	75.5	72.7	179 100	5.5	24.1	13.9	707	29.8	2.5	24 950	45 815	14.6
District 1	352 068	78.8	73.4	222 500	8.3	24.8	13.9	799	29.4	2.4	27 944	53 011	18.3
District 2	370 149	72.4	71.9	139 300	2.5	23.2	13.9	620	30.1	2.5	21 902	39 465	10.8
MARYLAND	2 380 605	89.4	67.0	301 400	18.6	25.4	12.9	1 131	30.8	2.4	33 772	68 854	32.8
District 1	343 317	78.9	78.6	297 900	18.2	25.4	13.3	960	33.4	1.9	32 222	66 890	31.4
District 2	290 940	93.3	59.2	230 100	6.3	25.0	13.0	1 013	29.2	2.6	27 536	56 215	21.2
District 3	306 087	91.8	65.5	289 600	15.6	24.6	13.3	1 164	30.3	2.4	36 005	70 113	33.1
District 4	274 323	93.6	63.1	312 800	16.5	28.3	11.7	1 215	31.4	3.0	32 929	71 863	33.8
District 5	288 936	91.6	74.9	324 600	15.2	25.9	12.2	1 279	29.5	1.7	35 146	83 020	40.5
District 6	299 008	90.4	76.9	288 700	13.8	24.4	13.0	881	29.5	1.1	31 762	69 501	32.3
District 7	290 919	82.9	54.6	264 100	20.3	24.7	13.5	952	33.1	2.7	28 157	51 012	24.8
District 8	287 075	94.4	62.3	459 300	44.5	24.8	12.5	1 450	31.2	3.7	45 691	85 926	43.6
MASSACHUSETTS	2 808 727	89.7	62.2	334 100	20.5	26.1	15.3	1 009	30.4	2.0	33 203	62 072	29.2
District 1	284 236	89.3	65.2	231 200	5.6	25.3	14.6	780	30.9	1.8	26 409	50 865	19.6
District 2	269 512	93.5	66.5	243 400	4.9	25.1	15.2	796	30.7	2.4	27 039	55 032	22.6
District 3	270 895	92	64.1	294 500	12.0	25.2	15.8	882	29.7	1.2	30 748	61 622	28.8
District 4	275 583	90.4	65.6	349 300	28.2	25.9	14.4	904	30.2	1.9	37 395	64 958	32.0
District 5	259 700	93.8	67.4	333 100	21.3	25.8	14.8	970	30.9	1.8	34 483	68 241	33.1
District 6	269 106	92.9	69.2	384 800	26.3	26.6	16.3	1 040	30.8	1.4	36 161	70 330	34.5
District 7	265 540	93.8	58.6	412 300	29.3	25.9	16.3	1 219	28.6	2.6	36 930	71 400	34.0
District 8	288 602	91.4	28.5	394 700	35.4	27.2	14.8	1 272	31.5	3.1	31 030	47 604	23.3
District 9	262 610	94.3	65.5	357 400	23.2	26.3	13.9	1 151	29.6	1.8	36 214	72 927	34.2
District 10	362 943	72.3	73.1	376 000	27.0	28.2	16.8	1 132	30.7	1.7	35 597	65 094	30.3
MICHIGAN	4 531 231	84	72.8	123 300	2.6	24.6	13.9	730	33.3	2.1	23 622	45 413	15.6
District 1	418 074	64.2	80.9	105 600	2.7	24.2	12.6	566	32.7	2.0	20 944	38 761	9.0
District 2	325 103	79.8	78.1	131 400	3.2	24.2	13.5	670	33.4	1.8	21 444	44 527	12.4
District 3	285 263	91.7	72.1	140 000	2.0	24.4	13.3	703	31.2	2.1	22 990	47 614	14.9
District 4	340 319	78.8	75.0	119 800	2.5	24.4	12.6	671	32.6	2.2	21 975	41 496	12.6
District 5	286 133	86.8	71.3	91 100	1.6	24.5	14.7	664	37.9	1.8	19 673	38 495	10.6
District 6	310 689	82.6	72.7	131 300	3.1	23.3	13.0	660	34.3	2.0	22 650	42 521	13.9
District 7	298 023	85	76.7	124 600	2.2	24.7	13.5	688	30.6	1.7	22 563	46 606	14.5
District 8	290 979	91.5	74.5	157 600	2.5	24.3	13.6	779	33.7	1.1	25 416	54 323	20.6
District 9	292 521	92.1	70.0	173 700	7.0	24.5	14.2	884	28.3	1.4	35 963	62 098	28.6
District 10	308 502	89	82.0	151 100	2.1	25.2	13.7	745	32.2	1.7	24 610	51 487	18.4
District 11	289 247	93.2	75.6	150 600	2.6	24.0	13.6	803	31.3	2.4	30 068	58 150	24.5
District 12	289 330	91	68.9	97 800	0.9	24.9	16.5	813	32.7	1.6	22 939	43 431	12.4
District 13	253 992	73.3	55.8	66 600	2.4	28.1	17.4	716	39.0	4.7	17 527	29 343	9.9
District 14	254 331	77.9	63.1	74 300	1.0	28.3	17.2	772	45.8	4.1	17 036	31 786	9.4
District 15	288 725	91.2	66.7	131 200	2.5	24.4	13.9	805	31.1	1.9	25 417	50 090	17.8
MINNESOTA	2 348 242	89.1	73.0	194 300	5.8	24.1	11.9	764	30.2	2.3	28 563	55 459	21.4
District 1	277 093	92.2	76.2	145 800	2.9	22.7	11.4	655	29.4	1.5	25 399	49 844	16.2
District 2	283 882	94.1	80.4	236 800	6.7	24.3	11.8	863	29.6	1.9	31 404	71 862	31.0
District 3	269 707	94.7	75.0	247 500	13.1	24.2	11.5	952	29.2	1.8	37 923	70 552	32.6
District 4	263 109	93.4	62.3	207 500	5.7	24.1	12.3	786	31.6	3.6	27 622	51 277	19.7
District 5	289 721	91.3	54.7	209 500	6.0	25.2	12.9	805	30.9	3.9	29 146	49 135	18.8
District 6	291 425	93.4	82.0	210 100	4.9	24.5	11.6	812	29.9	1.2	29 325	67 049	26.9
District 7	306 644	83.2	75.7	140 400	3.3	22.8	11.9	585	29.4	2.1	23 619	46 198	12.9
District 8	366 661	75.3	76.8	161 000	4.3	24.7	12.1	623	30.8	2.6	23 480	45 294	12.8

1. Specified owner-occupied units.   2. Median monthly owner costs is often in the minimum category—10.0 percent or less, which is indicated as 10.0 percent.   3. Specified renter-occupied units.   4. Overcrowded or lacking complete plumbing facilities.

Table E. Congressional Districts 112th Congress — **Poverty, Labor Force, Employment, and Social Security**

STATE District	Poverty, 2010 (percent) Persons below poverty level	Families below poverty level	Households receiving food stamps in past 12 months	Civilian labor force, 2010 Total	Unemployment Total	Rate[1]	Civilian employment,[2] 2010 Total	Percent Management, business, science, and arts occupations	Service, sales, and office	Construction and production	Persons under age 65 with no health insurance, 2010 (percent)	Social Security beneficiaries, December 2010 Number	Rate[3]	Supplemental Security Income recipients, December 2010
	54	55	56	57	58	59	60	61	62	63	64	65	66	67
KENTUCKY	19.0	14.5	16.6	2 044 016	228 045	11.2	1 815 971	32.3	41.2	26.5	17.5	894 473	206.1	192 076
District 1	18.0	13.3	16.1	302 681	34 089	11.3	268 592	26.9	39.7	33.4	19.2	161 247	234.7	28 957
District 2	16.8	12.6	13.8	357 586	37 451	10.5	320 135	29.1	40.4	30.6	15.9	150 884	198.5	25 853
District 3	17.2	12.6	13.6	376 961	42 440	11.3	334 521	37.0	42.7	20.3	15.2	134 181	185.9	23 368
District 4	16.2	12.3	13.6	361 303	39 187	10.8	322 116	34.2	41.8	23.9	15.4	136 995	184.8	22 843
District 5	26.9	21.7	27.7	246 455	27 977	11.4	218 478	27.5	41.2	31.3	21.2	175 087	261.3	65 987
District 6	19.5	14.8	16.1	399 030	46 901	11.8	352 129	36.3	41.1	22.6	18.6	136 079	179.2	25 068
LOUISIANA	18.7	14.5	15.3	2 187 678	220 155	10.1	1 967 523	31.4	43.8	24.9	20.2	790 617	174.4	174 731
District 1	12.5	9.7	10.5	350 823	36 110	10.3	314 713	37.6	42.0	20.3	18.8	122 955	179.0	18 079
District 2	27.2	22.6	20.9	251 916	35 248	14.0	216 668	30.4	48.9	20.6	23.4	78 315	158.7	26 250
District 3	17.9	14.7	16.4	304 233	31 444	10.3	272 789	27.3	39.2	33.6	19.0	113 284	177.7	23 931
District 4	18.9	15.3	16.8	311 412	31 737	10.2	279 675	28.2	45.1	26.6	20.7	121 158	181.6	27 486
District 5	22.1	17.7	17.1	281 242	27 821	9.9	253 421	29.9	45.1	25.0	26.6	116 958	181.5	29 911
District 6	15.3	9.4	12.0	370 583	33 148	8.9	337 435	34.3	43.3	22.5	16.4	116 271	159.8	23 648
District 7	19.8	15.1	15.4	317 469	24 647	7.8	292 822	30.2	44.1	25.6	18.1	121 676	179.8	25 426
MAINE	12.9	8.8	16.2	699 827	58 162	8.3	641 665	35.9	41.5	22.6	12.0	299 875	225.7	35 426
District 1	10.5	6.9	12.5	367 250	26 239	7.1	341 011	39.0	41.0	20.0	10.8	142 220	212.7	13 319
District 2	15.5	10.8	20.0	332 577	31 923	9.6	300 654	32.5	42.0	25.6	13.2	157 655	238.9	22 107
MARYLAND	9.9	6.6	8.4	3 164 140	278 125	8.8	2 886 015	44.1	40.1	15.8	12.6	850 361	147.3	107 636
District 1	8.9	5.1	7.7	390 130	33 918	8.7	356 212	41.5	40.2	18.2	9.1	142 644	191.7	10 116
District 2	12.0	8.5	11.0	387 724	35 986	9.3	351 738	35.9	44.5	19.7	13.7	113 664	162.2	16 583
District 3	9.6	6.3	6.4	399 253	28 681	7.2	370 572	49.0	37.8	13.3	12.0	104 875	145.7	12 411
District 4	8.9	6.3	8.0	415 125	43 995	10.6	371 130	42.6	42.7	14.7	15.0	77 114	108.0	12 059
District 5	6.6	4.3	6.3	426 194	36 278	8.5	389 916	43.7	39.5	16.8	12.2	94 396	123.0	8 436
District 6	7.7	5.5	7.5	396 166	28 019	7.1	368 147	42.3	39.7	18.1	8.5	125 988	170.5	9 659
District 7	18.2	13.7	16.6	323 364	40 947	12.7	282 417	43.3	43.0	13.6	13.6	102 954	156.0	29 103
District 8	8.2	4.9	4.8	426 184	30 301	7.1	395 883	53.1	34.9	12.0	16.8	88 726	121.9	9 269
MASSACHUSETTS	11.4	8.2	11.5	3 590 908	365 805	10.2	3 225 103	43.5	40.9	15.7	5.0	1 140 830	174.2	192 814
District 1	13.2	9.8	14.3	340 162	32 641	9.6	307 521	36.5	42.2	21.3	4.9	127 158	197.2	22 188
District 2	12.9	9.5	15.7	347 028	40 166	11.6	306 862	37.0	42.6	20.4	5.5	126 818	191.8	27 927
District 3	10.1	7.1	12.5	360 806	39 135	10.8	321 671	41.2	42.4	16.4	4.2	109 925	165.3	18 924
District 4	10.8	7.6	11.4	347 981	35 173	10.1	312 808	46.4	39.0	14.6	4.1	119 162	181.6	17 961
District 5	9.8	7.6	9.8	352 308	29 901	8.5	322 407	45.3	37.5	17.1	4.7	103 156	155.8	19 863
District 6	7.8	5.8	8.6	363 956	35 841	9.8	328 115	45.3	41.4	13.3	4.2	119 792	184.2	13 659
District 7	8.8	6.5	8.1	369 283	31 357	8.5	337 926	46.9	40.1	13.0	6.4	107 335	165.6	12 974
District 8	24.5	18.5	17.5	385 618	47 689	12.4	337 929	48.9	40.6	10.6	6.3	71 803	108.7	31 551
District 9	9.6	7.0	9.1	374 458	39 678	10.6	334 780	45.8	39.9	14.3	4.7	110 090	169.3	17 072
District 10	7.6	5.7	7.3	349 308	34 224	9.8	315 084	40.6	42.7	16.7	5.4	145 591	224.2	10 695
MICHIGAN	16.8	12.1	16.9	4 870 674	733 164	15.1	4 137 510	34.2	43.8	22.0	14.3	1 964 862	198.8	253 532
District 1	15.2	10.7	16.7	297 793	41 461	13.9	256 332	29.7	45.8	24.5	16.2	179 276	275.7	15 297
District 2	15.8	12.0	18.5	345 248	45 507	13.2	299 741	29.2	42.2	28.5	14.3	144 032	206.1	14 972
District 3	16.3	11.6	15.8	355 791	40 956	11.5	314 835	34.3	41.7	23.9	12.7	115 353	166.0	15 543
District 4	17.5	11.5	17.2	331 870	43 865	13.2	288 005	29.1	46.3	24.7	15.2	155 855	227.1	15 262
District 5	21.3	16.9	22.6	285 928	55 491	19.4	230 437	29.2	48.2	22.6	13.5	141 618	223.0	24 727
District 6	18.0	12.4	16.5	336 904	45 810	13.6	291 094	31.6	44.1	24.4	14.1	135 716	202.0	16 487
District 7	14.9	10.4	15.6	332 263	45 151	13.6	287 112	32.6	42.3	25.1	14.0	138 961	205.3	14 519
District 8	13.6	8.7	13.0	368 623	44 911	12.2	323 712	38.8	42.6	18.5	9.8	117 376	165.9	10 463
District 9	10.2	7.1	8.6	352 295	41 022	11.6	311 273	49.6	38.4	12.1	11.9	119 810	182.2	10 327
District 10	12.4	8.7	12.2	365 767	54 514	14.9	311 253	32.1	44.0	23.9	13.8	140 934	195.8	10 784
District 11	8.7	6.1	9.4	368 368	47 573	12.9	320 795	41.5	41.1	17.4	12.0	124 887	179.5	9 722
District 12	15.3	11.9	17.0	323 065	54 577	16.9	268 488	33.6	46.7	19.7	16.7	133 076	209.0	16 896
District 13	32.8	27.5	33.9	222 347	60 053	27.0	162 294	28.6	48.9	22.5	20.9	93 180	179.3	35 142
District 14	31.1	25.2	29.4	233 161	64 057	27.5	169 104	26.5	50.6	23.0	20.5	109 617	199.1	29 563
District 15	15.4	10.8	15.5	351 251	48 216	13.7	303 035	37.3	41.9	20.8	11.9	115 171	168.8	13 828
MINNESOTA	11.6	7.5	7.6	2 938 277	244 632	8.3	2 693 645	38.4	41.1	20.5	10.3	882 408	166.4	86 506
District 1	11.4	6.5	6.8	357 208	21 957	6.1	335 251	34.2	40.7	25.0	9.4	124 485	193.1	8 652
District 2	7.0	4.5	4.1	416 965	32 384	7.8	384 581	41.1	40.3	18.5	7.9	92 660	126.5	5 886
District 3	8.4	5.8	5.2	364 379	30 687	8.4	333 692	45.4	38.9	15.7	9.3	99 145	152.5	7 871
District 4	15.6	11.0	10.7	337 854	30 647	9.1	307 207	41.2	42.1	16.8	11.5	95 997	156.2	16 772
District 5	19.3	13.2	12.4	363 441	38 602	10.6	324 839	43.8	41.7	14.4	14.8	84 283	136.7	18 336
District 6	6.8	4.6	4.6	430 959	36 877	8.6	394 082	37.3	41.6	21.1	7.9	101 587	133.8	6 424
District 7	12.4	8.2	8.3	333 555	22 200	6.7	311 355	31.9	39.5	28.6	11.0	135 358	216.4	9 810
District 8	13.7	9.3	8.7	333 916	31 278	9.4	302 638	31.5	43.6	25.0	12.0	148 893	225.5	12 755

1. Percent of civilian labor force. 2. Persons 16 years old and over. 3. Per 1,000 resident population enumerated in the 2010 census.

Table E. Congressional Districts 112th Congress — **Agriculture**

STATE District	Farms		Land in farms		Farm Operators			Value of products sold				Government payments	
						Percent of farm operators				Percent of sales from			
	Number	Operated by family or individual (percent)	Acreage	Average size of farm (acres)	Total	Whose primary occupation is farming	Who live on the farm operated	Total ($1,000)	Average per farm	Crops	Livestock	Total ($1,000)	Percent of farms
	68	69	70	71	72	73	74	75	76	77	78	79	80
KENTUCKY	85 260	89.3	13 993 121	164	123 971	37.2	77.5	4 824 561	56 586	29.1	70.9	103 104	34.6
District 1	23 964	89.3	5 020 483	210	33 879	37.7	74.8	1 991 744	83 114	38.6	61.4	60 524	51.1
District 2	22 918	89.9	3 328 323	145	33 403	36.5	79.3	867 054	37 833	39.4	60.6	25 363	37.2
District 3	429	84.6	28 864	67	665	35.5	74.3	10 468	24 401	73.9	26.1	133	10.0
District 4	15 303	89.1	2 302 290	150	22 884	37.5	78.2	313 281	20 472	41.5	58.5	6 933	25.3
District 5	10 445	92.4	1 469 585	141	14 635	34.7	80.1	179 799	17 214	23.7	76.3	3 089	19.6
District 6	12 201	85.9	1 843 576	151	18 505	39.1	76.2	1 462 215	119 844	7.8	92.2	7 062	22.7
LOUISIANA	30 106	85.4	8 109 975	269	43 774	39.3	68.8	2 617 981	86 959	61.3	38.7	169 333	35.3
District 1	2 714	88.8	269 439	99	4 042	40.7	80.8	109 367	40 297	30.8	69.2	3 812	17.3
District 2	67	71.6	9 831	147	85	43.5	47.1	1 633	24 373	(D)	(D)	226	14.9
District 3	2 021	75.2	869 891	430	3 052	46.4	55.3	329 684	163 129	78.0	22.0	3 279	12.3
District 4	5 686	89.2	1 269 124	223	8 442	39.4	77.5	422 992	74 392	(D)	(D)	14 425	17.7
District 5	10 004	83.5	3 142 400	314	14 466	38.6	62.2	1 182 999	118 253	67.0	33.0	104 823	56.0
District 6	2 873	88.9	654 207	228	4 160	38.1	75.6	195 673	68 108	67.0	33.0	5 290	16.2
District 7	6 741	85.4	1 895 083	281	9 527	38.1	67.7	375 633	55 724	81.5	18.5	37 477	41.8
MAINE	8 136	85.5	1 347 566	166	13 063	39.7	81.9	617 190	75 859	52.9	47.1	8 815	17.9
District 1	2 829	83.6	271 549	96	4 605	41.2	85.0	126 534	44 727	38.3	61.7	2 391	8.0
District 2	5 307	86.5	1 076 017	203	8 458	38.9	80.2	490 655	92 454	56.7	43.3	6 424	23.2
MARYLAND	12 834	82.7	2 051 756	160	20 241	46.1	79.3	1 835 090	142 987	34.3	65.7	33 386	35.7
District 1	4 440	79.3	1 038 289	234	6 806	50.7	74.0	1 308 519	294 711	27.8	72.2	22 166	55.6
District 2	151	74.8	8 715	58	259	37.8	78.8	7 771	51 464	87.9	12.1	26	9.9
District 3	93	71.0	5 205	56	141	46.1	74.5	7 624	81 978	95.2	4.8	0	3.2
District 4	236	72.9	20 755	88	350	46.0	77.4	18 784	79 593	86.4	13.6	336	15.7
District 5	1 939	87.9	205 891	106	2 990	42.5	80.7	58 184	30 007	80.8	19.2	1 654	21.1
District 6	5 327	85.1	702 862	132	8 596	45.2	82.7	394 048	73 972	39.9	60.1	8 375	29.1
District 7	345	79.4	30 194	88	598	37.3	83.6	24 238	70 255	80.1	19.9	252	13.0
District 8	303	74.3	39 845	132	501	37.1	79.8	15 923	52 551	75.2	24.8	577	19.1
MASSACHUSETTS	7 691	82.1	517 879	67	12 265	44.3	74.7	489 820	63 687	74.4	25.6	4 603	7.7
District 1	2 843	85.1	263 885	93	4 581	43.1	81.0	150 896	53 076	61.4	38.6	1 934	9.1
District 2	1 002	86.6	66 518	66	1 588	42.9	81.9	50 708	50 607	53.0	47.0	558	8.6
District 3	569	81.2	30 099	53	896	41.3	77.0	41 199	72 406	84.0	16.0	347	5.6
District 4	993	80.3	52 648	53	1 553	48.0	75.1	80 664	81 233	93.9	6.1	660	8.1
District 5	624	78.7	30 837	49	995	49.4	70.3	66 195	106 082	87.2	12.8	191	3.5
District 6	464	78.7	25 318	55	766	42.4	76.6	26 389	56 873	65.7	34.3	266	4.3
District 7	75	73.3	2 397	32	140	50.0	59.3	10 415	138 867	(D)	(D)	(D)	1.3
District 8	5	80.0	129	26	7	71.4	57.1	173	34 600	(D)	(D)		0.0
District 9	148	77.0	8 618	58	218	50.5	71.1	4 365	29 493	(D)	(D)	(D)	7.4
District 10	968	76.7	37 430	39	1 521	46.2	50.0	58 814	60 758	78.1	21.9	612	8.6
MICHIGAN	56 014	86.9	10 031 807	179	85 339	41.8	81.2	5 758 219	102 710	57.9	42.1	118 871	41.5
District 1	7 541	88.3	1 394 362	185	11 499	40.0	81.0	323 259	42 867	45.1	54.9	8 152	34.7
District 2	5 987	85.1	881 541	147	9 209	41.7	80.7	1 015 927	169 689	49.1	50.9	7 288	23.8
District 3	3 286	87.9	530 232	161	5 015	39.1	83.4	445 182	135 478	40.7	59.3	6 578	42.4
District 4	9 429	88.3	1 742 086	185	14 278	41.6	81.4	861 789	91 398	52.5	47.5	19 494	47.2
District 5	2 834	85.4	602 886	213	4 244	46.0	77.6	280 324	98 915	82.5	17.5	7 954	51.9
District 6	6 317	86.3	1 066 950	169	9 702	42.4	80.7	878 750	139 109	71.9	28.1	13 635	33.7
District 7	8 983	87.8	1 604 376	179	13 440	37.8	81.5	663 253	73 834	63.2	36.8	27 942	53.5
District 8	3 841	85.8	661 961	172	6 050	41.3	85.1	329 610	85 814	51.4	48.6	8 249	37.7
District 9	62	66.1	4 022	65	102	31.4	58.8	3 795	61 210	97.4	2.6	31	14.5
District 10	5 764	85.9	1 255 181	218	8 752	50.4	81.6	761 837	132 172	54.9	45.1	15 494	48.4
District 11	279	77.8	15 133	54	491	36.9	69.0	14 811	53 086	93.0	7.0	68	7.5
District 12	32	71.9	2 095	65	59	28.8	23.7	1 910	59 688	58.1	41.9	10	15.6
District 13	15	73.3	659	44	23	30.4	47.8	115	7 667	(D)	(D)	(D)	13.3
District 14	16	81.3	679	42	24	66.7	45.8	31	1 938	(D)	(D)	(D)	18.8
District 15	1 628	86.7	269 644	166	2 451	42.3	79.9	172 623	106 034	94.1	5.9	3 968	41.5
MINNESOTA	80 992	86.5	26 917 962	332	119 650	45.6	76.2	13 180 466	162 738	53.5	46.5	445 861	70.0
District 1	22 184	85.8	7 509 493	339	32 543	50.8	76.2	5 151 480	232 216	49.5	50.5	146 361	78.9
District 2	6 979	86.8	1 454 811	208	10 455	41.6	78.6	885 548	126 888	52.9	47.1	28 288	66.4
District 3	557	83.5	63 222	114	837	42.8	81.7	42 408	76 136	82.4	17.6	920	36.4
District 4	57	75.4	2 380	42	104	52.9	36.5	(D)	(D)	(D)	(D)	1	5.3
District 5	20	75.0	1 923	96	32	12.5	31.3	(D)	(D)	(D)	(D)	16	25.0
District 6	6 438	88.1	1 094 375	170	9 945	44.1	84.9	717 229	111 406	33.6	66.4	15 926	54.6
District 7	33 697	85.0	14 475 509	430	48 910	45.9	70.0	5 779 300	171 508	61.9	38.1	240 420	79.5
District 8	11 060	91.5	2 316 249	209	16 824	38.2	87.3	584 392	52 838	28.4	71.6	13 929	36.0

1. Specified owner-occupied units. 2. Median monthly owner costs is often in the minimum category—10.0 percent or less, which is indicated as 10.0 percent. 3. Specified renter-occupied units. 4. Overcrowded or lacking complete plumbing facilities.

STATE District	Representative, 112th Congress	Land area,[1] 2010 (sq km)	Total persons	Per square kilometer	White	Black	American Indian, Alaska Native	Asian and Pacific Islander	Some other race	Two or more races	Hispanic or Latino[2]	Non-Hispanic White alone	Percent female	Percent foreign born	Percent born in state of residence
		1	2	3	4	5	6	7	8	9	10	11	12	13	14
MISSISSIPPI		121 531	2 967 297	24.4	59.1	37.0	0.5	0.9	1.3	1.1	2.7	58.0	51.4	2.1	71.9
District 1	Alan Nunnelee (R)	29 573	788 095	26.6	69.0	27.4	0.2	0.6	1.6	1.1	3.0	68.0	51.6	1.9	63.5
District 2	Bennie G. Thompson (D)	35 329	668 263	18.9	31.0	66.5	0.3	0.6	0.9	0.8	1.9	30.4	52.0	2.0	84.3
District 3	Gregg Harper (R)	34 127	756 924	22.2	61.1	34.8	1.1	0.9	1.1	0.9	2.3	60.2	51.5	1.8	78.9
District 4	Steven Palazzo (R)	22 502	754 015	33.5	71.7	23.2	0.4	1.5	1.5	1.7	3.7	70.0	50.7	2.6	62.5
MISSOURI		178 040	5 988 927	33.6	82.8	11.6	0.5	1.7	1.3	2.1	3.5	81.0	51.0	3.9	65.9
District 1	William Lacy Clay (D)	563	587 069	1 042.3	38.6	55.6	0.2	2.5	1.0	2.1	2.4	37.5	53.4	4.8	70.3
District 2	W. Todd Akin (R)	3 223	706 622	219.2	90.7	3.3	0.2	3.3	0.8	1.7	2.5	89.2	51.3	5.6	67.6
District 3	Russ Carnahan (D)	3 221	625 251	194.1	85.5	9.2	0.3	2.3	0.9	2.8	2.8	83.8	51.0	6.6	72.0
District 4	Vicky Hartzler (R)	37 553	679 375	18.1	91.9	3.5	0.6	0.8	1.1	2.0	3.2	90.2	49.8	2.7	62.8
District 5	Emanuel Cleaver (D)	1 323	633 887	479.2	65.3	25.3	0.5	1.8	4.0	3.1	8.7	61.6	51.7	6.0	57.8
District 6	Sam Graves (R)	33 674	693 974	20.6	90.3	4.3	0.5	1.5	1.3	2.2	4.2	87.9	50.5	3.3	64.6
District 7	Bill Long (R)	14 178	721 754	50.9	91.5	1.7	1.0	1.3	1.9	2.5	4.4	89.6	51.0	2.7	57.5
District 8	Jo Ann Emerson (R)	48 306	656 894	13.6	91.8	5.0	0.5	0.6	0.6	1.6	1.7	90.9	50.2	1.1	70.6
District 9	Blaine Luetkemeyer (R)	35 999	684 101	19.0	91.8	4.1	0.3	1.4	0.6	1.8	1.9	90.7	50.5	2.4	70.7
MONTANA		376 962	989 415	2.6	89.4	0.4	6.3	0.7	0.6	2.5	2.9	87.8	49.8	2.0	54.1
At Large	Denny Rehberg (R)	376 962	989 415	2.6	89.4	0.4	6.3	0.7	0.6	2.5	2.9	87.8	49.8	2.0	54.1
NEBRASKA		198 974	1 826 341	9.2	86.1	4.5	1.0	1.9	4.3	2.2	9.2	82.1	50.4	6.1	65.6
District 1	Jeff Fortenberry (R)	30 874	626 092	20.3	89.3	2.1	1.3	2.0	3.3	2.0	7.0	86.2	50.0	6.0	67.8
District 2	Lee Terry (R)	1 056	638 871	604.9	78.1	10.3	0.7	2.7	5.3	2.9	10.7	73.7	50.8	8.0	58.1
District 3	Adrian Smith (R)	167 043	561 378	3.4	91.8	0.7	1.0	0.7	4.4	1.4	9.8	87.2	50.3	4.1	71.6
NEVADA		284 332	2 700 551	9.5	66.2	8.1	1.2	7.8	12.0	4.7	26.5	54.1	49.5	18.8	24.3
District 1	Shelley Berkley (D)	458	820 134	1 789.4	55.0	13.9	0.8	6.8	18.3	5.2	37.2	39.4	49.1	24.4	24.6
District 2	Mark E. Amodei (R)	271 997	836 562	3.1	78.0	2.9	2.2	4.4	8.8	3.7	20.4	68.2	49.2	12.0	28.8
District 3	Joseph J. Heck (R)	11 876	1 043 855	87.9	65.4	7.7	0.7	11.4	9.7	5.0	23.0	54.4	50.0	19.9	20.6
NEW HAMPSHIRE		23 187	1 316 470	56.8	93.9	1.1	0.2	2.2	0.9	1.6	2.8	92.3	50.7	5.3	42.7
District 1	Frank Guinta (R)	6 333	657 984	103.9	93.9	1.3	0.2	2.0	0.9	1.7	2.8	92.3	50.8	5.4	42.6
District 2	Charles Bass (R)	16 854	658 486	39.1	93.8	1.0	0.3	2.3	1.0	1.6	2.8	92.3	50.6	5.2	42.7
NEW JERSEY		19 047	8 791 894	461.6	68.6	13.7	0.3	8.3	6.4	2.7	17.7	59.3	51.3	21.0	52.4
District 1	Robert E. Andrews (D)	859	669 169	779.0	69.4	18.2	0.3	3.7	5.8	2.6	12.1	65.0	51.7	8.1	55.0
District 2	Frank A. LoBiondo (R)	5 075	692 205	136.4	72.8	13.9	0.5	3.7	6.2	2.8	14.9	66.3	50.7	10.6	58.2
District 3	Jon Runyan (R)	2 373	680 341	286.7	82.0	9.7	0.2	3.9	1.9	2.3	6.4	78.4	51.5	8.7	56.9
District 4	Christopher H. Smith (R)	1 849	724 596	391.9	81.2	8.5	0.2	3.6	4.4	2.0	12.2	74.7	51.3	12.4	60.1
District 5	Scott Garrett (R)	2 836	666 551	235.0	84.9	2.1	0.2	9.1	1.8	1.8	7.6	79.9	51.4	15.6	54.6
District 6	Frank Pallone Jr. (D)	507	668 806	1 319.4	62.1	15.4	0.4	11.9	7.2	2.9	17.8	53.5	50.8	24.3	50.9
District 7	Leonard Lance (R)	1 532	672 885	439.3	76.1	5.7	0.2	12.6	3.2	2.2	11.2	69.0	51.2	20.3	56.7
District 8	Bill Pascrell Jr. (D)	276	660 424	2 392.5	61.6	14.3	0.5	6.6	13.2	3.7	33.2	45.7	51.9	29.1	50.6
District 9	Steven R. Rothman (D)	239	661 379	2 761.9	65.0	7.9	0.4	14.5	8.9	3.3	26.4	50.3	51.7	36.3	40.7
District 10	Vacant	172	634 343	3 687.9	26.8	57.5	0.4	4.5	7.8	3.1	20.4	17.1	52.7	27.0	51.7
District 11	Rodney P. Frelinghuysen (R)	1 555	674 349	433.8	83.0	2.9	0.1	9.3	2.6	2.0	10.3	76.1	51.1	17.9	58.3
District 12	Rush D. Holt (D)	1 629	701 881	430.9	68.4	11.7	0.2	15.0	2.5	2.2	8.0	63.8	51.5	21.6	48.5
District 13	Albio Sires (D)	146	684 965	4 693.6	54.7	13.2	0.7	8.9	17.7	4.8	50.6	27.4	49.8	41.5	38.7
NEW MEXICO		314 161	2 059 179	6.6	68.4	2.1	9.4	1.5	15.0	3.7	46.3	40.5	50.6	9.9	51.7
District 1	Martin Heinrich (D)	12 208	701 939	57.5	70.1	2.8	4.2	2.3	16.3	4.3	48.4	42.0	50.9	11.5	50.7
District 2	Steve Pearce (R)	179 859	663 956	3.7	72.9	1.9	5.6	0.9	15.7	3.1	51.8	39.8	50.1	11.7	49.3
District 3	Ben Ray Luján (D)	122 094	693 284	5.7	62.3	1.5	18.3	1.2	13.0	3.7	39.0	39.6	50.7	6.5	55.0
NEW YORK		122 057	19 378 102	158.8	65.7	15.9	0.6	7.3	7.4	3.0	17.6	58.3	51.6	22.2	63.6
District 1	Timothy H. Bishop (D)	1 676	705 559	420.9	85.6	4.9	0.4	3.3	3.8	2.1	12.6	77.9	50.6	10.0	80.2
District 2	Steve Israel (D)	618	679 893	1 099.7	73.9	10.6	0.4	4.7	7.6	2.8	21.0	62.9	51.0	19.7	72.4
District 3	Peter T. King (R)	470	645 508	1 374.7	87.1	3.1	0.2	4.9	2.8	1.8	10.1	80.7	51.5	14.2	79.1
District 4	Carolyn McCarthy (D)	233	663 407	2 852.5	61.5	19.7	0.3	6.8	8.7	2.9	20.2	52.3	51.7	25.4	67.0
District 5	Gary L. Ackerman (D)	171	670 130	3 921.1	47.0	4.8	0.5	32.7	11.6	3.4	25.6	35.7	51.1	48.1	45.8
District 6	Gregory W. Meeks (D)	102	651 764	6 400.6	16.9	51.8	1.0	13.3	11.2	5.8	19.0	10.1	52.9	44.3	46.3
District 7	Joseph Crowley (D)	68	667 632	9 792.8	39.6	19.8	0.8	16.4	18.8	4.6	44.4	20.7	52.1	41.6	48.4
District 8	Jerrold Nadler (D)	39	713 512	18 523.4	72.4	5.2	0.3	15.1	4.4	2.6	11.8	66.5	51.1	33.9	43.0
District 9	Robert L. Turner (R)	96	660 306	6 883.7	65.7	5.2	0.4	18.7	6.9	3.1	17.2	57.0	52.3	42.1	51.9
District 10	Edolphus Towns (D)	47	677 721	14 560.8	23.5	62.1	0.6	3.7	7.0	3.1	17.2	18.3	54.5	30.2	55.6
District 11	Yvette D. Clarke (D)	31	632 408	20 301.2	29.7	56.1	0.4	5.5	5.1	3.1	13.2	25.6	54.3	39.2	45.5
District 12	Nydia M. Velázquez (D)	48	672 358	13 960.6	44.3	10.9	1.0	18.4	20.9	4.6	44.6	26.8	50.6	40.0	43.2
District 13	Michael Grimm (R)	167	686 525	4 102.8	70.3	7.7	0.3	13.2	6.0	2.5	16.1	62.3	51.5	27.5	65.9

1. Dry land or land partially or temporarily covered by water.　2. May be of any race.

Table E. Congressional Districts 112th Congress — **Age and Education**

	Population and population characteristics, 2010 (cont.)										Education, 2010			
	Age (percent)										Enrollment[1]		Attainment[2] (percent)	
STATE District	Under 5 years	5 to 17 years	18 to 24 years	25 to 34 years	35 to 44 years	45 to 54 years	55 to 64 years	65 to 74 years	75 years and over	Median age	Total	Percent private	High school graduate or more	Bachelor's degree or more
	15	16	17	18	19	20	21	22	23	24	25	26	27	28
MISSISSIPPI	7.1	18.4	10.3	13.1	12.6	14.1	11.7	7.2	5.6	36.0	807 315	12.9	81.0	19.5
District 1	6.9	18.6	10.0	12.5	13.2	14.0	11.6	7.5	5.7	36.6	209 506	11.0	80.6	17.1
District 2	7.5	19.2	10.8	13.2	12.0	14.0	11.5	6.5	5.2	34.3	203 431	12.8	77.6	18.8
District 3	7.0	18.0	10.0	13.1	12.5	13.9	12.0	7.3	6.1	36.5	204 029	15.1	82.6	23.0
District 4	7.1	17.8	10.3	13.4	12.7	14.3	11.7	7.5	5.3	36.2	190 349	12.8	82.7	19.0
MISSOURI	6.5	17.3	9.8	12.9	12.5	14.8	12.1	7.5	6.5	37.9	1 571 470	19.0	86.9	25.6
District 1	6.5	17.5	10.9	13.8	11.9	14.4	11.8	6.8	6.5	36.1	168 612	24.0	85.3	26.1
District 2	6.2	19.0	7.7	11.6	13.3	16.3	12.5	7.2	6.3	39.5	200 181	28.4	93.4	42.7
District 3	6.3	15.6	9.3	15.3	13.2	15.5	12.0	6.5	6.1	37.6	155 605	29.7	87.3	29.1
District 4	6.6	17.4	10.0	11.9	12.0	14.4	12.4	8.6	6.8	38.8	169 917	14.0	86.0	18.2
District 5	7.1	17.2	9.5	14.6	12.7	14.7	11.4	6.6	6.3	36.3	160 907	18.6	86.7	26.9
District 6	6.7	17.9	9.0	12.9	13.2	15.0	12.0	7.2	6.2	37.9	178 713	13.6	90.1	24.3
District 7	6.6	17.1	10.8	12.8	12.2	13.9	11.9	8.1	6.6	37.3	188 668	14.3	86.4	21.6
District 8	6.4	16.9	9.5	11.7	12.0	14.6	12.7	9.0	7.3	39.8	160 482	10.7	78.5	15.6
District 9	6.3	16.9	12.0	12.4	12.1	14.7	11.9	7.4	6.2	37.1	188 385	17.2	87.1	25.2
MONTANA	6.3	16.3	9.6	12.4	11.4	15.1	14.0	8.2	6.7	39.8	243 290	12.3	91.7	28.8
At Large	6.3	16.3	9.6	12.4	11.4	15.1	14.0	8.2	6.7	39.8	243 290	12.3	91.7	28.8
NEBRASKA	7.2	17.9	10.0	13.4	12.1	14.2	11.7	6.7	6.8	36.2	513 227	17.9	90.4	28.6
District 1	7.1	17.4	11.2	13.3	12.0	14.0	11.6	6.6	6.7	35.8	179 898	17.6	91.0	28.2
District 2	7.8	18.6	10.2	15.6	13.1	13.8	10.6	5.5	4.8	33.4	192 328	21.6	90.8	36.2
District 3	6.7	17.7	8.4	11.1	11.1	14.7	13.0	8.3	9.0	40.6	141 001	13.2	89.1	20.9
NEVADA	6.9	17.7	9.2	14.3	14.2	13.9	11.7	7.3	4.7	36.3	674 712	10.4	84.7	21.7
District 1	7.8	19.3	9.6	14.8	14.8	13.4	10.2	6.1	4.0	33.9	201 264	8.7	78.5	16.6
District 2	6.6	17.0	9.3	12.5	12.7	14.5	13.4	8.6	5.4	38.9	215 091	9.4	86.6	22.0
District 3	6.5	17.0	8.8	16.4	14.9	13.9	11.5	7.2	4.7	36.5	258 357	12.7	87.5	25.0
NEW HAMPSHIRE	5.3	16.5	9.4	11.0	13.6	17.2	13.5	7.4	6.2	41.1	326 024	22.3	91.5	32.8
District 1	5.4	16.5	9.3	11.4	13.8	17.2	13.3	7.1	6.0	40.7	157 038	19.6	91.7	32.9
District 2	5.2	16.5	9.4	10.5	13.4	17.1	13.8	7.6	6.4	41.5	168 986	24.8	91.3	32.6
NEW JERSEY	6.2	17.3	8.7	12.6	14.1	15.7	11.9	7.0	6.5	39.0	2 298 400	19.5	88.0	35.4
District 1	6.4	17.5	9.6	13.2	13.6	15.4	11.8	6.5	5.9	37.6	181 464	17.9	86.9	25.5
District 2	6.0	17.3	8.9	11.6	13.3	15.9	12.6	7.7	6.7	39.9	169 363	13.5	85.5	22.5
District 3	5.3	16.7	7.4	10.5	13.1	16.1	13.2	9.0	8.8	43.0	167 622	18.8	91.5	33.6
District 4	7.0	18.2	8.2	11.4	12.9	14.9	11.6	7.8	8.1	39.4	190 198	30.3	89.8	29.4
District 5	5.2	19.3	7.2	8.5	14.0	18.0	13.1	7.5	7.2	42.5	178 485	20.3	93.3	44.0
District 6	6.4	15.9	11.5	14.3	14.0	14.9	11.5	6.1	5.4	36.4	182 797	16.2	87.6	35.9
District 7	5.8	18.6	6.7	10.7	14.7	17.8	12.5	6.7	6.6	41.0	172 179	20.5	91.9	47.7
District 8	6.7	17.8	9.7	13.1	14.1	14.6	11.4	6.3	6.2	37.0	178 235	16.1	84.8	33.9
District 9	6.0	14.6	8.2	15.2	14.7	15.0	12.2	7.1	7.0	39.1	153 289	20.8	87.6	35.5
District 10	7.0	18.0	10.6	14.5	14.3	14.4	10.6	5.9	4.6	34.9	181 022	14.8	81.8	22.5
District 11	5.5	18.8	6.8	10.0	14.7	17.5	12.6	7.2	6.7	41.5	179 519	23.1	93.9	48.9
District 12	5.5	17.8	8.5	10.7	14.3	16.6	12.4	7.0	7.1	40.6	194 750	23.0	92.4	48.9
District 13	7.2	14.8	10.4	20.6	15.5	12.9	9.1	5.2	4.3	33.4	169 477	16.9	76.5	29.7
NEW MEXICO	7.0	18.1	9.9	13.0	12.1	14.2	12.5	7.5	5.8	36.7	560 391	9.9	83.3	25.0
District 1	6.7	17.1	10.3	14.0	12.5	14.5	12.4	6.9	5.6	36.6	192 790	14.5	86.0	30.4
District 2	7.3	18.6	10.5	12.4	11.3	13.6	12.1	8.0	6.3	36.1	178 825	5.0	79.6	18.8
District 3	7.2	18.8	8.9	12.5	12.4	14.4	12.9	7.5	5.3	37.2	188 776	9.9	84.1	25.3
NEW YORK	6.0	16.4	10.2	13.7	13.5	14.9	11.9	7.0	6.5	38.0	5 032 081	23.3	84.9	32.5
District 1	5.7	17.7	9.1	11.0	14.2	16.2	12.4	7.5	6.3	40.0	179 250	15.1	91.8	34.0
District 2	5.9	19.0	8.2	11.1	14.3	16.5	11.6	7.1	6.3	39.5	181 058	14.6	88.4	33.9
District 3	5.1	17.4	8.0	10.4	13.6	17.5	13.0	7.4	7.7	42.2	164 551	22.6	92.4	37.2
District 4	5.9	17.6	9.4	11.8	13.3	15.5	12.3	6.9	7.3	39.3	179 056	26.5	85.4	36.1
District 5	5.6	14.7	8.7	14.1	14.2	15.1	12.3	7.5	7.8	39.9	162 166	23.7	81.3	37.2
District 6	6.4	17.6	10.8	14.0	13.7	14.9	11.1	6.6	5.0	35.9	186 970	21.0	79.2	22.6
District 7	6.2	15.7	9.8	15.6	14.7	14.2	11.0	6.8	6.0	36.7	153 878	19.1	76.7	24.1
District 8	6.3	11.8	10.5	20.2	14.4	12.4	11.2	6.7	6.5	35.7	154 249	54.5	86.4	54.7
District 9	6.0	14.4	8.8	14.1	13.5	14.5	13.1	7.6	8.0	39.9	152 386	30.7	86.6	37.6
District 10	7.5	18.8	11.4	15.6	13.3	13.1	10.0	5.9	4.4	32.7	205 158	27.6	80.7	25.1
District 11	6.8	16.0	10.1	17.6	14.4	13.5	10.9	6.2	4.6	34.7	176 110	23.2	82.8	32.2
District 12	6.3	14.6	11.5	21.5	14.9	12.3	9.2	5.3	4.3	32.8	163 535	20.0	69.8	28.6
District 13	6.0	16.2	9.2	13.7	14.1	15.0	12.4	7.0	6.4	38.6	171 470	24.5	83.8	29.0

1. All persons 3 years old and over enrolled in nursery school through college and graduate or professional school. 2. Persons 25 years old and over.

Table E. Congressional Districts 112th Congress — **Households and Group Quarters**

STATE District	Households, 2010						Group quarters, 2010					
	Number	Persons per household	Family households (percent)	Husband-wife family (percent)	Female family householder[1]	One person households (percent)	Total in group quarters	Percent 65 years and over	Persons in correctional institutions	Persons in nursing homes	Persons in college dormitories	Persons in military quarters
	29	30	31	32	33	34	35	36	37	38	39	40
MISSISSIPPI	1 115 768	2.58	69.0	45.4	18.5	26.3	91 964	16.0	34 273	16 496	26 472	3 938
District 1	299 632	2.58	70.3	49.1	16.2	25.4	18 629	23.6	2 924	4 603	7 786	0
District 2	240 529	2.65	68.9	36.9	26.3	27.0	22 979	11.8	14 750	4 075	8 476	8
District 3	290 731	2.52	67.8	46.4	16.6	27.6	30 571	17.2	9 775	4 554	5 828	601
District 4	284 876	2.58	69.1	47.7	16.1	25.4	19 785	14.6	6 824	3 264	4 382	3 329
MISSOURI	2 375 611	2.45	65.3	48.4	12.3	28.3	174 142	22.7	41 956	44 866	52 869	10 217
District 1	240 251	2.38	59.5	31.8	22.5	34.2	16 049	24.1	1 344	5 166	4 947	0
District 2	269 344	2.58	71.7	59.0	9.0	23.4	9 234	40.8	1 505	4 916	3 642	0
District 3	260 668	2.35	60.5	44.2	11.7	31.8	11 798	27.8	1 541	3 643	5 012	0
District 4	262 260	2.48	68.7	54.3	9.9	25.9	30 807	16.7	6 477	5 605	4 618	10 168
District 5	260 254	2.39	59.9	39.0	15.9	32.7	7 320	32.7	1 196	4 495	1 770	49
District 6	270 449	2.49	67.7	52.6	10.5	26.5	21 921	20.5	9 152	4 851	5 434	0
District 7	286 838	2.45	66.3	51.1	10.7	26.8	21 305	22.3	2 258	4 709	9 841	0
District 8	260 148	2.43	67.1	50.6	11.7	27.6	24 814	22.7	10 672	6 193	4 863	0
District 9	265 399	2.47	65.7	51.2	10.0	26.7	30 894	16.5	7 811	5 288	12 742	0
MONTANA	409 607	2.35	62.8	49.2	9.0	29.7	28 849	19.2	5 338	5 200	8 332	678
At Large	409 607	2.35	62.8	49.2	9.0	29.7	28 849	19.2	5 338	5 200	8 332	678
NEBRASKA	721 130	2.46	64.8	50.8	9.8	28.7	51 165	24.4	8 084	13 519	22 073	443
District 1	244 872	2.46	65.0	52.0	9.0	27.8	24 723	19.5	4 272	4 777	12 292	0
District 2	247 700	2.53	63.8	46.9	12.3	28.8	11 967	16.6	2 325	2 536	4 656	443
District 3	228 558	2.39	65.7	53.8	8.0	29.5	14 475	39.4	1 487	6 206	5 125	0
NEVADA	1 006 250	2.65	65.3	46.0	12.7	25.7	36 154	15.2	19 891	5 005	3 336	1 022
District 1	288 295	2.81	65.1	42.4	15.0	26.1	7 368	18.2	4 432	2 090	1 211	0
District 2	323 385	2.54	65.4	48.8	10.7	26.2	19 112	11.6	9 189	1 588	2 125	1 022
District 3	394 570	2.62	65.3	46.2	12.6	25.0	9 674	18.0	6 270	1 327	0	0
NEW HAMPSHIRE	518 973	2.46	66.3	52.1	9.7	25.6	40 104	19.5	4 851	7 767	22 820	454
District 1	260 415	2.46	65.8	51.5	9.9	25.8	16 923	20.7	1 640	3 762	10 357	454
District 2	258 558	2.46	66.8	52.8	9.5	25.5	23 181	18.6	3 211	4 005	12 463	0
NEW JERSEY	3 214 360	2.68	69.3	51.1	13.3	25.2	186 876	23.7	44 468	45 512	55 483	1 452
District 1	249 823	2.64	67.8	46.6	16.0	26.2	8 987	28.4	2 221	3 128	2 424	0
District 2	254 326	2.63	68.8	48.6	14.6	25.6	26 082	17.1	11 704	4 091	2 376	759
District 3	260 967	2.56	70.1	55.1	11.0	25.2	12 021	32.0	6 383	4 067	0	369
District 4	263 302	2.71	69.5	54.3	11.0	25.8	12 586	36.2	1 319	4 204	1 306	40
District 5	238 923	2.74	75.4	62.9	9.0	20.9	9 139	45.7	309	5 306	3 593	0
District 6	238 381	2.72	67.3	49.0	13.1	25.7	20 730	14.6	19	3 369	15 300	16
District 7	241 679	2.74	74.0	61.1	9.4	21.8	11 179	31.4	4 475	2 910	100	0
District 8	226 711	2.86	71.0	48.8	16.5	24.0	14 304	25.6	1 072	3 159	6 034	0
District 9	254 398	2.58	66.4	48.3	13.0	27.9	5 714	36.7	732	1 801	1 070	0
District 10	227 093	2.71	66.0	33.8	25.2	28.6	17 080	12.5	5 074	2 795	5 479	0
District 11	246 612	2.69	72.2	60.5	8.4	23.1	14 747	34.0	684	3 911	3 928	0
District 12	257 008	2.63	70.8	57.5	10.0	24.5	22 687	17.5	5 266	4 718	11 658	268
District 13	255 137	2.63	61.6	37.0	17.6	28.6	11 620	14.1	5 210	2 053	2 215	0
NEW MEXICO	791 395	2.55	65.5	45.3	14.0	28.0	42 629	14.3	17 907	5 567	8 478	1 789
District 1	281 431	2.45	62.1	42.1	13.8	30.1	7 831	15.8	4 489	1 768	2 750	530
District 2	246 715	2.62	68.5	47.9	14.4	25.9	20 743	11.4	9 874	2 263	3 613	815
District 3	263 249	2.59	66.5	46.2	13.8	27.6	14 055	17.6	3 544	1 536	2 115	444
NEW YORK	7 317 755	2.57	63.5	43.6	14.9	29.1	585 678	19.7	95 306	116 558	218 960	8 100
District 1	244 250	2.81	72.4	57.1	10.7	21.9	20 594	21.0	1 648	4 629	9 203	6
District 2	216 423	3.10	77.4	59.7	12.5	18.1	7 523	49.6	16	4 105	972	8
District 3	225 677	2.82	74.8	60.1	10.6	20.6	7 491	32.8	0	2 974	3 112	0
District 4	212 903	3.06	75.7	56.7	14.0	20.4	11 591	25.5	1 657	3 134	4 622	0
District 5	229 929	2.88	71.6	53.3	12.3	23.3	8 302	58.7	0	5 506	1 001	0
District 6	203 848	3.14	74.5	42.3	24.7	21.2	10 368	28.4	234	4 907	2 007	0
District 7	242 159	2.71	65.3	37.8	20.6	28.4	7 153	46.8	14	5 919	2 302	0
District 8	326 897	2.12	43.6	33.0	7.7	44.3	13 331	13.5	1 704	2 704	11 773	0
District 9	254 825	2.57	65.4	48.2	12.4	29.7	5 058	48.2	7	2 958	915	0
District 10	243 126	2.73	64.1	29.8	28.3	29.1	17 962	18.4	264	2 936	2 126	0
District 11	240 651	2.59	60.5	31.0	23.7	30.2	12 278	24.8	0	2 436	1 246	0
District 12	242 543	2.73	58.6	34.0	18.3	27.5	5 372	10.9	2 089	980	1 503	0
District 13	249 896	2.71	68.7	50.2	13.5	26.5	11 528	37.1	924	3 540	1 457	60

1. No spouse present.

1212 MS(District 1)—NY(District 13)

Items 29—40

Table E. Congressional Districts 112th Congress — **Housing and Money Income**

STATE District	Total	Percent occupied	Percent	Median value[1] (dollars)	Percent valued at $500,000 or more	With a mortgage	Without a mortgage[2]	Median rent[3]	Median rent as a percent of income	Sub-standard units[4] (percent)	Per capita income (dollars)	Median income (dollars)	Percent with income of $100,000 or more
	41	42	43	44	45	46	47	48	49	50	51	52	53
MISSISSIPPI	1 276 441	84.6	69.8	100 100	2.0	23.5	12.0	672	33.2	4.0	19 096	36 851	11.0
District 1	339 374	84.3	70.9	102 500	1.9	23.6	11.3	655	33.9	2.9	19 143	38 259	10.5
District 2	276 035	84	63.3	80 000	1.4	24.5	12.8	602	34.2	5.2	16 059	30 547	9.0
District 3	328 316	86.3	72.3	97 900	2.3	21.9	12.2	687	31.8	3.4	20 930	38 457	12.4
District 4	332 716	83.7	71.3	115 700	2.2	24.2	12.0	749	32.8	4.5	19 914	40 201	11.4
MISSOURI	2 714 017	86.6	69.0	139 000	3.4	22.6	11.7	682	30.1	2.2	23 920	44 301	15.2
District 1	279 936	85.7	58.8	113 600	3.4	24.7	13.1	738	33.2	2.2	22 358	37 440	12.5
District 2	281 367	94.4	80.5	218 100	7.8	21.6	11.7	822	26.8	1.4	34 736	70 146	32.6
District 3	291 513	89.2	67.6	161 900	3.4	22.7	11.7	691	30.6	1.9	26 626	48 868	16.9
District 4	325 801	79.6	72.3	119 400	2.2	22.7	11.3	628	27.8	3.2	20 635	42 113	11.0
District 5	299 490	85.4	61.1	130 800	2.8	23.5	13.0	732	32.5	2.3	24 170	43 525	15.1
District 6	299 052	88.8	71.3	137 300	2.3	22.0	12.1	689	27.3	1.7	24 726	50 464	17.3
District 7	329 954	85.5	66.9	118 300	2.7	22.7	11.4	631	30.6	2.2	20 638	38 404	10.2
District 8	299 484	84.8	69.2	96 200	1.8	21.5	10.9	554	31.2	2.8	18 759	35 288	8.1
District 9	307 420	87.3	71.9	135 200	3.7	22.6	11.1	654	29.3	2.6	22 240	41 829	13.2
MONTANA	483 006	83.4	69.7	181 200	6.3	24.1	11.3	642	28.3	2.8	23 552	42 666	13.0
At Large	483 006	83.4	69.7	181 200	6.3	24.1	11.3	642	28.3	2.8	23 552	42 666	13.0
NEBRASKA	797 677	90.2	67.4	127 600	2.0	21.4	12.6	669	27.7	2.2	24 744	48 408	15.7
District 1	267 027	92.2	67.3	133 600	2.2	21.3	12.1	654	27.7	2.5	24 357	49 602	16.1
District 2	268 793	92.5	64.2	146 600	2.6	22.0	12.9	765	29.2	2.1	27 280	52 306	19.9
District 3	261 857	85.7	71.0	94 800	1.1	20.6	12.9	569	24.9	1.9	22 271	43 757	10.6
NEVADA	1 175 070	84.2	57.2	174 800	5.9	28.1	12.2	952	31.6	5.0	25 284	51 001	18.5
District 1	345 027	80.7	48.3	144 600	3.0	29.1	12.5	885	32.3	8.0	21 248	43 916	14.2
District 2	373 704	86.4	62.1	190 000	8.5	26.6	12.8	871	31.9	3.7	26 350	49 352	18.6
District 3	456 339	85.1	59.4	186 300	5.3	28.4	11.4	1 089	30.7	3.8	27 494	57 239	21.6
NEW HAMPSHIRE	614 996	83.8	71.7	243 000	7.3	26.5	16.5	951	30.3	1.9	30 949	61 042	25.6
District 1	312 484	83.8	71.1	245 900	7.9	27.0	16.6	976	29.5	1.9	31 437	61 948	26.0
District 2	302 512	83.9	72.3	239 700	6.7	25.9	16.4	922	31.3	1.9	30 462	59 729	25.0
NEW JERSEY	3 554 909	89.2	66.4	339 200	21.7	28.7	18.9	1 114	32.4	4.1	33 555	67 681	32.5
District 1	268 839	93	69.0	214 200	3.7	28.3	19.3	943	35.1	1.8	28 109	58 089	23.7
District 2	344 069	73.4	73.6	235 300	10.2	28.9	18.1	974	35.6	2.6	26 790	55 993	23.5
District 3	308 568	82.9	82.4	273 700	11.0	27.3	18.2	1 280	35.5	1.2	34 159	70 743	32.1
District 4	289 918	90.9	76.9	302 000	15.8	28.9	19.4	1 181	35.9	2.6	31 663	64 265	30.5
District 5	252 578	93.2	82.4	425 900	36.7	28.6	19.5	1 216	32.3	1.1	41 858	90 587	45.2
District 6	258 644	89.9	62.4	344 500	15.7	28.8	18.5	1 184	31.6	5.1	30 902	69 417	32.5
District 7	248 869	95.5	79.6	408 900	33.5	26.6	17.6	1 305	28.3	2.1	44 400	94 843	47.7
District 8	239 429	92	56.1	379 900	21.7	31.4	20.3	1 101	35.9	11.3	30 183	60 473	29.3
District 9	270 566	93.3	51.8	389 600	25.3	30.8	21.9	1 206	31.8	3.8	31 380	61 224	28.5
District 10	256 981	86.2	39.9	297 900	11.8	35.0	20.7	968	32.5	10.0	22 687	45 313	17.9
District 11	258 698	93.8	78.7	444 200	40.3	27.8	17.7	1 281	29.5	1.3	45 407	93 514	46.6
District 12	274 657	93.8	76.2	384 700	29.5	27.3	17.6	1 155	29.2	1.9	41 719	86 685	44.3
District 13	283 093	88.6	30.6	334 300	17.5	34.3	22.3	1 064	30.2	10.2	26 477	49 264	20.9
NEW MEXICO	902 242	84.8	67.9	161 200	5.9	24.3	10.0	699	29.3	4.7	22 150	42 090	15.2
District 1	301 695	92.7	64.3	187 600	6.8	24.8	10.0	734	29.7	3.3	25 133	46 811	17.8
District 2	291 060	80.4	69.0	115 800	2.3	22.6	10.0	628	30.5	4.9	18 319	36 439	11.3
District 3	309 487	81.3	71.0	168 200	8.3	25.6	10.0	721	27.8	6.1	22 765	43 179	15.9
NEW YORK	8 108 211	88.8	54.3	296 500	24.4	26.3	15.5	1 020	31.7	5.5	30 011	54 148	24.8
District 1	301 738	80.5	79.3	381 400	26.0	30.0	18.8	1 371	36.2	2.5	34 715	80 674	37.9
District 2	228 777	95	80.3	416 400	31.6	30.7	19.8	1 387	32.4	3.2	35 585	84 909	42.7
District 3	232 945	94.1	82.4	440 800	33.0	29.8	19.9	1 478	31.8	2.1	39 751	92 064	46.2
District 4	222 945	94.7	76.9	433 500	31.4	31.2	19.6	1 323	36.2	3.6	34 156	82 102	41.4
District 5	244 350	93.8	55.3	594 200	62.6	31.4	15.5	1 318	33.8	9.1	32 044	61 429	30.2
District 6	225 690	92.7	51.1	421 400	24.8	35.5	14.4	1 141	34.0	8.7	22 122	55 769	22.9
District 7	249 146	92.5	32.9	418 400	32.6	32.0	15.8	1 112	31.8	10.2	22 090	45 918	15.6
District 8	347 075	87	28.8	752 800	77.4	24.8	15.0	1 363	29.7	8.9	53 920	63 146	35.7
District 9	267 845	92.5	49.5	512 800	52.0	29.9	16.9	1 197	32.6	6.3	28 464	54 716	23.9
District 10	269 947	88.7	30.9	495 100	48.9	34.8	16.7	1 008	31.1	11.0	21 144	41 602	18.1
District 11	262 942	91.4	24.9	581 300	59.5	29.6	15.9	1 105	32.9	10.8	26 012	45 070	20.2
District 12	272 513	89.7	19.4	593 400	64.2	33.5	19.8	1 111	32.0	14.9	23 516	41 891	17.1
District 13	268 368	92.5	60.8	481 200	45.7	29.5	17.4	1 129	33.8	5.3	28 652	60 445	29.8

1. Specified owner-occupied units. 2. Median monthly owner costs is often in the minimum category—10.0 percent or less, which is indicated as 10.0 percent. 3. Specified renter-occupied units. 4. Overcrowded or lacking complete plumbing facilities.

Table E. Congressional Districts 112th Congress — Poverty, Labor Force, Employment, and Social Security

| STATE District | Poverty, 2010 (percent) | | | Civilian labor force, 2010 | | | Civilian employment,[2] 2010 | | | | | Social Security beneficiaries, December 2010 | | |
	Persons below poverty level	Families below poverty level	Households receiving food stamps in past 12 months	Total	Unemployment Total	Unemployment Rate[1]	Total	Percent — Management, business, science, and arts occupations	Service, sales, and office	Construction and production	Persons under age 65 with no health insurance, 2010 (percent)	Number	Rate[3]	Supplemental Security Income recipients, December 2010
	54	55	56	57	58	59	60	61	62	63	64	65	66	67
MISSISSIPPI	22.4	17.8	16.4	1 340 288	165 085	12.3	1 175 203	31.0	41.7	27.3	20.8	596 637	201.1	125 507
District 1	20.4	15.5	14.2	359 213	44 626	12.4	314 587	29.6	39.6	30.8	20.1	167 079	212.0	28 688
District 2	29.8	25.0	23.8	290 449	46 722	16.1	243 727	28.2	45.8	26.0	23.6	130 585	195.4	43 506
District 3	19.5	15.5	14.1	342 948	33 073	9.6	309 875	35.3	40.9	23.8	18.0	151 095	199.6	29 243
District 4	20.8	16.5	15.0	347 678	40 664	11.7	307 014	30.1	41.4	28.4	21.8	147 878	196.1	24 070
MISSOURI	15.3	10.6	13.3	3 036 146	302 270	10.0	2 733 876	34.4	43.6	22.0	15.2	1 166 223	194.7	133 895
District 1	21.3	15.5	20.6	298 985	47 497	15.9	251 488	33.5	48.0	18.5	17.3	108 896	185.5	22 341
District 2	5.4	3.5	4.8	384 260	29 709	7.7	354 551	44.4	41.5	14.1	7.4	120 471	170.5	4 336
District 3	13.7	9.6	13.7	351 291	37 040	10.5	314 251	36.0	43.9	20.1	14.6	113 930	182.2	12 429
District 4	15.3	11.2	12.9	311 340	25 945	8.3	285 395	29.6	42.2	28.2	16.5	148 321	218.3	13 823
District 5	17.8	13.5	14.0	334 086	37 302	11.2	296 784	35.8	45.2	19.0	19.4	110 354	174.1	15 437
District 6	11.7	7.8	9.4	358 814	27 886	7.8	330 928	33.5	43.4	23.1	11.7	125 159	180.4	9 849
District 7	17.7	12.0	13.5	359 194	36 447	10.1	322 747	31.0	47.2	21.8	19.7	151 663	210.1	16 313
District 8	19.8	14.0	19.8	289 286	29 707	10.3	259 579	28.4	40.8	30.8	17.6	154 448	235.1	26 678
District 9	16.2	10.3	12.4	348 890	30 737	8.8	318 153	34.5	40.8	24.6	13.3	132 981	194.4	12 689
MONTANA	14.6	10.0	9.2	505 674	38 000	7.5	467 674	35.9	42.5	21.6	20.2	192 701	194.8	17 532
At Large	14.6	10.0	9.2	505 674	38 000	7.5	467 674	35.9	42.5	21.6	20.2	192 701	194.8	17 532
NEBRASKA	12.9	8.8	9.2	1 000 883	65 779	6.6	935 104	35.2	41.8	23.0	13.2	308 790	169.1	25 613
District 1	13.1	8.4	8.4	346 368	22 925	6.6	323 443	36.3	39.8	23.9	11.6	104 693	167.2	7 983
District 2	13.5	9.4	10.1	357 364	27 391	7.7	329 973	38.3	44.6	17.0	13.5	88 635	138.7	9 887
District 3	12.1	8.6	8.9	297 151	15 463	5.2	281 688	30.3	40.8	29.0	14.8	115 462	205.7	7 743
NEVADA	14.9	11.1	9.8	1 393 170	196 276	14.1	1 196 894	28.3	53.6	18.2	25.4	408 113	151.1	41 269
District 1	19.7	15.2	14.7	401 617	63 985	15.9	337 632	24.3	56.4	19.3	29.9	107 451	131.0	17 465
District 2	15.1	10.7	9.1	420 673	61 415	14.6	359 258	30.5	48.6	20.9	24.2	152 628	182.4	11 496
District 3	11.1	8.7	6.9	570 880	70 876	12.4	500 004	29.4	55.2	15.4	22.9	148 034	141.8	12 308
NEW HAMPSHIRE	8.3	5.3	8.3	742 209	57 634	7.8	684 575	38.9	41.2	20.0	12.8	254 752	193.5	17 910
District 1	7.7	5.4	8.4	375 347	28 094	7.5	347 253	38.0	42.4	19.6	13.7	124 485	189.2	8 693
District 2	8.9	5.1	8.2	366 862	29 540	8.1	337 322	39.8	39.9	20.4	11.8	130 267	197.8	9 217
NEW JERSEY	10.3	7.8	6.8	4 647 005	503 128	10.8	4 143 877	40.3	41.9	17.9	15.0	1 472 335	167.5	168 423
District 1	11.6	10.0	8.8	361 961	47 693	13.2	314 268	36.9	44.6	18.4	13.5	116 267	173.7	17 615
District 2	12.5	9.5	9.2	355 387	44 687	12.6	310 700	31.7	48.1	20.3	14.6	136 482	197.2	15 884
District 3	6.3	4.5	3.5	349 927	32 593	9.3	317 334	40.9	42.4	16.7	9.9	153 673	225.9	7 997
District 4	10.5	7.6	5.7	354 895	37 900	10.7	316 995	36.5	44.9	18.6	11.7	143 086	197.5	9 250
District 5	4.9	3.8	2.7	351 291	34 082	9.7	317 209	47.4	38.3	14.2	9.8	116 145	174.2	5 915
District 6	10.3	7.0	5.1	367 257	38 047	10.4	329 210	39.4	42.1	18.5	17.4	97 802	146.2	10 340
District 7	4.4	3.0	2.7	365 820	31 110	8.5	334 710	49.6	37.3	13.1	9.6	105 819	157.3	5 794
District 8	13.4	10.0	9.4	335 180	31 409	9.4	303 771	37.9	41.8	20.2	18.2	99 864	151.2	16 570
District 9	9.4	7.9	6.0	363 269	34 618	9.5	328 651	38.2	41.8	20.0	21.1	105 891	160.1	12 014
District 10	20.1	18.0	15.7	327 346	60 016	18.3	267 330	30.9	47.3	21.8	21.7	87 228	137.5	26 040
District 11	5.4	3.3	2.1	360 454	30 550	8.5	329 904	48.8	38.1	13.1	9.3	109 884	162.9	5 412
District 12	5.6	3.7	3.8	377 717	34 558	9.1	343 159	50.3	37.5	12.2	8.8	120 771	172.1	9 529
District 13	19.5	16.5	14.0	376 501	45 865	12.2	330 636	32.3	41.7	25.9	28.4	79 423	116.0	26 063
NEW MEXICO	20.4	15.7	13.0	959 218	90 942	9.5	868 276	35.5	44.0	20.4	22.4	360 242	174.9	60 487
District 1	18.0	14.7	11.7	358 143	31 161	8.7	326 982	40.0	42.8	17.2	19.9	113 036	161.0	16 883
District 2	22.7	17.6	15.9	289 104	31 953	11.1	257 151	29.7	44.0	26.3	23.7	125 335	188.8	22 409
District 3	20.8	15.0	11.7	311 971	27 828	8.9	284 143	35.7	45.3	19.0	23.8	121 871	175.8	21 195
NEW YORK	14.9	11.5	13.9	9 888 442	974 802	9.9	8 913 640	38.5	44.3	17.2	13.5	3 280 575	169.3	680 057
District 1	7.1	4.5	5.0	365 602	26 905	7.4	338 697	38.8	42.5	18.8	11.4	133 599	189.4	10 348
District 2	5.2	3.7	5.0	360 353	33 358	9.3	326 995	38.2	42.3	19.6	12.4	117 725	173.2	10 596
District 3	4.6	3.1	3.2	342 847	23 812	6.9	319 035	42.8	42.7	14.5	9.3	124 066	193.1	7 108
District 4	7.5	5.8	5.2	351 398	33 569	9.6	317 829	39.2	44.6	16.2	15.5	114 670	172.9	10 740
District 5	13.1	10.1	10.9	350 077	34 020	9.7	316 057	36.6	45.7	17.7	20.6	100 190	149.5	17 693
District 6	14.9	12.3	20.3	348 355	44 519	12.8	303 836	25.8	54.1	20.1	18.4	82 337	126.3	26 721
District 7	18.3	14.9	17.7	320 700	34 166	10.7	286 534	28.1	51.1	20.8	21.1	94 566	141.6	29 730
District 8	18.3	13.8	12.3	377 311	32 229	8.5	345 082	56.9	35.4	7.7	11.3	95 386	133.7	37 156
District 9	12.7	10.1	10.8	324 676	32 138	9.9	292 538	38.7	45.3	16.0	13.2	103 747	157.1	28 455
District 10	26.3	22.9	24.4	320 757	35 594	11.1	285 163	34.8	50.3	14.9	14.0	81 555	120.3	41 509
District 11	21.6	19.5	21.5	336 988	40 478	12.0	296 510	39.4	48.7	12.0	16.7	72 134	114.1	30 716
District 12	24.4	22.3	23.5	358 306	39 710	11.1	318 596	33.0	47.1	19.9	22.9	75 811	112.8	40 044
District 13	12.4	9.9	10.8	319 751	28 963	9.1	290 788	37.7	43.5	18.7	10.5	113 899	165.9	23 815

1. Percent of civilian labor force.　　2. Persons 16 years old and over.　　3. Per 1,000 resident population enumerated in the 2010 census.

Table E. Congressional Districts 112th Congress — **Agriculture**

STATE District	\: Agriculture, 2007 — Farms Number	Farms Operated by family or individual (percent)	Land in farms Acreage	Average size of farm (acres)	Farm Operators Total	Percent of farm operators Whose primary occupation is farming	Who live on the farm operated	Value of products sold Total ($1,000)	Average per farm	Percent of sales from Crops	Livestock	Government payments Total ($1,000)	Percent of farms
	68	69	70	71	72	73	74	75	76	77	78	79	80
MISSISSIPPI...................	41 959	86.6	11 456 241	273	60 669	35.9	68.5	4 876 781	116 227	34.2	65.8	231 382	41.0
District 1..............................	12 719	87.2	3 099 234	244	17 762	28.8	63.7	515 186	40 505	50.0	50.0	49 416	55.0
District 2..............................	9 068	77.4	4 859 239	536	13 366	40.0	54.5	1 691 439	186 528	74.8	25.2	151 762	56.3
District 3..............................	13 105	90.0	2 573 759	196	18 969	38.9	74.9	2 088 382	159 358	3.6	96.4	20 100	28.7
District 4..............................	7 067	91.3	924 009	131	10 572	37.4	82.6	581 774	82 323	12.1	87.9	10 105	18.7
MISSOURI	107 825	87.9	29 026 573	269	163 553	38.2	76.0	7 512 926	69 677	46.5	53.5	319 519	41.8
District 1..............................	73	72.6	8 349	114	111	38.7	53.2	3 429	46 973	98.7	1.3	31	20.5
District 2..............................	1 702	79.3	385 092	226	2 558	38.3	67.7	124 618	73 219	74.9	25.1	4 687	54.7
District 3..............................	1 432	86.8	283 002	198	2 147	34.6	77.9	36 976	25 821	48.6	51.4	1 317	29.7
District 4..............................	26 943	89.6	6 817 147	253	41 199	38.8	80.3	1 760 562	65 344	37.2	62.8	51 129	35.6
District 5..............................	611	83.6	94 011	154	931	34.9	76.7	21 409	35 039	77.4	22.6	504	21.1
District 6..............................	22 337	85.9	6 990 806	313	33 292	37.2	66.3	1 728 754	77 394	56.9	43.1	105 729	67.7
District 7..............................	12 488	91.2	2 076 703	166	19 419	37.9	86.5	1 081 603	86 611	8.2	91.8	9 113	14.9
District 8..............................	19 047	88.9	6 088 733	320	28 902	41.6	79.8	1 390 301	72 993	65.9	34.1	80 461	29.3
District 9..............................	23 192	86.3	6 282 730	271	34 994	36.0	71.6	1 365 273	58 868	52.8	47.2	66 549	49.3
MONTANA	29 524	76.6	61 388 462	2 079	46 903	47.1	75.4	2 803 062	94 942	45.4	54.6	221 977	44.3
At Large	29 524	76.6	61 388 462	2 079	46 903	47.1	75.4	2 803 062	94 942	45.4	54.6	221 977	44.3
NEBRASKA......................	47 712	83.5	45 480 358	953	71 924	55.9	71.2	15 506 035	324 992	44.1	55.9	387 340	73.2
District 1..............................	16 641	86.4	6 694 558	402	24 144	49.4	71.4	4 093 086	245 964	47.0	53.0	114 218	77.3
District 2..............................	426	82.9	98 590	231	662	42.9	75.5	52 204	122 545	95.1	4.9	1 437	49.5
District 3..............................	30 645	81.9	38 687 210	1 262	47 118	59.4	71.1	11 360 745	370 721	42.9	57.1	271 685	71.3
NEVADA	3 131	81.2	5 865 392	1 873	5 117	48.5	82.6	513 269	163 931	42.7	57.3	4 007	10.6
District 1..............................	52	71.2	1 315	25	78	44.9	65.4	1 637	31 481	(D)	(D)		0.0
District 2..............................	2 975	81.3	5 783 400	1 944	4 875	48.8	83.0	504 539	169 593	42.6	57.4	3 954	10.8
District 3..............................	104	83.7	80 677	776	164	40.2	78.7	7 093	68 202	(D)	(D)	53	9.6
NEW HAMPSHIRE	4 166	85.2	471 911	113	7 022	40.7	85.4	199 051	47 780	53.5	46.5	2 474	10.2
District 1..............................	1 460	84.2	115 574	79	2 466	40.3	86.3	47 650	32 637	69.2	30.8	606	8.2
District 2..............................	2 706	85.8	356 337	132	4 556	40.8	84.8	151 401	55 950	48.6	51.4	1 868	11.2
NEW JERSEY..................	10 327	84.0	733 450	71	16 182	42.6	78.8	986 885	95 564	86.3	13.7	6 988	8.3
District 1..............................	375	86.4	18 047	48	571	41.5	73.4	34 336	91 563	94.2	5.8	122	4.8
District 2..............................	2 686	85.1	252 773	94	4 169	47.3	78.5	471 147	175 408	93.5	6.5	2 908	11.6
District 3..............................	706	80.2	59 568	84	1 114	44.4	75.7	60 338	85 465	91.5	8.5	671	7.8
District 4..............................	1 181	79.3	68 692	58	1 917	48.0	77.0	119 235	100 961	78.5	21.6	587	5.3
District 5..............................	2 128	87.9	139 243	65	3 302	40.2	83.1	105 606	49 627	60.6	39.4	1 278	8.2
District 6..............................	108	78.7	4 304	40	172	45.9	60.5	23 521	217 787	88.8	11.2		0.0
District 7..............................	1 429	85.0	87 389	61	2 184	35.8	83.1	42 937	30 047	66.8	33.2	599	7.0
District 8..............................	15	40.0	175	12	37	43.2	10.8	5 642	376 133	99.9	0.1		0.0
District 9..............................	6	50.0	(D)	X	10	50.0	30.0	(D)	(D)	(D)	(D)		0.0
District 10..............................	7	71.4	83	12	15	26.7	46.7	(D)	(D)	(D)	(D)	(D)	(D)
District 11..............................	495	81.0	22 332	45	782	38.2	77.0	28 766	58 113	84.2	15.8	109	3.6
District 12..............................	1 190	82.4	80 773	68	1 908	39.5	76.3	95 270	80 059	90.8	9.2	715	9.9
District 13..............................	1	100.0	(D)	(D)	1	0.0	100.0	(D)	(D)	(D)	(D)	(D)	(D)
NEW MEXICO	20 930	86.9	43 238 049	2 066	32 109	44.2	72.5	2 175 080	103 922	25.4	74.6	43 377	15.9
District 1..............................	1 477	87.1	2 269 536	1 537	2 196	37.6	72.4	70 914	48 012	34.2	65.8	739	6.2
District 2..............................	7 559	84.2	21 591 388	2 856	11 838	43.0	73.9	1 155 121	152 814	29.5	70.5	14 137	14.3
District 3..............................	11 894	88.6	19 377 125	1 629	18 075	45.9	71.5	949 044	79 792	19.8	80.2	28 501	18.1
NEW YORK	36 352	84.2	7 174 743	197	57 984	50.3	83.4	4 418 634	121 551	35.3	64.7	62 652	29.1
District 1..............................	493	51.3	27 736	56	892	60.2	50.7	203 046	411 858	91.8	8.2	(D)	11.0
District 2..............................	86	48.8	6 487	75	148	51.4	53.4	39 453	458 756	96.2	3.8	(D)	1.2
District 3..............................	55	41.8	1 430	26	86	38.4	30.2	14 251	259 109	(D)	(D)	(D)	(D)
District 4..............................	10	30.0	39	4	17	29.4	17.6	1 982	198 200	(D)	(D)	(D)	(D)
District 5..............................	X	X	X	X	X	X	X	X	X	X	X	X	X
District 6..............................	2	0.0	(D)	(D)	11	0.0	0.0	(D)	(D)	(D)	(D)	(D)	0.0
District 7..............................	X	X	X	X	X	X	X	X	X	X	X	X	X
District 8..............................	X	X	X	X	X	X	X	X	X	X	X	X	X
District 9..............................	3	100.0	3	1	4	25.0	100.0	161	53 667	100.0	0.0		0.0
District 10..............................	X	X	X	X	X	X	X	X	X	X	X	X	X
District 11..............................	X	X	X	X	X	X	X	X	X	X	X	X	X
District 12..............................	X	X	X	X	X	X	X	X	X	X	X	X	X
District 13..............................	14	57.1	(D)	X	25	16.0	20.0	5 174	369 571	100.0	0.0		0.0

1. Specified owner-occupied units. 2. Median monthly owner costs is often in the minimum category—10.0 percent or less, which is indicated as 10.0 percent. 3. Specified renter-occupied units. 4. Overcrowded or lacking complete plumbing facilities.

Table E. Congressional Districts 112th Congress — **Land Area and Population Characteristics**

STATE District	Representative, 112th Congress	Land area,[1] 2010 (sq km)	Total persons	Per square kilometer	White	Black	American Indian, Alaska Native	Asian and Pacific Islander	Some other race	Two or more races	Hispanic or Latino[2]	Non-Hispanic White alone	Percent female	Percent foreign born	Percent born in state of residence
		1	2	3	4	5	6	7	8	9	10	11	12	13	14
NEW YORK—Cont'd															
District 14	Carolyn B. Maloney (D)	32	652 681	20 168.0	73.2	5.2	0.3	13.6	4.9	2.9	13.7	65.7	53.6	28.8	43.7
District 15	Charles B. Rangel (D)	27	639 873	24 078.1	34.5	31.8	1.0	4.5	22.5	5.6	46.1	20.9	52.4	33.0	45.1
District 16	José E. Serrano (D)	31	693 819	22 684.1	21.4	35.9	1.7	1.8	32.9	6.2	66.5	2.4	53.0	35.5	49.7
District 17	Eliot L. Engel (D)	328	678 558	2 066.5	46.9	32.7	0.6	4.9	11.3	3.5	25.6	37.2	53.0	31.5	54.8
District 18	Nita M. Lowey (D)	572	674 825	1 180.2	71.3	10.3	0.4	6.5	8.4	3.1	22.6	59.7	51.6	24.9	60.1
District 19	Nan Hayworth (R)	3 608	699 959	194.0	83.4	6.5	0.3	3.3	4.0	2.5	12.9	76.1	50.1	12.4	69.9
District 20	Christopher P. Gibson (R)	18 129	683 198	37.7	93.5	2.5	0.2	1.3	0.8	1.6	3.2	91.5	50.0	4.2	75.1
District 21	Paul Tonko (D)	5 000	679 193	135.8	81.7	9.6	0.3	3.5	2.1	2.7	5.4	79.2	51.4	7.5	77.8
District 22	Maurice D. Hinchey (D)	8 390	679 297	81.0	79.4	9.5	0.4	3.2	4.3	3.1	11.9	73.6	50.7	9.9	70.1
District 23	William L. Owens (D)	34 219	664 245	19.4	93.2	2.7	1.1	0.9	0.7	1.5	2.6	91.7	49.3	3.7	78.5
District 24	Richard Hanna (R)	15 946	657 222	41.2	91.3	3.9	0.3	1.6	1.0	1.9	3.3	89.5	50.3	4.9	81.1
District 25	Ann Marie Buerkle (R)	4 186	668 869	159.8	84.6	8.5	0.6	2.6	1.1	2.5	3.9	82.7	51.6	6.4	78.1
District 26	Kathleen C. Hochul (D)	7 068	674 804	95.5	90.9	4.0	0.4	2.3	0.8	1.6	2.8	89.3	51.0	6.1	82.6
District 27	Brian Higgins (D)	4 733	629 271	132.9	87.9	5.8	0.8	1.4	2.1	1.9	6.2	84.8	51.2	5.2	81.3
District 28	Louise McIntosh Slaughter (D)	1 380	611 838	443.4	61.3	30.2	0.6	2.2	2.8	2.9	7.7	58.1	52.3	7.2	75.6
District 29	Tom Reed (R)	14 642	663 727	45.3	91.3	3.3	0.6	2.5	0.6	1.7	2.3	89.5	50.7	4.6	76.9
NORTH CAROLINA		125 920	9 535 483	75.7	68.5	21.5	1.3	2.3	4.3	2.2	8.4	65.3	51.3	7.5	58.5
District 1	G. K. Butterfield (D)	18 643	635 936	34.1	44.2	49.6	0.8	0.7	2.9	1.6	5.2	42.6	52.0	3.4	73.4
District 2	Renee Ellmers (R)	10 235	741 576	72.5	60.2	28.4	0.8	1.2	6.7	2.6	12.4	55.9	50.8	7.5	60.1
District 3	Walter B. Jones (R)	15 977	735 979	46.1	75.4	16.7	0.5	1.4	3.5	2.5	7.4	72.4	49.9	5.1	53.2
District 4	David E. Price (D)	3 233	826 878	255.8	66.9	19.3	0.4	6.5	4.4	2.4	9.1	63.1	51.7	12.7	42.8
District 5	Virginia Foxx (R)	11 363	693 414	61.0	85.6	7.8	0.3	1.2	3.5	1.6	6.5	83.1	51.2	5.3	67.9
District 6	Howard Coble (R)	7 592	714 412	94.1	82.3	10.2	0.5	1.8	3.4	1.7	6.9	79.4	51.5	6.8	64.8
District 7	Mike McIntyre (D)	15 722	742 938	47.3	64.3	20.8	8.0	0.9	3.9	2.1	6.9	62.1	51.2	5.7	61.3
District 8	Larry Kissell (D)	8 492	709 449	83.5	58.3	28.4	1.9	2.3	6.1	2.9	11.5	54.3	51.3	8.4	58.0
District 9	Sue Wilkins Myrick (R)	2 552	852 377	334.0	75.5	15.1	0.4	3.2	3.7	2.1	8.2	71.7	51.6	9.3	47.0
District 10	Patrick T. McHenry (R)	8 546	689 468	80.7	84.7	8.8	0.3	1.9	2.6	1.7	5.5	82.3	50.7	4.3	68.4
District 11	Heath Shuler (D)	15 601	703 606	45.1	89.1	4.1	1.6	0.9	2.5	1.8	5.6	86.5	51.5	4.8	56.9
District 12	Melvin L. Watt (D)	2 122	736 346	347.0	42.4	43.9	0.5	3.5	7.2	2.5	12.4	38.6	51.9	11.1	58.4
District 13	Brad Miller (D)	5 840	753 104	129.0	60.1	28.5	0.6	2.7	5.5	2.5	10.6	56.2	51.3	11.3	55.3
NORTH DAKOTA		178 711	672 591	3.8	90.0	1.2	5.4	1.0	0.5	1.8	2.0	88.9	49.5	2.5	68.6
At Large	Rick Berg (R)	178 711	672 591	3.8	90.0	1.2	5.4	1.0	0.5	1.8	2.0	88.9	49.5	2.5	68.6
OHIO		105 829	11 536 504	109.0	82.7	12.2	0.2	1.7	1.1	2.1	3.1	81.1	51.2	4.1	75.1
District 1	Steve Chabot (R)	1 078	598 699	555.6	64.5	30.5	0.2	1.4	1.1	2.2	2.6	63.4	51.8	4.6	75.3
District 2	Jean Schmidt (R)	6 753	673 873	99.8	90.9	4.4	0.2	2.2	0.6	1.6	1.8	89.7	51.2	4.5	71.3
District 3	Michael R. Turner (R)	4 130	640 899	155.2	78.6	16.7	0.2	1.8	0.6	2.0	1.9	77.6	51.4	3.0	73.3
District 4	Jim Jordan (R)	11 954	632 771	52.9	91.5	5.1	0.2	0.7	0.6	1.8	2.0	90.3	49.9	1.2	82.0
District 5	Robert E. Latta (R)	15 856	627 799	39.6	94.4	1.5	0.2	0.6	1.6	1.6	5.1	91.6	50.7	1.9	80.9
District 6	Bill Johnson (R)	13 410	623 742	46.5	94.8	2.6	0.2	0.7	0.3	1.4	1.1	94.1	50.7	1.3	68.5
District 7	Steve Austria (R)	7 353	683 371	92.9	84.8	10.2	0.2	1.3	1.0	2.4	2.4	83.7	50.5	3.8	74.0
District 8	John A. Boehner (R)	5 205	663 644	127.5	88.4	6.1	0.2	1.9	1.4	2.1	3.1	86.9	51.0	3.8	72.2
District 9	Marcy Kaptur (D)	2 844	619 010	217.7	78.6	15.3	0.3	1.3	1.7	2.9	5.4	75.7	51.1	3.5	77.7
District 10	Dennis J. Kucinich (D)	504	599 205	1 188.7	83.5	8.8	0.2	2.2	2.9	2.4	7.5	80.0	51.8	8.3	75.3
District 11	Marcia L. Fudge (D)	348	540 432	1 551.5	34.7	59.8	0.2	2.4	1.0	2.0	2.6	33.6	53.7	5.6	72.3
District 12	Patrick J. Tiberi (R)	2 621	756 303	288.6	70.1	21.9	0.2	3.7	1.5	2.6	3.5	68.5	51.7	8.5	67.1
District 13	Betty Sutton (D)	1 372	649 102	473.3	82.2	12.1	0.2	1.8	1.3	2.4	4.6	79.6	51.7	4.2	77.2
District 14	Steven C. LaTourette (R)	4 637	648 128	139.8	92.1	3.7	0.1	1.8	0.9	1.5	2.3	90.8	51.1	4.7	75.8
District 15	Steve Stivers (R)	3 032	681 557	224.8	81.7	9.3	0.2	3.9	2.3	2.6	4.5	79.8	50.3	7.7	69.9
District 16	Jim Renacci (R)	4 481	644 691	143.9	91.8	5.0	0.2	0.8	0.4	1.8	1.5	90.8	51.3	2.2	80.2
District 17	Tim Ryan (D)	2 598	600 111	231.0	83.5	12.2	0.2	1.0	0.8	2.2	2.7	82.1	51.3	2.8	77.0
District 18	Bob Gibbs (R)	17 656	653 167	37.0	95.5	1.9	0.2	0.3	0.3	1.6	1.0	94.9	50.6	1.0	83.1
OKLAHOMA		177 660	3 751 351	21.1	72.2	7.4	8.6	1.8	4.1	5.9	8.9	68.7	50.5	5.5	60.8
District 1	John Sullivan (R)	4 490	754 310	168.0	70.7	9.2	6.9	2.2	5.0	6.0	9.8	67.1	51.2	6.8	58.7
District 2	Dan Boren (D)	53 169	729 887	13.7	67.5	3.5	18.8	0.6	1.7	7.9	4.1	66.0	50.3	2.1	60.4
District 3	Frank D. Lucas (R)	88 239	732 394	8.3	80.4	3.7	6.6	1.2	3.6	4.6	8.5	76.7	49.6	4.5	63.8
District 4	Tom Cole (R)	26 409	785 424	29.7	76.7	6.6	6.2	2.3	2.6	5.7	7.4	73.2	50.2	4.4	60.9
District 5	James Lankford (R)	5 353	749 336	140.0	65.3	13.9	4.8	2.8	7.7	5.4	14.5	60.2	51.2	9.6	60.4
OREGON		248 608	3 831 074	15.4	83.6	1.8	1.4	4.0	5.3	3.8	11.7	78.5	50.5	9.8	45.5
District 1	Suzanne Bonamici (D)	7 626	802 570	105.2	80.3	1.6	0.9	7.0	6.2	4.0	13.3	74.4	50.3	13.2	44.2
District 2	Greg Walden (R)	179 979	769 987	4.3	87.6	0.6	2.2	1.2	5.4	3.1	12.3	81.8	50.2	6.0	43.5
District 3	Earl Blumenauer (D)	2 633	762 155	289.5	76.8	5.2	1.1	7.0	5.4	4.5	11.2	72.4	50.7	14.0	46.0
District 4	Peter A. DeFazio (D)	44 478	739 234	16.6	89.6	0.7	1.4	2.1	2.5	3.8	6.8	86.1	50.7	4.8	44.9
District 5	Kurt Schrader (D)	13 892	757 128	54.5	84.2	0.9	1.4	2.8	7.2	3.5	14.9	77.9	50.6	10.5	49.0

1. Dry land or land partially or temporarily covered by water.   2. May be of any race.

Table E. Congressional Districts 112th Congress — **Age and Education**

	Population and population characteristics, 2010 (cont.)										Education, 2010			
	Age (percent)										Enrollment[1]		Attainment[2] (percent)	
STATE District	Under 5 years	5 to 17 years	18 to 24 years	25 to 34 years	35 to 44 years	45 to 54 years	55 to 64 years	65 to 74 years	75 years and over	Median age	Total	Percent private	High school graduate or more	Bachelor's degree or more
	15	16	17	18	19	20	21	22	23	24	25	26	27	28
NEW YORK—Cont'd														
District 14	4.4	8.0	10.3	24.7	14.8	12.0	11.2	7.7	6.9	36.4	114 621	47.4	91.5	64.1
District 15	5.5	14.0	12.8	17.7	14.1	13.4	10.5	6.6	5.5	35.0	177 543	32.2	75.1	37.4
District 16	8.5	21.3	12.8	14.9	13.3	12.8	8.4	4.8	3.2	29.7	214 358	13.3	60.5	9.6
District 17	7.3	18.3	9.8	13.4	13.1	13.9	11.0	6.7	6.4	35.9	194 559	32.5	83.7	31.4
District 18	6.0	18.2	8.3	11.3	13.9	15.5	12.1	7.3	7.4	39.8	181 682	27.5	87.7	48.6
District 19	5.9	19.1	8.5	9.9	14.1	17.2	12.5	6.9	5.9	40.1	197 481	23.7	90.0	37.2
District 20	5.0	16.3	8.5	10.3	13.2	16.8	14.2	8.6	7.1	42.8	157 676	18.5	90.1	29.2
District 21	5.5	15.7	11.7	12.6	12.4	15.0	12.7	6.9	7.5	39.0	179 111	21.6	88.7	30.6
District 22	5.5	15.6	13.4	11.9	12.3	15.0	12.3	7.2	6.7	38.2	191 918	21.5	85.7	27.1
District 23	6.0	16.3	12.1	11.8	12.6	15.5	12.3	7.4	6.1	38.5	171 999	14.8	86.5	20.6
District 24	5.4	16.1	10.8	11.1	12.1	15.5	13.2	8.0	7.7	40.7	167 550	14.8	87.0	22.2
District 25	5.8	17.3	9.9	11.3	12.6	15.9	12.7	7.2	7.3	40.0	175 525	19.9	89.8	32.3
District 26	5.1	16.4	10.7	10.7	12.6	16.2	13.0	7.5	7.8	41.1	176 929	14.9	91.1	30.8
District 27	5.5	16.1	9.9	11.9	12.4	15.6	12.9	7.9	7.8	40.7	155 436	14.6	87.9	24.5
District 28	6.2	16.6	11.8	13.5	11.9	14.6	11.9	6.7	6.9	36.8	169 087	21.2	85.8	25.6
District 29	5.5	17.0	10.2	10.5	12.2	15.6	13.4	8.1	7.5	40.9	176 769	25.0	90.7	30.9
NORTH CAROLINA	6.6	17.3	9.8	13.1	13.9	14.4	11.9	7.3	5.6	37.4	2 526 366	14.4	84.7	26.5
District 1	6.6	16.8	10.2	11.9	11.7	14.7	13.1	8.2	6.8	39.0	164 568	11.1	77.1	13.4
District 2	7.5	18.2	11.7	13.8	13.9	13.3	10.6	6.2	4.6	34.0	215 418	14.9	83.2	18.8
District 3	6.9	16.1	13.3	13.1	12.2	13.6	11.8	7.5	5.4	35.5	195 041	12.5	87.1	23.2
District 4	6.9	17.8	9.9	14.9	15.5	14.8	10.9	5.4	4.0	35.3	252 517	19.7	92.1	51.6
District 5	5.7	16.7	9.0	11.0	13.6	15.3	13.3	8.7	6.7	40.7	172 769	11.4	83.6	23.5
District 6	5.9	17.3	8.0	11.3	14.0	15.2	13.0	8.4	7.0	40.5	171 096	14.8	85.2	25.7
District 7	6.3	16.4	9.7	12.7	13.0	14.1	13.4	8.7	5.9	38.9	188 750	9.7	82.2	22.9
District 8	7.5	18.4	10.1	14.7	14.1	13.6	10.5	6.2	4.8	34.4	194 293	11.1	81.0	20.1
District 9	7.0	19.3	7.1	13.5	16.5	16.1	11.0	6.0	4.5	37.0	231 802	21.0	90.5	39.3
District 10	5.9	17.5	8.2	11.0	14.3	15.4	13.1	8.5	6.2	40.4	169 978	11.1	82.2	18.5
District 11	5.4	14.8	8.3	11.2	12.5	14.3	14.5	10.4	8.7	43.3	149 522	14.6	86.9	25.5
District 12	7.4	17.7	12.3	15.2	13.9	13.2	9.9	5.7	4.6	33.1	208 279	16.7	81.4	23.3
District 13	6.9	17.3	10.4	14.7	14.9	14.0	10.8	6.1	4.9	35.4	212 334	14.6	85.8	29.9
NORTH DAKOTA	6.6	15.7	12.0	13.5	11.2	14.4	12.2	7.0	7.5	37.0	169 128	10.7	90.3	27.6
At Large	6.6	15.7	12.0	13.5	11.2	14.4	12.2	7.0	7.5	37.0	169 128	10.7	90.3	27.6
OHIO	6.2	17.4	9.5	12.2	12.8	15.1	12.6	7.4	6.7	38.8	3 051 177	18.1	88.1	24.6
District 1	6.9	17.2	11.6	13.1	12.0	14.8	11.6	6.6	6.3	36.1	169 494	24.7	86.8	23.8
District 2	6.5	18.1	7.7	12.8	13.6	15.6	12.6	7.1	6.1	38.9	166 288	20.0	88.4	34.3
District 3	6.1	17.7	9.0	11.9	12.9	15.1	12.5	7.6	7.1	39.4	178 520	19.7	87.9	24.5
District 4	6.3	17.7	9.2	11.6	12.6	15.0	12.8	7.8	6.9	39.3	158 891	16.7	86.9	15.8
District 5	6.2	18.0	9.7	11.3	12.3	15.2	12.8	7.6	6.9	39.1	168 180	12.0	89.2	17.5
District 6	5.3	15.7	10.3	10.8	12.1	15.1	14.0	9.8	7.8	41.6	154 762	11.9	86.6	17.5
District 7	6.4	18.0	9.9	12.4	13.2	14.8	12.2	7.3	5.9	37.8	183 437	16.4	88.0	21.9
District 8	6.8	18.2	10.0	12.1	13.0	14.9	12.1	7.0	6.0	37.5	179 810	12.4	87.6	22.6
District 9	6.2	16.9	10.4	11.9	12.3	15.1	13.0	7.4	6.8	38.9	167 049	19.9	89.0	22.8
District 10	5.8	16.3	8.3	13.0	13.1	15.5	12.5	7.4	8.1	40.2	143 028	23.3	87.6	27.0
District 11	6.2	16.9	10.1	12.6	11.6	14.6	12.6	7.4	8.0	38.8	153 566	26.3	85.5	27.0
District 12	7.4	18.9	8.7	13.9	14.5	14.8	11.3	5.9	4.6	35.8	212 766	22.4	91.3	37.5
District 13	6.0	17.8	8.0	11.4	13.1	15.7	13.4	7.5	7.1	40.4	169 646	20.3	90.5	27.2
District 14	5.5	18.2	7.2	10.0	13.0	16.7	13.9	8.2	7.3	42.3	162 864	20.9	90.2	29.9
District 15	6.6	15.8	13.5	16.7	13.7	13.7	10.3	5.3	4.6	33.2	196 932	13.6	89.7	35.2
District 16	6.0	17.8	8.7	10.9	12.6	15.3	13.2	8.0	7.5	40.4	171 923	19.5	89.6	22.5
District 17	5.5	15.9	11.1	11.7	12.1	14.9	13.3	7.8	7.7	40.0	156 347	10.8	88.0	19.0
District 18	6.3	18.0	8.8	11.4	12.5	15.0	12.9	8.2	6.8	39.5	157 674	14.7	82.9	14.1
OKLAHOMA	7.0	17.7	10.2	13.5	12.3	14.0	11.7	7.5	6.0	36.2	993 212	10.6	86.2	22.9
District 1	7.3	18.3	9.4	14.0	13.0	14.1	11.6	6.7	5.8	35.8	198 236	15.7	88.5	27.4
District 2	6.6	17.8	8.9	11.6	12.0	14.2	12.8	9.2	6.9	39.3	178 577	5.8	83.1	15.1
District 3	6.8	17.5	10.8	12.8	11.8	14.2	11.9	7.8	6.4	36.9	197 735	8.1	86.2	22.0
District 4	6.9	17.5	11.3	14.2	12.4	13.9	11.3	7.1	5.4	35.1	209 975	8.6	88.0	22.7
District 5	7.6	17.6	10.4	14.9	12.4	13.7	11.2	6.6	5.7	34.6	208 689	14.3	85.3	27.3
OREGON	6.2	16.4	9.4	13.7	13.0	14.1	13.3	7.6	6.4	38.4	964 277	14.1	88.8	28.8
District 1	6.6	17.2	8.9	15.4	14.6	14.2	12.0	6.1	5.1	36.3	217 378	18.5	90.7	37.2
District 2	6.2	16.8	8.2	11.7	11.9	14.1	14.3	9.2	7.6	41.0	178 609	10.4	88.2	21.8
District 3	6.6	15.6	9.1	17.0	15.1	13.9	11.9	5.8	5.0	36.0	187 349	17.3	87.9	31.6
District 4	5.3	15.0	10.6	11.9	11.2	14.1	14.9	9.3	7.7	41.4	186 512	9.7	89.2	24.3
District 5	6.3	17.5	10.1	12.3	12.3	14.0	13.5	7.6	6.4	38.3	194 429	14.0	87.6	28.6

1. All persons 3 years old and over enrolled in nursery school through college and graduate or professional school.   2. Persons 25 years old and over.

STATE District		Households, 2010					Group quarters, 2010					
	Number	Persons per household	Family households (percent)	Husband-wife family (percent)	Female family householder[1]	One person households (percent)	Total in group quarters	Percent 65 years and over	Persons in correctional institutions	Persons in nursing homes	Persons in college dormitories	Persons in military quarters
	29	30	31	32	33	34	35	36	37	38	39	40
NEW YORK—Cont'd												
District 14	335 645	1.88	37.6	28.6	6.6	47.8	13 261	16.6	414	4 692	11 425	0
District 15	251 997	2.39	53.0	23.5	23.8	36.5	36 074	8.7	11 425	2 716	11 840	0
District 16	227 343	2.97	69.7	23.8	37.6	25.3	22 000	12.3	981	2 832	2 352	0
District 17	241 967	2.73	65.9	40.2	20.3	28.9	17 064	41.9	0	7 059	4 044	0
District 18	241 424	2.70	69.6	53.9	11.5	25.9	22 228	19.3	3 245	3 946	9 656	0
District 19	243 488	2.76	72.9	58.9	9.8	22.3	33 096	16.7	9 826	4 161	4 549	4 409
District 20	272 772	2.42	65.8	51.5	9.7	27.0	25 420	17.4	8 426	4 085	6 459	0
District 21	279 105	2.32	59.0	41.3	13.0	32.3	30 622	16.8	1 973	4 760	18 275	0
District 22	260 995	2.44	60.9	43.0	12.8	30.3	44 572	11.9	4 688	4 846	23 531	3
District 23	253 231	2.46	65.9	49.3	11.0	26.5	41 313	8.7	12 929	3 337	19 057	3 614
District 24	260 358	2.39	63.3	46.4	11.7	29.4	45 212	15.5	10 994	5 483	13 735	0
District 25	267 769	2.43	63.7	46.7	12.6	29.0	21 160	21.5	1 433	4 159	10 469	0
District 26	263 649	2.44	65.8	51.4	10.2	27.8	27 904	17.5	10 666	5 185	13 265	0
District 27	262 593	2.33	60.7	43.1	12.9	32.2	19 141	22.1	4 499	3 227	5 545	0
District 28	259 925	2.28	55.6	31.5	19.2	36.1	18 972	24.0	1 236	4 858	8 034	0
District 29	262 367	2.43	65.2	50.3	10.3	27.8	29 088	19.0	4 014	4 484	14 485	0
NORTH CAROLINA	3 745 155	2.48	66.7	48.4	13.7	27.0	257 246	16.6	61 680	46 638	89 795	26 326
District 1	251 591	2.43	65.4	40.4	20.2	29.7	20 282	17.7	10 052	4 942	2 870	3 621
District 2	271 902	2.61	69.1	48.3	15.6	25.0	39 168	10.4	7 387	3 845	13 982	5 444
District 3	283 662	2.48	69.1	52.6	12.1	24.7	28 640	8.1	4 759	3 108	5 163	16 722
District 4	324 883	2.48	64.8	50.7	10.6	27.1	25 514	10.3	1 118	2 282	15 199	0
District 5	282 500	2.41	67.7	52.7	10.7	26.8	14 079	26.6	2 028	3 491	4 967	0
District 6	288 300	2.45	69.1	53.7	11.1	25.9	8 884	30.4	1 633	2 858	2 769	0
District 7	296 567	2.44	66.3	46.6	14.7	27.1	18 696	16.5	7 435	3 585	5 424	538
District 8	268 583	2.58	67.7	45.7	16.7	26.3	18 634	17.8	6 914	3 655	4 779	0
District 9	329 467	2.57	68.9	53.6	11.4	25.1	4 455	45.2	715	2 736	1 206	1
District 10	270 889	2.50	70.2	52.8	12.3	25.2	11 642	22.8	4 726	3 128	2 397	0
District 11	296 556	2.31	64.6	49.8	10.4	29.2	18 679	27.2	2 999	5 519	6 755	0
District 12	281 845	2.50	62.3	37.0	19.9	29.8	24 587	12.4	4 490	4 338	16 986	0
District 13	298 410	2.45	62.6	43.3	14.6	29.4	23 986	15.4	7 424	3 151	7 298	0
NORTH DAKOTA	281 192	2.30	60.8	48.6	8.2	31.5	25 056	25.3	2 489	6 433	10 570	1 380
At Large	281 192	2.30	60.8	48.6	8.2	31.5	25 056	25.3	2 489	6 433	10 570	1 380
OHIO	4 603 435	2.44	65.0	47.2	13.1	28.9	306 266	24.0	76 590	83 019	106 042	571
District 1	243 608	2.39	59.9	37.6	17.4	33.2	16 258	22.7	1 860	4 593	7 060	0
District 2	269 010	2.48	66.9	51.8	10.7	27.4	7 045	51.5	811	4 509	712	0
District 3	259 051	2.39	64.5	46.3	13.7	30.0	21 642	23.1	6 214	5 443	6 456	0
District 4	243 854	2.49	68.4	52.1	11.4	26.4	27 709	18.0	13 689	5 113	4 912	0
District 5	244 496	2.51	69.0	54.3	10.0	25.4	15 388	29.7	1 422	4 914	6 786	0
District 6	249 767	2.40	66.4	50.6	11.0	27.9	25 143	23.8	7 084	5 420	10 627	0
District 7	260 570	2.52	68.6	50.5	13.1	25.5	27 835	14.4	11 487	4 019	8 019	547
District 8	253 573	2.56	69.3	52.1	12.3	24.9	16 987	23.6	1 168	3 845	7 393	0
District 9	250 394	2.39	63.4	43.4	15.0	30.1	13 481	22.7	5 838	5 126	5 890	0
District 10	255 531	2.31	59.1	40.9	13.6	34.5	8 135	53.3	121	5 304	1 820	0
District 11	234 266	2.22	55.3	28.3	22.3	39.0	21 249	20.9	3 012	4 822	6 448	0
District 12	298 648	2.49	65.4	47.1	13.8	27.9	13 327	24.5	598	3 885	6 561	0
District 13	260 492	2.45	66.3	48.2	13.6	28.3	9 503	37.2	1 286	4 556	2 103	0
District 14	254 680	2.51	69.3	55.1	10.0	25.8	12 200	40.4	1 891	4 440	1 338	24
District 15	274 464	2.39	57.7	41.6	11.4	31.1	24 619	8.3	9 536	2 376	11 351	0
District 16	252 864	2.49	68.4	52.8	11.2	26.6	14 816	30.5	814	5 304	6 824	0
District 17	245 139	2.37	62.9	43.2	14.6	30.2	15 538	17.2	5 313	3 908	7 638	0
District 18	253 028	2.52	68.8	52.5	11.2	26.0	15 391	31.2	4 446	5 442	4 104	0
OKLAHOMA	1 460 450	2.49	66.8	49.5	12.3	27.5	112 017	16.9	40 562	21 678	30 148	7 203
District 1	299 392	2.48	65.7	47.9	12.7	28.4	9 372	28.8	2 371	3 656	2 981	0
District 2	281 480	2.51	69.4	51.9	12.3	26.2	29 162	19.6	9 873	5 385	4 617	0
District 3	280 317	2.49	67.9	52.7	10.4	26.5	29 142	13.8	15 091	4 818	10 089	463
District 4	301 494	2.51	68.3	51.7	11.7	25.7	31 049	12.4	8 033	3 918	7 496	6 740
District 5	297 767	2.46	62.8	43.4	14.1	30.4	13 292	18.8	5 194	3 901	4 965	0
OREGON	1 518 938	2.47	63.4	48.3	10.5	27.4	86 642	18.0	22 203	11 491	23 704	178
District 1	316 857	2.47	62.8	49.2	9.3	28.7	17 905	16.5	5 150	2 060	5 092	127
District 2	307 014	2.45	66.2	50.9	10.5	26.6	18 652	19.1	8 762	2 660	1 775	13
District 3	300 491	2.49	59.3	42.6	11.7	28.2	13 409	21.8	1 556	2 481	3 682	0
District 4	306 072	2.37	62.4	47.3	10.4	27.9	14 589	21.8	1 312	2 067	4 551	21
District 5	288 504	2.55	66.6	51.6	10.4	25.7	22 087	13.5	5 423	2 223	8 604	17

1. No spouse present.

Table E. Congressional Districts 112th Congress — Housing and Money Income

STATE District	Housing units, 2010										Money income, 2010		
	Total	Occupied units									Households		
		Percent occupied	Owner-occupied					Renter-occupied		Sub-standard units[4] (percent)	Per capita income (dollars)	Median income (dollars)	Percent with income of $100,000 or more
			Percent	Median value[1] (dollars)	Percent valued at $500,000 or more	Median owner cost as a percent of income		Median rent[3]	Median rent as a percent of income				
						With a mortgage	Without a mortgage[2]						
	41	42	43	44	45	46	47	48	49	50	51	52	53
NEW YORK—Cont'd													
District 14	374 260	83.4	27.4	765 600	76.2	22.6	13.1	1 611	28.3	4.6	66 242	75 348	38.7
District 15	277 853	90.7	12.9	587 700	56.6	22.3	10.0	952	30.1	9.5	27 225	39 745	18.7
District 16	245 230	92.1	6.5	362 100	14.6	35.7	15.3	916	37.1	17.9	11 992	23 773	4.3
District 17	259 023	91.8	43.2	426 500	30.3	29.5	15.8	1 104	33.6	8.7	26 404	53 673	24.4
District 18	255 943	94.2	65.7	565 600	58.3	28.5	18.9	1 320	31.5	4.9	49 035	84 607	43.7
District 19	258 561	91.8	76.4	354 900	22.1	28.6	18.1	1 160	31.2	2.7	35 738	77 920	37.4
District 20	339 813	80.3	74.3	213 500	6.3	24.3	14.2	826	28.5	1.8	29 181	68 359	23.0
District 21	309 510	87.4	60.7	175 900	3.0	23.0	14.6	811	30.7	2.1	27 377	50 627	20.5
District 22	312 260	82.7	63.2	195 600	5.2	27.2	15.6	866	34.2	3.2	24 434	47 836	18.0
District 23	322 768	78.7	69.7	107 000	3.5	22.1	14.2	681	28.7	2.4	22 124	43 709	13.3
District 24	294 936	86.1	71.2	107 200	2.0	21.1	13.3	665	28.1	1.9	22 799	47 477	14.9
District 25	289 619	91.1	68.7	133 200	2.1	21.8	13.7	708	29.8	1.4	27 360	51 597	20.7
District 26	282 778	92.1	74.0	132 000	1.6	22.4	13.9	714	29.7	1.2	26 453	52 868	19.6
District 27	290 927	89.5	66.6	109 600	1.6	21.6	14.1	628	29.5	1.1	23 712	45 274	13.4
District 28	296 735	85.1	54.5	97 000	1.8	23.2	14.3	698	35.7	1.5	20 915	35 726	11.2
District 29	303 714	86.2	74.3	117 100	2.6	21.3	13.3	689	27.7	2.2	27 865	51 871	18.9
NORTH CAROLINA	4 333 479	84.7	67.2	154 200	5.6	24.0	12.5	731	31.3	2.8	23 432	43 326	14.6
District 1	291 475	83.4	61.3	94 500	2.1	25.6	16.1	642	34.4	3.0	17 690	32 370	7.3
District 2	297 471	87.4	65.8	130 800	1.9	23.5	14.1	746	33.5	3.3	19 177	41 233	11.1
District 3	361 964	78.1	66.7	155 100	5.4	24.8	13.2	771	30.7	1.6	23 907	45 390	14.1
District 4	349 870	90.9	64.7	246 200	10.7	22.1	10.0	850	29.8	1.9	32 454	63 543	28.9
District 5	331 931	83.3	73.5	144 400	4.1	23.1	11.5	658	33.1	1.9	22 835	40 801	12.8
District 6	313 401	90.6	73.0	155 500	4.9	23.8	12.1	677	27.4	2.9	24 372	46 040	14.8
District 7	366 583	78.5	67.8	152 600	7.3	25.7	13.7	734	33.0	3.6	21 797	40 171	12.4
District 8	308 647	85.2	64.7	130 700	2.5	24.6	14.0	736	31.0	3.7	20 029	41 256	12.1
District 9	353 233	92.1	72.5	202 100	10.6	23.4	11.5	823	29.9	2.0	32 329	59 081	25.9
District 10	312 570	84.2	73.7	126 100	5.3	23.1	11.8	643	30.5	2.2	20 796	40 262	10.3
District 11	382 655	77.5	71.1	166 700	6.3	24.6	10.7	698	31.0	2.4	22 299	39 650	10.0
District 12	327 772	85.4	54.6	127 800	2.9	25.9	13.6	714	32.6	4.0	19 298	38 266	9.5
District 13	335 907	86.6	62.4	159 400	5.2	24.1	11.9	748	30.3	3.5	23 968	43 866	15.4
NORTH DAKOTA	318 099	88.2	66.9	123 000	1.5	19.6	10.0	583	25.8	1.3	26 021	48 670	15.7
At Large	318 099	88.2	66.9	123 000	1.5	19.6	10.0	583	25.8	1.3	26 021	48 670	15.7
OHIO	5 128 113	88.2	68.4	134 400	2.2	23.4	13.1	685	31.1	1.8	23 975	45 090	15.3
District 1	278 676	84.6	58.5	130 000	1.9	24.1	14.7	662	34.7	3.0	22 499	39 847	13.5
District 2	293 604	89.3	73.6	162 500	5.4	23.7	13.8	742	28.2	1.1	30 289	56 052	22.7
District 3	289 527	85.5	66.7	129 500	2.6	24.0	14.0	679	32.1	1.3	23 631	43 212	14.3
District 4	273 149	89	71.3	115 300	1.2	22.7	11.8	635	28.0	1.9	21 062	43 186	10.7
District 5	265 874	89.6	75.5	116 400	1.2	22.2	12.0	614	28.7	1.5	22 051	45 123	12.5
District 6	278 632	87.7	74.3	98 800	1.2	22.3	11.8	585	32.8	1.2	20 628	38 543	10.4
District 7	286 495	90.2	67.3	135 500	1.5	23.0	11.7	714	30.5	2.2	23 100	46 633	14.9
District 8	280 902	90.5	71.3	135 700	1.5	22.8	12.9	714	31.5	2.2	23 739	48 985	16.0
District 9	291 150	84.5	67.0	122 600	2.0	23.9	13.2	646	32.5	NA	23 121	41 066	14.3
District 10	281 197	88.7	67.6	132 500	1.7	24.0	14.3	704	29.9	1.7	25 022	44 192	15.1
District 11	285 216	80.1	50.7	106 600	2.2	26.8	16.7	700	34.4	1.8	22 056	32 373	10.9
District 12	332 054	88.5	64.0	177 500	4.3	23.4	12.9	760	31.1	2.7	28 935	55 411	24.7
District 13	282 934	90.5	71.3	150 200	2.4	23.9	13.5	683	31.7	1.5	25 248	47 483	17.4
District 14	275 747	92.1	78.5	173 200	3.6	23.7	14.7	756	28.8	1.0	29 017	56 087	21.3
District 15	295 069	89.8	58.6	161 800	3.3	23.4	13.2	774	30.3	2.1	26 109	49 672	18.5
District 16	274 573	91.2	74.3	139 100	1.5	23.3	12.1	656	28.8	1.7	23 311	46 099	15.1
District 17	276 340	87.3	68.7	104 000	0.8	23.1	13.6	635	32.8	1.3	20 479	39 734	9.6
District 18	286 974	86.2	71.4	110 000	1.5	23.2	11.6	599	31.5	2.6	19 238	39 155	9.4
OKLAHOMA	1 666 205	86	67.8	111 400	2.1	21.9	11.2	659	28.9	3.0	22 254	42 072	13.3
District 1	332 678	89.5	65.6	134 300	2.7	22.1	11.5	702	29.3	2.9	25 216	45 677	16.2
District 2	338 604	82.7	72.7	86 700	1.5	21.6	11.1	570	28.0	3.5	18 581	37 011	8.5
District 3	324 810	84.4	69.4	97 000	1.6	20.8	11.0	594	27.1	2.9	21 140	41 509	12.2
District 4	335 876	86.8	68.6	115 800	1.5	21.8	10.9	699	29.0	2.8	22 213	45 876	13.9
District 5	334 237	86.6	63.0	119 300	3.2	22.9	11.5	689	30.3	3.1	23 965	41 262	15.0
OREGON	1 676 476	89.9	62.5	244 500	10.2	27.3	12.9	816	32.7	3.4	24 753	46 560	16.4
District 1	341 778	91.5	60.1	282 100	13.3	26.5	12.7	882	29.9	3.7	28 978	54 824	22.5
District 2	356 453	85.6	64.5	205 400	9.5	27.1	12.9	751	34.6	2.6	22 032	41 302	12.9
District 3	322 066	92.6	58.4	266 700	9.9	27.8	14.9	837	32.7	4.0	25 023	48 726	17.2
District 4	331 622	90.8	64.1	209 400	6.5	27.2	12.2	761	33.5	2.3	21 888	39 835	11.5
District 5	324 557	89.4	65.8	253 300	12.0	27.9	12.5	815	32.8	4.3	25 554	49 629	18.2

1. Specified owner-occupied units. 2. Median monthly owner costs is often in the minimum category—10.0 percent or less, which is indicated as 10.0 percent. 3. Specified renter-occupied units. 4. Overcrowded or lacking complete plumbing facilities.

Table E. Congressional Districts 112th Congress — Poverty, Labor Force, Employment, and Social Security

STATE District	Poverty, 2010 (percent) Persons below poverty level	Families below poverty level	Households receiving food stamps in past 12 months	Civilian labor force, 2010 Total	Unemployment Total	Rate[1]	Civilian employment,[2] 2010 Total	Percent Management, business, science, and arts occupations	Service, sales, and office	Construction and production	Persons under age 65 with no health insurance, 2010 (percent)	Social Security beneficiaries, December 2010 Number	Rate[3]	Supplemental Security Income recipients, December 2010
	54	55	56	57	58	59	60	61	62	63	64	65	66	67
NEW YORK—Cont'd														
District 14	11.1	6.7	6.2	399 486	31 479	7.9	368 007	59.3	34.5	6.2	11.4	96 127	147.3	14 024
District 15	24.0	20.0	24.7	331 606	41 186	12.4	290 420	43.7	44.5	11.8	17.1	89 209	139.4	49 115
District 16	38.9	36.8	51.4	301 099	57 665	19.2	243 434	15.3	62.0	22.7	18.3	71 512	103.1	66 931
District 17	17.2	14.3	16.8	334 697	37 720	11.3	296 977	38.1	47.1	14.7	14.8	102 065	150.4	25 497
District 18	7.9	5.6	4.4	353 040	27 681	7.8	325 359	47.7	39.7	12.5	12.8	115 213	170.7	11 394
District 19	7.3	4.7	4.8	349 661	29 566	8.5	320 095	42.3	41.4	16.3	10.3	118 092	168.7	8 589
District 20	7.9	5.2	7.4	361 137	31 763	8.8	329 374	38.0	41.4	20.5	10.9	149 560	218.9	14 788
District 21	14.7	11.3	12.5	359 991	33 753	9.4	326 238	40.7	44.4	14.9	11.3	129 959	191.3	18 201
District 22	16.9	11.3	13.8	339 099	34 777	10.3	304 322	36.3	43.8	19.9	13.2	136 183	200.5	20 283
District 23	14.6	10.7	14.8	310 758	32 532	10.5	278 226	31.9	42.4	25.7	12.1	136 099	204.9	19 393
District 24	13.8	9.1	13.3	320 389	28 698	9.0	291 691	35.0	42.8	22.3	10.8	140 394	213.6	19 315
District 25	12.4	8.4	10.3	343 726	27 086	7.9	316 640	39.5	42.0	18.4	10.4	136 149	203.6	17 936
District 26	10.0	6.7	8.5	348 698	27 385	7.9	321 313	38.2	41.8	20.0	7.8	139 338	206.5	10 805
District 27	14.7	10.7	14.5	325 847	31 350	9.6	294 497	32.8	47.1	20.2	10.3	141 185	224.4	20 466
District 28	23.6	18.8	22.9	294 229	35 929	12.2	258 300	33.9	46.2	19.9	11.3	125 108	204.5	32 521
District 29	11.6	7.5	9.1	337 858	26 771	7.9	311 087	38.5	40.9	20.6	10.7	144 097	217.1	16 168
NORTH CAROLINA	17.5	13.3	13.1	4 727 122	598 546	12.7	4 128 576	35.0	41.9	23.0	19.1	1 757 135	184.3	219 570
District 1	25.6	20.6	24.9	286 861	49 354	17.2	237 507	26.0	43.8	30.2	21.7	144 664	227.5	32 887
District 2	19.2	15.8	14.9	342 612	44 549	13.0	298 063	30.4	43.9	25.7	19.6	122 864	165.7	19 333
District 3	14.5	10.4	9.5	351 490	38 154	10.9	313 336	32.0	43.1	24.9	18.1	130 303	177.0	13 882
District 4	12.2	8.2	7.0	450 701	41 638	9.2	409 063	54.2	34.6	11.1	13.9	103 185	124.8	9 827
District 5	17.4	12.5	9.5	346 853	41 011	11.8	305 842	33.6	41.3	25.1	17.7	148 249	213.8	12 654
District 6	14.9	11.6	10.8	366 876	42 832	11.7	324 044	33.2	41.8	25.0	18.4	153 098	214.3	11 158
District 7	20.8	14.8	16.8	343 919	45 092	13.1	298 827	33.4	40.1	26.5	22.0	157 255	211.7	24 987
District 8	19.0	14.4	16.5	337 803	48 266	14.3	289 537	30.4	44.0	25.6	20.5	117 154	165.1	18 095
District 9	10.6	8.0	8.5	457 085	52 670	11.5	404 415	42.4	40.8	16.8	15.6	121 973	143.1	9 971
District 10	16.5	12.8	12.9	337 099	48 084	14.3	289 015	28.9	40.2	30.9	18.7	148 991	216.1	14 264
District 11	17.3	12.3	12.4	333 703	40 188	12.0	293 515	33.9	44.3	21.7	21.9	178 859	254.2	16 648
District 12	24.5	20.9	18.8	370 736	59 572	16.1	311 164	29.0	47.1	23.9	22.5	113 477	154.1	20 285
District 13	18.0	14.1	11.8	401 384	47 136	11.7	354 248	36.4	42.6	21.1	20.5	117 063	155.4	15 579
NORTH DAKOTA	13.0	7.8	8.2	377 605	14 710	3.9	362 895	34.6	41.3	24.0	11.3	120 098	178.6	8 277
At Large	13.0	7.8	8.2	377 605	14 710	3.9	362 895	34.6	41.3	24.0	11.3	120 098	178.6	8 277
OHIO	15.8	11.8	14.1	5 844 911	668 021	11.4	5 176 890	34.0	43.1	22.8	14.2	2 124 650	184.2	285 569
District 1	21.9	15.8	17.1	298 150	35 409	11.9	262 741	34.3	48.1	17.7	15.6	101 803	170.0	19 326
District 2	10.6	7.7	8.9	343 584	32 830	9.6	310 754	41.1	40.1	18.8	12.3	118 420	175.7	15 057
District 3	15.5	11.4	14.1	313 729	37 470	11.9	276 259	35.3	43.4	21.2	13.9	121 590	189.7	15 012
District 4	15.5	11.0	14.2	309 257	34 416	11.1	274 841	27.6	39.0	33.4	14.8	124 201	196.3	12 872
District 5	13.6	10.5	11.8	316 150	37 231	11.8	278 919	28.5	38.1	33.4	12.2	121 220	193.1	9 104
District 6	16.7	12.4	15.5	286 485	31 892	11.1	254 593	29.7	43.4	27.0	14.0	138 260	221.7	21 352
District 7	15.6	11.7	15.3	335 476	35 030	10.4	300 446	32.5	44.7	22.8	15.0	120 641	176.5	14 169
District 8	14.3	10.2	12.1	343 179	38 253	11.1	304 926	32.4	43.4	24.2	13.0	118 941	179.2	12 385
District 9	17.4	12.9	15.6	315 200	41 886	13.3	273 314	31.9	44.7	23.4	15.4	117 890	190.4	19 103
District 10	14.2	11.0	12.6	325 875	39 009	12.0	286 866	34.8	45.0	20.3	14.4	114 915	191.8	17 420
District 11	25.0	21.2	24.0	261 962	41 221	15.7	220 741	36.5	47.5	16.0	16.4	102 174	189.1	28 700
District 12	15.1	11.8	14.7	409 469	41 256	10.1	368 213	41.7	43.2	15.0	11.6	102 812	135.9	15 649
District 13	14.7	11.3	13.8	326 391	36 128	11.1	290 263	36.3	43.4	20.2	12.6	122 446	188.6	15 120
District 14	8.9	6.4	7.8	345 658	30 970	9.0	314 688	38.0	40.4	21.6	11.4	124 122	191.5	7 574
District 15	17.5	11.8	12.3	378 063	39 991	10.6	338 072	39.6	42.3	18.1	14.4	87 893	129.0	13 961
District 16	13.2	9.2	11.6	332 913	36 460	11.0	296 453	31.6	43.3	25.0	15.2	128 366	199.1	11 457
District 17	19.5	14.3	16.0	299 660	43 494	14.5	256 166	28.0	47.5	24.6	14.7	125 716	209.5	18 043
District 18	18.7	14.3	17.7	303 710	35 075	11.5	268 635	26.8	40.5	32.6	20.0	133 240	204.0	19 265
OKLAHOMA	16.9	12.7	13.7	1 815 022	148 418	8.2	1 666 604	32.2	43.1	24.7	21.7	705 364	188.0	93 855
District 1	15.3	11.3	11.5	386 770	32 088	8.3	354 682	34.4	44.1	21.5	21.1	130 079	172.4	15 649
District 2	19.6	15.3	17.3	318 999	30 939	9.7	288 060	28.4	42.0	29.6	25.2	170 283	233.3	26 997
District 3	16.1	10.9	12.0	352 794	26 096	7.4	326 698	30.7	41.6	27.8	21.7	141 681	193.4	14 886
District 4	15.1	11.1	12.2	374 426	28 468	7.6	345 958	32.5	43.3	24.2	18.4	137 989	175.7	16 004
District 5	18.6	15.0	15.4	382 033	30 827	8.1	351 206	34.1	44.3	21.7	22.3	125 332	167.3	20 319
OREGON	15.8	11.0	17.9	1 948 885	247 412	12.7	1 701 473	36.2	43.4	20.4	19.8	712 216	185.9	74 860
District 1	11.2	6.9	12.7	430 963	49 390	11.5	381 573	41.1	42.3	16.6	17.2	118 065	147.1	11 296
District 2	16.9	12.2	19.8	367 900	51 620	14.0	316 280	32.0	45.4	22.6	23.3	172 162	223.6	15 122
District 3	17.2	13.3	20.8	418 989	53 860	12.9	365 129	38.2	42.0	19.9	19.9	110 219	144.6	18 021
District 4	18.9	12.5	19.8	351 423	44 429	12.6	306 994	33.4	44.5	22.1	21.5	170 683	230.9	17 617
District 5	15.3	10.6	16.4	379 610	48 113	12.7	331 497	35.1	43.4	21.5	17.3	141 087	186.3	12 804

1. Percent of civilian labor force. 2. Persons 16 years old and over. 3. Per 1,000 resident population enumerated in the 2010 census.

Table E. Congressional Districts 112th Congress — **Agriculture**

STATE District	Farms		Land in farms		Farm Operators			Value of products sold				Government payments	
						Percent of farm operators				Percent of sales from			
	Number	Operated by family or individual (percent)	Acreage	Average size of farm (acres)	Total	Whose primary occupation is farming	Who live on the farm operated	Total ($1,000)	Average per farm	Crops	Livestock	Total ($1,000)	Percent of farms
	68	69	70	71	72	73	74	75	76	77	78	79	80
NEW YORK—Cont'd													
District 14	X	X	X	X	X	X	X	X	X	X	X	X	X
District 15	X	X	X	X	X	X	X	X	X	X	X	X	X
District 16	1	0.0	(D)	X	1	100.0	0.0	(D)	(D)	(D)	(D)	X	0.0
District 17	17	47.1	168	10	27	29.6	77.8	(D)	(D)	(D)	(D)	(D)	(D)
District 18	28	46.4	1 055	38	54	42.6	37.0	4 407	157 393	83.3	16.7	(D)	(D)
District 19	776	66.9	99 885	129	1 265	56.5	75.5	80 342	103 534	66.3	33.7	676	19.3
District 20	4 246	80.7	778 884	183	7 068	49.3	84.2	391 260	92 148	25.0	75.0	6 557	23.2
District 21	2 026	85.2	330 449	163	3 258	50.0	86.9	145 417	71 775	28.4	71.6	2 269	26.4
District 22	1 559	79.4	235 169	151	2 511	47.0	80.8	147 138	94 380	52.7	47.3	1 423	17.8
District 23	5 927	87.6	1 439 783	243	9 505	51.6	86.1	728 729	122 951	16.8	83.2	9 356	28.1
District 24	6 324	87.0	1 309 761	207	10 060	50.1	85.9	687 803	108 761	21.3	78.7	12 664	34.6
District 25	1 858	84.1	368 533	198	2 953	53.0	81.8	336 129	180 909	53.3	46.7	4 201	29.9
District 26	3 398	82.6	902 482	266	5 384	52.0	82.8	739 412	217 602	34.1	65.9	11 254	42.1
District 27	2 676	86.0	363 825	136	4 066	49.1	83.3	232 694	86 956	40.1	59.9	3 109	20.1
District 28	651	85.9	118 867	183	1 020	49.2	81.4	101 363	155 704	83.1	16.9	1 340	26.6
District 29	6 202	87.6	1 190 091	192	9 629	48.4	83.6	557 970	89 966	30.0	70.0	9 549	32.9
NORTH CAROLINA	52 913	86.5	8 474 671	160	76 832	42.8	76.1	10 313 628	194 917	25.3	74.7	147 334	26.2
District 1	4 378	78.8	1 726 917	394	6 185	52.6	62.3	1 400 944	319 996	43.6	56.4	59 335	66.5
District 2	4 905	86.8	870 059	177	7 065	45.1	77.5	1 337 344	272 649	21.9	78.1	14 298	33.6
District 3	3 398	80.5	1 107 876	326	4 852	54.5	66.9	1 700 397	500 411	30.7	69.3	28 698	50.1
District 4	1 424	81.1	137 866	97	2 094	42.2	80.6	71 607	50 286	58.6	41.4	1 372	22.0
District 5	9 489	89.7	950 965	100	14 123	39.9	79.3	972 920	102 531	15.8	84.2	3 512	11.4
District 6	4 921	90.2	481 673	98	7 139	40.9	82.3	478 083	97 152	17.3	82.7	2 060	13.8
District 7	4 809	83.5	1 045 148	217	6 595	51.7	68.8	2 520 862	524 197	14.6	85.4	18 430	41.5
District 8	3 226	87.0	554 937	172	4 666	41.0	73.9	917 331	284 356	7.8	92.2	7 642	28.7
District 9	1 229	87.6	140 803	115	1 919	40.4	81.2	318 414	259 084	42.4	57.6	1 213	15.1
District 10	5 301	87.6	449 206	85	7 793	35.7	77.3	216 435	40 829	40.5	59.5	3 459	17.7
District 11	5 893	88.6	415 181	70	8 676	37.4	81.3	210 015	35 638	66.4	33.6	1 943	8.8
District 12	1 191	88.9	127 907	107	1 768	37.6	81.4	62 908	52 819	59.0	41.0	1 004	17.5
District 13	2 749	87.1	466 133	170	3 957	40.4	77.3	106 370	38 694	59.5	40.5	4 372	27.5
NORTH DAKOTA	31 970	87.8	39 674 586	1 241	45 114	55.4	64.4	6 084 218	190 310	82.8	17.2	359 532	83.5
At Large	31 970	87.8	39 674 586	1 241	45 114	55.4	64.4	6 084 218	190 310	82.8	17.2	359 532	83.5
OHIO	75 861	87.5	13 966 563	184	114 172	40.3	80.0	7 070 212	93 200	58.1	41.9	232 184	50.2
District 1	527	88.0	51 116	97	869	41.2	74.0	25 142	47 708	69.9	30.1	704	24.5
District 2	5 090	89.0	698 102	137	7 755	36.4	79.0	157 028	30 850	72.5	27.5	8 087	42.2
District 3	3 549	87.8	656 624	185	5 470	39.3	78.3	228 806	64 471	85.0	15.0	12 440	59.9
District 4	9 576	86.6	2 166 029	226	14 190	39.6	77.0	1 191 884	124 466	60.2	39.8	45 962	69.6
District 5	12 572	84.8	3 145 610	250	18 248	39.8	72.7	1 588 365	126 341	69.7	30.3	65 491	80.0
District 6	7 811	91.8	1 065 139	136	11 688	38.2	85.8	228 382	29 239	34.7	65.3	5 632	21.6
District 7	4 985	86.6	1 204 288	242	7 639	41.2	79.7	535 241	107 370	81.2	18.8	24 064	55.2
District 8	5 456	86.9	1 024 076	188	8 211	42.8	80.1	1 104 892	202 510	30.6	69.4	21 046	63.0
District 9	1 973	84.7	350 078	177	2 968	40.2	77.9	227 206	115 158	88.2	11.8	5 873	56.4
District 10	61	60.7	1 198	20	101	54.5	73.3	9 058	148 492	(D)	(D)	(D)	3.3
District 11	12	58.3	562	47	17	29.4	58.8	769	64 083	(D)	(D)	(D)	(D)
District 12	1 654	86.4	290 016	175	2 508	40.7	79.9	222 870	134 746	55.5	44.5	5 286	39.6
District 13	586	79.5	40 375	69	949	44.7	79.2	38 582	65 840	92.5	7.5	(D)	17.2
District 14	2 884	85.5	306 851	106	4 470	44.0	84.9	204 298	70 838	75.3	24.7	2 366	22.3
District 15	1 912	85.2	507 981	266	2 850	42.8	77.9	246 614	128 982	81.9	18.1	10 435	62.5
District 16	4 552	86.2	570 855	125	6 992	45.1	85.4	477 088	104 808	30.9	69.1	7 024	34.3
District 17	1 385	90.0	143 005	103	2 115	39.1	83.2	49 697	35 882	65.4	34.6	1 339	25.2
District 18	11 276	90.6	1 734 658	154	17 132	39.9	84.8	534 288	47 383	37.8	62.2	16 102	30.5
OKLAHOMA	86 565	89.4	35 087 269	405	131 232	38.0	75.3	5 806 061	67 072	20.5	79.5	209 465	31.2
District 1	3 481	89.8	707 138	203	5 263	35.5	81.7	86 506	24 851	43.3	56.7	1 480	14.4
District 2	32 007	91.7	8 328 593	260	49 282	38.5	83.7	1 734 156	54 181	15.3	84.7	17 522	14.6
District 3	31 867	86.6	19 940 675	626	47 567	38.5	63.8	3 240 058	101 674	22.2	77.8	161 737	53.6
District 4	15 073	90.6	5 312 929	352	22 730	37.3	78.2	664 573	44 090	21.1	78.9	27 225	27.3
District 5	4 137	89.0	797 934	193	6 390	35.7	81.4	80 769	19 524	30.0	70.0	1 501	15.6
OREGON	38 553	85.1	16 399 647	425	64 503	41.7	85.3	4 386 143	113 769	67.9	32.1	76 491	13.3
District 1	4 922	85.2	387 935	79	8 100	37.7	85.4	(D)	(D)	(D)	(D)	2 843	12.0
District 2	14 424	83.6	13 871 879	962	24 189	45.8	83.4	1 881 562	130 447	54.6	45.4	65 760	22.4
District 3	2 118	87.1	84 923	40	3 535	40.5	87.9	(D)	(D)	(D)	(D)	283	2.1
District 4	9 888	87.8	1 361 577	138	16 642	38.7	87.7	521 521	52 743	68.7	31.3	4 111	5.7
District 5	7 201	83.5	693 333	96	12 037	40.4	85.1	1 080 499	150 048	72.8	27.2	3 494	9.5

1. Specified owner-occupied units.   2. Median monthly owner costs is often in the minimum category—10.0 percent or less, which is indicated as 10.0 percent.   3. Specified renter-occupied units.   4. Overcrowded or lacking complete plumbing facilities.

Table E. Congressional Districts 112th Congress — Land Area and Population Characteristics

STATE District	Representative, 112th Congress	Land area,[1] 2010 (sq km)	Total persons	Per square kilometer	White	Black	American Indian, Alaska Native	Asian and Pacific Islander	Some other race	Two or more races	Hispanic or Latino[2]	Non-Hispanic White alone	Percent female	Percent foreign born	Percent born in state of residence
		1	2	3	4	5	6	7	8	9	10	11	12	13	14
PENNSYLVANIA		115 883	12 702 379	109.6	81.9	10.8	0.2	2.7	2.4	1.9	5.7	79.5	51.3	5.8	74.0
District 1	Robert A. Brady (D)	151	655 146	4 324.9	31.8	48.1	0.7	6.6	9.8	3.2	19.3	25.7	52.7	12.0	66.3
District 2	Chaka Fattah (D)	151	630 277	4 161.0	32.1	57.3	0.3	5.9	1.8	2.5	4.8	30.4	54.0	8.9	67.4
District 3	Mike Kelly (R)	10 277	640 356	62.3	92.7	4.2	0.2	0.8	0.6	1.5	2.0	91.6	50.7	2.2	81.3
District 4	Jason Altmire (D)	3 366	647 418	192.4	93.1	3.5	0.1	1.7	0.2	1.3	1.1	92.3	51.7	2.9	81.1
District 5	Glenn Thompson (R)	28 554	651 762	22.8	94.9	1.9	0.2	1.5	0.5	1.0	1.5	94.0	49.7	2.4	80.8
District 6	Jim Gerlach (R)	2 096	726 465	346.6	82.6	7.8	0.2	3.7	3.4	2.2	7.8	79.2	51.1	8.2	69.8
District 7	Patrick Meehan (R)	749	673 623	899.3	81.7	9.9	0.1	5.7	0.8	1.8	2.7	80.1	51.6	10.0	72.4
District 8	Michael G. Fitzpatrick (R)	1 596	672 685	421.6	88.8	3.9	0.2	3.9	1.5	1.7	4.3	86.5	51.0	8.0	70.2
District 9	Bill Shuster (R)	18 524	666 810	36.0	95.2	2.1	0.1	0.5	0.8	1.2	1.9	94.4	50.1	1.6	80.7
District 10	Tom Marino (R)	16 939	669 257	39.5	94.5	2.6	0.2	0.7	0.7	1.3	2.7	92.9	50.0	2.8	71.7
District 11	Lou Barletta (R)	5 738	687 860	119.9	87.4	5.7	0.2	1.4	3.3	1.9	8.1	83.8	51.2	6.1	67.7
District 12	Mark Critz (D)	7 135	612 384	85.8	93.7	3.9	0.1	0.4	0.3	1.4	1.1	93.1	51.2	1.2	86.2
District 13	Allyson Y. Schwartz (D)	657	674 188	1 026.1	77.7	10.2	0.2	6.8	2.9	2.2	6.7	74.8	51.6	12.5	72.6
District 14	Michael F. Doyle (D)	419	584 493	1 395.1	69.4	24.5	0.2	2.7	0.6	2.5	1.9	68.5	52.3	4.4	79.9
District 15	Charles W. Dent (R)	2 174	721 828	332.1	83.3	5.4	0.3	2.6	5.8	2.5	13.7	77.3	51.3	7.4	63.2
District 16	Joseph R. Pitts (R)	3 323	723 977	217.9	84.8	4.8	0.3	1.8	6.0	2.2	13.3	79.4	51.0	7.2	70.0
District 17	Tim Holden (D)	6 045	681 835	112.8	85.3	8.4	0.2	1.7	2.4	2.0	6.0	82.6	50.7	3.7	79.8
District 18	Tim Murphy (R)	3 707	653 385	176.3	93.6	2.8	0.1	2.0	0.3	1.2	1.1	92.8	51.6	3.8	81.2
District 19	Todd Russell Platts (R)	4 282	728 630	170.1	89.6	4.5	0.2	1.8	2.0	1.9	5.0	87.3	50.8	4.2	67.3
RHODE ISLAND		2 678	1 052 567	393.0	81.4	5.7	0.6	3.0	6.0	3.3	12.4	76.4	51.7	12.8	59.3
District 1	David Cicilline (D)	831	519 021	624.8	81.8	6.1	0.5	2.6	5.4	3.6	11.0	76.7	52.0	12.5	56.1
District 2	James R. Langevin (D)	1 847	533 546	288.9	81.0	5.3	0.7	3.3	6.7	3.0	13.8	76.1	51.4	13.0	62.3
SOUTH CAROLINA		77 857	4 625 364	59.4	66.2	27.9	0.4	1.4	2.5	1.7	5.1	64.1	51.4	4.7	58.6
District 1	Tim Scott (R)	6 842	856 956	125.3	73.2	19.8	0.4	1.6	2.8	2.1	5.8	70.8	51.4	6.2	45.5
District 2	Joe Wilson (R)	12 317	825 324	67.0	65.6	27.2	0.4	1.7	3.1	2.0	6.9	62.7	50.7	5.8	52.8
District 3	Jeff Duncan (R)	13 902	722 675	52.0	75.7	19.5	0.3	0.8	2.2	1.5	4.1	74.1	51.1	3.5	62.5
District 4	Trey Gowdy (R)	5 549	770 226	138.8	73.0	19.5	0.3	1.9	3.5	1.8	7.0	70.0	51.6	7.2	57.3
District 5	Mick Mulvaney (R)	18 215	767 773	42.1	64.4	30.6	0.7	0.8	1.8	1.6	3.7	63.0	51.5	2.8	62.7
District 6	James E. Clyburn (D)	21 033	682 410	32.4	42.0	54.2	0.4	0.8	1.2	1.3	2.7	41.1	52.0	2.1	74.7
SOUTH DAKOTA		196 350	814 180	4.1	85.9	1.3	8.8	0.9	0.9	2.1	2.7	84.7	50.0	2.7	65.1
At Large	Kristi Noem (R)	196 350	814 180	4.1	85.9	1.3	8.8	0.9	0.9	2.1	2.7	84.7	50.0	2.7	65.1
TENNESSEE		106 798	6 346 105	59.4	77.6	16.7	0.3	1.5	2.2	1.7	4.6	75.6	51.3	4.5	61.0
District 1	David P. Roe (R)	10 607	684 093	64.5	93.8	2.2	0.3	0.6	1.6	1.4	3.3	92.4	51.1	2.6	61.6
District 2	John J. Duncan Jr. (R)	6 288	723 798	115.1	88.7	6.2	0.3	1.5	1.5	1.8	3.5	87.1	51.3	3.7	62.7
District 3	Chuck Fleischmann (R)	8 833	692 346	78.4	83.9	11.2	0.3	1.3	1.7	1.6	3.7	82.3	51.5	3.6	60.8
District 4	Scott DesJarlais (R)	25 998	688 008	26.5	92.4	4.1	0.3	0.4	1.2	1.5	2.7	91.1	50.8	1.8	66.7
District 5	Jim Cooper (D)	2 319	707 420	305.1	65.2	24.8	0.3	2.8	4.5	2.4	9.0	61.5	51.4	10.5	54.1
District 6	Diane Black (R)	14 194	788 754	55.6	86.0	7.6	0.3	1.6	2.7	1.8	5.4	83.8	50.7	4.9	61.2
District 7	Marsha Blackburn (R)	16 298	792 605	48.6	79.2	14.4	0.3	2.6	1.4	2.1	4.1	77.0	50.9	5.0	51.8
District 8	Stephen Fincher (R)	21 411	658 258	30.7	72.7	23.3	0.3	0.5	1.5	1.6	3.0	71.5	51.5	2.1	69.8
District 9	Steve Cohen (D)	850	610 823	718.5	28.8	63.5	0.2	1.9	4.1	1.3	6.6	26.9	52.3	6.5	62.7
TEXAS		676 587	25 145 561	37.2	70.4	11.8	0.7	3.9	10.5	2.7	37.6	45.3	50.4	16.4	60.5
District 1	Louie Gohmert (R)	22 014	723 464	32.9	71.2	17.7	0.6	0.9	7.7	1.9	15.1	64.8	51.0	8.0	71.1
District 2	Ted Poe (R)	4 925	782 375	158.9	63.1	21.6	0.5	3.5	8.8	2.5	22.5	51.1	50.2	12.0	61.7
District 3	Sam Johnson (R)	685	842 449	1 230.0	64.1	11.6	0.6	12.3	8.4	3.1	22.2	51.9	50.8	23.0	44.9
District 4	Ralph M. Hall (R)	24 474	846 142	34.6	78.8	10.4	0.9	2.2	5.4	2.4	13.1	72.1	50.5	7.7	63.6
District 5	Jeb Hensarling (R)	13 988	725 642	51.9	72.1	13.9	0.7	1.9	8.9	2.4	21.6	60.9	50.1	10.6	67.9
District 6	Joe Barton (R)	16 049	809 095	50.4	66.4	16.6	0.6	4.2	9.3	2.8	22.9	54.5	50.7	14.1	59.9
District 7	John Abney Culberson (R)	509	780 611	1 534.3	67.8	10.0	0.5	10.2	8.4	3.0	25.4	52.7	50.7	24.1	48.3
District 8	Kevin Brady (R)	21 028	833 770	39.7	82.4	7.8	0.7	1.5	5.6	2.0	15.4	73.7	49.3	8.7	63.2
District 9	Al Green (D)	395	733 796	1 856.3	32.8	35.8	0.8	11.0	16.0	3.7	42.4	10.4	50.6	36.7	48.5
District 10	Michael T. McCaul (R)	9 800	981 367	100.1	69.0	11.4	0.7	5.9	10.0	3.1	28.8	52.4	50.4	17.6	54.6
District 11	K. Michael Conaway (R)	90 614	710 682	7.8	81.2	4.0	0.8	0.8	10.9	2.3	36.3	57.8	50.2	9.1	71.0
District 12	Kay Granger (R)	5 613	831 100	148.1	76.4	6.8	0.7	3.0	10.3	2.8	28.8	59.8	50.5	13.4	59.2
District 13	Mac Thornberry (R)	103 860	672 781	6.5	81.0	5.9	0.9	1.7	8.1	2.4	23.4	67.2	49.1	8.3	65.8
District 14	Ron Paul (R)	18 189	779 704	42.9	75.5	9.1	0.6	3.5	8.7	2.5	29.0	57.0	49.8	10.4	66.3
District 15	Rubén Hinojosa (D)	27 763	787 124	28.4	85.7	1.5	0.4	0.9	9.8	1.6	82.5	15.0	50.4	20.5	68.1
District 16	Silvestre Reyes (D)	1 490	757 427	508.2	81.9	3.2	0.8	1.2	10.4	2.5	81.5	13.6	51.6	25.8	55.4
District 17	Bill Flores (R)	19 825	760 042	38.3	77.1	9.8	0.6	2.1	8.2	2.2	20.7	66.0	50.0	8.8	69.9
District 18	Sheila Jackson-Lee (D)	585	720 991	1 233.2	39.0	36.8	0.7	3.5	17.1	3.0	43.5	15.8	49.5	24.5	59.4
District 19	Randy Neugebauer (R)	65 378	698 130	10.7	78.7	5.7	0.8	1.4	11.0	2.5	33.8	58.0	50.0	7.9	73.8
District 20	Charles A. Gonzalez (D)	475	711 705	1 497.9	70.3	7.2	1.1	2.0	15.7	3.6	71.5	18.4	50.6	15.8	66.5
District 21	Lamar Smith (R)	13 261	856 954	64.6	79.4	6.7	0.6	3.9	6.4	3.0	28.1	59.8	51.1	10.1	57.0

1. Dry land or land partially or temporarily covered by water. 2. May be of any race.

Table E. Congressional Districts 112th Congress — **Age and Education**

STATE District	Population and population characteristics, 2010 (cont.)										Education, 2010			
	Age (percent)										Enrollment[1]		Attainment[2] (percent)	
	Under 5 years	5 to 17 years	18 to 24 years	25 to 34 years	35 to 44 years	45 to 54 years	55 to 64 years	65 to 74 years	75 years and over	Median age	Total	Percent private	High school graduate or more	Bachelor's degree or more
	15	16	17	18	19	20	21	22	23	24	25	26	27	28
PENNSYLVANIA	5.7	16.2	9.9	11.9	12.7	15.3	12.8	7.7	7.7	40.1	3 209 174	23.9	88.4	27.1
District 1	7.4	17.9	12.9	16.0	12.9	12.9	9.8	5.5	4.7	32.0	185 876	24.6	74.4	17.2
District 2	6.0	14.2	15.8	16.4	11.4	12.7	11.0	6.5	6.1	33.0	188 946	38.4	84.7	31.3
District 3	5.6	16.4	10.6	10.7	12.2	15.2	13.3	8.1	7.9	40.8	161 876	21.7	89.8	21.2
District 4	5.3	16.6	6.8	10.4	12.7	16.7	14.0	8.4	9.2	43.8	152 393	21.1	92.6	33.8
District 5	5.1	14.5	14.0	10.9	12.0	14.7	12.7	8.4	7.8	39.9	172 739	10.1	88.6	19.7
District 6	6.3	17.7	8.9	11.8	13.9	15.6	12.1	6.9	6.7	39.1	198 212	25.4	91.2	40.8
District 7	5.8	16.8	9.3	12.2	12.9	15.8	12.4	7.1	7.8	39.9	181 697	34.9	93.2	42.3
District 8	5.5	17.4	7.6	10.7	13.4	17.3	13.4	7.6	7.1	41.9	166 025	23.3	93.3	34.8
District 9	5.8	16.2	8.5	11.2	12.9	15.1	13.5	8.8	8.0	41.6	149 153	17.5	86.3	16.7
District 10	5.2	15.7	8.8	10.4	12.6	15.9	14.0	9.1	8.2	43.0	151 973	21.6	88.1	20.0
District 11	5.3	15.7	10.6	10.8	12.7	15.5	13.0	8.2	8.2	41.3	173 187	21.0	88.0	21.2
District 12	4.9	14.5	9.7	10.5	12.2	15.5	14.3	8.8	9.7	43.6	134 272	12.4	87.3	17.5
District 13	6.0	16.7	8.2	12.7	13.0	15.5	12.3	7.2	8.4	40.1	174 648	30.8	89.1	33.4
District 14	5.2	12.9	13.8	14.8	11.0	13.9	12.6	7.3	8.4	38.0	155 144	29.0	89.9	27.5
District 15	5.9	17.1	9.1	11.5	13.3	15.6	12.4	7.4	7.7	40.1	187 214	28.3	87.5	27.4
District 16	6.9	18.4	10.5	11.6	12.5	14.5	11.6	7.0	7.0	37.3	187 981	24.2	83.4	26.8
District 17	5.9	16.4	8.1	11.8	13.2	15.7	13.4	7.9	7.7	41.2	157 589	16.8	87.6	20.9
District 18	5.0	15.5	7.2	10.7	12.8	16.5	14.3	8.7	9.3	44.1	152 061	23.0	93.8	34.9
District 19	5.8	16.5	9.3	11.6	13.5	15.6	12.9	7.7	7.1	40.3	176 198	22.4	89.7	25.1
RHODE ISLAND	5.5	15.8	11.4	12.1	13.0	15.4	12.4	7.0	7.4	39.4	279 157	25.7	83.5	30.2
District 1	5.5	15.3	11.7	12.4	12.9	15.0	12.2	7.1	7.9	39.3	138 124	34.3	84.1	31.4
District 2	5.4	16.4	11.1	11.7	13.1	15.8	12.6	6.9	6.9	39.6	141 033	17.1	83.0	29.1
SOUTH CAROLINA	6.5	16.8	10.3	12.8	13.0	14.3	12.6	8.0	5.7	37.9	1 201 598	15.1	84.1	24.5
District 1	6.4	15.8	10.3	14.2	12.9	13.9	12.8	8.3	5.4	37.6	216 639	16.0	88.9	30.2
District 2	6.6	17.0	10.1	13.7	13.2	14.0	12.2	7.8	5.4	37.1	214 912	18.0	88.2	32.7
District 3	6.1	16.4	10.6	11.5	12.5	14.4	13.1	8.8	6.7	39.5	188 980	13.1	81.1	20.0
District 4	6.8	17.5	9.5	12.8	13.8	14.5	12.1	7.5	5.6	37.7	192 257	19.5	83.9	26.0
District 5	6.7	17.8	8.9	12.0	13.6	14.8	12.8	7.8	5.5	38.5	191 913	11.3	81.5	18.7
District 6	6.6	16.5	12.6	12.3	11.7	14.1	12.8	7.7	5.5	36.7	196 897	12.4	79.0	17.0
SOUTH DAKOTA	7.3	17.6	10.0	12.9	11.4	14.4	12.0	7.1	7.2	36.9	213 369	14.2	89.6	26.3
At Large	7.3	17.6	10.0	12.9	11.4	14.4	12.0	7.1	7.2	36.9	213 369	14.2	89.6	26.3
TENNESSEE	6.4	17.1	9.6	13.0	13.5	14.6	12.4	7.7	5.8	38.0	1 598 191	16.7	83.6	23.1
District 1	5.5	15.6	8.6	11.3	13.4	14.9	13.8	9.8	7.1	41.8	147 622	11.9	80.0	18.8
District 2	5.9	16.1	10.0	12.5	13.3	14.6	12.9	8.4	6.3	39.2	179 113	16.3	86.7	27.1
District 3	5.9	16.1	9.7	12.0	13.1	14.7	13.3	8.5	6.7	40.0	169 929	19.7	82.4	21.1
District 4	6.0	16.8	7.8	11.2	12.9	14.9	13.7	9.7	7.0	41.3	153 012	12.6	79.3	14.9
District 5	7.0	15.3	11.2	17.1	13.9	14.0	10.9	5.8	4.8	34.5	175 972	29.1	84.4	31.4
District 6	6.8	18.2	10.0	13.3	14.0	14.5	11.4	7.0	4.8	36.3	210 986	10.6	83.7	19.5
District 7	6.7	19.6	8.0	12.5	14.4	15.5	12.1	6.6	4.6	37.4	223 195	21.9	89.9	34.3
District 8	6.6	18.0	9.7	11.9	12.8	14.6	12.3	7.9	6.1	38.1	170 998	12.2	82.2	15.5
District 9	7.5	18.3	11.2	15.2	13.0	13.5	11.0	5.5	4.8	33.4	167 364	14.7	83.5	24.1
TEXAS	7.7	19.6	10.2	14.4	13.8	13.7	10.3	5.9	4.5	33.6	7 197 800	10.8	80.7	25.9
District 1	7.0	18.1	10.6	12.5	12.0	13.7	11.8	7.8	6.5	36.6	185 303	10.1	81.6	18.9
District 2	7.3	19.2	9.5	14.2	13.7	14.5	11.3	5.8	4.4	34.8	219 225	10.3	85.6	24.6
District 3	7.5	20.6	8.3	14.5	16.5	15.0	9.8	4.8	3.0	34.4	247 947	12.1	88.3	42.9
District 4	7.1	19.7	8.0	12.3	14.2	14.5	11.3	7.4	5.4	37.1	227 154	9.8	85.3	23.6
District 5	7.1	18.9	8.5	13.0	13.6	14.5	11.6	7.3	5.6	37.0	187 882	10.5	83.0	21.0
District 6	7.5	20.5	9.5	13.6	14.3	14.3	10.3	5.8	4.2	34.2	246 631	12.0	84.0	25.2
District 7	6.7	16.4	8.8	17.1	14.7	14.6	11.6	5.6	4.5	35.6	204 199	21.0	89.8	49.6
District 8	6.7	18.7	9.0	12.5	13.6	15.0	12.1	7.4	5.0	37.5	216 779	11.2	83.6	21.9
District 9	8.8	19.7	11.3	17.5	14.3	12.5	9.0	4.3	2.8	30.6	214 009	8.3	71.9	20.4
District 10	7.8	20.1	9.1	15.7	15.4	14.1	9.8	4.7	3.3	33.3	272 509	11.2	87.4	34.6
District 11	7.3	18.2	9.8	12.7	11.5	13.9	12.0	7.9	6.8	36.8	177 120	9.4	78.9	17.6
District 12	7.9	19.5	9.8	14.8	14.1	13.9	10.2	5.6	4.2	33.6	229 875	17.1	82.8	25.0
District 13	7.1	18.1	10.1	13.3	12.2	14.1	11.4	7.4	6.4	36.1	173 467	7.1	81.6	20.0
District 14	7.2	19.8	8.3	12.4	13.7	15.4	11.8	6.6	4.8	36.8	204 763	9.3	84.3	25.5
District 15	8.8	22.9	10.3	13.6	12.9	11.5	9.1	5.9	5.1	30.8	233 810	4.8	66.9	15.1
District 16	8.0	21.7	11.2	13.3	13.1	12.7	9.5	5.7	4.9	31.7	251 715	8.0	73.4	20.1
District 17	6.7	17.2	15.9	13.1	11.5	12.7	10.6	6.8	5.4	32.5	241 769	13.8	81.8	22.2
District 18	8.5	18.9	11.6	17.2	14.0	12.8	9.1	4.6	3.4	31.1	191 770	6.8	70.5	18.2
District 19	7.4	18.0	13.4	13.5	11.2	13.2	10.4	6.8	6.0	33.0	207 491	12.0	79.4	21.6
District 20	8.1	19.3	11.9	15.7	12.8	12.5	9.5	5.4	4.8	31.4	208 065	10.1	76.0	16.7
District 21	6.1	17.5	10.7	12.5	13.4	14.7	12.2	7.1	5.7	37.5	246 118	16.4	91.6	40.4

1. All persons 3 years old and over enrolled in nursery school through college and graduate or professional school.   2. Persons 25 years old and over.

Table E. Congressional Districts 112th Congress — Households and Group Quarters

STATE District	Households, 2010						Group quarters, 2010					
	Number	Persons per household	Family households (percent)	Husband-wife family (percent)	Female family householder[1]	One person households (percent)	Total in group quarters	Percent 65 years and over	Persons in correctional institutions	Persons in nursing homes	Persons in college dormitories	Persons in military quarters
	29	30	31	32	33	34	35	36	37	38	39	40
PENNSYLVANIA	5 018 904	2.45	65.0	48.2	12.2	28.6	426 113	21.0	97 820	87 775	177 332	259
District 1	244 591	2.60	60.0	26.2	26.9	31.3	16 842	9.9	3 479	1 848	8 724	14
District 2	261 874	2.29	50.8	24.0	21.7	38.2	18 889	14.9	557	4 685	19 070	0
District 3	254 238	2.41	65.1	49.3	11.2	28.7	28 835	16.4	6 229	4 604	13 921	11
District 4	265 843	2.40	67.5	53.8	9.9	28.0	12 602	49.6	562	4 914	2 532	6
District 5	258 223	2.37	63.5	49.9	9.1	28.2	36 950	11.8	12 778	4 696	19 980	0
District 6	273 354	2.57	68.4	53.9	10.4	25.2	24 860	19.2	4 301	4 514	11 693	0
District 7	257 565	2.53	66.7	51.7	11.0	27.4	21 506	19.9	3 405	4 314	11 362	0
District 8	252 595	2.63	71.8	57.9	9.7	23.0	15 923	44.4	1 041	4 093	1 569	0
District 9	263 373	2.45	68.6	54.5	9.5	26.1	21 885	25.5	8 381	5 051	3 725	6
District 10	265 853	2.41	66.8	52.5	9.7	27.6	32 267	18.2	12 365	4 991	8 579	0
District 11	272 161	2.43	64.6	46.9	12.4	29.1	24 122	22.1	5 600	6 018	11 849	1
District 12	255 439	2.30	63.7	47.4	11.5	30.7	14 270	16.8	7 477	3 436	9 909	0
District 13	259 070	2.54	67.1	49.9	12.5	27.7	20 063	37.3	7 540	6 110	399	121
District 14	263 770	2.11	50.4	30.3	15.8	39.9	27 362	12.5	4 586	3 282	15 715	0
District 15	275 273	2.55	68.6	52.3	11.7	25.3	26 737	28.4	2 022	5 850	9 792	0
District 16	263 679	2.67	70.0	55.4	10.4	23.8	19 255	24.3	1 132	4 997	11 299	0
District 17	273 262	2.42	66.0	49.8	11.5	28.1	20 466	24.3	8 150	5 070	1 847	63
District 18	274 826	2.33	65.6	53.0	9.0	29.5	18 054	39.8	1 467	4 543	3 932	0
District 19	283 915	2.48	68.6	54.3	10.0	25.2	25 225	19.1	6 748	4 759	11 435	37
RHODE ISLAND	413 600	2.44	62.8	44.5	13.5	29.6	42 663	18.5	3 783	8 420	24 687	1 385
District 1	208 384	2.38	60.9	42.9	13.5	31.3	23 736	21.0	350	5 467	14 727	1 385
District 2	205 216	2.51	64.6	46.1	13.5	27.9	18 927	15.2	3 433	2 953	9 960	0
SOUTH CAROLINA	1 801 181	2.49	67.5	47.2	15.6	26.5	139 154	13.0	41 649	19 020	46 463	19 413
District 1	345 283	2.45	65.4	47.5	13.4	26.2	14 189	16.0	1 386	2 219	5 020	2 987
District 2	319 613	2.48	67.7	49.4	13.9	26.4	29 396	7.8	11 096	2 531	498	15 815
District 3	283 500	2.47	68.5	49.6	14.2	26.2	26 147	16.1	6 554	3 781	10 640	0
District 4	299 799	2.50	68.2	49.1	14.4	26.8	19 181	14.6	4 877	3 089	9 668	0
District 5	293 980	2.55	70.2	47.8	17.3	25.4	16 558	20.8	8 264	4 128	3 723	611
District 6	259 006	2.51	65.4	38.5	21.8	28.5	33 683	9.1	9 472	3 272	16 914	0
SOUTH DAKOTA	322 282	2.42	64.2	50.1	9.7	29.4	34 050	21.1	6 327	7 005	10 248	597
At Large	322 282	2.42	64.2	50.1	9.7	29.4	34 050	21.1	6 327	7 005	10 248	597
TENNESSEE	2 493 552	2.48	67.3	48.7	13.9	26.9	153 472	19.8	46 957	33 041	53 136	1 544
District 1	281 852	2.37	67.3	50.8	11.6	27.7	13 616	26.7	4 573	4 466	4 176	0
District 2	293 768	2.41	66.0	50.6	11.2	27.6	17 546	20.8	1 821	3 593	9 048	0
District 3	277 113	2.43	67.4	50.1	12.8	27.2	15 323	21.1	2 776	4 012	8 575	3
District 4	272 781	2.47	70.4	53.5	12.0	25.4	11 116	31.4	5 913	4 684	1 684	0
District 5	287 586	2.37	58.6	39.5	14.4	32.5	30 188	8.6	6 542	2 451	13 996	0
District 6	298 006	2.60	70.5	53.4	12.2	23.3	12 717	26.3	2 928	3 801	4 870	0
District 7	292 501	2.66	74.6	59.4	11.4	21.3	13 216	23.6	6 983	3 713	1 087	1 250
District 8	253 112	2.52	69.2	47.5	16.6	26.1	20 460	20.1	8 115	4 412	5 727	291
District 9	236 833	2.51	61.1	30.3	24.6	32.2	19 290	10.1	7 306	1 909	3 973	0
TEXAS	8 922 933	2.75	69.9	50.6	14.1	24.2	581 139	14.9	267 405	94 278	119 834	35 260
District 1	270 801	2.58	69.5	51.1	13.7	25.7	23 481	18.0	8 197	5 362	8 696	0
District 2	277 601	2.73	72.1	52.4	14.4	23.1	29 690	8.8	19 101	2 465	1 950	4
District 3	307 039	2.73	70.4	54.3	11.5	24.0	2 505	50.1	52	1 945	387	0
District 4	307 036	2.70	73.8	57.0	12.1	22.2	12 048	24.8	9 800	5 055	2 237	0
District 5	260 927	2.69	71.7	52.6	13.9	23.7	22 988	13.9	17 768	3 702	1 365	0
District 6	288 086	2.77	72.3	53.2	13.9	22.5	12 104	26.4	5 022	3 474	2 137	0
District 7	326 548	2.37	59.1	45.1	9.9	33.6	6 906	29.5	21	2 353	2 901	0
District 8	300 376	2.68	72.5	56.3	11.4	22.4	27 463	10.2	22 675	2 774	2 615	0
District 9	251 735	2.90	67.6	40.0	20.3	25.8	4 268	30.0	154	1 386	1 520	0
District 10	352 057	2.76	69.9	53.7	11.4	23.4	11 499	23.1	2 110	2 651	4 135	0
District 11	267 618	2.57	69.5	52.3	12.2	26.0	28 790	17.8	11 102	3 898	3 521	1 924
District 12	300 073	2.72	69.7	52.1	12.3	24.6	26 432	16.8	6 975	3 070	3 667	202
District 13	251 590	2.53	68.3	51.5	11.8	26.9	37 424	10.5	22 079	4 155	2 367	5 487
District 14	279 530	2.73	72.8	55.7	12.1	22.4	20 656	17.8	11 942	3 120	992	36
District 15	236 117	3.24	78.6	55.0	17.9	17.9	23 664	12.5	17 106	2 991	1 161	0
District 16	245 234	3.02	76.1	50.1	20.5	20.3	11 597	9.5	6 503	1 482	491	5 683
District 17	278 213	2.61	66.3	49.3	12.1	24.5	36 997	13.1	11 480	5 037	15 364	0
District 18	247 664	2.81	64.6	36.8	20.7	28.1	11 957	3.6	12 136	707	5 679	0
District 19	257 781	2.58	67.1	49.2	12.8	26.1	38 138	11.7	13 316	4 160	10 842	621
District 20	247 818	2.78	66.5	40.0	19.8	27.0	19 947	12.8	4 883	2 850	2 173	9 787
District 21	333 389	2.49	65.9	51.2	10.7	27.1	23 767	16.2	840	4 692	14 712	3 793

1. No spouse present.

Table E. Congressional Districts 112th Congress — **Housing and Money Income**

STATE District	Housing units, 2010										Money income, 2010		
	Total	Occupied units									Households		
		Owner-occupied						Renter-occupied		Sub-standard units[4] (percent)	Per capita income (dollars)	Median income (dollars)	Percent with income of $100,000 or more
		Percent occupied	Percent	Median value[1] (dollars)	Percent valued at $500,000 or more	Median owner cost as a percent of income		Median rent[3]	Median rent as a percent of income				
						With a mortgage	Without a mortgage[2]						
	41	42	43	44	45	46	47	48	49	50	51	52	53
PENNSYLVANIA	5 568 820	88.6	70.1	165 500	5.4	23.8	13.7	763	30.4	1.6	26 374	49 288	18.6
District 1	275 206	85	53.1	112 600	3.5	26.9	16.2	811	36.0	4.2	17 832	31 259	8.7
District 2	305 358	84.8	49.9	150 600	5.0	25.5	15.8	845	33.7	2.8	23 403	34 512	14.7
District 3	284 903	88.6	71.1	114 000	1.9	22.0	12.4	611	30.4	1.5	21 801	42 639	12.3
District 4	284 817	91.3	76.2	145 800	4.2	21.6	13.1	677	28.8	0.8	31 269	54 578	21.9
District 5	320 825	79.2	71.3	105 500	2.3	22.6	12.4	630	29.4	1.5	20 448	40 730	9.6
District 6	289 178	94.6	72.8	257 700	14.2	24.3	14.7	972	29.2	1.8	36 218	69 222	33.5
District 7	270 385	93.9	72.4	280 900	13.7	24.6	15.9	1 002	29.0	1.1	35 343	69 135	33.1
District 8	263 480	92.6	79.2	299 800	15.7	26.4	15.1	1 043	33.2	1.2	34 087	70 008	32.3
District 9	297 419	87.8	75.4	130 800	1.9	22.6	12.3	610	27.1	2.0	21 956	45 090	12.1
District 10	327 417	78.7	75.2	146 400	3.3	24.6	13.6	629	28.8	1.6	23 018	44 684	13.3
District 11	323 326	82.2	70.2	143 100	2.2	25.5	14.4	656	29.3	1.2	22 499	43 561	13.6
District 12	290 584	86.9	71.2	94 100	1.2	20.7	13.1	560	29.2	1.0	21 090	38 581	9.3
District 13	269 760	93.3	71.5	242 600	8.5	25.1	14.3	958	32.7	1.3	29 891	58 857	25.7
District 14	305 271	83.7	57.1	83 800	2.1	21.5	13.9	650	30.4	1.2	23 392	36 084	11.1
District 15	290 297	93.4	71.0	219 800	5.4	24.7	14.5	855	32.9	1.8	27 333	55 099	21.6
District 16	282 630	95.3	68.1	203 500	6.7	24.8	12.8	835	31.6	2.4	26 143	52 893	20.7
District 17	297 328	90	72.3	153 700	2.3	23.1	13.3	721	28.4	1.2	25 261	50 798	17.1
District 18	288 608	92.3	76.5	150 700	2.6	21.2	12.8	713	26.7	0.9	30 272	56 507	21.6
District 19	302 028	95	75.8	186 200	3.5	24.4	13.9	793	28.9	1.6	27 662	56 357	21.0
RHODE ISLAND	463 416	86.8	60.8	254 500	10.3	27.7	15.4	868	30.9	2.6	27 667	52 254	21.4
District 1	232 020	87.9	56.4	264 600	11.4	27.3	14.9	846	30.4	2.6	28 589	50 272	21.9
District 2	231 396	85.7	65.3	246 100	9.4	28.0	16.1	896	31.5	2.6	26 791	54 390	20.9
SOUTH CAROLINA	2 140 337	82.3	68.7	138 100	5.5	23.5	12.0	728	32.2	2.7	22 128	42 018	13.5
District 1	458 464	74.2	68.2	184 900	10.1	26.6	13.1	866	33.2	3.9	25 352	46 879	16.5
District 2	375 860	83.4	70.4	155 600	8.0	22.8	11.4	832	30.9	1.6	26 115	50 887	17.1
District 3	331 666	84.7	71.2	113 800	3.6	21.8	11.0	653	33.6	2.5	20 463	38 471	10.8
District 4	333 135	87.3	69.0	141 700	4.0	22.9	10.7	667	29.5	2.3	23 183	43 238	15.4
District 5	333 923	86.1	69.8	117 400	2.7	23.4	11.6	651	30.0	2.6	19 685	38 867	12.0
District 6	307 289	80.8	62.8	98 100	3.3	23.7	14.6	667	35.7	3.0	16 588	31 502	7.5
SOUTH DAKOTA	364 031	87.6	68.0	129 700	2.6	21.9	10.9	591	26.9	2.7	23 647	45 904	14.2
At Large	364 031	87.6	68.0	129 700	2.6	21.9	10.9	591	26.9	2.7	23 647	45 904	14.2
TENNESSEE	2 815 087	86.7	68.1	139 000	4.0	23.7	11.4	697	31.4	2.5	22 463	41 461	13.6
District 1	336 189	84.1	71.4	122 400	2.6	23.4	10.9	569	29.5	2.0	20 786	35 625	9.8
District 2	325 875	90.4	69.0	151 800	4.5	23.0	11.0	683	30.3	1.4	23 959	42 095	13.9
District 3	311 696	87.2	69.1	135 700	3.7	23.0	11.3	668	29.6	2.3	22 416	40 620	13.2
District 4	315 858	85	74.7	112 300	3.3	23.6	11.4	569	31.9	2.4	19 268	36 301	9.2
District 5	315 114	88.1	57.9	170 900	5.6	24.8	12.2	775	32.5	2.9	25 460	44 587	15.4
District 6	328 053	87.9	70.9	146 400	2.4	24.1	11.2	703	31.0	2.8	20 867	43 712	12.7
District 7	317 307	89.4	76.1	185 600	8.0	23.7	10.9	870	29.7	2.2	27 924	58 253	25.3
District 8	288 502	85.1	68.2	99 500	1.8	22.6	12.1	634	31.5	2.2	19 512	37 427	9.6
District 9	276 493	82.4	52.9	108 100	3.9	25.3	13.3	780	35.8	4.4	20 971	37 508	12.3
TEXAS	9 996 209	87.4	63.6	128 100	3.8	23.4	12.5	801	30.2	5.8	23 863	48 615	19.3
District 1	308 525	86.7	69.4	101 800	2.0	21.6	11.8	710	31.2	4.9	21 623	41 351	13.3
District 2	304 497	89.6	68.3	128 100	1.6	22.3	12.6	845	30.1	4.7	25 124	53 617	23.3
District 3	326 851	91.6	62.8	191 100	5.0	22.8	12.7	894	28.3	4.1	31 754	66 068	31.8
District 4	349 673	86.8	74.5	128 100	3.1	23.0	12.8	745	29.7	3.4	24 633	51 584	19.9
District 5	298 299	85.5	69.2	115 400	2.1	23.5	12.9	779	31.7	5.0	22 032	46 131	15.7
District 6	324 237	88.5	65.9	131 100	1.7	23.4	13.0	844	31.9	5.2	23 471	51 287	19.2
District 7	355 207	88.8	55.8	208 100	16.3	23.0	11.2	979	26.5	3.6	41 804	70 229	33.1
District 8	347 614	85.3	74.8	125 700	4.1	22.2	12.2	783	27.4	5.1	25 725	52 247	20.9
District 9	291 737	83.5	44.0	106 200	0.7	28.4	14.0	758	32.3	11.2	17 416	37 185	10.3
District 10	380 528	90.1	66.5	164 100	5.1	23.6	12.7	918	30.7	4.3	28 598	60 802	26.8
District 11	318 396	81.4	69.9	96 400	3.4	22.0	11.9	661	29.0	4.4	22 828	41 947	14.6
District 12	331 602	90.8	65.3	124 500	3.3	23.7	13.1	836	29.1	3.9	24 691	51 049	19.4
District 13	295 496	84	67.7	89 300	1.7	21.5	11.6	653	28.9	4.5	21 291	42 368	12.6
District 14	335 439	81.1	71.5	141 100	2.7	22.2	12.8	793	29.7	4.6	27 241	56 312	27.0
District 15	278 441	82.3	69.0	78 500	1.4	22.6	12.3	604	31.3	10.6	15 183	35 394	11.2
District 16	261 055	91.7	61.8	110 400	1.1	24.9	12.0	666	30.7	7.5	17 208	36 185	12.6
District 17	309 229	86.3	62.4	114 300	2.3	22.7	12.8	782	34.4	4.7	20 324	42 093	13.6
District 18	290 647	83.4	48.6	100 900	1.3	25.7	14.6	768	32.9	8.8	18 715	36 991	12.3
District 19	289 561	85.1	63.9	90 600	1.7	21.2	11.6	703	31.6	4.7	20 495	41 039	13.0
District 20	275 562	88.3	51.7	94 800	1.0	24.3	11.6	730	29.4	6.7	17 335	38 859	8.9
District 21	375 048	89.8	64.5	186 800	10.9	22.5	12.3	892	30.2	3.5	32 752	58 329	26.3

1. Specified owner-occupied units.   2. Median monthly owner costs is often in the minimum category—10.0 percent or less, which is indicated as 10.0 percent.   3. Specified renter-occupied units.   4. Overcrowded or lacking complete plumbing facilities.

Table E. Congressional Districts 112th Congress — **Poverty, Labor Force, Employment, and Social Security**

STATE District	Poverty, 2010 (percent)			Civilian labor force, 2010			Civilian employment,[2] 2010				Persons under age 65 with no health insurance, 2010 (percent)	Social Security beneficiaries, December 2010		Supplemental Security Income recipients, December 2010
	Persons below poverty level	Families below poverty level	Households receiving food stamps in past 12 months	Total	Unemployment Total	Rate[1]	Total	Management, business, science, and arts occupations	Service, sales, and office	Construction and production		Number	Rate[3]	
	54	55	56	57	58	59	60	61	62	63	64	65	66	67
PENNSYLVANIA...............	13.4	9.3	11.4	6 463 490	620 700	9.6	5 842 790	36.1	42.0	21.9	11.9	2 577 714	202.9	358 197
District 1	31.6	27.2	29.5	290 666	51 074	17.6	239 592	29.8	50.7	19.5	18.0	95 852	146.3	53 616
District 2	26.3	19.2	19.5	298 873	41 853	14.0	257 020	43.8	44.5	11.7	14.7	103 111	163.6	39 471
District 3	16.0	11.3	13.9	312 550	28 600	9.2	283 950	29.3	43.3	27.4	12.3	143 754	224.5	21 212
District 4	9.8	6.9	9.6	335 313	22 991	6.9	312 322	40.3	40.6	19.1	8.2	144 910	223.8	12 402
District 5	17.0	10.5	11.6	309 998	26 818	8.7	283 180	30.8	39.5	29.7	12.9	145 387	223.1	17 343
District 6	7.4	4.7	6.1	393 058	29 344	7.5	363 714	44.6	39.1	16.3	9.1	123 570	170.1	9 679
District 7	6.9	4.7	5.0	364 430	28 932	7.9	335 498	46.4	38.6	15.1	8.5	124 183	184.4	8 738
District 8	6.1	4.0	4.0	373 680	33 728	9.0	339 952	41.7	41.1	17.1	7.8	125 577	186.7	7 242
District 9	12.6	8.9	11.3	327 867	28 605	8.7	299 262	28.8	40.6	30.6	15.0	148 028	222.0	18 311
District 10	12.1	8.3	10.3	329 887	28 990	8.8	300 897	29.5	43.0	27.5	13.0	154 393	230.7	15 813
District 11	15.7	11.0	12.9	339 391	40 069	11.8	299 322	30.0	45.2	24.8	13.7	157 894	229.5	18 822
District 12	15.5	11.3	16.1	294 046	30 587	10.4	263 459	28.1	44.6	27.4	11.8	158 675	259.1	18 455
District 13	9.9	7.2	8.0	360 431	39 961	11.1	320 470	40.4	42.1	17.4	12.3	129 406	191.9	18 455
District 14	18.8	12.9	17.2	298 276	32 289	10.8	265 987	36.6	47.8	15.6	12.9	118 000	201.9	26 030
District 15	11.8	8.9	9.9	370 909	39 861	10.7	331 048	36.8	41.3	21.8	11.2	141 062	195.4	15 434
District 16	12.9	9.6	10.3	376 672	31 167	8.3	345 505	33.7	39.3	27.0	15.6	133 781	184.8	14 891
District 17	12.1	9.0	10.8	349 141	29 592	8.5	319 549	33.3	41.1	25.5	11.5	138 516	203.2	13 654
District 18	6.7	4.5	6.4	340 598	24 138	7.1	316 460	41.6	40.1	18.3	7.6	148 500	227.3	11 115
District 19	8.7	6.1	7.3	397 704	32 101	8.1	365 603	35.3	40.0	24.7	9.8	143 115	196.4	10 941
RHODE ISLAND...............	14.0	9.2	14.5	551 014	60 050	10.9	490 964	36.3	44.3	19.4	14.0	203 660	193.5	32 809
District 1	13.9	8.6	14.7	265 916	25 602	9.6	240 314	37.6	44.3	18.1	12.7	102 230	197.0	16 086
District 2	14.2	9.7	14.3	285 098	34 448	12.1	250 650	35.0	44.3	20.7	15.2	101 430	190.1	16 723
SOUTH CAROLINA	18.2	13.8	14.5	2 241 088	286 053	12.8	1 955 035	32.2	44.1	23.8	20.2	924 726	199.9	112 094
District 1	16.2	11.9	11.3	446 558	50 944	11.4	395 614	33.4	47.9	18.7	21.1	163 396	190.7	13 895
District 2	14.0	10.0	11.3	410 224	42 971	10.5	367 253	37.1	42.7	20.2	18.0	143 851	174.3	13 761
District 3	18.5	13.9	14.6	336 927	43 735	13.0	293 192	28.9	41.1	30.0	19.0	166 114	229.9	16 811
District 4	16.0	12.3	11.7	381 520	41 668	10.9	339 852	33.8	42.1	24.1	20.7	153 945	199.9	16 406
District 5	19.8	15.6	18.2	365 999	55 264	15.1	310 735	29.3	43.1	27.5	19.7	155 338	202.3	21 151
District 6	26.0	20.9	21.9	299 860	51 471	17.2	248 389	28.2	46.9	24.9	22.8	142 082	208.2	30 070
SOUTH DAKOTA...............	14.4	9.2	10.2	435 452	26 258	6.0	409 194	35.3	41.7	23.0	14.4	153 508	188.5	13 812
At Large	14.4	9.2	10.2	435 452	26 258	6.0	409 194	35.3	41.7	23.0	14.4	153 508	188.5	13 812
TENNESSEE	17.7	13.4	17.0	3 081 522	346 693	11.3	2 734 829	33.4	42.6	24.0	16.5	1 251 947	197.3	174 486
District 1	21.0	15.4	17.8	317 264	34 770	11.0	282 494	30.5	44.3	25.2	17.4	175 044	255.9	22 084
District 2	13.5	9.2	13.3	355 661	33 778	9.5	321 883	35.4	42.9	21.7	14.4	149 406	206.4	16 834
District 3	17.3	13.5	17.5	338 993	38 713	11.4	300 280	31.9	43.1	25.0	15.9	154 268	222.8	20 528
District 4	19.2	14.6	20.2	301 927	34 797	11.5	267 130	29.5	40.1	30.5	16.6	170 414	247.7	23 510
District 5	19.3	14.8	16.3	377 040	39 196	10.4	337 844	36.8	44.9	18.3	19.3	104 541	147.8	15 175
District 6	16.3	11.8	15.2	392 347	43 529	11.1	348 818	31.7	42.5	25.8	16.7	140 440	178.1	15 583
District 7	10.8	8.3	10.1	386 498	36 644	9.5	349 854	42.8	38.1	19.2	10.6	125 320	158.1	12 845
District 8	18.7	14.8	19.9	310 665	40 301	13.0	270 364	27.9	43.2	28.8	17.3	140 389	213.3	22 104
District 9	25.5	20.7	25.4	301 127	44 965	14.9	256 162	30.4	45.9	23.7	21.5	92 125	150.8	25 823
TEXAS	17.9	13.8	12.9	12 363 612	1 091 761	8.8	11 271 851	34.3	42.9	22.9	26.2	3 440 442	136.8	616 968
District 1	17.7	13.1	14.1	336 550	29 708	8.8	306 842	28.5	44.8	26.7	27.3	141 424	195.5	22 168
District 2	15.6	12.3	11.8	383 391	36 796	9.6	346 595	34.2	42.3	23.4	24.9	113 608	145.2	17 733
District 3	11.1	7.9	5.3	467 419	35 214	7.5	432 205	43.8	40.8	15.3	22.4	80 563	95.6	10 770
District 4	13.3	9.7	11.5	416 459	36 404	8.7	380 055	35.9	40.7	23.4	22.6	147 434	174.2	19 316
District 5	15.4	11.7	10.9	344 797	29 469	8.5	315 328	30.7	42.6	26.7	25.6	125 185	172.5	16 047
District 6	14.1	10.9	11.5	422 845	39 958	9.4	382 887	32.9	43.4	23.7	23.6	108 415	134.0	14 875
District 7	10.5	8.2	4.6	450 764	27 423	6.1	423 341	49.6	35.6	14.9	21.8	88 440	113.3	9 078
District 8	14.1	10.7	11.4	392 753	34 564	8.8	358 189	32.5	40.9	26.6	22.4	144 509	173.3	17 268
District 9	23.6	20.3	15.9	373 610	43 042	11.5	330 568	23.2	51.2	25.7	38.9	65 793	89.7	25 155
District 10	13.3	9.8	8.2	514 255	37 406	7.3	476 849	42.6	39.0	18.3	21.0	102 513	104.5	12 940
District 11	17.5	13.9	13.9	329 741	21 789	6.6	307 952	27.0	44.6	28.5	28.0	132 408	186.3	17 003
District 12	14.8	11.3	9.7	427 180	41 642	9.7	385 538	33.5	39.7	26.7	25.0	108 167	130.1	13 165
District 13	16.6	12.5	11.6	319 898	22 914	7.2	296 984	30.8	43.2	26.0	25.6	118 554	176.2	14 129
District 14	14.8	11.7	12.2	380 789	32 150	8.4	348 639	38.0	38.2	23.9	22.0	116 472	149.4	15 295
District 15	29.5	24.7	28.1	316 091	32 164	10.2	283 927	27.6	50.0	22.4	34.5	109 704	139.4	38 747
District 16	23.7	20.1	22.9	321 269	29 328	9.1	291 941	28.9	49.0	22.1	32.5	104 970	138.6	27 299
District 17	21.4	14.1	13.2	361 987	30 695	8.5	331 292	33.0	42.8	24.2	21.6	121 862	160.3	16 748
District 18	27.5	24.1	18.6	354 580	39 198	11.1	315 382	25.6	43.5	30.8	33.5	82 324	114.2	28 186
District 19	19.7	14.1	12.6	329 212	23 275	7.1	305 937	29.6	46.1	24.3	24.6	115 103	164.9	16 821
District 20	21.4	17.3	17.9	332 397	31 189	9.4	301 208	27.4	50.1	22.4	27.1	104 770	147.2	28 709
District 21	12.0	7.8	7.1	445 810	34 017	7.6	411 793	44.2	41.0	14.8	16.8	138 500	161.6	11 939

1. Percent of civilian labor force.   2. Persons 16 years old and over.   3. Per 1,000 resident population enumerated in the 2010 census.

Table E. Congressional Districts 112th Congress — **Agriculture**

STATE District	Farms		Land in farms		Farm Operators			Value of products sold				Government payments	
						Percent of farm operators				Percent of sales from			
	Number	Operated by family or individual (percent)	Acreage	Average size of farm (acres)	Total	Whose primary occupation is farming	Who live on the farm operated	Total ($1,000)	Average per farm	Crops	Livestock	Total ($1,000)	Percent of farms
	68	69	70	71	72	73	74	75	76	77	78	79	80
PENNSYLVANIA	63 163	91.4	7 809 244	124	94 500	43.7	82.5	5 808 803	91 965	32.2	67.8	75 975	27.6
District 1	9	77.8	(D)	(D)	11	54.5	27.3	(D)	(D)	(D)	(D)	(D)	22.2
District 2	7	42.9	(D)	(D)	8	62.5	50.0	(D)	(D)	(D)	(D)	(D)	(D)
District 3	6 327	92.1	838 229	132	9 619	41.4	86.2	322 598	50 988	45.7	54.3	6 745	25.8
District 4	2 149	92.9	213 633	99	3 225	39.4	84.8	70 000	32 573	44.2	55.8	1 407	20.1
District 5	7 337	92.8	1 023 487	139	10 863	38.6	82.3	328 767	44 809	25.4	74.6	8 358	26.3
District 6	1 509	85.4	137 089	91	2 394	48.7	79.0	126 584	83 886	41.3	58.7	1 539	20.4
District 7	133	72.2	6 491	49	195	39.5	64.6	10 546	79 293	95.3	4.7	(D)	6.8
District 8	934	82.1	75 883	81	1 437	45.7	82.7	70 573	75 560	76.4	23.6	713	16.7
District 9	10 786	92.1	1 567 412	145	16 020	44.3	82.0	1 041 785	96 587	15.5	84.5	15 908	33.4
District 10	8 209	92.4	1 151 681	140	12 050	42.1	83.2	616 670	75 121	21.6	78.4	13 212	33.6
District 11	2 049	90.9	233 365	114	3 057	39.1	76.5	78 346	38 236	65.7	34.3	3 466	44.7
District 12	4 596	93.5	567 009	123	6 675	34.7	82.3	125 629	27 334	35.7	64.3	2 556	16.9
District 13	346	83.2	17 307	50	537	39.5	75.6	14 602	42 202	65.9	34.1	137	13.6
District 14	22	86.4	780	35	30	36.7	60.0	382	17 364	(D)	(D)	(D)	(D)
District 15	1 225	86.5	166 285	136	1 959	44.7	76.3	110 742	90 402	71.6	28.4	1 922	24.2
District 16	6 483	91.3	538 904	83	9 619	60.7	86.2	1 568 313	241 912	36.2	63.8	6 028	22.3
District 17	4 679	90.2	525 179	112	7 136	45.7	79.3	802 441	171 498	29.9	70.1	7 425	36.8
District 18	2 156	92.1	221 383	103	3 310	37.2	84.1	41 177	19 099	47.6	52.4	1 153	13.8
District 19	4 207	89.8	524 871	125	6 355	44.6	81.3	479 163	113 897	38.5	61.5	5 391	26.6
RHODE ISLAND	1 219	75.3	67 819	56	1 912	47.0	75.5	65 908	54 067	84.4	15.6	743	8.3
District 1	399	71.4	19 977	50	618	48.9	71.4	26 826	67 233	83.3	16.7	310	9.3
District 2	820	77.2	47 842	58	1 294	46.1	77.4	39 082	47 661	85.1	14.9	433	7.8
SOUTH CAROLINA	25 867	88.9	4 889 339	189	37 082	35.7	73.5	2 352 681	90 953	33.9	66.1	67 253	29.8
District 1	1 434	85.1	246 048	172	2 050	41.5	69.0	119 812	83 551	75.0	25.0	2 523	36.3
District 2	3 292	87.5	742 880	226	4 931	34.8	71.3	345 589	104 978	40.3	59.7	10 153	33.8
District 3	6 873	91.5	875 015	127	10 065	32.5	80.2	431 422	62 771	18.1	81.9	5 152	17.4
District 4	2 662	90.3	237 909	89	3 789	32.9	79.3	50 763	19 069	64.8	35.2	853	8.5
District 5	6 149	88.4	1 319 057	215	8 707	37.4	73.0	877 278	142 670	19.6	80.4	20 690	30.8
District 6	5 457	87.2	1 468 430	269	7 540	38.4	64.8	527 817	96 723	54.2	45.8	27 883	50.8
SOUTH DAKOTA	31 169	85.4	43 666 403	1 401	46 710	55.9	74.1	6 570 450	210 801	51.5	48.5	270 748	73.5
At Large	31 169	85.4	43 666 403	1 401	46 710	55.9	74.1	6 570 450	210 801	51.5	48.5	270 748	73.5
TENNESSEE	79 280	91.7	10 969 798	138	117 044	35.9	79.1	2 617 394	33 015	43.9	56.1	95 744	21.8
District 1	11 586	92.5	937 484	81	16 823	36.8	79.1	235 856	20 357	20.0	80.0	1 365	11.0
District 2	8 436	91.3	485 311	89	8 038	37.6	82.0	171 236	31 500	38.0	62.0	681	9.2
District 3	6 953	92.7	684 193	98	10 268	37.5	82.1	212 772	30 601	14.0	86.0	891	9.1
District 4	17 884	91.9	2 404 671	134	26 752	36.5	81.5	662 472	37 043	30.5	69.5	8 892	18.0
District 5	1 618	88.8	152 611	94	2 401	33.3	80.1	25 238	15 598	53.4	46.6	121	7.0
District 6	15 331	92.7	1 955 929	128	22 892	35.3	82.1	483 442	31 534	38.1	61.9	5 099	16.1
District 7	8 256	90.6	1 425 208	173	12 000	33.6	73.3	180 660	21 882	57.4	42.6	16 991	38.4
District 8	12 084	90.0	2 909 485	241	17 661	35.6	72.3	640 058	52 967	77.7	22.3	61 223	48.9
District 9	132	80.3	14 906	113	209	34.9	56.9	5 660	42 879	93.3	6.7	481	32.6
TEXAS	247 437	88.2	130 398 753	527	372 563	36.4	67.4	21 001 074	84 874	31.3	68.7	720 903	19.4
District 1	12 742	91.6	2 005 138	157	19 177	35.5	77.7	1 074 512	84 328	8.2	91.8	1 524	2.6
District 2	2 633	88.7	630 426	239	4 058	38.8	72.3	67 295	25 558	48.6	51.4	4 496	8.4
District 3	248	86.7	31 605	127	354	30.5	63.0	4 976	20 065	72.0	28.0	100	8.9
District 4	21 386	91.8	4 063 008	190	32 158	35.0	78.5	1 000 258	46 772	19.8	80.2	15 129	12.9
District 5	13 192	92.3	2 049 427	155	19 763	35.0	79.1	473 563	35 898	43.0	57.0	1 528	3.7
District 6	11 100	90.9	2 721 793	245	16 711	37.7	70.1	314 499	28 333	34.2	65.8	7 078	10.4
District 7	133	81.2	15 399	116	199	35.7	52.3	7 266	54 632	89.6	10.4	(D)	2.3
District 8	8 571	92.3	1 107 018	129	13 362	32.6	77.2	132 955	15 512	56.3	43.7	2 319	3.4
District 9	73	90.4	5 320	73	116	42.2	59.5	832	11 397	73.7	26.4	(D)	2.7
District 10	11 163	90.4	1 846 823	165	16 926	34.2	70.9	262 378	23 504	39.1	60.9	4 616	7.1
District 11	21 021	86.2	19 856 142	945	31 814	37.4	63.1	1 038 701	49 413	44.9	55.1	84 626	29.4
District 12	7 430	92.2	987 121	133	11 593	32.0	84.5	129 347	17 409	40.8	59.2	642	4.4
District 13	20 025	82.5	24 077 073	1 202	29 697	39.5	52.0	5 836 767	291 474	23.1	76.9	179 534	52.1
District 14	8 522	87.7	3 331 684	391	12 969	37.7	64.5	604 900	70 981	62.8	37.2	36 186	22.0
District 15	11 992	85.7	6 003 254	501	17 603	39.1	52.2	638 392	53 235	65.6	34.4	32 299	18.8
District 16	422	80.6	127 493	302	614	47.6	67.9	27 076	64 161	95.2	4.8	605	9.5
District 17	17 339	91.3	4 030 130	232	26 313	34.2	74.3	647 405	37 338	33.2	66.8	13 090	11.1
District 18	109	92.7	8 324	76	179	26.3	42.5	1 901	17 440	90.1	9.9	642	0.0
District 19	17 283	80.8	14 667 894	849	24 882	41.2	48.9	5 591 793	323 543	30.6	69.4	251 523	60.7
District 20	187	87.7	39 486	211	290	32.8	43.1	3 261	17 439	78.9	21.1	2	4.8
District 21	6 139	85.0	2 399 808	391	9 636	34.2	72.9	72 954	11 884	30.9	69.1	1 633	5.9

1. Specified owner-occupied units.   2. Median monthly owner costs is often in the minimum category—10.0 percent or less, which is indicated as 10.0 percent.   3. Specified renter-occupied units.   4. Overcrowded or lacking complete plumbing facilities.

STATE District	Representative, 112th Congress	Land area,[1] 2010 (sq km)	Population and population characteristics, 2010												
						Percent									
					Race alone										
			Total persons	Per square kilometer	White	Black	American Indian, Alaska Native	Asian and Pacific Islander	Some other race	Two or more races	Hispanic or Latino[2]	Non-Hispanic White alone	Percent female	Percent foreign born	Percent born in state of residence
		1	2	3	4	5	6	7	8	9	10	11	12	13	14
TEXAS—Cont'd															
District 22	Pete Olson (R)	2 471	910 877	368.6	61.2	14.2	0.5	12.8	8.4	2.9	26.9	44.5	50.7	19.4	56.3
District 23	Francisco "Quico" Canseco (R)	125 376	847 651	6.8	79.3	3.5	0.7	2.0	11.7	2.7	66.4	27.4	50.3	15.7	65.8
District 24	Kenny Marchant (R)	870	792 319	910.9	61.6	14.8	0.6	9.7	10.2	3.0	27.1	46.5	51.1	19.8	50.0
District 25	Lloyd Doggett (D)	15 911	814 381	51.2	71.8	7.9	0.9	2.4	14.0	3.1	38.8	49.8	49.6	13.7	63.4
District 26	Michael C. Burgess (R)	3 324	915 137	275.3	71.3	13.4	0.7	4.0	7.7	2.8	21.2	59.4	50.8	12.8	55.1
District 27	Blake Farenthold (R)	12 213	741 993	60.8	84.0	2.3	0.5	1.3	9.8	2.0	73.2	22.8	51.0	15.4	70.5
District 28	Henry Cuellar (D)	35 258	851 824	24.2	87.9	1.5	0.4	0.8	7.7	1.6	78.9	18.4	51.0	24.5	63.5
District 29	Gene Green (D)	593	677 032	1 140.9	58.8	10.1	1.0	1.2	25.3	3.6	76.0	12.5	49.2	33.4	56.9
District 30	Eddie Bernice Johnson (D)	814	706 469	867.7	36.2	41.5	0.6	1.3	17.9	2.5	39.7	16.7	50.3	19.9	62.7
District 31	John R. Carter (R)	18 426	902 101	49.0	71.8	12.5	0.7	3.8	7.3	3.8	21.7	59.7	50.8	9.2	53.6
District 32	Pete Sessions (R)	410	640 419	1 560.4	66.0	8.6	0.8	5.4	16.4	2.9	42.4	42.4	50.0	28.6	49.8
UTAH		212 818	2 763 885	13.0	86.1	1.1	1.2	2.9	6.0	2.7	13.0	80.4	49.8	8.0	62.3
District 1	Rob Bishop (R)	53 879	906 660	16.8	86.1	1.4	0.8	2.4	6.5	2.8	14.1	79.9	49.5	7.4	63.8
District 2	Jim Matheson (D)	118 168	890 993	7.5	88.5	0.9	2.1	2.6	3.4	2.5	8.7	84.2	50.0	7.0	60.5
District 3	Jason Chaffetz (R)	40 771	966 232	23.7	83.9	0.9	0.8	3.6	7.9	2.9	15.9	77.3	49.8	9.5	62.6
VERMONT		23 871	625 741	26.2	95.3	1.0	0.4	1.3	0.3	1.7	1.5	94.3	50.7	4.4	51.1
At Large	Peter Welch (D)	23 871	625 741	26.2	95.3	1.0	0.4	1.3	0.3	1.7	1.5	94.3	50.7	4.4	51.1
VIRGINIA		102 279	8 001 024	78.2	68.6	19.4	0.4	5.6	3.2	2.9	7.9	64.8	50.9	11.4	49.9
District 1	Robert J. Wittman (R)	9 745	786 237	80.7	71.0	19.9	0.4	2.8	2.5	3.4	6.7	67.8	51.0	7.1	46.3
District 2	Scott Rigell (R)	2 489	646 184	259.7	66.1	22.1	0.4	5.3	2.2	3.9	7.0	62.8	49.7	8.6	41.6
District 3	Robert C. "Bobby" Scott (D)	2 888	663 390	229.7	37.1	55.3	0.5	2.0	2.0	3.0	4.9	35.5	52.2	5.5	60.4
District 4	J. Randy Forbes (R)	11 607	738 639	63.6	59.7	33.7	0.4	2.0	1.8	2.4	4.5	57.9	50.7	4.4	61.2
District 5	Robert Hurt (R)	23 070	685 859	29.7	73.1	22.0	0.3	1.5	1.4	1.7	3.1	71.7	51.3	4.2	66.8
District 6	Bob Goodlatte (R)	14 574	704 056	48.3	84.8	11.3	0.3	1.5	1.9	1.9	4.3	81.2	51.7	4.7	66.2
District 7	Eric Cantor (R)	9 064	757 917	83.6	74.3	17.1	0.3	3.9	2.1	2.2	4.9	72.1	51.7	7.8	58.0
District 8	James P. Moran (D)	317	701 010	2 209.5	63.4	13.6	0.5	10.8	7.7	4.0	18.2	54.6	50.8	27.4	23.3
District 9	Morgan Griffith (R)	22 743	656 200	28.9	92.9	3.8	0.2	1.1	0.7	1.2	1.8	92.0	50.2	2.4	65.9
District 10	Frank R. Wolf (R)	4 785	869 437	181.7	70.3	7.5	0.3	12.5	5.7	3.7	13.5	63.7	50.3	21.7	36.2
District 11	Gerald E. Connolly (D)	996	792 095	795.1	62.9	11.5	0.4	15.0	5.9	4.4	15.6	54.9	50.7	26.5	29.2
WASHINGTON		172 119	6 724 540	39.1	77.3	3.6	1.5	7.8	5.2	4.7	11.2	72.5	50.2	13.1	46.9
District 1	Vacant	1 135	739 455	651.3	76.4	2.7	0.9	12.4	2.9	4.7	7.6	72.7	50.4	16.7	44.0
District 2	Rick Larsen (D)	16 946	760 041	44.8	84.4	1.4	2.1	3.8	4.2	4.0	9.6	80.2	50.1	10.0	50.8
District 3	Jaime Herrera Beutler (R)	19 443	779 348	40.1	86.6	1.6	1.1	3.9	2.9	4.0	7.4	83.1	50.6	8.2	42.4
District 4	Doc Hastings (R)	49 321	774 409	15.7	72.8	1.0	2.1	1.6	19.1	3.4	33.8	60.2	49.7	15.8	53.7
District 5	Cathy McMorris Rodgers (R)	59 212	723 609	12.2	87.8	1.4	2.4	2.4	2.3	3.6	6.3	84.7	50.3	6.0	52.2
District 6	Norman D. Dicks (D)	17 489	709 570	40.6	76.8	5.5	2.4	5.9	3.3	6.1	8.5	73.3	50.3	9.0	48.8
District 7	Jim McDermott (D)	366	704 225	1 925.6	67.3	8.4	0.9	14.8	3.3	5.2	8.0	63.8	50.0	18.7	39.7
District 8	David G. Reichert (R)	6 642	810 754	122.1	74.6	3.0	0.9	14.0	2.9	4.6	7.2	71.2	50.1	17.7	45.6
District 9	Adam Smith (D)	1 565	723 129	462.1	67.9	7.8	1.3	11.2	5.4	6.5	12.0	63.1	50.4	16.0	44.7
WEST VIRGINIA		62 259	1 852 994	29.8	93.9	3.4	0.2	0.7	0.5	1.5	1.2	93.2	50.7	1.2	71.1
District 1	David McKinley (R)	16 254	615 991	37.9	95.2	2.1	0.2	0.8	0.2	1.4	1.1	94.5	50.4	1.2	69.6
District 2	Shelley Moore Capito (R)	21 880	648 186	29.6	92.6	4.2	0.2	0.7	0.5	1.7	1.7	91.6	50.8	1.6	65.5
District 3	Nick J. Rahall II (D)	24 125	588 817	24.4	94.0	3.9	0.2	0.4	0.2	1.3	0.8	93.4	50.9	0.8	78.7
WISCONSIN		140 268	5 686 986	40.5	86.2	6.3	1.0	2.3	2.4	1.8	5.9	83.3	50.4	4.5	72.1
District 1	Paul Ryan (R)	4 339	728 042	167.8	86.8	5.4	0.4	1.7	3.6	2.1	9.0	82.2	50.5	5.3	67.0
District 2	Tammy Baldwin (D)	9 049	751 169	83.0	86.9	4.5	0.4	3.3	2.7	2.2	6.1	84.1	50.4	6.6	66.7
District 3	Ron Kind (D)	35 047	729 957	20.8	94.9	0.9	0.6	1.6	0.8	1.2	2.0	93.8	49.8	2.0	68.3
District 4	Gwen Moore (D)	290	669 015	2 307.9	49.4	35.9	0.8	3.3	7.2	3.4	16.7	41.9	51.6	9.1	67.8
District 5	F. James Sensenbrenner Jr. (R)	3 288	707 580	215.2	92.3	2.4	0.3	2.5	1.0	1.5	3.8	89.9	51.2	4.2	76.5
District 6	Thomas E. Petri (R)	14 541	705 102	48.5	93.2	1.5	0.5	2.0	1.5	1.3	4.0	91.1	49.5	3.3	80.9
District 7	Sean P. Duffy (R)	48 567	689 279	14.2	93.8	0.6	1.6	1.9	0.6	1.4	1.9	92.9	49.8	2.2	73.2
District 8	Reid Ribble (R)	25 146	706 840	28.1	90.2	1.2	3.1	1.9	2.0	1.6	4.3	88.5	50.1	3.2	77.0
WYOMING		251 470	563 626	2.2	90.7	0.8	2.4	0.9	3.0	2.2	8.9	85.9	49.0	2.8	41.5
At Large	Cynthia M. Lummis (R)	251 470	563 626	2.2	90.7	0.8	2.4	0.9	3.0	2.2	8.9	85.9	49.0	2.8	41.5

1. Dry land or land partially or temporarily covered by water.   2. May be of any race.

Table E. Congressional Districts 112th Congress — **Age and Education**

STATE District	Population and population characteristics, 2010 (cont.)										Education, 2010			
	Age (percent)										Enrollment[1]		Attainment[2] (percent)	
	Under 5 years	5 to 17 years	18 to 24 years	25 to 34 years	35 to 44 years	45 to 54 years	55 to 64 years	65 to 74 years	75 years and over	Median age	Total	Percent private	High school graduate or more	Bachelor's degree or more
	15	16	17	18	19	20	21	22	23	24	25	26	27	28
TEXAS—Cont'd														
District 22	7.5	20.4	8.5	13.8	14.9	15.1	11.0	5.2	3.5	34.8	276 964	12.2	87.4	33.3
District 23	7.8	21.2	10.6	13.3	13.6	13.2	10.2	5.9	4.3	32.8	260 926	10.7	75.5	23.4
District 24	7.2	19.5	9.1	15.7	15.2	15.3	10.1	4.7	3.0	33.9	227 973	13.3	87.1	35.8
District 25	7.3	17.1	12.8	17.1	13.8	12.9	10.0	5.1	4.0	32.3	238 408	10.5	83.0	33.1
District 26	7.9	20.7	9.8	13.8	15.4	14.2	9.6	5.1	3.5	33.4	282 743	11.1	87.1	33.2
District 27	7.9	21.4	10.5	13.2	12.5	12.8	10.4	6.2	5.1	32.6	225 229	6.4	71.4	17.5
District 28	8.8	23.9	10.1	13.1	13.5	11.8	8.9	5.6	4.3	30.4	280 844	5.8	66.7	16.2
District 29	9.9	22.7	11.4	15.7	13.5	11.7	8.1	4.1	3.0	28.7	202 229	5.3	55.7	7.1
District 30	8.5	19.6	10.6	17.3	14.2	12.8	9.0	4.7	3.3	31.2	176 565	11.4	71.2	19.2
District 31	8.3	19.7	10.2	15.6	14.5	13.0	9.3	5.4	4.0	32.4	260 899	11.2	89.5	27.9
District 32	8.0	17.7	10.2	17.2	14.2	13.0	9.5	5.3	4.9	33.0	177 419	17.7	77.3	37.6
UTAH	9.5	22.0	11.5	16.1	12.0	11.1	8.7	5.0	4.0	29.2	910 416	14.6	90.6	29.3
District 1	9.6	22.2	10.7	16.1	12.2	11.7	8.7	4.8	4.0	29.6	295 700	8.9	90.3	29.0
District 2	8.6	20.2	10.3	15.6	11.9	11.7	10.0	6.3	5.3	31.8	273 104	12.3	91.6	34.1
District 3	10.4	23.4	13.3	16.7	12.0	10.0	7.4	4.0	2.9	26.7	341 612	21.4	89.9	24.7
VERMONT	5.1	15.5	10.4	11.1	12.5	16.4	14.4	7.9	6.6	41.5	153 914	18.8	91.0	33.6
At Large	5.1	15.5	10.4	11.1	12.5	16.4	14.4	7.9	6.6	41.5	153 914	18.8	91.0	33.6
VIRGINIA	6.4	16.8	10.0	13.6	13.9	15.2	11.9	6.9	5.3	37.5	2 121 496	16.7	86.5	34.2
District 1	6.3	18.3	10.0	12.0	13.4	15.8	11.6	7.2	5.4	37.9	218 280	12.9	90.4	32.5
District 2	6.5	16.1	13.1	15.5	12.9	14.3	10.8	6.0	4.9	34.1	163 587	15.9	90.9	29.0
District 3	6.9	16.0	13.8	15.1	12.0	14.0	11.0	6.0	5.2	33.5	188 818	12.6	82.2	21.7
District 4	6.2	18.3	8.9	12.2	14.0	16.4	12.1	6.9	5.0	38.5	198 449	15.4	84.8	23.5
District 5	5.5	15.3	10.4	11.3	12.3	15.1	13.7	9.2	7.3	41.4	176 700	14.6	80.4	22.6
District 6	5.7	15.4	12.6	11.3	12.2	14.4	12.8	8.2	7.4	39.4	189 356	22.2	83.8	25.9
District 7	6.3	17.7	7.9	12.5	14.1	15.7	12.8	7.2	5.9	39.2	189 185	18.6	88.2	37.5
District 8	6.8	12.6	8.0	22.0	16.4	13.9	10.9	5.4	3.9	35.3	156 328	23.7	89.9	59.1
District 9	5.1	14.4	12.0	11.2	12.8	14.4	13.7	9.3	7.1	40.8	164 886	9.4	77.7	16.9
District 10	7.6	20.0	7.2	13.8	16.2	16.0	10.5	5.1	3.5	35.9	243 008	18.4	90.4	48.6
District 11	6.9	19.1	8.2	13.3	15.3	16.2	11.8	5.6	3.7	36.8	232 899	19.1	90.9	49.9
WASHINGTON	6.5	17.0	9.7	13.9	13.5	14.7	12.4	6.8	5.5	37.3	1 704 894	15.1	89.8	31.1
District 1	6.3	18.6	8.4	14.0	14.5	15.9	12.8	6.2	5.2	38.4	186 886	17.9	94.1	41.2
District 2	6.2	16.9	10.1	12.8	12.9	14.9	13.1	7.4	5.7	38.3	188 719	13.8	90.2	26.0
District 3	6.4	18.3	8.4	12.4	13.3	14.7	13.2	7.6	5.7	38.5	201 804	12.0	90.2	23.4
District 4	8.2	20.5	10.2	13.1	12.1	13.0	11.2	6.6	5.3	33.4	207 646	9.8	78.2	19.8
District 5	6.1	16.5	12.2	12.4	11.6	14.2	13.0	7.6	6.4	37.6	197 671	15.3	91.7	26.7
District 6	6.1	15.6	9.6	13.1	12.0	14.7	13.8	8.4	6.8	39.9	158 625	15.6	89.3	24.0
District 7	5.5	11.1	11.4	19.8	16.1	13.6	11.9	5.5	5.2	36.3	172 723	22.8	91.6	52.1
District 8	6.7	19.3	7.4	13.0	15.5	16.4	11.4	5.9	4.3	37.5	218 820	16.4	93.2	40.9
District 9	7.1	17.3	9.7	14.8	13.4	14.8	11.5	6.2	5.2	35.9	171 800	13.2	88.7	23.1
WEST VIRGINIA	5.6	15.3	9.1	11.9	12.8	14.9	14.3	8.8	7.2	41.3	427 552	10.7	83.2	17.5
District 1	5.3	14.6	11.2	11.9	12.5	14.6	13.9	8.7	7.5	40.8	153 193	9.9	86.9	19.6
District 2	5.9	16.2	7.8	11.9	13.2	15.4	14.1	8.7	6.8	41.3	145 163	12.1	82.9	18.2
District 3	5.7	15.0	8.4	12.0	12.8	14.7	14.9	9.0	7.5	41.9	129 196	10.0	79.8	14.7
WISCONSIN	6.3	17.3	9.7	12.7	12.8	15.4	12.3	7.0	6.6	38.5	1 498 366	16.9	90.1	26.3
District 1	6.2	18.2	8.2	12.2	13.5	16.2	12.3	6.9	6.4	39.2	193 365	15.7	90.2	25.2
District 2	6.2	16.1	12.0	14.6	13.1	14.5	11.8	6.1	5.5	35.8	212 595	12.6	92.6	38.1
District 3	6.3	17.0	11.7	11.9	12.1	14.9	12.3	7.2	6.7	37.8	199 474	12.8	90.3	23.6
District 4	8.0	18.5	13.1	16.2	12.5	12.5	9.6	4.7	4.8	31.0	205 891	23.9	81.4	21.0
District 5	5.7	17.7	7.0	11.3	13.1	16.8	13.4	7.4	7.5	41.6	181 752	25.0	95.1	40.5
District 6	5.9	16.7	8.7	12.0	12.9	16.0	12.7	7.7	7.4	40.5	173 526	16.3	88.9	18.9
District 7	6.0	16.6	8.3	11.2	12.1	16.0	13.5	8.6	7.8	41.8	158 818	12.2	89.8	19.5
District 8	6.2	17.3	8.3	12.1	12.8	16.0	12.6	7.8	6.9	40.1	172 945	16.6	91.1	22.7
WYOMING	7.1	16.9	10.0	13.8	11.9	14.8	13.0	7.0	5.4	36.8	141 936	7.5	92.3	24.1
At Large	7.1	16.9	10.0	13.8	11.9	14.8	13.0	7.0	5.4	36.8	141 936	7.5	92.3	24.1

1. All persons 3 years old and over enrolled in nursery school through college and graduate or professional school.   2. Persons 25 years old and over.

Table E. Congressional Districts 112th Congress — Households and Group Quarters

STATE District	Households, 2010						Group quarters, 2010					
	Number	Persons per household	Family households (percent)	Husband-wife family (percent)	Female family householder[1]	One person households (percent)	Total in group quarters	Percent 65 years and over	Persons in correctional institutions	Persons in nursing homes	Persons in college dormitories	Persons in military quarters
	29	30	31	32	33	34	35	36	37	38	39	40
TEXAS—Cont'd												
District 22	313 961	2.88	76.0	58.5	12.5	19.7	8 420	27.4	4 494	2 150	4	0
District 23	279 506	2.96	74.7	54.0	15.3	20.2	14 356	9.7	12 314	2 347	3 647	527
District 24	300 206	2.63	67.2	49.5	12.9	26.7	4 948	48.4	38	1 991	1 367	0
District 25	308 363	2.57	60.2	43.1	12.0	28.1	25 099	15.1	5 547	3 580	6 915	0
District 26	320 707	2.81	72.3	55.0	12.5	21.4	16 831	14.5	2 919	2 499	6 859	0
District 27	243 367	2.99	74.0	50.1	17.9	21.0	10 752	17.3	6 034	2 553	3 091	144
District 28	250 308	3.35	81.6	58.9	17.2	15.5	7 415	19.7	7 474	2 767	1 475	146
District 29	198 670	3.39	76.7	50.0	18.3	18.4	4 538	32.3	519	1 103	6	0
District 30	248 766	2.77	62.5	35.1	21.0	30.2	21 188	9.5	11 108	2 282	1 240	0
District 31	324 743	2.69	71.6	54.7	12.5	22.7	27 983	10.6	13 680	3 230	3 501	6 906
District 32	247 103	2.57	60.1	43.3	11.6	32.0	7 288	35.7	16	2 447	2 817	0
UTAH	877 692	3.10	75.2	61.0	9.7	18.7	46 152	10.4	12 666	5 854	15 666	523
District 1	295 733	3.02	74.3	59.9	9.9	20.2	12 062	10.9	2 609	1 702	3 440	523
District 2	306 392	2.86	71.4	57.9	9.4	21.8	13 234	14.7	7 488	2 817	3 267	0
District 3	275 567	3.44	80.5	65.9	9.9	13.6	20 856	6.1	2 569	1 335	8 959	0
VERMONT	256 442	2.34	62.5	48.5	9.6	28.2	25 329	15.0	1 592	3 588	16 895	5
At Large	256 442	2.34	62.5	48.5	9.6	28.2	25 329	15.0	1 592	3 588	16 895	5
VIRGINIA	3 056 058	2.54	67.0	50.2	12.4	26.0	239 834	12.0	65 240	30 324	84 048	37 568
District 1	289 503	2.64	72.0	55.8	11.8	22.2	30 336	13.5	4 086	2 980	9 167	3 088
District 2	239 597	2.54	67.2	48.6	14.0	24.9	13 394	5.0	1 946	2 162	4 442	28 197
District 3	262 994	2.42	59.6	33.0	21.5	31.0	29 857	8.9	6 005	2 856	10 718	3 484
District 4	267 909	2.65	73.1	52.5	15.8	22.2	28 662	11.0	19 559	2 935	2 942	555
District 5	275 330	2.38	65.7	48.1	13.1	28.1	35 110	13.2	11 174	3 918	12 206	0
District 6	280 074	2.39	64.4	48.2	11.9	28.6	39 643	12.3	5 456	4 600	20 480	1 398
District 7	295 528	2.52	68.7	52.9	11.6	25.4	11 790	19.6	4 306	2 628	3 874	0
District 8	305 812	2.27	51.9	39.8	8.5	36.8	7 089	23.6	944	1 604	1 084	760
District 9	268 825	2.34	65.1	50.2	10.4	28.1	28 163	12.4	8 729	3 493	12 908	0
District 10	301 333	2.87	74.2	60.6	9.3	19.9	7 553	25.4	1 828	1 552	1 380	0
District 11	269 153	2.91	75.8	61.8	9.8	18.4	8 237	17.1	1 207	1 596	4 847	86
WASHINGTON	2 620 076	2.51	64.4	49.2	10.5	27.2	139 375	18.6	31 960	22 156	35 534	12 385
District 1	289 401	2.52	66.6	53.3	9.1	25.6	10 192	29.9	2 525	2 406	628	2 217
District 2	296 320	2.52	66.5	51.0	9.7	26.0	13 111	19.4	1 905	2 636	3 876	2 504
District 3	300 870	2.56	67.9	51.8	11.0	24.9	8 305	30.3	2 455	1 922	713	14
District 4	270 745	2.82	71.0	53.2	12.0	22.8	10 938	21.3	4 294	2 469	2 537	4
District 5	287 291	2.43	63.1	48.0	10.5	28.6	28 279	12.3	5 842	3 157	13 048	513
District 6	285 128	2.41	63.1	45.7	12.2	28.9	24 773	16.7	8 177	3 517	2 465	3 477
District 7	317 699	2.14	45.6	34.2	8.0	39.4	31 152	11.8	1 991	2 729	11 804	362
District 8	297 785	2.71	72.9	59.4	9.0	20.6	4 321	41.6	389	947	4	0
District 9	274 837	2.58	65.9	47.3	13.1	26.5	10 110	20.4	4 382	2 373	459	3 294
WEST VIRGINIA	763 831	2.36	65.8	49.8	11.2	28.4	49 382	18.9	16 591	9 748	17 113	79
District 1	254 442	2.33	63.9	48.8	10.5	29.0	22 019	15.8	6 965	3 632	10 300	0
District 2	264 808	2.40	67.1	50.9	11.2	27.5	14 325	23.3	3 029	2 959	3 456	79
District 3	244 581	2.35	66.3	49.6	11.9	29.0	13 038	20.1	6 597	3 157	3 357	0
WISCONSIN	2 279 768	2.43	64.4	49.6	10.3	28.2	150 214	23.1	38 102	33 808	56 773	132
District 1	284 605	2.51	67.6	51.9	11.0	26.4	16 989	24.6	6 711	3 628	2 368	0
District 2	307 499	2.37	60.2	47.1	9.0	29.3	22 220	16.8	3 401	3 800	12 204	0
District 3	285 231	2.46	65.2	52.3	8.3	26.6	28 527	18.5	4 527	4 795	15 295	122
District 4	263 034	2.47	56.4	29.2	21.3	34.0	16 117	17.2	2 539	3 001	9 538	0
District 5	286 539	2.43	67.7	56.6	7.7	26.7	8 224	40.0	1 071	3 819	3 160	0
District 6	282 790	2.40	65.9	53.2	8.3	27.8	29 511	19.3	12 794	5 072	5 510	0
District 7	283 587	2.38	65.8	52.5	8.6	27.8	12 834	33.4	3 749	4 797	4 180	0
District 8	286 482	2.42	66.4	52.9	8.9	27.2	15 792	31.1	3 310	4 896	4 518	10
WYOMING	226 879	2.42	64.6	50.9	8.9	28.0	13 712	18.4	3 576	2 450	4 443	503
At Large	226 879	2.42	64.6	50.9	8.9	28.0	13 712	18.4	3 576	2 450	4 443	503

1. No spouse present.

STATE District	Housing units, 2010										Money income, 2010		
	Total	Occupied units									Households		
			Owner-occupied					Renter-occupied					
						Median owner cost as a percent of income							
		Percent occupied	Percent	Median value[1] (dollars)	Percent valued at $500,000 or more	With a mortgage	Without a mortgage[2]	Median rent[3]	Median rent as a percent of income	Sub-standard units[4] (percent)	Per capita income (dollars)	Median income (dollars)	Percent with income of $100,000 or more
	41	42	43	44	45	46	47	48	49	50	51	52	53
TEXAS—Cont'd													
District 22	334 745	92	72.0	161 200	3.5	23.7	11.2	940	28.5	4.0	29 266	67 196	31.4
District 23	306 974	88.3	70.7	113 800	3.9	22.8	12.5	760	28.8	6.7	21 329	47 330	18.8
District 24	322 198	92.3	56.4	167 800	6.0	23.5	12.4	893	27.9	4.2	30 110	57 031	25.9
District 25	344 775	88.2	57.5	168 500	5.2	24.8	12.6	877	33.5	5.5	24 165	47 216	17.9
District 26	340 873	92	69.8	159 100	4.1	23.0	13.3	816	33.5	3.7	27 515	61 158	27.8
District 27	280 872	84.3	63.0	92 000	1.4	25.4	13.1	726	33.1	9.2	17 789	36 960	13.7
District 28	284 661	87.3	70.5	96 600	1.2	23.8	12.8	670	30.9	13.4	15 987	39 839	12.2
District 29	222 750	86	58.0	87 600	0.5	27.6	13.2	735	33.1	13.3	14 054	36 154	8.0
District 30	280 241	87.7	47.5	97 300	2.4	26.1	14.6	808	31.7	8.4	19 436	37 668	13.0
District 31	358 538	86.9	62.6	146 000	1.9	23.3	12.2	883	27.3	3.0	24 535	55 532	19.2
District 32	271 938	89.2	48.8	176 200	16.9	25.9	13.8	839	28.7	8.7	31 683	49 919	21.8
UTAH	981 821	89.6	69.9	217 200	6.7	24.8	10.0	796	29.5	4.6	22 059	54 744	19.1
District 1	332 796	89.6	69.2	202 000	6.7	23.8	10.0	738	28.6	3.8	22 340	54 224	19.3
District 2	353 480	86.5	68.6	247 100	9.7	25.9	10.0	827	28.8	4.1	24 847	54 514	20.7
District 3	295 545	93.4	72.1	206 600	3.7	25.1	10.0	818	32.0	6.0	19 244	55 479	17.4
VERMONT	322 698	79.6	70.4	216 800	7.3	26.0	16.3	823	31.8	2.2	26 876	49 406	16.9
At Large	322 698	79.6	70.4	216 800	7.3	26.0	16.3	823	31.8	2.2	26 876	49 406	16.9
VIRGINIA	3 368 674	88.8	67.7	249 100	16.0	24.7	11.4	1 019	30.2	2.6	31 313	60 674	27.8
District 1	326 986	87.3	71.8	273 000	11.3	24.6	10.7	1 111	30.1	2.0	31 220	68 777	30.4
District 2	269 432	88.2	62.9	255 600	11.8	27.6	13.5	1 112	31.5	2.6	28 314	57 142	23.1
District 3	287 253	87.9	53.2	183 500	3.9	27.2	13.6	867	34.0	4.8	21 689	41 485	12.4
District 4	290 706	90.1	71.8	226 700	5.9	25.1	11.9	902	30.5	2.3	25 852	58 773	22.4
District 5	327 263	82.6	70.2	154 100	7.8	24.6	12.0	712	30.4	2.0	22 893	41 134	12.8
District 6	312 733	88	67.8	185 300	5.7	24.3	11.1	707	29.4	2.3	23 782	45 342	14.2
District 7	322 201	90.4	73.8	252 800	10.2	24.8	11.1	955	30.0	1.9	32 522	61 653	28.3
District 8	327 088	90.6	51.7	462 700	44.1	23.7	12.0	1 467	27.4	3.7	49 211	88 668	44.2
District 9	307 454	83.7	71.1	113 100	2.7	22.8	10.8	604	33.6	1.9	19 276	35 201	9.0
District 10	318 617	93.3	73.6	390 400	34.8	24.5	10.7	1 350	29.7	2.2	41 917	98 709	49.7
District 11	278 941	95.8	75.5	413 300	35.0	23.4	10.0	1 540	29.5	3.2	42 347	105 560	53.4
WASHINGTON	2 888 594	90.2	63.1	271 800	14.8	26.7	12.1	908	30.6	3.4	28 364	55 631	22.1
District 1	311 906	93	66.9	360 100	22.9	27.0	12.5	1 134	28.9	2.7	34 787	72 438	33.7
District 2	336 617	87.4	66.2	283 700	13.4	29.1	12.9	893	31.7	3.7	25 954	54 449	18.7
District 3	330 626	89.7	66.9	228 500	6.6	27.2	12.1	834	30.5	2.9	24 884	51 599	17.6
District 4	302 643	88.4	63.8	179 500	4.8	23.0	10.0	716	31.1	5.3	21 772	46 591	16.6
District 5	321 638	89.2	64.6	184 100	5.3	24.6	10.9	684	31.8	2.3	23 231	44 048	13.3
District 6	326 338	87.1	64.1	237 200	8.6	27.6	12.3	843	32.2	3.4	24 511	46 683	14.8
District 7	340 158	91.9	48.9	419 600	34.6	25.9	14.0	984	29.7	3.7	36 910	59 358	27.2
District 8	321 299	92.8	71.5	367 800	29.9	27.1	12.4	1 192	28.3	2.4	36 918	79 260	36.6
District 9	297 369	93.1	58.0	253 200	6.5	27.9	12.9	973	32.2	4.5	25 981	54 647	19.6
WEST VIRGINIA	882 213	84.1	74.6	95 100	1.6	20.1	10.0	571	29.7	1.8	20 953	38 218	10.5
District 1	289 312	86.1	75.0	93 600	1.5	19.2	10.0	589	30.7	1.6	21 689	37 859	11.0
District 2	305 723	84.8	74.8	117 700	2.1	20.8	10.0	583	28.4	2.0	22 259	41 921	12.0
District 3	287 178	81.4	74.0	79 200	1.1	20.4	10.0	541	30.1	1.7	18 744	33 922	8.5
WISCONSIN	2 625 477	86.8	68.7	169 400	3.8	24.5	14.0	715	29.8	2.2	25 458	49 001	16.3
District 1	314 083	89.7	70.3	190 700	3.3	24.8	14.5	766	29.4	1.7	26 677	55 165	20.2
District 2	333 301	92.1	64.2	207 800	5.5	25.0	12.9	788	31.5	1.8	28 611	54 199	20.2
District 3	318 869	89.9	71.6	151 800	3.7	23.9	14.1	644	29.7	2.5	23 600	46 668	14.1
District 4	292 463	89	46.1	137 600	0.9	27.5	17.5	731	34.3	4.1	18 338	34 138	7.8
District 5	302 224	94	74.6	242 700	9.0	24.3	14.0	812	28.4	1.1	34 128	64 869	28.5
District 6	323 786	87.2	73.1	148 600	1.8	23.7	14.1	637	26.4	1.9	23 991	48 999	13.0
District 7	368 859	78.4	74.8	137 400	2.3	23.9	13.1	598	29.1	2.4	23 058	43 591	11.5
District 8	371 892	77.5	73.1	154 800	2.8	24.2	14.0	644	27.0	2.3	24 665	47 469	14.1
WYOMING	262 286	84.9	69.7	180 100	6.3	22.0	10.0	693	25.3	2.8	27 616	53 512	19.4
At Large	262 286	84.9	69.7	180 100	6.3	22.0	10.0	693	25.3	2.8	27 616	53 512	19.4

1. Specified owner-occupied units.   2. Median monthly owner costs is often in the minimum category—10.0 percent or less, which is indicated as 10.0 percent.   3. Specified renter-occupied units.   4. Overcrowded or lacking complete plumbing facilities.

Table E. Congressional Districts 112th Congress — Poverty, Labor Force, Employment, and Social Security

STATE District	Poverty, 2010 (percent)			Civilian labor force, 2010			Civilian employment,[2] 2010					Persons under age 65 with no health insurance, 2010 (percent)	Social Security beneficiaries, December 2010		Supplemental Security Income recipients, December 2010
					Unemployment			Percent							
	Persons below poverty level	Families below poverty level	Households receiving food stamps in past 12 months	Total	Total	Rate[1]	Total	Management, business, science, and arts occupations	Service, sales, and office	Construction and production			Number	Rate[3]	
	54	55	56	57	58	59	60	61	62	63	64		65	66	67
TEXAS—Cont'd															
District 22	10.5	8.2	7.2	482 259	37 880	7.9	444 379	43.2	38.3	18.5	20.5		99 565	109.3	13 109
District 23	21.2	16.6	17.0	389 556	37 072	9.5	352 484	33.3	44.9	21.8	25.4		122 970	145.1	30 441
District 24	12.4	9.9	7.0	440 571	37 451	8.5	403 120	39.8	42.3	17.9	21.7		77 704	98.1	9 513
District 25	19.5	13.8	11.9	429 717	36 586	8.5	393 131	38.0	41.8	20.1	24.2		99 105	121.7	15 562
District 26	12.2	8.4	7.9	481 744	44 553	9.2	437 191	39.5	42.0	18.5	19.7		106 706	116.6	14 397
District 27	28.0	22.7	24.6	323 621	31 474	9.7	292 147	29.8	47.3	22.9	30.1		108 221	145.9	32 715
District 28	27.3	23.0	27.1	374 695	32 886	8.8	341 809	26.1	49.2	24.7	35.8		112 752	132.4	38 168
District 29	28.0	25.1	17.8	303 202	37 258	12.3	265 944	15.0	41.3	43.7	43.9		66 649	98.4	18 529
District 30	26.3	22.8	17.2	337 563	40 511	12.0	297 052	28.7	43.6	27.8	35.1		85 540	121.1	28 021
District 31	11.0	7.9	8.7	431 276	35 683	8.3	395 593	38.4	43.0	18.6	17.7		115 362	127.9	13 614
District 32	19.0	15.1	9.2	347 611	32 062	9.2	315 549	35.7	41.0	23.4	32.4		75 150	117.3	9 508
UTAH	13.2	9.7	8.9	1 355 406	126 342	9.3	1 229 064	35.3	42.5	22.1	16.8		324 136	117.3	28 106
District 1	12.6	9.7	9.7	448 804	38 352	8.5	410 452	35.1	41.0	23.9	15.9		102 313	112.8	10 200
District 2	12.6	9.4	7.6	429 488	41 708	9.7	387 780	39.1	41.9	18.9	17.3		128 274	144.0	8 688
District 3	14.2	10.0	9.4	477 114	46 282	9.7	430 832	32.2	44.4	23.4	17.1		93 549	96.8	9 218
VERMONT	12.7	8.4	13.2	350 829	28 397	8.1	322 432	38.5	41.1	20.4	9.4		128 619	205.5	15 265
At Large	12.7	8.4	13.2	350 829	28 397	8.1	322 432	38.5	41.1	20.4	9.4		128 619	205.5	15 265
VIRGINIA	11.1	7.7	8.6	4 141 905	327 706	7.9	3 814 199	42.1	39.6	18.3	14.7		1 284 823	160.6	148 501
District 1	7.6	5.2	5.4	387 453	26 931	7.0	360 522	40.7	41.3	18.0	11.7		124 156	157.9	8 938
District 2	9.4	6.6	5.6	322 682	24 289	7.5	298 393	36.6	42.9	20.4	14.5		89 518	138.5	9 232
District 3	19.9	15.2	16.8	336 178	43 685	13.0	292 493	31.1	46.2	22.7	18.0		112 301	169.3	25 069
District 4	10.0	7.4	11.6	367 632	29 485	8.0	338 147	36.1	41.3	22.5	14.4		125 090	169.4	16 328
District 5	16.5	11.4	13.3	323 393	34 210	10.6	289 183	35.0	41.3	23.7	16.3		159 083	231.9	18 883
District 6	15.6	9.7	10.8	353 171	28 988	8.2	324 183	32.9	42.3	24.8	15.7		148 128	210.4	14 622
District 7	8.5	6.6	7.0	406 325	33 218	8.2	373 107	44.1	39.9	16.0	12.6		128 081	169.0	9 627
District 8	7.9	5.7	3.8	432 807	23 162	5.4	409 645	57.6	33.4	9.1	16.0		63 363	90.4	7 564
District 9	19.1	12.6	13.9	286 063	28 234	9.9	257 829	31.5	40.4	28.1	16.8		171 430	261.2	24 256
District 10	6.4	4.3	4.2	483 207	26 946	5.6	456 261	51.2	35.1	13.7	12.6		86 075	99.0	6 971
District 11	5.4	3.7	3.6	442 994	28 558	6.4	414 436	51.3	36.8	11.9	15.0		77 598	98.0	7 011
WASHINGTON	13.4	9.2	13.3	3 440 495	370 226	10.8	3 070 269	38.5	40.8	20.6	16.1		1 089 887	162.1	137 546
District 1	7.8	5.4	7.9	410 306	40 852	10.0	369 454	46.3	38.1	15.6	12.4		100 828	136.4	8 734
District 2	12.3	8.3	13.0	384 318	43 610	11.3	340 708	34.1	42.1	23.8	15.7		134 369	176.8	13 707
District 3	14.0	9.9	16.2	378 709	50 516	13.3	328 193	35.1	41.1	23.8	15.4		145 183	186.3	16 878
District 4	19.4	14.6	19.1	367 929	35 472	9.6	332 457	28.8	40.3	30.8	24.0		123 665	159.7	17 155
District 5	15.6	10.3	16.8	349 243	36 532	10.5	312 711	34.5	45.9	19.6	17.2		138 885	191.9	18 763
District 6	15.1	9.5	15.5	330 617	42 070	12.7	288 547	32.4	45.1	22.5	18.2		144 806	204.1	21 008
District 7	15.4	9.0	9.8	429 591	40 789	9.5	388 802	51.7	36.4	12.0	15.0		89 933	127.7	16 983
District 8	7.5	5.2	7.8	433 433	37 151	8.6	396 282	46.9	36.3	16.8	11.2		102 846	126.9	9 000
District 9	14.5	11.1	14.5	356 349	43 234	12.1	313 115	30.9	45.4	23.8	16.5		109 372	151.2	15 318
WEST VIRGINIA	18.1	13.2	15.4	820 067	73 223	8.9	746 844	30.2	44.3	25.6	17.3		443 911	239.6	80 367
District 1	17.4	11.5	13.4	285 731	24 419	8.5	261 312	30.7	43.6	25.6	16.7		140 163	227.5	21 265
District 2	16.1	11.6	14.2	301 966	27 030	9.0	274 936	30.7	44.3	25.0	16.9		147 550	227.6	23 083
District 3	21.1	16.6	18.9	232 370	21 774	9.4	210 596	28.8	45.1	26.1	18.3		156 198	265.3	36 019
WISCONSIN	13.2	9.1	11.0	3 080 461	275 359	8.9	2 805 102	33.6	41.4	25.0	10.8		1 061 501	186.7	107 571
District 1	11.2	9.0	10.7	389 467	39 566	10.2	349 901	34.2	41.8	24.0	11.3		134 472	184.7	12 111
District 2	12.7	7.4	10.2	434 842	31 151	7.2	403 691	41.7	39.8	18.5	9.1		117 717	156.7	10 777
District 3	13.5	8.3	9.4	398 120	27 613	6.9	370 507	31.1	41.1	27.7	11.4		139 664	191.3	11 556
District 4	27.9	23.8	23.1	341 465	50 876	14.9	290 589	29.3	47.2	23.6	17.1		100 227	149.8	35 147
District 5	6.4	4.0	5.4	397 036	29 428	7.4	367 608	42.9	40.2	17.0	6.9		132 598	187.4	5 992
District 6	10.6	7.5	9.5	380 086	31 957	8.4	348 129	27.7	40.4	32.0	9.0		141 405	200.5	9 304
District 7	13.1	9.0	11.9	364 558	32 733	9.0	331 825	28.8	40.7	30.5	11.5		151 085	219.2	11 970
District 8	11.2	7.6	8.6	374 887	32 035	8.5	342 852	30.8	41.1	28.2	10.3		144 333	204.2	10 714
WYOMING	11.2	7.2	6.2	299 393	18 779	6.3	280 614	33.0	39.4	27.6	16.9		91 019	161.5	6 337
At Large	11.2	7.2	6.2	299 393	18 779	6.3	280 614	33.0	39.4	27.6	16.9		91 019	161.5	6 337

1. Percent of civilian labor force. 2. Persons 16 years old and over. 3. Per 1,000 resident population enumerated in the 2010 census.

Table E. Congressional Districts 112th Congress — **Agriculture**

STATE District	Farms — Number	Farms — Operated by family or individual (percent)	Land in farms — Acreage	Land in farms — Average size of farm (acres)	Farm Operators — Total	Percent of farm operators — Whose primary occupation is farming	Percent of farm operators — Who live on the farm operated	Value of products sold — Total ($1,000)	Value of products sold — Average per farm	Percent of sales from — Crops	Percent of sales from — Livestock	Government payments — Total ($1,000)	Government payments — Percent of farms
	68	69	70	71	72	73	74	75	76	77	78	79	80
TEXAS—Cont'd													
District 22	1 865	88.4	423 928	227	2 812	32.1	66.5	55 956	30 003	75.0	25.0	4 198	16.0
District 23	8 248	83.5	22 845 659	2 770	12 499	38.5	61.4	580 155	70 339	47.5	52.5	18 235	15.7
District 24	238	83.2	16 856	71	377	23.9	62.3	3 202	13 454	74.0	26.0	7	3.4
District 25	13 999	88.6	3 270 984	234	21 133	34.8	66.0	684 765	48 915	14.0	86.0	7 833	8.5
District 26	3 529	89.3	493 567	140	5 394	31.0	83.4	97 351	27 586	23.0	77.0	1 012	8.0
District 27	2 534	83.4	2 575 828	1 017	3 678	42.8	60.1	338 653	133 644	79.1	20.9	24 092	39.7
District 28	11 383	87.2	7 070 518	621	17 218	36.4	57.7	442 565	38 879	43.7	56.3	13 294	13.6
District 29	148	91.9	17 906	121	218	31.2	56.4	1 159	7 831	41.2	58.8	60	3.4
District 30	306	89.2	32 717	107	464	37.9	66.4	16 361	53 467	89.3	10.7	90	5.6
District 31	13 380	90.8	3 623 186	271	20 211	36.0	73.5	838 786	62 690	21.2	78.8	15 092	18.0
District 32	97	72.2	23 238	240	145	26.9	49.7	11 092	114 351	91.0	9.0	27	8.2
UTAH	16 700	81.5	11 094 700	664	26 424	34.9	67.0	1 415 678	84 771	26.3	73.7	22 759	17.7
District 1	5 405	79.6	3 138 183	581	8 548	33.1	69.7	438 713	81 168	30.4	69.6	10 569	22.1
District 2	6 348	82.8	6 191 169	975	10 325	35.7	67.6	263 396	41 493	34.9	65.1	5 554	13.3
District 3	4 947	81.9	1 765 348	357	7 551	35.7	63.2	713 569	144 243	20.6	79.4	6 636	18.6
VERMONT	6 984	83.7	1 233 313	177	11 392	45.6	84.2	673 713	96 465	14.7	85.3	6 773	19.3
At Large	6 984	83.7	1 233 313	177	11 392	45.6	84.2	673 713	96 465	14.7	85.3	6 773	19.3
VIRGINIA	47 383	86.9	8 103 925	171	71 281	39.4	78.9	2 906 188	61 334	29.5	70.5	54 940	20.8
District 1	2 703	82.8	592 666	219	4 111	43.2	80.2	163 591	60 522	72.0	28.0	7 428	28.6
District 2	573	72.9	184 195	321	916	47.1	60.2	255 679	446 211	(D)	(D)	3 153	37.7
District 3	557	80.4	132 013	237	839	42.4	82.4	37 525	67 370	78.1	21.9	2 500	26.0
District 4	3 244	84.0	797 762	246	4 763	43.3	76.5	305 661	94 223	51.5	48.5	19 997	39.7
District 5	10 350	87.4	1 994 011	193	16 151	39.1	78.7	404 888	39 120	28.8	71.2	8 484	25.4
District 6	7 665	86.9	1 187 211	155	11 778	41.3	82.3	900 897	117 534	7.2	92.8	4 492	16.3
District 7	4 594	85.6	733 550	160	7 051	39.4	81.1	359 689	78 295	34.4	65.6	2 939	16.7
District 8	35	68.6	1 578	45	57	26.3	64.9	91	2 600	(D)	(D)	7	22.9
District 9	13 678	90.2	1 974 427	144	20 244	36.7	76.3	361 284	26 414	19.2	80.8	4 805	18.0
District 10	3 693	84.0	478 901	130	5 921	38.5	82.6	107 190	29 025	47.4	52.6	1 031	7.9
District 11	291	82.5	27 611	95	450	32.7	83.6	9 695	33 316	(D)	(D)	105	6.9
WASHINGTON	39 284	82.9	14 972 789	381	63 645	41.9	80.3	6 792 856	172 917	70.0	30.0	138 272	17.6
District 1	684	83.8	18 014	26	1 198	38.6	80.4	(D)	(D)	(D)	(D)	226	2.8
District 2	4 986	85.0	322 150	65	8 161	38.9	84.4	706 872	141 571	46.3	53.7	2 531	9.8
District 3	5 893	88.7	385 509	65	9 612	37.2	86.5	306 266	51 971	29.0	71.0	1 018	3.6
District 4	11 952	80.5	5 833 631	488	19 009	47.0	76.3	4 004 098	335 015	75.5	24.5	46 663	18.9
District 5	10 300	78.8	8 120 730	788	16 516	42.8	76.0	1 409 474	136 842	83.4	16.6	86 992	36.5
District 6	2 333	87.9	192 588	83	3 940	36.9	85.4	94 842	40 652	29.6	70.4	487	3.9
District 7	159	83.6	2 732	17	242	55.8	75.6	(D)	(D)	(D)	(D)	(D)	1.3
District 8	2 098	87.1	66 431	32	3 510	37.6	86.8	91 878	43 793	34.4	65.6	334	2.6
District 9	879	86.8	31 004	35	1 457	36.7	88.1	97 848	111 317	46.5	53.5	(D)	1.7
WEST VIRGINIA	23 618	95.2	3 697 606	157	34 720	38.6	83.5	591 665	25 051	13.2	86.8	2 929	9.2
District 1	9 178	95.7	1 349 749	147	13 642	38.2	83.9	(D)	(D)	(D)	(D)	(D)	5.8
District 2	9 378	94.6	1 536 515	164	13 805	38.9	83.6	381 943	40 728	13.7	86.3	1 880	11.6
District 3	5 062	95.5	811 342	160	7 273	38.8	82.7	(D)	(D)	(D)	(D)	(D)	10.9
WISCONSIN	78 463	86.8	15 190 804	194	123 217	44.2	80.1	8 967 358	114 288	29.8	70.2	195 787	60.5
District 1	2 997	79.2	613 696	205	4 767	44.2	76.8	418 458	139 626	58.4	41.6	11 318	58.5
District 2	8 375	85.3	1 520 711	182	13 384	42.5	80.1	1 053 905	125 839	36.1	63.9	28 580	64.7
District 3	28 808	87.6	5 602 793	194	45 409	41.6	78.3	2 691 302	93 422	26.3	73.7	74 366	65.1
District 4	26	73.1	209	8	47	74.5	36.2	3 035	116 731	(D)	(D)	(D)	(D)
District 5	2 272	80.9	335 746	148	3 479	45.3	77.3	266 821	117 439	(D)	(D)	4 957	54.5
District 6	10 556	85.7	2 089 928	198	16 528	46.4	78.9	1 624 910	153 932	31.6	68.4	29 442	66.9
District 7	15 854	89.2	3 299 355	208	24 730	46.9	84.9	1 596 366	100 692	28.0	72.0	25 704	48.4
District 8	9 575	87.1	1 728 366	181	14 873	46.5	80.6	1 312 560	137 082	19.8	80.2	21 420	58.1
WYOMING	11 069	79.4	30 169 526	2 726	18 522	45.5	80.2	1 157 535	104 574	18.5	81.5	28 157	25.2
At Large	11 069	79.4	30 169 526	2 726	18 522	45.5	80.2	1 157 535	104 574	18.5	81.5	28 157	25.2

Appendixes

Appendixes

APPENDIX A
GEOGRAPHIC CONCEPTS AND CODES

GEOGRAPHIC AREAS COVERED

County and City Extra presents data for states (Table A), states and counties (Table B), metropolitan areas (Table C), cities with populations of 25,000 or more in 2010 (Table D), and congressional districts (Table E).

STATES AND COUNTIES

Data are presented for each of the 50 states, the District of Columbia, and the United States as a whole. The states are arranged alphabetically and counties in Table B are arranged alphabetically within each state. Data are presented for 3,143 counties and county equivalents.

County equivalents

In Louisiana, the primary divisions of the state are known as parishes rather than counties. In Alaska, the county equivalents are the organized boroughs, together with the census areas that were developed for general statistical purposes by the state of Alaska and the U.S. Census Bureau. Four states—Maryland, Missouri, Nevada, and Virginia—have one or more incorporated places that are legally independent of any county and thus constitute primary divisions of their states. Within each state, independent cities are listed alphabetically following the list of counties. The District of Columbia is not divided into counties or county equivalents—data for the entire district are presented as a county equivalent. New York City contains five counties: Bronx, Kings, New York, Queens, and Richmond.

County changes since the 2000 census

- Broomfield County, CO, was created from parts of Adams, Boulder, Jefferson, and Weld Counties, effective November 15, 2001. The boundaries of Broomfield County reflect the boundaries of Broomfield city legally in effect on that date.
- Clifton Forge city, VA, formerly an independent city, became a town within Alleghany County, effective July 1, 2001.
- Effective June 20, 2007, the Skagway-Hoonah-Angoon Census Area in Alaska was divided into the Skagway Municipality and the Hoonah-Angoon Census Area.
- In May and June, 2008, the Wrangell-Petersburg and Prince of Wales-Outer Ketchikan Census Areas were dissolved and replaced by Wrangell City and Borough, Petersburg Census Area, and Prince of Wales Census Area. Some territory from the Prince of Wales Outer Ketchikan Census Area became part of the existing Ketchikan Gateway Borough.

METROPOLITAN AREAS

Table C presents data for 366 metropolitan statistical areas and 29 metropolitan divisions, which are located within the 11 largest metropolitan statistical areas. The metropolitan statistical areas are listed alphabetically, and the metropolitan divisions are listed alphabetically under the metropolitan statistical area of which they are components.

The U.S. Office of Management and Budget (OMB) defines metropolitan and micropolitan statistical areas according to published standards. The major purpose of defining these areas is to enable all U.S. government agencies to use the same geographic definitions in tabulating and publishing data. The general concept of a metropolitan or micropolitan statistical area is that of a core area containing a substantial population nucleus, together with adjacent communities that have a high degree of economic and social integration with the core. Currently defined metropolitan and micropolitan statistical areas are based on application of the new 2000 standards to 2000 decennial census data. Current metropolitan and micropolitan statistical area definitions were announced by OMB effective December 1, 2009. New definitions based on the 2010 census are expected in 2013.

Standard definitions of metropolitan areas were first issued in 1949 by the Bureau of the Budget (the predecessor of OMB), under the designation ''standard metropolitan area'' (SMA). The term was changed to ''standard metropolitan statistical area'' (SMSA) in 1959, and to ''metropolitan statistical area'' (MSA) in 1983. The term ''metropolitan area'' (MA) was adopted in 1990 and referred collectively to metropolitan statistical areas (MSAs), consolidated metropolitan statistical areas (CMSAs), and primary metropolitan statistical areas (PMSAs). The term ''core based statistical area'', (CBSA) became effective in 2000 and refers collectively to metropolitan and micropolitan statistical areas.

The 2000 standards provide that each CBSA must contain at least one urban area of 10,000 or more population. Each metropolitan statistical area must have at least one urbanized area of 50,000 or more inhabitants. Each micropolitan statistical area must have at least one urban cluster of at least 10,000 but less than 50,000 people.

Under the standards, the county (or counties) in which at least 50 percent of the population resides within urban areas of 10,000 or more population, or that contain at least 5,000 people residing within a single urban area of 10,000 or more population, is identified as a ''central county'' (counties). Additional ''outlying counties'' are included in the CBSA if they meet specified requirements of commuting to or from the central counties. Counties or equivalent entities form the geographic ''building blocks'', for metropolitan and micropolitan statistical areas throughout the United States.

If specified criteria are met, a metropolitan statistical area containing a single core with a population of 2.5 million or more may be subdivided to form smaller groupings of counties referred to as ''metropolitan divisions.''

As of December 1, 2009, there were 366 metropolitan statistical areas and 576 micropolitan statistical areas in the United States. Table C includes the 366 metropolitan statistical areas and the 29 metropolitan divisions. The core based statistical areas (metropolitan and micropolitan) and metropolitan divisions (as of December 2009) are listed in Appendix C with their 2010 census population counts.

The largest city in each metropolitan or micropolitan statistical area is designated a ''principal city.'' Additional cities qualify if specified requirements are met concerning population size and employment. The title of each metropolitan or micropolitan statistical area consists of the names of up to three of its principal cities and the name of each state into which the metropolitan or micropolitan statistical area extends. Titles of metropolitan divisions also typically are based on principal city names, but in certain cases consist of county names. The principal city need not be an incorporated place if it meets the requirements of population size and employment. Usually such a principal city is a Census designated place in decennial census data, but it is not included in most other data sources and is not in Table D (cities) in this volume.

In view of the importance of cities and town in New England, the 2000 standards also provide for a set of geographic areas that are defined using cities and towns in the six New England states. These New England city and town areas (NECTAs) are not included in this volume.

Appendix B lists the 366 metropolitan statistical areas, together with their component metropolitan divisions, where appropriate, the component counties of each area, and their 2010 census populations Appendix C provides the same information but also includes the 576 micropolitan statistical aras. Maps showing the metropolitan and micropolitan areas within each state can be found in Appendix D.

CITIES

Table D presents data for 1,436 cities with 2010 census populations of 25,000 or more. Corresponding data for states are also provided. The states are arranged alphabetically and the cities are ordered alphabetically within each state.

As used in this volume, the term *city* refers to places that have been incorporated as cities, boroughs, towns, or villages under the laws of their respective states. Towns in the New England states and New York are treated as minor civil divisions (MCDs) and are not included in the cities database. For Hawaii, data for the census designated places (CDPs) are included in the cities table, since the Census Bureau does not recognize any incorporated places in Hawaii. CDPs are delineated by the Census Bureau, in cooperation with states and localities, as statistical counterparts of incorporated places for purposes of the decennial census. CDPs comprise densely settled concentrations of population that are identifiable by name but are not legally incorporated as places.

Appendix E lists the 1,436 cities followed by the county where each city is located. If a city includes portions of more than one county, the population in each part is specified.

A consolidated city is an incorporated place that has combined its government functions with a county or subcounty entity but contains one or more other semi-independent incorporated places that continue to function as local governments within the consolidated government. Each consolidated city contains a core city, the area of a consolidated city not included in another separately incorporated place. The census geographic term for this core is the ''balance'' of the consolidated city. Thus the ''balance'' is essentially the core city of the consolidated government. This volume includes the consolidated city data where possible, but some data sources include numbers only for the ''balance'' and others do not specify which entity is represented. All estimates from the American Community Survey include only the ''balance''.

Consolidated cities included in this volume are Milford, CT; Athens-Clarke County, GA; Augusta-Richmond County, GA; Indianapolis, IN; Louisville-Jefferson County, KY; Butte-Silver Bow, MT; and Nashville-Davidson, TN.

Appendix E lists these seven consolidated cities, followed by the component places and their 2010 census populations.

CONGRESSIONAL DISTRICTS

The congressional districts shown in this volume are the districts used for the election of the 112th Congress, which convened in January 2011. These are the districts that were established following the 2000 Census and are based on population data from that census. As a result of litigation, some boundaries in Texas and Georgia changed between the 109th and 110th Congresses. The new data from the 2010 Census will be used to draw boundaries for the 113th Congress. Data are shown for the 435 regular districts plus the District of Columbia, which has a non-voting delegate, but no representative. Corresponding data for each state also are included. States are listed alphabetically and districts numerically within each state. A map showing congressional districts for the 109th Congress is included in Appendix D.

GEOGRAPHIC CODES

Tables A, B, C, and D provide, in one or more columns at the beginning of the table, a geographic code or codes for each area.

In Table B (states and counties), a five-digit state and county code is given for each state and county. The first two digits indicate the state; the remaining three represent the county. Within each state, the counties are listed in order, beginning with 001, with even numbers usually omitted. Independent cities follow the counties and begin with the number 510. In the second column of Table B, a five-digit core based statistical area (CBSA) code is given for those counties that are within metropolitan and micropolitan areas. In Table A, a two-digit state code is provided. The state code is a sequential numbering, with some gaps, of the states and the District of Columbia in alphabetical order from Alabama (01) to Wyoming (56).

These codes have been established by the U.S. government as Federal Information Processing Standards and are often referred to as *FIPS codes*. They are used by U.S. government agencies and many other organizations for data presentation. The codes are provided in this volume for use in matching the data given here with other data sources in which counties are identified by FIPS code. The metro area codes will also enable the user to identify the metro area of which a county is a component. Table C (metropolitan areas) provides the same metro area codes for each metropolitan area, as well as metropolitan division codes where appropriate.

Table D (cities) provides, in the first column, a seven-digit state and place code. The first two digits identify the state and are the same as the FIPS codes described above. The remaining five digits are the place FIPS codes established by the U.S. government.

INDEPENDENT CITIES

The following independent cities are not included in any county; their data are presented separately in this volume.

MARYLAND
Baltimore (separate from Baltimore County)

MISSOURI
St. Louis (separate from St. Louis County)

NEVADA
Carson City

VIRGINIA

Alexandria	Manassas
Bedford	Manassas Park
Bristol	Martinsville
Buena Vista	Newport News
Charlottesville	Norfolk
Chesapeake	Norton
Colonial Heights	Petersburg
Covington	Poquoson
Danville	Portsmouth
Emporia	Radford
Fairfax	Richmond
Falls Church	Roanoke
Franklin	Salem
Fredericksburg	Staunton
Galax	Suffolk
Hampton	Virginia Beach
Harrisonburg	Waynesboro
Hopewell	Williamsburg
Lexington	Winchester
Lynchburg	

COUNTY TYPE

Table B (states and counties) provides, in the third column, a *county type* code that identifies each county by its metropolitan/ nonmetropolitan status and its size. These are the "rural-urban continuum codes" developed by the Economic Research Service of the U.S. Department of Agriculture.

The 2003 rural-urban continuum codes form a classification scheme that distinguishes metropolitan counties by size and non-metropolitan counties by degree of urbanization and proximity to metro areas. The standard OMB metro and nonmetro categories have been subdivided into three metro and six nonmetro categories, resulting in a nine-part county codification. This scheme was originally developed in 1974. The codes were updated in 1983 and 1993, and slightly revised in 1988. The 1988 revision was first published in 1990. This scheme allows researchers to break county data into finer residential groups, beyond metro and nonmetro, particularly for the analysis of trends in nonmetro areas that are related to population density and metro influence. The 2003 rural-urban continuum codes are not directly comparable with the codes from previous years because of the new methodology used in developing the 2003 metropolitan areas.

Metropolitan counties
1. Counties in metro areas of 1 million population or more.
2. Counties in metro areas of 250,000 to 1 million population.
3. Counties in metro areas of fewer than 250,000 population.

Nonmetropolitan counties
4. Urban population of 20,000 or more, adjacent to a metro area.
5. Urban population of 20,000 or more, not adjacent to a metro area.
6. Urban population of 2,500 to 19,999, adjacent to a metro area.
7. Urban population of 2,500 to 19,999, not adjacent to a metro area.
8. Completely rural or less than 2,500 urban population, adjacent to a metro area.
9. Completely rural or less than 2,500 urban population, not adjacent to a metro area.

APPENDIX B
METROPOLITAN STATISTICAL AREAS, METROPOLITAN DIVISIONS, AND COMPONENTS
(as defined December 2009)

Core based statistical area	State/County FIPS code	Title and Geographic Components	2010 Census Population	Core based statistical area	State/County FIPS code	Title and Geographic Components	2010 Census Population
10180		Abilene, TX Metro SA	165 252	11500		Anniston-Oxford, AL Metro SA	118 572
	48 059	Callahan County, TX	13 544		01 015	Calhoun County, AL	118 572
	48 253	Jones County, TX	20 202				
	48 441	Taylor County, TX	131 506	11540		Appleton, WI Metro SA	225 666
10420		Akron, OH Metro SA	703 200		55 015	Calumet County, WI	48 971
	39 133	Portage County, OH	161 419		55 087	Outagamie County, WI	176 695
	39 153	Summit County, OH	541 781	11700		Asheville, NC Metro SA	424 858
10500		Albany, GA Metro SA	157 308		37 021	Buncombe County, NC	238 318
	13 007	Baker County, GA	3 451		37 087	Haywood County, NC	59 036
	13 095	Dougherty County, GA	94 565		37 089	Henderson County, NC	106 740
	13 177	Lee County, GA	28 298		37 115	Madison County, NC	20 764
	13 273	Terrell County, GA	9 315	12020		Athens-Clarke County, GA Metro SA	192 541
	13 321	Worth County, GA	21 679		13 059	Clarke County, GA	116 714
10580		Albany-Schenectady-Troy, NY Metro SA	870 716		13 195	Madison County, GA	28 120
	36 001	Albany County, NY	304 204		13 219	Oconee County, GA	32 808
	36 083	Rensselaer County, NY	159 429		13 221	Oglethorpe County, GA	14 899
	36 091	Saratoga County, NY	219 607	12060		Atlanta-Sandy Springs-Marietta, GA Metro SA	5 268 860
	36 093	Schenectady County, NY	154 727		13 013	Barrow County, GA	69 367
	36 095	Schoharie County, NY	32 749		13 015	Bartow County, GA	100 157
					13 035	Butts County, GA	23 655
10740		Albuquerque, NM Metro SA	887 077		13 045	Carroll County, GA	110 527
	35 001	Bernalillo County, NM	662 564		13 057	Cherokee County, GA	214 346
	35 043	Sandoval County, NM	131 561		13 063	Clayton County, GA	259 424
	35 057	Torrance County, NM	16 383		13 067	Cobb County, GA	688 078
	35 061	Valencia County, NM	76 569		13 077	Coweta County, GA	127 317
					13 085	Dawson County, GA	22 330
10780		Alexandria, LA Metro SA	153 922		13 089	DeKalb County, GA	691 893
	22 043	Grant Parish, LA	22 309		13 097	Douglas County, GA	132 403
	22 079	Rapides Parish, LA	131 613		13 113	Fayette County, GA	106 567
10900		Allentown-Bethlehem-Easton, PA-NJ Metro SA	821 173		13 117	Forsyth County, GA	175 511
	34 041	Warren County, NJ	108 692		13 121	Fulton County, GA	920 581
	42 025	Carbon County, PA	65 249		13 135	Gwinnett County, GA	805 321
	42 077	Lehigh County, PA	349 497		13 143	Haralson County, GA	28 780
	42 095	Northampton County, PA	297 735		13 149	Heard County, GA	11 834
11020		Altoona, PA Metro SA	127 089		13 151	Henry County, GA	203 922
	42 013	Blair County, PA	127 089		13 159	Jasper County, GA	13 900
					13 171	Lamar County, GA	18 317
11100		Amarillo, TX Metro SA	249 881		13 199	Meriwether County, GA	21 992
	48 011	Armstrong County, TX	1 901		13 217	Newton County, GA	99 958
	48 065	Carson County, TX	6 182		13 223	Paulding County, GA	142 324
	48 375	Potter County, TX	121 073		13 227	Pickens County, GA	29 431
	48 381	Randall County, TX	120 725		13 231	Pike County, GA	17 869
					13 247	Rockdale County, GA	85 215
					13 255	Spalding County, GA	64 073
					13 297	Walton County, GA	83 768
11180		Ames, IA Metro SA	89 542	12100		Atlantic City-Hammonton, NJ Metro SA	274 549
	19 169	Story County, IA	89 542		34 001	Atlantic County, NJ	274 549
11260		Anchorage, AK Metro SA	380 821	12220		Auburn-Opelika, AL Metro SA	140 247
	02 020	Anchorage Municipality, AK	291 826		01 081	Lee County, AL	140 247
	02 170	Matanuska-Susitna Borough, AK	88 995	12260		Augusta-Richmond County, GA-SC Metro SA	556 877
11300		Anderson, IN Metro SA	131 636		13 033	Burke County, GA	23 316
	18 095	Madison County, IN	131 636		13 073	Columbia County, GA	124 053
					13 189	McDuffie County, GA	21 875
11340		Anderson, SC Metro SA	187 126		13 245	Richmond County, GA	200 549
	45 007	Anderson County, SC	187 126		45 003	Aiken County, SC	160 099
					45 037	Edgefield County, SC	26 985
11460		Ann Arbor, MI Metro SA	344 791				
	26 161	Washtenaw County, MI	344 791				

Core based statistical area	State/ County FIPS code	Title and Geographic Components	2010 Census Population	Core based statistical area	State/ County FIPS code	Title and Geographic Components	2010 Census Population
12420		Austin-Round Rock-San Marcos, TX Metro SA	1 716 289	13820		Birmingham-Hoover, AL Metro SA	1 128 047
	48 021	Bastrop County, TX	74 171		01 007	Bibb County, AL	22 915
	48 055	Caldwell County, TX	38 066		01 009	Blount County, AL	57 322
	48 209	Hays County, TX	157 107		01 021	Chilton County, AL	43 643
	48 453	Travis County, TX	1 024 266		01 073	Jefferson County, AL	658 466
	48 491	Williamson County, TX	422 679		01 115	St. Clair County, AL	83 593
					01 117	Shelby County, AL	195 085
12540		Bakersfield-Delano, CA Metro SA	839 631		01 127	Walker County, AL	67 023
	06 029	Kern County, CA	839 631	13900		Bismarck, ND Metro SA	108 779
					38 015	Burleigh County, ND	81 308
12580		Baltimore-Towson, MD Metro SA	2 710 489		38 059	Morton County, ND	27 471
	24 003	Anne Arundel County, MD	537 656				
	24 005	Baltimore County, MD	805 029	13980		Blacksburg-Christiansburg-Radford, VA Metro SA	162 958
	24 013	Carroll County, MD	167 134		51 071	Giles County, VA	17 286
	24 025	Harford County, MD	244 826		51 121	Montgomery County, VA	94 392
	24 027	Howard County, MD	287 085		51 155	Pulaski County, VA	34 872
	24 035	Queen Anne's County, MD	47 798		51 750	Radford clty, VA	16 408
	24 510	Baltimore city, MD	620 961				
				14020		Bloomington, IN Metro SA	192 714
12620		Bangor, ME Metro SA	153 923		18 055	Greene County, IN	33 165
	23 019	Penobscot County, ME	153 923		18 105	Monroe County, IN	137 974
					18 119	Owen County, IN	21 575
12700		Barnstable Town, MA Metro SA	215 888				
	25 001	Barnstable County, MA	215 888	14060		Bloomington-Normal, IL Metro SA	169 572
					17 113	McLean County, IL	169 572
12940		Baton Rouge, LA Metro SA	802 484				
	22 005	Ascension Parish, LA	107 215	14260		Boise City-Nampa, ID Metro SA	616 561
	22 033	East Baton Rouge Parish, LA	440 171		16 001	Ada County, ID	392 365
	22 037	East Feliciana Parish, LA	20 267		16 015	Boise County, ID	7 028
	22 047	Iberville Parish, LA	33 387		16 027	Canyon County, ID	188 923
	22 063	Livingston Parish, LA	128 026		16 045	Gem County, ID	16 719
	22 077	Pointe Coupee Parish, LA	22 802		16 073	Owyhee County, ID	11 526
	22 091	St. Helena Parish, LA	11 203	14460		Boston-Cambridge-Quincy, MA-NH Metro SA.	4 552 402
	22 121	West Baton Rouge Parish, LA	23 788			Boston-Quincy, MA Metro Div 14484	1 887 792
	22 125	West Feliciana Parish, LA	15 625		25 021	Norfolk County, MA	670 850
					25 023	Plymouth County, MA	494 919
12980		Battle Creek, MI Metro SA	136 146		25 025	Suffolk County, MA	722 023
	26 025	Calhoun County, MI	136 146			Cambridge-Newton-Framingham, MA Metro Div 15764	1 503 085
13020		Bay City, MI Metro SA	107 771		25 017	Middlesex County, MA	1 503 085
	26 017	Bay County, MI	107 771			Peabody, MA Metro Div 37764	743 159
					25 009	Essex County, MA	743 159
13140		Beaumont-Port Arthur, TX Metro SA	388 745			Rockingham County-Strafford County, NH Metro Div 40484	418 366
	48 199	Hardin County, TX	54 635		33 015	Rockingham County, NH	295 223
	48 245	Jefferson County, TX	252 273		33 017	Strafford County, NH	123 143
	48 361	Orange County, TX	81 837				
				14500		Boulder, CO Metro SA	294 567
13380		Bellingham, WA Metro SA	201 140		08 013	Boulder County, CO	294 567
	53 073	Whatcom County, WA	201 140				
				14540		Bowling Green, KY Metro SA	125 953
13460		Bend, OR Metro SA	157 733		21 061	Edmonson County, KY	12 161
	41 017	Deschutes County, OR	157 733		21 227	Warren County, KY	113 792
13740		Billings, MT Metro SA	158 050	14740		Bremerton-Silverdale, WA Metro SA	251 133
	30 009	Carbon County, MT	10 078		53 035	Kitsap County, WA	251 133
	30 111	Yellowstone County, MT	147 972				
13780		Binghamton, NY Metro SA	251 725	14860		Bridgeport-Stamford-Norwalk, CT Metro SA	916 829
	36 007	Broome County, NY	200 600		09 001	Fairfield County, CT	916 829
	36 107	Tioga County, NY	51 125				

Metropolitan Statistical Areas, Metropolitan Divisions, and Components (as defined December 2009)–*Continued*

Core based statistical area	State/ County FIPS code	Title and Geographic Components	2010 Census Population	Core based statistical area	State/ County FIPS code	Title and Geographic Components	2010 Census Population
15180		Brownsville-Harlingen, TX Metro SA................	406 220	16740		Charlotte-Gastonia-Rock Hill, NC-SC Metro SA..	1758 038
	48 061	Cameron County, TX....................................	406 220		37 007	Anson County, NC....................................	26 948
15260		Brunswick, GA Metro SA	112 370		37 025	Cabarrus County, NC	178 011
	13 025	Brantley County, GA.................................	18 411		37 071	Gaston County, NC	206 086
	13 127	Glynn County, GA.....................................	79 626		37 119	Mecklenburg County, NC	919 628
	13 191	McIntosh County, GA	14 333		37 179	Union County, NC....................................	201 292
15380		Buffalo-Niagara Falls, NY Metro SA	1135 509		45 091	York County, SC......................................	226 073
	36 029	Erie County, NY.......................................	919 040	16820		Charlottesville, VA Metro SA........................	201 559
	36 063	Niagara County, NY.................................	216 469		51 003	Albemarle County, VA	98 970
15500		Burlington, NC Metro SA..............................	151 131		51 065	Fluvanna County, VA...............................	25 691
	37 001	Alamance County, NC..............................	151 131		51 079	Greene County, VA	18 403
15540		Burlington-South Burlington, VT Metro SA	211 261		51 125	Nelson County, VA..................................	15 020
	50 007	Chittenden County, VT..............................	156 545		51 540	Charlottesville city, VA............................	43 475
	50 011	Franklin County, VT.................................	47 746	16860		Chattanooga, TN-GA Metro SA	528 143
	50 013	Grand Isle County, VT.............................	6 970		13 047	Catoosa County, GA................................	63 942
15940		Canton-Massillon, OH Metro SA....................	404 422		13 083	Dade County, GA	16 633
	39 019	Carroll County, OH	28 836		13 295	Walker County, GA..................................	68 756
	39 151	Stark County, OH	375 586		47 065	Hamilton County, TN	336 463
15980		Cape Coral-Fort Myers, FL Metro SA.............	618 754		47 115	Marion County, TN	28 237
	12 071	Lee County, FL..	618 754		47 153	Sequatchie County, TN	14 112
16020		Cape Girardeau-Jackson, MO-IL Metro SA.....	96 275	16940		Cheyenne, WY Metro SA...............................	91 738
	17 003	Alexander County, IL...............................	8 238		56 021	Laramie County, WY...............................	91 738
	29 017	Bollinger County, MO	12 363	16980		Chicago-Joliet-Naperville, IL-IN-WI Metro SA..	9461 105
	29 031	Cape Girardeau County, MO......................	75 674			Chicago-Joliet-Naperville, IL Metro Div 16974...	7883 147
16180		Carson City, NV Metro SA............................	55 274		17 031	Cook County, IL.......................................	5194 675
	32 510	Carson City, NV......................................	55 274		17 037	DeKalb County, IL	105 160
16220		Casper, WY Metro SA..................................	75 450		17 043	DuPage County, IL	916 924
	56 025	Natrona County, WY................................	75 450		17 063	Grundy County, IL...................................	50 063
16300		Cedar Rapids, IA Metro SA	257 940		17 089	Kane County, IL......................................	515 269
	19 011	Benton County, IA...................................	26 076		17 093	Kendall County, IL	114 736
	19 105	Jones County, IA.....................................	20 638		17 111	McHenry County, IL.................................	308 760
	19 113	Linn County, IA.......................................	211 226		17 197	Will County, IL..	677 560
16580		Champaign-Urbana, IL Metro SA...................	231 891			Gary, IN Metro Div 23844	708 070
	17 019	Champaign County, IL...............................	201 081		18 073	Jasper County, IN...................................	33 478
	17 053	Ford County, IL.......................................	14 081		18 089	Lake County, IN......................................	496 005
	17 147	Piatt County, IL.......................................	16 729		18 111	Newton County, IN	14 244
16620		Charleston, WV Metro SA.............................	304 284		18 127	Porter County, IN....................................	164 343
	54 005	Boone County, WV...................................	24 629			Lake County-Kenosha County, IL-WI Metro Div 29404...................................	869 888
	54 015	Clay County, WV.....................................	9 386		17 097	Lake County, IL.......................................	703 462
	54 039	Kanawha County, WV...............................	193 063		55 059	Kenosha County, WI................................	166 426
	54 043	Lincoln County, WV..................................	21 720	17020		Chico, CA Metro SA....................................	220 000
	54 079	Putnam County, WV.................................	55 486		06 007	Butte County, CA....................................	220 000
16700		Charleston-North Charleston-Summerville, SC Metro SA...	664 607				
	45 015	Berkeley County, SC	177 843				
	45 019	Charleston County, SC.............................	350 209				
	45 035	Dorchester County, SC............................	136 555				

Metropolitan Statistical Areas, Metropolitan Divisions, and Components (as defined December 2009)–*Continued*

Core based statistical area	State/County FIPS code	Title and Geographic Components	2010 Census Population	Core based statistical area	State/County FIPS code	Title and Geographic Components	2010 Census Population
17140		Cincinnati-Middletown, OH-KY-IN Metro SA....	2130 151	18020		Columbus, IN Metro SA	76 794
	18 029	Dearborn County, IN	50 047		18 005	Bartholomew County, IN	76 794
	18 047	Franklin County, IN	23 087				
	18 115	Ohio County, IN	6 128	18140		Columbus, OH Metro SA	1836 536
	21 015	Boone County, KY	118 811		39 041	Delaware County, OH	174 214
	21 023	Bracken County, KY	8 488		39 045	Fairfield County, OH	146 156
	21 037	Campbell County, KY	90 336		39 049	Franklin County, OH	1163 414
	21 077	Gallatin County, KY	8 589		39 089	Licking County, OH	166 492
	21 081	Grant County, KY	24 662		39 097	Madison County, OH	43 435
	21 117	Kenton County, KY	159 720		39 117	Morrow County, OH	34 827
	21 191	Pendleton County, KY	14 877		39 129	Pickaway County, OH	55 698
	39 015	Brown County, OH	44 846		39 159	Union County, OH	52 300
	39 017	Butler County, OH	368 130				
	39 025	Clermont County, OH	197 363	18580		Corpus Christi, TX Metro SA	428 185
	39 061	Hamilton County, OH	802 374		48 007	Aransas County, TX	23 158
	39 165	Warren County, OH	212 693		48 355	Nueces County, TX	340 223
					48 409	San Patricio County, TX	64 804
17300		Clarksville, TN-KY Metro SA	273 949				
	21 047	Christian County, KY	73 955	18700		Corvallis, OR Metro SA	85 579
	21 221	Trigg County, KY	14 339		41 003	Benton County, OR	85 579
	47 125	Montgomery County, TN	172 331				
	47 161	Stewart County, TN	13 324	18880		Crestview-Fort Walton Beach-Destin, FL Metro SA	180 822
17420		Cleveland, TN Metro SA	115 788		12 091	Okaloosa County, FL	180 822
	47 011	Bradley County, TN	98 963				
	47 139	Polk County, TN	16 825	19060		Cumberland, MD-WV Metro SA	103 299
					24 001	Allegany County, MD	75 087
17460		Cleveland-Elyria-Mentor, OH Metro SA	2077 240		54 057	Mineral County, WV	28 212
	39 035	Cuyahoga County, OH	1280 122				
	39 055	Geauga County, OH	93 389	19100		Dallas-Fort Worth-Arlington, TX Metro SA	6371 773
	39 085	Lake County, OH	230 041			Dallas-Plano-Irving, TX Metro Div 19124	4235 751
	39 093	Lorain County, OH	301 356		48 085	Collin County, TX	782 341
	39 103	Medina County, OH	172 332		48 113	Dallas County, TX	2368 139
					48 119	Delta County, TX	5 231
17660		Coeur d'Alene, ID Metro SA	138 494		48 121	Denton County, TX	662 614
	16 055	Kootenai County, ID	138 494		48 139	Ellis County, TX	149 610
					48 231	Hunt County, TX	86 129
17780		College Station-Bryan, TX Metro SA	228 660		48 257	Kaufman County, TX	103 350
	48 041	Brazos County, TX	194 851		48 397	Rockwall County, TX	78 337
	48 051	Burleson County, TX	17 187			Fort Worth-Arlington, TX Metro Div 23104	2136 022
	48 395	Robertson County, TX	16 622		48 251	Johnson County, TX	150 934
					48 367	Parker County, TX	116 927
17820		Colorado Springs, CO Metro SA	645 613		48 439	Tarrant County, TX	1809 034
	08 041	El Paso County, CO	622 263		48 497	Wise County, TX	59 127
	08 119	Teller County, CO	23 350				
				19140		Dalton, GA Metro SA	142 227
17860		Columbia, MO Metro SA	172 786		13 213	Murray County, GA	39 628
	29 019	Boone County, MO	162 642		13 313	Whitfield County, GA	102 599
	29 089	Howard County, MO	10 144				
				19180		Danville, IL Metro SA	81 625
17900		Columbia, SC Metro SA	767 598		17 183	Vermilion County, IL	81 625
	45 017	Calhoun County, SC	15 175				
	45 039	Fairfield County, SC	23 956	19260		Danville, VA Metro SA	106 561
	45 055	Kershaw County, SC	61 697		51 143	Pittsylvania County, VA	63 506
	45 063	Lexington County, SC	262 391		51 590	Danville city, VA	43 055
	45 079	Richland County, SC	384 504				
	45 081	Saluda County, SC	19 875	19340		Davenport-Moline-Rock Island, IA-IL Metro SA	379 690
17980		Columbus, GA-AL Metro SA	294 865		17 073	Henry County, IL	50 486
	01 113	Russell County, AL	52 947		17 131	Mercer County, IL	16 434
	13 053	Chattahoochee County, GA	11 267		17 161	Rock Island County, IL	147 546
	13 145	Harris County, GA	32 024		19 163	Scott County, IA	165 224
	13 197	Marion County, GA	8 742				
	13 215	Muscogee County, GA	189 885				

Metropolitan Statistical Areas,
Metropolitan Divisions,
and Components
(as defined December 2009)–*Continued*

Core based statistical area	State/ County FIPS code	Title and Geographic Components	2010 Census Population	Core based statistical area	State/ County FIPS code	Title and Geographic Components	2010 Census Population
19380		Dayton, OH Metro SA	841 502	20500		Durham-Chaspel Hill, NC Metro SA	504 357
	39 057	Greene County, OH	161 573		37 037	Chatham County, NC	63 505
	39 109	Miami County, OH	102 506		37 063	Durham County, NC	267 587
	39 113	Montgomery County, OH	535 153		37 135	Orange County, NC	133 801
	39 135	Preble County, OH	42 270		37 145	Person County, NC	39 464
19460		Decatur, AL Metro SA	153 829	20740		Eau Claire, WI Metro SA	161 151
	01 079	Lawrence County, AL	34 339		55 017	Chippewa County, WI	62 415
	01 103	Morgan County, AL	119 490		55 035	Eau Claire County, WI	98 736
19500		Decatur, IL Metro SA	110 768	20940		El Centro, CA Metro SA	174 528
	17 115	Macon County, IL	110 768		06 025	Imperial County, CA	174 528
19660		Deltona-Daytona Beach-Ormond Beach, FL Metro SA	494 593	21060		Elizabethtown, KY Metro SA	119 736
					21 093	Hardin County, KY	105 543
	12 127	Volusia County, FL	494 593		21 123	Larue County, KY	14 193
19740		Denver-Aurora-Broomfield, CO Metro SA.......	2543 482	21140		Elkhart-Goshen, IN Metro SA	197 559
	08 001	Adams County, CO	441 603		18 039	Elkhart County, IN	197 559
	08 005	Arapahoe County, CO	572 003				
	08 014	Broomfield County, CO...........................	55 889	21300		Elmira, NY Metro SA.......................................	88 830
	08 019	Clear Creek County, CO	9 088		36 015	Chemung County, NY	88 830
	08 031	Denver County, CO	600 158				
	08 035	Douglas County, CO	285 465	21340		El Paso, TX Metro SA	800 647
	08 039	Elbert County, CO	23 086		48 141	El Paso County, TX	800 647
	08 047	Gilpin County, CO..................................	5 441				
	08 059	Jefferson County, CO	534 543	21500		Erie, PA Metro SA..	280 566
	08 093	Park County, CO	16 206		42 049	Erie County, PA	280 566
19780		Des Moines-West Des Moines, IA Metro SA...	569 633	21660		Eugene-Springfield, OR Metro SA	351 715
	19 049	Dallas County, IA	66 135		41 039	Lane County, OR......................................	351 715
	19 077	Guthrie County, IA	10 954				
	19 121	Madison County, IA	15 679	21780		Evansville, IN-KY Metro SA	358 676
	19 153	Polk County, IA	430 640		18 051	Gibson County, IN	33 503
	19 181	Warren County, IA	46 225		18 129	Posey County, IN.....................................	25 910
					18 163	Vanderburgh County, IN...........................	179 703
19820		Detroit-Warren-Livonia, MI Metro SA.............	4296 250		18 173	Warrick County, IN	59 689
		Detroit-Livonia-Dearborn, MI Metro Div 19804	1820 584		21 101	Henderson County, KY	46 250
	26 163	Wayne County, MI..................................	1820 584		21 233	Webster County, KY	13 621
		Warren-Troy-Farmington Hills, MI Metro Div 47644	2475 666	21820		Fairbanks, AK Metro SA	97 581
	26 087	Lapeer County, MI..................................	88 319		02 090	Fairbanks North Star Borough, AK..............	97 581
	26 093	Livingston County, MI.............................	180 967				
	26 099	Macomb County, MI	840 978	22020		Fargo, ND-MN Metro SA.................................	208 777
	26 125	Oakland County, MI	1202 362		27 027	Clay County, MN......................................	58 999
	26 147	St. Clair County, MI	163 040		38 017	Cass County, ND	149 778
				22140		Farmington, NM Metro SA	130 044
20020		Dothan, AL Metro SA..................................	145 639		35 045	San Juan County, NM	130 044
	01 061	Geneva County, AL	26 790				
	01 067	Henry County, AL	17 302	22180		Fayetteville, NC Metro SA...............................	366 383
	01 069	Houston County, AL	101 547		37 051	Cumberland County, NC	319 431
					37 093	Hoke County, NC.....................................	46 952
20100		Dover, DE Metro SA	162 310				
	10 001	Kent County, DE.....................................	162 310	22220		Fayetteville-Springdale-Rogers, AR-MO Metro SA	463 204
20220		Dubuque, IA Metro SA	93 653		05 007	Benton County, AR...................................	221 339
	19 061	Dubuque County, IA	93 653		05 087	Madison County, AR.................................	15 717
					05 143	Washington County, AR............................	203 065
20260		Duluth, MN-WI Metro SA	279 771		29 119	McDonald County, MO	23 083
	27 017	Carlton County, MN	35 386				
	27 137	St. Louis County, MN	200 226	22380		Flagstaff, AZ Metro SA....................................	134 421
	55 031	Douglas County, WI................................	44 159		04 005	Coconino County, AZ	134 421

Metropolitan Statistical Areas, Metropolitan Divisions, and Components (as defined December 2009)–*Continued*

Core based statistical area	State/ County FIPS code	Title and Geographic Components	2010 Census Population	Core based statistical area	State/ County FIPS code	Title and Geographic Components	2010 Census Population
22420		Flint, MI Metro SA	425 790	24540		Greeley, CO Metro SA	252 825
	26 049	Genesee County, MI	425 790		08 123	Weld County, CO..	252 825
22500		Florence, SC Metro SA	205 566	24580		Green Bay, WI Metro SA	306 241
	45 031	Darlington County, SC..............................	68 681		55 009	Brown County, WI..	248 007
	45 041	Florence County, SC	136 885		55 061	Kewaunee County, WI.................................	20 574
					55 083	Oconto County, WI.......................................	37 660
22520		Florence-Muscle Shoals, AL Metro SA...........	147 137				
	01 033	Colbert County, AL....................................	54 428	24660		Greensboro-High Point, NC Metro SA............	723 801
	01 077	Lauderdale County, AL...............................	92 709		37 081	Guilford County, NC	488 406
					37 151	Randolph County, NC..................................	141 752
22540		Fond du Lac, WI Metro SA	101 633		37 157	Rockingham County, NC	93 643
	55 039	Fond du Lac County, WI	101 633				
				24780		Greenville-Mauldin-Easley, NC Metro SA........	189 510
22660		Fort Collins-Loveland, CO Metro SA	299 630		37 079	Greene County, NC.....................................	21 362
	08 069	Larimer County, CO...................................	299 630		37 147	Pitt County, NC...	168 148
22900		Fort Smith, AR-OK Metro SA.........................	298 592	24860		Greenville, SC Metro SA...............................	636 986
	05 033	Crawford County, AR.................................	61 948		45 045	Greenville County, SC................................	451 225
	05 047	Franklin County, AR	18 125		45 059	Laurens County, SC....................................	66 537
	05 131	Sebastian County, AR	125 744		45 077	Pickens County, SC....................................	119 224
	40 079	Le Flore County, OK..................................	50 384				
	40 135	Sequoyah County, OK	42 391	25060		Gulfport-Biloxi, MS Metro SA........................	248 820
					28 045	Hancock County, MS...................................	43 929
23060		Fort Wayne, IN Metro SA..............................	416 257		28 047	Harrison County, MS	187 105
	18 003	Allen County, IN..	355 329		28 131	Stone County, MS	17 786
	18 179	Wells County, IN..	27 636				
	18 183	Whitley County, IN.....................................	33 292	25180		Hagerstown-Martinsburg, MD-WV Metro SA ...	269 140
					24 043	Washington County, MD.............................	147 430
23420		Fresno, CA Metro SA....................................	930 450		54 003	Berkeley County, WV	104 169
	06 019	Fresno County, CA	930 450		54 065	Morgan County, WV	17 541
23460		Gadsden, AL Metro SA	104 430	25260		Hanford-Corcoran, CA Metro SA	152 982
	01 055	Etowah County, AL.....................................	104 430		06 031	Kings County, CA	152 982
23540		Gainesville, FL Metro SA	264 275	25420		Harrisburg-Carlisle, PA Metro SA	549 475
	12 001	Alachua County, FL....................................	247 336		42 041	Cumberland County, PA..............................	235 406
	12 041	Gilchrist County, FL...................................	16 939		42 043	Dauphin County, PA....................................	268 100
					42 099	Perry County, PA..	45 969
23580		Gainesville, GA Metro SA	179 684				
	13 139	Hall County, GA...	179 684	25500		Harrisonburg, VA Metro SA	125 228
					51 165	Rockingham County, VA	76 314
24020		Glens Falls, NY Metro SA.............................	128 923		51 660	Harrisonburg city, VA.................................	48 914
	36 113	Warren County, NY	65 707				
	36 115	Washington County, NY	63 216	25540		Hartford-West Hartford-East Hartford, CT Metro SA	1212 381
24140		Goldsboro, NC Metro SA	122 623		09 003	Hartford County, CT	894 014
	37 191	Wayne County, NC	122 623		09 007	Middlesex County, CT	165 676
					09 013	Tolland County, CT.....................................	152 691
24220		Grand Forks, ND-MN Metro SA.....................	98 461				
	27 119	Polk County, MN..	31 600	25620		Hattiesburg, MS Metro SA	142 842
	38 035	Grand Forks County, ND............................	66 861		28 035	Forrest County, MS	74 934
					28 073	Lamar County, MS......................................	55 658
24300		Grand Junction, CO Metro SA.......................	146 723		28 111	Perry County, MS	12 250
	08 077	Mesa County, CO......................................	146 723				
				25860		Hickory-Lenoir-Morganton, NC Metro SA........	365 497
24340		Grand Rapids-Wyoming, MI Metro SA	774 160		37 003	Alexander County, NC................................	37 198
	26 015	Barry County, MI	59 173		37 023	Burke County, NC.......................................	90 912
	26 067	Ionia County, MI..	63 905		37 027	Caldwell County, NC...................................	83 029
	26 081	Kent County, MI...	602 622		37 035	Catawba County, NC..................................	154 358
	26 123	Newaygo County, MI	48 460				
				25980		Hinesville-Fort Stewart, GA Metro SA	77 917
24500		Great Falls, MT Metro SA.............................	81 327		13 179	Liberty County, GA.....................................	63 453
	30 013	Cascade County, MT	81 327		13 183	Long County, GA..	14 464

Metropolitan Statistical Areas,
Metropolitan Divisions,
and Components
(as defined December 2009)–*Continued*

Core based statistical area	State/County FIPS code	Title and Geographic Components	2010 Census Population	Core based statistical area	State/County FIPS code	Title and Geographic Components	2010 Census Population
26100		Holland-Grand Haven, MI Metro SA	263 801	27140		Jackson, MS Metro SA	539 057
	26 139	Ottawa County, MI	263 801		28 029	Copiah County, MS	29 449
					28 049	Hinds County, MS	245 285
26180		Honolulu, HI Metro SA	953 207		28 089	Madison County, MS	95 203
	15 003	Honolulu County, HI	953 207		28 121	Rankin County, MS	141 617
					28 127	Simpson County, MS	27 503
26300		Hot Springs, AR Metro SA	96 024				
	05 051	Garland County, AR	96 024	27180		Jackson, TN Metro SA	115 425
					47 023	Chester County, TN	17 131
26380		Houma-Bayou Cane-Thibodaux, LA Metro SA	208 178		47 113	Madison County, TN	98 294
	22 057	Lafourche Parish, LA	96 318				
	22 109	Terrebonne Parish, LA	111 860	27260		Jacksonville, FL Metro SA	1345 596
					12 003	Baker County, FL	27 115
26420		Houston-Sugar Land-Baytown, TX Metro SA	5946 800		12 019	Clay County, FL	190 865
	48 015	Austin County, TX	28 417		12 031	Duval County, FL	864 263
	48 039	Brazoria County, TX	313 166		12 089	Nassau County, FL	73 314
	48 071	Chambers County, TX	35 096		12 109	St. Johns County, FL	190 039
	48 157	Fort Bend County, TX	585 375				
	48 167	Galveston County, TX	291 309	27340		Jacksonville, NC Metro SA	177 772
	48 201	Harris County, TX	4092 459		37 133	Onslow County, NC	177 772
	48 291	Liberty County, TX	75 643				
	48 339	Montgomery County, TX	455 746	27500		Janesville, WI Metro SA	160 331
	48 407	San Jacinto County, TX	26 384		55 105	Rock County, WI	160 331
	48 473	Waller County, TX	43 205				
				27620		Jefferson City, MO Metro SA	149 807
26580		Huntington-Ashland, WV-KY-OH Metro SA	287 702		29 027	Callaway County, MO	44 332
	21 019	Boyd County, KY	49 542		29 051	Cole County, MO	75 990
	21 089	Greenup County, KY	36 910		29 135	Moniteau County, MO	15 607
	39 087	Lawrence County, OH	62 450		29 151	Osage County, MO	13 878
	54 011	Cabell County, WV	96 319				
	54 099	Wayne County, WV	42 481	27740		Johnson City, TN Metro SA	198 716
					47 019	Carter County, TN	57 424
26620		Huntsville, AL Metro SA	417 593		47 171	Unicoi County, TN	18 313
	01 083	Limestone County, AL	82 782		47 179	Washington County, TN	122 979
	01 089	Madison County, AL	334 811				
				27780		Johnstown, PA Metro SA	143 679
26820		Idaho Falls, ID Metro SA	130 374		42 021	Cambria County, PA	143 679
	16 019	Bonneville County, ID	104 234				
	16 051	Jefferson County, ID	26 140	27860		Jonesboro, AR Metro SA	121 026
					05 031	Craighead County, AR	96 443
26900		Indianapolis-Carmel, IN Metro SA	1756 241		05 111	Poinsett County, AR	24 583
	18 011	Boone County, IN	56 640				
	18 013	Brown County, IN	15 242	27900		Joplin, MO Metro SA	175 518
	18 057	Hamilton County, IN	274 569		29 097	Jasper County, MO	117 404
	18 059	Hancock County, IN	70 002		29 145	Newton County, MO	58 114
	18 063	Hendricks County, IN	145 448				
	18 081	Johnson County, IN	139 654	28020		Kalamazoo-Portage, MI Metro SA	326 589
	18 097	Marion County, IN	903 393		26 077	Kalamazoo County, MI	250 331
	18 109	Morgan County, IN	68 894		26 159	Van Buren County, MI	76 258
	18 133	Putnam County, IN	37 963				
	18 145	Shelby County, IN	44 436	28100		Kankakee-Bradley, IL Metro SA	113 449
					17 091	Kankakee County, IL	113 449
26980		Iowa City, IA Metro SA	152 586				
	19 103	Johnson County, IA	130 882				
	19 183	Washington County, IA	21 704				
27060		Ithaca, NY Metro SA	101 564				
	36 109	Tompkins County, NY	101 564				
27100		Jackson, MI Metro SA	160 248				
	26 075	Jackson County, MI	160 248				

Metropolitan Statistical Areas, Metropolitan Divisions, and Components (as defined December 2009)–*Continued*

Core based statistical area	State/County FIPS code	Title and Geographic Components	2010 Census Population	Core based statistical area	State/County FIPS code	Title and Geographic Components	2010 Census Population
28140		Kansas City, MO-KS Metro SA	2035 334	29420		Lake Havasu City-Kingman, AZ Metro SA	200 186
	20 059	Franklin County, KS	25 992		04 015	Mohave County, AZ	200 186
	20 091	Johnson County, KS	544 179				
	20 103	Leavenworth County, KS	76 227	29460		Lakeland-Winter Haven, FL Metro SA	602 095
	20 107	Linn County, KS	9 656		12 105	Polk County, FL	602 095
	20 121	Miami County, KS	32 787				
	20 209	Wyandotte County, KS	157 505	29540		Lancaster, PA Metro SA	519 445
	29 013	Bates County, MO	17 049		42 071	Lancaster County, PA	519 445
	29 025	Caldwell County, MO	9 424				
	29 037	Cass County, MO	99 478	29620		Lansing-East Lansing, MI Metro SA	464 036
	29 047	Clay County, MO	221 939		26 037	Clinton County, MI	75 382
	29 049	Clinton County, MO	20 743		26 045	Eaton County, MI	107 759
	29 095	Jackson County, MO	674 158		26 065	Ingham County, MI	280 895
	29 107	Lafayette County, MO	33 381				
	29 165	Platte County, MO	89 322	29700		Laredo, TX Metro SA	250 304
	29 177	Ray County, MO	23 494		48 479	Webb County, TX	250 304
28420		Kennewick-Pasco-Richland, WA Metro SA	253 340	29740		Las Cruces, NM Metro SA	209 233
	53 005	Benton County, WA	175 177		35 013	Dona Ana County, NM	209 233
	53 021	Franklin County, WA	78 163				
				29820		Las Vegas-Paradise, NV Metro SA	1951 269
28660		Killeen-Temple-Fort Hood, TX Metro SA	405 300		32 003	Clark County, NV	1951 269
	48 027	Bell County, TX	310 235				
	48 099	Coryell County, TX	75 388	29940		Lawrence, KS Metro SA	110 826
	48 281	Lampasas County, TX	19 677		20 045	Douglas County, KS	110 826
28700		Kingsport-Bristol-Bristol, TN-VA Metro SA	309 544	30020		Lawton, OK Metro SA	124 098
	47 073	Hawkins County, TN	56 833		40 031	Comanche County, OK	124 098
	47 163	Sullivan County, TN	156 823				
	51 169	Scott County, VA	23 177	30140		Lebanon, PA Metro SA	133 568
	51 191	Washington County, VA	54 876		42 075	Lebanon County, PA	133 568
	51 520	Bristol city, VA	17 835				
				30300		Lewiston, ID-WA Metro SA	60 888
28740		Kingston, NY Metro SA	182 493		16 069	Nez Perce County, ID	39 265
	36 111	Ulster County, NY	182 493		53 003	Asotin County, WA	21 623
28940		Knoxville, TN Metro SA	698 030	30340		Lewiston-Auburn, ME Metro SA	107 702
	47 001	Anderson County, TN	75 129		23 001	Androscoggin County, ME	107 702
	47 009	Blount County, TN	123 010				
	47 093	Knox County, TN	432 226	30460		Lexington-Fayette, KY Metro SA	472 099
	47 105	Loudon County, TN	48 556		21 017	Bourbon County, KY	19 985
	47 173	Union County, TN	19 109		21 049	Clark County, KY	35 613
					21 067	Fayette County, KY	295 803
29020		Kokomo, IN Metro SA	98 688		21 113	Jessamine County, KY	48 586
	18 067	Howard County, IN	82 752		21 209	Scott County, KY	47 173
	18 159	Tipton County, IN	15 936		21 239	Woodford County, KY	24 939
29100		La Crosse, WI-MN Metro SA	133 665	30620		Lima, OH Metro SA	106 331
	27 055	Houston County, MN	19 027		39 003	Allen County, OH	106 331
	55 063	La Crosse County, WI	114 638				
				30700		Lincoln, NE Metro SA	302 157
29140		Lafayette, IN Metro SA	201 789		31 109	Lancaster County, NE	285 407
	18 007	Benton County, IN	8 854		31 159	Seward County, NE	16 750
	18 015	Carroll County, IN	20 155				
	18 157	Tippecanoe County, IN	172 780	30780		Little Rock-North Little Rock-Conway, AR Metro SA	699 757
29180		Lafayette, LA Metro SA	273 738		05 045	Faulkner County, AR	113 237
	22 055	Lafayette Parish, LA	221 578		05 053	Grant County, AR	17 853
	22 099	St. Martin Parish, LA	52 160		05 085	Lonoke County, AR	68 356
					05 105	Perry County, AR	10 445
29340		Lake Charles, LA Metro SA	199 607		05 119	Pulaski County, AR	382 748
	22 019	Calcasieu Parish, LA	192 768		05 125	Saline County, AR	107 118
	22 023	Cameron Parish, LA	6 839				

Metropolitan Statistical Areas, Metropolitan Divisions, and Components (as defined December 2009)–*Continued*

Core based statistical area	State/ County FIPS code	Title and Geographic Components	2010 Census Population	Core based statistical area	State/ County FIPS code	Title and Geographic Components	2010 Census Population
30860		Logan, UT-ID Metro SA	125 442	31700		Manchester-Nashua, NH Metro SA	400 721
	16 041	Franklin County, ID................................	12 786		33 011	Hillsborough County, NH............................	400 721
	49 005	Cache County, UT...................................	112 656				
				31740		Manhattan, KS Metro SA	127 081
30980		Longview, TX Metro SA	214 369		20 061	Geary County, KS....................................	34 362
	48 183	Gregg County, TX....................................	121 730		20 149	Pottawatomie County, KS........................	21 604
	48 401	Rusk County, TX	53 330		20 161	Riley County, KS	71 115
	48 459	Upshur County, TX.................................	39 309				
				31860		Mankato-North Mankato, MN Metro SA..........	96 740
31020		Longview, WA Metro SA	102 410		27 013	Blue Earth County, MN.............................	64 013
	53 015	Cowlitz County, WA.................................	102 410		27 103	Nicollet County, MN.................................	32 727
31100		Los Angeles-Long Beach-Santa Ana, CA Metro SA	12828 837	31900		Mansfield, OH Metro SA	124 475
		Los Angeles-Long Beach-Glendale, CA Metro Div 31084	9818 605		39 139	Richland County, OH................................	124 475
	06 037	Los Angeles County, CA	9818 605	32580		McAllen-Edinburg-Mission, TX Metro SA.........	774 769
		Santa Ana-Anaheim-Irvine, CA Metro Div 42044	3010 232		48 215	Hidalgo County, TX	774 769
	06 059	Orange County, CA	3010 232	32780		Medford, OR Metro SA	203 206
					41 029	Jackson County, OR................................	203 206
31140		Louisville-Jefferson County, KY-IN Metro SA..	1283 566	32820		Memphis, TN-MS-AR Metro SA......................	1316 100
	18 019	Clark County, IN.....................................	110 232		05 035	Crittenden County, AR.............................	50 902
	18 043	Floyd County, IN.....................................	74 578		28 033	DeSoto County, MS.................................	161 252
	18 061	Harrison County, IN................................	39 364		28 093	Marshall County, MS...............................	37 144
	18 175	Washington County, IN............................	28 262		28 137	Tate County, MS.....................................	28 886
	21 029	Bullitt County, KY....................................	74 319		28 143	Tunica County, MS..................................	10 778
	21 103	Henry County, KY...................................	15 416		47 047	Fayette County, TN.................................	38 413
	21 111	Jefferson County, KY..............................	741 096		47 157	Shelby County, TN	927 644
	21 163	Meade County, KY..................................	28 602		47 167	Tipton County, TN	61 081
	21 179	Nelson County, KY..................................	43 437				
	21 185	Oldham County, KY.................................	60 316	32900		Merced, CA Metro SA	255 793
	21 211	Shelby County, KY	42 074		06 047	Merced County, CA	255 793
	21 215	Spencer County, KY................................	17 061				
	21 223	Trimble County, KY	8 809	33100		Miami-Fort Lauderdale-Pompano Beach, FL Metro SA	5564 635
31180		Lubbock, TX Metro SA...................................	284 890			Fort Lauderdale-Pompano Beach-Deerfield Beach, FL Metro Div 22744	1748 066
	48 107	Crosby County, TX..................................	6 059		12 011	Broward County, FL.................................	1748 066
	48 303	Lubbock County, TX................................	278 831			Miami-Miami Beach-Kendall, FL Metro Div 33124	2496 435
31340		Lynchburg, VA Metro SA	252 634		12 086	Miami-Dade County, FL............................	2496 435
	51 009	Amherst County, VA	32 353			West Palm Beach-Boca Raton-Boynton Beach, FL Metro Div 48424	1320 134
	51 011	Appomattox County, VA	14 973		12 099	Palm Beach County, FL	1320 134
	51 019	Bedford County, VA.................................	68 676				
	51 031	Campbell County, VA	54 842	33140		Michigan City-La Porte, IN Metro SA.............	111 467
	51 515	Bedford city, VA.....................................	6 222		18 091	LaPorte County, IN..................................	111 467
	51 680	Lynchburg city, VA.................................	75 568				
31420		Macon, GA Metro SA	232 293	33260		Midland, TX Metro SA	136 872
	13 021	Bibb County, GA	155 547		48 329	Midland County, TX.................................	136 872
	13 079	Crawford County, GA..............................	12 630				
	13 169	Jones County, GA	28 669	33340		Milwaukee-Waukesha-West Allis, WI Metro SA...	1555 908
	13 207	Monroe County, GA................................	26 424		55 079	Milwaukee County, WI.............................	947 735
	13 289	Twiggs County, GA.................................	9 023		55 089	Ozaukee County, WI...............................	86 395
31460		Madera-Chowchilla, CA Metro SA	150 865		55 131	Washington County, WI............................	131 887
	06 039	Madera County, CA	150 865		55 133	Waukesha County, WI..............................	389 891
31540		Madison, WI Metro SA	568 593				
	55 021	Columbia County, WI...............................	56 833				
	55 025	Dane County, WI	488 073				
	55 049	Iowa County, WI	23 687				

Metropolitan Statistical Areas, Metropolitan Divisions, and Components (as defined December 2009)–*Continued*

Core based statistical area	State/County FIPS code	Title and Geographic Components	2010 Census Population	Core based statistical area	State/County FIPS code	Title and Geographic Components	2010 Census Population
33460		Minneapolis-St. Paul-Bloomington, MN-WI Metro SA	3279 833	34940		Naples-Marco Island, FL Metro SA.................	321 520
	27 003	Anoka County, MN	330 844		12 021	Collier County, FL................................	321 520
	27 019	Carver County, MN	91 042	34980		Nashville-Davidson—Murfreesboro—Franklin,	
	27 025	Chisago County, MN	53 887			TN Metro SA	1589 934
	27 037	Dakota County, MN	398 552		47 015	Cannon County, TN...........................	13 801
	27 053	Hennepin County, MN	1152 425		47 021	Cheatham County, TN........................	39 105
	27 059	Isanti County, MN............................	37 816		47 037	Davidson County, TN........................	626 681
	27 123	Ramsey County, MN	508 640		47 043	Dickson County, TN..........................	49 666
	27 139	Scott County, MN.............................	129 928		47 081	Hickman County, TN.........................	24 690
	27 141	Sherburne County, MN......................	88 499		47 111	Macon County, TN............................	22 248
	27 163	Washington County, MN.....................	238 136		47 147	Robertson County, TN.......................	66 283
	27 171	Wright County, MN...........................	124 700		47 149	Rutherford County, TN.......................	262 604
	55 093	Pierce County, WI	41 019		47 159	Smith County, TN.............................	19 166
	55 109	St. Croix County, WI.........................	84 345		47 165	Sumner County, TN..........................	160 645
					47 169	Trousdale County, TN	7 870
33540		Missoula, MT Metro SA......................	109 299		47 187	Williamson County, TN.......................	183 182
	30 063	Missoula County, MT........................	109 299		47 189	Wilson County, TN............................	113 993
33660		Mobile, AL Metro SA.........................	412 992	35300		New Haven-Milford, CT Metro SA	862 477
	01 097	Mobile County, AL	412 992		09 009	New Haven County, CT........................	862 477
33700		Modesto, CA Metro SA	514 453	35380		New Orleans-Metairie-Kenner, LA Metro SA...	1167 764
	06 099	Stanislaus County, CA.......................	514 453		22 051	Jefferson Parish, LA	432 552
					22 071	Orleans Parish, LA	343 829
33740		Monroe, LA Metro SA	176 441		22 075	Plaquemines Parish, LA	23 042
	22 073	Ouachita Parish, LA	153 720		22 087	St. Bernard Parish, LA.......................	35 897
	22 111	Union Parish, LA	22 721		22 089	St. Charles Parish, LA	52 780
					22 095	St. John the Baptist Parish, LA	45 924
33780		Monroe, MI Metro SA	152 021		22 103	St. Tammany Parish, LA	233 740
	26 115	Monroe County, MI	152 021				
				35620		New York-Northern NJ-Long Island, NY-NJ-	
33860		Montgomery, AL Metro SA..................	374 536			PA Metro SA	18897 109
	01 001	Autauga County, AL	54 571			Edison-New Brunswick, NJ Metro Div	
	01 051	Elmore County, AL	79 303			20764	2340 249
	01 085	Lowndes County, AL	11 299		34 023	Middlesex County, NJ........................	809 858
	01 101	Montgomery County, AL......................	229 363		34 025	Monmouth County, NJ........................	630 380
					34 029	Ocean County, NJ	576 567
34060		Morgantown, WV Metro SA	129 709		34 035	Somerset County, NJ	323 444
	54 061	Monongalia County, WV......................	96 189			Nassau-Suffolk, NY Metro Div 35004	2832 882
	54 077	Preston County, WV	33 520		36 059	Nassau County, NY...........................	1339 532
					36 103	Suffolk County, NY............................	1493 350
34100		Morristown, TN Metro SA...................	136 608			Newark-Union, NJ-PA Metro Div 35084.......	2147 727
	47 057	Grainger County, TN	22 657		34 013	Essex County, NJ.............................	783 969
	47 063	Hamblen County, TN	62 544		34 019	Hunterdon County, NJ........................	128 349
	47 089	Jefferson County, TN.........................	51 407		34 027	Morris County, NJ	492 276
					34 037	Sussex County, NJ...........................	149 265
34580		Mount Vernon-Anacortes, WA Metro SA	116 901		34 039	Union County, NJ	536 499
	53 057	Skagit County, WA	116 901		42 103	Pike County, PA	57 369
						New York-White Plains-Wayne, NY-NJ	
34620		Muncie, IN Metro SA..........................	117 671			Metro Div 35644	11576 251
	18 035	Delaware County, IN	117 671		34 003	Bergen County, NJ	905 116
					34 017	Hudson County, NJ	634 266
34740		Muskegon-Norton Shores, MI Metro SA.........	172 188		34 031	Passaic County, NJ	501 226
	26 121	Muskegon County, MI.........................	172 188		36 005	Bronx County, NY	1385 108
					36 047	Kings County, NY	2504 700
34820		Myrtle Beach-North Myrtle Beach-Conway, SC Metro SA	269 291		36 061	New York County, NY	1585 873
	45 051	Horry County, SC	269 291		36 079	Putnam County, NY	99 710
					36 081	Queens County, NY...........................	2230 722
34900		Napa, CA Metro SA	136 484		36 085	Richmond County, NY	468 730
	06 055	Napa County, CA..............................	136 484		36 087	Rockland County, NY	311 687
					36 119	Westchester County, NY	949 113

Metropolitan Statistical Areas, Metropolitan Divisions, and Components (as defined December 2009)–*Continued*

Core based statistical area	State/ County FIPS code	Title and Geographic Components	2010 Census Population	Core based statistical area	State/ County FIPS code	Title and Geographic Components	2010 Census Population
35660		Niles-Benton Harbor, MI Metro SA	156 813	37340		Palm Bay-Melbourne-Titusville, FL Metro SA..	543 376
	26 021	Berrien County, MI	156 813		12 009	Brevard County, FL	543 376
35840		North Port-Bradenton-Sarasota, FL Metro SA.	702 281	37380		Palm Coast, FL Metro SA	95 696
	12 081	Manatee County, FL	322 833		12 035	Flagler County, FL	95 696
	12 115	Sarasota County, FL	379 448	37460		Panama City-Lynn Haven-Panama City Beach, FL Metro SA	168 852
35980		Norwich-New London, CT Metro SA	274 055		12 005	Bay County, FL	168 852
	09 011	New London County, CT	274 055				
36100		Ocala, FL Metro SA	331 298	37620		Parkersburg-Marietta-Vienna, WV-OH Metro SA	162 056
	12 083	Marion County, FL	331 298		39 167	Washington County, OH	61 778
36140		Ocean City, NJ Metro SA	97 265		54 073	Pleasants County, WV	7 605
	34 009	Cape May County, NJ	97 265		54 105	Wirt County, WV	5 717
					54 107	Wood County, WV	86 956
36220		Odessa, TX Metro SA	137 130				
	48 135	Ector County, TX	137 130	37700		Pascagoula, MS Metro SA	162 246
36260		Ogden-Clearfield, UT Metro SA	547 184		28 039	George County, MS	22 578
	49 011	Davis County, UT	306 479		28 059	Jackson County, MS	139 668
	49 029	Morgan County, UT	9 469	37860		Pensacola-Ferry Pass-Brent, FL Metro SA	448 991
	49 057	Weber County, UT	231 236		12 033	Escambia County, FL	297 619
36420		Oklahoma City, OK Metro SA	1252 987		12 113	Santa Rosa County, FL	151 372
	40 017	Canadian County, OK	115 541	37900		Peoria, IL Metro SA	379 186
	40 027	Cleveland County, OK	255 755		17 123	Marshall County, IL	12 640
	40 051	Grady County, OK	52 431		17 143	Peoria County, IL	186 494
	40 081	Lincoln County, OK	34 273		17 175	Stark County, IL	5 994
	40 083	Logan County, OK	41 848		17 179	Tazewell County, IL	135 394
	40 087	McClain County, OK	34 506		17 203	Woodford County, IL	38 664
	40 109	Oklahoma County, OK	718 633	37980		Philadelphia-Camden-Wilmington, PA-NJ-DE-MD Metro SA	5965 343
36500		Olympia, WA Metro SA	252 264			Camden, NJ Metro Div 15804	1250 679
	53 067	Thurston County, WA	252 264		34 005	Burlington County, NJ	448 734
36540		Omaha-Council Bluffs, NE-IA Metro SA	865 350		34 007	Camden County, NJ	513 657
	19 085	Harrison County, IA	14 928		34 015	Gloucester County, NJ	288 288
	19 129	Mills County, IA	15 059			Philadelphia, PA Metro Div 37964	4008 994
	19 155	Pottawattamie County, IA	93 158		42 017	Bucks County, PA	625 249
	31 025	Cass County, NE	25 241		42 029	Chester County, PA	498 886
	31 055	Douglas County, NE	517 110		42 045	Delaware County, PA	558 979
	31 153	Sarpy County, NE	158 840		42 091	Montgomery County, PA	799 874
	31 155	Saunders County, NE	20 780		42 101	Philadelphia County, PA	1526 006
	31 177	Washington County, NE	20 234			Wilmington, DE-MD-NJ Metro Div 48864	705 670
36740		Orlando-Kissimmee-Sanford, FL Metro SA	2134 411		10 003	New Castle County, DE	538 479
	12 069	Lake County, FL	297 052		24 015	Cecil County, MD	101 108
	12 095	Orange County, FL	1145 956		34 033	Salem County, NJ	66 083
	12 097	Osceola County, FL	268 685	38060		Phoenix-Mesa-Glendale, AZ Metro SA	4192 887
	12 117	Seminole County, FL	422 718		04 013	Maricopa County, AZ	3817 117
					04 021	Pinal County, AZ	375 770
36780		Oshkosh-Neenah, WI Metro SA	166 994				
	55 139	Winnebago County, WI	166 994	38220		Pine Bluff, AR Metro SA	100 258
36980		Owensboro, KY Metro SA	114 752		05 025	Cleveland County, AR	8 689
	21 059	Daviess County, KY	96 656		05 069	Jefferson County, AR	77 435
	21 091	Hancock County, KY	8 565		05 079	Lincoln County, AR	14 134
	21 149	McLean County, KY	9 531				
37100		Oxnard-Thousand Oaks-Ventura, CA Metro SA	823 318				
	06 111	Ventura County, CA	823 318				

Metropolitan Statistical Areas, Metropolitan Divisions, and Components (as defined December 2009)–*Continued*

Core based statistical area	State/County FIPS code	Title and Geographic Components	2010 Census Population	Core based statistical area	State/County FIPS code	Title and Geographic Components	2010 Census Population
38300		Pittsburgh, PA Metro SA	2356 285	39540		Racine, WI Metro SA	195 408
	42 003	Allegheny County, PA	1223 348		55 101	Racine County, WI	195 408
	42 005	Armstrong County, PA	68 941				
	42 007	Beaver County, PA	170 539	39580		Raleigh-Cary, NC Metro SA	1130 490
	42 019	Butler County, PA	183 862		37 069	Franklin County, NC	60 619
	42 051	Fayette County, PA	136 606		37 101	Johnston County, NC	168 878
	42 125	Washington County, PA	207 820		37 183	Wake County, NC	900 993
	42 129	Westmoreland County, PA	365 169				
				39660		Rapid City, SD Metro SA	126 382
38340		Pittsfield, MA Metro SA	131 219		46 093	Meade County, SD	25 434
	25 003	Berkshire County, MA	131 219		46 103	Pennington County, SD	100 948
38540		Pocatello, ID Metro SA	90 656	39740		Reading, PA Metro SA	411 442
	16 005	Bannock County, ID	82 839		42 011	Berks County, PA	411 442
	16 077	Power County, ID	7 817				
				39820		Redding, CA Metro SA	177 223
38860		Portland-South Portland-Biddeford, ME Metro SA	514 098		06 089	Shasta County, CA	177 223
	23 005	Cumberland County, ME	281 674	39900		Reno-Sparks, NV Metro SA	425 417
	23 023	Sagadahoc County, ME	35 293		32 029	Storey County, NV	4 010
	23 031	York County, ME	197 131		32 031	Washoe County, NV	421 407
38900		Portland-Vancouver-Hillsboro, OR-WA Metro SA	2226 009	40060		Richmond, VA Metro SA	1258 251
	41 005	Clackamas County, OR	375 992		51 007	Amelia County, VA	12 690
	41 009	Columbia County, OR	49 351		51 033	Caroline County, VA	28 545
	41 051	Multnomah County, OR	735 334		51 036	Charles City County, VA	7 256
	41 067	Washington County, OR	529 710		51 041	Chesterfield County, VA	316 236
	41 071	Yamhill County, OR	99 193		51 049	Cumberland County, VA	10 052
	53 011	Clark County, WA	425 363		51 053	Dinwiddie County, VA	28 001
	53 059	Skamania County, WA	11 066		51 075	Goochland County, VA	21 717
					51 085	Hanover County, VA	99 863
					51 087	Henrico County, VA	306 935
38940		Port St. Lucie, FL Metro SA	424 107		51 097	King and Queen County, VA	6 945
	12 085	Martin County, FL	146 318		51 101	King William County, VA	15 935
	12 111	St. Lucie County, FL	277 789		51 109	Louisa County, VA	33 153
					51 127	New Kent County, VA	18 429
39100		Poughkeepsie-Newburgh-Middletown, NY Metro SA	670 301		51 145	Powhatan County, VA	28 046
	36 027	Dutchess County, NY	297 488		51 149	Prince George County, VA	35 725
	36 071	Orange County, NY	372 813		51 183	Sussex County, VA	12 087
					51 570	Colonial Heights city, VA	17 411
					51 670	Hopewell city, VA	22 591
39140		Prescott, AZ Metro SA	211 033		51 730	Petersburg city, VA	32 420
	04 025	Yavapai County, AZ	211 033		51 760	Richmond city, VA	204 214
39300		Providence-New Bedford-Fall River, RI-MA Metro SA	1600 852	40140		Riverside-San Bernardino-Ontario, CA Metro SA	4224 851
	25 005	Bristol County, MA	548 285		06 065	Riverside County, CA	2189 641
	44 001	Bristol County, RI	49 875		06 071	San Bernardino County, CA	2035 210
	44 003	Kent County, RI	166 158				
	44 005	Newport County, RI	82 888	40220		Roanoke, VA Metro SA	308 707
	44 007	Providence County, RI	626 667		51 023	Botetourt County, VA	33 148
	44 009	Washington County, RI	126 979		51 045	Craig County, VA	5 190
					51 067	Franklin County, VA	56 159
39340		Provo-Orem, UT Metro SA	526 810		51 161	Roanoke County, VA	92 376
	49 023	Juab County, UT	10 246		51 770	Roanoke city, VA	97 032
	49 049	Utah County, UT	516 564		51 775	Salem city, VA	24 802
39380		Pueblo, CO Metro SA	159 063	40340		Rochester, MN Metro SA	186 011
	08 101	Pueblo County, CO	159 063		27 039	Dodge County, MN	20 087
					27 109	Olmsted County, MN	144 248
39460		Punta Gorda, FL Metro SA	159 978		27 157	Wabasha County, MN	21 676
	12 015	Charlotte County, FL	159 978				

Metropolitan Statistical Areas, Metropolitan Divisions, and Components (as defined December 2009)–*Continued*

Core based statistical area	State/ County FIPS code	Title and Geographic Components	2010 Census Population	Core based statistical area	State/ County FIPS code	Title and Geographic Components	2010 Census Population
40380		Rochester, NY Metro SA..................................	1054 323	41500		Salinas, CA Metro SA..................................	415 057
	36 051	Livingston County, NY	65 393		06 053	Monterey County, CA	415 057
	36 055	Monroe County, NY............................	744 344				
	36 069	Ontario County, NY	107 931	41540		Salisbury, MD Metro SA............................	125 203
	36 073	Orleans County, NY............................	42 883		24 039	Somerset County, MD.........................	26 470
	36 117	Wayne County, NY..............................	93 772		24 045	Wicomico County, MD.........................	98 733
40420		Rockford, IL Metro SA...............................	349 431	41620		Salt Lake City, UT Metro SA.....................	1124 197
	17 007	Boone County, IL..............................	54 165		49 035	Salt Lake County, UT	1029 655
	17 201	Winnebago County, IL........................	295 266		49 043	Summit County, UT	36 324
					49 045	Tooele County, UT	58 218
40580		Rocky Mount, NC Metro SA........................	152 392				
	37 065	Edgecombe County, NC......................	56 552	41660		San Angelo, TX Metro SA........................	111 823
	37 127	Nash County, NC................................	95 840		48 235	Irion County, TX.................................	1 599
					48 451	Tom Green County, TX	110 224
40660		Rome, GA Metro SA	96 317				
	13 115	Floyd County, GA..............................	96 317	41700		San Antonio-New Braunfels, TX Metro SA......	2142 508
					48 013	Atascosa County, TX..........................	44 911
40900		Sacramento—Arden-Arcade—Roseville, CA Metro SA	2149 127		48 019	Bandera County, TX............................	20 485
	06 017	El Dorado County, CA........................	181 058		48 029	Bexar County, TX...............................	1714 773
	06 061	Placer County, CA..............................	348 432		48 091	Comal County, TX..............................	108 472
	06 067	Sacramento County, CA......................	1418 788		48 187	Guadalupe County, TX........................	131 533
	06 113	Yolo County, CA................................	200 849		48 259	Kendall County, TX............................	33 410
					48 325	Medina County, TX.............................	46 006
40980		Saginaw-Saginaw Township North, MI Metro SA..............................	200 169		48 493	Wilson County, TX..............................	42 918
	26 145	Saginaw County, MI............................	200 169	41740		San Diego-Carlsbad-San Marcos, CA Metro SA..............................	3095 313
41060		St. Cloud, MN Metro SA	189 093		06 073	San Diego County, CA	3095 313
	27 009	Benton County, MN............................	38 451				
	27 145	Stearns County, MN............................	150 642	41780		Sandusky, OH Metro SA............................	77 079
					39 043	Erie County, OH.................................	77 079
41100		St. George, UT Metro SA............................	138 115				
	49 053	Washington County, UT	138 115	41860		San Francisco-Oakland-Fremont, CA Metro SA..............................	4335 391
						Oakland-Fremont-Hayward, CA Metro Div 36084..............................	2559 296
41140		St. Joseph, MO-KS Metro SA........................	127 329		06 001	Alameda County, CA...........................	1510 271
	20 043	Doniphan County, KS.........................	7 945		06 013	Contra Costa County, CA.....................	1049 025
	29 003	Andrew County, MO	17 291			San Francisco-San Mateo-Redwood City, CA Metro Div 41884	1776 095
	29 021	Buchanan County, MO	89 201		06 041	Marin County, CA	252 409
	29 063	DeKalb County, MO............................	12 892		06 075	San Francisco County, CA	805 235
41180		St. Louis, MO-IL Metro SA........................	2812 896		06 081	San Mateo County, CA........................	718 451
	17 005	Bond County, IL................................	17 768				
	17 013	Calhoun County, IL............................	5 089	41940		San Jose-Sunnyvale-Santa Clara, CA Metro SA..............................	1836 911
	17 027	Clinton County, IL..............................	37 762		06 069	San Benito County, CA	55 269
	17 083	Jersey County, IL...............................	22 985		06 085	Santa Clara County, CA.......................	1781 642
	17 117	Macoupin County, IL..........................	47 765				
	17 119	Madison County, IL............................	269 282	42020		San Luis Obispo-Paso Robles, CA Metro SA .	269 637
	17 133	Monroe County, IL.............................	32 957		06 079	San Luis Obispo County, CA	269 637
	17 163	St. Clair County, IL............................	270 056				
	29 071	Franklin County, MO...........................	101 492	42060		Santa Barbara-Santa Maria-Goleta, CA Metro SA..............................	423 895
	29 099	Jefferson County, MO..........................	218 733		06 083	Santa Barbara County, CA...................	423 895
	29 113	Lincoln County, MO	52 566				
	29 183	St. Charles County, MO	360 485	42100		Santa Cruz-Watsonville, CA Metro SA	262 382
	29 189	St. Louis County, MO..........................	998 954		06 087	Santa Cruz County, CA........................	262 382
	29 219	Warren County, MO............................	32 513				
	29 221	Washington County, MO	25 195	42140		Santa Fe, NM Metro SA........................	144 170
	29 510	St. Louis city, MO..............................	319 294		35 049	Santa Fe County, NM..........................	144 170
41420		Salem, OR Metro SA	390 738				
	41 047	Marion County, OR............................	315 335				
	41 053	Polk County, OR................................	75 403				

Metropolitan Statistical Areas, Metropolitan Divisions, and Components (as defined December 2009)–*Continued*

Core based statistical area	State/ County FIPS code	Title and Geographic Components	2010 Census Population	Core based statistical area	State/ County FIPS code	Title and Geographic Components	2010 Census Population
42220		Santa Rosa-Petaluma, CA Metro SA..............	483 878	44140		Springfield, MA Metro SA................................	692 942
	06 097	Sonoma County, CA....................................	483 878		25 011	Franklin County, MA...................................	71 372
42340		Savannah, GA Metro SA................................	347 611		25 013	Hampden County, MA.................................	463 490
	13 029	Bryan County, GA.......................................	30 233		25 015	Hampshire County, MA...............................	158 080
	13 051	Chatham County, GA	265 128	44180		Springfield, MO Metro SA..............................	436 712
	13 103	Effingham County, GA.................................	52 250		29 043	Christian County, MO	77 422
42540		Scranton—Wilkes-Barre, PA Metro SA	563 631		29 059	Dallas County, MO	16 777
	42 069	Lackawanna County, PA	214 437		29 077	Greene County, MO	275 174
	42 079	Luzerne County, PA	320 918		29 167	Polk County, MO	31 137
	42 131	Wyoming County, PA	28 276		29 225	Webster County, MO	36 202
42660		Seattle-Tacoma-Bellevue, WA Metro SA.........	3439 809	44220		Springfield, OH Metro SA..............................	138 333
		Seattle-Bellevue-Everett, WA Metro Div 42644	2644 584		39 023	Clark County, OH	138 333
	53 033	King County, WA	1931 249	44300		State College, PA Metro SA	153 990
	53 061	Snohomish County, WA	713 335		42 027	Centre County, PA......................................	153 990
		Tacoma, WA Metro Div 45104	795 225	44600		Steubenville-Weirton, OH-WV Metro SA	124 454
	53 053	Pierce County, WA	795 225		39 081	Jefferson County, OH..................................	69 709
42680		Sebastian-Vero Beach, FL Metro SA..............	138 028		54 009	Brooke County, WV.....................................	24 069
	12 061	Indian River County, FL...............................	138 028		54 029	Hancock County, WV	30 676
43100		Sheboygan, WI Metro SA	115 507	44700		Stockton, CA Metro SA.................................	685 306
	55 117	Sheboygan County, WI.................................	115 507		06 077	San Joaquin County, CA	685 306
43300		Sherman-Denison, TX Metro SA	120 877	44940		Sumter, SC Metro SA	107 456
	48 181	Grayson County, TX	120 877		45 085	Sumter County, SC.....................................	107 456
43340		Shreveport-Bossier City, LA Metro SA	398 604	45060		Syracuse, NY Metro SA	662 577
	22 015	Bossier Parish, LA.....................................	116 979		36 053	Madison County, NY....................................	73 442
	22 017	Caddo Parish, LA	254 969		36 067	Onondaga County, NY	467 026
	22 031	De Soto Parish, LA.....................................	26 656		36 075	Oswego County, NY....................................	122 109
43580		Sioux City, IA-NE-SD Metro SA......................	143 577	45220		Tallahassee, FL Metro SA	367 413
	19 193	Woodbury County, IA	102 172		12 039	Gadsden County, FL....................................	46 389
	31 043	Dakota County, NE	21 006		12 065	Jefferson County, FL...................................	14 761
	31 051	Dixon County, NE.......................................	6 000		12 073	Leon County, FL...	275 487
	46 127	Union County, SD.......................................	14 399		12 129	Wakulla County, FL.....................................	30 776
43620		Sioux Falls, SD Metro SA.............................	228 261	45300		Tampa-St. Petersburg-Clearwater, FL Metro SA.............	2783 243
	46 083	Lincoln County, SD.....................................	44 828		12 053	Hernando County, FL...................................	172 778
	46 087	McCook County, SD....................................	5 618		12 057	Hillsborough County, FL...............................	1229 226
	46 099	Minnehaha County, SD	169 468		12 101	Pasco County, FL.......................................	464 697
	46 125	Turner County, SD......................................	8 347		12 103	Pinellas County, FL.....................................	916 542
43780		South Bend-Mishawaka, IN-MI Metro SA........	319 224	45460		Terre Haute, IN Metro SA	172 425
	18 141	St. Joseph County, IN	266 931		18 021	Clay County, IN	26 890
	26 027	Cass County, MI	52 293		18 153	Sullivan County, IN.....................................	21 475
43900		Spartanburg, SC Metro SA	284 307		18 165	Vermillion County, IN...................................	16 212
	45 083	Spartanburg County, SC	284 307		18 167	Vigo County, IN	107 848
44060		Spokane, WA Metro SA.................................	471 221	45500		Texarkana, TX-Texarkana, AR Metro SA........	136 027
	53 063	Spokane County, WA	471 221		05 091	Miller County, AR..	43 462
44100		Springfield, IL Metro SA................................	210 170		48 037	Bowie County, TX.......................................	92 565
	17 129	Menard County, IL......................................	12 705	45780		Toledo, OH Metro SA....................................	651 429
	17 167	Sangamon County, IL..................................	197 465		39 051	Fulton County, OH......................................	42 698
					39 095	Lucas County, OH......................................	441 815
					39 123	Ottawa County, OH.....................................	41 428
					39 173	Wood County, OH.......................................	125 488

Metropolitan Statistical Areas, Metropolitan Divisions, and Components (as defined December 2009)–*Continued*

Core based statistical area	State/County FIPS code	Title and Geographic Components	2010 Census Population	Core based statistical area	State/County FIPS code	Title and Geographic Components	2010 Census Population
45820		Topeka, KS Metro SA	233 870	47260		Virginia Beach-Norfolk-Newport News, VA-NC Metro SA	1671 683
	20 085	Jackson County, KS	13 462		37 053	Currituck County, NC	23 547
	20 087	Jefferson County, KS	19 126		51 073	Gloucester County, VA	36 858
	20 139	Osage County, KS	16 295		51 093	Isle of Wight County, VA	35 270
	20 177	Shawnee County, KS	177 934		51 095	James City County, VA	67 009
	20 197	Wabaunsee County, KS	7 053		51 115	Mathews County, VA	8 978
45940		Trenton-Ewing, NJ Metro SA	366 513		51 181	Surry County, VA	7 058
	34 021	Mercer County, NJ	366 513		51 199	York County, VA	65 464
46060		Tucson, AZ Metro SA	980 263		51 550	Chesapeake city, VA	222 209
	04 019	Pima County, AZ	980 263		51 650	Hampton city, VA	137 436
46140		Tulsa, OK Metro SA	937 478		51 700	Newport News city, VA	180 719
	40 037	Creek County, OK	69 967		51 710	Norfolk city, VA	242 803
	40 111	Okmulgee County, OK	40 069		51 735	Poquoson city , VA	12 150
	40 113	Osage County, OK	47 472		51 740	Portsmouth city, VA	95 535
	40 117	Pawnee County, OK	16 577		51 800	Suffolk city, VA	84 585
	40 131	Rogers County, OK	86 905		51 810	Virginia Beach city, VA	437 994
	40 143	Tulsa County, OK	603 403		51 830	Williamsburg city, VA	14 068
	40 145	Wagoner County, OK	73 085	47300		Visalia-Porterville, CA Metro SA	442 179
46220		Tuscaloosa, AL Metro SA	219 461		06 107	Tulare County, CA	442 179
	01 063	Greene County, AL	9 045	47380		Waco, TX Metro SA	234 906
	01 065	Hale County, AL	15 760		48 309	McLennan County, TX	234 906
	01 125	Tuscaloosa County, AL	194 656	47580		Warner Robins, GA Metro SA	139 900
46340		Tyler, TX Metro SA	209 714		13 153	Houston County, GA	139 900
	48 423	Smith County, TX	209 714	47900		Washington-Arlington-Alexandria, DC-VA-MD-WV Metro SA	5582 170
46540		Utica-Rome, NY Metro SA	299 397			Bethesda-Rockville-Frederick, MD Metro Div 13644	1205 162
	36 043	Herkimer County, NY	64 519		24 021	Frederick County, MD	233 385
	36 065	Oneida County, NY	234 878		24 031	Montgomery County, MD	971 777
46660		Valdosta, GA Metro SA	139 588			Washington-Arlington-Alexandria, DC-VA-MD-WV Metro Div 47894	4377 008
	13 027	Brooks County, GA	16 243		11 001	District of Columbia, DC	601 723
	13 101	Echols County, GA	4 034		24 009	Calvert County, MD	88 737
	13 173	Lanier County, GA	10 078		24 017	Charles County, MD	146 551
	13 185	Lowndes County, GA	109 233		24 033	Prince George's County, MD	863 420
46700		Vallejo-Fairfield, CA Metro SA	413 344		51 013	Arlington County, VA	207 627
	06 095	Solano County, CA	413 344		51 043	Clarke County, VA	14 034
47020		Victoria, TX Metro SA	115 384		51 059	Fairfax County, VA	1081 726
	48 057	Calhoun County, TX	21 381		51 061	Fauquier County, VA	65 203
	48 175	Goliad County, TX	7 210		51 107	Loudoun County, VA	312 311
	48 469	Victoria County, TX	86 793		51 153	Prince William County, VA	402 002
47220		Vineland-Millville-Bridgeton, NJ Metro SA	156 898		51 177	Spotsylvania County, VA	122 397
	34 011	Cumberland County, NJ	156 898		51 179	Stafford County, VA	128 961
					51 187	Warren County, VA	37 575
					51 510	Alexandria, VA	139 966
					51 600	Fairfax city, VA	22 565
					51 610	Falls Church city, VA	12 332
					51 630	Fredericksburg city, VA	24 286
					51 683	Manassas city, VA	37 821
					51 685	Manassas Park city, VA	14 273
					54 037	Jefferson County, WV	53 498
				47940		Waterloo-Cedar Falls, IA Metro SA	167 819
					19 013	Black Hawk County, IA	131 090
					19 017	Bremer County, IA	24 276
					19 075	Grundy County, IA	12 453
				48140		Wausau, WI Metro SA	134 063
					55 073	Marathon County, WI	134 063

Core based statistical area	State/County FIPS code	Title and Geographic Components	2010 Census Population	Core based statistical area	State/County FIPS code	Title and Geographic Components	2010 Census Population
48300		Wenatchee-East Wenatchee, WA Metro SA ...	110 884	49020		Winchester, VA-WVMetro SA	128 472
	53 007	Chelan County, WA	72 453		51 069	Frederick County, VA	78 305
	53 017	Douglas County, WA	38 431		51 840	Winchester city , VA	26 203
					54 027	Hampshire County, WV	23 964
48540		Wheeling, WV-OH Metro SA...........................	147 950				
	39 013	Belmont County, OH.....................................	70 400	49180		Winston-Salem, NC Metro SA	477 717
	54 051	Marshall County, WV...................................	33 107		37 059	Davie County, NC....................................	41 240
	54 069	Ohio County, WV..	44 443		37 067	Forsyth County, NC.................................	350 670
48620		Wichita, KS Metro SA	623 061		37 169	Stokes County, NC..................................	47 401
	20 015	Butler County, KS......................................	65 880		37 197	Yadkin County, NC..................................	38 406
	20 079	Harvey County, KS.....................................	34 684	49340		Worcester, MA Metro SA	798 552
	20 173	Sedgwick County, KS.................................	498 365		25 027	Worcester County, MA	798 552
	20 191	Sumner County, KS....................................	24 132				
48660		Wichita Falls, TX Metro SA...........................	151 306	49420		Yakima, WA Metro SA	243 231
	48 009	Archer County, TX......................................	9 054		53 077	Yakima County, WA	243 231
	48 077	Clay County, TX..	10 752	49620		York-Hanover, PA Metro SA	434 972
	48 485	Wichita County, TX....................................	131 500		42 133	York County, PA	434 972
48700		Williamsport, PA Metro SA...........................	116 111	49660		Youngstown-Warren-Boardman, OH-PA Metro SA	565 773
	42 081	Lycoming County, PA..................................	116 111		39 099	Mahoning County, OH.............................	238 823
48900		Wilmington, NC Metro SA	362 315		39 155	Trumbull County, OH.............................	210 312
	37 019	Brunswick County, NC..................................	107 431		42 085	Mercer County, PA	116 638
	37 129	New Hanover County, NC...........................	202 667	49700		Yuba City, CA Metro SA	166 892
	37 141	Pender County, NC	52 217		06 101	Sutter County, CA...................................	94 737
					06 115	Yuba County, CA....................................	72 155
				49740		Yuma, AZ Metro SA	195 751
					04 027	Yuma County, AZ	195 751

APPENDIX C
CORE BASED STATISTICAL AREAS
(Metropolitan and Micropolitan),
METROPOLITAN DIVISIONS, AND COMPONENTS
(as defined December 2009)

Core Based Statistical Area	State/County FIPS Code	Title and Geographic Components	2010 Census Population
10020		Abbeville, LA Micro SA	57 999
	22 113	Vermilion Parish, LA	57 999
10100		Aberdeen, SD Micro SA	40 602
	46 013	Brown County, SD	36 531
	46 045	Edmunds County, SD	4 071
10140		Aberdeen, WA Micro SA	72 797
	53 027	Grays Harbor County, WA	72 797
10180		Abilene, TX Metro SA	165 252
	48 059	Callahan County, TX	13 544
	48 253	Jones County, TX	20 202
	48 441	Taylor County, TX	131 506
10220		Ada, OK Micro SA	37 492
	40 123	Pontotoc County, OK	37 492
10300		Adrian, MI Micro SA	99 892
	26 091	Lenawee County, MI	99 892
10420		Akron, OH Metro SA	703 200
	39 133	Portage County, OH	161 419
	39 153	Summit County, OH	541 781
10460		Alamogordo, NM Micro SA	63 797
	35 035	Otero County, NM	63 797
10500		Albany, GA Metro SA	157 308
	13 007	Baker County, GA	3 451
	13 095	Dougherty County, GA	94 565
	13 177	Lee County, GA	28 298
	13 273	Terrell County, GA	9 315
	13 321	Worth County, GA	21 679
10540		Albany-Lebanon, OR Micro SA	116 672
	41 043	Linn County, OR	116 672
10580		Albany-Schenectady-Troy, NY Metro SA	870 716
	36 001	Albany County, NY	304 204
	36 083	Rensselaer County, NY	159 429
	36 091	Saratoga County, NY	219 607
	36 093	Schenectady County, NY	154 727
	36 095	Schoharie County, NY	32 749
10620		Albemarle, NC Micro SA	60 585
	37 167	Stanly County, NC	60 585
10660		Albert Lea, MN Micro SA	31 255
	27 047	Freeborn County, MN	31 255
10700		Albertville, AL Micro SA	93 019
	01 095	Marshall County, AL	93 019
10740		Albuquerque, NM Metro SA	887 077
	35 001	Bernalillo County, NM	662 564
	35 043	Sandoval County, NM	131 561
	35 057	Torrance County, NM	16 383
	35 061	Valencia County, NM	76 569
10760		Alexander City, AL Micro SA	53 155
	01 037	Coosa County, AL	11 539
	01 123	Tallapossa County, AL	41 616
10780		Alexandria, LA Metro SA	153 922
	22 043	Grant Parish, LA	22 309
	22 079	Rapides Parish, LA	131 613
10820		Alexandria, MN Micro SA	36 009
	27 041	Douglas County, MN	36 009
10860		Alice, TX Micro SA	40 838
	48 249	Jim Wells County, TX	40 838
10880		Allegan, MI Micro SA	111 408
	26 005	Allegan County, MI	111 408
10900		Allentown-Bethlehem-Easton, PA-NJ Metro SA	821 173
	34 041	Warren County, NJ	108 692
	42 025	Carbon County, PA	65 249
	42 077	Lehigh County, PA	349 497
	42 095	Northampton County, PA	297 735
10940		Alma, MI Micro SA	42 476
	26 057	Gratiot County, MI	42 476
10980		Alpena, MI Micro SA	29 598
	26 007	Alpena County, MI	29 598
11020		Altoona, PA Metro SA	127 089
	42 013	Blair County, PA	127 089
11060		Altus, OK Micro SA	26 446
	40 065	Jackson County, OK	26 446
11100		Amarillo, TX Metro SA	249 881
	48 011	Armstrong County, TX	1 901
	48 065	Carson County, TX	6 182
	48 375	Potter County, TX	121 073
	48 381	Randall County, TX	120 725
11140		Americus, GA Micro SA	37 829
	13 249	Schley County, GA	5 010
	13 261	Sumter County, GA	32 819
11180		Ames, IA Metro SA	89 542
	19 169	Story County, IA	89 542
11220		Amsterdam, NY Micro SA	50 219
	36 057	Montgomery County, NY	50 219
11260		Anchorage, AK Metro SA	380 821
	02 020	Anchorage Municipality, AK	291 826
	02 170	Matanuska-Susitna Borough, AK	88 995
11300		Anderson, IN Metro SA	131 636
	18 095	Madison County, IN	131 636
11340		Anderson, SC Metro SA	187 126
	45 007	Anderson County, SC	187 126
11380		Andrews, TX Micro SA	14 786
	48 003	Andrews County, TX	14 786
11420		Angola, IN Micro SA	34 185
	18 151	Steuben County, IN	34 185

Core Based Statistical Areas (Metropolitan and Micropolitan), Metropolitan Divisions, and Components (as defined December 2009)–*Continued*

Core Based Statistical Area	State/County FIPS Code	Title and Geographic Components	2010 Census Population	Core Based Statistical Area	State/County FIPS Code	Title and Geographic Components	2010 Census Population
11460		Ann Arbor, MI Metro SA	344 791	12060		Atlanta-Sandy Springs-Marietta, GA Metro SA	5268 860
	26 161	Washtenaw County, MI	344 791		13 013	Barrow County, GA	69 367
11500		Anniston-Oxford, AL Metro SA	118 572		13 015	Bartow County, GA	100 157
	01 015	Calhoun County, AL	118 572		13 035	Butts County, GA	23 655
11540		Appleton, WI Metro SA	225 666		13 045	Carroll County, GA	110 527
	55 015	Calumet County, WI	48 971		13 057	Cherokee County, GA	214 346
	55 087	Outagamie County, WI	176 695		13 063	Clayton County, GA	259 424
11580		Arcadia, FL Micro SA	34 862		13 067	Cobb County, GA	688 078
	12 027	DeSoto County, FL	34 862		13 077	Coweta County, GA	127 317
11620		Ardmore, OK Micro SA	56 980		13 085	Dawson County, GA	22 330
	40 019	Carter County, OK	47 557		13 089	DeKalb County, GA	691 893
	40 085	Love County, OK	9 423		13 097	Douglas County, GA	132 403
11660		Arkadelphia, AR Micro SA	22 995		13 113	Fayette County, GA	106 567
	05 019	Clark County, AR	22 995		13 117	Forsyth County, GA	175 511
11700		Asheville, NC Metro SA	424 858		13 121	Fulton County, GA	920 581
	37 021	Buncombe County, NC	238 318		13 135	Gwinnett County, GA	805 321
	37 087	Haywood County, NC	59 036		13 143	Haralson County, GA	28 780
	37 089	Henderson County, NC	106 740		13 149	Heard County, GA	11 834
	37 115	Madison County, NC	20 764		13 151	Henry County, GA	203 922
11740		Ashland, OH Micro SA	53 139		13 159	Jasper County, GA	13 900
	39 005	Ashland County, OH	53 139		13 171	Lamar County, GA	18 317
					13 199	Meriwether County, GA	21 992
					13 217	Newton County, GA	99 958
					13 223	Paulding County, GA	142 324
					13 227	Pickens County, GA	29 431
					13 231	Pike County, GA	17 869
					13 247	Rockdale County, GA	85 215
					13 255	Spalding County, GA	64 073
					13 297	Walton County, GA	83 768
11780		Ashtabula, OH Micro SA	101 497	12100		Atlantic City-Hammonton, NJ Metro SA	274 549
	39 007	Ashtabula County, OH	101 497		34 001	Atlantic County, NJ	274 549
11820		Astoria, OR Micro SA	37 039	12140		Auburn, IN Micro SA	42 223
	41 007	Clatsop County, OR	37 039		18 033	DeKalb County, IN	42 223
11860		Atchison, KS Micro SA	16 924	12180		Auburn, NY Micro SA	80 026
	20 005	Atchison County, KS	16 924		36 011	Cayuga County, NY	80 026
11900		Athens, OH Micro SA	64 757	12220		Auburn-Opelika, AL Metro SA	140 247
	39 009	Athens County, OH	64 757		01 081	Lee County, AL	140 247
11940		Athens, TN Micro SA	52 266	12260		Augusta-Richmond County, GA-SC Metro SA	556 877
	47 107	McMinn County, TN	52 266		13 033	Burke County, GA	23 316
					13 073	Columbia County, GA	124 053
11980		Athens, TX Micro SA	78 532		13 189	McDuffie County, GA	21 875
	48 213	Henderson County, TX	78 532		13 245	Richmond County, GA	200 549
					45 003	Aiken County, SC	160 099
12020		Athens-Clarke County, GA Metro SA	192 541		45 037	Edgefield County, SC	26 985
	13 059	Clarke County, GA	116 714				
	13 195	Madison County, GA	28 120	12300		Augusta-Waterville, ME Micro SA	122 151
	13 219	Oconee County, GA	32 808		23 011	Kennebec County, ME	122 151
	13 221	Oglethorpe County, GA	14 899				
				12380		Austin, MN Micro SA	39 163
					27 099	Mower County, MN	39 163
				12420		Austin-Round Rock-San Marcos, TX Metro SA	1716 289
					48 021	Bastrop County, TX	74 171
					48 055	Caldwell County, TX	38 066
					48 209	Hays County, TX	157 107
					48 453	Travis County, TX	1024 266
					48 491	Williamson County, TX	422 679
				12460		Bainbridge, GA Micro SA	27 842
					13 087	Decatur County, GA	27 842
				12540		Bakersfield-Delano, CA Metro SA	839 631
					06 029	Kern County, CA	839 631

Core Based Statistical Area	State/County FIPS Code	Title and Geographic Components	2010 Census Population	Core Based Statistical Area	State/County FIPS Code	Title and Geographic Components	2010 Census Population
12580		Baltimore-Towson, MD Metro SA	2710 489	13300		Beeville, TX Micro SA	31 861
	24 003	Anne Arundel County, MD........................	537 656		48 025	Bee County, TX..................................	31 861
	24 005	Baltimore County, MD	805 029				
	24 013	Carroll County, MD	167 134	13340		Bellefontaine, OH Micro SA	45 858
	24 025	Harford County, MD................................	244 826		39 091	Logan County, OH...............................	45 858
	24 027	Howard County, MD	287 085				
	24 035	Queen Anne's County, MD........................	47 798	13380		Bellingham, WA Metro SA	201 140
	24 510	Baltimore city, MD.................................	620 961		53 073	Whatcom County, WA	201 140
12620		Bangor, ME Metro SA	153 923	13420		Bemidji, MN Micro SA	44 442
	23 019	Penobscot County, ME............................	153 923		27 007	Beltrami County, MN	44 442
12660		Baraboo, WI Micro SA	61 976	13460		Bend, OR Metro SA	157 733
	55 111	Sauk County, WI....................................	61 976		41 017	Deschutes County, OR...........................	157 733
12700		Barnstable Town, MA Metro SA	215 888	13500		Bennettsville, SC Micro SA	28 933
	25 001	Barnstable County, MA............................	215 888		45 069	Marlboro County, SC	28 933
12740		Barre, VT Micro SA	59 534	13540		Bennington, VT Micro SA..........................	37 125
	50 023	Washington County, VT............................	59 534		50 003	Bennington County, VT	37 125
12780		Bartlesville, OK Micro SA.........................	50 976	13620		Berlin, NH-VTMicro SA	39 361
	40 147	Washington County, OK...........................	50 976		33 007	Coos County, NH.................................	33 055
					50 009	Essex County, VT................................	6 306
12820		Bastrop, LA Micro SA..............................	27 979				
	22 067	Morehouse Parish, LA	27 979	13660		Big Rapids, MI Micro SA	42 798
					26 107	Mecosta County, MI..............................	42 798
12860		Batavia, NY Micro SA	60 079				
	36 037	Genesee County, NY..............................	60 079	13700		Big Spring, TX Micro SA	35 012
					48 227	Howard County, TX...............................	35 012
12900		Batesville, AR Micro SA...........................	36 647				
	05 063	Independence County, AR	36 647	13740		Billings, MT Metro SA	158 050
					30 009	Carbon County, MT...............................	10 078
12940		Baton Rouge, LA Metro SA	802 484		30 111	Yellowstone County, MT..........................	147 972
	22 005	Ascension Parish, LA	107 215				
	22 033	East Baton Rouge Parish, LA	440 171	13780		Binghamton, NY Metro SA.........................	251 725
	22 037	East Feliciana Parish, LA	20 267		36 007	Broome County, NY...............................	200 600
	22 047	Iberville Parish, LA................................	33 387		36 107	Tioga County, NY	51 125
	22 063	Livingston Parish, LA..............................	128 026				
	22 077	Pointe Coupee Parish, LA	22 802	13820		Birmingham-Hoover, AL Metro SA................	1128 047
	22 091	St. Helena Parish, LA.............................	11 203		01 007	Bibb County, AL..................................	22 915
	22 121	West Baton Rouge Parish, LA	23 788		01 009	Blount County, AL................................	57 322
	22 125	West Feliciana Parish, LA	15 625		01 021	Chilton County, AL...............................	43 643
					01 073	Jefferson County, AL.............................	658 466
12980		Battle Creek, MI Metro SA........................	136 146		01 115	St. Clair County, AL	83 593
	26 025	Calhoun County, MI	136 146		01 117	Shelby County, AL	195 085
					01 127	Walker County, AL	67 023
13020		Bay City, MI Metro SA	107 771				
	26 017	Bay County, MI	107 771	13860		Bishop, CA Micro SA	18 546
					06 027	Inyo County, CA	18 546
13060		Bay City, TX Micro SA	36 702				
	48 321	Matagorda County, TX	36 702	13900		Bismarck, ND Metro SA	108 779
					38 015	Burleigh County, ND..............................	81 308
13100		Beatrice, NE Micro SA	22 311		38 059	Morton County, ND...............................	27 471
	31 067	Gage County, NE	22 311				
				13940		Blackfoot, ID Micro SA............................	45 607
13140		Beaumont-Port Arthur, TX Metro SA	388 745		16 011	Bingham County, ID	45 607
	48 199	Hardin County, TX.................................	54 635				
	48 245	Jefferson County, TX..............................	252 273	13980		Blacksburg-Christiansburg-Radford, VA Metro SA	162 958
	48 361	Orange County, TX................................	81 837		51 071	Giles County, VA	17 286
					51 121	Montgomery County, VA	94 392
13180		Beaver Dam, WI Micro SA.........................	88 759		51 155	Pulaski County, VA...............................	34 872
	55 027	Dodge County, WI	88 759		51 750	Radford city, VA..................................	16 408
13220		Beckley, WV Micro SA	78 859	14020		Bloomington, IN Metro SA	192 714
	54 081	Raleigh County, WV	78 859		18 055	Greene County, IN................................	33 165
					18 105	Monroe County, IN	137 974
13260		Bedford, IN Micro SA..............................	46 134		18 119	Owen County, IN..................................	21 575
	18 093	Lawrence County, IN...............................	46 134				

Core Based Statistical Areas (Metropolitan and Micropolitan), Metropolitan Divisions, and Components (as defined December 2009)–*Continued*

Core Based Statistical Area	State/ County FIPS Code	Title and Geographic Components	2010 Census Population	Core Based Statistical Area	State/ County FIPS Code	Title and Geographic Components	2010 Census Population
14060		Bloomington-Normal, IL Metro SA	169 572	14700		Branson, MO Micro SA	83 877
	17 113	McLean County, IL	169 572		29 209	Stone County, MO	32 202
14100		Bloomsburg-Berwick, PA Micro SA................	85 562		29 213	Taney County, MO	51 675
	42 037	Columbia County, PA	67 295	14740		Bremerton-Silverdale, WA Metro SA	251 133
	42 093	Montour County, PA	18 267		53 035	Kitsap County, WA	251 133
14140		Bluefield, WV-VA Micro SA	107 342	14780		Brenham, TX Micro SA	33 718
	51 185	Tazewell County, VA	45 078		48 477	Washington County, TX...............................	33 718
	54 055	Mercer County, WV	62 264	14820		Brevard, NC Micro SA..................................	33 090
14180		Blytheville, AR Micro SA..............................	46 480		37 175	Transylvania County, NC..............................	33 090
	05 093	Mississippi County, AR................................	46 480	14860		Bridgeport-Stamford-Norwalk, CT Metro SA....	916 829
14220		Bogalusa, LA Micro SA	47 168		09 001	Fairfield County, CT....................................	916 829
	22 117	Washington Parish, LA................................	47 168	14940		Brigham City, UT Micro SA...........................	49 975
14260		Boise City-Nampa, ID Metro SA	616 561		49 003	Box Elder County, UT..................................	49 975
	16 001	Ada County, ID	392 365	15020		Brookhaven, MS Micro SA............................	34 869
	16 015	Boise County, ID..	7 028		28 085	Lincoln County, MS	34 869
	16 027	Canyon County, ID......................................	188 923	15060		Brookings, OR Micro SA	22 364
	16 045	Gem County, ID..	16 719		41 015	Curry County, OR.......................................	22 364
	16 073	Owyhee County, ID.....................................	11 526	15100		Brookings, SD Micro SA	31 965
14300		Bonham, TX Micro SA	33 915		46 011	Brookings County, SD	31 965
	48 147	Fannin County, TX.......................................	33 915	15140		Brownsville, TN Micro SA	18 787
14340		Boone, IA Micro SA......................................	26 306		47 075	Haywood County, TN	18 787
	19 015	Boone County, IA..	26 306	15180		Brownsville-Harlingen, TX Metro SA...............	406 220
14380		Boone, NC Micro SA.....................................	51 079		48 061	Cameron County, TX...................................	406 220
	37 189	Watauga County, NC...................................	51 079	15220		Brownwood, TX Micro SA	38 106
14420		Borger, TX Micro SA	22 150		48 049	Brown County, TX	38 106
	48 233	Hutchinson County, TX................................	22 150	15260		Brunswick, GA Metro SA	112 370
14460		Boston-Cambridge-Quincy, MA-NH Metro SA.	4552 402		13 025	Brantley County, GA...................................	18 411
		Boston-Quincy, MA Metro Div 14484..........	1887 792		13 127	Glynn County, GA.......................................	79 626
	25 021	Norfolk County, MA	670 850		13 191	McIntosh County, GA	14 333
	25 023	Plymouth County, MA.................................	494 919	15340		Bucyrus, OH Micro SA	43 784
	25 025	Suffolk County, MA....................................	722 023		39 033	Crawford County, OH	43 784
		Cambridge-Newton-Framingham, MA Metro Div 15764......................................	1503 085	15380		Buffalo-Niagara Falls, NY Metro SA	1135 509
	25 017	Middlesex County, MA................................	1503 085		36 029	Erie County, NY...	919 040
		Peabody, MA Metro Div 37764....................	743 159		36 063	Niagara County, NY....................................	216 469
	25 009	Essex County, MA......................................	743 159	15420		Burley, ID Micro SA.....................................	43 021
		Rockingham County-Strafford County, NH Metro Div 40484	418 366		16 031	Cassia County, ID	22 952
	33 015	Rockingham County, NH..............................	295 223		16 067	Minidoka County, ID	20 069
	33 017	Strafford County, NH..................................	123 143	15460		Burlington, IA-IL Micro SA............................	47 656
14500		Boulder, CO Metro SA	294 567		17 071	Henderson County, IL..................................	7 331
	08 013	Boulder County, CO	294 567		19 057	Des Moines County, IA................................	40 325
14540		Bowling Green, KY Metro SA.........................	125 953	15500		Burlington, NC Metro SA..............................	151 131
	21 061	Edmonson County, KY.................................	12 161		37 001	Alamance County, NC..................................	151 131
	21 227	Warren County, KY.....................................	113 792	15540		Burlington-South Burlington, VT Metro SA	211 261
14580		Bozeman, MT Micro SA................................	89 513		50 007	Chittenden County, VT................................	156 545
	30 031	Gallatin County, MT....................................	89 513		50 011	Franklin County, VT....................................	47 746
14620		Bradford, PA Micro SA.................................	43 450		50 013	Grand Isle County, VT.................................	6 970
	42 083	McKean County, PA....................................	43 450	15580		Butte-Silver Bow, MT Micro SA	34 200
14660		Brainerd, MN Micro SA................................	91 067		30 093	Silver Bow County, MT................................	34 200
	27 021	Cass County, MN..	28 567				
	27 035	Crow Wing County, MN................................	62 500				

Core Based Statistical Area	State/ County FIPS Code	Title and Geographic Components	2010 Census Population	Core Based Statistical Area	State/ County FIPS Code	Title and Geographic Components	2010 Census Population
15620		Cadillac, MI Micro SA	47 584	16500		Centralia, WA Micro SA	75 455
	26 113	Missaukee County, MI	14 849		53 041	Lewis County, WA	75 455
	26 165	Wexford County, MI	32 735				
				16540		Chambersburg, PA Micro SA	149 618
15660		Calhoun, GA Micro SA	55 186		42 055	Franklin County, PA	149 618
	13 129	Gordon County, GA	55 186				
				16580		Champaign-Urbana, IL Metro SA	231 891
15700		Cambridge, MD Micro SA	32 618		17 019	Champaign County, IL	201 081
	24 019	Dorchester County, MD	32 618		17 053	Ford County, IL	14 081
					17 147	Piatt County, IL	16 729
15740		Cambridge, OH Micro SA	40 087	16620		Charleston, WV Metro SA	304 284
	39 059	Guernsey County, OH	40 087		54 005	Boone County, WV	24 629
					54 015	Clay County, WV	9 386
15780		Camden, AR Micro SA	31 488		54 039	Kanawha County, WV	193 063
	05 013	Calhoun County, AR	5 368		54 043	Lincoln County, WV	21 720
	05 103	Ouachita County, AR	26 120		54 079	Putnam County, WV	55 486
15820		Campbellsville, KY Micro SA	24 512				
	21 217	Taylor County, KY	24 512	16660		Charleston-Mattoon, IL Micro SA	64 921
					17 029	Coles County, IL	53 873
15860		Canon City, CO Micro SA	46 824		17 035	Cumberland County, IL	11 048
	08 043	Fremont County, CO	46 824				
				16700		Charleston-North Charleston-Summerville, SC Metro SA	664 607
15900		Canton, IL Micro SA	37 069		45 015	Berkeley County, SC	177 843
	17 057	Fulton County, IL	37 069		45 019	Charleston County, SC	350 209
15940		Canton-Massillon, OH Metro SA	404 422		45 035	Dorchester County, SC	136 555
	39 019	Carroll County, OH	28 836	16740		Charlotte-Gastonia-Rock Hill, NC-SC Metro SA	1758 038
	39 151	Stark County, OH	375 586		37 007	Anson County, NC	26 948
15980		Cape Coral-Fort Myers, FL Metro SA	618 754		37 025	Cabarrus County, NC	178 011
	12 071	Lee County, FL	618 754		37 071	Gaston County, NC	206 086
16020		Cape Girardeau-Jackson, MO-IL Metro SA	96 275		37 119	Mecklenburg County, NC	919 628
	17 003	Alexander County, IL	8 238		37 179	Union County, NC	201 292
	29 017	Bollinger County, MO	12 363		45 091	York County, SC	226 073
	29 031	Cape Girardeau County, MO	75 674				
				16820		Charlottesville, VA Metro SA	201 559
16060		Carbondale, IL Micro SA	60 218		51 003	Albemarle County, VA	98 970
	17 077	Jackson County, IL	60 218		51 065	Fluvanna County, VA	25 691
					51 079	Greene County, VA	18 403
16100		Carlsbad-Artesia, NM Micro SA	53 829		51 125	Nelson County, VA	15 020
	35 015	Eddy County, NM	53 829		51 540	Charlottesville city, VA	43 475
16180		Carson City, NV Metro SA	55 274	16860		Chattanooga, TN-GA Metro SA	528 143
	32 510	Carson City, NV	55 274		13 047	Catoosa County, GA	63 942
					13 083	Dade County, GA	16 633
16220		Casper, WY Metro SA	75 450		13 295	Walker County, GA	68 756
	56 025	Natrona County, WY	75 450		47 065	Hamilton County, TN	336 463
					47 115	Marion County, TN	28 237
16260		Cedar City, UT Micro SA	46 163		47 153	Sequatchie County, TN	14 112
	49 021	Iron County, UT	46 163				
				16900		Chester, SC Micro SA	33 140
16300		Cedar Rapids, IA Metro SA	257 940		45 023	Chester County, SC	33 140
	19 011	Benton County, IA	26 076				
	19 105	Jones County, IA	20 638	16940		Cheyenne, WY Metro SA	91 738
	19 113	Linn County, IA	211 226		56 021	Laramie County, WY	91 738
16340		Cedartown, GA Micro SA	41 475				
	13 233	Polk County, GA	41 475				
16380		Celina, OH Micro SA	40 814				
	39 107	Mercer County, OH	40 814				
16420		Central City, KY Micro SA	31 499				
	21 177	Muhlenberg County, KY	31 499				
16460		Centralia, IL Micro SA	39 437				
	17 121	Marion County, IL	39 437				

Core Based Statistical Areas (Metropolitan and Micropolitan), Metropolitan Divisions, and Components (as defined December 2009)–*Continued*

Core Based Statistical Area	State/County FIPS Code	Title and Geographic Components	2010 Census Population	Core Based Statistical Area	State/County FIPS Code	Title and Geographic Components	2010 Census Population
16980		Chicago-Joliet-Naperville, IL-IN-WI Metro SA..	9461 105	17420		Cleveland, TN Metro SA	115 788
		Chicago-Joliet-Naperville, IL Metro Div 16974	7883 147		47 011	Bradley County, TN	98 963
	17 031	Cook County, IL	5194 675		47 139	Polk County, TN	16 825
	17 037	DeKalb County, IL	105 160	17460		Cleveland-Elyria-Mentor, OH Metro SA	2077 240
	17 043	DuPage County, IL	916 924		39 035	Cuyahoga County, OH	1280 122
	17 063	Grundy County, IL	50 063		39 055	Geauga County, OH	93 389
	17 089	Kane County, IL	515 269		39 085	Lake County, OH	230 041
	17 093	Kendall County, IL	114 736		39 093	Lorain County, OH	301 356
	17 111	McHenry County, IL	308 760		39 103	Medina County, OH	172 332
	17 197	Will County, IL	677 560				
		Gary, IN Metro Div 23844	708 070	17500		Clewiston, FL Micro SA	39 140
	18 073	Jasper County, IN	33 478		12 051	Hendry County, FL	39 140
	18 089	Lake County, IN	496 005				
	18 111	Newton County, IN	14 244	17540		Clinton, IA Micro SA	49 116
	18 127	Porter County, IN	164 343		19 045	Clinton County, IA	49 116
		Lake County-Kenosha County, IL-WI Metro Div 29404	869 888	17580		Clovis, NM Micro SA	48 376
	17 097	Lake County, IL	703 462		35 009	Curry County, NM	48 376
	55 059	Kenosha County, WI	166 426				
				17660		Coeur d'Alene, ID Metro SA	138 494
17020		Chico, CA Metro SA	220 000		16 055	Kootenai County, ID	138 494
	06 007	Butte County, CA	220 000				
				17700		Coffeyville, KS Micro SA	35 471
17060		Chillicothe, OH Micro SA	78 064		20 125	Montgomery County, KS	35 471
	39 141	Ross County, OH	78 064				
				17740		Coldwater, MI Micro SA	45 248
17140		Cincinnati-Middletown, OH-KY-IN Metro SA....	2130 151		26 023	Branch County, MI	45 248
	18 029	Dearborn County, IN	50 047				
	18 047	Franklin County, IN	23 087	17780		College Station-Bryan, TX Metro SA	228 660
	18 115	Ohio County, IN	6 128		48 041	Brazos County, TX	194 851
	21 015	Boone County, KY	118 811		48 051	Burleson County, TX	17 187
	21 023	Bracken County, KY	8 488		48 395	Robertson County, TX	16 622
	21 037	Campbell County, KY	90 336				
	21 077	Gallatin County, KY	8 589	17820		Colorado Springs, CO Metro SA	645 613
	21 081	Grant County, KY	24 662		08 041	El Paso County, CO	622 263
	21 117	Kenton County, KY	159 720		08 119	Teller County, CO	23 350
	21 191	Pendleton County, KY	14 877				
	39 015	Brown County, OH	44 846	17860		Columbia, MO Metro SA	172 786
	39 017	Butler County, OH	368 130		29 019	Boone County, MO	162 642
	39 025	Clermont County, OH	197 363		29 089	Howard County, MO	10 144
	39 061	Hamilton County, OH	802 374				
	39 165	Warren County, OH	212 693	17900		Columbia, SC Metro SA	767 598
					45 017	Calhoun County, SC	15 175
17200		Claremont, NH Micro SA	43 742		45 039	Fairfield County, SC	23 956
	33 019	Sullivan County, NH	43 742		45 055	Kershaw County, SC	61 697
					45 063	Lexington County, SC	262 391
17220		Clarksburg, WV Micro SA	94 196		45 079	Richland County, SC	384 504
	54 017	Doddridge County, WV	8 202		45 081	Saluda County, SC	19 875
	54 033	Harrison County, WV	69 099				
	54 091	Taylor County, WV	16 895	17940		Columbia, TN Micro SA	80 956
					47 119	Maury County, TN	80 956
17260		Clarksdale, MS Micro SA	26 151				
	28 027	Coahoma County, MS	26 151	17980		Columbus, GA-AL Metro SA	294 865
					01 113	Russell County, AL	52 947
17300		Clarksville, TN-KY Metro SA	273 949		13 053	Chattahoochee County, GA	11 267
	21 047	Christian County, KY	73 955		13 145	Harris County, GA	32 024
	21 221	Trigg County, KY	14 339		13 197	Marion County, GA	8 742
	47 125	Montgomery County, TN	172 331		13 215	Muscogee County, GA	189 885
	47 161	Stewart County, TN	13 324				
				18020		Columbus, IN Metro SA	76 794
17340		Clearlake, CA Micro SA	64 665		18 005	Bartholomew County, IN	76 794
	06 033	Lake County, CA	64 665				
				18060		Columbus, MS Micro SA	59 779
17380		Cleveland, MS Micro SA	34 145		28 087	Lowndes County, MS	59 779
	28 011	Bolivar County, MS	34 145				
				18100		Columbus, NE Micro SA	32 237
					31 141	Platte County, NE	32 237

Core Based Statistical Areas (Metropolitan and Micropolitan), Metropolitan Divisions, and Components (as defined December 2009)–*Continued*

Core Based Statistical Area	State/County FIPS Code	Title and Geographic Components	2010 Census Population	Core Based Statistical Area	State/County FIPS Code	Title and Geographic Components	2010 Census Population
18140		Columbus, OH Metro SA	1836 536	18940		Crowley, LA Micro SA	61 773
	39 041	Delaware County, OH...................	174 214		22 001	Acadia Parish, LA........................	61 773
	39 045	Fairfield County, OH.....................	146 156				
	39 049	Franklin County, OH.....................	1163 414	18980		Cullman, AL Micro SA	80 406
	39 089	Licking County, OH......................	166 492		01 043	Cullman County, AL......................	80 406
	39 097	Madison County, OH.....................	43 435				
	39 117	Morrow County, OH......................	34 827	19020		Culpeper, VA Micro SA	46 689
	39 129	Pickaway County, OH....................	55 698		51 047	Culpeper County, VA.....................	46 689
	39 159	Union County, OH.........................	52 300				
				19060		Cumberland, MD-WV Metro SA......................	103 299
18180		Concord, NH Micro SA	146 445		24 001	Allegany County, MD.....................	75 087
	33 013	Merrimack County, NH...................	146 445		54 057	Mineral County, WV......................	28 212
18220		Connersville, IN Micro SA	24 277	19100		Dallas-Fort Worth-Arlington, TX Metro SA......	6371 773
	18 041	Fayette County, IN.......................	24 277			Dallas-Plano-Irving, TX Metro Div 19124.....	4235 751
					48 085	Collin County, TX.........................	782 341
18260		Cookeville, TN Micro SA	106 042		48 113	Dallas County, TX........................	2368 139
	47 087	Jackson County, TN......................	11 638		48 119	Delta County, TX.........................	5 231
	47 133	Overton County, TN......................	22 083		48 121	Denton County, TX........................	662 614
	47 141	Putnam County, TN.......................	72 321		48 139	Ellis County, TX..........................	149 610
					48 231	Hunt County, TX..........................	86 129
18300		Coos Bay, OR Micro SA	63 043		48 257	Kaufman County, TX......................	103 350
	41 011	Coos County, OR..........................	63 043		48 397	Rockwall County, TX.....................	78 337
						Fort Worth-Arlington, TX Metro Div 23104....	2136 022
18340		Corbin, KY Micro SA	35 637		48 251	Johnson County, TX......................	150 934
	21 235	Whitley County, KY.......................	35 637		48 367	Parker County, TX........................	116 927
					48 439	Tarrant County, TX.......................	1809 034
18380		Cordele, GA Micro SA.................................	23 439		48 497	Wise County, TX..........................	59 127
	13 081	Crisp County, GA.........................	23 439				
				19140		Dalton, GA Metro SA	142 227
18420		Corinth, MS Micro SA	37 057		13 213	Murray County, GA.......................	39 628
	28 003	Alcorn County, MS........................	37 057		13 313	Whitfield County, GA.....................	102 599
18460		Cornelia, GA Micro SA...............................	43 041	19180		Danville, IL Metro SA	81 625
	13 137	Habersham County, GA..................	43 041		17 183	Vermilion County, IL.....................	81 625
18500		Corning, NY Micro SA.................................	98 990	19220		Danville, KY Micro SA	53 174
	36 101	Steuben County, NY......................	98 990		21 021	Boyle County, KY.........................	28 432
					21 137	Lincoln County, KY.......................	24 742
18580		Corpus Christi, TX Metro SA	428 185				
	48 007	Aransas County, TX......................	23 158	19260		Danville, VA Metro SA	106 561
	48 355	Nueces County, TX.......................	340 223		51 143	Pittsylvania County, VA..................	63 506
	48 409	San Patricio County, TX.................	64 804		51 590	Danville city, VA.........................	43 055
18620		Corsicana, TX Micro SA..............................	47 735	19300		Daphne-Fairhope-Foley, AL Micro SA............	182 265
	48 349	Navarro County, TX......................	47 735		01 003	Baldwin County, AL.......................	182 265
18660		Cortland, NY Micro SA................................	49 336	19340		Davenport-Moline-Rock Island, IA-IL Metro SA	379 690
	36 023	Cortland County, NY......................	49 336		17 073	Henry County, IL..........................	50 486
					17 131	Mercer County, IL.........................	16 434
18700		Corvallis, OR Metro SA...............................	85 579		17 161	Rock Island County, IL	147 546
	41 003	Benton County, OR.......................	85 579		19 163	Scott County, IA..........................	165 224
18740		Coshocton, OH Micro SA..............................	36 901	19380		Dayton, OH Metro SA	841 502
	39 031	Coshocton County, OH..................	36 901		39 057	Greene County, OH.......................	161 573
					39 109	Miami County, OH........................	102 506
18820		Crawfordsville, IN Micro SA	38 124		39 113	Montgomery County, OH..................	535 153
	18 107	Montgomery County, IN.................	38 124		39 135	Preble County, OH	42 270
18860		Crescent City, CA Micro SA.........................	28 610	19460		Decatur, AL Metro SA	153 829
	06 015	Del Norte County, CA....................	28 610		01 079	Lawrence County, AL.....................	34 339
					01 103	Morgan County, AL.......................	119 490
18880		Crestview-Fort Walton Beach-Destin, FL Metro SA	180 822				
	12 091	Okaloosa County, FL.....................	180 822	19500		Decatur, IL Metro SA	110 768
					17 115	Macon County, IL.........................	110 768
18900		Crossville, TN Micro SA	56 053				
	47 035	Cumberland County, TN................	56 053	19540		Decatur, IN Micro SA	34 387
					18 001	Adams County, IN.........................	34 387

Core Based Statistical Areas (Metropolitan and Micropolitan), Metropolitan Divisions, and Components (as defined December 2009)–*Continued*

Core Based Statistical Area	State/ County FIPS Code	Title and Geographic Components	2010 Census Population	Core Based Statistical Area	State/ County FIPS Code	Title and Geographic Components	2010 Census Population
19580		Defiance, OH Micro SA	39 037	20100		Dover, DE Metro SA	162 310
	39 039	Defiance County, OH	39 037		10 001	Kent County, DE	162 310
19620		Del Rio, TX Micro SA	48 879	20140		Dublin, GA Micro SA	58 414
	48 465	Val Verde County, TX	48 879		13 167	Johnson County, GA	9 980
19660		Deltona-Daytona Beach-Ormond Beach, FL Metro SA	494 593		13 175	Laurens County, GA	48 434
				20180		DuBois, PA Micro SA	81 642
	12 127	Volusia County, FL	494 593		42 033	Clearfield County, PA	81 642
19700		Deming, NM Micro SA	25 095	20220		Dubuque, IA Metro SA	93 653
	35 029	Luna County, NM	25 095		19 061	Dubuque County, IA	93 653
19740		Denver-Aurora-Broomfield, CO Metro SA	2543 482	20260		Duluth, MN-WI Metro SA	279 771
	08 001	Adams County, CO	441 603		27 017	Carlton County, MN	35 386
	08 005	Arapahoe County, CO	572 003		27 137	St. Louis County, MN	200 226
	08 014	Broomfield County, CO	55 889		55 031	Douglas County, WI	44 159
	08 019	Clear Creek County, CO	9 088				
	08 031	Denver County, CO	600 158	20300		Dumas, TX Micro SA	21 904
	08 035	Douglas County, CO	285 465		48 341	Moore County, TX	21 904
	08 039	Elbert County, CO	23 086				
	08 047	Gilpln County, CO	5 441	20340		Duncan, OK Micro SA	45 048
	08 059	Jefferson County, CO	534 543		40 137	Stephens County, OK	45 048
	08 093	Park County, CO	16 206				
				20380		Dunn, NC Micro SA	114 678
19760		DeRidder, LA Micro SA	35 654		37 085	Harnett County, NC	114 678
	22 011	Beauregard Parish, LA	35 654				
				20420		Durango, CO Micro SA	51 334
19780		Des Moines-West Des Moines, IA Metro SA	569 633		08 067	La Plata County, CO	51 334
	19 049	Dallas County, IA	66 135				
	19 077	Guthrie County, IA	10 954	20460		Durant, OK Micro SA	42 416
	19 121	Madison County, IA	15 679		40 013	Bryan County, OK	42 416
	19 153	Polk County, IA	430 640				
	19 181	Warren County, IA	46 225	20500		Durham-Chaspel Hill, NC Metro SA	504 357
					37 037	Chatham County, NC	63 505
19820		Detroit-Warren-Livonia, MI Metro SA	4296 250		37 063	Durham County, NC	267 587
		Detroit-Livonia-Dearborn, MI Metro Div 19804	1820 584		37 135	Orange County, NC	133 801
	26 163	Wayne County, MI	1820 584		37 145	Person County, NC	39 464
		Warren-Troy-Farmington Hills, MI Metro Div 47644	2475 666	20540		Dyersburg, TN Micro SA	38 335
	26 087	Lapeer County, MI	88 319		47 045	Dyer County, TN	38 335
	26 093	Livingston County, MI	180 967				
	26 099	Macomb County, MI	840 978	20580		Eagle Pass, TX Micro SA	54 258
	26 125	Oakland County, MI	1202 362		48 323	Maverick County, TX	54 258
	26 147	St. Clair County, MI	163 040				
				20620		East Liverpool-Salem, OH Micro SA	107 841
19860		Dickinson, ND Micro SA	24 982		39 029	Columbiana County, OH	107 841
	38 007	Billings County, ND	783				
	38 089	Stark County, ND	24 199	20660		Easton, MD Micro SA	37 782
					24 041	Talbot County, MD	37 782
19900		Dillon, SC Micro SA	32 062				
	45 033	Dillon County, SC	32 062	20700		East Stroudsburg, PA Micro SA	169 842
					42 089	Monroe County, PA	169 842
19940		Dixon, IL Micro SA	36 031	20740		Eau Claire, WI Metro SA	161 151
	17 103	Lee County, IL	36 031		55 017	Chippewa County, WI	62 415
					55 035	Eau Claire County, WI	98 736
19980		Dodge City, KS Micro SA	33 848				
	20 057	Ford County, KS	33 848	20780		Edwards, CO Micro SA	59 507
					08 037	Eagle County, CO	52 197
20020		Dothan, AL Metro SA	145 639		08 065	Lake County, CO	7 310
	01 061	Geneva County, AL	26 790				
	01 067	Henry County, AL	17 302	20820		Effingham, IL Micro SA	34 242
	01 069	Houston County, AL	101 547		17 049	Effingham County, IL	34 242
20060		Douglas, GA Micro SA	50 731	20900		El Campo, TX Micro SA	41 280
	13 003	Atkinson County, GA	8 375		48 481	Wharton County, TX	41 280
	13 069	Coffee County, GA	42 356				

Core Based Statistical Areas (Metropolitan and Micropolitan), Metropolitan Divisions, and Components (as defined December 2009)–*Continued*

Core Based Statistical Area	State/ County FIPS Code	Title and Geographic Components	2010 Census Population	Core Based Statistical Area	State/ County FIPS Code	Title and Geographic Components	2010 Census Population
20940		El Centro, CA Metro SA	174 528	21780		Evansville, IN-KY Metro SA	358 676
	06 025	Imperial County, CA	174 528		18 051	Gibson County, IN	33 503
20980		El Dorado, AR Micro SA	41 639		18 129	Posey County, IN	25 910
	05 139	Union County, AR	41 639		18 163	Vanderburgh County, IN	179 703
					18 173	Warrick County, IN	59 689
21020		Elizabeth City, NC Micro SA	64 094		21 101	Henderson County, KY	46 250
	37 029	Camden County, NC	9 980		21 233	Webster County, KY	13 621
	37 139	Pasquotank County, NC	40 661				
	37 143	Perquimans County, NC	13 453	21820		Fairbanks, AK Metro SA	97 581
					02 090	Fairbanks North Star Borough, AK	97 581
21060		Elizabethtown, KY Metro SA	119 736	21860		Fairmont, MN Micro SA	20 840
	21 093	Hardin County, KY	105 543		27 091	Martin County, MN	20 840
	21 123	Larue County, KY	14 193				
				21900		Fairmont, WV Micro SA	56 418
21120		Elk City, OK Micro SA	22 119		54 049	Marion County, WV	56 418
	40 009	Beckham County, OK	22 119				
				21980		Fallon, NV Micro SA	24 877
21140		Elkhart-Goshen, IN Metro SA	197 559		32 001	Churchill County, NV	24 877
	18 039	Elkhart County, IN	197 559				
				22020		Fargo, ND-MN Metro SA	208 777
21220		Elko, NV Micro SA	50 805		27 027	Clay County, MN	58 999
	32 007	Elko County, NV	48 818		38 017	Cass County, ND	149 778
	32 011	Eureka County, NV	1 987				
				22060		Faribault-Northfield, MN Micro SA	64 142
21260		Ellensburg, WA Micro SA	40 915		27 131	Rice County, MN	64 142
	53 037	Kittitas County, WA	40 915				
				22100		Farmington, MO Micro SA	65 359
21300		Elmira, NY Metro SA	88 830		29 187	St. Francois County, MO	65 359
	36 015	Chemung County, NY	88 830				
				22140		Farmington, NM Metro SA	130 044
21340		El Paso, TX Metro SA	800 647		35 045	San Juan County, NM	130 044
	48 141	El Paso County, TX	800 647				
				22180		Fayetteville, NC Metro SA	366 383
21380		Emporia, KS Micro SA	36 480		37 051	Cumberland County, NC	319 431
	20 017	Chase County, KS	2 790		37 093	Hoke County, NC	46 952
	20 111	Lyon County, KS	33 690				
				22220		Fayetteville-Springdale-Rogers, AR-MO Metro SA	463 204
21420		Enid, OK Micro SA	60 580		05 007	Benton County, AR	221 339
	40 047	Garfield County, OK	60 580		05 087	Madison County, AR	15 717
					05 143	Washington County, AR	203 065
21460		Enterprise-Ozark, AL Micro SA	100 199		29 119	McDonald County, MO	23 083
	01 031	Coffee County, AL	49 948				
	01 045	Dale County, AL	50 251	22260		Fergus Falls, MN Micro SA	57 303
					27 111	Otter Tail County, MN	57 303
21500		Erie, PA Metro SA	280 566				
	42 049	Erie County, PA	280 566	22280		Fernley, NV Micro SA	51 980
					32 019	Lyon County, NV	51 980
21540		Escanaba, MI Micro SA	37 069				
	26 041	Delta County, MI	37 069	22300		Findlay, OH Micro SA	74 782
					39 063	Hancock County, OH	74 782
21580		Espanola, NM Micro SA	40 246				
	35 039	Rio Arriba County, NM	40 246	22340		Fitzgerald, GA Micro SA	27 172
					13 017	Ben Hill County, GA	17 634
21640		Eufaula, AL-GA Micro SA	29 970		13 155	Irwin County, GA	9 538
	01 005	Barbour County, AL	27 457				
	13 239	Quitman County, GA	2 513	22380		Flagstaff, AZ Metro SA	134 421
					04 005	Coconino County, AZ	134 421
21660		Eugene-Springfield, OR Metro SA	351 715				
	41 039	Lane County, OR	351 715	22420		Flint, MI Metro SA	425 790
					26 049	Genesee County, MI	425 790
21700		Eureka-Arcata-Fortuna, CA Micro SA	134 623				
	06 023	Humboldt County, CA	134 623	22500		Florence, SC Metro SA	205 566
					45 031	Darlington County, SC	68 681
21740		Evanston, WY Micro SA	21 118		45 041	Florence County, SC	136 885
	56 041	Uinta County, WY	21 118				

Core Based Statistical Areas (Metropolitan and Micropolitan), Metropolitan Divisions, and Components (as defined December 2009)–*Continued*

Core Based Statistical Area	State/County FIPS Code	Title and Geographic Components	2010 Census Population	Core Based Statistical Area	State/County FIPS Code	Title and Geographic Components	2010 Census Population
22520		Florence-Muscle Shoals, AL Metro SA............	147 137	23420		Fresno, CA Metro SA................................	930 450
	01 033	Colbert County, AL	54 428		06 019	Fresno County, CA.....................................	930 450
	01 077	Lauderdale County, AL................................	92 709				
				23460		Gadsden, AL Metro SA............................	104 430
22540		Fond du Lac, WI Metro SA	101 633		01 055	Etowah County, AL.....................................	104 430
	55 039	Fond du Lac County, WI	101 633				
				23500		Gaffney, SC Micro SA..............................	55 342
22580		Forest City, NC Micro SA..........................	67 810		45 021	Cherokee County, SC................................	55 342
	37 161	Rutherford County, NC..............................	67 810				
				23540		Gainesville, FL Metro SA........................	264 275
22620		Forrest City, AR Micro SA.........................	28 258		12 001	Alachua County, FL...................................	247 336
	05 123	St. Francis County, AR..............................	28 258		12 041	Gilchrist County, FL..................................	16 939
22660		Fort Collins-Loveland, CO Metro SA	299 630	23580		Gainesville, GA Metro SA	179 684
	08 069	Larimer County, CO..................................	299 630		13 139	Hall County, GA..	179 684
22700		Fort Dodge, IA Micro SA...........................	38 013	23620		Gainesville, TX Micro SA........................	38 437
	19 187	Webster County, IA	38 013		48 097	Cooke County, TX.....................................	38 437
22780		Fort Leonard Wood, MO Micro SA	52 274	23660		Galesburg, IL Micro SA...........................	70 626
	29 169	Pulaski County, MO...................................	52 274		17 095	Knox County, IL..	52 919
					17 187	Warren County, IL	17 707
22800		Fort Madison-Keokuk, IA-MO Micro SA...........	43 001				
	19 111	Lee County, IA...	35 862	23700		Gallup, NM Micro SA	71 492
	29 045	Clark County, MO.....................................	7 139		35 031	McKinley County, NM................................	71 492
22820		Fort Morgan, CO Micro SA	28 159	23780		Garden City, KS Micro SA.......................	36 776
	08 087	Morgan County, CO...................................	28 159		20 055	Finney County, KS....................................	36 776
22840		Fort Payne, AL Micro SA	71 109	23820		Gardnerville Ranchos, NV Micro SA.............	46 997
	01 049	DeKalb County, AL....................................	71 109		32 005	Douglas County, NV..................................	46 997
22860		Fort Polk South, LA Micro SA.....................	52 334	23860		Georgetown, SC Micro SA.......................	60 158
	22 115	Vernon Parish, LA	52 334		45 043	Georgetown County, SC............................	60 158
22900		Fort Smith, AR-OK Metro SA.......................	298 592	23900		Gettysburg, PA Micro SA.........................	101 407
	05 033	Crawford County, AR.................................	61 948		42 001	Adams County, PA....................................	101 407
	05 047	Franklin County, AR	18 125				
	05 131	Sebastian County, AR...............................	125 744	23940		Gillette, WY Micro SA	46 133
	40 079	Le Flore County, OK..................................	50 384		56 005	Campbell County, WY	46 133
	40 135	Sequoyah County, OK...............................	42 391				
				23980		Glasgow, KY Micro SA.............................	52 272
22980		Fort Valley, GA Micro SA..........................	27 695		21 009	Barren County, KY....................................	42 173
	13 225	Peach County, GA.....................................	27 695		21 169	Metcalfe County, KY.................................	10 099
23060		Fort Wayne, IN Metro SA...........................	416 257	24020		Glens Falls, NY Metro SA.......................	128 923
	18 003	Allen County, IN.......................................	355 329		36 113	Warren County, NY	65 707
	18 179	Wells County, IN.......................................	27 636		36 115	Washington County, NY............................	63 216
	18 183	Whitley County, IN....................................	33 292				
				24100		Gloversville, NY Micro SA.......................	55 531
23140		Frankfort, IN Micro SA	33 224		36 035	Fulton County, NY....................................	55 531
	18 023	Clinton County, IN....................................	33 224				
				24140		Goldsboro, NC Metro SA	122 623
23180		Frankfort, KY Micro SA	70 706		37 191	Wayne County, NC...................................	122 623
	21 005	Anderson County, KY................................	21 421				
	21 073	Franklin County, KY..................................	49 285	24180		Granbury, TX Micro SA...........................	59 672
					48 221	Hood County, TX......................................	51 182
23240		Fredericksburg, TX Micro SA.....................	24 837		48 425	Somervell County, TX...............................	8 490
	48 171	Gillespie County, TX.................................	24 837				
				24220		Grand Forks, ND-MN Metro SA....................	98 461
23300		Freeport, IL Micro SA	47 711		27 119	Polk County, MN.......................................	31 600
	17 177	Stephenson County, IL..............................	47 711		38 035	Grand Forks County, ND............................	66 861
23340		Fremont, NE Micro SA	36 691	24260		Grand Island, NE Micro SA....................	72 726
	31 053	Dodge County, NE.....................................	36 691		31 079	Hall County, NE..	58 607
					31 093	Howard County, NE	6 274
23380		Fremont, OH Micro SA.............................	60 944		31 121	Merrick County, NE	7 845
	39 143	Sandusky County, OH...............................	60 944				

Core Based Statistical Areas (Metropolitan and Micropolitan), Metropolitan Divisions, and Components (as defined December 2009)–*Continued*

Core Based Statistical Area	State/ County FIPS Code	Title and Geographic Components	2010 Census Population	Core Based Statistical Area	State/ County FIPS Code	Title and Geographic Components	2010 Census Population
24300		Grand Junction, CO Metro SA	146 723	25100		Guymon, OK Micro SA	20 640
	08 077	Mesa County, CO	146 723		40 139	Texas County, OK	20 640
24340		Grand Rapids-Wyoming, MI Metro SA	774 160	25180		Hagerstown-Martinsburg, MD-WV Metro SA	269 140
	26 015	Barry County, MI	59 173		24 043	Washington County, MD	147 430
	26 067	Ionia County, MI	63 905		54 003	Berkeley County, WV	104 169
	26 081	Kent County, MI	602 622		54 065	Morgan County, WV	17 541
	26 123	Newaygo County, MI	48 460				
				25220		Hammond, LA Micro SA	121 097
24380		Grants, NM Micro SA	27 213		22 105	Tangipahoa Parish, LA	121 097
	35 006	Cibola County, NM	27 213				
				25260		Hanford-Corcoran, CA Metro SA	152 982
24420		Grants Pass, OR Micro SA	82 713		06 031	Kings County, CA	152 982
	41 033	Josephine County, OR	82 713				
				25300		Hannibal, MO Micro SA	38 948
24460		Great Bend, KS Micro SA	27 674		29 127	Marion County, MO	28 781
	20 009	Barton County, KS	27 674		29 173	Ralls County, MO	10 167
24500		Great Falls, MT Metro SA	81 327	25340		Harriman, TN Micro SA	54 181
	30 013	Cascade County, MT	81 327		47 145	Roane County, TN	54 181
24540		Greeley, CO Metro SA	252 825	25380		Harrisburg, IL Micro SA	24 913
	08 123	Weld County, CO	252 825		17 165	Saline County, IL	24 913
24580		Green Bay, WI Metro SA	306 241	25420		Harrisburg-Carlisle, PA Metro SA	549 475
	55 009	Brown County, WI	248 007		42 041	Cumberland County, PA	235 406
	55 061	Kewaunee County, WI	20 574		42 043	Dauphin County, PA	268 100
	55 083	Oconto County, WI	37 660		42 099	Perry County, PA	45 969
24620		Greeneville, TN Micro SA	68 831	25460		Harrison, AR Micro SA	45 233
	47 059	Greene County, TN	68 831		05 009	Boone County, AR	36 903
					05 101	Newton County, AR	8 330
24660		Greensboro-High Point, NC Metro SA	723 801				
	37 081	Guilford County, NC	488 406	25500		Harrisonburg, VA Metro SA	125 228
	37 151	Randolph County, NC	141 752		51 165	Rockingham County, VA	76 314
	37 157	Rockingham County, NC	93 643		51 660	Harrisonburg city, VA	48 914
24700		Greensburg, IN Micro SA	25 740	25540		Hartford-West Hartford-East Hartford, CT Metro SA	1212 381
	18 031	Decatur County, IN	25 740		09 003	Hartford County, CT	894 014
24740		Greenville, MS Micro SA	51 137		09 007	Middlesex County, CT	165 676
	28 151	Washington County, MS	51 137		09 013	Tolland County, CT	152 691
24780		Greenville-Mauldin-Easley, NC Metro SA	189 510	25580		Hastings, NE Micro SA	37 906
	37 079	Greene County, NC	21 362		31 001	Adams County, NE	31 364
	37 147	Pitt County, NC	168 148		31 035	Clay County, NE	6 542
24820		Greenville, OH Micro SA	52 959	25620		Hattiesburg, MS Metro SA	142 842
	39 037	Darke County, OH	52 959		28 035	Forrest County, MS	74 934
					28 073	Lamar County, MS	55 658
24860		Greenville, SC Metro SA	636 986		28 111	Perry County, MS	12 250
	45 045	Greenville County, SC	451 225				
	45 059	Laurens County, SC	66 537	25660		Havre, MT Micro SA	16 096
	45 077	Pickens County, SC	119 224		30 041	Hill County, MT	16 096
24900		Greenwood, MS Micro SA	42 914	25700		Hays, KS Micro SA	28 452
	28 015	Carroll County, MS	10 597		20 051	Ellis County, KS	28 452
	28 083	Leflore County, MS	32 317				
				25720		Heber, UT Micro SA	23 530
24940		Greenwood, SC Micro SA	69 661		49 051	Wasatch County, UT	23 530
	45 047	Greenwood County, SC	69 661				
				25740		Helena, MT Micro SA	74 801
24980		Grenada, MS Micro SA	21 906		30 043	Jefferson County, MT	11 406
	28 043	Grenada County, MS	21 906		30 049	Lewis and Clark County, MT	63 395
25060		Gulfport-Biloxi, MS Metro SA	248 820	25760		Helena-West Helena, AR Micro SA	21 757
	28 045	Hancock County, MS	43 929		05 107	Phillips County, AR	21 757
	28 047	Harrison County, MS	187 105				
	28 131	Stone County, MS	17 786				

Core Based Statistical Areas (Metropolitan and Micropolitan), Metropolitan Divisions, and Components (as defined December 2009)–*Continued*

Core Based Statistical Area	State/ County FIPS Code	Title and Geographic Components	2010 Census Population	Core Based Statistical Area	State/ County FIPS Code	Title and Geographic Components	2010 Census Population
25780		Henderson, NC Micro SA................	45 422	26480		Humboldt, TN Micro SA..................	49 683
	37 181	Vance County, NC.........................	45 422		47 053	Gibson County, TN........................	49 683
25820		Hereford, TX Micro SA................	19 372	26500		Huntingdon, PA Micro SA..............	45 913
	48 117	Deaf Smith County, TX..................	19 372		42 061	Huntingdon County, PA..................	45 913
25860		Hickory-Lenoir-Morganton, NC Metro SA.......	365 497	26540		Huntington, IN Micro SA................	37 124
	37 003	Alexander County, NC....................	37 198		18 069	Huntington County, IN...................	37 124
	37 023	Burke County, NC..........................	90 912				
	37 027	Caldwell County, NC......................	83 029	26580		Huntington-Ashland, WV-KY-OH Metro SA.....	287 702
	37 035	Catawba County, NC......................	154 358		21 019	Boyd County, KY...........................	49 542
					21 089	Greenup County, KY......................	36 910
25900		Hilo, HI Micro SA..........................	185 079		39 087	Lawrence County, OH....................	62 450
	15 001	Hawaii County, HI.........................	185 079		54 011	Cabell County, WV........................	96 319
					54 099	Wayne County, WV.......................	42 481
25940		Hilton Head Island-Beaufort, SC Micro SA......	187 010				
	45 013	Beaufort County, SC......................	162 233	26620		Huntsville, AL Metro SA.................	417 593
	45 053	Jasper County, SC	24 777		01 083	Limestone County, AL....................	82 782
					01 089	Madison County, AL.......................	334 811
25980		Hinesville-Fort Stewart, GA Metro SA	77 917				
	13 179	Liberty County, GA........................	63 453	26660		Huntsville, TX Micro SA.................	67 861
	13 183	Long County, GA...........................	14 464		48 471	Walker County, TX........................	67 861
26020		Hobbs, NM Micro SA...................	64 727	26700		Huron, SD Micro SA......................	17 398
	35 025	Lea County, NM...........................	64 727		46 005	Beadle County, SD........................	17 398
26100		Holland-Grand Haven, MI Metro SA...............	263 801	26740		Hutchinson, KS Micro SA...............	64 511
	26 139	Ottawa County, MI.........................	263 801		20 155	Reno County, KS..........................	64 511
26140		Homosassa Springs, FL Micro SA	141 236	26780		Hutchinson, MN Micro SA...............	36 651
	12 017	Citrus County, FL..........................	141 236		27 085	McLeod County, MN.......................	36 651
26180		Honolulu, HI Metro SA	953 207	26820		Idaho Falls, ID Metro SA................	130 374
	15 003	Honolulu County, HI.......................	953 207		16 019	Bonneville County, ID.....................	104 234
					16 051	Jefferson County, ID......................	26 140
26220		Hood River, OR Micro SA..............	22 346				
	41 027	Hood River County, OR..................	22 346	26860		Indiana, PA Micro SA.....................	88 880
					42 063	Indiana County, PA........................	88 880
26260		Hope, AR Micro SA......................	31 606				
	05 057	Hempstead County, AR..................	22 609	26900		Indianapolis-Carmel, IN Metro SA	1756 241
	05 099	Nevada County, AR.......................	8 997		18 011	Boone County, IN..........................	56 640
					18 013	Brown County, IN..........................	15 242
26300		Hot Springs, AR Metro SA.............	96 024		18 057	Hamilton County, IN	274 569
	05 051	Garland County, AR	96 024		18 059	Hancock County, IN.......................	70 002
					18 063	Hendricks County, IN.....................	145 448
26340		Houghton, MI Micro SA..................	38 784		18 081	Johnson County, IN.......................	139 654
	26 061	Houghton County, MI......................	36 628		18 097	Marion County, IN.........................	903 393
	26 083	Keweenaw County, MI....................	2 156		18 109	Morgan County, IN	68 894
					18 133	Putnam County, IN........................	37 963
26380		Houma-Bayou Cane-Thibodaux, LA Metro SA.....	208 178		18 145	Shelby County, IN.........................	44 436
	22 057	Lafourche Parish, LA.....................	96 318				
	22 109	Terrebonne Parish, LA	111 860	26940		Indianola, MS Micro SA	29 450
					28 133	Sunflower County, MS....................	29 450
26420		Houston-Sugar Land-Baytown, TX Metro SA ..	5946 800				
	48 015	Austin County, TX..........................	28 417	26980		Iowa City, IA Metro SA...................	152 586
	48 039	Brazoria County, TX.......................	313 166		19 103	Johnson County, IA.......................	130 882
	48 071	Chambers County, TX.....................	35 096		19 183	Washington County, IA...................	21 704
	48 157	Fort Bend County, TX.....................	585 375				
	48 167	Galveston County, TX....................	291 309	27020		Iron Mountain, MI-WI Micro SA.......................	30 591
	48 201	Harris County, TX.........................	4092 459		26 043	Dickinson County, MI.....................	26 168
	48 291	Liberty County, TX.........................	75 643		55 037	Florence County, WI......................	4 423
	48 339	Montgomery County, TX..................	455 746				
	48 407	San Jacinto County, TX..................	26 384	27060		Ithaca, NY Metro SA	101 564
	48 473	Waller County, TX..........................	43 205		36 109	Tompkins County, NY.....................	101 564
26460		Hudson, NY Micro SA....................	63 096	27100		Jackson, MI Metro SA....................	160 248
	36 021	Columbia County, NY.....................	63 096		26 075	Jackson County, MI.......................	160 248

Core Based Statistical Area	State/County FIPS Code	Title and Geographic Components	2010 Census Population	Core Based Statistical Area	State/County FIPS Code	Title and Geographic Components	2010 Census Population
27140		Jackson, MS Metro SA	539 057	27900		Joplin, MO Metro SA	175 518
	28 029	Copiah County, MS	29 449		29 097	Jasper County, MO	117 404
	28 049	Hinds County, MS	245 285		29 145	Newton County, MO	58 114
	28 089	Madison County, MS	95 203				
	28 121	Rankin County, MS	141 617	27940		Juneau, AK Micro SA	31 275
	28 127	Simpson County, MS	27 503		02 110	Juneau City and Borough, AK	31 275
27180		Jackson, TN Metro SA	115 425	27980		Kahului-Wailuku, HI Micro SA	154 834
	47 023	Chester County, TN	17 131		15 009	Maui County, HI	154 834
	47 113	Madison County, TN	98 294				
				28020		Kalamazoo-Portage, MI Metro SA	326 589
27220		Jackson, WY-ID Micro SA	31 464		26 077	Kalamazoo County, MI	250 331
	16 081	Teton County, ID	10 170		26 159	Van Buren County, MI	76 258
	56 039	Teton County, WY	21 294				
				28060		Kalispell, MT Micro SA	90 928
27260		Jacksonville, FL Metro SA	1345 596		30 029	Flathead County, MT	90 928
	12 003	Baker County, FL	27 115				
	12 019	Clay County, FL	190 865	28100		Kankakee-Bradley, IL Metro SA	113 449
	12 031	Duval County, FL	864 263		17 091	Kankakee County, IL	113 449
	12 089	Nassau County, FL	73 314				
	12 109	St. Johns County, FL	190 039	28140		Kansas City, MO-KS Metro SA	2035 334
					20 059	Franklin County, KS	25 992
27300		Jacksonville, IL Micro SA	40 902		20 091	Johnson County, KS	544 179
	17 137	Morgan County, IL	35 547		20 103	Leavenworth County, KS	76 227
	17 171	Scott County, IL	5 355		20 107	Linn County, KS	9 656
					20 121	Miami County, KS	32 787
27340		Jacksonville, NC Metro SA	177 772		20 209	Wyandotte County, KS	157 505
	37 133	Onslow County, NC	177 772		29 013	Bates County, MO	17 049
					29 025	Caldwell County, MO	9 424
27380		Jacksonville, TX Micro SA	50 845		29 037	Cass County, MO	99 478
	48 073	Cherokee County, TX	50 845		29 047	Clay County, MO	221 939
					29 049	Clinton County, MO	20 743
27420		Jamestown, ND Micro SA	21 100		29 095	Jackson County, MO	674 158
	38 093	Stutsman County, ND	21 100		29 107	Lafayette County, MO	33 381
					29 165	Platte County, MO	89 322
27460		Jamestown-Dunkirk-Fredonia, NY Micro SA	134 905		29 177	Ray County, MO	23 494
	36 013	Chautauqua County, NY	134 905				
				28180		Kapaa, HI Micro SA	67 091
27500		Janesville, WI Metro SA	160 331		15 007	Kauai County, HI	67 091
	55 105	Rock County, WI	160 331				
				28260		Kearney, NE Micro SA	52 591
27540		Jasper, IN Micro SA	54 734		31 019	Buffalo County, NE	46 102
	18 037	Dubois County, IN	41 889		31 099	Kearney County, NE	6 489
	18 125	Pike County, IN	12 845				
				28300		Keene, NH Micro SA	77 117
27620		Jefferson City, MO Metro SA	149 807		33 005	Cheshire County, NH	77 117
	29 027	Callaway County, MO	44 332				
	29 051	Cole County, MO	75 990	28340		Kendallville, IN Micro SA	47 536
	29 135	Moniteau County, MO	15 607		18 113	Noble County, IN	47 536
	29 151	Osage County, MO	13 878				
				28380		Kennett, MO Micro SA	31 953
27660		Jennings, LA Micro SA	31 594		29 069	Dunklin County, MO	31 953
	22 053	Jefferson Davis Parish, LA	31 594				
				28420		Kennewick-Pasco-Richland, WA Metro SA	253 340
27700		Jesup, GA Micro SA	30 099		53 005	Benton County, WA	175 177
	13 305	Wayne County, GA	30 099		53 021	Franklin County, WA	78 163
27740		Johnson City, TN Metro SA	198 716	28500		Kerrville, TX Micro SA	49 625
	47 019	Carter County, TN	57 424		48 265	Kerr County, TX	49 625
	47 171	Unicoi County, TN	18 313				
	47 179	Washington County, TN	122 979	28540		Ketchikan, AK Micro SA	13 477
					02 130	Ketchikan Gateway Borough, AK	13 477
27780		Johnstown, PA Metro SA	143 679				
	42 021	Cambria County, PA	143 679	28580		Key West, FL Micro SA	73 090
					12 087	Monroe County, FL	73 090
27860		Jonesboro, AR Metro SA	121 026				
	05 031	Craighead County, AR	96 443	28620		Kill Devil Hills, NC Micro SA	33 920
	05 111	Poinsett County, AR	24 583		37 055	Dare County, NC	33 920

Core Based Statistical Areas (Metropolitan and Micropolitan), Metropolitan Divisions, and Components (as defined December 2009)–*Continued*

Core Based Statistical Area	State/County FIPS Code	Title and Geographic Components	2010 Census Population	Core Based Statistical Area	State/County FIPS Code	Title and Geographic Components	2010 Census Population
28660		Killeen-Temple-Fort Hood, TX Metro SA.........	405 300	29340		Lake Charles, LA Metro SA	199 607
	48 027	Bell County, TX...	310 235		22 019	Calcasieu Parish, LA	192 768
	48 099	Coryell County, TX..	75 388		22 023	Cameron Parish, LA	6 839
	48 281	Lampasas County, TX....................................	19 677				
				29380		Lake City, FL Micro SA	67 531
28700		Kingsport-Bristol-Bristol, TN-VA Metro SA.......	309 544		12 023	Columbia County, FL......................................	67 531
	47 073	Hawkins County, TN......................................	56 833				
	47 163	Sullivan County, TN	156 823	29420		Lake Havasu City-Kingman, AZ Metro SA	200 186
	51 169	Scott County, VA...	23 177		04 015	Mohave County, AZ..	200 186
	51 191	Washington County, VA	54 876				
	51 520	Bristol city, VA	17 835	29460		Lakeland-Winter Haven, FL Metro SA.............	602 095
					12 105	Polk County, FL..	602 095
28740		Kingston, NY Metro SA	182 493				
	36 111	Ulster County, NY..	182 493	29500		Lamesa, TX Micro SA....................................	13 833
					48 115	Dawson County, TX..	13 833
28780		Kingsville, TX Micro SA..................................	32 477				
	48 261	Kenedy County, TX	416	29540		Lancaster, PA Metro SA	519 445
	48 273	Kleberg County, TX	32 061		42 071	Lancaster County, PA.....................................	519 445
28820		Kinston, NC Micro SA	59 495	29580		Lancaster, SC Micro SA.................................	76 652
	37 107	Lenoir County, NC	59 495		45 057	Lancaster County, SC	76 652
28860		Kirksville, MO Micro SA	30 038	29620		Lansing-East Lansing, MI Metro SA	464 036
	29 001	Adair County, MO..	25 607		26 037	Clinton County, MI	75 382
	29 197	Schuyler County, MO	4 431		26 045	Eaton County, MI	107 759
					26 065	Ingham County, MI	280 895
28900		Klamath Falls, OR Micro SA...........................	66 380				
	41 035	Klamath County, OR......................................	66 380	29660		Laramie, WY Micro SA...................................	36 299
					56 001	Albany County, WY	36 299
28940		Knoxville, TN Metro SA	698 030				
	47 001	Anderson County, TN	75 129	29700		Laredo, TX Metro SA.....................................	250 304
	47 009	Blount County, TN...	123 010		48 479	Webb County, TX	250 304
	47 093	Knox County, TN	432 226				
	47 105	Loudon County, TN	48 556	29740		Las Cruces, NM Metro SA	209 233
	47 173	Union County, TN	19 109		35 013	Dona Ana County, NM	209 233
28980		Kodiak, AK Micro SA......................................	13 592	29780		Las Vegas, NM Micro SA................................	29 393
	02 150	Kodiak Island Borough, AK	13 592		35 047	San Miguel County, NM	29 393
29020		Kokomo, IN Metro SA.....................................	98 688	29820		Las Vegas-Paradise, NV Metro SA	1951 269
	18 067	Howard County, IN	82 752		32 003	Clark County, NV...	1951 269
	18 159	Tipton County, IN..	15 936				
				29860		Laurel, MS Micro SA	84 823
29060		Laconia, NH Micro SA....................................	60 088		28 061	Jasper County, MS...	17 062
	33 001	Belknap County, NH	60 088		28 067	Jones County, MS	67 761
29100		La Crosse, WI-MN Metro SA	133 665	29900		Laurinburg, NC Micro SA	36 157
	27 055	Houston County, MN	19 027		37 165	Scotland County, NC......................................	36 157
	55 063	La Crosse County, WI	114 638				
				29940		Lawrence, KS Metro SA.................................	110 826
29140		Lafayette, IN Metro SA...................................	201 789		20 045	Douglas County, KS	110 826
	18 007	Benton County, IN...	8 854				
	18 015	Carroll County, IN	20 155	29980		Lawrenceburg, TN Micro SA...........................	41 869
	18 157	Tippecanoe County, IN...................................	172 780		47 099	Lawrence County, TN.....................................	41 869
29180		Lafayette, LA Metro SA..................................	273 738	30020		Lawton, OK Metro SA.....................................	124 098
	22 055	Lafayette Parish, LA.....................................	221 578		40 031	Comanche County, OK....................................	124 098
	22 099	St. Martin Parish, LA	52 160				
				30060		Lebanon, MO Micro SA..................................	35 571
29220		La Follette, TN Micro SA................................	40 716		29 105	Laclede County, MO.......................................	35 571
	47 013	Campbell County, TN	40 716				
				30100		Lebanon, NH-VT Micro SA.............................	174 724
29260		La Grande, OR Micro SA................................	25 748		33 009	Grafton County, NH..	89 118
	41 061	Union County, OR	25 748		50 017	Orange County, VT...	28 936
					50 027	Windsor County, VT	56 670
29300		LaGrange, GA Micro SA.................................	67 044				
	13 285	Troup County, GA	67 044	30140		Lebanon, PA Metro SA	133 568
					42 075	Lebanon County, PA	133 568

Core Based Statistical Area	State/County FIPS Code	Title and Geographic Components	2010 Census Population	Core Based Statistical Area	State/County FIPS Code	Title and Geographic Components	2010 Census Population
30220		Levelland, TX Micro SA	22 935	30940		London, KY Micro SA	58 849
	48 219	Hockley County, TX	22 935		21 125	Laurel County, KY	58 849
30260		Lewisburg, PA Micro SA	44 947	30980		Longview, TX Metro SA	214 369
	42 119	Union County, PA	44 947		48 183	Gregg County, TX	121 730
					48 401	Rusk County, TX	53 330
30280		Lewisburg, TN Micro SA	30 617		48 459	Upshur County, TX	39 309
	47 117	Marshall County, TN	30 617				
				31020		Longview, WA Metro SA	102 410
30300		Lewiston, ID-WA Metro SA	60 888		53 015	Cowlitz County, WA	102 410
	16 069	Nez Perce County, ID	39 265				
	53 003	Asotin County, WA	21 623	31060		Los Alamos, NM Micro SA	17 950
					35 028	Los Alamos County, NM	17 950
30340		Lewiston-Auburn, ME Metro SA	107 702				
	23 001	Androscoggin County, ME	107 702	31100		Los Angeles-Long Beach-Santa Ana, CA Metro SA	12828 837
30380		Lewistown, PA Micro SA	46 682			Los Angeles-Long Beach-Glendale, CA Metro Div 31084	9818 605
	42 087	Mifflin County, PA	46 682		06 037	Los Angeles County, CA	9818 605
30420		Lexington, NE Micro SA	26 370			Santa Ana-Anaheim-Irvine, CA Metro Div 42044	3010 232
	31 047	Dawson County, NE	24 326		06 059	Orange County, CA	3010 232
	31 073	Gosper County, NE	2 044				
30460		Lexington-Fayette, KY Metro SA	472 099	31140		Louisville-Jefferson County, KY-IN Metro SA	1283 566
	21 017	Bourbon County, KY	19 985		18 019	Clark County, IN	110 232
	21 049	Clark County, KY	35 613		18 043	Floyd County, IN	74 578
	21 067	Fayette County, KY	295 803		18 061	Harrison County, IN	39 364
	21 113	Jessamine County, KY	48 586		18 175	Washington County, IN	28 262
	21 209	Scott County, KY	47 173		21 029	Bullitt County, KY	74 319
	21 239	Woodford County, KY	24 939		21 103	Henry County, KY	15 416
					21 111	Jefferson County, KY	741 096
30500		Lexington Park, MD Micro SA	105 151		21 163	Meade County, KY	28 602
	24 037	St. Mary's County, MD	105 151		21 179	Nelson County, KY	43 437
					21 185	Oldham County, KY	60 316
30580		Liberal, KS Micro SA	22 952		21 211	Shelby County, KY	42 074
	20 175	Seward County, KS	22 952		21 215	Spencer County, KY	17 061
					21 223	Trimble County, KY	8 809
30620		Lima, OH Metro SA	106 331				
	39 003	Allen County, OH	106 331	31180		Lubbock, TX Metro SA	284 890
					48 107	Crosby County, TX	6 059
30660		Lincoln, IL Micro SA	30 305		48 303	Lubbock County, TX	278 831
	17 107	Logan County, IL	30 305				
				31260		Lufkin, TX Micro SA	86 771
30700		Lincoln, NE Metro SA	302 157		48 005	Angelina County, TX	86 771
	31 109	Lancaster County, NE	285 407				
	31 159	Seward County, NE	16 750	31300		Lumberton, NC Micro SA	134 168
					37 155	Robeson County, NC	134 168
30740		Lincolnton, NC Micro SA	78 265				
	37 109	Lincoln County, NC	78 265	31340		Lynchburg, VA Metro SA	252 634
					51 009	Amherst County, VA	32 353
30780		Little Rock-North Little Rock-Conway, AR Metro SA	699 757		51 011	Appomattox County, VA	14 973
	05 045	Faulkner County, AR	113 237		51 019	Bedford County, VA	68 676
	05 053	Grant County, AR	17 853		51 031	Campbell County, VA	54 842
	05 085	Lonoke County, AR	68 356		51 515	Bedford city, VA	6 222
	05 105	Perry County, AR	10 445		51 680	Lynchburg city, VA	75 568
	05 119	Pulaski County, AR	382 748				
	05 125	Saline County, AR	107 118	31380		Macomb, IL Micro SA	32 612
					17 109	McDonough County, IL	32 612
30820		Lock Haven, PA Micro SA	39 238				
	42 035	Clinton County, PA	39 238	31420		Macon, GA Metro SA	232 293
					13 021	Bibb County, GA	155 547
30860		Logan, UT-ID Metro SA	125 442		13 079	Crawford County, GA	12 630
	16 041	Franklin County, ID	12 786		13 169	Jones County, GA	28 669
	49 005	Cache County, UT	112 656		13 207	Monroe County, GA	26 424
					13 289	Twiggs County, GA	9 023
30900		Logansport, IN Micro SA	38 966				
	18 017	Cass County, IN	38 966	31460		Madera-Chowchilla, CA Metro SA	150 865
					06 039	Madera County, CA	150 865

Core Based Statistical Areas (Metropolitan and Micropolitan), Metropolitan Divisions, and Components (as defined December 2009)–*Continued*

Core Based Statistical Area	State/ County FIPS Code	Title and Geographic Components	2010 Census Population	Core Based Statistical Area	State/ County FIPS Code	Title and Geographic Components	2010 Census Population
31500		Madison, IN Micro SA	32 428	32280		Martin, TN Micro SA	35 021
	18 077	Jefferson County, IN	32 428		47 183	Weakley County, TN	35 021
31540		Madison, WI Metro SA	568 593	32300		Martinsville, VA Micro SA	67 972
	55 021	Columbia County, WI	56 833		51 089	Henry County, VA	54 151
	55 025	Dane County, WI	488 073		51 690	Martinsville city, VA	13 821
	55 049	Iowa County, WI	23 687				
				32340		Maryville, MO Micro SA	23 370
31580		Madisonville, KY Micro SA	46 920		29 147	Nodaway County, MO	23 370
	21 107	Hopkins County, KY	46 920				
				32380		Mason City, IA Micro SA	51 749
31620		Magnolia, AR Micro SA	24 552		19 033	Cerro Gordo County, IA	44 151
	05 027	Columbia County, AR	24 552		19 195	Worth County, IA	7 598
31660		Malone, NY Micro SA	51 599	32460		Mayfield, KY Micro SA	37 121
	36 033	Franklin County, NY	51 599		21 083	Graves County, KY	37 121
31700		Manchester-Nashua, NH Metro SA	400 721	32500		Maysville, KY Micro SA	31 360
	33 011	Hillsborough County, NH	400 721		21 135	Lewis County, KY	13 870
					21 161	Mason County, KY	17 490
31740		Manhattan, KS Metro SA	127 081				
	20 061	Geary County, KS	34 362	32540		McAlester, OK Micro SA	45 837
	20 149	Pottawatomie County, KS	21 604		40 121	Pittsburg County, OK	45 837
	20 161	Riley County, KS	71 115				
				32580		McAllen-Edinburg-Mission, TX Metro SA	774 769
31820		Manitowoc, WI Micro SA	81 442		48 215	Hidalgo County, TX	774 769
	55 071	Manitowoc County, WI	81 442				
				32620		McComb, MS Micro SA	53 535
31860		Mankato-North Mankato, MN Metro SA	96 740		28 005	Amite County, MS	13 131
	27 013	Blue Earth County, MN	64 013		28 113	Pike County, MS	40 404
	27 103	Nicollet County, MN	32 727				
				32660		McMinnville, TN Micro SA	39 839
31900		Mansfield, OH Metro SA	124 475		47 177	Warren County, TN	39 839
	39 139	Richland County, OH	124 475				
				32700		McPherson, KS Micro SA	29 180
31920		Marble Falls, TX Micro SA	42 750		20 113	McPherson County, KS	29 180
	48 053	Burnet County, TX	42 750				
				32740		Meadville, PA Micro SA	88 765
31940		Marinette, WI-MI Micro SA	65 778		42 039	Crawford County, PA	88 765
	26 109	Menominee County, MI	24 029				
	55 075	Marinette County, WI	41 749	32780		Medford, OR Metro SA	203 206
					41 029	Jackson County, OR	203 206
31980		Marion, IN Micro SA	70 061				
	18 053	Grant County, IN	70 061	32820		Memphis, TN-MS-AR Metro SA	1316 100
					05 035	Crittenden County, AR	50 902
32020		Marion, OH Micro SA	66 501		28 033	DeSoto County, MS	161 252
	39 101	Marion County, OH	66 501		28 093	Marshall County, MS	37 144
					28 137	Tate County, MS	28 886
32060		Marion-Herrin, IL Micro SA	66 357		28 143	Tunica County, MS	10 778
	17 199	Williamson County, IL	66 357		47 047	Fayette County, TN	38 413
					47 157	Shelby County, TN	927 644
32100		Marquette, MI Micro SA	67 077		47 167	Tipton County, TN	61 081
	26 103	Marquette County, MI	67 077				
				32860		Menomonie, WI Micro SA	43 857
32140		Marshall, MN Micro SA	25 857		55 033	Dunn County, WI	43 857
	27 083	Lyon County, MN	25 857				
				32900		Merced, CA Metro SA	255 793
32180		Marshall, MO Micro SA	23 370		06 047	Merced County, CA	255 793
	29 195	Saline County, MO	23 370				
				32940		Meridian, MS Micro SA	107 449
32220		Marshall, TX Micro SA	65 631		28 023	Clarke County, MS	16 732
	48 203	Harrison County, TX	65 631		28 069	Kemper County, MS	10 456
					28 075	Lauderdale County, MS	80 261
32260		Marshalltown, IA Micro SA	40 648				
	19 127	Marshall County, IA	40 648	32980		Merrill, WI Micro SA	28 743
					55 069	Lincoln County, WI	28 743
32270		Marshfield-Wisconsin Rapids, WI Micro SA	74 749				
	55 141	Wood County, WI	74 749	33020		Mexico, MO Micro SA	25 529
					29 007	Audrain County, MO	25 529

Core Based Statistical Area	State/County FIPS Code	Title and Geographic Components	2010 Census Population	Core Based Statistical Area	State/County FIPS Code	Title and Geographic Components	2010 Census Population
33060		Miami, OK Micro SA...................................	31 848	33580		Mitchell, SD Micro SA	22 835
	40 115	Ottawa County, OK.................................	31 848		46 035	Davison County, SD	19 504
33100		Miami-Fort Lauderdale-Pompano Beach, FL			46 061	Hanson County, SD..............................	3 331
		Metro SA	5564 635	33620		Moberly, MO Micro SA	25 414
		Fort Lauderdale-Pompano Beach-Deerfield			29 175	Randolph County, MO	25 414
		Beach, FL Metro Div 22744	1748 066	33660		Mobile, AL Metro SA	412 992
	12 011	Broward County, FL...............................	1748 066		01 097	Mobile County, AL	412 992
		Miami-Miami Beach-Kendall, FL Metro Div					
		33124	2496 435	33700		Modesto, CA Metro SA	514 453
	12 086	Miami-Dade County, FL...........................	2496 435		06 099	Stanislaus County, CA...........................	514 453
		West Palm Beach-Boca Raton-Boynton		33740		Monroe, LA Metro SA	176 441
		Beach, FL Metro Div 48424	1320 134		22 073	Ouachita Parish, LA..............................	153 720
	12 099	Palm Beach County, FL...........................	1320 134		22 111	Union Parish, LA...................................	22 721
33140		Michigan City-La Porte, IN Metro SA..............	111 467	33780		Monroe, MI Metro SA...................................	152 021
	18 091	LaPorte County, IN.................................	111 467		26 115	Monroe County, MI...............................	152 021
33180		Middlesborough, KY Micro SA........................	28 691	33820		Monroe, WI Micro SA	36 842
	21 013	Bell County, KY.....................................	28 691		55 045	Green County, WI..................................	36 842
33220		Midland, MI Micro SA...................................	83 629	33860		Montgomery, AL Metro SA............................	374 536
	26 111	Midland County, MI.................................	83 629		01 001	Autauga County, AL	54 571
33260		Midland, TX Metro SA..................................	136 872		01 051	Elmore County, AL	79 303
	48 329	Midland County, TX	136 872		01 085	Lowndes County, AL	11 299
33300		Milledgeville, GA Micro SA............................	55 149		01 101	Montgomery County, AL.........................	229 363
	13 009	Baldwin County, GA...............................	45 720	33940		Montrose, CO Micro SA................................	41 276
	13 141	Hancock County, GA..............................	9 429		08 085	Montrose County, CO.............................	41 276
33340		Milwaukee-Waukesha-West Allis, WI Metro		33980		Morehead City, NC Micro SA.........................	66 469
		SA..	1555 908		37 031	Carteret County, NC..............................	66 469
	55 079	Milwaukee County, WI............................	947 735				
	55 089	Ozaukee County, WI...............................	86 395	34020		Morgan City, LA Micro SA	54 650
	55 131	Washington County, WI...........................	131 887		22 101	St. Mary Parish, LA..............................	54 650
	55 133	Waukesha County, WI............................	389 891	34060		Morgantown, WV Metro SA...........................	129 709
33380		Minden, LA Micro SA...................................	41 207		54 061	Monongalia County, WV.........................	96 189
	22 119	Webster Parish, LA................................	41 207		54 077	Preston County, WV..............................	33 520
33420		Mineral Wells, TX Micro SA..........................	28 111	34100		Morristown, TN Metro SA..............................	136 608
	48 363	Palo Pinto County, TX	28 111		47 057	Grainger County, TN.............................	22 657
33460		Minneapolis-St. Paul-Bloomington, MN-WI			47 063	Hamblen County, TN.............................	62 544
		Metro SA	3279 833		47 089	Jefferson County, TN............................	51 407
	27 003	Anoka County, MN	330 844	34140		Moscow, ID Micro SA	37 244
	27 019	Carver County, MN................................	91 042		16 057	Latah County, ID..................................	37 244
	27 025	Chisago County, MN..............................	53 887				
	27 037	Dakota County, MN................................	398 552	34180		Moses Lake, WA Micro SA	89 120
	27 053	Hennepin County, MN.............................	1152 425		53 025	Grant County, WA	89 120
	27 059	Isanti County, MN..................................	37 816				
	27 123	Ramsey County, MN...............................	508 640	34220		Moultrie, GA Micro SA	45 498
	27 139	Scott County, MN..................................	129 928		13 071	Colquitt County, GA..............................	45 498
	27 141	Sherburne County, MN...........................	88 499				
	27 163	Washington County, MN..........................	238 136	34260		Mountain Home, AR Micro SA........................	41 513
	27 171	Wright County, MN.................................	124 700		05 005	Baxter County, AR................................	41 513
	55 093	Pierce County, WI.................................	41 019				
	55 109	St. Croix County, WI..............................	84 345	34300		Mountain Home, ID Micro SA	27 038
33500		Minot, ND Micro SA	69 540		16 039	Elmore County, ID................................	27 038
	38 049	McHenry County, ND..............................	5 395				
	38 075	Renville County, ND...............................	2 470	34340		Mount Airy, NC Micro SA..............................	73 673
	38 101	Ward County, ND..................................	61 675		37 171	Surry County, NC.................................	73 673
33540		Missoula, MT Metro SA................................	109 299	34380		Mount Pleasant, MI Micro SA	70 311
	30 063	Missoula County, MT..............................	109 299		26 073	Isabella County, MI...............................	70 311

Core Based Statistical Areas (Metropolitan and Micropolitan), Metropolitan Divisions, and Components (as defined December 2009)–*Continued*

Core Based Statistical Area	State/ County FIPS Code	Title and Geographic Components	2010 Census Population	Core Based Statistical Area	State/ County FIPS Code	Title and Geographic Components	2010 Census Population
34420		Mount Pleasant, TX Micro SA	32 334	35100		New Bern, NC Micro SA	126 802
	48 449	Titus County, TX	32 334		37 049	Craven County, NC	103 505
34460		Mount Sterling, KY Micro SA	44 396		37 103	Jones County, NC	10 153
	21 011	Bath County, KY	11 591		37 137	Pamlico County, NC	13 144
	21 165	Menifee County, KY	6 306	35140		Newberry, SC Micro SA	37 508
	21 173	Montgomery County, KY	26 499		45 071	Newberry County, SC	37 508
34500		Mount Vernon, IL Micro SA	47 284	35220		New Castle, IN Micro SA	49 462
	17 065	Hamilton County, IL	8 457		18 065	Henry County, IN	49 462
	17 081	Jefferson County, IL	38 827				
				35260		New Castle, PA Micro SA	91 108
34540		Mount Vernon, OH Micro SA	60 921		42 073	Lawrence County, PA	91 108
	39 083	Knox County, OH	60 921				
				35300		New Haven-Milford, CT Metro SA	862 477
34580		Mount Vernon-Anacortes, WA Metro SA	116 901		09 009	New Haven County, CT	862 477
	53 057	Skagit County, WA	116 901				
				35340		New Iberia, LA Micro SA	73 240
34620		Muncie, IN Metro SA	117 671		22 045	Iberia Parish, LA	73 240
	18 035	Delaware County, IN	117 671				
				35380		New Orleans-Metairie-Kenner, LA Metro SA	1167 764
34660		Murray, KY Micro SA	37 191		22 051	Jefferson Parish, LA	432 552
	21 035	Calloway County, KY	37 191		22 071	Orleans Parish, LA	343 829
					22 075	Plaquemines Parish, LA	23 042
34700		Muscatine, IA Micro SA	54 132		22 087	St. Bernard Parish, LA	35 897
	19 115	Louisa County, IA	11 387		22 089	St. Charles Parish, LA	52 780
	19 139	Muscatine County, IA	42 745		22 095	St. John the Baptist Parish, LA	45 924
					22 103	St. Tammany Parish, LA	233 740
34740		Muskegon-Norton Shores, MI Metro SA	172 188				
	26 121	Muskegon County, MI	172 188	35420		New Philadelphia-Dover, OH Micro SA	92 582
					39 157	Tuscarawas County, OH	92 582
34780		Muskogee, OK Micro SA	70 990				
	40 101	Muskogee County, OK	70 990	35460		Newport, TN Micro SA	35 662
					47 029	Cocke County, TN	35 662
34820		Myrtle Beach-North Myrtle Beach-Conway, SC Metro SA	269 291	35500		Newton, IA Micro SA	36 842
	45 051	Horry County, SC	269 291		19 099	Jasper County, IA	36 842
34860		Nacogdoches, TX Micro SA	64 524	35580		New Ulm, MN Micro SA	25 893
	48 347	Nacogdoches County, TX	64 524		27 015	Brown County, MN	25 893
34900		Napa, CA Metro SA	136 484				
	06 055	Napa County, CA	136 484				
34940		Naples-Marco Island, FL Metro SA	321 520				
	12 021	Collier County, FL	321 520				
34980		Nashville-Davidson—Murfreesboro—Franklin, TN Metro S	1589 934				
	47 015	Cannon County, TN	13 801				
	47 021	Cheatham County, TN	39 105				
	47 037	Davidson County, TN	626 681				
	47 043	Dickson County, TN	49 666				
	47 081	Hickman County, TN	24 690				
	47 111	Macon County, TN	22 248				
	47 147	Robertson County, TN	66 283				
	47 149	Rutherford County, TN	262 604				
	47 159	Smith County, TN	19 166				
	47 165	Sumner County, TN	160 645				
	47 169	Trousdale County, TN	7 870				
	47 187	Williamson County, TN	183 182				
	47 189	Wilson County, TN	113 993				
35020		Natchez, MS-LA Micro SA	53 119				
	22 029	Concordia Parish, LA	20 822				
	28 001	Adams County, MS	32 297				
35060		Natchitoches, LA Micro SA	39 566				
	22 069	Natchitoches Parish, LA	39 566				

Core Based Statistical Area	State/ County FIPS Code	Title and Geographic Components	2010 Census Population	Core Based Statistical Area	State/ County FIPS Code	Title and Geographic Components	2010 Census Population
35620		New York-Northern NJ-Long Island, NY-NJ-PA Metro SA	18897 109	36100		Ocala, FL Metro SA	331 298
		Edison-New Brunswick, NJ Metro Div 20764	2340 249		12 083	Marion County, FL	331 298
	34 023	Middlesex County, NJ	809 858	36140		Ocean City, NJ Metro SA	97 265
	34 025	Monmouth County, NJ	630 380		34 009	Cape May County, NJ	97 265
	34 029	Ocean County, NJ	576 567				
	34 035	Somerset County, NJ	323 444	36180		Ocean Pines, MD Micro SA	51 454
		Nassau-Suffolk, NY Metro Div 35004	2832 882		24 047	Worcester County, MD	51 454
	36 059	Nassau County, NY	1339 532	36220		Odessa, TX Metro SA	137 130
	36 103	Suffolk County, NY	1493 350		48 135	Ector County, TX	137 130
		Newark-Union, NJ-PA Metro Div 35084	2147 727	36260		Ogden-Clearfield, UT Metro SA	547 184
	34 013	Essex County, NJ	783 969		49 011	Davis County, UT	306 479
	34 019	Hunterdon County, NJ	128 349		49 029	Morgan County, UT	9 469
	34 027	Morris County, NJ	492 276		49 057	Weber County, UT	231 236
	34 037	Sussex County, NJ	149 265	36300		Ogdensburg-Massena, NY Micro SA	111 944
	34 039	Union County, NJ	536 499		36 089	St. Lawrence County, NY	111 944
	42 103	Pike County, PA	57 369				
		New York-White Plains-Wayne, NY-NJ Metro Div 35644	11576 251	36340		Oil City, PA Micro SA	54 984
	34 003	Bergen County, NJ	905 116		42 121	Venango County, PA	54 984
	34 017	Hudson County, NJ	634 266				
	34 031	Passaic County, NJ	501 226	36380		Okeechobee, FL Micro SA	39 996
	36 005	Bronx County, NY	1385 108		12 093	Okeechobee County, FL	39 996
	36 047	Kings County, NY	2504 700				
	36 061	New York County, NY	1585 873	36420		Oklahoma City, OK Metro SA	1252 987
	36 079	Putnam County, NY	99 710		40 017	Canadian County, OK	115 541
	36 081	Queens County, NY	2230 722		40 027	Cleveland County, OK	255 755
	36 085	Richmond County, NY	468 730		40 051	Grady County, OK	52 431
	36 087	Rockland County, NY	311 687		40 081	Lincoln County, OK	34 273
	36 119	Westchester County, NY	949 113		40 083	Logan County, OK	41 848
35660		Niles-Benton Harbor, MI Metro SA	156 813		40 087	McClain County, OK	34 506
	26 021	Berrien County, MI	156 813		40 109	Oklahoma County, OK	718 633
35700		Nogales, AZ Micro SA	47 420	36460		Olean, NY Micro SA	80 317
	04 023	Santa Cruz County, AZ	47 420		36 009	Cattaraugus County, NY	80 317
35740		Norfolk, NE Micro SA	48 271	36500		Olympia, WA Metro SA	252 264
	31 119	Madison County, NE	34 876		53 067	Thurston County, WA	252 264
	31 139	Pierce County, NE	7 266				
	31 167	Stanton County, NE	6 129	36540		Omaha-Council Bluffs, NE-IA Metro SA	865 350
					19 085	Harrison County, IA	14 928
35820		North Platte, NE Micro SA	37 590		19 129	Mills County, IA	15 059
	31 111	Lincoln County, NE	36 288		19 155	Pottawattamie County, IA	93 158
	31 113	Logan County, NE	763		31 025	Cass County, NE	25 241
	31 117	McPherson County, NE	539		31 055	Douglas County, NE	517 110
					31 153	Sarpy County, NE	158 840
35840		North Port-Bradenton-Sarasota, FL Metro SA	702 281		31 155	Saunders County, NE	20 780
	12 081	Manatee County, FL	322 833		31 177	Washington County, NE	20 234
	12 115	Sarasota County, FL	379 448				
				36580		Oneonta, NY Micro SA	62 259
35860		North Vernon, IN Micro SA	28 525		36 077	Otsego County, NY	62 259
	18 079	Jennings County, IN	28 525				
				36620		Ontario, OR-ID Micro SA	53 936
35900		North Wilkesboro, NC Micro SA	69 340		16 075	Payette County, ID	22 623
	37 193	Wilkes County, NC	69 340		41 045	Malheur County, OR	31 313
35940		Norwalk, OH Micro SA	59 626	36660		Opelousas-Eunice, LA Micro SA	83 384
	39 077	Huron County, OH	59 626		22 097	St. Landry Parish, LA	83 384
35980		Norwich-New London, CT Metro SA	274 055	36700		Orangeburg, SC Micro SA	92 501
	09 011	New London County, CT	274 055		45 075	Orangeburg County, SC	92 501
36020		Oak Harbor, WA Micro SA	78 506	36740		Orlando-Kissimmee-Sanford, FL Metro SA	2134 411
	53 029	Island County, WA	78 506		12 069	Lake County, FL	297 052
					12 095	Orange County, FL	1145 956
36060		Oak Hill, WV Micro SA	46 039		12 097	Osceola County, FL	268 685
	54 019	Fayette County, WV	46 039		12 117	Seminole County, FL	422 718

Core Based Statistical Areas (Metropolitan and Micropolitan), Metropolitan Divisions, and Components (as defined December 2009)–*Continued*

Core Based Statis- tical Area	State/ County FIPS Code	Title and Geographic Components	2010 Census Population	Core Based Statis- tical Area	State/ County FIPS Code	Title and Geographic Components	2010 Census Population
36780		Oshkosh-Neenah, WI Metro SA	166 994	37620		Parkersburg-Marietta-Vienna, WV-OH Metro SA	162 056
	55 139	Winnebago County, WI	166 994		39 167	Washington County, OH	61 778
36820		Oskaloosa, IA Micro SA	22 381		54 073	Pleasants County, WV	7 605
	19 123	Mahaska County, IA	22 381		54 105	Wirt County, WV	5 717
36860		Ottawa-Streator, IL Micro SA	154 908		54 107	Wood County, WV	86 956
	17 011	Bureau County, IL	34 978	37660		Parsons, KS Micro SA	21 607
	17 099	La Salle County, IL	113 924		20 099	Labette County, KS	21 607
	17 155	Putnam County, IL	6 006	37700		Pascagoula, MS Metro SA	162 246
36900		Ottumwa, IA Micro SA	35 625		28 039	George County, MS	22 578
	19 179	Wapello County, IA	35 625		28 059	Jackson County, MS	139 668
36940		Owatonna, MN Micro SA	36 576	37740		Payson, AZ Micro SA	53 597
	27 147	Steele County, MN	36 576		04 007	Gila County, AZ	53 597
36980		Owensboro, KY Metro SA	114 752	37780		Pecos, TX Micro SA	13 783
	21 059	Daviess County, KY	96 656		48 389	Reeves County, TX	13 783
	21 091	Hancock County, KY	8 565	37800		Pella, IA Micro SA	33 309
	21 149	McLean County, KY	9 531		19 125	Marion County, IA	33 309
37020		Owosso, MI Micro SA	70 648	37820		Pendleton-Hermlston, OR Micro SA	87 062
	26 155	Shiawassee County, MI	70 648		41 049	Morrow County, OR	11 173
37060		Oxford, MS Micro SA	47 351		41 059	Umatilla County, OR	75 889
	28 071	Lafayette County, MS	47 351	37860		Pensacola-Ferry Pass-Brent, FL Metro SA	448 991
37100		Oxnard-Thousand Oaks-Ventura, CA Metro SA	823 318		12 033	Escambia County, FL	297 619
	06 111	Ventura County, CA	823 318		12 113	Santa Rosa County, FL	151 372
37140		Paducah, KY-IL Micro SA	98 762	37900		Peoria, IL Metro SA	379 186
	17 127	Massac County, IL	15 429		17 123	Marshall County, IL	12 640
	21 007	Ballard County, KY	8 249		17 143	Peoria County, IL	186 494
	21 139	Livingston County, KY	9 519		17 175	Stark County, IL	5 994
	21 145	McCracken County, KY	65 565		17 179	Tazewell County, IL	135 394
37220		Pahrump, NV Micro SA	43 946		17 203	Woodford County, IL	38 664
	32 023	Nye County, NV	43 946	37940		Peru, IN Micro SA	36 903
37260		Palatka, FL Micro SA	74 364		18 103	Miami County, IN	36 903
	12 107	Putnam County, FL	74 364	37980		Philadelphia-Camden-Wilmington, PA-NJ-DE-MD Metro SA	5965 343
37300		Palestine, TX Micro SA	58 458			Camden, NJ Metro Div 15804	1250 679
	48 001	Anderson County, TX	58 458		34 005	Burlington County, NJ	448 734
37340		Palm Bay-Melbourne-Titusville, FL Metro SA	543 376		34 007	Camden County, NJ	513 657
	12 009	Brevard County, FL	543 376		34 015	Gloucester County, NJ	288 288
37380		Palm Coast, FL Metro SA	95 696			Philadelphia, PA Metro Div 37964	4008 994
	12 035	Flagler County, FL	95 696		42 017	Bucks County, PA	625 249
37420		Pampa, TX Micro SA	23 464		42 029	Chester County, PA	498 886
	48 179	Gray County, TX	22 535		42 045	Delaware County, PA	558 979
	48 393	Roberts County, TX	929		42 091	Montgomery County, PA	799 874
37460		Panama City-Lynn Haven-Panama City Beach, FL Metro SA	168 852		42 101	Philadelphia County, PA	1526 006
	12 005	Bay County, FL	168 852			Wilmington, DE-MD-NJ Metro Div 48864	705 670
37500		Paragould, AR Micro SA	42 090		10 003	New Castle County, DE	538 479
	05 055	Greene County, AR	42 090		24 015	Cecil County, MD	101 108
37540		Paris, TN Micro SA	32 330		34 033	Salem County, NJ	66 083
	47 079	Henry County, TN	32 330	38020		Phoenix Lake-Cedar Ridge, CA Micro SA	55 365
37580		Paris, TX Micro SA	49 793		06 109	Tuolumne County, CA	55 365
	48 277	Lamar County, TX	49 793	38060		Phoenix-Mesa-Glendale, AZ Metro SA	4192 887
					04 013	Maricopa County, AZ	3817 117
					04 021	Pinal County, AZ	375 770
				38100		Picayune, MS Micro SA	55 834
					28 109	Pearl River County, MS	55 834

Core Based Statistical Areas (Metropolitan and Micropolitan), Metropolitan Divisions, and Components (as defined December 2009)–*Continued*

Core Based Statistical Area	State/County FIPS Code	Title and Geographic Components	2010 Census Population	Core Based Statistical Area	State/County FIPS Code	Title and Geographic Components	2010 Census Population
38180		Pierre, SD Micro SA	19 988	38900		Portland-Vancouver-Hillsboro, OR-WA Metro SA	2226 009
	46 065	Hughes County, SD	17 022		41 005	Clackamas County, OR	375 992
	46 117	Stanley County, SD	2 966		41 009	Columbia County, OR	49 351
38200		Pierre Part, LA Micro SA	23 421		41 051	Multnomah County, OR	735 334
	22 007	Assumption Parish, LA	23 421		41 067	Washington County, OR	529 710
38220		Pine Bluff, AR Metro SA	100 258		41 071	Yamhill County, OR	99 193
	05 025	Cleveland County, AR	8 689		53 011	Clark County, WA	425 363
	05 069	Jefferson County, AR	77 435		53 059	Skamania County, WA	11 066
	05 079	Lincoln County, AR	14 134	38940		Port St. Lucie, FL Metro SA	424 107
38260		Pittsburg, KS Micro SA	39 134		12 085	Martin County, FL	146 318
	20 037	Crawford County, KS	39 134		12 111	St. Lucie County, FL	277 789
38300		Pittsburgh, PA Metro SA	2356 285	39020		Portsmouth, OH Micro SA	79 499
	42 003	Allegheny County, PA	1223 348		39 145	Scioto County, OH	79 499
	42 005	Armstrong County, PA	68 941	39060		Pottsville, PA Micro SA	148 289
	42 007	Beaver County, PA	170 539		42 107	Schuylkill County, PA	148 289
	42 019	Butler County, PA	183 862	39100		Poughkeepsie-Newburgh-Middletown, NY Metro SA	670 301
	42 051	Fayette County, PA	136 606		36 027	Dutchess County, NY	297 488
	42 125	Washington County, PA	207 820		36 071	Orange County, NY	372 813
	42 129	Westmoreland County, PA	365 169	39140		Prescott, AZ Metro SA	211 033
38340		Pittsfield, MA Metro SA	131 219		04 025	Yavapai County, AZ	211 033
	25 003	Berkshire County, MA	131 219	39220		Price, UT Micro SA	21 403
38380		Plainview, TX Micro SA	36 273		49 007	Carbon County, UT	21 403
	48 189	Hale County, TX	36 273	39260		Prineville, OR Micro SA	20 978
38420		Platteville, WI Micro SA	51 208		41 013	Crook County, OR	20 978
	55 043	Grant County, WI	51 208	39300		Providence-New Bedford-Fall River, RI-MA Metro SA	1600 852
38460		Plattsburgh, NY Micro SA	82 128		25 005	Bristol County, MA	548 285
	36 019	Clinton County, NY	82 128		44 001	Bristol County, RI	49 875
38500		Plymouth, IN Micro SA	47 051		44 003	Kent County, RI	166 158
	18 099	Marshall County, IN	47 051		44 005	Newport County, RI	82 888
38540		Pocatello, ID Metro SA	90 656		44 007	Providence County, RI	626 667
	16 005	Bannock County, ID	82 839		44 009	Washington County, RI	126 979
	16 077	Power County, ID	7 817	39340		Provo-Orem, UT Metro SA	526 810
38580		Point Pleasant, WV-OH Micro SA	58 258		49 023	Juab County, UT	10 246
	39 053	Gallia County, OH	30 934		49 049	Utah County, UT	516 564
	54 053	Mason County, WV	27 324	39380		Pueblo, CO Metro SA	159 063
38620		Ponca City, OK Micro SA	46 562		08 101	Pueblo County, CO	159 063
	40 071	Kay County, OK	46 562	39420		Pullman, WA Micro SA	44 776
38700		Pontiac, IL Micro SA	38 950		53 075	Whitman County, WA	44 776
	17 105	Livingston County, IL	38 950	39460		Punta Gorda, FL Metro SA	159 978
38740		Poplar Bluff, MO Micro SA	42 794		12 015	Charlotte County, FL	159 978
	29 023	Butler County, MO	42 794	39500		Quincy, IL-MO Micro SA	77 314
38780		Portales, NM Micro SA	19 846		17 001	Adams County, IL	67 103
	35 041	Roosevelt County, NM	19 846		29 111	Lewis County, MO	10 211
38820		Port Angeles, WA Micro SA	71 404	39540		Racine, WI Metro SA	195 408
	53 009	Clallam County, WA	71 404		55 101	Racine County, WI	195 408
38860		Portland-South Portland-Biddeford, ME Metro SA	514 098	39580		Raleigh-Cary, NC Metro SA	1130 490
	23 005	Cumberland County, ME	281 674		37 069	Franklin County, NC	60 619
	23 023	Sagadahoc County, ME	35 293		37 101	Johnston County, NC	168 878
	23 031	York County, ME	197 131		37 183	Wake County, NC	900 993

Core Based Statistical Areas (Metropolitan and Micropolitan), Metropolitan Divisions, and Components (as defined December 2009)–*Continued*

Core Based Statistical Area	State/County FIPS Code	Title and Geographic Components	2010 Census Population	Core Based Statistical Area	State/County FIPS Code	Title and Geographic Components	2010 Census Population
39660		Rapid City, SD Metro SA	126 382	40220		Roanoke, VA Metro SA..................................	308 707
	46 093	Meade County, SD	25 434		51 023	Botetourt County, VA.............................	33 148
	46 103	Pennington County, SD.............................	100 948		51 045	Craig County, VA..............................	5 190
					51 067	Franklin County, VA..............................	56 159
39700		Raymondville, TX Micro SA	22 134		51 161	Roanoke County, VA..............................	92 376
	48 489	Willacy County, TX	22 134		51 770	Roanoke city, VA..............................	97 032
					51 775	Salem city, VA	24 802
39740		Reading, PA Metro SA	411 442				
	42 011	Berks County, PA	411 442	40260		Roanoke Rapids, NC Micro SA	76 790
					37 083	Halifax County, NC..............................	54 691
39780		Red Bluff, CA Micro SA	63 463		37 131	Northampton County, NC..............................	22 099
	06 103	Tehama County, CA	63 463				
				40300		Rochelle, IL Micro SA	53 497
39820		Redding, CA Metro SA	177 223		17 141	Ogle County, IL..............................	53 497
	06 089	Shasta County, CA	177 223				
				40340		Rochester, MN Metro SA..............................	186 011
39860		Red Wing, MN Micro SA..............................	46 183		27 039	Dodge County, MN..............................	20 087
	27 049	Goodhue County, MN.............................	46 183		27 109	Olmsted County, MN..............................	144 248
					27 157	Wabasha County, MN..............................	21 676
39900		Reno-Sparks, NV Metro SA	425 417				
	32 029	Storey County, NV.............................	4 010	40380		Rochester, NY Metro SA..............................	1054 323
	32 031	Washoe County, NV,.............................	421 407		36 051	Livingston County, NY..............................	65 393
					36 055	Monroe County, NY..............................	744 344
39940		Rexburg, ID Micro SA	50 778		36 069	Ontario County, NY..............................	107 931
	16 043	Fremont County, ID	13 242		36 073	Orleans County, NY..............................	42 883
	16 065	Madison County, ID.............................	37 536		36 117	Wayne County, NY..............................	93 772
39980		Richmond, IN Micro SA	68 917	40420		Rockford, IL Metro SA..............................	349 431
	18 177	Wayne County, IN	68 917		17 007	Boone County, IL..............................	54 165
					17 201	Winnebago County, IL..............................	295 266
40060		Richmond, VA Metro SA	1258 251				
	51 007	Amelia County, VA	12 690	40460		Rockingham, NC Micro SA	46 639
	51 033	Caroline County, VA	28 545		37 153	Richmond County, NC..............................	46 639
	51 036	Charles City County, VA.............................	7 256				
	51 041	Chesterfield County, VA..............................	316 236	40500		Rockland, ME Micro SA	39 736
	51 049	Cumberland County, VA.............................	10 052		23 013	Knox County, ME..............................	39 736
	51 053	Dinwiddie County, VA.............................	28 001				
	51 075	Goochland County, VA.............................	21 717	40540		Rock Springs, WY Micro SA	43 806
	51 085	Hanover County, VA.............................	99 863		56 037	Sweetwater County, WY..............................	43 806
	51 087	Henrico County, VA.............................	306 935				
	51 097	King and Queen County, VA.......................	6 945	40580		Rocky Mount, NC Metro SA..............................	152 392
	51 101	King William County, VA	15 935		37 065	Edgecombe County, NC..............................	56 552
	51 109	Louisa County, VA.............................	33 153		37 127	Nash County, NC..............................	95 840
	51 127	New Kent County, VA.............................	18 429				
	51 145	Powhatan County, VA.............................	28 046	40620		Rolla, MO Micro SA	45 156
	51 149	Prince George County, VA.............................	35 725		29 161	Phelps County, MO..............................	45 156
	51 183	Sussex County, VA.............................	12 087				
	51 570	Colonial Heights city, VA.............................	17 411	40660		Rome, GA Metro SA	96 317
	51 670	Hopewell city, VA.............................	22 591		13 115	Floyd County, GA..............................	96 317
	51 730	Petersburg city, VA.............................	32 420				
	51 760	Richmond city, VA.............................	204 214	40700		Roseburg, OR Micro SA	107 667
					41 019	Douglas County, OR..............................	107 667
40080		Richmond-Berea, KY Micro SA.........................	99 972				
	21 151	Madison County, KY.............................	82 916	40740		Roswell, NM Micro SA	65 645
	21 203	Rockcastle County, KY.............................	17 056		35 005	Chaves County, NM	65 645
40100		Rio Grande City-Roma, TX Micro SA..............	60 968	40760		Ruidoso, NM Micro SA..............................	20 497
	48 427	Starr County, TX	60 968		35 027	Lincoln County, NM	20 497
40140		Riverside-San Bernardino-Ontario, CA Metro SA	4224 851	40780		Russellville, AR Micro SA	83 939
					05 115	Pope County, AR..............................	61 754
	06 065	Riverside County, CA	2189 641		05 149	Yell County, AR	22 185
	06 071	San Bernardino County, CA.......................	2035 210				
				40820		Ruston, LA Micro SA	63 009
40180		Riverton, WY Micro SA	40 123		22 049	Jackson Parish, LA..............................	16 274
	56 013	Fremont County, WY.............................	40 123		22 061	Lincoln Parish, LA..............................	46 735
				40860		Rutland, VT Micro SA	61 642
					50 021	Rutland County, VT..............................	61 642

Core Based Statistical Area	State/ County FIPS Code	Title and Geographic Components	2010 Census Population	Core Based Statistical Area	State/ County FIPS Code	Title and Geographic Components	2010 Census Population
40900		Sacramento—Arden-Arcade—Roseville, CA Metro SA	2149 127	41620		Salt Lake City, UT Metro SA	1124 197
	06 017	El Dorado County, CA	181 058		49 035	Salt Lake County, UT	1029 655
	06 061	Placer County, CA	348 432		49 043	Summit County, UT	36 324
	06 067	Sacramento County, CA	1418 788		49 045	Tooele County, UT	58 218
	06 113	Yolo County, CA	200 849	41660		San Angelo, TX Metro SA	111 823
40940		Safford, AZ Micro SA	45 657		48 235	Irion County, TX	1 599
	04 009	Graham County, AZ	37 220		48 451	Tom Green County, TX	110 224
	04 011	Greenlee County, AZ	8 437	41700		San Antonio-New Braunfels, TX Metro SA	2142 508
40980		Saginaw-Saginaw Township North, MI Metro SA	200 169		48 013	Atascosa County, TX	44 911
	26 145	Saginaw County, MI	200 169		48 019	Bandera County, TX	20 485
41060		St. Cloud, MN Metro SA	189 093		48 029	Bexar County, TX	1714 773
	27 009	Benton County, MN	38 451		48 091	Comal County, TX	108 472
	27 145	Stearns County, MN	150 642		48 187	Guadalupe County, TX	131 533
					48 259	Kendall County, TX	33 410
41100		St. George, UT Metro SA	138 115		48 325	Medina County, TX	46 006
	49 053	Washington County, UT	138 115		48 493	Wilson County, TX	42 918
41140		St. Joseph, MO-KS Metro SA	127 329	41740		San Diego-Carlsbad-San Marcos, CA Metro SA	3095 313
	20 043	Doniphan County, KS	7 945		06 073	San Diego County, CA	3095 313
	29 003	Andrew County, MO	17 291	41780		Sandusky, OH Metro SA	77 079
	29 021	Buchanan County, MO	89 201		39 043	Erie County, OH	77 079
	29 063	DeKalb County, MO	12 892	41820		Sanford, NC Micro SA	57 866
41180		St. Louis, MO-IL Metro SA	2812 896		37 105	Lee County, NC	57 866
	17 005	Bond County, IL	17 768	41860		San Francisco-Oakland-Fremont, CA Metro SA	4335 391
	17 013	Calhoun County, IL	5 089			Oakland-Fremont-Hayward, CA Metro Div 36084	2559 296
	17 027	Clinton County, IL	37 762		06 001	Alameda County, CA	1510 271
	17 083	Jersey County, IL	22 985		06 013	Contra Costa County, CA	1049 025
	17 117	Macoupin County, IL	47 765			San Francisco-San Mateo-Redwood City, CA Metro Div 41884	1776 095
	17 119	Madison County, IL	269 282		06 041	Marin County, CA	252 409
	17 133	Monroe County, IL	32 957		06 075	San Francisco County, CA	805 235
	17 163	St. Clair County, IL	270 056		06 081	San Mateo County, CA	718 451
	29 071	Franklin County, MO	101 492	41940		San Jose-Sunnyvale-Santa Clara, CA Metro SA	1836 911
	29 099	Jefferson County, MO	218 733		06 069	San Benito County, CA	55 269
	29 113	Lincoln County, MO	52 566		06 085	Santa Clara County, CA	1781 642
	29 183	St. Charles County, MO	360 485				
	29 189	St. Louis County, MO	998 954				
	29 219	Warren County, MO	32 513				
	29 221	Washington County, MO	25 195				
	29 510	St. Louis city, MO	319 294				
41220		St. Marys, GA Micro SA	50 513	42020		San Luis Obispo-Paso Robles, CA Metro SA	269 637
	13 039	Camden County, GA	50 513		06 079	San Luis Obispo County, CA	269 637
41260		St. Marys, PA Micro SA	31 946	42060		Santa Barbara-Santa Maria-Goleta, CA Metro SA	423 895
	42 047	Elk County, PA	31 946		06 083	Santa Barbara County, CA	423 895
41420		Salem, OR Metro SA	390 738				
	41 047	Marion County, OR	315 335	42100		Santa Cruz-Watsonville, CA Metro SA	262 382
	41 053	Polk County, OR	75 403		06 087	Santa Cruz County, CA	262 382
41460		Salina, KS Micro SA	61 697	42140		Santa Fe, NM Metro SA	144 170
	20 143	Ottawa County, KS	6 091		35 049	Santa Fe County, NM	144 170
	20 169	Saline County, KS	55 606	42220		Santa Rosa-Petaluma, CA Metro SA	483 878
41500		Salinas, CA Metro SA	415 057		06 097	Sonoma County, CA	483 878
	06 053	Monterey County, CA	415 057	42300		Sault Ste. Marie, MI Micro SA	38 520
41540		Salisbury, MD Metro SA	125 203		26 033	Chippewa County, MI	38 520
	24 039	Somerset County, MD	26 470	42340		Savannah, GA Metro SA	347 611
	24 045	Wicomico County, MD	98 733		13 029	Bryan County, GA	30 233
41580		Salisbury, NC Micro SA	138 428		13 051	Chatham County, GA	265 128
	37 159	Rowan County, NC	138 428		13 103	Effingham County, GA	52 250

Core Based Statistical Areas (Metropolitan and Micropolitan), Metropolitan Divisions, and Components (as defined December 2009)–*Continued*

Core Based Statistical Area	State/ County FIPS Code	Title and Geographic Components	2010 Census Population	Core Based Statistical Area	State/ County FIPS Code	Title and Geographic Components	2010 Census Population
42380		Sayre, PA Micro SA	62 622	43180		Shelbyville, TN Micro SA	45 058
	42 015	Bradford County, PA..............................	62 622		47 003	Bedford County, TN.................................	45 058
42420		Scottsbluff, NE Micro SA............................	37 660	43220		Shelton, WA Micro SA	60 699
	31 007	Banner County, NE................................	690		53 045	Mason County, WA................................	60 699
	31 157	Scotts Bluff County, NE.......................	36 970	43260		Sheridan, WY Micro SA	29 116
42460		Scottsboro, AL Micro SA	53 227		56 033	Sheridan County, WY..............................	29 116
	01 071	Jackson County, AL.............................	53 227	43300		Sherman-Denison, TX Metro SA	120 877
42500		Scottsburg, IN Micro SA	24 181		48 181	Grayson County, TX................................	120 877
	18 143	Scott County, IN	24 181	43320		Show Low, AZ Micro SA	107 449
42540		Scranton—Wilkes-Barre, PA Metro SA	563 631		04 017	Navajo County, AZ.................................	107 449
	42 069	Lackawanna County, PA.........................	214 437	43340		Shreveport-Bossier City, LA Metro SA	398 604
	42 079	Luzerne County, PA	320 918		22 015	Bossier Parish, LA................................	116 979
	42 131	Wyoming County, PA	28 276		22 017	Caddo Parish, LA.................................	254 969
42580		Seaford, DE Micro SA	197 145		22 031	De Soto Parish, LA..............................	26 656
	10 005	Sussex County, DE	197 145	43380		Sidney, OH Micro SA	49 423
42620		Searcy, AR Micro SA	77 076		39 149	Shelby County, OH..............................	49 423
	05 145	White County, AR................................	77 076	43420		Sierra Vista-Douglas, AZ Micro SA................	131 346
42660		Seattle-Tacoma-Bellevue, WA Metro SA........	3439 809		04 003	Cochise County, AZ..............................	131 346
		Seattle-Bellevue-Everett, WA Metro Div 42644	2644 584	43460		Sikeston, MO Micro SA..............................	39 191
	53 033	King County, WA.................................	1931 249		29 201	Scott County, MO	39 191
	53 061	Snohomish County, WA.........................	713 335	43500		Silver City, NM Micro SA	29 514
		Tacoma, WA Metro Div 45104	795 225		35 017	Grant County, NM................................	29 514
	53 053	Pierce County, WA..............................	795 225	43540		Silverthorne, CO Micro SA	27 994
42680		Sebastian-Vero Beach, FL Metro SA..............	138 028		08 117	Summit County, CO.............................	27 994
	12 061	Indian River County, FL........................	138 028	43580		Sioux City, IA-NE-SD Metro SA.....................	143 577
42700		Sebring, FL Micro SA................................	98 786		19 193	Woodbury County, IA	102 172
	12 055	Highlands County, FL...........................	98 786		31 043	Dakota County, NE..............................	21 006
42740		Sedalia, MO Micro SA................................	42 201		31 051	Dixon County, NE.................................	6 000
	29 159	Pettis County, MO..............................	42 201		46 127	Union County, SD..............................	14 399
42780		Selinsgrove, PA Micro SA	39 702	43620		Sioux Falls, SD Metro SA	228 261
	42 109	Snyder County, PA................................	39 702		46 083	Lincoln County, SD..............................	44 828
42820		Selma, AL Micro SA	43 820		46 087	McCook County, SD..............................	5 618
	01 047	Dallas County, AL..............................	43 820		46 099	Minnehaha County, SD	169 468
42860		Seneca, SC Micro SA	74 273		46 125	Turner County, SD...............................	8 347
	45 073	Oconee County, SC.............................	74 273	43660		Snyder, TX Micro SA	16 921
42900		Seneca Falls, NY Micro SA	35 251		48 415	Scurry County, TX	16 921
	36 099	Seneca County, NY..............................	35 251	43700		Somerset, KY Micro SA	63 063
42940		Sevierville, TN Micro SA	89 889		21 199	Pulaski County, KY..............................	63 063
	47 155	Sevier County, TN	89 889	43740		Somerset, PA Micro SA	77 742
42980		Seymour, IN Micro SA	42 376		42 111	Somerset County, PA.............................	77 742
	18 071	Jackson County, IN	42 376	43780		South Bend-Mishawaka, IN-MI Metro SA........	319 224
43060		Shawnee, OK Micro SA	69 442		18 141	St. Joseph County, IN...........................	266 931
	40 125	Pottawatomie County, OK.......................	69 442		26 027	Cass County, MI..................................	52 293
43100		Sheboygan, WI Metro SA	115 507	43860		Southern Pines-Pinehurst, NC Micro SA........	88 247
	55 117	Sheboygan County, WI..........................	115 507		37 125	Moore County, NC.............................	88 247
43140		Shelby, NC Micro SA	98 078	43900		Spartanburg, SC Metro SA	284 307
	37 045	Cleveland County, NC...........................	98 078		45 083	Spartanburg County, SC	284 307
				43940		Spearfish, SD Micro SA..............................	24 097
					46 081	Lawrence County, SD.............................	24 097

Core Based Statistical Area	State/County FIPS Code	Title and Geographic Components	2010 Census Population	Core Based Statistical Area	State/County FIPS Code	Title and Geographic Components	2010 Census Population
43980		Spencer, IA Micro SA.................................	16 667	44740		Storm Lake, IA Micro SA	20 260
	19 041	Clay County, IA	16 667		19 021	Buena Vista County, IA	20 260
44020		Spirit Lake, IA Micro SA.............................	16 667	44780		Sturgis, MI Micro SA	61 295
	19 059	Dickinson County, IA	16 667		26 149	St. Joseph County, MI	61 295
44060		Spokane, WA Metro SA.............................	471 221	44860		Sulphur Springs, TX Micro SA......................	35 161
	53 063	Spokane County, WA	471 221		48 223	Hopkins County, TX.............................	35 161
44100		Springfield, IL Metro SA.............................	210 170	44900		Summerville, GA Micro SA	26 015
	17 129	Menard County, IL.............................	12 705		13 055	Chattooga County, GA	26 015
	17 167	Sangamon County, IL.............................	197 465	44940		Sumter, SC Metro SA	107 456
44140		Springfield, MA Metro SA.............................	692 942		45 085	Sumter County, SC.................................	107 456
	25 011	Franklin County, MA.............................	71 372				
	25 013	Hampden County, MA.............................	463 490	44980		Sunbury, PA Micro SA.................................	94 528
	25 015	Hampshire County, MA	158 080		42 097	Northumberland County, PA......................	94 528
44180		Springfield, MO Metro SA.............................	436 712	45000		Susanville, CA Micro SA.................................	34 895
	29 043	Christian County, MO.............................	77 422		06 035	Lassen County, CA.................................	34 895
	29 059	Dallas County, MO.............................	16 777				
	29 077	Greene County, MO.............................	275 174	45020		Sweetwater, TX Micro SA.............................	15 216
	29 167	Polk County, MO.............................	31 137		48 353	Nolan County, TX	15 216
	29 225	Webster County, MO.............................	36 202	45060		Syracuse, NY Metro SA.............................	662 577
44220		Springfield, OH Metro SA.............................	138 333		36 053	Madison County, NY.............................	73 442
	39 023	Clark County, OH.............................	138 333		36 067	Onondaga County, NY.............................	467 026
					36 075	Oswego County, NY.............................	122 109
44260		Starkville, MS Micro SA.............................	47 671				
	28 105	Oktibbeha County, MS.............................	47 671	45140		Tahlequah, OK Micro SA.............................	46 987
					40 021	Cherokee County, OK.............................	46 987
44300		State College, PA Metro SA	153 990				
	42 027	Centre County, PA.............................	153 990	45180		Talladega-Sylacauga, AL Micro SA	82 291
					01 121	Talladega County, AL.............................	82 291
44340		Statesboro, GA Micro SA.............................	70 217				
	13 031	Bulloch County, GA.............................	70 217	45220		Tallahassee, FL Metro SA.............................	367 413
					12 039	Gadsden County, FL.............................	46 389
44380		Statesville-Mooresville, NC Micro SA	159 437		12 065	Jefferson County, FL.............................	14 761
	37 097	Iredell County, NC.............................	159 437		12 073	Leon County, FL.............................	275 487
					12 129	Wakulla County, FL.............................	30 776
44420		Staunton-Waynesboro, VA Micro SA...............	118 502				
	51 015	Augusta County, VA.............................	73 750	45260		Tallulah, LA Micro SA	12 093
	51 790	Staunton city, VA.............................	23 746		22 065	Madison Parish, LA	12 093
	51 820	Waynesboro city, VA.............................	21 006	45300		Tampa-St. Petersburg-Clearwater, FL Metro SA.............................	2 783 243
44500		Stephenville, TX Micro SA	37 890		12 053	Hernando County, FL.............................	172 778
	48 143	Erath County, TX.............................	37 890		12 057	Hillsborough County, FL.............................	1 229 226
					12 101	Pasco County, FL.............................	464 697
44540		Sterling, CO Micro SA.............................	22 709		12 103	Pinellas County, FL.............................	916 542
	08 075	Logan County, CO.............................	22 709				
				45340		Taos, NM Micro SA.............................	32 937
44580		Sterling, IL Micro SA.............................	58 498		35 055	Taos County, NM.............................	32 937
	17 195	Whiteside County, IL.............................	58 498				
				45380		Taylorville, IL Micro SA.............................	34 800
44600		Steubenville-Weirton, OH-WV Metro SA	124 454		17 021	Christian County, IL.............................	34 800
	39 081	Jefferson County, OH.............................	69 709				
	54 009	Brooke County, WV.............................	24 069	45460		Terre Haute, IN Metro SA.............................	172 425
	54 029	Hancock County, WV.............................	30 676		18 021	Clay County, IN.............................	26 890
					18 153	Sullivan County, IN.............................	21 475
44620		Stevens Point, WI Micro SA.............................	70 019		18 165	Vermillion County, IN.............................	16 212
	55 097	Portage County, WI.............................	70 019		18 167	Vigo County, IN.............................	107 848
44660		Stillwater, OK Micro SA.............................	77 350				
	40 119	Payne County, OK.............................	77 350	45500		Texarkana, TX-Texarkana, AR Metro SA........	136 027
					05 091	Miller County, AR.............................	43 462
44700		Stockton, CA Metro SA.............................	685 306		48 037	Bowie County, TX.............................	92 565
	06 077	San Joaquin County, CA.............................	685 306				
				45520		The Dalles, OR Micro SA.............................	25 213
					41 065	Wasco County, OR.............................	25 213

Core Based Statistical Area	State/County FIPS Code	Title and Geographic Components	2010 Census Population	Core Based Statistical Area	State/County FIPS Code	Title and Geographic Components	2010 Census Population
45540		The Villages, FL Micro SA	93 420	46180		Tupelo, MS Micro SA....................................	136 268
	12 119	Sumter County, FL	93 420		28 057	Itawamba County, MS	23 401
45580		Thomaston, GA Micro SA	27 153		28 081	Lee County, MS....................................	82 910
	13 293	Upson County, GA..................................	27 153		28 115	Pontotoc County, MS............................	29 957
45620		Thomasville, GA Micro SA	44 720	46220		Tuscaloosa, AL Metro SA	219 461
	13 275	Thomas County, GA	44 720		01 063	Greene County, AL...............................	9 045
45640		Thomasville-Lexington, NC Micro SA	162 878		01 065	Hale County, AL...................................	15 760
	37 057	Davidson County, NC.............................	162 878		01 125	Tuscaloosa County, AL	194 656
45660		Tiffin, OH Micro SA	56 745	46260		Tuskegee, AL Micro SA	21 452
	39 147	Seneca County, OH	56 745		01 087	Macon County, AL................................	21 452
45700		Tifton, GA Micro SA	40 118	46300		Twin Falls, ID Micro SA	99 604
	13 277	Tift County, GA....................................	40 118		16 053	Jerome County, ID................................	22 374
45740		Toccoa, GA Micro SA	26 175		16 083	Twin Falls County, ID	77 230
	13 257	Stephens County, GA............................	26 175	46340		Tyler, TX Metro SA	209 714
45780		Toledo, OH Metro SA...................................	651 429		48 423	Smith County, TX	209 714
	39 051	Fulton County, OH	42 698	46380		Ukiah, CA Micro SA	87 841
	39 095	Lucas County, OH	441 815		06 045	Mendocino County, CA	87 841
	39 123	Ottawa County, OH	41 428	46420		Union, SC Micro SA	28 961
	39 173	Wood County, OH	125 488		45 087	Union County, SC	28 961
45820		Topeka, KS Metro SA	233 870	46460		Union City, TN-KY Micro SA	38 620
	20 085	Jackson County, KS	13 462		21 075	Fulton County, KY	6 813
	20 087	Jefferson County, KS.............................	19 126		47 131	Obion County, TN.................................	31 807
	20 139	Osage County, KS	16 295	46500		Urbana, OH Micro SA	40 097
	20 177	Shawnee County, KS	177 934		39 021	Champaign County, OH	40 097
	20 197	Wabaunsee County, KS	7 053	46540		Utica-Rome, NY Metro SA	299 397
45860		Torrington, CT Micro SA	189 927		36 043	Herkimer County, NY............................	64 519
	09 005	Litchfield County, CT	189 927		36 065	Oneida County, NY...............................	234 878
45900		Traverse City, MI Micro SA...........................	143 372	46620		Uvalde, TX Micro SA....................................	26 405
	26 019	Benzie County, MI	17 525		48 463	Uvalde County, TX	26 405
	26 055	Grand Traverse County, MI......................	86 986	46660		Valdosta, GA Metro SA	139 588
	26 079	Kalkaska County, MI..............................	17 153		13 027	Brooks County, GA...............................	16 243
	26 089	Leelanau County, MI..............................	21 708		13 101	Echols County, GA...............................	4 034
45940		Trenton-Ewing, NJ Metro SA	366 513		13 173	Lanier County, GA................................	10 078
	34 021	Mercer County, NJ................................	366 513		13 185	Lowndes County, GA.............................	109 233
45980		Troy, AL Micro SA	32 899	46700		Vallejo-Fairfield, CA Metro SA	413 344
	01 109	Pike County, AL....................................	32 899		06 095	Solano County, CA	413 344
46020		Truckee-Grass Valley, CA Micro SA...............	98 764	46740		Valley, AL Micro SA	34 215
	06 057	Nevada County, CA	98 764		01 017	Chambers County, AL	34 215
46060		Tucson, AZ Metro SA...................................	980 263	46780		Van Wert, OH Micro SA	28 744
	04 019	Pima County, AZ	980 263		39 161	Van Wert County, OH	28 744
46100		Tullahoma, TN Micro SA	100 210	46820		Vermillion, SD Micro SA...............................	13 864
	47 031	Coffee County, TN.................................	52 796		46 027	Clay County, SD	13 864
	47 051	Franklin County, TN...............................	41 052	46860		Vernal, UT Micro SA	32 588
	47 127	Moore County, TN	6 362		49 047	Uintah County, UT	32 588
46140		Tulsa, OK Metro SA	937 478	46900		Vernon, TX Micro SA	13 535
	40 037	Creek County, OK	69 967		48 487	Wilbarger County, TX	13 535
	40 111	Okmulgee County, OK.............................	40 069	46980		Vicksburg, MS Micro SA	48 773
	40 113	Osage County, OK	47 472		28 149	Warren County, MS...............................	48 773
	40 117	Pawnee County, OK	16 577				
	40 131	Rogers County, OK	86 905				
	40 143	Tulsa County, OK	603 403				
	40 145	Wagoner County, OK	73 085				

Core Based Statistical Areas (Metropolitan and Micropolitan), Metropolitan Divisions, and Components (as defined December 2009)–*Continued*

Core Based Statistical Area	State/ County FIPS Code	Title and Geographic Components	2010 Census Population	Core Based Statistical Area	State/ County FIPS Code	Title and Geographic Components	2010 Census Population
47020		Victoria, TX Metro SA	115 384	47780		Washington, IN Micro SA	31 648
	48 057	Calhoun County, TX	21 381		18 027	Daviess County, IN	31 648
	48 175	Goliad County, TX	7 210				
	48 469	Victoria County, TX	86 793	47820		Washington, NC Micro SA	47 759
					37 013	Beaufort County, NC	47 759
47080		Vidalia, GA Micro SA	36 346				
	13 209	Montgomery County, GA	9 123	47900		Washington-Arlington-Alexandria, DC-VA-MD-WV Metro SA	5582 170
	13 279	Toombs County, GA	27 223			Bethesda-Rockville-Frederick, MD Metro Div 13644	1205 162
47180		Vincennes, IN Micro SA	38 440		24 021	Frederick County, MD	233 385
	18 083	Knox County, IN	38 440		24 031	Montgomery County, MD	971 777
47220		Vineland-Millville-Bridgeton, NJ Metro SA	156 898			Washington-Arlington-Alexandria, DC-VA-MD-WV Metro Div 47894	4377 008
	34 011	Cumberland County, NJ	156 898		11 001	District of Columbia, DC	601 723
47260		Virginia Beach-Norfolk-Newport News, VA-NC Metro SA	1671 683		24 009	Calvert County, MD	88 737
	37 053	Currituck County, NC	23 547		24 017	Charles County, MD	146 551
	51 073	Gloucester County, VA	36 858		24 033	Prince George's County, MD	863 420
	51 093	Isle of Wight County, VA	35 270		51 013	Arlington County, VA	207 627
	51 095	James City County, VA	67 009		51 043	Clarke County, VA	14 034
	51 115	Mathews County, VA	8 978		51 059	Fairfax County, VA	1081 726
	51 181	Surry County, VA	7 058		51 061	Fauquier County, VA	65 203
	51 199	York County, VA	65 464		51 107	Loudoun County, VA	312 311
	51 550	Chesapeake city, VA	222 209		51 153	Prince William County, VA	402 002
	51 650	Hampton city, VA	137 436		51 177	Spotsylvania County, VA	122 397
	51 700	Newport News city, VA	180 719		51 179	Stafford County, VA	128 961
	51 710	Norfolk city, VA	242 803		51 187	Warren County, VA	37 575
	51 735	Poquoson city , VA	12 150		51 510	Alexandria city, VA	139 966
	51 740	Portsmouth city, VA	95 535		51 600	Fairfax city, VA	22 565
	51 800	Suffolk city, VA	84 585		51 610	Falls Church city, VA	12 332
	51 810	Virginia Beach city, VA	437 994		51 630	Fredericksburg city, VA	24 286
	51 830	Williamsburg city, VA	14 068		51 683	Manassas city, VA	37 821
47300		Visalia-Porterville, CA Metro SA	442 179		51 685	Manassas Park city, VA	14 273
	06 107	Tulare County, CA	442 179		54 037	Jefferson County, WV	53 498
47340		Wabash, IN Micro SA	32 888	47920		Washington Court House, OH Micro SA	29 030
	18 169	Wabash County, IN	32 888		39 047	Fayette County, OH	29 030
47380		Waco, TX Metro SA	234 906	47940		Waterloo-Cedar Falls, IA Metro SA	167 819
	48 309	McLennan County, TX	234 906		19 013	Black Hawk County, IA	131 090
					19 017	Bremer County, IA	24 276
47420		Wahpeton, ND-MN Micro SA	22 897		19 075	Grundy County, IA	12 453
	27 167	Wilkin County, MN	6 576	47980		Watertown, SD Micro SA	33 130
	38 077	Richland County, ND	16 321		46 029	Codington County, SD	27 227
					46 057	Hamlin County, SD	5 903
47460		Walla Walla, WA Micro SA	58 781	48020		Watertown-Fort Atkinson, WI Micro SA	83 686
	53 071	Walla Walla County, WA	58 781		55 055	Jefferson County, WI	83 686
47500		Walterboro, SC Micro SA	38 892	48060		Watertown-Fort Drum, NY Micro SA	116 229
	45 029	Colleton County, SC	38 892		36 045	Jefferson County, NY	116 229
47540		Wapakoneta, OH Micro SA	45 949	48100		Wauchula, FL Micro SA	27 731
	39 011	Auglaize County, OH	45 949		12 049	Hardee County, FL	27 731
47580		Warner Robins, GA Metro SA	139 900	48140		Wausau, WI Metro SA	134 063
	13 153	Houston County, GA	139 900		55 073	Marathon County, WI	134 063
47620		Warren, PA Micro SA	41 815	48180		Waycross, GA Micro SA	55 070
	42 123	Warren County, PA	41 815		13 229	Pierce County, GA	18 758
					13 299	Ware County, GA	36 312
47660		Warrensburg, MO Micro SA	52 595				
	29 101	Johnson County, MO	52 595	48220		Weatherford, OK Micro SA	27 469
					40 039	Custer County, OK	27 469
47700		Warsaw, IN Micro SA	77 358				
	18 085	Kosciusko County, IN	77 358	48300		Wenatchee-East Wenatchee, WA Metro SA	110 884
					53 007	Chelan County, WA	72 453
					53 017	Douglas County, WA	38 431

Appendix C

C-27

Core Based Statistical Area	State/ County FIPS Code	Title and Geographic Components	2010 Census Population	Core Based Statistical Area	State/ County FIPS Code	Title and Geographic Components	2010 Census Population
48460		West Plains, MO Micro SA	40 400	49300		Wooster, OH Micro SA................................	114 520
	29 091	Howell County, MO................................	40 400		39 169	Wayne County, OH................................	114 520
48500		West Point, MS Micro SA	20 634	49340		Worcester, MA Metro SA	798 552
	28 025	Clay County, MS................................	20 634		25 027	Worcester County, MA	798 552
48540		Wheeling, WV-OH Metro SA............................	147 950	49380		Worthington, MN Micro SA	21 378
	39 013	Belmont County, OH................................	70 400		27 105	Nobles County, MN	21 378
	54 051	Marshall County, WV................................	33 107	49420		Yakima, WA Metro SA	243 231
	54 069	Ohio County, WV................................	44 443		53 077	Yakima County, WA	243 231
48580		Whitewater, WI Micro SA	102 228				
	55 127	Walworth County, WI................................	102 228				
48620		Wichita, KS Metro SA	623 061				
	20 015	Butler County, KS................................	65 880				
	20 079	Harvey County, KS................................	34 684				
	20 173	Sedgwick County, KS................................	498 365				
	20 191	Sumner County, KS................................	24 132				
48660		Wichita Falls, TX Metro SA........................	151 306				
	48 009	Archer County, TX................................	9 054				
	48 077	Clay County, TX	10 752				
	48 485	Wichita County, TX................................	131 500				
48700		Williamsport, PA Metro SA........................	116 111				
	42 081	Lycoming County, PA................................	116 111				
48740		Willimantic, CT Micro SA	118 428				
	09 015	Windham County, CT	118 428				
48780		Williston, ND Micro SA................................	22 398				
	38 105	Williams County, ND................................	22 398				
48820		Willmar, MN Micro SA................................	42 239				
	27 067	Kandiyohi County, MN................................	42 239				
48900		Wilmington, NC Metro SA	362 315				
	37 019	Brunswick County, NC................................	107 431				
	37 129	New Hanover County, NC................................	202 667				
	37 141	Pender County, NC	52 217				
48940		Wilmington, OH Micro SA	42 040				
	39 027	Clinton County, OH................................	42 040				
48980		Wilson, NC Micro SA	81 234				
	37 195	Wilson County, NC................................	81 234				
49020		Winchester, VA-WVMetro SA	128 472				
	51 069	Frederick County, VA	78 305				
	51 840	Winchester city , VA................................	26 203				
	54 027	Hampshire County, WV................................	23 964				
49060		Winfield, KS Micro SA................................	36 311				
	20 035	Cowley County, KS................................	36 311				
49100		Winona, MN Micro SA................................	51 461				
	27 169	Winona County, MN	51 461				
49180		Winston-Salem, NC Metro SA	477 717				
	37 059	Davie County, NC................................	41 240				
	37 067	Forsyth County, NC................................	350 670				
	37 169	Stokes County, NC................................	47 401				
	37 197	Yadkin County, NC................................	38 406				
49260		Woodward, OK Micro SA	20 081				
	40 153	Woodward County, OK................................	20 081				

Core Based Statistical Area	State/ County FIPS Code	Title and Geographic Components	2010 Census Population	Core Based Statistical Area	State/ County FIPS Code	Title and Geographic Components	2010 Census Population
49460		Yankton, SD Micro SA	22 438				
	46 135	Yankton County, SD	22 438				
49540		Yazoo City, MS Micro SA	28 065				
	28 163	Yazoo County, MS..	28 065				
49620		York-Hanover, PA Metro SA	434 972				
	42 133	York County, PA	434 972				
49660		Youngstown-Warren-Boardman, OH-PA Metro SA	565 773				
	39 099	Mahoning County, OH	238 823				
	39 155	Trumbull County, OH	210 312				
	42 085	Mercer County, PA	116 638				
49700		Yuba City, CA Metro SA	166 892				
	06 101	Sutter County, CA..	94 737				
	06 115	Yuba County, CA..	72 155				
49740		Yuma, AZ Metro SA.......................................	195 751				
	04 027	Yuma County, AZ	195 751				
49780		Zanesville, OH Micro SA...............................	86 074				
	39 119	Muskingum County, OH	86 074				

APPENDIX D
MAPS OF CONGRESSIONAL DISTRICTS AND STATES

U.S. DEPARTMENT OF COMMERCE Economics and Statistics Administration U.S. Census Bureau
Prepared by the Geography Division

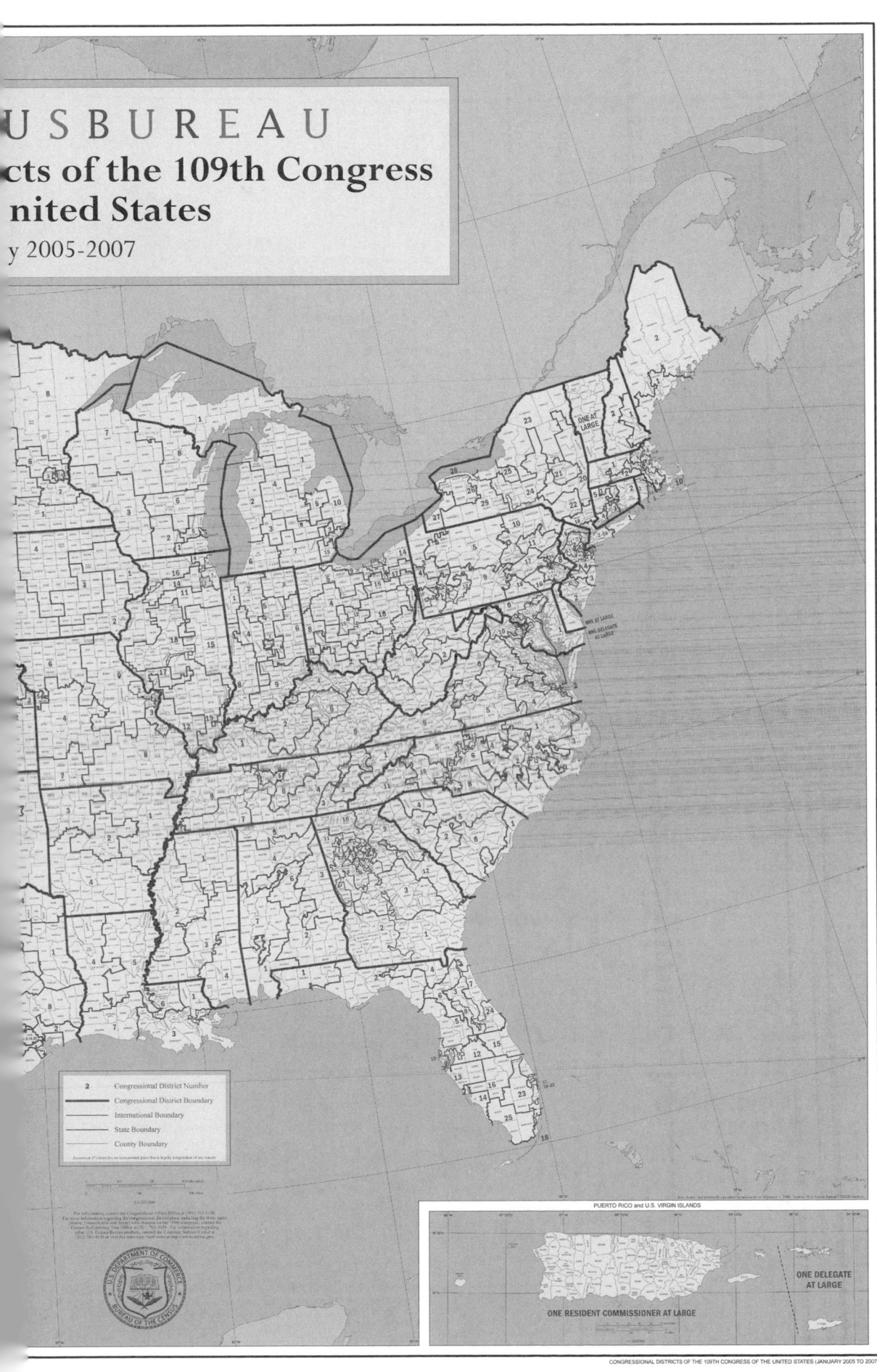

2	Congressional District Number
	Congressional District Boundary
	International Boundary
	State Boundary
	County Boundary

PUERTO RICO and U.S. VIRGIN ISLANDS

ONE RESIDENT COMMISSIONER AT LARGE

ONE DELEGATE
AT LARGE

CONGRESSIONAL DISTRICTS OF THE 109TH CONGRESS OF THE UNITED STATES (JANUARY 2005 TO 2007)

ALABAMA - Core Based Statistical Areas and Counties

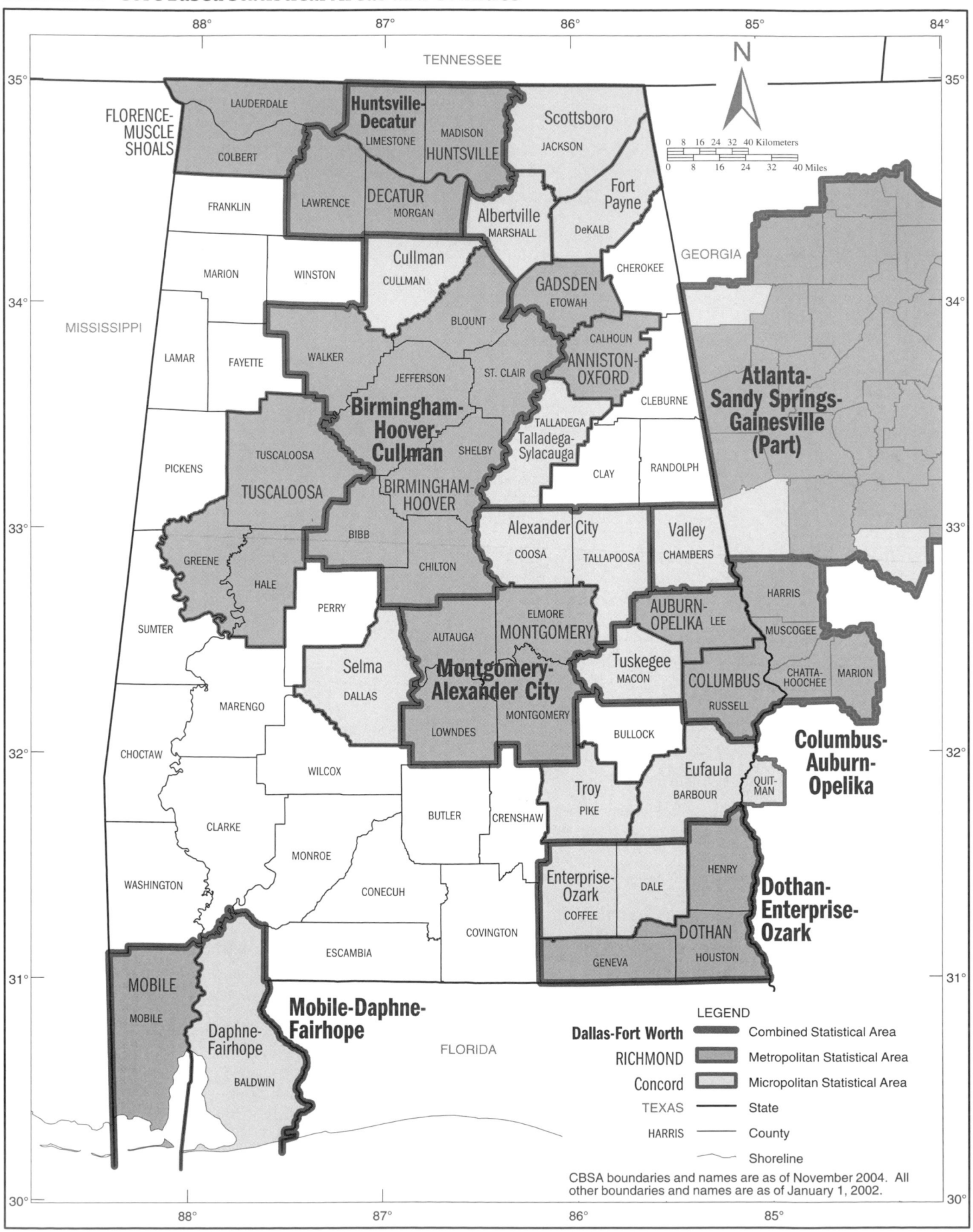

LEGEND

Dallas-Fort Worth — Combined Statistical Area

RICHMOND — Metropolitan Statistical Area

Concord — Micropolitan Statistical Area

TEXAS — State

HARRIS — County

Shoreline

CBSA boundaries and names are as of November 2004. All other boundaries and names are as of January 1, 2002.

ALASKA - Core Based Statistical Areas, Boroughs, and Census Areas

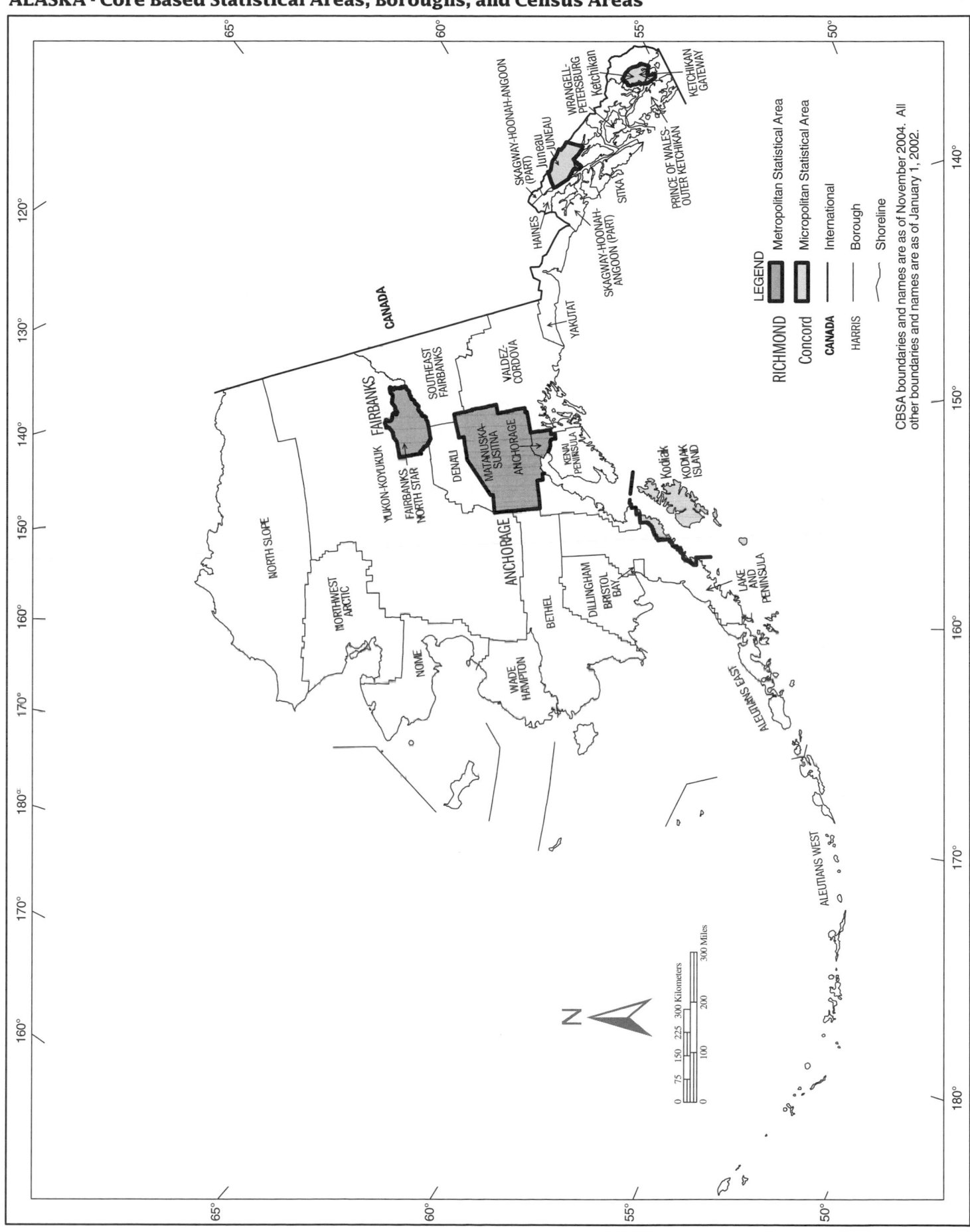

LEGEND

RICHMOND — Metropolitan Statistical Area

Concord — Micropolitan Statistical Area

CANADA — International

HARRIS — Borough

Shoreline

CBSA boundaries and names are as of November 2004. All other boundaries and names are as of January 1, 2002.

CANADA

SKAGWAY-HOONAH-ANGOON
WRANGELL-PETERSBURG
Ketchikan
KETCHIKAN GATEWAY
Juneau
JUNEAU
SKAGWAY-HOONAH-ANGOON (PART)
PRINCE OF WALES-OUTER KETCHIKAN
SITKA
HAINES
SKAGWAY-HOONAH-ANGOON (PART)
YAKUTAT
SOUTHEAST FAIRBANKS
VALDEZ-CORDOVA
FAIRBANKS
YUKON-KOYUKUK
FAIRBANKS NORTH STAR
DENALI
MATANUSKA-SUSITNA
ANCHORAGE
KENAI PENINSULA
Kodiak
KODIAK ISLAND
NORTH SLOPE
NORTHWEST ARCTIC
ANCHORAGE
DILLINGHAM
BRISTOL BAY
LAKE AND PENINSULA
NOME
BETHEL
WADE HAMPTON
ALEUTIANS EAST
ALEUTIANS WEST

N

0 75 150 225 300 Kilometers
0 100 200 300 Miles

U.S. DEPARTMENT OF COMMERCE Economics and Statistics Administration U.S. Census Bureau

Appendix D

D-5

ARIZONA - Core Based Statistical Areas and Counties

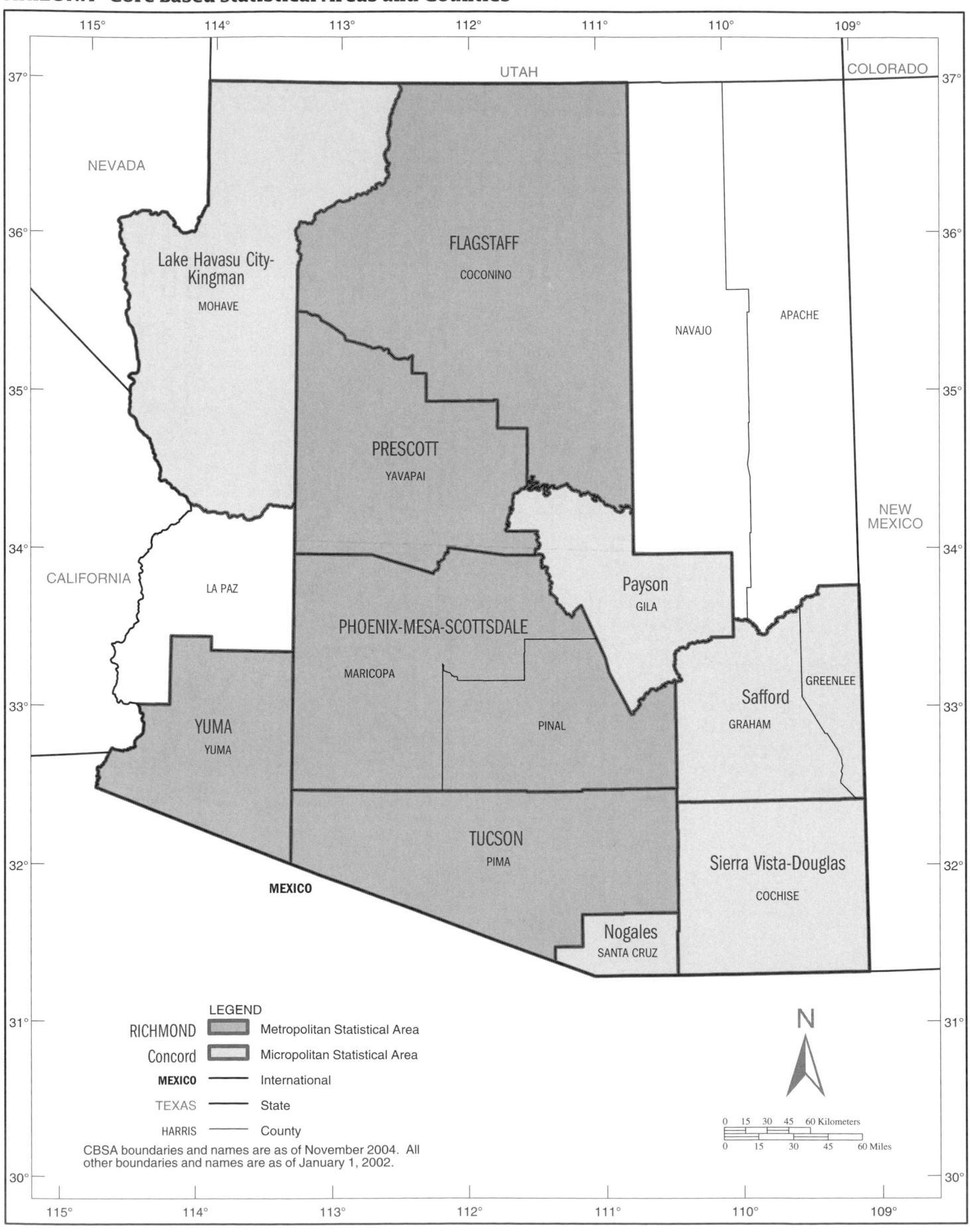

LEGEND

RICHMOND — Metropolitan Statistical Area

Concord — Micropolitan Statistical Area

MEXICO — International

TEXAS — State

HARRIS — County

CBSA boundaries and names are as of November 2004. All other boundaries and names are as of January 1, 2002.

ARKANSAS - Core Based Statistical Areas and Counties

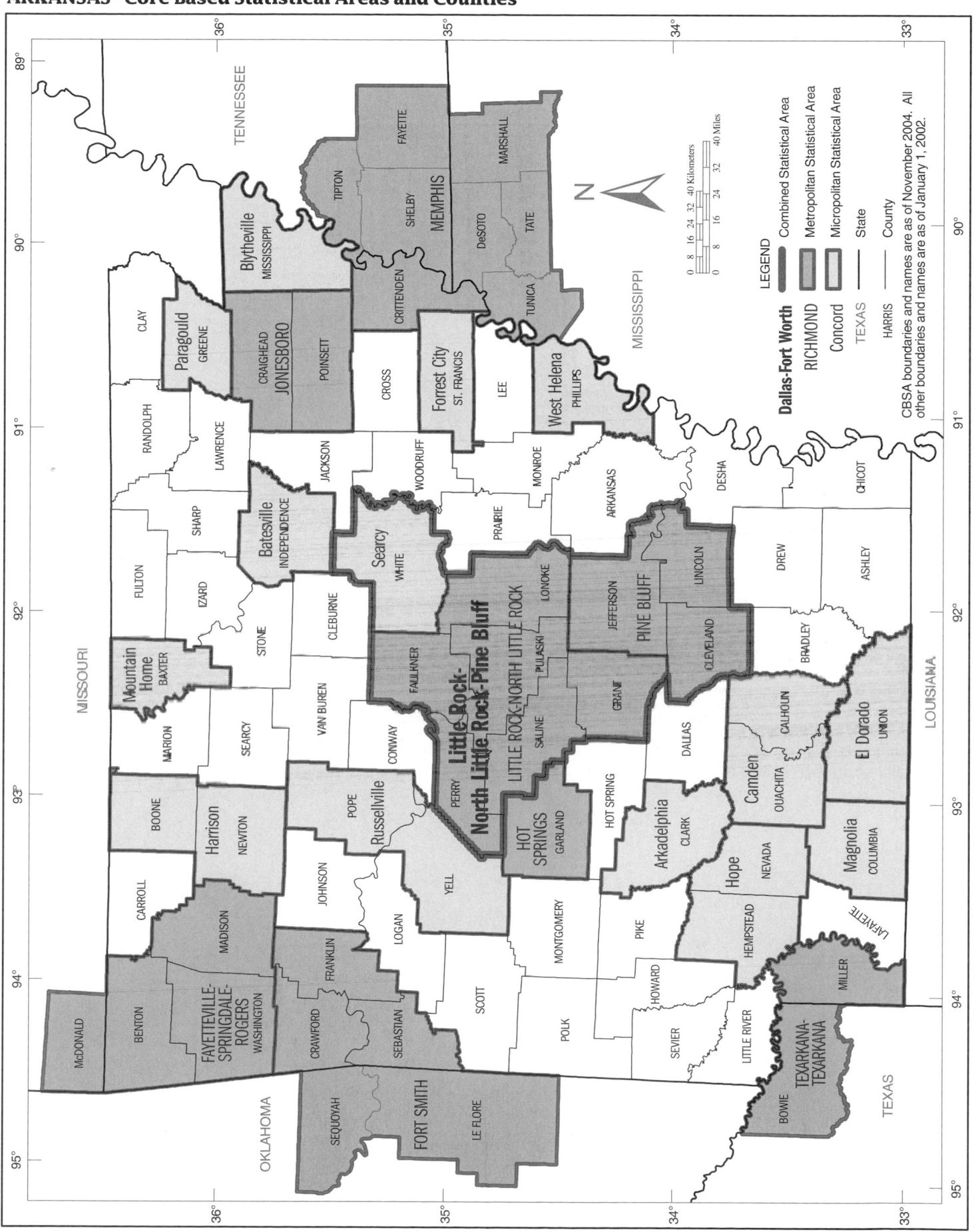

CALIFORNIA - Core Based Statistical Areas and Counties

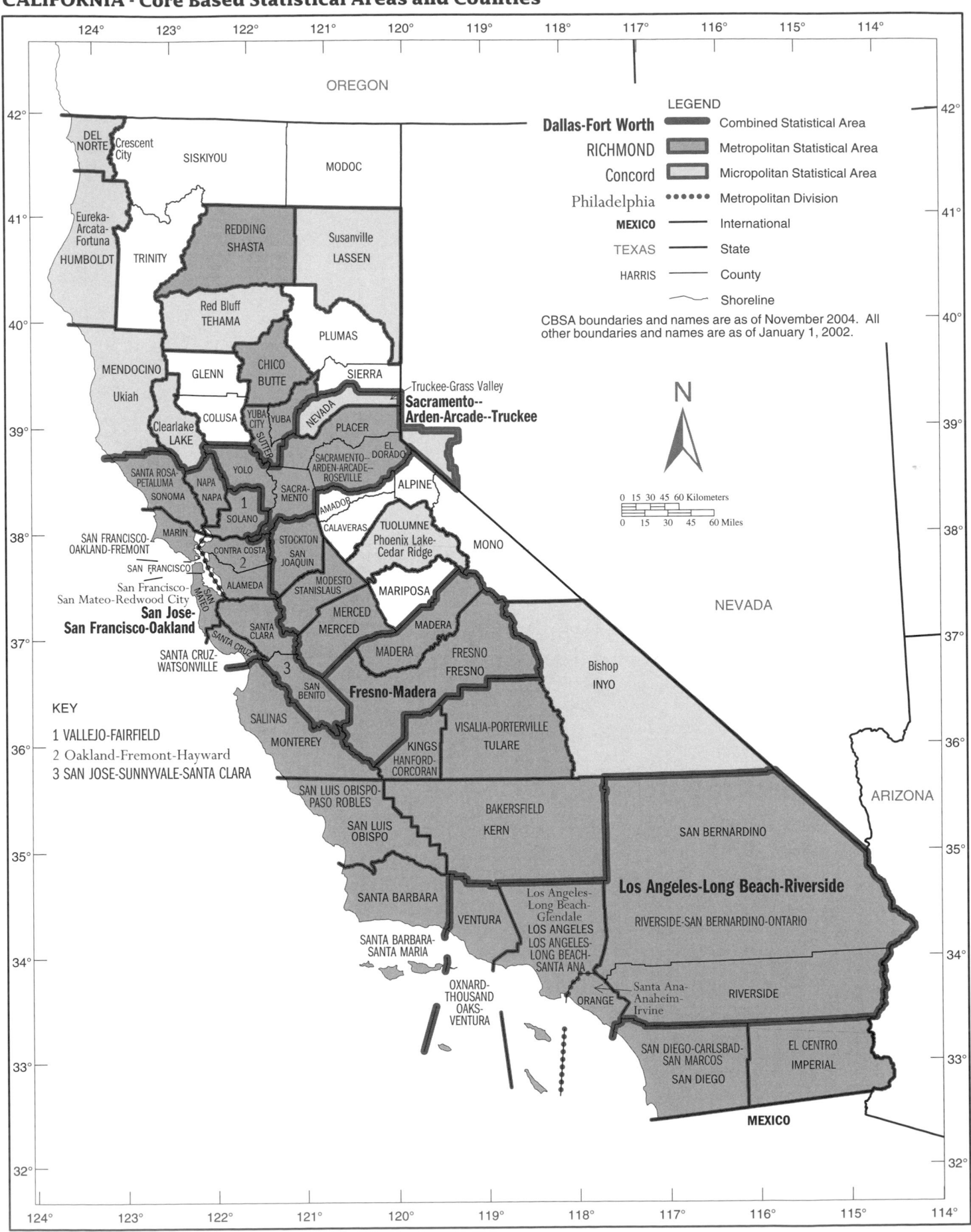

LEGEND

Dallas-Fort Worth	Combined Statistical Area
RICHMOND	Metropolitan Statistical Area
Concord	Micropolitan Statistical Area
Philadelphia	Metropolitan Division
MEXICO	International
TEXAS	State
HARRIS	County
	Shoreline

CBSA boundaries and names are as of November 2004. All other boundaries and names are as of January 1, 2002.

0 15 30 45 60 Kilometers
0 15 30 45 60 Miles

KEY

1 VALLEJO-FAIRFIELD
2 Oakland-Fremont-Hayward
3 SAN JOSE-SUNNYVALE-SANTA CLARA

COLORADO - Core Based Statistical Areas and Counties

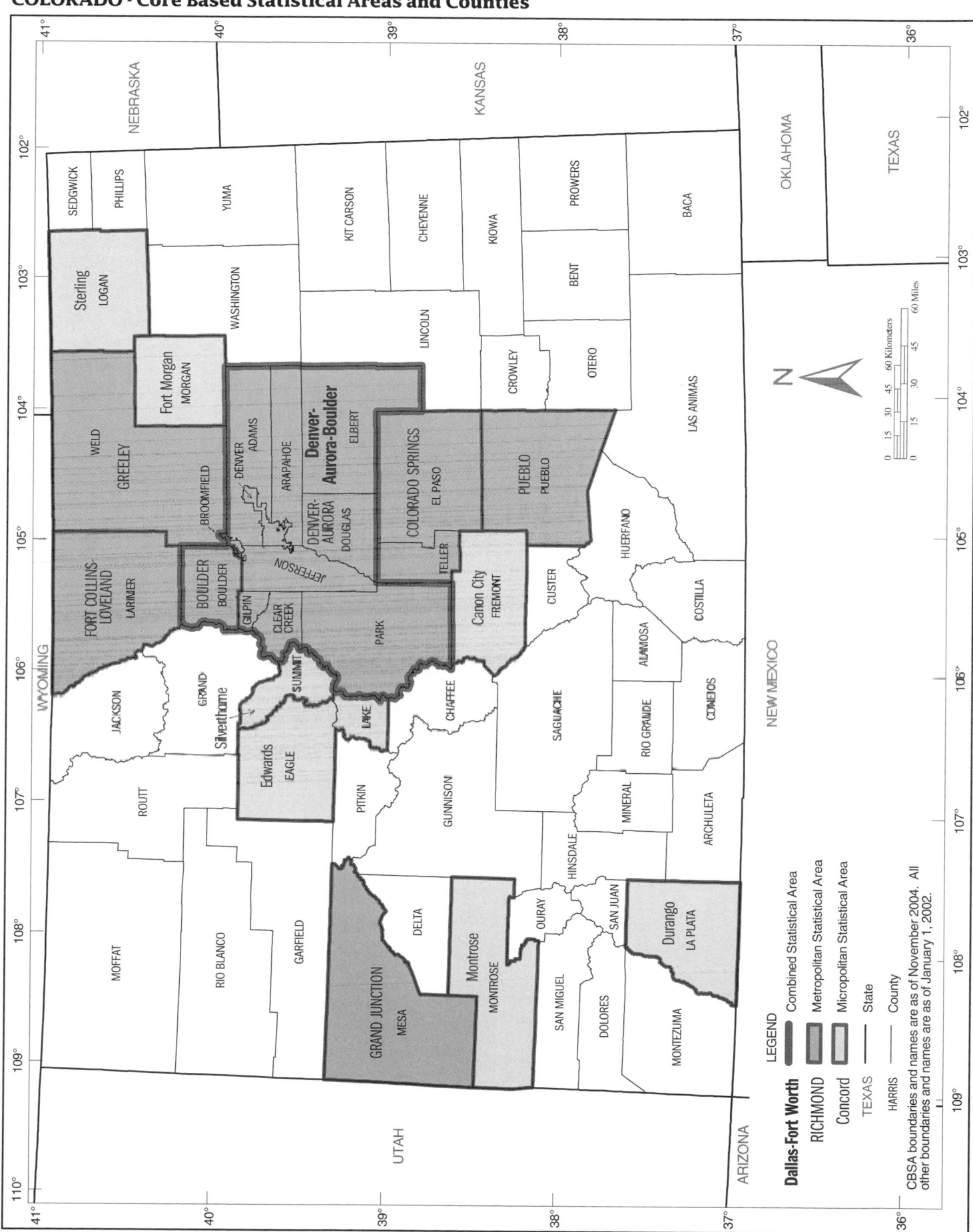

U.S. DEPARTMENT OF COMMERCE Economics and Statistics Administration U.S. Census Bureau

CONNECTICUT - Core Based Statistical Areas and Counties

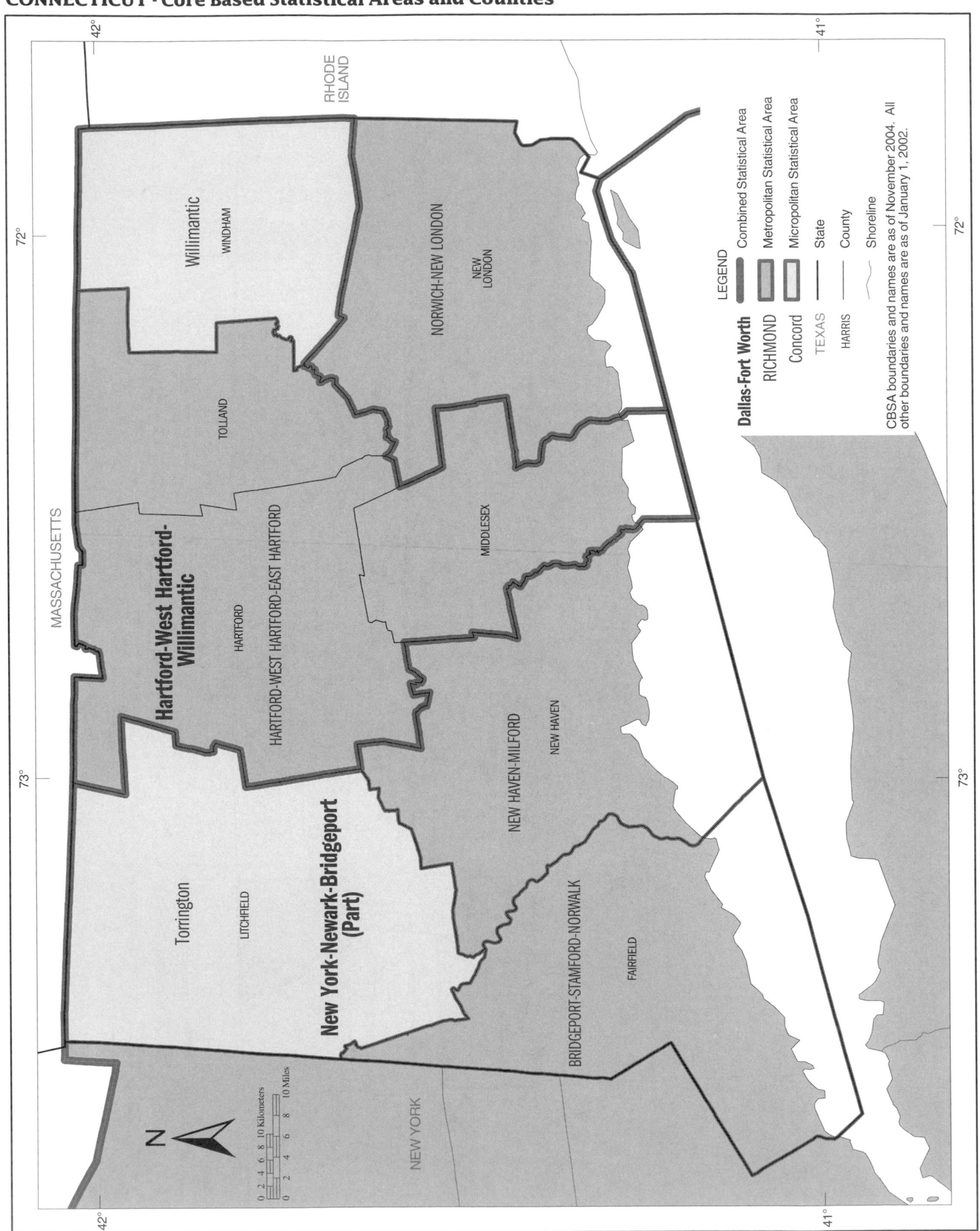

DELAWARE - Core Based Statistical Areas and Counties

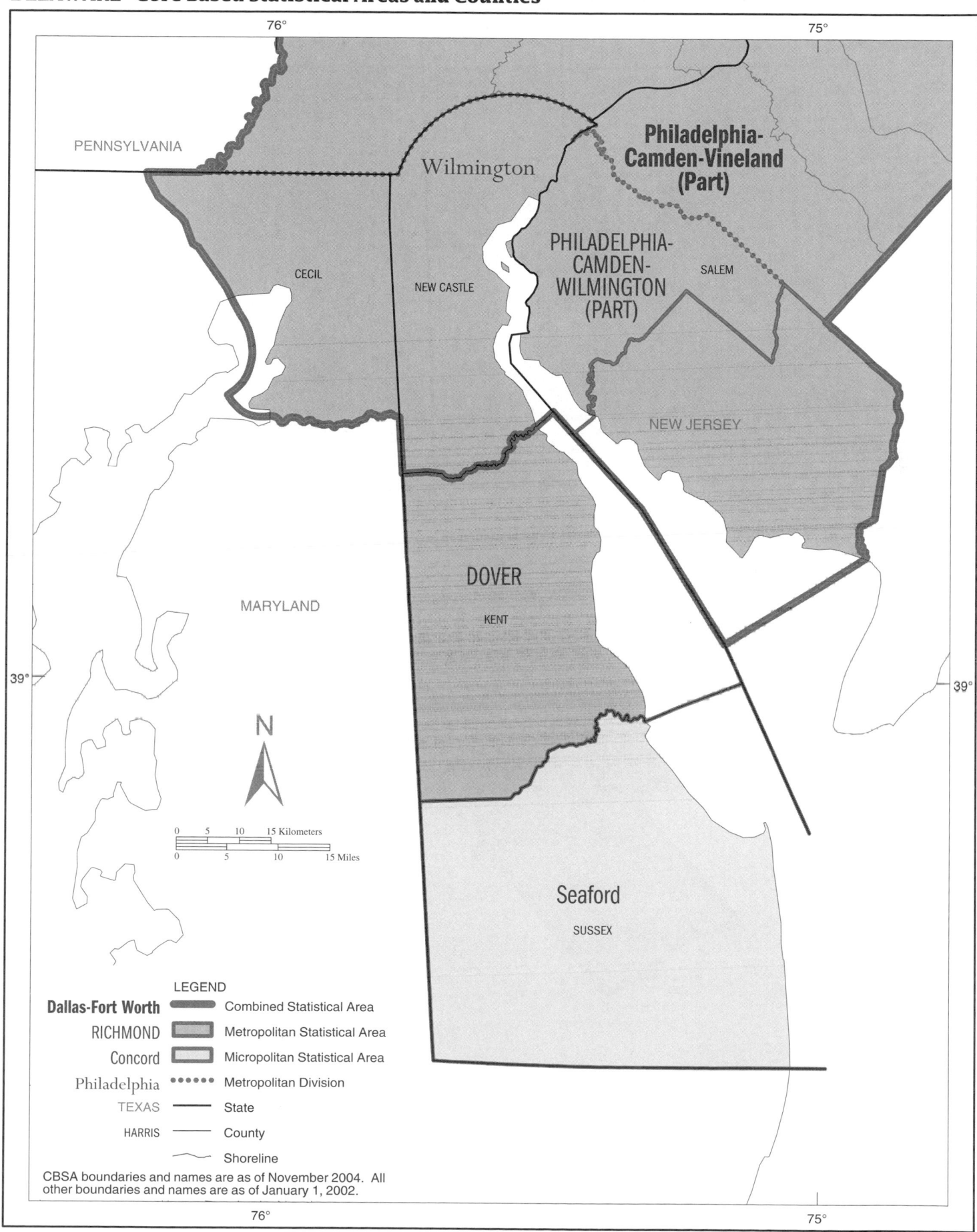

76°   75°

PENNSYLVANIA

Wilmington

**Philadelphia-
Camden-Vineland
(Part)**

CECIL

NEW CASTLE

**PHILADELPHIA-
CAMDEN-
WILMINGTON
(PART)**

SALEM

NEW JERSEY

MARYLAND

N

DOVER

KENT

39°   39°

0   5   10   15 Kilometers
0   5   10   15 Miles

Seaford

SUSSEX

LEGEND

Dallas-Fort Worth	Combined Statistical Area
RICHMOND	Metropolitan Statistical Area
Concord	Micropolitan Statistical Area
Philadelphia	•••••• Metropolitan Division
TEXAS	State
HARRIS	County
	Shoreline

CBSA boundaries and names are as of November 2004. All
other boundaries and names are as of January 1, 2002.

76°   75°

U.S. DEPARTMENT OF COMMERCE Economics and Statistics Administration U.S. Census Bureau

DISTRICT OF COLUMBIA - Core Based Statistical Areas, Counties, and Independent Cities

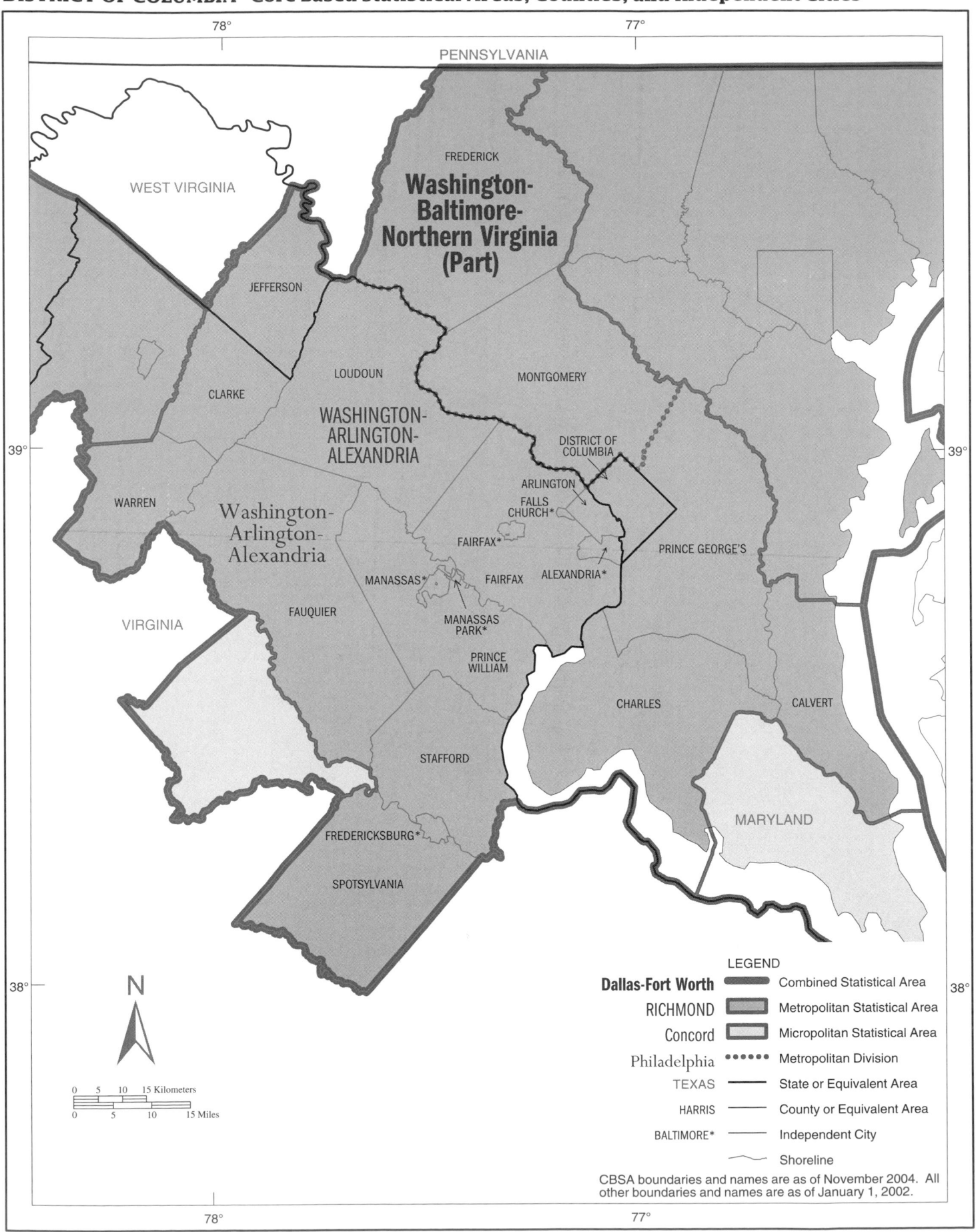

LEGEND

Dallas-Fort Worth ▬▬▬ Combined Statistical Area

RICHMOND ▬ Metropolitan Statistical Area

Concord ▭ Micropolitan Statistical Area

Philadelphia •••••• Metropolitan Division

TEXAS ▬▬ State or Equivalent Area

HARRIS ── County or Equivalent Area

BALTIMORE* ── Independent City

〰 Shoreline

CBSA boundaries and names are as of November 2004. All other boundaries and names are as of January 1, 2002.

FLORIDA - Core Based Statistical Areas and Counties

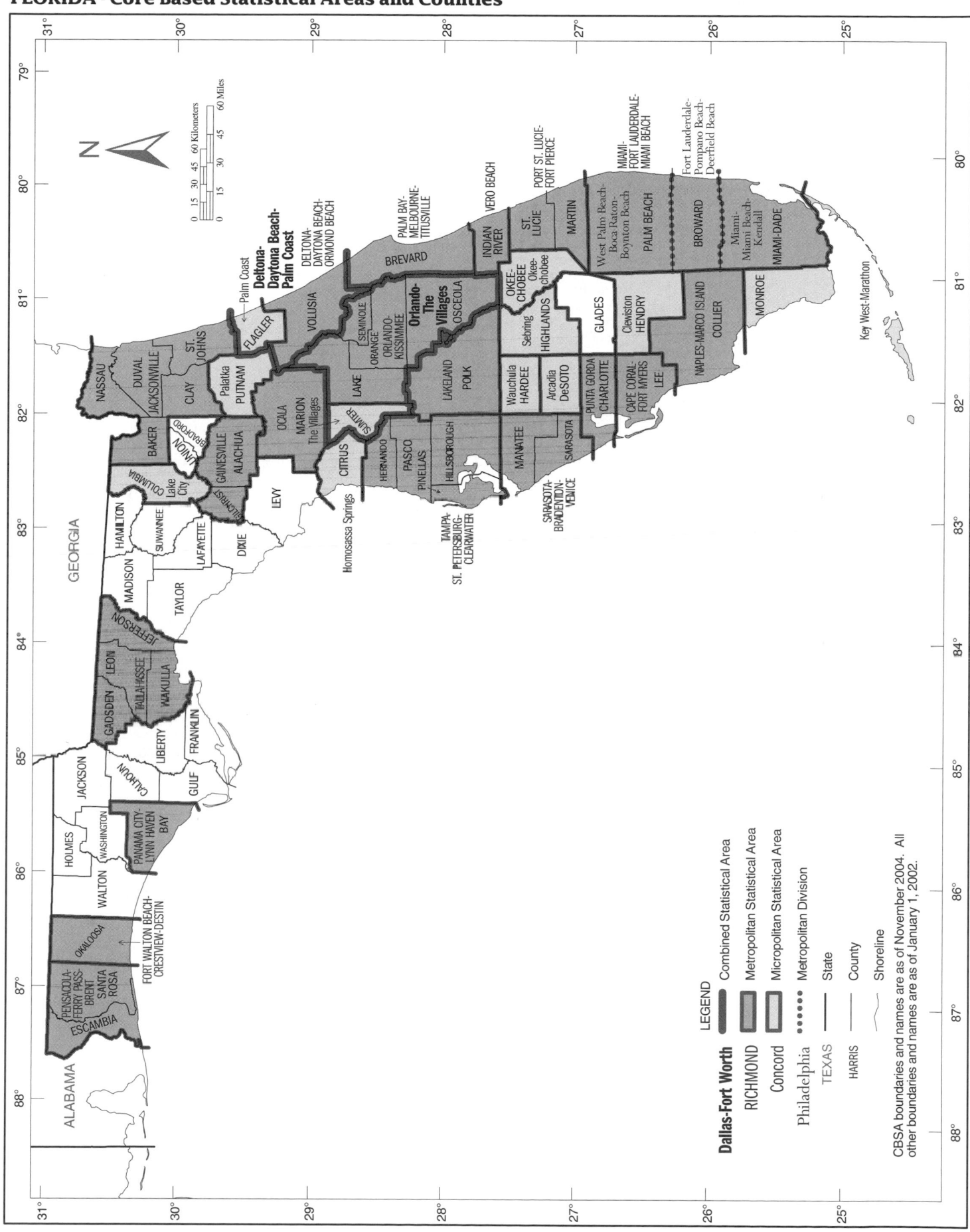

GEORGIA - Core Based Statistical Areas and Counties

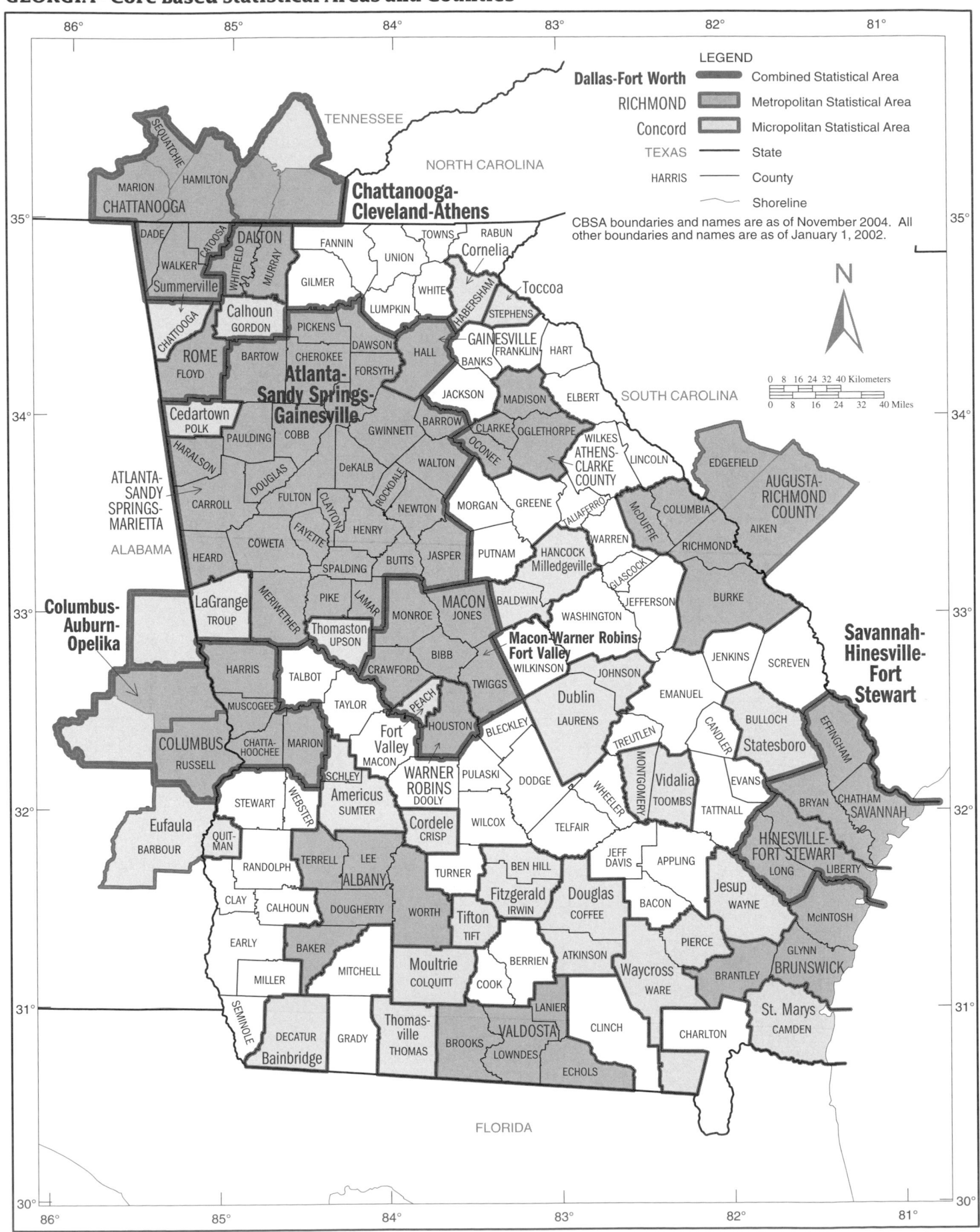

HAWAII - Core Based Statistical Areas and Counties

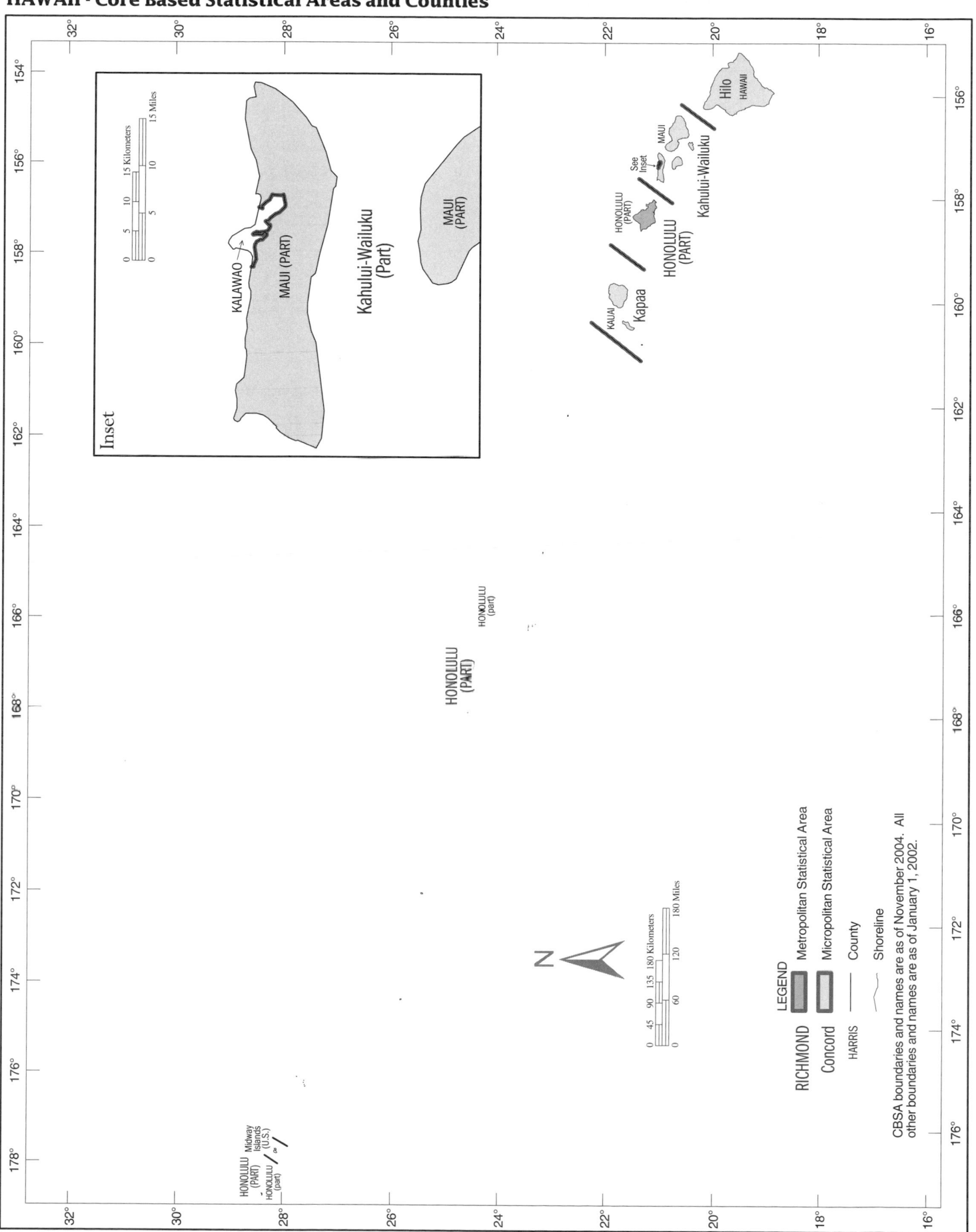

U.S. DEPARTMENT OF COMMERCE Economics and Statistics Administration U.S. Census Bureau

Appendix D

IDAHO - Core Based Statistical Areas and Counties

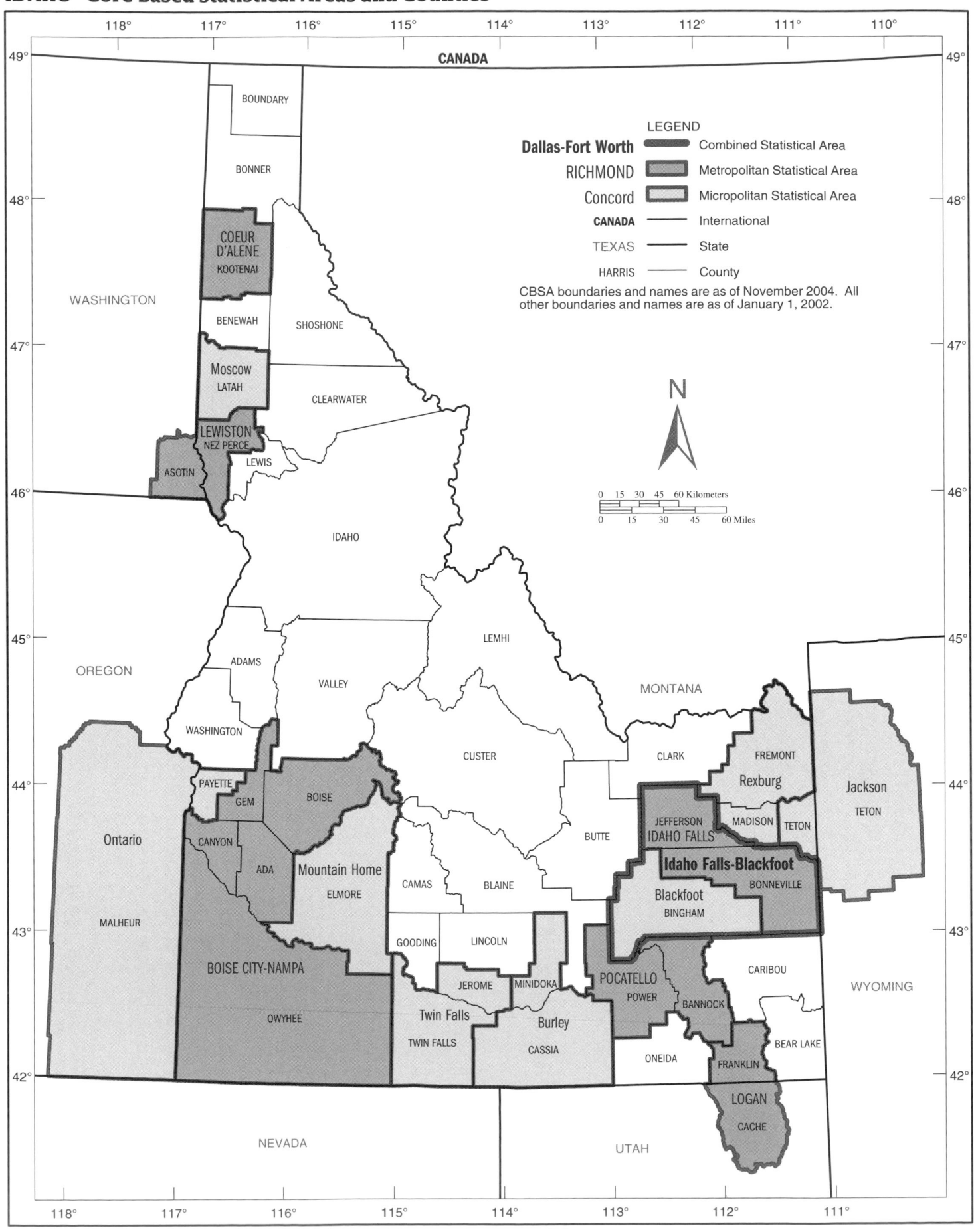

LEGEND

Dallas-Fort Worth Combined Statistical Area
RICHMOND Metropolitan Statistical Area
Concord Micropolitan Statistical Area
CANADA International
TEXAS State
HARRIS County

CBSA boundaries and names are as of November 2004. All other boundaries and names are as of January 1, 2002.

N

0 15 30 45 60 Kilometers
0 15 30 45 60 Miles

ILLINOIS - Core Based Statistical Areas, Counties, and Independent City

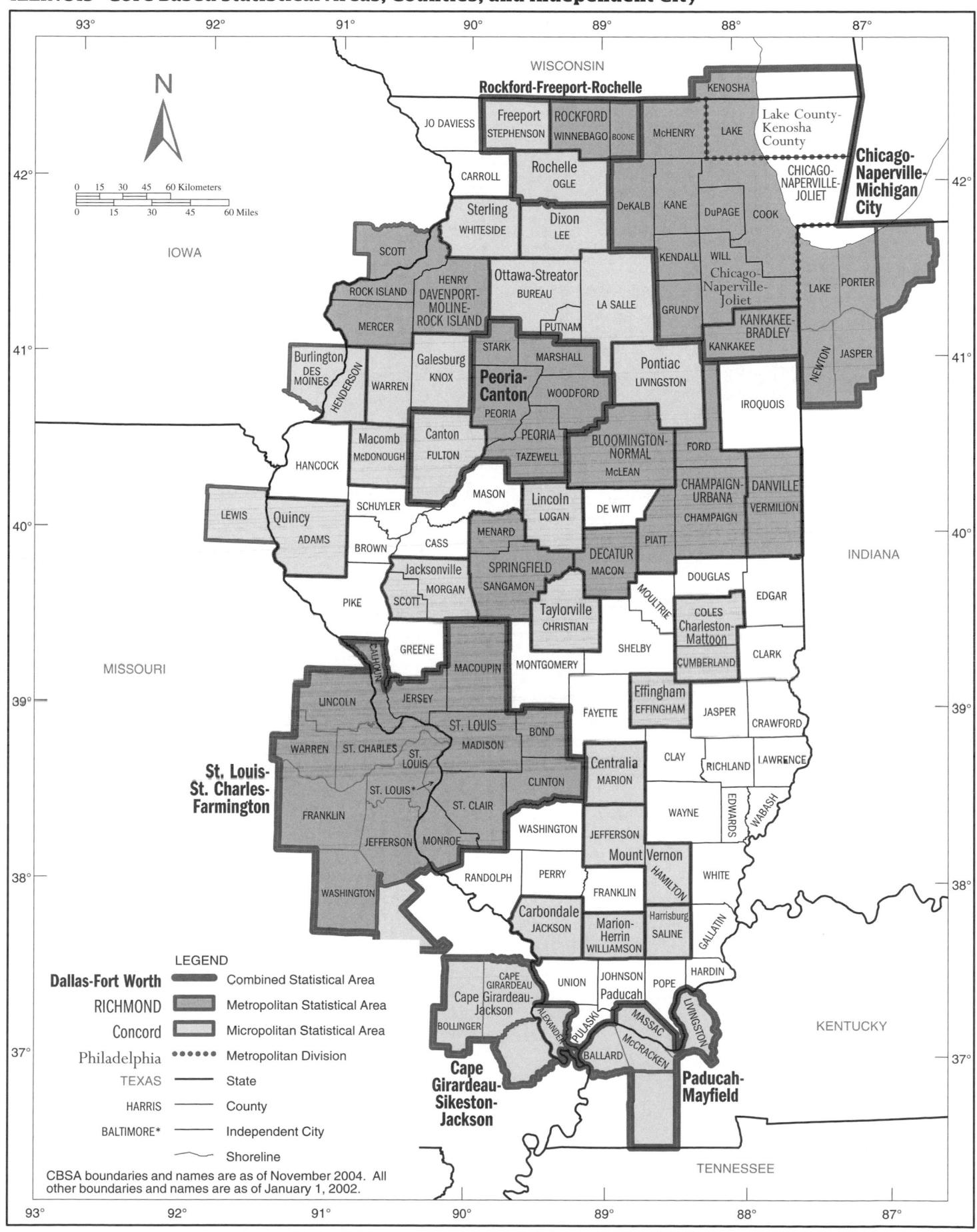

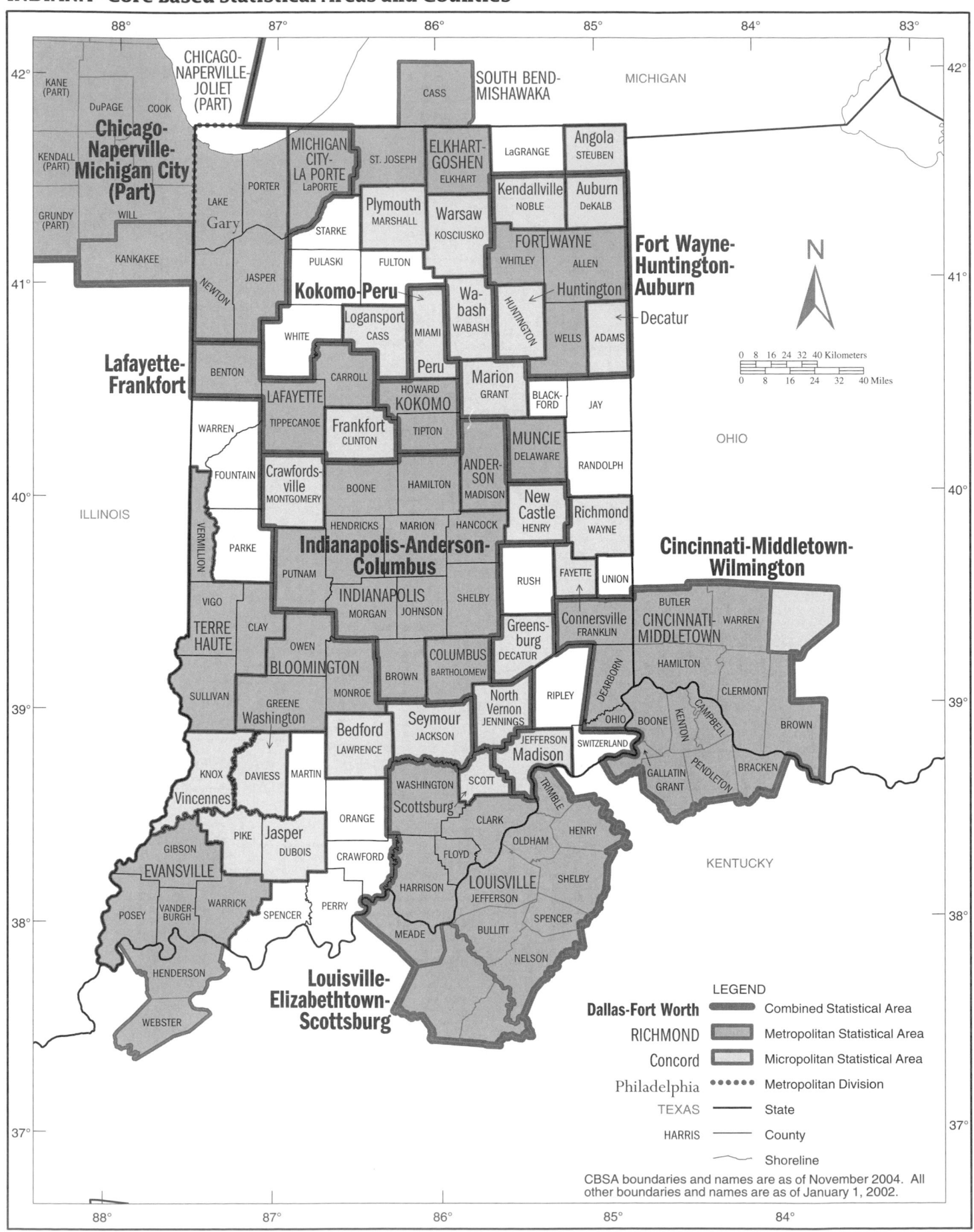

IOWA - Core Based Statistical Areas and Counties

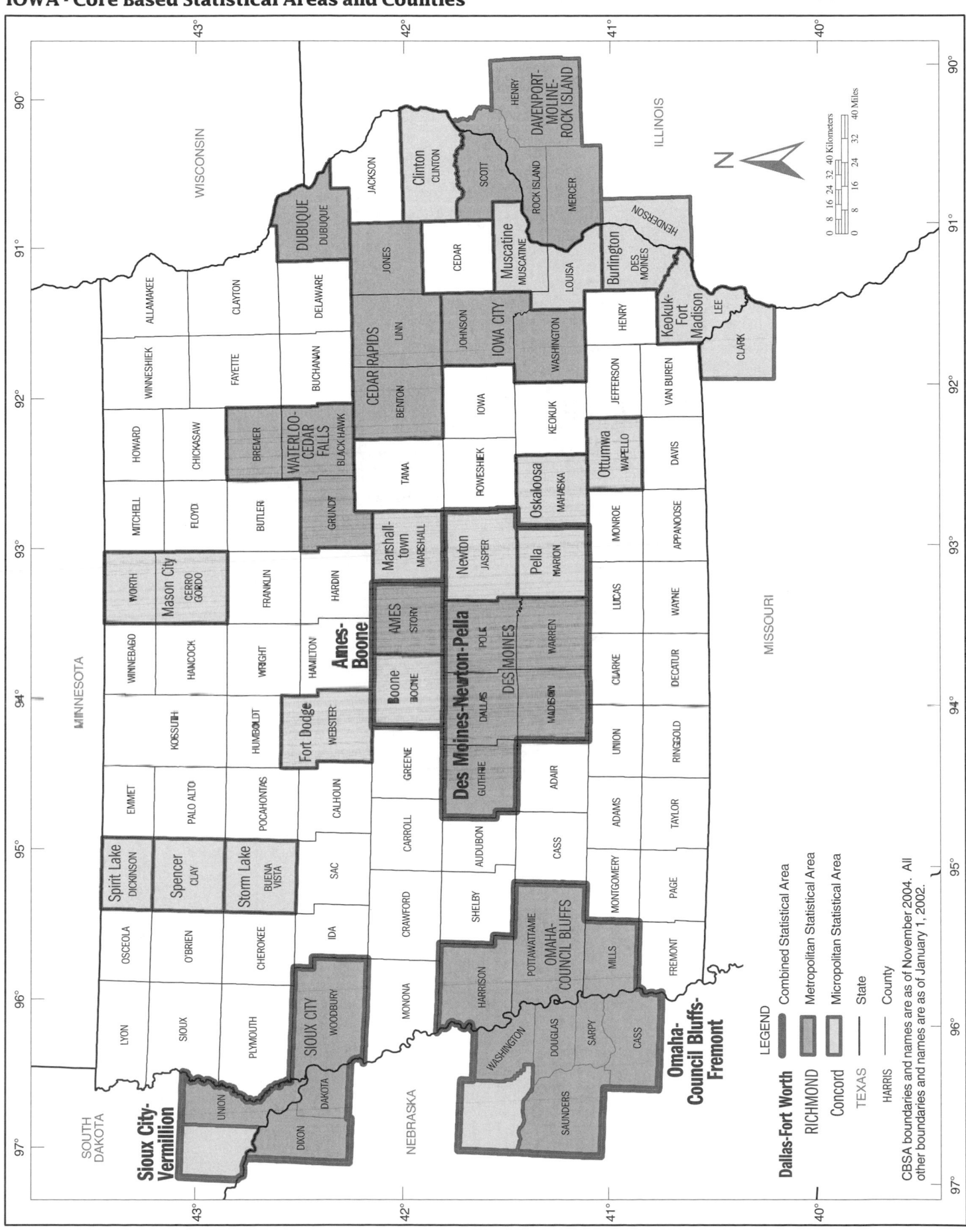

U.S. DEPARTMENT OF COMMERCE Economics and Statistics Administration U.S. Census Bureau

Appendix D

KANSAS - Core Based Statistical Areas and Counties

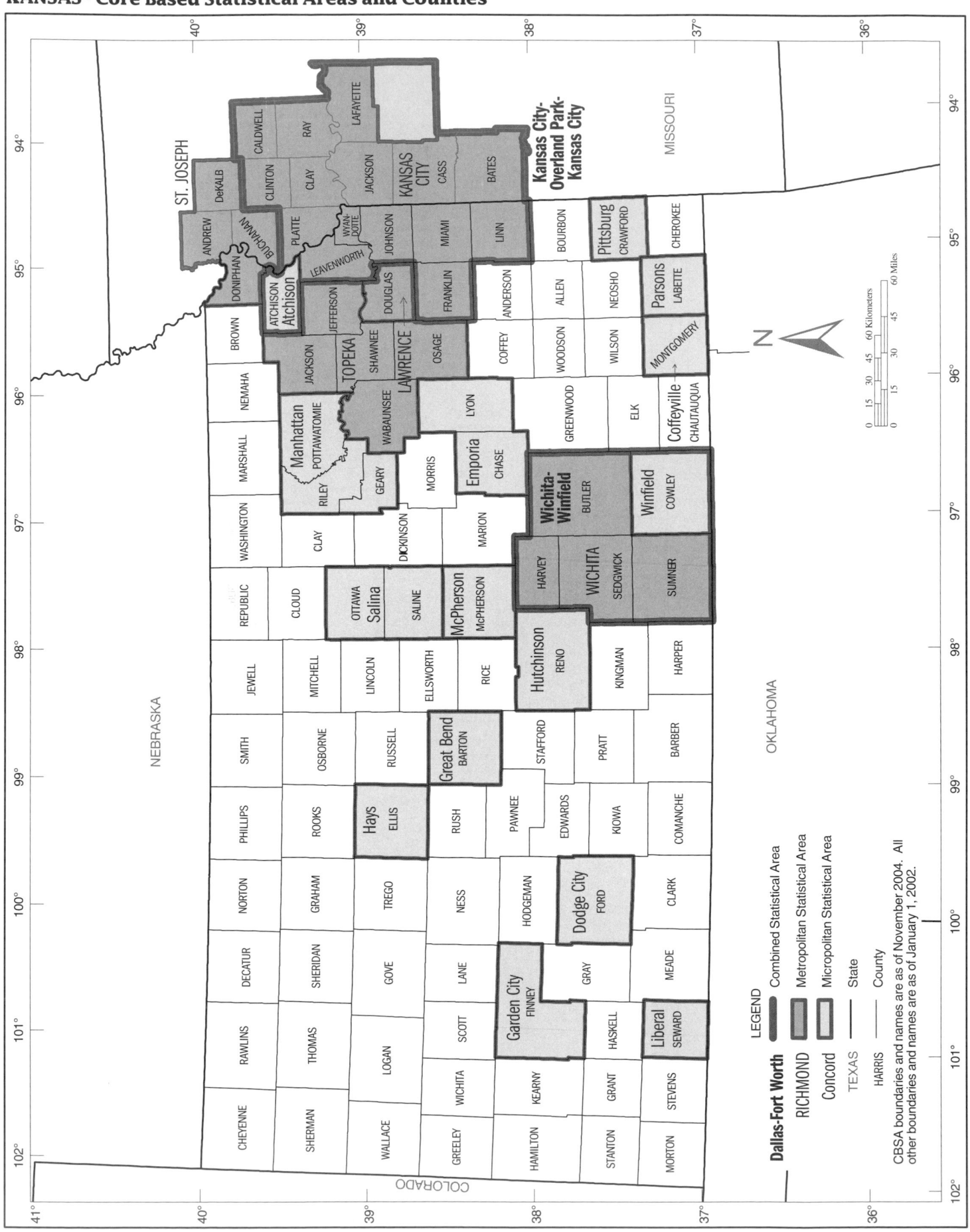

U.S. DEPARTMENT OF COMMERCE Economics and Statistics Administration U.S. Census Bureau

KENTUCKY - Core Based Statistical Areas and Counties

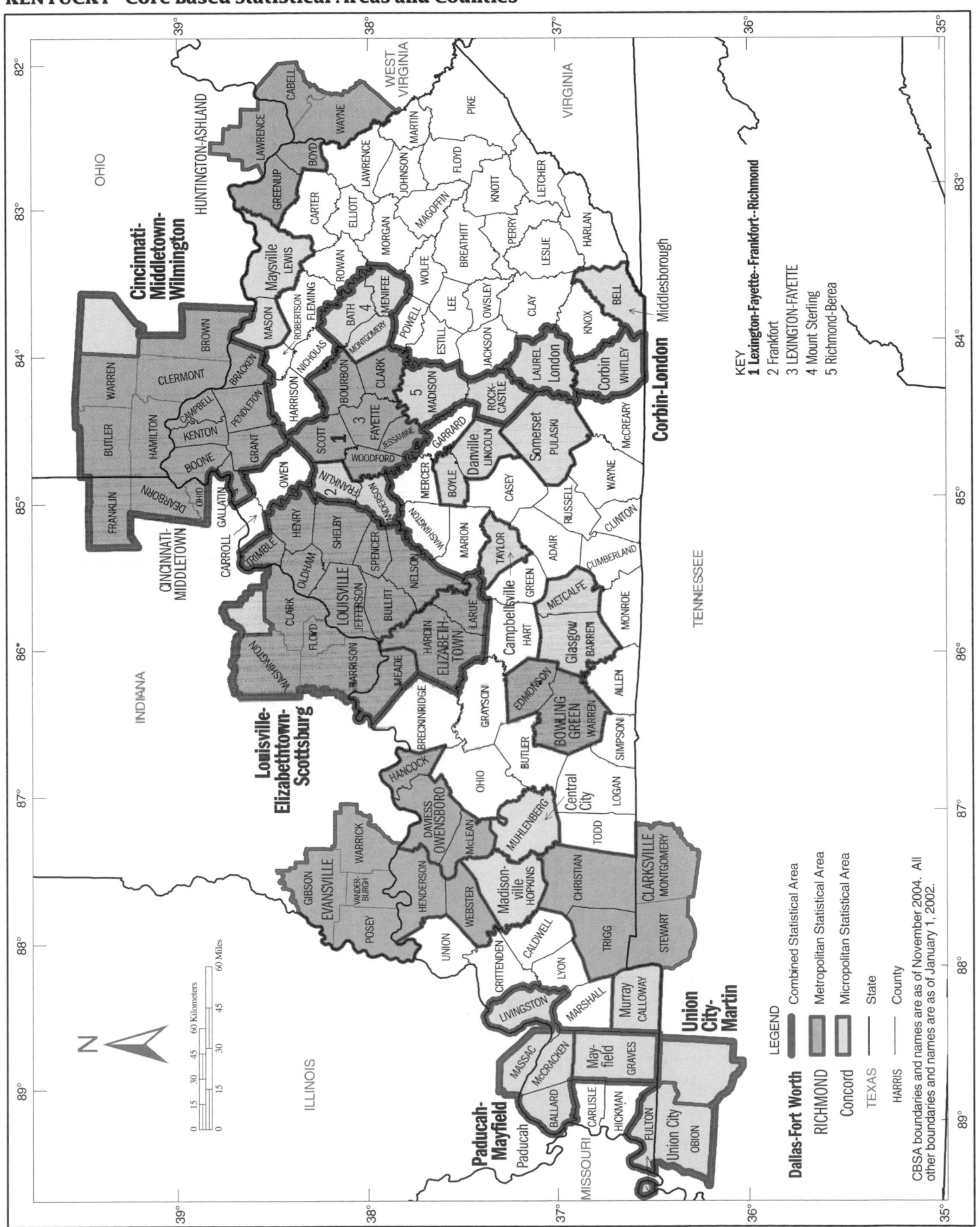

U.S. DEPARTMENT OF COMMERCE Economics and Statistics Administration U.S. Census Bureau

Appendix D

D-21

LOUISIANA - Core Based Statistical Areas and Parishes

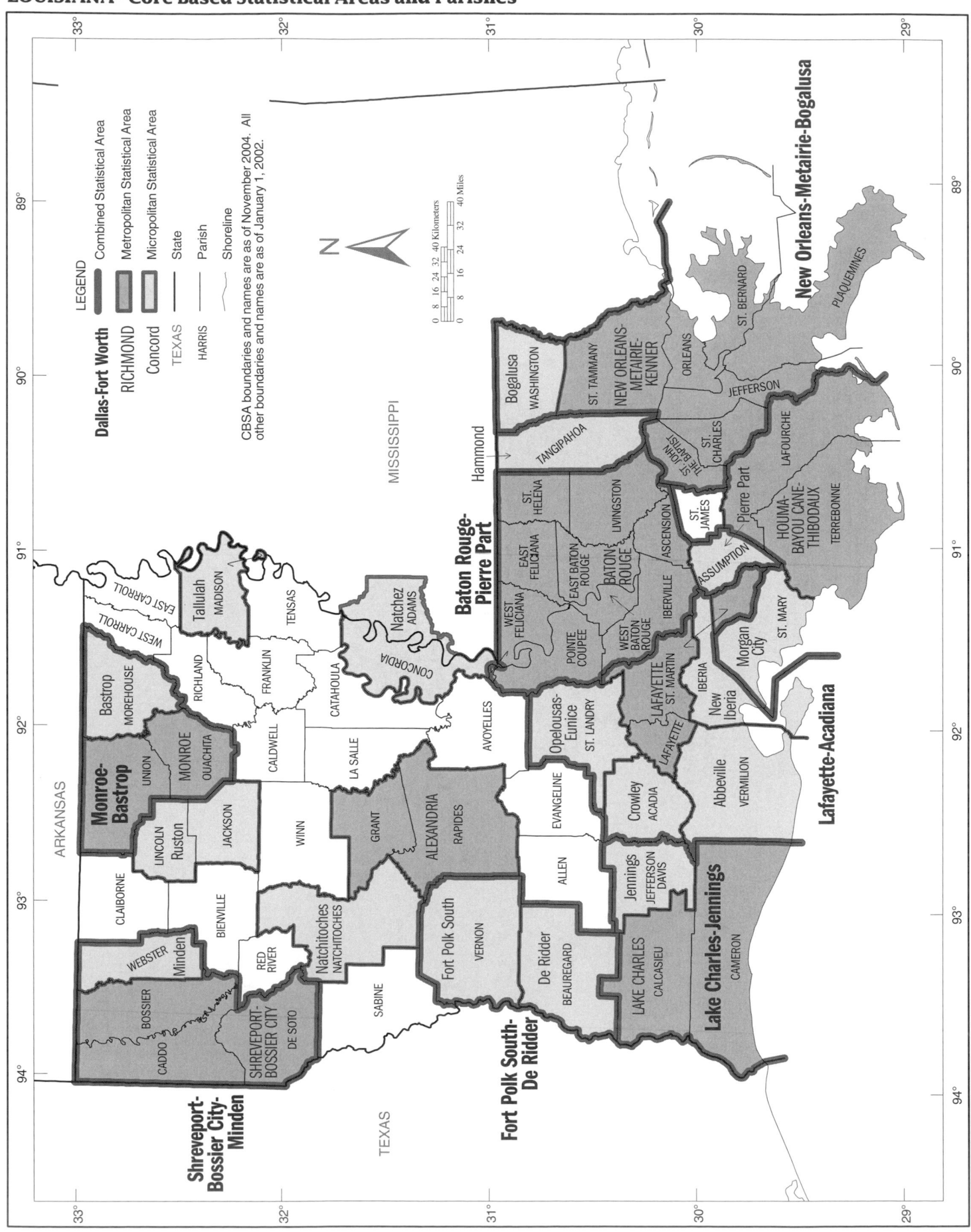

U.S. DEPARTMENT OF COMMERCE Economics and Statistics Administration U.S. Census Bureau

MAINE - Core Based Statistical Areas and Counties

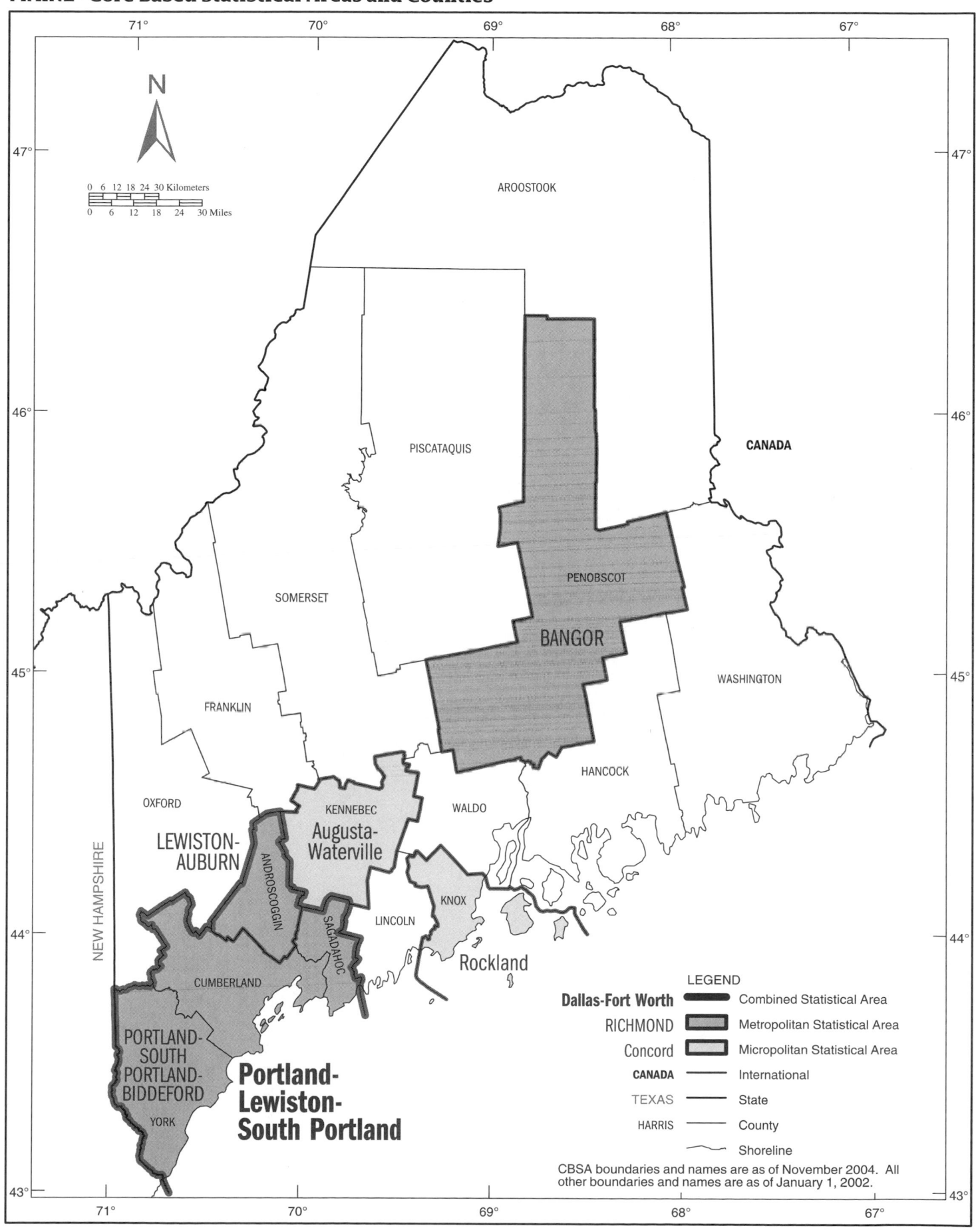

MARYLAND - Core Based Statistical Areas, District of Columbia, Counties, and Independent Cities

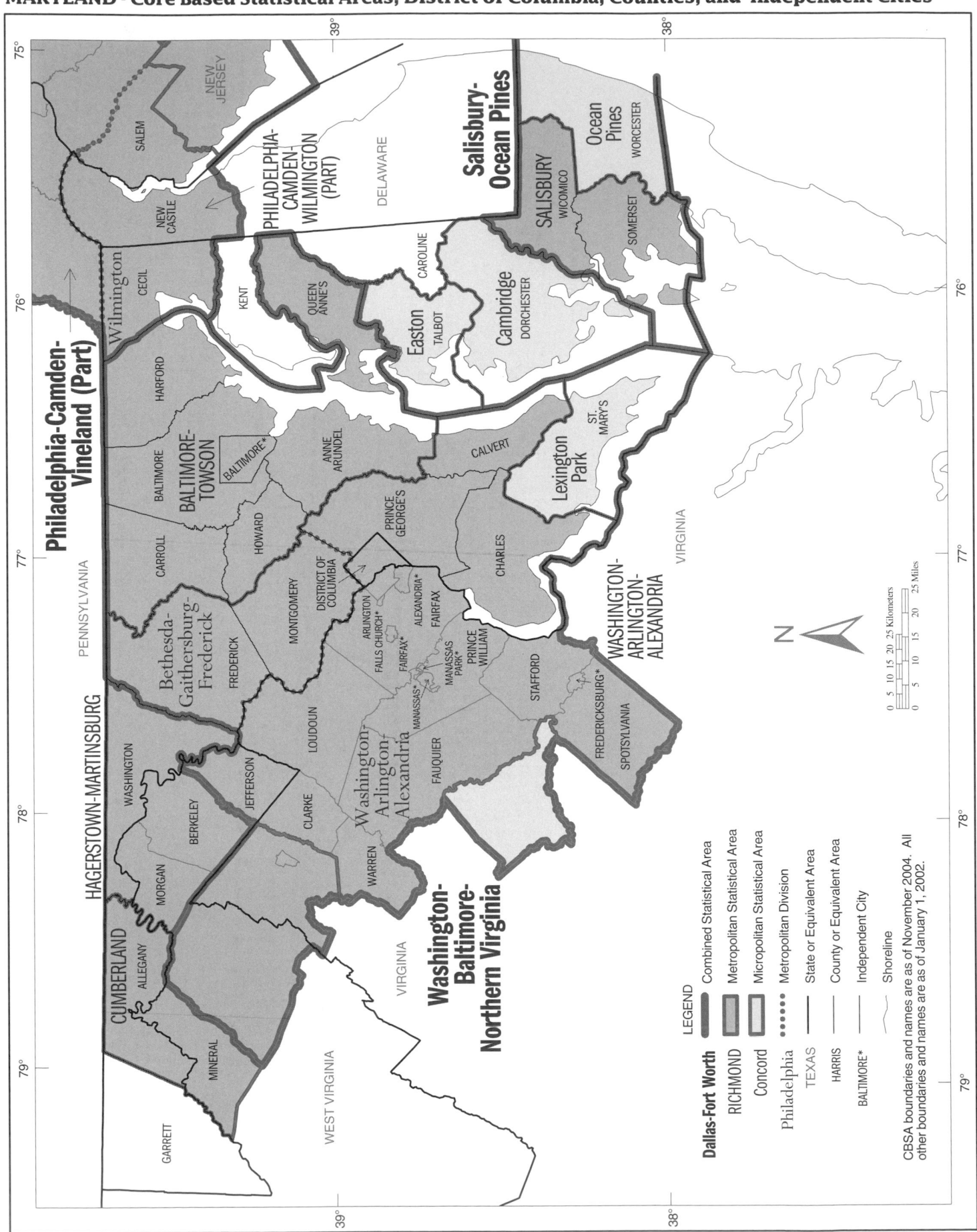

MASSACHUSETTS - Core Based Statistical Areas and Counties

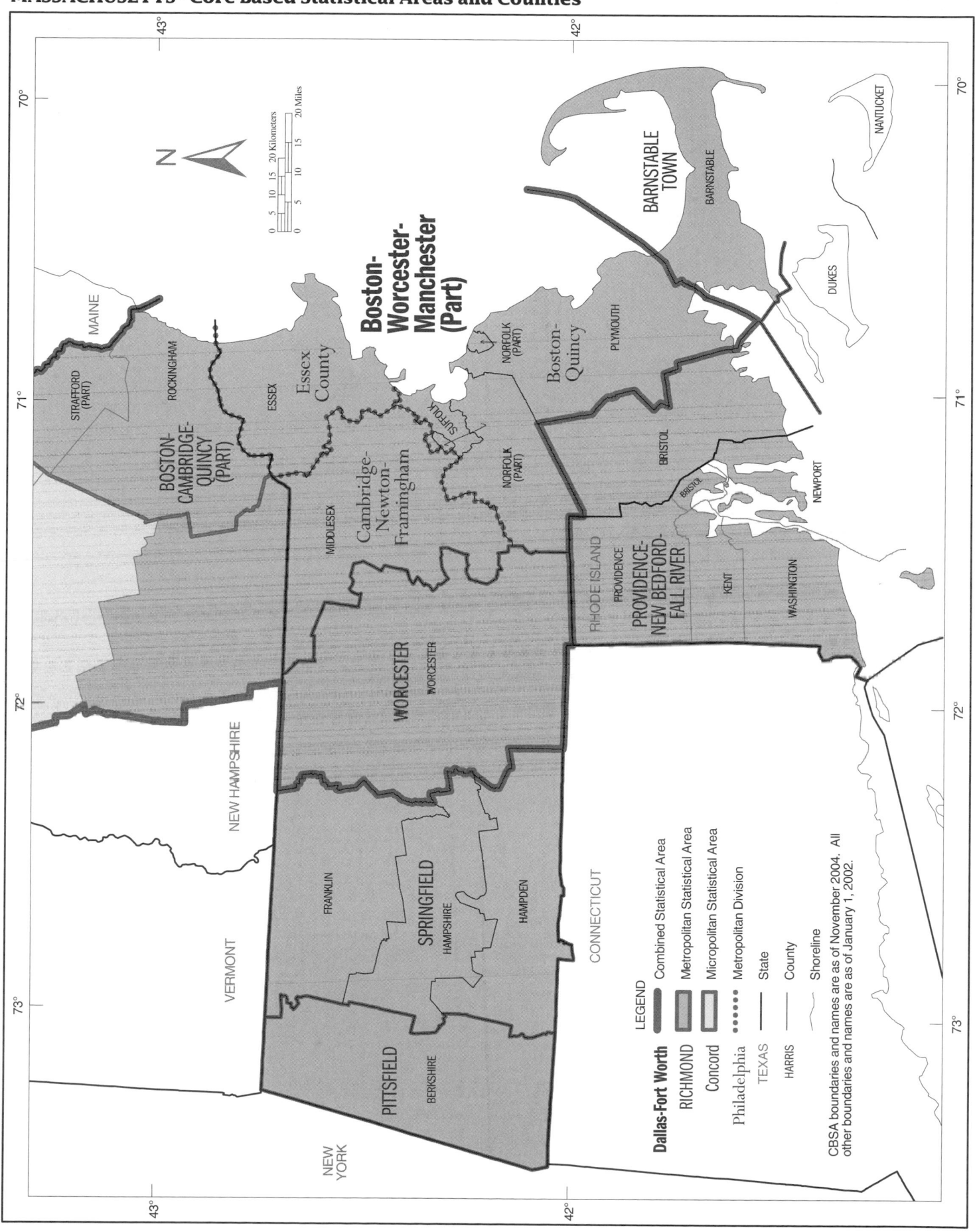

U.S. DEPARTMENT OF COMMERCE Economics and Statistics Administration U.S. Census Bureau

MICHIGAN - Core Based Statistical Areas and Counties

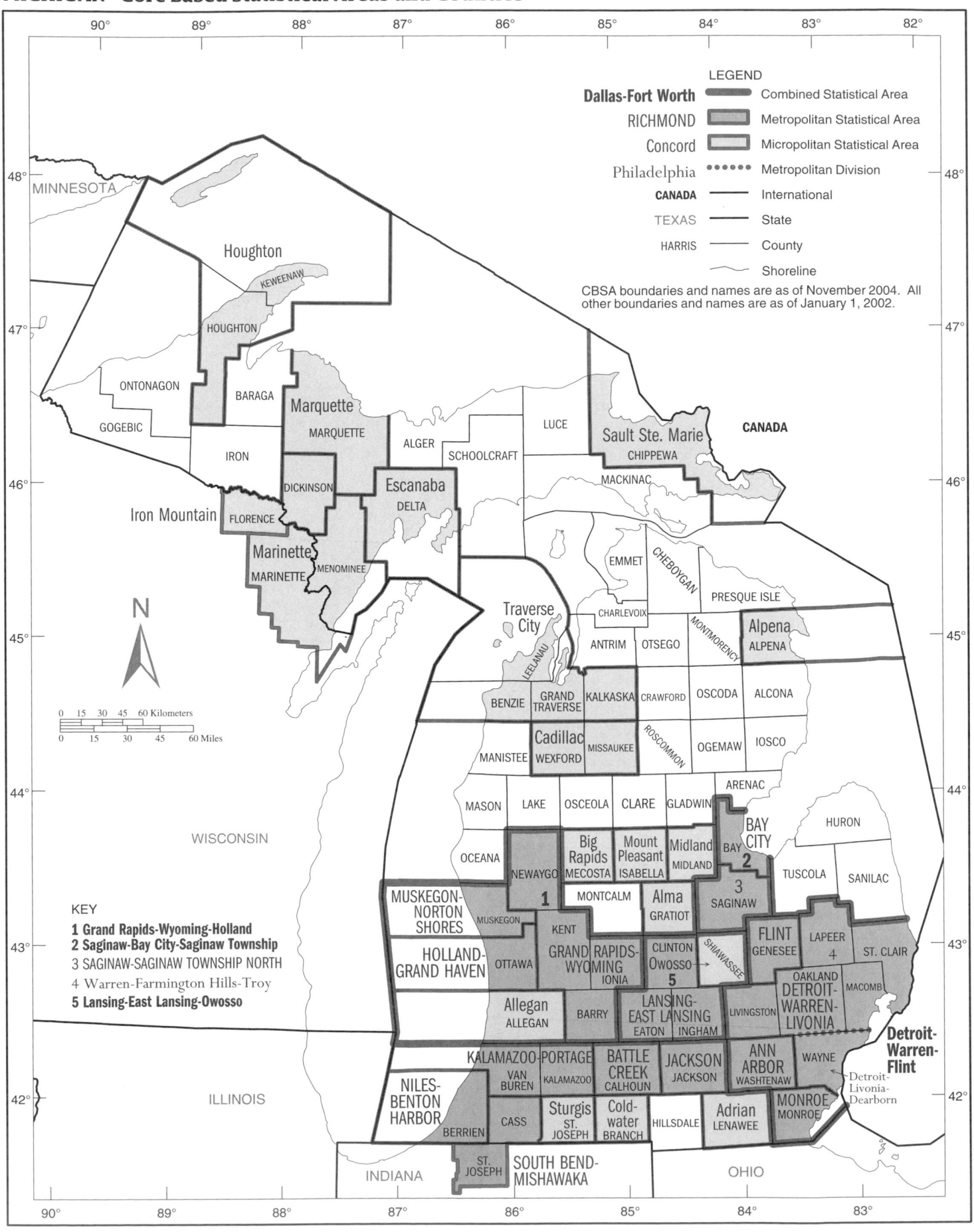

LEGEND

Dallas-Fort Worth — Combined Statistical Area
RICHMOND — Metropolitan Statistical Area
Concord — Micropolitan Statistical Area
Philadelphia — Metropolitan Division
CANADA — International
TEXAS — State
HARRIS — County
— Shoreline

CBSA boundaries and names are as of November 2004. All other boundaries and names are as of January 1, 2002.

KEY
1 **Grand Rapids-Wyoming-Holland**
2 **Saginaw-Bay City-Saginaw Township**
3 SAGINAW-SAGINAW TOWNSHIP NORTH
4 Warren-Farmington Hills-Troy
5 **Lansing-East Lansing-Owosso**

MINNESOTA - Core Based Statistical Areas and Counties

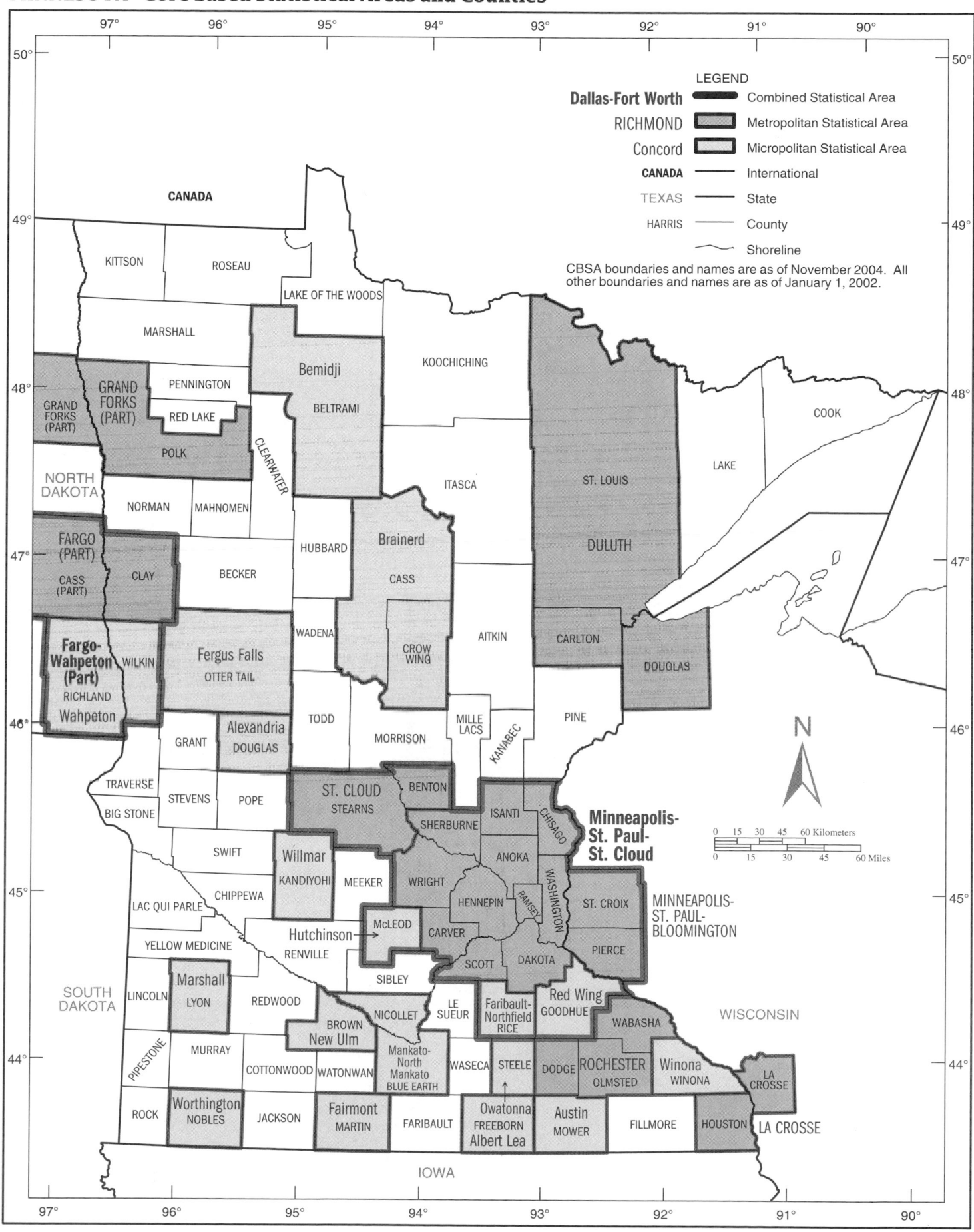

LEGEND

Dallas-Fort Worth	Combined Statistical Area
RICHMOND	Metropolitan Statistical Area
Concord	Micropolitan Statistical Area
CANADA	International
TEXAS	State
HARRIS	County
	Shoreline

CBSA boundaries and names are as of November 2004. All other boundaries and names are as of January 1, 2002.

MISSISSIPPI - Core Based Statistical Areas and Counties

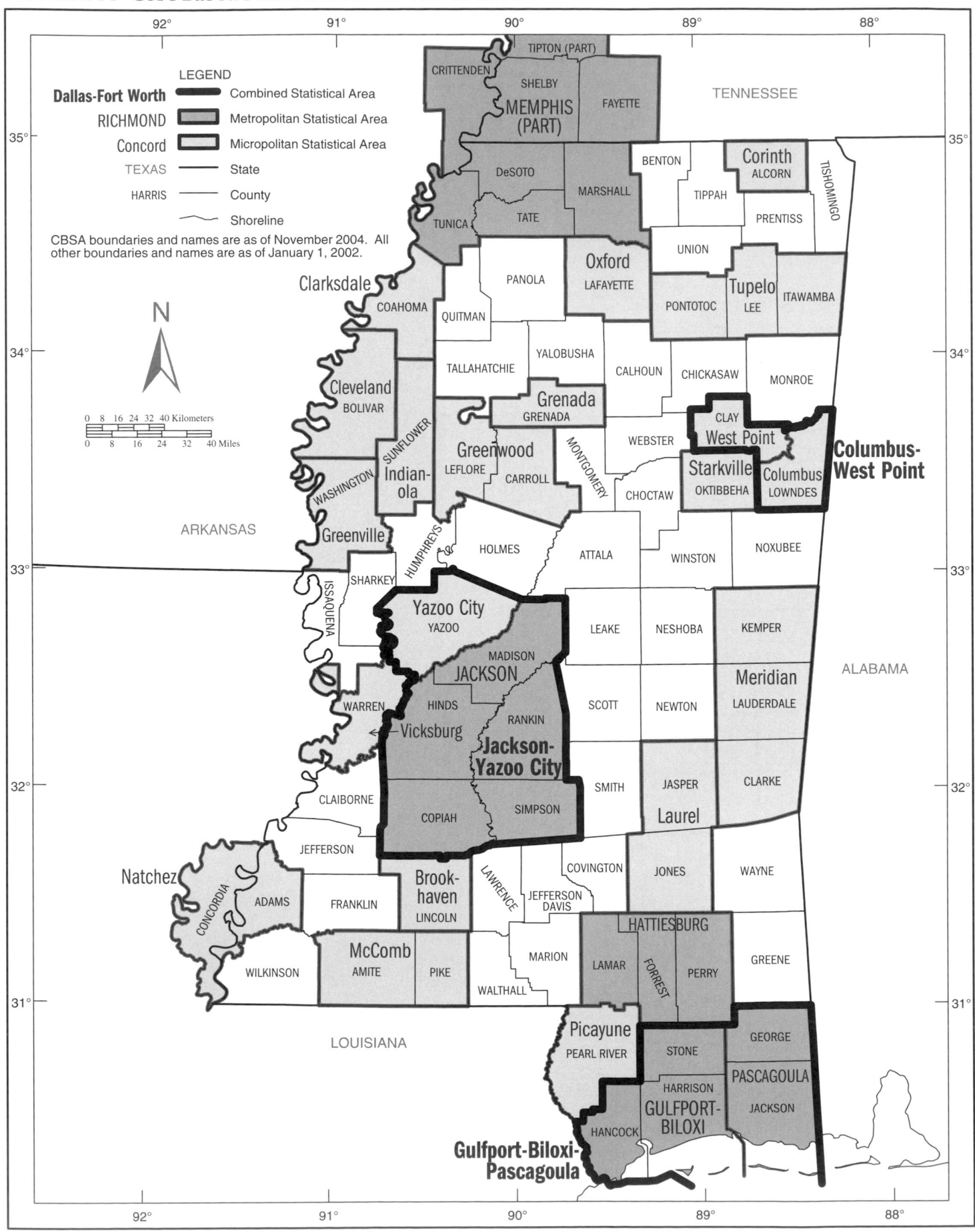

MISSOURI - Core Based Statistical Areas, Counties, and Independent City

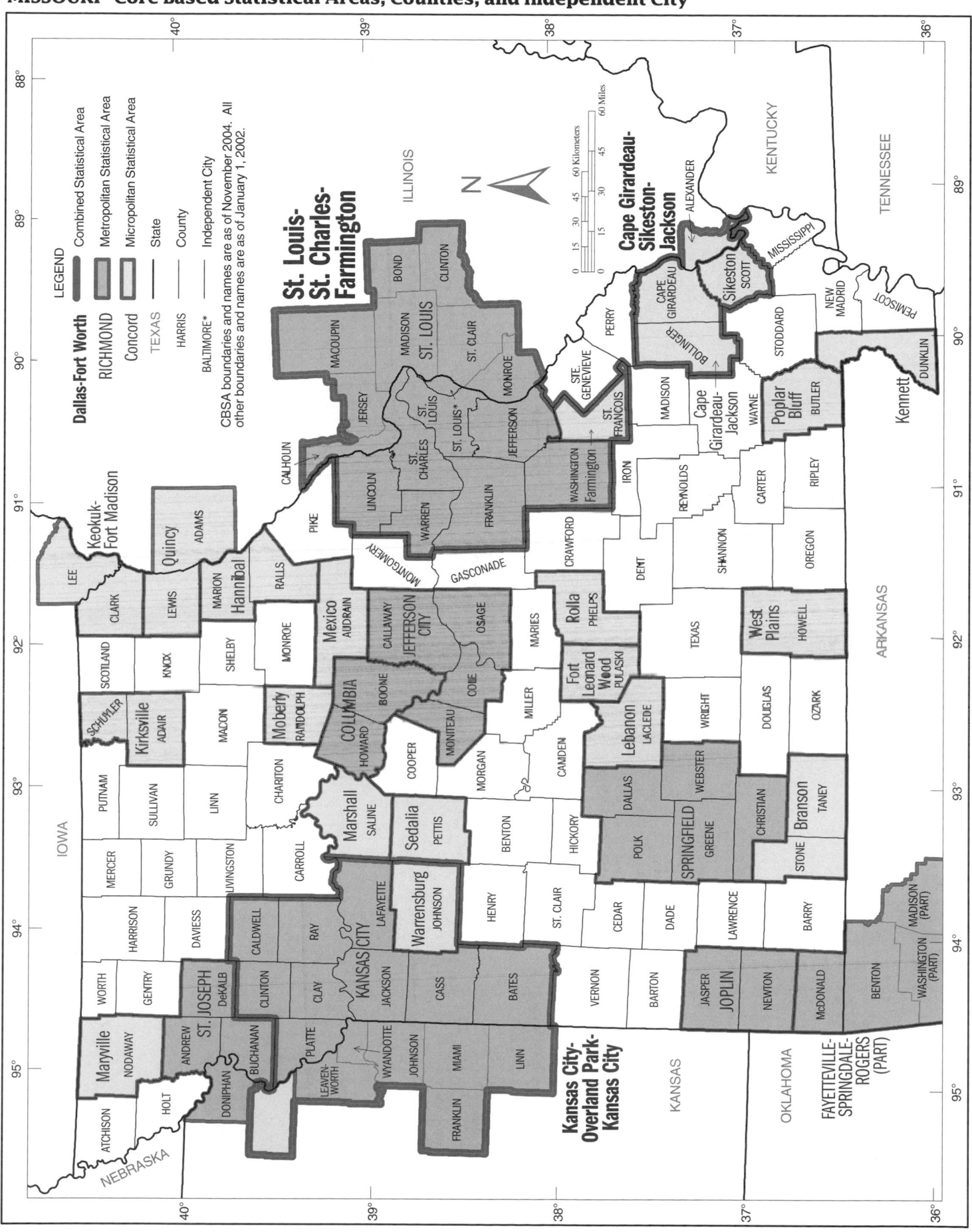

U.S. DEPARTMENT OF COMMERCE Economics and Statistics Administration U.S. Census Bureau

MONTANA - Core Based Statistical Areas and Counties

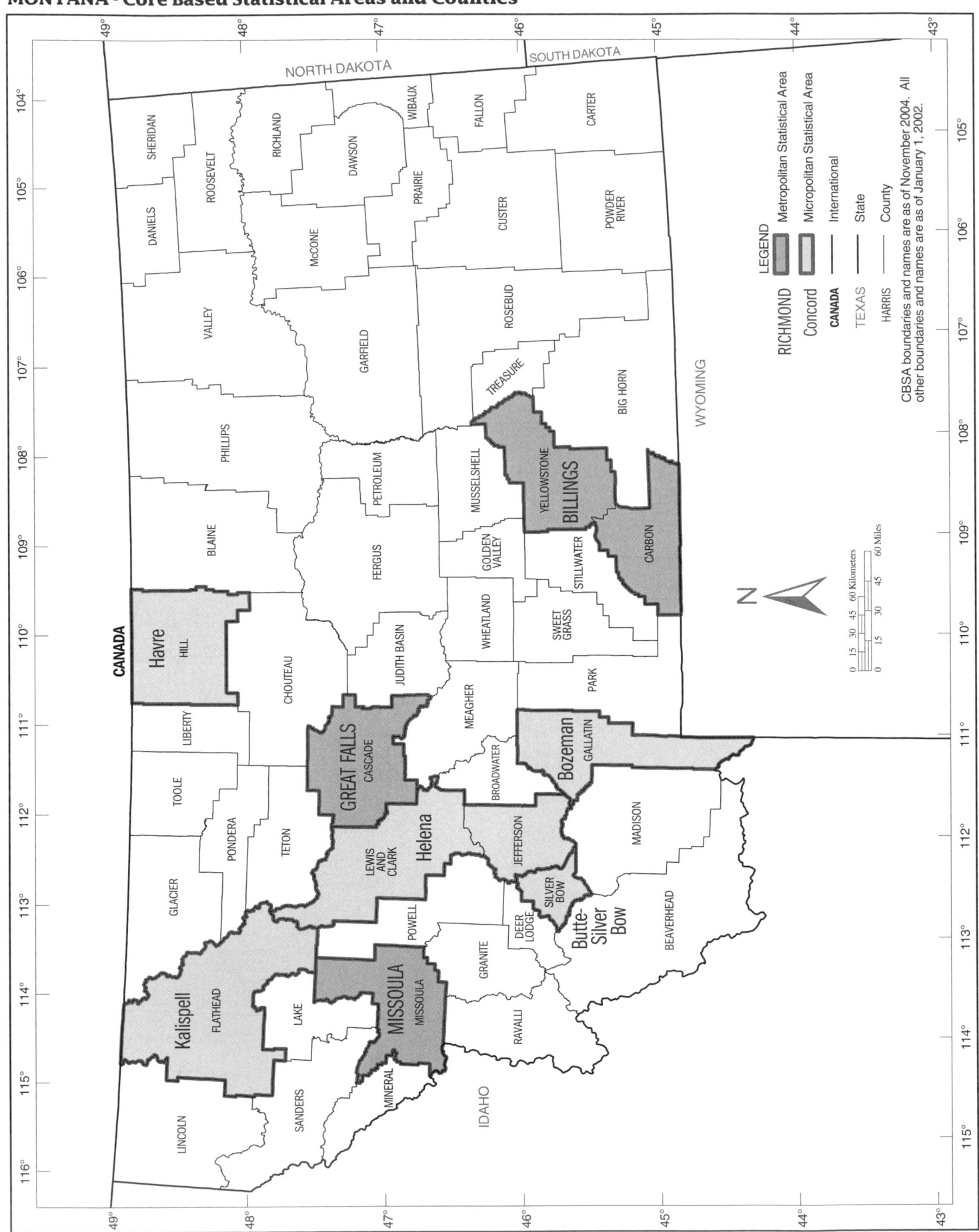

NEBRASKA - Core Based Statistical Areas and Counties

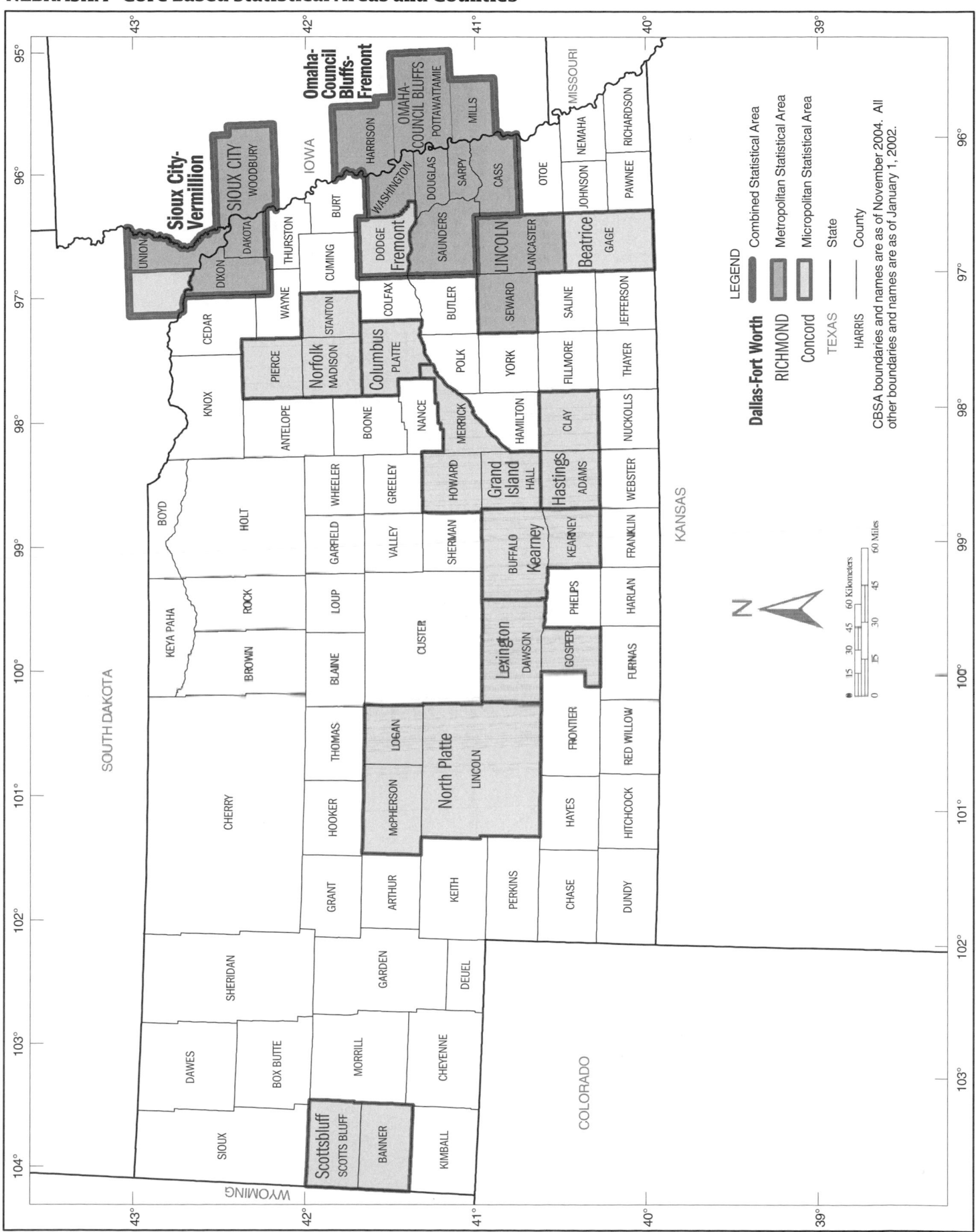

LEGEND

Combined Statistical Area
Metropolitan Statistical Area
Micropolitan Statistical Area
State
County

Dallas-Fort Worth
RICHMOND
Concord
TEXAS
HARRIS

CBSA boundaries and names are as of November 2004. All other boundaries and names are as of January 1, 2002.

U.S. DEPARTMENT OF COMMERCE Economics and Statistics Administration U.S. Census Bureau

NEVADA - Core Based Statistical Areas, Counties, and Independent City

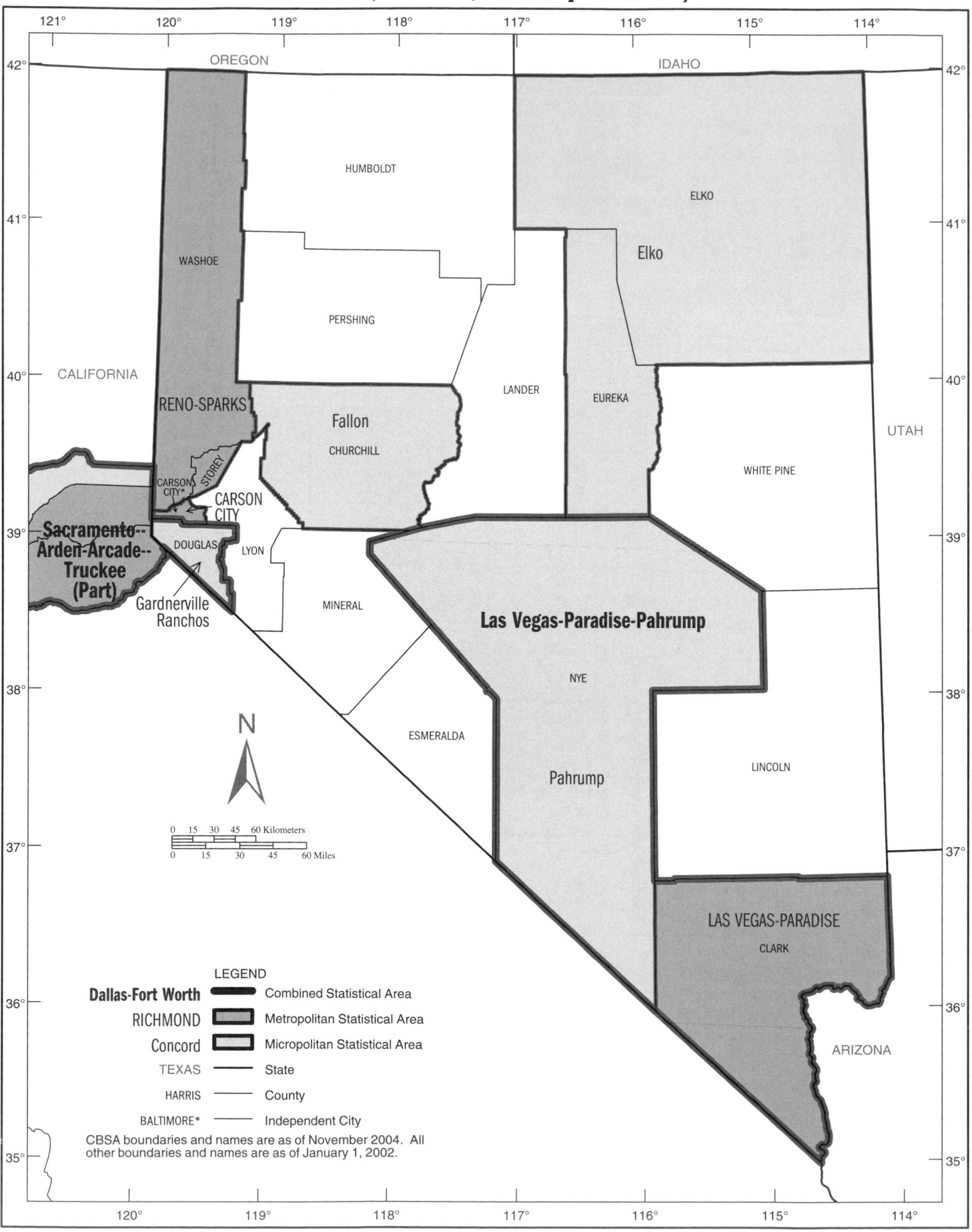

LEGEND

Dallas-Fort Worth ▬▬ Combined Statistical Area

RICHMOND ▬ Metropolitan Statistical Area

Concord ▭ Micropolitan Statistical Area

TEXAS ▬ State

HARRIS ▬ County

BALTIMORE* ▬ Independent City

CBSA boundaries and names are as of November 2004. All other boundaries and names are as of January 1, 2002.

NEW HAMPSHIRE - Core Based Statistical Areas and Counties

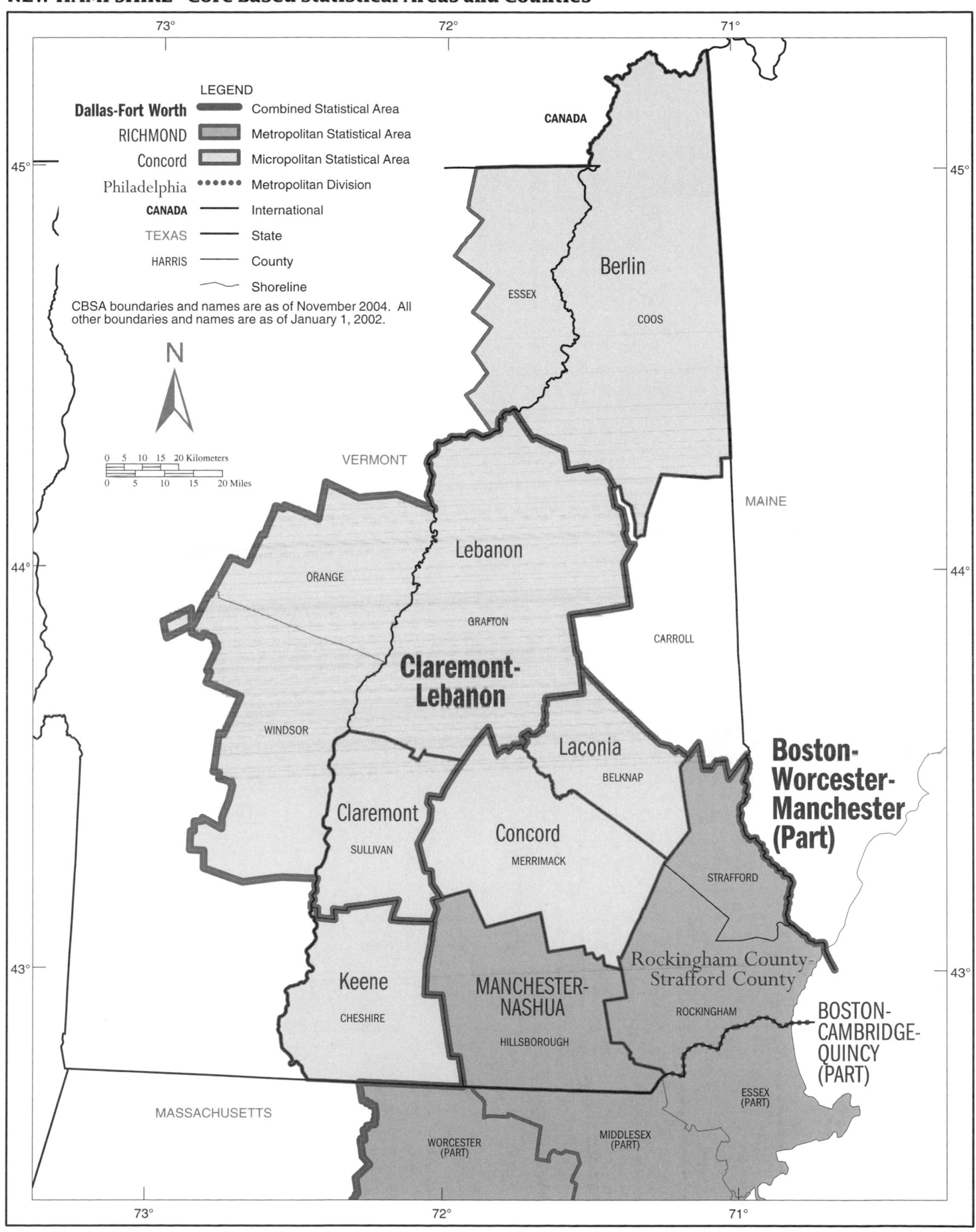

NEW JERSEY - Core Based Statistical Areas and Counties

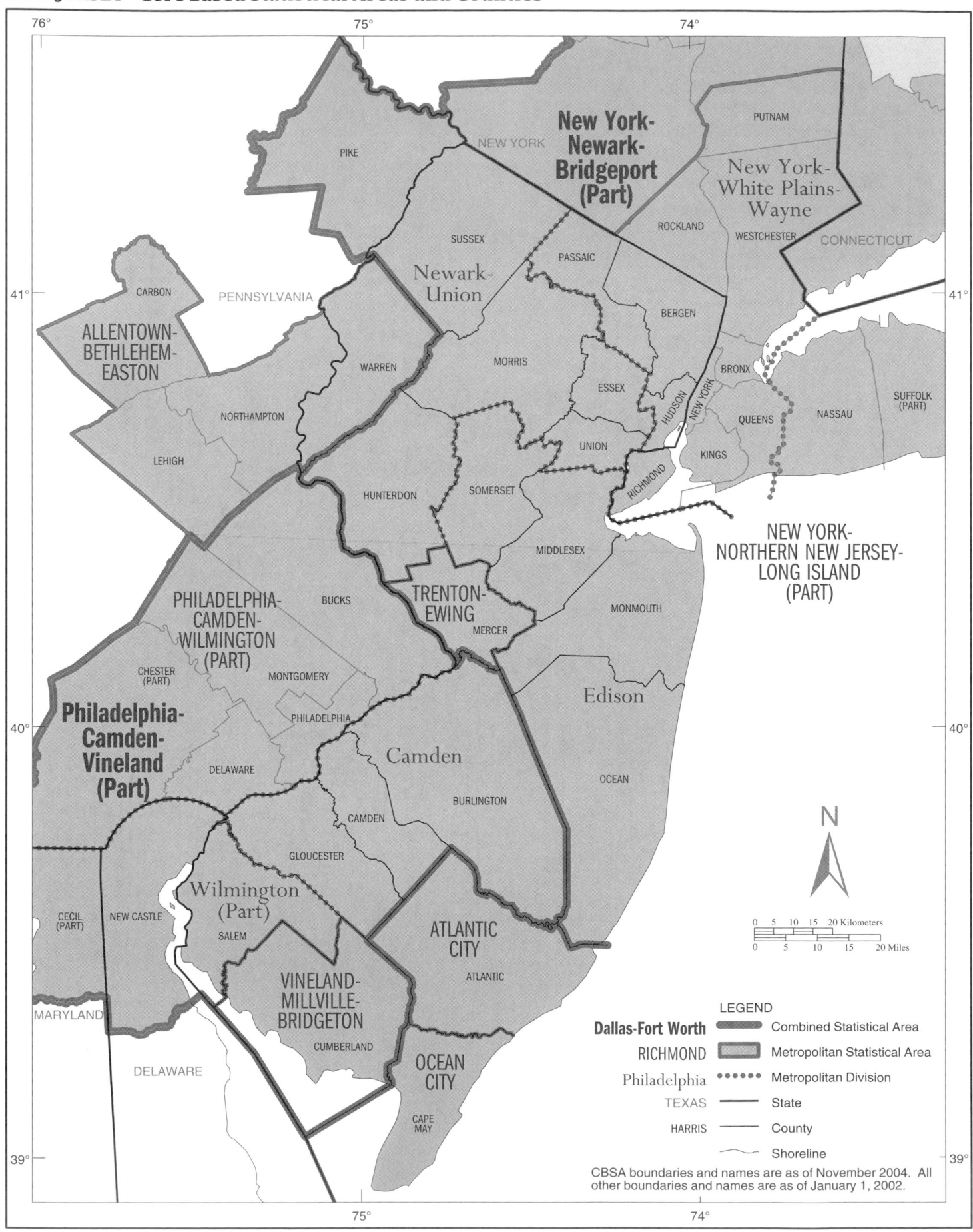

LEGEND

Dallas-Fort Worth — Combined Statistical Area

RICHMOND — Metropolitan Statistical Area

Philadelphia ••••• Metropolitan Division

TEXAS —— State

HARRIS — County

Shoreline

CBSA boundaries and names are as of November 2004. All other boundaries and names are as of January 1, 2002.

NEW MEXICO - Core Based Statistical Areas and Counties

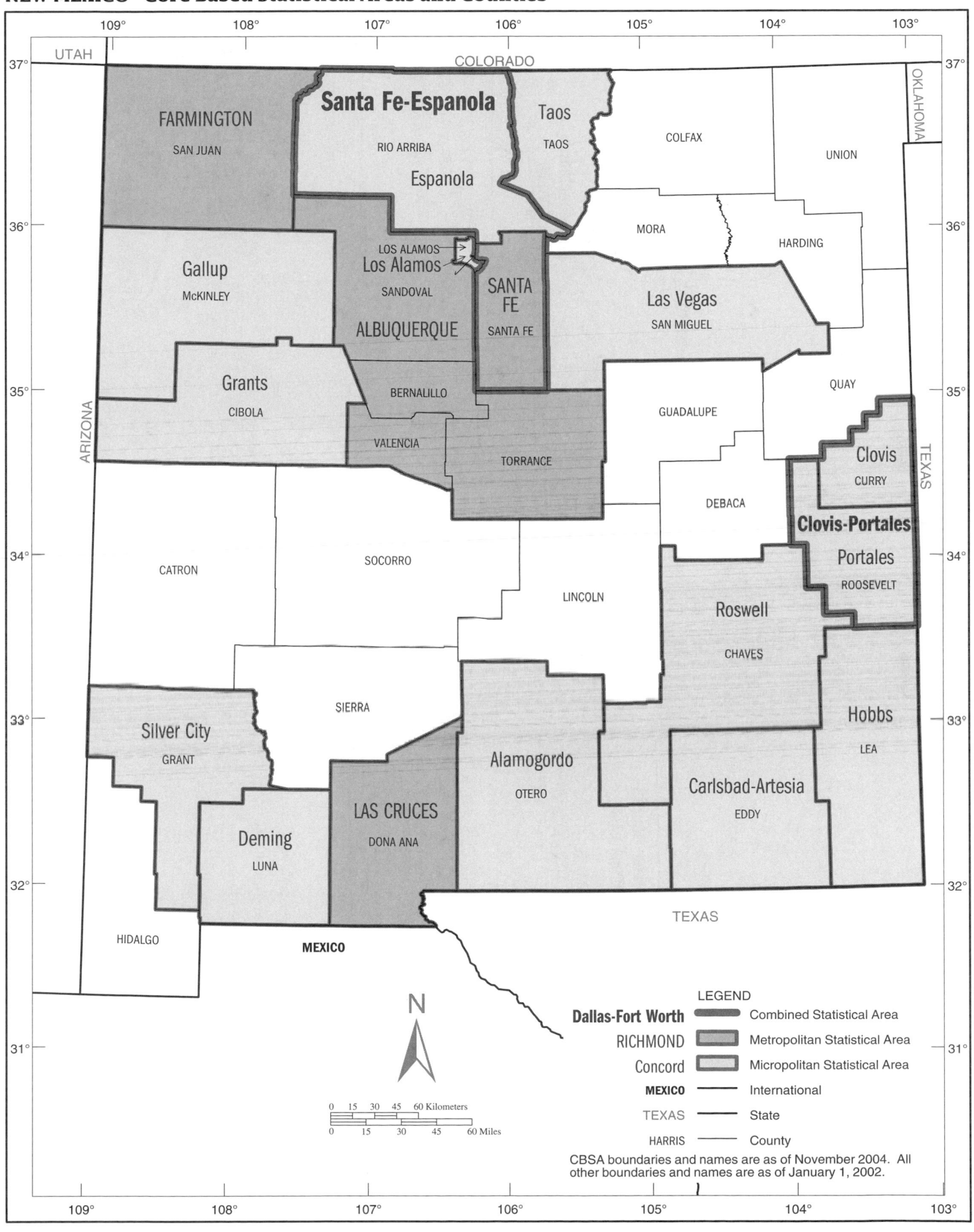

UTAH · COLORADO · OKLAHOMA · ARIZONA · TEXAS · MEXICO · TEXAS

FARMINGTON
SAN JUAN

Santa Fe-Espanola
RIO ARRIBA
Espanola

Taos
TAOS

COLFAX

UNION

MORA

HARDING

Gallup
McKINLEY

LOS ALAMOS
Los Alamos

SANDOVAL

ALBUQUERQUE

SANTA
FE
SANTA FE

Las Vegas
SAN MIGUEL

Grants
CIBOLA

BERNALILLO

VALENCIA

TORRANCE

QUAY

GUADALUPE

Clovis
CURRY

DEBACA

Clovis-Portales
Portales
ROOSEVELT

CATRON

SOCORRO

LINCOLN

Roswell
CHAVES

Silver City
GRANT

SIERRA

Hobbs
LEA

Alamogordo
OTERO

Carlsbad-Artesia
EDDY

LAS CRUCES
DONA ANA

Deming
LUNA

HIDALGO

MEXICO

TEXAS

N

0   15   30   45   60 Kilometers
0   15   30   45   60 Miles

LEGEND

Dallas-Fort Worth — Combined Statistical Area

RICHMOND — Metropolitan Statistical Area

Concord — Micropolitan Statistical Area

MEXICO — International

TEXAS — State

HARRIS — County

CBSA boundaries and names are as of November 2004. All other boundaries and names are as of January 1, 2002.

NEW YORK - Core Based Statistical Areas and Counties

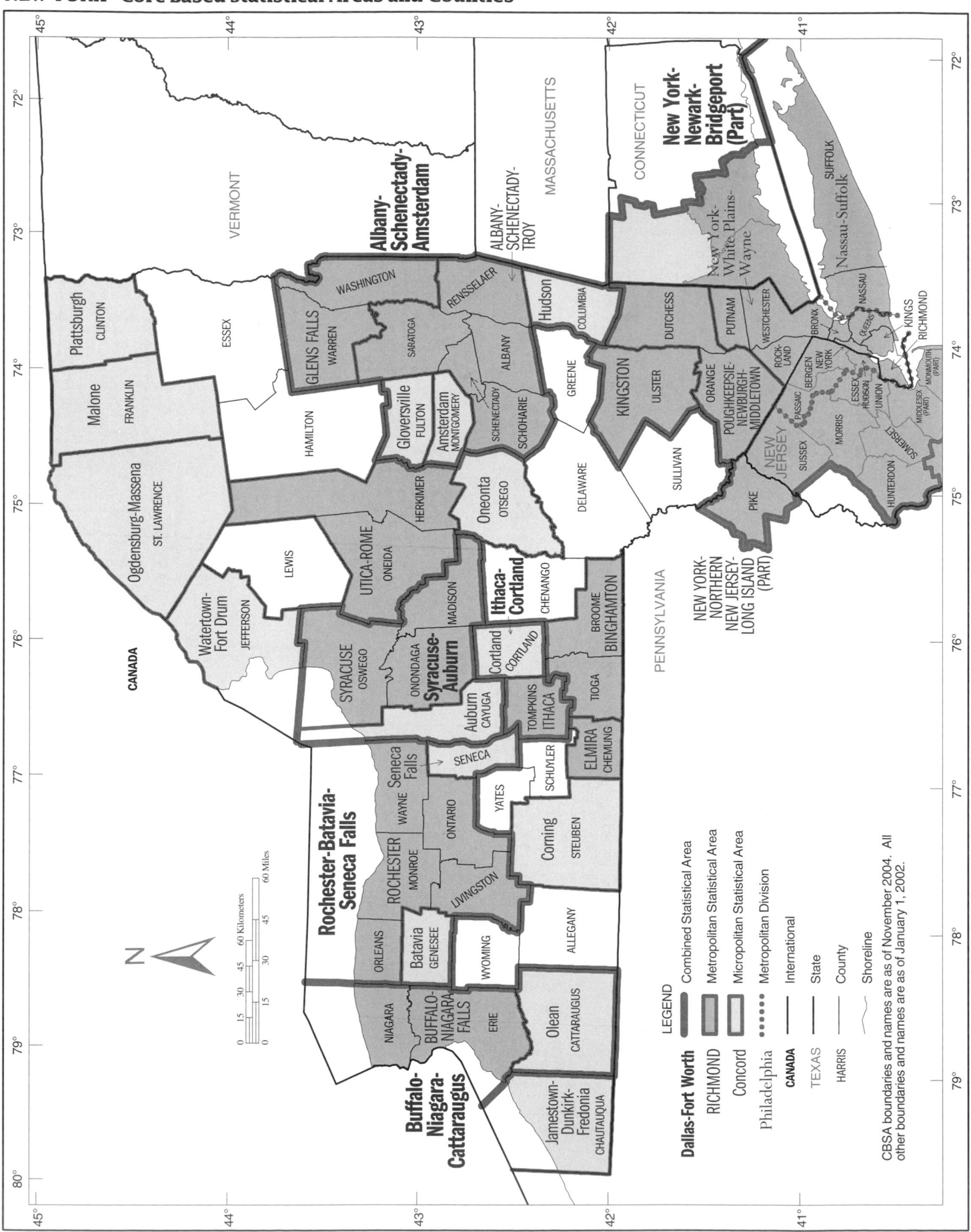

U.S. DEPARTMENT OF COMMERCE Economics and Statistics Administration U.S. Census Bureau

NORTH CAROLINA - Core Based Statistical Areas, Counties, and Independent Cities

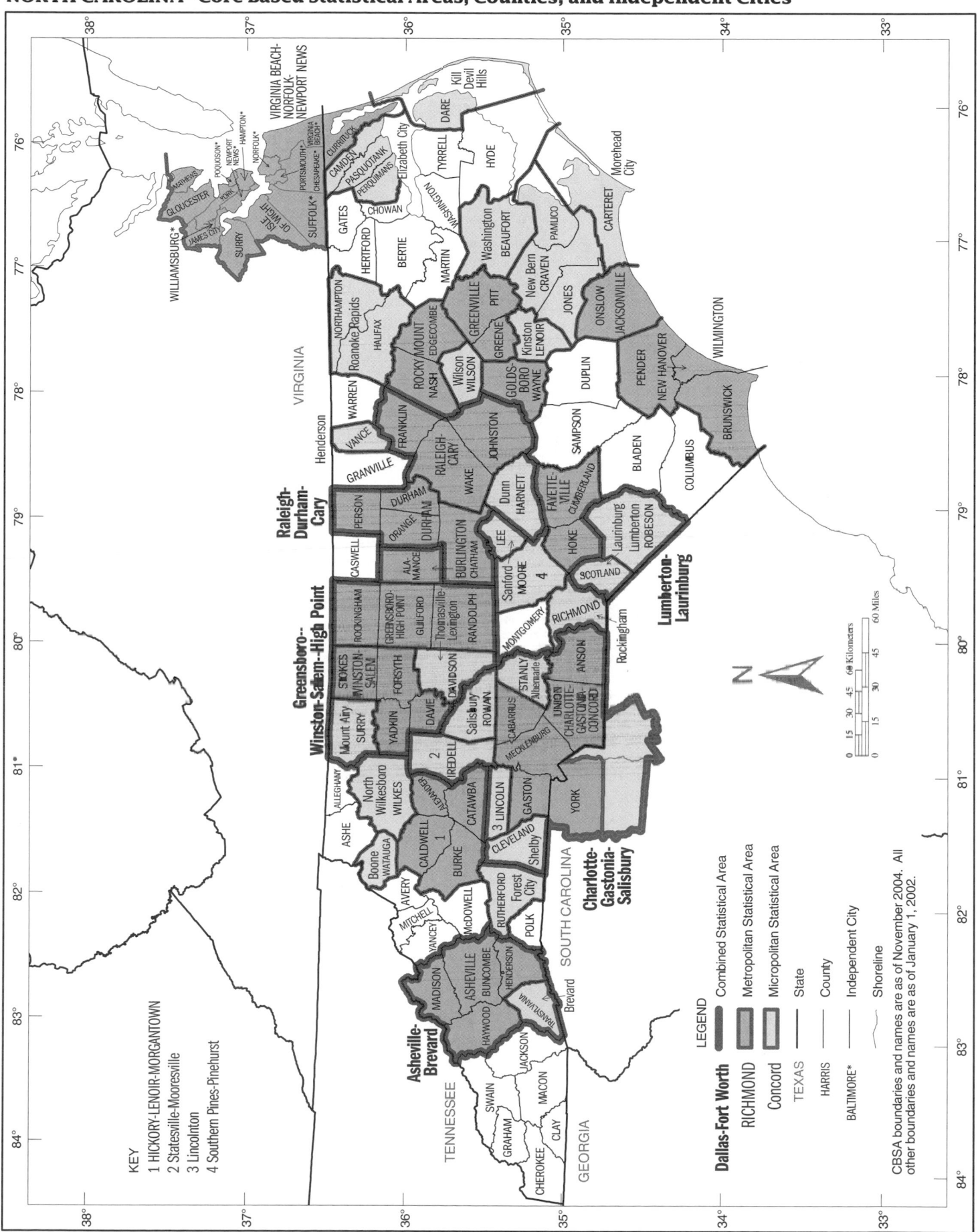

KEY
1 HICKORY-LENOIR-MORGANTOWN
2 STATESVILLE-MOORESVILLE
3 LINCOLNTON
4 SOUTHERN PINES-PINEHURST

LEGEND

Dallas-Fort Worth	Combined Statistical Area
RICHMOND	Metropolitan Statistical Area
Concord	Micropolitan Statistical Area
TEXAS	State
HARRIS	County
BALTIMORE*	Independent City
	Shoreline

CBSA boundaries and names are as of November 2004. All other boundaries and names are as of January 1, 2002.

NORTH DAKOTA - Core Based Statistical Areas and Counties

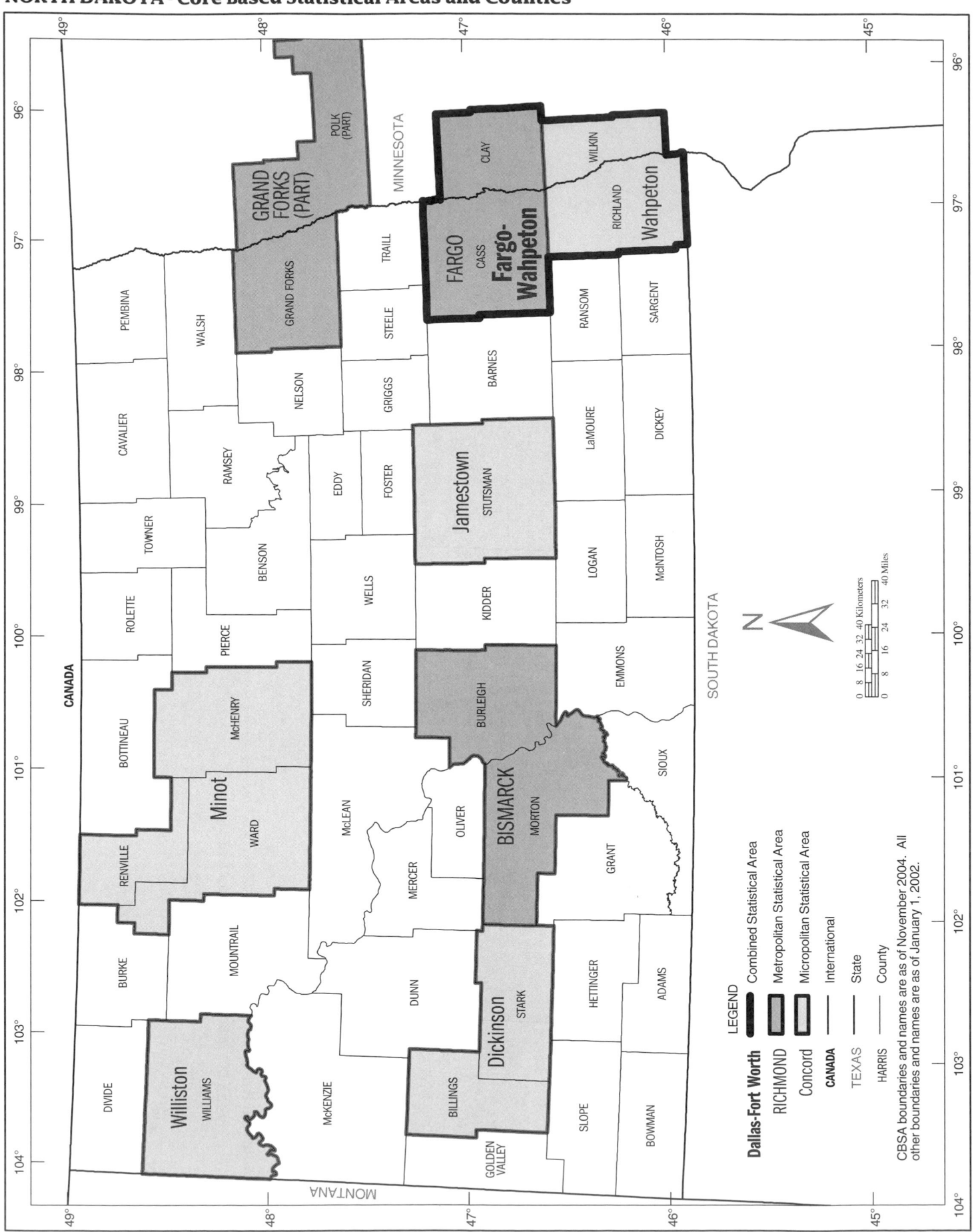

LEGEND

Dallas-Fort Worth ▬▬ Combined Statistical Area
RICHMOND Metropolitan Statistical Area
Concord Micropolitan Statistical Area
CANADA International
TEXAS State
HARRIS County

CBSA boundaries and names are as of November 2004. All other boundaries and names are as of January 1, 2002.

U.S. DEPARTMENT OF COMMERCE Economics and Statistics Administration U.S. Census Bureau

OHIO - Core Based Statistical Areas and Counties

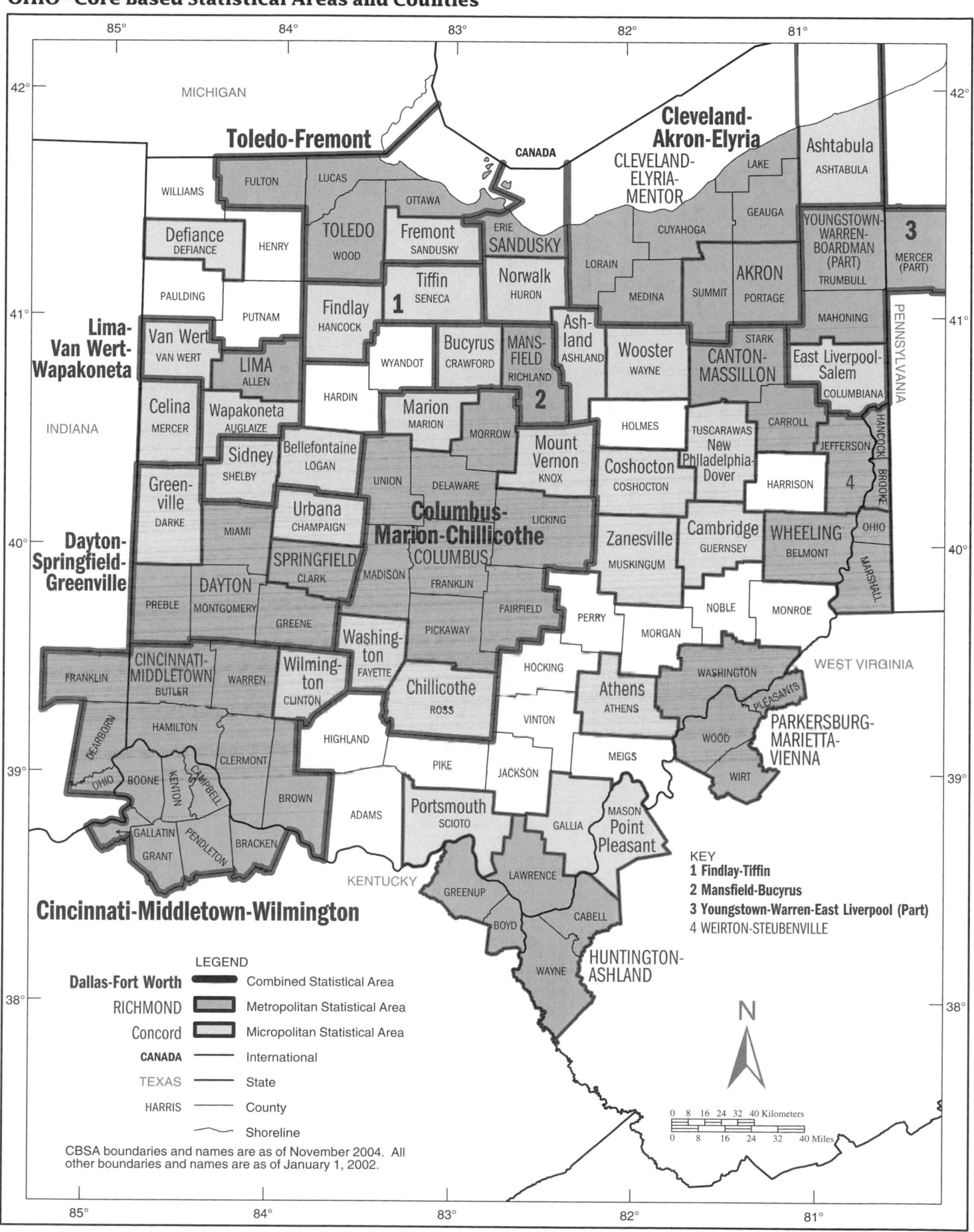

U.S. DEPARTMENT OF COMMERCE Economics and Statistics Administration U.S. Census Bureau

Appendix D

OKLAHOMA - Core Based Statistical Areas and Counties

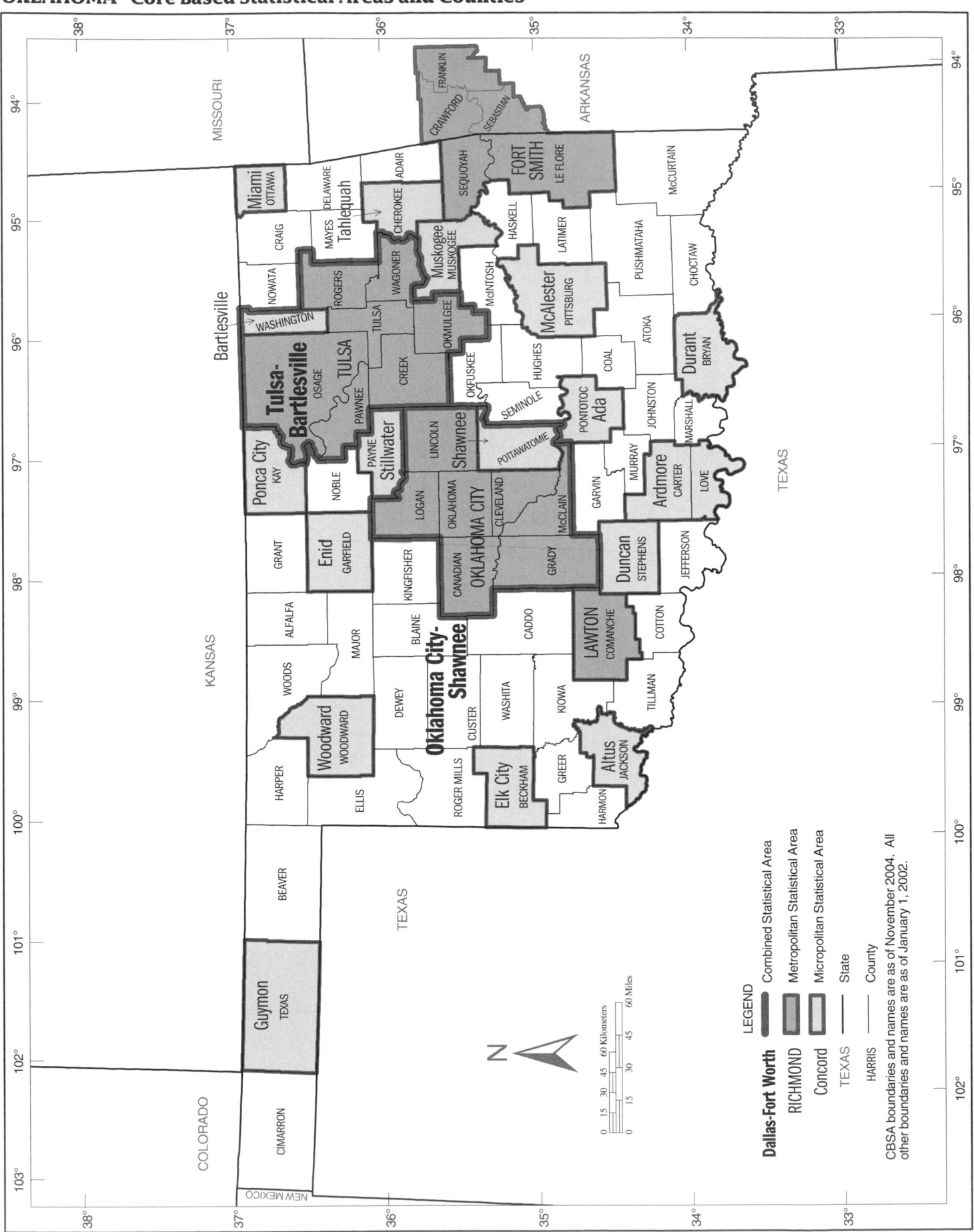

LEGEND

Dallas-Fort Worth Combined Statistical Area
RICHMOND Metropolitan Statistical Area
Concord Micropolitan Statistical Area
TEXAS State
HARRIS County

CBSA boundaries and names are as of November 2004. All other boundaries and names are as of January 1, 2002.

OREGON - Core Based Statistical Areas and Counties

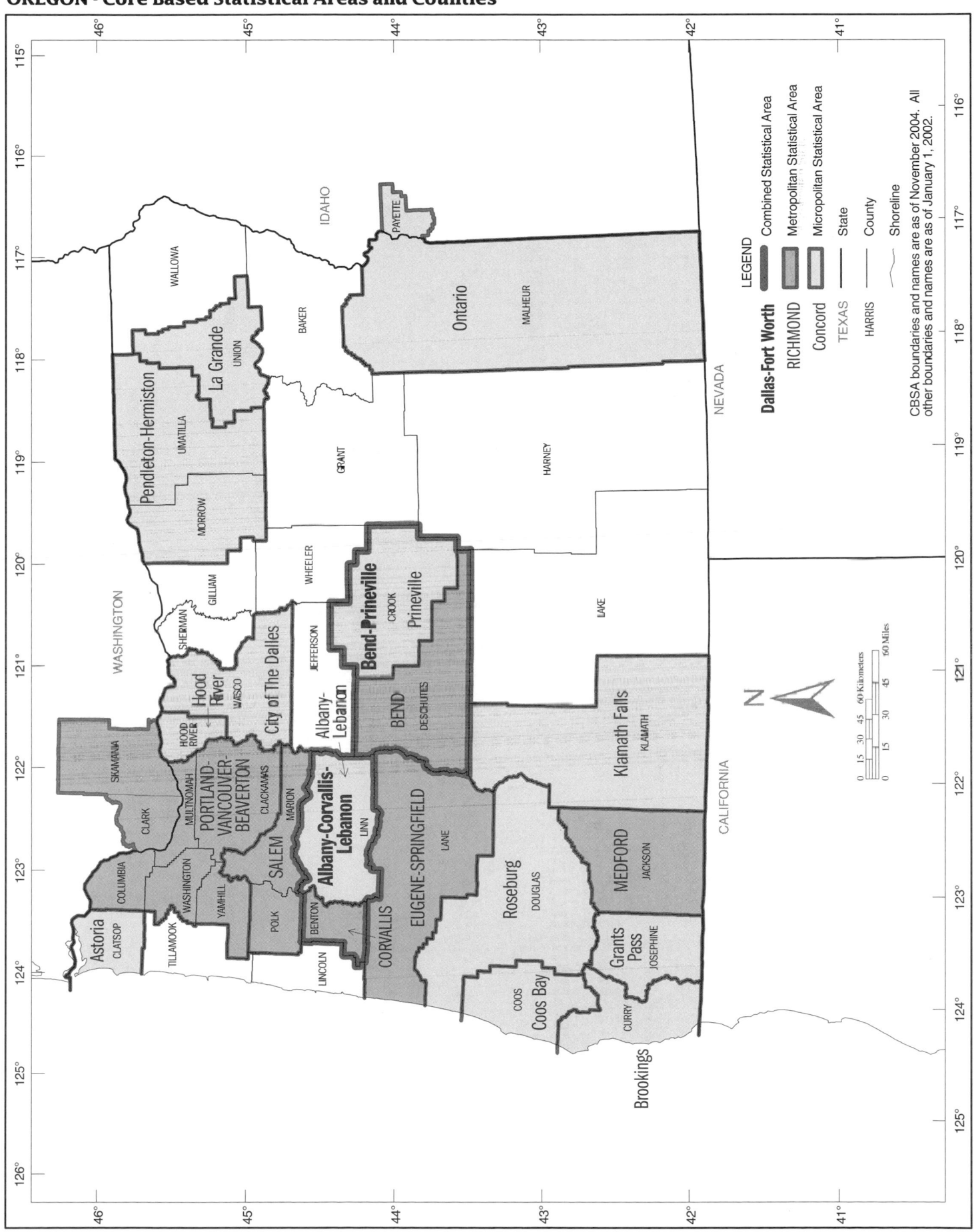

LEGEND

Combined Statistical Area
Metropolitan Statistical Area
Micropolitan Statistical Area
State
County
Shoreline

Dallas-Fort Worth
RICHMOND
Concord
TEXAS
HARRIS

CBSA boundaries and names are as of November 2004. All other boundaries and names are as of January 1, 2002.

PENNSYLVANIA - Core Based Statistical Areas and Counties

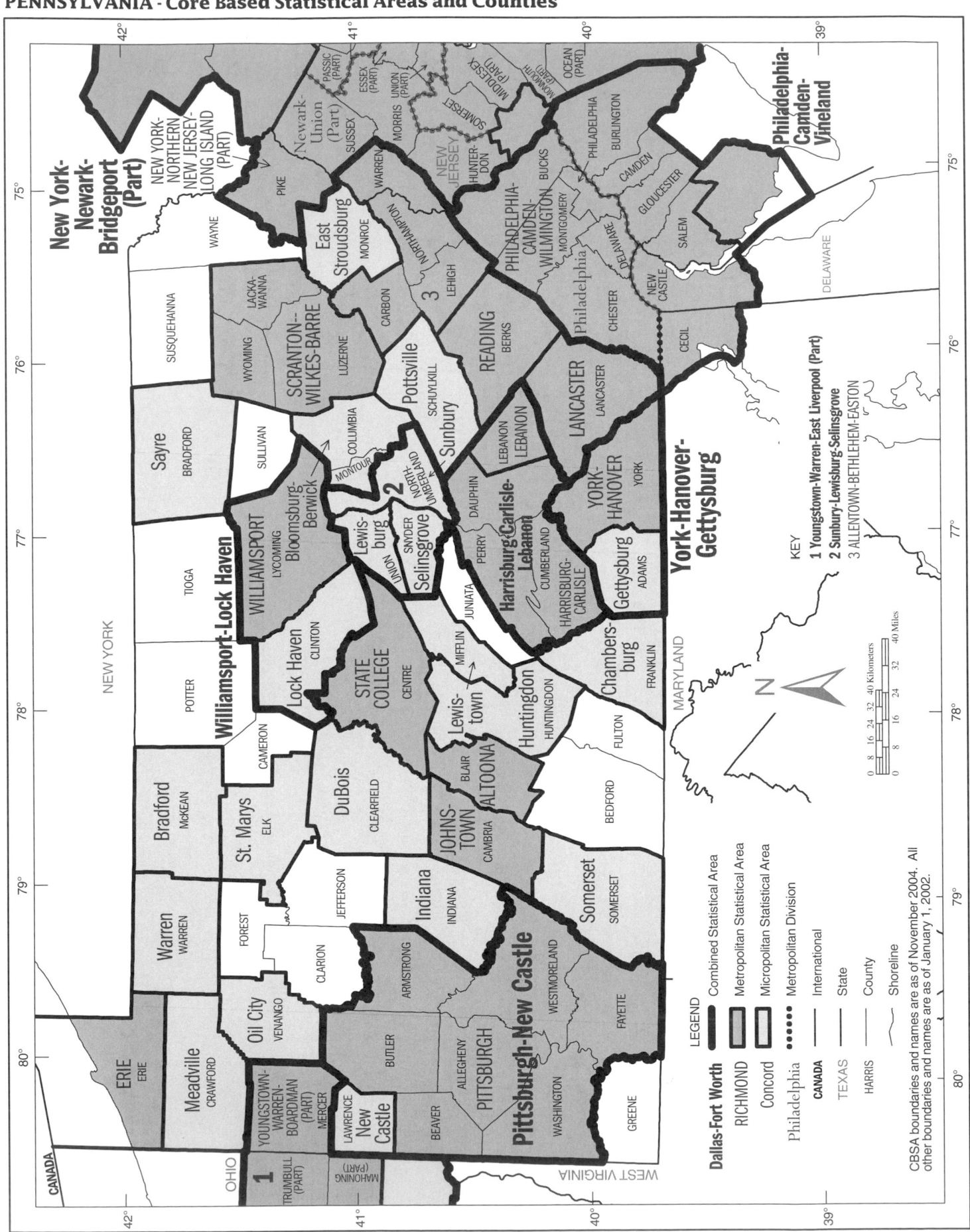

U.S. DEPARTMENT OF COMMERCE Economics and Statistics Administration U.S. Census Bureau

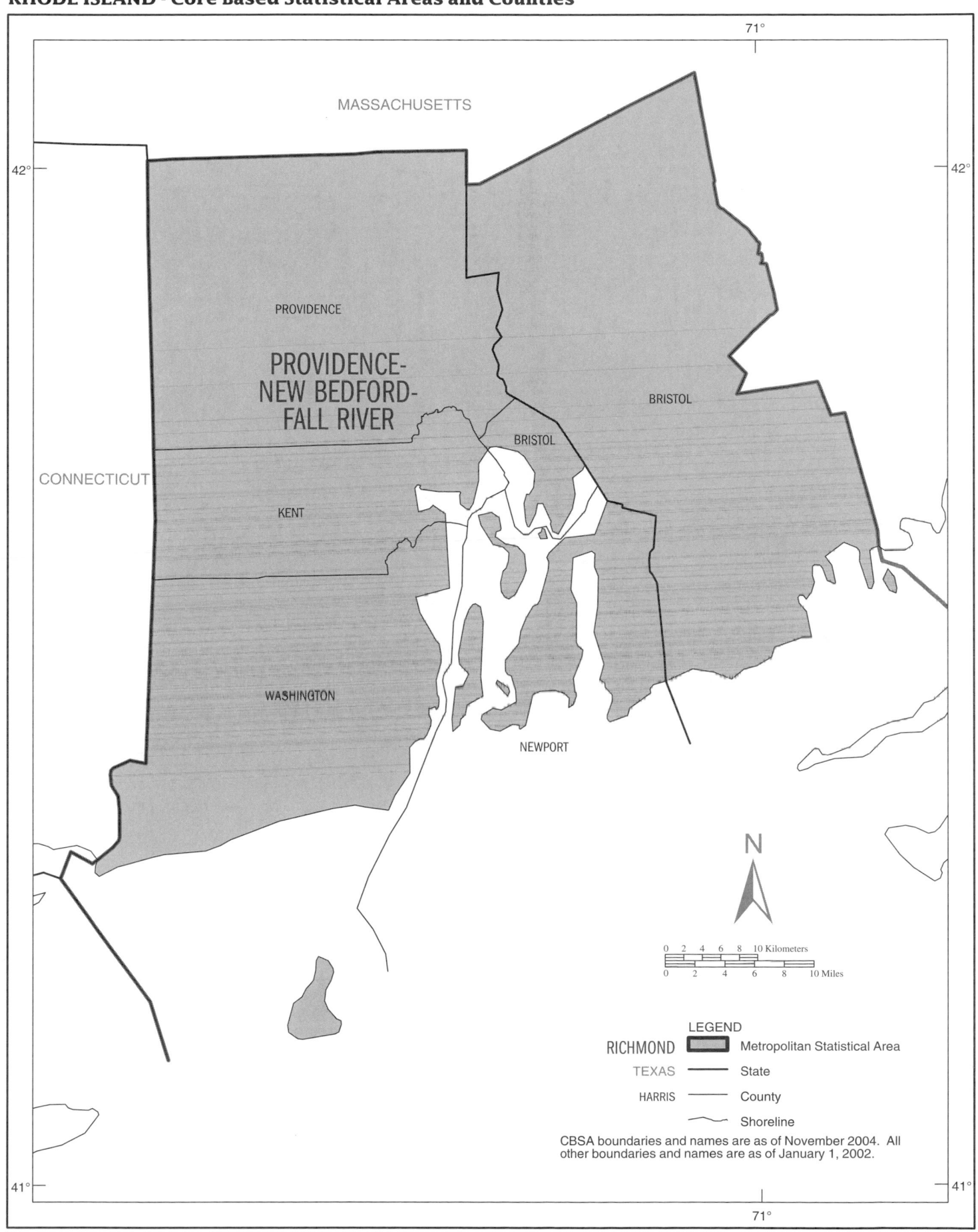

SOUTH CAROLINA - Core Based Statistical Areas and Counties

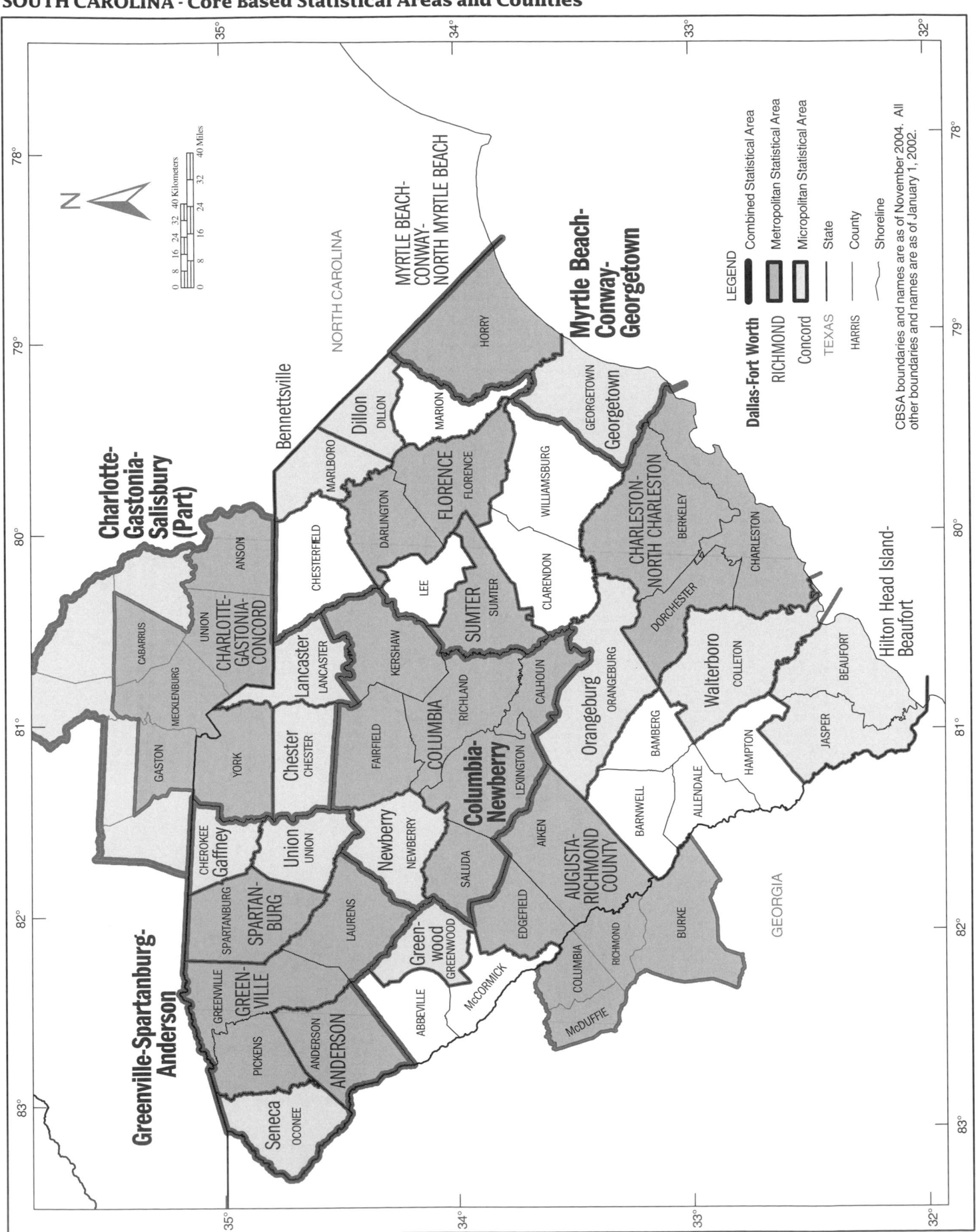

LEGEND

Combined Statistical Area
Dallas-Fort Worth

Metropolitan Statistical Area
RICHMOND

Micropolitan Statistical Area
Concord

State
TEXAS

County
HARRIS

Shoreline

CBSA boundaries and names are as of November 2004. All other boundaries and names are as of January 1, 2002.

NORTH CAROLINA

GEORGIA

Charlotte-Gastonia-Salisbury (Part)

CHARLOTTE-GASTONIA-CONCORD

Greenville-Spartanburg-Anderson

MYRTLE BEACH-CONWAY-NORTH MYRTLE BEACH

Myrtle Beach-Conway-Georgetown

Columbia-Newberry

Hilton Head Island-Beaufort

CHARLESTON-NORTH CHARLESTON

AUGUSTA-RICHMOND COUNTY

SOUTH DAKOTA - Core Based Statistical Areas and Counties

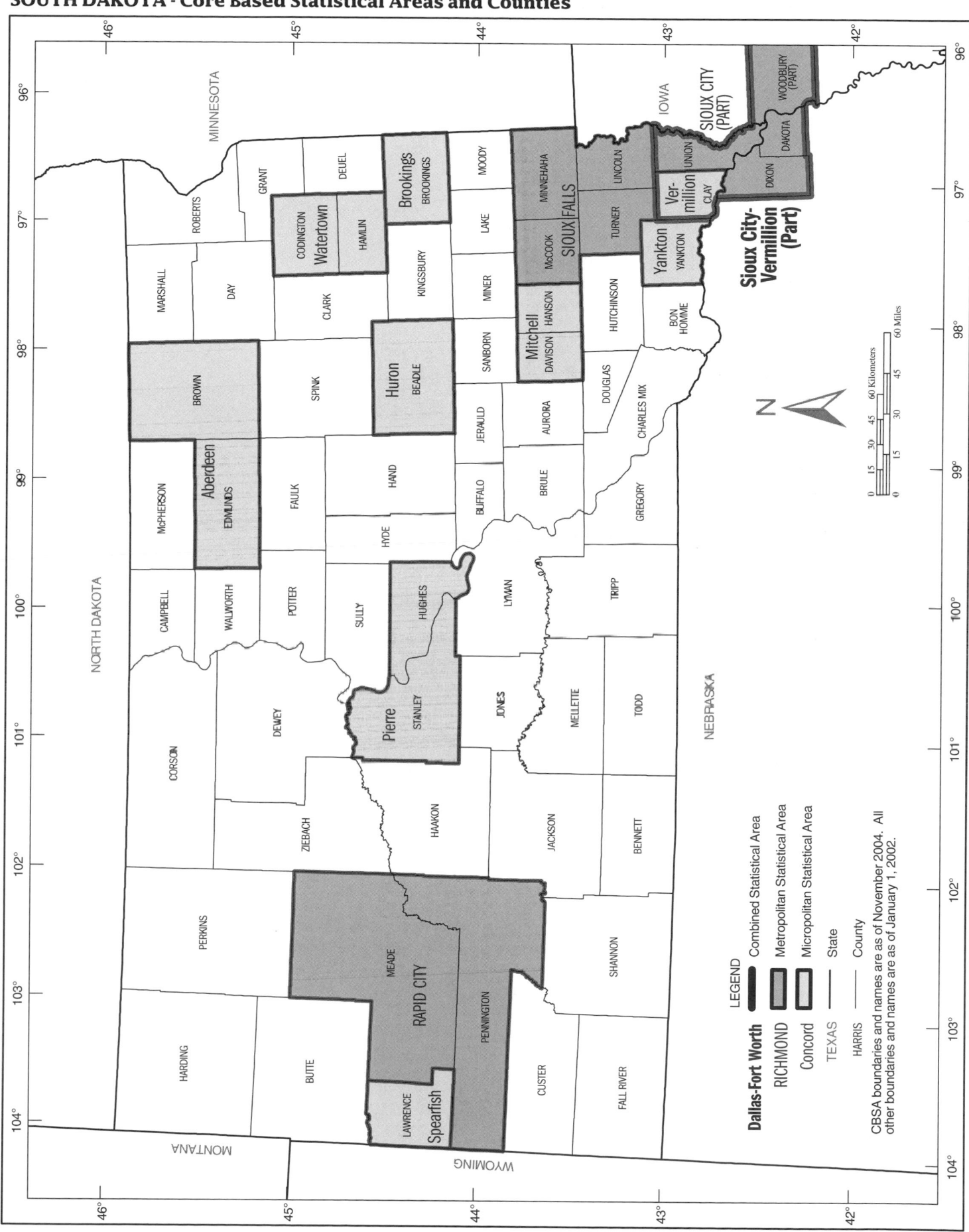

U.S. DEPARTMENT OF COMMERCE Economics and Statistics Administration U.S. Census Bureau

Appendix D

D-45

TENNESSEE - Core Based Statistical Areas, Counties, and Independent City

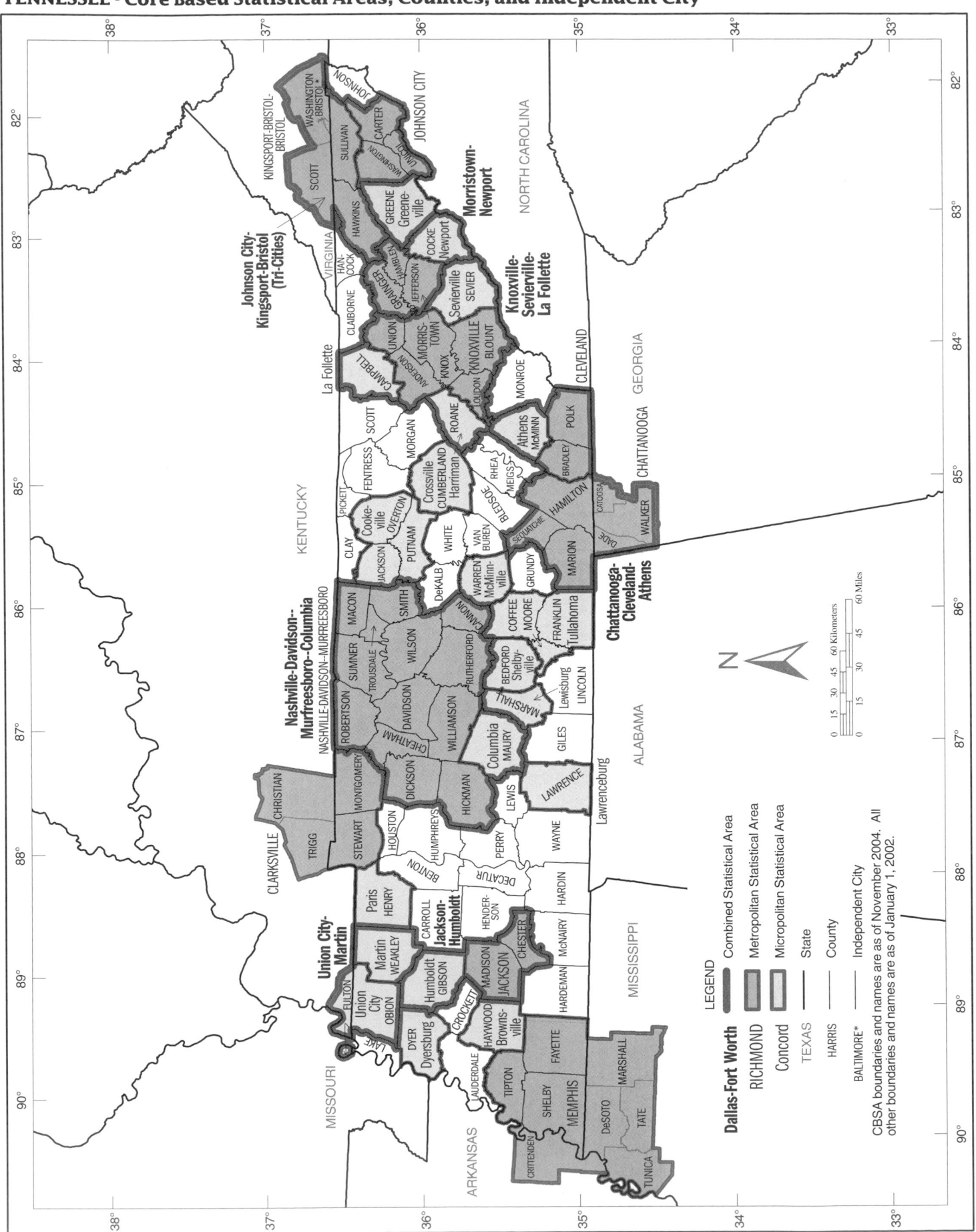

TEXAS - Core Based Statistical Areas and Counties

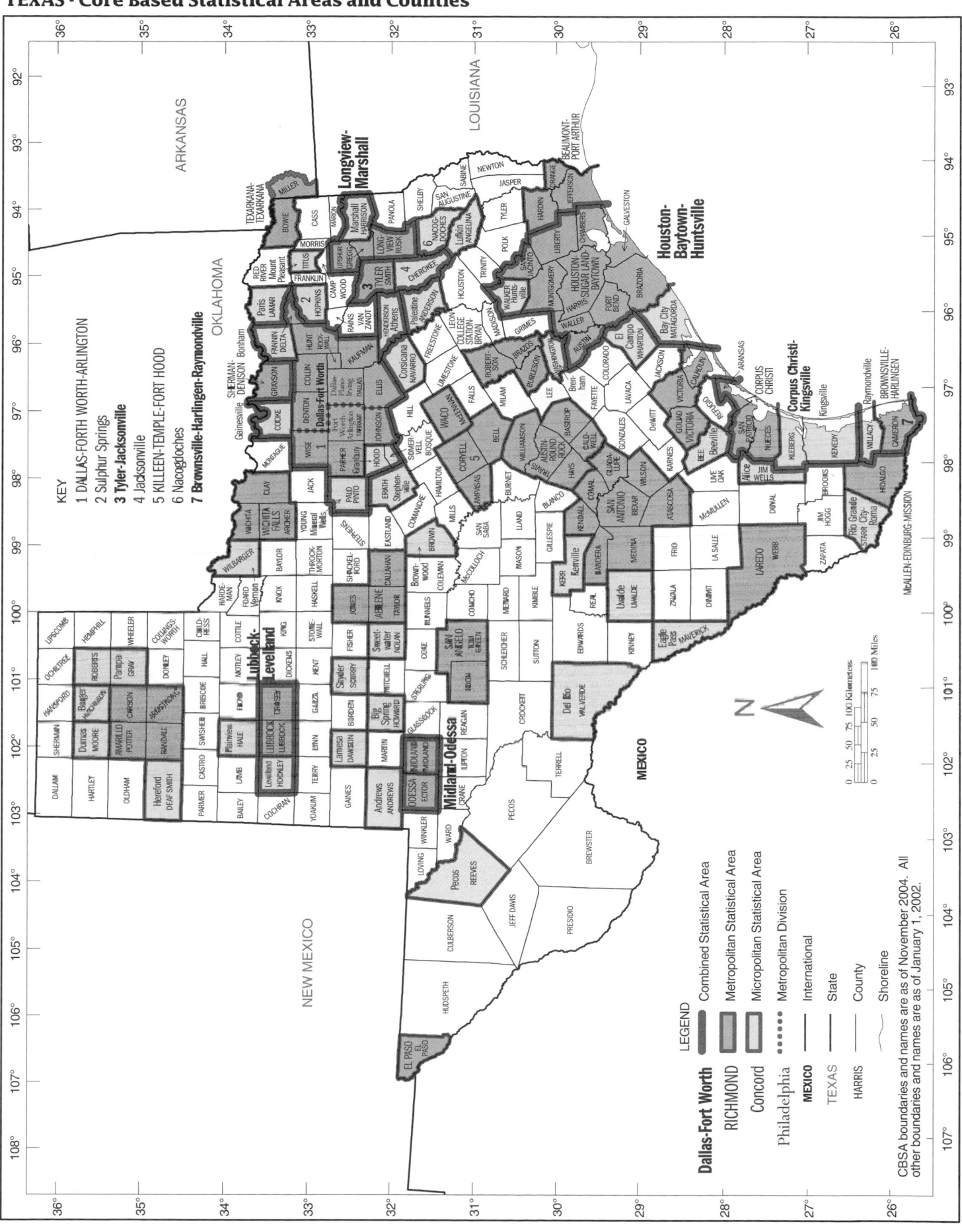

UTAH - Core Based Statistical Areas and Counties

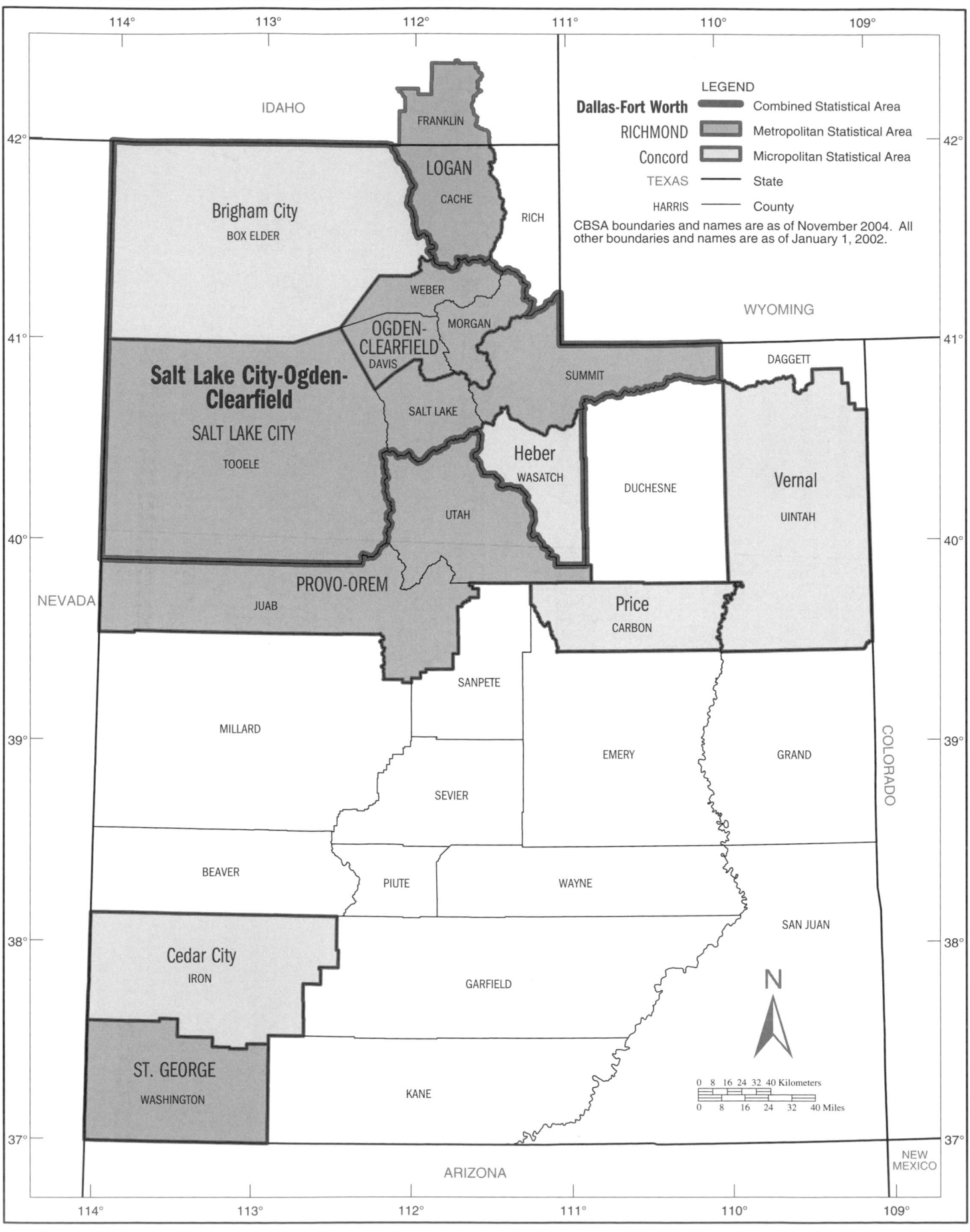

LEGEND

Dallas-Fort Worth	Combined Statistical Area
RICHMOND	Metropolitan Statistical Area
Concord	Micropolitan Statistical Area
TEXAS	State
HARRIS	County

CBSA boundaries and names are as of November 2004. All other boundaries and names are as of January 1, 2002.

VERMONT - Core Based Statistical Areas and Counties

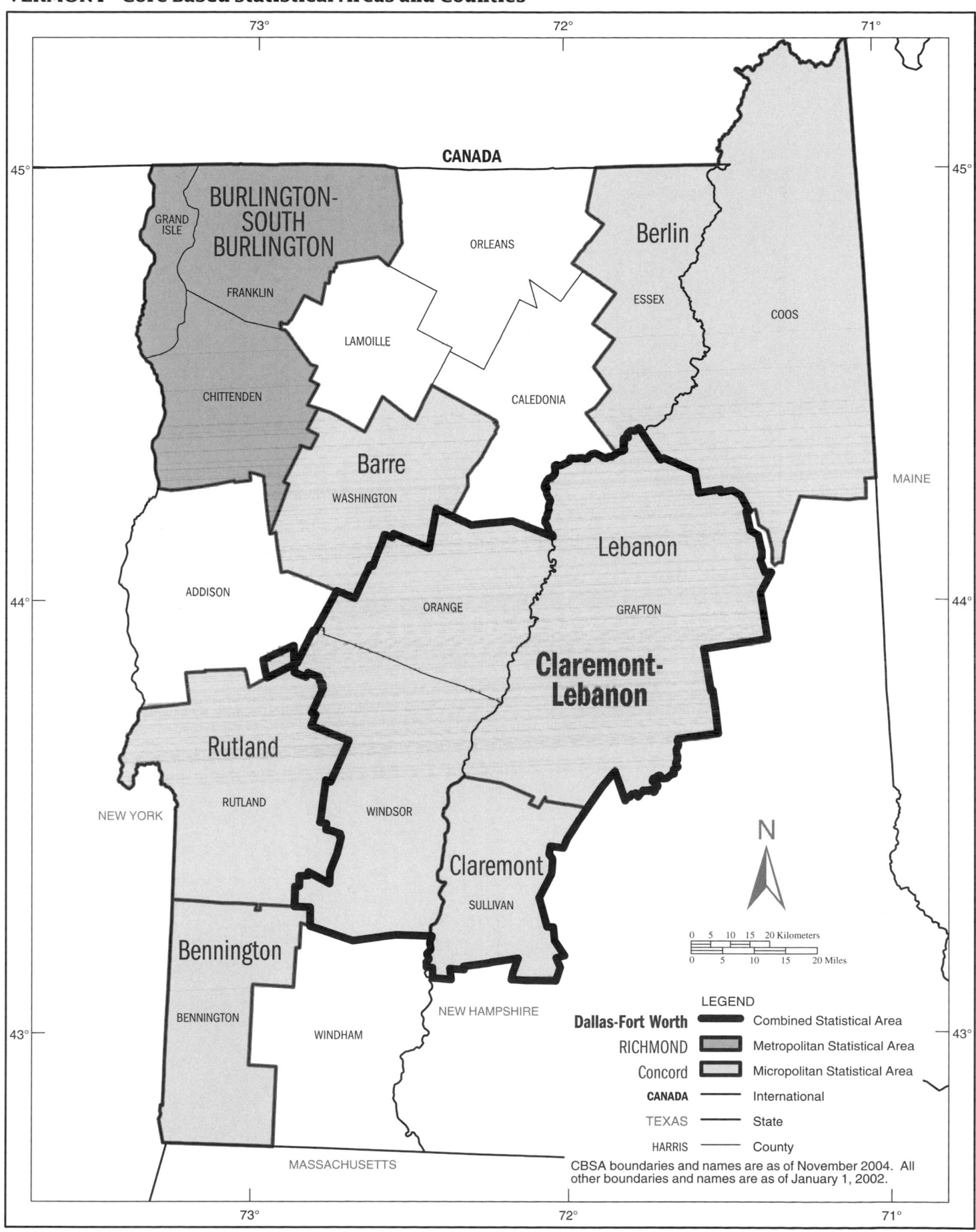

CANADA

73°   72°   71°

45°

BURLINGTON-
SOUTH
BURLINGTON

GRAND
ISLE

ORLEANS

Berlin

FRANKLIN

ESSEX

COOS

LAMOILLE

CHITTENDEN

CALEDONIA

MAINE

Barre

WASHINGTON

Lebanon

44°

ADDISON

ORANGE

GRAFTON

Claremont-
Lebanon

Rutland

RUTLAND

WINDSOR

NEW YORK

Claremont

SULLIVAN

0 5 10 15 20 Kilometers
0 5   10   15   20 Miles

Bennington

NEW HAMPSHIRE

43°

BENNINGTON

WINDHAM

LEGEND

Dallas-Fort Worth ▬▬▬ Combined Statistical Area

RICHMOND ▰ Metropolitan Statistical Area

Concord ▱ Micropolitan Statistical Area

CANADA ——— International

TEXAS ——— State

HARRIS ——— County

CBSA boundaries and names are as of November 2004. All
other boundaries and names are as of January 1, 2002.

MASSACHUSETTS

73°   72°   71°

VIRGINIA - Core Based Statistical Areas, District of Columbia, Counties, and Independent Cities

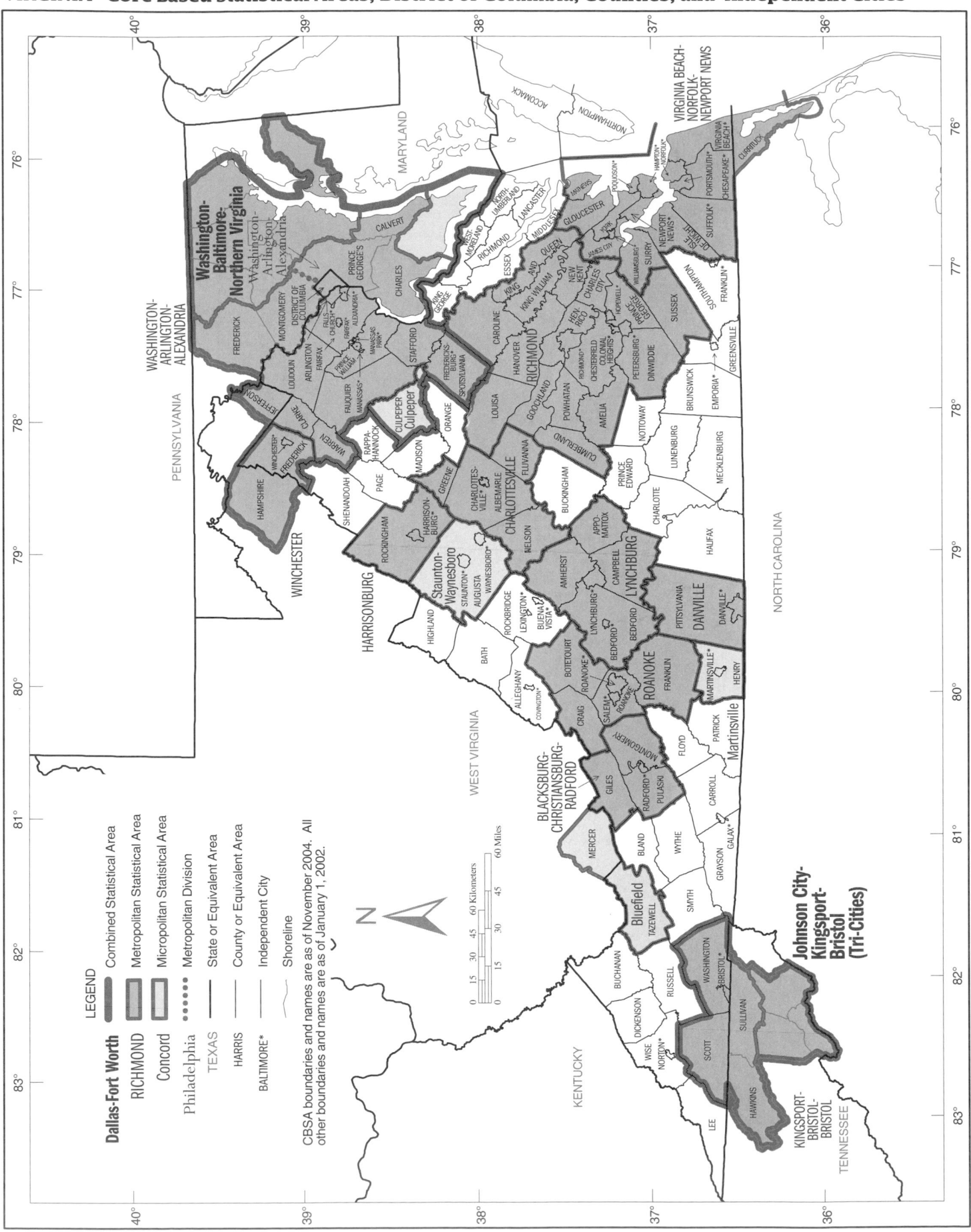

WASHINGTON - Core Based Statistical Areas and Counties

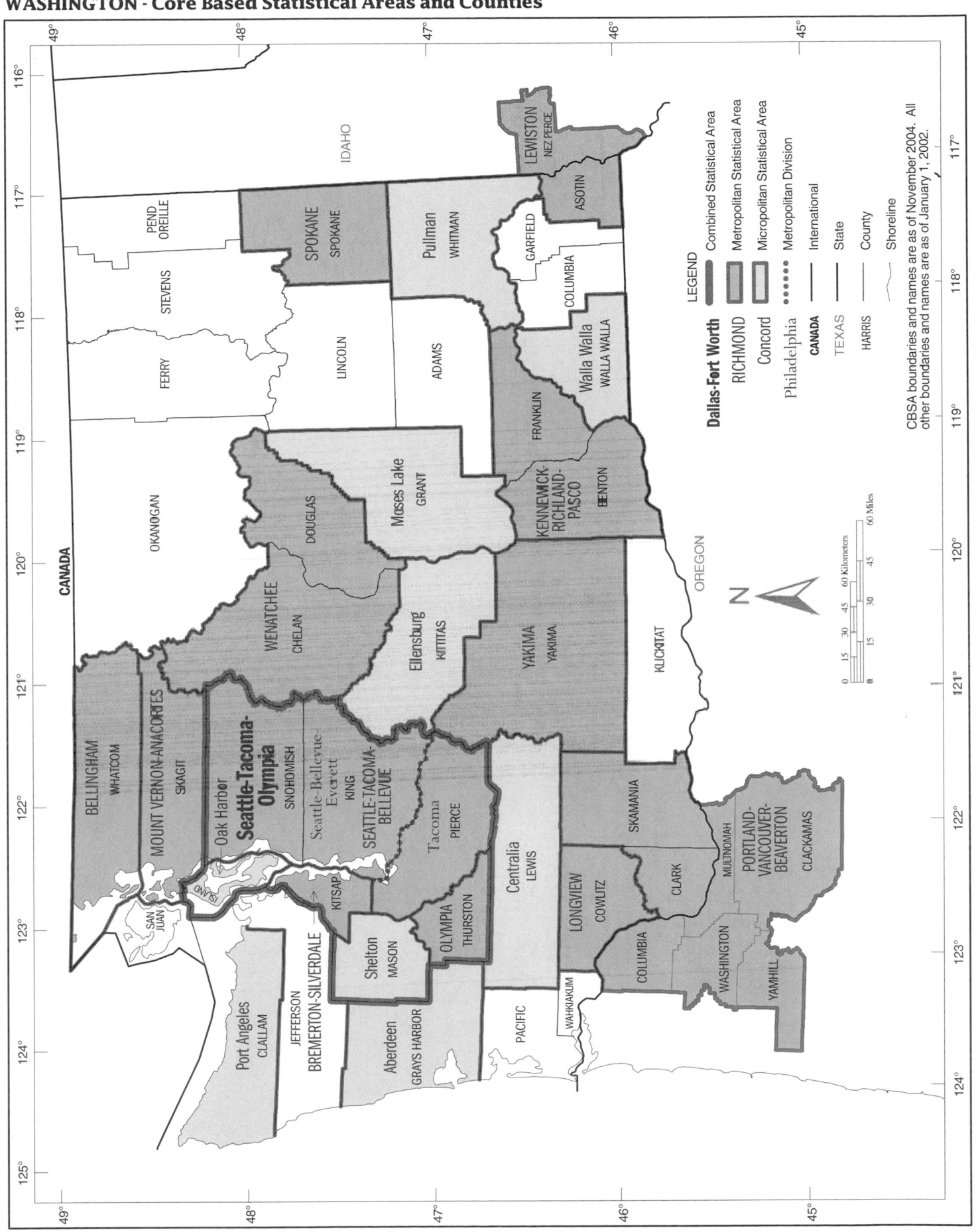

LEGEND

Combined Statistical Area — Dallas-Fort Worth
Metropolitan Statistical Area — RICHMOND
Micropolitan Statistical Area — Concord
Metropolitan Division — Philadelphia
International — CANADA
State — TEXAS
County — HARRIS
Shoreline

CBSA boundaries and names are as of November 2004. All other boundaries and names are as of January 1, 2002.

WEST VIRGINIA - Core Based Statistical Areas, District of Columbia, Counties, and Independent Cities

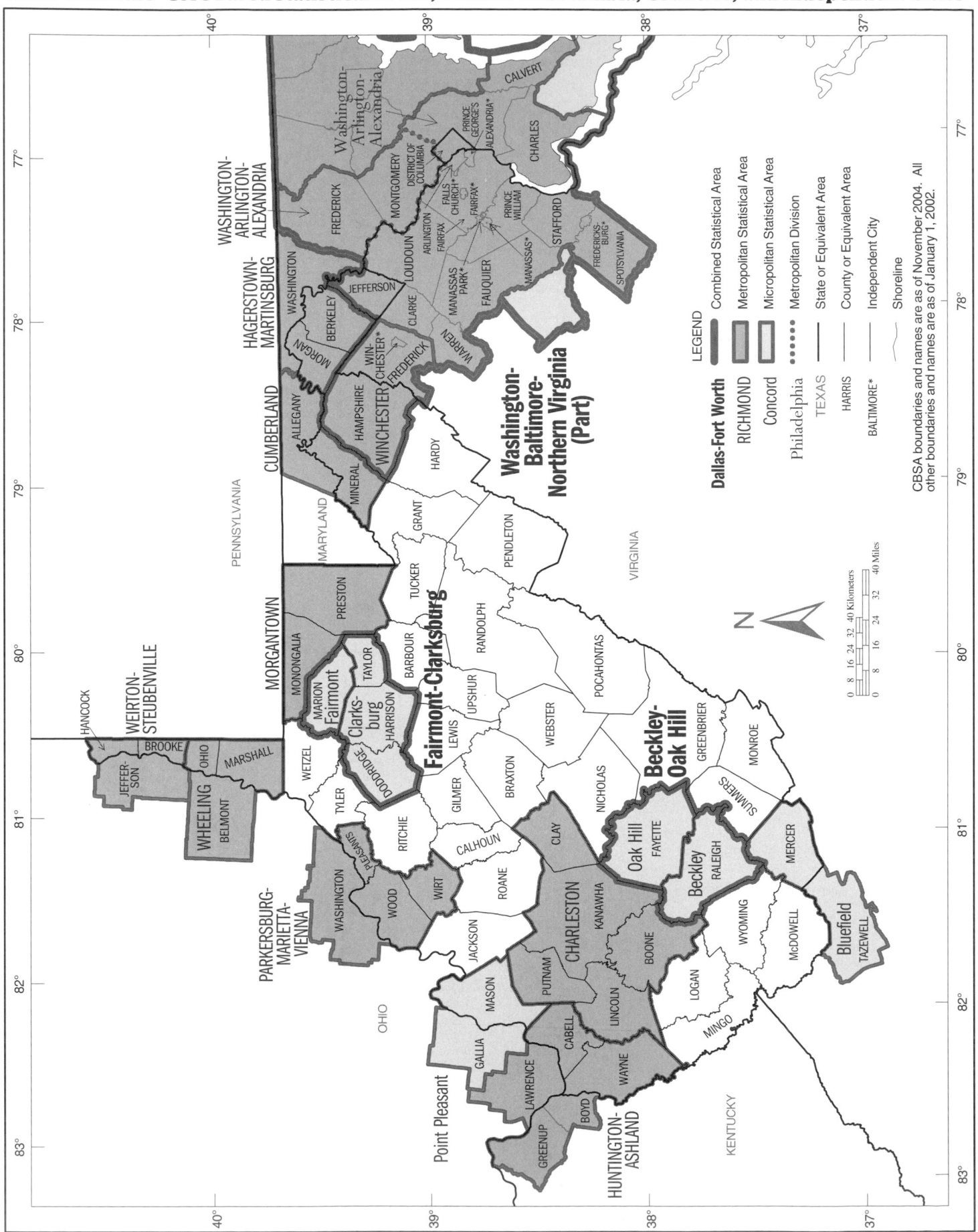

LEGEND

Combined Statistical Area
Metropolitan Statistical Area
Micropolitan Statistical Area
Metropolitan Division
State or Equivalent Area
County or Equivalent Area
Independent City
Shoreline

Dallas-Fort Worth
RICHMOND
Philadelphia
TEXAS
HARRIS
BALTIMORE*

Concord

CBSA boundaries and names are as of November 2004. All other boundaries and names are as of January 1, 2002.

0 8 16 24 32 40 Miles
0 8 16 24 32 40 Kilometers

WISCONSIN - Core Based Statistical Areas and Counties

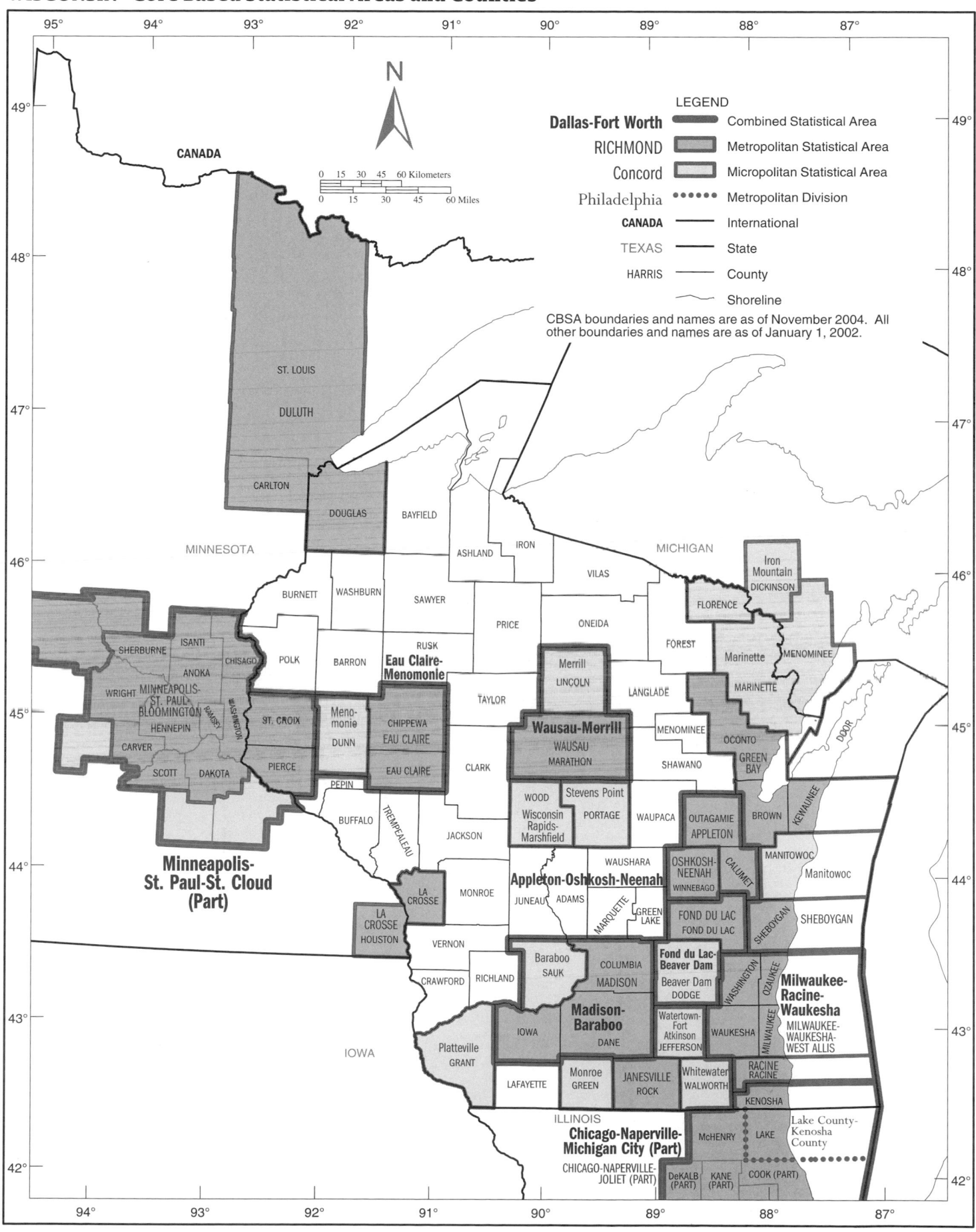

WYOMING - Core Based Statistical Areas and Counties

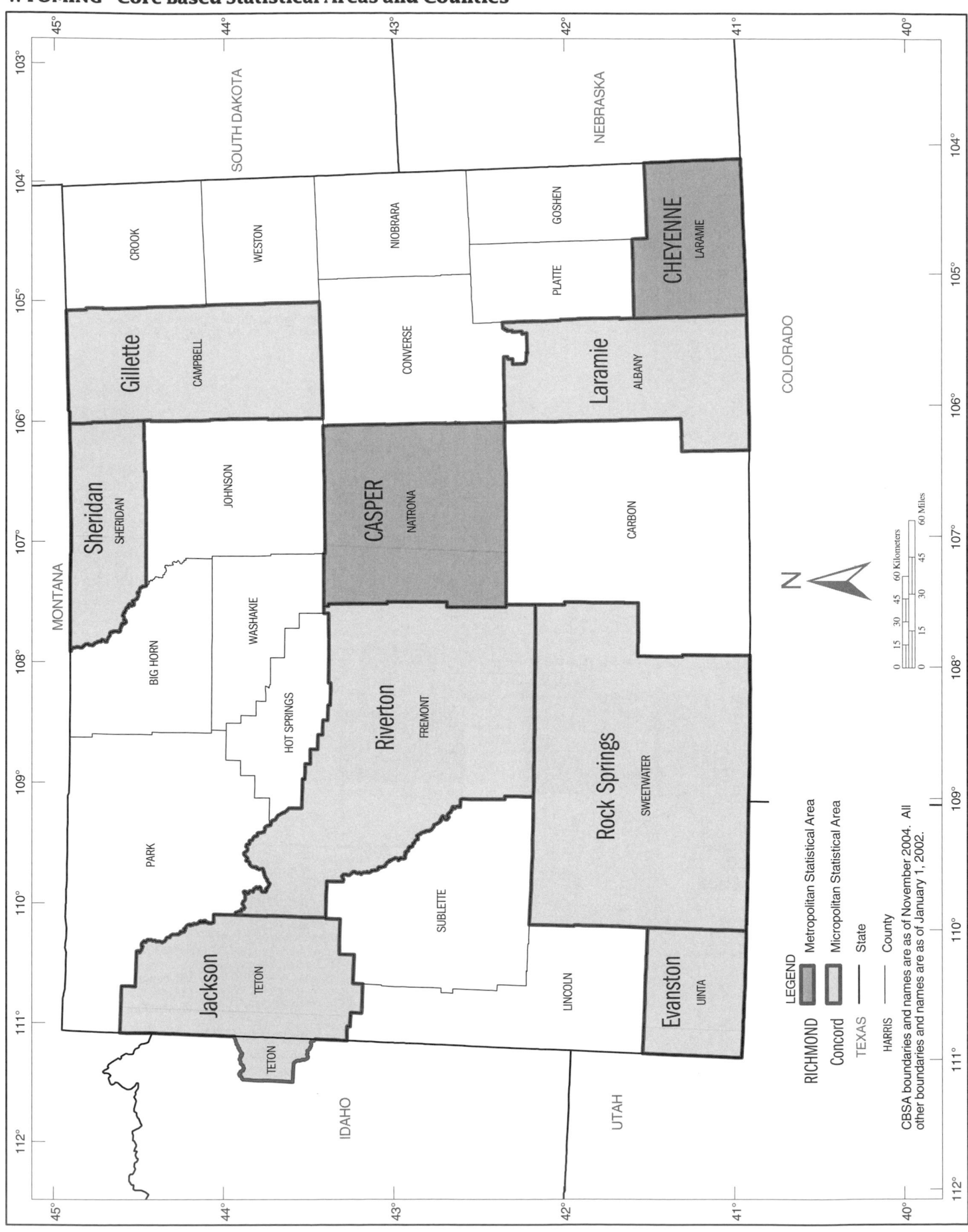

SOUTH DAKOTA

NEBRASKA

CROOK

WESTON

NIOBRARA

GOSHEN

PLATTE

CHEYENNE
LARAMIE

COLORADO

Gillette
CAMPBELL

CONVERSE

Laramie
ALBANY

Sheridan
SHERIDAN

MONTANA

JOHNSON

CASPER
NATRONA

CARBON

N

BIG HORN

WASHAKIE

HOT SPRINGS

Riverton
FREMONT

Rock Springs
SWEETWATER

PARK

SUBLETTE

Jackson
TETON

LINCOLN

Evanston
UINTA

TETON

IDAHO

UTAH

LEGEND

RICHMOND   Metropolitan Statistical Area

Concord   Micropolitan Statistical Area

TEXAS   State

HARRIS   County

CBSA boundaries and names are as of November 2004. All
other boundaries and names are as of January 1, 2002.

0 15 30 45 60 Kilometers

0 15 30 45 60 Miles

APPENDIX E
CITIES BY COUNTY

The following table is arranged alphabetically by state. Under each state heading are listed all cities with a 2010 census population over 25,000 along with their component counties and the population in each component.

State Code	Place Code	County Code	Geographic Area Name	2010 Census Population	State Code	Place Code	County Code	Geographic Area Name	2010 Census Population
01			**ALABAMA**	4 779 736	01	78552		Vestavia Hills city	34 033
01	00820		Alabaster city	30 352	01	78552	073	Jefferson County	34 019
01	00820	117	Shelby County	30 352	01	78552	117	Shelby County	14
01	03076		Auburn city	53 380	02			**ALASKA**	710 231
01	03076	081	Lee County	53 380	02	03000		Anchorage municipality	291 826
01	05980		Bessemer city	27 456	02	03000	020	Anchorage Municipality	291 826
01	05980	073	Jefferson County	27 456	02	24230		Fairbanks city	31 535
01	07000		Birmingham city	212 237	02	24230	090	Fairbanks North Star Borough	31 535
01	07000	073	Jefferson County	210 609	02	36400		Juneau city and borough	31 275
01	07000	117	Shelby County	1 628	02	36400	110	Juneau City and Borough	31 275
01	20104		Decatur city	55 683	04			**ARIZONA**	6 392 017
01	20104	083	Limestone County	84	04	02830		Apache Junction city	35 840
01	20104	103	Morgan County	55 599	04	02830	013	Maricopa County	294
01	21184		Dothan city	65 496	04	02830	021	Pinal County	35 546
01	21184	045	Dale County	887	04	04720		Avondale city	76 238
01	21184	067	Henry County	5	04	04720	013	Maricopa County	76 238
01	21184	069	Houston County	64 604	04	07940		Buckeye town	50 876
01	24184		Enterprise city	26 562	04	07940	013	Maricopa County	50 876
01	24184	031	Coffee County	26 139	04	08220		Bullhead City city	39 540
01	24184	045	Dale County	423	04	08220	015	Mohave County	39 540
01	26896		Florence city	39 319	04	10530		Casa Grande city	48 571
01	26896	077	Lauderdale County	39 319	04	10530	021	Pinal County	48 571
01	28696		Gadsden city	36 856	04	12000		Chandler city	236 123
01	28696	055	Etowah County	36 856	04	12000	013	Maricopa County	236 123
01	35800		Homewood city	25 167	04	22220		El Mirage city	31 797
01	35800	073	Jefferson County	25 167	04	22220	013	Maricopa County	31 797
01	35896		Hoover city	81 619	04	23620		Flagstaff city	65 870
01	35896	073	Jefferson County	58 582	04	23620	005	Coconino County	65 870
01	35896	117	Shelby County	23 037	04	23760		Florence town	25 536
01	37000		Huntsville city	180 105	04	23760	021	Pinal County	25 536
01	37000	083	Limestone County	1 521	04	27400		Gilbert town	208 453
01	37000	089	Madison County	178 584	04	27400	013	Maricopa County	208 453
01	45784		Madison city	42 938	04	27820		Glendale city	226 721
01	45784	083	Limestone County	3 453	04	27820	013	Maricopa County	226 721
01	45784	089	Madison County	39 485	04	28380		Goodyear city	65 275
01	50000		Mobile city	195 111	04	28380	013	Maricopa County	65 275
01	50000	097	Mobile County	195 111	04	37620		Kingman city	28 068
01	51000		Montgomery city	205 764	04	37620	015	Mohave County	28 068
01	51000	101	Montgomery County	205 764	04	39370		Lake Havasu City city	52 527
01	57048		Opelika city	26 477	04	39370	015	Mohave County	52 527
01	57048	081	Lee County	26 477	04	44270		Marana town	34 961
01	59472		Phenix City city	32 822	04	44270	019	Pima County	34 961
01	59472	081	Lee County	4 153	04	44270	021	Pinal County	0
01	59472	113	Russell County	28 669	04	44410		Maricopa city	43 482
01	62328		Prattville city	33 960	04	44410	021	Pinal County	43 482
01	62328	001	Autauga County	32 168	04	46000		Mesa city	439 041
01	62328	051	Elmore County	1 792	04	46000	013	Maricopa County	439 041
01	77256		Tuscaloosa city	90 468					
01	77256	125	Tuscaloosa County	90 468					

Cities by County–*Continued*

State Code	Place Code	County Code	Geographic Area Name	2010 Census Population	State Code	Place Code	County Code	Geographic Area Name	2010 Census Population
04	51600		Oro Valley town	41 011	05	41000		Little Rock city	193 524
04	51600	019	Pima County	41 011	05	41000	119	Pulaski County	193 524
04	54050		Peoria city	154 065	05	50450		North Little Rock city	62 304
04	54050	013	Maricopa County	154 058	05	50450	119	Pulaski County	62 304
04	54050	025	Yavapai County	7					
					05	53390		Paragould city	26 113
04	55000		Phoenix city	1 445 632	05	53390	055	Greene County	26 113
04	55000	013	Maricopa County	1 445 632					
					05	55310		Pine Bluff city	49 083
04	57380		Prescott city	39 843	05	55310	069	Jefferson County	49 083
04	57380	025	Yavapai County	39 843					
					05	60410		Rogers city	55 964
04	57450		Prescott Valley town	38 822	05	60410	007	Benton County	55 964
04	57450	025	Yavapai County	38 822					
					05	61670		Russellville city	27 920
04	58150		Queen Creek town	26 361	05	61670	115	Pope County	27 920
04	58150	013	Maricopa County	25 912					
04	58150	021	Pinal County	449	05	63800		Sherwood city	29 523
					05	63800	119	Pulaski County	29 523
04	62140		Sahuarita town	25 259					
04	62140	019	Pima County	25 259	05	66080		Springdale city	69 797
					05	66080	007	Benton County	6 054
04	63470		San Luis city	25 505	05	66080	143	Washington County	63 743
04	63470	027	Yuma County	25 505					
					05	68810		Texarkana city	29 919
04	65000		Scottsdale city	217 385	05	68810	091	Miller County	29 919
04	65000	013	Maricopa County	217 385					
					05	74540		West Memphis city	26 245
04	66820		Sierra Vista city	43 888	05	74540	035	Crittenden County	26 245
04	66820	003	Cochise County	43 888					
					06			**CALIFORNIA**	37 253 956
04	71510		Surprise city	117 517	06	00296		Adelanto city	31 765
04	71510	013	Maricopa County	117 517	06	00296	071	San Bernardino County	31 765
04	73000		Tempe city	161 719	06	00562		Alameda city	73 812
04	73000	013	Maricopa County	161 719	06	00562	001	Alameda County	73 812
04	77000		Tucson city	520 116	06	00884		Alhambra city	83 089
04	77000	019	Pima County	520 116	06	00884	037	Los Angeles County	83 089
04	85540		Yuma city	93 064	06	00947		Aliso Viejo city	47 823
04	85540	027	Yuma County	93 064	06	00947	059	Orange County	47 823
05			**ARKANSAS**	2 915 918	06	02000		Anaheim city	336 265
05	04840		Bella Vista town	26 461	06	02000	059	Orange County	336 265
05	04840	007	Benton County	26 461					
					06	02252		Antioch city	102 372
05	05290		Benton city	30 681	06	02252	013	Contra Costa County	102 372
05	05290	125	Saline County	30 681					
					06	02364		Apple Valley town	69 135
05	05320		Bentonville city	35 301	06	02364	071	San Bernardino County	69 135
05	05320	007	Benton County	35 301					
					06	02462		Arcadia city	56 364
05	15190		Conway city	58 908	06	02462	037	Los Angeles County	56 364
05	15190	045	Faulkner County	58 908					
					06	03064		Atascadero city	28 310
05	23290		Fayetteville city	73 580	06	03064	079	San Luis Obispo County	28 310
05	23290	143	Washington County	73 580					
					06	03162		Atwater city	28 168
05	24550		Fort Smith city	86 209	06	03162	047	Merced County	28 168
05	24550	131	Sebastian County	86 209					
					06	03386		Azusa city	46 361
05	33400		Hot Springs city	35 193	06	03386	037	Los Angeles County	46 361
05	33400	051	Garland County	35 193					
					06	03526		Bakersfield city	347 483
05	34750		Jacksonville city	28 364	06	03526	029	Kern County	347 483
05	34750	119	Pulaski County	28 364					
					06	03666		Baldwin Park city	75 390
05	35710		Jonesboro city	67 263	06	03666	037	Los Angeles County	75 390
05	35710	031	Craighead County	67 263					

State Code	Place Code	County Code	Geographic Area Name	2010 Census Population	State Code	Place Code	County Code	Geographic Area Name	2010 Census Population
06	03820		Banning city	29 603	06	13214		Chino Hills city	74 799
06	03820	065	Riverside County	29 603	06	13214	071	San Bernardino County	74 799
06	04758		Beaumont city	36 877	06	13392		Chula Vista city	243 916
06	04758	065	Riverside County	36 877	06	13392	073	San Diego County	243 916
06	04870		Bell city	35 477	06	13588		Citrus Heights city	83 301
06	04870	037	Los Angeles County	35 477	06	13588	067	Sacramento County	83 301
06	04982		Bellflower city	76 616	06	13756		Claremont city	34 926
06	04982	037	Los Angeles County	76 616	06	13756	037	Los Angeles County	34 926
06	04996		Bell Gardens city	42 072	06	14218		Clovis city	95 631
06	04996	037	Los Angeles County	42 072	06	14218	019	Fresno County	95 631
06	05108		Belmont city	25 835	06	14260		Coachella city	40 704
06	05108	081	San Mateo County	25 835	06	14260	065	Riverside County	40 704
06	05290		Benicia city	26 997	06	14890		Colton city	52 154
06	05290	095	Solano County	26 997	06	14890	071	San Bernardino County	52 154
06	06000		Berkeley city	112 580	06	15044		Compton city	96 455
06	06000	001	Alameda County	112 580	06	15044	037	Los Angeles County	96 455
06	06308		Beverly Hills city	34 109	06	16000		Concord city	122 067
06	06308	037	Los Angeles County	34 109	06	16000	013	Contra Costa County	122 067
06	08100		Brea city	39 282	06	16350		Corona city	152 374
06	08100	059	Orange County	39 282	06	16350	065	Riverside County	152 374
06	08142		Brentwood city	51 481	06	16532		Costa Mesa city	109 960
06	08142	013	Contra Costa County	51 481	06	16532	059	Orange County	109 960
06	08786		Buena Park city	80 530	06	16742		Covina city	47 796
06	08786	059	Orange County	80 530	06	16742	037	Los Angeles County	47 796
06	08954		Burbank city	103 340	06	17568		Culver City city	38 883
06	08954	037	Los Angeles County	103 340	06	17568	037	Los Angeles County	38 883
06	09066		Burlingame city	28 806	06	17610		Cupertino city	58 302
06	09066	081	San Mateo County	28 806	06	17610	085	Santa Clara County	58 302
06	09710		Calexico city	38 572	06	17750		Cypress city	47 802
06	09710	025	Imperial County	38 572	06	17750	059	Orange County	47 802
06	10046		Camarillo city	65 201	06	17918		Daly City city	101 123
06	10046	111	Ventura County	65 201	06	17918	081	San Mateo County	101 123
06	10345		Campbell city	39 349	06	17946		Dana Point city	33 351
06	10345	085	Santa Clara County	39 349	06	17946	059	Orange County	33 351
06	11194		Carlsbad city	105 328	06	17988		Danville town	42 039
06	11194	073	San Diego County	105 328	06	17988	013	Contra Costa County	42 039
06	11530		Carson city	91 714	06	18100		Davis city	65 622
06	11530	037	Los Angeles County	91 714	06	18100	113	Yolo County	65 622
06	12048		Cathedral City city	51 200	06	18394		Delano city	53 041
06	12048	065	Riverside County	51 200	06	18394	029	Kern County	53 041
06	12524		Ceres city	45 417	06	18996		Desert Hot Springs city	25 938
06	12524	099	Stanislaus County	45 417	06	18996	065	Riverside County	25 938
06	12552		Cerritos city	49 041	06	19192		Diamond Bar city	55 544
06	12552	037	Los Angeles County	49 041	06	19192	037	Los Angeles County	55 544
06	13014		Chico city	86 187	06	19766		Downey city	111 772
06	13014	007	Butte County	86 187	06	19766	037	Los Angeles County	111 772
06	13210		Chino city	77 983	06	20018		Dublin city	46 036
06	13210	071	San Bernardino County	77 983	06	20018	001	Alameda County	46 036

Cities by County—*Continued*

State Code	Place Code	County Code	Geographic Area Name	2010 Census Population	State Code	Place Code	County Code	Geographic Area Name	2010 Census Population
06	20956		East Palo Alto city	28 155	06	32548		Hawthorne city	84 293
06	20956	081	San Mateo County	28 155	06	32548	037	Los Angeles County	84 293
06	21712		El Cajon city	99 478	06	33000		Hayward city	144 186
06	21712	073	San Diego County	99 478	06	33000	001	Alameda County	144 186
06	21782		El Centro city	42 598	06	33182		Hemet city	78 657
06	21782	025	Imperial County	42 598	06	33182	065	Riverside County	78 657
06	22020		Elk Grove city	153 015	06	33434		Hesperia city	90 173
06	22020	067	Sacramento County	153 015	06	33434	071	San Bernardino County	90 173
06	22230		El Monte city	113 475	06	33588		Highland city	53 104
06	22230	037	Los Angeles County	113 475	06	33588	071	San Bernardino County	53 104
06	22300		El Paso de Robles (Paso Robles)	29 793	06	34120		Hollister city	34 928
06	22300	079	San Luis Obispo County	29 793	06	34120	069	San Benito County	34 928
06	22678		Encinitas city	59 518	06	36000		Huntington Beach city	189 992
06	22678	073	San Diego County	59 518	06	36000	059	Orange County	189 992
06	22804		Escondido city	143 911	06	36056		Huntington Park city	58 114
06	22804	073	San Diego County	143 911	06	36056	037	Los Angeles County	58 114
06	23042		Eureka city	27 191	06	36294		Imperial Beach city	26 324
06	23042	023	Humboldt County	27 191	06	36294	073	San Diego County	26 324
06	23182		Fairfield city	105 321	06	36448		Indio city	76 036
06	23182	095	Solano County	105 321	06	36448	065	Riverside County	76 036
06	24638		Folsom city	72 203	06	36546		Inglewood city	109 673
06	24638	067	Sacramento County	72 203	06	36546	037	Los Angeles County	109 673
06	24680		Fontana city	196 069	06	36770		Irvine city	212 375
06	24680	071	San Bernardino County	196 069	06	36770	059	Orange County	212 375
06	25338		Foster City city	30 567	06	39220		Laguna Hills city	30 344
06	25338	081	San Mateo County	30 567	06	39220	059	Orange County	30 344
06	25380		Fountain Valley city	55 313	06	39248		Laguna Niguel city	62 979
06	25380	059	Orange County	55 313	06	39248	059	Orange County	62 979
06	26000		Fremont city	214 089	06	39290		La Habra city	60 239
06	26000	001	Alameda County	214 089	06	39290	059	Orange County	60 239
06	27000		Fresno city	494 665	06	39486		Lake Elsinore city	51 821
06	27000	019	Fresno County	494 665	06	39486	065	Riverside County	51 821
06	28000		Fullerton city	135 161	06	39496		Lake Forest city	77 264
06	28000	059	Orange County	135 161	06	39496	059	Orange County	77 264
06	28168		Gardena city	58 829	06	39892		Lakewood city	80 048
06	28168	037	Los Angeles County	58 829	06	39892	037	Los Angeles County	80 048
06	29000		Garden Grove city	170 883	06	40004		La Mesa city	57 065
06	29000	059	Orange County	170 883	06	40004	073	San Diego County	57 065
06	29504		Gilroy city	48 821	06	40032		La Mirada city	48 527
06	29504	085	Santa Clara County	48 821	06	40032	037	Los Angeles County	48 527
06	30000		Glendale city	191 719	06	40130		Lancaster city	156 633
06	30000	037	Los Angeles County	191 719	06	40130	037	Los Angeles County	156 633
06	30014		Glendora city	50 073	06	40340		La Puente city	39 816
06	30014	037	Los Angeles County	50 073	06	40340	037	Los Angeles County	39 816
06	30378		Goleta city	29 888	06	40354		La Quinta city	37 467
06	30378	083	Santa Barbara County	29 888	06	40354	065	Riverside County	37 467
06	31960		Hanford city	53 967	06	40830		La Verne city	31 063
06	31960	031	Kings County	53 967	06	40830	037	Los Angeles County	31 063

Cities by County–*Continued*

State Code	Place Code	County Code	Geographic Area Name	2010 Census Population	State Code	Place Code	County Code	Geographic Area Name	2010 Census Population
06	40886		Lawndale city	32 769	06	48788		Montclair city	36 664
06	40886	037	Los Angeles County	32 769	06	48788	071	San Bernardino County	36 664
06	41124		Lemon Grove city	25 320	06	48816		Montebello city	62 500
06	41124	073	San Diego County	25 320	06	48816	037	Los Angeles County	62 500
06	41474		Lincoln city	42 819	06	48872		Monterey city	27 810
06	41474	061	Placer County	42 819	06	48872	053	Monterey County	27 810
06	41992		Livermore city	80 968	06	48914		Monterey Park city	60 269
06	41992	001	Alameda County	80 968	06	48914	037	Los Angeles County	60 269
06	42202		Lodi city	62 134	06	49138		Moorpark city	34 421
06	42202	077	San Joaquin County	62 134	06	49138	111	Ventura County	34 421
06	42524		Lompoc city	42 434	06	49270		Moreno Valley city	193 365
06	42524	083	Santa Barbara County	42 434	06	49270	065	Riverside County	193 365
06	43000		Long Beach city	462 257	06	49278		Morgan Hill city	37 882
06	43000	037	Los Angeles County	462 257	06	49278	085	Santa Clara County	37 882
06	43280		Los Altos city	28 976	06	49670		Mountain View city	74 066
06	43280	085	Santa Clara County	28 976	06	49670	085	Santa Clara County	74 066
06	44000		Los Angeles city	3 792 621	06	50076		Murrieta city	103 466
06	44000	037	Los Angeles County	3 792 621	06	50076	065	Riverside County	103 466
06	44028		Los Banos city	35 972	06	50258		Napa city	76 915
06	44028	047	Merced County	35 972	06	50258	055	Napa County	76 915
06	44112		Los Gatos town	29 413	06	50398		National City city	58 582
06	44112	085	Santa Clara County	29 413	06	50398	073	San Diego County	58 582
06	44574		Lynwood city	69 772	06	50916		Newark city	42 573
06	44574	037	Los Angeles County	69 772	06	50916	001	Alameda County	42 573
06	45022		Madera city	61 416	06	51182		Newport Beach city	85 186
06	45022	039	Madera County	61 416	06	51182	059	Orange County	85 186
06	45400		Manhattan Beach city	35 135	06	51560		Norco city	27 063
06	45400	037	Los Angeles County	35 135	06	51560	065	Riverside County	27 063
06	45484		Manteca city	67 096	06	52526		Norwalk city	105 549
06	45484	077	San Joaquin County	67 096	06	52526	037	Los Angeles County	105 549
06	46114		Martinez city	35 824	06	52582		Novato city	51 904
06	46114	013	Contra Costa County	35 824	06	52582	041	Marin County	51 904
06	46492		Maywood city	27 395	06	53000		Oakland city	390 724
06	46492	037	Los Angeles County	27 395	06	53000	001	Alameda County	390 724
06	46842		Menifee city	77 519	06	53070		Oakley city	35 432
06	46842	065	Riverside County	77 519	06	53070	013	Contra Costa County	35 432
06	46870		Menlo Park city	32 026	06	53322		Oceanside city	167 086
06	46870	081	San Mateo County	32 026	06	53322	073	San Diego County	167 086
06	46898		Merced city	78 958	06	53896		Ontario city	163 924
06	46898	047	Merced County	78 958	06	53896	071	San Bernardino County	163 924
06	47766		Milpitas city	66 790	06	53980		Orange city	136 416
06	47766	085	Santa Clara County	66 790	06	53980	059	Orange County	136 416
06	48256		Mission Viejo city	93 305	06	54652		Oxnard city	197 899
06	48256	059	Orange County	93 305	06	54652	111	Ventura County	197 899
06	48354		Modesto city	201 165	06	54806		Pacifica city	37 234
06	48354	099	Stanislaus County	201 165	06	54806	081	San Mateo County	37 234
06	48648		Monrovia city	36 590	06	55156		Palmdale city	152 750
06	48648	037	Los Angeles County	36 590	06	55156	037	Los Angeles County	152 750

State Code	Place Code	County Code	Geographic Area Name	2010 Census Population	State Code	Place Code	County Code	Geographic Area Name	2010 Census Population
06	55184		Palm Desert city	48 445	06	60466		Rialto city	99 171
06	55184	065	Riverside County	48 445	06	60466	071	San Bernardino County	99 171
06	55254		Palm Springs city	44 552	06	60620		Richmond city	103 701
06	55254	065	Riverside County	44 552	06	60620	013	Contra Costa County	103 701
06	55282		Palo Alto city	64 403	06	60704		Ridgecrest city	27 616
06	55282	085	Santa Clara County	64 403	06	60704	029	Kern County	27 616
06	55520		Paradise town	26 218	06	62000		Riverside city	303 871
06	55520	007	Butte County	26 218	06	62000	065	Riverside County	303 871
06	55618		Paramount city	54 098	06	62364		Rocklin city	56 974
06	55618	037	Los Angeles County	54 098	06	62364	061	Placer County	56 974
06	56000		Pasadena city	137 122	06	62546		Rohnert Park city	40 971
06	56000	037	Los Angeles County	137 122	06	62546	097	Sonoma County	40 971
06	56700		Perris city	68 386	06	62896		Rosemead city	53 764
06	56700	065	Riverside County	68 386	06	62896	037	Los Angeles County	53 764
06	56784		Petaluma city	57 941	06	62938		Roseville city	118 788
06	56784	097	Sonoma County	57 941	06	62938	061	Placer County	118 788
06	56924		Pico Rivera city	62 942	06	64000		Sacramento city	466 488
06	56924	037	Los Angeles County	62 942	06	64000	067	Sacramento County	466 488
06	57456		Pittsburg city	63 264	06	64224		Salinas city	150 441
06	57456	013	Contra Costa County	63 264	06	64224	053	Monterey County	150 441
06	57526		Placentia city	50 533	06	65000		San Bernardino city	209 924
06	57526	059	Orange County	50 533	06	65000	071	San Bernardino County	209 924
06	57764		Pleasant Hill city	33 152	06	65028		San Bruno city	41 114
06	57764	013	Contra Costa County	33 152	06	65028	081	San Mateo County	41 114
06	57792		Pleasanton city	70 285	06	65042		San Buenaventura (Ventura)	106 433
06	57792	001	Alameda County	70 285	06	65042	111	Ventura County	106 433
06	58072		Pomona city	149 058	06	65070		San Carlos city	28 406
06	58072	037	Los Angeles County	149 058	06	65070	081	San Mateo County	28 406
06	58240		Porterville city	54 165	06	65084		San Clemente city	63 522
06	58240	107	Tulare County	54 165	06	65084	059	Orange County	63 522
06	58520		Poway city	47 811	06	66000		San Diego city	1 307 402
06	58520	073	San Diego County	47 811	06	66000	073	San Diego County	1 307 402
06	59444		Rancho Cordova city	64 776	06	66070		San Dimas city	33 371
06	59444	067	Sacramento County	64 776	06	66070	037	Los Angeles County	33 371
06	59451		Rancho Cucamonga city	165 269	06	67000		San Francisco city	805 235
06	59451	071	San Bernardino County	165 269	06	67000	075	San Francisco County	805 235
06	59514		Rancho Palos Verdes city	41 643	06	67042		San Gabriel city	39 718
06	59514	037	Los Angeles County	41 643	06	67042	037	Los Angeles County	39 718
06	59587		Rancho Santa Margarita city	47 853	06	67112		San Jacinto city	44 199
06	59587	059	Orange County	47 853	06	67112	065	Riverside County	44 199
06	59920		Redding city	89 861	06	68000		San Jose city	945 942
06	59920	089	Shasta County	89 861	06	68000	085	Santa Clara County	945 942
06	59962		Redlands city	68 747	06	68028		San Juan Capistrano city	34 593
06	59962	071	San Bernardino County	68 747	06	68028	059	Orange County	34 593
06	60018		Redondo Beach city	66 748	06	68084		San Leandro city	84 950
06	60018	037	Los Angeles County	66 748	06	68084	001	Alameda County	84 950
06	60102		Redwood City city	76 815	06	68154		San Luis Obispo city	45 119
06	60102	081	San Mateo County	76 815	06	68154	079	San Luis Obispo County	45 119

Cities by County–*Continued*

State Code	Place Code	County Code	Geographic Area Name	2010 Census Population	State Code	Place Code	County Code	Geographic Area Name	2010 Census Population
06	68196		San Marcos city	83 781	06	75630		Suisun City city	28 111
06	68196	073	San Diego County	83 781	06	75630	095	Solano County	28 111
06	68252		San Mateo city	97 207	06	77000		Sunnyvale city	140 081
06	68252	081	San Mateo County	97 207	06	77000	085	Santa Clara County	140 081
06	68294		San Pablo city	29 139	06	78120		Temecula city	100 097
06	68294	013	Contra Costa County	29 139	06	78120	065	Riverside County	100 097
06	68364		San Rafael city	57 713	06	78148		Temple City city	35 558
06	68364	041	Marin County	57 713	06	78148	037	Los Angeles County	35 558
06	68378		San Ramon city	72 148	06	78582		Thousand Oaks city	126 683
06	68378	013	Contra Costa County	72 148	06	78582	111	Ventura County	126 683
06	69000		Santa Ana city	324 528	06	80000		Torrance city	145 438
06	69000	059	Orange County	324 528	06	80000	037	Los Angeles County	145 438
06	69070		Santa Barbara city	88 410	06	80238		Tracy city	82 922
06	69070	083	Santa Barbara County	88 410	06	80238	077	San Joaquin County	82 922
06	69084		Santa Clara city	116 468	06	80644		Tulare city	59 278
06	69084	085	Santa Clara County	116 468	06	80644	107	Tulare County	59 278
06	69088		Santa Clarita city	176 320	06	80812		Turlock city	68 549
06	69088	037	Los Angeles County	176 320	06	80812	099	Stanislaus County	68 549
06	69112		Santa Cruz city	59 946	06	80854		Tustin city	75 540
06	69112	087	Santa Cruz County	59 946	06	80854	059	Orange County	75 540
06	69196		Santa Maria city	99 553	06	80994		Twentynine Palms city	25 048
06	69196	083	Santa Barbara County	99 553	06	80994	071	San Bernardino County	25 048
06	70000		Santa Monica city	89 736	06	81204		Union City city	69 516
06	70000	037	Los Angeles County	89 736	06	81204	001	Alameda County	69 516
06	70042		Santa Paula city	29 321	06	81344		Upland city	73 732
06	70042	111	Ventura County	29 321	06	81344	071	San Bernardino County	73 732
06	70098		Santa Rosa city	167 815	06	81554		Vacaville city	92 428
06	70098	097	Sonoma County	167 815	06	81554	095	Solano County	92 428
06	70224		Santee city	53 413	06	81666		Vallejo city	115 942
06	70224	073	San Diego County	53 413	06	81666	095	Solano County	115 942
06	70280		Saratoga city	29 926	06	82590		Victorville city	115 903
06	70280	085	Santa Clara County	29 926	06	82590	071	San Bernardino County	115 903
06	70742		Seaside city	33 025	06	82954		Visalia city	124 442
06	70742	053	Monterey County	33 025	06	82954	107	Tulare County	124 442
06	72016		Simi Valley city	124 237	06	82996		Vista city	93 834
06	72016	111	Ventura County	124 237	06	82996	073	San Diego County	93 834
06	72520		Soledad city	25 738	06	83332		Walnut city	29 172
06	72520	053	Monterey County	25 738	06	83332	037	Los Angeles County	29 172
06	73080		South Gate city	94 396	06	83346		Walnut Creek city	64 173
06	73080	037	Los Angeles County	94 396	06	83346	013	Contra Costa County	64 173
06	73220		South Pasadena city	25 619	06	83542		Wasco city	25 545
06	73220	037	Los Angeles County	25 619	06	83542	029	Kern County	25 545
06	73262		South San Francisco city	63 632	06	83668		Watsonville city	51 199
06	73262	081	San Mateo County	63 632	06	83668	087	Santa Cruz County	51 199
06	73962		Stanton city	38 186	06	84200		West Covina city	106 098
06	73962	059	Orange County	38 186	06	84200	037	Los Angeles County	106 098
06	75000		Stockton city	291 707	06	84410		West Hollywood city	34 399
06	75000	077	San Joaquin County	291 707	06	84410	037	Los Angeles County	34 399

Cities by County–*Continued*

State Code	Place Code	County Code	Geographic Area Name	2010 Census Population	State Code	Place Code	County Code	Geographic Area Name	2010 Census Population
06	84550		Westminster city	89 701	08	31660		Grand Junction city	58 566
06	84550	059	Orange County	89 701	08	31660	077	Mesa County	58 566
06	84816		West Sacramento city	48 744	08	32155		Greeley city	92 889
06	84816	113	Yolo County	48 744	08	32155	123	Weld County	92 889
06	85292		Whittier city	85 331	08	43000		Lakewood city	142 980
06	85292	037	Los Angeles County	85 331	08	43000	059	Jefferson County	142 980
06	85446		Wildomar city	32 176	08	45255		Littleton city	41 737
06	85446	065	Riverside County	32 176	08	45255	005	Arapahoe County	39 328
					08	45255	035	Douglas County	28
06	85922		Windsor town	26 801	08	45255	059	Jefferson County	2 381
06	85922	097	Sonoma County	26 801					
					08	45970		Longmont city	86 270
06	86328		Woodland city	55 468	08	45970	013	Boulder County	86 240
06	86328	113	Yolo County	55 468	08	45970	123	Weld County	30
06	86832		Yorba Linda city	64 234	08	46465		Loveland city	66 859
06	86832	059	Orange County	64 234	08	46465	069	Larimer County	66 859
06	86972		Yuba City city	64 925	08	54330		Northglenn city	35 789
06	86972	101	Sutter County	64 925	08	54330	001	Adams County	35 777
					08	54330	123	Weld County	12
06	87042		Yucaipa city	51 367					
06	87042	071	San Bernardino County	51 367	08	57630		Parker town	45 297
					08	57630	035	Douglas County	45 297
08			**COLORADO**	5 029 196					
08	03455		Arvada city	106 433	08	62000		Pueblo city	106 595
08	03455	001	Adams County	2 849	08	62000	101	Pueblo County	106 595
08	03455	059	Jefferson County	103 584					
					08	77290		Thornton city	118 772
08	04000		Aurora city	325 078	08	77290	001	Adams County	118 772
08	04000	001	Adams County	39 871	08	77290	123	Weld County	0
08	04000	005	Arapahoe County	285 090					
08	04000	035	Douglas County	117	08	83835		Westminster city	106 114
					08	83835	001	Adams County	63 696
08	07850		Boulder city	97 385	08	83835	059	Jefferson County	42 418
08	07850	013	Boulder County	97 385					
					08	84440		Wheat Ridge city	30 166
08	08675		Brighton city	33 352	08	84440	059	Jefferson County	30 166
08	08675	001	Adams County	33 009					
08	08675	123	Weld County	343	09			**CONNECTICUT**	3 574 097
					09	08000		Bridgeport city	144 229
08	09280		Broomfield city	55 889	09	08000	001	Fairfield County	144 229
08	09280	014	Broomfield County	55 889					
					09	08420		Bristol city	60 477
08	12415		Castle Rock town	48 231	09	08420	003	Hartford County	60 477
08	12415	035	Douglas County	48 231					
					09	18430		Danbury city	80 893
08	12815		Centennial city	100 377	09	18430	001	Fairfield County	80 893
08	12815	005	Arapahoe County	100 377					
					09	37000		Hartford city	124 775
08	16000		Colorado Springs city	416 427	09	37000	003	Hartford County	124 775
08	16000	041	El Paso County	416 427					
					09	46450		Meriden city	60 868
08	16495		Commerce City city	45 913	09	46450	009	New Haven County	60 868
08	16495	001	Adams County	45 913					
					09	47290		Middletown city	47 648
08	20000		Denver city	600 158	09	47290	007	Middlesex County	47 648
08	20000	031	Denver County	600 158					
					09	49880		Naugatuck borough	31 862
08	24785		Englewood city	30 255	09	49880	009	New Haven County	31 862
08	24785	005	Arapahoe County	30 255					
					09	50370		New Britain city	73 206
08	27425		Fort Collins city	143 986	09	50370	003	Hartford County	73 206
08	27425	069	Larimer County	143 986					
					09	52000		New Haven city	129 779
08	27865		Fountain city	25 846	09	52000	009	New Haven County	129 779
08	27865	041	El Paso County	25 846					
					09	52280		New London city	27 620
					09	52280	011	New London County	27 620

Cities by County–*Continued*

State Code	Place Code	County Code	Geographic Area Name	2010 Census Population	State Code	Place Code	County Code	Geographic Area Name	2010 Census Population
09	55990		Norwalk city	85 603	12	14125		Cooper City city	28 547
09	55990	001	Fairfield County	85 603	12	14125	011	Broward County	28 547
09	56200		Norwich city	40 493	12	14250		Coral Gables city	46 780
09	56200	011	New London County	40 493	12	14250	086	Miami-Dade County	46 780
09	68100		Shelton city	39 559	12	14400		Coral Springs city	121 096
09	68100	001	Fairfield County	39 559	12	14400	011	Broward County	121 096
09	73000		Stamford city	122 643	12	15968		Cutler Bay town	40 286
09	73000	001	Fairfield County	122 643	12	15968	086	Miami-Dade County	40 286
09	76500		Torrington city	36 383	12	16335		Dania Beach city	29 639
09	76500	005	Litchfield County	36 383	12	16335	011	Broward County	29 639
09	80000		Waterbury city	110 366	12	16475		Davie town	91 992
09	80000	009	New Haven County	110 366	12	16475	011	Broward County	91 992
09	82800		West Haven city	55 564	12	16525		Daytona Beach city	61 005
09	82800	009	New Haven County	55 564	12	16525	127	Volusia County	61 005
10			**DELAWARE**	897 934	12	16725		Deerfield Beach city	75 018
10	21200		Dover city	36 047	12	16725	011	Broward County	75 018
10	21200	001	Kent County	36 047					
					12	16875		DeLand city	27 031
10	50670		Newark city	31 454	12	16875	127	Volusia County	27 031
10	50670	003	New Castle County	31 454					
					12	17100		Delray Beach city	60 522
10	77580		Wilmington city	70 851	12	17100	099	Palm Beach County	60 522
10	77580	003	New Castle County	70 851					
					12	17200		Deltona city	85 182
11			**DISTRICT OF COLUMBIA**	601 723	12	17200	127	Volusia County	85 182
11	50000		Washington city	601 723					
11	50000	001	District of Columbia	601 723	12	17935		Doral city	45 704
					12	17935	086	Miami-Dade County	45 704
12			**FLORIDA**	18 801 310					
12	00950		Altamonte Springs city	41 496	12	18575		Dunedin city	35 321
12	00950	117	Seminole County	41 496	12	18575	103	Pinellas County	35 321
12	01700		Apopka city	41 542	12	24000		Fort Lauderdale city	165 521
12	01700	095	Orange County	41 542	12	24000	011	Broward County	165 521
12	02681		Aventura city	35 762	12	24125		Fort Myers city	62 298
12	02681	086	Miami-Dade County	35 762	12	24125	071	Lee County	62 298
12	07300		Boca Raton city	84 392	12	24300		Fort Pierce city	41 590
12	07300	099	Palm Beach County	84 392	12	24300	111	St. Lucie County	41 590
12	07525		Bonita Springs city	43 914	12	25175		Gainesville city	124 354
12	07525	071	Lee County	43 914	12	25175	001	Alachua County	124 354
12	07875		Boynton Beach city	68 217	12	27322		Greenacres city	37 573
12	07875	099	Palm Beach County	68 217	12	27322	099	Palm Beach County	37 573
12	07950		Bradenton city	49 546	12	28452		Hallandale Beach city	37 113
12	07950	081	Manatee County	49 546	12	28452	011	Broward County	37 113
12	10275		Cape Coral city	154 305	12	30000		Hialeah city	224 669
12	10275	071	Lee County	154 305	12	30000	086	Miami-Dade County	224 669
12	11050		Casselberry city	26 241	12	32000		Hollywood city	140 768
12	11050	117	Seminole County	26 241	12	32000	011	Broward County	140 768
12	12875		Clearwater city	107 685	12	32275		Homestead city	60 512
12	12875	103	Pinellas County	107 685	12	32275	086	Miami-Dade County	60 512
12	12925		Clermont city	28 742	12	35000		Jacksonville city	821 784
12	12925	069	Lake County	28 742	12	35000	031	Duval County	821 784
12	13275		Coconut Creek city	52 909	12	35875		Jupiter town	55 156
12	13275	011	Broward County	52 909	12	35875	099	Palm Beach County	55 156

State Code	Place Code	County Code	Geographic Area Name	2010 Census Population	State Code	Place Code	County Code	Geographic Area Name	2010 Census Population
12	36950		Kissimmee city	59 682	12	54075		Palm Beach Gardens city	48 452
12	36950	097	Osceola County	59 682	12	54075	099	Palm Beach County	48 452
12	38250		Lakeland city	97 422	12	54200		Palm Coast city	75 180
12	38250	105	Polk County	97 422	12	54200	035	Flagler County	75 180
12	39075		Lake Worth city	34 910	12	54700		Panama City city	36 484
12	39075	099	Palm Beach County	34 910	12	54700	005	Bay County	36 484
12	39425		Largo city	77 648	12	55775		Pembroke Pines city	154 750
12	39425	103	Pinellas County	77 648	12	55775	011	Broward County	154 750
12	39525		Lauderdale Lakes city	32 593	12	55925		Pensacola city	51 923
12	39525	011	Broward County	32 593	12	55925	033	Escambia County	51 923
12	39550		Lauderhill city	66 887	12	56975		Pinellas Park city	49 079
12	39550	011	Broward County	66 887	12	56975	103	Pinellas County	49 079
12	43125		Margate city	53 284	12	57425		Plantation city	84 955
12	43125	011	Broward County	53 284	12	57425	011	Broward County	84 955
12	43975		Melbourne city	76 068	12	57550		Plant City city	34 721
12	43975	009	Brevard County	76 068	12	57550	057	Hillsborough County	34 721
12	45000		Miami city	399 457	12	58050		Pompano Beach city	99 845
12	45000	086	Miami-Dade County	399 457	12	58050	011	Broward County	99 845
12	45025		Miami Beach city	87 779	12	58575		Port Orange city	56 048
12	45025	086	Miami-Dade County	87 779	12	58575	127	Volusia County	56 048
12	45060		Miami Gardens city	107 167	12	58715		Port St. Lucie city	164 603
12	45060	086	Miami-Dade County	107 167	12	58715	111	St. Lucie County	164 603
12	45100		Miami Lakes town	29 361	12	60975		Riviera Beach city	32 488
12	45100	086	Miami-Dade County	29 361	12	60975	099	Palm Beach County	32 488
12	45975		Miramar city	122 041	12	62100		Royal Palm Beach village	34 140
12	45975	011	Broward County	122 041	12	62100	099	Palm Beach County	34 140
12	49425		North Lauderdale city	41 023	12	62625		St. Cloud city	35 183
12	49425	011	Broward County	41 023	12	62625	097	Osceola County	35 183
12	49450		North Miami city	58 786	12	63000		St. Petersburg city	244 769
12	49450	086	Miami-Dade County	58 786	12	63000	103	Pinellas County	244 769
12	49475		North Miami Beach city	41 523	12	63650		Sanford city	53 570
12	49475	086	Miami-Dade County	41 523	12	63650	117	Seminole County	53 570
12	49675		North Port city	57 357	12	64175		Sarasota city	51 917
12	49675	115	Sarasota County	57 357	12	64175	115	Sarasota County	51 917
12	50575		Oakland Park city	41 363	12	69700		Sunrise city	84 439
12	50575	011	Broward County	41 363	12	69700	011	Broward County	84 439
12	50750		Ocala city	56 315	12	70600		Tallahassee city	181 376
12	50750	083	Marion County	56 315	12	70600	073	Leon County	181 376
12	51075		Ocoee city	35 579	12	70675		Tamarac city	60 427
12	51075	095	Orange County	35 579	12	70675	011	Broward County	60 427
12	53000		Orlando city	238 300	12	71000		Tampa city	335 709
12	53000	095	Orange County	238 300	12	71000	057	Hillsborough County	335 709
12	53150		Ormond Beach city	38 137	12	71900		Titusville city	43 761
12	53150	127	Volusia County	38 137	12	71900	009	Brevard County	43 761
12	53575		Oviedo city	33 342	12	75812		Wellington village	56 508
12	53575	117	Seminole County	33 342	12	75812	099	Palm Beach County	56 508
12	54000		Palm Bay city	103 190	12	76582		Weston city	65 333
12	54000	009	Brevard County	103 190	12	76582	011	Broward County	65 333

Cities by County–*Continued*

State Code	Place Code	County Code	Geographic Area Name	2010 Census Population	State Code	Place Code	County Code	Geographic Area Name	2010 Census Population
12	76600		West Palm Beach city	99 919	13	55020		Newnan city	33 039
12	76600	099	Palm Beach County	99 919	13	55020	077	Coweta County	33 039
12	78250		Winter Garden city	34 568	13	59724		Peachtree City city	34 364
12	78250	095	Orange County	34 568	13	59724	113	Fayette County	34 364
12	78275		Winter Haven city	33 874	13	66668		Rome city	36 303
12	78275	105	Polk County	33 874	13	66668	115	Floyd County	36 303
12	78300		Winter Park city	27 852	13	67284		Roswell city	88 346
12	78300	095	Orange County	27 852	13	67284	121	Fulton County	88 346
12	78325		Winter Springs city	33 282	13	68516		Sandy Springs city	93 853
12	78325	117	Seminole County	33 282	13	68516	121	Fulton County	93 853
13			**GEORGIA**	9 687 653	13	69000		Savannah city	136 286
13	01052		Albany city	77 434	13	69000	051	Chatham County	136 286
13	01052	095	Dougherty County	77 434					
					13	71492		Smyrna city	51 271
13	01696		Alpharetta city	57 551	13	71492	067	Cobb County	51 271
13	01696	121	Fulton County	57 551					
					13	73256		Statesboro city	28 422
13	04000		Atlanta city	420 003	13	73256	031	Bulloch County	28 422
13	04000	089	DeKalb County	28 292					
13	04000	121	Fulton County	391 711	13	73704		Stockbridge city	25 636
					13	73704	151	Henry County	25 636
13	19000		Columbus city	189 885					
13	19000	215	Muscogee County	189 885	13	78800		Valdosta city	54 518
					13	78800	185	Lowndes County	54 518
13	21380		Dalton city	33 128					
13	21380	313	Whitfield County	33 128	13	80508		Warner Robins city	66 588
					13	80508	153	Houston County	66 224
13	23900		Douglasville city	30 961	13	80508	225	Peach County	364
13	23900	097	Douglas County	30 961					
					15			**HAWAII**	1 360 301
13	24600		Duluth city	26 600	15	06290		East Honolulu CDP	49 914
13	24600	135	Gwinnett County	26 600	15	06290	003	Honolulu County	49 914
13	24768		Dunwoody city	46 267	15	14650		Hilo CDP	43 263
13	24768	089	DeKalb County	46 267	15	14650	001	Hawaii County	43 263
13	25720		East Point city	33 712	15	22700		Kahului CDP	26 337
13	25720	121	Fulton County	33 712	15	22700	009	Maui County	26 337
13	31908		Gainesville city	33 804	15	23150		Kailua CDP	38 635
13	31908	139	Hall County	33 804	15	23150	003	Honolulu County	38 635
13	38964		Hinesville city	33 437	15	28250		Kaneohe CDP	34 597
13	38964	179	Liberty County	33 437	15	28250	003	Honolulu County	34 597
13	42425		Johns Creek city	76 728	15	51050		Mililani Town CDP	27 629
13	42425	121	Fulton County	76 728	15	51050	003	Honolulu County	27 629
13	43192		Kennesaw city	29 783	15	62600		Pearl City CDP	47 698
13	43192	067	Cobb County	29 783	15	62600	003	Honolulu County	47 698
13	44340		LaGrange city	29 588	15	71550		Urban Honolulu CDP	337 256
13	44340	285	Troup County	29 588	15	71550	003	Honolulu County	337 256
13	45488		Lawrenceville city	28 546	15	79700		Waipahu CDP	38 216
13	45488	135	Gwinnett County	28 546	15	79700	003	Honolulu County	38 216
13	49000		Macon city	91 351	16			**IDAHO**	1 567 582
13	49000	021	Bibb County	90 885	16	08830		Boise City city	205 671
13	49000	169	Jones County	466	16	08830	001	Ada County	205 671
13	49756		Marietta city	56 579	16	12250		Caldwell city	46 237
13	49756	067	Cobb County	56 579	16	12250	027	Canyon County	46 237
13	51670		Milton city	32 661	16	16750		Coeur d'Alene city	44 137
13	51670	121	Fulton County	32 661	16	16750	055	Kootenai County	44 137

Cities by County–*Continued*

State Code	Place Code	County Code	Geographic Area Name	2010 Census Population	State Code	Place Code	County Code	Geographic Area Name	2010 Census Population
16	39700		Idaho Falls city	56 813	17	09447		Buffalo Grove village	41 496
16	39700	019	Bonneville County	56 813	17	09447	031	Cook County	13 644
					17	09447	097	Lake County	27 852
16	46540		Lewiston city	31 894					
16	46540	069	Nez Perce County	31 894	17	09642		Burbank city	28 925
					17	09642	031	Cook County	28 925
16	52120		Meridian city	75 092					
16	52120	001	Ada County	75 092	17	10487		Calumet City city	37 042
					17	10487	031	Cook County	37 042
16	56260		Nampa city	81 557					
16	56260	027	Canyon County	81 557	17	11163		Carbondale city	25 902
					17	11163	077	Jackson County	25 902
16	64090		Pocatello city	54 255	17	11163	199	Williamson County	0
16	64090	005	Bannock County	54 239					
16	64090	077	Power County	16	17	11332		Carol Stream village	39 711
					17	11332	043	DuPage County	39 711
16	64810		Post Falls city	27 574					
16	64810	055	Kootenai County	27 574	17	11358		Carpentersville village	37 691
					17	11358	089	Kane County	37 691
16	67420		Rexburg city	25 484					
16	67420	065	Madison County	25 484	17	12385		Champaign city	81 055
					17	12385	019	Champaign County	81 055
16	82810		Twin Falls city	44 125					
16	82810	083	Twin Falls County	44 125	17	14000		Chicago city	2 695 598
					17	14000	031	Cook County	2 695 598
17			**ILLINOIS**	12 830 632	17	14000	043	DuPage County	0
17	00243		Addison village	36 942					
17	00243	043	DuPage County	36 942	17	14026		Chicago Heights city	30 276
					17	14026	031	Cook County	30 276
17	00685		Algonquin village	30 046					
17	00685	089	Kane County	8 433	17	14351		Cicero town	83 891
17	00685	111	McHenry County	21 613	17	14351	031	Cook County	83 891
17	01114		Alton city	27 865	17	15599		Collinsville city	25 579
17	01114	119	Madison County	27 865	17	15599	119	Madison County	22 573
					17	15599	163	St. Clair County	3 006
17	02154		Arlington Heights village	75 101					
17	02154	031	Cook County	75 101	17	17887		Crystal Lake city	40 743
17	02154	097	Lake County	0	17	17887	111	McHenry County	40 743
17	03012		Aurora city	197 899	17	18563		Danville city	33 027
17	03012	043	DuPage County	49 433	17	18563	183	Vermilion County	33 027
17	03012	089	Kane County	130 976					
17	03012	093	Kendall County	6 019	17	18823		Decatur city	76 122
17	03012	197	Will County	11 471	17	18823	115	Macon County	76 122
17	04013		Bartlett village	41 208	17	19161		DeKalb city	43 862
17	04013	031	Cook County	16 797	17	19161	037	DeKalb County	43 862
17	04013	043	DuPage County	24 411					
17	04013	089	Kane County	0	17	19642		Des Plaines city	58 364
					17	19642	031	Cook County	58 364
17	04078		Batavia city	26 045					
17	04078	043	DuPage County	0	17	20591		Downers Grove village	47 833
17	04078	089	Kane County	26 045	17	20591	043	DuPage County	47 833
17	04845		Belleville city	44 478	17	22255		East St. Louis city	27 006
17	04845	163	St. Clair County	44 478	17	22255	163	St. Clair County	27 006
17	05092		Belvidere city	25 585	17	23074		Elgin city	108 188
17	05092	007	Boone County	25 585	17	23074	031	Cook County	24 032
					17	23074	089	Kane County	84 156
17	05573		Berwyn city	56 657					
17	05573	031	Cook County	56 657	17	23256		Elk Grove Village village	33 127
					17	23256	031	Cook County	33 127
17	06613		Bloomington city	76 610	17	23256	043	DuPage County	0
17	06613	113	McLean County	76 610					
					17	23620		Elmhurst city	44 121
17	07133		Bolingbrook village	73 366	17	23620	031	Cook County	0
17	07133	043	DuPage County	1 571	17	23620	043	DuPage County	44 121
17	07133	197	Will County	71 795					
					17	24582		Evanston city	74 486
					17	24582	031	Cook County	74 486

Cities by County–*Continued*

State Code	Place Code	County Code	Geographic Area Name	2010 Census Population	State Code	Place Code	County Code	Geographic Area Name	2010 Census Population
17	27884		Freeport city	25 638	17	53234		Normal town	52 497
17	27884	177	Stephenson County	25 638	17	53234	113	McLean County	52 497
17	28326		Galesburg city	32 195	17	53481		Northbrook village	33 170
17	28326	095	Knox County	32 195	17	53481	031	Cook County	33 170
17	29730		Glendale Heights village	34 208	17	53559		North Chicago city	32 574
17	29730	043	DuPage County	34 208	17	53559	097	Lake County	32 574
17	29756		Glen Ellyn village	27 450	17	54638		Oak Forest city	27 962
17	29756	043	DuPage County	27 450	17	54638	031	Cook County	27 962
17	29938		Glenview village	44 692	17	54820		Oak Lawn village	56 690
17	29938	031	Cook County	44 692	17	54820	031	Cook County	56 690
17	30926		Granite City city	29 849	17	54885		Oak Park village	51 878
17	30926	119	Madison County	29 849	17	54885	031	Cook County	51 878
17	32018		Gurnee village	31 295	17	55249		O'Fallon city	28 281
17	32018	097	Lake County	31 295	17	55249	163	St. Clair County	28 281
17	32746		Hanover Park village	37 973	17	56640		Orland Park village	56 767
17	32746	031	Cook County	20 636	17	56640	031	Cook County	56 583
17	32746	043	DuPage County	17 337	17	56640	197	Will County	184
17	33383		Harvey city	25 282	17	56887		Oswego village	30 355
17	33383	031	Cook County	25 282	17	56887	093	Kendall County	30 355
17	34722		Highland Park city	29 763	17	57225		Palatine village	68 557
17	34722	097	Lake County	29 763	17	57225	031	Cook County	68 557
					17	57225	097	Lake County	0
17	35411		Hoffman Estates village	51 895					
17	35411	031	Cook County	51 895	17	57875		Park Ridge city	37 480
17	35411	089	Kane County	0	17	57875	031	Cook County	37 480
17	38570		Joliet city	147 433	17	58447		Pekin city	34 094
17	38570	093	Kendall County	9 749	17	58447	143	Peoria County	0
17	38570	197	Will County	137 684	17	58447	179	Tazewell County	34 094
17	38934		Kankakee city	27 537	17	59000		Peoria city	115 007
17	38934	091	Kankakee County	27 537	17	59000	143	Peoria County	115 007
17	41183		Lake in the Hills village	28 965	17	60287		Plainfield village	39 581
17	41183	111	McHenry County	28 965	17	60287	093	Kendall County	2 079
					17	60287	197	Will County	37 502
17	42028		Lansing village	28 331					
17	42028	031	Cook County	28 331	17	62367		Quincy city	40 633
					17	62367	001	Adams County	40 633
17	44407		Lombard village	43 165					
17	44407	043	DuPage County	43 165	17	65000		Rockford city	152 871
					17	65000	201	Winnebago County	152 871
17	45694		McHenry city	26 992					
17	45694	111	McHenry County	26 992	17	65078		Rock Island city	39 018
					17	65078	161	Rock Island County	39 018
17	48242		Melrose Park village	25 411					
17	48242	031	Cook County	25 411	17	65442		Romeoville village	39 680
					17	65442	197	Will County	39 680
17	49867		Moline city	43 483					
17	49867	161	Rock Island County	43 483	17	66040		Round Lake Beach village	28 175
					17	66040	097	Lake County	28 175
17	51089		Mount Prospect village	54 167					
17	51089	031	Cook County	54 167	17	66703		St. Charles city	32 974
					17	66703	043	DuPage County	543
17	51349		Mundelein village	31 064	17	66703	089	Kane County	32 431
17	51349	097	Lake County	31 064					
					17	68003		Schaumburg village	74 227
17	51622		Naperville city	141 853	17	68003	031	Cook County	74 227
17	51622	043	DuPage County	94 533	17	68003	043	DuPage County	0
17	51622	197	Will County	47 320					
					17	70122		Skokie village	64 784
17	53000		Niles village	29 803	17	70122	031	Cook County	64 784
17	53000	031	Cook County	29 803					

Cities by County–*Continued*

State Code	Place Code	County Code	Geographic Area Name	2010 Census Population	State Code	Place Code	County Code	Geographic Area Name	2010 Census Population
17	72000		Springfield city	116 250	18	28386		Goshen city	31 719
17	72000	167	Sangamon County	116 250	18	28386	039	Elkhart County	31 719
17	73157		Streamwood village	39 858	18	29898		Greenwood city	49 791
17	73157	031	Cook County	39 858	18	29898	081	Johnson County	49 791
17	75484		Tinley Park village	56 703	18	31000		Hammond city	80 830
17	75484	031	Cook County	49 236	18	31000	089	Lake County	80 830
17	75484	197	Will County	7 467					
					18	34114		Hobart city	29 059
17	77005		Urbana city	41 250	18	34114	089	Lake County	29 059
17	77005	019	Champaign County	41 250					
					18	38358		Jeffersonville city	44 953
17	77694		Vernon Hills village	25 113	18	38358	019	Clark County	44 953
17	77694	097	Lake County	25 113					
					18	40392		Kokomo city	45 468
17	79293		Waukegan city	89 078	18	40392	067	Howard County	45 468
17	79293	097	Lake County	89 078					
					18	40788		Lafayette city	67 140
17	80060		West Chicago city	27 086	18	40788	157	Tippecanoe County	67 140
17	80060	043	DuPage County	27 086					
					18	42426		Lawrence city	46 001
17	81048		Wheaton city	52 894	18	42426	097	Marion County	46 001
17	81048	043	DuPage County	52 894					
					18	46908		Marion city	29 948
17	81087		Wheeling village	37 648	18	46908	053	Grant County	29 948
17	81087	031	Cook County	37 642					
17	81087	097	Lake County	6	18	48528		Merrillville town	35 246
					18	48528	089	Lake County	35 246
17	82075		Wilmette village	27 087					
17	82075	031	Cook County	27 087	18	48798		Michigan City city	31 479
					18	48798	091	LaPorte County	31 479
17	83245		Woodridge village	32 971					
17	83245	031	Cook County	0	18	49932		Mishawaka city	48 252
17	83245	043	DuPage County	32 949	18	49932	141	St. Joseph County	48 252
17	83245	197	Will County	22					
					18	51876		Muncie city	70 085
18			**INDIANA**	6 483 802	18	51876	035	Delaware County	70 085
18	01468		Anderson city	56 129					
18	01468	095	Madison County	56 129	18	52326		New Albany city	36 372
					18	52326	043	Floyd County	36 372
18	05860		Bloomington city	80 405					
18	05860	105	Monroe County	80 405	18	54180		Noblesville city	51 969
					18	54180	057	Hamilton County	51 969
18	10342		Carmel city	79 191					
18	10342	057	Hamilton County	79 191	18	60246		Plainfield town	27 631
					18	60246	063	Hendricks County	27 631
18	14734		Columbus city	44 061					
18	14734	005	Bartholomew County	44 061	18	61092		Portage city	36 828
					18	61092	127	Porter County	36 828
18	16138		Crown Point city	27 317					
18	16138	089	Lake County	27 317	18	64260		Richmond city	36 812
					18	64260	177	Wayne County	36 812
18	19486		East Chicago city	29 698					
18	19486	089	Lake County	29 698	18	68220		Schererville town	29 243
					18	68220	089	Lake County	29 243
18	20728		Elkhart city	50 949					
18	20728	039	Elkhart County	50 949	18	71000		South Bend city	101 168
					18	71000	141	St. Joseph County	101 168
18	22000		Evansville city	117 429					
18	22000	163	Vanderburgh County	117 429	18	75428		Terre Haute city	60 785
					18	75428	167	Vigo County	60 785
18	23278		Fishers town	76 794					
18	23278	057	Hamilton County	76 794	18	78326		Valparaiso city	31 730
					18	78326	127	Porter County	31 730
18	25000		Fort Wayne city	253 691					
18	25000	003	Allen County	253 691	18	82700		Westfield town	30 068
					18	82700	057	Hamilton County	30 068
18	27000		Gary city	80 294					
18	27000	089	Lake County	80 294	18	82862		West Lafayette city	29 596
					18	82862	157	Tippecanoe County	29 596

Cities by County–*Continued*

State Code	Place Code	County Code	Geographic Area Name	2010 Census Population	State Code	Place Code	County Code	Geographic Area Name	2010 Census Population
19			**IOWA**	3 046 355	20	25325		Garden City city	26 658
19	01855		Ames city	58 965	20	25325	055	Finney County	26 658
19	01855	169	Story County	58 965					
					20	33625		Hutchinson city	42 080
19	02305		Ankeny city	45 582	20	33625	155	Reno County	42 080
19	02305	153	Polk County	45 582					
					20	36000		Kansas City city	145 786
19	06355		Bettendorf city	33 217	20	36000	209	Wyandotte County	145 786
19	06355	163	Scott County	33 217					
					20	38900		Lawrence city	87 643
19	09550		Burlington city	25 663	20	38900	045	Douglas County	87 643
19	09550	057	Des Moines County	25 663					
					20	39000		Leavenworth city	35 251
19	11755		Cedar Falls city	39 260	20	39000	103	Leavenworth County	35 251
19	11755	013	Black Hawk County	39 260					
					20	39075		Leawood city	31 867
19	12000		Cedar Rapids city	126 326	20	39075	091	Johnson County	31 867
19	12000	113	Linn County	126 326					
					20	39350		Lenexa city	48 190
19	14430		Clinton city	26 885	20	39350	091	Johnson County	48 190
19	14430	045	Clinton County	26 885					
					20	44250		Manhattan city	52 281
19	16860		Council Bluffs city	62 230	20	44250	149	Pottawatomie County	146
19	16860	155	Pottawattamie County	62 230	20	44250	161	Riley County	52 135
					20	52575		Olathe city	125 872
19	19000		Davenport city	99 685	20	52575	091	Johnson County	125 872
19	19000	163	Scott County	99 685					
					20	53775		Overland Park city	173 372
19	21000		Des Moines city	203 433	20	53775	091	Johnson County	173 372
19	21000	153	Polk County	203 419					
19	21000	181	Warren County	14	20	62700		Salina city	47 707
					20	62700	169	Saline County	47 707
19	22395		Dubuque city	57 637					
19	22395	061	Dubuque County	57 637	20	64500		Shawnee city	62 209
					20	64500	091	Johnson County	62 209
19	28515		Fort Dodge city	25 206					
19	28515	187	Webster County	25 206	20	71000		Topeka city	127 473
					20	71000	177	Shawnee County	127 473
19	38595		Iowa City city	67 862					
19	38595	103	Johnson County	67 862	20	79000		Wichita city	382 368
					20	79000	173	Sedgwick County	382 368
19	49485		Marion city	34 768					
19	49485	113	Linn County	34 768	21			**KENTUCKY**	4 339 367
					21	08902		Bowling Green city	58 067
19	49755		Marshalltown city	27 552	21	08902	227	Warren County	58 067
19	49755	127	Marshall County	27 552					
					21	17848		Covington city	40 640
19	50160		Mason City city	28 079	21	17848	117	Kenton County	40 640
19	50160	033	Cerro Gordo County	28 079					
					21	24274		Elizabethtown city	28 531
19	60465		Ottumwa city	25 023	21	24274	093	Hardin County	28 531
19	60465	179	Wapello County	25 023					
					21	27982		Florence city	29 951
19	73335		Sioux City city	82 684	21	27982	015	Boone County	29 951
19	73335	149	Plymouth County	6					
19	73335	193	Woodbury County	82 678	21	28900		Frankfort city	25 527
					21	28900	073	Franklin County	25 527
19	79950		Urbandale city	39 463					
19	79950	049	Dallas County	6 337	21	30700		Georgetown city	29 098
19	79950	153	Polk County	33 126	21	30700	209	Scott County	29 098
19	82425		Waterloo city	68 406					
19	82425	013	Black Hawk County	68 406	21	35866		Henderson city	28 757
					21	35866	101	Henderson County	28 757
19	83910		West Des Moines city	56 609					
19	83910	049	Dallas County	11 569	21	37918		Hopkinsville city	31 577
19	83910	153	Polk County	44 999	21	37918	047	Christian County	31 577
19	83910	181	Warren County	41					
					21	40222		Jeffersontown city	26 595
20			**KANSAS**	2 853 118	21	40222	111	Jefferson County	26 595
20	18250		Dodge City city	27 340					
20	18250	057	Ford County	27 340					

Cities by County–*Continued*

State Code	Place Code	County Code	Geographic Area Name	2010 Census Population	State Code	Place Code	County Code	Geographic Area Name	2010 Census Population
21	46027		Lexington-Fayette urban county	295 803	24	04000		Baltimore city	620 961
21	46027	067	Fayette County	295 803	24	04000	510	Baltimore city	620 961
21	56136		Nicholasville city	28 015	24	08775		Bowie city	54 727
21	56136	113	Jessamine County	28 015	24	08775	033	Prince George's County	54 727
21	58620		Owensboro city	57 265	24	18750		College Park city	30 413
21	58620	059	Daviess County	57 265	24	18750	033	Prince George's County	30 413
21	58836		Paducah city	25 024	24	30325		Frederick city	65 239
21	58836	145	McCracken County	25 024	24	30325	021	Frederick County	65 239
21	65226		Richmond city	31 364	24	31175		Gaithersburg city	59 933
21	65226	151	Madison County	31 364	24	31175	031	Montgomery County	59 933
22			**LOUISIANA**	4 533 372	24	36075		Hagerstown city	39 662
22	00975		Alexandria city	47 723	24	36075	043	Washington County	39 662
22	00975	079	Rapides Parish	47 723	24	45900		Laurel city	25 115
22	05000		Baton Rouge city	229 493	24	45900	033	Prince George's County	25 115
22	05000	033	East Baton Rouge Parish	229 493	24	67675		Rockville city	61 209
22	08920		Bossier City city	61 315	24	67675	031	Montgomery County	61 209
22	08920	015	Bossier Parish	61 315	24	69925		Salisbury city	30 343
22	13960		Central city	26 864	24	69925	045	Wicomico County	30 343
22	13960	033	East Baton Rouge Parish	26 864	25			**MASSACHUSETTS**	6 547 629
22	36255		Houma city	33 727	25	00840		Agawam Town city	28 438
22	36255	109	Terrebonne Parish	33 727	25	00840	013	Hampden County	28 438
22	39475		Kenner city	66 702	25	02690		Attleboro city	43 593
22	39475	051	Jefferson Parish	66 702	25	02690	005	Bristol County	43 593
22	40735		Lafayette city	120 623	25	03690		Barnstable Town city	45 193
22	40735	055	Lafayette Parish	120 623	25	03690	001	Barnstable County	45 193
22	41155		Lake Charles city	71 993	25	05595		Beverly city	39 502
22	41155	019	Calcasieu Parish	71 993	25	05595	009	Essex County	39 502
22	51410		Monroe city	48 815	25	07000		Boston city	617 594
22	51410	073	Ouachita Parish	48 815	25	07000	025	Suffolk County	617 594
22	54035		New Iberia city	30 617	25	07740		Braintree Town city	35 744
22	54035	045	Iberia Parish	30 617	25	07740	021	Norfolk County	35 744
22	55000		New Orleans city	343 829	25	09000		Brockton city	93 810
22	55000	071	Orleans Parish	343 829	25	09000	023	Plymouth County	93 810
22	70000		Shreveport city	199 311	25	11000		Cambridge city	105 162
22	70000	015	Bossier Parish	2 702	25	11000	017	Middlesex County	105 162
22	70000	017	Caddo Parish	196 609	25	13205		Chelsea city	35 177
22	70805		Slidell city	27 068	25	13205	025	Suffolk County	35 177
22	70805	103	St. Tammany Parish	27 068	25	13660		Chicopee city	55 298
23			**MAINE**	1 328 361	25	13660	013	Hampden County	55 298
23	02795		Bangor city	33 039	25	21990		Everett city	41 667
23	02795	019	Penobscot County	33 039	25	21990	017	Middlesex County	41 667
23	38740		Lewiston city	36 592	25	23000		Fall River city	88 857
23	38740	001	Androscoggin County	36 592	25	23000	005	Bristol County	88 857
23	60545		Portland city	66 194	25	23875		Fitchburg city	40 318
23	60545	005	Cumberland County	66 194	25	23875	027	Worcester County	40 318
23	71990		South Portland city	25 002	25	25172		Franklin Town city	31 635
23	71990	005	Cumberland County	25 002	25	25172	021	Norfolk County	31 635
24			**MARYLAND**	5 773 552	25	26150		Gloucester city	28 789
24	01600		Annapolis city	38 394	25	26150	009	Essex County	28 789
24	01600	003	Anne Arundel County	38 394					

Cities by County—*Continued*

State Code	Place Code	County Code	Geographic Area Name	2010 Census Population	State Code	Place Code	County Code	Geographic Area Name	2010 Census Population
25	29405		Haverhill city	60 879	25	76030		Westfield city	41 094
25	29405	009	Essex County	60 879	25	76030	013	Hampden County	41 094
25	30840		Holyoke city	39 880	25	77890		West Springfield Town city	28 391
25	30840	013	Hampden County	39 880	25	77890	013	Hampden County	28 391
25	34550		Lawrence city	76 377	25	78972		Weymouth Town city	53 743
25	34550	009	Essex County	76 377	25	78972	021	Norfolk County	53 743
25	35075		Leominster city	40 759	25	81035		Woburn city	38 120
25	35075	027	Worcester County	40 759	25	81035	017	Middlesex County	38 120
25	37000		Lowell city	106 519	25	82000		Worcester city	181 045
25	37000	017	Middlesex County	106 519	25	82000	027	Worcester County	181 045
25	37490		Lynn city	90 329	26			**MICHIGAN**	9 883 640
25	37490	009	Essex County	90 329	26	01380		Allen Park city	28 210
					26	01380	163	Wayne County	28 210
25	37875		Malden city	59 450					
25	37875	017	Middlesex County	59 450	26	03000		Ann Arbor city	113 934
					26	03000	161	Washtenaw County	113 934
25	38715		Marlborough city	38 499					
25	38715	017	Middlesex County	38 499	26	05920		Battle Creek city	52 347
					26	05920	025	Calhoun County	52 347
25	39835		Medford city	56 173					
25	39835	017	Middlesex County	56 173	26	06020		Bay City city	34 932
					26	06020	017	Bay County	34 932
25	40115		Melrose city	26 983					
25	40115	017	Middlesex County	26 983	26	12060		Burton city	29 999
					26	12060	049	Genesee County	29 999
25	40710		Methuen Town city	47 255					
25	40710	009	Essex County	47 255	26	21000		Dearborn city	98 153
					26	21000	163	Wayne County	98 153
25	45000		New Bedford city	95 072					
25	45000	005	Bristol County	95 072	26	21020		Dearborn Heights city	57 774
					26	21020	163	Wayne County	57 774
25	45560		Newton city	85 146					
25	45560	017	Middlesex County	85 146	26	22000		Detroit city	713 777
					26	22000	163	Wayne County	713 777
25	46330		Northampton city	28 549					
25	46330	015	Hampshire County	28 549	26	24120		East Lansing city	48 579
					26	24120	037	Clinton County	1 969
25	52490		Peabody city	51 251	26	24120	065	Ingham County	46 610
25	52490	009	Essex County	51 251					
					26	24290		Eastpointe city	32 442
25	53960		Pittsfield city	44 737	26	24290	099	Macomb County	32 442
25	53960	003	Berkshire County	44 737					
					26	27440		Farmington Hills city	79 740
25	55745		Quincy city	92 271	26	27440	125	Oakland County	79 740
25	55745	021	Norfolk County	92 271					
					26	29000		Flint city	102 434
25	56585		Revere city	51 755	26	29000	049	Genesee County	102 434
25	56585	025	Suffolk County	51 755					
					26	31420		Garden City city	27 692
25	59105		Salem city	41 340	26	31420	163	Wayne County	27 692
25	59105	009	Essex County	41 340					
					26	34000		Grand Rapids city	188 040
25	62535		Somerville city	75 754	26	34000	081	Kent County	188 040
25	62535	017	Middlesex County	75 754					
					26	38640		Holland city	33 051
25	67000		Springfield city	153 060	26	38640	005	Allegan County	7 016
25	67000	013	Hampden County	153 060	26	38640	139	Ottawa County	26 035
25	69170		Taunton city	55 874	26	40680		Inkster city	25 369
25	69170	005	Bristol County	55 874	26	40680	163	Wayne County	25 369
25	72600		Waltham city	60 632	26	41420		Jackson city	33 534
25	72600	017	Middlesex County	60 632	26	41420	075	Jackson County	33 534
25	73440		Watertown Town city	31 915	26	42160		Kalamazoo city	74 262
25	73440	017	Middlesex County	31 915	26	42160	077	Kalamazoo County	74 262

Cities by County—*Continued*

State Code	Place Code	County Code	Geographic Area Name	2010 Census Population
26	42820		Kentwood city	48 707
26	42820	081	Kent County	48 707
26	46000		Lansing city	114 297
26	46000	045	Eaton County	4 734
26	46000	065	Ingham County	109 563
26	47800		Lincoln Park city	38 144
26	47800	163	Wayne County	38 144
26	49000		Livonia city	96 942
26	49000	163	Wayne County	96 942
26	50560		Madison Heights city	29 694
26	50560	125	Oakland County	29 694
26	53780		Midland city	41 863
26	53780	017	Bay County	157
26	53780	111	Midland County	41 706
26	56020		Mount Pleasant city	26 016
26	56020	073	Isabella County	26 016
26	56320		Muskegon city	38 401
26	56320	121	Muskegon County	38 401
26	59440		Novi city	55 224
26	59440	125	Oakland County	55 224
26	59920		Oak Park city	29 319
26	59920	125	Oakland County	29 319
26	65440		Pontiac city	59 515
26	65440	125	Oakland County	59 515
26	65560		Portage city	46 292
26	65560	077	Kalamazoo County	46 292
26	65820		Port Huron city	30 184
26	65820	147	St. Clair County	30 184
26	69035		Rochester Hills city	70 995
26	69035	125	Oakland County	70 995
26	69800		Roseville city	47 299
26	69800	099	Macomb County	47 299
26	70040		Royal Oak city	57 236
26	70040	125	Oakland County	57 236
26	70520		Saginaw city	51 508
26	70520	145	Saginaw County	51 508
26	70760		St. Clair Shores city	59 715
26	70760	099	Macomb County	59 715
26	74900		Southfield city	71 739
26	74900	125	Oakland County	71 739
26	74960		Southgate city	30 047
26	74960	163	Wayne County	30 047
26	76460		Sterling Heights city	129 699
26	76460	099	Macomb County	129 699
26	79000		Taylor city	63 131
26	79000	163	Wayne County	63 131
26	80700		Troy city	80 980
26	80700	125	Oakland County	80 980
26	84000		Warren city	134 056
26	84000	099	Macomb County	134 056
26	86000		Westland city	84 094
26	86000	163	Wayne County	84 094
26	88900		Wyandotte city	25 883
26	88900	163	Wayne County	25 883
26	88940		Wyoming city	72 125
26	88940	081	Kent County	72 125
27			**MINNESOTA**	5 303 925
27	01486		Andover city	30 598
27	01486	003	Anoka County	30 598
27	01900		Apple Valley city	49 084
27	01900	037	Dakota County	49 084
27	06382		Blaine city	57 186
27	06382	003	Anoka County	57 186
27	06382	123	Ramsey County	0
27	06616		Bloomington city	82 893
27	06616	053	Hennepin County	82 893
27	07948		Brooklyn Center city	30 104
27	07948	053	Hennepin County	30 104
27	07966		Brooklyn Park city	75 781
27	07966	053	Hennepin County	75 781
27	08794		Burnsville city	60 306
27	08794	037	Dakota County	60 306
27	13114		Coon Rapids city	61 476
27	13114	003	Anoka County	61 476
27	13456		Cottage Grove city	34 589
27	13456	163	Washington County	34 589
27	17000		Duluth city	86 265
27	17000	137	St. Louis County	86 265
27	17288		Eagan city	64 206
27	17288	037	Dakota County	64 206
27	18116		Eden Prairie city	60 797
27	18116	053	Hennepin County	60 797
27	18188		Edina city	47 941
27	18188	053	Hennepin County	47 941
27	22814		Fridley city	27 208
27	22814	003	Anoka County	27 208
27	31076		Inver Grove Heights city	33 880
27	31076	037	Dakota County	33 880
27	35180		Lakeville city	55 954
27	35180	037	Dakota County	55 954
27	39878		Mankato city	39 309
27	39878	013	Blue Earth County	39 305
27	39878	079	Le Sueur County	4
27	39878	103	Nicollet County	0
27	40166		Maple Grove city	61 567
27	40166	053	Hennepin County	61 567
27	40382		Maplewood city	38 018
27	40382	123	Ramsey County	38 018

Cities by County–*Continued*

State Code	Place Code	County Code	Geographic Area Name	2010 Census Population	State Code	Place Code	County Code	Geographic Area Name	2010 Census Population
27	43000		Minneapolis city	382 578	28	36000		Jackson city	173 514
27	43000	053	Hennepin County	382 578	28	36000	049	Hinds County	172 891
					28	36000	089	Madison County	622
27	43252		Minnetonka city	49 734	28	36000	121	Rankin County	1
27	43252	053	Hennepin County	49 734					
					28	46640		Meridian city	41 148
27	43864		Moorhead city	38 065	28	46640	075	Lauderdale County	41 148
27	43864	027	Clay County	38 065					
					28	54040		Olive Branch city	33 484
27	47680		Oakdale city	27 378	28	54040	033	DeSoto County	33 484
27	47680	163	Washington County	27 378					
					28	55760		Pearl city	25 092
27	49300		Owatonna city	25 599	28	55760	121	Rankin County	25 092
27	49300	147	Steele County	25 599					
					28	69280		Southaven city	48 982
27	51730		Plymouth city	70 576	28	69280	033	DeSoto County	48 982
27	51730	053	Hennepin County	70 576					
					28	74840		Tupelo city	34 546
27	54214		Richfield city	35 228	28	74840	081	Lee County	34 546
27	54214	053	Hennepin County	35 228					
					29			**MISSOURI**	5 988 927
27	54880		Rochester city	106 769	29	03160		Ballwin city	30 404
27	54880	109	Olmsted County	106 769	29	03160	189	St. Louis County	30 404
27	55852		Roseville city	33 660	29	06652		Blue Springs city	52 575
27	55852	123	Ramsey County	33 660	29	06652	095	Jackson County	52 575
27	56896		St. Cloud city	65 842	29	11242		Cape Girardeau city	37 941
27	56896	009	Benton County	6 396	29	11242	031	Cape Girardeau County	37 941
27	56896	141	Sherburne County	6 785	29	11242	201	Scott County	0
27	56896	145	Stearns County	52 661					
					29	13600		Chesterfield city	47 484
27	57220		St. Louis Park city	45 250	29	13600	189	St. Louis County	47 484
27	57220	053	Hennepin County	45 250					
					29	15670		Columbia city	108 500
27	58000		St. Paul city	285 068	29	15670	019	Boone County	108 500
27	58000	123	Ramsey County	285 068					
					29	24778		Florissant city	52 158
27	58738		Savage city	26 911	29	24778	189	St. Louis County	52 158
27	58738	139	Scott County	26 911					
					29	27190		Gladstone city	25 410
27	59350		Shakopee city	37 076	29	27190	047	Clay County	25 410
27	59350	139	Scott County	37 076					
					29	31276		Hazelwood city	25 703
27	59998		Shoreview city	25 043	29	31276	189	St. Louis County	25 703
27	59998	123	Ramsey County	25 043					
					29	35000		Independence city	116 830
27	71032		Winona city	27 592	29	35000	047	Clay County	0
27	71032	169	Winona County	27 592	29	35000	095	Jackson County	116 830
27	71428		Woodbury city	61 961	29	37000		Jefferson City city	43 079
27	71428	163	Washington County	61 961	29	37000	027	Callaway County	22
28			**MISSISSIPPI**	2 967 297	29	37000	051	Cole County	43 057
28	06220		Biloxi city	44 054	29	37592		Joplin city	50 150
28	06220	047	Harrison County	44 054	29	37592	097	Jasper County	43 955
					29	37592	145	Newton County	6 195
28	14420		Clinton city	25 216					
28	14420	049	Hinds County	25 216	29	38000		Kansas City city	459 787
					29	38000	037	Cass County	197
28	29180		Greenville city	34 400	29	38000	047	Clay County	113 415
28	29180	151	Washington County	34 400	29	38000	095	Jackson County	302 499
					29	38000	165	Platte County	43 676
28	29700		Gulfport city	67 793					
28	29700	047	Harrison County	67 793	29	39044		Kirkwood city	27 540
					29	39044	189	St. Louis County	27 540
28	31020		Hattiesburg city	45 989					
28	31020	035	Forrest County	41 000	29	41348		Lee's Summit city	91 364
28	31020	073	Lamar County	4 989	29	41348	037	Cass County	1 917
					29	41348	095	Jackson County	89 447
28	33700		Horn Lake city	26 066					
28	33700	033	DeSoto County	26 066					

State Code	Place Code	County Code	Geographic Area Name	2010 Census Population	State Code	Place Code	County Code	Geographic Area Name	2010 Census Population
29	42032		Liberty city	29 149	32			**NEVADA**	2 700 551
29	42032	047	Clay County	29 149	32	09700		Carson City	55 274
					32	09700	510	Carson City	55 274
29	46586		Maryland Heights city	27 472					
29	46586	189	St. Louis County	27 472	32	31900		Henderson city	257 729
					32	31900	003	Clark County	257 729
29	54074		O'Fallon city	79 329					
29	54074	183	St. Charles County	79 329	32	40000		Las Vegas city	583 756
					32	40000	003	Clark County	583 756
29	60788		Raytown city	29 526					
29	60788	095	Jackson County	29 526	32	51800		North Las Vegas city	216 961
					32	51800	003	Clark County	216 961
29	64082		St. Charles city	65 794					
29	64082	183	St. Charles County	65 794	32	60600		Reno city	225 221
					32	60600	031	Washoe County	225 221
29	64550		St. Joseph city	76 780					
29	64550	021	Buchanan County	76 780	32	68400		Sparks city	90 264
					32	68400	031	Washoe County	90 264
29	65000		St. Louis city	319 294					
29	65000	510	St. Louis city	319 294	33			**NEW HAMPSHIRE**	1 316 470
					33	14200		Concord city	42 695
29	65126		St. Peters city	52 575	33	14200	013	Merrimack County	42 695
29	65126	183	St. Charles County	52 575					
					33	18820		Dover city	29 987
29	70000		Springfield city	159 498	33	18820	017	Strafford County	29 987
29	70000	043	Christian County	2					
29	70000	077	Greene County	159 496	33	45140		Manchester city	109 565
					33	45140	011	Hillsborough County	109 565
29	75220		University City city	35 371					
29	75220	189	St. Louis County	35 371	33	50260		Nashua city	86 494
					33	50260	011	Hillsborough County	86 494
29	78442		Wentzville city	29 070					
29	78442	183	St. Charles County	29 070	33	65140		Rochester city	29 752
					33	65140	017	Strafford County	29 752
29	79820		Wildwood city	35 517					
29	79820	189	St. Louis County	35 517	34			**NEW JERSEY**	8 791 894
					34	02080		Atlantic City city	39 558
30			**MONTANA**	989 415	34	02080	001	Atlantic County	39 558
30	06550		Billings city	104 170					
30	06550	111	Yellowstone County	104 170	34	03580		Bayonne city	63 024
					34	03580	017	Hudson County	63 024
30	08950		Bozeman city	37 280					
30	08950	031	Gallatin County	37 280	34	05170		Bergenfield borough	26 764
					34	05170	003	Bergen County	26 764
30	32800		Great Falls city	58 505					
30	32800	013	Cascade County	58 505	34	07600		Bridgeton city	25 349
					34	07600	011	Cumberland County	25 349
30	35600		Helena city	28 190					
30	35600	049	Lewis and Clark County	28 190	34	10000		Camden city	77 344
					34	10000	007	Camden County	77 344
30	50200		Missoula city	66 788					
30	50200	063	Missoula County	66 788	34	13690		Clifton city	84 136
					34	13690	031	Passaic County	84 136
31			**NEBRASKA**	1 826 341					
31	03950		Bellevue city	50 137	34	19390		East Orange city	64 270
31	03950	153	Sarpy County	50 137	34	19390	013	Essex County	64 270
31	17670		Fremont city	26 397	34	21000		Elizabeth city	124 969
31	17670	053	Dodge County	26 397	34	21000	039	Union County	124 969
31	19595		Grand Island city	48 520	34	21480		Englewood city	27 147
31	19595	079	Hall County	48 520	34	21480	003	Bergen County	27 147
31	25055		Kearney city	30 787	34	22470		Fair Lawn borough	32 457
31	25055	019	Buffalo County	30 787	34	22470	003	Bergen County	32 457
31	28000		Lincoln city	258 379	34	24420		Fort Lee borough	35 345
31	28000	109	Lancaster County	258 379	34	24420	003	Bergen County	35 345
31	37000		Omaha city	408 958	34	25770		Garfield city	30 487
31	37000	055	Douglas County	408 958	34	25770	003	Bergen County	30 487

Cities by County–*Continued*

State Code	Place Code	County Code	Geographic Area Name	2010 Census Population	State Code	Place Code	County Code	Geographic Area Name	2010 Census Population
34	28680		Hackensack city	43 010	35	16420		Clovis city	37 775
34	28680	003	Bergen County	43 010	35	16420	009	Curry County	37 775
34	32250		Hoboken city	50 005	35	25800		Farmington city	45 877
34	32250	017	Hudson County	50 005	35	25800	045	San Juan County	45 877
34	36000		Jersey City city	247 597	35	32520		Hobbs city	34 122
34	36000	017	Hudson County	247 597	35	32520	025	Lea County	34 122
34	36510		Kearny town	40 684	35	39380		Las Cruces city	97 618
34	36510	017	Hudson County	40 684	35	39380	013	Do⊠a Ana County	97 618
34	40350		Linden city	40 499	35	63460		Rio Rancho city	87 521
34	40350	039	Union County	40 499	35	63460	001	Bernalillo County	130
					35	63460	043	Sandoval County	87 391
34	41310		Long Branch city	30 719					
34	41310	025	Monmouth County	30 719	35	64930		Roswell city	48 366
					35	64930	005	Chaves County	48 366
34	46680		Millville city	28 400					
34	46680	011	Cumberland County	28 400	35	70500		Santa Fe city	67 947
					35	70500	049	Santa Fe County	67 947
34	51000		Newark city	277 140					
34	51000	013	Essex County	277 140	36			**NEW YORK**	19 378 102
					36	01000		Albany city	97 856
34	51210		New Brunswick city	55 181	36	01000	001	Albany County	97 856
34	51210	023	Middlesex County	55 181					
					36	03078		Auburn oity	27 687
34	55950		Paramus borough	26 342	36	03078	011	Cayuga County	27 687
34	55950	003	Bergen County	26 342					
					36	06607		Binghamton city	47 376
34	56550		Passaic city	69 781	36	06607	007	Broome County	47 376
34	56550	031	Passaic County	69 781					
					36	11000		Buffalo clty	261 310
34	57000		Paterson oity	146 199	36	11000	029	Erie County	261 010
34	57000	031	Passalo County	146 199					
					36	24229		Elmira clty	29 200
34	58200		Perth Amboy city	50 814	36	24229	015	Chemung County	29 200
34	58200	023	Middlesex County	50 814					
					36	27485		Freeport village	42 860
34	59190		Plainfield city	49 808	36	27485	059	Nassau County	42 860
34	59190	039	Union County	49 808					
					36	29113		Glen Cove city	26 964
34	61530		Rahway city	27 346	36	29113	059	Nassau County	26 964
34	61530	039	Union County	27 346					
					36	32402		Harrison village	27 472
34	65790		Sayreville borough	42 704	36	32402	119	Westchester County	27 472
34	65790	023	Middlesex County	42 704					
					36	33139		Hempstead village	53 891
34	74000		Trenton city	84 913	36	33139	059	Nassau County	53 891
34	74000	021	Mercer County	84 913					
					36	38077		Ithaca city	30 014
34	74630		Union City city	66 455	36	38077	109	Tompkins County	30 014
34	74630	017	Hudson County	66 455					
					36	38264		Jamestown city	31 146
34	76070		Vineland city	60 724	36	38264	013	Chautauqua County	31 146
34	76070	011	Cumberland County	60 724					
					36	42554		Lindenhurst village	27 253
34	79040		Westfield town	30 316	36	42554	103	Suffolk County	27 253
34	79040	039	Union County	30 316					
					36	43335		Long Beach city	33 275
34	79610		West New York town	49 708	36	43335	059	Nassau County	33 275
34	79610	017	Hudson County	49 708					
					36	47042		Middletown city	28 086
35			**NEW MEXICO**	2 059 179	36	47042	071	Orange County	28 086
35	01780		Alamogordo city	30 403					
35	01780	035	Otero County	30 403	36	49121		Mount Vernon city	67 292
					36	49121	119	Westchester County	67 292
35	02000		Albuquerque city	545 852					
35	02000	001	Bernalillo County	545 852	36	50034		Newburgh city	28 866
					36	50034	071	Orange County	28 866
35	12150		Carlsbad city	26 138					
35	12150	015	Eddy County	26 138					

Cities by County–*Continued*

State Code	Place Code	County Code	Geographic Area Name	2010 Census Population	State Code	Place Code	County Code	Geographic Area Name	2010 Census Population
36	50617		New Rochelle city	77 062	37	10740		Cary town	135 234
36	50617	119	Westchester County	77 062	37	10740	037	Chatham County	1 422
					37	10740	183	Wake County	133 812
36	51000		New York city	8 175 133					
36	51000	005	Bronx County	1 385 108	37	11800		Chapel Hill town	57 233
36	51000	047	Kings County	2 504 700	37	11800	063	Durham County	2 836
36	51000	061	New York County	1 585 873	37	11800	135	Orange County	54 397
36	51000	081	Queens County	2 230 722					
36	51000	085	Richmond County	468 730	37	12000		Charlotte city	731 424
					37	12000	119	Mecklenburg County	731 424
36	51055		Niagara Falls city	50 193					
36	51055	063	Niagara County	50 193	37	14100		Concord city	79 066
					37	14100	025	Cabarrus County	79 066
36	53682		North Tonawanda city	31 568					
36	53682	063	Niagara County	31 568	37	19000		Durham city	228 330
					37	19000	063	Durham County	228 300
36	55530		Ossining village	25 060	37	19000	135	Orange County	30
36	55530	119	Westchester County	25 060	37	19000	183	Wake County	0
36	59223		Port Chester village	28 967	37	22920		Fayetteville city	200 564
36	59223	119	Westchester County	28 967	37	22920	051	Cumberland County	200 564
36	59641		Poughkeepsie city	32 736	37	25480		Garner town	25 745
36	59641	027	Dutchess County	32 736	37	25480	183	Wake County	25 745
36	63000		Rochester city	210 565	37	25580		Gastonia city	71 741
36	63000	055	Monroe County	210 565	37	25580	071	Gaston County	71 741
36	63418		Rome city	33 725	37	26880		Goldsboro city	36 437
36	63418	065	Oneida County	33 725	37	26880	191	Wayne County	36 437
36	65255		Saratoga Springs city	26 586	37	28000		Greensboro city	269 666
36	65255	091	Saratoga County	26 586	37	28000	081	Guilford County	269 666
36	65508		Schenectady city	66 135	37	28080		Greenville city	84 554
36	65508	093	Schenectady County	66 135	37	28080	147	Pitt County	84 554
36	70420		Spring Valley village	31 347	37	31060		Hickory city	40 010
36	70420	087	Rockland County	31 347	37	31060	023	Burke County	66
					37	31060	027	Caldwell County	18
36	73000		Syracuse city	145 170	37	31060	035	Catawba County	39 926
36	73000	067	Onondaga County	145 170					
					37	31400		High Point city	104 371
36	75484		Troy city	50 129	37	31400	057	Davidson County	5 310
36	75484	083	Rensselaer County	50 129	37	31400	067	Forsyth County	8
					37	31400	081	Guilford County	99 042
36	76540		Utica city	62 235	37	31400	151	Randolph County	11
36	76540	065	Oneida County	62 235					
					37	33120		Huntersville town	46 773
36	76705		Valley Stream village	37 511	37	33120	119	Mecklenburg County	46 773
36	76705	059	Nassau County	37 511					
					37	33560		Indian Trail town	33 518
36	78608		Watertown city	27 023	37	33560	179	Union County	33 518
36	78608	045	Jefferson County	27 023					
					37	34200		Jacksonville city	70 145
36	81677		White Plains city	56 853	37	34200	133	Onslow County	70 145
36	81677	119	Westchester County	56 853					
					37	35200		Kannapolis city	42 625
37			**NORTH CAROLINA**	9 535 483	37	35200	025	Cabarrus County	33 194
37	01520		Apex town	37 476	37	35200	159	Rowan County	9 431
37	01520	183	Wake County	37 476					
					37	41960		Matthews town	27 198
37	02080		Asheboro city	25 012	37	41960	119	Mecklenburg County	27 198
37	02080	151	Randolph County	25 012					
					37	43920		Monroe city	32 797
37	02140		Asheville city	83 393	37	43920	179	Union County	32 797
37	02140	021	Buncombe County	83 393					
					37	44220		Mooresville town	32 711
37	09060		Burlington city	49 963	37	44220	097	Iredell County	32 711
37	09060	001	Alamance County	49 308					
37	09060	081	Guilford County	655	37	46340		New Bern city	29 524
					37	46340	049	Craven County	29 524

Cities by County—*Continued*

State Code	Place Code	County Code	Geographic Area Name	2010 Census Population	State Code	Place Code	County Code	Geographic Area Name	2010 Census Population
37	55000		Raleigh city	403 892	39	16014		Cleveland Heights city	46 121
37	55000	063	Durham County	1 067	39	16014	035	Cuyahoga County	46 121
37	55000	183	Wake County	402 825					
					39	18000		Columbus city	787 033
37	57500		Rocky Mount city	57 477	39	18000	041	Delaware County	7 245
37	57500	065	Edgecombe County	17 524	39	18000	045	Fairfield County	9 666
37	57500	127	Nash County	39 953	39	18000	049	Franklin County	770 122
37	58860		Salisbury city	33 662	39	19778		Cuyahoga Falls city	49 652
37	58860	159	Rowan County	33 662	39	19778	153	Summit County	49 652
37	59280		Sanford city	28 094	39	21000		Dayton city	141 527
37	59280	105	Lee County	28 094	39	21000	113	Montgomery County	141 527
37	67420		Thomasville city	26 757	39	21434		Delaware city	34 753
37	67420	057	Davidson County	26 493	39	21434	041	Delaware County	34 753
37	67420	151	Randolph County	264					
					39	22694		Dublin city	41 751
37	70540		Wake Forest town	30 117	39	22694	041	Delaware County	4 018
37	70540	069	Franklin County	899	39	22694	049	Franklin County	35 367
37	70540	183	Wake County	29 218	39	22694	159	Union County	2 366
37	74440		Wilmington city	106 476	39	25256		Elyria city	54 533
37	74440	129	New Hanover County	106 476	39	25256	093	Lorain County	54 533
37	74540		Wilson city	49 167	39	25704		Euclid city	48 920
37	74540	195	Wilson County	49 167	39	25704	035	Cuyahoga County	48 920
37	75000		Winston-Salem city	229 617	39	25914		Fairborn city	32 352
37	75000	067	Forsyth County	229 617	39	25914	057	Greene County	32 352
38			**NORTH DAKOTA**	672 591	39	25970		Fairfield city	42 510
38	07200		Bismarck city	61 272	39	25970	017	Butler County	42 510
38	07200	015	Burleigh County	61 272	39	25970	061	Hamilton County	0
38	25700		Fargo city	105 549	39	27048		Findlay city	41 202
38	25700	017	Cass County	105 549	39	27048	063	Hancock County	41 202
38	32060		Grand Forks city	52 838	39	29106		Gahanna city	33 248
38	32060	035	Grand Forks County	52 838	39	29106	049	Franklin County	33 248
38	53380		Minot city	40 888	39	29428		Garfield Heights city	28 849
38	53380	101	Ward County	40 888	39	29428	035	Cuyahoga County	28 849
38	84780		West Fargo city	25 830	39	31860		Green city	25 699
38	84780	017	Cass County	25 830	39	31860	153	Summit County	25 699
39			**OHIO**	11 536 504	39	32592		Grove City city	35 575
39	01000		Akron city	199 110	39	32592	049	Franklin County	35 575
39	01000	153	Summit County	199 110					
					39	33012		Hamilton city	62 477
39	03828		Barberton city	26 550	39	33012	017	Butler County	62 477
39	03828	153	Summit County	26 550					
					39	35476		Hilliard city	28 435
39	04720		Beavercreek city	45 193	39	35476	049	Franklin County	28 435
39	04720	057	Greene County	45 193					
					39	36610		Huber Heights city	38 101
39	07972		Bowling Green city	30 028	39	36610	057	Greene County	0
39	07972	173	Wood County	30 028	39	36610	109	Miami County	959
					39	36610	113	Montgomery County	37 142
39	09680		Brunswick city	34 255					
39	09680	103	Medina County	34 255	39	39872		Kent city	28 904
					39	39872	133	Portage County	28 904
39	12000		Canton city	73 007					
39	12000	151	Stark County	73 007	39	40040		Kettering city	56 163
					39	40040	057	Greene County	467
39	15000		Cincinnati city	296 943	39	40040	113	Montgomery County	55 696
39	15000	061	Hamilton County	296 943					
					39	41664		Lakewood city	52 131
39	16000		Cleveland city	396 815	39	41664	035	Cuyahoga County	52 131
39	16000	035	Cuyahoga County	396 815					

Cities by County-_Continued_

State Code	Place Code	County Code	Geographic Area Name	2010 Census Population	State Code	Place Code	County Code	Geographic Area Name	2010 Census Population
39	41720		Lancaster city	38 780	39	77588		Troy city	25 058
39	41720	045	Fairfield County	38 780	39	77588	109	Miami County	25 058
39	43554		Lima city	38 771	39	79002		Upper Arlington city	33 771
39	43554	003	Allen County	38 771	39	79002	049	Franklin County	33 771
39	44856		Lorain city	64 097	39	80892		Warren city	41 557
39	44856	093	Lorain County	64 097	39	80892	155	Trumbull County	41 557
39	47138		Mansfield city	47 821	39	83342		Westerville city	36 120
39	47138	139	Richland County	47 821	39	83342	041	Delaware County	7 792
					39	83342	049	Franklin County	28 328
39	47754		Marion city	36 837					
39	47754	101	Marion County	36 837	39	83622		Westlake city	32 729
					39	83622	035	Cuyahoga County	32 729
39	48188		Mason city	30 712					
39	48188	165	Warren County	30 712	39	86548		Wooster city	26 119
					39	86548	169	Wayne County	26 119
39	48244		Massillon city	32 149					
39	48244	151	Stark County	32 149	39	86772		Xenia city	25 719
					39	86772	057	Greene County	25 719
39	48790		Medina city	26 678					
39	48790	103	Medina County	26 678	39	88000		Youngstown city	66 982
					39	88000	099	Mahoning County	66 971
39	49056		Mentor city	47 159	39	88000	155	Trumbull County	11
39	49056	085	Lake County	47 159					
					39	88084		Zanesville city	25 487
39	49840		Middletown city	48 694	39	88084	119	Muskingum County	25 487
39	49840	017	Butler County	45 994					
39	49840	165	Warren County	2 700	40			**OKLAHOMA**	3 751 351
					40	04450		Bartlesville city	35 750
39	54040		Newark city	47 573	40	04450	113	Osage County	3
39	54040	089	Licking County	47 573	40	04450	147	Washington County	35 747
39	56882		North Olmsted city	32 718	40	09050		Broken Arrow city	98 850
39	56882	035	Cuyahoga County	32 718	40	09050	143	Tulsa County	80 634
					40	09050	145	Wagoner County	18 216
39	56966		North Ridgeville city	29 465					
39	56966	093	Lorain County	29 465	40	23200		Edmond city	81 405
					40	23200	109	Oklahoma County	81 405
39	57008		North Royalton city	30 444					
39	57008	035	Cuyahoga County	30 444	40	23950		Enid city	49 379
					40	23950	047	Garfield County	49 379
39	61000		Parma city	81 601					
39	61000	035	Cuyahoga County	81 601	40	41850		Lawton city	96 867
					40	41850	031	Comanche County	96 867
39	66390		Reynoldsburg city	35 893					
39	66390	045	Fairfield County	910	40	48350		Midwest City city	54 371
39	66390	049	Franklin County	26 157	40	48350	109	Oklahoma County	54 371
39	66390	089	Licking County	8 826					
					40	49200		Moore city	55 081
39	67468		Riverside city	25 201	40	49200	027	Cleveland County	55 081
39	67468	113	Montgomery County	25 201					
					40	50050		Muskogee city	39 223
39	70380		Sandusky city	25 793	40	50050	101	Muskogee County	39 223
39	70380	043	Erie County	25 793					
					40	52500		Norman city	110 925
39	71682		Shaker Heights city	28 448	40	52500	027	Cleveland County	110 925
39	71682	035	Cuyahoga County	28 448					
					40	55000		Oklahoma City city	579 999
39	74118		Springfield city	60 608	40	55000	017	Canadian County	44 541
39	74118	023	Clark County	60 608	40	55000	027	Cleveland County	63 723
					40	55000	109	Oklahoma County	471 671
39	74944		Stow city	34 837	40	55000	125	Pottawatomie County	64
39	74944	153	Summit County	34 837					
					40	56650		Owasso city	28 915
39	75098		Strongsville city	44 750	40	56650	131	Rogers County	2 614
39	75098	035	Cuyahoga County	44 750	40	56650	143	Tulsa County	26 301
39	77000		Toledo city	287 208	40	59850		Ponca City city	25 387
39	77000	095	Lucas County	287 208	40	59850	071	Kay County	25 387

Cities by County–*Continued*

State Code	Place Code	County Code	Geographic Area Name	2010 Census Population	State Code	Place Code	County Code	Geographic Area Name	2010 Census Population
40	66800		Shawnee city	29 857	41	74950		Tualatin city	26 054
40	66800	125	Pottawatomie County	29 857	41	74950	005	Clackamas County	2 862
40	70300		Stillwater city	45 688	41	74950	067	Washington County	23 192
40	70300	119	Payne County	45 688	41	80150		West Linn city	25 109
40	75000		Tulsa city	391 906	41	80150	005	Clackamas County	25 109
40	75000	113	Osage County	6 136	42			**PENNSYLVANIA**	12 702 379
40	75000	131	Rogers County	0	42	02000		Allentown city	118 032
40	75000	143	Tulsa County	385 613	42	02000	077	Lehigh County	118 032
40	75000	145	Wagoner County	157	42	02184		Altoona city	46 320
41			**OREGON**	3 831 074	42	02184	013	Blair County	46 320
41	01000		Albany city	50 158	42	06064		Bethel Park municipality	32 313
41	01000	003	Benton County	6 463	42	06064	003	Allegheny County	32 313
41	01000	043	Linn County	43 695	42	06088		Bethlehem city	74 982
41	05350		Beaverton city	89 803	42	06088	077	Lehigh County	19 343
41	05350	067	Washington County	89 803	42	06088	095	Northampton County	55 639
41	05800		Bend city	76 639	42	13208		Chester city	33 972
41	05800	017	Deschutes County	76 639	42	13208	045	Delaware County	33 972
41	15800		Corvallis city	54 462	42	21648		Easton city	26 800
41	15800	003	Benton County	54 462	42	21648	095	Northampton County	26 800
41	23850		Eugene city	156 185	42	24000		Erie city	101 786
41	23850	039	Lane County	156 185	42	24000	049	Erie County	101 786
41	30550		Grants Pass city	34 533	42	32800		Harrisburg city	49 528
41	30550	033	Josephine County	34 533	42	32800	043	Dauphin County	49 528
41	31250		Gresham city	105 594	42	33408		Hazleton city	25 340
41	31250	051	Multnomah County	105 594	42	33408	079	Luzerne County	25 340
41	34100		Hillsboro city	91 611	42	41216		Lancaster city	59 322
41	34100	067	Washington County	91 611	42	41216	071	Lancaster County	59 322
41	38500		Keizer city	36 478	42	42168		Lebanon city	25 477
41	38500	047	Marion County	36 478	42	42168	075	Lebanon County	25 477
41	40550		Lake Oswego city	36 619	42	50528		Monroeville municipality	28 386
41	40550	005	Clackamas County	34 066	42	50528	003	Allegheny County	28 386
41	40550	051	Multnomah County	2 544	42	54656		Norristown borough	34 324
41	40550	067	Washington County	9	42	54656	091	Montgomery County	34 324
41	45000		McMinnville city	32 187	42	60000		Philadelphia city	1 526 006
41	45000	071	Yamhill County	32 187	42	60000	101	Philadelphia County	1 526 006
41	47000		Medford city	74 907	42	61000		Pittsburgh city	305 704
41	47000	029	Jackson County	74 907	42	61000	003	Allegheny County	305 704
41	55200		Oregon City city	31 859	42	61536		Plum borough	27 126
41	55200	005	Clackamas County	31 859	42	61536	003	Allegheny County	27 126
41	59000		Portland city	583 776	42	63624		Reading city	88 082
41	59000	005	Clackamas County	744	42	63624	011	Berks County	88 082
41	59000	051	Multnomah County	581 485	42	69000		Scranton city	76 089
41	59000	067	Washington County	1 547	42	69000	069	Lackawanna County	76 089
41	61200		Redmond city	26 215	42	73808		State College borough	42 034
41	61200	017	Deschutes County	26 215	42	73808	027	Centre County	42 034
41	64900		Salem city	154 637	42	85152		Wilkes-Barre city	41 498
41	64900	047	Marion County	130 398	42	85152	079	Luzerne County	41 498
41	64900	053	Polk County	24 239	42	85312		Williamsport city	29 381
41	69600		Springfield city	59 403	42	85312	081	Lycoming County	29 381
41	69600	039	Lane County	59 403					
41	73650		Tigard city	48 035					
41	73650	067	Washington County	48 035					

Cities by County–*Continued*

State Code	Place Code	County Code	Geographic Area Name	2010 Census Population	State Code	Place Code	County Code	Geographic Area Name	2010 Census Population
42	87048		York city	43 718	45	70270		Summerville town	43 392
42	87048	133	York County	43 718	45	70270	015	Berkeley County	3 643
					45	70270	019	Charleston County	1 010
44			**RHODE ISLAND**	1 052 567	45	70270	035	Dorchester County	38 739
44	19180		Cranston city	80 387					
44	19180	007	Providence County	80 387	45	70405		Sumter city	40 524
					45	70405	085	Sumter County	40 524
44	22960		East Providence city	47 037					
44	22960	007	Providence County	47 037	46			**SOUTH DAKOTA**	814 180
					46	00100		Aberdeen city	26 091
44	54640		Pawtucket city	71 148	46	00100	013	Brown County	26 091
44	54640	007	Providence County	71 148					
					46	52980		Rapid City city	67 956
44	59000		Providence city	178 042	46	52980	103	Pennington County	67 956
44	59000	007	Providence County	178 042					
					46	59020		Sioux Falls city	153 888
44	74300		Warwick city	82 672	46	59020	083	Lincoln County	21 095
44	74300	003	Kent County	82 672	46	59020	099	Minnehaha County	132 793
44	80780		Woonsocket city	41 186	47			**TENNESSEE**	6 346 105
44	80780	007	Providence County	41 186	47	03440		Bartlett city	54 613
					47	03440	157	Shelby County	54 613
45			**SOUTH CAROLINA**	4 625 364					
45	00550		Aiken city	29 524	47	08280		Brentwood city	37 060
45	00550	003	Aiken County	29 524	47	08280	187	Williamson County	37 060
45	01360		Anderson city	26 686	47	08540		Bristol city	26 702
45	01360	007	Anderson County	26 686	47	08540	163	Sullivan County	26 702
45	13330		Charleston city	120 083	47	14000		Chattanooga city	167 674
45	13330	015	Berkeley County	8 095	47	14000	065	Hamilton County	167 674
45	13330	019	Charleston County	111 988					
					47	15160		Clarksville city	132 929
45	16000		Columbia city	129 272	47	15160	125	Montgomery County	132 929
45	16000	063	Lexington County	559					
45	16000	079	Richland County	128 713	47	15400		Cleveland city	41 285
					47	15400	011	Bradley County	41 285
45	25810		Florence city	37 056					
45	25810	041	Florence County	37 056	47	16420		Collierville town	43 965
					47	16420	047	Fayette County	0
45	29815		Goose Creek city	35 938	47	16420	157	Shelby County	43 965
45	29815	015	Berkeley County	35 933					
45	29815	019	Charleston County	5	47	16540		Columbia city	34 681
					47	16540	119	Maury County	34 681
45	30850		Greenville city	58 409					
45	30850	045	Greenville County	58 409	47	16920		Cookeville city	30 435
					47	16920	141	Putnam County	30 435
45	30985		Greer city	25 515					
45	30985	045	Greenville County	18 635	47	27740		Franklin city	62 487
45	30985	083	Spartanburg County	6 880	47	27740	187	Williamson County	62 487
45	34045		Hilton Head Island town	37 099	47	28540		Gallatin city	30 278
45	34045	013	Beaufort County	37 099	47	28540	165	Sumner County	30 278
45	48535		Mount Pleasant town	67 843	47	28960		Germantown city	38 844
45	48535	019	Charleston County	67 843	47	28960	157	Shelby County	38 844
45	49075		Myrtle Beach city	27 109	47	33280		Hendersonville city	51 372
45	49075	051	Horry County	27 109	47	33280	165	Sumner County	51 372
45	50875		North Charleston city	97 471	47	37640		Jackson city	65 211
45	50875	015	Berkeley County	0	47	37640	113	Madison County	65 211
45	50875	019	Charleston County	78 393					
45	50875	035	Dorchester County	19 078	47	38320		Johnson City city	63 152
					47	38320	019	Carter County	1 252
45	61405		Rock Hill city	66 154	47	38320	163	Sullivan County	367
45	61405	091	York County	66 154	47	38320	179	Washington County	61 533
45	68290		Spartanburg city	37 013	47	39560		Kingsport city	48 205
45	68290	083	Spartanburg County	37 013	47	39560	073	Hawkins County	2 854
					47	39560	163	Sullivan County	45 351

Cities by County–*Continued*

State Code	Place Code	County Code	Geographic Area Name	2010 Census Population	State Code	Place Code	County Code	Geographic Area Name	2010 Census Population
47	40000		Knoxville city	178 874	48	11428		Burleson city	36 690
47	40000	093	Knox County	178 874	48	11428	251	Johnson County	29 111
					48	11428	439	Tarrant County	7 579
47	41200		La Vergne city	32 588					
47	41200	149	Rutherford County	32 588	48	13024		Carrollton city	119 097
					48	13024	085	Collin County	2
47	41520		Lebanon city	26 190	48	13024	113	Dallas County	49 352
47	41520	189	Wilson County	26 190	48	13024	121	Denton County	69 743
47	46380		Maryville city	27 465	48	13492		Cedar Hill city	45 028
47	46380	009	Blount County	27 465	48	13492	113	Dallas County	44 477
					48	13492	139	Ellis County	551
47	48000		Memphis city	646 889					
47	48000	157	Shelby County	646 889	48	13552		Cedar Park city	48 937
					48	13552	453	Travis County	489
47	50280		Morristown city	29 137	48	13552	491	Williamson County	48 448
47	50280	063	Hamblen County	29 131					
47	50280	089	Jefferson County	6	48	15364		Cleburne city	29 337
					48	15364	251	Johnson County	29 337
47	51560		Murfreesboro city	108 755					
47	51560	149	Rutherford County	108 755	48	15976		College Station city	93 857
					48	15976	041	Brazos County	93 857
47	55120		Oak Ridge city	29 330					
47	55120	001	Anderson County	26 271	48	16432		Conroe city	56 207
47	55120	145	Roane County	3 059	48	16432	339	Montgomery County	56 207
47	69420		Smyrna town	39 974	48	16612		Coppell city	38 659
47	69420	149	Rutherford County	39 974	48	16612	113	Dallas County	37 905
					48	16612	121	Denton County	754
47	70580		Spring Hill city	29 036					
47	70580	119	Maury County	7 023	48	16624		Copperas Cove city	32 032
47	70580	187	Williamson County	22 013	48	16624	027	Bell County	0
					48	16624	099	Coryell County	31 457
48			**TEXAS**	25 145 561	48	16624	281	Lampasas County	575
48	01000		Abilene city	117 063					
48	01000	253	Jones County	5 145	48	17000		Corpus Christi city	305 215
48	01000	441	Taylor County	111 918	48	17000	007	Aransas County	0
					48	17000	273	Kleberg County	0
48	01924		Allen city	84 246	48	17000	355	Nueces County	305 215
48	01924	085	Collin County	84 246	48	17000	409	San Patricio County	0
48	03000		Amarillo city	190 695	48	19000		Dallas city	1 197 816
48	03000	375	Potter County	105 486	48	19000	085	Collin County	46 885
48	03000	381	Randall County	85 209	48	19000	113	Dallas County	1 124 296
					48	19000	121	Denton County	26 579
48	04000		Arlington city	365 438	48	19000	257	Kaufman County	0
48	04000	439	Tarrant County	365 438	48	19000	397	Rockwall County	56
48	05000		Austin city	790 390	48	19624		Deer Park city	32 010
48	05000	209	Hays County	2	48	19624	201	Harris County	32 010
48	05000	453	Travis County	754 691					
48	05000	491	Williamson County	35 697	48	19792		Del Rio city	35 591
					48	19792	465	Val Verde County	35 591
48	06128		Baytown city	71 802					
48	06128	071	Chambers County	4 116	48	19972		Denton city	113 383
48	06128	201	Harris County	67 686	48	19972	121	Denton County	113 383
48	07000		Beaumont city	118 296	48	20092		DeSoto city	49 047
48	07000	245	Jefferson County	118 296	48	20092	113	Dallas County	49 047
48	07132		Bedford city	46 979	48	21628		Duncanville city	38 524
48	07132	439	Tarrant County	46 979	48	21628	113	Dallas County	38 524
48	08236		Big Spring city	27 282	48	21892		Eagle Pass city	26 248
48	08236	227	Howard County	27 282	48	21892	323	Maverick County	26 248
48	10768		Brownsville city	175 023	48	22660		Edinburg city	77 100
48	10768	061	Cameron County	175 023	48	22660	215	Hidalgo County	77 100
48	10912		Bryan city	76 201	48	24000		El Paso city	649 121
48	10912	041	Brazos County	76 201	48	24000	141	El Paso County	649 121

Cities by County–*Continued*

State Code	Place Code	County Code	Geographic Area Name	2010 Census Population	State Code	Place Code	County Code	Geographic Area Name	2010 Census Population
48	24768		Euless city	51 277	48	38632		Keller city	39 627
48	24768	439	Tarrant County	51 277	48	38632	439	Tarrant County	39 627
48	25452		Farmers Branch city	28 616	48	39148		Killeen city	127 921
48	25452	113	Dallas County	28 616	48	39148	027	Bell County	127 921
48	26232		Flower Mound town	64 669	48	39352		Kingsville city	26 213
48	26232	121	Denton County	64 457	48	39352	273	Kleberg County	26 213
48	26232	439	Tarrant County	212	48	39952		Kyle city	28 016
48	27000		Fort Worth city	741 206	48	39952	209	Hays County	28 016
48	27000	121	Denton County	7 813					
48	27000	367	Parker County	7	48	40588		Lake Jackson city	26 849
48	27000	439	Tarrant County	733 386	48	40588	039	Brazoria County	26 849
48	27000	497	Wise County	0	48	41212		Lancaster city	36 361
48	27648		Friendswood city	35 805	48	41212	113	Dallas County	36 361
48	27648	167	Galveston County	25 510					
48	27648	201	Harris County	10 295	48	41440		La Porte city	33 800
					48	41440	201	Harris County	33 800
48	27684		Frisco city	116 989					
48	27684	085	Collin County	72 489	48	41464		Laredo city	236 091
48	27684	121	Denton County	44 500	48	41464	479	Webb County	236 091
48	28068		Galveston city	47 743	48	41980		League City city	83 560
48	28068	167	Galveston County	47 743	48	41980	167	Galveston County	81 998
					48	41980	201	Harris County	1 562
48	29000		Garland city	226 876					
48	29000	085	Collin County	266	48	42016		Leander city	26 521
48	29000	113	Dallas County	226 608	48	42016	453	Travis County	1 077
48	29000	397	Rockwall County	2	48	42016	491	Williamson County	25 444
48	29336		Georgetown city	47 400	48	42508		Lewisville city	95 290
48	29336	491	Williamson County	47 400	48	42508	113	Dallas County	841
					48	42508	121	Denton County	94 449
48	30464		Grand Prairie city	175 396					
48	30464	113	Dallas County	123 487	48	43012		Little Elm city	25 898
48	30464	139	Ellis County	45	48	43012	121	Denton County	25 898
48	30464	439	Tarrant County	51 864	48	43888		Longview city	80 455
48	30644		Grapevine city	46 334	48	43888	183	Gregg County	78 585
48	30644	113	Dallas County	0	48	43888	203	Harrison County	1 870
48	30644	121	Denton County	0					
48	30644	439	Tarrant County	46 334	48	45000		Lubbock city	229 573
					48	45000	303	Lubbock County	229 573
48	30920		Greenville city	25 557					
48	30920	231	Hunt County	25 557	48	45072		Lufkin city	35 067
					48	45072	005	Angelina County	35 067
48	31928		Haltom City city	42 409					
48	31928	439	Tarrant County	42 409	48	45384		McAllen city	129 877
					48	45384	215	Hidalgo County	129 877
48	32312		Harker Heights city	26 700					
48	32312	027	Bell County	26 700	48	45744		McKinney city	131 117
					48	45744	085	Collin County	131 117
48	32372		Harlingen city	64 849					
48	32372	061	Cameron County	64 849	48	46452		Mansfield city	56 368
					48	46452	139	Ellis County	95
48	35000		Houston city	2 099 451	48	46452	251	Johnson County	1 652
48	35000	157	Fort Bend County	38 124	48	46452	439	Tarrant County	54 621
48	35000	201	Harris County	2 057 280					
48	35000	339	Montgomery County	4 047	48	47892		Mesquite city	139 824
					48	47892	113	Dallas County	139 731
48	35528		Huntsville city	38 548	48	47892	257	Kaufman County	93
48	35528	471	Walker County	38 548					
					48	48072		Midland city	111 147
48	35576		Hurst city	37 337	48	48072	317	Martin County	0
48	35576	439	Tarrant County	37 337	48	48072	329	Midland County	111 147
48	37000		Irving city	216 290	48	48768		Mission city	77 058
48	37000	113	Dallas County	216 290	48	48768	215	Hidalgo County	77 058

Cities by County–*Continued*

State Code	Place Code	County Code	Geographic Area Name	2010 Census Population	State Code	Place Code	County Code	Geographic Area Name	2010 Census Population
48	48804		Missouri City city	67 358	48	65600		San Marcos city	44 894
48	48804	157	Fort Bend County	61 755	48	65600	055	Caldwell County	3
48	48804	201	Harris County	5 603	48	65600	187	Guadalupe County	0
					48	65600	209	Hays County	44 891
48	50256		Nacogdoches city	32 996					
48	50256	347	Nacogdoches County	32 996	48	66128		Schertz city	31 465
					48	66128	029	Bexar County	1 157
48	50820		New Braunfels city	57 740	48	66128	091	Comal County	845
48	50820	091	Comal County	47 586	48	66128	187	Guadalupe County	29 463
48	50820	187	Guadalupe County	10 154					
					48	66644		Seguin city	25 175
48	52356		North Richland Hills city	63 343	48	66644	187	Guadalupe County	25 175
48	52356	439	Tarrant County	63 343					
					48	67496		Sherman city	38 521
48	53388		Odessa city	99 940	48	67496	181	Grayson County	38 521
48	53388	135	Ector County	98 270					
48	53388	329	Midland County	1 670	48	68636		Socorro city	32 013
					48	68636	141	El Paso County	32 013
48	55080		Paris city	25 171					
48	55080	277	Lamar County	25 171	48	69032		Southlake city	26 575
					48	69032	121	Denton County	773
48	56000		Pasadena city	149 043	48	69032	439	Tarrant County	25 802
48	56000	201	Harris County	149 043					
					48	70808		Sugar Land city	78 817
48	56348		Pearland city	91 252	48	70808	157	Fort Bend County	78 817
48	56348	039	Brazoria County	86 706					
48	56348	157	Fort Bend County	721	48	72176		Temple city	66 102
48	56348	201	Harris County	3 825	48	72176	027	Bell County	66 102
48	57176		Pflugerville city	46 936	48	72368		Texarkana city	36 411
48	57176	453	Travis County	46 636	48	72368	037	Bowie County	36 411
48	57176	491	Williamson County	300					
					48	72392		Texas City city	45 099
48	57200		Pharr city	70 400	48	72392	071	Chambers County	0
48	57200	215	Hidalgo County	70 400	48	72392	167	Galveston County	45 099
48	58016		Plano city	259 841	48	72530		The Colony city	36 328
48	58016	085	Collin County	254 525	48	72530	121	Denton County	36 328
48	58016	121	Denton County	5 316					
					48	74144		Tyler city	96 900
48	58820		Port Arthur city	53 818	48	74144	423	Smith County	96 900
48	58820	245	Jefferson County	53 814					
48	58820	361	Orange County	4	48	75428		Victoria city	62 592
					48	75428	469	Victoria County	62 592
48	61796		Richardson city	99 223					
48	61796	085	Collin County	28 569	48	76000		Waco city	124 805
48	61796	113	Dallas County	70 654	48	76000	309	McLennan County	124 805
48	62828		Rockwall city	37 490	48	76816		Waxahachie city	29 621
48	62828	397	Rockwall County	37 490	48	76816	139	Ellis County	29 621
48	63284		Rosenberg city	30 618	48	76864		Weatherford city	25 250
48	63284	157	Fort Bend County	30 618	48	76864	367	Parker County	25 250
48	63500		Round Rock city	99 887	48	77272		Weslaco city	35 670
48	63500	453	Travis County	1 362	48	77272	215	Hidalgo County	35 670
48	63500	491	Williamson County	98 525					
					48	79000		Wichita Falls city	104 553
48	63572		Rowlett city	56 199	48	79000	485	Wichita County	104 553
48	63572	113	Dallas County	49 188					
48	63572	397	Rockwall County	7 011	48	80356		Wylie city	41 427
					48	80356	085	Collin County	39 957
48	64472		San Angelo city	93 200	48	80356	113	Dallas County	415
48	64472	451	Tom Green County	93 200	48	80356	397	Rockwall County	1 055
48	65000		San Antonio city	1 327 407	49			**UTAH**	2 763 885
48	65000	029	Bexar County	1 327 381	49	01310		American Fork city	26 263
48	65000	091	Comal County	0	49	01310	049	Utah County	26 263
48	65000	325	Medina County	26					
					49	07690		Bountiful city	42 552
48	65516		San Juan city	33 856	49	07690	011	Davis County	42 552
48	65516	215	Hidalgo County	33 856					

Cities by County–*Continued*

State Code	Place Code	County Code	Geographic Area Name	2010 Census Population	State Code	Place Code	County Code	Geographic Area Name	2010 Census Population
49	11320		Cedar City city	28 857	49	76680		Tooele city	31 605
49	11320	021	Iron County	28 857	49	76680	045	Tooele County	31 605
49	13850		Clearfield city	30 112	49	82950		West Jordan city	103 712
49	13850	011	Davis County	30 112	49	82950	035	Salt Lake County	103 712
49	16270		Cottonwood Heights city	33 433	49	83470		West Valley City city	129 480
49	16270	035	Salt Lake County	33 433	49	83470	035	Salt Lake County	129 480
49	20120		Draper city	42 274	50			**VERMONT**	625 741
49	20120	035	Salt Lake County	40 532	50	10675		Burlington city	42 417
49	20120	049	Utah County	1 742	50	10675	007	Chittenden County	42 417
49	36070		Holladay city	26 472	51			**VIRGINIA**	8 001 024
49	36070	035	Salt Lake County	26 472	51	01000		Alexandria city	139 966
					51	01000	510	Alexandria city	139 966
49	40360		Kaysville city	27 300					
49	40360	011	Davis County	27 300	51	07784		Blacksburg town	42 620
					51	07784	121	Montgomery County	42 620
49	43660		Layton city	67 311					
49	43660	011	Davis County	67 311	51	14968		Charlottesville city	43 475
					51	14968	540	Charlottesville city	43 475
49	44320		Lehi city	47 407					
49	44320	049	Utah County	47 407	51	16000		Chesapeake city	222 209
					51	16000	550	Chesapeake city	222 209
49	45860		Logan city	48 174					
49	45860	005	Cache County	48 174	51	21344		Danville city	43 055
					51	21344	590	Danville city	43 055
49	49710		Midvale city	27 964					
49	49710	035	Salt Lake County	27 964	51	35000		Hampton city	137 436
					51	35000	650	Hampton city	137 436
49	53230		Murray city	46 746					
49	53230	035	Salt Lake County	46 746	51	35624		Harrisonburg city	48 914
					51	35624	660	Harrisonburg city	48 914
49	55980		Ogden city	82 825					
49	55980	057	Weber County	82 825	51	44984		Leesburg town	42 616
					51	44984	107	Loudoun County	42 616
49	57300		Orem city	88 328					
49	57300	049	Utah County	88 328	51	47672		Lynchburg city	75 568
					51	47672	680	Lynchburg city	75 568
49	60930		Pleasant Grove city	33 509					
49	60930	049	Utah County	33 509	51	48952		Manassas city	37 821
					51	48952	683	Manassas city	37 821
49	62470		Provo city	112 488					
49	62470	049	Utah County	112 488	51	56000		Newport News city	180 719
					51	56000	700	Newport News city	180 719
49	64340		Riverton city	38 753					
49	64340	035	Salt Lake County	38 753	51	57000		Norfolk city	242 803
					51	57000	710	Norfolk city	242 803
49	65110		Roy city	36 884					
49	65110	057	Weber County	36 884	51	61832		Petersburg city	32 420
					51	61832	730	Petersburg city	32 420
49	65330		St. George city	72 897					
49	65330	053	Washington County	72 897	51	64000		Portsmouth city	95 535
					51	64000	740	Portsmouth city	95 535
49	67000		Salt Lake City city	186 440					
49	67000	035	Salt Lake County	186 440	51	67000		Richmond city	204 214
					51	67000	760	Richmond city	204 214
49	67440		Sandy city	87 461					
49	67440	035	Salt Lake County	87 461	51	68000		Roanoke city	97 032
					51	68000	770	Roanoke city	97 032
49	70850		South Jordan city	50 418					
49	70850	035	Salt Lake County	50 418	51	76432		Suffolk city	84 585
					51	76432	800	Suffolk city	84 585
49	71290		Spanish Fork city	34 691					
49	71290	049	Utah County	34 691	51	82000		Virginia Beach city	437 994
					51	82000	810	Virginia Beach city	437 994
49	72280		Springville city	29 466					
49	72280	049	Utah County	29 466	51	86720		Winchester city	26 203
					51	86720	840	Winchester city	26 203
49	75360		Taylorsville city	58 652					
49	75360	035	Salt Lake County	58 652					

Cities by County–*Continued*

State Code	Place Code	County Code	Geographic Area Name	2010 Census Population	State Code	Place Code	County Code	Geographic Area Name	2010 Census Population
53			**WASHINGTON**	6 724 540	53	56625		Pullman city	29 799
53	03180		Auburn city	70 180	53	56625	075	Whitman County	29 799
53	03180	033	King County	62 761					
53	03180	053	Pierce County	7 419	53	56695		Puyallup city	37 022
					53	56695	053	Pierce County	37 022
53	05210		Bellevue city	122 363					
53	05210	033	King County	122 363	53	57535		Redmond city	54 144
					53	57535	033	King County	54 144
53	05280		Bellingham city	80 885					
53	05280	073	Whatcom County	80 885	53	57745		Renton city	90 927
					53	57745	033	King County	90 927
53	07380		Bothell city	33 505					
53	07380	033	King County	17 090	53	58235		Richland city	48 058
53	07380	061	Snohomish County	16 415	53	58235	005	Benton County	48 058
53	07695		Bremerton city	37 729	53	61115		Sammamish city	45 780
53	07695	035	Kitsap County	37 729	53	61115	033	King County	45 780
53	08850		Burien city	33 313	53	62288		SeaTac city	26 909
53	08850	033	King County	33 313	53	62288	033	King County	26 909
53	17635		Des Moines city	29 673	53	63000		Seattle city	608 660
53	17635	033	King County	29 673	53	63000	033	King County	608 660
53	20750		Edmonds city	39 709	53	63960		Shoreline city	53 007
53	20750	061	Snohomish County	39 709	53	63960	033	King County	53 007
53	22640		Everett city	103 019	53	67000		Spokane city	208 916
53	22640	061	Snohomish County	103 019	53	67000	063	Spokane County	208 916
53	23515		Federal Way city	89 306	53	67167		Spokane Valley city	89 755
53	23515	033	King County	89 306	53	67167	063	Spokane County	89 755
53	33805		Issaquah city	30 434	53	70000		Tacoma city	198 397
53	33805	033	King County	30 434	53	70000	053	Pierce County	198 397
53	35275		Kennewick city	73 917	53	73465		University Place city	31 144
53	35275	005	Benton County	73 917	53	73465	053	Pierce County	31 144
53	35415		Kent city	92 411	53	74060		Vancouver city	161 791
53	35415	033	King County	92 411	53	74060	011	Clark County	161 791
53	35940		Kirkland city	48 787	53	75775		Walla Walla city	31 731
53	35940	033	King County	48 787	53	75775	071	Walla Walla County	31 731
53	36745		Lacey city	42 393	53	77105		Wenatchee city	31 925
53	36745	067	Thurston County	42 393	53	77105	007	Chelan County	31 925
53	37900		Lake Stevens city	28 069	53	80010		Yakima city	91 067
53	37900	061	Snohomish County	28 069	53	80010	077	Yakima County	91 067
53	38038		Lakewood city	58 163	54			**WEST VIRGINIA**	1 852 994
53	38038	053	Pierce County	58 163	54	14600		Charleston city	51 400
					54	14600	039	Kanawha County	51 400
53	40245		Longview city	36 648					
53	40245	015	Cowlitz County	36 648	54	39460		Huntington city	49 138
					54	39460	011	Cabell County	45 214
53	40840		Lynnwood city	35 836	54	39460	099	Wayne County	3 924
53	40840	061	Snohomish County	35 836					
					54	55756		Morgantown city	29 660
53	43955		Marysville city	60 020	54	55756	061	Monongalia County	29 660
53	43955	061	Snohomish County	60 020					
					54	62140		Parkersburg city	31 492
53	47560		Mount Vernon city	31 743	54	62140	107	Wood County	31 492
53	47560	057	Skagit County	31 743					
					54	86452		Wheeling city	28 486
53	51300		Olympia city	46 478	54	86452	051	Marshall County	276
53	51300	067	Thurston County	46 478	54	86452	069	Ohio County	28 210
53	53545		Pasco city	59 781					
53	53545	021	Franklin County	59 781					

Cities by County–*Continued*

State Code	Place Code	County Code	Geographic Area Name	2010 Census Population	State Code	Place Code	County Code	Geographic Area Name	2010 Census Population
55			**WISCONSIN**	5 686 986	55	72975		Sheboygan city	49 288
55	02375		Appleton city	72 623	55	72975	117	Sheboygan County	49 288
55	02375	015	Calumet County	11 088					
55	02375	087	Outagamie County	60 045	55	77200		Stevens Point city	26 717
55	02375	139	Winnebago County	1 490	55	77200	097	Portage County	26 717
55	06500		Beloit city	36 966	55	78600		Sun Prairie city	29 364
55	06500	105	Rock County	36 966	55	78600	025	Dane County	29 364
55	10025		Brookfield city	37 920	55	78650		Superior city	27 244
55	10025	133	Waukesha County	37 920	55	78650	031	Douglas County	27 244
55	22300		Eau Claire city	65 883	55	84250		Waukesha city	70 718
55	22300	017	Chippewa County	1 981	55	84250	133	Waukesha County	70 718
55	22300	035	Eau Claire County	63 902					
					55	84475		Wausau city	39 106
55	25950		Fitchburg city	25 260	55	84475	073	Marathon County	39 106
55	25950	025	Dane County	25 260					
					55	84675		Wauwatosa city	46 396
55	26275		Fond du Lac city	43 021	55	84675	079	Milwaukee County	46 396
55	26275	039	Fond du Lac County	43 021					
					55	85300		West Allis city	60 411
55	27300		Franklin city	35 451	55	85300	079	Milwaukee County	60 411
55	27300	079	Milwaukee County	35 451					
					55	85350		West Bend city	31 078
55	31000		Green Bay city	104 057	55	85350	131	Washington County	31 078
55	31000	009	Brown County	104 057					
					56			**WYOMING**	563 626
55	31175		Greenfield city	36 720	56	13150		Casper city	55 316
55	31175	079	Milwaukee County	36 720	56	13150	025	Natrona County	55 316
55	37825		Janesville city	63 575	56	13900		Cheyenne city	59 466
55	37825	105	Rock County	63 575	56	13900	021	Laramie County	59 466
55	39225		Kenosha city	99 218	56	31855		Gillette city	29 087
55	39225	059	Kenosha County	99 218	56	31855	005	Campbell County	29 087
55	40775		La Crosse city	51 320	56	45050		Laramie city	30 816
55	40775	063	La Crosse County	51 320	56	45050	001	Albany County	30 816
55	48000		Madison city	233 209	09			**CONNECTICUT**	3 574 097
55	48000	025	Dane County	233 209	09	47500		Milford city	52 759
								Milford city (balance)	51 271
55	48500		Manitowoc city	33 736		88050		Woodmont borough	1 488
55	48500	071	Manitowoc County	33 736					
					13			**GEORGIA**	9 687 653
55	51000		Menomonee Falls village	35 626	13	03436		Athens-Clark county	116 714
55	51000	133	Waukesha County	35 626	13	03440		Athens-Clark county (balance)	115 452
					13	09068		Bogart town	140
55	53000		Milwaukee city	594 833	13	83728		Winterville city	1 122
55	53000	079	Milwaukee County	594 833					
55	53000	131	Washington County	0	13	04200		Augusta-Richmond county	200 549
55	53000	133	Waukesha County	0	13	04204		Augusta-Richmond county (balance)	195 844
55	54875		Mount Pleasant village	26 197	13	09040		Blythe city	694
55	54875	101	Racine County	26 197	13	38040		Hephzibah city	4 011
55	55750		Neenah city	25 501					
55	55750	139	Winnebago County	25 501					
55	56375		New Berlin city	39 584					
55	56375	133	Waukesha County	39 584					
55	58800		Oak Creek city	34 451					
55	58800	079	Milwaukee County	34 451					
55	60500		Oshkosh city	66 083					
55	60500	139	Winnebago County	66 083					
55	66000		Racine city	78 860					
55	66000	101	Racine County	78 860					

State Code	Place Code	County Code	Geographic Area Name	2010 Census Population
18			**INDIANA**	6 483 802
18	36000		Indianapolis city	829 718
18	04204		Beech Grove city	0
18	13492		Clermont town	1 356
18	16156		Crows Nest town	73
18	16336		Cumberland town	2 597
18	34420		Homecroft town	722
18	36003		Indianapolis city (balance)	820 445
18	42426		Lawrence city	42
18	48456		Meridian Hills town	1 616
18	54612		North Crows Nest town	45
18	65556		Rocky Ripple town	606
18	72232		Spring Hill town	98
18	80234		Warren Park town	1 480
18	84374		Williams Creek town	407
18	85742		Wynnedale town	231
21			**KENTUCKY**	4 339 367
21	46003		Louisville/Jefferson County	741 096
21	01504		Anchorage city	2 348
21	02656		Audubon Park city	1 473
21	03376		Bancroft city	494
21	03556		Barbourmeade city	1 218
21	05068		Beechwood Village city	1 324
21	05392		Bellemeade city	865
21	05464		Bellewood city	321
21	07858		Blue Ridge Manor city	767
21	09532		Briarwood city	435
21	09847		Broeck Pointe city	272
21	10162		Brownsboro Farm city	648
21	10198		Brownsboro Village city	319
21	12066		Cambridge city	175
21	16395		Coldstream city	1 100
21	18270		Creekside city	305
21	18766		Crossgate city	225
21	22204		Douglass Hills city	5 484
21	22474		Druid Hills city	308
21	27262		Fincastle city	817
21	28342		Forest Hills city	444
21	31348		Glenview city	531
21	31402		Glenview Hills city	319
21	31420		Glenview Manor city	191
21	31870		Goose Creek city	294
21	32523		Graymoor-Devondale city	2 870
21	32986		Green Spring city	715
21	36102		Heritage Creek city	1 076
21	36374		Hickory Hill city	114
21	36865		Hills and Dales city	142
21	37576		Hollow Creek city	783
21	37630		Hollyvilla city	537
21	38170		Houston Acres city	507
21	38814		Hurstbourne city	4 216
21	38818		Hurstbourne Acres city	1 811
21	39304		Indian Hills city	2 868
21	40222		Jeffersontown city	26 595
21	42598		Kingsley city	381
21	43900		Langdon Place city	936
21	46540		Lincolnshire city	148
21	48006		Louisville/Jefferson County (balance)	597 337
21	48558		Lyndon city	11 002
21	48648		Lynnview city	914
21	49800		Manor Creek city	140
21	50412		Maryhill Estates city	179
21	51193		Meadowbrook Farm city	136
21	51258		Meadow Vale city	736
21	51294		Meadowview Estates city	363
21	51978		Middletown city	7 218
21	52842		Mockingbird Valley city	167
21	53328		Moorland city	431
21	54660		Murray Hill city	582
21	56550		Norbourne Estates city	441
21	56730		Northfield city	1 020
21	56928		Norwood city	370
21	57658		Old Brownsboro Place city	353
21	59322		Parkway Village city	650
21	61554		Plantation city	832
21	62370		Poplar Hills city	362
21	63264		Prospect city	4 636
21	65208		Richlawn city	405
21	65766		Riverwood city	446
21	66486		Rolling Fields city	646
21	66504		Rolling Hills city	959
21	67944		St. Matthews city	17 472
21	67998		St. Regis Park city	1 454
21	69384		Seneca Gardens city	696
21	70284		Shively city	15 264
21	72138		South Park View city	7
21	72770		Spring Mill city	287
21	72790		Spring Valley city	654
21	74064		Strathmoor Manor city	337
21	74082		Strathmoor Village city	648
21	75190		Sycamore city	160
21	75963		Ten Broeck city	103
21	76380		Thornhill city	178
21	80913		Watterson Park city	976
21	81372		Wellington city	565
21	81624		West Buechel city	1 230
21	82164		Westwood city	634
21	83208		Wildwood city	261
21	83784		Windy Hills city	2 385
21	84486		Woodland Hills city	696
21	84576		Woodlawn Park city	942
21	84891		Worthington Hills city	1 446
30			**MONTANA**	989 415
30	11390		Butte-Silver Bow	34 200
30	11397		Butte-Silver Bow (balance)	33 525
30	77650		Walkerville town	675
47			**TENNESSEE**	6 346 105
47	52004		Nashville-Davidson	626 681
47	04620		Belle Meade city	2 912
47	05140		Berry Hill city	537
47	27020		Forest Hills city	4 812
47	29920		Goodlettsville city	10 319
47	40720		Lakewood city	2 302
47	52006		Nashville-Davidson (balance)	601 222
47	54780		Oak Hill city	4 529
47	63140		Ridgetop city	48

APPENDIX F
SOURCE NOTES AND EXPLANATIONS

The following documentation is provided in the order in which items appear in the tables. Internet addresses are provided for the sources of the data. Some of the links refer to the specific data tables. Others provide information about the general data source.

TABLE A—STATES

Table A presents 355 items for the United States as a whole, for each individual state, and for the District of Columbia. The states are presented in alphabetical order.

LAND AREA, Items 1 and 4
Source: U.S. Census Bureau—Decennial Censuses and Population Estimates
http://www.census.gov/geo/www/2010census/
statearea_intpt.html

Land area measurements are shown to the nearest square kilometer. Land area includes dry land and land temporarily or partially covered by water, such as marshlands, swamps, and river floodplains.

POPULATION AND COMPONENTS OF CHANGE, Items 2–4, 31–41
Source: U.S. Census Bureau—Decennial Censuses and Population Estimates
http://www.census.gov/popest/estimates.html
http://2010.census.gov/2010census/data/

The population data for 2011 are Census Bureau estimates of the resident population as of July 1, 2011.

The population data for 1990, 2000, and 2010 are from the decennial censuses and represent the resident population as of April 1 of those years.

The change in population between 2010 and 2011 is made up of (a) natural increase—births minus deaths, and (b) net migration—the difference between the number of persons moving into a particular state and the number of persons moving out of the state. Net migration is composed of internal and international migration.

POPULATION PROJECTIONS, Items 42–44
Source: U.S. Census Bureau—Population Projections Branch
http://www.census.gov/population/www/projections/
index.html

Projections are estimates of the population for future dates. They illustrate plausible courses of future population change based on assumptions about future births, deaths, international migration, and domestic migration. Projected numbers are based on an estimated population consistent with the most recent decennial census as enumerated. The Census Bureau does not have a current set of state population projections and currently has no plans to produce them. This volume includes projections released in 2005, based on the 2000 census. The Census Bureau notes that these projections should be used with caution because population trends may have changed substantially since their release.

POPULATION AND POPULATION CHARACTERISTICS, Items 5–23 and 45–63
Source: U.S. Census Bureau—2010 and 2000 Censuses of Population and Housingand 2010 American Community Survey
http://2010.census.gov/2010census/data/
http://www.census.gov/acs/www/

Data on age, sex, race, and Hispanic origin are from the 2010 census. Data on place of birth are from the 2010 American Community Survey, a nationwide continuous survey designed to replace the long form questionnaire used in previous censuses.

Data on race were derived from answers to the question on race that was asked of all persons. The concept of race, as used by the Census Bureau, reflects self-identification by respondents according to the race or races with which they most closely identify. These categories are sociopolitical constructs and should not be interpreted as being scientific or anthropological in nature. Furthermore, the race categories include both racial and national origin groups.

On the 2000 and 2010 censuses, respondents were offered the option of selecting one or more races. This option was not available in prior censuses; thus, comparisons between censuses should be made with caution. In this table, Columns 5 through 8 refer to individuals who identified with each racial category, either alone or in combination with other races, and who had specified that they were not of Hispanic or Latino origin. Because respondents could include as many categories as they wished, and because the columns refer to the percentage of the population, the total will often exceed 100 percent. Columns 45 through 48 identify persons who specified one race only with those who claimed "some other race" combined with "two or more races" in Column 49.

The **White** population is defined as persons who indicated their race as White, as well as persons who did not classify themselves in one of the specific race categories listed on the questionnaire but entered a nationality such as Irish, German, Italian, Lebanese, Near Easterner, Arab, or Polish.

The **Black** population includes persons who indicated their race as "Black, African Am., or Negro," as well as persons who did not classify themselves in one of the specific race categories but reported entries such as African American, Afro American, Kenyan, Nigerian, or Haitian.

The **American Indian or Alaska Native** population includes persons who indicated their race as American Indian or Alaska Native, as well as persons who did not classify themselves in one of the specific race categories but reported entries such as Canadian Indian, French-American Indian, Spanish-American Indian, Eskimo, Aleut, Alaska Indian, or any of the American Indian or Alaska Native tribes.

The **Asian and Pacific Islander** population combines two census groupings: **Asian** and **Native Hawaiian or Other Pacific Islander**. The **Asian** population includes persons who indicated their race as Asian Indian, Chinese, Filipino, Japanese, Korean, Vietnamese, or "Other Asian," as well as persons who provided write-in entries of such groups as Cambodian, Laotian, Hmong, Pakistani, or Taiwanese. The **Native Hawaiian or Other Pacific Islander** population includes persons who indicated their race as "Native Hawaiian," "Guamanian or Chamorro," "Samoan," or "Other Pacific Islander," as well as persons who reported entries such as Part Hawaiian, American Samoan, Fijian, Melanesian, or Tahitian.

The Hispanic population is based on a question that asked respondents "Is this person Spanish/Hispanic/Latino?" Persons marking any one of the four Hispanic categories (i.e., Mexican, Puerto Rican, Cuban, or other Spanish) are collectively referred to as Hispanic.

In the 2000 and 2010 censuses, the Hispanic origin question was placed before the race question and specific instructions indicated that both questions should be answered. These changes were designed to improve accuracy and may affect comparability with 1990 data.

Age is defined as age at last birthday (number of completed years since birth), as of April 1 of the census year. The 2000 and 2010 censuses also asked for the specific date of birth of the respondent, and census procedures used the birth date for deriving age data. For this reason, it is likely that the data have fewer problems than data from prior censuses, such as the tendency of respondents to round ages or to report their ages on the date the questionnaire was filled out rather than on April 1.

The **median age** is the age that divides the population into two equal-size groups. Half of the population is older than the median age and half is younger. Median age is based on a standard distribution of the population by single years of age and is shown to the nearest tenth of a year.

The **female** population is shown as a percentage of total population.

The **foreign-born** population includes all persons who were not U.S. citizens at birth. Foreign-born persons are those who indicated they were either a U.S. citizen by naturalization or were not a citizen of the United States. Neither the census nor the American Community Survey asked about immigration status. The population surveyed included all persons who indicated that the United States was their usual place of residence. The foreign-born population consists of immigrants (legal permanent residents), temporary migrants (students), humanitarian migrants (refugees), and unauthorized migrants (persons illegally residing in the United States).

Percent born in state of residence is shown as a percentage of total population.

IMMIGRANTS, Item 24
Source: Department of Homeland Security, U.S. Citizenship and Immigration Services
http://www.dhs.gov/files/statistics/publications/LPR10.shtm

The number of immigrants by state of intended residence is summarized from the administrative records of the Citizenship and Immigration Services. This information is compiled from immigrant visas and forms granting legal permanent resident status.

An immigrant is an alien admitted to the United States as a lawful permanent resident. Immigrants are those persons lawfully accorded the privilege of residing permanently in the United States. They may be newly arrived individuals who were issued immigrant visas by the Department of State overseas, or they may be U.S. residents who were admitted to permanent resident status in 2010 by the U.S. Citizenship and Immigration Services.

HOUSEHOLDS, Items 25–30 and 64–68
Source: U.S. Census Bureau—2000 and 2010 Census of Population and Housing
http://2010.census.gov/2010census/data/
http://www.census.gov/main/www/cen2000.html

A **household** includes all of the persons who occupy a housing unit. Persons not living in households are classified as living in group quarters. A housing unit is a house, an apartment, a mobile home, a group of rooms, or a single room occupied (or, if vacant, intended for occupancy) as separate living quarters. Separate living quarters are those in which the occupants live separately from any other persons in the building and have direct access from the outside of the building or through a common hall. The occupants may be a single family, one person living alone, two or more families living together, or any other group of related or unrelated persons who share living quarters. The number of households is the same as the number of year-round occupied housing units.

The measure of **persons per household** is obtained by dividing the number of persons in households by the number of households or householders. One person in each household is designated as the householder. In most cases, this is the person, (or one of the persons) in whose name the house is owned, being bought, or rented. If there is no such person in the household, any adult household member 15 years old and over can be designated as the householder.

A **family** includes a householder and one or more other persons living in the same household who are related to the householder by birth, marriage, or adoption. All persons in a household who are related to the householder are regarded as members of his or her family. A **family household** may contain persons not related to the householder; thus, family households may include more members than families do. A household can contain only one family for the purposes of census tabulations. Not all households contain families, as a household may comprise a group of unrelated persons or one person living alone. Families are classified by type as either a "husband-wife family" or "other family" according to the presence of a spouse.

The category **female family householder** includes only female-headed family households with no spouse present.

HOUSING, Items 69–92
Source: U.S. Census Bureau—2000 Census of
Population and Housing and 2010 American
Community Survey
http://www.census.gov/main/www/cen2000.html
http://www.census.gov/acs/www/

Housing data for 2010 are from the American Community Survey, a nationwide continuous survey designed to replace the long form questionnaire used in previous censuses. A sample of households is surveyed to provide estimates. Housing data for 2000 are from the 2000 census.

A **housing unit** is a house, apartment, mobile home or trailer, group of rooms, or single room occupied or, if vacant, intended for occupancy as separate living quarters. Separate living quarters are those in which the occupants do not live and eat with any other person in the structure and which have direct access from the outside of the building or through a common hall. For vacant units, the criteria of separateness and direct access are applied to the intended occupants whenever possible. If that information cannot be obtained, the criteria are applied to the previous occupants.

The occupants of a housing unit may be a single family, one person living alone, two or more families living together, or any other group of related or unrelated persons who share living arrangements. Both occupied and vacant housing units are included in the housing inventory, although recreational vehicles, tents, caves, boats, railroad cars, and the like are included only if they are occupied as a person's usual place of residence.

A housing unit is classified as **occupied** if it is the usual place of residence of the person or group of persons living in it at the time of enumeration, or if the occupants are only temporarily absent (away on vacation). A household consists of all persons who occupy a housing unit as their usual place of residence.

Housing cost, as a percentage of income, is shown separately for owners with mortgages, owners without mortgages, and renters. Also shown is the percentage of mortgaged owners and renters who pay 30 percent or more of household income on selected monthly costs. Rent as a percent of income is a computed ratio of gross rent and monthly household income (total household income divided by 12). Selected owner costs include utilities and fuels, mortgage payments, insurance, taxes, etc. In each case, the ratio of housing cost to income is computed separately for each housing unit. The housing cost ratios for half of all units are above the median shown in this book, and half are below the median. Median monthly housing costs divides the monthly housing costs distribution into two equal parts, one-half of the cases falling below the median monthly housing costs and one-half above the median.

Median value is the dollar amount that divides the distribution of specified owner-occupied housing units into two equal parts, with half of all units below the median value and half above the median value. Value is defined as the respondent's estimate of what the house would sell for if it were for sale. Data are presented for single-family units on fewer than 10 acres of land that have no business or medical office on the property.

Median rent divides the distribution of renter-occupied housing units into two equal parts. The rent concept used in this volume is gross rent, which includes the amount of cash rent a renter pays (contract rent) plus the estimated average cost of utilities and fuels, if these are paid by the renter. The rent is the amount of rent only for living quarters and excludes any business or other space occupied. Single-family houses on lots of 10 or more acres of land are excluded.

Substandard units are occupied units that are overcrowded or lack complete plumbing facilities. For the purposes of this item, "overcrowded" is defined as having 1.01 persons or more per room. Complete plumbing facilities include hot and cold piped water, a flush toilet, and a bathtub or shower. These facilities must be located inside the housing unit, but do not have to be in the same room.

Different house includes all people 1 year old and over who, a year earlier, lived in a different house or apartment from the one they occupied at the time of interview.

BUILDING PERMITS, Items 93–95
Source: U.S. Census Bureau—Building Permits
Survey
http://www.census.gov/construction/bps/

These figures represent private residential construction authorized by building permits in approximately 20,000 places in the United States. Valuation represents the expected cost of construction as recorded on the building permit. This figure usually excludes the cost of on-site and off-site development and improvements, as well as the cost of heating, plumbing, electrical, and elevator installations.

National, state, and county totals were obtained by adding the data for permit-issuing places within each jurisdiction. These totals thus are limited to permits issued in the 20,000 place universe covered by the Census Bureau and may not include all permits issued within a state. Current surveys indicate that construction is undertaken for all but a very small percentage of housing units authorized by building permits.

Residential building permits include buildings with any number of housing units. Housing units exclude group quarters (such as dormitories and rooming houses), transient accommodations (such as transient hotels, motels, and tourist courts), "HUD-code" manufactured (mobile) homes, moved or relocated units, and housing units created in an existing residential or nonresidential structure.

MANUFACTURED HOUSING UNITS, Item 96
Source: U.S. Census Bureau—Manufactured Housing
Survey
http://www.census.gov/construction/mhs/
placbystate.html

The Manufactured Housing Survey involves a monthly sample of new mobile homes shipped by manufacturers. The dealer to whom the sampled unit was shipped is contacted by telephone and asked about the status of the unit. This is done each month until that unit is reported as placed.

A mobile home, often referred to as a manufactured housing unit, is defined as a movable dwelling, 8 feet or more wide and 40 feet or more long, that is designed to be towed on its own chassis (with transportation gear integral to the unit when it leaves the factory) and without need of a permanent foundation. These mobile homes include multiwides, which are counted as single units, and expandable mobile homes. Excluded are travel trailers, motor homes, and modular housing.

There was not an increase in placements due to Hurricane Katrina, as federally owned FEMA units are not included in the private placement data collected by the Manufactured Housing Survey.

BIRTHS AND DEATHS, Items 97–103

Source: U.S. Centers for Disease Control and Prevention, National Center for Health Statistics
http://www.cdc.gov/nchs/data/nvsr/nvsr60/ nvsr60_01.pdf

http://www.cdc.gov/nchs/data/nvsr/nvsr59/ nvsr59_10.pdf

The registration of births, deaths, and other vital events in the United States is primarily a state and local function. The civil laws of every state provide for continuous and permanent birth and death registration systems. Through the National Vital Statistics System, the National Center for Health Statistics (NCHS) obtains data on births and deaths from the registration offices of each state, New York City, and the District of Columbia.

Birth and death statistics are limited to events occurring during the year. The data are by place of residence and exclude events for nonresidents of the United States. Births or deaths occurring outside the United States are excluded.

Birth and death rates represent the number of births and deaths per 1,000 resident population enumerated as of April 1 for decennial census years and estimated as of July 1 for other years.

Figures for infant deaths include deaths of children under 1 year of age but exclude fetal deaths. The infant death rate is per 1,000 live births.

The rates of almost all causes of disease, injury, and death vary by age. Age adjustment is a technique for "removing" the effects of age from crude rates, in order to allow meaningful comparisons across populations with different underlying age structures. For example, comparing the crude death rate in Florida to that of California is misleading, since the relatively older population in Florida will lead to a higher crude death rate. For such a comparison, age-adjusted death rates are preferable.

The population estimates were developed by the Census Bureau's Population Division using a traditional cohort component method. Starting with a basic population from the 2000 census, each component of population change—births, deaths, domestic migration, and international migration—is estimated separately for each birth cohort by sex, race, and Hispanic or Latino origin.

Age-adjusted rates are calculated by applying the age-specific rates of various populations to a single standard population. In this volume, the standard population is 2000. The Centers for Disease Control and Prevention recently switched to the year 2000, after many years of using the year 1940 as the standard population for age-adjusted death rates. For this reason, the 2009 age-adjusted rates are close to the actual death rates.

PERSONS LACKING HEALTH INSURANCE, Items 104–105

Source: U.S. Census Bureau—Current Population Survey
http://www.census.gov/hhes/www/cpstables/032011/ health/toc.htm

The data on which these estimates are based were gathered in March 2010 from a national sample of about 60,000 households Data are available for states but not for counties or cities.

Those lacking coverage are the percentage of the population of each state who were not covered by private health plans purchased directly or provided by an employer, Medicaid, Medicare, or military health care.

MEDICARE ENROLLEES, Item 106

Source: U.S. Department of Health and Human Services, Centers for Medicare and Medicaid Services
http://www.cms.hhs.gov/DataCompendium/

The Centers for Medicare and Medicaid Services (CMS) administers Medicare, which provides health insurance to persons 65 years old and over, persons with permanent kidney failure, and certain persons with disabilities. Medicare has two parts: Hospital Insurance and Supplemental Medical Insurance. The numbers in this volume include persons enrolled in either or both parts of the program as of July 1 of the year shown for their state of residence.

CRIME, Items 107–110

Source: U.S. Federal Bureau of Investigation— Uniform Crime Reports
http://www.fbi.gov/ucr/ucr.htm

Crime data are as reported to the Federal Bureau of Investigation (FBI) by law enforcement agencies and have not been adjusted for underreporting. This may affect comparability between geographic areas or over time.

Through the voluntary contribution of crime statistics by law enforcement agencies across the United States, the Uniform Crime Reporting (UCR) Program provides periodic assessments of crime in the nation as measured by offenses that have come to the attention of the law enforcement community. The Committee on Uniform Crime Records of the International Association of Chiefs of Police initiated this voluntary national data-collection effort in 1930. The UCR Program contributors compile and submit their crime data either directly to the FBI or through state-level UCR Programs.

Seven offenses, because of their severity, frequency of occurrence, and likelihood of being reported to police, were initially selected to serve as an index for evaluating fluctuations in the volume of crime. These serious crimes were murder and nonnegligent manslaughter, forcible rape, robbery, aggravated assault, burglary, larceny-theft, and motor vehicle theft. By congressional mandate, arson was added as the eighth index offense in 1979. The totals shown in this volume do not include arson.

In 2004, the FBI discontinued the use of the Crime Index in the UCR Program and its publications, stating that the Crime Index was driven upward by the offense with the highest number of cases (in this case, larceny-theft) creating a bias against jurisdictions with a high number of larceny-thefts but a low number of other serious crimes, such as murder and forcible rape. The FBI is currently publishing a violent crime total and a property crime total until a more viable index is developed.

Violent crimes include four categories of offenses: (1) Murder and nonnegligent manslaughter, as defined in the UCR Program, is the willful (nonnegligent) killing of one human being by another. This offense excludes deaths caused by negligence, suicide, or accident; justifiable homicides; and attempts to murder or assaults to murder. (2) Forcible rape is the carnal knowledge of a female forcibly and against her will. Assaults or attempts to commit rape by force or threat of force are also included; however, statutory rape (without force) and other sex offenses are excluded. (3) Robbery is the taking or attempting to take anything of value from the care, custody, or control of a person or persons by force or threat of force or violence and/or by putting the victim in fear. (4) Aggravated assault is an unlawful attack by one person upon another for the purpose of inflicting severe or aggravated bodily injury. This type of assault is usually accompanied by the use of a weapon or by other means likely to produce death or great bodily harm. Attempts are included, since injury does not necessarily have to result when a gun, knife, or other weapon is used, as these incidents could and probably would result in a serious personal injury if the crime were successfully completed.

Property crimes include three categories: (1) Burglary, or breaking and entering, is the unlawful entry of a structure to commit a felony or theft, even though no force was used to gain entrance. (2) Larceny-theft is the unauthorized taking of the personal property of another, without the use of force. (3) Motor vehicle theft is the unauthorized taking of any motor vehicle.

Rates are based on population estimates provided by the FBI. For some states, reporting is not sufficiently complete to be representative of the state as a whole. The FBI has estimated state totals for those states.

ELEMENTARY AND SECONDARY SCHOOL ENROLLMENT, Items 111 and 112
Source: U.S. Department of Education, National Center for Education Statistics—Common Core of Data
http://www.nces.ed.gov/ccd/bat/

Data on public school enrollment is from the Common Core of Data 2009–2010 survey. Public school enrollment includes pre-kindergarten through grade 12 and ungraded students. The student/teacher ratio is calculated by dividing the number of students in all schools by the number of full-time equivalent teachers employed by all schools and agencies.

EDUCATIONAL ATTAINMENT, Items 113–116
Source: U.S. Census Bureau—2000 Current Population Survey and 2010 American Community Survey
http://www.census.gov/population/socdemo/education/p20-536/tab13.pdf
http://www.census.gov/acs/www/

Data on **educational attainment** are tabulated for the population 25 years old and over. The data were derived from a question that asked respondents for the highest level of school completed or the highest degree received. Persons who had passed a high school equivalency examination were considered high school graduates. Schooling received in foreign schools was to be reported as the equivalent grade or years in the regular American school system. Vocational and technical training, such as barber school training; business, trade, technical, and vocational schools; or other training for a specific trade are specifically excluded.

High school graduate or more. This category includes persons whose highest degree was a high school diploma or its equivalent, and those who reported any level higher than a high school diploma.

Bachelor's degree or more. This category includes persons who have received bachelor's degrees, master's degrees, professional school degrees (such as law school or medical school degrees), and doctoral degrees.

LOCAL GOVERNMENT EDUCATION EXPENDITURES, Items 117 and 118
Source: U.S. Department of Education, National Center for Education Statistics—Common Core of Data
http://www.nces.ed.gov/ccd/bat/

Total expenditure for education includes provision or support of schools and facilities for elementary and secondary education. It encompasses instructional, support, and auxiliary services (school lunch, student activities, and community service) offered by public school systems. Retirement benefits paid to former education employees and interest payments are not included. Current expenditure includes all components of total expenditure except capital outlay. Expenditure data are obtained by the Census Bureau through its annual survey of government finances and are supplied to the National Center for Education Statistics (NCES). Current expenditure per student is current expenditure divided by the number of students enrolled. The number of students enrolled is based on an annual ''membership'' count of students on or about October 1.

NCES uses the Common Core of Data (CCD) Survey system to acquire and maintain statistical data from each of the 50 states, the District of Columbia, and the outlying areas. State education agencies compile and submit data for approximately 94,000 schools and 17,000 local school districts. Typically, this results in varying interpretation of NCES definitions and different record keeping systems, leading to large amounts of missing data for several states; this absence is reflected in the data in this publication. The numbers in Table A reflect imputations and adjustments as published in *Revenues and Expenditures for Public Elementary and Secondary Education: School Year 2008–09 (Fiscal Year 2009).*

EXPORTS, Items 119–121
Source: U.S. Department of Commerce, International Trade Administration
http://www.census.gov/foreign-trade/statistics/state/origin_movement/index.html

The data on exports of goods by state of origin are based on the location of the exporter (the principal party responsible for exportation from the United States). Exporters are often intermediaries, so the data do not necessarily represent the states in which the goods were actually produced. The total includes re-exports of foreign goods.

INCOME AND POVERTY, Items 122–133
Source: U.S. Census Bureau—2010 American Community Survey
http://www.census.gov/acs/www/

The data on income were derived from answers to questions which were asked of the population 15 years old and over. **Total income** is the sum of the amounts reported separately for wage or salary income; net self-employment income; interest, dividends, or net rental or royalty income or income from estates and trusts; Social Security or railroad retirement income; Supplemental Security Income (SSI); public assistance or welfare payments; retirement, survivor, or disability pensions; and all other income. Receipts from the following sources are not included as income: capital gains; money received from the sale of property (unless the recipient was engaged in the business of selling such property); the value of income ''in kind'' from food stamps, public housing subsidies, medical care, employer contributions for individuals, etc.; withdrawal of bank deposits; money borrowed; tax refunds; exchange of money between relatives living in the same household; and gifts and lump-sum inheritances, insurance payments, and other types of lump-sum receipts.

Per capita income is the mean income computed for every man, woman, and child in a particular group. It is derived by dividing the aggregate income of a particular group by the total population in that group. Per capita income is rounded to the nearest whole dollar.

Household income includes the income of the householder and all other individuals 15 years old and over in the household, whether or not they are related to the householder. Since many households consist of only one person, average household income is usually less than average family income. Although the household income statistics cover the past 12 months, the characteristics of individuals and the composition of households refer to the time of enumeration. Thus, the income of the household does not include amounts received by individuals who were members of the household during all or part of the past 12 months if these individuals no longer resided in the household at the time of interview. Similarly, income amounts reported by individuals who did not reside in the household during the past 12 months but who were members of the household at the time of interview are included. However,

the composition of most households was the same during the past 12 months as at the time of interview.

Median income divides the income distribution into two equal parts, with half of all cases below the median income level and half of all cases above the median income level. For households and families, the median income is based on the distribution of the total number of households and families, including those with no income. Median income for households is computed on the basis of a standard distribution with a minimum value of less than $2,500 and a maximum value of $200,000 or more and is rounded to the nearest whole dollar.

For **family income**, the incomes of all household members 15 years old and over related to the householder are summed and treated as a single amount. Although the family income statistics cover the past 12 months, the characteristics of individuals and the composition of families refer to the time of interview. Thus, the income of the family does not include amounts received by individuals who were members of the family during all of part of the past 12 months if these individuals no longer resided with the family at the time of interview. Similarly, income amounts reported by individuals who did not reside with the family during the past 12 months but who were members of the family at the time of interview are included. However, the composition of most families was the same during the past 12 months as at the time of interview.

The **poverty status** data were derived from data collected on the number of persons in the household, each person's relationship to the householder, and the income data. The Social Security Administration (SSA) developed the original poverty definition in 1964, which federal interagency committees subsequently revised in 1969 and 1980. The Office of Management and Budget's (OMB) *Directive 14* prescribes the SSA's definition as the official poverty measure for federal agencies to use in their statistical work. Poverty statistics presented in American Community Survey products adhere to the standards defined by OMB in *Directive 14*.

The poverty thresholds vary depending on three criteria: size of family, number of children, and, for one- and two-person families, age of householder. In determining the poverty status of families and unrelated individuals, the Census Bureau uses thresholds (income cutoffs) arranged in a two-dimensional matrix. The matrix consists of family size (from one person to nine or more persons), cross-classified by presence and number of family members under 18 years old (from no children present to eight or more children present). Unrelated individuals and two-person families are further differentiated by age of reference person (under 65 years old and 65 years old and over). To determine a person's poverty status, the person's total family income in the last 12 months is compared to the poverty threshold appropriate for that person's family size and composition. If the total income of that person's family is less than the threshold appropriate for that family, then the person is considered poor or ''below the poverty level,'' together with every member of his or her family. If a person is not living with anyone related by birth, marriage, or adoption, then the person's own income is compared with his or her poverty threshold. The total number of persons below the poverty level is the sum of persons in families and the number of unrelated individuals with incomes below the poverty level in the last 12 months. The average poverty threshold for a four-person family was $22,314 in 2010.

The data on **poverty status of households** were derived from answers to the income questions. Since poverty is defined at the family level and not the household level, the poverty status of the household is determined by the poverty status of the householder. Households are classified as poor when the total income of the householder's family in the previous 12 months is below the appropriate poverty threshold. (For nonfamily householders, the person's income is compared with the appropriate threshold.) The income of persons living in the household who are unrelated to the householder is not considered when determining the poverty status of a household, nor does their presence affect the family size in determining the appropriate threshold. The poverty thresholds vary depending upon three criteria: size of family, number of children, and, for one- and two-person families, age of the householder.

Poverty status of children by **family type** is the percentage of children living in that particular type of family that has a family income below the poverty threshold based on family size and composition.

PERSONAL INCOME AND EARNINGS, Items 134–158

Source: U.S. Bureau of Economic Analysis, Regional Economic Accounts

http://www.bea.gov/regional/index.htm#state

Total personal income is the current income received by residents of an area from all sources. It is measured before deductions of income and other personal taxes but after deductions of personal contributions for Social Security, government retirement, and other social insurance programs. It consists of **wage and salary disbursements** (covering all employee earnings, including executive salaries, bonuses, commissions, payments-in-kind, incentive payments, and tips); various types of supplementary earnings, such as employers' contributions to pension funds (termed "other labor income" or "supplements to wages and salaries"); proprietors' income; rental income of persons; dividends; personal interest income; and government and business transfer payments.

Proprietors' income is the monetary income and income-in-kind of proprietorships and partnerships (including the independent professions), and the income of tax-exempt cooperatives. **Dividends** are cash payments by corporations to stockholders who are U.S. residents. **Interest** is the monetary and imputed interest income of persons from all sources. **Rent** is the monetary income of persons from the rental of real property, except the income of persons primarily engaged in the real estate business; the imputed net rental income of owner-occupants of nonfarm dwellings; and the royalties received by persons.

Transfer payments are income for which services are not currently rendered. They consist of both government and business transfer payments. Government transfer payments include payments under the following programs: Federal Old-Age, Survivors, and Disability Insurance ("Social Security"); Medicare and medical vendor payments; unemployment insurance; railroad and government retirement; federal- and state-government-insured workers' compensation; veterans' benefits, including veterans' life

insurance; food stamps; black lung payments; Supplemental Security Income; and Temporary Assistance for Needy Families. Government payments to nonprofit institutions, other than for work under research and development contracts, are also included. Business transfer payments consist primarily of liability payments for personal injury and of corporate gifts to nonprofit institutions.

Per capita personal income is based on resident population estimated as of July 1 of the year shown.

Personal tax payments include taxes paid by individuals to federal, state, and local governments. Personal taxes include individual income taxes, estate and gift taxes, motor vehicle license taxes, and personal property taxes. Personal contributions to social insurance ("Social Security taxes") are not included, nor are sales taxes.

Disposable personal income equals personal income less personal tax payments. It is a measure of the income available to persons for spending or saving.

Earnings cover wage and salary disbursements, other labor income, and proprietors' income.

The data for earnings obtained from the Bureau of Economic Analysis (BEA) are based on place of work. In computing personal income, BEA makes an "adjustment for residence" to earnings based on commuting patterns; thus, personal income is presented on a place-of-residence basis.

Farm earnings include the income of farm workers (wages and salaries and other labor income) and farm proprietors. Farm proprietors' income includes only the income of sole proprietorships and partnerships.

Farm earnings estimates are benchmarked to data collected in the Census of Agriculture and the revised Department of Agriculture state totals of income and expense items.

Goods-related industries include mining, construction, and manufacturing. **Service-related** and other industries includes private-sector earnings in forestry, related activities, and other; utilities; transportation and warehousing; information; wholesale trade; retail trade; finance and insurance; real estate and rental and leasing; and services, which includes professional, scientific, and technical services; management of companies and enterprises; administrative and waste services; educational services; health care and social assistance; arts, entertainment, and recreation; accommodation and food services; and other services, except public administration. Government earnings include all levels of government. Industries are categorized under the North American Industry Classification System (NAICS), and are not directly comparable to years prior to 2002.

GROSS STATE PRODUCT, Item 159

Source: U.S. Bureau of Economic Analysis, Regional Economic Accounts

http://www.bea.gov/regional/index.htm#state

Gross state product (GSP) for a state is derived as the sum of gross state product originating in all industries in the state. In concept, an industry's GSP, referred to as its "value added," is equivalent to its gross output (sales or receipts and other operating income, commodity taxes, and inventory changes) minus its intermediate inputs (consumption of goods and services purchased from other industries or imported from other countries). As such, it is often referred to as the state counterpart to the nation's gross domestic product (GDP). In practice, GSP estimates are measured as the sum of distributions by industry of the components of gross domestic income—that is, the sum of the costs incurred (such as compensation of employees, net interest, and indirect business taxes) and the profits earned in production.

SOCIAL SECURITY AND SUPPLEMENTAL SECURITY INCOME, Items 160–162
Source: U.S. Social Security Administration
http://www.ssa.gov/policy/docs/statcomps/oasdi_sc/

http://www.ssa.gov/policy/docs/statcomps/ssi_sc/

Social Security beneficiaries are persons receiving benefits under the Old-Age, Survivors, and Disability Insurance Program. These include retired or disabled workers covered by the program, their spouses and dependent children, and the surviving spouses and dependent children of deceased workers.

Supplemental Security Income (SSI) recipients are persons receiving SSI payments. The SSI program is a cash assistance program that provides monthly benefits to low-income aged, blind, or disabled persons.

Data are as of December of the year shown.

CIVILIAN EMPLOYMENT, Items 163–166
Source: U.S. Census Bureau—2010 American Community Survey
http://www.census.gov/acs/www/

The data on occupation were derived from answers to questions that were asked of all persons 15 years old and over who had worked in the past 5 years. **Occupation** describes the kind of work the person does on the job. For employed persons, the data refer to the person's job during the previous week. For those who worked two or more jobs, the data refer to the job at which the person worked the greatest number of hours. For unemployed persons, the data refer to their last job. The American Community Survey uses the occupational classification system that was developed for the 2000 census and modified in 2002 and again in 2010. This system consists of 539 specific occupational categories for employed persons arranged into 23 major occupational groups. This classification was developed based on the *Standard Occupational Classification (SOC) Manual: 2010*, published by the Executive Office of the President, Office of Management and Budget.

CIVILIAN LABOR FORCE AND UNEMPLOYMENT, Items 167–171
Source: U.S. Bureau of Labor Statistics—Local Areas Unemployment Statistics
http://www.bls.gov/lau/#tables

Data for the civilian labor force are the product of a federal-state cooperative program in which state employment security agencies prepare labor force and unemployment estimates under concepts, definitions, and technical procedures established by the Bureau of Labor Statistics (BLS). The **civilian labor force** consists of all civilians 16 years old and over who are either employed or unemployed.

Unemployment includes all persons who did not work during the survey week, made specific efforts to find a job during the prior four weeks, and were available for work during the survey week (except for temporary illness). Persons waiting to be called back to a job from which they had been laid off and those waiting to report to a new job within the next 30 days are included in unemployment figures.

PRIVATE NONFARM EMPLOYMENT AND EARNINGS, Items 172–183
Source: U.S. Bureau of Labor Statistics—Current Employment Survey
http://www.bls.gov/ces/#tables

Data for private nonfarm employment and earnings are compiled from payroll information reported monthly on a voluntary basis to the BLS and its cooperating state agencies. More than 350,000 establishments represent all industries except agriculture.

Employment is the annual average of monthly totals of persons who received pay for any part of the pay period including the 12th day of the month. Included are all full-time and part-time workers in nonfarm establishments. Not covered are government employees, proprietors, the self-employed, unpaid volunteers or family workers, farm workers, and domestic workers in households. The data by industry conform to the definitions established in the North American Industry Classification System (NAICS).

Earnings of **production workers** in **manufacturing** industries are derived from reports of gross payrolls and corresponding paid hours. Payroll is reported before deductions of any kinds. Total hours during the pay period include all hours worked (including overtime hours) and hours paid for holidays, vacations, and sick leave.

AGRICULTURE, ITEMS 184–202
Source: U.S. Department of Agriculture, National Agricultural Statistics Service—2007 Census of Agriculture
http://www.agcensus.usda.gov/Publications/2007/index.asp

The Census Bureau took a census of agriculture every 10 years from 1840 to 1920; since 1925, this census has been taken roughly once every 5 years. The 1997 Census of Agriculture was the first one conducted by the National Agricultural Statistics Service of the U.S. Department of Agriculture. Over time, the definition of a farm has varied. For recent censuses (including the 2007 census), a farm has been defined as any place from which $1,000 or more of agricultural products were produced and sold or normally would have been sold during the census year. Dollar figures are expressed in current dollars and have not been adjusted for inflation or deflation.

The term **operator** refers to a person who operates a farm by either doing the work or making day-to-day decisions about such activities as planting, harvesting, feeding, marketing, etc. The operator may be the owner, a member of the owner's household, a salaried manager, a tenant, a renter, or a sharecropper. If a person rents land to others or has land worked on shares by others, he/she is considered the operator only of the land that is retained for his/her own operation. The census collected information on the total number of operators, the total number of women operators, and demographic information for up to three operators per farm.

Government payments consists of direct payments as defined by the 2002 Farm Bill; payments from Conservation Reserve Program (CRP), Wetlands reserve Program (WRP), Farmable Wetlands Program (FWP), and Conservation Reserve Enhancement Program (CREP); loan deficiency payments; disaster payments; other conservation programs; and all other federal farm programs under which payments were made directly to farm operators. Commodity Credit Corporation (CCC) proceeds, amount from state and local federal crop insurance payments were not included in this category.

The acreage designated as **land in farms** consists primarily of agricultural land used for crops, pasture, or grazing. It also includes woodland and wasteland not actually under cultivation or used for pasture or grazing, provided that this land was part of the farm operator's total operation.

Land in farms is an operating-unit concept and includes all land owned and operated, as well as all land rented from others. Land used rent-free is classified as land rented from others. All land in Indian reservations used for growing crops or grazing livestock is classified as land in farms.

Irrigated land includes all land watered by any artificial or controlled means, such as sprinklers, flooding, furrows or ditches, sub-irrigation, and spreader dikes. Included are supplemental, partial, and preplant irrigation. Each acre was counted only once regardless of the number of times it was irrigated or harvested. Livestock lagoon waste water distributed by sprinkler or flood systems was also included.

Total cropland includes cropland harvested, cropland used only for pasture or grazing, cropland on which all crops failed or were abandoned, cropland in cultivated summer fallow, and cropland idle or used for cover crops or soil improvement but not harvested and not pastured or grazed.

Respondents were asked to report their estimate of the current market **value of land and buildings** owned, rented, or leased from others and rented and leased to others. Market value refers to the respondent's estimate of what the land and buildings would sell for under current market conditions.

The **value of machinery and equipment** was estimated by the respondent as the current market value of all cars, trucks, tractors, combines, balers, irrigation equipment, etc., used on the farm. This value is an estimate of what the machinery and equipment would sell for in its present condition and not the replacement of depreciated value. Share interests are reported at full value at the farm where the equipment and machinery are usually kept. Only equipment that was actually used in 2006 and 2007, or newly purchased but not yet used and physically located at the farm on December 31, 2007, is included.

Market **value of agricultural products sold** by farms represents the gross market value before taxes and the production expenses of all agricultural products sold or removed from the place in 2007, regardless of who received the payment. It is equivalent to total sales and it includes sales by the operator as well as the value of any share received by partners, landlords, contractors, and others associated with the operation. It includes value of direct sales and the value of commodities placed in the Commodity Credit Corporation (CCC) loan program. Market value of agricultural products sold does not include payments received for participation in other federal farm programs. Also, it does not include income from farm-related sources such as customwork and other agricultural services, or income from non-farm sources.

LAND USE, ITEMS 203 to 205
Source: U.S. Department of Agriculture, Natural Resources Conservation Service—2007 National Resources Inventory
http://www.nrcs.usda.gov/technical/NRI/

The National Resources Inventory (NRI) has been conducted every five years since 1982. The 2007 NRI is based on a sample of about 800,000 locations throughout the United States (excluding Alaska and the District of Columbia). Acreages for federal land and total surface area are established through geospatial processes and administrative records. Total surface area of the contiguous United States is 1,937.7 million acres.

Cropland includes cultivated and non-cultivated cropland. **Federally-owned lands** include military bases, national forests, wildlife refuges, parks, grassland game preserves, scenic waterways, wilderness areas, monuments, lakeshore, parkways, battlefields, Bureau of Land Management lands, and other federal lands. **Developed land** includes any built-up area greater than one fourth of an acre. Built-up areas include residential, industrial, commercial, and institutional land; construction sites; public administrative sites; railroad yards; cemeteries; airports; golf courses; sanitary landfills; sewage treatment plants; water control structures and spillways; other land used for such purpose; small parks (fewer than 10 acres of land) within urban and built-up areas; and highways, railroads, and other transportation facilities that are surrounded by urban areas. Also included are tracts of fewer than 10 acres that do not meet the above definition but are completely surrounded by urban and built-up land, as well as all highways, roads, railroads, and associated rights-of-way outside of urban and built-up areas (including private roads to farmsteads or ranch headquarters, logging roads, and other private roads).

WATER CONSUMPTION, Item 206
Source: U.S. Geological Survey, National Water Use Information Program—2005 Water Use Data
http://pubs.usgs.gov/circ/1344/

Every five years, the U.S. Geological Survey compiles national water-use estimates. This volume includes the total fresh and saline water withdrawals expressed as million gallons per day. Estimate of withdrawals of ground and surface water are given for the following categories of use: public water supplies, domestic, commercial, irrigation, livestock, industrial, mining, and thermoelectric power.

MANUFACTURES, Items 207–216

Source: U.S. Census Bureau— 2010 Annual Survey of Manufactures

http://www.census.gov/manufacturing/asm/

The Annual Survey of Manufactures (ASM) has been conducted annually every year since 1949, except for years ending in "2" and "7," at which time ASM data are included in the manufacturing sector of the Economic Census. The ASM provides statistics on employment, payroll, worker hours, payroll supplements, cost of materials, value added by manufacturing, capital expenditures, inventories, and energy consumption. It also provides estimates of value of shipments for over 1,400 classes of manufactured products. The Annual Survey of Manufactures includes approximately 50,000 establishments selected from the census universe of 350,000 manufacturing establishments.

The **all employees** number is the average number of production workers for the payroll periods including the 12th of March, May, August, and November plus the number of other employees in mid-March. Included are all persons on paid sick leave, paid holidays, and paid vacations during the pay period. Officers of corporations are included as employees, while proprietors and partners of unincorporated firms are excluded.

Payroll figures include the gross annual earnings of all employees on the payroll of operating manufacturing establishments. The definition, which is the same as the one used for calculating the federal withholding tax, includes all forms of compensation, such as salaries, wages, commissions, dismissal pay, bonuses, vacation and sick leave pay, and compensation-in-kind, prior to such deductions as employees' Social Security contributions, withholding taxes, group insurance, union dues, and savings bonds. The total includes salaries of officers of corporations; it excludes payments to proprietors or partners of unincorporated concerns. Also excluded are payments to members of armed forces and to pensioners carried on the active payrolls of manufacturing establishments.

Production workers include workers (up through the line-supervisor level) engaged in fabricating, processing, assembling, inspecting, receiving, storing, handling, packing, warehousing, shipping (but not delivering), maintenance, repair, janitorial and guard services, product development, auxiliary production for the plant's own use (for example, power plant), record keeping, and other services closely associated with these production operations at the establishment covered by the report. Employees above the working-supervisor level are excluded.

The number of production workers is the average for the payroll periods including the 12th of March, May, August, and November. Not included in this classification are all other employees, defined as non-production employees, including those engaged in factory supervision above the line-supervisor level.

Production worker hours cover hours worked or paid for at the manufacturing plant, including actual overtime hours (not straight-time equivalent hours). The data exclude hours paid for vacations, holidays, or sick leave when the employee is not at the establishment. Production wages represent all compensation paid to production workers.

Value added by manufacture is derived by subtracting the cost of materials, supplies, containers, fuel, purchased electricity, and contract work from the value of shipments (products manufactured plus receipts for services rendered). The result of this calculation is adjusted by the addition of value added by merchandising operations (the difference between the sales value and the cost of merchandise sold without further manufacture, processing, or assembly) plus the net change in finished goods and work-in-process between the beginning- and end-of-year inventories.

Value of shipments covers the received or receivable net selling values; free on board plant (excluding of freight and taxes), of all products shipped, both primary and secondary; and all miscellaneous receipts, such as receipts for contract work performed for others, installation and repair, sales of scrap, and sales of products bought and sold without further processing. Included are all items made by or for the establishments from material owned by it, whether sold, transferred to other plants of the same company, or shipped on consignment. The net selling value of products made in one plant on a contract basis from materials owned by another was reported by the plant providing the materials.

In the case of multi-unit companies, the manufacturer was asked to report the value of products transferred to other establishments of the same company at full economic or commercial value, including both the direct cost of production and a reasonable proportion of "all other costs" (including company overhead) and profit (interplant transfers).

The aggregate of the value of shipments figure for industry groups and for all manufacturing industries includes large amounts of duplications, as the products of some industries are used as materials by others. Estimates as to the overall extent of this duplication indicate that the value of manufactured products exclusive of such duplication (the value of finished manufactures) tends to approximate two-thirds of the total value of products reported in the census of manufactures.

Total capital expenditures (new and used) represents the total new and used capital expenditures reported by establishments in operation and any known plants under construction. These data include expenditures for (1) permanent additions and major alterations to manufacturing and mining establishments and (2) new and used machinery and equipment used for replacement and additions to plant capacity, if they are of the type for which depreciation, depletion accounts were ordinarily maintained.

Totals for expenditures include the costs of assets leased from nonmanufacturing concerns through capital leases. New facilities owned by the federal government but operated under contract by private companies and plant and equipment furnished to the manufacturer by communities and nonprofit organizations are excluded. These data exclude expenditures for land and mineral rights and cost of maintenance and repairs charged as current operating expenses.

For any equipment or structure transferred for the use for the reporting establishment by the parent company or one of its subsidiaries, the value at which it was transferred to the establishment was to be reported.

If an establishment changed ownership during the year, the cost of fixed assets (building and equipment) was to be reported.

2007 ECONOMIC CENSUS: OVERVIEW, Items 217–308

Source: U.S. Census Bureau
http://www.census.gov/econ/census07/

The Economic Census provides a detailed portrait of the nation's economy, from the national to the local level, once every five years. The 2007 Economic Census covers nearly all of the U.S. economy in its basic collection of establishment statistics. The 1997 Economic Census was the first major data source to use the new North American Industry Classification System (NAICS); therefore, data are not comparable to economic data from prior years, which were based on the Standard Industrial Classification (SIC) system.

NAICS, developed in cooperation with Canada and Mexico, classifies North America's economic activities at two, three, four, and five digit levels of detail; the U.S. version of NAICS further defines industries to a sixth digit. The Economic Census takes advantage of this hierarchy to publish data at these successive levels of detail: sector (two-digit); subsector (three-digit); industry group (four-digit); industry (five-digit); and U.S. industry (six-digit). Information in Table A is at the two-digit level, with a few three- and four-digit items.

Several key statistics are tabulated for all industries included in this volume: number of establishments (or companies); number of employees; payroll; and a measure of output (sales, receipts, revenue, value of shipments, or value of construction work done).

Number of establishments. An establishment is a single physical location at which business is conducted. It is not necessarily identical with a company or enterprise, which may consist of one establishment or more. Economic Census figures represent a summary of reports for individual establishments rather than companies. For cases in which a census report was received, separate information was obtained for each location where business was conducted. When administrative records of other federal agencies were used instead of a census report, no information was available on the number of locations operated. Each Economic Census establishment was tabulated according to the physical location at which the business was conducted. The count of establishments represents those in business at any time during 2007.

When two activities or more were carried on at a single location under a single ownership, all activities were generally grouped together as a single establishment. The entire establishment was classified on the basis of its major activity and all of its data were included in that classification. However, when distinct and separate economic activities (for which different industry classification codes were appropriate) were conducted at a single location under a single ownership, separate establishment reports for each of the different activities were obtained in the census.

Number of employees. Paid employees consist of the full time and part time employees, including salaried officers and executives of corporations. Included are employees on paid sick leave, paid holidays, and paid vacations; not included are proprietors and partners of unincorporated businesses. The definition of paid employees is the same as that used by the Internal Revenue Service (IRS) on form 941.

For some industries, the Economic Census gives codes representing the number of employees as a range of numbers (for example, "100 to 249 employees" or "1,000 to 2,499" employees). In this volume, those codes have been replaced by the standard suppression code "D".

Payroll. Payroll includes all forms of compensation, such as salaries, wages, commissions, dismissal pay, bonuses, vacation allowances, sick leave pay, and employee contributions to qualified pension plans paid during the year to all employees. For corporations, payroll includes amounts paid to officers and executives; for unincorporated businesses, it does not include profit or other compensation of proprietors or partners. Payroll is reported before deductions for Social Security, income tax, insurance, union dues, etc. This definition of payroll is the same as that used on IRS form 941.

Sales, shipments, receipts, revenue, or business done. This measure includes the total sales, shipments, receipts, revenue, or business done by establishments within the scope of the Economic Census. The definition of each of these items is specific to the economic sector measured.

CONSTRUCTION, Items 217–221

Source: U.S. Census Bureau—2007 Economic Census (See Overview of 2007 Economic Census prior to Item 217)

The Construction sector (sector 23) comprises establishments primarily engaged in the construction of buildings and other structures, heavy construction (except buildings), additions, alterations, reconstruction, installation, and maintenance and repairs. Establishments engaged in the demolition or wrecking of buildings and other structures, the clearing of building sites, and the sale of materials from demolished structures are also included. This sector also contains those establishments engaged in blasting, test drilling, landfill, leveling, earthmoving, excavating, land drainage, and other land preparation. The industries within this sector have been defined on the basis of their unique production processes. As with all industries, the production processes are distinguished by their use of specialized human resources and specialized physical capital. Construction activities are generally administered or managed at a relatively fixed place of business, but the actual construction work can be performed at one or more different project sites. This sector is divided into three subsectors of construction activities: (1) building construction and land subdivision and land development; (2) heavy construction (except buildings), such as highways, power plants, and pipelines; and (3) construction activity by special trade contractors.

WHOLESALE TRADE, Items 222–226

Source: U.S. Census Bureau—2007 Economic Census (See Overview of 2007 Economic Census prior to Item 217)

The Wholesale Trade sector (sector 42) comprises establishments engaged in wholesaling merchandise, generally without transformation, and rendering services incidental to the sale of merchandise. The wholesaling process is an intermediate step in the distribution of merchandise. Wholesalers are organized to sell or arrange the purchase or sale of (1) goods for resale (i.e., goods sold to other wholesalers or retailers), (2) capital or durable nonconsumer goods, and (3) raw and intermediate materials and supplies used in production.

Wholesalers sell merchandise to other businesses and normally operate from a warehouse or office. These warehouses and offices are characterized by having little or no display of merchandise. In addition, neither the design nor the location of the premises is intended to solicit walk in traffic. Wholesalers do not normally use advertising directed to the general public. Customers are generally first reached via telephone, in person marketing, or by specialized advertising that may include internet and other electronic means. Follow up orders are either vendor initiated or client initiated, are usually based on previous sales, and typically exhibit strong ties between sellers and buyers. In fact, transactions are often conducted between wholesalers and clients that have long standing business relationships.

This sector is made up of two main types of wholesalers: those that sell goods on their own account and those that arrange sales and purchases for others for a commission or fee.

(1) Establishments that sell goods on their own account are known as wholesale merchants, distributors, jobbers, drop shippers, import/export merchants, and sales branches. These establishments typically maintain their own warehouse, where they receive and handle goods for their customers. Goods are generally sold without transformation, but may include integral functions, such as sorting, packaging, labeling, and other marketing services.

(2) Establishments arranging for the purchase or sale of goods owned by others or purchasing goods on a commission basis are known as agents and brokers, commission merchants, import/ export agents and brokers, auction companies, and manufacturers' representatives. These establishments operate from offices and generally do not own or handle the goods they sell.

Some wholesale establishments may be connected with a single manufacturer and/or promote and sell that particular manufacturer's products to a wide range of other wholesalers or retailers. Other wholesalers may be connected to a retail chain or a limited number of retail chains and only provide a variety of products needed by that particular retail operation(s). These wholesalers may obtain the products from a wide range of manufacturers. Still other wholesalers may not take title to the goods but act as agents and brokers for a commission.

Although, in general, wholesaling normally denotes sales in large volumes, durable nonconsumer goods may be sold in single units. Sales of capital or durable nonconsumer goods used in the production of goods and services, such as farm machinery, medium- and heavy-duty trucks, and industrial machinery, are always included in Wholesale Trade.

RETAIL TRADE, Items 227–235
Source: U.S. Census Bureau—2007 Economic Census (See Overview of 2007 Economic Census prior to Item 217)

The Retail Trade sector (44–45) is made up of establishments engaged in retailing merchandise, generally without transformation, and rendering services incidental to the sale of merchandise.

The retailing process is the final step in the distribution of merchandise; retailers are, therefore, organized to sell merchandise in small quantities to the general public. This sector comprises two main types of retailers: store and nonstore retailers.

Store retailers operate fixed point of sale locations, located and designed to attract a high volume of walk in customers. In general, retail stores have extensive displays of merchandise and use mass media advertising to attract customers. They typically sell merchandise to the general public for personal or household consumption; some also serve business and institutional clients. These include establishments, such as office supply stores, computer and software stores, building materials dealers, plumbing supply stores, and electrical supply stores. Catalog showrooms, gasoline service stations, automotive dealers, and mobile home dealers are treated as store retailers.

In addition to retailing merchandise, some types of store retailers are also engaged in the provision of after sales services, such as repair and installation. For example, new automobile dealers, electronic and appliance stores, and musical instrument and supply stores often provide repair services. As a general rule, establishments engaged in retailing merchandise and providing after sales services are classified in this sector.

Nonstore retailers, like store retailers, are organized to serve the general public, although their retailing methods differ. The establishments of this subsector reach customers and market merchandise with methods, such as the broadcasting of ''infomercials,'' the broadcasting and publishing of direct response advertising, the publishing of paper and electronic catalogs, door to door solicitation, in home demonstration, selling from portable stalls (street vendors, except food), and distribution through vending machines. Establishments engaged in the direct sale (nonstore) of products, such as home heating oil dealers and home-delivery newspaper routes are included in this sector.

The buying of goods for resale is a characteristic of retail trade establishments that distinguishes them from establishments in the Agriculture, Manufacturing, and Construction sectors. For example, farms that sell their products at or from the point of production are classified in Agriculture instead of in Retail Trade. Similarly, establishments that both manufacture and sell their products to the general public are classified in Manufacturing instead of Retail Trade. However, establishments that engage in processing activities incidental to retailing are classified in retail.

Industries in the **Motor Vehicle and Parts Dealers** subsector (441) retail motor vehicle and parts merchandise from fixed point-of-sale locations. Establishments in this subsector typically operate from a showroom and/or an open lot where the vehicles are on display. The display of vehicles and the related parts require little by way of display equipment. Personnel generally include both sales and sales support staff familiar with the requirements for registering and financing a vehicle as well as a staff of parts experts and mechanics trained to provide vehicle repair and maintenance services. Specific industries have been included in this subsector to identify the type of vehicle being retailed. Sales of capital or durable nonconsumer goods, such as medium and heavy-duty trucks, are always included in the Wholesale Trade sector. These goods are virtually never sold through retail methods.

Industries in the **Food and Beverage Stores** subsector (445) usually retail food and beverage merchandise from fixed point-of-sale locations. Establishments in this subsector have special equipment (e.g., freezers, refrigerated display cases, and refrigerators) for displaying food and beverage goods. They have staff trained in the processing of food products to guarantee the proper storage and sanitary conditions, as mandated by regulatory authority.

Industries in the **Clothing and Clothing Accessories Stores** subsector (448) retail new clothing and clothing accessories merchandise from fixed point-of-sale locations. Establishments in this subsector have similar types of display equipment, as well as employees who are knowledgeable regarding fashion trends and who can match styles, colors, and combinations of clothing and accessories to the characteristics and tastes of the customer.

Industries in the **General Merchandise Stores** subsector (452) retail new general merchandise from fixed point-of-sale locations. Establishments in this subsector are unique in that they have the equipment and staff capable of retailing a large variety of goods from a single location. This includes a variety of display equipment and staff trained to provide information on many lines of products.

INFORMATION, Items 236–246

Source: U.S. Census Bureau—2007 Economic Census (See Overview of 2007 Economic Census prior to Item 217)

The Information sector (51) comprises establishments engaged in the following processes: (1) producing and distributing information and cultural products, (2) providing the means to transmit or distribute these products as well as data or communications, and (3) processing data.

The main components of this sector are the publishing industries, including software publishing; the motion picture and sound recording industries; the broadcasting and telecommunications industries; and the information services and data processing industries.

For the purpose of NAICS, the transformation of information into a commodity that is produced and distributed by a number of growing industries is at issue. The Information sector groups three types of establishments: (1) those engaged in producing and distributing information and cultural products; (2) those that provide the means to transmit or distribute these products as well as data or communications; and (3) those that process data. Cultural products are those that directly express attitudes, opinions, ideas, values, and artistic creativity; provide entertainment; or offer information and analysis concerning the past and present. Included in this definition are popular, mass produced products, as well as cultural products that normally have a more limited audience, such as poetry books, literary magazines, or classical records. These activities were formerly classified throughout the existing national classifications. Traditional publishing was in manufacturing; broadcasting in communications; software production in business services; film production in amusement services; and so forth.

Industries in the **Publishing Industries, Except Internet** subsector (511) include establishments engaged in the publishing of newspapers, magazines, other periodicals, and books, as well as database and software publishing. In general, these establishments, which are known as publishers, issue copies of works for which they usually possess copyright. Works may be in one or more formats, including traditional print format, CD ROM format, or online format. Publishers may publish works originally created by others for which they have obtained the rights and/or works that they have created in house. Software publishing is included here because the activity (creation of a copyrighted product and bringing it to market) is equivalent to the creation process for other types of intellectual products.

In NAICS, publishing—the reporting, writing, editing, and other processes that are required to create an edition of a book or a newspaper—is treated as a major economic activity in its own right, rather than as a subsidiary activity to printing, which is a manufacturing activity. Thus, publishing is classified in the Information sector, while printing remains in the NAICS Manufacturing sector. In part, the NAICS classification reflects the fact that publishing increasingly takes place in establishments that are physically separate from the associated printing establishments. More crucially, the NAICS classification of book and newspaper publishing is intended to portray their roles in a modern economy—roles that do not resemble manufacturing activities.

Music publishers are not included in the Publishing Industries subsector, but can be found in the Motion Picture and Sound Recording Industries subsector. Reproduction of prepackaged software is treated in NAICS as a manufacturing activity; online distribution of software products is in the Information sector, and custom design of software to client specifications is included in the Professional, Scientific, and Technical Services sector. These distinctions arise because of the different ways that software is created, reproduced, and distributed.

The Information sector does not include products, such as manifold business forms. Information is not the essential component of these items. Establishments producing these items are included in subsector 323, Printing and Related Support Activities.

Industries in the **Motion Picture and Sound Recording Industries** subsector (512) group establishments involved in the production and distribution of motion pictures and sound recordings. While producers and distributors of motion pictures and sound recordings issue works for sale as traditional publishers do, the processes are different enough to warrant placing the establishments engaged in these activities in separate subsectors. Production is typically a complex process that involves several distinct types of establishments engaged in activities, such as contracting with performers, creating the film or sound content, and providing technical postproduction services. Film distribution is often to exhibitors, such as theaters and broadcasters, rather than to a wholesale or retail distribution chain. When the product is in a mass produced form, NAICS treats production and distribution as the major economic activity, rather than as a subsidiary activity to the manufacture of such products.

This subsector does not include establishments primarily engaged in the wholesale distribution of video cassettes and sound recordings, such as compact discs and audio tapes; these establishments are included in the Wholesale Trade sector. Reproduction of video cassettes and sound recordings that is carried out separately from establishments engaged in production and distribution is treated in NAICS as a manufacturing activity.

Industries in the **Broadcasting, except Internet** subsector (515) include establishments that create content or acquire the right to distribute and subsequently broadcast content. The industry groups (Radio and Television Broadcasting and Cable and Other Subscription Programming) are based on differences in the methods of communication and the nature of services provided.

The Radio and Television Broadcasting industry group includes establishments that operate broadcasting studios and facilities for over-the-air or satellite delivery of radio and television programs, including entertainment, news, and talk programs. These establishments are often engaged in production and purchase of programs and generating revenues from the sale of air time to advertisers, as well as from donations, subsidies, and/or the sale of programs. The Cable and Other Subscription Programming industry group includes establishments that operate studios and facilities for the broadcasting of limited-format programs (such as news, sports, educational, and youth-oriented programs) that are typically narrowly-focused in nature; these programs are usually available on a subscription or fee basis. The distribution of cable and other subscription programming is included in subsector 517, Telecommunications.

Industries in the **Internet Publishing and Broadcasting and Web search portals** subsector (51913) consist of establishments that publish and/or broadcast content exclusively for the Internet. The unique combination of text, audio, video, and interactive features present in informational and/or cultural products on the Internet justifies the separation of internet publishers and broadcasters from the more traditional publishers included in subsector 511, Publishing Industries, Except Internet, and subsector 515, Broadcasting, Except Internet.

Industries in the **Telecommunications** subsector (517) include establishments that provide telecommunications and services related to that activity. The Telecommunications subsector is primarily engaged in operating, maintaining, and/or providing access to facilities for the transmission of voice, data, text, sound, and video. A transmission facility may be based on a single technology or a combination of technologies. Establishments primarily engaged as independent contractors in the maintenance and installation of broadcasting and telecommunications systems are classified in sector 23, Construction.

Industries in the **Internet Service Providers, Web Search Portals, and Data Processing Services** subsector (518) group establishments that provide: (1) access to the Internet; (2) search facilities for the Internet; and (3) data processing, hosting, and related services. The industry groups (Internet Service Providers and Web Search Portals, Data Processing Hosting, and Related Services) are based on differences in the processes used to access information and process information. The Internet Service Providers and Web Search Portals industry group includes establishments that provide access to the Internet or assist users in their navigations on the Web. The Data Processing, Hosting, and Related Services industry group includes establishments that process data. These establishments can transform data, prepare data for dissemination, or place data or content on the Internet for others. In addition, the shared use of computer resources is included in the Data Processing, Hosting, and Related Services industry group.

Establishments that are publishing exclusively on the Internet are included in subsector 516, Internet Publishing and Broadcasting; establishments that sell goods over the Internet are included in sector 44–45, Retail Trade.

UTILITIES, Items 247–252
Source: U.S. Census Bureau—2007 Economic Census (See Overview of 2007 Economic Census prior to Item 217)

The Utilities sector (22) comprises establishments engaged in the provision of the following utility services: electric power, natural gas, steam supply, water supply, and sewage removal. Within this sector, the specific activities associated with the utility services provided vary by utility: electric power includes generation, transmission, and distribution; natural gas includes distribution; steam supply includes provision and/or distribution; water supply includes treatment and distribution; and sewage removal includes collection, treatment, and disposal of waste through sewer systems and sewage treatment facilities.

Excluded from this sector are establishments primarily engaged in waste management. These services are classified in subsector 562, Waste Management and Remediation Services, which also collect, treat, and dispose of waste materials; however, establishments in this subsector do not use sewer systems or sewage treatment facilities.

TRANSPORTATION AND WAREHOUSING, Items 252–256
Source: U.S. Census Bureau—2007 Economic Census (See Overview of 2007 Economic Census prior to Item 217)

The Transportation and Warehousing sector (48–49) includes industries that provide transportation of passengers and cargo, warehousing and storage for goods, scenic and sightseeing transportation, and support activities related to modes of transportation. Establishments in these industries use transportation equipment or transportation related facilities as a productive asset. The type of equipment depends on the mode of transportation, which includes air, rail, water, road, and pipeline.

The transportation and warehousing sector distinguishes three basic types of activities: subsectors for each mode of transportation, a subsector for warehousing and storage, and a subsector for establishments providing support activities for transportation. In addition, there are subsectors for establishments that provide passenger transportation for scenic and sightseeing purposes, postal services, and courier services.

FINANCE AND INSURANCE, Items 257–261
Source: U.S. Census Bureau—2007 Economic Census (See Overview of 2007 Economic Census prior to Item 217)

The Finance and Insurance sector (52) comprises establishments primarily engaged in financial transactions (transactions involving the creation, liquidation, or change in ownership of financial assets) and/or in facilitating financial transactions. Three principal types of activities are identified:

(1) Raising funds by taking deposits and/or issuing securities and, in the process, incurring liabilities. Establishments engaged in this activity use raised funds to acquire financial assets by making loans and/or purchasing securities. Putting themselves at risk, they channel funds from lenders to borrowers and transform

or repackage the funds with respect to maturity, scale and risk. This activity is known as financial intermediation.

(2) Pooling of risk by underwriting insurance and annuities. Establishments engaged in this activity collect fees, insurance premiums, or annuity considerations; build up reserves; invest those reserves; and make contractual payments. Fees are based on the expected incidence of the insured risk and the expected return on investment.

(3) Providing specialized services facilitating or supporting financial intermediation, insurance, and employee benefit programs.

In addition, monetary authorities charged with monetary control are included in this sector.

REAL ESTATE AND RENTAL AND LEASING, Items 262–266
Source: U.S. Census Bureau—2007 Economic Census (See Overview of 2007 Economic Census prior to Item 217)

The Real Estate and Rental and Leasing sector (53) comprises establishments primarily engaged in renting, leasing, or otherwise allowing the use of tangible or intangible assets, and establishments providing related services. The major portion of this sector comprises establishments that rent, lease, or otherwise allow the use of their own assets by others. The assets may be tangible, such as real estate and equipment, or intangible, such as patents and trademarks.

This sector also includes establishments primarily engaged in managing real estate for others, selling, renting, and/or buying real estate for others, and appraising real estate. These activities are closely related to this sector's main activity. In addition, a substantial proportion of property management is self performed by lessors.

The main components of this sector are the real estate lessors industries; equipment lessors industries (including motor vehicles, computers, and consumer goods); and lessors of nonfinancial intangible assets (except copyrighted works).

PROFESSIONAL, SCIENTIFIC, AND TECHNICAL SERVICES, Items 267–275
Source: U.S. Census Bureau—2007 Economic Census (See Overview of 2007 Economic Census prior to Item 217)

The Professional, Scientific, and Technical Services sector (54) is made up of establishments that specialize in performing professional, scientific, and technical activities for others. These activities require a high degree of expertise and training. The establishments in this sector specialize according to expertise and provide services to clients in a variety of industries (and, in some cases, to households). Activities performed include legal advice and representation; accounting, bookkeeping, and payroll services; architectural, engineering, and specialized design services; computer services; consulting services; research services; advertising services; photographic services; translation and interpretation services; veterinary services; and other professional, scientific, and technical services.

This sector excludes establishments primarily engaged in providing a range of day to day office administrative services, such as financial planning, billing and record keeping, personnel services, and physical distribution and logistics services. These establishments are classified in sector 56, Administrative and Support and Waste Management and Remediation Services.

Legal Services is a NAICS industry group (5411) that includes establishments classified in the following NAICS industries: 54111, Offices of Lawyers, and 54119, Other Legal Services.

Accounting, Tax Preparation, Bookkeeping, and Payroll Services is a NAICS industry group (5412) that comprises establishments primarily engaged in providing services such as auditing of accounting records, designing accounting systems, preparing financial statements, developing budgets, preparing tax returns, processing payrolls, bookkeeping, and billing.

Architectural, Engineering, and Related Services is a NAICS industry group (5413) that includes establishments classified in the following NAICS industries: 54131, Architectural Services; 54133, Engineering Services; 54134, Drafting Services; 54135, Building Inspection Services; 54136, Geophysical Surveying and Mapping Services; 54137, Surveying and Mapping (Except Geophysical) Services; and 54138, Testing Laboratories.

Computer Systems Design and Related Services is a NAICS industry group (5415) that consists of establishments primarily engaged in providing expertise in the field of information technologies through one or more of the following activities: (1) writing, modifying, testing, and supporting software to meet the needs of a particular customer; (2) planning and designing computer systems that integrate computer hardware, software, and communication technologies; (3) on site management and operation of clients' computer systems and/or data processing facilities; and (4) other professional and technical computer related advice and services.

HEALTH CARE AND SOCIAL ASSISTANCE, Items 276–289
Source: U.S. Census Bureau—2007 Economic Census (See Overview of 2007 Economic Census prior to Item 217)

The Health Care and Social Assistance sector (62) consists of establishments that provide health care and social assistance services to individuals. The sector includes both health care and social assistance, because it is sometimes difficult to distinguish between the boundaries of these two activities. The industries in this sector are arranged on a continuum starting with those that provide medical care exclusively, continuing with those that provide health care and social assistance, and finishing with those that provide only social assistance. The services provided by establishments in this sector are delivered by trained professionals. All industries in the sector share this commonality of process—namely, labor inputs of health practitioners or social workers with the requisite expertise. Many of the industries in the sector are defined based on the educational degree held by the practitioners included in the industry.

In this volume, taxable and tax-exempt establishments are presented separately.

Excluded from this sector are aerobic classes, which can be found in subsector 713, Amusement, Gambling and Recreation Industries; and nonmedical diet and weight-reducing centers, which can be found in subsector 812, Personal and Laundry Services. Although these can be viewed as health services, they are not typically delivered by health practitioners.

Industries in the **Ambulatory Health Care Services** subsector (621) provide health care services directly or indirectly to ambulatory patients and do not typically provide inpatient services. Health practitioners in this subsector provide outpatient services, and facilities and equipment do not usually play the most significant part in this sector's production process.

Industries in the **Hospitals** subsector (622) provide medical, diagnostic, and treatment services, including physician, nursing, specialized accommodation, and other health services, to inpatients. Hospitals may provide outpatient services as a secondary activity. Many of the services provided by establishments in the Hospitals subsector require the use of specialized facilities and equipment, both of which form a significant and integral part of the production process.

ARTS, ENTERTAINMENT, AND RECREATION, Items 290–294

Source: U.S. Census Bureau—2007 Economic Census (See Overview of 2007 Economic Census prior to Item 217)

The Arts, Entertainment, and Recreation sector (71) includes a wide range of establishments that operate facilities or provide services that meet the diverse cultural, entertainment, and recreational interests of their patrons. This sector is made up of: (1) establishments that are involved in producing, promoting, or participating in live performances, events, or exhibits intended for public viewing; (2) establishments that preserve and exhibit objects and sites of historical, cultural, or educational interest; and (3) establishments that operate facilities or provide services that enable patrons to participate in recreational activities or pursue amusement, hobby, and leisure time interests.

Some establishments that provide cultural, entertainment, or recreational facilities and services are classified in other sectors. Excluded from this sector are: (1) establishments that provide both accommodations and recreational facilities—such as hunting and fishing camps and resort and casino hotels—are classified in subsector 721, Accommodation; (2) restaurants and night clubs that provide live entertainment in addition to the sale of food and beverages are classified in subsector 722, Food Services and Drinking Places; (3) motion picture theaters, libraries and archives, and publishers of newspapers, magazines, books, periodicals, and computer software are classified in sector 51, Information; and (4) establishments that use transportation equipment to provide recreational and entertainment services, such as those operating sightseeing buses, dinner cruises, or helicopter rides, are classified in subsector 487, Scenic and Sightseeing Transportation.

ACCOMMODATION AND FOOD SERVICES, Items 295–300

Source: U.S. Census Bureau—2007 Economic Census (See Overview of 2007 Economic Census prior to Item 217)

The Accommodation and Food Services sector (72) consists of establishments that provide customers with lodging and/or meals, snacks, and beverages for immediate consumption. The sector includes both accommodation and food services establishments because the two activities are often combined at the same establishment. Excluded from this sector are civic and social organizations, amusement and recreation parks, theaters, and other recreation or entertainment facilities providing food and beverage services.

Industries in the **Food Services and Drinking Places** subsector (722) prepare meals, snacks, and beverages to customer order for immediate on premises and off premises consumption. There is a wide range of establishments in these industries. Some provide food and drink only; while others provide various combinations of seating space, waiter/waitress services and incidental amenities, such as limited entertainment. The industries in the subsector are grouped based on the type and level of services provided. The industry groups are full service restaurants; limited service eating places; special food services, such as food service contractors, caterers, and mobile food services, and drinking places. Food services and drink activities at hotels and motels; amusement parks, theaters, casinos, country clubs, and similar recreational facilities; and civic and social organizations are included in this subsector only if these services are provided by a separate establishment primarily engaged in providing food and beverage services. Excluded from this subsector are establishments operating dinner cruises. These establishments are classified in subsector 487, Scenic and Sightseeing Transportation, because they utilize transportation equipment to provide scenic recreational entertainment.

OTHER SERVICES, EXCEPT PUBLIC ADMINISTRATION Items 301–308

Source: U.S. Census Bureau—2007 Economic Census (See Overview of 2007 Economic Census prior to Item 217)

The Other Services, Except Public Administration sector (81) comprises establishments engaged in providing services not specifically categorized elsewhere in the classification system. Establishments in this sector are primarily engaged in activities such as equipment and machinery repairing, promoting or administering religious activities, grant making, and advocacy; this sector also includes establishments that provide dry-cleaning and laundry services, personal care services, death care services, pet care services, photofinishing services, temporary parking services, and dating services.

Private households that employ workers on or about the premises in activities primarily concerned with the operation of the household are included in this sector.

Excluded from this sector are establishments primarily engaged in retailing new equipment and performing repairs and general maintenance on equipment. These establishments are classified in sector 44–45, Retail Trade.

Industries in the **Repair and Maintenance** subsector (811) restore machinery, equipment, and other products to working order. These establishments also typically provide general or routine maintenance (i.e., servicing) on such products to ensure they work efficiently; this maintenance also helps prevent breakdowns and make certain repairs unnecessary.

The NAICS structure for this subsector brings together most types of repair and maintenance establishments and categorizes them based on production processes (i.e., on the type of repair and maintenance activity performed, and the necessary skills, expertise, and processes required for different repair and maintenance establishments). This NAICS classification does not delineate between repair services provided to businesses versus those provided to households. Although some industries primarily serve either businesses or households, separation by class of customer is limited by the fact that many establishments serve both types. Establishments that repair computers and consumer electronics products are examples of such overlap.

The Repair and Maintenance subsector does not include all establishments engaged in repair and maintenance. For example, a substantial amount of repair is done by establishments that also manufacture machinery, equipment, and other goods. These establishments are included in the Manufacturing sector in NAICS. In addition, the repairing of transportation equipment is often provided by or based at transportation facilities, such as airports and seaports; these activities are included in the Transportation and Warehousing sector.

A particularly unique situation exists with repair of buildings. Plumbing, electrical installation and repair, painting and decorating, and other construction related establishments are often involved in performing installation or other work on new construction, while also providing repair services on existing structures. Although some establishments do specialize in repair, it is difficult to distinguish between these two types. Thus, all such establishments are included in the Construction sector.

Excluded from this subsector are establishments primarily engaged in rebuilding or remanufacturing machinery and equipment. These are classified in sector 31–33, Manufacturing. Also excluded are retail establishments that provide after sale services and repair. These are classified in sector 44–45, Retail Trade.

Industries in the **Personal and Laundry Services** subsector (812) include establishments that provide personal and laundry services to individuals, households, and businesses. Services performed include personal care services, death care services, laundry and dry-cleaning services, and a wide range of other personal services, such as pet care (except veterinary) services, photofinishing services, temporary parking services, and dating services.

The Personal and Laundry Services subsector is by no means all inclusive of the activities that could be termed personal services (i.e., those provided to individuals rather than businesses). There are many other sectors and subsectors that provide services to persons. Establishments providing legal, accounting, tax preparation, architectural, portrait photography, and similar professional services are classified in sector 54, Professional, Scientific, and Technical Services; those providing job placement, travel arrangement, home security, interior and exterior house cleaning, exterminating, lawn and garden care, and similar support services are classified in sector 56, Administrative and Support and Waste Management and Remediation Services; those providing health and social services are classified in sector 62, Health Care and Social Assistance; those providing amusement and recreation services are classified in sector 71, Arts, Entertainment and Recreation; those providing educational instruction are classified in sector 61, Educational Services; those providing repair services are classified in subsector 811, Repair and Maintenance; and those providing spiritual, civic, and advocacy services are classified in subsector 813, Religious, Grantmaking, Civic, Professional, and Similar Organizations.

Industries in the **Religious, Grantmaking, Civic, Professional, and Similar Organizations** subsector (813) include establishments that organize and promote religious activities, support various causes through grant making, advocate various social and political causes, and promote and defend the interests of their members. This category includes only tax-exempt establishments.

The industry groups within the subsector are defined in terms of their activities, separately grouping establishments that provide funding for specific causes or for a variety of charitable causes, establishments that advocate and actively promote causes and beliefs for the public good, and establishments that have an active membership structure to promote causes and represent the interests of their members. Establishments in this subsector may publish newsletters, books, and periodicals for distribution to their membership.

GOVERNMENT EMPLOYMENT, Items 309–311
Source: U.S. Bureau of Economic Analysis—Regional Economic Accounts
http://www.bea.gov/regional/index.htm#state

Employment is measured as the average annual sum of full-time and part-time jobs. The estimates are on a place-of-work basis. Data for federal civilian employment include civilian employees of the Department of Defense. Military employment includes all persons on active duty status.

FEDERAL FUNDS, Items 312–330
Source: U.S. Census Bureau—Consolidated Federal Funds Report
http://www.census.gov/govs/cffr/

Data on federal expenditure and obligations are obtained from a report prepared by the Census Bureau in accordance with the Consolidated Federal Funds Report (CFFR) Act of 1982 (P.L. 97-326). The data are for federal fiscal years beginning October 1 and ending the following September 30.

Salaries and wages represent actual federal expenditures during the fiscal year; the geographic distribution of these amounts by state and county was estimated based upon place of employment.

Procurement contract awards cover awards given by the United States Postal Service (USPS), as well as those given by all other federal agencies. Amounts provided by the USPS represent actual outlays for contractual commitments, while amounts for other agencies represent the value of obligations for contract actions and do not reflect actual federal government expenditures.

In general, only current-year contract actions are included; however, multiple-year obligations may be reported for contract actions of less than 3 years' duration.

Direct payments for individuals include Social Security benefits, federal government retirement, Medicare, Supplemental Security Income, unemployment compensation, food stamps, agricultural and housing assistance, and other categories not shown separately. All data represent actual expenditures during the fiscal year.

Direct housing assistance primarily includes the Low Income Housing Assistance Program.

Grants data represent the federal obligations incurred at the time the grant is awarded. The amounts reported do not represent actual expenditures, since obligations in one time period may not result in outlays during the same period. Moreover, initial amounts obligated may be adjusted at a later date, through either enhancements or de-obligations.

Medicaid and other health-related grants include a variety of grants from the Department of Health and Human Services for health services and research.

Nutrition and family welfare grants include a variety of grants from the Department of Health and Human Services for child welfare, special programs for the aging, and related areas. The school lunch program and other nutritional assistance programs administered by the Department of Agriculture are also included in this category.

Disasters and emergency preparedness grants include assistance to fire-fighting and rescue organizations; community assistance for earthquakes, floods, hurricanes and other disasters; domestic preparedness programs; and similar activities.

Housing and community development grants include Community Development Block Grants, housing demonstration programs, rental housing rehabilitation, and other housing programs.

Employment and training grants include various job training programs, welfare-to-work grants, occupational safety and health grants, and similar employment related funds.

Energy and environment grants include grants from the Department of Energy for energy development, energy conservation, and nuclear waste disposal, as well as grants from the Environmental Protection Agency for a variety of pollution control and waste management activities.

STATE GOVERNMENT FINANCES, Items 331–350
Source: U.S. Census Bureau—State Government Finances
http://www.census.gov/govs/state/

Data are from an annual survey conducted by the Census Bureau and pertain to state government fiscal years ending on June 30, except for four states with other ending dates: Alabama and Michigan (September 30), New York (March 31), and Texas (August 31).

The state government finance data presented in this publication may differ from data published by state governments because the Census Bureau may be using a different definition of which organizations are covered under the term, ''state government.''

For the purpose of Census Bureau statistics, the term ''state government'' refers not only to the executive, legislative, and judicial branches of a given state, but it also includes agencies, institutions, commissions, and public authorities that operate separately or somewhat autonomously from the central state government but where the state government maintains administrative or fiscal control over their activities as defined by the Census Bureau.

Total **general revenue** includes all revenue except utility, liquor stores, and insurance trust revenue. All tax revenue and intergovernmental revenue, even if designated for employee-retirement or local utility purpose, are classified as general revenue.

Intergovernmental revenue covers amounts received from the federal government as fiscal aid, reimbursements for performance of general government functions and specific services for the paying government, or in lieu of taxes. It excludes any amounts received from other governments from the sale of property, commodities, and utility services.

Taxes consist of compulsory contributions exacted by governments for public purposes. However, this category excludes employer and employee payments for retirement and social insurance purposes, which are classified as insurance trust revenue; it also excludes special assessments, which are classified as non-tax general revenue. Sales and gross receipts taxes do not include dealer discounts, or ''commissions'' allowed to merchants for collection of taxes from consumers. General sales taxes and selected taxes on sales of motor fuels, tobacco products, and other particular commodities and services are included.

General government expenditure includes capital outlay, a major portion of which is commonly financed by borrowing. Government revenue does not include receipts from borrowing. Among other things, this distorts the relationship between totals of revenue and expenditure figures that are presented and renders it useless as a direct measure of the degree of budgetary ''balance'' (as that term is generally applied).

Direct general expenditure comprises all expenditures of the state governments, excluding utility, liquor stores, insurance trust expenditures, and any intergovernmental payments.

State government expenditure for **education** is mainly for the provision and general support of schools and other educational facilities and services, including those for educational institutions beyond high school. They cover such related services as student transportation; school lunch and other cafeteria operations; school health, recreation, and library services; and dormitories, dining halls, and bookstores operated by public institutions of higher education.

Health and hospitals expenditure includes health research; clinics; nursing; immunization; other categorical, environmental, and general health services provided by health agencies; establishment and operation of hospital facilities; provision of hospital care; and support of other public and private hospitals.

Highways expenditure is for the provision and maintenance of highway facilities, including toll turnpikes, bridges, tunnels, and ferries, as well as regular roads, highways, and streets. Also included are expenditures for street lighting and for snow and ice removal. Not included are highway policing and traffic control, which are considered part of police protection

Public safety expenditure includes police and correctional institution expenditures.

Public welfare expenditure covers support of and assistance to needy persons; this aid is contingent upon the person's needs.

Included are cash assistance paid directly to needy persons under categorical (Old Age Assistance, Temporary Assistance for Needy Families, Aid to the Blind, and Aid to the Disabled) and other welfare programs; vendor payments made directly to private purveyors for medical care, burials, and other commodities and services provided under welfare programs; welfare institutions; and any intergovernmental or other direct expenditure for welfare purposes. Pensions to former employees and other benefits not contingent on need are excluded.

Natural resources, parks, and recreation includes expenditures for conservation, promotion, and development of natural resources (soil, water, energy, minerals, etc.) and the regulation of industries which develop, utilize, or affect natural resources. It also includes the provision and support of recreational and cultural-scientific facilities, such as golf courses, playgrounds, tennis courts, public beaches, swimming pools, play fields, parks, camping areas, recreational piers and marinas, galleries, museums, zoos, botanical gardens, auditoriums, stadiums, recreational centers, convention centers, exhibition halls, community music, drama, and celebrations.

Debt outstanding includes all long-term debt obligations of the government and its agencies (exclusive of utility debt) and all interest-bearing, short-term (repayable within one year) debt obligations remaining unpaid at the close of the fiscal year. It includes judgments, mortgages, and revenue bonds, as well as general obligation bonds, notes, and interest-bearing warrants. This category consists of non-interest-bearing, short-term obligations; inter-fund obligations; amounts owed in a trust or agency capacity; advances and contingent loans from other governments; and rights of individuals to benefit from government-administered employee-retirement funds.

VOTING AND REGISTRATION, Items 351 and 352
Source: U.S. Census Bureau—Current Population Survey
http://www.census.gov/hhes/www/socdemo/voting/index.html

These estimates are based on the November 2008 Voting and Registration Supplement to the Current Population Survey (CPS).

Voting rates are calculated using the voting-age population, which includes both citizens and noncitizens. Statistics from surveys are subject to sampling and nonsampling error. The CPS estimate of overall turnout differs from the ''official'' turnout reported by the Clerk of the House of Representatives.

ELECTION STATISTICS, Items 353–355
Source: Election Data Services, Inc. Washington, DC
(copyright)
http://www.electiondataservices.com/

© 2009 Election Data Services, Inc. All rights reserved. This material is proprietary and the subject of copyright protection and other intellectual property rights owned by or licensed to Election Data Services, Inc. The use of this material is subject to the terms of a License Agreement. You will be held liable for any unauthorized copying or disclosure of this material.

Election results show the percentage of the total vote cast for the Democratic and Republican candidates, as well as the combined percentage for all other candidates in the 2008 presidential election.

TABLE B—STATES AND COUNTIES

Table B presents 199 items for the United States as a whole, each individual state, and the District of Columbia; and every county, county equivalent, and independent city. The counties are presented in alphabetical order within each state, and the states are also presented in alphabetical order. Independent cities, which are found in Maryland, Missouri, Nevada, and Virginia, are placed in alphabetical order at the end of the list of counties for those states. The District of Columbia is included in Table B as both a county and a state. It is also included as a city in Table D.

LAND AREA, Items 1 and 4
Source: U.S. Census Bureau—2010 Census of Population and Housing
http://2010.census.gov/2010census/data/

Land area measurements are shown to the nearest square kilometer. Land area includes dry land and land temporarily or partially covered by water, such as marshlands, swamps, and river floodplains.

POPULATION, Items 2–4
Source: U.S. Census Bureau—2010 Census of Population and Housing
http://2010.census.gov/2010census/data/

The population data are from the 2010 census and represent the resident population as of April 1, 2010. The ranks are shown for counties (including independent cities and the District of Columbia).

POPULATION AND POPULATION CHARACTERISTICS, Items 5–19
Source: U.S. Census Bureau—2010 Census of Population and Housing
http://2010.census.gov/2010census/data/

The concept of race, as used by the Census Bureau, reflects self-identification by persons according to the race or races with which they most closely identify. These categories are sociopolitical constructs and should not be interpreted as being scientific or anthropological in nature. Furthermore, race categories include both racial and national origin groups.

Beginning with the 2000 census, respondents were offered the option of selecting one or more races. This option was not available in prior censuses; thus, comparisons between censuses should be made with caution. In Table B, Columns 5 through 8 refer to individuals who identified with each racial category, either alone or in combination with other races. The estimates exclude persons of Hispanic or Latino origin from all race groups. Because respondents could include as many categories as they wished, and because the columns refer to the percentage of the population, the total will often exceed 100 percent.

The **White** population is defined as persons who indicated their race as White, as well as persons who did not classify themselves in one of the specific race categories listed on the questionnaire but entered a nationality such as Irish, German, Italian, Lebanese, Near Easterner, Arab, or Polish.

The **Black** population includes persons who indicated their race as "Black, African Am., or Negro," as well as persons who did not classify themselves in one of the specific race categories but reported entries such as African American, Afro American, Kenyan, Nigerian, or Haitian.

The **American Indian or Alaska Native** population includes persons who indicated their race as American Indian or Alaska Native, as well as persons who did not classify themselves in one of the specific race categories but reported entries such as Canadian Indian, French-American Indian, Spanish-American Indian, Eskimo, Aleut, Alaska Indian, or any of the American Indian or Alaska Native tribes.

The **Asian and Pacific Islander** population combines two census groupings: **Asian** and **Native Hawaiian or Other Pacific Islander**. The **Asian** population includes persons who indicated their race as Asian Indian, Chinese, Filipino, Japanese, Korean, Vietnamese, or "Other Asian," as well as persons who provided write-in entries of such groups as Cambodian, Laotian, Hmong, Pakistani, or Taiwanese. The **Native Hawaiian or Other Pacific Islander** population includes persons who indicated their race as "Native Hawaiian," "Guamanian or Chamorro," "Samoan," or "Other Pacific Islander," as well as persons who reported entries such as Part Hawaiian, American Samoan, Fijian, Melanesian, or Tahitian.

The **Hispanic population** is based on a question that asked respondents "Is this person Spanish/Hispanic/Latino?" Persons marking any one of the four Hispanic categories (i.e., Mexican, Puerto Rican, Cuban, or other Spanish) are collectively referred to as Hispanic.

In the census, the Hispanic origin question was placed before the race question and specific instructions indicated that both questions should be answered. These changes were designed to improve accuracy and may affect comparability with data prior to the 2000 census.

Age is defined as age at last birthday (number of completed years since birth), as of April 1 of the census year. The census also asked for the specific date of birth of the respondent, and census procedures used the birth date for deriving age data. For this reason, it is likely that the data have fewer problems than data from censuses prior to 2000, such as the tendency of respondents to round ages or to report their ages on the date the questionnaire was filled out rather than on April 1.

The **female** population is shown as a percentage of total population.

POPULATION AND COMPONENTS OF CHANGE, Items 20–26
Source: U.S. Census Bureau—Decennial Censuses and Population Estimates
http://www.census.gov/main/www/cen2000.html
http://www.census.gov/popest/estimates.html
http://2010.census.gov/2010census/data/

The population data for 1990, 2000, and 2010 are from the decennial censuses and represent the resident population as of April 1 of those years. The components of change are based on Census Bureau estimates of the resident population as of July 1,

2009. The change in population between 2000 and 2009 is made up of (a) natural increase—births minus deaths, and (b) net migration—the difference between the number of persons moving into a particular area and the number of persons moving out of the area. Net migration is composed of internal and international migration.

Because the 2009 population estimates are based on a model that begins with a national population estimate, the county components of change do not always exactly add up to the difference between the 2000 census population and the 2009 estimates.

HOUSEHOLDS, Items 27–31
Source: U.S. Census Bureau—2010 Census of Population and Housing
http://2010.census.gov/2010census/data/

A **household** includes all of the persons who occupy a housing unit. (Persons not living in households are classified as living in group quarters.) A housing unit is a house, an apartment, a mobile home, a group of rooms, or a single room occupied (or, if vacant, intended for occupancy) as separate living quarters. Separate living quarters are those in which the occupants live separately from any other persons in the building and have direct access from the outside of the building or through a common hall. The occupants may be a single family, one person living alone, two or more families living together, or any other group of related or unrelated persons who share living quarters. The number of households is the same as the number of year-round occupied housing units.

A **family** includes a householder and one or more other persons living in the same household who are related to the householder by birth, marriage, or adoption. All persons in a household who are related to the householder are regarded as members of his or her family. A **family household** may contain persons not related to the householder; thus, family households may include more members than families do. A household can contain only one family for the purposes of census tabulations. Not all households contain families, as a household may comprise a group of unrelated persons or of one person living alone. Families are classified by type as either a "husband-wife family" or "other family," according to the presence or absence of a spouse.

The measure of **persons per household** is obtained by dividing the number of persons in households by the number of households or householders. One person in each household is designated as the householder. In most cases, this is the person (or one of the persons) in whose name the house is owned, being bought, or rented. If there is no such person in the household, any adult household member 15 years old and over can be designated as the householder.

The category **female family householder** includes only female-headed family households with no spouse present.

GROUP QUARTERS, Item 32
Source: U.S. Census Bureau—2010 Census of Population and Housing
http://2010.census.gov/2010census/data/

The Census Bureau classifies all persons not living in households as living in group quarters; this category includes both the institutional and noninstitutional populations. The institutionalized population includes persons under formally authorized, supervised care or custody in institutions, such as correctional institutions, nursing homes, mental (psychiatric) hospitals, and juvenile institutions. The noninstitutionalized population includes persons who live in group quarters other than institutions, such as college dormitories, military quarters, and group homes. This volume includes the total number of persons in group quarters.

DAYTIME POPULATION, Items 33 and 34
Source: U.S. Census Bureau—American Community Survey, 2006–2010
http://www.census.gov/acs/www/

Daytime population refers to the number of persons who are present in an area or place during normal business hours, including workers. This can be contrasted with the "resident" population, which is present during the evening and nighttime hours. The daytime population estimate is calculated by adding the total resident population and the total workers working in the area/place, and then subtracting the total workers living in the area/place from that result. Information on the expansion or contraction experienced by different communities between their nighttime and daytime populations is important for many planning purposes, especially those concerning transportation, disaster, and relief operations.

The employment/residence ratio is a measure of the total number of workers working in an area or place, relative to the total number of workers living in the area or place. It is often used as a rough indication of the jobs-workers balance in an area/place, although it does not take into account whether the resident workers possess the skills needed for the jobs available in their particular area/place. The employment/residence ratio is calculated by dividing the number of total workers working in an area/place by the number of total workers residing in the area/place.

BIRTHS AND DEATHS, Items 35–38
Source: U.S. Centers for Disease Control and Prevention, National Center for Health Statistics
http://wonder.cdc.gov/cmf-icd10.html

The registration of births, deaths, and other vital events in the United States is primarily a state and local function. The civil laws of every state provide for continuous and permanent birth and death registration systems. Through the National Vital Statistics System, the National Center for Health Statistics (NCHS) obtains data on births and deaths from the registration offices of each state, New York City, and the District of Columbia.

Birth and death statistics are limited to events occurring during the year. The data are by place of residence and exclude events for nonresidents of the United States. Births or deaths of Americans that occur outside the United States are excluded.

Birth and death rates represent the number of births and deaths per 1,000 resident population enumerated as of April 1 for decennial census years and estimated as of July 1 for other years.

In order to protect the privacy of individuals, the Centers for Disease Control and Prevention does not make county-level data available when the number of individual events falls below a threshold figure. Since a three-year time span allows more time for events to occur, cumulative data covering three years tend to be more complete than data for a single year. Also, an average for a three-year period may more accurately represent the trend level when the number of events for each year is small. For these reasons, the county data in this volume are presented as an average computed from data covering a three-year time span. State data in this table are presented on the same basis in order to maintain comparability. Even with the three-year average, death rates based on fewer than 20 deaths should be considered unreliable, and birth data are simply not available for smaller counties.

PERSONS UNDER 65 WITH NO HEALTH INSURANCE, Items 39 and 40
Source: U.S. Census Bureau—Small Area Health Insurance Estimates
http://www.census.gov/did/www/sahie/index.html

The Small Area Health Insurance Estimates (SAHIE) program develops model-based estimates of health insurance coverage for counties and states. This developmental program builds on the work of the Small Area Income and Poverty Estimates (SAIPE) program. The SAHIE program models health insurance coverage by combining survey data with population estimates and administrative records. The estimates are based on data from The Annual Social and Economic Supplement (ASEC) of the Current Population Survey (CPS); Demographic population estimates; Aggregated federal tax returns; Participation records for the Supplemental Nutrition Assistance Program (SNAP), formerly known as the Food Stamp program; County Business Patterns; Medicaid and Children's Health Insurance Program (CHIP) participation records; and Census 2000.

MEDICARE ENROLLMENT, Items 41–43
Source: U.S. Department of Health and Human Services, Centers for Medicare and Medicaid Services
http://www.cms.hhs.gov/MCRAdvPartDEnrolData/

http://www.cms.hhs.gov/DataCompendium/

The Centers for Medicare and Medicaid Services (CMS) administers Medicare, which provides health insurance to persons 65 years old and over, persons with permanent kidney failure, and certain persons with disabilities. Original Medicare has two parts: Hospital Insurance and Supplemental Medical Insurance. In recent years, Medicare has been expanded to include two new programs: Medicare Advantage plans and prescription drug coverage. Medicare Advantage Plans are health plan options that are approved by Medicare but run by private companies. Medicare prescription drug plans can be part of Medicare Advantage plans or stand-alone drug plans.

Persons who are **eligible for Medicare** can enroll in Part A (Hospital Insurance) at no charge, and can choose to pay a monthly premium to enroll in Part B. Most eligible persons are enrolled in Part A, and more than 90 percent of enrollees in Part A are also enrolled in Part B (Supplemental Medical Insurance.) This table includes persons who were eligible as of December 2010.

Medicare Advantage enrollees were enrolled in a Medicare Advantage plan of some type at the end of 2010. These include Private Fee for Service plans, Preferred Provider Organizations, Health Maintenance Organizations, Medical Savings Account

Plans, Demonstration plans, and Programs for All-Inclusive Care for the Elderly.

Persons enrolled in a **Medicare Prescription drug plan** were enrolled in stand-alone plans for prescription drug benefits. This number does not include Medicare enrollees who had prescription drug coverage through private or federal retiree health plans, through Medicare Advantage plans, or through Medicaid.

CRIME, Items 44–47
Source: U.S. Federal Bureau of Investigation— Uniform Crime Reports
http://www.fbi.gov/ucr/ucr.htm

Crime data are as reported to the Federal Bureau of Investigation (FBI) by law enforcement agencies and have not been adjusted for underreporting. This may affect comparability between geographic areas or over time.

Through the voluntary contribution of crime statistics by law enforcement agencies across the United States, the Uniform Crime Reporting (UCR) Program provides periodic assessments of crime in the nation as measured by offenses that have come to the attention of the law enforcement community. The Committee on Uniform Crime Records of the International Association of Chiefs of Police initiated this voluntary national data collection effort in 1930. The UCR Program contributors compile and submit their crime data either directly to the FBI or through state-level UCR Programs.

Seven offenses, because of their severity, frequency of occurrence, and likelihood of being reported to police, were initially selected to serve as an index for evaluating fluctuations in the volume of crime. These serious crimes were murder and nonnegligent manslaughter, forcible rape, robbery, aggravated assault, burglary, larceny-theft, and motor vehicle theft. By congressional mandate, arson was added as the eighth index offense in 1979. The totals shown in this volume do not include arson.

In 2004, the FBI discontinued the use of the Crime Index in the UCR Program and its publications, stating that the Crime Index was driven upward by the offense with the highest number of cases (in this case, larceny-theft), creating a bias against jurisdictions with a high number of larceny-thefts but a low number of other serious crimes, such as murder and forcible rape. The FBI is currently publishing a violent crime total and property crime total until a more viable index is developed. This book includes the crime total, as well as violent crime and property crime rates.

Violent crimes include four categories of offenses: (1) Murder and nonnegligent manslaughter, as defined in the UCR Program, is the willful (nonnegligent) killing of one human being by another. This offense excludes deaths caused by negligence, suicide, or accident; justifiable homicides; and attempts to murder or assaults to murder. (2) Forcible rape is the carnal knowledge of a female forcibly and against her will. Assaults or attempts to commit rape by force or threat of force are also included; however, statutory rape (without force) and other sex offenses are excluded. (3) Robbery is the taking or attempting to take anything of value from the care, custody, or control of a person or persons by force or threat of force or violence and/or by putting the victim in fear. (4) Aggravated assault is an unlawful attack by one person upon another for the purpose of inflicting severe or aggravated bodily injury. This type of assault is usually accompanied by the use of a weapon or by other means likely to produce death or great bodily harm. Attempts are included, since injury does not necessarily have to result when a gun, knife, or other weapon is used, as these incidents could and probably would result in a serious personal injury if the crime were successfully completed.

Property crimes include three categories: (1) Burglary, or breaking and entering, is the unlawful entry of a structure to commit a felony or theft, even though no force was used to gain entrance. (2) Larceny-theft is the unauthorized taking of the personal property of another, without the use of force. (3) Motor vehicle theft is the unauthorized taking of any motor vehicle.

Rates are based on population estimates provided by the FBI. The county totals published in this volume were obtained by aggregating individual reporting units within each county and MSA. If the population total for the units aggregated was less than 75 percent of the county's population (as estimated by the Census Bureau), the total was not considered representative of the county as a whole and was not published. State and U.S. totals include FBI estimates for those areas. State and U.S. totals in this table are the adjusted totals as published in the FBI's *Crime in the United States.*

EDUCATION—SCHOOL ENROLLMENT AND EDUCATIONAL ATTAINMENT, Items 48–51
Source: U.S. Census Bureau—American Community Survey, 2006–2010
http://www.census.gov/acs/www/

Persons were classified as enrolled in school if they reported attending a "regular" public or private school (or college) during the three months preceding the interview. The instructions were to include only nursery school, kindergarten, elementary school, and schooling which would lead to a high school diploma or a college degree as regular school. The Census Bureau defines a public school as "any school or college controlled and supported by a local, county, state, or federal government." Schools primarily supported and controlled by religious organizations or other private groups are defined as private schools.

Data on **educational attainment** are tabulated for the population 25 years old and over. The data were derived from a question that asked respondents for the highest level of school completed or the highest degree received. Persons who had passed a high school equivalency examination were considered high school graduates. Schooling received in foreign schools was to be reported as the equivalent grade or years in the regular American school system.

Vocational and technical training, such as barber school training; business, trade, technical, and vocational schools; or other training for a specific trade are specifically excluded.

High school graduate or less. This category includes persons whose highest degree was a high school diploma or its equivalent, and those who reported any level lower than a high school diploma.

Bachelor's degree or more. This category includes persons who have received bachelor's degrees, master's degrees, professional school degrees (such as law school or medical school degrees), and doctoral degrees.

LOCAL GOVERNMENT EDUCATION EXPENDITURES, Items 52 and 53
Source: U.S. Department of Education, National Center for Education Statistics—Common Core of Data
http://nces.ed.gov/ccd/f33agency.asp

Total expenditure for education includes provision or support of schools and facilities for elementary and secondary education. It encompasses instructional, support, and auxiliary services (school lunch, student activities, and community service) offered by public school systems. Retirement benefits paid to former education employees and interest payments are not included. Current expenditure includes all components of total expenditure except capital outlay. Expenditure data are obtained by the Census Bureau through its annual survey of government finances and are supplied to the National Center for Education Statistics (NCES). Current expenditure per student is current expenditure divided by the number of students enrolled. The number of students enrolled is based on an annual "membership" count of students on or about October 1.

NCES uses the Common Core of Data (CCD) Survey system to acquire and maintain statistical data from each of the 50 states, the District of Columbia, and the outlying areas. State education agencies compile and submit data for approximately 85,000 schools and 15,000 local school districts. Typically, this results in varying interpretation of NCES definitions and different record keeping systems, leading to large amounts of missing data for several states; this absence is reflected in the data in this publication. Schools and school districts are included in the county in which the school district offices (the local education agency) are located.

The state totals in this table are aggregated from the agencies in this file, sometimes resulting in different numbers from the state data in Table A.

MONEY INCOME, Items 54–57
Source: U.S. Census Bureau—American Community Survey, 2006–2010
http://www.census.gov/acs/www/

Total money income is the sum of the amounts reported separately for wage or salary income; net self-employment income; interest, dividends, or net rental or royalty income or income from estates and trusts; Social Security or railroad retirement income; Supplemental Security Income (SSI); public assistance or welfare payments; retirement, survivor, or disability pensions; and all other income. Receipts from the following sources are not included as income: capital gains; money received from the sale of property (unless the recipient was engaged in the business of selling such property); the value of income "in kind" from food stamps, public housing subsidies, medical care, employer contributions for individuals, etc.; withdrawal of bank deposits; money borrowed; tax refunds; exchange of money between relatives living in the same household; and gifts, lump-sum inheritances, insurance payments, and other types of lump-sum receipts.

Money income differs in definition from personal income (item 62). For example, money income does not include the pension rights, employer provided health insurance, food stamps, or Medicare payments that are included in personal income.

Per capita income is the mean income computed for every man, woman, and child in a particular group. It is derived by dividing the aggregate income of a particular group by the resident population in that group as estimated in the American Community Survey. Per capita income is rounded to the nearest whole dollar.

Household income includes the income of the householder and all other individuals 15 years old and over in the household, whether or not they are related to the householder. Since many households consist of only one person, median household income is usually less than median family income. Although the household income statistics cover the 12 months preceding the interview, the characteristics of individuals and the composition of households refer to the date of interview. Thus, the income of the household does not include amounts received by individuals who were no longer residing in the household at the time of interview. Similarly, income amounts reported by individuals who did not reside in the household during all of the past 12 months but who were members of the household at the time of interview are included. However, the composition of most households was the same during those 12 months as it was at the time of interview.

Median income divides the income distribution into two equal parts, with half of all cases below the median income level and half of all cases above the median income level. For households, the median income is based on the distribution of the total number of households, including those with no income. Median income for households is computed on the basis of a standard distribution with a minimum value of less than $2,500 and a maximum value of $200,000 or more and is rounded to the nearest whole dollar. Median income figures are calculated using linear interpolation if the width of the interval containing the estimate is $2,500 or less. If the width of the interval containing the estimate is greater than $2,500, Pareto interpolation is used.

Income amounts have been adjusted for inflation to represent the final year of multi-year estimates, in this case 2005–2009 estimates. The constant-dollar figures are based on an annual average Consumer Price Index from the Bureau of Labor Statistics. Constant-dollar figures are estimates representing an effort to remove the effects of price changes from statistical series reported in dollar terms. However, the estimates do not reflect the price and cost-of-living differences that may exist between areas.

INCOME AND POVERTY, Items 58–61
Source: U.S. Census Bureau—Small Area Income and Poverty Estimates Program
http://www.census.gov/did/www/saipe/index.html

The 2010 income and poverty estimates by county are constructed from statistical models that relate income and poverty to indicators based on summary data from federal income tax returns, data about participation in the Food Stamp program, and the previous census. A regression model predicts the number of people in poverty using county-level observations from the current year's American Community Survey (ACS) and administrative records and census data as the predictors. The 2005 estimates were the first to use the ACS. Prior year models were based on the Annual Social and Economic Supplement (ASEC) of the Current Population Survey (CPS). The ACS is a much larger survey than the ASEC, permitting income and poverty estimates based on a single year for many counties, Because of the differences between the two surveys, caution should be used when comparing these estimates with those from earlier years.

The **poverty status** data were derived from data collected on the number of persons in a household, each person's relationship to the householder, and income data. The Social Security Administration (SSA) developed the original poverty definition in 1964, which federal interagency committees subsequently revised in 1969 and 1980. The Office of Management and Budget's (OMB) *Directive 14* prescribes the SSA's definition as the official poverty measure for federal agencies to use in their statistical work. Poverty statistics presented in American Community Survey products adhere to the standards defined by OMB in *Directive 14*.

Poverty thresholds vary depending on three criteria: size of family, number of children, and, for one- and two-person families, age of householder. In determining the poverty status of families and unrelated individuals, the Census Bureau uses thresholds (income cutoffs) arranged in a two-dimensional matrix. The matrix consists of family size (from one person to nine or more persons), cross-classified by presence and number of family members under 18 years old (from no children present to eight or more children present). Unrelated individuals and two-person families are further differentiated by age of reference person (under 65 years old and 65 years old and over). To determine a person's poverty status, the person's total family income over the previous 12 months is compared with the poverty threshold appropriate for that person's family size and composition. If the total income of that person's family is less than the threshold appropriate for that family, then the person is considered poor or "below the poverty level," together with every member of his or her family. If a person is not living with anyone related by birth, marriage, or adoption, then the person's own income is compared with his or her poverty threshold. The total number of persons below the poverty level is the sum of persons in families and the number of unrelated individuals with incomes below the poverty level over the previous 12 months.

Poverty Thresholds in 2010 by Size of Family and Number of Related Children Under 18 Years

Size of family unit	Weighted average thresholds
One person (unrelated individual)	11,139
Under 65 years	11,344
65 years and over	10,458
Two people	14,218
Householder under 65 years	14,676
Householder 65 years and over	13,194
Three people	17,374
Four people	22,314
Five people	26,439
Six people	29,897
Seven people	34,009
Eight people	37,934
Nine people or more	45,220

Source: U.S. Census Bureau

PERSONAL INCOME AND EARNINGS, Items 62–83

Source: U.S. Bureau of Economic Analysis, Regional Economic Accounts
http://www.bea.gov/regional/index.htm#state

Total personal income is the current income received by residents of an area from all sources. It is measured before deductions of income and other personal taxes, but after deductions of personal contributions for Social Security, government retirement, and other social insurance programs. It consists of **wage and salary disbursements** (covering all employee earnings, including executive salaries, bonuses, commissions, payments-in-kind, incentive payments, and tips); various types of supplementary earnings, such as employers' contributions to pension funds (termed ''other labor income'' or ''supplements to wages and salaries''); proprietors' income; rental income of persons; dividends; personal interest income; and government and business transfer payments.

Per capita personal income is based on the resident population estimated as of July 1 of the year shown.

Proprietors' income is the monetary income and income-in-kind of proprietorships and partnerships (including the independent professions) and the income of tax-exempt cooperatives. **Dividends** are cash payments by corporations to stockholders who are U.S. residents. **Interest** is the monetary and imputed interest income of persons from all sources. **Rent** is the monetary income of persons from the rental of real property, except the income of persons primarily engaged in the real estate business; the imputed net rental income of owner-occupants of nonfarm dwellings; and the royalties received by persons.

Transfer payments are income for which services are not currently rendered. They consist of both government and business transfer payments. Government transfer payments include payments under the following programs: Federal Old-Age, Survivors, and Disability Insurance (''Social Security''); Medicare and medical vendor payments; unemployment insurance; railroad and government retirement; federal- and state-government-insured workers' compensation; veterans' benefits, including veterans' life insurance; food stamps; black lung payments; Supplemental Security Income; and Temporary Assistance for Needy Families. Government payments to nonprofit institutions, other than for work under research and development contracts, are also included. Business transfer payments consist primarily of liability payments for personal injury and of corporate gifts to nonprofit institutions.

Personal income differs in definition from money income (items 54–57). For example, personal income includes pension rights, employer-provided health insurance, food stamps, and Medicare. These are not included in the definition of money income.

Earnings cover wage and salary disbursements, other labor income, and proprietors' income.

The data for earnings obtained from the Bureau of Economic Analysis (BEA) are based on place of work. In computing personal income, BEA makes an ''adjustment for residence'' to earnings, based on commuting patterns; personal income is thus presented on a place-of-residence basis.

Farm earnings include the income of farm workers (wages and salaries and other labor income) and farm proprietors. Farm proprietors' income includes only the income of sole proprietorships and partnerships. Farm earnings estimates are benchmarked to data collected in the Census of Agriculture and the revised Department of Agriculture statistical totals of income and expense items.

Goods-related industries include mining, construction, and manufacturing. **Service-related** and other industries include private-sector earnings in agricultural services, forestry, and fisheries; transportation and public utilities; wholesale trade; retail trade; finance, insurance, and real estate; and services. Government earnings include all levels of government. Industries are categorized under the North American Industry Classification System (NAICS), and are not comparable to years prior to 2002.

SOCIAL SECURITY AND SUPPLEMENTAL SECURITY INCOME, Items 84–86

Source: U.S. Social Security Administration
http://www.ssa.gov/policy/docs/statcomps/oasdi_sc/
http://www.ssa.gov/policy/docs/statcomps/ssi_sc/

Social Security beneficiaries are persons receiving benefits under the Old-Age, Survivors, and Disability Insurance Program. These include retired or disabled workers covered by the program, their spouses and dependent children, and the surviving spouses and dependent children of deceased workers.

Supplemental Security Income (SSI) recipients are persons receiving SSI payments. The SSI program is a cash assistance program that provides monthly benefits to low-income aged, blind, or disabled persons.

Data are as of December of the year shown.

HOUSING, Items 87–96

Source: U.S. Census Bureau—2010 Census of Population and Housing
http://2010.census.gov/2010census/data/
Source: U.S. Census Bureau—American Community Survey, 2006–2010
http://www.census.gov/acs/www/

Housing data for 2010 are from the 2010 census. Housing unit characteristics for 2006–2010 are from the American Community Survey.

A **housing unit** is a house, apartment, mobile home or trailer, group of rooms, or single room occupied or, if vacant, intended for occupancy as separate living quarters. Separate living quarters are those in which the occupants do not live and eat with any other person in the structure and which have direct access from the outside of the building or through a common hall.

The occupants of a housing unit may be a single family, one person living alone, two or more families living together, or any other group of related or unrelated persons who share living quarters. Both occupied and vacant housing units are included in the housing inventory, although recreational vehicles, tents, caves, boats, railroad cars, and the like are included only if they are occupied as a person's usual place of residence.

A housing unit is classified as occupied if it is the usual place of residence of the person or group of persons living in it at the time of enumeration, or if the occupants are only temporarily absent (away on vacation). A household consists of all persons who occupy a housing unit as their usual place of residence. Vacant units for sale or rent include units rented or sold but not occupied and any other units held off the market.

Median value is the dollar amount that divides the distribution of specified owner-occupied housing units into two equal parts, with half of all units below the median value and half of all units above the median value. Value is defined as the respondent's estimate of what the house would sell for if it were for sale. Data are presented for single-family units on fewer than 10 acres of land that have no business or medical offices on the property.

Median rent divides the distribution of renter-occupied housing units into two equal parts. The rent concept used in this volume is gross rent, which includes the amount of cash rent a renter pays (contract rent) plus the estimated average cost of utilities and fuels, if these are paid by the renter. The rent is the amount of rent only for living quarters and excludes amounts paid for any business or other space occupied. Single-family houses on lots of 10 or more acres of land are also excluded.

Housing cost as a percentage of income is shown separately for owners with mortgages, owners without mortgages, and renters. Rent as a percentage of income is a computed ratio of gross rent and monthly household income (total household income in 1999 divided by 12). Selected owner costs include utilities and fuels, mortgage payments, insurance, taxes, etc. In each case, the ratio of housing cost to income is computed separately for each housing unit. The housing cost ratios for half of all units are above the median shown in this book, and half are below the median shown in the book.

Substandard units are occupied units that are overcrowded or lack complete plumbing facilities. For the purposes of this item, "overcrowded" is defined as having 1.01 persons or more per room. Complete plumbing facilities include hot and cold piped water, a flush toilet, and a bathtub or shower. These facilities must be located inside the housing unit, but do not have to be in the same room.

CIVILIAN LABOR FORCE AND UNEMPLOYMENT, Items 97–100

Source: U.S. Bureau of Labor Statistics—Local Area Unemployment Statistics
http://www.bls.gov/lau/#tables

Data for the civilian labor force are the product of a federal-state cooperative program in which state employment security agencies prepare labor force and unemployment estimates under concepts, definitions, and technical procedures established by the Bureau of Labor Statistics (BLS). The civilian labor force consists of all civilians 16 years old and over who are either employed or unemployed.

Unemployment includes all persons who did not work during the survey week, made specific efforts to find a job during the previous four weeks, and were available for work during the survey week (except for temporary illness). Persons waiting to be called back to a job from which they had been laid off and those waiting to report to a new job within the next 30 days are included in unemployment figures.

Table B includes annual average data for the year shown. The Local Area Unemployment Statistics data are periodically updated to reflect revised inputs, reestimation, and controlling to new statewide totals.

CIVILIAN EMPLOYMENT, Items 101–103

Source: U.S. Census Bureau—American Community Survey, 2006–2010
http://www.census.gov/acs/www/

Total employment includes all civilians 16 years old and over who were either (1) "at work"—those who did any work at all during the reference week as paid employees, worked in either their own business or profession, worked on their own farm, or worked 15 hours or more as unpaid workers in a family farm or business; or were (2) "with a job, but not at work" —those who had a job but were not at work that week due to illness, weather, industrial dispute, vacation, or other personal reasons.

The **occupational categories** are based on the occupational classification system that was developed for the 2000 census and revised in 2002 and 2010. This system consists of 539 specific occupational categories for employed persons arranged into 23 major occupational groups. This classification was developed based on the *Standard Occupational Classification (SOC) Manual: 2000*, published by the Executive Office of the President, Office of Management and Budget.

PRIVATE NONFARM EMPLOYMENT AND EARNINGS, Items 104–112

Source: U.S. Bureau of Labor Statistics—County Business Patterns
http://www.census.gov/econ/cbp/index.html

Data for private nonfarm employment and earnings are compiled from the payroll information reported monthly in the Census Bureau publication *County Business Patterns*. The estimates are based on surveys conducted by the Census Bureau and administrative records from the Internal Revenue Service (IRS).

The following types of employment are excluded from the tables: government employment, self-employed persons, farm workers, and domestic service workers. Railroad employment jointly covered by Social Security and railroad retirement programs, employment on oceanborne vessels, and employment in foreign countries are also excluded.

Annual payroll is the combined amount of wages paid, tips reported, and other compensation (including salaries, vacation allowances, bonuses, commissions, sick-leave pay, and the value of payments-in-kind such as free meals and lodging) paid to employees before deductions for Social Security, income tax, insurance, union dues, etc. All forms of compensation are included, regardless of whether they are subject to income tax or the Federal Insurance Contributions Act tax, with the exception of annuities, third-party sick pay, and supplemental unemployment compensation benefits (even if income tax was withheld). For corporations, total annual payroll includes compensation paid to officers and executives; for unincorporated businesses, it excludes profit or other compensation of proprietors or partners.

AGRICULTURE, ITEMS 113–132

Source: U.S. Department of Agriculture, National Agricultural Statistics Service—2007 Census of Agriculture
http://www.agcensus.usda.gov/Publications/2007/Index.asp

Data for the 2007 Census of Agriculture were collected in 2008, but pertain to the year 2007.

The Census Bureau took a census of agriculture every 10 years from 1840 to 1920; since 1925, this census has been taken roughly once every 5 years. The 1997 Census of Agriculture was the first one conducted by the National Agricultural Statistics Service of the U.S. Department of Agriculture. Over time, the definition of a farm has varied. For recent censuses (including the 2007 census), a farm has been defined as any place from which $1,000 or more of agricultural products were produced and sold or normally would have been sold during the census year. Dollar figures are expressed in current dollars and have not been adjusted for inflation or deflation.

The term **operator** refers to a person who operates a farm by either doing the work or making day-to-day decisions about such activities as planting, harvesting, feeding, marketing, etc. The operator may be the owner, a member of the owner's household, a salaried manager, a tenant, a renter, or a sharecropper. If a person rents land to others or has land worked on shares by others, he/she is considered the operator only of the land that is retained for his/her own operation. The census collected information on the total number of operators, the total number of women operators, and demographic information for up to three operators per farm.

The acreage designated as **land in farms** consists primarily of agricultural land used for crops, pasture, or grazing. It also includes woodland and wasteland not actually under cultivation or used for pasture or grazing, provided that this land was part of the farm operator's total operation. Land in farms is an operating-unit concept and includes all land owned and operated, as well as all land rented from others. Land used rent-free is classified as land rented from others. All land in Indian reservations used for growing crops or grazing livestock is classified as land in farms.

Irrigated land includes all land watered by any artificial or controlled means, such as sprinklers, flooding, furrows or ditches, sub-irrigation, and spreader dikes. Included are supplemental, partial, and preplant irrigation. Each acre was counted only once regardless of the number of times it was irrigated or harvested. Livestock lagoon waste water distributed by sprinkler or flood systems was also included.

Total cropland includes cropland harvested, cropland used only for pasture or grazing, cropland on which all crops failed or were abandoned, cropland in cultivated summer fallow, and cropland idle or used for cover crops or soil improvement but not harvested and not pastured or grazed.

Respondents were asked to report their estimate of the current market **value of land and buildings** owned, rented, or leased from others, and rented and leased to others. Market value refers to the respondent's estimate of what the land and buildings would sell for under current market conditions. If the value of land and buildings was not reported, it was estimated during processing by using the average value of land and buildings from similar farms in the same geographic area.

The **value of machinery and equipment** was estimated by the respondent as the current market value of all cars, trucks, tractors, combines, balers, irrigation equipment, etc., used on the farm. This value is an estimate of what the machinery and equipment would sell for in its present condition and not the replacement or depreciated value. Share interests are reported at full value at the farm where the equipment and machinery are usually kept. Only equipment that was actually used in 2006 and 2007, or newly purchased but not yet used and physically located at the farm on December 31, 2007, is included.

Market value of agricultural products sold by farms represents the gross market value before taxes and the production expenses of all agricultural products sold or removed from the place in 2007, regardless of who received the payment. It is equivalent to total sales and it includes sales by the operator as well as the value of any share received by partners, landlords, contractors, and others associated with the operation. It includes value of direct sales and the value of commodities placed in the Commodity Credit Corporation (CCC) loan program. Market value of agricultural products sold does not include payments received for participation in other federal farm programs. Also, it does not include income from farm-related sources such as customwork and other agricultural services, or income from non-farm sources.

Government payments consist of direct payments as defined by the 2002 Farm Bill;

payments from Conservation Reserve Program (CRP), Wetlands Reserve Program (WRP), Farmable Wetlands Program (FWP), and Conservation Reserve Enhancement Program (CREP); loan deficiency payments; disaster payments; other conservation programs; and all other federal farm programs under which payments were made directly to farm operators. Commodity Credit Corporation (CCC) proceeds, amount from State and local federal crop insurance payments were not included in this category.

WATER CONSUMPTION, Items 133–134

Source: U.S. Geological Survey, National Water Information System—2005 Water Use Data
http://water.usgs.gov/watuse/data/2005/index.html

Every ten years, the U.S. Geological Survey compiles county-level water-use estimates. This volume includes the total fresh and saline withdrawals expressed as million gallons per day. Estimate of withdrawals of ground and surface water are given for the following categories of use: public water supplies, domestic, commercial, irrigation, livestock, industrial, mining, and thermo-electric power. The number of gallons withdrawn per person is based on the county population but the water is not necessarily used locally, providing an indicator of counties that serve as major water sources.

2007 ECONOMIC CENSUS: OVERVIEW, Items 135–166

Source: U.S. Census Bureau
http://www.census.gov/econ/census07/

The Economic Census provides a detailed portrait of the nation's economy, from the national to the local level, once every five years. The 2007 Economic Census covers nearly all of the U.S. economy in its basic collection of establishment statistics. The 1997 Economic Census was the first major data source to use the new North American Industry Classification System (NAICS); therefore, data from this census are not comparable to economic data from prior years, which were based on the Standard Industrial Classification (SIC) system.

NAICS, developed in cooperation with Canada and Mexico, classifies North America's economic activities at two, three, four, and five digit levels of detail; the U.S. version of NAICS further defines industries to a sixth digit. The Economic Census takes advantage of this hierarchy to publish data at these successive levels of detail: sector (two-digit), subsector (three-digit), industry group (four-digit), industry (five-digit), and U.S. industry (six-digit). Information in Table A is at the two-digit level, with a few three- and four-digit items. The data in Table B are at the two-digit level.

Several key statistics are tabulated for all industries in this volume, including number of establishments (or companies), number of employees, payroll, and certain measures of output (sales, receipts, revenue, value of shipments, or value of construction work done).

Number of establishments. An establishment is a single physical location at which business is conducted. It is not necessarily identical with a company or enterprise, which may consist of one establishment or more. Economic Census figures represent a summary of reports for individual establishments rather than companies. For cases in which a census report was received, separate information was obtained for each location where business was conducted. When administrative records of other federal agencies were used instead of a census report, no information was available on the number of locations operated. Each Economic Census establishment was tabulated according to the physical location at which the business was conducted. The count of establishments represents those in business at any time during 2007.

When two activities or more were carried on at a single location under a single ownership, all activities were generally grouped together as a single establishment. The entire establishment was classified on the basis of its major activity and all of its data were included in that classification. However, when distinct and separate economic activities (for which different industry classification codes were appropriate) were conducted at a single location under a single ownership, separate establishment reports for each of the different activities were obtained in the census.

Number of employees. Paid employees consist of the full time and part time employees, including salaried officers and executives of corporations. Included are employees on paid sick leave, paid holidays, and paid vacations; not included are proprietors and partners of unincorporated businesses. The definition of paid employees is the same as that used by the Internal Revenue Service (IRS) on form 941.

For some industries, the Economic Census gives codes representing the number of employees as a range of numbers (for example, ''100 to 249 employees'' or ''1,000 to 2,499'' employees). In this volume, those codes have been replaced by the standard suppression code ''D''.

Payroll. Payroll includes all forms of compensation, such as salaries, wages, commissions, dismissal pay, bonuses, vacation allowances, sick leave pay, and employee contributions to qualified pension plans paid during the year to all employees. For corporations, payroll includes amounts paid to officers and executives; for unincorporated businesses, it does not include profit or other compensation of proprietors or partners. Payroll is reported before deductions for Social Security, income tax, insurance, union dues, etc. This definition of payroll is the same as that used by on IRS form 941.

Sales, shipments, receipts, revenue, or business done. This measure includes the total sales, shipments, receipts, revenue, or business done by establishments within the scope of the Economic Census. The definition of each of these items is specific to the economic sector measured.

WHOLESALE TRADE, Items 135–138

Source: U.S. Census Bureau—2007 Economic Census (See Overview of 2007 Economic Census prior to Item 135)

The Wholesale Trade sector (sector 42) comprises establishments engaged in wholesaling merchandise, generally without transformation, and rendering services incidental to the sale of merchandise. The wholesaling process is an intermediate step in the distribution of merchandise.

Wholesalers are organized to sell or arrange the purchase or sale of (1) goods for resale (i.e., goods sold to other wholesalers or retailers), (2) capital or durable nonconsumer goods, and (3) raw and intermediate materials and supplies used in production.

Wholesalers sell merchandise to other businesses and normally operate from a warehouse or office. These warehouses and offices are characterized by having little or no display of merchandise. In addition, neither the design nor the location of the premises is intended to solicit walk in traffic. Wholesalers do not normally use advertising directed to the general public. In general, customers are initially reached via telephone, in person marketing, or specialized advertising, which may include the Internet and other electronic means. Follow up orders are either vendor initiated or client initiated, are usually based on previous sales, and typically exhibit strong ties between sellers and buyers. In fact, transactions are often conducted between wholesalers and clients that have long standing business relationships.

This sector is made up of two main types of wholesalers: those that sell goods on their own account and those that arrange sales and purchases for others for a commission or fee.

(1) Establishments that sell goods on their own account are known as wholesale merchants, distributors, jobbers, drop shippers, import/export merchants, and sales branches. These establishments typically maintain their own warehouse, where they receive and handle goods for their customers. Goods are generally sold without transformation, but may include integral functions, such as sorting, packaging, labeling, and other marketing services.

(2) Establishments arranging for the purchase or sale of goods owned by others or purchasing goods on a commission basis are known as agents and brokers, commission merchants, import/export agents and brokers, auction companies, and manufacturers' representatives. These establishments operate from offices and generally do not own or handle the goods they sell.

Some wholesale establishments may be connected with a single manufacturer and promote and sell that particular manufacturer's products to a wide range of other wholesalers or retailers. Other wholesalers may be connected to a retail chain or a limited number of retail chains and only provide the products needed by the particular retail operation(s). These wholesalers may obtain the products from a wide range of manufacturers. Still other wholesalers may not take title to the goods, but act instead as agents and brokers for a commission.

Although wholesaling normally denotes sales in large volumes, durable nonconsumer goods may be sold in single units. Sales of capital or durable nonconsumer goods used in the production of goods and services, such as farm machinery, medium- and heavy-duty trucks, and industrial machinery, are always included in Wholesale Trade.

The county table includes only Merchant wholesalers, except manufacturers' sales branches and offices, establishments primarily engaged in buying and selling merchandise on their own account. Included here are such types of establishments as wholesale distributors and jobbers, importers, exporters, own-brand importers/marketers, terminal and country grain elevators, and farm products assemblers.

RETAIL TRADE, Items 139–142

Source: U.S. Census Bureau—2007 Economic Census (See Overview of 2007 Economic Census prior to Item 135)

The Retail Trade sector (44–45) is made up of establishments engaged in retailing merchandise, generally without transformation, and rendering services incidental to the sale of merchandise.

The retailing process is the final step in the distribution of merchandise; retailers are therefore organized to sell merchandise in small quantities to the general public. This sector comprises two main types of retailers: store and nonstore retailers.

Store retailers operate fixed point of sale locations, located and designed to attract a high volume of walk in customers. In general, retail stores have extensive displays of merchandise and use mass media advertising to attract customers. They typically sell merchandise to the general public for personal or household consumption; some also serve business and institutional clients. These include establishments such as office supply stores, computer and software stores, building materials dealers, plumbing supply stores, and electrical supply stores. Catalog showrooms, gasoline service stations, automotive dealers, and mobile home dealers are treated as store retailers.

In addition to retailing merchandise, some types of store retailers are also engaged in the provision of after sales services, such as repair and installation. For example, new automobile dealers, electronic and appliance stores, and musical instrument and supply stores often provide repair services. As a general rule, establishments engaged in retailing merchandise and providing after sales services are classified in this sector.

Nonstore retailers, like store retailers, are organized to serve the general public, although their retailing methods differ. The establishments of this subsector reach customers and market merchandise with methods including the broadcasting of ''infomercials,'' the broadcasting and publishing of direct response advertising, the publishing of paper and electronic catalogs, door to door solicitation, in home demonstration, selling from portable stalls (street vendors, except food), and distribution through vending machines. Establishments engaged in the direct sale (nonstore) of products, such as home heating oil dealers and home-delivery newspaper routes are included in this sector.

The buying of goods for resale is a characteristic of retail trade establishments that distinguishes them from establishments in the Agriculture, Manufacturing, and Construction sectors. For example, farms that sell their products at or from the point of production are classified in Agriculture instead of in Retail Trade. Similarly, establishments that both manufacture and sell their products to the general public are classified in Manufacturing instead of Retail Trade. However, establishments that engage in processing activities incidental to retailing are classified in Retail Trade.

REAL ESTATE AND RENTAL AND LEASING, Items 143–146

Source: U.S. Census Bureau—2007 Economic Census (See Overview of 2007 Economic Census prior to Item 135)

The Real Estate and Rental and Leasing sector (53) comprises establishments primarily engaged in renting, leasing, or otherwise allowing the use of tangible or intangible assets, and establishments providing related services. The major portion of this sector is made up of establishments that rent, lease, or otherwise allow the use of their own assets by others. The assets may be tangible, such as real estate and equipment, or intangible, such as patents and trademarks.

This sector also includes establishments primarily engaged in managing real estate for others, selling, renting, and/or buying real estate for others, and appraising real estate. These activities are closely related to this sector's main activity. In addition, a substantial proportion of property management is self performed by lessors.

The main components of this sector are the real estate lessors industries; equipment lessors industries (including motor vehicles, computers, and consumer goods); and lessors of nonfinancial intangible assets (except copyrighted works).

PROFESSIONAL, SCIENTIFIC, AND TECHNICAL SERVICES, Items 147–150

Source: U.S. Census Bureau—2007 Economic Census (See Overview of 2007 Economic Census prior to Item 135)

The Professional, Scientific, and Technical Services sector (54) is made up of establishments that specialize in performing professional, scientific, and technical activities for others. These activities require a high degree of expertise and training. The establishments in this sector specialize in one or more areas and provide services to clients in a variety of industries (and, in some cases, to households). Activities performed include legal advice and representation; accounting, bookkeeping, and payroll services; architectural, engineering, and specialized design services; computer services; consulting services; research services; advertising services; photographic services; translation and interpretation services; veterinary services; and other professional, scientific, and technical services.

Table B includes only those establishments subject to federal income tax.

This sector excludes establishments primarily engaged in providing a range of day to day office administrative services, such as financial planning, billing and record keeping, personnel services, and physical distribution and logistics services. These establishments are classified in sector 56, Administrative and Support and Waste Management and Remediation Services.

MANUFACTURING, Items 151–154

Source: U.S. Census Bureau—2007 Economic Census (See Overview of 2007 Economic Census prior to Item 135)

The Manufacturing sector (31–33) is made up of establishments engaged in the mechanical, physical, or chemical transformation of materials, substances, or components into new products. The assembling of component parts of manufactured products is considered manufacturing, except in cases in which the activity is appropriately classified in the Construction sector. Establishments in the Manufacturing sector are often described as plants, factories, or mills, and characteristically use power-driven machines and materials-handling equipment. However, establishments that transform materials or substances into new products by hand or in the worker's home, and establishments engaged in selling to the general public products made on the same premises from which they are sold (such as bakeries, candy stores, and custom tailors) may also be included in this sector. Manufacturing establishments may process materials or contract with other establishments to process their materials for them. Both types of establishments are included in the Manufacturing sector.

The materials, substances, or components transformed by manufacturing establishments are raw materials that are products of agriculture, forestry, fishing, mining, or quarrying, or are products of other manufacturing establishments. The materials used may be purchased directly from producers, obtained through customary trade channels, or secured without recourse to the market by transferring the product from one establishment to another, under the same ownership. The new product of a manufacturing establishment may be finished (in the sense that it is ready for utilization or consumption), or it may be semifinished to become an input for an establishment engaged in further manufacturing. For example, the product of the alumina refinery is the input used in the primary production of aluminum; primary aluminum is the input used in an aluminum wire drawing plant; and aluminum wire is the input used in a fabricated wire product manufacturing establishment.

Data are included for counties with 500 or more employees in the Manufacturing sector.

ACCOMMODATION AND FOOD SERVICES, Items 155–158

Source: U.S. Census Bureau—2007 Economic Census (See Overview of 2007 Economic Census prior to Item 135)

The Accommodation and Food Services sector (72) consists of establishments that provide customers with lodging and/or meals, snacks, and beverages for immediate consumption. This sector includes both accommodation and food services establishments because the two activities are often combined at the same establishment.

Excluded from this sector are civic and social organizations, amusement and recreation parks, theaters, and other recreation or entertainment facilities providing food and beverage services.

HEALTH CARE AND SOCIAL ASSISTANCE, Items 159-162

Source: U.S. Census Bureau—2007 Economic Census (See Overview of 2007 Economic Census prior to Item 135)

The Health Care and Social Assistance sector (62) consists of establishments that provide health care and social assistance services to individuals. The sector includes both health care and social assistance because it is sometimes difficult to distinguish between the boundaries of these two activities. The industries in this sector are arranged on a continuum, starting with establishments that provide medical care exclusively, continuing with those that provide health care and social assistance, and finishing with those that provide only social assistance. The services provided by establishments in this sector are delivered by trained professionals. All industries in the sector share this commonality of process—namely, labor inputs of health practitioners or social workers with the requisite expertise. Many of the industries in the sector are defined based on the educational degree held by the practitioners included in the industry.

Excluded from this sector are aerobic classes, which can be found in subsector 713, Amusement, Gambling, and Recreation Industries; and nonmedical diet and weight-reducing centers, which can be found in subsector 812, Personal and Laundry Services. Although these can be viewed as health services, they are not typically delivered by health practitioners.

OTHER SERVICES, EXCEPT PUBLIC ADMINISTRATION Items 163-166

Source: U.S. Census Bureau—2007 Economic Census (See Overview of 2007 Economic Census prior to Item 135)

The Other Services, Except Public Administration sector (81) comprises establishments engaged in providing services not specifically categorized elsewhere in the classification system. Establishments in this sector are primarily engaged in activities such as equipment and machinery repairing, promoting or administering religious activities, grant making, and advocacy; this sector also includes establishments that provide dry-cleaning and laundry services, personal care services, death care services, pet care services, photofinishing services, temporary parking services, and dating services.

Private households that employ workers on or about the premises in activities primarily concerned with the operation of the household are included in this sector.

Excluded from this sector are establishments primarily engaged in retailing new equipment and performing repairs and general maintenance on equipment. These establishments are classified in sector 44-45, Retail Trade.

FEDERAL FUNDS, Items 167-177

Source: U.S. Census Bureau—Consolidated Federal Funds Report
http://www.census.gov/govs/cffr/

Data on federal expenditure and obligations are obtained from a report prepared by the Census Bureau in accordance with the Consolidated Federal Funds Report (CFFR) Act of 1982 (P.L. 97-326). The data are for federal fiscal years beginning October 1 and ending the following September 30. Dollar amounts reported can reflect expenditures or obligations. In some cases, dollar amounts are negative, representing de-obligations of financial assistance that had previously been awarded. Such amounts generally appear in the grant categories.

Direct payments for individuals include Social Security benefits, federal government retirement, Medicare, Supplemental Security Income, food stamps, educational and housing assistance, and other categories not shown separately. All data represent actual expenditures during the fiscal year.

Salaries and wages represent actual federal expenditures during the fiscal year; the geographic distribution of these amounts by state and county was estimated based upon place of employment.

Procurement contract awards cover awards given by the United States Postal Service (USPS), as well as those given by all other federal agencies. Amounts provided by the USPS represent actual outlays for contractual commitments, while amounts for other agencies represent the value of obligations for contract actions and do not reflect actual federal government expenditures. In general, only current-year contract actions are included; however, multiple-year obligations may be reported for contract actions of less than three years' duration.

Grants data represent the federal obligations incurred at the time the grant is awarded. The amounts reported do not represent actual expenditures, since obligations in one time period may not result in outlays during the same period. Moreover, initial amounts obligated may be adjusted at a later date, through either enhancements or de-obligations. For many grants, this recipient is the state government even though grants monies are subsequently distributed to county, municipal, or township governments.

Medicaid and other health-related grants include a variety of grants from the Department of Health and Human Services for health services and research.

Nutrition and family welfare grants include a variety of grants from the Department of Health and Human Services for child welfare, special programs for the aging, and related areas. The school lunch program and other nutritional assistance programs administered by the Department of Agriculture are also included in this category.

Education grants include a variety of grant programs relating to elementary, secondary, and postsecondary education; adult education; vocational education; faculty training; and related areas.

BUILDING PERMITS, Items 178 and 179
Source: U.S. Census Bureau—Building Permits Survey
http://www.census.gov/const/www/permitsindex.html

These figures represent private residential construction authorized by building permits in approximately 20,000 places in the United States. Valuation represents the expected cost of construction as recorded on the building permit. This figure usually excludes the cost of on-site and off-site development and improvements, as well as the cost of heating, plumbing, electrical, and elevator installations.

National, state, and county totals were obtained by adding the data for permit-issuing places within each jurisdiction. Not all areas of the country require a building or zoning permit. The statistics only represent those areas that do require a permit. These totals thus are limited to permits issued in the 20,000 place universe covered by the Census Bureau and may not include all permits issued within a state. Current surveys indicate that construction is undertaken for all but a very small percentage of housing units authorized by building permits.

Residential building permits include buildings with any number of housing units. Housing units exclude group quarters (such as dormitories and rooming houses), transient accommodations (such as transient hotels, motels, and tourist courts), "HUD-code" manufactured (mobile) homes, moved or relocated units, and housing units created in an existing residential or nonresidential structure.

LOCAL GOVERNMENT FINANCES, Items 180–193
Source: U.S. Census Bureau—2007 Census of Governments
http://www.census.gov/govs/cog/

Data on local government finances are based on result of the 2007 Census of Governments. For each county area, the financial data comprise amounts for all local governments—not only the county government, but also any municipalities, townships, school districts, and special districts within the county. Statistics from governmental units located in two or more county areas are assigned to the county area containing the administrative office.

Revenue and expenditure items include all amounts of money received and paid out, respectively, by a government and its agencies (net of correcting transactions such as recoveries of refunds), with the exception of amounts for debt issuance and retirement and for loan and investment, agency, and private transactions.

Payments among the various funds and agencies of a particular government are excluded from revenue and expenditure items as representing internal transfers. Therefore, a government's contribution to a retirement fund that it administers is not counted as expenditure, nor is the receipt of this contribution by the retirement fund counted as revenue.

Total **general revenue** includes all revenue except utility, liquor stores, and insurance trust revenue. All tax revenue and intergovernmental revenue, even if designated for employee-retirement or local utility purpose, are classified as general revenue.

Intergovernmental revenue covers amounts received from the federal government as fiscal aid, reimbursements for performance of general government functions and specific services for the paying government, or in lieu of taxes. It excludes any amounts received from other governments from the sale of property, commodities, and utility services.

Taxes consist of compulsory contributions exacted by governments for public purposes. However, this category excludes employer and employee payments for retirement and social insurance purposes, which are classified as insurance trust revenue; it also excludes special assessments, which are classified as non-tax general revenue. Property taxes are taxes conditioned on ownership of property and assessed by its value. Sales and gross receipts taxes do not include dealer discounts, or "commissions" allowed to merchants for collection of taxes from consumers. General sales taxes and selected taxes on sales of motor fuels, tobacco products, and other particular commodities and services are included.

General government expenditure includes capital outlay, a major portion of which is commonly financed by borrowing. Government revenue does not include receipts from borrowing. Among other things, this distorts the relationship between totals of revenue and expenditure figures that are presented and renders it useless as a direct measure of the degree of budgetary "balance" (as that term is generally applied).

Direct general expenditure comprises all expenditures of the local governments, excluding utility, liquor stores, insurance trust expenditures, and any intergovernmental payments.

Local government expenditure for **education** is mainly for the provision and general support of schools and other educational facilities and services, including those for educational institutions beyond high school. They cover such related services as student transportation; school lunch and other cafeteria operations; school health, recreation, and library services; and dormitories, dining halls, and bookstores operated by public institutions of higher education.

Health and hospital expenditure includes health research; clinics; nursing; immunization; other categorical, environmental, and general health services provided by health agencies; establishment and operation of hospital facilities; provision of hospital care; and support of other public and private hospitals.

Police protection expenditure includes police activities such as patrols, communications, custody of persons awaiting trial, and vehicular inspection.

Public welfare expenditure covers support of and assistance to needy persons; this aid is contingent upon the person's needs. Included are cash assistance paid directly to needy persons under categorical (Old Age Assistance, Temporary Assistance for Needy Families, Aid to the Blind, and Aid to the Disabled) and other welfare programs; vendor payments made directly to private purveyors for medical care, burials, and other commodities and services provided under welfare programs; welfare institutions; and any intergovernmental or other direct expenditure for welfare purposes. Pensions to former employees and other benefits not contingent on need are excluded.

Highway expenditure is for the provision and maintenance of highway facilities, including toll turnpikes, bridges, tunnels, and ferries, as well as regular roads, highways, and streets. Also included are expenditures for street lighting and for snow and ice removal. Not included are highway policing and traffic control, which are considered part of police protection

Debt outstanding includes all long-term debt obligations of the government and its agencies (exclusive of utility debt) and all interest-bearing, short-term (repayable within one year) debt obligations remaining unpaid at the close of the fiscal year. It includes judgments, mortgages, and revenue bonds, as well as general obligation bonds, notes, and interest-bearing warrants. This category consists of non-interest-bearing, short-term obligations; inter-fund obligations; amounts owed in a trust or agency capacity; advances and contingent loans from other governments; and rights of individuals to benefit from government-administered employee-retirement funds.

GOVERNMENT EMPLOYMENT, Items 194–196

Source: U.S. Bureau of Economic Analysis—Regional Economic Accounts
http://www.bea.gov/regional/Index.htm#state

Employment is measured as the average annual sum of full-time and part-time jobs. The estimates are on a place-of-work basis. State and local government employment includes person employed in all state and local government agencies and enterprises. Data for federal civilian employment include civilian employees of the federal government, including civilian employees of the Department of Defense. Military employment includes all persons on active duty status.

ELECTION STATISTICS, Items 197–199

Source: Election Data Services, Inc. Washington, DC (copyright)
http://www.electiondataservices.com/
index.php?content=elecdata

© 2009 Election Data Services, Inc. All rights reserved. This material is proprietary and the subject of copyright protection and other intellectual property rights owned by or licensed to Election Data Services, Inc. The use of this material is subject to the terms of a License Agreement. You will be held liable for any unauthorized copying or disclosure of this material.

Election results show the percentage of the total vote cast for the Democratic and Republican candidates, as well as the combined percentage for all other candidates in the 2008 presidential election.

TABLE C—METROPOLITAN AREAS

Table C presents 199 items for the 366 metropolitan statistical areas (MSAs) and 29 metropolitan divisions in the United States. The metropolitan areas are presented in alphabetical order, and the metropolitan divisions are presented in alphabetical order within the appropriate metropolitan area. For many data items, the metropolitan area data have been aggregated from county data sources.

LAND AREA, Items 1 and 4
Source: U.S. Census Bureau—2010 Census of Population and Housing
http://2010.census.gov/2010census/data/

Land area measurements are shown to the nearest square kilometer. Land area includes dry land and land temporarily or partially covered by water, such as marshlands, swamps, and river floodplains.

POPULATION, Items 2–4
Source: U.S. Census Bureau—2010 Census of Population and Housing
http://2010.census.gov/2010census/data/

The population data are from the 2010 census and represent the resident population as of April 1, 2010.. The ranks are shown for metropolitan statistical areas, but exclude metropolitan divisions.

POPULATION AND POPULATION CHARACTERISTICS, Items 5–19
Source: U.S. Census Bureau—2010 Census of Population and Housing
http://2010.census.gov/2010census/data/

The concept of race, as used by the Census Bureau, reflects self-identification by persons according to the race or races with which they most closely identify. These categories are sociopolitical constructs and should not be interpreted as being scientific or anthropological in nature. Furthermore, race categories include both racial and national origin groups.

Beginning with the 2000 census, respondents were offered the option of selecting one or more races. This option was not available in prior censuses; thus, comparisons between censuses should be made with caution. In Table C, Columns 5 through 8 refer to individuals who identified with each racial category, either alone or in combination with other races. The estimates exclude persons of Hispanic or Latino origin from all race groups. Because respondents could include as many categories as they wished, and because the columns refer to the percentage of the population, the total will often exceed 100 percent.

The **White** population is defined as persons who indicated their race as White, as well as persons who did not classify themselves in one of the specific race categories listed on the questionnaire but entered a nationality such as Irish, German, Italian, Lebanese, Near Easterner, Arab, or Polish.

The **Black** population includes persons who indicated their race as "Black, African Am., or Negro," as well as persons who did not classify themselves in one of the specific race categories but reported entries such as African American, Afro American, Kenyan, Nigerian, or Haitian.

The **American Indian or Alaska Native** population includes persons who indicated their race as American Indian or Alaska Native, as well as persons who did not classify themselves in one of the specific race categories but reported entries such as Canadian Indian, French-American Indian, Spanish-American Indian, Eskimo, Aleut, Alaska Indian, or any of the American Indian or Alaska Native tribes.

The **Asian and Pacific Islander** population combines two census groupings: **Asian** and **Native Hawaiian or Other Pacific Islander**. The **Asian** population includes persons who indicated their race as Asian Indian, Chinese, Filipino, Japanese, Korean, Vietnamese, or "Other Asian," as well as persons who provided write-in entries of such groups as Cambodian, Laotian, Hmong, Pakistani, or Taiwanese. The **Native Hawaiian or Other Pacific Islander** population includes persons who indicated their race as "Native Hawaiian," "Guamanian or Chamorro," "Samoan," or "Other Pacific Islander," as well as persons who reported entries such as Part Hawaiian, American Samoan, Fijian, Melanesian, or Tahitian.

The **Hispanic population** is based on a complete-count question that asked respondents "Is this person Spanish/Hispanic/Latino?" Persons marking any one of the four Hispanic categories (i.e., Mexican, Puerto Rican, Cuban, or other Spanish) are collectively referred to as Hispanic.

In the 2000 census, the Hispanic origin question was placed before the race question and specific instructions indicated that both questions should be answered. These changes were designed to improve accuracy and may affect comparability with 1990 data.

Age is defined as age at last birthday (number of completed years since birth), as of April 1 of the census year. The 2000 census also asked for the specific date of birth of the respondent, and 2000 census procedures used the birth date for deriving age data. For this reason, it is likely that the 2000 data have fewer problems than data from prior censuses, such as the tendency of respondents to round ages or to report their ages on the date the questionnaire was filled out rather than on April 1.

The **female** population is shown as a percentage of total population.

POPULATION AND COMPONENTS OF CHANGE, Items 20–26
Source: U.S. Census Bureau—Decennial Censuses and Population Estimates
http://www.census.gov/main/www/cen2000.html
http://www.census.gov/popest/estimates.html
http://2010.census.gov/2010census/data/

The population data for 2000 and 2010 are from the decennial censuses and represent the resident population as of April 1 of those years. The components of change are based on Census Bureau estimates of the resident population as of July 1 of 2009. The change in population between 2000 and 2009 is made up of (a) natural increase—births minus deaths, and (b) net migration—the difference between the number of persons moving into a particular area and the number of persons moving out of the area. Net migration is composed of internal and international migration.

Because the 2009 population estimates are based on a model that begins with a national population estimate, the county and msa components of change do not always exactly add up to the difference between the 2000 census population and the 2009 estimates.

HOUSEHOLDS, Items 27–31
Source: U.S. Census Bureau—2010 Census of Population and Housing
http://2010.census.gov/2010census/data/

A **household** includes all of the persons who occupy a housing unit. (Persons not living in households are classified as living in group quarters.) A housing unit is a house, an apartment, a mobile home, a group of rooms, or a single room occupied (or, if vacant, intended for occupancy) as separate living quarters. Separate living quarters are those in which the occupants live separately from any other persons in the building and have direct access from the outside of the building or through a common hall. The occupants may be a single family, one person living alone, two or more families living together, or any other group of related or unrelated persons who share living quarters. The number of households is the same as the number of year-round occupied housing units.

A **family** includes a householder and one or more other persons living in the same household who are related to the householder by birth, marriage, or adoption. All persons in a household who are related to the householder are regarded as members of his or her family. A **family household** may contain persons not related to the householder; thus, family households may include more members than families do. A household can contain only one family for the purposes of census tabulations. Not all households contain families, as a household may comprise a group of unrelated persons or of one person living alone. Families are classified by type as either a ''husband-wife family'' or ''other family,'' according to the presence or absence of a spouse.

The measure of **persons per household** is obtained by dividing the number of persons in households by the number of households or householders. One person in each household is designated as the householder. In most cases, this is the person (or one of the persons) in whose name the house is owned, being bought, or rented. If there is no such person in the household, any adult household member 15 years old and over can be designated as the householder.

The category **female family householder** includes only female-headed family households with no spouse present.

GROUP QUARTERS, Item 32
Source: U.S. Census Bureau—2010 Census of Population and Housing
http://2010.census.gov/2010census/data/

The Census Bureau classifies all persons not living in households as living in group quarters; this category includes both the institutional and noninstitutional populations. The institutionalized population includes persons under formally authorized, supervised care or custody in institutions, such as correctional institutions, nursing homes, mental (psychiatric) hospitals, and juvenile institutions. The noninstitutionalized population includes persons who live in group quarters other than institutions, such as college dormitories, military quarters, and group homes. This volume includes the total number of persons in group quarters.

DAYTIME POPULATION, Items 33 and 34
Source: U.S. Census Bureau—American Community Survey, 2010
http://www.census.gov/acs/www/

Daytime population refers to the number of persons who are present in an area or place during normal business hours, including workers. This can be contrasted with the ''resident'' population, which is present during the evening and nighttime hours. The daytime population estimate is calculated by adding the total resident population and the total workers working in the area/place, and then subtracting the total workers living in the area/place from that result. Information on the expansion or contraction experienced by different communities between their nighttime and daytime populations is important for many planning purposes, especially those concerning transportation, disaster, and relief operations.

The employment/residence ratio is a measure of the total number of workers working in an area or place, relative to the total number of workers living in the area or place. It is often used as a rough indication of the jobs-workers balance in an area/place, although it does not take into account whether the resident workers possess the skills needed for the jobs available in their particular area/place. The employment/residence ratio is calculated by dividing the number of total workers working in an area/place by the number of total workers residing in the area/place.

BIRTHS AND DEATHS, Items 35–38
Source: U.S. Centers for Disease Control and Prevention, National Center for Health Statistics
http://wonder.cdc.gov/cmf-icd10.html

The registration of births, deaths, and other vital events in the United States is primarily a state and local function. The civil laws of every state provide for continuous and permanent birth and death registration systems. Through the National Vital Statistics System, the National Center for Health Statistics (NCHS) obtains data on births and deaths from the registration offices of each state, New York City, and the District of Columbia.

Birth and death statistics are limited to events occurring during the year. The data are by place of residence and exclude events for nonresidents of the United States. Births or deaths of Americans that occur outside the United States are excluded.

Birth and death rates represent the number of births and deaths per 1,000 resident population enumerated as of April 1 for decennial census years and estimated as of July 1 for other years.

In order to protect the privacy of individuals, the Centers for Disease Control and Prevention does not make county-level data available when the number of individual events falls below a threshold figure. Since a three-year time span allows more time for events to occur, cumulative data covering three years tend to be more complete than data for a single year. Also, an average for a three-year period may more accurately represent the trend level when the number of events for each year is small. For these reasons, the county data in this volume are presented as an average computed from data covering a three-year time span. State data in this table are presented on the same basis in order to maintain comparability. Even with the three-year average, death rates based on fewer than 20 deaths should be considered unreliable and birth rates are simply not available for smaller counties. The metropolitan area data are aggregated from the county data and sometimes the birth data are not available for one or more of the counties in the metropolitan area. If the aggregated birth data are based on less than 90 percent of a metropolitan area's population, we did not publish the number.

PERSONS UNDER 65 WITH NO HEALTH INSURANCE, Items 39 and 40
Source: U.S. Census Bureau—Small Area Health Insurance Estimates
http://www.census.gov/did/www/sahie/index.html

The Small Area Health Insurance Estimates (SAHIE) program develops model-based estimates of health insurance coverage for counties and states. This developmental program builds on the work of the Small Area Income and Poverty Estimates (SAIPE) program. The SAHIE program models health insurance coverage by combining survey data with population estimates and administrative records. The estimates are based on data from The Annual Social and Economic Supplement (ASEC) of the Current Population Survey (CPS); Demographic population estimates; Aggregated federal tax returns; Participation records for the Supplemental Nutrition Assistance Program (SNAP), formerly known as the Food Stamp program; County Business Patterns; Medicaid and Children's Health Insurance Program (CHIP) participation records; and Census 2000.

MEDICARE ENROLLMENT, Items 41–43
Source: U.S. Department of Health and Human Services, Centers for Medicare and Medicaid Services
http://www.cms.hhs.gov/MCRAdvPartDEnrolData/

http://www.cms.hhs.gov/DataCompendium/

The Centers for Medicare and Medicaid Services (CMS) administers Medicare, which provides health insurance to persons 65 years old and over, persons with permanent kidney failure, and certain persons with disabilities. Original Medicare has two parts: Hospital Insurance and Supplemental Medical Insurance. In recent years, Medicare has been expanded to include two new programs: Medicare Advantage plans and prescription drug coverage. Medicare Advantage Plans are health plan options that are approved by Medicare but run by private companies. Medicare prescription drug plans can be part of Medicare Advantage plans or stand-alone drug plans.

Persons who are **eligible for Medicare** can enroll in Part A (Hospital Insurance) at no charge, and can choose to pay a monthly premium to enroll in Part B. Most eligible persons are enrolled in Part A, and more than 90 percent of enrollees in Part A are also enrolled in Part B (Supplemental Medical Insurance.) This table includes persons who were eligible as of December 2010.

Medicare Advantage enrollees were enrolled in a Medicare Advantage plan of some type at the end of 2010. These include Private Fee For Service plans, Preferred Provider Organizations, Health Maintenance Organizations, Medical Savings Account Plans, Demonstration plans, and Programs for All-Inclusive Care for the Elderly.

Persons enrolled in a **Medicare Prescription drug plan** were enrolled in stand-alone plans for prescription drug benefits. This number does not include Medicare enrollees who had prescription drug coverage through private or federal retiree health plans, through Medicare Advantage plans, or through Medicaid.

CRIME, Items 44–47
Source: U.S. Federal Bureau of Investigation— Uniform Crime Reports http://www.fbi.gov/ucr/ucr.htm

Crime data are as reported to the Federal Bureau of Investigation (FBI) by law enforcement agencies and have not been adjusted for underreporting. This may affect comparability between geographic areas or over time.

Through the voluntary contribution of crime statistics by law enforcement agencies across the United States, the Uniform Crime Reporting (UCR) Program provides periodic assessments of crime in the nation as measured by offenses that have come to the attention of the law enforcement community. The Committee on Uniform Crime Records of the International Association of Chiefs of Police initiated this voluntary national data collection effort in 1930. The UCR Program contributors compile and submit their crime data either directly to the FBI or through state-level UCR Programs.

Seven offenses, because of their severity, frequency of occurrence, and likelihood of being reported to police, were initially selected to serve as an index for evaluating fluctuations in the volume of crime. These serious crimes were murder and nonnegligent manslaughter, forcible rape, robbery, aggravated assault, burglary, larceny-theft, and motor vehicle theft. By congressional mandate, arson was added as the eighth index offense in 1979. The totals shown in this volume do not include arson.

In 2004, the FBI discontinued the use of the Crime Index in the UCR Program and its publications, stating that the Crime Index was driven upward by the offense with the highest number of cases (in this case, larceny-theft), creating a bias against jurisdictions with a high number of larceny-thefts but a low number of other serious crimes, such as murder and forcible rape. The FBI is currently publishing a violent crime total and property crime total until a more viable index is developed. This book includes the crime total, as well as violent crime and property crime rates.

Violent crimes include four categories of offenses: (1) Murder and nonnegligent manslaughter, as defined in the UCR Program, is the willful (nonnegligent) killing of one human being by another. This offense excludes deaths caused by negligence, suicide, or accident; justifiable homicides; and attempts to murder or assaults to murder. (2) Forcible rape is the carnal knowledge of a female forcibly and against her will. Assaults or attempts to commit rape by force or threat of force are also included; however, statutory rape (without force) and other sex offenses are excluded. (3) Robbery is the taking or attempting to take anything of value from the care, custody, or control of a person or persons by force or threat of force or violence and/or by putting the victim in fear. (4) Aggravated assault is an unlawful attack by one person upon another for the purpose of inflicting severe or aggravated bodily injury. This type of assault is usually accompanied by the use of a weapon or by other means likely to produce death or great bodily harm. Attempts are included, since injury does not necessarily have to result when a gun, knife, or other weapon is used, as these incidents could and probably would result in a serious personal injury if the crime were successfully completed.

Property crimes include three categories: (1) Burglary, or breaking and entering, is the unlawful entry of a structure to commit a felony or theft, even though no force was used to gain entrance. (2) Larceny-theft is the unauthorized taking of the personal property of another, without the use of force. (3) Motor vehicle theft is the unauthorized taking of any motor vehicle.

Rates are based on population estimates provided by the FBI. The county totals published in this volume were obtained by aggregating individual reporting units within each county and MSA. If the population total for the units aggregated was less than 75 percent of the county's population (as estimated by the Census Bureau), the total was not considered representative of the county as a whole and was not published. State and U.S. totals include FBI estimates for those areas. State and U.S. totals in this table are the adjusted totals as published in the FBI's *Crime in the United States*.

EDUCATION—SCHOOL ENROLLMENT AND EDUCATIONAL ATTAINMENT, Items 48–51
Source: U.S. Census Bureau—American Community Survey, 2010
http://www.census.gov/acs/www/

Data on school enrollment and educational attainment were derived from a sample of the population. Persons were classified as enrolled in school if they reported attending a "regular" public or private school (or college) during the three months prior to the survey. The instructions were to "include only nursery school, kindergarten, elementary school, and schooling which would lead to a high school diploma or a college degree" as regular school. The Census Bureau defines a public school as "any school or college controlled and supported by a local, county, state, or federal government." Schools primarily supported and controlled by religious organizations or other private groups are defined as private schools.

Data on **educational attainment** are tabulated for the population 25 years old and over. The data were derived from a question that asked respondents for the highest level of school completed or the highest degree received. Persons who had passed a high school equivalency examination were considered high school graduates. Schooling received in foreign schools was to be reported as the equivalent grade or years in the regular American school system.

Vocational and technical training, such as barber school training; business, trade, technical, and vocational schools; or other training for a specific trade are specifically excluded.

High school graduate or less. This category includes persons whose highest degree was a high school diploma or its equivalent, and those who reported any level lower than a high school diploma.

Bachelor's degree or more. This category includes persons who have received bachelor's degrees, master's degrees, professional school degrees (such as law school or medical school degrees), and doctoral degrees.

LOCAL GOVERNMENT EDUCATION EXPENDITURES, Items 52 and 53
Source: U.S. Department of Education, National Center for Education Statistics—Common Core of Data
http://nces.ed.gov/ccd/f33agency.asp

Total expenditure for education includes provision or support of schools and facilities for elementary and secondary education. It encompasses instructional, support, and auxiliary services (school lunch, student activities, and community service) offered by public school systems. Retirement benefits paid to former education employees and interest payments are not included. Current expenditure includes all components of total expenditure except capital outlay. Expenditure data are obtained by the Census Bureau through its annual survey of government finances and are supplied to the National Center for Education Statistics (NCES). Current expenditure per student is current expenditure divided by the number of students enrolled. The number of students enrolled is based on an annual "membership" count of students on or about October 1.

NCES uses the Common Core of Data (CCD) Survey system to acquire and maintain statistical data from each of the 50 states, the District of Columbia, and the outlying areas. State education agencies compile and submit data for approximately 85,000 schools and 15,000 local school districts. Typically, this results in varying interpretation of NCES definitions and different record keeping systems, leading to large amounts of missing data for several states; this absence is reflected in the data in this publication. Schools and school districts are included in the county in which the school district offices (the local education agency) are located.

INCOME AND POVERTY Items 54–61
Source: U.S. Census Bureau—American Community Survey, 2010
http://www.census.gov/acs/www/

The data on income were derived from responses of a sample of persons 15 years old and over. **Total money income** is the sum of the amounts reported separately for wage or salary income; net self-employment income; interest, dividends, or net rental or royalty income or income from estates and trusts; Social Security or railroad retirement income; Supplemental Security Income (SSI); public assistance or welfare payments; retirement, survivor, or disability pensions; and all other income. Receipts from the following sources are not included as income: capital gains; money received from the sale of property (unless the recipient was engaged in the business of selling such property); the value of income "in kind" from food stamps, public housing subsidies, medical care, employer contributions for individuals, etc.; withdrawal of bank deposits; money borrowed; tax refunds; exchange of money between relatives living in the same household; and gifts, lump-sum inheritances, insurance payments, and other types of lump-sum receipts.

Money income differs in definition from personal income (item 62). For example, money income does not include the pension rights, employer provided health insurance, food stamps, or Medicare payments that are included in personal income.

Per capita income is the mean income computed for every man, woman, and child in a particular group. It is derived by dividing the aggregate income of a particular group by the resident population in that group in the survey year. Per capita income is rounded to the nearest whole dollar.

Household income includes the income of the householder and all other individuals 15 years old and over in the household, whether or not they are related to the householder. Since many households consist of only one person, median household income is usually less than median family income. Although the household income statistics cover the year preceding the survey, the characteristics of individuals and the composition of households refer to the date of the survey. Thus, the income of the household does not include amounts received by individuals who were members of the household during the year if these individuals were no longer residing in the household at the time of the survey. Similarly, income amounts reported by individuals who did not reside in the household during the year but who were members of the household at the time of the survey are included. However, the composition of most households was the same during the year as it was at the time of the survey.

Median income divides the income distribution into two equal parts, with half of all cases below the median income level and half of all cases above the median income level. For households, the median income is based on the distribution of the total number of households, including those with no income. Median income for households is computed on the basis of a standard distribution with a minimum value of less than $2,500 and a maximum value of $200,000 or more and is rounded to the nearest whole dollar. Median income figures are calculated using linear interpolation if the width of the interval containing the estimate is $2,500 or less. If the width of the interval containing the estimate is greater than $2,500, Pareto interpolation is used.

Income components were reported for the 12 months preceding the interview month. Monthly Consumer Price Indices (CPI) factors were used to inflation-adjust these components to a reference calendar year (January through December). For example, a household interviewed in March 2008 reports their income for March 2007 through February 2008. Their income is adjusted to the 2008 reference calendar year by multiplying their reported income by 2008 average annual CPI (January-December 2008) and then dividing by the average CPI for March 2007–February 2008. However, the estimates do not reflect the price and cost-of-living differences that may exist between areas.

The **poverty status** data were derived from data collected on the number of persons in a household, each person's relationship to the householder, and income data. The Social Security Administration (SSA) developed the original poverty definition in 1964, which federal interagency committees subsequently revised in 1969 and 1980. The Office of Management and Budget's (OMB) *Directive 14* prescribes the SSA's definition as the official poverty measure for federal agencies to use in their statistical work. Poverty statistics presented in American Community Survey products adhere to the standards defined by OMB in *Directive 14*.

Poverty thresholds vary depending on three criteria: size of family, number of children, and, for one- and two-person families, age of householder. In determining the poverty status of families and unrelated individuals, the Census Bureau uses thresholds (income cutoffs) arranged in a two-dimensional matrix. The matrix consists of family size (from one person to nine or more persons), cross-classified by presence and number of family members under 18 years old (from no children present to eight or more children present). Unrelated individuals and two-person families are further differentiated by age of reference person (under 65 years old and 65 years old and over). To determine a person's poverty status, the person's total family income over the previous 12 months is compared with the poverty threshold appropriate for that person's family size and composition. If the total income of that person's family is less than the threshold appropriate for that family, then the person is considered poor or "below the poverty level," together with every member of his or her family. If a person is not living with anyone related by birth, marriage, or adoption, then the person's own income is compared with his or her poverty threshold. The total number of persons below the poverty level is the sum of persons in families and the number of unrelated individuals with incomes below the poverty level over the previous 12 months.

Poverty Thresholds in 2010 by Size of Family and Number of Related Children Under 18 Years

Size of family unit	Weighted average thresholds
One person (unrelated individual)	11,139
Under 65 years	11,344
65 years and over	10,458
Two people	14,218
Householder under 65 years	14,676
Householder 65 years and over	13,194
Three people	17,374
Four people	22,314
Five people	26,439
Six people	29,897
Seven people	34,009
Eight people	37,934
Nine people or more	45,220

Source: U.S. Census Bureau

PERSONAL INCOME AND EARNINGS, Items 62–83

Source: U.S. Bureau of Economic Analysis, Regional Economic Accounts
http://www.bea.gov/regional/index.htm#state

Total personal income is the current income received by residents of an area from all sources. It is measured before deductions of income and other personal taxes, but after deductions of personal contributions for Social Security, government retirement, and other social insurance programs. It consists of **wage and salary disbursements** (covering all employee earnings, including executive salaries, bonuses, commissions, payments-in-kind, incentive payments, and tips); various types of supplementary earnings, such as employers' contributions to pension funds (termed "other labor income" or "supplements to wages and salaries"); proprietors' income; rental income of persons; dividends; personal interest income; and government and business transfer payments.

Per capita personal income is based on the resident population estimated as of July 1 of the year shown.

Proprietors' income is the monetary income and income-in-kind of proprietorships and partnerships (including the independent professions) and the income of tax-exempt cooperatives. **Dividends** are cash payments by corporations to stockholders who are U.S. residents. **Interest** is the monetary and imputed interest income of persons from all sources. **Rent** is the monetary income of persons from the rental of real property, except the income of persons primarily engaged in the real estate business; the imputed net rental income of owner-occupants of nonfarm dwellings; and the royalties received by persons.

Transfer payments are income for which services are not currently rendered. They consist of both government and business transfer payments. Government transfer payments include payments under the following programs: Federal Old-Age, Survivors, and Disability Insurance ("Social Security"); Medicare and medical vendor payments; unemployment insurance; railroad and government retirement; federal- and state-government-insured workers' compensation; veterans' benefits, including veterans' life insurance; food stamps; black lung payments; Supplemental Security Income; and Temporary Assistance for Needy Families. Government payments to nonprofit institutions, other than for work under research and development contracts, are also included. Business transfer payments consist primarily of liability payments for personal injury and of corporate gifts to nonprofit institutions.

Personal income differs in definition from money income (items 54–57). For example, personal income includes pension rights, employer-provided health insurance, food stamps, and Medicare. These are not included in the definition of money income.

Earnings cover wage and salary disbursements, other labor income, and proprietors' income.

The data for earnings obtained from the Bureau of Economic Analysis (BEA) are based on place of work. In computing personal income, BEA makes an "adjustment for residence" to earnings, based on commuting patterns; personal income is thus presented on a place-of-residence basis.

Farm earnings include the income of farm workers (wages and salaries and other labor income) and farm proprietors. Farm proprietors' income includes only the income of sole proprietorships and partnerships.

Farm earnings estimates are benchmarked to data collected in the Census of Agriculture and the revised Department of Agriculture statistical totals of income and expense items.

Goods-related industries include mining, construction, and manufacturing. **Service-related** and other industries include private-sector earnings in agricultural services, forestry, and fisheries; transportation and public utilities; wholesale trade; retail trade; finance, insurance, and real estate; and services. Government earnings include all levels of government. Industries are categorized under the North American Industry Classification System (NAICS), and are not comparable to years prior to 2002.

SOCIAL SECURITY AND SUPPLEMENTAL SECURITY INCOME, Items 84–86
Source: U.S. Social Security Administration
http://www.ssa.gov/policy/docs/statcomps/oasdi_sc/
http://www.ssa.gov/policy/docs/statcomps/ssi_sc/

Social Security beneficiaries are persons receiving benefits under the Old-Age, Survivors, and Disability Insurance Program. These include retired or disabled workers covered by the program, their spouses and dependent children, and the surviving spouses and dependent children of deceased workers.

Supplemental Security Income (SSI) recipients are persons receiving SSI payments. The SSI program is a cash assistance program that provides monthly benefits to low-income aged, blind, or disabled persons.

Data are as of December of the year shown.

HOUSING, Items 87–96
Source: U.S. Census Bureau—2010 Census of Population and Housing
U.S. Census Bureau—American Community Survey, 2010
http://2010.census.gov/2010census/data/
http://www.census.gov/acs/www/

The housing unit counts in columns 87 and 88 are from the 2010 census. The characteristics of occupied housing units in 2010 are from the American Community Survey.

A **housing unit** is a house, apartment, mobile home or trailer, group of rooms, or single room occupied or, if vacant, intended for occupancy as separate living quarters. Separate living quarters are those in which the occupants do not live and eat with any other person in the structure and which have direct access from the outside of the building through a common hall.

The occupants of a housing unit may be a single family, one person living alone, two or more families living together, or any other group of related or unrelated persons who share living quarters. Both occupied and vacant housing units are included in the housing inventory, although recreational vehicles, tents, caves, boats, railroad cars, and the like are included only if they are occupied as a person's usual place of residence.

A housing unit is classified as occupied if it is the usual place of residence of the person or group of persons living in it at the time of enumeration, or if the occupants are only temporarily absent (away on vacation). A household consists of all persons who occupy a housing unit as their usual place of residence. Vacant units for sale or rent include units rented or sold but not occupied and any other units held off the market.

Median value is the dollar amount that divides the distribution of specified owner-occupied housing units into two equal parts, with half of all units below the median value and half of all units above the median value. Value is defined as the respondent's estimate of what the house would sell for if it were for sale. Data are presented for single-family units on fewer than 10 acres of land that have no business or medical offices on the property.

Median rent divides the distribution of renter-occupied housing units into two equal parts. The rent concept used in this volume is gross rent, which includes the amount of cash rent a renter pays (contract rent) plus the estimated average cost of utilities and fuels, if these are paid by the renter. The rent is the amount of rent only for living quarters and excludes amounts paid for any business or other space occupied. Single-family houses on lots of 10 or more acres of land are also excluded.

Housing cost as a percentage of income is shown separately for owners with mortgages, owners without mortgages, and renters. Rent as a percentage of income is a computed ratio of gross rent and monthly household income (total household income in the past 12 months divided by 12). Selected owner costs include utilities and fuels, mortgage payments, insurance, taxes, etc. In each case, the ratio of housing cost to income is computed separately for each housing unit. The housing cost ratios for half of all units are above the median shown in this book, and half are below the median shown in the book.

Substandard units are occupied units that are overcrowded or lack complete plumbing facilities. For the purposes of this item, "overcrowded" is defined as having 1.01 persons or more per room. Complete plumbing facilities include hot and cold piped water, a flush toilet, and a bathtub or shower. These facilities must be located inside the housing unit, but do not have to be in the same room.

CIVILIAN LABOR FORCE AND UNEMPLOYMENT, Items 97–100
Source: U.S. Bureau of Labor Statistics—Local Area Unemployment Statistics
http://www.bls.gov/lau/#tables

Data for the civilian labor force are the product of a federal-state cooperative program in which state employment security agencies prepare labor force and unemployment estimates under concepts, definitions, and technical procedures established by the Bureau of Labor Statistics (BLS). The civilian labor force consists of all civilians 16 years old and over who are either employed or unemployed.

Unemployment includes all persons who did not work during the survey week, made specific efforts to find a job during the previous four weeks, and were available for work during the survey week (except for temporary illness). Persons waiting to be called back to a job from which they had been laid off and those waiting to report to a new job within the next 30 days are included in unemployment figures.

Table C includes annual average data for the year shown. The Local Area Unemployment Statistics data are periodically updated to reflect revised inputs, reestimation, and controlling to new statewide totals.

CIVILIAN EMPLOYMENT, Items 101–103
Source: U.S. Census Bureau—American Community Survey, 2010
http://www.census.gov/acs/www/

Total employment includes all civilians 16 years old and over who were either (1) "at work"—those who did any work at all during the reference week as paid employees, worked in either their own business or profession, worked on their own farm, or worked 15 hours or more as unpaid workers in a family farm or business; or were (2) "with a job, but not at work" —those who

had a job but were not at work that week due to illness, weather, industrial dispute, vacation, or other personal reasons.

The **occupational categories** are based on the occupational classification system that was developed for the 2000 census. This system consists of 509 specific occupational categories for employed persons arranged into 23 major occupational groups. This classification was developed based on the *Standard Occupational Classification (SOC) Manual: 2000*, published by the Executive Office of the President, Office of Management and Budget.

PRIVATE NONFARM EMPLOYMENT AND EARNINGS, Items 104–112
Source: U.S. Bureau of Labor Statistics—County Business Patterns
http://www.census.gov/econ/cbp/index.html

Data for private nonfarm employment and earnings are compiled from the payroll information reported monthly in the Census Bureau publication *County Business Patterns*. The estimates are based on surveys conducted by the Census Bureau and administrative records from the Internal Revenue Service (IRS).

The following types of employment are excluded from the tables: government employment, self-employed persons, farm workers, and domestic service workers. Railroad employment jointly covered by Social Security and railroad retirement programs, employment on oceanborne vessels, and employment in foreign countries are also excluded.

Annual payroll is the combined amount of wages paid, tips reported, and other compensation (including salaries, vacation allowances, bonuses, commissions, sick-leave pay, and the value of payments-in-kind such as free meals and lodging) paid to employees before deductions for Social Security, income tax, insurance, union dues, etc. All forms of compensation are included, regardless of whether they are subject to income tax or the Federal Insurance Contributions Act tax, with the exception of annuities, third-party sick pay, and supplemental unemployment compensation benefits (even if income tax was withheld). For corporations, total annual payroll includes compensation paid to officers and executives; for unincorporated businesses, it excludes profit or other compensation of proprietors or partners.

AGRICULTURE, ITEMS 113–132
Source: U.S. Department of Agriculture, National Agricultural Statistics Service—2007 Census of Agriculture
http://www.agcensus.usda.gov/Publications/2007/index.asp

Data for the 2007 Census of Agriculture were collected in 2008, but pertain to the year 2007.

The Census Bureau took a census of agriculture every 10 years from 1840 to 1920; since 1925, this census has been taken roughly once every 5 years. The 1997 Census of Agriculture was the first one conducted by the National Agricultural Statistics Service of the U.S. Department of Agriculture. Over time, the definition of a farm has varied. For recent censuses (including the 2007 census), a farm has been defined as any place from which $1,000 or more of agricultural products were produced and sold or normally would have been sold during the census year. Dollar figures are expressed in current dollars and have not been adjusted for inflation or deflation.

The term **operator** refers to a person who operates a farm by either doing the work or making day-to-day decisions about such activities as planting, harvesting, feeding, marketing, etc. The operator may be the owner, a member of the owner's household, a salaried manager, a tenant, a renter, or a sharecropper. If a person rents land to others or has land worked on shares by others, he/she is considered the operator only of the land that is retained for his/her own operation. The census collected information on the total number of operators, the total number of women operators, and demographic information for up to three operators per farm.

The acreage designated as **land in farms** consists primarily of agricultural land used for crops, pasture, or grazing. It also includes woodland and wasteland not actually under cultivation or used for pasture or grazing, provided that this land was part of the farm operator's total operation. Land in farms is an operating-unit concept and includes all land owned and operated, as well as all land rented from others. Land used rent-free is classified as land rented from others. All land in Indian reservations used for growing crops or grazing livestock is classified as land in farms.

Irrigated land includes all land watered by any artificial or controlled means, such as sprinklers, flooding, furrows or ditches, sub-irrigation, and spreader dikes. Included are supplemental, partial, and preplant irrigation. Each acre was counted only once regardless of the number of times it was irrigated or harvested. Livestock lagoon waste water distributed by sprinkler or flood systems was also included.

Total cropland includes cropland harvested, cropland used only for pasture or grazing, cropland on which all crops failed or were abandoned, cropland in cultivated summer fallow, and cropland idle or used for cover crops or soil improvement but not harvested and not pastured or grazed.

Respondents were asked to report their estimate of the current market **value of land and buildings** owned, rented, or leased from others, and rented and leased to others. Market value refers to the respondent's estimate of what the land and buildings would sell for under current market conditions. If the value of land and buildings was not reported, it was estimated during processing by using the average value of land and buildings from similar farms in the same geographic area.

The **value of machinery and equipment** was estimated by the respondent as the current market value of all cars, trucks, tractors, combines, balers, irrigation equipment, etc., used on the farm. This value is an estimate of what the machinery and equipment would sell for in its present condition and not the replacement or depreciated value. Share interests are reported at full value at the farm where the equipment and machinery are usually kept. Only equipment that was actually used in 2006 and 2007, or newly purchased but not yet used and physically located at the farm on December 31, 2007, is included.

Market value of agricultural products sold by farms represents the gross market value before taxes and the production expenses of all agricultural products sold or removed from the place in 2007, regardless of who received the payment. It is equivalent to total sales and it includes sales by the operator as well as the value of any share received by partners, landlords,

contractors, and others associated with the operation. It includes value of direct sales and the value of commodities placed in the Commodity Credit Corporation (CCC) loan program. Market value of agricultural products sold does not include payments received for participation in other federal farm programs. Also, it does not include income from farm-related sources such as customwork and other agricultural services, or income from nonfarm sources.

Government payments consists of direct payments as defined by the 2002 Farm Bill; payments from Conservation Reserve Program (CRP), Wetlands Reserve Program (WRP), Farmable Wetlands Program (FWP), and Conservation Reserve Enhancement Program (CREP); loan deficiency payments; disaster payments; other conservation programs; and all other federal farm programs under which payments were made directly to farm operators. Commodity Credit Corporation (CCC) proceeds, amount from State and local federal crop insurance payments were not included in this category.

WATER CONSUMPTION, Items 133–134
Source: U.S. Geological Survey, National Water Information System—2005 Water Use Data
http://water.usgs.gov/watuse/data/2005/index.html

Every ten years, the U.S. Geological Survey compiles county-level water-use estimates. This volume includes the total fresh and saline withdrawals expressed as million gallons per day. Estimate of withdrawals of ground and surface water are given for the following categories of use: public water supplies, domestic, commercial, irrigation, livestock, industrial, mining, and thermoelectric power. The number of gallons withdrawn per person is based on the metropolitan area population but the water is not necessarily used locally, providing an indicator of metropolitan areas that serve as major water sources.

2007 Economic CENSUS: OVERVIEW, Items 135–166
Source: U.S. Census Bureau
http://www.census.gov/econ/census07/

The Economic Census provides a detailed portrait of the nation's economy, from the national to the local level, once every five years. The 2007 Economic Census covers nearly all of the U.S. economy in its basic collection of establishment statistics. The 1997 Economic Census was the first major data source to use the new North American Industry Classification System (NAICS); therefore, data from this census are not comparable to economic data from prior years, which were based on the Standard Industrial Classification (SIC) system.

NAICS, developed in cooperation with Canada and Mexico, classifies North America's economic activities at two, three, four, and five digit levels of detail; the U.S. version of NAICS further defines industries to a sixth digit. The Economic Census takes advantage of this hierarchy to publish data at these successive levels of detail: sector (two-digit), subsector (three-digit), industry group (four-digit), industry (five-digit), and U.S. industry (six-digit). Information in Table A is at the two-digit level, with a few three- and four-digit items. The data in Tables B and C are at the two-digit level.

Several key statistics are tabulated for all industries in this volume, including number of establishments (or companies), number of employees, payroll, and certain measures of output (sales, receipts, revenue, value of shipments, or value of construction work done).

Number of establishments. An establishment is a single physical location at which business is conducted. It is not necessarily identical with a company or enterprise, which may consist of one establishment or more. Economic Census figures represent a summary of reports for individual establishments rather than companies. For cases in which a census report was received, separate information was obtained for each location where business was conducted. When administrative records of other federal agencies were used instead of a census report, no information was available on the number of locations operated. Each Economic Census establishment was tabulated according to the physical location at which the business was conducted. The count of establishments represents those in business at any time during 2002.

When two activities or more were carried on at a single location under a single ownership, all activities were generally grouped together as a single establishment. The entire establishment was classified on the basis of its major activity and all of its data were included in that classification. However, when distinct and separate economic activities (for which different industry classification codes were appropriate) were conducted at a single location under a single ownership, separate establishment reports for each of the different activities were obtained in the census.

Number of employees. Paid employees consist of the full time and part time employees, including salaried officers and executives of corporations. Included are employees on paid sick leave, paid holidays, and paid vacations; not included are proprietors and partners of unincorporated businesses. The definition of paid employees is the same as that used by the Internal Revenue Service (IRS) on form 941.

For some industries, the Economic Census gives codes representing the number of employees as a range of numbers (for example, ''100 to 249 employees'' or ''1,000 to 2,499'' employees). In this volume, those codes have been replaced by the standard suppression code ''D''.

Payroll. Payroll includes all forms of compensation, such as salaries, wages, commissions, dismissal pay, bonuses, vacation allowances, sick leave pay, and employee contributions to qualified pension plans paid during the year to all employees. For corporations, payroll includes amounts paid to officers and executives; for unincorporated businesses, it does not include profit or other compensation of proprietors or partners. Payroll is reported before deductions for Social Security, income tax, insurance, union dues, etc. This definition of payroll is the same as that used by on IRS form 941.

Sales, shipments, receipts, revenue, or business done. This measure includes the total sales, shipments, receipts, revenue, or business done by establishments within the scope of the Economic Census. The definition of each of these items is specific to the economic sector measured.

WHOLESALE TRADE, Items 135–138

Source: U.S. Census Bureau—2007 Economic Census (See Overview of 2007 Economic Census prior to Item 135)

The Wholesale Trade sector (sector 42) comprises establishments engaged in wholesaling merchandise, generally without transformation, and rendering services incidental to the sale of merchandise. The wholesaling process is an intermediate step in the distribution of merchandise.

Wholesalers are organized to sell or arrange the purchase or sale of (1) goods for resale (i.e., goods sold to other wholesalers or retailers), (2) capital or durable nonconsumer goods, and (3) raw and intermediate materials and supplies used in production.

Wholesalers sell merchandise to other businesses and normally operate from a warehouse or office. These warehouses and offices are characterized by having little or no display of merchandise. In addition, neither the design nor the location of the premises is intended to solicit walk in traffic. Wholesalers do not normally use advertising directed to the general public. In general, customers are initially reached via telephone, in person marketing, or specialized advertising, which may include the Internet and other electronic means. Follow up orders are either vendor initiated or client initiated, are usually based on previous sales, and typically exhibit strong ties between sellers and buyers. In fact, transactions are often conducted between wholesalers and clients that have long standing business relationships.

This sector is made up of two main types of wholesalers: those that sell goods on their own account and those that arrange sales and purchases for others for a commission or fee.

(1) Establishments that sell goods on their own account are known as wholesale merchants, distributors, jobbers, drop shippers, import/export merchants, and sales branches. These establishments typically maintain their own warehouse, where they receive and handle goods for their customers. Goods are generally sold without transformation, but may include integral functions, such as sorting, packaging, labeling, and other marketing services.

(2) Establishments arranging for the purchase or sale of goods owned by others or purchasing goods on a commission basis are known as agents and brokers, commission merchants, import/export agents and brokers, auction companies, and manufacturers' representatives. These establishments operate from offices and generally do not own or handle the goods they sell.

Some wholesale establishments may be connected with a single manufacturer and promote and sell that particular manufacturer's products to a wide range of other wholesalers or retailers. Other wholesalers may be connected to a retail chain or a limited number of retail chains and only provide the products needed by the particular retail operation(s). These wholesalers may obtain the products from a wide range of manufacturers. Still other wholesalers may not take title to the goods, but act instead as agents and brokers for a commission.

Although wholesaling normally denotes sales in large volumes, durable nonconsumer goods may be sold in single units. Sales of capital or durable nonconsumer goods used in the production of goods and services, such as farm machinery, medium- and heavy-duty trucks, and industrial machinery, are always included in Wholesale Trade.

The metropolitan area table includes only **Merchant wholesalers, except manufacturers' sales branches and offices,** establishments primarily engaged in buying and selling merchandise on their own account. Included here are such types of establishments as wholesale distributors and jobbers, importers, exporters, own-brand importers/marketers, terminal and country grain elevators, and farm products assemblers.

RETAIL TRADE, Items 139–142
Source: U.S. Census Bureau—2007 Economic Census (See Overview of 2007 Economic Census prior to Item 135)

The Retail Trade sector (44–45) is made up of establishments engaged in retailing merchandise, generally without transformation, and rendering services incidental to the sale of merchandise.

The retailing process is the final step in the distribution of merchandise; retailers are therefore organized to sell merchandise in small quantities to the general public. This sector comprises two main types of retailers: store and nonstore retailers.

Store retailers operate fixed point of sale locations, located and designed to attract a high volume of walk in customers. In general, retail stores have extensive displays of merchandise and use mass media advertising to attract customers. They typically sell merchandise to the general public for personal or household consumption; some also serve business and institutional clients. These include establishments such as office supply stores, computer and software stores, building materials dealers, plumbing supply stores, and electrical supply stores. Catalog showrooms, gasoline service stations, automotive dealers, and mobile home dealers are treated as store retailers.

In addition to retailing merchandise, some types of store retailers are also engaged in the provision of after sales services, such as repair and installation. For example, new automobile dealers, electronic and appliance stores, and musical instrument and supply stores often provide repair services. As a general rule, establishments engaged in retailing merchandise and providing after sales services are classified in this sector.

Nonstore retailers, like store retailers, are organized to serve the general public, although their retailing methods differ. The establishments of this subsector reach customers and market merchandise with methods including the broadcasting of "infomercials," the broadcasting and publishing of direct response advertising, the publishing of paper and electronic catalogs, door to door solicitation, in home demonstration, selling from portable stalls (street vendors, except food), and distribution through vending machines. Establishments engaged in the direct sale (nonstore) of products, such as home heating oil dealers and home-delivery newspaper routes are included in this sector.

The buying of goods for resale is a characteristic of retail trade establishments that distinguishes them from establishments in the Agriculture, Manufacturing, and Construction sectors. For example, farms that sell their products at or from the point of production are classified in Agriculture instead of in Retail Trade. Similarly, establishments that both manufacture and sell their products to the general public are classified in Manufacturing instead of Retail Trade. However, establishments that engage in processing activities incidental to retailing are classified in Retail Trade.

REAL ESTATE AND RENTAL AND LEASING, Items 143–146
Source: U.S. Census Bureau—2007 Economic Census (See Overview of 2007 Economic Census prior to Item 135)

The Real Estate and Rental and Leasing sector (53) comprises establishments primarily engaged in renting, leasing, or otherwise allowing the use of tangible or intangible assets, and establishments providing related services. The major portion of this sector is made up of establishments that rent, lease, or otherwise allow the use of their own assets by others. The assets may be tangible, such as real estate and equipment, or intangible, such as patents and trademarks.

This sector also includes establishments primarily engaged in managing real estate for others, selling, renting, and/or buying real estate for others, and appraising real estate. These activities are closely related to this sector's main activity. In addition, a substantial proportion of property management is self performed by lessors.

The main components of this sector are the real estate lessors industries; equipment lessors industries (including motor vehicles, computers, and consumer goods); and lessors of nonfinancial intangible assets (except copyrighted works).

PROFESSIONAL, SCIENTIFIC, AND TECHNICAL SERVICES, Items 147–150
Source: U.S. Census Bureau—2007 Economic Census (See Overview of 2007 Economic Census prior to Item 135)

The Professional, Scientific, and Technical Services sector (54) is made up of establishments that specialize in performing professional, scientific, and technical activities for others. These activities require a high degree of expertise and training. The establishments in this sector specialize in one or more areas and provide services to clients in a variety of industries (and, in some cases, to households). Activities performed include legal advice and representation; accounting, bookkeeping, and payroll services; architectural, engineering, and specialized design services; computer services; consulting services; research services; advertising services; photographic services; translation and interpretation services; veterinary services; and other professional, scientific, and technical services.

Table C includes only those establishments subject to federal income tax.

This sector excludes establishments primarily engaged in providing a range of day to day office administrative services, such as financial planning, billing and record keeping, personnel services, and physical distribution and logistics services. These establishments are classified in sector 56, Administrative and Support and Waste Management and Remediation Services.

MANUFACTURING, Items 151–154

Source: U.S. Census Bureau—2007 Economic Census (See Overview of 2007 Economic Census prior to Item 135)

The Manufacturing sector (31–33) is made up of establishments engaged in the mechanical, physical, or chemical transformation of materials, substances, or components into new products. The assembling of component parts of manufactured products is considered manufacturing, except in cases in which the activity is appropriately classified in the Construction sector. Establishments in the Manufacturing sector are often described as plants, factories, or mills, and characteristically use power-driven machines and materials-handling equipment. However, establishments that transform materials or substances into new products by hand or in the worker's home, and establishments engaged in selling to the general public products made on the same premises from which they are sold (such as bakeries, candy stores, and custom tailors) may also be included in this sector. Manufacturing establishments may process materials or contract with other establishments to process their materials for them. Both types of establishments are included in the Manufacturing sector.

The materials, substances, or components transformed by manufacturing establishments are raw materials that are products of agriculture, forestry, fishing, mining, or quarrying, or are products of other manufacturing establishments. The materials used may be purchased directly from producers, obtained through customary trade channels, or secured without recourse to the market by transferring the product from one establishment to another, under the same ownership. The new product of a manufacturing establishment may be finished (in the sense that it is ready for utilization or consumption), or it may be semifinished to become an input for an establishment engaged in further manufacturing. For example, the product of the alumina refinery is the input used in the primary production of aluminum; primary aluminum is the input used in an aluminum wire drawing plant; and aluminum wire is the input used in a fabricated wire product manufacturing establishment.

Data are included for counties with 500 or more employees in the Manufacturing sector.

ACCOMMODATION AND FOOD SERVICES, Items 155–158

Source: U.S. Census Bureau—2007 Economic Census (See Overview of 2007 Economic Census prior to Item 135)

The Accommodation and Food Services sector (72) consists of establishments that provide customers with lodging and/or meals, snacks, and beverages for immediate consumption. This sector includes both accommodation and food services establishments because the two activities are often combined at the same establishment.

Excluded from this sector are civic and social organizations, amusement and recreation parks, theaters, and other recreation or entertainment facilities providing food and beverage services.

HEALTH CARE AND SOCIAL ASSISTANCE, Items 159–162

Source: U.S. Census Bureau—2007 Economic Census (See Overview of 2007 Economic Census prior to Item 135)

The Health Care and Social Assistance sector (62) consists of establishments that provide health care and social assistance services to individuals. The sector includes both health care and social assistance because it is sometimes difficult to distinguish between the boundaries of these two activities. The industries in this sector are arranged on a continuum, starting with establishments that provide medical care exclusively, continuing with those that provide health care and social assistance, and finishing with those that provide only social assistance. The services provided by establishments in this sector are delivered by trained professionals. All industries in the sector share this commonality of process—namely, labor inputs of health practitioners or social workers with the requisite expertise. Many of the industries in the sector are defined based on the educational degree held by the practitioners included in the industry.

Excluded from this sector are aerobic classes, which can be found in subsector 713, Amusement, Gambling, and Recreation Industries; and nonmedical diet and weight-reducing centers, which can be found in subsector 812, Personal and Laundry Services. Although these can be viewed as health services, they are not typically delivered by health practitioners.

OTHER SERVICES, EXCEPT PUBLIC ADMINISTRATION Items 163–166

Source: U.S. Census Bureau—2007 Economic Census (See Overview of 2007 Economic Census prior to Item 135)

The Other Services, Except Public Administration sector (81) comprises establishments engaged in providing services not specifically categorized elsewhere in the classification system. Establishments in this sector are primarily engaged in activities such as equipment and machinery repairing, promoting or administering religious activities, grant making, and advocacy; this sector also includes establishments that provide dry-cleaning and laundry services, personal care services, death care services, pet care services, photofinishing services, temporary parking services, and dating services.

Private households that employ workers on or about the premises in activities primarily concerned with the operation of the household are included in this sector.

Excluded from this sector are establishments primarily engaged in retailing new equipment and performing repairs and general maintenance on equipment. These establishments are classified in sector 44–45, Retail Trade.

FEDERAL FUNDS, Items 167–177
Source: U.S. Census Bureau—Consolidated Federal Funds Report
http://www.census.gov/govs/cffr/

Data on federal expenditure and obligations are obtained from a report prepared by the Census Bureau in accordance with the Consolidated Federal Funds Report (CFFR) Act of 1982 (P.L. 97-326). The data are for federal fiscal years beginning October 1 and ending the following September 30. Dollar amounts reported can reflect expenditures or obligations. In some cases, dollar amounts are negative, representing de-obligations of financial assistance that had previously been awarded. Such amounts generally appear in the grant categories.

Direct payments for individuals include Social Security benefits, federal government retirement, Medicare, Supplemental Security Income, food stamps, educational and housing assistance, and other categories not shown separately. All data represent actual expenditures during the fiscal year.

Salaries and wages represent actual federal expenditures during the fiscal year; the geographic distribution of these amounts by state and county was estimated based upon place of employment.

Procurement contract awards cover awards given by the United States Postal Service (USPS), as well as those given by all other federal agencies. Amounts provided by the USPS represent actual outlays for contractual commitments, while amounts for other agencies represent the value of obligations for contract actions and do not reflect actual federal government expenditures. In general, only current-year contract actions are included; however, multiple-year obligations may be reported for contract actions of less than three years' duration.

Grants data represent the federal obligations incurred at the time the grant is awarded. The amounts reported do not represent actual expenditures, since obligations in one time period may not result in outlays during the same period. Moreover, initial amounts obligated may be adjusted at a later date, through either enhancements or de-obligations. For many grants, this recipient is the state government even though grants monies are subsequently distributed to county, municipal, or township governments.

Medicaid and other health-related grants include a variety of grants from the Department of Health and Human Services for health services and research.

Nutrition and family welfare grants include a variety of grants from the Department of Health and Human Services for child welfare, special programs for the aging, and related areas. The school lunch program and other nutritional assistance programs administered by the Department of Agriculture are also included in this category.

Education grants include a variety of grant programs relating to elementary, secondary, and postsecondary education; adult education; vocational education; faculty training; and related areas.

BUILDING PERMITS, Items 178 and 179
Source: U.S. Census Bureau—Building Permits Survey
http://www.census.gov/const/www/permitsindex.html

These figures represent private residential construction authorized by building permits in approximately 20,000 places in the United States. Valuation represents the expected cost of construction as recorded on the building permit. This figure usually excludes the cost of on-site and off-site development and improvements, as well as the cost of heating, plumbing, electrical, and elevator installations.

National, state, and county totals were obtained by adding the data for permit-issuing places within each jurisdiction. Not all areas of the country require a building or zoning permit. The statistics only represent those areas that do require a permit. These totals thus are limited to permits issued in the 20,000 place universe covered by the Census Bureau and may not include all permits issued within a state. Current surveys indicate that construction is undertaken for all but a very small percentage of housing units authorized by building permits.

Residential building permits include buildings with any number of housing units. Housing units exclude group quarters (such as dormitories and rooming houses), transient accommodations (such as transient hotels, motels, and tourist courts), ''HUD-code'' manufactured (mobile) homes, moved or relocated units, and housing units created in an existing residential or nonresidential structure.

LOCAL GOVERNMENT FINANCES, Items 180–193
Source: U.S. Census Bureau—2007 Census of Governments
http://www.census.gov/govs/cog/

Data on local government finances are based on result of the 2002 Census of Governments. For each county area, the financial data comprise amounts for all local governments—not only the county government, but also any municipalities, townships, school districts, and special districts within the county. Statistics from governmental units located in two or more county areas are assigned to the county area containing the administrative office.

Revenue and expenditure items include all amounts of money received and paid out, respectively, by a government and its agencies (net of correcting transactions such as recoveries of refunds), with the exception of amounts for debt issuance and retirement and for loan and investment, agency, and private transactions.

Payments among the various funds and agencies of a particular government are excluded from revenue and expenditure items as representing internal transfers. Therefore, a government's contribution to a retirement fund that it administers is not counted as expenditure, nor is the receipt of this contribution by the retirement fund counted as revenue.

Total **general revenue** includes all revenue except utility, liquor stores, and insurance trust revenue. All tax revenue and intergovernmental revenue, even if designated for employee-retirement or local utility purpose, are classified as general revenue.

Intergovernmental revenue covers amounts received from the federal government as fiscal aid, reimbursements for performance of general government functions and specific services for the paying government, or in lieu of taxes. It excludes any amounts received from other governments from the sale of property, commodities, and utility services.

Taxes consist of compulsory contributions exacted by governments for public purposes. However, this category excludes employer and employee payments for retirement and social insurance purposes, which are classified as insurance trust revenue; it also excludes special assessments, which are classified as non-tax general revenue. Property taxes are taxes conditioned on ownership of property and assessed by its value. Sales and gross receipts taxes do not include dealer discounts, or ''commissions'' allowed to merchants for collection of taxes from consumers. General sales taxes and selected taxes on sales of motor fuels, tobacco products, and other particular commodities and services are included.

General government expenditure includes capital outlay, a major portion of which is commonly financed by borrowing. Government revenue does not include receipts from borrowing. Among other things, this distorts the relationship between totals of revenue and expenditure figures that are presented and renders it useless as a direct measure of the degree of budgetary ''balance'' (as that term is generally applied).

Direct general expenditure comprises all expenditures of the local governments, excluding utility, liquor stores, insurance trust expenditures, and any intergovernmental payments.

Local government expenditure for **education** is mainly for the provision and general support of schools and other educational facilities and services, including those for educational institutions beyond high school. They cover such related services as student transportation; school lunch and other cafeteria operations; school health, recreation, and library services; and dormitories, dining halls, and bookstores operated by public institutions of higher education.

Health and hospital expenditure includes health research; clinics; nursing; immunization; other categorical, environmental, and general health services provided by health agencies; establishment and operation of hospital facilities; provision of hospital care; and support of other public and private hospitals.

Police protection expenditure includes police activities such as patrols, communications, custody of persons awaiting trial, and vehicular inspection.

Public welfare expenditure covers support of and assistance to needy persons; this aid is contingent upon the person's needs. Included are cash assistance paid directly to needy persons under categorical (Old Age Assistance, Temporary Assistance for Needy Families, Aid to the Blind, and Aid to the Disabled) and other welfare programs; vendor payments made directly to private purveyors for medical care, burials, and other commodities and services provided under welfare programs; welfare institutions; and any intergovernmental or other direct expenditure for welfare purposes. Pensions to former employees and other benefits not contingent on need are excluded.

Highway expenditure is for the provision and maintenance of highway facilities, including toll turnpikes, bridges, tunnels, and ferries, as well as regular roads, highways, and streets. Also included are expenditures for street lighting and for snow and ice removal. Not included are highway policing and traffic control, which are considered part of police protection

Debt outstanding includes all long-term debt obligations of the government and its agencies (exclusive of utility debt) and all interest-bearing, short-term (repayable within one year) debt obligations remaining unpaid at the close of the fiscal year. It includes judgments, mortgages, and revenue bonds, as well as general obligation bonds, notes, and interest-bearing warrants. This category consists of non-interest-bearing, short-term obligations; inter-fund obligations; amounts owed in a trust or agency capacity; advances and contingent loans from other governments; and rights of individuals to benefit from government-administered employee-retirement funds.

GOVERNMENT EMPLOYMENT, Items 194–196
Source: U.S. Bureau of Economic Analysis—Regional Economic Accounts
http://www.bea.gov/regional/index.htm#state

Employment is measured as the average annual sum of full-time and part-time jobs. The estimates are on a place-of-work basis. The estimates are on a place-of-work basis. State and local government employment includes person employed in all state and local government agencies and enterprises. Data for federal civilian employment include civilian employees of the federal government, including civilian employees of the Department of Defense. Military employment includes all persons on active duty status.

ELECTION STATISTICS, Items 197–199
Source: Election Data Services, Inc. Washington, DC (copyright)
http://www.electiondataservices.com/index.php?content=elecdata

© 2009 Election Data Services, Inc. All rights reserved. This material is proprietary and the subject of copyright protection and other intellectual property rights owned by or licensed to Election Data Services, Inc. The use of this material is subject to the terms of a License Agreement. You will be held liable for any unauthorized copying or disclosure of this material.

Election results show the percentage of the total vote cast for the Democratic and Republican candidates, as well as the combined percentage for all other candidates in the 2008 presidential election.

TABLE D—CITIES

Table D present 147 items of data for cities with populations of 25,000 or more at the time of the 2010 census.

LAND AREA, Items 1 and 4

Source: U.S. Census Bureau—2010 Census of Population and Housing
http://2010.census.gov/2010census/data/

Land area measurements are shown to the nearest square kilometer. Land area includes dry land and land temporarily or partially covered by water, such as marshlands, swamps, and river floodplains.

POPULATION, Items 2–4

Source: U.S. Census Bureau—2010 Census of Population and Housing
http://2010.census.gov/2010census/data/

The population data are from the 2010 census and represent the resident population as of April 1, 2010.

POPULATION AND POPULATION CHARACTERISTICS, Items 5–22

Source: U.S. Census Bureau—2010 Census of Population and Housing
http://2010.census.gov/2010census/data/

Data on race were derived from answers to the question on race that was asked of all persons. The concept of race, as used by the Census Bureau, reflects self-identification by respondents according to the race or races with which they most closely identify. These categories are sociopolitical constructs and should not be interpreted as being scientific or anthropological in nature. Furthermore, the race categories include both racial and national origin groups.

On the American Community Survey, respondents were offered the option of selecting one or more races. This option was not available prior to the 2000 census; thus, comparisons between censuses should be made with caution. In this table, Columns 5 through 9 refer to individuals who identified with each racial category, either alone or in combination with other races. Because respondents could include as many categories as they wished, and because the columns refer to the percentage of the population, the total will often exceed 100 percent.

The **White** population is defined as persons who indicated their race as White, as well as persons who did not classify themselves in one of the specific race categories listed on the questionnaire but entered a nationality such as Irish, German, Italian, Lebanese, Near Easterner, Arab, or Polish.

The **Black** population includes persons who indicated their race as "Black, African Am., or Negro," as well as persons who did not classify themselves in one of the specific race categories but reported entries such as African American, Afro American, Kenyan, Nigerian, or Haitian.

The **American Indian or Alaska Native** population includes persons who indicated their race as American Indian or Alaska Native, as well as persons who did not classify themselves in one of the specific race categories but reported entries such as Canadian Indian, French-American Indian, Spanish-American Indian, Eskimo, Aleut, Alaska Indian, or any of the American Indian or Alaska Native tribes.

The **Asian and Pacific Islander** population combines two census groupings: **Asian** and **Native Hawaiian or Other Pacific Islander**. Because two separate groups are combined, this category occasionally represents more than 100 percent of a city's population. The **Asian** population includes persons who indicated their race as Asian Indian, Chinese, Filipino, Japanese, Korean, Vietnamese, or "Other Asian," as well as persons who provided write-in entries of such groups as Cambodian, Laotian, Hmong, Pakistani, or Taiwanese. The **Native Hawaiian or Other Pacific Islander** population includes persons who indicated their race as "Native Hawaiian," "Guamanian or Chamorro," "Samoan," or "Other Pacific Islander," as well as persons who reported entries such as Part Hawaiian, American Samoan, Fijian, Melanesian, or Tahitian.

The **Some other race** category includes all persons who indicated "Some other race," as well as persons who wrote in a category not included in race categories describe above, including entries such as multiracial, mixed, interracial, or a Hispanic/Latino group such as Mexican, Puerto Rican, or Cuban in the "Some other race" write-in space.

The **Hispanic population** is based on a separate question that asked respondents "Is this person Spanish/Hispanic/Latino?" Persons marking any one of the four Hispanic categories (i.e., Mexican, Puerto Rican, Cuban, or other Spanish) are collectively referred to as Hispanic.

The Hispanic origin question was placed before the race question and specific instructions indicated that both questions should be answered.

The **foreign-born** population includes all persons who were not U.S. citizens at birth. Foreign-born persons are those who indicated they were either a U.S. citizen by naturalization or were not a citizen of the United States. The foreign-born population consists of immigrants (legal permanent residents), temporary migrants (students), humanitarian migrants (refugees), and unauthorized migrants (persons illegally residing in the United States).

Age is defined as age at last birthday (number of completed years since birth), at the time of the interview. The American Community Survey also asked for the specific date of birth of the respondent. Both age and date of birth are used in combination to calculate the most accurate age at the time of the interview.

The **female** population is shown as a percentage of total population.

POPULATION CHANGE, Items 23–26

Source: U.S. Census Bureau—Decennial Censuses
http://www.census.gov/main/www/cen2000.html
http://2010.census.gov/2010census/data/

The population data for 1990 and 2000 are from the decennial censuses and represent the resident population as of April 1 of those years.

The change in population from 1990 to 2000 is calculated from census data based on city boundaries as they existed in 1990

HOUSEHOLDS, Items 27–30
Source: U.S. Census Bureau—2010 Census of Population and Housing
http://2010.census.gov/2010census/data/

A **household** includes all of the persons who occupy a housing unit. (Persons not living in households are classified as living in group quarters.) A housing unit is a house, an apartment, a mobile home, a group of rooms, or a single room occupied (or, if vacant, intended for occupancy) as separate living quarters. Separate living quarters are those in which the occupants live separately from any other persons in the building and have direct access from the outside of the building or through a common hall. The occupants may be a single family, one person living alone, two or more families living together, or any other group of related or unrelated persons who share living quarters. The number of households is the same as the number of year-round occupied housing units.

A **family** includes a householder and one or more other persons living in the same household who are related to the householder by birth, marriage, or adoption. All persons in a household who are related to the householder are regarded as members of his or her family. A **family household** may contain persons not related to the householder; thus, family households may include more members than families do. A household can contain only one family for the purposes of census tabulations. Not all households contain families, as a household may comprise a group of unrelated persons or of one person living alone. Families are classified by type as either a "husband-wife family" or "other family," according to the presence or absence of a spouse.

The measure of **persons per household** is obtained by dividing the number of persons in households by the number of households or householders. One person in each household is designated as the householder. In most cases, this is the person (or one of the persons) in whose name the house is owned, being bought, or rented. If there is no such person in the household, any adult household member 15 years old and over can be designated as the householder.

The category **female family householder** includes only female-headed family households with no spouse present.

GROUP QUARTERS, Item 31–34
Source: U.S. Census Bureau—2010 Census of Population and Housing
http://2010.census.gov/2010census/data/

The Census Bureau classifies all persons not living in households as living in group quarters; this category includes both the institutional and noninstitutional populations. This volume includes the total number of persons in group quarters and in selected types of group quarters.

The **institutionalized population** includes persons who are primarily ineligible, unable, or unlikely to participate in the labor force while residents, including those in correctional institutions, skilled-nursing facilities, mental (psychiatric) hospitals, and juvenile institutions.

Nursing facilities include facilities licensed to provide medical care with 7-day, 24-hour coverage for people requiring long-term non-acute care. People in these facilities require nursing care, regardless of age. Included in this category are skilled-nursing facilities, intermediate-care facilities, long-term care rooms in wards or buildings on the grounds of hospitals, or long-term care rooms/nursing wings in congregate housing facilities. Also included are nursing, convalescent, and rest homes, such as soldiers', veterans', and fraternal or religious homes for the aged, with or without nursing care.

The **noninstitutionalized population** includes persons who live in group quarters other than institutions, such as college dormitories, military quarters, and group homes.

CRIME, Items 35–38
Source: U.S. Federal Bureau of Investigation— Uniform Crime Reports
http://www.fbi.gov/ucr/ucr.htm

Crime data are as reported to the Federal Bureau of Investigation (FBI) by law enforcement agencies and have not been adjusted for underreporting. This may affect comparability between geographic areas or over time.

Through the voluntary contribution of crime statistics by law enforcement agencies across the United States, the Uniform Crime Reporting (UCR) Program provides periodic assessments of crime in the nation as measured by offenses that have come to the attention of the law enforcement community. The Committee on Uniform Crime Records of the International Association of Chiefs of Police initiated this voluntary national data collection effort in 1930. The UCR Program contributors compile and submit their crime data either directly to the FBI or through state-level UCR Programs.

Seven offenses, because of their severity, frequency of occurrence, and likelihood of being reported to police, were initially selected to serve as an index for evaluating fluctuations in the volume of crime. These serious crimes were murder and nonnegligent manslaughter, forcible rape, robbery, aggravated assault, burglary, larceny-theft, and motor vehicle theft. By congressional mandate, arson was added as the eighth index offense in 1979. The totals shown in this volume do not include arson.

In 2004, the FBI discontinued the use of the Crime Index in the UCR Program and its publications, stating that the Crime Index was driven upward by the offense with the highest number of cases (in this case, larceny-theft), creating a bias against jurisdictions with a high number of larceny-thefts but a low number of other serious crimes, such as murder and forcible rape. The FBI is currently publishing a violent crime total and property crime total until a more viable index is developed. This book includes the total Crime Index, as well as violent crime and property crime rates.

Violent crimes include four categories of offenses: (1) Murder and nonnegligent manslaughter, as defined in the UCR Program, is the willful (nonnegligent) killing of one human being by another. This offense excludes deaths caused by negligence, suicide, or accident; justifiable homicides; and attempts to murder or assaults to murder. (2) Forcible rape is the carnal knowledge of a female forcibly and against her will. Assaults or attempts to commit rape by force or threat of force are also included; however, statutory rape (without force) and other sex offenses are excluded. (3) Robbery is the taking or attempting to take anything of value from the care, custody, or control of a person or persons by force or threat of force or violence and/or by putting the victim in fear. (4) Aggravated assault is an unlawful attack by one person upon another for the purpose of inflicting severe or aggravated bodily injury. This type of assault is usually accompanied by the use of a weapon or by other means likely to produce death or great bodily harm. Attempts are included, since injury does not necessarily have to result when a gun, knife, or other weapon is used, as these incidents could and probably would result in a serious personal injury if the crime were successfully completed.

Property crimes include three categories: (1) Burglary, or breaking and entering, is the unlawful entry of a structure to commit a felony or theft, even though no force was used to gain entrance. (2) Larceny-theft is the unauthorized taking of the personal property of another, without the use of force. (3) Motor vehicle theft is the unauthorized taking of any motor vehicle.

Rates are based on population estimates provided by the FBI. If a city is not in the UCR database, or if the population total for the units aggregated was less than 75 percent of the city's population (as estimated by the Census Bureau), the total was not considered representative of the city as a whole and was not published. State and U.S. totals include FBI estimates for those areas.

EDUCATIONAL ATTAINMENT, Items 39–41
Source: U.S. Census Bureau—American Community Survey, 2008-2010
http://www.census.gov/acs/www/

Data on **educational attainment** are tabulated for the population 25 years old and over. The data were derived from a question that asked respondents for the highest level of school completed or the highest degree received. Persons who had passed a high school equivalency examination were considered high school graduates. Schooling received in foreign schools was to be reported as the equivalent grade or years in the regular American school system.

Vocational and technical training, such as barber school training; business, trade, technical, and vocational schools; or other training for a specific trade are specifically excluded.

High school graduate or less. This category includes persons whose highest degree was a high school diploma or its equivalent, and those who reported any level lower than a high school diploma.

Bachelor's degree or more. This category includes persons who have received bachelor's degrees, master's degrees, professional school degrees (such as law school or medical school degrees), and doctoral degrees.

INCOME AND POVERTY, Items 42–46
Source: U.S. Census Bureau—American Community Survey, 2008–2010
http://www.census.gov/acs/www/

Total money income is the sum of the amounts reported separately for wage or salary income; net self-employment income; interest, dividends, or net rental or royalty income or income from estates and trusts; Social Security or railroad retirement income; Supplemental Security Income (SSI); public assistance or welfare payments; retirement, survivor, or disability pensions; and all other income. Receipts from the following sources are not included as income: capital gains; money received from the sale of property (unless the recipient was engaged in the business of selling such property); the value of income "in kind" from food stamps, public housing subsidies, medical care, employer contributions for individuals, etc.; withdrawal of bank deposits; money borrowed; tax refunds; exchange of money between relatives living in the same household; and gifts, lump-sum inheritances, insurance payments, and other types of lump-sum receipts.

Per capita income is the mean income computed for every man, woman, and child in a particular group. It is derived by dividing the aggregate income of a particular group by the resident population in that group in the survey year. Per capita income is rounded to the nearest whole dollar.

Household income includes the income of the householder and all other individuals 15 years old and over in the household, whether or not they are related to the householder. Since many households consist of only one person, median household income is usually less than median family income. Although the household income statistics cover the twelve months prior to the survey, the characteristics of individuals and the composition of households refer to the date of the interview. Thus, the income of the household does not include amounts received by individuals who were members of the household during all or part of the year if these individuals were no longer residing in the household at the time of the interview. Similarly, income amounts reported by individuals who did not reside in the household during full year but who were members of the household at the time of the interview are included. However, the composition of most households was the same during the year as it was at the time of the interview.

Median income divides the income distribution into two equal parts, with half of all cases below the median income level and half of all cases above the median income level. For households, the median income is based on the distribution of the total number of households, including those with no income. Median income for households is computed on the basis of a standard distribution with a minimum value of less than $2,500 and a maximum value of $200,000 or more and is rounded to the nearest whole dollar. Median income figures are calculated using linear interpolation if the width of the interval containing the estimate is $2,500 or less. If the width of the interval containing the estimate is greater than $2,500, Pareto interpolation is used.

Income components were reported for the 12 months preceding the interview month. Monthly Consumer Price Index (CPI) factors were used to inflation-adjust these components to a reference calendar year (January through December). For example, a household interviewed in March 2007 reports their income for March 2006 through February 2007. Their income is adjusted to the 2007 reference calendar year by multiplying their reported income by 2007 average annual CPI (January-December 2007) and then dividing by the average CPI for March 2006–February 2007. In addition, the 3-year estimates are inflation-adjusted to the final year. However, the estimates do not reflect the price and cost-of-living differences that may exist between areas.

The **poverty status** data were derived from data collected on the number of persons in a household, each person's relationship to the householder, and each person's income during the past twelve months. The Social Security Administration (SSA) developed the original poverty definition in 1964, which federal interagency committees subsequently revised in 1969 and 1980. The Office of Management and Budget's (OMB) *Directive 14* prescribes the SSA's definition as the official poverty measure for federal agencies to use in their statistical work.

Poverty thresholds vary depending on three criteria: size of family, number of children, and, for one- and two-person families, age of householder. In determining the poverty status of families and unrelated individuals, the Census Bureau uses thresholds (income cutoffs) arranged in a two-dimensional matrix. The matrix consists of family size (from one person to nine or more persons), cross-classified by presence and number of family members under 18 years old (from no children present to eight or more children present). Unrelated individuals and two-person families are further differentiated by age of reference person (under 65 years old and 65 years old and over). To determine a person's poverty status, the person's total family income over the previous 12 months is compared with the poverty threshold appropriate for that person's family size and composition. If the total income of that person's family is less than the threshold appropriate for that family, then the person is considered poor or "below the poverty level," together with every member of his or her family. If a person is not living with anyone related by birth, marriage, or adoption, then the person's own income is compared with his or her poverty threshold. The total number of persons below the poverty level is the sum of persons in families and the number of unrelated individuals with incomes below the poverty level.

Poverty Thresholds in 2010 by Size of Family and Number of Related Children Under 18 Years

Size of family unit	Weighted average thresholds
One person (unrelated individual)	11,139
Under 65 years	11,344
65 years and over	10,458
Two people	14,218
Householder under 65 years	14,676
Householder 65 years and over	13,194
Three people	17,374
Four people	22,314
Five people	26,439
Six people	29,897
Seven people	34,009
Eight people	37,934
Nine people or more	45,220

Source: U.S. Census Bureau

HOUSING, Items 47–57

Source: U.S. Census Bureau—2010 Census of Population and Housing http://2010.census.gov/2010census/data/Source: American Community Survey, 2008–2010 http://www.census.gov/acs/www/

The housing unit counts in columns 47 through 49 are from the 2010 census. The characteristics of occupied housing units are from the 2008–2010 American Community Survey.

A **housing unit** is a house, apartment, mobile home or trailer, group of rooms, or single room occupied or, if vacant, intended for occupancy as separate living quarters. Separate living quarters are those in which the occupants do not live and eat with any other person in the structure and which have direct access from the outside of the building through a common hall. For vacant units, the criteria of separateness and direct access are applied to the intended occupants whenever possible. If that information cannot be obtained, the criteria are applied to the previous occupants.

The occupants of a housing unit may be a single family, one person living alone, two or more families living together, or any other group of related or unrelated persons who share living quarters. Both occupied and vacant housing units are included in the housing inventory, although recreational vehicles, tents, caves, boats, railroad cars, and the like are included only if they are occupied as a person's usual place of residence.

A housing unit is classified as occupied if it is the usual place of residence of the person or group of persons living in it at the time of enumeration, or if the occupants are only temporarily absent (away on vacation). A household consists of all persons who occupy a housing unit as their usual place of residence. Vacant units for sale or rent include units rented or sold but not occupied and any other units held off the market.

The percent change represents the difference in the number of total housing units in a specified area from 1990 to 2000.

A housing unit is **owner occupied** if the owner or co-owner lives in the unit, even if it is mortgaged or not fully paid for. The owner or co-owner must live in the unit and is usually the first person listed on the census or ACS questionnaire.

All occupied housing units that are not owner occupied, whether they are rented for cash rent or occupied without payment of cash rent, are classified as **renter occupied**.

Median value is the dollar amount that divides the distribution of specified owner-occupied housing units into two equal parts, with half of all units below the median value and half of all units above the median value. Value is defined as the respondent's estimate of what the house would sell for if it were for sale. Data are presented for single-family units on fewer than 10 acres of land that have no business or medical offices on the property.

Median rent divides the distribution of renter-occupied housing units into two equal parts. The rent concept used in this volume is gross rent, which includes the amount of cash rent a renter pays (contract rent) plus the estimated average cost of utilities and fuels, if these are paid by the renter. The rent is the amount of rent only for living quarters and excludes amounts paid for any business or other space occupied. Single-family houses on lots of 10 or more acres of land are also excluded.

Housing cost as a percentage of income is shown separately for owners with mortgages, owners without mortgages, and renters. Rent as a percentage of income is a computed ratio of gross rent and monthly household income (total household income during the year divided by 12). Selected owner costs include utilities and fuels, mortgage payments, insurance, taxes, etc. In each case, the ratio of housing cost to income is computed separately for each housing unit. The housing cost ratios for half of all units are above the median shown in this book, and half are below the median shown in the book.

Substandard units are occupied units that are overcrowded or lack complete plumbing facilities. For the purposes of this item, "overcrowded" is defined as having 1.01 persons or more per room. Complete plumbing facilities include hot and cold piped water, a flush toilet, and a bathtub or shower. These facilities must be located inside the housing unit, but do not have to be in the same room.

PERCENT WITH NO VEHICLES AVAILABLE, Item 58

Source: U.S. Census Bureau—American Community Survey, 2008–2010
http://www.census.gov/acs/www/

The data on vehicles available show the number of passenger cars, vans, and pickup or panel trucks of one-ton capacity or less kept at home and available for the use of household members. Vehicles rented or leased for one month or more, company vehicles, and police and government vehicles are included if kept at home and used for non-business purposes. Dismantled or immobile vehicles are excluded. Vehicles kept at home but used only for business purposes also are excluded

MIGRATION, Items 59 and 60

Source: U.S. Census Bureau—American Community Survey, 2008–2010
http://www.census.gov/acs/www/

Residence one year ago is used in conjunction with location of current residence to determine the extent of residential mobility of the population and the resulting redistribution of the population across the various states, metropolitan areas, and regions of the country. **Same house** includes all people 1 year old and over who, a year before the survey date, lived in the same house or apartment that they occupied at the time of interview.

The **percent who lived outside this city** includes all persons who did not live in the listed city 1 year before the interview, whether their previous residence was in the same state, a different state, Puerto Rico, or abroad.

CIVILIAN LABOR FORCE AND UNEMPLOYMENT, Items 61–64

Source: U.S. Bureau of Labor Statistics—Local Areas Unemployment Statistics
http://www.bls.gov/lau/#tables

Data for the civilian labor force are the product of a federal-state cooperative program in which state employment security agencies prepare labor force and unemployment estimates under concepts, definitions, and technical procedures established by the Bureau of Labor Statistics (BLS). The civilian labor force consists of all civilians 16 years old and over who are either employed or unemployed.

Unemployment includes all persons who did not work during the survey week, made specific efforts to find a job during the previous four weeks, and were available for work during the survey week (except for temporary illness). Persons waiting to be called back to a job from which they had been laid off and those waiting to report to a new job within the next 30 days are included in unemployment figures.

Table D includes annual average data for the year shown. The Local Area Unemployment Statistics data are periodically updated to reflect revised inputs, reestimation, and controlling to new statewide totals.

CIVILIAN EMPLOYMENT, Items 65–68

Source: U.S. Census Bureau—American Community Survey, 2008–2010
http://www.census.gov/acs/www/

The **labor force** includes all persons 16 years old and over who were either (1) "at work"—those who did any work at all during the reference week as paid employees, worked in either their own business or profession, worked on their own farm, or worked 15 hours or more as unpaid workers in a family farm or business; or were (2) "with a job, but not at work" —those who had a job but were not at work that week due to illness, weather, industrial dispute, vacation, or other personal reasons.

Full-year, Full-Time Workers includes all people 16 years old and over who usually worked 35 hours or more per week for 50 to 52 weeks in the past 12 months.

Households with no workers includes households where all members "Did not work in the past 12 months." Workers include all people 16 years old and over who, for one or more weeks, did any work for pay or profit (including paid vacation and paid sick leave) or worked without pay on a family farm or in a family business. Weeks of active service in the Armed Forces are also included.

BUILDING PERMITS, Items 69–71

Source: U.S. Census Bureau—Building Permits Survey
http://www.census.gov/const/www/permitsindex.html

These figures represent private residential construction authorized by building permits in approximately 20,000 places in the United States. Valuation represents the expected cost of construction as recorded on the building permit. This figure usually excludes the cost of on-site and off-site development and improvements, as well as the cost of heating, plumbing, electrical, and elevator installations.

National, state, and county totals were obtained by adding the data for permit-issuing places within each jurisdiction. These totals thus are limited to permits issued in the 20,000 place universe covered by the Census Bureau and may not include all permits issued within a state. Current surveys indicate that construction is undertaken for all but a very small percentage of housing units authorized by building permits.

Residential building permits include buildings with any number of housing units. Housing units exclude group quarters (such as dormitories and rooming houses), transient accommodations (such as transient hotels, motels, and tourist courts), "HUD-code" manufactured (mobile) homes, moved or relocated units, and housing units created in an existing residential or nonresidential structure.

2007 Economic CENSUS: OVERVIEW, Items 72–107
Source: U.S. Census Bureau
http://www.census.gov/econ/census07/

The Economic Census provides a detailed portrait of the nation's economy, from the national to the local level, once every five years. The 2007 Economic Census covers nearly all of the U.S. economy in its basic collection of establishment statistics. The 1997 Economic Census was the first major data source to use the new North American Industry Classification System (NAICS); therefore, data from this census are not comparable to economic data from prior years, which were based on the Standard Industrial Classification (SIC) system.

NAICS, developed in cooperation with Canada and Mexico, classifies North America's economic activities at two, three, four, and five digit levels of detail; the U.S. version of NAICS further defines industries to a sixth digit. The Economic Census takes advantage of this hierarchy to publish data at these successive levels of detail: sector (two-digit), subsector (three-digit), industry group (four-digit), industry (five-digit), and U.S. industry (six-digit). Information in Table A is at the two-digit level, with a few three- and four-digit items. The data in Table D are at the two-digit level.

Several key statistics are tabulated for all industries in this volume, including number of establishments (or companies), number of employees, payroll, and certain measures of output (sales, receipts, revenue, value of shipments, or value of construction work done).

Number of establishments. An establishment is a single physical location at which business is conducted. It is not necessarily identical with a company or enterprise, which may consist of one establishment or more. Economic Census figures represent a summary of reports for individual establishments rather than companies. For cases in which a census report was received, separate information was obtained for each location where business was conducted. When administrative records of other federal agencies were used instead of a census report, no information was available on the number of locations operated. Each Economic Census establishment was tabulated according to the physical location at which the business was conducted. The count of establishments represents those in business at any time during 2002.

When two activities or more were carried on at a single location under a single ownership, all activities were generally grouped together as a single establishment. The entire establishment was classified on the basis of its major activity and all of its data were included in that classification. However, when distinct and separate economic activities (for which different industry classification codes were appropriate) were conducted at a single location under a single ownership, separate establishment reports for each of the different activities were obtained in the census.

Number of employees. Paid employees consist of the full time and part time employees, including salaried officers and executives of corporations. Included are employees on paid sick leave, paid holidays, and paid vacations; not included are proprietors and partners of unincorporated businesses. The definition of paid employees is the same as that used by the Internal Revenue Service (IRS) on form 941. For some industries, the Economic Census gives codes representing the number of employees as a range of numbers (for example, "100 to 249 employees" or "1,000 to 2,499" employees). In this volume, those codes have been replaced by the standard suppression code "D".

Payroll. Payroll includes all forms of compensation, such as salaries, wages, commissions, dismissal pay, bonuses, vacation allowances, sick leave pay, and employee contributions to qualified pension plans paid during the year to all employees. For corporations, payroll includes amounts paid to officers and executives; for unincorporated businesses, it does not include profit or other compensation of proprietors or partners. Payroll is reported before deductions for Social Security, income tax, insurance, union dues, etc. This definition of payroll is the same as that used by on IRS form 941.

Sales, shipments, receipts, revenue, or business done. This measure includes the total sales, shipments, receipts, revenue, or business done by establishments within the scope of the Economic Census. The definition of each of these items is specific to the economic sector measured.

WHOLESALE TRADE, Items 72–75
Source: U.S. Census Bureau—2007 Economic Census (See Overview of 2007 Economic Census prior to Item 72)

The Wholesale Trade sector (sector 42) comprises establishments engaged in wholesaling merchandise, generally without transformation, and rendering services incidental to the sale of merchandise. The wholesaling process is an intermediate step in the distribution of merchandise.

Wholesalers are organized to sell or arrange the purchase or sale of (1) goods for resale (i.e., goods sold to other wholesalers or retailers), (2) capital or durable nonconsumer goods, and (3) raw and intermediate materials and supplies used in production.

Wholesalers sell merchandise to other businesses and normally operate from a warehouse or office. These warehouses and offices are characterized by having little or no display of merchandise. In addition, neither the design nor the location of the premises is intended to solicit walk in traffic. Wholesalers do not normally use advertising directed to the general public. In general, customers are initially reached via telephone, in person marketing, or specialized advertising, which may include the Internet and other electronic means. Follow up orders are either vendor initiated or client initiated, are usually based on previous sales, and typically exhibit strong ties between sellers and buyers. In fact, transactions are often conducted between wholesalers and clients that have long standing business relationships.

This sector is made up of two main types of wholesalers: those that sell goods on their own account and those that arrange sales and purchases for others for a commission or fee.

(1) Establishments that sell goods on their own account are known as wholesale merchants, distributors, jobbers, drop shippers, import/export merchants, and sales branches. These establishments typically maintain their own warehouse, where they receive and handle goods for their customers. Goods are generally sold without transformation, but may include integral functions, such as sorting, packaging, labeling, and other marketing services.

(2) Establishments arranging for the purchase or sale of goods owned by others or purchasing goods on a commission basis are known as agents and brokers, commission merchants, import/export agents and brokers, auction companies, and manufacturers' representatives. These establishments operate from offices and generally do not own or handle the goods they sell.

Some wholesale establishments may be connected with a single manufacturer and promote and sell that particular manufacturer's products to a wide range of other wholesalers or retailers. Other wholesalers may be connected to a retail chain or a limited number of retail chains and only provide the products needed by the particular retail operation(s). These wholesalers may obtain the products from a wide range of manufacturers. Still other wholesalers may not take title to the goods, but act instead as agents and brokers for a commission.

Although wholesaling normally denotes sales in large volumes, durable nonconsumer goods may be sold in single units. Sales of capital or durable nonconsumer goods used in the production of goods and services, such as farm machinery, medium- and heavy-duty trucks, and industrial machinery, are always included in Wholesale Trade.

The city table includes only **Merchant wholesalers, except manufacturers' sales branches and offices,** establishments primarily engaged in buying and selling merchandise on their own account. Included here are such types of establishments as wholesale distributors and jobbers, importers, exporters, own-brand importers/marketers, terminal and country grain elevators, and farm products assemblers.

RETAIL TRADE, Items 76–79
Source: U.S. Census Bureau—2007 Economic Census (See Overview of 2007 Economic Census prior to Item 72)

The Retail Trade sector (44–45) is made up of establishments engaged in retailing merchandise, generally without transformation, and rendering services incidental to the sale of merchandise.

The retailing process is the final step in the distribution of merchandise; retailers are therefore organized to sell merchandise in small quantities to the general public. This sector comprises two main types of retailers: store and nonstore retailers.

Store retailers operate fixed point of sale locations, located and designed to attract a high volume of walk in customers. In general, retail stores have extensive displays of merchandise and use mass media advertising to attract customers. They typically sell merchandise to the general public for personal or household consumption; some also serve business and institutional clients. These include establishments such as office supply stores, computer and software stores, building materials dealers, plumbing

supply stores, and electrical supply stores. Catalog showrooms, gasoline service stations, automotive dealers, and mobile home dealers are treated as store retailers.

In addition to retailing merchandise, some types of store retailers are also engaged in the provision of after sales services, such as repair and installation. For example, new automobile dealers, electronic and appliance stores, and musical instrument and supply stores often provide repair services. As a general rule, establishments engaged in retailing merchandise and providing after sales services are classified in this sector.

Nonstore retailers, like store retailers, are organized to serve the general public, although their retailing methods differ. The establishments of this subsector reach customers and market merchandise with methods including the broadcasting of "infomercials," the broadcasting and publishing of direct response advertising, the publishing of paper and electronic catalogs, door to door solicitation, in home demonstration, selling from portable stalls (street vendors, except food), and distribution through vending machines. Establishments engaged in the direct sale (nonstore) of products, such as home heating oil dealers and home-delivery newspaper routes are included in this sector.

The buying of goods for resale is a characteristic of retail trade establishments that distinguishes them from establishments in the Agriculture, Manufacturing, and Construction sectors. For example, farms that sell their products at or from the point of production are classified in Agriculture instead of in Retail Trade. Similarly, establishments that both manufacture and sell their products to the general public are classified in Manufacturing instead of Retail Trade. However, establishments that engage in processing activities incidental to retailing are classified in Retail Trade.

REAL ESTATE AND RENTAL AND LEASING, Items 80–83
Source: U.S. Census Bureau—2007 Economic Census (See Overview of 2007 Economic Census prior to Item 72)

The Real Estate and Rental and Leasing sector (53) comprises establishments primarily engaged in renting, leasing, or otherwise allowing the use of tangible or intangible assets, and establishments providing related services. The major portion of this sector is made up of establishments that rent, lease, or otherwise allow the use of their own assets by others. The assets may be tangible, such as real estate and equipment, or intangible, such as patents and trademarks.

This sector also includes establishments primarily engaged in managing real estate for others, selling, renting, and/or buying real estate for others, and appraising real estate. These activities are closely related to this sector's main activity. In addition, a substantial proportion of property management is self performed by lessors.

The main components of this sector are the real estate lessors industries; equipment lessors industries (including motor vehicles, computers, and consumer goods); and lessors of nonfinancial intangible assets (except copyrighted works).

PROFESSIONAL, SCIENTIFIC, AND TECHNICAL SERVICES, Items 84–87

Source: U.S. Census Bureau—2007 Economic Census (See Overview of 2007 Economic Census prior to Item 72)

The Professional, Scientific, and Technical Services sector (54) is made up of establishments that specialize in performing professional, scientific, and technical activities for others. These activities require a high degree of expertise and training. The establishments in this sector specialize in one or more areas and provide services to clients in a variety of industries (and, in some cases, to households). Activities performed include legal advice and representation; accounting, bookkeeping, and payroll services; architectural, engineering, and specialized design services; computer services; consulting services; research services; advertising services; photographic services; translation and interpretation services; veterinary services; and other professional, scientific, and technical services.

Table D includes only those establishments subject to federal income tax.

This sector excludes establishments primarily engaged in providing a range of day to day office administrative services, such as financial planning, billing and record keeping, personnel services, and physical distribution and logistics services. These establishments are classified in sector 56, Administrative and Support and Waste Management and Remediation Services.

MANUFACTURING, Items 88–91

Source: U.S. Census Bureau—2007 Economic Census (See Overview of 2007 Economic Census prior to Item 72)

The Manufacturing sector (31–33) is made up of establishments engaged in the mechanical, physical, or chemical transformation of materials, substances, or components into new products. The assembling of component parts of manufactured products is considered manufacturing, except in cases in which the activity is appropriately classified in the Construction sector. Establishments in the Manufacturing sector are often described as plants, factories, or mills, and characteristically use power-driven machines and materials-handling equipment. However, establishments that transform materials or substances into new products by hand or in the worker's home, and establishments engaged in selling to the general public products made on the same premises from which they are sold (such as bakeries, candy stores, and custom tailors) may also be included in this sector. Manufacturing establishments may process materials or contract with other establishments to process their materials for them. Both types of establishments are included in the Manufacturing sector.

The materials, substances, or components transformed by manufacturing establishments are raw materials that are products of agriculture, forestry, fishing, mining, or quarrying, or are products of other manufacturing establishments. The materials used may be purchased directly from producers, obtained through customary trade channels, or secured without recourse to the market by transferring the product from one establishment to another, under the same ownership. The new product of a manufacturing establishment may be finished (in the sense that it is ready for utilization or consumption), or it may be semifinished to become an input for an establishment engaged in further manufacturing. For example, the product of the alumina refinery is the input used in the primary production of aluminum; primary aluminum is the input used in an aluminum wire drawing plant; and aluminum wire is the input used in a fabricated wire product manufacturing establishment.

Data are included for cities with 500 or more employees in the Manufacturing sector.

ACCOMMODATION AND FOOD SERVICES, Items 92–95

Source: U.S. Census Bureau—2007 Economic Census (See Overview of 2007 Economic Census prior to Item 72)

The Accommodation and Food Services sector (72) consists of establishments that provide customers with lodging and/or meals, snacks, and beverages for immediate consumption. This sector includes both accommodation and food services establishments because the two activities are often combined at the same establishment.

Excluded from this sector are civic and social organizations, amusement and recreation parks, theaters, and other recreation or entertainment facilities providing food and beverage services.

ARTS, ENTERTAINMENT, AND RECREATION, Items 96–99

Source: U.S. Census Bureau—2007 Economic Census (See Overview of 2007 Economic Census prior to Item 72)

The Arts, Entertainment, and Recreation sector (71) includes a wide range of establishments that operate facilities or provide services that meet the diverse cultural, entertainment, and recreational interests of their patrons. This sector is made up of: (1) establishments that are involved in producing, promoting, or participating in live performances, events, or exhibits intended for public viewing; (2) establishments that preserve and exhibit objects and sites of historical, cultural, or educational interest; and (3) establishments that operate facilities or provide services that enable patrons to participate in recreational activities or pursue amusement, hobby, and leisure time interests.

Some establishments that provide cultural, entertainment, or recreational facilities and services are classified in other sectors. Excluded from this sector are: (1) establishments that provide both accommodations and recreational facilities—such as hunting and fishing camps and resort and casino hotels—are classified in subsector 721, Accommodation; (2) restaurants and night clubs that provide live entertainment in addition to the sale of food and beverages are classified in subsector 722, Food Services and Drinking Places; (3) motion picture theaters, libraries and archives, and publishers of newspapers, magazines, books, periodicals, and computer software are classified in sector 51, Information; and (4) establishments that use transportation equipment to provide recreational and entertainment services, such as those operating sightseeing buses, dinner cruises, or helicopter rides, are classified in subsector 487, Scenic and Sightseeing Transportation.

Table D includes only those establishments subject to federal tax.

HEALTH CARE AND SOCIAL ASSISTANCE, Items 100–103

Source: U.S. Census Bureau—2007 Economic Census (See Overview of 2007 Economic Census prior to Item 72)

The Health Care and Social Assistance sector (62) consists of establishments that provide health care and social assistance services to individuals. The sector includes both health care and social assistance because it is sometimes difficult to distinguish between the boundaries of these two activities. The industries in this sector are arranged on a continuum, starting with establishments that provide medical care exclusively, continuing with those that provide health care and social assistance, and finishing with those that provide only social assistance. The services provided by establishments in this sector are delivered by trained professionals. All industries in the sector share this commonality of process—namely, labor inputs of health practitioners or social workers with the requisite expertise. Many of the industries in the sector are defined based on the educational degree held by the practitioners included in the industry.

Excluded from this sector are aerobic classes, which can be found in subsector 713, Amusement, Gambling, and Recreation Industries; and nonmedical diet and weight-reducing centers, which can be found in subsector 812, Personal and Laundry Services. Although these can be viewed as health services, they are not typically delivered by health practitioners.

Table D includes only those establishments subject to federal tax.

OTHER SERVICES, EXCEPT PUBLIC ADMINISTRATION Items 104–107

Source: U.S. Census Bureau—2007 Economic Census (See Overview of 2007 Economic Census prior to Item 72)

The Other Services, Except Public Administration sector (81) comprises establishments engaged in providing services not specifically categorized elsewhere in the classification system. Establishments in this sector are primarily engaged in activities such as equipment and machinery repairing, promoting or administering religious activities, grant making, and advocacy; this sector also includes establishments that provide dry-cleaning and laundry services, personal care services, death care services, pet care services, photofinishing services, temporary parking services, and dating services.

Private households that employ workers on or about the premises in activities primarily concerned with the operation of the household are included in this sector.

In Table D, only firms subject to federal tax are included.

Excluded from this sector are establishments primarily engaged in retailing new equipment and performing repairs and general maintenance on equipment. These establishments are classified in sector 44–45, Retail Trade.

FEDERAL FUNDS, Items 108–116

Source: U.S. Census Bureau—Consolidated Federal Funds Report
http://www.census.gov/govs/cffr/

Data on federal expenditure and obligations are obtained from a report prepared by the Census Bureau in accordance with the Consolidated Federal Funds Report (CFFR) Act of 1982 (P.L. 97-326). The data are for federal fiscal years beginning October 1 and ending the following September 30.

Only selected categories of data from the CFFR are identified at the city level. The city items shown in this book are "selected" federal funds and do not represent all federal funds received by individuals and entities within the city.

Dollar amounts reported can reflect expenditures or obligations. In some cases, dollar amounts are negative, representing de-obligations of financial assistance that had previously been awarded. Such amounts generally appear in the grant categories. Many categories are assigned only to state and county levels and never assigned to cities.

Procurement contract awards cover awards given by the United States Postal Service (USPS), as well as those given by all other federal agencies. Amounts provided by the USPS represent actual outlays for contractual commitments, while amounts for other agencies represent the value of obligations for contract actions and do not reflect actual federal government expenditures. In general, only current-year contract actions are included; however, multiple-year obligations may be reported for contract actions of less than three years' duration. The procurement contract data for cities are relatively complete.

Grants data represent the federal obligations incurred at the time the grant is awarded. The amounts reported do not represent actual expenditures, since obligations in one time period may not result in outlays during the same period. Moreover, initial amounts obligated may be adjusted at a later date, through either enhancements or de-obligations. All grant awards were reported by state, county, and city of the initial recipient. For many grants, this recipient is the state government even though grants monies are subsequently distributed to county, municipal, or township governments.

Medicaid and other health-related grants include a variety of grants from the Department of Health and Human Services for health services and research.

Nutrition and family welfare grants include a variety of grants from the Department of Health and Human Services for child welfare, special programs for the aging, and related areas. The school lunch program and other nutritional assistance programs administered by the Department of Agriculture are also included in this category.

Energy and environment grants include grants from the Department of Energy for energy development, energy conservation, and nuclear waste disposal, as well as grants from the Environmental Protection Agency for a variety of pollution control and waste management activities.

Disaster and emergency preparedness grants include assistance to fire-fighting and rescue organizations; community assistance for earthquakes, floods, hurricanes and other disasters; domestic preparedness programs; and similar activities.

Housing and community development grants include Community Development Block Grants, housing demonstration programs, rental housing rehabilitation, and other housing programs.

Employment and training grants include various job training programs, welfare-to-work grants, occupational safety and health grants, and similar employment related funds.

CITY GOVERNMENT FINANCES, Items 117–139
Source: U.S. Census Bureau—2007 Census of Governments
http://www.census.gov/govs/cog

Revenue and expenditure data are included in Table D for city governments only. The data do not include funds of any special district governments located in the city.

Total **general revenue** includes all revenue except utility, liquor stores, and insurance trust revenue. All tax revenue and intergovernmental revenue, even if designated for employee-retirement or local utility purpose, are classified as general revenue.

Intergovernmental revenue covers amounts received from other governments as fiscal aid in the form of shared revenues and grants-in-aid, as reimbursements for the performance of general government functions and specific services for the paying government (for example, care of prisoners or contractual research), or in lieu of taxes. It excludes any amounts received from other governments from the sale of property, commodities, and utility services. All intergovernmental revenue is classified as general revenue. Intergovernmental revenue from the state governments includes amounts originally from the federal government but channeled through the state.

Taxes consist of compulsory contributions exacted by governments for public purposes. However, this category excludes employer and employee payments for retirement and social insurance purposes, which are classified as insurance trust revenue. All tax revenue is classified as general revenue and comprises amounts received (including interest and penalties, but excluding protested amounts and refunds) from all taxes imposed by a government. Note that local government tax revenue excludes any amounts from shares of state-imposed and collected taxes, which are classified as intergovernmental revenue.

Property taxes are based on ownership of property and measured by its value. They include general property taxes related to property as a whole—real and personal, tangible or intangible—whether taxed at a single rate or at classified rates. Also included are taxes on selected types of property, such as motor vehicles or certain or all intangibles.

Sales and gross receipts taxes include "licenses" at more than nominal rates, based on volume or value of transfers of goods or services; taxes upon gross receipts or upon gross income; and related taxes based upon the use, storage, production (other than the severance of natural resources), importation, or consumption of goods. Dealer discounts "commissions," which are allowed to merchants for the collection of taxes from consumers, are excluded.

Total **general expenditure** includes all city expenditure other than specifically enumerated kinds of expenditure, including utility, liquor store, and employee-retirement and other insurance trust expenditures.

Capital outlays are direct expenditures for contract of force account construction or buildings, roads, and other improvements, and for purchases of equipment, land, and existing structures. They include amounts for additions, replacements, and major alterations to fixed work and structures. Expenditures for repair to such works and structures, however, is classified as current operation expenditure.

A major portion of capital outlay is commonly financed by borrowing, while governmental revenue does not include receipts from borrowing. Among other things, this distorts the relationship between the totals presented for revenue and expenditure and renders this relationship useless as a direct measure of the degree of budgetary "balance" (as that term is generally applied).

Public welfare expenditure covers support of and assistance to needy persons; this aid is contingent upon the person's needs. Included are cash assistance paid directly to needy persons; vendor payments made directly to private purveyors for medical care, burials, and other commodities and services provided under welfare programs; welfare institutions; and any intergovernmental or other direct expenditure for welfare purposes. Pensions to former employees and other benefits not contingent on need are excluded.

Highway expenditure is for the provision and maintenance of highway facilities, including toll turnpikes, bridges, tunnels, and ferries, as well as regular roads, highways, and streets. Also included are expenditures for street lighting and for snow and ice removal. Not included are highway policing and traffic control, which are considered part of police protection

Parking facilities include the construction, purchase, maintenance, and operation of public-use parking lots, garages, parking meters, and other distinctive parking facilities on a commercial basis.

Education is mainly for the provision and general support of schools and other educational facilities and services, including those for educational institutions beyond high school. Elementary and secondary education includes the provision of public kindergarten through high school education by local governments. It encompasses instructional, support, and auxiliary services (school lunch, student activities, and community services) offered by public school systems. Higher education consists of all local institutions of higher education.

Health expenditures include outpatient health services other than hospital care, such as public health administration; research and education; categorical health programs; treatment and immunization clinics; nursing; environmental health activities, such as air and water pollution control; ambulance service if provided separately from fire protection services; and other general public health activities, such as mosquito abatement. School health services provided by health agencies (rather than school agencies) are included here. Not included are sewage treatment operations, which are classified as part of sewerage and sanitation. **Hospital expenditures** include financing, construction, acquisition, maintenance and operation of hospital facilities, provision of hospital care, and support of public or private hospitals.

Police protection encompasses expenditures for the preservation of law and order, as well as for traffic safety. It includes police patrols and communications, crime prevention activities, detention and custody of persons awaiting trial, traffic safety, and vehicular inspection.

Sewerage and recreation include sanitary and storm sewers, sewage disposal facilities and services, and other government activities for such purposes. Street cleaning and the collection and disposal of garbage and other waste are also included.

Parks and recreation includes cultural and scientific activities, such as museums and art galleries; organized recreation, including playgrounds and playing fields, swimming pools, and bathing beaches; and municipal parks and special recreation facilities, such as auditoriums, stadiums, auto camps, recreation piers, and boat harbors.

Housing and community development includes city housing and redevelopment projects and the regulation, promotion, and support of private housing and redevelopment activities. Data from Arizona, Kentucky, Michigan, New Mexico, New York, and Virginia generally include municipal housing authorities. Housing authorities for other cities are usually classified as independent governments, and data from them are not included.

Interest on debt is the amount paid for the use of borrowed money.

Total **debt outstanding** is the total of debt obligations remaining unpaid on the date specified. **Debt issued during the year** is the amount of the outstanding debt that was recently borrowed.

CITY GOVERNMENT EMPLOYMENT, Item 140
Source: U.S. Census Bureau—Survey of Governments, 2010: Employment Statistics
http://www.census.gov/govs/apes/

The data are from an annual survey conducted by the Census Bureau and represent paid employment by city governments during March 2010. Full-time equivalent employment is a computed statistic representing the number of full-time employees that would have been employed if the hours worked by the part-time employees were converted to full-time equivalents.

CLIMATE, Items 141–147
Source: National Oceanic and Atmospheric Administration
http://cdo.ncdc.noaa.gov/cgi-bin/climatenormals/
climatenormals.pl

All climate data are average values for the 30-year period from 1961 to 1990.

Mean temperatures for January and July were determined by adding the average daily maximum temperatures and the average daily minimum temperatures and dividing by two.

Temperature limits represent average daily minimum for January and average daily maximum for July.

Annual precipitation values are the average annual water equivalent of all precipitation for the 30-year period.

Heating and cooling degree days are used as relative measures of the energy required for heating and cooling buildings. One heating degree day is accumulated for each whole degree that the mean daily temperature is below 65 degrees Fahrenheit (a mean daily temperature of 62 degrees Fahrenheit will produce three heating degree days). Cooling degree days are accumulated in similar fashion for deviations of the mean daily temperature above 65 degrees Fahrenheit.

TABLE E—CONGRESSIONAL DISTRICTS OF THE 112TH CONGRESS

Members of the House of Representatives are for the 112th Congress.

LAND AREA, Items 1 and 3

Source: U.S. Census Bureau—2010 Census of Population and Housing
http://2010.census.gov/2010census/data/

Land area measurements are shown to the nearest square kilometer. Land area includes dry land and land temporarily or partially covered by water, such as marshlands, swamps, and river floodplains.

POPULATION, Items 2–3

Source: U.S. Census Bureau—2010 Census of Population and Housing
http://2010.census.gov/2010census/data/

The population data are from the 2010 census and represent the resident population as of April 1, 2010.

POPULATION CHARACTERISTICS, Items 4–24

Source: U.S. Census Bureau—2010 Census of Population and Housing
http://2010.census.gov/2010census/data/
Source: U.S. Census Bureau—American Community Survey, 2010
http://www.census.gov/acs/www/

Data on age, sex, race, and Hispanic origin are from the 2010 census. Data on foreign-born residents and percent born in state of residence are from the 2010 American Community Survey.

Data on race were derived from answers to the question on race that was asked of all respondents. The concept of race, as used by the Census Bureau, reflects self-identification by people according to the race or races with which they most closely identify. These categories are sociopolitical constructs and should not be interpreted as being scientific or anthropological in nature. Furthermore, the race categories include both racial and national origin groups.

In Table E, Columns 4 through 8 refer to individuals who identified with each racial category alone, while column 9 includes persons who identified with two or more races.

The **White** population is defined as persons who indicated their race as White, as well as persons who did not classify themselves in one of the specific race categories listed on the questionnaire but entered a nationality such as Irish, German, Italian, Lebanese, Near Easterner, Arab, or Polish.

The **Black** population includes persons who indicated their race as "Black, African Am., or Negro," as well as persons who did not classify themselves in one of the specific race categories but reported entries such as African American, Afro American, Kenyan, Nigerian, or Haitian.

The **American Indian or Alaska Native** population includes persons who indicated their race as American Indian or Alaska Native, as well as persons who did not classify themselves in one of the specific race categories but reported entries such as Canadian Indian, French-American Indian, Spanish-American Indian, Eskimo, Aleut, Alaska Indian, or any of the American Indian or Alaska Native tribes.

The **Asian and Pacific Islander** population combines two census groupings: **Asian** and **Native Hawaiian or Other Pacific Islander**. The **Asian** population includes persons who indicated their race as Asian Indian, Chinese, Filipino, Japanese, Korean, Vietnamese, or "Other Asian," as well as persons who provided write-in entries of such groups as Cambodian, Laotian, Hmong, Pakistani, or Taiwanese. The **Native Hawaiian or Other Pacific Islander** population includes persons who indicated their race as "Native Hawaiian," "Guamanian or Chamorro," "Samoan," or "Other Pacific Islander," as well as persons who reported entries such as Part Hawaiian, American Samoan, Fijian, Melanesian, or Tahitian.

The **Hispanic population** is based on a question that asked respondents "Is this person Spanish/Hispanic/Latino?" Persons marking any one of the four Hispanic categories (i.e., Mexican, Puerto Rican, Cuban, or other Spanish) are collectively referred to as Hispanic.

The **Non-Hispanic White alone** number in Column 11 includes only those persons who were not Hispanic and whose race was "White only."

The **female** population is shown as a percentage of total population.

The **foreign-born** population includes all persons who were not U.S. citizens at birth. Foreign-born persons are those who indicated they were either a U.S. citizen by naturalization or were not a citizen of the United States. The foreign-born population consists of immigrants (legal permanent residents), temporary migrants (students), humanitarian migrants (refugees), and unauthorized migrants (persons illegally residing in the United States).

Percent born in state of residence is shown as a percentage of total population.

Age is defined as age at last birthday (number of completed years since birth).

EDUCATION—SCHOOL ENROLLMENT AND EDUCATIONAL ATTAINMENT, Items 25–28

Source: U.S. Census Bureau—American Community Survey, 2010
http://www.census.gov/acs/www/

Data on school enrollment and educational attainment were derived from a sample of the population. Persons were classified as enrolled in school if they reported attending a "regular" public or private school (or college) during the year. The instructions were to "include only nursery school, kindergarten, elementary school, and schooling which would lead to a high school diploma or a college degree" as regular school. The Census Bureau defines a public school as "any school or college controlled and supported by a local, county, state, or federal government." Schools primarily supported and controlled by religious organizations or other private groups are defined as private schools.